THIS

# HOLY BIBLE

IS PRESENTED TO

_____

BY

_____

_____

ON

_____

_____

**THY WORD IS A LAMP UNTO MY FEET,
AND A LIGHT UNTO MY PATH.**

PSALM 119:105

# HOLY BIBLE

# THE
# HOLY BIBLE

### CONTAINING
## THE OLD AND NEW TESTAMENTS
### TRANSLATED OUT OF THE ORIGINAL TONGUES
### AND WITH THE FORMER TRANSLATIONS
### DILIGENTLY COMPARED AND REVISED

## *Authorized King James Version*

### RED-LETTER EDITION

## THOMAS NELSON
*Since 1798*

**www.ThomasNelson.com**

The Holy Bible, King James Version

*KJV Thinline Reference Bible*

Copyright © 2017 by Thomas Nelson

Published by Thomas Nelson
Nashville, Tennessee 37214, U.S.A.

www.thomasnelsonbibles.com

Library of Congress Control Number: 2017935427

This Bible was set in the Thomas Nelson KJV Font,
created at the 2K/DENMARK type foundry.

*Printed in China*

17 18 19 20 21 22 23 24 25 /AMC/ 15 14 13 12 11 10 9 8 7 6 5 4 3 2 1

# TO THE MOST HIGH AND MIGHTY PRINCE

# JAMES

## BY THE GRACE OF GOD,

### KING OF GREAT BRITAIN, FRANCE, AND IRELAND, DEFENDER OF THE FAITH, &C.

#### THE TRANSLATORS OF THE BIBLE WISH GRACE, MERCY, AND PEACE, THROUGH JESUS CHRIST OUR LORD

Great and manifold were the blessings, most dread Sovereign, which Almighty God, the Father of all mercies, bestowed upon us the people of *England*, when first he sent Your Majesty's Royal Person to rule and reign over us. For whereas it was the expectation of many, who wished not well unto our *Sion*, that upon the setting of that bright *Occidental Star*, Queen *Elizabeth* of most happy memory, some thick and palpable clouds of darkness would so have overshadowed this Land, that men should have been in doubt which way they were to walk; and that it should hardly be known, who was to direct the unsettled State; the appearance of Your Majesty, as of the *Sun* in his strength, instantly dispelled those supposed and surmised mists, and gave unto all that were well affected exceeding cause of comfort; especially when we beheld the Government established in Your Highness, and Your hopeful Seed, by an undoubted Title, and this also accompanied with peace and tranquillity at home and abroad.

But among all our joys, there was no one that more filled our hearts, than the blessed continuance of the preaching of God's sacred Word among us; which is that inestimable treasure, which excelleth all the riches of the earth; because the fruit thereof extendeth itself, not only to the time spent in this transitory world, but directeth and disposeth men unto that eternal happiness which is above in heaven.

Then not to suffer this to fall to the ground, but rather to take it up, and to continue it in that state, wherein the famous Predecessor of Your Highness did leave it: nay, to go forward with the confidence and resolution of a Man in maintaining the truth of Christ, and propagating it far and near, is that which hath so bound and firmly knit the hearts of all Your Majesty's loyal and religious people unto You, that Your very name is precious among them: their eye doth behold You with comfort, and they bless You in their hearts, as that sanctified Person, who, under God, is the immediate Author of their true happiness. And this their contentment doth not diminish or decay, but every day increaseth and taketh strength, when they observe, that the zeal of Your Majesty toward the house of God doth not slack or go backward, but is more and more kindled, manifesting itself abroad in the farthest parts of *Christendom*, by writing in defence of the Truth, (which hath given such a blow unto that man of sin, as will not be healed,) and every day at home, by religious and learned discourse, by frequenting the house of God, by hearing the Word preached, by cherishing the Teachers thereof, by caring for the Church, as a most tender and loving nursing Father.

There are infinite arguments of this right Christian and religious affection in Your Majesty; but none is more forcible to declare it to others than the vehement and perpetuated desire of accomplishing

and publishing of this work, which now with all humility we present unto Your Majesty. For when Your Highness had once out of deep judgment apprehended how convenient it was, that out of the Original Sacred Tongues, together with comparing of the labours, both in our own, and other foreign Languages, of many worthy men who went before us, there should be one more exact Translation of the holy Scriptures into the *English Tongue*; Your Majesty did never desist to urge and to excite those to whom it was commended, that the work might be hastened, and that the business might be expedited in so decent a manner, as a matter of such importance might justly require.

And now at last, by the mercy of God, and the continuance of our labours, it being brought unto such a conclusion, as that we have great hopes that the Church of *England* shall reap good fruit thereby; we hold it our duty to offer it to Your Majesty, not only as to our King and Sovereign, but as to the principal Mover and Author of the work: humbly craving of Your most Sacred Majesty, that since things of this quality have ever been subject to the censures of ill-meaning and discontented persons, it may receive approbation and patronage from so learned and judicious a Prince as Your Highness is, whose allowance and acceptance of our labours shall more honour and encourage us, than all the calumniations and hard interpretations of other men shall dismay us. So that if, on the one side, we shall be traduced by Popish Persons at home or abroad, who therefore will malign us, because we are poor instruments to make God's holy Truth to be yet more and more known unto the people, whom they desire still to keep in ignorance and darkness; or if, on the other side, we shall be maligned by selfconceited Brethren, who run their own ways, and give liking unto nothing, but what is framed by themselves, and hammered on their anvil; we may rest secure, supported within by the truth and innocency of a good conscience, having walked the ways of simplicity and integrity, as before the Lord; and sustained without by the powerful protection of Your Majesty's grace and favour, which will ever give countenance to honest and Christian endeavours against bitter censures and uncharitable imputations.

The Lord of heaven and earth bless Your Majesty with many and happy days, that, as his heavenly hand hath enriched Your Highness with many singular and extraordinary graces, so You may be the wonder of the world in this latter age for happiness and true felicity, to the honour of that great GOD, and the good of his Church, through Jesus Christ our Lord and only Saviour.

# CONTENTS

## THE BOOKS OF THE OLD TESTAMENT

## THE BOOKS OF THE NEW TESTAMENT

# BOOK ABBREVIATIONS

OT = Old Testament; NT = New Testament

| | | | | | | |
|---|---|---|---|---|---|---|
| 1 Chr. | 1 Chronicles | OT | | Hos. | Hosea | OT |
| 1 Cor. | 1 Corinthians | NT | | Is. | Isaiah | OT |
| 1 John | 1 John | NT | | James | James | NT |
| 1 Kin. | 1 Kings | OT | | Jer. | Jeremiah | OT |
| 1 Pet. | 1 Peter | NT | | Job | Job | OT |
| 1 Sam. | 1 Samuel | OT | | Joel | Joel | OT |
| 1 Thess. | 1 Thessalonians | NT | | John | John | NT |
| 1 Tim. | 1 Timothy | NT | | Jon. | Jonah | OT |
| 2 Chr. | 2 Chronicles | OT | | Josh. | Joshua | OT |
| 2 Cor. | 2 Corinthians | NT | | Jude | Jude | NT |
| 2 John | 2 John | NT | | Judg. | Judges | OT |
| 2 Kin. | 2 Kings | OT | | Lam. | Lamentations | OT |
| 2 Pet. | 2 Peter | NT | | Lev. | Leviticus | OT |
| 2 Sam. | 2 Samuel | OT | | Luke | Luke | NT |
| 2 Thess. | 2 Thessalonians | NT | | Mal. | Malachi | OT |
| 2 Tim. | 2 Timothy | NT | | Mark | Mark | NT |
| 3 John | 3 John | NT | | Matt. | Matthew | NT |
| Acts | Acts | NT | | Mic. | Micah | OT |
| Amos | Amos | OT | | Nah. | Nahum | OT |
| Col. | Colossians | NT | | Neh. | Nehemiah | OT |
| Dan. | Daniel | OT | | Num. | Numbers | OT |
| Deut. | Deuteronomy | OT | | Obad. | Obadiah | OT |
| Eccl. | Ecclesiastes | OT | | Phil. | Philippians | NT |
| Eph. | Ephesians | NT | | Philem. | Philemon | NT |
| Esth. | Esther | OT | | Prov. | Proverbs | OT |
| Ex. | Exodus | OT | | Ps. | Psalms | OT |
| Ezek. | Ezekiel | OT | | Rev. | Revelation | NT |
| Ezra | Ezra | OT | | Rom. | Romans | NT |
| Gal. | Galatians | NT | | Ruth | Ruth | OT |
| Gen. | Genesis | OT | | Song | Song of Solomon | OT |
| Hab. | Habakkuk | OT | | Titus | Titus | NT |
| Hag. | Haggai | OT | | Zech. | Zechariah | OT |
| Heb. | Hebrews | NT | | Zeph. | Zephaniah | OT |

# SPECIAL ABBREVIATIONS

| | |
|---|---|
| Aram. | Aramaic |
| Bg. | the 1524-25 edition of the Hebrew Old Testament published by Daniel Bomberg |
| cf. | compare |
| ch., chs. | chapter, chapters |
| e.g. | for example |
| f., ff. | following verse, following verses |
| Gr. | Greek |
| Heb. | Hebrew |
| i.e. | that is |
| lit. | literally |
| LXX | Septuagint — an ancient translation of the Old Testament into Greek |
| ms., mss. | manuscript, manuscripts |
| MT | Masoretic Text — the traditional Hebrew Old Testament |
| Syr. | Syriac |
| Tg. | Targums — ancient Aramaic interpretations of the Old Testament |
| v., vv. | verse, verses |
| vss. | versions |
| Vg. | Vulgate — an ancient translation of the Bible into Latin, translated and edited by Jerome |

# THE
# OLD TESTAMENT

# THE FIRST BOOK OF MOSES CALLED
# GENESIS

The first part of Genesis focuses on the beginning and spread of sin in the world and culminates in the devastating flood in the days of Noah. The second part of the book focuses on God's dealings with one man, Abraham, through whom God promises to bring salvation and blessing to the world. Abraham and his descendants learn firsthand that it is always safe to trust the Lord in times of famine and feasting, blessing and bondage. From Abraham . . . to Isaac . . . to Jacob . . . to Joseph . . . God's promises begin to come to fruition in a great nation possessing a great land.

*Genesis* is a Greek word meaning "origin," "source," "generation," or "beginning." The original Hebrew title *Bereshith* means "In the Beginning."

The literary structure of Genesis is clear and is built around eleven separate units, each including the word *generations* in the phrase "These are the generations" or "The book of the generations": (1) Introduction to the Genealogies (1:1–2:3); (2) Heaven and Earth (2:4–4:26); (3) Adam (5:1–6:8); (4) Noah (6:9–9:29); (5) Sons of Noah (10:1–11:9); (6) Shem (11:10–26); (7) Terah (11:27–25:11); (8) Ishmael (25:12–18); (9) Isaac (25:19–35:29); (10) Esau (36:1–37:1); (11) Jacob (37:2–50:26).

## CHAPTER 1

I**N** the ᵃbeginning ᵇGod created the heaven and the earth.

2 And the earth was ᵃwithout form, and void; and darkness *was* upon the face of the deep. ᵇAnd the Spirit of God ¹moved upon the face of the waters.

3 ᵃAnd God said, ᵇLet there be ᶜlight: and there was light.

4 And God saw the light, that *it was* good: and God divided the light from the darkness.

5 And God called the light Day, and the ᵃdarkness he called Night. And the evening and the morning were the first day.

6 And God said, ᵃLet there be a ¹firmament in the midst of the waters, and let it divide the waters from the waters.

7 And God made the firmament, ᵃand divided the waters which *were* under the firmament from the waters which *were* ᵇabove the firmament: and it was so.

8 And God called the ¹firmament Heaven. And the evening and the morning were the second day.

9 And God said, ᵃLet the waters under the heaven be gathered together unto one place, and ᵇlet the dry *land* appear: and it was so.

10 And God called the dry *land* Earth; and the gathering together of the waters called he Seas: and God saw that *it was* good.

11 And God said, Let the earth ᵃbring forth grass, the herb yielding seed, *and* the ᵇfruit tree yielding fruit after his kind, whose seed *is* in itself, upon the earth: and it was so.

12 And the earth brought forth grass, *and* herb yielding seed after his kind, and the tree yielding fruit, whose seed *was* in itself, after his kind: and God saw that *it was* good.

13 And the evening and the morning were the third day.

14 And God said, Let there be ᵃlights in the firmament of the heaven to divide the day from the night; and let them be for signs, and for ᵇseasons, and for days, and years:

15 And let them be for lights in the firmament of the heaven to give light upon the earth: and it was so.

16 And God made two great ¹lights; the ᵃgreater light to rule the day, and the ᵇlesser light to rule the night: *he made* ᶜthe stars also.

17 And God set them in the firmament of the ᵃheaven to give light upon the earth,

18 And to ᵃrule over the day and over the night, and to divide the light from the darkness: and God saw that *it was* good.

19 And the evening and the morning were the fourth day.

20 And God said, Let the waters ¹bring forth abundantly the moving creature that hath life, and ²fowl *that* may fly above the earth in the ³open firmament of heaven.

21 And ᵃGod created great ¹whales, and every living creature that moveth, which the waters ²brought forth abundantly, after their kind, and every winged fowl after his kind: and God saw that *it was* good.

22 And God blessed them, saying, ᵃBe fruitful, and multiply, and fill the waters in the seas, and let fowl multiply in the earth.

23 And the evening and the morning were the fifth day.

24 And God said, Let the earth bring

### Cross-references

1:1 ᵃ [John 1:1–3]
ᵇ Acts 17:24
1:2 ᵃ Jer. 4:23  ᵇ Is. 40:13, 14  ¹ *was hovering over*
1:3 ᵃ Ps. 33:6, 9  ᵇ 2 Cor. 4:6  ᶜ [Heb. 11:3]
1:5 ᵃ Ps. 19:2; 33:6; 74:16; 104:20; 136:5
1:6 ᵃ Jer. 10:12  ¹ *expanse*
1:7 ᵃ Prov. 8:27–29  ᵇ Ps. 148:4
1:8 ¹ *expanse*
1:9 ᵃ Job 26:10  ᵇ Ps. 24:1, 2; 33:7; 95:5
1:11 ᵃ Heb. 6:7  ᵇ 2 Sam. 16:1
1:14 ᵃ Ps. 74:16; 136:5–9  ᵇ Ps. 104:19
1:16 ᵃ Ps. 136:8  ᵇ Ps. 8:3  ᶜ Job 38:7  ¹ *luminaries*
1:17 ᵃ Gen. 15:5
1:18 ᵃ Jer. 31:35
1:20 ¹ *abound with an abundance of living creatures*  ² *let birds fly* ³ *across the face of the expanse of heaven*
1:21 ᵃ Ps. 104:25–28  ¹ *sea creatures*  ² *abounded*
1:22 ᵃ Gen. 8:17

forth the living creature after his kind, cattle, and creeping thing, and beast of the earth after his kind: and it was so.

25 And God made the beast of the earth after his kind, and cattle after their kind, and every thing that creepeth upon the earth after his kind: and God saw that *it was* good.

26 And God said, ᵃLet us make man in our image, after our likeness: and ᵇlet them have dominion over the fish of the sea, and over the fowl of the air, and over the cattle, and over all the earth, and over every creeping thing that creepeth upon the earth.

27 So God created man ᵃin his *own* image, in the image of God created he him; ᵇmale and female created he them.

28 And God blessed them, and God said unto them, ᵃBe fruitful, and multiply, and ¹replenish the earth, and ᵇsubdue it: and have dominion over the fish of the sea, and over the fowl of the air, and over every living thing that ²moveth upon the earth.

29 And God said, Behold, I have given you every herb ¹bearing seed, which *is* upon the face of all the earth, and every tree, in the which *is* the fruit of a tree yielding seed; ᵃto you it shall be for ²meat.

30 And to ᵃevery beast of the earth, and to every ᵇfowl of the air, and to every thing that creepeth upon the earth, wherein *there is* ¹life, I have *given* every green herb for ²meat: and it was so.

31 And ᵃGod saw every thing that he had made, and, behold, *it was* very good. And the evening and the morning were the sixth day.

## CHAPTER 2

THUS the heavens and the earth were finished, and ᵃall the host of them.

2 ᵃAnd on the seventh day God ended his work which he had made; and he rested on the seventh day from all his work which he had made.

3 And God ᵃblessed the seventh day, and sanctified it: because that in it he had rested from all his work which God created and made.

4 ᵃThese¹ *are* the generations of the heavens and of the earth when they were created, in the day that the LORD God made the earth and the heavens,

5 And every ᵃplant of the field before it was in the earth, and every herb of the field before it grew: for the LORD God had not ᵇcaused it to rain upon the earth, and *there was* not a man ᶜto till the ground.

6 But there went up a mist from the earth, and watered the whole face of the ground.

7 And the LORD God formed man *of* the ᵃdust of the ground, and ᵇbreathed into his ᶜnostrils the breath of life; and ᵈman became a living soul.

8 And the LORD God planted ᵃa garden ᵇeastward in ᶜEden; and there he put the man whom he had formed.

9 And out of the ground made the LORD God to grow ᵃevery tree that is pleasant to the sight, and good for food; ᵇthe tree of life also in the midst of the garden, and the tree of knowledge of good and ᶜevil.

10 And a river went out of Eden to water the garden; and from thence it was parted, and became into four ¹heads.

11 The name of the first *is* Pison: that *is* it which compasseth ᵃthe whole land of Havilah, where *there is* gold;

12 And the gold of that land *is* good: ᵃthere *is* bdellium and the onyx stone.

13 And the name of the second river *is* Gihon: the same *is* it that compasseth the whole land of ¹Ethiopia.

14 And the name of the third river *is* ᵃHiddekel:¹ that *is* it which goeth toward the east of ²Assyria. And the fourth river *is* Euphrates.

15 And the LORD God took ¹the man, and put him into the garden of Eden to ²dress it and to keep it.

16 And the LORD God commanded the man, saying, Of every tree of the garden thou mayest freely eat:

17 But of the tree of the knowledge of good and evil, ᵃthou shalt not eat of it: for in the day that thou eatest thereof ᵇthou¹ shalt surely ᶜdie.

18 And the LORD God said, *It is* not good that the man should be alone; ᵃI will make him an ¹help meet for him.

19 ᵃAnd out of the ground the LORD God formed every beast of the field, and every fowl of the air; and ᵇbrought *them* unto ¹Adam to see what he would call them: and whatsoever Adam called every living creature, that *was* the name thereof.

20 And Adam gave names to all cattle, and to the fowl of the air, and to every beast of the field; but for Adam there was not found an ¹help meet for him.

21 And the LORD God caused a ᵃdeep sleep to fall upon Adam, and he slept: and he took one of his ribs, and closed up the flesh instead thereof;

22 And the rib, which the LORD God had taken from man, ¹made he a woman, ᵃand ᵇbrought her unto the man.

23 And Adam said, This *is* now ᵃbone of my bones, and flesh of my flesh: she shall be called ¹Woman, because she was ᵇtaken out of ²Man.

### Cross References (center column)

1:26 ᵃ Gen. 9:6; Ps. 100:3; Eccl. 7:29; [Eph. 4:24]; James 3:9 ᵇ Gen. 9:2; Ps. 8:6–8

1:27 ᵃ Gen. 5:2; 1 Cor. 11:7 ᵇ Matt. 19:4; [Mark 10:6–8]

1:28 ᵃ Gen. 9:1, 7; Lev. 26:9 ᵇ 1 Cor. 9:27 ¹ *fill* ² *move about*

1:29 ᵃ Gen. 9:3; Ps. 104:14, 15 ¹ *yielding* ² *food*

1:30 ᵃ Ps. 145:15 ᵇ Job 38:41 ¹ *a living soul* ² *food*

1:31 ᵃ [Ps. 104:24; 1 Tim. 4:4]

2:1 ᵃ Ps. 33:6

2:2 ᵃ Ex. 20:9–11; 31:17; Heb. 4:4, 10

2:3 ᵃ [Is. 58:13]

2:4 ᵃ Gen. 1:1; Ps. 90:1, 2 ¹ *This is the history*

2:5 ᵃ Gen. 1:11, 12 ᵇ Gen. 7:4; Job 5:10; 38:26–28 ᶜ Gen. 3:23

2:7 ᵃ Gen. 3:19, 23; Ps. 103:14 ᵇ Job 33:4 ᶜ Gen. 7:22 ᵈ 1 Cor. 15:45

2:8 ᵃ Is. 51:3 ᵇ Gen. 3:23, 24 ᶜ Gen. 4:16

2:9 ᵃ Ezek. 31:8 ᵇ [Gen. 3:22; Rev. 2:7; 22:2, 14] ᶜ [Deut. 1:39]

2:10 ¹ *riverheads*

2:11 ᵃ Gen. 25:18

2:12 ᵃ Num. 11:7

2:13 ¹ *Cush*

2:14 ᵃ Dan. 10:4 ¹ The *Tigris* ² Heb. *Ashshur*

2:15 ¹ *Adam* ² *tend or cultivate*

2:17 ᵃ Gen. 3:1, 3, 11, 17 ᵇ Gen. 3:3, 19; [Rom. 6:23] ᶜ Rom. 5:12; 1 Cor. 15:21, 22 ¹ Lit. *dying you shall die*

2:18 ᵃ 1 Cor. 11:8, 9; 1 Tim. 2:13 ¹ *helper comparable to him*

2:19 ᵃ Gen. 1:20, 24 ᵇ Ps. 8:6 ¹ *the man*

2:20 ¹ *helper comparable to him*

2:21 ᵃ Gen. 15:12; 1 Sam. 26:12

2:22 ᵃ Gen. 3:20; 1 Tim. 2:13 ᵇ Heb. 13:4 ¹ Lit. *he built into*

2:23 ᵃ Gen. 29:14 ᵇ 1 Cor. 11:8, 9 ¹ Heb. *Ishshah* ² Heb. *Ish*

24 [a]Therefore shall a man leave his father and his mother, and shall [b]cleave[1] unto his wife: and they shall be one flesh.

25 [a]And they were both naked, the man and his wife, and were not [b]ashamed.

## CHAPTER 3

Now [a]the serpent was [b]more [1]subtil than any beast of the field which the LORD God had made. And he said unto the woman, Yea, hath God said, Ye shall not eat of every tree of the garden?

2 And the woman said unto the serpent, We may eat of the [a]fruit of the trees of the garden:

3 But of the fruit of the tree which *is* in the midst of the garden, God hath said, Ye shall not eat of it, neither shall ye [a]touch it, lest ye die.

4 [a]And the serpent said unto the woman, Ye shall not surely die:

5 For God doth know that in the day ye eat thereof, then your eyes shall be opened, and ye shall be as [1]gods, knowing good and evil.

6 And when the woman [a]saw that the tree *was* good for food, and that it *was* [1]pleasant to the eyes, and a tree to be desired to make *one* wise, she took of the fruit thereof, [b]and did eat, and gave also unto her husband with her; and he did eat.

7 And the eyes of them both were opened, [a]and they knew that they *were* naked; and they sewed fig leaves together, and made themselves [1]aprons.

8 And they heard [a]the [1]voice of the LORD God walking in the garden in the [2]cool of the day: and Adam and his wife [b]hid themselves from the presence of the LORD God amongst the trees of the garden.

9 And the LORD God called unto Adam, and said unto him, Where *art* thou?

10 And he said, I heard thy voice in the garden, [a]and I was afraid, because I *was* naked; and I hid myself.

11 And he said, Who told thee that thou *wast* naked? Hast thou eaten of the tree, whereof I commanded thee that thou shouldest not eat?

12 And the man said, [a]The woman whom thou gavest *to be* with me, she gave me of the tree, and I did eat.

13 And the LORD God said unto the woman, What *is* this *that* thou hast done? And the woman said, [a]The serpent [b]beguiled me, and I did eat.

14 And the LORD God said unto the serpent, Because thou hast done this, thou *art* cursed above all cattle, and above every beast of the field; upon thy belly shalt thou go, and [a]dust shalt thou eat all the days of thy life:

15 And I will put enmity between thee and the woman, and between [a]thy seed and [b]her seed; [c]it[1] shall bruise thy head, and thou shalt bruise his heel.

16 Unto the woman he said, I will greatly multiply thy [1]sorrow and thy conception; [a]in sorrow thou shalt bring forth children; [b]and thy desire *shall be* [2]to thy husband, and he shall [c]rule over thee.

17 And unto Adam he said, [a]Because thou hast hearkened unto the voice of thy wife, and hast eaten of the tree, [b]of which I commanded thee, saying, Thou shalt not eat of it: [c]cursed *is* the ground for thy sake; [d]in [1]sorrow shalt thou eat *of* it all the days of thy life;

18 Thorns also and thistles shall it bring forth to thee; and [a]thou shalt eat the herb of the field;

19 [a]In the sweat of thy face shalt thou eat bread, till thou return unto the ground; for out of it wast thou taken: [b]for dust thou *art,* and [c]unto dust shalt thou return.

20 And Adam called his wife's name [a]Eve;[1] because she was the mother of all living.

21 Unto Adam also and to his wife did the LORD God make [1]coats of skins, and clothed them.

22 And the LORD God said, Behold, the man is become as one of us, to know good and evil: and now, lest he put forth his hand, and take also of the tree of life, and eat, and live for ever:

23 Therefore the LORD God sent him forth from the garden of Eden, [a]to till the ground from whence he was taken.

24 So [a]he drove out the man; and he placed [b]at the east of the garden of Eden [c]Cherubims, and a flaming sword which turned every way, to [1]keep the way of the tree of [d]life.

## CHAPTER 4

And Adam knew Eve his wife; and she conceived, and bare [1]Cain, and said, I have gotten a man from the LORD.

2 And she again bare his brother [1]Abel. And [a]Abel was a keeper of sheep, but Cain was a tiller of the ground.

3 And [1]in process of time it came to pass, that Cain brought of the fruit [a]of the ground an offering unto the LORD.

4 And Abel, he also brought of [a]the firstlings of his flock and of [b]the fat thereof. And the LORD had [c]respect unto Abel and to his offering:

5 But unto Cain and to his offering he had not respect. And Cain was very [1]wroth, and his countenance fell.

---

### Cross-references (center column)

2:24 [a] Matt. 19:5
[b] Mark 10:6–8
[1] *be joined*

2:25 [a] Gen. 3:7, 10
[b] Is. 47:3

3:1 [a] 1 Chr. 21:1
[b] 2 Cor. 11:3
[1] *cunning*

3:2 [a] Gen. 2:16, 17

3:3 [a] Ex. 19:12, 13

3:4 [a] [2 Cor. 11:3]

3:5 [1] *God*

3:6 [a] 1 John 2:16
[b] 1 Tim. 2:14 [1] Lit. *a desirable thing*

3:7 [a] Gen. 2:25 [1] *girding coverings*

3:8 [a] Job 38:1
[b] Job 31:33
[1] *sound* [2] *breeze*

3:10 [a] Gen. 2:25

3:12 [a] [Prov. 28:13]

3:13 [a] 2 Cor. 11:3
[1] *deceived*

3:14 [a] Deut. 28:15–20

3:15 [a] John 8:44
[b] Is. 7:14 [c] Rom. 16:20 [1] Lit. *he*

3:16 [a] John 16:21
[b] Gen. 4:7
[c] 1 Cor. 11:3 [1] *pain* [2] *toward*

3:17 [a] 1 Sam. 15:23 [b] Gen. 2:17
[c] Rom. 8:20–22
[d] Eccl. 2:23 [1] *toil*

3:18 [a] Ps. 104:14

3:19 [a] 2 Thess.

3:10 [b] Gen. 2:7; 5:5 [c] Job 21:26

3:20 [a] 2 Cor. 11:3
[1] *Life* or *Living*

3:21 [1] *tunics*

3:23 [a] Gen. 4:2; 9:20

3:24 [a] Ezek. 31:3, 11 [b] Gen. 2:8 [c] Ps. 104:4 [d] Gen. 2:9
[1] *guard*

4:1 [1] Lit. *Acquire*

4:2 [a] Luke 11:50, 51 [1] Lit. *Breath* or *Nothing*

4:3 [a] Num. 18:12
[1] Lit. *at the end of days*

4:4 [a] Num. 18:17
[b] Lev. 3:16 [c] Heb. 11:4

4:5 [1] *angry*

6 And the LORD said unto Cain, Why art thou wroth? and why is thy countenance fallen?

7 If thou doest well, shalt thou not be accepted? and if thou doest not well, sin lieth at the door. And [1]unto thee *shall be* his desire, and thou [2]shalt rule over him.

8 And Cain talked with Abel his brother: [1]and it came to pass, when they were in the field, that Cain rose up against Abel his brother, and [a]slew him.

9 And the LORD said unto Cain, Where *is* Abel thy brother? And he said, [a]I know not: *Am* I [b]my brother's keeper?

10 And he said, What hast thou done? the voice of thy brother's blood [a]crieth unto me from the ground.

11 And now *art* [a]thou cursed from the earth, which hath opened her mouth to receive thy brother's blood from thy hand;

12 When thou tillest the ground, it shall not henceforth yield unto thee her strength; a fugitive and a vagabond shalt thou be in the earth.

13 And Cain said unto the LORD, My [1]punishment *is* greater than I can bear.

14 Behold, thou hast driven me out this day from the face of the earth; and [a]from thy face shall I be [b]hid; and I shall be a fugitive and a vagabond in the earth; and it shall come to pass, [c]*that* every one that findeth me shall slay me.

15 And the LORD said unto him, [1]Therefore whosoever slayeth Cain, vengeance shall be taken on him [a]sevenfold. And the LORD set a [b]mark upon Cain, lest any finding him should kill him.

16 And Cain [a]went out from the [b]presence of the LORD, and dwelt in the land of [1]Nod, on the east of Eden.

17 And Cain knew his wife; and she conceived, and bare Enoch: and he builded a city, [a]and called the name of the city, after the name of his son, Enoch.

18 And unto Enoch was born Irad: and Irad begat Mehujael: and Mehujael begat Methusael: and Methusael begat Lamech.

19 And Lamech took unto him [a]two wives: the name of the one *was* Adah, and the name of the other Zillah.

20 And Adah bare Jabal: he was the father of such as dwell in tents, and *of such as have* [1]cattle.

21 And his brother's name *was* Jubal: he was the father of all such as handle the harp and [1]organ.

22 And Zillah, she also bare Tubal-cain, an [1]instructor of every artificer in brass and iron: and the sister of Tubal-cain *was* Naamah.

23 And Lamech said unto his wives, Adah and Zillah, Hear my voice; ye wives of Lamech, hearken unto my speech: for I have [1]slain a man to my wounding, and a young man [2]to my hurt.

24 [a]If Cain shall be avenged sevenfold, truly Lamech seventy and sevenfold.

25 And Adam knew his wife again; and she bare a son, and [a]called his name [1]Seth: For God, *said she,* hath appointed me another seed instead of Abel, whom Cain slew.

26 And to Seth, [a]to him also there was born a son; and he called his name [1]Enos: then began men [b]to call upon the name of the LORD.

## CHAPTER 5

THIS *is* the book of the [a]genera-tions[1] of Adam. In the day that God created man, in [b]the likeness of God made he him;

2 [a]Male and female created he them; and [b]blessed them, and called their name [1]Adam, in the day when they were created.

3 And Adam lived an hundred and thirty years, and begat *a son* [a]in his own likeness, after his image; and [b]called his name Seth:

4 [a]And the days of Adam after he had begotten Seth were eight hundred years: [b]and he begat sons and daughters:

5 And all the days that Adam lived were nine hundred and thirty years: [a]and he died.

6 And Seth lived an hundred and five years, and begat [a]Enos:[1]

7 And Seth lived after he begat Enos eight hundred and seven years, and begat sons and daughters:

8 And all the days of Seth were nine hundred and twelve years: and he died.

9 And Enos lived ninety years, and begat Cainan:

10 And Enos lived after he begat Cainan eight hundred and fifteen years, and begat sons and daughters:

11 And all the days of Enos were nine hundred and five years: and he died.

12 And Cainan lived seventy years, and begat [1]Mahalaleel:

13 And Cainan lived after he begat Mahalaleel eight hundred and forty years, and begat sons and daughters:

14 And all the days of Cainan were nine hundred and ten years: and he died.

15 And Mahalaleel lived sixty and five years, and begat Jared:

16 And Mahalaleel lived after he begat Jared eight hundred and thirty years, and begat sons and daughters:

17 And all the days of Mahalaleel

were eight hundred ninety and five years: and he died.

18 And Jared lived an hundred sixty and two years, and he begat ªEnoch:

19 And Jared lived after he begat Enoch eight hundred years, and begat sons and daughters:

20 And all the days of Jared were nine hundred sixty and two years: and he died.

21 And Enoch lived sixty and five years, and begat Methuselah:

22 And Enoch ªwalked with God after he begat Methuselah three hundred years, and begat sons and daughters:

23 And all the days of Enoch were three hundred sixty and five years:

24 And ªEnoch walked with God: and he *was* not; for God ᵇtook him.

25 And Methuselah lived an hundred eighty and seven years, and begat Lamech:

26 And Methuselah lived after he begat Lamech seven hundred eighty and two years, and begat sons and daughters:

27 And all the days of Methuselah were nine hundred sixty and nine years: and he died.

28 And Lamech lived an hundred eighty and two years, and begat a son:

29 And he called his name ªNoah,¹ saying, This *same* shall comfort us concerning our work and toil of our hands, because of the ground ᵇwhich the LORD hath cursed.

30 And Lamech lived after he begat Noah five hundred ninety and five years, and begat sons and daughters:

31 And all the days of Lamech were seven hundred seventy and seven years: and he died.

32 And Noah was five hundred years old: and Noah begat ªShem, Ham, ᵇand Japheth.

## CHAPTER 6

A ND it came to pass, ªwhen men began to multiply on the face of the earth, and daughters were born unto them,

2 That the sons of God saw the daughters of men that they *were* fair; and they ªtook them wives of all which they chose.

3 And the LORD said, ªMy spirit shall not always ᵇstrive¹ with man, ᶜfor that he also *is* flesh: yet his days shall be an hundred and twenty years.

4 There were ¹giants in the earth in those ªdays; and also after that, when the sons of God came in unto the daughters of men, and they bare *children* to them, the same *became* mighty men which *were* of old, men of renown.

5 And ¹GOD saw that the wickedness of man *was* great in the earth, and *that* every ªimagination² of the thoughts of his heart *was* only evil ³continually.

6 And ªit¹ repented the LORD that he had made man on the earth, and it ᵇgrieved him at his ᶜheart.

7 And the LORD said, I will ªdestroy man whom I have created from the face of the earth; both man, and beast, and the creeping thing, and the fowls of the air; for ¹it repenteth me that I have made them.

8 But Noah ªfound grace in the eyes of the LORD.

9¹ These *are* the generations of Noah: ªNoah was a just man *and* ²perfect in his generations, *and* Noah ᵇwalked with God.

10 And Noah begat three sons, ªShem, Ham, and Japheth.

11 The earth also was corrupt ªbefore God, and the earth was ᵇfilled with violence.

12 And God ªlooked upon the earth, and, behold, it was corrupt; for ᵇall flesh had corrupted his way upon the earth.

13 And God said unto Noah, ªThe end of all flesh is come before me; for the earth is filled with violence through them; ᵇand, behold, ᶜI will destroy them with the earth.

14 Make thee an ark of gopher wood; ¹rooms shalt thou make in the ark, and shalt pitch it within and without with pitch.

15 And this *is the fashion* which thou shalt make it *of:* The length of the ark *shall be* three hundred ¹cubits, the breadth of it fifty cubits, and the height of it thirty cubits.

16 A window shalt thou make ¹to the ark, and ²in a cubit shalt thou finish it above; and the door of the ark shalt thou set in the side thereof; *with* lower, second, and third *stories* shalt thou make it.

17 ªAnd, behold, I, even I, ¹do bring a ᵇflood of waters upon the earth, to destroy all flesh, wherein *is* the breath of life, from under heaven; *and* every thing that *is* in the earth shall ᶜdie.

18 But with thee will I establish my ªcovenant; and ᵇthou shalt come into the ark, thou, and thy sons, and thy wife, and thy sons' wives with thee.

19 And of every living thing of all flesh, ªtwo of every *sort* shalt thou bring into the ark, to keep *them* alive with thee; they shall be male and female.

20 Of fowls after their kind, and of ¹cattle after their kind, of every creeping thing of the earth after his kind, two of every *sort* ªshall come unto thee, to keep *them* alive.

### Cross references

5:18 ª Jude 14, 15
5:22 ª Gen. 6:9; 17:1; 24:40; 48:15
5:24 ª 2 Kin. 2:11 ᵇ Heb. 11:5
5:29 ª Luke 3:36 ᵇ Gen. 3:17–19; 4:11 ¹ Lit. *Rest*
5:32 ª Gen. 6:10; 7:13 ᵇ Gen. 10:21
6:1 ª Gen. 1:28
6:2 ª Deut. 7:3, 4
6:3 ª [Gal. 5:16, 17] ᵇ 2 Thess. 2:7 ᶜ Ps. 78:39 ¹ LXX, Syr., Tg., Vg. *abide*
6:4 ª Num. 13:32, 33 ¹ Heb. *nephilim, mighty or fallen ones*
6:5 ª Gen. 8:21 ¹ MT *LORD* ² *intent or thought* ³ Lit. *all the day*
6:6 ª 1 Sam. 15:11, 29 ᵇ Is. 63:10 ᶜ Mark 3:5 ¹ the *LORD was sorry*
6:7 ª Gen. 7:4, 23 ¹ *I am sorry*
6:8 ª Gen. 19:19
6:9 ª 2 Pet. 2:5 ᵇ Gen. 5:22, 24 ¹ *This is the genealogy* ² *blameless*
6:10 ª Gen. 5:32; 7:13
6:11 ª Rom. 2:13 ᵇ Ezek. 8:17
6:12 ª Ps. 14:2; 53:2, 3 ᵇ Ps. 14:1–3
6:13 ª 1 Pet. 4:7 ᵇ Gen. 6:17 ᶜ 2 Pet. 2:4–10
6:14 ¹ Lit. *compartments or nests*
6:15 ¹ A cubit is about 18 inches.
6:16 ¹ for ² *to a cubit from above you shall finish it*
6:17 ª 2 Pet. 2:5 ᵇ 2 Pet. 3:6 ᶜ Luke 16:22 ¹ *am bringing*
6:18 ª Gen. 8:20– 9:17; 17:7 ᵇ Gen. 7:1, 7, 13
6:19 ª Gen. 7:2, 8, 9, 14–16
6:20 ª Gen. 7:9, 15 ¹ *animals*

21 And take thou unto thee of all food that is eaten, and thou shalt gather *it* to thee; and it shall be for food for thee, and for them.

22 ªThus did Noah; ᵇaccording to all that ᶜGod commanded him, so did he.

## CHAPTER 7

AND the ªLORD said unto Noah, ᵇCome thou and all thy house into the ark; for ᶜthee have I seen righteous before me in this generation.

2 Of every ªclean beast thou shalt take to thee by sevens, the male and his female: ᵇand of beasts that *are* not clean by two, the male and his female.

3 Of fowls also of the air by sevens, the male and the female; to keep ¹seed alive upon the face of all the earth.

4 For ¹yet ªseven days, and I will cause it to rain upon the earth ᵇforty days and forty nights; and every living substance that I have made will I ²destroy from off the face of the earth.

5 ªAnd Noah did according unto all that the LORD commanded him.

6 And Noah *was* ªsix hundred years old when the flood of waters was upon the earth.

7 ªAnd Noah went in, and his sons, and his wife, and his sons' wives with him, into the ark, because of the waters of the flood.

8 Of clean beasts, and of beasts that *are* not clean, and of fowls, and of every thing that creepeth upon the earth,

9 There went in two and two unto Noah into the ark, the male and female, as God had commanded Noah.

10 And it came to pass after seven days, that the waters of the flood were upon the earth.

11 In the six hundredth year of Noah's life, in the second month, the seventeenth day of the month, the ªsame day were all ᵇthe fountains of the great deep broken up, and the ᶜwindows of heaven were opened.

12 ªAnd the rain was upon the earth forty days and forty nights.

13 In the selfsame day entered Noah, and Shem, and Ham, and Japheth, the sons of Noah, and Noah's wife, and the three wives of his sons with them, into the ark;

14 ªThey, and every beast after his kind, and all the cattle after their kind, and every creeping thing that creepeth upon the earth after his kind, and every fowl after his kind, every bird of every ᵇsort.

15 And they ªwent in unto Noah

6:22 ª Gen. 7:5; 12:4, 5  ᵇ Gen. 7:5, 9, 16  ᶜ [1 John 5:3]
7:1 ª Matt. 11:28  ᵇ Matt. 24:38  ᶜ Gen. 6:9
7:2 ª Lev. 11  ᵇ Lev. 10:10
7:3 ¹ *the species*
7:4 ª Gen. 7:10  ᵇ Gen. 7:12, 17 ¹ *after seven more days* ² Lit. *blot out*
7:5 ª Gen. 6:22
7:6 ª Gen. 5:4, 32
7:7 ª Matt. 24:38
7:11 ª Matt. 24:39  ᵇ Gen. 8:2  ᶜ Ps. 78:23
7:12 ª Gen. 7:4, 17
7:14 ª Gen. 6:19  ᵇ Gen. 1:21
7:15 ª Gen. 6:19, 20; 7:9
7:16 ª Gen. 7:2, 3
7:17 ª Gen. 7:4, 12; 8:6 ¹ *lifted* ² *rose high*
7:18 ª Ps. 104:26 ¹ *surface*
7:21 ª Gen. 6:7, 13, 17; 7:4 ¹ *the land*
7:22 ª Gen. 2:7 ¹ MT *the spirit of life*
7:23 ª 2 Pet. 2:5
7:24 ª Gen. 8:3, 4
8:1 ª Gen. 19:29  ᵇ Ex. 14:21; 15:10 ¹ *animals* ² *subsided*
8:2 ª Gen. 7:11  ᵇ Deut. 11:17  ᶜ Job 38:37
8:3 ª Gen. 7:24 ¹ *receded* ² *decreased*
8:6 ª Gen. 6:16

into the ark, two and two of all flesh, wherein *is* the breath of life.

16 And they that went in, went in male and female of all flesh, ªas God had commanded him: and the LORD shut him in.

17 ªAnd the flood was forty days upon the earth; and the waters increased, and ¹bare up the ark, and it ²was lift up above the earth.

18 And the waters prevailed, and were increased greatly upon the earth; ªand the ark went upon the ¹face of the waters.

19 And the waters prevailed exceedingly upon the earth; and all the high hills, that *were* under the whole heaven, were covered.

20 Fifteen cubits upward did the waters prevail; and the mountains were covered.

21 ªAnd all flesh died that moved upon ¹the earth, both of fowl, and of cattle, and of beast, and of every creeping thing that creepeth upon the earth, and every man:

22 All in ªwhose nostrils *was* the breath of ¹life, of all that *was* in the dry *land*, died.

23 And every living substance was destroyed which was upon the face of the ground, both man, and cattle, and the creeping things, and the fowl of the heaven; and they were destroyed from the earth: and ªNoah only remained *alive*, and they that *were* with him in the ark.

24 ªAnd the waters prevailed upon the earth an hundred and fifty days.

## CHAPTER 8

AND God ªremembered Noah, and every living thing, and all the ¹cattle that *was* with him in the ark: ᵇand God made a wind to pass over the earth, and the waters ²assuaged;

2 ªThe fountains also of the deep and the windows of heaven were ᵇstopped, and ᶜthe rain from heaven was restrained;

3 And the waters ¹returned from off the earth continually: and after the end ªof the hundred and fifty days the waters ²were abated.

4 And the ark rested in the seventh month, on the seventeenth day of the month, upon the mountains of Ararat.

5 And the waters decreased continually until the tenth month: in the tenth *month*, on the first *day* of the month, were the tops of the mountains seen.

6 And it came to pass at the end of forty days, that Noah opened ªthe window of the ark which he had made:

7 And he sent forth a raven, which went forth to and fro, until the wa-

ters were dried up from off the earth.

8 Also he sent forth a dove from him, to see if the waters were abated from off the face of the ground;

9 But the dove found no rest for the sole of her foot, and she returned unto him into the ark, for the waters *were* on the face of the whole earth: then he put forth his hand, and took her, and pulled her in unto him into the ark.

10 And he stayed yet other seven days; and again he sent forth the dove out of the ark;

11 And the dove came in to him in the evening; and, lo, in her mouth *was* an olive leaf 'pluckt off: so Noah knew that the waters were abated from off the earth.

12 And he stayed yet other seven days; and sent forth the dove; which returned not again unto him any more.

13 And it came to pass in the six hundredth and first year, in the first *month,* the first *day* of the month, the waters were dried up from off the earth: and Noah removed the covering of the ark, and looked, and, behold, the face of the ground was dry.

14 And in the second month, on the seven and twentieth day of the month, was the earth dried.

15 And God spake unto Noah, saying,

16 Go forth of the ark, ᵃthou, and thy wife, and thy sons, and thy sons' wives with thee.

17 Bring forth with thee every living thing that *is* with thee, of all flesh, *both* of fowl, and of cattle, and of every creeping thing that creepeth upon the earth; that they may breed abundantly in the earth, and ᵃbe fruitful, and multiply upon the earth.

18 And Noah went forth, and his sons, and his wife, and his sons' wives with him:

19 Every beast, every creeping thing, and every fowl, *and* whatsoever creepeth upon the earth, after their 'kinds, went forth out of the ark.

20 And Noah builded an ᵃaltar unto the LORD; and took of ᵇevery clean beast, and of every clean fowl, and offered ᶜburnt offerings on the altar.

21 And the LORD smelled ᵃa 'sweet savour; and the LORD said in his heart, I will not again ᵇcurse the ground any more for man's sake; ²for the ᶜimagination³ of man's heart *is* evil from his youth; ᵈneither will I again smite any more every thing living, as I have done.

22 ᵃWhile the earth remaineth, seedtime and harvest, and cold and heat, and summer and winter, and ᵇday and night shall not cease.

## CHAPTER 9

**A**ND God blessed Noah and his sons, and said unto them, ᵃBe fruitful, and multiply, and 'replenish the earth.

2 ᵃAnd the fear of you and the dread of you shall be upon every beast of the earth, and upon every fowl of the air, upon all that moveth *upon* the earth, and upon all the fishes of the sea; into your hand are they 'delivered.

3 ᵃEvery moving thing that liveth shall be 'meat for you; even as the ᵇgreen herb have I given you ᶜall things.

4 ᵃBut flesh with the life thereof, *which is* the blood thereof, shall ye not eat.

5 And surely your blood of your lives will I require; ᵃat the hand of every beast will I require it, and ᵇat the hand of man; at the hand of every ᶜman's brother will I require the life of man.

6 ᵃWhoso sheddeth man's blood, by man shall his blood be shed: ᵇfor in the image of God made he man.

7 And you, ᵃbe ye fruitful, and multiply; bring forth abundantly in the earth, and multiply therein.

8 And God spake unto Noah, and to his sons with him, saying,

9 And I, ᵃbehold, I establish ᵇmy covenant with you, and with your 'seed after you;

10 ᵃAnd with every living creature that *is* with you, of the fowl, of the cattle, and of every beast of the earth with you; from all that go out of the ark, to every beast of the earth.

11 And ᵃI will establish my covenant with you; neither shall all flesh be cut off any more by the waters of a flood; neither shall there any more be a flood to destroy the earth.

12 And God said, ᵃThis *is* the 'token of the covenant which I make between me and you and every living creature that *is* with you, for perpetual generations:

13 I do set ᵃmy 'bow in the cloud, and it shall be for a ²token of a covenant between me and the earth.

14 And it shall come to pass, when I bring a cloud over the earth, that the 'bow shall be seen in the cloud:

15 And ᵃI will remember my covenant, which *is* between me and you and every living creature of all flesh; and the waters shall no more become a flood to destroy all flesh.

16 And the 'bow shall be in the cloud; and I will look upon it, that I may remember ᵃthe everlasting covenant between God and every living creature of all flesh that *is* upon the earth.

17 And God said unto Noah, This *is*

### Center reference column

8:11 ¹ *freshly plucked*
8:16 ᵃ Gen. 7:13
8:17 ᵃ Gen. 1:22, 28; 9:1, 7
8:19 ¹ Lit. *families*
8:20 ᵃ Gen. 12:7; Ex. 29:18, 25 ᵇ Gen. 7:2; Lev. 11 ᶜ Gen. 22:2; Ex. 10:25
8:21 ᵃ Ex. 29:18, 25; Lev. 1:9; Ezek. 20:41; 2 Cor. 2:15; Eph. 5:2 ᵇ Gen. 3:17; 6:7, 13, 17; Is. 54:9 ᶜ Gen. 6:5; 11:6; Job 14:4; Ps. 51:5; Jer. 17:9; Rom. 1:21; 3:23; Eph. 2:1–3 ᵈ Gen. 9:11, 15 ¹ *soothing aroma* ² *although* ³ *intent or thought*
8:22 ᵃ Is. 54:9 ᵇ Ps. 74:16; Jer. 33:20, 25

9:1 ᵃ Gen. 1:28, 29; 8:17; 9:7, 19; 10:32 ¹ Lit. *fill*
9:2 ᵃ Gen. 1:26, 28; Ps. 8:6 ¹ Lit. *given*
9:3 ᵃ Deut. 12:15; 14:3, 9, 11; Acts 10:12, 13 ᵇ Rom. 14:14, 20; 1 Cor. 10:23, 26; Col. 2:16; [1 Tim. 4:3, 4] ᶜ Gen. 1:29 ¹ *food*
9:4 ᵃ Lev. 7:26; 17:10–16; 19:26; Deut. 12:16, 23; 15:23; 1 Sam. 14:33, 34; Acts 15:20, 29
9:5 ᵃ Ex. 21:28 ᵇ Gen. 4:9, 10; Ps. 9:12 ᶜ Acts 17:26
9:6 ᵃ Ex. 21:12–14; Lev. 24:17; Num. 35:33; Matt. 26:52 ᵇ Gen. 1:26, 27
9:7 ᵃ Gen. 9:1, 19
9:9 ᵃ Gen. 6:18 ᵇ Is. 54:9 ¹ *descendants*
9:10 ᵃ Ps. 145:9
9:11 ᵃ Gen. 8:21; Is. 54:9
9:12 ᵃ Gen. 9:13, 17; 17:11 ¹ *sign*
9:13 ᵃ Ezek. 1:28; Rev. 4:3 ¹ *rainbow* ² *sign*
9:14 ¹ *rainbow*
9:15 ᵃ Lev. 26:42, 45; Deut. 7:9; Ezek. 16:60
9:16 ᵃ Gen. 17:13, 19; 2 Sam. 23:5; Is. 55:3; Jer. 32:40; Heb. 13:20 ¹ *rainbow*

the ¹token of the covenant, which I have established between me and all flesh that *is* upon the earth.

18 And the sons of Noah, that went forth of the ark, were Shem, and Ham, and Japheth: ᵃand Ham *is* the father of Canaan.

19 ᵃThese *are* the three sons of Noah: ᵇand of them was the whole earth ¹overspread.

20 And Noah began *to be* ᵃan ¹husbandman, and he planted a vineyard:

21 And he drank of the wine, ᵃand was drunken; and he was uncovered within his tent.

22 And Ham, the father of Canaan, saw the nakedness of his father, and told his two brethren without.

23 ᵃAnd Shem and Japheth took a garment, and laid *it* upon both their shoulders, and went backward, and covered the nakedness of their father; and their faces *were* ¹backward, and they saw not their father's nakedness.

24 And Noah awoke from his wine, and knew what his younger son had done unto him.

25 And he said, ᵃCursed *be* Canaan; a ᵇservant of servants shall he be unto his brethren.

26 And he said, ᵃBlessed *be* the LORD God of Shem; and Canaan shall be his servant.

27 God shall ᵃenlarge Japheth, ᵇand he shall dwell in the tents of Shem; and Canaan shall be his servant.

28 And Noah lived after the flood three hundred and fifty years.

29 And all the days of Noah were nine hundred and fifty years: and he died.

## CHAPTER 10

Now ¹these *are* the generations of the sons of Noah, Shem, Ham, and Japheth: ᵃand unto them were sons born after the flood.

2 ᵃThe sons of Japheth; Gomer, and Magog, and Madai, and Javan, and Tubal, and Meshech, and Tiras.

3 And the sons of Gomer; Ashkenaz, and Riphath, and Togarmah.

4 And the sons of Javan; Elishah, and Tarshish, Kittim, and Dodanim.

5 By these were ᵃthe ¹isles of the Gentiles ²divided in their lands; every one ³after his tongue, after their families, ⁴in their nations.

6 ᵃAnd the sons of Ham; Cush, and Mizraim, and ¹Phut, and Canaan.

7 And the sons of Cush; Seba, and Havilah, and Sabtah, and Raamah, and Sabtechah: and the sons of Raamah; Sheba, and Dedan.

8 And Cush begat ᵃNimrod: he began to be a mighty one in the earth.

9 He was a mighty ᵃhunter ᵇbefore the LORD: wherefore it is said, Even

as Nimrod the mighty hunter before the LORD.

10 ᵃAnd the beginning of his kingdom was ᵇBabel, and Erech, and Accad, and Calneh, in the land of Shinar.

11 Out of that land ¹went ᵃforth Asshur, and builded Nineveh, and ²the city Rehoboth, and Calah,

12 And Resen between Nineveh and Calah: the same *is* ¹a great city.

13 And Mizraim begat Ludim, and Anamim, and Lehabim, and Naphtuhim,

14 And Pathrusim, and Casluhim, (ᵃout of whom came ¹Philistim,) and Caphtorim.

15 And Canaan begat ¹Sidon his firstborn, and ᵃHeth,

16 ᵃAnd the Jebusite, and the Amorite, and the ¹Girgasite,

17 And the Hivite, and the Arkite, and the Sinite,

18 And the Arvadite, and the Zemarite, and the Hamathite: and afterward were the families of the Canaanites spread abroad.

19 ᵃAnd the border of the Canaanites was from Sidon, as thou comest to Gerar, unto Gaza; as thou goest, unto Sodom, and Gomorrah, and Admah, and Zeboim, even unto Lasha.

20 These *are* the sons of Ham, after their families, after their tongues, in their countries, *and* in their nations.

21 Unto Shem also, the father of all the children of Eber, the ¹brother of Japheth the elder, even to him were *children* born.

22 The ᵃchildren¹ of Shem; Elam, and Asshur, and ᵇArphaxad, and Lud, and Aram.

23 And the ¹children of Aram; Uz, and Hul, and Gether, and ²Mash.

24 And Arphaxad begat ᵃSalah; and Salah begat Eber.

25 ᵃAnd unto Eber were born two sons: the name of one *was* ¹Peleg; for in his days was the earth divided; and his brother's name *was* Joktan.

26 And Joktan begat Almodad, and Sheleph, and Hazarmaveth, and Jerah,

27 And Hadoram, and Uzal, and Diklah,

28 And ¹Obal, and Abimael, and Sheba,

29 And Ophir, and Havilah, and Jobab: all these *were* the sons of Joktan.

30 And their dwelling was from Mesha, as thou goest unto Sephar a mount of the east.

31 These *are* the sons of Shem, after their families, ¹after their tongues, in their lands, after their nations.

32 ᵃThese *are* the families of the

9:17 ¹ *sign*
9:18 ᵃ Gen. 9:25–27; 10:6
9:19 ᵃ Gen. 5:32
ᵇ Gen. 9:1, 7; 10:32; 1 Chr. 1:4
¹ *populated*
9:20 ᵃ Gen. 3:19, 23; 4:2; Prov. 12:11; Jer. 31:24
¹ *farmer*
9:21 ᵃ Prov. 20:1; Eph. 5:18
9:23 ᵃ Ex. 20:12; Gal. 6:1 ¹ *turned away*
9:25 ᵃ Deut. 27:16; Josh. 9:23, 27
ᵇ Josh. 9:23; 1 Kin. 9:20, 21
9:26 ᵃ Gen. 14:20; 24:27; Ps. 144:15; Heb. 11:16
9:27 ᵃ Gen. 10:2–5; 39:3; Is. 66:19
ᵇ Luke 3:36; John 1:14; Eph. 2:13, 14; 3:6
10:1 ᵃ Gen. 9:1, 7, 19 ¹ *this is the genealogy*
10:2 ᵃ 1 Chr. 1:5–7
10:5 ᵃ Gen. 11:8; Ps. 72:10; Jer. 2:10; 25:22
¹ *coastland peoples* ² *separated into* ³ *according to his language* ⁴ *into*
10:6 ᵃ 1 Chr. 1:8–16
¹ Or *Put*
10:8 ᵃ Mic. 5:6
10:9 ᵃ Jer. 16:16; Mic. 7:2 ᵇ Gen. 21:20
10:10 ᵃ Mic. 5:6
ᵇ Gen. 11:9
10:11 ᵃ Gen. 25:18; 2 Kin. 19:36; Mic. 5:6 ¹ *he went to Assyria* ² Or *Rehoboth-Ir*
10:12 ¹ *the principal city*
10:14 ᵃ 1 Chr. 1:12
¹ *the Philistines*
10:15 ᵃ Gen. 23:3
¹ *Zidon*, 1 Chr. 1:13
10:16 ᵃ Gen. 14:7; 15:19–21; Deut. 7:1; Neh. 9:8
¹ *Girgashite*, 1 Chr. 1:14
10:19 ᵃ Gen. 13:12, 14, 15, 17; 15:18–21; Num. 34:2–12
10:21 ¹ Or *older brother of Japheth*
10:22 ᵃ Gen. 11:10–26; 1 Chr. 1:17–28 ᵇ Gen. 10:24; 11:10; Luke 3:36 ¹ Lit. *sons*
10:23 ¹ Lit. *sons* ˣ LXX *Meshech* and 1 Chr. 1:17
10:24 ᵃ Gen. 11:12; Luke 3:35　10:25 ᵃ 1 Chr. 1:19 ¹ Lit. *Division*　10:28 ¹ *Ebal*, 1 Chr. 1:22　10:31 ¹ *according to their languages*　10:32 ᵃ Gen. 10:1

sons of Noah, after their generations, in their nations: <sup>b</sup>and by these were the nations divided in the earth after the flood.

## CHAPTER 11

A<sup>ND</sup> the whole earth was of one <sup>1</sup>language, and of one speech.

2 And it came to pass, as they journeyed from the east, that they found a plain in the land <sup>a</sup>of Shinar; and they dwelt there.

3 And they said one to another, <sup>1</sup>Go to, let us make brick, and burn them thoroughly. And they had brick for stone, and <sup>2</sup>slime had they for morter.

4 And they said, Go to, let us build us a city and a tower, <sup>a</sup>whose top *may reach* unto heaven; and let us make us a <sup>b</sup>name, lest we <sup>c</sup>be scattered abroad <sup>1</sup>upon the face of the whole earth.

5 <sup>a</sup>And the LORD came down to see the city and the tower, which the children of men builded.

6 And the LORD said, Behold, <sup>a</sup>the people *is* one, and they have all <sup>b</sup>one language; and this they begin to do: and now nothing will be restrained from them, which they <sup>1</sup>have <sup>c</sup>imagined to do.

7 <sup>1</sup>Go to, <sup>a</sup>let us go down, and there <sup>b</sup>confound their language, that they may not understand one another's speech.

8 So <sup>a</sup>the LORD scattered them abroad from thence <sup>b</sup>upon<sup>1</sup> the face of all the earth: and they left off to build the city.

9 Therefore is the name of it called <sup>1</sup>Babel; <sup>a</sup>because the LORD did there <sup>2</sup>confound the language of all the earth: and from thence did the LORD scatter them abroad <sup>3</sup>upon the face of all the earth.

10 <sup>a</sup>These<sup>1</sup> *are* the generations of Shem: Shem *was* an hundred years old, and begat Arphaxad two years after the flood:

11 And Shem lived after he begat Arphaxad five hundred years, and begat sons and daughters.

12 And Arphaxad lived five and thirty years, <sup>a</sup>and begat Salah:

13 And Arphaxad lived after he begat Salah four hundred and three years, and begat sons and daughters.

14 And Salah lived thirty years, and begat Eber:

15 And Salah lived after he begat Eber four hundred and three years, and begat sons and daughters.

16 <sup>a</sup>And Eber lived four and thirty years, and begat <sup>b</sup>Peleg:

17 And Eber lived after he begat Peleg four hundred and thirty years, and begat sons and daughters.

18 And Peleg lived thirty years, and begat Reu:

19 And Peleg lived after he begat Reu two hundred and nine years, and begat sons and daughters.

20 And Reu lived two and thirty years, and begat <sup>a</sup>Serug:

21 And Reu lived after he begat Serug two hundred and seven years, and begat sons and daughters.

22 And Serug lived thirty years, and begat Nahor:

23 And Serug lived after he begat Nahor two hundred years, and begat sons and daughters.

24 And Nahor lived nine and twenty years, and begat <sup>a</sup>Terah:

25 And Nahor lived after he begat Terah an hundred and nineteen years, and begat sons and daughters.

26 And Terah lived seventy years, and <sup>a</sup>begat <sup>1</sup>Abram, Nahor, and Haran.

27 Now <sup>1</sup>these *are* the generations of Terah: Terah begat <sup>a</sup>Abram, Nahor, and Haran; and Haran begat Lot.

28 And Haran died before his father Terah in the land of his nativity, in Ur of the Chaldees.

29 And Abram and Nahor took them wives: the name of Abram's wife *was* <sup>a</sup>Sarai;<sup>1</sup> and the name of Nahor's wife, <sup>b</sup>Milcah, the daughter of Haran, the father of Milcah, and the father of Iscah.

30 But <sup>a</sup>Sarai was barren; she *had* no child.

31 And Terah <sup>a</sup>took Abram his son, and Lot the son of Haran his son's son, and Sarai his daughter in law, his son Abram's wife; and they went forth with them from <sup>b</sup>Ur of the Chaldees, to go into <sup>c</sup>the land of Canaan; and they came unto Haran, and dwelt there.

32 And the days of Terah were two hundred and five years: and Terah died in Haran.

## CHAPTER 12

N<sup>ow</sup> the <sup>a</sup>LORD had said unto Abram, Get thee <sup>b</sup>out of thy country, and from thy kindred, and from thy father's house, unto a land that I will shew thee:

2 <sup>a</sup>And I will make of thee a great nation, <sup>b</sup>and I will bless thee, and make thy name great; <sup>c</sup>and thou shalt be a blessing:

3 <sup>a</sup>And I will bless them that bless thee, and curse him that curseth thee: and in <sup>b</sup>thee shall all families of the earth be <sup>c</sup>blessed.

4 So Abram departed, as the LORD had spoken unto him; and Lot went with him: and Abram *was* seventy and five years old when he departed out of Haran.

5 And Abram took Sarai his wife, and Lot his brother's son, and all their

### Center column references

10:32<sup>b</sup> Gen. 9:19; 11:8
11:1 <sup>1</sup> Lit. *lip*
11:2 <sup>a</sup> Gen. 10:10; 14:1; Dan. 1:2
11:3 <sup>1</sup> *Come* <sup>2</sup> *asphalt*
11:4 <sup>a</sup> Deut. 1:28; 9:1; Ps. 107:26 <sup>b</sup> Gen. 6:4; 2 Sam. 8:13 <sup>c</sup> Deut. 4:27 <sup>1</sup> *over*
11:5 <sup>a</sup> Gen. 18:21; Ex. 3:8; 19:11, 18, 20
11:6 <sup>a</sup> Gen. 9:19; Acts 17:26 <sup>b</sup> Gen. 11:1 <sup>c</sup> Deut. 31:21; Ps. 2:1 <sup>1</sup> *propose*
11:7 <sup>a</sup> Gen. 1:26 <sup>b</sup> Gen. 42:23; Ex. 4:11; Deut. 28:49; Is. 33:19; Jer. 5:15 <sup>1</sup> *Come*
11:8 <sup>a</sup> Gen. 11:4; Deut. 32:8; Ps. 92:9; [Luke 1:51] <sup>b</sup> Gen. 10:25, 32 <sup>1</sup> *over*
11:9 <sup>a</sup> 1 Cor. 14:23 <sup>1</sup> *Babylon*, lit. *Confusion* <sup>2</sup> *confuse* <sup>3</sup> *over*
11:10 <sup>a</sup> Gen. 10:22–25; 1 Chr. 1:17 <sup>1</sup> *This is the genealogy*
11:12 <sup>a</sup> Luke 3:35
11:16 <sup>a</sup> 1 Chr. 1:19 <sup>b</sup> Luke 3:35
11:20 <sup>a</sup> Luke 3:35
11:24 <sup>a</sup> Gen. 11:31; Josh. 24:2; Luke 3:34
11:26 <sup>a</sup> Josh. 24:2; 1 Chr. 1:26 <sup>1</sup> *Called Abraham*, Gen. 17:5
11:27 <sup>a</sup> Gen. 11:31; 17:5 <sup>1</sup> *this is the genealogy*
11:29 <sup>a</sup> Gen. 17:15; 20:12 <sup>b</sup> Gen. 22:20, 23; 24:15 <sup>1</sup> *Called Sarah*, Gen. 17:15
11:30 <sup>a</sup> Gen. 16:1, 2
11:31 <sup>a</sup> Gen. 12:1 <sup>b</sup> Acts 7:4 <sup>c</sup> Gen. 10:19
12:1 <sup>a</sup> Acts 7:2, 3 <sup>b</sup> Gen. 13:9
12:2 <sup>a</sup> Deut. 26:5 <sup>b</sup> Gen. 22:17; 24:35 <sup>c</sup> Gen. 28:4
12:3 <sup>a</sup> Num. 24:9 <sup>b</sup> Acts 3:25 <sup>c</sup> Is. 41:27

¹substance that they had gathered, and ᵃthe ²souls that they had gotten ᵇin Haran; and they ᶜwent forth to go into the land of Canaan; and into the land of Canaan they came.

6 And Abram ᵃpassed through the land unto the place of ¹Sichem, ᵇunto ²the plain of Moreh. ᶜAnd the Canaanite *was* then in the land.

7 ᵃAnd the LORD appeared unto Abram, and said, ᵇUnto thy ¹seed will I give this land: and there builded he an ᶜaltar unto the LORD, who appeared unto him.

8 And he removed from thence unto a mountain on the east of Beth-el, and pitched his tent, *having* Beth-el on the west, and Hai on the east: and there he builded an altar unto the LORD, and ᵃcalled upon the name of the LORD.

9 And Abram journeyed, ᵃgoing on still toward the ¹south.

10 And there was ᵃa famine in the land: and Abram ᵇwent down into Egypt to sojourn there; for the famine *was* ᶜgrievous in the land.

11 And it came to pass, when he was come near to enter into Egypt, that he said unto Sarai his wife, Behold now, I know that thou *art* ᵃa ¹fair woman to look upon:

12 Therefore it shall come to pass, when the Egyptians shall see thee, that they shall say, ¹his *is* his wife: and they ᵃwill kill me, but they will save thee alive.

13 ᵃSay, I pray thee, thou *art* my ᵇsister: that it may be well with me for thy sake; and my soul shall live because of thee.

14 And it came to pass, that, when Abram was come into Egypt, the Egyptians beheld the woman that she *was* very fair.

15 The princes also of Pharaoh saw her, and commended her before Pharaoh: and the woman was taken into Pharaoh's house.

16 And he ᵃentreated¹ Abram well for her sake: and he ᵇhad sheep, and oxen, and ᵃhe asses, and menservants, and maidservants, and she asses, and camels.

17 And the LORD ᵃplagued Pharaoh and his house with great plagues because of Sarai Abram's wife.

18 And Pharaoh called Abram, and said, ᵃWhat *is* this *that* thou hast done unto me? why didst thou not tell me that she *was* thy wife?

19 Why saidst thou, She *is* my sister? so I might have taken her to me to wife: now therefore behold thy wife, take *her*, and go thy way.

20 ᵃAnd Pharaoh commanded *his* men concerning him: and they sent him away, and his wife, and all that he had.

---

**Cross-references (center column):**

12:5 ᵃ Gen. 14:14
ᵇ Gen. 11:31 ᶜ Gen. 13:18 ¹ *possessions* ² *people*
12:6 ᵃ Heb. 11:9 ᵇ Deut. 11:30 ᶜ Gen. 10:18, 19 ¹ Or *Shechem* ² Heb. *Alon Moreh, the terebinth tree of Moreh*
12:7 ᵃ Gen. 17:1; 18:1 ᵇ Gen. 13:15; 15:18; 17:8 ᶜ Gen. 13:4, 18; 22:9 ¹ *descendants*
12:8 ᵃ Gen. 4:26; 13:4; 21:33
12:9 ᵃ Gen. 13:1, 3; 20:1; 24:62 ¹ Heb. *Negev*
12:10 ᵃ Gen. 26:1 ᵇ Ps. 105:13 ᶜ Gen. 43:1
12:11 ᵃ Gen. 12:14; 26:7; 29:17 ¹ *beautiful*
12:12 ᵃ Gen. 20:11; 26:7
12:13 ᵃ Gen. 20:1–18; 26:6–11 ᵇ Gen. 20:12
12:16 ᵃ Gen. 20:14 ᵇ Gen. 13:2 ¹ *treated* ² *male donkeys*
12:17 ᵃ 1 Chr. 16:21
12:18 ᵃ Gen. 20:9, 10; 26:10
12:20 ᵃ [Prov. 21:1]

13:1 ᵃ Gen. 12:4; 14:12, 16 ᵇ Gen. 12:9 ¹ Heb. *Negev*
13:2 ᵃ Gen. 24:35; 26:14
13:3 ᵃ Gen. 12:8, 9 ¹ Or *Ai*
13:4 ᵃ Gen. 12:7, 8; 21:33 ᵇ Ps. 116:17
13:6 ᵃ Gen. 36:7 ¹ *support*
13:7 ᵃ Gen. 26:20 ᵇ Gen. 12:6; 15:20, 21 ¹ *livestock*
13:8 ᵃ 1 Cor. 6:7
13:9 ᵃ Gen. 20:15; 34:10 ᵇ Gen. 13:11, 14 ᶜ [Rom. 12:18]
13:10 ᵃ Gen. 19:17–29 ᵇ Gen. 19:24 ᶜ Gen. 2:8, 10 ᵈ Deut. 34:3
13:11 ¹ *for himself*
13:12 ᵃ Gen. 19:24, 25, 29 ᵇ Gen. 14:12, 19 ¹ *as far as*
13:13 ᵃ Gen. 18:20, 21 ᵇ Gen. 6:11; 39:9 ¹ *sinful*
13:14 ᵃ Gen. 13:11 ᵇ Gen. 28:14
13:15 ᵃ Acts 7:5 ᵇ 2 Chr. 20:7 ¹ *descendants*
13:16 ᵃ Gen. 22:17 ¹ *descendants*

---

## CHAPTER 13

AND Abram went up out of Egypt, he, and his wife, and all that he had, and ᵃLot with him, ᵇinto the ¹south.

2 ᵃAnd Abram *was* very rich in cattle, in silver, and in gold.

3 And he went on his journeys ᵃfrom the south even to Beth-el, unto the place where his tent had been at the beginning, between Beth-el and ¹Hai;

4 Unto the ᵃplace of the altar, which he had made there at the first: and there Abram ᵇcalled on the name of the LORD.

5 And Lot also, which went with Abram, had flocks, and herds, and tents.

6 And ᵃthe land was not able to ¹bear them, that they might dwell together: for their substance was great, so that they could not dwell together.

7 And there was ᵃa strife between the herdmen of Abram's ¹cattle and the herdmen of Lot's cattle: ᵇand the Canaanite and the Perizzite dwelled then in the land.

8 And Abram said unto Lot, ᵃLet there be no strife, I pray thee, between me and thee, and between my herdmen and thy herdmen; for we *be* brethren.

9 ᵃ*Is* not the whole land before thee? ᵇseparate thyself, I pray thee, from me: ᶜif *thou wilt take* the left hand, then I will go to the right; or if *thou depart* to the right hand, then I will go to the left.

10 And Lot lifted up his eyes, and beheld all ᵃthe plain of Jordan, that it *was* well watered every where, before the LORD ᵇdestroyed Sodom and Gomorrah, ᶜ*even* as the garden of the LORD, like the land of Egypt, as thou comest unto ᵈZoar.

11 Then Lot chose ¹him all the plain of Jordan; and Lot journeyed east: and they separated themselves the one from the other.

12 Abram dwelled in the land of Canaan, and Lot ᵃdwelled in the cities of the plain, and ᵇpitched *his* tent ¹toward Sodom.

13 But the men of Sodom ᵃ*were* wicked and ᵇsinners¹ before the LORD exceedingly.

14 And the LORD said unto Abram, after that Lot ᵃwas separated from him, Lift up now thine eyes, and look from the place where thou art ᵇnorthward, and southward, and eastward, and westward:

15 For all the land which thou seest, ᵃto thee will I give it, and ᵇto thy ¹seed for ever.

16 And ᵃI will make thy ¹seed as the dust of the earth: so that if a man can

number the dust of the earth, *then* shall thy seed also be numbered.

17 Arise, walk through the land in the length of it and in the breadth of it; for I will give it unto thee.

18 ªThen Abram removed *his* tent, and came and ᵇdwelt in ¹the plain of Mamre, ᶜwhich *is* in Hebron, and built there a ᵈaltar unto the LORD.

## CHAPTER 14

AND it came to pass in the days of Amraphel king ªof Shinar, Arioch king of Ellasar, Chedorlaomer king of ᵇElam, and Tidal king of ¹nations;

2 *That these* made war with Bera king of Sodom, and with Birsha king of Gomorrah, Shinab king of ªAdmah, and Shemeber king of Zeboiim, and the king of Bela, which is ᵇZoar.

3 All these were joined together in the vale of Siddim, ªwhich is the salt sea.

4 Twelve years ªthey served Chedorlaomer, and in the thirteenth year they rebelled.

5 And in the fourteenth year came Chedorlaomer, and the kings that *were* with him, and ¹smote ªthe Rephaims in Ashteroth Karnaim, and ᵇthe Zuzims in Ham, ᶜand the Emims in Shaveh Kiriathaim,

6 ªAnd the Horites in their mount Seir, unto El-paran, which *is* by the wilderness.

7 And they returned, and came to En-mishpat, which is Kadesh, and smote all the country of the Amalekites, and also the Amorites, that dwelt ªin Hazezon-tamar.

8 And there went out the king of Sodom, and the king of Gomorrah, and the king of Admah, and the king of Zeboiim, and the king of Bela (the same *is* Zoar;) and they joined battle with them in the vale of Siddim;

9 With Chedorlaomer the king of Elam, and with Tidal king of ¹nations, and Amraphel king of Shinar, and Arioch king of Ellasar; four kings ²with five.

10 And the vale of Siddim *was full of* ªslimepits;¹ and the kings of Sodom and Gomorrah fled, and fell there; and they that remained fled ᵇto the mountain.

11 And they took ªall the goods of Sodom and Gomorrah, and all their ¹victuals, and went their way.

12 And they took Lot, Abram's ªbrother's son, ᵇwho dwelt in Sodom, and his goods, and departed.

13 And there came one that had escaped, and told Abram the ªHebrew; for ᵇhe dwelt ¹in the ²plain of Mamre the Amorite, brother of Eshcol, and brother of Aner: ᶜand these *were* ³confederate with Abram.

14 And ªwhen Abram heard that ᵇhis

brother was taken captive, he armed his trained *servants,* ᶜborn in his own house, three hundred and eighteen, and pursued *them* ᵈunto Dan.

15 And he divided himself against them, he and his servants, by night, and ªsmote them, and pursued them unto Hobah, which *is* on the ¹left hand of Damascus.

16 And he ªbrought back all the goods, and also brought again his brother Lot, and his goods, and the women also, and the people.

17 And the king of Sodom ªwent out to meet him ᵇafter his return from the ¹slaughter of Chedorlaomer, and of the kings that *were* with him, at the valley of Shaveh, which *is* the ᶜking's ²dale.

18 And ªMelchizedek king of Salem brought forth ᵇbread and wine: and he *was* ᶜthe priest of ᵈthe most high God.

19 And he blessed him, and said, ªBlessed *be* Abram of the most high God, ᵇpossessor of heaven and earth:

20 And ªblessed be the most high God, which hath delivered thine enemies into thy hand. And he ᵇgave him ¹tithes of all.

21 And the king of Sodom said unto Abram, Give me the persons, and take the goods to thyself.

22 And Abram ªsaid to the king of Sodom, I ᵇhave lift up mine hand unto the LORD, the most high God, ᶜthe possessor of heaven and earth,

23 That ªI will not *take* from a thread even to a ¹shoelatchet, and that I will not take any thing that *is* thine, lest thou shouldest say, I have made Abram rich:

24 Save only that which the young men have eaten, and the portion of the men which went with me, Aner, Eshcol, and Mamre; let them take their portion.

## CHAPTER 15

AFTER these things the word of the LORD came unto Abram ªin a vision, saying, ᵇFear not, Abram: I *am* thy ᶜshield, *and* thy exceeding ᵈgreat reward.

2 ªAnd Abram said, Lord GOD, what wilt thou give me, ᵇseeing I go childless, and the ¹steward of my house *is* this Eliezer of Damascus?

3 And Abram said, Behold, to me thou hast given no seed: and, lo, ªone¹ born in my house is mine heir.

4 And, behold, the word of the LORD *came* unto him, saying, This shall not be thine heir; but he that ªshall come forth out of thine own bowels shall be thine heir.

5 And he brought him forth abroad, and said, Look now toward heaven, and ªtell¹ ᵇthe stars, if thou be able to

13:18 ª Gen. 26:17 ᵇ Gen. 14:13 ᶜ Gen. 23:2; 35:27 ᵈ Gen. 8:20; 22:8, 9 ¹ Heb. *Alon Mamre, terebinth trees of Mamre*

14:1 ª Gen. 10:10; 11:2 ᵇ Is. 11:11; 21:2 ¹ Heb. *Goyim*

14:2 ª Deut. 29:23 ᵇ Gen. 13:10; 19:22

14:3 ª Num. 34:12

14:4 ª Gen. 9:26

14:5 ª Gen. 15:20 ᵇ Deut. 2:20 ᶜ Deut. 2:10 ¹ *attacked*

14:6 ª Deut. 2:12, 22

14:7 ª 2 Chr. 20:2

14:9 ¹ Heb. *Goyim* ² *against*

14:10 ª Gen. 11:3 ᵇ Gen. 19:17, 30 ¹ *asphalt pits*

14:11 ª Gen. 14:16, 21 ¹ *provisions*

14:12 ª Gen. 11:27; 12:5 ᵇ Gen. 13:12

14:13 ª Gen. 39:14; 40:15 ᵇ Gen. 13:18 ᶜ Gen. 14:24; 21:27, 32 ¹ *by* ² Heb. *Alon Mamre, terebinth trees of Mamre* ³ *allies*

14:14 ª Gen. 19:29 ᵇ Gen. 13:8; 14:12

ᶜ Gen. 12:5; 15:3; 17:27 ᵈ Deut. 34:1

14:15 ª Is. 41:2, 3 ¹ *North*

14:16 ª Gen. 31:18

14:17 ª 1 Sam. 18:6 ᵇ 2 Sam. 18:18 ᶜ Heb. 7:1 ¹ *defeat* ² *valley*

14:18 ª Heb. 7:1–10 ᵇ Gen. 18:5 ᶜ Ps. 110:4 ᵈ Acts 16:17

14:19 ª Ruth 3:10 ᵇ Gen. 14:22

14:20 ª Gen. 24:27 ᵇ Heb. 7:4 ¹ Lit. *a tithe, a tenth*

14:22 ª Gen. 14:2, 8, 10 ᵇ Dan. 12:7 ᶜ Gen. 14:19

14:23 ª 2 Kin. 5:16 ¹ *sandal strap*

15:1 ª Dan. 10:1 ᵇ Gen. 21:17; 26:24 ᶜ Deut. 33:29 ᵈ Prov. 11:18

15:2 ª Gen. 17:18 ᵇ Acts 7:5 ¹ *heir*

15:3 ª Gen. 14:14 ¹ Lit. *a son of my house, a servant*

15:4 ª 2 Sam. 7:12

15:5 ª Ps. 147:4 ᵇ Jer. 33:22

number them: and he said unto him, [c]So shall thy [d]seed be.

6 And he [a]believed in the LORD; and he [b]counted it to him for righteousness.

7 And he said unto him, I *am* the LORD that [a]brought thee out of [b]Ur of the Chaldees, [c]to give thee this land to inherit it.

8 And he said, Lord GOD, [a]whereby shall I know that I shall inherit it?

9 And he said unto him, Take me an heifer of three years old, and a [1]she goat of three years old, and a ram of three years old, and a turtledove, and a young pigeon.

10 And he took unto him all these, and [a]divided[1] them in the [2]midst, and laid each piece one [3]against another: but [b]the birds divided he not.

11 And when the [1]fowls came down upon the carcases, Abram drove them away.

12 And when the sun was going down, [a]a deep sleep fell upon Abram; and, lo, an horror of great darkness fell upon him.

13 And he said unto Abram, Know of a surety [a]that thy seed shall be a stranger in a land *that is* not theirs, and shall serve them; and [b]they shall afflict them four hundred years;

14 And also that nation, whom they shall serve, [a]will I judge: and afterward [b]shall they come out with great [1]substance.

15 And [a]thou shalt [1]go [b]to thy fathers in peace; [c]thou shalt be buried in a good old age.

16 But [a]in the fourth generation they shall come hither again: for the iniquity [b]of the Amorites [c]*is* not yet [1]full.

17 And it came to pass, that, when the sun went down, and it was dark, behold [1]a smoking [2]furnace, and [3]a burning lamp that [a]passed between those pieces.

18 In the same day the LORD [a]made a covenant with Abram, saying, [b]Unto thy [1]seed have I given this land, from the river of Egypt unto the great river, the river Euphrates:

19 The Kenites, and the Kenizzites, and the Kadmonites,

20 And the Hittites, and the Perizzites, and the Rephaims,

21 And the Amorites, and the Canaanites, and the Girgashites, and the Jebusites.

## CHAPTER 16

Now Sarai Abram's wife [a]bare[1] him no children: and she had an [2]handmaid, [b]an Egyptian, whose name *was* [c]Hagar.

2 [a]And Sarai said unto Abram, Behold now, the LORD [b]hath restrained me from bearing: I pray thee, [c]go in unto my maid; it may be that I may [1]obtain children by her. And Abram [d]hearkened to the voice of Sarai.

3 And Sarai Abram's wife took Hagar her maid the Egyptian, after Abram [a]had dwelt ten years in the land of Canaan, and gave her to her husband Abram to be his wife.

4 And he went in unto Hagar, and she conceived: and when she saw that she had conceived, her mistress was [a]despised in her [1]eyes.

5 And Sarai said unto Abram, [1]My wrong *be* upon thee: I have given my maid into thy bosom; and when she saw that she had conceived, I was despised in her eyes: [a]the LORD judge between me and thee.

6 [a]But Abram said unto Sarai, Behold, thy maid *is* in thy hand; do to her [1]as it pleaseth thee. And when Sarai dealt [2]hardly with her, [b]she fled from her [3]face.

7 And the [a]angel of the LORD found her by a [1]fountain of water in the wilderness, [b]by the [1]fountain in the way to [c]Shur.

8 And he said, Hagar, Sarai's maid, whence camest thou? and whither wilt thou go? And she said, I flee from the face of my mistress Sarai.

9 And the angel of the LORD said unto her, Return to thy mistress, and [a]submit thyself under her hands.

10 And the angel of the LORD said unto her, [a]I will multiply thy [1]seed exceedingly, that it shall not be numbered for multitude.

11 And the angel of the LORD said unto her, Behold, thou *art* with child, [a]and shalt bear a son, and shalt call his name [1]Ishmael; because the LORD hath heard thy affliction.

12 [a]And he will be a wild man; his hand *will be* against every man, and every man's hand against him; [b]and he shall dwell in the presence of all his brethren.

13 And she called the name of the LORD that spake unto her, Thou [1]God seest me: for she said, Have I also here [2]looked after him [a]that seeth me?

14 Wherefore the well was called [a]Beer-lahai-roi;[1] behold, *it is* [b]between Kadesh and Bered.

15 And [a]Hagar bare Abram a son: and Abram called his son's name, which Hagar bare, Ishmael.

16 And Abram *was* fourscore and six years old, when Hagar bare Ishmael to Abram.

## CHAPTER 17

And when Abram was ninety years old and nine, the LORD [a]appeared to Abram, and said unto him, [b]I *am*

¹the Almighty God; ᶜwalk before me, and be thou ᵈperfect.²

2 And I will make my ᵃcovenant between me and thee, and ᵇwill multiply thee exceedingly.

3 And Abram fell on his face: and God talked with him, saying,

4 As for me, behold, my covenant *is* with thee, and thou shalt be ᵃa father of ¹many nations.

5 ¹Neither shall thy name any more be called ²Abram, but ᵃthy name shall be ³Abraham; ᵇfor a father of many nations have I made thee.

6 And I will make thee exceeding fruitful, and I will make ᵃnations of thee, and ᵇkings shall come out of thee.

7 And I will ᵃestablish my covenant between me and thee and thy ¹seed after thee in their generations for an everlasting covenant, ᵇto be a God unto thee, and to ᶜthy ¹seed after thee.

8 And ᵃI will give unto thee, and to thy seed after thee, the land ᵇwherein¹ thou art a stranger, all the land of Canaan, for an everlasting possession; and ᶜI will be their God.

9 And God said unto Abraham, ᵃThou shalt keep my covenant therefore, thou, and thy seed after thee ¹in their generations.

10 This *is* my covenant, which ye shall keep, between me and you and thy seed after thee; ᵃEvery man child among you shall be circumcised.

11 And ye shall circumcise the flesh of your foreskin; and it shall be ᵃa ¹token of the covenant betwixt me and you.

12 And he that is eight days old ᵃshall be circumcised among you, every ¹man child in your generations, he that is born in the house, or bought with money of any stranger, which *is* not of thy seed.

13 He that is born in thy house, and he that is bought with thy money, must needs be circumcised: and my covenant shall be in your flesh for an everlasting covenant.

14 And the uncircumcised man child whose flesh of his foreskin is not circumcised, that ¹soul ᵃshall be cut off from his people; he hath broken my covenant.

15 And God said unto Abraham, As for Sarai thy wife, thou shalt not call her name Sarai, but ¹Sarah *shall* her name *be*.

16 And I will bless her, ᵃand give thee a son also ¹of her: yea, I will bless her, and she shall be *a mother* ᵇof nations; ᶜkings of people shall be of her.

17 Then Abraham fell upon his face, ᵃand laughed, and said in his heart, Shall *a child* be born unto him that is an hundred years old? and shall Sarah, that is ninety years old, bear?

18 And Abraham ᵃsaid unto God, O that Ishmael might live before thee!

19 And God said, ᵃSarah thy wife shall bear thee a son indeed; and thou shalt call his name Isaac: and I will establish my ᵇcovenant with him for an everlasting covenant, *and* with his ¹seed after him.

20 And as for Ishmael, I have heard thee: Behold, I have blessed him, and will make him fruitful, and ᵃwill multiply him exceedingly; ᵇtwelve princes shall he beget, ᶜand I will make him a great nation.

21 But my ᵃcovenant will I establish with Isaac, ᵇwhich Sarah shall bear unto thee at this ᶜset time in the next year.

22 And he left off talking with him, and God went up from Abraham.

23 And Abraham took Ishmael his son, and all that were born in his house, and all that were bought with his money, every male among the men of Abraham's house; and circumcised the flesh of their foreskin in the selfsame day, as God had said unto him.

24 And Abraham *was* ninety years old and nine, when he was circumcised in the flesh of his foreskin.

25 And Ishmael his son *was* thirteen years old, when he was circumcised in the flesh of his foreskin.

26 In the selfsame day was Abraham circumcised, and Ishmael his son.

27 And ᵃall the men of his house, born in the house, and bought with money of the stranger, were circumcised with him.

## CHAPTER 18

AND the LORD appeared unto him ¹in ²the ᵃplains of Mamre: and he sat in the tent door in the heat of the day;

2 ᵃAnd he lift up his eyes and looked, and, lo, three men stood by him: ᵇand when he saw *them*, he ran to meet them from the tent door, and bowed himself ¹toward the ground,

3 And said, My Lord, if now I have found favour in thy sight, pass not ¹away, I pray thee, from thy servant:

4 Let ᵃa little water, I pray you, be ¹fetched, and wash your feet, and rest yourselves under the tree:

5 And ᵃI will ¹fetch a morsel of bread, and ᵇcomfort² ye your hearts; after that ye shall pass on: ᶜfor therefore ³are ye come to your servant. And they said, So do, as thou hast said.

6 And Abraham hastened into the tent unto Sarah, and said, Make ready quickly three measures of fine meal, knead *it*, and make cakes upon the hearth.

### Cross references

17:1 ᶜ 2 Kin. 20:3
ᵈ Deut. 18:13
¹ Heb. *El Shaddai*
² *blameless*
17:2 ᵃ Gen. 15:18
ᵇ Gen. 12:2; 13:16; 15:5; 18:18
17:4 ᵃ [Rom. 4:11, 12, 16] ¹ Lit. *multitude of nations*
17:5 ᵃ Neh. 9:7
ᵇ Rom. 4:17 ¹ *No longer* ² Lit. *Exalted Father*
³ Lit. *Father of a Multitude*
17:6 ᵃ Gen. 17:16; 35:11 ᵇ Matt. 1:6
17:7 ᵃ [Gal. 3:17]
ᵇ Gen. 26:24; 28:13 ᶜ Rom. 9:8
¹ *descendants*
17:8 ᵃ Acts 7:5
ᵇ Gen. 23:4;
28:4 ᶜ Lev. 26:12
¹ Lit. *of your sojournings*
17:9 ᵃ Ex. 19:5
¹ *throughout*
17:10 ᵃ Acts 7:8
17:11 ᵃ Ex. 12:13, 48
¹ *sign*
17:12 ᵃ Lev. 12:3
¹ *male*
17:14 ᵃ Ex. 4:24–26 ¹ *person*
17:15 ¹ Lit. *Princess*
17:16 ᵃ Gen.
18:10 ᵇ Gen.
35:11 ᶜ Gen. 17:6; 36:31 ¹ *by*
17:17 ᵃ Gen. 17:3; 18:12; 21:6

17:18 ᵃ Gen. 18:23
17:19 ᵃ Gen. 18:10;
21:2 ᵇ Gen. 22:16
¹ *descendants*
17:20 ᵃ Gen. 16:10
ᵇ Gen. 25:12–16
ᶜ Gen. 21:13, 18
17:21 ᵃ Gen. 26:2–5
ᵇ Gen. 21:2 ᶜ Gen. 18:14
17:27 ᵃ Gen. 18:19
18:1 ᵃ Gen. 13:18;
14:13 ¹ *by* ² Heb. *Alon Mamre*, terebinth trees of Mamre
18:2 ᵃ Heb. 13:2
ᵇ Gen. 19:1 ¹ *to*
18:3 ¹ *on by*
18:4 ᵃ Gen. 19:2;
24:32; 43:24
¹ *brought*
18:5 ᵃ Judg.
6:18, 19; 13:15, 16 ᵇ Judg. 19:5
ᶜ Gen. 19:8; 33:10
¹ *bring* ² *refresh*
³ *inasmuch as you have come*

7 And Abraham ran unto the herd, and fetcht a calf tender and good, and gave *it* unto a young man; and he hasted to ¹dress it.

8 And ᵃhe took butter, and milk, and the calf which he had ¹dressed, and set *it* before them; and he stood by them under the tree, and they did eat.

9 And they said unto him, Where *is* Sarah thy wife? And he said, Behold, ᵃin the tent.

10 And he said, I will certainly return unto thee ᵃaccording to the time of life; and, lo, ᵇSarah thy wife shall have a son. And Sarah heard *it* in the tent door, which *was* behind him.

11 Now ᵃAbraham and Sarah *were* old *and* well stricken in age; *and* ¹it ceased to be with Sarah ᵇafter the manner of women.

12 Therefore Sarah ᵃlaughed within herself, saying, ᵇAfter I am ¹waxed old shall I have pleasure, my ᶜlord being old also?

13 And the LORD said unto Abraham, Wherefore did Sarah laugh, saying, Shall I of a surety bear a child, which am old?

14 ᵃIs any thing too hard for the LORD? ᵇAt the time appointed I will return unto thee, according to the time of life, and Sarah shall have a son.

15 Then Sarah denied, saying, I laughed not; for she was afraid. And he said, Nay; but thou didst laugh.

16 And the men rose up from thence, and looked toward Sodom: and Abraham went with them ᵃto ¹bring them on the way.

17 And the LORD said, ᵃShall I hide from Abraham that thing which I do;

18 Seeing that Abraham shall surely become a great and mighty nation, and all the nations of the earth shall be ᵃblessed in him?

19 For I know him, ᵃthat he will command his children and his household after him, and they shall keep the way of the LORD, to do ¹justice and judgment; that the LORD may bring upon Abraham that which he hath spoken of him.

20 And the LORD said, Because ᵃthe cry of Sodom and Gomorrah is great, and because their ᵇsin is very grievous;

21 ᵃI will go down now, and see whether they have done altogether according to the cry of it, which is come unto me; and if not, ᵇI will know.

22 And the men turned their faces from thence, ᵃand went toward Sodom: but Abraham stood yet before the LORD.

23 And Abraham ᵃdrew near, and said, ᵇWilt thou also ᶜdestroy the ᵈrighteous with the wicked?

24 ¹Peradventure there be fifty righteous within the city: wilt thou also destroy and not spare the place for the fifty righteous that *are* therein?

25 That be far from thee to do after this manner, to slay the righteous with the wicked: and ᵃthat the righteous should be as the wicked, that be far from thee: ᵇShall not the Judge of all the earth do right?

26 And the LORD said, ᵃIf I find in Sodom fifty righteous within the city, then I will spare all the place for their sakes.

27 And Abraham answered and said, Behold now, I have taken upon me to speak unto the Lord, which *am* ᵃbut dust and ashes:

28 ¹Peradventure there shall lack five of the fifty righteous: wilt thou destroy all the city for *lack of* five? And he said, If I find there forty and five, I will not destroy *it*.

29 And he spake unto him yet again, and said, Peradventure there shall be forty found there. And he said, I will not do *it* for forty's sake.

30 And he said *unto him,* Oh let not the Lord be angry, and I will speak: Peradventure there shall thirty be found there. And he said, I will not do *it,* if I find thirty there.

31 And he said, Behold now, I have taken upon me to speak unto the Lord: Peradventure there shall be twenty found there. And he said, I will not destroy *it* for twenty's sake.

32 And he said, ᵃOh let not the Lord be angry, and I will speak yet but this once: Peradventure ten shall be found there. ᵇAnd he said, I will not destroy *it* for ten's sake.

33 And the LORD went his way, as soon as he had ¹left communing with Abraham: and Abraham returned unto his place.

## CHAPTER 19

AND there ᵃcame two angels to Sodom ¹at even; and ᵇLot sat in the gate of Sodom: and Lot seeing *them* rose up to meet them; and he bowed himself with his face toward the ground;

2 And he said, Behold now, my lords, ᵃturn in, I pray you, into your servant's house, and ¹tarry all night, and ᵇwash your feet, and ye shall rise up early, and go on your ways. And they said, ᶜNay; but we will abide in the ²street all night.

3 And he ¹pressed upon them greatly; and they turned in unto him, and entered into his house; ᵃand he made them a feast, and did bake ᵇunleavened bread, and they did eat.

4 But before they lay down, the men of the city, *even* the men of Sodom, ¹compassed the house round, both

18:7 ¹ *prepare*
18:8 ᵃ Gen. 19:3
¹ *prepared*
18:9 ᵃ Gen. 24:67
18:10 ᵃ 2 Kin. 4:16
ᵇ Rom. 9:9
18:11 ᵃ Gen. 17:17
ᵇ Gen. 31:35
¹ Sarah had passed the age of childbearing.
18:12 ᵃ Gen. 17:17
ᵇ Luke 1:18 ᶜ 1 Pet. 3:6 ¹ *grown*
18:14 ᵃ Jer. 32:17
ᵇ Gen. 17:21; 18:10
18:16 ᵃ Rom. 15:24
¹ *send*
18:17 ᵃ Ps. 25:14
18:18 ᵃ [Acts 3:25, 26]
18:19 ᵃ [Deut. 4:9, 10; 6:6, 7] ¹ *righteousness and justice*
18:20 ᵃ Gen. 4:10; 19:13 ᵇ Gen. 13:13
18:21 ᵃ Gen. 11:5 ᵇ Deut. 8:2; 13:3
18:22 ᵃ Gen. 18:16; 19:1
18:23 ᵃ [Heb. 10:22] ᵇ Num. 16:22 ᶜ Job 9:22 ᵈ Gen. 20:4
18:24 ¹ *Suppose*
18:25 ᵃ Is. 3:10, 11 ᵇ Deut. 1:16, 17; 32:4
18:26 ᵃ Jer. 5:1
18:27 ᵃ [Gen. 3:19]
18:28 ¹ *Suppose*
18:32 ᵃ Judg. 6:39 ᵇ James 5:16
18:33 ¹ *finished speaking*
19:1 ᵃ Gen. 18:2, 16, 22 ᵇ Gen. 18:1–5 ¹ *in the evening*
19:2 ᵃ Gen. 24:31; [Heb. 13:2] ᵇ Gen. 18:4; 24:32 ᶜ Luke 24:28 ¹ *spend the night* ² *open plaza*
19:3 ᵃ Gen. 18:6–8; Ex. 23:15; Num. 9:11; 28:17 ᵇ Ex. 12:8 ¹ *urged them*
19:4 ¹ *surrounded*

old and young, all the people from every quarter:

5 [a]And they called unto Lot, and said unto him, Where *are* the men which came in to thee this night? [b]bring them out unto us, that we [c]may [1]know them.

6 And [a]Lot went out at the door unto them, and shut the door after him,

7 And said, I pray you, brethren, do not so wickedly.

8 [a]Behold now, I have two daughters which have not known man; let me, I pray you, bring them out unto you, and do ye to them [1]as *is* good in your eyes: only unto these men do nothing; [b]for therefore came they under the shadow of my roof.

9 And they said, Stand back. And they said *again,* This one *fellow* [a]came in to [1]sojourn, [b]and he [2]will needs be a judge: now will we deal worse with thee, than with them. And they pressed sore upon the man, *even* Lot, and came near to break the door.

10 But the men put forth their hand, and pulled Lot into the house to them, and shut to the door.

11 And they [a]smote[1] the men that *were* at the door of the house with blindness, both small and great: so that they wearied themselves to find the door.

12 And the men said unto Lot, Hast thou here any besides? son in law, and thy sons, and thy daughters, and whatsoever thou hast in the city, [a]bring *them* out of this place:

13 For we will destroy this place, because the [a]cry of them [1]is waxen great before the face of the LORD; and [b]the LORD hath sent us to destroy it.

14 And Lot went out, and spake unto his sons in law, [a]which married his daughters, and said, [b]Up, get you out of this place; for the LORD will destroy this city. [c]But he seemed as one that [1]mocked unto his sons in law.

15 And when the morning arose, then the angels [1]hastened Lot, saying, [a]Arise, take thy wife, and thy two daughters, which are here; lest thou be consumed in the [2]iniquity of the city.

16 And while he lingered, the men [a]laid hold upon his hand, and upon the hand of his wife, and upon the hand of his two daughters; the [b]LORD being merciful unto him: [c]and they brought him forth, and set him [1]without the city.

17 And it came to pass, when they had brought them forth [1]abroad, that [2]he said, [a]Escape for thy life; [b]look not behind thee, neither stay thou in all the plain; escape [c]to the mountain, lest thou be [3]consumed.

18 And Lot said unto them, Oh, [a]not so, my Lord:

19 Behold now, thy servant hath found grace in thy sight, and thou hast magnified thy mercy, which thou hast shewed unto me in saving my life; and I cannot escape to the mountain, lest some evil take me, and I die:

20 Behold now, this city *is* near to flee unto, and it *is* a little one: Oh, let me escape thither, (*is* it not a little one?) and my soul shall live.

21 And he said unto him, See, [a]I have [1]accepted thee concerning this thing also, that I will not overthrow this city, for the which thou hast spoken.

22 Haste thee, escape thither; for [a]I cannot do any thing till thou [1]be come thither. Therefore [b]the name of the city was called [2]Zoar.

23 The sun was risen upon the earth when Lot entered into Zoar.

24 Then the LORD rained upon [a]Sodom and upon Gomorrah brimstone and [b]fire from the LORD out of heaven;

25 And he [1]overthrew those cities, and all the plain, and all the inhabitants of the cities, and [a]that which grew upon the ground.

26 But his wife looked back from behind him, and she became [a]a pillar of salt.

27 And Abraham gat up early in the morning to the place where [a]he [1]stood before the LORD:

28 And he looked toward Sodom and Gomorrah, and toward all the land of the plain, and beheld, and, lo, [a]the smoke of the country went up as the smoke of a furnace.

29 And it came to pass, when God destroyed the cities of the plain, that God [a]remembered Abraham, and sent Lot out of the midst of the overthrow, when he overthrew the cities in the which Lot dwelt.

30 And Lot went up out of Zoar, and [a]dwelt in the mountain, and his two daughters with him; for he feared to dwell in Zoar: and he dwelt in a cave, he and his two daughters.

31 And the firstborn said unto the younger, Our father *is* old, and *there is* not a man in the earth [a]to come in unto us after the [1]manner of all the earth:

32 Come, let us make our father drink wine, and we will lie with him, that we [a]may preserve [1]seed of our father.

33 And they made their father drink wine that night: and the firstborn went in, and lay with her father; and he perceived not when she lay down, nor when she arose.

34 And it came to pass on the morrow, that the firstborn said unto the

---

19:5 [a] Is. 3:9
[b] Judg. 19:22
[c] Gen. 4:1; Rom. 1:24, 27; Jude 7 [1] *know them carnally*
19:6 [a] Judg. 19:23
19:8 [a] Judg. 19:24
[b] Gen. 18:5 [1] *as you wish*
19:9 [a] 2 Pet. 2:7, 8 [b] Ex. 2:14 [1] *stay a little while* [2] *keeps acting as*
19:11 [a] Gen. 20:17 [1] *struck*
19:12 [a] Gen. 7:1; 2 Pet. 2:7, 9
19:13 [a] Gen. 18:20 [b] Lev. 26:30–33; Deut. 4:26; 28:45; 1 Chr. 21:15 [1] *has grown*
19:14 [a] Matt. 1:18 [b] Num. 16:21, 24, 26, 45; Rev. 18:4 [c] Ex. 9:21; Jer. 43:1, 2; Luke 17:28; 24:11 [1] *joked*
19:15 [a] Ps. 37:2; Rev. 18:4 [1] *urged Lot to hurry* [2] *punishment*
19:16 [a] Deut. 5:15; 6:21; 7:8; 2 Pet. 2:7 [b] Ex. 34:7; Ps. 32:10; 33:18, 19; Luke 18:13 [c] Ps. 34:22 [1] *outside*
19:17 [a] 1 Kin. 19:3; Jer. 48:6 [b] Gen. 19:26; Matt. 24:16–18; Luke 9:62; Phil. 3:13, 14 [c] Gen. 14:10 [1] *outside* [2] LXX, Syr., Vg. *they* [3] *destroyed*
19:18 [a] Acts 10:14
19:21 [a] Job 42:8, 9; Ps. 145:19 [1] *favoured thee*
19:22 [a] Ex. 32:10; Deut. 9:14 [b] Gen. 13:10; 14:2 [1] *arrive there* [2] Lit. *Insignificant*
19:24 [a] Deut. 29:23 [b] Lev. 10:2
19:25 [a] Ps. 107:34 [1] *devastated*
19:26 [a] Luke 17:32
19:27 [a] Gen. 18:22 [1] *had stood*
19:28 [a] Rev. 9:2; 18:9
19:29 [a] Gen. 8:1; 18:23
19:30 [a] Gen. 19:17, 19
19:31 [a] Gen. 16:2, 4; 38:8, 9 [1] *custom*
19:32 [a] [Mark 12:19] [1] *the lineage*

younger, Behold, I lay yesternight with my father: let us make him drink wine this night also; and go thou in, *and* lie with him, that we may preserve ¹seed of our father.

35 And they made their father drink wine that night also: and the younger arose, and lay with him; and he perceived not when she lay down, nor when she arose.

36 Thus were both the daughters of Lot with child by their father.

37 And the firstborn bare a son, and called his name Moab: ªthe same *is* the father of the Moabites unto this day.

38 And the younger, she also bare a son, and called his name Ben-ammi: ªthe same *is* the father of the children of Ammon unto this day.

## CHAPTER 20

A ND Abraham journeyed from ªthence toward the south country, and dwelled between ᵇKadesh and Shur, and ᶜsojourned in Gerar.

2 And Abraham said of Sarah his wife, ªShe *is* my sister: and Abimelech king of Gerar sent, and ᵇtook Sarah.

3 But ªGod came to Abimelech ᵇin a dream by night, and said to him, ᶜBehold, thou *art but* a dead man, for the woman which thou hast taken; for she *is* ¹a man's wife.

4 But Abimelech had not come near her: and he said, Lord, ªwilt thou slay also a righteous nation?

5 Said he not unto me, She *is* my sister? and she, even she herself said, He *is* my brother: ªin the ¹integrity of my heart and innocency of my hands have I done this.

6 And God said unto him in a dream, Yea, I know that thou didst this in the integrity of thy heart; for ªI also withheld thee from sinning ᵇagainst me: therefore suffered I thee not to touch her.

7 Now therefore restore the man *his* wife; ªfor he *is* a prophet, and he shall pray for thee, and thou shalt live: and if thou restore *her* not, ᵇknow thou that thou shalt surely die, thou, ᶜand all that *are* thine.

8 Therefore Abimelech rose early in the morning, and called all his servants, and told all these things in their ears: and the men were ¹sore afraid.

9 Then Abimelech called Abraham, and said unto him, What hast thou done unto us? and ¹what have I offended thee, ªthat thou hast brought on me and on my kingdom a great sin? thou hast done deeds unto me ᵇthat ought not to be done.

10 And Abimelech said unto Abraham, What sawest thou, that thou hast done this thing?

19:34 ¹ *the lineage*
19:37 ª Deut. 2:9
19:38 ª Deut. 2:19
20:1 ª Gen. 18:1
   ᵇ Gen. 12:9; 16:7,
14   ᶜ Gen. 26:1, 6
20:2 ª Gen. 12:11–13; 26:7 ᵇ Gen. 12:15
20:3 ª Ps. 105:14 ᵇ Job 33:15 ᶜ Gen.
20:7 ¹ Lit. *married to a husband*
20:4 ª Gen. 18:23–25
20:5 ª 2 Kin. 20:3 ¹ *innocence*
20:6 ª 1 Sam. 25:26, 34 ᵇ Gen. 39:9
20:7 ª 1 Sam. 7:5 ᵇ Gen. 2:17 ᶜ Num. 16:32, 33
20:8 ¹ *very*
20:9 ª Gen. 26:10; 39:9 ᵇ Gen. 34:7 ¹ *how have I sinned against*

20:11 ª Prov. 16:6 ᵇ Gen. 12:12; 26:7 ¹ *on account of my wife*
20:12 ª Gen. 11:29
20:13 ª Gen. 12:1–9, 11 ᵇ Gen. 12:13; 20:5
20:14 ª Gen. 12:16
20:15 ª Gen. 13:9; 34:10; 47:6
20:16 ª Gen. 26:11 ᵇ Gen. 24:65 ¹ *it vindicates you before all* ² *justified*
20:17 ª Job 42:9 ᵇ Gen. 21:2
20:18 ª Gen. 12:17
21:1 ª 1 Sam. 2:21 ᵇ [Gal. 4:23, 28]
21:2 ª Heb. 11:11, 12 ᵇ Gen. 17:21; 18:10, 14
21:3 ª Gen. 17:19, 21 ¹ Lit. *Laughter*
21:4 ª Acts 7:8 ᵇ Gen. 17:10, 12
21:5 ª Gen. 17:1, 17
21:6 ª Is. 54:1 ᵇ Luke 1:58 ¹ Lit. *made laughter for me*
21:7 ª Gen. 18:11, 12 ¹ *nurse children*
21:9 ª Gen. 16:1, 4, 15 ᵇ [Gal. 4:29] ¹ *scoffing*, lit. *laughing*

11 And Abraham said, Because I thought, Surely ªthe fear of God *is* not in this place; and ᵇthey will slay me ¹for my wife's sake.

12 And yet indeed ªshe *is* my sister; she *is* the daughter of my father, but not the daughter of my mother; and she became my wife.

13 And it came to pass, when ªGod caused me to wander from my father's house, that I said unto her, This *is* thy kindness which thou shalt shew unto me; at every place whither we shall come, ᵇsay of me, He *is* my brother.

14 And Abimelech ªtook sheep, and oxen, and menservants, and womenservants, and gave *them* unto Abraham, and restored him Sarah his wife.

15 And Abimelech said, Behold, ªmy land *is* before thee: dwell where it pleaseth thee.

16 And unto Sarah he said, Behold, I have given thy brother a thousand *pieces* of silver: ªbehold, ¹he *is* to thee ᵇa covering of the eyes, unto all that *are* with thee, and with all *other:* thus she was ²reproved.

17 So Abraham ªprayed unto God: and God ᵇhealed Abimelech, and his wife, and his maidservants; and they bare *children.*

18 For the LORD ªhad fast closed up all the wombs of the house of Abimelech, because of Sarah Abraham's wife.

## CHAPTER 21

A ND the LORD ªvisited Sarah as he had said, and the LORD did unto Sarah ᵇas he had spoken.

2 For Sarah ªconceived, and bare Abraham a son in his old age, ᵇat the set time of which God had spoken to him.

3 And Abraham called the name of his son that was born unto him, whom Sarah bare to him, ªIsaac.¹

4 And Abraham ªcircumcised his son Isaac being eight days old, ᵇas God had commanded him.

5 And ªAbraham was an hundred years old, when his son Isaac was born unto him.

6 And Sarah said, ªGod hath ¹made me to laugh, *so that* all that hear ᵇwill laugh with me.

7 And she said, Who would have said unto Abraham, that Sarah should ¹have given children suck? ªfor I have born *him* a son in his old age.

8 And the child grew, and was weaned: and Abraham made a great feast the *same* day that Isaac was weaned.

9 And Sarah saw the son of Hagar ªthe Egyptian, which she had born unto Abraham, ᵇmocking.¹

10 Wherefore she said unto Abraham, [a]Cast out this bondwoman and her son: for the son of this bondwoman shall not be heir with my son, *even* with Isaac.

11 And the thing was very [1]grievous in Abraham's sight [a]because of his son.

12 And God said unto Abraham, Let it not be grievous in thy sight because of the lad, and because of thy bondwoman; in all that Sarah hath said unto thee, hearken unto her voice; for [a]in Isaac shall thy seed be called.

13 And also of the son of the bondwoman will I make [a]a nation, because he *is* thy [1]seed.

14 And Abraham rose up early in the morning, and took bread, and a [1]bottle of water, and gave *it* unto Hagar, putting *it* on her shoulder, and the [2]child, and [a]sent her away: and she departed, and wandered in the wilderness of Beer-sheba.

15 And the water was [1]spent in the bottle, and she [2]cast the child under one of the shrubs.

16 And she went, and sat her down [1]over against *him* a good way off, as it were a bow shot: for she said, Let me not see the death of the child. And she sat over against *him,* and lift up her voice, and wept.

17 And [a]God heard the voice of the lad; and the [b]angel of God called to Hagar out of heaven, and said unto her, What aileth thee, Hagar? fear not; for God hath heard the voice of the lad where he *is.*

18 Arise, lift up the lad, and hold him [1]in thine hand; for [a]I will make him a great nation.

19 And [a]God opened her eyes, and she saw a well of water; and she went, and filled the [1]bottle with water, and gave the lad drink.

20 And God [a]was with the lad; and he grew, and dwelt in the wilderness, [b]and became an archer.

21 And he dwelt in the wilderness of Paran: and his mother [a]took him a wife out of the land of Egypt.

22 And it came to pass at that time, that [a]Abimelech and Phichol the chief captain of his host spake unto Abraham, saying, [b]God *is* with thee in all that thou doest:

23 Now therefore [a]swear[1] unto me here by God that thou wilt not deal falsely with me, nor with my [2]son, nor with my son's son: *but* according to the kindness that I have done unto thee, thou shalt do unto me, and to the land wherein thou hast sojourned.

24 And Abraham said, I will swear.

25 And Abraham reproved Abimelech because of a well of water, which

21:10 [a] Gal. 3:18; 4:30
21:11 [a] Gen. 17:18
[1] *distressing*
21:12 [a] [Rom. 9:7, 8]
21:13 [a] Gen. 16:10; 17:20; 21:18; 25:12–18
[1] *descendant*
21:14 [a] John 8:35
[1] *skin* [2] *youth*
21:15 [1] *used up* [2] *placed*
21:16 [1] *opposite*
21:17 [a] Ex. 3:7 [b] Gen. 22:11
21:18 [a] Gen. 16:10; 21:13; 25:12–16
[1] *with*
21:19 [a] Num. 22:31
[1] *skin*
21:20 [a] Gen. 28:15; 39:2, 3, 21 [b] Gen. 16:12
21:21 [a] Gen. 24:4
21:22 [a] Gen. 20:2, 14; 26:26 [b] Gen. 26:28
21:23 [a] Josh. 2:12
[1] *take an oath* [2] *offspring nor with my posterity*
21:25 [a] Gen. 26:15, 18, 20–22
21:26 [1] *know*
21:27 [a] Gen. 26:31; 31:44 [1] *treaty*
21:29 [a] Gen. 33:8
21:30 [a] Gen. 31:48, 52
21:31 [a] Gen. 21:14; 26:33 [1] Lit. *Well of the Oath* or *Well of the Seven*
21:33 [a] Gen. 4:26; 12:8; 13:4; 26:25 [b] Deut. 32:40; 33:27 [1] *tamarisk tree*
22:1 [a] Heb. 11:17 [1] *test*
22:2 [a] Gen. 22:12, 16 [b] John 5:20 [c] 2 Chr. 3:1 [d] Gen. 8:20; 31:54
22:3 [1] *donkey* [2] *split*
22:5 [a] [Heb. 11:19] [1] Lit. *young man* [2] *come back*
22:6 [a] John 19:17

Abimelech's servants [a]had violently taken away.

26 And Abimelech said, I [1]wot not who hath done this thing: neither didst thou tell me, neither yet heard I *of it,* but to day.

27 And Abraham took sheep and oxen, and gave them unto Abimelech; and both of them [a]made a [1]covenant.

28 And Abraham set seven ewe lambs of the flock by themselves.

29 And Abimelech said unto Abraham, [a]What *mean* these seven ewe lambs which thou hast set by themselves?

30 And he said, For *these* seven ewe lambs shalt thou take of my hand, that [a]they may be a witness unto me, that I have digged this well.

31 Wherefore he [a]called that place [1]Beer-sheba; because there they sware both of them.

32 Thus they made a covenant at Beer-sheba: then Abimelech rose up, and Phichol the chief captain of his host, and they returned into the land of the Philistines.

33 And *Abraham* planted a [1]grove in Beer-sheba, and [a]called there on the name of the LORD, [b]the everlasting God.

34 And Abraham sojourned in the Philistines' land many days.

## CHAPTER 22

AND it came to pass after these things, that [a]God did [1]tempt Abraham, and said unto him, Abraham: and he said, Behold, *here* I *am.*

2 And he said, Take now thy son, [a]thine only *son* Isaac, whom thou [b]lovest, and get thee [c]into the land of Moriah; and offer him there for a [d]burnt offering upon one of the mountains which I will tell thee of.

3 And Abraham rose up early in the morning, and saddled his [1]ass, and took two of his young men with him, and Isaac his son, and [2]clave the wood for the burnt offering, and rose up, and went unto the place of which God had told him.

4 Then on the third day Abraham lifted up his eyes, and saw the place afar off.

5 And Abraham said unto his young men, Abide ye here with the ass; and I and the [1]lad will go yonder and worship, and [a]come[2] again to you.

6 And Abraham took the wood of the burnt offering, and [a]laid *it* upon Isaac his son; and he took the fire in his hand, and a knife; and they went both of them together.

7 And Isaac spake unto Abraham his father, and said, My father: and he said, Here *am* I, my son. And he said, Behold the fire and the wood:

but where *is* the ¹lamb for a burnt offering?

8 And Abraham said, My son, God
will provide himself a ªlamb for a
ᵇburnt offering: so they went both of
them together.

9 And they came to the place which
God had told him of; and Abraham
built an altar there, and laid the wood
in order, and bound Isaac his son,
and ªlaid him on the altar upon the
wood.

10 And Abraham stretched forth his
hand, and took the knife to slay his
son.

11 And the ªangel of the LORD
called unto him out of heaven, and
said, Abraham, Abraham: and he
said, Here *am* I.

12 And he said, ªLay not thine hand
upon the lad, neither do thou any
thing unto him: for ᵇnow I know that
thou fearest God, seeing thou hast
not ᶜwithheld thy son, thine only *son*
from me.

13 And Abraham lifted up his eyes,
and looked, and behold behind *him* a
ram caught in a thicket by his horns:
and Abraham went and took the ram,
and offered him up for a burnt offering in the stead of his son.

14 And Abraham called the name of
that place ¹Jehovah-jireh: as it is said
*to* this day, In the mount of the LORD
It shall be ²seen.

15 And the angel of the LORD called
unto Abraham out of heaven the second time,

16 And said, ªBy myself have I
sworn, saith the LORD, for because
thou hast done this thing, and hast
not withheld thy son, thine only *son:*

17 That in blessing I will ªbless thee,
and in multiplying I will multiply thy
¹seed ᵇas the stars of the heaven, ᶜand
as the sand which *is* upon the sea
shore; and ᵈthy seed shall possess
the gate of his enemies;

18 ªAnd in thy seed shall all the
nations of the earth be blessed; ᵇbecause thou hast obeyed my voice.

19 So Abraham returned unto his
young men, and they rose up and
went together to ªBeer-sheba; and
Abraham dwelt at Beer-sheba.

20 And it came to pass after these
things, that it was told Abraham, saying, Behold, ªMilcah, she hath also
born children unto thy brother Nahor;

21 ªHuz his firstborn, and Buz his
brother, and Kemuel the father ᵇof
Aram,

22 And Chesed, and Hazo, and Pil-
dash, and Jidlaph, and Bethuel.

23 And ªBethuel begat ¹Rebekah:
these eight Milcah did bear to Nahor,
Abraham's brother.

24 And his concubine, whose name

*was* Reumah, she bare also Tebah, and
Gaham, and Thahash, and Maachah.

## CHAPTER 23

Aᴺᴰ Sarah was an hundred and
seven and twenty years old: *these
were* the years of the life of Sarah.

2 And Sarah died in ªKirjath-arba;
the same *is* ᵇHebron in the land
of Canaan: and Abraham came to
mourn for Sarah, and to weep for her.

3 And Abraham stood up from before his dead, and spake unto the
sons of ªHeth, saying,

4 ªI *am* a stranger and a sojourner
with you: ᵇgive me ¹a possession of
a buryingplace with you, that I may
bury my dead out of my sight.

5 And the children of Heth answered Abraham, saying unto him,

6 Hear us, my lord: thou *art* ªa
¹mighty prince among us: in the
choice of our ²sepulchres bury thy
dead; none of us shall withhold from
thee his sepulchre, but that thou
mayest bury thy dead.

7 And Abraham stood up, and
bowed himself to the people of the
land, *even* to the children of Heth.

8 And he ¹communed with them,
saying, If it be your mind that I
should bury my dead out of my
sight; hear me, and ²intreat for me to
Ephron the son of Zohar,

9 That he may give me the cave of
ªMachpelah, which he hath, which *is*
in the end of his field; for ¹as much
money as it is worth he shall give it
me ²for a possession of a buryingplace amongst you.

10 And Ephron dwelt among the
children of Heth: and Ephron the
Hittite answered Abraham in the ¹audience of the ²children of Heth, *even*
of all that ªwent in at the gate of his
city, saying,

11 ªNay, my lord, hear me: the
field give I thee, and the cave that
*is* therein, I give it thee; in the presence of the sons of my people give I it
thee: bury my dead.

12 And Abraham bowed down himself before the people of the land.

13 And he spake unto Ephron in the
audience of the people of the land,
saying, But if thou *wilt give it,* I pray
thee, hear me: I will give thee money
for the field; take *it* of me, and I will
bury my dead there.

14 And Ephron answered Abraham,
saying unto him,

15 My lord, hearken unto me: the
land *is worth* four hundred ªshekels
of silver; what is that ¹betwixt me and
thee? bury therefore thy dead.

16 And Abraham hearkened unto
Ephron; and Abraham ªweighed
to Ephron the silver, which he had
named in the ¹audience of the sons of

---

**Center column references:**

22:7 ¹ *goat*
22:8 ª John 1:29,
36 ᵇ Ex. 12:3–6
22:9 ª [Heb.
11:17–19]
22:11 ª Gen. 16:7–
11; 21:17, 18; 31:11
22:12 ª 1 Sam.
15:22 ᵇ James
2:21, 22 ᶜ Gen.
22:2, 16
22:14 ¹ Lit. *The
LORD Will Provide
or See* ² *provided*
22:16 ª Ps. 105:9
22:17 ª Gen. 17:16;
26:3, 24 ᵇ Gen.
15:5; 26:4 ᶜ Gen.
13:16; 32:12 ᵈ Gen.
24:60 ¹ *descen-
dants*
22:18 ª Gen. 12:3;
18:18; 26:4 ᵇ Gen.
18:19; 22:3, 10;
26:5
22:19 ª Gen. 21:31
22:20 ª Gen.
11:29; 24:15
22:21 ª Job 1:1
ᵇ Job 32:2
22:23 ª Gen. 24:15
¹ *Rebecca,* Rom.
9:10

23:2 ª Josh. 14:15;
15:13; 21:11 ᵇ Gen.
13:18; 23:19
23:3 ª Gen. 10:15;
15:20
23:4 ª [Gen. 17:8]
ᵇ Acts 7:5, 16
¹ *property for*
23:6 ª Gen. 13:2;
14:14; 24:35 ¹ Lit.
*Prince of God*
² *burial places*
23:8 ¹ *spoke*
² *meet for me
with*
23:9 ª Gen. 25:9
¹ *the full price*
² *as property for*
23:10 ª Gen. 23:18;
34:20, 24; Ruth
4:1, 4, 11 ¹ *pres-
ence* ² Lit. *sons*
23:11 ª 2 Sam.
24:21–24
23:15 ª Ex. 30:13;
Ezek. 45:12
¹ *between*
23:16 ª 2 Sam.
14:26; Jer. 32:9,
10; Zech. 11:12
¹ *hearing*

Heth, four hundred shekels of silver, [2]current *money* with the merchant.

17 And [a]the field of Ephron, which *was* in Machpelah, which *was* before Mamre, the field, and the cave which *was* therein, and all the trees that *were* in the field, that *were* in all the borders round about, were [1]made sure

18 Unto Abraham for a possession in the presence of the children of Heth, before all that went in at the gate of his city.

19 And after this, Abraham buried Sarah his wife in the cave of the field of Machpelah before Mamre: the same *is* Hebron in the land of Canaan.

20 And the field, and the cave that *is* therein, [a]were [1]made sure unto Abraham for a possession of a buryingplace by the sons of Heth.

## CHAPTER 24

AND Abraham [a]was old, *and* [1]well stricken in age: and the LORD [b]had blessed Abraham in all things.

2 And Abraham said [a]unto his eldest servant of his house, that [b]ruled over all that he had, [c]Put, I pray thee, thy hand under my thigh:

3 And I will make thee [a]swear[1] by the LORD, the God of heaven, and the God of the earth, that [b]thou shalt not take a wife unto my son of the daughters of the Canaanites, among whom I dwell:

4 [a]But thou shalt go [b]unto my country, and to my kindred, and take a wife unto my son Isaac.

5 And the servant said unto him, [1]Peradventure the woman will not be willing to follow me unto this land: must I [2]needs bring thy son again unto the land from whence thou camest?

6 And Abraham said unto him, Beware thou that thou [1]bring not my son thither again.

7 The LORD God of heaven, which [a]took me from my father's house, and from the land of my kindred, and which spake unto me, and that sware unto me, saying, [b]Unto thy [1]seed will I give this land; [c]he shall send his angel before thee, and thou shalt take a wife unto my son from thence.

8 And if the woman will not be willing to follow thee, then [a]thou shalt be clear from this my oath: only [1]bring not my son thither again.

9 And the servant put his hand under the thigh of Abraham his master, and sware to him concerning that matter.

10 And the servant took ten camels of the camels of his master, and departed; [a]for all [1]the goods of his master *were* in his hand: and he arose, and went to Mesopotamia, unto [b]the city of Nahor.

11 And he made his camels to kneel down without the city by a well of water at the time of the evening, *even* the time [a]that women go out to draw *water*.

12 And he [a]said, O LORD God of my master Abraham, I pray thee, [b]send[1] me good speed this day, and shew kindness unto my master Abraham.

13 Behold, [a]I stand *here* by the well of water; and [b]the daughters of the men of the city come out to draw water:

14 And let it come to pass, that the damsel to whom I shall say, Let down thy pitcher, I pray thee, that I may drink; and she shall say, Drink, and I will give thy camels drink also: *let the same be* she *that* thou hast appointed for thy servant Isaac; and [a]thereby shall I know that thou hast shewed kindness unto my master.

15 And it came to pass, [a]before he had done speaking, that, behold, [b]Rebekah[1] came out, who was born to Bethuel, son of [c]Milcah, the wife of Nahor, Abraham's brother, with her pitcher upon her shoulder.

16 And the damsel [a]*was* very [1]fair to look upon, a virgin, neither had any man known her: and she went down to the well, and filled her pitcher, and came up.

17 And the servant ran to meet her, and said, Let me, I pray thee, drink a little water of thy pitcher.

18 [a]And she said, Drink, my lord: and she hasted, and let down her pitcher upon her hand, and gave him drink.

19 And when she had done giving him drink, she said, I will draw *water* for thy camels also, until they have done drinking.

20 And she hasted, and emptied her pitcher into the trough, and ran again unto the well to draw *water*, and drew for all his camels.

21 And the man wondering at her held his peace, [1]to wit whether [a]the LORD had made his journey prosperous or not.

22 And it came to pass, as the camels had done drinking, that the man took a golden [a]earring[1] of half a shekel weight, and two bracelets for her hands of ten *shekels* weight of gold;

23 And said, Whose daughter *art* thou? tell me, I pray thee: is there room *in* thy father's house for us to lodge in?

24 And she said unto him, [a]I *am* the daughter of Bethuel the son of Milcah, which she bare unto Nahor.

25 She said moreover unto him, We have both straw and [1]provender enough, and room to lodge in.

26 And the man [a]bowed down his head, and worshipped the LORD.

23:16 [2] *currency of the merchants*

23:17 [a] Gen. 25:9; 49:29–32; 50:13; Acts 7:16
[1] *deeded*

23:20 [a] Jer. 32:10, 11 [1] *deeded to*

24:1 [a] Gen. 18:11; 21:5 [b] Gen. 12:2; 13:2; 24:35; Ps. 112:3; Prov. 10:22; [Gal. 3:9]
[1] *advanced*

24:2 [a] Gen. 15:2 [b] Gen. 24:10; 39:4–6 [c] Gen. 47:29; 1 Chr. 29:24

24:3 [a] Gen. 14:19, 22 [b] Gen. 26:35; 28:2; Ex. 34:16; Deut. 7:3; 2 Cor. 6:14–17 [1] *take an oath*

24:4 [a] Gen. 28:2 [b] Gen. 12:1; Heb. 11:15

24:5 [1] *Perhaps* [2] *take*

24:6 [1] *take*

24:7 [a] Gen. 12:1; 24:3 [b] Gen. 12:7; 13:15; 15:18; 17:8; Ex. 32:13; Deut. 1:8; 34:4; Acts 7:5 [c] Gen. 16:7; 21:17; 22:11; Ex. 23:20, 23; 33:2; Heb. 1:4, 14 [1] *descendants*

24:8 [a] Josh. 2:17–20 [1] *take*

24:10 [a] Gen. 24:2, 22 [b] Gen. 11:31, 32; 22:20; 27:43; 29:5 [1] Lit. *good things*

24:11 [a] Ex. 2:16; 1 Sam. 9:11

24:12 [a] Gen. 24:27, 42, 48; 26:24; 32:9; Ex. 3:6, 15 [b] Gen. 27:20; Neh. 1:11; Ps. 37:5 [1] *give me success*

24:13 [a] Gen. 24:43 [b] Ex. 2:16

24:14 [a] Judg. 6:17, 37; 1 Sam. 14:10; 16:7; 20:7; 2 Kin. 20:9; Prov. 16:33; Acts 1:26

24:15 [a] Is. 65:24 [b] Gen. 24:45; 25:20 [c] Gen. 22:20, 23 [1] *Rebecca*, Rom. 9:10

24:16 [a] Gen. 12:11; 26:7; 29:17 [1] *beautiful*

24:18 [a] Gen. 24:14, 46; [1 Pet. 3:8, 9]

24:21 [a] Gen.

24:12–14, 27, 52 [1] *so as to know*

24:22 [a] Gen. 24:47; Ex. 32:2, 3; Is. 3:19–21 [1] *nose ring*

24:24 [a] Gen. 22:23; 24:15

24:25 [1] *food*    24:26 [a] Gen. 24:48, 52; Ex. 4:31

27 And he said, [a]Blessed *be* the LORD God of my master Abraham, who hath not [1]left destitute my master of [b]his [2]mercy and his truth: I *being* in the way, the LORD [c]led me to the house of my master's brethren.

28 And the damsel ran, and told *them of* her mother's house these things.

29 And Rebekah had a brother, and his name *was* [a]Laban: and Laban ran out unto the man, unto the well.

30 And it came to pass, when he saw the [1]earring and bracelets upon his sister's hands, and when he heard the words of Rebekah his sister, saying, Thus spake the man unto me; that he came unto the man; and, behold, he stood by the camels at the well.

31 And he said, Come in, [a]thou blessed of the LORD; wherefore standest thou [1]without? for I have prepared the house, and [2]room for the camels.

32 And the man came into the house: and he [1]ungirded his camels, and [a]gave straw and [2]provender for the camels, and water to [b]wash his feet, and the men's feet that *were* with him.

33 And there was set [1]*meat* before him to eat: but he said, [a]I will not eat, until I have told mine errand. And he said, Speak on.

34 And he said, I *am* Abraham's servant.

35 And the LORD [a]hath blessed my master greatly; and he is become great: and he hath given him flocks, and herds, and silver, and gold, and menservants, and maidservants, and camels, and [1]asses.

36 And Sarah my master's wife [a]bare a son to my master when she was old: and [b]unto him hath he given all that he hath.

37 And my master [a]made me swear, saying, Thou shalt not take a wife to my son of the daughters of the Canaanites, in whose land I dwell:

38 [a]But thou shalt go unto my father's house, and to my kindred, and take a wife unto my son.

39 [a]And I said unto my master, [1]Peradventure the woman will not follow me.

40 [a]And he said unto me, The LORD, [b]before whom I walk, will send his angel with thee, and [1]prosper thy way; and thou shalt take a wife for my son of my kindred, and of my father's house:

41 [a]Then shalt thou be clear from *this* my oath, when thou comest to my kindred; and if they give not thee *one,* thou shalt be clear from my oath.

42 And I came this day unto the well, and said, [a]O LORD God of my master Abraham, if now thou do prosper my way which I go:

43 [a]Behold, I stand by the well of water; and it shall come to pass, that when the virgin cometh forth to draw *water,* and I say to her, Give me, I pray thee, a little water of thy pitcher to drink;

44 And she say to me, Both drink thou, and I will also draw for thy camels: *let* the same *be* the woman whom the LORD hath appointed out for my master's son.

45 [a]And before I had [1]done [b]speaking in mine heart, behold, Rebekah came forth with her pitcher on her shoulder; and she went down unto the well, and drew *water:* and I said unto her, Let me drink, I pray thee.

46 And she made haste, and let down her pitcher from her *shoulder,* and said, Drink, and I will give thy camels drink also: so I drank, and she made the camels drink also.

47 And I asked her, and said, Whose daughter *art* thou? And she said, The daughter of Bethuel, Nahor's son, whom Milcah bare unto him: and I put the [1]earring upon her face, and the bracelets upon her hands.

48 [a]And I bowed down my head, and worshipped the LORD, and blessed the LORD God of my master Abraham, which had led me in the [1]right way to [b]take my master's brother's daughter unto his son.

49 And now if ye will [a]deal kindly and truly with my master, tell me: and if not, tell me; that I may turn to the right hand, or to the left.

50 Then Laban and Bethuel answered and said, [a]The thing proceedeth from the LORD: we cannot [b]speak unto thee bad or good.

51 Behold, Rebekah [a]*is* before thee, take *her,* and go, and let her be thy master's son's wife, as the LORD hath spoken.

52 And it came to pass, that, when Abraham's servant heard their words, [a]he worshipped the LORD, *bowing himself* to the earth.

53 And the servant brought forth [a]jewels[1] of silver, and jewels of gold, and [2]raiment, and gave *them* to Rebekah: he gave also to her brother and to her mother [b]precious things.

54 And they did eat and drink, he and the men that *were* with him, and tarried all night; and they rose up in the morning, and he said, [a]Send me away unto my master.

55 And her brother and her mother said, Let the damsel [1]abide with us *a few* days, at the least ten; after that she shall go.

56 And he said unto them, [1]Hinder me not, seeing the LORD hath prospered my way; send me away that I may go to my master.

24:27 [a] Gen. 24:12, 42, 48; Ex. 18:10; Ruth 4:14; 1 Sam. 25:32, 39; 2 Sam. 18:28; Luke 1:68 [b] Gen. 32:10; Ps. 98:3 [c] Gen. 24:21, 48 [1] forsaken [2] lovingkindness

24:29 [a] Gen. 29:5, 13

24:30 [1] nose ring

24:31 [a] Gen. 26:29; Judg. 17:2; Ruth 3:10; Ps. 115:15 [1] outside [2] a place

24:32 [a] Gen. 43:24; Judg. 19:21 [b] Gen. 19:2; John 13:5, 13–15 [1] unloaded [2] feed

24:33 [a] Job 23:12; John 4:34; Eph. 6:5–7 [1] Food

24:35 [a] Gen. 13:2; 24:1 [1] donkeys

24:36 [a] Gen. 21:1–7 [b] Gen. 21:10; 25:5

24:37 [a] Gen. 24:2–4

24:38 [a] Gen. 24:4

24:39 [a] Gen. 24:5 [1] Perhaps

24:40 [a] Gen. 24:7 [b] Gen. 5:22, 24; 17:1; 1 Kin. 8:23 [1] make your way successful

24:41 [a] Gen. 24:8

24:42 [a] Gen. 24:12

24:43 [a] Gen. 24:13

24:45 [a] Gen. 24:15 [b] 1 Sam. 1:13 [1] finished

24:47 [1] nose ring on her nose

24:48 [a] Gen. 24:26, 52 [b] Gen. 22:23; 24:27; Ps. 32:8; 48:14; Is. 48:17 [1] true

24:49 [a] Gen. 47:29; Josh. 2:14

24:50 [a] Ps. 118:23; Matt. 21:42; Mark 12:11 [b] Gen. 31:24, 29

24:51 [a] Gen. 20:15

24:52 [a] Gen. 24:26, 48

24:53 [a] Gen. 24:10, 22; Ex. 3:22; 11:2; 12:35 [b] 2 Chr. 21:3; Ezra 1:6 [1] jewelry [2] clothing

24:54 [a] Gen. 24:56, 59; 30:25

24:55 [1] stay

24:56 [1] Delay

57 And they said, We will call the damsel, and ¹enquire at her mouth.

58 And they called Rebekah, and said unto her, Wilt thou go with this man? And she said, I will go.

59 And they sent away Rebekah their sister, ᵃand her nurse, and Abraham's servant, and his men.

60 And they blessed Rebekah, and said unto her, Thou *art* our sister, be thou ᵃ*the mother* of thousands of ¹millions, and ᵇlet thy ²seed possess the gate of those which hate them.

61 And Rebekah arose, and her damsels, and they rode upon the camels, and followed the man: and the servant took Rebekah, and went his way.

62 And Isaac came from the way of the ᵃwell Lahai-roi; for he dwelt in the south country.

63 And Isaac went out ᵃto meditate in the field at the eventide: and he lifted up his eyes, and saw, and, behold, the camels *were* coming.

64 And Rebekah lifted up her eyes, and when she saw Isaac, ᵃshe ¹lighted off the camel.

65 For she *had* said unto the servant, What man *is* this that walketh in the field to meet us? And the servant *had* said, It *is* my master: therefore she took a vail, and covered herself.

66 And the servant told Isaac all things that he had done.

67 And Isaac brought her into his mother Sarah's tent, and ᵃtook Rebekah, and she became his wife; and he loved her: and Isaac ᵇwas comforted after his mother's *death.*

## CHAPTER 25

THEN again Abraham took a wife, and her name *was* ᵃKeturah.

2 And ᵃshe bare him Zimran, and Jokshan, and Medan, and Midian, and Ishbak, and Shuah.

3 And Jokshan begat Sheba, and Dedan. And the sons of Dedan were Asshurim, and Letushim, and Leummim.

4 And the sons of Midian; Ephah, and Epher, and Hanoch, and Abidah, and Eldaah. All these *were* the children of Keturah.

5 And ᵃAbraham gave all that he had unto Isaac.

6 But unto the sons of the concubines, which Abraham had, Abraham gave gifts, and ᵃsent them away from Isaac his son, while he yet lived, eastward, unto ᵇthe east country.

7 And these *are* the days of the years of Abraham's life which he lived, an hundred threescore and fifteen years.

8 Then Abraham ¹gave up the ghost, and ᵃdied in a good old age, an old man, and full *of years;* and ᵇwas gathered to his people.

9 And ᵃhis sons Isaac and Ishmael buried him in the cave of ᵇMachpelah, in the field of Ephron the son of Zohar the Hittite, which *is* before Mamre;

10 ᵃThe field which Abraham purchased of the sons of Heth: ᵇthere was Abraham buried, and Sarah his wife.

11 And it came to pass after the death of Abraham, that God blessed his son Isaac; and Isaac dwelt by the ᵃwell Lahai-roi.

12 Now ¹these *are* the ᵃgenerations of Ishmael, Abraham's son, whom Hagar the Egyptian, Sarah's ²handmaid, bare unto Abraham:

13 And ᵃthese *are* the names of the sons of Ishmael, by their names, according to their generations: the firstborn of Ishmael, Nebajoth; and Kedar, and Adbeel, and Mibsam,

14 And Mishma, and Dumah, and Massa,

15 ¹Hadar, and Tema, Jetur, Naphish, and Kedemah:

16 These *are* the sons of Ishmael, and these *are* their names, by their towns, and by their ¹castles; ᵃtwelve princes according to their nations.

17 And these *are* the years of the life of Ishmael, an hundred and thirty and seven years: and ᵃhe ¹gave up the ghost and died; and was gathered unto his people.

18 ᵃAnd they dwelt from Havilah unto Shur, that *is* before Egypt, as thou goest toward Assyria: *and* he ¹died ᵇin the presence of all his brethren.

19 And ¹these *are* the ᵃgenerations of Isaac, Abraham's son: ᵇAbraham begat Isaac:

20 And Isaac was forty years old when he took Rebekah to wife, ᵃthe daughter of Bethuel the Syrian of Padan-aram, ᵇthe sister to Laban the Syrian.

21 And Isaac ¹intreated the LORD for his wife, because she *was* barren: ᵃand the LORD was intreated of him, and ᵇRebekah his wife conceived.

22 And the children struggled together within her; and she said, If *it be* ¹so, why *am* I thus? ᵃAnd she went to enquire of the LORD.

23 And the LORD said unto her, ᵃTwo nations *are* in thy womb, and two manner of people shall be separated from thy bowels; and ᵇthe one people shall be stronger than *the other* people; and ᶜthe elder shall serve the younger.

24 And when her days to be delivered were fulfilled, behold, *there were* twins in her womb.

25 And the first came out red, ᵃall over like an hairy garment; and they called his name ¹Esau.

### Cross-references (center column)

24:57 ¹ *ask her personally*
24:59 ᵃ Gen. 35:8
24:60 ᵃ Gen. 17:16 ᵇ Gen. 22:17; 28:14 ¹ *ten thousands* ² *descendants*
24:62 ᵃ Gen. 16:14; 25:11
24:63 ᵃ Josh. 1:8; Ps. 1:2; 77:12; 119:15, 27, 48; 143:5; 145:5
24:64 ᵃ Josh. 15:18 ¹ *dismounted from*
24:67 ᵃ Gen. 25:20; 29:20; Prov. 18:22 ᵇ Gen. 23:1, 2; 38:12
25:1 ᵃ 1 Chr. 1:32, 33
25:2 ᵃ 1 Chr. 1:32, 33
25:5 ᵃ Gen. 24:35, 36
25:6 ᵃ Gen. 21:14 ᵇ Judg. 6:3
25:8 ᵃ Gen. 15:15; 47:8, 9 ᵇ Gen. 25:17; 35:29; 49:29, 33 ¹ *breathed his last*
25:9 ᵃ Gen. 35:29; 50:13 ᵇ Gen. 23:9, 17; 49:30
25:10 ᵃ Gen. 23:3–16 ᵇ Gen. 49:31
25:11 ᵃ Gen. 16:14
25:12 ᵃ Gen. 11:10, 27; 16:15 ¹ *this is the genealogy* ² *maidservant*
25:13 ᵃ 1 Chr. 1:29–31
25:15 ¹ MT *Hadad*
25:16 ᵃ Gen. 17:20 ¹ *settlements or camps*
25:17 ᵃ Gen. 25:8; 49:33 ¹ *breathed his last*
25:18 ᵃ 1 Sam. 15:7 ᵇ Gen. 16:12 ¹ Lit. *fell*
25:19 ᵃ Gen. 36:1, 9 ᵇ Matt. 1:2 ¹ *this is the genealogy*
25:20 ᵃ Gen. 22:23; 24:15, 29, 67 ᵇ Gen. 24:29
25:21 ᵃ 1 Chr. 5:20 ᵇ Rom. 9:10–13 ¹ *pleaded with*
25:22 ᵃ 1 Sam. 1:15; 9:9; 10:22 ¹ *well*
25:23 ᵃ Gen. 17:4–6, 16; 24:60 ᵇ 2 Sam. 8:14 ᶜ Rom. 9:12
25:25 ᵃ Gen. 27:11, 16, 23 ¹ Lit. *Hairy*

26 And after that came his brother out, and ªhis hand took hold on Esau's heel; and ᵇhis name was called ¹Jacob: and Isaac *was* threescore years old when she bare them.

27 And the boys grew: and Esau was ªa ¹cunning hunter, a man of the field; and Jacob *was* ᵇa ²plain man, ᶜdwelling in tents.

28 And Isaac loved Esau, because he did ªeat of *his* venison: ᵇbut Rebekah loved Jacob.

29 And Jacob ¹sod pottage: and Esau came from the field, and he *was* faint:

30 And Esau said to Jacob, Feed me, I pray thee, with that same red *pottage;* for I *am* faint: therefore was his name called ¹Edom.

31 And Jacob said, Sell me this day thy birthright.

32 And Esau said, Behold, I *am* at the point to die: and ªwhat profit shall this birthright do to me?

33 And Jacob said, Swear to me this day; and he sware unto him: and ªhe sold his birthright unto Jacob.

34 Then Jacob gave Esau bread and ¹pottage of lentiles; and ªhe did eat and drink, and rose up, and went his way: thus Esau ᵇdespised *his* birthright.

## CHAPTER 26

AND there was a famine in the land, beside ªthe first famine that was in the days of Abraham. And Isaac went unto ᵇAbimelech king of the Philistines unto Gerar.

2 And the LORD appeared unto him, and said, ªGo not down into Egypt; dwell in ᵇthe land which I shall tell thee of:

3 ªSojourn in this land, and ᵇI will be with thee, and ᶜwill bless thee; for unto thee, and unto thy seed, ᵈI will give all these countries, and I will perform ᵉthe oath which I sware unto Abraham thy father;

4 And ªI will make thy ¹seed to multiply as the stars of heaven, and will give unto thy seed all these ²countries; ᵇand in thy seed shall all the nations of the earth be blessed;

5 ªBecause that Abraham obeyed my voice, and kept my charge, my commandments, my statutes, and my laws.

6 And Isaac dwelt in Gerar:

7 And the men of the place asked *him* of his wife; and ªhe said, She *is* my sister: for ᵇhe feared to say, *She is* my wife; lest, *said he,* the men of the place should kill me for Rebekah; because she ᶜ*was* ¹fair to look upon.

8 And it came to pass, when he had been there a long time, that Abimelech king of the Philistines looked out at a window, and saw, and, behold,

Isaac *was* ¹sporting with Rebekah his wife.

9 And Abimelech called Isaac, and said, Behold, ¹of a surety she *is* thy wife: and how saidst thou, She *is* my sister? And Isaac said unto him, Because I said, Lest I die ²for her.

10 And Abimelech said, What *is* this thou hast done unto us? one of the people might ¹lightly have lien with thy wife, and ªthou shouldest have brought guiltiness upon us.

11 And Abimelech charged all *his* people, saying, He that ªtoucheth this man or his wife shall surely be put to death.

12 Then Isaac sowed in that land, and ¹received in the same year ªan hundredfold: and the LORD ᵇblessed him.

13 And the man ªwaxed¹ great, and ²went forward, and grew until he became very great:

14 For he had possession of flocks, and possession of herds, and ¹great store of servants: and the Philistines ªenvied him.

15 For all the wells ªwhich his father's servants had digged in the days of Abraham his father, the Philistines had stopped them, and filled them with earth.

16 And Abimelech said unto Isaac, Go from us; for ªthou art much mightier than we.

17 And Isaac departed thence, and ¹pitched his tent in the valley of Gerar, and dwelt there.

18 And Isaac digged again the wells of water, which they had digged in the days of Abraham his father; for the Philistines had stopped them after the death of Abraham: ªand he called their names after the names by which his father had called them.

19 And Isaac's servants digged in the valley, and found there a well of ¹springing water.

20 And the herdmen of Gerar ªdid¹ strive with Isaac's herdmen, saying, The water *is* ours: and he called the name of the well ²Esek; because they strove with him.

21 And they digged another well, and strove for that also: and he called the name of it ¹Sitnah.

22 And he ¹removed from thence, and digged another well; and for that they strove not: and he called the name of it ²Rehoboth; and he said, For now the LORD ³hath made room for us, and we shall ªbe fruitful in the land.

23 And he went up from thence to Beer-sheba.

24 And the LORD ªappeared unto him the same night, and said, ᵇI *am*

25:26 ª Hos. 12:3 ᵇ Gen. 27:36 ¹ *Supplanter* or *Deceitful,* lit. *One Who Takes the Heel*
25:27 ª Gen. 27:3, 5 ᵇ Job 1:1, 8 ᶜ Heb. 11:9 ¹ *skilful* ² *mild,* lit. *complete*
25:28 ª Gen. 27:4, 19, 25, 31 ᵇ Gen. 27:6–10
25:29 ¹ *cooked a stew*
25:30 ¹ Lit. *Red*
25:32 ª Mark 8:36, 37
25:33 ª Heb. 12:16
25:34 ª Eccl. 8:15 ᵇ Heb. 12:16, 17 ¹ *stew*
26:1 ª Gen. 12:10 ᵇ Gen. 20:1, 2
26:2 ª Gen. 12:7; 17:1; 18:1; 35:9 ᵇ Gen. 12:1
26:3 ª Heb. 11:9 ᵇ Gen. 28:13, 15 ᶜ Gen. 12:2 ᵈ Gen. 12:7; 13:15; 15:18 ᵉ Gen. 22:16
26:4 ª Gen. 15:5; 22:17 ᵇ Gen. 12:3; 22:18 ¹ *descendants* ² Lit. *lands*
26:5 ª Gen. 22:16, 18
26:7 ª Gen. 12:13; 20:2, 12, 13 ᵇ Prov. 29:25 ᶜ Gen. 12:11; 24:16; 29:17 ¹ *beautiful*
26:8 ¹ *caressing*
26:9 ¹ *obviously* ² *on account of*
26:10 ª Gen. 20:9 ¹ *soon*
26:11 ª Ps. 105:15
26:12 ª Matt. 13:8, 23; Mark 4:8 ᵇ Gen. 24:1; 25:3, 11; 26:3; Job 42:12; Prov. 10:22 ¹ *reaped*
26:13 ª Gen. 24:35; [Prov. 10:22] ¹ *grew* ² *continued prospering until*
26:14 ª Gen. 37:11; Eccl. 4:4 ¹ *a great number*
26:15 ª Gen. 21:25, 30
26:16 ª Ex. 1:9
26:17 ¹ *camped*
26:18 ª Gen. 21:31
26:19 ¹ *running*
26:20 ª Gen. 21:25 ¹ *quarreled* ² Lit. *Quarrel*
26:21 ¹ Lit. *Enmity*
26:22 ª Gen. 17:6; 28:3; 41:52; Ex. 1:7 ¹ *moved* ² Lit. *Spaciousness* ³ *has enlarged*
26:24 ª Gen. 26:2 ᵇ Gen. 17:7, 8; 24:12; Ex. 3:6; Acts 7:32

the God of Abraham thy father: cfear not, for dI *am* with thee, and will bless thee, and multiply thy 1seed for my servant Abraham's sake.

25 And he abuilded an altar there, and bcalled upon the name of the LORD, and pitched his tent there: and there Isaac's servants digged a well.

26 Then Abimelech went to him from Gerar, and Ahuzzath one of his friends, aand Phichol the chief captain of his army.

27 And Isaac said unto them, Wherefore come ye to me, aseeing ye hate me, and have bsent me away from you?

28 And they said, We saw certainly that the LORD awas with thee: and we said, Let there be now an oath betwixt us, *even* betwixt us and thee, and let us make a 1covenant with thee;

29 That thou wilt do us no 1hurt, as we have not touched thee, and as we have done unto thee nothing but good, and have sent thee away in peace: athou *art* now the blessed of the LORD.

30 aAnd he made them a feast, and they did eat and drink.

31 And they rose up 1betimes in the morning, and asware one to another: and Isaac sent them away, and they departed from him in peace.

32 And it came to pass the same day, that Isaac's servants came, and told him concerning the well which they had digged, and said unto him, We have found water.

33 And he called it 1Shebah: atherefore the name of the city *is* 2Beersheba unto this day.

34 aAnd Esau was forty years old when he took to wife Judith the daughter of Beeri the Hittite, and Bashemath the daughter of Elon the Hittite:

35 Which awere a grief of mind unto Isaac and to Rebekah.

## CHAPTER 27

AND it came to pass, that when Isaac was aold, and bhis eyes were dim, so that he could not see, he called Esau his eldest son, and said unto him, My son: and he said unto him, Behold, *here am* I.

2 And he said, Behold now, I am old, I aknow not the day of my death:

3 aNow therefore take, I pray thee, thy weapons, thy quiver and thy bow, and go out to the field, and 1take me *some* venison;

4 And make me 1savoury meat, such as I love, and bring *it* to me, that I may eat; that my soul amay bless thee before I die.

5 And Rebekah heard when Isaac spake to Esau his son. And Esau went

to the field to hunt *for* venison, *and* to bring *it.*

6 And Rebekah spake unto Jacob her son, saying, Behold, I heard thy father speak unto Esau thy brother, saying,

7 Bring me 1venison, and make me 2savoury meat, that I may eat, and bless thee before the LORD before my death.

8 Now therefore, my son, aobey my voice according to that which I command thee.

9 Go now to the flock, and fetch me from thence two good kids of the goats; and I will make them asavoury meat for thy father, such as he loveth:

10 And thou shalt bring *it* to thy father, that he may eat, and that he amay bless thee before his death.

11 And Jacob said to Rebekah his mother, Behold, aEsau my brother *is* a hairy man, and I *am* a 1smooth man:

12 My father 1peradventure will afeel me, and I shall seem to him as a deceiver; and I shall bring ba curse upon me, and not a blessing.

13 And his mother said unto him, aUpon me *be* thy curse, my son: only obey my voice, and go fetch me *them.*

14 And he went, and fetched, and brought *them* to his mother: and his mother amade 1savoury meat, such as his father loved.

15 And Rebekah took agoodly1 raiment of her eldest son Esau, which *were* with her in the house, and put them upon Jacob her younger son:

16 And she put the skins of the kids of the goats upon his hands, and upon the 1smooth of his neck:

17 And she gave the savoury meat and the bread, which she had prepared, into the hand of her son Jacob.

18 And he came unto his father, and said, My father: and he said, Here *am* I; who *art* thou, my son?

19 And Jacob said unto his father, I *am* Esau thy firstborn; I have done according as thou 1badest me: arise, I pray thee, sit and eat of my 2venison, athat thy soul may bless me.

20 And Isaac said unto his son, How *is it* that thou hast found *it* so quickly, my son? And he said, Because the LORD thy God brought *it* to me.

21 And Isaac said unto Jacob, Come near, I pray thee, that I amay feel thee, my son, whether thou *be* my very son Esau or not.

22 And Jacob went near unto Isaac his father; and he felt him, and said, The voice *is* Jacob's voice, but the hands *are* the hands of Esau.

23 And he 1discerned him not, because ahis hands were hairy, as his brother Esau's hands: so he blessed him.

### Cross references (center column)

26:24 c Gen. 15:1
d Gen. 26:3, 4
1 *descendants*

26:25 a Gen. 12:7, 8; 13:4, 18; 22:9; 33:20 b Gen. 21:33; Ps. 116:17

26:26 a Gen. 21:22

26:27 a Judg. 11:7
b Gen. 26:16

26:28 a Gen. 21:22, 23 1 *treaty*

26:29 a Gen. 24:31; Ps. 115:15
1 *harm*

26:30 a Gen. 19:3

26:31 a Gen. 21:31
1 *early*

26:33 a Gen. 21:31; 28:10 1 Lit. *Oath* or *Seven* 2 Lit. *Well of the Oath* or *Well of the Seven*

26:34 a Gen. 28:8; 36:2

26:35 a Gen. 27:46; 28:1, 8

27:1 a Gen. 35:28
b Gen. 48:10; 1 Sam. 3:2

27:2 a [Prov. 27:1; James 4:14]

27:3 a Gen. 25:27, 28 1 *hunt game for me*

27:4 a Gen. 27:19, 25, 27, 31; 48:9, 15, 16; 49:28; Deut. 33:1; Heb. 11:20 1 *tasty food*

27:7 1 *game* 2 *tasty food*

27:8 a Gen. 27:13, 43

27:9 a Gen. 27:4

27:10 a Gen. 27:4; 48:16

27:11 a Gen. 25:25
1 *smooth*-skinned

27:12 a Gen. 27:21, 22 b Gen. 9:25; Deut. 27:18 1 *perhaps*

27:13 a Gen. 43:9; 1 Sam. 25:24; 2 Sam. 14:9; Matt. 27:25

27:14 a Prov. 23:3; Luke 21:34 1 *tasty food*

27:15 a Gen. 27:27 1 *choice clothes*

27:16 1 *smooth part*

27:19 a Gen. 27:4 1 *told* 2 *game*

27:21 a Gen. 27:12

27:23 a Gen. 27:16 1 *recognized*

24 And he said, *Art* thou ¹my very son Esau? And he said, I *am*.

25 And he said, Bring *it* near to me, and I will eat of my son's venison, ᵃthat my soul may bless thee. And he brought *it* near to him, and he did eat: and he brought him wine, and he drank.

26 And his father Isaac said unto him, Come near now, and kiss me, my son.

27 And he came near, and ᵃkissed him: and he smelled the smell of his ¹raiment, and blessed him, and said, See, ᵇthe smell of my son *is* as the smell of a field which the LORD hath blessed:

28 Therefore ᵃGod give thee of ᵇthe dew of heaven, and ᶜthe fatness of the earth, and ᵈplenty of ¹corn and wine:

29 ᵃLet ¹people serve thee, and nations bow down to thee: be ²lord over thy brethren, and ᵇlet thy mother's sons bow down to thee: ᶜcursed *be* every one that curseth thee, and blessed *be* he that blesseth thee.

30 And it came to pass, as soon as Isaac had made an end of blessing Jacob, and Jacob ¹was yet scarce gone out from the presence of Isaac his father, that Esau his brother came in from his hunting.

31 And he also had made ¹savoury meat, and brought it unto his father, and said unto his father, Let my father arise, and ᵃeat of his son's venison, that thy soul may bless me.

32 And Isaac his father said unto him, Who *art* thou? And he said, I *am* thy son, thy firstborn Esau.

33 And Isaac trembled very exceedingly, and said, Who? where *is* he that hath ¹taken venison, and brought *it* me, and I have eaten of all before thou camest, and have blessed him? yea, ᵃ*and* he shall be blessed.

34 And when Esau heard the words of his father, ᵃhe cried with a great and exceeding bitter cry, and said unto his father, Bless me, *even* me also, O my father.

35 And he said, Thy brother came with ¹subtilty, and hath taken away thy blessing.

36 And he said, ᵃIs not he rightly named ¹Jacob? for he hath supplanted me these two times: he took away my birthright; and, behold, now he hath taken away my blessing. And he said, Hast thou not reserved a blessing for me?

37 And Isaac answered and said unto Esau, ᵃBehold, I have made him thy ¹lord, and all his brethren have I given to him for servants; and ᵇwith ²corn and wine have I sustained him: and what shall I do now unto thee, my son?

38 And Esau said unto his father, Hast thou but one blessing, my father? bless me, *even* me also, O my father. And Esau lifted up his voice, ᵃand wept.

39 And Isaac his father answered and said unto him, Behold, ᵃthy dwelling shall be ¹the fatness of the earth, and of the dew of heaven from above;

40 And by thy sword shalt thou live, and ᵃshalt serve thy brother; and ᵇit shall come to pass when thou shalt have ¹the dominion, that thou shalt break his yoke from off thy neck.

41 And Esau ᵃhated Jacob because of the blessing wherewith his father blessed him: and Esau said in his heart, ᵇThe days of mourning for my father are at hand; ᶜthen will I slay my brother Jacob.

42 And these words of Esau her elder son were told to Rebekah: and she sent and called Jacob her younger son, and said unto him, Behold, thy brother Esau, ¹as touching thee, doth ᵃcomfort himself, ²*purposing* to kill thee.

43 Now therefore, my son, obey my voice; and arise, flee thou to Laban my brother ᵃto Haran;

44 And ¹tarry with him a ᵃfew days, until thy brother's fury turn away;

45 Until thy brother's anger turn away from thee, and he forget *that* which thou hast done to him: then I will send, and fetch thee from thence: why should I be ¹deprived also of you both in one day?

46 And Rebekah said to Isaac, ᵃI am weary of my life because of the daughters of Heth: ᵇif Jacob take a wife of the daughters of Heth, such as these *which are* of the daughters of the land, what good shall my life do me?

## CHAPTER 28

AND Isaac called Jacob, and ᵃblessed him, and ¹charged him, and said unto him, ᵇThou shalt not take a wife of the daughters of Canaan.

2 ᵃArise, go to ᵇPadan-aram, to the house of ᶜBethuel thy mother's father; and take thee a wife from thence of the daughters of ᵈLaban thy mother's brother.

3 ᵃAnd God Almighty bless thee, and make thee ᵇfruitful, and multiply thee, that thou mayest be ¹a multitude of people;

4 And give thee ᵃthe blessing of Abraham, to thee, and to thy ¹seed with thee; that thou mayest inherit the land ᵇwherein² thou art a stranger, which God gave unto Abraham.

### Cross-references

27:24 ¹ *really my son*

27:25 ᵃ Gen. 27:4, 10, 19, 31

27:27 ᵃ Gen. 29:13 ᵇ Song 4:11; Hos. 14:6 ¹ *clothing*

27:28 ᵃ Heb. 11:20 ᵇ Gen.

27:39; Deut. 33:13, 28; 2 Sam. 1:21; Ps. 133:3; Prov. 3:20; Mic. 5:7; Zech. 8:12 ᶜ Gen. 45:18; Num. 18:12 ᵈ Deut. 7:13; 33:28 ¹ *grain*

27:29 ᵃ Gen. 9:25; 25:23; Is. 45:14; 49:7; 60:12, 14 ᵇ Gen. 37:7, 10; 49:8 ᶜ Gen. 12:2, 3; Zeph. 2:8, 9 ¹ *peoples* ² *master*

27:30 ¹ *had scarcely*

27:31 ᵃ Gen. 27:4 ¹ *tasty food*

27:33 ᵃ Gen. 25:23; 28:3, 4; Num. 23:20; Rom. 11:29 ¹ *hunted game*

27:34 ᵃ [Heb. 12:17]

27:35 ¹ *deceit*

27:36 ᵃ Gen. 25:26, 32–34 ¹ Lit. *Supplanter*

27:37 ᵃ 2 Sam. 8:14 ᵇ Gen. 27:28, 29 ¹ *master* ² *grain*

27:38 ᵃ Heb. 12:17

27:39 ᵃ Gen. 27:28; Heb. 11:20 ¹ *of the fertility*

27:40 ᵃ Gen. 25:23; 27:29; 2 Sam. 8:14; [Obad. 18–20] ᵇ 2 Kin. 8:20–22 ¹ *become restless*

27:41 ᵃ Gen. 26:27; 32:3–11; 37:4, 5, 8 ᵇ Gen. 50:2–4, 10 ᶜ Obad. 10

27:42 ᵃ Ps. 64:5 ¹ *concerning you* ² *by intending*

27:43 ᵃ Gen. 11:31; 35:20; 28:2, 5

27:44 ᵃ Gen. 31:41 ¹ *stay*

27:45 ¹ *bereaved*

27:46 ᵃ Gen. 26:34, 35; 28:8 ᵇ Gen. 24:3

28:1 ᵃ Gen. 27:33 ᵇ Gen. 24:3 ¹ *commanded*

28:2 ᵃ Hos. 12:12 ᵇ Gen. 25:20 ᶜ Gen. 22:23 ᵈ Gen. 24:29; 27:43; 29:5

28:3 ᵃ Gen. 17:16; 35:11; 48:3 ᵇ Gen. 26:4, 24 ¹ *an assembly* 28:4 ᵃ Gen. 12:2, 3; 22:17 ᵇ Gen. 17:8; 23:4; 36:7 ¹ *descendants* ² *of your sojournings*

5 And Isaac sent away Jacob: and he went to Padan-aram unto Laban, son of Bethuel the Syrian, the brother of Rebekah, Jacob's and Esau's mother.

6 When Esau saw that Isaac had blessed Jacob, and sent him away to Padan-aram, to take him a wife from thence; and that as he blessed him he gave him a charge, saying, Thou shalt not take a wife of the daughters of Canaan;

7 And that Jacob obeyed his father and his mother, and was gone to Padan-aram;

8 And Esau seeing ªthat the daughters of Canaan pleased not Isaac his father;

9 Then went Esau unto Ishmael, and ªtook ¹unto the wives which he had ᵇMahalath the daughter of Ishmael Abraham's son, ᶜthe sister of Nebajoth, to be his wife.

10 And Jacob ªwent out from Beersheba, and went toward ᵇHaran.

11 And he ¹lighted upon a certain place, and ²tarried there all night, because the sun was set; and he took ³of the stones of that place, and ⁴put *them for* his pillows, and lay down in that place to sleep.

12 And he ªdreamed, and behold a ladder set up on the earth, and the top of it reached to heaven: and behold ᵇthe angels of God ascending and descending on it.

13 ªAnd, behold, the LORD stood above it, and said, ᵇI *am* the LORD God of Abraham thy father, and the God of Isaac: ᶜthe land whereon thou liest, to thee will I give it, and to thy ¹seed;

14 And thy ªseed¹ shall be as the dust of the earth, and thou shalt spread abroad ᵇto the west, and to the east, and to the north, and to the south: and in thee and ᶜin thy seed shall all the families of the earth be blessed.

15 And, behold, ªI *am* with thee, and will ᵇkeep thee in all *places* whither thou goest, and will ᶜbring thee again into this land; for ᵈI will not leave thee, ᵉuntil I have done *that* which I have spoken to thee of.

16 And Jacob awaked out of his sleep, and he said, Surely the LORD is in ªthis place; and I knew *it* not.

17 And he was afraid, and said, How ¹dreadful *is* this place! this *is* none other but the house of God, and this *is* the gate of heaven.

18 And Jacob rose up early in the morning, and took the stone that he had put ¹*for* his pillows, and ªset it up *for* a pillar, ᵇand poured oil upon the top of it.

19 And he called the name of ªthat place ¹Beth-el: but the name of that city *was called* Luz at the first.

20 ªAnd Jacob vowed a vow, saying, If ᵇGod will be with me, and will keep me in this way that I go, and will give me ᶜbread to eat, and raiment to put on,

21 So that ªI come again to my father's house in peace; ᵇthen shall the LORD be my God:

22 And this stone, which I have set *for* a pillar, ªshall be God's house: ᵇand of all that thou shalt give me I will surely give ¹the tenth unto thee.

## CHAPTER 29

THEN Jacob went on his journey, ªand came into the land of the people of the east.

2 And he looked, and behold a ªwell in the field, and, lo, there *were* three flocks of sheep lying by it; for out of that well they watered the flocks: and a great stone *was* upon the well's mouth.

3 And thither were all the flocks gathered: and they rolled the stone from the well's mouth, and watered the sheep, and put the stone again upon the well's mouth in his place.

4 And Jacob said unto them, My brethren, whence *be* ye? And they said, Of ªHaran *are* we.

5 And he said unto them, Know ye ªLaban the son of Nahor? And they said, We know *him.*

6 And he said unto them, ªIs he well? And they said, He is well: and, behold, Rachel his daughter ᵇcometh with the sheep.

7 And he said, Lo, *it is* yet ¹high day, neither *is it* time that the cattle should be gathered together: water ye the sheep, and go *and* feed *them.*

8 And they said, We cannot, until all the flocks be gathered together, and *till* they roll the stone from the well's mouth; then we water the sheep.

9 And while he yet spake with them, ªRachel came with her father's sheep: for she kept them.

10 And it came to pass, when Jacob saw Rachel the daughter of Laban his mother's brother, and the sheep of Laban his mother's brother, that Jacob went near, and ªrolled the stone from the well's mouth, and watered the flock of Laban his mother's brother.

11 And Jacob ªkissed Rachel, and lifted up his voice, and wept.

12 And Jacob told Rachel that he *was* ªher father's ¹brother, and that he *was* Rebekah's son: ᵇand she ran and told her father.

13 And it came to pass, when Laban heard the tidings of Jacob his sister's son, that ªhe ran to meet him, and embraced him, and kissed him, and brought him to his house. And he told Laban all these things.

### Cross-references (center column)

28:8 ª Gen. 24:3; 26:34, 35; 27:46
28:9 ª Gen. 26:34, 35 ᵇ Gen. 36:2, 3 ᶜ Gen. 25:13 ¹ *in addition to*
28:10 ª Hos. 12:12 ᵇ Gen. 12:4, 5; 27:43; 29:4
28:11 ¹ *came to* ² *stayed* ³ *one of* ⁴ Lit. *put it at his head*
28:12 ª Gen. 31:10; 41:1 ᵇ John 1:51
28:13 ª Gen. 35:1; 48:3 ᵇ Gen. 26:24 ᶜ Gen. 13:15, 17; 26:3; 35:12 ¹ *descendants*
28:14 ª Gen. 13:16; 22:17 ᵇ Gen. 13:14, 15 ᶜ Gen. 12:3; 18:18; 22:18; 26:4 ¹ *descendants*
28:15 ª Gen. 26:3, 24; 31:3 ᵇ Gen. 48:16 ᶜ Gen. 35:6; 48:21 ᵈ Deut. 7:9; 31:6, 8 ᵉ Num. 23:19
28:16 ª Ex. 3:5
28:17 ¹ *awesome*
28:18 ª Gen. 31:13, 45 ᵇ Lev. 8:10–12 ¹ Lit. *at his head*
28:19 ª Judg. 1:23, 26 ¹ Lit. *House of God*
28:20 ª Judg. 11:30 ᵇ Gen. 28:15 ᶜ 1 Tim. 6:8
28:21 ª Judg. 11:31 ᵇ Deut. 26:17
28:22 ª Gen. 35:7, 14 ᵇ Gen. 14:20 ¹ *a tithe*
29:1 ª Num. 23:7
29:2 ª Gen. 24:10, 11
29:4 ª Gen. 11:31; 28:10
29:5 ª Gen. 24:24, 29; 28:2
29:6 ª Gen. 43:27 ᵇ Gen. 24:11; Ex. 2:16, 17
29:7 ¹ *Early in the day*
29:9 ª Ex. 2:16
29:10 ª Ex. 2:17
29:11 ª Gen. 33:4; 45:14, 15
29:12 ª Gen. 13:8; 14:14, 16; 28:5 ᵇ Gen. 24:28 ¹ *relative*
29:13 ª Gen. 24:29–31; Luke 15:20

14 And Laban said to him, [a]Surely thou *art* my bone and my flesh. And he abode with him the space of a month.

15 And Laban said unto Jacob, Because thou *art* my brother, shouldest thou therefore serve me for [1]nought? tell me, [a]what *shall* thy wages *be?*

16 And Laban had two daughters: the name of the elder *was* Leah, and the name of the younger *was* Rachel.

17 Leah *was* [1]tender eyed; but Rachel was [a]beautiful [2]and well favoured.

18 And Jacob loved Rachel; and said, [a]I will serve thee seven years for Rachel thy younger daughter.

19 And Laban said, *It is* better that I give her to thee, than that I should give her to another man: abide with me.

20 And Jacob [a]served seven years for Rachel; and they seemed unto him *but* a few days, [1]for the love he had [2]to her.

21 And Jacob said unto Laban, Give *me* my wife, for my days are fulfilled, that I may [a]go in unto her.

22 And Laban gathered together all the men of the place, and [a]made a feast.

23 And it came to pass in the evening, that he took Leah his daughter, and brought her to him; and he went in unto her.

24 And Laban gave unto his daughter Leah [a]Zilpah his maid *for* an handmaid.

25 And it came to pass, that in the morning, behold, it *was* Leah: and he said to Laban, What *is* this thou hast done unto me? did not I serve with thee for Rachel? wherefore then hast thou [a]beguiled[1] me?

26 And Laban said, It must not be so done in our [1]country, to give the younger before the firstborn.

27 [a]Fulfil her week, and we will give thee this also for the service which thou shalt serve with me yet seven other years.

28 And Jacob did so, and fulfilled her week: and he gave him Rachel his daughter [1]to wife also.

29 And Laban gave to Rachel his daughter [a]Bilhah his handmaid to be her maid.

30 And [1]he went in also unto Rachel, and he [a]loved also Rachel more than Leah, and served with him [b]yet seven other years.

31 And when the LORD [a]saw that Leah *was* [1]hated, he [b]opened her womb: but Rachel *was* barren.

32 And Leah conceived, and bare a son, and she called his name [1]Reuben: for she said, Surely the LORD hath [a]looked upon my affliction; now therefore my husband will love me.

33 And she conceived again, and bare a son; and said, Because the LORD hath heard that I *was* [1]hated, he hath therefore given me this *son* also: and she called his name [2]Simeon.

34 And she conceived again, and bare a son; and said, Now this time will my husband [1]be joined unto me, because I have born him three sons: therefore was his name called [2]Levi.

35 And she conceived again, and bare a son: and she said, Now will I praise the LORD: therefore she called his name [a]Judah;[1] and [2]left bearing.

## CHAPTER 30

AND when Rachel saw that [a]she bare Jacob no children, Rachel [b]envied her sister; and said unto Jacob, Give me children, [c]or else I die.

2 And Jacob's anger was kindled against Rachel: and he said, [a]*Am* I in God's stead, who hath withheld from thee the fruit of the womb?

3 And she said, Behold [a]my maid Bilhah, go in unto her; [b]and she shall bear [1]upon my knees, [c]that I may also [2]have children by her.

4 And she gave him Bilhah her handmaid [a]to[1] wife: and Jacob went in unto her.

5 And Bilhah conceived, and bare Jacob a son.

6 And Rachel said, God hath [a]judged [1]me, and hath also heard my voice, and hath given me a son: therefore called she his name [2]Dan.

7 And Bilhah Rachel's maid conceived again, and bare Jacob a second son.

8 And Rachel said, With [1]great wrestlings have I wrestled with my sister, and I have prevailed: and she called his name [2]Naphtali.

9 When Leah saw that she had left bearing, she took Zilpah her maid, and [a]gave her Jacob [1]to wife.

10 And Zilpah Leah's maid bare Jacob a son.

11 And Leah said, A [1]troop cometh: and she called his name [2]Gad.

12 And Zilpah Leah's maid bare Jacob a second son.

13 And Leah said, Happy am I, for the daughters [a]will call me blessed: and she called his name [1]Asher.

14 And Reuben went in the days of wheat harvest, and found mandrakes in the field, and brought them unto his mother Leah. Then Rachel said to Leah, [a]Give me, I pray thee, of thy son's mandrakes.

15 And she said unto her, [a]*Is it* a small matter that thou hast taken my husband? and wouldest thou take away my son's mandrakes also? And Rachel said, Therefore he shall lie

---

29:14 [a] Gen. 2:23; 37:27; Judg. 9:2; 2 Sam. 5:1; 19:12, 13
29:15 [a] Gen. 30:28; 31:41 [1] *nothing*
29:17 [a] Gen. 12:11, 14; 26:7 [1] *delicate or soft* [2] *of form and appearance*
29:18 [a] Gen. 31:41; 2 Sam. 3:14; Hos. 12:12
29:20 [a] Gen. 30:26; Hos. 12:12 [1] *because of* [2] *for*
29:21 [a] Judg. 15:1
29:22 [a] Judg. 14:10; John 2:1, 2
29:24 [a] Gen. 30:9, 10
29:25 [a] Gen. 27:35; 31:7; 1 Sam. 28:12 [1] *deceived*
29:26 [1] Lit. *place*
29:27 [a] Gen. 31:41; Judg. 14:2
29:28 [1] *as*
29:29 [a] Gen. 30:3–5
29:30 [a] Gen. 29:17–20; Deut. 21:15–17 [b] Gen. 30:26; 31:41; Hos. 12:12 [1] *Jacob*
29:31 [a] Ps. 127:3 [b] Gen. 30:1 [1] *unloved*
29:32 [a] Gen. 16:11; 31:42; Ex. 3:7; 4:31; Deut. 26:7; Ps. 25:18 [1] *Lit. See, a Son*
29:33 [1] *unloved* [2] Lit. *Heard*
29:34 [1] *become attached to* [2] Lit. *Attached*
29:35 [a] Gen. 49:8; Matt. 1:2 [1] Lit. *Praise* [2] *stopped*
30:1 [a] Gen. 16:1, 2; 29:31 [b] Gen. 37:11 [c] 1 Sam. 1:5, 6; [Job 5:2]
30:2 [a] Gen. 16:2; 1 Sam. 1:5
30:3 [a] Gen. 16:2 [b] Gen. 50:23; Job 3:12 [c] Gen. 16:2; 3 [1] *to be upon* [2] Lit. *be built up*
30:4 [a] Gen. 16:3, 4 [1] *as*
30:6 [a] Gen. 18:25; Ps. 35:24; 43:1; Lam. 3:59 [1] *my case* [2] Lit. *Judge*
30:8 [1] Lit. *wrestlings of God* [2] Lit. *My Wrestling*
30:9 [a] Gen. 30:4 [1] *as*
30:11 [1] *fortune* [2] Lit. *Troop or Fortune*
30:13 [a] Prov. 31:28; Luke 1:48 [1] Lit. *Happy*
30:14 [a] Gen. 25:30  30:15 [a] [Num. 16:9, 13]

with thee to night for thy son's mandrakes.

16 And Jacob came out of the field in the evening, and Leah went out to meet him, and said, Thou must come in unto me; for surely I have hired thee with my son's mandrakes. And he lay with her that night.

17 And God hearkened unto Leah, and she conceived, and bare Jacob the fifth son.

18 And Leah said, God hath given me my hire, because I have given my maiden to my husband: and she called his name [1]Issachar.

19 And Leah conceived again, and bare Jacob the sixth son.

20 And Leah said, God hath endued me *with* a good [1]dowry; now will my husband dwell with me, because I have born him six sons: and she called his name [2]Zebulun.

21 And afterwards she bare a [a]daughter, and called her name [1]Dinah.

22 And God [a]remembered Rachel, and God hearkened to her, and [b]opened her womb.

23 And she conceived, and bare a son; and said, God hath taken away [a]my reproach:

24 And she called his name [1]Joseph; and said, [a]The LORD shall add to me another son.

25 And it came to pass, when Rachel had born Joseph, that Jacob said unto Laban, [a]Send me away, that I may go unto [b]mine own place, and to my country.

26 Give *me* my wives and my children, [a]for whom I have served thee, and let me go: for thou knowest my service which I have done thee.

27 And Laban said unto him, I pray thee, if I have found favour in thine eyes, [1]*tarry: for* [a]I have learned by experience that the LORD hath blessed me for thy sake.

28 And he said, [a]Appoint[1] me thy wages, and I will give *it*.

29 And he said unto him, [a]Thou knowest how I have served thee, and how thy [2]cattle was with me.

30 For *it was* little which thou hadst before I *came*, and it is *now* increased unto a multitude; and the LORD hath blessed thee [1]since my coming: and now when shall I [a]provide for mine own house also?

31 And he said, What shall I give thee? And Jacob said, Thou shalt not give me any thing: if thou wilt do this thing for me, I will again feed *and* keep thy flock:

32 I will pass through all thy flock to day, removing from thence all the speckled and spotted [1]cattle, and all the brown cattle among the sheep, and the spotted and speckled among

the goats: and [a]*of*[2] *such* shall be my hire.

33 So shall my [a]righteousness answer for me in time to come, when it shall come [1]for my hire before thy face: every one that *is* not speckled and spotted among the goats, and brown among the sheep, that shall be counted stolen with me.

34 And Laban said, Behold, I would it might be according to thy word.

35 And he removed that day the he goats that were [a]ringstraked[1] and spotted, and all the she goats that were speckled and spotted, *and* every one that had *some* white in it, and all the brown among the sheep, and gave *them* into the hand of his sons.

36 And he set three days' journey [1]betwixt himself and Jacob: and Jacob fed the rest of Laban's flocks.

37 And [a]Jacob took him rods of green poplar, and of the hazel and chesnut tree; and [1]pilled white [2]strakes in them, and made the white appear which *was* in the rods.

38 And he set the rods which he had [1]pilled before the flocks in the gutters in the watering troughs when the flocks came to drink, that they should conceive when they came to drink.

39 And the flocks conceived before the rods, and brought forth cattle [1]ringstraked, speckled, and spotted.

40 And Jacob did separate the lambs, and set the faces of the flocks toward the [1]ringstraked, and all the brown in the flock of Laban; and he put his own flocks by themselves, and put them not [2]unto Laban's cattle.

41 And it came to pass, whensoever the stronger [1]cattle did conceive, that Jacob laid the rods before the eyes of the cattle in the gutters, that they might conceive among the rods.

42 But when the cattle were feeble, he put *them* not in: so the feebler were Laban's, and the stronger Jacob's.

43 And the man [a]increased[1] exceedingly, and [b]had [2]much cattle, and maidservants, and menservants, and camels, and [3]asses.

## CHAPTER 31

AND [1]he heard the words of Laban's sons, saying, Jacob hath taken away all that *was* our father's; and of *that* which *was* our father's hath he gotten all this [a]glory.[2]

2 And Jacob beheld the [a]countenance of Laban, and, behold, it *was* [1]not [b]toward him as before.

3 And the LORD said unto Jacob, [a]Return unto the land of thy fathers, and to thy kindred; and I will [b]be with thee.

---

**Center column notes:**

30:18 [1] Lit. *Hire*
30:20 [1] *endowment* [2] Lit. *Dwelling*
30:21 [a] Gen. 34:1 [1] Lit. *Judgment*
30:22 [a] Gen. 19:29; 1 Sam. 1:19, 20 [b] Gen. 29:31
30:23 [a] 1 Sam. 1:6; Is. 4:1; Luke 1:25
30:24 [a] Gen. 35:16–18 [1] Lit. *He Will Add*
30:25 [a] Gen. 24:54, 56 [b] Gen. 18:33
30:26 [a] Gen. 29:18–20, 27, 30; Hos. 12:12
30:27 [a] Gen. 26:24; 39:3; Is. 61:9 [1] *stay*
30:28 [a] Gen. 29:15; 31:7, 41 [1] *Name me*
30:29 [a] Gen. 31:6, 38–40; Matt. 24:45; Titus 2:10 [1] Jacob [2] *livestock*
30:30 [a] [1 Tim. 5:8] [1] Lit. *at my foot*
30:32 [1] *sheep*

[a] Gen. 31:8
[2] these *shall be my wages*
30:33 [a] Ps. 37:6 [1] *about my wages*
30:35 [a] Gen. 31:9–12 [1] *streaked*
30:36 [1] *between*
30:37 [a] Gen. 31:9–12 [1] *peeled* [2] *strips*
30:38 [1] *peeled*
30:39 [1] *streaked*
30:40 [1] *streaked* [2] *with*
30:41 [1] *livestock*
30:43 [a] Gen. 12:16; 30:30 [b] Gen. 13:2; 24:35; 26:13, 14 [1] *prospered* [2] *large flocks* [3] *donkeys*
31:1 [a] Ps. 49:16 [1] Jacob [2] *wealth*
31:2 [a] Gen. 4:5 [b] Deut. 28:54 [1] *not favourable*
31:3 [a] Gen. 28:15, 20, 21; 32:9 [b] Gen. 46:4

4 And Jacob sent and called Rachel and Leah to the field unto his flock,

5 And said unto them, [a]I see your father's [1]countenance, that it *is* [2]not toward me as before; but the God of my father [b]hath been with me.

6 And [a]ye know that with all my [1]power I have served your father.

7 And your father hath deceived me, and [a]changed my wages [b]ten times; but God [c]suffered[1] him not to hurt me.

8 If he said thus, [a]The speckled shall be thy wages; then all the [1]cattle bare speckled: and if he said thus, The [2]ringstraked shall be thy hire; then bare all the cattle ringstraked.

9 Thus God hath [a]taken away the cattle of your father, and given *them* to me.

10 And it came to pass at the time that the [1]cattle conceived, that I lifted up mine eyes, and saw in a dream, and, behold, the rams which leaped upon the [1]cattle *were* [2]ringstraked, speckled, and [3]grisled.

11 And [a]the angel of God spake unto me in a dream, *saying,* Jacob: And I said, Here *am* I.

12 And he said, Lift up now thine eyes, and see, all the rams which leap upon the cattle *are* [1]ringstraked, speckled, and [2]grisled: for [a]I have seen all that Laban doeth unto thee.

13 I *am* the God of Beth-el, [d]where thou anointedst the pillar, *and* where thou vowedst a vow unto me: now [b]arise, get thee out from this land, and return unto the land of thy kindred.

14 And Rachel and Leah answered and said unto him, [a]*Is there* yet any portion or inheritance for us in our father's house?

15 Are we not [1]counted of him strangers? for [a]he hath sold us, and hath [2]quite devoured also our money.

16 For all the riches which God hath taken from our father, that *is* ours, and our children's: now then, whatsoever God hath said unto thee, do.

17 Then Jacob rose up, and set his sons and his wives upon camels;

18 And he carried away all his [1]cattle, and all his goods which he had gotten, the [1]cattle [2]of his getting, which he had gotten in Padan-aram, for to go to Isaac his father in the land of [a]Canaan.

19 And Laban went to shear his sheep: and Rachel had stolen the [a]images[1] that *were* her father's.

20 And Jacob stole away unawares to Laban the Syrian, in that he told him not that he [1]fled.

21 So he fled with all that he had; and he rose up, and passed over the river, and [a]set his face *toward* the [1]mount Gilead.

22 And it was told Laban on the third day that Jacob was fled.

23 And he took [a]his brethren with him, and pursued after him seven days' journey; and they overtook him in the [1]mount Gilead.

24 And God [a]came to Laban the Syrian in a dream by night, and said unto him, Take heed that thou [b]speak not to Jacob either good or bad.

25 Then Laban overtook Jacob. Now Jacob had pitched his tent in the mount: and Laban with his brethren pitched in the mount of Gilead.

26 And Laban said to Jacob, What hast thou done, that thou hast stolen away unawares to me, and [a]carried away my daughters, as captives *taken* with the sword?

27 Wherefore didst thou flee away secretly, and steal away from me; and didst not tell me, that I might have sent thee away with [1]mirth, and with songs, with [2]tabret, and with harp?

28 And hast not [1]suffered me [a]to kiss my sons and my daughters? [b]thou hast now done foolishly in *so* doing.

29 It is in [1]the power of my hand to do you hurt: but the [a]God of your father spake unto me [b]yesternight,[2] saying, Take thou heed that thou speak not to Jacob either good or bad.

30 And now, *though* thou wouldest needs be gone, because thou [1]sore longedst after thy father's house, *yet* wherefore hast thou [a]stolen my gods?

31 And Jacob answered and said to Laban, Because I was [a]afraid: for I said, [1]Peradventure thou wouldest take by force thy daughters from me.

32 With whomsoever thou findest thy gods, [a]let him not live: before our brethren [1]discern thou what *is* thine with me, and take *it* [2]to thee. For Jacob knew not that Rachel had stolen them.

33 And Laban went into Jacob's tent, and into Leah's tent, and into the two maidservants' tents; but he found *them* not. Then went he out of Leah's tent, and entered into Rachel's tent.

34 Now Rachel had taken the [1]images, and put them in the camel's [2]furniture, and sat upon them. And Laban searched all the tent, but found *them* not.

35 And she said to her father, Let it not displease my lord that I cannot [a]rise up before thee; for the custom of women *is* upon me. And he searched, but found not the [1]images.

36 And Jacob was [1]wroth, and [2]chode with Laban: and Jacob answered and said to Laban, What *is* my [3]trespass? what *is* my sin, that thou hast so hotly pursued after me?

---

**Center column references:**

31:5 [a] Gen. 31:2,
3   [b] Is. 41:10
[1] Lit. *face* [2] *not favourable*

31:6 [a] Gen. 30:29;
31:38–41 [1] *might*

31:7 [a] Gen. 29:25;
31:41 [b] Num. 14:22
[c] Job 1:10 [1] *did not allow him*

31:8 [a] Gen. 30:32
[1] *flocks* [2] *streaked*

31:9 [a] Gen. 31:1, 16

31:10 [1] *flocks*
[2] *streaked* [3] *gray-spotted*

31:11 [a] Gen. 16:7–
11; 22:11, 15; 31:13;
48:16

31:12 [a] Ex. 3:7
[1] *streaked* [2] *gray-spotted*

31:13 [a] Gen. 28:16–
22; 35:1, 6, 15
[b] Gen. 31:3; 32:9

31:14 [a] Gen. 2:24

31:15 [a] Gen. 29:15,
20, 23, 27 [1] *considered by him as* [2] *completely consumed*

31:18 [a] Gen. 17:8;
33:18; 35:27 [1] *livestock* [2] *which he acquired*

31:19 [a] Judg. 17:5
[1] *household idols,* Heb. *teraphim*

31:20 [1] *was fleeing*

31:21 [a] 2 Kin. 12:17
[1] *mountains of*

31:23 [a] Gen. 13:8
[1] *mountains of*

31:24 [a] Gen. 20:3;
31:29; 46:2–4
[b] Gen. 24:50;
31:7, 29

31:26 [a] 1 Sam. 30:2

31:27 [1] *joy*
[2] *timbrel*

31:28 [a] Gen. 31:55;
Ruth 1:9, 14; 1 Kin.
19:20; Acts 20:37
[b] 1 Sam. 13:13
[1] *allowed*

31:29 [a] Gen. 28:13;
31:5, 24, 42, 53
[b] Gen. 31:24 [1] *my power* [2] *last night*

31:30 [a] Gen.
31:19; Josh. 24:2;
Judg. 17:5; 18:24
[1] *greatly long for*

31:31 [a] Gen. 26:7;
32:7, 11 [1] *Perhaps*

31:32 [a] Gen. 44:9
[1] *identify* [2] *with*

31:34 [1] *household idols,* Heb. *teraphim* [2] *saddle*

31:35 [a] Ex.
20:12; Lev. 19:32
[1] *household idols,* Heb. *teraphim*

31:36 [1] *angry*
[2] *rebuked* [3] *transgression*

37 Whereas thou hast searched all my stuff, what hast thou found of all thy household stuff? set *it* here before my brethren and thy brethren, that they may judge betwixt us both.

38 This twenty years *have* I *been* with thee; thy ewes and thy she goats have not cast their young, and the rams of thy flock have I not eaten.

39 ªThat which was torn *of beasts* I brought not unto thee; I bare the loss of it; of ᵇmy hand didst thou require it, *whether* stolen by day, or stolen by night.

40 *Thus* I was; in the day the drought consumed me, and the frost by night; and my sleep departed from mine eyes.

41 Thus have I been twenty years in thy house; I ªserved thee fourteen years for thy two daughters, and six years for thy ¹cattle: and ᵇthou hast changed my wages ten times.

42 ªExcept the God of my father, the God of Abraham, and ᵇthe fear of Isaac, had been with me, surely thou hadst sent me away now empty. ᶜGod hath seen mine affliction and the labour of my hands, and ᵈrebuked *thee* ¹yesternight.

43 And Laban answered and said unto Jacob, *These* daughters *are* my daughters, and *these* children *are* my children, and ¹*these* cattle *are* my cattle, and all that thou seest is mine: and what can I do this day unto these my daughters, or unto their children which they have born?

44 Now therefore come thou, ªlet us make a ¹covenant, I ᵇand thou; and let it be for a witness between me and thee.

45 And Jacob ªtook a stone, and set it up *for* a pillar.

46 And Jacob said unto his brethren, Gather stones; and they took stones, and made an heap: and they did eat there upon the heap.

47 And Laban called it ¹Jegar-sahadutha: but Jacob called it ²Galeed.

48 And Laban said, ªThis ¹heap *is* a witness between me and thee this day. Therefore was the name of it called Galeed;

49 And ªMizpah;¹ for he said, The LORD watch between me and thee, when we are absent one from another.

50 If thou shalt afflict my daughters, or if thou shalt take *other* wives beside my daughters, ¹no man *is* with us; see, God *is* witness betwixt me and thee.

51 And Laban said to Jacob, Behold this heap, and behold *this* pillar, which I have cast betwixt me and thee;

52 This heap *be* witness, and *this* pillar *be* witness, that I will not pass

---

31:39 ª Ex. 22:10
ᵇ Ex. 22:10–13
31:41 ª Gen. 29:20,
27–30 ᵇ Gen. 31:7
¹ *flock*
31:42 ª Gen. 31:5,
29, 53; Ps. 124:1,
2 ᵇ Gen. 31:53; Is.
8:13 ᶜ Gen. 29:32;
Ex. 3:7 ᵈ Gen.
31:24, 29; 1 Chr.
12:17 ¹ *last night*
31:43 ¹ *flock*
31:44 ª Gen. 21:27,
32; 26:28 ᵇ Josh.
24:27 ¹ *treaty*
31:45 ª Gen.
28:18; 35:14; Josh.
24:26, 27
31:47 ¹ Aram.
for *The Heap of
Witness* ² Heb.
for *The Heap of
Witness*
31:48 ª Josh.
24:27 ¹ *pile of
stones*
31:49 ª Judg.
10:17; 11:29;
1 Sam. 7:5, 6
¹ Lit. *Watch*
31:50 ¹ *although
no man*

31:52 ¹ *beyond*
31:53 ª Gen.
16:5 ᵇ Gen. 21:23
ᶜ Gen. 31:42 ¹ Or
*Fear,* a reference
to God
31:55 ª Gen.
29:11, 13; 31:28, 43
ᵇ Gen. 28:1 ᶜ Gen.
18:33; 30:25;
Num. 24:25
32:1 ª Num. 22:31
32:2 ª Josh. 5:14
¹ *camp.* ² Lit.
*Double Camp*
32:3 ª Gen. 14:6;
33:14, 16 ᵇ Gen.
25:30; 36:6–9
¹ Lit. *field*
32:4 ª Prov. 15:1
32:5 ª Gen. 30:43
ᵇ Gen. 33:8, 15
¹ *donkeys*
32:6 ª Gen. 33:1
32:7 ª Gen. 32:11;
35:3 ¹ *companies*
32:8 ¹ *attacks*
32:9 ª [Ps. 50:15]
ᵇ Gen. 28:13; 31:42
ᶜ Gen. 31:3, 13
32:10 ª Gen. 24:27
ᵇ Job 8:7 ¹ *loving-
kindnesses*
² *companies*
32:11 ª Ps. 59:1,
2 ᵇ Hos. 10:14
¹ *attack*

---

¹over this heap to thee, and that thou shalt not pass ¹over this heap and this pillar unto me, for harm.

53 The God of Abraham, and the God of Nahor, the God of their father, ªjudge betwixt us. And Jacob ᵇsware by ᶜthe ¹fear of his father Isaac.

54 Then Jacob offered sacrifice upon the mount, and called his brethren to eat bread: and they did eat bread, and tarried all night in the mount.

55 And early in the morning Laban rose up, and ªkissed his sons and his daughters, and ᵇblessed them: and Laban departed, and ᶜreturned unto his place.

## CHAPTER 32

AND Jacob went on his way, and ªthe angels of God met him.

2 And when Jacob saw them, he said, This *is* God's ªhost:¹ and he called the name of that place ²Mahanaim.

3 And Jacob sent messengers before him to Esau his brother ªunto the land of Seir, ᵇthe ¹country of Edom.

4 And he commanded them, saying, ªThus shall ye speak unto my lord Esau; Thy servant Jacob saith thus, I have sojourned with Laban, and stayed there until now:

5 And ªI have oxen, and ¹asses, flocks, and menservants, and womenservants: and I have sent to tell my lord, that ᵇI may find grace in thy sight.

6 And the messengers returned to Jacob, saying, We came to thy brother Esau, and also ªhe cometh to meet thee, and four hundred men with him.

7 Then Jacob was greatly afraid and ªdistressed: and he divided the people that *was* with him, and the flocks, and herds, and the camels, into two ¹bands;

8 And said, If Esau come to the one company, and ¹smite it, then the other company which is left shall escape.

9 ªAnd Jacob said, ᵇO God of my father Abraham, and God of my father Isaac, the LORD ᶜwhich saidst unto me, Return unto thy country, and to thy kindred, and I will deal well with thee:

10 I am not worthy of the least of all the ªmercies,¹ and of all the truth, which thou hast shewed unto thy servant; for with ᵇmy staff I passed over this Jordan; and now I am become two ²bands.

11 ªDeliver me, I pray thee, from the hand of my brother, from the hand of Esau: for I fear him, lest he will come and ¹smite me, *and* ᵇthe mother with the children.

12 And athou saidst, I will surely do thee good, and make thy 1seed as the bsand of the sea, which cannot be numbered for multitude.

13 And he lodged there that same night; and took of that which 1came to his hand aa present for Esau his brother;

14 Two hundred she goats, and twenty he goats, two hundred ewes, and twenty rams,

15 Thirty 1milch camels with their colts, forty 2kine, and ten bulls, twenty 3she asses, and ten foals.

16 And he delivered *them* into the hand of his servants, every drove by themselves; and said unto his servants, Pass over before me, and put a 1space betwixt drove and drove.

17 And he commanded the foremost, saying, When Esau my brother meeteth thee, and asketh thee, saying, Whose *art* thou? and whither goest thou? and whose *are* these before thee?

18 Then thou shalt say, *They be* thy servant Jacob's; it *is* a present sent unto my lord Esau: and, behold, also he *is* behind us.

19 And so commanded he the second, and the third, and all that followed the droves, saying, On this manner shall ye speak unto Esau, when ye find him.

20 And say ye moreover, Behold, thy servant Jacob *is* behind us. For he said, I will aappease him with the present that goeth before me, and afterward I will see his face; 1peradventure he will accept 2of me.

21 So went the present over before him: and himself lodged that night in the 1company.

22 And he rose up that night, and took his two wives, and his two womenservants, and his eleven sons, aand passed over the ford Jabbok.

23 And he took them, and sent them over the brook, and sent over that he had.

24 And Jacob was left alone; and there awrestled a man with him until the 1breaking of the day.

25 And when he saw that he prevailed not against him, he 1touched the 2hollow of his 3thigh; and athe 2hollow of Jacob's 3thigh was out of joint, as he wrestled with him.

26 And ahe said, Let me go, for the day breaketh. And he said, 1I will not let thee go, except thou bless me.

27 And he said unto him, What *is* thy name? And he said, Jacob.

28 And he said, aThy name shall be called no more Jacob, but 1Israel: 2for as a prince hast thou bpower with God and cwith men, and hast prevailed.

29 And Jacob asked *him*, and said, Tell *me*, I pray thee, thy name. And he

**Marginal notes (left column):**

32:12 a Gen. 28:13–15 b Gen. 22:17 1 *descendants*

32:13 a Gen. 43:11 1 *he had received*

32:15 1 *milk* 2 *cows* 3 *female donkeys*

32:16 1 *distance between successive droves*

32:20 a [Prov. 21:14] 1 *perhaps* 2 Lit. *my face*

32:21 1 *camp*

32:22 a Deut. 3:16

32:24 a Hos. 12:2–4 1 *dawn*

32:25 2 Cor. 12:7 1 *struck* 2 *socket* 3 *hip*

32:26 a Luke 24:28 b Hos. 12:4

32:28 a Gen. 35:10 b Hos. 12:3, 4 c Gen. 25:31; 27:33 1 Lit. *Prince with God* 2 *for you have struggled with God*

said, aWherefore *is* it *that* thou dost ask after my name? And he bblessed him there.

30 And Jacob called the name of the place 1Peniel: for aI have seen God face to face, and my life is preserved.

31 And as he passed over 1Penuel the sun rose upon him, and he 2halted upon his thigh.

32 Therefore the children of Israel eat not *of* the 1sinew which shrank, which *is* upon the 2hollow of the 3thigh, unto this day: because he 4touched the hollow of Jacob's thigh in the 1sinew that shrank.

## CHAPTER 33

AND Jacob lifted up his eyes, and looked, and, behold, aEsau came, and with him four hundred men. And he divided the children unto Leah, and unto Rachel, and unto the two 1handmaids.

2 And he put the handmaids and their children foremost, and Leah and her children after, and Rachel and Joseph 1hindermost.

3 And he passed over before them, and abowed himself to the ground seven times, until he came near to his brother.

4 aAnd Esau ran to meet him, and embraced him, band fell on his neck, and kissed him: and they wept.

5 And he lifted up his eyes, and saw the women and the children; and said, Who *are* those with thee? And he said, The children awhich God hath graciously given thy servant.

6 Then the 1handmaidens came near, they and their children, and they bowed themselves.

7 And Leah also with her children came near, and bowed themselves: and after came Joseph near and Rachel, and they bowed themselves.

8 And he said, What *meanest* thou by aall this 1drove which I met? And he said, *These are* bto find 2grace in the sight of my lord.

9 And Esau said, I have enough, my brother; keep that thou hast unto thyself.

10 And Jacob said, Nay, I pray thee, if now I have found 1grace in thy sight, then receive my present at my hand: for therefore I ahave seen thy face, as though I had seen the face of God, and thou wast pleased with me.

11 Take, I pray thee, amy blessing that is brought to thee; because God hath dealt bgraciously with me, and because I have 1enough. cAnd he urged him, and he took *it*.

12 And he said, Let us take our journey, and let us go, and I will go before thee.

13 And he said unto him, My lord knoweth that the children *are* 1tender,

**Marginal notes (right column):**

32:29 a Judg. 13:17, 18 b Gen. 35:9

32:30 a Gen. 16:13 1 Lit. *Face of God*

32:31 1 Lit. *Face of God* 2 *limped on his hip*

32:32 1 *muscle* 2 *socket* 3 *hip* 4 *struck*

33:1 a Gen. 32:6 1 *maidservants*

33:2 1 *last*

33:3 a Gen. 18:2; 42:6

33:4 a Gen. 32:28 b Gen. 45:14, 15

33:5 a Gen. 48:9; [Ps. 127:3]; Is. 8:18

33:6 1 *maidservants*

33:8 a Gen. 32:13–16 b Gen. 32:5 1 *company* 2 *favour*

33:10 a Gen. 43:3; 2 Sam. 3:13; 14:24, 28, 32 1 *favour*

33:11 a Judg. 1:15; 1 Sam. 25:27; 30:26 b Gen. 30:43; Ex. 33:19 c 2 Kin. 5:23 1 Lit. *all*

33:13 1 *weak*

and the flocks and herds [2]with young *are* with me: and if men should [3]overdrive them one day, all the flock will die.

14 Let my lord, I pray thee, pass over before his servant: and I will lead on [1]softly, according as the [2]cattle that goeth before me and the children be able to endure, until I come unto my lord [a]unto Seir.

15 And Esau said, Let me now leave with thee *some* of the [1]folk that *are* with me. And he said, [2]What needeth it? [a]let me find grace in the sight of my lord.

16 So Esau returned that day on his way unto Seir.

17 And Jacob journeyed to [a]Succoth, and built him an house, and made [1]booths for his cattle: therefore the name of the place is called [2]Succoth.

18 And Jacob came [1]to [a]Shalem, a city of [b]Shechem, which *is* in the land of Canaan, when he came from Padan-aram; and pitched his tent before the city.

19 And [a]he bought a parcel of a field, where he had [1]spread his tent, at the hand of the children of Hamor, Shechem's father, for an hundred [2]pieces of money.

20 And he erected there an altar, and [a]called it [1]El-elohe-Israel.

## CHAPTER 34

A ND [a]Dinah the daughter of Leah, which she bare unto Jacob, went out to see the daughters of the land.

2 And when Shechem the son of Hamor the Hivite, prince of the country, saw her, he [a]took her, and lay with her, and [1]defiled her.

3 And his soul [1]clave unto Dinah the daughter of Jacob, and he loved the damsel, and spake kindly unto the [2]damsel.

4 And Shechem [a]spake unto his father Hamor, saying, Get me this damsel [1]to wife.

5 And Jacob heard that he had defiled Dinah his daughter: now his sons were with his [1]cattle in the field: and Jacob [a]held[2] his peace until they were come.

6 And Hamor the father of Shechem went out unto Jacob to [1]commune with him.

7 And the sons of Jacob came out of the field when they heard *it:* and the men were grieved, and they were very [1]wroth, because he [a]had [2]wrought folly in Israel in lying with Jacob's daughter; [b]which thing ought not to be done.

8 And Hamor communed with them, saying, The soul of my son Shechem longeth for your daughter: I pray you give her him to wife.

9 And make ye marriages with us, *and* give your daughters unto us, and take our daughters unto you.

10 And ye shall dwell with us: and the land shall be before you; dwell and trade ye therein, and [1]get you possessions therein.

11 And Shechem said unto her father and unto her brethren, Let me find [1]grace in your eyes, and what ye shall say unto me I will give.

12 Ask me [1]never so much [a]dowry[2] and gift, and I will give according as ye shall say unto me: but give me the damsel [3]to wife.

13 And the sons of Jacob answered Shechem and Hamor his father [a]deceitfully, and said, because he had defiled Dinah their sister:

14 And they said unto them, We cannot do this thing, to give our sister to one that is [a]uncircumcised; for [b]that *were* a reproach unto us:

15 But in this will we consent unto you: If ye will be as we *be,* that every male of you be circumcised;

16 Then will we give our daughters unto you, and we will take your daughters to us, and we will dwell with you, and we will become one people.

17 But if ye will not hearken unto us, to be circumcised; then will we take our daughter, and we will be gone.

18 And their words pleased Hamor, and Shechem Hamor's son.

19 And the young man [1]deferred not to do the thing, because he had delight in Jacob's daughter: and he *was* [a]more honourable than all the house of his father.

20 And Hamor and Shechem his son came unto the [a]gate of their city, and communed with the men of their city, saying,

21 These men *are* peaceable with us; therefore let them dwell in the land, and trade therein; for the land, behold, *it is* large enough for them; let us take their daughters to us for wives, and let us give them our daughters.

22 Only [1]herein will the men consent unto us for to dwell with us, to be one people, if every male among us be circumcised, as they *are* circumcised.

23 *Shall* not their [1]cattle and their [2]substance and every [3]beast of theirs *be* ours? only let us consent unto them, and they will dwell with us.

24 And unto Hamor and unto Shechem his son hearkened all that [a]went out of the gate of his city; and every male was circumcised, all that went out of the gate of his city.

25 And it came to pass on the third day, when they were [1]sore, that two

### Cross-references (center column)

33:13 [2] *which are nursing* [3] *drive them hard*
33:14 [a] Gen. 32:3; 36:8 [1] *slowly* [2] *livestock*
33:15 [a] Gen. 34:11; 47:25; Ruth 2:13 [1] *people* [2] *What need is there?*
33:17 [a] Josh. 13:27; Judg. 8:5; Ps. 60:6 [1] *shelters* [2] Lit. *Booths*
33:18 [a] John 3:23 [b] Gen. 12:6; 35:4; Josh. 24:1; Judg. 9:1; Ps. 60:6 [1] *safely to the city of*
33:19 [a] Josh. 24:32; John 4:5 [1] *pitched* [2] Heb. *qesitah*
33:20 [a] Gen. 35:7 [1] Lit. *God, the God of Israel*
34:1 [a] Gen. 30:21
34:2 [a] Gen. 20:2 [1] *violated*
34:3 [1] *was strongly attracted to* [2] *young woman*
34:4 [a] Judg. 14:2 [1] *as a wife*
34:5 [a] 2 Sam. 13:22 [1] *livestock* [2] *kept silent*
34:6 [1] *speak*
34:7 [a] Deut. 22:20–30; Josh. 7:15; Judg. 20:6 [b] Deut. 23:17; 2 Sam. 13:12 [1] *angry* [2] *done a disgraceful thing*
34:10 [1] *acquire*
34:11 [1] *favour*
34:12 [a] Ex. 22:16, 17; Deut. 22:29 [1] *ever* [2] *bride-price* [3] *as a wife*
34:13 [a] Gen. 31:7; Ex. 8:29
34:14 [a] Ex. 12:48 [b] Josh. 5:2–9
34:19 [a] 1 Chr. 4:9 [1] *did not delay*
34:20 [a] Ruth 4:1, 11
34:22 [1] *on this condition*
34:23 [1] *livestock* [2] *property* [3] *animal*
34:24 [a] Gen. 23:10, 18
34:25 [1] *in pain*

of the sons of Jacob, [a]Simeon and Levi, Dinah's brethren, took each man his sword, and came upon the city boldly, and slew all the males.

26 And they [a]slew Hamor and Shechem his son with the edge of the sword, and took Dinah out of Shechem's house, and went out.

27 The sons of Jacob came upon the slain, and [1]spoiled the city, because they had defiled their sister.

28 They took their sheep, and their oxen, and their [1]asses, and that which *was* in the city, and that which *was* in the field,

29 And all their wealth, and all their little ones, and their wives took they captive, and [1]spoiled even all that *was* in the house.

30 And Jacob said to Simeon and Levi, [a]Ye have [b]troubled me [c]to make me [1]to stink among the inhabitants of the land, among the Canaanites and the Perizzites: [d]and I *being* few in number, they shall gather themselves together against me, and slay me; and I shall be destroyed, I and my house.

31 And they said, Should he deal with our sister as with an harlot?

## CHAPTER 35

AND God said unto Jacob, Arise, go up to [a]Beth-el, and dwell there: and make there an altar unto God, [b]that appeared unto thee [c]when thou fleddest from the face of Esau thy brother.

2 Then Jacob said unto his household, and to all that *were* with him, Put away [b]the [1]strange gods that *are* among you, and [c]be [2]clean, and change your garments:

3 And let us arise, and go up to Beth-el; and I will make there an altar unto God, [a]who answered me in the day of my distress, [b]and was with me in the way which I went.

4 And they gave unto Jacob all the [1]strange gods which *were* in their hand, and *all their* [a]earrings which *were* in their ears; and Jacob hid them under [b]the [2]oak which *was* by Shechem.

5 And they journeyed: and [a]the terror of God was upon the cities that *were* round about them, and they did not pursue after the sons of Jacob.

6 So Jacob came to [a]Luz, which *is* in the land of Canaan, that *is*, Beth-el, he and all the people that *were* with him.

7 And he [a]built there an altar, and called the place [1]El-beth-el: because [b]there God appeared unto him, when he fled from the face of his brother.

8 But [a]Deborah Rebekah's nurse died, and she was buried [1]beneath Beth-el under an [2]oak: and the name of it was called [3]Allon-bachuth.

9 And [a]God appeared unto Jacob again, when he came out of Padanaram, and [b]blessed him.

10 And God said unto him, Thy name *is* Jacob: [a]thy name shall not be called any more Jacob, [b]but Israel shall be thy name: and he called his name Israel.

11 And God said unto him, [a]I *am* God Almighty: [b]be fruitful and multiply; [c]a nation and a company of nations shall be of thee, and kings shall come out of thy loins;

12 And the [a]land which I gave Abraham and Isaac, to thee I will give it, and to thy [1]seed after thee will I give the land.

13 And God [a]went[1] up from him in the place where he talked with him.

14 And Jacob [a]set up a pillar in the place where he talked with him, *even* a pillar of stone: and he poured a drink offering thereon, and he poured oil thereon.

15 And Jacob called the name of the place where God spake with him, [a]Beth-el.

16 And they journeyed from Beth-el; and there was but a little way to come to Ephrath: and Rachel [1]travailed, and she had hard labour.

17 And it came to pass, when she was in hard labour, that the midwife said unto her, Fear not; [a]thou shalt have this son also.

18 And it came to pass, as her soul was in departing, (for she died) that she called his name [1]Ben-oni: but his father called him [2]Benjamin.

19 And [a]Rachel died, and was buried in the way to [b]Ephrath, which *is* Beth-lehem.

20 And Jacob set a pillar upon her grave: that *is* the pillar of Rachel's grave [a]unto this day.

21 And Israel journeyed, and spread his tent beyond [a]the tower of [1]Edar.

22 And it came to pass, when Israel dwelt in that land, that Reuben went and [a]lay with Bilhah his father's concubine: and Israel heard *it*. Now the sons of Jacob were twelve:

23 The sons of Leah; [a]Reuben, Jacob's firstborn, and Simeon, and Levi, and Judah, and Issachar, and Zebulun:

24 The sons of Rachel; Joseph, and Benjamin:

25 And the sons of Bilhah, Rachel's handmaid; Dan, and Naphtali:

26 And the sons of Zilpah, Leah's handmaid; Gad, and Asher: these *are* the sons of Jacob, which were born to him in Padan-aram.

27 And Jacob came unto Isaac his father unto [a]Mamre, unto the [b]city[1] of Arbah, which *is* Hebron, where Abraham and Isaac sojourned.

### Center column references

34:25 [a] Gen. 29:33, 34; 42:24; 49:5-7
34:26 [a] Gen. 49:5, 6
34:27 [1] plundered
34:28 [1] donkeys
34:29 [1] plundered
34:30 [a] Gen. 49:6 [b] Josh. 7:25 [c] Ex. 5:21 [d] Deut. 4:27 [1] obnoxious
35:1 [a] Gen. 28:19; 31:13 [b] Gen. 28:13 [c] Gen. 27:43
35:2 [a] Josh. 24:15 [b] Josh. 24:2, 14, 23 [c] Ex. 19:10, 14 [1] foreign [2] purify yourselves
35:3 [a] Gen. 32:7, 24 [b] Gen. 28:15, 20; 31:3, 42
35:4 [a] Hos. 2:13 [b] Josh. 24:26 [1] foreign [2] terebinth tree
35:5 [a] Ex. 15:16; 23:27
35:6 [a] Gen. 28:19, 22; 48:3
35:7 [a] Eccl. 5:4 [b] Gen. 28:13 [1] Lit. God of the House of God
35:8 [a] Gen. 24:59 [1] below [2] terebinth tree [3] Lit. Terebinth of Weeping
35:9 [a] Josh. 5:13 [b] Gen. 32:29
35:10 [a] Gen. 17:5 [b] Gen. 32:28
35:11 [a] Ex. 6:3 [b] Gen. 9:1, 7 [c] Gen. 17:5, 6, 16; 28:3; 48:4 [1] descendants
35:12 [a] Gen. 12:7; 13:15; 26:3, 4; 28:13; 48:4 [1] descendants
35:13 [a] Gen. 17:22; 18:33 [1] departed
35:14 [a] Gen. 28:18, 19; 31:45
35:15 [a] Gen. 28:19
35:16 [1] travailed in childbirth
35:17 [a] Gen. 30:24; 1 Sam. 4:20
35:18 [1] Lit. Son of My Sorrow [2] Lit. Son of the Right Hand
35:19 [a] Gen. 48:7 [b] Ruth 1:2; 4:11; Mic. 5:2; Matt. 2:6
35:20 [a] 1 Sam. 10:2
35:21 [a] Mic. 4:8 [1] Or Eder
35:22 [a] Gen. 49:4; 1 Chr. 5:1
35:23 [a] Gen. 29:31-35; 30:18-20; 46:8; Ex. 1:1-4
35:27 [a] Gen. 13:18; 18:1; 23:19 [b] Josh. 14:15 [1] Heb. Kirjath-haarbah

28 And the days of Isaac were an hundred and fourscore years.

29 And Isaac [1]gave up the ghost, and died, and [a]was [2]gathered unto his people, *being* old and full of days: and [b]his sons Esau and Jacob buried him.

## CHAPTER 36

Now [1]these *are* the generations of Esau, [a]who *is* Edom.

2 [a]Esau took his wives of the daughters of Canaan; Adah the daughter of Elon the [b]Hittite, and [c]Aholibamah[1] the daughter of Anah the daughter of Zibeon the Hivite;

3 And [a]Bashemath[1] Ishmael's daughter, sister of Nebajoth.

4 And [a]Adah bare to Esau Eliphaz; and Bashemath bare Reuel;

5 And [1]Aholibamah bare Jeush, and Jaalam, and Korah: these *are* the sons of Esau, which were born unto him in the land of Canaan.

6 And Esau took his wives, and his sons, and his daughters, and all the persons of his house, and his cattle, and all his [1]beasts, and all his [2]substance, which he had got in the land of Canaan; and went into the country [3]from the face of his brother Jacob.

7 [a]For their [1]riches were more than that they might dwell together; and [b]the land wherein they were strangers could not [2]bear them because of their cattle.

8 Thus dwelt Esau in [a]mount Seir: [b]Esau *is* Edom.

9 And [1]these *are* the generations of Esau the father of the Edomites in mount Seir:

10 These *are* the names of Esau's sons; [a]Eliphaz the son of Adah the wife of Esau, Reuel the son of [1]Bashemath the wife of Esau.

11 And the sons of Eliphaz were Teman, Omar, [1]Zepho, and Gatam, and Kenaz.

12 And Timna was concubine to Eliphaz Esau's son; and she bare to Eliphaz [a]Amalek: these *were* the sons of Adah Esau's wife.

13 And these *are* the sons of Reuel; Nahath, and Zerah, Shammah, and Mizzah: these were the sons of [1]Bashemath Esau's wife.

14 And these were the sons of [1]Aholibamah, the daughter of Anah the daughter of Zibeon, Esau's wife: and she bare to Esau Jeush, and Jaalam, and Korah.

15 These *were* [1]dukes of the sons of Esau: the sons of Eliphaz the firstborn *son* of Esau; [2]duke Teman, duke Omar, duke Zepho, duke Kenaz,

16 Duke Korah, duke Gatam, *and* duke Amalek: these *are* the dukes *that came* of Eliphaz in the land of Edom; these *were* the sons of Adah.

17 And these *are* the sons of Reuel Esau's son; duke Nahath, duke Zerah, duke Shammah, duke Mizzah: these *are* the dukes *that came* of Reuel in the land of Edom; these *are* the sons of Bashemath Esau's wife.

18 And these *are* the sons of [1]Aholibamah Esau's wife; duke Jeush, duke Jaalam, duke Korah: these *were* the dukes *that came* of Aholibamah the daughter of Anah, Esau's wife.

19 These *are* the sons of Esau, who *is* Edom, and these *are* their dukes.

20 [a]These *are* the sons of Seir [b]the Horite, who inhabited the land; Lotan, and Shobal, and Zibeon, and Anah,

21 And Dishon, and Ezer, and Dishan: these *are* the [1]dukes of the Horites, the children of Seir in the land of Edom.

22 And the children of Lotan were Hori and [1]Hemam; and Lotan's sister *was* Timna.

23 And the children of Shobal *were* these; [1]Alvan, and Manahath, and Ebal, [2]Shepho, and Onam.

24 And these *are* the children of Zibeon; both Ajah, and Anah: this *was that* Anah that found [a]the [1]mules in the wilderness, as he fed the [2]asses of Zibeon his father.

25 And the children of Anah *were* these; Dishon, and [1]Aholibamah the daughter of Anah.

26 And these *are* the children of [1]Dishon; [2]Hemdan, and Eshban, and Ithran, and Cheran.

27 The children of Ezer *are* these; Bilhan, and Zaavan, and [1]Akan.

28 The children of Dishan *are* these; [a]Uz, and Aran.

29 These *are* the [1]dukes *that came* of the Horites; [2]duke Lotan, duke Shobal, duke Zibeon, duke Anah,

30 Duke Dishon, duke Ezer, duke Dishan: these *are* the dukes *that came* of Hori, among their dukes in the land of Seir.

31 And [a]these *are* the kings that reigned in the land of Edom, before there reigned any king over the children of Israel.

32 And Bela the son of Beor reigned in Edom: and the name of his city *was* Dinhabah.

33 And Bela died, and Jobab the son of Zerah of Bozrah reigned in his stead.

34 And Jobab died, and Husham of the land of Temani reigned in his stead.

35 And Husham died, and Hadad the son of Bedad, who smote Midian in the field of Moab, reigned in his stead: and the name of his city *was* Avith.

36 And Hadad died, and Samlah of Masrekah reigned in his stead.

---

**Cross-references (center column):**

35:29 [a] Gen. 15:15; 25:8; 49:33 [b] Gen. 25:9; 49:31 [1] *breathed his last* [2] Joined his ancestors

36:1 [a] Gen. 25:30 [1] *this is the genealogy*

36:2 [a] Gen. 26:34; 28:9 [b] 2 Kin. 7:6 [c] Gen. 36:25 [1] Or *Oholibamah*

36:3 [a] Gen. 28:9 [1] Heb. *Basemath*

36:4 [a] 1 Chr. 1:35

36:5 [1] Or *Oholibamah*

36:6 [1] *animals* [2] *goods* [3] *away from the presence of*

36:7 [a] Gen. 13:6, 11 [b] Gen. 17:8; 28:4; Heb. 11:9 [1] *possessions were too great for them to* [2] *support*

36:8 [a] Gen. 32:3; Deut. 2:5; Josh. 24:4 [b] Gen. 36:1, 19

36:9 [1] *this is the genealogy*

36:10 [a] 1 Chr. 1:35 [1] Heb. *Basemath*

36:11 [1] *Zephi*, 1 Chr. 1:36

36:12 [a] Ex. 17:8–16; Num. 24:20; Deut. 25:17–19; 1 Sam. 15:2, 3

36:13 [1] Heb. *Basemath*

36:14 [1] Or *Oholibamah*

36:15 [1] *chiefs* [2] *chief*

36:18 [1] Or *Oholibamah*

36:20 [a] 1 Chr. 1:38–42 [b] Gen. 14:6; Deut. 2:12, 22

36:21 [1] *chiefs*

36:22 [1] *Homam*, 1 Chr. 1:39

36:23 [1] *Alian*, 1 Chr. 1:40 [2] *Shephi*, 1 Chr. 1:40

36:24 [a] Lev. 19:19 [1] *water* [2] *donkeys*

36:25 [1] Or *Oholibamah*

36:26 [1] Heb. *Dishan* [2] *Amran*, 1 Chr. 1:41

36:27 [1] *Jakan*, 1 Chr. 1:42; Heb. *Jaakan*

36:28 [a] Job 1:1

36:29 [1] *chiefs* [2] *chief*

36:31 [a] Gen. 17:6, 16; 35:11; 1 Chr. 1:43

37 And Samlah died, and Saul of [a]Rehoboth *by* the river reigned in his stead.

38 And Saul died, and Baal-hanan the son of Achbor reigned in his stead.

39 And Baal-hanan the son of Achbor died, and [1]Hadar reigned in his stead: and the name of his city *was* [2]Pau; and his wife's name *was* Mehetabel, the daughter of Matred, the daughter of Mezahab.

40 And these *are* the names of the [1]dukes *that came* of Esau, according to their families, after their places, by their names; [2]duke Timnah, duke [3]Alvah, duke Jetheth,

41 Duke [1]Aholibamah, duke Elah, duke Pinon,

42 Duke Kenaz, duke Teman, duke Mibzar,

43 Duke Magdiel, duke Iram: these *be* the dukes of Edom, according to their [1]habitations in the land of their possession: he *is* Esau the father of the Edomites.

## CHAPTER 37

AND Jacob dwelt in the land [a]wherein his father was a [1]stranger, in the land of Canaan.

2 [1]These *are* the generations of Jacob. Joseph, *being* seventeen years old, was feeding the flock with his brethren; and the lad *was* with the sons of Bilhah, and with the sons of Zilpah, his father's wives: and Joseph brought unto his father [a]their[2] evil report.

3 Now Israel loved Joseph more than all his children, because he *was* [a]the son of his old age: and he [b]made him a [1]coat of *many* colours.

4 And when his brethren saw that their father loved him more than all his brethren, they [a]hated him, and could not speak peaceably unto him.

5 And Joseph dreamed a dream, and he told *it* his brethren: and they hated him yet the more.

6 And he said unto them, Hear, I pray you, this dream which I have dreamed:

7 For, [a]behold, we *were* binding sheaves in the field, and, lo, my sheaf arose, and also stood upright; and, behold, your sheaves stood round about, and [1]made obeisance to my sheaf.

8 And his brethren said to him, Shalt thou indeed reign over us? or shalt thou indeed have dominion over us? And they hated him yet the more for his dreams, and for his words.

9 And he dreamed yet another dream, and told it his brethren, and said, Behold, I have dreamed a dream more; and, behold, [a]the sun and the moon and the eleven stars [1]made obeisance to me.

10 And he told *it* to his father, and to his brethren: and his father rebuked him, and said unto him, What *is* this dream that thou hast dreamed? Shall I and thy mother and [a]thy brethren indeed come to bow down ourselves to thee to the earth?

11 And [a]his brethren envied him; but his father [b]observed[1] the saying.

12 And his brethren went to feed their father's flock in [a]Shechem.

13 And Israel said unto Joseph, Do not thy brethren feed *the flock* in Shechem? come, and I will send thee unto them. And he said to him, Here am I.

14 And he said to him, Go, I pray thee, see whether it be well with thy brethren, and well with the flocks; and bring me word again. So he sent him out of the vale of [a]Hebron, and he came to Shechem.

15 And a certain man found him, and, behold, *he was* wandering in the field: and the man asked him, saying, What seekest thou?

16 And he said, I seek my brethren: [a]tell me, I pray thee, where they feed *their flocks.*

17 And the man said, They are departed hence; for I heard them say, Let us go to Dothan. And Joseph went after his brethren, and found them in [a]Dothan.

18 And when they saw him afar off, even before he came near unto them, [a]they conspired against him to slay him.

19 And they said one to another, Behold, this [1]dreamer cometh.

20 [a]Come now therefore, and let us slay him, and cast him into some pit, and we will say, Some [1]evil beast hath devoured him: and we shall see what will become of his dreams.

21 And [a]Reuben heard *it,* and he delivered him out of their hands; and said, Let us not kill him.

22 And Reuben said unto them, Shed no blood, *but* cast him into this pit that *is* in the wilderness, and lay no hand upon him; that he might [1]rid him out of their hands, to deliver him to his father again.

23 And it came to pass, when Joseph was come unto his brethren, that they [a]stript Joseph out of his [1]coat, *his* coat of *many* colours that *was* on him;

24 And they took him, and cast him into a pit: and the pit *was* empty, *there was* no water in it.

25 [a]And they sat down to eat [1]bread: and they lifted up their eyes and looked, and, behold, a company of [b]Ishmeelites came from Gilead with their camels bearing spicery

36:37 [a] Gen. 10:11
36:39 [1] Sam., Syr. Hadad, 1 Chr. 1:50
[2] *Pai,* 1 Chr. 1:50
36:40 [1] chiefs
[2] chief [3] Aliah, 1 Chr. 1:51
36:41 [1] Or Oholibamah
36:43 [1] dwelling places
37:1 [a] Gen. 17:8; 23:4; 28:4; 36:7; Heb. 11:9 [1] sojourner, a temporary resident
37:2 [a] Gen. 35:25, 26; 1 Sam. 2:22–24 [1] This is the genealogy [2] a bad report of them
37:3 [a] Gen. 44:20 [b] Gen. 37:23, 32; Judg. 5:30; 1 Sam. 2:19 [1] tunic
37:4 [a] Gen. 27:41; 49:23; 1 Sam. 17:28; John 15:18–20
37:7 [a] Gen. 42:6, 9; 43:26; 44:14 [1] bowed down
37:9 [a] Gen. 46:29; 47:25

[1] bowed down
37:10 [a] Gen. 27:29
37:11 [a] Matt. 27:17, 18; Acts 7:9 [b] Dan. 7:28; Luke 2:19, 51 [1] kept the matter in mind
37:12 [a] Gen. 33:18–20
37:14 [a] Gen. 13:18; 23:2, 19; 35:27; Josh. 14:14, 15; Judg. 1:10
37:16 [a] Song 1:7
37:17 [a] 2 Kin. 6:13
37:18 [a] 1 Sam. 19:1; Ps. 31:13; 37:12, 32; Matt. 21:38; 26:3, 4; 27:1; Mark 14:1; John 11:53; Acts 23:12
37:19 [1] Lit. master of dreams
37:20 [a] Gen. 37:22; Prov. 1:11 [1] wild
37:21 [a] Gen. 42:22
37:22 [1] deliver
37:23 [a] Matt. 27:28 [1] tunic
37:25 [a] Prov. 30:20 [b] Gen. 16:11, 12; 37:28, 36; 39:1 [1] a meal

and <sup>c</sup>balm and myrrh, going to carry *it* down to Egypt.

26 And Judah said unto his brethren, What profit *is it* if we slay our brother, and <sup>a</sup>conceal his blood?

27 Come, and let us sell him to the Ishmeelites, and <sup>a</sup>let not our hand be upon him; for he *is* <sup>b</sup>our brother *and* <sup>c</sup>our flesh. And his brethren ¹were content.

28 Then there passed by <sup>a</sup>Midianites merchantmen; and they ¹drew and lifted up Joseph out of the pit, <sup>b</sup>and sold Joseph to the Ishmeelites for <sup>c</sup>twenty *pieces* of silver: and they brought Joseph into Egypt.

29 And Reuben returned unto the pit; and, behold, Joseph *was* not in the pit; and he <sup>a</sup>rent¹ his clothes.

30 And he returned unto his brethren, and said, The ¹child <sup>a</sup>*is* not; and I, whither shall I go?

31 And they took <sup>a</sup>Joseph's ¹coat, and killed a kid of the goats, and dipped the coat in the blood;

32 And they sent the ¹coat of *many* colours, and they brought *it* to their father; and said, This have we found: ²know now whether it *be* thy son's coat or no.

33 And he ¹knew it, and said, *It is* my son's ²coat; an <sup>a</sup>evil³ beast hath devoured him; Joseph is without doubt ⁴rent in pieces.

34 And Jacob <sup>a</sup>rent¹ his clothes, and put sackcloth upon his loins, and <sup>b</sup>mourned for his son many days.

35 And all his sons and all his daughters <sup>a</sup>rose up to comfort him; but he refused to be comforted; and he said, For <sup>b</sup>I will go down into the grave unto my son mourning. Thus his father wept for him.

36 And <sup>a</sup>the Midianites sold him into Egypt unto Potiphar, an officer of Pharaoh's, *and* captain of the guard.

### CHAPTER 38

AND it came to pass at that time, that Judah went down from his brethren, and <sup>a</sup>turned in to a certain Adullamite, whose name *was* Hirah.

2 And Judah <sup>a</sup>saw there a daughter of a certain Canaanite, whose name *was* ¹Shuah; and he ²took her, and went in unto her.

3 And she conceived, and bare a son; and she called his name <sup>a</sup>Er.

4 And she conceived again, and bare a son; and she called his name <sup>a</sup>Onan.

5 And she yet again conceived, and bare a son; and called his name <sup>a</sup>Shelah: and he was at Chezib, when she bare him.

6 And Judah <sup>a</sup>took a wife for Er his firstborn, whose name *was* <sup>b</sup>Tamar.

7 And <sup>a</sup>Er, Judah's firstborn, was

wicked in the sight of the LORD; <sup>b</sup>and the LORD ¹slew him.

8 And Judah said unto Onan, Go in unto <sup>a</sup>thy brother's wife, and marry her, and raise up seed to thy brother.

9 And Onan knew that the seed should not be <sup>a</sup>his; and it came to pass, when he went in unto his brother's wife, that he spilled *it* on the ground, lest that he should give seed to his brother.

10 And the thing which he did ¹displeased the LORD: wherefore he slew <sup>a</sup>him also.

11 Then said Judah to Tamar his daughter in law, <sup>a</sup>Remain a widow at thy father's house, till Shelah my son be grown: for he said, ¹Lest peradventure he die also, as his brethren *did*. And Tamar went and dwelt <sup>b</sup>in her father's house.

12 And in process of time the daughter of Shuah Judah's wife died; and Judah <sup>a</sup>was comforted, and went up unto his sheepshearers to Timnath, he and his friend Hirah the Adullamite.

13 And it was told Tamar, saying, Behold thy father in law goeth up <sup>a</sup>to Timnath to shear his sheep.

14 And she put her widow's garments off from her, and covered her with a vail, and wrapped herself, and <sup>a</sup>sat in an open place, which *is* by the way to Timnath; for she saw <sup>b</sup>that Shelah was grown, and she was not given unto him to wife.

15 When Judah saw her, he thought her *to be* an harlot; because she had covered her face.

16 And he turned unto her by the way, and said, Go to, I pray thee, let me come in unto thee; (for he knew not that she *was* his daughter in law.) And she said, What wilt thou give me, that thou mayest come in unto me?

17 And he said, <sup>a</sup>I will send *thee* a kid from the flock. And she said, <sup>b</sup>Wilt thou give *me* a pledge, till thou send *it?*

18 And he said, What pledge shall I give thee? And she said, <sup>a</sup>Thy signet, and thy ¹bracelets, and thy staff that *is* in thine hand. And he gave *it* her, and came in unto her, and she conceived by him.

19 And she arose, and went away, and <sup>a</sup>laid by her vail from her, and put on the garments of her widowhood.

20 And Judah sent the kid by the hand of his friend the Adullamite, to receive *his* pledge from the woman's hand: but he found her not.

21 Then he asked the men of that place, saying, Where *is* the harlot, that *was* ¹openly by the way side? And they said, There was no harlot in this *place*.

22 And he returned to Judah, and said, I cannot find her; and also the

37:25 <sup>c</sup> Jer. 8:22
37:26 <sup>a</sup> Gen. 37:20
37:27 <sup>a</sup> 1 Sam.
18:17 <sup>b</sup> Gen. 42:21
<sup>c</sup> Gen. 29:14
¹ *listened*
37:28 <sup>a</sup> Gen.
37:25; Judg. 6:1–
3; 8:22, 24 <sup>b</sup> Gen.
45:4, 5; Ps. 105:17;
Acts 7:9 <sup>c</sup> Matt.
27:9 ¹ *pulled him up*
37:29 <sup>a</sup> Gen.
37:34; 44:13; Job
1:20 ¹ *tore his clothes* in grief
37:30 <sup>a</sup> Gen.
42:13, 36 ¹ *lad*
37:31 <sup>a</sup> Gen. 37:3,
23 ¹ *tunic*
37:32 ¹ *tunic* ² *do you know*
37:33 <sup>a</sup> Gen. 37:20
¹ *recognized* ² *tunic* ³ *wild* ⁴ *torn*
37:34 <sup>a</sup> Gen.
37:29; 2 Sam.
3:31 <sup>b</sup> Gen. 50:10
¹ *tore*
37:35 <sup>a</sup> 2 Sam.
12:17 <sup>b</sup> Gen. 25:8;
35:29; 42:38;
44:29, 31
37:36 <sup>a</sup> Gen. 39:1
38:1 <sup>a</sup> 2 Kin. 4:8
38:2 <sup>a</sup> Gen. 34:2
¹ Heb. *Shua;* 1 Chr.
2:3 ² *married*
38:3 <sup>a</sup> Gen. 46:12;
Num. 26:19
38:4 <sup>a</sup> Gen. 46:12;
Num. 26:19
38:5 <sup>a</sup> Num. 26:20
38:6 <sup>a</sup> Gen. 21:21
<sup>b</sup> Ruth 4:12
38:7 <sup>a</sup> Gen. 46:12;
Num. 26:19

<sup>b</sup> 1 Chr. 2:3 ¹ *killed*
38:8 <sup>a</sup> Deut. 25:5,
6; Matt. 22:24
38:9 <sup>a</sup> Deut. 25:6
38:10 <sup>a</sup> Gen.
46:12; Num. 26:19
¹ Lit. *was evil in the eyes of*
38:11 <sup>a</sup> Ruth 1:12,
13 <sup>b</sup> Lev. 22:13
¹ *Lest he die*
38:12 <sup>a</sup> 2 Sam.
13:39
38:13 <sup>a</sup> Josh. 15:10,
57; Judg. 14:1
38:14 <sup>a</sup> Prov. 7:12
<sup>b</sup> Gen. 38:11, 26
38:17 <sup>a</sup> Judg. 15:1;
Ezek. 16:33 <sup>b</sup> Gen.
38:20
38:18 <sup>a</sup> Gen. 38:25;
41:42 ¹ *cord*
38:19 <sup>a</sup> Gen. 38:14
38:21 ¹ *in full view*

men of the place said, *that* there was no harlot in this *place.*

23 And Judah said, Let her take *it* to her, lest we be shamed: behold, I sent this kid, and thou hast not found her.

24 And it came to pass about three months after, that it was told Judah, saying, Tamar thy daughter in law hath [a]played the harlot; and also, behold, she *is* with child by [1]whoredom. And Judah said, Bring her forth, [b]and let her be burnt.

25 When she *was* brought forth, she sent to her father in law, saying, By the man, whose these *are, am* I with child: and she said, [a]Discern, I pray thee, whose *are* these, the signet, and [1]bracelets, and staff.

26 And Judah [a]acknowledged *them,* and said, [b]She hath been more righteous than I; because that [c]I gave her not to Shelah my son. And he knew her again [d]no more.

27 And it came to pass in the time of her travail, that, behold, twins *were* in her womb.

28 And it came to pass, when she travailed, that *the one* put out *his* hand: and the midwife took and bound upon his hand a scarlet thread, saying, This came out first.

29 And it came to pass, as he drew back his hand, that, behold, his brother came out: and she said, How hast thou broken forth? *this* breach *be* upon thee: therefore his name was called [a]Pharez.[1]

30 And afterward came out his brother, that had the scarlet thread upon his hand: and his name was called [a]Zarah.[1]

## CHAPTER 39

AND Joseph was brought [a]down to Egypt; and [b]Potiphar, an officer of Pharaoh, captain of the guard, an Egyptian, [c]bought him of the hands of the Ishmeelites, which had brought him down thither.

2 And [a]the LORD was with Joseph, and he was a [1]prosperous man; and he was in the house of his master the Egyptian.

3 And his master saw that the LORD *was* with him, and that the LORD [a]made all that he did [1]to prosper in his hand.

4 And Joseph [a]found [1]grace in his sight, and he served him: and he made him [b]overseer over his house, and all *that* he had he put into his [2]hand.

5 And it came to pass from the time *that* he had made him overseer in his house, and over all that he had, that [a]the LORD blessed the Egyptian's house for Joseph's sake; and the blessing of the LORD was upon all that he had in the house, and in the field.

6 And he left all that he had in Joseph's [1]hand; and he knew not [2]ought he had, [3]save the bread which he did eat. And Joseph [a]was [4]a goodly *person,* and well favoured.

7 And it came to pass after these things, that his master's wife [1]cast her eyes upon Joseph; and she said, [a]Lie with me.

8 But he refused, and said unto his master's wife, Behold, my master [1]wotteth not what *is* [2]with me in the house, and he hath committed all that he hath to my hand;

9 *There is* none greater in this house than I; neither hath he kept back any thing from me but thee, because thou *art* his wife: [a]how then can I do this great wickedness, and [b]sin against God?

10 And it came to pass, as she spake to Joseph day by day, that he [1]hearkened [a]not unto her, to lie by her, *or* to be with her.

11 And it came to pass about this time, that *Joseph* went into the house to do his [1]business; and *there was* none of the men of the house there within.

12 And she [a]caught him by his garment, saying, Lie with me: and he left his garment in her hand, and fled, and got him out.

13 And it came to pass, when she saw that he had left his garment in her hand, and was fled [1]forth,

14 That she called unto the men of her house, and spake unto them, saying, See, he hath brought in an [a]Hebrew unto us to [1]mock us; he came in unto me to lie with me, and I cried with a loud voice:

15 And it came to pass, when he heard that I lifted up my voice and cried, that he left his garment with me, and fled, and got him out.

16 And she laid up his garment by her, until his lord came home.

17 And she [a]spake unto him according to these words, saying, The Hebrew servant, which thou hast brought unto us, came in unto me to mock me:

18 And it came to pass, as I lifted up my voice and cried, that he left his garment with me, and fled out.

19 And it came to pass, when his master heard the words of his wife, which she spake unto him, saying, After this manner did thy servant to me; that [1]his [a]wrath was kindled.

20 And Joseph's master took him, and [a]put him into the [b]prison, a place where the king's prisoners *were* bound: and he was there in the prison.

21 But the LORD was with Joseph, and shewed him [1]mercy, and [a]gave[2] him favour in the sight of the keeper of the prison.

---

38:24 [a] Judg. 19:2 [b] Lev. 20:14; 21:9; Deut. 22:21 [1] *harlotry*

38:25 [a] Gen. 37:32; 38:18 [1] *cord*

38:26 [a] Gen. 37:33 [b] 1 Sam. 24:17 [c] Gen. 38:14 [d] Job 34:31, 32

38:29 [a] Gen. 46:12; Num. 26:20; Ruth 4:12; 1 Chr. 2:4; Matt. 1:3 [1] Lit. *Breach* or *Breakthrough*

38:30 [a] Gen. 46:12; 1 Chr. 2:4; Matt. 1:3 [1] *Zerah,* 1 Chr. 2:4

39:1 [a] Gen. 12:10; 43:15 [b] Gen. 37:36; Ps. 105:17 [c] Gen. 37:28; 45:4

39:2 [a] Gen. 26:24, 28; 28:15; 35:3; 39:3, 21, 23; 1 Sam. 16:18; 18:14, 28; Acts 7:9 [1] *successful*

39:3 [a] Ps. 1:3 [1] *to be a success*

39:4 [a] Gen. 18:3; 19:19; 39:21 [b] Gen. 24:2, 10; 39:8, 22; 41:40 [1] *favour* [2] *care*

39:5 [a] Gen. 18:26; 30:27; 2 Sam. 6:11

39:6 [a] Gen. 29:17; 1 Sam. 16:12 [1] *care* [2] *anything* [3] *except* [4] *handsome in form and appearance*

39:7 [a] 2 Sam. 13:11 [1] *cast longing eyes*

39:8 [1] *knows* [2] *in the house* except *through me*

39:9 [a] Lev. 20:10; Prov. 6:29, 32 [b] Gen. 20:6; 42:18; 2 Sam. 12:13; Ps. 51:4

39:10 [a] Prov. 1:10 [1] *did not heed her*

39:11 [1] *work*

39:12 [a] Prov. 7:13

39:13 [1] *outside*

39:14 [a] Gen. 14:13; 41:12 [1] *laugh at*

39:17 [a] Ex. 23:1; Ps. 120:3; Prov. 26:28

39:19 [a] Prov. 6:34, 35 [1] *his anger was aroused*

39:20 [a] Ps. 105:18; [1 Pet. 2:19] [b] Gen. 40:3, 15; 41:14

39:21 [a] Gen. 39:2; Ex. 3:21; Ps. 105:19; [Prov. 16:7]; Dan. 1:9; Acts 7:9, 10 [1] *lovingkindness* [2] *caused him to be viewed with favour by*

22 And the keeper of the prison [a]committed to Joseph's hand all the prisoners that *were* in the prison; and whatsoever they did there, [1]he was the doer *of it.*

23 The keeper of the prison [1]looked not to any thing *that was* under his hand; because [a]the LORD was with him, and *that* which he did, the LORD made *it* to prosper.

## CHAPTER 40

AND it came to pass after these things, *that* the [a]butler of the king of Egypt and *his* baker had offended their lord the king of Egypt.

2 And Pharaoh was [a]wroth[1] against two *of* his officers, against the chief of the butlers, and against the chief of the bakers.

3 [a]And he put them [1]in ward in the house of the captain of the guard, into the prison, the place where Joseph *was* [2]bound.

4 And the captain of the guard charged Joseph with them, and he served them: and they continued [1]a season in ward.

5 And they [a]dreamed a dream both of them, each man his dream in one night, each man according to the interpretation of his dream, the butler and the baker of the king of Egypt, which *were* bound in the prison.

6 And Joseph came in unto them in the morning, and looked upon them, and, behold, they *were* [1]sad.

7 And he asked Pharaoh's officers that *were* with him in the ward of his lord's house, saying, [a]Wherefore look ye *so* sadly to day?

8 And they said unto him, [a]We have dreamed a dream, and *there is* no interpreter of it. And Joseph said unto them, [b]*Do* not interpretations *belong* to God? tell me *them,* I pray you.

9 And the chief butler told his dream to Joseph, and said to him, In my dream, behold, a vine *was* before me;

10 And in the vine *were* three branches: and it *was* as though it budded, *and* her blossoms shot forth; and the clusters thereof brought forth ripe grapes:

11 And Pharaoh's cup *was* in my hand: and I took the grapes, and pressed them into Pharaoh's cup, and I gave the cup into Pharaoh's hand.

12 And Joseph said unto him, [a]This *is* the interpretation of it: The three branches [b]are three days:

13 Yet within three days shall Pharaoh [a]lift up thine head, and restore thee unto thy [1]place: and thou shalt deliver Pharaoh's cup into his hand, after the former manner when thou wast his butler.

39:22 [a] Gen. 39:4; 40:3, 4 [1] *it was his doing*

39:23 [a] Gen. 39:2, 3 [1] *did not look into*

40:1 [a] Gen. 40:11, 13; Neh. 1:11

40:2 [a] Prov. 16:14 [1] *angry*

40:3 [a] Gen. 39:1, 20, 23; 41:10 [1] *in custody* [2] *confined*

40:4 [1] *in custody for a while*

40:5 [a] Gen. 37:5; 41:1

40:6 [1] *dejected*

40:7 [a] Neh. 2:2

40:8 [a] Gen. 41:15 [b] [Gen. 41:16; Dan. 2:11, 20–22, 27, 28, 47]

40:12 [a] Gen. 40:18; 41:12, 25; Judg. 7:14; Dan. 2:36; 4:18, 19 [b] Gen. 40:18; 42:17

40:13 [a] 2 Kin. 25:27; Ps. 3:3; Jer. 52:31 [1] *position*

40:14 [a] 1 Sam. 25:31; Luke 23:42 [b] Gen. 24:49; 47:29; Josh. 2:12; 1 Sam. 20:14, 15; 2 Sam. 9:1; 1 Kin. 2:7

40:15 [a] Gen. 37:26–28 [b] Gen. 39:20

40:16 [1] *baskets of white bread*

40:17 [1] *baked goods*

40:18 [a] Gen. 40:12

40:19 [a] Gen. 40:13 [b] Deut. 21:22

40:20 [a] Matt. 14:6–10 [b] Mark 6:21 [c] Gen. 40:13, 19

40:21 [a] Gen. 40:13 [b] Neh. 2:1

40:22 [a] Gen. 40:19

40:23 [a] Eccl. 9:15, 16

41:1 [a] Gen. 40:5

41:2 [1] *cows, fine-looking and fat*

41:3 [1] *cows* [2] *ugly and gaunt* [3] *bank*

41:4 [1] *ugly and gaunt cows* [2] *fine-looking and fat cows*

41:5 [1] *heads of grain* [2] *plump*

41:6 [a] Ex. 10:13 [1] *heads of grain* [2] *blighted*

41:7 [1] *heads* [2] *plump*

14 But [a]think on me when it shall be well with thee, and [b]shew kindness, I pray thee, unto me, and make mention of me unto Pharaoh, and bring me out of this house:

15 For indeed I was [a]stolen away out of the land of the Hebrews: [b]and here also have I done nothing that they should put me into the dungeon.

16 When the chief baker saw that the interpretation was good, he said unto Joseph, I also *was* in my dream, and, behold, *I had* three [1]white baskets on my head:

17 And in the uppermost basket *there was* of all manner of [1]bakemeats for Pharaoh; and the birds did eat them out of the basket upon my head.

18 And Joseph answered and said, [a]This *is* the interpretation thereof: The three baskets *are* three days:

19 [a]Yet within three days shall Pharaoh lift up thy head from off thee, and shall [b]hang thee on a tree; and the birds shall eat thy flesh from off thee.

20 And it came to pass the third day, *which was* Pharaoh's [a]birthday, that he [b]made a feast unto all his servants: and he [c]lifted up the head of the chief butler and of the chief baker among his servants.

21 And he [a]restored the chief butler unto his butlership again; and [b]he gave the cup into Pharaoh's hand:

22 But he [a]hanged the chief baker: as Joseph had interpreted to them.

23 Yet did not the chief butler remember Joseph, but [a]forgat him.

## CHAPTER 41

AND it came to pass at the end of two full years, that [a]Pharaoh dreamed: and, behold, he stood by the river.

2 And, behold, there came up out of the river seven well favoured [1]kine and fatfleshed; and they fed in a meadow.

3 And, behold, seven other [1]kine came up after them out of the river, [2]ill favoured and leanfleshed; and stood by the *other* kine upon the [3]brink of the river.

4 And the [1]ill favoured and leanfleshed kine did eat up the seven [2]well favoured and fat kine. So Pharaoh awoke.

5 And he slept and dreamed the second time: and, behold, seven [1]ears of corn came up upon one stalk, [2]rank and good.

6 And, behold, seven thin [1]ears and [2]blasted with the [a]east wind sprung up after them.

7 And the seven thin [1]ears devoured the seven [2]rank and full ears.

*Joseph Remembered*

And Pharaoh awoke, and, behold, *it was* a dream.

8 And it came to pass in the morning [a]that his spirit was troubled; and he sent and called for all [b]the magicians of Egypt, and all the [c]wise men thereof: and Pharaoh told them his dream; but *there was* none that could interpret them unto Pharaoh.

9 Then spake the [a]chief butler unto Pharaoh, saying, I do remember my faults this day:

10 Pharaoh was [a]wroth[1] with his servants, [b]and put me in [2]ward in the captain of the guard's house, *both* me and the chief baker:

11 And [a]we dreamed a dream in one night, I and he; we dreamed each man according to the interpretation of his dream.

12 And *there was* there with us a young man, [a]an Hebrew, [b]servant to the captain of the guard; and we told him, and he [c]interpreted to us our dreams; to each man according to his dream he did interpret.

13 And it came to pass, [a]as he interpreted to us, so it was; me he restored unto mine office, and him he hanged.

14 [a]Then Pharaoh sent and called Joseph, and they [b]brought him hastily [c]out of the dungeon: and he shaved *himself,* and [d]changed his [1]raiment, and came in unto Pharaoh.

15 And Pharaoh said unto Joseph, I have dreamed a dream, and *there is* none that can interpret it: [a]and I have heard say of thee, *that* thou canst understand a dream to interpret it.

16 And Joseph answered Pharaoh, saying, [a]*It is* not in me: [b]God shall give Pharaoh an answer of peace.

17 And Pharaoh said unto Joseph, [a]In my dream, behold, I stood upon the bank of the river:

18 And, behold, there came up out of the river seven [1]kine, [2]fatfleshed and well favoured; and they fed in a meadow:

19 And, behold, seven other [1]kine came up after them, poor and very [2]ill favoured and leanfleshed, such as I never saw in all the land of Egypt for [3]badness:

20 And the [1]lean and the ill favoured kine did eat up the first seven fat [2]kine:

21 And when they had eaten them up, it could not be known that they had eaten them; but they *were* still [1]ill favoured, as at the beginning. So I awoke.

22 And I saw in my dream, and, behold, seven [1]ears came up in one stalk, full and good:

23 And, behold, seven [1]ears, withered, thin, *and* [2]blasted with the east wind, sprung up after them:

24 And the thin [1]ears devoured the seven good ears: and [a]I told *this* unto the magicians; but *there was* none that could declare *it* to me.

25 And Joseph said unto Pharaoh, The dream of Pharaoh *is* one: [a]God hath shewed Pharaoh what he *is* about to do.

26 The seven good [1]kine *are* seven years; and the seven good [2]ears *are* seven years: the dream *is* one.

27 And the seven thin and [1]ill favoured kine that came up after them *are* seven years; and the seven empty [2]ears [3]blasted with the east wind shall be [a]seven years of famine.

28 [a]This *is* the thing which I have spoken unto Pharaoh: What God *is* about to do he sheweth unto Pharaoh.

29 Behold, there come [a]seven years of great plenty throughout all the land of Egypt:

30 And there shall [a]arise after them seven years of famine; and all the plenty shall be forgotten in the land of Egypt; and the famine [b]shall [1]consume the land;

31 And the plenty shall not be known in the land by reason of that famine following; for it *shall be* very grievous.

32 And for that the dream was [1]doubled unto Pharaoh twice; *it is* because the [a]thing *is* established by God, and God will shortly bring it to pass.

33 Now therefore let Pharaoh look out a man [1]discreet and wise, and set him over the land of Egypt.

34 Let Pharaoh do *this,* and let him appoint [1]officers over the land, and [a]take up the [2]fifth part of the land of Egypt in the seven plenteous years.

35 And [a]let them gather all the food of those good years that come, and lay up [1]corn under the [2]hand of Pharaoh, and let them keep food in the cities.

36 And that food shall be for [1]store to the land against the seven years of famine, which shall be in the land of Egypt; that the land [a]perish not through the famine.

37 And [a]the thing was good in the eyes of Pharaoh, and in the eyes of all his servants.

38 And Pharaoh said unto his servants, Can we find *such a one* as this *is,* a man [a]in whom the Spirit of God *is?*

39 And Pharaoh said unto Joseph, Forasmuch as God hath shewed thee all this, *there is* none [1]so discreet and wise as thou *art:*

40 [a]Thou shalt be [1]over my house, and according unto thy word shall all my people be ruled: only in the throne will I be greater than thou.

---

41:8 [a] Dan. 2:1, 3; 4:5, 19 [b] Ex. 7:11, 22 [c] Matt. 2:1
41:9 [a] Gen. 40:1, 14, 23
41:10 [a] Gen. 40:2, 3 [b] Gen. 39:20 [1] *angry* [2] *custody*
41:11 [a] Gen. 40:5
41:12 [a] Gen. 39:14; 43:32 [b] Gen. 37:36 [c] Gen. 40:12
41:13 [a] Gen. 40:21, 22
41:14 [a] Ps. 105:20 [b] Dan. 2:25 [c] [1 Sam. 2:8] [d] 2 Kin. 25:27–29 [1] *clothing*
41:15 [a] Dan. 5:16
41:16 [a] Dan. 2:30 [b] Dan. 2:22, 28, 47
41:17 [a] Gen. 41:1
41:18 [1] *cows* [2] *fine-looking and fat*
41:19 [1] *cows* [2] *ugly and gaunt* [3] *ugliness*
41:20 [1] *gaunt and ugly cows* [2] *cows*
41:21 [1] *ugly*
41:22 [1] *heads of grain*
41:23 [1] *heads* [2] *blighted*
41:24 [a] Is. 8:19 [1] *heads*
41:25 [a] Dan. 2:28, 29, 45
41:26 [1] *cows* [2] *heads of grain*
41:27 [a] 2 Kin. 8:1 [1] *ugly cows* [2] *heads* [3] *blighted*
41:28 [a] [Gen. 41:25, 32]
41:29 [a] Gen. 41:47
41:30 [a] Gen. 41:54, 56 [b] Gen. 47:13 [1] *deplete the food of*
41:32 [a] Num. 23:19 [1] *repeated*
41:33 [1] *discerning*
41:34 [a] [Prov. 6:6 8] [1] *overseers* [2] *fifth part of the produce of*
41:35 [a] Gen. 41:48 [1] *grain* [2] *authority*
41:36 [a] Gen. 47:15, 19 [1] *a reserve for*
41:37 [a] Acts 7:10
41:38 [a] Num. 27:18
41:39 [1] *as discerning*
41:40 [d] Ps. 105:21 [1] *in charge of*

---

38

41 And Pharaoh said unto Joseph, See, I have <sup>a</sup>set thee over all the land of Egypt.

42 And Pharaoh <sup>a</sup>took off his <sup>1</sup>ring from his hand, and put it upon Joseph's hand, and <sup>b</sup>arrayed him in <sup>2</sup>vestures of fine linen, <sup>c</sup>and put a gold chain about his neck;

43 And he made him to ride in the second <sup>a</sup>chariot which he had; <sup>b</sup>and they cried before him, Bow the knee: and he made him *ruler* <sup>c</sup>over all the land of Egypt.

44 And Pharaoh said unto Joseph, I *am* Pharaoh, and <sup>1</sup>without thee shall no man lift up his hand or foot in all the land of Egypt.

45 And Pharaoh called Joseph's name <sup>1</sup>Zaphnath-paaneah; and he gave him to wife <sup>a</sup>Asenath the daughter of Poti-pherah priest of On. And Joseph went out over *all* the land of Egypt.

46 And Joseph *was* thirty years old when he <sup>a</sup>stood before Pharaoh king of Egypt. And Joseph went out from the presence of Pharaoh, and went throughout all the land of Egypt.

47 And in the seven plenteous years the earth brought forth <sup>1</sup>by handfuls.

48 And he gathered up all the food of the seven years, which were in the land of Egypt, and laid up the food in the cities: the food of the field, which *was* round about every city, laid he up in the same.

49 And Joseph gathered <sup>1</sup>corn <sup>a</sup>as the sand of the sea, very much, until he <sup>2</sup>left numbering; for *it was* without number.

50 <sup>a</sup>And unto Joseph were born two sons before the years of famine came, which Asenath the daughter of Poti-pherah priest of On bare unto him.

51 And Joseph called the name of the firstborn <sup>1</sup>Manasseh: For God, *said he,* hath made me forget all my toil, and all my <sup>a</sup>father's house.

52 And the name of the second called he <sup>1</sup>Ephraim: For God hath caused me to be <sup>a</sup>fruitful in the land of my affliction.

53 And the seven years of plenteousness, that was in the land of Egypt, were ended.

54 <sup>a</sup>And the seven years of <sup>1</sup>dearth began to come, <sup>b</sup>according as Joseph had said: and the dearth was in all lands; but in all the land of Egypt there was bread.

55 And when all the land of Egypt was famished, the people cried to Pharaoh for bread: and Pharaoh said unto all the Egyptians, Go unto Joseph; <sup>a</sup>what he saith to you, do.

56 And the famine was over all the face of the earth: And Joseph opened <sup>1</sup>all the storehouses, and <sup>a</sup>sold unto the Egyptians; and the famine <sup>2</sup>waxed sore in the land of Egypt.

57 <sup>a</sup>And all countries came into Egypt to Joseph for to <sup>b</sup>buy <sup>1</sup>corn; because that the famine was *so* <sup>2</sup>sore in all lands.

## CHAPTER 42

Now when <sup>a</sup>Jacob saw that there was <sup>1</sup>corn in Egypt, Jacob said unto his sons, Why do ye look one upon another?

2 And he said, Behold, I have heard that there is <sup>1</sup>corn in Egypt: get you down thither, and buy for us from thence; that we may <sup>a</sup>live, and not die.

3 And Joseph's ten brethren went down to buy <sup>1</sup>corn in Egypt.

4 But Benjamin, Joseph's brother, Jacob sent not with his brethren; for he said, <sup>a</sup>Lest peradventure <sup>1</sup>mischief befall him.

5 And the sons of Israel came to buy <sup>1</sup>corn among those that came: for the famine was <sup>a</sup>in the land of Canaan.

6 And Joseph *was* the governor <sup>a</sup>over the land, *and* he *it was* that sold to all the people of the land: and Joseph's <sup>1</sup>brethren came, and <sup>b</sup>bowed down themselves before him *with* their faces to the earth.

7 And Joseph saw his brethren, and he knew them, but <sup>1</sup>made himself <sup>a</sup>strange unto them, and spake <sup>2</sup>roughly unto them; and he said unto them, Whence come ye? And they said, From the land of Canaan to buy food.

8 And Joseph knew his brethren, but they knew not him.

9 And Joseph <sup>a</sup>remembered the dreams which he dreamed of them, and said unto them, Ye *are* spies; to see the <sup>1</sup>nakedness of the land ye are come.

10 And they said unto him, Nay, my lord, but to buy food are thy servants come.

11 We *are* all one man's sons; we *are* <sup>1</sup>true *men,* thy servants are no spies.

12 And he said unto them, Nay, but to see the nakedness of the land ye are come.

13 And they said, Thy servants *are* twelve <sup>1</sup>brethren, the sons of one man in the land of Canaan; and, behold, the youngest *is* this day with our father, and one <sup>a</sup>*is* <sup>2</sup>not.

14 And Joseph said unto them, That *is it* that I spake unto you, saying, Ye *are* spies:

15 Hereby ye shall be <sup>1</sup>proved: <sup>a</sup>By the life of Pharaoh ye shall not go forth hence, except your youngest brother come hither.

16 Send one of you, and let him fetch your brother, and ye shall be

41:41 <sup>a</sup> Dan. 6:3
41:42 <sup>a</sup> Esth. 3:10 <sup>b</sup> Esth. 8:2, 15 <sup>c</sup> Dan. 5:7, 16, 29 <sup>1</sup> signet ring <sup>2</sup> garments
41:43 <sup>a</sup> Gen. 46:29 <sup>b</sup> Esth. 6:9 <sup>c</sup> Gen. 42:6
41:44 <sup>1</sup> without your consent
41:45 <sup>a</sup> Gen. 46:20 <sup>1</sup> Probably Egyptian for God speaks and he lives
41:46 <sup>a</sup> 1 Sam. 16:21
41:47 <sup>1</sup> Abundantly
41:49 <sup>a</sup> Gen. 22:17 <sup>1</sup> grain <sup>2</sup> stopped counting
41:50 <sup>a</sup> Gen. 46:20; 48:5
41:51 <sup>a</sup> Ps. 45:10 <sup>1</sup> Lit. Making Forgetful
41:52 <sup>a</sup> Gen. 17:6; 28:3; 49:22 <sup>1</sup> Lit. Fruitfulness
41:54 <sup>a</sup> Acts 7:11 <sup>b</sup> Gen. 41:30 <sup>1</sup> famine
41:55 <sup>a</sup> John 2:5
41:56 <sup>a</sup> Gen. 42:6 <sup>1</sup> Lit. all that was in them

<sup>2</sup> became severe
41:57 <sup>a</sup> Ezek. 29:12 <sup>b</sup> Gen. 27:28, 37; 42:3 <sup>1</sup> Grain <sup>2</sup> severe
42:1 <sup>a</sup> Acts 7:12 <sup>1</sup> grain
42:2 <sup>a</sup> Gen. 43:8; Ps. 33:18, 19; Is. 38:1 <sup>1</sup> grain
42:3 <sup>1</sup> grain
42:4 <sup>a</sup> Gen. 42:38 <sup>1</sup> some calamity
42:5 <sup>a</sup> Gen. 12:10; 26:1; 41:57; Acts 7:11 <sup>1</sup> Grain
42:6 <sup>a</sup> Gen. 41:41, 55 <sup>b</sup> Gen. 37:7–10; 41:43; Is. 60:14 <sup>1</sup> brothers
42:7 <sup>a</sup> Gen. 45:1, 2 <sup>1</sup> acted as a stranger to them <sup>2</sup> harshly
42:9 <sup>a</sup> Gen. 37:5–9 <sup>1</sup> exposed parts
42:11 <sup>1</sup> honest
42:13 <sup>a</sup> Gen. 37:30; 42:32; 44:20; Lam. 5:7 <sup>1</sup> brothers <sup>2</sup> no more
42:15 <sup>a</sup> 1 Sam. 1:26; 17:55 <sup>1</sup> tested

[1]kept in prison, that your words may be [2]proved, whether *there be any* truth in you: or else by the life of Pharaoh surely ye *are* spies.

17 And he put them all together into [1]ward [a]three days.

18 And Joseph said unto them the third day, This do, and live; [a]*for* I fear God:

19 If ye *be* true *men,* let one of your brethren be bound in the house of your prison: go ye, carry [1]corn for the famine of your houses:

20 But [a]bring your youngest brother unto me; so shall your words be verified, and ye shall not die. And they did so.

21 And they said one to another, [a]We *are* verily guilty concerning our brother, in that we saw the anguish of his soul, when he [1]besought us, and we would not hear; [b]therefore is this distress come upon us.

22 And Reuben answered them, saying, [a]Spake I not unto you, saying, Do not sin against the [1]child; and ye would not hear? therefore, behold, also his blood is [b]required.

23 And they knew not that Joseph understood *them;* for he spake unto them by an interpreter.

24 And he turned himself [1]about from them, and [a]wept; and returned to them again, and [2]communed with them, and took from them [b]Simeon, and bound him before their eyes.

25 Then Joseph [a]commanded to fill their sacks with [1]corn, and to [b]restore every man's money into his sack, and to give them provision for the way: and [c]thus did he unto them.

26 And they [1]laded their [2]asses with the [3]corn, and departed thence.

27 And as [a]one of them opened his sack to give his [1]ass [2]provender in the inn, he [3]espied his money; for, behold, it *was* in his sack's mouth.

28 And he said unto his brethren, My money is restored; and, lo, *it is* even in my sack: and [1]their heart failed *them,* and they were afraid, saying one to another, What *is* this *that* God hath done unto us?

29 And they came unto Jacob their father unto the land of Canaan, and told him all that befell unto them; saying,

30 The man, *who is* the lord of the land, [a]spake [1]roughly to us, and took us for spies of the country.

31 And we said unto him, We *are* [1]true *men;* we are no spies:

32 We *be* twelve brethren, sons of our father; one *is* not, and the youngest *is* this day with our father in the land of Canaan.

33 And the man, the lord of the country, said unto us, [a]Hereby shall I know that ye *are* [1]true *men;* leave

one of your brethren *here* with me, and take *food for* the famine of your households, and be gone:

34 And bring your [a]youngest brother unto me: then shall I know that ye *are* no spies, but *that* ye *are* true *men: so* will I deliver you your brother, and ye shall [b]traffick[1] in the land.

35 And it came to pass as they emptied their sacks, that, behold, [a]every man's bundle of money *was* in his sack: and when *both* they and their father saw the bundles of money, they were afraid.

36 And Jacob their father said unto them, Me have ye [a]bereaved *of my children:* Joseph *is* not, and Simeon *is* not, and ye will take [b]Benjamin *away:* all these things are against me.

37 And Reuben spake unto his father, saying, Slay my two sons, if I bring him not to thee: deliver him into my hand, and I will bring him to thee again.

38 And he said, My son shall not go down with you; for [a]his brother is dead, and he is left alone: [b]if[1]mischief befall him [2]by the way in the which ye go, then shall ye [c]bring down my gray hairs with sorrow to the grave.

## CHAPTER 43

AND the famine *was* [a]sore[1] in the land.

2 And it came to pass, when they had eaten up the [1]corn which they had brought out of Egypt, their father said unto them, Go [a]again, buy us a little food.

3 And Judah spake unto him, saying, The man did solemnly [1]protest unto us, saying, Ye shall not see my face, except your [a]brother *be* with you.

4 If thou wilt send our brother with us, we will go down and buy thee food:

5 But if thou wilt not send *him,* we will not go down: for the man said unto us, Ye shall not see my face, except your brother *be* with you.

6 And Israel said, Wherefore dealt ye *so* [1]ill with me, *as* to tell the man whether ye had yet a brother?

7 And they said, The man asked us [1]straitly of our state, and of our kindred, saying, *Is* your father yet alive? have ye *another* brother? and we told him according to [2]the tenor of these words: could we [3]certainly know that he would say, Bring your brother down?

8 And Judah said unto Israel his father, Send the lad with me, and we will arise and go; that we may [a]live, and not die, both we, and thou, *and* also our little ones.

9 I will be surety for him; of my hand shalt thou require him: [a]if I

### Cross-references (center column)

42:16 [1] Lit. *bound*
[2] *tested*
42:17 [a] Gen. 40:4, 7, 12 [1] *prison*
42:18 [a] Gen. 22:12; 39:9; Ex. 1:17; Lev. 25:43; Neh. 5:15; Prov. 1:7; 9:10
42:19 [1] *grain*
42:20 [a] Gen.
42:34; 43:5; 44:23
42:21 [a] Gen. 37:26–28; 44:16; 45:3; Job 36:8, 9; Hos. 5:15  [b] Prov. 21:13; Matt. 7:2 [1] *pleaded with*
42:22 [a] Gen. 37:21, 22, 29  [b] Gen. 9:5, 6; 1 Kin. 2:32; 2 Chr. 24:22; Ps. 9:12; Luke 11:50, 51 [1] *boy*
42:24 [a] Gen. 43:30; 45:14, 15 [b] Gen. 34:25, 30; 43:14, 23 [1] *away* [2] *talked*
42:25 [a] Gen. 44:1  [b] Gen. 43:12 [c] [Matt. 5:44; Rom. 12:17, 20, 21; 1 Pet. 3:9] [1] *grain*
42:26 [1] *loaded* [2] *donkeys* [3] *grain*
42:27 [a] Gen. 43:21, 22 [1] *donkey* [2] *feed* [3] *saw*
42:28 [1] *their hearts sank*
42:30 [a] Gen. 42:7 [1] *harshly*
42:31 [1] *honest*
42:33 [a] Gen. 42:15, 19, 20 [1] *honest*
42:34 [a] Gen. 42:20; 43:3, 5 [b] Gen. 34:10 [1] *trade*
42:35 [a] Gen. 43:12, 15, 21
42:36 [a] Gen. 43:14 [b] Gen. 35:18; [Rom. 8:28, 31]
42:38 [a] Gen. 37:29; 42:13; 44:20, 28 [b] Gen. 42:4; 44:29 [c] Gen. 37:35; 44:31 [1] *calamity should come to* [2] *along*
43:1 [a] Gen. 41:54, 57; 42:5; 45:6, 11 [1] *severe*
43:2 [a] Gen. 42:2; 44:25 [1] *grain*
43:3 [a] Gen. 42:20; 43:5; 44:23 [1] Lit. *warn*
43:6 [1] *wickedly*
43:7 [1] *pointedly about ourselves* [2] Lit. *these words* [3] *possibly*
43:8 [a] Gen. 42:2; 47:19
43:9 [a] Gen. 42:37; 44:32; Philem. 18

bring him not unto thee, and set him before thee, then let me bear the blame for ever:

10 For except we had lingered, surely now we had returned this second time.

11 And their father Israel said unto them, If *it must be* so now, do this; take [1]of the best fruits in the land in your vessels, and [a]carry down the man a present, a little [b]balm, and a little honey, spices, and myrrh, [2]nuts, and almonds:

12 And take double money in your hand; and the money [a]that was brought again in the mouth of your sacks, carry *it* again in your hand; peradventure it *was* an oversight:

13 Take also your brother, and arise, go again unto the man:

14 And God [a]Almighty [b]give you mercy before the man, that he may send away your other brother, and Benjamin. [c]If I be bereaved *of my children,* I am bereaved.

15 And the men took that present, and they took double money in their hand, and Benjamin; and rose up, and went [a]down to Egypt, and stood before Joseph.

16 And when Joseph saw Benjamin with them, he said to the [a]ruler of his house, Bring *these* men home, and [1]slay, and make ready; for *these* men shall [2]dine with me at noon.

17 And the man did as Joseph [1]bade; and the man brought the men into Joseph's house.

18 And the men were [a]afraid, because they were brought into Joseph's house; and they said, Because of the money that was returned in our sacks at the first time are we brought in; that he may [1]seek occasion against us, and fall upon us, and take us [2]for bondmen, and our [3]asses.

19 And they came near to the steward of Joseph's house, and they communed with him at the door of the house,

20 And said, O sir, [a]we came indeed down at the first time to buy food:

21 And [a]it came to pass, when we came to the [1]inn, that we opened our sacks, and, behold, *every* man's money *was* in the mouth of his sack, our money in full weight: and we have brought it again in our hand.

22 And other money have we brought down in our hands to buy food: we cannot tell who put our money in our sacks.

23 And he said, Peace *be* to you, fear not: your God, and the God of your father, hath given you treasure in your sacks: I had your money. And he brought [a]Simeon out unto them.

24 And the man brought the men into Joseph's house, and [a]gave *them*

water, and they washed their feet; and he gave their [1]asses [2]provender.

25 And they made ready the present [1]against Joseph came at noon: for they heard that they should eat bread there.

26 And when Joseph came home, they brought him the present which *was* in their hand into the house, and [a]bowed themselves to him to the earth.

27 And he asked them of *their* [1]welfare, and said, *Is* your father well, the old man [a]of whom ye spake? *Is* he yet alive?

28 And they answered, Thy servant our father *is* in good health, he *is* yet alive. [a]And they bowed down their heads, and [1]made obeisance.

29 And he lifted up his eyes, and saw his brother Benjamin, [a]his mother's son, and said, *Is* this your younger brother, [b]of whom ye spake unto me? And he said, God be gracious unto thee, my son.

30 And Joseph made haste; for [a]his [b]bowels did yearn upon his brother: and he sought *where* to weep; and he entered into *his* chamber, and [b]wept there.

31 And he washed his face, and went out, and [1]refrained himself, and said, [2]Set on [a]bread.

32 And they [1]set on for him by himself, and for them by themselves, and for the Egyptians, which did eat with him, by themselves: because the Egyptians [2]might not eat bread with the [a]Hebrews; for that *is* [b]an abomination unto the Egyptians.

33 And they sat before him, the firstborn according to his [a]birthright, and the youngest according to his youth: and the men [1]marvelled one at another.

34 And he took *and sent* [1]messes unto them from before him: but Benjamin's [2]mess was [a]five times so much as any of theirs. And they drank, and were merry with him.

## CHAPTER 44

AND he commanded [1]the [a]steward of his house, saying, [b]Fill the men's sacks *with* food, as much as they can carry, and put every man's money in his sack's mouth.

2 And put my cup, the silver cup, in the sack's mouth of the youngest, and his [1]corn money. And he did according to the word that Joseph had spoken.

3 As soon as the morning was light, the men were sent away, they and their [1]asses.

4 *And* when they were gone out of the city, *and* not *yet* far off, Joseph said unto his steward, Up, follow after the men; and when thou

43:11 [a] Gen. 32:20; 33:10; 43:25, 26; [Prov. 18:16] [b] Gen. 37:25; Jer. 8:22; Ezek. 27:17 [1] *some of* [2] *pistachio nuts*

43:12 [a] Gen. 42:25, 35; 43:21, 22

43:14 [a] Gen. 17:1; 28:3; 35:11; 48:3 [b] Gen. 39:21; Ps. 106:46 [c] Gen. 42:36; Esth. 4:16

43:15 [a] Gen. 39:1; 46:3, 6

43:16 [a] Gen. 24:2; 39:4; 44:1 [1] *slaughter an animal* [2] Lit. *eat*

43:17 [1] *ordered*

43:18 [a] Gen. 42:28 [1] Lit. *roll himself upon us* [2] *as slaves* [3] *donkeys*

43:20 [a] Gen. 42:3, 10

43:21 [a] Gen. 42:27, 35 [1] *encampment*

43:23 [a] Gen. 42:24

43:24 [a] Gen. 18:4; 19:2; 24:32 [1] *donkeys* [2] *feed*

43:25 [1] *for Joseph's coming*

43:26 [a] Gen. 37:7, 10; 42:6; 44:14

43:27 [a] Gen. 29:6; 42:11, 13; 43:7; 45:3; 2 Kin. 4:26 [1] *well-being*

43:28 [a] Gen. 37:7, 10 [1] *prostrated themselves*

43:29 [a] Gen. 35:17, 18 [b] Gen. 42:13

43:30 [a] 1 Kin. 3:26 [b] Gen. 42:24; 45:2, 14, 15; 46:29 [1] *heart yearned for*

43:31 [a] Gen. 43:25 [1] *restrained* [2] *Serve the bread*

43:32 [a] Gen. 41:12; Ex. 1:15 [b] Gen. 46:34; Ex. 8:26 [1] *set a place for him* [2] *could not eat food*

43:33 [a] Gen. 27:36; 42:7; Deut. 21:16, 17 [1] *looked with astonishment at*

43:34 [a] Gen. 35:24; 45:22 [1] *servings* [2] *serving*

44:1 [a] Gen. 43:16 [b] Gen. 42:25 [1] Lit. *the one over his house*

44:2 [1] *grain*

44:3 [1] *donkeys*

dost overtake them, say unto them, Wherefore have ye <sup>a</sup>rewarded<sup>1</sup> evil for good?

5 *Is* not this *it* in which my lord drinketh, and whereby indeed he <sup>1</sup>divineth? ye have done evil in so doing.

6 And he overtook them, and he spake unto them these same words.

7 And they said unto him, Wherefore saith my lord these words? <sup>1</sup>God forbid that thy servants should do according to this thing:

8 Behold, <sup>a</sup>the money, which we found in our sacks' mouths, we brought again unto thee out of the land of Canaan: how then should we steal out of thy lord's house silver or gold?

9 With whomsoever of thy servants it be found, <sup>a</sup>both let him die, and we also will be my lord's <sup>1</sup>bondmen.

10 And he said, Now also *let* it *be* according unto your words: he with whom it is found shall be my <sup>1</sup>servant; and ye shall be blameless.

11 Then they speedily took down every man his sack to the ground, and opened every man his sack.

12 And he searched, *and* began at the eldest, and <sup>1</sup>left at the youngest: and the cup was found in Benjamin's sack.

13 Then they <sup>a</sup>rent<sup>1</sup> their clothes, and laded every man his <sup>2</sup>ass, and returned to the city.

14 And Judah and his brethren came to Joseph's house; for he *was* yet there: and they <sup>a</sup>fell before him on the ground.

15 And Joseph said unto them, What deed *is* this that ye have done? <sup>1</sup>wot ye not that such a man as I can certainly <sup>2</sup>divine?

16 And Judah said, What shall we say unto my lord? what shall we speak? or how shall we clear ourselves? God hath <sup>a</sup>found out the iniquity of thy servants: behold, <sup>b</sup>we *are* my lord's servants, both we, and *he* also with whom the cup is found.

17 And he said, <sup>a</sup>God<sup>1</sup> forbid that I should do so: *but* the man in whose hand the cup is found, he shall be my servant; and as for you, get you up in peace unto your father.

18 Then Judah came near unto him, and said, Oh my lord, let thy servant, I pray thee, speak a word in my lord's ears, and <sup>a</sup>let not thine anger burn against thy servant: for thou *art* even as Pharaoh.

19 My lord asked his servants, saying, Have ye a father, or a brother?

20 And we said unto my lord, We have a father, an old man, and <sup>a</sup>a child of his old age, <sup>1</sup>a little one; and his brother is <sup>b</sup>dead, and he <sup>c</sup>alone is left of his mother, and his <sup>d</sup>father loveth him.

21 And thou saidst unto thy servants, <sup>a</sup>Bring him down unto me, that I may set mine eyes upon him.

22 And we said unto my lord, The lad cannot leave his father: for *if* he should leave his father, *his father* would die.

23 And thou saidst unto thy servants, <sup>a</sup>Except your youngest brother come down with you, ye shall see my face no more.

24 And it came to pass when we came up unto thy servant my father, we told him the words of my lord.

25 And <sup>a</sup>our father said, Go again, *and* buy us a little food.

26 And we said, We cannot go down: if our youngest brother be with us, then will we go down: for we may not see the man's face, except our youngest brother *be* with us.

27 And thy servant my father said unto us, Ye know that <sup>a</sup>my wife bare me two *sons:*

28 And the one went out from me, and I said, <sup>a</sup>Surely he is torn in pieces; and I saw him not since:

29 And if ye <sup>a</sup>take <sup>1</sup>this also from me, and <sup>2</sup>mischief befall him, ye shall bring down my gray hairs with sorrow to the grave.

30 Now therefore when I come to thy servant my father, and the lad *he* not with us; seeing that <sup>a</sup>his life is bound up in the lad's life;

31 It shall come to pass, when he seeth that the lad *is* not *with us,* that he will die: and thy servants shall bring down the gray hairs of thy servant our father with sorrow to the grave.

32 For thy servant became surety for the lad unto my father, saying, <sup>a</sup>If I bring him not unto thee, then I shall bear the blame to my father for ever.

33 Now therefore, I pray thee, <sup>a</sup>let thy servant <sup>1</sup>abide instead of the lad <sup>2</sup>a bondman to my lord; and let the lad go up with his brethren.

34 For how shall I go up to my father, and the lad *be* not with me? lest peradventure I see the evil that shall come on my father.

## CHAPTER 45

THEN Joseph could not <sup>1</sup>refrain himself before all them that stood by him; and he cried, Cause every man to go out from me. And there stood no man with him, <sup>a</sup>while Joseph made himself known unto his brethren.

2 And he <sup>a</sup>wept aloud: and the Egyptians and the house of Pharaoh heard.

3 And Joseph said unto his brethren, <sup>a</sup>I *am* Joseph; doth my father yet live? And his brethren could not answer him; for they were <sup>1</sup>troubled at his presence.

4 And Joseph said unto his brethren, Come near to me, I pray you. And they came near. And he said, I *am* Joseph your brother, [a]whom ye sold into Egypt.

5 Now therefore be not grieved, nor angry with yourselves, that ye sold me hither: [a]for God did send me before you to preserve life.

6 For these two years *hath* the [a]famine *been* in the land: and yet *there are* five years, in the which *there shall* neither *be* [1]earing nor harvest.

7 And God [a]sent me before you to preserve you a [1]posterity in the earth, and to save your lives by a great deliverance.

8 So now *it was* not you *that* sent me hither, but [a]God: and he hath made me [b]a father to Pharaoh, and lord of all his house, and a [c]ruler throughout all the land of Egypt.

9 Haste ye, and go up to my father, and say unto him, Thus saith thy son Joseph, God hath made me lord of all Egypt: come down unto me, [1]tarry not:

10 And [a]thou shalt dwell in the land of Goshen, and thou shalt be near unto me, thou, and thy children, and thy children's children, and thy flocks, and thy herds, and all that thou hast:

11 And there will I [a]nourish[1] thee; for yet *there are* five years of famine; lest thou, and thy household, and all that thou hast, come to poverty.

12 And, behold, your eyes see, and the eyes of my brother Benjamin, that *it is* [a]my mouth that speaketh unto you.

13 And ye shall tell my father of all my glory in Egypt, and of all that ye have seen; and ye shall haste and [a]bring down my father hither.

14 And he fell upon his brother Benjamin's neck, and wept; and Benjamin wept upon his neck.

15 Moreover he [a]kissed all his brethren, and wept upon them: and after that his brethren talked with him.

16 And the [1]fame thereof was heard in Pharaoh's house, saying, Joseph's brethren are come: and it pleased Pharaoh well, and his servants.

17 And Pharaoh said unto Joseph, Say unto thy brethren, This do ye; [1]lade your beasts, and go, get you unto the land of Canaan;

18 And [1]take your father and your households, and come unto me: and I will give you the good of the land of Egypt, and ye shall eat [a]the [2]fat of the land.

19 Now thou art commanded, this do ye; take you wagons out of the land of Egypt for your little ones, and for your wives, and bring your father, and come.

20 Also [1]regard not your stuff; for the good of all the land of Egypt *is* yours.

21 And the children of Israel did so: and Joseph gave them [a]wagons,[1] according to the commandment of Pharaoh, and gave them provision for the way.

22 To all of them he gave each man [a]changes of [1]raiment; but to Benjamin he gave three hundred *pieces* of silver, and [b]five changes of raiment.

23 And to his father he sent after this *manner;* ten [1]asses [2]laden with the good things of Egypt, and ten she asses laden with [3]corn and bread and [4]meat for his father [5]by the way.

24 So he sent his brethren away, and they departed: and he said unto them, See that ye [1]fall not out by the way.

25 And they went up out of Egypt, and came into the land of Canaan unto Jacob their father,

26 And told him, saying, Joseph *is* yet alive, and he *is* governor over all the land of Egypt. [a]And Jacob's heart fainted, for he believed them not.

27 And they told him all the words of Joseph, which he had said unto them: and when he saw the wagons which Joseph had sent to carry him, the spirit [a]of Jacob their father revived:

28 And Israel said, *It is* enough; Joseph my son *is* yet alive: I will go and see him before I die.

## CHAPTER 46

A ND Israel took his journey with all that he had, and came to [a]Beer-sheba, and offered sacrifices [b]unto the God of his father Isaac.

2 And God spake unto Israel [a]in the visions of the night, and said, Jacob, Jacob. And he said, Here *am* I.

3 And he said, I *am* God, [a]the God of thy father: fear not to go down into Egypt; for I will there [b]make of thee a great nation:

4 [a]I will go down with thee into Egypt; and I will also surely [b]bring thee up *again:* and [c]Joseph [1]shall put his hand upon thine eyes.

5 And [a]Jacob rose up from Beer-sheba: and the sons of Israel carried Jacob their father, and their little ones, and their wives, in the wagons [b]which Pharaoh had sent to carry him.

6 And they took their [1]cattle, and their goods, which they had gotten in the land of Canaan, and came into Egypt, [a]Jacob, and all his [2]seed with him:

7 His sons, and his sons' sons with him, his daughters, and his sons' daughters, and all his seed brought he with him into Egypt.

45:4 [a] Gen. 37:28; 39:1; Ps. 105:17
45:5 [a] Gen. 45:7, 8; 50:20; Ps. 105:16, 17
45:6 [a] Gen. 43:1; 47:4, 13 [1] plowing
45:7 [a] Gen. 45:5; 50:20 [1] remnant
45:8 [a] [Rom. 8:28] [b] Judg. 17:10; Is. 22:21 [c] Gen. 41:43; 42:6
45:9 [1] do not delay
45:10 [a] Gen. 46:28, 34; 47:1, 6; Ex. 9:26
45:11 [a] Gen. 47:12 [1] provide for
45:12 [a] Gen. 42:23
45:13 [a] Gen. 46:6–28; Acts 7:14
45:15 [a] Gen. 48:10
45:16 [1] report
45:17 [1] load
45:18 [a] Gen. 27:28; 47:6; Deut. 32:9–14 [1] bring [2] best
45:20 [1] do not be concerned about your things
45:21 [a] Gen. 45:19; 46:5 [1] carts
45:22 [a] 2 Kin. 5:5 [b] Gen. 43:34 [1] clothing
45:23 [1] donkeys [2] loaded [3] grain [4] food [5] for
45:24 [1] be not troubled
45:26 [a] Job 29:24
45:27 [a] Judg. 15:19
46:1 [a] Gen. 21:31, 33; 26:32, 33; 28:10 [b] Gen. 26:24, 25; 28:13; 31:42; 32:9
46:2 [a] Gen. 15:1; 22:11; 31:11
46:3 [a] Gen. 17:1; 28:13 [b] Deut. 26:5
46:4 [a] Gen. 28:15; 31:3; 48:21 [b] Gen. 15:16; 50:12, 24, 25 [c] Gen. 50:1 [1] Will close your eyes when you die
46:5 [a] Acts 7:15 [b] Gen. 45:19–21
46:6 [a] Deut. 26:5 [1] livestock [2] descendants

8 And ᵃthese *are* the names of the children of Israel, which came into Egypt, Jacob, and his sons: ᵇReuben, Jacob's firstborn.

9 And the ᵃsons of Reuben; Hanoch, and ¹Phallu, and Hezron, and Carmi.

10 And ᵃthe sons of Simeon; ¹Jemuel, and Jamin, and Ohad, and ²Jachin, and ³Zohar, and Shaul the son of a Canaanitish woman.

11 And the sons of ᵃLevi; Gershon, Kohath, and Merari.

12 And the sons of ᵃJudah; Er, and Onan, and Shelah, and ¹Pharez, and ²Zarah: but ᵇEr and Onan died in the land of Canaan. And ᶜthe sons of Pharez were Hezron and Hamul.

13 And the sons of Issachar; Tola, and ¹Phuvah, and ²Job, and Shimron.

14 And the ᵃsons of Zebulun; Sered, and Elon, and Jahleel.

15 These *be* the ᵃsons of Leah, which she bare unto Jacob in Padanaram, with his daughter Dinah: all the ¹souls of his sons and his daughters *were* thirty and three.

16 And the sons of Gad; ¹Ziphion, and Haggi, Shuni, and ²Ezbon, Eri, and ³Arodi, and Areli.

17 ᵃAnd the sons of Asher; Jimnah, and Ishuah, and Isui, and Beriah, and Serah their sister: and the sons of Beriah; Heber, and Malchiel.

18 ᵃThese *are* the sons of Zilpah, ᵇwhom Laban gave to Leah his daughter, and these she bare unto Jacob, *even* sixteen ¹souls.

19 The ᵃsons of Rachel ᵇJacob's wife; Joseph, and Benjamin.

20 ᵃAnd unto Joseph in the land of Egypt were born Manasseh and Ephraim, which Asenath the daughter of Poti-pherah priest of On bare unto him.

21 ᵃAnd the sons of Benjamin *were* Belah, and Becher, and Ashbel, Gera, and Naaman, ᵇEhi, and Rosh, ᶜMuppim, and ¹Huppim, and Ard.

22 These *are* the sons of Rachel, which were born to Jacob: all the souls *were* fourteen.

23 And the sons of Dan; ¹Hushim.

24 ᵃAnd the sons of Naphtali; ¹Jahzeel, and Guni, and Jezer, and ²Shillem.

25 ᵃThese *are* the sons of Bilhah, ᵇwhich Laban gave unto Rachel his daughter, and she bare these unto Jacob: all the souls *were* seven.

26 ᵃAll the ¹souls that came with Jacob into Egypt, which came out of his loins, ᵇbesides Jacob's sons' wives, all the souls *were* threescore and six;

27 And the sons of Joseph, which were born him in Egypt, *were* two souls: ᵃall the souls of the house of Jacob, which came into Egypt, *were* threescore and ten.

28 And he sent Judah before him unto Joseph, ᵃto direct his face unto Goshen; and they came ᵇinto the land of Goshen.

29 And Joseph made ready his ᵃchariot, and went up to meet Israel his father, to Goshen, and presented himself unto him; and he ᵇfell on his neck, and wept on his neck a good while.

30 And Israel said unto Joseph, ᵃNow let me die, since I have seen thy face, because thou *art* yet alive.

31 And Joseph said unto his brethren, and unto his father's house, ᵃI will go up, and ¹shew Pharaoh, and say unto him, My brethren, and my father's house, which *were* in the land of Canaan, are come unto me;

32 And the men *are* ᵃshepherds, for their ¹trade hath been to feed ²cattle; and they have brought their flocks, and their herds, and all that they have.

33 And it shall come to pass, when Pharaoh shall call you, and shall say, ᵃWhat *is* your occupation?

34 That ye shall say, Thy servants' ᵃtrade¹ hath been ²about cattle ᵇfrom our youth even until now, both we, *and* also our fathers: that ye may dwell in the land of Goshen; for every shepherd *is* ᶜan ³abomination unto the Egyptians.

## CHAPTER 47

THEN Joseph ᵃcame and told Pharaoh, and said, My father and my brethren, and their flocks, and their herds, and all that they have, are come out of the land of Canaan; and, behold, they *are* in ᵇthe land of Goshen.

2 And he took some of his ¹brethren, *even* five men, and ᵃpresented them unto Pharaoh.

3 And Pharaoh said unto his brethren, ᵃWhat *is* your occupation? And they said unto Pharaoh, ᵇThy servants *are* shepherds, both we, *and* also our fathers.

4 They said moreover unto Pharaoh, ᵃFor to sojourn in the land are we come; for thy servants have no pasture for their flocks; ᵇfor the famine *is* ¹sore in the land of Canaan: now therefore, we pray thee, let thy servants ᶜdwell in the land of Goshen.

5 And Pharaoh spake unto Joseph, saying, Thy father and thy brethren are come unto thee:

6 ᵃThe land of Egypt *is* before thee; in the best of the land make thy father and brethren to dwell; ᵇin the land of Goshen let them dwell: and if thou knowest *any* men of activity

---

46:8 ᵃ Ex. 1:1–4
ᵇ Num. 26:4, 5
46:9 ᵃ Ex. 6:14
¹ *Pallu*, Num. 26:5
46:10 ᵃ Ex. 6:15
¹ *Nemuel*, 1 Chr.
4:24  ² *Jarib*,
1 Chr. 4:24
³ *Zerah*, 1 Chr. 4:24
46:11 ᵃ 1 Chr. 6:1, 16
46:12 ᵃ 1 Chr. 2:3;
4:21  ᵇ Gen. 38:3,
7, 10  ᶜ Gen. 38:29
¹ Or *Perez*  ² Or
*Zerah*
46:13 ¹ *Puah*,
1 Chr. 7:1
² *Jashub*, 1 Chr. 7:1
46:14 ᵃ Num. 26:26
46:15 ᵃ 1 Chr. 35:23;
49:31 ¹ *persons*
46:16 ¹ 1 Sam.,
LXX *Zephon*,
and Num. 26:15
² *Ozni*, Num.
26:16  ³ *Arod*,
Num. 26:17
46:17 ᵃ 1 Chr. 7:30
46:18 ᵃ Gen.
30:10; 37:2  ᵇ Gen.
29:24 ¹ *persons*
46:19 ᵃ Gen. 35:24
ᵇ Gen. 44:27
46:20 ᵃ Gen.
41:45, 50–52; 48:1
46:21 ᵃ 1 Chr. 7:6;
8:1  ᵇ Num. 26:38
ᶜ Num. 26:39
¹ *Hupham*, Num.
26:39
46:23 ¹ *Shuham*,
Num. 26:42
46:24 ᵃ Num.
26:48 ¹ *Jahziel*,
1 Chr. 7:13  ² *Shallum*, 1 Chr. 7:13
46:25 ᵃ Gen. 30:5,
7  ᵇ Gen. 29:29
46:26 ᵃ Ex. 1:5
ᵇ Gen. 35:11 ¹ *persons who went*
46:27 ᵃ Deut. 10:22
46:28 ᵃ Gen. 31:21
ᵇ Gen. 47:1
46:29 ᵃ Gen. 41:43
ᵇ Gen. 45:14, 15
46:30 ᵃ Luke
2:29, 30
46:31 ᵃ Gen. 47:1
¹ *tell*
46:32 ᵃ Gen.
47:3 ¹ *occupation*
² *livestock*
46:33 ᵃ Gen.
47:2, 3
46:34 ᵃ Gen. 47:3
ᵇ Gen. 30:35;
34:5; 37:17  ᶜ Gen.
43:32; Ex. 8:26
¹ *occupation*
² *with livestock*
³ *loathsome*
47:1 ᵃ Gen. 46:31
ᵇ Gen. 45:10;
46:28; 50:8
47:2 ᵃ Acts
7:13 ¹ *brothers*

47:3 ᵃ Gen. 46:33; Jon. 1:8  ᵇ Gen. 46:32, 34; Ex. 2:17,
19   47:4 ᵃ Gen. 15:13; Deut. 26:5; Ps. 105:23  ᵇ Gen.
43:1; Acts 7:11  ᶜ Gen. 46:34 ¹ *severe*   47:6 ᵃ Gen. 20:15;
45:10, 18; 47:11  ᵇ Gen. 47:4 ¹ *competent men*

among them, then make them rulers over my cattle.

7 And Joseph brought in Jacob his father, and set him before Pharaoh: and Jacob [a]blessed Pharaoh.

8 And Pharaoh said unto Jacob, How old *art* thou?

9 And Jacob said unto Pharaoh, [a]The days of the years of my [1]pilgrimage *are* an [b]hundred and thirty years: [c]few and evil have the days of the years of my life been, and [d]have not attained unto the days of the years of the life of my fathers in the days of their pilgrimage.

10 And Jacob [a]blessed Pharaoh, and went out from before Pharaoh.

11 And Joseph placed his father and his brethren, and gave them a possession in the land of Egypt, in the best of the land, in the land of [a]Rameses, [b]as Pharaoh had commanded.

12 And Joseph [1]nourished [a]his father, and his brethren, and all his father's household, with bread, according to *their* families.

13 And *there was* no bread in all the land; for the famine *was* very [1]sore, [a]so that the land of Egypt and *all* the land of Canaan [2]fainted by reason of the famine.

14 [a]And Joseph gathered up all the money that was found in the land of Egypt, and in the land of Canaan, for the [1]corn which they bought: and Joseph brought the money into Pharaoh's house.

15 And when money failed in the land of Egypt, and in the land of Canaan, all the Egyptians came unto Joseph, and said, Give us bread: for [a]why should we die in thy presence? for the money faileth.

16 And Joseph said, Give your [1]cattle: and I will [2]give you for your cattle, if money fail.

17 And they brought their [1]cattle unto Joseph: and Joseph gave them bread in *exchange* for horses, and for the flocks, and for the cattle of the herds, and for the [2]asses: and he [3]fed them with bread for all their cattle for that year.

18 When that year was ended, they came unto him the second year, and said unto him, We will not hide *it* from my lord, how that our money is spent; my lord also hath our herds of [1]cattle; there is [2]not ought left in the sight of my lord, but our bodies, and our lands:

19 Wherefore shall we die before thine eyes, both we and our land? buy us and our land for bread, and we and our land will be servants unto Pharaoh: and give *us* seed, that we may [a]live, and not die, that the land be not desolate.

20 And Joseph [a]bought all the land of Egypt for Pharaoh; for the Egyptians sold every man his field, because the famine [1]prevailed over them: so the land became Pharaoh's.

21 And as for the people, he [1]removed them to cities from *one* end of the borders of Egypt even to the *other* end thereof.

22 [a]Only the land of the [b]priests bought he not; for the priests had [1]a portion *assigned them* of Pharaoh, and did eat their [2]portion which Pharaoh gave them: wherefore they sold not their lands.

23 Then Joseph said unto the people, Behold, I have bought you this day and your land for Pharaoh: lo, *here is* seed for you, and ye shall sow the land.

24 And it shall come to pass in the increase, that ye shall give the fifth *part* unto Pharaoh, and four parts shall be your own, for seed of the field, and for your food, and for them of your households, and for food for your little ones.

25 And they said, Thou hast saved [a]our lives: let us find [1]grace in the sight of my lord, and we will be Pharaoh's servants.

26 And Joseph made it a law over the land of Egypt unto this day, *that* Pharaoh should have the fifth *part;* [a]except the land of the priests only, *which* became not Pharaoh's.

27 And Israel [a]dwelt in the land of Egypt, in the country of Goshen; and they had possessions therein, and [b]grew, and multiplied exceedingly.

28 And Jacob lived in the land of Egypt seventeen years: so the whole age of Jacob was an hundred forty and seven years.

29 And the time [a]drew nigh that Israel must die: and he called his son Joseph, and said unto him, If now I have found grace in thy sight, [b]put, I pray thee, thy hand under my thigh, and [c]deal kindly and truly with me; [d]bury me not, I pray thee, in Egypt:

30 But [a]I will lie with my fathers, and thou shalt carry me out of Egypt, and [b]bury me in their buryingplace. And he said, I will do as thou hast said.

31 And he said, Swear unto me. And he sware unto him. And [a]Israel bowed himself upon the bed's head.

## CHAPTER 48

A ND it came to pass after these things, that *one* told Joseph, Behold, thy father *is* sick: and he took with him his two sons, [a]Manasseh and Ephraim.

2 And *one* told Jacob, and said, Behold, thy son Joseph cometh unto thee: and Israel [1]strengthened himself, and sat upon the bed.

47:7 [a] Gen. 47:10; 48:15, 20; 2 Sam. 14:22; 1 Kin. 8:66; Heb. 7:7

47:9 [a] Ps. 39:12; [Heb. 11:9, 13] [b] Gen. 47:28 [c] [Job 14:1] [d] Gen. 5:5; 11:10, 11; 25:7, 8; 35:28 [1] Lit. sojourning

47:10 [a] Gen. 47:7

47:11 [a] Ex. 1:11; 12:37 [b] Gen. 47:6, 27

47:12 [a] Gen. 45:11; 50:21 [1] provided

47:13 [a] Gen. 41:30; Acts 7:11 [1] severe [2] languished

47:14 [a] Gen. 41:56; 42:6 [1] grain

47:15 [a] Gen. 47:19

47:16 [1] livestock [2] give you bread

47:17 [1] livestock [2] donkeys [3] supplied or refreshed

47:18 [1] livestock [2] nothing

47:19 [a] Gen. 43:8

47:20 [a] Jer. 32:43 [1] was severe upon them

47:21 [1] moved

47:22 [a] Lev. 25:34; Ezra 7:24 [b] Gen. 41:45 [1] rations allotted [2] rations

47:25 [a] Gen. 33:15 [1] favour

47:26 [a] Gen. 47:22

47:27 [a] Gen. 47:11 [b] Gen. 17:6; 26:4; 35:11; 46:3; Ex. 1:7; Deut. 26:5; Acts 7:17

47:29 [a] Deut. 31:14; 1 Kin. 2:1 [b] Gen. 24:2–4 [c] Gen. 24:49; Josh. 2:14 [d] Gen. 50:25

47:30 [a] 2 Sam. 19:37 [b] Gen. 49:29; 50:5–13; Heb. 11:21

47:31 [a] Gen. 48:2; 1 Kin. 1:47; Heb. 11:21

48:1 [a] Gen. 41:51, 56; 46:20; 50:23; Josh. 14:4

48:2 [1] collected his strength

3 And Jacob said unto Joseph, God [a]Almighty appeared unto me at [b]Luz in the land of Canaan, and blessed me,

4 And said unto me, Behold, I will [a]make thee fruitful, and multiply thee, and I will make of thee a multitude of people; and will [b]give this land to thy [1]seed after thee [c]*for* an everlasting possession.

5 And now thy [a]two sons, Ephraim and Manasseh, which were born unto thee in the land of Egypt before I came unto thee into Egypt, *are* mine; as Reuben and Simeon, they shall be mine.

6 And thy [1]issue, which [2]thou begettest after them, shall be thine, *and* shall be called after the name of their brethren in their inheritance.

7 And as for me, when I came from Padan, [a]Rachel died [1]by me in the land of Canaan in the way, when yet *there was* but a little way to come unto Ephrath: and I buried her there [2]in the way of Ephrath; the same *is* Beth-lehem.

8 And Israel beheld Joseph's sons, and said, Who *are* these?

9 And Joseph said unto his father, They *are* my sons, whom God hath given me in this *place*. And he said, Bring them, I pray thee, unto me, and [a]I will bless them.

10 Now [a]the eyes of Israel were dim [1]for age, *so that* he could not see. And he brought them near unto him; and he [b]kissed them, and embraced them.

11 And Israel said unto Joseph, [a]I had not thought to see thy face: and, lo, God hath shewed me also thy [1]seed.

12 And Joseph brought them out from [1]between his knees, and he bowed himself with his face to the earth.

13 And Joseph took them both, Ephraim in his right hand toward Israel's left hand, and Manasseh in his left hand toward Israel's right hand, and brought *them* near unto him.

14 And Israel stretched out his right hand, and [a]laid *it* upon Ephraim's head, who *was* the younger, and his left hand upon Manasseh's head, [b]guiding his hands [1]wittingly; for Manasseh *was* the [c]firstborn.

15 And [a]he blessed Joseph, and said, God, [b]before whom my fathers Abraham and Isaac did walk, the God which fed me all my life long unto this day,

16 The Angel [a]which redeemed me from all evil, bless the lads; and let [b]my name be named on them, and the name of my fathers Abraham and Isaac; and let them [c]grow into a multitude in the midst of the earth.

17 And when Joseph saw that his father [a]laid his right hand upon the head of Ephraim, it displeased him: and he held up his father's hand, to remove it from Ephraim's head unto Manasseh's head.

18 And Joseph said unto his father, Not so, my father: for this *is* the firstborn; put thy right hand upon his head.

19 And his father refused, and said, [a]I know *it,* my son, I know *it:* he also shall become a people, and he also shall be great: but truly [b]his younger brother shall be greater than he, and his seed shall become a multitude of nations.

20 And he blessed them that day, saying, [a]In thee shall Israel bless, saying, God make thee as Ephraim and as Manasseh: and he set Ephraim before Manasseh.

21 And Israel said unto Joseph, Behold, I die: but [a]God shall be with you, and bring you again unto the land of your fathers.

22 Moreover [a]I have given to thee one [1]portion above thy brethren, which I took out of the hand [b]of the Amorite with my sword and with my bow.

## CHAPTER 49

AND Jacob called unto his sons, and said, Gather yourselves together, that I may [a]tell you *that* which shall befall you [b]in the last days.

2 Gather yourselves together, and hear, ye sons of Jacob; and hearken unto Israel your father.

3 Reuben, thou *art* [a]my firstborn, my might, and the beginning of my strength, the excellency of dignity, and the excellency of power:

4 Unstable as water, thou shalt not excel; because thou [a]wentest up to thy father's bed; then defiledst thou *it:* he went up to my couch.

5 Simeon and Levi *are* brethren; instruments of [1]cruelty *are in* their habitations.

6 O my soul, [a]come not thou into their [1]secret; [b]unto their assembly, mine honour, be not thou united: [c]for in their anger they slew a man, and in their selfwill they [2]digged down a wall.

7 Cursed *be* their anger, for *it was* fierce; and their wrath, for it *was* cruel: [a]I will divide them in Jacob, and scatter them in Israel.

8 [a]Judah, thou *art he* whom thy brethren shall praise: [b]thy hand *shall be* [1]in the neck of thine enemies; [c]thy father's children shall bow down before thee.

9 Judah *is* [a]a lion's whelp: from the prey, my son, thou art gone up: [b]he [1]stooped down, he [2]couched as a lion,

48:3 [a] Gen. 43:14; 49:25 [b] Gen. 28:13, 19; 35:6, 9
48:4 [a] Gen. 46:3 [b] Gen. 35:12; Ex. 6:8 [c] Gen. 17:8 [1] descendants
48:5 [a] Gen. 41:50; 46:20; 48:8; Josh. 13:7; 14:4
48:6 [1] offspring [2] are born to you
48:7 [a] Gen. 35:9, 16, 19, 20 [1] beside [2] on
48:9 [a] Gen. 27:4; 47:15
48:10 [a] Gen. 27:1; 1 Sam. 3:2 [b] Gen. 27:27; 45:15; 50:1 [1] with
48:11 [a] Gen. 45:26 [1] offspring
48:12 [1] beside
48:14 [a] Matt. 19:15; Mark 10:16 [b] Gen. 48:19 [c] Gen. 41:51, 52; Josh. 17:1 [1] knowingly
48:15 [a] Gen. 47:7, 10; 49:24; [Heb. 11:21] [b] Gen. 17:1; 24:40; 2 Kin. 20:3
48:16 [a] Gen. 22:11, 15–18; 28:13–15; 31:11; [Ps. 34:22; 121:7] [b] Amos 9:12; Acts 15:17 [c] Num. 26:34, 37

48:17 [a] Gen. 48:14
48:19 [a] Gen. 48:14 [b] Num. 1:33, 35; Deut. 33:17
48:20 [a] Ruth 4:11, 12
48:21 [a] Gen. 28:15; 46:4; 50:24
48:22 [a] Josh. 24:32 [b] Gen. 34:28 [1] Lit. shoulder
49:1 [a] Deut. 33:1, 6–25 [b] Is. 2:2; 39:6
49:3 [a] Gen. 29:32
49:4 [a] Gen. 35:22
49:5 [1] violence
49:6 [a] Prov. 1:15, 16 [b] Ps. 26:9 [c] Gen. 34:26 [1] council [2] hamstrung an ox
49:7 [a] Josh. 19:1, 9; 21:1–42
49:8 [a] Deut. 33:7 [b] Ps. 18:40 [c] 1 Chr. 5:2 [1] on
49:9 [a] [Rev. 5:5] [b] Num. 23:24; 24:9 [1] crouches [2] lies down

and as an old lion; who shall rouse him up?

10 ªThe¹ sceptre shall not depart from Judah, nor ᵇa lawgiver from between his feet, ᶜuntil Shiloh come; ᵈand unto him *shall* the ²gathering of the people *be.*

11 Binding his ¹foal unto the vine, and his ²ass's colt unto the choice vine; he washed his garments in wine, and his clothes in the blood of grapes:

12 His eyes *shall be* ¹red with wine, and his teeth ²white with milk.

13 ªZebulun shall dwell at the haven of the sea; and he *shall be* for an haven of ships; and his border *shall* ¹be unto ᵇZidon.

14 ªIssachar *is* a strong ¹ass ²couching down between two burdens:

15 And he saw that rest *was* good, and the land that *it was* pleasant; and bowed ªhis shoulder to ¹bear, and became a ²servant unto tribute.

16 ªDan shall judge his people, as one of the tribes of Israel.

17 ªDan shall be a serpent by the way, ¹an adder in the path, that biteth the horse heels, so that his rider shall fall backward.

18 ªI have waited for thy salvation, O LORD.

19 ªGad,¹ a troop shall overcome him: but he shall ²overcome at the last.

20 ªOut of Asher his bread *shall be* ¹fat, and he shall yield royal dainties.

21 ªNaphtali *is* a ¹hind let loose: he giveth ¹goodly words.

22 Joseph *is* a fruitful bough, *even* a fruitful bough by a well; *whose* branches run over the wall:

23 The archers have ªsorely¹ grieved him, and shot *at him,* and hated him:

24 But his ªbow ¹abode in strength, and the arms of his hands were made strong by the hands of ᵇthe mighty *God* of Jacob; (ᶜfrom thence ᵈ*is* the shepherd, ᵉthe stone of Israel:)

25 ªEven by the God of thy father, who shall help thee; ᵇand by the Almighty, ᶜwho shall bless thee with blessings of heaven above, blessings of the deep that lieth ¹under, blessings of the breasts, and of the womb:

26 The blessings of thy father have ¹prevailed above the blessings of my ²progenitors ªunto the utmost bound of the everlasting hills: ᵇthey shall be on the head of Joseph, and on the crown of the head of him that was separate from his brethren.

27 Benjamin shall ªravin¹ *as* a wolf: in the morning he shall devour the prey, ᵇand at night he shall divide the ²spoil.

28 All these *are* the twelve tribes of Israel: and this *is it* that their father spake unto them, and blessed them; every one according to his blessing he blessed them.

29 And he charged them, and said unto them, I ªam to be gathered unto my people: ᵇbury me with my fathers ᶜin the cave that *is* in the field of Ephron the Hittite,

30 In the cave that *is* in the field of Machpelah, which *is* before Mamre, in the land of Canaan, ªwhich Abraham bought with the field of Ephron the Hittite for a possession of a buryingplace.

31 ªThere they buried Abraham and Sarah his wife; ᵇthere they buried Isaac and Rebekah his wife; and there I buried Leah.

32 The purchase of the field and of the cave that *is* therein *was* from the children of Heth.

33 And when Jacob had made an end of commanding his sons, he ¹gathered up his feet into the bed, and ²yielded up the ghost, and was gathered unto his people.

## CHAPTER 50

AND Joseph ªfell upon his father's face, and ᵇwept upon him, and kissed him.

2 And Joseph commanded his servants the physicians to ªembalm his father: and the physicians embalmed Israel.

3 And forty days were fulfilled for him; for so are fulfilled the days of those which are embalmed: and the Egyptians ªmourned¹ for him threescore and ten days.

4 And when the days of his mourning were past, Joseph spake unto ªthe house of Pharaoh, saying, If now I have found ¹grace in your eyes, speak, I pray you, in the ears of Pharaoh, saying,

5 ªMy father made me swear, saying, Lo, I ¹die: in my grave ᵇwhich I have digged for me in the land of Canaan, there shalt thou bury me. Now therefore let me go up, I pray thee, and bury my father, and I will come again.

6 And Pharaoh said, Go up, and bury thy father, according as he made thee swear.

7 And Joseph went up to bury his father: and with him went up all the servants of Pharaoh, the elders of his house, and all the elders of the land of Egypt,

8 And all the house of Joseph, and his brethren, and his father's house: only their little ones, and their flocks, and their herds, they left in the land of Goshen.

9 And there went up with him both chariots and horsemen: and it was a very great company.

10 And they came to the threshingfloor of Atad, which *is* beyond Jordan,

---

**Cross-references and notes:**

49:10 ª Num. 24:17 ᵇ Ps. 60:7 ᶜ Is. 11:1 ᵈ Ps. 2:6–9; 72:8–11 ¹ A symbol of kingship ² obedience
49:11 ¹ donkey ² donkey's
49:12 ¹ darker than ² whiter than
49:13 ª Deut. 33:18, 19 ᵇ Gen. 10:19 ¹ adjoin Sidon
49:14 ª 1 Chr. 12:32 ¹ donkey ² lying down
49:15 ª 1 Sam. 10:9 ¹ bear a burden ² band of slaves
49:16 ª Deut. 33:22
49:17 ª Judg. 18:27 ¹ a viper by
49:18 ª Is. 25:9
49:19 ª Deut. 33:20 ¹ Lit. Troop ² Heb. gad, lit. raid
49:20 ª Deut. 33:24 ¹ rich
49:21 ª Deut. 33:23 ¹ deer ² Lit. beautiful
49:23 ª Gen. 37:4, 24 ¹ bitterly
49:24 ª Job 29:20 ᵇ Ps. 132:2, 5 ᶜ Gen. 45:11; 47:12 ᵈ [Ps. 23:1; 80:1] ᵉ Is. 28:16 ¹ remained
49:25 ª Gen. 28:13; 32:9; 35:3; 43:23; 50:17 ᵇ Gen. 17:1; 35:11 ᶜ Deut. 33:13 ¹ beneath
49:26 ª Deut. 33:15 ᵇ Deut. 33:16 ¹ excelled ² ancestors
49:27 ª Judg. 20:21, 25 ᵇ Zech. 14:1 ¹ is a ravenous wolf ² plunder
49:29 ª Gen. 15:15; 25:8; 35:29 ᵇ Gen. 47:30 ᶜ Gen. 23:16–20; 50:13
49:30 ª Gen. 23:3–20
49:31 ª Gen. 23:19, 20; 25:9 ᵇ Gen. 35:29; 50:13
49:33 ¹ drew up ² breathed his last
50:1 ª Gen. 46:4, 29 ᵇ 2 Kin. 13:14
50:2 ª Gen. 50:26
50:3 ª Deut. 34:8 ¹ Lit. wept
50:4 ª Esth. 4:2 ¹ favour
50:5 ª Gen. 47:29–31 ᵇ Is. 22:16 ¹ am dying

and there they [a]mourned with a great and very [1]sore lamentation: [b]and he [2]made a mourning for his father seven days.

11 And when the inhabitants of the land, the Canaanites, saw the mourning in the floor of Atad, they said, This *is* a grievous mourning to the Egyptians: wherefore the name of it was called [1]Abel-mizraim, which *is* beyond Jordan.

12 And his sons did unto him according as he commanded them:

13 For [a]his sons carried him into the land of Canaan, and buried him in the cave of the field of Machpelah, which Abraham [b]bought with the field for a possession of a buryingplace of Ephron the Hittite, before Mamre.

14 And Joseph returned into Egypt, he, and his brethren, and all that went up with him to bury his father, after he had buried his father.

15 And when Joseph's brethren saw that their father was dead, [a]they said, Joseph will [1]peradventure hate us, and [2]will certainly requite us all the evil which we did unto him.

16 And they sent a messenger unto Joseph, saying, Thy father did command before he died, saying,

17 So shall ye say unto Joseph, Forgive, I pray thee now, the trespass of thy brethren, and their sin; [a]for they did unto thee evil: and now, we pray thee, forgive the trespass of the ser-

vants of [b]the God of thy father. And Joseph wept when they spake unto him.

18 And his brethren also went and [a]fell down before his face; and they said, Behold, we *be* thy servants.

19 And Joseph said unto them, [a]Fear not: [b]for *am* I in the place of God?

20 [a]But as for you, ye [1]thought evil against me; *but* [b]God meant it unto good, to bring to pass, as *it is* this day, to save much people alive.

21 Now therefore fear ye not: [a]I will [1]nourish you, and your little ones. And he comforted them, and spake kindly [2]unto them.

22 And Joseph dwelt in Egypt, he, and his father's house: and Joseph lived an hundred and ten years.

23 And Joseph saw Ephraim's children [a]of the third *generation:* [b]the children also of Machir the son of Manasseh [c]were brought up upon Joseph's knees.

24 And Joseph said unto his brethren, [1]I die: and [a]God will surely visit you, and bring you out of this land unto the land [b]which he sware to Abraham, to Isaac, and to Jacob.

25 And [a]Joseph took an oath of the children of Israel, saying, God will surely [1]visit you, and [b]ye shall carry up my [c]bones from hence.

26 So Joseph died, *being* an hundred and ten years old: and they embalmed him, and he was put in a coffin in Egypt.

---

**Center column references:**

50:10 [a] Acts 8:2 [b] 1 Sam. 31:13 [1] *solemn* [2] *observed*

50:11 [1] Lit. *Mourning of Egypt*

50:13 [a] Acts 7:16 [b] Gen. 23:16–20

50:15 [a] [Job 15:21] [1] *perhaps* [2] *may fully repay us*

50:17 [a] [Prov. 28:13] [b] Gen. 49:25

50:18 [a] Gen. 37:7–10; 41:43; 44:14

50:19 [a] Gen. 45:5 [b] 2 Kin. 5:7

50:20 [a] Ps. 56:5 [b] [Acts 3:13–15] [1] *intended*

50:21 [a] [Matt. 5:44] [1] *provide for* [2] Lit. *to their hearts*

50:23 [a] Job 42:16 [b] Num. 26:29; 32:39 [c] Gen. 30:3

50:24 [a] Ex. 3:16, 17 [b] Gen. 26:3; 35:12; 46:4 [1] *I am dying*

50:25 [a] Ex. 13:19 [b] Deut. 1:8; 30:1–8 [c] Ex. 13:19 [1] *visit to help*

# THE SECOND BOOK OF MOSES CALLED
# EXODUS

Exodus is the record of Israel's birth as a nation. Within the protective "womb" of Egypt, the Jewish family of seventy rapidly multiplies. At the right time, accompanied with severe "birth pains," an infant nation, numbering between two and three million people, is brought into the world where it is divinely protected, fed, and nurtured.

The Hebrew title, *We'elleh Shemoth,* "Now These *Are* the Names," comes from the first phrase in 1:1. Exodus begins with "Now" to show it as a continuation of Genesis. The Greek title is *Exodus,* a word meaning "exit," "departure," or "going out." The Septuagint uses this word to describe the book by its key event (see 19:1, "gone forth out"). In Luke 9:31 and in Second Peter 1:15, the word *exodus* speaks of physical death (Jesus and Peter). This embodies Exodus's theme of redemption, because redemption is accomplished only through death. The Latin title is *Liber Exodus,* "Book of Departure," taken from the Greek title.

## CHAPTER 1

Now ᵃthese *are* the names of the children of Israel, which came into Egypt; every man and his household came with Jacob.

2 Reuben, Simeon, Levi, and Judah,

3 Issachar, Zebulun, and Benjamin,

4 Dan, and Naphtali, Gad, and Asher.

5 And all ¹the souls that came out of the loins of Jacob were ᵃseventy souls: for Joseph was in Egypt *already.*

6 And ᵃJoseph died, and all his brethren, and all that generation.

7 ᵃAnd the children of Israel were fruitful, and increased abundantly, and multiplied, and ¹waxed exceeding mighty; and the land was filled with them.

8 Now there arose up a new king over Egypt, ᵃwhich ¹knew not Joseph.

9 And he said unto his people, Behold, the people of the children of Israel *are* more and ᵃmightier than we:

10 ᵃCome on, let us ᵇdeal ¹wisely with them; lest they multiply, and it come to pass, that, ²when there falleth out any war, they join also unto our enemies, and fight against us, and *so* ³get them up out of the land.

11 Therefore they did set over them taskmasters ᵃto afflict them with their ᵇburdens. And they built for Pharaoh ᶜtreasure cities, Pithom ᵈand Raamses.

12 But the more they afflicted them, the more they multiplied and grew. And they were ¹grieved because of the children of Israel.

13 And the Egyptians made the children of Israel to ᵃserve with ¹rigour:

14 And they ᵃmade their lives bitter with hard bondage, ᵇin morter, and in brick, and in all manner of service in the field: all their service, wherein

they made them serve, *was* with rigour.

15 And the king of Egypt spake to the ᵃHebrew midwives, of which the name of the one *was* Shiphrah, and the name of the other Puah:

16 And he said, When ye do the office of a midwife to the Hebrew women, and see *them* upon the stools; if it *be* a ᵃson, then ye shall kill him: but if it *be* a daughter, then she shall live.

17 But the midwives ᵃfeared God, and did not ᵇas the king of Egypt commanded them, but saved the men children alive.

18 And the king of Egypt called for the midwives, and said unto them, Why have ye done this thing, and have saved the men children alive?

19 And ᵃthe midwives said unto Pharaoh, Because the Hebrew women *are* not as the Egyptian women; for they ¹*are* lively, and are delivered ere the midwives come in unto them.

20 ᵃTherefore God dealt well with the midwives: and the people multiplied, and ¹waxed very mighty.

21 And it came to pass, because the midwives feared God, ᵃthat he ¹made them houses.

22 And Pharaoh ¹charged all his people, saying, ᵃEvery son that is born ye shall cast into the river, and every daughter ye shall save alive.

## CHAPTER 2

And there went ᵃa man of the house of Levi, and took *to wife* a daughter of Levi.

2 And the woman conceived, and bare a son: and ᵃwhen she saw him that he *was a* goodly *child,* she hid him three months.

3 And when she could not longer hide him, she took for him an ark of ᵃbulrushes, and daubed it with

1:1 ᵃ Gen. 46:8–27
1:5 ᵃ Gen. 46:26, 27 ¹ *those who were descendants of*
1:6 ᵃ Gen. 50:26
1:7 ᵃ Acts 7:17 ¹ *became very numerous*
1:8 ᵃ Acts 7:18, 19 ¹ *did not know Joseph*
1:9 ᵃ Gen. 26:16
1:10 ᵃ Ps. 83:3, 4 ᵇ Acts 7:19 ¹ *shrewdly toward* ² *in the event of war* ³ *go up out of*
1:11 ᵃ Ex. 3:7; 5:6 ᵇ Ex. 1:14; 2:11; 5:4–9; 6:6 ᶜ 1 Kin. 9:19 ᵈ Gen. 47:11
1:12 ¹ *in dread*
1:13 ᵃ Gen. 15:13 ¹ *harshness*
1:14 ᵃ Num. 20:15 ᵇ Ps. 81:6
1:15 ᵃ Ex. 2:6
1:16 ᵃ Acts 7:19
1:17 ᵃ Prov. 16:6 ᵇ Dan. 3:16, 18
1:19 ᵃ Josh. 2:4 ¹ *Bear quickly, easily, lit. have vigour of life*
1:20 ᵃ [Prov. 11:18] ¹ *became very numerous*
1:21 ᵃ 1 Sam. 2:35 ¹ *provided households for them*
1:22 ᵃ Acts 7:19 ¹ *commanded*
2:1 ᵃ Ex. 6:16–20
2:2 ᵃ Acts 7:20
2:3 ᵃ Is. 18:2

49

[b]slime and with [c]pitch, and put the child therein; and she laid *it* in the [1]flags [d]by the river's brink.

4 [a]And his sister stood afar off, to [1]wit what would be done to him.

5 And the [a]daughter of Pharaoh came down to wash *herself* at the river; and her maidens walked along by the river's side; and when she saw the ark among the flags, she sent her maid to fetch it.

6 And when she had opened *it,* she saw the child: and, behold, the babe wept. And she had compassion on him, and said, This *is one* of the Hebrews' children.

7 Then said his sister to Pharaoh's daughter, Shall I go and call to thee a nurse of the Hebrew women, that she may nurse the child for thee?

8 And Pharaoh's daughter said to her, Go. And the maid went and called the child's mother.

9 And Pharaoh's daughter said unto her, Take this child away, and nurse it for me, and I will give *thee* thy wages. And the woman took the child, and nursed it.

10 And the child grew, and she brought him unto Pharaoh's daughter, and he became [a]her son. And she called his name [1]Moses: and she said, Because I drew him out of the water.

11 And it came to pass in those days, [a]when Moses was grown, that he went out unto his brethren, and looked on their burdens: and he [1]spied an Egyptian [2]smiting an Hebrew, one of his brethren.

12 And he looked this way and that way, and when he saw that *there was* no man, he [a]slew the Egyptian, and hid him in the sand.

13 And [a]when he went out the second day, behold, two men of the Hebrews [b]strove[1] together: and he said to him that did the wrong, [2]Wherefore smitest thou thy fellow?

14 And he said, [a]Who made thee a prince and a judge over us? intendest thou to kill me, as thou killedst the Egyptian? And Moses [b]feared, and said, Surely this thing is known.

15 Now when Pharaoh heard this thing, he sought to slay Moses. But [a]Moses fled from [1]the face of Pharaoh, and dwelt in the land of [b]Midian: and he sat down by [c]a well.

16 [a]Now the priest of Midian had seven daughters: [b]and they came and drew *water,* and filled the [c]troughs to water their father's flock.

17 And the [a]shepherds came and [b]drove them away: but Moses stood up and helped them, and [c]watered their flock.

18 And when they came to [a]Reuel[1] their father, [b]he said, How *is it that* ye are come so soon to day?

### Center column references

2:3 [b] Gen. 14:10
[c] Gen. 6:14 [d] Is. 19:6 [1] *reeds*
2:4 [a] Num. 26:59
[1] *know*
2:5 [a] Acts 7:21
2:10 [a] Acts 7:21
[1] Heb. *Mosheh, Drawn Out*
2:11 [a] Heb. 11:24–26 [1] *saw* [2] *beating*
2:12 [a] Acts 7:24, 25
2:13 [a] Acts 7:26–28
[b] Prov. 25:8 [1] *were fighting* [2] *Why are you striking your companion*
2:14 [a] Acts 7:27, 28 [b] Judg. 6:27
2:15 [a] Acts 7:29
[b] Ex. 3:1 [c] Gen. 24:11; 29:2 [1] *the presence of*
2:16 [a] Ex. 3:1; 4:18; 18:12 [b] Gen. 24:11, 13, 19; 29:6–10
[c] Gen. 30:38
2:17 [a] Gen. 47:3
[b] Gen. 26:19–21
[c] Gen. 29:3, 10
2:18 [a] Num. 10:29
[b] Ex. 3:1; 4:18
[1] *Jethro,* Ex. 3:1
2:20 [a] Gen. 31:54; 43:25
2:21 [a] Ex. 4:25; 18:2
2:22 [a] Ex. 4:20; 18:3, 4 [b] Acts 7:29
[1] Lit. *Stranger There* [2] *sojourner, temporary dweller*
2:23 [a] Acts 7:34
[b] Deut. 26:7
[c] James 5:4
[1] *groaned because*
2:24 [a] Ex. 6:5
[b] Gen. 15:13; 22:16–18; 26:2–5; 28:13–15 [c] Gen. 12:1–3; 15:14; 17:1–14
2:25 [a] Ex. 4:31 [b] Ex. 3:7 [1] *acknowledged them*
3:1 [a] Ex. 4:18 [b] Ex. 2:16 [c] Ex. 18:5
[d] Ex. 17:6
3:2 [a] Deut. 33:16
3:3 [a] Acts 7:31
3:4 [a] Deut. 33:16
3:5 [a] Josh. 5:15
[1] *Do not draw near this place*
3:6 [a] [Matt. 22:32]
[b] 1 Kin. 19:13
3:7 [a] Ex. 2:23–25
[b] Ex. 1:11 [c] Gen. 18:21; Ex. 2:25
[1] *pain*
3:8 [a] Gen. 15:13–16; 46:4; 50:24, 25 [b] Ex. 6:6–8; 12:51 [c] Num. 13:27; Deut. 1:25; 8:7–9; Josh. 3:17 [d] Ex. 3:17; 13:5; Jer. 11:5; Ezek. 20:6 [e] Gen. 15:19–21; Josh. 24:11

19 And they said, An Egyptian delivered us out of the hand of the shepherds, and also drew *water* enough for us, and watered the flock.

20 And he said unto his daughters, And where *is* he? why *is it that* ye have left the man? call him, that he may [a]eat bread.

21 And Moses was content to dwell with the man: and he gave Moses [a]Zipporah his daughter.

22 And she bare *him* a son, and he called his name [a]Gershom:[1] for he said, I have been [b]a [2]stranger in a strange land.

23 And it came to pass [a]in process of time, that the king of Egypt died: and the children of Israel [b]sighed[1] by reason of the bondage, and they cried, and [c]their cry came up unto God by reason of the bondage.

24 And God [a]heard their groaning, and God [b]remembered his [c]covenant with Abraham, with Isaac, and with Jacob.

25 And God [a]looked upon the children of Israel, and God [b]had[1] respect unto *them.*

## CHAPTER 3

Now Moses kept the flock of [a]Jethro his father in law, [b]the priest of Midian: and he led the flock to the backside of the desert, and came [c]to the mountain of God, *even* to [d]Horeb.

2 And [a]the angel of the LORD appeared unto him in a flame of fire out of the midst of a bush: and he looked, and, behold, the bush burned with fire, and the bush *was* not consumed.

3 And Moses said, I will now turn aside, and see this [a]great sight, why the bush is not burnt.

4 And when the LORD saw that he turned aside to see, God called [a]unto him out of the midst of the bush, and said, Moses, Moses. And he said, Here *am* I.

5 And he said, [1]Draw not nigh hither: [a]put off thy shoes from off thy feet, for the place whereon thou standest *is* holy ground.

6 Moreover he said, [a]I *am* the God of thy father, the God of Abraham, the God of Isaac, and the God of Jacob. And Moses hid his face; for [b]he was afraid to look upon God.

7 And the LORD said, [a]I have surely seen the affliction of my people which *are* in Egypt, and have heard their cry [b]by reason of their taskmasters; [c]for I know their [1]sorrows;

8 And [a]I am come down to [b]deliver them out of the hand of the Egyptians, and to bring them up out of that land [c]unto a good land and a large, unto a land [d]flowing with milk and honey; unto the place of [e]the Canaanites, and

the Hittites, and the Amorites, and the Perizzites, and the Hivites, and the Jebusites.

9 Now therefore, behold, [a]the cry of the children of Israel is come unto me: and I have also seen the [b]oppression wherewith the Egyptians oppress them.

10 [a]Come now therefore, and I will send thee unto Pharaoh, that thou mayest bring forth my people the children of Israel out of Egypt.

11 And Moses said unto God, [a]Who *am* I, that I should go unto Pharaoh, and that I should bring forth the children of Israel out of Egypt?

12 And he said, [a]Certainly I will be with thee; and this *shall be* a [b]token unto thee, that I have sent thee: When thou hast brought forth the people out of Egypt, ye shall serve God upon this mountain.

13 And Moses said unto God, Behold, *when* I come unto the children of Israel, and shall say unto them, The God of your fathers hath sent me unto you; and they shall say to me, What *is* his name? what shall I say unto them?

14 And God said unto Moses, I AM THAT I AM: and he said, Thus shalt thou say unto the children of Israel, [a]I AM hath sent me unto you.

15 And God said moreover unto Moses, Thus shalt thou say unto the children of Israel, The LORD God of your fathers, the God of Abraham, the God of Isaac, and the God of Jacob, hath sent me unto you: this *is* [a]my name for ever, and this *is* my memorial unto all generations.

16 Go, and [a]gather the elders of Israel together, and say unto them, The LORD God of your fathers, the God of Abraham, of Isaac, and of Jacob, appeared unto me, saying, [b]I have surely visited you, and *seen* that which is done to you in Egypt:

17 And I have said, [a]I will bring you up out of the affliction of Egypt unto the land of the Canaanites, and the Hittites, and the Amorites, and the Perizzites, and the Hivites, and the Jebusites, unto a land flowing with milk and honey.

18 And [a]they shall [1]hearken to thy voice: and [b]thou shalt come, thou and the elders of Israel, unto the king of Egypt, and ye shall say unto him, The LORD God of the Hebrews hath [c]met with us: and now let us go, we beseech thee, three days' journey into the wilderness, that we may sacrifice to the LORD our God.

19 And I am sure that the king of Egypt [a]will not let you go, no, not by a mighty hand.

20 And I will [a]stretch out my hand, and [1]smite Egypt with [b]all my wonders which I will do in the midst

*Reference column:*

3:9 [a] Ex. 2:23
[b] Ex. 1:11, 13, 14

3:10 [a] Gen. 15:13, 14; Ex. 12:40, 41; [Mic. 6:4]; Acts 7:6, 7

3:11 [a] Ex. 4:10; 6:12; 1 Sam. 18:18

3:12 [a] Gen. 31:3; Ex. 4:12, 15; 33:14–16; Deut. 31:23; Josh. 1:5; Is. 43:2; Rom. 8:31 [b] Ex. 4:8; 19:3

3:14 [a] [Ex. 6:3; John 8:24, 28, 58; Heb. 13:8; Rev. 1:8; 4:8]

3:15 [a] Ps. 30:4; 97:12; 102:12; 135:13; [Hos. 12:5]

3:16 [a] Ex. 4:29
[b] Gen. 50:24; Ex. 2:25; 4:31; Ps. 33:18; Luke 1:68

3:17 [a] Gen. 15:13–21; 46:4; 50:24, 25

3:18 [a] Ex. 4:31
[b] Ex. 5:1, 3
[c] Num. 23:3, 4, 15, 16 [1] *heed*

3:19 [a] Ex. 5:2

3:20 [a] Ex. 6:6; 9:15 [b] Deut. 6:22; Neh. 9:10; Ps. 105:27; 135:9; Jer. 32:20; Acts 7:36 [1] *strike*

thereof: and [c]after that he will let you go.

21 And [a]I will give this people favour in the sight of the Egyptians: and it shall come to pass, that, when ye go, ye shall not go empty:

22 [a]But every woman shall borrow of her neighbour, and of her that sojourneth in her house, [b]jewels of silver, and jewels of gold, and raiment: and ye shall put *them* upon your sons, and upon your daughters; and [c]ye shall [1]spoil the Egyptians.

## CHAPTER 4

A ND Moses answered and said, But, behold, they will not believe me, nor hearken unto my voice: for they will say, The LORD hath not appeared unto thee.

2 And the LORD said unto him, What *is* that in thine hand? And he said, A rod.

3 And he said, Cast it on the ground. And he cast it on the ground, and it became a serpent; and Moses fled from before it.

4 And the LORD said unto Moses, Put forth thine hand, and take it by the tail. And he put forth his hand, and caught it, and it became a rod in his hand:

5 That they may [a]believe that the [b]LORD God of their fathers, the God of Abraham, the God of Isaac, and the God of Jacob, hath appeared unto thee.

6 And the LORD said furthermore unto him, Put now thine hand into thy bosom. And he put his hand into his bosom: and when he took it out, behold, his hand *was* leprous [a]as snow.

7 And he said, Put thine hand into thy bosom again. And he put his hand into his bosom again; and plucked it out of his bosom, and, behold, [a]it was turned again as his *other* flesh.

8 And it shall come to pass, if they will not believe thee, neither hearken to the voice of the [a]first sign, that they will believe the voice of the latter sign.

9 And it shall come to pass, if they will not believe also these two signs, neither hearken unto thy voice, that thou shalt take of the water of the [1]river, and pour *it* upon the dry *land:* and [a]the water which thou takest out of the river shall become blood upon the dry *land.*

10 And Moses said unto the LORD, O my Lord, I *am* not eloquent, neither [1]heretofore, nor since thou hast spoken unto thy servant: but [a]I *am* slow of speech, and [2]of a slow tongue.

11 And the LORD said unto him, [a]Who hath made man's mouth? or who maketh the dumb, or deaf, or

*Reference column:*

[c] Ex. 11:1; 12:31–37

3:21 [a] Ex. 11:3; 12:36; 1 Kin. 8:50; Ps. 105:37; 106:46; [Prov. 16:7]

3:22 [a] Ex. 11:2
[b] Ex. 33:6 [c] Job 27:17; Prov. 13:22; [Ezek. 39:10] [1] *plunder*

4:5 [a] Ex. 4:31; 19:9 [b] Gen. 28:13; 48:15; Ex. 3:6, 15

4:6 [a] Num. 12:10; 2 Kin. 5:27

4:7 [a] Num. 12:13–15; Deut. 32:39

4:8 [a] Ex. 7:6–13

4:9 [a] Ex. 7:19, 20 [1] The Nile

4:10 [a] Ex. 3:11; 4:1; 6:12 [1] *before* [2] *heavy or dull of*

4:11 [a] Ps. 94:9; 146:8

the seeing, or the blind? have not I the LORD?

12 Now therefore go, and I will be <sup>a</sup>with thy mouth, and teach thee what thou shalt say.

13 And he said, O my Lord, <sup>a</sup>send, I pray thee, by the hand *of him whom* thou wilt send.

14 And <sup>a</sup>the anger of the LORD was kindled against Moses, and he said, *Is* not Aaron the Levite thy <sup>b</sup>brother? I know that he can speak well. And also, behold, <sup>c</sup>he cometh forth to meet thee: and when he seeth thee, he will be glad in his heart.

15 And <sup>a</sup>thou shalt speak unto him, and <sup>b</sup>put words in his mouth: and I will be with thy mouth, and with his mouth, and <sup>c</sup>will teach you what ye shall do.

16 And he shall be thy spokesman unto the people: and he shall be, *even* he shall be <sup>1</sup>to thee instead of a mouth, and <sup>a</sup>thou shalt be to him instead of God.

17 And thou shalt take this rod in thine hand, wherewith thou shalt do signs.

18 And Moses went and returned to <sup>a</sup>Jethro his father in law, and said unto him, Let me go, I pray thee, and return unto my brethren which *are* in Egypt, and see whether they be yet alive. And Jethro said to Moses, <sup>b</sup>Go in peace.

19 And the LORD said unto Moses in <sup>a</sup>Midian, Go, return into <sup>b</sup>Egypt: for <sup>c</sup>all the men are dead which sought thy life.

20 And Moses <sup>a</sup>took his wife and his sons, and set them upon an ass, and he returned to the land of Egypt: and Moses took <sup>b</sup>the rod of God in his hand.

21 And the LORD said unto Moses, When thou goest to return into Egypt, see that thou do all those <sup>a</sup>wonders before Pharaoh, which I have put in thine hand: but <sup>b</sup>I will harden his heart, that he shall not let the people go.

22 And thou shalt <sup>a</sup>say unto Pharaoh, Thus saith the LORD, <sup>b</sup>Israel *is* my son, <sup>c</sup>*even* my firstborn:

23 And I say unto thee, Let my son go, that he may serve me: and if thou refuse to let him go, behold, <sup>a</sup>I will slay thy son, *even* thy firstborn.

24 And it came to pass by the way in the <sup>a</sup>inn, that the LORD <sup>b</sup>met him, and sought to <sup>c</sup>kill him.

25 Then <sup>a</sup>Zipporah took <sup>b</sup>a sharp stone, and cut off the foreskin of her son, and <sup>1</sup>cast *it* at his feet, and said, Surely a bloody husband *art* thou to me.

26 So he let him go: then she said, <sup>1</sup>A bloody husband *thou art*, because of the circumcision.

27 And the LORD said to Aaron, Go into the wilderness <sup>a</sup>to meet Moses. And he went, and met him in <sup>b</sup>the mount of God, and kissed him.

28 And Moses <sup>a</sup>told Aaron all the words of the LORD who had sent him, and all the <sup>b</sup>signs which he had commanded him.

29 And Moses and Aaron <sup>a</sup>went and gathered together all the elders of the children of Israel:

30 <sup>a</sup>And Aaron spake all the words which the LORD had spoken unto Moses, and did the signs in the sight of the people.

31 And the people <sup>a</sup>believed: and when they heard that the LORD had <sup>b</sup>visited the children of Israel, and that he <sup>c</sup>had looked upon their affliction, then <sup>d</sup>they bowed their heads and worshipped.

## CHAPTER 5

AND afterward Moses and Aaron went in, and told Pharaoh, Thus saith the LORD God of Israel, Let my people go, that they may <sup>1</sup>hold <sup>a</sup>a feast unto me in the wilderness.

2 And Pharaoh said, <sup>a</sup>Who *is* the LORD, that I should obey his voice to let Israel go? I know not the LORD, <sup>b</sup>neither will I let Israel go.

3 And they said, <sup>a</sup>The God of the Hebrews hath <sup>b</sup>met with us: let us go, we pray thee, three days' journey into the desert, and sacrifice unto the LORD our God; lest he fall upon us with <sup>c</sup>pestilence, or with the sword.

4 And the king of Egypt said unto them, Wherefore do ye, Moses and Aaron, let the people from their works? get <sup>1</sup>you unto your <sup>a</sup>burdens.

5 And Pharaoh said, Behold, the people of the land now *are* <sup>a</sup>many, and ye make them rest from their burdens.

6 And Pharaoh commanded the same day the <sup>a</sup>taskmasters of the people, and their officers, saying,

7 Ye shall no more give the people straw to make <sup>a</sup>brick, as heretofore: let them go and gather straw for themselves.

8 And the <sup>1</sup>tale of the bricks, which they did make heretofore, ye shall lay upon them; ye shall not diminish *ought* thereof: for they *be* idle; therefore they cry, saying, Let us go *and* sacrifice to our God.

9 Let there more work be laid upon the men, that they may labour therein; and let them not regard <sup>1</sup>vain words.

10 And the taskmasters of the people went out, and their officers, and they spake to the people, saying, Thus saith Pharaoh, I will not give you straw.

11 Go ye, get you straw where ye can find it: yet <sup>1</sup>not ought of your work shall be diminished.

### Cross references

4:12 <sup>a</sup> Is. 50:4
4:13 <sup>a</sup> Jon. 1:3
4:14 <sup>a</sup> Num. 11:1, 33 <sup>b</sup> Num. 26:59 <sup>c</sup> Ex. 4:27
4:15 <sup>a</sup> Ex. 4:12, 30; 7:1, 2 <sup>b</sup> Num. 23:5, 12 <sup>c</sup> Deut. 5:31
4:16 <sup>a</sup> Ex. 7:1, 2 <sup>1</sup> *your spokesman*
4:18 <sup>a</sup> Ex. 2:21; 3:1; 4:18 <sup>b</sup> Judg. 18:6
4:19 <sup>a</sup> Ex. 3:1; 18:1 <sup>b</sup> Gen. 46:3, 6 <sup>c</sup> Ex. 2:15, 23
4:20 <sup>a</sup> Ex. 18:2–5 <sup>b</sup> Num. 20:8, 9, 11
4:21 <sup>a</sup> Ex. 3:20; 11:9, 10 <sup>b</sup> John 12:40
4:22 <sup>a</sup> Ex. 5:1 <sup>b</sup> Hos. 11:1 <sup>c</sup> Jer. 31:9
4:23 <sup>a</sup> Ex. 11:5; 12:29
4:24 <sup>a</sup> Gen. 42:27 <sup>b</sup> Num. 22:22 <sup>c</sup> Gen. 17:14
4:25 <sup>a</sup> Ex. 2:21; 18:2 <sup>b</sup> Josh. 5:2, 3 <sup>1</sup> Lit. *made it touch*
4:26 <sup>1</sup> *You are a husband of blood*
4:27 <sup>a</sup> Ex. 4:14 <sup>b</sup> Ex. 3:1; 18:5; 24:13
4:28 <sup>a</sup> Ex. 4:15, 16 <sup>b</sup> Ex. 4:8, 9
4:29 <sup>a</sup> Ex. 3:16; 12:21
4:30 <sup>a</sup> Ex. 4:15, 16
4:31 <sup>a</sup> Ex. 3:18; 4:8, 9; 19:9 <sup>b</sup> Gen. 50:24 <sup>c</sup> Ex. 2:25; 3:7 <sup>d</sup> Gen. 24:26
5:1 <sup>a</sup> Ex. 3:18; 7:16; 10:9 <sup>1</sup> *keep a pilgrim-feast*
5:2 <sup>a</sup> 2 Kin. 18:35 <sup>b</sup> Ex. 3:19; 7:14
5:3 <sup>a</sup> Ex. 3:18; 7:16 <sup>b</sup> Num. 23:3 <sup>c</sup> Ex. 9:15
5:4 <sup>a</sup> Ex. 1:11; 2:11; 6:6 <sup>1</sup> *back to your labour*
5:5 <sup>a</sup> Ex. 1:7, 9
5:6 <sup>a</sup> Ex. 1:11; 3:7; 5:10, 13, 14
5:7 <sup>a</sup> Ex. 1:14
5:8 <sup>1</sup> *quota*
5:9 <sup>1</sup> *false*
5:11 <sup>1</sup> *none*

12 So the people were scattered abroad throughout all the land of Egypt to gather stubble instead of straw.

13 And the taskmasters ¹hasted *them,* saying, Fulfil your works, *your* daily tasks, as when there was straw.

14 And the ªofficers of the children of Israel, which Pharaoh's taskmasters had set over them, were ᵇbeaten, *and* demanded, Wherefore have ye not fulfilled your task in making brick both yesterday and to day, as heretofore?

15 Then the officers of the children of Israel came and cried unto Pharaoh, saying, Wherefore dealest thou thus with thy servants?

16 There is no straw given unto thy servants, and they say to us, Make brick: and, behold, thy servants *are* beaten; but the fault *is* in thine own people.

17 But he said, Ye *are* idle, *ye are* idle: therefore ye say, Let us go *and* do sacrifice unto the LORD.

18 Go therefore now, *and* work; for there shall no straw be given you, yet shall ye deliver the ¹tale of bricks.

19 And the officers of the children of Israel did see *that* they *were* ¹in evil *case,* after it was said, Ye shall not ²minish *ought* from your bricks of your daily task.

20 And they met Moses and Aaron, who stood in the way, as they came forth from Pharaoh:

21 ªAnd they said unto them, The LORD look upon you, and judge; because ye have made our ¹savour to be abhorred in the eyes of Pharaoh, and in the eyes of his servants, to put a sword in their hand to slay us.

22 And Moses returned unto the LORD, and said, Lord, wherefore hast thou ¹so evil entreated this people? why *is* it *that* thou hast sent me?

23 For since I came to Pharaoh to speak in thy name, he hath done evil to this people; neither hast thou delivered thy people at all.

## CHAPTER 6

THEN the LORD said unto Moses, Now shalt thou see what I will do to Pharaoh: for ªwith a strong hand shall he let them go, and with a strong hand ᵇshall he drive them out of his land.

2 And God spake unto Moses, and said unto him, I *am* ¹the LORD:

3 And I ªappeared unto Abraham, unto Isaac, and unto Jacob, by *the name of* ᵇGod Almighty, but by my name ᶜJEHOVAH¹ was I not known to them.

4 ªAnd I have also ¹established my covenant with them, ᵇto give them the land of Canaan, the land of their ²pilgrimage, ᶜwherein they were ³strangers.

5 And ªI have also heard the groaning of the children of Israel, whom the Egyptians keep in bondage; and I have remembered my covenant.

6 Wherefore say unto the children of Israel, ªI *am* the LORD, and ᵇI will bring you out from under the burdens of the Egyptians, and I will rid you out of their bondage, and I will ᶜredeem you ¹with a stretched out arm, and with great judgments:

7 And I will ªtake you to me for a people, and ᵇI will be to you a God: and ye shall know that I *am* the LORD your God, which bringeth you out ᶜfrom under the burdens of the Egyptians.

8 And I will bring you in unto the land, concerning the which I did ªswear¹ to give it to Abraham, to Isaac, and to Jacob; and I will give it you for an heritage: I *am* the LORD.

9 And Moses spake so unto the children of Israel: ªbut they hearkened not unto Moses for ᵇanguish¹ of spirit, and for cruel bondage.

10 And the LORD spake unto Moses, saying,

11 Go in, speak unto Pharaoh king of Egypt, that he let the children of Israel go out of his land.

12 And Moses spake before the LORD, saying, Behold, the children of Israel have not hearkened unto me; how then shall Pharaoh hear me, ªwho ¹*am* of uncircumcised lips?

13 And the LORD spake unto Moses and unto Aaron, and gave them ¹a ªcharge unto the children of Israel, and unto Pharaoh king of Egypt, to bring the children of Israel out of the land of Egypt.

14 These *be* the heads of their fathers' houses: ªThe sons of Reuben the firstborn of Israel; Hanoch, and Pallu, Hezron, and Carmi: these *be* the families of Reuben.

15 ªAnd the sons of Simeon; Jemuel, and Jamin, and Ohad, and Jachin, and Zohar, and Shaul the son of a Canaanitish woman: these *are* the families of Simeon.

16 And these *are* the names of ªthe sons of Levi according to their generations; Gershon, and Kohath, and Merari: and the years of the life of Levi *were* an hundred thirty and seven years.

17 ªThe sons of Gershon; Libni, and Shimi, according to their families.

18 And ªthe sons of Kohath; Amram, and Izhar, and Hebron, and Uzziel: and the years of the life of Kohath *were* an hundred thirty and three years.

19 And ªthe sons of Merari; Mahali and Mushi: these *are* the families of Levi according to their ¹generations.

### Center reference column

5:13 ¹ forced them to hurry
5:14 ª Ex. 5:6 ᵇ Is. 10:24
5:18 ¹ quota
5:19 ¹ in trouble ² diminish any
5:21 ª Ex. 6:9; 14:11; 15:24; 16:2 ¹ Lit. scent to stink
5:22 ¹ brought trouble on
6:1 ª Ex. 3:19 ᵇ Ex. 12:31, 33, 39
6:2 ¹ Heb. YHWH
6:3 ª Gen. 17:1; 35:9; 48:3 ᵇ Gen. 28:3; 35:11 ᶜ Ex. 3:14, 15; 15:3; Ps. 68:4; 83:18; Is. 52:6; Jer. 16:21; Ezek. 37:6, 13; John 8:58 ¹ Heb. YHWH
6:4 ª Gen. 12:7; 15:18; 17:4, 7, 8; 26:3; 28:4, 13 ᵇ Gen. 47:9; Lev. 25:23 ᶜ Gen. 28:4 ¹ made or ratified ² sojournings ³ sojourners, temporary dwellers
6:5 ª Ex. 2:24; [Job 34:28]; Acts 7:34
6:6 ª Ex. 13:3, 14; 20:2; Deut. 6:12 ᵇ Ex. 3:17; 7:4; 12:51; 16:6; 18:1; Deut. 26:8; Ps. 136:11 ᶜ Ex. 15:13; Deut. 7:8; 1 Chr. 17:21; Neh. 1:10 ¹ with mighty power
6:7 ª Ex. 19:5; Deut. 4:20; 7:6; 2 Sam. 7:24 ᵇ Gen. 17:7; Ex. 29:45, 46; Lev. 26:12, 13, 45; Deut. 29:13; Rev. 21:7 ᶜ Ex. 5:4, 5
6:8 ª Gen. 15:18; 26:3; Num. 14:30; Neh. 9:15; Ezek. 20:5, 6 ¹ Lit. lift up my hand
6:9 ª Ex. 5:21 ᵇ Ex. 2:23; Num. 21:4 ¹ Lit. shortness
6:12 ª Ex. 4:10; 6:30; Jer. 1:6 ¹ does not speak well
6:13 ª Num. 27:19, 23; Deut. 31:14 ¹ an instruction
6:14 ª Gen. 46:9; Num. 26:5–11; 1 Chr. 5:3
6:15 ª Gen. 46:10; Num. 26:12–14; 1 Chr. 4:24
6:16 ª Gen. 46:11; Num. 3:17; 1 Chr. 6:16–30
6:17 ª 1 Chr. 6:17  6:18 ª 1 Chr. 6:2, 18  6:19 ª 1 Chr. 6:19; 23:21 ¹ families

20 And [a]Amram took him [b]Jochebed his father's sister to wife; and she bare him [c]Aaron and Moses: and the years of the life of Amram *were* an hundred and thirty and seven years.

21 And [a]the sons of Izhar; Korah, and Nepheg, and Zichri.

22 And [a]the sons of Uzziel; Mishael, and Elzaphan, and Zithri.

23 And Aaron took him Elisheba, daughter of [a]Amminadab, sister of Naashon, to wife; and she bare him [b]Nadab, and Abihu, [c]Eleazar, and Ithamar.

24 And [a]the sons of Korah; Assir, and Elkanah, and Abiasaph: these *are* the families of the Korhites.

25 And Eleazar Aaron's son took him *one* of the daughters of Putiel to wife; and [a]she bare him Phinehas: these *are* the heads of the fathers of the Levites according to their families.

26 These *are* that Aaron and Moses, to whom the LORD said, Bring out the children of Israel from the land of Egypt according to their armies.[1]

27 These *are* they which spake to Pharaoh king of Egypt, [a]to bring out the children of Israel from Egypt: these *are* that Moses and Aaron.

28 And it came to pass on the day *when* the LORD spake unto Moses in the land of Egypt,

29 That the LORD spake unto Moses, saying, I *am* the LORD: [a]speak thou unto Pharaoh king of Egypt all that I say unto thee.

30 And Moses said before the LORD, Behold, [a]I *am* [1]of uncircumcised lips, and how shall Pharaoh hearken unto me?

## CHAPTER 7

AND the LORD said unto Moses, See, I have made thee [a]a god to Pharaoh: and Aaron thy brother shall be [b]thy prophet.

2 Thou [a]shalt speak all that I command thee: and Aaron thy brother shall speak unto Pharaoh, that he send the children of Israel out of his land.

3 And [a]I will harden Pharaoh's heart, and [b]multiply my [c]signs and my wonders in the land of Egypt.

4 But [a]Pharaoh shall not hearken unto you, [b]that I may lay my hand upon Egypt, and bring forth mine [1]armies, *and* my people the children of Israel, out of the land of Egypt [c]by great judgments.

5 And the Egyptians [a]shall know that I *am* the LORD, when I [b]stretch forth mine hand upon Egypt, and [c]bring out the children of Israel from among them.

6 And Moses and Aaron [a]did as the LORD commanded them, so did they.

7 And Moses *was* [a]fourscore years old, and [b]Aaron fourscore and three years old, when they spake unto Pharaoh.

8 And the LORD spake unto Moses and unto Aaron, saying,

9 When Pharaoh shall speak unto you, saying, [a]Shew a miracle for you: then thou shalt say unto Aaron, [b]Take thy rod, and cast *it* before Pharaoh, *and* it shall become a serpent.

10 And Moses and Aaron went in unto Pharaoh, and they did so [a]as the LORD had commanded: and Aaron cast down his rod before Pharaoh, and before his servants, and it [b]became a serpent.

11 Then Pharaoh also [a]called the wise men and [b]the sorcerers: now the [1]magicians of Egypt, they also [c]did in like manner with their [2]enchantments.

12 For they cast down every man his rod, and they became serpents: but Aaron's rod swallowed up their rods.

13 And he hardened Pharaoh's heart, that he hearkened not unto them; as the LORD had said.

14 And the LORD said unto Moses, [a]Pharaoh's heart *is* hardened, he refuseth to let the people go.

15 Get thee unto Pharaoh in the morning; lo, he goeth out unto the [a]water; and thou shalt stand by the river's brink [1]against he come; and [b]the rod which was turned to a serpent shalt thou take in thine hand.

16 And thou shalt say unto him, [a]The LORD God of the Hebrews hath sent me unto thee, saying, Let my people go, [b]that they may [1]serve me in the wilderness: and, behold, hitherto thou wouldest not hear.

17 Thus saith the LORD, In this [a]thou shalt know that I *am* the LORD: behold, I will smite with the rod that *is* in mine hand upon the waters which *are* in the river, and [b]they shall be turned [c]to blood.

18 And the fish that *is* in the river shall die, and the river shall stink; and the Egyptians shall [a]lothe[1] to drink of the water of the river.

19 And the LORD spake unto Moses, Say unto Aaron, Take thy rod, and [a]stretch out thine hand upon the waters of Egypt, upon their streams, upon their rivers, and upon their ponds, and upon all their pools of water, that they may become blood; and *that* there may be blood throughout all the land of Egypt, both in *vessels of* wood, and in *vessels of* stone.

20 And Moses and Aaron did so, as the LORD commanded; and he [a]lifted up the rod, and smote the waters that *were* in the river, in the sight of

### Cross references

6:20 [a] Ex. 2:1, 2; Num. 3:19 [b] Num. 26:59 [c] Num. 26:59

6:21 [a] Num. 16:1; 1 Chr. 6:37, 38

6:22 [a] Lev. 10:4

6:23 [a] Ruth 4:19, 20; 1 Chr. 2:10; Matt. 1:4 [b] Lev. 10:1; Num. 3:2; 26:60 [c] Ex. 28:1

6:24 [a] Num. 26:11

6:25 [a] Num. 25:7, 11; Josh. 24:33

6:26 [a] Ex. 7:4; 12:17, 51; Num. 33:1 [1] hosts

6:27 [a] Ex. 6:13; 32:7; 33:1; Ps. 77:20

6:29 [a] Ex. 6:11; 7:2

6:30 [a] Ex. 4:10; 6:12; Jer. 1:6 [1] one who does not speak well

7:1 [a] Ex. 4:16; Jer. 1:10 [b] Ex. 4:15, 16

7:2 [a] Ex. 4:15; Deut. 18:18

7:3 [a] Ex. 4:21; 9:12 [b] Ex. 11:9; Acts 7:36 [c] Ex. 4:7; Deut. 4:34

7:4 [a] Ex. 3:19, 20; 10:1; 11:9 [b] Ex. 9:14 [c] Ex. 6:6; 12:12 [1] hosts

7:5 [a] Ex. 7:17; 8:22; 14:4, 18; Ps. 9:16 [b] Ex. 9:15 [c] Ex. 3:20; 6:6; 12:51

7:6 [a] Ex. 7:2

7:7 [a] Deut. 29:5; 31:2; 34:7; Acts 7:23, 30 [b] Num. 33:39

7:9 [a] Ex. 10:1; Is. 7:11; John 2:18; 6:30 [b] Ex. 4:2, 3, 17

7:10 [a] Ex. 7:9 [b] Ex. 4:3

7:11 [a] Gen. 41:8 [b] Dan. 2:2; 2 Tim. 3:8 [c] Ex. 7:22; 8:7, 18; 2 Tim. 3:9; Rev. 13:13, 14 [1] soothsayers [2] secret arts

7:14 [a] Ex. 8:15; 10:1, 20, 27

7:15 [a] Ex. 2:5; 8:20 [b] Ex. 4:2, 3; 7:10 [1] to meet him

7:16 [a] Ex. 3:13, 18; 4:22 [b] Ex. 3:12, 18; 4:23; 5:1, 3; 8:1 [1] worship

7:17 [a] Ex. 5:2; 7:5; 10:2; Ps. 9:16; Ezek. 25:17 [b] Ex. 4:9; 7:20 [c] Rev. 11:6; 16:4, 6

7:18 [a] Ex. 7:24 [1] be weary of

7:19 [a] Ex. 8:5, 6, 16; 9:22; 10:12, 21; 14:21, 26

7:20 [a] Ex. 17:5

Pharaoh, and in the sight of his servants; and all the [b]waters that *were* in the river were turned to blood.

21 And the fish that *was* in the river died; and the river stank, and the Egyptians [a]could not drink of the water of the river; and there was blood throughout all the land of Egypt.

22 [a]And the magicians of Egypt did [b]so with their [1]enchantments: and Pharaoh's heart was hardened, neither did he hearken unto them; [c]as the LORD had said.

23 And Pharaoh turned and went into his house, neither [1]did he set his heart to this also.

24 And all the Egyptians digged round about the river for water to drink; for they could not drink of the water of the river.

25 And seven days were fulfilled, after that the LORD had smitten the river.

## CHAPTER 8

AND the LORD spake unto Moses, Go unto Pharaoh, and say unto him, Thus saith the LORD, Let my people go, [a]that they may serve me.

2 And if thou [a]refuse to let *them* go, behold, I will [1]smite all thy [2]borders with [b]frogs:

3 And the river shall bring forth frogs abundantly, which shall go up and come into thine house, and into thy [a]bedchamber, and upon thy bed, and into the house of thy servants, and upon thy people, and into thine ovens, and into thy [1]kneadingtroughs:

4 And the frogs shall come up both on thee, and upon thy people, and upon all thy servants.

5 And the LORD spake unto Moses, Say unto Aaron, [a]Stretch forth thine hand with thy rod over the streams, over the rivers, and over the ponds, and cause frogs to come up upon the land of Egypt.

6 And Aaron stretched out his hand over the waters of Egypt; and [a]the frogs came up, and covered the land of Egypt.

7 [a]And the magicians did so with their [1]enchantments, and brought up frogs upon the land of Egypt.

8 Then Pharaoh called for Moses and Aaron, and said, [a]Intreat[1] the LORD, that he may take away the frogs from me, and from my people; and I will let the people [b]go, that they may do sacrifice unto the LORD.

9 And Moses said unto Pharaoh, Glory over me: when shall I intreat for thee, and for thy servants, and for thy people, to destroy the frogs from thee and thy houses, *that* they may remain in the river only?

10 And he said, To morrow. And he said, *Be it* according to thy word: that

thou mayest know that [a]*there is* none like unto the LORD our God.

11 And the frogs shall depart from thee, and from thy houses, and from thy servants, and from thy people; they shall remain in the river only.

12 And Moses and Aaron went out from Pharaoh: and Moses [a]cried unto the LORD because of the frogs which he had brought against Pharaoh.

13 And the LORD did according to the word of Moses; and the frogs died out of the houses, out of the villages, and out of the fields.

14 And they gathered them together upon heaps: and the land stank.

15 But when Pharaoh saw that there was [a]respite,[1] [b]he hardened his heart, and [2]hearkened not unto them; as the LORD had said.

16 And the LORD said unto Moses, Say unto Aaron, Stretch out thy rod, and smite the dust of the land, that it may become [1]lice throughout all the land of Egypt.

17 And they did so; for Aaron stretched out his hand with his rod, and smote the dust of the earth, and [a]it became lice in man, and in beast; all the dust of the land became lice throughout all the land of Egypt.

18 And [a]the magicians did so with their [1]enchantments to bring forth lice, but they [b]could not: so there were lice upon man, and upon beast.

19 Then the magicians said unto Pharaoh, This *is* [a]the[1] finger of God: and Pharaoh's [b]heart was hardened, and he hearkened not unto them; as the LORD had said.

20 And the LORD said unto Moses, [a]Rise up early in the morning, and stand before Pharaoh; lo, he cometh forth to the water; and say unto him, Thus saith the LORD, [b]Let my people go, that they may serve me.

21 Else, if thou wilt not let my people go, behold, I will send swarms *of flies* upon thee, and upon thy servants, and upon thy people, and into thy houses: and the houses of the Egyptians shall be full of swarms *of flies,* and also the ground whereon they *are.*

22 And [a]I will [1]sever in that day the land of [b]Goshen, in which my people dwell, that no swarms *of flies* shall be there; to the end thou mayest [c]know that I *am* the LORD in the midst of the [d]earth.

23 And I will put a [1]division between my people and thy people: to morrow shall this [a]sign be.

24 And the LORD did so; and [a]there came a [1]grievous swarm *of flies* into the house of Pharaoh, and *into* his servants' houses, and into all the land of Egypt: the land was [2]corrupted by reason of the swarm *of flies.*

7:20 [b] Ps. 78:44; 105:29, 30
7:21 [a] Ex. 7:18
7:22 [a] Ex. 7:11 [b] Ex. 8:7 [c] Ex. 3:19; 7:3 [1] *secret arts*
7:23 [1] *was his heart moved by this*
8:1 [a] Ex. 3:12, 18; 4:23; 5:1, 3
8:2 [a] Ex. 7:14; 9:2 [b] Rev. 16:13 [1] *strike* [2] *territories*
8:3 [a] Ps. 105:30 [1] *dough*
8:5 [a] Ex. 7:19
8:6 [a] Ps. 78:45; 105:30
8:7 [a] Ex. 7:11, 22 [1] *secret arts*
8:8 [a] Ex. 8:28; 9:28; 10:17; Num. 21:7; 1 Kin. 13:6 [b] Ex. 10:8, 24 [1] *Pray to*
8:10 [a] Ex. 9:14; 15:11; Deut. 4:35, 39; 33:26; 2 Sam. 7:22; 1 Chr. 17:20; Ps. 86:8; Is. 46:9; [Jer. 10:6, 7]
8:12 [a] Ex. 8:30; 9:33; 10:18; 32:11; [James 5:16–18]
8:15 [a] Eccl. 8:11 [b] Ex. 7:14, 22; 9:34; 1 Sam. 6:6 [1] *relief* [2] *did not listen*
8:16 [1] *gnats*
8:17 [a] Ps. 105:31
8:18 [a] Ex. 7:11, 12; 8:7 [b] Dan. 5:8; 2 Tim. 3:8, 9 [1] *secret arts*
8:19 [a] Ex. 7:5; 10:7; 1 Sam. 6:3, 9; Ps. 8:3; Luke 11:20 [b] Ex. 8:15 [1] *an act of God*
8:20 [a] Ex. 7:15; 9:13 [b] Ex. 3:18; 4:23; 5:1, 3; 8:1
8:22 [a] Ex. 9:4, 6, 26; 10:23; 11:6, 7; 12:13 [b] Gen. 50:8 [c] Ex. 7:5, 17; 10:2; 14:4 [d] Ex. 9:29 [1] *set apart*
8:23 [a] Ex. 4:8 [1] Lit. *ransom*
8:24 [a] Ps. 78:45; 105:31 [1] *thick swarms* [2] *destroyed*

25 And Pharaoh called for Moses and for Aaron, and said, Go ye, sacrifice to your God in the land.

26 And Moses said, It is not meet so to do; for we shall sacrifice ªthe abomination of the Egyptians to the LORD our God: lo, shall we sacrifice the abomination of the Egyptians before their eyes, and will they not ¹stone us?

27 We will go ªthree days' journey into the wilderness, and sacrifice to the LORD our God, as ᵇhe shall command us.

28 And Pharaoh said, I will let you go, that ye may sacrifice to the LORD your God in the wilderness; only ye shall not go very far away: ªintreat¹ for me.

29 And Moses said, Behold, I go out from thee, and I will intreat the LORD that the swarms *of flies* may depart from Pharaoh, from his servants, and from his people, to morrow: but let not Pharaoh ªdeal deceitfully any more in not letting the people go to sacrifice to the LORD.

30 And Moses went out from Pharaoh, and ªintreated the LORD.

31 And the LORD did according to the word of Moses; and he removed the swarms *of flies* from Pharaoh, from his servants, and from his people; there remained not one.

32 And Pharaoh ªhardened his heart at this time also, neither would he let the people go.

## CHAPTER 9

THEN the LORD said unto Moses, ªGo in unto Pharaoh, and tell him, Thus saith the LORD God of the Hebrews, Let my people go, that they may ᵇserve me.

2 For if thou ªrefuse to let *them* go, and wilt hold them still,

3 Behold, the ªhand of the LORD is upon thy cattle which *is* in the field, upon the horses, upon the asses, upon the camels, upon the oxen, and upon the sheep: *there shall be* a very ¹grievous murrain.

4 And ªthe LORD shall ¹sever between the cattle of Israel and the cattle of Egypt: and there shall nothing die of all *that is* the children's of Israel.

5 And the LORD appointed a set time, saying, To morrow the LORD shall do this thing in the land.

6 And the LORD did that thing on the morrow, and ªall the cattle of Egypt died: but of the cattle of the children of Israel died not one.

7 And Pharaoh sent, and, behold, there was not one of the cattle of the Israelites dead. And the ªheart of Pharaoh was hardened, and he did not let the people go.

8 And the LORD said unto Moses and unto Aaron, Take to you handfuls of ashes of the furnace, and let Moses sprinkle it toward the heaven in the sight of Pharaoh.

9 And it shall become small dust in all the land of Egypt, and shall be ªa boil breaking forth *with* ¹blains upon man, and upon beast, throughout all the land of Egypt.

10 And they took ashes of the furnace, and stood before Pharaoh; and Moses sprinkled it up toward heaven; and it became ªa boil breaking forth *with* blains upon man, and upon beast.

11 And the ªmagicians could not stand before Moses because of the ᵇboils; for the boil was upon the magicians, and upon all the Egyptians.

12 And the LORD hardened the heart of Pharaoh, and he ªhearkened not unto them; ᵇas the LORD had spoken unto Moses.

13 And the LORD said unto Moses, ªRise up early in the morning, and stand before Pharaoh, and say unto him, Thus saith the LORD God of the Hebrews, Let my people go, that they may ᵇserve me.

14 For I will at this time send all my plagues upon thine heart, and upon thy servants, and upon thy people; ªthat thou mayest know that *there is* none like me in all the earth.

15 For now I will ªstretch out my hand, that I may smite thee and thy people with ᵇpestilence; and thou shalt be cut off from the earth.

16 And in very deed for ªthis *cause* have I raised thee up, for to ᵇshew *in* thee my power; and that my ᶜname may be declared throughout all the earth.

17 As yet exaltest thou thyself against my people, that thou wilt not let them go?

18 Behold, to morrow about this time I will cause it to rain a very ¹grievous hail, such as hath not been in Egypt since the ²foundation thereof even until now.

19 Send therefore now, *and* gather thy cattle, and all that thou hast in the field; *for upon* every man and beast which shall be found in the field, and shall not be brought home, the hail shall come down upon them, and they shall die.

20 He that ªfeared the word of the LORD among the ᵇservants of Pharaoh made his servants and his cattle flee into the houses:

21 And he that regarded not the word of the LORD left his servants and his cattle in the field.

22 And the LORD said unto Moses, Stretch forth thine hand toward heaven, that there may be ªhail in

all the land of Egypt, upon man, and upon beast, and upon every herb of the field, throughout the land of Egypt.

23 And Moses stretched forth his rod toward heaven: and ªthe LORD sent thunder and hail, and the fire ran along upon the ground; and the LORD rained hail upon the land of Egypt.

24 So there was hail, and fire mingled with the hail, very grievous, such as there was none like it in all the land of Egypt since it became a nation.

25 And the ªhail smote throughout all the land of Egypt all that *was* in the field, both man and beast; and the hail smote every herb of the field, and brake every tree of the field.

26 ªOnly in the land of Goshen, where the children of Israel *were,* was there no hail.

27 And Pharaoh sent, and ªcalled for Moses and Aaron, and said unto them, ᵇI have sinned this time: ᶜthe LORD *is* righteous, and I and my people *are* wicked.

28 ªIntreat¹ the LORD (for *it is* enough) that there be no *more* ²mighty thunderings and hail; and I will let you ᵇgo, and ye shall stay no longer.

29 And Moses said unto him, As soon as I am gone out of the city, I will ªspread abroad my hands unto the LORD; *and* the thunder shall cease, neither shall there be any more hail; that thou mayest know how that the ᵇearth *is* the LORD's.

30 But as for thee and thy servants, ªI know that ye will not yet fear the LORD God.

31 And the flax and the barley was smitten: ªfor the barley *was* in the ear, and the flax *was* bolled.

32 But the wheat and the ¹rie were not smitten: for they *were* ²not grown up.

33 And Moses went out of the city from Pharaoh, and ªspread abroad his hands unto the LORD: and the thunders and hail ceased, and the rain was not poured upon the earth.

34 And when Pharaoh saw that the rain and the hail and the thunders were ceased, he sinned yet more, and hardened his heart, he and his servants.

35 And ªthe heart of Pharaoh was hardened, neither would he let the children of Israel go; as the LORD had spoken by Moses.

## CHAPTER 10

A ND the LORD said unto Moses, Go in unto Pharaoh: ªfor I have hardened his heart, and the heart of his servants, ᵇthat I might shew these my signs before him:

2 And that ªthou mayest tell in the ears of thy son, and of thy son's son, what things I have wrought in Egypt, and my signs which I have done among them; that ye may ᵇknow how that I *am* the LORD.

3 And Moses and Aaron came in unto Pharaoh, and said unto him, Thus saith the LORD God of the Hebrews, How long wilt thou refuse to ªhumble thyself before me? let my people go, that they may ᵇserve me.

4 Else, if thou refuse to let my people go, behold, to morrow will I bring the ªlocusts into thy ¹coast:

5 And they shall cover the face of the earth, that one cannot be able to see the earth: and ªthey shall eat the residue of that which is escaped, which remaineth unto you from the hail, and shall eat every tree which groweth for you out of the field:

6 And they shall ªfill thy houses, and the houses of all thy servants, and the houses of all the Egyptians; which neither thy fathers, nor thy fathers' fathers have seen, since the day that they were upon the earth unto this day. And he turned himself, and went out from Pharaoh.

7 And Pharaoh's ªservants said unto him, How long shall this man be ᵇa snare unto us? let the men go, that they may serve the LORD their God: knowest thou not yet that Egypt is destroyed?

8 And Moses and Aaron were brought again unto Pharaoh: and he said unto them, Go, serve the LORD your God: *but* who *are* they that shall go?

9 And Moses said, We will go with our young and with our old, with our sons and with our daughters, with our flocks and with our herds will we go; for ªwe *must hold* a feast unto the LORD.

10 And he said unto them, Let the LORD be so with you, as I will let you go, and your little ones: look *to it;* for evil *is* before you.

11 Not so: go now ye *that are* men, and serve the LORD; for that ye did desire. And they were driven ªout from Pharaoh's presence.

12 And the LORD said unto Moses, ªStretch out thine hand over the land of Egypt for the locusts, that they may come up upon the land of Egypt, and ᵇeat every herb of the land, *even* all that the hail hath left.

13 And Moses stretched forth his rod over the land of Egypt, and the LORD brought an east wind upon the land all that day, and all *that* night; *and* when it was morning, the east wind brought the locusts.

14 And ªthe locusts went up over all the land of Egypt, and rested in

### Cross-references (center column)

9:23 ª Josh. 10:11
9:25 ª Ps. 78:47, 48; 105:32, 33
9:26 ª Ex. 8:22, 23; 9:4, 6; 10:23; 11:7; 12:13
9:27 ª Ex. 8:8
ᵇ Ex. 9:34; 10:16, 17 ᶜ 2 Chr. 12:6
9:28 ª Ex. 8:8, 28; 10:17 ᵇ Ex. 8:25; 10:8, 24 ¹ *Pray to* ² *sounds of God*
9:29 ª Is. 1:15 ᵇ Ps. 24:1
9:30 ª [Is. 26:10]
9:31 ª Ruth 1:22; 2:23
9:32 ¹ *spelt* ² *Late in ripening, lit. darkened*
9:33 ª Ex. 8:12; 9:29
9:35 ª Ex. 4:21
10:1 ª John 12:40 ᵇ Ex. 7:4; 9:16

10:2 ª Joel 1:3 ᵇ Ex. 7:5, 17; 8:22
10:3 ª [1 Kin. 21:29] ᵇ Ex. 4:23; 8:1; 9:1
10:4 ª Rev. 9:3 ¹ *territory*
10:5 ª Ex. 9:32
10:6 ª Ex. 8:3, 21
10:7 ª Ex. 7:5; 8:19; 9:20; 12:33 ᵇ Ex. 23:33; Josh. 23:13; 1 Sam. 18:21; Eccl. 7:26; 1 Cor. 7:35
10:9 ª Ex. 5:1; 7:16
10:11 ª Ex. 10:28
10:12 ª Ex. 7:19 ᵇ Ex. 10:5, 15
10:14 ª Deut. 28:38; Ps. 78:46; 105:34

all the coasts of Egypt: very ¹grievous *were they;* ᵇbefore them there were no such locusts as they, neither after them shall be such.

15 For they ªcovered the face of the whole earth, so that the land was darkened; and they ᵇdid eat every herb of the land, and all the fruit of the trees which the hail had left: and there remained not any green thing in the trees, or in the herbs of the field, through all the land of Egypt.

16 Then Pharaoh called ªfor Moses and Aaron in haste; and he said, ᵇI have sinned against the LORD your God, and against you.

17 Now therefore forgive, I pray thee, my sin only this once, and ªintreat¹ the LORD your God, that he may take away from me this death only.

18 And he ªwent out from Pharaoh, and intreated the LORD.

19 And the LORD turned a mighty strong west wind, which took away the locusts, and cast them ªinto the Red sea; there remained not one locust in all the ¹coasts of Egypt.

20 But the LORD ªhardened Pharaoh's heart, so that he would not let the children of Israel go.

21 And the LORD said unto Moses, ªStretch out thine hand toward heaven, that there may be darkness over the land of Egypt, ¹even darkness *which* may be felt.

22 And Moses stretched forth his hand toward heaven; and there was a ªthick darkness in all the land of Egypt ᵇthree days:

23 They saw not one another, neither rose any from his place for three days: ªbut all the children of Israel had light in their dwellings.

24 And Pharaoh called unto Moses, and ªsaid, Go ye, serve the LORD; only let your flocks and your herds be stayed: let your ᵇlittle ones also go with you.

25 And Moses said, Thou must give ¹us also sacrifices and burnt offerings, that we may sacrifice unto the LORD our God.

26 Our ªcattle also shall go with us; there shall not an hoof be left behind; for thereof must we take to serve the LORD our God; and we know not with what we must serve the LORD, until we come thither.

27 But the LORD ªhardened Pharaoh's heart, and he would not let them go.

28 And Pharaoh said unto him, ªGet thee from me, take heed to thyself, see my face no more; for in *that* day thou seest my face thou shalt die.

29 And Moses said, Thou hast spoken well, ªI will see thy face again no more.

## Center column references

10:14 ᵇ Joel 1:4,
7; 2:1–11; Rev. 9:3
¹ *severe*
10:15 ª Ex. 10:5
ᵇ Ps. 105:35
10:16 ª Ex. 8:8
ᵇ Ex. 9:27
10:17 ª Ex. 8:8, 28;
9:28; 1 Kin. 13:6
¹ *pray to*
10:18 ª Ex. 8:30
10:19 ª Joel 2:20
¹ *territory*
10:20 ª Ex. 4:21;
10:1; 11:10
10:21 ª Ex. 9:22
¹ Lit. *that one may feel the darkness*
10:22 ª Ps. 105:28;
Rev. 16:10 ᵇ Ex. 3:18
10:23 ª Ex. 8:22, 23
10:24 ª Ex. 8:8, 25;
10:8 ᵇ Ex. 10:10
10:25 ¹ Lit. *into our hands*
10:26 ª Ex. 10:9
10:27 ª Ex. 4:21;
10:1, 20; 14:4, 8
10:28 ª Ex. 10:11
10:29 ª Ex. 11:8;
Heb. 11:27

11:1 ª Ex. 12:31, 33,
39 ᵇ Ex. 6:1; 12:39
11:2 ª Ex. 3:22;
12:35, 36 ¹ *ask*
11:3 ª Ex. 3:21;
12:36; Ps. 106:46
ᵇ Deut. 34:10–12;
2 Sam. 7:9; Esth. 9:4
11:4 ª Ex. 12:12,
23, 29
11:5 ª Ex. 4:23;
12:12, 29; Ps. 78:51;
105:36; 135:8;
136:10; Amos 4:10
11:6 ª Ex. 12:30;
Amos 5:17 ᵇ Ex. 10:14
11:7 ª Ex. 8:22
ᵇ Josh. 10:21 ¹ Lit. *sharpen*
11:8 ª Ex. 12:31–33
ᵇ Heb. 11:27
11:9 ª Ex. 3:19; 7:4;
10:1 ᵇ Ex. 7:3; 9:16
11:10 ª Rom. 2:5
12:2 ª Deut. 16:1
12:3 ª Josh. 4:19

## The Plague of Darkness

### CHAPTER 11

AND the LORD said unto Moses, Yet will I bring one plague *more* upon Pharaoh, and upon Egypt; ªafterwards he will let you go hence: ᵇwhen he shall let *you* go, he shall surely thrust you out hence altogether.

2 Speak now in the ears of the people, and let every man ¹borrow of his neighbour, and every woman of her neighbour, ªjewels of silver, and jewels of gold.

3 ªAnd the LORD gave the people favour in the sight of the Egyptians. Moreover the man ᵇMoses *was* very great in the land of Egypt, in the sight of Pharaoh's servants, and in the sight of the people.

4 And Moses said, Thus saith the LORD, ªAbout midnight will I go out into the midst of Egypt:

5 And ªall the firstborn in the land of Egypt shall die, from the firstborn of Pharaoh that sitteth upon his throne, even unto the firstborn of the maidservant that *is* behind the mill; and all the firstborn of beasts.

6 ªAnd there shall be a great cry throughout all the land of Egypt, ᵇsuch as there was none like it, nor shall be like it any more.

7 ªBut against any of the children of Israel ᵇshall not a dog ¹move his tongue, against man or beast: that ye may know how that the LORD doth put a difference between the Egyptians and Israel.

8 And ªall these thy servants shall come down unto me, and bow down themselves unto me, saying, Get thee out, and all the people that follow thee: and after that I will go out. ᵇAnd he went out from Pharaoh in a great anger.

9 And the LORD said unto Moses, ªPharaoh shall not hearken unto you; that ᵇmy wonders may be multiplied in the land of Egypt.

10 And Moses and Aaron did all these wonders before Pharaoh: ªand the LORD hardened Pharaoh's heart, so that he would not let the children of Israel go out of his land.

### CHAPTER 12

AND the LORD spake unto Moses and Aaron in the land of Egypt, saying,

2 ªThis month *shall be* unto you the beginning of months: it *shall be* the first month of the year to you.

3 Speak ye unto all the congregation of Israel, saying, In the ªtenth *day* of this month they shall take to them every man a lamb, according to the house of *their* fathers, a lamb for an house:

4 And if the household be too little for the lamb, let him and his neighbour

next unto his house take *it* according to the number of the 'souls; every man according to his eating shall make your count for the lamb.

5 Your lamb shall be ªwithout¹ blemish, a male ²of the first year: ye shall take *it* out from the sheep, or from the goats:

6 And ye shall keep it up until the ªfourteenth day of the same month: and the whole assembly of the congregation of Israel shall kill it in the evening.

7 And they shall take of the blood, and strike *it* on the two side posts and on the upper door post of the houses, wherein they shall eat it.

8 And they shall eat the flesh in that ªnight, ᵇroast with fire, and ᶜunleavened bread; *and* with bitter *herbs* they shall eat it.

9 Eat not of it raw, nor ¹sodden at all with water, but ªroast *with* fire; his head with his legs, and with the ²purtenance thereof.

10 ªAnd ye shall let nothing of it remain until the morning; and that which remaineth of it until the morning ye shall burn with fire.

11 And thus shall ye eat it; *with* ¹your loins girded, your shoes on your feet, and your staff in your hand; and ye shall eat it in haste: ªit *is* the LORD's passover.

12 For I ªwill pass through the land of Egypt this night, and will smite all the firstborn in the land of Egypt, both man and beast; and ᵇagainst all the gods of Egypt I will execute judgment: ᶜI *am* the LORD.

13 And the blood shall be to you for a ¹token upon the houses where ye *are:* and when I see the blood, I will pass over you, and the plague shall not be upon you to destroy *you,* when I smite the land of Egypt.

14 And this day shall be unto you ªfor a memorial; and ye shall keep it a ᵇfeast to the LORD throughout your generations; ye shall keep it a feast ᶜby an ordinance for ever.

15 ªSeven days shall ye eat unleavened bread; even the first day ye shall put away leaven out of your houses: for whosoever eateth leavened bread from the first day until the seventh day, ᵇthat ¹soul shall be ²cut off from Israel.

16 And in the first day *there shall be* ªan holy convocation, and in the seventh day there shall be an holy convocation to you; no manner of work shall be done in them, ¹save *that* which every man must eat, that only may be done of you.

17 And ye shall observe *the feast of* unleavened bread; for ªin this selfsame day have I brought your ¹armies ᵇout of the land of Egypt: therefore

shall ye observe this day ²in your generations by an ordinance for ever.

18 ªIn the first *month,* on the fourteenth day of the month at even, ye shall eat unleavened bread, until the one and twentieth day of the month at even.

19 ªSeven days shall there be no leaven found in your houses: for whosoever eateth that which is leavened, even that ¹soul shall be cut off from the congregation of Israel, whether he be a stranger, or born in the land.

20 Ye shall eat nothing leavened; in all your habitations shall ye eat unleavened bread.

21 Then ªMoses called for all the ᵇelders of Israel, and said unto them, ᶜDraw out and take you a lamb according to your families, and kill the passover.

22 ªAnd ye shall take a bunch of hyssop, and dip *it* in the blood that *is* in the bason, and ᵇstrike the lintel and the two side posts with the blood that *is* in the bason; and none of you shall go out at the door of his house until the morning.

23 ªFor the LORD will pass through to smite the Egyptians; and when he seeth the ᵇblood upon the ¹lintel, and on the two side posts, the LORD will pass over the door, and ᶜwill not suffer ᵈthe destroyer to come in unto your houses to smite *you.*

24 And ye shall ªobserve this thing for an ordinance to thee and to thy sons for ever.

25 And it shall come to pass, when ye be come to the land which the LORD will give you, ªaccording as he hath promised, that ye shall keep this service.

26 ªAnd it shall come to pass, when your children shall say unto you, What mean ye by this service?

27 That ye shall say, ªIt *is* the sacrifice of the LORD's passover, who passed over the houses of the children of Israel in Egypt, when he smote the Egyptians, and delivered our houses. And the people ᵇbowed the head and worshipped.

28 And the children of Israel went away, and ªdid as the LORD had commanded Moses and Aaron, so did they.

29 ªAnd it came to pass, that at midnight ᵇthe LORD smote all the firstborn in the land of Egypt, from the firstborn of Pharaoh that sat on his throne unto the firstborn of the captive that *was* ¹in the dungeon; and all the firstborn of ᶜcattle.

30 And Pharaoh rose up in the night, he, and all his servants, and all the Egyptians; and there was a great cry in Egypt; for *there was* not a house where *there was* not one dead.

---

**Center column references:**

12:4 ¹ *persons*
12:5 ª [1 Pet. 1:19]
¹ *perfect or sound*
² *a year old*
12:6 ª Lev. 23:5
12:8 ª Num. 9:12   ᵇ Deut. 16:7
ᶜ 1 Cor. 5:8
12:9 ª Deut. 16:7
¹ *boiled* ² *entrails*
12:10 ª Ex. 16:19; 23:18; 34:25
12:11 ª Ex. 12:13, 21, 27, 43  ¹ *a belt on your waist*
12:12 ª Ex. 11:4, 5  ᵇ Num. 33:4
ᶜ Ex. 6:2
12:13 ¹ *sign*
12:14 ª Ex. 13:9
ᵇ Lev. 23:4, 5  ᶜ Ex. 12:17, 24; 13:10
12:15 ª Lev. 23:6
ᵇ Gen. 17:14  ¹ *person* ² *put away*
12:16 ª Lev. 23:2, 7, 8  ¹ *except*
12:17 ª Ex. 12:14; 13:3, 10  ᵇ Num. 33:1  ¹ *hosts*

² *throughout*
12:18 ª Lev. 23:5–8
12:19 ª Ex. 12:15; 23:15; 34:18
¹ *person*
12:21 ª [Heb. 11:28]  ᵇ Ex. 3:16
ᶜ Num. 9:4
12:22 ª Heb. 11:28
ᵇ Ex. 12:7
12:23 ª Ex. 11:4; 12:12, 13  ᵇ Ex. 24:8  ᶜ Rev. 7:3; 9:4  ᵈ Heb. 11:28
¹ Crosspiece at top of door
12:24 ª Ex. 12:14, 17; 13:5, 10
12:25 ª Ex. 3:8, 17
12:26 ª Ex. 10:2; 13:8, 14, 15
12:27 ª Ex. 12:11
ᵇ Ex. 4:31
12:28 ª [Heb. 11:28]
12:29 ª Ex. 11:4, 5  ᵇ Num. 8:17; 33:4  ᶜ Ex. 9:6  ¹ *in prison*

---

**31** And he [a]called for Moses and Aaron by night, and said, Rise up, *and* get you forth from among my people, [b]both ye and the children of Israel; and go, serve the LORD, as ye have [c]said.

**32** [a]Also take your flocks and your herds, as ye have said, and be gone; and bless me also.

**33** [a]And the Egyptians were [b]urgent upon the people, that they might send them out of the land in haste; for they said, We *be* all dead *men.*

**34** And the people took their dough before it was leavened, their [1]kneadingtroughs being bound up in their clothes upon their shoulders.

**35** And the children of Israel did according to the word of Moses; and they [1]borrowed of the Egyptians [a]jewels of silver, and jewels of gold, and raiment:

**36** [a]And the LORD gave the people favour in the sight of the Egyptians, so that they [1]lent unto them *such things as they* [2]*required.* And [b]they [3]spoiled the Egyptians.

**37** And [a]the children of Israel journeyed from [b]Rameses to Succoth, about [c]six hundred thousand on foot *that were* men, beside children.

**38** And a [a]mixed multitude went up also with them; and flocks, and herds, *even* very much [b]cattle.

**39** And they baked unleavened cakes of the dough which they brought forth out of Egypt, for it was not leavened; because [a]they were thrust out of Egypt, and could not tarry, neither had they prepared for themselves any victual.

**40** Now the [1]sojourning of the children of Israel, who dwelt in Egypt, *was* [a]four hundred and thirty years.

**41** And it came to pass at the end of the four hundred and thirty years, even the selfsame day it came to pass, that [a]all the hosts of the LORD went out from the land of Egypt.

**42** It *is* [a]a [1]night to be much observed unto the LORD for bringing them out from the land of Egypt: this *is* that night of the LORD to be observed of all the children of Israel in their generations.

**43** And the LORD said unto Moses and Aaron, This *is* [a]the ordinance of the passover: There shall no stranger eat thereof:

**44** But every man's servant that is bought for money, when thou hast [a]circumcised him, then shall he eat thereof.

**45** [a]A foreigner and an hired servant shall not eat thereof.

**46** In one house shall it be eaten; thou shalt not carry forth ought of the flesh abroad out of the house; [a]neither shall ye break a bone thereof.

**47** [a]All the congregation of Israel shall keep it.

**48** And [a]when a stranger shall [1]sojourn with thee, and will keep the passover to the LORD, let all his males be circumcised, and then let him come near and keep it; and he shall be as one that is born in the land: for no uncircumcised person shall eat thereof.

**49** [a]One law shall be to him that is homeborn, and unto the stranger that [1]sojourneth among you.

**50** Thus did all the children of Israel; as the LORD commanded Moses and Aaron, so did they.

**51** [a]And it came to pass the selfsame day, *that* the LORD did bring the children of Israel out of the land of Egypt [b]by their armies.

## CHAPTER 13

**A**ND the LORD spake unto Moses, saying,

**2** [a]Sanctify[1] unto me all the firstborn, whatsoever openeth the womb among the children of Israel, *both* of man and of beast: it *is* mine.

**3** And Moses said unto the people, [a]Remember this day, in which ye came out from Egypt, out of the house of [1]bondage; for [b]by strength of hand the LORD brought you out from this *place:* [c]there shall no leavened bread be eaten.

**4** [a]This day came ye out in the month Abib.

**5** And it shall be when the LORD shall [a]bring thee into the [b]land of the Canaanites, and the Hittites, and the Amorites, and the Hivites, and the Jebusites, which he [c]sware unto thy fathers to give thee, a land flowing with milk and honey, [d]that thou shalt keep this service in this month.

**6** [a]Seven days thou shalt eat unleavened bread, and in the seventh day *shall be* a feast to the LORD.

**7** Unleavened bread shall be eaten seven days; and there shall [a]no leavened bread be seen with thee, neither shall there be leaven seen with thee in all thy quarters.

**8** And thou shalt [a]shew thy son in that day, saying, This *is done* because of that *which* the LORD did unto me when I came forth out of Egypt.

**9** And it shall be for [a]a sign unto thee upon thine hand, and for a memorial between thine eyes, that the LORD's law may be in thy mouth: for with a strong hand hath the LORD brought thee out of Egypt.

**10** [a]Thou shalt therefore keep this [1]ordinance in his season from year to year.

**11** And it shall be when the LORD shall [a]bring thee into the land of the [b]Canaanites, as he sware unto thee

### Center reference column

12:31 [a] Ex. 10:28, 29 [b] Ex. 8:25; 11:1 [c] Ex. 10:9
12:32 [a] Ex. 10:9, 26
12:33 [a] Ex. 10:7 [b] Ps. 105:38
12:34 [1] *dough*
12:35 [a] Ex. 3:21, 22; 11:2, 3 [1] *asked from*
12:36 [a] Ex. 3:21 [b] Gen. 15:14 [1] *granted* [2] *requested* [3] *plundered*
12:37 [a] Num. 33:3, 5 [b] Gen. 47:11 [c] Ex. 38:26
12:38 [a] Num. 11:4 [b] Deut. 3:19
12:39 [a] Ex. 6:1; 11:1; 12:31–33
12:40 [a] Acts 7:6 [1] *time of stay*
12:41 [a] Ex. 3:8, 10; 6:6; 7:4
12:42 [a] Deut. 16:1, 6 [1] *night of vigil*
12:43 [a] Num. 9:14
12:44 [a] Gen. 17:12, 13
12:45 [a] Lev. 22:10
12:46 [a] [John 19:33, 36]
12:47 [a] Ex. 12:6
12:48 [a] Num. 9:14 [1] *stay for a while*
12:49 [a] Num. 15:15, 16 [1] *stays temporarily*
12:51 [a] Ex. 12:41; 20:2 [b] Ex. 6:26
13:2 [a] Luke 2:23 [1] *Set apart*
13:3 [a] Deut. 16:3 [b] Ex. 3:20; 6:1 [c] Ex. 12:8, 19 [1] Lit. *slaves*
13:4 [a] Ex. 12:2; 23:15; 34:18
13:5 [a] Ex. 3:8, 17 [b] Gen. 17:8 [c] Ex. 6:8 [d] Ex. 12:25, 26
13:6 [a] Ex. 12:15–20
13:7 [a] Ex. 12:19
13:8 [a] Ex. 10:2; 12:26; 13:14
13:9 [a] Deut. 6:8; 11:18
13:10 [a] Ex. 12:14, 24 [1] *regulation*
13:11 [a] Ex. 13:5 [b] Num. 21:3

and to thy fathers, and shall give it thee,

12 ªThat thou shalt ¹set apart unto the LORD all that openeth the ²matrix, and every firstling that cometh of a beast which thou hast; the males *shall be* the LORD's.

13 And ªevery firstling of an ass thou shalt redeem with a lamb; and if thou wilt not redeem it, then thou shalt break his neck: and all the firstborn of man among thy children ᵇshalt thou redeem.

14 ªAnd it shall be when thy son asketh thee in time to come, saying, What *is* this? that thou shalt say unto him, ᵇBy strength of hand the LORD brought us out from Egypt, from the house of bondage:

15 And it came to pass, when Pharaoh would hardly let us go, that ªthe LORD slew all the firstborn in the land of Egypt, both the firstborn of man, and the firstborn of beast: therefore I sacrifice to the LORD all that openeth the matrix, being males; but all the firstborn of my children I redeem.

16 And it shall be for ªa token upon thine hand, and for frontlets between thine eyes: for by strength of hand the LORD brought us forth out of Egypt.

17 And it came to pass, when Pharaoh had let the people go, that God led them not *through* the way of the land of the Philistines, although that *was* near; for God said, Lest peradventure the people ªrepent¹ when they see war, and ᵇthey return to Egypt:

18 But God ªled the people about, *through* the way of the wilderness of the Red sea: and the children of Israel went up ¹harnessed out of the land of Egypt.

19 And Moses took the ªbones of ᵇJoseph with him: for he had ¹straitly sworn the children of Israel, saying, ᶜGod will surely ²visit you; and ye shall carry up my bones away hence with you.

20 And ªthey took their journey from ᵇSuccoth, and encamped in Etham, in the edge of the wilderness.

21 And ªthe LORD went before them by day in a pillar of a cloud, to lead them the way; and by night in a pillar of fire, to give them light; to go by day and night:

22 He took not away the pillar of the cloud by day, nor the pillar of fire by night, *from* before the people.

## CHAPTER 14

AND the LORD spake unto Moses, saying,

2 Speak unto the children of Israel, ªthat they turn and encamp before

ᵇPi-hahiroth, between ᶜMigdol and the sea, over against Baal-zephon: before it shall ye encamp by the sea.

3 For Pharaoh will say of the children of Israel, ªThey *are* entangled in the land, the wilderness hath shut them in.

4 And ªI will harden Pharaoh's heart, that he shall follow after them; and I ᵇwill be honoured upon Pharaoh, and upon all his host; ᶜthat the Egyptians may know that I *am* the LORD. And they did so.

5 And it was told the king of Egypt that the people fled: and ªthe heart of Pharaoh and of his servants was turned against the people, and they said, Why have we done this, that we have let Israel go from serving us?

6 And he ¹made ready his chariot, and took his people with him:

7 And he took ªsix hundred chosen chariots, and all the chariots of Egypt, and captains over every one of them.

8 And the LORD ªhardened the heart of Pharaoh king of Egypt, and he pursued after the children of Israel: and ᵇthe children of Israel went out with an high hand.

9 But the ªEgyptians pursued after them, all the horses *and* chariots of Pharaoh, and his horsemen, and his army, and overtook them encamping by the sea, beside Pi-hahiroth, before Baal-zephon.

10 And when Pharaoh drew nigh, the children of Israel lifted up their eyes, and, behold, the Egyptians marched after them; and they were ¹sore afraid: and the children of Israel ªcried out unto the LORD.

11 ªAnd they said unto Moses, Because *there were* no graves in Egypt, hast thou taken us away to die in the wilderness? wherefore hast thou dealt thus with us, to carry us forth out of Egypt?

12 ª*Is* not this the word that we did tell thee in Egypt, saying, Let us alone, that we may serve the Egyptians? For *it had been* better for us to serve the Egyptians, than that we should die in the wilderness.

13 And Moses said unto the people, ªFear ye not, ᵇstand still, and see the ᶜsalvation¹ of the LORD, which he will shew to you to day: for the Egyptians whom ye have seen to day, ye shall ᵈsee them again no more for ever.

14 ªThe LORD shall fight for you, and ye ¹shall ᵇhold your peace.

15 And the LORD said unto Moses, Wherefore criest thou unto me? speak unto the children of Israel, that they go forward:

16 But ªlift thou up thy rod, and stretch out thine hand over the sea, and divide it: and the children of Israel

### Center column references

13:12 ª Lev. 27:26 ¹ Lit. *cause to pass over* ² *womb*
13:13 ª Ex. 34:20 ᵇ Num. 3:46, 47; 18:15, 16
13:14 ª Deut. 6:20 ᵇ Ex. 13:3, 9
13:15 ª Ex. 12:29
13:16 ª Ex. 13:9
13:17 ª Ex. 14:11 ᵇ Deut. 17:16 ¹ *change their minds*
13:18 ª Num. 33:6 ¹ *in orderly ranks*
13:19 ª Gen. 50:24, 25 ᵇ Ex. 1:6; Deut. 33:13–17 ᶜ Ex. 4:31 ¹ *placed under solemn oath* ² *pay attention to*
13:20 ª Num. 33:6–8 ᵇ Ex. 12:37
13:21 ª Deut. 1:33
14:2 ª Ex. 13:18

ᵇ Num. 33:7 ᶜ Jer. 44:1
14:3 ª Ps. 71:11
14:4 ª Ex. 4:21; 7:3; 14:17 ᵇ Ex. 9:16; 14:17, 18, 23 ᶜ Ex. 7:5; 14:25
14:5 ª Ps. 105:25
14:6 ¹ Lit. *harnessed*
14:7 ª Ex. 15:4
14:8 ª Ex. 14:4 ᵇ Num. 33:3
14:9 ª Josh. 24:6
14:10 ª Neh. 9:9 ¹ *very*
14:11 ª Ps. 106:7, 8
14:12 ª Ex. 5:21; 6:9
14:13 ª 2 Chr. 20:15, 17 ᵇ Ps. 46:10, 11 ᶜ Ex. 14:30; 15:2 ᵈ Deut. 28:68 ¹ *deliverance*
14:14 ª Deut. 1:30; 3:22 ᵇ [Is. 30:15] ¹ *be quiet*
14:16 ª Num. 20:8, 9, 11

shall go on dry *ground* through the midst of the sea.

17 And I, behold, I will ªharden the hearts of the Egyptians, and they shall follow them: and I will ᵇget¹ me honour upon Pharaoh, and upon all his host, upon his chariots, and upon his horsemen.

18 And the Egyptians shall know that I *am* the LORD, when I have gotten me honour upon Pharaoh, upon his chariots, and upon his horsemen.

19 And the angel of God, ªwhich went before the camp of Israel, removed and went behind them; and the pillar of the cloud went from before their face, and stood behind them:

20 And it came between the camp of the Egyptians and the camp of Israel; and it was a cloud and darkness *to them,* but it gave light by night *to these:* so that the one came not near the other all the night.

21 And Moses stretched out his hand over the sea; and the LORD caused the sea to go *back* by a strong east wind all that night, and ªmade the sea dry *land,* and the waters were ᵇdivided.

22 And ªthe children of Israel went into the midst of the sea upon the dry *ground:* and the waters *were* ᵇa wall unto them on their right hand, and on their left.

23 And the Egyptians pursued, and went in after them to the midst of the sea, *even* all Pharaoh's horses, his chariots, and his horsemen.

24 And it came to pass, that in the morning ªwatch ᵇthe LORD looked unto the host of the Egyptians through the pillar of fire and of the cloud, and ¹troubled the host of the Egyptians,

25 And took off their chariot wheels, that they drave them heavily: so that the Egyptians said, Let us flee from the face of Israel; for the LORD ªfighteth for them against the Egyptians.

26 And the LORD said unto Moses, Stretch out thine hand over the sea, that the waters may come again upon the Egyptians, upon their chariots, and upon their horsemen.

27 And Moses stretched forth his hand over the sea, and the sea ªreturned ¹to his strength when the morning appeared; and the Egyptians fled against it; and the LORD ᵇoverthrew² the Egyptians in the midst of the sea.

28 And the waters returned, and ªcovered the chariots, and the horsemen, *and* all the host of Pharaoh that came into the sea after them; there remained not so much as one of them.

29 But ªthe children of Israel walked upon dry *land* in the midst of the sea; and the waters *were* a wall unto them on their right hand, and on their left.

30 Thus the LORD ªsaved¹ Israel that day out of the hand of the Egyptians; and Israel ᵇsaw the Egyptians dead upon the sea shore.

31 And Israel saw that great ¹work which the LORD did upon the Egyptians: and the people ²feared the LORD, and ªbelieved the LORD, and his servant Moses.

## CHAPTER 15

THEN sang ªMoses and the children of Israel this song unto the LORD, and spake, saying, I will ᵇsing unto the LORD, for he hath triumphed gloriously: the horse and his rider hath he thrown into the sea.

2 The LORD *is* my strength and ªsong, and he is become my salvation: he *is* my God, and I will ᵇprepare¹ him an habitation; my ᶜfather's God, and I ᵈwill exalt him.

3 The LORD *is* a man of ªwar: the LORD *is* his ᵇname.

4 ªPharaoh's chariots and his host hath he cast into the sea: ᵇhis chosen captains also are drowned in the Red sea.

5 The depths have covered them: ªthey sank into the bottom as a stone.

6 ªThy right hand, O LORD, is become glorious in power: thy right hand, O LORD, hath dashed in pieces the enemy.

7 And in the greatness of thine ªexcellency thou hast overthrown them that rose up against thee: thou sentest forth thy ᵇwrath, *which* ᶜconsumed them ᵈas stubble.

8 And ªwith the blast of thy nostrils the waters were gathered together, ᵇthe floods stood upright as an heap, *and* the depths ¹were congealed in the heart of the sea.

9 ªThe enemy said, I will pursue, I will overtake, I will ᵇdivide the spoil; my lust shall be satisfied upon them; I will draw my sword, my hand shall destroy them.

10 Thou didst blow with thy wind, the sea covered them: they sank as lead in the mighty waters.

11 ªWho *is* like unto thee, O LORD, among the ¹gods? who *is* like thee, ᵇglorious in holiness, fearful *in* ᶜpraises, ᵈdoing wonders?

12 Thou stretchedst out thy right hand, the earth swallowed them.

13 Thou in thy mercy hast ªled forth the people *which* thou hast redeemed: thou hast guided *them* in thy strength unto ᵇthy holy habitation.

14 ªThe people shall hear, *and* be afraid: ᵇsorrow¹ shall take hold on the inhabitants of ²Palestina.

14:17 ª Ex. 14:8
ᵇ Ex. 14:4 ¹ *gain honour over*

14:19 ª [Is. 63:9]

14:21 ª Ps. 66:6;
106:9; 136:13, 14
ᵇ Is. 63:12, 13

14:22 ª Ex. 15:19
ᵇ Ex. 14:29; 15:8

14:24 ª Judg.
7:19 ᵇ Ex. 13:21
¹ *confused*

14:25 ª Ex. 7:5;
14:4, 14, 18

14:27 ª Josh. 4:18
ᵇ Ex. 15:1, 7 ¹ *to its full depth* ² Lit. *shook off*

14:28 ª Ps. 78:53;
106:11

14:29 ª Ps. 66:6;
78:52, 53

14:30 ª Ps. 106:8,
10 ᵇ Ps. 58:10;
59:10 ¹ *delivered*

14:31 ª John 2:11;
11:45 ¹ Lit. *hand with which the LORD worked against* ² *stood in awe of*

15:1 ª Ps. 106:12
ᵇ Is. 12:1–6

15:2 ª Is. 12:2
ᵇ Gen. 28:21, 22
ᶜ Ex. 3:6, 15, 16
ᵈ Is. 25:1 ¹ *praise him*

15:3 ª Rev. 19:11
ᵇ Ps. 24:8; 83:18

15:4 ª Ex. 14:28
ᵇ Ex. 14:7

15:5 ª Neh. 9:11

15:6 ª Ps. 17:7;
118:15

15:7 ª Deut. 33:26
ᵇ Ps. 78:49, 50
ᶜ Ps. 59:13 ᵈ Is.
5:24

15:8 ª Ex. 14:21,
22, 29 ᵇ Ps. 78:13
¹ *became firm*

15:9 ª Judg. 5:30
ᵇ Is. 53:12

15:11 ª 1 Kin. 8:23
ᵇ Is. 6:3 ᶜ 1 Chr.
16:25 ᵈ Ps. 77:11,
14 ¹ *mighty ones*

15:13 ª [Ps. 77:20]
ᵇ Ps. 78:54

15:14 ª Josh.
2:9 ᵇ Ps. 48:6
¹ *anguish* ² Or *Philistia*

15 [a]Then [b]the dukes of Edom shall be amazed; [c]the mighty men of Moab, trembling shall take hold upon them; [d]all the inhabitants of Canaan shall [e]melt away.

16 [a]Fear and dread shall fall upon them; by the greatness of thine arm they shall be [b]*as* still as a stone; till thy people pass over, O LORD, till the people pass over, [c]*which* thou hast purchased.

17 Thou shalt bring them in, and [a]plant them in the [b]mountain of thine inheritance, *in* the place, O LORD, *which* thou hast made for thee to dwell in, *in* the [c]Sanctuary, O Lord, *which* thy hands have established.

18 [a]The LORD shall reign for ever and ever.

19 For the [a]horse of Pharaoh went in with his chariots and with his horsemen into the sea, and [b]the LORD brought again the waters of the sea upon them; but the children of Israel went on dry *land* in the midst of the sea.

20 And Miriam [a]the prophetess, [b]the sister of Aaron, [c]took a timbrel in her hand; and all the women went out after her [d]with timbrels and with dances.

21 And Miriam [a]answered them, [b]Sing ye to the LORD, for he hath triumphed gloriously; the horse and his rider hath he thrown into the sea.

22 So Moses brought Israel from the Red sea, and they went out into the wilderness of [a]Shur; and they went three days in the wilderness, and found no [b]water.

23 And when they came to [a]Marah, they could not drink of the waters of Marah, for they *were* bitter: therefore the name of it was called [1]Marah.

24 And the people [a]murmured against Moses, saying, What shall we drink?

25 And he cried unto the LORD; and the LORD shewed him a tree, [a]*which* when he had cast into the waters, the waters were made sweet: there he [b]made for them a statute and an [1]ordinance, and there [c]he [2]proved them,

26 And said, [a]If thou wilt diligently hearken to the voice of the LORD thy God, and wilt do that which is right in his sight, and wilt give ear to his commandments, and keep all his statutes, I will put none of these [b]diseases upon thee, which I have brought upon the Egyptians: for I *am* the LORD [c]that healeth thee.

27 [a]And they came to Elim, where *were* twelve wells of water, and threescore and ten palm trees: and they encamped there by the waters.

## CHAPTER 16

AND they [a]took their journey from Elim, and all the congregation of

the children of Israel came unto the wilderness of Sin, which *is* between Elim and [b]Sinai, on the fifteenth day of the second month after their departing out of the land of Egypt.

2 And the whole congregation of the children of Israel [a]murmured[1] against Moses and Aaron in the wilderness:

3 And the children of Israel said unto them, [a]Would to God we had died by the hand of the LORD in the land of Egypt, [b]when we sat by the [1]flesh pots, *and* when we did eat bread to the full; for ye have brought us forth into this wilderness, to kill this whole assembly with hunger.

4 Then said the LORD unto Moses, Behold, I will rain [a]bread from heaven for you; and the people shall go out and gather [1]a certain rate every day, that I may [b]prove[2] them, whether they will [c]walk in my law, or no.

5 And it shall come to pass, that on the sixth day they shall prepare *that* which they bring in; and [a]it shall be twice as much as they gather daily.

6 And Moses and Aaron said unto all the children of Israel, [a]At even, then ye shall know that the LORD hath brought you out from the land of Egypt:

7 And in the morning, then ye shall see [a]the glory of the LORD; for that he [b]heareth your [1]murmurings against the LORD: and [c]what *are* we, that ye murmur against us?

8 And Moses said, *This shall be,* when the LORD shall give you in the evening flesh to eat, and in the morning bread to the full; for that the LORD heareth your murmurings which ye [1]murmur against him: and what *are* we? your murmurings *are* not against us, but [a]against the LORD.

9 And Moses spake unto Aaron, Say unto all the congregation of the children of Israel, [a]Come near before the LORD: for he hath heard your [1]murmurings.

10 And it came to pass, as Aaron spake unto the whole congregation of the children of Israel, that they looked toward the wilderness, and, behold, the glory of the LORD [a]appeared in the cloud.

11 And the LORD spake unto Moses, saying,

12 [a]I have heard the [1]murmurings of the children of Israel: speak unto them, saying, [b]At even ye shall eat flesh, and [c]in the morning ye shall be filled with bread; and ye shall know that I *am* the LORD your God.

13 And it came to pass, that at even [a]the quails came up, and covered the camp: and in the morning [b]the dew lay round about the host.

### Center reference column

15:15 [a] Gen. 36:15, 40 [b] Deut. 2:4
[c] Num. 22:3, 4
[d] Josh. 5:1 [e] Josh. 2:9–11, 24

15:16 [a] Josh. 2:9
[b] 1 Sam. 25:37
[c] Jer. 31:11

15:17 [a] Ps. 44:2; 80:8, 15 [b] Ps. 2:6; 78:54, 68
[c] Ps. 68:16; 76:2; 132:13, 14

15:18 [a] Is. 57:15
15:19 [a] Ex. 14:23
[b] Ex. 14:28

15:20 [a] Judg. 4:4
[b] Num. 26:59
[c] 1 Sam. 18:6
[d] Judg. 11:34; 21:21

15:21 [a] 1 Sam. 18:7
[b] Ex. 15:1

15:22 [a] Gen. 16:7; 20:1; 25:18
[b] Num. 20:2

15:23 [a] Num. 33:8
[1] Lit. *Bitter*

15:24 [a] Ex. 14:11; 16:2

15:25 [a] 2 Kin. 2:21 [b] Josh. 24:25 [c] Deut. 8:2, 16 [1] *regulation*
[2] *tested*

15:26 [a] Deut. 7:12, 15 [b] Deut. 28:27, 58, 60 [c] Ex. 23:25

15:27 [a] Num. 33:9

16:1 [a] Num. 33:10, 11 [b] Ex. 12:6, 51; 19:1

16:2 [a] 1 Cor. 10:10
[1] *grumbled*

16:3 [a] Lam. 4:9
[1] *pots of meat*

16:4 [a] [John 6:31–35] [b] Ex. 15:25; Deut. 8:2, 16 [c] Judg. 2:22
[1] Lit. *the portion of a day in its day*
[2] *test*

16:5 [a] Ex. 16:22, 29; Lev. 25:21

16:6 [a] Ex. 6:7

16:7 [a] Ex. 16:10, 12; Is. 35:2; 40:5; John 11:4, 40
[b] Num. 14:27;
17:5 [c] Num. 16:11
[1] *grumblings*

16:8 [a] 1 Sam. 8:7; Luke 10:16; [Rom. 13:2]; 1 Thess. 4:8
[1] *grumble*

16:9 [a] Num. 16:16
[1] *grumblings*

16:10 [a] Ex. 13:21; 16:7; Num. 16:19; 1 Kin. 8:10

16:12 [a] Ex. 16:8; Num. 14:27 [b] Ex. 16:6 [c] Ex. 16:7;
1 Kin. 20:28; Joel 3:17 [1] *grumblings*

16:13 [a] Num. 11:31; Ps. 78:27–29; 105:40 [b] Num. 11:9

14 And when the dew that lay was gone up, behold, upon the face of the wilderness _there lay_ a small round [a]thing, _as_ small as the [b]hoar frost on the ground.

15 And when the children of Israel saw _it,_ they said one to another, [1]It _is_ manna: for they [2]wist not what it _was._ And Moses said unto them, [a]This _is_ the bread which the LORD hath given you to eat.

16 This _is_ the thing which the LORD hath commanded, Gather of it every man [a]according to his eating, an [b]omer for every man, _according to_ the number of your persons; take ye every man for _them_ which _are_ in his tents.

17 And the children of Israel did so, and gathered, some more, some less.

18 And when they did [1]mete _it_ with an omer, [a]he that gathered much had nothing over, and he that gathered little had no lack; they gathered every man according to his eating.

19 And Moses said, Let no man [a]leave of it till the morning.

20 Notwithstanding they [1]hearkened not unto Moses; but some of them left of it until the morning, and it bred worms, and stank: and Moses was [2]wroth with them.

21 And they gathered it every morning, every man according to his eating: and when the sun waxed hot, it melted.

22 And it came to pass, _that_ on the sixth day they gathered twice as much bread, two omers for one _man:_ and all the rulers of the congregation came and told Moses.

23 And he said unto them, This _is that_ which the LORD hath said, To morrow _is_ [a]the rest of the holy sabbath unto the LORD: bake _that_ which ye will bake _to day,_ and [1]seethe that ye will [1]seethe; and that which remaineth over lay up for you to be kept until the morning.

24 And they laid it up till the morning, as Moses bade: and it did not [a]stink, neither was there any worm therein.

25 And Moses said, Eat that to day; for to day _is_ a sabbath unto the LORD: to day ye shall not find it in the field.

26 [a]Six days ye shall gather it; but on the seventh day, _which is_ the sabbath, in it there shall be none.

27 And it came to pass, _that_ there went out _some_ of the people on the seventh day for to gather, and they found none.

28 And the LORD said unto Moses, How long [a]refuse [1]ye to keep my commandments and my laws?

29 See, for that the LORD hath given you the sabbath, therefore he giveth you on the sixth day the bread of two days; abide ye every man in his place,

let no man go out of his place on the seventh day.

30 So the people rested on the seventh day.

31 And the house of Israel called the name thereof [1]Manna: and [a]it _was_ like coriander seed, white; and the taste of it _was_ like wafers _made_ with honey.

32 And Moses said, This _is_ the thing which the LORD commandeth, Fill an omer of it to be kept for your generations; that they may see the bread wherewith I have fed you in the wilderness, when I brought you forth from the land of Egypt.

33 And Moses said unto Aaron, [a]Take a pot, and put an omer full of manna therein, and lay it up before the LORD, to be kept for your generations.

34 As the LORD commanded Moses, so Aaron laid it up [a]before the Testimony, to be kept.

35 And the children of Israel did [a]eat manna [b]forty years, [c]until they came to a land inhabited; they did eat manna, until they came unto the borders of the land of Canaan.

36 Now an omer _is_ the tenth _part_ of an ephah.

## CHAPTER 17

AND [a]all the congregation of the children of Israel journeyed from the wilderness of [b]Sin, after their journeys, according to the commandment of the LORD, and [1]pitched in Rephidim: and _there was_ no water for the people to [c]drink.

2 [a]Wherefore the people did [1]chide with Moses, and said, Give us water that we may drink. And Moses said unto them, Why chide ye with me? wherefore do ye [b]tempt[2] the LORD?

3 And the people thirsted there for water; and the people [a]murmured against Moses, and said, Wherefore _is_ this _that_ thou hast brought us up out of Egypt, to kill us and our children and our [b]cattle with thirst?

4 And Moses [a]cried unto the LORD, saying, What shall I do unto this people? they be almost ready to [b]stone[1] me.

5 And the LORD said unto Moses, [a]Go on before the people, and take with thee of the elders of Israel; and thy rod, wherewith [b]thou [1]smotest the river, take in thine hand, and go.

6 [a]Behold, I will stand before thee there upon the rock in Horeb; and thou shalt smite the rock, and there shall come water out of it, that the people may drink. And Moses did so in the sight of the elders of Israel.

7 And he called the name of the place [a]Massah,[1] and [2]Meribah, because of the [3]chiding of the children

of Israel, and because they [4]tempted the LORD, saying, Is the LORD among us, or not?

8 [a]Then came Amalek, and fought with Israel in Rephidim.

9 And Moses said unto Joshua, Choose us out men, and go out, fight with Amalek: to morrow I will stand on the top of the hill with [a]the rod of God in mine hand.

10 So Joshua did as Moses had said to him, and fought with Amalek: and Moses, Aaron, and Hur went up to the top of the hill.

11 And it came to pass, when Moses [a]held up his hand, that Israel prevailed: and when he let down his hand, Amalek prevailed.

12 But Moses' hands *were* [1]heavy; and they took a stone, and put *it* under him, and he sat thereon; and Aaron and Hur [2]stayed up his hands, the one on the one side, and the other on the other side; and his hands were steady until the going down of the sun.

13 And Joshua [1]discomfited Amalek and his people with the edge of the sword.

14 And the LORD said unto Moses, [a]Write this *for* a memorial in a book, and rehearse *it* in the ears of Joshua: for [b]I will utterly put out the remembrance of Amalek from under heaven.

15 And Moses built an altar, and called the name of it [1]Jehovah-nissi:

16 For he said, Because [1]the LORD hath [a]sworn *that* the LORD *will have* war with Amalek from generation to generation.

## CHAPTER 18

WHEN [a]Jethro, the priest of Midian, Moses' father in law, heard of all that [b]God had done for Moses, and for Israel his people, *and* that the LORD had brought Israel out of Egypt;

2 Then Jethro, Moses' father in law, took [a]Zipporah, Moses' wife, after he had sent her back,

3 And her [a]two sons; of which the [b]name of the one *was* [1]Gershom; for he said, I have been [2]an alien in a strange land:

4 And the name of the other *was* [1]Eliezer; for the God of my father, *said he, was* mine [a]help, and delivered me from the sword of Pharaoh:

5 And Jethro, Moses' father in law, came with his sons and his wife unto Moses into the wilderness, where he encamped at [a]the mount of God:

6 And he said unto Moses, I thy father in law Jethro am come unto thee, and thy wife, and her two sons with her.

7 And Moses [a]went out to meet his father in law, and did [1]obeisance,

and [b]kissed him; and they asked each other of *their* welfare; and they came into the tent.

8 And Moses told his father in law all that the LORD had done unto Pharaoh and to the Egyptians for Israel's sake, *and* all the [1]travail that had come upon them by the way, and *how* the LORD [a]delivered them.

9 And Jethro rejoiced for all the [a]goodness which the LORD had done to Israel, whom he had delivered out of the hand of the Egyptians.

10 And Jethro said, [a]Blessed *be* the LORD, who hath delivered you out of the hand of the Egyptians, and out of the hand of Pharaoh, who hath delivered the people from under the hand of the Egyptians.

11 Now I know that the LORD *is* [a]greater than all gods: [b]for in the thing wherein they [1]dealt [c]proudly *he was* above them.

12 And Jethro, Moses' father in law, took a burnt [a]offering and sacrifices for God: and Aaron came, and all the elders of Israel, [b]to eat bread with Moses' father in law before God.

13 And it came to pass on the morrow, that Moses [a]sat to judge the people: and the people stood by Moses from the morning unto the evening.

14 And when Moses' father in law saw all that he did to the people, he said, What *is* this thing that thou doest to the people? why [1]sittest thou thyself alone, and all the people stand by thee from morning unto even?

15 And Moses said unto his father in law, Because [a]the people come unto me to enquire of God:

16 When they have [a]a [1]matter, they come unto me; and I judge between one and another, and I do make *them* know the statutes of God, and his laws.

17 And Moses' father in law said unto him, The thing that thou doest *is* not good.

18 Thou wilt surely wear away, both thou, and this people that *is* with thee: for this thing *is* too [1]heavy for thee; [a]thou art not able to perform it thyself alone.

19 Hearken now unto my voice, I will give thee [1]counsel, and God shall be with thee: Be thou for the people to [a]God-ward, that thou mayest [b]bring the causes unto God:

20 And thou shalt [a]teach them ordinances and laws, and shalt shew them the way wherein they must walk, and [b]the work that they must do.

21 Moreover thou shalt provide out of all the people [a]able men, such as [b]fear God, [c]men of truth, [d]hating covetousness; and place *such* over them, *to be* rulers of thousands, *and* rulers

## Cross References

17:7 [4] tested
17:8 [a] Gen. 36:12
17:9 [a] Ex. 4:20
17:11 [a] [James 5:16]
17:12 [1] weary of holding up [2] supported
17:13 [1] defeated
17:14 [a] Ex. 24:4; 34:27 [b] 1 Sam. 15:3
17:15 [1] Heb. YHWH Nissi, The LORD Is My Banner
17:16 [a] Gen. 22:14–16 [1] Lit. a hand is upon the throne of the LORD
18:1 [a] Ex. 2:16, 18; 3:1 [b] [Ps. 106:2, 8]
18:2 [a] Ex. 2:21; 4:20–26
18:3 [a] Acts 7:29 [b] Ex. 2:22 [1] Lit. Sojourner There [2] a stranger in a foreign
18:4 [a] Gen. 49:25 [1] Lit. My God Is Help
18:5 [a] Ex. 3:1, 12; 4:27; 24:13
18:7 [a] Gen. 18:2 [1] bowed down
[b] Ex. 4:27
18:8 [a] Ex. 15:6, 16 [1] hardship
18:9 [a] [Is. 63:7–14]
18:10 [a] Gen. 14:20
18:11 [a] 2 Chr. 2:5 [b] Ex. 1:10, 16, 22; 5:2, 7 [c] Luke 1:51 [1] behaved
18:12 [a] Ex. 24:5 [b] Deut. 12:7
18:13 [a] Matt. 23:2
18:14 [1] do you sit alone as judge
18:15 [a] Lev. 24:12
18:16 [a] Ex. 24:14 [1] difficulty
18:18 [a] Num. 11:14, 17 [1] much
18:19 [a] Ex. 4:16; 20:19 [b] Num. 9:8; 27:5 [1] advice
18:20 [a] Deut. 5:1 [b] Deut. 1:18
18:21 [a] Acts 6:3 [b] 2 Sam. 23:3 [c] Ezek. 18:8 [d] Deut. 16:19

of hundreds, rulers of fifties, and rulers of tens:

22 And let them judge the people at all seasons: [a]and it shall be, *that* every great matter they shall bring unto thee, but every small matter they shall judge: so shall it be easier for thyself, and [b]they shall bear *the burden* with thee.

23 If thou shalt do this thing, and God command thee *so,* then thou shalt be able to endure, and all this people shall also go to their [a]place in peace.

24 So Moses hearkened to the voice of his father in law, and did all that he had said.

25 And [a]Moses chose able men out of all Israel, and made them heads over the people, rulers of thousands, rulers of hundreds, rulers of fifties, and rulers of tens.

26 And they judged the people at all seasons: the [a]hard[1] [2]causes they brought unto Moses, but every small matter they judged themselves.

27 And Moses let his father in law depart; and [a]he went his way into his own land.

## CHAPTER 19

IN the third month, when the children of Israel were gone forth out of the land of Egypt, the same day [a]came they *into* the wilderness of Sinai.

2 For they were departed from [a]Rephidim, and were come *to* the desert of Sinai, and had pitched in the wilderness; and there Israel camped before [b]the mount.

3 And [a]Moses went up unto God, and the LORD [b]called unto him out of the mountain, saying, Thus shalt thou say to the house of Jacob, and tell the children of Israel;

4 [a]Ye have seen what I did unto the Egyptians, and *how* [b]I [1]bare you on eagles' wings, and brought you unto myself.

5 Now [a]therefore, if ye will obey my voice indeed, and [b]keep my covenant, then [c]ye shall be a [1]peculiar treasure unto me above all people: for all the earth *is* [d]mine:

6 And ye shall be unto me a [a]kingdom of priests, and an [b]holy nation. These *are* the words which thou shalt speak unto the children of Israel.

7 And Moses came and called for the [a]elders of the people, and [1]laid before their faces all these words which the LORD commanded him.

8 And [a]all the people answered together, and said, All that the LORD hath spoken we will do. And Moses returned the words of the people unto the LORD.

9 And the LORD said unto Moses, Lo, I come unto thee [a]in a thick cloud,

[b]that the people may hear when I speak with thee, and believe thee for ever. And Moses told the words of the people unto the LORD.

10 And the LORD said unto Moses, Go unto the people, and [a]sanctify[1] them to day and to morrow, and let them wash their clothes,

11 And be ready against the third day: for the third day the LORD will come down in the sight of all the people upon mount Sinai.

12 And thou shalt set bounds unto the people round about, saying, Take heed to yourselves, *that ye* go *not* up into the mount, or touch the border of it: [a]whosoever toucheth the mount shall be surely put to death:

13 There shall not an hand touch it, but he shall surely be stoned, or shot through; whether *it be* beast or man, it shall not live: when the trumpet soundeth long, they shall come up to the mount.

14 And Moses went down from the mount unto the people, and sanctified the people; and they washed their clothes.

15 And he said unto the people, Be ready against the third day: [a]come not [1]at *your* wives.

16 And it came to pass on the third day in the morning, that there were [a]thunders and lightnings, and a thick cloud upon the mount, and the voice of the trumpet exceeding loud; so that all the people that *was* in the camp [b]trembled.[1]

17 And [a]Moses brought forth the people out of the camp to meet with God; and they stood at the nether part of the mount.

18 And [a]mount Sinai was altogether on a smoke, because the LORD descended upon [b]it in fire: [c]and the smoke thereof ascended as the smoke of a furnace, and the [d]whole mount quaked greatly.

19 And when the voice of the trumpet sounded long, and waxed louder and louder, [a]Moses spake, and [b]God answered him by a voice.

20 And the LORD came down upon mount Sinai, on the top of the mount: and the LORD called Moses *up* to the top of the mount; and Moses went up.

21 And the LORD said unto Moses, Go down, [1]charge the people, lest they break through unto the LORD [a]to gaze, and many of them perish.

22 And let the [a]priests also, which come near to the LORD, [b]sanctify[1] themselves, lest the LORD [c]break forth upon them.

23 And Moses said unto the LORD, The people cannot come up to mount Sinai: for thou chargedst us, saying, [a]Set bounds about the mount, and [1]sanctify it.

### Cross references

18:22 [a] Deut. 1:17
[b] Num. 11:17
18:23 [a] Ex. 16:29
18:25 [a] Deut. 1:15
18:26 [a] Job 29:16
[1] *difficult* [2] *cases*
18:27 [a] Num. 10:29, 30
19:1 [a] Num. 33:15
19:2 [a] Ex. 17:1
[b] Ex. 3:1, 12; 18:5
19:3 [a] Acts 7:38
[b] Ex. 3:4
19:4 [a] Deut. 29:2 [b] Is. 63:9
[1] *sustained*
19:5 [a] Ex. 15:26; 23:22 [b] Deut. 5:2
[c] Ps. 135:4 [d] Ex. 9:29 [1] *special*
19:6 [a] [1 Pet. 2:5, 9] [b] Deut. 7:6; 14:21; 26:19
19:7 [a] Ex. 4:29, 30 [1] *set*
19:8 [a] Deut. 5:27; 26:17
19:9 [a] Ex. 19:16; 20:21; 24:15

[b] Deut. 4:12, 36
19:10 [a] Lev. 11:44, 45 [1] *consecrate*
19:12 [a] Heb. 12:20
19:15 [a] [1 Cor. 7:5]
[1] *near to*
19:16 [a] Heb. 12:18, 19 [b] Heb. 12:21
[1] *In awe*
19:17 [a] Deut. 4:10
19:18 [a] Deut. 4:11
[b] Ex. 3:2; 24:17
[c] Gen. 15:17; 19:28 [d] Ps. 68:8
19:19 [a] Heb. 12:21
[b] Ps. 81:7
19:21 [a] 1 Sam. 6:19
[1] *warn*
19:22 [a] Ex. 19:24; 24:5 [1] Lev. 10:3; 21:6–8 [c] 2 Sam. 6:7, 8 [1] *consecrate*
19:23 [a] Ex. 19:12
[1] *set it apart*

24 And the LORD said unto him, Away, get thee down, and thou shalt come up, thou, and Aaron with thee: but let not the priests and the people break through to come up unto the LORD, lest he break forth upon them.

25 So Moses went down unto the people, and spake unto them.

## CHAPTER 20

AND God spake ᵃall these words, saying,

2 ᵃI *am* the LORD thy God, which have brought thee out of the land of Egypt, ᵇout of the house of ¹bondage.

3 ᵃThou shalt have no other gods before me.

4 ᵃThou shalt not make unto thee any graven image, or any likeness *of any thing* that *is* in heaven above, or that *is* in the earth beneath, or that *is* in the water under the earth:

5 ᵃThou shalt not ¹bow down thyself to them, nor serve them: ᵇfor I the LORD thy God *am* a jealous God, ᶜvisiting² the iniquity of the fathers upon the children unto the third and fourth *generation* of them that hate me;

6 And ᵃshewing mercy unto thousands of them that love me, and keep my commandments.

7 ᵃThou shalt not take the name of the LORD thy God in vain; for the LORD ᵇwill not hold him guiltless that taketh his name in vain.

8 ᵃRemember the sabbath day, to keep it holy.

9 ᵃSix days shalt thou labour, and do all thy work:

10 But the ᵃseventh day *is* the sabbath of the LORD thy God: *in it* thou shalt not do any work, thou, nor thy son, nor thy daughter, nor thy manservant, nor thy maidservant, nor thy cattle, ᵇnor thy stranger that *is* within thy gates:

11 For ᵃin six days the LORD made heaven and earth, the sea, and all that in them *is,* and rested the seventh day: wherefore the LORD blessed the sabbath day, and hallowed it.

12 ᵃHonour thy father and thy mother: that thy days may be ᵇlong upon the land which the LORD thy God giveth thee.

13 ᵃThou shalt not kill.

14 ᵃThou shalt not commit ᵇadultery.

15 ᵃThou shalt not steal.

16 ᵃThou shalt not bear false witness against thy neighbour.

17 ᵃThou shalt not covet thy neighbour's house, ᵇthou shalt not covet thy neighbour's wife, nor his manservant, nor his maidservant, nor his ox, nor his ass, nor any thing that *is* thy neighbour's.

18 And ᵃall the people ᵇsaw the thunderings, and the lightnings, and

the noise of the trumpet, and the mountain ᶜsmoking: and when the people saw *it,* they ¹removed, and stood afar off.

19 And they said unto Moses, ᵃSpeak thou with us, and we will hear: but ᵇlet not God speak with us, lest we die.

20 And Moses said unto the people, ᵃFear not: ᵇfor God is come to ¹prove you, and ᶜthat his fear may be before your faces, that ye sin not.

21 And the people stood afar off, and Moses drew near unto ᵃthe thick darkness where God *was.*

22 And the LORD said unto Moses, Thus thou shalt say unto the children of Israel, Ye have seen that I have talked with you ᵃfrom heaven.

23 Ye shall not make ᵃwith me gods of silver, neither shall ye make unto you gods of gold.

24 An altar of ᵃearth thou shalt make unto me, and shalt sacrifice thereon thy burnt offerings, and thy peace offerings, ᵇthy sheep, and thine oxen: in all ᶜplaces where I ¹record my name I will come unto thee, and I will ᵈbless thee.

25 And ᵃif thou wilt make me an altar of stone, thou shalt not build it of hewn stone: for if thou ᵇlift up thy tool upon it, thou hast ¹polluted it.

26 Neither shalt thou go up by steps unto mine altar, that thy ᵃnakedness be not discovered thereon.

## CHAPTER 21

Now these *are* the ¹judgments which thou shalt ᵃset before them.

2 ᵃIf thou buy an Hebrew servant, six years he shall serve: and in the seventh he shall go out free for nothing.

3 If he came in by himself, he shall go out by himself: if he were married, then his wife shall go out with him.

4 If his master have given him a wife, and she have born him sons or daughters; the wife and her children shall be her master's, and he shall go out by himself.

5 ᵃAnd if the servant shall plainly say, I love my master, my wife, and my children; I will not go out free:

6 Then his master shall bring him unto the ᵃjudges; he shall also bring him to the door, or unto the door post; and his master shall bore his ear through with an aul; and he shall serve him for ever.

7 And if a man ᵃsell his daughter to be a maidservant, she shall not go out as the menservants do.

8 If she ¹please not her master, who hath betrothed her to himself, then shall he let her be redeemed: to sell her unto a ²strange nation he shall have no power, seeing he hath dealt deceitfully with her.

---

*Reference column:*

20:1 ᵃ Deut. 5:22
20:2 ᵃ Hos. 13:4
ᵇ Ex. 13:3 ¹ Lit. *slaves*
20:3 ᵃ Jer. 25:6; 35:15
20:4 ᵃ Deut. 4:15–19; 27:15
20:5 ᵃ Is. 44:15, 19 ᵇ Deut. 4:24 ᶜ Num. 14:18, 33 ¹ *worship* ² *punishing*
20:6 ᵃ Deut. 7:9
20:7 ᵃ Lev. 19:12 ᵇ Mic. 6:11
20:8 ᵃ Lev. 26:2
20:9 ᵃ Luke 13:14
20:10 ᵃ Gen. 2:2, 3 ᵇ Neh. 13:16–19
20:11 ᵃ Ex. 31:17
20:12 ᵃ Lev. 19:3 ᵇ Deut. 5:16, 33; 6:2; 11:8, 9
20:13 ᵃ Rom. 13:9
20:14 ᵃ Matt. 5:27 ᵇ Deut. 5:18
20:15 ᵃ Lev. 19:11, 13
20:16 ᵃ Deut. 5:20
20:17 ᵃ [Eph. 5:3, 5] ᵇ [Matt. 5:28]
20:18 ᵃ Heb. 12:18, 19 ᵇ Rev. 1:10, 12
ᶜ Ex. 19:16, 18 ¹ *trembled*
20:19 ᵃ Heb. 12:19 ᵇ Deut. 5:5, 23–27
20:20 ᵃ [Is. 41:10, 13] ᵇ [Deut. 13:3] ᶜ Is. 8:13 ¹ *test*
20:21 ᵃ Ex. 19:16
20:22 ᵃ Deut. 4:36; 5:24, 26
20:23 ᵃ Ex. 32:1, 2, 4
20:24 ᵃ Ex. 20:25; 27:1–8 ᵇ Ex. 24:5 ᶜ 2 Chr. 6:6 ᵈ Gen. 12:2 ¹ *cause to be remembered*
20:25 ᵃ Deut. 27:5 ᵇ Josh. 8:30, 31 ¹ *profaned*
20:26 ᵃ Ex. 28:42, 43
21:1 ᵃ Deut. 4:14; 6:1 ¹ *ordinances*
21:2 ᵃ Jer. 34:14
21:5 ᵃ Deut. 15:16, 17
21:6 ᵃ Ex. 12:12; 22:8, 9
21:7 ᵃ Neh. 5:5
21:8 ¹ Lit. *be evil in the eyes of* ² *foreign people*

9 And if he have betrothed her unto his son, he shall deal with her after the manner of daughters.

10 If he take him another *wife;* her food, her raiment, [a]and her duty of marriage, shall he not diminish.

11 And if he do not these three unto her, then shall she go out free without money.

12 [a]He that smiteth a man, so that he die, shall be surely put to death.

13 And [a]if a man lie not in wait, but God [b]deliver *him* into his hand; then [c]I will appoint thee a place whither he shall flee.

14 But if a man come [a]presumptuously[1] upon his neighbour, to slay him with [2]guile; [b]thou shalt take him from mine altar, that he may die.

15 And he that smiteth his father, or his mother, shall be surely put to death.

16 And [a]he that [1]stealeth a man, and [b]selleth him, or if he be [c]found in his hand, he shall surely be put to death.

17 And [a]he that curseth his father, or his mother, shall surely be put to death.

18 And if men strive together, and one smite another with a stone, or with *his* fist, and he die not, but keepeth *his* bed:

19 If he rise again, and walk abroad [a]upon his staff, then shall he that smote *him* be [1]quit: only he shall pay *for* the loss of his time, and shall cause *him* to be thoroughly healed.

20 And if a man smite his servant, or his maid, with a rod, and he die under his hand; he shall be surely punished.

21 Notwithstanding, if he continue a day or two, he shall not be punished: for he *is* his [a]money.

22 If men [1]strive, and hurt a woman with child, so that [2]her fruit depart *from her,* and yet no mischief follow: he shall be surely punished, according as the woman's husband will lay upon him; and he shall [a]pay as the judges *determine.*

23 And if *any* [1]mischief follow, then thou shalt give life for life,

24 [a]Eye for eye, tooth for tooth, hand for hand, foot for foot,

25 Burning for burning, wound for wound, stripe for stripe.

26 And if a man smite the eye of his servant, or the eye of his maid, that it perish; he shall let him go free for his eye's sake.

27 And if he smite out his manservant's tooth, or his maidservant's tooth; he shall let him go free for his tooth's sake.

28 If an ox gore a man or a woman, that they die: then [a]the ox shall be surely [1]stoned, and his flesh shall not be eaten; but the owner of the ox *shall be* [2]quit.

29 But if the ox [1]were wont to push with his horn in time past, and it hath been [2]testified to his owner, and he hath not kept him in, but that he hath killed a man or a woman; the ox shall be stoned, and his owner also shall be put to death.

30 If there be laid on him a sum of money, then he shall give for [a]the ransom of his life whatsoever is laid upon him.

31 Whether he have gored a son, or have gored a daughter, according to this judgment shall it be done unto him.

32 If the ox shall push a manservant or a maidservant; he shall give unto their master [a]thirty shekels of silver, and the [b]ox shall be stoned.

33 And if a man shall open a pit, or if a man shall dig a pit, and not cover it, and an ox or an ass fall therein;

34 The owner of the pit shall make *it* good, *and* give money unto the owner of them; and the dead *beast* shall be his.

35 And if one man's ox hurt another's, that he die; then they shall sell the live ox, and divide the money of it; and the dead *ox* also they shall divide.

36 Or if it be known that the ox hath used to push in time past, and his owner hath not kept him in; he shall surely pay ox for ox; and the dead shall be his own.

## CHAPTER 22

IF a man shall steal an ox, or a sheep, and kill it, or sell it; he shall [a]restore five oxen for an ox, and four sheep for a sheep.

2 If a thief be found [a]breaking [1]up, and be smitten that he die, *there shall* [b]no blood *be shed* for him.

3 If the sun be risen upon him, *there shall be* blood *shed* for him; *for* he should make full restitution; if he have nothing, then he shall be [a]sold[1] for his theft.

4 If the theft be certainly [a]found in his hand alive, whether it be ox, or ass, or sheep; he shall [b]restore double.

5 If a man shall cause a field or vineyard to be eaten, and shall put in his beast, and shall feed in another man's field; of the best of his own field, and of the best of his own vineyard, shall he make restitution.

6 If fire break out, and catch in thorns, so that the stacks of corn, or the standing corn, or the field, be consumed *therewith;* he that kindled the fire shall surely make restitution.

7 If a man shall [a]deliver unto his neighbour money or stuff to keep, and it be stolen out of the man's house; [b]if the thief be found, let him pay double.

---

**Cross-references (center column):**

21:10 [a] [1 Cor. 7:3, 5]
21:12 [a] [Matt. 26:52]
21:13 [a] Deut. 19:4, 5 [b] 1 Sam. 24:4, 10, 18 [c] Num. 35:11
21:14 [a] Deut. 19:11, 12 [b] 1 Kin. 2:28–34 [1] *acts with premeditation* [2] *craftiness*
21:16 [a] Deut. 24:7 [b] Gen. 37:28 [c] Ex. 22:4 [1] *kidnaps*
21:17 [a] Mark 7:10
21:19 [a] 2 Sam. 3:29 [1] *free from responsibility, acquitted*
21:21 [a] Lev. 25:44–46
21:22 [a] Ex. 18:21, 22; 21:30 [1] *fight* [2] *she gives birth prematurely*
21:23 [1] *harm*
21:24 [a] Lev. 24:20
21:28 [a] Gen. 9:5 [1] *put to death by stoning* [2] *acquitted*
21:29 [1] *tended* [2] *made known*
21:30 [a] Ex. 21:22; Num. 35:31
21:32 [a] Zech. 11:12, 13; Matt. 26:15; 27:3, 9 [b] Ex. 21:28
22:1 [a] 2 Sam. 12:6; Prov. 6:31; Luke 19:8
22:2 [a] Job 24:16; Matt. 6:19; 24:43; 1 Pet. 4:15 [b] Num. 35:27 [1] *in*
22:3 [a] Ex. 21:2; Matt. 18:25 [1] *sold as a slave*
22:4 [a] Ex. 21:16 [b] Prov. 6:31
22:7 [a] Lev. 6:1–7 [b] Ex. 22:4

8 If the thief be not found, then the master of the house shall be brought unto the ªjudges, *to see* whether he ¹have put his hand unto his neighbour's goods.

9 For all manner of trespass, *whether it be* for ox, for ass, for sheep, for raiment, *or* for any manner of lost thing, which *another* challengeth to be his, the ªcause of both parties shall come before the judges; *and* whom the judges shall condemn, he shall pay double unto his neighbour.

10 If a man deliver unto his neighbour an ass, or an ox, or a sheep, or any beast, to keep; and it die, or be hurt, or driven away, no man seeing *it*:

11 *Then* shall an ªoath of the LORD be between them both, that he hath not put his hand unto his neighbour's goods; and the owner of it shall accept *thereof,* and he shall not make *it* good.

12 And ªif it be stolen from him, he shall make restitution unto the owner thereof.

13 If it be ªtorn in pieces, *then* let him bring it *for* witness, *and* he shall not make good that which was torn.

14 And if a man borrow ¹ought of his neighbour, and it be hurt, or die, the owner thereof *being* not with it, he shall surely make *it* good.

15 *But* if the owner thereof *be* with it, he shall not make *it* good: if it *be* an hired *thing,* it came for his hire.

16 And ªif a man entice a maid that is not betrothed, and lie with her, he shall surely endow her to be his wife.

17 If her father utterly refuse to give her unto him, he shall pay money according to the ªdowry of virgins.

18 ªThou shalt not ¹suffer a witch to live.

19 ªWhosoever lieth with a beast shall surely be put to death.

20 ªHe that sacrificeth unto *any* god, save unto the LORD only, he shall be utterly destroyed.

21 ªThou shalt neither vex a ¹stranger, nor oppress him: for ye were strangers in the land of Egypt.

22 ªYe shall not afflict any widow, or fatherless child.

23 If thou afflict them in any wise, and they ªcry at all unto me, I will surely ᵇhear their cry;

24 And my ªwrath shall wax hot, and I will kill you with the sword; and ᵇyour wives shall be widows, and your children fatherless.

25 ªIf thou lend money to *any of* my people *that is* poor by thee, thou shalt not be to him as an ¹usurer, neither shalt thou lay upon him ᵇusury.²

26 ªIf thou at all take thy neighbour's raiment to pledge, thou shalt deliver it unto him by that the sun goeth down:

27 For that *is* his covering only, it *is* his raiment for his skin: wherein shall he sleep? and it shall come to pass, when he crieth unto me, that I will hear; for I *am* ªgracious.

28 ªThou shalt not revile the ¹gods, nor curse the ᵇruler of thy people.

29 Thou shalt not delay *to offer* ªthe first of thy ripe fruits, and of thy liquors: ᵇthe firstborn of thy sons shalt thou give unto me.

30 ªLikewise shalt thou do with thine oxen, *and* with thy sheep: ᵇseven days it shall be with his dam; on the eighth day thou shalt give it me.

31 And ye shall be ªholy men unto me: ᵇneither shall ye eat *any* flesh *that is* torn of beasts in the field; ye shall cast it to the dogs.

## CHAPTER 23

THOU ªshalt not raise a false report: put not thine hand with the wicked to be an ᵇunrighteous witness.

2 ªThou shalt not follow a multitude to *do* evil; ᵇneither shalt thou speak in a cause to ¹decline after many to ²wrest *judgment:*

3 Neither shalt thou countenance a ªpoor man in his cause.

4 ªIf thou meet thine enemy's ox or his ass going astray, thou shalt surely bring it back to him again.

5 ªIf thou see the ass of him that hateth thee lying under his burden, and wouldest ¹forbear to help him, thou shalt surely help with him.

6 ªThou shalt not ¹wrest the judgment of thy poor in his cause.

7 ªKeep thee far from a false matter; ᵇand the innocent and righteous slay thou not: for ᶜI will not justify the wicked.

8 And ªthou shalt take no ¹gift: for the gift blindeth the wise, and perverteth the words of the righteous.

9 Also ªthou shalt not oppress a ¹stranger: for ye know the heart of a stranger, seeing ye were strangers in the land of Egypt.

10 And ªsix years thou shalt sow thy land, and shalt gather in the fruits thereof:

11 But the seventh *year* thou shalt let it rest and lie still; that the poor of thy people may eat: and what they leave the beasts of the field shall eat. In like manner thou shalt deal with thy vineyard, *and* with thy ¹oliveyard.

12 ªSix days thou shalt do thy work, and on the seventh day thou shalt rest: that thine ox and thine ass may rest, and the son of thy handmaid, and the stranger, may be refreshed.

13 And in all *things* that I have said unto you ªbe circumspect: and ᵇmake no mention of the name of other

22:8 ª Ex. 21:6, 22; 22:28; Deut. 17:8, 9; 19:17 ¹ Lit. *has stretched forth his hand into*
22:9 ª Deut. 25:1; 2 Chr. 19:10
22:11 ª Heb. 6:16
22:12 ª Gen. 31:39
22:13 ª Gen. 31:39
22:14 ¹ *anything*
22:16 ª Deut.
22:28, 29
22:17 ª Gen. 34:12; 1 Sam. 18:25
22:18 ª Lev. 19:31; 20:6, 27; Deut. 18:10, 11; 1 Sam. 28:3–10; Jer. 27:9, 10 ¹ *permit*
22:19 ª Lev. 18:23; 20:15, 16; Deut. 27:21
22:20 ª Ex. 32:8; 34:15; Lev. 17:7; Num. 25:2; Deut. 17:2, 3, 5; 1 Kin. 18:40; 2 Kin. 10:25
22:21 ª Ex. 23:9; Deut. 10:19; Zech. 7:10 ¹ *sojourner*
22:22 ª Deut. 24:17, 18; Prov. 23:10, 11; Jer. 7:6, 7; [James 1:27]
22:23 ª [Luke 18:7] ᵇ Deut. 10:17, 18; Ps. 18:6
22:24 ª Ps. 69:24 ᵇ Ps. 109:9
22:25 ª Lev. 25:35–37 ᵇ Ps. 15:5 ¹ *money lender* ² *interest*
22:26 ª Deut. 24:6, 10–13
22:27 ª Ex. 34:6, 7
22:28 ª Eccl. 10:20 ᵇ Acts 23:5 ¹ *God*
22:29 ª Ex. 23:16, 19 ᵇ Ex. 13:2, 12, 15
22:30 ª Deut. 15:19 ᵇ Lev. 22:27
22:31 ª Lev. 11:44; 19:2 ᵇ Ezek. 4:14
23:1 ª Ps. 101:5 ᵇ Deut. 19:16–21
23:2 ª Gen. 7:1 ᵇ Lev. 19:5 ¹ *turn aside* ² *pervert*
23:3 ª Deut. 1:17; 16:19
23:4 ª [Rom. 12:20]
23:5 ª Deut. 22:4 ¹ *refrain from helping it*
23:6 ª Eccl. 5:8 ¹ *pervert*
23:7 ª Eph. 4:25 ᵇ Matt. 27:4 ᶜ Rom. 1:18
23:8 ª Prov. 15:27; 17:8, 23 ¹ *bribe*
23:9 ª Ex. 22:21 ¹ *sojourner*
23:10 ª Lev. 25:1–7 23:11 ¹ *olive grove* 23:12 ª Luke 13:14 23:13 ª 1 Tim. 4:16 ᵇ Josh. 23:7

gods, neither let it be heard out of thy mouth.

14 [a]Three times thou shalt keep a feast unto me in the year.

15 [a]Thou shalt keep the feast of unleavened bread: (thou shalt eat unleavened bread seven days, as I commanded thee, in the time appointed of the month Abib; for in it thou camest out from Egypt: [b]and none shall appear before me empty:)

16 [a]And the feast of harvest, the firstfruits of thy labours, which thou hast sown in the field: and [b]the feast of ingathering, *which is* in the end of the year, when thou hast gathered in thy labours out of the field.

17 [a]Three times in the year all thy males shall appear before the Lord [1]GOD.

18 [a]Thou shalt not offer the blood of my sacrifice with leavened bread; [b]neither shall the fat of my [1]sacrifice remain until the morning.

19 [a]The first of the firstfruits of thy land thou shalt bring into the house of the LORD thy God. [b]Thou shalt not [1]seethe a kid in his mother's milk.

20 [a]Behold, I send an Angel before thee, to keep thee in the way, and to bring thee into the place which I have prepared.

21 Beware of him, and obey his voice, [a]provoke him not; for he will [b]not pardon your transgressions: for [c]my name *is* in him.

22 But if thou shalt indeed obey his voice, and do all that I speak; then [a]I will be an enemy unto thine enemies, and an adversary unto thine adversaries.

23 [a]For mine Angel shall go before thee, and [b]bring thee in unto the Amorites, and the Hittites, and the Perizzites, and the Canaanites, the Hivites, and the Jebusites: and I will [1]cut them off.

24 Thou shalt not [a]bow down to their gods, nor serve them, [b]nor do after their works: [c]but thou shalt utterly overthrow them, and [1]quite break down their images.

25 And ye shall [a]serve the LORD your God, and [b]he shall bless thy bread, and thy water; and [c]I will take sickness away from the midst of thee.

26 [a]There shall nothing cast their young, nor be barren, in thy land: the number of thy days I will [b]fulfill.

27 I will send [a]my fear before thee, and will [b]destroy all the people to whom thou shalt come, and I will make all thine enemies turn their backs unto thee.

28 And [a]I will send hornets before thee, which shall drive out the Hivite, the Canaanite, and the Hittite, from before thee.

29 [a]I will not drive them out from before thee in one year; lest the land become desolate, and the beast of the field multiply against thee.

30 By little and little I will drive them out from before thee, until thou be increased, and inherit the land.

31 And [a]I will set thy [1]bounds from the Red sea even unto the sea of the Philistines, and from the desert unto the [2]river: for I will [b]deliver the inhabitants of the land into your hand; and thou shalt drive them out before thee.

32 [a]Thou shalt make no [1]covenant with them, nor with their gods.

33 They shall not dwell in thy land, lest they make thee sin against me: for if thou serve their gods, [a]it will surely be a snare unto thee.

## CHAPTER 24

AND he said unto Moses, Come up unto the LORD, thou, and Aaron, [a]Nadab, and Abihu, [b]and seventy of the elders of Israel; and worship ye afar off.

2 And Moses alone shall come near the LORD: but they shall not come nigh; neither shall the people go up with him.

3 And Moses came and told the people all the words of the LORD, and all the [1]judgments: and all the people answered with one voice, and said, [a]All the words which the LORD hath said will we do.

4 And Moses [a]wrote all the words of the LORD, and rose up early in the morning, and builded an altar under the hill, and twelve [b]pillars, according to the twelve tribes of Israel.

5 And he sent young men of the children of Israel, which offered [a]burnt offerings, and sacrificed peace offerings of oxen unto the LORD.

6 And Moses [a]took half of the blood, and put *it* in basons; and half of the blood he sprinkled on the altar.

7 And he [a]took the book of the covenant, and read in the audience of the people: and they said, All that the LORD hath said will we do, and be obedient.

8 And Moses took the blood, and sprinkled *it* on the people, and said, Behold [a]the blood of the covenant, which the LORD hath made with you concerning all these words.

9 Then went up Moses, and Aaron, Nadab, and Abihu, and seventy of the elders of Israel:

10 And they [a]saw the God of Israel: and *there was* under his feet as it were a paved work of a [b]sapphire stone, and as it were the [c]body of heaven in *his* clearness.

11 And upon the nobles of the children of Israel he [a]laid[1] not his hand:

also <sup>b</sup>they saw God, and did <sup>c</sup>eat and drink.

12 And the LORD said unto Moses, <sup>a</sup>Come up to me into the mount, and be there: and I will give thee <sup>b</sup>tables of stone, and a law, and commandments which I have written; that thou mayest teach them.

13 And Moses rose up, and <sup>a</sup>his minister Joshua: and Moses went up into the mount of God.

14 And he said unto the elders, Tarry ye here for us, until we come again unto you: and, behold, Aaron and <sup>a</sup>Hur *are* with you: if any man have any matters to do, let him come unto them.

15 And Moses went up into the mount, and <sup>a</sup>a cloud covered the mount.

16 And <sup>a</sup>the glory of the LORD abode upon mount Sinai, and the cloud covered it six days: and the seventh day he called unto Moses out of the midst of the cloud.

17 And the sight of the glory of the LORD *was* like <sup>a</sup>devouring fire on the top of the mount in the eyes of the children of Israel.

18 And Moses went into the midst of the cloud, and gat him up into the mount: and <sup>a</sup>Moses was in the mount forty days and forty nights.

## CHAPTER 25

AND the LORD spake unto Moses, saying,

2 Speak unto the children of Israel, that they bring me an <sup>1</sup>offering: <sup>a</sup>of every man that giveth it willingly with his heart ye shall take my offering.

3 And this *is* the offering which ye shall take of them; gold, and silver, and brass,

4 And blue, and purple, and scarlet, and fine linen, and goats' *hair*,

5 And rams' skins dyed red, and <sup>1</sup>badgers' skins, and shittim wood,

6 <sup>a</sup>Oil for the light, <sup>b</sup>spices for anointing oil, and for sweet incense,

7 Onyx stones, and stones to be set in the <sup>a</sup>ephod, and in the breastplate.

8 And let them make me a <sup>a</sup>sanctuary;<sup>1</sup> that <sup>b</sup>I may dwell among them.

9 According to all that I shew thee, *after* the pattern of the tabernacle, and the pattern of all the instruments thereof, even so shall ye make *it*.

10 <sup>a</sup>And they shall make an ark *of* shittim wood: two cubits and a half *shall be* the length thereof, and a cubit and a half the breadth thereof, and a cubit and a half the height thereof.

11 And thou shalt overlay it with pure gold, within and without shalt thou overlay it, and shalt make upon it a crown of <sup>a</sup>gold round about.

12 And thou shalt cast four rings of gold for it, and put *them* in the four

corners thereof; and two rings *shall be* in the one side of it, and two rings in the other side of it.

13 And thou shalt make staves *of* shittim wood, and overlay them with gold.

14 And thou shalt put the staves into the rings by the sides of the ark, that the ark may be borne with them.

15 <sup>a</sup>The staves shall be in the rings of the ark: they shall not be taken from it.

16 And thou shalt put into the ark <sup>a</sup>the testimony which I shall give thee.

17 And <sup>a</sup>thou shalt make a mercy seat *of* pure gold: two cubits and a half *shall be* the length thereof, and a cubit and a half the breadth thereof.

18 And thou shalt make two cherubims *of* gold, *of* beaten work shalt thou make them, in the two ends of the mercy seat.

19 And make one cherub on the one end, and the other cherub on the other end: *even* of the mercy seat shall ye make the cherubims on the two ends thereof.

20 And <sup>a</sup>the cherubims shall stretch forth *their* wings on high, covering the mercy seat with their wings, and their faces *shall look* one to another; toward the mercy seat shall the faces of the cherubims be.

21 <sup>a</sup>And thou shalt put the mercy seat above upon the ark; and <sup>b</sup>in the ark thou shalt put the testimony that I shall give thee.

22 And <sup>a</sup>there I will meet with thee, and I will <sup>1</sup>commune with thee from above the mercy seat, from <sup>b</sup>between the two cherubims which *are* upon the ark of the testimony, of all *things* which I will give thee in commandment unto the children of Israel.

23 <sup>a</sup>Thou shalt also make a table of shittim wood: two cubits *shall be* the length thereof, and a cubit the breadth thereof, and a cubit and a half the height thereof.

24 And thou shalt overlay it with pure gold, and make thereto a crown of gold round about.

25 And thou shalt make unto it a border of an hand breadth round about, and thou shalt make a golden crown to the border thereof round about.

26 And thou shalt make for it four rings of gold, and put the rings in the four corners that *are* on the four feet thereof.

27 Over against the border shall the rings be for places of the staves to bear the table.

28 And thou shalt make the staves of shittim wood, and overlay them with gold, that the table may be borne with them.

### Cross references

24:11 <sup>b</sup> Gen. 32:30
<sup>c</sup> 1 Cor. 10:18
24:12 <sup>a</sup> Ex. 24:2, 15
<sup>b</sup> Ex. 31:18; 32:15
24:13 <sup>a</sup> Ex. 32:17
24:14 <sup>a</sup> Ex. 17:10, 12
24:15 <sup>a</sup> Ex. 19:9
24:16 <sup>a</sup> Ex. 16:10; 33:18
24:17 <sup>a</sup> Deut. 4:26, 36; 9:3
24:18 <sup>a</sup> Ex. 34:28
25:2 <sup>a</sup> Ex. 35:4–9, 21 <sup>1</sup> *heave offering*
25:5 <sup>1</sup> Or *dolphin*
25:6 <sup>a</sup> Ex. 27:20
<sup>b</sup> Ex. 30:23
25:7 <sup>a</sup> Ex. 28:4, 6–14
25:8 <sup>a</sup> Ex. 36:1, 3, 4; Lev. 4:6; 10:4; 21:12; Heb. 9:1, 2
<sup>b</sup> Ex. 29:45; 1 Kin. 6:13; [2 Cor. 6:16; Heb. 3:6; Rev. 2:13] <sup>1</sup> *sacred place*
25:10 <sup>a</sup> Ex. 37:1–9; Deut. 10:3; Heb. 9:4
25:11 <sup>a</sup> Ex. 37:2; Heb. 9:4
25:15 <sup>a</sup> Num. 4:6; 1 Kin. 8:8
25:16 <sup>a</sup> Ex. 16:34; 31:18; Deut. 10:2; 31:26; 1 Kin. 8:9; Heb. 9:4
25:17 <sup>a</sup> Ex. 37:6; Heb. 9:5
25:20 <sup>a</sup> 1 Kin. 8:7; 1 Chr. 28:18; Heb. 9:5
25:21 <sup>a</sup> Ex. 26:34; 40:20 <sup>b</sup> Ex. 25:16
25:22 <sup>a</sup> Ex. 29:42, 43; 30:6, 36; Lev. 16:2; Num. 17:4
<sup>b</sup> Num. 7:89; 1 Sam. 4:4; 2 Sam. 6:2; 2 Kin. 19:15; Ps. 80:1; Is. 37:16 <sup>1</sup> *speak*
25:23 <sup>a</sup> Ex. 37:10–16; 1 Kin. 7:48; 2 Chr. 4:8; Heb. 9:2

29 And thou shalt make [a]the dishes thereof, and spoons thereof, and covers thereof, and bowls thereof, [1]to cover withal: *of* pure gold shalt thou make them.

30 And thou shalt set upon the table [a]shewbread before me alway.

31 [a]And thou shalt make a candlestick *of* pure gold: *of* beaten work shall the candlestick be made: his shaft, and his branches, his bowls, his knops, and his flowers, shall be of the same.

32 And six branches shall come out of the sides of it; three branches of the candlestick out of the one side, and three branches of the candlestick out of the other side:

33 [a]Three bowls made like unto almonds, *with* a knop and a flower in one branch; and three bowls made like almonds in the other branch, *with* a knop and a flower: so in the six branches that come out of the candlestick.

34 And [a]in the candlestick *shall be* four bowls made like unto almonds, *with* their knops and their flowers.

35 And *there shall be* a knop under two branches of the same, and a knop under two branches of the same, and a knop under two branches of the same, according to the six branches that proceed out of the candlestick.

36 Their knops and their branches shall be of the same: all it *shall be* one beaten work *of* pure gold.

37 And thou shalt make the seven lamps thereof: and [a]they shall [1]light the lamps thereof, that they may [b]give light [2]over against it.

38 And the tongs thereof, and the snuffdishes thereof, *shall be of* pure gold.

39 *Of* a talent of pure gold shall he make it, with all these vessels.

40 And [a]look that thou make *them* after their pattern, which was shewed thee in the mount.

### CHAPTER 26

M OREOVER [a]thou shalt make the tabernacle *with* ten curtains *of* fine twined linen, and blue, and purple, and scarlet: *with* cherubims of [1]cunning work shalt thou make them.

2 The length of one curtain *shall be* eight and twenty cubits, and the breadth of one curtain four cubits: and every one of the curtains shall [1]have one measure.

3 The five curtains shall be coupled together one to another; and *other* five curtains *shall be* coupled one to another.

4 And thou shalt make loops of blue upon the edge of the one curtain from the selvedge in the coupling; and likewise shalt thou make in the

uttermost edge of *another* curtain, in the coupling of the second.

5 Fifty loops shalt thou make in the one curtain, and fifty loops shalt thou make in the edge of the curtain that *is* in the coupling of the second; that the loops may take hold one of another.

6 And thou shalt make fifty [1]taches of gold, and couple the curtains together with the taches: and it shall be one tabernacle.

7 And [a]thou shalt make curtains of goats' *hair* to be a covering upon the tabernacle: eleven curtains shalt thou make.

8 The length of one curtain *shall be* thirty cubits, and the breadth of one curtain four cubits: and the eleven curtains *shall be all* of one measure.

9 And thou shalt couple five curtains by themselves, and six curtains by themselves, and shalt double the sixth curtain in the forefront of the tabernacle.

10 And thou shalt make fifty loops on the edge of the one curtain *that is* outmost in the coupling, and fifty loops in the edge of the curtain which coupleth the second.

11 And thou shalt make fifty taches of brass, and put the taches into the loops, and couple the tent together, that it may be one.

12 And the remnant that remaineth of the curtains of the tent, the half curtain that remaineth, shall hang over the backside of the tabernacle.

13 And a cubit on the one side, and a cubit on the other side of that which remaineth in the length of the curtains of the tent, it shall hang over the sides of the tabernacle on this side and on that side, to cover it.

14 And [a]thou shalt make a covering for the tent *of* rams' skins dyed red, and a covering above *of* badgers' skins.

15 And thou shalt [a]make boards for the tabernacle *of* shittim wood standing up.

16 Ten cubits *shall be* the length of a board, and a cubit and a half *shall be* the breadth of one board.

17 Two [1]tenons *shall there be* in one board, set in order one against another: thus shalt thou make for all the boards of the tabernacle.

18 And thou shalt make the boards for the tabernacle, twenty boards on the south side southward.

19 And thou shalt make forty sockets of silver under the twenty boards; two sockets under one board for his two tenons, and two sockets under another board for his two tenons.

20 And for the second side of the tabernacle on the north side *there shall be* twenty boards:

25:29 [a] Ex. 37:16; Num. 4:7 [1] *for pouring*

25:30 [a] Ex. 39:36; 40:23; Lev. 24:5–9

25:31 [a] Ex. 37:17–24; 1 Kin. 7:49; Zech. 4:2; Heb. 9:2; Rev. 1:12

25:33 [a] Ex. 37:19

25:34 [a] Ex. 37:20–22

25:37 [a] Ex. 27:21; 30:8; Lev. 24:3, 4; 2 Chr. 13:11 [b] Num. 8:2 [1] *arrange* [2] *in front of*

25:40 [a] Ex. 25:9; 26:30; Num. 8:4; 1 Chr. 28:11, 19; Acts 7:44; [Heb. 8:5]

26:1 [a] Ex. 36:8–19 [1] *artistic designs*

26:2 [1] *be the same measurement*

26:6 [1] *clasps*

26:7 [a] Ex. 36:14

26:14 [a] Ex. 35:7, 23; 36:19

26:15 [a] Ex. 36:20–34

26:17 [1] *projections for joining*

21 And their forty sockets *of* silver; two sockets under one board, and two sockets under another board.

22 And for the sides of the tabernacle westward thou shalt make six boards.

23 And two boards shalt thou make for the corners of the tabernacle in the two sides.

24 And they shall be ¹coupled together beneath, and they shall be coupled together above the head of it unto one ring: thus shall it be for them both; they shall be for the two corners.

25 And they shall be eight boards, and their sockets *of* silver, sixteen sockets; two sockets under one board, and two sockets under another board.

26 And thou shalt make bars *of* shittim wood; five for the boards of the one side of the tabernacle,

27 And five bars for the boards of the other side of the tabernacle, and five bars for the boards of the side of the tabernacle, for the two sides westward.

28 And the ªmiddle bar in the midst of the boards shall reach from end to end.

29 And thou shalt overlay the boards with gold, and make their rings *of* gold *for* places for the bars: and thou shalt overlay the bars with gold.

30 And thou shalt ¹rear up the tabernacle ªaccording to the fashion thereof which was shewed thee in the mount.

31 And ªthou shalt make a vail *of* blue, and purple, and scarlet, and fine twined linen of cunning work: with cherubims shall it be made:

32 And thou shalt hang it upon four pillars of shittim *wood* overlaid with gold: their hooks *shall be of* gold, upon the four sockets of silver.

33 And thou shalt hang up the vail under the taches, that thou mayest bring in thither within the vail ªthe ark of the testimony: and the vail shall divide unto you between ᵇthe holy *place* and the most holy.

34 And ªthou shalt put the mercy seat upon the ark of the testimony in the most holy *place*.

35 And ªthou shalt set the table ¹without the vail, and ᵇthe candlestick over against the table on the side of the tabernacle toward the south: and thou shalt put the table on the north side.

36 And ªthou shalt make an hanging for the door of the tent, *of* blue, and purple, and scarlet, and fine twined linen, wrought with needlework.

37 And thou shalt make for the hanging ªfive pillars *of* shittim *wood*,

---

**Center reference column:**

26:24 ¹ Lit. *doubled*
26:28 ª Ex. 36:33
26:30 ª Ex. 25:9, 40; 27:8; 39:32; Num. 8:4; Acts 7:44; [Heb. 8:2, 5] ¹ *raise*
26:31 ª Ex. 27:21; 36:35–38; Lev. 16:2; 2 Chr. 3:14; Matt. 27:51; Heb. 9:3; 10:20
26:33 ª Ex. 25:10–16; 40:21 ᵇ Lev. 16:2; Heb. 9:2, 3
26:34 ª Ex. 25:17–22; 40:20; Heb. 9:5
26:35 ª Ex. 40:22; Heb. 9:2 ᵇ Ex. 40:24 ¹ *outside*
26:36 ª Ex. 36:37
26:37 ª Ex. 36:38

27:1 ª Ex. 38:1; Ezek. 43:13
27:8 ª Ex. 25:40; 26:30; Acts 7:44; [Heb. 8:5]
27:9 ª Ex. 38:9–20

---

and overlay them with gold, *and* their hooks *shall be of* gold: and thou shalt cast five sockets of brass for them.

## CHAPTER 27

AND thou shalt make ªan altar *of* shittim wood, five cubits long, and five cubits broad; the altar shall be foursquare: and the height thereof *shall be* three cubits.

2 And thou shalt make the horns of it upon the four corners thereof: his horns shall be of the same: and thou shalt overlay it with brass.

3 And thou shalt make his pans to receive his ashes, and his shovels, and his basons, and his fleshhooks, and his firepans: all the vessels thereof thou shalt make *of* brass.

4 And thou shalt make for it a grate of network *of* brass; and upon the net shalt thou make four brasen rings in the four corners thereof.

5 And thou shalt put it under the compass of the altar beneath, that the net may be even to the midst of the altar.

6 And thou shalt make staves for the altar, staves *of* shittim wood, and overlay them with brass.

7 And the staves shall be put into the rings, and the staves shall be upon the two sides of the altar, to bear it.

8 Hollow with boards shalt thou make it: ªas it was shewed thee in the mount, so shall they make *it*.

9 And ªthou shalt make the court of the tabernacle: for the south side southward *there shall be* hangings for the court *of* fine twined linen of an hundred cubits long for one side:

10 And the twenty pillars thereof and their twenty sockets *shall be of* brass; the hooks of the pillars and their fillets *shall be of* silver.

11 And likewise for the north side in length *there shall be* hangings of an hundred *cubits* long, and his twenty pillars and their twenty sockets *of* brass; the hooks of the pillars and their fillets *of* silver.

12 And *for* the breadth of the court on the west side *shall be* hangings of fifty cubits: their pillars ten, and their sockets ten.

13 And the breadth of the court on the east side eastward *shall be* fifty cubits.

14 The hangings of one side *of the gate shall be* fifteen cubits: their pillars three, and their sockets three.

15 And on the other side *shall be* hangings fifteen *cubits:* their pillars three, and their sockets three.

16 And for the gate of the court *shall be* an hanging of twenty cubits, *of* blue, and purple, and scarlet, and fine twined linen, wrought with

needlework: *and* their pillars *shall be* four, and their sockets four.

17 All the pillars round about the court *shall be* filleted with silver; their ªhooks *shall be of* silver, and their sockets *of* brass.

18 The length of the court *shall be* an hundred cubits, and the breadth fifty ¹every where, and the height five cubits *of* fine twined linen, and their sockets *of* brass.

19 All the vessels of the tabernacle in all the service thereof, and all the pins thereof, and all the pins of the court, *shall be of* brass.

20 And ªthou shalt command the children of Israel, that they bring thee pure oil olive beaten for the light, to cause the lamp to ¹burn always.

21 In the tabernacle of the congregation ªwithout the vail, which *is* before the testimony, ᵇAaron and his sons shall ¹order it from evening to morning before the LORD: ᶜ*it shall be* a statute for ever unto their generations on the behalf of the children of Israel.

## CHAPTER 28

A ND take thou unto thee ªAaron thy brother, and his sons with him, from among the children of Israel, that he may minister unto me in the priest's ᵇoffice, *even* Aaron, ᶜNadab and Abihu, ᵈEleazar and Ithamar, Aaron's sons.

2 And ªthou shalt make ¹holy garments for Aaron thy brother for glory and for beauty.

3 And ªthou shalt speak unto all *that are* wise hearted, ᵇwhom I have filled with the spirit of wisdom, that they may make Aaron's garments to consecrate him, that he may minister unto me in the priest's office.

4 And these *are* the garments which they shall make; ªa breastplate, and ᵇan ¹ephod, and ᶜa robe, and ᵈa broidered coat, a ²mitre, and ᵉa ³girdle: and they shall make holy garments for Aaron thy brother, and his sons, that he may minister unto me in the priest's office.

5 And they shall take gold, and blue, and purple, and scarlet, and fine linen.

6 ªAnd they shall make the ephod *of* gold, *of* blue, and *of* purple, *of* scarlet, and fine twined linen, with ¹cunning work.

7 It shall have the two shoulderpieces thereof joined at the two edges thereof; and *so* it shall be joined together.

8 And the ¹curious girdle of the ephod, which *is* upon it, shall be of the same, according to the work thereof; *even of* gold, *of* blue, and

---

27:17 ª Ex. 38:19
27:18 ¹ *throughout*

27:20 ª Ex. 35:8, 28; Lev. 24:1–4
¹ Lit. *ascend*

27:21 ª Ex. 26:31, 33　ᵇ Ex. 30:8;
1 Sam. 3:3; 2 Chr. 13:11　ᶜ Ex. 28:43;
29:9; Lev. 3:17; 16:34; Num. 18:23; 19:21;
1 Sam. 30:25
¹ *tend*

28:1 ª Num. 3:10; 18:7　ᵇ Ps. 99:6;
Heb. 5:4　ᶜ Ex. 24:1, 9; Lev. 10:1
ᵈ Ex. 6:23; Lev. 10:6, 16

28:2 ª Ex. 29:5, 29; 31:10; 39:1–31;
Lev. 8:7–9, 30
¹ *sacred*

28:3 ª Ex. 31:6; 36:1　ᵇ Ex. 31:3;
35:30, 31; Is. 11:2; Eph. 1:17

28:4 ª Ex. 28:15
ᵇ Ex. 28:6　ᶜ Ex. 28:31　ᵈ Ex. 28:39　ᵉ Lev. 8:7
¹ *ornamented vest*
² *turban* ³ *sash*

28:6 ª Ex. 39:2–7;
Lev. 8:7　¹ *artistic*

28:8 ¹ *intricately woven band*

28:9 ª Ex. 35:27
¹ *engrave*

28:10 ª Gen. 29:31–30:24;
35:16–18

28:11 ª Ex. 35:35
¹ *settings*

28:12 ª Ex. 28:29, 30; 39:6, 7　ᵇ Lev. 24:7; Num. 31:54;
Josh. 4:7; Zech. 6:14; 1 Cor. 11:24

28:15 ª Ex. 39:8–21

28:17 ª Ex. 39:10
¹ *emerald*

28:18 ¹ *turquoise*
² *sapphire*

28:19 ¹ *jacinth or amber*

28:20 ¹ *yellow jasper* ² *onyx or carnelian*
³ *settings*

28:22 ¹ *braided*

---

purple, and scarlet, and fine twined linen.

9 And thou shalt take two onyx ªstones, and ¹grave on them the names of the children of Israel:

10 Six of their names on one stone, and *the other* six names of the rest on the other stone, according to their ªbirth.

11 With the work of an ªengraver in stone, *like* the engravings of a signet, shalt thou engrave the two stones with the names of the children of Israel: thou shalt make them to be set in ¹ouches of gold.

12 And thou shalt put the two stones upon the shoulders of the ephod *for* stones of memorial unto the children of Israel: and ªAaron shall bear their names before the LORD upon his two shoulders ᵇfor a memorial.

13 And thou shalt make ouches *of* gold;

14 And two chains *of* pure gold at the ends; *of* wreathen work shalt thou make them, and fasten the wreathen chains to the ouches.

15 And ªthou shalt make the breastplate of judgment with cunning work; after the work of the ephod thou shalt make it; *of* gold, *of* blue, and *of* purple, and *of* scarlet, and *of* fine twined linen, shalt thou make it.

16 Foursquare it shall be *being* doubled; a span *shall be* the length thereof, and a span *shall be* the breadth thereof.

17 ªAnd thou shalt set in it settings of stones, *even* four rows of stones: *the first* row *shall be* a sardius, a topaz, and a ¹carbuncle: *this shall be* the first row.

18 And the second row *shall be* an ¹emerald, a sapphire, and a ²diamond.

19 And the third row a ¹ligure, an agate, and an amethyst.

20 And the fourth row a ¹beryl, and an ²onyx, and a jasper: they shall be set in gold in their ³inclosings.

21 And the stones shall be with the names of the children of Israel, twelve, according to their names, *like* the engravings of a signet; every one with his name shall they be according to the twelve tribes.

22 And thou shalt make upon the breastplate chains at the ends *of* ¹wreathen work *of* pure gold.

23 And thou shalt make upon the breastplate two rings of gold, and shalt put the two rings on the two ends of the breastplate.

24 And thou shalt put the two wreathen *chains* of gold in the two rings *which are* on the ends of the breastplate.

25 And *the other* two ends of the two wreathen *chains* thou shalt fasten in

the two ouches, and put *them* on the shoulderpieces of the ephod before it.

26 And thou shalt make two rings of gold, and thou shalt put them upon the two ends of the breastplate in the border thereof, which *is* in the side of the ephod inward.

27 And two *other* rings of gold thou shalt make, and shalt put them on the two sides of the ephod underneath, toward the forepart thereof, over against the *other* coupling thereof, above the ¹curious girdle of the ephod.

28 And they shall bind the breastplate by the rings thereof unto the rings of the ephod with a lace of blue, that *it* may be above the curious girdle of the ephod, and that the breastplate be not loosed from the ephod.

29 And Aaron shall ªbear the names of the children of Israel in the breastplate of judgment upon his heart, when he goeth in unto the holy *place,* for a memorial before the LORD continually.

30 And ªthou shalt put in the breastplate of judgment the ¹Urim and the Thummim; and they shall be upon Aaron's heart, when he goeth in before the LORD: and Aaron shall bear the judgment of the children of Israel upon his heart before the LORD continually.

31 And ªthou shalt make the robe of the ephod all *of* blue.

32 And there shall be an hole in the top of it, in the midst thereof: it shall have a binding of woven work round about the hole of it, as it were the hole of an habergeon, that it be not rent.

33 And *beneath* upon the hem of it thou shalt make pomegranates *of* blue, and *of* purple, and *of* scarlet, round about the hem thereof; and bells of gold between them round about:

34 A golden bell and a pomegranate, a golden bell and a pomegranate, upon the hem of the robe round about.

35 And it shall be upon Aaron to minister: and his sound shall be heard when he goeth in unto the holy *place* before the LORD, and when he cometh out, that he die not.

36 And ªthou shalt make a plate *of* pure gold, and grave upon it, *like* the engravings of a signet, HOLINESS TO THE LORD.

37 And thou shalt put it on a blue lace, that it may be upon the mitre; upon the forefront of the mitre it shall be.

38 And it shall be upon Aaron's forehead, that Aaron may ªbear the iniquity of the holy things, which the children of Israel shall hallow in all their ¹holy gifts; and it shall be always

upon his forehead, that they may be ᵇaccepted before the LORD.

39 And thou shalt ªembroider the coat of fine linen, and thou shalt make the mitre *of* fine linen, and thou shalt make the girdle *of* needlework.

40 ªAnd for Aaron's sons thou shalt make coats, and thou shalt make for them girdles, and ¹bonnets shalt thou make for them, for glory and for ᵇbeauty.

41 And thou shalt put them upon Aaron thy brother, and his sons with him; and shalt ªanoint them, and ᵇconsecrate them, and ¹sanctify them, that they may minister unto me in the priest's office.

42 And thou shalt make them ªlinen breeches to cover their ¹nakedness; from the loins even unto the thighs they shall ²reach:

43 And ªthey shall be upon Aaron, and upon his sons, when they come in unto the tabernacle of the congregation, or when they come near ªunto the altar to minister in the holy *place;* that they ᵇbear¹ not iniquity, and die: ᶜ*it shall be* a statute for ever unto him and his seed after him.

## CHAPTER 29

AND this *is* the thing that thou shalt do unto them to hallow them, to minister unto me in the priest's office: ªTake one young bullock, and two rams without blemish,

2 And ªunleavened bread, and cakes unleavened tempered with oil, and wafers unleavened anointed with oil: *of* wheaten flour shalt thou make them.

3 And thou shalt put them into one basket, and bring them in the basket, with the bullock and the two rams.

4 And Aaron and his sons thou shalt bring unto the door of the tabernacle of the congregation, ªand shalt wash them with water.

5 ªAnd thou shalt take the garments, and put upon Aaron the coat, and the robe of the ephod, and the ephod, and the breastplate, and gird him with ᵇthe curious girdle of the ephod:

6 ªAnd thou shalt put the mitre upon his head, and put the holy crown upon the mitre.

7 Then shalt thou take the anointing ªoil, and pour *it* upon his head, and anoint him.

8 And ªthou shalt bring his sons, and put coats upon them.

9 And thou shalt gird them with girdles, Aaron and his sons, and put the bonnets on them: and ªthe priest's office shall be theirs for a perpetual statute: and thou shalt ᵇconsecrate Aaron and his sons.

28:27 ¹ *intricately woven band*

28:29 ª Ex. 28:12
28:30 ª Lev. 8:8; Num. 27:21; Deut. 33:8; 1 Sam. 28:6; Ezra 2:63; Neh. 7:65 ¹ Lit. *Lights and the Perfections*
28:31 ª Ex. 39:22–26
28:36 ª Ex. 39:30, 31; Lev. 8:9; Zech. 14:20
28:38 ª Ex. 28:43; Lev. 10:17; 22:9, 16; Num. 18:1; [Is. 53:11]; Ezek. 4:4–6; [John 1:29; Heb. 9:28; 1 Pet. 2:24] ¹ *sacred*

b Lev. 1:4; 22:27; 23:11; Is. 56:7
28:39 ª Ex. 35:35; 39:27–29
28:40 ª Ex. 28:4; 39:27–29, 41; Ezek. 44:17, 18 ᵇ Ex. 28:2 ¹ *hats*
28:41 ª Ex. 29:7–9; 30:30; 40:15; Lev. 10:7 ᵇ Ex. 29:9; Lev. 8; Heb. 7:28 ¹ *set them apart*
28:42 ª Ex. 39:28; Lev. 6:10; 16:4; Ezek. 44:18 ¹ *bare flesh* ² Lit. *be*
28:43 ª Ex. 20:26 ᵇ Lev. 5:1, 17; 20:19, 20; 22:9; Num. 9:13; 18:22 ᶜ Ex. 27:21; Lev. 17:7 ¹ *do not incur guilt*

29:1 ª Lev. 8; [Heb. 7:26–28]
29:2 ª Lev. 2:4; 6:19–23
29:4 ª Ex. 40:12; Lev. 8:6; [Heb. 10:22]
29:5 ª Ex. 28:2; Lev. 8:7 ᵇ Ex. 28:8
29:6 ª Ex. 28:36, 37; Lev. 8:9
29:7 ª Ex. 25:6; 30:25–31; Lev. 8:12; 10:7; 21:10; Num. 35:25; Ps. 133:2
29:8 ª Ex. 28:39, 40; Lev. 8:13
29:9 ª Ex. 40:15; Num. 3:10; 18:7; 25:13; Deut. 18:5 ᵇ Ex. 28:41; Lev. 8

10 And thou shalt cause a bullock to be brought before the tabernacle of the congregation: and [a]Aaron and his sons shall put their hands upon the head of the bullock.

11 And thou shalt kill the bullock before the LORD, *by* the door of the tabernacle of the congregation.

12 And thou shalt take of the blood of the bullock, and put *it* upon [a]the horns of the altar with thy finger, and [b]pour all the blood beside the bottom of the altar.

13 And [a]thou shalt take all the fat that covereth the inwards, and the caul *that is* above the liver, and the two kidneys, and the fat that *is* upon them, and burn *them* upon the altar.

14 But [a]the flesh of the bullock, and his skin, and his dung, shalt thou burn with fire [1]without the camp: it *is* a sin offering.

15 [a]Thou shalt also take one ram; and Aaron and his sons shall [b]put their hands upon the head of the ram.

16 And thou shalt slay the ram, and thou shalt take his blood, and [a]sprinkle *it* round about upon the altar.

17 And thou shalt cut the ram in pieces, and wash the inwards of him, and his legs, and put *them* unto his pieces, and [1]unto his head.

18 And thou shalt burn the whole ram upon the altar: it *is* a [a]burnt offering unto the LORD: it *is* a sweet [1]savour, an offering made by fire unto the LORD.

19 [a]And thou shalt take the other ram; and Aaron and his sons shall put their hands upon the head of the ram.

20 Then shalt thou kill the ram, and take of his blood, and put *it* upon the tip of the right ear of Aaron, and upon the tip of the right ear of his sons, and upon the thumb of their right hand, and upon the great toe of their right foot, and sprinkle the blood upon the altar round about.

21 And thou shalt take of the blood that *is* upon the altar, and of [a]the anointing oil, and sprinkle *it* upon Aaron, and upon his garments, and upon his sons, and upon the garments of his sons with him: and [b]he shall be hallowed, and his garments, and his sons, and his sons' garments with him.

22 Also thou shalt take of the ram the fat and the rump, and the fat that covereth the inwards, and the caul *above* the liver, and the two kidneys, and the fat that *is* upon them, and the right shoulder; for it *is* a ram of consecration:

23 [a]And one loaf of bread, and one cake of oiled bread, and one wafer out of the basket of the unleavened bread that *is* before the LORD:

24 And thou shalt put all in the hands of Aaron, and in the hands of his sons; and shalt [a]wave them *for* a wave offering before the LORD.

25 [a]And thou shalt receive them of their hands, and burn *them* upon the altar for a burnt offering, for a sweet savour before the LORD: it *is* an offering made by fire unto the LORD.

26 And thou shalt take [a]the breast of the ram of Aaron's consecration, and wave it *for* a wave offering before the LORD: and it shall be thy part.

27 And thou shalt sanctify [a]the breast of the wave offering, and the shoulder of the heave offering, which is waved, and which is [1]heaved up, of the ram of the consecration, *even* of *that* which *is* for Aaron, and of *that* which is for his sons:

28 And it shall be Aaron's and his sons' [a]by a statute for ever from the children of Israel: for it *is* an heave offering: and [b]it shall be an heave offering from the children of Israel of the sacrifice of their peace offerings, *even* their heave offering unto the LORD.

29 And the [a]holy garments of Aaron [b]shall be his sons' after him, [c]to be anointed therein, and to be consecrated in them.

30 *And* [a]that son that is priest in his stead shall put them on [b]seven days, when he cometh into the tabernacle of the congregation to minister in the [1]holy *place.*

31 And thou shalt take the ram of the consecration, and [a]seethe[1] his flesh in the holy place.

32 And Aaron and his sons shall eat the flesh of the ram, and the [a]bread that *is* in the basket, *by* the door of the tabernacle of the congregation.

33 And [a]they shall eat those things wherewith the atonement was made, to consecrate *and* to sanctify them: [b]but a stranger shall not eat *thereof,* because they *are* holy.

34 And if ought of the flesh of the consecrations, or of the bread, remain unto the morning, then [a]thou shalt burn the remainder with fire: it shall not be eaten, because it *is* holy.

35 And thus shalt thou do unto Aaron, and to his sons, according to all *things* which I have commanded thee: [a]seven days shalt thou consecrate them.

36 And thou [a]shalt offer every day a bullock *for* a sin offering for atonement: and thou shalt cleanse the altar, when thou hast made an atonement for it, [b]and thou shalt anoint it, to sanctify it.

37 Seven days thou shalt make an atonement for the altar, and sanctify it; and it shall be an altar most holy: [a]whatsoever[1] toucheth the altar shall be holy.

29:10 [a] Lev. 1:4; 8:14

29:12 [a] Lev. 8:15 [b] Ex. 27:2; 30:2; Lev. 4:7

29:13 [a] Lev. 1:8; 3:3, 4

29:14 [a] Lev. 4:11, 12, 21; Heb. 13:11 [1] outside

29:15 [a] Lev. 8:18 [b] Lev. 1:4–9

29:16 [a] Lev. 24:6; Lev. 1:5, 11

29:17 [1] with

29:18 [a] Ex. 20:24 [1] aroma

29:19 [a] Lev. 8:22

29:21 [a] Ex. 30:25, 31; Lev. 8:30 [b] Ex. 28:41; 29:1; [Heb. 9:22]

29:23 [a] Lev. 8:26

29:24 [a] Lev. 7:30; 10:14

29:25 [a] Lev. 8:28

29:26 [a] Lev. 7:31, 34; 8:29

29:27 [a] Lev. 7:31, 34; Num. 18:11, 18; Deut. 18:3 [1] raised

29:28 [a] Lev. 10:15 [b] Lev. 3:1; 7:34

29:29 [a] Ex. 28:2 [b] Num. 20:26, 28 [c] Ex. 28:41; 30:30; Num. 18:8

29:30 [a] Num. 20:28 [b] Lev. 8:35 [1] sanctuary

29:31 [a] Lev. 8:31 [1] boil

29:32 [a] Matt. 12:4

29:33 [a] Lev. 10:14, 15, 17 [b] Ex. 12:43; Lev. 22:10

29:34 [a] Ex. 12:10; 23:18; 34:25; Lev. 7:18; 8:32

29:35 [a] Lev. 8:33–35

29:36 [a] Heb. 10:11 [b] Ex. 30:26–29; 40:10, 11

29:37 [a] Num. 4:15; Hag. 2:11–13; Matt. 23:19 [1] everything that

**38** Now this *is that* which thou shalt offer upon the altar; [a]two lambs of the first year [b]day by day continually.

**39** The one lamb thou shalt offer [a]in the morning; and the other lamb thou shalt offer [1]at even:

**40** And with the one lamb a tenth deal of flour mingled with the fourth part of an hin of beaten oil; and the fourth part of an hin of wine *for* a drink offering.

**41** And the other lamb thou shalt [a]offer [1]at even, and shalt do thereto according to the meat offering of the morning, and according to the drink offering thereof, for a sweet savour, an offering made by fire unto the LORD.

**42** *This shall be* [a]a continual burnt offering throughout your generations *at* the door of the tabernacle of the congregation before the LORD: [b]where I will meet you, to speak there unto thee.

**43** And there I will meet with the children of Israel, and *the tabernacle* [a]shall be sanctified by my glory.

**44** And I will sanctify the tabernacle of the congregation, and the altar: I will [a]sanctify also both Aaron and his sons, to minister to me in the priest's office.

**45** And [a]I will dwell among the children of Israel, and will [b]be their God.

**46** And they shall know that [a]I *am* the LORD their God, that [b]brought them forth out of the land of Egypt, that I may dwell among them: I *am* the LORD their God.

### CHAPTER 30

A ND thou shalt make [a]an altar to burn incense upon: *of* shittim wood shalt thou make it.

**2** A cubit *shall be* the length thereof, and a cubit the breadth thereof; foursquare shall it be: and two cubits *shall be* the height thereof: the horns thereof *shall be* of the same.

**3** And thou shalt overlay it with pure gold, the top thereof, and the sides thereof round about, and the horns thereof; and thou shalt make unto it a [1]crown of gold round about.

**4** And two golden rings shalt thou make to it under the crown of it, by the two corners thereof, upon the two sides of it shalt thou make *it;* and they shall be for places for the staves to bear it withal.

**5** And thou shalt make the staves *of* shittim wood, and overlay them with gold.

**6** And thou shalt put it before the [a]vail that *is* by the ark of the testimony, before the [b]mercy seat that *is* over the testimony, where I will meet with thee.

**7** And Aaron shall burn thereon [a]sweet incense every morning: when

[b]he dresseth the lamps, he shall burn incense upon it.

**8** And when Aaron lighteth the lamps [1]at even, he shall burn incense upon it, a perpetual incense before the LORD throughout your generations.

**9** Ye shall offer no [a]strange incense thereon, nor burnt sacrifice, nor meat offering; neither shall ye pour drink offering thereon.

**10** And [a]Aaron shall make an atonement upon the horns of it once in a year with the blood of the sin offering of atonements: once in the year shall he make atonement upon it throughout your generations: it *is* most holy unto the LORD.

**11** And the LORD spake unto Moses, saying,

**12** [a]When thou takest the sum of the children of Israel after their number, then shall they give every man [b]a [1]ransom for his soul unto the LORD, when thou numberest them; that there be no [c]plague among them, when *thou* numberest them.

**13** [a]This they shall give, every one that passeth among them that are numbered, half a shekel after the shekel of the sanctuary: ([b]a shekel *is* twenty gerahs:) [c]an half shekel *shall be* the offering of the LORD.

**14** Every one that passeth among them that are numbered, from twenty years old and above, shall give an [1]offering unto the LORD.

**15** The [a]rich shall not give more, and the poor shall not give less than half a shekel, when *they* give an offering unto the LORD, to make an atonement for your souls.

**16** And thou shalt take the atonement money of the children of Israel, and [a]shalt [1]appoint it for the service of the tabernacle of the congregation; that it may be [b]a memorial unto the children of Israel before the LORD, to make an atonement for your souls.

**17** And the LORD spake unto Moses, saying,

**18** [a]Thou shalt also make a [1]laver *of* brass, and his foot *also of* brass, to wash *withal:* and thou shalt [b]put it between the tabernacle of the congregation and the altar, and thou shalt put water therein.

**19** For Aaron and his sons [a]shall wash their hands and their feet thereat:

**20** When they go into the tabernacle of the congregation, they shall wash with water, that they die not; or when they come near to the altar to minister, to burn offering made by fire unto the LORD:

**21** So they shall wash their hands and their feet, that they die not: and [a]it shall be a [1]statute for ever to them,

29:38 [a] Num. 28:3–31; 29:6–38; 1 Chr. 16:40; Ezra 3:3 [b] Dan. 12:11

29:39 [a] Ezek. 46:13–15 [1] *at twilight*

29:41 [a] 1 Kin. 18:29, 36; 2 Kin. 16:15; Ezra 9:4, 5; Ps. 141:2 [1] *at twilight*

29:42 [a] Ex. 30:8 [b] Ex. 25:22; 33:7, 9; Num. 17:4

29:43 [a] Ex. 40:34; 1 Kin. 8:11; 2 Chr. 5:14; Ezek. 43:5; Hag. 2:7, 9

29:44 [a] Lev. 21:15

29:45 [a] Ex. 25:8; Lev. 26:12; Num. 5:3; Deut. 12:11; Zech. 2:10; [John 14:17, 23; Rev. 21:3] [b] Gen. 17:8; Lev. 11:45

29:46 [a] Ex. 16:12; 20:2; Deut. 4:35 [b] Lev. 11:45

30:1 [a] Ex. 37:25–29

30:3 [1] *moulding*

30:6 [a] Ex. 26:31–35 [b] Ex. 25:21, 22

30:7 [a] Ex. 30:34; 1 Sam. 2:28; 1 Chr. 23:13; Luke 1:9

[b] Ex. 27:20, 21

30:8 [1] *at twilight*

30:9 [a] Lev. 10:1

30:10 [a] Lev. 16:3–34

30:12 [a] Ex. 38:25, 26; Num. 1:2; 26:2; 2 Sam. 24:2 [b] Num. 31:50; [Matt. 20:28; 1 Pet. 1:18, 19] [c] 2 Sam. 24:15 [1] *price of a life*

30:13 [a] Matt. 17:24 [b] Lev. 27:25; Num. 3:47; Ezek. 45:12 [c] Ex. 38:26

30:14 [1] *contribution*

30:15 [a] Job 34:19; Prov. 22:2; [Eph. 6:9]

30:16 [a] Ex. 38:25–31 [b] Num. 16:40 [1] *give*

30:18 [a] Ex. 38:8; 1 Kin. 7:38 [b] Ex. 40:30 [1] *basin*

30:19 [a] Ex. 40:31, 32; Ps. 26:6; Is. 52:11; John 13:8, 10; Heb. 10:22

30:21 [a] Ex. 28:43 [1] *requirement*

*even* to him and to his [2]seed throughout their generations.

22 Moreover the LORD spake unto Moses, saying,

23 Take thou also unto thee [a]principal spices, of pure [b]myrrh five hundred *shekels,* and of sweet cinnamon half so much, *even* two hundred and fifty *shekels,* and of sweet [c]calamus two hundred and fifty *shekels,*

24 And of [a]cassia five hundred *shekels,* after the shekel of the sanctuary, and of oil olive an [b]hin:

25 And thou shalt make it an oil of holy ointment, an ointment compound after the art of the [1]apothecary: it shall be [a]an holy anointing oil.

26 [a]And thou shalt anoint the tabernacle of the congregation therewith, and the ark of the testimony,

27 And the table and all his vessels, and the candlestick and his vessels, and the altar of incense,

28 And the altar of burnt offering with all his vessels, and the laver and [1]his foot.

29 And thou shalt [1]sanctify them, that they may be most holy: [a]whatsoever[2] toucheth them shall be holy.

30 [a]And thou shalt anoint Aaron and his sons, and consecrate them, that *they* may minister unto me in the priest's office.

31 And thou shalt speak unto the children of Israel, saying, This shall be an holy anointing oil unto me throughout your generations.

32 Upon man's flesh shall it not be poured, neither shall ye make *any other* like it, after the composition of it: [a]it *is* holy, *and* it shall be holy unto you.

33 [a]Whosoever [1]compoundeth *any* like it, or whosoever putteth *any* of it upon a stranger, [b]shall even be [2]cut off from his people.

34 And the LORD said unto Moses, [a]Take unto thee sweet spices, stacte, and onycha, and galbanum; *these* sweet spices with pure frankincense: of each shall there be a like *weight:*

35 And thou shalt make it a perfume, a confection [a]after the art of the [1]apothecary, [2]tempered together, pure *and* holy:

36 And thou shalt beat *some* of it very small, and put of it before the testimony in the tabernacle of the congregation, [a]where I will meet with thee: [b]it shall be unto you most holy.

37 And *as for* the perfume which thou shalt make, [a]ye shall not make to yourselves according to [1]the composition thereof: it shall be unto thee holy for the LORD.

38 [a]Whosoever shall make like unto that, to smell thereto, shall even be cut off from his people.

## Reference Column

30:21 [2] *descendants*
30:23 [a] Song 4:14; Ezek. 27:22 [b] Ps. 45:8; Prov. 7:17 [c] Song 4:14
30:24 [a] Ps. 45:8 [b] Ex. 29:40
30:25 [a] Ex. 37:29; 40:9 [1] *perfumer*
30:26 [a] Lev. 8:10
30:28 [a] *its base*
30:29 [a] Ex. 29:37; Num. 4:15; Hag. 2:11–13 [1] *consecrate* [2] *everything that*
30:30 [a] Lev. 8:12
30:32 [a] Ex. 30:25, 37
30:33 [a] Ex. 30:38 [b] Gen. 17:14 [1] *mixes* [2] *By death*
30:34 [a] Ex. 25:6; 37:29
30:35 [a] Ex. 30:25 [1] *perfumer* [2] *salted*
30:36 [a] Ex. 29:42 [b] Lev. 2:3
30:37 [a] Ex. 30:32 [1] Lit. *its proportion*
30:38 [a] Ex. 30:33

31:2 [a] Ex. 35:30– 36:1 [b] 1 Chr. 2:20
31:3 [a] 1 Kin. 7:14
31:4 [1] *artistic*
31:5 [1] *cutting jewels for setting*
31:6 [a] Ex. 35:34 [b] Ex. 28:3; 35:10, 35; 36:1 [1] *gifted artisans*
31:7 [a] Ex. 36:8 [b] Ex. 37:1–5 [c] Ex. 37:6–9
31:8 [a] Ex. 37:10–16 [b] Ex. 37:17–24
31:9 [a] Ex. 38:1–7 [b] Ex. 38:8
31:10 [a] Ex. 39:1, 41 [1] *woven garments*
31:11 [a] Ex. 30:23– 33 [b] Ex. 30:34–38
31:13 [a] Ezek. 20:12, 20 [b] Lev. 20:8 [1] *set you apart*
31:14 [a] Ex. 20:8 [b] Num. 15:32–36 [1] *profanes* [2] *person* [3] *By death*
31:15 [a] Ex. 20:9–11 [b] Gen. 2:2
31:17 [a] Ex. 31:13 [b] Gen. 1:31; 2:2, 3

## CHAPTER 31

AND the LORD spake unto Moses, saying,

2 [a]See, I have called by name Bezaleel the [b]son of Uri, the son of Hur, of the tribe of Judah:

3 And I have [a]filled him with the spirit of God, in wisdom, and in understanding, and in knowledge, and in all manner of workmanship,

4 To devise [1]cunning works, to work in gold, and in silver, and in brass,

5 And in [1]cutting of stones, to set *them,* and in carving of timber, to work in all manner of workmanship.

6 And I, behold, I have given with him [a]Aholiab, the son of Ahisamach, of the tribe of Dan: and in the hearts of all that are [b]wise[1] hearted I have put wisdom, that they may make all that I have commanded thee;

7 [a]The tabernacle of the congregation, and [b]the ark of the testimony, and [c]the mercy seat that *is* thereupon, and all the furniture of the tabernacle,

8 And [a]the table and his furniture, and [b]the pure candlestick with all his furniture, and the altar of incense,

9 And [a]the altar of burnt offering with all his furniture, and [b]the laver and his foot,

10 And [a]the [1]cloths of service, and the holy garments for Aaron the priest, and the garments of his sons, to minister in the priest's office,

11 [a]And the anointing oil, and [b]sweet incense for the holy *place:* according to all that I have commanded thee shall they do.

12 And the LORD spake unto Moses, saying,

13 Speak thou also unto the children of Israel, saying, [a]Verily my sabbaths ye shall keep: for it *is* a sign between me and you throughout your generations; that *ye* may know that I *am* the LORD that doth [b]sanctify[1] you.

14 [a]Ye shall keep the sabbath therefore; for it *is* holy unto you: every one that [1]defileth it shall surely be put to death: for [b]whosoever doeth *any* work therein, that [2]soul shall be [3]cut off from among his people.

15 [a]Six days may work be done; but in the [b]seventh *is* the sabbath of rest, holy to the LORD: whosoever doeth *any* work in the sabbath day, he shall surely be put to death.

16 Wherefore the children of Israel shall keep the sabbath, to observe the sabbath throughout their generations, *for* a perpetual covenant.

17 It *is* [a]a sign between me and the children of Israel for ever: for [b]in six days the LORD made heaven and earth, and on the seventh day he rested, and was refreshed.

18 And he gave unto Moses, when he had made an end of communing with him upon mount Sinai, [a]two tables of testimony, tables of stone, written with the finger of God.

## CHAPTER 32

A ND when the people saw that Moses [a]delayed to come down out of the mount, the people [b]gathered themselves together unto Aaron, and said unto him, [c]Up, make us [1]gods, which shall [d]go before us; for *as for* this Moses, the man that [e]brought us up out of the land of Egypt, we [2]wot not what is become of him.

2 And Aaron said unto them, Break off the [a]golden earrings, which *are* in the ears of your wives, of your sons, and of your daughters, and bring *them* unto me.

3 And all the people brake off the golden earrings which *were* in their ears, and brought *them* unto Aaron.

4 [a]And he received *them* at their hand, and fashioned it with a graving tool, after he had made it a molten calf: and they said, These *be* thy gods, O Israel, which [b]brought thee up out of the land of Egypt.

5 And when Aaron saw *it,* he built an altar before it; and Aaron made [a]proclamation, and said, To morrow *is* a feast to the LORD.

6 And they rose up early on the morrow, and offered burnt offerings, and brought peace offerings; and the people [a]sat down to eat and to drink, and rose up to play.

7 And the LORD said unto Moses, [a]Go, get thee down; for thy people, which thou broughtest out of the land of Egypt, [b]have corrupted *themselves:*

8 They have turned aside quickly out of the way which [a]I commanded them: they have made them a molten calf, and have worshipped it, and have sacrificed thereunto, and said, [b]These *be* thy gods, O Israel, which have brought thee up out of the land of Egypt.

9 And the LORD said unto Moses, [a]I have seen this people, and, behold, it *is* a [1]stiffnecked people:

10 Now therefore [a]let me alone, that [b]my wrath may wax hot against them, and that I may [1]consume them: and [c]I will make of thee a great nation.

11 [a]And Moses besought [1]the LORD his God, and said, LORD, why doth thy wrath wax hot against thy people, which thou hast brought forth out of the land of Egypt with great power, and with a mighty hand?

12 [a]Wherefore should the Egyptians speak, and say, For [1]mischief did he bring them out, to slay them

in the mountains, and to consume them from the face of the earth? Turn from thy fierce wrath, and [b]repent[2] of this evil against thy people.

13 Remember Abraham, Isaac, and Israel, thy servants, to whom thou [a]swarest by thine own self, and saidst unto them, [b]I will multiply your seed as the stars of heaven, and all this land that I have spoken of will I give unto your seed, and they shall inherit *it* for ever.

14 And the LORD [a]repented[1] of the evil which he thought to do unto his people.

15 [a]Moses turned, and went down from the mount, and the two tables of the testimony *were* in his hand: the tables *were* written on both their sides; on the one side and on the other *were* they written.

16 And the [a]tables *were* the work of God, and the writing *was* the writing of God, graven upon the tables.

17 And when Joshua heard the noise of the people as they shouted, he said unto Moses, *There is* a noise of war in the camp.

18 And he said, *It is* not the voice of *them that* shout for mastery, neither *is it* the voice of *them that* cry for being overcome: *but* the [1]noise of *them that* sing do I hear.

19 And it came to pass, as soon as he came nigh unto the camp, that [a]he saw the calf, and the dancing: and Moses' anger waxed hot, and he cast the tables out of his hands, and brake them beneath the mount.

20 [a]And he took the calf which they had made, and burnt *it* in the fire, and ground *it* to powder, and [1]strawed *it* upon the water, and made the children of Israel drink *of it.*

21 And Moses said unto Aaron, [a]What did this people unto thee, that thou hast brought so great a sin upon them?

22 And Aaron said, Let not the anger of my lord [1]wax hot: [a]thou knowest the people, that they *are set* on [2]mischief.

23 For they said unto me, Make us gods, which shall go before us: for *as for* this Moses, the man that brought us up out of the land of Egypt, we [1]wot not what is become of him.

24 And I said unto them, Whosoever hath any gold, let them break *it* off. So they gave *it* me: then I cast it into the fire, and there came out this calf.

25 And when Moses saw that the people *were* [a]naked; (for Aaron [b]had made them naked unto *their* shame among their enemies:)

26 Then Moses stood in the gate of the camp, and said, Who *is* on the LORD's side? *let him come* unto me.

### Cross references

31:18 [a] [Ex. 24:12; 32:15, 16; Deut. 4:13; 5:22; 2 Cor. 3:3]
32:1 [a] Ex. 24:18; Deut. 9:9–12 [b] Ex. 17:1–3 [c] Acts 7:40 [d] Ex. 13:21 [e] Ex. 32:8 [1] *a god* [2] *know*
32:2 [a] Ex. 11:2; 35:22; Judg. 8:24–27
32:4 [a] Ex. 20:3, 4, 23; Deut. 9:16; Judg. 17:3, 4; 1 Kin. 12:28; Neh. 9:18; Ps. 106:19; Acts 7:41 [b] Ex. 29:45, 46
32:5 [a] Lev. 23:2, 4, 21, 37; 2 Kin. 10:20; 2 Chr. 30:5
32:6 [a] Ex. 32:17–19; Num. 25:2; 1 Cor. 10:7
32:7 [a] Deut. 9:8–21; Dan. 9:14 [b] Gen. 6:11, 12
32:8 [a] Ex. 20:3, 4, 23; Deut. 32:17 [b] 1 Kin. 12:28
32:9 [a] Ex. 33:3, 5; 34:9; Deut. 9:6; 2 Chr. 30:8; Is. 48:4; [Acts 7:51] [1] *stubborn*
32:10 [a] Deut. 9:14, 19 [b] Ex. 22:24 [c] Num. 14:12 [1] *destroy*
32:11 [a] Deut. 9:18, 26–29 [1] Lit. *the face of the LORD*
32:12 [a] Num. 14:13–19; Deut. 9:28; Josh. 7:9 [1] *harm*

32:14 [b] Ex. 32:14 [2] *relent from this harm*
32:13 [a] Gen. 22:16–18; [Heb. 6:13] [b] Gen. 12:7; 13:15; 15:7, 18; 22:17; 26:4; 35:11, 12; Ex. 13:5, 11; 33:1
32:14 [a] 2 Sam. 24:16 [1] *relented from the harm*
32:15 [a] Deut. 9:15
32:16 [a] Ex. 31:18
32:18 [1] *voice*
32:19 [a] Deut. 9:16, 17
32:20 [a] Num. 5:17, 24; Deut. 9:21 [1] *scattered*
32:21 [a] Gen. 26:10
32:22 [a] Ex. 14:11; Deut. 9:24 [1] *became* [2] *evil*
32:23 [1] *know*
32:25 [a] Ex. 33:4, 5 [b] 2 Chr. 28:19

And all the sons of Levi gathered themselves together unto him.

27 And he said unto them, Thus saith the LORD God of Israel, Put every man his sword by his side, *and* go in and out from gate to gate throughout the camp, and [a]slay every man his brother, and every man his companion, and every man his neighbour.

28 And the children of Levi did according to the word of Moses: and there fell of the people that day about three thousand men.

29 [a]For Moses had said, [1]Consecrate yourselves to day to the LORD, even every man upon his son, and upon his brother; that he may bestow upon you a blessing this day.

30 And it came to pass on the morrow, that Moses said unto the people, [a]Ye have sinned a great sin: and now I will go up unto the LORD; [b]peradventure[1] I shall [c]make an atonement for your sin.

31 And Moses [a]returned unto the LORD, and said, Oh, this people have sinned a great sin, and have [b]made them gods of gold.

32 Yet now, if thou wilt forgive their sin—; and if not, [a]blot me, I pray thee, [b]out of thy book which thou hast written.

33 And the LORD said unto Moses, [a]Whosoever hath sinned against me, him will I [b]blot out of my book.

34 Therefore now go, lead the people unto *the place* of which I have [a]spoken unto thee: [b]behold, mine Angel shall go before thee: nevertheless [c]in the day when I [d]visit[1] I will [2]visit their sin upon them.

35 And the LORD plagued the people, because [a]they made the calf, which Aaron made.

## CHAPTER 33

A ND the LORD said unto Moses, Depart, *and* go up hence, thou [a]and the people which thou hast brought up out of the land of Egypt, unto the land which I sware unto Abraham, to Isaac, and to Jacob, saying, [b]Unto thy seed will I give it:

2 [a]And I will send an angel before thee; [b]and I will drive out the Canaanite, the Amorite, and the Hittite, and the Perizzite, the Hivite, and the Jebusite:

3 [a]Unto a land flowing with milk and honey: for I will not go up in the midst of thee; for thou *art* a [b]stiffnecked[1] people: lest [c]I [2]consume thee in the way.

4 And when the people heard these evil tidings, [a]they mourned: [b]and no man did put on him his ornaments.

5 For the LORD had said unto Moses, Say unto the children of Israel,

Ye *are* a stiffnecked people: I will come up into the midst of thee in a moment, and consume thee: therefore now put off thy [1]ornaments from thee, that I may [a]know what to do unto thee.

6 And the children of Israel stripped themselves of their ornaments by the mount Horeb.

7 And Moses took the tabernacle, and pitched it [1]without the camp, afar off from the camp, and [a]called it the Tabernacle of the congregation. And it came to pass, *that* every one which [b]sought the LORD went out unto the tabernacle of the congregation, which *was* without the camp.

8 And it came to pass, when Moses went out unto the tabernacle, *that* all the people rose up, and stood every man [a]at his tent door, and looked after Moses, until he was gone into the tabernacle.

9 And it came to pass, as Moses entered into the tabernacle, the cloudy pillar descended, and stood *at* the door of the tabernacle, and *the* [1]LORD [a]talked with Moses.

10 And all the people saw the cloudy pillar stand *at* the tabernacle door: and all the people rose up and [a]worshipped, every man *in* his tent door.

11 And [a]the LORD spake unto Moses face to face, as a man speaketh unto his friend. And he turned again into the camp: but [b]his servant Joshua, the son of Nun, a young man, departed not out of the tabernacle.

12 And Moses said unto the LORD, See, [a]thou sayest unto me, Bring up this people: and thou hast not let me know whom thou wilt send with me. Yet thou hast said, [b]I know thee by name, and thou hast also found grace in my sight.

13 Now therefore, I pray thee, [a]if I have found grace in thy sight, [b]shew me now thy way, that I may know thee, that I may find grace in thy sight: and consider that this nation *is* [c]thy people.

14 And he said, [a]My presence shall go *with thee*, and I will give thee [b]rest.

15 And he said unto him, [a]If thy presence go not *with me*, carry us not up hence.

16 For wherein shall it be known here that I and thy people have found grace in thy sight? [a]*is it* not in that thou goest with us? so [b]shall we be separated, I and thy people, from all the people that *are* upon the face of the earth.

17 And the LORD said unto Moses, [a]I will do this thing also that thou hast spoken: for thou hast found grace in my sight, and I know thee by name.

### Center reference column

32:27 [a] Num. 25:5–13

32:29 [a] Ex. 28:41; 1 Sam. 15:18, 22; Prov. 21:3; Zech. 13:3 [1] Lit. *Fill your hand today*

32:30 [a] 1 Sam. 12:20, 23 [b] 2 Sam. 16:12 [c] Num. 25:13 [1] *perhaps I can*

32:31 [a] Deut. 9:18 [b] Ex. 20:23

32:32 [a] Ps. 69:28; Is. 4:3; Mal. 3:16; Rom. 9:3 [b] Dan. 12:1; Phil. 4:3; Rev. 3:5; 21:27

32:33 [a] Lev. 23:30; [Ezek. 18:4; 33:2, 14, 15] [b] Ex. 17:14; Deut. 29:20; Ps. 9:5; Rev. 3:5; 21:27

32:34 [a] Ex. 3:17 [b] Ex. 23:20; Josh. 5:14 [c] Deut. 32:35; Rom. 2:5, 6 [d] Ps. 89:32 [1] *visit for punishment* [2] *visit punishment upon them for their sin*

32:35 [a] Neh. 9:18

33:1 [a] Ex. 32:1, 7, 13; Josh. 3:17 [b] Gen. 12:7

33:2 [a] Ex. 32:34; Josh. 5:14 [b] Ex. 23:27–31; Josh. 24:11

33:3 [a] Ex. 3:8 [b] Num. 16:21, 45 [c] Ex. 32:9; 33:5 [1] *stubborn* [2] *destroy*

33:4 [a] Num. 14:1, 39 [b] Ezra 9:3; Esth. 4:1, 4; Ezek. 24:17, 23

33:5 [a] [Ps. 139:23] [1] *jewels*

33:7 [a] Ex. 29:42, 43 [b] Deut. 4:29 [1] *outside*

33:8 [a] Num. 16:27

33:9 [a] Ex. 25:22; 31:18; Ps. 99:7 [1] Lit. *He*

33:10 [a] Ex. 4:31

33:11 [a] Num. 12:8; Deut. 34:10 [b] Ex. 24:13

33:12 [a] Ex. 3:10; 32:34 [b] Ex. 33:17; John 10:14, 15; 2 Tim. 2:19

33:13 [a] Ex. 34:9 [b] Ps. 25:4; 27:11; 86:11; 119:33 [c] Deut. 9:26, 29

33:14 [a] Is. 63:9 [b] Josh. 21:44; 22:4

33:15 [a] Ex. 33:3

33:16 [a] Num. 14:14 [b] Ex. 34:10

33:17 [a] [James 5:16]

18 And he said, I beseech thee, shew me [a]thy glory.

19 And he said, I will make all my [a]goodness pass before thee, and I will proclaim the name of the LORD before thee; [b]and will be gracious to whom I will be [c]gracious, and will shew mercy on whom I will shew mercy.

20 And he said, Thou canst not see my face: for [a]there shall no man see me, and live.

21 And the LORD said, Behold, there is a place by me, and thou shalt stand upon a rock:

22 And it shall come to pass, while my glory passeth by, that I will put thee [a]in a clift of the rock, and will [b]cover thee with my hand while I pass by:

23 And I will take away mine hand, and thou shalt see my back parts: but my face shall [a]not be seen.

## CHAPTER 34

AND the LORD said unto Moses, [a]Hew[1] thee two tables of stone like unto the first: and [b]I will write upon these tables the words that were in the first tables, which thou brakest.

2 And be ready in the morning, and come up in the morning unto mount Sinai, and present thyself there to me [a]in the top of the mount.

3 And no man shall [a]come up with thee, neither let any man be seen throughout all the mount; neither let the flocks nor herds feed before that mount.

4 And he hewed two tables of stone like unto the first; and Moses rose up early in the morning, and went up unto mount Sinai, as the LORD had commanded him, and took in his hand the two tables of stone.

5 And the LORD descended in the [a]cloud, and stood with him there, and [b]proclaimed the name of the LORD.

6 And the LORD passed by before him, and proclaimed, The LORD, The LORD [a]God, merciful and gracious, longsuffering, and abundant in [b]goodness and [c]truth,

7 [a]Keeping mercy for thousands, [b]forgiving iniquity and transgression and sin, and [c]that will by no means clear the guilty; visiting the iniquity of the fathers upon the children, and upon the children's children, unto the third and to the fourth generation.

8 And Moses made haste, and [a]bowed his head toward the earth, and worshipped.

9 And he said, If now I have found grace in thy sight, O Lord, [a]let my Lord, I pray thee, go among us; for it is a [b]stiffnecked[1] people; and pardon our iniquity and our sin, and take us for [c]thine inheritance.

10 And he said, Behold, [a]I make a covenant: before all thy people I will [b]do [1]marvels, such as have not been done in all the earth, nor in any nation: and all the people among which thou art shall see the work of the LORD: for it is [c]a [2]terrible thing that I will do with thee.

11 [a]Observe thou that which I command thee this day: behold, [b]I drive out before thee the Amorite, and the Canaanite, and the Hittite, and the Perizzite, and the Hivite, and the Jebusite.

12 [a]Take heed to thyself, lest thou make a covenant with the inhabitants of the land whither thou goest, lest it be for a snare in the midst of thee:

13 But ye shall [a]destroy their altars, break their images, and [b]cut down their groves:

14 For thou shalt worship [a]no other god: for the LORD, whose [b]name is Jealous, is a [c]jealous God:

15 Lest thou make a covenant with the inhabitants of the land, and they [a]go[1] a whoring after their gods, and do sacrifice unto their gods, and one [b]call thee, and thou [c]eat of his sacrifice;

16 And thou take of [a]their daughters unto thy sons, and their daughters [b]go a whoring after their gods, and make thy sons go a whoring after their gods.

17 [a]Thou shalt make thee no molten gods.

18 The feast of [a]unleavened bread shalt thou keep. Seven days thou shalt eat unleavened bread, as I commanded thee, in the time of the [b]month Abib: for in the month Abib thou camest out from Egypt.

19 [a]All that openeth the [1]matrix is mine; and every firstling among thy cattle, whether ox or sheep, that is male.

20 But [a]the firstling of an ass thou shalt redeem with a lamb: and if thou redeem him not, then shalt thou break his neck. All the firstborn of thy sons thou shalt redeem. And none shall appear before me [b]empty.

21 [a]Six days thou shalt work, but on the seventh day thou shalt rest: [1]in earing time and in harvest thou shalt rest.

22 And thou shalt observe the feast of weeks, of the firstfruits of wheat harvest, and the feast of ingathering at the year's end.

23 [a]Thrice in the year shall all your men children appear before the Lord GOD, the God of Israel.

24 For I will [a]cast out the nations before thee, and enlarge thy borders:

### Cross references

33:18 [a] [1 Tim. 6:16]
33:19 [a] Ex. 34:6, 7 [b] [Rom. 9:15, 16, 18] [c] [Rom. 4:4, 16]
33:20 [a] [Gen. 32:30]
33:22 [a] Is. 2:21 [b] Ps. 91:1, 4
33:23 [a] [John 1:18]
34:1 [a] [Ex. 24:12; 31:18; 32:15, 16, 19] [b] Deut. 10:2, 4 [1] Cut out
34:2 [a] Ex. 19:11, 18, 20
34:3 [a] Ex. 19:12, 13; 24:9–11
34:5 [a] Ex. 19:9 [b] Ex. 33:19
34:6 [a] Neh. 9:17 [b] Rom. 2:4 [c] Ps. 108:4
34:7 [a] Ex. 20:6 [b] Ps. 103:3, 4 [c] Job 10:14
34:8 [a] Ex. 4:31
34:9 [a] Ex. 33:12–16
[b] Ex. 33:3 [c] Ps. 33:12; 94:14 [1] stubborn
34:10 [a] Deut. 5:2 [b] Ps. 77:14 [c] Ps. 145:6 [1] wonderful acts [2] awesome
34:11 [a] Deut. 6:25 [b] Ex. 23:20–33; 33:2
34:12 [a] Ex. 23:32, 33
34:13 [a] Deut. 12:3 [b] 2 Kin. 18:4
34:14 [a] [Ex. 20:3–5] [b] [Is. 9:6; 57:15] [c] [Deut. 4:24]
34:15 [a] Judg. 2:17 [b] Num. 25:1, 2 [c] 1 Cor. 8:4, 7, 10 [1] play the harlot with
34:16 [a] Gen. 28:1 [b] Num. 25:1, 2
34:17 [a] Ex. 20:4, 23; 32:8
34:18 [a] Ex. 12:15, 16 [b] Ex. 12:2; 13:4
34:19 [a] Ex. 13:2; 22:29 [1] womb
34:20 [a] Ex. 13:13 [b] Ex. 22:29; 23:15; Deut. 16:16
34:21 [a] Ex. 20:9; 23:12; 31:15; 35:2; Lev. 23:3; Deut. 5:13 [1] at plowing time
34:23 [a] Ex. 23:14–17
34:24 [a] [Ex. 33:2]; Josh. 11:23; 1 Kin. 4:21; 2 Chr. 36:14–16; Ps. 78:55

neither shall any man desire thy land, when thou shalt go up to appear before the LORD thy God thrice in the year.

25 Thou shalt not offer the blood of my sacrifice with leaven; [a]neither shall the sacrifice of the feast of the passover be left unto the morning.

26 [a]The first of the firstfruits of thy land thou shalt bring unto the house of the LORD thy God. Thou shalt not [1]seethe a kid in his mother's milk.

27 And the LORD said unto Moses, Write thou [a]these words: for [1]after the tenor of these words I have made a covenant with thee and with Israel.

28 [a]And he was there with the LORD forty days and forty nights; he did neither eat bread, nor drink water. And [b]he wrote upon the tables the words of the covenant, the [1]ten commandments.

29 And it came to pass, when Moses came down from mount Sinai with the [a]two tables of testimony in Moses' hand, when he came down from the mount, that Moses [1]wist not that [b]the skin of his face shone while he talked with him.

30 And when Aaron and all the children of Israel saw Moses, behold, the skin of his face shone; and they were afraid to come nigh him.

31 And Moses called unto them; and Aaron and all the rulers of the congregation returned unto him: and Moses talked with them.

32 And afterward all the children of Israel came nigh: [a]and he gave them in commandment all that the LORD had spoken with him in mount Sinai.

33 And [i]till Moses had done speaking with them, he put [a]a vail on his face.

34 But [a]when Moses went in before the LORD to speak with him, he took the vail off, until he came out. And he came out, and spake unto the children of Israel that which he was commanded.

35 And the children of Israel saw the face of Moses, that the skin of Moses' face shone: and Moses put the vail upon his face again, until he went in to speak with him.

## CHAPTER 35

AND Moses gathered all the congregation of the children of Israel together, and said unto them, [a]These are the words which the LORD hath commanded, that ye should do them.

2 [a]Six days shall work be done, but on the seventh day there shall be to you an holy day, a sabbath of rest to the LORD: whosoever doeth work therein shall be put to [b]death.

3 [a]Ye shall kindle no fire throughout your habitations upon the sabbath day.

34:25 [a] Ex. 12:10
34:26 [a] Ex. 23:19; Deut. 26:2 [1] boil
34:27 [a] Ex. 17:14; 24:4; Deut. 31:9 [1] according to
34:28 [a] Ex. 24:18 [b] Ex. 34:1, 4; Deut. 4:31; 10:2, 4 [1] Lit. ten words
34:29 [a] Ex. 32:15 [b] Matt. 17:2; 2 Cor. 3:7 [1] did not know
34:32 [a] Ex. 24:3
34:33 [a] [2 Cor. 3:13, 14]
34:34 [a] [2 Cor. 3:13–16]
35:1 [a] Ex. 34:32
35:2 [a] Ex. 20:9, 10; Lev. 23:3; Deut. 5:13 [b] Num. 15:32–36
35:3 [a] Ex. 12:16; 16:23

35:4 [a] Ex. 25:1, 2
35:5 [a] Ex. 25:2; 1 Chr. 29:14; Mark 12:41–44; 2 Cor. 8:10–12; 9:7 [b] Ex. 38:24
35:6 [a] Ex. 36:8 [b] Ex. 36:14
35:8 [a] Ex. 25:6; 30:23–25
35:10 [a] Ex. 31:2–6; 36:1, 2 [1] skilful
35:11 [a] Ex. 26:1, 2; 36:14
35:12 [a] Ex. 25:10–22
35:13 [a] Ex. 25:23 [b] Ex. 25:30; Lev. 24:5, 6
35:14 [a] Ex. 25:31
35:15 [a] Ex. 30:1 [b] Ex. 30:25 [c] Ex. 30:34–38
35:16 [a] Ex. 27:1–8
35:17 [a] Ex. 27:9–18
35:19 [a] Ex. 31:10; 39:1, 41 [1] woven garments
35:21 [a] Ex. 25:2; 35:5, 22, 26, 29; 36:2 [b] Ex. 35:24 [1] Lit. lifted up
35:22 [a] Ex. 32:2, 3 [b] Ex. 11:2
35:23 [a] 1 Chr. 29:8

4 And Moses spake unto all the congregation of the children of Israel, saying, [a]This is the thing which the LORD commanded, saying,

5 Take ye from among you an offering unto the LORD: [a]whosoever is of a willing heart, let him bring it, an offering of the LORD; [b]gold, and silver, and brass,

6 And [a]blue, and purple, and scarlet, and fine linen, and [b]goats' hair,

7 And rams' skins dyed red, and badgers' skins, and shittim wood,

8 And oil for the light, [a]and spices for anointing oil, and for the sweet incense,

9 And onyx stones, and stones to be set for the ephod, and for the breastplate.

10 And [a]every [1]wise hearted among you shall come, and make all that the LORD hath commanded;

11 [a]The tabernacle, his tent, and his covering, his taches, and his boards, his bars, his pillars, and his sockets,

12 [a]The ark, and the staves thereof, with the mercy seat, and the vail of the covering,

13 The [a]table, and his staves, and all his vessels, [b]and the shewbread,

14 [a]The candlestick also for the light, and his furniture, and his lamps, with the oil for the light,

15 [a]And the incense altar, and his staves, [b]and the anointing oil, and [c]the sweet incense, and the hanging for the door at the entering in of the tabernacle,

16 [a]The altar of burnt offering, with his brasen grate, his staves, and all his vessels, the laver and his foot,

17 [a]The hangings of the court, his pillars, and their sockets, and the hanging for the door of the court,

18 The pins of the tabernacle, and the pins of the court, and their cords,

19 [a]The [1]cloths of service, to do service in the holy place, the holy garments for Aaron the priest, and the garments of his sons, to minister in the priest's office.

20 And all the congregation of the children of Israel departed from the presence of Moses.

21 And they came, every one [a]whose heart [1]stirred him up, and every one whom his spirit made willing, and they [b]brought the LORD's offering to the work of the tabernacle of the congregation, and for all his service, and for the holy garments.

22 And they came, both men and women, as many as were willing hearted, and brought bracelets, and [a]earrings, and rings, and tablets, all [b]jewels of gold: and every man that offered offered an offering of gold unto the LORD.

23 And [a]every man, with whom was

82

found blue, and purple, and scarlet, and fine linen, and goats' *hair*, and red skins of rams, and badgers' skins, brought *them*.

24 Every one that did offer an offering of silver and brass brought the LORD's offering: and every man, with whom was found shittim wood for any work of the service, brought *it*.

25 And all the women that were [a]wise[1] hearted did spin with their hands, and brought that which they had spun, *both* of blue, and of purple, *and* of scarlet, and of fine linen.

26 And all the women whose heart [1]stirred them up in wisdom spun goats' *hair*.

27 And [a]the rulers brought onyx stones, and stones to be set, for the ephod, and for the breastplate;

28 And [a]spice, and oil for the light, and for the anointing oil, and for the sweet incense.

29 The children of Israel brought a [a]willing[1] offering unto the LORD, every man and woman, whose heart made them willing to bring for all manner of work, which the LORD had commanded to be made by the hand of Moses.

30 And Moses said unto the children of Israel, See, [a]the LORD hath called by name Bezaleel the son of Uri, the son of Hur, of the tribe of Judah;

31 And he hath filled him with the spirit of God, in wisdom, in understanding, and in knowledge, and in all manner of workmanship;

32 And to devise [1]curious works, to work in gold, and in silver, and in brass,

33 And in the cutting of stones, to set *them*, and in carving of wood, to make any manner of [1]cunning work.

34 And he hath put in his heart that he may teach, *both* he, and [a]Aholiab, the son of Ahisamach, of the tribe of Dan.

35 Them hath he [a]filled with wisdom of heart, to work all manner of work, of the engraver, and of the cunning workman, and of the embroiderer, in blue, and in purple, in scarlet, and in fine linen, and of the weaver, *even* of them that do any work, and of those that devise cunning work.

## CHAPTER 36

THEN wrought Bezaleel and Aholiab, and every [a]wise hearted man, in whom the LORD put wisdom and understanding to know how to work all manner of work for the service of the [b]sanctuary,[1] according to all that the LORD had commanded.

2 And Moses called Bezaleel and Aholiab, and every wise hearted

man, in whose heart the LORD had put wisdom, *even* every one [a]whose heart [1]stirred him up to come unto the work to do it:

3 And they received of Moses all the [a]offering, which the children of Israel [b]had brought for the work of the service of the sanctuary, to make it *withal*. And they brought yet unto him free offerings every morning.

4 And all the wise men, that wrought all the work of the sanctuary, came every man from his work which they made;

5 And they spake unto Moses, saying, [a]The people bring much more than enough for the service of the work, which the LORD commanded to make.

6 And Moses gave commandment, and they caused it to be proclaimed throughout the camp, saying, Let neither man nor woman make any more work for the offering of the sanctuary. So the people were restrained from bringing.

7 For the stuff they had was sufficient for all the work to make it, and too [a]much.

8 [a]And every [1]wise hearted man among them that wrought the work of the tabernacle made ten curtains *of* fine twined linen, and blue, and purple, and scarlet: *with* cherubims of [2]cunning work made he them.

9 The length of one curtain *was* twenty and eight cubits, and the breadth of one curtain four cubits: the curtains *were* all of one size.

10 And he coupled the five curtains one unto another: and *the other* five curtains he coupled one unto another.

11 And he made loops of blue on the edge of one curtain [1]from the selvedge in the coupling: likewise he made in the uttermost side of *another* curtain, in the coupling of the second.

12 [a]Fifty loops made he in one curtain, and fifty loops made he in the edge of the curtain which *was* in the coupling of the second: the loops held one *curtain* to another.

13 And he made fifty [1]taches of gold, and coupled the curtains one unto another with the taches: so it became one tabernacle.

14 [a]And he made curtains *of* goats' *hair* for the tent over the tabernacle: eleven curtains he made them.

15 The length of one curtain *was* thirty cubits, and four cubits *was* the breadth of one curtain: the eleven curtains *were* of one size.

16 And he coupled five curtains by themselves, and six curtains by themselves.

17 And he made fifty loops upon the uttermost edge of the curtain in

the ¹coupling, and fifty loops made he upon the edge of the curtain which coupleth the second.

18 And he made fifty taches *of* brass to couple the tent together, that it might be one.

19 ³And he made a covering for the tent *of* rams' skins dyed red, and a covering *of* ¹badgers' skins above *that.*

20 ³And he made boards for the tabernacle *of* shittim wood, standing up.

21 The length of a board *was* ten cubits, and the breadth of a board one cubit and a half.

22 One board had two ¹tenons, ³equally distant one from another: thus did he make for all the boards of the tabernacle.

23 And he made boards for the tabernacle; twenty boards for the south side southward:

24 And forty sockets of silver he made under the twenty boards; two sockets under one board for his two tenons, and two sockets under another board for his two tenons.

25 And for the other side of the tabernacle, *which is* toward the north corner, he made twenty boards,

26 And their forty sockets of silver; two sockets under one board, and two sockets under another board.

27 And for the sides of the tabernacle westward he made six boards.

28 And two boards made he for the corners of the tabernacle in the two sides.

29 And they were ¹coupled beneath, and coupled together at the head thereof, to one ring: thus he did to both of them in both the corners.

30 And there were eight boards; and their sockets *were* sixteen sockets of silver, under every board two sockets.

31 And he made ³bars of shittim wood; five for the boards of the one side of the tabernacle,

32 And five bars for the boards of the other side of the tabernacle, and five bars for the boards of the tabernacle for the sides westward.

33 And he made the middle bar to ¹shoot through the boards from the one end to the other.

34 And he overlaid the boards with gold, and made their rings *of* gold *to be* places for the bars, and overlaid the bars with gold.

35 And he made ³a vail *of* blue, and purple, and scarlet, and fine twined linen: *with* cherubims made he it of cunning work.

36 And he made thereunto four pillars *of* shittim *wood,* and overlaid them with gold: their hooks *were of* gold; and he cast for them four sockets of silver.

36:17 ¹ *one set*
36:19 ³ Ex. 26:14
¹ Or *dolphin skins*
36:20 ³ Ex. 26:15–29
36:22 ³ Ex. 26:17
¹ Projections for joining
36:29 ¹ *twined*
36:31 ³ Ex. 26:26–29
36:33 ¹ *pass*
36:35 ³ Ex. 26:31–37

37 And he made an ³hanging¹ for the tabernacle door *of* blue, and purple, and scarlet, and fine twined linen, ²of needlework;

38 And the five pillars of it with their hooks: and he overlaid their ¹chapiters and their fillets with gold: but their five sockets *were of* brass.

## CHAPTER 37

AND ³Bezaleel made ᵇthe ark *of* shittim wood: two cubits and a half *was* the length of it, and a cubit and a half the breadth of it, and a cubit and a half the height of it:

2 And he overlaid it with pure gold ¹within and without, and made a ²crown of gold to it round about.

3 And he cast for it four rings of gold, *to be set* by the four corners of it; even two rings upon the one side of it, and two rings upon the other side of it.

4 And he made staves *of* shittim wood, and overlaid them with gold.

5 And he put the staves into the rings by the sides of the ark, to bear the ark.

6 And he made the ³mercy seat *of* pure gold: two cubits and a half *was* the length thereof, and one cubit and a half the breadth thereof.

7 And he made two cherubims *of* gold, beaten out of one piece made he them, on the two ends of the mercy seat;

8 One cherub on the end on this side, and another cherub on the *other* end on that side: out of the mercy seat made he the cherubims on the two ends thereof.

9 ³And the cherubims spread out *their* wings on high, *and* covered with their wings over the mercy seat, with their faces one to another; *even* to the mercy seatward were the faces of the cherubims.

10 And he made ³the table *of* shittim wood: two cubits *was* the length thereof, and a cubit the breadth thereof, and a cubit and a half the height thereof:

11 And he overlaid it with pure gold, and made thereunto a crown of gold round about.

12 Also he made thereunto a border of an handbreadth round about; and made a crown of gold for the border thereof round about.

13 And he cast for it four rings of gold, and put the rings upon the four corners that *were* in the four feet thereof.

14 Over against the border were the rings, the places for the staves to bear the table.

15 And he made the staves *of* shittim wood, and overlaid them with gold, to bear the table.

36:37 ³ Ex. 26:36
¹ *screen* ² *made by a weaver in colours*
36:38 ¹ *capitals*
37:1 ³ Ex. 35:30; 36:1 ᵇ Ex. 25:10–20
37:2 ¹ *inside and outside* ² *moulding*
37:6 ³ Ex. 25:17
37:9 ³ Ex. 25:20
37:10 ³ Ex. 25:23–29

16 And he made the vessels which were upon the table, his [a]dishes, and his spoons, and his bowls, and his covers to cover [1]withal, of pure gold.

17 And he made the [a]candlestick of pure gold: of beaten work made he the candlestick; his shaft, and his branch, his bowls, his knops, and his flowers, were of the same:

18 And six branches going out of the sides thereof; three branches of the candlestick out of the one side thereof, and three branches of the candlestick out of the other side thereof:

19 Three bowls made after the fashion of almonds in one branch, a knop and a flower; and three bowls made like almonds in another branch, a knop and a flower: so throughout the six branches going out of the candlestick.

20 And in the candlestick were four bowls made like almonds, his knops, and his flowers:

21 And a knop under two branches of the same, and a knop under two branches of the same, and a knop under two branches of the same, according to the six branches going out of it.

22 Their knops and their branches were of the same: all of it was one beaten work of pure gold.

23 And he made his seven lamps, and his [a]snuffers, and his snuffdishes, of pure gold.

24 Of a talent of pure gold made he it, and all the vessels thereof.

25 [a]And he made the incense altar of shittim wood: the length of it was a cubit, and the breadth of it a cubit; it was foursquare; and two cubits was the height of it; the horns thereof were of the same.

26 And he overlaid it with pure gold, both the top of it, and the sides thereof round about, and the horns of it: also he made unto it a crown of gold round about.

27 And he made two rings of gold for it under the crown thereof, by the two corners of it, upon the two sides thereof, to be places for the staves to bear it [1]withal.

28 And he [a]made the staves of shittim wood, and overlaid them with gold.

29 And he made [a]the holy anointing oil, and the pure incense of sweet spices, according to the work of the [1]apothecary.

## CHAPTER 38

AND [a]he made the altar of burnt offering of shittim wood: five cubits was the length thereof, and five cubits the breadth thereof; it was foursquare; and three cubits the height thereof.

37:16 [a] Ex. 25:29
[1] with them
37:17 [a] Ex. 25:31–39
37:23 [a] Num. 4:9
37:25 [a] Ex. 30:1–5
37:27 [1] with them
37:28 [a] Ex. 30:5
37:29 [a] Ex. 30:23–25 [1] perfumer
38:1 [a] Ex. 27:1–8

2 And he made the horns thereof on the four corners of it; the horns thereof were of the same: and he overlaid it with brass.

3 And he made all the vessels of the altar, the pots, and the shovels, and the basons, and the fleshhooks, and the firepans: all the vessels thereof made he of brass.

4 And he made for the altar a brasen grate of network under the compass thereof beneath unto the midst of it.

5 And he cast four rings for the four ends of the grate of brass, to be places for the staves.

6 And he made the staves of shittim wood, and overlaid them with brass.

7 And he put the staves into the rings on the sides of the altar, to bear it withal; he made the altar hollow with boards.

8 And he made [a]the laver of brass, and the foot of it of brass, of the [1]lookingglasses of the women assembling, which assembled at the door of the tabernacle of the congregation.

9 And he made [a]the court: on the south side southward the hangings of the court were of fine twined linen, an hundred cubits:

10 Their pillars were twenty, and their brasen sockets twenty; the hooks of the pillars and their fillets were of silver.

11 And for the north side the hangings were an hundred cubits, their pillars were twenty, and their sockets of brass twenty; the hooks of the pillars and their fillets of silver.

12 And for the west side were hangings of fifty cubits, their pillars ten, and their sockets ten; the hooks of the pillars and their fillets of silver.

13 And for the east side eastward fifty cubits.

14 The hangings of the one side of the gate were fifteen cubits; their pillars three, and their sockets three.

15 And for the other side of the court gate, on this hand and that hand, were hangings of fifteen cubits; their pillars three, and their sockets three.

16 All the hangings of the court round about were of fine twined linen.

17 And the sockets for the pillars were of brass; the hooks of the pillars and their fillets of silver; and the overlaying of their [1]chapiters of silver; and all the pillars of the court were filleted with silver.

18 And the hanging for the gate of the court was needlework, of blue, and purple, and scarlet, and fine twined linen: and twenty cubits was the length, and the height in the breadth was five cubits, [1]answerable to the hangings of the court.

19 And their pillars were four, and their sockets of brass four; their hooks

38:8 [a] Ex. 30:18
[1] mirrors
38:9 [a] Ex. 27:9–19
38:17 [1] capitals
38:18 [1] corresponding

*of* silver, and the overlaying of their ¹chapiters and their fillets *of* silver.

20 And all the ªpins of the tabernacle, and of the court round about, *were of* brass.

21 This is the ¹sum of the tabernacle, *even* of ªthe tabernacle of testimony, as it was counted, according to the commandment of Moses, *for* the service of the Levites, ᵇby the hand of ᶜIthamar, son to Aaron the priest.

22 And ªBezaleel the son of Uri, the son of Hur, of the tribe of Judah, made all that the LORD commanded Moses.

23 And with him *was* ªAholiab, son of Ahisamach, of the tribe of Dan, an engraver, and a ¹cunning workman, and an embroiderer in blue, and in purple, and in scarlet, and fine linen.

24 All the gold that was occupied for the work in all the work of the holy *place,* even the gold of the ªoffering, was twenty and nine talents, and seven hundred and thirty shekels, after ᵇthe shekel of the sanctuary.

25 And the silver of them that were ªnumbered of the congregation *was* an hundred talents, and a thousand seven hundred and threescore and fifteen shekels, after the shekel of the sanctuary:

26 ªA bekah for ¹every man, *that is,* half a shekel, after the shekel of the sanctuary, for every one that went to be numbered, from twenty years old and upward, for ᵇsix hundred thousand and three thousand and five hundred and fifty *men.*

27 And of the hundred talents of silver were cast ªthe sockets of the sanctuary, and the sockets of the vail; an hundred sockets of the hundred talents, a talent for a socket.

28 And of the thousand seven hundred seventy and five *shekels* he made hooks for the pillars, and overlaid their ¹chapiters, and ªfilleted them.

29 And the brass of the offering *was* seventy talents, and two thousand and four hundred shekels.

30 And therewith he made the sockets to the door of the tabernacle of the congregation, and the brasen altar, and the brasen grate for it, and all the vessels of the altar,

31 And the sockets of the court round about, and the sockets of the court gate, and all the pins of the tabernacle, and all the pins of the court round about.

## CHAPTER 39

AND of the ªblue, and purple, and scarlet, they made ᵇcloths¹ of service, to do service in the ²holy *place,* and made the holy garments for Aaron; ᶜas the LORD commanded Moses.

### Cross References

38:19 ¹ *capitals*
38:20 ª Ex. 27:19
38:21 ª Num. 1:50, 53; 9:15; 10:11; 17:7, 8; 2 Chr. 24:6; Acts 7:44 ᵇ Num. 4:28, 33 ᶜ Ex. 28:1; Lev. 10:6, 16 ¹ *inventory*
38:22 ª Ex. 31:2, 6; 1 Chr. 2:18–20
38:23 ª Ex. 31:6; 36:1 ¹ *designer*
38:24 ª Ex. 35:5, 22 ᵇ Ex. 30:13, 24; Lev. 5:15; 27:3, 25; Num. 3:47; 18:16
38:25 ª Ex. 30:11–16; Num. 1:2
38:26 ª Ex. 30:13, 15 ᵇ Ex. 12:37; Num. 1:46; 26:51 ¹ Lit. *a head*
38:27 ª Ex. 26:19, 21, 25, 32
38:28 ª Ex. 27:17 ¹ *capitals*
39:1 ª Ex. 25:4; 35:23 ᵇ Ex. 31:10; 35:19 ᶜ Ex. 28:4 ¹ *woven garments* ² *sanctuary*

39:2 ª Ex. 28:6–14 ᵇ Lev. 8:7
39:3 ¹ *artistic designs*
39:6 ª Ex. 28:9–11 ¹ *settings*
39:7 ª Ex. 28:12, 29; Josh. 4:7
39:8 ª Ex. 28:15–30
39:10 ª Ex. 28:17 ¹ *ruby*
39:13 ¹ *settings*
39:14 ª Rev. 21:12
39:15 ¹ *braided cords*
39:16 ¹ *settings*
39:18 ¹ *settings*

2 ªAnd he made the ᵇephod *of* gold, blue, and purple, and scarlet, and fine twined linen.

3 And they did beat the gold into thin plates, and cut *it into* wires, to work *it* in the blue, and in the purple, and in the scarlet, and in the fine linen, *with* ¹cunning work.

4 They made shoulderpieces for it, to couple *it* together: by the two edges was it coupled together.

5 And the curious girdle of his ephod, that *was* upon it, *was* of the same, according to the work thereof; *of* gold, blue, and purple, and scarlet, and fine twined linen; as the LORD commanded Moses.

6 ªAnd they wrought onyx stones inclosed in ¹ouches of gold, graven, as signets are graven, with the names of the children of Israel.

7 And he put them on the shoulders of the ephod, *that they should be* stones for a ªmemorial to the children of Israel; as the LORD commanded Moses.

8 ªAnd he made the breastplate *of* cunning work, like the work of the ephod; *of* gold, blue, and purple, and scarlet, and fine twined linen.

9 It was foursquare; they made the breastplate double: a span *was* the length thereof, and a span the breadth thereof, *being* doubled.

10 ªAnd they set in it four rows of stones: *the first* row *was* a ¹sardius, a topaz, and a carbuncle: this *was* the first row.

11 And the second row, an emerald, a sapphire, and a diamond.

12 And the third row, a ligure, an agate, and an amethyst.

13 And the fourth row, a beryl, an onyx, and a jasper: *they were* inclosed in ¹ouches of gold in their inclosings.

14 And the stones *were* according to the names of the children of Israel, ªtwelve, according to their names, *like* the engravings of a signet, every one with his name, according to the twelve tribes.

15 And they made upon the breastplate chains at the ends, *of* ¹wreathen work *of* pure gold.

16 And they made two ¹ouches *of* gold, and two gold rings; and put the two rings in the two ends of the breastplate.

17 And they put the two wreathen chains of gold in the two rings on the ends of the breastplate.

18 And the two ends of the two wreathen chains they fastened in the two ¹ouches, and put them on the shoulderpieces of the ephod, before it.

19 And they made two rings of gold, and put *them* on the two ends of the breastplate, upon the border of it,

which *was* on the side of the ephod inward.

20 And they made two *other* golden rings, and put them on the two sides of the ephod underneath, toward the forepart of it, over against the *other* coupling thereof, above the ¹curious girdle of the ephod.

21 And they did bind the breastplate by his rings unto the rings of the ephod with a lace of blue, that it might be above the curious girdle of the ephod, and that the breastplate ¹might not be loosed from the ephod; as the LORD commanded Moses.

22 ªAnd he made the ᵇrobe of the ephod *of* woven work, all *of* blue.

23 And *there was* an hole in the midst of the robe, as the hole of an habergeon, *with* a band round about the hole, that it should not rend.

24 And they made upon the hems of the robe pomegranates *of* blue, and purple, and scarlet, *and* twined *linen.*

25 And they made ªbells *of* pure gold, and put the bells between the pomegranates upon the hem of the robe, round about between the pomegranates;

26 A bell and a pomegranate, a bell and a pomegranate, round about the hem of the robe to ¹minister *in;* as the LORD commanded Moses.

27 ªAnd they made coats *of* fine linen *of* woven work for Aaron, and for his sons,

28 ªAnd a mitre *of* fine linen, and goodly bonnets *of* fine linen, and ᵇlinen breeches *of* fine twined linen,

29 ªAnd a girdle *of* fine twined linen, and blue, and purple, and scarlet, *of* needlework; as the LORD commanded Moses.

30 ªAnd they made the plate of the holy crown *of* pure gold, and wrote upon it a writing, *like to* the engravings of a signet, ᵇHOLINESS TO THE LORD.

31 And they tied unto it a lace of blue, to fasten *it* on high upon the mitre; as the LORD commanded Moses.

32 Thus was all the work of the tabernacle of the tent of the congregation ªfinished: and the children of Israel did ᵇaccording to all that the LORD commanded Moses, so did they.

33 And they brought the tabernacle unto Moses, the tent, and all his furniture, his taches, his boards, his bars, and his pillars, and his sockets,

34 And the covering of rams' skins dyed red, and the covering of badgers' skins, and the vail of the covering,

35 The ark of the testimony, and the staves thereof, and the mercy seat,

36 The table, *and* all the vessels thereof, and the ªshewbread,

37 The pure candlestick, *with* the lamps thereof, *even with* the lamps to be set in order, and all the vessels thereof, and the oil for light,

38 And the golden altar, and the anointing oil, and the sweet incense, and the hanging for the tabernacle door,

39 The brasen altar, and his grate of brass, his staves, and all his vessels, the laver and his foot,

40 The hangings of the court, his pillars, and his sockets, and the hanging for the court gate, his cords, and his pins, and all the vessels of the service of the tabernacle, for the tent of the congregation,

41 The ¹cloths of service to do service in the holy *place,* and the holy garments for Aaron the priest, and his sons' garments, to ²minister in the priest's office.

42 According to all that the LORD commanded Moses, so the children of Israel ªmade all the work.

43 And Moses did look upon all the work, and, behold, they had done it as the LORD had commanded, even so had they done it: and Moses ªblessed them.

## CHAPTER 40

AND the LORD ªspake unto Moses, saying,

2 On the first day of the ªfirst month shalt thou set up ᵇthe tabernacle of the tent of the congregation.

3 And ªthou shalt put therein the ark of the testimony, and ¹cover the ark with the vail.

4 And ªthou shalt bring in the table, and ᵇset in order the things that are to be set in order upon it; ᶜand thou shalt bring in the candlestick, and ¹light the lamps thereof.

5 ªAnd thou shalt set the altar of gold for the incense before the ark of the testimony, and put the hanging of the door to the tabernacle.

6 And thou shalt set the ªaltar of the burnt offering before the door of the tabernacle of the tent of the congregation.

7 And ªthou shalt set the laver between the tent of the congregation and the altar, and shalt put water therein.

8 And thou shalt set up the court round about, and hang up the hanging at the court gate.

9 And thou shalt take the anointing oil, and ªanoint the tabernacle, and all that *is* therein, and shalt hallow it, and all the vessels thereof: and it shall be holy.

10 And thou shalt ªanoint the altar of the burnt offering, and all his vessels,

---

**Cross-reference column:**

39:20 ¹ *intricately woven band*
39:21 ¹ *should not fall off*
39:22 ª Ex. 28:31–35 ᵇ Ex. 29:5; Lev. 8:7
39:25 ª Ex. 28:33
39:26 ¹ *serve*
39:27 ª Ex. 28:39, 40
39:28 ª Ex. 28:4, 39; Lev. 8:9; Ezek. 44:18 ᵇ Ex. 28:42; Lev. 6:10
39:29 ª Ex. 28:39
39:30 ª Ex. 28:36, 37 ᵇ Zech. 14:20
39:32 ª Ex. 40:17 ᵇ Ex. 25:40; 39:42, 43
39:36 ª Ex. 25:23–30
39:41 ¹ *woven garments* ² *serve*
39:42 ª Ex. 35:10
39:43 ª Lev. 9:22, 23; Num. 6:23–26; Josh. 22:6; 2 Sam. 6:18; 1 Kin. 8:14; 2 Chr. 30:27
40:1 ª Ex. 25:1–31:18
40:2 ª Ex. 12:2; 13:4 ᵇ Ex. 26:1, 30; 40:17
40:3 ª Ex. 26:33; 40:21; Lev. 16:2; Num. 4:5 ¹ *partition off*
40:4 ª Ex. 26:35; 40:22 ᵇ Ex. 25:30; 40:23 ᶜ Ex. 40:24, 25 ¹ *set up*
40:5 ª Ex. 40:26
40:6 ª Ex. 39:39
40:7 ª Ex. 30:18; 40:30
40:9 ª Ex. 30:26; Lev. 8:10
40:10 ª Ex. 30:26–30

and ¹sanctify the altar: and ᵇit shall be an altar most holy.

11 And thou shalt anoint the laver and his foot, and sanctify it.

12 ᵃAnd thou shalt bring Aaron and his sons unto the door of the tabernacle of the congregation, and wash them with water.

13 And thou shalt put upon Aaron the holy ᵃgarments, ᵇand anoint him, and sanctify him; that he may minister unto me in the priest's office.

14 And thou shalt bring his sons, and clothe them with coats:

15 And thou shalt anoint them, as thou didst anoint their father, that they may minister unto me in the priest's office: for their anointing shall surely be ᵃan everlasting priesthood throughout their generations.

16 Thus did Moses: according to all that the LORD commanded him, so did he.

17 And it came to pass in the first month in the second year, on the first *day* of the month, *that* the ᵃtabernacle was ¹reared up.

18 And Moses reared up the tabernacle, and fastened his sockets, and set up the boards thereof, and put in the bars thereof, and reared up his pillars.

19 And he spread abroad the tent over the tabernacle, and put the covering of the tent above upon it; as the LORD commanded Moses.

20 And he took and put ᵃthe testimony into the ark, and set the staves on the ark, and put the mercy seat above upon the ark:

21 And he brought the ark into the tabernacle, and ᵃset up the vail of the covering, and covered the ark of the testimony; as the LORD commanded Moses.

22 ᵃAnd he put the table in the tent of the congregation, upon the side of the tabernacle northward, without the vail.

23 ᵃAnd he set the bread in order upon it before the LORD; as the LORD had commanded Moses.

24 ᵃAnd he put the candlestick in the tent of the congregation, over

against the table, on the side of the tabernacle southward.

25 And ᵃhe lighted the lamps before the LORD; as the LORD commanded Moses.

26 ᵃAnd he put the golden altar in the tent of the congregation before the vail:

27 ᵃAnd he burnt sweet incense thereon; as the LORD commanded Moses.

28 ᵃAnd he set up the hanging *at* the door of the tabernacle.

29 ᵃAnd he put the altar of burnt offering *by* the door of the tabernacle of the tent of the congregation, and ᵇoffered upon it the burnt offering and the meat offering; as the LORD commanded Moses.

30 ᵃAnd he set the laver between the tent of the congregation and the altar, and put water there, to wash *withal.*

31 And Moses and Aaron and his sons ᵃwashed their hands and their feet thereat:

32 When they went into the tent of the congregation, and when they came near unto the altar, they washed; ᵃas the LORD commanded Moses.

33 ᵃAnd he reared up the court round about the tabernacle and the altar, and set up the hanging of the court gate. So Moses ᵇfinished the work.

34 ᵃThen a ᵇcloud covered the tent of the congregation, and the ᶜglory of the LORD filled the tabernacle.

35 And Moses ᵃwas not able to enter into the tent of the congregation, because the cloud abode thereon, and the glory of the LORD filled the tabernacle.

36 And when the cloud was taken up from over the tabernacle, the children of Israel ¹went onward in all their journeys:

37 But ᵃif the cloud were not taken up, then they journeyed not till the day that it was taken up.

38 For ᵃthe cloud of the LORD *was* upon the tabernacle by day, and fire was on it by night, in the sight of all the house of Israel, throughout all their journeys.

40:10 ᵇ Ex. 29:36, 37 ¹ *consecrate*
40:12 ᵃ Ex. 29:4–9; Lev. 8:1–13
40:13 ᵃ Ex. 29:5; 39:1, 41 ᵇ [Ex. 28:41]; Lev. 8:12
40:15 ᵃ Ex. 29:9; Num. 25:13
40:17 ᵃ Ex. 40:2; Num. 7:1 ¹ *raised*
40:20 ᵃ Ex. 25:16; Deut. 10:5; 1 Kin. 8:9; 2 Chr. 5:10; Heb. 9:4
40:21 ᵃ Ex. 26:33
40:22 ᵃ Ex. 26:35
40:23 ᵃ Ex. 40:4; Lev. 24:5, 6
40:24 ᵃ Ex. 26:35
40:25 ᵃ Ex. 25:37; 30:7, 8; 40:4; Lev. 24:3, 4
40:26 ᵃ Ex. 30:1, 6; 40:5
40:27 ᵃ Ex. 30:7
40:28 ᵃ Ex. 26:36; 40:5
40:29 ᵃ Ex. 40:6 ᵇ Ex. 29:38–42
40:30 ᵃ Ex. 30:18; 40:7
40:31 ᵃ Ex. 30:19, 20; John 13:8
40:32 ᵃ Ex. 30:19
40:33 ᵃ Ex. 27:9–18; 40:8 ᵇ [Heb. 3:2–5]
40:34 ᵃ Ex. 29:43; Lev. 16:2; Num. 9:15; 2 Chr. 5:13; Is. 6:4 ᵇ 1 Kin. 8:10, 11 ᶜ Lev. 9:6, 23
40:35 ᵃ [Lev. 16:2]; 1 Kin. 8:11; 2 Chr. 5:13, 14
40:36 ᵃ Ex. 13:21, 22; Num. 9:17; Neh. 9:19 ¹ Lit. *journeyed*
40:37 ᵃ Num. 9:19–22
40:38 ᵃ Ex. 13:21; Num. 9:15; Ps. 78:14; Is. 4:5

# THE THIRD BOOK OF MOSES CALLED
# LEVITICUS

Leviticus is God's guidebook for His newly redeemed people, showing them how to worship, serve, and obey a holy God. Fellowship with God through sacrifice and obedience show the awesome holiness of the God of Israel. Indeed, " 'Ye shall be holy: for I the LORD your God *am* holy' " (19:2).

Leviticus focuses on the worship and walk of the nation of God. In Exodus, Israel was redeemed and established as a kingdom of priests and a holy nation. Leviticus shows how God's people are to fulfill their priestly calling.

The Hebrew title is *Wayyiqra,* "And He Called." The Talmud refers to Leviticus as the "Law of the Priests," and the "Law of the Offerings." The Greek title appearing in the Septuagint is *Leuitikon,* "That Which Pertains to the Levites." From this word, the Latin Vulgate derived its name *Leviticus* which was adopted as the English title. This title is slightly misleading because the book does not deal with the Levites as a whole but more with the priests, a segment of the Levites.

## CHAPTER 1

AND the LORD ªcalled unto Moses, and spake unto him ᵇout of the tabernacle of the congregation, saying,

2 Speak unto the children of Israel, and say unto them, ªIf any man of you bring an offering unto the LORD, ye shall bring your offering of the cattle, *even* of the herd, and of the flock.

3 If his offering *be* a burnt sacrifice of the herd, let him offer a male ªwithout blemish: he shall offer it of his own voluntary will at the door of the tabernacle of the congregation before the LORD.

4 ªAnd he shall put his hand upon the head of the burnt offering; and it shall be ᵇaccepted for him ᶜto make atonement for him.

5 And he shall kill the ªbullock before the LORD: ᵇand the priests, Aaron's sons, shall bring the blood, ᶜand sprinkle the blood round about upon the altar that *is by* the door of the tabernacle of the congregation.

6 And he shall ªflay ¹the burnt offering, and cut it into his pieces.

7 And the sons of Aaron the priest shall put ªfire upon the altar, and ᵇlay the wood in order upon the fire:

8 And the priests, Aaron's sons, shall lay the parts, the head, and the fat, in order upon the wood that *is* on the fire which *is* upon the altar:

9 But his inwards and his legs shall he wash in water: and the priest shall burn all on the altar, *to be* a burnt sacrifice, an offering made by fire, of a ªsweet¹ savour unto the LORD.

10 And if his offering *be* of the flocks, *namely,* of the sheep, or of the goats, for a burnt sacrifice; he shall bring it a male ªwithout blemish.

11 ªAnd he shall kill it on the side of the altar northward before the LORD:

and the priests, Aaron's sons, shall sprinkle his blood round about upon the altar.

12 And he shall cut it into his pieces, with his head and his fat: and the priest shall lay them in order on the wood that *is* on the fire which *is* upon the altar:

13 But he shall wash the inwards and the legs with water: and the priest shall bring *it* all, and burn *it* upon the altar: it *is* a burnt sacrifice, an ªoffering made by fire, of a sweet savour unto the LORD.

14 And if the burnt sacrifice for his offering to the LORD *be* of fowls, then he shall bring his offering of ªturtledoves, or of young pigeons.

15 And the priest shall bring it unto the altar, and ¹wring off his head, and burn *it* on the altar; and the blood thereof shall be wrung out at the side of the altar:

16 And he shall pluck away his crop with his feathers, and cast it ªbeside the altar on the east part, by the place of the ashes:

17 And he shall cleave it with the wings thereof, *but* ªshall not divide *it* asunder: and the priest shall burn it upon the altar, upon the wood that *is* upon the fire: ᵇit *is* a burnt sacrifice, an offering made by fire, of a ¹sweet savour unto the LORD.

## CHAPTER 2

AND when any will offer ªa ¹meat offering unto the LORD, his offering shall be *of* fine flour; and he shall pour oil upon it, and put ᵇfrankincense thereon:

2 And he shall bring it to Aaron's sons the priests: and he shall take thereout his handful of the flour thereof, and of the oil thereof, with all the frankincense thereof; and the

---

**Cross references (center column):**

1:1 ª Ex. 19:3; 25:22
ᵇ Ex. 40:34
1:2 ª Lev. 22:18, 19
1:3 ª Eph. 5:27
1:4 ª Lev. 3:2, 8, 13; 4:15  ᵇ [Rom. 12:1]
ᶜ 2 Chr. 29:23, 24
1:5 ª Mic. 6:6
ᵇ 2 Chr. 35:11
ᶜ [Heb. 12:24]
1:6 ª Lev. 7:8  ¹ *skin*
1:7 ª Mal. 1:10
ᵇ Gen. 22:9
1:9 ª Gen. 8:21
¹ *pleasing aroma*
1:10 ª Lev. 1:3
1:11 ª Lev. 1:5

1:13 ª Num. 15:4–7; 28:12–14
1:14 ª Lev. 5:7, 11; 12:8
1:15 ¹ *nip or pinch off*
1:16 ª Lev. 6:10
1:17 ª Gen. 15:10; Lev. 5:8  ᵇ Lev. 1:9, 13  ¹ *pleasing aroma*
2:1 ª Lev. 6:14; 9:17; Num. 15:4
ᵇ Lev. 5:11  ¹ *grain or meal*

priest shall burn ᵃthe memorial of it upon the altar, *to be* an offering made by fire, of a sweet savour unto the LORD:

3 And ᵃthe remnant of the meat offering *shall be* Aaron's and his ᵇsons': ᶜ*it is* a thing most holy of the offerings of the LORD made by fire.

4 And if thou bring an oblation of a meat offering baken in the oven, *it shall be* unleavened cakes of fine flour mingled with oil, or unleavened wafers ᵃanointed¹ with oil.

5 And if thy oblation *be* a meat offering *baken* in a ¹pan, it shall be *of* fine flour unleavened, mingled with oil.

6 Thou shalt part it in pieces, and pour oil thereon: it *is* a meat offering.

7 And if thy oblation *be* a meat offering *baken* in the ᵃfryingpan, it shall be made *of* fine flour with oil.

8 And thou shalt bring the meat offering that is made of these things unto the LORD: and when it is presented unto the priest, he shall bring it unto the altar.

9 And the priest shall take from the meat offering ᵃa ¹memorial thereof, and shall burn *it* upon the altar: *it is* an ᵇoffering made by fire, of a sweet savour unto the LORD.

10 And ᵃthat which is left of the meat offering *shall be* Aaron's and his sons': *it is* a thing most holy of the offerings of the LORD made by fire.

11 No meat offering, which ye shall bring unto the LORD, shall be made with ᵃleaven: for ye shall burn no leaven, nor any honey, in any offering of the LORD made by fire.

12 ᵃAs for the ¹oblation of the firstfruits, ye shall offer them unto the LORD: but they shall not be burnt on the altar for a sweet savour.

13 And every oblation of thy meat offering ᵃshalt thou season with salt; neither shalt thou suffer ᵇthe salt of the covenant of thy God to be lacking from thy meat offering: ᶜwith all thine offerings thou shalt offer salt.

14 And if thou offer a meat offering of thy firstfruits unto the LORD, ᵃthou shalt offer for the meat offering of thy firstfruits green ears of corn dried by the fire, *even* corn beaten out of ᵇfull ears.

15 And ᵃthou shalt put oil upon it, and lay frankincense thereon: it *is* a meat offering.

16 And the priest shall burn ᵃthe ¹memorial of it, *part* of the beaten corn thereof, and *part* of the oil thereof, with all the frankincense thereof: *it is* an offering made by fire unto the LORD.

## CHAPTER 3

A ND if his oblation *be* a ᵃsacrifice of peace offering, if he offer *it* of the herd; whether *it be* a male or female, he shall offer it ᵇwithout ¹blemish before the LORD.

2 And ᵃhe shall lay his hand upon the head of his offering, and kill it *at* the door of the tabernacle of the congregation: and Aaron's sons the priests shall ᵇsprinkle the blood upon the altar round about.

3 And he shall offer of the sacrifice of the peace offering an offering made by fire unto the LORD; ᵃthe ¹fat that covereth the inwards, and all the fat that *is* upon the inwards,

4 And the two kidneys, and the fat that *is* on them, which *is* by the flanks, and the ¹caul above the liver, with the kidneys, it shall he take away.

5 And Aaron's sons ᵃshall burn it on the altar upon the ᵇburnt sacrifice, which *is* upon the wood that *is* on the fire: *it is* an ᶜoffering made by fire, of a ᵈsweet savour unto the LORD.

6 And if his offering for a sacrifice of peace offering unto the LORD *be* of the flock; male or female, ᵃhe shall offer it without blemish.

7 If he offer a ᵃlamb for his offering, then shall he ᵇoffer it ᶜbefore the LORD.

8 And he shall lay his hand upon the head of his offering, and kill it before the tabernacle of the congregation: and Aaron's sons shall sprinkle the blood thereof round about upon the altar.

9 And he shall offer of the sacrifice of the peace offering an offering made by fire unto the LORD; the fat thereof, *and* the whole rump, it shall he take off hard by the backbone; and the fat that covereth the inwards, and all the fat that *is* upon the inwards,

10 And the two kidneys, and the fat that *is* upon them, which *is* by the flanks, and the caul above the liver, with the kidneys, it shall he take away.

11 And the priest shall burn it upon the altar: *it is* ᵃthe food of the offering made by fire unto the LORD.

12 And if his ᵃoffering *be* a goat, then ᵇhe shall offer it before the LORD.

13 And he shall lay his hand upon the head of it, and kill it before the tabernacle of the congregation: and the sons of Aaron shall sprinkle the blood thereof upon the altar round about.

14 And he shall offer thereof his offering, *even* an offering made by fire unto the LORD; the fat that covereth the inwards, and all the fat that *is* upon the inwards,

15 And the two kidneys, and the fat that *is* upon them, which *is* by the flanks, and the caul above the liver, with the kidneys, it shall he take away.

### Cross references

2:2 ᵃ Lev. 2:9; 5:12; 6:15; 24:7; Acts 10:4
2:3 ᵃ Lev. 7:9 ᵇ Lev. 6:6; 10:12, 13 ᶜ Ex. 29:37; Num. 18:9
2:4 ᵃ Ex. 29:2 ¹ spread
2:5 ¹ flat plate or griddle
2:7 ᵃ Lev. 7:9
2:9 ᵃ Lev. 2:2, 16; 5:12; 6:15 ᵇ Ex. 29:18 ¹ memorial portion
2:10 ᵃ Lev. 2:3; 6:16
2:11 ᵃ Ex. 23:18; 34:25; Lev. 6:16, 17; [Matt. 16:12; Mark 8:15; Luke 12:1; 1 Cor. 5:8; Gal. 5:9]
2:12 ᵃ Ex. 22:29; 34:22; Lev. 23:10, 11, 17, 18 ¹ offering
2:13 ᵃ [Mark 9:49, 50; Col. 4:6] ᵇ Num. 18:19; 2 Chr. 13:5 ᶜ Ezek. 43:24
2:14 ᵃ Lev. 23:10, 14 ᵇ 2 Kin. 4:42
2:15 ᵃ Lev. 2:1
2:16 ᵃ Lev. 2:2 ¹ memorial portion
3:1 ᵃ Lev. 7.11, 29

ᵇ Lev. 1:3; 22:20–24 ¹ defect or imperfection
3:2 ᵃ Ex. 29:10, 11, 16, 20; Lev. 1:4, 5; 16:21 ᵇ Lev. 1:5
3:3 ᵃ Ex. 29:13, 22; Lev. 1:8; 3:16; 4:8, 9 ¹ fat that covers the entrails
3:4 ¹ fatty lobe attached to
3:5 ᵃ Ex. 29:13; Lev. 6:12; 7:28–34 ᵇ 2 Chr. 35:14 ᶜ Num. 28:3–10 ᵈ Num. 15:8–10
3:6 ᵃ Lev. 3:1; 22:20–24
3:7 ᵃ Num. 15:4, 5 ᵇ 1 Kin. 8:62 ᶜ Lev. 17:8, 9
3:11 ᵃ Lev. 21:6, 8, 17, 21, 22; 22:25; Num. 28:2; [Ezek. 44:7; Mal. 1:7, 12]
3:12 ᵃ Num. 15:6–11 ᵇ Lev. 3:1, 7

16 And the priest shall burn them upon the altar: *it is* the food of the offering made by fire for a sweet savour: [a]all the fat *is* the LORD's.

17 *It shall be* a [a]perpetual[1] statute for your generations throughout all your dwellings, that ye eat neither fat nor [b]blood.

## CHAPTER 4

AND the LORD spake unto Moses, saying,

2 Speak unto the children of Israel, saying, [a]If a soul shall sin [1]through ignorance against any of the commandments of the LORD *concerning things* which ought not to be done, and shall do against any of them:

3 [a]If the priest that is anointed do sin according to the sin of the people; then let him bring for his sin, which he hath sinned, [b]a young bullock without blemish unto the LORD for a [c]sin offering.

4 And he shall bring the bullock [a]unto the door of the tabernacle of the congregation before the LORD; and shall lay his hand upon the bullock's head, and kill the bullock before the LORD.

5 And the priest that is anointed [a]shall take of the bullock's blood, and bring it to the tabernacle of the congregation:

6 And the priest shall dip his finger in the blood, and sprinkle of the blood seven times before the LORD, before the [a]vail of the sanctuary.

7 And the priest shall [a]put *some* of the blood upon the horns of the altar of sweet incense before the LORD, which *is* in the tabernacle of the congregation; and shall pour [b]all the blood of the bullock at the bottom of the altar of the burnt offering, which *is at* the door of the tabernacle of the congregation.

8 And he shall take off from it all the fat of the bullock for the sin offering; the fat that covereth the inwards, and all the fat that *is* upon the inwards,

9 And the two kidneys, and the fat that *is* upon them, which *is* by the flanks, and the caul above the liver, with the kidneys, it shall he take away,

10 [a]As it was taken off from the bullock of the sacrifice of peace offerings: and the priest shall burn them upon the altar of the burnt offering.

11 [a]And the skin of the bullock, and all his flesh, with his head, and with his legs, and his inwards, and his dung,

12 Even the whole bullock shall he carry forth [1]without the camp unto a clean place, [a]where the ashes are poured out, and [b]burn him on the

wood with fire: where the ashes are poured out shall he be burnt.

13 And [a]if the whole congregation of Israel sin through ignorance, [b]and the thing be hid from the eyes of the assembly, and they have done *somewhat against* any of the commandments of the LORD *concerning things* which should not be done, and are guilty;

14 When the sin, which they have sinned against it, is known, then the congregation shall offer a young bullock for the sin, and bring him before the tabernacle of the congregation.

15 And the elders of the congregation [a]shall lay their hands upon the head of the bullock before the LORD: and the bullock shall be killed before the LORD.

16 [a]And the priest that is anointed shall bring of the bullock's blood to the tabernacle of the congregation:

17 And the priest shall dip his finger *in some* of the blood, and sprinkle *it* seven times before the LORD, *even* before the vail.

18 And he shall put *some* of the blood upon the horns of the altar which *is* before the LORD, that *is* in the tabernacle of the congregation, and shall pour out all the blood at the bottom of the altar of the burnt offering, which *is at* the door of the tabernacle of the congregation.

19 And he shall take all his fat from him, and burn *it* upon the altar.

20 And he shall do with the bullock as he did [a]with the bullock for a sin offering, so shall he do with this: [b]and the priest shall make an [1]atonement for them, and it shall be forgiven them.

21 And he shall carry forth the bullock [1]without the camp, and burn him as he burned the first bullock: it *is* a sin offering for the congregation.

22 When a [1]ruler hath sinned, and [a]done *somewhat* through ignorance *against* any of the commandments of the LORD his God *concerning things* which should not be done, and is guilty;

23 Or [a]if his sin, wherein he hath sinned, [1]come to his knowledge; he shall bring his offering, a kid of the goats, a male without blemish:

24 And [a]he shall lay his hand upon the head of the goat, and kill it in the place where they kill the burnt offering before the LORD: it *is* a sin offering.

25 [a]And the priest shall take of the blood of the sin offering with his finger, and put *it* upon the horns of the altar of burnt offering, and shall pour out his blood at the bottom of the altar of burnt offering.

26 And he shall burn all his fat upon the altar, as [a]the fat of the sacrifice

---

3:16 [a] Lev. 7:23–25; 1 Sam. 2:15; 2 Chr. 7:7
3:17 [a] Lev. 6:18; 7:36; 17:7; 23:14 [b] Gen. 9:4; Lev. 7:23, 26; 17:10, 14; 1 Sam. 14:33 [1] *never-ending*
4:2 [a] Lev. 5:15–18; Num. 15:22–30; 1 Sam. 14:27; Acts 3:17 [1] *unintentionally or through error*
4:3 [a] Ex. 40:15; Lev. 8:12 [b] Lev. 3:1; 9:2 [c] Lev. 9:7
4:4 [a] Lev. 1:3, 4; 4:15; Num. 8:12
4:5 [a] Lev. 16:14; Num. 19:4
4:6 [a] Ex. 40:21, 26
4:7 [a] Lev. 4:18, 25, 30, 34; 8:15; 9:9; 16:18 [b] Ex. 40:5, 6; Lev. 5:9
4:10 [a] Lev. 3:3–5
4:11 [a] Ex. 29:14; Lev. 9:11; Num. 19:5
4:12 [a] Lev. 4:21; 6:10, 11; 16:27 [b] [Heb. 13:11, 12] [1] *outside*

4:13 [a] Num. 15:24–26; Josh. 7:11 [b] Lev. 5:2–4, 17
4:15 [a] Lev. 1:3, 4
4:16 [a] Lev. 4:5; [Heb. 9:12–14]
4:20 [a] Lev. 4:3 [b] Lev. 1:4; Num. 19:5 [1] *covering or propitiation*
4:21 [1] *outside*
4:22 [a] Lev. 4:2, 13, 27 [1] *leader*
4:23 [a] Lev. 4:14; 5:4 [1] Lit. *is made known to him*
4:24 [a] Lev. 4:4; [Is. 53:6]
4:25 [a] Lev. 4:7, 18, 30, 34
4:26 [a] Lev. 3:3–5

of peace offerings: [b]and the priest shall make [1]an atonement for him as concerning his sin, and it shall be forgiven him.

27 And [a]if [1]any one of the [2]common people sin through ignorance, while he doeth *somewhat against* any of the commandments of the LORD *concerning things* which ought not to be done, and be guilty;

28 Or [a]if his sin, which he hath sinned, come to his knowledge: then he shall bring his offering, a kid of the goats, a female without blemish, for his sin which he hath sinned.

29 [a]And he shall lay his hand upon the head of the sin offering, and [1]slay the sin offering in the place of the burnt offering.

30 And the priest shall take of the blood thereof with his finger, and put *it* upon the horns of the altar of burnt offering, and shall pour out all the blood thereof at the bottom of the altar.

31 And [a]he shall take away all the fat thereof, [b]as the fat is taken away from off the sacrifice of peace offerings; and the priest shall burn *it* upon the altar for a [c]sweet savour unto the LORD; [d]and the priest shall make an atonement for him, and it shall be forgiven him.

32 And if he bring a lamb for a sin offering, [a]he shall bring it a female without blemish.

33 And he shall [a]lay his hand upon the head of the sin offering, and slay it for a sin offering in the place where they kill the burnt offering.

34 And the priest shall take of the blood of the sin offering with his finger, and put *it* upon the horns of the altar of burnt offering, and shall pour out all the blood thereof at the bottom of the altar:

35 And he shall take away all the fat thereof, as the fat of the lamb is taken away from the sacrifice of the peace offerings; and the priest shall burn them upon the altar, [a]according to the offerings made by fire unto the LORD: [b]and the priest shall make an atonement for his sin that he hath committed, and it shall be forgiven him.

## CHAPTER 5

AND if a soul sin, and [a]hear the voice of swearing, and *is* a witness, whether he hath seen or known *of it;* if he do not [1]utter *it,* then he shall [b]bear his [2]iniquity.

2 Or [a]if a soul touch any unclean thing, whether *it be* a carcase of an unclean beast, or a carcase of unclean cattle, or the carcase of unclean creeping things, and *if* it be hidden from him; he also shall be [1]unclean, and [b]guilty.

3 Or if he touch [a]the uncleanness of man, whatsoever uncleanness *it be* that a man shall be defiled withal, and [1]it be hid from him; when he knoweth *of it,* then he shall be guilty.

4 Or if a soul [1]swear, pronouncing with *his* lips [a]to do evil, or [b]to do good, whatsoever *it be* that a man shall pronounce with an oath, and it be hid from him; when he knoweth *of it,* then he shall be guilty in one of these.

5 And it shall be, when he shall be guilty in one of these *things,* that he shall [a]confess that he hath sinned in that *thing:*

6 And he shall bring his trespass offering unto the LORD for his sin which he hath sinned, a female from the flock, a lamb or a kid of the goats, for a sin offering; and the priest shall make an atonement for him concerning his sin.

7 And [a]if he be not able to bring a lamb, then he shall bring for his trespass, which he hath committed, two [b]turtledoves, or two young pigeons, unto the LORD; one for a sin offering, and the other for a burnt offering.

8 And he shall bring them unto the priest, who shall offer *that* which *is* for the sin offering first, and [a]wring off his head from his neck, but shall not divide *it* [1]asunder:

9 And he shall sprinkle of the blood of the sin offering upon the side of the altar; and the [a]rest of the blood shall be wrung out at the bottom of the altar: it *is* a sin offering.

10 And he shall offer the second *for* a burnt offering, according to the [a]manner:[1] and [b]the priest shall make an atonement for him for his sin which he hath sinned, and it shall be forgiven him.

11 But if he be [a]not able to bring two turtledoves, or two young pigeons, then he that sinned shall bring for his offering the tenth part of an ephah of fine flour for a sin offering; [b]he shall put no oil upon it, neither shall he put *any* frankincense thereon: for it *is* a sin offering.

12 Then shall he bring it to the priest, and the priest shall take his handful of it, [a]even a [1]memorial thereof, and burn *it* on the altar, [b]according to the offerings made by fire unto the LORD: it *is* a sin offering.

13 [a]And the priest shall make an atonement for him [1]as touching his sin that he hath sinned in one of these, and it shall be forgiven him: and [b]*the remnant* shall be the priest's, as a meat offering.

14 And the LORD spake unto Moses, saying,

15 [a]If a soul commit a trespass, and sin through ignorance, in the holy

---

**Center cross-reference column:**

4:26 [b] Lev. 4:20; Num. 15:28
[1] covering or propitiation
4:27 [a] Lev. 4:2; Num. 15:27 [1] one soul [2] Lit. people of the land
4:28 [a] Lev. 4:23
4:29 [a] Lev. 1:4; 4:4, 24 [1] kill
4:31 [a] Lev. 3:14 [b] Lev. 3:3, 4 [c] Gen. 8:21; Ex. 29:18; Lev. 1:9, 13; 2:2, 9, 12 [d] Lev. 4:26
4:32 [a] Lev. 4:28
4:33 [a] Lev. 1:4; Num. 8:12
4:35 [a] Lev. 3:5 [b] Lev. 4:26, 31
5:1 [a] Prov. 29:24; [Jer. 23:10] [b] Lev. 5:17; 7:18; 17:16; 19:8; 20:17; Num. 9:13 [1] tell [2] guilt
5:2 [a] Lev. 11:24, 28, 31, 39; Num. 19:11–16; Deut. 14:8 [b] Lev. 5:17 [1] defiled

5:3 [a] Lev. 5:12, 13, 15 [1] he is unaware of it
5:4 [a] 1 Sam. 25:22; Acts 23:12 [b] [Matt. 5:33–37]; Mark 6:23; [James 5:12] [1] vows
5:5 [a] Lev. 16:21; 26:40; Num. 5:7; Ezra 10:11, 12; Ps. 32:5; Prov. 28:13
5:7 [a] Lev. 12:6, 8; 14:21 [b] Lev. 1:14
5:8 [a] Lev. 1:15–17 [1] apart
5:9 [a] Lev. 4:7, 18, 30, 34
5:10 [a] Lev. 1:14–17 [b] Lev. 4:20, 26; 5:13, 16 [1] prescribed manner
5:11 [a] Lev. 14:21–32 [b] Lev. 2:1, 2; 6:15; Num. 5:15
5:12 [a] Lev. 2:2 [b] Lev. 4:35 [1] memorial portion
5:13 [a] Lev. 4:26 [b] Lev. 2:3; 6:17, 26 [1] concerning his sin
5:15 [a] Lev. 4:2; 22:14; Num. 5:5–8

---

things of the LORD; then [b]he shall bring for his trespass unto the LORD a ram without blemish out of the flocks, with thy [1]estimation by shekels of silver, after [c]the shekel of the sanctuary, for a trespass offering:

16 And he shall make amends for the harm that he hath done in the holy thing, and [a]shall add the fifth part thereto, and give it unto the priest: [b]and the priest shall make an atonement for him with the ram of the trespass offering, and it shall be forgiven him.

17 And if a soul sin, and commit any of these things which are forbidden to be done by the commandments of the LORD; [a]though[1] he wist *it* not, yet is he [b]guilty, and shall [2]bear his iniquity.

18 [a]And he shall bring a ram without blemish out of the flock, with thy estimation, for a trespass offering, unto the priest: and the priest shall make an atonement for him concerning his ignorance wherein he erred and wist *it* not, and it shall be forgiven him.

19 It *is* a trespass offering: [a]he hath certainly trespassed against the LORD.

## CHAPTER 6

AND the LORD spake unto Moses, saying,

2 If a [1]soul sin, and [a]commit a trespass against the LORD, and [b]lie[2] unto his neighbour in that [c]which was delivered him to keep, [3]or in fellowship, [4]or in a thing taken away by violence, or hath [d]deceived his neighbour;

3 Or [a]have found that which was lost, and lieth concerning it, and [b]sweareth falsely; in any of all these that a man doeth, sinning therein:

4 Then it shall be, because he hath sinned, and is guilty, that he shall [1]restore [a]that which he took violently away, or the thing which he hath deceitfully gotten, or that which was delivered him to keep, or the lost thing which he found,

5 Or all that about which he hath sworn falsely; he shall even [a]restore it in the principal, and shall add the fifth part more thereto, *and* give it unto him to whom it [1]appertaineth, in the day of his trespass offering.

6 And he shall bring his trespass offering unto the LORD, [a]a ram without blemish out of the flock, with thy [1]estimation, for a trespass offering, unto the priest:

7 [a]And the priest shall make an atonement for him before the LORD: and it shall be forgiven him for any thing of all that he hath done in trespassing therein.

8 And the LORD spake unto Moses, saying,

9 Command Aaron and his sons, saying, This *is* the [a]law of the burnt offering: It *is* the burnt offering, because of the burning upon the altar all night unto the morning, and the fire of the altar shall be burning in it.

10 [a]And the priest shall put on his linen garment, and his linen breeches shall he put upon his flesh, and take up the ashes which the fire hath consumed with the burnt offering on the altar, and he shall put them [b]beside the altar.

11 And [a]he shall put off his garments, and put on other garments, and carry forth the ashes [1]without the camp [b]unto a clean place.

12 And the fire upon the altar shall be burning in it; it shall not be put out: and the priest shall burn wood on it every morning, and lay the burnt offering in order upon it; and he shall burn thereon [a]the fat of the peace offerings.

13 The fire shall ever be burning upon the [a]altar; it shall never go out.

14 And this *is* the law of the [1]meat offering: the sons of Aaron shall offer it before the LORD, before the altar.

15 And he shall take of it his handful, of the flour of the [1]meat offering, and of the oil thereof, and all the frankincense which *is* upon the meat offering, and shall burn *it* upon the altar *for* a [2]sweet savour, *even* the memorial [3]of it, unto the LORD.

16 And the remainder thereof shall Aaron and his sons eat: with unleavened bread shall it be eaten in the holy place; in the court of the tabernacle of the congregation they shall eat it.

17 It shall not be baken with leaven. I have given it *unto them for* their [1]portion of my offerings made by fire; it *is* most holy, as *is* the sin offering, and as the [a]trespass offering.

18 [a]All the males among the children of Aaron shall eat of it. [b]*It shall be* a statute for ever in your generations concerning the offerings of the LORD made by fire: [c]every one that toucheth them shall be holy.

19 And the LORD spake unto Moses, saying,

20 [a]This *is* the offering of Aaron and of his sons, which they shall offer unto the LORD in the day when he is anointed; the tenth part of an [b]ephah of fine flour for a [1]meat offering perpetual, half of it in the morning, and half thereof at night.

21 In a [a]pan it shall be made with oil; *and when it is* baken, thou shalt bring it in: *and* the baken pieces of the meat offering shalt thou offer *for* a [1]sweet savour unto the LORD.

22 And the priest of his sons [a]that is anointed in his stead shall offer it: *it*

---

**Cross references (center column):**

5:15 [b] Ezra 10:19
[c] Ex. 30:13; Lev. 27:25 [1] *evaluation in shekels*

5:16 [a] Lev. 6:5; 22:14; 27:13, 15, 27, 31; Num. 5:7
[b] Lev. 4:26

5:17 [a] Lev. 4:2, 13, 22, 27 [b] Lev. 5:1, 2 [1] *does not know it* [2] *punishment*

5:18 [a] Lev. 5:15

5:19 [a] Ezra 10:2

6:2 [a] Num. 5:6
[b] Lev. 19:11; Acts 5:4; Col. 3:9 [c] Ex. 22:7, 10 [d] Prov. 24:28 [1] *person* [2] *deceives his associates* [3] *or an entrusted security* [4] *or about a robbery*

6:3 [a] Ex. 23:4; Deut. 22:1–4
[b] Ex. 22:11; Lev. 19:12; Jer. 7:9; Zech. 5:4

6:4 [a] Lev. 24:18, 21 [1] *return*

6:5 [a] Lev. 5:16; Num. 5:7, 8; 2 Sam. 12:6 [1] *belongs*

6:6 [a] Lev. 1:3; 5:15 [1] *valuation or appraisal*

6:7 [a] Lev. 4:26

6:9 [a] Ex. 29:38–42; Num. 28:3–10

6:10 [a] Ex. 28:39–43; Lev. 16:4; Ezek. 44:17, 18
[b] Lev. 1:16

6:11 [a] Ezek. 44:19 [b] Lev. 4:12 [1] *outside*

6:12 [a] Lev. 3:3, 5, 9, 14

6:13 [a] Lev. 1:7

6:14 [1] *grain* or *meal*

6:15 [1] *grain* or *meal* [2] *pleasing aroma* [3] *to the LORD*

6:17 [a] Lev. 7:7 [1] *share*

6:18 [a] Lev. 6:29; 7:6; Num. 18:10; 1 Cor. 9:13 [b] Lev. 3:17 [c] Ex. 29:37; Lev. 22:3–7; Num. 4:15; Hag. 2:11–13

6:20 [a] Ex. 29:2 [b] Ex. 16:36 [1] *meal* or *grain*

6:21 [a] Lev. 2:5; 7:9 [1] *pleasing aroma*

6:22 [a] Lev. 4:3

---

*is* a statute for ever unto the LORD; [b]it shall be [1]wholly burnt.

23 For every meat offering for the priest shall be wholly burnt: it shall not be eaten.

24 And the LORD spake unto Moses, saying,

25 Speak unto Aaron and to his sons, saying, This *is* the law of the sin offering: [a]In the place where the burnt offering is killed shall the sin offering be killed before the LORD: it *is* most holy.

26 [a]The priest that offereth it for sin shall eat it: in the holy place shall it be eaten, in the court of the tabernacle of the congregation.

27 [a]Whatsoever[1] shall touch the flesh thereof [2]shall be holy: and when there is sprinkled of the blood thereof upon any garment, thou shalt wash that whereon it was sprinkled in the holy place.

28 But the earthen vessel wherein it is [1]sodden [a]shall be broken: and if it be sodden in a brasen pot, it shall be both scoured, and rinsed in water.

29 All the males among the priests shall eat thereof: it *is* most holy.

30 [a]And no sin offering, whereof *any* of the blood is brought into the tabernacle of the congregation to reconcile *withal* in the [1]holy [b]place, shall be [c]eaten: it shall be [d]burnt in the fire.

## CHAPTER 7

LIKEWISE [a]this *is* the [1]law of the trespass offering: it *is* most holy.

2 In the place where they kill the burnt offering shall they kill the trespass offering: and the blood thereof shall he sprinkle round about upon the altar.

3 And he shall offer of it all the fat thereof; the rump, and the fat that covereth the inwards,

4 And the two kidneys, and the fat that *is* on them, which *is* by the flanks, and the caul *that is* above the liver, with the kidneys, it shall he take away:

5 And the priest shall burn them upon the altar *for* an offering made by fire unto the LORD: it *is* a trespass offering.

6 [a]Every male among the priests shall eat thereof: it shall be eaten in the holy place: [b]it *is* most holy.

7 As the sin offering *is*, so *is* [a]the trespass offering: *there is* one law for [1]them: the priest that maketh atonement therewith shall have *it*.

8 And the priest that offereth any man's burnt offering, *even* the priest shall have [1]to himself the skin of the burnt offering which he hath offered.

9 And [a]all the [1]meat offering that is baken in the oven, and all that is [2]dressed in the fryingpan, and in

[3]the pan, shall be the priest's that offereth it.

10 And every meat offering, mingled with oil, and dry, shall all the sons of Aaron have, one *as much as* another.

11 And [a]this *is* the law of the sacrifice of peace offerings, which he shall offer unto the LORD.

12 If he offer it for a thanksgiving, then he shall offer with the sacrifice of thanksgiving unleavened cakes mingled with oil, and unleavened wafers [a]anointed with oil, and cakes mingled with oil, of fine flour, fried.

13 Besides the cakes, he shall offer *for* his offering [a]leavened bread with the sacrifice of thanksgiving of his peace offerings.

14 And of it he shall offer [1]one out of the whole oblation *for* an heave offering unto the LORD, [a]*and* it shall be the priest's that sprinkleth the blood of the peace offerings.

15 [a]And the flesh of the sacrifice of his peace offerings for thanksgiving shall be eaten the same day that it is offered; he shall not leave any of it until the morning.

16 But [a]if the sacrifice of his offering *be* a vow, or a voluntary offering, it shall be eaten the same day that he offereth his sacrifice: and on the morrow also the remainder of it shall be eaten:

17 But the remainder of the flesh of the sacrifice on the third day shall be burnt with fire.

18 And if *any* of the flesh of the sacrifice of his peace offerings be eaten at all on the third day, it shall not be [1]accepted, neither shall it be [a]imputed unto him that offereth it: it shall be an [b]abomination, and the soul that eateth of it shall bear his [2]iniquity.

19 And the flesh that toucheth any unclean *thing* shall not be eaten; it shall be burnt with fire: and as for the flesh, all that be [1]clean shall eat thereof.

20 But the soul that eateth *of* the flesh of the sacrifice of peace offerings, that *pertain* unto the [a]LORD, [b]having his uncleanness upon him, even that soul [c]shall be cut off from his people.

21 Moreover the soul that shall touch any unclean *thing, as* [a]the uncleanness of man, or *any* [b]unclean beast, or any [c]abominable unclean *thing,* and eat of the flesh of the sacrifice of peace offerings, which *pertain* unto the LORD, even that soul [d]shall be cut off from his people.

22 And the LORD spake unto Moses, saying,

23 Speak unto the children of Israel, saying, [a]Ye shall eat no manner of fat, of ox, or of sheep, or of goat.

---

**Center column references:**

6:22 [b] Ex. 29:25
[1] completely

6:25 [a] Lev. 1:1, 3, 5, 11

6:26 [a] [Lev. 10:17, 18]; Num. 18:9, 10; [Ezek. 44:28, 29]

6:27 [a] Ex. 29:37; Num. 4:15; Hag. 2:11–13 [1] *Every-thing that* [2] *must*

6:28 [a] Lev. 11:33; 15:12 [1] *boiled*

6:30 [a] Lev. 4:7, 11, 12, 18, 21; 10:18; 16:27; [Heb. 13:11, 12] [b] Ex. 26:33 [c] Lev. 6:16, 23, 26 [d] Lev. 16:27 [1] *Most Holy Place* or *Holy of Holies*

7:1 [a] Lev. 5:14–6:7 [1] Heb. *torah*

7:6 [a] Lev. 6:16–18, 29; Num. 18:9 [b] Lev. 2:3

7:7 [a] Lev. 6:24–30; 14:13 [1] *them both*

7:8 [1] *for*

7:9 [a] Lev. 2:3, 10; Num. 18:9; Ezek. 44:29 [1] *grain* or *meal* [2] *prepared*

3 *a griddle*

7:11 [a] Lev. 3:1; 22:18, 21; Ezek. 45:15

7:12 [a] Lev. 2:4; Num. 6:15

7:13 [a] Lev. 2:12; 23:17, 18; Amos 4:5

7:14 [a] Num. 18:8, 11, 19 [1] *one cake from each offering*

7:15 [a] Lev. 22:29, 30

7:16 [a] Lev. 19:5–8

7:18 [a] Num. 18:27 [b] Lev. 11:10, 11, 41; 19:7; [Prov. 15:8] [1] *pleasing* [2] *guilt*

7:19 [1] *pure*

7:20 [a] [Heb. 2:17] [b] Lev. 5:3; 15:3; 22:3–7; Num. 19:13; [1 Cor. 11:28] [c] Gen. 17:14; Ex. 31:14

7:21 [a] Lev. 5:2, 3, 5 [b] Lev. 11:24, 28 [c] Ezek. 4:14 [d] Lev. 7:20

7:23 [a] Lev. 3:17; 17:10–15; Deut. 14:21; Ezek. 4:14; 44:31

---

24 And the fat of the beast that dieth of itself, and the fat of that which is torn with beasts, may be used in any other use: but ye shall in no wise eat of it.

25 For whosoever eateth the fat of the beast, of which men offer an offering made by fire unto the LORD, even the ¹soul that eateth *it* shall be cut off from his people.

26 ᵃMoreover ye shall eat no manner of blood, *whether it be* of fowl or of beast, in any of your dwellings.

27 Whatsoever ¹soul *it be* that eateth any manner of blood, even that soul shall be cut off from his people.

28 And the LORD spake unto Moses, saying,

29 Speak unto the children of Israel, saying, ᵃHe that offereth the sacrifice of his peace offerings unto the LORD shall bring his ¹oblation unto the LORD of the sacrifice of his peace offerings.

30 ᵃHis own hands shall bring the offerings of the LORD made by fire, the fat with the breast, it shall he bring, that the ᵇbreast may be waved *for* a wave offering before the LORD.

31 ᵃAnd the priest shall burn the fat upon the altar: but the ᵇbreast shall be Aaron's and his sons'.

32 And ᵃthe right shoulder shall ye give unto the priest *for* an heave offering of the sacrifices of your peace offerings.

33 He among the sons of Aaron, that offereth the blood of the peace offerings, and the fat, shall have the right shoulder for *his* part.

34 For ᵃthe wave breast and the heave shoulder have I taken of the children of Israel from off the sacrifices of their peace offerings, and have given them unto Aaron the priest and unto his sons by a statute for ever from among the children of Israel.

35 This *is the portion* of the anointing of Aaron, and of the anointing of his sons, out of the offerings of the LORD made by fire, in the day *when* he presented them to ¹minister unto the LORD in the priest's office;

36 Which the LORD commanded to be given them of the children of Israel, ᵃin the day that he anointed them, *by* a statute for ever throughout their generations.

37 This *is* the law ᵃof the burnt offering, ᵇof the ¹meat offering, ᶜand of the sin offering, ᵈand of the trespass offering, ᵉand of the consecrations, and ᶠof the sacrifice of the peace offerings;

38 Which the LORD commanded Moses in mount Sinai, in the day that he commanded the children of Israel ᵃto offer their oblations unto the LORD, in the wilderness of Sinai.

## CHAPTER 8

AND the LORD spake unto Moses, saying,

2 ᵃTake Aaron and his sons with him, and ᵇthe garments, and ᶜthe anointing oil, and a ᵈbullock for the sin offering, and two ᵉrams, and a basket of unleavened bread;

3 And gather thou all the congregation together ¹unto the door of the tabernacle of the ²congregation.

4 And Moses did as the LORD commanded him; and the assembly was gathered together unto the door of the tabernacle of the congregation.

5 And Moses said unto the congregation, This *is* the thing which the LORD commanded to be done.

6 And Moses brought Aaron and his sons, and ᵃwashed them with water.

7 And he ᵃput upon him the coat, and girded him with the girdle, and clothed him with the robe, and put the ephod upon him, and he girded him with the curious girdle of the ephod, and bound *it* unto him therewith.

8 And he put the breastplate upon him: also he ᵃput in the breastplate the ¹Urim and the Thummim.

9 ᵃAnd he put the mitre upon his head; also upon the mitre, *even* upon his forefront, did he put the golden plate, the holy crown; as the LORD commanded Moses.

10 ᵃAnd Moses took the anointing oil, and anointed the tabernacle and all that *was* therein, and sanctified them.

11 And he sprinkled thereof upon the altar seven times, and anointed the altar and all his vessels, both the laver and his foot, to ¹sanctify them.

12 And he ᵃpoured of the anointing oil upon Aaron's head, and anointed him, to sanctify him.

13 ᵃAnd Moses brought Aaron's sons, and put coats upon them, and girded them with girdles, and put ¹bonnets upon them; as the LORD commanded Moses.

14 ᵃAnd he brought the bullock for the sin offering: and Aaron and his sons ᵇlaid their hands upon the head of the bullock for the sin offering.

15 And he slew *it;* ᵃand Moses took the blood, and put *it* upon the horns of the altar round about with his finger, and purified the altar, and poured the blood at the bottom of the altar, and sanctified it, to make ¹reconciliation upon it.

16 ᵃAnd he took all the fat that *was* upon the inwards, and the caul *above* the liver, and the two kidneys, and their fat, and Moses burned *it* upon the altar.

17 But the bullock, and his hide, his flesh, and his dung, he burnt with fire ¹without the camp; as the LORD ᵃcommanded Moses.

18 ᵃAnd he brought the ram for the burnt offering: and Aaron and his sons laid their hands upon the head of the ram.

19 And he killed *it;* and Moses sprinkled the blood upon the altar round about.

20 And he cut the ram into pieces; and Moses ᵃburnt the head, and the pieces, and the fat.

21 And he washed the inwards and the legs in water; and Moses burnt the whole ram upon the altar: it *was* a burnt sacrifice for a ¹sweet savour, *and* an offering made by fire unto the LORD; ᵃas the LORD commanded Moses.

22 And ᵃhe brought the other ram, the ram of consecration: and Aaron and his sons laid their hands upon the head of the ram.

23 And he slew *it;* and Moses took of the ᵃblood of it, and put *it* upon the tip of Aaron's right ear, and upon the thumb of his right hand, and upon the great toe of his right foot.

24 And he brought Aaron's sons, and Moses put of the ᵃblood upon the tip of their right ear, and upon the thumbs of their right hands, and upon the great toes of their right feet: and Moses sprinkled the blood upon the altar round about.

25 ᵃAnd he took the fat, and the rump, and all the fat that *was* upon the inwards, and the caul *above* the liver, and the two kidneys, and their fat, and the right shoulder:

26 ᵃAnd out of the basket of unleavened bread, that *was* before the LORD, he took one unleavened cake, and a cake of oiled bread, and one wafer, and put *them* on the fat, and upon the right shoulder:

27 And he put all ᵃupon Aaron's hands, and upon his sons' hands, and waved them *for* a wave offering before the LORD.

28 ᵃAnd Moses took them from off their hands, and burnt *them* on the altar upon the burnt offering: they *were* consecrations for a sweet savour: it *is* an offering made by fire unto the LORD.

29 And ᵃMoses took the ᵇbreast, and waved it *for* a wave offering before the LORD: for of the ram of consecration it was Moses' ᶜpart; as the LORD commanded Moses.

30 And ᵃMoses took of the anointing oil, and of the blood which *was* upon the altar, and sprinkled *it* upon Aaron, *and* upon his garments, and upon his sons, and upon his sons' garments with him; and sanctified Aaron, *and*

8:17 ᵃ Ex. 29:14;
Lev. 4:11, 12
¹ outside

8:18 ᵃ Ex. 29:15

8:20 ᵃ Lev. 1:8

8:21 ᵃ Ex. 29:18
¹ pleasing aroma

8:22 ᵃ Ex. 29:19,
31; Lev. 8:2

8:23 ᵃ Ex. 29:20,
21; Lev. 14:14

8:24 ᵃ [Heb. 9:13,
14, 18–23]

8:25 ᵃ Ex. 29:22

8:26 ᵃ Ex. 29:23

8:27 ᵃ Ex. 29:24;
Lev. 7:30, 34

8:28 ᵃ Ex. 29:25

8:29 ᵃ Ps. 99:6
ᵇ Ex. 29:27 ᶜ Ex.
29:26

8:30 ᵃ Ex. 29:21;
30:30; Num. 3:3

8:31 ᵃ Ex. 29:31, 32

8:32 ᵃ Ex. 29:34

8:33 ᵃ Ex. 29:30,
35; Lev. 10:7; Ezek.
43:25, 26

8:34 ᵃ [Heb. 7:16]

8:35 ᵃ Num.
1:53; 3:7; 9:19;
Deut. 11:1; 1 Kin.
2:3; Ezek. 48:11
¹ office

9:1 ᵃ Ezek. 43:27

9:2 ᵃ Ex. 29:21;
Lev. 4:1–12

9:3 ᵃ Lev. 4:23, 28;
Ezra 6:17; 10:19

9:4 ᵃ Lev. 2:4
ᵇ Ex. 29:43; Lev.
9:6, 23 ¹ grain or
meal

9:5 ¹ in the presence of

9:7 ᵃ Lev. 4:3;
1 Sam. 3:14; [Heb.
5:3–5; 7:27] ᵇ Lev.
4:16, 20; Heb. 5:1

his garments, and his sons, and his sons' garments with him.

31 And Moses said unto Aaron and to his sons, ᵃBoil the flesh *at* the door of the tabernacle of the congregation: and there eat it with the bread that *is* in the basket of consecrations, as I commanded, saying, Aaron and his sons shall eat it.

32 ᵃAnd that which remaineth of the flesh and of the bread shall ye burn with fire.

33 And ye shall not go out of the door of the tabernacle of the congregation *in* seven days, until the days of your consecration be at an end: for ᵃseven days shall he consecrate you.

34 ᵃAs he hath done this day, *so* the LORD hath commanded to do, to make an atonement for you.

35 Therefore shall ye abide *at* the door of the tabernacle of the congregation day and night seven days, and ᵃkeep ¹the charge of the LORD, that ye die not: for so I am commanded.

36 So Aaron and his sons did all things which the LORD commanded by the hand of Moses.

## CHAPTER 9

AND ᵃit came to pass on the eighth day, *that* Moses called Aaron and his sons, and the elders of Israel;

2 And he said unto Aaron, Take thee a young ᵃcalf for a sin offering, and a ram for a burnt offering, without blemish, and offer *them* before the LORD.

3 And unto the children of Israel thou shalt speak, saying, ᵃTake ye a kid of the goats for a sin offering; and a calf and a lamb, *both* of the first year, without blemish, for a burnt offering;

4 Also a bullock and a ram for peace offerings, to sacrifice before the LORD; and ᵃa ¹meat offering mingled with oil: for ᵇto day the LORD will appear unto you.

5 And they brought *that* which Moses commanded before the tabernacle of the congregation: and all the congregation drew near and stood ¹before the LORD.

6 And Moses said, This *is* the thing which the LORD commanded that ye should do: and the glory of the LORD shall appear unto you.

7 And Moses said unto Aaron, Go unto the altar, and ᵃoffer thy sin offering, and thy burnt offering, and make an atonement for thyself, and for the people: and ᵇoffer the offering of the people, and make an atonement for them; as the LORD commanded.

8 Aaron therefore went unto the altar, and slew the calf of the sin offering, which *was* for himself.

9 And the sons of Aaron brought the blood unto him: and he dipped his

finger in the blood, and put *it* upon the horns of the altar, and poured out the blood at the bottom of the altar:

10 [a]But the fat, and the kidneys, and the caul above the liver of the sin offering, he burnt upon the altar; as the LORD commanded Moses.

11 [a]And the flesh and the hide he burnt with fire [1]without the camp.

12 And he slew the burnt offering; and Aaron's sons presented unto him the blood, [a]which he sprinkled round about upon the altar.

13 [a]And they presented the burnt offering unto him, with the pieces thereof, and the head: and he burnt *them* upon the altar.

14 [a]And he did wash the inwards and the legs, and burnt *them* upon the burnt offering on the altar.

15 [a]And he brought the people's offering, and took the goat, which *was* the sin offering for the people, and slew it, and offered it for sin, as the first.

16 And he brought the burnt offering, and offered it [a]according to the [1]manner.

17 And he brought [1]the meat offering, and took an handful thereof, and burnt *it* upon the altar, [a]beside the burnt sacrifice of the morning.

18 He slew also the bullock and the ram *for* [a]a sacrifice of peace offerings, which *was* for the people: and Aaron's sons presented unto him the blood, which he sprinkled upon the altar round about,

19 And the fat of the bullock and of the ram, the rump, and that which covereth *the inwards,* and the kidneys, and the caul *above* the liver:

20 And they put the fat upon the breasts, [a]and he burnt the fat upon the altar:

21 And the breasts and the right shoulder Aaron waved [a]*for* a wave offering before the LORD; as Moses commanded.

22 And Aaron lifted up his hand toward the people, and [a]blessed them, and came down from offering of the sin offering, and the burnt offering, and peace offerings.

23 And Moses and Aaron went into the tabernacle of the congregation, and came out, and blessed the people: and the glory of the LORD appeared unto all the people.

24 And [a]there came a fire out from before the LORD, and consumed upon the altar the burnt offering and the fat: *which* when all the people saw, they [b]shouted, and fell on their [c]faces.

## CHAPTER 10

A ND [a]Nadab and Abihu, the sons of Aaron, [b]took either of them his censer, and put fire therein, and

put incense thereon, and offered [c]strange fire before the LORD, which he commanded them not.

2 And there [a]went out fire from the LORD, and devoured them, and they died before the LORD.

3 Then Moses said unto Aaron, This *is it* that the LORD spake, saying, I will be sanctified in them [a]that come nigh me, and before all the people I will be glorified. And Aaron held his peace.

4 And Moses called Mishael and Elzaphan, the sons of Uzziel the uncle of Aaron, and said unto them, Come near, [a]carry your brethren from [1]before the sanctuary out of the camp.

5 So they went near, and carried them in their coats out of the camp; as Moses had said.

6 And Moses said unto Aaron, and unto Eleazar and unto Ithamar, his sons, [1]Uncover not your heads, neither rend your clothes; lest ye die, and [a]lest wrath come upon all the people: but let your brethren, the whole house of Israel, [2]bewail the burning which the LORD hath kindled.

7 [a]And ye shall not go out from the door of the tabernacle of the congregation, lest ye die: [b]for the anointing oil of the LORD *is* upon you. And they did according to the word of Moses.

8 And the LORD spake unto Aaron, saying,

9 [a]Do not drink wine nor strong drink, thou, nor thy sons with thee, when ye go into the tabernacle of the congregation, lest ye die: *it shall be* a statute for ever throughout your generations:

10 And that ye may [a]put difference between holy and unholy, and between unclean and clean;

11 [a]And that ye may teach the children of Israel all the statutes which the LORD hath spoken unto them by the hand of Moses.

12 And Moses spake unto Aaron, and unto Eleazar and unto Ithamar, his sons that were left, Take [a]the [1]meat offering that remaineth of the offerings of the LORD made by fire, and eat it without leaven beside the altar: for [b]it *is* most holy:

13 And ye shall eat it in the [a]holy place, because it *is* [1]thy due, and thy sons' due, of the sacrifices of the LORD made by fire: for [b]so I am commanded.

14 And [a]the wave breast and heave shoulder shall ye eat in a clean place; thou, and thy sons, and thy [b]daughters with thee: for *they be* thy due, and thy sons' [c]due, *which* are given out of the sacrifices of peace offerings of the children of Israel.

15 [a]The heave shoulder and the wave breast shall they bring with the

---

*Center column cross-references:*

9:10 [a] Ex. 23:18;
Lev. 8:16
9:11 [a] Lev. 4:11, 12;
8:17 [1] *outside*
9:12 [a] Lev. 1:5; 8:19
9:13 [a] Lev. 8:20
9:14 [a] Lev. 8:21
9:15 [a] [Is. 53:10;
Heb. 2:17; 5:3]
9:16 [a] Lev. 1:1–13
[1] *prescribed
manner*
9:17 [a] Ex. 29:38, 39
[1] *grain* or *meal*
9:18 [a] Lev. 3:1–11
9:20 [a] Lev. 3:5, 16
9:21 [a] Ex. 29:24,
26, 27; Lev.
7:30–34
9:22 [a] Num.
6:22–26; Deut.
21:5; Luke 24:50
9:24 [a] Gen. 4:4;
Judg. 6:21; 2 Chr.
7:1; Ps. 20:3
[b] Ezra 3:11 [c] 1 Kin.
18:38, 39
10:1 [a] Ex. 24:1,
9; Num. 3:2–4;
1 Chr. 24:2 [b] Lev.
16:12

[c] Ex. 30:9; 1 Sam.
2:17
10:2 [a] Gen. 19:24;
Num. 11:1; 16:35;
Rev. 20:9
10:3 [a] Ex. 19:22;
Lev. 21:6; Is. 52:11;
Ezek. 20:41
10:4 [a] Acts 5:6, 10
[1] *in front of*
10:6 [a] Num. 1:53;
16:22, 46; 18:5;
Josh. 7:1; 22:18, 20;
2 Sam. 24:1 [1] An
act of mourning
[2] *weep bitterly in
mourning*
10:7 [a] Lev. 8:33;
21:12 [b] Lev. 8:30
10:9 [a] Gen. 9:21;
[Prov. 20:1; 31:5];
Is. 28:7; Ezek.
44:21; Hos. 4:11;
Luke 1:15; [Eph.
5:18]; 1 Tim. 3:3;
Titus 1:7
10:10 [a] Lev. 11:47;
20:25; Ezek.
22:26; 44:23
10:11 [a] Deut. 24:8;
Neh. 8:2, 8; Jer.
18:18; Mal. 2:7
10:12 [a] Num.
18:9 [b] Lev. 21:22
[1] *grain or meal*
10:13 [a] Num. 18:10
[b] Lev. 2:3; 6:16
[1] *your portion*
10:14 [a] Ex. 29:24,
26, 27; Lev.
7:30–34; Num.
18:11 [b] Lev. 22:13
[c] Num. 18:10
10:15 [a] Lev. 7:29,
30, 34

offerings made by fire of the fat, to wave *it for* a wave offering before the LORD; and it shall be thine, and thy sons' with thee, by a statute for ever; as the LORD hath commanded.

16 And Moses diligently sought athe goat of the sin offering, and, behold, it was burnt: and he was angry with Eleazar and Ithamar, the sons of Aaron *which were* left *alive,* saying,

17 aWherefore have ye not eaten the sin offering in the holy place, seeing it *is* most holy, and *God* hath given it you to bear bthe 1iniquity of the congregation, to make atonement for them before the LORD?

18 Behold, athe blood of it was not brought in within the holy *place:* ye should indeed have eaten it in the holy *place,* bas I commanded.

19 And Aaron said unto Moses, Behold, athis day have they offered their sin offering and their burnt offering before the LORD; and such things have 1befallen me: and *if* I had eaten the sin offering to day, bshould it have been accepted in the sight of the LORD?

20 And when Moses heard *that,* he was content.

## CHAPTER 11

AND the LORD spake unto Moses and to Aaron, saying unto them,

2 Speak unto the children of Israel, saying, aThese *are* the beasts which ye shall eat among all the beasts that *are* on the earth.

3 Whatsoever parteth the hoof, and is clovenfooted, *and* cheweth the cud, among the beasts, that shall ye eat.

4 Nevertheless these shall ye anot eat of them that chew the cud, or of them that divide the hoof: *as* the camel, because he cheweth the cud, but divideth not the hoof; he *is* 1unclean unto you.

5 And the 1coney, because he cheweth the cud, but divideth not the hoof; he *is* 2unclean unto you.

6 And the hare, because he cheweth the cud, but divideth not the hoof; *is* unclean unto you.

7 And the swine, though he divide the hoof, and be clovenfooted, yet he cheweth not the cud; ahe *is* unclean to you.

8 Of their flesh shall ye not eat, and their carcase shall ye not touch; athey *are* unclean to you.

9 aThese shall ye eat of all that *are* in the waters: whatsoever hath fins and scales in the waters, in the seas, and in the rivers, them shall ye eat.

10 And all that have not fins and scales in the seas, and in the rivers, of all that move in the waters, and of any living thing which *is* in the waters,

they *shall be* an aabomination1 unto you:

11 They shall be even an abomination unto you; ye shall not eat of their flesh, but ye shall have their carcases in abomination.

12 Whatsoever hath no fins nor scales in the waters, that *shall be* an abomination unto you.

13 aAnd these *are they which* ye shall have in abomination among the fowls; they shall not be eaten, they *are* an abomination: the eagle, and the 1ossifrage, and the 2ospray,

14 And the 1vulture, and the kite after his kind;

15 Every raven after his kind;

16 And the owl, and the night hawk, and the cuckow, and the hawk after his kind,

17 And the little owl, and the cormorant, and the great owl,

18 And the swan, and the pelican, and the gier eagle,

19 And the stork, the heron after her kind, and the lapwing, and the bat.

20 All fowls that creep, going upon *all* four, *shall be* an abomination unto you.

21 Yet these may ye eat of every flying creeping thing that goeth upon *all* four, which have legs above their feet, to leap withal upon the earth;

22 *Even* these of them ye may eat; athe locust after his kind, and the bald locust after his kind, and the beetle after his kind, and the grasshopper after his kind.

23 But all *other* flying creeping things, which have four feet, *shall be* an abomination unto you.

24 And 1for these ye shall be unclean: whosoever toucheth the carcase of them shall be unclean until the even.

25 And whosoever beareth *ought* of the carcase of them ashall wash his clothes, and be unclean until the even.

26 *The carcases* of every beast which divideth the hoof, and *is* not clovenfooted, nor cheweth the cud, *are* unclean unto you: every one that toucheth them shall be unclean.

27 And whatsoever goeth upon his paws, among all manner of beasts that go on *all* four, those *are* unclean unto you: whoso toucheth their carcase shall be unclean until the even.

28 And he that beareth the carcase of them shall wash his clothes, and be unclean until the even: they *are* unclean unto you.

29 These also *shall be* unclean unto you among the creeping things that creep upon the earth; the weasel, and athe mouse, and the tortoise after his kind,

### Cross references (center column)

10:16 a Lev. 9:3, 15
10:17 a Lev. 6:24–30 b Ex. 28:38; Lev. 22:16; Num. 18:1 1 *guilt*
10:18 a Lev. 6:30 b Lev. 6:26, 30
10:19 a Lev. 9:8, 12 b [Is. 1:11–15]; Jer. 6:20; 14:12; Hos. 9:4; [Mal. 1:10, 13; 3:1–4] 1 *happened to*
11:2 a Deut. 14:4; Ezek. 4:14; Dan. 1:8; [Matt. 15:11]; Acts 10:12, 14; [Rom. 14:14; Heb. 9:10; 13:9]
11:4 a Acts 10:14 1 *impure*
11:5 1 *rock hyrax or rock badger* 2 *impure*
11:7 a Is. 65:4; 66:3, 17; Mark 5:1–17
11:8 a Is. 52:11; [Mark 7:2, 15, 18]; Acts 10:14, 15; 15:29
11:9 a Deut. 14:9
11:10 a Lev. 7:18, 21; Deut. 14:3 1 *detestable*
11:13 a Deut. 14:12–19; Is. 66:17 1 *vulture* 2 *buzzard*
11:14 1 *kite, and falcon*
11:22 a Matt. 3:4; Mark 1:6
11:24 1 *by these you shall become impure*
11:25 a Lev. 14:8; 15:5; Num. 19:10, 21, 22; 31:24; Zech. 13:1; [Heb. 9:10; 10:22; Rev. 7:14]
11:29 a Is. 66:17

30 And the ferret, and the chameleon, and the lizard, and the snail, and the mole.

31 These *are* unclean to you among all that creep: whosoever doth [a]touch them, when they be dead, shall be unclean until the even.

32 And upon whatsoever *any* of them, when they are dead, doth fall, it shall be [1]unclean; whether *it be* any vessel of wood, or raiment, or skin, or sack, whatsoever vessel *it be*, wherein *any* work is done, [a]it must be put into water, and it shall be unclean until the even; so it shall be [2]cleansed.

33 And every [a]earthen vessel, whereinto *any* of them falleth, whatsoever *is* in it shall be unclean; and [b]ye shall break it.

34 Of all meat which may be eaten, *that* on which *such* water cometh shall be unclean: and all drink that may be drunk in every *such* vessel shall be unclean.

35 And every *thing* whereupon *any part* of their carcase falleth shall be unclean; *whether it be* oven, or ranges for pots, they shall be broken down: *for* they *are* unclean, and shall be unclean unto you.

36 Nevertheless a [1]fountain or [2]pit, *wherein there is* plenty of water, shall be clean: but that which toucheth their carcase shall be unclean.

37 And if *any part* of their carcase fall upon any sowing seed which is to be sown, it *shall be* clean.

38 But if *any* water be put upon the seed, and *any part* of their carcase fall thereon, it *shall be* [1]unclean unto you.

39 And if any beast, of which ye may eat, die; he that toucheth the carcase thereof shall be [a]unclean until the even.

40 And [a]he that eateth of the carcase of it shall wash his clothes, and be unclean until the even: he also that beareth the carcase of it shall wash his clothes, and be unclean until the even.

41 And every creeping thing that creepeth upon the earth *shall be* [1]an abomination; it shall not be eaten.

42 Whatsoever goeth upon the belly, and whatsoever goeth upon *all* four, or whatsoever hath more feet among all creeping things that creep upon the earth, them ye shall not eat; for they *are* an abomination.

43 [a]Ye shall not make [1]yourselves [2]abominable with any creeping thing that creepeth, neither shall ye make yourselves unclean with them, that ye should be defiled thereby.

44 For I *am* the LORD your [a]God: ye shall therefore sanctify yourselves, and [b]ye shall be holy; for I *am* holy:

neither shall ye defile yourselves with any manner of creeping thing that creepeth upon the earth.

45 [a]For I *am* the LORD that bringeth you up out of the land of Egypt, to be your God: [b]ye shall therefore be holy, for I *am* holy.

46 This *is* the law [1]of the beasts, and of the fowl, and of every living creature that moveth in the waters, and of every creature that creepeth upon the earth:

47 [a]To [1]make a difference between the unclean and the clean, and between the beast that may be eaten and the beast that may not be eaten.

## CHAPTER 12

AND the LORD spake unto Moses, saying,

2 Speak unto the children of Israel, saying, If a [a]woman have conceived seed, and born a man child: then [b]she shall be [1]unclean seven days; [c]according to the days of the separation for her infirmity shall she be unclean.

3 And in the [a]eighth day the flesh of his foreskin shall be circumcised.

4 And she shall then continue in the blood of her purifying three and thirty days; she shall touch no [1]hallowed thing, nor come into the sanctuary, until the days of her purifying be fulfilled.

5 But if she bear a maid child, then she shall be unclean two weeks, as in her separation: and she shall continue in the blood of her purifying threescore and six days.

6 And [a]when the days of her purifying are fulfilled, for a son, or for a daughter, she shall bring a [b]lamb [1]of the first year for a burnt offering, and a young pigeon, or a turtledove, for a [c]sin offering, unto the door of the tabernacle of the congregation, unto the priest:

7 Who shall offer it before the LORD, and make [1]an atonement for her; and she shall be cleansed from the issue of her blood. This *is* the law for her that hath born a male or a female.

8 [a]And if she be not able to bring a lamb, then she shall bring two turtles, or two young pigeons; the one for the burnt offering, and the other for a sin offering: [b]and the priest shall make an atonement for her, and she shall be [1]clean.

## CHAPTER 13

AND the LORD spake unto Moses and Aaron, saying,

2 When a man shall have in the skin of his flesh a [1]rising, [a]a scab, or bright spot, and it be in the skin of his flesh *like* the [2]plague of leprosy; [b]then he shall be brought unto Aaron

11:31 [a] Hag. 2:13
11:32 [a] Lev. 15:12
[1] impure [2] clean
11:33 [a] Lev. 6:28
[b] Lev. 15:12; Ps. 2:9; Jer. 48:38;
[2 Tim. 2:21]; Rev. 2:27
11:36 [1] spring
[2] cistern
11:38 [1] impure
11:39 [a] Hag. 2:11–13
11:40 [a] Ex. 22:31;
Lev. 17:15; 22:8;
Deut. 14:21; Ezek. 4:14; 44:31
11:41 [1] detestable
11:43 [a] Lev. 20:25
[1] Lit. your souls
[2] impure
11:44 [a] Ex. 6:7;
Lev. 22:33; 25:38;
26:45 [b] Ex. 19:6;
Lev. 19:2; 20:7, 26;
[Amos 3:3]; Matt.
5:48; 1 Thess.
4:7; 1 Pet. 1:15, 16;
[Rev. 22:11, 14]

11:45 [a] Ex. 6:7;
20:2; Lev. 22:33;
25:38; 26:45; Ps.
105:43–45; Hos.
11:1 [b] Lev. 11:44
11:46 [1] concerning
11:47 [a] Lev. 10:10;
Ezek. 44:23; Mal.
3:18 [1] distinguish
between
12:2 [a] Lev. 15:19;
[Job 14:4; Ps.
51:5] [b] Ex. 22:30;
Lev. 8:33; 13:4;
Luke 2:22 [c] Lev.
18:19 [1] impure
12:3 [a] Gen. 17:12;
Luke 1:59; 2:21;
John 7:22, 23;
Gal. 5:3
12:4 [1] consecrated
12:6 [a] Luke 2:22
[b] [John 1:29;
1 Pet. 1:18, 19]
[c] Lev. 5:7 [1] Lit. a
son of his year
12:7 [1] a propitiation
12:8 [a] Lev. 5:7;
Luke 2:22–24
[b] Lev. 4:26 [1] pure
13:2 [a] Deut. 28:27;
Is. 3:17 [b] Deut.
17:8, 9; 24:8;
Mal. 2:7; Luke
17:14 [1] swelling
[2] Exact identity is
unclear.

the priest, or unto one of his sons the priests:

3 And the priest shall look on the ¹plague in the skin of the flesh: and *when* the hair in the plague is turned white, and the plague in sight *be* deeper than the skin of his flesh, it *is* a plague of leprosy: and the priest shall look on him, and pronounce him ²unclean.

4 If the bright spot *be* white in the skin of his flesh, and in sight *be* not deeper than the skin, and the hair thereof be not turned white; then the priest shall ¹shut up *him that hath* the plague ᵃseven days:

5 And the priest shall look on him the seventh day: and, behold, *if* the plague in his sight ¹be at a stay, *and* the plague spread not in the skin; then the priest shall ²shut him up seven days more:

6 And the priest shall look on him again the seventh day: and, behold, *if* the plague *be* somewhat dark, *and* the plague spread not in the skin, the priest shall pronounce him clean: it *is but* a scab: and he ᵃshall wash his clothes, and be clean.

7 But if the scab spread much abroad in the skin, after that he hath been seen of the priest for his cleansing, he shall be seen of the priest again:

8 And *if* the priest see that, behold, the scab spreadeth in the skin, then the priest shall pronounce him ¹unclean: it *is* a leprosy.

9 When the plague of leprosy is in a man, then he shall be brought unto the priest;

10 ᵃAnd the priest shall see *him:* and, behold, *if* the ¹rising *be* white in the skin, and it have turned the hair white, and *there be* ²quick raw flesh in the rising;

11 It *is* an old leprosy in the skin of his flesh, and the priest shall pronounce him ¹unclean, and shall not shut him up: for he *is* unclean.

12 And if a leprosy break out abroad in the skin, and the leprosy cover all the skin of *him that hath* the plague from his head even to his foot, wheresoever the priest looketh;

13 Then the priest shall consider: and, behold, *if* the leprosy have covered all his flesh, he shall pronounce *him* clean *that hath* the plague: it is all turned ᵃwhite: he *is* clean.

14 But when raw flesh appeareth in him, he shall be unclean.

15 And the priest shall see the raw flesh, and pronounce him to be unclean: *for* the raw flesh *is* unclean: it *is* a leprosy.

16 Or if the raw flesh turn again, and be changed unto white, he shall come unto the priest;

17 And the priest shall see him: and, behold, *if* the plague be turned into white; then the priest shall pronounce *him* clean *that hath* the plague: he *is* clean.

18 The flesh also, in which, *even* in the skin thereof, was a ᵃboil, and is healed,

19 And in the place of the boil there be a white ¹rising, or a bright spot, white, and somewhat reddish, and it be shewed to the priest;

20 And if, when the priest seeth it, behold, it *be* in sight ¹lower than the skin, and the hair thereof be turned white; the priest shall pronounce him unclean: it *is* a plague of leprosy broken out of the boil.

21 But if the priest look on it, and, behold, *there be* no white hairs therein, and *if* it *be* not lower than the skin, but *be* somewhat dark; then the priest shall ¹shut him up seven days:

22 And if it spread much abroad in the skin, then the priest shall pronounce him unclean: it *is* a ¹plague.

23 But if the bright spot ¹stay in his place, *and* spread not, it *is* a burning boil; and the priest shall pronounce him clean.

24 Or if there be *any* flesh, in the skin whereof *there is* a ¹hot ᵃburning, and the ²quick *flesh* that burneth have a white bright spot, somewhat reddish, or white;

25 Then the priest shall look upon it: and, behold, *if* the hair in the bright spot be turned white, and it *be in* sight deeper than the skin; it *is* a leprosy broken out of the burning: wherefore the priest shall pronounce him unclean: it *is* the ¹plague of leprosy.

26 But if the priest look on it, and, behold, *there be* no white hair in the bright spot, and it *be* no ¹lower than the *other* skin, but *be* somewhat dark; then the priest shall ²shut him up seven days:

27 And the priest shall look upon him the seventh day: *and* if it be spread much abroad in the skin, then the priest shall pronounce him unclean: it *is* the plague of leprosy.

28 And if the bright spot stay in his place, *and* spread not in the skin, but it *be* somewhat dark; it *is* a rising of the burning, and the priest shall pronounce him clean: for it *is* an inflammation of the burning.

29 If a man or woman have a plague upon the head or the beard;

30 Then the priest shall see the plague: and, behold, if it *be* in sight deeper than the skin; *and there be* in it a yellow thin hair; then the priest shall pronounce him unclean: it *is* a dry scall, *even* a leprosy upon the head or beard.

---

13:3 ¹ *sore*
² *defiled*

13:4 ᵃ Lev. 14:8
¹ *isolate*

13:5 ¹ *has not spread* ² *isolate*

13:6 ᵃ Lev. 11:25; 14:8; [John 13:8, 10]

13:8 ¹ *defiled*

13:10 ᵃ Num. 12:10, 12; 2 Kin. 5:27; 2 Chr. 26:19, 20 ¹ *a spot of* ² *swelling*

13:11 ¹ *defiled*

13:13 ᵃ Ex. 4:6

13:18 ᵃ Ex. 9:9; 15:26

13:19 ¹ *swelling*

13:20 ¹ *deeper*

13:21 ¹ *isolate*

13:22 ¹ *infection or leprous sore*

13:23 ¹ *remains*

13:24 ᵃ Is. 3:24 ¹ Lit. *burning of fire* ² *raw*

13:25 ¹ *infection*

13:26 ¹ *deeper* ² *isolate*

31 And if the priest look on the plague of the scall, and, behold, it *be* not in sight deeper than the skin, and *that there is* no black hair in it; then the priest shall shut up *him that hath* the plague of the scall seven days:

32 And in the seventh day the priest shall look on the plague: and, behold, *if* the scall spread not, and there be in it no yellow hair, and the scall *be* not in sight deeper than the skin;

33 He shall be shaven, but the scall shall he not shave; and the priest shall shut up *him that hath* the scall seven days more:

34 And in the seventh day the priest shall look on the scall: and, behold, *if* the scall be not spread in the skin, nor *be* in sight deeper than the skin; then the priest shall pronounce him clean: and he shall wash his clothes, and be clean.

35 But if the scall spread much in the skin after his cleansing;

36 Then the priest shall look on him: and, behold, if the scall be spread in the skin, the priest shall not seek for yellow hair; he *is* unclean.

37 But if the scall be in his sight at a stay, and *that* there is black hair grown up therein; the scall is healed, he *is* clean: and the priest shall pronounce him clean.

38 If a man also or a woman have in the skin of their flesh bright spots, *even* white bright spots;

39 Then the priest shall look: and, behold, *if* the bright spots in the skin of their flesh *be* darkish white; it *is* a freckled spot *that* groweth in the skin; he *is* clean.

40 And the man whose hair is fallen off his head, he *is* bald; *yet is* he clean.

41 And he that hath his hair fallen off from the part of his head toward his face, he *is* forehead bald: *yet is* he clean.

42 And if there be in the bald head, or bald [a]forehead, a white reddish sore; it *is* a leprosy sprung up in his bald head, or his bald forehead.

43 Then the priest shall look upon it: and, behold, *if* the rising of the sore *be* white reddish in his bald head, or in his bald forehead, as the leprosy appeareth in the skin of the flesh;

44 He is a leprous man, he *is* unclean: the priest shall pronounce him [1]utterly unclean; his plague *is* in his [a]head.

45 And the leper in whom the plague *is,* his clothes shall be [1]rent, and his head [a]bare, and he shall [b]put a covering upon his upper lip, and shall cry, [c]Unclean, unclean.

46 All the days wherein the plague *shall be* in him he shall be defiled; he *is* unclean: he shall [1]dwell alone;

[a]without[2] the camp *shall* his habitation *be.*

47 The garment also that the [1]plague of leprosy is in, *whether it be* a woollen garment, or a linen garment;

48 Whether *it be* in the warp, or woof; of linen, or of woollen; whether in a skin, or in any thing made of [1]skin;

49 And if the plague be greenish or reddish in the garment, or in the skin, either in the warp, or in the woof, or in any thing of [1]skin; it *is* a [2]plague of leprosy, and shall be shewed unto the priest:

50 And the priest shall look upon the plague, and shut up *it that hath* the plague seven days:

51 And he shall look on the plague on the seventh day: if the plague be spread in the garment, either in the warp, or in the woof, or in a skin, *or* in any work that is made of skin; the plague *is* [a]a [1]fretting leprosy; it *is* unclean.

52 He shall therefore burn that garment, whether warp or woof, in woollen or in linen, or any thing of skin, wherein the plague is: for it *is* a fretting leprosy; it shall be burnt in the fire.

53 And if the priest shall look, and, behold, the plague be not spread in the garment, either in the warp, or in the woof, or in any thing of skin;

54 Then the priest shall command that they wash *the thing* wherein the plague *is,* and he shall shut it up seven days more:

55 And the priest shall look on the plague, after that it is washed: and, behold, *if* the plague have not changed his colour, and the plague be not spread; it *is* unclean; thou shalt burn it in the fire; it *is* fret inward, *whether* it *be* bare within or without.

56 And if the priest look, and, behold, the plague *be* somewhat dark after the washing of it; then he shall [1]rend it out of the garment, or out of the skin, or out of the warp, or out of the woof:

57 And if it appear still in the garment, either in the warp, or in the woof, or in any thing of skin; it *is* a spreading *plague:* thou shalt burn that wherein the plague *is* with fire.

58 And the garment, either warp, or woof, or whatsoever thing of skin *it be,* which thou shalt wash, if the plague be departed from them, then it shall be washed the second time, and shall be clean.

59 This *is* the law of the plague of leprosy in a garment of woollen or linen, either in the warp, or woof, or any thing of skins, to pronounce it clean, or to pronounce it unclean.

---

13:42 [a] 2 Chr. 26:19

13:44 [a] Is. 1:5 [1]*altogether defiled*

13:45 [a] Lev. 10:6; 21:10 [b] Ezek. 24:17, 22; Mic. 3:7 [c] Is. 6:5; 64:6; Lam. 4:15; Luke 5:8 [1]*torn*

13:46 [1]*live*

[a] Num. 5:1-4; 12:14; 2 Kin. 7:3; 15:5; 2 Chr. 26:21; Ps. 38:11; Luke 17:12 [2] *outside*

13:47 [1] Exact identity is unclear.

13:48 [1] *leather*

13:49 [1] *leather* [2] *leprous mark*

13:51 [a] Lev. 14:44 [1] *active*

13:56 [1] *tear*

## CHAPTER 14

AND the LORD spake unto Moses, saying,

2 This shall be the law of the ¹leper in the day of his cleansing: He ᵃshall be brought unto the priest:

3 And the priest shall go forth out of the camp; and the priest shall look, and, behold, *if* the plague of leprosy be healed in the leper;

4 Then shall the priest command to take for him that is to be cleansed two birds alive *and* clean, and ᵃcedar wood, and ᵇscarlet, and ᶜhyssop:

5 And the priest shall command that one of the birds be killed in an earthen vessel over running water:

6 As for the living bird, he shall take it, and the cedar wood, and the scarlet, and the hyssop, and shall dip them and the living bird in the blood of the bird *that was* killed over the running water:

7 And he shall ᵃsprinkle upon him that is to be cleansed from the leprosy ᵇseven times, and shall pronounce him clean, and shall let the living bird loose into to the open field.

8 And he that is to be cleansed ᵃshall wash his clothes, and shave off all his hair, and ᵇwash himself in water, that he may be clean: and after that he shall come into the camp, and ᶜshall ¹tarry abroad out of his tent seven days.

9 But it shall be on the ᵃseventh day, that he shall shave all his hair off his head and his beard and his eyebrows, even all his hair he shall shave off: and he shall wash his clothes, also he shall wash his flesh in water, and he shall be clean.

10 And on the eighth day ᵃhe shall take two he lambs without blemish, and one ewe lamb ¹of the first year without blemish, and three tenth deals of fine flour *for* ᵇa meat offering, mingled with oil, and one log of oil.

11 And the priest that maketh *him* clean shall present the man that is to be made clean, and those things, before the LORD, *at* the door of the tabernacle of the congregation:

12 And the priest shall take one he lamb, and ᵃoffer him for a trespass offering, and the log of oil, and ᵇwave them *for* a wave offering before the LORD:

13 And he shall slay the lamb ᵃin the place where he shall kill the sin offering and the burnt offering, in the holy place: for ᵇas the sin offering *is* the priest's, *so is* the trespass offering: ᶜit *is* most holy:

14 And the priest shall take *some* of the blood of the trespass offering, and the priest shall put *it* ᵃupon the tip of the right ear of him that is to be

cleansed, and upon the thumb of his right hand, and upon the great toe of his right foot:

15 And the priest shall take *some* of the log of oil, and pour *it* into the palm of his own left hand:

16 And the priest shall dip his right finger in the oil that *is* in his left hand, and shall ᵃsprinkle of the oil with his finger seven times before the LORD:

17 And of the rest of the oil that *is* in his hand shall the priest put upon the tip of the right ear of him that is to be cleansed, and upon the thumb of his right hand, and upon the great toe of his right foot, upon the blood of the trespass offering:

18 And the remnant of the oil that *is* in the priest's hand he shall pour upon the head of him that is to be cleansed: ᵃand the priest shall make ¹an atonement for him before the LORD.

19 And the priest shall offer ᵃthe sin offering, and make an atonement for him that is to be cleansed from his uncleanness; and afterward he shall kill the burnt offering:

20 And the priest shall offer the burnt offering and the ¹meat offering upon the altar: and the priest shall make an atonement for him, and he shall be ᵃclean.

21 And ᵃif he *be* poor, and cannot get so much; then he shall take one lamb *for* a trespass offering to be waved, to make an atonement for him, and one tenth ¹deal of fine flour mingled with oil for a meat offering, and a log of oil;

22 ᵃAnd two turtledoves, or two young pigeons, such as he is able to get; and the one shall be a sin offering, and the other a burnt offering.

23 ᵃAnd he shall bring them on the eighth day for his cleansing unto the priest, unto the door of the tabernacle of the congregation, before the LORD.

24 ᵃAnd the priest shall take the lamb of the trespass offering, and the log of oil, and the priest shall wave them *for* a wave offering before the LORD:

25 And he shall kill the lamb of the trespass offering, ᵃand the priest shall take *some* of the blood of the trespass offering, and put *it* upon the tip of the right ear of him that is to be cleansed, and upon the thumb of his right hand, and upon the great toe of his right foot:

26 And the priest shall pour of the oil into the palm of his own left hand:

27 And the priest shall sprinkle with his right finger *some* of the oil that *is* in his left hand seven times before the LORD:

28 And the priest shall put of the oil that *is* in his hand upon the tip

### Center reference column

14:2 ᵃ Matt. 8:2, 4; Mark 1:40, 44; Luke 5:12, 14; 17:14 ¹ Medical identity is unclear.

14:4 ᵃ Lev. 14:6, 49, 51, 52; Num. 19:6; Heb. 9:19 ᵇ Ex. 25:4 ᶜ Ex. 12:22; Ps. 51:7

14:7 ᵃ Num. 19:18, 19; [Heb. 9:13, 21; 12:24] ᵇ 2 Kin. 5:10, 14; Ps. 51:2

14:8 ᵃ Lev. 11:25; 13:6; Num. 8:7 ᵇ Lev. 11:25; [Eph. 5:26; Heb. 10:22; Rev. 1:5, 6] ᶜ Lev. 13:5; Num. 5:2, 3; 12:14, 15; 2 Chr. 26:21 ¹ *stay outside*

14:9 ᵃ Num. 19:19

14:10 ᵃ Matt. 8:4; Mark 1:44; Luke 5:14 ᵇ Lev. 2:1; Num. 15:4 ¹ *one year old*

14:12 ᵃ Lev. 5:6, 18; 6:6; 14:19 ᵇ Ex. 29:22–24, 26

14:13 ᵃ Lev. 29:11; Lev. 1:5, 11; 4:4, 24 ᵇ Lev. 6:24–30; 7:7 ᶜ Lev. 2:3; 7:6; 21:22

14:14 ᵃ Ex. 29:20; Lev. 8:23, 24

14:16 ᵃ Lev. 4:6

14:18 ᵃ Lev. 4:26; 5:6; Num. 15:28; [Heb. 2:17] ¹ *propitiation*

14:19 ᵃ Lev. 5:1, 6; 12:7; [2 Cor. 5:21]

14:20 ᵃ Lev. 14:8, 9 ¹ *meal or grain*

14:21 ᵃ Lev. 5:7, 11; 12:8; 27:8 ¹ *ephah, measure*

14:22 ᵃ Lev. 12:8; 15:14, 15

14:23 ᵃ Lev. 14:10, 11

14:24 ᵃ Lev. 14:12

14:25 ᵃ Lev. 14:14, 17

of the right ear of him that is to be cleansed, and upon the thumb of his right hand, and upon the great toe of his right foot, upon the place of the blood of the trespass offering:

29 And the rest of the oil that *is* in the priest's hand he shall put upon the head of him that is to be cleansed, to make an atonement for him before the LORD.

30 And he shall offer the one of [a]the turtledoves, or of the young pigeons, such as he can get;

31 *Even* such as he is able to get, the one *for* a sin offering, and the other *for* a burnt offering, with the meat offering: and the priest shall make an atonement for him that is to be cleansed before the LORD.

32 This *is* the law *of him* in whom *is* the plague of leprosy, [1]whose hand is not able to get [a]*that which pertaineth* to his cleansing.

33 And the LORD spake unto Moses and unto Aaron, saying,

34 [a]When ye be come into the land of Canaan, which I give to you for a possession, and [b]I put the [1]plague of leprosy in a house of the land of your possession;

35 And he that owneth the house shall come and tell the priest, saying, It seemeth to me *there is* as it were [a]a plague in the house:

36 Then the priest shall command that they empty the house, before the priest go *into it* to see the plague, that all that *is* in the house be not made unclean: and afterward the priest shall go in to see the house:

37 And he shall look on the plague, and, behold, *if* the plague *be* in the walls of the house with hollow strakes, greenish or reddish, which in sight *are* [1]lower than the wall;

38 Then the priest shall go out of the house to the door of the house, and [1]shut up the house seven days:

39 And the priest shall come again the seventh day, and shall look: and, behold, *if* the plague be spread in the walls of the house;

40 Then the priest shall command that they take away the stones in which the plague *is,* and they shall cast them into an unclean place without the city:

41 And he shall cause the house to be scraped within round about, and they shall pour out the dust that they scrape off without the city into an unclean place:

42 And they shall take other stones, and put *them* in the place of those stones; and he shall take other morter, and shall plaister the house.

43 And if the plague come again, and break out in the house, after that he hath taken away the stones, and

after he hath scraped the house, and after it is plaistered;

44 Then the priest shall come and look, and, behold, *if* the plague be spread in the house, it *is* [a]a [1]fretting leprosy in the house: it *is* unclean.

45 And he shall break down the house, the stones of it, and the timber thereof, and all the morter of the house; and he shall carry *them* forth out of the city into an unclean place.

46 Moreover he that goeth into the house all the while that it is shut up shall be [1]unclean [a]until the even.

47 And he that lieth in the house shall [a]wash his clothes; and he that eateth in the house shall wash his clothes.

48 And if the priest shall come in, and look *upon it,* and, behold, the plague hath not spread in the house, after the house was plaistered: then the priest shall pronounce the house clean, because the plague is healed.

49 And [a]he shall take to cleanse the house two birds, and cedar wood, and scarlet, and hyssop:

50 And he shall kill the one of the birds in an earthen vessel over running water:

51 And he shall take the cedar wood, and the hyssop, and the scarlet, and the living bird, and dip them in the blood of the slain bird, and in the running water, and sprinkle the house seven times:

52 And he shall [1]cleanse the house with the blood of the bird, and with the running water, and with the living bird, and with the cedar wood, and with the hyssop, and with the scarlet:

53 But he shall let go the living bird out of the city into the open fields, and [a]make an atonement for the house: and it shall be clean.

54 This *is* the law for all manner of [a]plague of leprosy, and scall,

55 And for the [a]leprosy of a garment, [b]and of a house,

56 And [a]for a rising, and for a scab, and for a bright spot:

57 To [a]teach when *it is* unclean, and when *it is* clean: this *is* the law of leprosy.

## CHAPTER 15

AND the LORD spake unto Moses and to Aaron, saying,

2 Speak unto the children of Israel, and say unto them, [a]When any man hath a [1]running issue out of his flesh, *because of* his issue he *is* unclean.

3 And this shall be his uncleanness in his issue: whether his flesh run with his issue, or his flesh be stopped from his issue, it *is* his uncleanness.

4 Every bed, whereon he lieth that hath the issue, is [1]unclean: and every

14:30 [a] Lev. 14:22; 15:14, 15
14:32 [a] Lev. 14:10
[1] who cannot afford
14:34 [a] Gen. 12:7; 13:17; 17:8; Num. 32:22; Deut. 7:1; 32:49 [b] [Prov. 3:33]
[1] Exact identity is unclear.
14:35 [a] [Ps. 91:9, 10; Prov. 3:33; Zech. 5:4]
14:37 [1] deeper than the surface
14:38 [1] quarantine

14:44 [a] Lev. 13:51; [Zech. 5:4]
[1] active
14:46 [a] Lev. 11:24; 15:5 [1] defiled
14:47 [a] Lev. 14:8
14:49 [a] Lev. 14:4
14:52 [1] ceremonially cleanse
14:53 [a] Lev. 14:20
14:54 [a] Lev. 13:30; 26:21
14:55 [a] Lev. 13:47–52 [b] Lev. 14:34
14:56 [a] Lev. 13:2
14:57 [a] Lev. 11:47; 20:25; Deut. 24:8; Ezek. 44:23
15:2 [a] Lev. 22:4; Num. 5:2; 2 Sam. 3:29 [1] discharge
15:4 [1] defiled

thing, whereon he sitteth, shall be unclean.

5 And whosoever ªtoucheth his bed shall ᵇwash his clothes, ᶜand bathe *himself* in water, and be unclean until the even.

6 And he that sitteth on *any* thing whereon he sat that hath the ªissue shall wash his clothes, and bathe *himself* in water, and be unclean until the even.

7 And he that toucheth the flesh of him that hath the issue shall wash his clothes, and bathe *himself* in water, and be unclean until the even.

8 And if he that hath the issue ªspit upon him that is clean; then he shall wash his clothes, and bathe *himself* in water, and be unclean until the even.

9 And what saddle soever he rideth upon that hath the issue shall be unclean.

10 And whosoever toucheth any thing that was under him shall be unclean until the even: and he that beareth *any of* those things shall wash his clothes, and bathe *himself* in water, and be unclean until the even.

11 And whomsoever he toucheth that hath the ¹issue, and hath not rinsed his hands in water, he shall wash his clothes, and bathe *himself* in water, and be unclean until the even.

12 And the ªvessel of earth, that he toucheth which hath the issue, shall be broken: and every vessel of wood shall be rinsed in water.

13 And when he that hath an issue is cleansed of his issue; then ªhe shall number to himself seven days for his cleansing, and wash his clothes, and bathe his flesh in running water, and shall be clean.

14 And on the eighth day he shall take to him ªtwo turtledoves, or two young pigeons, and come before the LORD unto the door of the tabernacle of the congregation, and give them unto the priest:

15 And the priest shall offer them, ªthe one *for* a sin offering, and the other *for* a burnt offering; ᵇand the priest shall make ¹an atonement for him before the LORD for his issue.

16 And ªif any man's seed of copulation go out from him, then he shall wash all his flesh in water, and be unclean until the even.

17 And every garment, and every skin, whereon is the seed of copulation, shall be washed with water, and be unclean until the even.

18 The woman also with whom man shall lie *with* seed of copulation, they shall *both* bathe *themselves* in water, and ªbe unclean until the even.

19 And ªif a woman have ¹an issue, *and* her issue in her flesh be blood, she shall be ²put apart seven days: and whosoever toucheth her shall be unclean until the even.

20 And every thing that she lieth upon in her separation shall be unclean: every thing also that she sitteth upon shall be unclean.

21 And whosoever toucheth her bed shall wash his clothes, and bathe *himself* in water, and be unclean until the even.

22 And whosoever toucheth any thing that she sat upon shall wash his clothes, and bathe *himself* in water, and be unclean until the even.

23 And if it *be* on *her* bed, or on any thing whereon she sitteth, when he toucheth it, he shall be unclean until the even.

24 And ªif any man lie with her at all, and her ¹flowers be upon him, he shall be ²unclean seven days; and all the bed whereon he lieth shall be unclean.

25 And if ªa woman have an issue of her blood many days out of the time of her separation, or if it run beyond the time of her separation; all the days of the issue of her uncleanness shall be as the days of her separation: she *shall be* unclean.

26 Every bed whereon she lieth all the days of her issue shall be unto her as the bed of her separation: and whatsoever she sitteth upon shall be unclean, as the uncleanness of her separation.

27 And whosoever toucheth those things shall be unclean, and shall wash his clothes, and bathe *himself* in water, and be unclean until the even.

28 But ªif she be cleansed of her issue, then she shall number to herself seven days, and after that she shall be clean.

29 And on the eighth day she shall take unto her two turtles, or two young pigeons, and bring them unto the priest, to the door of the tabernacle of the congregation.

30 And the priest shall offer the one *for* a sin offering, and the other *for* a ªburnt offering; and the priest shall make an atonement for her before the LORD for the issue of her uncleanness.

31 Thus shall ye ªseparate the children of Israel from their uncleanness; that they die not in their uncleanness, when they ᵇdefile my tabernacle that *is* among them.

32 ªThis *is* the law of him that hath an issue, ᵇand *of him* whose seed goeth from him, and is defiled therewith;

33 ªAnd of her that is sick of her ¹flowers, and of him that hath an issue, of the man, ᵇand of the woman,

[c]and of him that lieth with her that is unclean.

## CHAPTER 16

AND the LORD spake unto Moses [a]after the death of the two sons of Aaron, when they offered before the LORD, and died;

2 And the LORD said unto Moses, Speak unto Aaron thy brother, that he [a]come not at [1]all times into the holy *place* within the vail before the mercy seat, which *is* upon the ark; that he die not: for [b]I will appear in the cloud upon the mercy seat.

3 [1]Thus shall Aaron [a]come into the holy *place:* [b]with a young bullock for a sin offering, and a ram for a burnt offering.

4 He shall put on the [a]holy linen coat, and he shall have the linen breeches upon his flesh, and shall be girded with a linen girdle, and with the linen [1]mitre shall he be attired: these *are* holy garments; therefore [b]shall he wash his flesh in water, and *so* put them on.

5 And he shall take of [a]the congregation of the children of Israel two kids of the goats for a sin offering, and one ram for a burnt offering.

6 And Aaron shall offer his bullock of the sin offering, which *is* for himself, and [a]make an atonement for himself, and for his house.

7 And he shall take the two goats, and present them before the LORD *at* the door of the tabernacle of the congregation.

8 And Aaron shall cast lots upon the two goats; one lot for the LORD, and the other lot for the scapegoat.

9 And Aaron shall bring the goat upon which the LORD's lot fell, and offer him *for* a sin offering.

10 But the goat, on which the lot fell to be the scapegoat, shall be presented alive before the LORD, to make [a]an atonement with him, *and* to let him go for a scapegoat into the wilderness.

11 And Aaron shall bring the bullock of the sin offering, which *is* for [a]himself, and shall make an atonement for himself, and for his house, and shall kill the bullock of the sin offering which *is* for himself:

12 And he shall take [a]a censer full of burning coals of fire from off the altar before the LORD, and his hands full of [b]sweet incense beaten small, and bring *it* within the vail:

13 [a]And he shall put the incense upon the fire before the LORD, that the cloud of the incense may cover the [b]mercy seat that *is* upon the testimony, that he [c]die not:

14 And [a]he shall take of the blood of the bullock, and [b]sprinkle *it* with his

---

15:33 [c] Lev. 15:24

16:1 [a] Lev. 10:1, 2; 2 Sam. 6:6–8

16:2 [a] Ex. 30:10; Lev. 16:34; 23:27; [Heb. 6:19; 9:7, 8, 12; 10:19] [b] Ex. 25:21, 22; 40:34; 1 Kin. 8:10–12 [1] *any time*

16:3 [a] Lev. 4:1–12; 16:6; [Heb. 9:7, 12, 24, 25] [b] Lev. 4:3 [1] Lit. *With this*

16:4 [a] Ex. 28:39, 42, 43; Lev. 6:10; Ezek. 44:17, 18 [b] Ex. 30:20; Lev. 8:6, 7 [1] *turban*

16:5 [a] Lev. 4:14; Num. 29:11; 2 Chr. 29:21; Ezra 6:17; Ezek. 45:22, 23

16:6 [a] Lev. 9:7; [Heb. 5:3; 7:27, 28; 9:7]

16:10 [a] [Is. 53:5, 6; Rom. 3:25; Heb. 7:27; 9:23, 24; 1 John 2:2]

16:11 [a] [Heb. 7:27; 9:7]

16:12 [a] Lev. 10:1; Num. 16:7, 18; Is. 6:6, 7; Rev. 8:5 [b] Ex. 30:34–38

16:13 [a] Ex. 30:7, 8; Num. 16:7, 18, 46 [b] Ex. 25:21 [c] Ex. 28:43; Lev. 22:9; Num. 4:15, 20

16:14 [a] Lev. 4:5; [Heb. 9:25; 10:4] [b] Lev. 4:6, 17

16:15 [a] [Heb. 2:17] [b] [Heb. 6:19; 7:27; 9:3, 7, 12]

16:16 [a] Ex. 29:36; 30:10; Ezek. 45:18; [Heb. 9:22–24]

16:17 [a] Ex. 34:3; Luke 1:10

16:18 [a] Ex. 29:36

16:19 [a] Lev. 16:14; Ezek. 43:20 [1] *set it apart*

16:20 [1] *atoning for*

16:21 [a] Lev. 5:5; 26:40 [b] [Is. 53:6]

16:22 [a] Lev. 8:14; [Is. 53:6, 11, 12; John 1:29; Heb. 9:28; 1 Pet. 2:24] [b] Lev. 14:7 [1] *shall carry* [2] Lit. *solitary*

16:23 [a] Lev. 6:11; 16:4; Ezek. 42:14; 44:19

16:24 [1] *a propitiation*

16:25 [a] Lev. 1:8; 4:10

---

finger upon the mercy seat eastward; and before the mercy seat shall he sprinkle of the blood with his finger seven times.

15 [a]Then shall he kill the goat of the sin offering, that *is* for the people, and bring his blood [b]within the vail, and do with that blood as he did with the blood of the bullock, and sprinkle it upon the mercy seat, and before the mercy seat:

16 And he shall [a]make an atonement for the holy *place,* because of the uncleanness of the children of Israel, and because of their transgressions in all their sins: and so shall he do for the tabernacle of the congregation, that remaineth among them in the midst of their uncleanness.

17 And there shall be [a]no man in the tabernacle of the congregation when he goeth in to make an atonement in the holy *place,* until he come out, and have made an atonement for himself, and for his household, and for all the congregation of Israel.

18 And he shall go out unto the altar that *is* before the LORD, and make an atonement for [a]it; and shall take of the blood of the bullock, and of the blood of the goat, and put *it* upon the horns of the altar round about.

19 And he shall sprinkle of the blood upon it with his finger seven times, and cleanse it, and [a]hallow[1] it from the uncleanness of the children of Israel.

20 And when he hath made an end of [1]reconciling the holy *place,* and the tabernacle of the congregation, and the altar, he shall bring the live goat:

21 And Aaron shall lay both his hands upon the head of the live goat, and [a]confess over him all the iniquities of the children of Israel, and all their transgressions in all their sins, [b]putting them upon the head of the goat, and shall send *him* away by the hand of a fit man into the wilderness:

22 And the goat [1]shall [a]bear upon him all their iniquities unto a land [2]not inhabited: and he shall [b]let go the goat in the wilderness.

23 And Aaron shall come into the tabernacle of the congregation, [a]and shall put off the linen garments, which he put on when he went into the holy *place,* and shall leave them there:

24 And he shall wash his flesh with water in the holy place, and put on his garments, and come forth, and offer his burnt offering, and the burnt offering of the people, and make [1]an atonement for himself, and for the people.

25 And [a]the fat of the sin offering shall he burn upon the altar.

26 And he that let go the goat for the scapegoat shall wash his clothes,

[a]and bathe his flesh in water, and afterward come into the camp.

27 [a]And the bullock *for* the sin offering, and the goat *for* the sin offering, whose blood was brought in to make atonement in the holy *place,* shall *one* carry forth [1]without the camp; and they shall burn in the fire their skins, and their flesh, and their dung.

28 And he that burneth them shall wash his clothes, and bathe his flesh in water, and afterward he shall come into the camp.

29 And *this* shall be a statute for ever unto you: *that* [a]in the seventh month, on the tenth *day* of the month, ye shall [1]afflict your souls, and do no work at all, *whether it be* one of your own country, or a stranger that sojourneth among you:

30 For on that day shall *the priest* make [1]an atonement for you, to [a]cleanse you, *that* ye may be clean from all your sins before the LORD.

31 [a]It *shall be* a [1]sabbath of rest unto you, and ye shall afflict your souls, by a statute for ever.

32 [a]And the priest, whom he shall anoint, and whom he shall [b]consecrate to minister in the priest's office in his father's stead, shall make the atonement, and shall put on the linen clothes, *even* the holy garments:

33 And he shall make [1]an atonement for [2]the holy sanctuary, and he shall make an atonement for the tabernacle of the congregation, and for the altar, and he shall make an atonement for the priests, and for all the people of the congregation.

34 [a]And this shall be an everlasting statute unto you, to make an atonement for the children of Israel for all their sins [b]once a year. And he did as the LORD commanded Moses.

## CHAPTER 17

AND the LORD spake unto Moses, saying,

2 Speak unto Aaron, and unto his sons, and unto all the children of Israel, and say unto them; This *is* the thing which the LORD hath commanded, saying,

3 What man soever *there be* of the house of Israel, [a]that killeth an ox, or lamb, or goat, in the camp, or that killeth *it* [1]out of the camp,

4 And bringeth it not unto the door of the tabernacle of the congregation, to offer an offering unto the LORD before the tabernacle of the LORD; blood shall be [a]imputed unto that man; he hath shed blood; and that man shall be [1]cut off from among his people:

5 To the end that the children of Israel may bring their sacrifices, [a]which

### Cross references

16:26 [a] Lev. 15:5
16:27 [a] Lev. 4:12, 21; 6:30; Heb. 13:11 [1] *outside*
16:29 [a] Ex. 30:10; Lev. 23:27–32; Num. 29:7 [1] *humble*
16:30 [a] Ps. 51:2; Jer. 33:8; [Eph. 5:26; Heb. 9:13, 14; 1 John 1:7, 9] [1] *a propitiation*
16:31 [a] Lev. 23:27, 32; Ezra 8:21; Is. 58:3, 5; Dan. 10:12 [1] *sabbath of solemn rest*
16:32 [a] Lev. 4:3, 5, 16; 21:10 [b] Ex. 29:29, 30; Num. 20:26, 28
16:33 [1] *a propitiation* [2] *the Most Holy Place*
16:34 [a] Lev. 23:31; Num. 29:7 [b] Ex. 30:10; [Heb. 9:7, 25, 28]
17:3 [a] Deut. 12:5, 15, 21 [1] *outside*
17:4 [a] Rom. 5:13 [1] *put to death*
17:5 [a] Gen. 21:33; 22:2; 31:54; Deut. 12:1–27; Ezek. 20:28
17:6 [a] Lev. 3:2 [b] Ex. 29:13, 18; Num. 18:17
17:7 [a] Ex. 22:20; 32:8; 34:15; Deut. 32:17; 2 Chr. 11:15; Ps. 106:37; 1 Cor. 10:20 [b] Ex. 34:15; Deut. 31:16; Ezek. 23:8 [1] *Demons having the form of a goat or satyr*
17:8 [a] Lev. 1:2, 3; 18:26
17:9 [a] Lev. 14:23 [1] *put to death*
17:10 [a] Gen. 9:4; Lev. 3:17; 7:26, 27; Deut. 12:16, 23–25; 15:23; 1 Sam. 14:33 [b] Lev. 20:3, 5, 6 [1] *any blood* [2] *person*
17:11 [a] Gen. 9:4; Lev. 17:14 [b] [Matt. 26:28; Rom. 3:25; Eph. 1:7; Col. 1:14, 20; 1 Pet. 1:2; 1 John 1:7] [c] [Heb. 9:22]
17:12 [1] *person among*
17:13 [a] Lev. 7:26 [b] Deut. 12:16, 24 [c] Ezek. 24:7
17:14 [a] Gen. 9:4; Lev. 17:11; Deut. 12:23
17:15 [a] Ex. 22:31; Lev. 7:24; 22:8; Deut. 14:21; Ezek. 4:14; 44:31

they offer in the open field, even that they may bring them unto the LORD, unto the door of the tabernacle of the congregation, unto the priest, and offer them *for* peace offerings unto the LORD.

6 And the priest [a]shall sprinkle the blood upon the altar of the LORD *at* the door of the tabernacle of the congregation, and [b]burn the fat for a sweet savour unto the LORD.

7 And they shall no more offer their sacrifices [a]unto [1]devils, after whom they [b]have gone a whoring. This shall be a statute for ever unto them throughout their generations.

8 And thou shalt say unto them, Whatsoever man *there be* of the house of Israel, or of the strangers which sojourn among you, [a]that offereth a burnt offering or sacrifice,

9 And bringeth it not unto the door of the tabernacle of the [a]congregation, to offer it unto the LORD; even that man shall be [1]cut off from among his people.

10 [a]And whatsoever man *there be* of the house of Israel, or of the strangers that sojourn among you, that eateth [1]any manner of blood; [b]I will even set my face against that [2]soul that eateth blood, and will cut him off from among his people.

11 For the [a]life of the flesh *is* in the blood: and I have given it to you upon the altar [b]to make an atonement for your souls: for [c]it *is* the blood *that* maketh an atonement for the soul.

12 Therefore I said unto the children of Israel, No [1]soul of you shall eat blood, neither shall any stranger that sojourneth among you eat blood.

13 And whatsoever man *there be* of the children of Israel, or of the strangers that sojourn among you, which hunteth and catcheth any [a]beast or fowl that may be eaten; he shall even [b]pour out the blood thereof, and [c]cover it with dust.

14 [a]For *it is* the life of all flesh; the blood of it *is* for the life thereof: therefore I said unto the children of Israel, Ye shall eat the blood of no manner of flesh: for the life of all flesh *is* the blood thereof: whosoever eateth it shall be cut off.

15 [a]And every soul that eateth that which died [1]*of itself,* or that which was torn *with beasts, whether it be* one of your own country, or a stranger, [b]he shall both wash his clothes, and [c]bathe *himself* in water, and be unclean until the even: then shall he be clean.

16 But if he wash *them* not, nor bathe his flesh; then [a]he shall bear his [1]iniquity.

[b] Lev. 11:25  [c] Lev. 15:5  [1] *naturally*  17:16 [a] Lev. 5:1  [1] *guilt*

## CHAPTER 18

A ND the LORD spake unto Moses, saying,

2 Speak unto the children of Israel, and say unto them, [a]I am the LORD your God.

3 [a]After [1]the doings of the land of Egypt, wherein ye dwelt, shall ye not do: and [b]after the doings of the land of Canaan, whither I bring you, shall ye not do: neither shall ye walk in their [2]ordinances.

4 [a]Ye shall do my judgments, and keep mine ordinances, to walk therein: I *am* the LORD your God.

5 Ye shall therefore keep my statutes, and my judgments: which if a man [1]do, he shall live [2]in them: I *am* the LORD.

6 None of you shall approach to any that is near of kin to him, to uncover *their* nakedness: I *am* the LORD.

7 The nakedness of thy father, or the nakedness of thy mother, shalt thou not uncover: she *is* thy mother; thou shalt not uncover her nakedness.

8 The nakedness of thy [a]father's wife shalt thou not uncover: it *is* thy father's nakedness.

9 [a]The nakedness of thy sister, the daughter of thy father, or daughter of thy mother, *whether she be* born at home, or born abroad, *even* their nakedness thou shalt not uncover.

10 The nakedness of thy son's daughter, or of thy daughter's daughter, *even* their nakedness thou shalt not uncover: for theirs *is* thine own nakedness.

11 The nakedness of thy father's wife's daughter, begotten of thy father, she *is* thy sister, thou shalt not uncover her nakedness.

12 [a]Thou shalt not uncover the nakedness of thy father's sister: she *is* thy father's near kinswoman.

13 Thou shalt not uncover the nakedness of thy mother's sister: for she *is* thy mother's near kinswoman.

14 [a]Thou shalt not uncover the nakedness of thy father's brother, thou shalt not approach to his wife: she *is* thine aunt.

15 Thou shalt not uncover the nakedness of thy daughter in law: she *is* thy son's wife; thou shalt not uncover her nakedness.

16 Thou shalt not uncover the nakedness of thy brother's wife: it *is* thy brother's nakedness.

17 Thou shalt not uncover the nakedness of a woman and her [a]daughter, neither shalt thou take her son's daughter, or her daughter's daughter, to uncover her nakedness; *for* they *are* her near kinswomen: it *is* wickedness.

18 Neither shalt thou take a wife to her sister, [a]to [1]vex *her,* to uncover her

nakedness, beside the other in her life *time.*

19 Also thou shalt not approach unto a woman to uncover her nakedness, as [a]long as she is put apart [1]for her [b]uncleanness.

20 [a]Moreover thou shalt not lie carnally with thy [b]neighbour's wife, to defile thyself with her.

21 And thou shalt not let any of thy seed [a]pass through [b]*the fire* to [c]Molech, neither shalt thou profane the name of thy God: I *am* the LORD.

22 Thou shalt not lie with [a]mankind, as with womankind: it *is* abomination.

23 Neither shalt thou lie with any [a]beast to defile thyself therewith: neither shall any woman stand before a beast to lie down thereto: it *is* [1]confusion.

24 [a]Defile not ye yourselves in any of these things: [b]for in all these the nations are defiled which I cast out before you:

25 And [a]the land is defiled: therefore I do [b]visit[1] the iniquity thereof upon it, and the land itself [c]vomiteth out her inhabitants.

26 [a]Ye shall therefore [1]keep my statutes and my judgments, and shall not commit *any* of these abominations; *neither* any of your own nation, nor any stranger that sojourneth among you:

27 (For all these abominations have the men of the land done, which *were* before you, and the land is defiled;)

28 That [a]the land spue not you out also, when ye defile it, as it spued out the nations that *were* before you.

29 For whosoever shall commit any of these abominations, even the [1]souls that commit *them* shall be [2]cut off from among their people.

30 Therefore shall ye keep mine [1]ordinance, [a]that *ye* commit not *any one* of these abominable customs, which were committed before you, and that ye defile not yourselves therein: [b]I *am* the LORD your God.

## CHAPTER 19

A ND the LORD spake unto Moses, saying,

2 Speak unto all the congregation of the children of Israel, and say unto them, [a]Ye shall be holy: for I the LORD your God *am* holy.

3 [a]Ye shall [1]fear every man his mother, and his father, and [b]keep my sabbaths: I *am* the LORD your God.

4 [a]Turn ye not unto idols, [b]nor make to yourselves [1]molten gods: I *am* the LORD your God.

5 And [a]if ye offer a sacrifice of peace offerings unto the LORD, ye shall offer it at your own will.

6 It shall be eaten the same day ye offer it, and on the morrow: and if

### Center column cross-references

18:2 [a] Ex. 6:7;
Lev. 11:44, 45;
19:3; Ezek. 20:5,
7, 19, 20
18:3 [a] Josh. 24:14;
Ezek. 20:7, 8
[b] Ex. 23:24; Lev.
18:24–30; 20:23;
Deut. 12:30, 31
[1] *what is done in*
[2] *statutes*
18:4 [a] Ezek. 20:19
18:5 [1] *does* [2] *by*
18:8 [a] Gen. 35:22
18:9 [a] Lev. 18:11;
20:17; Deut. 27:22
18:12 [a] Lev. 20:19
18:14 [a] Lev. 20:20
18:17 [a] Lev. 20:14
18:18 [a] 1 Sam. 1:6,
8 [1] *be a rival*

18:19 [a] Ezek. 18:6
[b] Lev. 15:24; 20:18
[1] *in her customary
impurity*
18:20 [a] [Prov.
6:25–33] [b] Lev.
20:10
18:21 [a] Lev. 20:2–5
[b] 2 Kin. 16:3
[c] 1 Kin. 11:7, 33
18:22 [a] Lev. 20:13
18:23 [a] Ex. 22:19
[1] *perversion*
18:24 [a] Matt.
15:18–20 [b] Deut.
18:12
18:25 [a] Num.
35:33, 34 [b] Jer.
5:9 [c] Lev. 18:28;
20:22 [1] *bring
judgment for*
18:26 [a] Lev. 18:5,
30 [1] *obey*
18:28 [a] Jer. 9:19
18:29 [1] *persons*
[2] *put to death*
18:30 [a] Lev. 18:3;
22:9 [b] Lev. 18:2
[1] *charge*
19:2 [a] Lev. 11:44;
20:7, 26
19:3 [a] Ex. 20:12
[b] Ex. 16:23; 20:8;
31:13 [1] *revere*
19:4 [a] Ex. 20:4
[b] Ex. 34:17
[1] *moulded*
19:5 [a] Lev. 7:16

107

ought remain until the third day, it shall be burnt in the fire.

7 And if it be eaten at all on the third day, it *is* abominable; it shall not be accepted.

8 Therefore *every one* that eateth it shall bear his iniquity, because he hath profaned the hallowed thing of the LORD: and that soul shall be cut off from among his people.

9 And [a]when ye reap the harvest of your land, thou shalt not wholly reap the corners of thy field, neither shalt thou gather the gleanings of thy harvest.

10 And thou shalt not glean thy vineyard, neither shalt thou gather *every* grape of thy vineyard; thou shalt leave them for the poor and stranger: I *am* the LORD your God.

11 [a]Ye shall not steal, neither deal falsely, [b]neither lie one to another.

12 And ye shall not [a]swear by my name falsely, [b]neither shalt thou profane the name of thy God: I *am* the LORD.

13 [a]Thou shalt not defraud thy neighbour, neither rob *him:* [b]the wages of him that is hired shall not abide with thee all night until the morning.

14 Thou shalt not curse the deaf, [a]nor put a stumblingblock before the blind, but shalt fear thy God: I *am* the LORD.

15 Ye shall do no unrighteousness in [a]judgment: thou shalt not [b]respect the person of the poor, nor honour the person of the mighty: *but* in righteousness shalt thou judge thy neighbour.

16 Thou shalt not go up and down *as* a [a]talebearer among thy people: neither shalt thou [b]stand against the [1]blood of thy neighbour: I *am* the LORD.

17 [a]Thou shalt not hate thy brother in thine heart: [b]thou shalt [1]in any wise rebuke thy neighbour, and not [2]suffer sin upon him.

18 [a]Thou shalt not [1]avenge, nor bear any grudge against the children of thy people, [b]but thou shalt love thy neighbour as thyself: I *am* the LORD.

19 Ye shall keep my statutes. Thou shalt not let thy [1]cattle gender with a diverse kind: thou shalt not sow thy field with mingled seed: neither shall a garment mingled of linen and woollen come upon thee.

20 And whosoever lieth carnally with a woman, that *is* a [a]bondmaid, betrothed to an husband, and not at all redeemed, nor freedom given her; she shall be [1]scourged; they shall not be put to death, because she was not free.

21 And he shall bring his trespass offering unto the LORD, unto the door

of the tabernacle of the congregation, *even* a ram for a trespass offering.

22 And the priest shall make [1]an atonement for him with the ram of the trespass offering before the LORD for his sin which he hath done: and the sin which he hath done shall be forgiven him.

23 And when ye shall come into the land, and shall have planted all manner of trees for food, then ye shall count the fruit thereof as [1]uncircumcised: three years shall it be as uncircumcised unto you: it shall not be eaten of.

24 But in the fourth year all the fruit thereof shall be [1]holy to praise the LORD *withal.*

25 And in the fifth year shall ye eat of the fruit thereof, that it may yield unto you the increase thereof: I *am* the LORD your God.

26 Ye shall not eat *any thing* with the blood: neither shall ye use [1]enchantment, nor [2]observe times.

27 Ye shall not round the corners of your heads, neither shalt thou mar the corners of thy beard.

28 Ye shall not [a]make any cuttings in your flesh for the dead, nor print any marks upon you: I *am* the LORD.

29 [a]Do not prostitute thy daughter, to cause her to be a whore; lest the land fall to whoredom, and the land become full of wickedness.

30 Ye shall [1]keep my sabbaths, and [a]reverence my sanctuary: I *am* the LORD.

31 [1]Regard not them that have familiar spirits, neither seek after [a]wizards, to be defiled by them: I *am* the LORD your God.

32 [a]Thou shalt [1]rise up before [2]the hoary head, and honour the face of the old man, and [b]fear thy God: I *am* the LORD.

33 And [a]if a stranger sojourn with thee in your land, ye shall not [1]vex him.

34 [a]*But* the stranger that dwelleth with you shall be unto you as one [1]born among you, and [b]thou shalt love him as thyself; for ye were strangers in the land of Egypt: I *am* the LORD your God.

35 Ye shall [1]do no unrighteousness in judgment, in meteyard, in weight, or in measure.

36 [a]Just balances, just weights, a just ephah, and a just hin, shall ye have: I *am* the LORD your God, which brought you out of the land of Egypt.

37 [a]Therefore shall ye observe all my statutes, and all my judgments, and do them: I *am* the LORD.

## CHAPTER 20

AND the LORD spake unto Moses, saying,

### Center column references

19:9 [a] Deut. 24:19–22

19:11 [a] Ex. 20:15, 16 [b] Eph. 4:25

19:12 [a] Deut. 5:11 [b] Lev. 18:21

19:13 [a] Ex. 22:7–15, 21–27 [b] Deut. 24:15

19:14 [a] Deut. 27:18

19:15 [a] Deut. 16:19 [b] Ex. 23:3, 6

19:16 [a] Prov. 11:13; 18:8; 20:19 [b] 1 Kin. 21:7–19 [1] *life*

19:17 [a] [1 John 2:9, 11; 3:15] [b] Matt. 18:15 [1] *surely reprove* [2] *bear sin because of him*

19:18 [a] [Deut. 32:35] [b] Mark 12:31 [1] *take vengeance*

19:19 [1] *livestock breed with another kind*

19:20 [a] Deut. 22:23–27 [1] *punished*

19:22 [1] *propitiation*

19:23 [1] *unclean*

19:24 [1] *holy, a praise to*

19:26 [1] *practise divination* [2] *soothsaying*

19:28 [a] 1 Kin. 18:28; Jer. 16:6

19:29 [a] Lev. 21:9; Deut. 22:21; 23:17, 18

19:30 [a] Lev. 26:2; Eccl. 5:1 [1] *observe*

19:31 [a] Lev. 20:6, 27; Deut. 18:11; 1 Sam. 28:3; Is. 8:19 [1] *Give no regard to mediums*

19:32 [a] Prov. 23:22; Lam. 5:12; 1 Tim. 5:1 [b] Lev. 19:14 [1] *rise to give honour* [2] *grayheaded*

19:33 [a] Ex. 22:21; Deut. 24:17, 18 [1] *mistreat*

19:34 [a] Ex. 12:48 [b] Deut. 10:19 [1] *native*

19:35 [1] *do no injustice*

19:36 [a] Deut. 25:13–15; Prov. 20:10

19:37 [a] Lev. 18:4, 5; Deut. 4:5, 6; 5:1; 6:25

2 [a]Again, thou shalt say to the children of Israel, [b]Whosoever *he be* of the children of Israel, or of the strangers that [1]sojourn in Israel, that giveth *any* of his seed unto Molech; he shall surely be put to death: the people of the land shall [c]stone him with stones.

3 And [a]I will set my face against that man, and will [1]cut him off from among his people; because he hath given of his seed unto Molech, to defile my sanctuary, and to profane my holy name.

4 And if the people of the land do any ways [1]hide their eyes from the man, when he giveth of his seed unto Molech, and kill him not:

5 Then I will set my face against that man, and against his family, and will cut him off, and all that go a whoring after him, to commit whoredom with Molech, from among their people.

6 And [a]the [1]soul that turneth after such as have familiar spirits, and after wizards, to go a whoring after them, I will even set my face against that soul, and will cut him off from among his people.

7 [a]Sanctify[1] yourselves therefore, and be ye holy: for I *am* the LORD your God.

8 And ye shall keep [a]my statutes, and do them: [b]I *am* the LORD which [1]sanctify you.

9 For [a]every one that curseth his father or his mother shall be surely put to death: he hath cursed his father or his mother; [b]his blood *shall be* upon him.

10 And [a]the man that committeth adultery with *another* man's wife, *even he* that committeth adultery with his neighbour's wife, the adulterer and the adulteress shall surely be put to death.

11 And the man that lieth with his [a]father's wife hath uncovered his father's nakedness: both of them shall surely be put to death; their blood *shall be* upon them.

12 And if a man lie with his [a]daughter in law, both of them shall surely be put to death: they have [1]wrought confusion; their blood *shall be* upon them.

13 [a]If a man also lie with mankind, as he lieth with a woman, both of them have committed an abomination: they shall surely be put to death; their blood *shall be* upon them.

14 And if a man take a wife and her [a]mother, it *is* wickedness: they shall be burnt with fire, both he and they; that there be no wickedness among you.

15 And if a man lie with a [a]beast, he shall surely be put to death: and ye shall slay the beast.

16 And if a woman approach unto any beast, and lie down thereto, thou shalt kill the woman, and the beast: they shall surely be put to death; their blood *shall be* upon them.

17 And if a man shall take his [a]sister, his father's daughter, or his mother's daughter, and see her nakedness, and she see his nakedness; it *is* a wicked thing; and they shall be [1]cut off in the sight of their people: he hath uncovered his sister's nakedness; he shall [2]bear his iniquity.

18 [a]And if a man shall lie with a woman [1]having her sickness, and shall uncover her nakedness; he hath [2]discovered her fountain, and she hath uncovered the fountain of her blood: and both of them shall be [3]cut off from among their people.

19 And thou shalt not uncover the nakedness of thy [a]mother's sister, nor of thy [b]father's sister: for he uncovereth his near kin: they shall bear their iniquity.

20 And if a man shall lie with his [a]uncle's wife, he hath uncovered his uncle's nakedness: they shall bear their sin; they shall die childless.

21 And if a man shall take his [a]brother's wife, it *is* an [1]unclean thing: he hath uncovered his brother's nakedness; they shall be childless.

22 Ye shall therefore keep all my [a]statutes, and all my judgments, and do them: that the land, whither I bring you to dwell therein, [b]spue you not out.

23 [a]And ye shall not walk in the manners of the nation, which I cast out before you: for they committed all these things, and [b]therefore I abhorred them.

24 But [a]I have said unto you, Ye shall inherit their land, and I will give it unto you to possess it, a land that floweth with milk and honey: I *am* the LORD your God, [b]which have [1]separated you from *other* people.

25 [a]Ye shall therefore [1]put difference between clean beasts and unclean, and between unclean fowls and clean: [b]and ye shall not make your souls [2]abominable by beast, or by fowl, or by any manner of living thing that creepeth on the ground, which I have separated from you as [3]unclean.

26 And ye shall be holy unto me: [a]for I the LORD *am* holy, and have severed you from *other* people, that ye should be mine.

27 [a]A man also or woman that hath a familiar spirit, or that is a wizard, shall surely be put to death: they shall stone them with stones: their blood *shall be* upon them.

20:2 [a] Lev. 18:2
[b] Lev. 18:21; 2 Kin. 23:10; 2 Chr. 33:6; Jer. 7:31 [c] Deut. 17:2–5 [1] *stays a while*
20:3 [a] Lev. 17:10 [1] *put him to death*
20:4 [1] *disregard*
20:6 [a] Lev. 19:31; 1 Sam. 28:7–25 [1] *person that turns to mediums*
20:7 [a] Lev. 19:2; Heb. 12:14 [1] *Consecrate yourselves*
20:8 [a] Lev. 19:19, 37 [b] Ex. 31:13; Deut. 14:2; Ezek. 37:28 [1] *sets you apart*
20:9 [a] Ex. 21:17; Deut. 27:16; Prov. 20:20; Matt. 15:4 [b] 2 Sam. 1:16
20:10 [a] Ex. 20:14; Lev. 18:20; Deut. 5:18; 22:22; John 8:4, 5
20:11 [a] Lev. 18:7, 8; Deut. 27:20
20:12 [a] Lev. 18:15 [1] *committed perversion*
20:13 [a] Lev. 18:22; Deut. 23:17; Judg. 19:22
20:14 [a] Lev. 18:17
20:15 [a] Lev. 18:23; Deut. 27:21
20:17 [a] Lev. 18:9; Deut. 27:22 [1] *put to death* [2] *guilt*
20:18 [a] Lev. 15:24; 18:19 [1] *during her customary impurity* [2] Lit. *made bare* [3] *put to death*
20:19 [a] Lev. 18:13 [b] Lev. 18:12
20:20 [a] Lev. 18:14
20:21 [a] Lev. 18:16; Matt. 14:3, 4 [1] *impure thing*
20:22 [a] Lev. 18:26; 19:37 [b] Lev. 18:25, 28; 2 Chr. 36:14–16
20:23 [a] Lev. 18:3, 24 [b] Deut. 9:5
20:24 [a] Ex. 3:17; 6:8; 13:5; 33:1–3 [b] Ex. 19:5; 33:16; Lev. 20:26; Deut. 7:6; 14:2; 1 Kin. 8:53 [1] *set you apart*
20:25 [a] Lev. 10:10; 11:1–47; Deut. 14:3–21 [b] Lev. 11:43 [1] *distinguish* [2] *detestable or loathsome* [3] *defiled*
20:26 [a] Lev. 19:2; 1 Pet. 1:16
20:27 [a] Lev. 19:31; 1 Sam. 28:9

## CHAPTER 21

AND the LORD said unto Moses, Speak unto the priests the sons of Aaron, and say unto them, ªThere shall none be defiled for the dead among his people:

2 But for his kin, that is near unto him, *that is,* for his mother, and for his father, and for his son, and for his daughter, and for his brother,

3 And for his sister a virgin, that is nigh unto him, which hath had no husband; for her may he be defiled.

4 *But* he shall not defile himself, *being* a ¹chief man among his people, to profane himself.

5 ªThey shall not make baldness upon their head, neither shall they shave off the corner of their beard, nor make any cuttings in their flesh.

6 They shall be ªholy unto their God, and not profane the name of their God: for the offerings of the LORD made by fire, *and* the ᵇbread of their God, they do offer: ᶜtherefore they shall be holy.

7 ªThey shall not take a wife *that is* a whore, or profane; neither shall they take a woman ᵇput away from her husband: for he *is* holy unto his God.

8 Thou shalt ¹sanctify him therefore; for he offereth the bread of thy God: he shall be holy unto thee: for ªI the LORD, which ᵇsanctify you, *am* holy.

9 And the daughter of any priest, if she profane herself by playing the whore, she profaneth her father: she shall be ªburnt with fire.

10 And *he that is* the high priest among his brethren, upon whose head the anointing oil was ªpoured, and that is consecrated to put on the garments, ¹shall not ᵇuncover his head, nor rend his clothes;

11 Neither shall he go ªin to any dead body, nor defile himself for his father, or for his mother;

12 ªNeither shall he go out of the sanctuary, nor profane the sanctuary of his God; for the ᵇcrown¹ of the anointing oil of his God *is* upon him: I *am* the LORD.

13 And he shall take a wife in her virginity.

14 A widow, or a divorced woman, or profane, *or* an harlot, these shall he not take: but he shall take a virgin of his own people to wife.

15 Neither shall he profane his seed among his people: for I the LORD do sanctify him.

16 And the LORD spake unto Moses, saying,

17 Speak unto Aaron, saying, Whosoever *he be* of thy seed in their generations that hath ¹any blemish, let him not approach to offer the bread of his God.

21:1 ª Lev. 19:28; Ezek. 44:25
21:4 ¹ Lit. *master or husband*
21:5 ª Lev. 19:27; Deut. 14:1; Ezek. 44:20
21:6 ª Ex. 22:31 ᵇ Lev. 3:11 ᶜ Is. 52:11
21:7 ª Ezek. 44:22 ᵇ Deut. 24:1, 2
21:8 ª Lev. 11:44, 45 ᵇ Lev. 8:12, 30 ¹ *set him apart*
21:9 ª Deut. 22:21
21:10 ª Lev. 8:12 ᵇ Lev. 10:6, 7 ¹ *in mourning uncover his head*
21:11 ª Num. 19:14
21:12 ª Lev. 10:7 ᵇ Ex. 29:6, 7 ¹ *consecration*
21:17 ¹ *any defect*

18 For whatsoever man *he be* that hath a ªblemish, he shall not approach: a blind man, or a lame, or he that hath a flat nose, or any thing ᵇsuperfluous,

19 Or a man that is brokenfooted, or brokenhanded,

20 Or ¹crookbackt, or a dwarf, or that hath a blemish in his eye, or be scurvy, or scabbed, or hath his stones broken;

21 No man that hath a blemish of the seed of Aaron the priest shall come nigh to offer the offerings of the LORD made by fire: he hath a blemish; he shall not come nigh to offer the bread of his God.

22 He shall eat the bread of his God, *both* of the most holy, and of the holy.

23 Only he shall not go ¹in unto the ªvail, nor come nigh unto the altar, because he hath a blemish; that ᵇhe profane not my sanctuaries: for I the LORD do sanctify them.

24 And Moses told *it* unto Aaron, and to his sons, and unto all the children of Israel.

## CHAPTER 22

AND the LORD spake unto Moses, saying,

2 Speak unto Aaron and to his sons, that they ªseparate¹ themselves from the holy things of the children of Israel, and that they ᵇprofane not my holy name *in those things* which they ᶜhallow unto me: I *am* the LORD.

3 Say unto them, Whosoever *he be* of all your seed among your generations, that ¹goeth unto the holy things, which the children of Israel hallow unto the LORD, ªhaving² that soul shall be cut off from my presence: I *am* the LORD.

4 What man soever of the seed of Aaron *is* a ªleper, or hath ᵇa running issue; he shall not eat of the holy things, ᶜuntil he be clean. And ᵈwhoso toucheth any thing *that is* unclean *by* the dead, or ᵉa man whose seed goeth from him;

5 Or ªwhosoever toucheth any creeping thing, whereby he may be made unclean, or ᵇa man of whom he may take uncleanness, whatsoever uncleanness he hath;

6 The ¹soul which hath touched any such shall be unclean until even, and shall not eat of the holy things, unless he ªwash his flesh with water.

7 And when the sun is down, he shall be clean, and shall afterward eat of the holy things; because ªit *is* his food.

8 ªThat which dieth of itself, or is torn *with beasts,* he shall not eat to defile himself therewith: I *am* the LORD.

21:18 ª Lev. 22:19–25 ᵇ Lev. 22:23
21:20 ¹ *hunchbacked*
21:23 ª Lev. 16:2 ᵇ Lev. 21:12 ¹ *near to*
22:2 ª Num. 6:3 ᵇ Lev. 18:21 ᶜ Ex. 28:38; Lev. 16:19; 25:10; Num. 18:32; Deut. 15:19 ¹ *keep apart from*
22:3 ª Lev. 7:20, 21; Num. 19:13 ¹ *goes near* ² *while he has defilement*
22:4 ª Num. 5:2 ᵇ Lev. 15:2 ᶜ Lev. 14:2; 15:13 ᵈ Lev. 11:24–28, 39, 40; Num. 19:11 ᵉ Lev. 15:16, 17
22:5 ª Lev. 11:23–28 ᵇ Lev. 15:7, 19
22:6 ª Lev. 15:5 ¹ *person*
22:7 ª Lev. 21:22; Num. 18:11, 13
22:8 ª Ex. 22:31; Lev. 7:24; 11:39, 40; 17:15; Ezek. 44:31

9 They shall therefore keep <sup>a</sup>mine <sup>1</sup>ordinance, <sup>b</sup>lest they bear sin for it, and die therefore, if they profane it: I the LORD do sanctify them.

10 <sup>a</sup>There shall no stranger eat *of* <sup>1</sup>the holy thing: a sojourner of the priest, or an hired servant, shall not eat of the holy thing.

11 But if the priest <sup>a</sup>buy *any* soul with his money, he shall eat of it, and he that is born in his house: they shall eat of his meat.

12 If the priest's daughter also be *married* unto a stranger, she may not eat of an offering of the holy things.

13 But if the priest's daughter be a widow, or divorced, and have no child, and is returned unto her father's house, as in her youth, she shall eat of her father's meat: but there shall no stranger eat thereof.

14 And if a man eat *of* the holy thing <sup>1</sup>unwittingly, then he shall put the fifth *part* thereof unto it, and shall give *it* unto the priest with the holy thing.

15 And they shall not profane the <sup>a</sup>holy things of the children of Israel, which they offer unto the LORD;

16 Or <sup>1</sup>suffer them to bear the iniquity of trespass, when they eat their holy things: for I the LORD do sanctify them.

17 And the LORD spake unto Moses, saying,

18 Speak unto Aaron, and to his sons, and unto all the children of Israel, and say unto them, <sup>a</sup>Whatsoever *he be* of the house of Israel, or of the strangers in Israel, that will offer his <sup>1</sup>oblation for all his vows, and for all his freewill offerings, which they will offer unto the LORD for a burnt offering;

19 <sup>a</sup>*Ye shall offer* at your own will a male without blemish, of the beeves, of the sheep, or of the goats.

20 <sup>a</sup>*But* whatsoever hath a blemish, *that* shall ye not offer: for it shall not be acceptable for you.

21 And <sup>a</sup>whosoever offereth a sacrifice of peace offerings unto the LORD <sup>b</sup>to accomplish *his* vow, or a freewill offering in beeves or sheep, it shall be perfect to be accepted; there shall be no blemish therein.

22 <sup>a</sup>Blind, or broken, or maimed, or having <sup>1</sup>a wen, or scurvy, or scabbed, ye shall not offer these unto the LORD, nor make <sup>b</sup>an offering by fire of them upon the altar unto the LORD.

23 Either a bullock or a lamb that hath <sup>1</sup>any thing <sup>a</sup>superfluous or lacking in his parts, that mayest thou offer *for* a freewill offering; but for a vow it shall not be accepted.

24 Ye shall not offer unto the LORD that which is bruised, or crushed, or broken, or cut; neither shall ye make *any offering thereof* in your land.

25 Neither <sup>a</sup>from a stranger's hand shall ye offer <sup>b</sup>the bread of your God of any of these; because their <sup>c</sup>corruption *is* in them, *and* blemishes *be* in them: they shall not be accepted for you.

26 And the LORD spake unto Moses, saying,

27 <sup>a</sup>When a bullock, or a sheep, or a goat, is brought forth, then it shall be seven days <sup>1</sup>under the dam; and from the eighth day and thenceforth it shall be accepted for an offering made by fire unto the LORD.

28 And *whether it be* cow or <sup>1</sup>ewe, ye shall not kill it <sup>a</sup>and her young both in one day.

29 And when ye will <sup>a</sup>offer a sacrifice of thanksgiving unto the LORD, offer *it* <sup>1</sup>at your own will.

30 On the same day it shall be eaten up; ye shall leave <sup>a</sup>none of it until the morrow: I *am* the LORD.

31 <sup>a</sup>Therefore shall ye keep my commandments, and do them: I *am* the LORD.

32 <sup>a</sup>Neither shall ye profane my holy name; but <sup>b</sup>I will be <sup>1</sup>hallowed among the children of Israel: I *am* the LORD which <sup>c</sup>hallow you,

33 <sup>a</sup>That brought you out of the land of Egypt, to be your God: I *am* the LORD.

## CHAPTER 23

AND the LORD spake unto Moses, saying,

2 Speak unto the children of Israel, and say unto them, *Concerning* the feasts of the LORD, which ye shall proclaim *to be* <sup>a</sup>holy convocations, *even* these *are* my feasts.

3 <sup>a</sup>Six days shall work be done: but the seventh day *is* the sabbath of rest, an holy convocation; ye shall do no work *therein:* it *is* the sabbath of the LORD in all your dwellings.

4 <sup>a</sup>These *are* the feasts of the LORD, *even* holy convocations, which ye shall proclaim in their seasons.

5 <sup>a</sup>In the fourteenth *day* of the first month at even *is* the LORD's passover.

6 And on the fifteenth day of the same month *is* the feast of unleavened bread unto the LORD: seven days ye must eat unleavened bread.

7 <sup>a</sup>In the first day ye shall have an holy convocation: ye shall do no <sup>1</sup>servile work therein.

8 But ye shall offer an offering made by fire unto the LORD seven days: in the seventh day *is* an holy convocation: ye shall do no servile work *therein.*

9 And the LORD spake unto Moses, saying,

10 Speak unto the children of Israel, and say unto them, <sup>a</sup>When ye

### Center column references

22:9 <sup>a</sup> Lev. 18:30
<sup>b</sup> Ex. 28:43; Lev. 22:16; Num. 18:22
<sup>1</sup> *charge*

22:10 <sup>a</sup> Ex. 29:33; Lev. 22:13; Num. 3:10 <sup>1</sup> *offering*

22:11 <sup>a</sup> Ex. 12:44

22:14 <sup>1</sup> *unintentionally*

22:15 <sup>a</sup> Num. 18:32

22:16 <sup>1</sup> *allow them to bear the guilt*

22:18 <sup>a</sup> Lev. 1:2, 3, 10 <sup>1</sup> *offering for any*

22:19 <sup>a</sup> Lev. 1:3; Deut. 15:21

22:20 <sup>a</sup> Deut. 15:21; 17:1; Mal. 1:8, 14; [Eph. 5:27; Heb. 9:14; 1 Pet. 1:19]

22:21 <sup>a</sup> Lev. 3:1, 6 <sup>b</sup> Num. 15:3, 8; Ps. 61:8; 65:1; Eccl. 5:4, 5

22:22 <sup>a</sup> Lev. 22:20; Mal. 1:8 <sup>b</sup> Lev. 1:9, 13; 3:3, 5 <sup>1</sup> *an ulcer or running sore*

22:23 <sup>a</sup> Lev. 21:18 <sup>1</sup> *a limb too long or too short*

22:25 <sup>a</sup> Num. 15:15, 16 <sup>b</sup> Lev. 21:6, 17 <sup>c</sup> Mal. 1:14

22:27 <sup>a</sup> Ex. 22:30 <sup>1</sup> *with its mother*

22:28 <sup>a</sup> Deut. 22:6, 7 <sup>1</sup> *female sheep*

22:29 <sup>a</sup> Lev. 7:12; Ps. 107:22; 116:17; Amos 4:5 <sup>1</sup> *of your own free will*

22:30 <sup>a</sup> Lev. 7:15

22:31 <sup>a</sup> Lev. 19:37; Num. 15:40; Deut. 4:40

22:32 <sup>a</sup> Lev. 18:21 <sup>b</sup> Lev. 10:3; Matt. 6:9; Luke 11:2 <sup>c</sup> Lev. 20:8 <sup>1</sup> *treated as holy*

22:33 <sup>a</sup> Lev. 19:36, 37; Num. 15:40; Deut. 4:40

23:2 <sup>a</sup> Ex. 12:16

23:3 <sup>a</sup> Ex. 20:9; 23:12; 31:15; Lev. 19:3; Deut. 5:13, 14; Luke 13:14

23:4 <sup>a</sup> Ex. 23:14–16; Lev. 23:2, 37

23:5 <sup>a</sup> Ex. 12:1–28; Num. 9:1–5; 28:16–25; Deut. 16:1–8; Josh. 5:10

23:7 <sup>a</sup> Ex. 12:16; Num. 28:18, 25 <sup>1</sup> *labourious*

23:10 <sup>a</sup> Ex. 23:19; 34:26

be come into the land which I give unto you, and shall reap the harvest thereof, then ye shall bring a sheaf of ᵇthe firstfruits of your harvest unto the priest:

11 And he shall ªwave the sheaf before the LORD, to be accepted for you: on the morrow after the sabbath the priest shall wave it.

12 And ye shall offer that day when ye wave the sheaf an he lamb without blemish of the first year for a burnt offering unto the LORD.

13 And the ¹meat offering thereof *shall be* two tenth deals of fine flour mingled with oil, an offering made by fire unto the LORD *for* a ²sweet savour: and the drink offering thereof *shall be* of wine, the fourth *part* of an hin.

14 And ye shall *eat* neither bread, nor parched corn, nor green ears, until the selfsame day that ye have brought an offering unto your God: *it shall be* a statute for ever throughout your generations in all your dwellings.

15 And ye shall count unto you from the morrow after the sabbath, from the day that ye brought the sheaf of the wave offering; seven sabbaths shall be complete:

16 Even unto the morrow after the seventh sabbath shall ye number ªfifty days; and ye shall offer ᵇa new meat offering unto the LORD.

17 Ye shall bring out of your habitations two wave loaves of two tenth deals: they shall be of fine flour; they shall be baken with leaven; *they are* ªthe firstfruits unto the LORD.

18 And ye shall offer with the bread seven lambs without blemish of the first year, and one young bullock, and two rams: they shall be *for* a burnt offering unto the LORD, with their meat offering, and their drink offerings, *even* an offering made by fire, of sweet savour unto the LORD.

19 Then ye shall sacrifice ªone kid of the goats for a sin offering, and two lambs of the first year for a sacrifice of ᵇpeace offerings.

20 And the priest shall wave them with the bread of the firstfruits *for* a wave offering before the LORD, with the two lambs: ªthey shall be holy to the LORD for the priest.

21 And ye shall proclaim on the selfsame day, *that* it may be an holy convocation unto you: ye shall do no servile work *therein: it shall be* a statute for ever in all your dwellings throughout your generations.

22 And ªwhen ye reap the harvest of your land, thou shalt not make clean riddance of the corners of thy field when thou reapest, neither shalt thou gather any gleaning of thy harvest: thou shalt leave them unto the poor,

23:10 ᵇ [Rom. 11:16]; James 1:18; Rev. 14:4
23:11 ª Ex. 29:24
23:13 ¹ *grain* or *meal* ² *sweet* or *pleasing aroma*
23:16 ª Acts 2:1 ᵇ Num. 28:26
23:17 ª Ex. 23:16, 19; Num. 15:17–21
23:19 ª Lev. 4:23, 28; Num. 28:30; [2 Cor. 5:21] ᵇ Lev. 3:1
23:20 ª Lev. 14:13; Num. 18:12; Deut. 18:4
23:22 ª Lev. 19:9, 10; Deut. 24:19– 22; Ruth 2:2, 15

23:24 ª Num. 29:1 ᵇ Lev. 25:9
23:27 ª Lev. 16:1– 34; 25:9; Num. 29:7 ¹ *the day of atonement*
23:28 ª Lev. 16:34
23:29 ª Is. 22:12; Jer. 31:9; Ezek. 7:16 ᵇ Gen. 17:14; Lev. 13:46; Num. 5:2 ¹ *person*
23:30 ª Lev. 20:3–6 ¹ *person*
23:32 ¹ *humble yourselves* ² *observe*
23:34 ª Ex. 23:16; Num. 29:12; Deut. 16:13–16; Ezra 3:4; Neh. 8:14; Zech. 14:16– 19; John 7:2
23:36 ª Num. 29:12–34 ᵇ Num. 29:35–38; Neh. 8:18; John 7:37 ᶜ Deut. 16:8; 2 Chr. 7:8
23:37 ª Lev. 23:2, 4
23:38 ª Num. 29:39

and to the stranger: I *am* the LORD your God.

23 And the LORD spake unto Moses, saying,

24 Speak unto the children of Israel, saying, In the ªseventh month, in the first *day* of the month, shall ye have a sabbath, ᵇa memorial of blowing of trumpets, an holy convocation.

25 Ye shall do no servile work *therein:* but ye shall offer an offering made by fire unto the LORD.

26 And the LORD spake unto Moses, saying,

27 ªAlso on the tenth *day* of this seventh month *there shall be* ¹a day of atonement: it shall be an holy convocation unto you; and ye shall afflict your souls, and offer an offering made by fire unto the LORD.

28 And ye shall do no work in that same day: for it *is* a day of atonement, ªto make an atonement for you before the LORD your God.

29 For whatsoever ¹soul *it be* that shall not be ªafflicted in that same day, ᵇhe shall be cut off from among his people.

30 And whatsoever ¹soul *it be* that doeth any work in that same day, ªthe same soul will I destroy from among his people.

31 Ye shall do no manner of work: *it shall be* a statute for ever throughout your generations in all your dwellings.

32 It *shall be* unto you a sabbath of rest, ¹and ye shall afflict your souls: in the ninth *day* of the month at even, from even unto even, shall ye ²celebrate your sabbath.

33 And the LORD spake unto Moses, saying,

34 Speak unto the children of Israel, saying, ªThe fifteenth day of this seventh month *shall be* the feast of tabernacles *for* seven days unto the LORD.

35 On the first day *shall be* an holy convocation: ye shall do no servile work *therein.*

36 Seven days ye shall offer an ªoffering made by fire unto the LORD: ᵇon the eighth day shall be an holy convocation unto you; and ye shall offer an offering made by fire unto the LORD: it *is* a ᶜsolemn assembly; *and* ye shall do no servile work *therein.*

37 ªThese *are* the feasts of the LORD, which ye shall proclaim *to be* holy convocations, to offer an offering made by fire unto the LORD, a burnt offering, and a meat offering, a sacrifice, and drink offerings, every thing upon his day:

38 ªBeside the sabbaths of the LORD, and beside your gifts, and beside all your vows, and beside all your

freewill offerings, which ye give unto the LORD.

39 Also in the fifteenth day of the seventh month, when ye have [a]gathered in the fruit of the land, ye shall keep a feast unto the LORD seven days: on the first day *shall be* a sabbath, and on the eighth day *shall be* a sabbath.

40 And [a]ye shall take you on the first day the [1]boughs of goodly trees, branches of palm trees, and the boughs of thick trees, and willows of the brook; [b]and ye shall rejoice before the LORD your God seven days.

41 [a]And ye shall keep it a feast unto the LORD seven days in the year. *It shall be* a statute for ever in your generations: ye shall celebrate it in the seventh month.

42 [a]Ye shall dwell in [1]booths seven days; [b]all that are Israelites born shall dwell in booths:

43 [a]That your generations may [b]know that I made the children of Israel to dwell in booths, when [c]I brought them out of the land of Egypt: I *am* the LORD your God.

44 And Moses [a]declared unto the children of Israel the feasts of the LORD.

## CHAPTER 24

AND the LORD spake unto Moses, saying,

2 [a]Command the children of Israel, that they bring unto thee pure olive beaten for the light, to cause the lamps to burn continually.

3 [1]Without the vail of the testimony, in the tabernacle of the congregation, shall Aaron order it from the evening unto the morning before the LORD continually: *it shall be* a statute for ever in your generations.

4 He shall [1]order the lamps upon [a]the pure candlestick before the LORD continually.

5 And thou shalt take fine flour, and bake twelve [a]cakes thereof: two tenth deals shall be in one cake.

6 And thou shalt set them in two rows, six on a row, [a]upon the [1]pure table before the LORD.

7 And thou shalt put pure frankincense upon *each* row, that it may be on the bread for a [a]memorial, *even* an offering made by fire unto the LORD.

8 [a]Every sabbath he shall set it in order before the LORD continually, *being taken* from the children of Israel by an everlasting covenant.

9 And [a]it shall be Aaron's and his sons'; [b]and they shall eat it in the holy place: for it *is* most holy unto him of the offerings of the LORD made by fire by a perpetual statute.

10 And the son of an Israelitish woman, whose father *was* an Egyptian, went out among the children of

Israel: and this son of the Israelitish *woman* and a man of Israel [1]strove together in the camp;

11 And the Israelitish woman's son [a]blasphemed the name *of the LORD,* and [b]cursed. And they [c]brought him unto Moses: (and his mother's name *was* Shelomith, the daughter of Dibri, of the tribe of Dan:)

12 And they [a]put him [1]in ward, [b]that [2]the mind of the LORD might be shewed them.

13 And the LORD spake unto Moses, saying,

14 Bring forth him that hath cursed without the camp; and let all that heard *him* [a]lay their hands upon his head, and let all the congregation stone him.

15 And thou shalt speak unto the children of Israel, saying, Whosoever curseth his God [a]shall [1]bear his sin.

16 And he that [a]blasphemeth the name of the LORD, he shall surely be put to death, *and* all the congregation shall certainly stone him: as well the stranger, as he that is born in the land, when he blasphemeth the name *of the LORD,* shall be put to death.

17 [a]And he that killeth any man shall surely be put to death.

18 [a]And he that killeth a beast shall make it good; [1]beast for beast.

19 And if a man [1]cause a blemish in his neighbour; as [a]he hath done, so shall it be done to him;

20 Breach for [a]breach, [b]eye for eye, tooth for tooth: as he hath caused a blemish in a man, so shall it be done to him *again.*

21 And he that killeth a beast, he shall restore it: and he that killeth a man, he shall be put to death.

22 Ye shall have [a]one [1]manner of law, as well for the stranger, as for one of your own country: for I *am* the LORD your God.

23 And Moses spake to the children of Israel, that they should bring forth him that had cursed out of the camp, and stone him with stones. And the children of Israel did as the LORD commanded Moses.

## CHAPTER 25

AND the LORD spake unto Moses in mount [a]Sinai, saying,

2 Speak unto the children of Israel, and say unto them, When ye come into the land which I give you, then shall the land [a]keep a sabbath unto the LORD.

3 Six years thou shalt sow thy field, and six years thou shalt prune thy vineyard, and gather in the fruit thereof;

4 But in the [a]seventh year shall be a sabbath of [b]rest unto the land, a sabbath for the LORD: thou shalt

### Center column cross-references

23:39 [a] Ex. 23:16; Deut. 16:13
23:40 [a] Neh. 8:15 [b] Deut. 12:7; 16:14, 15 [1] Lit. *fruit*
23:41 [a] Num. 29:12; Neh. 8:18
23:42 [a] [Is. 4:6] [b] Neh. 8:14–16 [1] *tabernacles, shelters made of boughs*
23:43 [a] Deut. 31:13 [b] Ex. 10:2 [c] Lev. 22:33
23:44 [a] Lev. 23:2
24:2 [a] Ex. 27:20, 21
24:3 [1] *Outside*
24:4 [a] Ex. 25:31; 31:8; 37:17 [1] Lit. *arrange* or *set in order*
24:5 [a] Ex. 25:30; 39:36; 40:23
24:6 [a] 1 Kin. 7:48 [1] *table of pure gold*
24:7 [a] Lev. 2:2, 9, 16
24:8 [a] 1 Chr. 9:32
24:9 [a] Matt. 12:4 [b] Ex. 29:33
24:10 [1] *fought*
24:11 [a] Ex. 22:28 [b] Is. 8:21 [c] Ex. 18:22, 26
24:12 [a] Num. 15:34 [b] Num. 27:5 [1] *in custody* or *under guard* [2] Lit. *it might be declared to them from the mouth of the LORD*
24:14 [a] Deut. 13:9; 17:7
24:15 [a] Lev. 20:17 [1] *be responsible for*
24:16 [a] [Mark 3:28, 29]
24:17 [a] Ex. 21:12
24:18 [a] Lev. 24:21 [1] Lit. *living being for living being*
24:19 [a] Ex. 21:24 [1] *causes a disfigurement*
24:20 [a] Ex. 21:23 [b] [Matt. 5:38, 39]
24:22 [a] Ex. 12:49 [1] *standard of judgment*
25:1 [a] Lev. 26:46
25:2 [a] Lev. 26:34, 35
25:4 [b] [Heb. 4:9]

neither sow thy field, nor prune thy vineyard.

5 <sup>a</sup>That which groweth of its own accord of thy harvest thou shalt not reap, neither gather the grapes of thy vine undressed: *for* it is a year of rest <sup>1</sup>unto the land.

6 And the sabbath of the land shall be meat for you; for thee, and for thy servant, and for thy maid, and for thy hired servant, and for thy stranger that sojourneth with thee,

7 And for thy cattle, and for the beast that *are* in thy land, shall all the increase thereof be meat.

8 And thou shalt number seven sabbaths of years unto thee, seven times seven years; and the space of the seven sabbaths of years shall be unto thee forty and nine years.

9 Then shalt thou cause the trumpet of the jubile to sound on the tenth *day* of the seventh month, <sup>a</sup>in the day of atonement shall ye make the trumpet sound throughout all your land.

10 And ye shall hallow the fiftieth year, and <sup>a</sup>proclaim liberty throughout *all* the land unto all the inhabitants thereof: it shall be a jubile unto you; <sup>b</sup>and ye shall return every man unto his possession, and ye shall return every man unto his family.

11 A jubile shall that fiftieth year be unto you: <sup>a</sup>ye shall not sow, neither reap that which groweth of itself in it, nor gather *the grapes* in it of thy vine undressed.

12 For it *is* the jubile; it shall be holy unto you: <sup>a</sup>ye shall eat the increase thereof out of the field.

13 <sup>a</sup>In the year of this jubile ye shall return every man unto his possession.

14 And if thou sell ought unto thy neighbour, or buyest *ought* of thy neighbour's hand, ye shall not <sup>a</sup>oppress one another:

15 <sup>a</sup>According to the number of years after the jubile thou shalt buy of thy neighbour, *and* according unto the number of years of the fruits he shall sell unto thee:

16 According to the multitude of years thou shalt increase the price thereof, and according to the fewness of years thou shalt diminish the price of it: for *according* to the number *of the years* of the fruits doth he sell unto thee.

17 <sup>a</sup>Ye shall not therefore <sup>1</sup>oppress one another; <sup>b</sup>but thou shalt fear thy God: for I *am* the LORD your God.

18 <sup>a</sup>Wherefore ye shall do my statutes, and keep my judgments, and do them; <sup>b</sup>and ye shall dwell in the land in safety.

19 And the land shall yield her fruit, and <sup>a</sup>ye shall eat your fill, and dwell therein in safety.

20 And if ye shall say, <sup>a</sup>What shall we eat the seventh year? behold, <sup>b</sup>we shall not sow, nor gather in our increase:

21 Then I will <sup>a</sup>command my blessing upon you in the <sup>b</sup>sixth year, and it shall bring forth fruit for three years.

22 <sup>a</sup>And ye shall sow the eighth year, and eat *yet* of <sup>b</sup>old fruit until the ninth year; until her fruits come in ye shall eat *of* the old *store.*

23 The land shall not be sold <sup>1</sup>for ever: for <sup>a</sup>the land *is* mine; for ye *are* <sup>b</sup>strangers and sojourners with me.

24 And in all the land of your possession ye shall grant a redemption for the land.

25 <sup>a</sup>If thy brother be waxen poor, and hath sold away *some* of his possession, and if <sup>b</sup>any of his kin come to redeem it, then shall he redeem that which his brother sold.

26 And if the man have none to redeem it, and himself be able to redeem it;

27 Then <sup>a</sup>let him count the years of the sale thereof, and restore the overplus unto the man to whom he sold it; that he may return unto his possession.

28 But if he be not able to restore *it* to him, then that which is sold shall remain in the hand of him that hath bought it until the year of jubile: <sup>a</sup>and in the jubile it shall go out, and he shall return unto his possession.

29 And if a man sell a dwelling house in a walled city, then he may redeem it within a whole year after it is sold; *within* a full year may he redeem it.

30 And if it be not redeemed within the space of a full year, then the house that *is* in the walled city shall be established for ever to him that bought it throughout his generations: it shall not go out in the jubile.

31 But the houses of the villages which have no wall round about them shall be counted as the fields of the country: they may be redeemed, and they shall go out in the jubile.

32 Notwithstanding <sup>a</sup>the cities of the Levites, *and* the houses of the cities of their possession, may the Levites redeem at any time.

33 And if a man <sup>1</sup>purchase of the Levites, then the house that was sold, and the city of his possession, shall go out in *the year of* jubile: for the houses of the cities of the Levites *are* their possession among the children of Israel.

34 But <sup>a</sup>the field of the suburbs of their cities may not be <sup>b</sup>sold; for it *is* their perpetual possession.

35 And if thy brother be waxen poor, and <sup>1</sup>fallen in decay with thee; then thou shalt <sup>a</sup>relieve<sup>2</sup> him: *yea,*

---

25:5 <sup>a</sup> 2 Kin. 19:29
<sup>1</sup> *for*

25:9 <sup>a</sup> Lev. 23:24, 27

25:10 <sup>a</sup> Is. 61:2; 63:4; Jer. 34:8, 15, 17; [Luke 4:19]
<sup>b</sup> Lev. 25:13, 28, 54; Num. 36:4

25:11 <sup>a</sup> Lev. 25:5

25:12 <sup>a</sup> Lev. 25:6, 7

25:13 <sup>a</sup> Lev. 25:10; 27:24; Num. 36:4

25:14 <sup>a</sup> Lev. 19:13

25:15 <sup>a</sup> Lev. 27:18, 23

25:17 <sup>a</sup> Lev. 25:14; Prov. 14:31; 22:22; Jer. 7:5, 6; 1 Thess. 4:6 <sup>b</sup> Lev. 19:14, 32; 25:43
<sup>1</sup> *mistreat*

25:18 <sup>a</sup> Lev. 19:37
<sup>b</sup> Lev. 26:5; Deut. 12:10; Ps. 4:8; Jer. 23:6

25:19 <sup>a</sup> Lev. 26:5; Ezek. 34:25

25:20 <sup>a</sup> Matt. 6:25, 31 <sup>b</sup> Lev. 25:4, 5

25:21 <sup>a</sup> Deut. 28:8 <sup>b</sup> Ex. 16:29

25:22 <sup>a</sup> 2 Kin. 19:29 <sup>b</sup> Lev. 26:10; Josh. 5:11

25:23 <sup>a</sup> Ex. 19:5; 2 Chr. 7:20 <sup>b</sup> Gen. 23:4; Ex. 6:4; 1 Chr. 29:15; Ps. 39:12; Heb. 11:13; 1 Pet. 2:11
<sup>1</sup> *permanently*

25:25 <sup>a</sup> Ruth 2:20; 4:4, 6 <sup>b</sup> Num. 5:8; Ruth 3:2, 9, 12; [Job 19:25]; Jer. 32:7, 8

25:27 <sup>a</sup> Lev. 25:50–52

25:28 <sup>a</sup> Lev. 25:10, 13

25:32 <sup>a</sup> Num. 35:1–8; Josh. 21:2

25:33 <sup>1</sup> *purchases a house from one of*

25:34 <sup>a</sup> Num. 35:2–5 <sup>b</sup> Acts 4:36, 37

25:35 <sup>a</sup> Deut. 15:7–11; 24:14, 15; Luke 6:35; 1 John 3:17 <sup>1</sup> Lit. *his hand fails* <sup>2</sup> *help*

*though he be* a stranger, or a sojourner; that he may live with thee.

36 ᵃTake thou no ¹usury of him, or increase: but ᵇfear thy God; that thy brother may live with thee.

37 Thou shalt not give him thy money upon usury, nor lend him thy victuals for increase.

38 ᵃI *am* the LORD your God, which brought you forth out of the land of Egypt, to give you the land of Canaan, *and* to be your God.

39 And if thy brother *that dwelleth* by thee be waxen poor, and be sold unto thee; thou shalt not compel him to serve as a bondservant:

40 *But* as an hired servant, *and* as a sojourner, he shall be with thee, *and* shall serve thee unto the year of jubile:

41 And *then* shall he depart from thee, *both* he and his children ᵃwith him, and shall return unto his own family, and unto the possession of his fathers shall he return.

42 For they *are* ᵃmy servants, which I brought forth out of the land of Egypt: they shall not be sold as ¹bondmen.

43 ᵃThou shalt not rule over him ᵇwith ¹rigour; but ᶜshalt fear thy God.

44 Both thy bondmen, and thy bondmaids, which thou shalt have, *shall be* of the heathen that are round about you; of them shall ye buy bondmen and bondmaids.

45 Moreover of ᵃthe children of the strangers that do sojourn among you, of them shall ye buy, and of their families that *are* with you, which they begat in your land: and they shall be your possession.

46 And ᵃye shall take them as an inheritance for your children after you, to inherit *them for* a possession; they shall be your ¹bondmen for ever: but over your brethren the children of Israel, ye shall not rule one over another with rigour.

47 And if a sojourner or stranger wax rich by thee, and thy brother *that dwelleth* by him wax poor, and sell himself unto the stranger *or* sojourner by thee, or to the stock of the stranger's family:

48 After that he is sold he may be redeemed again; one of his brethren may redeem him:

49 Either his uncle, or his uncle's son, may redeem him, or *any* that is nigh of kin unto him of his family may redeem him; or if he be able, he may redeem himself.

50 And he shall reckon with him that bought him from the year that he was sold to him unto the year of jubile: and the price of his sale shall be according unto the number of years, ᵃaccording to the time of an hired servant shall it be with him.

25:36 ᵃ Ex. 22:25; Deut. 23:19, 20 ᵇ Neh. 5:9 ¹ *interest*

25:38 ᵃ Lev. 11:45; 22:32, 33

25:41 ᵃ Ex. 21:3

25:42 ᵃ Lev. 25:55; [Rom. 6:22; 1 Cor. 7:22, 23] ¹ *slaves*

25:43 ᵃ Eph. 6:9; Col. 4:1 ᵇ Ex. 1:13, 14; Lev. 25:46, 53; Ezek. 34:4 ᶜ Ex. 1:17; Deut. 25:18; Mal. 3:5 ¹ *severity*

25:45 ᵃ [Is. 56:3, 6, 7]

25:46 ᵃ Is. 14:2 ¹ *permanent slaves*

25:50 ᵃ Job 7:1; Is. 16:14

26:1 ᵃ Ex. 20:4, 5; Deut. 4:15–18; 5:8 ¹ *sacred pillar* ² *engraved stone*

26:2 ᵃ Lev. 19:30 ¹ *observe*

26:3 ᵃ Deut. 28:1–14 ¹ *perform*

26:4 ᵃ Is. 30:23 ᵇ Ps. 67:6

26:5 ᵃ Deut. 11:15; Joel 2:19, 26; Amos 9:13 ᵇ Lev. 25:18, 19; Ezek. 34:25

26:6 ᵃ Is. 45:7 ᵇ Job 11:19; Ps. 4:8; Zeph. 3:13 ᶜ 2 Kin. 17:25; Hos. 2:18 ᵈ Ezek. 14:17 ¹ *eliminate wild beasts*

26:8 ᵃ Deut. 32:30; Judg. 7:7–12

26:9 ᵃ Ex. 2:25; 2 Kin. 13:23 ᵇ Gen. 17:6, 7; Ps. 107:38 ᶜ Gen. 17:1–7 ¹ *confirm*

26:10 ᵃ Lev. 25:22

26:11 ᵃ Ex. 25:8; 29:45, 46; Josh. 22:19; Ps. 76:2; Ezek. 37:26; Rev. 21:3 ¹ *dwelling*

51 If *there be* yet many years *behind,* according unto them he shall give again the price of his redemption out of the money that he was bought for.

52 And if there remain but few years unto the year of jubile, then he shall count with him, *and* according unto his years shall he give him again the price of his redemption.

53 *And* as a yearly hired servant shall he be with him: *and the other* shall not rule with rigour over him in thy sight.

54 And if he be not redeemed in these *years,* then he shall go out in the year of jubile, *both* he, and his children with him.

55 For unto me the children of Israel *are* servants; they *are* my servants whom I brought forth out of the land of Egypt: I *am* the LORD your God.

## CHAPTER 26

Y E shall make you ᵃno idols nor graven image, neither rear you up a ¹standing image, neither shall ye set up *any* ²image of stone in your land, to bow down unto it: for I *am* the LORD your God.

2 ᵃYe shall ¹keep my sabbaths, and reverence my sanctuary: I *am* the LORD.

3 ᵃIf ye walk in my statutes, and keep my commandments, and ¹do them;

4 ᵃThen I will give you rain in due season, ᵇand the land shall yield her increase, and the trees of the field shall yield their fruit.

5 ᵃAnd your threshing shall reach unto the vintage, and the vintage shall reach unto the sowing time: and ye shall eat your bread to the full, and ᵇdwell in your land safely.

6 And ᵃI will give peace in the land, and ᵇye shall lie down, and none shall make *you* afraid: and I will ¹rid ᶜevil beasts out of the land, neither shall ᵈthe sword go through your land.

7 And ye shall chase your enemies, and they shall fall before you by the sword.

8 And ᵃfive of you shall chase an hundred, and an hundred of you shall put ten thousand to flight: and your enemies shall fall before you by the sword.

9 For I will ᵃhave respect unto you, and ᵇmake you fruitful, and multiply you, and ¹establish my ᶜcovenant with you.

10 And ye shall eat ᵃold store, and bring forth the old because of the new.

11 ᵃAnd I will set my ¹tabernacle among you: and my soul shall not abhor you.

12 <sup>a</sup>And I will walk among you, and will be your God, and ye shall be my people.

13 I *am* the LORD your God, which brought you forth out of the land of Egypt, that ye should not be their <sup>1</sup>bondmen; and I have broken the bands of your <sup>a</sup>yoke, and made you <sup>2</sup>go upright.

14 But if ye will not hearken unto me, and will not do all these commandments;

15 And if ye shall despise my statutes, or if your soul abhor my judgments, so that ye will not do all my commandments, *but* that ye break my covenant:

16 I also will do this unto you; I will even appoint over you terror, <sup>a</sup>consumption,<sup>1</sup> and the <sup>2</sup>burning ague, that shall <sup>b</sup>consume the eyes, and <sup>c</sup>cause sorrow of heart: and <sup>d</sup>ye shall sow your seed <sup>3</sup>in vain, for your enemies shall eat it.

17 And I will <sup>1</sup>set <sup>a</sup>my face against you, and <sup>b</sup>ye shall be slain before your enemies: <sup>c</sup>they that hate you shall reign over you; and ye shall <sup>d</sup>flee when none pursueth you.

18 And if ye will not yet for all this <sup>1</sup>hearken unto me, then I will punish you <sup>a</sup>seven times more for your sins.

19 And I will <sup>a</sup>break the pride of your power; and I <sup>b</sup>will make your heaven as iron, and your earth as brass:

20 And your <sup>a</sup>strength shall be spent in vain: for your <sup>b</sup>land shall not yield her increase, neither shall the trees of the land yield their fruits.

21 And if ye walk contrary unto me, and will not hearken unto me; I will bring seven times more plagues upon you according to your sins.

22 <sup>a</sup>I will also send wild beasts among you, which shall rob you of your children, and destroy your cattle, and make you few in number; and <sup>b</sup>your *high* ways shall be desolate.

23 And if ye <sup>a</sup>will not be reformed by me by these things, but will walk contrary unto me;

24 <sup>a</sup>Then will I also walk contrary unto you, and will punish you yet seven times for your sins.

25 And <sup>a</sup>I will bring a sword upon you, that shall avenge the quarrel of *my* covenant: and when ye are gathered together within your cities, <sup>b</sup>I will send the pestilence among you; and ye shall be delivered into the hand of the enemy.

26 <sup>a</sup>*And* when I have broken the staff of your bread, ten women shall bake your bread in one oven, and they shall deliver *you* your bread again by weight: and <sup>b</sup>ye shall eat, and not be satisfied.

27 And if ye will not for all this hearken unto me, but walk contrary unto me;

28 Then I will walk contrary unto you also in fury; and I, even I, will chastise you seven times for your sins.

29 <sup>a</sup>And ye shall <sup>1</sup>eat the flesh of your sons, and the flesh of your daughters shall ye eat.

30 And <sup>a</sup>I will destroy your high places, and cut down your images, and cast your carcases upon the carcases of your idols, and my soul shall abhor you.

31 And I will make your <sup>a</sup>cities waste, and <sup>b</sup>bring your sanctuaries unto desolation, and I will not <sup>c</sup>smell the <sup>1</sup>savour of your sweet odours.

32 <sup>a</sup>And I will bring the land into desolation: and your enemies which dwell therein shall be astonished at it.

33 And <sup>a</sup>I will scatter you among the heathen, and will draw out a sword after you: and your land shall be desolate, and your cities waste.

34 <sup>a</sup>Then shall the land enjoy her sabbaths, as long as it lieth desolate, and ye *be* in your enemies' land; *even* then shall the land rest, and enjoy her sabbaths.

35 As long as it lieth desolate it shall rest; because it did not rest in your <sup>a</sup>sabbaths, when ye dwelt upon it.

36 And upon them that are left *alive* of you I will <sup>1</sup>send a <sup>a</sup>faintness into their hearts in the lands of their enemies; and the sound of a shaken leaf shall chase them; and they shall flee, as fleeing from a sword; and they shall fall when none pursueth.

37 And <sup>a</sup>they shall fall one upon another, as it were before a sword, when none pursueth: and <sup>b</sup>ye shall have no power to stand before your enemies.

38 And ye shall <sup>a</sup>perish among the heathen, and the land of your enemies shall eat you up.

39 And they that are left of you <sup>a</sup>shall <sup>1</sup>pine away in their iniquity in your enemies' lands; and also in the iniquities of their <sup>b</sup>fathers shall they pine away with them.

40 <sup>a</sup>If they shall confess their iniquity, and the iniquity of their fathers, with their trespass which they trespassed against me, and that also they have walked contrary unto me;

41 And *that* I also have walked contrary unto them, and have brought them into the land of their enemies; if then their <sup>a</sup>uncircumcised hearts be <sup>b</sup>humbled, and they then <sup>c</sup>accept of the punishment of their iniquity:

42 Then will I <sup>a</sup>remember my covenant with Jacob, and also my covenant with Isaac, and also my

26:12 <sup>a</sup> Deut. 23:14; [2 Cor. 6:16]

26:13 <sup>a</sup> Gen. 27:40 <sup>1</sup> slaves <sup>2</sup> walk erect

26:16 <sup>a</sup> Deut. 28:22 <sup>b</sup> 1 Sam. 2:33 <sup>c</sup> Ezek. 24:23; 33:10 <sup>d</sup> Judg. 6:3–6 <sup>1</sup> a wasting disease <sup>2</sup> fever <sup>3</sup> without profit

26:17 <sup>a</sup> Ps. 34:16 <sup>b</sup> Deut. 28:25 <sup>c</sup> Ps. 106:41 <sup>d</sup> Prov. 28:1 <sup>1</sup> oppose you

26:18 <sup>a</sup> 1 Sam. 2:5 <sup>1</sup> obey me

26:19 <sup>a</sup> Is. 25:11 <sup>b</sup> Deut. 28:23

26:20 <sup>a</sup> Ps. 127:1 <sup>b</sup> Gen. 4:12

26:22 <sup>a</sup> Deut. 32:24 <sup>b</sup> Judg. 5:6

26:23 <sup>a</sup> Amos 4:6–12

26:24 <sup>a</sup> Lev. 26:28, 41

26:25 <sup>a</sup> Ezek. 5:17 <sup>b</sup> Deut. 28:21

26:26 <sup>a</sup> Ps. 105:16 <sup>b</sup> Mic. 6:14

26:29 <sup>a</sup> 2 Kin. 6:28, 29 <sup>1</sup> In a time of famine

26:30 <sup>a</sup> 2 Chr. 34:3

26:31 <sup>a</sup> 2 Kin. 25:4, 10 <sup>b</sup> Ps. 74:7 <sup>c</sup> Is. 1:11–15 <sup>1</sup> fragrance of your pleasing aromas

26:32 <sup>a</sup> Jer. 9:11; 18:16

26:33 <sup>a</sup> Deut. 4:27

26:34 <sup>a</sup> 2 Chr. 36:21

26:35 <sup>a</sup> Lev. 25:2

26:36 <sup>a</sup> Ezek. 21:7, 12, 15 <sup>1</sup> make them fearful

26:37 <sup>a</sup> 1 Sam. 14:15, 16 <sup>b</sup> Josh. 7:12, 13

26:38 <sup>a</sup> Deut. 4:26

26:39 <sup>a</sup> Ezek. 4:17; 33:10 <sup>b</sup> Ex. 34:7 <sup>1</sup> waste or rot

26:40 <sup>a</sup> Neh. 9:2

26:41 <sup>a</sup> Acts 7:51 <sup>b</sup> 2 Chr. 12:6, 7, 12 <sup>c</sup> Dan. 9:7

26:42 <sup>a</sup> Ex. 2:24; 6:5

covenant with Abraham will I remember; and I will ᵇremember the land.

43 ᵃThe land also shall be left of them, and shall enjoy her sabbaths, while she lieth desolate without them: and they shall accept of the punishment of their iniquity: because, even because they ᵇdespised my judgments, and because their soul abhorred my statutes.

44 And yet for all that, when they be in the land of their enemies, ᵃI will not cast them away, neither will I abhor them, to destroy them utterly, and to break my covenant with them: for I *am* the LORD their God.

45 But I will ᵃfor their sakes remember the covenant of their ancestors, ᵇwhom I brought forth out of the land of Egypt ᶜin the sight of the heathen, that I might be their God: I *am* the LORD.

46 ᵃThese *are* the statutes and judgments and laws, which the LORD made between him and the children of Israel ᵇin mount Sinai by the hand of Moses.

## CHAPTER 27

AND the LORD spake unto Moses, saying,

2 Speak unto the children of Israel, and say unto them, ᵃWhen a man shall make a ¹singular vow, the persons *shall be* for the LORD by thy ²estimation.

3 And thy estimation shall be of the male from twenty years old even unto sixty years old, even thy ¹estimation shall be fifty shekels of silver, ᵃafter the shekel of the sanctuary.

4 And if it *be* a female, then thy estimation shall be thirty shekels.

5 And if *it be* from five years old even unto twenty years old, then thy estimation shall be of the male twenty shekels, and for the female ten shekels.

6 And if *it be* from a month old even unto five years old, then thy estimation shall be of the male five shekels of silver, and for the female thy estimation *shall be* three shekels of silver.

7 And if *it be* from sixty years old and above; if *it be* a male, then thy estimation shall be fifteen shekels, and for the female ten shekels.

8 But if he be poorer than thy estimation, then he shall present himself before the priest, and the priest shall value ᵃhim; according to his ability that vowed shall the priest value him.

9 And if *it be* a beast, whereof men bring an offering unto the LORD, all that *any man* giveth of such unto the LORD shall be holy.

10 He shall not alter it, nor change it, a good for a bad, or a bad for a good:

and if he shall at all change beast for beast, then it and the exchange thereof shall be ᵃholy.

11 And if *it be* any unclean beast, of which they do not offer a sacrifice unto the LORD, then he shall present the beast before the priest:

12 And the priest shall value it, whether it be good or bad: as thou valuest it, *who art* the priest, so shall it be.

13 ᵃBut if he will at all redeem it, then he shall add a fifth *part* thereof unto thy estimation.

14 And when a man shall ¹sanctify his house *to be* holy unto the LORD, then the priest shall estimate it, whether it be good or bad: as the priest shall estimate it, so shall it stand.

15 And if he that sanctified it will ¹redeem his house, then he shall add the fifth *part* of the money of thy estimation unto it, and it shall be his.

16 And if a man shall ¹sanctify unto the LORD *some part* of a field of his possession, then thy estimation shall be according to the seed thereof: an homer of barley seed *shall be valued* at fifty shekels of silver.

17 If he sanctify his field from the year of jubile, according to thy estimation it shall stand.

18 But if he sanctify his field after the jubile, then the priest shall ᵃreckon unto him the money according to the years that remain, even unto the year of the jubile, and it shall be ¹abated from thy estimation.

19 And if he that sanctified the field will in any wise redeem it, then he shall add the fifth *part* of the money of thy estimation unto it, and it shall be assured to him.

20 And if he will not redeem the field, or if he have sold the field to another man, it shall not be redeemed any more.

21 But the field, ᵃwhen it goeth out in the jubile, shall be holy unto the LORD, as a field ᵇdevoted; ᶜthe possession thereof shall be the priest's.

22 And if *a man* sanctify unto the LORD a field which he hath bought, which *is* not of the fields of ᵃhis possession;

23 Then the priest shall reckon unto him the worth of thy estimation, *even* unto the year of the jubile: and he shall give thine estimation in that day, *as* a holy thing unto the LORD.

24 ᵃIn the year of the jubile the field shall return unto him of whom it was bought, *even* to him to whom the possession of the land *did belong*.

25 And all thy estimations shall be according to the shekel of the sanctuary: ᵃtwenty gerahs shall be the shekel.

### Cross-references (center column)

26:42 ᵇ Ps. 136:23
26:43 ᵃ Lev. 26:34, 35 ᵇ Lev. 26:15
26:44 ᵃ Deut. 4:31; 2 Kin. 13:23; Jer. 30:11; [Rom. 11:1–36]
26:45 ᵃ [Rom. 11:28] ᵇ Lev. 22:33; 25:38 ᶜ Ps. 98:2; Ezek. 20:9, 14, 22
26:46 ᵃ Lev. 27:34; Deut. 6:1; 12:1; [John 1:17] ᵇ Lev. 25:1
27:2 ᵃ Lev. 7:16; Num. 6:2; Deut. 23:21–23; Judg. 11:30, 31, 39 ¹ Lit. *difficult* or *extraordinary* ² *evaluation*
27:3 ᵃ Ex. 30:13; Lev. 27:25; Num. 3:47; 18:16 ¹ *appraisal* or *valuation*
27:8 ᵃ Lev. 5:11; 14:21–24
27:10 ᵃ Lev. 27:33
27:13 ᵃ Lev. 6:5; 22:14; 27:15, 19
27:14 ¹ *set apart*
27:15 ¹ *buy back*
27:16 ¹ *set apart*
27:18 ᵃ Lev. 25:15, 16, 28 ¹ *deducted*
27:21 ᵃ Lev. 25:10, 28, 31 ᵇ Lev. 27:28 ᶜ Num. 18:14; Ezek. 44:29
27:22 ᵃ Lev. 25:10, 25
27:24 ᵃ Lev. 25:10–13, 28
27:25 ᵃ Ex. 30:13; Lev. 27:3; Num. 3:47; 18:16; Ezek. 45:12

26 Only the [a]firstling[1] of the beasts, which should be the LORD's firstling, no man shall sanctify it; whether *it be* ox, or sheep: it *is* the LORD's.

27 And if *it be* of an unclean beast, then he shall redeem *it* according to thine estimation, and [a]shall add a fifth *part* of it thereto: or if it be not redeemed, then it shall be sold according to thy estimation.

28 [a]Notwithstanding[1] no [2]devoted thing, that a man shall devote unto the LORD of all that he hath, *both* of man and beast, and of the field of his possession, shall be sold or redeemed: every devoted thing *is* most holy unto the LORD.

29 [a]None devoted, which shall be devoted of men, shall be redeemed; *but* shall surely be put to death.

30 And [a]all the tithe of the land,

*whether* of the seed of the land, *or* of the fruit of the tree, *is* the LORD's: *it is* holy unto the LORD.

31 [a]And if a man will at all redeem *ought* of his tithes, he shall add thereto the fifth *part* thereof.

32 And concerning the tithe of the herd, or of the flock, *even* of whatsoever [a]passeth under the rod, the tenth shall be holy unto the LORD.

33 He shall not search whether it be good or bad, [a]neither shall he change it: and if he change it at all, then both it and the change thereof shall be holy; it shall not be redeemed.

34 [a]These *are* the commandments, which the LORD commanded Moses for the children of Israel in mount [b]Sinai.

27:26 [a] Ex. 13:2, 12; 22:30 [1] *firstborn among the animals*

27:27 [a] Lev. 27:11, 12

27:28 [a] Lev. 27:21; Num. 18:14; Josh. 6:17–19 [1] *Nevertheless* [2] *dedicated to God*

27:29 [a] Num. 21:2

27:30 [a] Gen. 28:22; Num. 18:21, 24; 2 Chr. 31:5, 6, 12; Neh. 13:12; Mal. 3:8

27:31 [a] Lev. 27:13

27:32 [a] Jer. 33:13; Ezek. 20:37; Mic. 7:14

27:33 [a] Lev. 27:10

27:34 [a] Lev. 26:46; Deut. 4:5; Mal. 4:4 [b] Ex. 19:1–6, 25; [Heb. 12:18–29]

118

# THE FOURTH BOOK OF MOSES CALLED
# NUMBERS

Numbers is the book of wanderings. It takes its name from the two numberings of the Israelites—the first at Mount Sinai and the second on the plains of Moab. Most of the book, however, describes Israel's experiences as they wander in the wilderness. The lesson of Numbers is clear. While it may be necessary to pass through wilderness experiences, one does not have to live there. For Israel, an eleven-day journey became a forty-year agony.

The title of Numbers comes from the first word in the Hebrew text, *Wayyedabber*, "And He Said." Jewish writings, however, usually refer to it by the fifth Hebrew word in 1:1, *Bemidbar*, "In the Wilderness," which more nearly indicates the content of the book. The Greek title in the Septuagint is *Arithmoi*, "Numbers." The Latin Vulgate followed this title and translated it *Liber Numeri*, "Book of Numbers." These titles are based on the two numberings: the generation of Exodus (Num. 1) and the generation that grew up in the wilderness and conquered Canaan (Num. 26). Numbers has also been called the "Book of the Journeyings," the "Book of the Murmurings," and the "Fourth Book of Moses."

## CHAPTER 1

AND the LORD spake unto Moses ªin the wilderness of Sinai, ᵇin the tabernacle of the ¹congregation, on the ᶜfirst *day* of the second month, in the second year after they were come out of the land of Egypt, saying,

2 ªTake ¹ye the sum of all the congregation of the children of Israel, after their families, by the house of their fathers, with the number of *their* names, every male ᵇby their polls;

3 From ªtwenty years old and upward, all that are able to go forth to war in Israel: thou and Aaron shall number them by their armies.

4 And with you there shall be a man of every tribe; every one head of the house of his fathers.

5 And these *are* the names of the men that shall stand with you: of *the tribe of* Reuben; Elizur the son of Shedeur.

6 Of Simeon; Shelumiel the son of Zurishaddai.

7 Of Judah; Nahshon the son of Amminadab.

8 Of Issachar; Nethaneel the son of Zuar.

9 Of Zebulun; Eliab the son of Helon.

10 Of the children of Joseph: of Ephraim; Elishama the son of Ammihud: of Manasseh; Gamaliel the son of Pedahzur.

11 Of Benjamin; Abidan the son of Gideoni.

12 Of Dan; Ahiezer the son of Ammishaddai.

13 Of Asher; Pagiel the son of Ocran.

14 Of Gad; Eliasaph the son of ªDeuel.¹

15 Of Naphtali; Ahira the son of Enan.

16 ªThese *were* the ᵇrenowned¹ of the congregation, ²princes of the tribes of their fathers, ᶜheads of thousands in Israel.

17 And Moses and Aaron took these men which are ¹expressed ªby *their* names:

18 And they assembled all the congregation together on the first *day* of the second month, and they declared their ªpedigrees after their families, by the house of their fathers, according to the number of the names, from twenty years old and upward, by their polls.

19 As the LORD commanded Moses, so he numbered them in the wilderness of Sinai.

20 And the ªchildren of Reuben, Israel's eldest son, by their generations, after their families, by the house of their fathers, according to the number of the names, by their polls, every male from twenty years old and upward, all that were able to go forth to war;

21 Those that were numbered of them, *even* of the tribe of Reuben, *were* forty and six thousand and five hundred.

22 Of the ªchildren of Simeon, by their generations, after their families, by the house of their fathers, those that were numbered of them, according to the number of the names, by their polls, every male from twenty years old and upward, all that were able to go forth to war;

23 Those that were numbered of them, *even* of the tribe of Simeon, *were* fifty and nine thousand and three hundred.

24 Of the ªchildren of Gad, by their

1:1 ª Ex. 19:1; Num. 10:11, 12 ᵇ Ex. 25:22 ᶜ Ex. 40:2, 17; Num. 9:1; 10:11 ¹ *meeting*

1:2 ª Ex. 30:12; Num. 26:2, 63, 64; 2 Sam. 24:2; 1 Chr. 21:2 ᵇ Ex. 30:12, 13; 38:26 ¹ *a census*

1:3 ª Ex. 30:14; 38:26

1:14 ª Num. 7:42 ¹ *Reuel*, Num. 2:14

1:16 ª Ex. 18:21; Num. 7:2; 1 Chr. 27:16–22 ᵇ Num. 16:2 ᶜ Ex. 18:21, 25; Jer. 5:5; Mic. 3:1, 9; 5:2 ¹ *chosen* ² *leaders*

1:17 ª Is. 43:1 ¹ *designated*

1:18 ª Ezra 2:59; Heb. 7:3

1:20 ª Num. 2:10, 11; 26:5–11; 32:6, 15, 21, 29

1:22 ª Num. 2:12, 13; 26:12–14

1:24 ª Gen. 30:11; Num. 26:15–18; Josh. 4:12; Jer. 49:1

generations, after their families, by the house of their fathers, according to the number of the names, from twenty years old and upward, all that were able to go forth to war;

25 Those that were numbered of them, *even* of the tribe of Gad, *were* forty and five thousand six hundred and fifty.

26 Of the ªchildren of Judah, by their generations, after their families, by the house of their fathers, according to the number of the names, from twenty years old and upward, all that were able to go forth to war;

27 Those that were numbered of them, *even* of the tribe of Judah, *were* ªthreescore and fourteen thousand and six hundred.

28 Of the ªchildren of Issachar, by their generations, after their families, by the house of their fathers, according to the number of the names, from twenty years old and upward, all that were able to go forth to war;

29 Those that were numbered of them, *even* of the tribe of Issachar, *were* fifty and four thousand and four hundred.

30 Of the ªchildren of Zebulun, by their generations, after their families, by the house of their fathers, according to the number of the names, from twenty years old and upward, all that were able to go forth to war;

31 Those that were numbered of them, *even* of the tribe of Zebulun, *were* fifty and seven thousand and four hundred.

32 Of the children of Joseph, *namely,* of the ªchildren of Ephraim, by their generations, after their families, by the house of their fathers, according to the number of the names, from twenty years old and upward, all that were able to go forth to war;

33 Those that were numbered of them, *even* of the tribe of Ephraim, *were* forty thousand and five hundred.

34 Of the ªchildren of Manasseh, by their generations, after their families, by the house of their fathers, according to the number of the names, from twenty years old and upward, all that were able to go forth to war;

35 Those that were numbered of them, *even* of the tribe of Manasseh, *were* thirty and two thousand and two hundred.

36 Of the ªchildren of Benjamin, by their generations, after their families, by the house of their fathers, according to the number of the names, from twenty years old and upward, all that were able to go forth to war;

37 Those that were numbered of them, *even* of the tribe of Benjamin, *were* thirty and five thousand and four hundred.

38 Of the ªchildren of Dan, by their generations, after their families, by the house of their fathers, according to the number of the names, from twenty years old and upward, all that were able to go forth to war;

39 Those that were numbered of them, *even* of the tribe of Dan, *were* threescore and two thousand and seven hundred.

40 Of the ªchildren of Asher, by their generations, after their families, by the house of their fathers, according to the number of the names, from twenty years old and upward, all that were able to go forth to war;

41 Those that were numbered of them, *even* of the tribe of Asher, *were* forty and one thousand and five hundred.

42 Of the children of Naphtali, throughout their generations, after their families, by the house of their fathers, according to the number of the names, from twenty years old and upward, all that were able to go forth to war;

43 Those that were numbered of them, *even* of the tribe of Naphtali, *were* fifty and three thousand and four hundred.

44 ªThese *are* those that were numbered, which Moses and Aaron numbered, and the ¹princes of Israel, *being* twelve men: each one was ²for the house of his fathers.

45 So were all those that were numbered of the children of Israel, by the house of their fathers, from twenty years old and upward, all that were able to go forth to war in Israel;

46 Even all they that were numbered were ªsix hundred thousand and three thousand and five hundred and fifty.

47 But ªthe Levites after the tribe of their fathers were not numbered among them.

48 For the LORD had spoken unto Moses, saying,

49 ªOnly thou shalt not number the tribe of Levi, neither take the sum of them among the children of Israel:

50 ªBut thou shalt appoint the Levites over the tabernacle of testimony, and over all the vessels thereof, and over all things that *belong* to it: they shall bear the tabernacle, and all the vessels thereof; and they shall minister unto it, ᵇand shall encamp round about the tabernacle.

51 ªAnd when the tabernacle ¹setteth forward, the Levites shall take it down: and when the tabernacle is to be ²pitched, the Levites shall set it ᵇup: ᶜand the stranger that ³cometh nigh shall be put to death.

52 And the children of Israel shall pitch their tents, ªevery man by his

*Center column references:*

1:26 ª Gen. 29:35; Num. 26:19–22; 2 Sam. 24:9; Ps. 78:68; Matt. 1:2
1:27 ª 2 Chr. 17:14
1:28 ª Num. 2:5, 6
1:30 ª Num. 2:7, 8; 26:26, 27
1:32 ª Gen. 48:1–22; Num. 26:28–37; Deut. 33:13–17; Jer. 7:15; Obad. 19
1:34 ª Num. 2:20, 21; 26:28–34
1:36 ª Gen. 49:27; Num. 26:38–41; 2 Chr. 17:17; Rev. 7:8
1:38 ª Gen. 30:6; 46:23; Num. 2:25, 26; 26:42, 43
1:40 ª Num. 2:27, 28; 26:44–47
1:44 ª Num. 26:64 ¹ *leaders* ² *representing*
1:46 ª Ex. 12:37; 38:26; Num. 2:32; 26:51, 63; Heb. 11:12; Rev. 7:4–8
1:47 ª Num. 2:33; 3:14–22; 26:57–62; 1 Chr. 6:1–47; 21:6
1:49 ª Num. 2:33; 26:62
1:50 ª Ex. 38:21; Num. 3:7, 8; 4:15, 25–27, 33 ᵇ Num. 3:23, 29, 35, 38
1:51 ª Num. 4:5–15; 10:17, 21 ᵇ Num. 10:21 ᶜ Num. 3:10, 38; 4:15, 19, 20; 18:22 ¹ *goes* ² *set up* ³ *comes near*
1:52 ª Num. 2:2, 34; 24:2

own camp, and every man by his own standard, throughout their hosts.

53 [a]But the Levites shall pitch round about the tabernacle of testimony, that there be no [b]wrath upon the congregation of the children of Israel: and the Levites shall [c]keep[1] the charge of the tabernacle of testimony.

54 And the children of Israel did according to all that the LORD commanded Moses, so did they.

## CHAPTER 2

AND the LORD spake unto Moses and unto Aaron, saying,

2 [a]Every man of the children of Israel shall pitch by his own standard, with the [1]ensign of their father's house: [b]far[2] off about the tabernacle of the congregation shall they pitch.

3 And on the [a]east side toward the rising of the sun shall they of the standard of the camp of Judah [1]pitch throughout their armies: and [b]Nahshon the son of Amminadab *shall be* captain of the children of Judah.

4 And his host, and those that were numbered of them, *were* threescore and fourteen thousand and six hundred.

5 And those that do [1]pitch next unto him *shall be* the tribe of Issachar: and Nethaneel the son of Zuar *shall be* captain of the children of Issachar.

6 And his host, and those that were numbered thereof, *were* fifty and four thousand and four hundred.

7 *Then* the tribe of Zebulun: and Eliab the son of Helon *shall be* captain of the children of Zebulun.

8 And his host, and those that were numbered thereof, *were* fifty and seven thousand and four hundred.

9 All that were numbered in the camp of Judah *were* an hundred thousand and fourscore thousand and six thousand and four hundred, throughout their armies. [a]These shall first [1]set forth.

10 On the [a]south side *shall be* the standard of the camp of Reuben according to their armies: and the captain of the children of Reuben *shall be* Elizur the son of Shedeur.

11 And his host, and those that were numbered thereof, *were* forty and six thousand and five hundred.

12 And those which pitch by him *shall be* the tribe of Simeon: and the captain of the children of Simeon *shall be* Shelumiel the son of Zurishaddai.

13 And his host, and those that were numbered of them, *were* fifty and nine thousand and three hundred.

14 Then the tribe of Gad: and the captain of the sons of Gad *shall be* Eliasaph the son of [1]Reuel.

15 And his host, and those that were numbered of them, *were* forty and five thousand and six hundred and fifty.

16 All that were numbered in the camp of Reuben *were* an hundred thousand and fifty and one thousand and four hundred and fifty, throughout their armies. [a]And they shall [1]set forth in the second rank.

17 [a]Then the tabernacle of the congregation shall set forward with the [1]camp of the Levites [b]in the midst of the [2]camp: as they encamp, so shall they set forward, every man in his place by their [3]standards.

18 On the west side *shall be* the standard of the camp of Ephraim according to their armies: and the captain of the sons of Ephraim *shall be* Elishama the son of Ammihud.

19 And his host, and those that were numbered of them, *were* forty thousand and five hundred.

20 And by him *shall be* the tribe of Manasseh: and the captain of the children of Manasseh *shall be* Gamaliel the son of Pedahzur.

21 And his host, and those that were numbered of them, *were* thirty and two thousand and two hundred.

22 Then the tribe of Benjamin: and the captain of the sons of Benjamin *shall be* Abidan the son of Gideoni.

23 And his host, and those that were numbered of them, *were* thirty and five thousand and four hundred.

24 All that were numbered of the camp of Ephraim *were* an hundred thousand and eight thousand and an hundred, throughout their armies. [a]And they shall [1]go forward in the third rank.

25 The [1]standard of the camp of Dan *shall be* on the north side by their armies: and the captain of the children of Dan *shall be* Ahiezer the son of Ammishaddai.

26 And his host, and those that were numbered of them, *were* threescore and two thousand and seven hundred.

27 And those that encamp by him *shall be* the tribe of Asher: and the captain of the children of Asher *shall be* Pagiel the son of Ocran.

28 And his host, and those that were numbered of them, *were* forty and one thousand and five hundred.

29 Then the tribe of Naphtali: and the captain of the children of Naphtali *shall be* Ahira the son of Enan.

30 And his host, and those that were numbered of them, *were* fifty and three thousand and four hundred.

31 All they that were numbered in the camp of Dan *were* an hundred thousand and fifty and seven thousand and six hundred. [a]They shall [1]go hindmost with their [2]standards.

1:53 [a] Num. 1:50 [b] Lev. 10:6; Num. 8:19; 16:46; 18:5; 1 Sam. 6:19 [c] Num. 8:24; 18:2–4; 1 Chr. 23:32 [1] *have in their care*

2:2 [a] Num. 1:52; 24:2 [b] Josh. 3:4 [1] *emblem* or *banner* [2] *some distance from*

2:3 [a] Num. 10:5 [b] Num. 1:7; 7:12; 10:14; Ruth 4:20; 1 Chr. 2:10; Matt. 1:4; Luke 3:32, 33 [1] *make camp according to their*

2:5 [1] *camp*

2:9 [a] Num. 10:14 [1] *break camp*

2:10 [a] Num. 10:6

2:14 [1] *Deuel,* Num. 1:14; 7:42

2:16 [a] Num. 10:18 [1] *be second to break camp*

2:17 [a] Num. 10:17, 21 [b] Num. 1:53 [1] *company* [2] *whole company* [3] *banners*

2:24 [a] Num. 10:22 [1] *be third to break camp*

2:25 [1] *banner*

2:31 [a] Num. 10:25 [1] *break camp last* [2] *banners*

32 These *are* those which were numbered of the children of Israel by the house of their fathers: [a]all those that were numbered of the camps throughout their hosts *were* six hundred thousand and three thousand and five hundred and fifty.

33 But [a]the Levites were not numbered among the children of Israel; as the LORD commanded Moses.

34 And the children of Israel [a]did according to all that the LORD commanded Moses: [b]so they pitched by their [1]standards, and so they set forward, every one after their families, according to the house of their fathers.

## CHAPTER 3

THESE also *are* [1]the [a]generations of Aaron and Moses in the day *that* the LORD spake with Moses in mount Sinai.

2 And these *are* the names of the sons of Aaron; Nadab the [a]firstborn, and [b]Abihu, Eleazar, and Ithamar.

3 These *are* the names of the sons of Aaron, [a]the priests which were anointed, [1]whom he consecrated to minister in the priest's office.

4 [a]And Nadab and Abihu died before the LORD, when they offered strange fire before the LORD, in the wilderness of Sinai, and they had no children: and Eleazar and Ithamar ministered in the priest's office in the sight of Aaron their father.

5 And the LORD spake unto Moses, saying,

6 [a]Bring the tribe of Levi near, and present them before Aaron the priest, that they may [1]minister unto him.

7 And they shall [1]keep his charge, and the charge of the whole congregation before the tabernacle of the congregation, to do [a]the service of the tabernacle.

8 And they shall keep all the instruments of the tabernacle of the congregation, and the charge of the children of Israel, to do the service of the tabernacle.

9 And [a]thou shalt give the Levites unto Aaron and to his sons: they *are* wholly given unto him out of the children of Israel.

10 And thou shalt appoint Aaron and his sons, [a]and they shall [1]wait on their priest's office: [b]and the stranger that cometh nigh shall be put to death.

11 And the LORD spake unto Moses, saying,

12 And I, behold, [a]I have taken the Levites from among the children of Israel instead of all the firstborn that openeth the matrix among the children of Israel: therefore the Levites shall be [b]mine;

### Cross references

2:32 [a] Ex. 38:26; Num. 1:46; 11:21
2:33 [a] Num. 1:47; 26:57–62
2:34 [a] Num. 1:54 [b] Num. 24:2, 5, 6 [1] *banners*
3:1 [a] Ex. 6:16–27 [1] *the records of*
3:2 [a] Ex. 6:23 [b] Lev. 10:1, 2; Num. 26:60, 61; 1 Chr. 24:2
3:3 [a] Ex. 28:41; Lev. 8 [1] *Lit. whose hands he filled*
3:4 [a] Lev. 10:1, 2; Num. 26:61; 1 Chr. 24:2
3:6 [a] Num. 8:6–22; 18:1–7; Deut. 10:8; 33:8–11 [1] *serve him*
3:7 [a] Num. 1:50; 8:11, 15, 24, 26 [1] *attend to his needs and the needs of*
3:9 [a] Num. 8:19; 18:6, 7
3:10 [a] Ex. 29:9; Num. 18:7 [b] Num. 1:51; 3:38; 16:40 [1] *attend to their*
3:12 [a] Num. 3:41; 8:16; 18:6 [b] Ex. 13:2; Num. 3:45; 8:14
3:13 [a] Ex. 13:2; Lev. 27:26; Num. 8:16, 17; Neh. 10:36; Luke 2:23 [b] Ex. 13:12, 15; Num. 8:17
3:15 [a] Num. 3:39; 26:62 [1] *Take a census of*
3:16 [1] Lit. *mouth*
3:17 [a] Gen. 46:11; Ex. 6:16–22; Num. 26:57; 1 Chr. 6:1, 16; 23:6
3:18 [a] Num. 4:38–41 [b] Ex. 6:17
3:19 [a] Num. 4:34–37 [b] Ex. 6:18
3:20 [a] Ex. 6:19; Num. 4:42–45
3:23 [a] Num. 1:53 [1] *camp*
3:25 [a] Num. 4:24–26 [b] Ex. 25:9 [c] Ex. 26:1 [d] Ex. 26:7, 14 [e] Ex. 26:36
3:26 [a] Ex. 27:9, 12, 14, 15 [b] Ex. 27:16 [c] Ex. 35:18
3:27 [a] 1 Chr. 26:23
3:28 [1] *taking care of*
3:29 [a] Ex. 6:18; Num. 1:53

### The Sons of Aaron

13 Because [a]all the firstborn *are* mine; [b]for on the day that I smote all the firstborn in the land of Egypt I hallowed unto me all the firstborn in Israel, both man and beast: mine shall they be: I *am* the LORD.

14 And the LORD spake unto Moses in the wilderness of Sinai, saying,

15 [1]Number the children of Levi after the house of their fathers, by their families: [a]every male from a month old and upward shalt thou number them.

16 And Moses numbered them according to the [1]word of the LORD, as he was commanded.

17 [a]And these were the sons of Levi by their names; Gershon, and Kohath, and Merari.

18 And these *are* the names of the sons of [a]Gershon by their families; [b]Libni, and Shimei.

19 And the sons of [a]Kohath by their families; [b]Amram, and Izehar, Hebron, and Uzziel.

20 [a]And the sons of Merari by their families; Mahli, and Mushi. These *are* the families of the Levites according to the house of their fathers.

21 Of Gershon *was* the family of the Libnites, and the family of the Shimites: these *are* the families of the Gershonites.

22 Those that were numbered of them, according to the number of all the males, from a month old and upward, *even* those that were numbered of them *were* seven thousand and five hundred.

23 [a]The families of the Gershonites shall [1]pitch behind the tabernacle westward.

24 And the chief of the house of the father of the Gershonites *shall be* Eliasaph the son of Lael.

25 And [a]the charge of the sons of Gershon in the tabernacle of the congregation *shall be* [b]the tabernacle, and [c]the tent, [d]the covering thereof, and [e]the hanging for the door of the tabernacle of the congregation,

26 And [a]the hangings of the court, and [b]the curtain for the door of the court, which *is* by the tabernacle, and by the altar round about, and [c]the cords of it for all the service thereof.

27 [a]And of Kohath *was* the family of the Amramites, and the family of the Izeharites, and the family of the Hebronites, and the family of the Uzzielites: these *are* the families of the Kohathites.

28 In the number of all the males, from a month old and upward, *were* eight thousand and six hundred, [1]keeping the charge of the sanctuary.

29 [a]The families of the sons of Kohath shall pitch on the side of the tabernacle southward.

30 And the chief of the house of the father of the families of the Kohathites *shall be* Elizaphan the son of [a]Uzziel.

31 And [a]their [1]charge *shall be* [b]the ark, and [c]the table, and [d]the candlestick, and [e]the altars, and the vessels of the sanctuary wherewith they minister, and [f]the hanging, and all the service thereof.

32 And Eleazar the son of Aaron the priest *shall be* chief over the chief of the Levites, *and have* the oversight of them that keep the charge of the sanctuary.

33 Of Merari *was* the family of the Mahlites, and the family of the Mushites: these *are* the families of Merari.

34 And those that were numbered of them, according to the number of all the males, from a month old and upward, *were* six thousand and two hundred.

35 And the chief of the house of the father of the families of Merari *was* Zuriel the son of Abihail: [a]these shall pitch on the side of the tabernacle northward.

36 And [a]under the [1]custody and charge of the sons of Merari *shall be* the boards of the tabernacle, and the bars thereof, and the pillars thereof, and the sockets thereof, and all the vessels thereof, and all that serveth thereto,

37 And the pillars of the court round about, and their sockets, and their pins, and their cords.

38 [a]But those that encamp before the tabernacle toward the east, *even* before the tabernacle of the congregation eastward, *shall be* Moses, and Aaron and his sons, [b]keeping the charge of the sanctuary [c]for the charge of the children of Israel; and [d]the stranger that [1]cometh nigh shall be put to death.

39 [a]All that were numbered of the Levites, which Moses and Aaron numbered at the commandment of the LORD, throughout their families, all the males from a month old and upward, *were* twenty and two thousand.

40 And the LORD said unto Moses, [a]Number[1] all the firstborn of the males of the children of Israel from a month old and upward, and take the number of their names.

41 [a]And thou shalt take the Levites for me (I *am* the LORD) instead of all the firstborn among the children of Israel; and the cattle of the Levites instead of all the firstlings among the cattle of the children of Israel.

42 And Moses numbered, as the LORD commanded him, all the firstborn among the children of Israel.

43 And all the firstborn males by the number of names, from a month

old and upward, of those that were numbered of them, were twenty and two thousand two hundred and threescore and thirteen.

44 And the LORD spake unto Moses, saying,

45 [a]Take the Levites instead of all the firstborn among the children of Israel, and the cattle of the Levites instead of their cattle; and the Levites shall be mine: I *am* the LORD.

46 And for those that are to be [a]redeemed of the two hundred and threescore and thirteen of the firstborn of the children of Israel, [b]which are more than the Levites;

47 Thou shalt even take [a]five shekels apiece [b]by the poll, after the shekel of the sanctuary shalt thou take *them:* ([c]the shekel *is* twenty gerahs:)

48 And thou shalt give the money, wherewith the odd number of them is to be redeemed, unto Aaron and to his sons.

49 And Moses took the redemption money of them that were over and above them that were redeemed by the Levites:

50 Of the firstborn of the children of Israel took he the money; [a]a thousand three hundred and threescore and five *shekels,* after the shekel of the sanctuary:

51 And Moses [a]gave the money of them that were redeemed unto Aaron and to his sons, according to the word of the LORD, as the LORD commanded Moses.

## CHAPTER 4

AND the LORD spake unto Moses and unto Aaron, saying,

2 [1]Take the sum of the sons of [a]Kohath from among the sons of Levi, after their families, by the house of their fathers,

3 [a]From thirty years old and upward even until fifty years old, all that enter into the host, to do the work in the tabernacle of the congregation.

4 [a]This *shall be* the service of the sons of Kohath in the tabernacle of the congregation, *about* [b]the most holy things:

5 And when the camp setteth forward, Aaron shall come, and his sons, and they shall take down [a]the covering vail, and cover the [b]ark of testimony with it:

6 And shall put thereon the covering of badgers' skins, and shall spread over *it* a cloth wholly of [a]blue, and shall put in [b]the staves thereof.

7 And upon the [a]table of shewbread they shall spread a cloth of blue, and put thereon the dishes, and the spoons, and the bowls, and [1]covers

3:30 [a] Lev. 10:4
3:31 [a] Num. 4:15
[b] Ex. 25:10  [c] Ex. 25:23  [d] Ex. 25:31
[e] Ex. 27:1; 30:1
[f] Ex. 26:31–33
[1] *duty*
3:35 [a] Num. 1:53; 2:25
3:36 [a] Num. 4:31, 32  [1] *duty of appointed*
3:38 [a] Num. 1:53  [b] Num. 18:5  [c] Num. 3:7, 8  [d] Num. 3:10  [1] *came near*
3:39 [a] Num. 3:43; 4:48; 26:62
3:40 [a] Num. 3:15  [1] *Take a census of*
3:41 [a] Num. 3:12, 45

3:45 [a] Num. 3:12, 41
3:46 [a] Ex. 13:13, 15; Num. 18:15, 16  [b] Num. 3:39, 43
3:47 [a] Lev. 27:6; Num. 18:16  [b] Num. 1:2, 18, 20  [c] Ex. 30:13
3:50 [a] Num. 3:46, 47
3:51 [a] Num. 3:48
4:2 [a] Num. 3:27–32  [1] *Take a census*
4:3 [a] Num. 4:23, 30, 35; 8:24; 1 Chr. 23:3, 24, 27; Ezra 3:8
4:4 [a] Num. 4:15  [b] Num. 4:19
4:5 [a] Ex. 26:31; Heb. 9:3  [b] Ex. 25:10, 16
4:6 [a] Ex. 39:1  [b] Ex. 25:13; 1 Kin. 8:7, 8
4:7 [a] Ex. 25:23, 29, 30  [1] *jars for the drink offering*

to cover withal: and the ᵇcontinual² bread shall be thereon:

8 And they shall spread upon them a cloth of scarlet, and cover the same with a covering of badgers' skins, and shall put in the staves thereof.

9 And they shall take a cloth of blue, and cover the ᵃcandlestick of the light, ᵇand his lamps, and his tongs, and his snuffdishes, and all the oil vessels thereof, wherewith they minister unto it:

10 And they shall put it and all the vessels thereof within a covering of badgers' skins, and shall put *it* upon a bar.

11 And upon ᵃthe golden altar they shall spread a cloth of blue, and cover it with a covering of badgers' skins, and shall put to the staves thereof:

12 And they shall take all the ᵃinstruments of ministry, wherewith they minister in the sanctuary, and put *them* in a cloth of blue, and cover them with a covering of badgers' skins, and shall put *them* on a bar:

13 And they shall take away the ashes from the altar, and spread a purple cloth thereon:

14 And they shall put upon it all the vessels thereof, wherewith they minister about it, *even* the censers, the fleshhooks, and the shovels, and the ˡbasons, all the vessels of the altar; and they shall spread upon it a covering of badgers' skins, and put to the staves of it.

15 And when Aaron and his sons have made an end of covering the sanctuary, and all the vessels of the sanctuary, as the camp is to set forward; after that, ᵃthe sons of Kohath shall come to bear *it:* ᵇbut they shall not touch *any* holy thing, lest they die. ᶜThese *things are* the burden of the sons of Kohath in the tabernacle of the congregation.

16 And to the office of Eleazar the son of Aaron the priest *pertaineth* ᵃthe oil for the light, and the ᵇsweet incense, and ᶜthe daily meat offering, and the ᵈanointing oil, *and* the oversight of all the tabernacle, and of all that therein *is,* in the sanctuary, and in the vessels thereof.

17 And the LORD spake unto Moses and unto Aaron, saying,

18 Cut ye not off the tribe of the families of the Kohathites from among the Levites:

19 But thus do unto them, that they may live, and not die, when they approach unto ᵃthe most holy things: Aaron and his sons shall go in, and ˡappoint them every one to his service and to his burden:

20 ᵃBut they shall not go in to see when the holy things are covered, lest they die.

4:7 ᵇ Lev. 24:5–9
² shew bread
4:9 ᵃ Ex. 25:31
ᵇ Ex. 25:37, 38
4:11 ᵃ Ex. 30:1–5
4:12 ᵃ Ex. 25:9;
1 Chr. 9:29
4:14 ˡ bowls
4:15 ᵃ Num. 7:9;
10:21; Deut. 31:9;
Josh. 4:10; 2 Sam.
6:13; 1 Chr. 15:2,
15  ᵇ 2 Sam. 6:6,
7; 1 Chr. 13:9, 10
ᶜ Num. 3:31
4:16 ᵃ Ex. 25:6;
Lev. 24:2  ᵇ Ex.
30:34  ᶜ Ex. 29:38
ᵈ Ex. 30:23–25
4:19 ᵃ Num. 4:4
ˡ assign
4:20 ᵃ Ex. 19:21;
1 Sam. 6:19

21 And the LORD spake unto Moses, saying,

22 Take also the sum of the sons of ᵃGershon, throughout the houses of their fathers, by their families;

23 ᵃFrom thirty years old and upward until fifty years old shalt thou number them; all that enter in to perform the service, to do the work in the tabernacle of the congregation.

24 This *is* the ᵃservice of the families of the Gershonites, to serve, and ˡfor burdens:

25 ᵃAnd they shall bear the ᵇcurtains of the tabernacle, and the tabernacle of the congregation, his covering, and the covering of the ᶜbadgers' skins that *is* above upon it, and the hanging for the door of the tabernacle of the congregation,

26 And the hangings of the court, and the hanging for the door of the gate of the court, which *is* by the tabernacle and by the altar round about, and their cords, and all the instruments of their service, and all that is made for them: so shall they serve.

27 At the ˡappointment of Aaron and his sons shall be all the service of the sons of the Gershonites, in all their burdens, and in all their service: and ye shall ²appoint unto them in charge all their burdens.

28 This *is* the service of the families of the sons of Gershon in the tabernacle of the congregation: and their ˡcharge *shall be* ᵃunder the hand of Ithamar the son of Aaron the priest.

29 As for the sons of ᵃMerari, thou shalt number them after their families, by the house of their fathers;

30 ᵃFrom thirty years old and upward even unto fifty years old shalt thou number them, every one that entereth into the service, to do the work of the tabernacle of the congregation.

31 And ᵃthis *is* ˡthe charge of their ᵇburden, according to all their service in the tabernacle of the congregation; ᶜthe boards of the tabernacle, and the bars thereof, and the pillars thereof, and sockets thereof,

32 And the pillars of the court round about, and their sockets, and their pins, and their cords, with all their ˡinstruments, and with all their service: and by name ye shall ᵃreckon the instruments of the charge of their burden.

33 This *is* the service of the families of the sons of Merari, according to all their service, in the tabernacle of the congregation, under the hand of Ithamar the son of Aaron the priest.

34 ᵃAnd Moses and Aaron and the chief of the congregation numbered the sons of the Kohathites after their

4:22 ᵃ Num. 3:22
4:23 ᵃ Num. 4:3;
1 Chr. 23:3, 24, 27
4:24 ᵃ Num. 7:7
ˡ to carry
4:25 ᵃ Num. 3:25,
26  ᵇ Ex. 36:8
ᶜ Ex. 26:14
4:27 ˡ command
² assign
4:28 ᵃ Num. 4:33
ˡ duties
4:29 ᵃ Num.
3:33–37
4:30 ᵃ Num. 4:3;
8:24–26
4:31 ᵃ Num. 3:36,
37  ᵇ Num. 7:8
ᶜ Ex. 26:15  ˡ what
they must carry
4:32 ᵃ Ex. 25:9;
38:21  ˡ furnishings
4:34 ᵃ Num. 4:2

families, and after the house of their fathers,

35 From thirty [a]years old and upward even unto fifty years old, every one that entereth into the service, for the work in the tabernacle of the congregation:

36 And those that were numbered of them by their families were two thousand seven hundred and fifty.

37 These *were* they that were numbered of the families of the Kohathites, all that might do service in the tabernacle of the congregation, which Moses and Aaron did number according to the commandment of the LORD by the hand of Moses.

38 And those that were numbered of the sons of Gershon, throughout their families, and by the house of their fathers,

39 From thirty years old and upward even unto fifty years old, every one that entereth into the service, for the work in the tabernacle of the congregation,

40 Even those that were numbered of them, throughout their families, by the house of their fathers, were two thousand and six hundred and thirty.

41 [a]These *are* they that were numbered of the families of the sons of Gershon, of all that might do service in the tabernacle of the congregation, whom Moses and Aaron did number according to the commandment of the LORD.

42 And those that were numbered of the families of the sons of Merari, throughout their families, by the [1]house of their fathers,

43 From thirty years old and upward even unto fifty years old, every one that entereth into the service, for the work in the tabernacle of the congregation,

44 Even those that were numbered of them after their families, were three thousand and two hundred.

45 These *be* those that were numbered of the families of the sons of Merari, whom Moses and Aaron numbered [a]according to the word of the LORD by the hand of Moses.

46 All those that were [a]numbered of the Levites, whom Moses and Aaron and the chief of Israel numbered, after their families, and after the house of their fathers,

47 [a]From thirty years old and upward even unto fifty years old, every one that came to do the service of the ministry, and the service of the burden in the tabernacle of the congregation,

48 Even those that were numbered of them, were eight thousand and five hundred and fourscore.

49 According to the commandment of the LORD they were numbered by the hand of Moses, [a]every one according to his service, and according to his [1]burden: thus were they numbered of him, [b]as the LORD commanded Moses.

## CHAPTER 5

AND the LORD spake unto Moses, saying,

2 Command the children of Israel, that they put out of the camp every [a]leper, and every one that hath [1]an [b]issue, and whosoever is [c]defiled [2]by the dead:

3 Both male and female shall ye put out, [1]without the camp shall ye put them; that they defile not their camps, [a]in the midst whereof I dwell.

4 And the children of Israel did so, and put them out without the camp: as the LORD spake unto Moses, so did the children of Israel.

5 And the LORD spake unto Moses, saying,

6 Speak unto the children of Israel, [a]When a man or woman shall commit any sin that men commit, [1]to do a trespass against the LORD, and that person be guilty;

7 [a]Then they shall confess their sin which they have done: and he shall [1]recompense his trespass [b]with the principal thereof, and add unto it the fifth *part* thereof, and give *it* unto *him* against whom he hath trespassed.

8 But if the man have no [1]kinsman to recompense the trespass unto, let the trespass be recompensed unto the LORD, *even* to the priest; beside [a]the ram of the atonement, whereby an atonement shall be made for him.

9 And every [a]offering[1] of all the holy things of the children of Israel, which they bring unto the priest, shall be [b]his.

10 And every man's hallowed things shall be his: whatsoever any man giveth the priest, it shall be [a]his.

11 And the LORD spake unto Moses, saying,

12 Speak unto the children of Israel, and say unto them, If any man's wife go aside, and [1]commit a trespass against him,

13 And a man [a]lie with her carnally, and it be hid from the eyes of her husband, and be kept close, and she be defiled, and *there be* no witness against her, neither she be [b]taken *with the manner;*

14 And the spirit of jealousy come upon him, and he be [a]jealous of his wife, and she be defiled: or if the spirit of jealousy come upon him, and he be jealous of his wife, and she be not defiled:

---

4:35 [a] Num. 4:47
4:41 [a] Num. 4:22
4:42 [1] *household*
4:45 [a] Num. 4:29
4:46 [a] Num. 3:39; 26:57–62; 1 Chr. 23:3–23
4:47 [a] Num. 4:3, 23, 30

4:49 [a] Num. 4:15, 24, 31 [b] Num. 4:1, 21 [1] *task*
5:2 [a] Lev. 13:3, 8, 46; Num. 12:10, 14, 15 [b] Lev. 15:2 [c] Lev. 21:1; Num. 9:6, 10; 19:11, 13; 31:19 [1] *a discharge* [2] *by contact with*
5:3 [a] Lev. 26:11, 12; Num. 35:34; [2 Cor. 6:16] [1] *outside*
5:6 [a] Lev. 5:14–6:7 [1] *acting unfaithfully*
5:7 [a] Lev. 5:5; 26:40, 41; Josh. 7:19; Ps. 32:5; 1 John 1:9 [b] Lev. 6:4, 5 [1] *make restitution for*
5:8 [a] Lev. 5:15; 6:6, 7; 7:7 [1] *relative to receive restitution for*
5:9 [a] Ex. 29:28; Lev. 6:17, 18, 26; 7:6–14 [b] Lev. 7:32–34; 10:14, 15 [1] *heave offering*
5:10 [a] Lev. 10:13
5:12 [1] *acts unfaithfully*
5:13 [a] Lev. 18:20; 20:10 [b] John 8:4
5:14 [a] Prov. 6:34; Song 8:6

15 Then shall the man bring his wife unto the priest, and he shall [a]bring her offering for her, the tenth *part* of an ephah of barley meal; he shall pour no oil upon it, nor put frankincense thereon; for it *is* an offering of jealousy, an offering of memorial, [b]bringing iniquity to remembrance.

16 And the priest shall bring her near, and set her before the LORD:

17 And the priest shall take holy water in an earthen vessel; and of the dust that is in the floor of the tabernacle the priest shall take, and put *it* into the water:

18 And the priest shall set the woman before the [a]LORD, and uncover the woman's head, and put the offering of memorial in her hands, which *is* the jealousy offering: and the priest shall have in his hand the bitter water that causeth the curse:

19 And the priest shall charge her by an oath, and say unto the woman, If no man have lain with thee, and if thou hast not gone aside to uncleanness *with another* instead of thy husband, be thou free from this bitter water that causeth the curse:

20 But if thou hast gone aside to *another* instead of thy husband, and if thou be defiled, and some man have lain with thee beside thine husband:

21 Then the priest shall [a]charge the woman with an oath of cursing, and the priest shall say unto the woman, [b]The LORD make thee a curse and an oath among thy people, when the LORD doth make thy thigh to [1]rot, and thy belly to swell;

22 And this water that causeth the curse [a]shall go into thy bowels, to make *thy* belly to swell, and *thy* thigh to rot: [b]And the woman shall say, Amen, amen.

23 And the priest shall write these curses in a book, and he shall blot *them* out with the bitter water:

24 And he shall cause the woman to drink the bitter water that causeth the curse: and the water that causeth the curse shall enter into her, *and become* bitter.

25 [a]Then the priest shall take the jealousy offering out of the woman's hand, and shall [b]wave the offering before the LORD, and offer it upon the altar:

26 And the priest shall take an handful of the offering, *even* the memorial thereof, and burn *it* upon the altar, and afterward shall cause the woman to drink the water.

27 And when he hath made her to drink the water, then it shall come to pass, *that,* if she be defiled, and have done trespass against her husband, that the water that causeth the [a]curse shall enter into her, *and become* bitter,

and her belly shall swell, and her thigh shall rot: and the woman [b]shall be a curse among her people.

28 And if the woman be not defiled, but be clean; then she shall be free, and shall conceive seed.

29 This *is* the law of jealousies, when a wife goeth aside to *another* [a]instead of her husband, and is defiled;

30 Or when the spirit of jealousy cometh upon him, and he be jealous over his wife, and shall set the woman before the LORD, and the priest shall execute upon her all this law.

31 Then shall the man be guiltless from iniquity, and this woman [a]shall bear her [1]iniquity.

## CHAPTER 6

AND the LORD spake unto Moses, saying,

2 Speak unto the children of Israel, and say unto them, When either man or woman shall [a]separate[1] *themselves* to vow a vow of a [2]Nazarite, to separate *themselves* unto the LORD:

3 [a]He shall separate *himself* from wine and strong drink, and shall drink no vinegar of wine, or vinegar of strong drink, neither shall he drink any liquor of grapes, nor eat moist grapes, or dried.

4 All the days of his [1]separation shall he eat nothing that is made of the [2]vine tree, from the kernels even to the husk.

5 All the days of the vow of his separation there shall no [a]razor come upon his head: until the days be fulfilled, in the which he separateth *himself* unto the LORD, he shall be holy, *and* shall let the locks of the hair of his head grow.

6 All the days that he separateth *himself* unto the LORD [a]he shall [1]come at no dead body.

7 [a]He shall not [1]make himself unclean for his father, or for his mother, for his brother, or for his sister, when they die: because the [2]consecration of his God is upon his head.

8 [a]All the days of his separation he *is* holy unto the LORD.

9 And if any man die very suddenly by him, and he hath defiled the head of his consecration; then he shall [a]shave his head in the day of his cleansing, on the seventh day shall he shave it.

10 And [a]on the eighth day he shall bring two turtles, or two young pigeons, to the priest, to the door of the tabernacle of the congregation:

11 And the priest shall offer the one for a sin offering, and the other for a burnt offering, and make an atonement for him, for that he sinned by

5:15 [a] Lev. 5:11
[b] 1 Kin. 17:18;
Ezek. 29:16; Heb.
10:3
5:18 [a] Heb. 13:4
5:21 [a] Josh. 6:26;
1 Sam. 14:24; Neh.
10:29 [b] Jer. 29:22
[1] Lit. *fall away*
5:22 [a] Ps. 109:18
[b] Deut. 27:15–26
5:25 [a] Lev. 8:27
[b] Lev. 2:2, 9
5:26 [a] Lev. 2:2, 9
5:27 [a] Deut. 28:37;
Is. 65:15; Jer. 24:9;
29:18, 22; 42:18

[b] Num. 5:21
5:29 [a] Num. 5:19
5:31 [a] Lev. 20:17,
19, 20 [1] *guilt*
6:2 [a] Lev. 27:2;
Judg. 13:5; [Lam.
4:7; Amos 2:11,
12]; Acts 21:23;
Rom. 1:1 [1] *consecrates an offering*
[2] Heb. *Nazir*
6:3 [a] Lev. 10:9;
Amos 2:12; Luke
1:15
6:4 [1] *separation
as a Nazarite*
[2] *grapevine*
6:5 [a] Judg. 13:5;
16:17; 1 Sam. 1:11
6:6 [a] Lev. 21:1–3,
11; Num. 19:11–22
[1] *go near*
6:7 [a] Lev. 21:1,
2, 11; Num. 9:6
[1] *By touching
a dead body*
[2] *separation*
6:8 [a] [2 Cor.
6:17, 18]
6:9 [a] Lev. 14:8, 9;
Acts 18:18; 21:24
6:10 [a] Lev. 5:7;
14:22; 15:14, 29

the dead, and shall hallow his head that same day.

12 And he shall consecrate unto the LORD the days of his separation, and shall bring a lamb of the first year [a]for a trespass offering: but the days that were before shall be [1]lost, because his separation was defiled.

13 And this *is* the law of the Nazarite, [a]when the days of his separation are fulfilled: he shall be brought unto the door of the tabernacle of the congregation:

14 And he shall offer his offering unto the LORD, one he lamb of the first year without blemish for a burnt offering, and one ewe lamb of the first year without blemish [a]for a sin offering, and one ram without blemish [b]for peace offerings,

15 And a basket of unleavened bread, [a]cakes of fine flour mingled with oil, and wafers of unleavened bread [b]anointed with oil, and their meat offering, and their [c]drink offerings.

16 And the priest shall bring *them* before the LORD, and shall offer his sin offering, and his burnt offering:

17 And he shall offer the ram *for* a sacrifice of peace offerings unto the LORD, with the basket of unleavened bread: the priest shall offer also his meat offering, and his drink offering.

18 [a]And the Nazarite shall shave the head of his separation *at* the door of the tabernacle of the congregation, and shall take the hair of the head of his separation, and put *it* in the fire which *is* under the sacrifice of the peace offerings.

19 And the priest shall take the [a]sodden[1] shoulder of the ram, and one [b]unleavened cake out of the basket, and one unleavened wafer, and [c]shall put *them* upon the hands of the Nazarite, after *the hair of* his separation is shaven:

20 And the priest shall wave them *for* a wave offering before the LORD: [a]this *is* holy for the priest, with the wave breast and heave shoulder: and after that the Nazarite may drink wine.

21 This *is* the law of the Nazarite who hath vowed, *and of* his offering unto the LORD for his separation, beside *that* that his hand shall get: according to the vow which he vowed, so he must do after the law of his separation.

22 And the LORD spake unto Moses, saying,

23 Speak unto Aaron and unto his sons, saying, On this wise ye shall bless the children of Israel, saying unto them,

24 The LORD [a]bless thee, and [b]keep thee:

25 The LORD [a]make his face shine upon thee, and [b]be gracious unto thee:

26 [a]The LORD [1]lift up his countenance upon thee, and [b]give thee peace.

27 [a]And they shall [1]put my name upon the children of Israel; and [b]I will bless them.

## CHAPTER 7

AND it came to pass on the day that Moses had fully [a]set up the tabernacle, and had [b]anointed it, and sanctified it, and all the instruments thereof, both the altar and all the vessels thereof, and had anointed them, and sanctified them;

2 That [a]the princes of Israel, heads of the house of their fathers, who *were* the princes of the tribes, and [1]were over them that were numbered, offered:

3 And they brought their offering before the LORD, six covered wagons, and twelve oxen; a wagon for two of the princes, and for each one an ox: and they brought them before the tabernacle.

4 And the LORD spake unto Moses, saying,

5 Take *it* of them, that they may be [1]to do the service of the tabernacle of the congregation; and thou shalt give them unto the Levites, to every man according to his service.

6 And Moses took the wagons and the oxen, and gave them unto the Levites.

7 Two wagons and four oxen [a]he gave unto the sons of Gershon, according to their service:

8 [a]And four wagons and eight oxen he gave unto the sons of Merari, according unto their service, under the hand of Ithamar the son of Aaron the priest.

9 But unto the sons of Kohath he gave none: because [a]the service of the sanctuary belonging unto them [b]*was that* they should bear upon their shoulders.

10 And the princes offered [1]for [a]dedicating of the altar in the day that it was anointed, even the princes offered their offering before the altar.

11 And the LORD said unto Moses, They shall offer their offering, each prince on his day, for the dedicating of the altar.

12 And he that offered his offering the first day was [a]Nahshon the son of Amminadab, of the tribe of Judah:

13 And his offering *was* one silver charger, the weight thereof *was* an hundred and thirty *shekels,* one silver bowl of seventy shekels, after [a]the shekel of the sanctuary; both of them *were* full of fine flour mingled with oil for a [b]meat offering:

6:12 [a] Lev. 5:6 [1] *void*
6:13 [a] Acts 21:26
6:14 [a] Lev. 4:2, 27, 32 [b] Lev. 3:6
6:15 [a] Lev. 2:4 [b] Ex. 29:2 [c] Num. 15:5, 7, 10
6:18 [a] Num. 6:9; Acts 21:23, 24
6:19 [a] 1 Sam. 2:15 [b] Ex. 29:23, 24 [c] Lev. 7:30 [1] *boiled*
6:20 [a] Ex. 29:27, 28
6:24 [a] Deut. 28:3–6 [b] Ps. 121:7; John 7:11
6:25 [a] Ps. 31:16; 67:1; 80:3, 7, 19; 119:135; Dan. 9:17 [b] Gen. 43:29; Ex. 33:19; Mal. 1:9
6:26 [a] Ps. 4:6; 89:15 [b] Lev. 26:6; Is. 26:3, 12; John 14:27; Phil. 4:7 [1] Look on you with favour
6:27 [a] Deut. 28:10; 2 Sam. 7:23; 2 Chr. 7:14; Is. 43:7; Dan. 9:18, 19 [b] Ex. 20:24; Num. 23:20; Ps. 5:12; 67:7; 115:12, 13; Eph. 1:3 [1] *invoke*
7:1 [a] Ex. 40:17–33 [b] Lev. 8:10, 11
7:2 [a] Num. 1:4 [1] Lit. *who stood*
7:5 [1] *used for*
7:7 [a] Num. 4:24–28
7:8 [a] Num. 4:29–33
7:9 [a] Num. 4:15 [b] Num. 4:6–14
7:10 [a] Num. 7:1; Deut. 20:5; 1 Kin. 8:63; 2 Chr. 7:5, 9; Ezra 6:16; Neh. 12:27 [1] *the dedication offering*
7:12 [a] Num. 2:3
7:13 [a] Ex. 30:13 [b] Lev. 2:1

14 One spoon of ten *shekels* of gold, full of ªincense:

15 ªOne young bullock, one ram, one lamb ᵇof the first year, for a burnt offering:

16 One kid of the goats for a ªsin offering:

17 And for ªa sacrifice of peace offerings, two oxen, five rams, five he goats, five lambs of the first year: this *was* the offering of Nahshon the son of Amminadab.

18 On the second day Nethaneel the son of Zuar, prince of Issachar, did offer:

19 He offered *for* his offering one silver ¹charger, the weight whereof *was* an hundred and thirty *shekels*, one silver bowl of seventy shekels, after the shekel of the sanctuary; both of them full of fine flour mingled with oil for a meat offering:

20 One spoon of gold of ten *shekels*, full of incense:

21 One young bullock, one ram, one lamb of the first year, for a burnt offering:

22 One kid of the goats for a sin offering:

23 And for a sacrifice of peace offerings, two oxen, five rams, five he goats, five lambs of the first year: this *was* the offering of Nethaneel the son of Zuar.

24 On the third day Eliab the son of Helon, prince of the children of Zebulun, *did offer:*

25 His offering *was* one silver charger, the weight whereof *was* an hundred and thirty *shekels*, one silver bowl of seventy shekels, after the shekel of the sanctuary; both of them full of fine flour mingled with oil for a meat offering:

26 One golden spoon of ten *shekels*, full of incense:

27 One young bullock, one ram, one lamb of the first year, for a burnt offering:

28 One kid of the goats for a sin offering:

29 And for a sacrifice of peace offerings, two oxen, five rams, five he goats, five lambs of the first year: this *was* the offering of Eliab the son of Helon.

30 On the fourth day ªElizur the son of Shedeur, prince of the children of Reuben, *did offer:*

31 His offering *was* one silver charger of the weight of an hundred and thirty *shekels*, one silver bowl of seventy shekels, after the shekel of the sanctuary; both of them full of fine flour mingled with oil for a ¹meat offering:

32 One golden spoon of ten *shekels*, full of incense:

33 One young bullock, one ram, one

*cross-references (center column):*

7:14 ª Ex. 30:34
7:15 ª Lev. 1:2
   ᵇ Ex. 12:5
7:16 ª Lev. 4:23
7:17 ª Lev. 3:1
7:19 ¹ *platter*
7:30 ª Num. 1:5;
2:10
7:31 ¹ *grain or meal*

7:36 ª Num. 1:6;
2:12; 7:41
7:37 ¹ *grain or meal*
7:42 ª Num. 1:14;
2:14; 10:20
¹ *Reuel*, Num. 2:14
7:45 ª Ps. 40:6
7:48 ª Num. 1:10;
2:18; 1 Chr. 7:26

lamb of the first year, for a burnt offering:

34 One kid of the goats for a sin offering:

35 And for a sacrifice of peace offerings, two oxen, five rams, five goats, five lambs of the first year: this *was* the offering of Elizur the son of Shedeur.

36 On the fifth day ªShelumiel the son of Zurishaddai, prince of the children of Simeon, *did offer:*

37 His offering *was* one silver charger, the weight whereof *was* an hundred and thirty *shekels,* one silver bowl of seventy shekels, after the shekel of the sanctuary; both of them full of fine flour mingled with oil for a ¹meat offering:

38 One golden spoon of ten *shekels,* full of incense:

39 One young bullock, one ram, one lamb of the first year, for a burnt offering:

40 One kid of the goats for a sin offering:

41 And for a sacrifice of peace offerings, two oxen, five rams, five he goats, five lambs of the first year: this *was* the offering of Shelumiel the son of Zurishaddai.

42 On the sixth day ªEliasaph the son of ¹Deuel, prince of the children of Gad, *offered:*

43 His offering *was* one silver charger of the weight of an hundred and thirty *shekels,* a silver bowl of seventy shekels, after the shekel of the sanctuary; both of them full of fine flour mingled with oil for a meat offering:

44 One golden spoon of ten *shekels,* full of incense:

45 One young bullock, one ram, one lamb of the first year, for ªa burnt offering:

46 One kid of the goats for a sin offering:

47 And for a sacrifice of peace offerings, two oxen, five rams, five he goats, five lambs of the first year: this *was* the offering of Deuel.

48 On the seventh day ªElishama the son of Ammihud, prince of the children of Ephraim, *offered:*

49 His offering *was* one silver charger, the weight whereof *was* an hundred and thirty *shekels,* one silver bowl of seventy shekels, after the shekel of the sanctuary; both of them full of fine flour mingled with oil for a meat offering:

50 One golden spoon of ten *shekels,* full of incense:

51 One young bullock, one ram, one lamb of the first year, for a burnt offering:

52 One kid of the goats for a sin offering:

53 And for a sacrifice of peace of-ferings, two oxen, five rams, five he goats, five lambs of the first year: this *was* the offering of Elishama the son of Ammihud.

54 On the eighth day *offered* [a]Gamaliel the son of Pedahzur, prince of the children of Manasseh:

55 His offering *was* one silver charger of the weight of an hundred and thirty *shekels,* one silver bowl of seventy shekels, after the shekel of the sanctuary; both of them full of fine flour mingled with oil for a meat offering:

56 One golden spoon of ten *shekels,* full of incense:

57 One young bullock, one ram, one lamb of the first year, for a burnt of-fering:

58 One kid of the goats for a sin of-fering:

59 And for a sacrifice of peace of-ferings, two oxen, five rams, five he goats, five lambs of the first year: this *was* the offering of Gamaliel the son of Pedahzur.

60 On the ninth day [a]Abidan the son of Gideoni, prince of the children of Benjamin, *offered:*

61 His offering *was* one silver charger, the weight whereof *was* an hundred and thirty *shekels,* one sil-ver bowl of seventy shekels, after the shekel of the sanctuary; both of them full of fine flour mingled with oil for a meat offering:

62 One golden spoon of ten *shekels,* full of incense:

63 One young bullock, one ram, one lamb of the first year, for a burnt of-fering:

64 One kid of the goats for a sin of-fering:

65 And for a sacrifice of peace of-ferings, two oxen, five rams, five he goats, five lambs of the first year: this *was* the offering of Abidan the son of Gideoni.

66 On the tenth day [a]Ahiezer the son of Ammishaddai, prince of the children of Dan, *offered:*

67 His offering *was* one silver charger, the weight whereof *was* an hundred and thirty *shekels,* one sil-ver bowl of seventy shekels, after the shekel of the sanctuary; both of them full of fine flour mingled with oil for a meat offering:

68 One golden spoon of ten *shekels,* full of incense:

69 One young bullock, one ram, one lamb of the first year, for a burnt of-fering:

70 One kid of the goats for a sin of-fering:

71 And for a sacrifice of peace of-ferings, two oxen, five rams, five he goats, five lambs of the first year: this

*was* the offering of Ahiezer the son of Ammishaddai.

72 On the eleventh day [a]Pagiel the son of Ocran, prince of the children of Asher, *offered:*

73 His offering *was* one silver charger, the weight whereof *was* an hundred and thirty *shekels,* one sil-ver bowl of seventy shekels, after the shekel of the sanctuary; both of them full of fine flour mingled with oil for a meat offering:

74 One golden spoon of ten *shekels,* full of incense:

75 One young bullock, one ram, one lamb of the first year, for a burnt of-fering:

76 One kid of the goats for a sin of-fering:

77 And for a sacrifice of peace of-ferings, two oxen, five rams, five he goats, five lambs of the first year: this *was* the offering of Pagiel the son of Ocran.

78 On the twelfth day [a]Ahira the son of Enan, prince of the children of Naphtali, *offered:*

79 His offering *was* one silver charger, the weight whereof *was* an hundred and thirty *shekels,* one sil-ver bowl of seventy shekels, after the shekel of the sanctuary; both of them full of fine flour mingled with oil for a meat offering:

80 One golden spoon of ten *shekels,* full of incense:

81 One young bullock, one ram, one lamb of the first year, for a burnt of-fering:

82 One kid of the goats for a sin of-fering:

83 And for a sacrifice of peace of-ferings, two oxen, five rams, five he goats, five lambs of the first year: this *was* the offering of Ahira the son of Enan.

84 This *was* [a]the dedication of the altar, in the day when it was anointed, by the princes of Israel: twelve charg-ers of silver, twelve silver bowls, twelve spoons of gold:

85 Each charger of silver *weighing* an hundred and thirty *shekels,* each bowl seventy: all the silver vessels *weighed* two thousand and four hun-dred *shekels,* after the shekel of the sanctuary:

86 The golden spoons *were* twelve, full of incense, *weighing* ten *shekels* apiece, after the shekel of the sanctu-ary: all the gold of the spoons *was* an hundred and twenty *shekels.*

87 All the oxen for the burnt offering *were* twelve bullocks, the rams twelve, the lambs of the first year twelve, with their meat offering: and the kids of the goats for sin offering twelve.

88 And all the oxen for the sacrifice of the peace offerings *were* twenty

7:54 [a] Num. 1:10; 2:20
7:60 [a] Num. 1:11; 2:22
7:66 [a] Num. 1:12; 2:25
7:72 [a] Num. 1:13; 2:27
7:78 [a] Num. 1:15; 2:29
7:84 [a] Num. 7:10

and four bullocks, the rams sixty, the he goats sixty, the lambs of the first year sixty. This *was* the dedication of the altar, after that it was ªanointed.

89 And when Moses was gone into the tabernacle of the congregation ªto speak with ¹him, then he heard ᵇthe voice of one speaking unto him from off the mercy seat that *was* upon the ark of testimony, from ᶜbetween the two cherubims: and he spake unto him.

### CHAPTER 8

A ND the LORD spake unto Moses, saying,

2 Speak unto Aaron, and say unto him, When thou ªlightest the lamps, the seven ᵇlamps shall give light over against the candlestick.

3 And Aaron did so; he lighted the lamps thereof over against the candlestick, as the LORD commanded Moses.

4 ªAnd this work of the candlestick *was of* beaten gold, unto the shaft thereof, unto the flowers thereof, *was* ᵇbeaten work: ᶜaccording unto the pattern which the LORD had shewed Moses, so he made the candlestick.

5 And the LORD spake unto Moses, saying,

6 Take the Levites from among the children of Israel, and cleanse them.

7 And thus shalt thou do unto them, to cleanse them: Sprinkle ªwater of purifying upon them, and ᵇlet them ¹shave all their flesh, and let them wash their clothes, and *so* make themselves clean.

8 Then let them take a young bullock with ªhis ¹meat offering, *even* fine flour mingled with oil, and another young bullock shalt thou take for a sin offering.

9 ªAnd thou shalt bring the Levites before the tabernacle of the congregation: ᵇand thou shalt gather the whole assembly of the children of Israel together:

10 And thou shalt bring the Levites before the LORD: and the children of Israel ªshall ¹put their hands upon the Levites:

11 And Aaron shall ¹offer the Levites before the LORD *for* an ªoffering² of the children of Israel, that they may ³execute the service of the LORD.

12 ªAnd the Levites shall lay their hands upon the heads of the bullocks: and thou shalt offer the one *for* a sin offering, and the other *for* a burnt offering, unto the LORD, to make an atonement for the Levites.

13 And thou shalt set the Levites before Aaron, and before his sons,

7:88 ª Num. 7:1, 10
7:89 ª [Ex. 33:9, 11]; Num. 12:8
ᵇ Ex. 25:21, 22
ᶜ Ps. 80:1; 99:1
¹ God

8:2 ª Lev. 24:2–4
ᵇ Ex. 25:37; 40:25
8:4 ª Ex. 25:31
ᵇ Ex. 25:18  ᶜ Ex. 25:40; Acts 7:44
8:7 ª Num. 19:9, 13, 17, 20; Ps. 51:2, 7; [Heb. 9:13, 14]
ᵇ Lev. 14:8, 9  ¹ Lit. *cause a razor to pass over*
8:8 ª Lev. 2:1; Num. 15:8–10
¹ *grain* or *meal*
8:9 ª Ex. 29:4; 40:12  ᵇ Lev. 8:3
8:10 ª Lev. 1:4
¹ *lay*
8:11 ª Num. 18:6  ¹ *present*
² *wave offering*
³ *perform*
8:12 ª Ex. 29:10

8:14 ª Num. 16:9
ᵇ Num. 3:12, 45; 16:9
8:15 ª Num. 8:11, 13
8:16 ª Num. 3:9
ᵇ Ex. 13:2; Num. 3:12, 45
8:17 ª Ex. 12:2, 12, 13, 15; Num. 3:13; Luke 2:23  ¹ *set them apart*
8:18 ¹ *instead of*
8:19 ª Num. 3:9
ᵇ Num. 1:53; 16:46; 18:5; 2 Chr. 26:16
8:21 ª Num. 8:7  ¹ *purified themselves*
8:22 ª Num. 8:15
ᵇ Num. 8:5
8:24 ª Num. 4:3; 1 Chr. 23:3, 24, 27
¹ *enter to perform service in the work*
8:25 ¹ *stop performing this work*
8:26 ª Num. 1:53
¹ *regarding their duties*

and offer them *for* an offering unto the LORD.

14 Thus shalt thou ªseparate the Levites from among the children of Israel: and the Levites shall be ᵇmine.

15 And after that shall the Levites go in to do the service of the tabernacle of the congregation: and thou shalt cleanse them, and ªoffer them *for* an offering.

16 For they *are* ªwholly given unto me from among the children of Israel; ᵇinstead of such as open every womb, *even instead of* the firstborn of all the children of Israel, have I taken them unto me.

17 ªFor all the firstborn of the children of Israel *are* mine, *both* man and beast: on the day that I smote every firstborn in the land of Egypt I ¹sanctified them for myself.

18 And I have taken the Levites ¹for all the firstborn of the children of Israel.

19 And ªI have given the Levites *as* a gift to Aaron and to his sons from among the children of Israel, to do the service of the children of Israel in the tabernacle of the congregation, and to make an atonement for the children of Israel: ᵇthat there be no plague among the children of Israel, when the children of Israel come nigh unto the sanctuary.

20 And Moses, and Aaron, and all the congregation of the children of Israel, did to the Levites according unto all that the LORD commanded Moses concerning the Levites, so did the children of Israel unto them.

21 ªAnd the Levites ¹were purified, and they washed their clothes; and Aaron offered them *as* an offering before the LORD; and Aaron made an atonement for them to cleanse them.

22 ªAnd after that went the Levites in to do their service in the tabernacle of the congregation before Aaron, and before his sons: ᵇas the LORD had commanded Moses concerning the Levites, so did they unto them.

23 And the LORD spake unto Moses, saying,

24 This *is it* that *belongeth* unto the Levites: ªfrom twenty and five years old and upward they shall ¹go in to wait upon the service of the tabernacle of the congregation:

25 And from the age of fifty years they shall ¹cease waiting upon the service *thereof,* and shall serve no more:

26 But shall minister with their brethren in the tabernacle of the congregation, ªto keep the charge, and shall do no service. Thus shalt thou do unto the Levites ¹touching their charge.

## CHAPTER 9

AND the LORD spake unto Moses in the wilderness of Sinai, in the first month of the second year after they were come out of the land of Egypt, saying,

2 Let the children of Israel also keep ªthe passover at his appointed ᵇseason.

3 In the fourteenth day of this month, ¹at even, ye shall keep it ²in his appointed season: according to all the ³rites of it, and according to all the ceremonies thereof, shall ye keep it.

4 And Moses spake unto the children of Israel, that they should keep the passover.

5 And ªthey kept the passover on the fourteenth day of the first month at even in the wilderness of Sinai: according to all that the LORD commanded Moses, so did the children of Israel.

6 And there were certain men, who were ªdefiled by the dead body of a man, that they could not keep the passover on that day: ᵇand they came before Moses and before Aaron on that day:

7 And those men said unto him, We *are* defiled by the dead body of a man: wherefore are we ¹kept back, that we may not offer an offering of the LORD in his appointed season among the children of Israel?

8 And Moses said unto them, Stand still, and ªI will hear what the LORD will command concerning you.

9 And the LORD spake unto Moses, saying,

10 Speak unto the children of Israel, saying, If any man of you or of your ¹posterity shall be unclean by reason of a dead body, or *be* in a journey afar off, yet he shall keep the passover unto the LORD.

11 ªThe fourteenth day of the second month at even they shall keep it, *and* ᵇeat it with unleavened bread and bitter *herbs*.

12 ªThey shall leave none of it unto the morning, ᵇnor break any bone of it: ᶜaccording to all the ¹ordinances of the passover they shall keep it.

13 But the man that *is* clean, and is not in a journey, and forbeareth to keep the passover, even the same soul ªshall be cut off from among his people: because he ᵇbrought not the offering of the LORD ¹in his appointed season, that man shall ᶜbear his sin.

14 And if a stranger shall ¹sojourn among you, and will keep the passover unto the LORD; according to the ordinance of the passover, and according to the manner thereof, so shall he do: ªye shall have one ²ordinance, both for the stranger, and for him that was born in the land.

9:2 ª Ex. 12:1–16; Lev. 23:5; Num. 28:16; Deut. 16:1, 2
ᵇ 2 Chr. 30:1–15; Luke 22:7; [1 Cor. 5:7, 8]
9:3 ¹ *at twilight* ² *at its appointed time* ³ *statutes*
9:5 ª Josh. 5:10
9:6 ª Num. 5:2; 19:11–22; John 18:28 ᵇ Ex. 18:15, 19, 26; Num. 27:2
9:7 ¹ *kept from presenting the offering*
9:8 ª Ex. 18:22; Num. 27:5
9:10 ¹ *descendants*
9:11 ª 2 Chr. 30:2, 15 ᵇ Ex. 12:8
9:12 ª Ex. 12:10 ᵇ Ex. 12:46; [John 19:36] ᶜ Ex. 12:43 ¹ *statutes*
9:13 ª Gen. 17:14; Ex. 12:15, 47 ᵇ Num. 9:7 ᶜ Num. 5:31 ¹ *at its appointed time*
9:14 ª Ex. 12:49; Lev. 24:22; Num. 15:15, 16, 29 ¹ *stay for a while* ² *statute*

15 And ªon the day that the tabernacle was reared up the cloud ᵇcovered the tabernacle, *namely,* the tent of the testimony: and ᶜat even there was upon the tabernacle as it were the appearance of fire, until the morning.

16 So it was alway: the cloud covered it *by day,* and the appearance of fire by night.

17 And when the cloud ªwas ¹taken up from the tabernacle, then after that the children of Israel journeyed: and in the place where the cloud abode, there the children of Israel pitched their tents.

18 At the ¹commandment of the LORD the children of Israel journeyed, and at the commandment of the LORD they ²pitched: ªas long as the cloud abode upon the tabernacle they rested in their tents.

19 And when the cloud ¹tarried long upon the tabernacle many days, then the children of Israel ªkept the charge of the LORD, and journeyed not.

20 And *so* it was, when the cloud was a few days upon the tabernacle; according to the commandment of the LORD they abode in their tents, and according to the commandment of the LORD they journeyed.

21 And *so* it was, when the cloud abode from even unto the morning, and *that* the cloud was taken up in the morning, then they journeyed: whether *it was* by day or by night that the cloud was taken up, they journeyed.

22 Or *whether it were* two days, or a month, or a year, that the cloud tarried upon the tabernacle, remaining thereon, the children of Israel ªabode¹ in their tents, and journeyed not: but when it was taken up, they journeyed.

23 At the commandment of the LORD they rested in the tents, and at the commandment of the LORD they journeyed: they ªkept the charge of the LORD, at the commandment of the LORD by the hand of Moses.

## CHAPTER 10

AND the LORD spake unto Moses, saying,

2 Make thee two trumpets of silver; of a whole piece shalt thou make them: that thou mayest use them for the ªcalling of the assembly, and for the journeying of the camps.

3 And when ªthey shall blow with them, all the assembly shall assemble themselves to thee at the door of the tabernacle of the congregation.

4 And if they blow *but* with one *trumpet,* then the princes, *which are* ªheads of the thousands of Israel, shall gather themselves unto thee.

9:15 ª Ex. 40:33, 34; Neh. 9:12, 19; Ps. 78:14 ᵇ Is. 4:5 ᶜ Ex. 13:21, 22; 40:38
9:17 ª Ex. 40:36–38; Num. 10:11, 12, 33, 34; Ps. 80:1 ¹ *lifted up*
9:18 ª 1 Cor. 10:1 ¹ Lit. *mouth of* ² *encamped*
9:19 ª Num. 1:53; 3:8 ¹ *continued*
9:22 ª Ex. 40:36, 37 ¹ *remained encamped*
9:23 ª Num. 9:19
10:2 ª Is. 1:13
10:3 ª Jer. 4:5; Joel 2:15
10:4 ª Ex. 18:21; Num. 1:16; 7:2

5 When ye blow an ªalarm, then ᵇthe camps that lie on the east parts shall go forward.

6 When ye blow an alarm the second time, then the camps that lie ªon the south side shall ¹take their journey: they shall blow an alarm for their journeys.

7 But when the congregation is to be gathered together, ªye shall blow, but ye shall not ᵇsound an alarm.

8 ªAnd the sons of Aaron, the priests, shall blow with the trumpets; and they shall be to you for an ¹ordinance for ever throughout your generations.

9 And ªif ye go to war in your land against the enemy that ᵇoppresseth you, then ye shall blow an alarm with the trumpets; and ye shall be ᶜremembered before the LORD your God, and ye shall be saved from your enemies.

10 Also ªin the day of your gladness, and in your ¹solemn days, and in the beginnings of your months, ye shall blow with the trumpets over your burnt offerings, and over the sacrifices of your peace offerings; that they may be to you ᵇfor a memorial before your God: I *am* the LORD your God.

11 And it came to pass on the twentieth *day* of the second month, in the second year, that the cloud ªwas taken up from off the tabernacle of the testimony.

12 And the children of Israel took ªtheir journeys out of the ᵇwilderness of Sinai; and the cloud rested in the ᶜwilderness of Paran.

13 And they first took their journey ªaccording to the commandment of the LORD by the hand of Moses.

14 ªIn the first *place* went the ¹standard of the camp of the children of Judah according to their armies: and over his host *was* ᵇNahshon the son of Amminadab.

15 And over the host of the tribe of the children of Issachar *was* Nethaneel the son of Zuar.

16 And over the host of the tribe of the children of Zebulun *was* Eliab the son of Helon.

17 And ªthe tabernacle was taken down; and the sons of Gershon and the sons of Merari set forward, ᵇbearing¹ the tabernacle.

18 And ªthe standard of the camp of Reuben ¹set forward according to their ²armies: and over his host *was* Elizur the son of Shedeur.

19 And over the host of the tribe of the children of Simeon *was* Shelumiel the son of Zurishaddai.

20 And over the host of the tribe of the children of Gad *was* Eliasaph the son of Deuel.

21 And the Kohathites set forward, bearing the ªsanctuary: and ¹the other

did set up the tabernacle ²against they came.

22 And ªthe standard of the camp of the children of Ephraim set forward according to their armies: and over his host *was* Elishama the son of Ammihud.

23 And over the host of the tribe of the children of Manasseh *was* Gamaliel the son of Pedahzur.

24 And over the host of the tribe of the children of Benjamin *was* Abidan the son of Gideoni.

25 And ªthe standard of the camp of the children of Dan set forward, *which* ¹*was* the rereward of all the camps throughout their hosts: and over his host *was* Ahiezer the son of Ammishaddai.

26 And over the host of the tribe of the children of Asher *was* Pagiel the son of Ocran.

27 And over the host of the tribe of the children of Naphtali *was* Ahira the son of Enan.

28 ªThus ¹*were* the journeyings of the children of Israel according to their armies, when they set forward.

29 And Moses said unto ªHobab, the son of ᵇRaguel¹ the Midianite, Moses' father in law, We are journeying unto the place of which the LORD said, ᶜI will give it you: come thou with us, and ᵈwe will do thee good: for ᶜthe LORD hath ²spoken good concerning Israel.

30 And he said unto him, I will not go; but I will depart to mine own land, and to my kindred.

31 And ¹he said, Leave us not, I pray thee; forasmuch as thou knowest how we are to encamp in the wilderness, and thou ²mayest be to us ªinstead of eyes.

32 And it shall be, if thou go with us, yea, it shall be, that ªwhat goodness the LORD shall do unto us, the same will we do unto thee.

33 And they departed from ªthe mount of the LORD three days' journey: and the ark of the covenant of the LORD ᵇwent before them in the three days' journey, to search out a resting place for them.

34 And ªthe cloud of the LORD *was* upon them by day, when they went out of the camp.

35 And it came to pass, when the ark set forward, that Moses said, ªRise up, LORD, and let thine enemies be scattered; and let them that hate thee flee before thee.

36 And when it rested, he said, Return, O LORD, unto the many thousands of Israel.

## CHAPTER 11

AND ªwhen the people complained, it displeased the LORD: and the

### Cross references (center column)

10:5 ª Joel 2:1 ᵇ Num. 2:3
10:6 ª Num. 2:10 ¹ *begin*
10:7 ª Num. 10:3 ᵇ Joel 2:1
10:8 ª Num. 31:6; Josh. 6:4; 1 Chr. 15:24; 2 Chr. 13:12 ¹ *statute*
10:9 ª Num. 31:6; Josh. 6:5; 2 Chr. 13:14 ᵇ Judg. 2:18; 4:3; 6:9; 10:8, 12 ᶜ Gen. 8:1; Ps. 106:4
10:10 ª Lev. 23:24; Num. 29:1; 1 Chr. 15:24; 2 Chr. 5:12; Ps. 81:3 ᵇ Lev. 23:24; Num. 10:9 ¹ Lit. *appointed*
10:11 ª Num. 9:17
10:12 ª Ex. 19:1; Num. 1:1; 9:5 ᵇ Ex. 40:36 ᶜ Gen. 21:21; Num. 12:16; Deut. 1:1
10:13 ª Num. 10:5, 6
10:14 ª Num. 2:3–9 ᵇ Num. 1:7 ¹ *banner*
10:17 ª Num. 1:51 ᵇ Num. 4:21–32; 7:7–9 ¹ *carrying*
10:18 ª Num. 2:10–16 ¹ *set out* ² *army*
10:21 ª Num. 4:4–20; 7:9 ¹ The Gershonites and the Merarites ² *for their arrival*
10:22 ª Num. 2:18–24
10:25 ª Num. 2:25–31; Josh. 6:9 ¹ *formed the rear guard*
10:28 ª Num. 2:34 ¹ *was the order of march*
10:29 ª Judg. 4:11 ᵇ Ex. 2:18; 3:1; 18:12 ᶜ Gen. 12:7; Ex. 6:4–8 ᵈ Judg. 1:16 ᵉ Gen. 32:12; Ex. 3:8 ¹ Heb. *Reuel*; Ex. 2:18 ² *promised good things*
10:31 ª Job 29:15 ¹ Moses ² *can be our eyes* (act as our guide)
10:32 ª Ex. 18:9; Lev. 19:34; Judg. 1:16
10:33 ª Ex. 3:1; Deut. 1:6 ᵇ Deut. 1:33; Josh. 3:3–6; Ezek. 20:6
10:34 ª Ex. 13:21; Neh. 9:12, 19
10:35 ª Ps. 68:1, 2; 132:8; Is. 17:12–14
11:1 ª Num. 14:2; 16:11; 17:5; Deut. 9:22

LORD heard *it;* ᵇand his anger was ¹kindled; and the ᶜfire of the LORD burnt among them, and consumed *them that were* in the ²uttermost parts of the camp.

2 And the people ᵃcried unto Moses; and when Moses ᵇprayed unto the LORD, the fire was ¹quenched.

3 And he called the name of the place ¹Taberah: because the fire of the LORD burnt among them.

4 And the ᵃmixt multitude that *was* among them ¹fell a ᵇlusting: and the children of Israel also wept again, and said, ᶜWho shall give us flesh to eat?

5 ᵃWe remember the fish, which we did eat in Egypt freely; the cucumbers, and the melons, and the leeks, and the onions, and the garlick:

6 But now ᵃour ¹soul *is* dried away: *there is* nothing at all, beside this manna, *before* our eyes.

7 And ᵃthe manna *was* as coriander seed, and the colour thereof as the colour of bdellium.

8 *And* the people went about, and gathered *it,* and ground *it* in mills, or beat *it* in a mortar, and baked *it* in pans, and made cakes of it: and ᵃthe taste of it was as the taste of fresh oil.

9 And ᵃwhen the dew fell upon the camp in the night, the manna fell upon it.

10 Then Moses heard the people weep throughout their families, every man in the door of his tent: and ᵃthe anger of the LORD was ¹kindled greatly; Moses also was displeased.

11 ᵃAnd Moses said unto the LORD, Wherefore hast thou afflicted thy servant? and wherefore have I not found favour in thy sight, that thou layest the ¹burden of all this people upon me?

12 Have I conceived all this people? have I begotten them, that thou shouldest say unto me, ᵃCarry them in thy bosom, as a ᵇnursing father beareth the sucking child, unto the land which thou ᶜswarest¹ unto their fathers?

13 ᵃWhence should I have ¹flesh to give unto all this people? for they weep unto me, saying, Give us flesh, that we may eat.

14 ᵃI am not able to bear all this people alone, because *it is* too heavy for me.

15 And if thou ¹deal thus with me, kill me, I pray thee, ²out of hand, if I have found favour in thy sight; and let me not ᵃsee my wretchedness.

16 And the LORD said unto Moses, Gather unto me ᵃseventy men of the elders of Israel, whom thou knowest to be the elders of the people, and ᵇofficers over them; and bring them unto the tabernacle of the congregation, that they may stand there with thee.

17 And I will come down and talk with thee there: and ᵃI will take of

the spirit which *is* upon thee, and will put it upon them; and they shall bear the burden of the people with thee, that thou bear *it* not thyself alone.

18 And say thou unto the people, ¹Sanctify yourselves against to morrow, and ye shall eat ²flesh: for ye have wept ᵃin the ears of the LORD, saying, Who shall give us flesh to eat? for *it was* well with us in Egypt: therefore the LORD will give you flesh, and ye shall eat.

19 Ye shall not eat one day, nor two days, nor five days, neither ten days, nor twenty days;

20 ᵃ*But* even a whole month, until it come out at your nostrils, and it be loathsome unto you: because that ye have ᵇdespised the LORD which *is* among you, and have wept before him, saying, ᶜWhy came we forth out of Egypt?

21 And Moses said, ᵃThe people, among whom I *am, are* six hundred thousand footmen; and thou hast said, I will give them flesh, that they may eat a whole month.

22 ᵃShall the flocks and the herds be slain for them, to ¹suffice them? or shall all the fish of the sea be gathered together for them, to suffice them?

23 And the LORD said unto Moses, ᵃIs¹ the LORD's hand waxed short? thou shalt see now whether my ᵇword shall come to pass unto thee or not.

24 And Moses went out, and told the people the words of the LORD, and ᵃgathered the seventy men of the elders of the people, and set them round about the tabernacle.

25 And the LORD came down in a cloud, and spake unto him, and took of the spirit that *was* upon him, and gave *it* unto the seventy elders: and it came to pass, *that,* ᵃwhen the spirit rested upon them, ᵇthey prophesied, and did not ¹cease.

26 But there remained two *of the* men in the camp, the name of the one *was* Eldad, and the name of the other Medad: and the spirit rested upon them; and they *were* of them that were written, but ᵃwent not out unto the tabernacle: and they prophesied in the camp.

27 And there ran a young man, and told Moses, and said, Eldad and Medad do prophesy in the camp.

28 And Joshua the son of Nun, the servant of Moses, *one* of his young men, answered and said, My lord Moses, ᵃforbid them.

29 And Moses said unto him, ¹Enviest thou for my sake? ᵃwould God that all the LORD's people were prophets, *and* that the LORD would put his spirit upon them!

30 And Moses gat him into the camp, he and the elders of Israel.

---

**Center column references:**

11:1 ᵇ Ps. 78:21
ᶜ Lev. 10:2; 2 Kin. 1:12 ¹ *aroused*
² *outskirts*

11:2 ᵃ Num. 12:11, 13; 21:7 ᵇ [James 5:16] ¹ *extinguished*

11:3 ¹ Lit. *Burning*

11:4 ᵃ Ex. 12:38
ᵇ 1 Cor. 10:6 ᶜ [Ps. 78:18] ¹ *yielded to intense craving*

11:5 ᵃ Ex. 16:3

11:6 ᵃ Num. 21:5 ¹ *whole being is dried up*

11:7 ᵃ Ex. 16:14, 31

11:8 ᵃ Ex. 16:31

11:9 ᵃ Ex. 16:13, 14

11:10 ᵃ Ps. 78:21 ¹ *aroused*

11:11 ᵃ Ex. 5:22; Deut. 1:12 ¹ *responsibility*

11:12 ᵃ Is. 40:11 ᵇ Is. 49:23; 1 Thess. 2:7 ᶜ Gen. 26:3 ¹ *solemnly promised*

11:13 ᵃ Matt. 15:33; Mark 8:4 ¹ *meat*

11:14 ᵃ Ex. 18:18; Deut. 1:12

11:15 ᵃ Rev. 3:17 ¹ *treat me like this, please kill me* ² *at once*

11:16 ᵃ Ex. 18:25; 24:1, 9 ᵇ Deut. 16:18

11:17 ᵃ 1 Sam. 10:6; 2 Kin. 2:15; [Joel 2:28]

11:18 ᵃ Ex. 16:7 ¹ *Set yourselves apart* ² *meat*

11:20 ᵃ Ps. 78:29; 106:15 ᵇ 1 Sam. 10:19 ᶜ Num. 21:5

11:21 ᵃ Gen. 12:2; Ex. 12:37; Num. 1:46; 2:32

11:22 ᵃ 2 Kin. 7:2 ¹ *provide enough*

11:23 ᵃ Is. 50:2; 59:1 ᵇ Num. 23:19 ¹ *Is the LORD's power limited?*

11:24 ᵃ Num. 11:16

11:25 ᵃ 2 Kin. 2:15 ᵇ 1 Sam. 10:5, 6, 10; Joel 2:28; Acts 2:17, 18; 1 Cor. 14:1 ¹ *do it again*

11:26 ᵃ Jer. 36:5

11:28 ᵃ [Mark 9:38–40; Luke 9:49]

11:29 ᵃ 1 Cor. 14:5 ¹ *Are you jealous for*

31 And there went forth a ªwind from the LORD, and brought quails from the sea, and let *them* fall by the camp, as it were a day's journey on this side, and as it were a day's journey on the other side, round about the camp, and as it were two cubits *high* upon the face of the earth.

32 And the people stood up all that day, and all *that* night, and all the next day, and they gathered the quails: he that gathered least gathered ten ªhomers: and they spread *them* all abroad for themselves round about the camp.

33 And while the ªflesh[1] *was* yet between their teeth, ere it was chewed, ²the wrath of the LORD was kindled against the people, and the LORD ³smote the people with a very great plague.

34 And he called the name of that place ¹Kibroth-hattaavah: because there they buried the people that ²lusted.

35 ªAnd the people journeyed from Kibroth-hattaavah unto Hazeroth; and abode at Hazeroth.

## CHAPTER 12

AND ªMiriam and Aaron ¹spake ᵇagainst Moses because of the ²Ethiopian woman whom he had married: for ᶜhe had married an Ethiopian woman.

2 And they said, Hath the LORD indeed spoken only by ªMoses? ᵇhath he not spoken also by us? And the LORD ᶜheard *it.*

3 (Now the man Moses *was* very meek, above all the men which *were* upon the face of the earth.)

4 ªAnd the LORD spake suddenly unto Moses, and unto Aaron, and unto Miriam, Come out ye three unto the tabernacle of the congregation. And they three came out.

5 ªAnd the LORD came down in the pillar of the cloud, and stood *in* the door of the tabernacle, and called Aaron and Miriam: and they both came forth.

6 And he said, Hear now my words: If there be a prophet among you, *I* the LORD will make myself known unto him ªin a vision, *and* will speak unto him ᵇin a dream.

7 ªMy servant Moses *is* not so, ᵇwho *is* faithful in all ᶜmine house.

8 With him will I speak ªmouth to mouth, even ᵇapparently,¹ and not in ²dark speeches; and ᶜthe similitude of the LORD shall he behold: wherefore then ᵈwere ye not afraid to speak against my servant Moses?

9 And the anger of the LORD was kindled against them; and he departed.

10 And the cloud departed from off

11:31 ª Ex. 16:13;
Ps. 78:26–28;
105:40

11:32 ª Ex. 16:36;
Ezek. 45:11

11:33 ª Ps. 78:29–
31; 106:15 ¹ *meat*
² *the anger of
the LORD was
aroused* ³ *struck*

11:34 ¹ Lit. *Graves
of Craving*
² *yielded to
craving*

11:35 ª Num. 33:17

12:1 ª Num. 20:1
ᵇ Num. 11:1 ᶜ Ex.
2:21 ¹ *criticized*
² *Cushite*

12:2 ª Num. 16:3
ᵇ Mic. 6:4 ᶜ Ezek.
35:12, 13

12:4 ª [Ps. 76:9]

12:5 ª Ex. 19:9;
34:5

12:6 ª Gen. 46:2
ᵇ Gen. 31:10

12:7 ª Josh. 1:1
ᵇ Heb. 3:2, 5
ᶜ 1 Tim. 1:12

12:8 ª Deut.
34:10 ᵇ [1 Cor.
13:12] ᶜ Ex.
33:19–23 ᵈ 2 Pet.
2:10 ¹ *plainly or
appearing* ² *dark
sayings or riddles*

12:10 ª Deut. 24:9
ᵇ 2 Kin. 5:27; 15:5

12:11 ª 2 Sam.
19:19; 24:10 ¹ *lay
the penalty for
this*

12:12 ª Ps. 88:4

12:13 ª Ps. 103:3

12:14 ª Deut.
25:9 ᵇ Lev. 13:46
¹ *exiled*

12:15 ª Deut. 24:9

12:16 ª Num.
11:35; 33:17, 18

13:2 ª Deut. 1:22;
9:23 ¹ *spy out*

13:3 ª Num. 12:16;
32:8

13:6 ª Num. 34:19
ᵇ Josh. 14:6, 7

13:8 ¹ Heb.
*Hoshea*

the tabernacle; and, ªbehold, Miriam *became* ᵇleprous, *white* as snow: and Aaron looked upon Miriam, and, behold, *she was* leprous.

11 And Aaron said unto Moses, Alas, my lord, I beseech thee, ªlay¹ not the sin upon us, wherein we have done foolishly, and wherein we have sinned.

12 Let her not be ªas one dead, of whom the flesh is half consumed when he cometh out of his mother's womb.

13 And Moses cried unto the LORD, saying, ªHeal her now, O God, I beseech thee.

14 And the LORD said unto Moses, If her father had but ªspit in her face, should she not be ashamed seven days? let her be ᵇshut¹ out from the camp seven days, and after that let her be received in *again.*

15 ªAnd Miriam was shut out from the camp seven days: and the people journeyed not till Miriam was brought in *again.*

16 And afterward the people removed from ªHazeroth, and pitched in the wilderness of Paran.

## CHAPTER 13

AND the LORD spake unto Moses, saying,

2 ªSend thou men, that they may ¹search the land of Canaan, which I give unto the children of Israel: of every tribe of their fathers shall ye send a man, every one a ruler among them.

3 And Moses by the commandment of the LORD sent them ªfrom the wilderness of Paran: all those men *were* heads of the children of Israel.

4 And these *were* their names: of the tribe of Reuben, Shammua the son of Zaccur.

5 Of the tribe of Simeon, Shaphat the son of Hori.

6 ªOf the tribe of Judah, ᵇCaleb the son of Jephunneh.

7 Of the tribe of Issachar, Igal the son of Joseph.

8 Of the tribe of Ephraim, ¹Oshea the son of Nun.

9 Of the tribe of Benjamin, Palti the son of Raphu.

10 Of the tribe of Zebulun, Gaddiel the son of Sodi.

11 Of the tribe of Joseph, *namely,* of the tribe of Manasseh, Gaddi the son of Susi.

12 Of the tribe of Dan, Ammiel the son of Gemalli.

13 Of the tribe of Asher, Sethur the son of Michael.

14 Of the tribe of Naphtali, Nahbi the son of Vophsi.

15 Of the tribe of Gad, Geuel the son of Machi.

16 These *are* the names of the men which Moses sent to [1]spy out the land. And Moses called [a]Oshea[2] the son of Nun Jehoshua.

17 And Moses sent them to spy out the land of Canaan, and said unto them, Get you up this *way* southward, and go up into [a]the mountain:

18 And see [1]the land, what it *is;* and the people that dwelleth therein, whether they *be* strong or weak, few or many;

19 And what the land *is* that they dwell in, whether it *be* good or bad; and what cities *they be* that they dwell in, whether in tents, or in strong holds;

20 And what the land *is,* whether it *be* [1]fat or lean, whether there be wood therein, or not. And [a]be ye of good courage, and bring of the fruit of the land. Now the time *was* the time of the firstripe grapes.

21 So they went up, and searched the land [a]from the wilderness of Zin unto [b]Rehob, as men come to [c]Hamath.

22 And they ascended by the south, and came unto [a]Hebron; where Ahiman, Sheshai, and Talmai, the children of [b]Anak, *were*. (Now Hebron was built seven years before Zoan in Egypt.)

23 [a]And they came unto the [1]brook of Eshcol, and cut down from thence a branch with one cluster of grapes, and they bare it between two upon a staff; and *they brought* of the pomegranates, and of the figs.

24 The place was called the brook [1]Eshcol, because of the cluster of grapes which the children of Israel cut down from thence.

25 And they returned from searching of the land after forty days.

26 And they went and came to Moses, and to Aaron, and to all the congregation of the children of Israel, unto the wilderness of Paran, to [a]Kadesh; and brought back word unto them, and unto all the congregation, and shewed them the fruit of the land.

27 And they told him, and said, We came unto the land whither thou sentest us, and [1]surely [2]it floweth with [a]milk and honey; [b]and this *is* the fruit of it.

28 Nevertheless the [a]people *be* strong that dwell in the land, and the cities *are* walled, *and* very great: and moreover we saw the children of [b]Anak there.

29 [a]The Amalekites dwell in the land of the south: and the Hittites, and the Jebusites, and the Amorites, dwell in the mountains: and the Canaanites dwell by the sea, and by the coast of Jordan.

30 And [a]Caleb stilled the people before Moses, and said, Let us go up at once, and [1]possess it; for we are well able to overcome it.

31 [a]But the men that went up with him said, We be not able to go up against the people; for they *are* stronger than we.

32 And they [a]brought up an [1]evil report of the land which they had searched unto the children of Israel, saying, The land, through which we have gone to search it, *is* a land that [2]eateth up the inhabitants thereof; and [b]all the people that we saw in it *are* men of a great stature.

33 And there we saw the [a]giants,[1] the sons of Anak, *which come* of the giants: and we were in our own sight [b]as [2]grasshoppers, and so we were [c]in their sight.

## CHAPTER 14

AND all the congregation lifted up their voice, and cried; and the people [a]wept that night.

2 [a]And all the children of Israel [1]murmured against Moses and against Aaron: and the whole congregation said unto them, Would God that we had died in the land of Egypt! or would God we had died in this wilderness!

3 And wherefore hath the LORD brought us unto this land, to [1]fall by the sword, that our wives and our [a]children should be a prey? were it not better for us to return into Egypt?

4 And they said one to another, [a]Let us make a captain, and [b]let us return into Egypt.

5 Then Moses and Aaron [1]fell on their faces before all the assembly of the congregation of the children of Israel.

6 And Joshua the son of Nun, and Caleb the son of Jephunneh, *which were* of them that searched the land, [1]rent their clothes:

7 And they spake unto all the company of the children of Israel, saying, [a]The land, which we passed through to search it, *is* an exceeding good land.

8 If the LORD [a]delight in us, then he will bring us into this land, and give it us; [b]a land which floweth with milk and honey.

9 Only [a]rebel not ye against the LORD, [b]neither fear ye the people of the land; for [c]they *are* [1]bread for us: their [2]defence is departed from them, [d]and the LORD *is* with us: fear them not.

10 [a]But all the congregation bade stone them with stones. And [b]the glory of the LORD appeared in the tabernacle of the congregation before all the children of Israel.

---

**Center column references:**

13:16 [a] Ex. 17:9
[1] *secretly search*
[2] Heb. *Hoshea*
13:17 [a] Judg. 1:9
13:18 [1] *what the land is like*
13:20 [a] Deut. 31:6, 7, 23 [1] *fertile or barren*
13:21 [a] Num. 20:1; 27:14; 33:36 [b] Josh. 19:28 [c] Josh. 13:5
13:22 [a] Josh. 15:13, 14 [b] Josh. 11:21, 22
13:23 [a] Deut. 1:24, 25 [1] *valley or wadi*
13:24 [1] Lit. *Cluster*
13:26 [a] Deut. 1:19
13:27 [a] Ex. 3:8, 17; 13:5; 33:3 [b] Deut. 1:25 [1] *truly* [2] *it has an abundance of food*
13:28 [a] Deut. 1:28; 9:1, 2 [b] Josh. 11:21, 22
13:29 [a] Judg. 6:3
13:30 [a] Num. 14:6, 24 [1] *take possession of*
13:31 [a] Deut. 1:28; 9:1–3
13:32 [a] Num. 14:36, 37 [b] Amos 2:9 [1] *bad* [2] *devours*
13:33 [a] Deut. 1:28; 9:2 [b] Is. 40:22 [c] 1 Sam. 17:42 [1] Heb. *nephilim* [2] *Mere insects*
14:1 [a] Deut. 1:45
14:2 [a] Ex. 16:2; 17:3 [1] *grumbled*
14:3 [a] Deut. 1:39 [1] *be killed in battle*
14:4 [a] Neh. 9:17 [b] Acts 7:39
14:5 [1] *prostrated themselves*
14:6 [1] *tore*
14:7 [a] Num. 13:27
14:8 [a] Deut. 10:15 [b] Num. 13:27
14:9 [a] Deut. 1:26; 9:7, 23, 24 [b] Deut. 7:18 [c] Num. 24:8 [d] Deut. 20:1, 3, 4; 31:6–8 [1] *food for our consumption* [2] *protection*
14:10 [a] Ex. 17:4 [b] Ex. 16:10

---

11 And the LORD said unto Moses, How long will this people [a]provoke[1] me? and how long will it be ere they [b]believe me, for all the [2]signs which I have shewed among them?

12 I will smite them with the pestilence, and disinherit them, and will [a]make of thee a greater nation and mightier than they.

13 And [a]Moses said unto the LORD, [b]Then the Egyptians shall hear *it,* (for thou broughtest up this people in thy might from among them;)

14 And they will tell *it* to the inhabitants of this land: *for* they have [a]heard that thou LORD *art* among this people, that thou LORD art seen face to face, and *that* thy cloud standeth over them, and *that* thou goest before them, by day time in a pillar of a cloud, and in a pillar of fire by night.

15 Now *if* thou shalt kill *all* this people as one man, then the nations which have heard the fame of thee will speak, saying,

16 Because the LORD was not [a]able to bring this people into the land which he sware unto them, therefore he hath slain them in the wilderness.

17 And now, I beseech thee, let the power of my Lord be great, according as thou hast spoken, saying,

18 The LORD *is* [a]longsuffering, and of great mercy, forgiving iniquity and transgression, and by no means clearing *the guilty,* [b]visiting the iniquity of the fathers upon the children unto the third and fourth *generation.*

19 [a]Pardon, I beseech thee, the iniquity of this people [b]according unto the greatness of thy mercy, and [c]as thou hast forgiven this people, from Egypt even until now.

20 And the LORD said, I have pardoned [a]according to thy word:

21 But *as* truly *as* I live, [a]all the earth shall be filled with the glory of the LORD.

22 [a]Because all those men which have seen my glory, and my miracles, which I did in Egypt and in the wilderness, and have [1]tempted me now [b]these ten times, and have not hearkened to my voice;

23 Surely they shall not [a]see the land which I [1]sware unto their fathers, neither shall any of them that provoked me see it:

24 But my servant [a]Caleb, because he had another spirit with him, and [b]hath followed me fully, him will I bring into the land whereinto he went; and his seed shall possess it.

25 (Now the Amalekites and the Canaanites dwelt in the valley.) To morrow turn you, and [a]get you into the wilderness by the way of the Red sea.

26 And the LORD spake unto Moses and unto Aaron, saying,

27 [a]How long *shall I bear with* this evil congregation, which [1]murmur against me? [b]I have heard the murmurings of the children of Israel, which they murmur against me.

28 Say unto them, [a]*As truly as* I live, saith the LORD, as ye have spoken in mine ears, so will I do to you:

29 Your carcases shall fall in this wilderness; and [a]all that were numbered of you, according to your [1]whole number, from twenty years old and upward, which have murmured against me.

30 Doubtless ye shall not come into the land, *concerning* which I [1]sware to make you dwell therein, [a]save Caleb the son of Jephunneh, and Joshua the son of Nun.

31 [a]But your little ones, which ye said should be a prey, them will I bring in, and they shall [1]know the land which [b]ye have despised.

32 But *as for* you, [a]your carcases, they shall [1]fall in this wilderness.

33 And your children shall [a]wander[1] in the wilderness [b]forty years, and [c]bear your whoredoms, until your carcases be wasted in the wilderness.

34 [a]After the number of the days in which ye searched the land, *even* [b]forty days, each day for a year, shall ye bear your [1]iniquities, *even* forty years, [c]and ye shall know my [2]breach of promise.

35 [a]I the LORD have said, I will surely do it unto all [b]this evil congregation, that are gathered together against me: in this wilderness they shall be consumed, and there they shall die.

36 And the men, which Moses sent to [1]search the land, who returned, and made all the congregation to murmur against him, by bringing up a [2]slander upon the land,

37 Even those men that did bring up the evil report upon the land, [a]died by the plague before the LORD.

38 [a]But Joshua the son of Nun, and Caleb the son of Jephunneh, *which were* of the men that went to search the land, lived *still.*

39 And Moses told these sayings unto all the children of Israel: [a]and the people mourned greatly.

40 And they rose up early in the morning, and gat them up into the top of the mountain, saying, Lo, [a]we *be here,* and will go up unto the place which the LORD hath promised: for we have sinned.

41 And Moses said, Wherefore now do ye [1]transgress the commandment of the LORD? but [2]it shall not prosper.

42 [a]Go not up, for the LORD *is* not among you; that ye be not [1]smitten before your enemies.

43 For the Amalekites and the Canaanites *are* there before you, and ye

---

14:11 [a] Heb. 3:8
[b] Deut. 9:23
[1] *despise* [2] *miraculous signs*

14:12 [a] Ex. 32:10

14:13 [a] Ps. 106:23
[b] Ex. 32:12

14:14 [a] Deut. 2:25

14:16 [a] Deut. 9:28

14:18 [a] Ex. 34:6, 7
[b] Ex. 20:5

14:19 [a] Ex. 32:32;
34:9 [b] Ps. 51:1;
106:45 [c] Ps. 78:38

14:20 [a] Mic.
7:18–20

14:21 [a] Ps. 72:19

14:22 [a] Deut. 1:35
[b] Gen. 31:7 [1] *put me to the test*

14:23 [a] Num.
26:65; 32:11 [1] *solemnly promised*

14:24 [a] Josh. 14:6,
8, 9 [b] Num. 32:12

14:25 [a] Deut. 1:40

14:27 [a] Ex.
16:28 [b] Ex. 16:12
[1] *grumbled*

14:28 [a] Heb.
3:16–19

14:29 [a] Num. 1:45,
46; 26:64 [1] *entire*

14:30 [a] Deut.
1:36–38 [1] *solemnly promised*

14:31 [a] Deut. 1:39
[b] Ps. 106:24 [1] *be acquainted with*

14:32 [a] Num.
26:64, 65; 32:13
[1] *die*

14:33 [a] Ps. 107:40
[b] Deut. 2:14
[c] Ezek. 23:35 [1] *be shepherds*

14:34 [a] Num.
13:25 [b] Ezek. 4:6
[c] [Heb. 4:1] [1] *guilt* [2] *rejection or opposition*

14:35 [a] Num.
23:19 [b] 1 Cor. 10:5

14:36 [1] *spy out*
[2] *bad report*

14:37 [a] [1 Cor.
10:10]

14:38 [a] Josh.
14:6, 10

14:39 [a] Ex. 33:4

14:40 [a] Deut.
1:41–44

14:41 [1] *overstep the command* [2] *it shall not succeed*

14:42 [a] Deut. 1:42;
31:17 [1] *defeated*

shall fall by the sword: [a]because ye are turned away from the LORD, therefore the LORD will not be with you.

44 [a]But they presumed to go up unto the hill top: nevertheless the ark of the covenant of the LORD, and Moses, departed not out of the camp.

45 Then the Amalekites came down, and the Canaanites which dwelt in that hill, and smote them, and [1]discomfited them, *even* unto [a]Hormah.

## CHAPTER 15

A ND the LORD spake unto Moses, saying,

2 [a]Speak unto the children of Israel, and say unto them, When ye be come into the land [1]of your habitations, which I give unto you,

3 And [a]will make an offering by fire unto the LORD, a burnt offering, or a sacrifice [b]in performing a vow, or in a freewill offering, or [c]in your [1]solemn feasts, to make a [d]sweet[2] savour unto the LORD, of the herd, or of the flock:

4 Then [a]shall he that offereth his offering unto the LORD bring [b]a meat offering of a tenth deal of flour mingled [c]with the fourth *part* of an hin of oil.

5 [a]And the fourth *part* of an hin of wine for a drink offering shalt thou prepare with the burnt offering or sacrifice, for one [b]lamb.

6 [a]Or for a ram, thou shalt prepare *for* a [1]meat offering two tenth deals of flour mingled with the third *part* of an hin of oil.

7 And for a drink offering thou shalt offer the third *part* of an hin of wine, *for* a sweet savour unto the LORD.

8 And when thou preparest a bullock *for* a burnt offering, or *for* a sacrifice in [1]performing a vow, or [a]peace offerings unto the LORD:

9 Then shall he bring [a]with a bullock a meat offering of three tenth deals of flour mingled with half an hin of oil.

10 And thou shalt bring for a drink offering half an hin of wine, *for* an offering made by fire, of a sweet savour unto the LORD.

11 [a]Thus shall it be done for one bullock, or for one ram, or for a lamb, or a kid.

12 According to the number that ye shall prepare, so shall ye do to every one according to their number.

13 All that are born of the country shall do these things after this manner, in offering an offering made by fire, of a sweet savour unto the LORD.

14 And if a stranger [1]sojourn with you, or whosoever *be* among you in your generations, and will offer an offering made by fire, of a sweet savour unto the LORD; as ye do, so he shall do.

15 [a]One [1]ordinance *shall be both* for you of the congregation, and also for the stranger that sojourneth *with you,* an ordinance for ever in your generations: as ye *are,* so shall the stranger be before the LORD.

16 One law and one manner shall be for you, and for the stranger that sojourneth with you.

17 And the LORD spake unto Moses, saying,

18 [a]Speak unto the children of Israel, and say unto them, When ye come into the land whither I bring you,

19 Then it shall be, that, when ye eat of [a]the bread of the land, ye shall offer up an heave offering unto the LORD.

20 [a]Ye shall offer up a cake of the first of your dough *for* an heave offering: as *ye do* [b]the heave offering of the threshingfloor, so shall ye heave it.

21 Of the first of your dough ye shall give unto the LORD an heave offering in your generations.

22 And [a]if ye [1]have erred, and not observed all these commandments, which the LORD hath spoken unto Moses,

23 *Even* all that the LORD hath commanded you by the hand of Moses, from the day that the LORD commanded *Moses,* and henceforward among your generations;

24 Then it shall be, [a]if *ought* be committed by ignorance [1]without the knowledge of the congregation, that all the congregation shall offer one young bullock for a burnt offering, for a sweet savour unto the LORD, [b]with his meat offering, and his drink offering, according to the [2]manner, and [c]one kid of the goats for a sin offering.

25 [a]And the priest shall make an atonement for all the congregation of the children of Israel, and it shall be forgiven them; for it *is* ignorance: and they shall bring their offering, a sacrifice made by fire unto the LORD, and their sin offering before the LORD, for their ignorance:

26 And it shall be forgiven all the congregation of the children of Israel, and the stranger that sojourneth among them; seeing all the people *were* in ignorance.

27 And [a]if any soul sin through ignorance, then he shall bring a she goat of the first year for a sin offering.

28 [a]And the priest shall make an atonement for the soul that sinneth ignorantly, when he sinneth by ignorance before the LORD, to make an atonement for him; and it shall be forgiven him.

29 [a]Ye shall have one law for him that sinneth through ignorance, *both*

### Cross references (center column)

14:43 [a] 2 Chr. 15:2
14:44 [a] Deut. 1:43
14:45 [a] Num. 21:3 [1] *drove them back*
15:2 [a] Lev. 23:10; Num. 15:18; Deut. 7:1 [1] *you are to inhabit*
15:3 [a] Lev. 1:2, 3 [b] Lev. 7:16; 22:18, 21 [c] Lev. 23:2, 8, 12, 38; Num. 28:18, 19, 27; Deut. 16:10 [d] Gen. 8:21; Ex. 29:18; Lev. 1:9 [1] Lit. *appointed* [2] *pleasing aroma*
15:4 [a] Lev. 2:1; 6:14 [b] Ex. 29:40; Lev. 23:13 [c] Lev. 14:10; Num. 28:5
15:5 [a] Num. 28:7, 14 [b] Lev. 1:10; 3:6; Num. 15:11; 28:4, 5
15:6 [a] Num. 28:12, 14 [1] *grain or meal*
15:8 [a] Lev. 7:11 [1] *fulfilling a special vow*
15:9 [a] Num. 28:12, 14
15:11 [a] Num. 28
15:14 [1] *stays temporarily*
15:15 [a] Ex. 12:49; Num. 9:14; 15:29 [1] *statute*
15:18 [a] Num. 15:2; Deut. 26:1
15:19 [a] Josh. 5:11, 12
15:20 [a] Ex. 34:26; Lev. 23:10, 14, 17; Deut. 26:2, 10; Prov. 3:9, 10 [b] Lev. 2:14; 23:10, 16
15:22 [a] Lev. 4:2 [1] *sin unintentionally*
15:24 [a] Lev. 4:13 [b] Num. 15:8–10 [c] Lev. 4:23 [1] Lit. *away from the eyes* [2] *ordinance*
15:25 [a] Lev. 4:20; [Heb. 2:17]
15:27 [a] Lev. 4:27–31
15:28 [a] Lev. 4:35
15:29 [a] Num. 15:15

*for* him that is born among the children of Israel, and for the stranger that sojourneth among them.

30 aBut the ¹soul that doeth *ought* ²presumptuously, *whether he be* born in the land, or a stranger, the same ³reproacheth the LORD; and that soul shall ⁴be cut off from among his people.

31 Because he hath ªdespised the word of the LORD, and hath broken his commandment, that ¹soul shall utterly be cut off; his ²iniquity *shall be* upon him.

32 And while the children of Israel were in the wilderness, ªthey found a man that gathered sticks upon the sabbath day.

33 And they that found him gathering sticks brought him unto Moses and Aaron, and unto all the congregation.

34 And they put him ªin ¹ward, because it was not ²declared what should be done to him.

35 And the LORD said unto Moses, ªThe man shall be surely put to death: all the congregation shall ᵇstone him with stones without the camp.

36 And all the congregation brought him without the camp, and stoned him with stones, and he died; as the LORD commanded Moses.

37 And the LORD spake unto Moses, saying,

38 Speak unto the children of Israel, and bid ªthem that they make them fringes in the borders of their garments throughout their generations, and that they put upon the fringe of the borders a ribband of blue:

39 And it shall be unto you for a fringe, that ye may look upon it, and ªremember all the commandments of the LORD, and do them; and that ye ᵇseek¹ not after your own heart and your own eyes, after which ye use ᶜto go ²a whoring:

40 That ye may remember, and do all my commandments, and be ªholy unto your God.

41 I *am* the LORD your God, which brought you out of the land of Egypt, to be your God: I *am* the LORD your God.

## CHAPTER 16

Now ªKorah, the son of Izhar, the son of Kohath, the son of Levi, and ᵇDathan and Abiram, the sons of Eliab, and On, the son of Peleth, sons of Reuben, took *men:*

2 And they rose up before Moses, with certain of the children of Israel, two hundred and fifty princes of the assembly, ªfamous in the congregation, men of renown:

3 And ªthey gathered themselves together against Moses and against Aaron, and said unto them, Ye ¹take too much upon you, seeing ᵇall the congregation *are* holy, every one of them, ᶜand the LORD *is* among them: wherefore then ²lift ye up yourselves above the congregation of the LORD?

4 And when Moses heard *it,* he ªfell upon his face:

5 And he spake unto Korah and unto all his company, saying, Even to morrow the LORD will shew who *are* ªhis, and *who is* ᵇholy; and will cause *him* to come near unto him: even *him* whom he hath chosen will he cause to ᶜcome near unto him.

6 This do; Take you censers, Korah, and all his company;

7 And put fire therein, and put incense in them before the LORD to morrow: and it shall be *that* the man whom the LORD doth choose, he *shall be* holy: *ye take* too much upon you, ye sons of Levi.

8 And Moses said unto Korah, Hear, I pray you, ye sons of Levi:

9 *Seemeth it but* ªa small thing unto you, that the God of Israel hath ᵇseparated¹ you from the congregation of Israel, to bring you near to himself to do the service of the tabernacle of the LORD, and to stand before the congregation to minister unto them?

10 And he hath brought thee near *to him,* and all thy brethren the sons of Levi with thee: and seek ye the priesthood also?

11 For which cause *both* thou and all thy company *are* gathered together against the LORD: ªand what *is* Aaron, that ye ¹murmur against him?

12 And Moses sent to call Dathan and Abiram, the sons of Eliab: which said, We will not come up:

13 *Is it* a small thing that thou hast brought us up out of a ªland that floweth with milk and honey, to kill us in the wilderness, except thou ᵇmake thyself altogether a prince over us?

14 Moreover ªthou hast not brought us into ᵇa land that floweth with milk and honey, or given us inheritance of fields and vineyards: wilt thou put out the eyes of these men? we will not come up.

15 And Moses was very ¹wroth, and said unto the LORD, ªRespect² not thou their offering: ᵇI have not taken one ass from them, neither have I hurt one of them.

16 And Moses said unto Korah, Be thou and all thy company ªbefore the LORD, thou, and they, and Aaron, to morrow:

17 And take every man his censer, and put incense in them, and bring ye before the LORD every man his censer, two hundred and fifty censers; thou also, and Aaron, each *of you* his censer.

### Cross references (center column)

15:30 ª Num. 14:40–44; Deut. 1:43; 17:12; Ps. 19:13; Heb. 10:26 ¹ *person* ² *defiantly, lit. with a high hand* ³ *brings reproach or blasphemes* ⁴ *die*

15:31 ª 2 Sam. 12:9; Prov. 13:13 ¹ *person* ² *guilt*

15:32 ª Ex. 31:14, 15; 35:2, 3

15:34 ª Lev. 24:12 ¹ *under guard or custody* ² *explained*

15:35 ª Ex. 31:14, 15 ᵇ Lev. 24:14; Deut. 21:21; 1 Kin. 21:13; Acts 7:58

15:38 ª Deut. 22:12; Matt. 23:5

15:39 ª Ps. 103:18 ᵇ Deut. 29:19 ᶜ Ps. 73:27; 106:39; James 4:4 ¹ *follow* ² *into harlotry*

15:40 ª [Lev. 11:44, 45; Rom. 12:1; Col. 1:22; 1 Pet. 1:15, 16]

16:1 ª Ex. 6:21 ᵇ Num. 26:9; Deut. 11:6

16:2 ª Num. 1:16; 96:9

16:3 ª Num. 12:2; 14:2; Ps. 106:16

ᵇ Ex. 19:6 ᶜ Ex. 29:45 ¹ *assume too much for yourselves* ² *do you exalt yourselves*

16:4 ª Num. 14:5; 20:6

16:5 ª [2 Tim. 2:19] ᵇ Lev. 21:6–8, 12 ᶜ Ezek. 40:46; 44:15, 16

16:9 ª 1 Sam. 18:23; Is. 7:13 ᵇ Num. 3:41, 45; 8:13–16; Deut. 10:8 ¹ *set you apart*

16:11 ª Ex. 16:7, 8 ¹ *grumble*

16:13 ª Ex. 16:3; Num. 11:4–6 ᵇ Ex. 2:14; Acts 7:27, 35

16:14 ª Num. 14:1–4 ᵇ Ex. 3:8; Lev. 20:24

16:15 ª Gen. 4:4, 5 ᵇ 1 Sam. 12:3; Acts 20:33 ¹ *angry* ² *Do not graciously regard*

16:16 ª 1 Sam. 12:3, 7

18 And they took every man his censer, and put fire in them, and laid incense thereon, and stood in the door of the tabernacle of the congregation with Moses and Aaron.

19 And Korah gathered all the congregation against them unto the door of the tabernacle of the congregation: and ᵃthe glory of the LORD appeared unto all the congregation.

20 And the LORD spake unto Moses and unto Aaron, saying,

21 ᵃSeparate yourselves from among this congregation, that I may ᵇconsume them in a moment.

22 And they ᵃfell¹ upon their faces, and said, O God, ᵇthe God of the spirits of all flesh, shall one man sin, and wilt thou be wroth with all the ᶜcongregation?

23 And the LORD spake unto Moses, saying,

24 Speak unto the congregation, saying, ¹Get you up from about the tabernacle of Korah, Dathan, and Abiram.

25 And Moses rose up and went unto Dathan and Abiram; and the elders of Israel followed him.

26 And he spake unto the congregation, saying, ᵃDepart, I pray you, from the tents of these wicked men, and touch nothing of theirs, lest ye be consumed in all their sins.

27 So they gat up from the tabernacle of Korah, Dathan, and Abiram, on every side: and Dathan and Abiram came out, and stood in the door of their tents, and their wives, and their sons, and their little ᵃchildren.

28 And Moses said, ᵃHereby ye shall know that the LORD hath sent me to do all these works; for I have not done them ᵇof mine own ¹mind.

29 If these men die ¹the common death of all men, or if they be ᵃvisited ²after the visitation of all men; then the LORD hath not sent me.

30 But if the LORD ¹make ᵃa new thing, and the earth open her mouth, and swallow them up, with all that appertain unto them, and they ᵇgo down ²quick into the pit; then ye shall understand that these men have provoked the LORD.

31 ᵃAnd it came to pass, as he had made an end of speaking all these words, that the ground clave asunder that was under them:

32 And the earth opened her mouth, and swallowed them up, and their houses, and ᵃall the men that appertained unto Korah, and all their goods.

33 They, and all that appertained to them, went down alive into the pit, and the earth closed upon them: and they perished from among the congregation.

34 And all Israel that were round about them fled at the cry of them: for they said, Lest the earth swallow us up also.

35 And there ᵃcame out a fire from the LORD, and consumed the two hundred and fifty men that offered incense.

36 And the LORD spake unto Moses, saying,

37 Speak unto Eleazar the son of Aaron the priest, that he take up the censers out of the burning, and scatter thou the fire yonder; for ᵃthey are ¹hallowed.

38 The censers of these ᵃsinners¹ against their own souls, let them make them broad plates for a covering of the altar: for they offered before the LORD, therefore they are hallowed: ᵇand they shall be a sign unto the children of Israel.

39 And Eleazar the priest took the brasen censers, wherewith they that were burnt had offered; and they were made broad plates for a covering of the altar:

40 To be a ¹memorial unto the children of Israel, ᵃthat no stranger, which is not of the seed of Aaron, come near to offer incense before the LORD; that he be not as Korah, and as his company: as the LORD said to him by the hand of Moses.

41 But on the morrow ᵃall the congregation of the children of Israel ¹murmured against Moses and against Aaron, saying, Ye have killed the people of the LORD.

42 And it came to pass, when the congregation was gathered against Moses and against Aaron, that they looked toward the tabernacle of the congregation: and, behold, ᵃthe cloud covered it, and the glory of the LORD appeared.

43 And Moses and Aaron came before the tabernacle of the congregation.

44 And the LORD spake unto Moses, saying,

45 Get you up from among this congregation, that I may consume them as in a moment. And they fell upon their faces.

46 And Moses said unto Aaron, Take a censer, and put fire therein from off the altar, and put on incense, and go quickly unto the congregation, and make ¹an atonement for them: ᵃfor there is wrath gone out from the LORD; the plague is begun.

47 And Aaron took as Moses commanded, and ran into the midst of the congregation; and, behold, the plague was begun among the people: and he put on incense, and made an atonement for the people.

## Cross References

16:19 ᵃ Ex. 16:7, 10; Lev. 9:6, 23; Num. 14:10
16:21 ᵃ Gen. 19:17; Jer. 51:6 ᵇ Ex. 32:10; 33:5
16:22 ᵃ Num. 14:5 ᵇ Num. 27:16; Job 12:10; Eccl. 12:7; Heb. 12:9 ᶜ Gen. 18:23–32; 20:4 ¹ prostrated themselves
16:24 ¹ Get away from
16:26 ᵃ Gen. 19:12, 14, 15, 17
16:27 ᵃ Ex. 20:5; Num. 26:11
16:28 ᵃ Ex. 3:12; John 5:36 ᵇ Num. 24:13; John 5:30 ¹ will
16:29 ᵃ Ex. 20:5; Job 35:15; Is. 10:3 ¹ a natural death like all ² by the common fate of
16:30 ᵃ Job 31:3; Is. 28:21 ᵇ [Ps. 55:15] ¹ creates ² alive
16:31 ᵃ Num. 26:10; Ps. 106:17
16:32 ᵃ Num. 26:11; 1 Chr. 6:22, 37
16:35 ᵃ Lev. 10:2; Num. 11:1–3; 26:10; Ps. 106:18
16:37 ᵃ Lev. 27:28 ¹ holy
16:38 ᵃ Prov. 20:2; Hab. 2:10 ᵇ Num. 17:10; Ezek. 14:8 ¹ men who sinned at the cost of their own lives
16:40 ᵃ Num. 3:10; 2 Chr. 26:18 ¹ reminder
16:41 ᵃ Num. 14:2; Ps. 106:25 ¹ grumbled
16:42 ᵃ Ex. 40:34
16:46 ᵃ Lev. 10:6; Num. 18:5 ¹ propitiation

48 And he stood between the dead and the living; and [a]the plague was [1]stayed.

49 Now they that died in the plague were fourteen thousand and seven hundred, beside them that died about the matter of Korah.

50 And Aaron returned unto Moses unto the door of the tabernacle of the congregation: and the plague was stayed.

## CHAPTER 17

AND the LORD spake unto Moses, saying,

2 Speak unto the children of Israel, and take of every one of them a rod according to the house of *their* fathers, of all their princes according to the house of their fathers twelve rods: write thou every man's name upon his rod.

3 And thou shalt write Aaron's name upon the rod of Levi: for one rod *shall be* for the head of the house of their fathers.

4 And thou shalt lay them up in the tabernacle of the congregation before the [a]testimony, [b]where I will meet with you.

5 And it shall come to pass, *that* the man's rod, [a]whom I shall choose, shall blossom: and I will [1]make to cease from me the [2]murmurings of the children of Israel, [b]whereby they murmur against you.

6 And Moses spake unto the children of Israel, and every one of their princes gave him a rod apiece, for each prince one, according to their fathers' houses, *even* twelve rods: and the rod of Aaron *was* among their rods.

7 And Moses laid up the rods before the LORD in [a]the tabernacle of witness.

8 And it came to pass, that on the morrow Moses went into the tabernacle of witness; and, behold, the [a]rod of Aaron for the house of Levi was budded, and brought forth buds, and bloomed blossoms, and yielded almonds.

9 And Moses brought out all the rods from before the LORD unto all the children of Israel: and they looked, and took every man his rod.

10 And the LORD said unto Moses, Bring [a]Aaron's rod again before the testimony, to be kept [b]for a token against the rebels; [c]and thou shalt [1]quite take away their murmurings from me, that they die not.

11 And Moses did *so:* as the LORD commanded him, so did he.

12 And the children of Israel spake unto Moses, saying, Behold, we die, we perish, we all perish.

13 [a]Whosoever cometh any thing near unto the tabernacle of the LORD shall die: shall we [1]be consumed with dying?

## CHAPTER 18

AND the LORD said unto Aaron, [a]Thou and thy sons and thy father's house with thee shall [b]bear[1] the [2]iniquity of the sanctuary: and thou and thy sons with thee shall bear the iniquity of your priesthood.

2 And thy brethren also of the [a]tribe of Levi, the tribe of thy father, bring thou with thee, that they may be [b]joined unto thee, and minister unto thee: but thou and thy sons with thee *shall minister* before the tabernacle of [1]witness.

3 And they shall [1]keep thy charge, and [a]the charge of all the tabernacle: [b]only they shall not come nigh the vessels of the sanctuary and the altar, [c]that neither they, nor ye also, die.

4 And they shall be joined unto thee, and keep the charge of the tabernacle of the congregation, for all the service of the tabernacle: [a]and a stranger shall not come nigh unto you.

5 And ye shall keep [a]the charge of the sanctuary, and the charge of the altar: [b]that there be no wrath any more upon the children of Israel.

6 And I, behold, I have [a]taken your brethren the Levites from among the children of Israel: [b]to you *they are* given *as* a gift for the LORD, to do the service of the tabernacle of the congregation.

7 Therefore [a]thou and thy sons with thee shall keep your priest's office for every thing of the altar, and [b]within the vail; and ye shall serve: I have given your priest's office *unto you as* a [c]service[1] of gift: and the stranger that cometh nigh shall be put to death.

8 And the LORD spake unto Aaron, Behold, [a]I also have given thee the [1]charge of mine heave offerings of all the hallowed things of the children of Israel; unto thee have I given them [b]by reason of the anointing, and to thy sons, by an ordinance for ever.

9 This shall be thine of the most holy things, *reserved* from the fire: every oblation of theirs, every [a]meat[1] offering of theirs, and every [b]sin offering of theirs, and every [c]trespass offering of theirs, which they shall render unto me, *shall be* most holy for thee and for thy sons.

10 [a]In the most holy *place* shalt thou eat it; every male shall eat it: it shall be holy unto thee.

11 And this *is* thine; [a]the heave offering of their gift, with all the wave offerings of the children of Israel: I have given them unto thee, and to thy sons and to thy daughters with

16:48 [a] Num. 25:8; Ps. 106:30 [1] *stopped*
17:4 [a] Ex. 25:16 [b] Ex. 25:22; 29:42, 43; 30:36; Num. 17:7
17:5 [a] Num. 16:5 [b] Num. 16:11 [1] *rid myself* [2] *grumbling*
17:7 [a] Ex. 38:21; Num. 1:50, 51; 9:15; 18:2; Acts 7:44
17:8 [a] [Ezek. 17:24]; Heb. 9:4
17:10 [a] Heb. 9:4 [b] Num. 16:38; Deut. 9:7, 24 [c] Num. 17:5 [1] *put away*
17:13 [a] Num. 1:51, 53; 18:4, 7 [1] *all utterly die*
18:1 [a] Num. 17:13 [b] Ex. 28:38; Lev. 10:17; 22:16 [1] *be responsible for* [2] *guilt related to*
18:2 [a] Gen. 29:34; Num. 1:47 [b] Num. 3:5–10 [1] *testimony*
18:3 [a] Num. 3:25, 31, 36 [b] Num. 16:40 [c] Num. 4:15 [1] *attend to your service*
18:4 [a] Num. 3:10
18:5 [a] Ex. 27:21; 30:7; Lev. 24:3 [b] Num. 8:19; 16:46
18:6 [a] Num. 3:12, 45 [b] Num. 3:9
18:7 [a] Num. 3:10; 18:5 [b] Heb. 9:3, 6 [c] Matt. 10:8; 1 Pet. 5:2, 3 [1] *gift of service*
18:8 [a] Lev. 6:16, 18; 7:28–34; Num. 5:9 [b] Ex. 29:29; 40:13, 15 [1] *custody*
18:9 [a] Lev. 2:2, 3; 10:12, 13 [b] Lev. 6:25, 26 [c] Lev. 7:7; Num. 5:8–10 [1] *grain or meal*
18:10 [a] Lev. 6:16, 26
18:11 [a] Ex. 29:27, 28; Deut. 18:3–5

thee, by a statute for ever: [b]every one that is [1]clean in thy house shall eat of it.

12 [a]All the [b]best of the oil, and all the best of the wine, and of the wheat, [b]the firstfruits of them which they shall offer unto the LORD, them have I given thee.

13 *And* whatsoever is first ripe in the land, [a]which they shall bring unto the LORD, shall be thine; every one that is clean in thine house shall eat *of* it.

14 [a]Every thing [1]devoted in Israel shall be thine.

15 Every thing that openeth [a]the matrix in all flesh, which they bring unto the LORD, *whether it be* of men or beasts, shall be thine: nevertheless [b]the firstborn of man shalt thou surely redeem, and the firstling of unclean beasts shalt thou redeem.

16 And those that are to be redeemed from a month old shalt thou redeem, [a]according to thine estimation, for the money of five shekels, after the shekel of the sanctuary, which *is* [b]twenty gerahs.

17 [a]But the firstling of a cow, or the firstling of a sheep, or the firstling of a goat, thou shalt not redeem; they *are* holy: [b]thou shalt sprinkle their blood upon the altar, and shalt burn their fat *for* an offering made by fire, for a sweet savour unto the LORD.

18 And the flesh of them shall be thine, as the [a]wave[1] breast and as the right shoulder are thine.

19 All the heave offerings of the holy things, which the children of Israel offer unto the LORD, have I given thee, and thy sons and thy daughters with thee, by a statute for ever: [a]it *is* a covenant of salt for ever before the LORD unto thee and to thy seed with thee.

20 And the LORD spake unto Aaron, Thou shalt have [a]no inheritance in their land, neither shalt thou have any part among them: [b]I *am* thy part and thine inheritance among the children of Israel.

21 And, behold, [a]I have given the children of Levi all the tenth in Israel for [1]an inheritance, for their service which they serve, *even* [b]the service of the tabernacle of the congregation.

22 [a]Neither must the children of Israel henceforth come nigh the tabernacle of the congregation, [b]lest they bear sin, and die.

23 But the Levites shall [1]do the service of the tabernacle of the congregation, and they shall bear their iniquity: *it shall be* a statute for ever throughout your generations, that among the children of Israel they have no inheritance.

24 But the tithes of the children of Israel, which they offer *as* an heave

---

18:11 [b] Lev. 22:1–16
[1] *purified*
18:12 [a] Ex. 23:19;
Neh. 10:35, 36
[b] Ex. 22:29; Lev.
23:20 [1] Lit. *fat*
18:13 [a] Ex. 22:29;
23:19; 34:26
18:14 [a] Lev. 27:1–
33 [1] *consecrated*
18:15 [a] Ex. 13:2
[b] Ex. 13:12–15;
Num. 3:46; Luke
2:22–24
18:16 [a] Lev. 27:6
[b] Ex. 30:13
18:17 [a] Deut. 15:19
[b] Lev. 3:2, 5
18:18 [a] Ex. 29:26–
28; Lev. 7:31–36
[1] *breast of the
wave offering*
18:19 [a] Lev. 2:13;
2 Chr. 13:5; [Mark
9:49, 50]
18:20 [a] Deut. 10:8,
9; 12:12; 14:27–29;
18:1, 2; Josh. 13:14,
33 [b] Ps. 16:5;
Ezek. 44:28
18:21 [a] Lev. 27:30–
33; Deut. 14:22–
29; Neh. 10:37;
12:44; Mal. 3:8–
10; [Heb. 7:4–10]
[b] Num. 3:7, 8 [1] *a
possession*
18:22 [a] Num. 1:51
[b] Lev. 22:9
18:23 [1] *perform*

18:24 [1] *for a
possession*
18:26 [a] Neh. 10:38
18:27 [a] Num.
15:20; [2 Cor.
8:12]
18:29 [1] Lit. *fat*
18:30 [1] *reckoned
or accounted*
18:31 [a] [Matt.
10:10; Luke 10:7];
1 Cor. 9:13; [1 Tim.
5:18] [1] *wages*
18:32 [a] Lev. 19:8;
22:16; Ezek. 22:26
[b] Lev. 22:2, 15
[1] *lifted up*
19:2 [a] Lev. 22:20–
25 [b] Deut. 21:3;
1 Sam. 6:7 [1] *stat-
ute* [2] *blemish, in
which there is no
defect*
19:3 [a] Lev. 4:12,
21; Num. 19:9;
Heb. 13:11
19:4 [a] Lev. 4:6;
Heb. 9:13
19:5 [a] Ex. 29:14;
Lev. 4:11, 12; 9:11
19:6 [a] Lev. 14:4,
6, 49 [b] Ex. 12:22;
1 Kin. 4:33

---

offering unto the LORD, I have given to the Levites [1]to inherit: therefore I have said unto them, Among the children of Israel they shall have no inheritance.

25 And the LORD spake unto Moses, saying,

26 Thus speak unto the Levites, and say unto them, When ye take of the children of Israel the tithes which I have given you from them for your inheritance, then ye shall offer up an heave offering of it for the LORD, [a]even a tenth *part* of the tithe.

27 And *this* your heave offering shall be reckoned unto you, as though *it were* the corn of the [a]threshingfloor, and as the fulness of the winepress.

28 Thus ye also shall offer an heave offering unto the LORD of all your tithes, which ye receive of the children of Israel; and ye shall give thereof the LORD's heave offering to Aaron the priest.

29 Out of all your gifts ye shall offer every heave offering of the LORD, of all the [1]best thereof, *even* the hallowed part thereof out of it.

30 Therefore thou shalt say unto them, When ye have heaved the best thereof from it, then it shall be [1]counted unto the Levites as the increase of the threshingfloor, and as the increase of the winepress.

31 And ye shall eat it in every place, ye and your households: for it *is* [a]your [1]reward for your service in the tabernacle of the congregation.

32 And ye shall [a]bear no sin by reason of it, when ye have [1]heaved from it the best of it: neither shall ye [b]pollute the holy things of the children of Israel, lest ye die.

## CHAPTER 19

AND the LORD spake unto Moses and unto Aaron, saying,

2 This *is* the [1]ordinance of the law which the LORD hath commanded, saying, Speak unto the children of Israel, that they bring thee a red heifer without [2]spot, wherein *is* no [a]blemish, [b]*and* upon which never came yoke:

3 And ye shall give her unto Eleazar the priest, that he may bring her [a]forth without the camp, and *one* shall slay her before his face:

4 And Eleazar the priest shall take of her blood with his finger, and [a]sprinkle of her blood directly before the tabernacle of the congregation seven times:

5 And *one* shall burn the heifer in his sight; [a]her skin, and her flesh, and her blood, with her dung, shall he burn:

6 And the priest shall take [a]cedar wood, and [b]hyssop, and scarlet, and

cast *it* into the midst of the burning of the heifer.

7 ᵃThen the priest shall wash his clothes, and he shall bathe his flesh in water, and afterward he shall come into the camp, and the priest shall be unclean until the even.

8 And he that burneth her shall wash his clothes in water, and bathe his flesh in water, and shall be unclean until the even.

9 And a man *that is* clean shall gather up ᵃthe ashes of the heifer, and lay *them* up ¹without the camp in a clean place, and it shall be kept for the congregation of the children of Israel ᵇfor a water of ²separation: it *is* a purification for sin.

10 And he that gathereth the ashes of the heifer shall wash his clothes, and be unclean until the even: and it shall be unto the children of Israel, and unto the stranger that sojourneth among them, for a statute for ever.

11 ᵃHe that toucheth the dead body of any ¹man shall be unclean seven days.

12 ᵃHe shall purify himself with it on the third day, and on the seventh day he shall be clean: but if he purify not himself the third day, then the seventh day he shall not be clean.

13 Whosoever toucheth the dead body of any man that is dead, and purifieth ᵃnot himself, ᵇdefileth the tabernacle of the LORD; and that ¹soul shall be cut off from Israel: because ᶜthe water of separation was not sprinkled upon him, he shall be unclean; ᵈhis uncleanness *is* yet upon him.

14 This *is* the law, when a man dieth in a tent: all that come into the tent, and all that *is* in the tent, shall be unclean seven days.

15 And every ᵃopen vessel, which hath no covering bound upon it, *is* unclean.

16 And ᵃwhosoever toucheth one that is slain with a sword in the open fields, or a dead body, or a bone of a man, or a grave, shall be unclean seven days.

17 And for an unclean *person* they shall take of the ᵃashes of the burnt heifer of purification for sin, and ¹running water shall be put thereto in a vessel:

18 And a clean person shall take ᵃhyssop, and dip *it* in the water, and sprinkle *it* upon the tent, and upon all the vessels, and upon the persons that were there, and upon him that touched a bone, or one slain, or one dead, or a grave:

19 And the clean *person* shall sprinkle upon the unclean on the third day, ᵃand on the seventh day: and on

the seventh day he shall purify himself, and wash his clothes, and bathe himself in water, and shall be clean at even.

20 But the man that shall be unclean, and shall not purify himself, that ¹soul shall be cut off from among the congregation, because he hath ᵃdefiled the sanctuary of the LORD: the water of separation hath not been sprinkled upon him; he *is* unclean.

21 And it shall be a perpetual statute unto them, that he that sprinkleth the water of separation shall wash his clothes; and he that toucheth the water of separation shall be unclean until even.

22 And ᵃwhatsoever the unclean *person* toucheth shall be unclean; and ᵇthe soul that toucheth *it* shall be unclean until even.

## CHAPTER 20

THEN ᵃcame the children of Israel, *even* the whole congregation, into the desert of Zin in the first month: and the people abode in ᵇKadesh; and ᶜMiriam died there, and was buried there.

2 ᵃAnd there was no water for the congregation: ᵇand they gathered themselves together against Moses and against Aaron.

3 And the people ᵈchode¹ with Moses, and spake, saying, Would God that we had died ᵇwhen our brethren died before the LORD!

4 And ᵃwhy have ye brought up the congregation of the LORD into this wilderness, that we and our cattle should die there?

5 And wherefore have ye made us to come up out of Egypt, to bring us in unto this evil place? it *is* no place of seed, or of figs, or of vines, or of pomegranates; neither *is* there any water to drink.

6 And Moses and Aaron went from the presence of the assembly unto the door of the tabernacle of the congregation, and ᵃthey ¹fell upon their faces: and ᵇthe glory of the LORD appeared unto them.

7 And the LORD spake unto Moses, saying,

8 ᵃTake the rod, and gather thou the assembly together, thou, and Aaron thy brother, and speak ye unto the rock before their eyes; and it shall give forth his water, and ᵇthou shalt bring forth to them water out of the rock: so thou shalt give the congregation and their beasts drink.

9 And Moses took the rod ᵃfrom before the LORD, as he commanded him.

10 And Moses and Aaron gathered the congregation together before the

19:7 ᵃ Lev. 11:25; 15:5; 16:26, 28
19:9 ᵃ [Heb. 9:13, 14] ᵇ Num. 19:13, 20, 21 ¹ *outside* ² Lit. *impurity*
19:11 ᵃ Lev. 21:1, 11; Num. 5:2; 6:6; 9:6, 10; 31:19; Lam. 4:14; Hag. 2:13 ¹ Lit. *soul of man*
19:12 ᵃ Num. 19:19; 31:19
19:13 ᵃ Lev. 22:3–7 ᵇ Lev. 15:31 ᶜ Num. 8:7; 19:9 ᵈ Lev. 7:20; 22:3 ¹ *person*
19:15 ᵃ Lev. 11:32; Num. 31:20
19:16 ᵃ Num. 19:11; 31:19
19:17 ᵃ Num. 19:9 ¹ Lit. *living*
19:18 ᵃ Ps. 51:7
19:19 ᵃ Lev. 14:9

19:20 ᵃ Num. 19:13 ¹ *person*
19:22 ᵃ Hag. 2:11–13 ᵇ Lev. 15:5
20:1 ᵃ Num. 13:21; 33:36 ᵇ Num. 13:26 ᶜ Ex. 15:20; Num. 26:59
20:2 ᵃ Ex. 17:1 ᵇ Num. 16:19, 42
20:3 ᵃ Ex. 17:2; Num. 14:2 ᵇ Num. 11:1, 33; 14:37; 16:31–35, 49 ¹ *contended*
20:4 ᵃ Ex. 17:3
20:6 ᵃ Num. 14:5; 16:4, 22, 45 ᵇ Num. 14:10 ¹ *prostrated themselves*
20:8 ᵃ Ex. 4:17, 20; 17:5, 6 ᵇ Neh. 9:15; Ps. 78:15, 16; 105:41; Is. 43:20; 48:21; [1 Cor. 10:4]
20:9 ᵃ Num. 17:10

rock, and he said unto them, ªHear now, ye rebels; must we fetch you water out of this rock?

11 And Moses lifted up his hand, and with his rod he smote the rock twice: and ªthe water came out abundantly, and the congregation drank, and their beasts *also.*

12 And the LORD spake unto Moses and Aaron, Because ªye believed me not, to ᵇsanctify¹ me in the eyes of the children of Israel, therefore ye shall not bring this congregation into the land which I have given them.

13 ªThis *is* the water of ¹Meribah; because the children of Israel strove with the LORD, and he was ²sanctified in them.

14 ªAnd Moses sent messengers from Kadesh unto the king of ᵇEdom, ᶜThus saith thy brother Israel, Thou knowest all the ¹travail that hath befallen us:

15 ªHow our fathers went down into Egypt, ᵇand we have dwelt in Egypt a long time; ᶜand the Egyptians ¹vexed us, and our fathers:

16 And ªwhen we cried unto the LORD, he heard our voice, and ᵇsent an angel, and hath brought us forth out of Egypt: and, behold, we *are* in Kadesh, a city in the uttermost of thy border:

17 ªLet us pass, I pray thee, through thy country: we will not pass through the fields, or through the vineyards, neither will we drink *of* the water of the wells: we will go by the king's *high* way, we will not turn to the right hand nor to the left, until we have passed thy borders.

18 And ªEdom said unto him, Thou shalt not pass by me, lest I come out against thee with the sword.

19 And the children of Israel said unto him, We will go by the high way: and if I and my cattle drink of thy water, ªthen I will pay for it: I will only, without *doing* any thing *else,* ¹go through on my feet.

20 And he said, ªThou shalt not go through. And Edom came out against him with much people, and with a strong hand.

21 Thus Edom ªrefused to give Israel passage through his border: wherefore Israel ᵇturned away from him.

22 And the children of Israel, *even* the whole congregation, journeyed from ªKadesh, ᵇand came unto mount Hor.

23 And the LORD spake unto Moses and Aaron in mount Hor, by the coast of the land of Edom, saying,

24 Aaron shall ¹be ªgathered unto his people: for he shall not enter into the land which I have given unto the children of Israel, because ye rebelled

against my word at the water of Meribah.

25 ªTake Aaron and Eleazar his son, and bring them up unto mount Hor:

26 And strip Aaron of his garments, and put them upon Eleazar his son: and Aaron shall be gathered *unto his people,* and shall die there.

27 And Moses did as the LORD commanded: and they went up into mount Hor in the sight of all the congregation.

28 ªMoses stripped Aaron of his garments, and put them upon Eleazar his son; and ᵇAaron died there in the top of the mount: and Moses and Eleazar came down from the mount.

29 And when all the congregation saw that Aaron was dead, they mourned for Aaron ªthirty days, *even* all the house of Israel.

## CHAPTER 21

AND *when* ªking Arad the Canaanite, which dwelt in the south, heard tell that Israel came by the way of the spies; then he fought against Israel, and took *some* of them prisoners.

2 ªAnd Israel ¹vowed a vow unto the LORD, and said, If thou wilt indeed deliver this people into my hand, then ᵇI will utterly destroy their cities.

3 And the LORD hearkened to the voice of Israel, and delivered up the Canaanites; and they utterly destroyed them and their cities: and he called the name of the place ¹Hormah.

4 And they journeyed from mount Hor by the way of the Red sea, to ªcompass the land of Edom: and the soul of the people was much ¹discouraged because of the way.

5 And the people ªspake against God, and against Moses, Wherefore have ye brought us up out of Egypt to die in the wilderness? for *there is* no bread, neither *is there any* water; and our soul ¹loatheth this light bread.

6 And ªthe LORD sent ᵇfiery serpents among the people, and they bit the people; and much people of Israel died.

7 ªTherefore the people came to Moses, and said, We have ᵇsinned, for we have spoken against the LORD, and against thee; ᶜpray unto the LORD, that he take away the serpents from us. And Moses prayed for the people.

8 And the LORD said unto Moses, ªMake thee a ᵇfiery serpent, and set it upon a pole: and it shall come to pass, that every one that is bitten, when he looketh upon it, shall live.

20:10 ª Ps. 106:33
20:11 ª Ex. 17:6;
Deut. 8:15; Ps.
78:16; Is. 48:21;
[1 Cor. 10:4]
20:12 ª Num.
20:28; 27:14;
Deut. 1:37; 3:26,
27; 34:5 ᵇ Lev.
10:3; Ezek. 20:41;
36:23; 1 Pet. 3:15
¹ *hallow*
20:13 ª Deut.
33:8; Ps. 106:32
¹ Lit. *Contention*
² *hallowed
among*
20:14 ª Judg.
11:16, 17 ᵇ Gen.
36:31–39 ᶜ Deut.
2:4; Obad. 10–12
¹ *hardship*
20:15 ª Gen. 46:6;
Acts 7:15 ᵇ Ex.
12:40 ᶜ Ex. 1:11;
Deut. 26:6; Acts
7:19 ¹ *did evil to*
20:16 ª Ex. 2:23;
3:7 ᵇ Ex. 3:2;
14:19
20:17 ª Num.
21:22
20:18 ª Num.
24:18; Ps. 137:7;
Ezek. 25:12, 13;
Obad. 10–15
20:19 ª Deut. 2:6,
28 ¹ *pass through
on foot*
20:20 ª Judg. 11:17
20:21 ª Deut. 2:27,
30 ᵇ Deut. 2:8;
Judg. 11:18
20:22 ª Num.
33:37 ᵇ Num. 21:4
20:24 ª Gen.
25:8; Deut. 32:50
¹ *die and join his
ancestors*
20:25 ª Num.
33:38; Deut.
32:50
20:28 ª Ex. 29:29,
30; Deut. 10:6
ᵇ Num. 33:38
20:29 ª Num. 50:3,
10; Deut. 34:8
21:1 ª Num. 33:40;
Josh. 12:14; Judg.
1:16
21:2 ª Gen. 28:20;
Judg. 11:30
ᵇ Deut. 2:34
¹ *made a vow*
21:3 ¹ Lit. *Utter
Destruction*
21:4 ª Judg. 11:18
¹ *impatient*
21:5 ª Num. 20:4,
5 ¹ *detests*
21:6 ª 1 Cor. 10:9
ᵇ Deut. 8:15
21:7 ª Num. 11:2;
Ps. 78:34; Is.
26:16; Hos. 5:15
ᵇ Lev. 26:40 ᶜ Ex.
8:8; 1 Sam. 12:19;
1 Kin. 13:6; Acts 8:24 21:8 ª [John 3:14, 15] ᵇ Is. 14:29;
30:6

9 And ᵃMoses made a serpent of brass, and put it upon a pole, and it came to pass, that if a serpent had bitten any man, when he ⁱbeheld the serpent of brass, he lived.

10 And the children of Israel set forward, and ᵃpitchedⁱ in Oboth.

11 And they journeyed from Oboth, and pitched at Ije-abarim, in the wilderness which *is* before Moab, toward the sunrising.

12 ᵃFrom thence they removed, and pitched in the valley of Zared.

13 From thence they removed, and pitched on the other side of Arnon, which *is* in the wilderness that cometh out of the coasts of the Amorites: for ᵃArnon *is* the border of Moab, between Moab and the Amorites.

14 Wherefore it is said in the book of the wars of the LORD, ⁱWhat he did in the Red sea, and in the brooks of Arnon,

15 And at the stream of the brooks that goeth down to the dwelling of ᵃAr, and lieth upon the border of Moab.

16 And from thence *they went* ᵃto Beer: that *is* the well whereof the LORD spake unto Moses, Gather the people together, and I will give them water.

17 ᵃThen Israel sang this song, Spring up, O well; sing ye unto it:

18 The princes digged the well, the nobles of the people digged it, by *the direction of* the ᵃlawgiver, with their staves. And from the wilderness *they went* to Mattanah:

19 And from Mattanah to Nahaliel: and from Nahaliel to Bamoth:

20 And from Bamoth *in* the valley, that *is* in the ⁱcountry of Moab, to the top of Pisgah, which looketh ᵃtoward ²Jeshimon.

21 And ᵃIsrael sent messengers unto Sihon king of the Amorites, saying,

22 ᵃLet me pass through thy land: we will not turn into the fields, or into the vineyards; we will not drink *of* the waters of the well: *but* we will go along by the king's *high* way, until we be past thy borders.

23 ᵃAnd Sihon would not suffer Israel to pass through his border: but Sihon gathered all his people together, and ⁱwent out against Israel into the wilderness: ᵇand he came to Jahaz, and fought against Israel.

24 And ᵃIsrael smote him with the edge of the sword, and ⁱpossessed his land from Arnon unto Jabbok, even unto the children of Ammon: for the border of the children of Ammon *was* strong.

25 And Israel took all these cities: and Israel ᵃdwelt in all the cities of the Amorites, in Heshbon, and in all the villages thereof.

26 For Heshbon *was* the city of Sihon the king of the Amorites, who had fought against the former king of Moab, and taken all his land out of his hand, even unto Arnon.

27 Wherefore they that speak in ⁱproverbs say, Come into Heshbon, let the city of Sihon be built and prepared:

28 For there is ᵃa fire gone out of Heshbon, a flame from the city of Sihon: it hath consumed ᵇAr of Moab, *and* the lords of the ᶜhigh places of Arnon.

29 Woe to thee, ᵃMoab! thou art undone, O people of ᵇChemosh: he hath given his ᶜsons that escaped, and his ᵈdaughters, into captivity unto Sihon king of the Amorites.

30 We have shot at them; Heshbon is perished even ᵃunto Dibon, and we have laid them waste even unto Nophah, which *reacheth* unto ᵇMedeba.

31 Thus Israel dwelt in the land of the Amorites.

32 And Moses sent to ⁱspy out ᵃJaazer, and they took the villages thereof, and drove out the Amorites that *were* there.

33 ᵃAnd they turned and went up by the way of ᵇBashan: and Og the king of Bashan went out against them, he, and all his people, to the battle ᶜat Edrei.

34 And the LORD said unto Moses, ᵃFear him not: for I have ⁱdelivered him into thy hand, and all his people, and his land; and ᵇthou shalt do to him as thou didst unto Sihon king of the Amorites, which dwelt at Heshbon.

35 ᵃSo they ⁱsmote him, and his sons, and all his people, until there was none left him alive: and they possessed his land.

## CHAPTER 22

AND ᵃthe children of Israel set forward, and ⁱpitched in the plains of Moab on this side Jordan *by* Jericho.

2 And ᵃBalak the son of Zippor saw all that Israel had done to the Amorites.

3 And ᵃMoab was ⁱsore afraid of the people, because they *were* many: and Moab was ²distressed because of the children of Israel.

4 And Moab said unto ᵃthe elders of Midian, Now shall this company ⁱlick up all *that are* round about us, as the ox licketh up the grass of the field. And Balak the son of Zippor *was* king of the Moabites at that time.

5 ᵃHe sent messengers therefore unto Balaam the son of Beor to ᵇPethor, which *is* by the ⁱriver of the

21:9 ᵃ 2 Kin. 18:4; John 3:14, 15 ⁱ *looked at*
21:10 ᵃ Num. 33:43, 44 ⁱ *camped*
21:12 ᵃ Deut. 2:13
21:13 ᵃ Num. 22:36; Judg. 11:18
21:14 ⁱ *Waheb in Suphah*, ancient unknown places
21:15 ᵃ Num. 21:28; Deut. 2:9, 18, 29
21:16 ᵃ Judg. 9:21
21:17 ᵃ Ex. 15:1
21:18 ᵃ Is. 33:22
21:20 ᵃ Num. 23:28 ⁱ *field* ² Lit. *Wasteland*
21:21 ᵃ Num. 32:33; Deut. 2:26–37; Judg. 11:19
21:22 ᵃ Num. 20:16, 17
21:23 ᵃ Deut. 29:7 ᵇ Deut. 2:32; Judg. 11:20 ⁱ *attacked*
21:24 ᵃ Deut. 2:33; Josh. 12:1; Neh. 9:22; Ps. 135:10; 136:19; Amos 2:9 ⁱ *took possession of*
21:25 ᵃ Amos 2:10
21:27 ⁱ *parables*
21:28 ᵃ Jer. 48:45, 46 ᵇ Deut. 2:9, 18; Is. 15:1 ᶜ Num. 22:41; 33:52
21:29 ᵃ Jer. 48:46 ᵇ Judg. 11:24; 1 Kin. 11:33; 2 Kin. 23:13 ᶜ Is. 15:2, 5 ᵈ Is. 16:2
21:30 ᵃ Num. 32:3, 34; Jer. 48:18, 22 ᵇ Is. 15:2
21:32 ᵃ Num. 32:1, 3, 35; Jer. 48:32 ⁱ *secretly search*
21:33 ᵃ Deut. 29:7 ᵇ Deut. 3:1 ᶜ Josh. 13:12
21:34 ᵃ Deut. 3:2 ᵇ Num. 21:24; Ps. 135:10; 136:20 ⁱ *given you victory over him*
21:35 ᵃ Deut. 3:3, 4; 29:7; Josh. 13:12 ⁱ *defeated*
22:1 ᵃ Num. 33:48, 49 ⁱ *camped*
22:2 ᵃ Josh. 24:9; Judg. 11:25; Mic. 6:5; Rev. 2:14
22:3 ᵃ Ex. 15:15 ⁱ *exceedingly* ² *sick with dread*
22:4 ᵃ Num. 25:15–18; 31:1–3; Josh. 13:21 ⁱ *consume*
22:5 ᵃ Num. 31:8, 16; Deut. 23:4; Josh. 13:22; 24:9; Neh. 13:1, 2; Mic. 6:5; 2 Pet. 2:15; Jude 11; Rev. 2:14 ᵇ Deut. 23:4 ⁱ The Euphrates

land of the [2]children of his people, to call him, saying, Behold, there is a people come out from Egypt: behold, they cover the face of the earth, and they [3]abide over against me:

6 [a]Come now therefore, I pray thee, [b]curse me this people; for they *are* too mighty for me: peradventure I shall prevail, *that* we may smite them, and *that* I may drive them out of the land: for I [1]wot that he whom thou blessest *is* blessed, and he whom thou cursest is cursed.

7 And the elders of Moab and the elders of Midian departed with [a]the [1]rewards of divination in their hand; and they came unto Balaam, and spake unto him the words of Balak.

8 And he said unto them, [a]Lodge here this night, and I will bring you word again, as the LORD shall speak unto me: and the princes of Moab abode with Balaam.

9 [a]And God came unto Balaam, and said, What men *are* these with thee?

10 And Balaam said unto God, Balak the son of Zippor, king of Moab, hath sent unto me, *saying*,

11 Behold, *there is* a people come out of Egypt, which covereth the face of the earth: come now, curse me them; peradventure I shall be able to [1]overcome them, and drive them out.

12 And God said unto Balaam, Thou shalt not go with them; thou shalt not curse the people: for [a]they *are* blessed.

13 And Balaam rose up in the morning, and said unto the princes of Balak, Get you into your land: for the LORD refuseth to give me [1]leave to go with you.

14 And the princes of Moab rose up, and they went unto Balak, and said, Balaam refuseth to come with us.

15 And Balak sent yet again princes, more, and more [1]honourable than they.

16 And they came to Balaam, and said to him, Thus saith Balak the son of Zippor, Let nothing, I pray thee, hinder thee from coming unto me:

17 For I will [a]promote thee unto very great honour, and I will do whatsoever thou sayest unto me: [b]come therefore, I pray thee, curse me this people.

18 And Balaam answered and said unto the servants of Balak, [a]If Balak would give me his house full of silver and gold, [b]I cannot go beyond the word of the LORD my God, to do less or more.

19 Now therefore, I pray you, [a]tarry ye also here this night, that I may know what the LORD will say unto me more.

20 [a]And God came unto Balaam at night, and said unto him, If the men

come to call thee, rise up, *and* go with them; but [b]yet the word which I shall say unto thee, that shalt thou do.

21 And Balaam rose up in the morning, and saddled his ass, and went with the princes of Moab.

22 And God's anger was [1]kindled because he went: [a]and the angel of the LORD stood in the way [2]for an adversary against him. Now he was riding upon his ass, and his two servants *were* with him.

23 And [a]the ass saw the angel of the LORD standing in the way, and his sword drawn in his hand: and the ass turned aside out of the way, and went into the field: and Balaam smote the ass, to turn her into the way.

24 But the angel of the LORD stood in a path of the vineyards, a wall *being* on this side, and a wall on that side.

25 And when the ass saw the angel of the LORD, she thrust herself unto the wall, and crushed Balaam's foot against the wall: and he smote her again.

26 And the angel of the LORD went further, and stood in a narrow place, where *was* no way to turn either to the right hand or to the left.

27 And when the ass saw the angel of the LORD, she fell down under Balaam: and Balaam's anger was kindled, and he smote the ass with a staff.

28 And the LORD [a]opened the mouth of the ass, and she said unto Balaam, What have I done unto thee, that thou hast smitten me these three times?

29 And Balaam said unto the ass, Because thou hast [1]mocked me: I would there were a sword in mine hand, [a]for now would I kill thee.

30 [a]And the ass said unto Balaam, *Am* not I thine ass, upon which thou hast ridden ever since *I was* thine unto this day? was I ever [1]wont to do so unto thee? And he said, Nay.

31 Then the LORD [a]opened the eyes of Balaam, and he saw the angel of the LORD standing in the way, and his sword drawn in his hand: and he bowed down his head, and fell flat on his face.

32 And the angel of the LORD said unto him, Wherefore hast thou smitten thine ass these three times? behold, I went out [1]to withstand thee, because *thy* way is [a]perverse[2] before me:

33 And the ass saw me, and turned from me these three times: unless she had turned from me, surely now also I had slain thee, and saved her alive.

34 And Balaam said unto the angel of the LORD, [a]I have sinned; for I knew not that thou stoodest in the way against me: now therefore, if

## Cross-references (center column)

22:5 [2] Or *the people of Amau* [3] *are settling next to*
22:6 [a] Num. 22:17; 23:7, 8 [b] Num. 22:12; 24:9 [1] *know*
22:7 [a] 1 Sam. 9:7, 8 [1] *diviner's fee*
22:8 [a] Num. 22:19
22:9 [a] Gen. 20:3
22:11 [1] *overpower*
22:12 [a] Num. 23:20; [Rom. 11:28]
22:13 [1] *permission*
22:15 [1] *distinguished*
22:17 [a] Num. 24:11 [b] Num. 22:6
22:18 [a] Num. 22:38; 24:13 [b] 1 Kin. 22:14; 2 Chr. 18:13
22:19 [a] Num. 22:8
22:20 [a] Num. 22:9

[b] Num. 22:35; 23:5, 12, 16, 26; 24:13
22:22 [a] Ex. 4:24 [1] *aroused* [2] *as*
22:23 [a] Josh. 5:13; 2 Kin. 6:17; Dan. 10:7; Acts 22:9
22:28 [a] 2 Pet. 2:16
22:29 [a] [Prov. 12:10; Matt. 15:19] [1] *abused*
22:30 [a] 2 Pet. 2:16 [1] *accustomed*
22:31 [a] Gen. 21:19; 2 Kin. 6:17; Luke 24:16, 31
22:32 [a] [2 Pet. 2:14, 15] [1] *as an adversary* [2] *contrary*
22:34 [a] 1 Sam. 15:24, 30; 26:21; 2 Sam. 12:13

it ¹displease thee, I will get me back again.

35 And the angel of the LORD said unto Balaam, Go with the men: ᵃbut only the word that I shall speak unto thee, that thou shalt speak. So Balaam went with the princes of Balak.

36 And when Balak heard that Balaam was come, ᵃhe went out to meet him unto a city of Moab, ᵇwhich *is* in the border of Arnon, which *is* in the utmost coast.

37 And Balak said unto Balaam, Did I not earnestly send unto thee to call thee? wherefore camest thou not unto me? am I not able indeed ᵃto promote thee to honour?

38 And Balaam said unto Balak, Lo, I am come unto thee: have I now any power at all to say any thing? ᵃthe word that God putteth in my mouth, that shall I speak.

39 And Balaam went with Balak, and they came unto Kirjath-huzoth.

40 And Balak offered oxen and sheep, and sent to Balaam, and to the princes that *were* with him.

41 And it came to pass on the morrow, that Balak took Balaam, and brought him up into the ᵃhigh places of Baal, that thence he might see the ¹utmost *part* of the people.

## CHAPTER 23

A ND Balaam said unto Balak, ᵃBuild me here seven altars, and prepare me here seven oxen and seven rams.

2 And Balak did as Balaam had spoken; and Balak and Balaam ᵃoffered on *every* altar a bullock and a ram.

3 And Balaam said unto Balak, ᵃStand by thy burnt offering, and I will go: ¹peradventure the LORD will come ᵇto meet me: and whatsoever he sheweth me I will tell thee. And he went to ²an high place.

4 ᵃAnd God met Balaam: and he said unto him, I have prepared seven altars, and I have offered upon *every* altar a bullock and a ram.

5 And the LORD ᵃput a word in Balaam's mouth, and said, Return unto Balak, and thus thou shalt speak.

6 And he returned unto him, and, lo, he stood by his burnt sacrifice, he, and all the princes of Moab.

7 And he ᵃtook¹ up his parable, and said, Balak the king of Moab hath brought me from Aram, out of the mountains of the east, *saying,* ᵇCome, curse me Jacob, and come, ᶜdefy Israel.

8 ᵃHow shall I curse, whom God hath not cursed? or how shall I defy, *whom* the LORD hath not defied?

9 For from the top of the rocks I see him, and from the hills I behold him: lo, ᵃthe people shall dwell alone, and

---

22:34 ¹ Lit. *is evil in your eyes*
22:35 ᵃ Num. 22:20
22:36 ᵃ Gen. 14:17 ᵇ Num. 21:13
22:37 ᵃ Num. 22:17; 24:11
22:38 ᵃ Num. 23:26; 24:13; 1 Kin. 22:14; 2 Chr. 18:13
22:41 ᵃ Num. 21:28; Deut. 12:2 ¹ *farthest extent*
23:1 ᵃ Num. 23:29
23:2 ᵃ Num. 23:14, 30
23:3 ᵃ Num. 23:15 ᵇ Num. 23:4, 16 ¹ *perhaps* ² *a desolate height*
23:4 ᵃ Num. 23:16
23:5 ᵃ Num. 22:20, 35, 38; 23:16; Deut. 18:18; Jer. 1:9
23:7 ᵃ Deut. 23:4; Job 27:1; 29:1; Ps. 78:2 ᵇ Num. 22:6, 11, 17 ᶜ 1 Sam. 17:10 ¹ *began his oracle or prophetic discourse*
23:8 ᵃ Num. 22:12
23:9 ᵃ Deut. 32:8; 33:28; Josh. 11:23

ᵇ Ex. 33:16; Ezra 9:2; [Eph. 2:14] ¹ *not reckoning itself*
23:10 ᵃ Gen. 13:16; 22:17; 28:14; 2 Chr. 1:9 ᵇ Ps. 116:15 ¹ *dust cloud* ² Lit. *my soul*
23:11 ᵃ Num. 22:11
23:12 ᵃ Num. 22:38
23:14 ᵃ Num. 23:1, 2
23:16 ᵃ Num. 22:35; 23:5
23:18 ᵃ Judg. 3:20
23:19 ᵃ 1 Sam. 15:29; Mal. 3:6; James 1:17 ᵇ Num. 11:23; 1 Kin. 8:56
23:20 ᵃ Gen. 12:2; 22:17; Num. 22:12
23:21 ᵃ Ps. 32:2; [Rom. 4:7, 8] ᵇ Ps. 89:15–18 ¹ *trouble*
23:22 ᵃ Num. 24:8 ᵇ Deut. 33:17; Job 39:10
23:23 ¹ *sorcery or enchantment* ² *fortune-telling* ᵃ Ps. 31:19; 44:1
23:24 ᵃ Gen. 49:9 ᵇ Gen. 49:27; Josh. 11:23

---

ᵇshall¹ not be reckoned among the nations.

10 ᵃWho can count the ¹dust of Jacob, and the number of the fourth *part* of Israel? Let ²me die ᵇthe death of the righteous, and let my last end be like his!

11 And Balak said unto Balaam, What hast thou done unto me? ᵃI took thee to curse mine enemies, and, behold, thou hast blessed *them* altogether.

12 And he answered and said, ᵃMust I not take heed to speak that which the LORD hath put in my mouth?

13 And Balak said unto him, Come, I pray thee, with me unto another place, from whence thou mayest see them: thou shalt see but the utmost part of them, and shalt not see them all: and curse me them from thence.

14 And he brought him into the field of Zophim, to the top of Pisgah, ᵃand built seven altars, and offered a bullock and a ram on *every* altar.

15 And he said unto Balak, Stand here by thy burnt offering, while I meet *the* LORD yonder.

16 And the LORD met Balaam, and ᵃput a word in his mouth, and said, Go again unto Balak, and say thus.

17 And when he came to him, behold, he stood by his burnt offering, and the princes of Moab with him. And Balak said unto him, What hath the LORD spoken?

18 And he took up his parable, and said, ᵃRise up, Balak, and hear; hearken unto me, thou son of Zippor:

19 ᵃGod *is* not a man, that he should lie; neither the son of man, that he should repent: hath he ᵇsaid, and shall he not do *it?* or hath he spoken, and shall he not make it good?

20 Behold, I have received *commandment* to bless: and ᵃhe hath blessed; and I cannot reverse it.

21 ᵃHe hath not beheld iniquity in Jacob, neither hath he seen ¹perverseness in Israel: the LORD his God *is* with him, ᵇand the shout of a king *is* among them.

22 ᵃGod brought them out of Egypt; he hath as it were ᵇthe strength of an unicorn.

23 Surely *there is* no ¹enchantment against Jacob, neither *is there* any ²divination against Israel: according to this time it shall be said of Jacob and of Israel, ᵃWhat hath God wrought!

24 Behold, the people shall rise up ᵃas a great lion, and lift up himself as a young lion: ᵇhe shall not lie down until he eat *of* the prey, and drink the blood of the slain.

25 And Balak said unto Balaam, Neither curse them at all, nor bless them at all.

26 But Balaam answered and said unto Balak, Told not I thee, saying, [a]All that the LORD speaketh, that I must do?

27 And Balak said unto Balaam, Come, I pray thee, I will bring thee unto another place; peradventure it will please God that thou mayest curse me them from thence.

28 And Balak brought Balaam unto the top of Peor, that looketh [a]toward [1]Jeshimon.

29 And Balaam said unto Balak, Build me here seven altars, and prepare me here seven bullocks and seven rams.

30 And Balak did as Balaam had said, and offered a bullock and a ram on *every* altar.

## CHAPTER 24

A ND when Balaam saw that it pleased the LORD to bless Israel, he went not, as at [a]other times, [1]to seek for enchantments, but he set his face toward the wilderness.

2 And Balaam lifted up his eyes, and he saw Israel [a]abiding *in his tents* according to their tribes; and [b]the spirit of God came upon him.

3 [a]And he took up his parable, and said, Balaam the son of Beor hath said, and the man whose eyes are [1]open hath said:

4 He hath said, which heard the words of God, which saw the vision of the Almighty, [a]falling *into a trance,* but having his eyes open:

5 How goodly are thy tents, O Jacob, *and* thy tabernacles, O Israel!

6 As the valleys are they spread forth, [a]as gardens by the river's side, as the trees of lign aloes [b]which the LORD hath planted, *and* as cedar trees beside the waters.

7 He shall pour the water out of his buckets, and his seed *shall be* [a]in many waters, and his king shall be higher than [b]Agag, and his [c]kingdom shall be exalted.

8 [a]God brought him forth out of Egypt; he hath as it were the strength of an unicorn: he shall [b]eat up the nations his enemies, and shall [c]break their bones, and [d]pierce *them* through with his arrows.

9 [a]He couched, he lay down as a lion, and as a great lion: who shall stir him up? [b]Blessed *is* he that blesseth thee, and cursed *is* he that curseth thee.

10 And Balak's anger was kindled against Balaam, and he [a]smote his hands together: and Balak said unto Balaam, [b]I called thee to curse mine enemies, and, behold, thou hast altogether blessed *them* these three times.

11 Therefore now flee thou to thy place: [a]I thought to promote thee

unto great honour; but, lo, the LORD hath kept thee back from honour.

12 And Balaam said unto Balak, Spake I not also to thy messengers which thou sentest unto me, saying,

13 If Balak would give me his house full of silver and gold, I cannot go beyond the commandment of the LORD, to do *either* good or bad of mine own mind; *but* what the LORD saith, that will I speak?

14 And now, behold, I go unto my people: come *therefore, and* [a]I will advertise thee what this people shall do to thy people in the [b]latter days.

15 And he took up his parable, and said, Balaam the son of Beor hath said, and the man whose eyes are open hath said:

16 He hath said, which heard the words of God, and knew the knowledge of the most High, *which* saw the vision of the Almighty, falling *into a trance,* but having his eyes open:

17 [a]I shall see him, but not now: I shall behold him, but not nigh: there shall come [b]a Star out of Jacob, and [c]a Sceptre shall rise out of Israel, and shall [1]smite the corners of Moab, and destroy all the [2]children of Sheth.

18 And [a]Edom shall be a possession, Seir also shall be a possession for his enemies; and Israel shall do [1]valiantly.

19 [a]Out of Jacob shall come he that [1]shall have dominion, and shall destroy him that remaineth of the city.

20 And when he looked on Amalek, he took up his parable, and said, Amalek *was* the first [1]of the nations; but his latter end *shall be* that he perish for ever.

21 And he looked on the Kenites, and took up his parable, and said, Strong is thy dwellingplace, and thou puttest thy nest in a rock.

22 Nevertheless the Kenite shall be wasted, until Asshur shall carry thee away captive.

23 And he took up his parable, and said, Alas, who shall live when God doeth this!

24 And ships *shall come* from the coast of [a]Chittim,[1] and shall afflict Asshur, and shall afflict [b]Eber, and [2]he also shall perish for ever.

25 And Balaam rose up, and went and [a]returned to his place: and Balak also went his way.

## CHAPTER 25

A ND Israel [1]abode in [a]Shittim,[2] and the [b]people began to commit [3]whoredom with the daughters of Moab.

2 And [a]they called the people unto [b]the sacrifices of their gods: and the people did eat, and [c]bowed down to their gods.

### Cross references

23:26 [a] Num. 22:38
23:28 [a] Num. 21:20 [1] Lit. *Wasteland*
24:1 [a] Num. 23:3, 15 [1] *to use sorcery or enchantments*
24:2 [a] Num. 2:2, 34 [b] Num. 11:25; 1 Sam. 10:10; 19:20, 23; 2 Chr. 15:1
24:3 [a] Num. 23:7, 18 [1] *opened*
24:4 [a] Ezek. 1:28
24:6 [a] Ps. 1:3; Jer. 17:8 [b] Ps. 104:16
24:7 [a] Jer. 51:13; Rev. 17:1, 15 [b] 1 Sam. 15:8, 9 [c] 2 Sam. 5:12; 1 Chr. 14:2
24:8 [a] Num. 23:22 [b] Num. 14:9; 23:24 [c] Ps. 2:9; Jer. 50:17 [d] Ps. 45:5
24:9 [a] Gen. 49:9; Num. 23:24 [b] Gen. 12:3; 27:29
24:10 [a] Ezek. 21:14, 17 [b] Num. 23:11; Neh. 13:2
24:11 [a] Num. 22:17, 37
24:14 [a] [Mic. 6:5] [b] Gen. 49:1; Deut. 4:30; Dan. 2:28
24:17 [a] Rev. 1:7; Matt. 1:2; Luke 3:34 [b] Matt. 2:2 [c] Gen. 49:10 [1] *shatter the forehead* [2] *sons of tumult*
24:18 [a] 2 Sam. 8:14 [1] *mightily*
24:19 [a] Gen. 49:10; Amos 9:11, 12 [1] *shall rule*
24:20 [1] *among*
24:24 [a] Gen. 10:4; Ezek. 27:6; Dan. 11:30 [1] *Cyprus* [b] Gen. 10:21, 25 [2] Amalek
24:25 [a] Num. 21:34; 31:8
25:1 [a] Num. 33:49; Josh. 2:1 [b] Rev. 2:14 [1] *remained* [2] *Acacia Grove* [3] *harlotry*
25:2 [a] Josh. 22:17; Hos. 9:10 [b] Ex. 34:15; Deut. 32:38; 1 Cor. 10:20 [c] Ex. 20:5

3 And Israel joined himself unto Baal-peor: and [a]the anger of the LORD was [1]kindled against Israel.

4 And the LORD said unto Moses, [a]Take all the heads of the people, and hang them up before the LORD against the sun, [b]that the fierce anger of the LORD may be turned away from Israel.

5 And Moses said unto [a]the judges of Israel, [b]Slay ye every one his men that were joined unto Baal-peor.

6 And, behold, one of the children of Israel came and brought unto his brethren a Midianitish woman in the sight of Moses, and in the sight of all the congregation of the children of Israel, [a]who *were* weeping *before* the door of the tabernacle of the congregation.

7 And [a]when Phinehas, [b]the son of Eleazar, the son of Aaron the priest, saw *it,* he rose up from among the congregation, and took a javelin in his hand;

8 And he went after the man of Israel into the tent, and thrust both of them through, the man of Israel, and the woman through her belly. So [a]the plague was [b]stayed from the children of Israel.

9 And [a]those that died in the plague were twenty and four thousand.

10 And the LORD spake unto Moses, saying,

11 [a]Phinehas, the son of Eleazar, the son of Aaron the priest, hath turned my wrath away from the children of Israel, while he was zealous for my sake among them, that I consumed not the children of Israel in [b]my jealousy.

12 Wherefore say, [a]Behold, I give unto him my [b]covenant of peace:

13 And he shall have it, and [a]his seed after him, *even* the covenant of [b]an everlasting priesthood; because he was [c]zealous for his God, and [d]made [1]an atonement for the children of Israel.

14 Now the name of the Israelite that was slain, *even* that was slain with the Midianitish woman, *was* Zimri, the son of Salu, a prince of a chief house among the Simeonites.

15 And the name of the Midianitish woman that was slain *was* Cozbi, the daughter of [a]Zur; he *was* head over a people, *and* of a chief house in Midian.

16 And the LORD spake unto Moses, saying,

17 [a]Vex[1] the Midianites, and smite them:

18 For they vex you with their [a]wiles,[1] wherewith they have [2]beguiled you in the matter of Peor, and in the matter of Cozbi, the daughter of a prince of Midian, their sister, which was slain in the day of the plague for Peor's sake.

## Cross References (center column)

25:3 [a] Ps. 106:28, 29 [1] aroused
25:4 [a] Deut. 4:3 [b] Num. 25:11; Deut. 13:17
25:5 [a] Ex. 18:21 [b] Deut. 13:6, 9
25:6 [a] Joel 2:17
25:7 [a] Ps. 106:30 [b] Ex. 6:25
25:8 [a] Ps. 106:30 [b] Num. 16:46–48
25:9 [a] Deut. 4:3
25:11 [a] Ps. 106:30 [b] [Ex. 20:5]; Deut. 32:16, 21; 1 Kin. 14:22; Ps. 78:58; Ezek. 16:38
25:12 [a] [Mal. 2:4, 5; 3:1] [b] Is. 54:10; Ezek. 34:25; 37:26; Mal. 2:5
25:13 [a] 1 Chr. 6:4 [b] Ex. 40:15 [c] Acts 22:3; Rom. 10:2 [d] [Heb. 2:17] [1] propitiation
25:15 [a] Num. 31:8; Josh. 13:21
25:17 [a] Num. 31:1–3 [1] Be hostile toward
25:18 [a] Num. 31:16; Rev. 2:14 [1] tricks or schemes [2] seduced
26:1 [a] Num. 25:9
26:2 [a] Ex. 30:12; 38:25, 26; Num. 1:2; 14:29 [b] Num. 1:3 [1] a census
26:3 [a] Num. 22:1; 31:12; 33:48; 35:1
26:4 [a] Num. 1:1
26:5 [a] Gen. 46:8; Ex. 6:14; 1 Chr. 5:1–3
26:9 [a] Num. 1:16; 16:1, 2 [1] contended
26:10 [a] Num. 16:32–35 [b] Num. 16:38–40; 1 Cor. 10:6; 2 Pet. 2:6
26:11 [a] Ex. 6:24; 1 Chr. 6:22, 23
26:12 [1] Jemuel, Gen. 46:10; Ex. 6:15 [2] Jarib, 1 Chr. 4:24
26:13 [1] Zohar, Gen. 46:10
26:15 [1] Ziphion, Gen. 46:16
26:16 [1] Ezbon, Gen. 46:16
26:17 [1] Arodi, Gen. 46:16

## CHAPTER 26

AND it came to pass after the [a]plague, that the LORD spake unto Moses and unto Eleazar the son of Aaron the priest, saying,

2 [a]Take [1]the sum of all the congregation of the children of Israel, [b]from twenty years old and upward, throughout their fathers' house, all that are able to go to war in Israel.

3 And Moses and Eleazar the priest spake with them [a]in the plains of Moab by Jordan *near* Jericho, saying,

4 Take the sum of the people, from twenty years old and upward; as the LORD [a]commanded Moses and the children of Israel, which went forth out of the land of Egypt.

5 [a]Reuben, the eldest son of Israel: the children of Reuben; Hanoch, *of whom cometh* the family of the Hanochites: of Pallu, the family of the Palluites:

6 Of Hezron, the family of the Hezronites: of Carmi, the family of the Carmites.

7 These *are* the families of the Reubenites: and they that were numbered of them were forty and three thousand and seven hundred and thirty.

8 And the sons of Pallu; Eliab.

9 And the sons of Eliab; Nemuel, and Dathan, and Abiram. This *is that* Dathan and Abiram, *which were* [a]famous in the congregation, who [1]strove against Moses and against Aaron in the company of Korah, when they strove against the LORD:

10 [a]And the earth opened her mouth, and swallowed them up together with Korah, when that company died, what time the fire devoured two hundred and fifty men: [b]and they became a sign.

11 Notwithstanding [a]the children of Korah died not.

12 The sons of Simeon after their families: of [1]Nemuel, the family of the Nemuelites: of Jamin, the family of the Jaminites: of [2]Jachin, the family of the Jachinites:

13 Of [1]Zerah, the family of the Zarhites: of Shaul, the family of the Shaulites.

14 These *are* the families of the Simeonites, twenty and two thousand and two hundred.

15 The children of Gad after their families: of [1]Zephon, the family of the Zephonites: of Haggi, the family of the Haggites: of Shuni, the family of the Shunites:

16 Of [1]Ozni, the family of the Oznites: of Eri, the family of the Erites:

17 Of [1]Arod, the family of the Arodites: of Areli, the family of the Arelites.

18 These *are* the families of the children of Gad according to those that

were numbered of them, forty thousand and five hundred.

19 ªThe sons of Judah *were* Er and Onan: and Er and Onan died in the land of Canaan.

20 And ªthe sons of Judah after their families were; of Shelah, the family of the Shelanites: of Pharez, the family of the Pharzites: of Zerah, the family of the Zarhites.

21 And the sons of Pharez were; of Hezron, the family of the Hezronites: of Hamul, the family of the Hamulites.

22 These *are* the families of Judah according to those that were numbered of them, threescore and sixteen thousand and five hundred.

23 *Of* the sons of Issachar after their families: *of* Tola, the family of the Tolaites: of ¹Pua, the family of the Punites:

24 Of ¹Jashub, the family of the Jashubites: of Shimron, the family of the Shimronites.

25 These *are* the families of Issachar according to those that were numbered of them, threescore and four thousand and three hundred.

26 ªOf the sons of Zebulun after their families: of Sered, the family of the Sardites: of Elon, the family of the Elonites: of Jahleel, the family of the Jahleelites.

27 These *are* the families of the Zebulunites according to those that were numbered of them, threescore thousand and five hundred.

28 ªThe sons of Joseph after their families *were* Manasseh and Ephraim.

29 Of the sons of ªManasseh: of ᵇMachir, the family of the Machirites: and Machir begat Gilead: of Gilead *come* the family of the Gileadites.

30 These *are* the sons of Gilead: *of* ¹Jeezer, the family of the Jeezerites: of Helek, the family of the Helekites:

31 And *of* Asriel, the family of the Asrielites: and *of* Shechem, the family of the Shechemites:

32 And *of* Shemida, the family of the Shemidaites: and *of* Hepher, the family of the Hepherites.

33 And ªZelophehad the son of Hepher had no sons, but daughters: and the names of the daughters of Zelophehad *were* Mahlah, and Noah, Hoglah, Milcah, and Tirzah.

34 These *are* the families of Manasseh, and those that were numbered of them, fifty and two thousand and seven hundred.

35 These *are* the sons of Ephraim after their families: of Shuthelah, the family of the Shuthalhites: of ¹Becher, the family of the Bachrites: of Tahan, the family of the Tahanites.

36 And these *are* the sons of Shuthelah: of Eran, the family of the Eranites.

37 These *are* the families of the sons of Ephraim according to those that were numbered of them, thirty and two thousand and five hundred. These *are* the sons of Joseph after their families.

38 ªThe sons of Benjamin after their families: of Bela, the family of the Belaites: of Ashbel, the family of the Ashbelites: of ᵇAhiram, the family of the Ahiramites:

39 Of ªShupham,¹ the family of the Shuphamites: of Hupham, the family of the Huphamites.

40 And the sons of Bela were Ard and Naaman: ªof Ard, the family of the Ardites: *and* of Naaman, the family of the Naamites.

41 These *are* the sons of Benjamin after their families: and they that were numbered of them *were* forty and five thousand and six hundred.

42 These *are* the sons of Dan after their families: of ¹Shuham, the family of the Shuhamites. These *are* the families of Dan after their families.

43 All the families of the Shuhamites, according to those that were numbered of them, *were* threescore and four thousand and four hundred.

44 ªOf the children of Asher after their families: of Jimna, the family of the Jimnites: of Jesui, the family of the Jesuites: of Beriah, the family of the Beriites.

45 Of the sons of Beriah: of Heber, the family of the Heberites: of Malchiel, the family of the Malchielites.

46 And the name of the daughter of Asher *was* Sarah.

47 These *are* the families of the sons of Asher according to those that were numbered of them; *who were* fifty and three thousand and four hundred.

48 ªOf the sons of Naphtali after their families: of Jahzeel, the family of the Jahzeelites: of Guni, the family of the Gunites:

49 Of Jezer, the family of the Jezerites: of ªShillem, the family of the Shillemites.

50 These *are* the families of Naphtali according to their families: and they that were numbered of them *were* forty and five thousand and four hundred.

51 ªThese *were* the numbered of the children of Israel, six hundred thousand and a thousand seven hundred and thirty.

52 And the LORD spake unto Moses, saying,

53 ªUnto these the land shall be ᵇdivided for an inheritance according to the number of names.

54 ªTo many thou shalt give the ¹more inheritance, and to few thou shalt give the ²less inheritance: to every one shall his inheritance be given

---

**Cross references (center column):**

26:19 ª Gen. 38:2; 46:12

26:20 ª 1 Chr. 2:3

26:23 ¹ Heb. *Puvah,* Gen. 46:13

26:24 ¹ *Job,* Gen. 46:13

26:26 ª Gen. 46:14

26:28 ª Gen. 46:20; Deut. 33:16

26:29 ª Josh. 17:1
ᵇ 1 Chr. 7:14, 15

26:30 ¹ *Abiezer,* Josh. 17:2

26:33 ª Num. 27:1; 36:11

26:35 ¹ *Bered,* 1 Chr. 7:20

26:38 ª Gen. 46:21; 1 Chr. 7:6
ᵇ Gen. 46:21; 1 Chr. 8:1, 2

26:39 ¹ 1 Chr. 7:12 ¹ MT *Shephupham; Shephuphan,* 1 Chr. 8:5

26:40 ¹ 1 Chr. 8:3

26:42 ¹ *Hushim,* Gen. 46:23

26:44 ª Gen. 46:17; 1 Chr. 7:30

26:48 ª Gen. 46:24; 1 Chr. 7:13

26:49 ¹ 1 Chr. 7:13

26:51 ª Ex. 12:37; 38:26; Num. 1:46; 11:21

26:53 ª Josh. 11:23; 14:1 ᵇ Num. 33:54

26:54 ª Num. 33:54 ¹ *larger* ² *smaller*

according to those that were numbered of him.

55 Notwithstanding the land shall be [a]divided by lot: according to the names of the tribes of their fathers they shall inherit.

56 According to the lot shall the possession thereof be divided between many and few.

57 [a]And these *are* they that were numbered of the Levites after their families: of Gershon, the family of the Gershonites: of Kohath, the family of the Kohathites: of Merari, the family of the Merarites.

58 These *are* the families of the Levites: the family of the Libnites, the family of the Hebronites, the family of the Mahlites, the family of the Mushites, the family of the Korathites. And Kohath begat Amram.

59 And the name of Amram's wife *was* [a]Jochebed, the daughter of Levi, whom *her mother* bare to Levi in Egypt: and she bare unto Amram Aaron and Moses, and Miriam their sister.

60 [a]And unto Aaron was born Nadab, and Abihu, Eleazar, and Ithamar.

61 And [a]Nadab and Abihu died, when they offered [1]strange fire before the LORD.

62 [a]And those that were numbered of them were twenty and three thousand, all males from a month old and upward: [b]for they were not numbered among the children of Israel, because there was [c]no inheritance given them among the children of Israel.

63 These *are* they that were numbered by Moses and Eleazar the priest, who numbered the children of Israel [a]in the plains of Moab by Jordan *near* Jericho.

64 [a]But among these there was not a man of them whom Moses and Aaron the priest numbered, when they numbered the children of Israel in the [b]wilderness of Sinai.

65 For the LORD had said of them, They [a]shall surely die in the wilderness. And there was not left a man of them, [b]save Caleb the son of Jephunneh, and Joshua the son of Nun.

## CHAPTER 27

THEN came the daughters of [a]Zelophehad, the son of Hepher, the son of Gilead, the son of Machir, the son of Manasseh, of the families of Manasseh the son of Joseph: and these *are* the names of his daughters; Mahlah, Noah, and Hoglah, and Milcah, and Tirzah.

2 And they stood before Moses, and before Eleazar the priest, and before the princes and all the congregation, *by* the door of the tabernacle of the congregation, saying,

3 Our father [a]died in the wilderness, and he was not in the company of them that gathered themselves together against the LORD [b]in the company of Korah; but died in his own sin, and had no sons.

4 Why should the name of our father be [a]done[1] away from among his family, because he hath no son? [b]Give unto us *therefore* a [2]possession among the brethren of our father.

5 And Moses [a]brought their cause before the LORD.

6 And the LORD spake unto Moses, saying,

7 The daughters of Zelophehad speak right: [a]thou shalt surely give them a possession of an inheritance among their father's brethren; and thou shalt cause the inheritance of their father to pass unto them.

8 And thou shalt speak unto the children of Israel, saying, If a man die, and have no son, then ye shall cause his inheritance to pass unto his daughter.

9 And if he have no daughter, then ye shall give his inheritance unto his brethren.

10 And if he have no brethren, then ye shall give his inheritance unto his father's brethren.

11 And if his father have no brethren, then ye shall give his inheritance unto his kinsman that is next to him of his family, and he shall possess it: and it shall be unto the children of Israel [a]a statute of judgment, as the LORD commanded Moses.

12 And the LORD said unto Moses, [a]Get thee up into this mount Abarim, and see the land which I have given unto the children of Israel.

13 And when thou hast seen it, thou also [a]shalt [1]be gathered unto thy people, as Aaron thy brother was gathered.

14 For ye [a]rebelled against my commandment in the desert of Zin, in the strife of the congregation, to [1]sanctify me at the water before their eyes: that *is* the [b]water of Meribah in Kadesh in the wilderness of Zin.

15 And Moses spake unto the LORD, saying,

16 Let the LORD, [a]the God of the spirits of all flesh, set a man over the congregation,

17 [a]Which may go out before them, and which may go in before them, and which may lead them out, and which may bring them in; that the congregation of the LORD be not [b]as sheep which have no shepherd.

18 And the LORD said unto Moses, Take thee Joshua the son of Nun, a man [a]in whom *is* the spirit, and [b]lay thine hand upon him;

### Cross references (center column)

26:55 [a] Num. 33:54; 34:13; Josh. 11:23; 14:2

26:57 [a] Gen. 46:11; Ex. 6:16–19; Num. 3:15; 1 Chr. 6:1, 16

26:59 [a] Ex. 2:1, 2; 6:20

26:60 [a] Num. 3:2

26:61 [a] Lev. 10:1, 2; Num. 3:3, 4; 1 Chr. 24:2 [1] *foreign or profane*

26:62 [a] Num. 3:39 [b] Num. 1:49 [c] Num. 18:20, 23, 24

26:63 [a] Num. 26:3

26:64 [a] Num. 14:29–35; Deut. 2:14–16; Heb. 3:17 [b] Num. 1:1–46

26:65 [a] Num. 14:26–35; [1 Cor. 10:5, 6] [b] Num. 14:30

27:1 [a] Num. 26:33; 36:1, 11; Josh. 17:3

27:3 [a] Num. 14:35; 26:64, 65 [b] Num. 16:1, 2

27:4 [a] Deut. 25:6 [b] Josh. 17:4 [1] *removed* [2] *inheritance*

27:5 [a] Ex. 18:13–26

27:7 [a] Num. 36:2; Josh. 17:4

27:11 [a] Num. 35:29

27:12 [a] Num. 33:47; Deut. 3:23–27; 32:48–52; 34:1–4

27:13 [a] Num. 20:12, 24, 28; 31:2; Deut. 10:6; 34:5, 6 [1] *die and join your ancestors*

27:14 [a] Num. 20:12, 24; Deut. 1:37; 32:51; Ps. 106:32, 33 [b] Ex. 17:7 [1] *hallow*

27:16 [a] Num. 16:22; Heb. 12:9

27:17 [a] Deut. 31:2; 1 Sam. 8:20; 18:13; 2 Chr. 1:10 [b] 1 Kin. 22:17; Zech. 10:2; Matt. 9:36; Mark 6:34

27:18 [a] Gen. 41:38; Judg. 3:10; 1 Sam. 16:13, 18 [b] Deut. 34:9

19 And set him before Eleazar the priest, and before all the congregation; and [a]give[1] him a charge in their sight.

20 And [a]thou shalt put *some* of thine honour upon him, that all the congregation of the children of Israel [b]may be obedient.

21 [a]And he shall stand before Eleazar the priest, who shall ask *counsel* for him [b]after the judgment of Urim before the LORD: [c]at his word shall they go out, and at his word they shall come in, *both* he, and all the children of Israel with him, even all the congregation.

22 And Moses did as the LORD commanded him: and he took Joshua, and set him before Eleazar the priest, and before all the congregation:

23 And he laid his hands upon him, [a]and [1]gave him a charge, as the LORD commanded by the hand of Moses.

## CHAPTER 28

AND the LORD spake unto Moses, saying,

2 Command the children of Israel, and say unto them, My offering, *and* [a]my bread for my sacrifices made by fire, *for* a sweet savour unto me, shall ye observe to offer unto me [1]in their due season.

3 And thou shalt say unto them, [a]This *is* the offering made by fire which ye shall offer unto the LORD; two lambs of the first year without spot day by day, *for* a continual burnt offering.

4 The one lamb shalt thou offer in the morning, and the other lamb shalt thou offer at even;

5 And [a]a tenth *part* of an ephah of flour for a [b]meat offering, mingled with the fourth *part* of an hin of beaten oil.

6 *It is* [a]a continual burnt offering, which was ordained in mount Sinai for a sweet savour, a sacrifice made by fire unto the LORD.

7 And the drink offering thereof *shall be* the fourth *part* of an hin for the one lamb: [a]in the holy *place* shalt thou cause the strong wine to be poured unto the LORD *for* a drink offering.

8 And the other lamb shalt thou offer at even: as the [1]meat offering of the morning, and as the drink offering thereof, thou shalt offer *it,* a sacrifice made by fire, of a [2]sweet savour unto the LORD.

9 And on the sabbath day two lambs of the first year without spot, and two tenth deals of flour *for* a meat offering, mingled with oil, and the drink offering thereof:

10 *This is* [a]the burnt offering of every

sabbath, beside the continual burnt offering, and his drink offering.

11 And [a]in the beginnings of your months ye shall offer a burnt offering unto the LORD; two young bullocks, and one ram, seven lambs of the first year without spot;

12 And [a]three tenth deals of flour *for* a meat offering, mingled with oil, for one bullock; and two tenth deals of flour *for* a meat offering, mingled with oil, for one ram;

13 And a several tenth deal of flour mingled with oil *for* a meat offering unto one lamb; *for* a burnt offering of a sweet savour, a sacrifice made by fire unto the LORD.

14 And their drink offerings shall be half an hin of wine unto a bullock, and the third *part* of an hin unto a ram, and a fourth *part* of an hin unto a lamb: this *is* the burnt offering of every month throughout the months of the year.

15 And [a]one kid of the goats for a sin offering unto the LORD shall be offered, beside the continual burnt offering, and his drink offering.

16 [a]And in the fourteenth day of the first month *is* the passover of the LORD.

17 [a]And in the fifteenth day of this month *is* the feast: seven days shall unleavened bread be eaten.

18 In the [a]first day *shall be* an holy [1]convocation; ye shall do no manner of [2]servile work *therein:*

19 But ye shall offer a sacrifice made by fire *for* a burnt offering unto the LORD; two young bullocks, and one ram, and seven lambs of the first year: [a]they shall be unto you without blemish:

20 And their meat offering *shall be* of flour mingled with oil: three tenth deals shall ye offer for a bullock, and two tenth deals for a ram;

21 A several tenth deal shalt thou offer for every lamb, throughout the seven lambs:

22 And [a]one goat *for* a sin offering, to make [1]an atonement for you.

23 Ye shall offer these beside the burnt offering in the morning, which *is* for a continual burnt offering.

24 After this manner ye shall offer daily, throughout the seven days, the meat of the sacrifice made by fire, of a sweet savour unto the LORD: it shall be offered beside the continual burnt offering, and his drink offering.

25 And [a]on the seventh day ye shall have an holy convocation; ye shall do no servile work.

26 Also [a]in the day of the firstfruits, when ye bring a new meat offering unto the LORD, after your weeks *be out,* ye shall have a holy convocation; ye shall do no servile work:

27:19 [a] Deut. 3:28; 31:3, 7, 8, 23 [1] *commission him*
27:20 [a] Num. 11:17 [b] Josh. 1:16–18
27:21 [a] Judg. 20:18, 23, 26; 1 Sam. 23:9; 30:7 [b] Ex. 28:30; 1 Sam. 28:6 [c] Josh. 9:14; 1 Sam. 22:10
27:23 [a] Deut. 3:28; 31:7, 8 [1] *commissioned him*
28:2 [a] Lev. 3:11; 21:6, 8; [Mal. 1:7, 12] [1] *at their appointed time*
28:3 [a] Ex. 29:38–42
28:5 [a] Ex. 16:36; Num. 15:4 [b] Lev. 2:1
28:6 [a] Ex. 29:42; Amos 5:25
28:7 [a] Ex. 29:42
28:8 [1] *grain or meal* [2] *pleasing aroma*
28:10 [a] Ezek. 46:4
28:11 [a] Num. 10:10; 1 Sam. 20:5; 1 Chr. 23:31; 2 Chr. 2:4; Ezra 3:5; Neh. 10:33; Is. 1:13, 14; Ezek. 45:17; 46:6, 7; Hos. 2:11; Col. 2:16
28:12 [a] Num. 15:4–12
28:15 [a] Num. 15:24; 28:3, 22
28:16 [a] Ex. 12:1–20; Lev. 23:5–8; Num. 9:2–5; Deut. 16:1–8; Ezek. 45:21
28:17 [a] Lev. 23:6
28:18 [a] Ex. 12:16; Lev. 23:7 [1] *assembly or gathering* [2] *labourious*
28:19 [a] Lev. 22:20; Num. 28:31; 29:8; Deut. 15:21
28:22 [a] Num. 28:15 [1] *a propitiation*
28:25 [a] Ex. 12:16; 13:6; Lev. 23:8
28:26 [a] Ex. 23:16; 34:22; Lev. 23:10–21; Deut. 16:9–12; Acts 2:1

27 But ye shall offer the burnt offering for a sweet savour unto the LORD; [a]two young bullocks, one ram, seven lambs of the first year;

28 And their [1]meat offering of flour mingled with oil, three tenth deals unto one bullock, two tenth deals unto one ram,

29 A several tenth deal unto one lamb, throughout the seven lambs;

30 *And* one kid of the goats, to make [1]an atonement for you.

31 Ye shall offer *them* beside the continual burnt offering, and his meat offering, ([a]they shall be unto you [1]without blemish) and their drink offerings.

## CHAPTER 29

AND in the seventh month, on the first *day* of the month, ye shall have an holy convocation; ye shall do no servile work: [a]it is a day of blowing the trumpets unto you.

2 And ye shall offer a burnt offering for a sweet savour unto the LORD; one young bullock, one ram, *and* seven lambs of the first year without blemish:

3 And their meat offering *shall be of* flour mingled with oil, three tenth deals for a bullock, *and* two tenth deals for a ram,

4 And one tenth deal for one lamb, throughout the seven lambs:

5 And one kid of the goats *for* a sin offering, to make an atonement for you:

6 Beside [a]the burnt offering of the month, and his meat offering, and [b]the daily burnt offering, and his meat offering, and their drink offerings, [c]according unto their manner, for a sweet savour, a sacrifice made by fire unto the LORD.

7 And [a]ye shall have on the tenth *day* of this seventh month an holy convocation; and ye shall [b]afflict your souls: ye shall not do any work *therein:*

8 But ye shall offer a burnt offering unto the LORD *for* a sweet savour; one young bullock, one ram, *and* seven lambs of the first year; [a]they shall be unto you without blemish:

9 And their meat offering *shall be of* flour mingled with oil, three tenth deals to a bullock, *and* two tenth deals to one ram,

10 A several tenth deal for one lamb, throughout the seven lambs:

11 One kid of the goats *for* a sin offering; beside [a]the sin offering of atonement, and the continual burnt offering, and the meat offering of it, and their drink offerings.

12 And [a]on the fifteenth day of the seventh month ye shall have an holy convocation; ye shall do no servile work, and ye shall keep a feast unto the LORD seven days:

13 And [a]ye shall offer a burnt offering, a sacrifice made by fire, of a sweet savour unto the LORD; thirteen young bullocks, two rams, *and* fourteen lambs of the first year; they shall be without blemish:

14 And their meat offering *shall be of* flour mingled with oil, three tenth deals unto every bullock of the thirteen bullocks, two tenth deals to each ram of the two rams,

15 And a several tenth deal to each lamb of the fourteen lambs:

16 And one kid of the goats *for* a sin offering; beside the continual burnt offering, his meat offering, and his drink offering.

17 And on the [a]second day *ye shall offer* twelve young bullocks, two rams, fourteen lambs of the first year without spot:

18 And their meat offering and their drink offerings for the bullocks, for the rams, and for the lambs, *shall be* according to their number, [a]after the manner:

19 And one kid of the goats *for* a sin offering; beside the continual burnt offering, and the meat offering thereof, and their drink offerings.

20 And on the third day eleven bullocks, two rams, fourteen lambs of the first year without blemish;

21 And their meat offering and their drink offerings for the bullocks, for the rams, and for the lambs, *shall be* according to their number, [a]after the manner:

22 And one goat *for* a sin offering; beside the continual burnt offering, and his meat offering, and his drink offering.

23 And on the fourth day ten bullocks, two rams, *and* fourteen lambs of the first year without blemish:

24 Their meat offering and their drink offerings for the bullocks, for the rams, and for the lambs, *shall be* according to their number, [1]after the manner:

25 And one kid of the goats *for* a sin offering; beside the continual burnt offering, his meat offering, and his drink offering.

26 And on the fifth day nine bullocks, two rams, *and* fourteen lambs of the first year without spot:

27 And their meat offering and their drink offerings for the bullocks, for the rams, and for the lambs, *shall be* according to their number, after the manner:

28 And one goat *for* a sin offering; beside the continual burnt offering, and his meat offering, and his drink offering.

28:27 [a] Lev. 23:18, 19
28:28 [1] *grain or meal*
28:30 [1] *a propitiation*
28:31 [a] Num. 28:3, 19 [1] *without defect*
29:1 [a] Ex. 23:16; 34:22; Lev. 23:23–25
29:6 [a] Num. 28:11–15 [b] Num. 28:3 [c] Num. 15:11, 12
29:7 [a] Lev. 16:29–34; 23:26–32 [b] Ps. 35:13; Is. 58:5
29:8 [a] Num. 28:19
29:11 [a] Lev. 16:3, 5
29:12 [a] Lev. 23:33–35; Deut. 16:13–15; Ezek. 45:25
29:13 [a] Ezra 3:4
29:17 [a] Lev. 23:36
29:18 [a] Num. 15:12; 28:7, 14; 29:3, 4, 9, 10
29:21 [a] Num. 29:18
29:24 [1] *according to the ordinance*

29 And on the sixth day eight bullocks, two rams, *and* fourteen lambs of the first year without blemish:

30 And their meat offering and their drink offerings for the bullocks, for the rams, and for the lambs, *shall be* according to their number, after the manner:

31 And one goat *for* a sin offering; beside the continual burnt offering, his meat offering, and his drink offering.

32 And on the seventh day seven bullocks, two rams, *and* fourteen lambs of the first year without blemish:

33 And their meat offering and their drink offerings for the bullocks, for the rams, and for the lambs, *shall be* according to their number, after the manner:

34 And one goat *for* a sin offering; beside the continual burnt offering, his meat offering, and his drink offering.

35 On the eighth day ye shall have a ªsolemn[1] assembly: ye shall do no servile work *therein:*

36 But ye shall offer a burnt offering, a sacrifice made by fire, of a sweet savour unto the LORD: one bullock, one ram, seven lambs of the first year without blemish:

37 Their meat offering and their drink offerings for the bullock, for the ram, and for the lambs, *shall be* according to their number, after the manner:

38 And one goat *for* a sin offering; beside the continual burnt offering, and his meat offering, and his drink offering.

39 These *things* ye shall [1]do unto the LORD in your ªset[2] feasts, beside your ᵇvows, and your freewill offerings, for your burnt offerings, and for your meat offerings, and for your drink offerings, and for your peace offerings.

40 And Moses told the children of Israel according to all that the LORD commanded Moses.

## CHAPTER 30

AND Moses spake unto ªthe heads of the tribes concerning the children of Israel, saying, This *is* the thing which the LORD hath commanded.

2 ªIf a man vow a vow unto the LORD, or ᵇswear an oath [1]to bind his soul with a bond; he shall not break his word, he shall ᶜdo according to all that proceedeth out of his mouth.

3 If a woman also vow a vow unto the LORD, and bind *herself* by a bond, *being* in her father's house in her youth;

4 And her father hear her vow, and her bond wherewith she hath bound

her soul, and her father [1]shall hold his peace at her: then all her vows shall stand, and every bond wherewith she hath bound her soul shall stand.

5 But if her father [1]disallow her in the day that he heareth; not any of her vows, or of her bonds wherewith she hath bound her soul, shall stand: and the LORD shall forgive her, because her father disallowed her.

6 And if she had at all an husband, [1]when she vowed, or uttered ought out of her lips, wherewith she bound her soul;

7 And her husband heard *it*, and [1]held his peace at her in the day that he heard *it*: then her vows shall stand, and her bonds wherewith she bound her soul shall stand.

8 But if her husband ªdisallowed[1] her on the day that he heard *it*; then he shall make her vow which she vowed, and that which she uttered with her lips, wherewith she bound her soul, of none effect: and the LORD shall forgive her.

9 But every vow of a widow, and of her that is divorced, wherewith they have bound their souls, shall stand against her.

10 And if she vowed in her husband's house, or bound her soul by a bond with an oath;

11 And her husband heard *it*, and held his peace at her, *and* disallowed her not: then all her vows shall stand, and every bond wherewith she bound her soul shall stand.

12 But if her husband hath utterly made them void on the day he heard *them; then* whatsoever proceeded out of her lips concerning her vows, or concerning the bond of her soul, shall not stand: her husband hath made them [1]void; and the LORD shall forgive her.

13 Every vow, and every binding oath to afflict the soul, her husband may establish it, or her husband may make it void.

14 But if her husband altogether hold his peace at her from day to day; then he establisheth all her vows, or all her bonds, which *are* upon her: he confirmeth them, because he held his peace at her in the day that he heard *them*.

15 But if he shall any ways make them void after that he hath heard *them;* then he shall bear her [1]iniquity.

16 These *are* the statutes, which the LORD commanded Moses, between a man and his wife, between the father and his daughter, *being yet* in her youth in her father's house.

## CHAPTER 31

AND the LORD spake unto Moses, saying,

### Cross references (center column)

29:35 ª Lev. 23:36
[1] *day of restraint*
29:39 ª Lev. 23:1–44; 1 Chr. 23:31; 2 Chr. 31:3; Ezra 3:5; Neh. 10:33; Is. 1:14 ᵇ Lev. 7:16; 22:18, 21, 23; 23:38 [1] *present* [2] *appointed*
30:1 ª Num. 1:4, 16; 7:2
30:2 ª Lev. 27:2; Deut. 23:21–23; Judg. 11:30, 31, 35; Eccl. 5:4 ᵇ Lev. 5:4; Matt. 14:9; Acts 23:14 ᶜ Job 22:27; Ps. 22:25; 50:14; 66:13, 14; Nah. 1:15 [1] *binding himself by some agreement*
30:4 [1] *says nothing to interfere*
30:5 [1] *overrules*
30:6 [1] *while bound by her vows*
30:7 [1] *makes no response*
30:8 ª [Gen. 3:16] [1] *overrules*
30:12 [1] *annulled or invalidated*
30:15 [1] *guilt*

153

2 [a]Avenge[1] the children of Israel [2]of the Midianites: afterward shalt thou [b]be gathered unto thy people.

3 And Moses spake unto the people, saying, Arm some of yourselves unto the war, and let them go against the Midianites, and avenge the LORD of [a]Midian.

4 Of every tribe a thousand, throughout all the tribes of Israel, shall ye send to the war.

5 So there were delivered out of the thousands of Israel, a thousand of *every* tribe, twelve thousand armed for war.

6 And Moses sent them to the war, a thousand of *every* tribe, them and Phinehas the son of Eleazar the priest, to the war, with the holy instruments, and [a]the trumpets to blow in his hand.

7 And they warred against the Midianites, as the LORD commanded Moses; and [a]they slew all the [b]males.

8 And they slew the kings of Midian, beside the rest of them that were slain; *namely,* [a]Evi, and Rekem, and [b]Zur, and Hur, and Reba, five kings of Midian: [c]Balaam also the son of Beor they slew with the sword.

9 And the children of Israel took *all* the women of Midian captives, and their little ones, and took the spoil of all their cattle, and all their flocks, and all their goods.

10 And they burnt all their cities wherein they dwelt, and all their goodly castles, with fire.

11 And [a]they took all the spoil, and all the prey, *both* of men and of beasts.

12 And they brought the captives, and the prey, and the spoil, unto Moses, and Eleazar the priest, and unto the congregation of the children of Israel, unto the camp at the plains of Moab, which *are* by Jordan *near* Jericho.

13 And Moses, and Eleazar the priest, and all the princes of the congregation, went forth to meet them without the camp.

14 And Moses was [1]wroth with the officers of the host, *with* the captains over thousands, and captains over hundreds, which came from the battle.

15 And Moses said unto them, Have ye saved [a]all the women alive?

16 Behold, [a]these caused the children of Israel, through the [b]counsel of Balaam, to commit trespass against the LORD in the matter of Peor, and [c]there was a plague among the congregation of the LORD.

17 Now therefore [a]kill every male among the little ones, and kill every woman that hath known man [b]by lying with him.

18 But all the women children, that have not known a man by lying with him, keep alive [a]for yourselves.

19 And [a]do ye abide without the camp seven days: whosoever hath killed any person, and [b]whosoever hath touched any slain, purify *both* yourselves and your captives on the third day, and on the seventh day.

20 And purify all *your* raiment, and all that is made of skins, and all work of goats' *hair,* and all things made of wood.

21 And Eleazar the priest said unto the men of war which went to the battle, This *is* the [1]ordinance of the law which the LORD commanded Moses;

22 Only the gold, and the silver, the brass, the iron, the tin, and the lead,

23 Every thing that may abide the fire, ye shall make *it* go through the fire, and it shall be clean: nevertheless it shall be purified [a]with the water of separation: and all that abideth not the fire ye shall make go through the water.

24 [a]And ye shall wash your clothes on the seventh day, and ye shall be clean, and afterward ye shall come into the camp.

25 And the LORD spake unto Moses, saying,

26 Take the sum of the [1]prey that was [2]taken, *both* of man and of beast, thou, and Eleazar the priest, and the chief fathers of the congregation:

27 And [a]divide the prey into two parts; between them that took the war upon them, who went out to battle, and between all the congregation:

28 And levy a [1]tribute unto the LORD of the men of war which went out to battle: [a]one[2] soul of five hundred, *both* of the persons, and of the beeves, and of the asses, and of the sheep:

29 Take *it* of their half, and [a]give *it* unto Eleazar the priest, *for* an heave offering of the LORD.

30 And of the children of Israel's half, thou shalt take [a]one portion of fifty, of the persons, of the beeves, of the asses, and of the [1]flocks, of all manner of beasts, and give them unto the Levites, [b]which [2]keep the charge of the tabernacle of the LORD.

31 And Moses and Eleazar the priest did as the LORD commanded Moses.

32 And the booty, *being* the rest of the prey which the men of war had caught, was six hundred thousand and seventy thousand and five thousand sheep,

33 And threescore and twelve thousand beeves,

34 And threescore and one thousand asses,

---

**Cross-references (center column):**

31:2 [a] Num. 25:17
[b] Num. 25:12, 13
[1] *Take vengeance*
[2] *on*

31:3 [a] Josh. 13:21

31:6 [a] Num. 10:9

31:7 [a] Deut. 20:13; Judg. 21:11; 1 Sam. 27:9; 1 Kin. 11:15, 16 [b] Gen. 34:25

31:8 [a] Josh. 13:21
[b] Num. 25:15
[c] Num. 31:16; Josh. 13:22

31:11 [a] Deut. 20:14

31:14 [1] *angry*

31:15 [a] Deut. 20:14

31:16 [a] Num. 25:2
[b] Num. 24:14; 2 Pet. 2:15; Rev. 2:14 [c] Num. 25:9

31:17 [a] Deut. 7:2; 20:16–18; Judg. 21:11 [1] *intimately*

31:18 [a] Deut. 21:10–14

31:19 [a] Num. 5:2
[b] Num. 19:11–22

31:21 [1] *statute*

31:23 [a] Num. 19:9, 17

31:24 [a] Lev. 11:25

31:26 [1] *plunder*
[2] *captured*

31:27 [a] Josh. 22:8; 1 Sam. 30:24

31:28 [a] Num. 31:30, 47 [1] *tax* [2] *one for every*

31:29 [a] Deut. 18:1–5

31:30 [a] Num. 31:42–47 [b] Num. 3:7, 8, 25, 31, 36; 18:3, 4 [1] *sheep* [2] *perform the service*

35 And thirty and two thousand persons in all, of women that had not known man by lying with him.

36 And the half, *which was* the portion of them that went out to war, was in number three hundred thousand and seven and thirty thousand and five hundred sheep:

37 And the LORD's [1]tribute of the sheep was six hundred and three-score and fifteen.

38 And the beeves *were* thirty and six thousand; of which the LORD's tribute *was* threescore and twelve.

39 And the asses *were* thirty thousand and five hundred; of which the LORD's tribute *was* threescore and one.

40 And the persons *were* sixteen thousand; of which the LORD's tribute *was* thirty and two persons.

41 And Moses gave the tribute, *which was* the LORD's heave offering, unto Eleazar the priest, [a]as the LORD commanded Moses.

42 And of the children of Israel's half, which Moses divided from the men that warred,

43 (Now the half *that pertained unto* the congregation was three hundred thousand and thirty thousand *and* seven thousand and five hundred sheep,

44 And thirty and six thousand beeves,

45 And thirty thousand asses and five hundred,

46 And sixteen thousand persons;)

47 Even [a]of the children of Israel's half, Moses took one portion of fifty, *both* of man and of beast, and gave them unto the Levites, which kept the charge of the tabernacle of the LORD; as the LORD commanded Moses.

48 And the officers which *were* over thousands of the host, the captains of thousands, and captains of hundreds, came near unto Moses:

49 And they said unto Moses, Thy servants have taken the sum of the men of war which *are* under our [1]charge, and there lacketh not one man of us.

50 We have therefore brought an [1]oblation for the LORD, what every man hath [2]gotten, of jewels of gold, chains, and bracelets, rings, earrings, and [3]tablets, [a]to make an [4]atonement for our souls before the LORD.

51 And Moses and Eleazar the priest took the gold of them, *even* all wrought jewels.

52 And all the gold of the offering that they offered up to the LORD, of the captains of thousands, and of the captains of hundreds, was sixteen thousand seven hundred and fifty shekels.

53 (For [a]the men of war had taken spoil, every man for himself.)

54 And Moses and Eleazar the priest took the gold of the captains of thousands, and of hundreds, and brought it into the tabernacle of the congregation, [a]for a memorial for the children of Israel before the LORD.

## CHAPTER 32

Now the children of Reuben and the children of Gad had a very great multitude of cattle: and when they saw the land of [a]Jazer, and the land of [b]Gilead, that, behold, the place *was* a place for cattle;

2 The children of Gad and the children of Reuben came and spake unto Moses, and to Eleazar the priest, and unto the princes of the congregation, saying,

3 Ataroth, and Dibon, and Jazer, and [a]Nimrah, and [b]Heshbon, and Elealeh, and [c]Shebam, and Nebo, and [d]Beon,

4 *Even* the country [a]which the LORD [1]smote before the congregation of Israel, *is* a land for cattle, and thy servants have cattle:

5 Wherefore, said they, if we have found [1]grace in thy sight, let this land be given unto thy servants for a possession, *and* bring us not over Jordan.

6 And Moses said unto the children of Gad and to the children of Reuben, Shall your brethren go to war, and shall ye sit here?

7 And wherefore [a]discourage ye the heart of the children of Israel from going over into the land which the LORD hath given them?

8 Thus did your fathers, [a]when I sent them from Kadesh-barnea [b]to see the land.

9 For [a]when they went up unto the valley of Eshcol, and saw the land, they discouraged the heart of the children of Israel, that they should not go into the land which the LORD had given them.

10 [a]And the LORD's anger was [1]kindled the same time, and he [2]sware, saying,

11 Surely none of the men that came up out of Egypt, [a]from twenty years old and upward, shall see the land which I sware unto Abraham, unto Isaac, and unto Jacob; because [b]they have not [1]wholly followed me:

12 Save Caleb the son of Jephunneh the Kenezite, and Joshua the son of Nun: [a]for they have wholly followed the LORD.

13 And the LORD's anger was [1]kindled against Israel, and he made them [a]wander in the wilderness forty years, until [b]all the generation, that had done evil in the sight of the LORD, was [2]consumed.

---

**Cross-references (center column):**

31:37 [1] *tax*

31:41 [a] Num. 5:9, 10; 18:8, 19

31:47 [a] Num. 31:30

31:49 [1] *command*

31:50 [a] Ex. 30:12–16 [1] *offering* [2] Lit. *found* [3] *necklaces* [4] *propitiation*

31:53 [a] Num. 31:32; Deut. 20:14

31:54 [a] Ex. 30:16

32:1 [a] Num. 21:32; Josh. 13:25; 2 Sam. 24:5 [b] Deut. 3:13

32:3 [a] Num. 32:36 [b] Josh. 13:17, 26 [c] Num. 32:38 [d] Num. 32:38

32:4 [a] Num. 21:24, 34, 35 [1] *defeated*

32:5 [1] *favour*

32:7 [a] Num. 13:27–14:4

32:8 [a] Num. 13:3, 26 [b] Deut. 1:19–25

32:9 [a] Num. 13:24, 31; Deut. 1:24, 28

32:10 [a] Num. 14:11; Deut. 1:34–36 [1] *aroused* [2] *swore an oath*

32:11 [a] Num. 14:28, 29; 26:63–65; Deut. 1:35 [b] Num. 14:24, 30 [1] *fully*

32:12 [a] Num. 14:6–9, 24, 30; Deut. 1:36; Josh. 14:8, 9

32:13 [a] Num. 14:33–35 [b] Num. 26:64, 65 [1] *aroused* [2] *destroyed*

14 And, behold, ye are risen up in your fathers' stead, ¹an increase of sinful men, to augment yet the ªfierce anger of the LORD toward Israel.

15 For if ye ªturn away from after him, he will yet again leave them in the wilderness; and ye shall destroy all this people.

16 And they came near unto him, and said, We will build sheepfolds here for our cattle, and cities for our little ones:

17 But ªwe ourselves will go ready armed before the children of Israel, until we have brought them unto their place: and our little ones shall dwell in the fenced cities because of the inhabitants of the land.

18 ªWe will not return unto our houses, until the children of Israel have ¹inherited every man his inheritance.

19 For we will not inherit with them on yonder side Jordan, or forward; ªbecause our inheritance is fallen to us on this side Jordan eastward.

20 And ªMoses said unto them, If ye will do this thing, if ye will go armed before the LORD to war,

21 And will go all of you armed over Jordan before the LORD, until he hath driven out his enemies from before him,

22 And ªthe land be subdued before the LORD: then afterward ᵇye shall return, and be ¹guiltless before the LORD, and before Israel; and ᶜthis land shall be your possession before the LORD.

23 But if ye will not do so, behold, ye have sinned against the LORD: and be sure ªyour sin will find you out.

24 ªBuild you cities for your little ones, and folds for your sheep; and do that which ¹hath proceeded out of your mouth.

25 And the children of Gad and the children of Reuben spake unto Moses, saying, Thy servants will do as my lord commandeth.

26 ªOur little ones, our wives, our flocks, and all our cattle, shall be there in the cities of Gilead:

27 ªBut thy servants will pass over, every man armed for war, before the LORD to battle, as my lord saith.

28 So ªconcerning them Moses commanded Eleazar the priest, and Joshua the son of Nun, and the chief fathers of the tribes of the children of Israel:

29 And Moses said unto them, If the children of Gad and the children of Reuben will pass with you over Jordan, every man armed to battle, before the LORD, and the land shall be subdued before you; then ye shall give them the land of Gilead for a possession:

30 But if they will not pass over with you armed, they shall have possessions among you in the land of Canaan.

31 And the children of Gad and the children of Reuben answered, saying, As the LORD hath said unto thy servants, so will we do.

32 We will pass over armed before the LORD into the land of Canaan, that the possession of our inheritance on this side Jordan *may be* ours.

33 And ªMoses gave unto them, *even* to the children of Gad, and to the children of Reuben, and unto half the tribe of Manasseh the son of Joseph, ᵇthe kingdom of Sihon king of the Amorites, and the kingdom of Og king of Bashan, the land, with the cities thereof in the coasts, *even* the cities of the country round about.

34 And the children of Gad ªbuilt ªDibon, and Ataroth, and ᵇAroer,

35 And Atroth, Shophan, and ªJaazer, and Jogbehah,

36 And ªBeth-nimrah, and Beth-haran, ᵇfenced cities: and folds for sheep.

37 And the children of Reuben ªbuilt Heshbon, and Elealeh, and Kirjathaim,

38 And ªNebo, and ᵇBaal-meon, (ᶜtheir names being changed,) and Shibmah: and gave other names unto the cities which they builded.

39 And the children of ªMachir the son of Manasseh went to Gilead, and took it, and dispossessed the Amorite which *was* in it.

40 And Moses ªgave Gilead unto Machir the son of Manasseh; and he dwelt therein.

41 And ªJair the son of Manasseh went and took the small towns thereof, and called them ᵇHavoth-jair.¹

42 And Nobah went and took Kenath, and the villages thereof, and called it Nobah, after his own name.

## CHAPTER 33

THESE *are* the journeys of the children of Israel, which went forth out of the land of Egypt with their armies under the ªhand of Moses and Aaron.

2 And Moses wrote their goings out according to their journeys by the commandment of the LORD: and these *are* their journeys according to their goings out.

3 And they ªdeparted from Rameses in ᵇthe first month, on the fifteenth day of the first month; on the morrow after the passover the children of Israel went out ᶜwith ¹an high hand in the sight of all the Egyptians.

4 For the Egyptians buried all *their* firstborn, ªwhich the LORD had smitten among them: ᵇupon their gods also the LORD executed judgments.

### Cross references

32:14 ª Num. 11:1; Deut. 1:34 ¹ *a brood*

32:15 ª Deut. 30:17, 18; Josh. 22:16–18; 2 Chr. 7:19; 15:2

32:17 ª Josh. 4:12, 13

32:18 ª Josh. 22:1–4 ¹ *possessed*

32:19 ª Josh. 12:1; 13:8

32:20 ª Deut. 3:18; Josh. 1:14

32:22 ª Deut. 3:20; Josh. 11:23 ᵇ Josh. 22:4 ᶜ Deut. 3:12, 15, 16, 18; Josh. 1:15; 13:8, 32; 22:4, 9 ¹ *blameless*

32:23 ª Gen. 4:7; 44:16; Josh. 7:1–26; Is. 59:12; [Gal. 6:7]

32:24 ª Num. 32:16 ¹ *you said you would do*

32:26 ª Josh. 1:14

32:27 ª Josh. 4:12

32:28 ª Josh. 1:13

32:33 ª Deut. 3:8–17; 29:8; Josh. 12:1–6; 13:8–31; 22:4 ᵇ Num. 21:24, 33, 35

32:34 ª Num. 33:45, 46 ᵇ Deut. 2:36

32:35 ª Num. 32:1, 3

32:36 ª Num. 32:3 ᵇ Num. 32:24

32:37 ª Num. 21:27

32:38 ª Is. 46:1 ᵇ Ezek. 25:9 ᶜ Ex. 23:13; Josh. 23:7

32:39 ª Gen. 50:23; Num. 27:1; 36:1

32:40 ª Deut. 3:12, 13, 15; Josh. 13:31

32:41 ª Deut. 3:14; Josh. 13:30 ᵇ Judg. 10:4; 1 Kin. 4:13 ¹ Lit. *Towns of Jair*

33:1 ª Ps. 77:20

33:3 ª Ex. 12:37 ᵇ Ex. 12:2; 13:4 ᶜ Ex. 14:8 ¹ *boldness*

33:4 ª Ex. 12:29 ᵇ [Ex. 12:12; 18:11]; Is. 19:1

5 ªAnd the children of Israel removed from Rameses, and ¹pitched in Succoth.

6 And they departed from ªSuccoth, and pitched in Etham, which *is* in the edge of the wilderness.

7 And ªthey removed from Etham, and turned again unto Pi-hahiroth, which *is* before Baal-zephon: and they pitched before Migdol.

8 And they departed from before ¹Pi-hahiroth, and ªpassed through the midst of the sea into the wilderness, and went three days' journey in the wilderness of Etham, and pitched in Marah.

9 And they removed from Marah, and ªcame unto Elim: and in Elim *were* twelve fountains of water, and threescore and ten palm trees; and they pitched there.

10 And they removed from Elim, and encamped by the Red sea.

11 And they removed from the Red sea, and encamped in the ªwilderness of Sin.

12 And they took their journey out of the wilderness of Sin, and encamped in Dophkah.

13 And they departed from Dophkah, and encamped in Alush.

14 And they removed from Alush, and encamped at ªRephidim, where was no water for the people to drink.

15 And they departed from Rephidim, and pitched in the ªwilderness of Sinai.

16 And they removed from the desert of Sinai, and pitched ªat ¹Kibroth-hattaavah.

17 And they departed from Kibroth-hattaavah, and ªencamped at Hazeroth.

18 And they departed from Hazeroth, and pitched in ªRithmah.

19 And they departed from Rithmah, and pitched at Rimmon-parez.

20 And they departed from Rimmon-parez, and pitched in Libnah.

21 And they removed from Libnah, and pitched at Rissah.

22 And they journeyed from Rissah, and pitched in Kehelathah.

23 And they went from Kehelathah, and pitched in mount Shapher.

24 And they removed from mount Shapher, and encamped in Haradah.

25 And they removed from Haradah, and pitched in Makheloth.

26 And they removed from Makheloth, and encamped at Tahath.

27 And they departed from Tahath, and pitched at Tarah.

28 And they removed from Tarah, and pitched in Mithcah.

29 And they went from Mithcah, and pitched in Hashmonah.

30 And they departed from Hashmonah, and ªencamped at Moseroth.

31 And they departed from Moseroth, and pitched in Bene-jaakan.

32 And they removed from ªBene-jaakan, and ᵇencamped at Hor-hagidgad.

33 And they went from Hor-hagidgad, and pitched in Jotbathah.

34 And they removed from Jotbathah, and encamped at Ebronah.

35 And they departed from Ebronah, ªand encamped at Ezion-gaber.

36 And they removed from Ezion-gaber, and pitched in the ªwilderness of Zin, which *is* Kadesh.

37 And they removed from ªKadesh, and pitched in mount Hor, in the edge of the land of Edom.

38 And ªAaron the priest went up into mount Hor at the commandment of the LORD, and died there, in the fortieth year after the children of Israel were come out of the land of Egypt, in the first *day* of the fifth month.

39 And Aaron *was* an hundred and twenty and three years old when he died in mount Hor.

40 And ªking Arad the Canaanite, which dwelt in the south in the land of Canaan, heard of the coming of the children of Israel.

41 And they departed from mount Hor, and pitched in Zalmonah.

42 And they departed from Zalmonah, and pitched in Punon.

43 And they departed from Punon, and ªpitched in Oboth.

44 And ªthey departed from Oboth, and pitched in ¹Ije-abarim, in the border of Moab.

45 And they departed from ¹Iim, and pitched ªin Dibon-gad.

46 And they removed from Dibon-gad, and encamped in ªAlmon-diblathaim.

47 And they removed from Almon-diblathaim, ªand pitched in the mountains of Abarim, before Nebo.

48 And they departed from the mountains of Abarim, and ªpitched in the plains of Moab by Jordan *near* Jericho.

49 And they pitched by Jordan, from Beth-jesimoth *even* unto ªAbel-shittim¹ in the plains of Moab.

50 And the LORD spake unto Moses in the plains of Moab by Jordan *near* Jericho, saying,

51 Speak unto the children of Israel, and say unto them, ªWhen ye are passed over Jordan into the land of Canaan;

52 ªThen ye shall drive out all the inhabitants of the land from before you, and destroy all their pictures, and destroy all their molten images, and quite pluck down all their ¹high places:

53 And ye shall dispossess *the inhabitants of* the land, and dwell

---

**Cross-references (center column):**

33:5 ª Ex. 12:37
¹ *camped*
33:6 ª Ex. 13:20
33:7 ª Ex. 14:1, 2, 9
33:8 ª Ex. 14:22; 15:22, 23 ¹ Heb. *Hahiroth*
33:9 ª Ex. 15:27
33:11 ª Ex. 16:1
33:14 ª Ex. 17:1; 19:2
33:15 ª Ex. 16:1; 19:1, 2
33:16 ª Num. 11:34 ¹ Lit. *The Graves of Craving*
33:17 ª Num. 11:35
33:18 ª Num. 12:16
33:30 ª Deut. 10:6

33:32 ª Deut. 10:6 ᵇ Deut. 10:7
33:35 ª Deut. 2:8; 1 Kin. 9:26; 22:48
33:36 ª Num. 20:1; 27:14
33:37 ª Num. 20:22, 23; 21:4
33:38 ª Num. 20:25, 28; Deut. 10:6; 32:50
33:40 ª Num. 21:1
33:43 ª Num. 21:10
33:44 ª Num. 21:11 ¹ *Heaps of Abarim*
33:45 ª Num. 32:34 ¹ Or *Ijim*, the same as *Ije-abarim*
33:46 ª Jer. 48:22; Ezek. 6:14
33:47 ª Num. 21:20; Deut. 32:49
33:48 ª Num. 22:1; 31:12; 35:1
33:49 ª Num. 25:1; Josh. 2:1 ¹ *the Abel Acacia Grove*
33:51 ª Deut. 7:1, 2; 9:1; Josh. 3:17
33:52 ª Ex. 23:24, 33; 34:13; Deut. 7:2, 5; 12:3; Judg. 2:2; Ps. 106:34–36 ¹ *Places of pagan worship*

therein: for I have given you the land to [a]possess it.

54 And [a]ye shall divide the land by lot for an inheritance among your families: *and* to the more ye shall give the [1]more inheritance, and to the fewer ye shall give the [2]less inheritance: every man's *inheritance* shall be in the place where his lot falleth; according to the tribes of your fathers ye shall inherit.

55 But if ye will not drive out the inhabitants of the land from before you; then it shall come to pass, that those which ye let remain of them *shall be* [a]pricks[1] in your eyes, and thorns in your sides, and shall [2]vex you in the land wherein ye dwell.

56 Moreover it shall come to pass, *that* I shall do unto you, as I thought to do unto them.

### CHAPTER 34

AND the LORD spake unto Moses, saying,

2 Command the children of Israel, and say unto them, When ye come into [a]the land of Canaan; (this *is* the land that shall fall unto you for an inheritance, *even* the land of Canaan with the coasts thereof:)

3 Then [a]your south quarter shall be from the wilderness of Zin along by the coast of Edom, and your south border shall be the outmost coast of [b]the salt sea eastward:

4 And your border shall turn from the south [a]to the ascent of Akrabbim, and pass on to Zin: and the going forth thereof shall be from the south [b]to Kadesh-barnea, and shall go on to [c]Hazar-addar, and pass on to Azmon:

5 And the border [1]shall fetch a compass from Azmon [a]unto the river of Egypt, and the goings out of it shall be at the sea.

6 And *as for* the [a]western border, ye shall even have the great sea for a border: this shall be your west border.

7 And this shall be your north border: from the great sea ye shall point out for you [a]mount Hor:

8 From mount Hor ye shall point out *your border* [a]unto the entrance of Hamath; and the goings forth of the border shall be to [b]Zedad:

9 And the border shall go on to Ziphron, and the goings out of it shall be at [a]Hazar-enan: this shall be your north border.

10 And ye shall point out your east border from Hazar-enan to Shepham:

11 And the coast shall go down from Shepham [a]to Riblah, on the east side of Ain; and the border shall descend, and shall reach unto the [1]side of the sea [b]of Chinnereth eastward:

12 And the border shall go down to Jordan, and the goings out of it shall be at [a]the salt sea: this shall be your land with the coasts thereof round about.

13 And Moses commanded the children of Israel, saying, [a]This *is* the land which ye shall inherit by lot, which the LORD commanded to give unto the nine tribes, and to the half tribe:

14 [a]For the tribe of the children of Reuben according to the house of their fathers, and the tribe of the children of Gad according to the house of their fathers, have received *their inheritance;* and half the tribe of Manasseh have received their inheritance:

15 The two tribes and the half tribe have received their inheritance on this side Jordan *near* Jericho eastward, toward the sunrising.

16 And the LORD spake unto Moses, saying,

17 These *are* the names of the men which shall divide the land unto you: [a]Eleazar the priest, and Joshua the son of Nun.

18 And ye shall take one [a]prince of every tribe, to divide the land by inheritance.

19 And the names of the men *are* these: Of the tribe of Judah, Caleb the son of Jephunneh.

20 And of the tribe of the children of Simeon, Shemuel the son of Ammihud.

21 Of the tribe of Benjamin, Elidad the son of Chislon.

22 And the prince of the tribe of the children of Dan, Bukki the son of Jogli.

23 The prince of the children of Joseph, for the tribe of the children of Manasseh, Hanniel the son of Ephod.

24 And the prince of the tribe of the children of Ephraim, Kemuel the son of Shiphtan.

25 And the prince of the tribe of the children of Zebulun, Elizaphan the son of Parnach.

26 And the prince of the tribe of the children of Issachar, Paltiel the son of Azzan.

27 And the prince of the tribe of the children of Asher, Ahihud the son of Shelomi.

28 And the prince of the tribe of the children of Naphtali, Pedahel the son of Ammihud.

29 These *are they* whom the LORD commanded to [1]divide the inheritance unto the children of Israel in the land of Canaan.

### CHAPTER 35

AND the LORD spake unto Moses in [a]the plains of Moab by Jordan *near* Jericho, saying,

## Cross references (center column)

33:53 [a] Deut. 11:31; Josh. 21:43
33:54 [a] Num. 26:53–56 [1] *larger* [2] *smaller*
33:55 [a] Josh. 23:13; Judg. 2:3 [1] *irritants* [2] *harass*
34:2 [a] Gen. 17:8; Deut. 1:7, 8; Ps. 78:54, 55; 105:11
34:3 [a] Josh. 15:1–3; Ezek. 47:13, 19 [b] Gen. 14:3; Josh. 15:2
34:4 [a] Josh. 15:3 [b] Num. 13:26; 32:8 [c] Josh. 15:3, 4
34:5 [a] Gen. 15:18; Josh. 15:4, 47; 1 Kin. 8:65; Is. 27:12 [1] *shall turn from*
34:6 [a] Ex. 23:31; Josh. 15:12; Ezek. 47:20
34:7 [a] Num. 33:37
34:8 [a] Num. 13:21; Josh. 13:5; 2 Kin. 14:25 [b] Ezek. 47:15
34:9 [a] Ezek. 47:17
34:11 [a] 2 Kin. 23:33; Jer. 39:5, 6 [b] Deut. 3:17; Josh. 11:2; 12:3; 13:27; 19:35; Matt. 14:34; Luke 5:1 [1] *Lit. shoulder*
34:12 [a] Num. 34:3
34:13 [a] Gen. 15:18; Num. 26:52–56; Deut. 11:24; Josh. 14:1–5
34:14 [a] Num. 32:33
34:17 [a] Josh. 14:1, 2; 19:51
34:18 [a] Num. 1:4, 16
34:29 [1] *apportion the inheritance*
35:1 [a] Num. 33:50

2 ªCommand the children of Israel, that they give unto the Levites of the inheritance of their possession cities to dwell in; and ye shall give *also* unto the Levites ᵇsuburbs for the cities round about.

3 And the cities shall they have to dwell in; and the suburbs of them shall be for their cattle, and for their goods, and for all their beasts.

4 And the suburbs of the cities, which ye shall give unto the Levites, *shall reach* from the wall of the city and outward a thousand cubits round about.

5 And ye shall measure from without the city on the east side two thousand cubits, and on the south side two thousand cubits, and on the west side two thousand cubits, and on the north side two thousand cubits; and the city *shall be* in the midst: this shall be to them the suburbs of the cities.

6 And among the cities which ye shall give unto the Levites *there shall be* ªsix cities for refuge, which ye shall appoint for the manslayer, that he may flee thither: and to ¹them ye shall add forty and two cities.

7 *So* all the cities which ye shall give to the Levites *shall be* ªforty and eight cities: them *shall ye give* with their suburbs.

8 And the cities which ye shall give *shall be* ªof the possession of the children of Israel: ᵇfrom *them that have* many ye shall give many; but from *them that have* few ye shall give few: every one shall give of his cities unto the Levites according to his inheritance which ¹he inheriteth.

9 And the LORD spake unto Moses, saying,

10 Speak unto the children of Israel, and say unto them, ªWhen ye be come over Jordan into the land of Canaan;

11 Then ªye shall appoint you cities to be cities of refuge for you; that the slayer may flee thither, which killeth any person ¹at unawares.

12 ªAnd they shall be unto you cities for refuge from the avenger; that the manslayer die not, until he stand before the congregation in judgment.

13 And of these cities which ye shall give ªsix cities shall ye have for refuge.

14 ªYe shall give three cities on this side Jordan, and three cities shall ye give in the land of Canaan, *which* shall be cities of refuge.

15 These six cities shall be a refuge, *both* for the children of Israel, and ªfor the stranger, and for the sojourner among them: that every one that killeth any person unawares may flee thither.

16 ªAnd if he smite him with an instrument of iron, so that he die, he *is* a murderer: the murderer shall surely be put to death.

17 And if he smite him with throwing a stone, wherewith he may die, and he die, he *is* a murderer: the murderer shall surely be put to death.

18 Or *if* he smite him with an hand weapon of wood, wherewith he may die, and he die, he *is* a murderer: the murderer shall surely be put to death.

19 ªThe ¹revenger of blood himself shall slay the murderer: when he meeteth him, he shall slay him.

20 But ªif he ¹thrust him of hatred, or hurl at him ᵇby laying of wait, that he die;

21 Or in enmity smite him with his hand, that he die: he that smote *him* shall surely be put to death; *for* he *is* a murderer: the revenger of blood shall slay the murderer, when he meeteth him.

22 But if he thrust him suddenly ªwithout enmity, or have cast upon him any thing without ¹laying of wait,

23 Or with any stone, wherewith a man may die, seeing *him* not, and cast *it* upon him, that he die, and *was* not his enemy, neither sought his harm:

24 Then ªthe congregation shall judge between the slayer and the revenger of blood according to these judgments:

25 And the congregation shall deliver the slayer out of the hand of the revenger of blood, and the congregation shall restore him to the city of his refuge, whither he was fled: and ªhe shall abide in it unto the death of the high priest, ᵇwhich was anointed with the holy oil.

26 But if the slayer shall at any time ¹come without the border of the city of his refuge, whither he was fled;

27 And the revenger of blood find him without the borders of the city of his refuge, and the revenger of blood kill the slayer; ¹he shall not be guilty of blood:

28 Because he should have remained in the city of his refuge until the death of the high priest: but after the death of the high priest the slayer shall return into the land of his possession.

29 So these *things* shall be for ªa statute of judgment unto you throughout your generations in all your dwellings.

30 Whoso killeth any person, the murderer shall be put to death by the ªmouth of witnesses: but one witness ¹shall not testify against any person *to cause him* to die.

31 Moreover ye shall take no ¹satisfaction for the life of a murderer, which *is* guilty of death: but he shall be surely put to death.

---

**Center column notes:**

35:2 ª Josh. 14:3, 4; 21:2, 3; Ezek. 45:1; 48:10–20
ᵇ Lev. 25:22–34

35:6 ª Deut. 4:41; Josh. 20:2, 7, 8; 21:3, 13 ¹ *these*

35:7 ª Josh. 21:41

35:8 ª Josh. 21:3
ᵇ Num. 26:54; 33:54 ¹ *each inherits*

35:10 ª Deut. 19:2; Josh. 20:1–9

35:11 ª Ex. 21:13; Num. 35:22–25; Deut. 19:1–13 ¹ *accidentally*

35:12 ª Deut. 19:6; Josh. 20:3, 5, 6

35:13 ª Num. 35:6

35:14 ª Deut. 4:41; Josh. 20:8

35:15 ª Num. 15:16

35:16 ª Ex. 21:12, 14; Lev. 24:17; Deut. 19:11, 12

35:19 ª Num. 35:21, 24, 27; Deut. 19:6, 12 ¹ *blood avenger*, a family member who is to avenge the victim

35:20 ª Gen. 4:8; 2 Sam. 3:27; 20:10; 1 Kin. 2:31, 32 ᵇ Ex. 21:14; Deut. 19:11, 12 ¹ *pushes*

35:22 ª Ex. 21:13 ¹ *lying in wait*

35:24 ª Num. 35:12; Josh. 20:6

35:25 ª Josh. 20:6 ᵇ Ex. 29:7; Lev. 4:3; 21:10

35:26 ¹ *goes outside*

35:27 ¹ *there shall be no bloodguiltiness*

35:29 ª Num. 27:11

35:30 ª Deut. 17:6; 19:15; Matt. 18:16; John 7:51; 8:17, 18; 2 Cor. 13:1; Heb. 10:28 ¹ *is not sufficient testimony*

35:31 ¹ *ransom*

32 And ye shall take no satisfaction for him that is fled to the city of his refuge, that he should come again to dwell in the land, until the death of the priest.

33 So ye shall not pollute the land wherein ye *are:* for blood ᵃit defileth the land: and ¹the land cannot be cleansed of the blood that is shed therein, but ᵇby the blood of him that shed it.

34 ᵃDefile not therefore the land which ye shall inhabit, wherein I dwell: for ᵇI the LORD dwell among the children of Israel.

## CHAPTER 36

A ND the chief fathers of the families of the ᵃchildren of Gilead, the son of Machir, the son of Manasseh, of the families of the sons of Joseph, came near, and ᵇspake before Moses, and before the princes, the chief fathers of the children of Israel:

2 And they said, ᵃThe LORD commanded my lord to give the land for an inheritance by lot to the children of Israel: and ᵇmy lord was commanded by the LORD to give the inheritance of Zelophehad our brother unto his daughters.

3 And if they be married to any of the sons of the *other* tribes of the children of Israel, then shall their inheritance be ᵈtaken from the inheritance of our fathers, and shall be put to the inheritance of the tribe ¹whereunto they are received: so shall it be taken from the lot of our inheritance.

4 And when ᵃthe jubile of the children of Israel shall be, then shall their inheritance be put unto the inheritance of the tribe whereunto they are received: so shall their inheritance be taken away from the inheritance of the tribe of our fathers.

5 And Moses commanded the children of Israel according to the word of the LORD, saying, The tribe of the sons of Joseph ᵃhath said well.

6 This *is* the thing which the LORD doth command concerning the daughters of Zelophehad, saying, Let them ¹marry to whom they think best; ᵃonly to the family of the tribe of their father shall they marry.

7 So shall not the inheritance of the children of Israel remove from tribe to tribe: for every one of the children of Israel shall ᵃkeep¹ himself to the inheritance of the tribe of his fathers.

8 And ᵃevery daughter, that possesseth an inheritance in any tribe of the children of Israel, shall be wife unto one of the family of the tribe of her father, that the children of Israel may enjoy every man the inheritance of his fathers.

9 Neither shall the inheritance remove from *one* tribe to another tribe; but every one of the tribes of the children of Israel shall keep himself to his own inheritance.

10 Even as the LORD commanded Moses, so did the daughters of Zelophehad:

11 ᵃFor Mahlah, Tirzah, and Hoglah, and Milcah, and Noah, the daughters of Zelophehad, were married unto their father's brothers' sons:

12 *And* they were married into the families of the sons of Manasseh the son of Joseph, and their inheritance remained in the tribe of the family of their father.

13 These *are* the commandments and the judgments, which the LORD commanded by the hand of Moses unto the children of Israel ᵃin the plains of Moab by Jordan *near* Jericho.

35:33 ᵃ Deut. 21:7, 8; Ps. 106:38 ᵇ Gen. 9:6 ¹ *no expiation can be made for the land for the blood that is shed*

35:34 ᵃ Lev. 18:24, 25; Deut. 21:23 ᵇ Ex. 29:45, 46

36:1 ᵃ Num. 26:29 ᵇ Num. 27:1–11

36:2 ᵃ Num. 26:55; 33:54; Josh. 17:4 ᵇ Num. 27:1, 5–7

36:3 ᵃ Num. 27:4 ¹ *into which they married*

36:4 ᵃ Lev. 25:10

36:5 ᵃ Num. 27:7

36:6 ᵃ Num. 36:11, 12 ¹ Lit. *be wives*

36:7 ᵃ 1 Kin. 21:3 ¹ *keep the inheritance of*

36:8 ᵃ 1 Chr. 23:22

36:11 ᵃ Num. 26:33; 27:1

36:13 ᵃ Num. 26:3; 33:50

# THE FIFTH BOOK OF MOSES CALLED
# DEUTERONOMY

Deuteronomy, Moses' "Upper Desert Discourse," consists of a series of farewell messages by Israel's 120-year-old leader. It is addressed to the new generation destined to possess the Land of Promise—those who survived the forty years of wilderness wandering.

Like Leviticus, Deuteronomy contains a vast amount of legal detail, but its emphasis is on the laymen rather than the priests. Moses reminds the new generation of the importance of obedience if they are to learn from the sad example of their parents.

The Hebrew title of Deuteronomy is *Haddebharim*, "The Words," taken from the opening phrase in 1:1, "These *be* the words." The parting words of Moses to the new generation are given in oral and written form so that they will endure to all generations. Deuteronomy has been called "five-fifths of the Law" since it completes the five books of Moses. The Jewish people have also called it *Mishneh Hattorah*, "Repetition of the Law," which is translated in the Septuagint as *To Deuteronomion Touto*, "This Second Law." Deuteronomy, however, is not a second law but an adaptation and expansion of much of the original law given on Mount Sinai. The English title comes from the Greek title *Deuteronomion*, "Second Law." Deuteronomy has also been appropriately called the "Book of Remembrance."

## CHAPTER 1

THESE *be* the words which Moses spake unto all Israel [a]on this side Jordan in the [1]wilderness, in the plain over against the [2]Red *sea,* between Paran, and Tophel, and Laban, and Hazeroth, and Dizahab.

2 *(There are* eleven days' *journey* from Horeb by the way of mount Seir [a]unto Kadesh-barnea.)

3 And it came to pass [a]in the fortieth year, in the eleventh month, on the first *day* of the month, *that* Moses spake unto the children of Israel, according unto all that the LORD had given him in commandment unto them;

4 [a]After he had slain Sihon the king of the Amorites, which dwelt in Heshbon, and Og the king of Bashan, which dwelt at Astaroth [b]in Edrei:

5 On this side Jordan, in the land of Moab, began Moses to declare this law, saying,

6 The LORD our God spake unto us [a]in Horeb, saying, Ye have dwelt long [b]enough in this mount:

7 Turn you, and take your journey, and go to the mount of the Amorites, and unto all *the* [1]places nigh thereunto, in the [2]plain, in the hills, and in the vale, and in the south, and by the sea side, to the land of the Canaanites, and unto Lebanon, unto the great river, the river Euphrates.

8 Behold, I have set the land before you: go in and possess the land which the LORD [1]sware unto your fathers, [a]Abraham, Isaac, and Jacob, to give unto them and to their seed after them.

9 And [a]I spake unto you at that time, saying, I am not able to bear you myself alone:

10 The LORD your God hath multiplied you, and, behold, [a]ye *are* this day as the stars of heaven for multitude.

11 ([a]The LORD God of your fathers make you a thousand times so many more as ye *are,* and bless you, [b]as he hath promised you!)

12 [a]How can I myself alone bear your [1]cumbrance, and your burden, and your strife?

13 Take you wise men, and understanding, and known among your tribes, and I will make them [1]rulers over you.

14 And ye answered me, and said, The thing which thou hast spoken *is* good *for us* to do.

15 So I took [a]the chief of your tribes, wise men, and known, and [1]made them heads over you, captains over thousands, and captains over hundreds, and captains over fifties, and captains over tens, and officers among your tribes.

16 And I charged your judges at that time, saying, [1]Hear *the causes* between your brethren, and [a]judge righteously between *every* man and his [b]brother, and the stranger *that is* with him.

17 [a]Ye shall not [1]respect persons in judgment; *but* ye shall hear the small as well as the great; ye shall not be afraid of the face of man; for [b]the judgment *is* God's: and the [2]cause that is too hard for you, [c]bring *it* unto me, and I will hear it.

1:1 [a] Deut. 4:44–46; Josh. 9:1, 10
[1] Heb. *arabah*
[2] Heb. *Suph*
1:2 [a] Num. 13:26; 32:8; Deut. 9:23
1:3 [a] Num. 33:38
1:4 [a] Num. 21:23, 24, 33–35; Deut. 2:26–35; Josh. 13:10; Neh. 9:22
[b] Josh. 13:12
1:6 [a] Ex. 3:1, 12
[b] Ex. 19:1, 2
1:7 [1] *neighbouring places* [2] Heb. *arabah*
1:8 [a] Gen. 12:7; 15:5; 22:17; 26:3; 28:13 [1] *promised*

1:9 [a] Ex. 18:18, 24
1:10 [a] Gen. 15:5; 22:17
1:11 [a] 2 Sam. 24:3
[b] Gen. 15:5
1:12 [a] 1 Kin. 3:8, 9 [1] *problems*
1:13 [1] Lit. *heads*
1:15 [a] Ex. 18:25 [1] *appointed*
1:16 [a] Deut. 16:18
[b] Lev. 24:22 [1] *Hear the cases*
1:17 [a] Prov. 24:23–26 [b] 2 Chr. 19:6 [c] Ex. 18:22, 26 [1] *show partiality* [2] *case*

18 And I commanded you at that time all the things which ye should do.

19 And when we departed from Horeb, [a]we went through all that great and terrible wilderness, which ye saw by the way of the mountain of the Amorites, as the LORD our God commanded us; and [b]we came to Kadesh-barnea.

20 And I said unto you, Ye are come unto the mountain of the Amorites, which the LORD our God doth give unto us.

21 Behold, the LORD thy God hath set the land before thee: go up *and* possess *it*, as the LORD God of thy fathers hath said unto thee; [a]fear not, neither be discouraged.

22 And ye came near unto me every one of you, and said, We will send men before us, and they shall [1]search us out the land, and bring us word again by what way we must go up, and into what cities we shall come.

23 And the saying pleased me well: and [a]I took twelve men of you, one of a tribe:

24 [a]And they turned and went up into the mountain, and came unto the valley of Eshcol, and searched it out.

25 And they took of the fruit of the land in their hands, and brought *it* down unto us, and brought us word again, and said, It *is* a [a]good land which the LORD our God doth give us.

26 [a]Notwithstanding ye would not go up, but rebelled against the commandment of the LORD your God:

27 And ye [a]murmured[1] in your tents, and said, Because the LORD [b]hated us, he hath brought us forth out of the land of Egypt, to deliver us into the hand of the Amorites, to destroy us.

28 [1]Whither shall we go up? our brethren have [2]discouraged our heart, saying, [a]The people *is* greater and taller than we; the cities *are* great and walled up to heaven; and moreover we have seen the sons of the [b]Anakims there.

29 Then I said unto you, Dread not, [a]neither be afraid of them.

30 [a]The LORD your God which goeth before you, he shall fight for you, according to all that he did for you in Egypt before your eyes;

31 And in the wilderness, where thou hast seen how that the LORD thy God [1]bare thee, as a [a]man doth bear his son, in all the way that ye went, until ye came into this place.

32 Yet in this thing [a]ye did not believe the LORD your God,

33 [a]Who went in the way before you, [b]to [1]search you out a place to pitch your tents *in,* in fire by night, to shew you by what way ye should go, and in a cloud by day.

34 And the LORD heard the voice of your words, and was [1]wroth, [a]and [2]sware, saying,

35 [a]Surely there shall not one of these men of this evil generation see that good land, which I [1]sware to give unto your fathers,

36 [a]Save Caleb the son of Jephunneh; he shall see it, and to him will I give the land that he [1]hath trodden upon, and to his children, because [b]he hath [2]wholly followed the LORD.

37 [a]Also the LORD was angry with me for your sakes, saying, Thou also shalt not go in thither.

38 [a]*But* Joshua the son of Nun, [b]which standeth before thee, he shall go in thither: [c]encourage him: for he shall cause Israel to inherit it.

39 [a]Moreover your little ones, which [b]ye said should be [1]a prey, and your children, which in that day [c]had no knowledge between good and evil, they shall go in thither, and unto them will I give it, and they shall possess it.

40 [a]But *as for* you, turn you, and take your journey into the wilderness by the way of the Red sea.

41 Then ye answered and said unto me, [a]We have sinned against the LORD, we will go up and fight, according to all that the LORD our God commanded us. And when ye had girded on every man his weapons of war, ye were ready to go up into the hill.

42 And the LORD said unto me, Say unto them, [a]Go not up, neither fight; for I *am* not among you; lest ye be [1]smitten before your enemies.

43 So I spake unto you; and ye would not hear, but [a]rebelled against the commandment of the LORD, and [b]went [1]presumptuously up into the hill.

44 And the Amorites, which dwelt in that mountain, came out against you, and chased you, [a]as bees do, and destroyed you in Seir, *even* unto Hormah.

45 And ye returned and wept before the LORD; but the LORD [1]would not hearken to your voice, nor give ear unto you.

46 [a]So ye abode in Kadesh many days, according unto the days that ye abode *there.*

## CHAPTER 2

THEN we turned, and [a]took our journey into the wilderness by the way of the Red sea, [b]as the LORD spake unto me: and we [1]compassed mount Seir many days.

2 And the LORD spake unto me, saying,

3 Ye have compassed this mountain [a]long enough: turn you northward.

1:19 [a] Deut. 2:7; 8:15; 32:10 [b] Num. 13:26

1:21 [a] Josh. 1:6, 9

1:22 [1] *search out the land for us*

1:23 [a] Num. 13:2, 3

1:24 [a] Num. 13:21–25

1:25 [a] Num. 13:27

1:26 [a] Num. 14:1–4

1:27 [a] Ps. 106:25 [b] Deut. 9:28 [1] *grumbled*

1:28 [a] Deut. 9:1, 2 [b] Num. 13:28 [1] *Where can* [2] Lit. *melted*

1:29 [a] Num. 14:9

1:30 [a] Ex. 14:14

1:31 [a] Is. 46:3, 4; 63:9 [1] *carried*

1:32 [a] Jude 5

1:33 [a] Ex. 13:21 [b] Num. 10:33 [1] *search out a place for you*

1:34 [a] Deut. 2:14, 15 [1] *angry* [2] *took an oath*

1:35 [a] Num. 14:22, 23 [1] *promised*

1:36 [a] [Josh. 14:9] [b] Num. 32:11, 12 [1] *have walked* [2] *fully*

1:37 [a] Deut. 3:26; 4:21; 34:4

1:38 [a] Num. 14:30 [b] 1 Sam. 16:22 [c] Deut. 31:7, 23

1:39 [a] Num. 14:31 [b] Num. 14:3 [c] Is. 7:15, 16 [1] *victims*

1:40 [a] Num. 14:25

1:41 [a] Num. 14:40

1:42 [a] Num. 14:41–43 [1] *defeated*

1:43 [a] Num. 14:44 [b] Deut. 17:12, 13 [1] *wilfully*

1:44 [a] Num. 14:45; Ps. 118:12

1:45 [1] *would not listen*

1:46 [a] Num. 13:25; 20:1, 22; Deut. 2:7, 14

2:1 [a] Deut. 1:40 [b] Num. 14:25 [1] *skirted or circled around*

2:3 [a] Deut. 2:7, 14

4 And command thou the people, saying, [a]Ye *are* to pass through the [1]coast of [b]your brethren the children of Esau, which dwell in Seir; and they shall be afraid of you: [2]take ye good heed unto yourselves therefore:

5 Meddle not with them; for I will not give you of their land, no, not so much as a foot breadth; [a]because I have given mount Seir unto Esau *for* a possession.

6 Ye shall buy meat of them for money, that ye may eat; and ye shall also buy water of them for money, that ye may drink.

7 For the LORD thy God hath blessed thee in all the works of thy hand: he knoweth thy [1]walking through this great wilderness: [a]these forty years the LORD thy God *hath been* with thee; thou hast lacked nothing.

8 And when we passed by from our brethren the children of Esau, which dwelt in Seir, through the way of the plain from [a]Elath, and from Eziongaber, we [b]turned and passed by the way of the wilderness of Moab.

9 And the LORD said unto me, [1]Distress not the Moabites, neither contend with them in battle: for I will not give thee of their land *for* a possession; because I have given [a]Ar unto [b]the children of Lot *for* a possession.

10 [a]The Emims dwelt therein in times past, a people great, and many, and tall, as [b]the Anakims;

11 Which also were accounted [1]giants, as the Anakims; but the Moabites call them Emims.

12 [a]The [1]Horims also dwelt in Seir beforetime; but the children of Esau [2]succeeded them, when they had destroyed them from before them, and dwelt in their [3]stead; as Israel did unto the land of his possession, which the LORD gave unto them.

13 Now rise up, *said I,* and get you over [a]the [1]brook Zered. And we went over the brook Zered.

14 And the space in which we came [a]from Kadesh-barnea, until we were come over the brook Zered, *was* thirty and eight years; [b]until all the generation of the men of war were [1]wasted out from among the host, [c]as the LORD sware unto them.

15 For indeed the hand of the LORD was against them, to destroy them from among the host, until they [1]were consumed.

16 So it came to pass, when all the men of war were consumed and dead from among the people,

17 That the LORD spake unto me, saying,

18 Thou art to pass over through Ar, the coast of Moab, this day:

19 And *when* thou comest nigh over against the children of Ammon,

distress them not, nor meddle with them: for I will not give thee of the land of the children of Ammon *any* possession; because I have given it unto [a]the children of Lot *for* a possession.

20 (That also was accounted a land of giants: [1]giants dwelt therein in old time; and the Ammonites call them [a]Zamzummims;

21 [a]A people great, and many, and tall, as the Anakims; but the LORD destroyed them before them; and they [1]succeeded them, and dwelt in their stead:

22 As he did to the children of Esau, [a]which dwelt in Seir, when he destroyed [b]the Horims from before them; and they succeeded them, and dwelt in their stead even unto this day:

23 And [a]the Avims which dwelt in Hazerim, *even* unto Azzah, [b]the Caphtorims, which came forth out of Caphtor, destroyed them, and dwelt in their stead.)

24 Rise ye up, take your journey, and [a]pass over the river Arnon: behold, I have given into thine hand [b]Sihon the Amorite, king of Heshbon, and his land: [1]begin to possess *it,* and contend with him in battle.

25 [a]This day will I begin to put the dread of thee and the fear of thee upon the nations *that are* [1]under the whole heaven, who shall hear report of thee, and shall [b]tremble, and be in anguish because of thee.

26 And I [a]sent messengers out of the wilderness of Kedemoth unto Sihon king of Heshbon [b]with words of peace, saying,

27 [a]Let me pass through thy land: I will go along by the high way, I will neither turn unto the right hand nor to the left.

28 Thou shalt sell me meat for money, that I may eat; and give me water for money, that I may drink: [a]only I will pass through on my feet;

29 ([a]As the children of Esau which dwell in Seir, and the Moabites which dwell in Ar, did unto me;) until I shall pass over Jordan into the land which the LORD our God giveth us.

30 [a]But Sihon king of Heshbon would not let us pass by him: for [b]the LORD thy God [c]hardened his spirit, and made his heart obstinate, that he might deliver him into thy hand, as *appeareth* this day.

31 And the LORD said unto me, Behold, I have begun to [a]give Sihon and his land before thee: begin to possess, that thou mayest inherit his land.

32 [a]Then Sihon came out against us, he and all his people, to fight at Jahaz.

2:4 [a] Num. 20:14–21 [b] Deut. 23:7 [1] *territory* [2] *watch yourselves carefully*

2:5 [a] Gen. 36:8; Josh. 24:4

2:7 [a] Deut. 8:2–4; [Matt. 6:8, 32] [1] Lit. *goings*

2:8 [a] Judg. 11:18; 1 Kin. 9:26 [b] Num. 21:4

2:9 [a] Num. 21:15, 28; Deut. 2:18, 29 [b] Gen. 19:36–38 [1] *Do not harass*

2:10 [a] Gen. 14:5 [b] Num. 13:22, 33; Deut. 9:2

2:11 [1] Heb. *rephaim*

2:12 [a] Gen. 14:6; 36:20; Deut. 2:22 [1] *Horites* [2] *dispossessed* [3] *place*

2:13 [a] Num. 21:12 [1] *valley or wadi*

2:14 [a] Num. 13:26 [b] Num. 14:33; 26:64; Deut. 1:34, 35 [c] Num. 14:35; Ezek. 20:15 [1] *consumed*

2:15 [1] *perished*

2:19 [a] Gen. 19:38; Num. 21:24

2:20 [a] Gen. 14:5 [1] Heb. *rephaim*

2:21 [a] Deut. 2:10 [1] *dispossessed*

2:22 [a] Gen. 36:8; Deut. 2:5 [b] Gen. 14:6; 36:20–30

2:23 [a] Josh. 13:3 [b] Gen. 10:14; 1 Chr. 1:12; Jer. 47:4; Amos 9:7

2:24 [a] Num. 21:13, 14; Judg. 11:18 [b] Deut. 1:4 [1] *take possession of it*

2:25 [a] Ex. 23:27; Deut. 11:25; Josh. 2:9 [b] Ex. 15:14–16 [1] *everywhere under the heavens*

2:26 [a] Num. 21:21–32; Deut. 1:4; Judg. 11:19–21 [b] Deut. 20:10

2:27 [a] Num. 21:21, 22; Judg. 11:19

2:28 [a] Num. 20:19

2:29 [a] Num. 20:18; Deut. 23:3, 4; Judg. 11:17

2:30 [a] Num. 21:23 [b] Josh. 11:20 [c] Ex. 4:21

2:31 [a] Deut. 1:3, 8

2:32 [a] Num. 21:23

33 And [a]the LORD our God delivered him [1]before us; and [b]we [2]smote him, and his sons, and all his people.

34 And we took all his cities at that time, and [a]utterly destroyed the men, and the women, and the little ones, of every city, we left none to remain:

35 [1]Only the cattle we took for a prey unto ourselves, and the spoil of the cities which we took.

36 [a]From Aroer, which *is* by the brink of the river of Arnon, and *from* the [b]city that *is* by the river, even unto Gilead, there was not one city too strong for us: [c]the LORD our God delivered all unto us:

37 Only unto the land of the children of Ammon thou camest not, *nor* unto any place of the river [a]Jabbok, nor unto the cities in the mountains, nor unto [b]whatsoever the LORD our God forbad us.

## CHAPTER 3

THEN we turned, and went up the way to Bashan: and [a]Og the king of Bashan came out against us, he and all his people, to battle [b]at Edrei.

2 And the LORD said unto me, Fear him not: for I will deliver him, and all his people, and his land, into thy hand; and thou shalt do unto him as thou didst unto [a]Sihon king of the Amorites, which dwelt at Heshbon.

3 So the LORD our God delivered into our hands Og also, the king of Bashan, and all his people: and we [1]smote him until none was left to him remaining.

4 And we took all his cities at that time, there was not a city which we took not from them, threescore cities, [a]all the region of Argob, the kingdom of Og in Bashan.

5 All these cities *were* [1]fenced with high walls, gates, and bars; beside unwalled towns a great many.

6 And we utterly destroyed them, as we did unto Sihon king [a]of Heshbon, utterly destroying the men, women, and children, of every city.

7 But all the cattle, and the spoil of the cities, we took for [1]a prey to ourselves.

8 And we took at that time out of the hand of the two kings of the Amorites the [a]land that *was* on this side Jordan, from the river of Arnon unto mount [b]Hermon;

9 *(Which* [a]Hermon the Sidonians call Sirion; and the Amorites call it Shenir;)

10 [a]All the cities of the plain, and all Gilead, and [b]all Bashan, unto Salchah and Edrei, cities of the kingdom of Og in Bashan.

11 [a]For only Og king of Bashan remained of the remnant of [b]giants;[1] behold, his bedstead *was* a bedstead

of iron; *is* it not in [c]Rabbath of the children of Ammon? nine cubits *was* the length thereof, and four cubits the breadth of it, after the cubit of a man.

12 And this [a]land, *which* we possessed at that time, [b]from Aroer, which *is* by the river Arnon, and half mount Gilead, and [c]the cities thereof, gave I unto the Reubenites and to the Gadites.

13 [a]And the rest of Gilead, and all Bashan, *being* the kingdom of Og, gave I unto the half tribe of Manasseh; all the region of Argob, with all Bashan, which was called the land of [1]giants.

14 [a]Jair the son of Manasseh took all the country of Argob [b]unto the coasts of Geshuri and Maachathi; and [c]called[1] them after his own name, Bashan-havoth-jair, unto this day.

15 And I gave [a]Gilead unto Machir.

16 And unto the Reubenites [a]and unto the Gadites I gave from Gilead even unto the river Arnon half the valley, and the border even unto the river Jabbok, [b]which *is* the border of the children of Ammon;

17 The plain also, and Jordan, and the coast *thereof,* from Chinnereth [a]even unto the sea of the plain, [b]*even* the salt sea, [1]under Ashdoth-pisgah eastward.

18 And I commanded you at that time, saying, The LORD your God hath given you this land to possess it: [a]ye shall pass over armed before your brethren the children of Israel, all *that are* [1]meet for the war.

19 But your wives, and your little ones, and your cattle, *(for* I know that ye have much cattle,) shall abide in your cities which I have given you;

20 Until the LORD have given [a]rest unto your brethren, as well as unto you, and *until* they also possess the land which the LORD your God hath given them beyond Jordan: and *then* shall ye [b]return every man unto his possession, which I have given you.

21 And [a]I commanded Joshua at that time, saying, Thine eyes have seen all that the LORD your God hath done unto these two kings: so shall the LORD do unto all the kingdoms whither thou passest.

22 Ye shall not fear them: for [a]the LORD your God he shall fight for you.

23 And I besought the LORD at that time, saying,

24 O Lord GOD, thou hast begun to shew thy servant [a]thy greatness, and thy [1]mighty hand: for [b]what God *is there* in heaven or in earth, that can do according to thy works, and according to thy might?

25 I pray thee, let me go over, and see [a]the good land that *is* beyond

2:33 [a] Ex. 23:31; Deut. 7:2 [b] Num. 21:24 [1] *over to us* [2] *defeated*
2:34 [a] Lev. 27:28
2:35 [1] *We took only the livestock as plunder*
2:36 [a] Deut. 3:12; 4:48; Josh. 13:9 [b] Josh. 13:9, 16 [c] Ps. 44:3
2:37 [a] Gen. 32:22; Num. 21:24; Deut. 3:16 [b] Deut. 2:5, 9, 19
3:1 [a] Num. 21:33–35; Deut. 29:7 [b] Deut. 1:4
3:2 [a] Num. 21:34; Josh. 13:21
3:3 [1] *attacked*
3:4 [a] Deut. 3:13, 14
3:5 [1] *fortified*
3:6 [a] Deut. 2:24, 34, 35
3:7 [1] *booty*
3:8 [a] Num. 32:33; Josh. 12:6; 13:8–12 [b] Deut. 4:48; 1 Chr. 5:23
3:9 [a] 1 Chr. 5:23
3:10 [a] Deut. 4:49 [b] Josh. 12:5; 13:11
3:11 [a] Amos 2:9 [b] Gen. 14:5; Deut. 2:11, 20 [c] 2 Sam. 12:26; Jer. 49:2; Ezek. 21:20 [1] Heb. *rephaim*
3:12 [a] Num. 32:33; Josh. 12:6; 13:8–12 [b] Deut. 2:36; Josh. 12:2 [c] Num. 34:14
3:13 [a] Josh. 13:29–31; 17:1 [1] Heb. *rephaim*
3:14 [a] 1 Chr. 2:22 [b] Josh. 13:13 [c] Num. 32:41 [1] *Or called Bashan after his own name, Havoth-jair; lit. Towns of Jair*
3:15 [a] Num. 32:39, 40
3:16 [a] 2 Sam. 24:5 [b] Num. 21:24
3:17 [a] Num. 34:11, 12 [b] Gen. 14:3 [1] *below the slopes of Pisgah*
3:18 [a] Num. 32:20 [1] *men of valour*
3:20 [a] Deut. 12:9, 10 [b] Josh. 22:4
3:21 [a] [Num. 27:22, 23]
3:22 [a] Ex. 14:14
3:23 [a] [2 Cor. 12:8, 9]
3:24 [a] Deut. 5:24; 11:2 [b] 2 Sam. 7:22 [1] *strong*
3:25 [a] Deut. 4:22

Jordan, that goodly mountain, and Lebanon.

26 But the LORD ᵃwas ¹wroth with me ²for your sakes, and would not hear me: and the LORD said unto me, Let it suffice thee; speak no more unto me of this matter.

27 ᵃGet thee up into the top of Pisgah, and lift up thine eyes westward, and northward, and southward, and eastward, and behold *it* with thine eyes: for thou shalt not go over this Jordan.

28 But ᵃcharge¹ Joshua, and encourage him, and strengthen him: for he shall go over before this people, and he shall cause them to inherit the land which thou shalt see.

29 So we abode in ᵃthe valley over against Beth-peor.

## CHAPTER 4

Now therefore hearken, O Israel, unto ᵃthe statutes and unto the judgments, which I teach you, for to do *them,* that ye may live, and go in and ¹possess the land which the LORD God of your fathers giveth you.

2 ᵃYe shall not add unto the word which I command you, neither shall ye ¹diminish *ought* from it, that ye may keep the commandments of the LORD your God which I command you.

3 Your eyes have seen what the LORD did because of ᵃBaal-peor: for all the men that followed Baal-peor, the LORD thy God hath destroyed them from among you.

4 But ye that ¹did cleave unto the LORD your God *are* alive every one of you this day.

5 Behold, I have taught you statutes and judgments, even as the LORD my God commanded me, that ye should do so in the land whither ye go to possess it.

6 Keep therefore and do *them;* for this *is* ᵃyour wisdom and your understanding in the sight of the nations, which shall hear all these statutes, and say, Surely this great nation *is* a wise and understanding people.

7 For ᵃwhat nation *is there so* great, who *hath* ᵇGod¹ *so* nigh unto them, as the LORD our God *is* in all *things that* we call upon him *for?*

8 And what nation *is there so* great, that hath statutes and judgments *so* righteous as all this law, which I set before you this day?

9 Only take heed to thyself, and ᵃkeep ¹thy soul diligently, lest thou ᵇforget the things which thine eyes have seen, and lest they depart from thy heart all the days of thy life: but ᶜteach them thy sons, and thy sons' sons;

10 *Specially* ᵃthe day that thou stoodest before the LORD thy God in

Horeb, when the LORD said unto me, Gather me the people together, and I will make them hear my words, that they may learn to fear me all the days that they shall live upon the earth, and *that* they may teach their children.

11 And ye came near and stood under the mountain; and the mountain burned with fire unto the midst of heaven, with darkness, clouds, and thick darkness.

12 ᵃAnd the LORD spake unto you out of the midst of the fire: ye heard the voice of the words, but saw no ¹similitude; ᵇonly *ye heard* a voice.

13 ᵃAnd he declared unto you his covenant, which he commanded you to perform, *even* ᵇten commandments; and ᶜhe wrote them upon two tables of stone.

14 And ᵃthe LORD commanded me at that time to teach you statutes and judgments, that ye might ¹do them in the land whither ye go over to possess it.

15 ᵃTake ye therefore good heed unto yourselves; for ye saw no ¹manner of ᵇsimilitude on the day *that* the LORD spake unto you in Horeb out of the midst of the fire:

16 Lest ye ᵃcorrupt¹ *yourselves,* and ᵇmake you a graven image, the ²similitude of any figure, ᶜthe likeness of male or female,

17 The likeness of any beast that *is* on the earth, the likeness of any winged fowl that flieth in the air,

18 The likeness of any thing that creepeth on the ground, the likeness of any fish that *is* in the waters beneath the earth:

19 And lest thou ᵃlift up thine eyes unto heaven, and when thou seest the sun, and the moon, and the stars, *even* ᵇall the host of heaven, shouldest be driven to ᶜworship them, and serve them, which the LORD thy God hath ¹divided unto all nations under the whole heaven.

20 But the LORD hath taken you, and ᵃbrought you forth out of the iron furnace, *even* out of Egypt, to be unto him a ᵇpeople of inheritance, as *ye are* this day.

21 Furthermore ᵃthe LORD was angry with me for your sakes, and sware that ᵇI should not go over Jordan, and that I should not go in unto that good land, which the LORD thy God giveth thee *for* an inheritance:

22 But ᵃI must die in this land, ᵇI must not go over Jordan: but ye shall go over, and ¹possess ᶜthat good land.

23 Take heed unto yourselves, lest ye forget the covenant of the LORD your God, which he made with you, ᵃand make you a graven image, *or* the likeness of any *thing,* which the LORD thy God hath forbidden thee.

24 For [a]the LORD thy God *is* a consuming fire, *even* [b]a jealous God.

25 When thou shalt beget children, and children's children, and ye shall have remained long in the land, and shall [1]corrupt *yourselves,* and make a graven image, *or* the likeness of any *thing, or* [a]shall do evil in the sight of the LORD thy God, to provoke him to anger:

26 [a]I call heaven and earth to witness against you this day, that ye shall soon utterly perish from off the land whereunto ye go over Jordan to possess it; ye shall not [1]prolong *your* days upon it, but shall utterly be destroyed.

27 And the LORD [a]shall scatter you among the nations, and ye shall be left few in number among the heathen, whither the LORD shall lead you.

28 And [a]there ye shall serve gods, the work of men's hands, wood and stone, [b]which neither see, nor hear, nor eat, nor smell.

29 [a]But if from thence thou shalt seek the LORD thy God, thou shalt find *him,* if thou seek him with all thy heart and with all thy soul.

30 When thou art in [1]tribulation, and all these things are come upon thee, *even* in the [a]latter days, if thou [b]turn to the LORD thy God, and shalt be obedient unto his voice;

31 (For the LORD thy God *is* a merciful God;) he will not forsake thee, neither [a]destroy thee, nor forget the covenant of thy fathers which he sware unto them.

32 For [a]ask now of the days that are past, which were before thee, since the day that God created man upon the earth, and *ask* [b]from the one side of heaven unto the other, whether there hath been *any such thing* as this great thing *is,* or hath been heard like it?

33 [a]Did *ever* people hear the voice of God speaking out of the midst of the fire, as thou hast heard, and live?

34 Or hath God [1]assayed to go *and* take him a nation from the midst of *another* nation, [a]by [2]temptations, [b]by signs, and by wonders, and by war, and [c]by a mighty hand, and [d]by a stretched out arm, [e]and by great [3]terrors, according to all that the LORD your God did for you in Egypt before your eyes?

35 Unto thee it was shewed, that thou mightest know that the LORD he *is* God; [a]*there is* none else beside him.

36 [a]Out of heaven he made thee to hear his voice, that he might instruct thee: and upon earth he shewed thee his great fire; and thou heardest his words out of the midst of the fire.

37 And because [a]he loved thy fathers, therefore he chose their [1]seed

after them, and [b]brought thee out in his sight with his mighty power out of Egypt;

38 [a]To drive out nations from before thee greater and mightier than thou *art,* to bring thee in, to give thee their land *for* an inheritance, as *it is* this day.

39 Know therefore this day, and consider *it* in thine heart, that [a]the LORD he *is* God in heaven above, and upon the earth beneath: *there is* none else.

40 [a]Thou shalt keep therefore his statutes, and his commandments, which I command thee this day, that [1]it may go well with thee, and with thy children after thee, and that thou mayest [2]prolong *thy* days upon the earth, which the LORD thy God giveth thee, for ever.

41 Then Moses [a]severed[1] three cities on this side Jordan toward the sunrising;

42 [a]That the [1]slayer might flee [2]thither, which should kill his neighbour [3]unawares, and hated him not in times past; and that fleeing unto one of these cities he might live:

43 *Namely,* [a]Bezer in the wilderness, in the plain country, of the Reubenites; and Ramoth in Gilead, of the Gadites; and Golan in Bashan, of the Manassites.

44 And this *is* the law which Moses set before the children of Israel:

45 These *are* the testimonies, and the statutes, and the judgments, which Moses spake unto the children of Israel, after they came forth out of Egypt,

46 On this side Jordan, [a]in the valley over against Beth-peor, in the land of Sihon king of the Amorites, who dwelt at Heshbon, whom Moses and the children of Israel [b]smote,[1] after they were come forth out of Egypt:

47 And they possessed his land, and the land [a]of Og king of Bashan, two kings of the Amorites, which *were* on this side Jordan toward the [1]sunrising;

48 [a]From Aroer, which *is* by the bank of the river Arnon, even unto mount Sion, which *is* [b]Hermon,

49 And all the plain on this side Jordan eastward, even unto the sea of the plain, under the [a]springs of Pisgah.

## CHAPTER 5

AND Moses called all Israel, and said unto them, Hear, O Israel, the statutes and judgments which I speak in your ears this day, that ye may learn them, and [1]keep, and do them.

2 [a]The LORD our God made a covenant with us in Horeb.

4:24 [a] Deut. 9:3
[b] Ex. 20:5; 34:14
4:25 [a] 2 Kin. 17:17
[1] *act corruptly*
4:26 [a] Deut. 30:18, 19 [1] *live long in it*
4:27 [a] Deut. 28:62
4:28 [a] Jer. 16:13
[b] Ps. 115:4–7; 135:15–17
4:29 [a] [2 Chr. 15:4]
4:30 [a] Hos. 3:5 [b] Joel 2:12
[1] *distress*
4:31 [a] Jer. 30:11
4:32 [a] Job 8:8
[b] Matt. 24:31
4:33 [a] Deut. 5:24–26
4:34 [a] Deut. 7:19
[b] Ex. 7:3 [c] Ex. 13:3
[d] Ex. 6:6 [e] Deut. 26:8 [1] *tried* [2] *trials* [3] *calamities*
4:35 [a] Mark 12:32
4:36 [a] Heb. 12:19, 25
4:37 [a] Deut. 7:7, 8; 10:15; 33:3
[1] *descendants*

[b] Ex. 13:3, 9, 14
4:38 [a] Deut. 7:1
4:39 [a] Josh. 2:11
4:40 [a] Lev. 22:31
[1] *you may prosper* [2] *live long in the land*
4:41 [a] Num. 35:6
[1] *set apart*
4:42 [a] Deut. 19:4 [1] *manslayer* [2] *there* [3] *unintentionally*
4:43 [a] Josh. 20:8
4:46 [a] Deut. 3:29
[b] Num. 21:24
[1] *defeated*
4:47 [a] Num. 21:33–35 [1] *east*
4:48 [a] Deut. 2:36; 3:12 [b] Deut. 3:9
4:49 [a] Deut. 3:17
5:1 [1] *be careful to observe them*
5:2 [a] Ex. 19:5

3 The LORD [a]made not this covenant with our fathers, but with us, *even* us, who *are* all of us here alive this day.

4 [a]The LORD talked with you face to face in the mount out of the midst of the fire,

5 ([a]I stood between the LORD and you at that time, to [1]shew you the word of the LORD: for [b]ye were afraid by reason of the fire, and went not up into the mount;) saying,

6 [a]I *am* the LORD thy God, which brought thee out of the land of Egypt, from the house of [1]bondage.

7 [a]Thou shalt have none other gods [1]before me.

8 [a]Thou shalt not make thee *any* graven image, *or* any likeness *of any thing* that *is* in heaven above, or that *is* in the earth beneath, or that *is* in the waters beneath the earth:

9 Thou shalt not [a]bow[1] down thyself unto them, nor serve them: for I the LORD thy God *am* a jealous God, [2]visiting the iniquity of the fathers upon the children unto the third and fourth *generation* of them that hate me,

10 [a]And shewing mercy unto thousands of them that love me and keep my commandments.

11 [a]Thou shalt not take the name of the LORD thy God in vain: for the LORD will not hold *him* [1]guiltless that taketh his name in vain.

12 [a]Keep the sabbath day to [1]sanctify it, as the LORD thy God hath commanded thee.

13 [a]Six days thou shalt labour, and do all thy work:

14 But the seventh day *is* the [a]sabbath of the LORD thy God: *in it* thou shalt not do any work, thou, nor thy son, nor thy daughter, nor thy manservant, nor thy maidservant, nor thine ox, nor thine ass, nor any of thy cattle, nor thy stranger that *is* within thy gates; that thy manservant and thy maidservant may rest as well as thou.

15 [a]And remember that thou wast a servant in the land of Egypt, and *that* the LORD thy God brought thee out thence [b]through a mighty hand and by a stretched out arm: therefore the LORD thy God commanded thee to [1]keep the sabbath day.

16 [a]Honour thy father and thy mother, as the LORD thy God hath commanded thee; [b]that thy days may be prolonged, and that it may go well with [c]thee, in the land which the LORD thy God giveth thee.

17 [a]Thou shalt not kill.

18 [a]Neither shalt thou commit adultery.

19 [a]Neither shalt thou steal.

20 [a]Neither shalt thou bear false witness against thy neighbour.

21 [a]Neither shalt thou desire thy neighbour's wife, neither shalt thou covet thy neighbour's house, his field, or his manservant, or his maidservant, his ox, or his ass, or any *thing* that *is* thy neighbour's.

22 These words the LORD spake unto all your assembly in the mount out of the midst of the fire, of the cloud, and of the thick darkness, with a great voice: and he added no more. And [a]he wrote them in two tables of stone, and delivered them unto me.

23 [a]And it came to pass, when ye heard the voice out of the midst of the darkness, (for the mountain did burn with fire,) that ye came near unto me, *even* all the heads of your tribes, and your elders;

24 And ye said, Behold, the LORD our God hath shewed us his glory and his greatness, and [a]we have heard his voice out of the midst of the fire: we have seen this day that God doth talk with man, and he [b]liveth.[1]

25 Now therefore why should we die? for this great fire will consume us: [a]if we hear the voice of the LORD our God any more, then we shall die.

26 [a]For who *is there of* all flesh, that hath heard the voice of the living God speaking out of the midst of the fire, as we *have,* and lived?

27 Go thou near, and hear all that the LORD our God shall say: and [a]speak thou unto us all that the LORD our God shall speak unto thee; and we will hear *it,* and do *it.*

28 And the LORD heard the voice of your words, when ye spake unto me; and the LORD said unto me, I have heard the voice of the words of this people, which they have spoken unto thee: [a]they have well said all that they have spoken.

29 [a]O that there were such an heart in them, that they would fear me, and [b]keep all my commandments always, [c]that it might be well with them, and with their children for ever!

30 Go say to them, Get you into your tents again.

31 But as for thee, stand thou here by me, [a]and I will speak unto thee all the commandments, and the statutes, and the judgments, which thou shalt teach them, that they may do *them* in the land which I give them to possess it.

32 Ye shall [1]observe to do therefore as the LORD your God hath commanded you: [a]ye shall not turn aside to the right hand or to the left.

33 Ye shall walk in [a]all the ways which the LORD your God hath commanded you, that ye may live, [b]and *that it may be* well with you, and *that* ye may prolong *your* days in the land which ye shall possess.

---

**Cross-references (center column):**

5:3 [a] Heb. 8:9
5:4 [a] Ex. 19:9
5:5 [a] Gal. 3:19
[b] Ex. 19:16 [1] *declare to*
5:6 [a] Ex. 20:2–17 [1] *slavery*
5:7 [a] Hos. 13:4 [1] *besides me*
5:8 [a] Ex. 20:4
5:9 [a] Ex. 34:7, 14–16 [1] *worship them* [2] *punishing*
5:10 [a] Dan. 9:4
5:11 [a] Ex. 20:7 [1] *innocent*
5:12 [a] Ex. 20:8 [1] *keep it holy*
5:13 [a] Ex. 23:12; 35:2
5:14 [a] [Heb. 4:4]
5:15 [a] Deut. 15:15 [b] Deut. 4:34, 37 [1] *observe*
5:16 [a] Lev. 19:3 [b] Deut. 6:2 [c] Deut. 4:40
5:17 [a] Matt. 5:21
5:18 [a] Ex. 20:14
5:19 [a] [Rom. 13:9]
5:20 [a] Ex. 20:16; 23:1; Matt. 19:18
5:21 [a] Ex. 20:17; [Rom. 7:7; 13:9]
5:22 [a] Ex. 24:12; 31:18; Deut. 4:13
5:23 [a] Ex. 20:18, 19
5:24 [a] Ex. 19:19 [b] Deut. 4:33; Judg. 13:22 [1] *still lives*
5:25 [a] Ex. 20:18, 19; Deut. 18:16
5:26 [a] Deut. 4:33
5:27 [a] Ex. 20:19; Heb. 12:19
5:28 [a] Deut. 18:17
5:29 [a] Deut. 32:29; Ps. 81:13; Is. 48:18 [b] Deut. 11:1 [c] Deut. 4:40
5:31 [a] [Gal. 3:19]
5:32 [a] Deut. 17:20; 28:14; Josh. 1:7; 23:6; Prov. 4:27 [1] *be careful*
5:33 [a] Deut. 10:12; Ps. 119:3; Jer. 7:23; Luke 1:6 [b] Deut. 4:40; Eph. 6:3

## CHAPTER 6

Now these are [a]the commandments, the statutes, and the judgments, which the LORD your God commanded to teach you, that ye might do *them* in the land whither ye go to possess it:

2 [a]That thou mightest [1]fear the LORD thy God, to keep all his statutes and his commandments, which I command thee, thou, and thy son, and thy son's son, all the days of thy life; [b]and that thy days may be prolonged.

3 Hear therefore, O Israel, and [1]observe to do *it;* that it may be well with thee, and that ye may [a]increase[2] mightily, [b]as the LORD God of thy fathers hath promised thee, in [c]the land that floweth with milk and honey.

4 [a]Hear, O Israel: The LORD our God *is* one LORD:

5 And [a]thou shalt love the LORD thy God with all thine heart, and [b]with all thy soul, and with all thy might.

6 And [a]these words, which I command thee this day, shall be in thine heart:

7 And [a]thou shalt teach them diligently unto thy children, and shalt talk of them when thou sittest in thine house, and when thou walkest by the way, and when thou liest down, and when thou risest up.

8 [a]And thou shalt bind them for a sign upon thine hand, and they shall be as frontlets between thine eyes.

9 [a]And thou shalt write them upon the posts of thy house, and on thy gates.

10 And it shall be, when the LORD thy God shall have brought thee into the land which he [1]sware unto thy fathers, to Abraham, to Isaac, and to Jacob, to give thee great and goodly cities, [a]which thou buildedst not,

11 And houses full of all good *things,* which thou filledst not, and wells digged, which thou diggedst not, vineyards and olive trees, which thou plantedst not; [a]when thou shalt have eaten and be full;

12 *Then* beware lest thou forget the [a]LORD, which brought thee forth out of the land of Egypt, from the house of bondage.

13 Thou shalt [a]fear the LORD thy God, and serve him, and [b]shalt swear by his name.

14 Ye shall not go after other gods, [a]of the gods of the people which *are* round about you;

15 (For [a]the LORD thy God *is* a jealous God [b]among you) lest the anger of the LORD thy God be kindled against thee, and destroy thee from off the face of the earth.

16 [a]Ye shall not [1]tempt the LORD your God, [b]as ye tempted *him* in Massah.

17 Ye shall [a]diligently keep the commandments of the LORD your God, and his testimonies, and his statutes, which he hath commanded thee.

18 And thou [a]shalt do *that which is* right and good in the sight of the LORD: that it may be well with thee, and that thou mayest go in and possess the good land which the LORD sware unto thy fathers,

19 [a]To cast out all thine enemies from before thee, as the LORD hath spoken.

20 *And* [a]when thy son asketh thee in time to come, saying, What *mean* the testimonies, and the statutes, and the judgments, which the LORD our God hath commanded you?

21 Then thou shalt say unto thy son, We were Pharaoh's [1]bondmen in Egypt; and the LORD brought us out of Egypt [a]with a mighty hand:

22 And the LORD shewed signs and wonders, great and [1]sore, upon Egypt, upon Pharaoh, and upon all his household, before our eyes:

23 And he brought us out from thence, that he might bring us in, to give us the land which he [1]sware unto our fathers.

24 And the LORD commanded us to [1]do all these [2]statutes, [a]to fear the LORD our God, [b]for our good always, that [c]he might preserve us alive, as *it is* [3]at this day.

25 And [a]it shall be our righteousness, if we [1]observe to do all these commandments before the LORD our God, as he hath commanded us.

## CHAPTER 7

When the LORD thy God shall bring thee into the land whither thou goest to [a]possess it, and hath cast out many [b]nations before thee, the [c]Hittites, and the Girgashites, and the Amorites, and the Canaanites, and the Perizzites, and the Hivites, and the Jebusites, seven nations greater and mightier than thou;

2 And when the LORD thy God shall deliver [a]them before thee; thou shalt smite them, *and* utterly destroy them; [b]thou shalt make no covenant with them, nor shew mercy unto them:

3 [a]Neither shalt thou make marriages with them; thy daughter thou shalt not give unto his son, nor his daughter shalt thou take unto thy son.

4 For they will turn away thy son from following me, that they may serve other gods: [a]so will the anger of the LORD be kindled against you, and destroy thee suddenly.

5 But thus shall ye deal with them; ye shall [a]destroy their altars, and break

### Cross References

6:1 [a] Deut. 12:1
6:2 [a] Ex. 20:20; 13; [Ps. 111:10; 128:1; Eccl. 12:13] [b] Deut. 4:40 [1] *stand in awe of*
6:3 [a] Deut. 7:13 [b] Gen. 22:17 [c] Ex. 3:8, 17 [1] *be careful to observe* [2] *multiply greatly*
6:4 [a] Deut. 4:35; Mark 12:29; John 17:3; [1 Cor. 8:4, 6]
6:5 [a] Matt. 22:37; Mark 12:30; Luke 10:27 [b] 2 Kin. 23:25
6:6 [a] Deut. 11:18–20; Ps. 119:11, 98
6:7 [a] Deut. 4:9; 11:19; [Eph. 6:4]
6:8 [a] Ex. 12:14; 13:9, 16; Deut. 11:18; Prov. 3:3; 6:21; 7:3
6:9 [a] Deut. 11:20; Is. 57:8
6:10 [a] Deut. 9:1; 19:1; Josh. 24:13; Ps. 105:44 [1] *promised*
6:11 [a] Deut. 8:10; 11:15; 14:29
6:12 [a] Deut. 8:11–18
6:13 [a] Deut. 13:4; Matt. 4:10; Luke 4:8 [b] Deut. 5:11; [Is. 45:23; Jer. 4:2]
6:14 [a] Deut. 13:7
6:15 [a] Ex. 20:5; Deut. 4:24 [b] Ex. 33:3
6:16 [a] Matt. 4:7; Luke 4:12 [b] [1 Cor. 10:9] [1] *test*
6:17 [a] Deut. 11:22; Ps. 119:4
6:18 [a] Ex. 15:26; Deut. 8:7–10
6:19 [a] Num. 33:52, 53
6:20 [a] Ex. 13:8, 14
6:21 [a] Ex. 13:3 [1] *slaves*
6:22 [1] *severe*
6:23 [1] *promised*
6:24 [a] Deut. 6:2 [b] Deut. 10:12, 13; Job 35:7, 8; Jer. 32:39 [c] Deut. 4:1 [1] *observe* [2] *ordinances* [3] *today*
6:25 [a] Deut. 24:13; [Rom. 10:3, 5] [1] *are careful to observe*
7:1 [a] Deut. 6:10 [b] Gen. 15:19–21 [c] Ex. 33:2
7:2 [a] Num. 31:17; Deut. 20:16–18 [b] Ex. 23:32, 33; Josh. 2:14
7:3 [a] Ex. 34:15, 16;

Josh. 23:12; 1 Kin. 11:2; Ezra 9:2   7:4 [a] Deut. 6:15
7:5 [a] Ex. 23:24; 34:13; Deut. 12:3

down their images, and cut down their ¹groves, and burn their ²graven images with fire.

6 For thou *art* an ¹holy people unto the LORD thy God: ªthe LORD thy God hath chosen thee to be a special ²people unto himself, above all people that *are* upon the face of the earth.

7 The LORD did not set his ªlove upon you, nor choose you, because ye were more in number than any people; for ye *were* ᵇthe fewest of all people:

8 But ªbecause the LORD loved you, and because he would keep ᵇthe oath which he had sworn unto your fathers, ᶜhath the LORD brought you out with a mighty hand, and redeemed you out of the house of ¹bondmen, from the hand of Pharaoh king of Egypt.

9 Know therefore that the LORD thy God, he *is* God, ªthe faithful God, ᵇwhich keepeth covenant and mercy with them that love him and keep his commandments to a thousand generations;

10 And repayeth them that hate him to their face, to destroy them: he will not ¹be ªslack to him that hateth him, he will repay him to his face.

11 Thou shalt therefore keep the commandments, and the statutes, and the judgments, which I command thee this day, to do them.

12 Wherefore it shall come to pass, if ye ¹hearken to these judgments, and keep, and do them, that the LORD thy God shall keep unto thee the covenant and the mercy which he sware unto thy fathers:

13 And he will ªlove thee, and bless thee, and ¹multiply thee: ᵇhe will also bless the fruit of thy womb, and the fruit of thy land, thy corn, and thy wine, and thine oil, the increase of thy ²kine, and the flocks of thy sheep, in the land which he ³sware unto thy fathers to give thee.

14 Thou shalt be blessed above all people: there shall not be male or female ªbarren among you, or among your cattle.

15 And the LORD will take away from thee all sickness, and will put none of the ªevil diseases of Egypt, which thou knowest, upon thee; but will lay them upon all *them* that hate thee.

16 And thou shalt ¹consume all the people which the LORD thy God shall deliver thee; thine eye shall have no pity upon them: neither shalt thou serve their gods; for that *will* ªbe a snare unto thee.

17 If thou shalt say in thine heart, These nations *are* ¹more than I; how can I dispossess them?

18 Thou shalt not be afraid of them: *but* shalt well ªremember what the

LORD thy God did unto Pharaoh, and unto all Egypt;

19 ªThe great ¹temptations which thine eyes saw, and the signs, and the wonders, and the mighty hand, and the stretched out arm, whereby the LORD thy God brought thee out: so shall the LORD thy God do unto all the people of whom thou art afraid.

20 ªMoreover the LORD thy God will send the hornet among them, until they that are left, and hide themselves from thee, be destroyed.

21 Thou shalt not be affrighted at them: for the LORD thy God *is* among you, a mighty God and ¹terrible.

22 And the LORD thy God will put out those nations before thee ªby little ¹and little: thou mayest not ²consume them at once, lest the beasts of the field increase upon thee.

23 But the LORD thy God shall deliver them unto thee, and shall destroy them with a mighty destruction, until they be destroyed.

24 And ªhe shall deliver their kings into thine hand, and thou shalt destroy their name from under heaven: ᵇthere shall no man be able to stand ¹before thee, until thou have destroyed them.

25 The ¹graven images of their gods shall ye burn with fire: thou shalt not ªdesire² the silver or gold *that is* on them, nor take *it* unto thee, lest thou be snared therein: for it *is* an abomination to the LORD thy God.

26 Neither shalt thou bring an abomination into thine house, lest thou be a cursed thing like it: *but* thou shalt utterly detest it, and thou shalt utterly abhor it; ªfor it *is* ¹a cursed thing.

## CHAPTER 8

ALL the commandments which I command thee this day ªshall ye ¹observe to do, that ye may live, and ᵇmultiply,² and go in and possess the land which the LORD ³sware unto your fathers.

2 And thou shalt remember all the way which the LORD thy God ªled thee these forty years in the wilderness, to humble thee, *and* ᵇto ¹prove thee, ᶜto know what *was* in thine heart, whether thou wouldest keep his commandments, or no.

3 And he humbled thee, and ªsuffered thee to hunger, and ᵇfed thee with manna, which thou knewest not, neither did thy fathers know; that he might make thee know that man doth ᶜnot live by bread only, but by every *word* that proceedeth out of the mouth of the LORD doth man live.

4 ªThy raiment ¹waxed not old upon thee, neither did thy foot swell, these forty years.

---

**7:5** ¹ Heb. *asherim, wooden images* of Canaanite deities
² *carved*

**7:6** ª Ex. 19:5, 6; Amos 3:2; 1 Pet. 2:9 ¹ *set apart*
² *treasure*

**7:7** ª Deut. 4:37
ᵇ Deut. 10:22

**7:8** ª Deut. 10:15
ᵇ Luke 1:55, 72, 73 ᶜ Ex. 13:3, 14 ¹ *slavery*

**7:9** ª 1 Cor. 1:9; 2 Thess. 3:3; 2 Tim. 2:13 ᵇ Ex. 20:6; Deut. 5:10; Neh. 1:5; Dan. 9:4

**7:10** ª [2 Pet. 3:10] ¹ *delay with him who*

**7:12** ¹ *listen*

**7:13** ª Ps. 146:8; Prov. 15:9; John 14:21 ᵇ Deut. 28:4 ¹ *cause you to increase* ² *cattle* ³ *promised*

**7:14** ª Ex. 23:26

**7:15** ª Ex. 9:14; 15:26; Deut. 28:27, 60

**7:16** ª Ex. 23:33; Judg. 8:27; Ps. 106:36 ¹ *destroy*

**7:17** ¹ *greater*

**7:18** ª Ps. 105:5

**7:19** ª Deut. 4:34; 29:3 ¹ *trials*

**7:20** ª Ex. 23:28; Josh. 24:12

**7:21** ¹ *awesome*

**7:22** ª Ex. 23:29, 30 ¹ *by* ² *destroy*

**7:24** ª Josh. 10:24, 42; 12:1–24 ᵇ Josh. 23:9 ¹ *against*

**7:25** ª Prov. 23:6 ¹ *carved* ² *covet*

**7:26** ª Deut. 13:17 ¹ *devoted or banned*

**8:1** ª Deut. 4:1; 6:24 ᵇ Deut. 30:16 ¹ *be careful to observe* ² *increase in number* ³ *promised*

**8:2** ª Deut. 1:3; 2:7; 29:5; Ps. 136:16; Amos 2:10 ᵇ Ex. 16:4 ᶜ [John 2:25] ¹ *test*

**8:3** ª Ex. 16:2, 3 ᵇ Ex. 16:12, 14, 35 ᶜ Matt. 4:4; Luke 4:4

**8:4** ª Deut. 29:5; Neh. 9:21 ¹ *did not wear out*

---

5 [a]Thou shalt also [1]consider in thine heart, that, as a man chasteneth his son, *so* the LORD thy God chasteneth thee.

6 Therefore thou shalt keep the commandments of the LORD thy God, [a]to walk in his ways, and to fear him.

7 For the LORD thy God bringeth thee into a good land, [a]a land of brooks of water, of fountains and depths that spring out of valleys and hills;

8 A land of wheat, and barley, and vines, and fig trees, and pomegranates; a land of oil olive, and honey;

9 A land wherein thou shalt eat bread without scarceness, thou shalt not lack any *thing* in it; a land whose stones *are* iron, and out of whose hills thou mayest dig brass.

10 [a]When thou hast eaten and art full, then thou shalt bless the LORD thy God for the good land which he hath given thee.

11 Beware that thou forget not the LORD thy God, in not keeping his commandments, and his judgments, and his statutes, which I command thee this day:

12 [a]Lest *when* thou hast eaten and art [1]full, and hast built [2]goodly houses, and dwelt *therein;*

13 And *when* thy herds and thy flocks multiply, and thy silver and thy gold is [1]multiplied, and all that thou hast is multiplied;

14 [a]Then thine heart [1]be lifted up, and thou [b]forget the LORD thy God, which brought thee forth out of the land of Egypt, from the house of bondage;

15 Who [a]led thee through that great and terrible wilderness, [b]*wherein were* fiery serpents, and scorpions, and drought, where *there was* no water; [c]who brought thee forth water out of the rock of flint;

16 Who fed thee in the wilderness with [a]manna, which thy fathers knew not, that he might humble thee, and that he might [1]prove thee, [b]to do thee good at thy latter end;

17 And thou say in thine heart, My power and the might of *mine* hand hath gotten me this wealth.

18 But thou shalt remember the LORD thy God: [a]for *it is* he that giveth thee power to get wealth, [b]that he may [1]establish his covenant which he sware unto thy fathers, as *it is* this day.

19 And it shall be, if thou do at all forget the LORD thy God, and walk after other gods, and serve them, and worship them, [a]I testify against you this day that ye shall surely perish.

20 As the nations which the LORD destroyeth before your face, [a]so shall

8:5 [a] 2 Sam. 7:14;
Ps. 89:30–33;
Prov. 3:11, 12; Heb.
12:5–11; Rev. 3:19
[1] *know*

8:6 [a] [Deut. 5:33]

8:7 [a] Deut. 11:9–
12; Jer. 2:7

8:10 [a] Deut.
6:11, 12

8:12 [a] Deut. 28:47;
Prov. 30:9; Hos.
13:6 [1] *satisfied*
[2] *beautiful*

8:13 [1] *increased*

8:14 [a] 1 Cor. 4:7
[b] Deut. 8:11; Ps.
106:21 [1] *becomes
proud*

8:15 [a] Is. 63:12–14
[b] Num. 21:6 [c] Ex.
17:6; Num. 20:11

8:16 [a] Ex. 16:15
[b] Jer. 24:5, 6;
[Heb. 12:11] [1] *test*

8:18 [a] Prov. 10:22;
Hos. 2:8 [b] Deut.
7:8, 12 [1] *confirm*

8:19 [a] Deut. 4:26;
30:18

8:20 [a] [Dan.
9:11, 12]

ye perish; because ye would not be obedient unto the voice of the LORD your God.

## CHAPTER 9

HEAR, O Israel: Thou *art* to pass over Jordan this day, to go in to possess nations greater and mightier than thyself, cities great and [1]fenced up to heaven,

2 A people great and tall, the [a]children of the Anakims, whom thou knowest, and *of whom* thou hast heard *say,* Who can stand before the children of Anak!

3 Understand therefore this day, that the LORD thy God *is* he which [a]goeth over before thee; *as* a [b]consuming fire [c]he shall destroy them, and he shall bring them down before thy face: [d]so shalt thou drive them out, and destroy them quickly, as the LORD hath said unto thee.

4 [a]Speak not thou in thine heart, after that the LORD thy God hath cast them out from before thee, saying, [1]For my righteousness the LORD hath brought me in to possess this land: but [b]for[2] the wickedness of these nations the LORD doth drive them out from before thee.

5 [a]Not for thy righteousness, or for the uprightness of thine heart, dost thou go to possess their land: but for the wickedness of these nations the LORD thy God doth drive them out from before thee, and that he may [1]perform the [b]word which the LORD sware unto thy fathers, Abraham, Isaac, and Jacob.

6 Understand therefore, that the LORD thy God giveth thee not this good land to possess it for thy righteousness; for thou *art* a [a]stiffnecked[1] people.

7 Remember, *and* forget not, how thou [a]provokedst the LORD thy God to wrath in the wilderness: [b]from the day that thou didst depart out of the land of Egypt, until ye came unto this place, ye have been rebellious against the LORD.

8 Also [a]in Horeb ye provoked the LORD to wrath, so that the LORD was angry with you to have destroyed you.

9 [a]When I was gone up into the mount to receive the tables of stone, *even* the tables of the covenant which the LORD made with you, then I [1]abode in the mount forty days and [b]forty nights, I neither did eat bread nor drink water:

10 [a]And the LORD delivered unto me two tables of stone written with the finger of God; and on them *was written* according to all the words, which the LORD spake with you in the mount out of the midst of the fire [b]in the day of the assembly.

9:1 [1] *fortified*

9:2 [a] Num. 13:22,
28, 33; Josh.
11:21, 22

9:3 [a] Deut.
1:33; 31:3; Josh.
3:11; 5:14; John
10:4 [b] Deut.
4:24; Heb. 12:29
[c] Deut. 7:24 [d] Ex.
23:31

9:4 [a] Deut. 8:17;
[Rom. 11:6, 20;
1 Cor. 4:4, 7]
[b] Gen. 15:16; Lev.
18:3, 24–30; Deut.
12:31; 18:9–14
[1] *Because of*
[2] *because of*

9:5 [a] [Titus 3:5]
[b] Gen. 50:24
[1] *fulfil*

9:6 [a] Ex. 34:9;
Deut. 31:27
[1] *stubborn or
rebellious*

9:7 [a] Num. 14:22
[b] Ex. 14:11

9:8 [a] Ex. 32:1–8;
Ps. 106:19

9:9 [a] Ex. 24:12,
15; Deut. 5:2–
22 [b] Ex. 24:18
[1] *stayed on*

9:10 [a] Ex. 31:18;
Deut. 4:13 [b] Ex.
19:17

11 And it came to pass at the end of forty days and forty nights, *that* the LORD gave me the two tables of stone, *even* the tables of the covenant.

12 And the LORD said unto me, [a]Arise, get thee down quickly from hence; for thy people which thou hast brought forth out of Egypt have [1]corrupted *themselves;* they are [b]quickly turned aside out of the way which I commanded them; they have made them a [2]molten image.

13 Furthermore [a]the LORD spake unto me, saying, I have seen this people, and, behold, [b]it *is* a [1]stiffnecked people:

14 [a]Let me alone, that I may destroy them, and [b]blot out their name from under heaven: [c]and I will make of thee a nation mightier and greater than they.

15 [a]So I turned and came down from the mount, and [b]the mount burned with fire: and the two tables of the covenant *were* in my two hands.

16 And [a]I looked, and, behold, ye had sinned against the LORD your God, *and* had made you a molten calf: ye had turned aside quickly out of the way which the LORD had commanded you.

17 And I took the two tables, and cast them out of my two hands, and [a]brake them before your eyes.

18 And I [a]fell[1] down before the LORD, as at the first, forty days and forty nights: I did neither eat bread, nor drink water, because of all your sins which ye sinned, in doing wickedly in the sight of the LORD, to provoke him to anger.

19 [a]For I was afraid of the anger and hot displeasure, wherewith the LORD was wroth against you to destroy you. [b]But the LORD [1]hearkened unto me at that time also.

20 And the LORD was very angry with Aaron to have destroyed him: and I prayed for Aaron also the same time.

21 And I took your sin, the calf which ye had made, and burnt it with fire, and stamped it, *and* ground *it* very small, *even* until it was as small as dust: and I [a]cast the dust thereof into the brook that descended out of the mount.

22 And at [a]Taberah, and at [b]Massah, and at [c]Kibroth-hattaavah, ye [1]provoked the LORD to wrath.

23 Likewise [a]when the LORD sent you from Kadesh-barnea, saying, Go up and possess the land which I have given you; then ye rebelled against the commandment of the LORD your God, and [b]ye believed him not, nor hearkened to his voice.

24 [a]Ye have been rebellious against the LORD from the day that I knew you.

25 [a]Thus I [1]fell down before the LORD forty days and forty nights, as I fell down *at the first;* because the LORD had said he would destroy you.

26 I prayed therefore unto the LORD, and said, O Lord GOD, destroy not thy people and [a]thine inheritance, which thou hast redeemed through thy greatness, which thou hast brought forth out of Egypt with a mighty hand.

27 Remember thy servants, Abraham, Isaac, and Jacob; look not unto the stubbornness of this people, nor to their wickedness, nor to their sin:

28 Lest the land whence thou broughtest us out say, Because the LORD was not able to bring them into the land which he promised them, and because he hated them, he hath brought them out to slay them in the wilderness.

29 Yet they *are* thy people and thine inheritance, which thou broughtest out by thy mighty power and by thy stretched out arm.

## CHAPTER 10

AT that time the LORD said unto me, [1]Hew thee two tables of stone like unto the first, and come up unto me into the mount, and make thee an [a]ark of wood.

2 And I will write on the tables the words that were in the first tables which thou brakest, and [a]thou shalt put them in the ark.

3 And I made an ark *of* shittim wood, and hewed two tables of stone like unto the first, and went up into the mount, having the two tables in mine hand.

4 And he wrote on the tables, according to the first writing, the ten [1]commandments, [a]which the LORD spake unto you in the mount out of the midst of the fire in the day of the assembly: and the LORD gave them unto me.

5 And I turned myself and [a]came down from the mount, and [b]put the tables in the ark which I had made; [c]and there they be, as the LORD commanded me.

6 And the children of Israel took their journey from Beeroth of the children of Jaakan to Mosera: there Aaron [a]died, and there he was buried; and Eleazar his son ministered in the priest's office [1]in his stead.

7 [a]From thence they journeyed unto Gudgodah; and from Gudgodah to Jotbath, a land of [1]rivers of waters.

8 At that time [a]the LORD [1]separated the tribe of Levi, [b]to bear the ark of the covenant of the LORD, [c]to stand

9:12 [a] Ex. 32:7, 8 [b] Deut. 31:29 [1] *acted corruptly* [2] *moulded*
9:13 [a] Ex. 32:9 [b] Deut. 9:6 [1] *stubborn* or *rebellious*
9:14 [a] Ex. 32:10 [b] Deut. 29:20 [c] Num. 14:12
9:15 [a] Ex. 32:15–19 [b] Ex. 19:18
9:16 [a] Ex. 32:19
9:17 [a] Ex. 32:19
9:18 [a] Ex. 34:28; Ps. 106:23 [1] *prostrated myself*
9:19 [a] Ex. 32:10, 11; Heb. 12:21 [b] Ex. 32:14 [1] *listened*
9:21 [a] Ex. 32:20
9:22 [a] Num. 11:1, 3 [b] Ex. 17:7 [c] Num. 11:4, 34 [1] *caused to be angry*
9:23 [a] Num. 13:3 [b] Ps. 106:24, 25
9:24 [a] Deut. 9:7; 31:27
9:25 [a] Deut. 9:18 [1] *prostrated myself*
9:26 [a] Deut. 32:9
10:1 [a] Ex. 25:10 [1] *Cut out*
10:2 [a] Ex. 25:16, 21
10:4 [a] Ex. 20:1; 34:28 [1] Lit. *words*
10:5 [a] Ex. 34:29 [b] Ex. 40:20 [c] 1 Kin. 8:9
10:6 [a] Num. 20:25–28; 33:38 [1] *in his place*
10:7 [a] Num. 33:32–34 [1] *brooks of*
10:8 [a] Num. 3:6 [b] Num. 4:5, 15; 10:21 [c] Deut. 18:5 [1] *set apart*

171

before the LORD to minister unto him, and [d]to bless in his name, unto this day.

9 [a]Wherefore Levi hath no part nor inheritance with his brethren; the LORD *is* his inheritance, according as the LORD thy God promised him.

10 And [a]I stayed in the mount, according to the first time, forty days and forty nights; and [b]the LORD hearkened unto me at that time also, *and* the LORD would not destroy thee.

11 [a]And the LORD said unto me, Arise, [1]take *thy* journey before the people, that they may go in and possess the land, which I sware unto their fathers to give unto them.

12 And now, Israel, [a]what doth the LORD thy God require of thee, but to fear the LORD thy God, to walk in all his ways, and to [b]love him, and to serve the LORD thy God with all thy heart and with all thy soul,

13 To keep the commandments of the LORD, and his statutes, which I command thee this day [a]for thy [1]good?

14 Behold, the heaven and the heaven of heavens *is* the [a]LORD's thy God, the earth *also,* with all that therein *is.*

15 [1]Only the LORD had a delight in thy fathers to love them, and he chose their [2]seed after them, *even* you above all people, as *it is* this day.

16 Circumcise therefore the foreskin of your [a]heart, and be no more [b]stiffnecked.[1]

17 For the [b]LORD your God *is* [a]God of gods, and Lord of lords, [1]a great God, [c]a mighty, and a terrible, which [d]regardeth not persons, nor taketh reward:

18 [a]He doth execute the judgment of the fatherless and widow, and loveth the stranger, in giving him food and raiment.

19 Love ye therefore the stranger: for ye were strangers in the land of Egypt.

20 [a]Thou shalt fear the LORD thy God; him shalt thou serve, and to him shalt thou [1]cleave, and swear by his name.

21 He *is* thy praise, and he *is* thy God, that hath done for thee these great and [1]terrible things, which thine eyes have seen.

22 Thy fathers went down into Egypt with threescore and ten persons; and now the LORD thy God hath made thee as the stars of heaven for multitude.

## CHAPTER 11

THEREFORE thou shalt love the LORD thy God, and keep his charge, and his statutes, and his judgments, and his commandments, alway.

2 And know ye this day: for *I speak* not with your children which have not known, and which have not seen the [1]chastisement of the LORD your God, his greatness, his mighty hand, and his stretched out arm,

3 And his miracles, and his acts, which he did in the midst of Egypt unto Pharaoh the king of Egypt, and unto all his land;

4 And what he did unto the army of Egypt, unto their horses, and to their chariots; [a]how he made the water of the Red sea to overflow them as they pursued after you, and *how* the LORD hath destroyed them unto this day;

5 And what he did unto you in the wilderness, until ye came into this place;

6 And [a]what he did unto Dathan and Abiram, the sons of Eliab, the son of Reuben: how the earth opened her mouth, and swallowed them up, and their households, and their tents, and all the substance that *was* [1]in their possession, in the midst of all Israel:

7 But your eyes have [a]seen all the great [1]acts of the LORD which he did.

8 Therefore shall ye keep all the commandments which I command you this day, that ye may [a]be strong, and go in and possess the land, whither ye go to possess it;

9 And [a]that ye may prolong *your* days in the land, [b]which the LORD [1]sware unto your fathers to give unto them and to their seed, [c]a land that floweth with milk and honey.

10 For the land, whither thou goest in to possess it, *is* not as the land of Egypt, from whence ye came out, where thou sowedst thy seed, and wateredst *it* with thy foot, as a garden of [1]herbs:

11 [a]But the land, whither ye go to possess it, *is* a land of hills and valleys, *and* drinketh water of the rain of heaven:

12 A land which the LORD thy God careth for: [a]the eyes of the LORD thy God *are* always upon it, from the beginning of the year even unto the end of the year.

13 And it shall come to pass, if ye shall [1]hearken diligently unto my commandments which I command you this day, to love the LORD your God, and to serve him with all your heart and with all your soul,

14 That [a]I will give *you* the rain of your land in his due season, [b]the first rain and the latter rain, that thou mayest gather in thy [1]corn, and thy wine, and thine oil.

15 [a]And I will send grass in thy fields for thy cattle, that thou mayest [b]eat and be [1]full.

16 Take heed to yourselves, [a]that your heart be not deceived, and ye

10:8 [d] Num. 6:23
10:9 [a] Num. 18:20, 24; Deut. 18:1, 2; Ezek. 44:28
10:10 [a] Ex. 34:28; Deut. 9:18 [b] Ex. 32:14
10:11 [a] Ex. 33:1 [1] *begin*
10:12 [a] Mic. 6:8 [b] Deut. 6:5; Matt. 22:37; 1 Tim. 1:5
10:13 [a] Deut. 6:24 [1] *benefit* or *welfare*
10:14 [a] [Neh. 9:6; Ps. 68:33; 115:16]
10:15 [1] *The LORD delighted only in thy fathers* [2] *descendants*
10:16 [a] Lev. 26:41; Deut. 30:6; Jer. 4:4; Rom. 2:28, 29 [b] Deut. 9:6, 13 [1] *stubborn* or *rebellious*
10:17 [a] Deut. 4:35, 39; Is. 44:8; 46:9; Dan. 2:47; 1 Cor. 8:5, 6 [b] Rev. 19:16 [c] Deut. 7:21 [d] Acts 10:34 [1] *the great God, mighty and awesome who shows no partiality, nor takes a bribe*
10:18 [a] Ex. 22:22–24; Ps. 68.5; 146:9
10:20 [a] Matt. 4:10 [1] *hold fast*
10:21 [1] *awesome*
11:2 [1] *discipline*
11:4 [a] Ex. 14:28; Ps. 106:11
11:6 [a] Num. 16:1–35; Ps. 106:16–18 [1] Lit. *at their feet*
11:7 [a] Deut. 10:21; 29:2 [1] *works*
11:8 [a] Deut. 31:6, 7, 23; Josh. 1:6, 7
11:9 [a] Deut. 4:40; 5:16, 33; 6:2; Prov. 10:27 [b] Deut. 9:5 [c] Ex. 3:8 [1] *promised*
11:10 [1] *vegetables*
11:11 [a] Deut. 8:7
11:12 [a] 1 Kin. 9:3
11:13 [1] *obey*
11:14 [a] Lev. 26:4; Deut. 28:12 [b] Joel 2:23; James 5:7 [1] *grain*
11:15 [a] Ps. 104:14 [b] Deut. 6:11; Joel 2:19 [1] *satisfied*
11:16 [a] Deut. 29:18; Job 31:27

turn aside, and ᵇserve other gods, and worship them;

17 And *then* ᵃthe LORD's ¹wrath be ²kindled against you, and he ᵇshut up the heaven, that there be no rain, and that the land yield not her fruit; and *lest* ᶜye perish quickly from off the good land which the LORD giveth you.

18 Therefore ᵃshall ye ¹lay up these my words in your heart and in your ᵇsoul, and ᶜbind them for a sign upon your hand, that they may be as frontlets between your eyes.

19 ᵃAnd ye shall teach them your children, speaking of them when thou sittest in thine house, and when thou walkest by the way, when thou liest down, and when thou risest up.

20 ᵃAnd thou shalt write them upon the door posts of thine house, and upon thy gates:

21 That ᵃyour days may be multiplied, and the days of your children, in the land which the LORD sware unto your fathers to give them, as ᵇthe days of heaven upon the earth.

22 For if ᵃye shall diligently keep all these commandments which I command you, to do them, to love the LORD your God, to walk in all his ways, and ᵇto ¹cleave unto him;

23 Then will the LORD ᵃdrive out all these nations from before you, and ye shall ᵇpossess greater nations and mightier than yourselves.

24 ᵃEvery place whereon the soles of your feet shall tread shall be yours: ᵇfrom the wilderness and Lebanon, from the river, the river Euphrates, even unto the ¹uttermost sea shall your coast be.

25 There shall no man be able to ᵃstand ¹before you: *for* the LORD your God shall lay the fear of you and the ᵇdread of you upon all the land that ye shall tread upon, as he hath said unto you.

26 ᵃBehold, I set before you this day a blessing and a curse;

27 ᵃA blessing, if ye obey the commandments of the LORD your God, which I command you this day:

28 And a ᵃcurse, if ye will not obey the commandments of the LORD your God, but turn aside out of the way which I command you this day, to go after other gods, which ye have not known.

29 And it shall come to pass, when the LORD thy God hath brought thee in unto the land ¹whither thou goest to possess it, that thou shalt put the ᵃblessing upon mount Gerizim, and the ᵇcurse upon mount Ebal.

30 *Are* they not on the other side Jordan, ¹by the way where the sun goeth down, in the land of the Canaanites,

which dwell in the champaign over against Gilgal, ᵃbeside the ²plains of Moreh?

31 For ye shall pass over Jordan to go in to possess the land which the LORD your God giveth you, and ye shall possess it, and dwell therein.

32 And ye shall observe to do all the statutes and judgments which I set before you this day.

## CHAPTER 12

THESE ᵃ*are* the statutes and judgments, which ye shall observe to do in the land, which the LORD God of thy fathers giveth thee to possess ᵇall¹ the days that ye live upon the earth.

2 ᵃYe shall utterly destroy all the places, wherein the nations which ye shall ¹possess served their gods, ᵇupon the high mountains, and upon the hills, and under every green tree:

3 And ᵃye shall ¹overthrow their altars, and break their pillars, and burn their ²groves with fire; and ye shall ³hew down the graven images of their gods, and destroy the names of them out of that place.

4 Ye shall not do ᵃso unto the LORD your God.

5 But unto the ᵃplace which the LORD your God shall choose out of all your tribes to put his name there, *even* ¹unto his ᵇhabitation shall ye seek, and thither thou shalt come:

6 And ᵃthither ye shall bring your burnt offerings, and your sacrifices, and your tithes, and heave offerings of your hand, and your vows, and your freewill offerings, and the ᵇfirstlings of your herds and of your flocks:

7 And ᵃthere ye shall eat before the LORD your God, and ᵇye shall rejoice in all that ye ¹put your hand unto, ye and your households, wherein the LORD thy God hath blessed thee.

8 Ye shall not do ¹after all *the things* that we do here this day, ᵃevery man whatsoever *is* right in his own eyes.

9 For ye are not as yet come to the ᵃrest¹ and to the inheritance, which the LORD your God giveth you.

10 But *when* ye go over Jordan, and dwell in the land which the LORD your God giveth you to inherit, and *when* he giveth you ᵃrest from all your enemies round about, so that ye dwell in safety;

11 Then there shall be a place which the LORD your God shall choose to cause his name to dwell there; thither shall ye bring all that I command you; your burnt offerings, and your sacrifices, your tithes, and the heave offering of your hand, and all your choice ¹vows which ye vow unto the LORD:

### Center column references

11:16 ᵇ Deut. 8:19

11:17 ᵃ Deut. 6:15; 9:19 ᵇ Deut. 28:24; 1 Kin. 8:35; 2 Chr. 6:26; 7:13 ᶜ Deut. 4:26; 2 Chr. 36:14–20 ¹ *anger* ² *aroused*

11:18 ᵃ Deut. 6:6–9 ᵇ Ps. 119:2, 34 ᶜ Deut. 6:8 ¹ Lit. *put*

11:19 ᵃ Deut. 4:9, 10; 6:7; Prov. 22:6

11:20 ᵃ Deut. 6:9

11:21 ᵃ Deut. 4:40 ᵇ Ps. 72:5; 89:29; Prov. 3:2; 4:10; 9:11

11:22 ᵃ Deut. 11:1 ᵇ Deut. 10:20 ¹ *hold fast*

11:23 ᵃ Deut. 4:38 ᵇ Deut. 9:1

11:24 ᵃ Josh. 1:3; 14:9 ᵇ Gen. 15:18; Ex. 23:31; Deut. 1:7, 8 ¹ The Mediterranean

11:25 ᵃ Deut. 7:24 ᵇ Ex. 23:27; Deut. 2:25; Josh. 2:9–11 ¹ *against*

11:26 ᵃ Deut. 30:1, 15, 19

11:27 ᵃ Deut. 28:1–14

11:28 ᵃ Deut. 28:15–68

11:29 ᵃ Deut. 27:12, 13; Josh. 8:33 ᵇ Deut. 27:13–26 ¹ *which*

11:30 ᵃ Gen. 12:6 ¹ *toward the setting sun* ² *terebinth trees of*

12:1 ᵃ Deut. 6:1 ᵇ Deut. 4:9, 10; 1 Kin. 8:40 ¹ *as long as*

12:2 ᵃ Ex. 34:13 ᵇ 2 Kin. 16:4; 17:10, 11 ¹ *dispossess*

12:3 ᵃ Num. 33:52; Deut. 7:5; Judg. 2:2 ¹ *destroy* ² Heb. *asherim, wooden images* ³ *cut*

12:4 ᵃ Deut. 12:31

12:5 ᵇ Ex. 20:24 ᵇ Ex. 15:13; 1 Sam. 2:29 ¹ *for his dwelling*

12:6 ᵃ Lev. 17:3, 4 ᵇ Deut. 14:23

12:7 ᵃ Deut. 14:26 ᵇ Deut. 12:12, 18 ¹ *undertake*

12:8 ᵃ Judg. 17:6; 21:25 ¹ *as we are doing today*

12:9 ᵃ Deut. 3:20; 25:19; Ps. 95:11 ¹ *place of rest*

12:10 ᵃ Josh. 11:23

12:11 ¹ *offerings*

12 And ªye shall rejoice before the LORD your God, ye, and your sons, and your daughters, and your menservants, and your maidservants, and the ᵇLevite that *is* within your gates; forasmuch as he hath no part nor inheritance with you.

13 Take heed to thyself that thou offer not thy burnt offerings in every place that thou seest:

14 But in the place which the LORD shall choose in one of thy tribes, there thou shalt offer thy burnt offerings, and there thou shalt do all that I command thee.

15 ¹Notwithstanding ªthou mayest kill and eat flesh in all thy gates, whatsoever thy ²soul lusteth after, according to the blessing of the LORD thy God which he hath given thee: ᵇthe unclean and the clean may eat thereof, ᶜas of the roebuck, and as of the hart.

16 ªOnly ye shall not eat the blood; ye shall pour it upon the earth as water.

17 Thou mayest not eat within thy gates the tithe of thy ¹corn, or of thy wine, or of thy oil, or the firstlings of thy herds or of thy flock, nor any of thy ²vows which thou vowest, nor thy freewill offerings, or ³heave offering of thine hand:

18 But thou must eat them before the LORD thy God in the place which the LORD thy God shall choose, thou, and thy son, and thy daughter, and thy manservant, and thy maidservant, and the Levite that *is* within thy gates: and thou shalt rejoice before the LORD thy God in all that thou ¹puttest thine hands unto.

19 ¹Take heed to thyself that thou forsake not the Levite as long as thou livest upon the earth.

20 When the LORD thy God shall ªenlarge thy border, as he hath promised thee, and thou shalt say, I will eat ¹flesh, because thy soul longeth to eat ¹flesh; thou mayest eat ²flesh, whatsoever thy soul lusteth after.

21 If the place which the LORD thy God hath chosen to put his name there be too far from ªthee, then thou shalt kill of thy herd and of thy flock, which the LORD hath given thee, as I have commanded thee, and thou shalt eat in thy gates whatsoever thy soul lusteth after.

22 Even as the ¹roebuck and the ²hart is eaten, so thou shalt eat them: the unclean and the clean shall eat *of* them alike.

23 Only be sure that thou eat not the blood: ªfor the blood *is* the life; and thou mayest not eat the life with the flesh.

24 Thou shalt not eat it; thou shalt pour it upon the earth as water.

25 Thou shalt not eat it; ªthat it may go well with thee, and with thy children after thee, ᵇwhen thou shalt do *that which is* right in the sight of the LORD.

26 Only thy ªholy things which thou hast, and thy ¹vows, thou shalt take, and go unto the place which the LORD shall choose:

27 And ªthou shalt offer thy burnt offerings, the flesh and the blood, upon the altar of the LORD thy God: and the blood of thy sacrifices shall be poured out upon the altar of the LORD thy God, and thou shalt eat the flesh.

28 Observe and hear all these words which I command thee, ªthat it may go well with thee, and with thy children after thee for ever, when thou doest *that which is* good and right in the sight of the LORD thy God.

29 When ªthe LORD thy God shall cut off the nations from before thee, whither thou goest to possess them, and thou ¹succeedest them, and dwellest in their land:

30 Take heed to thyself that thou be not ¹snared by following them, after that they be destroyed from before thee; and that thou enquire not after their gods, saying, How did these nations serve their gods? even so will I do likewise.

31 ªThou shalt not do so unto the LORD thy God: for ¹every abomination to the LORD, which he hateth, have they done unto their gods; for ᵇeven their sons and their daughters they have burnt in the fire to their gods.

32 What thing soever I command you, ¹observe to do it: ªthou shalt not add thereto, nor ²diminish from it.

## CHAPTER 13

IF there arise among you a prophet, or a ªdreamer of dreams, ᵇand giveth thee a sign or a wonder,

2 And ªthe sign or the wonder come to pass, whereof he spake unto thee, saying, Let us go after other gods, which thou hast not known, and let us serve them;

3 Thou shalt not ¹hearken unto the words of that prophet, or that dreamer of dreams: for the LORD your God ªproveth² you, to know whether ye love the LORD your God with all your heart and with all your soul.

4 Ye shall ªwalk¹ after the LORD your God, and fear him, and keep his commandments, and obey his voice, and ye shall serve him, and ᵇcleave² unto him.

5 And ªthat prophet, or that dreamer of dreams, shall be put to death; because he hath spoken to turn *you*

### Cross References

12:12 ª Deut. 12:18; 26:11 ᵇ Deut. 10:9; 14:29
12:15 ª Deut. 12:21 ᵇ Deut. 12:22 ᶜ Deut. 14:5 ¹ *However* ² *heart desires*
12:16 ª Gen. 9:4; Lev. 7:26; 17:10–12; 1 Sam. 14:33; Acts 15:20, 29
12:17 ¹ *grain* ² *offerings* ³ *contribution*
12:18 ¹ *undertake*
12:19 ¹ *Be careful*
12:20 ª Gen. 15:18; Ex. 34:24; Deut. 11:24; 19:8 ¹ *meat* ² *as much meat as your heart desires*
12:21 ª Deut. 14:24
12:22 ¹ *gazelle* ² *deer*
12:23 ª Gen. 9:4; Lev. 17:10–14; Deut. 12:16
12:25 ª Deut. 4:40; 6:18; Is. 3:10 ᵇ Ex. 15:26; 1 Kin. 11:38
12:26 ª Num. 5:9, 10; 18:19 ¹ *vowed offerings*
12:27 ª Lev. 1:5, 9, 13, 17
12:28 ª Deut. 12:25
12:29 ª Ex. 23:23; Deut. 19:1; Josh. 23:4 ¹ *displace*
12:30 ¹ *ensnared to follow*
12:31 ª Lev. 18:3, 26, 30; 20:1, 2 ᵇ Deut. 18:10; Ps. 106:37; Jer. 32:35 ¹ *everything detestable*
12:32 ª Deut. 4:2; 13:18; Josh. 1:7; Prov. 30:6; Rev. 22:18, 19 ¹ *be careful to observe it* ² *take away*
13:1 ª Num. 12:6; Jer. 23:28; Zech. 10:2 ᵇ Matt. 24:24; Mark 13:22; 2 Thess. 2:9
13:2 ª Deut. 18:22
13:3 ª Ex. 20:20; Deut. 8:2, 16 ¹ *listen* ² *is testing*
13:4 ª Deut. 10:12, 20; 2 Kin. 23:3 ᵇ Deut. 30:20 ¹ *follow* ² *hold fast to*
13:5 ª Deut. 18:20; Jer. 14:15

away from the LORD your God, which brought you out of the land of Egypt, and redeemed you out of the house of bondage, to [1]thrust thee out of the way which the LORD thy God commanded thee to walk in. [b]So shalt thou [2]put the evil away from the midst of thee.

6 [a]If thy brother, the son of thy mother, or thy son, or thy daughter, or [b]the wife [1]of thy bosom, or thy friend, [c]which *is* as thine own soul, entice thee secretly, saying, Let us go and serve other gods, which thou hast not known, thou, nor thy fathers;

7 *Namely*, of the gods of the people which *are* round about you, [1]nigh unto thee, or far off from thee, from the *one* end of the earth even unto the *other* end of the earth;

8 Thou shalt [a]not [1]consent unto him, nor hearken unto him; neither shall thine eye pity him, neither shalt thou spare, neither shalt thou conceal him:

9 But thou shalt surely kill him; thine hand shall be first upon him to put him to [a]death, and afterwards the hand of all the people.

10 And thou shalt stone him with stones, that he die; because he hath sought to thrust thee away from the LORD thy God, which brought thee out of the land of Egypt, from the house of bondage.

11 And all Israel shall hear, and [a]fear, and shall [1]do no more any such wickedness as this is among you.

12 [a]If thou shalt hear *say* in one of thy cities, which the LORD thy God hath given thee to dwell there, saying,

13 *Certain* men, [1]the children of Belial, are gone out from among you, and have [2]withdrawn the inhabitants of their city, saying, Let us go and serve other gods, which ye have not known;

14 Then shalt thou enquire, and make search, and ask diligently; and, behold, *if it be* truth, *and* the thing certain, *that* such [1]abomination is wrought among you;

15 Thou shalt surely [1]smite the inhabitants of that city with the edge of the sword, destroying it utterly, and all that *is* therein, and the cattle thereof, with the edge of the sword.

16 And thou shalt gather all the [1]spoil of it into the midst of the street thereof, and shalt [a]burn with fire the city, and all the spoil thereof [2]every whit, for the LORD thy God: and it shall be [b]an [3]heap for ever; it shall not be built again.

17 And [a]there shall [1]cleave [2]nought of the cursed thing to thine hand: that the LORD may [b]turn from the fierceness of his anger, and shew thee mercy, and have compassion upon thee, and [3]multiply thee, as he hath sworn unto thy fathers;

18 When thou shalt [1]hearken to the voice of the LORD thy God, [a]to keep all his commandments which I command thee this day, to do *that which is* right in the eyes of the LORD thy God.

## CHAPTER 14

YE *are* [a]the children of the LORD your God: [b]ye shall not cut yourselves, nor [1]make any baldness between your eyes for the dead.

2 [a]For thou *art* an holy people unto the LORD thy God, and the LORD hath chosen thee to be a [1]peculiar people unto himself, above all the nations that *are* upon the earth.

3 [a]Thou shalt not eat any [1]abominable thing.

4 [a]These *are* the beasts which ye shall eat: the ox, the sheep, and the goat,

5 The [1]hart, and the [2]roebuck, and the [3]fallow deer, and the wild goat, and the [4]pygarg, and the [5]wild ox, and the [6]chamois.

6 And every beast that parteth the hoof, and cleaveth the cleft into two claws, *and* cheweth the cud among the beasts, that ye shall eat.

7 Nevertheless these ye shall not eat of them that chew the cud, or of them that divide the cloven hoof; *as* the camel, and the hare, and the coney: for they chew the cud, but divide not the hoof; *therefore* they *are* unclean unto you.

8 And the swine, because it divideth the hoof, yet cheweth not the cud, it *is* unclean unto you: ye shall not eat of their flesh, [a]nor touch their dead carcase.

9 [a]These ye shall eat of all that *are* in the waters: all that have fins and scales shall ye eat:

10 And whatsoever hath not fins and scales ye may not eat; it *is* unclean unto you.

11 *Of* all clean birds ye shall eat.

12 [a]But these *are they* of which ye shall not eat: the eagle, and the ossifrage, and the ospray,

13 And the glede, and the kite, and the vulture after his kind,

14 And every raven after his kind,

15 And the owl, and the night hawk, and the cuckow, and the hawk after his kind,

16 The little owl, and the great owl, and the swan,

17 And the pelican, and the gier eagle, and the cormorant,

18 And the stork, and the heron after her kind, and the lapwing, and the bat.

19 And [a]every [1]creeping thing that flieth *is* unclean unto you: [b]they shall not be eaten.

20 *But of* all clean fowls ye may eat.

21 [a]Ye shall not eat *of* any thing that

### Center reference column

13:5 [b] Deut. 17:5,
7; 1 Cor. 5:13
[1] *entice you from*
[2] *exterminate*
13:6 [a] Deut.
17:2 [a] Gen. 16:5
[c] 1 Sam. 18:1, 3
[1] *you cherish*
13:7 [1] *near to*
13:8 [a] Deut. 7:16;
Prov. 1:10 [1] *yield*
13:9 [a] Lev. 24:14;
Deut. 17:7
13:11 [a] Deut. 17:13
[1] *not again do*
13:12 [a] Judg.
20:1–48
13:13 [1] *reprobate
or worthless*
[2] *enticed*
13:14 [1] *detestable
action*
13:15 [1] *strike*
13:16 [a] Josh. 6:24
[b] Josh. 8:28; Is.
17:1; 25:2; Jer.
49:2 [1] *plunder*
[2] *completely* [3] Lit.
*a mound or ruin*
13:17 [a] Josh.
6:18 [b] Josh.
7:26 [1] *remain*
[2] *none of the
accursed thing in*
[3] *increase*

13:18 [a] Deut.
12:25, 28, 32
[1] *listen*
14:1 [a] [Rom. 8:16;
Gal. 3:26] [b] Lev.
19:28; 21:1–5
[1] *shave the front
of your head*
14:2 [a] Lev. 20:26;
Deut. 7:6; [Rom.
12:1] [1] *special
treasure*
14:3 [a] Ezek. 4:14
[1] *detestable*
14:4 [a] Lev. 11:2–45
14:5 [1] *deer*
[2] *gazelle* [3] *roe
deer* [4] *mountain
goat* [5] *antelope*
[6] *mountain sheep*
14:8 [a] Lev.
11:26, 27
14:9 [a] Lev. 11:9
14:12 [a] Lev. 11:13
14:19 [a] Lev.
11:20 [b] Lev. 11:23
[1] *swarming*
14:21 [a] Lev. 17:15;
22:8; Ezek. 4:14;
44:31

dieth of itself: thou shalt give it unto the stranger that *is* in thy gates, that he may eat it; or thou mayest sell it unto an alien: ᵇfor thou *art* an holy people unto the LORD thy God. ᶜThou shalt not ¹seethe a kid in his mother's milk.

22 ᵃThou shalt truly tithe all the increase of thy seed, that the field bringeth forth year by year.

23 ᵃAnd thou shalt eat before the LORD thy God, in the place which he shall choose to place his name there, the tithe of thy corn, of thy wine, and of thine oil, and ᵇthe firstlings of thy herds and of thy flocks; that thou mayest learn to ¹fear the LORD thy God always.

24 And if the ¹way be too long for thee, so that thou art not able to carry it; *or* ᵃif the place be too far from thee, which the LORD thy God shall choose to set his name there, when the LORD thy God hath blessed thee:

25 Then shalt thou ¹turn *it* into money, and bind up the money in thine hand, and shalt go unto the place which the LORD thy God shall choose:

26 And thou shalt ¹bestow that money for whatsoever ²thy soul lusteth after, for oxen, or for sheep, or for wine, or for strong drink, or for whatsoever thy soul desireth: and thou shalt eat there before the LORD thy God, and thou shalt ᵃrejoice, thou, and thine household,

27 And the ᵃLevite that *is* within thy gates; thou shalt not ¹forsake him; for he hath no part nor inheritance with thee.

28 ᵃAt the end of three years thou shalt bring forth all the ᵇtithe of thine increase the same year, and shalt ¹lay *it* up within thy gates:

29 And the Levite, (because he hath no part nor inheritance with thee,) and the stranger, and the fatherless, and the widow, which *are* within thy gates, shall come, and shall eat and be satisfied; that the LORD thy God may bless thee in all the work of thine hand which thou doest.

## CHAPTER 15

AT the end of ᵃ*every* seven years thou shalt make a ¹release.

2 And this *is* the manner of the release: Every creditor that lendeth *ought* unto his neighbour shall ¹release *it;* he shall not ²exact *it* of his neighbour, or of his brother; because it is called the LORD's release.

3 Of a foreigner thou mayest exact *it again:* but *that* which is thine with thy brother thine hand shall release;

4 ¹Save when there shall be no poor among you; for the LORD shall greatly ᵃbless thee in the land which

14:21 ᵇ Deut. 14:2
ᶜ Ex. 23:19; 34:26
¹ boil a young goat
14:22 ᵃ Lev. 27:30; Deut. 12:6, 17; Neh. 10:37
14:23 ᵃ Deut. 12:5–7 ᵇ Deut. 15:19, 20 ¹ stand in awe of
14:24 ᵃ Deut. 12:5, 21 ¹ journey
14:25 ¹ exchange it for
14:26 ᵃ Deut. 12:7 ¹ spend ² your heart desires
14:27 ᵃ Deut. 12:12 ¹ neglect
14:28 ᵃ Deut. 26:12; Amos 4:4 ᵇ Num. 18:21–24 ¹ store it
15:1 ᵃ Ex. 21:2; 23:10, 11; Lev. 25:4; Jer. 34:14 ¹ remission of debts
15:2 ¹ cancel the debt ² require
15:4 ᵃ Deut. 7:13 ¹ Except

15:5 ¹ obey
15:6 ᵃ Deut. 28:12, 44
15:7 ᵃ Ex. 23:6; Lev. 25:35–37; Deut. 24:12–14; [1 John 3:17] ¹ towns
15:8 ᵃ Matt. 5:42; Gal. 2:10 ¹ freely
15:9 ᵃ Deut. 28:54, 56 ᵇ Ex. 22:23; Deut. 24:15; Job 34:28; Ps. 12:5; James 5:4 ᶜ [Matt. 25:41, 42]
15:10 ᵃ 2 Cor. 9:5, 7 ᵇ Deut. 14:29; Ps. 41:1; Prov. 22:9
15:11 ᵃ Matt. 26:11; Mark 14:7; John 12:8 ¹ freely
15:12 ᵃ Ex. 21:2–6; Jer. 34:14 ᵇ Lev. 25:39–46
15:13 ¹ set him free ² empty-handed
15:14 ᵃ Prov. 10:22
15:15 ᵃ Deut. 5:15 ¹ slave
15:16 ᵃ Ex. 21:5, 6

the LORD thy God giveth thee *for* an inheritance to possess it:

5 Only if thou carefully ¹hearken unto the voice of the LORD thy God, to observe to do all these commandments which I command thee this day.

6 For the LORD thy God blesseth thee, as he promised thee: and ᵃthou shalt lend unto many nations, but thou shalt not borrow; and thou shalt reign over many nations, but they shall not reign over thee.

7 If there be among you a poor man of one of thy brethren within any of thy ¹gates in thy land which the LORD thy God giveth thee, ᵃthou shalt not harden thine heart, nor shut thine hand from thy poor brother:

8 But ᵃthou shalt open thine hand ¹wide unto him, and shalt surely lend him sufficient for his need, *in that* which he wanteth.

9 Beware that there be not a thought in thy wicked heart, saying, The seventh year, the year of release, is at hand; and thine ᵃeye be evil against thy poor brother, and thou givest him nought; and ᵇhe cry unto the LORD against thee, and ᶜit be sin unto thee.

10 Thou shalt surely give him, and ᵃthine heart shall not be grieved when thou givest unto him: because that ᵇfor this thing the LORD thy God shall bless thee in all thy works, and in all that thou puttest thine hand unto.

11 For ᵃthe poor shall never cease out of the land: therefore I command thee, saying, Thou shalt open thine hand ¹wide unto thy brother, to thy poor, and to thy needy, in thy land.

12 *And* ᵃif thy brother, an Hebrew man, or an Hebrew woman, be ᵇsold unto thee, and serve thee six years; then in the seventh year thou shalt let him go free from thee.

13 And when thou ¹sendest him out free from thee, thou shalt not let him go away ²empty:

14 Thou shalt furnish him liberally out of thy flock, and out of thy floor, and out of thy winepress: *of that* wherewith the LORD thy God hath ᵃblessed thee thou shalt give unto him.

15 And ᵃthou shalt remember that thou wast a ¹bondman in the land of Egypt, and the LORD thy God redeemed thee: therefore I command thee this thing to day.

16 And it shall be, ᵃif he say unto thee, I will not go away from thee; because he loveth thee and thine house, because he is well with thee;

17 Then thou shalt take an aul, and thrust *it* through his ear unto the door, and he shall be thy servant for ever. And also unto thy maidservant thou shalt do likewise.

18 It shall not seem hard unto thee, when thou sendest him away free from thee; for he hath been worth [a]a double hired servant *to thee,* in serving thee six years: and the LORD thy God shall bless thee in all that thou doest.

19 [a]All the firstling males that come of thy herd and of thy flock thou shalt [1]sanctify unto the LORD thy God: thou shalt do no work with the firstling of thy bullock, nor shear the firstling of thy sheep.

20 [a]Thou shalt eat *it* before the LORD thy God year by year in the place which the LORD shall choose, thou and thy household.

21 [a]And if there be *any* blemish therein, *as if it be* lame, or blind, *or have* any ill blemish, thou shalt not sacrifice it unto the LORD thy God.

22 Thou shalt eat it within thy gates: [a]the unclean and the clean *person shall eat it* alike, as the roebuck, and as the hart.

23 Only thou shalt not eat the blood thereof; thou shalt pour it upon the ground as water.

## CHAPTER 16

OBSERVE the [a]month of Abib, and keep the passover unto the LORD thy God: for [b]in the month of Abib the LORD thy God brought thee forth out of Egypt by night.

2 Thou shalt therefore sacrifice the passover unto the LORD thy God, of the flock and [a]the herd, in the [b]place which the LORD shall choose to place his name there.

3 Thou shalt eat no leavened bread with it; [a]seven days shalt thou eat unleavened bread therewith, *even* the bread of affliction; for thou camest forth out of the land of Egypt in haste: that thou mayest [b]remember the day when thou camest forth out of the land of Egypt all the days of thy life.

4 [a]And there shall be no leavened bread seen with thee in all thy coast seven days; neither shall there *any thing* of the flesh, which thou sacrificedst the first day at even, remain [1]all night until the [b]morning.

5 Thou mayest not sacrifice the passover within any of thy gates, which the LORD thy God giveth thee:

6 But at the place which the LORD thy God shall choose to place his name in, there thou shalt sacrifice the passover [a]at even, at the going down of the sun, [1]at the season that thou camest forth out of Egypt.

7 And thou shalt roast and eat *it* [a]in the place which the LORD thy God shall choose: and thou shalt turn in the morning, and go unto thy tents.

8 Six days thou shalt eat unleavened bread: and [a]on the seventh day

shall *be* [1]a solemn assembly to the LORD thy God: thou shalt do no work *therein.*

9 Seven weeks shalt thou number unto thee: begin to number the seven weeks from *such time as* thou beginnest *to put* the sickle to the [1]corn.

10 And thou shalt keep the [a]feast of weeks unto the LORD thy God with a tribute of a freewill offering of thine hand, which thou shalt give *unto the LORD thy God,* [b]according as the LORD thy God hath blessed thee:

11 And [a]thou shalt rejoice before the LORD thy God, thou, and thy son, and thy daughter, and thy manservant, and thy maidservant, and the Levite that *is* within thy gates, and the stranger, and the fatherless, and the widow, that *are* among you, in the place which the LORD thy God hath chosen to place his name there.

12 [a]And thou shalt remember that thou wast a [1]bondman in Egypt: and thou shalt [2]observe and do these statutes.

13 [a]Thou shalt observe the feast of tabernacles seven days, after that thou hast gathered [1]in thy corn and thy wine:

14 And [a]thou shalt rejoice in thy feast, thou, and thy son, and thy daughter, and thy manservant, and thy maidservant, and the Levite, the stranger, and the fatherless, and the widow, that *are* within thy [1]gates.

15 [a]Seven days shalt thou keep a [1]solemn feast unto the LORD thy God in the place which the LORD thy God shall choose: because the LORD thy God shall bless thee in all thine increase, and in all the works of thine hands, therefore thou shalt surely rejoice.

16 [a]Three times in a year shall all thy males appear before the LORD thy God in the place which he shall choose; in the feast of unleavened bread, and in the feast of weeks, and in the feast of tabernacles: and [b]they shall not appear before the LORD [1]empty:

17 Every man *shall give* as he is able, [a]according to the blessing of the LORD thy God which he hath given thee.

18 [a]Judges and officers shalt thou make thee in all thy [1]gates, which the LORD thy God giveth thee, throughout thy tribes: and they shall judge the people with just judgment.

19 [a]Thou shalt not [1]wrest judgment; [b]thou shalt not [2]respect persons, [c]neither take a [3]gift: for a gift doth blind the eyes of the wise, and [4]pervert the words of the righteous.

20 That which is altogether just shalt thou follow, that thou mayest [a]live, and inherit the land which the LORD thy God giveth thee.

---

15:18 [a] Is. 16:14
15:19 [a] Ex. 13:2, 12 [1] *set apart* or *consecrate*
15:20 [a] Lev. 7:15–18; Deut. 12:5; 14:23
15:21 [a] Lev. 22:19–25; Deut. 17:1
15:22 [a] Deut. 12:15, 16, 22
16:1 [a] Ex. 12:2 [b] Ex. 13:4
16:2 [a] Num. 28:19 [b] Deut. 12:5, 26; 15:20
16:3 [a] Num. 29:12 [b] Ex. 13:3; Deut. 4:9
16:4 [a] Ex. 13:7 [b] Num. 9:12 [1] *overnight*
16:6 [a] Ex. 12:7–10 [1] *at the time*
16:7 [a] 2 Kin. 23:23
16:8 [a] Ex. 12:16; 13:6; Lev. 23:8, 36
[1] *day of restraint*
16:9 [a] *grain*
16:10 [a] Ex. 34:22; Lev. 23:15, 16; Num. 28:26 [b] 1 Cor. 16:2
16:11 [a] Deut. 16:14
16:12 [a] Deut. 15:15 [1] *slave* [2] *be careful to observe*
16:13 [a] Ex. 23:16 [1] *from your threshingfloor and from your winepress*
16:14 [a] Neh. 8:9 [1] *towns*
16:15 [a] Lev. 23:39–41 [1] *pilgrim feast*
16:16 [a] Ex. 23:14–17; 34:22–24 [b] Ex. 23:15 [1] *empty-handed*
16:17 [a] Lev. 14:30, 31; Deut. 16:10
16:18 [a] Ex. 23:1–8; Deut. 1:16, 17; John 7:24 [1] *towns*
16:19 [a] Ex. 23:2, 6 [b] Deut. 1:17 [c] Ex. 23:8 [1] *pervert* [2] *show partiality* [3] *bribe* [4] *twist*
16:20 [a] Ezek. 18:5–9

177

21 ᵃThou shalt not plant thee ¹a grove of any trees near unto the altar of the LORD thy God, which thou shalt make thee.

22 ᵃNeither shalt thou set thee up *any* ¹image; which the LORD thy God hateth.

## CHAPTER 17

THOU ᵃshalt not sacrifice unto the LORD thy God *any* bullock, or sheep, wherein is blemish, *or* any ¹evilfavouredness: for that *is* an ²abomination unto the LORD thy God.

2 ᵃIf there be found among you, within any of thy ¹gates which the LORD thy God giveth thee, man or woman, that hath wrought wickedness in the sight of the LORD thy God, ᵇin transgressing his covenant,

3 And hath gone and served other gods, and worshipped them, either ᵃthe sun, or moon, or any of the host of heaven, ᵇwhich I have not commanded;

4 ᵃAnd it be told thee, and thou hast heard *of it*, and enquired diligently, and, behold, *it be* true, *and* the thing certain, *that* such ¹abomination is wrought in Israel:

5 Then shalt thou bring forth that man or that woman, which have committed that wicked thing, unto thy gates, *even* that man or that woman, and ᵈshalt stone them with stones, till they ᵇdie.

6 At the mouth of two witnesses, or three ᵃwitnesses, shall he that is worthy of death be put to death; *but* at the mouth of one witness he shall not be put to death.

7 The hands of the witnesses shall be first upon him to put him to death, and afterward the hands of all the people. So thou shalt put the evil away from among ᵃyou.

8 ᵃIf there arise a matter too hard for thee in judgment, between blood and blood, between plea and plea, and between stroke and stroke, *being* matters of controversy within thy gates: then shalt thou arise, and get thee up into the ᵇplace which the LORD thy God shall choose;

9 And ᵃthou shalt come unto the priests the Levites, and ᵇunto the judge that shall be in those days, and enquire; ᶜand they shall shew thee the sentence of judgment:

10 And thou shalt do according to the sentence, which they of that place which the LORD shall choose shall shew thee; and thou shalt observe to do according to all that they ¹inform thee:

11 According to the sentence of the law which they shall teach thee, and according to the judgment which they shall tell thee, thou shalt do:

thou shalt not ¹decline from the sentence which they shall shew thee, *to* the right hand, nor *to* the left.

12 And ᵃthe man that will do presumptuously, and will not ¹hearken unto the priest that standeth to minister there before the LORD thy God, or unto the judge, even that man shall die: and thou shalt put away the evil from Israel.

13 ᵃAnd all the people shall hear, and fear, and do no more presumptuously.

14 When thou art come unto the land which the LORD thy God giveth thee, and shalt possess it, and shalt dwell therein, and shalt say, ᵃI will set a king over me, like as all the nations that *are* about me;

15 Thou shalt in any wise set *him* king over thee, ᵃwhom the LORD thy God shall choose: *one* ᵇfrom among thy brethren shalt thou set king over thee: thou mayest not set a stranger over thee, which *is* not thy brother.

16 But he shall not multiply ᵃhorses to himself, nor cause the people ᵇto return to Egypt, to the end that he should multiply horses: forasmuch as ᶜthe LORD hath said unto you, ᵈYe shall henceforth return no more that way.

17 Neither shall he multiply wives to himself, that his heart turn not away: neither shall he greatly multiply to himself silver and ᵃgold.

18 And it shall be, when he sitteth upon the throne of his kingdom, that he shall write him a copy of this law in a book out of *that which is* ᵃbefore the priests the Levites:

19 And ᵃit shall be with him, and he shall read therein all the days of his life: that he may learn to ¹fear the LORD his God, to keep all the words of this law and these statutes, to do them:

20 That his heart be not ¹lifted up above his brethren, and that he ᵃturn not aside from the commandment, *to* the right hand, or *to* the left: to the end that he may ²prolong *his* days in his kingdom, he, and his children, in the midst of Israel.

## CHAPTER 18

THE priests the Levites, *and* all the tribe of Levi, shall have no ¹part nor ᵃinheritance with Israel: they shall eat the offerings of the LORD made by fire, and his inheritance.

2 Therefore shall they have no inheritance among their brethren: the LORD *is* their inheritance, as he hath said unto them.

3 And this shall be the priest's ᵃdue¹ from the people, from them that offer a sacrifice, whether *it be* ox or sheep; and they shall give unto

16:21 ᵃ Ex. 34:13
¹ *any tree, as a*
*wooden image*
16:22 ᵃ Lev. 26:1
¹ *idol*

17:1 ᵃ Deut. 15:21;
Mal. 1:8, 13 ¹ *de-*
*fect,* lit. *evil thing*
² *detestable thing*
17:2 ᵃ Deut.
13:6 ᵇ Josh. 7:11
¹ *towns*
17:3 ᵃ Deut. 4:19
ᵇ Jer. 7:22
17:4 ᵃ Deut. 13:12,
14 ¹ *a detestable*
*thing*
17:5 ᵃ Lev. 24:14–
16; Josh. 7:25
ᵇ Deut. 13:6–18
17:6 ᵃ Num.
35:30; Deut. 19:15;
Matt. 18:16; John
8:17; 2 Cor. 13:1;
1 Tim. 5:19; Heb.
10:28
17:7 ᵃ Deut. 13:5;
19:19; 1 Cor. 5:13
17:8 ᵃ Deut.
1:17; 2 Chr. 19:10
ᵇ Deut. 12:5; 16:2
17:9 ᵃ Jer. 18:18
ᵇ Deut. 19:17–19
ᶜ Ezek. 44:24
17:10 ¹ *instruct*

17:11 ¹ *turn aside*
17:12 ᵃ Num.
15:30; Deut. 1:43
¹ *heed*
17:13 ᵃ Deut. 13:11
17:14 ᵃ 1 Sam. 8:5,
19, 20; 10:19
17:15 ᵃ 1 Sam. 9:15,
16; 10:24; 16:12,
13; 1 Chr. 22:8–10;
Hos. 8:4 ᵇ Jer.
30:21
17:16 ᵃ 1 Kin. 4:26;
10:26–29; Ps. 20:7
ᵇ Is. 31:1; Ezek.
17:15 ᶜ Ex. 13:17, 18;
Hos. 11:5 ᵈ Deut.
28:68
17:17 ᵃ 1 Kin. 10:14
17:18 ᵃ Deut.
31:24–26
17:19 ᵃ Ps. 119:97,
98 ¹ *stand in*
*awe of*
17:20 ᵃ Deut. 5:32;
1 Kin. 15:5 ¹ *proud*
² *continue long*
18:1 ᵃ Deut.
10:9; 1 Cor. 9:13
¹ *portion*
18:3 ᵃ Lev. 7:32–
34; Num. 18:11, 12;
1 Sam. 2:13–16, 29
¹ *right*

the priest the shoulder, and the two cheeks, and the maw.

4 ᵃThe firstfruit *also* of thy corn, of thy wine, and of thine oil, and the first of the fleece of thy sheep, shalt thou give him.

5 For ᵃthe LORD thy God hath chosen him out of all thy tribes, ᵇto stand to minister in the name of the LORD, him and his sons for ever.

6 And if a Levite come from any of thy ¹gates out of all Israel, where he ᵃsojourned,² and come with all the desire of his mind ᵇunto the place which the LORD shall choose;

7 Then he shall minister in the name of the LORD his God, ᵃas all his brethren the Levites *do,* which stand there before the LORD.

8 They shall have ¹like ᵃportions to eat, beside that which cometh of the sale of his ²patrimony.

9 When thou art come into the land which the LORD thy God giveth thee, ᵃthou shalt not learn to do after the ¹abominations of those nations.

10 There shall not be found among you *any one* that maketh his son or his daughter ᵃto ¹pass through the fire, ᵇ*or* that useth divination, *or* an observer of times, or an enchanter, or a witch,

11 ᵃOr a charmer, or a consulter with familiar spirits, or a wizard, or a ᵇnecromancer.

12 For all that do these things *are* an ¹abomination unto the LORD: and ᵃbecause of these abominations the LORD thy God doth drive them out from before thee.

13 Thou shalt be ¹perfect with the LORD thy God.

14 For these nations, which thou shalt ¹possess, hearkened unto observers of times, and unto diviners: but as for thee, the LORD thy God hath not ²suffered thee so *to do.*

15 ᵃThe LORD thy God will raise up unto thee a Prophet from the midst of thee, of thy brethren, like unto me; unto him ye shall hearken;

16 According to all that thou desiredst of the LORD thy God in Horeb ᵃin the day of the assembly, saying, ᵇLet me not hear again the voice of the LORD my God, neither let me see this great fire any more, that I die not.

17 And the LORD said unto me, ᵃThey have well *spoken that* which they have spoken.

18 ᵃI will raise them up a Prophet from among their brethren, like unto thee, and ᵇwill put my words in his mouth; ᶜand he shall speak unto them all that I shall command him.

19 ³And it shall come to pass, *that* whosoever will not hearken unto my words which he shall speak in my name, I will require *it* of him.

20 But ᵃthe prophet, which shall presume to speak a word in my name, which I have not commanded him to speak, or ᵇthat shall speak in the name of other gods, even that prophet shall die.

21 And if thou say in thine heart, How shall we know the word which the LORD hath not spoken?

22 ᵃWhen a prophet speaketh in the name of the LORD, ᵇif the thing follow not, nor come to pass, that *is* the thing which the LORD hath not spoken, *but* the prophet hath spoken it ᶜpresumptuously: thou shalt not be afraid of him.

## CHAPTER 19

WHEN the LORD thy God ᵃhath cut off the nations, whose land the LORD thy God giveth thee, and thou ¹succeedest them, and dwellest in their cities, and in their houses;

2 ᵃThou shalt separate three cities for thee in the midst of thy land, which the LORD thy God giveth thee to possess it.

3 Thou shalt prepare ¹thee a way, and divide the ²coasts of thy land, which the LORD thy God giveth thee to inherit, into three parts, that every slayer may flee thither.

4 And ᵃthis *is* the case of the slayer, which shall flee thither, that he may live: Whoso killeth his neighbour ¹ignorantly, whom he hated not in time past;

5 As when a man goeth into the wood with his neighbour to ¹hew wood, and his hand ²fetcheth a stroke with the axe to cut down the tree, and the head slippeth from the ³helve, and ⁴lighteth upon his neighbour, that he die; he shall flee unto one of those cities, and live:

6 ᵃLest the avenger of the blood pursue the slayer, while his heart is hot, and overtake him, because the way is long, and slay him; whereas he *was* not worthy of death, inasmuch as he hated him not in time past.

7 Wherefore I command thee, saying, Thou shalt separate three cities for thee.

8 And if the LORD thy God ᵃenlarge thy coast, as he hath sworn unto thy ᵇfathers, and give thee all the land which he promised to give unto thy fathers;

9 If thou shalt keep all these commandments to do them, which I command thee this day, to love the LORD thy God, and to walk ever in his ways; ᵃthen shalt thou add three cities more for thee, beside these three:

10 That ᵃinnocent blood be not shed in thy land, which the LORD thy

---

18:4 ᵃ Ex. 22:29
18:5 ᵃ Ex. 28:1
ᵇ Deut. 10:8
18:6 ᵃ Num. 35:2
ᵇ Deut. 12:5; 14:23
¹ *towns* ² *resides*
18:7 ᵃ Num. 1:50;
2 Chr. 31:2
18:8 ᵃ Lev.
27:30–33; Num.
18:21–24; 2 Chr.
31:4; Neh. 12:44
¹ *equal* ² *inheritance*
18:9 ᵃ Lev. 18:26,
27, 30; Deut.
12:29, 30; 20:16–
18 ¹ *detestable things*
18:10 ᵃ Lev. 18:21;
Deut. 12:31 ᵇ Ex.
22:18; Lev. 19:26,
31; 20:6, 27; Is.
8:19 ¹ Be burned
as an offering to
an idol
18:11 ᵃ Lev. 20:27
ᵇ 1 Sam. 28:7
18:12 ᵃ Lev. 18:24;
Deut. 9:4 ¹ *detestable thing*
18:13 ¹ *blameless*
18:14 ¹ *dispossess*
² *appointed such for you*
18:15 ᵃ Matt. 21:11;
Luke 1:76; 2:25–
34; 7:16; 24:19;
Acts 3:22
18:16 ᵃ Deut.
5:23–27 ᵇ Ex.
20:18, 19; Heb.
12:19
18:17 ᵃ Deut. 5:28
18:18 ᵃ Deut.
34:10; John 1:45;
Acts 3:22 ᵇ Num.
23:5; Is. 49:2;
51:16; John 17:8
ᶜ [John 4:25;
8:28]
18:19 ᵃ Acts 3:23;
[Heb. 12:25]
18:20 ᵃ Deut.
13:5; Jer. 14:14,
15; Zech. 13:2–5
ᵇ Deut. 13:1–3;
Jer. 2:8
18:22 ᵃ Jer. 28:9
ᵇ Deut. 13:2
ᶜ Deut. 18:20
19:1 ᵃ Deut. 12:29
¹ *dispossessed*
19:2 ᵃ Ex. 21:13;
Num. 35:10–15;
Deut. 4:41; Josh.
20:2
19:3 ¹ *yourselves
roads* ² *territory*
19:4 ᵃ Num. 35:9–
34; Deut. 4:42
¹ *unintentionally,*
lit. *without knowledge*
19:5 ¹ *cut timber*
² *swings* ³ *handle*
⁴ *strikes*
19:6 ᵃ Num. 35:12
19:8 ᵃ Deut. 12:20 ᵇ Gen. 15:18–21　19:9 ᵃ Josh. 20:7–9
19:10 ᵃ Num. 35:33; Deut. 21:1–9

God giveth thee *for* an inheritance, and *so* blood be upon thee.

11 But ªif any man hate his neighbour, and lie in wait for him, and rise up against him, and smite him mortally that he die, and fleeth into one of these cities:

12 Then the elders of his city shall send and fetch him thence, and deliver him into the hand of the avenger of blood, that he may die.

13 ªThine eye shall not pity him, ᵇbut thou shalt ¹put away *the guilt of* innocent blood from Israel, that it may go well with thee.

14 ªThou shalt not remove thy neighbour's landmark, which they of old time have set in thine inheritance, which thou shalt inherit in the land that the LORD thy God giveth thee to possess it.

15 ªOne witness shall not rise up against a man for any iniquity, or for any sin, in any sin that he sinneth: at the mouth of two witnesses, or at the mouth of three witnesses, shall the matter be established.

16 If a false witness ªrise up against any man to testify against him *that which is* wrong;

17 Then both the men, between whom the controversy *is,* shall stand before the LORD, ªbefore the priests and the judges, which shall be in those days;

18 And the judges shall make diligent inquisition: and, behold, *if* the witness *be* a false witness, *and* hath testified falsely against his brother;

19 ªThen shall ye do unto him, as he had thought to have done unto his brother: so ᵇshalt thou put the evil away from among you.

20 ªAnd those which remain shall hear, and fear, and shall henceforth commit no more any such evil among you.

21 ªAnd thine eye shall not pity; *but* ᵇlife *shall go* for life, eye for eye, tooth for tooth, hand for hand, foot for foot.

## CHAPTER 20

WHEN thou goest out to battle against thine enemies, and seest ªhorses, and chariots, *and* a people more than thou, be not ᵇafraid of them: for the LORD thy God *is* ᶜwith thee, which brought thee up out of the land of Egypt.

2 And it shall be, when ye are come nigh unto the battle, that the priest shall approach and speak unto the people,

3 And shall say unto them, Hear, O Israel, ye approach this day unto battle against your enemies: let not your hearts faint, fear not, and do not tremble, ncithcr bc yc terrified because of them;

4 For the LORD your God *is* he that goeth with you, ªto fight for you against your enemies, to save you.

5 And the officers shall speak unto the people, saying, What man *is there* that hath built a new house, and hath not ªdedicated it? let him go and return to his house, lest he die in the battle, and another man dedicate it.

6 And what man *is he* that hath planted a vineyard, and hath not *yet* eaten of it? let him *also* go and return unto his house, lest he die in the battle, and another man eat of it.

7 ªAnd what man *is there* that hath betrothed a wife, and hath not taken her? let him go and return unto his house, lest he die in the battle, and another man take her.

8 And the officers shall speak further unto the people, and they shall say, ªWhat man *is there that is* fearful and fainthearted? let him go and return unto his house, lest his brethren's heart faint as well as his heart.

9 And it shall be, when the officers have made an end of speaking unto the people, that they shall make captains of the armies to lead the people.

10 When thou comest nigh unto a city to fight against it, ªthen ¹proclaim peace unto it.

11 And it shall be, if it make thee answer of peace, and open unto thee, then it shall be, *that* all the people *that is* found therein shall be ¹tributaries unto thee, and they shall serve thee.

12 And if it will make no peace with thee, but will make war against thee, then thou shalt besiege it:

13 And when the LORD thy God hath delivered it into thine hands, ªthou shalt smite every male thereof with the edge of the sword:

14 But the ªwomen, and the little ones, and ªthe cattle, and all that is in the city, *even* all the ¹spoil thereof, shalt thou take unto thyself; and ᵇthou shalt eat the spoil of thine enemies, which the LORD thy God hath given thee.

15 Thus shalt thou do unto all the cities *which are* very far off from thee, which *are* not of the cities of these nations.

16 But ªof the cities of these people, which the LORD thy God doth give thee *for* an inheritance, thou shalt save alive nothing that breatheth:

17 But thou shalt utterly destroy them; *namely,* the Hittites, and the Amorites, the Canaanites, and the Perizzites, the Hivites, and the Jebusites; as the LORD thy God hath commanded thee:

18 That ªthey teach you not to do after all their ¹abominations, which they have done unto their gods; so

---

19:11 ª Num. 35:16, 24; Deut. 27:24; [1 John 3:15]
19:13 ª Deut. 13:8 ᵇ Num. 35:33, 34; 1 Kin. 2:31 ¹ *purge the blood of the innocent*
19:14 ª Deut. 27:17; Job 24:2; Prov. 22:28; Hos. 5:10
19:15 ª Num. 35:30; Deut. 17:6; Matt. 18:16; John 8:17; 2 Cor. 13:1; 1 Tim. 5:19; Heb. 10:28
19:16 ª Ex. 23:1; Ps. 27:12; 35:11
19:17 ª Deut. 17:8–11; 21:5
19:19 ª Prov. 19:5; Dan. 6:24 ᵇ Deut. 13:5; 17:7; 21:21; 22:21
19:20 ª Deut. 17:13; 21:21
19:21 ª Deut. 19:13 ᵇ Ex. 21:23, 24; Lev. 24:20; Matt. 5:38, 39
20:1 ª Ps. 20:7; Is. 31:1 ᵇ Deut. 7:18 ᶜ Num. 23:21; Deut. 5:6; 31:6, 8; 2 Chr. 13:12; 32:7, 8; Ps. 23:4; Is. 41:10

20:4 ª Deut. 1:30; 3:22; Josh. 23:10
20:5 ª Neh. 12:27
20:7 ª Deut. 24:5
20:8 ª Judg. 7:3
20:10 ª 2 Sam. 10:19 ¹ *proclaim an offer of*
20:11 ¹ *servants, placed under tribute*
20:13 ª Num. 31:7
20:14 ª Josh. 8:2 ᵇ 1 Sam. 14:30 ¹ *plunder*
20:16 ª Ex. 23:31–33; Num. 21:2, 3; Deut. 7:1–5; Josh. 11:14
20:18 ª Ex. 34:12–16; Deut. 7:4; 12:30; 18:9 ¹ *detestable things*

should ye [b]sin against the LORD your God.

19 When thou shalt besiege a city a long time, in making war against it to take it, thou shalt not destroy the trees thereof by forcing an axe against them: for thou mayest eat of them, and thou shalt not cut them down (for the tree of the field *is* man's *life*) to employ *them* in the siege:

20 Only the trees which thou knowest that they *be* not trees for [1]meat, thou shalt destroy and cut them down; and thou shalt build bulwarks against the city that maketh war with thee, until it be subdued.

## CHAPTER 21

IF *one* be found slain in the land which the LORD thy God giveth thee to possess it, lying in the field, *and* it be not known who hath slain him:

2 Then thy elders and thy judges shall come forth, and they shall measure unto the cities which *are* round about him that is slain:

3 And it shall be, *that* the city *which is* next unto the slain man, even the elders of that city shall take an heifer, which hath not been [1]wrought with, *and* which hath not drawn in the [a]yoke;

4 And the elders of that city shall bring down the heifer unto a rough valley, which is neither eared nor sown, and shall strike off the heifer's neck there in the valley:

5 And the priests the sons of Levi shall come near; for [a]them the LORD thy God hath chosen to minister unto him, and to bless in the name of the LORD; and [b]by their word shall every controversy and every [1]stroke be *tried:*

6 And all the elders of that city, *that are* next unto the slain *man,* [a]shall wash their hands over the heifer that is beheaded in the valley:

7 And they shall answer and say, Our hands have not shed this blood, neither have our eyes seen *it.*

8 Be merciful, O LORD, unto thy people Israel, whom thou hast redeemed, [a]and lay not innocent blood unto thy people of Israel's charge. And the blood shall be forgiven them.

9 So [a]shalt thou put away the *guilt of* innocent blood from among you, when thou shalt do *that which is* right in the sight of the LORD.

10 When thou goest forth to war against thine enemies, and the LORD thy God hath delivered them into thine hands, and thou hast taken them captive,

11 And seest among the captives a beautiful woman, and hast a desire unto her, that thou wouldest have her to thy [a]wife;

20:18 [b] Ex. 23:33; 2 Kin. 21:3–15; Ps. 106:34–41
20:20 [1] food
21:3 [a] Num. 19:2 [1] worked
21:5 [a] Deut. 10:8; 1 Chr. 23:13 [b] Deut. 17:8, 9 [1] assault
21:6 [a] Ps. 19:12; 26:6; Matt. 27:24
21:8 [a] Deut. 19:10, 13; Jon. 1:14
21:9 [a] Deut. 19:13
21:11 [a] Num. 31:18

21:12 [a] Lev. 14:8, 9; Num. 6:9 [1] trim
21:13 [a] Ps. 45:10 [1] mourn
21:14 [a] Gen. 34:2; Deut. 22:29; Judg. 19:24
21:15 [a] Gen. 29:33
21:16 [a] 1 Chr. 5:2; 26:10
21:17 [a] 2 Kin. 2:9 [b] Gen. 49:3 [c] Gen. 25:31, 33
21:21 [a] Deut. 13:5; 19:19, 20; 22:21, 24 [b] Deut. 13:11 [1] the evil person
21:22 [a] Deut. 22:26; Matt. 26:66; Mark 14:64; Acts 23:29 [1] is put
21:23 [a] Josh. 8:29; 10:26, 27; John 19:31 [b] Lev. 18:25; Num. 35:34 [c] Gal. 3:13
22:1 [a] Ex. 23:4 [1] ignore them

12 Then thou shalt bring her home to thine house; and she shall [a]shave her head, and [1]pare her nails;

13 And she shall put the raiment of her captivity from off her, and shall remain in thine house, and [a]bewail[1] her father and her mother a full month: and after that thou shalt go in unto her, and be her husband, and she shall be thy wife.

14 And it shall be, if thou have no delight in her, then thou shalt let her go whither she will; but thou shalt not sell her at all for money, thou shalt not make merchandise of her, because thou hast [a]humbled her.

15 If a man have two wives, one beloved, [a]and another hated, and they have born him children, *both* the beloved and the hated; and *if* the firstborn son be hers that was hated:

16 Then it shall be, [a]when he maketh his sons to inherit *that* which he hath, *that* he may not make the son of the beloved firstborn before the son of the hated, *which is indeed* the firstborn:

17 But he shall acknowledge the son of the hated *for* the firstborn, [a]by giving him a double portion of all that he hath: for he [b]*is* the beginning of his strength; [c]the right of the firstborn *is* his.

18 If a man have a stubborn and rebellious son, which will not obey the voice of his father, or the voice of his mother, and *that,* when they have chastened him, will not hearken unto them:

19 Then shall his father and his mother lay hold on him, and bring him out unto the elders of his city, and unto the gate of his place;

20 And they shall say unto the elders of his city, This our son *is* stubborn and rebellious, he will not obey our voice; *he is* a glutton, and a drunkard.

21 And all the men of his city shall stone him with stones, that he die: [a]so shalt thou put [1]evil away from among you; [b]and all Israel shall hear, and fear.

22 And if a man have committed a sin [a]worthy of death, and he [1]be to be put to death, and thou hang him on a tree:

23 [a]His body shall not remain all night upon the tree, but thou shalt in any wise bury him that day; (for [b]he that is hanged *is* accursed of God;) that [c]thy land be not defiled, which the LORD thy God giveth thee *for* an inheritance.

## CHAPTER 22

THOU [a]shalt not see thy brother's ox or his sheep go astray, and [1]hide thyself from them: thou shalt in

any case bring them ²again unto thy brother.

2 And if thy brother *be* not nigh unto thee, or if thou know him not, then thou shalt bring it unto thine own house, and it shall be with thee until thy brother seek after it, and thou shalt restore it to him again.

3 In like manner shalt thou do with his ass; and so shalt thou do with his raiment; and with all lost thing of thy brother's, which he hath lost, and thou hast found, shalt thou do likewise: thou ¹mayest not hide thyself.

4 ªThou shalt not see thy brother's ass or his ox fall down by the way, and hide thyself from them: thou shalt surely help him to lift *them* up again.

5 The woman shall not wear that which pertaineth unto a man, neither shall a man put on a woman's garment: for all that do so *are* ¹abomination unto the LORD thy God.

6 If a bird's nest chance to be before thee in the way in any tree, or on the ground, *whether they be* young ones, or eggs, and the ¹dam sitting upon the young, or upon the eggs, ªthou shalt not take the dam with the young:

7 *But* thou shalt in any wise let the dam go, and take the young to thee; ªthat it may be well with thee, and *that* thou mayest prolong *thy* days.

8 When thou buildest a new house, then thou shalt make a battlement for thy roof, that thou bring not ¹blood upon thine house, if any man fall from thence.

9 ªThou shalt not sow thy vineyard with ¹divers seeds: lest the fruit of thy seed which thou hast sown, and the fruit of thy vineyard, be defiled.

10 ªThou shalt not plow with an ox and an ass together.

11 ªThou shalt not wear a garment of ¹divers sorts, *as* of woollen and linen together.

12 Thou shalt make thee ªfringes upon the four ¹quarters of thy ²vesture, wherewith thou coverest *thyself.*

13 If any man take a wife, and go in unto her, and ªhate her,

14 And give occasions of speech against her, and bring up an evil name upon her, and say, I took this woman, and when I came to her, I found her not a maid:

15 Then shall the father of the damsel, and her mother, take and bring forth *the tokens of* the damsel's virginity unto the elders of the city in the gate:

16 And the damsel's father shall say unto the elders, I gave my daughter unto this man to wife, and he hateth her;

17 And, lo, he hath given occasions of speech *against her,* saying, I found not thy daughter a maid; and yet these *are the tokens of* my daughter's virginity. And they shall spread the cloth before the elders of the city.

18 And the elders of that city shall take that man and chastise him;

19 And they shall ¹amerce him in an hundred *shekels* of silver, and give *them* unto the father of the damsel, because he hath brought up ²an evil name upon a virgin of Israel: and she shall be his wife; he may not put her away all his days.

20 But if this thing be true, *and the tokens of* virginity be not found for the damsel:

21 Then they shall bring out the damsel to the door of her father's house, and the men of her city shall stone her with ªstones that she die: because she hath ᵇwrought¹ folly in Israel, to play the whore in her father's house: ᶜso shalt thou ²put evil away from among you.

22 ªIf a man be found lying with a woman married to an husband, then they shall both of them die, *both* the man that lay with the woman, and the woman: so shalt thou put away evil from Israel.

23 If a damsel *that is* a virgin be ªbetrothed unto an husband, and a man find her in the city, and lie with her;

24 Then ye shall bring them both out unto the gate of that city, and ye shall stone them with stones that they die; the damsel, because she cried not, *being* in the city; and the man, because he hath ªhumbled his neighbour's wife: ᵇso thou shalt put away evil from among you.

25 But if a man find a betrothed damsel in the field, and the man force her, and lie with her: then the man only that lay with her shall die:

26 But unto the damsel thou shalt do nothing; *there is* in the damsel no sin *worthy* of death: for as when a man riseth against his neighbour, and slayeth him, even so *is* this matter:

27 For he found her in the field, *and* the betrothed damsel cried, and *there was* none to save her.

28 ªIf a man find a damsel *that is* a virgin, which is not betrothed, and lay hold on her, and lie with her, and they be found;

29 Then the man that lay with her shall give unto the damsel's father ªfifty *shekels* of silver, and she shall be his wife; ᵇbecause he hath humbled her, he may not put her away all his days.

30 ªA man shall not take his father's wife, nor ᵇdiscover his father's skirt.

---

22:1 ² *back*

22:3 ¹ *may not avoid responsibility*

22:4 ª Ex. 23:5

22:5 ¹ *detestable*

22:6 ª Lev. 22:28
¹ *mother*

22:7 ª Deut. 4:40

22:8 ¹ *bloodguiltiness*

22:9 ª Lev. 19:19
¹ *different*

22:10 ª [2 Cor. 6:14–16]

22:11 ª Lev. 19:19
¹ *different*

22:12 ª Num. 15:37–41; Matt. 23:5 ¹ *corners*
² *clothing*

22:13 ª Deut. 21:15; 24:3

22:19 ¹ *fine* ² *a bad*

22:21 ª Deut. 21:21
ᵇ Gen. 34:7; Judg. 20:5–10; 2 Sam. 13:12, 13 ᶜ Deut. 13:5 ¹ *done a disgraceful thing* ² *purge the evil person*

22:22 ª Lev. 20:10; Num. 5:22–27; Ezek. 16:38; [Matt. 5:27, 28]; John 8:5; [1 Cor. 6:9; Heb. 13:4]

22:23 ª Lev. 19:20–22; Matt. 1:18, 19

22:24 ª Deut. 21:14 ᵇ Deut. 22:21, 22; 1 Cor. 5:2, 13

22:28 ª Ex. 22:16, 17

22:29 ª Ex. 22:16, 17 ᵇ Deut. 22:24

22:30 ª Deut. 18:8; 20:11; Deut. 27:20; 1 Cor. 5:1 ᵇ Ruth 3:9; Ezek. 16:8

## CHAPTER 23

HE that is wounded in the stones, or hath his privy member cut off, shall [a]not enter into the congregation of the LORD.

2 A bastard shall not enter into the congregation of the LORD; even to his tenth generation shall he not enter into the congregation of the LORD.

3 [a]An Ammonite or Moabite shall not enter into the congregation of the LORD; even to their tenth generation shall they not enter into the congregation of the LORD for ever:

4 [a]Because they met you not with bread and with water in the way, when ye came forth out of Egypt; and [b]because they hired against thee Balaam the son of Beor of Pethor of [1]Mesopotamia, to curse thee.

5 Nevertheless the LORD thy God would not hearken unto Balaam; but the LORD thy God turned the curse into a blessing unto thee, because the LORD thy God [a]loved thee.

6 [a]Thou shalt not seek their peace nor their prosperity all thy days for ever.

7 Thou shalt not abhor an Edomite; [a]for he *is* thy brother: thou shalt not abhor an Egyptian; because [b]thou wast a stranger in his land.

8 The children that are begotten of them shall enter into the congregation of the LORD in their third generation.

9 When the host goeth forth against thine enemies, then keep thee from every wicked thing.

10 [a]If there be among you any man, that is not clean by reason of uncleanness that chanceth him by night, then shall he go abroad out of the camp, he shall not come within the camp:

11 But it shall be, when evening cometh on, [a]he shall wash *himself* with water: and when the sun is down, he shall come into the camp *again*.

12 Thou shalt have a place also [1]without the camp, whither thou shalt go forth abroad:

13 And thou shalt have a paddle upon thy weapon; and it shall be, when thou wilt ease thyself abroad, thou shalt dig therewith, and shalt turn back and cover that which cometh from thee:

14 For the LORD thy God [a]walketh in the midst of thy camp, to deliver thee, and to give up thine enemies before thee; therefore shall thy camp be holy: that he see no unclean thing in thee, and turn away from thee.

15 [a]Thou shalt not [1]deliver unto his master the servant which is escaped from his master unto thee:

16 He shall dwell with thee, *even* among you, in that place which he

shall choose in one of thy gates, where it [1]liketh him best: [a]thou shalt not oppress him.

17 There shall be no whore [a]of the daughters of Israel, nor [b]a sodomite of the sons of Israel.

18 Thou shalt not bring the hire of a whore, or the price of a dog, into the house of the LORD thy God for any vow: for even both these *are* [1]abomination unto the LORD thy God.

19 [a]Thou shalt not [1]lend upon usury to thy brother; usury of money, usury of victuals, usury of any thing that is lent upon usury:

20 [a]Unto a stranger thou mayest lend upon usury; but unto thy brother thou shalt not lend upon usury: [b]that the LORD thy God may bless thee in all that thou settest thine hand to in the land whither thou goest to possess it.

21 [a]When thou shalt vow a vow unto the LORD thy God, thou shalt not [1]slack to pay it: for the LORD thy God will surely require it of thee; and it would be sin in thee.

22 But if thou shalt [1]forbear to vow, it shall be no sin in thee.

23 [a]That which is gone out of thy lips thou shalt keep and perform; *even* a freewill offering, according as thou hast vowed unto the LORD thy God, which thou hast promised with thy mouth.

24 When thou comest into thy neighbour's vineyard, then thou mayest eat grapes thy fill at thine own pleasure; but thou shalt not put *any* in thy vessel.

25 When thou comest into the standing corn of thy neighbour, [a]then thou mayest pluck the ears with thine hand; but thou shalt not [1]move a sickle unto thy neighbour's standing corn.

## CHAPTER 24

WHEN a [a]man hath taken a wife, and married her, and it come to pass that she find no favour in his eyes, because he hath found some [1]uncleanness in her: then let him write her a [b]bill of divorcement, and give *it* in her hand, and send her out of his house.

2 And when she is departed out of his house, she may go and be another man's *wife*.

3 And *if* the latter husband hate her, and write her a bill of divorcement, and giveth *it* in her hand, and sendeth her out of his house; or if the latter husband die, which took her *to be* his wife;

4 [a]Her former husband, which sent her away, may not take her again to be his wife, after that she is defiled; for that *is* [1]abomination before the

---

23:1 [a] Lev. 21:20; 22:24

23:3 [a] Neh. 13:1, 2

23:4 [a] Deut. 2:27–30 [b] Num. 22:5, 6; 23:7; Josh. 24:9; 2 Pet. 2:15; Jude 11. [1] Heb. *Aram-naharaim*

23:5 [a] Deut. 4:37

23:6 [a] Ezra 9:12

23:7 [a] Gen. 25:24–26; Deut. 2:4, 8; Amos 1:11; Obad. 10, 12 [b] Ex. 22:21; 23:9; Lev. 19:34; Deut. 10:19

23:10 [a] Lev. 15:16

23:11 [a] Lev. 15:5

23:12 [1] *outside*

23:14 [a] Lev. 26:12; Deut. 7:21

23:15 [a] 1 Sam. 30:15 [1] *give back*

23:16 [a] Ex. 22:21; Prov. 22:22 [1] *pleases*

23:17 [a] Lev. 19:29; Deut. 22:21 [b] Gen. 19:5; 2 Kin. 23:7

23:18 [1] *detestable*

23:19 [a] Ex. 22:25; Lev. 25:35–37; Neh. 5:2–7; Ps. 15:5 [1] *charge interest*

23:20 [a] Deut. 15:3 [b] Deut. 15:10

23:21 [a] Num. 30:1, 2; Job 22:27; Ps. 61:8; Eccl. 5:4, 5; Matt. 5:33 [1] *delay*

23:22 [1] *abstain from vowing*

23:23 [a] Num. 30:2; Ps. 66:13, 14

23:25 [a] Matt. 12:1; Mark 2:23; Luke 6:1 [1] *use*

24:1 [a] [Matt. 5:31; 19:7; Mark 10:4] [b] [Jer. 3:8] [1] *indecency, lit. nakedness of a thing*

24:4 [a] [Jer. 3:1] [1] *a detestable thing*

---

LORD: and thou shalt not cause the land to sin, which the LORD thy God giveth thee *for* an inheritance.

5 [a]When a man hath taken a new wife, he shall not go out to war, neither shall he be charged with any business: *but* he shall be free at home one year, and shall [b]cheer up his wife which he hath taken.

6 No man shall take the [1]nether or the upper millstone to pledge: for he taketh *a man's* [2]life to pledge.

7 If a man be [a]found [1]stealing any of his brethren of the children of Israel, and [2]maketh merchandise of him, or selleth him; then that thief shall die; [b]and thou shalt put evil away from among you.

8 Take heed in [a]the plague of leprosy, that thou observe diligently, and do according to all that the priests the Levites shall teach you: as I commanded them, *so* ye shall observe to do.

9 [a]Remember what the LORD thy God did [b]unto Miriam by the way, after that ye were come forth out of Egypt.

10 When thou dost [a]lend thy brother any thing, thou shalt not go into his house to [1]fetch his pledge.

11 Thou shalt stand abroad, and the man to whom thou dost lend shall bring out the pledge abroad unto thee.

12 And if the man *be* poor, thou shalt not [1]sleep with his pledge:

13 [a]In any case thou shalt deliver him the pledge again when the sun goeth down, that he may sleep in his own raiment, and [b]bless thee: and [c]it shall be righteousness unto thee before the LORD thy God.

14 Thou shalt not [a]oppress an hired servant *that is* poor and needy, *whether he be* of thy brethren, or of thy strangers that *are* in thy land within thy gates:

15 [1]At his day [a]thou shalt give *him* his [2]hire, neither shall the sun go down upon it; for he *is* poor, and setteth his heart upon it: [b]lest he cry against thee unto the LORD, and it be sin unto thee.

16 [a]The fathers shall not be put to death for the children, neither shall the children be put to death for the fathers: every man shall be put to death for his own sin.

17 [a]Thou shalt not pervert the [1]judgment of the stranger, *nor* of the fatherless; [b]nor take a widow's raiment to pledge:

18 But [a]thou shalt remember that thou wast a [1]bondman in Egypt, and the LORD thy God redeemed thee thence: therefore I command thee to do this thing.

19 [a]When thou cuttest down thine harvest in thy field, and hast forgot a sheaf in the field, thou shalt not go again to fetch it: it shall be for the stranger, for the fatherless, and for the widow: that the LORD thy God may [b]bless thee in all the work of thine hands.

20 When thou beatest thine olive tree, thou shalt not go over the boughs again: it shall be for the stranger, for the fatherless, and for the widow.

21 When thou gatherest the grapes of thy vineyard, thou shalt not glean *it* afterward: it shall be for the stranger, for the fatherless, and for the widow.

22 And thou shalt remember that thou wast a bondman in the land of Egypt: therefore I command thee to do this thing.

## CHAPTER 25

IF there be a [a]controversy[1] between men, and they come unto [2]judgment, that *the judges* may judge them; then they [b]shall justify the righteous, and condemn the wicked.

2 And it shall be, if the wicked man *be* [a]worthy to be beaten, that the judge shall cause him to lie down, [b]and to be beaten [1]before his face, according to his fault, by a certain number.

3 [a]Forty stripes he may give him, *and* not exceed: lest, *if* he should exceed, and beat him above these with many stripes, then thy brother [1]should [b]seem vile unto thee.

4 [a]Thou shalt not muzzle the ox when he [1]treadeth out *the corn.*

5 [a]If brethren dwell together, and one of them die, and have no child, the wife of the dead shall not marry without unto a stranger: her husband's brother shall go in unto her, and take her to him to wife, and perform the duty of an husband's brother unto her.

6 And it shall be, *that* the firstborn which she beareth [a]shall succeed in the name of his brother *which is* dead, that [b]his name be not put out of Israel.

7 And if the man like not to take his brother's wife, then let his brother's wife go up to the [a]gate unto the elders, and say, My husband's brother refuseth to raise up unto his brother a name in Israel, he will not perform the duty of my husband's brother.

8 Then the elders of his city shall call him, and speak unto him: and *if* he stand *to it,* and say, [a]I like not to take her;

9 Then shall his brother's wife come unto him in the presence of the elders, and [a]loose[1] his shoe from off his foot, and spit in his face, and shall answer and say, So shall it be done

### Cross References (center column)

24:5 [a] Deut. 20:7
[b] Prov. 5:18
24:6 [1] *lower*
[2] *living in*
24:7 [a] Ex. 21:16
[b] Deut. 19:19
[1] *kidnapping*
[2] *mistreats*
24:8 [a] Lev. 13:2; 14:2
24:9 [a] [1 Cor. 10:6]
[b] Num. 12:10
24:10 [a] Matt. 5:42
[1] *get*
24:12 [1] *keep his pledge overnight*
24:13 [a] Ex. 22:26; Ezek. 18:7 [b] Job 29:11; 2 Tim. 1:18
[c] Deut. 6:25; Ps. 106:31; Dan. 4:27
24:14 [a] Lev. 19:13; Deut. 15:7–18; [Prov. 14:31]; Amos 4:1; [Mal. 3:5; 1 Tim. 5:18]
24:15 [a] Lev. 19:13; Jer. 22:13 [b] Ex. 22:23; Deut. 15:9; Job 35:9; James 5:4 [1] *Each day*
[2] *wages*
24:16 [a] 2 Kin. 14:6; 2 Chr. 25:4; Jer. 31:29, 30; Ezek. 18:20
24:17 [a] Ex. 23:6
[b] Ex. 22:26 [1] *justice due*
24:18 [a] Deut. 24:22 [1] *slave*
24:19 [a] Lev. 19:9, 10

[b] Deut. 15:10; Ps. 41:1; Prov. 19:17
25:1 [a] Deut. 17:8–13; 19:17; Ezek. 44:24 [b] Prov. 17:15 [1] *dispute*
[2] *court*
25:2 [a] Prov. 19:29; Luke 12:48 [b] Matt. 10:17 [1] *in his presence*
25:3 [a] 2 Cor. 11:24
[b] Job 18:3 [1] *would be humiliated in your sight*
25:4 [a] [Prov. 12:10; 1 Cor. 9:9; 1 Tim. 5:18] [1] *threshes out the grain*
25:5 [a] Matt. 22:24; Mark 12:19; Luke 20:28
25:6 [a] Gen. 38:9
[b] Ruth 4:5, 10
25:7 [a] Ruth 4:1, 2
25:8 [a] Ruth 4:6
25:9 [a] Ruth 4:7, 8 [1] *remove his sandal*

unto that man that will not [b]build up his brother's house.

10 And his name shall be called in Israel, The house of him that hath his shoe loosed.

11 When men strive together one with another, and the wife of the one draweth near for to deliver her husband out of the hand of him that smiteth him, and putteth forth her hand, and taketh him by the secrets:

12 Then thou shalt cut off her hand, [a]thine eye shall not pity *her*.

13 [a]Thou shalt not have in thy bag [1]divers weights, a great and a small.

14 Thou shalt not have in thine house [1]divers measures, a great and a small.

15 *But* thou shalt have a perfect and just weight, a perfect and just measure shalt thou have: [a]that thy days may be lengthened in the land which the LORD thy God giveth thee.

16 For [a]all that do such things, *and* all that do unrighteously, *are* [1]an abomination unto the LORD thy God.

17 [a]Remember what Amalek did unto thee by the way, when ye were come forth out of Egypt;

18 How he met thee by the way, and smote [1]the hindmost of thee, *even* all *that were* feeble behind thee, when thou *wast* faint and weary; and he [a]feared not God.

19 Therefore it shall be, [a]when the LORD thy God hath given thee rest from all thine enemies round about, in the land which the LORD thy God giveth thee *for* an inheritance to possess it, *that* thou shalt [b]blot out the remembrance of Amalek from under heaven; thou shalt not forget *it*.

## CHAPTER 26

AND it shall be, when thou *art* come in unto the land which the LORD thy God giveth thee *for* an inheritance, and possessest it, and dwellest therein;

2 [a]That thou shalt take of the first of all the fruit of the earth, which thou shalt bring of thy land that the LORD thy God giveth thee, and shalt put *it* in a basket, and shalt [b]go unto the place which the LORD thy God shall choose to place his name there.

3 And thou shalt go unto the priest that shall be in those days, and say unto him, I [1]profess this day unto the LORD thy God, that I am come unto the country which the LORD sware unto our fathers for to give us.

4 And the priest shall take the basket out of thine hand, and set it down before the altar of the LORD thy God.

5 And thou shalt speak and say before the LORD thy God, [a]A [1]Syrian [b]ready to perish *was* my father, and [c]he went down into Egypt, and

sojourned there with a [d]few, and became there a nation, [e]great, mighty, and populous:

6 And the [a]Egyptians [1]evil entreated us, and afflicted us, and laid upon us hard bondage:

7 And [a]when we cried unto the LORD God of our fathers, the LORD heard our voice, and looked on our affliction, and our labour, and our oppression:

8 And [a]the LORD brought us forth out of Egypt with a mighty hand, and with an outstretched arm, and [b]with great [1]terribleness, and with signs, and with wonders:

9 And he hath brought us into this place, and hath given us this land, *even* [a]a land that floweth with milk and honey.

10 And now, behold, I have brought the firstfruits of the land, which thou, O LORD, hast given me. And thou shalt set it before the LORD thy God, and worship before the LORD thy God:

11 And [a]thou shalt rejoice in every good *thing* which the LORD thy God hath given unto thee, and unto thine house, thou, and the Levite, and the stranger that *is* among you.

12 When thou hast made an end of tithing all the [a]tithes of thine increase the third year, *which is* [b]the year of tithing, and hast given *it* unto the Levite, the stranger, the fatherless, and the widow, that they may eat within thy gates, and be filled;

13 Then thou shalt say before the LORD thy God, I have brought away the [1]hallowed things out of *mine* house, and also have given them unto the Levite, and unto the stranger, to the fatherless, and to the widow, according to all thy commandments which thou hast commanded me: I have not transgressed thy commandments, [a]neither have I forgotten *them*:

14 [a]I have not eaten thereof in my mourning, neither have I taken away *ought* thereof [1]for *any* unclean *use*, nor given *ought* thereof for the dead: *but* I have hearkened to the voice of the LORD my God, *and* have done according to all that thou hast commanded me.

15 [a]Look down from thy holy [1]habitation, from heaven, and bless thy people Israel, and the land which thou hast given us, as thou swarest unto our fathers, [b]a land that floweth with milk and honey.

16 This day the LORD thy God hath commanded thee to do these statutes and judgments: thou shalt therefore keep and do them with all thine heart, and with all thy soul.

17 Thou hast [a]avouched[1] the LORD this day to be thy God, and to walk

### Center column references

25:9 [b] Ruth 4:11
25:12 [a] Deut. 7:2; 19:13
25:13 [a] Lev. 19:35–37; Prov. 11:1; 20:23; Ezek. 45:10; Mic. 6:11 [1] differing
25:14 [1] differing
25:15 [a] Ex. 20:12
25:16 [a] Prov. 11:1; [1 Thess. 4:6] [1] detestable
25:17 [a] Ex. 17:8–16; 1 Sam. 15:1–3
25:18 [a] [Ps. 36:1]; Rom. 3:18 [1] your rear ranks
25:19 [a] 1 Sam. 15:3 [b] Ex. 17:14
26:2 [a] Ex. 22:29; 23:16, 19; Num. 18:13; Deut. 16:10; Prov. 3:9 [b] Deut. 12:5
26:3 [1] declare
26:5 [a] Gen. 25:20; Hos. 12:12 [b] Gen. 43:1, 2; 45:7, 11 [c] Gen. 46:1, 6; Acts 7:15 [1] Or Aramean

d Gen. 46:27; Deut. 10:22
e Deut. 1:10

26:6 [a] Ex. 1:8–11, 14 [1] mistreated
26:7 [a] Ex. 2:23–25; 3:9; 4:31
26:8 [a] Ex. 12:37, 51; 13:3, 14, 16; Deut. 5:15 [b] Deut. 4:34; 34:11, 12 [1] awesomeness
26:9 [a] Ex. 3:8, 17
26:11 [a] Deut. 12:7; 16:11; Eccl. 3:12, 13; 5:18–20
26:12 [a] Lev. 27:30; Num. 18:24 [b] Deut. 14:28, 29
26:13 [a] Ps. 119:141, 153, 176 [1] holy tithe
26:14 [a] Lev. 7:20; Jer. 16:7; Hos. 9:4 [1] while I was unclean
26:15 [a] Ps. 80:14; Is. 63:15; Zech. 2:13 [b] Ex. 3:8 [1] abode
26:17 [a] Ex. 20:19 [1] proclaimed

in his ways, and to keep his statutes, and his commandments, and his judgments, and to [b]hearken unto his voice:

18 And [a]the LORD hath avouched thee this day to be his [1]peculiar people, as he hath promised thee, and that *thou* shouldest keep all his commandments;

19 And to [1]make thee [a]high above all nations which he hath made, in praise, and in name, and in honour; and that thou mayest be [b]an [2]holy people unto the LORD thy God, as he hath spoken.

## CHAPTER 27

A ND Moses with the elders of Israel commanded the people, saying, Keep all the commandments which I command you this day.

2 And it shall be on the day [a]when ye shall pass over Jordan unto the land which the LORD thy God giveth thee, that [b]thou shalt set thee up great stones, and plaister them with plaister:

3 And thou shalt write upon them all the words of this law, when thou art passed over, that thou mayest go in unto the land which the LORD thy God giveth thee, [a]a land that floweth with milk and honey; as the LORD God of thy fathers hath promised thee.

4 Therefore it shall be when ye be gone over Jordan, *that* ye shall set up these stones, which I command you this day, [a]in mount Ebal, and thou shalt plaister them with plaister.

5 And there shalt thou build an altar unto the LORD thy God, an altar of stones: [a]thou shalt not [1]lift up *any* iron *tool* upon them.

6 Thou shalt build the altar of the LORD thy God of [1]whole stones: and thou shalt offer burnt offerings thereon unto the LORD thy God:

7 And thou shalt offer peace offerings, and shalt eat there, and [a]rejoice before the LORD thy God.

8 And thou shalt [a]write upon the stones all the words of this law very plainly.

9 And Moses and the priests the Levites spake unto all Israel, saying, Take heed, and hearken, O Israel; [a]this day thou art become the people of the LORD thy God.

10 Thou shalt therefore obey the voice of the LORD thy God, and do his commandments and his statutes, which I command thee this day.

11 And Moses charged the people the same day, saying,

12 These shall stand [a]upon mount Gerizim to bless the people, when ye are come over Jordan; Simeon, and Levi, and Judah, and Issachar, and Joseph, and Benjamin:

13 And [a]these shall stand upon mount Ebal to curse; Reuben, Gad, and Asher, and Zebulun, Dan, and Naphtali.

14 And [a]the Levites shall speak, and say unto all the men of Israel with a loud voice,

15 [a]Cursed *be* the man that maketh *any* graven or molten image, [1]an abomination unto the LORD, the work of the hands of the craftsman, and [2]putteth *it* in *a* secret *place*. [b]And all the people shall answer and say, Amen.

16 [a]Cursed *be* he that [1]setteth light by his father or his mother. And all the people shall say, Amen.

17 [a]Cursed *be* he that [1]removeth his neighbour's [2]landmark. And all the people shall say, Amen.

18 [a]Cursed *be* he that maketh the blind to wander out of the way. And all the people shall say, Amen.

19 [a]Cursed *be* he that perverteth the [1]judgment of the stranger, fatherless, and widow. And all the people shall say, Amen.

20 [a]Cursed *be* he that lieth with his father's wife; because he uncovereth his father's skirt. And all the people shall say, Amen.

21 [a]Cursed *be* he that lieth with any manner of beast. And all the people shall say, Amen.

22 [a]Cursed *be* he that lieth with his sister, the daughter of his father, or the daughter of his mother. And all the people shall say, Amen.

23 [a]Cursed *be* he that lieth with his mother in law. And all the people shall say, Amen.

24 [a]Cursed *be* he that [1]smiteth his neighbour secretly. And all the people shall say, Amen.

25 [a]Cursed *be* he that taketh [1]reward to slay an innocent person. And all the people shall say, Amen.

26 [a]Cursed *be* he that confirmeth not *all* the words of this law to do them. And all the people shall say, Amen.

## CHAPTER 28

A ND it shall come to pass, [a]if thou shalt hearken diligently unto the voice of the LORD thy God, to observe *and* to do all his commandments which I command thee this day, that the LORD thy God [b]will set thee on high above all nations of the earth:

2 And all these blessings shall come on thee, and [a]overtake thee, if thou shalt hearken unto the voice of the LORD thy God.

3 [a]Blessed *shalt* thou *be* in the city, and blessed *shalt* thou *be* [b]in the field.

4 Blessed *shall be* [a]the [1]fruit of thy body, and the fruit of thy ground, and

### Cross references (center column)

26:17 [b] Deut. 15:5
26:18 [a] Ex. 6:7; 19:5; Deut. 7:6; 14:2; 28:9; [Titus 2:14; 1 Pet. 2:9] [1] special
26:19 [a] Deut. 4:7, 8; 28:1 [b] Ex. 19:6; Deut. 7:6; 28:9; Is. 62:12; [1 Pet. 2:9] [1] set [2] consecrated
27:2 [a] Josh. 4:1 [b] Josh. 8:32
27:3 [a] Ex. 3:8
27:4 [a] Deut. 11:29; Josh. 8:30, 31
27:5 [a] Ex. 20:25; Josh. 8:31 [1] use
27:6 [1] uncut
27:7 [a] Deut. 26:11
27:8 [a] Josh. 8:32
27:9 [a] Deut. 26:18
27:12 [a] Josh. 8:33

27:13 [a] Deut. 11:29
27:14 [a] Deut. 33:10
27:15 [a] Ex. 20:4, 23; 34:17 [b] Num. 5:22 [1] a detestable thing [2] sets it up
27:16 [a] Ezek. 22:7 [1] treats with contempt
27:17 [a] Deut. 19:14 [1] moves [2] boundary marker
27:18 [a] Lev. 19:14
27:19 [a] Ex. 22:21, 22; 23:9 [1] justice due
27:20 [a] Deut. 22:30
27:21 [a] Lev. 18:23; 20:15, 16
27:22 [a] Lev. 18:9
27:23 [a] Lev. 18:17; 20:14
27:24 [a] Ex. 20:13; 21:12 [1] attacks
27:25 [a] Ex. 23:7 [1] a bribe
27:26 [a] Gal. 3:10
28:1 [a] Ex. 15:26 [b] Deut. 26:19
28:2 [a] Deut. 28:15
28:3 [a] Ps. 128:1, 4 [b] Gen. 39:5
28:4 [a] Gen. 22:17 [1] offspring

the fruit of thy cattle, the increase of thy ²kine, and the flocks of thy sheep.

5 Blessed *shall be* thy basket and thy ¹store.

6 ªBlessed *shalt* thou *be* when thou comest in, and blessed *shalt* thou *be* when thou goest out.

7 The LORD ªshall cause thine enemies that rise up against thee to be ¹smitten before thy face: they shall come out against thee one way, and flee before thee seven ways.

8 The LORD shall ªcommand the blessing upon thee in thy storehouses, and in all that thou ᵇsettest thine hand unto; and he shall bless thee in the land which the LORD thy God giveth thee.

9 ªThe LORD shall establish thee an holy people unto himself, as he hath sworn unto thee, if thou shalt keep the commandments of the LORD thy God, and walk in his ways.

10 And all people of the earth shall see that thou art ªcalled by the name of the LORD; and they shall be ᵇafraid of thee.

11 And ªthe LORD shall ¹make thee plenteous in goods, in the fruit of thy body, and in the fruit of thy cattle, and in the fruit of thy ground, in the land which the LORD ²sware unto thy fathers to give thee.

12 The LORD shall open unto thee his good ¹treasure, the heaven ªto give the rain unto thy land in his season, and ᵇto bless all the work of thine hand: and ᶜthou shalt lend unto many nations, and thou shalt not borrow.

13 And the LORD shall make ªthee the head, and not the tail; and thou shalt be above only, and thou shalt not be beneath; if that thou ¹hearken unto the commandments of the LORD thy God, which I command thee this day, ²to observe and to do *them:*

14 ³And thou shalt not ¹go aside from any of the words which I command thee this day, *to* the right hand, or *to* the left, to go after other gods to serve them.

15 But it shall come to pass, ªif thou wilt not ¹hearken unto the voice of the LORD thy God, to ²observe to do all his commandments and his statutes which I command thee this day; that all these curses shall come upon thee, and overtake thee:

16 Cursed *shalt* thou *be* in the city, and cursed *shalt* thou *be* in the field.

17 Cursed *shall be* thy basket and thy ¹store.

18 Cursed *shall be* the ¹fruit of thy body, and the fruit of thy land, the increase of thy ²kine, and the flocks of thy sheep.

19 Cursed *shalt* thou *be* when thou comest in, and cursed *shalt* thou *be* when thou goest out.

20 The LORD shall send upon thee ªcursing, ᵇvexation,¹ and ᶜrebuke, in all that thou settest thine hand unto for to do, until thou be destroyed, and until thou perish quickly; because of the wickedness of thy doings, whereby thou hast forsaken me.

21 The LORD shall make the ¹pestilence cleave unto thee, until he have consumed thee from off the land, whither thou goest to possess it.

22 ªThe LORD shall smite thee with a consumption, and with a fever, and with an inflammation, and with an extreme burning, and with the sword, and with ᵇblasting,¹ and with mildew; and they shall pursue thee until thou perish.

23 And ªthy heaven that *is* over thy head shall be ¹brass, and the earth that *is* under thee *shall be* iron.

24 The LORD shall make the rain of thy land powder and dust: from heaven shall it come down upon thee, until thou be destroyed.

25 ªThe LORD shall cause thee to be ¹smitten before thine enemies: thou shalt go out one way against them, and flee seven ways before them: and shalt be ²removed into all the kingdoms of the earth.

26 And ªthy carcase shall be meat unto all fowls of the air, and unto the beasts of the earth, and no man shall ¹fray *them* away.

27 The LORD will smite thee with ªthe ¹botch of Egypt, and with ᵇthe ²emerods, and with the scab, and with the itch, whereof thou canst not be healed.

28 The LORD shall smite thee with madness, and blindness, and ªastonishment¹ of heart:

29 And thou shalt ªgrope at noonday, as the blind gropeth in darkness, and thou shalt not prosper in thy ways: and thou shalt be only oppressed and ¹spoiled evermore, and no man shall save *thee.*

30 ªThou shalt betroth a wife, and another man shall lie with her: ᵇthou shalt build an house, and thou shalt not dwell therein: ᶜthou shalt plant a vineyard, and shalt not gather the grapes thereof.

31 Thine ox *shall be* slain before thine eyes, and thou shalt not eat thereof: thine ass *shall be* violently taken away from before thy face, and shall not be restored to thee: thy sheep *shall be* given unto thine enemies, and thou shalt have none to rescue *them.*

32 Thy sons and thy daughters *shall be* given unto ªanother people, and thine eyes shall look, and ᵇfail *with longing* for them all the day long: and *there shall be* ¹no might in thine ᶜhand.

33 ªThe fruit of thy land, and all thy labours, shall a nation which thou knowest not eat up; and thou shalt be only oppressed and crushed alway:

34 So that thou shalt be ¹mad for the sight of thine eyes which thou shalt see.

35 The LORD shall smite thee in the knees, and in the legs, with a sore ¹botch that cannot be healed, from the sole of thy foot unto the top of thy head.

36 The LORD shall ªbring thee, and thy king which thou shalt set over thee, unto a nation which neither thou nor thy fathers have known; and ᵇthere shalt thou serve other gods, wood and stone.

37 And thou shalt become ªan ¹astonishment, a proverb, ᵇand a byword, among all nations whither the LORD shall lead thee.

38 ªThou shalt carry much seed out into the field, and shalt gather *but* little in; for ᵇthe locust shall ¹consume it.

39 Thou shalt plant vineyards, and dress *them,* but shalt neither drink *of* the ªwine, nor gather *the grapes;* for the worms shall eat them.

40 Thou shalt have olive trees throughout all thy coasts, but thou shalt not anoint *thyself* with the oil; for thine ¹olive shall cast *his fruit.*

41 Thou shalt beget sons and daughters, but thou shalt not enjoy them; for ªthey shall go into captivity.

42 All thy trees and fruit of thy land shall the locust ¹consume.

43 The stranger that *is* within thee shall get up above thee very high; and thou shalt come down very low.

44 He shall lend to thee, and thou shalt not lend to him: he shall be the head, and thou shalt be the tail.

45 Moreover all these curses shall come upon thee, and shall pursue thee, and overtake thee, till thou be destroyed; because thou ¹hearkenedst not unto the voice of the LORD thy God, to keep his commandments and his statutes which he commanded thee:

46 And they shall be upon ªthee for a sign and for a wonder, and upon thy seed for ever.

47 ªBecause thou servedst not the LORD thy God with joyfulness, and with gladness of heart, ᵇfor the abundance of all *things;*

48 Therefore shalt thou serve thine enemies which the LORD shall send against thee, in ªhunger, and in thirst, and in nakedness, and in want of all *things:* and he ᵇshall put a yoke of iron upon thy neck, until he have destroyed thee.

49 ªThe LORD shall bring a nation against thee from far, from the end of

the earth, ᵇ*as swift* as the eagle flieth; a nation whose ¹tongue thou shalt not understand;

50 A nation of fierce countenance, ªwhich shall not ¹regard the person of the old, nor shew favour to the young:

51 And he shall eat the fruit of thy cattle, and the fruit of thy land, until thou be destroyed: which *also* shall not leave thee *either* corn, wine, or oil, *or* the increase of thy kine, or flocks of thy sheep, until he have destroyed thee.

52 And he shall ªbesiege thee in all thy gates, until thy high and ¹fenced walls come down, wherein thou trustedst, throughout all thy land: and he shall besiege thee in all thy gates throughout all thy land, which the LORD thy God hath given thee.

53 And ªthou shalt eat the ¹fruit of thine own body, the flesh of thy sons and of thy daughters, which the LORD thy God hath given thee, in the siege, and in the ²straitness, wherewith thine enemies shall distress thee:

54 *So that* the man *that is* ¹tender among you, and very ²delicate, ªhis³ eye shall be evil toward his brother, and toward ᵇthe wife of his bosom, and toward the remnant of his children which he shall leave:

55 So that he will not give to any of them of the flesh of his children whom he shall eat: because he hath nothing left him in the siege, and in the straitness, wherewith thine enemies shall distress thee in all thy gates.

56 The ¹tender and ²delicate woman among you, which would not adventure to set the sole of her foot upon the ground for delicateness and tenderness, ³her eye shall be evil toward the husband of her bosom, and toward her son, and toward her daughter,

57 And toward her ¹young one that cometh out ªfrom between her feet, and toward her children which she shall bear: for she shall eat them for want of all *things* secretly in the siege and straitness, wherewith thine enemy shall distress thee in thy gates.

58 If thou wilt not observe to do all the words of this law that are written in this book, that thou mayest fear ªthis glorious and fearful name, THE LORD THY GOD;

59 Then the LORD will make thy plagues ªwonderful,¹ and the plagues of thy seed, *even* great plagues, and of long continuance, and sore sicknesses, and of long continuance.

60 Moreover he will bring upon thee all ªthe diseases of Egypt, which thou wast afraid of; and they shall cleave unto thee.

28:33 ª Lev. 26:16; Jer. 5:15, 17
28:34 ¹ driven mad because of
28:35 ¹ boils
28:36 ª 2 Kin. 17:4, 6; 24:12, 14; 25:7, 11; 2 Chr. 36:1–21; Jer. 39:1–9 ᵇ Deut. 4:28; Jer. 16:13
28:37 ª 1 Kin. 9:7, 8; Jer. 24:9; 25:9 ᵇ Ps. 44:14 ¹ thing of horror
28:38 ª Mic. 6:15; Hag. 1:6 ᵇ Ex. 10:4; Joel 1:4 ¹ devour
28:39 ¹ Zeph. 1:13
28:40 ¹ olives shall drop off
28:41 ª Lam. 1:5
28:42 ¹ possess
28:45 ª did not listen
28:46 ª Num. 26:10; Is. 8:18; Ezek. 14:8
28:47 ª Deut. 12:7; Neh. 9:35–37 ᵇ Deut. 32:15
28:48 ª Lam. 4:4–6 ᵇ Jer. 28:13, 14
28:49 ª Is. 5:26–30; 7:18–20; Jer. 5:15
ᵇ Jer. 48:40; 49:22; Lam. 4:19; Hos. 8:1 ¹ language
28:50 ª 2 Chr. 36:17 ¹ respect
28:52 ª 2 Kin. 25:1, 2, 4 ¹ fortified
28:53 ª Lev. 26:29; 2 Kin. 6:28, 29; Jer. 19:9; Lam. 2:20; 4:10 ¹ offspring ² desperate straits
28:54 ª Deut. 15:9 ᵇ Deut. 13:6 ¹ sensitive ² refined ³ he shall be hostile toward
28:56 ¹ sensitive ² refined ³ she shall be hostile toward
28:57 ª Gen. 49:10 ¹ placenta or afterbirth
28:58 ª Ex. 6:3
28:59 ª Dan. 9:12 ¹ extraordinary
28:60 ª Deut. 7:15

**61** Also every sickness, and every plague, which *is* not written in the book of this law, them will the LORD bring upon thee, until thou be destroyed.

**62** And ye ªshall be left few in number, whereas ye were ᵇas the stars of heaven for multitude; because thou wouldest not obey the voice of the LORD thy God.

**63** And it shall come to pass, *that* as the LORD ªrejoiced over you to do you good, and to multiply you; so the LORD ᵇwill rejoice over you to destroy you, and to bring you to 'nought; and ye shall be ᶜplucked² from off the land whither thou goest to possess it.

**64** And the LORD ªshall scatter thee among all people, from the one end of the earth even unto the other; and ᵇthere thou shalt serve other gods, which neither thou nor thy fathers have known, *even* wood and stone.

**65** And ªamong these nations shalt thou find no 'ease, neither shall the sole of thy foot have rest: ᵇbut the LORD shall give thee there ²a trembling heart, and failing of eyes, and ᶜsorrow of mind:

**66** And thy life shall hang in doubt before thee; and thou shalt fear day and night, and shalt have none assurance of thy life:

**67** ªIn the morning thou shalt say, Would God it were even! and at even thou shalt say, Would God it were morning! for the fear of thine heart wherewith thou shalt fear, and ᵇfor the sight of thine eyes which thou shalt see.

**68** And the LORD ªshall bring thee into Egypt again with ships, by the way whereof I spake unto thee, ᵇThou shalt see it no more again: and there ye shall be sold unto your enemies for 'bondmen and bondwomen, and no man shall buy *you*.

### CHAPTER 29

**T**HESE *are* the words of the covenant, which the LORD commanded Moses to make with the children of Israel in the land of Moab, beside the ªcovenant which he made with them in Horeb.

**2** And Moses called unto all Israel, and said unto them, ªYe have seen all that the LORD did before your eyes in the land of Egypt unto Pharaoh, and unto all his servants, and unto all his land;

**3** ªThe great 'temptations which thine eyes have seen, the signs, and those great miracles:

**4** Yet ªthe LORD hath not given you an heart to 'perceive, and eyes to see, and ears to hear, unto this day.

**5** ªAnd I have led you forty years in the wilderness: ᵇyour clothes are not

28:62 ª Deut. 4:27
ᵇ Deut. 10:22;
Neh. 9:23
28:63 ª Deut.
30:9; Jer. 32:41
ᵇ Prov. 1:26; [Is.
1:24] ᶜ Jer. 12:14;
45:4 ¹ *nothing*
² *torn*
28:64 ª Lev.
26:33; Deut. 4:27,
28; Neh. 1:8; Jer.
16:13; Amos 9:9
ᵇ Deut. 28:36
28:65 ª Lam. 1:3;
Amos 9:4 ᵇ Lev.
26:36 ᶜ Lev.
26:16 ¹ *rest* ² *an anxious*
28:67 ª Job 7:4
ᵇ Deut. 28:34
28:68 ª Jer. 43:7;
Hos. 8:13 ᵇ Deut.
17:16 ¹ *male and female slaves*
29:1 ª Lev. 26:46;
Deut. 5:2, 3
29:2 ª Ex. 19:4;
Deut. 11:7
29:3 ª Deut. 4:34;
7:19 ¹ *trials*
29:4 ª [Is. 6:9,
10; Ezek. 12:2];
Matt. 13:14; [Acts
28:26, 27]; Rom.
11:8; [Eph. 4:18]
¹ *understand*
29:5 ª Deut. 1:3;
8:2 ᵇ Deut. 8:4

29:6 ª Ex. 16:12;
Deut. 8:3
29:7 ª Num.
21:23, 24; Deut.
2:26–3:3
29:8 ª Num.
32:33; Deut.
3:12, 13
29:9 ª Deut.
4:6; 1 Kin. 2:3
ᵇ Josh. 1:7
29:11 ª Josh. 9:21,
23, 27
29:12 ª Neh. 10:29
29:13 ª Deut. 28:9
ᵇ Ex. 6:7 ᶜ Gen.
17:7, 8
29:14 ª [Jer. 31:31;
Heb. 8:7, 8]
29:15 ª Acts 2:39
29:17 ¹ *detestable things*
29:18 ª Deut.
11:16 ᵇ Heb. 12:15
ᶜ Deut. 32:32;
Acts 8:23
29:19 ª Jer. 3:17;
7:24 ᵇ Is. 30:1
¹ *stubbornness*
29:20 ª Ezek. 14:7
ᵇ Ps. 74:1 ᶜ Ps.
79:5; Ezek. 23:25
¹ *burn*

waxen old upon you, and thy shoe is not waxen old upon thy foot.

**6** ªYe have not eaten bread, neither have ye drunk wine or strong drink: that ye might know that I *am* the LORD your God.

**7** And when ye came unto this place, ªSihon the king of Heshbon, and Og the king of Bashan, came out against us unto battle, and we smote them:

**8** And we took their land, and ªgave it for an inheritance unto the Reubenites, and to the Gadites, and to the half tribe of Manasseh.

**9** ªKeep therefore the words of this covenant, and do them, that ye may ᵇprosper in all that ye do.

**10** Ye stand this day all of you before the LORD your God; your captains of your tribes, your elders, and your officers, *with* all the men of Israel,

**11** Your little ones, your wives, and thy stranger that *is* in thy camp, from ªthe hewer of thy wood unto the drawer of thy water:

**12** That thou shouldest enter into covenant with the LORD thy God, and ªinto his oath, which the LORD thy God maketh with thee this day:

**13** That he may ªestablish thee to day for a people unto himself, and *that* he may be unto thee a God, ᵇas he hath said unto thee, and ᶜas he hath sworn unto thy fathers, to Abraham, to Isaac, and to Jacob.

**14** Neither with you only ªdo I make this covenant and this oath;

**15** But with *him* that standeth here with us this day before the LORD our God, ªand also with *him* that *is* not here with us this day:

**16** (For ye know how we have dwelt in the land of Egypt; and how we came through the nations which ye passed by;

**17** And ye have seen their 'abominations, and their idols, wood and stone, silver and gold, which *were* among them:)

**18** Lest there should be among you man, or woman, or family, or tribe, ªwhose heart turneth away this day from the LORD our God, to go *and* serve the gods of these nations; ᵇlest there should be among you a root that beareth ᶜgall and wormwood;

**19** And it come to pass, when he heareth the words of this curse, that he bless himself in his heart, saying, I shall have peace, though I walk ªin the 'imagination of mine heart, ᵇto add drunkenness to thirst:

**20** ªThe LORD will not spare him, but then ᵇthe anger of the LORD and ᶜhis jealousy shall 'smoke against that man, and all the curses that are written in this book shall lie upon

him, and the LORD [d]shall blot out his name from under heaven.

21 And the LORD [a]shall separate him unto evil out of all the tribes of Israel, according to all the curses of the covenant that are written in this book of the [b]law:

22 So that the generation to come of your children that shall rise up after you, and the stranger that shall come from a far land, shall say, when they [a]see the plagues of that land, and the sicknesses which the LORD hath laid upon it;

23 *And that* the whole land thereof *is* brimstone, [a]and salt, *and* burning, *that* it is not sown, nor beareth, nor any grass groweth therein, [b]like the overthrow of Sodom, and Gomorrah, Admah, and Zeboim, which the LORD overthrew in his anger, and in his wrath:

24 Even all nations shall say, [a]Wherefore hath the LORD done thus unto this land? what *meaneth* the heat of this great anger?

25 Then men shall say, Because they have forsaken the covenant of the LORD God of their fathers, which he made with them when he brought them forth out of the land of Egypt:

26 For they went and served other gods, and worshipped them, gods whom they knew not, and *whom* he had not given unto them:

27 And the anger of the LORD was kindled against this land, [a]to bring upon it all the curses that are written in this book:

28 And the LORD [a]rooted[1] them out of their land in anger, and in wrath, and in great indignation, and cast them into another land, as *it is* this day.

29 The secret *things belong* unto the LORD our God: but those *things which are* revealed *belong* unto us and to our children for ever, that *we* may do all the words of this law.

## CHAPTER 30

AND [a]it shall come to pass, when [b]all these things are come upon thee, the blessing and the [c]curse, which I have set before thee, and [d]thou shalt [1]call *them* to mind among all the nations, whither the LORD thy God hath driven thee,

2 And shalt [a]return unto the LORD thy God, and shalt obey his voice according to all that I command thee this day, thou and thy children, with all thine heart, and with all thy soul;

3 [a]That then the LORD thy God will [1]turn thy captivity, and have compassion upon thee, and will return and [b]gather thee from all the nations, whither the LORD thy God hath scattered thee.

29:20 [d] Ex. 32:33; Deut. 9:14; 2 Kin. 14:27

29:21 [a] [Matt. 24:51] [b] Deut. 30:10

29:22 [a] Jer. 19:8; 49:17; 50:13

29:23 [a] Jer. 17:6; Zeph. 2:9 [b] Gen. 19:24, 25; Is. 1:9; Jer. 20:16; Hos. 11:8

29:24 [a] 1 Kin. 9:8; Jer. 22:8

29:27 [a] Dan. 9:11

29:28 [a] 1 Kin. 14:15; 2 Chr. 7:20; Ps. 52:5; Prov. 2:22 [1] *uprooted*

30:1 [a] Lev. 26:40 [b] Deut. 28:2 [c] Deut. 28:15–45 [d] Deut. 4:29, 30 [1] Lit. *cause them to return to your heart*

30:2 [a] Deut. 4:29, 30; Neh. 1:9; Is. 55:7; Jer. 3:40; Joel 2:12

30:3 [a] Ps. 106:45; Jer. 29:14; Lam. 3:22, 32 [b] Ps. 147:2; Jer. 32:37; Ezek. 34:13 [1] *bring you back from*

30:4 [a] Deut. 28:64; Neh. 1:9; Is. 62:11

30:6 [a] Deut. 10:16; Jer. 32:39; Ezek. 11:19

30:7 [a] Is. 54:15–17; Jer. 30:16, 20

30:8 [a] Zeph. 3:20

30:9 [a] Deut. 28:11 [b] Deut. 28:63; Jer. 32:41 [1] *abound* [2] *offspring*

30:11 [a] Is. 45:19 [1] *too mysterious for thee*

30:12 [a] Prov. 30:4; Rom. 10:6–8

30:14 [a] Rom. 10:8

30:15 [a] Deut. 30:1, 19

30:18 [a] Deut. 4:26; 8:19 [1] *announce*

4 [a]If *any* of thine be driven out unto the outmost *parts* of heaven, from thence will the LORD thy God gather thee, and from thence will he fetch thee:

5 And the LORD thy God will bring thee into the land which thy fathers possessed, and thou shalt possess it; and he will do thee good, and multiply thee above thy fathers.

6 And [a]the LORD thy God will circumcise thine heart, and the heart of thy seed, to love the LORD thy God with all thine heart, and with all thy soul, that thou mayest live.

7 And the LORD thy God will put all these [a]curses upon thine enemies, and on them that hate thee, which persecuted thee.

8 And thou shalt [a]return and obey the voice of the LORD, and do all his commandments which I command thee this day.

9 [a]And the LORD thy God will make thee [1]plenteous in every work of thine hand, in the [2]fruit of thy body, and in the fruit of thy cattle, and in the fruit of thy land, for good: for the LORD will again [b]rejoice over thee for good, as he rejoiced over thy fathers:

10 If thou shalt hearken unto the voice of the LORD thy God, to keep his commandments and his statutes which are written in this book of the law, *and* if thou turn unto the LORD thy God with all thine heart, and with all thy soul.

11 For this commandment which I command thee this day, [a]it *is* not [1]hidden from thee, neither *is* it far off.

12 [a]It *is* not in heaven, that thou shouldest say, Who shall go up for us to heaven, and bring it unto us, that we may hear it, and do it?

13 Neither *is* it beyond the sea, that thou shouldest say, Who shall go over the sea for us, and bring it unto us, that we may hear it, and do it?

14 But the word *is* very nigh unto thee, in thy [a]mouth, and in thy heart, that thou mayest do it.

15 See, [a]I have set before thee this day life and good, and death and evil;

16 In that I command thee this day to love the LORD thy God, to walk in his ways, and to keep his commandments and his statutes and his judgments, that thou mayest live and multiply: and the LORD thy God shall bless thee in the land whither thou goest to possess it.

17 But if thine heart turn away, so that thou wilt not hear, but shalt be drawn away, and worship other gods, and serve them;

18 [a]I [1]denounce unto you this day, that ye shall surely perish, *and that* ye shall not prolong *your* days upon

the land, whither thou passest over Jordan to go to possess it.

19 [a]I call heaven and earth [1]to record this day against you, *that* [b]I have set before you life and death, blessing and cursing: therefore choose life, that both thou and thy seed may live:

20 That thou mayest love the LORD thy God, *and* that thou mayest obey his voice, and that thou mayest cleave unto him: for he *is* thy [a]life, and the length of thy days: that thou mayest dwell in the land which the LORD sware unto thy fathers, to Abraham, to Isaac, and to Jacob, to give them.

## CHAPTER 31

AND Moses went and spake these words unto all Israel.

2 And he said unto them, I [a]*am* an hundred and twenty years old this day; I can no more [b]go out and come in: also the LORD hath said unto me, [c]Thou shalt not go over this Jordan.

3 The LORD thy God, [a]he will go over before thee, *and* he will destroy these nations from before thee, and thou shalt [1]possess them: *and* [b]Joshua, he shall go over before thee, [c]as the LORD hath said.

4 [a]And the LORD shall do unto them [b]as he did to Sihon and to Og, kings of the Amorites, and unto the land of them, whom he destroyed.

5 And [a]the LORD shall give them up before your face, that ye may do unto them according unto all the commandments which I have commanded you.

6 [a]Be strong and of a good courage, [b]fear not, nor be afraid of them: for the LORD thy God, [c]he *it is* that doth go with thee; [d]he will not fail thee, nor forsake thee.

7 And Moses called unto Joshua, and said unto him in the sight of all Israel, [a]Be strong and of a good courage: for thou must go with this people unto the land which the LORD hath sworn unto their fathers to give them; and thou shalt cause them to inherit it.

8 And the LORD, [a]he *it is* that doth go before thee; [b]he will be with thee, he will not fail thee, neither forsake thee: fear not, neither be dismayed.

9 And Moses wrote this law, [a]and delivered it unto the priests the sons of Levi, [b]which bare the ark of the covenant of the LORD, and unto all the elders of Israel.

10 And Moses commanded them, saying, At the end of *every* seven years, in the [1]solemnity of the [a]year of release, [b]in the feast of tabernacles,

11 When all Israel is come to [a]appear before the LORD thy God in the [b]place which he shall choose, [c]thou

shalt read this law before all Israel in their hearing.

12 [a]Gather the people together, men, and women, and children, and thy stranger that *is* within thy gates, that they may hear, and that they may learn, and fear the LORD your God, and observe to do all the words of this law:

13 And *that* their children, [a]which have not known *any thing*, [b]may hear, and learn to fear the LORD your God, as long as ye live in the land whither ye go over Jordan to possess it.

14 And the LORD said unto Moses, [a]Behold, thy days approach that thou must die: call Joshua, and present yourselves in the tabernacle of the congregation, that [b]I may give him a [1]charge. And Moses and Joshua went, and presented themselves in the tabernacle of the congregation.

15 And [a]the LORD appeared in the tabernacle in a pillar of a cloud: and the pillar of the cloud stood over the door of the tabernacle.

16 And the LORD said unto Moses, Behold, thou shalt [1]sleep with thy fathers; and this people will [a]rise up, and [b]go[2] a whoring after the gods of the strangers of the land, whither they go *to be* among them, and will [c]forsake me, and [d]break my covenant which I have made with them.

17 Then my anger shall be [a]kindled against them in that day, and [b]I will forsake them, and I will [c]hide my face from them, and they shall be [1]devoured, and many evils and troubles shall befall them; so that they will say in that day, [d]Are not these evils come upon us, because our God *is* [e]not among us?

18 And [a]I will surely hide my face in that day for all the evils which they shall have wrought, in that they are turned unto other gods.

19 Now therefore write ye this song for you, and teach it the children of Israel: put it in their mouths, that this song may be [a]a witness for me against the children of Israel.

20 For when I shall have brought them into the land which I sware unto their fathers, that floweth with milk and honey; and they shall have eaten and filled themselves, [a]and [1]waxen fat; [b]then will they turn unto other gods, and serve them, and provoke me, and break my covenant.

21 And it shall come to pass, [a]when many evils and troubles are befallen them, that this song shall testify against them as a witness; for it shall not be forgotten out of the mouths of their seed: for [b]I know [1]their imagination [c]which they go about, even now, before I have brought them into the land which I sware.

30:19 [a] Deut. 4:26
[b] Deut. 30:15 [1] *as witnesses*

30:20 [a] Ps. 27:1;
[John 11:25; 14:6;
Col. 3:4]

31:2 [a] Ex. 7:7; Deut. 34:7 [b] Num. 27:17;
1 Kin. 3:7 [c] Num. 20:12

31:3 [a] Deut. 9:3; Josh. 11:23
[b] Num. 27:18
[c] Num. 27:21
[1] *dispossess*

31:4 [a] Deut. 3:21
[b] Num. 21:24, 33

31:5 [a] Deut. 7:2;
20:10–20

31:6 [a] Josh. 10:25; 1 Chr. 22:13 [b] Deut. 1:29 [c] Deut. 20:4
[d] Josh. 1:5; Heb. 13:5

31:7 [a] Num. 27:19;
Deut. 31:23;
Josh. 1:6

31:8 [a] Ex. 13:21
[b] Deut. 31:6; Josh. 1:5; 1 Chr. 28:20;
Heb. 13:5

31:9 [a] Deut. 17:18;
31:25, 26 [b] Num. 4:5, 6, 15; Deut. 10:8; 31:25, 26;
Josh. 3:3

31:10 [a] Deut. 15:1,
2 [b] Lev. 23:34;
Deut. 16:13 [1] *appointed time*

31:11 [a] Deut. 16:16 [b] Deut. 12:5 [c] Josh. 8:34;
2 Kin. 23:2

31:12 [a] Deut. 4:10

31:13 [a] Deut. 11:2
[b] Ps. 78:6, 7

31:14 [a] Num. 27:13 [b] Num. 27:19; Deut. 3:28
[1] *commission*

31:15 [a] Ex. 33:9

31:16 [a] Deut. 29:22
[b] Ex. 34:15; Deut. 4:25–28; Judg. 2:11, 12, 17 [c] Deut. 32:15 [d] Judg. 2:20
[1] *die and join your ancestors* [2] *play the harlot*

31:17 [a] Judg. 2:14;
6:13 [b] 2 Chr. 15:2 [c] Deut. 32:20 [d] Judg. 6:13 [e] Num. 14:42
[1] *consumed*

31:18 [a] Deut. 31:17;
[Is. 1:15, 16]

31:19 [a] Deut. 31:22, 26

31:20 [a] Deut. 32:15–17 [b] Deut. 31:16 [1] *grown*

31:21 [a] Deut. 31:17 [b] Hos. 5:3
[c] Amos 5:25, 26
[1] *the inclination of their behaviour*

22 Moses therefore wrote this song the same day, and taught it the children of Israel.

23 [a]And he gave Joshua the son of Nun a charge, and said, [b]Be strong and of a good courage: for thou shalt bring the children of Israel into the land which I sware unto them: and I will be with thee.

24 And it came to pass, when Moses had made an end of writing the words of this law in a book, until they were finished,

25 That Moses commanded the Levites, which bare the ark of the covenant of the LORD, saying,

26 Take this book of the law, [a]and put it in the side of the ark of the covenant of the LORD your God, that it may be there [b]for a witness against thee.

27 [a]For I know thy rebellion, and thy [b]stiff neck: behold, while I am yet alive with you this day, ye have been rebellious against the LORD; and how much more after my death?

28 Gather unto me all the elders of your tribes, and your officers, that I may speak these words in their [1]ears, [a]and call heaven and earth to [2]record against them.

29 For I know that after my death ye will utterly [a]corrupt *yourselves,* and turn aside from the way which I have commanded you; and [b]evil will befall you [c]in the latter days; because ye will do evil in the sight of the LORD, to provoke him to anger through the work of your hands.

30 And Moses spake in the ears of all the congregation of Israel the words of this song, until they were ended.

## CHAPTER 32

GIVE [a]ear, O ye heavens, and I will speak; and hear, O [b]earth, the words of my mouth.

2 [a]My [1]doctrine shall drop as the rain, my speech shall distil as the dew, [b]as the small rain upon the tender herb, and as the showers upon the grass:

3 Because I will [1]publish the [a]name of the LORD: [b]ascribe ye greatness unto our God.

4 *He is* [a]the Rock, [b]his work *is* perfect: for all his ways *are* judgment: [c]a God of truth and [d]without iniquity, just and right *is* he.

5 [a]They have corrupted themselves, [1]their spot *is* not *the spot* of his children: *they are* a [b]perverse and crooked generation.

6 Do ye thus [a]requite[1] the LORD, O foolish people and unwise? *is* not he [b]thy father *that* hath [c]bought thee? hath he not [d]made thee, and established thee?

7 [a]Remember the days of old, consider the years of many generations: [b]ask thy father, and he will shew thee; thy elders, and they will tell thee.

8 When the Most High [a]divided to the nations their inheritance, when he [b]separated the sons of Adam, he set the bounds of the people according to the number of the [1]children of Israel.

9 For [a]the LORD's portion *is* his people; Jacob *is* the lot of his inheritance.

10 He found him [a]in a desert land, and in the waste howling wilderness; he [1]led him about, he instructed him, he [b]kept him as the [2]apple of his eye.

11 [a]As an eagle stirreth up her nest, fluttereth over her young, spreadeth abroad her wings, taketh them, beareth them on her wings:

12 *So* the LORD alone did lead him, and *there was* no strange god with him.

13 [a]He made him ride on the high places of the earth, that he might eat the increase of the fields; and he made him to suck honey out of the rock, and oil out of the flinty rock;

14 Butter of kine, and milk of sheep, [a]with fat of lambs, and rams of the breed of Bashan, and goats, with the fat of kidneys of wheat; and thou didst drink the pure [b]blood of the grape.

15 But Jeshurun [1]waxed fat, and kicked: [a]thou art waxen fat, thou art grown thick, thou art covered *with fatness;* then he [b]forsook God *which* [c]made him, and [2]lightly esteemed the [d]Rock of his salvation.

16 [a]They provoked him to jealousy with strange *gods,* with [1]abominations provoked they him to anger.

17 [a]They sacrificed unto devils, not to God; to gods whom they knew not, to new *gods* [1]that came newly up, whom your fathers [2]feared not.

18 [a]Of the Rock *that* begat thee thou art unmindful, and hast [b]forgotten God that formed thee.

19 [a]And when the LORD saw *it,* he [1]abhorred *them,* because of the provoking of his sons, and of his daughters.

20 And he said, I will hide my face from them, I will see what their end *shall be:* for they *are* a very [1]froward generation, [a]children in whom *is* no faith.

21 [a]They have moved me to jealousy with *that which is* not God; they have provoked me to anger [b]with their [1]vanities: and [c]I will move them to jealousy with *those which are* not a people; I will provoke them to anger with a foolish nation.

22 For [a]a fire is kindled in mine anger, and shall burn unto the [1]lowest

---

*Center column references:*

31:23 [a] Num. 27:23; Deut. 31:14 [b] Deut. 31:7

31:26 [a] 2 Kin. 22:8 [b] Deut. 31:19

31:27 [a] Deut. 9:7, 24 [b] Ex. 32:9; Deut. 9:6, 13

31:28 [a] Deut. 30:19 [1] *hearing* [2] *witness*

31:29 [a] Judg. 2:19 [b] Deut. 28:15 [c] Gen. 49:1

32:1 [a] Deut. 4:26 [b] Jer. 6:19

32:2 [a] Is. 55:10, 11 [b] Ps. 72:6 [1] *teaching*

32:3 [a] Deut. 28:58 [b] 1 Chr. 29:11 [1] *proclaim*

32:4 [a] Ps. 18:2 [b] 2 Sam. 22:31 [c] Is. 65:16 [d] Job 34:10

32:5 [a] Deut. 4:25; 31:29 [b] Phil. 2:15 [1] *they are not his children because of their blemish*

32:6 [a] Ps. 116:12 [b] Is. 63:16 [c] Ps. 74:2 [d] Deut. 32:15 [1] *repay*

32:7 [a] Ps. 44:1 [b] Ps. 78:5–8

32:8 [a] Acts 17:26 [b] Gen. 11:8 [1] LXX, DSS *angels of God;* Symmachus, Lat. *sons of God*

32:9 [a] Ex. 19:5

32:10 [a] Jer. 2:6 [b] Ps. 17:8 [1] *encircled* [2] *pupil*

32:11 [a] Is. 31:5

32:13 [a] Is. 58:14

32:14 [a] Ps. 81:16 [b] Gen. 49:11

32:15 [a] Deut. 31:20 [b] Is. 1:4 [c] Is. 51:13 [d] Ps. 95:1 [1] *grew* [2] *scornfully*

32:16 [a] 1 Cor. 10:22 [1] *detestable acts*

32:17 [a] Rev. 9:20 [1] *new arrivals* [2] *dreaded*

32:18 [a] Is. 17:10 [b] Jer. 2:32

32:19 [a] Judg. 2:14 [1] *spurned*

32:20 [a] Matt. 17:17 [1] *perverse*

32:21 [a] Ps. 78:58 [b] Ps. 31:6 [c] Rom. 10:19 [1] *foolish idols*

32:22 [a] Lam. 4:11 [1] *lowest part of*

[2] hell, and shall consume the earth with her increase, and set on fire the foundations of the mountains.

23 I will [a]heap [1]mischiefs upon them; [b]I will spend mine arrows upon them.

24 *They shall be* burnt with hunger, and devoured with burning heat, and with bitter destruction: I will also send the [a]teeth of beasts upon them, with the poison of serpents of the dust.

25 The sword without, and terror within, shall destroy both the young man and the virgin, the suckling *also* with the man of gray hairs.

26 [a]I said, I [1]would scatter them into corners, I would make the remembrance of them to cease from among men:

27 Were it not that I feared the wrath of the enemy, lest their adversaries should behave themselves strangely, *and* lest they should say, [a]Our hand *is* high, and the LORD hath not done all this.

28 For they *are* a nation void of counsel, neither *is there any* understanding in them.

29 [a]O that they were wise, *that* they understood this, *that* they would consider their [b]latter end!

30 How should one chase a thousand, and two put ten thousand to flight, except their Rock [a]had sold them, and the LORD had shut them up?

31 For their rock *is* not as our Rock, [a]even our enemies themselves *being* judges.

32 For [a]their vine *is* of the vine of Sodom, and of the fields of Gomorrah: their grapes *are* grapes of gall, their clusters *are* bitter:

33 Their wine *is* [a]the poison of dragons, and the cruel [b]venom of asps.

34 *Is* not this [a]laid up in store with me, *and* sealed up among my treasures?

35 [a]To me *belongeth* vengeance, and recompence; their foot shall slide in *due* time: [b]for the day of their calamity *is* at hand, and the things that shall come upon them make haste.

36 [a]For the LORD shall judge his people, [b]and [1]repent himself for his servants, when he seeth that *their* power is gone, and [c]*there is* none shut up, or left.

37 And he shall say, [a]Where *are* their gods, *their* rock in whom they [1]trusted,

38 Which did eat the fat of their sacrifices, *and* drank the wine of their drink offerings? let them rise up and help you, *and* be your protection.

39 See now that [a]I, *even* I, *am* he, and [b]*there is* no god with me: [c]I kill, and I make alive; I wound, and I heal:

**Marginal references (center column):**

32:22 [2] Heb. *Sheol*
32:23 [a] Ex. 32:12; [b] Ps. 7:12, 13; [1] *disasters*
32:24 [a] Lev. 26:22
32:26 [a] Ezek. 20:23 [1] *will dash them in pieces*
32:27 [a] Is. 10:12–15
32:29 [a] [Luke 19:42] [b] Deut. 31:29
32:30 [a] Judg. 2:14
32:31 [a] [1 Sam. 4:7, 8]
32:32 [a] Is. 1:8–10
32:33 [a] Ps. 58:4; [b] Rom. 3:13
32:34 [a] [Jer. 2:22]
32:35 [a] Heb. 10:30; [b] 2 Pet. 2:3
32:36 [a] Ps. 135:14; [b] Jer. 31:20; [c] 2 Kin. 14:26 [1] *have compassion on*
32:37 [a] Judg. 10:14 [1] *sought refuge*
32:39 [a] Is. 41:4; 43:10 [b] Is. 45:5; [c] 1 Sam. 2:6

32:41 [a] Is. 1:24; 66:16 [1] *sharpen*
32:43 [a] Rom. 15:10 [b] Rev. 6:10; 19:2 [c] Ps. 65:3; 79:9; 85:1
32:44 [1] Joshua
32:46 [a] Ezek. 40:4; 44:5; [b] Deut. 11:19
32:47 [a] Deut. 8:3; 30:15–20 [1] *futile*
32:49 [a] Num. 27:12–14
32:50 [a] Num. 20:25, 28; 33:38 [1] *join your ancestors*
32:51 [a] Num. 20:11–13 [b] Lev. 10:3 [1] *contention at Kadesh* [2] *did not hallow me*
32:52 [a] Deut. 34:1–5
33:1 [a] Gen. 49:28 [b] Ps. 90
33:2 [a] Ps. 68:8, 17 [b] Deut. 2:1, 4

neither *is there any* that can deliver out of my hand.

40 For I lift up my hand to heaven, and say, I live for ever.

41 [a]If I [1]whet my glittering sword, and mine hand take hold on judgment; I will render vengeance to mine enemies, and will reward them that hate me.

42 I will make mine arrows drunk with blood, and my sword shall devour flesh; *and that* with the blood of the slain and of the captives, from the beginning of revenges upon the enemy.

43 [a]Rejoice, O ye nations, *with* his people: for he will [b]avenge the blood of his servants, and will render vengeance to his adversaries, and [c]will be merciful unto his land, *and* to his people.

44 And Moses came and spake all the words of this song in the ears of the people, he, and [1]Hoshea the son of Nun.

45 And Moses made an end of speaking all these words to all Israel:

46 And he said unto them, [a]Set your hearts unto all the words which I testify among you this day, which ye shall command your [b]children to observe to do, all the words of this law.

47 For it *is* not a [1]vain thing for you; because it *is* your [a]life: and through this thing ye shall prolong *your* days in the land, whither ye go over Jordan to possess it.

48 And the LORD spake unto Moses that selfsame day, saying,

49 [a]Get thee up into this mountain Abarim, *unto* mount Nebo, which *is* in the land of Moab, that *is* over against Jericho; and behold the land of Canaan, which I give unto the children of Israel for a possession:

50 And die in the mount whither thou goest up, and [b]be gathered unto thy people; as [a]Aaron thy brother died in mount Hor, and was gathered unto his people:

51 Because [a]ye trespassed against me among the children of Israel at the waters of [1]Meribah-Kadesh, in the wilderness of Zin; because ye [b]sanctified[2] me not in the midst of the children of Israel.

52 [a]Yet thou shalt see the land before *thee;* but thou shalt not go thither unto the land which I give the children of Israel.

## CHAPTER 33

AND this *is* [a]the blessing, wherewith Moses [b]the man of God blessed the children of Israel before his death.

2 And he said, [a]The LORD came from Sinai, and rose up from [b]Seir unto them; he shined forth from

cmount Paran, and he came with dten thousands of saints: from his right hand *went* a fiery law for them.

3 Yea, ahe loved the people; ball his saints *are* in his hand: and they csat down at thy feet; *every one* shall dreceive of thy words.

4 aMoses 1commanded us a law, b*even* the inheritance of the congregation of Jacob.

5 And he was aking in bJeshurun, when the heads of the people *and* the tribes of Israel were gathered together.

6 Let aReuben live, and not die; and let *not* his men be few.

7 And this *is the blessing* of aJudah: and he said, Hear, LORD, the voice of Judah, and bring him unto his people: blet his hands be sufficient for him; and be thou can help *to him* from his enemies.

8 And of aLevi he said, b*Let* thy 1Thummim and thy Urim *be* with thy holy one, cwhom thou didst prove at Massah, *and with* whom thou didst strive at the waters of Meribah;

9 aWho said unto his father and to his mother, I have not bseen him; cneither did he acknowledge his brethren, nor knew his own children: for dthey have observed thy word, and kept thy covenant.

10 aThey shall teach Jacob thy judgments, and Israel thy law: they shall put incense before thee, band whole burnt sacrifice upon thine altar.

11 Bless, LORD, his substance, and aaccept the work of his hands: smite through the loins of them that rise against him, and of them that hate him, that they rise not again.

12 *And* of Benjamin he said, The beloved of the LORD shall dwell in safety by him; *and the LORD* shall cover him all the day long, and he shall dwell between his shoulders.

13 And of Joseph he said, aBlessed of the LORD *be* his land, for the precious things of heaven, for the bdew, and for the deep that coucheth beneath,

14 And for the precious fruits *brought forth* by the sun, and for the precious things put forth by the moon,

15 And for the chief things of athe ancient mountains, and for the precious things bof the lasting hills,

16 And for the precious things of the earth and fulness thereof, and *for* the good will of ahim that dwelt in the bush: let *the blessing* bcome upon the head of Joseph, and upon the top of the head of him *that was* separated from his brethren.

17 His glory *is like* the afirstling of his bullock, and his horns *are like* the bhorns of unicorns: with them che shall push the people together to the ends of the earth: and dthey *are*

the ten thousands of Ephraim, and they *are* the thousands of Manasseh.

18 And of Zebulun he said, aRejoice, Zebulun, in thy going out; and, Issachar, in thy tents.

19 They shall acall the people unto the mountain; there bthey shall offer sacrifices of righteousness: for they shall suck *of* the abundance of the seas, and *of* treasures hid in the sand.

20 And of Gad he said, Blessed *be* he that aenlargeth Gad: he dwelleth as a lion, and teareth the arm with the crown of the head.

21 And ahe provided the first part for himself, because there, *in* a portion of the lawgiver, *was* he 1seated; and bhe came with the heads of the people, he executed the justice of the LORD, and his judgments with Israel.

22 And of Dan he said, Dan is a lion's whelp: ahe shall leap from Bashan.

23 And of Naphtali he said, O Naphtali, asatisfied with favour, and full with the blessing of the LORD: bpossess thou the west and the south.

24 And of Asher he said, aLet Asher *be* blessed with children; let him be acceptable to his brethren, and let him bdip his foot in oil.

25 Thy shoes *shall be* airon and brass; and as thy days, *so shall* thy strength *be.*

26 *There is* anone like unto the God of bJeshurun, cwho rideth upon the heaven in thy help, and in his excellency on the sky.

27 The eternal God *is thy* arefuge, and underneath *are* the everlasting arms: and bhe shall thrust out the enemy from before thee; and shall say, Destroy *them.*

28 aIsrael then shall dwell in safety balone: cthe fountain of Jacob *shall be* upon a land of corn and wine; also his dheavens shall drop down dew.

29 aHappy *art* thou, O Israel: bwho *is* like unto thee, O people saved by the LORD, cthe shield of thy help, and who *is* the sword of thy 1excellency! and thine enemies dshall 2be found liars unto thee; and ethou shalt 3tread upon their 4high places.

## CHAPTER 34

AND Moses went up from the plains of Moab aunto the mountain of Nebo, to the top of Pisgah, that *is* over against Jericho. And the LORD shewed him all the land of Gilead, unto Dan,

2 And all Naphtali, and the land of Ephraim, and Manasseh, and all the land of Judah, unto 1the utmost sea,

3 And the south, and the plain of

### Center column references

33:2 c Num. 10:12
d Dan. 7:10
33:3 a Hos. 11:1
b 1 Sam. 2:9
c [Luke 10:39]
d Prov. 2:1
33:4 a John 1:17;
7:19 b Ps. 119:111
1 *charged us with*
33:5 a Ex. 15:18
b Deut. 32:15
33:6 a Gen.
49:3, 4
33:7 a Gen. 49:8–
12 b Gen. 49:8
c Ps. 146:5
33:8 a Gen.
49:5 b Ex. 28:30
c Ps. 81:7 1 Lit.
*Perfections and thy Lights*
33:9 a [Num.
25:5–8] b [Gen.
29:32] c Ex.
32:26–28 d Mal.
2:5, 6
33:10 a Lev. 10:11;
Deut. 31:9–13;
Mal. 2:7 b Lev.
1:9; Ps. 51:19
33:11 a 2 Sam.
24:23; Ezek.
20:40
33:13 a Gen.
49:22–26 b Gen.
27:28
33:15 a Gen. 49:26
b Hab. 3:6
33:16 a Ex. 3:2–4;
Acts 7:30–35
b Gen. 49:26
33:17 a 1 Chr. 5:1
b Num. 23:22
c 1 Kin. 22:11; Ps.
44:5 d Gen. 48:19
33:18 a Gen.
49:13–15
33:19 a Ex. 15:17;
Ps. 2:6; Is. 2:3
b Ps. 4:5; 51:19
33:20 a 1 Chr. 12:8
33:21 a Num.
32:16, 17 b Josh.
4:12 1 *was reserved*
33:22 a Gen.
49:16, 17; Josh.
19:47
33:23 a Gen. 49:21
b Josh. 19:32
33:24 a Gen.
49:20 b Job 29:6
33:25 a Deut. 8:9
33:26 a Ex. 15:11;
Deut. 4:35; Ps.
86:8; Jer. 10:6
b Deut. 32:15
c Deut. 10:14; Ps.
68:3, 33, 34; 104:3
33:27 a [Ps. 90:1;
91:2, 9] b Deut.
9:3–5
33:28 a Deut.
33:12; Jer. 23:6;
33:16 b Deut. 8:7,
8 c Num. 23:9
d Gen. 27:28
33:29 a Ps. 144:15

b Deut. 4:32–34; 2 Sam. 7:23 c Gen. 15:1; Ps. 115:9 d Ps. 18:44; 66:3 e Num. 33:52 1 *majesty* 2 *submit to you* 3 *tread down* 4 Places of pagan worship 34:1 a Num. 27:12; Deut. 32:49 34:2 1 The Mediterranean

the valley of Jericho, [a]the city of palm trees, unto Zoar.

4 And the LORD said unto him, [a]This *is* the land which I sware unto Abraham, unto Isaac, and unto Jacob, saying, I will give it unto thy seed: [b]I have caused thee to see *it* with thine eyes, but thou shalt not go over thither.

5 [a]So Moses the servant of the LORD died there in the land of Moab, according to the word of the LORD.

6 And he buried him in a valley in the land of Moab, over against Bethpeor: but [a]no man knoweth [1]of his sepulchre unto this day.

7 [a]And Moses *was* an hundred and twenty years old when he died: [b]his [1]eye was not dim, nor his natural force [2]abated.

34:3 [a] 2 Chr. 28:15
34:4 [a] Gen. 12:7
[b] Deut. 3:27
34:5 [a] Num. 20:12; Deut. 32:50; Josh. 1:1, 2
34:6 [a] Jude 9
[1] *his grave to this day*
34:7 [a] Deut. 31:2
[b] Gen. 27:1; 48:10
[1] *eyesight was not weakened*
[2] *reduced*
34:8 [a] Gen. 50:3, 10
34:9 [a] Is. 11:2
[b] Num. 27:18, 23
34:10 [a] Deut. 18:15, 18 [b] Ex. 33:11; Num. 12:8; Deut. 5:4
34:11 [a] Deut. 7:19

8 And the children of Israel wept for Moses in the plains of Moab [a]thirty days: so the days of weeping *and* mourning for Moses were ended.

9 And Joshua the son of Nun was full of the [a]spirit of wisdom; for [b]Moses had laid his hands upon him: and the children of Israel hearkened unto him, and did as the LORD commanded Moses.

10 And there [a]arose not a prophet since in Israel like unto Moses, [b]whom the LORD knew face to face,

11 In all [a]the signs and the wonders, which the LORD sent him to do in the land of Egypt to Pharaoh, and to all his servants, and to all his land,

12 And in all that mighty hand, and in all the great terror which Moses shewed in the sight of all Israel.

# THE BOOK OF
# JOSHUA

Joshua, the first of the twelve historical books (Joshua–Esther), forges a link between the Pentateuch and the remainder of Israel's history. Through three major military campaigns involving more than thirty enemy armies, the people of Israel learn a crucial lesson under Joshua's capable leadership: victory comes through faith in God and obedience to His word, rather than through military might or numerical superiority.

The title of this book is appropriately named after its central figure, Joshua. His original name is *Hoshea*, "Salvation" (Num. 13:8); but Moses evidently changes it to *Yehoshua*, "Yahweh Is Salvation" (Num. 13:16). He is also called *Yeshua*, a shortened form of *Yehoshua*. This is the Hebrew equivalent of the Greek name *Iesous* (Jesus). Thus, the Greek title given to the book in the Septuagint is *Iesous Naus*, "Joshua the Son of Nun." The Latin title is *Liber Josue*, the "Book of Joshua."

Joshua's name is symbolic of the fact that although he is the leader of the Israelite nation during the conquest, the Lord is the Conqueror.

## CHAPTER 1

Now after the death of Moses the servant of the LORD it came to pass, that the LORD spake unto Joshua the son of Nun, Moses' ªminister, saying,

2 ªMoses my servant is dead; now therefore arise, go over this Jordan, thou, and all this people, unto the land which I do give to them, *even* to the children of Israel.

3 ªEvery place that the sole of your foot shall tread upon, that have I given unto you, as I said unto Moses.

4 ªFrom the wilderness and this Lebanon even unto the great river, the river Euphrates, all the land of the Hittites, and unto the great sea toward the going down of the sun, shall be your coast.

5 ªThere shall not any man be able to stand before thee all the days of thy life: ᵇas I was with Moses, *so* ᶜI will be with thee: ᵈI will not fail thee, nor forsake thee.

6 ªBe strong and of a good courage: for unto this people ¹shalt thou divide for an inheritance the land, which I sware unto their fathers to give them.

7 Only be thou strong and very courageous, that thou mayest observe to do according to all the law, ªwhich Moses my servant commanded thee: ᵇturn not from it *to* the right hand or *to* the left, that thou mayest ¹prosper whithersoever thou goest.

8 ªThis book of the law shall ¹not depart out of thy mouth; but ᵇthou shalt meditate therein day and night, that thou mayest observe to do according to all that is written therein: for then thou shalt make thy way prosperous, and then thou shalt have good success.

9 ªHave not I commanded thee? Be strong and of a good courage; ᵇbe not afraid, neither be thou dismayed: for the LORD thy God *is* with thee whithersoever thou goest.

10 Then Joshua commanded the officers of the people, saying,

11 Pass through the host, and command the people, saying, Prepare you victuals; for ªwithin three days ye shall pass over this Jordan, to go in to possess the land, which the LORD your God giveth you to possess it.

12 And to the Reubenites, and to the Gadites, and to half the tribe of Manasseh, spake Joshua, saying,

13 Remember ªthe word which Moses the servant of the LORD commanded you, saying, The LORD your God hath given you rest, and hath given you this land.

14 Your wives, your little ones, and your cattle, shall remain in the land which Moses gave you on this side Jordan; but ye shall ¹pass before your brethren armed, all the mighty men of valour, and help them;

15 Until the LORD have given your brethren rest, as *he hath given* you, and they also have possessed the land which the LORD your God giveth them: ªthen ye shall return unto the land of your possession, and enjoy it, which Moses the LORD's servant gave you on this side Jordan toward the sunrising.

16 And they answered Joshua, saying, All that thou commandest us we will do, and whithersoever thou sendest us, we will go.

17 According as we hearkened unto Moses in all things, so will we hearken unto thee: only the LORD thy God ªbe with thee, as he was with Moses.

18 Whosoever *he be* that doth rebel against thy commandment, and will

## Cross-references

1:1 ª Ex. 24:13; Num. 13:16; 14:6, 29, 30, 37, 38; Deut. 1:38; Acts 7:45
1:2 ª Num. 12:7; Deut. 34:5
1:3 ª Deut. 11:24; Josh. 11:23
1:4 ª Gen. 15:18; Ex. 23:31; Num. 34:3–12
1:5 ª Deut. 7:24 ᵇ Ex. 3:12 ᶜ Deut. 31:8, 23 ᵈ Deut. 31:6, 7; Heb. 13:5
1:6 ª Deut. 31:7, 23 ¹ *you shall give as a possession*
1:7 ª Num. 27:23; Deut. 31:7; Josh. 11:15 ᵇ Deut. 5:32 ¹ *have success or act wisely*
1:8 ª Deut. 17:18, 19; 31:24, 26; Josh. 8:34 ᵇ Deut. 29:9; Ps. 1:1–3 ¹ *be constantly in*
1:9 ª Deut. 31:7 ᵇ Ps. 27:1
1:11 ª Deut. 9:1; Josh. 3:17
1:13 ª Num. 32:20–28
1:14 ¹ *cross over ahead of*
1:15 ª Josh. 22:1–4
1:17 ª 1 Sam. 20:13; 1 Kin. 1:37

196

not hearken unto thy words in all that thou commandest him, he shall be put to death: only be strong and of a good courage.

## CHAPTER 2

AND Joshua the son of Nun sent [a]out of [1]Shittim two men to spy secretly, saying, Go view the land, even Jericho. And they went, and [b]came into an harlot's house, named [c]Rahab, and [2]lodged there.

2 And [a]it was told the king of Jericho, saying, Behold, there came men in [1]hither to night of the children of Israel to search out the country.

3 And the king of Jericho sent unto Rahab, saying, Bring forth the men that are come to thee, which are entered into thine house: for they be come to search out all the country.

4 [a]And the woman took the two men, and hid them, and said thus, There came men unto me, but I [1]wist not [2]whence they *were:*

5 And it came to pass *about the time* of shutting of the gate, when it was dark, that the men went out: [1]whither the men went I [2]wot not: pursue after them quickly; for ye shall overtake them.

6 But [a]she had brought them up to the roof of the house, and hid them with the stalks of flax, which she had laid in order upon the roof.

7 And the men pursued after them the way to Jordan unto the fords: and as soon as they which pursued after them were gone out, they shut the gate.

8 And before they were laid down, she came up unto them upon the roof;

9 And she said unto the men, [a]I know that the LORD hath given you the land, and that [b]your[1] terror is fallen upon us, and that all the inhabitants of the land [c]faint because of you.

10 For we have heard how the LORD [a]dried up the water of the Red sea for you, when ye came out of Egypt; and [b]what ye did unto the two kings of the Amorites, that *were* on the other side Jordan, Sihon and Og, whom ye [c]utterly destroyed.

11 And as soon as we had [a]heard *these things,* [b]our hearts did melt, neither did there remain any more courage in any man, because of you: for [c]the LORD your God, he *is* God in heaven above, and in earth beneath.

12 Now therefore, I pray you, [a]swear unto me by the LORD, since I have shewed you kindness, that ye will also shew kindness unto [b]my father's house, and [c]give me [1]a true token:

13 And *that* ye will save [a]alive my father, and my mother, and my brethren,

and my sisters, and all that they have, and deliver our lives from death.

14 And the men answered her, Our life for yours, if [1]ye utter not this our business. And it shall be, when the LORD hath given us the land, that [a]we will deal kindly and truly with thee.

15 Then she [a]let them down by a cord through the window: for her house *was* upon the town wall, and she dwelt upon the wall.

16 And she said unto them, Get you to the mountain, lest the pursuers meet you; and hide yourselves there three days, until the pursuers be returned: and afterward may ye go your way.

17 And the men said unto her, We *will be* [a]blameless[1] of this thine oath which thou hast made us swear.

18 [a]Behold, *when* we come into the land, thou shalt bind this line of scarlet thread in the window which thou didst let us down by: [b]and thou shalt [1]bring thy father, and thy mother, and thy brethren, and all thy father's household, home unto thee.

19 And it shall be, *that* whosoever shall go out of the doors of thy house into the street, his blood *shall be* upon his head, and we *will be* [1]guiltless: and whosoever shall be with thee in the house, [a]his[2] blood *shall be* on our head, if *any* hand be upon him.

20 And if thou utter this our business, then we will be [1]quit of thine oath which thou hast made us to swear.

21 And she said, According unto your words, so *be* it. And she sent them away, and they departed: and she bound the scarlet line in the window.

22 And they went, and came unto the mountain, and abode there three days, until the pursuers were returned: and the pursuers sought *them* throughout all the way, but found *them* not.

23 So the two men returned, and descended from the mountain, and passed over, and came to Joshua the son of Nun, and told him all *things* that befell them:

24 And they said unto Joshua, Truly [a]the LORD hath delivered into our hands all the land; for even all the inhabitants of the country [1]do faint because of us.

## CHAPTER 3

AND Joshua rose early in the morning; and they removed [a]from [1]Shittim, and came to Jordan, he and all the children of Israel, and lodged there before they passed over.

2 And it came to pass [a]after three days, that the officers went through the host;

---

2:1 [a] Num. 25:1; Josh. 3:1  [b] Heb. 11:31; James 2:25  [c] Matt. 1:5  [1] Lit. *Acacia Grove*  [2] Lit. *lay down there*

2:2 [a] Josh. 2:22  [1] *here*

2:4 [a] 2 Sam. 17:19, 20  [1] *knew*  [2] *where they were from*

2:5 [1] *where*  [2] *know*

2:6 [a] Ex. 1:17; 2 Sam. 17:19

2:9 [a] Deut. 1:8  [b] Gen. 35:5; Ex. 23:27; Deut. 2:25; 11:25; Josh. 9:9, 10  [c] Ex. 15:15; Josh. 5:1  [1] *terror of you*

2:10 [a] Ex. 14:21; Josh. 4:23  [b] Num. 21:21–35  [c] Deut. 20:17; Josh. 6:21

2:11 [a] Ex. 15:14, 15  [b] Josh. 5:1; 7:5; Ps. 22:14; Is. 13:7  [c] Deut. 4:39

2:12 [a] 1 Sam. 20:14, 15, 17  [b] 1 Tim. 5:8  [c] Ex. 12:13; Josh. 2:18  [1] *a pledge of faithfulness*

2:13 [a] Josh. 6:23–25

2:14 [a] Gen. 47:29; Judg. 1:24; [Matt. 5:7]  [1] *none of you tell this business of ours*

2:15 [a] Acts 9:25

2:17 [a] Ex. 20:7  [1] *free from obligation to*

2:18 [a] Josh. 2:12  [b] Josh. 6:23  [1] Lit. *gather*

2:19 [a] 1 Kin. 2:32; Matt. 27:25  [1] *free from obligation to*  [2] *guilt of his bloodshed*

2:20 [1] *free from obligation to*

2:24 [a] Ex. 23:31; Josh. 6:2; 21:44  [1] *are fainthearted*

3:1 [a] Josh. 2:1  [1] Lit. *Acacia Grove*

3:2 [a] Josh. 1:10, 11

---

3 And they commanded the people, saying, [a]When ye see the ark of the covenant of the LORD your God, [b]and the priests the Levites [1]bearing it, then ye shall remove from your place, and go after it.

4 [a]Yet there shall be a space between you and it, about two thousand cubits by measure: come not near unto it, that ye may know the way by which ye must go: for ye have not passed *this* way [1]heretofore.

5 And Joshua said unto the people, [a]Sanctify[1] yourselves: for to morrow the LORD will do wonders among you.

6 And Joshua spake unto the priests, saying, [a]Take up the ark of the covenant, and pass over before the people. And they took up the ark of the covenant, and went before the people.

7 And the LORD said unto Joshua, This day will I begin to [a]magnify[1] thee in the sight of all Israel, that they may know that, [b]as I was with Moses, *so* I will be with thee.

8 And thou shalt command [a]the priests that bear the ark of the covenant, saying, When ye are come to the brink of the water of Jordan, [b]ye shall stand still in Jordan.

9 And Joshua said unto the children of Israel, Come hither, and hear the words of the LORD your God.

10 And Joshua said, Hereby ye shall know that [a]the living God *is* among you, and *that* he will without fail [b]drive out from before you the [c]Canaanites, and the Hittites, and the Hivites, and the Perizzites, and the Girgashites, and the Amorites, and the Jebusites.

11 Behold, the ark of the covenant of [a]the Lord of all the earth passeth over before you into Jordan.

12 Now therefore [a]take you twelve men out of the tribes of Israel, out of every tribe a man.

13 And it shall come to pass, [a]as soon as the soles of the feet of the priests that bear the ark of the LORD, [b]the Lord of all the earth, shall rest in the waters of Jordan, *that* the waters of Jordan shall be cut off *from* the waters that come down from above; and they [c]shall stand [1]upon an heap.

14 And it came to pass, when the people removed from their tents, to pass over Jordan, and the priests bearing the [a]ark of the covenant before the people;

15 And as they that bare the ark were come unto Jordan, and [a]the feet of the priests that bare the ark were dipped in the brim of the water, (for [b]Jordan overfloweth all his banks [c]all the time of harvest,)

16 That the waters which came down from above stood *and* rose up

upon an heap very far [1]from the city Adam, that *is* beside [a]Zaretan: and those that came down [b]toward the sea of the plain, *even* [c]the salt sea, failed, *and* were cut off: and the people passed over right against Jericho.

17 And the priests that bare the ark of the covenant of the LORD stood firm on dry ground in the midst of Jordan, [a]and all the Israelites passed over on dry ground, until all the people were passed [1]clean over Jordan.

## CHAPTER 4

AND it came to pass, when all the people were [1]clean passed [a]over Jordan, that the LORD spake unto Joshua, saying,

2 [a]Take you twelve men out of the people, out of every tribe a man,

3 And command ye them, saying, Take you hence out of the midst of Jordan, out of the place where [a]the priests' feet stood firm, twelve stones, and ye shall carry them over with you, and leave them in [b]the lodging place, where ye shall lodge this night.

4 Then Joshua called the twelve men, whom he had prepared of the children of Israel, out of every tribe a man:

5 And Joshua said unto them, Pass over before the ark of the LORD your God into the midst of Jordan, and take you up every man of you a stone upon his shoulder, according unto the number of the tribes of the children of Israel:

6 That this may be [a]a sign among you, *that* [b]when your children ask *their fathers* in time to come, saying, [1]What *mean* ye by these stones?

7 Then ye shall answer them, That [a]the waters of Jordan were cut off before the ark of the covenant of the LORD; when it passed over Jordan, the waters of Jordan were cut off: and these stones shall be for [b]a memorial unto the children of Israel for ever.

8 And the children of Israel did so as Joshua commanded, and took up twelve stones out of the midst of Jordan, as the LORD spake unto Joshua, according to the number of the tribes of the children of Israel, and carried them over with them unto the place where they lodged, and laid them down there.

9 And Joshua set up twelve stones in the midst of Jordan, in the place where the feet of the priests which bare the ark of the covenant stood: and they are there unto this day.

10 For the priests which bare the ark stood in the midst of Jordan, until every thing was finished that the LORD commanded Joshua to speak

### Cross references (center column)

3:3 [a] Num. 10:33
[b] Deut. 31:9, 25
[1] *carrying*

3:4 [a] Ex. 19:12
[1] *before*

3:5 [a] Ex. 19:10, 14, 15; Lev. 20:7; Num. 11:18; Josh. 7:13; 1 Sam. 16:5; Job 1:5; Joel 2:16
[1] *Consecrate*

3:6 [a] Num. 4:15

3:7 [a] Josh. 4:14; 1 Chr. 29:25; 2 Chr. 1:1 [b] Josh. 1:5, 9 [1] *make you great*

3:8 [a] Josh. 3:3
[b] Josh. 3:17

3:10 [a] Deut. 5:26; Josh. 11:23; 1 Sam. 17:26; 2 Kin. 19:4; Hos. 1:10; Matt. 16:16; 1 Thess. 1:9
[b] Ex. 33:2; Deut. 7:1; 18:12; Ps. 44:2 [c] Acts 13:19

3:11 [a] Josh. 3:13; Job 41:11; Ps. 24:1; Mic. 4:13; Zech. 4:14; 6:5

3:12 [a] Josh. 4:2, 4

3:13 [a] Josh. 3:15, 16 [b] Josh. 3:11 [c] Ps. 78:13; 114:3 [1] *in a heap*

3:14 [a] Ps. 132:8; Acts 7:44, 45

3:15 [a] Josh. 3:13 [b] 1 Chr. 12:15; Jer. 12:5; 49:19 [c] Josh. 4:18; 5:10, 12

3:16 [a] 1 Kin. 4:12; 7:46 [b] Deut. 3:17 [c] Gen. 14:3; Num. 34:3 [1] *at Adam*

3:17 [a] Gen. 50:24; Ex. 3:8; 6:1–8; 14:21, 22, 29; 33:1; Deut. 6:10; Heb. 11:29 [1] *completely*

4:1 [a] Deut. 27:2; Josh. 3:17 [1] *completely*

4:2 [a] Josh. 3:12

4:3 [a] Josh. 3:13 [b] Josh. 4:19, 20

4:6 [a] Deut. 27:2; Ps. 103:2 [b] Ex. 12:26; 13:14; Deut. 6:20 [1] *What do these stones mean to you?*

4:7 [a] Josh. 3:13, 16 [b] Ex. 16:14; Num. 16:40

unto the people, according to all that Moses commanded Joshua: and the people [1]hasted and passed over.

11 And it came to pass, when all the people were [1]clean passed over, that the [a]ark of the LORD passed over, and the priests, in the presence of the people.

12 And [a]the children of Reuben, and the children of Gad, and half the tribe of Manasseh, passed over armed before the children of Israel, as Moses spake unto them:

13 About forty thousand [1]prepared for war passed over before the LORD unto battle, to the plains of Jericho.

14 On that day the LORD [a]magnified[1] Joshua in the sight of all Israel; and they [2]feared him, as they feared Moses, all the days of his life.

15 And the LORD spake unto Joshua, saying,

16 Command the priests that bear [a]the ark of the testimony, that they come up out of Jordan.

17 Joshua therefore commanded the priests, saying, Come ye up out of Jordan.

18 And it came to pass, when the priests that bare the ark of the covenant of the LORD were come up out of the midst of Jordan, *and* the soles of the priests' feet were lifted up unto the dry land, that the waters of Jordan returned unto their place, [a]and flowed over all his banks, as *they did* before.

19 And the people came up out of Jordan on the tenth *day* of the first month, and encamped [a]in Gilgal, in the east border of Jericho.

20 And [a]those twelve stones, which they took out of Jordan, did Joshua [1]pitch in Gilgal.

21 And he spake unto the children of Israel, saying, [a]When your children shall ask their fathers in time to come, saying, What *mean* these stones?

22 Then ye shall let your children know, saying, [a]Israel came over this Jordan on [b]dry land.

23 For the LORD your God dried up the waters of Jordan from before you, until ye were passed over, as the LORD your God did to the Red sea, [a]which he dried up from before us, until we were gone over:

24 [a]That all the people of the earth might know the hand of the LORD, that it *is* [b]mighty: that ye might [c]fear[1] the LORD your God [2]for ever.

## CHAPTER 5

AND it came to pass, when all the kings of the Amorites, which *were* on the side of Jordan westward, and all the kings of the Canaanites, [a]which *were* by the sea, [b]heard that

the LORD had dried up the waters of Jordan from before the children of Israel, until [1]we were passed over, that [2]their heart melted, [c]neither was there spirit in them any more, because of the children of Israel.

2 At that time the LORD said unto Joshua, Make thee [a]sharp knives, and circumcise again the children of Israel the second time.

3 And Joshua made him sharp knives, and circumcised the children of Israel at [1]the hill of the foreskins.

4 And this *is* the cause why Joshua did circumcise: [a]All the people that came out of Egypt, *that were* males, *even* all the men of war, died in the wilderness by the way, after they came out of Egypt.

5 Now all the people that came out were circumcised: but all the people *that were* born in the wilderness by the way as they came forth out of Egypt, *them* they had not circumcised.

6 For the children of Israel walked [a]forty years in the wilderness, till all the people *that were* men of war, which came out of Egypt, were [1]consumed, because they obeyed not the voice of the LORD: unto whom the LORD sware that [b]he would not shew them the land, which the LORD sware unto their fathers that he would give us, [c]a land that [2]floweth with milk and honey.

7 And [a]their children, *whom* he raised up in their [1]stead, them Joshua circumcised: for they were uncircumcised, because they had not circumcised them by the way.

8 And it came to pass, when they had done circumcising all the people, that they abode in their places in the camp, [a]till they were [1]whole.

9 And the LORD said unto Joshua, This day have I rolled away [a]the reproach of Egypt from off you. Wherefore the name of the place is called [b]Gilgal[1] unto this day.

10 And the children of Israel encamped in Gilgal, and kept the passover [a]on the fourteenth day of the month at even in the plains of Jericho.

11 And they did eat of the [1]old corn of the land on the morrow after the passover, unleavened cakes, and [2]parched *corn* in the selfsame day.

12 And [a]the manna ceased on the morrow after they had eaten of the old corn of the land; neither had the children of Israel manna any more; but they did eat of the fruit of the land of Canaan that year.

13 And it came to pass, when Joshua was by Jericho, that he lifted up his eyes and looked, and, behold, there stood [a]a man [1]over against him [b]with his sword drawn in his hand:

### Center References

4:10 [1] *hurried*
4:11 [a] Josh. 3:11;
6:11 [1] *completely*
4:12 [a] Num. 32:17, 20, 27, 28; Josh. 1:14
4:13 [1] *equipped*
4:14 [a] Josh. 3:7; 1 Chr. 29:25 [1] Lit. *made Joshua great* [2] *revered*
4:16 [a] Ex. 25:16, 22
4:18 [a] Josh. 3:15; 1 Chr. 12:15
4:19 [a] Josh. 5:9
4:20 [a] Deut. 11:30; Josh. 4:3; 5:9, 10 [1] *set up*
4:21 [a] Josh. 4:6
4:22 [a] Ex. 12:26, 27; 13:8–14; Deut. 26:5–9 [b] Josh. 3:17
4:23 [a] Ex. 14:21
4:24 [a] 1 Kin. 8:42; 2 Kin. 19:19; Ps. 106:8 [b] Ex. 15:16; 1 Chr. 29:12; Ps. 89:13 [c] Ex. 14:31; Deut. 6:2; Ps. 76:7; Jer. 10:7 [1] *stand in awe of* [2] Lit. *all the days*
5:1 [a] Num. 13:29 [b] Ex. 15:14, 15 [c] Josh. 2:10, 11; 9:9; 1 Kin. 10:5 [1] Qr., some Heb. mss. and editions, LXX, Syr., Tg., Vg. *they* [2] *their courage failed*
5:2 [a] Ex. 4:25
5:3 [1] Heb. *Gibeath-haaraloth*
5:4 [a] Num. 14:29; 26:64, 65; Deut. 2:14–16
5:6 [a] Num. 14:33; Deut. 1:3; 29:5 [b] Num. 14:23, 29–35; 26:23–65; Heb. 3:11 [c] Ex. 3:8 [1] *destroyed* [2] *is abundant in good food*
5:7 [a] Num. 14:31; Deut. 1:39 [1] *place*
5:8 [a] Gen. 34:25 [1] *healed*
5:9 [a] Gen. 34:14 [b] Josh. 4:19 [1] Lit. *Rolling*
5:10 [a] Ex. 12:6; Num. 9:5
5:11 [1] *produce* [2] *roasted grain*
5:12 [a] Ex. 16:35
5:13 [a] Gen. 18:1, 2; 32:24, 30; Ex. 23:23; Num. 22:31; Zech. 1:8; Acts 1:10 [b] Num. 22:23; 1 Chr. 21:16 [1] *opposite*

and Joshua went unto him, and said unto him, *Art* thou for us, or for our adversaries?

14 And he said, Nay; but *as* captain of the host of the LORD am I now come. And Joshua ªfell on his face to the earth, and did ᵇworship, and said unto him, What saith my lord unto his servant?

15 And the captain of the LORD's host said unto Joshua, ªLoose thy shoe from off thy foot; for the place whereon thou standest *is* holy. And Joshua did so.

## CHAPTER 6

Now ªJericho was ¹straitly shut up because of the children of Israel: none went out, and none came in.

2 And the LORD said unto Joshua, See, ªI have given into thine hand Jericho, and the ᵇking thereof, *and* the mighty men of valour.

3 And ye shall ¹compass the city, all *ye* men of war, *and* go round about the city once. Thus shalt thou do six days.

4 And seven priests shall bear before the ark seven ªtrumpets of rams' horns: and the seventh day ye shall compass the city ᵇseven times, and ᶜthe priests shall blow with the trumpets.

5 And it shall come to pass, that when they make a long *blast* with the ram's horn, *and* when ye hear the sound of the trumpet, all the people shall shout with a great shout; and the wall of the city shall fall down flat, and the people shall ¹ascend up every man straight before him.

6 And Joshua the son of Nun called the priests, and said unto them, Take up the ark of the covenant, and let seven priests bear seven trumpets of rams' horns before the ark of the LORD.

7 And he said unto the people, Pass on, and compass the city, and let him that is armed pass on before the ark of the LORD.

8 And it came to pass, when Joshua had spoken unto the people, that the seven priests bearing the seven trumpets of rams' horns passed on before the LORD, and blew with the trumpets: and the ark of the covenant of the LORD followed them.

9 And the armed men went before the priests that blew with the trumpets, ªand the ¹rereward came after the ark, *the priests* going on, and blowing with the trumpets.

10 And Joshua had commanded the people, saying, Ye shall not shout, nor make any noise with your voice, neither shall *any* word proceed out of your mouth, until the day I bid you shout; then shall ye shout.

11 So the ªark of the LORD compassed the city, going about *it* once: and they came into the camp, and ¹lodged in the camp.

12 And Joshua rose early in the morning, ªand the priests took up the ark of the LORD.

13 And seven priests bearing seven trumpets of rams' horns before the ark of the LORD went on continually, and blew with the trumpets: and the armed men went before them; but the ¹rereward came after the ark of the LORD, *the priests* going on, and blowing with the trumpets.

14 And the second day they compassed the city once, and returned into the camp: so they did six days.

15 And it came to pass on the seventh day, that they rose early about the dawning of the day, and compassed the city after the same manner seven times: only on that day they compassed the city seven times.

16 And it came to pass at the seventh time, when the priests blew with the trumpets, Joshua said unto the people, Shout; for the LORD hath given you the city.

17 And the city shall be ªaccursed,¹ *even* it, and all that *are* therein, to the LORD: only ᵇRahab the harlot shall live, she and all that *are* with her in the house, because ᶜshe hid the messengers that we sent.

18 And ye, ªin any wise keep *yourselves* from the accursed thing, lest ye make *yourselves* accursed, when ye take of the accursed thing, and make the camp of Israel a curse, ᵇand trouble it.

19 But all the silver, and gold, and vessels of brass and iron, *are* ¹consecrated unto the LORD: they ²shall come into the treasury of the LORD.

20 So the people shouted when *the priests* blew with the trumpets: and it came to pass, when the people heard the sound of the trumpet, and the people shouted with a great shout, that ªthe wall fell down flat, so that the people went up into the city, every man straight before him, and they took the city.

21 And they ªutterly destroyed all that *was* in the city, both man and woman, young and old, and ox, and sheep, and ass, with the edge of the sword.

22 But Joshua had said unto the two men that had spied out the country, Go into the harlot's house, and bring out thence the woman, and all that she hath, ªas ye sware unto her.

23 And the young men that were spies went in, and brought out Rahab, ªand her father, and her mother, and her brethren, and all that she had; and they brought out all her

¹kindred, and left them ²without the camp of Israel.

24 And they burnt the city with fire, and all that *was* therein: only the silver, and the gold, and the vessels of brass and of iron, they put into the treasury of the house of the LORD.

25 And Joshua saved Rahab the harlot alive, and her father's household, and all that she had; and ªshe dwelleth in Israel *even* unto this day; because she hid the messengers, which Joshua sent to spy out Jericho.

26 And Joshua ¹adjured *them* at that time, saying, ªCursed *be* the man before the LORD, that riseth up and buildeth this city Jericho: he shall lay the foundation thereof in his firstborn, and in his youngest *son* shall he set up the gates of it.

27 So the LORD was with Joshua; and his fame was ¹noised throughout all the country.

## CHAPTER 7

**B**UT the children of Israel ¹committed a ªtrespass in the ᵇaccursed thing: for ᶜAchan, the son of Carmi, the son of Zabdi, the son of Zerah, of the tribe of Judah, took of the accursed thing: and the anger of the LORD was ²kindled against the children of Israel.

2 And Joshua sent men from Jericho to Ai, which *is* beside Beth-aven, on the east side of Beth-el, and spake unto them, saying, Go up and ¹view the country. And the men went up and viewed Ai.

3 And they returned to Joshua, and said unto him, Let not all the people go up; but let about two or three thousand men go up and smite Ai; *and* ¹make not all the people to labour thither; for they *are but* few.

4 So there went up thither of the people about three thousand men: ªand they fled before the men of Ai.

5 And the men of Ai ¹smote of them about thirty and six men: for they chased them *from* before the gate *even* unto Shebarim, and smote them ²in the going down: wherefore ªthe ³hearts of the people melted, and became as water.

6 And Joshua ªrent¹ his clothes, and fell to the earth upon his face before the ark of the LORD until the eventide, he and the elders of Israel, and ᵇput dust upon their heads.

7 And Joshua said, Alas, O Lord ¹GOD, ªwherefore hast thou at all brought this people over Jordan, to deliver us into the hand of the Amorites, to destroy us? would to God we had been content, and dwelt on the other side Jordan!

8 O Lord, what shall I say, when Israel turneth their ¹backs before their enemies!

9 For the Canaanites and all the inhabitants of the land shall hear *of it,* and shall ¹environ us round, and ªcut off our name from the earth: and ᵇwhat wilt thou do unto thy great name?

10 And the LORD said unto Joshua, Get thee up; wherefore liest thou thus upon thy face?

11 Israel hath sinned, and they have also transgressed my covenant which I commanded them: ªfor they have even taken of the ¹accursed thing, and have also stolen, and ᵇdissembled² also, and they have put *it* even among their own stuff.

12 ªTherefore the children of Israel could not stand before their enemies, *but* turned *their* backs before their enemies, because ᵇthey were ¹accursed: neither will I be with you any more, except ye destroy the accursed from among you.

13 Up, ªsanctify¹ the people, and say, ᵇSanctify yourselves against to morrow: for thus saith the LORD God of Israel, *There is* an accursed thing in the midst of thee, O Israel: thou canst not stand before thine enemies, until ye take away the accursed thing from among you.

14 In the morning therefore ye shall be brought according to your tribes: and it shall be, *that* the tribe which ªthe LORD taketh shall come according to the families *thereof;* and the family which the LORD shall take shall come by households; and the household which the LORD shall take shall come man by man.

15 ªAnd it shall be, *that* he that is taken with the accursed thing shall be burnt with fire, he and all that he hath: because he hath ᵇtransgressed¹ the covenant of the LORD, and because he ᶜhath ²wrought folly in Israel.

16 So Joshua rose up early in the morning, and brought Israel by their tribes: and the tribe of Judah was taken:

17 And he brought the family of Judah; and he took the family of the Zarhites: and he brought the family of the Zarhites man by man; and Zabdi was taken:

18 And he brought his household man by man; and Achan, the son of Carmi, the son of Zabdi, the son of Zerah, of the tribe of Judah, ªwas taken.

19 And Joshua said unto Achan, My son, ªgive, I pray thee, glory to the LORD God of Israel, ᵇand make confession unto him; and ᶜtell me now what thou hast done; hide *it* not from me.

20 And Achan answered Joshua, and said, Indeed ªI have sinned against the LORD God of Israel, and thus and thus have I done:

### Cross references (center column)

6:23 ¹ *relatives* ² *outside*

6:25 ª [Matt. 1:5]

6:26 ª 1 Kin. 16:34 ¹ *warned*

6:27 ¹ *spread*

7:1 ª Josh. 7:20, 21 ᵇ Josh. 6:17–19 ᶜ Josh. 22:20 ¹ *acted unfaithfully regarding the devoted things* ² *burned*

7:2 ¹ *spy out*

7:3 ¹ *do not weary all the people*

7:4 ª Lev. 26:17; Deut. 28:25

7:5 ª Lev. 26:36; Josh. 2:9, 11 ¹ *struck down* ² *on the descent* ³ *the people's courage failed*

7:6 ª Gen. 37:29, 34 ᵇ 1 Sam. 4:12 ¹ *tore*

7:7 ª Ex. 17:3; Num. 21:5 ¹ Heb. YHWH (LORD)

7:8 ¹ Lit. *necks*

7:9 ª Deut. 32:26 ᵇ Ex. 32:12; Num. 14:13 ¹ *surround us*

7:11 ª Josh. 6:17–19 ᵇ Acts 5:1, 2 ¹ *things devoted to the LORD* ² *deceived*

7:12 ª Judg. 2:14 ᵇ Deut. 7:26; [Hag. 2:13, 14] ¹ *devoted to destruction*

7:13 ª Ex. 19:10 ᵇ Josh. 3:5 ¹ *consecrate*

7:14 ª [Prov. 16:33]

7:15 ª 1 Sam. 14:38, 39 ᵇ Josh. 7:11 ᶜ Gen. 34:7; Judg. 20:6 ¹ *overstepped* ² *done a disgraceful thing*

7:18 ª 1 Sam. 14:42

7:19 ª 1 Sam. 6:5; Jer. 13:16; John 9:24 ᵇ Num. 5:6, 7; 2 Chr. 30:22; Ezra 10:10, 11; Ps. 32:5; Prov. 28:13; Jer. 3:12, 13; Dan. 9:4 ᶜ 1 Sam. 14:43

7:20 ª Num. 22:34; 1 Sam. 15:24

21 When I saw among the spoils a goodly Babylonish garment, and two hundred shekels of silver, and a wedge of gold of fifty shekels weight, then I ¹coveted them, and took them; and, behold, they *are* hid in the earth in the midst of my tent, and the silver under it.

22 So Joshua sent messengers, and they ran unto the tent; and, behold, *it was* hid in his tent, and the silver under it.

23 And they took them out of the midst of the tent, and brought them unto Joshua, and unto all the children of Israel, and laid them out before the LORD.

24 And Joshua, and all Israel with him, took Achan the son of Zerah, and the silver, and the garment, and the wedge of gold, and his sons, and his daughters, and his oxen, and his asses, and his sheep, and his tent, and ªall that he had: and they brought them unto ᵇthe valley of Achor.

25 And Joshua said, ªWhy hast thou troubled us? the LORD shall trouble thee this day. ᵇAnd all Israel stoned him with stones, and burned them with fire, after they had stoned them with stones.

26 And they ªraised over him a great heap of stones unto this day. So ᵇthe LORD turned from the fierceness of his anger. Wherefore the name of that place was called, ᶜThe valley of ¹Achor, unto this day.

## CHAPTER 8

A ND the LORD said unto Joshua, ªFear not, neither be thou dismayed: take all the people of war with thee, and arise, go up to Ai: see, ᵇI have given into thy hand the king of Ai, and his people, and his city, and his land:

2 And thou shalt do to Ai and her king as thou didst unto ªJericho and her king: only ᵇthe spoil thereof, and the cattle thereof, shall ye take ¹for a prey unto yourselves: lay thee an ambush for the city behind it.

3 So Joshua arose, and all the people of war, to go up against Ai: and Joshua chose out thirty thousand mighty men of valour, and sent them away by night.

4 And he commanded them, saying, Behold, ªye shall lie in wait against the city, *even* behind the city: go not very far from the city, but be ye all ready:

5 And I, and all the people that *are* with me, will approach unto the city: and it shall come to pass, when they come out against us, as at the first, that ªwe will flee before them,

6 (For they will come out after us) till we have drawn them from the

### Cross-references

7:21 ¹ *desired*
7:24 ª Num. 16:32, 33; Dan. 6:24 ᵇ Josh. 7:26; 15:7
7:25 ª Josh. 6:18; 1 Chr. 2:7; [Gal. 5:12] ᵇ Deut. 17:5
7:26 ª Josh. 8:29; 2 Sam. 18:17; Lam. 3:53 ᵇ Deut. 13:17 ᶜ Josh. 7:24; Is. 65:10; Hos. 2:15 ¹ Lit. *Trouble*
8:1 ª Deut. 1:21; 7:18; 31:8; Josh. 1:9; 10:8 ᵇ Josh. 6:2
8:2 ª Josh. 6:21 ᵇ Deut. 20:14; Josh. 8:27 ¹ *as booty for*
8:4 ª Judg. 20:29
8:5 ª Josh. 7:5; Judg. 20:32

city; for they will say, They flee before us, as at the first: therefore we will flee before them.

7 Then ye shall rise up from the ambush, and seize upon the city: for the LORD your God will deliver it into your hand.

8 And it shall be, when ye have taken the city, *that* ye shall set the city on fire: according to the commandment of the LORD shall ye do. ªSee, I have commanded you.

9 Joshua therefore sent them forth: and they went to lie in ambush, and abode between Beth-el and Ai, on the west side of Ai: but Joshua lodged that night among the people.

10 And Joshua rose up early in the morning, and ¹numbered the people, and went up, he and the elders of Israel, before the people to Ai.

11 ªAnd all the people, *even the people* of war that *were* with him, went up, and drew nigh, and came before the city, and ¹pitched on the north side of Ai: now *there was* a valley between them and Ai.

12 And he took about five thousand men, and set them to lie in ambush between Beth-el and Ai, on the west side of ¹the city.

13 And when they had set the people, *even* all the host that *was* on the north of the city, and ¹their liers in wait on the west of the city, Joshua went that night into the midst of the valley.

14 And it came to pass, when the king of Ai saw *it*, that they ¹hasted and rose up early, and the men of the city went out against Israel to battle, he and all his people, at a time appointed, before the plain; but he ªwist² not that *there were* liers in ambush against him behind the city.

15 And Joshua and all Israel ªmade as if they were beaten before them, and fled by the way of the wilderness.

16 And all the people that *were* in Ai were called together to pursue after them: and they pursued after Joshua, and were drawn away from the city.

17 And there was not a man left in Ai or Beth-el, that went not out after Israel: and they left the city open, and pursued after Israel.

18 And the LORD said unto Joshua, Stretch out the spear that *is* in thy hand toward Ai; for I will give it into thine hand. And Joshua stretched out the spear that *he had* in his hand toward the city.

19 And the ambush arose quickly out of their place, and they ran as soon as he had stretched out his hand: and they entered into the city, and took it, and ¹hasted and set the city on fire.

20 And when the men of Ai looked behind them, they saw, and, behold,

### Cross-references (right column)

8:8 ª 2 Sam. 13:28
8:10 ¹ *mustered*
8:11 ª Josh. 8:5 ¹ *camped*
8:12 ¹ Ai
8:13 ¹ *its rear guard*
8:14 ª Judg. 20:34; Eccl. 9:12 ¹ *hurried* ² *did not know*
8:15 ª Judg. 20:36
8:19 ¹ *hurried*

the smoke of the city ascended up to heaven, and they had no power to flee this way or that way: and the people that fled to the wilderness turned back upon the pursuers.

21 And when Joshua and all Israel saw that the ambush had taken the city, and that the smoke of the city ascended, then they turned again, and slew the men of Ai.

22 And the other issued out of the city against them; so they were in the midst of Israel, some on this side, and some on that side: and they ¹smote them, so that they ᵃlet none of them remain or escape.

23 And the king of Ai they took alive, and brought him to Joshua.

24 And it came to pass, when Israel had made an end of slaying all the inhabitants of Ai in the field, in the wilderness wherein they chased them, and when they were all fallen ¹on the edge of the sword, until they were consumed, that all the Israelites returned unto Ai, and ²smote it with the edge of the sword.

25 And *so* it was, *that* all that fell that day, both of men and women, *were* twelve thousand, *even* all the men of Ai.

26 For Joshua drew not his hand back, wherewith he stretched out the spear, until he had ᵃutterly destroyed all the inhabitants of Ai.

27 ᵃOnly the cattle and the spoil of that city Israel took for a prey unto themselves, according unto the word of the LORD which he ᵇcommanded Joshua.

28 And Joshua burnt Ai, and made it ᵃan heap for ever, *even* a desolation unto this day.

29 ᵃAnd the king of Ai he hanged on a tree until eventide: ᵇand as soon as the sun was down, Joshua commanded that they should take his carcase down from the tree, and cast it at the entering of the gate of the city, and ᶜraise thereon a great heap of stones, *that remaineth* unto this day.

30 Then Joshua built an altar unto the LORD God of Israel ᵃin mount Ebal,

31 As Moses the servant of the LORD commanded the children of Israel, as it is written in the book of the law of Moses, ᵃan altar of whole stones, over which no man hath ¹lift up *any* iron: and ᵇthey offered thereon burnt offerings unto the LORD, and sacrificed peace offerings.

32 And ᵃhe wrote there upon the stones a copy of the law of Moses, which he wrote in the presence of the children of Israel.

33 And all Israel, and their elders, and officers, and their judges, stood

on ¹this side the ark and on that side before the priests the Levites, ᵃwhich bare the ark of the covenant of the LORD, as well ᵇthe stranger, as he that was born among them; half of them over against mount Gerizim, and half of them over against mount Ebal; ᶜas Moses the servant of the LORD had commanded before, that they should bless the people of Israel.

34 And afterward ᵃhe read all the words of the law, ᵇthe blessings and cursings, according to all that is written in the ᶜbook of the law.

35 There was not a word of all that Moses commanded, which Joshua read not before all the congregation of Israel, ᵃwith the women, and the little ones, ᵇand the strangers that were ¹conversant among them.

## CHAPTER 9

AND it came to pass, when ᵃall the kings which *were* on this side Jordan, in the hills, and in the valleys, and in all the coasts of ᵇthe great sea over against Lebanon, ᶜthe Hittite, and the Amorite, the Canaanite, the Perizzite, the Hivite, and the Jebusite, heard *thereof;*

2 That they ᵃgathered themselves together, to fight with Joshua and with Israel, with one ¹accord.

3 And when the inhabitants of ᵃGibeon ᵇheard what Joshua had done unto Jericho and to Ai,

4 They did work ¹willily, and went and ²made as if they had been ambassadors, and took old sacks upon their asses, and wine bottles, old, and ³rent, and ⁴bound up;

5 And old shoes and ¹clouted upon their feet, and old garments upon them; and all the bread of their provision was dry *and* mouldy.

6 And they went to Joshua ᵃunto the camp at Gilgal, and said unto him, and to the men of Israel, We be come from a far country: now therefore make ye a ¹league with us.

7 And the men of Israel said unto the ᵃHivites, ¹Peradventure ye dwell among us; and ᵇhow shall we make a ²league with you?

8 And they said unto Joshua, ᵃWe *are* thy servants. And Joshua said unto them, Who *are* ye? and from whence come ye?

9 And they said unto him, ᵃFrom a very far country thy servants are come because of the name of the LORD thy God: for we have ᵇheard the fame of him, and all that he did in Egypt,

10 And ᵃall that he did to the two kings of the Amorites, that *were* beyond Jordan, to Sihon king of Heshbon, and to Og king of Bashan, which *was* at Ashtaroth.

---

8:22 ᵃ Deut. 7:2
¹ struck them down
8:24 ¹ Or by
² struck
8:26 ᵃ Josh. 6:21
8:27 ᵃ Num. 31:22, 26 ᵇ Josh. 8:2
8:28 ᵃ Deut. 13:16
8:29 ᵃ Josh. 10:26 ᵇ Deut. 21:22, 23; Josh. 10:27 ᶜ Josh. 7:26; 10:27
8:30 ᵃ Deut. 27:4–8
8:31 ᵃ Ex. 20:25; Deut. 27:5, 6 ᵇ Ex. 20:24 ¹ wielded any iron tool
8:32 ᵃ Deut. 27:2, 3, 8

8:33 ᵃ Deut. 31:9, 25 ᵇ Deut. 31:12 ᶜ Deut. 11:29; 27:12 ¹ either side of the ark
8:34 ᵃ Deut. 31:11; Neh. 8:3 ᵇ Deut. 28:2, 15, 45; 29:20, 21; 30:19 ᶜ Josh. 1:8
8:35 ᵃ Ex. 12:38; Deut. 31:12 ᵇ Josh. 8:33 ¹ living
9:1 ᵃ Num. 13:29; Josh. 3:10 ᵇ Num. 34:6 ᶜ Ex. 3:17; 23:23
9:2 ᵃ Josh. 10:5; Ps. 83:3, 5 ¹ mouth
9:3 ᵃ Josh. 9:17, 22; 10:2; 21:17; 2 Sam. 21:1, 2 ᵇ Josh. 6:27
9:4 ¹ craftily ² acted as envoys ³ torn ⁴ mended, lit. tied up
9:5 ¹ patched
9:6 ᵃ Josh. 5:10 ¹ covenant or treaty
9:7 ᵃ Josh. 9:1; 11:19 ᵇ Ex. 23:32; Deut. 7:2 ¹ Perhaps you are living in our midst ² covenant
9:8 ᵃ Deut. 20:11; 2 Kin. 10:5
9:9 ᵃ Deut. 20:15 ᵇ Ex. 15:14; Josh. 2:9, 10; 5:1
9:10 ᵃ Num. 21:24, 33

11 Wherefore our elders and all the inhabitants of our country spake to us, saying, Take victuals with you for the journey, and go to meet them, and say unto them, We *are* your servants: therefore now make ye a [1]league with us.

12 This our bread we took hot *for* our provision out of our houses on the day we came forth to go unto you; but now, behold, it is dry, and it is mouldy:

13 And these bottles of wine, which we filled, *were* new; and, behold, they be [1]rent: and these our garments and our shoes are become old by reason of the very long journey.

14 And the men took of their victuals, [a]and asked not *counsel* at the mouth of the LORD.

15 And Joshua [a]made peace with them, and made a [1]league with them, to let them live: and the princes of the congregation sware unto them.

16 And it came to pass at the end of three days after they had made a league with them, that they heard that they *were* their neighbours, and *that* they dwelt among them.

17 And the children of Israel journeyed, and came unto their cities on the third day. Now their cities *were* [a]Gibeon, and Chephirah, and Beeroth, and Kirjath-jearim.

18 And the children of Israel [1]smote them not, [a]because the princes of the congregation had sworn unto them by the LORD God of Israel. And all the congregation [2]murmured against the princes.

19 But all the princes said unto all the congregation, We have sworn unto them by the LORD God of Israel: now therefore we may not touch them.

20 This we will do to them; we will even let them live, lest [a]wrath be upon us, because of the oath which we sware unto them.

21 And the princes said unto them, Let them live; but let them be [a]hewers of wood and drawers of water unto all the congregation; as the princes had [b]promised them.

22 And Joshua called for them, and he spake unto them, saying, [1]Wherefore have ye beguiled us, saying, [a]We *are* very far from you; when [b]ye dwell among us?

23 Now therefore ye *are* [a]cursed, and there shall none of you be freed from being bondmen, and hewers of wood and drawers of water for the house of my God.

24 And they answered Joshua, and said, Because it was certainly told thy servants, how that the LORD thy God [a]commanded his servant Moses to give you all the land, and to destroy

all the inhabitants of the land from before you, therefore [b]we were sore afraid of our lives because of you, and have done this thing.

25 And now, behold, we *are* [a]in thine hand: as it seemeth good and right unto thee to do unto us, do.

26 And so did he unto them, and delivered them out of the hand of the children of Israel, that they slew them not.

27 And Joshua made them that day [a]hewers of wood and drawers of water for the congregation, and for the altar of the LORD, even unto this day, [b]in the place which he should choose.

## CHAPTER 10

N ow it came to pass, when Adoni-zedek king of Jerusalem had [a]heard how Joshua had taken [b]Ai, and had utterly destroyed it; [c]as he had done to Jericho and her king, so he had done to [d]Ai and her king; and [e]how the inhabitants of Gibeon had made peace with Israel, and were among them;

2 That they [a]feared greatly, because Gibeon *was* a great city, as one of the royal cities, and because it *was* greater than Ai, and all the men thereof *were* mighty.

3 Wherefore Adoni-zedek king of Jerusalem sent unto Hoham king of Hebron, and unto Piram king of Jarmuth, and unto Japhia king of Lachish, and unto Debir king of Eglon, saying,

4 Come up unto me, and help me, that we may [1]smite Gibeon: for [a]it hath made peace with Joshua and with the children of Israel.

5 Therefore the five kings of the [a]Amorites, the king of Jerusalem, the king of Hebron, the king of Jarmuth, the king of Lachish, the king of Eglon, [b]gathered themselves together, and went up, they and all their hosts, and encamped before Gibeon, and made war against it.

6 And the men of Gibeon sent unto Joshua to the camp [a]to Gilgal, saying, [1]Slack not thy hand from thy servants; come up to us quickly, and save us, and help us: for all the kings of the Amorites that dwell in the mountains are gathered together against us.

7 So Joshua ascended from Gilgal, he, and [a]all the people of war with him, and all the mighty men of valour.

8 And the LORD said unto Joshua, [a]Fear them not: for I have delivered them into thine hand; [b]there shall not a man of them [c]stand before thee.

9 Joshua therefore came unto them suddenly, *and* went up from Gilgal all night.

### Center column notes

9:11 [1] *covenant or treaty*
9:13 [1] *torn*
9:14 [a] Num. 27:21; Is. 30:1
9:15 [a] 2 Sam. 21:2 [1] *treaty*
9:17 [a] Josh. 18:25
9:18 [a] Ps. 15:4 [1] *attack* [2] *complained*
9:20 [a] 2 Sam. 21:1, 2, 6; Ezek. 17:13, 15
9:21 [a] Deut. 29:11 [b] Josh. 9:15
9:22 [a] Josh. 9:6, 9 [b] Josh. 9:16 [1] *Why have you deceived us*
9:23 [a] Gen. 9:25
9:24 [a] Ex. 23:31–33; Deut. 7:1, 2

[b] Ex. 15:14
9:25 [a] Gen. 16:6
9:27 [a] Josh. 9:21, 23 [b] Deut. 12:5
10:1 [a] Josh. 9:1 [b] Josh. 8:1 [c] Josh. 6:21 [d] Josh. 8:22, 26, 28 [e] Josh. 9:15
10:2 [a] Ex. 15:14–16; Deut. 11:25; 1 Chr. 14:17
10:4 [a] Josh. 9:15; 10:1 [1] *attack*
10:5 [a] Num. 13:29 [b] Josh. 9:2
10:6 [a] Josh. 5:10; 9:6 [1] *Do not forsake your servants*
10:7 [a] Josh. 8:1
10:8 [a] Josh. 11:6; Judg. 4:14 [b] Josh. 1:5, 9 [c] Josh. 21:44

10 And the LORD ᵃdiscomfited them before Israel, and slew them with a great slaughter at Gibeon, and chased them along the way that goeth up ᵇto Beth-horon, and smote them to ᶜAzekah, and unto Makkedah.

11 And it came to pass, as they fled from before Israel, *and* were in the going down to Beth-horon, ᵃthat the LORD cast down great stones from heaven upon them unto Azekah, and they died: *they were* more which died with hailstones than *they* whom the children of Israel slew with the sword.

12 Then spake Joshua to the LORD in the day when the LORD delivered up the Amorites before the children of Israel, and he said in the sight of Israel, ᵃSun, stand thou still upon Gibeon; and thou, Moon, in the valley of ᵇAjalon.

13 And the sun stood still, and the moon stayed, until the people had avenged themselves upon their enemies. ᵃ*Is* not this written in the book of Jasher? So the sun stood still in the midst of heaven, and ¹hasted not to go down about a whole day.

14 And there was ᵃno day like that before it or after it, that the LORD ¹hearkened unto the voice of a man: for ᵇthe LORD fought for Israel.

15 ᵃAnd Joshua returned, and all Israel with him, unto the camp to Gilgal.

16 But these five kings fled, and hid themselves in a cave at Makkedah.

17 And it was told Joshua, saying, The five kings are found hid in a cave at Makkedah.

18 And Joshua said, Roll great stones upon the mouth of the cave, and set men by it for to ¹keep them:

19 And, ¹stay ye not, *but* pursue after your enemies, and ²smite the hindmost of them; ³suffer them not to enter into their cities: for the LORD your God hath delivered them into your hand.

20 And it came to pass, when Joshua and the children of Israel had made an end of slaying them with a very great slaughter, till they ¹were consumed, that the rest *which* remained of them entered into ²fenced cities.

21 And all the people returned to the camp to Joshua at Makkedah in peace: ᵃnone ¹moved his tongue against any of the children of Israel.

22 Then said Joshua, Open the mouth of the cave, and bring out those five kings unto me out of the cave.

23 And they did so, and brought forth those five kings unto him out of the cave, the king of Jerusalem, the king of Hebron, the king of Jarmuth,

the king of Lachish, *and* the king of Eglon.

24 And it came to pass, when they brought out those kings unto Joshua, that Joshua called for all the men of Israel, and said unto the captains of the men of war which went with him, Come near, put your feet upon the necks of these kings. And they came near, and ᵃput their feet upon the necks of them.

25 And Joshua said unto them, ᵃFear not, nor be dismayed, be strong and of good courage: for ᵇthus shall the LORD do to all your enemies against whom ye fight.

26 And afterward Joshua ¹smote them, and slew them, and hanged them on five trees: and they ᵃwere hanging upon the trees until the evening.

27 And it came to pass at the time of the going down of the sun, *that* Joshua commanded, and they ᵃtook them down off the trees, and cast them into the cave wherein they had been hid, and laid great stones in the cave's mouth, *which remain* until this very day.

28 And that day Joshua took Makkedah, and ¹smote it with the edge of the sword, and the king thereof he utterly ᵃdestroyed, them, and all the souls that *were* therein; he let none remain: and he did to the king of Makkedah ᵇas he did unto the king of Jericho.

29 Then Joshua passed from Makkedah, and all Israel with him, unto ᵃLibnah, and fought against Libnah:

30 And the LORD delivered it also, and the king thereof, into the hand of Israel; and he smote it with the edge of the sword, and all the ¹souls that *were* therein; he let none remain in it; but did unto the king thereof as he did unto the king of Jericho.

31 And Joshua passed from Libnah, and all Israel with him, unto Lachish, and encamped against it, and fought against it:

32 And the LORD delivered Lachish into the hand of Israel, which took it on the second day, and smote it with the edge of the sword, and all the souls that *were* therein, according to all that he had done to Libnah.

33 Then Horam king of Gezer came up to help Lachish; and Joshua smote him and his people, until he had left him none remaining.

34 And from Lachish Joshua passed unto Eglon, and all Israel with him; and they encamped against it, and fought against it:

35 And they took it on that day, and smote it with the edge of the sword, and all the souls that *were* therein he

### Center column references

10:10 ᵃ Judg. 4:15;
1 Sam. 7:10, 12; Is.
28:21 ᵇ Josh. 16:3,
5 ᶜ Josh. 15:35
¹ *routed*

10:11 ᵃ Is. 30:30;
Rev. 16:21

10:12 ᵃ Is. 28:21;
Hab. 3:11 ᵇ Judg.
12:12

10:13 ᵃ 2 Sam. 1:18
¹ *did not hasten*

10:14 ᵃ Is. 38:7,
8 ᵇ Ex. 14:14;
Deut. 1:30; 20:4;
Josh. 10:42; 23:3
¹ *heeded*

10:15 ᵃ Josh. 10:43

10:18 ¹ *guard*

10:19 ¹ *stay
not yourselves*
² *attack their rear
ranks* ³ *do not
allow*

10:20 ¹ *had finished* ² *fortified*

10:21 ᵃ Ex. 11:7
¹ Lit. *sharpened
his tongue*

10:24 ᵃ Ps. 107:40;
Is. 26:5, 6; Mal.
4:3

10:25 ᵃ Deut.
31:6–8; Josh. 1:9
ᵇ Deut. 3:21; 7:19

10:26 ᵃ Josh.
8:29; 2 Sam. 21:9
¹ *struck*

10:27 ᵃ Deut.
21:22, 23; Josh.
8:29

10:28 ᵃ Deut. 7:2,
16 ᵇ Josh. 6:21
¹ *struck*

10:29 ᵃ Josh.
15:42; 21:13; 2 Kin.
8:22; 19:8

10:30 ¹ *people*

utterly destroyed that day, according to all that he had done to Lachish.

36 And Joshua went up from Eglon, and all Israel with him, unto ªHebron; and they fought against it:

37 And they took it, and smote it with the edge of the sword, and the king thereof, and all the cities thereof, and all the souls that *were* therein; he left none remaining, according to all that he had done to Eglon; but destroyed it utterly, and all the souls that *were* therein.

38 And Joshua returned, and all Israel with him, to ªDebir; and fought against it:

39 And he took it, and the king thereof, and all the cities thereof; and they smote them with the edge of the sword, and utterly destroyed all the souls that *were* therein; he left none remaining: as he had done to Hebron, so he did to Debir, and to the king thereof; as he had done also to Libnah, and to her king.

40 So Joshua ªsmote all the ᵃcountry of the hills, and of the south, and of the vale, and of the springs, and ᵇall their kings: he left none remaining, but ᶜutterly destroyed all that breathed, as the LORD God of Israel commanded.

41 And Joshua smote them from ªKadesh-barnea even unto ᵇGaza, ʳand all the country of Goshen, even unto Gibeon.

42 And all these kings and their land did Joshua take at one time, ᵃbecause the LORD God of Israel fought for Israel.

43 And Joshua returned, and all Israel with him, unto the camp to Gilgal.

## CHAPTER 11

AND it came to pass, when Jabin king of Hazor had heard *those things,* that he ᵃsent to Jobab king of Madon, and to the king ᵇof Shimron, and to the king of Achshaph,

2 And to the kings that *were* on the north of the mountains, and of the plains south of ªChinneroth, and in the valley, and in the borders ᵇof Dor on the west,

3 *And to* the Canaanite on the east and on the west, and *to* the ªAmorite, and the Hittite, and the Perizzite, and the Jebusite in the mountains, ᵇand *to* the Hivite under ᶜHermon ᵈin the land of Mizpeh.

4 And they went out, they and all their hosts with them, much people, ªeven as the sand that *is* upon the sea shore in multitude, with horses and chariots very many.

5 And when all these kings were ¹met together, they came and ²pitched together at the waters of Merom, to fight against Israel.

6 And the LORD said unto Joshua, ªBe not afraid because of them: for to morrow about this time will I deliver them up all slain before Israel: thou shalt ᵇhough¹ their horses, and burn their chariots with fire.

7 So Joshua came, and all the people of war with him, against them by the waters of Merom suddenly; and they fell upon them.

8 And the LORD delivered them into the hand of Israel, who ¹smote them, and chased them unto ²great ªZidon, and unto ᵇMisrephoth-maim,³ and unto the valley of Mizpeh eastward; and they smote them, until they left them none remaining.

9 And Joshua did unto them as the LORD bade him: he ¹houghed their horses, and burnt their chariots with fire.

10 And Joshua at that time turned back, and took Hazor, and ¹smote the king thereof with the sword: for Hazor beforetime was the head of all those kingdoms.

11 And they ¹smote all the ²souls that *were* therein with the edge of the sword, ªutterly destroying *them:* there was not any left to ᵇbreathe: and he burnt Hazor with fire.

12 And all the cities of those kings, and all the kings of them, did Joshua take, and smote them with the edge of the sword, *and* he utterly destroyed them, ªas Moses the servant of the LORD commanded.

13 But *as for* the cities that ¹stood still in their ²strength, Israel burned none of them, save Hazor only; *that* did Joshua burn.

14 And all the ªspoil of these cities, and the cattle, the children of Israel took for a prey unto themselves; but every man they ¹smote with the edge of the sword, until they had destroyed them, neither left they any to breathe.

15 ªAs the LORD commanded Moses his servant, so ᵇdid Moses command Joshua, and ᶜso did Joshua; ¹he left nothing undone of all that the LORD commanded Moses.

16 So Joshua took all that land, ªthe hills, and all the south country, ᵇand all the land of Goshen, and the valley, and the ¹plain, and the mountain of Israel, and the valley of the same;

17 ªEven from ¹the mount Halak, that goeth up to Seir, even unto Baal-gad in the valley of Lebanon under mount Hermon: and ᵇall their kings he took, and smote them, and slew them.

18 Joshua made war a long time with all those kings.

19 There was not a city that made peace with the children of Israel, save ªthe Hivites the inhabitants of Gibeon: all *other* they took in battle.

### Center column notes

10:36 ª Num. 13:22; Josh. 14:13–15; 15:13; Judg. 1:10, 20; 2 Sam. 5:1, 3, 5, 13; 2 Chr. 11:10

10:38 ª Josh. 15:15; Judg. 1:11; 1 Chr. 6:58

10:40 ª Deut. 1:7 ᵇ Deut. 7:24 ᶜ Deut. 20:16, 17 ¹ *conquered*

10:41 ª Num. 13:26; Deut. 9:23 ᵇ Gen. 10:19; Josh. 11:22 ᶜ Josh. 11:16; 15:51

10:42 ª Josh. 10:14

11:1 ª Josh. 10:3 ᵇ Josh. 19:15

11:2 ª Num. 34:11 ᵇ Josh. 17:11; Judg. 1:27; 1 Kin. 4:11

11:3 ª Josh. 9:1 ᵇ Deut. 7:1; Judg. 3:3, 5; 1 Kin. 9:20 ᶜ Josh. 11:17; 13:5, 11 ᵈ Gen. 31:49

11:4 ª Gen. 22:17; 32:12; Judg. 7:12; 1 Sam. 13:5

11:5 ¹ Lit. *assembled by appointment* ² *camped*

11:6 ª Josh. 10:8 ᵇ 2 Sam. 8:4 ¹ *hamstring*

11:8 ª Gen. 49:13 ᵇ Josh. 13:6 ¹ *defeated* ² Or *Sidon-rabbah* ³ Or *Brook Misrephoth,* lit. *Burnings of Water*

11:9 ¹ *hamstrung*

11:10 ¹ *struck*

11:11 ª Deut. 20:16 ᵇ Josh. 10:40 ¹ *struck* ² *people*

11:12 ª Num. 33:50–56

11:13 ¹ *stood on* ² *mounds,* Heb. *tel,* a heap of successive city ruins

11:14 ª Deut. 20:14–18 ¹ *struck*

11:15 ª Ex. 34:10–17 ᵇ Deut. 31:7, 8 ᶜ Josh. 1:7 ¹ Lit. *he turned aside from nothing*

11:16 ª Josh. 12:8 ᵇ Josh. 10:40, 41 ¹ Heb. *arabah,* the Jordan plain

11:17 ª Josh. 12:7 ᵇ Deut. 7:24 ¹ *the smooth* or *bald mountain*

11:19 ª Josh. 9:3–7

20 For ᵃit was of the LORD to ¹harden their hearts, that they should come against Israel in battle, that he might destroy them utterly, *and* that they might ²have no favour, but that he might destroy them, ᵇas the LORD commanded Moses.

21 And at that time came Joshua, and cut off ᵃthe Anakims from the mountains, from Hebron, from Debir, from Anab, and from all the mountains of Judah, and from all the mountains of Israel: Joshua destroyed them utterly with their cities.

22 There was none of the Anakims left in the land of the children of Israel: only ᵃin Gaza, in Gath, ᵇand in Ashdod, there remained.

23 So Joshua took the whole land, ᵃaccording to all that the LORD said unto Moses; and Joshua gave it for an inheritance unto Israel ᵇaccording to their divisions by their tribes. And the land ᶜrested from war.

## CHAPTER 12

Now these *are* the kings of the land, which the children of Israel ¹smote, and possessed their land on the other side Jordan toward the rising of the sun, ᵃfrom the river Arnon ᵇunto mount Hermon, and all the plain on the east:

2 ᵃSihon king of the Amorites, who dwelt in Heshbon, *and* ruled from Aroer, which *is* upon the bank of the river Arnon, and from the middle of the river, and from half Gilead, even unto the river Jabbok, *which is* the border of the children of Ammon;

3 And ᵃfrom the plain to the ¹sea of Chinneroth on the east, and unto the sea of the ²plain, *even* the ³salt sea on the east, ᵇthe way to Beth-jeshimoth; and from ⁴the south, under ᶜAshdoth-pisgah:⁵

4 And ᵃthe coast of Og king of Bashan, *which was* of ᵇthe remnant of the giants, ᶜthat dwelt at Ashtaroth and at Edrei,

5 And reigned in ᵃmount Hermon, ᵇand in Salcah, and in all Bashan, ᶜunto the border of the Geshurites and the Maachathites, and half Gilead, the border of Sihon king of Heshbon.

6 ᵃThem did Moses the servant of the LORD and the children of Israel ¹smite: and ᵇMoses the servant of the LORD gave it *for* a possession unto the Reubenites, and the Gadites, and the half tribe of Manasseh.

7 And these *are* the kings of the country ᵃwhich Joshua and the children of Israel smote on this side Jordan on the west, from Baal-gad in the valley of Lebanon even unto the mount Halak, that goeth up to ᵇSeir; which Joshua ᶜgave unto the tribes of Israel *for* a possession according to their divisions;

8 ᵃIn the mountains, and in the valleys, and in the plains, and in the springs, and in the wilderness, and in the south country; ᵇthe Hittites, the Amorites, and the Canaanites, the Perizzites, the Hivites, and the Jebusites:

9 ᵃThe king of Jericho, one; ᵇthe king of Ai, which *is* beside Beth-el, one;

10 ᵃThe king of Jerusalem, one; the king of Hebron, one;

11 The king of Jarmuth, one; the king of Lachish, one;

12 The king of Eglon, one; ᵃthe king of Gezer, one;

13 ᵃThe king of Debir, one; the king of Geder, one;

14 The king of Hormah, one; the king of Arad, one;

15 ᵃThe king of Libnah, one; the king of Adullam, one;

16 ᵃThe king of Makkedah, one; ᵇthe king of Beth-el, one;

17 The king of Tappuah, one; ᵃthe king of Hepher, one;

18 The king of Aphek, one; the king of ¹Lasharon, one;

19 The king of Madon, one; ᵃthe king of Hazor, one;

20 The king of ᵃShimron-meron, one; the king of Achshaph, one;

21 The king of Taanach, one; the king of Megiddo, one;

22 ᵃThe king of Kedesh, one; the king of Jokneam of Carmel, one;

23 The king of Dor in the ᵃcoast of Dor, one; the king of ᵇthe nations of Gilgal, one;

24 The king of Tirzah, one: ᵃall the kings thirty and one.

## CHAPTER 13

Now Joshua ᵃwas old *and* stricken in years; and the LORD said unto him, Thou art old *and* stricken in years, and there remaineth yet very much land to be possessed.

2 ᵃThis *is* the land that yet remaineth: ᵇall the borders of the Philistines, and all ᶜGeshuri,

3 ᵃFrom Sihor, which *is* before Egypt, even unto the borders of Ekron northward, *which* is counted to the Canaanite: ᵇfive lords of the Philistines; the Gazathites, and the Ashdothites, the Eshkalonites, the Gittites, and the Ekronites; also ᶜthe Avites:

4 From the south, all the land of the Canaanites, and Mearah that *is* beside the Sidonians, ᵃunto Aphek, to the borders of ᵇthe Amorites:

5 And the land of ᵃthe ¹Giblites, and all Lebanon, toward the sunrising, ᵇfrom Baal-gad under mount Hermon unto the entering into Hamath.

6 All the inhabitants of the hill country from Lebanon unto ᵃMisrephoth-maim,¹ *and* all the Sidonians, them

[b]will I drive out from before the children of Israel: only [c]divide[2] thou it by lot unto the Israelites for an inheritance, as I have commanded thee.

7 Now therefore divide this land for an inheritance unto the nine tribes, and the half tribe of Manasseh,

8 With whom the Reubenites and the Gadites have received their inheritance, [a]which Moses gave them, [b]beyond Jordan eastward, *even* as Moses the servant of the LORD gave them;

9 From Aroer, that *is* upon the bank of the river Arnon, and the city that *is* in the midst of the river, [a]and all the plain of Medeba unto Dibon;

10 And [a]all the cities of Sihon king of the Amorites, which reigned in Heshbon, unto the border of the children of Ammon;

11 [a]And Gilead, and the border of the Geshurites and Maachathites, and all mount Hermon, and all Bashan unto Salcah;

12 All the kingdom of Og in Bashan, which reigned in Ashtaroth and in Edrei, who remained of [a]the remnant of the giants: [b]for these [1]did Moses smite, and cast them out.

13 Nevertheless the children of Israel expelled [a]not the Geshurites, nor the Maachathites: but the Geshurites and the Maachathites dwell among the Israelites until this day.

14 [a]Only unto the tribe of Levi he gave [1]none inheritance; the sacrifices of the LORD God of Israel made by fire *are* their inheritance, [b]as he said unto them.

15 [a]And Moses gave unto the tribe of the children of Reuben *inheritance* according to their families.

16 And their coast was [a]from Aroer, that *is* on the bank of the river Arnon, [b]and the city that *is* in the midst of the river, [c]and all the plain by Medeba;

17 [a]Heshbon, and all her cities that *are* in the plain; Dibon, and Bamothbaal, and Beth-baal-meon,

18 [a]And Jahaza, and Kedemoth, and Mephaath,

19 [a]And Kirjathaim, and [b]Sibmah, and Zareth-shahar in the mount of the valley,

20 And Beth-peor, and [a]Ashdothpisgah, and Beth-jeshimoth,

21 [a]And all the cities of the plain, and all the kingdom of Sihon king of the Amorites, which reigned in Heshbon, [b]whom Moses smote [c]with the princes of Midian, Evi, and Rekem, and Zur, and Hur, and Reba, *which were* dukes of Sihon, dwelling in the country.

22 [a]Balaam also the son of Beor, the [1]soothsayer, did the children of Israel slay with the sword among them that were slain by them.

23 And the border of the children of Reuben was Jordan, and the border *thereof.* This *was* the inheritance of the children of Reuben after their families, the cities and the villages thereof.

24 [a]And Moses gave *inheritance* unto the tribe of Gad, *even* unto the children of Gad according to their families.

25 [a]And their coast was Jazer, and all the cities of Gilead, [b]and half the land of the children of Ammon, unto Aroer that *is* before [c]Rabbah;

26 And from Heshbon unto Ramathmizpeh, and Betonim; and from Mahanaim unto the border of Debir;

27 And in the valley, [a]Beth-aram, and Beth-nimrah, [b]and Succoth, and Zaphon, the rest of the kingdom of Sihon king of Heshbon, Jordan and *his* border, *even* unto the edge [c]of the [1]sea of Chinnereth on the other side Jordan eastward.

28 This *is* the inheritance of the children of Gad after their families, the cities, and their villages.

29 [a]And Moses gave *inheritance* unto the half tribe of Manasseh: and *this* was *the possession* of the half tribe of the children of Manasseh by their families.

30 And their coast was from Mahanaim, all Bashan, all the kingdom of Og king of Bashan, and [a]all the towns of Jair, which *are* in Bashan, threescore cities:

31 And half Gilead, and [a]Ashtaroth, and Edrei, cities of the kingdom of Og in Bashan, *were pertaining* unto the [b]children of Machir the son of Manasseh, *even* to the one half of the children of Machir by their families.

32 These *are the countries* which Moses did [1]distribute for inheritance in the plains of Moab, on the other side Jordan, by Jericho, eastward.

33 [a]But unto the tribe of Levi Moses gave not *any* inheritance: the LORD God of Israel *was* their inheritance, [b]as he said unto them.

## CHAPTER 14

AND these *are the countries* which the children of Israel inherited in the land of Canaan, [a]which Eleazar the priest, and Joshua the son of Nun, and the heads of the fathers of the tribes of the children of Israel, distributed for inheritance to them.

2 [a]By lot *was* their inheritance, as the LORD commanded by the hand of Moses, for the nine tribes, and *for* the half tribe.

3 [a]For Moses had given the inheritance of two tribes and an half tribe on the other side Jordan: but unto the Levites he gave none inheritance among them.

13:6 [b] Josh. 23:13
[c] Josh. 14:1, 2
[2] *apportion*

13:8 [a] Num. 32:33
[b] Josh. 12:1–6

13:9 [a] Num. 21:30

13:10 [a] Num. 21:24, 25

13:11 [a] Josh. 12:5

13:12 [a] Deut. 3:11
[b] Num. 21:24, 34, 35  [1] *Moses defeated and dispossessed*

13:13 [a] Josh. 13:11

13:14 [a] Josh. 14:3, 4  [b] Josh. 13:33
[1] *no land as a possession*

13:15 [a] Num. 34:14
13:16 [a] Josh. 12:2
[b] Num. 21:28
[c] Num. 21:30

13:17 [a] Num. 21:28, 30

13:18 [a] Num. 21:23
13:19 [a] Num. 32:37
[b] Num. 32:38

13:20 [a] Deut. 3:17
13:21 [a] Deut. 3:10
[b] Num. 21:24
[c] Num. 31:8

13:22 [a] Num. 22:5; 31:8  [1] *diviner*

13:24 [a] Num. 34:14; 1 Chr. 5:11
13:25 [a] Num. 32:1, 35  [b] Judg. 11:13, 15  [c] Deut. 3:11; 2 Sam. 11:1; 12:26

13:27 [a] Num. 32:36  [b] Gen. 33:17; 1 Kin. 7:46
[c] Num. 34:11; Deut. 3:17  [1] *Sea of Galilee*

13:29 [a] Num. 34:14; 1 Chr. 5:23

13:30 [a] Num. 32:41; 1 Chr. 2:23
13:31 [a] Josh. 9:10; 12:4; 13:12; 1 Chr. 6:71  [b] Num. 32:39, 40; Josh. 17:1

13:32 [1] *apportion*

13:33 [a] Deut. 18:1; Josh. 13:14; 18:7
[b] Num. 18:20; Deut. 10:9; 18:1, 2

14:1 [a] Num. 34:16–29

14:2 [a] Num. 26:55; 33:54; 34:13; Ps. 16:5

14:3 [a] Num. 32:33; Josh. 13:8, 32, 33

4 For <sup>a</sup>the children of Joseph were two tribes, Manasseh and Ephraim: therefore they gave no part unto the Levites in the land, save <sup>b</sup>cities to dwell *in,* with their suburbs for their cattle and for their substance.

5 <sup>a</sup>As the LORD commanded Moses, so the children of Israel did, and they divided the land.

6 Then the children of Judah came unto Joshua in Gilgal: and Caleb the son of Jephunneh the <sup>a</sup>Kenezite said unto him, Thou knowest <sup>b</sup>the thing that the LORD said unto Moses the man of God concerning me and <sup>c</sup>thee in Kadesh-barnea.

7 Forty years old *was* I when Moses the servant of the LORD <sup>a</sup>sent me from Kadesh-barnea to <sup>1</sup>espy out the land; and I brought him word again as *it was* in mine heart.

8 Nevertheless <sup>a</sup>my brethren that went up with me made the <sup>1</sup>heart of the people melt: but I <sup>2</sup>wholly <sup>b</sup>followed the LORD my God.

9 And Moses sware on that day, saying, <sup>a</sup>Surely the land <sup>b</sup>whereon thy feet have trodden shall be thine inheritance, and thy children's for ever, because thou hast wholly followed the LORD my God.

10 And now, behold, the LORD hath kept me <sup>a</sup>alive, <sup>b</sup>as he said, these forty and five years, even since the LORD spake this word unto Moses, while *the children of* Israel <sup>1</sup>wandered in the wilderness: and now, lo, I *am* this day fourscore and five years old.

11 <sup>a</sup>As yet I *am as* strong this day as *I was* in the day that Moses sent me: as my strength *was* then, even so *is* my strength now, for war, both <sup>b</sup>to go out, and to come in.

12 Now therefore give me this mountain, whereof the LORD spake in that day; for thou heardest in that day how <sup>a</sup>the Anakims *were* there, and *that* the cities *were* great *and* fenced: <sup>b</sup>if so be the LORD *will be* with me, then <sup>c</sup>I shall be able to drive them out, as the LORD said.

13 And Joshua <sup>a</sup>blessed him, <sup>b</sup>and gave unto Caleb the son of Jephunneh Hebron for an inheritance.

14 <sup>a</sup>Hebron therefore became the inheritance of Caleb the son of Jephunneh the Kenezite unto this day, because that he <sup>b</sup>wholly followed the LORD God of Israel.

15 And <sup>a</sup>the name of Hebron before *was* Kirjath-arba; *which Arba was* a great man among the Anakims. <sup>b</sup>And the land had rest from war.

## CHAPTER 15

THIS then was <sup>1</sup>the lot of the tribe of the children of Judah by their families; <sup>a</sup>*even* to the border of Edom the <sup>b</sup>wilderness of Zin southward

*was* the uttermost part of the south coast.

2 And their <sup>a</sup>south border was from the shore of the salt sea, from the bay that looketh southward:

3 And it went out to the south side <sup>a</sup>to <sup>1</sup>Maaleh-acrabbim, and passed along to Zin, and ascended up on the south side unto Kadesh-barnea, and passed along to Hezron, and went up to Adar, and fetched a compass to Karkaa:

4 *From thence* it passed <sup>a</sup>toward Azmon, and went out unto the river of Egypt; and the goings out of that coast were at the sea: this shall be your south coast.

5 And the east border *was* the salt sea, *even* unto the end of Jordan. And their <sup>a</sup>border in the north quarter *was* from the bay of the sea at the uttermost part of Jordan:

6 And the border went up to Beth-hogla, and passed along by the north of <sup>a</sup>Beth-arabah; and the border went up <sup>b</sup>to the stone of Bohan the son of Reuben:

7 And the border went up toward <sup>a</sup>Debir from <sup>b</sup>the valley of Achor, and so northward, looking toward Gilgal, that *is* before the going up to Adummim, which *is* on the south side of the river: and the border passed toward the waters of En-shemesh, and the goings out thereof were at <sup>c</sup>En-rogel:

8 And the border went up <sup>a</sup>by the valley of the son of Hinnom unto the south side of the <sup>b</sup>Jebusite; the same *is* Jerusalem: and the border went up to the top of the mountain that *lieth* before the valley of Hinnom westward, which *is* at the end of the valley <sup>c</sup>of the <sup>1</sup>giants northward:

9 And the border was drawn from the top of the hill unto <sup>a</sup>the fountain of the water of Nephtoah, and went out to the cities of mount Ephron; and the border was drawn <sup>b</sup>to Baalah, which *is* <sup>c</sup>Kirjath-jearim:

10 And the border <sup>1</sup>compassed from Baalah westward unto mount Seir, and passed along unto the side of mount Jearim, which *is* Chesalon, on the north side, and went down to Beth-shemesh, and passed on to <sup>a</sup>Timnah:

11 And the border went out unto the side of <sup>a</sup>Ekron northward: and the border was drawn to Shicron, and passed along to mount Baalah, and went out unto Jabneel; and the <sup>1</sup>goings out of the border were at the sea.

12 And the west border *was* to the great sea, and the coast *thereof.* This *is* the coast of the children of Judah round about according to their families.

13 <sup>a</sup>And unto Caleb the son of Jephunneh he gave a part among the

### Center column references

14:4 <sup>a</sup> Gen. 41:51; 46:20; 48:1, 5; Num. 26:28; 2 Chr. 30:1 <sup>b</sup> Num. 35:2–8; Josh. 21:1–42

14:5 <sup>a</sup> Num. 35:2; Josh. 21:2

14:6 <sup>a</sup> Num. 32:11, 12 <sup>b</sup> Num. 14:24, 30 <sup>c</sup> Num. 13:26

14:7 <sup>a</sup> Num. 13:6, 17; 14:6 <sup>1</sup> *spy*

14:8 <sup>a</sup> Num. 13:31, 32; Deut. 1:28 <sup>b</sup> Num. 14:24; Deut. 1:36 <sup>1</sup> *courage of the people fail* <sup>2</sup> *fully*

14:9 <sup>a</sup> Num. 14:23, 24 <sup>b</sup> Num. 13:22; Deut. 1:36

14:10 <sup>a</sup> Num. 14:24, 30, 38 <sup>b</sup> Josh. 5:6; Neh. 9:21 <sup>1</sup> Lit. *walked*

14:11 <sup>a</sup> Deut. 34:7 <sup>b</sup> Deut. 31:2

14:12 <sup>a</sup> Num. 13:28, 33 <sup>b</sup> Rom. 8:31 <sup>c</sup> Josh. 15:14; Judg. 1:20

14:13 <sup>a</sup> Josh. 22:6 <sup>b</sup> Josh. 10:37; 15:13

14:14 <sup>a</sup> Josh. 21:12 <sup>b</sup> Josh. 14:8, 9

14:15 <sup>a</sup> Gen. 23:2; Josh. 15:13 <sup>b</sup> Josh. 11:23

15:1 <sup>a</sup> Num. 34:3 <sup>b</sup> Num. 33:36 <sup>1</sup> *allotment*

15:2 <sup>a</sup> Num. 34:3, 4

15:3 <sup>a</sup> Num. 34:4 <sup>1</sup> *of the Ascent of Acrabbim*

15:4 <sup>a</sup> Num. 34:5

15:5 <sup>a</sup> Josh. 18:15–19

15:6 <sup>a</sup> Josh. 18:19, 21 <sup>b</sup> Josh. 18:17

15:7 <sup>a</sup> Josh. 13:26 <sup>b</sup> Josh. 7:26 <sup>c</sup> 2 Sam. 17:17; 1 Kin. 1:9

15:8 <sup>a</sup> Josh. 18:16; 2 Kin. 23:10; Jer. 19:2, 6 <sup>b</sup> Josh. 1:21; 19:10 <sup>c</sup> Josh. 18:16 <sup>1</sup> Heb. *rephaim*

15:9 <sup>a</sup> Josh. 18:15 <sup>b</sup> 1 Chr. 13:6 <sup>c</sup> Judg. 18:12

15:10 <sup>a</sup> Gen. 38:13; Judg. 14:1 <sup>1</sup> *turned*

15:11 <sup>a</sup> Josh. 19:43 <sup>1</sup> *end of*

15:12 <sup>a</sup> Num. 34:6, 7; Josh. 15:47

15:13 <sup>a</sup> Josh. 14:13

children of bJudah, according to the commandment of the LORD to Joshua, *even* cthe 1city of Arba the father of Anak, which *city is* Hebron.

14 And Caleb drove thence athe three sons of Anak, bSheshai, and Ahiman, and Talmai, the children of Anak.

15 And ahe went up thence to the inhabitants of Debir: and the name of Debir before *was* Kirjath-sepher.

16 aAnd Caleb said, He that 1smiteth Kirjath-sepher, and taketh it, to him will I give Achsah my daughter to wife.

17 And aOthniel the bson of Kenaz, the brother of Caleb, took it: and he gave him cAchsah his daughter to wife.

18 aAnd it came to pass, as she came *unto him,* that she moved him to ask of her father a field: and bshe lighted off *her* ass; and Caleb said unto her, What wouldest thou?

19 Who answered, Give me a ablessing; for thou hast given me a south land; give me also springs of water. And he gave her the upper springs, and the 1nether springs.

20 This *is* the inheritance of the tribe of the children of Judah according to their families.

21 And the uttermost cities of the tribe of the children of Judah toward the coast of Edom southward were Kabzeel, and aEder, and Jagur,

22 And Kinah, and Dimonah, and Adadah,

23 And Kedesh, and Hazor, and Ithnan,

24 aZiph, and Telem, and Bealoth,

25 And Hazor, Hadattah, and Kerioth, *and* Hezron, which *is* Hazor,

26 Amam, and Shema, and Moladah,

27 And Hazar-gaddah, and Heshmon, and Beth-palet,

28 And Hazar-shual, and aBeersheba, and Bizjothjah,

29 Baalah, and Iim, and Azem,

30 And Eltolad, and Chesil, and aHormah,

31 And aZiklag, and Madmannah, and Sansannah,

32 And Lebaoth, and Shilhim, and Ain, and aRimmon: all the cities *are* twenty and nine, with their villages:

33 *And* in the valley, aEshtaol, and Zoreah, and Ashnah,

34 And Zanoah, and En-gannim, Tappuah, and Enam,

35 Jarmuth, and aAdullam, Socoh, and Azekah,

36 And Sharaim, and Adithaim, and Gederah, and Gederothaim; fourteen cities with their villages:

37 Zenan, and Hadashah, and Migdal-gad,

38 And Dilean, and Mizpeh, aand Joktheel,

39 aLachish, and Bozkath, and bEglon,

40 And Cabbon, and 1Lahmam, and Kithlish,

41 And Gederoth, Beth-dagon, and Naamah, and Makkedah; sixteen cities with their villages:

42 aLibnah, and Ether, and Ashan,

43 And Jiphtah, and Ashnah, and Nezib,

44 And Keilah, and Achzib, and Mareshah; nine cities with their villages:

45 Ekron, with her towns and her villages:

46 From Ekron even unto the sea, all that *lay* near aAshdod, with their villages:

47 Ashdod with her towns and her villages, Gaza with her towns and her villages, unto athe river of Egypt, and bthe great sea, and the border *thereof:*

48 And in the mountains, Shamir, and Jattir, and Socoh,

49 And Dannah, and Kirjath-sannah, which *is* Debir,

50 And Anab, and Eshtemoh, and Anim,

51 aAnd Goshen, and Holon, and Giloh; eleven cities with their villages:

52 Arab, and Dumah, and Eshean,

53 And Janum, and Beth-tappuah, and Aphekah,

54 And Humtah, and aKirjath-arba, which *is* Hebron, and Zior; nine cities with their villages:

55 aMaon, Carmel, and Ziph, and Juttah,

56 And Jezreel, and Jokdeam, and Zanoah,

57 Cain, Gibeah, and Timnah; ten cities with their villages:

58 Halhul, Beth-zur, and Gedor,

59 And Maarath, and Beth-anoth, and Eltekon; six cities with their villages:

60 aKirjath-baal, which *is* Kirjath-jearim, and Rabbah; two cities with their villages:

61 In the wilderness, Beth-arabah, Middin, and Secacah,

62 And Nibshan, and the city of Salt, and aEn-gedi; six cities with their villages:

63 As for the Jebusites the inhabitants of Jerusalem, athe children of Judah could not drive them out: bbut the Jebusites dwell with the children of Judah at Jerusalem unto this day.

## CHAPTER 16

AND the lot of the children of Joseph 1fell from Jordan by Jericho, unto the water of Jericho on the east, to the awilderness that goeth up from Jericho throughout mount Beth-el,

2 And goeth out from Beth-el to Luz, and passeth along unto the borders of Archi to Ataroth,

---

15:13 b Num. 13:6 c Josh. 14:15
1 Heb. *Kirjath-arba*
15:14 a Judg. 1:10, 20 b Num. 13:22
15:15 a Josh. 10:38; Judg. 1:11
15:16 a Judg. 1:12
1 *attacks*
15:17 a Judg. 1:13; 3:9 b Num. 32:12; Josh. 14:6 c Judg. 1:12
15:18 a Judg. 1:14 b Gen. 24:64; 1 Sam. 25:23
15:19 a Gen. 33:11
1 *lower*
15:21 a Gen. 35:21
15:24 a 1 Sam. 23:14
15:28 a Gen. 21:31; Josh. 19:2
15:30 a Josh. 19:4
15:31 a Josh. 19:5; 1 Sam. 27:6; 30:1
15:32 a Judg. 20:45, 47
15:33 a Judg. 13:25; 16:31
15:35 a 1 Sam. 22:1
15:38 a 2 Kin. 14:7
15:39 a 2 Kin. 14:19 b Josh. 10:3
15:40 1 Or *Lahmas*
15:42 a Josh. 21:13
15:46 a Josh. 11:22
15:47 a Josh. 15:4 b Num. 34:6
15:51 a Josh. 10:41; 11:16
15:54 a Josh. 14:15
15:55 a 1 Sam. 23:24, 25
15:60 a Josh. 18:14; 1 Sam. 7:1, 2
15:62 a 1 Sam. 23:29; Ezek. 47:10
15:63 a Judg. 1:8, 21; 2 Sam. 5:6; 1 Chr. 11:4 b Judg. 1:21
16:1 a Josh. 8:15; 18:12 1 Lit. *went out*
16:2 a Josh. 18:13; Judg. 1:26

3 And goeth down westward to the coast of Japhleti, [a]unto the coast of Beth-horon the nether, and to [b]Gezer: and [1]the goings out thereof are at the sea.

4 [a]So the children of Joseph, Manasseh and Ephraim, took their [1]inheritance.

5 [a]And the border of the children of Ephraim according to their families was *thus:* even the border of their inheritance on the east side was [b]Ataroth-addar, [c]unto Beth-horon the upper;

6 And the border went out toward the sea to [a]Michmethah on the north side; and the border went about eastward unto Taanath-shiloh, and passed by it on the east to Janohah;

7 And it went down from Janohah to Ataroth, and to [1]Naarath, and came to Jericho, and went out at Jordan.

8 The border went out from [a]Tappuah westward unto the [b]river Kanah; and [1]the goings out thereof were at the sea. This *is* the inheritance of the tribe of the children of Ephraim by their families.

9 And [a]the separate cities for the children of Ephraim *were* among the inheritance of the children of Manasseh, all the cities with their villages.

10 [a]And they drave not out the Canaanites that dwelt in Gezer: but the Canaanites dwell among the Ephraimites unto this day, and [1]serve under tribute.

## CHAPTER 17

THERE was also a lot for the tribe of Manasseh; for he *was* the [a]firstborn of Joseph; *to wit,* for [b]Machir the firstborn of Manasseh, the father of Gilead: because he was a man of war, therefore he had [c]Gilead and Bashan.

2 There was also *a lot* for [a]the rest of the children of Manasseh by their families; [b]for the children of Abiezer, and for the children of Helek, [c]and for the children of Asriel, and for the children of Shechem, [d]and for the children of Hepher, and for the children of Shemida: these *were* the male children of Manasseh the son of Joseph by their families.

3 But [a]Zelophehad, the son of Hepher, the son of Gilead, the son of Machir, the son of Manasseh, had no sons, but daughters: and these *are* the names of his daughters, Mahlah, and Noah, Hoglah, Milcah, and Tirzah.

4 And they came near before [a]Eleazar the priest, and before Joshua the son of Nun, and before the princes, saying, [b]The LORD commanded Moses to give us [1]an inheritance among our brethren. Therefore according to the commandment of the LORD he gave them an inheritance among the brethren of their father.

5 And there fell ten portions to [a]Manasseh, beside the land of Gilead and Bashan, which *were* on the other side Jordan;

6 Because the daughters of Manasseh had an inheritance among his sons: and the rest of Manasseh's sons had the land of Gilead.

7 And the coast of Manasseh was from Asher to [a]Michmethah, that *lieth* before Shechem; and the border went along on the right hand unto the inhabitants of En-tappuah.

8 *Now* Manasseh had the land of Tappuah: but [a]Tappuah on the border of Manasseh *belonged* to the children of Ephraim;

9 And the [1]coast descended unto the [2]river Kanah, southward of the river: [a]these cities of Ephraim *are* among the cities of Manasseh: the coast of Manasseh also *was* on the north side of the river, and the outgoings of it were at the sea:

10 Southward *it was* Ephraim's, and northward *it was* Manasseh's, and the sea is [1]his border; and they met together in Asher on the north, and in Issachar on the east.

11 [a]And Manasseh had in Issachar and in Asher [b]Beth-shean and her towns, and Ibleam and her towns, and the inhabitants of Dor and her towns, and the inhabitants of En-dor and her towns, and the inhabitants of Taanach and her towns, and the inhabitants of Megiddo and her towns, *even* three countries.

12 Yet [a]the children of Manasseh could not drive out *the inhabitants of* those cities; but the Canaanites would dwell in that land.

13 Yet it came to pass, when the children of Israel [1]were waxen strong, that they put the Canaanites to [a]tribute;[2] but did not utterly drive them out.

14 [a]And the children of Joseph spake unto Joshua, saying, Why hast thou given me *but* [b]one [1]lot and one portion to inherit, seeing I *am* [c]a great people, forasmuch as the LORD hath blessed me hitherto?

15 And Joshua answered them, If thou *be* a great people, *then* get thee up to the wood *country,* and cut down for thyself there in the land of the Perizzites and of the giants, if mount Ephraim be too [1]narrow for thee.

16 And the children of Joseph said, The hill is not enough for us: and all the Canaanites that dwell in the land of the valley have [a]chariots of iron, *both they* who *are* of Beth-shean and

16:3 [a] Josh. 18:13; 1 Kin. 9:17; 2 Chr. 8:5 [b] Josh. 21:21; 1 Kin. 9:15; 1 Chr. 7:28 [1] *it ended at*
16:4 [a] Josh. 17:14 [1] *possession*
16:5 [a] Judg. 1:29; 1 Chr. 7:28, 29 [b] Josh. 18:13 [c] 2 Chr. 8:5
16:6 [a] Josh. 17:7
16:7 [1] *Naaran,* 1 Chr. 7:28
16:8 [a] Josh. 17:8 [b] Josh. 17:9 [1] *it ended at*
16:9 [a] Josh. 17:9
16:10 [a] Josh. 15:63; 17:12, 13; Judg. 1:29; 1 Kin. 9:16 [1] *have become forced labourers*
17:1 [a] Gen. 41:51; 46:20; 48:18 [b] Gen. 50:23; Judg. 5:14 [c] Deut. 3:15
17:2 [a] Num. 26:29–33 [b] 1 Chr. 7:18 [c] Num. 26:31 [d] Num. 26:32
17:3 [a] Num. 26:33; 27:1; 36:2
17:4 [a] Josh. 14:1 [b] Num. 27:2–11 [1] *a possession*
17:5 [a] Josh. 22:7
17:7 [a] Josh. 16:6
17:8 [a] Josh. 16:8
17:9 [a] Josh. 16:9 [1] *border* [2] *brook or wadi*
17:10 [1] *its*
17:11 [a] 1 Chr. 7:29 [b] Judg. 1:27; 1 Sam. 31:10; 1 Kin. 4:12
17:12 [a] Judg. 1:19, 27, 28
17:13 [a] Josh. 16:10 [1] *grew strong* [2] *forced labour*
17:14 [a] Josh. 16:4 [b] Gen. 48:22 [c] Gen. 48:19; Num. 26:34, 37 [1] *allotment*
17:15 [1] *confined*
17:16 [a] Josh. 17:18; Judg. 1:19; 4:3

her towns, and *they* who *are* [b]of the valley of Jezreel.

17 And Joshua spake unto the house of Joseph, *even* to Ephraim and to Manasseh, saying, Thou *art* a great people, and hast great power: thou shalt not have one [1]lot *only:*

18 But the mountain shall be thine; for it *is* a wood, and thou shalt cut it down: and the [1]outgoings of it shall be thine: for thou shalt drive out the Canaanites, [a]though they have iron chariots, *and* though they *be* strong.

## CHAPTER 18

AND the whole congregation of the children of Israel assembled together [a]at Shiloh, and [b]set up the tabernacle of the congregation there. And the land was subdued before them.

2 And there remained among the children of Israel seven tribes, which had not yet received their inheritance.

3 And Joshua said unto the children of Israel, [a]How long *are* ye slack to go to possess the land, which the LORD God of your fathers hath given you?

4 Give out from among you three men for *each* tribe: and I will send them, and they shall rise, and go through the land, and [1]describe it according to the inheritance of them; and they shall come *again* to me.

5 And they shall divide it into seven parts: [a]Judah shall abide in their [1]coast on the south, and the [b]house of Joseph shall abide in their [1]coasts on the north.

6 Ye shall therefore [1]describe the land *into* seven parts, and bring *the description* hither to me, [a]that I may cast lots for you here before the LORD our God.

7 [a]But the Levites have no part among you; for the priesthood of the LORD *is* their inheritance: [b]and Gad, and Reuben, and half the tribe of Manasseh, have received their inheritance beyond Jordan on the east, which Moses the servant of the LORD gave them.

8 And the men arose, and went away: and Joshua charged them that went to [1]describe the land, saying, Go and walk [a]through the land, and describe it, and come again to me, that I may here cast lots for you before the LORD in Shiloh.

9 And the men went and passed through the land, and [1]described it by cities into seven parts in a book, and came *again* to Joshua to the host at Shiloh.

10 And Joshua cast [a]lots for them in Shiloh before the LORD: and there [b]Joshua divided the land unto the children of Israel according to their [1]divisions.

11 [a]And the lot of the tribe of the children of Benjamin came up according to their families: and the [1]coast of their lot came forth between the children of Judah and the children of Joseph.

12 [a]And their border on the north side was from Jordan; and the border went up to the side of Jericho on the north side, and went up through the mountains westward; and the goings out thereof were at the wilderness of Beth-aven.

13 And the border went over from thence toward Luz, to the side of Luz, [a]which *is* Beth-el, southward; and the border descended to Ataroth-adar, near the hill that *lieth* on the south side [b]of the nether Beth-horon.

14 And the border [1]was drawn *thence,* and compassed the corner of the sea southward, from the hill that *lieth* before Beth-horon southward; and [2]the goings out thereof were at [a]Kirjath-baal, which *is* Kirjath-jearim, a city of the children of Judah: this *was* the west [3]quarter.

15 And the south [1]quarter *was* from the end of Kirjath-jearim, and the border went out on the west, and went out to [a]the well of waters of Nephtoah:

16 And the border came down to the end of the mountain that *lieth* before [a]the valley of the son of Hinnom, *and* which *is* in the valley of the [1]giants on the north, and descended to the valley of Hinnom, to the side of Jebusi on the south, and descended to [b]En-rogel,

17 And was drawn from the north, and went forth to En-shemesh, and went forth toward Geliloth, which *is* [1]over against the going up of Adummim, and descended to [a]the stone of Bohan the son of Reuben,

18 And passed along toward the side over against [1]Arabah northward, and went down unto [1]Arabah:

19 And the border passed along to the side of Beth-hoglah northward: and the [1]outgoings of the border were at the north bay of the [a]salt sea at the south end of Jordan: this *was* the south coast.

20 And Jordan was the border of it on the east side. This *was* the inheritance of the children of Benjamin, by the coasts thereof round about, according to their families.

21 Now the cities of the tribe of the children of Benjamin according to their families were Jericho, and Beth-hoglah, and the valley of Keziz,

22 And Beth-arabah, and Zemaraim, and Beth-el,

23 And Avim, and Parah, and Ophrah,

24 And Chephar-haammonai, and Ophni, and Gaba; twelve cities with their villages:

17:16 [b] Josh. 19:18; 1 Kin. 4:12
17:17 [1] allotment
17:18 [a] Deut. 20:1 [1] farthest extent
18:1 [a] Josh. 19:51; 21:2; 22:9; Jer. 7:12 [b] Judg. 18:31; 1 Sam. 1:3, 24; 4:3, 4
18:3 [a] Judg. 18:9 [1] will ye neglect to
18:4 [1] survey
18:5 [a] Josh. 15:1 [b] Josh. 16:1–17:18 [1] territory
18:6 [a] Josh. 14:2; 18:10 [1] survey
18:7 [a] Num. 18:7, 20; Josh. 13:33 [b] Josh. 13:8
18:8 [a] Gen. 13:17 [1] survey
18:9 [1] wrote the survey in a book in seven parts by cities
18:10 [a] Acts 13:19 [b] Num. 34:16–29; Josh. 19:51 [1] portions

18:11 [a] Judg. 1:21 [1] territory
18:12 [a] Josh. 16:1
18:13 [a] Gen. 28:19; Josh. 16:2; Judg. 1:23 [b] Josh. 16:3
18:14 [a] Josh. 15:9 [1] extended from there around the west side southward [2] it ended at [3] side
18:15 [a] Josh. 15:9 [1] side
18:16 [a] Josh. 15:8 [b] Josh. 15:7 [1] Heb. rephaim
18:17 [a] Josh. 15:6 [1] before the ascent of
18:18 [1] Or Beth-arabah, Josh. 15:6
18:19 [a] Josh. 15:2, 5 [1] border ended at

25 ᵃGibeon, and ᵇRamah, and Beeroth,

26 And Mizpeh, and Chephirah, and Mozah,

27 And Rekem, and Irpeel, and Taralah,

28 And Zelah, Eleph, and ᵃJebusi, which *is* Jerusalem, Gibeath, *and* Kirjath; fourteen cities with their villages. This *is* the inheritance of the children of Benjamin according to their families.

## CHAPTER 19

AND the ᵃsecond lot came forth to Simeon, *even* for the tribe of the children of Simeon according to their families: ᵇand their inheritance was within the inheritance of the children of Judah.

2 And ᵃthey had in their inheritance Beer-sheba, or Sheba, and Moladah,

3 And Hazar-shual, and Balah, and Azem,

4 And Eltolad, and Bethul, and Hormah,

5 And Ziklag, and Beth-marcaboth, and Hazar-susah,

6 And Beth-lebaoth, and Sharuhen; thirteen cities and their villages:

7 Ain, Remmon, and Ether, and Ashan; four cities and their villages:

8 And all the villages that *were* round about these cities to Baalath-beer, ᵃRamath of the south. This *is* the inheritance of the tribe of the children of Simeon according to their families.

9 Out of the portion of the children of Judah *was* the inheritance of the children of Simeon: for the ¹part of the children of Judah was ²too much for them: ᵃtherefore the children of Simeon had their inheritance within the inheritance of ³them.

10 And the third lot came up for the children of Zebulun according to their families: and the border of their inheritance was unto Sarid:

11 ᵃAnd their border went up toward the sea, and Maralah, and reached to Dabbasheth, and reached to the river that *is* ᵇbefore Jokneam;

12 And turned from Sarid eastward toward the sunrising unto the border of Chisloth-tabor, and then goeth out to ᵃDaberath, and goeth up to Japhia,

13 And from thence passeth on along on the east to ᵃGittah-hepher, to Ittah-kazin, and goeth out to Remmon-methoar to Neah;

14 And the border ¹compasseth it on the north side to Hannathon: and ²the outgoings thereof are in the valley of Jiphthah-el:

15 And Kattath, and Nahallal, and Shimron, and Idalah, and Beth-lehem: twelve cities with their villages.

16 This *is* the inheritance of the

children of Zebulun according to their families, these cities with their villages.

17 *And* the fourth lot came out to Issachar, for the children of Issachar according to their families.

18 And their border was toward Jezreel, and Chesulloth, and Shunem,

19 And Haphraim, and Shihon, and Anaharath,

20 And Rabbith, and Kishion, and Abez,

21 And Remeth, and En-gannim, and En-haddah, and Beth-pazzez;

22 And the coast reacheth to Tabor, and Shahazimah, and ᵃBeth-shemesh; and the outgoings of their border were at Jordan: sixteen cities with their villages.

23 This *is* the inheritance of the tribe of the children of Issachar according to their families, the cities and their villages.

24 ᵃAnd the fifth lot came out for the tribe of the children of Asher according to their families.

25 And their border was Helkath, and Hali, and Beten, and Achshaph,

26 And Alammelech, and Amad, and Misheal; and reacheth to ᵃCarmel westward, and to Shihor-libnath;

27 And turneth toward the sunrising to Beth-dagon, and reacheth to Zebulun, and to the valley of Jiphthah-el toward the north side of Beth-emek, and Neiel, and goeth out to ᵃCabul on the left hand,

28 And Hebron, and Rehob, and Hammon, and Kanah, ᵃeven unto great Zidon;

29 And *then* the coast turneth to Ramah, and to the strong city Tyre; and the coast turneth to Hosah; and the outgoings thereof are at the sea from the coast to ᵃAchzib:

30 Ummah also, and Aphek, and Rehob: twenty and two cities with their villages.

31 This *is* the inheritance of the tribe of the children of Asher according to their families, these cities with their villages.

32 ᵃThe sixth lot came out to the children of Naphtali, *even* for the children of Naphtali according to their families.

33 And their coast was from Heleph, from Allon to Zaanannim, and Adami, Nekeb, and Jabneel, unto Lakum; and ¹the outgoings thereof were at Jordan:

34 And *then* ᵃthe coast turneth westward to Aznoth-tabor, and goeth out from thence to Hukkok, and reacheth to Zebulun on the south side, and reacheth to Asher on the west side, and to Judah upon Jordan toward the sunrising.

### Center column references

18:25 ᵃ Josh. 11:19; 21:17; 1 Kin. 3:4, 5
ᵇ Jer. 31:15
18:28 ᵃ Josh. 15:8, 63
19:1 ᵃ Judg. 1:3
ᵇ Josh. 19:9
19:2 ᵃ 1 Chr. 4:28
19:8 ᵃ 1 Sam. 30:27
19:9 ᵃ Josh. 19:1
¹ *portion* ² *too large* ³ *that people*
19:11 ᵃ Gen. 49:13
ᵇ Josh. 12:22
19:12 ᵃ 1 Chr. 6:72
19:13 ᵃ 2 Kin. 14:25
19:14 ¹ *went around* ² *it ended in*
19:22 ᵃ Josh. 15:10; Judg. 1:33
19:24 ᵃ Judg. 1:31, 32
19:26 ᵃ 1 Sam. 15:12; 1 Kin. 18:20; Is. 33:9; 35:2; Jer. 46:18
19:27 ᵃ 1 Kin. 9:13
19:28 ᵃ Gen. 10:19; Josh. 11:8; Judg. 1:31; Acts 27:3
19:29 ᵃ Judg. 1:31
19:32 ᵃ Josh. 19:32–39; Judg. 1:33
19:33 ¹ *it ended in*
19:34 ᵃ Deut. 33:23

35 And the fenced cities *are* Ziddim, Zer, and Hammath, Rakkath, and Chinnereth,

36 And Adamah, and Ramah, and Hazor,

37 And ªKedesh, and Edrei, and En-hazor,

38 And Iron, and Migdal-el, Horem, and Beth-anath, and Beth-shemesh; nineteen cities with their villages.

39 This *is* the inheritance of the tribe of the children of Naphtali according to their families, the cities and their villages.

40 ªAnd the seventh lot came out for the tribe of the children of Dan according to their families.

41 And the coast of their inheritance was Zorah, and ªEshtaol, and Ir-shemesh,

42 And ªShaalabbin, and ᵇAjalon, and Jethlah,

43 And Elon, and Thimnathah, and ªEkron,

44 And Eltekeh, and Gibbethon, and Baalath,

45 And Jehud, and Bene-berak, and Gath-rimmon,

46 And Me-jarkon, and Rakkon, with the border ¹before Japho.

47 And the ªcoast of the children of Dan went out *too little* for them: therefore the children of Dan went up to fight against Leshem, and took it, and ¹smote it with the edge of the sword, and ²possessed it, and dwelt therein, and called Leshem, ᵇDan, after the name of Dan their father.

48 This *is* the inheritance of the tribe of the children of Dan according to their families, these cities with their villages.

49 When they had ¹made an end of dividing the land for inheritance by their coasts, the children of Israel gave an inheritance to Joshua the son of Nun among them:

50 According to the word of the LORD they gave him the city which he asked, *even* ªTimnath-ᵇserah in mount Ephraim: and he built the city, and dwelt therein.

51 ªThese *are* the inheritances, which Eleazar the priest, and Joshua the son of Nun, and the heads of the fathers of the tribes of the children of Israel, divided for an inheritance by lot ᵇin Shiloh before the LORD, at the door of the tabernacle of the congregation. So they made an end of dividing the country.

## CHAPTER 20

THE LORD also spake unto Joshua, saying,

2 Speak to the children of Israel, saying, ªAppoint¹ out for you cities of refuge, whereof I spake unto you by the hand of Moses:

3 That the slayer that killeth *any* person ¹unawares *and* ²unwittingly may flee thither: and they shall be your refuge from the avenger of blood.

4 And when he that doth flee unto one of those cities shall stand at the entering of the gate of the city, and shall ¹declare his cause in the ears of the elders of that city, they shall take him into the city unto them, and give him a place, that he may dwell among them.

5 ªAnd if the avenger of blood pursue after him, then they shall not deliver the slayer up into his hand; because he smote his neighbour ¹unwittingly, and hated him not beforetime.

6 And he shall dwell in that city, ªuntil he stand before the congregation for judgment, *and* until the death of the high priest that shall be in those days: then shall the slayer return, and come unto his own city, and unto his own house, unto the city from whence he fled.

7 And they appointed ªKedesh in Galilee in mount Naphtali, and ᵇShechem in mount Ephraim, and ᶜKirjath-arba, which *is* Hebron, in ᵈthe mountain of Judah.

8 And on the other side Jordan by Jericho eastward, they assigned ᵈBezer in the wilderness upon the plain out of the tribe of Reuben, and ᵇRamoth in Gilead out of the tribe of Gad, and ᶜGolan in Bashan out of the tribe of Manasseh.

9 ªThese were the cities appointed for all the children of Israel, and for the stranger that ¹sojourneth among them, that whosoever killeth *any* person ²at unawares might flee thither, and not die by the hand of the avenger of blood, ᵇuntil he stood before the congregation.

## CHAPTER 21

THEN came near the heads of the fathers of the ªLevites unto ᵇEleazar the priest, and unto Joshua the son of Nun, and unto the heads of the fathers of the tribes of the children of Israel;

2 And they spake unto them at ªShiloh in the land of Canaan, saying, ᵇThe LORD commanded by the hand of Moses to give us cities to dwell in, with the suburbs thereof for our cattle.

3 And the children of Israel gave unto the Levites out of their inheritance, at the commandment of the LORD, these cities and their suburbs.

4 And the lot came out for the families of the Kohathites: and ªthe children of Aaron the priest, *which were* of the Levites, ᵇhad by lot out of the

tribe of Judah, and out of the tribe of Simeon, and out of the tribe of Benjamin, thirteen cities.

5 And [a]the rest of the children of Kohath *had* by lot out of the families of the tribe of Ephraim, and out of the tribe of Dan, and out of the half tribe of Manasseh, ten cities.

6 And [a]the children of Gershon *had* by lot out of the families of the tribe of Issachar, and out of the tribe of Asher, and out of the tribe of Naphtali, and out of the half tribe of Manasseh in Bashan, thirteen cities.

7 [a]The children of Merari by their families *had* out of the tribe of Reuben, and out of the tribe of Gad, and out of the tribe of Zebulun, twelve cities.

8 [a]And the children of Israel gave by lot unto the Levites these cities with their suburbs, [b]as the LORD commanded by the hand of Moses.

9 And they gave out of the tribe of the children of Judah, and out of the tribe of the children of Simeon, these cities which are *here* [1]mentioned by name,

10 Which the children of Aaron, *being* of the families of the Kohathites, *who were* of the children of Levi, had: for theirs was the first lot.

11 [a]And they gave them [1]the city of Arba the father of [b]Anak, [c]which *city is* Hebron, in the hill *country* of Judah, with the suburbs thereof round about it.

12 But [a]the fields of the city, and the villages thereof, gave they to Caleb the son of Jephunneh for his possession.

13 Thus [a]they gave to the children of Aaron the priest [b]Hebron with her suburbs, *to be* a city of refuge for the slayer; [c]and Libnah with her suburbs,

14 And [a]Jattir with her suburbs, [b]and Eshtemoa with her suburbs,

15 And [a]Holon with her suburbs, [b]and Debir with her suburbs,

16 And [a]Ain with her suburbs, [b]and Juttah with her suburbs, *and* [c]Bethshemesh with her suburbs; nine cities out of those two tribes.

17 And out of the tribe of Benjamin, [a]Gibeon with her suburbs, [b]Geba with her suburbs,

18 Anathoth with her suburbs, and [a]Almon with her suburbs; four cities.

19 All the cities of the children of Aaron, the priests, *were* thirteen cities with their suburbs.

20 [a]And the families of the children of Kohath, the Levites which remained of the children of Kohath, even they had the cities of their [1]lot out of the tribe of Ephraim.

21 For they gave them [a]Shechem with her suburbs in mount Ephraim, *to be* a city of refuge for the slayer; and [b]Gezer with her suburbs,

22 And Kibzaim with her suburbs, and Beth-horon with her suburbs; four cities.

23 And out of the tribe of Dan, Eltekeh with her suburbs, Gibbethon with her suburbs,

24 [a]Aijalon with her suburbs, Gathrimmon with her suburbs; four cities.

25 And out of the half tribe of Manasseh, Tanach with her suburbs, and Gath-rimmon with her suburbs; two cities.

26 All the cities *were* ten with their suburbs for the families of the children of Kohath that remained.

27 [a]And unto the children of Gershon, of the families of the Levites, out of the *other* half tribe of Manasseh *they gave* [b]Golan in Bashan with her suburbs, *to be* a city of refuge for the slayer; and Beesh-terah with her suburbs; two cities.

28 And out of the tribe of Issachar, Kishon with her suburbs, Dabareh with her suburbs,

29 Jarmuth with her suburbs, Engannim with her suburbs; four cities.

30 And out of the tribe of Asher, Mishal with her suburbs, Abdon with her suburbs,

31 Helkath with her suburbs, and Rehob with her suburbs; four cities.

32 And out of the tribe of Naphtali, [a]Kedesh in Galilee with her suburbs, *to be* a city of refuge for the slayer; and Hammoth-dor with her suburbs, and Kartan with her suburbs; three cities.

33 All the cities of the Gershonites according to their families *were* thirteen cities with their suburbs.

34 [a]And unto the families of the children of Merari, the rest of the Levites, out of the tribe of Zebulun, Jokneam with her suburbs, and Kartah with her suburbs,

35 Dimnah with her suburbs, Nahalal with her suburbs; four cities.

36 And out of the tribe of Reuben, [a]Bezer with her suburbs, and Jahazah with her suburbs,

37 Kedemoth with her suburbs, and Mephaath with her suburbs; four cities.

38 And out of the tribe of Gad, [a]Ramoth in Gilead with her suburbs, *to be* a city of refuge for the slayer; and Mahanaim with her suburbs,

39 Heshbon with her suburbs, Jazer with her suburbs; four cities in all.

40 So all the cities for the children of Merari by their families, which were remaining of the families of the Levites, were *by* their lot twelve cities.

41 [a]All the cities of the Levites within the possession of the children of Israel *were* forty and eight cities with their suburbs.

---

21:5 [a] Josh. 21:20
21:6 [a] Josh. 21:27
21:7 [a] Josh. 21:34
21:8 [a] Josh. 21:3
   [b] Num. 35:2
21:9 [1] Lit. *called*
21:11 [a] Josh. 20:7; 1 Chr. 6:55
   [b] Josh. 14:15; 15:13, 14 [c] Josh. 20:7; Luke 1:39
   [1] *Kirjath-arba*
21:12 [a] Josh. 14:14; 1 Chr. 6:56
21:13 [a] 1 Chr. 6:57
   [b] Josh. 15:54; 20:2, 7 [c] Josh. 15:42; 2 Kin. 8:22
21:14 [a] Josh. 15:48
   [b] Josh. 15:50
21:15 [a] 1 Chr. 6:58
   [b] Josh. 15:49
21:16 [a] 1 Chr. 6:59
   [b] Josh. 15:55
   [c] Josh. 15:10
21:17 [a] Josh. 18:25
   [b] Josh. 18:24
21:18 [a] 1 Chr. 6:60
21:20 [a] 1 Chr. 6:66
   [1] *allotment*
21:21 [a] Josh. 20:7
   [b] Judg. 1:29

21:24 [a] Josh. 10:12
21:27 [a] Josh. 21:6; 1 Chr. 6:71 [b] Josh. 20:8
21:32 [a] Josh. 20:7
21:34 [a] Josh. 21:7; 1 Chr. 6:77–81
21:36 [a] Deut. 4:43; Josh. 20:8
21:38 [a] Josh. 20:8
21:41 [a] Num. 35:7

42 [1]These cities were every one with their suburbs round about them: thus *were* all these cities.

43 And the LORD gave unto Israel [a]all the land which he sware to give unto their fathers; and they [b]possessed it, and dwelt therein.

44 [a]And the LORD gave them [b]rest round about, according to all that he sware unto their fathers: and [c]there stood not a man of all their enemies [1]before them; the LORD delivered all their enemies into their hand.

45 [a]There[1] failed not ought of any good thing which the LORD had spoken unto the house of Israel; all came to pass.

## CHAPTER 22

THEN Joshua called the Reubenites, and the Gadites, and the half tribe of Manasseh,

2 And said unto them, Ye have kept [a]all that Moses the servant of the LORD commanded you, [b]and have obeyed my voice in all that I commanded you:

3 Ye have not [1]left your brethren these many days unto this day, but have kept the charge of the commandment of the LORD your God.

4 And now the LORD your God hath given [a]rest unto your brethren, as he promised them: therefore now return ye, and get you unto your tents, *and* unto the land of your possession, [b]which Moses the servant of the LORD gave you on the other side Jordan.

5 But [a]take[1] diligent heed to do the commandment and the law, which Moses the servant of the LORD charged you, [b]to love the LORD your God, and to walk in all his ways, and to keep his commandments, and to [2]cleave unto him, and to serve him with all your heart and with all your soul.

6 So Joshua [a]blessed them, and sent them away: and they went unto their tents.

7 Now to the *one* half of the tribe of Manasseh Moses had given *possession* in Bashan: [a]but unto the *other* half thereof gave Joshua among their brethren on this side Jordan westward. And when Joshua sent them away also unto their tents, then he blessed them,

8 And he spake unto them, saying, Return with much riches unto your tents, and with very much cattle, with silver, and with gold, and with brass, and with iron, and with very much raiment: [a]divide the [1]spoil of your enemies with your brethren.

9 And the children of Reuben and the children of Gad and the half tribe of Manasseh returned, and departed from the children of Israel out of Shiloh, which *is* in the land of Canaan, to go unto [a]the country of Gilead, to the land of their possession, whereof they were possessed, according to the word of the LORD by the hand of Moses.

10 And when they came unto the borders of Jordan, that *are* in the land of Canaan, the children of Reuben and the children of Gad and the half tribe of Manasseh built there an altar by Jordan, a great [1]altar to see to.

11 And the children of Israel [a]heard say, Behold, the children of Reuben and the children of Gad and the half tribe of Manasseh have built an altar [1]over against the land of Canaan, in the [2]borders of Jordan, at the passage of the children of Israel.

12 And when the children of Israel heard *of it*, [a]the whole congregation of the children of Israel gathered themselves together at Shiloh, to go up to war against them.

13 And the children of Israel [a]sent unto the children of Reuben, and to the children of Gad, and to the half tribe of Manasseh, into the land of Gilead, [b]Phinehas the son of Eleazar the priest,

14 And with him ten princes, of each chief house a prince throughout all the tribes of Israel; and [a]each one *was* an head of the house of their fathers among the [1]thousands of Israel.

15 And they came unto the children of Reuben, and to the children of Gad, and to the half tribe of Manasseh, unto the land of Gilead, and they spake with them, saying,

16 Thus saith the whole congregation of the LORD, What [a]trespass[1] *is* this that ye have committed against the God of Israel, to turn away this day from following the LORD, in that ye have builded you an altar, [b]that ye might rebel this day against the LORD?

17 *Is* the iniquity [a]of Peor [1]too little for us, from which we are not cleansed until this day, although there was a plague in the congregation of the LORD,

18 But that ye must turn away this day from following the LORD? and it will be, *seeing* ye rebel to day against the LORD, that to morrow [a]he will be [1]wroth with the whole congregation of Israel.

19 [1]Notwithstanding, if the land of your possession *be* unclean, *then* pass ye over unto the land of the possession of the LORD, [a]wherein the LORD's tabernacle dwelleth, and take possession among us: but rebel not against the LORD, nor rebel against us, in building you an altar [2]beside the altar of the LORD our God.

---

21:42 [1] *Every one of these cities had its common-land surrounding it*

21:43 [a] Gen. 12:7; 26:3, 4; 28:4, 13, 14   [b] Num. 33:53; Josh. 1:11

21:44 [a] Deut. 7:23, 24; Josh. 11:23; 22:4   [b] Josh. 1:13, 15; 11:23   [c] Deut. 7:24   [1] *against*

21:45 [a] [Num. 23:19]; Josh. 23:14; 1 Kin. 8:56   [1] *Not a word failed of*

22:2 [a] Num. 32:20–22; Deut. 3:18   [b] Josh. 1:12–18

22:3 [1] *forsaken*

22:4 [a] Josh. 21:44   [b] Num. 32:33

22:5 [a] Deut. 6:6, 17; 11:22; Jer. 12:16   [b] Deut. 10:12; 11:13, 22   [1] *be very careful to do*   [2] *hold fast*

22:6 [a] Gen. 47:7; Ex. 39:43; Num. 14:13; 2 Sam. 6:18; Luke 24:50

22:7 [a] Josh. 17:1–13

22:8 [a] Num. 31:27; 1 Sam. 30:24   [1] *plunder*

22:9 [a] Num. 32:1, 26, 29

22:10 [1] *impressive altar*

22:11 [a] Deut. 13:12–18; Judg. 20:12, 13   [1] *on the frontier of*   [2] *region of Jordan on the side of*

22:12 [a] Josh. 18:1; Judg. 20:1

22:13 [a] Deut. 13:14; Judg. 20:12   [b] Ex. 6:25; Num. 25:7, 11–13

22:14 [a] Num. 1:4   [1] *divisions*

22:16 [a] Deut. 12:5–14   [b] Lev. 17:8, 9   [1] *treachery*

22:17 [a] Num. 25:1–9; Deut. 4:3   [1] *not enough*

22:18 [a] Num. 16:22   [1] *angry*

22:19 [a] Josh. 18:1   [1] *Nevertheless*   [2] *in addition to*

20 [a]Did not Achan the son of Zerah [1]commit a trespass in the [2]accursed thing, and wrath fell on all the congregation of Israel? and that man perished not alone in his iniquity.

21 Then the children of Reuben and the children of Gad and the half tribe of Manasseh answered, and said unto the heads of the [1]thousands of Israel,

22 The LORD [a]God of gods, the LORD God of gods, he [b]knoweth, and Israel he shall know; if *it be* in rebellion, or if in transgression against the LORD, (save us not this day,)

23 That we have built us an altar to turn from following the LORD, or if to offer thereon burnt offering or meat offering, or if to offer peace offerings thereon, let the LORD himself [a]require[1] *it;*

24 And if we have not *rather* done it [1]for fear of *this* thing, saying, In time to come your children might speak unto our children, saying, What have ye to do with the LORD God of Israel?

25 For the LORD hath made Jordan a border between us and you, ye children of Reuben and children of Gad; ye have no part in the LORD: so shall your children make our children [1]cease from fearing the LORD.

26 Therefore we said, Let us now prepare to build us an altar, not for burnt offering, nor for sacrifice:

27 But *that* it *may be* [a]a [1]witness between us, and you, and our generations after us, that we might [b]do the service of the LORD before him with our burnt offerings, and with our sacrifices, and with our peace offerings; that your children may not say to our children in time to come, Ye have no part in the LORD.

28 Therefore said we, that it shall be, when they should *so* say to us or to our generations in time to come, that we may say *again,* Behold the pattern of the altar of the LORD, which our fathers made, not for burnt offerings, nor for sacrifices; but it *is* a witness between us and you.

29 God forbid that we should rebel against the LORD, and turn this day from following the LORD, [a]to build an altar for burnt offerings, for meat offerings, or for sacrifices, [1]beside the altar of the LORD our God that *is* before his tabernacle.

30 And when Phinehas the priest, and the princes of the congregation and heads of the [1]thousands of Israel which *were* with him, heard the words that the children of Reuben and the children of Gad and the children of Manasseh spake, it pleased them.

31 And Phinehas the son of Eleazar the priest said unto the children of Reuben, and to the children of Gad,

and to the children of Manasseh, This day we perceive that the LORD is [a]among us, because ye have not committed this trespass against the LORD: now ye have delivered the children of Israel out of the hand of the LORD.

32 And Phinehas the son of Eleazar the priest, and the princes, returned from the children of Reuben, and from the children of Gad, out of the land of Gilead, unto the land of Canaan, to the children of Israel, and brought them word again.

33 And the thing pleased the children of Israel; and the children of Israel [a]blessed God, and did not intend to go up against them in battle, to destroy the land wherein the children of Reuben and Gad dwelt.

34 And the children of Reuben and the children of Gad called the altar [1]Ed: for it *shall be* a witness between us that the LORD *is* God.

## CHAPTER 23

AND it came to pass a long time after that the LORD [a]had given rest unto Israel from all their enemies round about, that Joshua [b]waxed[1] old *and* stricken in age.

2 And Joshua [a]called for all Israel, *and* for their elders, and for their heads, and for their judges, and for their officers, and said unto them, I am old *and* stricken in age:

3 And ye have seen all that the [a]LORD your God hath done unto all these nations because of you; for the [b]LORD your God *is* he that hath fought for you.

4 Behold, [a]I have divided unto you by lot these nations that remain, to be an inheritance for your tribes, from Jordan, with all the nations that I have cut off, even unto the great sea westward.

5 And the LORD your God, [a]he shall expel them from before you, and drive them from out of your sight; and ye shall possess their land, [b]as the LORD your God hath promised unto you.

6 [a]Be ye therefore very courageous to keep and to do all that is written in the book of the law of Moses, [b]that ye turn not aside therefrom *to* the right hand or *to* the left;

7 That ye [a]come[1] not among these nations, these that remain among you; neither [b]make mention of the name of their gods, nor cause to [c]swear *by them,* neither [d]serve them, nor bow yourselves unto them:

8 But [a]cleave[1] unto the LORD your God, as ye have done unto this day.

9 [a]For the LORD hath [1]driven out from before you great nations and strong: but *as for* you, no man hath

### Cross references (center column)

22:20 [a] Josh. 7:1–26  [1] *act unfaithfully*  [2] *devoted thing*

22:21 [1] *divisions*

22:22 [a] Deut. 4:35; 10:17; Is. 44:8; 45:5; 46:9; [1 Cor. 8:5, 6]  [b] [Job 10:7; 23:10; Jer. 12:3; 2 Cor. 11:11, 31]

22:23 [a] Deut. 18:19; 1 Sam. 20:16  [1] *require an account*

22:24 [1] *from fear, for a reason*

22:25 [1] *stop standing in awe of*

22:27 [a] Gen. 31:48; Josh. 22:34; 24:27  [b] Deut. 12:5, 14  [1] *testimony*

22:29 [a] Deut. 12:13, 14  [1] *besides*

22:30 [1] *divisions*

22:31 [a] Ex. 25:8; Lev. 26:11, 12; 2 Chr. 15:2; Zech. 8:23

22:33 [a] 1 Chr. 29:20; Neh. 8:6; Dan. 2:19; Luke 2:28

22:34 [1] Lit. *Witness*

23:1 [a] Josh. 21:44; 22:4  [b] Josh. 13:1; 24:29  [1] *was old, advanced in age*

23:2 [a] Deut. 31:28

23:3 [a] Ps. 44:3  [b] Ex. 14:14; Deut. 1:30; Josh. 10:14, 42

23:4 [a] Josh. 13:2, 6; 18:10

23:5 [a] Ex. 23:30; 33:2  [b] Num. 33:53

23:6 [a] Josh. 1:7  [b] Deut. 5:32

23:7 [a] Deut. 7:2, 3  [b] Ex. 23:13  [c] Deut. 6:13; 10:20  [d] Ex. 20:5  [1] *not associate with*

23:8 [a] Deut. 10:20  [1] *hold fast*

23:9 [a] Deut. 7:24; 11:23  [1] *dispossessed*

been able to stand ²before you unto this day.

10 ªOne man of you shall chase a thousand: for the LORD your God, he *it is* that fighteth for you, ᵇas he hath promised you.

11 ªTake ¹good heed therefore unto yourselves, that ye love the LORD your God.

12 Else if ye do in any wise ªgo back, and cleave unto the remnant of these nations, *even* these that remain among you, and shall ᵇmake marriages with them, and ¹go in unto them, and they to you:

13 Know for a certainty that ªthe LORD your God will no more drive out *any of* these nations from before you; ᵇbut they shall be snares and traps unto you, and scourges in your sides, and thorns in your eyes, until ye perish from off this good land which the LORD your God hath given you.

14 And, behold, this day ªI *am* going the way of all the earth: and ye know in all your hearts and in all your souls, that ᵇnot one thing hath failed of all the good things which the LORD your God spake concerning you; all are come to pass unto you, *and* not one thing hath failed thereof.

15 ªTherefore it shall come to pass, *that* as all good things are come upon you, which the LORD your God promised you; so shall the LORD bring upon you ᵇall evil things, until he have destroyed you from off this good land which the LORD your God hath given you.

16 When ye have transgressed the covenant of the LORD your God, which he commanded you, and have gone and served other gods, and bowed yourselves to them; then shall the ªanger of the LORD be kindled against you, and ye shall perish quickly from off the good land which he hath given unto you.

## CHAPTER 24

AND Joshua gathered all the tribes of Israel to ªShechem, and ᵇcalled for the elders of Israel, and for their heads, and for their judges, and for their officers; and they ᶜpresented themselves before God.

2 And Joshua said unto all the people, Thus saith the LORD God of Israel, ªYour fathers dwelt on the other side of ¹the flood in old time, *even* Terah, the father of Abraham, and the father of Nachor: and ᵇthey served other gods.

3 And ªI took your father Abraham from the other side of the ¹flood, and led him throughout all the land of Canaan, and multiplied his ²seed, and ᵇgave him Isaac.

23:9 ² *against*
23:10 ª Lev. 26:8
ᵇ Ex. 14:14
23:11 ª Josh. 22:5
¹ *diligent*
23:12 ª [2 Pet. 2:20, 21] ᵇ Deut. 7:3, 4 ¹ *associate with*
23:13 ª Judg. 2:3
ᵇ Ex. 23:33; 34:12
23:14 ª 1 Kin. 2:2
ᵇ Josh. 21:45 ¹ *I am going to die.*
23:15 ª Deut. 28:63 ᵇ Deut. 28:15–68
23:16 ª Deut. 4:24–28
24:1 ª Gen. 35:4
ᵇ Josh. 23:2
ᶜ 1 Sam. 10:19
24:2 ª Gen. 11:7–32 ᵇ Josh. 24:14
¹ The Euphrates, Heb. *Hannahar*
24:3 ª Gen. 12:1; Acts 7:2, 3 ᵇ [Ps. 127:3]
¹ The Euphrates, Heb. *Hannahar*
² *descendants*

24:4 ª Gen. 25:24–26 ᵇ Deut. 2:5 ᶜ Gen. 46:1, 3, 6
24:5 ª Ex. 3:10
ᵇ Ex. 7–10
24:6 ª Ex. 12:37, 51; 14:2–31
24:7 ª Ex. 14:20
ᵇ Deut. 4:34
ᶜ Josh. 5:6 ¹ *long time*
24:8 ª Num. 21:21–35
24:9 ª Judg. 11:25
ᵇ Num. 22:2–14
24:10 ª Deut. 23:5
ᵇ Num. 23:11, 20; 24:10
24:11 ª Josh. 3:14, 17 ᵇ Josh. 6:1; 10:1
24:12 ª Ex. 23:28
ᵇ Ps. 44:3
24:13 ª Deut. 6:10, 11
24:14 ª 1 Sam. 12:24 ᵇ 2 Cor. 1:12 ᶜ Ezek. 20:18
ᵈ Ezek. 20:7, 8
¹ The Euphrates, Heb. *Hannahar*
24:15 ª 1 Kin. 18:21 ᵇ Josh. 24:2
ᶜ Ex. 23:24, 32
ᵈ Gen. 18:19 ¹ The Euphrates, Heb. *Hannahar*

4 And I gave unto Isaac ªJacob and Esau: and I gave unto ᵇEsau mount Seir, to possess it; ᶜbut Jacob and his children went down into Egypt.

5 ªI sent Moses also and Aaron, and ᵇI plagued Egypt, according to that which I did among them: and afterward I brought you out.

6 And I ªbrought your fathers out of Egypt: and ye came unto the sea; and the Egyptians pursued after your fathers with chariots and horsemen unto the Red sea.

7 And when they cried unto the LORD, he put ªdarkness between you and the Egyptians, and brought the sea upon them, and covered them; and ᵇyour eyes have seen what I have done in Egypt: and ye dwelt in the wilderness ᶜa ¹long season.

8 And I brought you into the land of the Amorites, which dwelt on the other side Jordan; ªand they fought with you: and I gave them into your hand, that ye might possess their land; and I destroyed them from before you.

9 Then ªBalak the son of Zippor, king of Moab, arose and warred against Israel, and ᵇsent and called Balaam the son of Beor to curse you:

10 ªBut I would not hearken unto Balaam; ᵇtherefore he blessed you still: so I delivered you out of his hand.

11 And ªye went over Jordan, and came unto Jericho: and ᵇthe men of Jericho fought against you, the Amorites, and the Perizzites, and the Canaanites, and the Hittites, and the Girgashites, the Hivites, and the Jebusites; and I delivered them into your hand.

12 And ªI sent the hornet before you, which drave them out from before you, *even* the two kings of the Amorites; *but* ᵇnot with thy sword, nor with thy bow.

13 And I have given you a land for which ye did not labour, and ªcities which ye built not, and ye dwell in them; of the vineyards and oliveyards which ye planted not do ye eat.

14 ªNow therefore fear the LORD, and serve him in ᵇsincerity and in truth: and ᶜput away the gods which your fathers served on the other side of the ¹flood, and ᵈin Egypt; and serve ye the LORD.

15 And if it seem evil unto you to serve the LORD, ªchoose you this day whom ye will serve; whether ᵇthe gods which your fathers served that *were* on the other side of the ¹flood, or ᶜthe gods of the Amorites, in whose land ye dwell: ᵈbut as for me and my house, we will serve the LORD.

16 And the people answered and said, God forbid that we should forsake the LORD, to serve other gods;

17 For the LORD our God, he *it is* that brought us up and our fathers out of the land of Egypt, from the house of bondage, and which did those great signs in our sight, and preserved us in all the way wherein we went, and among all the people through whom we passed:

18 And the LORD drave out from before us all the people, even the Amorites which dwelt in the land: ªtherefore will we also serve the LORD; for he *is* our God.

19 And Joshua said unto the people, ªYe cannot serve the LORD: for he *is* an ᵇholy God; he *is* ᶜa jealous God; ᵈhe will not forgive your transgressions nor your sins.

20 ªIf ye forsake the LORD, and serve strange gods, ᵇthen he will turn and do you ¹hurt, and consume you, after that he hath done you good.

21 And the people said unto Joshua, Nay; but we will serve the LORD.

22 And Joshua said unto the people, Ye *are* witnesses against yourselves that ªye have chosen you the LORD, to serve him. And they said, We *are* witnesses.

23 Now therefore ªput away, *said he*, the strange gods which *are* among you, and ᵇincline your heart unto the LORD God of Israel.

24 And the people ªsaid unto Joshua, The LORD our God will we serve, and his voice will we obey.

25 So Joshua ªmade¹ a covenant with the people that day, and ²set them a statute and an ordinance ᵇin Shechem.

26 And Joshua ªwrote these words in the book of the law of God, and took ᵇa great stone, and ᶜset it up there ᵈunder an oak, that *was* by the sanctuary of the LORD.

27 And Joshua said unto all the people, Behold, this stone shall be ªa witness unto us; for ᵇit hath heard all the words of the LORD which he spake unto us: it shall be therefore a witness unto you, lest ye deny your God.

28 So ªJoshua let the people depart, every man unto his inheritance.

29 ªAnd it came to pass after these things, that Joshua the son of Nun, the servant of the LORD, died, *being* an hundred and ten years old.

30 And they buried him in the border of his inheritance in ªTimnathserah, which *is* in mount Ephraim, on the north side of the hill of Gaash.

31 And ªIsrael served the LORD all the days of Joshua, and all the days of the elders that ¹overlived Joshua, and which had ᵇknown all the works of the LORD, that he had done for Israel.

32 And ªthe bones of Joseph, which the children of Israel brought up out of Egypt, buried they in Shechem, in a ¹parcel of ground ᵇwhich Jacob bought of the sons of Hamor the father of Shechem for an hundred ²pieces of silver: and it became the inheritance of the children of Joseph.

33 And ªEleazar the son of Aaron died; and they buried him in a hill that ¹pertained to ᵇPhinehas his son, which was given him in mount Ephraim.

---

24:18 ª Ps. 116:16
24:19 ª Matt. 6:24
ᵇ 1 Sam. 6:20
ᶜ Ex. 20:5 ᵈ Ex. 23:21
24:20 ª Ezra 8:22
ᵇ Deut. 4:24–26
¹ *harm*
24:22 ª Ps. 119:173
24:23 ª Gen. 35:2
ᵇ 1 Kin. 8:57, 58
24:24 ª Deut. 5:24–27
24:25 ª Ex. 15:25
ᵇ Josh. 24:1 ¹ Lit. *cut a covenant*
² *made for them*
24:26 ª Deut. 31:24 ᵇ Judg. 9:6 ᶜ Gen. 28:18
ᵈ Gen. 35:4
24:27 ª Gen. 31:48
ᵇ Deut. 32:1
24:28 ª Judg. 2:6, 7
24:29 ª Judg. 2:8
24:30 ª Josh. 19:50
24:31 ª Judg. 2:7 ᵇ Deut. 11:2
¹ *outlived*
24:32 ª Gen. 50:25 ᵇ Gen. 33:19 ¹ *plot*
² Heb. *qesitah* (an unknown ancient measure of weight)
24:33 ª Ex. 28:1 ᵇ Ex. 6:25
¹ *belonged*

# THE BOOK OF JUDGES

The Book of Judges stands in stark contrast to Joshua. In Joshua an obedient people conquered the land through trust in the power of God. In Judges, however, a disobedient and idolatrous people are defeated time and time again because of their rebellion against God.

In seven distinct cycles of sin to salvation, Judges shows how Israel had set aside God's law and in its place substituted "*that which was* right in his own eyes" (21:25). The recurring result of abandonment from God's law is corruption from within and oppression from without. During the nearly four centuries spanned by this book, God raises up military champions to throw off the yoke of bondage and to restore the nation to pure worship. But all too soon the "sin cycle" begins again as the nation's spiritual temperature grows steadily colder.

The Hebrew title is *Shophetim*, meaning "judges," "rulers," "deliverers," or "saviors." *Shophet* not only carries the idea of maintaining justice and settling disputes, but it is also used to mean "liberating" and "delivering." First the judges deliver the people; then they rule and administer justice. The Septuagint used the Greek equivalent of this word, *Kritai* ("Judges"). The Latin Vulgate called it *Liber Judicum*, the "Book of Judges." This book could also appropriately be titled the "Book of Failure."

## CHAPTER 1

Now after the [a]death of Joshua it
came to pass, that the children of
Israel [b]asked the LORD, saying, Who
shall go up for us against the [c]Ca-
naanites first, to fight against them?
2 And the LORD said, [a]Judah shall
go up: behold, I have delivered the
land into his hand.
3 And Judah said unto [a]Simeon his
brother, Come up with me into my
[1]lot, that we may fight against the Canaanites; and [b]I likewise will go with
thee into thy lot. So Simeon went
with him.
4 And Judah went up; and the
LORD delivered the Canaanites and
the Perizzites into their hand: and
they slew of them in [a]Bezek ten thousand men.
5 And they found Adoni-bezek in
Bezek: and they fought against him,
and they slew the Canaanites and the
Perizzites.
6 But Adoni-bezek fled; and they
pursued after him, and caught him,
and cut off his thumbs and his great
toes.
7 And Adoni-bezek said, Threescore
and ten kings, having their thumbs
and their great toes cut off, gathered
*their meat* under my table: [a]as I have
done, so God hath requited me. And
they brought him to Jerusalem, and
there he died.
8 Now [a]the children of Judah had
fought against Jerusalem, and had
taken it, and smitten it with the edge
of the sword, and set the city on fire.
9 [a]And afterward the children of
Judah went down to fight against
the Canaanites, that dwelt in the
mountain, and in the south, and in
the valley.
10 And Judah [1]went against the
Canaanites that dwelt in [a]Hebron:
(now the name of Hebron before *was*
[b]Kirjath-arba:) and they slew Sheshai, and Ahiman, and Talmai.
11 [a]And from thence he went
against the inhabitants of Debir:
and the name of Debir before *was*
Kirjath-sepher:
12 [a]And Caleb said, He that [1]smiteth
Kirjath-sepher, and taketh it, to him
will I give Achsah my daughter [2]to
wife.
13 And Othniel the son of Kenaz,
[a]Caleb's younger brother, took it: and
he gave him Achsah his daughter to
wife.
14 [a]And it came to pass, when she
came *to him,* that she moved him
to ask of her father a field: and she
lighted from off *her* ass; and Caleb
said unto her, What wilt thou?
15 And she said unto him, [a]Give me
a blessing: for thou hast given me a
south land; give me also springs of
water. And Caleb gave her the upper
springs and the nether springs.
16 [a]And the children of the Kenite,
Moses' father in law, went up out [b]of
the city of palm trees with the children of Judah into the wilderness
of Judah, which *lieth* in the south
of [c]Arad; [d]and they went and dwelt
among the people.
17 [a]And Judah went with Simeon
his brother, and they slew the Canaanites that inhabited Zephath, and
utterly destroyed it. And the name of
the city was called [b]Hormah.
18 Also Judah took [a]Gaza with [1]the

1:1 [a] Josh. 24:29 [b] Num. 27:21; Judg. 20:18 [c] Josh. 17:12, 13
1:2 [a] Gen. 49:8, 9; Rev. 5:5
1:3 [a] Josh. 19:1 [b] Judg. 1:17 [1] *allotted territory*
1:4 [a] 1 Sam. 11:8
1:7 [a] Lev. 24:19; 1 Sam. 15:33; [James 2:13]
1:8 [a] Josh. 15:63; Judg. 1:21
1:9 [a] Josh. 10:36; 11:21; 15:13
1:10 [a] Josh. 15:13–19 [b] Josh. 14:15 [1] *attacked*
1:11 [a] Josh. 15:15
1:12 [a] Josh. 15:16, 17 [1] *attacks* [2] *as wife*
1:13 [a] Judg. 3:9
1:14 [a] Josh. 15:18, 19
1:15 [a] Gen. 33:11
1:16 [a] Num. 10:29–32; Judg. 4:11, 17; 1 Sam. 15:6; 1 Chr. 2:55 [b] Deut. 34:3; Judg. 3:13 [c] Josh. 12:14 [d] 1 Sam. 15:6
1:17 [a] Judg. 1:3 [b] Num. 21:3; Josh. 19:4
1:18 [a] Josh. 11:22 [1] *its territory*

coast thereof, and Askelon with the coast thereof, and Ekron with the coast thereof.

19 And the LORD was with Judah; and he drave out *the inhabitants of* the mountain; but could not drive out the inhabitants of the valley, because they had [a]chariots of iron.

20 [a]And they gave Hebron unto Caleb, as Moses said: and he [1]expelled thence the [b]three sons of Anak.

21 [a]And the children of Benjamin did not drive out the Jebusites that inhabited Jerusalem; but the Jebusites dwell with the children of Benjamin in Jerusalem unto this day.

22 And the [1]house of Joseph, they also went up against Beth-el: [a]and the LORD *was* with them.

23 And the [1]house of Joseph [a]sent to [2]descry Beth-el. (Now the name of the city before *was* [b]Luz.)

24 And the spies saw a man come forth out of the city, and they said unto him, Shew us, we pray thee, the entrance into the city, and [a]we will shew thee mercy.

25 And when he shewed them the entrance into the city, they [1]smote the city with the edge of the sword; but they let go the man and all his family.

26 And the man went into the land of the Hittites, and built a city, and called the name thereof Luz: which *is* the name thereof unto this day.

27 [a]Neither did Manasseh drive out *the inhabitants of* Beth-shean and her towns, nor [b]Taanach and her towns, nor the inhabitants of [c]Dor and her towns, nor the inhabitants of Ibleam and her towns, nor the inhabitants of Megiddo and her towns: but the Canaanites [1]would dwell in that land.

28 And it came to pass, when Israel was strong, that they put the Canaanites to [1]tribute, and did not utterly drive them out.

29 [a]Neither did Ephraim drive out the Canaanites that dwelt in Gezer; but the Canaanites dwelt in Gezer among them.

30 Neither did [a]Zebulun drive out the inhabitants of Kitron, nor the inhabitants of Nahalol; but the Canaanites dwelt among them, and became [1]tributaries.

31 [a]Neither did Asher drive out the inhabitants of Accho, nor the inhabitants of Zidon, nor of Ahlab, nor of Achzib, nor of Helbah, nor of Aphik, nor of Rehob:

32 But the Asherites [a]dwelt among the Canaanites, the inhabitants of the land: for they did not drive them out.

33 [a]Neither did Naphtali drive out the inhabitants of Beth-shemesh, nor

the inhabitants of Beth-anath; but he dwelt among the Canaanites, the inhabitants of the land: nevertheless the inhabitants of Beth-shemesh and of Beth-anath became tributaries unto them.

34 And the Amorites forced the children of Dan into the mountain: for they would not suffer them to come down to the valley:

35 But the Amorites would dwell in mount Heres [a]in Aijalon, and in [1]Shaalbim: yet the hand of the house of Joseph [2]prevailed, so that they became [3]tributaries.

36 And the coast of the Amorites *was* [a]from the going up to Akrabbim, from the rock, and upward.

## CHAPTER 2

AND an angel of the LORD came up from Gilgal to Bochim, and said, [a]I made you to go up out of Egypt, and [b]have brought you unto the land which I sware unto your fathers; and [c]I said, I will never break my covenant with you.

2 And [a]ye shall make no [1]league with the inhabitants of this land; [b]ye shall throw down their altars: [c]but ye have not obeyed my voice: why have ye done this?

3 Wherefore I also said, I will not drive them out from before you; but they shall be [a]*as thorns* in your sides, and [b]their gods shall [1]be a [c]snare unto you.

4 And it came to pass, when the angel of the LORD spake these words unto all the children of Israel, that the people lifted up their voice, and wept.

5 And they called the name of that place [1]Bochim: and they sacrificed there unto the LORD.

6 And when [a]Joshua had let the people go, the children of Israel went every man unto his inheritance to possess the land.

7 [a]And the people served the LORD all the days of Joshua, and all the days of the elders that outlived Joshua, who had seen all the great works of the LORD, that he did for Israel.

8 And [a]Joshua the son of Nun, the servant of the LORD, died, *being* an hundred and ten years old.

9 [a]And they buried him in the border of his inheritance in [b]Timnathheres, in the mount of Ephraim, on the north side of the hill Gaash.

10 And also all that generation [1]were gathered unto their fathers: and there arose another generation after them, which [a]knew not the LORD, nor yet the works which he had done for Israel.

11 And the children of Israel did [a]evil in the sight of the LORD, and served Baalim:

1:19 [a] Josh. 17:16, 18; Judg. 4:3, 13
1:20 [a] Num. 14:24; Josh. 14:9, 14 [b] Josh. 15:14; Judg. 1:10 [1] *drove out from there*
1:21 [a] Josh. 15:63; Judg. 1:8
1:22 [a] Judg. 1:19 [1] *family*
1:23 [a] Josh. 2:1; 7:2 [b] Gen. 28:19 [1] *family* [2] *spy out*
1:24 [a] Josh. 2:12, 14
1:25 [1] *struck*
1:27 [a] Josh. 17:11–13 [b] Josh. 21:25 [c] Josh. 17:11 [1] *were determined to dwell*
1:28 [1] *forced labour*
1:29 [a] Josh. 16:10; 1 Kin. 9:16
1:30 [a] Josh. 19:10–16 [1] *forced labourers*
1:31 [a] Josh. 19:24–31
1:32 [a] Ps. 106:34, 35
1:33 [a] Josh. 19:32–39
1:35 [a] Josh. 19:42 [1] *Shaalabbin, Josh.* 19:42 [2] *became stronger* [3] *forced labourers*
1:36 [a] Num. 34:4; Josh. 15:3
2:1 [a] Ex. 20:2; Judg. 6:8, 9 [b] Deut. 1:8 [c] Gen. 17:7, 8; Lev. 26:42, 44; Deut. 7:9; Ps. 89:34
2:2 [a] Ex. 23:32; Deut. 7:2 [b] Ex. 34:12, 13; Deut. 12:3 [c] Ps. 106:34 [1] *treaty or covenant*
2:3 [a] Num. 33:55; Josh. 23:13 [b] Judg. 3:6 [c] Ex. 23:33; Deut. 7:16; Ps. 106:36 [1] *entrap*
2:5 [1] Lit. *Weeping*
2:6 [a] Josh. 22:6; 24:28–31
2:7 [a] Josh. 24:31
2:8 [a] Josh. 24:29
2:9 [a] Josh. 24:30 [b] Josh. 19:49, 50
2:10 [a] Ex. 5:2; 1 Sam. 2:12; Gal. 4:8; [Titus 1:16] [1] *died and joined their ancestors*
2:11 [a] Judg. 3:7, 12; 4:1; 6:1

12 And they [a]forsook the LORD God of their fathers, which brought them out of the land of Egypt, and followed [b]other gods, of the gods of the people that *were* round about them, and [c]bowed themselves unto them, and provoked the LORD to anger.

13 And they forsook the LORD, [a]and served [1]Baal and [2]Ashtaroth.

14 [a]And the anger of the LORD was hot against Israel, and he [b]delivered them into the hands of [1]spoilers that spoiled them, and [c]he sold them into the hands of their enemies round about, so that they [d]could not any longer stand before their enemies.

15 Whithersoever they went out, the hand of the LORD was against them for evil, as the LORD had said, and as the LORD had [a]sworn unto them: and they were greatly distressed.

16 Nevertheless [a]the LORD raised up judges, [1]which delivered them out of the hand of those that [2]spoiled them.

17 And yet they would not hearken unto their judges, but they [a]went[1] a whoring after other gods, and bowed themselves unto them: they turned quickly out of the way which their fathers walked in, obeying the commandments of the LORD; *but* they did not so.

18 And when the LORD raised them up judges, then [a]the LORD was with the judge, and delivered them out of the hand of their enemies all the days of the judge: [b]for [1]it repented the LORD because of their groanings by reason of them that oppressed them and [2]vexed them.

19 And it came to pass, [a]when the judge was dead, *that* they returned, and [1]corrupted *themselves* more than their fathers, in following other gods to serve them, and to bow down unto them; they ceased not from their own doings, nor from their stubborn way.

20 And the anger of the LORD was hot against Israel; and he said, Because that this people hath [a]transgressed my covenant which I commanded their fathers, and have not hearkened unto my voice;

21 I also will not henceforth drive out any from before them of the nations which Joshua [a]left when he died:

22 [a]That through them I may [b]prove[1] Israel, whether they will keep the way of the LORD to walk therein, as their fathers did keep *it*, or not.

23 Therefore the LORD left those nations, without driving them out [1]hastily; neither delivered he them into the hand of Joshua.

## CHAPTER 3

Now these *are* [a]the nations which the LORD left, to [1]prove Israel by them, *even* as many of Israel as had not [2]known all the wars of Canaan;

2 Only that the generations of the children of Israel might [1]know, to teach them war, at the least such as before knew nothing thereof;

3 *Namely*, [a]five lords of the Philistines, and all the Canaanites, and the Sidonians, and the Hivites that dwelt in mount Lebanon, from mount Baal-hermon unto the entering in of Hamath.

4 And they were to [1]prove Israel by them, to [2]know whether they would hearken unto the commandments of the LORD, which he commanded their fathers by the hand of Moses.

5 [a]And the children of Israel dwelt among the Canaanites, Hittites, and Amorites, and Perizzites, and Hivites, and Jebusites:

6 And [a]they took their daughters to be their wives, and gave their daughters to their sons, and served their gods.

7 And the children of Israel did [a]evil in the sight of the LORD, and [b]forgat the LORD their God, and served [1]Baalim and [2]the groves.

8 Therefore the anger of the LORD was hot against Israel, and he [a]sold them into the hand of [b]Chushan-rishathaim king of Mesopotamia: and the children of Israel served Chushan-rishathaim eight years.

9 And when the children of Israel [a]cried unto the LORD, the LORD [b]raised up a deliverer to the children of Israel, who delivered them, *even* [c]Othniel the son of Kenaz, Caleb's younger brother.

10 And [a]the Spirit of the LORD came upon him, and he judged Israel, and went out to war: and the LORD delivered Chushan-rishathaim king of Mesopotamia into his hand; and his hand prevailed against Chushan-rishathaim.

11 And the land had rest forty years. And Othniel the son of Kenaz died.

12 [a]And the children of Israel did evil again in the sight of the LORD: and the LORD strengthened [b]Eglon the king of Moab against Israel, because they had done evil in the sight of the LORD.

13 And he gathered unto him the children of Ammon and [a]Amalek, and went and [1]smote Israel, and [2]possessed [b]the city of palm trees.

14 So the children of Israel [a]served Eglon the king of Moab eighteen years.

15 But when the children of Israel [a]cried unto the LORD, the LORD raised them up a deliverer, Ehud the son of Gera, a Benjamite, a man

---

2:12 [a] Deut. 31:16; Judg. 8:33; 10:6 [b] Deut. 6:14 [c] Ex. 20:5

2:13 [a] Judg. 10:6; Ps. 106:36 [1] Name of a Canaanite god [2] Canaanite goddesses

2:14 [a] Deut. 31:17; Judg. 3:8; Ps. 106:40–42 [b] 2 Kin. 17:20 [c] Is. 50:1 [d] Lev. 26:37; Josh. 7:12, 13 [1] plunderers who despoiled

2:15 [a] Lev. 26:14–26; Deut. 28:15–68

2:16 [a] Judg. 3:9, 10, 15; Ps. 106:43–45 [1] and they delivered [2] plundered

2:17 [a] Ex. 34:15 [1] played the harlot with

2:18 [a] Josh. 1:5 [b] Gen. 6:6 [1] the LORD was moved to pity by [2] harassed

2:19 [a] Judg. 3:12 [1] behaved more corruptly

2:20 [a] [Josh. 23:16]

9:91 [a] Josh. 93:4, 5, 13

2:22 [a] Judg. 3:1, 4 [b] Deut. 8:2, 16; 13:3 [1] test

2:23 [1] immediately

3:1 [a] Judg. 1:1; 2:21, 22 [1] test [2] experienced

3:2 [1] be taught to know

3:3 [a] Josh. 13:3

3:4 [1] test [2] find out

3:5 [a] Ps. 106:35

3:6 [a] Ex. 34:15, 16; Deut. 7:3, 4; Josh. 23:12

3:7 [a] Judg. 2:11 [b] Deut. 32:18 [1] Baals, name or symbol of Canaanite gods [2] Asherahs, names or symbols of Canaanite goddesses

3:8 [a] Deut. 32:30; Judg. 2:14 [b] Hab. 3:7

3:9 [a] Judg. 3:15 [b] Judg. 2:16 [c] Judg. 1:13

3:10 [a] Num. 27:18; 1 Sam. 11:6; 2 Chr. 15:1

3:12 [a] Judg. 2:19 [b] 1 Sam. 12:9

3:13 [a] Judg. 5:14 [b] Deut. 34:3; Judg. 1:16; 2 Chr. 28:15 [1] struck [2] took possession    3:14 [a] Deut. 28:48    3:15 [a] Ps. 78:34

[b]lefthanded: and by him the children of Israel sent a present unto Eglon the king of Moab.

16 But Ehud made him a dagger which had two edges, of a cubit length; and he [1]did gird it under his raiment upon his right thigh.

17 And he brought the present unto Eglon king of Moab: and Eglon *was* a very fat man.

18 And when he had [1]made an end to offer the present, he sent away the people that [2]bare the present.

19 But he himself turned again [a]from the [1]quarries that *were* by Gilgal, and said, I have a secret [2]errand unto thee, O king: [3]who said, Keep silence. And all that [4]stood by him went out from him.

20 And Ehud came unto him; and he was sitting in a summer parlour, which he had for himself alone. And Ehud said, I have a message from God unto thee. And he arose out of *his* seat.

21 And Ehud put forth his left hand, and took the dagger from his right thigh, and thrust it into his belly:

22 And the [1]haft also went in after the blade; and the fat closed upon the blade, so that he could not draw the dagger out of his belly; and the dirt came out.

23 Then Ehud went forth through the porch, and shut the doors of the parlour upon him, and locked them.

24 When he was gone out, [1]his servants came; and when they saw that, behold, the doors of the parlour *were* locked, they said, [2]Surely he [a]covereth his feet in his summer chamber.

25 And they [1]tarried till they were [a]ashamed: and, behold, he opened not the doors of the parlour; therefore they took a key, and opened *them*: and, behold, their lord *was* fallen down dead on the earth.

26 And Ehud escaped while they tarried, and passed beyond the [1]quarries, and escaped unto Seirath.

27 And it came to pass, when he was come, that [a]he blew a trumpet in the [b]mountain of Ephraim, and the children of Israel went down with him from the mount, and he [1]before them.

28 And he said unto them, Follow after me: for [a]the LORD hath delivered your enemies the Moabites into your hand. And they went down after him, and took the [b]fords of Jordan toward Moab, and suffered not a man to pass over.

29 And they slew of Moab at that time about ten thousand men, all [1]lusty, and all men of valour; and there escaped not a man.

30 So Moab was [1]subdued that day under the hand of Israel. And [a]the land had rest fourscore years.

31 And after him was [a]Shamgar the son of Anath, which slew of the Philistines six hundred men [b]with an ox goad: [c]and he also delivered [d]Israel.

## CHAPTER 4

AND [a]the children of Israel again did [b]evil in the sight of the LORD, when Ehud was dead.

2 And the LORD [a]sold them into the hand of Jabin king of Canaan, that reigned in [b]Hazor; the captain of whose host *was* [c]Sisera, which dwelt in [d]Harosheth of the Gentiles.

3 And the children of Israel cried unto the LORD: for he had nine hundred [a]chariots of iron; and twenty years [b]he mightily oppressed the children of Israel.

4 And Deborah, a prophetess, the wife of Lapidoth, she judged Israel at that time.

5 [a]And she dwelt under the palm tree of Deborah between Ramah and Beth-el in mount Ephraim: and the children of Israel came up to her for judgment.

6 And she sent and called [a]Barak the son of Abinoam out [b]of Kedesh-naphtali, and said unto him, Hath not the LORD God of Israel commanded, *saying,* Go and [1]draw toward mount [c]Tabor, and take with thee ten thousand men of the children of Naphtali and of the children of Zebulun?

7 And [a]I will draw unto thee to the [b]river Kishon Sisera, the captain of Jabin's army, with his chariots and his multitude; and I will deliver him into thine hand.

8 And Barak said unto her, If thou wilt go with me, then I will go: but if thou wilt not go with me, *then* I will not go.

9 And she said, I will surely go with thee: notwithstanding the journey that thou takest shall [1]not be for thine honour; for the LORD shall [a]sell Sisera into the hand of a woman. And Deborah arose, and went with Barak to Kedesh.

10 And Barak called [a]Zebulun and Naphtali to Kedesh; and he went up with ten thousand men [b]at[1] his feet: and Deborah went up with him.

11 Now Heber [a]the Kenite, *which was* of the children of [b]Hobab the father in law of Moses, had [1]severed himself from the Kenites, and pitched his tent unto the plain of Zaanaim, [c]which *is* by Kedesh.

12 And they shewed Sisera that Barak the son of Abinoam was gone up to mount Tabor.

13 And Sisera gathered together all his chariots, *even* nine hundred chariots of iron, and all the people that *were* with him, from Harosheth of the Gentiles unto the river of Kishon.

---

3:15 [b] Judg. 20:16
3:16 [1] *fastened*
3:18 [1] *finished offering* [2] *carried*
3:19 [a] Josh. 4:20
[1] *stone images*
[2] *message for you*
[3] *He* [4] *attended him*
3:22 [1] *handle*
3:24 [a] 1 Sam.
24:3 [1] *Eglon's*
[2] *He is probably attending to his needs in the cool chamber.*
3:25 [a] 2 Kin. 2:17; 8:11 [1] *waited*
3:26 [1] *stone images*
3:27 [a] Judg. 6:34; 1 Sam. 13:3 [b] Josh. 17:15 [1] *led*
3:28 [a] Judg. 7:9, 15; 1 Sam. 17:47 [b] Josh. 2:7; Judg. 12:5
3:29 [1] *stout*
3:30 [a] Judg. 3:11 [1] *defeated*

3:31 [a] Judg. 5:6 [b] 1 Sam. 17:47 [c] Judg. 2:16 [d] 1 Sam. 4:1
4:1 [a] Judg. 2:19 [b] Judg. 2:11
4:2 [a] Judg. 2:14 [b] Josh. 11:1, 10 [c] 1 Sam. 12:9; Ps. 83:9 [d] Judg. 4:13, 16
4:3 [a] Deut. 20:1; Judg. 1:19 [b] Ps. 106:42
4:5 [a] Gen. 35:8
4:6 [a] Heb. 11:32 [b] Josh. 19:37; 21:32 [c] Judg. 8:18 [1] *deploy troops*
4:7 [a] Ex. 14:4 [b] Judg. 5:21; 1 Kin. 18:40; Ps. 83:9, 10
4:9 [a] Judg. 2:14 [1] *be no glory for you*
4:10 [a] Judg. 5:18 [b] Ex. 11:8; 1 Kin. 20:10 [1] *under his command*
4:11 [a] Judg. 1:16 [b] Num. 10:29 [c] Judg. 4:6 [1] *separated*

14 And Deborah said unto Barak, [1]Up; for this *is* the day in which the LORD hath delivered Sisera into thine hand: [a]is not the LORD gone out before thee? So Barak went down from mount Tabor, and ten thousand men after him.

15 And the LORD [1]discomfited Sisera, and all *his* chariots, and all *his* host, with the edge of the sword before Barak; so that Sisera lighted down off *his* chariot, and fled away on his feet.

16 But Barak pursued after the chariots, and after the host, unto Harosheth of the Gentiles: and all the [1]host of Sisera fell [2]upon the edge of the sword; *and* there was not a man [a]left.

17 Howbeit Sisera fled away [1]on his feet to the tent of [a]Jael the wife of Heber the Kenite: for *there was* peace between Jabin the king of Hazor and the house of Heber the Kenite.

18 And Jael went out to meet Sisera, and said unto him, Turn in, my lord, turn in to me; fear not. And when he had turned in unto her into the tent, she covered him with a [1]mantle.

19 And he said unto her, Give me, I pray thee, a little water to drink; for I am thirsty. And she opened [a]a bottle of milk, and gave him drink, and covered him.

20 Again he said unto her, Stand in the door of the tent, and it shall be, when any man doth come and enquire of thee, and say, Is there any man here? that thou shalt say, No.

21 Then Jael Heber's wife [a]took a [1]nail of the tent, and took an hammer in her hand, and went softly unto him, and [2]smote the nail into his temples, and fastened it into the ground: for he was fast asleep and weary. So he died.

22 And, behold, as Barak pursued Sisera, Jael came out to meet him, and said unto him, Come, and I will shew thee the man whom thou seekest. And when he came into her *tent*, behold, Sisera lay dead, and the nail *was* in his temples.

23 So God subdued on that day Jabin the king of Canaan before the children of Israel.

24 And the hand of the children of Israel prospered, and prevailed against Jabin the king of Canaan, until they had destroyed Jabin king of Canaan.

## CHAPTER 5

THEN [a]sang Deborah and Barak the son of Abinoam on that day, saying,

2 Praise ye the LORD [1]for the [a]avenging of Israel, [b]when the people willingly [2]offered themselves.

3 [a]Hear, O ye kings; give ear, O ye princes; I, *even* [b]I, will sing unto the LORD; I will sing *praise* to the LORD God of Israel.

4 LORD, [a]when thou wentest out of Seir, when thou marchedst out of [b]the field of Edom, the earth trembled, and the heavens dropped, the clouds also dropped water.

5 [a]The mountains [1]melted from before the LORD, *even* [b]that Sinai from before the LORD God of Israel.

6 In the days of [a]Shamgar the son of Anath, in the days of [b]Jael, [c]the highways were [1]unoccupied, and the travellers walked through byways.

7 [1]The inhabitants of the villages ceased, they ceased in Israel, until that I Deborah arose, that I arose a mother in Israel.

8 They chose [a]new gods; then *was* war in the gates: was there a shield or spear seen among forty thousand in Israel?

9 My heart *is* [1]toward the governors of Israel, that offered themselves willingly among the people. Bless ye the LORD.

10 Speak, ye that ride on white [a]asses, ye that sit in judgment, and walk by the way.

11 They that are delivered from the noise of archers in the places of drawing water, there shall they [1]rehearse the righteous acts of the LORD, *even* the righteous acts *toward the inhabitants* of his villages in Israel: then shall the people of the LORD go down to the gates.

12 [a]Awake, awake, Deborah: awake, awake, utter a song: arise, Barak, and lead thy captivity captive, thou son of Abinoam.

13 Then [1]he made him that remaineth have dominion over the nobles among the people: the LORD made me have dominion over the mighty.

14 Out of Ephraim [1]*was there* a root of them against [a]Amalek; after thee, Benjamin, among thy people; out of Machir came down [2]governors, and out of Zebulun [3]they that handle the pen of the writer.

15 And the [1]princes of Issachar *were* with Deborah; even Issachar, and also Barak: he was sent [2]on foot into the valley. For the divisions of Reuben *there were* great [3]thoughts of heart.

16 Why [1]abodest thou among the sheepfolds, to hear the [2]bleatings of the flocks? For the divisions of Reuben *there were* great searchings of heart.

17 [a]Gilead abode beyond Jordan: and why did Dan remain in ships? [b]Asher continued on the sea shore, and abode in his [1]breaches.

### Center column notes

4:14 [a] Deut. 9:3; 31:3; 2 Sam. 5:24; Ps. 68:7; Is. 52:12 [1] *Arise!*

4:15 [1] *routed*

4:16 [a] Ex. 14:28; Ps. 83:9 [1] *army* [2] *by*

4:17 [a] Judg. 5:6 [1] *on foot*

4:18 [1] *blanket or rug*

4:19 [a] Judg. 5:24–27

4:21 [a] Judg. 5:24–27 [1] *tent peg* [2] *drove the peg*

5:1 [a] Ex. 15:1; Judg. 4:4

5:2 [a] Ps. 18:47 [b] 2 Chr. 17:16 [1] *when leaders lead in Israel* [2] *volunteered*

5:3 [a] Deut. 32:1, 3 [b] Ps. 27:6

5:4 [a] Deut. 33:2; Ps. 68:7 [b] Ps. 68:8

5:5 [a] Ps. 97:5 [b] Ex. 19:18 [1] *gushed*

5:6 [a] Judg. 3:31 [b] Judg. 4:17 [c] Is. 33:8 [1] *deserted*

5:7 [1] *Village life ceased*

5:8 [a] Deut. 32:17

5:9 [1] *with the rulers*

5:10 [a] Judg. 10:4; 12:14

5:11 [1] *recount*

5:12 [a] Ps. 57:8

5:13 [1] *the survivors came down, the people against the nobles; the LORD came down against the mighty*

5:14 [a] Judg. 3:13 [1] *were those whose roots were in Amalek* [2] *rulers* [3] *those who bear the recruiter's staff*

5:15 [1] *rulers* [2] *under his command* [3] *resolves*

5:16 [1] *did you sit between* [2] *pipings for*

5:17 [a] Josh. 22:9 [b] Josh. 19:99, 31 [1] *inlets*

18 ᵃZebulun and Naphtali *were* a people *that* ¹jeoparded their lives unto the death in the ²high places of the field.

19 The kings came *and* fought, then fought the kings of Canaan in ᵃTaanach by the waters of Megiddo; they took no ¹gain of money.

20 They fought from heaven; the stars in their courses fought against Sisera.

21 ᵃThe river of Kishon swept them away, that ancient river, the river Kishon. O my soul, ¹thou hast trodden down strength.

22 Then ¹were the horsehoofs broken by the means of the pransings, the pransings of their mighty ones.

23 Curse ye Meroz, said the angel of the LORD, curse ye bitterly the inhabitants thereof; because they came not to the help of the LORD, to the help of the LORD against the mighty.

24 Blessed above women shall Jael the wife of Heber the Kenite be, ᵃblessed shall she be above women in the tent.

25 He asked water, *and* she gave *him* milk; she brought forth butter in a lordly dish.

26 She put her hand to the nail, and her right hand to the workmen's hammer; and with the hammer she smote Sisera, she smote off his head, when she had pierced and stricken through his temples.

27 At her feet he bowed, he fell, he lay down: at her feet he bowed, he fell: where he bowed, there he fell down ᵃdead.

28 The mother of Sisera looked out at a window, and cried through the lattice, Why is his chariot *so* long in coming? why tarry the wheels of his chariots?

29 Her ¹wise ladies answered her, yea, she ²returned answer to herself,

30 Have they not ¹sped? have they *not* divided the prey; to every man a damsel or two; to Sisera a prey of divers colours, a prey of divers colours of needlework, of divers colours of needlework on both sides, *meet* for the necks of *them that take* the spoil?

31 So let all thine enemies ᵃperish, O LORD: but *let* them that love him *be* ᵇas the ᶜsun when he goeth forth in his ᵈmight. And the land had rest forty years.

## CHAPTER 6

AND the children of Israel did ᵃevil in the sight of the LORD: and the LORD delivered them into the hand of ᵇMidian seven years.

2 And the hand of Midian prevailed against Israel: *and* because of the Midianites the children of Israel made them the dens which *are* in the

mountains, and ᵃcaves, and strong holds.

3 And *so* it was, when Israel had sown, that the Midianites came up, and the Amalekites, and the ᵃchildren of the east, even they came up against them;

4 And they encamped against them, and ᵃdestroyed the ¹increase of the earth, till thou come unto Gaza, and left no sustenance for Israel, neither sheep, nor ox, nor ᵇass.

5 For they came up with their cattle and their tents, and they came as grasshoppers for multitude; *for* both they and their camels were ¹without number: and they entered into the land to destroy it.

6 And Israel was greatly impoverished because of the Midianites; and the children of Israel ᵃcried unto the LORD.

7 And it came to pass, when the children of Israel cried unto the LORD because of the Midianites,

8 That the LORD sent a prophet unto the children of Israel, which said unto them, Thus saith the LORD God of Israel, I brought you up from Egypt, and brought you forth out of the ᵃhouse of ¹bondage;

9 And I delivered you out of the hand of the Egyptians, and out of the hand of all that oppressed you, and ᵃdrave them out from before you, and gave you their land;

10 And I said unto you, I *am* the LORD your God; ᵃfear not the gods of the Amorites, in whose land ye dwell: but ye have not obeyed my ᵇvoice.

11 And there came an angel of the LORD, and sat under an oak which *was* in Ophrah, that *pertained* unto Joash ᵃthe Abiezrite: and his son ᵇGideon threshed wheat by the winepress, to hide *it* from the Midianites.

12 And the ᵃangel of the LORD appeared unto him, and said unto him, The LORD *is* ᵇwith thee, thou mighty man of valour.

13 And Gideon said unto him, Oh ¹my Lord, if the LORD be with us, why then is all this ²befallen us? and ᵃwhere *be* all his miracles ᵇwhich our fathers told us of, saying, Did not the LORD bring us up from Egypt? but now the LORD hath ᶜforsaken us, and delivered us into the hands of the Midianites.

14 And the LORD looked upon him, and said, ᵃGo in this ¹thy might, and thou shalt save Israel from the hand of the Midianites: ᵇhave not I sent thee?

15 And he said unto him, Oh ¹my Lord, wherewith shall I save Israel? behold, ᵃmy family *is* poor in Manasseh, and I *am* the least in my father's house.

5:18 ᵃ Judg. 4:6, 10 ¹ *jeopardized* ² *heights of the battlefield*

5:19 ᵃ Judg. 1:27 ¹ *plunder of silver*

5:21 ᵃ Judg. 4:7 ¹ *march on in strength*

5:22 ¹ *the horses' hooves pounded, the galloping, galloping of his steeds*

5:24 ᵃ [Luke 1:28]

5:27 ᵃ Judg. 4:18–21

5:29 ¹ *wisest* ² *answers herself*

5:30 ¹ *found*

5:31 ᵃ Ps. 92:9 ᵇ 2 Sam. 23:4 ᶜ Ps. 37:6; 89:36, 37 ᵈ Ps. 19:5

6:1 ᵃ Judg. 2:11 ᵇ Num. 22:4; 31:1–3

6:2 ᵃ 1 Sam. 13:6; Heb. 11:38

6:3 ᵃ Judg. 7:12

6:4 ᵃ Lev. 26:16 ᵇ Deut. 28:31 ¹ *produce*

6:5 ¹ *innumerable*

6:6 ᵃ Ps. 50:15; Hos. 5:15

6:8 ᵃ Josh. 24:17 ¹ *slavery*

6:9 ᵃ Ps. 44:2, 3

6:10 ᵃ 2 Kin. 17:35, 37, 38; Jer. 10:2 ᵇ Judg. 2:1, 2

6:11 ᵃ Josh. 17:2; Judg. 6:15 ᵇ Judg. 7:1; Heb. 11:32

6:12 ᵃ Judg. 13:3; Luke 1:11, 28 ᵇ Josh. 1:5

6:13 ᵃ [Is. 59:1] ᵇ Josh. 4:6, 21; Ps. 44:1 ᶜ Deut. 31:17; 2 Chr. 15:2; Ps. 44:9–16 ¹ Heb. *adoni,* used to refer to a man ² *happened to us*

6:14 ᵃ 1 Sam. 12:11 ᵇ Josh. 1:9 ¹ *strength of yours*

6:15 ᵃ 1 Sam. 9:21 ¹ Heb. *Adonai,* used of God

16 And the LORD said unto him, <sup>a</sup>Surely I will be with thee, and thou shalt <sup>1</sup>smite the Midianites as one man.

17 And he said unto him, If now I have found grace in thy sight, then <sup>a</sup>shew<sup>1</sup> me a sign <sup>2</sup>that thou talkest with me.

18 <sup>a</sup>Depart not hence, I pray thee, until I come unto thee, and bring forth my <sup>1</sup>present, and set *it* before thee. And he said, I will tarry until thou come again.

19 <sup>a</sup>And Gideon went in, and made ready a kid, and unleavened cakes of an ephah of flour: the flesh he put in a basket, and he put the broth in a pot, and brought *it* out unto him under the oak, and presented *it*.

20 And the angel of God said unto him, Take the flesh and the unleavened cakes, and <sup>a</sup>lay *them* upon this rock, and <sup>b</sup>pour out the broth. And he did so.

21 Then the angel of the LORD put forth the end of the staff that *was* in his hand, and touched the flesh and the unleavened cakes; and <sup>a</sup>there rose up fire out of the rock, and consumed the flesh and the unleavened cakes. Then the angel of the LORD departed out of his sight.

22 And when Gideon <sup>a</sup>perceived that he *was* an angel of the LORD, Gideon said, Alas, O Lord GOD! <sup>b</sup>for because I have seen an angel of the LORD face to face.

23 And the LORD said unto him, <sup>a</sup>Peace *be* unto thee; fear not: thou shalt not die.

24 Then Gideon built an altar there unto the LORD, and called it <sup>1</sup>Jehovah-shalom: unto this day it *is* yet <sup>a</sup>in Ophrah of the Abiezrites.

25 And it came to pass the same night, that the LORD said unto him, Take thy father's young bullock, even the second bullock of seven years old, and <sup>a</sup>throw<sup>1</sup> down the altar of <sup>b</sup>Baal that thy father hath, and <sup>c</sup>cut down <sup>2</sup>the grove that *is* by it:

26 And build an altar unto the LORD thy God upon the top of this <sup>1</sup>rock, in the <sup>2</sup>ordered place, and take the second bullock, and offer a burnt sacrifice with the wood of the grove which thou shalt cut down.

27 Then Gideon took ten men of his servants, and did as the LORD had said unto him: and *so* it was, because he feared his father's household, and the men of the city, that he could not do *it* by day, that he did *it* by night.

28 And when the men of the city arose early in the morning, behold, the altar of Baal was cast down, and the grove was cut down that *was* by it, and the second bullock was offered upon the altar *that was* built.

---

<sup>a</sup> Ex. 3:12;
Josh. 1:5  <sup>1</sup> *defeat*

6:17 <sup>a</sup> Judg. 6:36,
37; 2 Kin. 20:8; Ps.
86:17; Is. 7:11; 38:7,
8  <sup>1</sup> *give me some
evidence*  <sup>2</sup> *that
it is you who talk
with me*

6:18 <sup>a</sup> Gen. 18:3, 5
<sup>1</sup> *offering*

6:19 <sup>a</sup> Gen. 18:6–8

6:20 <sup>a</sup> Judg. 13:19
<sup>b</sup> 1 Kin. 18:33, 34

6:21 <sup>a</sup> Lev. 9:24

6:22 <sup>a</sup> Gen. 32:30;
Ex. 33:20; Judg.
13:21, 22  <sup>b</sup> Gen.
16:13

6:23 <sup>a</sup> Dan. 10:19

6:24 <sup>a</sup> Judg. 8:32
<sup>1</sup> Lit. *The LORD Is
Peace*

6:25 <sup>a</sup> Judg.
2:2  <sup>b</sup> Judg.
3:7  <sup>c</sup> Ex. 34:13;
Deut. 7:5  <sup>1</sup> *tear*
<sup>2</sup> Heb. *asherah*, a
wooden image
for a Canaanite
goddess

6:26 <sup>1</sup> *strong
hold*  <sup>2</sup> *proper
arrangement*

6:30 <sup>1</sup> *torn*
6:31 <sup>1</sup> *contend*
<sup>2</sup> *by morning*
6:32 <sup>a</sup> Judg.
7:1; 1 Sam. 12:11;
2 Sam. 11:21  <sup>1</sup> Lit.
*Let Baal Plead*

6:33 <sup>a</sup> Judg. 6:3
<sup>b</sup> Josh. 17:16; Hos.
1:5  <sup>1</sup> *encamped*

6:34 <sup>a</sup> Judg. 3:10;
1 Chr. 12:18; 2 Chr.
24:20  <sup>b</sup> Num.
10:3; Judg. 3:27
<sup>1</sup> *the Abiezrites
gathered behind
him*

6:35 <sup>a</sup> Judg. 5:17;
7:23  <sup>b</sup> Judg. 4:6,
10; 5:18  <sup>1</sup> *gathered behind*

6:37 <sup>a</sup> [Ex. 4:3–7]

6:39 <sup>a</sup> Gen. 18:32

7:1 <sup>a</sup> Judg. 6:32
<sup>1</sup> *encamped*
<sup>2</sup> *camp*

---

29 And they said one to another, Who hath done this thing? And when they enquired and asked, they said, Gideon the son of Joash hath done this thing.

30 Then the men of the city said unto Joash, Bring out thy son, that he may die: because he hath <sup>1</sup>cast down the altar of Baal, and because he hath cut down the grove that *was* by it.

31 And Joash said unto all that stood against him, Will ye <sup>1</sup>plead for Baal? will ye save him? he that will plead for him, let him be put to death <sup>2</sup>whilst *it is yet* morning: if he *be* a god, let him plead for himself, because *one* hath cast down his altar.

32 Therefore on that day he called him <sup>a</sup>Jerub-baal,<sup>1</sup> saying, Let Baal plead against him, because he hath thrown down his altar.

33 Then all <sup>a</sup>the Midianites and the Amalekites and the children of the east were gathered together, and went over, and <sup>1</sup>pitched in <sup>b</sup>the valley of Jezreel.

34 But <sup>a</sup>the Spirit of the LORD came upon Gideon, and he <sup>b</sup>blew a trumpet; and <sup>1</sup>Abiezer was gathered after him.

35 And he sent messengers throughout all Manasseh; who also <sup>1</sup>was gathered after him: and he sent messengers unto <sup>a</sup>Asher, and unto <sup>b</sup>Zebulun, and unto Naphtali; and they came up to meet them.

36 And Gideon said unto God, If thou wilt save Israel by mine hand, as thou hast said,

37 <sup>a</sup>Behold, I will put a fleece of wool in the floor; *and* if the dew be on the fleece only, and *it be* dry upon all the earth *beside*, then shall I know that thou wilt save Israel by mine hand, as thou hast said.

38 And it was so: for he rose up early on the morrow, and thrust the fleece together, and wringed the dew out of the fleece, a bowl full of water.

39 And Gideon said unto God, <sup>a</sup>Let not thine anger be hot against me, and I will speak but this once: let me prove, I pray thee, but this once with the fleece; let it now be dry only upon the fleece, and upon all the ground let there be dew.

40 And God did so that night: for it was dry upon the fleece only, and there was dew on all the ground.

## CHAPTER 7

THEN <sup>a</sup>Jerub-baal, who *is* Gideon, and all the people that *were* with him, rose up early, and <sup>1</sup>pitched beside the well of Harod: so that the <sup>2</sup>host of the Midianites were on the north side of them, by the hill of Moreh, in the valley.

2 And the LORD said unto Gideon, The people that *are* with thee *are* too

many for me to give the Midianites into their hands, lest Israel ªvaunt themselves against me, saying, Mine own hand hath saved me.

3 Now therefore go to, proclaim in the ears of the people, saying, ªWhosoever *is* fearful and afraid, let him return and depart early from mount Gilead. And there returned of the people twenty and two thousand; and there remained ten thousand.

4 And the LORD said unto Gideon, The people *are* yet *too* many; bring them down unto the water, and I ¹try them for thee there: and it shall be, *that* of whom I say unto thee, This shall go with thee, the same shall go with thee; and of whomsoever I say unto thee, This shall not go with thee, the same shall not go.

5 So he brought down the people unto the water: and the LORD said unto Gideon, Every one that lappeth of the water with his tongue, as a dog lappeth, him shalt thou set by himself; likewise every one that boweth down upon his knees to drink.

6 And the number of them that lapped, *putting* their hand to their mouth, were three hundred men: but all the rest of the people bowed down upon their knees to drink water.

7 And the LORD said unto Gideon, ªBy the three hundred men that lapped will I save you, and deliver the Midianites into thine hand: and let all the *other* people go every man unto his ¹place.

8 So the people took victuals in their hand, and their trumpets: and he sent all *the rest of* Israel every man unto his tent, and retained those three hundred men: and the ¹host of Midian was beneath him in the valley.

9 And it came to pass the same ªnight, that the LORD said unto him, Arise, get thee down unto the host; for I have delivered it into thine hand.

10 But if thou fear to go down, go thou with Phurah thy servant down to the host:

11 And thou shalt ªhear what they say; and afterward ¹shall thine hands be strengthened to go down unto the host. Then went he down with Phurah his servant unto the outside of the armed men that *were* in the host.

12 And the Midianites and the Amalekites and ªall the children of the east lay along in the valley like grasshoppers for ᵇmultitude; and their camels *were* ¹without number, as the sand by the sea side for multitude.

13 And when Gideon was come, behold, *there was* a man that told a dream unto his fellow, and said, Behold, I dreamed a dream, and, lo, a

cake of barley bread tumbled into the host of Midian, and came unto a tent, and smote it that it fell, and over-turned it, that the tent lay along.

14 And his fellow answered and said, This *is* nothing else save the sword of Gideon the son of Joash, a man of Israel: *for* into his hand hath ªGod delivered Midian, and all the host.

15 And it was *so,* when Gideon heard the telling of the dream, and the interpretation thereof, that he worshipped, and returned into the ¹host of Israel, and said, Arise; for the LORD hath delivered into your hand the host of Midian.

16 And he divided the three hundred men *into* three companies, and he put a trumpet in every man's hand, with empty pitchers, and ¹lamps within the pitchers.

17 And he said unto them, Look on me, and do likewise: and, behold, when I come to the outside of the camp, it shall be *that,* as I do, so shall ye do.

18 When I blow with a trumpet, I and all that *are* with me, then blow ye the trumpets also on every side of all the camp, and say, *The sword* of the LORD, and of Gideon.

19 So Gideon, and the hundred men that *were* with him, came unto the outside of the camp in the beginning of the middle watch; and they had but newly set the watch: and they blew the trumpets, and brake the pitchers that *were* in their hands.

20 And the three companies blew the trumpets, and brake the pitchers, and held the lamps in their left hands, and the trumpets in their right hands to blow *withal:* and they cried, The sword of the LORD, and of Gideon.

21 And they ªstood every man in his place round about the camp: ᵇand all the ¹host ran, and cried, and fled.

22 And the three hundred ªblew the trumpets, and ᵇthe LORD set ᶜevery man's sword against his ¹fellow, even throughout ²all the host: and the host fled to Beth-shittah in Zererath, *and* to the border of ᵈAbel-meholah, unto Tabbath.

23 And the men of Israel gathered themselves together out of ªNaphtali, and out of Asher, and out of all Manasseh, and pursued after the Midianites.

24 And Gideon sent messengers throughout all ªmount Ephraim, saying, Come down against the Midianites, and ¹take before them the waters unto Beth-barah and Jordan. Then all the men of Ephraim gathered themselves together, and ᵇtook the waters unto ᶜBeth-barah and Jordan.

---

**Cross-references (center column):**

7:2 ª Deut. 8:17; Is. 10:13
7:3 ª Deut. 20:8
7:4 ¹ *test*
7:7 ª 1 Sam. 14:6 ¹ *home*
7:8 ¹ *camp*
7:9 ª Gen. 46:2, 3; Judg. 6:25
7:11 ª Gen. 24:14; 1 Sam. 14:9, 10 ¹ *you will be encouraged*
7:12 ª Judg. 6:3, 33; 8:10 ᵇ Judg. 6:5 ¹ *innumerable*

7:14 ª Judg. 6:14, 16
7:15 ¹ *camp*
7:16 ¹ *torches*
7:21 ª Ex. 14:13, 14; 2 Chr. 20:17 ᵇ 2 Kin. 7:7 ¹ *army*
7:22 ª Josh. 6:4, 16, 20 ᵇ Ps. 83:9; Is. 9:4 ᶜ 1 Sam. 14:20; 2 Chr. 20:23 ᵈ 1 Kin. 4:12 ¹ *companion* ² *the whole camp*
7:23 ª Judg. 6:35
7:24 ª Judg. 3:27 ᵇ Judg. 3:28 ᶜ John 1:28 ¹ *seize from them the watering places as far as*

25 And they took [a]two princes of the Midianites, [b]Oreb and Zeeb; and they slew Oreb upon the rock Oreb, and Zeeb they slew at the winepress of Zeeb, and pursued Midian, and brought the heads of Oreb and Zeeb to Gideon on the [c]other side Jordan.

## CHAPTER 8

AND [a]the men of Ephraim said unto him, Why hast thou served us thus, that thou calledst us not, when thou wentest to fight with the Midianites? And they did [1]chide with him sharply.

2 And he said unto them, What have I done now in comparison of you? *Is* not the [1]gleaning of the grapes of Ephraim better than [2]the vintage of [a]Abiezer?

3 [a]God hath delivered into your hands the princes of Midian, Oreb and Zeeb: and what was I able to do in comparison of you? Then their [b]anger was [1]abated toward him, when he had said that.

4 And Gideon came [a]to Jordan, *and* passed over, he, and [b]the three hundred men that *were* with him, faint, yet pursuing *them*.

5 And he said unto the men of [a]Succoth, Give, I pray you, loaves of bread unto the people that follow me; for they *be* faint, and I am pursuing after Zebah and Zalmunna, kings of Midian.

6 And the princes of Succoth said, [a]*Are*[1] the hands of Zebah and Zalmunna now in thine hand, that [b]we should give bread unto thine army?

7 And Gideon said, Therefore when the LORD hath delivered Zebah and Zalmunna into mine hand, [a]then I will tear your flesh with the thorns of the wilderness and with briers.

8 And he went up thence [a]to Penuel, and spake unto them likewise: and the men of Penuel answered him as the men of Succoth had answered *him*.

9 And he spake also unto the men of Penuel, saying, When I [a]come again in peace, [b]I will break down this tower.

10 Now Zebah and Zalmunna *were* in Karkor, and their hosts with them, about fifteen thousand *men*, all that were left of [a]all the [1]hosts of the children of the east: for there fell [b]an hundred and twenty thousand men that drew sword.

11 And Gideon went up by the way of them that dwelt in tents on the east of [a]Nobah and Jogbehah, and [1]smote the host: for the host was [b]secure.

12 And when Zebah and Zalmunna fled, he pursued after them, and [a]took the two kings of Midian, Zebah

and Zalmunna, and [1]discomfited all the host.

13 And Gideon the son of Joash returned from battle before the sun *was up,*

14 And caught a young man of the men of Succoth, and enquired of him: and he [1]described unto him the princes of Succoth, and the elders thereof, *even* threescore and seventeen men.

15 And he came unto the men of Succoth, and said, Behold Zebah and Zalmunna, with whom ye did [a]upbraid[1] me, saying, *Are* the hands of Zebah and Zalmunna now in thine hand, that we should give bread unto thy men *that are* weary?

16 [a]And he took the elders of the city, and thorns of the wilderness and briers, and with them he [1]taught the men of Succoth.

17 [a]And he beat down the tower of [b]Penuel, and slew the men of the city.

18 Then said he unto Zebah and Zalmunna, What manner of men *were they* whom ye slew at [a]Tabor? And they answered, As thou *art,* so *were* they; each one resembled the children of a king.

19 And he said, They *were* my brethren, *even* the sons of my mother: *as* the LORD liveth, if ye had saved them alive, I would not slay you.

20 And he said unto Jether his firstborn, Up, *and* slay them. But the youth drew not his sword: for he feared, because he *was* yet a youth.

21 Then Zebah and Zalmunna said, Rise thou, and fall upon us: for as the man *is, so is* his strength. And Gideon arose, and [a]slew Zebah and Zalmunna, and took away the [1]ornaments that *were* on their camels' necks.

22 Then the men of Israel said unto Gideon, [a]Rule thou over us, both thou, and thy son, and thy son's son also: for thou hast [b]delivered us from the hand of Midian.

23 And Gideon said unto them, I will not rule over you, neither shall my son rule over you: [a]the LORD shall rule over you.

24 And Gideon said unto them, I would [1]desire a request of you, that ye would give me every man the earrings of his [2]prey. (For they had golden earrings, [a]because they *were* Ishmaelites.)

25 And they answered, We will willingly give *them*. And they spread a garment, and did cast therein every man the earrings of his prey.

26 And the weight of the golden earrings that he requested was a thousand and seven hundred *shekels* of gold; beside ornaments, and collars, and purple raiment that *was* on

7:25 [a] Judg. 8:3
[b] Ps. 83:11; Is. 10:26 [c] Judg. 8:4

8:1 [a] Judg. 12:1; 2 Sam. 19:41 [1] *reprimand*

8:2 [a] Judg. 6:11 [1] *few grapes left after the harvest* [2] *the whole harvest*

8:3 [a] Judg. 7:24, 25 [b] Prov. 15:1 [1] *subsided*

8:4 [a] Judg. 7:25 [b] Judg. 7:6

8:5 [a] Gen. 33:17; Ps. 60:6

8:6 [a] 1 Kin. 20:11; Judg. 8:15 [b] 1 Sam. 25:11 [1] *Have they already been captured?* lit. *Is the palm*

8:7 [a] Judg. 8:16

8:8 [a] Gen. 32:30, 31; 1 Kin. 12:25

8:9 [a] 1 Kin. 22:27 [b] Judg. 8:17

8:10 [a] Judg. 7:12 [b] Judg. 6:5 [1] *army*

8:11 [a] Num. 32:35, 42 [b] Judg. 18:27; [1 Thess. 5:3] [1] *attacked the army while the camp felt secure*

8:12 [a] Ps. 83:11

[1] *routed the whole army*

8:14 [1] Lit. *wrote down for him*

8:15 [a] Judg. 8:6 [1] *ridiculed*

8:16 [a] Judg. 8:7 [1] *disciplined*

8:17 [a] Judg. 8:9 [b] 1 Kin. 12:25

8:18 [a] Judg. 4:6; Ps. 89:12

8:21 [a] Ps. 83:11 [1] *crescent ornaments*

8:22 [a] [Judg. 9:8] [b] Judg. 3:9; 9:17

8:23 [a] 1 Sam. 8:7; 10:19; 12:12; Ps. 10:16

8:24 [a] Gen. 37:25, 28 [1] *like to make* [2] *plunder*

the kings of Midian, and beside the chains that *were* about their camels' necks.

27 And Gideon [a]made an ephod thereof, and put it in his city, *even* [b]in Ophrah: and all Israel [c]went[1] thither a whoring after it: which thing became [d]a snare unto Gideon, and to his house.

28 Thus was Midian subdued before the children of Israel, so that they lifted up their heads no more. [a]And the country was in quietness forty years in the days of Gideon.

29 And [a]Jerub-baal the son of Joash went and dwelt in his own house.

30 And Gideon had [a]threescore and ten sons of his body begotten: for he had many wives.

31 [a]And his concubine that *was* in Shechem, she also bare him a son, whose name he called Abimelech.

32 And Gideon the son of Joash died [a]in a good old age, and was buried in the sepulchre of Joash his father, [b]in Ophrah of the Abiezrites.

33 And it came to pass, [a]as soon as Gideon was dead, that the children of Israel turned again, and [b]went[1] a whoring after Baalim, [c]and made Baal-berith their god.

34 And the children of Israel [a]remembered not the LORD their God, who had delivered them out of the hands of all their enemies on every side:

35 [a]Neither shewed they kindness to the house of Jerub-baal, *namely,* Gideon, according to all the goodness which he had shewed unto Israel.

## CHAPTER 9

AND Abimelech the son of Jerub-baal went to Shechem unto [a]his mother's brethren, and [1]communed with them, and with all the family of the house of his mother's father, saying,

2 Speak, I pray you, in the [1]ears of all the men of Shechem, [2]Whether *is* better for you, either that all the sons of Jerub-baal, *which are* [a]threescore and ten persons, reign over you, or that one reign over you? remember also that I *am* your [b]bone[3] and your flesh.

3 And his mother's brethren spake of him in the ears of all the men of Shechem all these words: and their hearts inclined to follow Abimelech; for they said, He *is* our [a]brother.

4 And they gave him threescore and ten *pieces* of silver out of the house of [a]Baal-berith, wherewith Abimelech hired [b]vain[1] and light persons, which followed him.

5 And he went unto his father's house [a]at Ophrah, and [b]slew his brethren the sons of Jerub-baal,

**Cross references (center column):**

8:27 [a] Judg. 17:5
[b] Judg. 6:11, 24
[c] [Ps. 106:39]
[d] Deut. 7:16
[1] *played the harlot with it there*
8:28 [a] Judg. 5:31
8:29 [a] Judg. 6:32; 7:1
8:30 [a] Judg. 9:2, 5
8:31 [a] Judg. 9:1
8:32 [a] Gen. 25:8; Job 5:26 [b] Judg. 6:24; 8:27
8:33 [a] Judg. 2:19 [b] Judg. 2:17 [c] Judg. 9:4, 46 [1] *played the harlot with the Baals*
8:34 [a] Deut. 4:9; Judg. 3:7; Ps. 78:11, 42; 106:13, 21
8:35 [a] Judg. 9:16–18
9:1 [a] Judg. 8:31, 35 [1] *conferred*
9:2 [a] Judg. 8:30; 9:5, 18 [b] Gen. 29:14 [1] *hearing* [2] *Which* [3] *own flesh and bone*
9:3 [a] Gen. 29:15
9:4 [a] Judg. 8:33 [b] Judg. 11:3; 2 Chr. 13:7; Acts 17:5 [1] *worthless and reckless*
9:5 [a] Judg. 6:24 [b] Judg. 8:30; 9:2, 18; 2 Kin. 11:1, 2

9:7 [a] Deut. 11:29; 27:12; Josh. 8:33; John 4:20 [1] *Listen*
9:8 [a] 2 Kin. 14:9 [b] Judg. 8:22, 23
9:9 [a] [John 5:23]
9:13 [a] Ps. 104:15
9:15 [a] Is. 30:2; Dan. 4:12; Hos. 14:7 [b] Num. 21:28; Judg. 9:20; Ezek. 19:14 [c] 2 Kin. 14:9; Is. 2:13; Ezek. 31:3
9:16 [a] Judg. 8:35 [1] *as he deserves*
9:17 [a] Judg. 7 [b] Judg. 8:22
9:18 [a] Judg. 8:30, 35; 9:2, 5, 6 [b] Judg. 8:31
9:19 [a] Is. 8:6; [Phil. 3:3]
9:20 [a] Judg. 9:15, 45, 56, 57

*being* threescore and ten persons, upon one stone: notwithstanding yet Jotham the youngest son of Jerubbaal was left; for he hid himself.

6 And all the men of Shechem gathered together, and all the house of Millo, and went, and made Abimelech king, by the plain of the pillar that *was* in Shechem.

7 And when they told *it* to Jotham, he went and stood in the top of [a]mount Gerizim, and lifted up his voice, and cried, and said unto them, [1]Hearken unto me, ye men of Shechem, that God may hearken unto you.

8 [a]The trees went forth *on a time* to anoint a king over them; and they said unto the olive tree, [b]Reign thou over us.

9 But the olive tree said unto them, Should I leave my fatness, [a]wherewith by me they honour God and man, and go to be promoted over the trees?

10 And the trees said to the fig tree, Come thou, *and* reign over us.

11 But the fig tree said unto them, Should I forsake my sweetness, and my good fruit, and go to be promoted over the trees?

12 Then said the trees unto the vine, Come thou, *and* reign over us.

13 And the vine said unto them, Should I leave my wine, [a]which cheereth God and man, and go to be promoted over the trees?

14 Then said all the trees unto the bramble, Come thou, *and* reign over us.

15 And the bramble said unto the trees, If in truth ye anoint me king over you, *then* come *and* put your trust in my [a]shadow: and if not, [b]let fire come out of the bramble, and devour the [c]cedars of Lebanon.

16 Now therefore, if ye have done truly and sincerely, in that ye have made Abimelech king, and if ye have dealt well with Jerub-baal and his house, and have done unto him [a]according[1] to the deserving of his hands;

17 (For my [a]father fought for you, and adventured his life far, and [b]delivered you out of the hand of Midian:

18 [a]And ye are risen up against my father's house this day, and have slain his sons, threescore and ten persons, upon one stone, and have made Abimelech, the son of his [b]maidservant, king over the men of Shechem, because he *is* your brother;)

19 If ye then have dealt truly and sincerely with Jerub-baal and with his house this day, *then* [a]rejoice ye in Abimelech, and let him also rejoice in you:

20 But if not, [a]let fire come out from Abimelech, and devour the men

of Shechem, and the house of Millo; and let fire come out from the men of Shechem, and from the house of Millo, and devour Abimelech.

21 And Jotham ran away, and fled, and went to <sup>a</sup>Beer, and dwelt there, for fear of Abimelech his brother.

22 When Abimelech had reigned three years over Israel,

23 Then <sup>a</sup>God sent <sup>1</sup>an <sup>b</sup>evil spirit between Abimelech and the men of Shechem; and the men of Shechem <sup>c</sup>dealt treacherously with Abimelech:

24 <sup>a</sup>That the cruelty *done* to the threescore and ten sons of Jerubbaal might come, and their <sup>b</sup>blood be laid upon Abimelech their brother, which slew them; and upon the men of Shechem, which aided him in the killing of his brethren.

25 And the men of Shechem set <sup>1</sup>liers in wait for him in the top of the mountains, and they robbed all that came along that way by them: and it was told Abimelech.

26 And Gaal the son of Ebed came with his brethren, and went over to Shechem: and the men of Shechem put their confidence in him.

27 And they went out into the fields, and gathered their vineyards, and trode *the grapes,* and <sup>1</sup>made merry, and went into <sup>a</sup>the house of their god, and did eat and drink, and cursed Abimelech.

28 And Gaal the son of Ebed said, <sup>a</sup>Who *is* Abimelech, and who *is* Shechem, that we should serve him? *is* not *he* the son of Jerub-baal? and Zebul his officer? serve the men of <sup>b</sup>Hamor the father of Shechem: for why should we serve him?

29 And <sup>a</sup>would to God this people were under my hand! then would I remove Abimelech. And he said to Abimelech, Increase thine army, and come out.

30 And when Zebul the ruler of the city heard the words of Gaal the son of Ebed, his anger was <sup>1</sup>kindled.

31 And he sent messengers unto Abimelech <sup>1</sup>privily, saying, Behold, Gaal the son of Ebed and his brethren be come to Shechem; and, behold, they fortify the city against thee.

32 Now therefore <sup>1</sup>up by night, thou and the people that *is* with thee, and <sup>2</sup>lie in wait in the field:

33 And it shall be, *that* in the morning, as soon as the sun is up, thou shalt rise early, and set upon the city: and, behold, *when* he and the people that *is* with him come out against thee, then mayest thou do to them <sup>1</sup>as thou shalt find occasion.

34 And Abimelech rose up, and all the people that *were* with him, by night, and they laid wait against Shechem in four companies.

9:21 <sup>a</sup> Num. 21:16
9:23 <sup>a</sup> 1 Kin. 12:15; Is. 19:14 <sup>b</sup> 1 Sam. 16:14; 18:9, 10; 1 Kin. 22:22; 2 Chr. 18:22 <sup>c</sup> Is. 33:1 <sup>1</sup> *a spirit of ill will*
9:24 <sup>a</sup> 1 Kin. 2:32; Esth. 9:25; Matt. 23:35, 36 <sup>b</sup> Num. 35:33
9:25 <sup>1</sup> *men in ambush*
9:27 <sup>a</sup> Judg. 9:4 <sup>1</sup> *rejoiced*
9:28 <sup>a</sup> 1 Sam. 25:10; 1 Kin. 12:16 <sup>b</sup> Gen. 34:2, 6; Josh. 24:32
9:29 <sup>a</sup> 2 Sam. 15:4
9:30 <sup>1</sup> *aroused*
9:31 <sup>1</sup> *secretly*
9:32 <sup>1</sup> *get up* <sup>2</sup> *set up an ambush*
9:33 <sup>1</sup> *as your hand can find*

35 And Gaal the son of Ebed went out, and stood in the entering of the gate of the city: and Abimelech rose up, and the people that *were* with him, from <sup>1</sup>lying in wait.

36 And when Gaal saw the people, he said to Zebul, Behold, there come people down from the top of the mountains. And Zebul said unto him, Thou seest the shadow of the mountains as *if they were* men.

37 And Gaal spake again and said, See there come people down by the middle of the land, and another company come along <sup>1</sup>by the plain of Meonenim.

38 Then said Zebul unto him, Where *is* now thy mouth, wherewith thou <sup>a</sup>saidst, Who *is* Abimelech, that we should serve him? *is* not this the people that thou hast despised? go out, I pray now, and fight with them.

39 And Gaal went out before the men of Shechem, and fought with Abimelech.

40 And Abimelech chased him, and he fled before him, and many were overthrown *and* wounded, *even* unto the <sup>1</sup>entering of the gate.

41 And Abimelech dwelt at Arumah: and Zebul <sup>1</sup>thrust out Gaal and his brethren, that they should not dwell in Shechem.

42 And it came to pass on the morrow, that the people went out into the field; and they told Abimelech.

43 And he took the people, and divided them into three companies, and <sup>1</sup>laid wait in the field, and looked, and, behold, the people *were* come forth out of the city; and he rose up against them, and <sup>2</sup>smote them.

44 And Abimelech, and the company that *was* with him, rushed forward, and stood <sup>1</sup>in the entering of the gate of the city: and the two *other* companies ran upon all *the people* that *were* in the fields, and slew them.

45 And Abimelech fought against the city all that day; and <sup>a</sup>he took the city, and slew the people that *was* therein, and <sup>b</sup>beat<sup>1</sup> down the city, and sowed it with salt.

46 And when all the men of the tower of Shechem heard *that,* they entered into <sup>1</sup>an hold of the house <sup>a</sup>of the god Berith.

47 And it was told Abimelech, that all the men of the tower of Shechem were gathered together.

48 And Abimelech gat him up to mount <sup>a</sup>Zalmon, he and all the people that *were* with him; and Abimelech took an axe in his hand, and cut down a bough from the trees, and took it, and laid *it* on his shoulder, and said unto the people that *were* with him, What ye have seen me do, make haste, *and* do as I *have done.*

9:35 <sup>1</sup> *the ambush*
9:37 <sup>1</sup> *Or from the Diviners' Terebinth Tree*
9:38 <sup>a</sup> Judg. 9:28, 29
9:40 <sup>1</sup> *entrance*
9:41 <sup>1</sup> *exiled*
9:43 <sup>1</sup> *set an ambush* <sup>2</sup> *attacked*
9:44 <sup>1</sup> *at the entrance*
9:45 <sup>a</sup> Judg. 9:20 <sup>b</sup> Deut. 29:23; 2 Kin. 3:25 <sup>1</sup> *demolished*
9:46 <sup>a</sup> Judg. 8:33 <sup>1</sup> *a fortified room*
9:48 <sup>a</sup> Ps. 68:14

**49** And all the people likewise cut down every man his bough, and followed Abimelech, and put *them* to the ¹hold, and set the hold on fire upon them; so that all the men of the tower of Shechem died also, about a thousand men and women.

**50** Then went Abimelech to Thebez, and ¹encamped against Thebez, and took it.

**51** But there was a strong tower within the city, and thither fled all the men and women, and all they of the city, and shut *it* to them, and ¹gat them up to the top of the tower.

**52** And Abimelech came unto the tower, and fought against it, and went hard unto the door of the tower to burn it with fire.

**53** And a certain woman ᵃcast a piece of a millstone upon Abimelech's head, and ¹all to brake his skull.

**54** Then ᵃhe called hastily unto the young man his armourbearer, and said unto him, Draw thy sword, and slay me, that men say not of me, A woman slew him. And his young man thrust him through, and he died.

**55** And when the men of Israel saw that Abimelech was dead, they departed every man unto his ¹place.

**56** ᵃThus God ¹rendered the wickedness of Abimelech, which he did unto his father, in slaying his seventy brethren:

**57** And all the evil of the men of Shechem did God render upon their heads: and upon them came ᵃthe curse of Jotham the son of Jerub-baal.

### CHAPTER 10

**A**ND after Abimelech there ᵃarose to ¹defend Israel Tola the son of Puah, the son of Dodo, a man of Issachar; and he dwelt in Shamir in mount Ephraim.

**2** And he judged Israel twenty and three years, and died, and was buried in Shamir.

**3** And after him arose Jair, a Gileadite, and judged Israel twenty and two years.

**4** And he had thirty sons that ᵃrode on thirty ass colts, and they had thirty cities, ᵇwhich are called ¹Havoth-jair unto this day, which *are* in the land of Gilead.

**5** And Jair died, and was buried in Camon.

**6** And ᵃthe children of Israel did evil again in the sight of the LORD, and ᵇserved ¹Baalim, and Ashtaroth, and ᶜthe gods of Syria, and the gods of ᵈZidon, and the gods of Moab, and the gods of the children of Ammon, and the gods of the Philistines, and forsook the LORD, and served not him.

**7** And the anger of the LORD was hot against Israel, and he ᵃsold them

into the hands of the ᵇPhilistines, and into the hands of the children of ᶜAmmon.

**8** And that year they ¹vexed and oppressed the children of Israel: eighteen years, all the children of Israel that *were* on the other side Jordan in the ᵃland of the Amorites, which *is* in Gilead.

**9** Moreover the children of Ammon passed over Jordan to fight also against Judah, and against Benjamin, and against the house of Ephraim; so that Israel was ¹sore distressed.

**10** ᵃAnd the children of Israel cried unto the LORD, saying, We have ᵇsinned against thee, both because we have forsaken our God, and also served Baalim.

**11** And the LORD said unto the children of Israel, *Did* not *I deliver you* ᵃfrom the Egyptians, and ᵇfrom the Amorites, ᶜfrom the children of Ammon, and ᵈfrom the Philistines?

**12** ᵃThe Zidonians also, ᵇand the Amalekites, and the Maonites, ᶜdid oppress you; and ye cried to me, and I delivered you out of their hand.

**13** ᵃYet ye have forsaken me, and served other gods: wherefore I will deliver you no more.

**14** Go and ᵃcry¹ unto the gods which ye have chosen; let them deliver you in the time of your ²tribulation.

**15** And the children of Israel said unto the LORD, We have sinned: ᵃdo thou unto us ¹whatsoever seemeth good unto thee; deliver us only, we pray thee, this day.

**16** ᵃAnd they put away the ¹strange gods from among them, and served the LORD: and ᵇhis soul was ²grieved for the misery of Israel.

**17** Then the children of Ammon were gathered together, and encamped in Gilead. And the children of Israel assembled themselves together, and encamped in ᵃMizpeh.

**18** And the people *and* princes of Gilead said one to another, What man *is he* that will begin to fight against the children of Ammon? he shall ᵃbe head over all the inhabitants of Gilead.

### CHAPTER 11

**N**OW ᵃJephthah the Gileadite was ᵇa mighty man of valour, and he *was* the son of an harlot: and Gilead begat Jephthah.

**2** And Gilead's wife bare him sons; and his wife's sons grew up, and they ¹thrust out Jephthah, and said unto him, Thou shalt ᵃnot inherit in our father's house; for thou *art* the son of a strange woman.

**3** Then Jephthah fled from his brethren, and dwelt in the land of ᵃTob: and there were gathered ᵇvain¹

---

**Center column cross-references:**

9:49 ¹ *fortified room*
9:50 ¹ *besieged*
9:51 ¹ *they went up*
9:53 ᵃ 2 Sam. 11:21
¹ *crushed his skull*
9:54 ᵃ 1 Sam. 31:4
9:55 ¹ *home*
9:56 ᵃ Judg. 9:24; Job 31:3; Prov. 5:22 ¹ *repaid*
9:57 ᵃ Judg. 9:20
10:1 ᵃ Judg. 2:16 ¹ *save*
10:4 ᵃ Judg. 5:10; 12:14 ᵇ Deut. 3:14 ¹ Lit. *The Towns of Jair,* Num. 32:41; Deut. 3:14
10:6 ᵃ Judg. 2:11; 3:7; 6:1; 13:1 ᵇ Judg. 13:1 ᶜ Judg. 2:12 ᵈ 1 Kin. 11:33; Ps. 106:36 ¹ *Baals and Ashtoreths*
10:7 ᵃ Judg. 2:14; 4:2; 1 Sam. 12:9

b Judg. 13:1
c Judg. 3:13

10:8 ᵃ Num. 32:33 ¹ *harassed,* lit. *shattered*
10:9 ¹ *severely*
10:10 ᵃ Judg. 6:6; 1 Sam. 12:10 ᵇ Deut. 1:41
10:11 ᵃ Ex. 14:30 ᵇ Num. 21:21, 24, 25 ᶜ Judg. 3:12, 13 ᵈ Judg. 3:31
10:12 ᵃ Judg. 1:31; 5:19 ᵇ Judg. 6:3; 7:12 ᶜ Ps. 106:42, 43
10:13 ᵃ [Deut. 32:15; Judg. 2:12; Jer. 2:13]
10:14 ᵃ Deut. 32:37, 38 ¹ *cry out* ² *distress*
10:15 ᵃ 1 Sam. 3:18; 2 Sam. 15:26 ¹ *whatever seems best to you*
10:16 ᵃ 2 Chr. 7:14; Jer. 18:7, 8 ᵇ Ps. 106:44, 45; Is. 63:9 ¹ *foreign* ² *could no longer endure the misery*
10:17 ᵃ Gen. 31:49; Judg. 11:11, 29
10:18 ᵃ Judg. 11:8, 11

11:1 ᵃ Heb. 11:32 ᵇ Judg. 6:12; 2 Kin. 5:1
11:2 ᵃ Gen. 21:10; Deut. 23:2 ¹ *drove*
11:3 ᵃ 2 Sam. 10:6, 8 ᵇ 1 Sam. 22:2 ¹ *worthless*

---

men to Jephthah, and went out with him.

4 And it came to pass in process of time, that the [a]children of Ammon made war against Israel.

5 And it was so, that when the children of Ammon made war against Israel, the elders of Gilead went to fetch Jephthah out of the land of Tob:

6 And they said unto Jephthah, Come, and be our captain, that we may fight with the children of Ammon.

7 And Jephthah said unto the elders of Gilead, [a]Did not ye hate me, and expel me out of my father's house? and why are ye come unto me now when ye are in [1]distress?

8 [a]And the elders of Gilead said unto Jephthah, Therefore we [b]turn again to thee now, that thou mayest go with us, and fight against the children of Ammon, and be [c]our head over all the inhabitants of Gilead.

9 And Jephthah said unto the elders of Gilead, If ye bring me home again to fight against the children of Ammon, and the LORD deliver them before me, shall I be your head?

10 And the elders of Gilead said unto Jephthah, [a]The LORD be witness between us, if we do not so according to thy words.

11 Then Jephthah went with the elders of Gilead, and the people made him [a]head and captain over them: and Jephthah [1]uttered all his words [b]before the LORD in Mizpeh.

12 And Jephthah sent messengers unto the king of the children of Ammon, saying, [a]What hast thou to do with me, that thou art come against me to fight in my land?

13 And the king of the children of Ammon answered unto the messengers of Jephthah, [a]Because Israel took away my land, when they came up out of Egypt, from [b]Arnon even unto [c]Jabbok, and unto Jordan: now therefore restore those *lands* again peaceably.

14 And Jephthah sent messengers again unto the king of the children of Ammon:

15 And said unto him, Thus saith Jephthah, [a]Israel took not away the land of Moab, nor the land of the children of Ammon:

16 But when Israel came up from Egypt, and walked through the wilderness unto the Red sea, and [a]came to Kadesh;

17 Then [a]Israel sent messengers unto the king of Edom, saying, [1]Let me, I pray thee, pass through thy land: [b]but the king of Edom would not [2]hearken *thereto*. And in like manner they sent unto the [c]king of Moab: but he would not *consent:* and Israel [d]abode in Kadesh.

18 Then they [a]went along through the wilderness, and [b]compassed the land of Edom, and the land of Moab, and came by the east side of the land of Moab, and pitched on the other side of Arnon, but came not within the border of Moab: for Arnon *was* the border of Moab.

19 And [a]Israel sent messengers unto Sihon king of the Amorites, the king of Heshbon; and Israel said unto him, [b]Let us pass, we pray thee, through thy land into my place.

20 [a]But Sihon trusted not Israel to pass through his [1]coast: but Sihon gathered all his people together, and [2]pitched in Jahaz, and fought against Israel.

21 And the LORD God of Israel [a]delivered Sihon and all his people into the hand of Israel, and they [b]smote[1] them: so Israel possessed all the land of the Amorites, the inhabitants of that country.

22 And they possessed [a]all the [1]coasts of the Amorites, from Arnon even unto Jabbok, and from the wilderness even unto Jordan.

23 So now the LORD God of Israel hath [1]dispossessed the Amorites from before his people Israel, and shouldest thou possess it?

24 Wilt not thou possess that which [a]Chemosh thy god giveth thee to possess? So whomsoever [b]the LORD our God shall drive out from before us, them will we possess.

25 And now *art* thou any thing better than [a]Balak the son of Zippor, king of Moab? did he ever strive against Israel, or did he ever fight against them,

26 While Israel dwelt in [a]Heshbon and her towns, and in [b]Aroer and her towns, and in all the cities that *be* along by the [1]coasts of Arnon, three hundred years? why therefore did ye not recover *them* within that time?

27 Wherefore I have not sinned against thee, but thou doest me wrong to war against me: the LORD [a]the Judge [b]be judge this day between the children of Israel and the children of Ammon.

28 Howbeit the king of the children of Ammon [1]hearkened not unto the words of Jephthah which he sent him.

29 Then [a]the Spirit of the LORD came upon Jephthah, and he passed over Gilead, and Manasseh, and passed over Mizpeh of Gilead, and from Mizpeh of Gilead he passed over *unto* the children of Ammon.

30 And Jephthah [a]vowed a vow unto the LORD, and said, If thou shalt without fail deliver the children of Ammon into mine hands,

31 Then it shall be, that whatsoever cometh forth of the doors of my

---

11:4 [a] Judg. 10:9, 17

11:7 [a] Gen. 26:27 [1] trouble

11:8 [a] Judg. 10:18 [b] [Luke 17:4] [c] Judg. 10:18 [1] return

11:10 [a] Gen. 31:49, 50; Jer. 29:23; 42:5

11:11 [a] Judg. 11:8 [b] Judg. 10:17; 20:1; 1 Sam. 10:17 [1] spoke

11:12 [a] 2 Sam. 16:10

11:13 [a] Num. 21:24–26 [b] Josh. 13:9 [c] Gen. 32:22

11:15 [a] Deut. 2:9, 19

11:16 [a] Num. 13:26; 20:1

11:17 [a] Num. 20:14 [b] Num. 20:14–21 [c] Josh. 24:9 [d] Num. 20:1 [1] Please let me pass [2] heed

11:18 [a] Deut. 2:9, 18, 19 [b] Num. 21:4

11:19 [a] Num. 21:21; Deut. 2:26–36 [b] Num. 21:22; Deut. 2:27

11:20 [a] Num. 21:23; Deut. 2:27 [1] territory [2] encamped

11:21 [a] Josh. 24:8 [b] Num. 21:24, 25 [1] defeated

11:22 [a] Deut. 2:36, 37 [1] territory

11:23 [1] driven out

11:24 [a] Num. 21:29; 1 Kin. 11:7; Jer. 48:7 [b] [Deut. 9:4, 5; Josh. 3:10]

11:25 [a] Num. 22:2; Josh. 24:9; Mic. 6:5

11:26 [a] Num. 21:25, 26 [b] Deut. 2:36 [1] banks

11:27 [a] Gen. 18:25 [b] Gen. 16:5; 31:53; [1 Sam. 24:12, 15]

11:28 [1] heed

11:29 [a] Judg. 3:10

11:30 [a] Gen. 28:20; Num. 30:2; 1 Sam. 1:11

---

house to meet me, when I return in peace from the children of Ammon, [a]shall surely be the LORD's, [b]and I will offer it up for a burnt offering.

32 So Jephthah passed over unto the children of Ammon to fight against them; and the LORD delivered them into his hands.

33 And he [1]smote them from Aroer, even till thou come to [a]Minnith, *even* twenty cities, and unto the [2]plain of the vineyards, with a very great slaughter. Thus the children of Ammon were subdued before the children of Israel.

34 And Jephthah came to [a]Mizpeh unto his house, and, behold, [b]his daughter came out to meet him with timbrels and with dances: and she *was his* only child; beside her he had neither son nor daughter.

35 And it came to pass, when he saw her, that he [a]rent[1] his clothes, and said, Alas, my daughter! thou hast brought me very low, and thou art one of them that trouble me: for I [b]have [2]opened my mouth unto the LORD, and [c]I cannot [3]go back.

36 And she said unto him, My father, *if* thou hast opened thy mouth unto the LORD, [a]do to me according to that which hath proceeded out of thy mouth; forasmuch as [b]the LORD hath taken vengeance for thee of thine enemies, *even* of the children of Ammon.

37 And she said unto her father, Let this thing be done for me: let me alone two months, that I may go up and down upon the mountains, and [1]bewail my virginity, I and my [2]fellows.

38 And he said, Go. And he sent her away *for* two months: and she went with her companions, and bewailed her virginity upon the mountains.

39 And it came to pass at the end of two months, that she returned unto her father, who [a]did with her *according* to his vow which he had vowed: and she [1]knew no man. And it [2]was a custom in Israel,

40 *That* the daughters of Israel went yearly [1]to lament the daughter of Jephthah the Gileadite four days in a year.

## CHAPTER 12

AND [a]the men of Ephraim [1]gathered themselves together, and went northward, and said unto Jephthah, Wherefore passedst thou over to fight against the children of Ammon, and didst not call us to go with thee? we will burn thine house upon thee with fire.

2 And Jephthah said unto them, I and my people were [1]at great strife with the children of Ammon; and

11:31 [a] Lev. 27:2, 3, 28; 1 Sam. 1:11 [b] Ps. 66:13
11:33 [a] Ezek. 27:17 [1] *defeated* [2] Heb. *Abel-keramim*
11:34 [a] Judg. 10:17; 11:11 [b] Ex. 15:20; 1 Sam. 18:6; Ps. 68:25; Jer. 31:4
11:35 [a] Gen. 37:29, 34 [b] Eccl. 5:2, 4, 5 [c] Num. 30:2 [1] *tore* [2] *given my word* [3] *go back on it*
11:36 [a] Num. 30:2 [b] 2 Sam. 18:19, 31
11:37 [1] *lament* [2] *companions*
11:39 [a] Judg. 11:31 [1] She remained a virgin. [2] *became*
11:40 [1] *commemorate*
12:1 [a] Judg. 8:1 [1] *were summoned*
12:2 [1] *in a great struggle*

12:3 [a] 1 Sam. 19:5; 28:21; Job 13:14 [1] *took* [2] *crossed*
12:4 [a] 1 Sam. 25:10
12:5 [a] Josh. 22:11
12:6 [a] Ps. 69:2, 15 [1] Lit. *a flowing stream* (used as a test of dialect) [2] Shibboleth as enunciated in a different dialect [3] Lit. *speak so*
12:9 [1] *elsewhere*
12:14 [a] Judg. 5:10; 10:4
12:15 [a] Judg. 3:13, 27; 5:14
13:1 [a] Judg. 2:11 [b] Judg. 10:7; 1 Sam. 12:9
13:2 [a] Josh. 19:41; Judg. 16:31

when I called you, ye delivered me not out of their hands.

3 And when I saw that ye delivered *me* not, I [a]put[1] my life in my hands, and [2]passed over against the children of Ammon, and the LORD delivered them into my hand: wherefore then are ye come up unto me this day, to fight against me?

4 Then Jephthah gathered together all the men of Gilead, and fought with Ephraim: and the men of Gilead smote Ephraim, because they said, Ye Gileadites [a]*are* fugitives of Ephraim among the Ephraimites, *and* among the Manassites.

5 And the Gileadites took the [a]passages of Jordan before the Ephraimites: and it was *so*, that when those Ephraimites which were escaped said, Let me go over; that the men of Gilead said unto him, Art thou an Ephraimite? If he said, Nay;

6 Then said they unto him, Say now [a]Shibboleth:[1] and he said [2]Sibboleth: for he could not [3]frame to pronounce *it* right. Then they took him, and slew him at the passages of Jordan: and there fell at that time of the Ephraimites forty and two thousand.

7 And Jephthah judged Israel six years. Then died Jephthah the Gileadite, and was buried in *one of* the cities of Gilead.

8 And after him Ibzan of Bethlehem judged Israel.

9 And he had thirty sons, and thirty daughters, *whom* he sent abroad, and took in thirty daughters from [1]abroad for his sons. And he judged Israel seven years.

10 Then died Ibzan, and was buried at Beth-lehem.

11 And after him Elon, a Zebulonite, judged Israel; and he judged Israel ten years.

12 And Elon the Zebulonite died, and was buried in Aijalon in the country of Zebulun.

13 And after him Abdon the son of Hillel, a Pirathonite, judged Israel.

14 And he had forty sons and thirty nephews, that [a]rode on threescore and ten ass colts: and he judged Israel eight years.

15 And Abdon the son of Hillel the Pirathonite died, and was buried in Pirathon in the land of Ephraim, [a]in the mount of the Amalekites.

## CHAPTER 13

AND the children of Israel [a]did evil again in the sight of the LORD; and the LORD delivered them [b]into the hand of the Philistines forty years.

2 And there was a certain man of [a]Zorah, of the family of the Danites, whose name *was* Manoah; and his wife *was* barren, and bare not.

3 And the [a]angel of the LORD appeared unto the woman, and said unto her, Behold now, thou *art* barren, and bearest not: but thou shalt conceive, and bear a son.

4 Now therefore [b]beware, I pray thee, and [a]drink not wine nor strong drink, and eat not any unclean *thing:*

5 For, lo, thou shalt conceive, and bear a son; and no [a]razor shall come on his head: for the child shall be [b]a Nazarite unto God from the womb: and he shall [c]begin to deliver Israel out of the hand of the Philistines.

6 Then the woman came and told her husband, saying, [a]A man of God came unto me, and his [b]countenance[1] *was* like the countenance of an angel of God, very [2]terrible: but I [c]asked him not whence he *was,* neither told he me his name:

7 But he said unto me, Behold, thou shalt conceive, and bear a son; and now drink no wine nor strong drink, neither eat any unclean *thing:* for the child shall be a Nazarite to God from the womb to the day of his death.

8 Then Manoah intreated the LORD, and said, O my Lord, let the man of God which thou didst send come again unto us, and teach us what we shall do unto the child that shall be born.

9 And God [1]hearkened to the voice of Manoah; and the angel of God came again unto the woman as she sat in the field: but Manoah her husband *was* not with her.

10 And the woman made haste, and ran, and [1]shewed her husband, and said unto him, Behold, the man hath appeared unto me, that came unto me the *other* day.

11 And Manoah arose, and went after his wife, and came to the man, and said unto him, *Art* thou the man that spakest unto the woman? And he said, I *am.*

12 And Manoah said, Now let thy words come to pass. [1]How shall we order the child, and *how* shall we do unto him?

13 And the angel of the LORD said unto Manoah, Of all that I said unto the woman let her beware.

14 She may not eat of any *thing* that cometh of the vine, [a]neither let her drink wine or strong drink, nor eat any unclean *thing:* all that I commanded her let her observe.

15 And Manoah said unto the angel of the LORD, I pray thee, [a]let us detain thee, until we shall have made ready a kid for thee.

16 And the angel of the LORD said unto Manoah, Though thou detain me, I will not eat of thy bread: and if thou wilt offer a burnt offering, thou

must offer it unto the LORD. For Manoah knew not that he *was* an angel of the LORD.

17 And Manoah said unto the angel of the LORD, What *is* thy name, that when thy sayings come to pass we may do thee honour?

18 And the angel of the LORD said unto him, [a]Why askest thou thus after my name, seeing it *is* [1]secret?

19 So Manoah took a kid with a meat offering, [a]and offered *it* upon a rock unto the LORD: and *the angel* did [1]wonderously; and Manoah and his wife looked on.

20 For it came to pass, when the flame went up toward heaven from off the altar, that the angel of the LORD ascended in the flame of the altar. And Manoah and his wife looked on *it,* and [a]fell on their faces to the ground.

21 But the angel of the LORD did no more appear to Manoah and to his wife. [a]Then Manoah knew that he *was* an angel of the LORD.

22 And Manoah said unto his wife, [a]We shall surely die, because we have seen God.

23 But his wife said unto him, If the LORD were pleased to kill us, he would not have received a burnt offering and a meat offering at our hands, neither would he have shewed us all these *things,* nor would as at this time have told us *such things* as these.

24 And the woman bare a son, and called his name [a]Samson: and [b]the child grew, and the LORD blessed him.

25 [a]And the Spirit of the LORD began to move [1]him at times in the [2]camp of Dan [b]between Zorah and [c]Eshtaol.

## CHAPTER 14

AND Samson went down [a]to Timnath, and [b]saw a woman in Timnath of the daughters of the Philistines.

2 And he came up, and told his father and his mother, and said, I have seen a woman in Timnath of the daughters of the Philistines: now therefore [a]get her for me [1]to wife.

3 Then his father and his mother said unto him, *Is there* never a woman among the daughters of [a]thy brethren, or among all my people, that thou goest to take a wife of the [b]uncircumcised Philistines? And Samson said unto his father, Get her for me; for she [1]pleaseth me well.

4 But his father and his mother knew not that it *was* [a]of the LORD, that he sought an occasion against the Philistines: for at that time [b]the Philistines had dominion over Israel.

5 Then went Samson down, and his father and his mother, to Timnath,

13:3 [a] Judg. 6:12
13:4 [a] Num. 6:2, 3, 20; Judg. 13:4; Luke 1:15 [1] *please be careful*
13:5 [a] Num. 6:5; 1 Sam. 1:11 [b] Num. 6:2 [c] 1 Sam. 7:13; 2 Sam. 8:1; 1 Chr. 18:1
13:6 [a] Gen. 32:24–30 [b] Matt. 28:3; Luke 9:29; Acts 6:15 [c] Judg. 13:17, 18 [1] *appearance* [2] *awesome*
13:9 [1] *listened*
13:10 [1] *told*
13:12 [1] *What will be the boy's rule of life, and his work?*
13:14 [a] Num. 6:3, 4; Judg. 13:4
13:15 [a] Gen. 18:5; Judg. 6:18
13:18 [a] Gen. 32:29 [1] *wonderful*
13:19 [a] Judg. 6:19–21 [1] *a wondrous thing*
13:20 [a] Lev. 9:24; 1 Chr. 21:16; Ezek. 1:28; Matt. 17:6
13:21 [a] Judg. 6:22
13:22 [a] Gen. 32:30; Ex. 33:20; Deut. 5:26; Judg. 6:22, 23
13:24 [a] Heb. 11:32 [b] 1 Sam. 3:19; Luke 1:80
13:25 [a] Judg. 3:10; 1 Sam. 11:6; Matt. 4:1 [b] Josh. 15:33; Judg. 18:11 [c] Judg. 16:31 [1] *on him at* [2] Heb. *Mahaneh-dan*
14:1 [a] Gen. 38:13; Josh. 15:10, 57 [b] Gen. 34:2
14:2 [a] Gen. 21:21 [1] *as a wife*
14:3 [a] Gen. 24:3, 4 [b] Gen. 34:14; Ex. 34:16; Deut. 7:3 [1] Lit. *is right in my eyes*
14:4 [a] Josh. 11:20; 1 Kin. 12:15; 2 Kin. 6:33; 2 Chr. 10:15 [b] Deut. 28:48; Judg. 13:1

and came to the vineyards of Timnath: and, behold, a young lion roared against him.

6 And ªthe Spirit of the LORD came mightily upon him, and he ¹rent him as he would have rent a kid, and *he had* nothing in his hand: but he told not his father or his mother what he had done.

7 And he went down, and talked with the woman; and she pleased Samson well.

8 And after a time he returned to take her, and he turned aside to see the carcase of the lion: and, behold, *there was* a swarm of bees and honey in the carcase of the lion.

9 And he took thereof in his hands, and went on eating, and came to his father and mother, and he gave them, and they did eat: but he told not them that he had taken the honey out of the ªcarcase of the lion.

10 So his father went down unto the woman: and Samson made there a feast; for so used the young men to do.

11 And it came to pass, when they saw him, that they brought thirty companions to be with him.

12 And Samson said unto them, I will now ªput forth a riddle unto you: if ye can certainly declare it me ᵇwithin the seven days of the feast, and find *it* out, then I will give you thirty ¹sheets and thirty ᶜchange of garments:

13 But if ye cannot declare *it* me, then shall ye give me thirty sheets and thirty change of garments. And they said unto him, ªPut forth thy riddle, that we may hear it.

14 And he said unto them, Out of the eater came forth meat, and out of the strong came forth sweetness. And they could not in three days expound the riddle.

15 And it came to pass on the seventh day, that they said unto Samson's wife, ªEntice thy husband, that he may declare unto us the riddle, ᵇlest we burn thee and thy father's house with fire: have ye called us to take ¹that we have? *is it* not *so?*

16 And Samson's wife wept before him, and said, ªThou dost but hate me, and lovest me not: thou hast put forth a riddle unto the children of my people, and hast not told *it* me. And he said unto her, Behold, I have not told *it* my father nor my mother, and shall I tell *it* thee?

17 And she wept before him the seven days, while their feast lasted: and it came to pass on the seventh day, that he told her, because she ¹lay sore upon him: and she told the riddle to the children of her people.

18 And the men of the city said unto

14:6 ª Judg. 3:10
¹ tore apart
14:9 ª Lev. 11:27
14:12 ª 1 Kin. 10:1;
Ezek. 17:2 ᵇ Gen.
29:27 ᶜ Gen.
45:22; 2 Kin. 5:22
¹ linen garments
14:13 ª Ezek. 17:2
14:15 ª Judg.
16:5 ᵇ Judg. 15:6
¹ what is ours
14:16 ª Judg. 16:15
14:17 ¹ pressured
him so much

14:18 ¹ A proverbial expression
implying a
conspiracy with
his wife
14:19 ª Judg. 3:10;
13:25 ¹ explained
14:20 ª Judg. 15:2
ᵇ John 3:29 ¹ best
man
15:1 ª Gen. 38:17
15:2 ª Judg. 14:20
15:3 ¹ blameless
regarding ² harm
15:4 ¹ torches
15:6 ª Judg. 14:15
15:8 ª 2 Chr. 11:6
¹ attacked
15:9 ª Judg. 15:19
¹ encamped
15:10 ¹ imprison

him on the seventh day before the sun went down, What *is* sweeter than honey? and what *is* stronger than a lion? And he said unto them, ¹If ye had not plowed with my heifer, ye had not found out my riddle.

19 And ªthe Spirit of the LORD came upon him, and he went down to Ashkelon, and slew thirty men of them, and took their spoil, and gave change of garments unto them which ¹expounded the riddle. And his anger was kindled, and he went up to his father's house.

20 But Samson's wife ªwas *given* to his companion, whom he had used as ᵇhis ¹friend.

## CHAPTER 15

BUT it came to pass within a while after, in the time of wheat harvest, that Samson visited his wife with a ªkid; and he said, I will go in to my wife into the chamber. But her father would not suffer him to go in.

2 And her father said, I verily thought that thou hadst utterly ªhated her; therefore I gave her to thy companion: *is* not her younger sister fairer than she? take her, I pray thee, instead of her.

3 And Samson said concerning them, Now shall I be ¹more blameless than the Philistines, though I do them a ²displeasure.

4 And Samson went and caught three hundred foxes, and took ¹firebrands, and turned tail to tail, and put a firebrand in the midst between two tails.

5 And when he had set the brands on fire, he let *them* go into the standing corn of the Philistines, and burnt up both the shocks, and also the standing corn, with the vineyards *and* olives.

6 Then the Philistines said, Who hath done this? And they answered, Samson, the son in law of the Timnite, because he had taken his wife, and given her to his companion. ªAnd the Philistines came up, and burnt her and her father with fire.

7 And Samson said unto them, Though ye have done this, yet will I be avenged of you, and after that I will cease.

8 And he ¹smote them hip and thigh with a great slaughter: and he went down and dwelt in the top of the rock ªEtam.

9 Then the Philistines went up, and ¹pitched in Judah, and spread themselves ªin Lehi.

10 And the men of Judah said, Why are ye come up against us? And they answered, To ¹bind Samson are we come up, to do to him as he hath done to us.

11 Then three thousand men of Judah went to the top of the rock Etam, and said to Samson, Knowest thou not that the Philistines *are* <sup>a</sup>rulers over us? what *is* this *that* thou hast done unto us? And he said unto them, As they did unto me, so have I done unto them.

12 And they said unto him, We are come down to bind thee, that we may deliver thee into the hand of the Philistines. And Samson said unto them, Swear unto me, that ye will not fall upon me yourselves.

13 And they spake unto him, saying, No; but we will bind thee fast, and deliver thee into their hand: but surely we will not kill thee. And they bound him with two <sup>a</sup>new cords, and brought him up from the rock.

14 *And* when he came unto Lehi, the Philistines shouted against him: and <sup>a</sup>the Spirit of the LORD came mightily upon him, and the cords that *were* upon his arms became as flax that was burnt with fire, and his bands <sup>1</sup>loosed from off his hands.

15 And he found a <sup>1</sup>new jawbone of an ass, and put forth his hand, and took it, and <sup>a</sup>slew a thousand men therewith.

16 And Samson said, With the jawbone of an ass, heaps upon heaps, with the jaw of an ass have I slain a thousand men.

17 And it came to pass, when he had made an end of speaking, that he cast away the jawbone out of his hand, and called that place <sup>1</sup>Ramath-lehi.

18 And he was sore athirst, and called on the LORD, and said, <sup>a</sup>Thou hast given this great deliverance into the hand of thy servant: and now shall I die for thirst, and fall into the hand of the uncircumcised?

19 But God clave an hollow place that *was* in the <sup>1</sup>jaw, and there came water thereout; and when he had drunk, <sup>a</sup>his spirit came again, and he revived: wherefore he called the name thereof <sup>2</sup>En-hakkore, which *is* in Lehi unto this day.

20 And <sup>a</sup>he judged Israel <sup>b</sup>in the days of the Philistines <sup>c</sup>twenty years.

## CHAPTER 16

THEN went Samson to <sup>a</sup>Gaza, and saw there an harlot, and went in unto her.

2 *And it was told* the Gazites, saying, Samson is come hither. And they <sup>a</sup>compassed *him* in, and laid wait for him all night in the gate of the city, and were quiet all the night, saying, In the morning, when it is day, we shall kill him.

3 And Samson lay till midnight, and arose at midnight, and took the doors of the gate of the city, and the two posts, and went away with them, bar and all, and put *them* upon his shoulders, and carried them up to the top of an hill that *is* before Hebron.

4 And it came to pass afterward, that he loved a woman in the valley of Sorek, whose name *was* Delilah.

5 And the <sup>a</sup>lords of the Philistines came up unto her, and said unto her, <sup>b</sup>Entice him, and see wherein his great strength *lieth,* and by what *means* we may prevail against him, that we may bind him to afflict him: and we will give thee every one of us eleven hundred *pieces* of silver.

6 And Delilah said to Samson, Tell me, I pray thee, wherein thy great strength *lieth,* and wherewith thou mightest be bound to afflict thee.

7 And Samson said unto her, If they bind me with seven <sup>1</sup>green withs that were never dried, then shall I be weak, and be as another man.

8 Then the lords of the Philistines brought up to her seven green withs which had not been dried, and she bound him with them.

9 Now *there were* men lying in wait, abiding with her in the chamber. And she said unto him, The Philistines *be* upon thee, Samson. And he brake the <sup>1</sup>withs, as a thread of <sup>2</sup>tow is broken when it toucheth the fire. So his strength was not known.

10 And Delilah said unto Samson, Behold, thou hast mocked me, and told me lies: now tell me, I pray thee, wherewith thou mightest be bound.

11 And he said unto her, If they bind me fast with <sup>a</sup>new ropes that never were <sup>1</sup>occupied, then shall I be weak, and be as another man.

12 Delilah therefore took new ropes, and bound him therewith, and said unto him, The Philistines *be* upon thee, Samson. And *there were* <sup>1</sup>liers in wait abiding in the chamber. And he brake them from off his arms like a thread.

13 And Delilah said unto Samson, Hitherto thou hast mocked me, and told me lies: tell me wherewith thou mightest be bound. And he said unto her, If thou weavest the seven locks of my head with the web.

14 And she fastened *it* with the <sup>1</sup>pin, and said unto him, The Philistines *be* upon thee, Samson. And he awaked out of his sleep, and <sup>2</sup>went away with the pin of the beam, and with the web.

15 And she said unto him, <sup>a</sup>How canst thou say, I love thee, when thine heart *is* not with me? thou hast mocked me these three times, and hast not told me wherein thy great strength *lieth.*

### Cross References

15:11 <sup>a</sup> Lev. 26:25; Deut. 28:43; Judg. 13:1; 14:4; Ps. 106:40–42
15:13 <sup>a</sup> Judg. 16:11, 12
15:14 <sup>a</sup> Judg. 3:10; 14:6 <sup>1</sup> broke loose
15:15 <sup>a</sup> Lev. 26:8; Josh. 23:10; Judg. 3:31 <sup>1</sup> Lit. *fresh*
15:17 <sup>1</sup> Lit. *Jawbone Heights*
15:18 <sup>a</sup> Ps. 3:7
15:19 <sup>a</sup> Gen. 45:27; Is. 40:29 <sup>1</sup> Heb. *Lehi* <sup>2</sup> Lit. *Spring of the Caller*
15:20 <sup>a</sup> Judg. 10:2; 12:7–14 <sup>b</sup> Judg. 16:31 <sup>c</sup> Judg. 13:1
16:1 <sup>a</sup> Josh. 15:47
16:2 <sup>a</sup> 1 Sam. 23:26; Ps. 118:10–12
16:5 <sup>a</sup> Josh. 13:3 <sup>b</sup> Judg. 14:15
16:7 <sup>1</sup> fresh bowstrings
16:9 <sup>1</sup> bowstrings <sup>2</sup> yarn
16:11 <sup>a</sup> Judg. 15:13 <sup>1</sup> used
16:12 <sup>1</sup> men in hiding
16:14 <sup>1</sup> batten of a loom <sup>2</sup> pulled out the batten and the web from the loom
16:15 <sup>a</sup> Judg. 14:16

16 And it came to pass, when she pressed him daily with her words, and urged him, *so* that his soul was [1]vexed unto death;

17 That he [a]told her all his heart, and said unto her, [b]There hath not come a razor upon mine head; for I *have been* a Nazarite unto God from my mother's womb: if I be shaven, then my strength will go from me, and I shall become weak, and be like any *other* man.

18 And when Delilah saw that he had told her all his heart, she sent and called for the lords of the Philistines, saying, Come up this once, for he hath shewed me all his heart. Then the lords of the Philistines came up unto her, and brought money in their hand.

19 [a]And she made him sleep upon her knees; and she called for a man, and she caused him to shave off the seven locks of his head; and she began to afflict him, and his strength went from him.

20 And she said, The Philistines *be* upon thee, Samson. And he awoke out of his sleep, and said, I will go out as at other times before, and shake myself. And he [1]wist not that the LORD [a]was departed from him.

21 But the Philistines took him, and [1]put out his [a]eyes, and brought him down to Gaza, and bound him with fetters of brass; and he did grind in the prison house.

22 Howbeit the hair of his head began to grow again after he was shaven.

23 Then the lords of the Philistines gathered them together for to offer a great sacrifice unto [a]Dagon their god, and to rejoice: for they said, Our god hath delivered Samson our enemy into our hand.

24 And when the people saw him, they [a]praised their god: for they said, Our god hath delivered into our hands our enemy, and the destroyer of our country, which slew many of us.

25 And it came to pass, when their hearts were [a]merry, that they said, Call for Samson, that he may [1]make us sport. And they called for Samson out of the prison house; and he [2]made them sport: and they set him between the pillars.

26 And Samson said unto the lad that held him by the hand, Suffer me that I may feel the pillars whereupon the house standeth, that I may lean upon them.

27 Now the house was full of men and women; and all the lords of the Philistines *were* there; and *there were* upon the [a]roof about three thousand men and women, that beheld while Samson [1]made sport.

28 And Samson called unto the LORD, and said, O Lord GOD, [a]remember me, I pray thee, and strengthen me, I pray thee, only this once, O God, that I may [1]be at once avenged of the Philistines for my two eyes.

29 And Samson took hold of the two middle pillars upon which the house stood, and [1]on which it was borne up, of the one with his right hand, and of the other with his left.

30 And Samson said, Let me die with the Philistines. And he bowed himself with *all his* might; and the house fell upon the lords, and upon all the people that *were* therein. So the dead which he slew at his death were more than *they* which he slew in his life.

31 Then his brethren and all the house of his father came down, and took him, and brought *him* up, and [a]buried him between Zorah and Eshtaol in the buryingplace of Manoah his father. And he judged Israel [b]twenty years.

## CHAPTER 17

AND there was a man of mount Ephraim, whose name *was* [a]Micah.

2 And he said unto his mother, The eleven hundred *shekels* of silver that were taken from thee, about which thou [a]cursedst,[1] and spakest of also in mine ears, behold, the silver *is* with me; I took it. And his mother said, [b]Blessed *be thou* of the LORD, my son.

3 And when he had restored the eleven hundred *shekels* of silver to his mother, his mother said, I had wholly dedicated the silver unto the LORD from my hand for my son, to [a]make a graven image and a molten image: now therefore I will restore it unto thee.

4 Yet he restored the money unto his mother; and his mother [a]took two hundred *shekels* of silver, and gave them to the [1]founder, who made thereof a graven image and a molten image: and they were in the house of Micah.

5 And the man Micah had an [a]house[1] of gods, and made an [b]ephod, and [c]teraphim,[2] and consecrated one of his sons, who became his priest.

6 [a]In those days *there was* no king in Israel, [b]but every man did *that which was* right in his own eyes.

7 And there was a young man out of [a]Beth-lehem-judah of the family of Judah, who *was* a Levite, and he [b]sojourned[1] there.

8 And the man departed out of the city from Beth-lehem-judah to [1]sojourn where he could find *a place:* and he came to mount Ephraim to the house of Micah, as he journeyed.

16:16 [1] *impatient to the point of*
16:17 [a] [Mic. 7:5]
[b] Num. 6:5; Judg. 13:5
16:19 [a] Prov. 7:26, 27
16:20 [a] Num. 14:9, 42, 43; [Josh. 7:12]; 1 Sam. 16:14; 18:12; 28:15, 16; 2 Chr. 15:2 [1] *knew*
16:21 [a] 2 Kin. 25:7 [1] Lit. *bored out*
16:23 [a] 1 Sam. 5:2
16:24 [a] Dan. 5:4
16:25 [a] Judg. 9:27 [1] *perform for us* [2] *performed for them*
16:27 [a] Deut. 22:8 [1] *performed*
16:28 [a] Jer. 15:15 [1] *with one blow take vengeance on*
16:29 [1] *he braced himself against them*
16:31 [a] Judg. 13:25 [b] Judg. 15:20
17:1 [a] Judg. 18:2
17:2 [a] Lev. 5:1 [b] Gen. 14:19 [1] *put a curse*
17:3 [a] Ex. 20:4, 23; 34:17; Lev. 19:4
17:4 [a] Is. 46:6 [1] *silversmith*
17:5 [a] Judg. 18:24 [b] Judg. 8:27; 18:14 [c] Gen. 31:19, 30; Hos. 3:4 [1] *shrine* [2] *household idols*
17:6 [a] Judg. 18:1; 19:1 [b] Deut. 12:8; Judg. 21:25
17:7 [a] Josh. 19:15; Judg. 19:1; Ruth 1:1, 2; Mic. 5:2; Matt. 2:1, 5, 6 [b] Deut. 18:6 [1] *lived there temporarily*
17:8 [1] *live temporarily*

9 And Micah said unto him, Whence comest thou? And he said unto him, I *am* a Levite of Beth-lehem-judah, and I go to ¹sojourn where I may find *a place.*

10 And Micah said unto him, Dwell with me, ªand be unto me a ᵇfather and a priest, and I will give thee ten *shekels* of silver by the year, and a suit of apparel, and thy victuals. So the Levite went in.

11 And the Levite was content to dwell with the man; and the young man was unto him as one of his sons.

12 And Micah ªconsecrated¹ the Levite; and the young man ᵇbecame his priest, and was in the house of Micah.

13 Then said Micah, Now know I that the LORD will do me good, seeing I have a Levite to *my* ªpriest.

## CHAPTER 18

IN ªthose days *there was* no king in Israel: and in those days ᵇthe tribe of the Danites sought them an inheritance to dwell in; for unto that day *all their* inheritance had not fallen unto them among the tribes of Israel.

2 And the children of Dan sent of their family five men from their coasts, men of valour, from ªZorah, and from Eshtaol, ᵇto spy out the land, and to search it; and they said unto them, Go, search the land: who when they came to mount Ephraim, to the ᶜhouse of Micah, they lodged there.

3 When they *were* by the house of Micah, they knew the voice of the young man the Levite: and they turned in thither, and said unto him, Who brought thee hither? and what makest thou in this *place?* and what hast thou here?

4 And he said unto them, Thus and thus dealeth Micah with me, and hath ªhired me, and I am his priest.

5 And they said unto him, ªAsk¹ counsel, we pray thee, ᵇof God, that we may know whether our way which we go shall be prosperous.

6 And the priest said unto them, ªGo in peace: ¹before the LORD *is* your way wherein ye go.

7 Then the five men departed, and came to ªLaish, and saw the people that *were* therein, ᵇhow they dwelt ¹careless, after the manner of the Zidonians, quiet and secure; and *there was* no ²magistrate in the land, that might put *them* to shame in any thing; and they *were* far from the ᶜZidonians, and had no business with *any* man.

8 And ¹they came unto their brethren to ªZorah and Eshtaol: and their brethren said unto them, What *say* ye?

17:9 ¹ *live temporarily*
17:10 ª Judg. 18:19
ᵇ Gen. 45:8; Job 29:16
17:12 ª Judg. 17:5
ᵇ Judg. 18:30
¹ Lit. *filled the hand of*
17:13 ª Judg. 18:4
18:1 ª Judg. 17:6; 19:1; 21:25 ᵇ Josh. 19:40–48
18:2 ª Judg. 13:25
ᵇ Num. 13:17; Josh. 2:1 ᶜ Judg. 17:1
18:4 ª Judg. 17:10, 12
18:5 ª 1 Kin. 22:5; [Is. 30:1]; Hos. 4:12 ᵇ Judg. 1:1; 17:5; 18:14 ¹ *Please inquire of God*
18:6 ª 1 Kin. 22:6 ¹ *may the presence of the LORD be with you on your way*
18:7 ª Josh. 19:47 ᵇ Judg. 18:27–29 ᶜ Judg. 10:12 ¹ *safely or securely* ² *rulers*
18:8 ª Judg. 18:2 ¹ *the spies*
18:9 ª Num. 13:30; Josh. 2:23, 24 ᵇ 1 Kin. 22:3
18:10 ª Judg. 18:7, 27 ᵇ Deut. 8:9
18:11 ¹ *armed*
18:12 ª Josh. 15:60 ᵇ Judg. 13:25 ¹ *encamped* ² Lit. *Camp of Dan*
18:13 ª Judg. 18:2
18:14 ª 1 Sam. 14:28 ᵇ Judg. 17:5
18:15 ¹ *aside there* ² *greeted*
18:16 ª Judg. 18:11
18:17 ª Judg. 18:2, 14 ᵇ Judg. 17:4, 5
18:19 ª Job 21:5; 29:9; 40:4; Mic. 7:16 ᵇ Judg. 17:10 ¹ *Be quiet, put thy hand over*

9 And they said, ªArise, that we may go up against them: for we have seen the land, and, behold, it *is* very good: and *are* ye ᵇstill? be not slothful to go, *and* to enter to possess the land.

10 When ye go, ye shall come unto a people ªsecure, and to a large land: for God hath given it into your hands; ᵇa place where *there is* no want of any thing that *is* in the earth.

11 And there went from thence of the family of the Danites, out of Zorah and out of Eshtaol, six hundred men ¹appointed with weapons of war.

12 And they went up, and ¹pitched in ªKirjath-jearim, in Judah: wherefore they called that place ᵇMahaneh-dan² unto this day: behold, *it is* behind Kirjath-jearim.

13 And they passed thence unto mount Ephraim, and came unto ªthe house of Micah.

14 ªThen answered the five men that went to spy out the country of Laish, and said unto their brethren, Do ye know that ᵇthere is in these houses an ephod, and teraphim, and a graven image, and a molten image? now therefore consider what ye have to do.

15 And they turned ¹thitherward, and came to the house of the young man the Levite, *even* unto the house of Micah, and ²saluted him.

16 And the ªsix hundred men appointed with their weapons of war, which *were* of the children of Dan, stood by the entering of the gate.

17 And ªthe five men that went to spy out the land went up, *and* came in thither, *and* took ᵇthe graven image, and the ephod, and the teraphim, and the molten image: and the priest stood in the entering of the gate with the six hundred men *that were* appointed with weapons of war.

18 And these went into Micah's house, and fetched the carved image, the ephod, and the teraphim, and the molten image. Then said the priest unto them, What do ye?

19 And they said unto him, ¹Hold thy peace, ªlay thine hand upon thy mouth, and go with us, ᵇand be to us a father and a priest: *is it* better for thee to be a priest unto the house of one man, or that thou be a priest unto a tribe and a family in Israel?

20 And the priest's heart was glad, and he took the ephod, and the teraphim, and the graven image, and went in the midst of the people.

21 So they turned and departed, and put the little ones and the cattle and the carriage before them.

22 *And* when they were a good way from the house of Micah, the men

that *were* in the houses near to Micah's house were gathered together, and overtook the children of Dan.

23 And they cried unto the children of Dan. And they turned their faces, and said unto Micah, [a]What aileth thee, that thou comest with such a company?

24 And he said, Ye have [a]taken away my [1]gods which I made, and the priest, and ye are gone away: and what have I more? and what *is* this *that* ye say unto me, What aileth thee?

25 And the children of Dan said unto him, Let not thy voice be heard among us, lest [1]angry fellows run upon thee, and thou lose thy life, with the lives of thy household.

26 And the children of Dan went their way: and when Micah saw that they *were* too strong for him, he turned and went back unto his house.

27 And they took *the things* which Micah had made, and the priest which he had, and came unto Laish, unto a people *that were* at quiet and secure: [a]and they [1]smote them with the edge of the sword, and burnt the city with fire.

28 And *there was* no deliverer, because it *was* [a]far from Zidon, and they had [1]no business with *any* man; and it was in the valley that *lieth* [b]by Beth-rehob. And they built a city, and dwelt therein.

29 And [a]they called the name of the city [b]Dan, after the name of Dan their father, who was born unto Israel: howbeit the name of the city *was* Laish at the first.

30 And the children of Dan set up the graven image: and Jonathan, the son of Gershom, the son of [1]Manasseh, he and his sons were priests to the tribe of Dan [a]until the day of the captivity of the land.

31 And they set them up Micah's graven image, which he made, [a]all the time that the house of God was in Shiloh.

## CHAPTER 19

AND it came to pass in those days, [a]when *there was* no king in Israel, that there was a certain Levite sojourning on the side of mount Ephraim, who took to him a concubine out of [b]Beth-lehem-judah.

2 And his concubine played the [1]whore against him, and went away from him unto her father's house to Beth-lehem-judah, and was there four whole months.

3 And her husband arose, and went after her, to [a]speak [1]friendly unto her, *and* to bring her again, having his servant with him, and a couple of

18:23 [a] 2 Kin. 6:28
18:24 [a] Gen. 31:30; Judg. 17:5
[1] *idols*
18:25 [1] Lit. *bitter of soul*
18:27 [a] Josh. 19:47
[1] *struck*
18:28 [a] Judg. 18:7 [b] Num. 13:21; 2 Sam. 10:6
[1] *no ties*
18:29 [a] Josh. 19:47 [b] Judg. 20:1; 1 Kin. 12:29, 30; 15:20
18:30 [a] 2 Kin. 15:29 [1] LXX, Vg. read *Moses*
18:31 [a] Deut. 12:1–32; Josh. 18:1, 8; Judg. 19:18; 21:12
19:1 [a] Judg. 17:6; 18:1; 21:25 [b] Judg. 17:7; Ruth 1:1
19:2 [1] *harlot*
19:3 [a] Gen. 34:3; 50:21 [1] *kindly*, lit. *to her heart*
19:5 [a] Gen. 18:5; Judg. 19:8; Ps. 104:15 [1] *Refresh*
19:9 [1] Lit. *to your tent*
19:10 [a] Josh. 18:28; 1 Chr. 11:4, 5
19:11 [a] Josh. 15:8, 63; Judg. 1:21; 2 Sam. 5:6
19:12 [a] Josh. 18:28
19:13 [a] Josh. 18:25 [1] *spend the night*
19:15 [1] *spend the night*

asses: and she brought him into her father's house: and when the father of the damsel saw him, he rejoiced to meet him.

4 And his father in law, the damsel's father, retained him; and he abode with him three days: so they did eat and drink, and lodged there.

5 And it came to pass on the fourth day, when they arose early in the morning, that he rose up to depart: and the damsel's father said unto his son in law, [a]Comfort[1] thine heart with a morsel of bread, and afterward go your way.

6 And they sat down, and did eat and drink both of them together: for the damsel's father had said unto the man, Be content, I pray thee, and tarry all night, and let thine heart be merry.

7 And when the man rose up to depart, his father in law urged him: therefore he lodged there again.

8 And he arose early in the morning on the fifth day to depart: and the damsel's father said, Comfort thine heart, I pray thee. And they tarried until afternoon, and they did eat both of them.

9 And when the man rose up to depart, he, and his concubine, and his servant, his father in law, the damsel's father, said unto him, Behold, now the day draweth toward evening, I pray you tarry all night: behold, the day groweth to an end, lodge here, that thine heart may be merry; and to morrow get you early on your way, that thou mayest go [1]home.

10 But the man would not tarry that night, but he rose up and departed, and came over against [a]Jebus, which *is* Jerusalem; and *there were* with him two asses saddled, his concubine also *was* with him.

11 *And* when they *were* by Jebus, the day was far spent; and the servant said unto his master, Come, I pray thee, and let us turn in into this city [a]of the Jebusites, and lodge in it.

12 And his master said unto him, We will not turn aside hither into the city of a stranger, that *is* not of the children of Israel; we will pass over [a]to Gibeah.

13 And he said unto his servant, Come, and let us draw near to one of these places to [1]lodge all night, in Gibeah, or in [a]Ramah.

14 And they passed on and went their way; and the sun went down upon them *when they were* by Gibeah, which *belongeth* to Benjamin.

15 And they turned aside thither, to go in *and* to [1]lodge in Gibeah: and when he went in, he sat him down in a street of the city: for *there was* no

man that [a]took them into his house to [2]lodging.

16 And, behold, there came an old man from [a]his work out of the field at even, which *was* also of mount Ephraim; and he sojourned in Gibeah: but the men of the place *were* Benjamites.

17 And when he had lifted up his eyes, he saw a [1]wayfaring man in the street of the city: and the old man said, Whither goest thou? and whence comest thou?

18 And he said unto him, We *are* passing from Beth-lehem-judah toward the side of mount Ephraim; from thence *am* I: and I went to Beth-lehem-judah, but I *am now* going to [a]the house of the LORD; and there *is* no man that [1]receiveth me to house.

19 Yet there is both straw and provender for our asses; and there is bread and wine also for me, and for thy handmaid, and for the young man *which is* with thy servants: *there is* no want of any thing.

20 And the old man said, [a]Peace *be* with thee; howsoever *let* all thy wants *lie* upon me; [b]only lodge not in the street.

21 [a]So he brought him into his house, and gave [1]provender unto the asses: [b]and they washed their feet, and did eat and drink.

22 *Now* as they were [1]making their [a]hearts merry, behold, [b]the men of the city, certain [c]sons[2] of Belial, beset the house round about, *and* beat at the door, and spake to the master of the house, the old man, saying, [d]Bring forth the man that came into thine house, that we may know him.

23 And [a]the man, the master of the house, went out unto them, and said unto them, Nay, my brethren, *nay,* I pray you, do not *so* wickedly; seeing that this man is come into mine house, [b]do[1] not this folly.

24 [a]Behold, *here is* my daughter a maiden, and [1]his concubine; them I will bring out now, and [b]humble ye them, and do with them [2]what seemeth good unto you: but unto this man do not so vile a thing.

25 But the men would not hearken to him: so the man took his concubine, and brought her forth unto them; and they [a]knew her, and abused her all the night until the morning: and when the day began to spring, they let her go.

26 Then came the woman in the dawning of the day, and fell down at the door of the man's house where her lord *was,* till it was light.

27 And her lord rose up in the morning, and opened the doors of the house, and went out to go his

way: and, behold, the woman his concubine was fallen down *at* the door of the house, and her hands *were* upon the threshold.

28 And he said unto her, [1]Up, and let us be going. But [a]none answered. Then the man took her *up* upon an ass, and the man rose up, and gat him unto his place.

29 And when he was come into his house, he took a knife, and laid hold on his concubine, and [a]divided[1] her, [2]together with her bones, into twelve pieces, and sent her into all the coasts of Israel.

30 And it was so, that all that saw it said, There was no such deed done nor seen from the day that the children of Israel came up out of the land of Egypt unto this day: consider of it, [a]take [1]advice, and [2]speak *your minds.*

## CHAPTER 20

THEN [a]all the children of Israel went out, and the congregation was gathered together as one man, from [b]Dan even to [c]Beer-sheba, with the land of Gilead, unto the LORD [d]in Mizpeh.

2 And the chief of all the people, *even* of all the tribes of Israel, presented themselves in the assembly of the people of God, four hundred thousand footmen [a]that drew sword.

3 (Now the children of Benjamin heard that the children of Israel were gone up to Mizpeh.) Then said the children of Israel, Tell *us,* [1]how was this wickedness?

4 And the Levite, the husband of the woman that was slain, answered and said, [a]I came into Gibeah that *belongeth* to Benjamin, I and my concubine, to [1]lodge.

5 [a]And the men of Gibeah rose against me, and beset the house round about upon me by night, *and* thought to have slain me: [b]and my concubine have they [1]forced, that she is dead.

6 And [a]I took my concubine, and cut her in pieces, and sent her throughout all the country of the inheritance of Israel: for they [b]have committed lewdness and [1]folly in Israel.

7 Behold, ye *are* all children of Israel; [a]give here your advice and counsel.

8 And all the people arose as one man, saying, We will not any *of us* go to his tent, neither will we any *of us* turn into his house.

9 But now this *shall be* the thing which we will do to Gibeah; *we will* go up [a]by lot against it;

10 And we will take ten men of an hundred throughout all the tribes of Israel, and an hundred of a thousand,

---

**Center cross-reference column:**

19:15 [a] Matt. 25:43
[2] *spend the night*
19:16 [a] Ps. 104:23
19:17 [1] *traveller*
19:18 [a] Josh. 18:1;
Judg. 18:31; 20:18;
1 Sam. 1:3, 7 [1] *will take me into his house*
19:20 [a] Gen. 43:23; Judg. 6:23; 1 Sam. 25:6 [b] Gen. 19:2
19:21 [a] Gen. 24:32; 43:24 [b] Gen. 18:4; John 13:5 [1] *fodder*
19:22 [a] Judg. 16:25; 19:6, 9 [b] Gen. 19:4, 5; Judg. 20:5; Hos. 9:9; 10:9 [c] Deut. 13:13; 1 Sam. 2:12; 1 Kin. 21:10; [2 Cor. 6:15] [d] Gen. 19:5; [Rom. 1:26, 27] [1] *enjoying themselves* [2] *perverted men*
19:23 [a] Gen. 19:6, 7 [b] Gen. 34:7; Deut. 22:21; Judg. 20:6, 10; 2 Sam. 13:12 [1] *do not commit this outrage*
19:24 [a] Gen. 19:8 [b] Gen. 34:2; Deut. 21:14 [1] *the man's* [2] *as you please*
19:25 [a] Gen. 4:1

19:28 [a] Judg. 20:5 [1] *Arise*
19:29 [a] Judg. 20:6; 1 Sam. 11:7 [1] *dismembered* [2] *limb by limb*
19:30 [a] Judg. 20:7; Prov. 13:10 [1] *counsel* [2] *speak up!*
20:1 [a] Josh. 22:12; Judg. 20:11; 21:5 [b] Judg. 18:29; 1 Sam. 3:20; 2 Sam. 3:10; 24:2 [c] Josh. 19:2 [d] Judg. 10:17; 1 Sam. 7:5
20:2 [a] Judg. 8:10
20:3 [1] *how did this wicked deed happen*
20:4 [a] Judg. 19:15 [1] *spend the night*
20:5 [a] Judg. 19:22 [b] Judg. 19:25, 26 [1] *ravished*
20:6 [a] Judg. 19:29 [b] Josh. 7:15 [1] *outrage*
20:7 [a] Judg. 19:30
20:9 [a] Judg. 1:3

and a thousand out of ten thousand, to [1]fetch victual for the people, that they may do, when they come to Gibeah of Benjamin, according to all the [2]folly that they have wrought in Israel.

11 So all the men of Israel were gathered against the city, [1]knit together as one man.

12 [a]And the tribes of Israel sent men through all the tribe of Benjamin, saying, What wickedness *is* this that is done among you?

13 Now therefore deliver *us* the men, [a]the [1]children of Belial, which *are* in Gibeah, that we may put them to death, and [b]put away evil from Israel. But the children of Benjamin would not hearken to the voice of their brethren the children of Israel:

14 But the children of Benjamin gathered themselves together out of the cities unto Gibeah, to go out to battle against the children of Israel.

15 And the [a]children of Benjamin were numbered at that time out of the cities twenty and six thousand men that drew sword, beside the inhabitants of Gibeah, which were numbered seven hundred chosen men.

16 Among all this people *there were* seven hundred chosen men [a]lefthanded; every one could sling stones at an hair *breadth*, and not miss.

17 And the men of Israel, beside Benjamin, were numbered four hundred thousand men that drew sword: all these *were* men of war.

18 And the children of Israel arose, and [a]went up to [1]the house of God, and [b]asked counsel of God, and said, Which of us shall go up first to the battle against the children of Benjamin? And the LORD said, [c]Judah *shall go up* first.

19 And the children of Israel rose up in the morning, and encamped against Gibeah.

20 And the men of Israel went out to battle against Benjamin; and the men of Israel put themselves in array to fight against them at Gibeah.

21 And [a]the children of Benjamin came forth out of Gibeah, and destroyed down to the ground of the Israelites that day twenty and two thousand men.

22 And the people the men of Israel encouraged themselves, and set their battle again in array in the place where they put themselves in array the first day.

23 ([a]And the children of Israel went up and wept before the LORD until even, and asked counsel of the LORD, saying, Shall I go up again to battle against the children of Benjamin my brother? And the LORD said, Go up against him.)

24 And the children of Israel came near against the children of Benjamin the second day.

25 And [a]Benjamin went forth against them out of Gibeah the second day, and destroyed down to the ground of the children of Israel again eighteen thousand men; all these drew the sword.

26 Then all the children of Israel, and all the people, [a]went up, and came unto [1]the house of God, and wept, and sat there before the LORD, and fasted that day until even, and offered burnt offerings and peace offerings before the LORD.

27 And the children of Israel enquired of the LORD, (for [a]the ark of the covenant of God *was* there in those days,

28 [a]And Phinehas, the son of Eleazar, the son of Aaron, [b]stood before it in those days,) saying, Shall I yet again go out to battle against the children of Benjamin my brother, or shall I cease? And the LORD said, Go up; for to morrow I will deliver them into thine hand.

29 And Israel [a]set [1]liers in wait round about Gibeah.

30 And the children of Israel went up against the children of Benjamin on the third day, and put themselves in array against Gibeah, as at other times.

31 And the children of Benjamin went out against the people, *and* were drawn away from the city; and they began to smite of the people, *and* kill, as at other times, in the highways, of which [a]one goeth up to [1]the house of God, and the other to Gibeah in the field, about thirty men of Israel.

32 And the children of Benjamin said, They *are* smitten down before us, as at the first. But the children of Israel said, Let us flee, and draw them from the city unto the highways.

33 And all the men of Israel rose up out of their place, and put themselves in array at Baal-tamar: and the [1]liers in wait of Israel came forth out of their places, *even* out of the meadows of Gibeah.

34 And there came against Gibeah ten thousand chosen men out of all Israel, and the battle was [1]sore: [a]but they knew not that [2]evil *was* near them.

35 And the LORD [1]smote Benjamin before Israel: and the children of Israel destroyed of the Benjamites that day twenty and five thousand and an hundred men: all these drew the sword.

### Cross references

20:10 [1] *make provisions* [2] *vileness*
20:11 [1] *united*
20:12 [a] Deut. 13:14; Josh. 22:13, 16
20:13 [a] Deut. 13:13; Judg. 19:22 [b] Deut. 17:12; 1 Cor. 5:13 [1] *perverted men*
20:15 [a] Num. 1:36, 37; 2:23; 26:41
20:16 [a] Judg. 3:15; 1 Chr. 12:2
20:18 [a] Judg. 20:23, 26 [b] Num. 27:21 [c] Judg. 1:1, 2 [1] Heb. *Beth-el*
20:21 [a] [Gen. 49:27]
20:23 [a] Judg. 20:26, 27
20:25 [a] Judg. 20:21
20:26 [a] Judg. 20:18, 23; 21:2 [1] Heb. *Beth-el*
20:27 [a] Josh. 18:1; 1 Sam. 1:3; 3:3; 4:3, 4
20:28 [a] Num. 25:7, 13; Josh. 24:33 [b] Deut. 10:8; 18:5
20:29 [a] Josh. 8:4 [1] *set an ambush*
20:31 [a] Judg. 21:19 [1] Heb. *Beth-el*
20:33 [1] *men in ambush*
20:34 [a] Josh. 8:14; Job 21:13; Is. 47:11 [1] *fierce* [2] *disaster*
20:35 [1] *defeated*

**36** So the children of Benjamin saw that they were smitten: [a]for the men of Israel gave place to the Benjamites, because they trusted unto the liers in wait which they had set beside Gibeah.

**37** [a]And the [1]liers in wait hasted, and rushed upon Gibeah; and the [2]liers in wait drew *themselves* along, and smote all the city with the edge of the sword.

**38** Now there was an appointed [1]sign between the men of Israel and the liers in wait, that they should make a great flame with [a]smoke rise up out of the city.

**39** And when the men of Israel retired in the battle, Benjamin began [1]to smite *and* kill of the men of Israel about thirty persons: for they said, Surely they are smitten down before us, as *in* the first battle.

**40** But when the flame began to arise up out of the city with a pillar of smoke, the Benjamites [a]looked behind them, and, behold, the flame of the city ascended up to heaven.

**41** And when the men of Israel [1]turned again, the men of Benjamin were amazed: for they saw that [2]evil was come upon them.

**42** Therefore they [1]turned *their backs* before the men of Israel unto the way of the wilderness; but the battle overtook them; and them which *came* out of the cities they destroyed in the midst of them.

**43** *Thus* they inclosed the Benjamites round about, *and* chased them, *and* [1]trode them down with ease over against Gibeah toward the [2]sunrising.

**44** And there fell of Benjamin eighteen thousand men; all these *were* men of valour.

**45** And they turned and fled toward the wilderness unto the rock of [a]Rimmon: and they [1]gleaned of them in the highways five thousand men; and pursued hard after them unto Gidom, and slew two thousand men of them.

**46** So that all which fell that day of Benjamin were twenty and five thousand men that drew the sword; all these *were* [1]men of valour.

**47** [a]But six hundred men turned and fled to the wilderness unto the rock Rimmon, and abode in the rock Rimmon four months.

**48** And the men of Israel [1]turned again upon the children of Benjamin, and smote them with the edge of the sword, as well the [2]men of *every* city, as the beast, and [3]all that came to hand: also they set on fire all the cities that they came to.

## CHAPTER 21

**N**ow [a]the men of Israel had sworn in Mizpeh, saying, There shall not

20:36 [a] Josh. 8:15
20:37 [a] Josh. 8:19
[1] *men in ambush quickly rushed*
[2] *men in ambush spread out*
20:38 [a] Josh. 8:20
[1] *signal*
20:39 [1] Lit. *to strike the slain ones of*
20:40 [a] Josh. 8:20
20:41 [1] *turned back* [2] *disaster*
20:42 [1] *fled*
20:43 [1] *trampled* [2] *east*
20:45 [a] Josh. 15:32; 1 Chr. 6:77; Zech. 14:10 [1] *cut down*
20:46 [1] *valiant warriors*
20:47 [a] Judg. 21:13
20:48 [1] *turned back against* [2] *men and beasts* [3] *all who were found*
21:1 [a] Judg. 20:1

21:2 [a] Judg. 20:18, 26 [1] Heb. *Beth-el* [2] *bitterly*
21:4 [a] Deut. 12:5; 2 Sam. 24:25
21:5 [a] Judg. 20:1–3
21:6 [1] *grieved*
21:8 [a] 1 Sam. 11:1; 31:11
21:9 [1] *counted*
21:10 [a] Num. 31:17; Judg. 5:23; 1 Sam. 11:7 [1] *most valiant*
21:11 [a] Num. 31:17; Deut. 20:13, 14
21:12 [a] Josh. 18:1; Judg. 18:31
21:13 [a] Judg. 20:47 [1] *announce peace*
21:14 [1] *they had not found enough for them*
21:15 [a] Judg. 21:6 [1] *were grieved*

any of us give his daughter unto Benjamin to wife.

**2** And the people came [a]to [1]the house of God, and abode there till even before God, and lifted up their voices, and wept [2]sore;

**3** And said, O LORD God of Israel, why is this come to pass in Israel, that there should be to day one tribe lacking in Israel?

**4** And it came to pass on the morrow, that the people rose early, and [a]built there an altar, and offered burnt offerings and peace offerings.

**5** And the children of Israel said, Who *is there* among all the tribes of Israel that came not up with the congregation unto the LORD? [a]For they had made a great oath concerning him that came not up to the LORD to Mizpeh, saying, He shall surely be put to death.

**6** And the children of Israel [1]repented them for Benjamin their brother, and said, There is one tribe cut off from Israel this day.

**7** How shall we do for wives for them that remain, seeing we have sworn by the LORD that we will not give them of our daughters to wives?

**8** And they said, What one *is there* of the tribes of Israel that came not up to Mizpeh to the LORD? And, behold, there came none to the camp from [a]Jabesh-gilead to the assembly.

**9** For the people were [1]numbered, and, behold, *there were* none of the inhabitants of Jabesh-gilead there.

**10** And the congregation sent thither twelve thousand men of the [1]valiantest, and commanded them, saying, [a]Go and smite the inhabitants of Jabesh-gilead with the edge of the sword, with the women and the children.

**11** And this *is* the thing that ye shall do, [a]Ye shall utterly destroy every male, and every woman that hath lain by man.

**12** And they found among the inhabitants of Jabesh-gilead four hundred young virgins, that had known no man by lying with any male: and they brought them unto the camp to [a]Shiloh, which *is* in the land of Canaan.

**13** And the whole congregation sent *some* to speak to the children of Benjamin [a]that *were* in the rock Rimmon, and to [1]call peaceably unto them.

**14** And Benjamin came again at that time; and they gave them wives which they had saved alive of the women of Jabesh-gilead: and yet [1]so they sufficed them not.

**15** And the people [a]repented[1] them for Benjamin, because that the LORD had made a breach in the tribes of Israel.

**16** Then the elders of the congregation said, How shall we do for wives for them that remain, seeing the women are destroyed out of Benjamin?

**17** And they said, *There must be* an inheritance for them that be escaped of Benjamin, that a tribe be not destroyed out of Israel.

**18** Howbeit we may not give them wives of our daughters: ªfor the children of Israel have sworn, saying, Cursed *be* he that giveth a wife to Benjamin.

**19** Then they said, Behold, *there is* a ªfeast of the LORD in ᵇShiloh yearly *in a place* which *is* on the north side of Beth-el, on the east side of the ᶜhighway that goeth up from Beth-el to Shechem, and on the south of Lebonah.

**20** Therefore they commanded the children of Benjamin, saying, Go and lie in wait in the vineyards;

**21** And see, and, behold, if the daughters of Shiloh come out ªto dance in dances, then come ye out of the vineyards, and catch you every

man his wife of the daughters of Shiloh, and go to the land of Benjamin.

**22** And it shall be, when their fathers or their brethren come unto us to complain, that we will say unto them, ¹Be favourable unto them for our sakes: because we reserved not to each man his wife in the war: for ye did not give unto them at this time, *that* ye should be guilty.

**23** And the children of Benjamin did so, and took *them* wives, according to their number, of them that danced, whom they caught: and they went and returned unto their inheritance, and ªrepaired¹ the cities, and dwelt in them.

**24** And the children of Israel departed thence at that time, every man to his tribe and to his family, and they went out from thence every man to his inheritance.

**25** ªIn those days *there was* no king in Israel: ᵇevery man did *that which was* right in his own eyes.

21:18 ª Judg. 11:35; 21:1
21:19 ª Lev. 23:2 ᵇ Deut. 12:5; Josh. 18:1; Judg. 18:31; 1 Sam. 1:3 ᶜ Judg. 20:31
21:21 ª Ex. 15:20; Judg. 11:34; 1 Sam. 18:6

21:22 ¹ *Be kind*
21:23 ª Judg. 20:48 ¹ *rebuilt*
21:25 ª Judg. 17:6; 18:1; 19:1 ᵇ Deut. 12:8; Judg. 17:6

# THE BOOK OF
# RUTH

**R**uth is a cameo story of love, devotion, and redemption set in the dark context of the days of the judges. It is the story of a Moabite woman who forsakes her pagan heritage in order to cling to the people of Israel and to the God of Israel. Because of her *faithfulness* in a time of national *faithlessness*, God rewards her by giving her a new husband (Boaz), a son (Obed), and a privileged position in the lineage of David and Christ (she is the great-grandmother of David).

*Ruth* is the Hebrew title of this book. This name may be a Moabite modification of the Hebrew word *reuit*, meaning "friendship" or "association." The Septuagint entitles the book *Routh*, the Greek equivalent of the Hebrew name. The Latin title is *Ruth*, a transliteration of *Routh*.

## CHAPTER 1

**N**ow it came to pass in the days when ᵃthe judges ¹ruled, that there was ᵇa famine in the land. And a certain man of ᶜBeth-lehem-judah went to ²sojourn in the country of ᵈMoab, he, and his wife, and his two sons.

2 And the name of the man *was* Elimelech, and the name of his wife Naomi, and the name of his two sons Mahlon and Chilion, ᵃEphrathites of Beth-lehem-judah. And they came ᵇinto the country of Moab, and ¹continued there.

3 And Elimelech Naomi's husband died; and she was left, and her two sons.

4 And they took them wives of the women of Moab; the name of the one *was* Orpah, and the name of the other Ruth: and they ¹dwelled there about ten years.

5 And Mahlon and Chilion died also both of them; and the woman was left of her two sons and her husband.

6 Then she arose with her daughters in law, that she might return from the country of Moab: for she had heard in the country of Moab how that the LORD had ᵃvisited¹ his people in ᵇgiving them bread.

7 Wherefore she went forth out of the place where she was, and her two daughters in law with her; and they went on the way to return unto the land of Judah.

8 And Naomi said unto her two daughters in law, ᵃGo, return each to her mother's house: ᵇthe LORD deal kindly with you, as ye have dealt ᶜwith the dead, and with me.

9 The LORD grant you that ye may find ᵃrest, each *of you* in the house of her husband. Then she kissed them; and they lifted up their voice, and wept.

10 And they said unto her, Surely we will return with thee unto thy people.

11 And Naomi said, Turn again, my daughters: why will ye go with me? *are* there yet *any more* sons in my womb, ᵃthat they may be your husbands?

12 Turn again, my daughters, go *your way;* for I am too old to have an husband. If I should say, I have hope, *if* I should have an husband also to night, and should also bear sons;

13 Would ye tarry for them till they were grown? would ye ¹stay for them from having husbands? nay, my daughters; for it grieveth me much for your sakes that ᵃthe hand of the LORD is gone out against me.

14 And they lifted up their voice, and wept again: and Orpah kissed her mother in law; but Ruth ᵃclave¹ unto her.

15 And she said, Behold, thy sister in law is gone back unto ᵃher people, and unto her gods: ᵇreturn thou after thy sister in law.

16 And Ruth said, ᵃIntreat¹ me not to leave thee, *or* to ²return from following after thee: for whither thou goest, I will go; and where thou lodgest, I will lodge: ᵇthy people *shall be* my people, and thy God my God:

17 Where thou diest, will I die, and there will I be buried: ᵃthe LORD do so to me, and more also, *if ought* but death part thee and me.

18 ᵃWhen she saw that she ¹was stedfastly minded to go with her, then she left speaking unto her.

19 So they two went until they came to Beth-lehem. And it came to pass, when they were come to Bethlehem, that ᵃall the city was ¹moved about them, and they said, ᵇ*Is* this Naomi?

20 And she said unto them, Call me not ¹Naomi, call me ²Mara: for the Almighty hath dealt very bitterly with me.

21 I went out full, ᵃand the LORD hath brought me home again empty:

244

why *then* call ye me Naomi, seeing the LORD hath testified against me, and 'the Almighty hath afflicted me?

22 So Naomi returned, and Ruth the Moabitess, her daughter in law, with her, which returned out of the country of Moab: and they came to Beth-lehem [a]in the beginning of barley harvest.

## CHAPTER 2

A ND Naomi had a [a]kinsman of her husband's, a mighty man of wealth, of the family of [b]Elimelech; and his name *was* [c]Boaz.

2 And Ruth the Moabitess said unto Naomi, Let me now go to the [a]field, and glean 'ears of corn after *him* in whose sight I shall find grace. And she said unto her, Go, my daughter.

3 And she went, and came, and gleaned in the field after the reapers: and 'her hap was to light on a part of the field *belonging* unto Boaz, who *was* of the kindred of Elimelech.

4 And, behold, Boaz came from [a]Beth-lehem, and said unto the reapers, [b]The LORD *be* with you. And they answered him, The LORD bless thee.

5 Then said Boaz unto his servant that was set over the reapers, Whose damsel *is* this?

6 And the servant that was set over the reapers answered and said, It *is* the Moabitish damsel [a]that came back with Naomi out of the country of Moab:

7 And she said, I pray you, let me glean and gather after the reapers among the sheaves: so she came, and hath continued even from the morning until now, 'that she tarried a little in the house.

8 Then said Boaz unto Ruth, Hearest thou not, my daughter? Go not to glean in another field, neither go 'from hence, but abide here [2]fast by my maidens:

9 *Let* thine eyes *be* on the field that they do reap, and go thou after them: have I not charged the young men that they shall not touch thee? and when thou art athirst, go unto the vessels, and drink of *that* which the young men have drawn.

10 Then she [a]fell on her face, and bowed herself to the ground, and said unto him, Why have I found [b]grace in thine eyes, that thou shouldest 'take knowledge of me, seeing I *am* a stranger?

11 And Boaz answered and said unto her, It hath fully been shewed me, [a]all that thou hast done unto thy mother in law since the death of thine husband: and *how* thou hast left thy father and thy mother, and the land of thy nativity, and art come

unto a people which thou knewest not heretofore.

12 [a]The LORD 'recompense thy work, and a full reward be given thee of the LORD God of Israel, [b]under whose wings thou art come to trust.

13 Then she said, [a]Let me find favour in thy sight, my lord; for that thou hast comforted me, and for that thou hast spoken 'friendly unto thine handmaid, [b]though I be not like unto one of thine handmaidens.

14 And Boaz said unto her, At mealtime come thou hither, and eat of the bread, and dip thy morsel in the vinegar. And she sat beside the reapers: and he reached her parched *corn,* and she did eat, and [a]was sufficed, and left.

15 And when she was risen up to 'glean, Boaz commanded his young men, saying, Let her glean even among the sheaves, and [2]reproach her not:

16 And let fall also *some* of the handfuls of purpose for her, and leave *them,* that she may glean *them,* and rebuke her not.

17 So she gleaned in the field until even, and beat out that she had gleaned: and it was about an ephah of [a]barley.

18 And she took *it* up, and went into the city: and her mother in law saw what she had gleaned: and she brought forth, and gave to her [a]that' she had reserved after she was sufficed.

19 And her mother in law said unto her, Where hast thou gleaned to day? and where 'wroughtest thou? blessed be he that [2]did [a]take knowledge of thee. And she [3]shewed her mother in law with whom she had wrought, and said, The man's name with whom I wrought to day *is* Boaz.

20 And Naomi said unto her daughter in law, [a]Blessed *be* he of the LORD, who [b]hath not left off his kindness to the living and to the dead. And Naomi said unto her, The man *is* near of kin unto us, [c]one of our 'next kinsmen.

21 And Ruth the Moabitess said, He said unto me also, Thou shalt 'keep fast by my young men, until they have ended all my harvest.

22 And Naomi said unto Ruth her daughter in law, *It is* good, my daughter, that thou go out with his maidens, that 'they meet thee not in any other field.

23 So she kept fast by the maidens of Boaz to glean unto the end of barley harvest and of wheat harvest; and dwelt with her mother in law.

## CHAPTER 3

T HEN Naomi her mother in law said unto her, My daughter, [a]shall

### Cross references (center column)

1:21 [1] Heb. *Shaddai*
1:22 [a] Ruth 2:23; 2 Sam. 21:9
2:1 [a] Ruth 3:2, 12 [b] Ruth 1:2 [c] Ruth 4:21
2:2 [a] Lev. 19:9, 10; 23:22; Deut. 24:19 [1] heads of grain
2:3 [1] she happened to come to
2:4 [a] Ruth 1:1 [b] Ps. 129:7, 8; Luke 1:28; 2 Thess. 3:16
2:6 [a] Ruth 1:22
2:7 [1] though she rested
2:8 [1] from here [2] close
2:10 [a] 1 Sam. 25:23 [b] 1 Sam. 1:18 [1] take notice
2:11 [a] Ruth 1:14–18

2:12 [a] 1 Sam. 24:19; Ps. 58:11 [b] Ruth 1:16; Ps. 17:8; 36:7; 57:1; 61:4; 63:7; 91:4 [1] repay
2:13 [a] Gen. 33:15; 1 Sam. 1:18 [b] 1 Sam. 25:41 [1] kindly, lit. to the heart
2:14 [a] Ruth 2:18
2:15 [1] gather after the reapers [2] rebuke
2:17 [a] Ruth 1:22
2:18 [a] Ruth 2:14 [1] what she had kept back after she had been satisfied
2:19 [a] Ruth 2:10; [Ps. 41:1] [1] did you work [2] noticed [3] told
2:20 [a] Ruth 3:10; 2 Sam. 2:5 [b] Prov. 17:17 [c] Ruth 3:9; 4:4, 6 [1] near
2:21 [1] stay close
2:22 [1] men do not encounter
3:1 [a] 1 Cor. 7:36; 1 Tim. 5:8

I not seek [b]rest[1] for thee, that it may be well with thee?

2 And now *is* not Boaz of our kindred, [a]with whose maidens thou wast? Behold, he winnoweth barley to night in the threshingfloor.

3 Wash thyself therefore, [a]and anoint thee, and put thy [1]raiment upon thee, and get thee down to the floor: *but* make not thyself known unto the man, until he shall have done eating and drinking.

4 And it shall be, when he lieth down, that thou shalt mark the place where he shall lie, and thou shalt go in, and uncover his feet, and lay thee down; and he will tell thee what thou shalt do.

5 And she said unto her, All that thou sayest unto me I will do.

6 And she went down unto the floor, and did according to all that her mother in law bade her.

7 And when Boaz had eaten and drunk, and [a]his heart was [1]merry, he went to lie down at the end of the heap of [2]corn: and she came softly, and uncovered his feet, and laid her down.

8 And it came to pass at midnight, that the man was [1]afraid, and turned himself: and, behold, a woman lay at his feet.

9 And he said, Who *art* thou? And she answered, I *am* Ruth thine handmaid: [a]spread therefore thy [1]skirt over thine handmaid; for thou *art* [b]a [2]near kinsman.

10 And he said, [a]Blessed *be* thou of the LORD, my daughter: *for* thou hast shewed more kindness in the latter end than [b]at the beginning, inasmuch as thou followedst not young men, whether poor or rich.

11 And now, my daughter, fear not; I will do to thee all that thou [1]requirest: for all the city of my people doth know that thou *art* [a]a virtuous woman.

12 And now it is true that I *am* thy [a]near kinsman: howbeit [b]there is a kinsman nearer than I.

13 Tarry this night, and it shall be in the morning, *that* if he will [a]perform unto thee the part of a kinsman, well; let him do the kinsman's part: but if he will not do the part of a kinsman to thee, then will I do the part of a kinsman to thee, [b]as the LORD liveth: lie down until the morning.

14 And she lay at his feet until the morning: and she rose up before one could [1]know another. And he said, [a]Let it not be known that a woman came into the floor.

15 Also he said, Bring the [1]vail that *thou hast* upon thee, and hold it. And when she held it, he measured six *measures* of barley, and laid *it* on her: and [2]she went into the city.

16 And when she came to her mother in law, she said, [1]Who *art* thou, my daughter? And she told her all that the man had done to her.

17 And she said, These six *measures* of barley gave he me; for he said to me, Go not empty unto thy mother in law.

18 Then said she, [a]Sit still, my daughter, until thou know how the matter will [1]fall: for the man will not [2]be in rest, until he have finished the thing this day.

## CHAPTER 4

THEN went Boaz up to the gate, and sat him down there: and, behold, [a]the kinsman of whom Boaz spake came by; unto whom he said, Ho, [1]such a one! turn aside, sit down here. And he turned aside, and sat down.

2 And he took ten men of [a]the elders of the city, and said, Sit ye down here. And they sat down.

3 And he said unto the kinsman, Naomi, that is come again out of the country of Moab, selleth a parcel of land, [a]which *was* our brother Elimelech's:

4 And I thought to [1]advertise thee, saying, [a]Buy *it* [b]before[2] the inhabitants, and before the elders of my people. If thou wilt redeem *it,* redeem *it:* but if thou wilt not redeem *it, then* tell me, that I may know: [c]for *there is* none to redeem *it* beside thee; and I *am* after thee. And he said, I will redeem *it.*

5 Then said Boaz, What day thou buyest the field [1]of the hand of Naomi, thou must buy *it* also of Ruth the Moabitess, the wife of the dead, [a]to raise up the name of the dead upon his inheritance.

6 [a]And the kinsman said, I cannot redeem *it* for myself, lest I [1]mar mine own inheritance: redeem thou my [2]right to thyself; for I cannot redeem *it.*

7 [a]Now this *was the manner* in former time in Israel concerning redeeming and concerning [1]changing, for to confirm all things; a man plucked off his shoe, and gave *it* to his neighbour: and this *was* [2]a testimony in Israel.

8 Therefore the kinsman said unto Boaz, Buy *it* for thee. So he drew off his shoe.

9 And Boaz said unto the elders, and *unto* all the people, Ye *are* witnesses this day, that I have bought all that *was* Elimelech's, and all that *was* Chilion's and Mahlon's, of the hand of Naomi.

10 Moreover Ruth the Moabitess, the wife of Mahlon, have I purchased to be my wife, to raise up the name of

---

*Center column references:*

3:1 [b] Ruth 1:9
[1] *security*

3:2 [a] Ruth 2:3, 8

3:3 [a] 2 Sam. 14:2
[1] *best garment*

3:7 [a] Judg. 19:6, 9, 22; 2 Sam. 13:28; Esth. 1:10 [1] *cheerful* [2] *grain*

3:8 [1] *startled*

3:9 [a] Ezek. 16:8
[b] Ruth 2:20;
3:12 [1] *garment corner or wing*
[2] *redeemer*

3:10 [a] Ruth 2:20
[b] Ruth 1:8

3:11 [a] Prov. 12:4; 31:10–31 [1] *request*

3:12 [a] Ruth 3:9
[b] Ruth 4:1

3:13 [a] Deut. 25:5–10; Ruth 4:5, 10; Matt. 22:24
[b] Judg. 8:19; Jer. 4:2; 12:16

3:14 [a] [Rom. 12:17; 14:16; 1 Cor. 10:32; 2 Cor. 8:21; 1 Thess. 5:22]
[1] *recognize*

3:15 [1] *shawl*
[2] Many Heb. mss., Syr., Vg. *she;* MT, LXX, Tg. *he*

3:16 [1] *How are you?*

3:18 [a] [Ps. 37:3, 5]
[1] *turn out* [2] *rest*

4:1 [a] Ruth 3:12
[1] Lit. *so and so*

4:2 [a] 1 Kin. 21:8; Prov. 31:23

4:3 [a] Lev. 25:25

4:4 [a] Jer. 32:7, 8 [b] Gen. 23:18
[c] Lev. 25:25
[1] *inform* [2] *in the presence of*

4:5 [a] Gen. 38:8; Deut. 25:5, 6; Ruth 3:13; Matt. 22:24 [1] *from*

4:6 [a] Ruth 3:12, 13; Job 19:14
[1] *ruin* [2] *right of redemption*

4:7 [a] Deut. 25:7–10 [1] *exchanging*
[2] *an attestation*

the dead upon his inheritance, [a]that the name of the dead be not cut off from among his brethren, and from the gate of his place: ye *are* witnesses this day.

11 And all the people that *were* in the gate, and the elders, said, *We are* witnesses. [a]The LORD make the woman [1]that is come into thine house like Rachel and like Leah, which two did [b]build the house of Israel: and do thou worthily in [c]Ephrath, and be famous in [d]Beth-lehem:

12 And let thy house be like the house of [a]Pharez, [b]whom Tamar bare unto Judah, of [c]the [1]seed which the LORD shall give thee of this young woman.

13 So Boaz [a]took Ruth, and she was his wife: and when he went in unto her, [b]the LORD gave her conception, and she bare a son.

14 And [a]the women said unto Naomi, Blessed *be* the LORD, which hath not left thee this day without a [1]kinsman, that his name may be famous in Israel.

15 And he shall be unto thee a restorer of *thy* life, and a [1]nourisher of thine old age: for thy daughter in law, which loveth thee, which is [a]better to thee than seven sons, hath born him.

16 And Naomi took the child, and laid it in her bosom, and became nurse unto it.

17 [a]And the women her neighbours gave it a name, saying, There is a son born to Naomi; and they called his name Obed: he *is* the father of Jesse, the father of David.

18 [a]Now these *are* the generations of Pharez: [b]Pharez begat Hezron,

19 And Hezron begat Ram, and Ram begat Amminadab,

20 And Amminadab begat [a]Nahshon, and Nahshon begat [b]Salmon,[1]

21 And Salmon begat Boaz, and Boaz begat Obed,

22 And Obed begat Jesse, and Jesse begat [a]David.

---

4:10 [a] Deut. 25:6
4:11 [a] Ps. 127:3; 128:3 [b] Gen. 29:25–30; Deut. 25:9 [c] Gen. 35:16–18 [d] 1 Sam. 16:4–13; Mic. 5:2; Matt. 2:1–8 [1] *who*
4:12 [a] 1 Chr. 2:4; Matt. 1:3 [b] Gen. 38:6–29 [c] 1 Sam. 2:20 [1] *offspring*
4:13 [a] Ruth 3:11 [b] Gen. 29:31; 33:5; Matt. 1:5
4:14 [a] Luke 1:58; [Rom. 12:15] [1] *redeemer*
4:15 [a] 1 Sam. 1:8 [1] *sustainer*
4:17 [a] Luke 1:58
4:18 [a] 1 Chr. 2:4, 5; Matt. 1:1–7 [b] Num. 26:20, 21
4:20 [a] Num. 1:7 [b] Matt. 1:4 [1] Heb. *Salmah*
4:22 [a] 1 Chr. 2:15; Matt. 1:6

# THE FIRST BOOK OF

# SAMUEL

The Book of First Samuel describes the transition of leadership in Israel from judges to kings. Three characters are prominent in the book: Samuel, the last judge and first prophet; Saul, the first king of Israel; and David, the king-elect, anointed but not yet recognized as Saul's successor.

The books of First and Second Samuel were originally one book in the Hebrew Bible, known as the "Book of Samuel" or simply "Samuel." This name has been variously translated "The Name of God," "His Name Is God," "Heard of God," and "Asked of God." The Septuagint divides Samuel into two books even though it is one continuous account. This division artificially breaks up the history of David. The Greek (Septuagint) title is *Bibloi Basileion*, "Books of Kingdoms," referring to the later kingdoms of Israel and Judah. First Samuel is called *Basileion Alpha*, "First Kingdoms." Second Samuel and First and Second Kings are called "Second, Third, and Fourth Kingdoms." The Latin Vulgate originally called the books of Samuel and Kings *Libri Regum*, "Books of the Kings." Later the Latin Bible combined the Hebrew and Greek titles for the first of these books, calling it *Liber I Samuelis*, the "First Book of Samuel," or simply "First Samuel."

## CHAPTER 1

Now there was a certain man of Ramathaim-zophim, of ᵃmount Ephraim, and his name *was* ᵇEl-kanah, the son of Jeroham, the son of ¹Elihu, the son of ²Tohu, the son of Zuph, ᶜan Ephrathite:

2 And he had ᵃtwo wives; the name of the one *was* Hannah, and the name of the other Peninnah: and Peninnah had children, but Hannah had no children.

3 And this man went up out of his city ᵃyearly ᵇto worship and to sacrifice unto the LORD of hosts in ᶜShiloh. And the two sons of Eli, Hophni and Phinehas, the priests of the LORD, *were* there.

4 And when the time was that Elkanah ᵃoffered, he gave to Peninnah his wife, and to all her sons and her daughters, portions:

5 But unto Hannah he gave a ¹worthy portion; for he loved Hannah: ᵃbut the LORD had shut up her womb.

6 And her adversary also ᵃprovoked her ¹sore, for to make her ²fret, because the LORD had shut up her womb.

7 And *as* he did so year by year, when she went up to the house of the LORD, so she provoked her; therefore she wept, and did not eat.

8 Then said Elkanah her husband to her, Hannah, why weepest thou? and why eatest thou not? and why is thy heart grieved? *am* not I ᵃbetter to thee than ten sons?

9 So Hannah rose up after they had eaten in Shiloh, and after they had drunk. Now Eli the priest sat upon a seat by a post of ᵃthe ¹temple of the LORD.

1:1 ᵃ Josh. 17:17, 18; 24:33  ᵇ 1 Chr. 6:27, 33–38
ᶜ Ruth 1:2  ¹ *Eliel*, 1 Chr. 6:34
² *Toah*, 1 Chr. 6:34
1:2 ᵃ Deut. 21:15–17
1:3 ᵃ Luke 2:41  ᵇ Deut. 19:5–7; 16:16  ᶜ Josh. 18:1
1:4 ᵃ Deut. 12:17, 18
1:5 ᵃ Gen. 16:1; 30:1, 2  ¹ *double portion*
1:6 ᵃ Job 24:21  ¹ *severely*  ² *miserable*
1:8 ᵃ Ruth 4:15
1:9 ᵃ 1 Sam. 3:3  ¹ *tabernacle*, lit. *palace* or *temple*

1:10 ᵃ Job 7:11  ¹ *in anguish*, lit. *greatly*
1:11 ᵃ Num. 30:6–11  ᵇ Ps. 25:18  ᶜ Gen. 8:1  ᵈ Num. 6:5
1:15 ᵃ Ps. 42:4; 62:8
1:16 ᵃ Deut. 13:13  ¹ *wicked woman*
1:17 ᵃ Mark 5:34  ᵇ Ps. 20:3–5
1:18 ᵃ Ruth 2:13  ᵇ Rom. 15:13

10 ᵃAnd she *was* in bitterness of soul, and prayed unto the LORD, and wept ¹sore.

11 And she ᵃvowed a vow, and said, O LORD of hosts, if thou wilt indeed ᵇlook on the affliction of thine handmaid, and ᶜremember me, and not forget thine handmaid, but wilt give unto thine handmaid a man child, then I will give him unto the LORD all the days of his life, and there ᵈshall no razor come upon his head.

12 And it came to pass, as she continued praying before the LORD, that Eli marked her mouth.

13 Now Hannah, she spake in her heart; only her lips moved, but her voice was not heard: therefore Eli thought she had been drunken.

14 And Eli said unto her, How long wilt thou be drunken? put away thy wine from thee.

15 And Hannah answered and said, No, my lord, I *am* a woman of a sorrowful spirit: I have drunk neither wine nor strong drink, but have ᵃpoured out my soul before the LORD.

16 Count not thine handmaid for a ¹daughter of ᵃBelial: for out of the abundance of my complaint and grief have I spoken hitherto.

17 Then Eli answered and said, ᵃGo in peace: and ᵇthe God of Israel grant *thee* thy petition that thou hast asked of him.

18 And she said, ᵃLet thine handmaid find grace in thy sight. So the woman ᵇwent her way, and did eat, and her countenance was no more *sad.*

19 And they rose up in the morning early, and worshipped before the LORD, and returned, and came to

their house to Ramah: and Elkanah [a]knew Hannah his wife; and the LORD [b]remembered her.

20 Wherefore it came to pass, when the time was come about after Hannah had conceived, that she bare a son, and called his name [1]Samuel, *saying,* Because I have asked him of the LORD.

21 And the man Elkanah, and all his house, [a]went up to offer unto the LORD the yearly sacrifice, and his vow.

22 But Hannah went not up; for she said unto her husband, *I will not go up* until the child be weaned, and *then* I will [a]bring him, that he may appear before the LORD, and there [b]abide [c]for ever.

23 And [a]Elkanah her husband said unto her, Do what seemeth thee good; tarry until thou have weaned him; [1]only the LORD establish his word. So the woman abode, and [2]gave her son suck until she weaned him.

24 And when she had weaned him, she [a]took him up with her, with three bullocks, and one ephah of flour, and a bottle of wine, and brought him unto [b]the house of the LORD in Shiloh: and the child *was* young.

25 And they slew a bullock, and [a]brought the child to Eli.

26 And she said, Oh my lord, [a]*as* thy soul liveth, my lord, I *am* the woman that stood by thee here, praying unto the LORD.

27 [a]For this child I prayed; and the LORD hath given me my petition which I asked of him:

28 Therefore also I have [1]lent him to the LORD; as long as he liveth he shall be lent to the LORD. And he [a]worshipped the LORD there.

## CHAPTER 2

AND Hannah [a]prayed, and said, [b]My heart rejoiceth in the LORD, [c]mine [1]horn is exalted in the LORD: my mouth [2]is enlarged over mine enemies; because I [d]rejoice in thy salvation.

2 [a]*There is* none holy as the LORD: for *there is* [b]none beside thee: neither *is there* any [c]rock like our God.

3 Talk no more so exceeding proudly; [a]let *not* [1]arrogancy come out of your mouth: for the LORD *is* a God of [b]knowledge, and by him actions are weighed.

4 [a]The bows of the mighty men *are* broken, and they that stumbled are girded with strength.

5 *They that were* full have hired out themselves for bread; and *they that were* hungry [1]ceased: so that [a]the barren hath born seven; and [b]she that hath many children is waxed feeble.

6 [a]The LORD killeth, and maketh alive: he bringeth down to the grave, and bringeth up.

7 The LORD [a]maketh poor, and maketh rich: [b]he bringeth low, and lifteth up.

8 [a]He raiseth up the poor out of the dust, *and* lifteth up the beggar from the dunghill, [b]to set *them* among princes, and to make them inherit the throne of glory: [c]for the pillars of the earth *are* the LORD's, and he hath set the world upon them.

9 [a]He will keep the feet of his saints, and the [b]wicked shall be silent in darkness; for by strength shall no man prevail.

10 The adversaries of the LORD shall be [a]broken to pieces; [b]out of heaven shall he thunder upon them: [c]the LORD shall judge the ends of the earth; and [d]he shall give [e]strength unto his king, and [f]exalt the [1]horn of his anointed.

11 And Elkanah went to Ramah to his house. And the child did [1]minister unto the LORD before Eli the priest.

12 Now the sons of Eli *were* [a]sons[1] of Belial; [b]they knew not the LORD.

13 And the priest's custom with the people *was, that,* when any man offered sacrifice, the priest's servant came, while the flesh was in seething, with a fleshhook of three teeth in his hand;

14 And he struck *it* into the pan, or kettle, or caldron, or pot; all that the fleshhook brought up the priest took for himself. So they did in [a]Shiloh unto all the Israelites that came thither.

15 Also before they [a]burnt the fat, the priest's servant came, and said to the man that sacrificed, Give flesh to roast for the priest; for he will not have [1]sodden flesh of thee, but raw.

16 And *if* any man said unto him, Let them not fail to burn the fat [1]presently, and *then* take as much as thy soul desireth; then he would answer him, *Nay;* but thou shalt give *it me* now: and if not, I will take *it* by force.

17 Wherefore the sin of the young men was very great [a]before the LORD: for men [b]abhorred[1] the offering of the LORD.

18 [a]But Samuel ministered before the LORD, *being* a child, [b]girded with a linen ephod.

19 Moreover his mother made him a little coat, and brought *it* to him from year to year, when she [a]came up with her husband to offer the yearly sacrifice.

20 And Eli [a]blessed Elkanah and his wife, and said, The LORD give thee seed of this woman for the [1]loan which is [b]lent[2] to the LORD. And they went unto their own home.

### Cross references

1:19 [a] Gen. 4:1 [b] Gen. 21:1; 30:22
1:20 [1] Lit. *Heard by God*
1:21 [a] 1 Sam. 1:3
1:22 [a] Luke 2:22 [b] 1 Sam. 1:11, 28 [c] Ex. 21:6
1:23 [a] Num. 30:7, 10, 11 [1] *only let* [2] *nursed her son*
1:24 [a] Num. 15:9, 10 [b] Josh. 18:1
1:25 [a] Luke 2:22
1:26 [a] 2 Kin. 2:2, 4, 6; 4:30
1:27 [a] [Matt. 7:7]
1:28 [a] Gen. 24:26, 52 [1] *granted*
2:1 [a] Phil. 4:6 [b] Luke 1:46–55 [c] Ps. 75:10; 89:17, 24; 92:10; 112:9 [d] Ps. 9:14; 13:5; 35:9 [1] *strength* [2] *smiles at*
2:2 [a] Ex. 15:11 [b] Deut. 4:35 [c] Deut. 32:4, 30, 31
2:3 [a] Ps. 94:4 [b] 1 Sam. 16:7 [1] *arrogance*
2:4 [a] Ps. 37:15; 46:9
2:5 [a] Ps. 113:9 [b] Is. 54:1 [1] *ceased to hunger*
2:6 [a] Deut. 32:39
2:7 [a] Deut. 8:17, 18 [b] Ps. 75:7
2:8 [a] Luke 1:52 [b] Job 36:7 [c] Job 38:4–6
2:9 [a] [1 Pet. 1:5] [b] [Rom. 3:19]
2:10 [a] Ps. 2:9 [b] Ps. 18:13, 14 [c] Ps. 96:13; 98:9 [d] [Matt. 28:18] [e] Ps. 21:1, 7 [f] Ps. 89:24 [1] *Strength*
2:11 [1] *serve*
2:12 [a] Deut. 13:13 [b] Judg. 2:10 [1] *worthless men*
2:14 [a] 1 Sam. 1:3
2:15 [a] Lev. 3:3–5, 16 [1] *boiled*
2:16 [1] *first*
2:17 [a] Gen. 6:11 [b] [Mal. 2:7–9] [1] *despised*
2:18 [a] 1 Sam. 2:11; 3:1 [b] Ex. 28:4
2:19 [a] 1 Sam. 1:3, 21
2:20 [a] Gen. 14:19 [b] 1 Sam. 1:11, 27, 28 [1] *gift* [2] *granted*

21 And the LORD <sup>a</sup>visited<sup>1</sup> Hannah, so that she conceived, and bare three sons and two daughters. And the child Samuel <sup>b</sup>grew before the LORD.

22 Now Eli was very old, and heard all that his sons did unto all Israel; and how they lay with <sup>a</sup>the women that assembled *at* the door of the tabernacle of the congregation.

23 And he said unto them, Why do ye such things? for I hear of your evil dealings by all this people.

24 Nay, my sons; for *it is* no good report that I hear: ye make the LORD's people to transgress.

25 If one man sin against another, <sup>1</sup>the <sup>a</sup>judge shall judge him: but if a man <sup>b</sup>sin against the LORD, who shall intreat for him? Notwithstanding they hearkened not unto the voice of their father, <sup>c</sup>because the LORD would slay them.

26 And the child Samuel <sup>a</sup>grew on, and was <sup>b</sup>in favour both with the LORD, and also with men.

27 And there came a <sup>a</sup>man of God unto Eli, and said unto him, Thus saith the LORD, <sup>b</sup>Did I plainly appear unto the house of thy father, when they were in Egypt in Pharaoh's house?

28 And did I <sup>a</sup>choose him out of all the tribes of Israel *to be* my priest, to offer upon mine altar, to burn incense, to wear an ephod before me? and <sup>b</sup>did I give unto the house of thy father all the offerings made by fire of the children of Israel?

29 Wherefore <sup>a</sup>kick ye at my sacrifice and at mine offering, which I have commanded *in my* <sup>b</sup>habitation; and honourest thy sons above <sup>c</sup>me, to make yourselves fat with the <sup>1</sup>chiefest of all the offerings of Israel my people?

30 Wherefore the LORD God of Israel saith, <sup>a</sup>I said indeed *that* thy house, and the house of thy father, should walk before me for ever: but now the LORD saith, <sup>b</sup>Be it far from me; for them that honour me I will honour, and <sup>c</sup>they that despise me shall be lightly esteemed.

31 Behold, <sup>a</sup>the days come, that I will cut off thine <sup>1</sup>arm, and the arm of thy father's house, that there shall not be an old man in thine house.

32 And thou shalt see an enemy *in my* habitation, in all *the wealth* which *God* shall give Israel: and there shall not be <sup>a</sup>an old man in thine house for ever.

33 And the man of thine, *whom* I shall not cut off from mine altar, *shall be* to consume thine eyes, and to grieve thine heart: and all <sup>1</sup>the increase of thine house shall die in the flower of their age.

34 And this *shall be* <sup>a</sup>a sign unto thee, that shall come upon thy two

sons, on Hophni and Phinehas; <sup>b</sup>in one day they shall die both of them.

35 And <sup>a</sup>I will raise me up a faithful priest, *that* shall do according to *that* which *is* in mine heart and in my mind: and <sup>b</sup>I will build him a sure house; and he shall walk before <sup>c</sup>mine anointed for ever.

36 <sup>a</sup>And it shall come to pass, *that* every one that is left in thine house shall come *and* <sup>1</sup>crouch to him for a piece of silver and a morsel of bread, and shall say, <sup>2</sup>Put me, I pray thee, into one of the priests' offices, that I may eat a piece of bread.

## CHAPTER 3

AND <sup>a</sup>the child Samuel ministered unto the LORD before Eli. And <sup>b</sup>the word of the LORD was <sup>1</sup>precious in those days; *there was* no open vision.

2 And it came to pass at that time, when Eli *was* laid down in his place, and his eyes began to wax <sup>a</sup>dim, *that* he could not see;

3 And ere <sup>a</sup>the lamp of God went out in the <sup>1</sup>temple of the LORD, where the ark of God *was,* and Samuel was laid down *to sleep;*

4 That the LORD called Samuel: and he answered, Here *am* I.

5 And he ran unto Eli, and said, Here *am* I; for thou calledst me. And he said, I called not; lie down again. And he went and lay down.

6 And the LORD called yet again, Samuel. And Samuel arose and went to Eli, and said, Here *am* I; for thou didst call me. And he answered, I called not, my son; lie down again.

7 Now Samuel <sup>a</sup>did not yet know the LORD, neither was the word of the LORD yet revealed unto him.

8 And the LORD called Samuel again the third time. And he arose and went to Eli, and said, Here *am* I; for thou didst call me. And Eli perceived that the LORD had called the child.

9 Therefore Eli said unto Samuel, Go, lie down: and it shall be, if he call thee, that thou shalt say, <sup>a</sup>Speak, LORD; for thy servant heareth. So Samuel went and lay down in his place.

10 And the LORD came, and stood, and called as at other times, Samuel, Samuel. Then Samuel answered, Speak; for thy servant heareth.

11 And the LORD said to Samuel, Behold, I will do a thing in Israel, <sup>a</sup>at which both the ears of every one that heareth it shall tingle.

12 In that day I will perform against Eli <sup>a</sup>all *things* which I have spoken concerning his house: when I begin, I will also make an end.

13 <sup>a</sup>For I have told him that I will <sup>b</sup>judge his house for ever for the iniquity which he knoweth; because <sup>c</sup>his

### Center cross-reference column

2:21 <sup>a</sup> Gen. 21:1 <sup>b</sup> Judg. 13:24; 1 Sam. 2:26; 3:19–21; Luke 1:80; 2:40 <sup>1</sup> *attended to*

2:22 <sup>a</sup> Ex. 38:8

2:25 <sup>a</sup> Deut. 1:17; 25:1, 2 <sup>b</sup> Num. 15:30 <sup>c</sup> Josh. 11:20 <sup>1</sup> MT *God*

2:26 <sup>a</sup> 1 Sam. 2:21 <sup>b</sup> Prov. 3:4

2:27 <sup>a</sup> Deut. 33:1; Judg. 13:6; 1 Sam. 9:6; 1 Kin. 13:1 <sup>b</sup> Ex. 4:14–16; 12:1

2:28 <sup>a</sup> Ex. 28:1, 4; Num. 16:5 <sup>b</sup> Lev. 2:3, 10; 6:16; 7:7, 8, 34, 35; Num. 5:9

2:29 <sup>a</sup> Deut. 32:15 <sup>b</sup> Deut. 12:5; Ps. 26:8 <sup>c</sup> Matt. 10:37 <sup>1</sup> *best*

2:30 <sup>a</sup> Ex. 29:9; Num. 25:13 <sup>b</sup> Jer. 18:9, 10 <sup>c</sup> Ps. 91:14; Mal. 2:9–12

2:31 <sup>a</sup> 1 Sam. 4:11–18; 22:18, 19; 1 Kin. 2:27, 35 <sup>1</sup> *strength*

2:32 <sup>a</sup> Zech. 8:4

2:33 <sup>1</sup> *the descendants*

2:34 <sup>a</sup> 1 Sam. 10:7–9; 1 Kin. 13:3

b 1 Sam. 4:11, 17

2:35 <sup>a</sup> 1 Kin. 2:35; Ezek. 44:15; [Heb. 2:17; 7:26–28] <sup>b</sup> 2 Sam. 7:11, 27; 1 Kin. 11:38 <sup>c</sup> Ps. 18:50

2:36 <sup>a</sup> 1 Kin. 2:27 <sup>1</sup> *bow down* <sup>2</sup> *Please assign*

3:1 <sup>a</sup> 1 Sam. 2:11, 18 <sup>b</sup> Ps. 74:9; Ezek. 7:26; Amos 8:11, 12 <sup>1</sup> *rare*

3:2 <sup>a</sup> Gen. 27:1; 48:10; 1 Sam. 4:15

3:3 <sup>a</sup> Ex. 27:20, 21 <sup>1</sup> *tabernacle,* lit. *palace* or *temple*

3:7 <sup>a</sup> 1 Sam. 2:12; Acts 19:2; 1 Cor. 13:11

3:9 <sup>a</sup> 1 Kin. 2:17

3:11 <sup>a</sup> 2 Kin. 21:12; Jer. 19:3

3:12 <sup>a</sup> 1 Sam. 2:27–36; Ezek. 12:25; Luke 21:33

3:13 <sup>a</sup> 1 Sam. 2:29–31 <sup>b</sup> 1 Sam. 2:22; Ezek. 7:3; 18:30 <sup>c</sup> 1 Sam. 2:12, 17, 22

sons made themselves vile, and he
[d]restrained[1] them not.
14 And therefore I have sworn unto
the house of Eli, that the iniquity of
Eli's house [a]shall not be [1]purged with
sacrifice nor offering for ever.
15 And Samuel lay until the morning, and opened the doors of the
house of the LORD. And Samuel
feared to shew Eli the vision.
16 Then Eli called Samuel, and said,
Samuel, my son. And he answered,
Here *am* I.
17 And he said, What *is* the thing
that *the LORD* hath said unto thee? I
pray thee hide *it* not from me: [a]God
do so to thee, and more also, if thou
hide *any* thing from me of all the
things that he said unto thee.
18 And Samuel told him [1]every
whit, and hid nothing from him. And
he said, [a]It *is* the LORD: let him do
what seemeth him good.
19 And Samuel [a]grew, and [b]the
LORD was with him, [c]and did let none
of his words [1]fall to the ground.
20 And all Israel [a]from Dan even to
Beer-sheba knew that Samuel *was*
[1]established *to be* a prophet of the
LORD.
21 And the LORD appeared again in
Shiloh: for the LORD revealed himself
to Samuel in Shiloh by [a]the word of
the LORD.

## CHAPTER 4

AND the word of Samuel came to
all Israel. Now Israel went out
against the Philistines to battle, and
[1]pitched beside [a]Eben-ezer: and the
Philistines pitched in Aphek.
2 And the [a]Philistines put themselves in array against Israel: and
when they joined battle, Israel was
[1]smitten before the Philistines: and
they slew of the army in the field
about four thousand men.
3 And when the people were come
into the camp, the elders of Israel
said, Wherefore hath the LORD smitten us to day before the Philistines?
[a]Let us [1]fetch the ark of the covenant
of the LORD out of Shiloh unto us,
that, when it cometh among us, it
may save us out of the hand of our
enemies.
4 So the people sent to Shiloh, that
they might bring from thence the
ark of the covenant of the LORD of
hosts, [a]which dwelleth *between* [b]the
cherubims: and the [c]two sons of Eli,
Hophni and Phinehas, *were* there
with the ark of the covenant of God.
5 And when the ark of the covenant
of the LORD came into the camp, all
Israel shouted with a great shout, so
that the earth rang again.
6 And when the Philistines heard
the noise of the shout, they said,
What *meaneth* the noise of this great
shout in the camp of the Hebrews?
And they understood that the ark of
the LORD was come into the camp.
7 And the Philistines were afraid,
for they said, God is come into the
camp. And they said, [a]Woe unto us!
for there hath not been such a thing
heretofore.
8 Woe unto us! who shall deliver
us out of the hand of these mighty
[1]Gods? these *are* the [1]Gods that
[2]smote the Egyptians with all the
plagues in the wilderness.
9 [a]Be strong, and [1]quit yourselves
like men, O ye Philistines, that ye be
not servants unto the Hebrews, [b]as
they have been to you: [2]quit yourselves like men, and fight.
10 And the Philistines fought, and
[a]Israel was [1]smitten, and they fled every man into his tent: and there was
a very great slaughter; for there fell of
Israel thirty thousand footmen.
11 And [a]the ark of God was taken;
and [b]the two sons of Eli, Hophni and
Phinehas, were slain.
12 And there ran a man of Benjamin out of the army, and [a]came to
Shiloh the same day with his clothes
[1]rent, and [b]with earth upon his head.
13 And when he came, lo, Eli sat
upon [a]a seat by the wayside watching:
for his heart [1]trembled for the ark of
God. And when the man came into the
city, and told *it*, all the city cried out.
14 And when Eli heard the noise of
the crying, he said, What *meaneth*
the noise of this tumult? And the
man came in hastily, and told Eli.
15 Now Eli was ninety and eight
years old; and [a]his eyes [1]were dim,
that he could not see.
16 And the man said unto Eli, I *am*
he that came out of the army, and I
fled to day out of the army. And he
said, [a]What [1]is there done, my son?
17 And the messenger answered
and said, Israel is fled before the Philistines, and there hath been also a
great slaughter among the people,
and thy two sons also, Hophni and
Phinehas, are dead, and the ark of
God is taken.
18 And it came to pass, when he
made mention of the ark of God, that
he fell from off the seat backward
by the side of the gate, and his neck
brake, and he died: for he was an old
man, and heavy. And he had judged
Israel forty years.
19 And his daughter in law, Phinehas' wife, was with child, *near* to be
delivered: and when she heard the tidings that the ark of God was taken,
and that her father in law and her
husband were dead, she bowed herself and [1]travailed; for her pains came
upon her.

3:13 [d] 1 Sam. 2:23, 25 [1] Lit. *rebuked*
3:14 [a] Num. 15:30, 31; Is. 22:14; Heb. 10:4, 26–31 [1] *atoned for*
3:17 [a] Ruth 1:17
3:18 [a] Gen. 24:50; Ex. 34:5–7; Lev. 10:3; Is. 39:8; Acts 5:39 [1] *everything*
3:19 [a] 1 Sam. 2:21 [b] Gen. 21:22; 28:15; 39:2, 21, 23 [c] 1 Sam. 9:6 [1] *fail*
3:20 [a] Judg. 20:1 [1] *confirmed*
3:21 [a] 1 Sam. 3:1, 4
4:1 [a] 1 Sam. 7:12 [1] *encamped*
4:2 [a] 1 Sam. 12:9 [1] *defeated*
4:3 [a] Num. 10:35; Josh. 6:6–21 [1] *bring*
4:4 [a] Ex. 25:18–21; 1 Sam. 6:2; Ps. 80:1 [b] Num. 7:89 [c] 1 Sam. 2:12
4:7 [a] Ex. 15:14
4:8 [1] *gods* [2] *struck*
4:9 [a] 1 Cor. 16:13 [b] Judg. 13:1; 1 Sam. 14:21 [1] *conduct* [2] Lit. *be men*
4:10 [a] Lev. 26:17; Deut. 28:15, 25; 1 Sam. 4:2; 2 Sam. 18:17; 19:8; 2 Kin. 14:12; 2 Chr. 25:22 [1] *defeated*
4:11 [a] 1 Sam. 2:32; Ps. 78:60, 61 [b] 1 Sam. 2:34; Ps. 78:64
4:12 [a] 2 Sam. 1:2 [b] Josh. 7:6; 2 Sam. 13:19; 15:32; Neh. 9:1; Job 2:12 [1] *torn*
4:13 [a] 1 Sam. 1:9; 4:18 [1] *trembled with anxiety*
4:15 [a] 1 Sam. 3:2; 1 Kin. 14:4 [1] Lit. *were fixed*
4:16 [a] 2 Sam. 1:4 [1] *happened*
4:19 [1] *gave birth*

20 And about the time of her death [a]the women that stood by her said unto her, Fear not; for thou hast born a son. But she answered not, neither did she [1]regard *it*.

21 And she named the child [a]I-chabod,[1] saying, [b]The glory is departed from Israel: because the ark of God was taken, and because of her father in law and her husband.

22 And she said, The glory is departed from Israel: for the ark of God is taken.

## CHAPTER 5

A ND the Philistines took the ark of God, and brought it [a]from Ebenezer unto Ashdod.

2 When the Philistines took the ark of God, they brought it into the house of [a]Dagon,[1] and set it by Dagon.

3 And when they of Ashdod arose early on the morrow, behold, [1]Dagon *was* [a]fallen upon his face to the earth before the ark of the LORD. And they took Dagon, and [b]set him in his place again.

4 And when they arose early on the morrow morning, behold, Dagon *was* fallen upon his face to the ground before the ark of the LORD; and [a]the head of Dagon and both the palms of his hands *were* cut off upon the threshold; [1]only *the stump of* Dagon was left to him.

5 Therefore neither the priests of Dagon, nor any that come into Dagon's house, [a]tread on the threshold of Dagon in Ashdod unto this day.

6 But the [a]hand of the LORD was heavy upon them of Ashdod, and he [b]destroyed them, and [1]smote them with [c]emerods, *even* Ashdod and the [d]coasts thereof.

7 And when the men of Ashdod saw that *it was* so, they said, The ark of the [a]God of Israel shall not abide with us: for his hand is sore upon us, and upon Dagon our god.

8 They sent therefore and gathered all the [a]lords of the Philistines unto them, and said, What shall we do with the ark of the God of Israel? And they answered, Let the ark of the God of Israel be carried about unto [b]Gath. And they carried the ark of the God of Israel about *thither*.

9 And it was *so,* that, after they had carried it about, [a]the hand of the LORD was against the city with a very great destruction: and he smote the men of the city, both small and great, and [1]they had emerods in their secret parts.

10 Therefore they sent the ark of God to Ekron. And it came to pass, as the ark of God came to Ekron, that the Ekronites cried out, saying, They have brought about the ark of the

God of Israel to us, to slay us and our people.

11 So they sent and gathered together all the lords of the Philistines, and said, Send away the ark of the God of Israel, and let it go again to his own place, that it slay us not, and our people: for there was a deadly destruction throughout all the city; the hand of God was very heavy there.

12 And the men that died not were [1]smitten with the [2]emerods: and the [a]cry of the city went up to heaven.

## CHAPTER 6

A ND the ark of the LORD was in the country of the Philistines seven months.

2 And the Philistines [a]called for the priests and the diviners, saying, What shall we do to the ark of the LORD? tell us wherewith we shall send it to his place.

3 And they said, If ye send away the ark of the God of Israel, send it not [a]empty; but in any wise return him [b]a trespass offering: then ye shall be healed, and it shall be known to you why his hand is not removed from you.

4 Then said they, What *shall be* the trespass offering which we shall return to him? They answered, [a]Five golden [1]emerods, and five golden mice, *according to* the number of the lords of the Philistines: for one plague *was* on [2]you all, and on your lords.

5 Wherefore ye shall make images of your emerods, and images of your mice that [a]mar the land; and ye shall [b]give glory unto the God of Israel: peradventure he will [c]lighten[1] his hand from off you, and from off [d]your gods, and from off your land.

6 Wherefore then do ye harden your hearts, [a]as the Egyptians and Pharaoh hardened their hearts? when he [1]had wrought wonderfully among them, [b]did they not let the people go, and they departed?

7 Now therefore make [a]a new cart, and take two milch [1]kine, [b]on which there hath come no yoke, and tie the kine to the cart, and bring their calves home from them:

8 And take the ark of the LORD, and lay it upon the cart; and put [a]the jewels of gold, which ye return him *for* a trespass offering, in a coffer by the side thereof; and send it away, that it may go.

9 And see, if it goeth up by the way of his own coast to [a]Beth-shemesh, *then* he hath done [1]us this great evil: but if not, then [b]we shall know that *it is* not his hand *that* smote us; it *was* a [2]chance *that* happened to us.

10 And the men did so; and took two [1]milch kine, and tied them to

### Cross references

4:20 [a] Gen. 35:16–19 [1] *pay attention*

4:21 [a] 1 Sam. 14:3 [b] Ps. 26:8; 78:61; [Jer. 2:11] [1] Lit. *Inglorious*

5:1 [a] 1 Sam. 4:1; 7:12

5:2 [a] Judg. 16:23–30; 1 Chr. 10:8–10 [1] A Philistine idol

5:3 [a] Is. 19:1; 46:1, 2 [b] Is. 46:7 [1] A Philistine idol

5:4 [a] Jer. 50:2; Ezek. 6:4, 6; Mic. 1:7 [1] Lit. *only Dagon*

5:5 [a] Zeph. 1:9

5:6 [a] Ex. 9:3; Deut. 2:15; 1 Sam. 5:7; 7:13; Ps. 32:4; 145:20; 147:6 [b] 1 Sam. 6:5 [c] Deut. 28:27; Ps. 78:66 [d] Josh. 15:46, 47 [1] *struck them with tumours* (probably bubonic plague)

5:7 [a] 1 Sam. 6:5

5:8 [a] 1 Sam. 6:4 [b] Josh. 11:22

5:9 [a] Deut. 2:15; 1 Sam. 5:11; 7:13; 12:15 [1] MT *tumours broke out on them*

5:12 [a] 1 Sam. 9:16; Jer. 14:2 [1] *stricken* [2] *tumours*

6:2 [a] Gen. 41:8; Ex. 7:11; Is. 2:6; 47:13; Dan. 2:2; 5:7

6:3 [a] Ex. 23:15; Deut. 16:16 [b] Lev. 5:15, 16

6:4 [a] 1 Sam. 5:6, 9, 12; 6:17 [1] *tumours* [2] Lit. *them*

6:5 [a] 1 Sam. 5:6 [b] Josh. 7:19; 1 Chr. 16:28, 29; Is. 42:12; Jer. 13:16; Mal. 2:2; Rev. 14:7 [c] 1 Sam. 5:6, 11; Ps. 39:10 [d] 1 Sam. 5:3, 4, 7 [1] *ease*

6:6 [a] Ex. 7:13; 8:15; 9:34; 14:17 [b] Ex. 12:31 [1] *did mighty things*

6:7 [a] 2 Sam. 6:3 [b] Num. 19:2; Deut. 21:3, 4 [1] *cows*

6:8 [a] 1 Sam. 6:4, 5

6:9 [a] Josh. 15:10; 21:16 [b] 1 Sam. 6:3 [1] *this calamity to us* [2] *by chance*

6:10 [1] *milk cows*

the cart, and shut up their calves at home:

11 And they laid the ark of the LORD upon the cart, and the [1]coffer with the mice of gold and the images of their emerods.

12 And the [1]kine took the straight way to the way of Beth-shemesh, *and* went along the [a]highway, lowing as they went, and turned not aside *to* the right hand or *to* the left; and the lords of the Philistines went after them unto the border of Beth-shemesh.

13 And *they of* Beth-shemesh *were* reaping their [a]wheat harvest in the valley: and they lifted up their eyes, and saw the ark, and rejoiced to see *it.*

14 And the cart came into the field of Joshua, a Beth-shemite, and stood there, where *there was* a great stone: and they clave the wood of the cart, and offered the kine a burnt offering unto the LORD.

15 And the Levites took down the ark of the LORD, and the coffer that *was* with it, wherein the jewels of gold *were,* and put *them* on the great stone: and the men of Beth-shemesh offered burnt offerings and sacrificed sacrifices the same day unto the LORD.

16 And when [a]the five lords of the Philistines had seen *it,* they returned to Ekron the same day.

17 [a]And these *are* the golden emerods which the Philistines returned *for* a trespass offering unto the LORD; for Ashdod one, for Gaza one, for Askelon one, for [b]Gath one, for Ekron one;

18 And the golden mice, *according to* the number of all the cities of the Philistines *belonging* to the five lords, *both* of fenced cities, and of country villages, even unto the great *stone of* Abel, whereon they set down the ark of the LORD: *which stone remaineth* unto this day in the field of Joshua, the Beth-shemite.

19 And [a]he [1]smote the men of Bethshemesh, because they had looked into the ark of the LORD, even he [b]smote[2] of the people fifty thousand and threescore and ten men: and the people lamented, because the LORD had smitten *many* of the people with a great slaughter.

20 And the men of Beth-shemesh said, [a]Who is able to stand before this holy LORD God? and to whom shall he go up from us?

21 And they sent messengers to the inhabitants of [a]Kirjath-jearim, saying, The Philistines have brought again the ark of the LORD; come ye down, *and* [1]fetch it up to you.

## CHAPTER 7

A ND the men of [a]Kirjath-jearim came, and fetched up the ark

6:11 [1] *chest*
6:12 [a] Num. 20:19
[1] *cows*
6:13 [a] 1 Sam. 12:17
6:16 [a] Josh. 13:3;
Judg. 3:3
6:17 [a] 1 Sam. 6:4
[b] 1 Sam. 5:8
6:19 [a] Ex. 19:21;
Num. 4:5, 15, 16,
20 [b] 2 Sam. 6:7
[1] *struck* [2] *struck
seventy men of
the people and
fifty oxen of a
man*
6:20 [a] Lev. 11:44,
45; Ps. 24:3, 4;
Mal. 3:2; Rev. 6:17
6:21 [a] Josh. 9:17;
15:9, 60; 18:14;
Judg. 18:12; 1 Chr.
13:5, 6 [1] *take*
7:1 [a] 1 Sam. 6:21;
Ps. 132:6

[b] 2 Sam. 6:3, 4
[c] Lev. 21:8
7:3 [a] Deut. 30:2–
10 [b] Gen. 35:2
[c] Judg. 2:13 [d] Job
11:13 [e] Luke 4:8
[1] *foreign* [2] Images of Canaanite goddesses
7:4 [a] Judg. 2:11;
10:16 [1] *Baals,*
images of
Canaanite
gods [2] Images
of Canaanite
goddesses
7:5 [a] Judg. 10:17;
20:1 [b] 1 Sam.
12:17–19
7:6 [a] 2 Sam. 14:14
[b] Neh. 9:1, 2
[c] 1 Sam. 12:10
7:8 [a] Is. 37:4
7:9 [a] Lev. 22:27
[b] 1 Sam. 12:18
[1] *answered*
7:10 [a] 2 Sam.
22:14, 15 [1] *confused* [2] *overcome*
7:11 [1] *struck them
down*
7:12 [a] Josh. 4:9;
24:26 [1] Lit. Stone
of Help
7:13 [a] Judg. 13:1
[b] 1 Sam. 13:5

of the LORD, and brought it into the house of [b]Abinadab in the hill, and [c]sanctified Eleazar his son to keep the ark of the LORD.

2 And it came to pass, while the ark abode in Kirjath-jearim, that the time was long; for it was twenty years: and all the house of Israel lamented after the LORD.

3 And Samuel spake unto all the house of Israel, saying, If ye do [a]return unto the LORD with all your hearts, *then* [b]put away the [1]strange gods and [c]Ashtaroth[2] from among you, and [d]prepare your hearts unto the LORD, and [e]serve him only: and he will deliver you out of the hand of the Philistines.

4 Then the children of Israel did put away [a]Baalim[1] and [2]Ashtaroth, and served the LORD only.

5 And Samuel said, [a]Gather all Israel to Mizpeh, and [b]I will pray for you unto the LORD.

6 And they gathered together to Mizpeh, [a]and drew water, and poured *it* out before the LORD, and [b]fasted on that day, and said there, [c]We have sinned against the LORD. And Samuel judged the children of Israel in Mizpeh.

7 And when the Philistines heard that the children of Israel were gathered together to Mizpeh, the lords of the Philistines went up against Israel. And when the children of Israel heard *it,* they were afraid of the Philistines.

8 And the children of Israel said to Samuel, [a]Cease not to cry unto the LORD our God for us, that he will save us out of the hand of the Philistines.

9 And Samuel took a [a]sucking lamb, and offered *it for* a burnt offering wholly unto the LORD: and [b]Samuel cried unto the LORD for Israel; and the LORD [1]heard him.

10 And as Samuel was offering up the burnt offering, the Philistines drew near to battle against Israel: [a]but the LORD thundered with a great thunder on that day upon the Philistines, and [1]discomfited them; and they were [2]smitten before Israel.

11 And the men of Israel went out of Mizpeh, and pursued the Philistines, and [1]smote them, until *they* came under Beth-car.

12 Then Samuel [a]took a stone, and set *it* between Mizpeh and Shen, and called the name of it [1]Ebenezer, saying, Hitherto hath the LORD helped us.

13 [a]So the Philistines were subdued, and they [b]came no more into the coast of Israel: and the hand of the LORD was against the Philistines all the days of Samuel.

14 And the cities which the Philistines had taken from Israel were

restored to Israel, from Ekron even unto Gath; and the coasts thereof did Israel [1]deliver out of the hands of the Philistines. And there was peace between Israel and the Amorites.

15 And Samuel [a]judged Israel all the days of his life.

16 And he went from year to year in circuit to Beth-el, and Gilgal, and Mizpeh, and judged Israel in all those places.

17 And [a]his return *was* to Ramah; for there *was* his house; and there he judged Israel; and there he [b]built an altar unto the LORD.

## CHAPTER 8

A ND it came to pass, when Samuel was [a]old, that he [b]made his [c]sons judges over Israel.

2 Now the name of his firstborn was Joel; and the name of his second, Abiah: *they were* judges in Beer-sheba.

3 And his sons [a]walked not in his ways, but turned aside [b]after [1]lucre, and [c]took bribes, and perverted [2]judgment.

4 Then all the elders of Israel gathered themselves together, and came to Samuel unto Ramah,

5 And said unto him, Behold, thou art old, and thy sons walk not in thy ways: now [a]make us a king to judge us like all the nations.

6 But the thing [a]displeased Samuel, when they said, Give us a king to judge us. And Samuel [b]prayed unto the LORD.

7 And the LORD said unto Samuel, [1]Hearken unto the voice of the people in all that they say unto thee: for [a]they have not rejected thee, but [b]they have rejected me, that I should not reign over them.

8 According to all the works which they have done since the day that I brought them up out of Egypt even unto this day, wherewith they have forsaken me, and served other gods, so do they also unto thee.

9 Now therefore [1]hearken unto their voice: howbeit yet [2]protest solemnly unto them, and [a]shew them the manner of the king that shall reign over them.

10 And Samuel told all the words of the LORD unto the people that asked of him a king.

11 And he said, [a]This will be the manner of the king that shall reign over you: He will take your [b]sons, and appoint *them* for himself, for his [c]chariots, and *to be* his horsemen; and *some* shall run before his chariots.

12 And he will [a]appoint him captains over thousands, and captains over fifties; and *will set them* to [1]ear

his ground, and to reap his harvest, and to make his instruments of war, and instruments of his chariots.

13 And he will take your daughters *to be* confectionaries, and *to be* cooks, and *to be* bakers.

14 And [a]he will take your fields, and your vineyards, and your oliveyards, *even* the best *of them,* and give *them* to his servants.

15 And he will take the tenth of your seed, and of your vineyards, and give to his officers, and to his servants.

16 And he will take your menservants, and your maidservants, and your goodliest young men, and your asses, and put *them* to his work.

17 He will take the tenth of your sheep: and ye shall be his servants.

18 And ye shall cry out in that day because of your king which ye shall have chosen you; and the LORD [a]will not hear you in that day.

19 Nevertheless the people [a]refused to obey the voice of Samuel; and they said, Nay; but we will have a king over us;

20 That we also may be [a]like all the nations; and that our king may judge us, and go out before us, and fight our battles.

21 And Samuel heard all the words of the people, and he [1]rehearsed them in the ears of the LORD.

22 And the LORD said to Samuel, [a]Hearken unto their voice, and make them a king. And Samuel said unto the men of Israel, Go ye every man unto his city.

## CHAPTER 9

N OW there was a man of Benjamin, whose name *was* [a]Kish, the son of Abiel, the son of Zeror, the son of Bechorath, the son of Aphiah, a Benjamite, a mighty man of [1]power.

2 And he had a son, whose name *was* Saul, a choice young man, and [1]a goodly: and *there was* not among the children of Israel a goodlier person than he: [a]from his shoulders and upward *he was* [2]higher than any of the people.

3 And the asses of Kish Saul's father were lost. And Kish said to Saul his son, Take now one of the servants with thee, and arise, go seek the asses.

4 And he passed through mount Ephraim, and passed through the land of [a]Shalisha, but they found *them* not: then they passed through the land of Shalim, and *there they were* not: and he passed through the land of the Benjamites, but they found *them* not.

5 *And* when they were come to the land of [a]Zuph, Saul said to his servant that *was* with him, Come, and let [b]us

### Cross references (center column)

7:14 [1] *recovered their territory*
7:15 [a] 1 Sam. 12:11
7:17 [a] 1 Sam. 8:4
[b] Judg. 21:4
8:1 [a] 1 Sam. 12:2
[b] Deut. 16:18, 19
[c] Judg. 10:4
8:3 [a] Jer. 22:15–17
[b] Ex. 18:21 [c] Ex. 23:6–8 [1] *dishonest gain* [2] *justice*
8:5 [a] Deut. 17:14, 15
8:6 [a] 1 Sam. 12:17
[b] 1 Sam. 7:9
8:7 [a] Ex. 16:8
[b] 1 Sam. 10:19
[1] *Heed*
8:9 [a] 1 Sam. 8:11–18 [1] *heed* [2] *solemnly forewarn*
8:11 [a] Deut. 17:14–20 [b] 1 Sam. 14:52
[c] 2 Sam. 15:1
8:12 [a] 1 Sam. 22:7
[1] *plow*
8:14 [a] 1 Kin. 21:7
8:18 [a] Prov. 1:25–28; Is. 1:15; Mic. 3:4
8:19 [a] Is. 66:4; Jer. 44:16
8:20 [a] 1 Sam. 8:5
8:21 [1] *repeated them in the hearing of*
8:22 [a] 1 Sam. 8:7; Hos. 13:11
9:1 [a] 1 Sam. 14:51; 1 Chr. 8:33; 9:36–39 [1] *strength or wealth*
9:2 [a] 1 Sam. 10:23 [1] *handsome* [2] *taller*
9:4 [a] 2 Kin. 4:42
9:5 [a] 1 Sam. 1:1
[b] 1 Sam. 10:2

return; lest my father ¹leave *caring* for the asses, and take thought for us.

6 And he said unto him, Behold now, *there is* in this city ªa man of God, and *he is* an honourable man; ᵇall that he saith cometh surely to pass: now let us go thither; peradventure he can shew us our way that we should go.

7 Then said Saul to his servant, But, behold, *if* we go, ªwhat shall we bring the man? for the bread is ¹spent in our vessels, and *there is* not a present to bring to the man of God: what have we?

8 And the servant answered Saul again, and said, Behold, I have here at hand the fourth part of a shekel of silver: *that* will I give to the man of God, to tell us our way.

9 (Beforetime in Israel, when a man ªwent to ¹enquire of God, thus he spake, Come, and let us go to the seer: for *he that is* now *called* a Prophet was beforetime called ᵇa Seer.)

10 Then said Saul to his servant, ¹Well said; come, let us go. So they went unto the city where the man of God *was*.

11 *And* as they went up the hill to the city, ªthey found young maidens going out to draw water, and said unto them, Is the seer here?

12 And they answered them, and said, He is; behold, *he is* before you: make haste now, for he came to day to the city; for ªthere is a sacrifice of the people to day ᵇin the high place:

13 As soon as ye be come into the city, ye shall straightway find him, before he go up to the high place to eat: for the people will not eat until he come, because he doth bless the sacrifice; *and* afterwards they ¹eat that be bidden. Now therefore get you up; for about this time ye shall find him.

14 And they went up into the city: *and* when they were come into the city, behold, Samuel came out against them, for to go up to the high place.

15 ªNow the Lᴏʀᴅ had told Samuel in his ear a day before Saul came, saying,

16 To morrow about this time ªI will send thee a man out of the land of Benjamin, ᵇand thou shalt anoint him *to be* ¹captain over my people Israel, that he may save my people out of the hand of the Philistines: for I have ᶜlooked upon my people, because their cry is come unto me.

17 And when Samuel saw Saul, the Lᴏʀᴅ said unto him, ªBehold the man whom I spake to thee of! this same shall reign over my people.

18 Then Saul drew near to Samuel in the gate, and said, Tell me, I pray thee, where the seer's house *is*.

19 And Samuel answered Saul, and said, I *am* the seer: go up before me unto the high place; for ye shall eat with me to day, and to morrow I will let thee go, and will tell thee all that *is* in thine heart.

20 And as for ªthine asses that were lost three days ago, set not thy mind on them; for they are found. And ¹on whom ᵇis all the desire of Israel? *Is it* not on thee, and on all thy father's house?

21 And Saul answered and said, ªAm not I a Benjamite, of the ᵇsmallest of the tribes of Israel? and ᶜmy family the least of all the families of the tribe of Benjamin? wherefore then speakest thou so to me?

22 And Samuel took Saul and his servant, and brought them into the parlour, and made them sit in the chiefest place among them that were bidden, which *were* about thirty persons.

23 And Samuel said unto the cook, Bring the portion which I gave thee, of which I said unto thee, Set it by thee.

24 And the cook took up ªthe shoulder, and *that* which *was* upon it, and set *it* before Saul. And *Samuel* said, Behold that which is left! set *it* before thee, *and* eat: for unto this time hath it been kept for thee since I said, I have invited the people. So Saul did eat with Samuel that day.

25 And when they were come down from the high place into the city, *Samuel* ¹communed with Saul upon ªthe top of the house.

26 And they arose early: and it came to pass about the spring of the day, that Samuel called Saul to the top of the house, saying, Up, that I may send thee away. And Saul arose, and they went out both of them, he and Samuel, abroad.

27 *And* as they were going down to the end of the city, Samuel said to Saul, ¹Bid the servant ²pass on before us, (and he passed on,) but stand thou still ³a while, that I may ⁴shew thee the word of God.

## CHAPTER 10

THEN ªSamuel took a ¹vial of oil, and poured *it* upon his head, ᵇand kissed him, and said, *Is it* not because ᶜthe Lᴏʀᴅ hath anointed thee *to be* captain over ᵈhis inheritance?

2 When thou art departed from me to day, then thou shalt find two men by ªRachel's sepulchre in the border of Benjamin ᵇat Zelzah; and they will say unto thee, The asses which thou wentest to seek are found: and, lo, thy father hath ¹left the care of the asses, and sorroweth for ᶜyou, saying, What shall I do for my son?

### Center column references

9:5 ¹ *cease caring about*

9:6 ª Deut. 33:1; 1 Kin. 13:1; 2 Kin. 5:8  ᵇ 1 Sam. 3:19

9:7 ª Judg. 6:18; 13:17; 1 Kin. 14:3; 2 Kin. 4:42; 8:8
¹ *all gone*

9:9 ª Gen. 25:22
ᵇ 2 Sam. 24:11; 2 Kin. 17:13; 1 Chr. 26:28; 29:29; 2 Chr. 16:7, 10; Is. 30:10; Amos 7:12
¹ *seek guidance*

9:10 ¹ Lit. *Your word is good*

9:11 ª Gen. 24:11, 15; 29:8, 9; Ex. 2:16

9:12 ª Gen. 31:54; 1 Sam. 16:2
ᵇ 1 Sam. 7:17; 10:5; 1 Kin. 3:2

9:13 ¹ *who are invited will eat*

9:15 ª 1 Sam. 15:1

9:16 ª Deut. 17:15
ᵇ 1 Sam. 10:1  ᶜ Ex. 2:23–25; 3:7, 9
¹ *prince or ruler*

9:17 ª 1 Sam. 16:12; Hos. 13:11

9:20 ª 1 Sam. 9:3
ᵇ 1 Sam. 8:5, 19; 12:13  ¹ *for whom*

9:21 ª 1 Sam. 15:17
ᵇ Judg. 20:46–48; Ps. 68:27
ᶜ Judg. 6:15

9:24 ª Ex. 29:22, 27; Lev. 7:32, 33; Num. 18:18; Ezek. 24:4

9:25 ª Deut. 22:8; 2 Sam. 11:2; Luke 5:19; Acts 10:9
¹ *spoke*

9:27 ¹ *Tell* ² *go on ahead of us* ³ *now* ⁴ *announce to you*

10:1 ª Ex. 30:23–33; 1 Sam. 9:16; 16:13; 2 Kin. 9:3, 6
ᵇ Ps. 2:12  ᶜ 2 Sam. 5:2; Acts 13:21
ᵈ Ex. 34:9; Deut. 32:9; Ps. 78:71
¹ *flask*

10:2 ª Gen. 35:16–20; 48:7  ᵇ Josh. 18:28  ¹ 1 Sam. 9:3–5  ¹ *ceased caring about the donkeys*

3 Then shalt thou go on forward from thence, and thou shalt come to the plain of Tabor, and there shall meet thee three men going up ᵃto God to Beth-el, one carrying three kids, and another carrying three loaves of bread, and another carrying a bottle of wine:

4 And they will ¹salute thee, and give thee two *loaves* of bread; which thou shalt receive of their hands.

5 After that thou shalt come to the hill of God, ᵃwhere *is* the garrison of the Philistines: and it shall come to pass, when thou art come thither to the city, that thou shalt meet a company of prophets coming down ᵇfrom the high place with a psaltery, and a tabret, and a pipe, and a harp, before them; ᶜand they shall prophesy:

6 And ᵃthe Spirit of the LORD will come upon thee, and ᵇthou shalt prophesy with them, and shalt be turned into another man.

7 And let it be, when these ᵃsigns are come unto thee, *that* thou do as ¹occasion serve thee; for ᵇGod *is* with thee.

8 And thou shalt go down before me ᵃto Gilgal; and, behold, I will come down unto thee, to offer burnt offerings, *and* to sacrifice sacrifices of peace offerings: ᵇseven days shalt thou tarry, till I come to thee, and shew thee what thou shalt do.

9 And it was so, that when he had turned his back to go from Samuel, God ¹gave him another heart: and all those signs came to pass that day.

10 And ᵃwhen they came thither to the hill, behold, ᵇa company of prophets met him; and the Spirit of God came upon him, and he prophesied among them.

11 And it came to pass, when all that knew him beforetime saw that, behold, he prophesied among the prophets, then the people said one to another, What *is* this *that* is come unto the son of Kish? ᵃ*Is* Saul also among the prophets?

12 And one of the same place answered and said, But ᵃwho *is* their father? Therefore it became a proverb, *Is* Saul also among the prophets?

13 And when he had made an end of prophesying, he came to the high place.

14 And Saul's ᵃuncle said unto him and to his servant, Whither went ye? And he said, To seek the asses: and when we saw that *they were* no where, we came to Samuel.

15 And Saul's uncle said, Tell me, I pray thee, what Samuel said unto you.

16 And Saul said unto his uncle, He told us plainly that the asses were

10:3 ᵃ Gen. 28:22; 35:1, 3, 7
10:4 ¹ *ask you about your welfare*
10:5 ᵃ 1 Sam. 13:2, 3   ᵇ 1 Sam. 19:12, 20; 2 Kin. 2:3, 5, 15   ᶜ Ex. 15:20, 21; 2 Kin. 3:15; 1 Chr. 25:1–6; 1 Cor. 14:1
10:6 ᵃ Num. 11:25, 29; Judg. 14:6; 1 Sam. 16:13   ᵇ 1 Sam. 10:10; 19:23, 24
10:7 ᵃ Ex. 4:8; Luke 2:12   ᵇ Josh. 1:5; Judg. 6:12; 1 Sam. 3:19; [Heb. 13:5]   ¹ *the occasion demands*
10:8 ᵃ 1 Sam. 11:14, 15; 13:8   ᵇ 1 Sam. 13:8–10
10:9 ¹ *changed his heart*
10:10 ᵃ 1 Sam. 10:5   ᵇ 1 Sam. 19:20
10:11 ᵃ 1 Sam. 19:24; Amos 7:14, 15; Matt. 13:54–57; John 7:15; Acts 4:13
10:12 ᵃ John 5:30, 36
10:14 ᵃ 1 Sam. 14:50
10:16 ᵃ 1 Sam. 9:20
10:17 ᵃ Judg. 20:1   ᵇ 1 Sam. 7:5, 6
10:18 ᵃ Judg. 6:8, 9; 1 Sam. 8:8; 12:6, 8
10:19 ᵃ 1 Sam. 8:7, 19; 12:12   ¹ *clans*
10:20 ᵃ Acts 1:24, 26
10:22 ᵃ 1 Sam. 23:2, 4, 10, 11
10:23 ᵃ 1 Sam. 9:2   ¹ *brought*   ² *taller*
10:24 ᵃ Deut. 17:15; 1 Sam. 9:16; 2 Sam. 21:6   ᵇ 1 Kin. 1:25, 39   ¹ *Long live the king,* lit. *May the king live*
10:25 ᵃ Deut. 17:14–20; 1 Sam. 8:11–18
10:26 ᵃ Judg. 20:14
10:27 ᵃ 1 Sam. 11:12   ᵇ Deut. 13:13; 1 Sam. 25:17   ᶜ 2 Sam. 8:2; 1 Kin. 4:21; 10:25; 2 Chr. 17:5; Matt. 2:11   ¹ *rebels*   ² *kept silent*
11:1 ᵃ 1 Sam. 12:12   ᵇ Judg. 21:8; 1 Sam. 31:11   ᶜ Gen. 26:28; 1 Kin. 20:34; Job 41:4; Ezek. 17:13   ¹ *besieged*

found. But of the matter of the kingdom, whereof Samuel spake, he told him not.

17 And Samuel called the people together ᵃunto the LORD ᵇto Mizpeh;

18 And said unto the children of Israel, ᵃThus saith the LORD God of Israel, I brought up Israel out of Egypt, and delivered you out of the hand of the Egyptians, and out of the hand of all kingdoms, *and* of them that oppressed you:

19 ᵃAnd ye have this day rejected your God, who himself saved you out of all your adversities and your tribulations; and ye have said unto him, *Nay,* but set a king over us. Now therefore present yourselves before the LORD by your tribes, and by your ¹thousands.

20 And when Samuel had ᵃcaused all the tribes of Israel to come near, the tribe of Benjamin was taken.

21 When he had caused the tribe of Benjamin to come near by their families, the family of Matri was taken, and Saul the son of Kish was taken: and when they sought him, he could not be found.

22 Therefore they ᵃenquired of the LORD further, if the man should yet come thither. And the LORD answered, Behold, he hath hid himself among the stuff.

23 And they ran and ¹fetched him thence: and when he stood among the people, ᵃhe was ²higher than any of the people from his shoulders and upward.

24 And Samuel said to all the people, See ye him ᵃwhom the LORD hath chosen, that *there is* none like him among all the people? And all the people shouted, and said, ᵇGod¹ save the king.

25 Then Samuel told the people ᵃthe manner of the kingdom, and wrote *it* in a book, and laid *it* up before the LORD. And Samuel sent all the people away, every man to his house.

26 And Saul also went home ᵃto Gibeah; and there went with him a band of men, whose hearts God had touched.

27 ᵃBut the ᵇchildren¹ of Belial said, How shall this man save us? And they despised him, ᶜand brought him no presents. But ²he held his peace.

## CHAPTER 11

THEN ᵃNahash the Ammonite came up, and ¹encamped against ᵇJabesh-gilead: and all the men of Jabesh said unto Nahash, ᶜMake a covenant with us, and we will serve thee.

2 And Nahash the Ammonite answered them, On this *condition* will I make *a covenant* with you, that I may

thrust out all your right eyes, and [1]lay it *for* [a]a reproach upon all Israel.

3 And the elders of Jabesh said unto him, Give us seven days' respite, that we may send messengers unto all the coasts of Israel: and then, if *there be* no man to [1]save us, we will come out to thee.

4 Then came the messengers [a]to Gibeah of Saul, and told the tidings in the ears of the people: and [b]all the people lifted up their voices, and wept.

5 And, behold, Saul came after the herd out of the field; and Saul said, What *aileth* the people that they weep? And they told him the tidings of the men of Jabesh.

6 [a]And the Spirit of God came upon Saul when he heard those tidings, and his anger was kindled greatly.

7 And he took a yoke of oxen, and [a]hewed them in pieces, and sent *them* throughout all the coasts of Israel by the hands of messengers, saying, [b]Whosoever cometh not forth after Saul and after Samuel, so shall it be done unto his oxen. And the fear of the LORD fell on the people, and they came out [1]with one consent.

8 And when he numbered them in [a]Bezek, the children [b]of Israel were three hundred thousand, and the men of Judah thirty thousand.

9 And they said unto the messengers that came, Thus shall ye say unto the men of Jabesh-gilead, To morrow, by *that time* the sun be hot, ye shall have help. And the messengers came and shewed *it* to the men of Jabesh; and they were glad.

10 Therefore the men of Jabesh said, To morrow we will come out unto you, and ye shall do with us all that seemeth good unto you.

11 And it was *so* on the morrow, that [a]Saul put the people [b]in three companies; and they came into the midst of the host in the morning watch, and slew the Ammonites until the heat of the day: and it came to pass, that they which remained were scattered, so that two of them were not left together.

12 And the people said unto Samuel, [a]Who *is* he that said, Shall Saul reign over us? [b]bring the men, that we may put them to death.

13 And Saul said, [a]There shall not a man be put to death this day: for to day [b]the LORD hath [1]wrought salvation in Israel.

14 Then said Samuel to the people, Come, and let us go [a]to Gilgal, and renew the kingdom there.

15 And all the people went to Gilgal; and there they made Saul king [a]before the LORD in Gilgal; and [b]there they sacrificed sacrifices of peace of-

ferings before the LORD; and there Saul and all the men of Israel rejoiced greatly.

## CHAPTER 12

AND Samuel said unto all Israel, Behold, I have [1]hearkened unto [a]your voice in all that ye said unto me, and [b]have made a king over you.

2 And now, behold, the king [a]walketh before you: [b]and I am old and grayheaded; and, behold, my sons *are* with you: and I have walked before you from my childhood unto this day.

3 Behold, here I *am:* witness against me before the LORD, and before [a]his anointed: [b]whose ox have I taken? or whose ass have I taken? or whom have I defrauded? whom have I oppressed? or of whose hand have I received *any* [c]bribe to [d]blind mine eyes therewith? and I will restore it you.

4 And they said, [a]Thou hast not defrauded us, nor oppressed us, neither hast thou taken [1]ought of any man's hand.

5 And he said unto them, The LORD *is* witness against you, and his anointed *is* witness this day, [a]that ye have not found ought [b]in my hand. And they answered, *He is* witness.

6 And Samuel said unto the people, [a]*It is* the LORD that [1]advanced Moses and Aaron, and that brought your fathers up out of the land of Egypt.

7 Now therefore stand still, that I may [a]reason with you before the LORD of all the [b]righteous acts of the LORD, which he did to you and to your fathers.

8 [a]When Jacob was come into Egypt, and your fathers [b]cried unto the LORD, then the LORD [c]sent Moses and Aaron, which brought forth your fathers out of Egypt, and made them dwell in this place.

9 And when they [a]forgat the LORD their God, he sold them into the hand of [b]Sisera, captain of the host of Hazor, and into the hand of the [c]Philistines, and into the hand of the king of [d]Moab, and they fought against them.

10 And they cried unto the LORD, and said, [a]We have sinned, because we have forsaken the LORD, [b]and have served [1]Baalim and [2]Ashtaroth: but now deliver us out of the hand of our enemies, and we will serve thee.

11 And the LORD sent [1]Jerub-baal, and Bedan, and [a]Jephthah, and [b]Samuel, and delivered you out of the hand of your enemies on every side, and ye dwelled [2]safe.

12 And when ye saw that [a]Nahash the king of the children of Ammon came against you, [b]ye said unto me,

---

11:2 [a] Gen. 34:14; 1 Sam. 17:26; Ps. 44:13 [1] *bring reproach*

11:3 [1] *deliver*

11:4 [a] 1 Sam. 10:26; 15:34; 2 Sam. 21:6 [b] Gen. 27:38; Judg. 2:4; 20:23, 26; 21:2; 1 Sam. 30:4

11:6 [a] Judg. 3:10; 6:34; 11:29; 13:25; 14:6; 1 Sam. 10:10; 16:13

11:7 [a] Judg. 19:29 [b] Judg. 21:5, 8, 10 [1] Lit. *as one man*

11:8 [a] Judg. 1:5 [b] 2 Sam. 24:9

11:11 [a] 1 Sam. 31:11 [b] Judg. 7:16, 20

11:12 [a] 1 Sam. 10:27 [b] Luke 19:27

11:13 [a] 1 Sam. 10:27; 2 Sam. 19:22 [b] Ex. 14:13, 30; 1 Sam. 19:5 [1] *accomplished*

11:14 [a] 1 Sam. 7:16; 10:8

11:15 [a] 1 Sam. 10:17 [b] Josh. 8:31; 1 Sam. 10:8

12:1 [a] 1 Sam. 8:5, 7, 9, 20, 22 [b] 1 Sam. 10:24; 11:14, 15 [1] *listened*

12:2 [a] Num. 27:17 [b] 1 Sam. 8:1, 5

12:3 [a] 1 Sam. 10:1; 24:6 [b] Num. 16:15 [c] Ex. 23:8 [d] Deut. 16:19

12:4 [a] Lev. 19:13 [1] *anything*

12:5 [a] Acts 23:9; 24:20 [b] Ex. 22:4

12:6 [a] Mic. 6:4 [1] *raised up*

12:7 [a] Is. 1:18 [b] Judg. 5:11

12:8 [a] Gen. 46:5, 6 [b] Ex. 2:23–25 [c] Ex. 3:10; 4:14–16

12:9 [a] Judg. 3:7 [b] Judg. 4:2 [c] Judg. 3:31; 10:7; 13:1 [d] Judg. 3:12–30

12:10 [a] Judg. 10:10 [b] Judg. 2:13; 3:7 [1] *Baals,* images of Canaanite gods [2] Images of Canaanite goddesses

12:11 [a] Judg. 11:1 [b] 1 Sam. 7:13 [1] *Gideon,* Judg. 6:32 [2] *in safety*

12:12 [a] 1 Sam. 11:1, 2 [b] 1 Sam. 8:5, 19, 20

Nay; but a king shall reign over us: when <sup>c</sup>the LORD your God *was* your king.

13 Now therefore <sup>a</sup>behold the king <sup>b</sup>whom ye have chosen, *and* whom ye have desired! and, behold, <sup>c</sup>the LORD hath set a king over you.

14 If ye will <sup>a</sup>fear the LORD, and serve him, and obey his voice, and not rebel against the commandment of the LORD, then shall both ye and also the king that reigneth over you continue following the LORD your God:

15 But if ye will <sup>a</sup>not obey the voice of the LORD, but <sup>b</sup>rebel against the commandment of the LORD, then shall the hand of the LORD be against you, as *it was* against your fathers.

16 Now therefore <sup>a</sup>stand and see this great thing, which the LORD will do before your eyes.

17 *Is it* not <sup>a</sup>wheat harvest to day? <sup>b</sup>I will call unto the LORD, and he shall send thunder and <sup>c</sup>rain; that ye may perceive and see that <sup>d</sup>your wickedness *is* great, which ye have done in the sight of the LORD, in asking you a king.

18 So Samuel called unto the LORD; and the LORD sent thunder and rain that day: and <sup>a</sup>all the people greatly feared the LORD and Samuel.

19 And all the people said unto Samuel, <sup>a</sup>Pray for thy servants unto the LORD thy God, that we die not: for we have added unto all our sins *this* evil, to ask us a king.

20 And Samuel said unto the people, Fear not: ye have done all this wickedness: <sup>a</sup>yet turn not aside from following the LORD, but serve the LORD with all your heart;

21 And <sup>a</sup>turn ye not aside: <sup>b</sup>for *then should ye go* after <sup>1</sup>vain *things,* which cannot profit nor deliver; for they *are* vain.

22 For <sup>a</sup>the LORD will not forsake <sup>b</sup>his people <sup>c</sup>for his great name's sake: because <sup>d</sup>it hath pleased the LORD to make you his people.

23 Moreover as for me, God forbid that I should sin against the LORD <sup>a</sup>in ceasing to pray for you: but <sup>b</sup>I will teach you the <sup>c</sup>good and the right way:

24 <sup>a</sup>Only fear the LORD, and serve him in truth with all your heart: for <sup>b</sup>consider how <sup>c</sup>great *things* he hath done for you.

25 But if ye shall still do wickedly, <sup>a</sup>ye shall be <sup>1</sup>consumed, <sup>b</sup>both ye and your king.

## CHAPTER 13

SAUL reigned one year; and when he had reigned two years over Israel,

2 Saul chose him three thousand *men* of Israel; *whereof* two thousand

were with Saul in <sup>a</sup>Michmash and in mount Beth-el, and a thousand were with <sup>b</sup>Jonathan in <sup>c</sup>Gibeah of Benjamin: and the rest of the people he sent every man to his tent.

3 And Jonathan <sup>1</sup>smote <sup>a</sup>the garrison of the Philistines that *was* in <sup>b</sup>Geba, and the Philistines heard *of it.* And Saul blew the trumpet throughout all the land, saying, Let the Hebrews hear.

4 And all Israel heard say *that* Saul had smitten a garrison of the Philistines, and *that* Israel also <sup>1</sup>was had in abomination with the Philistines. And the people were called together after Saul to Gilgal.

5 And the Philistines gathered themselves together to fight with Israel, thirty thousand chariots, and six thousand horsemen, and people <sup>a</sup>as the sand which *is* on the sea shore in multitude: and they came up, and <sup>1</sup>pitched in Michmash, eastward from <sup>b</sup>Beth-aven.

6 When the men of Israel saw that they were in a <sup>1</sup>strait, (for the people were distressed,) then the people <sup>a</sup>did hide themselves in caves, and in thickets, and in rocks, and in high places, and in pits.

7 And *some of* the Hebrews went over Jordan to the <sup>a</sup>land of Gad and Gilead. As for Saul, he *was* yet in Gilgal, and all the people followed him trembling.

8 <sup>a</sup>And he tarried seven days, according to the set time that Samuel *had appointed:* but Samuel came not to Gilgal; and the people were scattered from him.

9 And Saul said, Bring hither a burnt offering to me, and peace offerings. And he offered the burnt offering.

10 And it came to pass, that as soon as he had made an end of offering the burnt offering, behold, Samuel came; and Saul went out to meet him, that he might <sup>1</sup>salute him.

11 And Samuel said, What hast thou done? And Saul said, Because I saw that the people were scattered from me, and *that* thou camest not within the days appointed, and *that* the Philistines gathered themselves together at Michmash;

12 Therefore said I, The Philistines will come down now upon me to Gilgal, and I have not made supplication unto the LORD: I <sup>1</sup>forced myself therefore, and offered a burnt offering.

13 And Samuel said to Saul, <sup>a</sup>Thou hast done foolishly: <sup>b</sup>thou hast not kept the commandment of the LORD thy God, which he commanded thee: for now would the LORD have established thy kingdom upon Israel for ever.

14 ªBut now thy kingdom shall not continue: ᵇthe LORD hath sought him a man ᶜafter his own heart, and the LORD hath commanded him *to be* captain over his people, because thou hast ᵈnot kept *that* which the LORD commanded thee.

15 And Samuel arose, and gat him up from Gilgal unto Gibeah of Benjamin. And Saul numbered the people *that were* present with him, ªabout six hundred men.

16 And Saul, and Jonathan his son, and the people *that were* present with them, abode in ¹Gibeah of Benjamin: but the Philistines encamped in Michmash.

17 And the ¹spoilers came out of the camp of the Philistines in three companies: one company turned unto the way *that leadeth to* ªOphrah, unto the land of Shual:

18 And another company turned the way *to* ªBeth-horon: and another company turned *to* the way of the border that looketh to the valley of ᵇZeboim toward the wilderness.

19 Now ªthere was no smith found throughout all the land of Israel: for the Philistines said, Lest the Hebrews make *them* swords or spears:

20 But all the Israelites went down to the Philistines, to sharpen every man his share, and his coulter, and his axe, and his mattock.

21 ¹Yet they had a file for the mattocks, and for the coulters, and for the forks, and for the axes, and to sharpen the goads.

22 So it came to pass in the day of battle, that ªthere was neither sword nor spear found in the hand of any of the people that *were* with Saul and Jonathan: but with Saul and with Jonathan his son was there found.

23 ªAnd the garrison of the Philistines went out to the passage of Michmash.

## CHAPTER 14

Now it came to ¹pass upon a day, that Jonathan the son of Saul said unto the young man that ²bare his armour, Come, and let us go over to the Philistines' garrison, that *is* on the other side. But he told not his father.

2 And Saul tarried in the uttermost part of ªGibeah under a pomegranate tree which *is* in Migron: and the people that *were* with him *were* about six hundred men;

3 And ªAhiah, the son of Ahitub, ᵇIchabod's brother, the son of Phinehas, the son of Eli, the LORD's priest in Shiloh, ᶜwearing an ephod. And the people knew not that Jonathan was gone.

4 And between the ¹passages, by which Jonathan sought to go over

13:14 ª 1 Sam. 15:28; 31:6
ᵇ 1 Sam. 16:1 ᶜ Ps. 89:20; Acts 7:46;
13:22 ᵈ 1 Sam. 15:11, 19
13:15 ª 1 Sam. 13:2, 6, 7; 14:2
13:16 ¹ Heb. *Geba*
13:17 ª Josh. 18:23 ¹ *raiders*
13:18 ª Josh. 16:3; 18:13, 14 ᵇ Gen. 14:2; Neh. 11:34
13:19 ª Judg. 5:8; 2 Kin. 24:14; Jer. 24:1; 29:2
13:21 ¹ *And the charge for a sharpening was a pim* (about two-thirds of a shekel weight) *for the mattocks ...*
13:22 ª Judg. 5:8
13:23 ª 1 Sam. 14:1, 4
14:1 ¹ *one day* ² *carried*
14:2 ª 1 Sam. 13:15, 16
14:3 ª 1 Sam. 22:9, 11, 20 ᵇ 1 Sam. 4:21 ᶜ 1 Sam. 2:28
14:4 ¹ *passes*

ª 1 Sam. 13:23
14:5 ¹ *front of one faced north opposite*
14:6 ª 1 Sam. 17:26, 36; Jer. 9:25, 26 ᵇ Judg. 7:4, 7; 1 Sam. 17:46, 47; 2 Chr. 14:11; [Ps. 115:3; 135:6; Zech. 4:6; Matt. 19:26; Rom. 8:31] ¹ *nothing restrains*
14:8 ¹ *show*
14:9 ¹ Lit. *Stand still*
14:10 ª Gen. 24:14; Judg. 6:36–40
14:11 ª 1 Sam. 13:6; 14:22 ¹ *showed*
14:12 ¹ *teach you something*
14:13 ª Lev. 26:8; Josh. 23:10
14:14 ¹ Lit. *half the area plowed by a yoke of oxen in a day*
14:15 ª Deut. 28:7; 2 Kin. 7:6, 7; Job 18:11 ᵇ 1 Sam. 13:17 ᶜ Gen. 35:5 ¹ *terror*
14:16 ª 1 Sam. 14:20 ¹ Lit. *went here and there*

ªunto the Philistines' garrison, *there was* a sharp rock on the one side, and a sharp rock on the other side: and the name of the one *was* Bozez, and the name of the other Seneh.

5 The ¹forefront of the one *was* situate northward over against Michmash, and the other southward over against Gibeah.

6 And Jonathan said to the young man that bare his armour, Come, and let us go over unto the garrison of these ªuncircumcised: it may be that the LORD will work for us: for ¹*there is* no restraint to the LORD ᵇto save by many or by few.

7 And his armourbearer said unto him, Do all that *is* in thine heart: turn thee; behold, I *am* with thee according to thy heart.

8 Then said Jonathan, Behold, we will pass over unto *these* men, and we will ¹discover ourselves unto them.

9 If they say thus unto us, ¹Tarry until we come to you; then we will stand still in our place, and will not go up unto them.

10 But if they say thus, Come up unto us; then we will go up: for the LORD hath delivered them into our hand: and ªthis *shall be* a sign unto us.

11 And both of them ¹discovered themselves unto the garrison of the Philistines: and the Philistines said, Behold, the Hebrews come forth out of the holes where they had ªhid themselves.

12 And the men of the garrison answered Jonathan and his armourbearer, and said, Come up to us, and we will ¹shew you a thing. And Jonathan said unto his armourbearer, Come up after me: for the LORD hath delivered them into the hand of Israel.

13 And Jonathan climbed up upon his hands and upon his feet, and his armourbearer after him: and they ªfell before Jonathan; and his armourbearer slew after him.

14 And that first slaughter, which Jonathan and his armourbearer made, was about twenty men, within as it were an ¹half acre of land, *which* a yoke *of oxen might plow.*

15 And ªthere was ¹trembling in the host, in the field, and among all the people: the garrison, and ᵇthe spoilers, they also trembled, and the earth quaked: so it was ᶜa very great trembling.

16 And the watchmen of Saul in Gibeah of Benjamin looked; and, behold, the multitude melted away, and they ªwent ¹on beating down *one another.*

17 Then said Saul unto the people that *were* with him, Number now, and see who is gone from us. And when they had numbered, behold,

Jonathan and his armourbearer *were* not *there.*

18 And Saul said unto Ahiah, Bring hither the ark of God. For the ark of God was at that time with the children of Israel.

19 And it came to pass, while Saul ªtalked unto the priest, that the ¹noise that *was* in the host of the Philistines went on and increased: and Saul said unto the priest, Withdraw thine hand.

20 And Saul and all the people that *were* with him assembled themselves, and they came to the battle: and, behold, ªevery man's sword was against his fellow, *and there was* a very great ¹discomfiture.

21 Moreover the Hebrews *that* were with the Philistines before that time, which went up with them into the camp *from the country* round about, even they also *turned* to be with the Israelites that *were* with Saul and Jonathan.

22 Likewise all the men of Israel which ªhad hid themselves in mount Ephraim, *when* they heard that the Philistines fled, even they also followed hard after them in the battle.

23 ªSo the LORD saved Israel that day: and the battle passed over ᵇunto Beth-aven.

24 And the men of Israel were distressed that day: for Saul had ªadjured¹ the people, saying, Cursed *be* the man that eateth *any* food until evening, that I may be avenged on mine enemies. So none of the people tasted *any* food.

25 ªAnd all *they of* the land came to a wood; and there was ᵇhoney upon the ground.

26 And when the people were come into the wood, behold, the honey dropped; but no man put his hand to his mouth: for the people feared the oath.

27 But Jonathan heard not when his father charged the people with the oath: wherefore he put forth the end of the rod that *was* in his hand, and dipped it in an honeycomb, and put his hand to his mouth; and his ¹eyes were enlightened.

28 Then answered one of the people, and said, Thy father ¹straitly charged the people with an oath, saying, Cursed *be* the man that eateth *any* food this day. And the people were faint.

29 Then said Jonathan, My father hath troubled the land: see, I pray you, how mine eyes have been enlightened, because I tasted a little of this honey.

30 How much more, if ¹haply the people had eaten freely to day of the ²spoil of their enemies which they found? for ³had there not been now

a much greater slaughter among the Philistines?

31 And they ¹smote the Philistines that day from Michmash to Aijalon: and the people were very faint.

32 And the people ¹flew upon the spoil, and took sheep, and oxen, and calves, and slew *them* on the ground: and the people did eat *them* ªwith the blood.

33 Then they told Saul, saying, Behold, the people sin against the LORD, in that they eat with the blood. And he said, Ye have ¹transgressed: roll a great stone unto me this day.

34 And Saul said, Disperse yourselves among the people, and say unto them, Bring me hither every man his ox, and every man his sheep, and slay *them* here, and eat; and sin not against the LORD in eating with the blood. And all the people brought every man his ox with him that night, and slew *them* there.

35 And Saul ªbuilt an altar unto the LORD: the same was the first altar that he built unto the LORD.

36 And Saul said, Let us go down after the Philistines by night, and ¹spoil them until the morning light, and let us not leave a man of them. And they said, Do whatsoever seemeth good unto thee. Then said the priest, Let us draw near hither unto God.

37 And Saul ªasked counsel of God, Shall I go down after the Philistines? wilt thou deliver them into the hand of Israel? But ᵇhe answered him not that day.

38 And Saul said, ªDraw ye near hither, all the chief of the people: and know and see wherein this sin hath been this day.

39 For, ªas the LORD liveth, which saveth Israel, though it be in Jonathan my son, he shall surely die. But *there was* not a man among all the people *that* answered him.

40 Then said he unto all Israel, Be ye on one side, and I and Jonathan my son will be on the other side. And the people said unto Saul, Do what seemeth good unto thee.

41 Therefore Saul said unto the LORD God of Israel, ªGive a perfect *lot.* ᵇAnd Saul and Jonathan were taken: but the people escaped.

42 And Saul said, Cast *lots* between me and Jonathan my son. And Jonathan was taken.

43 Then Saul said to Jonathan, ªTell me what thou hast done. And Jonathan told him, and said, ᵇI did but taste a little honey with the end of the rod that *was* in mine hand, *and,* lo, I must die.

44 And Saul answered, ªGod do so and more also: ᵇfor thou shalt surely die, Jonathan.

45 And the people said unto Saul,
Shall Jonathan die, who hath [1]wrought
this great salvation in Israel? God forbid: [a]*as* the LORD liveth, there shall not
one hair of his head fall to the ground;
for he hath wrought [b]with God this
day. So the people rescued Jonathan,
that he died not.
46 Then Saul went up from following the Philistines: and the Philistines went to their own place.
47 So Saul took the kingdom over
Israel, and fought against all his enemies on every side, against Moab,
and against the children of [a]Ammon,
and against Edom, and against the
kings of [b]Zobah, and against the
Philistines: and whithersoever he
turned himself, he [1]vexed *them.*
48 And he gathered [1]an host, and
[a]smote[2] the Amalekites, and delivered Israel out of the hands of them
that [3]spoiled them.
49 Now [a]the sons of Saul were Jonathan, and [1]Ishui, and Melchi-shua:
and the names of his two daughters
*were these;* the name of the firstborn
Merab, and the name of the younger
[b]Michal:
50 And the name of Saul's wife *was*
Ahinoam, the daughter of Ahimaaz:
and the name of the captain of his
host *was* Abner, the son of Ner, Saul's
[a]uncle.
51 [a]And Kish *was* the father of Saul;
and Ner the father of Abner *was* the
son of Abiel.
52 And there was [1]sore war against
the Philistines all the days of Saul: and
when Saul saw any strong man, or any
valiant man, [a]he took him unto him.

## CHAPTER 15

SAMUEL also said unto Saul, [a]The
LORD sent me to anoint thee *to
be* king over his people, over Israel:
now therefore hearken thou unto the
voice of the words of the LORD.
2 Thus saith the LORD of hosts, I remember *that* which Amalek did to Israel, [a]how he laid *wait* for him in the
way, when he came up from Egypt.
3 Now go and [a]smite[1] Amalek, and
[b]utterly destroy all that they have,
and spare them not; but slay both
man and woman, infant and suckling, ox and sheep, camel and ass.
4 And Saul gathered the people
together, and numbered them in Te-
laim, two hundred thousand footmen, and ten thousand men of Judah.
5 And Saul came to a city of Amalek, and laid wait in the valley.
6 And Saul said unto [a]the Kenites,
[b]Go, depart, get you down from
among the Amalekites, lest I destroy you with them: for [c]ye shewed
kindness to all the children of Israel,
when they came up out of Egypt. So
the Kenites departed from among
the Amalekites.
7 [a]And Saul smote the Amalekites
from [b]Havilah *until* thou comest to
[c]Shur, that *is* over against Egypt.
8 And [a]he took Agag the king of the
Amalekites alive, and [b]utterly destroyed all the people with the edge
of the sword.
9 But Saul and the people [a]spared
Agag, and the best of the sheep, and
of the oxen, and of the fatlings, and
the lambs, and all *that was* good,
and would not utterly destroy them:
but every thing *that was* [1]vile and
refuse, that they destroyed utterly.
10 Then came the word of the LORD
unto Samuel, saying,
11 [a]It[1] repenteth me that I have set
up Saul *to be* king: for he is [b]turned
back from following me, [c]and hath
not performed my commandments.
And it [d]grieved Samuel; and he cried
unto the LORD all night.
12 And when Samuel rose early to
meet Saul in the morning, it was told
Samuel, saying, Saul came to [a]Car-
mel, and, behold, he set him up a
place, and is gone about, and passed
on, and gone down to Gilgal.
13 And Samuel came to Saul: and
Saul said unto him, [a]Blessed *be* thou
of the LORD: I have performed the
commandment of the LORD.
14 And Samuel said, What *meaneth*
then this bleating of the sheep in
mine ears, and the lowing of the oxen
which I hear?
15 And Saul said, They have brought
them from the Amalekites: [a]for the
people spared the best of the sheep
and of the oxen, to sacrifice unto the
LORD thy God; and the rest we have
utterly destroyed.
16 Then Samuel said unto Saul,
Stay, and I will tell thee what the
LORD hath said to me this night. And
he said unto him, Say on.
17 And Samuel said, [a]When thou
*wast* little in thine own sight, *wast*
thou not *made* the head of the tribes
of Israel, and the LORD anointed thee
king over Israel?
18 And the LORD sent thee on a journey, and said, Go and utterly destroy
the sinners the Amalekites, and fight
against them until they be [1]consumed.
19 Wherefore then didst thou not
obey the voice of the LORD, but didst
[1]fly upon the spoil, and didst evil in
the sight of the LORD?
20 And Saul said unto Samuel, Yea,
[a]I have obeyed the voice of the LORD,
and have gone the way which the
LORD sent me, and have brought Agag
the king of Amalek, and have utterly
destroyed the Amalekites.
21 [a]But the people took of the [1]spoil,
sheep and oxen, the chief of the things

14:45 [a] 2 Sam. 14:11; 1 Kin. 1:52; Luke 21:18; Acts 27:34 [b] [2 Cor. 6:1; Phil. 2:12, 13] [1] *accomplished*
14:47 [a] 1 Sam. 11:1–13 [b] 2 Sam. 10:6 [1] *harassed*
14:48 [a] Ex. 17:16; 1 Sam. 15:3–7 [1] *an army* [2] *attacked* [3] *plundered*
14:49 [a] 1 Sam. 31:2; 1 Chr. 8:33 [b] 1 Sam. 18:17–20, 27; 19:12 [1] Heb. *Jishui; Abinadab,* 1 Chr. 8:33; 9:39
14:50 [a] 1 Sam. 10:14
14:51 [a] 1 Sam. 9:1, 21
14:52 [a] 1 Sam. 8:11 [1] *fierce*
15:1 [a] 1 Sam. 9:16; 10:1
15:2 [a] Ex. 17:8, 14; Num. 24:20; Deut. 25:17–19
15:3 [a] Deut. 25:19 [b] Lev. 27:28, 29; Num. 24:20; Deut. 20:16–18; Josh. 6:17–21 [1] *attack*
15:6 [a] Num. 24:21; Judg. 1:16; 4:11–22; 1 Chr. 2:55 [b] Gen. 18:25; 19:12, 14; Rev. 18:4 [c] Ex. 18:10, 19; Num. 10:29, 32
15:7 [a] 1 Sam. 14:48 [b] Gen. 2:11; 25:17, 18 [c] Gen. 16:7; Ex. 15:22; 1 Sam. 27:8
15:8 [a] 1 Sam. 15:32, 33 [b] 1 Sam. 27:8, 9
15:9 [a] 1 Sam. 15:3, 15, 19 [1] *despised and worthless*
15:11 [a] Gen. 6:6, 7 [b] 1 Kin. 9:6 [c] 1 Sam. 13:13; 15:3, 9 [d] 1 Sam. 15:35; 16:1 [1] *I greatly regret*
15:12 [a] Josh. 15:55
15:13 [a] Judg. 17:2
15:15 [a] [Gen. 3:12, 13]; 1 Sam. 15:9, 21
15:17 [a] 1 Sam. 9:21; 10:22
15:18 [1] *exterminated*
15:19 [1] *swoop down on the plunder*
15:20 [a] 1 Sam. 15:13
15:21 [a] 1 Sam. 15:15 [1] *plunder*

which should have been utterly destroyed, to sacrifice unto the LORD thy God in Gilgal.

22 And Samuel said, ªHath the LORD *as great* delight in burnt offerings and sacrifices, as in obeying the voice of the LORD? Behold, ᵇto obey *is* better than sacrifice, *and* to hearken than the fat of rams.

23 For rebellion *is as* the sin of ¹witchcraft, and stubbornness *is as* iniquity and idolatry. Because thou hast rejected the word of the LORD, ªhe hath also rejected thee from *being* king.

24 ªAnd Saul said unto Samuel, I have sinned: for I have transgressed the commandment of the LORD, and thy words: because I ᵇfeared the people, and obeyed their voice.

25 Now therefore, I pray thee, pardon my sin, and turn again with me, that I may worship the LORD.

26 And Samuel said unto Saul, I will not return with thee: ªfor thou hast rejected the word of the LORD, and the LORD hath rejected thee from being king over Israel.

27 And as Samuel turned about to go away, ªhe ¹laid hold upon the skirt of his mantle, and it ²rent.

28 And Samuel said unto him, ªThe LORD hath ¹rent the kingdom of Israel from thee this day, and hath given it to a neighbour of thine, *that is* better than thou.

29 And also the Strength of Israel ªwill not lie nor ¹repent: for he *is* not a man, that he should repent.

30 Then he said, I have sinned: *yet* ªhonour me now, I pray thee, before the elders of my people, and before Israel, and turn again with me, that I may worship the LORD thy God.

31 So Samuel ¹turned again after Saul; and Saul worshipped the LORD.

32 Then said Samuel, Bring ye hither to me Agag the king of the Amalekites. And Agag came unto him ¹delicately. And Agag said, Surely the bitterness of death is past.

33 And Samuel said, ªAs thy sword hath made women childless, so shall thy mother be childless among women. And Samuel hewed Agag in pieces before the LORD in Gilgal.

34 Then Samuel went to ªRamah; and Saul went up to his house to ᵇGibeah of Saul.

35 And ªSamuel came no more to see Saul until the day of his death: nevertheless Samuel mourned for Saul: and the LORD ¹repented that he had made Saul king over Israel.

## CHAPTER 16

ND the LORD said unto Samuel, ªHow long wilt thou mourn for Saul, seeing I have rejected him from

reigning over Israel? ᵇfill thine horn with oil, and go, I will send thee to ᶜJesse the Beth-lehemite: for ᵈI have ¹provided me a king among his sons.

2 And Samuel said, How can I go? if Saul hear *it,* he will kill me. And the LORD said, Take an heifer with thee, and say, ªI am come to sacrifice to the LORD.

3 And call Jesse to the sacrifice, and I will shew thee what thou shalt do: and thou shalt anoint unto me *him* whom I name unto thee.

4 And Samuel did that which the LORD spake, and came to Bethlehem. And the elders of the town ªtrembled at his coming, and said, ᵇComest thou peaceably?

5 And he said, Peaceably: I am come to sacrifice unto the LORD: ªsanctify¹ yourselves, and come with me to the sacrifice. And he sanctified Jesse and his sons, and called them to the sacrifice.

6 And it came to pass, when they were come, that he looked on ªEliab, and ᵇsaid, Surely the LORD's anointed *is* before him.

7 But the LORD said unto Samuel, ªLook not on his countenance, or on the height of his stature; because I have ¹refused him: ᵇfor *the LORD seeth* not as man seeth; for man ᶜlooketh on the outward appearance, but the LORD looketh on the ᵈheart.

8 Then Jesse called Abinadab, and made him pass before Samuel. And he said, Neither hath the LORD chosen this.

9 Then Jesse made Shammah to pass by. And he said, Neither hath the LORD chosen this.

10 Again, Jesse made seven of his sons to pass before Samuel. And Samuel said unto Jesse, The LORD hath not chosen these.

11 And Samuel said unto Jesse, Are here all *thy* children? And he said, There remaineth yet the youngest, and, behold, he keepeth the ªsheep. And Samuel said unto Jesse, Send and ¹fetch him: for we will not sit down till he come hither.

12 And he sent, and brought him in. Now he *was* ªruddy, ¹*and* withal of a ᵇbeautiful countenance, and goodly to look to. ᶜAnd the LORD said, Arise, anoint him: for this *is* he.

13 Then Samuel took the horn of oil, and anointed him in the midst of his brethren: and ªthe Spirit of the LORD came upon David from that day forward. So Samuel rose up, and went to Ramah.

14 ªBut the Spirit of the LORD departed from Saul, and ᵇan evil spirit from the LORD troubled him.

15 And Saul's servants said unto

### Center column references

15:22 ª [Is. 1:11–17]
ᵇ [Hos. 6:6]
15:23 ª 1 Sam. 13:14; 16:1 ¹ *divination*
15:24 ª Josh. 7:20
ᵇ [Is. 51:12, 13]
15:26 ª 1 Sam. 2:30
15:27 ª 1 Kin. 11:30, 31 ¹ *seized the edge of his robe* ² *tore*
15:28 ª 1 Kin. 11:31 ¹ *torn*
15:29 ª Num. 23:19 ¹ *relent*
15:30 ª [John 5:44; 12:43]
15:31 ¹ *turned back*
15:32 ¹ *cautiously*
15:33 ª [Gen. 9:6]
15:34 ª 1 Sam. 7:17 ᵇ 1 Sam. 11:4
15:35 ª 1 Sam. 19:24 ¹ *regretted*
16:1 ª 1 Sam. 15:23, 35
ᵇ 1 Sam. 9:16; 10:1
ᶜ Ruth 4:18–22
ᵈ Ps. 78:70, 71; Acts 13:22 ¹ Lit. *seen*
16:2 ª 1 Sam. 9:12
16:4 ª 1 Sam. 21:1 ᵇ 1 Kin. 2:13; 2 Kin. 9:22
16:5 ª Gen. 35:2; Ex. 19:10 ¹ *consecrate*
16:6 ª 1 Sam. 17:13, 28 ᵇ 1 Kin. 12:26
16:7 ª Ps. 147:10 ᵇ Is. 55:8, 9
ᶜ 2 Cor. 10:7 ᵈ 1 Kin. 8:39 ¹ *rejected*
16:11 ª 2 Sam. 7:8; Ps. 78:70–72 ¹ *bring*
16:12 ª 1 Sam. 17:42 ᵇ Gen. 39:6; Ex. 2:2; Acts 7:20 ᶜ 1 Sam. 9:17 ¹ *with bright eyes and good-looking*
16:13 ª Num. 27:18; 1 Sam. 10:6, 9, 10
16:14 ª Judg. 16:20; 1 Sam. 11:6; 18:12; 28:15 ᵇ Judg. 9:23; 1 Sam. 16:15, 16; 18:10; 19:9; 1 Kin. 22:19–22

him, Behold now, an evil spirit from God troubleth thee.

16 Let our lord now command thy servants, *which are* before thee, to seek out a man, *who is* a cunning player on an harp: and it shall come to pass, when the [1]evil spirit from God is upon thee, that he shall [a]play with his hand, and thou shalt be well.

17 And Saul said unto his servants, [1]Provide me now a man that can play well, and bring *him* to me.

18 Then answered one of the servants, and said, Behold, I have seen a son of Jesse the Beth-lehemite, *that is* [1]cunning in playing, and a mighty valiant man, and a man of war, and prudent in [2]matters, and a [3]comely person, and [a]the LORD *is* with him.

19 Wherefore Saul sent messengers unto Jesse, and said, Send me David thy son, which *is* with the sheep.

20 And Jesse [a]took an ass *laden* with bread, and a bottle of wine, and a kid, and sent *them* by David his son unto Saul.

21 And David came to Saul, and [a]stood before him: and he loved him greatly; and he became his armourbearer.

22 And Saul sent to Jesse, saying, Let David, I pray thee, stand before me; for he hath found favour in my sight.

23 And it came to pass, when the *evil* spirit from God was upon Saul, that David took an harp, and played with his hand: so Saul was refreshed, and was well, and the [1]evil spirit departed from him.

## CHAPTER 17

Now the Philistines gathered together their armies to battle, and were gathered together at [a]Shochoh, which *belongeth* to Judah, and pitched between Shochoh and Azekah, in Ephes-dammim.

2 And Saul and the men of Israel were gathered together, and [1]pitched by the valley of Elah, and [2]set the battle in array against the Philistines.

3 And the Philistines stood on a mountain on the one side, and Israel stood on a mountain on the other side: and *there was* a valley between them.

4 And there went out a champion out of the camp of the Philistines, named [a]Goliath, of [b]Gath, whose height *was* six cubits and a span.

5 And *he had* an helmet of brass upon his head, and he *was* [1]armed with a coat of mail; and the weight of the coat *was* five thousand shekels of brass.

6 And *he had* greaves of brass upon his legs, and a [1]target of brass between his shoulders.

16:16 [a] 1 Sam. 18:10; 19:9; 2 Kin. 3:15 [1] *distressing*
16:17 [1] Lit. *Look for*
16:18 [a] 1 Sam. 3:19; 18:12, 14 [1] *skilful* [2] *speech* [3] *handsome*
16:20 [a] 1 Sam. 10:4, 27; Prov. 18:16
16:21 [a] Gen. 41:46; Prov. 22:29
16:23 [1] *distressing*
17:1 [a] Josh. 15:35; 2 Chr. 28:18
17:2 [1] *encamped* [2] *drew up in battle array*
17:4 [a] 2 Sam. 21:19 [b] Josh. 11:21, 22
17:5 [1] Lit. *clothed with scaled body armour*
17:6 [1] *javelin of bronze*
17:8 [a] 1 Sam. 8:17 [1] *to line up for battle*
17:9 [a] 1 Sam. 11:1
17:10 [a] 1 Sam. 17:26, 36, 45; 2 Sam. 21:21
17:12 [a] Ruth 4:22; 1 Sam. 16:1, 18; 17:58 [b] Gen. 35:19 [c] 1 Sam. 16:10, 11; 1 Chr. 2:13-15 [1] *was advanced in years*
17:13 [a] 1 Sam. 16:6, 8, 9; 1 Chr. 2:13
17:15 [a] 1 Sam. 16:11, 19; 2 Sam. 7:8
17:18 [a] Gen. 37:13, 14 [1] *see how your brothers are* [2] *bring back news*
17:20 [1] *camp* [2] *army*
17:22 [1] *supplies* [2] *supply keeper* [3] *greeted*

7 And the staff of his spear *was* like a weaver's beam; and his spear's head *weighed* six hundred shekels of iron: and one bearing a shield went before him.

8 And he stood and cried unto the armies of Israel, and said unto them, Why are ye come out [1]to set *your* battle in array? *am* not I a Philistine, and ye [a]servants to Saul? choose you a man for you, and let him come down to me.

9 If he be able to fight with me, and to kill me, then will we be your servants: but if I prevail against him, and kill him, then shall ye be our servants, and [a]serve us.

10 And the Philistine said, I [a]defy the armies of Israel this day; give me a man, that we may fight together.

11 When Saul and all Israel heard those words of the Philistine, they were dismayed, and greatly afraid.

12 Now David *was* [a]the son of that [b]Ephrathite of Beth-lehem-judah, whose name *was* Jesse; and he had [c]eight sons: and the man [1]went among men *for* an old man in the days of Saul.

13 And the three eldest sons of Jesse went *and* followed Saul to the battle: and the [a]names of his three sons that went to the battle *were* Eliab the firstborn, and next unto him Abinadab, and the third Shammah.

14 And David *was* the youngest: and the three eldest followed Saul.

15 But David went and returned from Saul [a]to feed his father's sheep at Beth-lehem.

16 And the Philistine drew near morning and evening, and presented himself forty days.

17 And Jesse said unto David his son, Take now for thy brethren an ephah of this parched *corn,* and these ten loaves, and run to the camp to thy brethren;

18 And carry these ten cheeses unto the captain of *their* thousand, and [a]look[1] how thy brethren fare, and [2]take their pledge.

19 Now Saul, and they, and all the men of Israel, *were* in the valley of Elah, fighting with the Philistines.

20 And David rose up early in the morning, and left the sheep with a keeper, and took, and went, as Jesse had commanded him; and he came to the [1]trench, as the [2]host was going forth to the fight, and shouted for the battle.

21 For Israel and the Philistines had put the battle in array, army against army.

22 And David left his [1]carriage in the hand of the [2]keeper of the carriage, and ran into the army, and came and [3]saluted his brethren.

23 And as he talked with them, behold, there came up the champion, the Philistine of Gath, Goliath by name, out of the armies of the Philistines, and spake ªaccording to the same words: and David heard *them.*

24 And all the men of Israel, when they saw the man, fled from him, and were sore afraid.

25 And the men of Israel said, Have ye seen this man that is come up? surely to defy Israel is he come up: and it shall be, *that* the man who killeth him, the king will enrich him with great riches, and ªwill give him his daughter, and make his father's house free in Israel.

26 And David spake to the men that stood by him, saying, What shall be done to the man that killeth this Philistine, and taketh away ªthe reproach from Israel? for who *is* this ᵇuncircumcised Philistine, that he should ᶜdefy the armies of ᵈthe living God?

27 And the people answered him after this manner, saying, ªSo shall it be done to the man that killeth him.

28 And Eliab his eldest brother heard when he spake unto the men; and Eliab's ªanger was kindled against David, and he said, Why camest thou down hither? and with whom hast thou left those few sheep in the wilderness? I know thy pride, and the ¹naughtiness of thine heart; for thou art come down that thou mightest see the battle.

29 And David said, What have I now done? ªIs¹ there not a cause?

30 And he turned from him toward another, and ªspake after the same manner: and the people answered him again ¹after the former manner.

31 And when the words were heard which David spake, they ¹rehearsed *them* before Saul: and he sent for him.

32 And David said to Saul, ªLet no man's heart fail because of him; ᵇthy servant will go and fight with this Philistine.

33 And Saul said to David, ªThou art not able to go against this Philistine to fight with him: for thou *art but* a youth, and he a man of war from his youth.

34 And David said unto Saul, Thy servant kept his father's sheep, and there came a ªlion, and a bear, and took a lamb out of the flock:

35 And I went out after him, and ¹smote him, and delivered *it* out of his mouth: and when he arose against me, I caught *him* by his beard, and smote him, and slew him.

36 Thy servant slew both the lion and the bear: and this uncircumcised Philistine shall be as one of them,

seeing he hath defied the armies of the living God.

37 David said moreover, ªThe LORD that delivered me out of the paw of the lion, and out of the paw of the bear, he will deliver me out of the hand of this Philistine. And Saul said unto David, Go, and ᵇthe LORD be with thee.

38 And Saul ¹armed David with his armour, and he put an helmet of brass upon his head; also he armed him with a coat of mail.

39 And David girded his sword upon his armour, and he ¹assayed to go; for he had not ²proved *it.* And David said unto Saul, I cannot go with these; for I have not proved *them.* And David put them off him.

40 And he took his staff in his hand, and chose him five smooth stones out of the brook, and put them in a shepherd's bag which he had, even in a scrip; and his sling *was* in his hand: and he drew near to the Philistine.

41 And the Philistine came on and drew near unto David; and the man that bare the shield *went* before him.

42 And when the Philistine looked about, and saw David, he ªdisdained¹ him: for he was *but* a youth, and ᵇruddy, and of a fair countenance.

43 And the Philistine said unto David, ªAm I a dog, that thou comest to me with ¹staves? And the Philistine cursed David by his gods.

44 And the Philistine ªsaid to David, Come to me, and I will give thy flesh unto the fowls of the air, and to the beasts of the field.

45 Then said David to the Philistine, Thou comest to me with a sword, and with a spear, and with a shield: ªbut I come to thee in the name of the LORD of hosts, the God of the armies of Israel, whom thou hast ᵇdefied.

46 This day will the LORD deliver thee into mine hand; and I will ¹smite thee, and take thine head from thee; and I will give ªthe carcases of the host of the Philistines this day unto the fowls of the air, and to the wild beasts of the earth; ᵇthat all the earth may know that there is a God in Israel.

47 And all this assembly shall know that the LORD ªsaveth not with sword and spear: for ᵇthe battle *is* the LORD's, and he will give you into our hands.

48 And it came to pass, when the Philistine arose, and came and drew nigh to meet David, that David ¹hasted, and ªran toward the army to meet the Philistine.

49 And David put his hand in his bag, and took thence a stone, and slang *it,* and smote the Philistine in his forehead, that the stone sunk into his forehead; and he fell upon his face to the earth.

264

50 So David prevailed over the Philistine with a ªsling and with a stone, and smote the Philistine, and slew him; but *there was* no sword in the hand of David.

51 Therefore David ran, and stood upon the Philistine, and took his ªsword, and drew it out of the sheath thereof, and slew him, and cut off his head therewith. And when the Philistines saw their champion was dead, ᵇthey fled.

52 And the men of Israel and of Judah arose, and shouted, and pursued the Philistines, ¹until thou come to the valley, and to the gates of Ekron. And the wounded of the Philistines fell down by the way to ªShaaraim, even unto Gath, and unto Ekron.

53 And the children of Israel returned from chasing after the Philistines, and they ¹spoiled their tents.

54 And David took the head of the Philistine, and brought it to Jerusalem; but he put his armour in his tent.

55 And when Saul saw David go forth against the Philistine, he said unto ªAbner, the captain of the host, Abner, ᵇwhose son *is* this youth? And Abner said, *As* thy soul liveth, O king, I cannot tell.

56 And the king said, Enquire thou whose son the stripling *is.*

57 And as David returned from the slaughter of the Philistine, Abner took him, and brought him before Saul ªwith the head of the Philistine in his hand.

58 And Saul said to him, Whose son *art* thou, *thou* young man? And David answered, ª*I am* the son of thy servant Jesse the Beth-lehemite.

## CHAPTER 18

AND it came to pass, when he had made an end of speaking unto Saul, that ªthe ¹soul of Jonathan was knit with the soul of David, ᵇand Jonathan loved him as his own soul.

2 And Saul took him that day, ªand would let him go no more home to his father's house.

3 Then Jonathan and David made a ªcovenant, because he loved him as his own soul.

4 And Jonathan ¹stripped himself of the robe that *was* upon him, and gave it to David, and his garments, even to his sword, and to his bow, and to his girdle.

5 And David went out whithersoever Saul sent him, *and* ᵇbehaved himself wisely: and Saul set him over the men of war, and he was accepted in the sight of all the people, and also in the sight of Saul's servants.

6 And it came to pass as they came, when David was returned from the slaughter of the ¹Philistine, that ªthe women came out of all cities of Israel, singing and dancing, to meet king Saul, with tabrets, with joy, and with ²instruments of musick.

7 And the women ªanswered *one another* as they played, and said, ᵇSaul hath slain his thousands, and David his ten thousands.

8 And Saul was very ¹wroth, and the saying ªdispleased him; and he said, They have ascribed unto David ten thousands, and to me they have ascribed *but* thousands: and *what* can he have more but ᵇthe kingdom?

9 And Saul ¹eyed David from that day and forward.

10 And it came to pass on the morrow, that ªthe evil spirit from God came upon Saul, ᵇand he prophesied in the midst of the house: and David ᶜplayed with his hand, as at other times: ᵈand *there was* a javelin in Saul's hand.

11 And Saul ªcast the javelin; for he said, I will smite David even to the wall *with it.* And David ¹avoided out of his presence twice.

12 And Saul was ªafraid of David, because ᵇthe LORD was with him, and was ᶜdeparted from Saul.

13 Therefore Saul removed ¹him from him, and made him his captain over a thousand; and ªhe went out and came in before the people.

14 And David behaved himself wisely in all his ways; and ªthe LORD *was* with him.

15 Wherefore when Saul saw that he behaved himself very wisely, he was afraid of him.

16 But ªall Israel and Judah loved David, because he went out and came in before them.

17 And Saul said to David, Behold my elder daughter Merab, ªher will I give thee to wife: only be thou valiant for me, and fight ᵇthe LORD's battles. For Saul said, ᶜLet not mine hand be upon him, but let the hand of the Philistines be upon him.

18 And David said unto Saul, ªWho *am* I? and what *is* my life, *or* my father's family in Israel, that I should be son in law to the king?

19 But it came to pass at the time when Merab Saul's daughter should have been given to David, that she was given unto ªAdriel the ᵇMeholathite to wife.

20 ªAnd Michal Saul's daughter loved David: and they told Saul, and the thing pleased him.

21 And Saul said, I will give him her, that she may ¹be a snare to him, and that ªthe hand of the Philistines may be against him. Wherefore Saul said to David, Thou shalt ᵇthis day be my son in law in *the one of* the twain.

---

**Center column references:**

17:50 ª Judg. 3:31;
15:15; 20:16
17:51 ¹ 1 Sam.
21:9; 2 Sam. 23:21
ᵇ Heb. 11:34
17:52 ª Josh. 15:36
¹ *as far as*
17:53 ¹ *plundered*
17:55 ª 1 Sam.
14:50 ᵇ 1 Sam.
16:21, 22
17:57 ª 1 Sam. 17:54
17:58 ª 1 Sam. 17:12
18:1 ª Gen. 44:30
ᵇ Deut. 13:6;
1 Sam. 20:17;
2 Sam. 1:26 ¹ *life of Jonathan was bound up with the life of*
18:2 ª 1 Sam. 17:15
18:3 ª 1 Sam.
20:8–17
18:4 ¹ *took off*
18:5 ¹ *prospered*
18:6 ª Ex. 15:20,
21; Judg. 11:34;
Ps. 68:25; 149:3
¹ *Philistines*
² *three-stringed instruments*
18:7 ª Ex. 15:21
ᵇ 1 Sam. 21:11; 29:5
18:8 ª Eccl. 4:4
ᵇ 1 Sam. 15:28
¹ *angry*
18:9 ¹ *viewed with suspicion*
18:10 ª 1 Sam. 16:14
ᵇ 1 Sam. 19:24;
1 Kin. 18:29; Acts
16:16 ᶜ 1 Sam.
16:23 ᵈ 1 Sam.
19:9, 10
18:11 ª 1 Sam. 19:10;
20:33 ¹ *escaped*
18:12 ª 1 Sam. 18:15,
29 ᵇ 1 Sam. 16:13,
18 ᶜ 1 Sam. 16:14;
28:15
18:13 ª Num. 27:17;
1 Sam. 18:16; 29:6;
2 Sam. 5:2 ¹ *his presence*
18:14 ª Gen. 39:2,
3, 23; Josh. 6:27;
1 Sam. 16:18
18:16 ª Num.
27:16, 17; 1 Sam.
18:5; 2 Sam. 5:2;
1 Kin. 3:7
18:17 ª 1 Sam.
14:49; 17:25
ᵇ Num. 32:20, 27,
29; 1 Sam. 25:28
ᶜ 1 Sam. 18:21, 25;
2 Sam. 12:9
18:18 ª 1 Sam. 9:21;
18:23; 2 Sam. 7:18
18:19 ª 2 Sam.
21:8 ᵇ Judg. 7:22;
2 Sam. 21:8; 1 Kin.
19:16
18:20 ª 1 Sam.
18:28
18:21 ª 1 Sam. 18:17
ᵇ 1 Sam. 18:26 ¹ *be bait for*

22 And Saul commanded his servants, *saying,* [1]Commune with David secretly, and say, Behold, the king hath delight in thee, and all his servants love thee: now therefore be the king's son in law.

23 And Saul's servants spake those words in the ears of David. And David said, Seemeth it to you *a* light *thing* to be a king's son in law, seeing that I *am* a poor man, and lightly esteemed?

24 And the servants of Saul told him, saying, [1]On this manner spake David.

25 And Saul said, Thus shall ye say to David, The king desireth not any [a]dowry, but an hundred foreskins of the Philistines, to be [b]avenged of the king's enemies. But Saul [c]thought to make David fall by the hand of the Philistines.

26 And when his servants told David these words, it pleased David well to be the king's son in law: and [a]the days were not expired.

27 Wherefore David arose and went, he and [a]his men, and slew of the Philistines two hundred men; and [b]David brought their foreskins, and they gave them in full [1]tale to the king, that he might be the king's son in law. And Saul gave him Michal his daughter to wife.

28 And Saul saw and knew that the LORD *was* with David, and *that* Michal Saul's daughter loved him.

29 And Saul was yet the more afraid of David; and Saul became David's enemy [1]continually.

30 Then the princes of the Philistines [a]went forth: and it came to pass, after they went forth, *that* David [b]behaved himself more wisely than all the servants of Saul; so that his name [1]was much set by.

## CHAPTER 19

AND Saul spake to Jonathan his son, and to all his servants, that they should kill [a]David.

2 But Jonathan Saul's son [a]delighted much in David: and Jonathan told David, saying, Saul my father seeketh to kill thee: now therefore, I pray thee, take heed to thyself until the morning, and abide in a secret *place,* and hide thyself:

3 And I will go out and stand beside my father in the field where thou *art,* and I will commune with my father of thee; and what I see, that I will tell [a]thee.

4 And Jonathan [a]spake good of David unto Saul his father, and said unto him, Let not the king [b]sin against his servant, against David; because he hath not sinned against thee, and because his works *have been* to thee-ward very good:

5 For he did put his [a]life in his hand, and [b]slew the Philistine, and [c]the LORD wrought a great salvation for all Israel: thou sawest *it,* and didst rejoice: [d]wherefore then wilt thou [e]sin against innocent blood, to slay David without a cause?

6 And Saul hearkened unto the voice of Jonathan: and Saul sware, *As* the LORD liveth, he shall not be slain.

7 And Jonathan called David, and Jonathan shewed him all those things. And Jonathan brought David to Saul, and he was in his presence, [a]as in times past.

8 And there was war again: and David went out, and fought with the Philistines, and [a]slew them with a great slaughter; and they fled from him.

9 And [a]the evil spirit from the LORD was upon Saul, as he sat in his house with his javelin in his hand: and David [1]played with *his* hand.

10 And Saul sought to [1]smite David even to the wall with the javelin; but he slipped away out of Saul's presence, and he smote the javelin into the wall: and David fled, and escaped that night.

11 [a]Saul also sent messengers unto David's house, to watch him, and to slay him in the morning: and Michal David's wife told him, saying, If thou save not thy life to night, to morrow thou shalt be slain.

12 So Michal [a]let David down through a window: and he went, and fled, and escaped.

13 And Michal took [1]an image, and laid *it* in the bed, and put a pillow of goats' *hair* for his bolster, and covered *it* with a cloth.

14 And when Saul sent messengers to take David, she said, He *is* sick.

15 And Saul sent the messengers *again* to see David, saying, Bring him up to me in the bed, that I may slay him.

16 And when the messengers were come in, behold, *there was* an image in the bed, with a pillow of goats' *hair* for his bolster.

17 And Saul said unto Michal, Why hast thou deceived me so, and sent away mine enemy, that he is escaped? And Michal answered Saul, He said unto me, Let me go; [a]why should I kill thee?

18 So David fled, and escaped, and came to [a]Samuel to [b]Ramah, and told him all that Saul had done to him. And he and Samuel went and dwelt in Naioth.

19 And it was told Saul, saying, Behold, David *is* at Naioth in Ramah.

20 And [a]Saul sent messengers to take David: [b]and when they saw the company of the prophets prophesying, and Samuel standing *as* ap-

18:22 [1] *Communicate*
18:24 [1] Lit. *According to these words*
18:25 [a] Gen. 34:12; Ex. 22:17 [b] 1 Sam. 14:24 [c] 1 Sam. 18:17
18:26 [a] 1 Sam. 18:21
18:27 [a] 1 Sam. 18:13 [b] 2 Sam. 3:14 [1] *count*
18:29 [1] Lit. *all the days*
18:30 [a] 2 Sam. 11:1 [b] 1 Sam. 18:5 [1] *became highly esteemed*
19:1 [a] 1 Sam. 8:8, 9
19:2 [a] 1 Sam. 18:1
19:3 [a] 1 Sam. 20:8–13
19:4 [a] 1 Sam. 20:32; [Prov. 31:8, 9] [b] Gen. 42:22; [Prov. 17:13]; Jer. 18:20
19:5 [a] Judg. 9:17; 12:3 [b] 1 Sam. 17:49, 50 [c] 1 Sam. 11:13; 1 Chr. 11:14 [d] 1 Sam. 20:32 [e] [Deut. 19:10–13]
19:7 [a] 1 Sam. 16:21; 18:2, 10, 13
19:8 [a] 1 Sam. 18:27; 23:5
19:9 [a] 1 Sam. 16:14; 18:10, 11 [1] *played music*
19:10 [1] *pin*
19:11 [a] Judg. 16:2; Ps. 59:title
19:12 [a] Josh. 2:15; Acts 9:25; 2 Cor. 11:33
19:13 [1] *household idols,* Heb. *teraphim*
19:17 [a] 2 Sam. 2:22
19:18 [a] 1 Sam. 16:13 [b] 1 Sam. 7:17
19:20 [a] 1 Sam. 19:11, 14; John 7:32 [b] 1 Sam. 10:5, 6, 10; [1 Cor. 14:3, 24, 25]

pointed over them, the Spirit of God was upon the messengers of Saul, and they also ᶜprophesied.

21 And when it was told Saul, he sent other messengers, and they prophesied likewise. And Saul sent messengers again the third time, and they prophesied also.

22 Then went he also to Ramah, and came to a great well that *is* in Sechu: and he asked and said, Where *are* Samuel and David? And *one* said, Behold, *they be* at Naioth in Ramah.

23 And he went thither to Naioth in Ramah: and ᵃthe Spirit of God was upon him also, and he went on, and prophesied, until he came to Naioth in Ramah.

24 ᵃAnd he stripped off his clothes also, and prophesied before Samuel in like manner, and lay down ᵇnaked all that day and all that night. Wherefore they say, ᶜ*Is* Saul also among the prophets?

## CHAPTER 20

ᴀND David fled from Naioth in Ramah, and came and said before Jonathan, What have I done? what *is* mine iniquity? and what *is* my sin before thy father, that he seeketh my life?

2 And he said unto him, God forbid; thou shalt not die: behold, my father will do nothing either great or small, ¹but that he will shew it me: and why should my father hide this thing from me? it *is* not *so*.

3 And David sware moreover, and said, Thy father certainly knoweth that I have found grace in thine eyes; and he saith, Let not Jonathan know this, lest he be grieved: but ᵃtruly *as* the LORD liveth, and *as* thy soul liveth, *there is* but a step between me and death.

4 Then said Jonathan unto David, Whatsoever thy soul desireth, I will even do *it* for thee.

5 And David said unto Jonathan, Behold, to morrow *is* the ᵃnew moon, and I should not fail to sit with the king ¹at meat: but let me go, that I may ᵇhide myself in the field unto the third *day* at even.

6 If thy father at all miss me, then say, David earnestly asked *leave* of me that he might run ᵃto Beth-lehem his city: for *there is* a yearly sacrifice there for all the family.

7 ᵃIf he say thus, *It is* well; thy servant shall have peace: but if he be very wroth, *then* be sure that ᵇevil is determined by him.

8 Therefore thou shalt ᵃdeal kindly with thy servant; for ᵇthou hast brought thy servant into a covenant of the LORD with thee: notwithstanding, ᶜif there be in me iniquity, slay

me thyself; for why shouldest thou bring me to thy father?

9 And Jonathan said, Far be it from thee: for if I knew certainly that evil were determined by my father to come upon thee, then would not I tell it thee?

10 Then said David to Jonathan, Who shall tell me? or what *if* thy father answer thee roughly?

11 And Jonathan said unto David, Come, and let us go out into the field. And they went out both of them into the field.

12 And Jonathan said unto David, O LORD God of Israel, when I have ¹sounded my father about to morrow any time, *or* the third *day,* and, behold, *if there be* good toward David, and I then send not unto thee, and shew it thee;

13 ᵃThe LORD do so and much more to Jonathan: but if it please my father *to do* thee evil, then I will shew it thee, and send thee away, that thou mayest go in peace: and ᵇthe LORD be with thee, as he hath ᶜbeen with my father.

14 And thou shalt not only while yet I live shew me the kindness of the LORD, that I die not:

15 But *also* ᵃthou shalt not cut off thy kindness from my ¹house for ever: no, not when the LORD hath cut off the enemies of David every one from the face of the earth.

16 So Jonathan made *a covenant* with the ¹house of David, *saying,* ᵃLet the LORD even require *it* at the hand of David's enemies.

17 And Jonathan caused David to ¹swear again, because he loved him: ᵃfor he loved him as he loved his own soul.

18 Then Jonathan said to David, ᵃTo morrow *is* the new moon: and thou shalt be missed, because thy seat will be empty.

19 And *when* thou hast stayed three days, *then* thou shalt go down quickly, and come to ᵃthe place where thou didst hide thyself ¹when the business was *in hand,* and shalt remain by the stone Ezel.

20 And I will shoot three arrows on the side *thereof,* as though I shot at a mark.

21 And, behold, I will send a lad, *saying,* Go, find out the arrows. If I expressly say unto the lad, Behold, the arrows *are* on this side of thee, take them; then come thou: for *there is* peace to thee, and no hurt; ᵃas the LORD liveth.

22 But if I say thus unto the young man, Behold, the arrows *are* beyond thee; go thy way: for the LORD hath sent thee away.

23 And *as touching* ᵃthe matter which thou and I have spoken of,

### Center reference column

19:20 ᶜ Num. 11:25; Joel 2:28

19:23 ᵃ 1 Sam. 10:10

19:24 ᵃ Is. 20:2 ᵇ Mic. 1:8 ᶜ 1 Sam. 10:10–12

20:2 ¹ *without first telling me*

20:3 ᵃ 1 Sam. 27:1; 2 Kin. 2:6

20:5 ᵃ Num. 10:10; 28:11–15 ᵇ 1 Sam. 19:2, 3 ¹ *to eat*

20:6 ᵃ 1 Sam. 16:4; 17:12; John 7:42

20:7 ᵃ Deut. 1:23; 2 Sam. 17:4 ᵇ 1 Sam. 25:17; Esth. 7:7

20:8 ᵃ Josh. 2:14 ᵇ 1 Sam. 18:3; 20:16; 23:18 ᶜ 2 Sam. 14:32

20:12 ¹ *searched out*

20:13 ᵃ Ruth 1:17; 1 Sam. 3:17 ᵇ Josh. 1:5; 1 Sam. 17:37; 18:12; 1 Chr. 22:11, 16 ᶜ 1 Sam. 10:7

20:15 ᵃ 1 Sam. 24:21; 2 Sam. 9:1, 3, 7; 21:7 ¹ *family*

20:16 ᵃ Deut. 23:21; 1 Sam. 25:22; 31:2; 2 Sam. 4:7; 21:8 ¹ *family*

20:17 ᵃ 1 Sam. 18:1 ¹ *vow*

20:18 ᵃ 1 Sam. 20:5, 24

20:19 ᵃ 1 Sam. 19:2 ¹ *on the day of the deed*

20:21 ᵃ Jer. 4:2

20:23 ᵃ 1 Sam. 20:14, 15

behold, the LORD *be* between thee and me for ever.

24 So David hid himself in the field: and when the new moon was come, the king sat him down to eat meat.

25 And the king sat upon his seat, as at other times, *even* upon a seat by the wall: and Jonathan arose, and Abner sat by Saul's side, and David's place was empty.

26 Nevertheless Saul spake not any thing that day: for he thought, Something hath befallen him, he *is* not clean; surely he *is* ᵃnot¹ clean.

27 And it came to pass on the morrow, *which was* the second *day* of the month, that David's place was empty: and Saul said unto Jonathan his son, Wherefore cometh not the son of Jesse to meat, neither yesterday, nor to day?

28 And Jonathan ᵃanswered Saul, David earnestly asked *leave* of me *to go* to Bethlehem:

29 And he said, Let me go, I pray thee; for our family hath a sacrifice in the city; and my brother, he hath commanded me *to be there:* and now, if I have found favour in thine eyes, let me get away, I pray thee, and see my brethren. Therefore he cometh not unto the king's table.

30 Then Saul's anger was kindled against Jonathan, and he said unto him, Thou son of the perverse rebellious *woman,* do not I know that thou hast chosen the son of Jesse to thine own ¹confusion, and unto the confusion of thy mother's nakedness?

31 For as long as the son of Jesse liveth upon the ground, thou shalt not be established, nor thy kingdom. Wherefore now send and fetch him unto me, for he ¹shall surely die.

32 And Jonathan answered Saul his father, and said unto him, ᵃWherefore shall he be slain? what hath he done?

33 And Saul ᵃcast a javelin at him to ¹smite him: ᵇwhereby Jonathan knew that it was determined of his father to slay David.

34 So Jonathan arose from the table in fierce anger, and did eat no meat the second day of the month: for he was grieved for David, because his father had done him shame.

35 And it came to pass in the morning, that Jonathan went out into the field at the time appointed with David, and a little lad with him.

36 And he said unto his lad, Run, find out now the arrows which I shoot. *And* as the lad ran, he shot an arrow beyond him.

37 And when the lad was come to the place of the arrow which Jonathan had shot, Jonathan cried after the lad, and said, *Is* not the arrow beyond thee?

38 And Jonathan cried after the lad, Make speed, haste, ¹stay not. And Jonathan's lad gathered up the arrows, and came to his master.

39 But the lad knew not any thing: only Jonathan and David knew the matter.

40 And Jonathan gave his ¹artillery unto his lad, and said unto him, Go, carry *them* to the city.

41 *And* as soon as the lad was gone, David arose out of *a place* toward the south, and fell on his face to the ground, and bowed himself three times: and they kissed one another, and wept one with another, until David exceeded.

42 And Jonathan said to David, ᵃGo in peace, forasmuch as we have sworn both of us in the name of the LORD, saying, The LORD be between me and thee, and between my seed and thy seed for ever. And he arose and departed: and Jonathan went into the city.

## CHAPTER 21

THEN came David to Nob to Ahimelech the priest: and ᵃAhimelech was ᵇafraid ¹at the meeting of David, and said unto him, Why *art* thou alone, and no man with thee?

2 And David said unto Ahimelech the priest, The king hath ¹commanded me a business, and hath said unto me, Let no man know any thing of the business whereabout I send thee, and what I have commanded thee: and I have ²appointed *my* servants to such and such a place.

3 Now therefore ¹what is under thine hand? give *me* five *loaves of* bread in mine hand, or ²what there is present.

4 And the priest answered David, and said, *There is* no ¹common bread under mine hand, but there is ᵃhallowed² bread; ᵇif the young men have kept themselves at least from women.

5 And David answered the priest, and said unto him, Of a truth women *have been* kept from us about these three days, since I came out, and the ᵃvessels¹ of the young men are holy, and *the bread is* in a manner common, yea, though it were ²sanctified this day ᵇin the vessel.

6 So the priest ᵃgave him hallowed *bread:* for there was no bread there but the shewbread, ᵇthat was taken from before the LORD, to put hot bread in the day when it was taken away.

7 Now a certain man of the servants of Saul *was* there that day, detained before the LORD; and his name *was* ᵃDoeg, an Edomite, the chiefest of the herdmen that *belonged* to Saul.

### Cross references

20:26 ᵃ Lev. 7:20, 21; 15:5 ¹ *unclean*
20:28 ᵃ 1 Sam. 20:6
20:30 ¹ *shame*
20:31 ¹ Lit. *is a son of death*
20:32 ᵃ Gen. 31:36; 1 Sam. 19:5; [Prov. 31:9]; Matt. 27:23; Luke 23:22
20:33 ᵃ 1 Sam. 18:11; 19:10 ᵇ 1 Sam. 20:7 ¹ Lit. *strike him down*
20:38 ¹ *do not delay*
20:40 ¹ *weapons*
20:42 ᵃ 1 Sam. 1:17
21:1 ᵃ 1 Sam. 14:3; Mark 2:26 ᵇ 1 Sam. 16:4 ¹ *when he met*
21:2 ¹ *ordered me on some business* ² *directed*
21:3 ¹ *what do you have on hand* ² *whatever can be found*
21:4 ᵃ Ex. 25:30; Lev. 24:5–9; Matt. 12:4 ᵇ Ex. 19:15 ¹ *ordinary* ² *holy*
21:5 ᵃ Ex. 19:14, 15; 1 Thess. 4:4 ᵇ Lev. 8:26 ¹ *The young men are ceremonially undefiled.* ² *consecrated*
21:6 ᵃ Matt. 12:3, 4; Mark 2:25, 26; Luke 6:3, 4 ᵇ Lev. 24:8, 9
21:7 ᵃ 1 Sam. 14:47; 22:9; Ps. 52:title

8 And David said unto Ahimelech, And is there not here under thine hand spear or sword? for I have neither brought my sword nor my weapons with me, because the king's business required haste.

9 And the priest said, The sword of Goliath the Philistine, whom thou slewest in [a]the valley of Elah, [b]behold, it *is here* wrapped in a cloth behind the ephod: if thou wilt take that, take *it*: for *there is* no other save that here. And David said, *There is* none like that; give it me.

10 And David arose, and fled that day for fear of Saul, and went to Achish the king of Gath.

11 And [a]the servants of Achish said unto him, [b]*Is* not this David the king of the land? did they not sing one to another of him in dances, saying, Saul hath slain his thousands, and David his ten thousands?

12 And David [a]laid[1] up these words in his heart, and was [2]sore afraid of Achish the king of Gath.

13 And [a]he changed his behaviour before them, and [1]feigned himself mad in their hands, and [2]scrabbled on the doors of the gate, and let his spittle fall down upon his beard.

14 Then said Achish unto his servants, Lo, ye see the man is [1]mad: wherefore *then* have ye brought him to me?

15 Have I need of mad men, that ye have brought this *fellow* to play the mad man in my presence? shall this *fellow* come into my house?

## CHAPTER 22

DAVID therefore departed thence, and [a]escaped [b]to the cave Adullam: and when his brethren and all his father's house heard *it,* they went down [1]thither to him.

2 [a]And every one *that was* in distress, and every one that *was* in debt, and every one *that was* [1]discontented, gathered themselves unto him; and he became a captain over them: and there were with him about [b]four hundred men.

3 And David went thence to Mizpeh of [a]Moab: and he said unto the king of Moab, Let my father and my mother, [1]I pray thee, come forth, *and be* with you, till I know what God will do for me.

4 And he brought them before the king of Moab: and they dwelt with him all the while that David was [1]in the hold.

5 And the prophet [a]Gad said unto David, Abide not in the hold; depart, and get thee into the land of Judah. Then David departed, and came into the forest of Hareth.

6 When Saul heard that David was

discovered, and the men that *were* with him, (now Saul abode in [a]Gibeah under a [1]tree in Ramah, having his spear in his hand, and all his servants *were* standing about him;)

7 Then Saul said unto his servants that stood about him, Hear now, ye Benjamites; will the son of Jesse [a]give every one of you fields and vineyards, *and* make you all captains of thousands, and captains of hundreds;

8 That all of you have conspired against me, and *there is* none that sheweth me that [a]my son hath made a league with the son of Jesse, and *there is* none of you that is sorry for me, or sheweth unto me that my son hath stirred up my servant against me, to lie in wait, as at this day?

9 Then answered [a]Doeg the Edomite, which was set over the servants of Saul, and said, I saw the son of Jesse coming to Nob, to [b]Ahimelech the son of [c]Ahitub.

10 [a]And he enquired of the LORD for him, and [b]gave him [1]victuals, and gave him the sword of Goliath the Philistine.

11 Then the king sent to call Ahimelech the priest, the son of Ahitub, and all his father's house, the priests that *were* in Nob: and they came all of them to the king.

12 And Saul said, Hear now, thou son of Ahitub. And he answered, Here I *am,* my lord.

13 And Saul said unto him, Why have ye conspired against me, thou and the son of Jesse, in that thou hast given him bread, and a sword, and hast enquired of God for him, that he should rise against me, to lie in wait, as at this day?

14 Then Ahimelech answered the king, and said, And who *is so* [a]faithful among all thy servants as David, which is the king's son in law, and goeth at thy bidding, and is honourable in thine house?

15 Did I then begin to enquire of God for him? be it far from me: let not the king impute *any* thing unto his servant, *nor* to all the house of my father: for thy servant knew nothing of all this, less or more.

16 And the king said, Thou shalt surely die, Ahimelech, thou, and all [a]thy father's house.

17 And the king said unto the [1]footmen that stood about him, Turn, and slay the priests of the LORD; because their hand also *is* with David, and because they knew when he fled, and did not shew it to me. But the servants of the king [a]would not put forth their hand to fall upon the priests of the LORD.

18 And the king said to Doeg, Turn thou, and fall upon the priests. And

*Cross references (center column):*

21:9 [a] 1 Sam. 17:2, 50 [b] 1 Sam. 31:10
21:11 [a] Ps. 56:title [b] 1 Sam. 18:6–8; 29:5
21:12 [a] Luke 2:19 [1] took these words to heart [2] very much
21:13 [a] Ps. 34:title [1] feigned madness [2] scratched
21:14 [1] insane
22:1 [a] Ps. 57:title; 142:title [b] Josh. 12:15; 15:35; 2 Sam. 23:13 [1] there
22:2 [a] Judg. 11:3 [b] 1 Sam. 25:13 [1] Lit. bitter of soul
22:3 [a] 2 Sam. 8:2 [1] please, come here
22:4 [1] strong hold
22:5 [a] 2 Sam. 24:11; 1 Chr. 21:9; 29:29; 2 Chr. 29:25

22:6 [a] 1 Sam. 15:34 [1] tamarisk tree
22:7 [a] 1 Sam. 8:14
22:8 [a] 1 Sam. 18:3; 20:16, 30
22:9 [a] 1 Sam. 21:7; 22:22; Ps. 52:title [b] 1 Sam. 21:1 [c] 1 Sam. 14:3
22:10 [a] Num. 27:21; 1 Sam. 10:22 [b] 1 Sam. 21:6, 9 [1] provisions
22:14 [a] 1 Sam. 19:4, 5; 20:32; 24:11
22:16 [a] Deut. 24:16
22:17 [a] Ex. 1:17 [1] guards

Doeg the Edomite turned, and he [1]fell upon the priests, and [a]slew on that day fourscore and five persons that did wear a linen ephod.

19 [a]And Nob, the city of the priests, [1]smote he with the edge of the sword, both men and women, children and sucklings, and oxen, and asses, and sheep, with the edge of the sword.

20 [a]And one of the sons of Ahimelech the son of Ahitub, named Abiathar, [b]escaped, and fled after David.

21 And Abiathar shewed David that Saul had slain the LORD's priests.

22 And David said unto Abiathar, I knew *it* that day, when Doeg the Edomite *was* there, that he would surely tell Saul: I have [1]occasioned *the death* of all the persons of thy father's [2]house.

23 Abide thou with me, fear not: [a]for he that seeketh my life seeketh thy life: but with me thou *shalt be* [1]in safeguard.

## CHAPTER 23

THEN they told David, saying, Behold, the Philistines fight against [a]Keilah, and they rob the threshing-floors.

2 Therefore David [a]enquired of the LORD, saying, Shall I go and [1]smite these Philistines? And the LORD said unto David, Go, and smite the Philistines, and save Keilah.

3 And David's men said unto him, Behold, we be afraid here in Judah: how much more then if we come to Keilah against the armies of the Philistines?

4 Then David enquired of the LORD yet again. And the LORD answered him and said, Arise, go down to Keilah; for I will deliver the Philistines into thine hand.

5 So David and his men went to Keilah, and [a]fought with the Philistines, and brought away their cattle, and smote them with a great slaughter. So David saved the inhabitants of Keilah.

6 And it came to pass, when Abiathar the son of Ahimelech [a]fled to David to Keilah, *that* he came down *with* an ephod in his hand.

7 And it was told Saul that David was come to Keilah. And Saul said, God hath delivered him into mine hand; for he is shut in, by entering into a town that hath gates and bars.

8 And Saul called all the people together to war, to go down to Keilah, to besiege David and his men.

9 And David knew that Saul secretly [1]practised mischief against him; and [a]he said to Abiathar the priest, Bring hither the ephod.

10 Then said David, O LORD God of Israel, thy servant hath certainly

heard that Saul seeketh to come to Keilah, [a]to destroy the city for my sake.

11 Will the men of Keilah deliver me up into his hand? will Saul come down, as thy servant hath heard? O LORD God of Israel, I beseech thee, tell thy servant. And the LORD said, He will come down.

12 Then said David, Will the men of Keilah [1]deliver me and my men into the hand of Saul? And the LORD said, They will deliver *thee* up.

13 Then David and his men, [a]*which were* about six hundred, arose and departed out of Keilah, and went whithersoever they could go. And it was told Saul that David was escaped from Keilah; and he forbare to go forth.

14 And David [1]abode in the wilderness in strong holds, and remained in [a]a mountain in the wilderness of [b]Ziph. And Saul [c]sought him every day, but God delivered him not into his hand.

15 And David saw that Saul was come out to seek his life: and David *was* in the wilderness of Ziph [1]in a wood.

16 And Jonathan Saul's son arose, and went to David into the wood, and [1]strengthened his hand in God.

17 And he said unto him, [a]Fear not: for the hand of Saul my father shall not find thee; and thou shalt be king over Israel, and I shall be next unto thee; and [b]that also Saul my father knoweth.

18 And they two [a]made a covenant before the LORD: and David abode in the wood, and Jonathan went to his house.

19 Then [a]came up the Ziphites to Saul to Gibeah, saying, Doth not David hide himself with us in strong holds in the wood, in the hill of Hachilah, which *is* on the south of Jeshimon?

20 Now therefore, O king, come down according to all the desire of thy soul to come down; and [a]our part *shall be* to deliver him into the king's hand.

21 And Saul said, Blessed *be* ye of the LORD; for ye have compassion on me.

22 Go, I pray you, prepare yet, and know and see his place where his [1]haunt is, *and* who hath seen him there: for it is told me *that* he dealeth very [2]subtilly.

23 See therefore, and take knowledge of all the lurking places where he hideth himself, and come ye again to me with the certainty, and I will go with you: and it shall come to pass, if he be in the land, that I will search him out throughout all the [1]thousands of Judah.

---

22:18 [a] 1 Sam. 2:31
[1] *attacked*

22:19 [a] Josh. 21:1–45; 1 Sam. 22:9, 11
[1] *struck*

22:20 [a] 1 Sam. 23:6, 9; 30:7;
1 Kin. 2:26, 27
[b] 1 Sam. 2:33

22:22 [1] *caused*
[2] *family*

22:23 [a] 1 Kin. 2:26
[1] *safe*

23:1 [a] Josh. 15:44;
Neh. 3:17, 18

23:2 [a] 1 Sam. 22:10; 23:4, 6, 9;
28:6; 30:8; 2 Sam. 5:19, 23 [1] *attack*

23:5 [a] 1 Sam. 19:8;
2 Sam. 5:20

23:6 [a] 1 Sam. 22:20

23:9 [a] Num. 27:21;
1 Sam. 23:6; 30:7
[1] *plotted evil*

23:10 [a] 1 Sam. 22:19

23:12 [1] Lit. *shut me and my men up*

23:13 [a] 1 Sam. 22:2; 25:13

23:14 [a] Ps. 11:1
[b] Josh. 15:55;
2 Chr. 11:8 [c] Ps. 32:7; 54:3, 4
[1] *stayed*

23:15 [1] *in Horesh*

23:16 [1] *encouraged him*

23:17 [a] [Ps. 27:1–3; Heb. 13:6]
[b] 1 Sam. 20:31; 24:20

23:18 [a] 1 Sam. 18:3; 20:12–17, 42; 2 Sam. 9:1; 21:7

23:19 [a] 1 Sam. 26:1; Ps. 54:title

23:20 [a] Ps. 54:3

23:22 [1] *hideout*
[2] *craftily*

23:23 [1] *clans*

---

24 And they arose, and went to Ziph before Saul: but David and his men *were* in the wilderness ᵃof Maon, in the plain on the south of Jeshimon.

25 Saul also and his men went to seek *him.* And they told David: wherefore he came down ¹into a rock, and abode in the wilderness of Maon. And when Saul heard *that,* he pursued after David in the wilderness of Maon.

26 And Saul went on this side of the mountain, and David and his men on that side of the mountain: ᵃand David made haste to get away for fear of Saul; for Saul and his men ᵇcompassed¹ David and his men round about to take them.

27 ᵃBut there came a messenger unto Saul, saying, Haste thee, and come; for the Philistines have invaded the land.

28 Wherefore Saul returned from pursuing after David, and went against the Philistines: therefore they called that place ¹Sela-hammahlekoth.

29 And David went up from thence, and dwelt in strong holds at ᵃEn-gedi.

## CHAPTER 24

Aᴺᴅ it came to pass, ᵃwhen Saul was returned from following the Philistines, that it was told him, saying, Behold, David *is* in the wilderness of En-gedi.

2 Then Saul took three thousand chosen men out of all Israel, and ᵃwent to seek David and his men upon the rocks of the wild goats.

3 And he came to the sheepcotes by the way, where *was* a cave; and ᵃSaul went in to ᵇcover¹ his feet: and ᶜDavid and his men remained in the sides of the cave.

4 ᵃAnd the men of David said unto him, Behold the day of which the LORD said unto thee, Behold, I will deliver thine enemy into thine hand, that thou mayest do to him as it shall seem good unto thee. Then David arose, and cut off ¹the skirt of Saul's robe privily.

5 And it came to pass afterward, that ᵃDavid's heart smote him, because he had cut off Saul's skirt.

6 And he said unto his men, ᵃThe LORD forbid that I should do this thing unto my master, the LORD's anointed, to stretch forth mine hand against him, seeing he *is* the anointed of the LORD.

7 So David ᵃstayed¹ his servants with these words, and suffered them not to rise against Saul. But Saul rose up out of the cave, and went on *his* way.

8 David also arose afterward, and went out of the cave, and cried after

Saul, saying, My lord the king. And when Saul looked behind him, David stooped with his face to the earth, and bowed himself.

9 And David said to Saul, ᵃWherefore hearest thou men's words, saying, Behold, David seeketh thy hurt?

10 Behold, this day thine eyes have seen how that the LORD had delivered thee to day into mine hand in the cave: and *some* bade *me* kill thee: but *mine eye* spared thee; and I said, I will not put forth mine hand against my lord; for he *is* the LORD's anointed.

11 Moreover, my father, see, yea, see the ¹skirt of thy robe in my hand: for in that I cut off the ¹skirt of thy robe, and killed thee not, know thou and see that *there is* ᵃneither evil nor ²transgression in mine hand, and I have not sinned against thee; yet thou ᵇhuntest my ³soul to take it.

12 ᵃThe LORD judge between me and thee, and the LORD avenge me ¹of thee: but mine hand shall not be upon thee.

13 As saith the proverb of the ancients, ᵃWickedness proceedeth from the wicked: but mine hand shall not be upon thee.

14 After whom is the king of Israel come out? after whom dost thou pursue? ᵃafter a dead dog, after ᵇa flea.

15 ᵃThe LORD therefore be judge, and judge between me and thee, and ᵇsee, and ᶜplead my cause, and deliver me out of thine hand.

16 And it came to pass, when David had made an end of speaking these words unto Saul, that Saul said, ᵃ*Is* this thy voice, my son David? And Saul lifted up his voice, and wept.

17 ᵃAnd he said to David, Thou *art* ᵇmore righteous than I: for ᶜthou hast rewarded me good, whereas I have rewarded thee evil.

18 And thou hast shewed this day how that thou hast dealt well with me: forasmuch as when ᵃthe LORD had delivered me into thine hand, thou killedst me not.

19 For if a man find his enemy, will he let him ¹go well away? wherefore the LORD reward thee good for that thou hast done unto me this day.

20 And now, behold, ᵃI know well that thou shalt surely be king, and that the kingdom of Israel shall be established in thine hand.

21 ᵃSwear now therefore unto me by the LORD, ᵇthat thou wilt not cut off my seed after me, and that thou wilt not destroy my name out of my father's house.

22 And David sware unto Saul. And Saul went home; but David and his men gat them up unto ᵃthe ¹hold.

---

23:24 ᵃ Josh. 15:55; 1 Sam. 25:2
23:25 ¹ *to the rock*
23:26 ᵃ Ps. 31:22
ᵇ Ps. 17:9 ¹ *were encircling*
23:27 ᵃ 2 Kin. 19:9
23:28 ¹ Lit. *Rock of Escaping*
23:29 ᵃ Josh. 15:62; 2 Chr. 20:2
24:1 ᵃ 1 Sam. 23:19, 28, 29
24:2 ᵃ 1 Sam. 26:2; Ps. 38:12
24:3 ᵃ 1 Sam. 24:10 ᵇ Judg. 3:24 ᶜ Ps. 57:title; 142:title ¹ *attend to his needs*
24:4 ᵃ 1 Sam. 26:8–11 ¹ *a corner of Saul's robe secretly*
24:5 ᵃ 2 Sam. 24:10
24:6 ᵃ 1 Sam. 26:11
24:7 ᵃ Ps. 7:4; [Matt. 5:44; Rom. 12:17, 19] ¹ *restrained*

24:9 ᵃ Ps. 141:6; [Prov. 16:28; 17:9]
24:11 ᵃ Judg. 11:27; Ps. 7:3; 35:7 ᵇ 1 Sam. 26:20 ¹ *corner* ² *rebellion* ³ *life*
24:12 ᵃ Gen. 16:5; Judg. 11:27; 1 Sam. 26:10–23; Job 5:8 ¹ *on thee*
24:13 ᵃ [Matt. 7:16–20]
24:14 ᵃ 1 Sam. 17:43; 2 Sam. 9:8 ᵇ 1 Sam. 26:20
24:15 ᵃ 1 Sam. 24:12 ᵇ 2 Chr. 24:22 ᶜ Ps. 35:1; 43:1; 119:154; Mic. 7:9
24:16 ᵃ 1 Sam. 26:17
24:17 ¹ 1 Sam. 26:21 ᵇ Gen. 38:26 ᶜ [Matt. 5:44]
24:18 ᵃ 1 Sam. 26:23
24:19 ¹ *get away safely*
24:20 ᵃ 1 Sam. 23:17
24:21 ᵃ Gen. 21:23; 1 Sam. 20:14–17 ᵇ 2 Sam. 21:6–8
24:22 ᵃ 1 Sam. 23:29 ¹ *strong hold*

---

## CHAPTER 25

AND [a]Samuel died; and all the Israelites were gathered together, and [b]lamented him, and buried him in his house at Ramah. And David arose, and went down [c]to the wilderness of [1]Paran.

2 And *there was* a man [a]in Maon, whose [1]possessions *were* in [b]Carmel; and the man *was* very great, and he had three thousand sheep, and a thousand goats: and he was shearing his sheep in Carmel.

3 Now the name of the man *was* Nabal; and the name of his wife Abigail: and *she was* a woman of good understanding, and of a beautiful countenance: but the man *was* [1]churlish and evil in his doings; and he *was* of the house of [a]Caleb.

4 And David heard in the wilderness that Nabal did [a]shear his sheep.

5 And David sent out ten young men, and David said unto the young men, Get you up to Carmel, and go to Nabal, and greet him in my name:

6 And thus shall ye say to him that liveth *in prosperity,* [a]Peace *be* both to thee, and peace *be* to thine house, and peace *be* unto all that thou hast.

7 And now I have heard that thou hast shearers: now thy shepherds which were with us, we hurt them not, [a]neither was there ought missing unto them, all the while they were in Carmel.

8 Ask thy young men, and they will shew thee. Wherefore [1]let the young men find favour in thine eyes: for we come in [a]a good day: give, I pray thee, whatsoever cometh to thine hand unto thy servants, and to thy son David.

9 And when David's young men came, they spake to Nabal according to all those words in the name of David, and ceased.

10 And Nabal answered David's servants, and said, [a]Who *is* David? and who *is* the son of Jesse? there be many servants now a days that break away every man from his master.

11 [a]Shall I then take my bread, and my water, and my [1]flesh that I have killed for my shearers, and give *it* unto men, whom I know not whence they *be?*

12 So David's young men turned their way, and went again, and came and told him all those sayings.

13 And David said unto his men, Gird ye on every man his sword. And they girded on every man his sword; and David also girded on his sword: and there went up after David about four hundred men; and two hundred [a]abode by the stuff.

14 But one of the young men told Abigail, Nabal's wife, saying, Behold,

David sent messengers out of the wilderness to [1]salute our master; and he [2]railed on them.

15 But the men *were* very good unto us, and [a]we were not hurt, neither missed we any thing, as long as we [1]were conversant with them, when we were in the fields:

16 They were [a]a wall unto us both by night and day, all the while we were with them keeping the sheep.

17 Now therefore know and consider what thou wilt do; for [a]evil[1] is determined against our master, and against all his household: for he *is* such a [2]son of [b]Belial, that *a man* cannot speak to him.

18 Then Abigail made haste, and [a]took two hundred loaves, and two bottles of wine, and five sheep ready dressed, and five measures of [1]parched *corn,* and an hundred clusters of raisins, and two hundred cakes of figs, and laid *them* on asses.

19 And she said unto her servants, [a]Go on before me; behold, I come after you. But she told not her husband Nabal.

20 And it was *so, as* she rode on the ass, that she came down by the covert of the hill, and, behold, David and his men came down against her; and she met them.

21 Now David had said, Surely in vain have I kept all that this *fellow* hath in the wilderness, so that nothing was missed of all that *pertained* unto him: and he hath [a]requited[1] me evil for good.

22 [a]So and more also do God unto the enemies of David, if I [b]leave of all that *pertain* to him by the morning light [c]any that pisseth against the wall.

23 And when Abigail saw David, she hasted, and [a]lighted off the ass, and fell before David on her face, and bowed herself to the ground,

24 And fell at his feet, and said, Upon me, my lord, *upon* me *let this* iniquity *be:* and [1]let thine handmaid, I pray thee, speak in thine audience, and hear the words of thine handmaid.

25 Let not my lord, I pray thee, regard this man of Belial, *even* Nabal: for as his name *is,* so *is* he; [1]Nabal *is* his name, and folly *is* with him: but I thine handmaid saw not the young men of my lord, whom thou didst send.

26 Now therefore, my lord, [a]as the LORD liveth, and *as* thy soul liveth, seeing the LORD hath [b]withholden[1] thee from coming to *shed* blood, and from [2]avenging[2] thyself with thine own hand, now [d]let thine enemies, and they that seek [3]evil to my lord, be as Nabal.

---

### Cross-references (center column)

25:1 [a] 1 Sam. 28:3
[b] Num. 20:29;
Deut. 34:8 [c] Gen.
21:21; Num. 10:12;
13:3 [1] LXX, *Maon*
25:2 [a] 1 Sam.
23:24 [b] Josh.
15:55 [1] *business*
25:3 [a] Josh. 15:13;
1 Sam. 30:14
[1] *harsh*
25:4 [a] Gen. 38:13;
2 Sam. 13:23
25:6 [a] Judg.
19:20; 1 Chr. 12:18;
Ps. 122:7; Luke
10:5
25:7 [a] 1 Sam.
25:15, 21
25:8 [a] Neh. 8:10–
12; Esth. 8:17; 9:19,
22 [1] *be gracious
to the young men*
25:10 [a] Judg. 9:28
25:11 [a] Judg. 8:6,
15 [1] Lit. *slaughter*
25:13 [a] 1 Sam.
30:24

25:14 [1] *greet* [2] *reviled or scolded*
25:15 [a] 1 Sam.
25:7, 21 [1] *accompanied them*
25:16 [a] Ex. 14:22;
Job 1:10
25:17 [a] 1 Sam.
20:7 [b] Deut.
13:13; Judg. 19:22
[1] *harm* [2] *wicked man*
25:18 [a] Gen. 32:13;
[Prov. 18:16; 21:14]
[1] *roasted grain*
25:19 [a] Gen.
32:16, 20
25:21 [a] 1 Sam.
24:17; Ps. 109:5;
[Prov. 17:13]
[1] *repaid*
25:22 [a] Ruth 1:17;
1 Sam. 3:17; 20:13,
16 [b] 1 Sam. 25:34
[c] 1 Kin. 14:10;
21:21; 2 Kin. 9:8
25:23 [a] Josh.
15:18; Judg. 1:14
25:24 [1] *please
let your maidservant speak in
your ears*
25:25 [1] Lit. *Fool*
25:26 [a] 2 Kin.
2:2 [b] Gen. 20:6;
1 Sam. 25:33
[c] [Rom. 12:19]
[d] 2 Sam. 18:32
[1] *held you back*
[2] Lit. *delivering
yourself* [3] *harm
for*

27 And ᵃthis ¹blessing which thine handmaid hath brought unto my lord, let it even be given unto the young men that follow my lord.

28 I pray thee, forgive the trespass of thine handmaid: for ᵃthe LORD will certainly make my lord ¹a sure house; because my lord ᵇfighteth the battles of the LORD, and ᶜevil hath not been found in thee *all* thy days.

29 Yet a man is risen to pursue thee, and to seek thy soul: but the soul of my lord shall be ᵃbound ¹in the bundle of life with the LORD thy God; and the souls of thine enemies, them shall he ᵇsling out, *as out* of the middle of a sling.

30 And it shall come to pass, when the LORD shall have done to my lord according to all the good that he hath spoken concerning thee, and shall have appointed thee ᵃruler over Israel;

31 That this shall be no grief unto thee, nor offence of heart unto my lord, either that thou hast shed blood causeless, or that my lord hath avenged himself: but when the LORD shall have dealt well with my lord, then remember thine handmaid.

32 And David said to Abigail, ᵃBlessed *be* the LORD God of Israel, which sent thee this day to meet me:

33 And blessed *be* thy advice, and blessed *be* thou, which hast ᵃkept me this day from coming to *shed* blood, and from avenging myself with mine own hand.

34 For in very deed, *as* the LORD God of Israel liveth, which hath ᵃkept me back from hurting thee, ¹except thou hadst hasted and come to meet me, surely there had ᵇnot been left unto Nabal by the morning light any ²that pisseth against the wall.

35 So David received of her hand *that* which she had brought him, and said unto her, ᵃGo up in peace to thine house; see, I have ¹hearkened to thy voice, and have ᵇaccepted thy person.

36 And Abigail came to Nabal; and, behold, ᵃhe held a feast in his house, like the feast of a king; and Nabal's heart *was* merry within him, for he *was* very drunken: wherefore she told him nothing, less or more, until the morning light.

37 But it came to pass in the morning, when the wine was gone out of Nabal, and his wife had told him these things, that his heart died within him, and he became *as* a stone.

38 And it came to pass about ten days *after,* that the LORD ᵃsmote Nabal, that he died.

39 And when David heard that Nabal was dead, he said, ᵃBlessed *be* the

---

**Center column references:**

25:27 ᵃ Gen. 33:11; 1 Sam. 30:26; 2 Kin. 5:15 ¹ *gift*

25:28 ᵃ 2 Sam. 7:11–16, 27; 1 Kin. 9:5; 1 Chr. 17:10, 25 ᵇ 1 Sam. 18:17 ᶜ 1 Sam. 24:11; Ps. 7:3 ¹ *an enduring*

25:29 ᵃ [Ps. 66:9; Col. 3:3] ᵇ Jer. 10:18 ¹ *the living*

25:30 ᵃ 1 Sam. 13:14; 15:28

25:32 ᵃ Gen. 24:27; Ex. 18:10; 1 Kin. 1:48; Ps. 41:13; 72:18; 106:48; Luke 1:68

25:33 ᵃ 1 Sam. 25:26

25:34 ᵃ 1 Sam. 25:26 ᵇ 1 Sam. 25:22 ¹ *if you had not hastened* ² *males*

25:35 ᵃ 1 Sam. 20:42; 2 Sam. 15:9; 2 Kin. 5:19; Luke 7:50; 8:48 ᵇ Gen. 19:21 ¹ *heeded*

25:36 ᵃ 2 Sam. 13:28; Prov. 20:1; Is. 5:11; Dan. 5:1; [Hos. 4:11]

25:38 ᵃ 1 Sam. 26:10; 2 Sam. 6:7; Ps. 104:29

25:39 ᵃ 1 Sam. 25:32

ᵇ 1 Sam. 24:15; Prov. 22:23 ᶜ 1 Sam. 25:26, 34 ᵈ 1 Kin. 2:44 ¹ *proposed to*

25:41 ᵃ [Prov. 15:33]; Luke 7:38, 44

25:42 ¹ Lit. *at her feet*

25:43 ᵃ Josh. 15:56 ᵇ 1 Sam. 27:3; 30:5

25:44 ᵃ 1 Sam. 18:20; 2 Sam. 3:14 ᵇ Is. 10:30 ¹ *Phaltiel,* 2 Sam. 3:15

26:1 ᵃ 1 Sam. 23:19; Ps. 54:title

26:2 ᵃ 1 Sam. 13:2; 24:2

26:4 ¹ *had indeed come*

26:5 ᵃ 1 Sam. 14:50, 51; 17:55 ¹ *encamped* ² *camp*

26:6 ᵃ 1 Chr. 2:16 ᵇ 2 Sam. 2:13 ᶜ Judg. 7:10, 11 ᵈ 2 Sam. 2:18, 24

26:7 ¹ *the camp* ² *head*

26:8 ᵃ 1 Sam. 24:4 ¹ *strike*

---

LORD, that hath ᵇpleaded the cause of my reproach from the hand of Nabal, and hath ᶜkept his servant from evil: for the LORD hath ᵈreturned the wickedness of Nabal upon his own head. And David sent and ¹communed with Abigail, to take her to him to wife.

40 And when the servants of David were come to Abigail to Carmel, they spake unto her, saying, David sent us unto thee, to take thee to him to wife.

41 And she arose, and bowed herself on *her* face to the earth, and said, Behold, *let* thine handmaid *be* a servant to ᵃwash the feet of the servants of my lord.

42 And Abigail hasted, and arose, and rode upon an ass, with five damsels of hers that went ¹after her; and she went after the messengers of David, and became his wife.

43 David also took Ahinoam ᵃof Jezreel; ᵇand they were also both of them his wives.

44 But Saul had given ᵃMichal his daughter, David's wife, to ¹Phalti the son of Laish, which *was* of ᵇGallim.

## CHAPTER 26

AND the Ziphites came unto Saul to Gibeah, saying, ᵃDoth not David hide himself in the hill of Hachilah, *which is* before Jeshimon?

2 Then Saul arose, and went down to the wilderness of Ziph, having ᵃthree thousand chosen men of Israel with him, to seek David in the wilderness of Ziph.

3 And Saul pitched in the hill of Hachilah, which *is* before Jeshimon, by the way. But David abode in the wilderness, and he saw that Saul came after him into the wilderness.

4 David therefore sent out spies, and understood that Saul ¹was come in very deed.

5 And David arose, and came to the place where Saul had ¹pitched: and David beheld the place where Saul lay, and ᵃAbner the son of Ner, the captain of his host: and Saul lay in the ²trench, and the people pitched round about him.

6 Then answered David and said to Ahimelech the Hittite, and to Abishai ᵃthe son of Zeruiah, brother to ᵇJoab, saying, Who will ᶜgo down with me to Saul to the camp? And ᵈAbishai said, I will go down with thee.

7 So David and Abishai came to the people by night: and, behold, Saul lay sleeping within ¹the trench, and his spear stuck in the ground at his ²bolster: but Abner and the people lay round about him.

8 Then said Abishai to David, ᵃGod hath delivered thine enemy into thine hand this day: now therefore let me ¹smite him, I pray thee, with

the spear even to the earth ²at once, and I will not *smite* him the second time.

9 And David said to Abishai, Destroy him not: ᵃfor who can stretch forth his hand against the LORD's anointed, and be guiltless?

10 David said furthermore, *As* the LORD liveth, ᵃthe LORD shall smite him; or ᵇhis day shall come to die; or he shall ᶜdescend into battle, and perish.

11 ᵃThe LORD forbid that I should stretch forth mine hand against the LORD's anointed: but, I pray thee, take thou now the spear that *is* at his ¹bolster, and the cruse of water, and let us go.

12 So David took the spear and the cruse of water from Saul's bolster; and they gat them away, and no man saw *it,* nor knew *it,* neither awaked: for they *were* all asleep; because ᵃa deep sleep from the LORD was fallen upon them.

13 Then David went over to the other side, and stood on the top of an hill afar off; a great space *being* between them:

14 And David cried to the people, and to Abner the son of Ner, saying, Answerest thou not, Abner? Then Abner answered and said, Who *art* thou *that* criest to the king?

15 And David said to Abner, *Art* not thou a *valiant* man? and who *is* like to thee in Israel? wherefore then hast thou not ¹kept thy lord the king? for there came one of the people in to destroy the king thy lord.

16 This thing *is* not good that thou hast done. *As* the LORD liveth, ye *are* worthy to die, because ye have not ¹kept your master, the LORD's anointed. And now see where the king's spear *is,* and the cruse of water that *was* at his bolster.

17 And Saul knew David's voice, and said, ᵃ*Is* this thy voice, my son David? And David said, *It is* my voice, my lord, O king.

18 And he said, ᵃWherefore doth my lord thus pursue after his servant? for what have I done? or what evil *is* in mine hand?

19 Now therefore, I pray thee, let my lord the king hear the words of his servant. If the LORD have ᵃstirred thee up against me, let him accept an offering: but if *they* be the children of men, cursed *be* they before the LORD; ᵇfor they have driven me out this day from abiding in the ᶜinheritance of the LORD, saying, Go, serve other gods.

20 Now therefore, let not my blood fall to the earth before the face of the LORD: for the king of Israel is come out to seek ᵃa flea, as when one doth hunt a partridge in the mountains.

21 Then said Saul, ᵃI have sinned: return, my son David: for I will no more do thee harm, because my soul was precious in thine eyes this day: behold, I have played the fool, and have erred exceedingly.

22 And David answered and said, Behold the king's spear! and let one of the young men come over and fetch it.

23 ᵃThe LORD ᵇrender to every man his righteousness and his faithfulness: for the LORD delivered thee into *my* hand to day, but I would not stretch forth mine hand against the LORD's anointed.

24 And, behold, as thy life was much ¹set by this day in mine eyes, so let my life be much set by in the eyes of the LORD, and let him deliver me out of all tribulation.

25 Then Saul said to David, Blessed *be* thou, my son David: thou shalt both do great *things,* and also shalt still ᵃprevail. So David went on his way, and Saul returned to his place.

## CHAPTER 27

AND David said in his heart, I shall now perish one day by the hand of Saul: *there is* nothing better for me than that I should speedily escape into the land of the Philistines; and Saul should ¹despair of me, to seek me any more in any ²coast of Israel: so shall I escape out of his hand.

2 And David arose, ᵃand he passed over with the six hundred men that *were* with him ᵇunto Achish, the son of Maoch, king of Gath.

3 And David dwelt with Achish at Gath, he and his men, every man with his household, *even* David ᵃwith his two wives, Ahinoam the Jezreelitess, and Abigail the Carmelitess, Nabal's wife.

4 And it was told Saul that David was fled to Gath: and he sought no more again for him.

5 And David said unto Achish, If I have now found grace in thine eyes, let them give me a place in some town in the country, that I may dwell there: for why should thy servant dwell in the royal city with thee?

6 Then Achish gave him Ziklag that day: wherefore ᵃZiklag pertaineth unto the kings of Judah unto this day.

7 And ¹the time that David ᵃdwelt in the country of the Philistines was a full year and four months.

8 And David and his men went up, and invaded ᵃthe Geshurites, ᵇand the ¹Gezrites, and the ᶜAmalekites: for those *nations were* ²of old the inhabitants of the land, ᵈas thou goest to Shur, even unto the land of Egypt.

9 And David ¹smote the land, and left neither man nor woman alive,

---

26:8 ² *one time*
26:9 ª 1 Sam. 24:6, 7; 2 Sam. 1:14, 16
26:10 ª [Deut. 32:35]; 1 Sam. 25:26, 38; [Luke 18:7; Rom. 12:19; Heb. 10:30] ᵇ Gen. 47:29; Deut. 31:14; [Job 7:1; 14:5]; Ps. 37:13 ᶜ 1 Sam. 31:6
26:11 ª 1 Sam. 24:6–12; [Rom. 12:17, 19] ¹ *head*
26:12 ª Gen. 2:21; 15:12; Is. 29:10
26:15 ¹ *guarded*
26:16 ¹ *guarded*
26:17 ª 1 Sam. 24:16
26:18 ª 1 Sam. 24:9, 11–14
26:19 ª 2 Sam. 16:11; 24:1 ᵇ Deut. 4:27, 28 ᶜ 2 Sam. 14:16; 20:19
26:20 ª 1 Sam. 24:14

26:21 ª Ex. 9:27; 1 Sam. 15:24, 30; 24:17; 2 Sam. 12:13
26:23 ª 1 Sam. 24:19; Ps. 7:8; 18:20; 62:12 ᵇ 2 Sam. 22:21
26:24 ¹ *valued*
26:25 ª Gen. 32:28; 1 Sam. 24:20
27:1 ¹ *despair of searching for me any more* ² *territory*
27:2 ª 1 Sam. 25:13 ᵇ 1 Sam. 21:10; 1 Kin. 2:39
27:3 ª 1 Sam. 25:42, 43
27:6 ª Josh. 15:31; 19:5; 1 Chr. 12:1; Neh. 11:28
27:7 ª 1 Sam. 29:3 ¹ Lit. *the number of days*
27:8 ª Josh. 13:2, 13 ᵇ Josh. 16:10; Judg. 1:29 ᶜ Ex. 17:8, 16; 1 Sam. 15:7, 8 ᵈ Gen. 25:18; Ex. 15:22 ¹ MT, *Girzites* ² *from ancient times*
27:9 ¹ *attacked*

and took away the sheep, and the oxen, and the asses, and the camels, and the apparel, and returned, and came to Achish.

10 And Achish said, Whither have ye made a road to day? And David said, Against the south of Judah, and against the south of ᵃthe Jerahmeelites, and against the south of ᵇthe Kenites.

11 And David saved neither man nor woman alive, to bring *tidings* to Gath, saying, Lest they should tell on us, saying, So did David, and ¹so *will be* his manner all the while he dwelleth in the country of the Philistines.

12 And Achish believed David, saying, He hath made his people Israel utterly to abhor him; therefore he shall be my servant for ever.

### CHAPTER 28

AND ᵃit came to pass in those days, that the Philistines gathered their armies together for warfare, to fight with Israel. And Achish said unto David, Know thou assuredly, that thou shalt go out with me to battle, thou and thy men.

2 And David said to Achish, Surely thou shalt know what thy servant can do. And Achish said to David, Therefore will I make thee ¹keeper of mine head for ever.

3 Now ᵃSamuel was dead, and all Israel had lamented him, and buried him in ᵇRamah, even in his own city. And Saul had put away ᶜthose¹ that had familiar spirits, and the wizards, out of the land.

4 And the Philistines gathered themselves together, and came and ¹pitched in ᵃShunem: and Saul gathered all Israel together, and they pitched in ᵇGilboa.

5 And when Saul saw the host of the Philistines, he was ᵃafraid, and his heart greatly trembled.

6 And when Saul enquired of the LORD, ᵃthe LORD answered him not, neither by ᵇdreams, nor ᶜby Urim, nor by prophets.

7 Then said Saul unto his servants, Seek me a woman that ¹hath a familiar spirit, ᵃthat I may go to her, and enquire of her. And his servants said to him, Behold, *there is* a woman that hath a familiar spirit at En-dor.

8 And Saul disguised himself, and put on other raiment, and he went, and two men with him, and they came to the woman by night: and ᵃhe said, ¹I pray thee, divine unto me by the familiar spirit, and ²bring me *him* up, whom I shall name unto thee.

9 And the woman said unto him, Behold, thou knowest what Saul hath done, how he hath ᵃcut off those that have familiar spirits, and the wizards,

out of the land: wherefore then layest thou a snare for my life, to cause me to die?

10 And Saul sware to her by the LORD, saying, *As* the LORD liveth, there shall no punishment happen to thee for this thing.

11 Then said the woman, Whom shall I bring up unto thee? And he said, Bring me up Samuel.

12 And when the woman saw Samuel, she cried with a loud voice: and the woman spake to Saul, saying, Why hast thou deceived me? for thou *art* Saul.

13 And the king said unto her, Be not afraid: for what sawest thou? And the woman said unto Saul, I saw ᵃgods¹ ascending out of the earth.

14 And he said unto her, What form *is* he of? And she said, An old man cometh up; and he *is* covered with ᵃa mantle. And Saul perceived that it *was* Samuel, and he stooped with *his* face to the ground, and bowed himself.

15 And Samuel said to Saul, Why hast thou ᵃdisquieted me, to bring me up? And Saul answered, I am ¹sore distressed; for the Philistines make war against me, and ᵇGod is departed from me, and ᶜanswereth me no more, neither by prophets, nor by dreams: therefore I have called thee, that thou mayest make known unto me what I shall do.

16 Then said Samuel, Wherefore then dost thou ask of me, seeing the LORD is departed from thee, and is become thine enemy?

17 And the LORD hath done to ¹him, ᵃas he spake by me: for the LORD hath rent the kingdom out of thine hand, and given it to thy neighbour, *even* to David:

18 ᵃBecause thou obeyedst not the voice of the LORD, nor executedst his fierce wrath upon ᵇAmalek, therefore hath the LORD done this thing unto thee this day.

19 Moreover the LORD will also deliver Israel with thee into the hand of the Philistines: and to morrow *shalt* thou and thy sons *be* with ᵃme: the LORD also shall deliver the host of Israel into the hand of the Philistines.

20 Then Saul fell straightway ¹all along on the earth, and was sore afraid, because of the words of Samuel: and there was no strength in him; for he had eaten no bread all the day, nor all the night.

21 And the woman came unto Saul, and saw that he was ¹sore troubled, and said unto him, Behold, thine handmaid hath obeyed thy voice, and I have ᵃput my life in my hand, and have hearkened unto thy words which thou spakest unto me.

### Center column references

27:10 ᵃ 1 Chr. 2:9, 25 ᵇ Judg. 1:16
27:11 ¹ *this was his behaviour*
28:1 ᵃ 1 Sam. 29:1, 2
28:2 ¹ *one of my chief guardians*
28:3 ᵃ 1 Sam. 25:1 ᵇ 1 Sam. 1:19 ᶜ Ex. 22:18; Lev. 19:31; 20:27; Deut. 18:10, 11; 1 Sam. 15:23; 28:9 ¹ *the mediums and the spiritists*
28:4 ᵃ Josh. 19:18; 1 Sam. 28:4; 1 Kin. 1:3; 2 Kin. 4:8 ᵇ 1 Sam. 31:1 ¹ *encamped*
28:5 ᵃ Job 18:11; [Is. 57:20]
28:6 ᵃ 1 Sam. 14:37; Prov. 1:28; Lam. 2:9 ᵇ Num. 12:6; Joel 2:28 ᶜ Ex. 28:30; Num. 27:21; Deut. 33:8
28:7 ᵃ 1 Chr. 10:13 ¹ *is a medium*
28:8 ᵃ Deut. 18:10, 11; 1 Chr. 10:13; Is. 8:19 ¹ *please conduct a seance for me,* ² *bring up for me*
28:9 ᵃ 1 Sam. 28:3
28:13 ᵃ Ex. 22:28; Ps. 138:1 ¹ *a spirit*
28:14 ᵃ 1 Sam. 15:27; 2 Kin. 2:8, 13
28:15 ᵃ Is. 14:9 ᵇ 1 Sam. 16:14; 18:12 ᶜ 1 Sam. 28:6 ¹ *deeply*
28:17 ᵃ 1 Sam. 15:28 ¹ *David*
28:18 ᵃ 1 Sam. 13:9–13; 15:1–26; 1 Kin. 20:42; 1 Chr. 10:13; Jer. 48:10 ᵇ 1 Sam. 15:3–9
28:19 ᵃ 1 Sam. 31:1–6; Job 3:17–19
28:20 ¹ *full length on the ground*
28:21 ᵃ Judg. 12:3; 1 Sam. 19:5; Job 13:14 ¹ *severely*

22 Now therefore, I pray thee, hearken thou also unto the voice of thine handmaid, and let me set a morsel of bread before thee; and eat, that thou mayest have strength, when thou goest on thy way.

23 But he refused, and said, I will not eat. But his servants, together with the woman, 'compelled him; and he hearkened unto their voice. So he arose from the earth, and sat upon the bed.

24 And the woman had a fat calf in the house; and she 'hasted, and killed it, and took flour, and kneaded *it*, and did bake unleavened bread thereof:

25 And she brought *it* before Saul, and before his servants; and they did eat. Then they rose up, and went away that night.

## CHAPTER 29

Now ªthe Philistines gathered together all their armies ᵇto Aphek: and the Israelites 'pitched by a fountain which *is* in Jezreel.

2 And the ªlords of the Philistines passed on by hundreds, and by thousands: but ᵇDavid and his men passed on in the 'rereward with Achish.

3 Then said the princes of the Philistines, What *do* these Hebrews *here?* And Achish said unto the princes of the Philistines, *Is* not this David, the servant of Saul the king of Israel, which hath been with me ªthese days, or these years, and I have ᵇfound no fault in him since he 'fell *unto me* unto this day?

4 And the princes of the Philistines were wroth with him; and the princes of the Philistines said unto him, ªMake this fellow return, that he may go again to his place which thou hast appointed him, and let him not go down with us to ᵇbattle, lest ᶜin the battle he be an adversary to us: for 'wherewith should he reconcile himself unto his master? *should it* not *be* with the heads of these ᵈmen?

5 *Is* not this David, ªof whom they sang one to another in dances, saying, ᵇSaul slew his thousands, and David his ten thousands?

6 Then Achish called David, and said unto him, Surely, *as* the LORD liveth, thou hast been upright, and ªthy going out and thy coming in with me in the 'host *is* good in my sight: for ᵇI have not found evil in thee since the day of thy coming unto me unto this day: nevertheless the lords favour thee not.

7 Wherefore now return, and go in peace, that thou displease not the lords of the Philistines.

8 And David said unto Achish, But what have I done? and what hast thou found in thy servant so long as

I have been with thee unto this day, that I may not go fight against the enemies of my lord the king?

9 And Achish answered and said to David, I know that thou *art* good in my sight, ªas an angel of God: notwithstanding ᵇthe princes of the Philistines have said, He shall not go up with us to the battle.

10 Wherefore now rise up early in the morning with thy master's servants ªthat are come with thee: and as soon as ye be up early in the morning, and have light, depart.

11 So David and his men rose up early to depart in the morning, to return into the land of the Philistines. ªAnd the Philistines went up to Jezreel.

## CHAPTER 30

AND it came to pass, when David and his men were come to ªZiklag on the third day, that the ᵇAmalekites had invaded the south, and Ziklag, and smitten Ziklag, and burned it with fire;

2 And had taken the ªwomen captives, that *were* therein: they slew not any, either great or small, but carried *them* away, and went on their way.

3 So David and his men came to the city, and, behold, *it was* burned with fire; and their wives, and their sons, and their daughters, were taken captives.

4 Then David and the people that *were* with him lifted up their voice and wept, until they had no more power to weep.

5 And David's two ªwives were taken captives, Ahinoam the Jezreelitess, and Abigail the wife of Nabal the Carmelite.

6 And David was greatly distressed; for ªthe people spake of stoning him, because the soul of all the people was 'grieved, every man for his sons and for his daughters: ᵇbut David encouraged himself in the LORD his God.

7 ªAnd David said to Abiathar the priest, Ahimelech's son, I pray thee, bring me hither the ephod. And ᵇAbiathar brought thither the ephod to David.

8 ªAnd David enquired at the LORD, saying, Shall I pursue after this troop? shall I overtake them? And he answered him, Pursue: for thou shalt surely overtake *them*, and without fail recover *all*.

9 So David went, he and the six hundred men that *were* with him, and came to the brook Besor, where those that were left behind stayed.

10 But David pursued, he and four hundred men: ªfor two hundred abode behind, which were so faint that they could not go over the brook Besor.

### Center column references

28:23 ¹ *urged*
28:24 ¹ *hastened*
29:1 ª 1 Sam. 28:1
ᵇ Josh. 12:18;
19:30; 1 Sam. 4:1;
1 Kin. 20:30 ¹ *encamped*
29:2 ª 1 Sam. 6:4;
7:7 ᵇ 1 Sam. 28:1,
2 ¹ *rear*
29:3 ª 1 Sam. 27:7
ᵇ 1 Sam. 27:1–6;
1 Chr. 12:19, 20;
Dan. 6:5 ¹ *defected to me*
29:4 ª 1 Sam.
27:6 ᵇ 1 Sam.
14:21 ᶜ 1 Sam.
29:9 ᵈ 1 Chr. 12:19,
20 ¹ *with what could he*
29:5 ª 1 Sam. 21:11
ᵇ 1 Sam. 18:7
29:6 ª 2 Sam.
3:25; 2 Kin. 19:27
ᵇ 1 Sam. 29:3
¹ *army*

29:9 ª 2 Sam.
14:17, 20; 19:27
ᵇ 1 Sam. 29:4
29:10 ª 1 Chr.
12:19, 22
29:11 ª 2 Sam. 4:4
30:1 ª 1 Sam. 27:6
ᵇ 1 Sam. 15:7; 27:8
30:2 ª 1 Sam.
27:2, 3
30:5 ª 1 Sam.
25:42, 43
30:6 ª Ex. 17:4;
John 8:59
ᵇ 1 Sam. 23:16; Is.
25:4; Hab. 3:17–19
¹ *Lit. bitter*
30:7 ª 1 Sam.
23:2–9 ᵇ 1 Sam.
23:6
30:8 ª 1 Sam. 23:2,
4; Ps. 50:15; 91:15
30:10 ª 1 Sam.
30:9, 21

11 And they found an Egyptian in the field, and brought him to David, and gave him bread, and he did eat; and they made him drink water;

12 And they gave him a piece of a a cake of figs, and two clusters of raisins: and b when he had eaten, his [1]spirit came again to him: for he had eaten no bread, nor drunk *any* water, three days and three nights.

13 And David said unto him, To whom *belongest* thou? and whence *art* thou? And he said, I *am* a young man of Egypt, servant to an Amalekite; and my master left me, because three days [1]agone I fell sick.

14 We made an invasion *upon* the south of a the Cherethites, and upon *the coast* which *belongeth* to Judah, and upon the south b of Caleb; and we burned Ziklag with fire.

15 And David said to him, Canst thou bring me down to this company? And he said, Swear unto me by God, that thou wilt neither kill me, nor deliver me into the hands of my a master, and I will bring thee down to this company.

16 And when he had brought him down, behold, *they were* spread abroad upon all the earth, a eating and drinking, and dancing, because of all the great spoil that they had taken out of the land of the Philistines, and out of the land of Judah.

17 And David smote them from the twilight even unto the evening of the next day: and there escaped not a man of them, save four hundred young men, which rode upon camels, and fled.

18 And David recovered all that the Amalekites had carried away: and David rescued his two wives.

19 And there was nothing lacking to them, neither small nor great, neither sons nor daughters, neither spoil, nor any *thing* that they had taken to them: a David recovered all.

20 And David took all the flocks and the herds, *which* they drave before those *other* cattle, and said, This *is* David's spoil.

21 And David came to the a two hundred men, which were so [1]faint that they could not follow David, whom they had made also to abide at the brook Besor: and they went forth to meet David, and to meet the people that *were* with him: and when David came near to the people, he [2]saluted them.

22 Then answered all the wicked men and [1]*men* a of Belial, of those that went with David, and said, Because they went not with us, we will not give them *ought* of the spoil that we have recovered, save to every man his wife and his children, that they may lead *them* away, and depart.

23 Then said David, Ye shall not do so, my brethren, with that which the LORD hath given us, who hath preserved us, and delivered the company that came against us into our hand.

24 For who will [1]hearken unto you in this matter? but a as his part *is* that goeth down to the battle, so *shall* his part *be* that [2]tarrieth by the stuff: they shall [3]part alike.

25 And it was *so* from that day forward, that he made it a statute and an ordinance for Israel unto this day.

26 And when David came to Ziklag, he sent of the [1]spoil unto the elders of Judah, *even* to his friends, saying, Behold a present for you of the spoil of the enemies of the LORD;

27 To *them* which *were* in Beth-el, and to *them* which *were* in a south Ramoth, and to *them* which *were* in b Jattir,

28 And to *them* which *were* in a Aroer, and to *them* which *were* in b Siphmoth, and to *them* which *were* in c Eshtemoa,

29 And to *them* which *were* in Rachal, and to *them* which *were* in the cities of a the Jerahmeelites, and to *them* which *were* in the cities of the b Kenites,

30 And to *them* which *were* in a Hormah, and to *them* which *were* in [1]Chor-ashan, and to *them* which *were* in Athach,

31 And to *them* which *were* in a Hebron, and to all the places where David himself and his men were [1]wont to b haunt.

## CHAPTER 31

Now a the Philistines fought against Israel: and the men of Israel fled from before the Philistines, and fell down slain in mount b Gilboa.

2 And the Philistines followed hard upon Saul and upon his sons; and the Philistines slew a Jonathan, and Abinadab, and Melchi-shua, Saul's sons.

3 And a the battle [1]went sore against Saul, and the archers [2]hit him; and he was sore wounded of the archers.

4 a Then said Saul unto his armourbearer, Draw thy sword, and thrust me through therewith; lest b these uncircumcised come and thrust me through, and [1]abuse me. But his armourbearer would not; c for he was sore afraid. Therefore Saul took a sword, and d fell upon it.

5 And when his armourbearer saw that Saul was dead, he fell likewise upon his sword, and died with him.

6 So Saul died, and his three sons, and his armourbearer, and all his men, that same day together.

7 And when the men of Israel that *were* on the other side of the valley,

### Center column notes

30:12 a 1 Sam. 25:18; 1 Kin. 20:7
b Judg. 15:19;
1 Sam. 14:27
[1] strength came back

30:13 [1] ago

30:14 a 2 Sam. 8:18; 1 Kin. 1:38, 44; Ezek. 25:16; Zeph. 2:5 b Josh. 14:13; 15:13

30:15 a Deut. 23:15

30:16 [1] 1 Thess. 5:3

30:19 a 1 Sam. 30:8

30:21 a 1 Sam. 30:10 [1] weary
[2] greeted them

30:22 a Deut. 13:13; Judg. 19:22
[1] worthless men

30:24 a Num. 31:27; Josh. 22:8
[1] heed you [2] stays by the supplies
[3] share

30:26 [1] booty

30:27 a Josh. 19:8
b Josh. 15:48; 21:14

30:28 a Josh. 13:16
b 1 Chr. 27:27
c Josh. 15:50

30:29 a 1 Sam. 27:10 b Judg. 1:16;
1 Sam. 15:6; 27:10

30:30 a Num. 14:45; 21:3; Josh. 19:14; 15:30; 19:4; Judg. 1:17 [1] Or Borashan

30:31 a Num. 13:22; Josh. 14:13–15; 21:11–13; 2 Sam. 2:1
b 1 Sam. 23:22
[1] accustomed to rove

31:1 a 1 Chr. 10:1–12
b 1 Sam. 28:4

31:2 a 1 Sam. 14:49; 1 Chr. 8:33

31:3 a 2 Sam. 1:6
[1] became intense
[2] Lit. found

31:4 a Judg. 9:54; 1 Chr. 10:4
b Judg. 14:3;
1 Sam. 14:6; 17:26, 36 c 2 Sam. 1:14
d 2 Sam. 1:6, 10
[1] torture

and *they* that *were* on the other side Jordan, saw that the men of Israel fled, and that Saul and his sons were dead, they forsook the cities, and fled; and the Philistines came and dwelt in them.

8 And it came to pass on the morrow, when the Philistines came to strip the slain, that they found Saul and his three sons fallen in mount Gilboa.

9 And they cut off his head, and stripped off his armour, and sent into the land of the Philistines round about, to ªpublish *it in* the house of their idols, and among the people.

31:9 ª Judg. 16:23,
24; 2 Sam. 1:20
31:10 ª 1 Sam.
21:9 ᵇ Judg.
2:13; 1 Sam. 7:3
ᶜ 2 Sam. 21:12
ᵈ Judg. 1:27
¹ *Beth-shean,*
Josh. 17:11 and
elsewhere
31:11 ª 1 Sam.
11:1–13
31:12 ª 2 Sam.
2:4–7 ᵇ 2 Chr.
16:14
31:13 ª 2 Sam. 2:4,
5; 21:12–14 ᵇ Gen.
50:10

10 ªAnd they put his armour in the house of ᵇAshtaroth: and ᶜthey fastened his body to the wall of ᵈBeth-shan.¹

11 ªAnd when the inhabitants of Jabesh-gilead heard of that which the Philistines had done to Saul;

12 ªAll the valiant men arose, and went all night, and took the body of Saul and the bodies of his sons from the wall of Beth-shan, and came to Jabesh, and ᵇburnt them there.

13 And they took their bones, and ªburied *them* under a tree at Jabesh, ᵇand fasted seven days.

# THE SECOND BOOK OF
# SAMUEL

The Book of Second Samuel records the highlights of David's reign, first over the territory of Judah, and finally over the entire nation of Israel. It traces the ascension of David to the throne, his climactic sins of adultery and murder, and the shattering consequences of those sins upon his family and the nation.

See First Samuel for details on the titles of the books of Samuel. The Hebrew title for both books (originally one) is "Samuel." The Greek title for Second Samuel is *Basileion Beta*, "Second Kingdoms." The Latin title is *Liber II Samuelis*, the "Second Book of Samuel," or simply "Second Samuel."

## CHAPTER 1

**N**ow it came to pass after the ᵃdeath of Saul, when David was returned from ᵇthe slaughter of the Amalekites, and David had abode two days in Ziklag;

2 It came even to pass on the third day, that, behold, ᵃa man came out of the camp from Saul ᵇwith his clothes ¹rent, and earth upon his head: and *so* it was, when he came to David, that he ᶜfell to the earth, and ²did obeisance.

3 And David said unto him, From whence comest thou? And he said unto him, Out of the camp of Israel am I escaped.

4 And David said unto him, ᵃHow went the matter? I pray thee, tell me. And he answered, That the people are fled from the battle, and many of the people also are fallen and dead; and Saul and ᵇJonathan his son are dead also.

5 And David said unto the young man that told him, How knowest thou that Saul and Jonathan his son be dead?

6 And the young man that told him said, As I ¹happened by chance upon ᵃmount Gilboa, behold, ᵇSaul leaned upon his spear; and, lo, the chariots and horsemen followed hard after him.

7 And when he looked behind him, he saw me, and called unto me. And I answered, Here *am* I.

8 And he said unto me, Who *art* thou? And I answered him, I *am* an Amalekite.

9 He said unto me again, ¹Stand, I pray thee, upon me, and slay me: for ²anguish is come upon me, because my life *is* yet whole in me.

10 So I stood upon him, and ᵃslew him, because I was sure that he could not live after that he was fallen: and I took the crown that *was* upon his head, and the bracelet that *was* on his arm, and have brought them hither unto my lord.

11 Then David took hold on his clothes, and ᵃrent¹ them; and likewise all the men that *were* with him:

12 And they ᵃmourned, and wept, and ᵇfasted until even, for Saul, and for Jonathan his son, and for the ᶜpeople of the LORD, and for the house of Israel; because they were fallen by the sword.

13 And David said unto the young man that told him, Whence *art* thou? And he answered, I *am* the son of a stranger, an Amalekite.

14 And David said unto him, ¹How ᵃwast thou not ᵇafraid to ᶜstretch forth thine hand to destroy the LORD's anointed?

15 And ᵃDavid called one of the young men, and said, Go near, *and* fall upon him. And he ¹smote him that he died.

16 And David said unto him, ᵃThy blood *be* upon thy head; for ᵇthy¹ mouth hath testified against thee, saying, I have slain the LORD's anointed.

17 And David lamented with this lamentation over Saul and over Jonathan his son:

18 (ᵃAlso he bade them teach the children of Judah *the use of* the bow: behold, *it is* written ᵇin the book of ¹Jasher.)

19 The beauty of Israel is slain upon thy high places: ᵃhow are the mighty fallen!

20 ᵃTell *it* not in Gath, ¹publish *it* not in the streets of ᵇAskelon; lest ᶜthe daughters of the Philistines rejoice, lest the daughters of ᵈthe uncircumcised triumph.

21 Ye ᵃmountains of Gilboa, ᵇ*let there be* no dew, neither *let there be* rain, upon you, nor fields of offerings: for there the shield of the mighty is ¹vilely cast away, the shield of Saul, *as though he had* not *been* ᶜanointed with oil.

22 From the blood of the slain, from the fat of the mighty, ᵃthe bow of Jonathan turned not back, and the sword of Saul returned not empty.

### Cross-references

1:1 ᵃ 1 Sam. 31:6
ᵇ 1 Sam. 30:1, 17, 26
1:2 ᵃ 2 Sam. 4:10
ᵇ 1 Sam. 4:12
ᶜ 1 Sam. 25:23
¹ *torn* ² *prostrated himself*
1:4 ᵃ 1 Sam. 4:16; 31:3 ᵇ 1 Sam. 31:2
1:6 ᵃ 1 Sam. 31:1 ᵇ 1 Sam. 31:2–4 ¹ *happened to be*
1:9 ¹ *Please stand over me and kill me* ² *agony*
1:10 ᵃ Judg. 9:54; 2 Kin. 11:12

1:11 ᵃ 2 Sam. 3:31; 13:31 ¹ *tore*
1:12 ᵃ 2 Sam. 3:31 ᵇ 1 Sam. 31:13 ᶜ 2 Sam. 6:21
1:14 ᵃ Num. 12:8 ᵇ 1 Sam. 31:4 ᶜ 1 Sam. 24:6; 26:9 ¹ *Why were you not*
1:15 ᵃ 2 Sam. 4:10, 12 ¹ *struck him so that*
1:16 ᵃ 1 Sam. 26:9; 2 Sam. 3:28; 1 Kin. 2:32–37 ᵇ 2 Sam. 1:10; Luke 19:22 ¹ *your own*
1:18 ᵃ 1 Sam. 31:3 ᵇ Josh. 10:13 ¹ *Lit. the upright*
1:19 ᵃ 2 Sam. 1:27
1:20 ᵃ 1 Sam. 27:2; 31:8–13; Mic. 1:10 ᵇ 1 Sam. 6:17; Jer. 25:20 ᶜ Ex. 15:20; Judg. 11:34; 1 Sam. 18:6 ᵈ 1 Sam. 31:4 ¹ *proclaim*
1:21 ᵃ 1 Sam. 31:1 ᵇ Ezek. 31:15 ᶜ 1 Sam. 10:1 ¹ *Lit. defiled*
1:22 ᵃ Deut. 32:42; 1 Sam. 18:4

23 Saul and Jonathan *were* lovely and pleasant in their lives, and in their ªdeath they were not divided: they were swifter than eagles, they were ᵇstronger than lions.

24 Ye daughters of Israel, weep over Saul, who clothed you in scarlet, with *other* delights, who put on ornaments of gold upon your apparel.

25 How are the mighty fallen in the midst of the battle! O Jonathan, *thou wast* slain in thine high places.

26 I am distressed for thee, my brother Jonathan: very pleasant hast thou been unto me: ªthy love to me was wonderful, passing the love of women.

27 ªHow are the mighty fallen, and the weapons of war perished!

### CHAPTER 2

AND it came to pass after this, that David ªenquired of the LORD, saying, Shall I go up into any of the cities of Judah? And the LORD said unto him, Go up. And David said, Whither shall I go up? And he said, Unto ᵇHebron.

2 So David went up thither, and his ªtwo wives also, Ahinoam the Jezreelitess, and Abigail Nabal's wife the Carmelite.

3 And ªhis men that *were* with him did David bring up, every man with his household: and they dwelt in the cities of Hebron.

4 ªAnd the men of Judah came, and there they ᵇanointed David king over the house of Judah. And they told David, saying, *That* ᶜthe men of Jabeshgilead *were they* that buried Saul.

5 And David sent messengers unto the men of Jabesh-gilead, and said unto them, ªBlessed *be* ye of the LORD, that ye have shewed this kindness unto your lord, *even* unto Saul, and have buried him.

6 And now ªthe LORD shew kindness and truth unto you: and I also will ¹requite you this kindness, because ye have done this thing.

7 Therefore now let your hands be strengthened, and be ye valiant: for your master Saul is dead, and also the house of Judah have anointed me king over them.

8 But ªAbner the son of Ner, captain of Saul's host, took ¹Ish-bosheth the son of Saul, and brought him over to ᵇMahanaim;

9 And made him king over ªGilead, and over the ᵇAshurites, and over ᶜJezreel, and over Ephraim, and over Benjamin, and over all Israel.

10 Ish-bosheth Saul's son *was* forty years old when he began to reign over Israel, and reigned two years. But the house of Judah followed David.

11 And ªthe ¹time that David was king in Hebron over the house of Judah was seven years and six months.

12 And Abner the son of Ner, and the servants of Ish-bosheth the son of Saul, went out from Mahanaim to ªGibeon.

13 And ªJoab the son of Zeruiah, and the servants of David, went out, and met together by ᵇthe pool of Gibeon: and they sat down, the one on the one side of the pool, and the other on the other side of the pool.

14 And Abner said to Joab, Let the young men now arise, and ¹play before us. And Joab said, Let them arise.

15 Then there arose and went over by number twelve of Benjamin, which *pertained* to Ish-bosheth the son of Saul, and twelve of the servants of David.

16 And they caught every one his fellow by the head, and *thrust* his sword in his fellow's side; so they fell down together: wherefore that place was called ¹Helkath-hazzurim, which *is* in Gibeon.

17 And there was a very ¹sore battle that day; and Abner was beaten, and the men of Israel, before the servants of David.

18 And there were ªthree sons of Zeruiah there, Joab, and Abishai, and Asahel: and Asahel *was* ᵇas light of foot ᶜas a wild ¹roe.

19 And Asahel pursued after Abner; and in going he turned not to the right hand nor to the left from following Abner.

20 Then Abner looked behind him, and said, *Art* thou Asahel? And he answered, I *am.*

21 And Abner said to him, Turn thee aside to thy right hand or to thy left, and lay thee hold on one of the young men, and take thee his armour. But Asahel would not turn aside from following of him.

22 And Abner said again to Asahel, Turn thee aside from following me: wherefore should I ¹smite thee to the ground? how then should I hold up my face to Joab thy brother?

23 Howbeit he refused to turn aside: wherefore Abner with the hinder end of the spear smote him ªunder the fifth *rib*, that the spear came out behind him; and he fell down there, and died in the same place: and it came to pass, *that* as many as came to the place where Asahel fell down and died stood ᵇstill.

24 Joab also and Abishai pursued after Abner: and the sun went down when they were come to the hill of Ammah, that *lieth* before Giah by the way of the wilderness of Gibeon.

25 And the children of Benjamin gathered themselves together after

**Center column cross-references:**

1:23 ª 1 Sam. 31:2–4
ᵇ Judg. 14:18
1:26 ª 1 Sam. 18:1–4; 19:2; 20:17
1:27 ª 2 Sam. 1:19, 25
2:1 ª Judg. 1:1; 1 Sam. 23:2, 4, 9; 30:7, 8 ᵇ 1 Sam. 30:31; 2 Sam. 2:11; 5:1–3; 1 Kin. 2:11
2:2 ª 1 Sam. 25:42, 43; 30:5
2:3 ª 1 Sam. 27:2, 3; 30:1; 1 Chr. 12:1
2:4 ª 1 Sam. 30:26; 2 Sam. 2:11; 5:5; 19:14, 41–43 ᵇ 1 Sam. 16:13; 2 Sam. 5:3
ᶜ 1 Sam. 31:11–13
2:5 ª Ruth 2:20; 3:10
2:6 ª Ex. 34:6; 2 Tim. 1:16, 18
¹ repay
2:8 ª 1 Sam. 14:50; 2 Sam. 3:6 ᵇ Gen. 32:2; Josh. 21:38; 2 Sam. 17:24
¹ *Esh-baal,* 1 Chr. 8:33; 9:39
2:9 ª Josh. 22:9
ᵇ Judg. 1:32
ᶜ 1 Sam. 29:1
2:11 ª 2 Sam. 5:5; 1 Kin. 2:11 ¹ Lit. *number of days*
2:12 ª Josh. 10:2–12; 18:25
2:13 ª 1 Sam. 26:6; 2 Sam. 8:16; 1 Chr. 2:16; 11:6 ᵇ Jer. 41:12
2:14 ¹ *compete*
2:16 ¹ Lit. *The Field of Sharp Swords*
2:17 ¹ *fierce*
2:18 ª 1 Chr. 2:16 ᵇ 1 Chr. 12:8; Hab. 3:19 ᶜ Ps. 18:33
¹ *gazelle*
2:22 ¹ *strike you*
2:23 ª 2 Sam. 3:27; 4:6; 20:10
ᵇ 2 Sam. 20:12

Abner, and became one [1]troop, and stood on the top of an hill.

26 Then Abner called to Joab, and said, Shall the sword devour for ever? knowest thou not that it will be bitterness in the latter end? how long shall it be then, [1]ere thou bid the people return from [2]following their brethren?

27 And Joab said, *As* God liveth, [1]unless [a]thou hadst spoken, surely then in the morning the people [2]had gone up every one from following his brother.

28 So Joab blew a trumpet, and all the people stood still, and pursued after Israel no more, neither fought they any more.

29 And Abner and his men walked all that night through the plain, and passed over Jordan, and went through all Bithron, and they came to Mahanaim.

30 And Joab returned from following Abner: and when he had gathered all the people together, there lacked of David's servants nineteen men and Asahel.

31 But the servants of David had [1]smitten of Benjamin, and of Abner's men, *so that* three hundred and threescore men died.

32 And they took up Asahel, and buried him in the sepulchre of his father, which *was in* [a]Beth-lehem. And Joab and his men went all night, and they came to Hebron at break of day.

### CHAPTER 3

Now there was long [a]war between the house of Saul and the house of David: but David [1]waxed stronger and stronger, and the house of Saul waxed weaker and weaker.

2 And [a]unto David were sons born in Hebron: and his firstborn was Amnon, [b]of Ahinoam the Jezreelitess;

3 And his second, [1]Chileab, of Abigail the wife of Nabal the Carmelite; and the third, [a]Absalom the son of Maacah the daughter of Talmai king [b]of Geshur;

4 And the fourth, [a]Adonijah the son of Haggith; and the fifth, Shephatiah the son of Abital;

5 And the sixth, Ithream, by Eglah David's wife. These were born to David in Hebron.

6 And it came to pass, while there was war between the house of Saul and the house of David, that Abner [1]made himself strong for the house of Saul.

7 And Saul had a concubine, whose name *was* [a]Rizpah, the daughter of Aiah: and *Ish-bosheth* said to Abner, Wherefore hast thou [b]gone in unto my father's concubine?

8 Then was Abner very [1]wroth for

the words of Ish-bosheth, and said, *Am* I [a]a dog's head, [2]which against Judah [3]do shew kindness this day unto the house of Saul thy father, to his brethren, and to his friends, and have not delivered thee into the hand of David, [4]that thou chargest me to day with a fault concerning this woman?

9 [a]So do God to Abner, and more also, except, [b]as the LORD hath sworn to David, even so I do to him;

10 To [1]translate the kingdom from the [2]house of Saul, and to set up the throne of David over Israel and over Judah, [a]from Dan even to Beer-sheba.

11 And he could not answer Abner a word again, because he feared him.

12 And Abner sent messengers to David on his behalf, saying, Whose *is* the land? saying *also,* Make thy [1]league with me, and, behold, my hand *shall be* with thee, to bring about all Israel unto thee.

13 And [1]he said, Well; I will make a league with thee: but one thing I require of thee, that is, [a]Thou shalt not see my face, except thou first bring [b]Michal Saul's daughter, when thou comest to see my face.

14 And David sent messengers to [a]Ish-bosheth Saul's son, saying, Deliver *me* my wife Michal, which I espoused to me [b]for an hundred foreskins of the Philistines.

15 And Ish-bosheth sent, and took her from *her* husband, *even* from [1]Phaltiel the son of Laish.

16 And her husband went with her [1]along weeping behind her to [a]Bahurim. Then said Abner unto him, Go, return. And he returned.

17 And Abner had communication with the elders of Israel, saying, Ye sought for David in times past *to be* king over you:

18 Now then do *it:* [a]for the LORD hath spoken of David, saying, By the hand of my servant David I will save my people Israel out of the hand of the Philistines, and out of the hand of all their enemies.

19 And Abner also spake [1]in the ears of [a]Benjamin: and Abner went also to speak in the ears of David in Hebron all that seemed good to Israel, and that seemed good to the whole house of Benjamin.

20 So Abner came to David to Hebron, and twenty men with him. And David made Abner and the men that *were* with him a feast.

21 And Abner said unto David, I will arise and go, and [a]will gather all Israel unto my lord the king, that they may make a league with thee, and that thou mayest [b]reign over all that thine heart desireth. And David sent Abner away; and he went in peace.

**Center column notes:**

2:25 [1] *band or unit*

2:26 [1] *until you tell the people to* [2] *pursuing*

2:27 [a] 2 Sam. 2:14 [1] *if you had not spoken* [2] *would have given up*

2:31 [1] *struck down*

2:32 [a] 1 Sam. 20:6

3:1 [a] 1 Kin. 14:30; [Ps. 46:9] [1] *grew*

3:2 [a] 1 Chr. 3:1–4 [b] 1 Sam. 25:42, 43

3:3 [a] 2 Sam. 15:1–10 [b] Josh. 13:13; 1 Sam. 27:8; 2 Sam. 13:37; 14:32; 15:8 [1] *Daniel,* 1 Chr. 3:1

3:4 [a] 1 Kin. 1:5

3:6 [1] *was strengthening his hold on the house*

3:7 [a] 2 Sam. 21:8–11 [b] 2 Sam. 16:21

3:8 [1] *angry at*

a Deut. 23:18; 1 Sam. 24:14; 2 Sam. 9:8; 16:9 [2] *that belongs to Judah* [3] *today I show loyalty to* [4] *and you charge me*

3:9 [a] Ruth 1:17; 1 Kin. 19:2 [b] 1 Sam. 15:28; 16:1, 12; 28:17; 1 Chr. 12:23

3:10 [a] Judg. 20:1; 1 Sam. 3:20; 2 Sam. 17:11; 1 Kin. 4:25 [1] *transfer* [2] *family*

3:12 [1] Lit. *covenant*

3:13 [a] Gen. 43:3 [b] 1 Sam. 18:20; 19:11; 25:44; 2 Sam. 6:16 [1] *David*

3:14 [a] 2 Sam. 2:10 [b] 1 Sam. 18:25–27

3:15 [1] *Phalti,* 1 Sam. 25:44

3:16 [1] Lit. *going and weeping* [a] 2 Sam. 16:5; 19:16

3:18 [a] 2 Sam. 3:9

3:19 [a] 1 Sam. 10:20, 21; 1 Chr. 12:29 [1] *in the hearing of*

3:21 [a] 2 Sam. 3:10, 12 [b] 1 Kin. 11:37

22 And, behold, the servants of David and Joab came from *pursuing* a troop, and brought in a great ¹spoil with them: but Abner *was* not with David in Hebron; for he had sent him away, and he was gone in peace.

23 When Joab and all the host that *was* with him were come, they told Joab, saying, Abner the son of Ner came to the king, and he hath sent him away, and he is gone in peace.

24 Then Joab came to the king, and said, What hast thou done? behold, Abner came unto thee; why *is* it *that* thou hast sent him away, and he is quite gone?

25 Thou knowest Abner the son of Ner, that he came to deceive thee, and to know ᵃthy going out and thy coming in, and to know all that thou doest.

26 And when Joab was come out from David, he sent messengers after Abner, which brought him again from the well of Sirah: but David knew *it* not.

27 And when Abner was returned to Hebron, Joab ᵃtook him aside in the gate to speak with him ¹quietly, and ²smote him there ᵇunder the fifth *rib,* that he died, for the blood of ᶜAsahel his brother.

28 And afterward when David heard *it,* he said, I and my kingdom *are* ¹guiltless before the LORD for ever from the blood of Abner the son of Ner:

29 ᵃLet it ¹rest on the head of Joab, and on all his father's house; and let there ²not fail from the ³house of Joab one ᵇthat hath ⁴an issue, or that is a leper, or that leaneth on a staff, or that falleth on the sword, or that lacketh bread.

30 So Joab and Abishai his brother slew Abner, because he had slain their brother ᵃAsahel at Gibeon in the battle.

31 And David said to Joab, and to all the people that *were* with him, ᵃRend your clothes, and ᵇgird you with sackcloth, and mourn before Abner. And king David *himself* followed the bier.

32 And they buried Abner in Hebron: and the king lifted up his voice, and wept at the grave of Abner; and all the people wept.

33 And the king lamented over Abner, and said, Died Abner as a ᵃfool dieth?

34 Thy hands *were* not bound, nor thy feet put into fetters: as a man falleth before wicked men, *so* fellest thou. And all the people wept again over him.

35 And when all the people came ᵃto cause David to eat meat while it was yet day, David sware, saying, ᵇSo

do God to me, and more also, if I taste bread, or ought else, ᶜtill the sun be down.

36 And all the people took notice *of it,* and it pleased them: as whatsoever the king did pleased all the people.

37 For all the people and all Israel understood that day that it was ¹not of the king to slay Abner the son of Ner.

38 And the king said unto his servants, Know ye not that there is a prince and a great man fallen this day in Israel?

39 And I *am* this day weak, though anointed king; and these men the sons of Zeruiah ᵃbe too ¹hard for me: ᵇthe LORD shall reward the doer of evil according to his wickedness.

## CHAPTER 4

A ND when Saul's ¹son heard that Abner was dead in Hebron, ᵃhis² hands were feeble, and all the Israelites were ᵇtroubled.

2 And Saul's son had two men *that were* captains of bands: the name of the one *was* Baanah, and the name of the other Rechab, the sons of Rimmon a Beerothite, of the children of Benjamin: (for ᵃBeeroth also was ¹reckoned to Benjamin.

3 And the Beerothites fled to ᵃGittaim, and were sojourners there until this day.)

4 And ᵃJonathan, Saul's son, had a son *that was* lame of *his* feet. He was five years old when the tidings came of Saul and Jonathan ᵇout of Jezreel, and his nurse took him up, and fled: and it came to pass, as she made haste to flee, that he fell, and became lame. And his name *was* ᶜMephibosheth.¹

5 And the sons of Rimmon the Beerothite, Rechab and Baanah, went, and came about the heat of the day to the ᵃhouse of Ish-bosheth, who lay on a bed at noon.

6 And they came thither into the midst of the house, *as though* they would ¹have fetched wheat; and they ²smote him ᵃunder the fifth *rib:* and Rechab and Baanah his brother escaped.

7 For when they came into the house, he lay on his bed in his bedchamber, and they ¹smote him, and slew him, and beheaded him, and took his head, and ²gat them away through the plain all night.

8 And they brought the head of Ish-bosheth unto David to Hebron, and said to the king, Behold the head of Ish-bosheth the son of Saul thine enemy, ᵃwhich sought thy life; and the LORD hath avenged my lord the king this day of Saul, and of his seed.

---

**3:22** ¹ *booty*

**3:25** ᵃ Deut. 28:6; 1 Sam. 29:6; Is. 37:28

**3:27** ᵃ 2 Sam. 20:9, 10; 1 Kin. 2:5 ᵇ 2 Sam. 4:6 ᶜ 2 Sam. 2:23 ¹ *privately* ² *stabbed*

**3:28** ¹ *innocent*

**3:29** ᵃ Deut. 21:6– 9; 1 Kin. 2:32, 33 ᵇ Lev. 15:2 ¹ Lit. *whirl* ² *never fail to be in* ³ *family* ⁴ *a discharge*

**3:30** ᵃ 2 Sam. 2:23

**3:31** ᵃ Josh. 7:6; 2 Sam. 1:2, 11 ᵇ Gen. 37:34

**3:33** ᵃ 2 Sam. 13:12, 13

**3:35** ᵃ 2 Sam. 12:17; Jer. 16:7, 8 ᵇ Ruth 1:17

ᶜ Judg. 20:26; 2 Sam. 1:12

**3:37** ¹ *not the king's intent*

**3:39** ᵃ 2 Sam. 19:5–7 ᵇ 1 Kin. 2:5, 6, 32–34; 2 Tim. 4:14 ¹ *harsh*

**4:1** ᵃ Ezra 4:4; Is. 13:7 ᵇ Matt. 2:3 ¹ Ish-bosheth ² *he lost heart,* lit. *his hands dropped*

**4:2** ᵃ Josh. 18:25 ¹ *considered part*

**4:3** ᵃ Neh. 11:33

**4:4** ᵃ 2 Sam. 9:3 ᵇ 1 Sam. 29:1, 11 ᶜ 2 Sam. 9:6 ¹ *Merib-baal,* 1 Chr. 8:34; 9:40

**4:5** ᵃ 2 Sam. 2:8, 9

**4:6** ᵃ 2 Sam. 2:23; 20:10 ¹ *get* ² *stabbed*

**4:7** ¹ *struck* ² *they escaped*

**4:8** ᵃ 1 Sam. 19:2, 10, 11; 23:15; 25:29

9 And David answered Rechab and Baanah his brother, the sons of Rimmon the Beerothite, and said unto them, *As* the LORD liveth, [a]who hath redeemed my soul out of all adversity,

10 When [a]one told me, saying, Behold, Saul is dead, thinking to have brought good tidings, I took hold of him, and slew him in Ziklag, who *thought* that I would have given him a reward for his tidings:

11 How much more, when wicked men have slain a righteous person in his own house upon his bed? shall I not therefore now [a]require his [1]blood of your hand, and [2]take you away from the earth?

12 And David [a]commanded his young men, and they slew them, and cut off their hands and their feet, and hanged *them* up over the pool in Hebron. But they took the head of Ish-bosheth, and buried *it* in the [b]sepulchre of Abner in Hebron.

## CHAPTER 5

THEN [a]came all the tribes of Israel to David unto Hebron, and spake, saying, Behold, [b]we *are* thy bone and thy flesh.

2 Also in time past, when Saul was king over us, [a]thou[1] wast he that leddest out and broughtest in Israel: and the LORD said to thee, [b]Thou shalt feed my people Israel, and thou shalt be a captain over Israel.

3 [a]So all the elders of Israel came to the king to Hebron; [b]and king David made a league with them in Hebron [c]before the LORD: and they anointed David king over Israel.

4 David *was* [a]thirty years old when he began to reign, [b]*and* he reigned forty years.

5 In Hebron he reigned over Judah [a]seven years and six months: and in Jerusalem he reigned thirty and three years over all Israel and Judah.

6 [a]And the king and his men went to Jerusalem unto [b]the Jebusites, the inhabitants of the land: which spake unto David, saying, [1]Except thou take away the blind and the lame, thou shalt not come in hither: thinking, David cannot come in hither.

7 Nevertheless David took the strong hold of Zion: [a]the same *is* the city of David.

8 And David said on that day, Whosoever [1]getteth up to the gutter, and smiteth the Jebusites, and the lame and the blind, *that are* hated of David's soul, [a]*he shall be chief and captain.* Wherefore they said, The blind and the lame shall not come into the house.

9 So David dwelt in the fort, and called it [a]the city of David. And David built round about from Millo and inward.

10 And David went on, and grew great, and [a]the LORD God of hosts *was* with [b]him.

11 And [a]Hiram [b]king of Tyre sent messengers to David, and cedar trees, and carpenters, and masons: and they built David an house.

12 And David [1]perceived that the LORD had established him king over Israel, and that he had [a]exalted his kingdom for his people Israel's [b]sake.

13 And [a]David took *him* more concubines and wives out of Jerusalem, after he was come from Hebron: and there were yet sons and daughters born to David.

14 And [a]these *be* the names of those that were born unto him in Jerusalem; [1]Shammuah, and Shobab, and Nathan, and [b]Solomon,

15 Ibhar also, and [1]Elishua, and Nepheg, and Japhia,

16 And Elishama, and Eliada, and Eliphalet.

17 [a]But when the Philistines heard that they had anointed David king over Israel, all the Philistines came up to seek David; and David heard *of it,* [b]and went down to the [1]hold.

18 The Philistines also came and spread themselves in [a]the valley of Rephaim.

19 And David [a]enquired of the LORD, saying, Shall I go up to the Philistines? wilt thou deliver them into mine hand? And the LORD said unto David, Go up: for I will doubtless deliver the Philistines into thine hand.

20 And David came to [a]Baal-perazim, and David smote them there, and said, The LORD hath [1]broken forth upon mine enemies before me, as the breach of waters. Therefore he called the name of that place [2]Baal-perazim.

21 And there they left their [1]images, and David and his men [a]burned[2] them.

22 [a]And the Philistines came up yet again, and spread themselves in the valley of Rephaim.

23 And when [a]David enquired of the LORD, he said, Thou shalt not go up; *but* [1]fetch a compass behind them, and come upon them over against the mulberry trees.

24 And let it be, when thou [a]hearest the sound of a going in the tops of the mulberry trees, that then thou shalt bestir thyself: for then [b]shall the LORD go out before thee, to smite the host of the Philistines.

25 And David did so, as the LORD had commanded him; and smote the Philistines from [a]Geba until thou come to [b]Gazer.

4:9 [a] Gen. 48:16; 1 Kin. 1:29; Ps. 31:7
4:10 [a] 2 Sam. 1:2–16
4:11 [a] [Gen. 9:5, 6; Ps. 9:12] [1] *bloodshed* [2] Lit. *consume you*
4:12 [a] 2 Sam. 1:15 [b] 2 Sam. 3:32
5:1 [a] 1 Chr. 11:1–3 [b] Gen. 29:14; Judg. 9:2; 2 Sam. 19:12, 13
5:2 [a] 1 Sam. 18:5, 13, 16 [b] 1 Sam. 16:1 [1] *you were the one who led Israel out and brought them in*
5:3 [a] 2 Sam. 3:17; 1 Chr. 11:3 [b] 2 Sam. 2:4; 3:21; 2 Kin. 11:17 [c] Judg. 11:11; 1 Sam. 23:18
5:4 [a] Gen. 41:46; Num. 4:3; Luke 3:23 [b] 1 Kin. 2:11; 1 Chr. 26:31; 29:27
5:5 [a] 2 Sam. 2:11; 1 Chr. 3:4; 29:27
5:6 [a] Judg. 1:21 [b] Josh. 15:63; Judg. 1:8; 19:11, 12 [1] *You will not come in here; but the blind and the lame will repel you*
5:7 [a] 2 Sam. 6:12, 16; 1 Kin. 2:10; 8:1; 9:24
5:8 [a] 1 Chr. 11:6–9 [1] *climbs up the water shaft, and defeats*
5:9 [a] 2 Sam. 5:7; 1 Kin. 9:15, 24
5:10 [a] 1 Sam. 17:45 [b] 1 Sam. 18:12, 28
5:11 [a] 1 Kin. 5:1–18 [b] 1 Chr. 14:1
5:12 [a] Num. 24:7 [b] Is. 45:4 [1] *knew*
5:13 [a] [Deut. 17:17]; 1 Chr. 3:9
5:14 [a] 1 Chr. 3:5–8 [b] 2 Sam. 12:24 [1] *Shimea,* 1 Chr. 3:5
5:15 [1] *Elishama,* 1 Chr. 3:6
5:17 [a] 1 Chr. 11:16 [b] 2 Sam. 23:14 [1] *stronghold*
5:18 [a] Gen. 14:5; Josh. 15:8; 1 Chr. 11:15; Is. 17:5
5:19 [a] 1 Sam. 23:2; 2 Sam. 2:1
5:20 [a] 1 Chr. 14:11; Is. 28:21 [1] *broken up my* [2] Lit. *Master of Breakthroughs*
5:21 [a] Deut. 7:5, 25 [1] *idols* [2] *carried them away*
5:22 [a] 1 Chr. 14:13 5:23 [a] 2 Sam. 5:19 [1] *circle around* 5:24 [a] 2 Kin. 7:6; 1 Chr. 14:15 [b] Judg. 4:14 5:25 [a] 1 Chr. 14:16 [b] Josh. 16:10

## CHAPTER 6

A GAIN, David gathered together all *the* [1]chosen *men* of Israel, thirty thousand.

2 And [a]David arose, and went with all the people that *were* with him from [1]Baale of Judah, to bring up from thence the ark of God, whose name is called by the name of the LORD of hosts [b]that dwelleth *between* the cherubims.

3 And they set the ark of God upon a new cart, and brought it out of the house of Abinadab that *was* in [a]Gibeah: and Uzzah and Ahio, the sons of Abinadab, drave the new cart.

4 And they brought it out of [a]the house of Abinadab which *was* at Gibeah, accompanying the ark of God: and Ahio went before the ark.

5 And David and all the house of Israel [a]played before the LORD on all manner of *instruments made of* fir wood, even on harps, and on psalteries, and on timbrels, and on cornets, and on cymbals.

6 And when they came to [a]Nachon's threshingfloor, Uzzah put forth [b]*his hand* to the ark of God, and took hold of it; for the oxen [1]shook *it.*

7 And the anger of the LORD was kindled against Uzzah; and God smote him there for *his* [1]error; and there he died by the ark of God.

8 And David was displeased, [1]because the LORD had made a breach upon Uzzah: and he called the name of the place [2]Perez-uzzah to this day.

9 And [a]David was afraid of the LORD that day, and said, How shall the ark of the LORD come to me?

10 So David would not remove the ark of the LORD unto him into the [a]city of David: but David carried it aside into the house of Obed-edom the [b]Gittite.

11 [a]And the ark of the LORD continued in the house of Obed-edom the Gittite three months: and the LORD [b]blessed Obed-edom, and all his household.

12 And it was told king David, saying, The LORD hath blessed the house of Obed-edom, and all that *pertaineth* unto him, because of the ark of God. [a]So David went and brought up the ark of God from the house of Obed-edom into the city of David with gladness.

13 And it was *so,* that when [a]they that bare the ark of the LORD had gone six paces, he sacrificed [b]oxen and fatlings.

14 And David [a]danced[1] before the LORD with all *his* might; and David *was* girded [b]with a linen ephod.

15 [a]So David and all the house of Israel brought up the ark of the LORD

with shouting, and with the sound of the trumpet.

16 And as the ark of the LORD came into the city of David, [a]Michal Saul's daughter looked through a window, and saw king David leaping and dancing before the LORD; and she despised him in her heart.

17 And [a]they brought in the ark of the LORD, and set it in [b]his place, in the midst of the tabernacle that David had [1]pitched for it: and David [c]offered burnt offerings and peace offerings before the LORD.

18 And as soon as David had made an end of offering burnt offerings and peace offerings, [a]he blessed the people in the name of the LORD of hosts.

19 [a]And he [1]dealt among all the people, *even* among the whole multitude of Israel, as well to the women as men, to every one a cake of bread, and a good piece *of flesh,* and a flagon *of wine.* So all the people departed every one to his house.

20 [a]Then David returned to bless his household. And Michal the daughter of Saul came out to meet David, and said, How glorious was the king of Israel to day, who [b]uncovered himself to day in the eyes of the handmaids of his servants, as one of the [c]vain[1] fellows [2]shamelessly uncovereth himself!

21 And David said unto Michal, *It was* before the LORD, [a]which chose me before thy father, and before all his house, to appoint me ruler over the [b]people of the LORD, over Israel: therefore will I play before the LORD.

22 And I will yet be more [1]vile than thus, and will be [2]base in mine own sight: and of the maidservants which thou hast spoken of, of them shall I be had in honour.

23 Therefore Michal the daughter of Saul had no child [a]unto the day of her death.

## CHAPTER 7

A ND it came to pass, [a]when the king sat in his house, and the LORD had given him rest round about from all his enemies;

2 That the king said unto Nathan the prophet, See now, I dwell in [a]an house of cedar, [b]but the ark of God dwelleth [1]within [c]curtains.

3 And Nathan said to the king, Go, do all that *is* in thine [a]heart; for the LORD *is* with thee.

4 And it came to pass that night, that the word of the LORD came unto Nathan, saying,

5 Go and tell my servant David, Thus saith the LORD, [a]Shalt thou build me an house for me to dwell in?

6 Whereas I have not dwelt in *any* house [a]since the time that I brought

### Center column cross-references

6:1 [1] *choice*
6:2 [a] 1 Chr. 13:5, 6
[b] Ex. 25:22; 1 Sam. 4:4; Ps. 80:1
[1] *Baalah (Kirjath-jearim),* Josh. 15:9; 1 Chr. 13:6
6:3 [a] 1 Sam. 26:1
6:4 [a] 1 Sam. 7:1; 1 Chr. 13:7
6:5 [a] 1 Sam. 18:6, 7
6:6 [a] 1 Chr. 13:9
[b] Num. 4:15, 19, 20 [1] *stumbled*
6:7 [1] *irreverence*
6:8 [1] *because of the LORD's outburst against* [2] Lit. *Outburst Against Uzzah*
6:9 [a] Deut. 9:19; Ps. 119:120; Luke 5:8
6:10 [a] 2 Sam. 5:7 [b] 1 Chr. 13:13; 26:4–8
6:11 [a] 1 Chr. 13:14 [b] Gen. 30:27; 39:5
6:12 [a] 1 Chr. 15:25–16:3
6:13 [a] Num. 4:15; Josh. 3:3; 1 Sam. 6:15; 2 Sam. 15:24; 1 Chr. 15:2, 15 [b] 1 Kin. 8:5
6:14 [a] Ps. 30:11; 149:3 [b] 1 Sam. 2:18, 28 [1] *whirled about*
6:15 [a] 1 Chr. 15:28
6:16 [a] 2 Sam. 3:14
6:17 [a] 1 Chr. 16:1 [b] 1 Chr. 15:1; 2 Chr. 1:4 [c] 1 Kin. 8:5, 62, 63 [1] *erected*
6:18 [a] 1 Kin. 8:14, 15, 55
6:19 [a] 1 Chr. 16:3 [1] *distributed*
6:20 [a] Ps. 30:title [b] 2 Sam. 6:14, 16 [c] Judg. 9:4 [1] *base* [2] *openly*
6:21 [a] 1 Sam. 13:14; 15:28 [b] 2 Kin. 11:17
6:22 [1] *undignified* [2] *humble*
6:23 [a] Is. 22:14
7:1 [a] 1 Chr. 17:1–27
7:2 [a] 2 Sam. 5:11 [b] Acts 7:46 [c] Ex. 26:1 [1] *inside tent curtains*
7:3 [a] 1 Kin. 8:17, 18
7:5 [a] 1 Kin. 5:3, 4; 8:19
7:6 [a] 1 Kin. 8:16

up the children of Israel out of Egypt, even to this day, but have ¹walked in ᵇa tent and in a tabernacle.

7 In all *the places* wherein I have ᵃwalked with all the children of Israel spake I a word with any of the tribes of Israel, whom I commanded ᵇto feed my people Israel, saying, Why build ye not me an house of cedar?

8 Now therefore so shalt thou say unto my servant David, Thus saith the LORD of hosts, ᵃI took thee from the ¹sheepcote, from following the sheep, to be ruler over my people, over Israel:

9 And ᵃI was with thee whithersoever thou wentest, ᵇand have ¹cut off all thine enemies out of thy sight, and have made thee a great name, like unto the name of the great *men* that *are* in the earth.

10 Moreover I will appoint a place for my people Israel, and will ᵃplant them, that they may dwell in a place of their own, and move no more; ᵇneither shall the children of wickedness afflict them any more, as beforetime,

11 And as ᵃsince the time that I commanded judges *to be* over my people Israel, and have ¹caused thee to rest from all thine enemies. Also the LORD ²telleth thee ᵇthat he will make thee an house.

12 And ᵃwhen thy days be fulfilled, and thou ᵇshalt sleep with thy fathers, ᶜI will set up thy seed after thee, which shall proceed out of thy bowels, and I will establish his kingdom.

13 ᵃHe shall build an house for my name, and I will ᵇstablish the throne of his kingdom for ever.

14 ᵃI will be his father, and he shall be ᵇmy son. If he commit iniquity, I will chasten him with the rod of men, and with the ¹stripes of the children of men:

15 But my mercy shall not depart away from him, ᵃas I took *it* from Saul, whom I put away before thee.

16 And ᵃthine house and thy kingdom shall be established for ever before thee: thy throne shall be established for ever.

17 According to all these words, and according to all this vision, so did Nathan speak unto David.

18 Then went king David in, and sat before the LORD, and he said, ᵃWho *am* I, O Lord GOD? and what *is* my house, that thou hast brought me hitherto?

19 And this was yet a small thing in thy sight, O Lord GOD; but thou hast spoken also of thy servant's house for a great while to come. ᵃAnd *is* this the manner of man, O Lord GOD?

20 And what can David say more unto thee? for thou, Lord GOD, ᵃknowest thy servant.

7:6 ᵇ Ex. 40:18, 34
¹ moved about
7:7 ᵃ Lev. 26:11, 12
ᵇ 2 Sam. 5:2
7:8 ᵃ 1 Sam. 16:11,
12 ¹ sheepfold
7:9 ᵃ 2 Sam. 5:10
ᵇ 1 Sam. 31:6
¹ destroyed
7:10 ᵃ Ps. 44:2;
80:8 ᵇ Ps. 89:22,
23
7:11 ᵃ Judg. 2:14–
16 ᵇ 2 Sam. 7:27
¹ given you rest
² declares to you
7:12 ᵃ 1 Kin. 2:1
ᵇ Deut. 31:16 ᶜ Ps.
132:11
7:13 ᵃ 1 Kin. 5:5;
8:19 ᵇ [Is. 9:7;
49:8]
7:14 ᵃ [Heb. 1:5]
ᵇ [Ps. 2:7; 89:26,
27, 30] ¹ strokes
7:15 ᵃ 1 Sam. 15:23,
28; 16:14
7:16 ᵃ 2 Sam. 7:13
7:18 ᵃ Ex. 3:11
7:19 ᵃ [Is. 55:8, 9]
7:20 ᵃ John 21:17

7:22 ᵃ Deut. 10:17
ᵇ Ex. 15:11 ᶜ Ex.
10:2 ¹ MT O Lord
GOD
7:23 ᵃ Ps. 147:20
ᵇ Deut. 9:26;
33:29 ¹ awesome
7:24 ᵃ [Deut.
26:18] ᵇ Ps. 48:14
¹ made your
people Israel your
very own
7:28 ᵃ John 17:17
7:29 ᵃ 2 Sam.
22:51
8:1 ¹ attacked
² Lit. The Bridle of
the Mother City
8:2 ᵃ Num.
24:17 ᵇ 2 Sam.
12:31 ᶜ 1 Kin. 4:21
¹ defeated
8:3 ᵃ 1 Sam. 14:47
ᵇ 2 Sam. 10:15–
19 ¹ defeated
² territory
8:4 ᵃ Josh. 11:6, 9
¹ thousand, 1 Chr.
18:4 ² hamstrung

21 For thy word's sake, and according to thine own heart, hast thou done all these great things, to make thy servant know *them.*

22 Wherefore ᵃthou art great, ¹O LORD God: for ᵇthere *is* none like thee, neither *is there any* God beside thee, according to all that we have heard with our ᶜears.

23 And ᵃwhat one nation in the earth *is* like thy people, *even* like Israel, whom God went to redeem for a people to himself, and to make him a name, and to do for you great things and ¹terrible, for thy land, before ᵇthy people, which thou redeemedst to thee from Egypt, *from* the nations and their gods?

24 For ᵃthou hast ¹confirmed to thyself thy people Israel *to be* a people unto thee for ever: ᵇand thou, LORD, art become their God.

25 And now, O LORD God, the word that thou hast spoken concerning thy servant, and concerning his house, establish *it* for ever, and do as thou hast said.

26 And let thy name be magnified for ever, saying, The LORD of hosts *is* the God over Israel: and let the house of thy servant David be established before thee.

27 For thou, O LORD of hosts, God of Israel, hast revealed to thy servant, saying, I will build thee an house: therefore hath thy servant found in his heart to pray this prayer unto thee.

28 And now, O Lord GOD, thou *art* that God, and ᵃthy words be true, and thou hast promised this goodness unto thy servant:

29 Therefore now let it please thee to bless the house of thy servant, that it may continue for ever before thee: for thou, O Lord GOD, hast spoken *it:* and with thy blessing let the house of thy servant be blessed ᵃfor ever.

## CHAPTER 8

AND after this it came to pass, that David ¹smote the Philistines, and subdued them: and David took ²Metheg-ammah out of the hand of the Philistines.

2 And ᵃhe ¹smote Moab, and measured them with a line, casting them down to the ground; even with two lines measured he to put to death, and with one full line to keep alive. And *so* the Moabites became David's ᵇservants, *and* ᶜbrought gifts.

3 David ¹smote also Hadadezer, the son of Rehob, king of ᵃZobah, as he went to recover ᵇhis ²border at the river Euphrates.

4 And David took from him a thousand *chariots,* and seven ¹hundred horsemen, and twenty thousand footmen: and David ᵃhoughed² all

the chariot *horses,* but reserved of them *for* an hundred chariots.

5 ªAnd when the Syrians of Damascus came to ¹succour Hadadezer king of Zobah, David slew of the Syrians two and twenty thousand men.

6 Then David put garrisons in Syria of Damascus: and the Syrians became servants to David, *and* brought gifts. ªAnd the LORD preserved David whithersoever he went.

7 And David took ªthe shields of gold that were on the servants of Hadadezer, and brought them to Jerusalem.

8 And from ¹Betah, and from ªBerothai,² cities of Hadadezer, king David took exceeding much brass.

9 When ¹Toi king of ªHamath heard that David had ²smitten all the host of Hadadezer,

10 Then Toi sent ¹Joram his son unto king David, to ²salute him, and to bless him, because he had fought against Hadadezer, and ³smitten him: for Hadadezer had wars with Toi. And *Joram* brought with him vessels of silver, and ⁴vessels of gold, and vessels of brass:

11 Which also king David ªdid dedicate unto the LORD, with the silver and gold that he had dedicated of all nations which he subdued;

12 Of Syria, and of Moab, and of the children of Ammon, and of the ªPhilistines, and of Amalek, and of the spoil of Hadadezer, son of Rehob, king of Zobah.

13 And David ¹gat *him* a ªname when he returned from ²smiting of the ³Syrians in ᵇthe valley of salt, ᶜ*being* eighteen thousand *men.*

14 And he put garrisons in Edom; throughout all Edom put he garrisons, and ªall they of Edom became David's servants. And the LORD preserved David whithersoever he went.

15 And David reigned over all Israel; and David executed judgment and justice unto all his people.

16 ªAnd Joab the son of Zeruiah *was* over the ¹host; and ᵇJehoshaphat the son of Ahilud *was* recorder;

17 And ªZadok the son of Ahitub, and Ahimelech the son of Abiathar, *were* the priests; and ¹Seraiah *was* the ²scribe;

18 ªAnd Benaiah the son of Jehoiada *was over* both the ᵇCherethites and the Pelethites; and David's sons were ¹chief rulers.

## CHAPTER 9

AND David said, Is there yet any that is left of the house of Saul, that I may ªshew him ¹kindness for Jonathan's ªsake?

2 And *there was* of the house of Saul a servant whose name *was* ªZiba. And

8:5 ª 1 Kin. 11:23–25 ¹ help
8:6 ª 2 Sam. 7:9; 8:14
8:7 ª 1 Kin. 10:16
8:8 ª Ezek. 47:16 ¹ Tibhath, 1 Chr. 18:8 ² Chun, 1 Chr. 18:8
8:9 ª 1 Kin. 8:65 ¹ Tou, 1 Chr. 18:9 ² defeated all the army
8:10 ¹ Hadoram, 1 Chr. 18:10 ² Lit. ask of his welfare ³ defeated ⁴ articles
8:11 ª 1 Kin. 7:51
8:12 ª 2 Sam. 5:17–25
8:13 ª 2 Sam. 7:9 ᵇ 2 Kin. 14:7 ᶜ 1 Chr. 18:12 ¹ made himself ² killing ³ Edomites, 1 Chr. 18:12
8:14 ª Gen. 27:29, 37–40
8:16 ª 2 Sam. 19:13; 20:23 ᵇ 1 Kin. 4:3 ¹ army
8:17 ª 1 Chr. 6:4–8; 24:3 ¹ Shavsha, 1 Chr. 18:16 ² secretary
8:18 ª 1 Chr. 18:17 ᵇ 1 Sam. 30:14 ¹ Lit. priests
9:1 ª 1 Sam. 18:3; 20:14–16 ¹ covenant faithfulness
9:2 ª 2 Sam. 16:1–4; 19:17, 29
9:3 ª 1 Sam. 20:14 ᵇ 2 Sam. 4:4
9:4 ª 2 Sam. 17:27–29
9:6 ª 2 Sam. 16:4; 19:24–30 ¹ Merib-baal ² prostrated himself
9:8 ª 2 Sam. 16:9
9:9 ª 2 Sam. 16:4; 19:29 ¹ belonged
9:10 ª 2 Sam. 9:7, 11, 13; 19:28 ᵇ 2 Sam. 19:17 ¹ work
9:12 ª 1 Chr. 8:34
9:13 ª 2 Sam. 9:7, 10, 11; 1 Kin. 2:7; 2 Kin. 25:29 ᵇ 2 Sam. 9:3
10:1 ª 2 Sam. 11:1; 1 Chr. 19:1
10:2 ª 2 Sam. 9:1; 1 Kin. 2:7 ᵇ 1 Sam. 11:1

when they had called him unto David, the king said unto him, *Art* thou Ziba? And he said, Thy servant *is* he.

3 And the king said, *Is* there not yet any of the house of Saul, that I may shew ªthe kindness of God unto him? And Ziba said unto the king, Jonathan hath yet a son, *which is* ᵇlame on *his* feet.

4 And the king said unto him, Where *is* he? And Ziba said unto the king, Behold, he *is* in the house of ªMachir, the son of Ammiel, in Lodebar.

5 Then king David sent, and fetched him out of the house of Machir, the son of Ammiel, from Lo-debar.

6 Now when ªMephibosheth,¹ the son of Jonathan, the son of Saul, was come unto David, he fell on his face, and ²did reverence. And David said, Mephibosheth. And he answered, Behold thy servant!

7 And David said unto him, Fear not: for I will surely shew thee kindness for Jonathan thy father's sake, and will restore thee all the land of Saul thy father; and thou shalt eat bread at my table continually.

8 And he bowed himself, and said, What *is* thy servant, that thou shouldest look upon such ªa dead dog as I *am?*

9 Then the king called to Ziba, Saul's servant, and said unto him, ªI have given unto thy master's son all that ¹pertained to Saul and to all his house.

10 Thou therefore, and thy sons, and thy servants, shall ¹till the land for him, and thou shalt bring in *the fruits,* that thy master's son may have food to eat: but Mephibosheth thy master's son ªshall eat bread alway at my table. Now Ziba had ᵇfifteen sons and twenty servants.

11 Then said Ziba unto the king, According to all that my lord the king hath commanded his servant, so shall thy servant do. As for Mephibosheth, *said the king,* he shall eat at my table, as one of the king's sons.

12 And Mephibosheth had a young son, ªwhose name *was* Micha. And all that dwelt in the house of Ziba *were* servants unto Mephibosheth.

13 So Mephibosheth dwelt in Jerusalem: ªfor he did eat continually at the king's table; and ᵇwas lame on both his feet.

## CHAPTER 10

AND it came to pass after this, that the ªking of the children of Ammon died, and Hanun his son reigned in his stead.

2 Then said David, I will shew ªkindness unto Hanun the son of ᵇNahash, as his father shewed kindness unto me. And David sent to comfort him

by the hand of his servants for his father. And David's servants came into the land of the children of Ammon.

3 And the princes of the children of Ammon said unto Hanun their lord, Thinkest thou that David doth honour thy father, that he hath sent comforters unto thee? hath not David *rather* sent his servants unto thee, to search the city, and to spy it out, and to overthrow it?

4 Wherefore Hanun took David's servants, and shaved off the one half of their beards, and cut off their garments in the middle, [a]*even* to their buttocks, and sent them away.

5 When they told *it* unto David, he sent to meet them, because the men were greatly [1]ashamed: and the king said, Tarry at Jericho until your beards be grown, and *then* return.

6 And when the children of Ammon saw that they [a]stank[1] before David, the children of Ammon sent and hired [b]the Syrians of [c]Bethrehob, and the Syrians of Zoba, twenty thousand footmen, and of king [d]Maacah a thousand men, and of [e]Ish-tob twelve thousand men.

7 And when David heard of *it,* he sent Joab, and all the host of [a]the mighty men.

8 And the children of Ammon came out, and [1]put the battle in array at the entering in of the gate: and [a]the Syrians of Zoba, and of Rehob, and Ish-tob, and Maacah, *were* by themselves in the field.

9 When Joab saw that the front of the battle was against him before and behind, he chose of all the choice *men* of Israel, and put *them* in array against the Syrians:

10 And the rest of the people he delivered into the hand of [a]Abishai his brother, that he might put *them* in array against the children of Ammon.

11 And he said, If the Syrians be too strong for me, then thou shalt help me: but if the children of Ammon be too strong for thee, then I will come and help thee.

12 [a]Be of good courage, and let us [b]play the men for our people, and for the cities of our God: and [c]the LORD do that which seemeth him good.

13 And Joab drew nigh, and the people that *were* with him, unto the battle against the Syrians: and they fled before him.

14 And when the children of Ammon saw that the Syrians were fled, then fled they also before Abishai, and entered into the city. So Joab returned from the children of Ammon, and came to [a]Jerusalem.

15 And when the Syrians saw that they [1]were smitten before Israel, they gathered themselves together.

16 And [1]Hadarezer sent, and brought out the Syrians that *were* beyond [2]the river: and they came to Helam; and [3]Shobach the captain of the host of Hadarezer *went* before them.

17 And when it was told David, he gathered all Israel together, and passed over Jordan, and came to Helam. And the Syrians set themselves in array against David, and fought with him.

18 And the Syrians fled before Israel; and David slew *the men of* seven hundred chariots of the Syrians, and forty thousand [a]horsemen, and [1]smote Shobach the captain of their host, who died there.

19 And when all the kings *that were* servants to [1]Hadarezer saw that they were smitten before Israel, they made peace with Israel, and [a]served them. So the Syrians feared to help the children of Ammon any more.

## CHAPTER 11

A ND it came to pass, [1]after the year was expired, at the [a]time when kings go forth *to battle,* that [b]David sent Joab, and his servants with him, and all Israel; and they destroyed the children of Ammon, and besieged [c]Rabbah. But David tarried still at Jerusalem.

2 And it came to pass in an eveningtide, that David arose from off his bed, [a]and walked upon the roof of the king's house: and from the roof he [b]saw a woman washing herself; and the woman *was* very beautiful to look upon.

3 And David sent and enquired after the woman. And *one* said, *Is* not this [1]Bath-sheba, the daughter of [2]Eliam, the wife [a]of Uriah the [b]Hittite?

4 And David sent messengers, and took her; and she came in unto him, and [a]he lay with her; for she was [b]purified from her uncleanness: and she returned unto her house.

5 And the woman conceived, and sent and told David, and said, I *am* with child.

6 And David sent to Joab, *saying,* Send me Uriah the Hittite. And Joab sent Uriah to David.

7 And when Uriah was come unto him, David [1]demanded *of him* how Joab did, and how the people did, and how the war prospered.

8 And David said to Uriah, Go down to thy house, and [a]wash thy feet. And Uriah departed out of the king's house, and there followed him [1]a mess *of meat* from the king.

9 But Uriah slept at the [a]door of the king's house with all the servants of his lord, and went not down to his house.

### Cross references (margin)

10:4 [a] Is. 20:4; 47:2
10:5 [1] *humiliated*
10:6 [a] Gen. 34:30; Ex. 5:21 [b] 2 Sam. 8:3, 5 [c] Judg. 18:28 [d] Deut. 3:14; Josh. 13:11, 13 [e] Judg. 11:3, 5 [1] *had made themselves repulsive*
10:7 [a] 2 Sam. 23:8
10:8 [a] 2 Sam. 10:6 [1] *put themselves in battle array*
10:10 [a] 1 Sam. 26:6; 2 Sam. 3:30
10:12 [a] Deut. 31:6; Josh. 1:6, 7, 9; Neh. 4:14 [b] 1 Sam. 4:9; 1 Cor. 16:13 [c] 1 Sam. 3:18 [1] *be strong*
10:14 [a] 2 Sam. 11:1
10:15 [1] *had been defeated*

10:16 [1] Or *Hadadezer* [2] The Euphrates [3] *Shophach,* 1 Chr. 19:16
10:18 [a] 1 Chr. 19:18 [1] *struck*
10:19 [a] 2 Sam. 8:6 [1] Or *Hadadezer*
11:1 [a] 1 Kin. 20:22–26 [b] 1 Chr. 20:1 [c] 2 Sam. 12:26; Jer. 49:2, 3; Amos 1:14 [1] *in the spring of the year*
11:2 [a] Deut. 22:8; 1 Sam. 9:25; Matt. 24:17; Acts 10:9 [b] Gen. 34:2; [Ex. 20:17]; Job 31:1; [Matt. 5:28]
11:3 [a] 2 Sam. 23:39 [b] 1 Sam. 26:6 [1] *Bath-shuah,* 1 Chr. 3:5 [2] *Ammiel,* 1 Chr. 3:5
11:4 [a] [Lev. 20:10; Deut. 22:22]; Ps. 51:title; [James 1:14, 15] [b] Lev. 15:19, 28
11:7 [1] *asked*
11:8 [a] Gen. 18:4; 19:2 [1] *a gift of food*
11:9 [a] 1 Kin. 14:27, 28

287

10 And when they had told David, saying, Uriah went not down unto his house, David said unto Uriah, Camest thou not from *thy* journey? why *then* didst thou not go down unto thine house?

11 And Uriah said unto David, ªThe ark, and Israel, and Judah, abide in tents; and ᵇmy lord Joab, and the servants of my lord, are encamped in the open fields; shall I then go into mine house, to eat and to drink, and to lie with my wife? *as* thou livest, and *as* thy soul liveth, I will not do this thing.

12 And David said to Uriah, Tarry here to day also, and to morrow I will let thee depart. So Uriah abode in Jerusalem that day, and the morrow.

13 And when David had called him, he did eat and drink before him; and he made him ªdrunk: and at even he went out to lie on his bed ᵇwith the servants of his lord, but went not down to his house.

14 And it came to pass in the morning, that David ªwrote a letter to Joab, and sent *it* by the hand of Uriah.

15 And he wrote in the letter, saying, Set ye Uriah in the forefront of the ¹hottest battle, and ²retire ye from him, that he may ªbe ³smitten, and die.

16 And it came to pass, when Joab observed the city, that he assigned Uriah unto a place where he knew that valiant men *were*.

17 And the men of the city went out, and fought with Joab: and there fell *some* of the people of the servants of David; and Uriah the Hittite died also.

18 Then Joab sent and told David all the things concerning the war;

19 And charged the messenger, saying, When thou hast made an end of telling the matters of the war unto the king,

20 And if so be that the king's wrath arise, and he say unto thee, Wherefore approached ye so ¹nigh unto the city when ye did fight? knew ye not that they would shoot from the wall?

21 Who smote ªAbimelech the son of ¹Jerubbesheth? did not a woman cast a piece of a millstone upon him from the wall, that he died in Thebez? why went ye nigh the wall? then say thou, Thy servant Uriah the Hittite is dead also.

22 So the messenger went, and came and shewed David all that Joab had sent him for.

23 And the messenger said unto David, Surely the men prevailed against us, and came out unto us into the field, and we were upon them even unto the entering of the gate.

24 And the shooters shot from off the wall upon thy servants; and *some*

of the king's servants be dead, and thy servant Uriah the Hittite is dead also.

25 Then David said unto the messenger, Thus shalt thou say unto Joab, Let not this thing ¹displease thee, for the sword devoureth one as well as another: make thy battle more strong against the city, and overthrow it: and encourage thou him.

26 And when the wife of Uriah heard that Uriah her husband was dead, she mourned for her husband.

27 And when the mourning was past, David sent and ¹fetched her to his house, and she ¹became his wife, and bare him a son. But the thing that David had done ᵇdispleased² the LORD.

## CHAPTER 12

AND the LORD sent Nathan unto David. And ªhe came unto him, and ᵇsaid unto him, There were two men in one city; the one rich, and the other poor.

2 The rich *man* had exceeding many flocks and herds:

3 But the poor *man* had nothing, save one little ewe lamb, which he had bought and nourished up: and it grew up together with him, and with his children; it did eat of his own ¹meat, and drank of his own cup, and lay in his bosom, and was unto him as a daughter.

4 And there came a traveller unto the rich man, and he ¹spared to take of his own flock and of his own herd, to dress for the wayfaring man that was come unto him; but took the poor man's lamb, and ²dressed it for the man that was come to him.

5 And David's anger was greatly kindled against the man; and he said to Nathan, *As* the LORD liveth, the man that hath done this *thing* ¹shall surely die:

6 And he shall restore the lamb ªfourfold, because he did this thing, and because he had no pity.

7 And Nathan said to David, Thou *art* the man. Thus saith the LORD God of Israel, I ªanointed thee king over Israel, and I delivered thee out of the hand of Saul;

8 And I gave thee thy master's house, and thy master's wives into thy bosom, and gave thee the house of Israel and of Judah; and if *that had been* too little, I would moreover have given unto thee ¹such and such things.

9 ªWherefore hast thou ᵇdespised the commandment of the LORD, to do evil in his sight? ᶜthou hast killed Uriah the Hittite with the sword, and hast taken his wife *to be* thy wife,

and hast slain him with the sword of the children of Ammon.

10 Now therefore ªthe sword shall never depart from thine house; because thou hast despised me, and hast taken the wife of Uriah the Hittite to be thy wife.

11 Thus saith the LORD, Behold, I will raise up ¹evil against thee out of thine own house, and I will ªtake thy wives before thine eyes, and give *them* unto thy neighbour, and he shall lie with thy wives in the sight of this sun.

12 For thou didst *it* secretly: ªbut I will do this thing before all Israel, and before the sun.

13 ªAnd David said unto Nathan, ᵇI have sinned against the LORD. And Nathan said unto David, The LORD also hath ᶜput away thy sin; thou shalt not die.

14 Howbeit, because by this deed thou hast given great occasion to the enemies of the LORD ªto blaspheme, the child also *that is* born unto thee shall surely die.

15 And Nathan departed unto his house. And the ªLORD struck the child that Uriah's wife bare unto David, and it was very sick.

16 David therefore ¹besought God for the child; and David fasted, and went in, and ªlay all night upon the earth.

17 And the elders of his house arose, *and went* to him, to raise him up from the earth: but he would not, neither did he eat bread with them.

18 And it came to pass on the seventh day, that the child died. And the servants of David feared to tell him that the child was dead: for they said, Behold, while the child was yet alive, we spake unto him, and he would not hearken unto our voice: how will he then ¹vex himself, if we tell him that the child is dead?

19 But when David saw that his servants whispered, David perceived that the child was dead: therefore David said unto his servants, Is the child dead? And they said, He is dead.

20 Then David arose from the earth, and washed, and ªanointed *himself,* and changed his apparel, and came into the house of the LORD, and ᵇworshipped: then he came to his own house; and when he ¹required, they set bread before him, and he did eat.

21 Then said his servants unto him, What thing *is* this that thou hast done? thou didst fast and weep for the child, *while it was* alive; but when the child was dead, thou didst rise and eat bread.

22 And he said, While the child was yet alive, I fasted and wept: ªfor I

said, Who can tell *whether* ¹God will be gracious to me, that the child may live?

23 But now he is dead, wherefore should I fast? can I bring him back again? I shall go ªto him, but ᵇhe shall not return to me.

24 And David comforted Bathsheba his wife, and went in unto her, and lay with her: and ªshe bare a son, and ᵇhe called his name Solomon: and the LORD loved him.

25 And he sent by the hand of Nathan the prophet; and he called his name ¹Jedidiah, because of the LORD.

26 And ªJoab fought against ᵇRabbah of the children of Ammon, and took the royal city.

27 And Joab sent messengers to David, and said, I have fought against Rabbah, and have taken the city of waters.

28 Now therefore gather the rest of the people together, and encamp against the city, and take it: lest I take the city, and it be called after my name.

29 And David gathered all the people together, and went to Rabbah, and fought against it, and took it.

30 ªAnd he took their king's crown from off his head, the weight whereof *was* a talent of gold with the precious stones: and it was *set* on David's head. And he brought forth the ¹spoil of the city in great abundance.

31 And he brought forth the people that *were* therein, and put *them* under saws, and under harrows of iron, and under axes of iron, and made them ¹pass through the brickkiln: and thus did he unto all the cities of the children of Ammon. So David and all the people returned unto Jerusalem.

## CHAPTER 13

AND it came to pass after this, ªthat Absalom the son of David had a ¹fair sister, whose name *was* ᵇTamar; and ᶜAmnon the son of David loved her.

2 And Amnon was so ¹vexed, that he fell sick for his sister Tamar; for she *was* a virgin; and Amnon ²thought it hard for him to do any thing to her.

3 But Amnon had a friend, whose name was Jonadab, ªthe son of Shimeah David's brother: and Jonadab *was* a very ¹subtil man.

4 And he said unto him, Why *art* thou, *being* the king's son, ¹lean from day to day? wilt thou not tell me? And Amnon said unto him, I love Tamar, my brother Absalom's sister.

5 And Jonadab said unto him, Lay thee down on thy bed, and ¹make thyself sick: and when thy father cometh to see thee, say unto him, I pray thee,

---

**Center column cross-references:**

12:10 ª 2 Sam. 13:28; 18:14; 1 Kin. 2:25; [Amos 7:9]
12:11 ª Deut. 28:30; 2 Sam. 16:21, 22 ¹ *adversity*
12:12 ª 2 Sam. 16:22
12:13 ª 1 Sam. 15:24 ᵇ 2 Sam. 24:10; Job 7:20; Ps. 51; Luke 18:13 ᶜ 2 Sam. 24:10; Job 7:21; [Ps. 32:1–5; Prov. 28:13; Mic. 7:18]; Zech. 3:4
12:14 ª Is. 52:5; [Ezek. 36:20, 23]; Rom. 2:24
12:15 ª 1 Sam. 25:38
12:16 ª 2 Sam. 13:31 ¹ *pleaded with*
12:18 ¹ *harm*
12:20 ª Ruth 3:3; Matt. 6:17 ᵇ Job 1:20 ¹ *requested*
12:22 ª Is. 38:1–5; Joel 2:14; Jon. 3:9
¹ MT LORD
12:23 ª Gen. 37:35 ᵇ Job 7:8–10
12:24 ª Matt. 1:6 ᵇ 1 Chr. 22:9
12:25 ¹ Lit. *Beloved of the LORD*
12:26 ª 1 Chr. 20:1 ᵇ Deut. 3:11; 2 Sam. 11:1
12:30 ª 1 Chr. 20:2 ¹ *plunder*
12:31 ¹ *cross over to*
13:1 ª 2 Sam. 3:2, 3; 1 Chr. 3:2 ᵇ 1 Chr. 3:9 ᶜ 2 Sam. 3:2 ¹ *lovely*
13:2 ¹ *distressed* ² *saw it was improper*
13:3 ª 1 Sam. 16:9 ¹ *crafty*
13:4 ¹ *becoming thinner*
13:5 ¹ *pretend to be ill*

let my sister Tamar come, and give me ²meat, and ³dress the meat in my sight, that I may see *it,* and eat *it* at her hand.

6 So Amnon lay down, and ¹made himself sick: and when the king was come to see him, Amnon said unto the king, I pray thee, let Tamar my sister come, and ªmake me a couple of cakes in my sight, that I may eat at her hand.

7 Then David sent home to Tamar, saying, Go now to thy brother Amnon's house, and ¹dress him meat.

8 So Tamar went to her brother Amnon's house; and he was laid down. And she took flour, and kneaded *it,* and made cakes in his sight, and did bake the cakes.

9 And she took a pan, and poured *them* out before him; but he refused to eat. And Amnon said, ªHave ¹out all men from me. And they went out every man from him.

10 And Amnon said unto Tamar, Bring the ¹meat into the ²chamber, that I may eat of thine hand. And Tamar took the cakes which she had made, and brought *them* into the chamber to Amnon her brother.

11 And when she had brought *them* unto him to eat, ªhe took hold of her, and said unto her, Come lie with me, my sister.

12 And she answered him, Nay, my brother, do not ¹force me; for ªno such thing ought to be done in Israel: do not thou this ᵇfolly.²

13 And I, whither shall I cause my shame to go? and as for thee, thou shalt be as one of the fools in Israel. Now therefore, I pray thee, speak unto the king; ªfor he will not withhold me from thee.

14 Howbeit he would not hearken unto her voice: but, being stronger than she, ªforced her, and lay with her.

15 Then Amnon hated her ¹exceedingly; so that the hatred wherewith he hated her *was* greater than the love wherewith he had loved her. And Amnon said unto her, Arise, be gone.

16 And she said unto him, ¹*There is* no cause: this evil in sending me away *is* greater than the other that thou didst unto me. But he would not ²hearken unto her.

17 Then he called his servant that ministered unto him, and said, Put now this *woman* out from me, and bolt the door after her.

18 And *she had* ªa garment of divers colours upon her: for with such robes were the king's daughters *that were* virgins apparelled. Then his servant brought her out, and bolted the door after her.

19 And Tamar put ªashes on her head, and ¹rent her garment of divers

colours that *was* on her, and ᵇlaid her hand on her head, and went on crying.

20 And Absalom her brother said unto her, Hath Amnon thy brother been with thee? but ¹hold now thy peace, my sister: he *is* thy brother; ²regard not this thing. So Tamar remained desolate in her brother Absalom's house.

21 But when king David heard of all these things, he was very ¹wroth.

22 And Absalom spake unto his brother Amnon ªneither good nor bad: for Absalom ᵇhated Amnon, because he had forced his sister Tamar.

23 And it came to pass after two full years, that Absalom ªhad sheepshearers in Baal-hazor, which *is* beside Ephraim: and Absalom invited all the king's sons.

24 And Absalom came to the king, and said, Behold now, thy servant hath sheepshearers; let the king, I beseech thee, and his servants go with thy servant.

25 And the king said to Absalom, Nay, my son, let us not all now go, lest we be ¹chargeable unto thee. And he ²pressed him: howbeit he would not go, but blessed him.

26 Then said Absalom, If not, I pray thee, let my brother Amnon go with us. And the king said unto him, Why should he go with thee?

27 But Absalom ¹pressed him, that he let Amnon and all the king's sons go with him.

28 Now Absalom had commanded his servants, saying, Mark ye now when Amnon's ªheart *is* merry with wine, and when I say unto you, ¹Smite Amnon; then kill him, fear not: have not I commanded you? be courageous, and be ²valiant.

29 And the servants of Absalom ªdid unto Amnon as Absalom had commanded. Then all the king's sons arose, and every man ¹gat him up upon ᵇhis mule, and fled.

30 And it came to pass, while they were in the way, that tidings came to David, saying, Absalom hath slain all the king's sons, and there is not one of them left.

31 Then the king arose, and ªtare¹ his garments, and ᵇlay on the earth; and all his servants stood by with their clothes rent.

32 And ªJonadab, the son of Shimeah David's brother, answered and said, Let not my lord suppose *that* they have slain all the young men the king's sons; for Amnon only is dead: for by the ¹appointment of Absalom this hath been determined from the day that he forced his sister Tamar.

33 Now therefore ªlet not my lord the king take the thing to his heart,

13:5 ² *food* ³ *prepare the food*

13:6 ª Gen. 18:6
¹ *pretended to be ill*

13:7 ¹ *prepare food for him*

13:9 ª Gen. 45:1
¹ *every one go out*

13:10 ¹ *food*
² *bedroom*

13:11 ª Gen. 39:12; [Deut. 27:22]; Ezek. 22:11

13:12 ª [Lev. 18:9–11; 20:17] ᵇ Gen. 34:7; Judg. 19:23; 20:6 ¹ Lit. *humble me* ² *disgraceful thing*

13:13 ª Gen. 20:12

13:14 ª Lev. 18:9; [Deut. 22:25; 27:22]; 2 Sam. 12:11

13:15 ¹ Lit. *with a very great hatred*

13:16 ¹ *No, indeed* ² *listen*

13:18 ª Gen. 37:3; Judg. 5:30; Ps. 45:13–14

13:19 ª Josh. 7:6; 2 Sam. 1:2; Job 2:12; 42:6 ¹ *tore*

ᵇ Jer. 2:37

13:20 ¹ *now keep silent* ² *do not take this thing to heart*

13:21 ¹ *angry*

13:22 ª Gen. 24:50; 31:24 ᵇ [Lev. 19:17, 18; 1 John 2:9, 11; 3:10, 12, 15]

13:23 ª Gen. 38:12, 13; 1 Sam. 25:4

13:25 ¹ *a burden to* ² *urged*

13:27 ¹ *urged*

13:28 ª Judg. 19:6, 9, 22; Ruth 3:7; 1 Sam. 25:36; Esth. 1:10 ¹ *Strike* ² Lit. *sons of valour*

13:29 ª 2 Sam. 12:10 ᵇ 2 Sam. 18:9; 1 Kin. 1:33, 38 ¹ *mounted*

13:31 ª 2 Sam. 1:11 ᵇ 2 Sam. 12:16 ¹ *tore*

13:32 ª 2 Sam. 13:3–5 ¹ *command*

13:33 ª 2 Sam. 19:19

to think that all the king's sons are dead: for Amnon only is dead.

34 [a]But Absalom fled. And the young man that kept the watch lifted up his eyes, and looked, and, behold, there came much people by the way of the hill side behind him.

35 And Jonadab said unto the king, Behold, the king's sons come: as thy servant said, so it is.

36 And it came to pass, as soon as he had [1]made an end of speaking, that, behold, the king's sons came, and lifted up their voice and wept: and the king also and all his servants wept very [2]sore.

37 But Absalom fled, and went to [a]Talmai, the son of Ammihud, king of Geshur. And *David* mourned for his son every day.

38 So Absalom fled, and went to [a]Geshur, and was there three years.

39 And *the soul* of king David longed to go forth unto Absalom: for he was [a]comforted concerning Amnon, seeing he was dead.

### CHAPTER 14

Now Joab the son of Zeruiah perceived that the king's heart *was* [a]toward[1] Absalom.

2 And Joab sent to [a]Tekoah, and fetched thence a wise woman, and said unto her, I pray thee, [1]feign thyself to be a mourner, [b]and put on now mourning apparel, and anoint not thyself with oil, but be as a woman that had a long time mourned for the dead:

3 And come to the king, and speak on this manner unto him. So Joab [a]put the words in her mouth.

4 And when the woman of Tekoah spake to the king, she [a]fell on her face to the ground, and [1]did obeisance, and said, [b]Help, O king.

5 And the king said unto her, What [1]aileth thee? And she answered, [a]I *am* indeed a widow woman, and mine husband is dead.

6 And thy handmaid had two sons, and they two [1]strove together in the field, and *there was* none to part them, but the one [2]smote the other, and slew him.

7 And, behold, the whole family is risen against thine handmaid, and they said, Deliver him that smote his brother, that we may kill him, [a]for the life of his brother whom he slew; and we will destroy the heir also: and so they shall [1]quench my coal which is left, and shall not leave to my husband *neither* name nor [2]remainder upon the earth.

8 And the king said unto the woman, Go to thine house, and I will give charge concerning thee.

9 And the woman of Tekoah said unto the king, My lord, O king, [a]the

[1]iniquity *be* on me, and on my father's house: [b]and the king and his throne *be* guiltless.

10 And the king said, Whosoever saith *ought* unto thee, bring him to me, and he shall not touch thee any more.

11 Then said she, I pray thee, let the king remember the LORD thy God, [1]that thou wouldest not suffer [a]the revengers of blood to destroy any more, lest they destroy my son. And he said, [b]As the LORD liveth, there shall not one hair of thy son fall to the earth.

12 Then the woman said, Let thine handmaid, I pray thee, speak *one* word unto my lord the king. And he said, Say on.

13 And the woman said, Wherefore then hast thou thought such a thing against [a]the people of God? for the king doth speak this thing as one which is [1]faulty, in that the king doth not fetch home again [b]his banished.

14 For we [a]must needs die, and *are* as water spilt on the ground, which cannot be gathered up again; neither doth God [b]respect[1] *any* person: yet doth he [c]devise means, that his banished be not [2]expelled from him.

15 Now therefore that I am come to speak of this thing unto my lord the king, *it is* because the people have made me afraid: and thy handmaid said, I will now speak unto the king; it may be that the king will perform the request of his handmaid.

16 For the king will hear, to deliver his handmaid out of the hand of the man *that would* destroy me and my son together out of the [a]inheritance of God.

17 Then thine handmaid said, The word of my lord the king shall now be [1]comfortable: for [a]as an angel of God, so *is* my lord the king to [b]discern good and bad: therefore the LORD thy God will be with thee.

18 Then the king answered and said unto the woman, Hide not from me, I pray thee, the thing that I shall ask thee. And the woman said, Let my lord the king now speak.

19 And the king said, *Is not* the hand of Joab with thee in all this? And the woman answered and said, *As* thy soul liveth, my lord the king, none can turn to the right hand or to the left from ought that my lord the king hath spoken: for thy servant Joab, he bade me, and [a]he put all these words in the mouth of thine handmaid:

20 To fetch about this form of speech hath thy servant Joab done this thing: and my lord *is* wise, [a]according to the wisdom of an angel of God, to know all *things* that *are* in the earth.

---

13:34 [a] 2 Sam. 13:37, 38
13:36 [1] finished [2] bitterly
13:37 [a] 2 Sam. 3:3; 1 Chr. 3:2
13:38 [a] 2 Sam. 14:23, 32; 15:8
13:39 [a] Gen. 38:12; 2 Sam. 12:19, 23
14:1 [a] 2 Sam.
13:39 [1] concerned about
14:2 [a] 2 Sam. 23:26; 2 Chr. 11:6; Amos 1:1 [b] Ruth 3:3 [1] pretend
14:3 [a] Ex. 4:15; 2 Sam. 14:19
14:4 [a] 1 Sam. 20:41; 25:23; 2 Sam. 1:2 [b] 2 Kin. 6:26, 28 [1] showed respect
14:5 [a] [Zech. 7:10] [1] troubles
14:6 [1] fought [2] struck
14:7 [a] Num. 35:19; Deut. 19:12, 13 [1] extinguish my ember [2] remnant
14:9 [a] Gen. 27:13; 43:9; 1 Sam. 25:24; Matt. 27:25

[b] 2 Sam. 3:28, 29; 1 Kin. 2:33 [1] guilt
14:11 [a] Num. 35:19, 21; [Deut. 19:4–10] [b] 1 Sam. 14:45; 1 Kin. 1:52; Matt. 10:30; Acts 27:34 [1] and do not permit the avenger of blood
14:13 [a] Judg. 20:2 [b] 2 Sam. 13:37, 38 [1] guilty
14:14 [a] Job 30:23; 34:15; [Heb. 9:27] [b] Job 34:19; Matt. 22:16; Acts 10:34; Rom. 2:11 [c] Num. 35:15 [1] take away a life [2] cast out
14:16 [a] Deut. 32:9; 1 Sam. 26:19; 2 Sam. 20:19
14:17 [a] 1 Sam. 29:9; 2 Sam. 19:27 [b] 1 Kin. 3:9 [1] comforting
14:19 [a] 2 Sam. 14:3
14:20 [a] 2 Sam. 14:17; 19:27

21 And the king said unto Joab, Behold now, I have ¹done this thing: go therefore, bring the young man Absalom again.

22 And Joab fell to the ground on his face, and bowed himself, and ¹thanked the king: and Joab said, To day thy servant knoweth that I have found grace in thy sight, my lord, O king, in that the king hath fulfilled the request of his servant.

23 So Joab arose ᵃand went to Geshur, and brought Absalom to Jerusalem.

24 And the king said, Let him turn to his own house, and let him ᵃnot see my face. So Absalom returned to his own house, and saw not the king's face.

25 But in all Israel there was none to be so much praised as Absalom for his beauty: ᵃfrom the sole of his foot even to the crown of his head there was no blemish in him.

26 And when he ¹polled his head, (for it was at every year's end that he polled *it:* because *the hair* was heavy on him, therefore he polled it:) he weighed the hair of his head at two hundred shekels after the king's weight.

27 And ᵃunto Absalom there were born three sons, and one daughter, whose name *was* Tamar: she was a woman of a fair countenance.

28 So Absalom dwelt two full years in Jerusalem, ᵃand saw not the king's face.

29 Therefore Absalom sent for Joab, to have sent him to the king; but he would not come to him: and when he sent again the second time, he would not come.

30 Therefore he said unto his servants, See, Joab's field is near mine, and he hath barley there; go and set it on fire. And Absalom's servants set the field on fire.

31 Then Joab arose, and came to Absalom unto *his* house, and said unto him, Wherefore have thy servants set my field on fire?

32 And Absalom answered Joab, Behold, I sent unto thee, saying, Come hither, that I may send thee to the king, to say, Wherefore am I come from Geshur? it *had been* good for me *to have been* there still: now therefore let me see the king's face; and ᵃif there be *any* iniquity in me, let him kill me.

33 So Joab came to the king, and told him: and when he had called for Absalom, he came to the king, and bowed himself on his face to the ground before the king: and the king ᵃkissed Absalom.

## CHAPTER 15

AND ᵃit came to pass after this, that Absalom ᵇprepared him chariots

and horses, and fifty men to run before him.

2 And Absalom rose up early, and stood beside the way of the gate: and it was so, that when any man that had a ᵃcontroversy¹ came to the king ²for judgment, then Absalom called unto him, and said, Of what city *art* thou? And he said, Thy servant *is* of one of the tribes of Israel.

3 And Absalom said unto him, See, thy ¹matters *are* good and right; but *there is* no man ²deputed of the king to hear thee.

4 Absalom said moreover, ᵃOh that I were made judge in the land, that every man which hath any suit or cause might come unto me, and I would do him justice!

5 And it was *so,* that when any man came nigh *to him* to ¹do him obeisance, he put forth his hand, and took him, and ᵃkissed him.

6 And on this manner did Absalom to all Israel that came to the king for judgment: ᵃso Absalom stole the hearts of the men of Israel.

7 And it came to pass ᵃafter ¹forty years, that Absalom said unto the king, I pray thee, let me go and pay my vow, which I have vowed unto the LORD, in ᵇHebron.

8 ᵃFor thy servant ᵇvowed a vow ᶜwhile I abode at Geshur in Syria, saying, If the LORD shall bring me again indeed to Jerusalem, then I will serve the LORD.

9 And the king said unto him, Go in peace. So he arose, and went to Hebron.

10 But Absalom sent spies throughout all the tribes of Israel, saying, As soon as ye hear the sound of the trumpet, then ye shall say, Absalom ᵃreigneth in Hebron.

11 And with Absalom went two hundred men out of Jerusalem, *that were* ᵃcalled;¹ and they ᵇwent ²in their simplicity, and they knew not any thing.

12 And Absalom sent for Ahithophel the Gilonite, ᵃDavid's counsellor, from his city, *even* from ᵇGiloh, while he offered sacrifices. And the conspiracy was strong; for the people ᶜincreased continually with Absalom.

13 And there came a messenger to David, saying, ᵃThe hearts of the men of Israel are ¹after Absalom.

14 And David said unto all his servants that *were* with him at Jerusalem, Arise, and let us ᵃflee; ¹for we shall not *else* escape from Absalom: make speed to depart, lest he overtake us suddenly, and bring ²evil upon us, and ³smite the city with the edge of the sword.

15 And the king's servants said unto the king, Behold, thy servants

### Cross references

14:21 ¹ *granted*
14:22 ¹ Lit. *blessed*
14:23 ᵃ 2 Sam. 13:37, 38
14:24 ᵃ Gen. 43:3; 2 Sam. 3:13
14:25 ᵃ Deut. 28:35; Job 2:7; Is. 1:6
14:26 ¹ *cut the hair of*
14:27 ᵃ 2 Sam. 13:1; 18:18
14:28 ᵃ 2 Sam. 14:24
14:32 ᵃ 1 Sam. 20:8; [Prov. 28:13]
14:33 ᵃ Gen. 33:4; 45:15; Luke 15:20
15:1 ᵃ 2 Sam. 12:11 ᵇ 1 Kin. 1:5

15:2 ᵃ Deut. 19:17 ¹ *lawsuit* ² *for a decision*
15:3 ¹ *case or claim* ² *deputy*
15:4 ᵃ Judg. 9:29
15:5 ᵃ 2 Sam. 14:33; 20:9 ¹ *bow down to him*
15:6 ᵃ [Rom. 16:18]
15:7 ᵃ [Deut. 23:21] ᵇ 2 Sam. 3:2, 3 ¹ LXX, Syr., and Josephus *four*
15:8 ᵃ 1 Sam. 16:2 ᵇ Gen. 28:20, 21 ᶜ 2 Sam. 13:38
15:10 ᵃ 1 Kin. 1:34; 2 Kin. 9:13
15:11 ᵃ 1 Sam. 16:3, 5 ᵇ Gen. 20:5 ¹ *invited* ² *innocently*
15:12 ᵃ 2 Sam. 16:15; 1 Chr. 27:33; Ps. 41:9; 55:12–14 ᵇ Josh. 15:51 ᶜ Ps. 3:1
15:13 ᵃ Judg. 9:3; 2 Sam. 15:6 ¹ *with*
15:14 ᵃ 2 Sam. 12:11; Ps. 3:title ¹ *or else* ² *disaster* ³ *strike*

*are ready to do* whatsoever my lord the king ¹shall appoint.

16 And ªthe king went forth, and all his household after him. And the king left ᵇten women, *which were* concubines, to keep the house.

17 And the king went forth, and all the people after him, and ¹tarried in a place that was far off.

18 And all his servants passed on ¹beside him; ªand all the Cherethites, and all the Pelethites, and all the Gittites, ᵇsix hundred men which came after him from Gath, passed on before the king.

19 Then said the king to ªIttai the Gittite, Wherefore goest thou also with us? return to thy place, and abide with the king: for thou *art a* ¹stranger, and also an exile.

20 Whereas thou camest *but* yesterday, should I this day make thee ¹go up and down with us? seeing I go ªwhither I may, return thou, and take back thy brethren: mercy and truth *be* with thee.

21 And Ittai answered the king, and said, ªAs the LORD liveth, and *as* my lord the king liveth, surely in what place my lord the king shall be, whether in death or life, even there also will thy servant be.

22 And David said to Ittai, Go and pass over. And Ittai the Gittite passed over, and all his men, and all the little ones that *were* with him.

23 And all the country wept with a loud voice, and all the people ¹passed over: the king also himself passed over the brook Kidron, and all the people passed over, toward the way of the ªwilderness.

24 And lo ªZadok also, and all the Levites *were* with him, bearing the ᵇark of the covenant of God: and they set down the ark of God; and ᶜAbiathar went up, until all the people had done passing out of the city.

25 And the king said unto Zadok, Carry back the ark of God into the city: if I shall find ¹favour in the eyes of the LORD, he ªwill bring me again, and shew me *both* it, and ᵇhis habitation:

26 But if he thus say, I have no ªdelight in thee; behold, *here am* I, ᵇlet him do to me as seemeth good unto him.

27 The king said also unto Zadok the priest, *Art not* thou a ªseer?¹ return into the city in peace, and ᵇyour two sons with you, Ahimaaz thy son, and Jonathan the son of Abiathar.

28 See, ªI will ¹tarry in the plain of the wilderness, until there come word from you to ²certify me.

29 Zadok therefore and Abiathar carried the ark of God again to Jerusalem: and they tarried there.

30 And David went up by the ascent of *mount* Olivet, and wept as he went up, and ªhad his head covered, and he went ᵇbarefoot: and all the people that *was* with him ᶜcovered every man his head, and they went up, ᵈweeping as they went up.

31 And *one* told David, saying, ªAhithophel *is* among the conspirators with Absalom. And David said, O LORD, I pray thee, ᵇturn the counsel of Ahithophel into foolishness.

32 And it came to pass, that *when* David was come to the top *of the mount,* where he worshipped God, behold, Hushai the ªArchite came to meet him ᵇwith his coat rent, and earth upon his head:

33 Unto whom David said, If thou passest on with me, then thou shalt be ªa burden unto me:

34 But if thou return to the city, and say unto Absalom, ªI will be thy servant, O king; *as* I *have been* thy father's servant hitherto, so *will* I now also *be* thy servant: then mayest thou for me defeat the counsel of Ahithophel.

35 And *hast thou* not there with thee Zadok and Abiathar the priests? therefore it shall be, *that* what thing soever thou shalt hear out of the king's house, thou shalt tell *it* to ªZadok and Abiathar the priests.

36 Behold, *they have* there ªwith them their two sons, Ahimaaz Zadok's *son,* and Jonathan Abiathar's *son;* and by them ye shall send unto me every thing that ye can hear.

37 So Hushai ªDavid's friend came into the city, ᵇand Absalom came into Jerusalem.

## CHAPTER 16

AND ªwhen David was a little past the top *of the hill,* behold, ᵇZiba the servant of Mephibosheth met him, with a couple of asses saddled, and upon them two hundred *loaves* of bread, and an hundred bunches of raisins, and an hundred of summer fruits, and a ¹bottle of wine.

2 And the king said unto Ziba, What meanest thou by these? And Ziba said, The asses *be* for the king's household to ride on; and the bread and summer fruit for the young men to eat; and the wine, ªthat such as be faint in the wilderness may drink.

3 And the king said, And where *is* thy ªmaster's son? ᵇAnd Ziba said unto the king, Behold, he abideth at Jerusalem: for he said, To day shall the house of Israel restore ¹me the kingdom of my father.

4 Then said the king to Ziba, Behold, thine *are* all that *pertained* unto Mephibosheth. And Ziba said, I humbly beseech thee *that* I may find ¹grace in thy sight, my lord, O king.

### Center column references

15:15 ¹ commands
15:16 ª Ps. 3:title
ᵇ 2 Sam. 12:11;
16:21, 22
15:17 ¹ stopped at a house
15:18 ª 2 Sam. 8:18
ᵇ 1 Sam. 23:13;
25:13; 30:1, 9 ¹ Lit. by his hand
15:19 ª 2 Sam. 18:2
¹ foreigner
15:20 ª 1 Sam. 23:13 ¹ wander
15:21 ª Ruth 1:16, 17; [Prov. 17:17]
15:23 ª 2 Sam. 15:28; 16:2
¹ crossed over
15:24 ª 2 Sam. 8:17 ᵇ Num. 4:15; 1 Sam. 4:4
ᶜ 1 Sam. 22:20
15:25 ª [Ps. 43:3] ᵇ Ex. 15:13; Jer. 25:30 ¹ grace
15:26 ª Num. 14:8; 2 Sam. 22:20; 1 Kin. 10:9; 2 Chr. 9:8; Is. 62:4
ᵇ 1 Sam. 3:18
15:27 ª 1 Sam. 9:6–9 ᵇ 2 Sam. 17:17–20
¹ prophet
15:28 ª Josh. 5:10; 2 Sam. 17:16
¹ wait ² inform

15:30 ª 2 Sam. 19:4; Esth. 6:12; Ezek. 24:17, 23
ᵇ Is. 20:2–4 ᶜ Jer. 14:3, 4 ᵈ [Ps. 126:6]
15:31 ª Ps. 3:1, 2; 55:12 ᵇ 2 Sam. 16:23; 17:14, 23
15:32 ª Josh. 16:2 ᵇ 2 Sam. 1:2
15:33 ª 2 Sam. 19:35
15:34 ª 2 Sam. 16:19
15:35 ª 2 Sam. 17:15, 16
15:36 ª 2 Sam. 15:27
15:37 ª 2 Sam. 16:16; 1 Chr. 27:33
ᵇ 2 Sam. 16:15
16:1 ª 2 Sam. 15:30, 32 ᵇ 2 Sam. 9:2; 19:17, 29
¹ skin
16:2 ª 2 Sam. 15:23; 17:29
16:3 ª 2 Sam. 9:9, 10 ᵇ 2 Sam. 19:27
¹ to me
16:4 ¹ favour

5 And when king David came to [a]Bahurim, behold, thence came out a man of the family of the house of Saul, whose name *was* [b]Shimei, the son of Gera: he came forth, and cursed [1]still as he came.

6 And he cast stones at David, and at all the servants of king David: and all the people and all the mighty men *were* on his right hand and on his left.

7 And thus said Shimei when he cursed, Come out, come out, thou [1]bloody man, and thou [a]man[2] of Belial:

8 The LORD hath [a]returned[1] upon thee all [b]the blood of the house of Saul, in whose [2]stead thou hast reigned; and the LORD hath delivered the kingdom into the hand of Absalom thy son: and, behold, thou *art taken* in thy mischief, because thou *art* a [3]bloody man.

9 Then said Abishai the son of Zeruiah unto the king, Why should this [a]dead dog [b]curse my lord the king? let me go over, I pray thee, and take off his head.

10 And the king said, [a]What have I to do with you, ye sons of Zeruiah? so let him curse, because [b]the LORD hath said unto him, Curse David. [c]Who shall then say, Wherefore hast thou done so?

11 And David said to Abishai, and to all his servants, Behold, [a]my son, which [b]came forth of [1]my bowels, seeketh my life: how much more now *may this* Benjamite *do it?* let him alone, and let him curse; for the LORD hath bidden him.

12 It may be that the LORD will look on mine affliction, and that the LORD will [a]requite[1] me [b]good for his cursing this day.

13 And as David and his men went by the way, Shimei went along on the hill's side over against him, and cursed as he went, and threw stones at him, and [1]cast dust.

14 And the king, and all the people that *were* with him, came weary, and refreshed themselves there.

15 And [a]Absalom, and all the people the men of Israel, came to Jerusalem, and Ahithophel with him.

16 And it came to pass, when Hushai the Archite, [a]David's friend, was come unto Absalom, that [b]Hushai said unto Absalom, God save the king, [1]God save the king.

17 And Absalom said to Hushai, *Is* this thy [1]kindness to thy friend? [a]why wentest thou not with thy friend?

18 And Hushai said unto Absalom, Nay; but whom the LORD, and this people, and all the men of Israel, choose, his will I be, and with him will I abide.

19 And again, [a]whom should I serve? *should I* not *serve* in the presence of

his son? as I have served in thy father's presence, so will I be in thy presence.

20 Then said Absalom to [a]Ahithophel, Give counsel among you what we shall do.

21 And Ahithophel said unto Absalom, Go in unto thy father's [a]concubines, which he hath left to keep the house; and all Israel shall hear that thou [b]art abhorred of thy father: then shall [c]the hands of all that *are* with thee be strong.

22 So they spread Absalom a tent upon the top of the house; and Absalom went in unto his father's concubines [a]in the sight of all Israel.

23 And the counsel of Ahithophel, which he counselled in those days, *was* as if a man had enquired at the oracle of God: so *was* all the counsel of Ahithophel [a]both with David and with Absalom.

## CHAPTER 17

MOREOVER Ahithophel said unto Absalom, Let me now choose out twelve thousand men, and I will arise and pursue after David this night:

2 And I will come upon him while he *is* [a]weary and weak handed, and will make him [1]afraid: and all the people that *are* with him shall flee; and I will [b]smite[2] the king only:

3 And I will bring back all the people unto thee: [1]the man whom thou seekest *is* as if all returned: *so* all the people shall be in peace.

4 And the saying pleased Absalom well, and all the [a]elders of Israel.

5 Then said Absalom, Call now Hushai the Archite also, and let us hear likewise what he [a]saith.

6 And when Hushai was come to Absalom, Absalom spake unto him, saying, Ahithophel hath spoken after this manner: shall we do *after* his saying? if not; speak thou.

7 And Hushai said unto Absalom, The counsel that Ahithophel hath given *is* not good at this time.

8 For, said Hushai, thou knowest thy father and his men, that they *be* mighty men, and they *be* [1]chafed in their minds, as [a]a bear robbed of her whelps in the field: and thy father *is* a man of war, and will not [2]lodge with the people.

9 Behold, he *is* hid now in some pit, or in some *other* place: and it will come to pass, when some of them be overthrown at the first, that whosoever heareth it will say, There is a slaughter among the people that follow Absalom.

10 And he also *that is* valiant, whose heart *is* as the heart of a lion, shall utterly [a]melt: for all Israel knoweth that thy father *is* a mighty man, and *they* which be with him *are* valiant men.

---

16:5 [a] 2 Sam. 3:16
[b] 2 Sam. 19:21;
1 Kin. 2:8, 9, 44–
46 [1] *continuously*
16:7 [a] Deut. 13:13
[1] *bloodthirsty*
[2] *reprobate*

16:8 [a] Judg. 9:24,
56, 57; 1 Kin. 2:32,
33  [b] 2 Sam. 1:16;
3:28, 29; 4:11, 12
[1] *brought* [2] *place*
[3] *bloodthirsty*

16:9 [a] 1 Sam.
24:14; 2 Sam. 9:8
[b] Ex. 22:28

16:10 [a] 2 Sam.
3:39; 19:22; [1 Pet.
2:23] [b] 2 Kin.
18:25; [Lam. 3:38]
[c] [Rom. 9:20]

16:11 [a] 2 Sam. 12:11
[b] Gen. 15:4 [1] *my
own body*

16:12 [a] Deut. 23:5;
Neh. 13:2; Prov.
20:22 [b] Deut.
23:5; [Rom. 8:28;
Heb. 12:10, 11]
[1] *repay*

16:13 [1] *kicked up
dust,* lit. *dusted
him with dust*

16:15 [a] 2 Sam.
15:12, 37

16:16 [a] 2 Sam.
15:37 [b] 2 Sam.
15:34 [1] *Long live
the king*

16:17 [a] 2 Sam.
19:25; [Prov. 17:17]
[1] *loyalty*

16:19 [a] 2 Sam.
15:34

16:20 [a] 2 Sam.
15:12

16:21 [a] 2 Sam.
15:16; 20:3 [b] Gen.
34:30; 1 Sam.
13:4 [c] 2 Sam. 2:7;
Zech. 8:13

16:22 [a] 2 Sam.
12:11, 12

16:23 [a] 2 Sam.
15:12

17:2 [a] Deut.
25:18; 2 Sam.
16:14 [b] Zech. 13:7
[1] *tremble with
fear* [2] *strike*

17:3 [1] *When all
return except the
man whom you
seek*

17:4 [a] 2 Sam. 5:3;
19:11

17:5 [a] 2 Sam.
15:32–34

17:8 [a] Hos. 13:8
[1] *enraged* [2] *camp*

17:10 [a] Josh. 2:11

---

11 Therefore I counsel that all Israel be ¹generally gathered unto thee, ªfrom Dan even to Beer-sheba, ᵇas the sand that *is* by the sea for multitude; and that thou go to battle in thine own person.

12 So shall we come upon him in some place where he shall be found, and we will light upon him as the dew falleth on the ground: and of him and of all the men that *are* with him there shall not be left so much as one.

13 Moreover, if he ¹be gotten into a city, then shall all Israel bring ropes to that city, and we will ªdraw it into the river, until there be not one small stone found there.

14 And Absalom and all the men of Israel said, The counsel of Hushai the Archite *is* better than the counsel of Ahithophel. For ªthe LORD had ¹appointed to defeat the good counsel of Ahithophel, to the intent that the LORD might bring evil upon Absalom.

15 ªThen said Hushai unto Zadok and to Abiathar the priests, Thus and thus did Ahithophel counsel Absalom and the elders of Israel; and thus and thus have I counselled.

16 Now therefore send quickly, and tell David, saying, ¹Lodge not this night ªin the plains of the wilderness, but speedily ²pass over; lest the king be swallowed up, and all the people that *are* with him.

17 ªNow Jonathan and Ahimaaz ᵇstayed by ᶜEn-rogel; for they ¹might not be seen to come into the city: and a ²wench went and told them; and they went and told king David.

18 Nevertheless a lad saw them, and told Absalom: but they went both of them away quickly, and came to a man's house ªin Bahurim, which had a well in his court; ¹whither they went down.

19 ªAnd the woman took and spread a covering over the well's mouth, and spread ground ¹corn thereon; and the thing was not known.

20 And when Absalom's servants came to the woman to the house, they said, Where *is* Ahimaaz and Jonathan? And ªthe woman said unto them, They be gone over the brook of water. And when they had sought and could not find *them,* they returned to Jerusalem.

21 And it came to pass, after they were departed, that they came up out of the well, and went and told king David, and said unto David, ªArise, and ¹pass quickly over the water: for thus hath Ahithophel counselled against you.

22 Then David arose, and all the people that *were* with him, and they ¹passed over Jordan: by the morning light there lacked not one of them that was not gone over Jordan.

23 And when Ahithophel saw that his counsel was not followed, he saddled *his* ¹ass, and arose, and ²gat him home to ªhis house, to his city, and ³put his ᵇhousehold in order, and ᶜhanged himself, and died, and was buried in the ⁴sepulchre of his father.

24 Then David came to ªMahanaim. And Absalom passed over Jordan, he and all the men of Israel with him.

25 And Absalom made ªAmasa captain of the host instead of Joab: which Amasa *was* a man's son, whose name *was* ¹Ithra an Israelite, that went in to ᵇAbigail the daughter of Nahash, sister to Zeruiah Joab's mother.

26 So Israel and Absalom ¹pitched in the land of Gilead.

27 And it came to pass, when David was come to Mahanaim, that ªShobi the son of Nahash of Rabbah of the children of Ammon, and ᵇMachir the son of Ammiel of Lo-debar, and ᶜBarzillai the Gileadite of Rogelim,

28 Brought beds, and basons, and earthen vessels, and wheat, and barley, and flour, and parched ¹corn, and beans, and lentiles, and parched ²pulse,

29 And honey, and butter, and sheep, and cheese of ¹kine, for David, and for the people that *were* with him, to eat: for they said, The people *is* hungry, and weary, and thirsty, ªin the wilderness.

## CHAPTER 18

AND David ¹numbered the people that *were* with him, and ªset captains of thousands and captains of hundreds over them.

2 And David sent forth a third part of the people under the hand of Joab, ªand a third part under the hand of Abishai the son of Zeruiah, Joab's brother, and a third part under the hand of ᵇIttai the Gittite. And the king said unto the people, I will surely go forth with you myself also.

3 ªBut the people answered, Thou shalt not go forth: for if we flee away, they will not care ¹for us; neither if half of us die, will they care for us: but now *thou art* worth ten thousand of us: therefore now *it is* better that thou ²succour us out of the city.

4 And the king said unto them, What seemeth you best I will do. And the king stood by the gate side, and all the people came out by hundreds and by thousands.

5 And the king commanded Joab and Abishai and Ittai, saying, *Deal* gently for my sake with the young man, *even* with Absalom. ªAnd all the people heard when the king gave

---

17:11 ª Judg. 20:1; 2 Sam. 3:10
ᵇ Gen. 22:17; Josh. 11:4; 1 Kin. 20:10
¹ *fully*

17:13 ª Mic. 1:6
¹ *has withdrawn*

17:14 ª 2 Sam. 15:31, 34 ¹ *purposed*

17:15 ª 2 Sam. 15:35, 36

17:16 ª 2 Sam. 15:28 ¹ *Do not spend the night*
² *cross*

17:17 ª 2 Sam. 15:27, 36; 1 Kin. 1:42, 43 ᵇ Josh. 2:4–6 ᶜ Josh. 15:7; 18:16 ¹ *dared*
² *maidservant*

17:18 ª 2 Sam. 3:16; 16:5 ¹ *they went down into it*

17:19 ª Josh. 2:4–6 ¹ *grain*

17:20 ª Ex. 1:19; [Lev. 19:11]; Josh. 2:3–5

17:21 ª 2 Sam. 17:15, 16 ¹ *cross*

17:22 ¹ *crossed*

17:23 ª 2 Sam. 15:12 ᵇ 2 Kin. 20:1 ᶜ Matt. 27:5
¹ *donkey* ² *he went* ³ Lit. *gave charge to* ⁴ *tomb*

17:24 ª Gen. 32:2; Josh. 13:26; 2 Sam. 2:8; 19:32

17:25 ª 2 Sam. 19:13; 20:9–12; 1 Kin. 2:5, 32 ᵇ 1 Chr. 2:16 ¹ *Jether,* 1 Chr. 2:17

17:26 ¹ *encamped*

17:27 ª 1 Sam. 11:1; 2 Sam. 10:1; 12:29 ᵇ 2 Sam. 9:4 ᶜ 2 Sam. 19:31, 32; 1 Kin. 2:7

17:28 ¹ *grain* ² *seeds*

17:29 ª 2 Sam. 16:2, 14 ¹ *the herd*

18:1 ª Ex. 18:25; Num. 31:14; 1 Sam. 22:7 ¹ *organized*

18:2 ª Judg. 7:16; 1 Sam. 11:11 ᵇ 2 Sam. 15:19–22

18:3 ª 2 Sam. 21:17 ¹ *about* ² *help*

18:5 ª 2 Sam. 18:12

all the captains charge concerning Absalom.

6 So the people went out into the field against Israel: and the battle was in the [a]wood[1] of Ephraim;

7 Where the people of Israel were slain before the servants of David, and there was there a great slaughter that day of twenty thousand *men.*

8 For the battle was there scattered over the face of all the country: and the [1]wood devoured more people that day than the sword devoured.

9 And Absalom met the servants of David. And Absalom rode upon a mule, and the mule went under the thick boughs of a great oak, and [a]his head caught hold of the oak, and he was [1]taken up between the heaven and the earth; and the mule that *was* under him went away.

10 And a certain man saw *it,* and told Joab, and said, Behold, I saw Absalom hanged in an oak.

11 And Joab said unto the man that told him, And, behold, thou sawest *him,* and why didst thou not [1]smite him there to the ground? and I would have given thee ten *shekels* of silver, and a girdle.

12 And the man said unto Joab, Though I should receive a thousand *shekels* of silver in mine hand, *yet* would I not put forth mine hand against the king's son: [d]for in our hearing the king charged thee and Abishai and Ittai, saying, Beware that none *touch* the young man Absalom.

13 Otherwise I should have [1]wrought falsehood against mine own life: for there is no matter hid from the king, and thou thyself wouldest have set thyself against *me.*

14 Then said Joab, I [1]may not tarry thus with thee. And he took three [2]darts in his hand, and thrust them through the heart of Absalom, while he *was* yet alive in the midst of the [3]oak.

15 And ten young men that bare Joab's armour [1]compassed about and [2]smote Absalom, and slew him.

16 And Joab blew the trumpet, and the people returned from pursuing after Israel: for Joab held back the people.

17 And they took Absalom, and cast him into a great pit in the wood, and [a]laid a very great heap of stones upon him: and all Israel [b]fled every one to his tent.

18 Now Absalom in his lifetime had taken and reared up for himself a pillar, which *is* in [a]the king's dale: for he said, [b]I have no son to keep my name in remembrance: and he called the pillar after his own name: and it is called unto this day, Absalom's [1]place.

**19** Then said [a]Ahimaaz the son of Zadok, Let me now run, and bear the king tidings, how that the LORD hath [1]avenged him of his enemies.

20 And Joab said unto him, Thou shalt not bear tidings this day; but thou shalt bear tidings another day: but this day thou shalt bear no tidings, because the king's son is dead.

21 Then said Joab to Cushi, Go tell the king what thou hast seen. And Cushi bowed himself unto Joab, and ran.

22 Then said Ahimaaz the son of Zadok yet again to Joab, But [1]howsoever, let me, I pray thee, also run after Cushi. And Joab said, Wherefore wilt thou run, my son, seeing that thou hast no [2]tidings ready?

23 But howsoever, *said he,* let me run. And he said unto him, Run. Then Ahimaaz ran by the way of the plain, and [1]overran Cushi.

24 And David sat between the [a]two gates: and the watchman went up to the roof over the gate unto the wall, and lifted up his eyes, and looked, and behold a man running alone.

25 And the watchman cried, and told the king. And the king said, If he *be* alone, *there is* [1]tidings in his mouth. And he came [2]apace, and drew near.

26 And the watchman saw another man running: and the watchman called unto the [1]porter, and said, Behold *another* man running alone. And the king said, He also bringeth tidings.

27 And the watchman said, [1]Me thinketh the running of the foremost is like the running of Ahimaaz the son of Zadok. And the king said, He *is* a good man, and cometh with [a]good tidings.

28 And Ahimaaz called, and said unto the king, [1]All is well. And he fell down to the earth upon his face before the king, and said, [a]Blessed *be* the LORD thy God, which hath delivered up the men that lifted up their hand against my lord the king.

29 And the king said, Is the young man Absalom safe? And Ahimaaz answered, When Joab sent the king's servant, and *me* thy servant, I saw a great tumult, but I knew not what *it was.*

30 And the king said *unto him,* Turn aside, *and* stand here. And he turned aside, and stood still.

31 And, behold, Cushi came; and Cushi said, Tidings, my lord the king: for the LORD hath [1]avenged thee this day of all them that rose up against thee.

32 And the king said unto Cushi, *Is* the young man Absalom safe? And Cushi answered, The enemies of my

---

18:6 [a] Josh. 17:15, 18; 2 Sam. 17:26  [1] *forest*

18:8 [1] *forest*

18:9 [a] 2 Sam. 14:26  [1] *left hanging*

18:11 [1] *strike*

18:12 [a] 2 Sam. 18:5

18:13 [1] *dealt falsely*

18:14 [1] *cannot linger with you*  [2] *spears*  [3] *terebinth tree*

18:15 [1] *surrounded*  [2] *struck*

18:17 [a] Deut. 21:20, 21; Josh. 7:26; 8:29  [b] 2 Sam. 19:8; 20:1, 22

18:18 [a] Gen. 14:17  [b] 2 Sam. 14:27  [1] *monument*

18:19 [a] 2 Sam. 15:36; 17:17  [1] *vindicated*

18:22 [1] Lit. *be what may*  [2] *news*

18:23 [1] *outran*

18:24 [a] Judg. 5:11; 2 Sam. 13:34; 2 Kin. 9:17

18:25 [1] *news*  [2] *rapidly*

18:26 [1] *gatekeeper*

18:27 [a] 1 Kin. 1:42  [1] Lit. *I see the running*

18:28 [a] 2 Sam. 16:12  [1] Lit. *Peace*

18:31 [1] *vindicated*

lord the king, and all that rise against thee to do *thee* ¹hurt, be as *that* young man *is.*

33 And the king was much moved, and went up to the chamber over the gate, and wept: and as he went, thus he said, ªO my son Absalom, my son, my son Absalom! would God I had died for thee, O Absalom, my son, ᵇmy son!

## CHAPTER 19

A ND it was told Joab, Behold, the king weepeth and ªmourneth for Absalom.

2 And the victory that day was *turned* into ªmourning unto all the people: for the people heard say that day how the king was grieved for his son.

3 And the people ¹gat them by stealth that day ªinto the city, as people being ashamed steal away when they flee in battle.

4 But the king ªcovered his face, and the king cried with a loud voice, ᵇO my son Absalom, O Absalom, my son, my son!

5 And ªJoab came into the house to the king, and said, ¹Thou hast shamed this day the faces of all thy servants, which this day have saved thy life, and the lives of thy sons and of thy daughters, and the lives of thy wives, and the lives of thy concubines;

6 In that thou lovest thine enemies, and hatest thy friends. For thou hast declared this day, that thou ¹regardest neither princes nor servants: for this day I perceive, that if Absalom had lived, and all we had died this day, then it had pleased thee well.

7 Now therefore arise, go forth, and speak ¹comfortably unto thy servants: for I swear by the LORD, if thou go not forth, there will not ²tarry one with thee this night: and that will be worse unto thee than all the evil that befell thee from thy youth until now.

8 Then the king arose, and sat in the ªgate. And they told unto all the people, saying, Behold, the king doth sit in the gate. And all the people came before the king: for Israel had ᵇfled every man to his tent.

9 And all the people were ¹at strife throughout all the tribes of Israel, saying, The king saved us out of the hand of our ªenemies, and he delivered us out of the hand of the ᵇPhilistines; and now he is ᶜfled out of the land for Absalom.

10 And Absalom, whom we anointed over us, is dead in battle. Now therefore why speak ye not a word of bringing the king back?

11 And king David sent to ªZadok and to Abiathar the priests, saying, Speak unto the elders of Judah, say-

ing, Why are ye the last to bring the king back to his house? seeing the speech of all Israel is come to the king, *even* to his house.

12 Ye *are* my brethren, ye *are* ªmy bones and my flesh: wherefore then are ye the last to bring back the king?

13 ªAnd say ye to Amasa, *Art* thou not of my bone, and of my flesh? ᵇGod do so to me, and more also, if thou be not captain of the host before me ¹continually in the ²room of Joab.

14 And he ¹bowed the heart of all the men of Judah, ªeven as *the heart of* one man; so that they sent *this word* unto the king, Return thou, and all thy servants.

15 So the king returned, and came to Jordan. And Judah came to ªGilgal, to go to meet the king, to conduct the king ᵇover Jordan.

16 And ªShimei the son of Gera, a Benjamite, which *was* of Bahurim, hasted and came down with the men of Judah to meet king David.

17 And *there were* a thousand men of ªBenjamin with him, and ᵇZiba the servant of the house of Saul, and his fifteen sons and his twenty servants with him; and they went over Jordan before the king.

18 And there went over a ferry boat to carry over the king's household, and to do what he thought good. And Shimei the son of Gera fell down before the king, as he was come over Jordan;

19 And said unto the king, ªLet not my lord ¹impute iniquity unto me, neither do thou remember ᵇthat which thy servant did ²perversely the day that my lord the king went out of Jerusalem, that the king should ᶜtake it to his heart.

20 For thy servant doth know that I have sinned: therefore, behold, I am come the first this day of all ªthe house of Joseph to go down to meet my lord the king.

21 But Abishai the son of Zeruiah answered and said, Shall not Shimei be put to death for this, ªbecause he ᵇcursed the LORD's anointed?

22 And David said, ªWhat have I to do with you, ye sons of Zeruiah, that ye should this day be adversaries unto me? ᵇshall there any man be put to death this day in Israel? for do not I know that I *am* this day king over Israel?

23 Therefore ªthe king said unto Shimei, Thou shalt not die. And the king sware unto him.

24 And ªMephibosheth the son of Saul came down to meet the king, and had neither dressed his feet, nor trimmed his beard, nor washed his clothes, from the day the king departed until the day he came *again* in peace.

18:32 ¹ *harm*
18:33 ª 2 Sam. 12:10 ᵇ 2 Sam. 19:4
19:1 ª Jer. 14:2
19:2 ª Esth. 4:3
19:3 ª 2 Sam. 17:24, 27; 19:32 ¹ *went by stealth*
19:4 ª 2 Sam. 15:30 ᵇ 2 Sam. 18:33
19:5 ª 2 Sam. 18:14 ¹ *You have disgraced*
19:6 ¹ *have no respect for*
19:7 ¹ Lit. *to the heart of* ² *stay*
19:8 ª 2 Sam. 15:2; 18:24 ᵇ 2 Sam. 18:17
19:9 ª 2 Sam. 8:1–14 ᵇ 2 Sam. 3:18 ᶜ 2 Sam. 15:14 ¹ *in a dispute*
19:11 ª 2 Sam. 15:24
19:12 ª 2 Sam. 5:1; 1 Chr. 11:1
19:13 ª 2 Sam. 17:25; 1 Chr. 2:17 ᵇ Ruth 1:17 ¹ *permanently* ² *place*
19:14 ª Judg. 20:1 ¹ *swayed*
19:15 ª Josh. 5:9; 1 Sam. 11:14, 15 ᵇ 2 Sam. 17:22
19:16 ª 2 Sam. 16:5; 1 Kin. 2:8
19:17 ª 2 Sam. 3:19; 1 Kin. 12:21 ᵇ 2 Sam. 9:2, 10; 16:1, 2
19:19 ª 1 Sam. 22:15 ᵇ 2 Sam. 16:5, 6 ᶜ 2 Sam. 13:33 ¹ *charge me with iniquity* ² *rebelliously*
19:20 ª Judg. 1:22; 1 Kin. 11:28
19:21 ª [Ex. 22:28] ᵇ [1 Sam. 26:9]
19:22 ª 2 Sam. 3:39; 16:10 ᵇ 1 Sam. 11:13
19:23 ª 1 Kin. 2:8, 9, 37, 46
19:24 ª 2 Sam. 9:6; 21:7

25 And it came to pass, when he was come to Jerusalem to meet the king, that the king said unto him, <sup>a</sup>Wherefore wentest not thou with me, Mephibosheth?

26 And he answered, My lord, O king, my servant deceived me: for thy servant said, I will saddle me an ass, that I may ride thereon, and go to the king; because thy servant *is* lame.

27 And <sup>a</sup>he hath slandered thy servant unto my lord the king; <sup>b</sup>but my lord the king *is* as an angel of God: do therefore *what is* good in thine eyes.

28 For all *of* my father's house were but dead men before my lord the king: <sup>a</sup>yet didst thou set thy servant among them that did eat at thine own table. What right therefore have I yet to <sup>1</sup>cry any more unto the king?

29 And the king said unto him, Why speakest thou any more of thy matters? I have said, Thou and Ziba divide the land.

30 And Mephibosheth said unto the king, Yea, let him take all, forasmuch as my lord the king is come again in peace unto his own house.

31 And <sup>a</sup>Barzillai the Gileadite came down from Rogelim, and went over Jordan with the king, to conduct him over Jordan.

32 Now Barzillai was a very aged man, *even* fourscore years old: and <sup>a</sup>he had provided the king <sup>1</sup>of sustenance while he lay at Mahanaim; for he *was* a very great man.

33 And the king said unto Barzillai, Come thou over with me, and I will feed thee with me in Jerusalem.

34 And Barzillai said unto the king, How long have I to live, that I should go up with the king unto Jerusalem?

35 I *am* this day <sup>a</sup>fourscore years old: *and* can I discern between good and <sup>1</sup>evil? can thy servant taste what I eat or what I drink? can I hear any more the voice of singing men and singing women? wherefore then should thy servant be yet a burden unto my lord the king?

36 Thy servant will go a little way over Jordan with the king: and why should the king <sup>1</sup>recompense it me with such a reward?

37 Let thy servant, I pray thee, turn back again, that I may die in mine own city, *and be buried* by the grave of my father and of my mother. But behold thy servant <sup>a</sup>Chimham; let him go over with my lord the king; and do to him what shall seem good unto thee.

38 And the king answered, Chimham shall go over with me, and I will do to him that which shall seem good unto thee: and whatsoever thou shalt <sup>1</sup>require of me, *that* will I do for thee.

39 And all the people went over Jordan. And when the king was come

over, the king <sup>a</sup>kissed Barzillai, and blessed him; and he returned unto his own place.

40 Then the king went on to Gilgal, and <sup>1</sup>Chimham went on with him: and all the people of Judah conducted the king, and also half the people of Israel.

41 And, behold, all the men of Israel came to the king, and said unto the king, Why have our brethren the men of Judah stolen thee away, and <sup>a</sup>have brought the king, and his household, and all David's men with him, over Jordan?

42 And all the men of Judah answered the men of Israel, Because the king *is* <sup>a</sup>near of kin to us: wherefore then be ye angry for this matter? have we eaten at all of the king's *cost?* or hath he given us any gift?

43 And the men of Israel answered the men of Judah, and said, We have <sup>a</sup>ten parts in the king, and we have also more *right* in David than ye: why then did ye despise us, that our advice should not be first had in bringing back our king? And <sup>b</sup>the words of the men of Judah were <sup>1</sup>fiercer than the words of the men of Israel.

## CHAPTER 20

A<sup>ND</sup> there happened to be there <sup>1</sup>a man of Belial, whose name *was* Sheba, the son of Bichri, a Benjamite: and he blew a trumpet, and said, <sup>a</sup>We have no part in David, neither have we inheritance in the son of Jesse: <sup>b</sup>every man to his tents, O Israel.

2 So every man of Israel went up from after David, *and* followed Sheba the son of Bichri: but the <sup>a</sup>men of Judah clave unto their king, from Jordan even to Jerusalem.

3 And David came to his house at Jerusalem; and the king took the ten women <sup>a</sup>his concubines, whom he had left to keep the house, and put them in <sup>1</sup>ward, and fed them, but went not in unto them. So they were shut up unto the day of their death, living in widowhood.

4 Then said the king to Amasa, <sup>a</sup>Assemble me the men of Judah within three days, and be thou here present.

5 So Amasa went to assemble *the men of* Judah: but he <sup>1</sup>tarried longer than the set time which he had appointed him.

6 And David said to <sup>a</sup>Abishai, Now shall Sheba the son of Bichri do us more harm than *did* Absalom: take thou <sup>b</sup>thy lord's servants, and pursue after him, lest he <sup>1</sup>get him fenced cities, and escape us.

7 And there went out after him Joab's men, and the <sup>a</sup>Cherethites, and the Pelethites, and <sup>b</sup>all the mighty men: and they went out of

---

19:25 <sup>a</sup> 2 Sam. 16:7
19:27 <sup>a</sup> 2 Sam. 16:3, 4 <sup>b</sup> 2 Sam. 14:17, 20
19:28 <sup>a</sup> 2 Sam. 9:7–13 <sup>1</sup> *complain*
19:31 <sup>a</sup> 2 Sam. 17:27–29; 1 Kin. 2:7
19:32 <sup>a</sup> 2 Sam. 17:27–29 <sup>1</sup> *with supplies*
19:35 <sup>a</sup> Ps. 90:10 <sup>1</sup> *bad*
19:36 <sup>1</sup> *repay me*
19:37 <sup>a</sup> 2 Sam. 19:40; Jer. 41:17
19:38 <sup>1</sup> *request*

19:39 <sup>a</sup> Gen. 31:55; Ruth 1:14; 2 Sam. 14:33
19:40 <sup>1</sup> MT *Chimhan*
19:41 <sup>a</sup> 2 Sam. 19:15
19:42 <sup>a</sup> 2 Sam. 19:12
19:43 <sup>a</sup> 1 Kin. 11:30, 31 <sup>b</sup> Judg. 8:1; 12:1 <sup>1</sup> *harsher*
20:1 <sup>a</sup> 2 Sam. 19:43; 1 Kin. 12:16 <sup>b</sup> 1 Sam. 13:2; 2 Sam. 18:17; 2 Chr. 10:16 <sup>1</sup> *a rebel*
20:2 <sup>a</sup> 2 Sam. 19:14
20:3 <sup>a</sup> 2 Sam. 15:16; 16:21, 22 <sup>1</sup> *seclusion*
20:4 <sup>a</sup> 2 Sam. 17:25; 19:13
20:5 <sup>1</sup> *delayed*
20:6 <sup>a</sup> 2 Sam. 21:17 <sup>b</sup> 2 Sam. 11:11; 1 Kin. 1:33 <sup>1</sup> *finds fortified cities for himself*
20:7 <sup>a</sup> 2 Sam. 8:18; 1 Kin. 1:38, 44 <sup>b</sup> 2 Sam. 15:18

Jerusalem, to pursue after Sheba the son of Bichri.

8 When they *were* at the great stone which *is* in Gibeon, Amasa went before them. And Joab's garment that he had put on was girded unto him, and upon it a ¹girdle *with* a sword fastened upon his loins in the sheath thereof; and as he ²went forth it fell out.

9 ³And Joab said to Amasa, *Art* thou in health, my brother? And Joab took Amasa by the beard with the right hand to kiss him.

10 But Amasa took no heed to the sword that *was* in Joab's hand: so ³he smote him therewith ᵇin the fifth *rib*, and shed out his bowels to the ground, and struck him not again; and he died. So Joab and Abishai his brother pursued after Sheba the son of Bichri.

11 And one of Joab's men stood by him, and said, He that favoureth Joab, and he that *is* for David, *let him go* after Joab.

12 And Amasa wallowed in blood in the midst of the highway. And when the man saw that all the people stood still, he removed Amasa out of the highway into the field, and cast a cloth upon him, when he saw that every one that came by him stood still.

13 When he was removed out of the highway, all the people went on after Joab, to pursue after Sheba the son of Bichri.

14 And he went through all the tribes of Israel unto ᵃAbel, and to Beth-maachah, and all the Berites: and they were gathered together, and went also after ¹him.

15 And they came and besieged him in Abel of Beth-maachah, and they ᵃcast up a ¹bank against the city, and it stood ²in the trench: and all the people that *were* with Joab battered the wall, to throw it down.

16 Then cried a wise woman out of the city, Hear, hear; say, I pray you, unto Joab, Come near hither, that I may speak with thee.

17 And when he was come near unto her, the woman said, *Art* thou Joab? And he answered, I *am* he. Then she said unto him, Hear the words of thine handmaid. And he answered, I do hear.

18 Then she spake, saying, They ¹were wont to speak in old time, saying, They shall surely ask *counsel* at Abel: and so they ended *the matter.*

19 I *am one of them that are* peaceable *and* faithful in Israel: thou seekest to destroy a city and a mother in Israel: why wilt thou swallow up ᵃthe inheritance of the LORD?

20 And Joab answered and said, Far be it, far be it from me, that I should swallow up or destroy.

21 The matter *is* not so: but a man of mount Ephraim, Sheba the son of Bichri by name, hath lifted up his hand against the king, *even* against David: deliver him only, and I will depart from the city. And the woman said unto Joab, Behold, his head shall be thrown to thee over the wall.

22 Then the woman went unto all the people ᵃin her wisdom. And they cut off the head of Sheba the son of Bichri, and cast *it* out to Joab. And he blew a trumpet, and they ¹retired from the city, every man to his tent. And Joab returned to Jerusalem unto the king.

23 Now ᵃJoab *was* over all the host of Israel: and Benaiah the son of Jehoiada *was* over the Cherethites and over the Pelethites:

24 And Adoram *was* ᵃover the tribute: and ᵇJehoshaphat the son of Ahilud *was* recorder:

25 And Sheva *was* scribe: and ᵃZadok and Abiathar *were* the priests:

26 ᵃAnd Ira also the Jairite was ¹a chief ruler about David.

## CHAPTER 21

THEN there was a famine in the days of David three years, year after year; and David ᵃenquired of the LORD. And the LORD answered, *It is* for Saul, and for *his* ¹bloody house, because he slew the Gibeonites.

2 And the king called the Gibeonites, and said unto them; (now the Gibeonites *were* not of the children of Israel, but ᵃof the remnant of the Amorites; and the children of Israel had sworn unto them: and Saul sought to slay them ᵇin his zeal to the children of Israel and Judah.)

3 Wherefore David said unto the Gibeonites, What shall I do for you? and wherewith shall I make the atonement, that ye may bless ᵃthe inheritance of the LORD?

4 And the Gibeonites said unto him, We will have no silver nor gold of Saul, nor of his house; neither for us shalt thou kill any man in Israel. And he said, What ye shall say, *that* will I do for you.

5 And they answered the king, The man that consumed us, and that ¹devised against us *that* we should be destroyed from remaining in any of the ²coasts of Israel,

6 Let seven men of his sons be delivered ᵃunto us, and we will hang them up unto the LORD ᵇin Gibeah of Saul, ᶜwhom the LORD did choose. And the king said, I will give *them.*

7 But the king spared ᵃMephibosheth, the son of Jonathan the son of Saul, because of ᵇthe LORD's oath that *was* between them, between David and Jonathan the son of Saul.

---

20:8 ¹ *belt* ² *was going forward*
20:9 ᵃ Matt. 26:49; Luke 22:47
20:10 ᵃ 2 Sam. 3:27; 1 Kin. 2:5 ᵇ 2 Sam. 2:23
20:14 ᵃ 1 Kin. 15:20; 2 Kin. 15:29; 2 Chr. 16:4 ¹ Sheba
20:15 ᵃ 2 Kin. 19:32; Ezek. 4:2 ¹ *siege mound* ² *by the rampart*
20:18 ¹ *used to talk in former times*
20:19 ᵃ 1 Sam. 26:19; 2 Sam. 14:16; 21:3

20:22 ᵃ 2 Sam. 20:16; [Eccl. 9:13–16] ¹ *withdrew*
20:23 ᵃ 2 Sam. 8:16–18; 1 Kin. 4:3–6
20:24 ᵃ 1 Kin. 4:6 ᵇ 2 Sam. 8:16; 1 Kin. 4:3
20:25 ᵃ 2 Sam. 8:17; 1 Kin. 4:4
20:26 ᵃ 2 Sam. 8:18 ¹ *David's priest*
21:1 ᵃ Num. 27:21; 2 Sam. 5:19 ¹ *bloodthirsty*
21:2 ᵃ Josh. 9:3, 15–20 ᵇ [Ex. 34:11–16]
21:3 ᵃ 1 Sam. 26:19; 2 Sam. 20:19
21:5 ¹ *plotted* ² *territories*
21:6 ᵃ Num. 25:4 ᵇ 1 Sam. 10:26 ᶜ 1 Sam. 10:24; [Hos. 13:11]
21:7 ᵃ 2 Sam. 4:4; 9:10 ᵇ 1 Sam. 18:3; 20:12–17; 23:18; 2 Sam. 9:1–7

8 But the king took the two sons of ªRizpah the daughter of Aiah, whom she bare unto Saul, Armoni and Mephibosheth; and the five sons of ¹Michal the daughter of Saul, whom she ²brought up for Adriel the son of Barzillai the Meholathite:

9 And he delivered them into the hands of the Gibeonites, and they hanged them in the hill ªbefore the LORD: and they fell *all* seven together, and were put to death in the days of harvest, in the first *days*, in the beginning of barley harvest.

10 And ªRizpah the daughter of Aiah took sackcloth, and spread it for her upon the rock, ᵇfrom the beginning of harvest until water dropped upon them out of heaven, and suffered neither the birds of the air to rest on them by day, nor the beasts of the field by night.

11 And it was told David what Rizpah the daughter of Aiah, the concubine of Saul, had done.

12 And David went and took the bones of Saul and the bones of Jonathan his son from the men of ªJabeshgilead, which had stolen them from the street of ¹Beth-shan, where the ᵇPhilistines had hanged them, when the Philistines had slain Saul in Gilboa:

13 And he brought up from thence the bones of Saul and the bones of Jonathan his son; and they gathered the bones of them that were hanged.

14 And the bones of Saul and Jonathan his son buried they in the country of Benjamin in ªZelah, in the sepulchre of Kish his father: and they performed all that the king commanded. And after that ᵇGod ¹was intreated for the land.

15 Moreover the Philistines had yet war again with Israel; and David went down, and his servants with him, and fought against the Philistines: and David waxed faint.

16 And Ishbi-benob, which *was* of the sons of ¹the ªgiant, the weight of whose ²spear *weighed* three hundred *shekels* of brass in weight, he being girded with a new *sword*, thought ³to have slain David.

17 But ªAbishai the son of Zeruiah ¹succoured him, and ²smote the Philistine, and killed him. Then the men of David sware unto him, saying, ᵇThou shalt go no more out with us to battle, that thou quench not the ᶜlight of Israel.

18 ªAnd it came to pass after this, that there was again a battle with the Philistines at Gob: then ᵇSibbechai the Hushathite slew ¹Saph, which *was* of the sons of ²the giant.

19 And there was again a battle in Gob with the Philistines, where ªElhanan the son of ¹Jaare-oregim, a

Beth-lehemite, slew ᵇ*the brother of* Goliath the Gittite, the staff of whose spear *was* like a weaver's beam.

20 And ªthere was yet a battle in Gath, where was a man of *great* stature, that had on every hand six fingers, and on every foot six toes, four and twenty in number; and he also was born to ¹the giant.

21 And when he ªdefied Israel, Jonathan the son of ¹Shimeah the brother of David slew him.

22 ªThese four were born to ¹the giant in Gath, and fell by the hand of David, and by the hand of his servants.

## CHAPTER 22

AND David ªspake unto the LORD the words of this song in the day *that* the LORD had ᵇdelivered him out of the hand of all his enemies, and out of the hand of Saul:

2 And he ªsaid, ᵇThe LORD *is* my rock, and my ᶜfortress, and my deliverer;

3 The God of my rock; ªin him will I trust: *he is* my ᵇshield, and the ᶜhorn of my salvation, my ᵈhigh² tower, and my ᵉrefuge, my saviour; thou savest me from violence.

4 I will call on the LORD, *who is* worthy to be praised: so shall I be saved from mine enemies.

5 When the waves of death compassed me, the floods of ¹ungodly men ²made me afraid;

6 The ªsorrows of ¹hell ²compassed me about; the snares of death ³prevented me;

7 In my distress ªI called upon the LORD, and cried to my God: and he did ᵇhear my voice out of his temple, and my cry *did enter* into his ears.

8 Then ªthe earth shook and trembled; ᵇthe foundations of heaven moved and shook, because he was ¹wroth.

9 There went up a smoke out of his nostrils, and ªfire out of his mouth devoured: coals were kindled by it.

10 He ªbowed the heavens also, and came down; and ᵇdarkness *was* under his feet.

11 And he rode upon a cherub, and did fly: and he was seen ªupon the wings of the wind.

12 And he made ªdarkness ¹pavilions round about him, dark waters, *and* thick clouds of the skies.

13 Through the brightness before him were coals of fire kindled.

14 The LORD ªthundered from heaven, and the most High uttered his voice.

15 And he sent out ªarrows, and scattered them; lightning, and ¹discomfited them.

16 And the channels of the sea ªappeared, the foundations of the world

### Center reference column

21:8 ª 2 Sam. 3:7 ¹ Merab, 1 Sam. 18:19; 25:44 ² Lit. bore to Adriel

21:9 ª 2 Sam. 6:17

21:10 ª 2 Sam. 3:7; 21:8 ᵇ Deut. 21:23

21:12 ª 1 Sam. 31:11–13 ᵇ 1 Sam. 31:8 ¹ Beth-shean, Josh. 17:11

21:14 ª Josh. 18:28 ᵇ 2 Sam. 24:25 ¹ heeded the prayer

21:16 ª 2 Sam. 21:18–22 ¹ Or Rapha ² bronze spear ³ he could kill

21:17 ª 2 Sam. 20:6–10 ᵇ 2 Sam. 18:3 ᶜ 1 Kin. 11:36 ¹ came to his aid ² struck

21:18 ª 1 Chr. 20:4–8 ᵇ 1 Chr. 11:29; 27:11 ¹ Sippai, 1 Chr. 20:4 ² Or Rapha

21:19 ª 2 Sam. 23:24 ᵇ 1 Chr. 20:5 ¹ Or Jair, 1 Chr. 20:5

21:20 ª 1 Chr. 20:6 ¹ Or Rapha

21:21 ª 1 Sam. 17:10 ¹ Shammah, 1 Sam. 16:9

21:22 ª 1 Chr. 20:8 ¹ Or Rapha

22:1 ª Ex. 15:1 ᵇ Ps. 18:title; 34:19

22:2 ª Ps. 18 ᵇ Deut. 32:4 ᶜ Ps. 91:2

22:3 ª Heb. 2:13 ᵇ Gen. 15:1 ᶜ Luke 1:69 ᵈ Prov. 18:10 ᵉ Ps. 9:9; 46:1, 7, 11 ¹ Strength ² stronghold

22:5 ¹ ungodliness ² overwhelmed

22:6 ª Ps. 116:3 ¹ Heb. Sheol ² surrounded ³ confronted

22:7 ª Ps. 116:4; 120:1 ᵇ Ex. 3:7

22:8 ª Judg. 5:4 ᵇ Job 26:11 ¹ angry

22:9 ª Heb. 12:29

22:10 ª Is. 64:1 ᵇ Ex. 20:21

22:11 ª Ps. 104:3

22:12 ª Job 36:29 ¹ canopies

22:14 ª Job 37:2–5

22:15 ª Deut. 32:23 ¹ vanquished

22:16 ª Nah. 1:4

were ¹discovered, at the ᵇrebuking of the LORD, at the blast of the breath of his nostrils.

17 ᵃHe sent from above, he took me; he drew me out of many waters;

18 He delivered me from my strong enemy, *and* from them that hated me: for they were too strong for me.

19 They ¹prevented me in the day of my calamity: but the LORD was my ᵃstay.²

20 ᵃHe brought me forth also into a large place: he delivered me, because he ᵇdelighted in me.

21 ᵃThe LORD rewarded me according to my righteousness: according to the ᵇcleanness of my hands hath he recompensed me.

22 For I have ᵃkept the ways of the LORD, and have not wickedly departed from my God.

23 For all his ᵃjudgments *were* before me: and *as for* his statutes, I did not depart from them.

24 I was also ᵃupright before him, and have kept myself from mine iniquity.

25 Therefore ᵃthe LORD hath ¹recompensed me according to my righteousness; according to my cleanness in his eye sight.

26 With ᵃthe merciful thou wilt shew thyself merciful, *and* with the upright man thou wilt shew thyself upright.

27 With the pure thou wilt shew thyself pure; and ᵃwith the ¹froward thou wilt shew thyself ²unsavoury.

28 And the ᵃafflicted people thou wilt save: but thine eyes *are* upon ᵇthe haughty, *that* thou mayest bring *them* down.

29 For thou *art* my ᵃlamp, O LORD: and the LORD will lighten my darkness.

30 For by thee I ¹have run through a troop: by my God ²have I leaped over a ᵃwall.

31 *As for* God, ᵃhis way *is* perfect; ᵇthe word of the LORD *is* ¹tried: he *is* a ²buckler to all them that trust in him.

32 For ᵃwho *is* God, save the LORD? and who *is* a rock, save our God?

33 God *is* my ᵃstrength *and* power: and he ᵇmaketh my way ᶜperfect.

34 He maketh my feet ᵃlike ¹hinds' *feet:* and ᵇsetteth me upon my high places.

35 He teacheth my hands ¹to war; so that a bow of ²steel is broken by mine arms.

36 Thou hast also given me the shield of thy salvation: and thy gentleness hath made me great.

37 Thou hast ᵃenlarged my steps under me; so that my feet did not slip.

38 I have pursued mine enemies, and destroyed them; and turned not again until I had consumed them.

39 And I have consumed them, and wounded them, that they could not arise: yea, they are fallen ᵃunder my feet.

40 For thou hast ᵃgirded me with strength to battle: ᵇthem that rose up against me hast thou ¹subdued under me.

41 Thou hast also ¹given me the ᵃnecks of mine enemies, that I might destroy them that hate me.

42 They looked, but *there was* none to save; *even* ᵃunto the LORD, but he answered them not.

43 Then did I beat them as small ᵃas the dust of the earth, I did stamp them ᵇas the mire of the street, *and* did ¹spread them abroad.

44 ᵃThou also hast delivered me from the ¹strivings of my people, thou hast kept me *to be* ᵇhead of the heathen: ᶜa people *which* I knew not shall serve me.

45 ¹Strangers shall submit themselves unto me: as soon as they hear, they shall be obedient unto me.

46 Strangers shall fade away, and they shall be afraid ᵃout of their ¹close places.

47 The LORD liveth; and blessed *be* my rock; and exalted be the God of the ᵃrock of my salvation.

48 It *is* God that avengeth me, and that ᵃbringeth down the people under me,

49 And that bringeth me forth from mine enemies: thou also hast lifted me up on high above them that rose up against me: thou hast delivered me from the ᵃviolent man.

50 Therefore I will give thanks unto thee, O LORD, among ᵃthe ¹heathen, and I will sing praises unto thy ᵇname.

51 ᵃ*He is* the tower of salvation for his king: and sheweth mercy to his ᵇanointed, unto David, and ᶜto his seed for evermore.

## CHAPTER 23

Now these *be* the last words of David. David the son of Jesse said, ᵃand the man *who was* raised up on high, ᵇthe anointed of the God of Jacob, and the sweet psalmist of Israel, said,

2 ᵃThe Spirit of the LORD spake by me, and his word *was* in my tongue.

3 The God of Israel said, ᵃthe Rock of Israel spake to me, He that ruleth over men *must be* just, ruling ᵇin the fear of God.

4 And ᵃ*he shall be* as the light of the morning, *when* the sun riseth, *even* a morning without clouds; *as* the tender grass *springing* out of the earth by clear shining after rain.

22:16 ᵃ Ex. 15:8
¹ *uncovered*
22:17 ᵃ Ps. 144:7
22:19 ᵃ Is. 10:20
¹ *confronted*
² *support*
22:20 ᵃ Ps. 31:8; 118:5 ᵇ 2 Sam. 15:26
22:21 ᵃ 1 Sam. 26:23 ᵇ Ps. 24:4
22:22 ᵃ Ps. 119:3
22:23 ᵃ [Deut. 6:6–9; 7:12]
22:24 ᵃ [Eph. 1:4]
22:25 ᵃ 2 Sam. 22:21 ¹ *rewarded*
22:26 ᵃ [Matt. 5:7]
22:27 ᵃ [Lev. 26:23, 24] ¹ *devious* ² *shrewd*
22:28 ᵃ Ps. 72:12 ᵇ Job 40:11
22:29 ᵃ Ps. 119:105; 132:17
22:30 ᵃ 2 Sam. 5:6–8 ¹ *can run against* ² *I can leap*
22:31 ᵃ [Matt. 5:48] ᵇ Ps. 12:6 ¹ *proven* ² *shield*
22:32 ᵃ Is. 45:5, 6
22:33 ᵃ Ps. 27:1 ᵇ [Heb. 13:21] ᶜ Ps. 101:2, 6
22:34 ᵃ 2 Sam. 2:18 ᵇ Is. 33:16 ¹ *the feet of deer*
22:35 ¹ Lit. *for the war* ² *bronze is bent by*
22:37 ᵃ Prov. 4:12
22:39 ᵃ Mal. 4:3
22:40 ᵃ [Ps. 18:32] ᵇ [Ps. 44:5] ¹ Lit. *caused to bow down*
22:41 ᵃ Gen. 49:8 ¹ *given me victory over*
22:42 ᵃ 1 Sam. 28:6
22:43 ᵃ Ps. 18:42 ᵇ Is. 10:6 ¹ *scatter*
22:44 ᵃ 2 Sam. 3:1 ᵇ Deut. 28:13 ᶜ [Is. 55:5] ¹ *contentions*
22:45 ¹ *Foreigners*
22:46 ᵃ [Mic. 7:17] ¹ *hideouts*
22:47 ᵃ Ps. 89:26
22:48 ᵃ Ps. 144:2
22:49 ᵃ Ps. 140:1, 4, 11
22:50 ᵃ 2 Sam. 8:1–14 ᵇ Rom. 15:9 ¹ *nations* or *Gentiles*
22:51 ᵃ Ps. 144:10 ᵇ Ps. 89:20 ᶜ 2 Sam. 7:12–16
23:1 ᵃ 2 Sam. 7:8, 9 ᵇ 1 Sam. 16:12, 13
23:2 ᵃ [2 Pet. 1:21] 23:3 ᵃ [Deut. 32:4] ᵇ Ex. 18:21 23:4 ᵃ Ps. 89:36

5 Although my house *be* not so with God; [a]yet he hath made with me an everlasting covenant, ordered in all *things*, and sure: for *this is* all my salvation, and all *my* desire, [1]although he make *it* not to grow.

6 But *the* [1]*sons* of Belial *shall be* all of them as thorns thrust away, because they cannot be taken with hands:

7 But the man *that* shall touch them must be [1]fenced with iron and the staff of a spear; and they shall be utterly burned with fire in the *same* place.

8 These *be* the names of the mighty men whom David had: The Tachmonite [1]that sat in the seat, chief among the captains; the same *was* Adino the Eznite: *he lift up his spear* against eight hundred, whom he slew at one time.

9 And after him *was* [a]Eleazar the son of [1]Dodo the Ahohite, *one* of the three mighty men with David, when they defied the Philistines *that* were there gathered together to battle, and the men of Israel were gone away:

10 He arose, and [1]smote the Philistines until his hand was [a]weary, and his hand [2]clave unto the sword: and the LORD wrought a great victory that day; and the people returned after him only to [b]spoil.[3]

11 And after him *was* [a]Shammah the son of Agee the Hararite. [b]And the Philistines were gathered together into a troop, where was a piece of ground full of lentiles: and the people fled from the Philistines.

12 But he stood in the midst of the ground, and defended it, and slew the Philistines: and the LORD wrought a great victory.

13 And [a]three of the thirty [1]chief went down, and came to David in the harvest time unto [b]the cave of Adullam: and the troop of the Philistines [2]pitched in [c]the valley of Rephaim.

14 And David *was* then in [a]an[1] hold, and the garrison of the Philistines *was* then *in* Beth-lehem.

15 And David longed, and said, Oh that one would give me drink of the water of the well of Beth-lehem, which *is* by the gate!

16 And the three mighty men brake through the host of the Philistines, and drew water out of the well of Beth-lehem, that *was* by the gate, and took *it*, and brought *it* to David: nevertheless he would not drink thereof, but poured it out unto the LORD.

17 And he said, Be it far from me, O LORD, that I should do this: *is not this* [a]the blood of the men that went in jeopardy of their lives? therefore he would not drink it. These things did these three mighty men.

18 And [a]Abishai, the brother of Joab, the son of Zeruiah, was chief among three. And he lifted up his spear against three hundred, *and* slew *them*, and had the name among three.

19 Was he not most honourable of three? therefore he was their captain: howbeit he attained not unto the *first* three.

20 And Benaiah the son of Jehoiada, the son of a valiant man, of [a]Kabzeel, [1]who had done many acts, [b]he slew two lionlike men of Moab: he went down also and slew a lion in the midst of a pit in time of snow:

21 And he slew an Egyptian, [1]a goodly man: and the Egyptian had a spear in his hand; but he went down to him with a staff, and plucked the spear out of the Egyptian's hand, and slew him with his own spear.

22 These *things* did Benaiah the son of Jehoiada, and had the name among three mighty men.

23 He was more [1]honourable than the thirty, but he attained not to the *first* three. And David set him [a]over his guard.

24 [a]Asahel the brother of Joab *was* one of the thirty; Elhanan the son of Dodo of Beth-lehem,

25 [a]Shammah the Harodite, Elika the Harodite,

26 Helez the Paltite, Ira the son of Ikkesh the Tekoite,

27 Abiezer the Anethothite, Mebunnai the Hushathite,

28 Zalmon the Ahohite, Maharai the Netophathite,

29 Heleb the son of Baanah, a Netophathite, Ittai the son of Ribai out of Gibeah of the children of Benjamin,

30 Benaiah the Pirathonite, Hiddai of the brooks of [a]Gaash,

31 Abi-albon the Arbathite, Azmaveth the Barhumite,

32 Eliahba the Shaalbonite, of the sons of Jashen, Jonathan,

33 [a]Shammah the Hararite, Ahiam the son of Sharar the [1]Hararite,

34 Eliphelet the son of Ahasbai, the son of the Maachathite, Eliam the son of [a]Ahithophel the Gilonite,

35 [1]Hezrai the Carmelite, Paarai the Arbite,

36 Igal the son of Nathan of [a]Zobah, Bani the Gadite,

37 Zelek the Ammonite, Nahari the Beerothite, armourbearer to Joab the son of Zeruiah,

38 [a]Ira an Ithrite, Gareb an Ithrite,

39 [a]Uriah the Hittite: thirty and seven in all.

## CHAPTER 24

AND [a]again the anger of the LORD was [1]kindled against Israel, and he moved David against them to say, [b]Go, [2]number Israel and Judah.

### Cross References

23:5 [a] Ps. 89:29 [1] will he not make it increase
23:6 [1] rebellious
23:7 [1] armed, lit. filled
23:8 [1] Heb. Josheb-bashshebeth, lit. One Who Sits in the Seat
23:9 [a] 1 Chr. 11:12; 27:4 [1] Dodai, 1 Chr. 27:4
23:10 [a] Judg. 8:4 [b] 1 Sam. 30:24, 25 [1] attacked [2] stuck [3] plunder
23:11 [a] 1 Chr. 11:27 [b] 1 Chr. 11:13, 14
23:13 [a] 1 Chr. 11:15 [b] 1 Sam.
22:1 [c] 2 Sam. 5:18 [1] chief men [2] encamped
23:14 [a] 1 Sam. 22:4, 5 [1] the stronghold
23:17 [a] [Lev. 17:10]
23:18 [a] 2 Sam. 21:17; 1 Chr. 11:20
23:20 [a] Josh. 15:21 [b] Ex. 15:15 [1] Lit. great of acts
23:21 [1] Lit. a man of appearance
23:23 [a] 2 Sam. 8:18; 20:23 [1] honoured
23:24 [a] 2 Sam. 2:18; 1 Chr. 27:7
23:25 [a] 1 Chr. 11:27
23:30 [a] Judg. 2:9
23:33 [a] 2 Sam. 23:11 [1] Or Ararite
23:34 [a] 2 Sam. 15:12
23:35 [1] Hezro, 1 Chr. 11:37
23:36 [a] 2 Sam. 8:3
23:38 [a] 1 Cor. 11:28
23:39 [a] 2 Sam. 11:3, 6
24:1 [a] 2 Sam. 21:1, 2 [b] Num. 26:2; 1 Chr. 27:23, 24 [1] aroused [2] take a census of

2 For the king said to Joab the captain of the host, which *was* with him, Go now through all the tribes of Israel, [a]from Dan even to Beer-sheba, and [1]number ye the people, that [b]I may know the number of the people.

3 And Joab said unto the king, Now the LORD thy God [a]add unto the people, how many soever they be, an hundredfold, and that the eyes of my lord the king may see *it:* but why doth my lord the king [1]delight in this thing?

4 Notwithstanding the king's word [1]prevailed against Joab, and against the captains of the host. And Joab and the captains of the host went out from the presence of the king, to number the people of Israel.

5 And they passed over Jordan, and [1]pitched in [a]Aroer, on the right side of the city that *lieth* in the midst of the [2]river of Gad, and toward [b]Jazer:

6 Then they came to Gilead, and to the land of Tahtim-hodshi; and they came to [a]Dan-jaan, and about to [b]Zidon,

7 And came to the [1]strong hold of [a]Tyre, and to all the cities of the [b]Hivites, and of the Canaanites: and they went out to the south of Judah, *even* to Beer-sheba.

8 So when they had gone through all the land, they came to Jerusalem at the end of nine months and twenty days.

9 And Joab gave up the sum of the number of the people unto the king: [a]and there were in Israel eight hundred thousand valiant men that drew the sword; and the men of Judah *were* five hundred thousand men.

10 And [a]David's [1]heart smote him after that he had numbered the people. And [b]David said unto the LORD, [c]I have sinned greatly in that I have done: and now, I beseech thee, O LORD, take away the iniquity of thy servant; for I have [d]done very foolishly.

11 For when David was up in the morning, the word of the LORD came unto the prophet [a]Gad, David's [b]seer, saying,

12 Go and say unto David, Thus saith the LORD, I offer thee three *things;* choose thee one of them, that I may *do it* unto thee.

13 So Gad came to David, and told him, and said unto him, Shall [a]seven[1] years of famine come unto thee in thy land? or wilt thou flee three months before thine enemies, while they pursue thee? or that there be three days' [2]pestilence in thy land? now [3]advise, and see what answer I shall return to him that sent me.

14 And David said unto Gad, I am in [1]a great strait: let us fall now into the hand of the LORD; [a]for his mercies *are* great: and [b]let me not fall into the hand of man.

15 So [a]the LORD sent a [1]pestilence upon Israel from the morning even to the time appointed: and there died of the people from Dan even to Beer-sheba seventy thousand men.

16 [a]And when the angel stretched out his hand upon Jerusalem to destroy it, [b]the LORD [1]repented him of the evil, and said to the angel that destroyed the people, It is enough: [2]stay now thine hand. And the angel of the LORD was by the threshing-place of [3]Araunah the Jebusite.

17 And David spake unto the LORD when he saw the angel that [1]smote the people, and said, Lo, [a]I have sinned, and I have done wickedly: but these sheep, what have they done? let thine hand, I pray thee, be against me, and against my father's house.

18 And Gad came that day to David, and said unto him, [a]Go up, rear an altar unto the LORD in the threshingfloor of Araunah the Jebusite.

19 And David, according to the saying of Gad, went up as the LORD commanded.

20 And Araunah looked, and saw the king and his servants coming on toward him: and Araunah went out, and bowed himself before the king on his face upon the ground.

21 And Araunah said, Wherefore is my lord the king come to his servant? [a]And David said, To buy the threshingfloor of thee, to build an altar unto the LORD, that [b]the plague may be [1]stayed from the people.

22 And Araunah said unto David, Let my lord the king take and offer up what *seemeth* good unto him: [a]behold, *here be* oxen for burnt sacrifice, and threshing instruments and *other* instruments of the oxen for wood.

23 All these *things* did Araunah, *as* a king, give unto the king. And Araunah said unto the king, The LORD thy God [a]accept thee.

24 And the king said unto Araunah, Nay; but I will surely buy *it* of thee at a price: neither will I offer burnt offerings unto the LORD my God of that which doth cost me nothing. So [a]David bought the threshingfloor and the oxen for fifty shekels of silver.

25 And David built there an altar unto the LORD, and offered burnt offerings and peace offerings. [a]So the LORD [1]was intreated for the land, and [b]the plague was stayed from Israel.

24:2 [a] Judg. 20:1; 2 Sam. 3:10 [b] [Jer. 17:5] [1] count

24:3 [a] Deut. 1:11 [1] desire

24:4 [1] overruled

24:5 [a] Deut. 2:36; Josh. 13:9, 16 [b] Num. 32:1, 3 [1] camped [2] ravine

24:6 [a] Josh. 19:47; Judg. 18:29 [b] Josh. 19:28; Judg. 18:28

24:7 [a] Josh. 19:29 [b] Josh. 11:3; Judg. 3:3 [1] fortress

24:9 [a] 1 Chr. 21:5

24:10 [a] 1 Sam. 24:5 [b] 2 Sam. 23:1 [c] 2 Sam. 12:13 [d] 1 Sam. 13:13; [2 Chr. 16:9] [1] conscience bothered

24:11 [a] 1 Sam. 22:5 [b] 1 Sam. 9:9; 1 Chr. 29:29

24:13 [a] Ezek. 14:21 [1] three in 1 Chr. 21:12 [2] plague [3] consider

24:14 [a] [Ps. 51:1; 103:8, 13, 14; 119:156; 130:4, 7] [b] [Is. 47:6; Zech. 1:15] [1] great distress

24:15 [a] 1 Chr. 21:14 [1] plague

24:16 [a] Ex. 12:23; 2 Kin. 19:35; Acts 12:23 [b] Gen. 6:6; 1 Sam. 15:11 [1] relented from the destruction [2] restrain [3] Ornan, 1 Chr. 21:15

24:17 [a] 2 Sam. 7:8; 1 Chr. 21:17; Ps. 74:1 [1] struck

24:18 [a] 1 Chr. 21:18

24:21 [a] Gen. 23:8–16 [b] Num. 16:48, 50 [1] withdrawn

24:22 [a] 1 Sam. 6:14; 1 Kin. 19:21

24:23 [a] [Ezek. 20:40, 41]

24:24 [a] 1 Chr. 21:24, 25

24:25 [a] 2 Sam. 21:14 [b] 2 Sam. 24:21 [1] heeded the prayers

# THE FIRST BOOK OF THE
# KINGS

The first half of First Kings traces the life of Solomon. Under his leadership Israel rises to the peak of her size and glory. Solomon's great accomplishments, including the unsurpassed splendor of the temple which he constructs in Jerusalem, bring him worldwide fame and respect. However, Solomon's zeal for God diminishes in his later years, as pagan wives turn his heart away from worship in the temple of God. As a result, the king with the divided heart leaves behind a divided kingdom. For the next century, the Book of First Kings traces the twin histories of two sets of kings and two nations of disobedient people who are growing indifferent to God's prophets and precepts.

Like the two books of Samuel, the two books of Kings were originally one in the Hebrew Bible. The original title was *Melechim*, "Kings," taken from the first word in 1:1, *Vehamelech*, "Now king." The Septuagint artificially divided the book of Kings in the middle of the story of Ahaziah into two books. It called the books of Samuel "First and Second Kingdoms" and the books of Kings "Third and Fourth Kingdoms." The Septuagint may have divided Samuel, Kings, and Chronicles into two books each because the Greek required a greater amount of scroll space than did the Hebrew. The Latin title for these books is *Liber Regum Tertius et Quartus*, "Third and Fourth Books of Kings."

## CHAPTER 1

Now king David was [a]old *and* stricken in [1]years; and they covered him with clothes, but he [2]gat no heat.

2 Wherefore his servants said unto him, Let there be sought for my lord the king a young [1]virgin: and let her [2]stand before the king, and let her [3]cherish him, and let her lie in thy bosom, that my lord the king may get heat.

3 So they sought for a fair damsel throughout all the coasts of Israel, and found [a]Abishag a [b]Shunammite, and brought her to the king.

4 And the damsel *was* very fair, and cherished the king, and ministered to him: but the king knew her not.

5 Then [a]Adonijah the [1]son of Haggith exalted himself, saying, I will [2]be king: and [b]he prepared him chariots and horsemen, and fifty men to run before him.

6 And his father had not [1]displeased him at any time in saying, Why hast thou done so? and he also *was a* very [2]goodly *man;* [a]and *his mother* bare him after Absalom.

7 And he conferred with [a]Joab the son of Zeruiah, and with [b]Abiathar the priest: and [c]they following Adonijah helped *him.*

8 But [a]Zadok the priest, and [b]Benaiah the son of Jehoiada, and [c]Nathan the prophet, and [d]Shimei, and Rei, and [e]the mighty men which *belonged* to David, were not with Adonijah.

9 And Adonijah slew sheep and oxen and fat cattle by the stone of [1]Zoheleth, which *is* by [a]En-rogel,[2] and called all his brethren the king's sons,

1:1 [a] 1 Chr. 23:1
[1] About seventy years old [2] *could not get warm*
1:2 [1] *woman* [2] *serve* [3] *care for*
1:3 [a] 1 Kin. 2:17
[b] Josh. 19:18;
1 Sam. 28:4
1:5 [a] 2 Sam. 3:4
[b] 2 Sam. 15:1 [1] *the fourth son* [2] Lit. *reign*
1:6 [a] 2 Sam. 3:3, 4; 1 Chr. 3:2
[1] *rebuked* [2] *good-looking*
1:7 [a] 1 Chr. 11:6
[b] 2 Sam. 20:25
[c] 1 Kin. 2:22, 28
1:8 [a] 1 Kin. 2:35 [b] 1 Kin. 2:25; 2 Sam. 8:18 [c] 2 Sam. 12:1 [d] 1 Kin. 4:18
[e] 2 Sam. 23:8
1:9 [a] Josh. 15:7; 18:16; 2 Sam. 17:17
[1] Lit. *Serpent* [2] A spring in the Kidron Valley to the south of Jerusalem

1:10 [a] 2 Sam. 12:24
1:11 [a] 2 Sam. 3:4
[1] *has become king*
1:13 [a] 1 Kin. 1:30; 1 Chr. 22:9–13
1:16 [1] *homage* [2] *is your wish*
1:17 [a] 1 Kin. 1:13, 30
1:19 [a] 1 Kin. 1:7–9, 25

and all the men of Judah the king's servants:

10 But Nathan the prophet, and Benaiah, and the mighty men, and [a]Solomon his brother, he called not.

11 Wherefore Nathan spake unto Bath-sheba the mother of Solomon, saying, Hast thou not heard that Adonijah the son of [a]Haggith [1]doth reign, and David our lord knoweth *it* not?

12 Now therefore come, let me, I pray thee, give thee counsel, that thou mayest save thine own life, and the life of thy son Solomon.

13 Go and get thee in unto king David, and say unto him, Didst not thou, my lord, O king, swear unto thine handmaid, saying, [a]Assuredly Solomon thy son shall reign after me, and he shall sit upon my throne? why then doth Adonijah reign?

14 Behold, while thou yet talkest there with the king, I also will come in after thee, and confirm thy words.

15 And Bath-sheba went in unto the king into the chamber: and the king was very old; and Abishag the Shunammite ministered unto the king.

16 And Bath-sheba bowed, and did [1]obeisance unto the king. And the king said, What [2]wouldest thou?

17 And she said unto him, My lord, [a]thou swarest by the LORD thy God unto thine handmaid, *saying,* Assuredly Solomon thy son shall reign after me, and he shall sit upon my throne.

18 And now, behold, Adonijah reigneth; and now, my lord the king, thou knowest *it* not:

19 [a]And he hath slain oxen and fat cattle and sheep in abundance, and

hath called all the sons of the king, and Abiathar the priest, and Joab the captain of the host: but Solomon thy servant hath he not called.

20 And thou, my lord, O king, the eyes of all Israel *are* upon thee, that thou shouldest tell them who shall sit on the throne of my lord the king after him.

21 Otherwise it shall come to pass, when my lord the king [a]shall sleep with his fathers, that I and my son Solomon shall be [1]counted offenders.

22 And, lo, while she yet talked with the king, Nathan the prophet also came in.

23 And they told the king, saying, Behold Nathan the prophet. And when he was come in before the king, he bowed himself before the king with his face to the ground.

24 And Nathan said, My lord, O king, hast thou said, Adonijah shall reign after me, and he shall sit upon my throne?

25 [a]For he is gone down this day, and hath slain oxen and fat cattle and sheep in abundance, and hath called all the king's sons, and the captains of the host, and Abiathar the priest; and, behold, they eat and drink before him, and say, [b]God[1] save king Adonijah.

26 But me, *even* me thy servant, and Zadok the priest, and Benaiah the son of Jehoiada, and thy servant Solomon, hath he not called.

27 Is this thing done by my lord the king, and thou hast not shewed *it* unto thy servant, who should sit on the throne of my lord the king after him?

28 Then king David answered and said, Call me Bath-sheba. And she came into the king's presence, and stood before the king.

29 And the king sware, and said, [a]As the LORD liveth, that hath redeemed my soul out of all distress,

30 [a]Even as I sware unto thee by the LORD God of Israel, saying, Assuredly Solomon thy son shall reign after me, and he shall sit upon my throne in my stead; even so will I certainly do this day.

31 Then Bath-sheba bowed with *her* face to the earth, and did [1]reverence to the king, and said, [a]Let my lord king David live for ever.

32 And king David said, Call me Zadok the priest, and Nathan the prophet, and Benaiah the son of Jehoiada. And they came before the king.

33 The king also said unto them, [a]Take with you the servants of your lord, and cause Solomon my son to ride upon mine own [b]mule, and bring him down to [c]Gihon:[1]

34 And let Zadok the priest and Nathan the prophet [a]anoint him there king over Israel: and [b]blow ye with the trumpet, and say, [1]God save king Solomon.

35 Then ye shall come up after him, that he may come and sit upon my throne; for he shall be king in my stead: and I have appointed him to be ruler over Israel and over Judah.

36 And Benaiah the son of Jehoiada answered the king, and said, [a]Amen: the LORD God of my lord the king say so *too.*

37 [a]As the LORD hath been with my lord the king, even so be he with Solomon, and [b]make his throne greater than the throne of my lord king David.

38 So Zadok the priest, and Nathan the prophet, [a]and Benaiah the son of Jehoiada, and the [b]Cherethites, and the Pelethites, went down, and caused Solomon to ride upon king David's mule, and brought him to Gihon.

39 And Zadok the priest took an horn of [a]oil out of the tabernacle, and [b]anointed Solomon. And they blew the trumpet; [c]and all the people said, [1]God save king Solomon.

40 And all the people [1]came up after him, and the people [2]piped with pipes, and rejoiced with great joy, so that the earth [3]rent with the sound of them.

41 And Adonijah and all the guests that *were* with him heard *it* as they had made an end of eating. And when Joab heard the sound of the trumpet, he said, Wherefore *is this* noise of the city being in an uproar?

42 And while he yet spake, behold, [a]Jonathan the son of Abiathar the priest came: and Adonijah said unto him, Come in; for [b]thou *art* a [1]valiant man, and bringest good tidings.

43 And Jonathan answered and said to Adonijah, Verily our lord king David hath made Solomon king.

44 And the king hath sent with him Zadok the priest, and Nathan the prophet, and Benaiah the son of Jehoiada, and the Cherethites, and the Pelethites, and they have caused him to ride upon the king's mule:

45 And Zadok the priest and Nathan the prophet have anointed him king in Gihon: and they are come up from thence rejoicing, so that the city rang again. This *is* the noise that ye have heard.

46 And also Solomon [a]sitteth on the throne of the kingdom.

47 And moreover the king's servants came to bless our lord king David, saying, [a]God make the name of Solomon better than thy name, and make his throne greater than thy throne. [b]And the king bowed himself upon the bed.

1:21 [a] Deut. 31:16; 2 Sam. 7:12; 1 Kin. 2:10 [1] *counted as*

1:25 [a] 1 Kin. 1:9, 19 [b] 1 Sam. 10:24 [1] *Long live king Adonijah*

1:29 [a] 2 Sam. 4:9; 12:5

1:30 [a] 1 Kin. 1:13, 17

1:31 [a] Neh. 2:3; Dan. 2:4; 3:9 [1] *homage*

1:33 [a] 2 Sam. 20:6 [b] Esth. 6:8 [c] 2 Chr. 32:30; 33:14 [1] A spring east of Jerusalem in the Kidron Valley

1:34 [a] 1 Sam. 10:1; 16:3, 12; 2 Sam. 2:4; 5:3; 1 Kin. 19:16; 2 Kin. 9:3; 11:12; 1 Chr. 29:22 [b] 2 Sam. 15:10; 2 Kin. 9:13; 11:14 [1] *Long live king Solomon*

1:36 [a] Jer. 28:6

1:37 [a] Josh. 1:5, 17; 1 Sam. 20:13 [b] 1 Kin. 1:47

1:38 [a] 2 Sam. 8:18; 23:20–23 [b] 2 Sam. 20:7; 1 Chr. 18:17

1:39 [a] Ex. 30:23, 25, 32; Ps. 89:20 [b] 1 Chr. 29:22 [c] 1 Sam. 10:24 [1] *Long live king Solomon*

1:40 [1] *went up* [2] *played on flutes* [3] *was split*

1:42 [a] 2 Sam. 17:17, 20 [b] 2 Sam. 18:27 [1] *prominent*

1:46 [a] 1 Kin. 2:12; 1 Chr. 29:23

1:47 [a] 1 Kin. 1:37 [b] Gen. 47:31

48 And also thus said the king, Blessed *be* the LORD God of Israel, which hath [a]given *one* to sit on my throne this day, mine eyes even seeing [b]*it.*

49 And all the guests that *were* with Adonijah were afraid, and rose up, and went every man his way.

50 And Adonijah feared because of Solomon, and arose, and went, and [a]caught[1] hold on the horns of the altar.

51 And it was told Solomon, saying, Behold, Adonijah feareth king Solomon: for, lo, he hath caught hold on the horns of the altar, saying, Let king Solomon swear unto me to day that he will not slay his servant with the sword.

52 And Solomon said, If he will shew himself a worthy man, [a]there shall not an hair of him fall to the earth: but if wickedness shall be found in him, he shall die.

53 So king Solomon sent, and they brought him down from the altar. And he came and [1]bowed himself to king Solomon: and Solomon said unto him, Go to thine house.

## CHAPTER 2

Now [a]the days of David drew nigh that he should die; and he [1]charged Solomon his son, saying,

2 [a]I go the way of all the earth: [b]be thou strong therefore, and shew thyself a man;

3 And keep the charge of the LORD thy God, to walk in his ways, to keep his statutes, and his commandments, and his judgments, and his testimonies, as it is written in the law of Moses, that thou mayest [a]prosper in all that thou doest, and [1]whithersoever thou turnest thyself:

4 That the LORD may [a]continue his word which he spake concerning me, saying, [b]If thy children take heed to their way, to [c]walk before me in truth with all their heart and with all their soul, [d]there shall not fail thee (said he) a man on the throne of Israel.

5 Moreover thou knowest also what Joab the son of Zeruiah [a]did to me, *and* what he did to the two captains of the hosts of Israel, unto [b]Abner the son of Ner, and unto [c]Amasa the son of Jether, whom he slew, and shed the blood of war in peace, and put the blood of war upon his girdle that *was* about his loins, and in his shoes that *were* on his feet.

6 Do therefore [a]according to thy wisdom, and let not his [1]hoar head go down to the grave in peace.

7 But shew kindness unto the sons of [a]Barzillai the Gileadite, and let them be of those that [b]eat at thy table: for so [c]they came to me when I fled because of Absalom thy brother.

8 And, behold, *thou hast* with thee [a]Shimei the son of Gera, a Benjamite of Bahurim, which cursed me with a grievous curse in the day when I went to Mahanaim: but [b]he came down to meet me at Jordan, and [c]I [1]sware to him by the LORD, saying, I will not put thee to death with the sword.

9 Now therefore [a]hold him not guiltless: for thou *art* a wise man, and knowest what thou oughtest to do unto him; but his [1]hoar head [b]bring thou down to the grave with blood.

10 So [a]David [1]slept with his fathers, and was buried in [b]the city of David.

11 And the days that David [a]reigned over Israel *were* forty years: seven years reigned he in Hebron, and thirty and three years reigned he in Jerusalem.

12 [a]Then sat Solomon upon the throne of David his father; and his kingdom was [b]established [1]greatly.

13 And Adonijah the son of Haggith came to Bath-sheba the mother of Solomon. And she said, [a]Comest thou peaceably? And he said, Peaceably.

14 He said moreover, I have somewhat to say unto thee. And she said, Say on.

15 And he said, Thou knowest that the kingdom was [a]mine, and *that* all Israel set their faces on me, that I should reign: howbeit the kingdom is turned about, and is become my brother's: for [b]it was his from the LORD.

16 And now I ask one petition of thee, [1]deny me not. And she said unto him, Say on.

17 And he said, Speak, I pray thee, unto Solomon the king, (for he will not say thee nay,) that he give me [a]Abishag the Shunammite to wife.

18 And Bath-sheba said, Well; I will speak for thee unto the king.

19 Bath-sheba therefore went unto king Solomon, to speak unto him for Adonijah. And the king rose up to meet her, and [a]bowed himself unto her, and sat down on his throne, and caused a seat to be set for the king's mother; [b]and she sat on his right hand.

20 Then she said, I desire one small petition of thee; *I pray thee,* say me not nay. And the king said unto her, Ask on, my mother: for I will not say thee nay.

21 And she said, Let Abishag the Shunammite be given to Adonijah thy brother to wife.

22 And king Solomon answered and said unto his mother, And why dost thou ask Abishag the Shunammite for Adonijah? ask for him the

### Cross references

1:48 [a] 1 Kin. 3:6; [Ps. 132:11, 12] [b] 2 Sam. 7:12
1:50 [a] Ex. 27:2; 30:10; 1 Kin. 2:28 [1] took hold of
1:52 [a] 1 Sam. 14:45; 2 Sam. 14:11; Acts 27:34
1:53 [1] fell before
2:1 [a] Gen. 47:29; Deut. 31:14 [1] commanded
2:2 [a] Josh. 23:14 [b] Deut. 31:7, 23; 1 Chr. 22:13
2:3 [a] [Deut. 29:9; Josh. 1:7]; 1 Chr. 22:12, 13 [1] wherever you turn
2:4 [a] 2 Sam. 7:25 [b] [Ps. 132:12] [c] 2 Kin. 20:3 [d] 2 Sam. 7:12, 13; 1 Kin. 8:25
2:5 [a] 2 Sam. 3:39; 18:5, 12, 14 [b] 2 Sam. 3:27; 1 Kin. 2:32 [c] 2 Sam. 20:10
2:6 [a] 1 Kin. 2:9; Prov. 20:26 [1] gray hair
2:7 [a] 2 Sam. 19:31–39 [b] 2 Sam. 9:7, 10; 19:28 [c] 2 Sam. 17:17–29
2:8 [a] 2 Sam. 16:5–13 [b] 2 Sam. 19:18 [c] 2 Sam. 19:23 [1] swore
2:9 [a] Ex. 20:7; Job 9:28 [b] Gen. 42:38; 44:31 [1] gray hair
2:10 [a] 1 Kin. 1:21; Acts 2:29; 13:36 [b] 2 Sam. 5:7; 1 Kin. 3:1 [1] Died and joined his ancestors
2:11 [a] 2 Sam. 5:4, 5; 1 Chr. 3:4; 29:26, 27
2:12 [a] 1 Kin. 1:46; 1 Chr. 29:23 [b] 1 Kin. 2:46; 2 Chr. 1:1 [1] firmly
2:13 [a] 1 Sam. 16:4, 5
2:15 [a] 1 Sam. 1:11, 18 [b] 1 Chr. 22:9, 10; 28:5–7; [Dan. 2:21]
2:16 [1] do not refuse me, lit. turn not away my face
2:17 [a] 1 Kin. 1:3, 4
2:19 [a] [Ex. 20:12] [b] Ps. 45:9

kingdom also; for he *is* mine [a]elder brother; even for him, and for [b]Abiathar the priest, and for Joab the son of Zeruiah.

23 Then king Solomon sware by the LORD, saying, [a]God do so to me, and more also, if Adonijah have not spoken this word against his own life.

24 Now therefore, *as* the LORD liveth, which hath established me, and set me on the throne of David my father, and who hath made me an house, as he [a]promised, Adonijah shall be put to death this day.

25 And king Solomon sent by the hand of [a]Benaiah the son of Jehoiada; and he fell upon him that he died.

26 And unto Abiathar the priest said the king, Get thee to [a]Anathoth, unto thine own fields; for [1]thou *art* worthy of death: but I will not at this time put thee to death, [b]because thou barest the ark of the Lord GOD before David my father, and because thou hast been afflicted in all wherein my father was afflicted.

27 So Solomon thrust out Abiathar from being priest unto the LORD; that he might [a]fulfil the word of the LORD, which he spake concerning the house of Eli in Shiloh.

28 Then tidings came to Joab: for Joab [a]had turned after Adonijah, though he turned not after Absalom. And Joab fled unto the tabernacle of the LORD, and [b]caught[1] hold on the horns of the altar.

29 And it was told king Solomon that Joab was fled unto the tabernacle of the LORD; and, behold, *he is* by the altar. Then Solomon sent Benaiah the son of Jehoiada, saying, Go, [a]fall upon him.

30 And Benaiah came to the tabernacle of the LORD, and said unto him, Thus saith the king, [a]Come forth. And he said, Nay; but I will die here. And Benaiah brought the king word again, saying, Thus said Joab, and thus he answered me.

31 And the king said unto him, [a]Do as he hath said, and fall upon him, and bury him; [b]that thou mayest take away the innocent blood, which Joab shed, from me, and from the house of my father.

32 And the LORD [a]shall return his [1]blood upon his own head, who fell upon two men more righteous [b]and better than he, and slew them with the sword, my father David not knowing *thereof, to wit,* [c]Abner the son of Ner, captain of the host of Israel, and [d]Amasa the son of Jether, captain of the host of Judah.

33 Their blood shall therefore return upon the head of Joab, and [a]upon the head of his seed for ever: [b]but upon David, and upon his seed,

and upon his house, and upon his throne, shall there be peace for ever from the LORD.

34 So Benaiah the son of Jehoiada went up, and fell upon him, and slew him: and he was buried in his own house in the wilderness.

35 And the king put Benaiah the son of Jehoiada in his room over the host: and [a]Zadok the priest did the king put in the room of [b]Abiathar.

36 And the king sent and called for [a]Shimei, and said unto him, Build thee an house in Jerusalem, and dwell there, and [1]go not forth thence any whither.

37 For it shall be, *that* on the day thou goest out, and passest over [a]the brook Kidron, thou shalt know for certain that thou shalt surely die: [b]thy [1]blood shall be upon thine own head.

38 And Shimei said unto the king, The saying *is* good: as my lord the king hath said, so will thy servant do. And Shimei dwelt in Jerusalem many days.

39 And it came to pass at the end of three years, that two of the servants of Shimei ran away unto [a]Achish son of Maachah king of Gath. And they told Shimei, saying, Behold, thy servants *be* in Gath.

40 And Shimei arose, and saddled his ass, and went to Gath to Achish to seek his servants: and Shimei went, and brought his servants from Gath.

41 And it was told Solomon that Shimei had gone from Jerusalem to Gath, and was come again.

42 And the king sent and called for Shimei, and said unto him, Did I not make thee to swear by the LORD, and [1]protested unto thee, saying, Know for a certain, on the day thou goest out, and walkest abroad any whither, that thou shalt surely die? and thou saidst unto me, The word *that* I have heard *is* good.

43 Why then hast thou not kept the oath of the LORD, and the commandment that I have charged thee with?

44 The king said moreover to Shimei, Thou knowest [a]all the wickedness which thine heart [1]is privy to, that thou didst to David my father: therefore the LORD shall [b]return thy wickedness upon thine own head;

45 And king Solomon *shall be* blessed, and [a]the throne of David shall be established before the LORD for ever.

46 So the king commanded Benaiah the son of Jehoiada; which went out, and fell upon him, that he died. And the [a]kingdom was established in the hand of Solomon.

## CHAPTER 3

AND [a]Solomon made [1]affinity with Pharaoh king of Egypt, and took

---

**Center column references:**

2:22 [a] 1 Kin. 1:6; 2:15; 1 Chr. 3:2, 5
[b] 1 Kin. 1:7
2:23 [a] Ruth 1:17
2:24 [a] 2 Sam. 7:11, 13; 1 Chr. 22:10
2:25 [a] 2 Sam. 8:18; 1 Kin. 4:4
2:26 [a] Josh. 21:18; Jer. 1:1 [b] 1 Sam. 22:23; 23:6; 2 Sam. 15:14, 29
[1] Lit. *you are a man of death*
2:27 [a] 1 Sam. 2:31–35
2:28 [a] 1 Kin. 1:7 [b] 1 Kin. 1:50
[1] *took hold of*
2:29 [a] 1 Kin. 2:5, 6
2:30 [a] [Ex. 21:14]
2:31 [a] [Ex. 21:14]
[b] [Num. 35:33; Deut. 19:13; 21:8, 9]
2:32 [a] [Gen. 9:6]; Judg. 9:24, 57
[b] 2 Chr. 21:13, 14 [c] 2 Sam. 3:27
[d] 2 Sam. 20:9, 10
[1] *bloodshed*
2:33 [a] 2 Sam. 3:29
[b] [Prov. 25:5]

2:35 [a] 1 Sam. 2:35; 1 Kin. 4:4; 1 Chr. 6:53; 24:3; 29:22
[b] 1 Kin. 2:27
2:36 [a] 2 Sam. 16:5–13; 1 Kin. 2:8 [1] *do not go out from there anywhere*
2:37 [a] 2 Sam. 15:23; 2 Kin. 23:6; John 18:1 [b] Lev. 20:9; Josh. 2:19; 2 Sam. 1:16; Ezek. 18:13 [1] *bloodshed*
2:39 [a] 1 Sam. 27:2
2:42 [1] *warn you*
2:44 [a] 2 Sam. 16:5–13 [b] 1 Sam. 25:39; 2 Kin. 11:1, 12–16; Ps. 7:16; Ezek. 17:19 [1] *acknowledges*
2:45 [a] 2 Sam. 7:13; [Prov. 25:5]
2:46 [a] 1 Kin. 2:12; 2 Chr. 1:1

3:1 [a] 1 Kin. 7:8; 9:24 [1] *a treaty or an alliance*

Pharaoh's daughter, and brought her binto the city of David, until he had made an end of building his cown house, and dthe house of the LORD, and ethe wall of Jerusalem round about.

2 aOnly1 the people sacrificed in high places, because there was no house built unto the name of the LORD, until those days.

3 And Solomon aloved the LORD, bwalking in the statutes of David his father: only he sacrificed and burnt incense in high places.

4 And athe king went to Gibeon to sacrifice there; bfor that *was* the great high place: a thousand burnt offerings did Solomon offer upon that altar.

5 aIn Gibeon the LORD appeared to Solomon bin a dream by night: and God said, Ask what I shall give thee.

6 aAnd Solomon said, Thou hast shewed unto thy servant David my father great mercy, according as he bwalked before thee in truth, and in righteousness, and in uprightness of heart with thee; and thou hast kept for him this great kindness, that thou chast given him a son to sit on his throne, as *it is* this day.

7 And now, O LORD my God, thou hast made thy servant king instead of David my father: and I *am but* a alittle child: I know not how bto go out or come in.

8 And thy servant *is* in the midst of thy people which thou ahast chosen, a great people, bthat cannot be numbered nor counted for multitude.

9 aGive therefore thy servant an 1understanding heart bto judge thy people, that I may cdiscern between good and bad: for who is able to judge this thy so great a people?

10 And the speech pleased the Lord, that Solomon had asked this thing.

11 And God said unto him, Because thou hast asked this thing, and hast anot asked for thyself long life; neither hast asked riches for thyself, nor hast asked the life of thine enemies; but hast asked for thyself understanding to discern 1judgment;

12 aBehold, I have done according to thy words: blo, I have given thee a wise and an understanding heart; so that there was none like thee before thee, neither after thee shall any arise like unto thee.

13 And I have also agiven thee that which thou hast not asked, both briches, and honour: so that there shall not be 1any among the kings like unto thee all thy days.

14 And aif thou wilt walk in my ways, to keep my statutes and my commandments, bas thy father David did walk, then I will clengthen1 thy days.

15 And Solomon aawoke; and, behold, *it was* a dream. And he came to Jerusalem, and stood before the ark of the covenant of the LORD, and offered up burnt offerings, and offered peace offerings, and bmade a feast to all his servants.

16 Then came there two women, *that were* harlots, unto the king, and astood before him.

17 And the one woman said, O my lord, I and this woman dwell in one house; and I was delivered of a child with her in the house.

18 And it came to pass the third day after that I was delivered, that this woman was delivered also: and we *were* together; *there was* no 1stranger with us in the house, save we two in the house.

19 And this woman's child died in the night; because she 1overlaid it.

20 And she arose at midnight, and took my son from beside me, while thine handmaid slept, and laid it in her bosom, and laid her dead child in my bosom.

21 And when I rose in the morning to give my child suck, behold, it was dead: but when I had considered it in the morning, behold, it was not my son, which I did bear.

22 And the other woman said, Nay; but the living *is* my son, and the dead *is* thy son. And this said, No; but the dead *is* thy son, and the living *is* my son. Thus they spake before the king.

23 Then said the king, The one saith, This *is* my son that liveth, and thy son *is* the dead: and the other saith, Nay; but thy son *is* the dead, and my son *is* the living.

24 And the king said, Bring me a sword. And they brought a sword before the king.

25 And the king said, Divide the living child in two, and give half to the one, and half to the other.

26 Then spake the woman whose 1the living child *was* unto the king, for aher2 bowels yearned upon her son, and she said, O my lord, give her the living child, and in no wise slay it. But the other said, Let it be neither mine nor thine, *but* divide *it*.

27 Then the king answered and said, Give her the living child, and in no wise slay it: she *is* the mother thereof.

28 And all Israel heard of the judgment which the king had judged; and they feared the king: for they saw that the awisdom of God *was* in him, to do judgment.

## CHAPTER 4

So king Solomon was king over all Israel.

2 And these *were* the princes which

---

Cross-references:

3:1 b 2 Sam. 5:7
c 1 Kin. 7:1; d 1 Kin.
6 e 1 Kin. 9:15, 19
3:2 a [Deut.
12:2–5, 13, 14];
1 Kin. 11:7; 22:43
1 Meanwhile
3:3 a [Rom. 8:28]
b [1 Kin. 3:6, 14]
3:4 a 1 Kin. 9:2;
2 Chr. 1:3 b 1 Chr.
16:39; 21:29
3:5 a 1 Kin. 9:2;
11:9; 2 Chr. 1:7
b Num. 12:6;
Matt. 1:20; 2:13
3:6 a 2 Chr.
1:8 b 1 Kin. 2:4;
9:4; 2 Kin. 20:3
c 2 Sam. 7:8–17;
1 Kin. 1:48
3:7 a 1 Chr. 22:5;
Jer. 1:6, 7 b Num.
27:17; 2 Sam. 5:2
3:8 a [Ex. 19:6;
Deut. 7:6] b Gen.
13:6; 15:5; 22:17
3:9 a 2 Chr. 1:10;
[James 1:5] b Ps.
72:1, 2 c 2 Sam.
14:17; Is. 7:15;
[Heb. 5:14] 1 Lit.
hearing
3:11 a [James 4:3]
1 justice
3:12 a [1 John 5:14,
15] b 1 Kin. 4:29–
31; 5:12; 10:24;
Eccl. 1:16
3:13 a [Matt. 6:33;
Eph. 3:20] b 1 Kin.
4:21, 24; 10:23;
1 Chr. 29:12 1 any
one
3:14 a [1 Kin. 6:12]
b 1 Kin. 15:5 c Ps.
91:16; Prov. 3:2
1 prolong
3:15 a Gen. 41:7
b Gen. 40:20;
1 Kin. 8:65; Esth.
1:3; Dan. 5:1;
Mark 6:21
3:16 a Num. 27:2
3:18 1 no one
3:19 1 lay on him
3:26 a Gen. 43:30;
Is. 49:15; Jer.
31:20; Hos. 11:8
1 son was living
2 she yearned
with compassion
for her son
3:28 a 1 Kin. 3:9,
11, 12; 2 Chr. 1:12;
Dan. 1:17; [Col.
2:2, 3]

he had; Azariah the son of Zadok the priest,

3 Elihoreph and Ahiah, the sons of Shisha, ¹scribes; ªJehoshaphat the son of Ahilud, the recorder.

4 And ªBenaiah the son of Jehoiada *was* over the host: and Zadok and ᵇAbiathar *were* the priests:

5 And Azariah the son of Nathan *was* over ªthe officers: and Zabud the son of Nathan *was* ᵇprincipal ¹officer, *and* ᶜthe king's friend:

6 And Ahishar *was* over the household: and ªAdoniram the son of Abda *was* over the ¹tribute.

7 And Solomon had twelve ¹officers over all Israel, which provided ²victuals for the king and his household: each man his month in a year made provision.

8 And these *are* their names: ¹The son of Hur, in mount Ephraim:

9 The son of Dekar, in Makaz, and in Shaalbim, and Beth-shemesh, and Elon-beth-hanan:

10 The son of Hesed, in Aruboth; to him *pertained* Sochoh, and all the land of Hepher:

11 The son of Abinadab, in all the region of Dor; which had Taphath the daughter of Solomon to wife:

12 Baana the son of Ahilud; *to him pertained* Taanach and Megiddo, and all Beth-shean, which *is* by Zartanah beneath Jezreel, from Beth-shean to Abel-meholah, *even* unto *the place that is* beyond Jokneam:

13 The son of Geber, in Ramothgilead; to him *pertained* ªthe towns of Jair the son of Manasseh, which *are* in Gilead; to him *also pertained* ᵇthe region of Argob, which *is* in Bashan, threescore great cities with walls and brasen bars:

14 Ahinadab the son of Iddo ¹*had* Mahanaim:

15 ªAhimaaz *was* in Naphtali; he also took Basmath the daughter of Solomon to wife:

16 Baanah the son of ªHushai *was* in Asher and in Aloth:

17 Jehoshaphat the son of Paruah, in Issachar:

18 ªShimei the son of Elah, in Benjamin:

19 Geber the son of Uri *was* in the country of Gilead, *in* ªthe country of Sihon king of the Amorites, and of Og king of Bashan; and *he was* the only officer which *was* in the land.

20 Judah and Israel *were* many, ªas the sand which *is* by the sea in multitude, ᵇeating and drinking, and ¹making merry.

21 And ªSolomon reigned over all kingdoms from ᵇthe¹ river unto the land of the Philistines, and unto the border of Egypt: ᶜthey brought pres-

ents, and served Solomon all the days of his life.

22 ªAnd Solomon's ¹provision for one day was thirty ²measures of fine flour, and threescore measures of meal,

23 Ten fat oxen, and twenty oxen out of the pastures, and an hundred sheep, beside harts, and roebucks, and fallowdeer, and fatted fowl.

24 For he had dominion over all *the region* on this side ¹the river, from Tiphsah even to Azzah, over ªall the kings on this side the river: and ᵇhe had peace on all sides round about him.

25 And Judah and Israel ªdwelt¹ safely, ᵇevery man under his vine and under his fig tree, ᶜfrom Dan even to Beer-sheba, all the days of Solomon.

26 And ªSolomon had forty thousand stalls of ᵇhorses for his chariots, and twelve thousand horsemen.

27 And ªthose officers provided victual for king Solomon, and for all that came unto king Solomon's table, every man in his month: they lacked nothing.

28 Barley also and straw for the horses and ¹dromedaries brought they unto the place where *the officers* were, every man according to his charge.

29 And ªGod gave Solomon wisdom and understanding exceeding much, and largeness of heart, even as the sand that *is* on the sea shore.

30 And Solomon's wisdom excelled the wisdom of all the children ªof the east country, and all ᵇthe wisdom of Egypt.

31 For he was ªwiser than all men; ᵇthan Ethan the Ezrahite, ᶜand Heman, and Chalcol, and Darda, the sons of Mahol: and his fame was in all nations round about.

32 And ªhe spake three thousand proverbs: and his ᵇsongs were a thousand and five.

33 And he spake of trees, from the cedar tree that *is* in Lebanon even unto the hyssop that springeth out of the wall: he spake also of beasts, and of fowl, and of creeping things, and of fishes.

34 And ªthere came of all people to hear the wisdom of Solomon, from all kings of the earth, which had heard of his wisdom.

## CHAPTER 5

AND ªHiram king of Tyre sent his servants unto Solomon; for he had heard that they had anointed him king in the room of his father: ᵇfor Hiram was ever a lover of David.

2 And ªSolomon sent to Hiram, saying,

3 ªThou knowest how that David my father could not build an house

### Center column references

4:3 ª 2 Sam. 8:16; 20:24 ¹ *secretaries*

4:4 ª 1 Kin. 2:35 ᵇ 1 Kin. 2:27

4:5 ª 1 Kin. 4:7 ᵇ 2 Sam. 8:18; 20:26 ᶜ 2 Sam. 15:37; 16:16; 1 Chr. 27:33 ¹ *a priest*

4:6 ª 1 Kin. 5:14 ¹ *labour force*

4:7 ¹ *governors* ² *food*

4:8 ¹ Heb. *Ben-hur*

4:13 ª Num. 32:41; 1 Chr. 2:22 ᵇ Deut. 3:4

4:14 ¹ *in*

4:15 ª 2 Sam. 15:27

4:16 ª 2 Sam. 15:32; 1 Chr. 27:33

4:18 ª 1 Kin. 1:8

4:19 ª Deut. 3:8–10

4:20 ª Gen. 22:17; 32:12; 1 Kin. 3:8; [Prov. 14:28] ᵇ Ps. 72:3, 7; Mic. 4:4 ¹ *rejoicing*

4:21 ª Ex. 34:24; 2 Chr. 9:26; Ps. 72:8 ᵇ Gen. 15:18; Josh. 1:4 ᶜ Ps. 68:29 ¹ The Euphrates

4:22 ª Neh. 5:18 ¹ Lit. *bread* ² Heb. *kor*

4:24 ª Ps. 72:11 ᵇ 1 Kin. 5:4; 1 Chr. 22:9 ¹ The Euphrates

4:25 ª [Jer. 23:6] ᵇ [Mic. 4:4; Zech. 3:10] ᶜ Judg. 20:1 ¹ *lived in safety*

4:26 ª 1 Kin. 10:26; 2 Chr. 1:14 ᵇ [Deut. 17:16]

4:27 ª 1 Kin. 4:7

4:28 ¹ *swift steeds*

4:29 ª 1 Kin. 3:12

4:30 ª Gen. 25:6 ᵇ Is. 19:11, 12; Acts 7:22

4:31 ª 1 Kin. 3:12 ᵇ 1 Chr. 15:19; Ps. 89:title ᶜ 1 Chr. 2:6; Ps. 88:title

4:32 ª Prov. 1:1; 10:1; 25:1; Eccl. 12:9 ᵇ Song 1:1

4:34 ª 1 Kin. 10:1; 2 Chr. 9:1, 23

5:1 ª 1 Kin. 5:10, 18; 2 Chr. 2:3 ᵇ 2 Sam. 5:11; 1 Chr. 14:1

5:2 ª 2 Chr. 2:3

5:3 ª 1 Chr. 28:2, 3

unto the name of the LORD his God [b]for the wars which were about him on every side, until the LORD put [1]them under the soles of his feet.

4 But now the LORD my God hath given me [a]rest[1] on every side, *so that there is* neither adversary nor [2]evil occurrent.

5 [a]And, behold, [1]I purpose to build an house unto the name of the LORD my God, [b]as the LORD spake unto David my father, saying, Thy son, whom I will set upon thy throne in thy room, he shall build an house unto my name.

6 Now therefore command thou that they hew me [a]cedar trees out of Lebanon; and my servants shall be with thy servants: and unto thee will I [1]give hire for thy servants according to all that thou shalt [2]appoint: for thou knowest that *there is* not among us any that [3]can skill to hew timber like unto the Sidonians.

7 And it came to pass, when Hiram heard the words of Solomon, that he rejoiced greatly, and said, Blessed *be* the LORD this day, which hath given unto David a wise son over this great people.

8 And Hiram sent to Solomon, saying, I have considered the things which thou sentest to me for: *and* I will do all thy desire concerning timber of cedar, and concerning timber of fir.

9 My servants shall bring *them* down [a]from Lebanon unto the sea: and I will convey them by sea in [1]floats unto the place that thou shalt [2]appoint me, and will [3]cause them to be discharged there, and thou shalt receive *them:* and thou shalt [4]accomplish my desire, [b]in giving food for my household.

10 So Hiram gave Solomon cedar trees and fir trees *according to* all his desire.

11 [a]And Solomon gave Hiram twenty thousand [1]measures of wheat *for* food to his household, and twenty [1]measures of pure oil: thus gave Solomon to Hiram year by year.

12 And the LORD gave Solomon wisdom, [a]as he promised him: and there was peace between Hiram and Solomon; and they two made a [1]league together.

13 And king Solomon raised a [1]levy out of all Israel; and the [1]levy was thirty thousand men.

14 And he sent them to Lebanon, ten thousand a month [1]by courses: a month they were in Lebanon, *and* two months at home: and [a]Adoniram *was* over the [2]levy.

15 [a]And Solomon had threescore and ten thousand that bare burdens, and fourscore thousand [1]hewers in the mountains;

16 Beside the [a]chief of Solomon's officers which *were* over the work, three thousand and three hundred, which [1]ruled over the people that wrought in the work.

17 And the king commanded, and they brought great stones, costly stones, *and* [a]hewed stones, to lay the foundation of the [1]house.

18 And Solomon's builders and Hiram's builders did hew *them,* and the [1]stonesquarers: so they prepared timber and stones to build the [2]house.

## CHAPTER 6

AND [a]it came to pass in the four hundred and eightieth year after the children of Israel were come out of the land of Egypt, in the fourth year of Solomon's reign over Israel, in the month [1]Zif, which *is* the second month, that [b]he began to build the house of the LORD.

2 And [a]the house which king Solomon built for the LORD, the length thereof *was* threescore cubits, and the breadth thereof twenty *cubits,* and the height thereof thirty cubits.

3 And the porch before the [1]temple of the house, twenty cubits *was* the length thereof, according to the breadth of the house; *and* ten cubits *was* the breadth thereof before the house.

4 And for the house he made [a]windows of narrow lights.

5 And against the wall of the [1]house he built [a]chambers round about, *against* the walls of the house round about, *both* of the [2]temple [b]and of the [3]oracle: and he made chambers round about:

6 The [1]nethermost chamber *was* five cubits broad, and the middle *was* six cubits broad, and the third *was* seven cubits broad: for without *in the wall* of the [2]house he made [3]narrowed rests round about, that *the beams* should not be fastened in the walls of the house.

7 And [a]the house, when it was in building, was built of stone made ready before it was brought thither: so that there was neither hammer nor axe *nor* any tool of iron heard in the house, while it was in building.

8 The door for the middle chamber *was* in the right side of the house: and they went up with winding stairs into the middle *chamber,* and out of the middle into the third.

9 [a]So he built the [1]house, and finished it; and covered the house [2]with beams and boards of cedar.

10 And *then* he built chambers against all the house, five cubits high: and they rested on the house with timber of cedar.

5:3 [b] 1 Chr. 22:8; 28:3 [1] *his foes*
5:4 [a] 1 Kin. 4:24; 1 Chr. 22:9 [1] *peace* [2] *misfortune*
5:5 [a] 2 Chr. 2:4 [b] 2 Sam. 7:12, 13; 1 Kin. 6:38; 1 Chr. 17:12; 22:10; 28:6; 2 Chr. 6:2 [1] Lit. *I am saying*
5:6 [a] 2 Chr. 2:8, 10 [1] *pay wages* [2] *say* [3] *has*
5:9 [a] Ezra 3:7 [b] Ezek. 27:17; Acts 12:20 [1] *rafts* [2] *indicate to* [3] *have them broken apart* [4] *fulfil*
5:11 [a] 2 Chr. 2:10 [1] Heb. *kor*
5:12 [a] 1 Kin. 3:12 [1] *treaty*
5:13 [1] *labour force*
5:14 [a] 1 Kin. 12:18 [1] *in shifts* [2] *labour force*
5:15 [a] 1 Kin. 9:20–22; 2 Chr. 2:17, 18 [1] *who quarried stone*
5:16 [a] 1 Kin. 9:23 [1] *supervised*
5:17 [a] 1 Kin. 6:7; 1 Chr. 22:2 [1] *temple*
5:18 [1] Or *Gebalites* [2] *temple*
6:1 [a] 2 Chr. 3:1, 2 [b] Acts 7:47 [1] Or *Ayyar* (April or May)
6:2 [a] Ezek. 41:1
6:3 [1] Heb. *heykal;* here the main room of the temple; elsewhere called *the holy place,* Ex. 26:33
6:4 [a] Ezek. 40:16; 41:16
6:5 [a] Ezek. 41:6 [b] 1 Kin. 6:16, 19–21, 31 [1] *temple* [2] *sanctuary* [3] Heb. *debir;* here the inner room of the temple; elsewhere called *the most holy place,* 1 Kin. 6:16
6:6 [1] *lowest* [2] *temple* [3] *narrow ledges*
6:7 [a] Ex. 20:25; Deut. 27:5, 6
6:9 [a] 1 Kin. 6:14, 38 [1] *temple* [2] *panelled*

11 And the word of the LORD came to Solomon, saying,

12 *Concerning* this ¹house which thou art in building, ᵃif thou wilt walk in my statutes, and execute my judgments, and keep all my commandments to walk in them; then will I perform my ²word with thee, ᵇwhich I spake unto David thy father:

13 And ᵃI will dwell among the children of Israel, and will not ᵇforsake my people Israel.

14 So Solomon built the house, and finished it.

15 And he built the walls of the house within with boards of cedar, ¹both the floor of the house, and the walls of the cieling: *and* he covered *them* on the inside with wood, and covered the floor of the house with planks of fir.

16 And he built twenty cubits on the sides of the house, both the floor and the walls with boards of cedar: he even built *them* for it within, *even* for the oracle, *even* for the ᵃmost holy *place.*

17 And the house, that *is,* the temple before it, was forty cubits *long.*

18 And the cedar of the house within *was* carved with ¹knops and open flowers: all *was* cedar; there was no stone seen.

19 And the ¹oracle he prepared in the house within, to set there the ark of the covenant of the LORD.

20 And the oracle in the forepart *was* twenty cubits in length, and twenty cubits in breadth, and twenty cubits in the height thereof: and he overlaid it with pure gold; and *so* covered the altar *which was of* cedar.

21 So Solomon overlaid the house within with pure gold: and he made a partition by the chains of gold before the oracle; and he overlaid it with gold.

22 And the whole house he overlaid with gold, until he had finished all the house: also ᵃthe whole altar that *was* by the oracle he overlaid with gold.

23 And within the oracle ᵃhe made two cherubims *of* olive ¹tree, *each* ten cubits high.

24 And five cubits *was* the one wing of the cherub, and five cubits the other wing of the cherub: from the uttermost part of the one wing unto the uttermost part of the other *were* ten cubits.

25 And the other cherub *was* ten cubits: both the cherubims *were* of one measure and one size.

26 The height of the one cherub *was* ten cubits, and so *was it* of the other cherub.

27 And he set the cherubims within the inner ¹house: and ᵃthey stretched forth the wings of the cherubims, so that the wing of the one touched the *one* wall, and the wing of the other cherub touched the other wall; and their wings touched one another in the midst of the house.

28 And he overlaid the cherubims with gold.

29 And he carved all the walls of the house round about with carved ᵃfigures of cherubims and palm trees and open flowers, within and without.

30 And the floor of the house he overlaid with gold, within and without.

31 And for the entering of the oracle he made doors *of* olive tree: the lintel *and* side posts *were* ¹a fifth part *of the wall.*

32 The two doors also *were of* olive tree; and he carved upon them carvings of cherubims and palm trees and open flowers, and overlaid *them* with gold, and spread gold upon the cherubims, and upon the palm trees.

33 So also made he for the door of the ¹temple posts *of* olive tree, ²a fourth part *of the wall.*

34 And the two doors *were of* ¹fir tree: the ᵃtwo ²leaves of the one door *were* folding, and the two ³leaves of the other door *were* folding.

35 And he carved *thereon* cherubims and palm trees and open flowers: and covered *them* with gold fitted upon the carved work.

36 And he built the ᵃinner court with three rows of hewed stone, and a row of cedar beams.

37 ᵃIn the fourth year was the foundation of the house of the LORD laid, in the month ¹Zif:

38 And in the eleventh year, in the month ¹Bul, which *is* the eighth month, was the house finished ²throughout all the parts thereof, and according to all the fashion of it. So was he ᵃseven years in building it.

## CHAPTER 7

BUT Solomon was building his own house ᵃthirteen years, and he finished all his house.

2 He built also the ᵃhouse of the forest of Lebanon; the length thereof *was* an ¹hundred cubits, and the breadth thereof ²fifty cubits, and the height thereof thirty cubits, upon four rows of cedar pillars, with cedar beams upon the pillars.

3 And *it was* ¹covered with cedar above upon the beams, that *lay* on forty five pillars, fifteen *in* a row.

4 And *there were* windows *in* three rows, and ¹light *was* against light *in* three ²ranks.

5 And all the ¹doors and posts *were* square, with the windows: and light *was* against light *in* three ranks.

### Center column references

6:12 ᵃ 1 Kin. 2:4; 9:4 ᵇ [2 Sam. 7:13; 1 Chr. 22:10] ¹ temple ² promise
6:13 ᵃ Ex. 25:8; Lev. 26:11; [2 Cor. 6:16; Rev. 21:3] ᵇ [Deut. 31:6]
6:15 ¹ from the floor of the temple to the ceiling
6:16 ᵃ Ex. 26:33; Lev. 16:2; 1 Kin. 8:6; 2 Chr. 3:8; Ezek. 45:3; Heb. 9:3
6:18 ¹ gourds
6:19 ¹ Heb. *debir*; 1 Kin. 6:5
6:22 ᵃ Ex. 30:1, 3, 6
6:23 ᵃ Ex. 37:7–9; 2 Chr. 3:10–12 ¹ wood
6:27 ᵃ Ex. 25:20; 37:9; 1 Kin. 8:7; 2 Chr. 5:8 ¹ room
6:29 ᵃ Ex. 36:8, 35
6:31 ¹ Or *five-sided*
6:33 ¹ sanctuary ² Or four-sided
6:34 ᵃ Ezek. 41:23–25 ¹ cypress ² panels were one swinging door ³ panels were the other swinging door
6:36 ᵃ 1 Kin. 7:12; Jer. 36:10
6:37 ᵃ 1 Kin. 6:1 ¹ April or May
6:38 ᵃ 2 Sam. 7:13; 1 Kin. 5:5; 6:1; 8:19 ¹ October or November ² in all its details according to all its plans
7:1 ᵃ 1 Kin. 3:1; 9:10; 2 Chr. 8:1
7:2 ᵃ 1 Kin. 10:17, 21; 2 Chr. 9:16 ¹ About 150 feet ² About 75 feet
7:3 ¹ above the beams
7:4 ¹ window was opposite window ² rows
7:5 ¹ doorways

6 And he made a [1]porch of pillars; the length thereof *was* fifty cubits, and the breadth thereof thirty cubits: and the [2]porch *was* before them: and the *other* pillars and [3]the thick beam *were* before them.

7 Then he made a porch for the throne where he might judge, *even* the porch of judgment: and *it was* covered with cedar [1]from one side of the floor to the other.

8 And his house where he dwelt *had* another court within the porch, *which* was of the like work. Solomon made also an house for Pharaoh's daughter, [a]whom he had taken *to wife*, like unto this [1]porch.

9 All these *were of* costly stones, according to the measures of hewed stones, sawed with saws, within and without, even from the foundation unto the coping, and *so* on the outside toward the great court.

10 And the foundation *was of* costly stones, even great stones, stones of ten cubits, and stones of eight cubits.

11 And above *were* costly stones, after the measures of hewed stones, and cedars.

12 And the great court round about *was* with three rows of hewed stones, and a row of cedar beams, both for the [a]inner court of the house of the LORD, [b]and for the porch of the house.

13 And king Solomon sent and fetched [1]Hiram out of Tyre.

14 [a]He *was* a widow's son of the tribe of Naphtali, and [b]his father *was* a man of Tyre, a worker in [1]brass: and [c]he was filled with wisdom, and understanding, and [2]cunning to work all works in brass. And he came to king Solomon, and wrought all his work.

15 For he [1]cast [a]two pillars of [2]brass, of eighteen cubits high apiece: and a line of twelve cubits [3]did compass either of them about.

16 And he made two [1]chapiters *of* molten brass, to set upon the tops of the pillars: the height of the one chapiter *was* five cubits, and the height of the other chapiter *was* five cubits:

17 *And* nets of checker work, and wreaths of chain work, for the chapiters which *were* upon the top of the pillars; seven for the one chapiter, and seven for the other chapiter.

18 And he made the pillars, and two rows round about upon the one network, to cover the chapiters that *were* upon the top, with pomegranates: and so did he for the other chapiter.

19 And the chapiters that *were* upon the top of the pillars *were* of lily work in the porch, four cubits.

20 And the chapiters upon the two pillars *had pomegranates* also above, [1]over against the belly which *was* by the network: and the pomegranates *were* [a]two hundred in rows round about upon the other chapiter.

21 [a]And he set up the pillars in the porch of the temple: and he set up the right pillar, and called the name thereof [1]Jachin: and he set up the left pillar, and called the name thereof [2]Boaz.

22 And upon the top of the pillars *was* lily work: so was the work of the pillars finished.

23 And he made [a]a [1]molten sea, ten cubits from the one brim to the other: *it was* round all about, and his height *was* five cubits: and a line of thirty cubits did compass it round about.

24 And under the brim of it round about *there were* knops compassing it, ten in a cubit, [a]compassing the sea round about: the knops *were* cast in two rows, when it was cast.

25 It stood upon [a]twelve oxen, three looking toward the north, and three looking toward the west, and three looking toward the south, and three looking toward the east: and the sea *was set* above upon them, and all their [1]hinder parts *were* inward.

26 And it *was* an hand breadth thick, and the brim thereof was wrought like the brim of a cup, with flowers of lilies: it contained [a]two thousand baths.

27 And he made ten [1]bases of brass; four cubits *was* the length of one base, and four cubits the breadth thereof, and three cubits the height of it.

28 And the work of the bases *was* on this *manner:* they had borders, and the borders *were* between the ledges:

29 And on the borders that *were* between the ledges *were* lions, oxen, and cherubims: and upon the ledges *there was* a base above: and beneath the lions and oxen *were* [1]certain additions made of thin work.

30 And every base had four brasen wheels, and [1]plates of brass: and the four corners thereof had [2]undersetters: under the laver *were* undersetters molten, at the side of every addition.

31 And the mouth of it within the chapiter and above *was* a cubit: but the mouth thereof *was* round *after* the work of the base, a cubit and an half: and also upon the mouth of it *were* [1]gravings with their borders, foursquare, not round.

32 And under the borders *were* four wheels; and the axletrees of the wheels *were joined* to the base: and

---

**Cross references / footnotes (center column):**

7:6 [1] *hall* [2] *portico with pillars* [3] *a canopy*

7:7 [1] *from floor to ceiling*

7:8 [a] 1 Kin. 3:1; 9:24; 11:1; 2 Chr. 8:11 [1] *hall*

7:12 [a] 1 Kin. 6:36 [b] John 10:23; Acts 3:11

7:13 [1] *Huram,* 2 Chr. 2:13, 14

7:14 [a] 2 Chr. 2:14 [b] 2 Chr. 4:16 [c] Ex. 31:3; 36:1 [1] *bronze* [2] *skill in working*

7:15 [a] 2 Kin. 25:17; 2 Chr. 3:15; 4:12; Jer. 52:21 [1] *fashioned* [2] *bronze* [3] *measured the circumference of each of them*

7:16 [1] *capitals of cast bronze*

7:20 [a] 2 Chr. 3:16; 4:13; Jer. 52:23 [1] *by the convex surface*

7:21 [a] 2 Chr. 3:17 [1] *Lit. He Shall Establish* [2] *Lit. In It Is Strength*

7:23 [a] 2 Kin. 25:13; 2 Chr. 4:2; Jer. 52:17 [1] *sea of cast metal*

7:24 [a] 2 Chr. 4:3

7:25 [a] 2 Chr. 4:4, 5; Jer. 52:20 [1] *back*

7:26 [a] 2 Chr. 4:5

7:27 [1] *carts or stands*

7:29 [1] *wreaths of plaited work*

7:30 [1] *axles of bronze* [2] *supports*

7:31 [1] *engravings*

the height of a wheel *was* a cubit and half a cubit.

33 And the work of the wheels *was* like the work of a chariot wheel: their axletrees, and their [1]naves, and their [2]felloes, and their spokes, *were* all [3]molten.

34 And *there were* four undersetters to the four corners of one base: *and* the undersetters *were* of the very base itself.

35 And in the top of the base *was there* a round compass of half a cubit high: and on the top of the base the ledges thereof and the borders thereof *were* of the same.

36 For on the plates of the ledges thereof, and on the borders thereof, he graved cherubims, lions, and palm trees, [1]according to the proportion of every one, and additions round about.

37 After this *manner* he made the ten bases: all of them had [1]one casting, one measure, *and* one size.

38 Then [a]made he ten lavers of brass: one laver contained forty baths: *and* every laver was four cubits: *and* upon every one of the ten bases one laver.

39 And he put five bases on the right side of the house, and five on the left side of the house: and he set the sea on the right side of the house eastward over against the south.

40 [a]And Hiram made the lavers, and the shovels, and the basons. So Hiram [1]made an end of doing all the work that he made king Solomon for the house of the LORD:

41 The two pillars, and the *two* bowls of the chapiters that *were* on the top of the two pillars; and the two [a]networks, to cover the two bowls of the chapiters which *were* upon the top of the pillars;

42 And [a]four hundred pomegranates for the two networks, *even* two rows of pomegranates for one network, to cover the two bowls of the chapiters that *were* [1]upon the pillars;

43 And the ten bases, and ten lavers on the bases;

44 And one sea, and twelve oxen under the sea;

45 [a]And the pots, and the shovels, and the basons: and all these vessels, which Hiram made to king Solomon for the house of the LORD, *were of* [1]bright brass.

46 [a]In the plain of Jordan did the king cast them, in the clay ground between [b]Succoth and [c]Zarthan.

47 And Solomon left all the vessels *unweighed,* because they were exceeding many: neither was the weight of the brass found [a]out.

48 And Solomon made all the vessels that *pertained* unto the house of

the LORD: [a]the altar of gold, and [b]the table of gold, whereupon [c]the shewbread *was,*

49 And the candlesticks of pure gold, five on the right *side,* and five on the left, before the oracle, with the flowers, and the lamps, and the tongs *of* gold,

50 And the bowls, and the snuffers, and the basons, and the spoons, and the [1]censers *of* pure gold; and the hinges *of* gold, *both* for the doors of the inner house, the most holy *place, and* for the doors of the house, *to wit,* of the temple.

51 So was ended all the work that king Solomon made for the house of the LORD. And Solomon brought in the things [a]which David his father had dedicated; *even* the silver, and the gold, and the vessels, did he put among the treasures of the house of the LORD.

## CHAPTER 8

THEN [a]Solomon assembled the elders of Israel, and all the heads of the tribes, the chief of the fathers of the children of Israel, unto king Solomon in Jerusalem, [b]that they might bring [c]up the ark of the covenant of the LORD out of the city of David, which *is* Zion.

2 And all the men of Israel assembled themselves unto king Solomon at the [a]feast in the month [1]Ethanim, which *is* the seventh month.

3 And all the elders of Israel came, [a]and the priests took up the ark.

4 And they brought up the ark of the LORD, [a]and the [1]tabernacle of the congregation, and all the holy vessels that *were* in the tabernacle, even those did the priests and the Levites bring up.

5 And king Solomon, and all the congregation of Israel, that were assembled unto him, *were* with him before the ark, [a]sacrificing sheep and oxen, that could not be told nor numbered for multitude.

6 And the priests [a]brought in the ark of the covenant of the LORD unto [b]his place, into the oracle of the house, to the most holy *place, even* [c]under the wings of the cherubims.

7 For the cherubims spread forth *their* two wings over the place of the ark, and the cherubims covered the ark and the staves thereof above.

8 And [1]they [a]drew out the staves, that the [2]ends of the staves were seen out in the holy *place* [b]before the oracle, and they were not seen without: and there they are unto this day.

9 [a]*There was* nothing in the ark [b]save the two tables of stone, which Moses [c]put there at Horeb, [d]when the LORD made *a covenant* with the

7:33 [1] rims  [2] hubs  [3] cast metal

7:36 [1] wherever there was a clear space

7:37 [1] the same

7:38 [a] Ex. 30:18; 2 Chr. 4:6

7:40 [a] 2 Chr. 4:11–5:1  [1] finished

7:41 [a] 1 Kin. 7:17, 18

7:42 [a] 1 Kin. 7:20  [1] on the tops of

7:45 [a] Ex. 27:3; 2 Chr. 4:16  [1] burnished bronze

7:46 [a] 2 Chr. 4:17  [b] Gen. 33:17; Josh. 13:27  [c] Josh. 3:16

7:47 [a] 1 Chr. 22:3, 14

7:48 [a] Ex. 37:25, 26; 2 Chr. 4:8  [b] Ex. 37:10, 11  [c] Lev. 24:5–8

7:50 [1] firepans

7:51 [a] 2 Sam. 8:11; 1 Chr. 18:11; 2 Chr. 5:1

8:1 [a] Num. 1:4; 7:2; 2 Chr. 5:2–14  [b] 2 Sam. 6:12–17; 1 Chr. 15:25–29  [c] 2 Sam. 5:7; 6:12, 16

8:2 [a] Lev. 23:34; 1 Kin. 8:65; 2 Chr. 7:8–10  [1] September or October

8:3 [a] Num. 4:15; 7:9

8:4 [a] 2 Chr. 1:3  [1] tent of meeting

8:5 [a] 2 Sam. 6:13

8:6 [a] 2 Sam. 6:17  [b] 1 Kin. 6:19  [c] 1 Kin. 6:27

8:8 [a] Ex. 25:13–15; 37:4, 5  [1] the poles extended so that  [2] Lit. heads of the poles  [3] in front of the inner sanctuary

8:9 [a] Ex. 25:21  [b] Deut. 10:5  [c] Ex. 24:7, 8; 40:20  [d] Ex. 34:27, 28

children of Israel, when they came out of the land of Egypt.

10 And it came to pass, when the priests were come out of the holy *place*, that the cloud <sup>a</sup>filled the house of the LORD,

11 So that the priests could not stand to minister because of the cloud: for the <sup>a</sup>glory of the LORD had filled the house of the LORD.

12 <sup>a</sup>Then spake Solomon, The LORD said that he would dwell <sup>b</sup>in the thick <sup>1</sup>darkness.

13 <sup>a</sup>I have surely built thee <sup>1</sup>an house to dwell in, <sup>b</sup>a<sup>2</sup> settled place for thee to abide in for ever.

14 And the king turned his face about, and <sup>a</sup>blessed all the congregation of Israel: (and all the congregation of Israel stood;)

15 And he said, <sup>a</sup>Blessed *be* the LORD God of Israel, which <sup>b</sup>spake with his mouth unto David my father, and hath with his hand fulfilled *it*, saying,

16 Since the day that I brought forth my people Israel out of Egypt, I chose no city out of all the tribes of Israel to build an house, that <sup>a</sup>my name might be therein; but I chose <sup>b</sup>David to be over my people Israel.

17 And <sup>a</sup>it was in the heart of David my father to build an house for the name of the LORD God of Israel.

18 <sup>a</sup>And the LORD said unto David my father, Whereas it was in thine heart to build an house unto my name, thou didst well that it was in thine heart.

19 Nevertheless <sup>a</sup>thou shalt not build the house; but thy son that shall come forth out of thy loins, he shall build the house unto my name.

20 And the LORD hath performed his word that he spake, and I <sup>1</sup>am risen up in the room of David my father, and sit on the throne of Israel, <sup>a</sup>as the LORD promised, and have built an house for the name of the LORD God of Israel.

21 And I have set there a place for the ark, wherein *is* <sup>a</sup>the covenant of the LORD, which he made with our fathers, when he brought them out of the land of Egypt.

22 And Solomon stood before <sup>a</sup>the altar of the LORD in the presence of all the congregation of Israel, and <sup>b</sup>spread forth his hands toward heaven:

23 And he said, LORD God of Israel, <sup>a</sup>*there is* no God like thee, in heaven above, or on earth beneath, <sup>b</sup>who <sup>1</sup>keepest covenant and mercy with thy servants that <sup>c</sup>walk before thee with all their heart:

24 Who hast kept with thy servant David my father that thou promisedst him: thou spakest also with

thy mouth, and hast fulfilled *it* with thine hand, as *it is* this day.

25 Therefore now, LORD God of Israel, keep with thy servant David my father that thou promisedst him, saying, <sup>a</sup>There shall not fail thee a man in my sight to sit on the throne of Israel; <sup>1</sup>so that thy children take heed to their way, that they walk before me as thou hast walked before me.

26 <sup>a</sup>And now, O God of Israel, let thy word, I pray thee, be verified, which thou spakest unto thy servant David my father.

27 But <sup>a</sup>will God indeed dwell on the earth? behold, the heaven and heaven of <sup>b</sup>heavens cannot contain thee; how much less this house that I have builded?

28 Yet <sup>1</sup>have thou respect unto the prayer of thy servant, and to his supplication, O LORD my God, to hearken unto the cry and to the prayer, which thy servant prayeth before thee to day:

29 That thine eyes may be open toward this <sup>1</sup>house night and day, *even* toward the place of which thou hast said, <sup>a</sup>My name shall be <sup>b</sup>there: that thou mayest hearken unto the prayer which thy servant shall make <sup>c</sup>toward this place.

30 <sup>a</sup>And hearken thou to the supplication of thy servant, and of thy people Israel, when they shall pray toward this place: and hear thou in heaven thy dwelling place: and when thou hearest, forgive.

31 If any man trespass against his neighbour, and <sup>a</sup>an<sup>1</sup> oath be laid upon him to cause him to swear, and the oath come before thine altar in this house:

32 Then hear thou in heaven, and do, and judge thy servants, <sup>a</sup>condemning the wicked, to bring his way upon his head; and justifying the righteous, to give him according to his righteousness.

33 <sup>a</sup>When thy people Israel be smitten down before the enemy, because they have sinned against thee, and <sup>b</sup>shall turn again to thee, and confess thy name, and pray, and make supplication unto thee in this house:

34 Then hear thou in heaven, and forgive the sin of thy people Israel, and bring them again unto the land which thou gavest unto their <sup>a</sup>fathers.

35 <sup>a</sup>When heaven is shut up, and there is no rain, because they have sinned against thee; if they pray toward this place, and confess thy name, and turn from their sin, when thou afflictest them:

36 Then hear thou in heaven, and forgive the sin of thy servants, and of thy people Israel, that thou <sup>a</sup>teach

## Center reference column

8:10 <sup>a</sup> Ex. 40:34, 35

8:11 <sup>a</sup> 2 Chr. 7:1, 2

8:12 <sup>a</sup> 2 Chr. 6:1
<sup>b</sup> Ps. 18:11; 97:2
<sup>1</sup> *cloud*

8:13 <sup>a</sup> 2 Sam. 7:13
<sup>b</sup> Ps. 132:14 <sup>1</sup> *an exalted house* <sup>2</sup> *a place*

8:14 <sup>a</sup> 2 Sam. 6:18

8:15 <sup>a</sup> Luke 1:68
<sup>b</sup> 2 Sam. 7:2, 12, 13, 25

8:16 <sup>a</sup> 1 Kin. 8:29
<sup>b</sup> 2 Sam. 7:8

8:17 <sup>a</sup> 2 Sam. 7:2, 3

8:18 <sup>a</sup> 2 Chr. 6:8, 9

8:19 <sup>a</sup> 2 Sam. 7:5, 12, 13

8:20 <sup>a</sup> 1 Chr. 28:5, 6 <sup>1</sup> *filled the place*

8:21 <sup>a</sup> Deut. 31:26

8:22 <sup>a</sup> 2 Chr. 6:12
<sup>b</sup> Ezra 9:5

8:23 <sup>a</sup> Ex. 15:11
<sup>b</sup> [Neh. 1:5]
<sup>c</sup> [Gen. 17:1]
<sup>1</sup> *keeps your covenant*

8:25 <sup>a</sup> 1 Kin. 2:4; 9:5 <sup>1</sup> *only if*

8:26 <sup>a</sup> 2 Sam. 7:25

8:27 <sup>a</sup> [Acts 7:49; 17:24] <sup>b</sup> 2 Cor. 12:2

8:28 <sup>1</sup> *regard the prayer*

8:29 <sup>a</sup> Deut. 12:11
<sup>b</sup> 1 Kin. 9:3 <sup>c</sup> Dan. 6:10 <sup>1</sup> *temple*

8:30 <sup>a</sup> Neh. 1:6

8:31 <sup>a</sup> Ex. 22:8–11
<sup>1</sup> *he is forced to take an oath and he comes and takes an oath before your altar*

8:32 <sup>a</sup> Deut. 25:1

8:33 <sup>a</sup> Lev. 26:17; Deut. 28:25 <sup>b</sup> Lev. 26:39, 40

8:34 <sup>a</sup> [Lev. 26:40–42; Deut. 30:1–3]

8:35 <sup>a</sup> Lev. 26:19; Deut. 28:23

8:36 <sup>a</sup> Ps. 25:4; 27:11; 94:12

them ᵇthe good way wherein they should walk, and give rain upon thy land, which thou hast given to thy people for an inheritance.

37 ªIf there be in the land famine, if there be pestilence, ¹blasting, mildew, locust, *or* if there be caterpiller; if their enemy besiege them in the land ²of their cities; whatsoever plague, whatsoever sickness *there be;*

38 What prayer and supplication soever be *made* by any man, *or* by all thy people Israel, which shall know every man the plague of his own heart, and spread forth his hands toward this house:

39 Then hear thou in heaven thy dwelling place, and forgive, and do, and give to every man according to his ways, whose heart thou knowest; (for thou, *even* thou only, ªknowest the hearts of all the children of men;)

40 ªThat they may fear thee all the days that they live in the land which thou gavest unto our fathers.

41 Moreover concerning a stranger, that *is* not of thy people Israel, but cometh out of a far country for thy name's sake;

42 (For they shall hear of thy great name, and of thy ªstrong hand, and of thy stretched out arm;) when he shall come and pray toward this house;

43 Hear thou in heaven thy dwelling place, and do according to all that the stranger calleth to thee for: ªthat all people of the earth may know thy name, to ᵇfear thee, as *do* thy people Israel; and that they may know that this house, which I have builded, is called by thy name.

44 If thy people go out to battle against their enemy, whithersoever thou shalt send them, and shall pray unto the LORD toward the city which thou hast chosen, and *toward* the house that I have built for thy name:

45 Then hear thou in heaven their prayer and their supplication, and maintain their ¹cause.

46 If they sin against thee, ª(for *there is* no man that sinneth not,) and thou be angry with them, and deliver them to the enemy, so that they carry them away captives ᵇunto the land of the enemy, far or near;

47 ªYet if they shall ¹bethink themselves in the land whither they were carried captives, and repent, and make supplication unto thee in the land of them that carried them captives, ᵇsaying, We have sinned, and have done ²perversely, we have committed wickedness;

48 And *so* ªreturn unto thee with all their heart, and with all their soul, in the land of their enemies, which led them away captive, and ᵇpray unto thee toward their land, which

thou gavest unto their fathers, the city which thou hast chosen, and the house which I have built for thy name:

49 Then hear thou their prayer and their supplication in heaven thy dwelling place, and maintain their ¹cause,

50 And forgive thy people that have sinned against thee, and all their transgressions wherein they have transgressed against thee, and ªgive them compassion before them who carried them captive, that they may have compassion on them:

51 For ªthey *be* thy people, and thine inheritance, which thou broughtest forth out of Egypt, ᵇfrom the midst of the furnace of iron:

52 ªThat thine eyes may be open unto the supplication of thy servant, and unto the supplication of thy people Israel, to hearken unto them in all that they call for unto thee.

53 For thou didst separate them from among all the people of the earth, *to be* thine inheritance, ªas thou spakest by the hand of Moses thy servant, when thou broughtest our fathers out of Egypt, O Lord GOD.

54 ªAnd it was *so,* that when Solomon had made an end of praying all this prayer and supplication unto the LORD, he arose from before the altar of the LORD, from kneeling on his knees with his hands spread up to heaven.

55 And he stood, ªand blessed all the congregation of Israel with a loud voice, saying,

56 Blessed *be* the LORD, that hath given ªrest¹ unto his people Israel, according to all that he promised: ᵇthere hath not failed one word of all his good promise, which he promised by the hand of Moses his servant.

57 The LORD our God be with us, as he was with our fathers: ªlet him not leave us, nor forsake us:

58 That he may ªincline our hearts unto him, to walk in all his ways, and to keep his commandments, and his statutes, and his judgments, which he commanded our fathers.

59 And let these my words, wherewith I have made supplication before the LORD, be nigh unto the LORD our God day and night, that he maintain the cause of his servant, and the cause of his people Israel at all times, ¹as the matter shall require:

60 ªThat all the people of the earth may know that ᵇthe LORD *is* God, *and that there is* none else.

61 Let your ªheart therefore be ¹perfect with the LORD our God, to walk in his statutes, and to keep his commandments, as at this day.

62 And ªthe king, and all Israel with him, offered sacrifice before the LORD.

---

**Center column cross-references:**

8:36 ᵇ 1 Sam. 12:23

8:37 ª Lev. 26:16, 25, 26; Deut. 28:21, 22, 27, 38, 42, 52 ¹ *blight* ² *in their gates*

8:39 ª [1 Sam. 16:7; 1 Chr. 28:9; Jer. 17:10]; Acts 1:24

8:40 ª [Ps. 130:4]

8:42 ª Ex. 13:3; Deut. 3:24

8:43 ª [Ex. 9:16; 1 Sam. 17:46; 2 Kin. 19:19] ᵇ Ps. 102:15

8:45 ¹ *justice*

8:46 ª 2 Chr. 6:36; Ps. 130:3; Prov. 20:9; Eccl. 7:20; [Rom. 3:23; 1 John 1:8, 10] ᵇ Lev. 26:34, 44; Deut. 28:36, 64; 2 Kin. 17:6, 18; 25:21

8:47 ª [Lev. 26:40–42]; Neh. 9:2 ᵇ Ezra 9:6, 7; Neh. 1:6; Ps. 106:6; Dan. 9:5 ¹ *come to themselves* ² *wrong*

8:48 ª Jer. 29:12–14 ᵇ Dan. 6:10; Jon. 2:4

8:49 ¹ *justice*

8:50 ª [2 Chr. 30:9]; Ezra 7:6; Ps. 106:46; Acts 7:10

8:51 ª Ex. 32:11, 12; Deut. 9:26–29; Neh. 1:10; [Rom. 11:28, 29] ᵇ Deut. 4:20; Jer. 11:4

8:52 ª 1 Kin. 8:29

8:53 ª Ex. 19:5, 6

8:54 ª 2 Chr. 7:1

8:55 ª 2 Sam. 6:18

8:56 ª 1 Chr. 22:18 ᵇ Deut. 12:10 ¹ *peace*

8:57 ª Deut. 31:6

8:58 ª Ps. 119:36

8:59 ¹ *as each day may require*

8:60 ª 1 Sam. 17:46 ᵇ Deut. 4:35, 39

8:61 ª Deut. 18:13 ¹ Lit. *at peace with*

8:62 ª 2 Chr. 7:4–10

63 And Solomon offered a sacrifice of peace offerings, which he offered unto the LORD, two and twenty thousand oxen, and an hundred and twenty thousand sheep. So the king and all the children of Israel dedicated the house of the LORD.

64 [a]The same day did the king [1]hallow the middle of the court that *was* before the house of the LORD: for there he offered burnt offerings, and meat offerings, and the fat of the peace offerings: because the [b]brasen altar that *was* before the LORD *was* too little to receive the burnt offerings, and [2]meat offerings, and the fat of the peace offerings.

65 And at that time Solomon held [a]a feast, and all Israel with him, a great congregation, from [b]the entering in of Hamath unto [c]the river of Egypt, before the LORD our God, [d]seven days and seven days, *even* fourteen days.

66 [a]On the eighth day he sent the people away: and they [1]blessed the king, and went unto their tents joyful and glad of heart for all the goodness that the LORD had done for David his servant, and for Israel his people.

## CHAPTER 9

AND [a]it came to pass, when Solomon had finished the building of the house of the LORD, [b]and the king's house, and [c]all Solomon's desire which he was pleased to do,

2 That the LORD appeared to Solomon the second time, [a]as he had appeared unto him at Gibeon.

3 And the LORD said unto him, [a]I have heard thy prayer and thy supplication, that thou hast made before me: I have [1]hallowed this house, which thou hast built, [b]to put my name there for ever; [c]and mine eyes and mine heart shall be there perpetually.

4 And if thou wilt [a]walk before me, [b]as David thy father walked, in integrity of heart, and in uprightness, to do according to all that I have commanded thee, *and* wilt [c]keep my statutes and my judgments:

5 Then I will establish the throne of thy kingdom upon Israel for ever, [a]as I promised to David thy father, saying, There shall not fail thee a man upon the throne of Israel.

6 [a]*But* if ye shall at all [1]turn from following me, ye or your children, and will not keep my commandments *and* my statutes which I have set before you, but go and serve other gods, and worship them:

7 [a]Then will I [1]cut off Israel out of the land which I have given them; and this house, which I have hallowed [b]for my name, will I cast out of my sight; [c]and Israel shall be a proverb and a byword among all people:

8 And [a]at this house, *which* [1]is high, every one that passeth by it shall be astonished, and shall hiss; and they shall say, [b]Why hath the LORD done thus unto this land, and to this house?

9 And they shall answer, Because they forsook the LORD their God, who brought forth their fathers out of the land of Egypt, and have taken hold upon other gods, and have worshipped them, and served them: therefore hath the LORD brought upon them all this [a]evil.

10 And [a]it came to pass at the end of twenty years, when Solomon had built the two houses, the house of the LORD, and the king's house,

11 [a](Now Hiram the king of Tyre had furnished Solomon with cedar trees and fir trees, and with gold, according to all his desire,) that then king Solomon gave Hiram twenty cities in the land of Galilee.

12 And Hiram came out from Tyre to see the cities which Solomon had given him; and they pleased him not.

13 And he said, What cities *are* these which thou hast given me, my brother? [a]And he called them the land of [1]Cabul unto this day.

14 And Hiram sent to the king sixscore talents of gold.

15 And this *is* the reason of [a]the [1]levy which king Solomon raised; for to build the house of the LORD, and his own house, and [b]Millo, and the wall of Jerusalem, and [c]Hazor, and [d]Megiddo, and [e]Gezer.

16 *For* Pharaoh king of Egypt had gone up, and taken Gezer, and burnt it with fire, [a]and slain the Canaanites that dwelt in the city, and given it *for* a present unto his daughter, Solomon's wife.

17 And Solomon built Gezer, and [a]Beth-horon the nether,

18 And [a]Baalath, and Tadmor in the wilderness, in the land,

19 And all the cities of store that Solomon had, and cities for [a]his chariots, and cities for his [b]horsemen, and that which Solomon [c]desired to build in Jerusalem, and in Lebanon, and in all the land of his dominion.

20 [a]*And* all the people *that were* left of the Amorites, Hittites, Perizzites, Hivites, and Jebusites, which *were* not of the children of Israel,

21 Their children [a]that were left after them in the land, [b]whom the children of Israel also were not able utterly to destroy, [c]upon those did Solomon [1]levy a tribute of [d]bondservice unto this day.

22 But of the children of Israel did Solomon [a]make no [1]bondmen: but they *were* men of war, and his servants, and his princes, and his

### Cross references (center column)

8:64 [a] 2 Chr. 7:7
[b] 2 Chr. 4:1 [1] consecrate [2] grain or meal
8:65 [a] Lev. 23:34 [b] Num. 34:8 [c] Gen. 15:18 [d] 2 Chr. 7:8
8:66 [a] 2 Chr. 7:9 [1] thanked
9:1 [a] 2 Chr. 7:11 [b] 1 Kin. 7:1 [c] 2 Chr. 8:6
9:2 [a] 1 Kin. 3:5; 11:9
9:3 [a] Ps. 10:17 [b] 1 Kin. 8:29 [c] Deut. 11:12 [1] sanctified
9:4 [a] Gen. 17:1 [b] 1 Kin. 11:4, 6; 15:5 [c] 1 Kin. 8:61
9:5 [a] 2 Sam. 7:12, 16
9:6 [a] 2 Sam. 7:14–16 [1] turn back
9:7 [a] [Lev. 18:24–29] [b] [Jer. 7:4–14] [c] Ps 44:14 [1] destroy

9:8 [a] 2 Chr. 7:21 [b] [Deut. 29:24–26] [1] will be high
9:9 [a] [Deut. 29:25–28]
9:10 [a] 2 Chr. 8:1
9:11 [a] 1 Kin. 5:1
9:13 [a] Josh. 19:27 [1] Lit. Good for Nothing
9:15 [a] 1 Kin. 5:13 [b] 2 Sam. 5:9; 1 Kin. 9:24 [c] Josh. 11:1; 19:36 [d] Josh. 17:11 [e] Josh. 16:10 [1] labour force
9:16 [a] Josh. 16:10; Judg. 1:29
9:17 [a] Josh. 10:10; 16:3; 21:22; 2 Chr. 8:5
9:18 [a] Josh. 19:44; 2 Chr. 8:4
9:19 [a] 1 Kin. 10:26; 2 Chr. 1:14 [b] 1 Kin. 4:26 [c] 1 Kin. 9:1
9:20 [a] 2 Chr. 8:7
9:21 [a] Judg. 1:21–36; 3:1 [b] Josh. 15:63; 17:12, 13 [c] Judg. 1:28, 35 [d] Ezra 2:55, 58; Neh. 7:57 [1] tax
9:22 [a] [Lev. 25:39] [1] forced labourers

captains, and rulers of his chariots, and his horsemen.

23 These *were* the chief of the officers that *were* over Solomon's work, [a]five hundred and fifty, which bare rule over the people that wrought in the work.

24 But [a]Pharaoh's daughter came up out of the city of David unto [b]her house which *Solomon* had built for her: [c]then did he build Millo.

25 [a]And three times in a year did Solomon offer burnt offerings and peace offerings upon the altar which he built unto the LORD, and he burnt incense upon the altar that *was* before the LORD. So he finished the house.

26 And [a]king Solomon made a navy of ships in [b]Ezion-geber, which *is* beside Eloth, on the shore of the Red sea, in the land of Edom.

27 [a]And Hiram sent in the navy his servants, shipmen that had knowledge of the sea, with the servants of Solomon.

28 And they came to [a]Ophir, and fetched from thence gold, four hundred and twenty talents, and brought *it* to king Solomon.

## CHAPTER 10

AND when the [a]queen of Sheba heard of the fame of Solomon concerning the name of the LORD, she came [b]to prove him with hard questions.

2 And she came to Jerusalem with a very great [1]train, with camels that bare spices, and very much gold, and precious stones: and when she was come to Solomon, she communed with him of all that was in her heart.

3 And Solomon [1]told her all her questions: there was not *any* thing [2]hid from the king, which he told her not.

4 And when the queen of Sheba had seen all Solomon's wisdom, and the house that he had built,

5 And the [1]meat of his table, and the [2]sitting of his servants, and the [3]attendance of his ministers, and their apparel, and his cupbearers, [a]and [4]his ascent by which he went up unto the house of the LORD; there was no more spirit in her.

6 And she said to the king, It was a true report that I heard in mine own land of thy [1]acts and of thy wisdom.

7 Howbeit I believed not the words, until I came, and mine eyes had seen *it:* and, behold, the half was not told me: thy wisdom and prosperity exceedeth the fame which I heard.

8 [a]Happy *are* thy men, happy *are* these thy servants, which stand continually before thee, *and* that hear thy wisdom.

9 [a]Blessed be the LORD thy God, which [b]delighted in thee, to set thee on the throne of Israel: because the LORD loved Israel for ever, therefore made he thee king, [c]to do [1]judgment and justice.

10 And she [a]gave the king an hundred and twenty talents of gold, and of spices very great store, and precious stones: there [1]came no more such abundance of spices as these which the queen of Sheba gave to king Solomon.

11 [a]And the navy also of Hiram, that brought gold from Ophir, brought in from Ophir great plenty of [1]almug trees, and precious stones.

12 [a]And the king made of the almug trees [1]pillars for the house of the LORD, and for the king's house, harps also and [2]psalteries for singers: there came no such [b]almug trees, nor were seen unto this day.

13 And king Solomon gave unto the queen of Sheba all her desire, whatsoever she asked, beside *that* which Solomon gave her of his royal bounty. So she turned and went to her own country, she and her servants.

14 Now the weight of gold that came to Solomon in one year was six hundred threescore and six talents of gold,

15 Beside *that he had* of the [a]merchantmen, and of the [1]traffick of the spice merchants, and of [b]all the kings of Arabia, and of the governors of the country.

16 And king Solomon made two hundred targets *of* beaten gold: six hundred *shekels* of gold went to one target.

17 And *he made* [a]three hundred shields *of* beaten gold; three [1]pound of gold went to one shield: and the king put them in the [b]house of the forest of Lebanon.

18 [a]Moreover the king made a great throne of ivory, and overlaid it with the best gold.

19 The throne had six steps, and the top of the throne *was* round [1]behind: and *there were* [2]stays on either side on the place of the seat, and two lions stood beside the stays.

20 And twelve lions stood there on the one side and on the other upon the six steps: there was not the like made in any kingdom.

21 [a]And all king Solomon's drinking vessels *were of* gold, and all the vessels of the house of the forest of Lebanon *were of* pure gold; none *were of* silver: it was [1]nothing accounted of in the days of Solomon.

22 For the king had at sea [1]a navy of [a]Tharshish with the [2]navy of Hiram: once in three years came the [b]navy of Tharshish, bringing gold, and silver, ivory, and apes, and [3]peacocks.

### Cross references (center column)

9:23 [a] 2 Chr. 8:10
9:24 [a] 1 Kin. 3:1 [b] 1 Kin. 7:8
[c] 2 Sam. 5:9; 1 Kin. 11:27; 2 Chr. 32:5
9:25 [a] Ex. 23:14–17; Deut. 16:16; 2 Chr. 8:12, 13
9:26 [a] 2 Chr. 8:17, 18 [b] Num. 33:35; Deut. 2:8; 1 Kin. 22:48
9:27 [a] 1 Kin. 5:6, 9; 10:11
9:28 [a] Job 22:24
10:1 [a] 2 Chr. 9:1; Matt. 12:42; Luke 11:31 [b] Judg. 14:12; Ps. 49:4; Prov. 1:6
10:2 [1] *retinue* or *company*
10:3 [1] *answered* [2] *too difficult for*
10:5 [a] 1 Chr. 26:16; 2 Chr. 9:4 [1] *food* [2] *seating* [3] *service of his attendants* [4] *entryway*
10:6 [1] *words*
10:8 [a] Prov. 8:34

10:9 [a] 1 Kin. 5:7 [b] 2 Sam. 22:20 [c] 2 Sam. 8:15; Ps. 72:2; [Prov. 8:15] [1] *justice and righteousness*
10:10 [a] Ps. 72:10, 15 [1] *never again came*
10:11 [a] 1 Kin. 9:27, 28; Job 22:24 [1] *algum,* 2 Chr. 9:10, 11
10:12 [a] 2 Chr. 9:11 [b] 2 Chr. 9:10 [1] *steps or supports* [2] *stringed instruments*
10:15 [a] 2 Chr. 1:16 [b] 2 Chr. 9:24; Ps. 72:10 [1] *income of traders*
10:17 [a] 1 Kin. 14:26 [b] 1 Kin. 7:2 [1] Heb. *mina*
10:18 [a] 1 Kin. 10:22; 2 Chr. 9:17; Ps. 45:8
10:19 [1] *at the back* [2] *armrests*
10:21 [a] 2 Chr. 9:20 [1] *for this was accounted as nothing*
10:22 [a] Gen. 10:4; 2 Chr. 20:36 [b] 1 Kin. 9:26–28; 22:48; Ps. 72:10 [1] *merchant ships* [2] *fleet* [3] Or *monkeys*

**23** So ᵃking Solomon exceeded all the kings of the earth for riches and for wisdom.

**24** And all the earth ¹sought to Solomon, to hear his wisdom, which God had put in his heart.

**25** And they brought every man his present, vessels of silver, and vessels of gold, and garments, and armour, and spices, horses, and mules, a rate year by year.

**26** ᵃAnd Solomon ᵇgathered together chariots and horsemen: and he had a thousand and four hundred chariots, and twelve thousand horsemen, whom he ¹bestowed in the cities for chariots, and with the king at Jerusalem.

**27** ᵃAnd the king ¹made silver *to be* in Jerusalem as stones, and cedars made he *to be* as the sycomore trees that *are* in the vale, for abundance.

**28** ᵃAnd Solomon had horses brought out of Egypt, and linen yarn: the king's merchants received the linen yarn at a price.

**29** And a chariot came up and went out of Egypt for six hundred *shekels* of silver, and an horse for an hundred and fifty: ᵃand so for all the kings of the Hittites, and for the kings of Syria, did they bring *them* ¹out by their means.

## CHAPTER 11

**B**UT ᵃking Solomon loved ᵇmany strange women, ¹together with the daughter of Pharaoh, women of the Moabites, Ammonites, Edomites, Zidonians, *and* Hittites;

**2** Of the nations *concerning* which the LORD said unto the children of Israel, ᵃYe shall not go in to them, neither shall they come in unto you: *for* surely they will turn away your heart after their gods: Solomon ¹clave unto these in love.

**3** And he had seven hundred wives, princesses, and three hundred concubines: and his wives turned away his heart.

**4** For it came to pass, when Solomon was old, ᵃ*that* his wives turned away his heart after other gods: and his ᵇheart was not ¹perfect with the LORD his God, ᶜas *was* the heart of David his father.

**5** For Solomon went after ᵃAshtoreth the goddess of the Zidonians, and after ᵇMilcom¹ the abomination of the ᶜAmmonites.

**6** And Solomon did evil in the sight of the LORD, and ¹went not fully after the LORD, as *did* David his father.

**7** ᵃThen did Solomon build ¹an high place for ᵇChemosh, the abomination of Moab, in ᶜthe hill that *is* before Jerusalem, and for Molech, the abomination of the children of Ammon.

10:23 ᵃ 1 Kin. 3:12, 13; 4:30; 2 Chr. 1:12
10:24 ¹ sought the presence of
10:26 ᵃ 1 Kin. 4:26; 2 Chr. 1:14; 9:25 ᵇ [Deut. 17:16]; 1 Kin. 9:19 ¹ stationed
10:27 ᵃ [Deut. 17:17]; 2 Chr. 1:15– 17 ¹ made silver as common in
10:28 ᵃ [Deut. 17:16]; 2 Chr. 1:16; 9:28
10:29 ᵃ Josh. 1:4; 2 Kin. 7:6, 7 ¹ through their agents, lit. by their hands
11:1 ᵃ [Neh. 13:26] ᵇ [Deut. 17:17]; 1 Kin. 3:1 ¹ as well as
11:2 ᵃ Ex. 34:16; [Deut. 7:3, 4] ¹ clung
11:4 ᵃ [Deut. 17:17; Neh. 13:26] ᵇ 1 Kin. 8:61 ᶜ 1 Kin. 9:4 ¹ Lit. at peace with
11:5 ᵃ Judg. 2:13; 1 Kin. 11:33 ᵇ [Lev. 20:2–5] ᶜ 2 Kin. 23:13 ¹ Or Molech
11:6 ¹ did not fully follow
11:7 ᵃ Num. 33:52 ᵇ Num. 21:29; Judg. 11:24 ᶜ 2 Kin. 23:13 ¹ A place for pagan worship

**8** And likewise did he for all his strange wives, which burnt incense and sacrificed unto their gods.

**9** And the LORD was angry with Solomon, because his heart was turned from the LORD God of Israel, ᵃwhich had appeared unto him twice,

**10** And ᵃhad commanded him concerning this thing, that he should not go after other gods: but he kept not that which the LORD commanded.

**11** Wherefore the LORD said unto Solomon, Forasmuch as ¹this is done of thee, and thou hast not kept my covenant and my statutes, which I have commanded thee, ᵃI will surely ²rend the kingdom from thee, and will give it to thy ᵇservant.

**12** Notwithstanding in thy days I will not do it for David thy father's sake: *but* I will ¹rend it out of the hand of thy son.

**13** ᵃHowbeit I will not ¹rend away all the kingdom; *but* will give ᵇone tribe to thy son ᶜfor David my servant's sake, and for Jerusalem's sake ᵈwhich I have chosen.

**14** And the LORD ᵃstirred¹ up an adversary unto Solomon, Hadad the Edomite: he *was* of the king's seed in Edom.

**15** ᵃFor it came to pass, when David was in Edom, and Joab the captain of the host was gone up to bury the slain, ᵇafter he had ¹smitten every male in Edom;

**16** (For six months did Joab remain there with all Israel, until he had cut off every male in Edom:)

**17** That Hadad fled, he and certain Edomites of his father's servants with him, to go into Egypt; Hadad *being* yet a little child.

**18** And they arose out of Midian, and came to Paran: and they took men with them out of Paran, and they came to Egypt, unto Pharaoh king of Egypt; which gave him an house, and ¹appointed him victuals, and gave him land.

**19** And Hadad found great favour in the sight of Pharaoh, so that he gave him to wife the sister of his own wife, the sister of Tahpenes the queen.

**20** And the sister of Tahpenes bare him Genubath his son, whom Tahpenes weaned in Pharaoh's house: and Genubath was in Pharaoh's household among the sons of Pharaoh.

**21** ᵃAnd when Hadad heard in Egypt that David ¹slept with his fathers, and that Joab the captain of the host was dead, Hadad said to Pharaoh, ²Let me depart, that I may go to mine own country.

**22** Then Pharaoh said unto him, But what hast thou lacked with me, that, behold, thou seekest to go to thine own country? And he answered,

11:9 ᵃ 1 Kin. 3:5; 9:2
11:10 ᵃ 1 Kin. 6:12; 9:6, 7
11:11 ᵃ 1 Kin. 11:31; 12:15, 16 ᵇ 1 Kin. 11:31, 37 ¹ you have done this ² tear away
11:12 ¹ tear
11:13 ᵃ 2 Sam. 7:15; 1 Chr. 17:13; Ps. 89:33 ᵇ 1 Kin. 12:20 ᶜ 2 Sam. 7:15, 16 ᵈ Deut. 12:11; 1 Kin. 9:3; 14:21 ¹ tear
11:14 ᵃ 1 Chr. 5:26 ¹ raised up
11:15 ᵃ 2 Sam. 8:14; 1 Chr. 18:12, 13 ᵇ Num. 24:18, 19; [Deut. 20:13] ¹ killed
11:18 ¹ apportioned food
11:21 ᵃ 1 Kin. 2:10, 34 ¹ rested in death ² Lit. Send me away

Nothing: howbeit let me go in ¹any wise.

23 And God ¹stirred him up *another* adversary, Rezon the son of Eliadah, which fled from his lord ªHadadezer king of Zobah:

24 And he gathered men unto him, and became captain over a band, ªwhen David slew them *of Zobah:* and they went to Damascus, and dwelt therein, and reigned in Damascus.

25 And he was an adversary to Israel all the days of Solomon, beside the ¹mischief that Hadad *did:* and he abhorred Israel, and reigned over Syria.

26 And ªJeroboam the son of Nebat, an Ephrathite of Zereda, Solomon's servant, whose mother's name *was* Zeruah, a widow woman, ᵇeven he ᶜlifted¹ up *his* hand against the king.

27 And this *was* the cause that he lifted up *his* hand against the king: ªSolomon built Millo, *and* ¹repaired the breaches of the city of David his father.

28 And the man Jeroboam *was* a mighty man of valour: and Solomon seeing the young man that he was ªindustrious, he made him ruler over all the ¹charge of the house of Joseph.

29 And it came to pass at that time when Jeroboam went out of Jerusalem, that the prophet ªAhijah the Shilonite found him in the way; and he had clad himself with a new garment; and they two *were* alone in the field:

30 And Ahijah caught the new garment that *was* on him, and ªrent¹ it *in* twelve pieces:

31 And he said to Jeroboam, Take thee ten pieces: for ªthus saith the LORD, the God of Israel, Behold, I will ¹rend the kingdom out of the hand of Solomon, and will give ten tribes to thee:

32 (But he shall have one tribe for my servant David's sake, and for Jerusalem's sake, the city which I have chosen out of all the tribes of Israel:)

33 ªBecause that they have forsaken me, and have worshipped Ashtoreth the goddess of the Zidonians, Chemosh the god of the Moabites, and Milcom the god of the children of Ammon, and have not walked in my ways, to do *that which is* right in mine eyes, and *to keep* my statutes and my judgments, as *did* David his father.

34 Howbeit I will not take the whole kingdom out of his hand: but I will make him prince all the days of his life for David my servant's sake, whom I chose, because he kept my commandments and my statutes:

35 But ªI will take the kingdom out of his son's hand, and will give it unto thee, *even* ten tribes.

---

**Reference column:**

11:22 ¹ *anyway*
11:23 ª 2 Sam. 8:3; 10:16 ¹ *raised up*
11:24 ª 2 Sam. 8:3; 10:8, 18
11:25 ¹ *trouble*
11:26 ª 1 Kin. 12:2 ᵇ 1 Kin. 11:11; 2 Chr. 13:6 ᶜ 2 Sam. 20:21 ¹ *rebelled*
11:27 ª 1 Kin. 9:15, 24 ¹ Lit. *closed up*
11:28 ª [Prov. 22:29] ¹ *labour force*
11:29 ª 1 Kin. 12:15; 14:2; 2 Chr. 9:29
11:30 ª 1 Sam. 15:27, 28; 24:5 ¹ *tore*
11:31 ª 1 Kin. 11:11, 13 ¹ *tear*
11:33 ª 1 Sam. 7:3; 1 Kin. 11:5–8
11:35 ª 1 Kin. 12:16, 17

11:36 ª [1 Kin. 15:4; 2 Kin. 8:19] ¹ *lamp*
11:37 ¹ *heart desires*
11:38 ª Deut. 31:8; Josh. 1:5 ᵇ 2 Sam. 7:11, 27
11:40 ª 1 Kin. 11:17; 14:25; 2 Chr. 12:2–9
11:41 ª 2 Chr. 9:29
11:42 ª 2 Chr. 9:30
11:43 ª 1 Kin. 2:10; 2 Chr. 9:31 ᵇ 1 Kin. 14:21; 2 Chr. 10:1 ¹ *rested in death*
12:1 ª 2 Chr. 10:1 ᵇ Judg. 9:6
12:2 ª 1 Kin. 11:26 ᵇ 1 Kin. 11:40
12:4 ª 1 Sam. 8:11–18; 1 Kin. 4:7; 5:13–15 ¹ *heavy* or *hard*
12:7 ª 2 Chr. 10:7; [Prov. 15:1]

---

36 And unto his son will I give one tribe, that ªDavid my servant may have a ¹light alway before me in Jerusalem, the city which I have chosen me to put my name there.

37 And I will take thee, and thou shalt reign according to all that ¹thy soul desireth, and shalt be king over Israel.

38 And it shall be, if thou wilt hearken unto all that I command thee, and wilt walk in my ways, and do *that is* right in my sight, to keep my statutes and my commandments, as David my servant did; that ªI will be with thee, and ᵇbuild thee a sure house, as I built for David, and will give Israel unto thee.

39 And I will for this afflict the seed of David, but not for ever.

40 Solomon sought therefore to kill Jeroboam. And Jeroboam arose, and fled into Egypt, unto ªShishak king of Egypt, and was in Egypt until the death of Solomon.

41 And ªthe rest of the acts of Solomon, and all that he did, and his wisdom, *are* they not written in the book of the acts of Solomon?

42 ªAnd the time that Solomon reigned in Jerusalem over all Israel *was* forty years.

43 ªAnd Solomon ¹slept with his fathers, and was buried in the city of David his father: and Rehoboam his son reigned in his ᵇstead.

## CHAPTER 12

AND ªRehoboam went to ᵇShechem: for all Israel were come to Shechem to make him king.

2 And it came to pass, when ªJeroboam the son of Nebat, who was yet in ᵇEgypt, heard *of it,* (for he was fled from the presence of king Solomon, and Jeroboam dwelt in Egypt;)

3 That they sent and called him. And Jeroboam and all the congregation of Israel came, and spake unto Rehoboam, saying,

4 Thy father made our ªyoke ¹grievous: now therefore make thou the grievous service of thy father, and his heavy yoke which he put upon us, lighter, and we will serve thee.

5 And he said unto them, Depart yet *for* three days, then come again to me. And the people departed.

6 And king Rehoboam consulted with the old men, that stood before Solomon his father while he yet lived, and said, How do ye advise that I may answer this people?

7 And they spake unto him, saying, ªIf thou wilt be a servant unto this people this day, and wilt serve them, and answer them, and speak good words to them, then they will be thy servants for ever.

8 But he forsook the counsel of the old men, which they had given him, and consulted with the young men that were grown up with him, *and* which stood before him:

9 And he said unto them, What counsel give ye that we may answer this people, who have spoken to me, saying, Make the yoke which thy father did put upon us lighter?

10 And the young men that were grown up with him spake unto him, saying, Thus shalt thou speak unto this people that spake unto thee, saying, Thy father made our yoke heavy, but make thou *it* lighter unto us; thus shalt thou say unto them, My little *finger* shall be thicker than my father's loins.

11 And now whereas my father did lade you with a heavy yoke, I will add to your yoke: my father hath chastised you with whips, but I will chastise you with scorpions.

12 So Jeroboam and all the people came to Rehoboam the third day, as the king had ¹appointed, saying, Come to me again the third day.

13 And the king answered the people ¹roughly, and ²forsook the old men's ³counsel that they gave him;

14 And spake to them ¹after the counsel of the young men, saying, My father made your yoke heavy, and I will add to your yoke: my father *also* chastised you with whips, but I will chastise you with ²scorpions.

15 Wherefore the king ¹hearkened not unto the people; for ᵃthe ²cause was from the LORD, that he might perform his saying, which the LORD ᵇspake by Ahijah the Shilonite unto Jeroboam the son of Nebat.

16 So when all Israel saw that the king hearkened not unto them, the people answered the king, saying, ᵃWhat portion have we in David? neither *have we* inheritance in the son of Jesse: to your tents, O Israel: now see to thine own house, David. So Israel departed unto their tents.

17 But ᵃ*as for* the children of Israel which dwelt in the cities of Judah, Rehoboam reigned over them.

18 Then king Rehoboam ᵃsent Adoram, who *was* ¹over the tribute; and all Israel stoned him with stones, that he died. Therefore king Rehoboam made speed to get him up to his chariot, to flee to Jerusalem.

19 So ᵃIsrael rebelled against the house of David unto this day.

20 And it came to pass, when all Israel heard that Jeroboam was come again, that they sent and called him unto the congregation, and made him king over all ᵃIsrael: there was none that followed the house of David, but the tribe of Judah ᵇonly.

21 And when ᵃRehoboam was come to Jerusalem, he assembled all the house of Judah, with the tribe of ᵇBenjamin, an hundred and fourscore thousand chosen men, which were warriors, to fight against the house of Israel, ¹to bring the kingdom again to Rehoboam the son of Solomon.

22 But ᵃthe word of God came unto Shemaiah the man of God, saying,

23 Speak unto Rehoboam, the son of Solomon, king of Judah, and unto all the house of Judah and Benjamin, and to the remnant of the people, saying,

24 Thus saith the LORD, Ye shall not go up, nor fight against your brethren the children of Israel: return every man to his house; ᵃfor this thing is from me. They hearkened therefore to the word of the LORD, and ¹returned to depart, according to the word of the LORD.

25 Then Jeroboam ᵃbuilt¹ Shechem in mount Ephraim, and dwelt therein; and went out from thence, and built ᵇPenuel.

26 And Jeroboam said in his heart, Now shall the kingdom return to the house of David:

27 If this people ᵃgo up to do sacrifice in the house of the LORD at Jerusalem, then shall the heart of this people turn again unto their lord, *even* unto Rehoboam king of Judah, and they shall kill me, and go again to Rehoboam king of Judah.

28 Whereupon the king took counsel, and ᵃmade two calves *of* gold, and said unto them, It is too much for you to go up to Jerusalem: ᵇbehold thy gods, O Israel, which brought thee up out of the land of Egypt.

29 And he set the one in ᵃBeth-el, and the other put he in ᵇDan.

30 And this thing became ᵃa sin: for the people went *to worship* before the one, *even* unto Dan.

31 And he made ¹an house of high places, ᵃand made priests ²of the lowest of the people, which were not of the sons of Levi.

32 And Jeroboam ¹ordained a feast in the eighth month, on the fifteenth day of the month, like unto ᵃthe feast that *is* in Judah, and he ²offered upon the altar. So did he in Beth-el, sacrificing unto the calves that he had made: ᵇand he placed in Beth-el the priests of the high places which he had made.

33 So he offered upon the altar which he had made in Beth-el the fifteenth day of the eighth month, *even* in the month which he had ᵃdevised of his own heart; and ¹ordained a feast unto the children of Israel: and he offered upon the altar, and ᵇburnt incense.

## CHAPTER 13

AND, behold, there ᵃcame a man of God out of Judah ᵇby the word of the LORD unto Beth-el: ᵇand Jeroboam stood by the altar to burn incense.

2 And he ¹cried against the altar ²in the word of the LORD, and said, O altar, altar, thus saith the LORD; Behold, a child shall be born unto the house of David, ᵃJosiah by name; and upon thee shall he ³offer the priests of the high places that burn incense upon thee, and men's bones shall be ᵇburnt upon thee.

3 And he gave ᵃa sign the same day, saying, This *is* the sign which the LORD hath spoken; Behold, the altar shall be ¹rent, and the ashes that *are* upon it shall be poured out.

4 And it came to pass, when king Jeroboam heard the saying of the man of God, which had cried against the altar in Beth-el, that he ¹put forth his hand from the altar, saying, Lay hold on him. And his hand, which he put forth against him, dried up, so that he could not pull it in again to him.

5 The altar also was ¹rent, and the ashes poured out from the altar, according to the sign which the man of God had given by the word of the LORD.

6 And the king answered and said unto the man of God, ᵃIntreat¹ now the face of the LORD thy God, and pray for me, that my hand may be restored me again. And the man of God besought the LORD, and the king's hand was ²restored him again, and became as *it was* before.

7 And the king said unto the man of God, Come home with me, and refresh thyself, and ᵃI will give thee a reward.

8 And the man of God said unto the king, ᵃIf thou wilt give me half thine house, I will not go in with thee, neither will I eat bread nor drink water in this place:

9 For so was it charged me by the word of the LORD, saying, ᵃEat no bread, nor drink water, nor turn again by the same way that thou camest.

10 So he went another way, and returned not by the way that he came to Beth-el.

11 Now there dwelt an ᵃold prophet in Beth-el; and his ¹sons came and told him all the works that the man of God had done that day in Beth-el: the words which he had spoken unto the king, them they told also to their father.

12 And their father said unto them, What way went he? For his sons had seen what way the man of God went, which came from Judah.

13 And he said unto his sons, Saddle me the ass. So they saddled him the ass: and he rode thereon,

14 And went after the man of God, and found him sitting under an oak: and he said unto him, *Art* thou the man of God that camest from Judah? And he said, I *am.*

15 Then he said unto him, Come home with me, and eat bread.

16 And he said, ᵃI may not return with thee, nor go in with thee: neither will I eat bread nor drink water with thee in this place:

17 For ¹it was said to me ᵃby the word of the LORD, Thou shalt eat no bread nor drink water there, nor turn again to go by the way that thou camest.

18 He said unto him, I *am* a prophet also as thou *art;* and an angel spake unto me by the word of the LORD, saying, Bring him back with thee into thine house, that he may eat bread and drink water. *But* he lied unto him.

19 So he went back with him, and did eat bread in his house, and drank water.

20 And it came to pass, as they sat at the table, that the word of the LORD came unto the prophet that brought him back:

21 And he cried unto the man of God that came from Judah, saying, Thus saith the LORD, Forasmuch as thou hast disobeyed the mouth of the LORD, and hast not kept the commandment which the LORD thy God commanded thee,

22 But camest back, and hast eaten bread and drunk water in the ᵃplace, of the which *the LORD* did say to thee, Eat no bread, and drink no water; ¹thy carcase shall not come unto the sepulchre of thy fathers.

23 And it came to pass, after he had eaten bread, and after he had drunk, that he saddled for him the ass, *to wit,* for the prophet whom he had brought back.

24 And when he was gone, ᵃa lion met him by the way, and slew him: and his carcase was cast in the way, and the ass stood by it, the lion also stood by the carcase.

25 And, behold, men passed by, and saw the carcase cast in the way, and the lion standing by the carcase: and they came and told *it* in the city where the old prophet dwelt.

26 And when the prophet that brought him back from the way heard *thereof,* he said, It *is* the man of God, who was disobedient unto the word of the LORD: therefore the LORD hath delivered him unto the lion, which ¹hath torn him, and slain him, according to the word of the LORD, which he spake unto him.

### Cross References

13:1 ᵃ 2 Kin. 23:17
ᵇ 1 Kin. 12:32, 33
¹ *at the LORD's command*
13:2 ᵃ 2 Kin. 23:15, 16 ᵇ [Lev. 26:30]
¹ *cried out* ² *at the LORD's command* ³ *sacrifice*
13:3 ᵃ Ex. 4:1–5; Judg. 6:17; Is. 7:14; 38:7; John 2:18; 1 Cor. 1:22 ¹ *split apart*
13:4 ¹ *stretched out*
13:5 ¹ *split apart*
13:6 ᵃ Ex. 8:8; 9:28; 10:17; Num. 21:7; Jer. 37:3; Acts 8:24; [James 5:16] ¹ *Intreat the favour* ² *restored to*
13:7 ᵃ 1 Sam. 9:7; 2 Kin. 5:15
13:8 ᵃ Num. 22:18; 24:13; 1 Kin. 13:16, 17
13:9 ᵃ [1 Cor. 5:11]
13:11 ᵃ 1 Kin. 13:25 ¹ Lit. *son*

13:16 ᵃ 1 Kin. 13:8, 9
13:17 ᵃ 1 Kin. 20:35; 1 Thess. 4:15 ¹ Lit. *a command came to me by*
13:22 ᵃ 1 Kin. 13:9 ¹ *your corpse will not come to the tomb of*
13:24 ᵃ 1 Kin. 20:36
13:26 ¹ *tore him apart and killed him*

27 And he spake to his sons, saying, Saddle me the ass. And they saddled *him.*

28 And he went and found his carcase cast in the way, and the ass and the lion standing by the carcase: the lion had not eaten the carcase, nor [1]torn the ass.

29 And the prophet took up the carcase of the man of God, and laid it upon the ass, and brought it back: and the old prophet came to the city, to mourn and to bury him.

30 And he laid his carcase in his own [1]grave; and they mourned over him, *saying,* [a]Alas, my brother!

31 And it came to pass, after he had buried him, that he spake to his sons, saying, When I am dead, then bury me in the sepulchre wherein the man of God *is* buried; [a]lay my bones beside his bones:

32 [a]For the [1]saying which he [2]cried by the word of the LORD against the altar in Beth-el, and against all the [3]houses of the high places which *are* in the cities of [b]Samaria, shall surely come to pass.

33 [a]After this thing Jeroboam returned not from his evil way, but [1]made again of the lowest of the people priests of the high places: whosoever would, he consecrated him, and he became *one* of the priests of the high places.

34 [a]And this thing became sin unto the house of Jeroboam, even [b]to cut *it* off, and to destroy *it* from off the face of the earth.

## CHAPTER 14

At that time Abijah the son of Jeroboam fell sick.

2 And Jeroboam said to his wife, Arise, I pray thee, and disguise thyself, that thou be not known to be the wife of Jeroboam; and get thee to Shiloh: behold, there *is* Ahijah the prophet, which told me that [a]*I should be* king over this people.

3 [a]And take [1]with thee ten loaves, and [2]cracknels, and a [3]cruse of honey, and go to him: he shall tell thee what shall become of the child.

4 And Jeroboam's wife did so, and arose, [a]and went to Shiloh, and came to the house of Ahijah. But Ahijah could not see; for his eyes were [1]set by reason of his age.

5 And the LORD said unto Ahijah, Behold, the wife of Jeroboam cometh to ask a thing of thee for her son; for he *is* sick: thus and thus shalt thou say unto her: for it shall be, when she cometh in, that she shall [1]feign herself *to be* another *woman.*

6 And it was *so,* when Ahijah heard the sound of her feet, as she came in at the door, that he said, Come in, thou wife of Jeroboam; why feignest thou thyself *to be* another? for I *am* sent to thee *with* [1]heavy *tidings.*

7 Go, tell Jeroboam, Thus saith the LORD God of Israel, [a]Forasmuch as I exalted thee from among the people, and made thee prince over my people Israel,

8 And [a]rent[1] the kingdom away from the house of David, and gave it thee: and *yet* thou hast not been as my servant David, [b]who kept my commandments, and who followed me with all his heart, to do *that* only *which was* right in mine eyes;

9 But hast done evil above all that were before thee: [a]for thou hast gone and made thee other gods, and molten images, to provoke me to anger, and [b]hast cast me behind thy back:

10 Therefore, behold, [a]I will bring [1]evil upon the house of Jeroboam, and [b]will [2]cut off from Jeroboam [3]him that pisseth against the wall, [c]*and* him that is shut up and left in Israel, and will take away the remnant of the house of Jeroboam, as a man taketh away dung, till it be all gone.

11 [a]Him that dieth of Jeroboam in the city shall the dogs eat; and him that dieth in the field shall the fowls of the air eat: for the LORD hath spoken *it.*

12 Arise thou therefore, get thee to thine own house: *and* [a]when thy feet enter into the city, the child shall die.

13 And all Israel shall mourn for him, and bury him: for he only of Jeroboam [1]shall come to the grave, because in him [a]there is found *some* good thing toward the LORD God of Israel in the house of Jeroboam.

14 [a]Moreover the LORD shall raise him up a king over Israel, who shall cut off the house of Jeroboam [1]that day: but what? even now.

15 For the LORD shall [1]smite Israel, as a reed is shaken in the water, and he shall [a]root up Israel out of this [b]good land, which he gave to their fathers, and shall scatter them [c]beyond [2]the river, [d]because they have made their [3]groves, provoking the LORD to anger.

16 And he shall give Israel up because of the sins of Jeroboam, [a]who did sin, and who made Israel to sin.

17 And Jeroboam's wife arose, and departed, and came to [a]Tirzah: *and* [b]when she came to the threshold of the door, the child died;

18 And they buried him; and all Israel mourned for him, [a]according to the word of the LORD, which he spake by the hand of his servant Ahijah the prophet.

19 And the rest of the acts of Jeroboam, how he [a]warred, and how he reigned, behold, they *are* written

13:28 [1] *torn apart*
13:30 [a] Jer. 22:18 [1] *tomb*
13:31 [a] Ruth 1:17; 2 Kin. 23:17, 18
13:32 [a] 1 Kin. 13:2; 2 Kin. 23:16, 19 [b] 1 Kin. 16:24; John 4:5; Acts 8:14 [1] Lit. *word* [2] *cried out* [3] *shrines*
13:33 [a] 1 Kin. 12:31, 32; 2 Chr. 11:15; 13:9 [1] *again made priests from every class of people*
13:34 [a] 1 Kin. 12:30; 2 Kin. 17:21 [b] [1 Kin. 14:10; 15:29, 30]
14:2 [a] 1 Kin. 11:29–31
14:3 [a] 1 Sam. 9:7, 8; 1 Kin. 13:7; 2 Kin. 4:42 [1] Lit. *in your hand* [2] *cakes* [3] *jar*
14:4 [a] 1 Kin. 11:29 [1] *glazed*
14:5 [1] *pretend to be*
14:6 [1] *bad news*
14:7 [a] 1 Kin. 16:2
14:8 [a] 1 Kin. 11:31 [b] 1 Kin. 11:33, 38; 15:5 [1] *tore*
14:9 [a] 1 Kin. 12:28 [b] Ps. 50:17
14:10 [a] 1 Kin. 15:29 [b] 1 Kin. 21:21 [c] Deut. 32:36 [1] *disaster* [2] *destroy* [3] *every male in Israel, bond and free*
14:11 [a] 1 Kin. 16:4; 21:24
14:12 [a] 1 Kin. 14:17
14:13 [a] 2 Chr. 12:12; 19:3 [1] *will be buried*
14:14 [a] 1 Kin. 15:27–29 [1] *this day*
14:15 [a] 2 Kin. 17:6 [b] [Josh. 23:15, 16] [c] 2 Kin. 15:29 [d] [Ex. 34:13, 14] [1] *strike* [2] The Euphrates [3] *wooden images,* Heb. *asherim*
14:16 [a] 1 Kin. 12:30; 13:34; 15:30, 34; 16:2
14:17 [a] Song 6:4 [b] 1 Kin. 14:12
14:18 [a] 1 Kin. 14:13
14:19 [a] 2 Chr. 13:2–20

in the book of the chronicles of the kings of Israel.

20 And the days which Jeroboam reigned *were* two and twenty years: and he slept with his fathers, and [a]Nadab his son reigned in his stead.

21 And Rehoboam the son of Solomon reigned in Judah. [a]Rehoboam *was* forty and one years old when he began to reign, and he reigned seventeen years in Jerusalem, the city [b]which the LORD did choose out of all the tribes of Israel, to put his name there. [c]And their mother's name *was* Naamah an Ammonitess.

22 [a]And Judah did evil in the sight of the LORD, and they [b]provoked him to jealousy with their sins which they had committed, above all that their fathers had done.

23 For they also built them [a]high[1] places, and [b]images,[2] [c]and [3]groves, on every high hill, and [d]under every green tree.

24 [a]And there were also [1]sodomites in the land: *and* they did according to all the [b]abominations of the nations which the LORD cast out before the children of [c]Israel.

25 [a]And it came to pass in the fifth year of king Rehoboam, *that* Shishak king of Egypt came up against Jerusalem:

26 [a]And he took away the treasures of the house of the LORD, and the treasures of the king's house; he even took away all: and he took away all the shields of gold [b]which Solomon had made.

27 And king Rehoboam made in their stead [1]brasen shields, and [2]committed *them* unto the hands of the [3]chief of the guard, which kept the door of the king's house.

28 And it was *so,* when the king went into the house of the LORD, that the guard bare them, and brought them back into the guard chamber.

29 [a]Now the rest of the acts of Rehoboam, and all that he did, *are* they not written in the book of the chronicles of the kings of Judah?

30 And there was [a]war between Rehoboam and Jeroboam all *their* days.

31 [a]And Rehoboam [1]slept with his fathers, and was buried with his fathers in the city of David. [b]And his mother's name *was* Naamah an Ammonitess. And [c]Abijam[2] his son reigned in his stead.

## CHAPTER 15

Now [a]in the eighteenth year of king Jeroboam the son of Nebat reigned Abijam over Judah.

2 Three years reigned he in Jerusalem. [a]And his mother's name *was* [b]Maachah, the daughter of [c]Abishalom.

3 And he walked in all the sins of his father, which he had done before him: and [a]his heart was not [1]perfect with the LORD his God, as the heart of David his father.

4 Nevertheless [a]for David's sake did the LORD his God give him a lamp in Jerusalem, to set up his son after him, and to establish Jerusalem:

5 Because David [a]did *that which was* right in the eyes of the LORD, and turned not aside from any *thing* that he commanded him all the days of his life, [b]save only in the matter of Uriah the Hittite.

6 [a]And there was war between Rehoboam and Jeroboam all the days of his life.

7 [a]Now the rest of the acts of Abijam, and all that he did, *are* they not written in the book of the chronicles of the kings of Judah? And there was war between Abijam and Jeroboam.

8 [a]And Abijam [1]slept with his fathers; and they buried him in the city of David: and Asa his son reigned in his stead.

9 And in the twentieth year of Jeroboam king of Israel reigned Asa over Judah.

10 And forty and one years reigned he in Jerusalem. And his [1]mother's name *was* Maachah, the daughter of Abishalom.

11 [a]And Asa did *that which was* right in the eyes of the LORD, as *did* David his father.

12 [a]And he [1]took away the sodomites out of the land, and removed all the idols that his fathers had made.

13 And also [a]Maachah his mother, even her he removed from being queen, because she had made [1]an idol in a grove; and Asa [2]destroyed her idol, and [b]burnt *it* by the brook Kidron.

14 [a]But the [1]high places were not removed: nevertheless Asa's [b]heart was perfect with the LORD all his days.

15 And he brought in the things which his father [a]had dedicated, and the things which himself had dedicated, into the house of the LORD, silver, and gold, and vessels.

16 And there was war between Asa and Baasha king of Israel all their days.

17 And [a]Baasha king of Israel went up against Judah, and built [b]Ramah, [c]that he might not [1]suffer any to go out or come in to Asa king of Judah.

18 Then Asa took all the silver and the gold *that were* left in the treasures of the house of the LORD, and the treasures of the king's house, and delivered them into the hand of his servants: and king Asa sent them to [a]Ben-hadad, the son of Tabrimon, the son of Hezion, king of Syria, that dwelt at [b]Damascus, saying,

### Cross references (center column)

14:20 [a] 1 Kin. 15:25
14:21 [a] 2 Chr. 12:13
[b] 1 Kin. 11:32, 36
[c] 1 Kin. 14:31
14:22 [a] 2 Chr. 12:1, 14 [b] Deut. 32:21
14:23 [a] Deut. 12:2 [b] [Deut. 16:22] [c] [2 Kin. 17:9, 10] [d] Is. 57:5
[1] Places for pagan worship [2] *sacred pillars* [3] *wooden images*
14:24 [a] Deut. 23:17 [b] Deut. 20:18 [c] [Deut. 9:4, 5]
[1] *ritual sodomites*
14:25 [a] 1 Kin. 11:40
14:26 [a] 2 Chr. 12:9–11 [b] 1 Kin. 10:17
14:27 [1] *bronze* [2] *entrusted* [3] *captains of the guards* or *runners*
14:29 [a] 2 Chr. 12:15, 16
14:30 [a] 1 Kin. 12:21–24; 15:6
14:31 [a] 2 Chr. 12:16 [b] 1 Kin. 14:21 [c] 2 Chr. 12:16
[1] *rested in death* [2] *Abijah,* 2 Chr. 12:16
15:1 [a] 2 Chr. 13:1
15:2 [a] 2 Chr. 11:20–22 [b] 2 Chr. 13:2 [c] 2 Chr. 11:21
15:3 [a] Ps. 119:80
[1] Lit. *at peace with*
15:4 [a] 2 Sam. 21:17
15:5 [a] 1 Kin. 9:4; 14:8 [b] 2 Sam. 11:3, 15–17; 12:9, 10
15:6 [a] 1 Kin. 14:30
15:7 [a] 2 Chr. 13:2–22
15:8 [a] 2 Chr. 14:1
[1] *rested in death*
15:10 [1] *grandmother's*
15:11 [a] 2 Chr. 14:2
15:12 [a] 1 Kin. 14:24; 22:46
[1] *banished the ritual sodomites*
15:13 [a] 2 Chr. 15:16–18 [b] Ex. 32:20 [1] *an obscene image of Asherah* [2] *cut down her obscene image*
15:14 [a] 1 Kin. 3:2; 22:43 [b] 1 Kin. 8:61; 15:3 [1] *Places for pagan worship*
15:15 [a] 1 Kin. 7:51
15:17 [a] 2 Chr. 16:1–6 [b] Josh. 18:25 [c] 1 Kin. 12:26–29 [1] *allow*
15:18 [a] 2 Chr. 16:2 [b] 1 Kin. 11:23, 24

19 *There is* [1]a league between me and thee, *and* between my father and thy father: behold, I have sent unto thee a present of silver and gold; come and break thy league with Baasha king of Israel, that he may depart from me.

20 So Ben-hadad hearkened unto king Asa, and [a]sent the captains of the hosts which he had against the cities of Israel, and smote [b]Ijon, and [c]Dan, and [d]Abel-beth-maachah, and all Cinneroth, with all the land of Naphtali.

21 And it came to pass, when Baasha heard *thereof,* that he left off building of Ramah, and dwelt in [a]Tirzah.

22 [a]Then king Asa made a proclamation throughout all Judah; none *was* exempted: and they took away the stones of Ramah, and the timber thereof, wherewith Baasha had builded; and king Asa built with them [b]Geba of Benjamin, and [c]Mizpah.

23 The rest of all the acts of Asa, and all his might, and all that he did, and the cities which he built, *are* they not written in the book of the chronicles of the kings of Judah? Nevertheless [a]in the time of his old age he was diseased in his feet.

24 And Asa [1]slept with his fathers, and was buried with his fathers in the city of David his father: [a]and [b]Jehoshaphat his son reigned in his stead.

25 And [a]Nadab the son of Jeroboam began to reign over Israel in the second year of Asa king of Judah, and reigned over Israel two years.

26 And he did evil in the sight of the LORD, and walked in the way of his father, and in [a]his sin wherewith he made Israel to sin.

27 [a]And Baasha the son of Ahijah, of the house of Issachar, conspired against him; and Baasha [1]smote him at [b]Gibbethon, which *belonged* to the Philistines; for Nadab and all Israel laid siege to Gibbethon.

28 Even in the third year of Asa king of Judah did Baasha slay him, and reigned in his stead.

29 And it came to pass, when he reigned, *that* he smote all the house of Jeroboam; he left not to Jeroboam any that breathed, until he had destroyed him, according unto [a]the saying of the LORD, which he spake by his servant Ahijah the Shilonite:

30 [a]Because of the sins of Jeroboam which he sinned, and which he made Israel sin, by his provocation wherewith he provoked the LORD God of Israel to anger.

31 Now the rest of the acts of Nadab, and all that he did, *are* they not written in the book of the chronicles of the kings of Israel?

32 [a]And there was war between Asa and Baasha king of Israel all their days.

33 In the third year of Asa king of Judah began Baasha the son of Ahijah to reign over all Israel in Tirzah, twenty and four years.

34 And he did evil in the sight of the LORD, and walked in [a]the way of Jeroboam, and in his sin wherewith he made Israel to sin.

## CHAPTER 16

THEN the word of the LORD came to [a]Jehu the son of [b]Hanani against [c]Baasha, saying,

2 [a]Forasmuch as I [1]exalted thee out of the dust, and made thee prince over my people Israel; and [b]thou hast walked in the way of Jeroboam, and hast made my people Israel to sin, to provoke me to anger with their sins;

3 Behold, I will [a]take[1] away the posterity of Baasha, and the posterity of his house; and will make thy house like [b]the house of Jeroboam the son of Nebat.

4 [a]Him that dieth of Baasha in the city shall the dogs eat; and him that dieth of his in the fields shall the fowls of the air eat.

5 Now the rest of the acts of Baasha, and what he did, and his might, [a]are* they not written in the book of the chronicles of the kings of Israel?

6 So Baasha [1]slept with his fathers, and was buried in [a]Tirzah: and Elah his son reigned in his stead.

7 And also by the hand of the prophet [a]Jehu the son of Hanani came the word of the LORD against Baasha, and against his house, even for all the evil that he did in the sight of the LORD, in provoking him to anger with the work of his hands, in being like the house of Jeroboam; and because [b]he killed him.

8 In the twenty and sixth year of Asa king of Judah began Elah the son of Baasha to reign over Israel in Tirzah, two years.

9 [a]And his servant Zimri, captain of half *his* chariots, conspired against him, as he was in Tirzah, drinking himself drunk in the house of Arza [b]steward[1] of *his* house in Tirzah.

10 And Zimri went in and [1]smote him, and killed him, in the twenty and seventh year of Asa king of Judah, and reigned in his stead.

11 And it came to pass, when he began to reign, as soon as he sat on his throne, *that* he slew all the house of Baasha: he left him [a]not one [1]that pisseth against a wall, neither of his kinsfolks, nor of his friends.

12 Thus did Zimri destroy all the house of Baasha, [a]according to the word of the LORD, which he spake against Baasha by Jehu the prophet,

**13** For all the sins of Baasha, and the sins of Elah his son, by which they sinned, and by which they made Israel to sin, in provoking the LORD God of Israel to anger [a]with their [1]vanities.

**14** Now the rest of the acts of Elah, and all that he did, *are* they not written in the book of the chronicles of the kings of Israel?

**15** In the twenty and seventh year of Asa king of Judah did Zimri reign seven days in Tirzah. And the people *were* encamped [a]against Gibbethon, which *belonged* to the Philistines.

**16** And the people *that were* encamped heard say, Zimri hath conspired, and hath also slain the king: wherefore all Israel made Omri, the captain of the host, king over Israel that day in the camp.

**17** And Omri went up from Gibbethon, and all Israel with him, and they besieged Tirzah.

**18** And it came to pass, when Zimri saw that the city was [1]taken, that he went into the palace of the king's house, and burnt the king's house [2]over him with fire, and died,

**19** For his sins which he sinned in doing evil in the sight of the LORD, [a]in walking in the [b]way of Jeroboam, and in his sin which he did, to make Israel to sin.

**20** Now the rest of the acts of Zimri, and his treason that he wrought, *are* they not written in the book of the chronicles of the kings of Israel?

**21** Then were the people of Israel divided into two parts: half of the people followed Tibni the son of Ginath, to make him king; and half followed Omri.

**22** But the people that followed Omri prevailed against the people that followed Tibni the son of Ginath: so Tibni died, and Omri reigned.

**23** In the thirty and first year of Asa king of Judah began Omri to reign over Israel, twelve years: six years reigned he in [a]Tirzah.

**24** And he bought the hill Samaria of Shemer for two talents of silver, and built on the hill, and called the name of the city which he built, after the name of Shemer, owner of the hill, [a]Samaria.[1]

**25** But [a]Omri wrought evil in the eyes of the LORD, and did worse than all that *were* before him.

**26** For he [a]walked in all the way of Jeroboam the son of Nebat, and in his sin wherewith he made Israel to sin, to provoke the LORD God of Israel to anger with their [b]vanities.[1]

**27** Now the rest of the acts of Omri which he did, and his might that he shewed, *are* they not written in the book of the chronicles of the kings of Israel?

**28** So Omri slept with his fathers, and was buried in Samaria: and Ahab his son reigned in his stead.

**29** And in the thirty and eighth year of Asa king of Judah began Ahab the son of Omri to reign over Israel: and Ahab the son of Omri reigned over Israel in Samaria twenty and two years.

**30** And Ahab the son of Omri did evil in the sight of the LORD [1]above all that *were* before him.

**31** And it came to pass, as if it had been a light thing for him to walk in the sins of Jeroboam the son of Nebat, [a]that he took to wife Jezebel the daughter of Ethbaal king of the [b]Zidonians, [c]and went and served Baal, and worshipped him.

**32** And he reared up an altar for Baal in [a]the house of Baal, which he had built in Samaria.

**33** [a]And Ahab made a [1]grove; and Ahab [b]did more to provoke the LORD God of Israel to anger than all the kings of Israel that were before him.

**34** In his days did Hiel the Bethelite build Jericho: he laid the foundation thereof [1]in Abiram his firstborn, and set up the gates thereof in his youngest *son* Segub, [a]according to the word of the LORD, which he spake by Joshua the son of Nun.

## CHAPTER 17

AND [1]Elijah the Tishbite, *who was* of the [a]inhabitants of Gilead, said unto Ahab, [b]*As* the LORD God of Israel liveth, [c]before whom I stand, [d]there shall not be dew nor rain [e]these years, [2]but according to my word.

**2** And the word of the LORD came unto him, saying,

**3** Get thee hence, and turn thee eastward, and hide thyself by the brook Cherith, that *is* before Jordan.

**4** And it shall be, *that* thou shalt drink of the brook; and I have commanded the [a]ravens to feed thee there.

**5** So he went and did according unto the word of the LORD: for he went and dwelt by the brook Cherith, that *is* before Jordan.

**6** And the ravens brought him bread and flesh in the morning, and bread and flesh in the evening; and he drank of the brook.

**7** And it came to pass after a while, that the brook dried up, because there had been no rain in the land.

**8** And the word of the LORD came unto him, saying,

**9** Arise, get thee to [a]Zarephath, which *belongeth* to [b]Zidon, and dwell there: behold, I have commanded a widow woman there to [1]sustain thee.

**10** So he arose and went to Zarephath. And when he came to the gate

---

16:13 [a] Deut. 32:21; 1 Sam. 12:21; [Is. 41:29; Jon. 2:8; 1 Cor. 8:4; 10:19] [1] *idols*
16:15 [a] 1 Kin. 15:27
16:18 [1] *captured* [2] *down upon himself*
16:19 [a] 1 Kin. 15:26, 34 [b] 1 Kin. 12:25–33
16:23 [a] 1 Kin. 15:21; 2 Kin. 15:14
16:24 [a] 1 Kin. 13:32; 2 Kin. 17:24; John 4:4 [1] Heb. *Shomeron*
16:25 [a] Mic. 6:16
16:26 [a] 1 Kin. 16:19 [b] 1 Kin. 16:13 [1] *idols*
16:30 [1] *more than all*
16:31 [a] Deut. 7:3 [b] Judg. 18:7; 1 Kin. 11:1–5 [c] 1 Kin. 21:25, 26; 2 Kin. 10:18; 17:16
16:32 [a] 2 Kin. 10:21, 26, 27
16:33 [a] 2 Kin. 13:6 [b] 1 Kin. 14:9; 16:29, 30; 21:25 [1] *wooden image*
16:34 [a] Josh. 6:26 [1] *at the cost of the life of*
17:1 [a] Judg. 12:4 [b] 1 Kin. 18:10; 22:14; 2 Kin. 3:14; 5:20 [c] Deut. 10:8 [d] 1 Kin. 18:1; James 5:17 [e] Luke 4:25 [1] Heb. *Elijahu* [2] *except at*
17:4 [a] Job 38:41
17:9 [a] Obad. 20; Luke 4:25, 26 [b] 2 Sam. 24:6 [1] *provide for*

of the city, behold, the widow woman *was* there gathering of sticks: and he called to her, and said, Fetch me, I pray thee, a little water in a vessel, that I may drink.

11 And as she was going to fetch *it,* he called to her, and said, Bring me, I pray thee, a morsel of bread in thine hand.

12 And she said, *As* the LORD thy God liveth, I have not a cake, but an handful of meal in a barrel, and a little oil in a ¹cruse: and, behold, I *am* gathering two sticks, that I may go in and ²dress it for me and my son, that we may eat it, and ªdie.

13 And Elijah said unto her, Fear not; go *and* do as thou hast said: but make me thereof a little cake first, and bring *it* unto me, and after make for thee and for thy son.

14 For thus saith the LORD God of Israel, The barrel of ¹meal shall not waste, neither shall the ²cruse of oil fail, until the day *that* the LORD sendeth rain upon the earth.

15 And she went and did according to the saying of Elijah: and she, and he, and her house, did eat *many* days.

16 *And* the barrel of meal wasted not, neither did the cruse of oil fail, according to the word of the LORD, which he spake by Elijah.

17 And it came to pass after these things, *that* the son of the woman, the mistress of the house, fell sick; and his sickness was so ¹sore, that ²there was no breath left in him.

18 And she said unto Elijah, ªWhat have I to do with thee, O thou man of God? art thou come unto me to call my sin to remembrance, and to slay my son?

19 And he said unto her, Give me thy son. And he took him out of her ¹bosom, and carried him up into a ²loft, where he abode, and laid him upon his own bed.

20 And he cried unto the LORD, and said, O LORD my God, hast thou also brought evil upon the widow with whom I ¹sojourn, by slaying her son?

21 ªAnd he stretched himself upon the child three times, and cried unto the LORD, and said, O LORD my God, I pray thee, let this child's soul come into him again.

22 And the LORD heard the voice of Elijah; and the soul of the child came into him again, and he ªrevived.

23 And Elijah took the child, and brought him down out of the ¹chamber into the house, and delivered him unto his mother: and Elijah said, See, thy son liveth.

24 And the woman said to Elijah, Now by this ªI know that thou *art* a man of God, *and* that the word of the LORD in thy mouth *is* truth.

---

17:12 ª Deut. 28:23, 24 ¹ *pitcher or water jar* ² *prepare*

17:14 ¹ *flour shall not be used up* ² *jar*

17:17 ¹ *severe* ² He died

17:18 ª Luke 5:8

17:19 ¹ *arms* ² *upper room*

17:20 ¹ *lodge*

17:21 ª 2 Kin. 4:34, 35; Acts 20:10

17:22 ª Luke 7:14, 15; Heb. 11:35

17:23 ¹ *upper room*

17:24 ª John 2:11; 3:2; 16:30

18:1 ª 1 Kin. 17:1; Luke 4:25; James 5:17 ᵇ Deut. 28:12 ¹ *present yourself*

18:2 ¹ *severe*

18:3 ¹ Heb. *Obadyahu* ² *in charge of*

18:4 ¹ *massacred*

18:7 ª 2 Kin. 1:6–8 ¹ *Is that you*

18:12 ª 2 Kin. 2:16; Ezek. 3:12, 14; Matt. 4:1; Acts 8:39

18:15 ¹ *present*

18:17 ª 1 Kin. 21:20 ᵇ Josh. 7:25; Acts 16:20 ¹ *Is that you, O troubler?*

---

## CHAPTER 18

AND it came to pass *after* ªmany days, that the word of the LORD came to Elijah in the third year, saying, Go, ¹shew thyself unto Ahab; and ᵇI will send rain upon the earth.

2 And Elijah went to shew himself unto Ahab. And *there was* a ¹sore famine in Samaria.

3 And Ahab called ¹Obadiah, which *was* ²the governor of *his* house. (Now Obadiah feared the LORD greatly:

4 For it was *so,* when Jezebel ¹cut off the prophets of the LORD, that Obadiah took an hundred prophets, and hid them by fifty in a cave, and fed them with bread and water.)

5 And Ahab said unto Obadiah, Go into the land, unto all fountains of water, and unto all brooks: peradventure we may find grass to save the horses and mules alive, that we lose not all the beasts.

6 So they divided the land between them to pass throughout it: Ahab went one way by himself, and Obadiah went another way by himself.

7 And as Obadiah was in the way, behold, Elijah met him: and he ªknew him, and fell on his face, and said, ¹*Art* thou that my lord Elijah?

8 And he answered him, I *am:* go, tell thy lord, Behold, Elijah *is here.*

9 And he said, What have I sinned, that thou wouldest deliver thy servant into the hand of Ahab, to slay me?

10 *As* the LORD thy God liveth, there is no nation or kingdom, whither my lord hath not sent to seek thee: and when they said, *He is* not *there;* he took an oath of the kingdom and nation, that they found thee not.

11 And now thou sayest, Go, tell thy lord, Behold, Elijah *is here.*

12 And it shall come to pass, *as soon as* I am gone from thee, that ªthe Spirit of the LORD shall carry thee whither I know not; and *so* when I come and tell Ahab, and he cannot find thee, he shall slay me: but I thy servant fear the LORD from my youth.

13 Was it not told my lord what I did when Jezebel slew the prophets of the LORD, how I hid an hundred men of the LORD's prophets by fifty in a cave, and fed them with bread and water?

14 And now thou sayest, Go, tell thy lord, Behold, Elijah *is here:* and he shall slay me.

15 And Elijah said, *As* the LORD of hosts liveth, before whom I stand, I will surely ¹shew myself unto him to day.

16 So Obadiah went to meet Ahab, and told him: and Ahab went to meet Elijah.

17 And it came to pass, when Ahab saw Elijah, that Ahab said unto him, ª*Art*¹ thou he that ᵇtroubleth Israel?

18 And he answered, I have not troubled Israel; but thou, and thy father's house, [a]in that ye have forsaken the commandments of the LORD, and thou hast followed Baalim.

19 Now therefore send, *and* gather to me all Israel unto mount [a]Carmel, and the prophets of Baal four hundred and fifty, [b]and the prophets of the [1]groves four hundred, which [2]eat at Jezebel's table.

20 So Ahab sent unto all the children of Israel, and [a]gathered the prophets together unto mount Carmel.

21 And Elijah came unto all the people, and said, [a]How long [1]halt ye between two opinions? if the LORD *be* God, follow him: but if Baal, [b]*then* follow him. And the people answered him not a word.

22 Then said Elijah unto the people, [a]I, *even* I only, remain a prophet of the LORD; [b]but Baal's prophets *are* four hundred and fifty men.

23 Let them therefore give us two bullocks; and let them choose one bullock for themselves, and cut it in pieces, and lay *it* on wood, and put no fire *under:* and I will dress the other bullock, and lay *it* on wood, and put no fire *under:*

24 And call ye on the name of your gods, and I will call on the name of the LORD: and the God that [a]answereth by fire, let him be God. And all the people answered and said, [1]It is well spoken.

25 And Elijah said unto the prophets of Baal, Choose you one bullock for yourselves, and dress *it* first; for ye *are* many; and call on the name of your gods, but put no fire *under.*

26 And they took the bullock which was given them, and they dressed *it,* and called on the name of Baal from morning even until noon, saying, O Baal, [1]hear us. But *there was* [a]no voice, nor any that answered: and they [2]leaped upon the altar which was made.

27 And it came to pass at noon, that Elijah mocked them, and said, Cry [1]aloud: for he *is* a god; either he is [2]talking, or he is [3]pursuing, or he is [4]in a journey, *or* peradventure he sleepeth, and must be awaked.

28 And they cried aloud, and [a]cut themselves after their manner with knives and [1]lancets, till the blood gushed out upon them.

29 And it came to pass, when midday was past, [a]and they prophesied until the *time* of the offering of the *evening* sacrifice, that *there was* [b]neither voice, nor any to answer, [1]nor any that regarded.

30 And Elijah said unto all the people, Come near unto me. And all the people came near unto him. [a]And he

repaired the altar of the LORD *that was* broken down.

31 And Elijah took twelve stones, according to the number of the tribes of the sons of Jacob, unto whom the word of the LORD came, saying, [a]Israel shall be thy name:

32 And with the stones he built an altar [a]in the name of the LORD: and he made a trench about the altar, as great as would contain two [1]measures of seed.

33 And he [a]put the wood in order, and cut the bullock in pieces, and laid *him* on the wood, and said, Fill four [1]barrels with water, and [b]pour *it* on the burnt sacrifice, and on the wood.

34 And he said, Do *it* the second time. And they did *it* the second time. And he said, Do *it* the third time. And they did *it* the third time.

35 And the water ran round about the altar; and he filled [a]the trench also with water.

36 And it came to pass at *the time of* the offering of the *evening* sacrifice, that Elijah the prophet came near, and said, LORD [a]God of Abraham, Isaac, and of Israel, [b]let it be known this day that thou *art* God in Israel, and *that* I *am* thy servant, and *that* [c]I have done all these things at thy word.

37 Hear me, O LORD, hear me, that this people may know that thou *art* the LORD God, and *that* thou hast turned their heart back again.

38 Then [a]the fire of the LORD fell, and consumed the burnt sacrifice, and the wood, and the stones, and the dust, and licked up the water that *was* in the trench.

39 And when all the people saw *it,* they fell on their faces: and they said, [a]The LORD, he *is* the God; the LORD, he *is* the God.

40 And Elijah said unto them, [a]Take[1] the prophets of Baal; let not one of them escape. And they took them: and Elijah brought them down to the brook [b]Kishon, and [c]slew them there.

41 And Elijah said unto Ahab, Get thee up, eat and drink; for *there is* a sound of abundance of rain.

42 So Ahab went up to eat and to drink. And Elijah went up to the top of Carmel; [a]and he cast himself down upon the earth, and put his face between his knees,

43 And said to his servant, Go up now, look toward the sea. And he went up, and looked, and said, There *is* nothing. And he said, Go again seven times.

44 And it came to pass at the seventh time, that he said, Behold, there ariseth a little cloud out of the sea, like a man's hand. And he said, Go up,

---

*Cross-references (center column):*

18:18 [a] 1 Kin. 16:30–33; [2 Chr. 15:2]
18:19 [a] Josh. 19:26; 2 Kin. 2:25 [b] 1 Kin. 16:33 [1] Heb. *Asherah,* a Canaanite goddess [2] *are provided for by Jezebel*
18:20 [a] 1 Kin. 22:6
18:21 [a] 2 Kin. 17:41; [Matt. 6:24] [b] Josh. 24:15 [1] *will you falter*
18:22 [a] 1 Kin. 19:10, 14 [b] 1 Kin. 18:19
18:24 [a] 1 Kin. 18:38; 1 Chr. 21:26 [1] Lit. *The word is good*
18:26 [a] Ps. 115:5; Jer. 10:5; [1 Cor. 8:4] [1] *answer* [2] *leaped in dancing around,* lit. *limped about*
18:27 [1] *with a loud voice* [2] *meditating* [3] *busy* [4] *on a journey*
18:28 [a] [Lev. 19:28; Deut. 14:1] [1] *swords*
18:29 [a] Ex. 29:39, 41 [b] 1 Kin. 18:26 [1] *no one paid attention*
18:30 [a] 1 Kin. 19:10, 14; 2 Chr. 33:16
18:31 [a] Gen. 32:28; 35:10; 2 Kin. 17:34
18:32 [a] [Ex. 20:25; Col. 3:17] [1] Heb. *seah*
18:33 [a] Gen. 22:9; Lev. 1:6–8 [b] Judg. 6:20 [1] *waterpots*
18:35 [a] 1 Kin. 18:32, 38
18:36 [a] Gen. 28:13; Ex. 3:6; 4:5; [Matt. 22:32] [b] 1 Kin. 8:43; 2 Kin. 19:19 [c] Num. 16:28
18:38 [a] Gen. 15:17; Lev. 9:24; 10:1, 2; Judg. 6:21; 2 Kin. 1:12; 1 Chr. 21:26; 2 Chr. 7:1; Job 1:16
18:39 [a] 1 Kin. 18:21, 24
18:40 [a] 2 Kin. 10:25 [b] Judg. 4:7; 5:21 [c] [Deut. 13:5; 18:20] [1] Lit. *Seize*
18:42 [a] James 5:17, 18

say unto Ahab, ¹Prepare *thy chariot,* and get thee down, that the rain stop thee not.

45 And it came to pass in the mean while, that the heaven was black with clouds and wind, and there was a great rain. And Ahab rode, and went to Jezreel.

46 And the ᵃhand of the LORD was on Elijah; and he ᵇgirded¹ up his loins, and ran before Ahab to the entrance of Jezreel.

## CHAPTER 19

AND Ahab told Jezebel all that Elijah had done, and withal how he had ᵃslain all the prophets with the sword.

2 Then Jezebel sent a messenger unto Elijah, saying, ᵃSo let the gods do *to me,* and more also, if I make not thy life as the life of one of them by to morrow about this time.

3 And when he saw *that,* he arose, and ¹went for his life, and came to Beer-sheba, which *belongeth* to Judah, and left his servant there.

4 But he himself went a day's journey into the wilderness, and came and sat down under a ¹juniper tree: and he ᵃrequested for himself that he might die; and said, It is enough; now, O LORD, take away my life; for I *am* not better than my fathers.

5 And as he lay and slept under a juniper tree, behold, then an angel touched him, and said unto him, Arise *and* eat.

6 And he looked, and, behold, *there was* a cake baken on the ¹coals, and a ²cruse of water at his head. And he did eat and drink, and laid him down again.

7 And the angel of the LORD came again the second time, and touched him, and said, Arise *and* eat; because the journey *is* too great for thee.

8 And he arose, and did eat and drink, and went in the strength of that ¹meat forty days and ᵃforty nights unto ᵇHoreb the mount of God.

9 And he came thither unto a cave, and ¹lodged there; and, behold, the word of the LORD *came* to him, and he said unto him, What doest thou here, Elijah?

10 And he said, ᵃI have been very ᵇjealous¹ for the LORD God of hosts: for the children of Israel have forsaken thy covenant, thrown down thine altars, and ᶜslain thy prophets with the sword; and ᵈI, *even* I only, am left; and they seek my life, to take it away.

11 And he said, Go forth, and stand ᵃupon the mount before the LORD. And, behold, the LORD ᵇpassed by, and ᶜa great and strong wind ¹rent the mountains, and brake in pieces

the rocks before the LORD; *but* the LORD *was* not in the wind: and after the wind an earthquake; *but* the LORD *was* not in the earthquake:

12 And after the earthquake a fire; *but* the LORD *was* not in the fire: and after the fire a ¹still small voice.

13 And it was *so,* when Elijah heard *it,* that ᵃhe wrapped his face in his mantle, and went out, and stood in the entering in of the cave. ᵇAnd, behold, *there came* a voice unto him, and said, What doest thou here, Elijah?

14 ᵃAnd he said, I have been very ¹jealous for the LORD God of hosts: because the children of Israel have forsaken thy covenant, thrown down thine altars, and slain thy prophets with the sword; and I, *even* I only, am left; and they seek my life, to take it away.

15 And the LORD said unto him, Go, return on thy way to the wilderness of Damascus: ᵃand when thou comest, anoint Hazael *to be* king over Syria:

16 And ᵃJehu the son of Nimshi shalt thou anoint *to be* king over Israel: and ᵇElisha the son of Shaphat of Abel-meholah shalt thou anoint *to be* prophet in thy room.

17 And ᵃit shall come to pass, *that* him that escapeth the sword of Hazael shall Jehu ᵇslay: and him that escapeth from the sword of Jehu ᶜshall Elisha slay.

18 ᵃYet I have ¹left *me* seven thousand in Israel, all the knees which have not bowed unto Baal, ᵇand every mouth which hath not kissed him.

19 So he departed thence, and found Elisha the son of Shaphat, who *was* plowing *with* twelve yoke *of oxen* before him, and he with the twelfth: and Elijah passed by him, and cast his ᵃmantle upon him.

20 And he left the oxen, and ran after Elijah, and said, ᵃLet me, I pray thee, kiss my father and my mother, and *then* I will follow thee. And he said unto him, Go back again: for what have I done to thee?

21 And ¹he returned from him, and took a yoke of oxen, and slew them, and ᵃboiled their flesh ²with the instruments of the oxen, and gave unto the people, and they did eat. Then he arose, and went after Elijah, and ministered unto him.

## CHAPTER 20

AND ᵃBen-hadad the king of Syria gathered all his host together: and *there were* thirty and two kings with him, and horses, and chariots: and he went up and besieged ᵇSamaria, and warred against it.

### Center reference column

18:44 ¹ Lit. *Bind or Harness*
18:46 ᵃ 2 Kin. 3:15; Is. 8:11; Ezek. 3:14
ᵇ 2 Kin. 4:29; 9:1; Jer. 1:17; 1 Pet. 1:13 ¹ *tucked the skirts of his robe in his belt in preparation for quick travel*
19:1 ᵃ 1 Kin. 18:40
19:2 ᵃ Ruth 1:17; 1 Kin. 20:10; 2 Kin. 6:31
19:3 ¹ *ran*
19:4 ᵃ Num. 11:15; Jer. 20:14–18; Jon. 4:3, 8 ¹ *broom tree*
19:6 ¹ *hot stones* ² *jar*
19:8 ᵃ Ex. 24:18; 34:28; Deut. 9:9–11, 18; Matt. 4:2 ᵇ Ex. 3:1; 4:27 ¹ *food*
19:9 ¹ *spent the night*
19:10 ᵃ Rom. 11:3 ᵇ Num. 25:11, 13; Ps. 69:9 ᶜ 1 Kin. 18:4 ᵈ 1 Kin. 18:22; Rom. 11:3 ¹ *zealous*
19:11 ᵃ Ex. 19:20; 24:12, 18 ᵇ Ex. 33:21, 22 ᶜ Ezek. 1:4; 37:7 ¹ *tore into*
19:12 ¹ *delicate whispering voice*
19:13 ᵃ Ex. 3:6; Is. 6:2 ᵇ 1 Kin. 19:9
19:14 ᵃ 1 Kin. 19:10 ¹ *zealous*
19:15 ᵃ 2 Kin. 8:8–15
19:16 ᵃ 2 Kin. 9:1–10 ᵇ 1 Kin. 19:19–21; 2 Kin. 2:9–15
19:17 ᵃ 2 Kin. 8:12; 13:3, 22 ᵇ 2 Kin. 9:14–10:28 ᶜ [Hos. 6:5]
19:18 ᵃ Rom. 11:4 ᵇ Hos. 13:2 ¹ *reserved*
19:19 ᵃ 1 Sam. 28:14; 2 Kin. 2:8, 13, 14
19:20 ᵃ [Matt. 8:21, 22; Luke 9:61, 62]; Acts 20:37
19:21 ᵃ 2 Sam. 24:22 ¹ *Elisha* ² *using the oxen's equipment*
20:1 ᵃ 1 Kin. 15:18, 20; 2 Kin. 6:24 ᵇ 1 Kin. 16:24; 2 Kin. 6:24

2 And he sent messengers to Ahab king of Israel into the city, and said unto him, Thus saith Ben-hadad,

3 Thy silver and thy gold *is* mine; thy wives also and thy children, *even* the goodliest, *are* mine.

4 And the king of Israel answered and said, My lord, O king, according to thy saying, I *am* thine, and all that I have.

5 And the messengers came again, and said, Thus speaketh Ben-hadad, saying, Although I have sent unto thee, saying, Thou shalt deliver me thy silver, and thy gold, and thy wives, and thy children;

6 Yet I will send my servants unto thee to morrow about this time, and they shall search thine house, and the houses of thy servants; and it shall be, *that* whatsoever is [1]pleasant in thine eyes, they shall put *it* in their hand, and take *it* away.

7 Then the king of Israel called all the elders of the land, and said, Mark, I pray you, and see how this *man* seeketh [1]mischief: for he sent unto me for my wives, and for my children, and for my silver, and for my gold; and I denied him not.

8 And all the elders and all the people said unto him, Hearken not *unto him,* nor consent.

9 Wherefore he said unto the messengers of Ben-hadad, Tell my lord the king, All that thou didst send for to thy servant at the first I will do: but this thing I may not do. And the messengers departed, and brought him word again.

10 And Ben-hadad sent unto him, and said, [a]The gods do so unto me, and more also, if the dust of Samaria shall suffice for handfuls for all the people [1]that follow me.

11 And the king of Israel answered and said, Tell *him,* Let not him that girdeth on *his harness* [a]boast himself as he that putteth it off.

12 And it came to pass, when *Ben-hadad* heard this message, as he *was* [a]drinking, he and the kings in the [1]pavilions, that he said unto his servants, [2]Set *yourselves in array.* And they set *themselves in array* against the city.

13 And, behold, there came a prophet unto Ahab king of Israel, saying, Thus saith the LORD, Hast thou seen all this great multitude? behold, [a]I will deliver it into thine hand this day; and thou shalt know that I *am* the LORD.

14 And Ahab said, By whom? And he said, Thus saith the LORD, *Even* by the young men of the princes of the provinces. Then he said, Who shall order the battle? And he answered, Thou.

15 Then he [1]numbered the young men of the princes of the provinces, and they were two hundred and thirty two: and after them he numbered all the people, *even* all the children of Israel, *being* seven thousand.

16 And they went out at noon. But Ben-hadad *was* [a]drinking himself drunk in the pavilions, he and the kings, the thirty and two kings that helped him.

17 And the young men of the princes of the provinces went out first; and Ben-hadad sent out, and they told him, saying, There are men come out of Samaria.

18 And he said, Whether they be come out for peace, take them alive; or whether they be come out for war, take them alive.

19 So these young men of the princes of the provinces came out of the city, and the army which followed them.

20 And [1]they slew every one his man: and the Syrians fled; and Israel pursued them: and Ben-hadad the king of Syria escaped on an horse with the horsemen.

21 And the king of Israel went out, and [1]smote the horses and chariots, and slew the Syrians with a great slaughter.

22 And the prophet came to the king of Israel, and said unto him, Go, strengthen thyself, and [1]mark, and see what thou doest: [a]for [2]at the return of the year the king of Syria will come up against thee.

23 And the servants of the king of Syria said unto him, Their gods *are* gods of the hills; therefore they were stronger than we; but let us fight against them in the plain, and surely we shall be stronger than they.

24 And do this thing, Take the kings away, every man out of his place, and put captains in their [1]rooms:

25 And [1]number thee an army, like the army that [2]thou hast lost, horse for horse, and chariot for chariot: and we will fight against them in the plain, *and* surely we shall be stronger than they. And he hearkened unto their voice, and did so.

26 And it came to pass at the return of the year, that Ben-hadad numbered the Syrians, and went up to [a]Aphek, to fight against Israel.

27 And the children of Israel were [1]numbered, and were all [2]present, and went against them: and the children of Israel [3]pitched before them like two little flocks of kids; but the Syrians filled the [a]country.

28 And there came a [a]man of God, and spake unto the king of Israel, and said, Thus saith the LORD, Because the Syrians have said, The LORD *is*

---

20:6 [1] *pleasing*
20:7 [1] *trouble*
20:10 [a] 1 Kin. 19:2; 2 Kin. 6:31 [1] Lit. *at my feet*
20:11 [a] Prov. 27:1; [Eccl. 7:8]
20:12 [a] 1 Kin. 20:16 [1] *booths or shelters* [2] *Get ready to attack*
20:13 [a] 1 Kin. 20:28
20:15 [1] *mustered*
20:16 [a] 1 Kin. 16:9; 20:12; [Prov. 20:1]
20:20 [1] *each one killed his man*
20:21 [1] *attacked*
20:22 [a] 2 Sam. 11:1; 1 Kin. 20:26 [1] *take note* [2] *in the spring*
20:24 [1] *places*
20:25 [1] *muster* [2] Lit. *fell from you*
20:26 [a] Josh. 13:4; 2 Kin. 13:17
20:27 [1] *mustered* [2] *given provisions* [3] *encamped* [a] Judg. 6:3–5; 1 Sam. 13:5–8
20:28 [a] 1 Kin. 17:18

God of the hills, but he *is* not God of the valleys, therefore [b]will I deliver all this great multitude into thine hand, and ye shall know that I *am* the LORD.

29 And they [1]pitched one over against the other seven days. And *so* it was, that in the seventh day the battle was joined: and the children of Israel slew of the Syrians an hundred thousand footmen in one day.

30 But the rest fled to Aphek, into the city; and *there* a wall fell upon twenty and seven thousand of the men *that were* left. And Ben-hadad fled, and came into the city, into an inner chamber.

31 And his servants said unto him, Behold now, we have heard that the kings of the house of Israel *are* merciful kings: let us, I pray thee, [a]put sackcloth on our loins, and ropes upon our heads, and go out to the king of Israel: peradventure he will save thy life.

32 So they girded sackcloth on their loins, and *put* ropes on their heads, and came to the king of Israel, and said, Thy servant Ben-hadad saith, I pray thee, let me live. And he said, *Is* he yet alive? he *is* my brother.

33 Now the men did diligently observe whether [1]*any thing would come* from him, and did hastily catch *it:* and they said, Thy brother Ben-hadad. Then he said, Go ye, bring him. Then Ben-hadad came forth to him; and he caused him to come up into the chariot.

34 And *Ben-hadad* said unto him, [a]The cities, which my father took from thy father, I will restore; and thou shalt make streets for thee in Damascus, as my father made in Samaria. Then *said Ahab,* I will send thee away with this covenant. So he made a covenant with him, and sent him away.

35 And a certain man of [a]the sons of the prophets said unto his neighbour [b]in the word of the LORD, [1]Smite me, I pray thee. And the man refused to smite him.

36 Then said he unto him, Because thou hast not obeyed the voice of the LORD, behold, as soon as thou art departed from me, a lion shall slay thee. And as soon as he was departed from him, [a]a lion found him, and slew him.

37 Then he found another man, and said, [1]Smite me, I pray thee. And the man smote him, so that in smiting he wounded *him.*

38 So the prophet departed, and waited for the king by the way, and disguised himself with ashes upon his face.

39 And [a]as the king passed by, he cried unto the king: and he said, Thy

servant went out into the midst of the battle; and, behold, a man turned aside, and brought a man unto me, and said, [1]Keep this man: if by any means he be missing, then [b]shall thy life be for his life, or else thou shalt [2]pay a talent of silver.

40 And as thy servant was busy here and there, he was gone. And the king of Israel said unto him, So *shall* thy judgment *be;* thyself hast decided *it.*

41 And he hasted, and took the ashes away from his face; and the king of Israel discerned him that he *was* of the prophets.

42 And he said unto him, Thus saith the LORD, [a]Because thou hast let go out of *thy* hand a man whom I appointed to utter destruction, therefore thy life shall go for his life, and thy people for his people.

43 And the king of Israel [a]went to his house [1]heavy and displeased, and came to Samaria.

## CHAPTER 21

AND it came to pass after these things, *that* Naboth the Jezreelite had a vineyard, which *was* in [a]Jezreel, hard by the palace of Ahab king of Samaria.

2 And Ahab spake unto Naboth, saying, Give me thy [a]vineyard, that I may have it for a garden of herbs, because it *is* near unto my house: and I will give thee for it a better vineyard than it; *or,* if it seem good to thee, I will give thee the worth of it in money.

3 And Naboth said to Ahab, The LORD forbid it me, [a]that I should give the inheritance of my fathers unto thee.

4 And Ahab came into his house [1]heavy and displeased because of the word which Naboth the Jezreelite had spoken to him: for he had said, I will not give thee the inheritance of my fathers. And he laid him down upon his bed, and turned away his face, and would eat no bread.

5 But [a]Jezebel his wife came to him, and said unto him, Why is thy spirit so sad, that thou eatest no bread?

6 And he said unto her, Because I spake unto Naboth the Jezreelite, and said unto him, Give me thy vineyard for money; or else, if it please thee, I will give thee *another* vineyard for it: and he answered, I will not give thee my vineyard.

7 And Jezebel his wife said unto him, Dost thou now govern the kingdom of Israel? arise, *and* eat bread, and let thine heart be merry: I will give thee the vineyard of Naboth the Jezreelite.

8 So she wrote letters in Ahab's name, and sealed *them* with his seal,

20:28 [b]1 Kin. 20:13
20:29 [1] *encamped opposite each other*
20:31 [a] Gen. 37:34; 2 Sam. 3:31
20:33 [1] *any sign of mercy would*
20:34 [a] 1 Kin. 15:20
20:35 [a] 2 Kin. 2:3, 5, 7, 15   [b] 1 Kin. 13:17, 18 [1] *Strike me please*
20:36 [a] 1 Kin. 13:24
20:37 [1] *Strike me please*
20:39 [a] 2 Sam. 12:1

[b] 2 Kin. 10:24 [1] *Guard* [2] *Lit. weigh*
20:42 [a] 1 Kin. 22:31–37
20:43 [a] 1 Kin. 21:4 [1] *sullen*
21:1 [a] Judg. 6:33; 1 Kin. 18:45, 46
21:2 [a] 1 Sam. 8:14
21:3 [a] [Lev. 25:23; Num. 36:7; Ezek. 46:18]
21:4 [1] *sullen*
21:5 [a] 1 Kin. 19:1, 2

and sent the letters unto the elders and to the nobles that *were* in his city, dwelling with Naboth.

9 And she wrote in the letters, saying, Proclaim a fast, and ¹set Naboth ²on high among the people:

10 And set two men, ¹sons of Belial, before him, to bear witness against him, saying, Thou didst ᵃblaspheme God and the king. And *then* carry him out, and ᵇstone him, that he may die.

11 And the men of his city, *even* the elders and the nobles who were the inhabitants in his city, did as Jezebel had sent unto them, *and* as it *was* written in the letters which she had sent unto them.

12 ᵃThey proclaimed a fast, and set Naboth on high among the people.

13 And there came in two men, children of Belial, and sat before him: and the men of Belial ᵃwitnessed against him, *even* against Naboth, in the presence of the people, saying, Naboth did blaspheme God and the king. ᵇThen they carried him forth out of the city, and stoned him with stones, that he died.

14 Then they sent to Jezebel, saying, Naboth is stoned, and is dead.

15 And it came to pass, when Jezebel heard that Naboth was stoned, and was dead, that Jezebel said to Ahab, Arise, take possession of the vineyard of Naboth the Jezreelite, which he refused to give thee for money: for Naboth is not alive, but dead.

16 And it came to pass, when Ahab heard that Naboth was dead, that Ahab rose up to go down to the vineyard of Naboth the Jezreelite, to take possession of it.

17 ᵃAnd the word of the LORD came to ᵇElijah the Tishbite, saying,

18 Arise, go down to meet Ahab king of Israel, ᵃwhich *is* in Samaria: behold, *he is* in the vineyard of Naboth, whither he is gone down to possess it.

19 And thou shalt speak unto him, saying, Thus saith the LORD, Hast thou killed, and also taken possession? And thou shalt speak unto him, saying, Thus saith the LORD, ᵃIn the place where dogs licked the blood of Naboth shall dogs lick thy blood, even thine.

20 And Ahab said to Elijah, ᵃHast thou found me, O mine enemy? And he answered, I have found *thee:* because ᵇthou hast sold thyself to work evil in the sight of the LORD.

21 Behold, ᵃI will bring ¹evil upon thee, and will take away thy ᵇposterity, and will cut off from Ahab ᶜhim² that pisseth against the wall, and ᵈhim that is shut up and left in Israel,

22 And will make thine house like the house of ᵃJeroboam the son of

Nebat, and like the house of ᵇBaasha the son of Ahijah, for the provocation wherewith thou hast provoked *me* to anger, and made Israel to sin.

23 And ᵃof Jezebel also spake the LORD, saying, The dogs shall eat Jezebel by the wall of Jezreel.

24 ᵃHim that dieth of Ahab in the city the dogs shall eat; and him that dieth in the field shall the fowls of the air eat.

25 But ᵃthere was none like unto Ahab, which did sell himself to work wickedness in the sight of the LORD, ᵇwhom Jezebel his wife ¹stirred up.

26 And he did very abominably in following idols, according to all *things* ᵃas did the Amorites, whom the LORD cast out before the children of Israel.

27 And it came to pass, when Ahab heard those words, that he rent his clothes, and ᵃput sackcloth upon his flesh, and fasted, and lay in sackcloth, and ¹went softly.

28 And the word of the LORD came to Elijah the Tishbite, saying,

29 Seest thou how Ahab humbleth himself before me? because he ᵃhumbleth himself before me, I will not bring the evil in his days: *but* ᵇin his son's days will I bring the evil upon his house.

### CHAPTER 22

AND they continued three years without war between Syria and Israel.

2 And it came to pass in the third year, that ᵃJehoshaphat the king of Judah came down to the king of Israel.

3 And the king of Israel said unto his servants, Know ye that ᵃRamoth in Gilead *is* ours, and we ¹*be* still, *and* take it not out of the hand of the king of Syria?

4 And he said unto Jehoshaphat, Wilt thou go with me to battle to Ramoth-gilead? And Jehoshaphat said to the king of Israel, ᵃI *am* as thou *art,* my people as thy people, my horses as thy horses.

5 And Jehoshaphat said unto the king of Israel, ᵃEnquire, I pray thee, ¹at the word of the LORD to day.

6 Then the king of Israel ᵃgathered ¹the prophets together, about four hundred men, and said unto them, Shall I go against Ramoth-gilead to battle, or shall I forbear? And they said, Go up; for the Lord shall deliver *it* into the hand of the king.

7 And ᵃJehoshaphat said, *Is there* not here a prophet of the LORD besides, that we might enquire of him?

8 And the king of Israel said unto Jehoshaphat, *There is* yet one man, Micaiah the son of Imlah, by whom

---

21:9 ¹ *seat* ² Lit. *at the head*

21:10 ᵃ [Ex. 22:28; Lev. 24:15, 16]; Acts 6:11 ᵇ [Lev. 24:14] ¹ *scoundrels*

21:12 ᵃ Is. 58:4

21:13 ᵃ [Ex. 20:16; 23:1, 7] ᵇ 2 Kin. 9:26; 2 Chr. 24:21; Acts 7:58, 59; Heb. 11:37

21:17 ᵃ [Ps. 9:12] ᵇ 1 Kin. 19:1

21:18 ᵃ 1 Kin. 13:32; 2 Chr. 22:9

21:19 ᵃ 1 Kin. 22:38; 2 Kin. 9:26

21:20 ᵃ 1 Kin. 18:17 ᵇ 1 Kin. 21:25; 2 Kin. 17:17; [Rom. 7:14]

21:21 ᵃ 1 Kin. 14:10; 2 Kin. 9:8 ᵇ 2 Kin. 10:10 ᶜ 1 Sam. 25:22 ᵈ 1 Kin. 14:10 ¹ *calamity* ² *every male in Israel, both bond and free*

21:22 ᵃ 1 Kin. 15:29

ᵇ 1 Kin. 16:3, 11

21:23 ᵃ 2 Kin. 9:10, 30–37

21:24 ᵃ 1 Kin. 14:11; 16:4

21:25 ᵃ 1 Kin. 16:30–33; 21:20 ᵇ 1 Kin. 16:31 ¹ *incited*

21:26 ᵃ Gen. 15:16; [Lev. 18:25–30]; 2 Kin. 21:11

21:27 ᵃ Gen. 37:34; 2 Sam. 3:31; 2 Kin. 6:30 ¹ *went about mourning*

21:29 ᵃ [2 Kin. 22:19] ᵇ 2 Kin. 9:25; 10:11, 17

22:2 ᵃ 1 Kin. 15:24; 2 Chr. 18:2

22:3 ᵃ Deut. 4:43; Josh. 21:38; 1 Kin. 4:13 ¹ *hesitate*

22:4 ᵃ 2 Kin. 3:7

22:5 ᵃ 2 Kin. 3:11 ¹ *for*

22:6 ᵃ 1 Kin. 18:19 ¹ *the false prophets*

22:7 ᵃ 2 Kin. 3:11

---

we may enquire of the LORD: but I hate him; for he doth not prophesy good concerning me, but evil. And Jehoshaphat said, Let not the king say so.

9 Then the king of Israel called an officer, and said, Hasten *hither* Micaiah the son of Imlah.

10 And the king of Israel and Jehoshaphat the king of Judah sat each on his throne, having put on their robes, [1]in a void place in the entrance of the gate of Samaria; and all the prophets prophesied before them.

11 And Zedekiah the son of Chenaanah made him [a]horns of iron: and he said, Thus saith the LORD, With these shalt thou [b]push the Syrians, until thou have consumed them.

12 And all the prophets prophesied so, saying, Go up to Ramoth-gilead, and prosper: for the LORD shall deliver *it* into the king's hand.

13 And the messenger that was gone to call Micaiah spake unto him, saying, Behold now, the words of the prophets *declare* good unto the king with [1]one mouth: let thy word, I pray thee, be like the word of one of them, and speak *that which is* good.

14 And Micaiah said, *As* the LORD liveth, [a]what the LORD saith unto me, that will I speak.

15 So he came to the king. And the king said unto him, Micaiah, shall we go against Ramoth-gilead to battle, or shall we [1]forbear? And he answered him, Go, and prosper: for the LORD shall deliver *it* into the hand of the king.

16 And the king said unto him, How many times shall I [1]adjure thee that thou tell me nothing but *that which is* true in the name of the LORD?

17 And he said, I saw all Israel [a]scattered upon the hills, as sheep that have not a shepherd: and the LORD said, These have no master: let them return every man to his house in peace.

18 And the king of Israel said unto Jehoshaphat, Did I not tell thee that he would prophesy no good concerning me, but evil?

19 And [1]he said, Hear thou therefore the word of the LORD: [a]I saw the LORD sitting on his throne, [b]and all the host of heaven standing by him on his right hand and on his left.

20 And the LORD said, Who shall persuade Ahab, that he may go up and fall at Ramoth-gilead? And one said on this manner, and another said on that manner.

21 And there came forth a spirit, and stood before the LORD, and said, I will persuade him.

22 And the LORD said unto him, Wherewith? And he said, I will go forth, and I will be a lying spirit in the mouth of all his prophets. And he said, [a]Thou shalt persuade *him,* and prevail also: go forth, and do so.

23 [a]Now therefore, behold, the LORD hath put a lying spirit in the mouth of all these thy prophets, and the LORD hath [1]spoken evil concerning thee.

24 But Zedekiah the son of Chenaanah went near, and [a]smote[1] Micaiah on the cheek, and said, [b]Which way went the Spirit of the LORD from me to speak unto thee?

25 And Micaiah said, Behold, thou shalt see in that day, when thou shalt go into an [a]inner chamber to hide thyself.

26 And the king of Israel said, Take Micaiah, and carry him back unto Amon the governor of the city, and to Joash the king's son;

27 And say, Thus saith the king, Put this *fellow* in the [a]prison, and feed him with bread of affliction and with water of affliction, until I come in peace.

28 And Micaiah said, If thou return at all in peace, [a]the LORD hath not spoken by me. And he said, Hearken, O people, every one of you.

29 So the king of Israel and Jehoshaphat the king of Judah went up to Ramoth-gilead.

30 And the king of Israel said unto Jehoshaphat, I will disguise myself, and enter into the battle; but put thou on thy robes. And the king of Israel [a]disguised himself, and went into the battle.

31 But the [a]king of Syria commanded his thirty and two [b]captains that had rule over his chariots, saying, Fight neither with small nor great, save only with the king of Israel.

32 And it came to pass, when the captains of the chariots saw Jehoshaphat, that they said, Surely it *is* the king of Israel. And they turned aside to fight against him: and Jehoshaphat [a]cried out.

33 And it came to pass, when the captains of the chariots perceived that it *was* not the king of Israel, that they turned back from pursuing him.

34 And a *certain* man drew a bow [1]at a venture, and [2]smote the king of Israel between the joints of [3]the harness: wherefore he said unto the driver of his chariot, [4]Turn thine hand, and carry me out of the host; for I am wounded.

35 And the battle increased that day: and the king was [1]stayed up in his chariot against the Syrians, and died at even: and the blood ran out of the wound [2]into the midst of the chariot.

36 And there went a proclamation

## Cross references (center column)

22:10 [1] *at the threshingfloor at*
22:11 [a] Zech. 1:18–21 [b] Deut. 33:17
22:13 [1] *one accord*
22:14 [a] Num. 22:38; 24:13
22:15 [1] *refrain*
22:16 [1] *make you swear*
22:17 [a] Num. 27:17; 1 Kin. 22:34–36; 2 Chr. 18:16; Matt. 9:36; Mark 6:34
22:19 [a] Is. 6:1; Ezek. 1:26–28; Dan. 7:9 [b] Job 1:6; 2:1; Ps. 103:20; Dan. 7:10; Zech. 1:10; [Matt. 18:10; Heb. 1:7, 14] [1] *Micaiah*
22:22 [a] Judg. 9:23; 1 Sam. 16:14; 18:10; 19:9; Job 12:16; [Ezek. 14:9; 2 Thess. 2:11]
22:23 [a] [Ezek. 14:9] [1] *declared disaster*
22:24 [a] Jer. 20:2 [b] 2 Chr. 18:23 [1] *struck*
22:25 [a] 1 Kin. 20:30
22:27 [a] 2 Chr. 16:10; 18:25–27
22:28 [a] Num. 16:29; Deut. 18:20–22
22:30 [a] 2 Chr. 35:22
22:31 [a] 1 Kin. 20:1 [b] 1 Kin. 20:24; 2 Chr. 18:30
22:32 [a] 2 Chr. 18:31
22:34 [1] *at random* [2] *struck* [3] *his armour* [4] *Turn around and take me out of the battle*
22:35 [1] *propped* [2] *onto the floor*

throughout the host about the going down of the sun, saying, Every man to his city, and every man to his own country.

37 So the king died, and was brought to Samaria; and they buried the king in Samaria.

38 And *one* washed the chariot in the pool of Samaria; and the dogs licked up his blood; [1]and they washed his armour; according [a]unto the word of the LORD which he spake.

39 Now the rest of the acts of Ahab, and all that he did, and [a]the ivory house which he made, and all the cities that he built, *are* they not written in the book of the chronicles of the kings of Israel?

40 So Ahab [1]slept with his fathers; and [a]Ahaziah his son reigned in his stead.

41 And [a]Jehoshaphat the son of Asa began to reign over Judah in the fourth year of Ahab king of Israel.

42 Jehoshaphat *was* thirty and five years old when he began to reign; and he reigned twenty and five years in Jerusalem. And his mother's name *was* Azubah the daughter of Shilhi.

43 And [a]he walked in all the ways of Asa his father; he turned not aside from it, doing *that which was* right in the eyes of the LORD: nevertheless [b]the [1]high places were not taken away; *for* the people offered and burnt incense yet in the high places.

44 And [a]Jehoshaphat made [b]peace with the king of Israel.

45 Now the rest of the acts of Jehoshaphat, and his might that he shewed, and how he warred, *are* they not written [a]in the book of the chronicles of the kings of Judah?

46 [a]And the remnant of the sodomites, which remained in the days of his father Asa, he took out of the land.

47 [a]*There was* then no king in Edom: a deputy *was* king.

48 [a]Jehoshaphat [b]made [1]ships of Tharshish to go to [c]Ophir for gold: [d]but they went not; for the ships were [2]broken at [e]Ezion-geber.

49 Then said Ahaziah the son of Ahab unto Jehoshaphat, Let my servants go with thy servants in the ships. But Jehoshaphat would not.

50 And [a]Jehoshaphat [1]slept with his fathers, and was buried with his fathers in the city of David his father: and Jehoram his son reigned in his stead.

51 [a]Ahaziah the son of Ahab began to reign over Israel in Samaria the seventeenth year of Jehoshaphat king of Judah, and reigned two years over Israel.

52 And he did evil in the sight of the LORD, and [a]walked in the way of his father, and in the way of his mother, and in the way of Jeroboam the son of Nebat, who made Israel to sin:

53 For [a]he served Baal, and worshipped him, and provoked to anger the LORD God of Israel, [b]according[1] to all that his father had done.

22:38 [a] 1 Kin. 21:19
[1] MT *while the harlots bathed*
22:39 [a] Amos 3:15
22:40 [a] 2 Kin. 1:2, 18 [1] *rested in death with*
22:41 [a] 2 Chr. 20:31
22:43 [a] 2 Chr. 17:3; 20:32, 33 [b] 2 Kin. 12:3 [1] Places for pagan worship
22:44 [a] 2 Chr. 19:2 [b] 2 Chr. 18:1

22:45 [a] 2 Chr. 20:34
22:46 [a] 1 Kin. 14:24; 15:12
22:47 [a] 2 Sam. 8:14
22:48 [a] 2 Chr. 20:35-37 [b] 1 Kin. 10:22 [c] 1 Kin. 9:28 [d] 2 Chr. 20:37 [e] 1 Kin. 9:26 [1] Or *merchant ships* [2] *wrecked*
22:50 [a] 2 Chr. 21:1 [1] *rested in death*
22:51 [a] 1 Kin. 22:40
22:52 [a] 1 Kin. 15:26; 21:25
22:53 [a] Judg. 2:11 [b] 1 Kin. 16:30-32 [1] *in the same way*

# THE SECOND BOOK OF THE
# KINGS

The Book of Second Kings continues the drama begun in First Kings—the tragic history of two nations on a collision course with captivity. The author systematically traces the reigning monarchs of Israel and Judah, first by carrying one nation's history forward, then retracing the same period for the other nation.

Nineteen consecutive evil kings rule in Israel, leading to the captivity by Assyria. The picture is somewhat brighter in Judah, where godly kings occasionally emerge to reform the evils of their predecessors. In the end, however, sin outweighs righteousness and Judah is marched off to Babylon.

## CHAPTER 1

THEN Moab ªrebelled against Israel ᵇafter the death of Ahab.

2 And ªAhaziah fell down through a lattice in his upper chamber that *was* in Samaria, and was ¹sick: and he sent messengers, and said unto them, Go, enquire of ᵇBaal-zebub² the god of ᶜEkron whether I shall recover of this ³disease.

3 But the angel of the LORD said to Elijah the Tishbite, Arise, go up to meet the messengers of the king of Samaria, and say unto them, *Is it* not because *there is* not a God in Israel, *that* ye go to enquire of Baal-zebub the god of Ekron?

4 Now therefore thus saith the LORD, Thou shalt not come down from that bed on which thou art gone up, but shalt surely die. And Elijah departed.

5 And when the messengers turned back unto ¹him, he said unto them, Why are ye now ²turned back?

6 And they said unto him, There came a man up to meet us, and said unto us, Go, turn again unto the king that sent you, and say unto him, Thus saith the LORD, *Is it* not because *there is* not a God in Israel, *that* thou sendest to enquire of Baal-zebub the god of Ekron? therefore thou shalt not come down from that bed on which thou art gone up, but shalt surely die.

7 And he said unto them, What ¹manner of man *was he* which came up to meet you, and told you these words?

8 And they answered him, He *was* ªan hairy man, and girt with a girdle of leather about his loins. And he said, ᵇIt *is* Elijah the Tishbite.

9 Then the king sent unto him a captain of fifty with his fifty. And he went up to him: and, behold, he sat on the top of an hill. And he spake unto him, Thou man of God, the king hath said, Come down.

10 And Elijah answered and said to the captain of fifty, If I *be* a man of

God, then ªlet fire come down from heaven, and consume thee and thy fifty. And there came down fire from heaven, and consumed him and his fifty.

11 Again also he sent unto him another captain of fifty with his fifty. And he answered and said unto him, O man of God, thus hath the king said, Come down quickly.

12 And Elijah answered and said unto them, If I *be* a man of God, let fire come down from heaven, and consume thee and thy fifty. And the fire of God came down from heaven, and consumed him and his fifty.

13 And he sent again a captain of the third fifty with his fifty. And the third captain of fifty went up, and came and ¹fell on his knees before Elijah, and besought him, and said unto him, O man of God, I pray thee, let my life, and the life of these fifty thy servants, ªbe precious in thy sight.

14 Behold, there came fire down from heaven, and burnt up the two captains of the former fifties with their fifties: therefore let my life now be precious in thy sight.

15 And the angel of the LORD said unto Elijah, Go down with him: be not afraid of him. And he arose, and went down with him unto the king.

16 And he said unto him, Thus saith the LORD, Forasmuch as thou hast sent messengers to enquire of Baal-zebub the god of Ekron, *is it* not because *there is* no God in Israel to enquire of his word? therefore thou shalt not come down off that bed on which thou art gone up, but shalt surely die.

17 So ¹he died according to the word of the LORD which Elijah had spoken. And ªJehoram² reigned in his stead in the second year of Jehoram the son of Jehoshaphat king of Judah; because he had no son.

18 Now the rest of the acts of Ahaziah which he did, *are* they not written in the book of the chronicles of the kings of Israel?

1:1 ª 2 Sam. 8:2
ᵇ 2 Kin. 3:5
1:2 ª 1 Kin. 22:40
ᵇ 2 Kin. 1:3, 6, 16;
Matt. 10:25; Mark
3:22 ᶜ 1 Sam.
5:10 ¹ *injured*
² Lit. *Lord of Flies*
³ *injury*
1:5 ¹ Ahaziah
² *come back*
1:7 ¹ *kind*
1:8 ª Zech. 13:4;
Matt. 3:4; Mark
1:6 ᵇ 1 Kin. 18:7

1:10 ª 1 Kin. 18:36–
38; Luke 9:54
1:13 ª 1 Sam. 26:21;
Ps. 72:14 ¹ Lit.
*bowed down*
1:17 ª 1 Kin. 22:50;
2 Kin. 8:16; Matt.
1:8 ¹ Ahaziah
² The son of Ahab
king of Israel,
2 Kin. 3:1

## CHAPTER 2

A ND it came to pass, when the LORD would [a]take up Elijah into heaven by a whirlwind, that Elijah went with [b]Elisha from Gilgal.

2 And Elijah said unto Elisha, [a]Tarry here, I pray thee; for the LORD hath sent me to Beth-el. And Elisha said unto him, *As* the LORD liveth, and [b]*as* thy soul liveth, I will not leave thee. So they went down to Beth-el.

3 And [a]the sons of the prophets that *were* at Beth-el came forth to Elisha, and said unto him, Knowest thou that the LORD will take away thy master [1]from thy head to day? And he said, Yea, I know *it;* hold ye your peace.

4 And Elijah said unto him, Elisha, tarry here, I pray thee; for the LORD hath sent me to Jericho. And he said, *As* the LORD liveth, and *as* thy soul liveth, I will not leave thee. So they came to Jericho.

5 And the sons of the prophets that *were* at Jericho came to Elisha, and said unto him, Knowest thou that the LORD will take away thy master from thy head to day? And he answered, Yea, I know *it;* [1]hold ye your peace.

6 And Elijah said unto him, Tarry, I pray thee, here; for the LORD hath sent me to Jordan. And he said, *As* the LORD liveth, and *as* thy soul liveth, I will not leave thee. And they two went on.

7 And fifty men of the sons of the prophets went, and stood [1]to view afar off: and they two stood by Jordan.

8 And Elijah took his mantle, and wrapped *it* together, and smote the waters, and [a]they were divided hither and thither, so that they two went over on dry [b]ground.

9 And it came to pass, when they were gone over, that Elijah said unto Elisha, Ask what I shall do for thee, before I be taken away from thee. And Elisha said, I pray thee, let a double portion of thy spirit be upon me.

10 And he said, Thou hast asked a hard thing: *nevertheless,* if thou see me *when I am* taken from thee, it shall be so unto thee; but if not, it shall not be *so.*

11 And it came to pass, as they still went on, and talked, that, behold, *there appeared* [a]a chariot of fire, and horses of fire, and [1]parted them both asunder; and Elijah [b]went up by a whirlwind into heaven.

12 And Elisha saw *it,* and he cried, [a]My father, my father, the chariot of Israel, and the horsemen thereof. And he saw him no more: and he took hold of his own clothes, and [1]rent them in two pieces.

13 He took up also the mantle of Elijah that fell from him, and went back, and stood by the bank of Jordan;

14 And he took the mantle of Elijah that fell from him, and smote the waters, and said, Where *is* the LORD God of Elijah? and when he also had smitten the waters, [a]they parted hither and thither: and Elisha went over.

15 And when the sons of the prophets [1]which *were* [a]to view at Jericho saw him, they said, The spirit of Elijah doth rest on Elisha. And they came to meet him, and bowed themselves to the ground before him.

16 And they said unto him, Behold now, there be with thy servants fifty strong men; let them go, we pray thee, and seek thy master: [a]lest peradventure the Spirit of the LORD hath taken him up, and cast him upon some mountain, or into some valley. And he said, Ye shall not send.

17 And when they urged him till he was [a]ashamed, he said, Send. They sent therefore fifty men; and they sought three days, but found him not.

18 And when they came again to him, (for he tarried at Jericho,) he said unto them, Did I not say unto you, Go not?

19 And the men of the city said unto Elisha, Behold, I pray thee, the situation of this city *is* pleasant, as my lord seeth: but the water *is* [1]naught, and the ground barren.

20 And he said, Bring me a new cruse, and put salt therein. And they brought *it* to him.

21 And he went forth unto the spring of the waters, and [a]cast the salt in there, and said, Thus saith the LORD, I have [1]healed these waters; there shall not be from thence any more death or barren *land.*

22 So the waters were [a]healed unto this day, according to the saying of Elisha which he spake.

23 And he went up from thence unto Beth-el: and as he was going up by the way, there came forth [1]little children out of the city, and mocked him, and said unto him, Go up, thou bald head; go up, thou bald head.

24 And he turned back, and looked on them, and [a]cursed[1] them in the name of the LORD. And there came forth two she bears out of the wood, and [2]tare forty and two children of them.

25 And he went from thence to [a]mount Carmel, and from thence he returned to Samaria.

## CHAPTER 3

N OW [a]Jehoram the son of Ahab began to reign over Israel in Samaria the eighteenth year of Jehoshaphat king of Judah, and reigned twelve years.

2 And he wrought evil in the sight of the LORD; but not like his father,

**Cross-references (center column):**

2:1 [a] Gen. 5:24; [Heb. 11:5] [b] 1 Kin. 19:16–21

2:2 [a] Ruth 1:15, 16 [b] 1 Sam. 1:26; 2 Kin. 2:4, 6; 4:30

2:3 [a] 1 Kin. 20:35; 2 Kin. 2:5, 7, 15; 4:1, 38; 9:1 [1] *from over you*

2:5 [1] *keep silent*

2:7 [1] *facing them at a distance*

2:8 [a] Ex. 14:21, 22; Josh. 3:16; 2 Kin. 2:14 [b] Josh. 3:17

2:11 [a] 2 Kin. 6:17; Ps. 104:4 [b] Gen. 5:24; Heb. 11:5 [1] *separated the two of them*

2:12 [a] 2 Kin. 13:14 [1] *tore*

2:14 [a] 2 Kin. 2:8

2:15 [a] 2 Kin. 2:7 [1] *who were at Jericho opposite him*

2:16 [a] 1 Kin. 18:12; Ezek. 8:3; Acts 8:39

2:17 [a] 2 Kin. 8:11

2:19 [1] *bad*

2:21 [a] Ex. 15:25, 26; 2 Kin. 4:41; 6:6; John 9:6 [1] *purified*

2:22 [a] Ezek. 47:8, 9

2:23 [1] *youths*

2:24 [a] Deut. 27:13–26 [1] *pronounced a curse on* [2] *mauled*

2:25 [a] 1 Kin. 18:19, 20; 2 Kin. 4:25

3:1 [a] 2 Kin. 1:17

and like his mother: for he put away the [1]image of Baal [a]that his father had made.

3 Nevertheless he [1]cleaved unto [a]the sins of Jeroboam the son of Nebat, which made Israel to sin; he departed not therefrom.

4 And Mesha king of Moab was a [1]sheepmaster, and [a]rendered[2] unto the king of Israel an hundred thousand [b]lambs, and an hundred thousand rams, with the wool.

5 But it came to pass, when [a]Ahab was dead, that the king of Moab rebelled against the king of Israel.

6 And king Jehoram went out of Samaria the same time, and [1]numbered all Israel.

7 And he went and sent to Jehoshaphat the king of Judah, saying, The king of Moab hath rebelled against me: wilt thou go with me against Moab to battle? And he said, I will go up: [a]I *am* as thou *art,* my people as thy people, *and* my horses as thy horses.

8 And he said, Which way shall we go up? And he answered, The way through the wilderness of Edom.

9 So the king of Israel went, and the king of Judah, and the king of Edom: and they [1]fetched a compass of seven days' journey: and there was no water for the host, and for the cattle that followed them.

10 And the king of Israel said, Alas! that the LORD hath called these three kings together, to deliver them into the hand of Moab!

11 But [a]Jehoshaphat said, *Is there* not here a prophet of the LORD, that we may enquire of the LORD by him? And one of the king of Israel's servants answered and said, Here *is* Elisha the son of [1]Shaphat, which [b]poured water on the hands of Elijah.

12 And Jehoshaphat said, The word of the LORD is with him. So the king of Israel and Jehoshaphat and the king of Edom [a]went down to him.

13 And Elisha said unto the king of Israel, [a]What have I to do with thee? [b]get thee to [c]the prophets of thy father, and to the [d]prophets of thy mother. And the king of Israel said unto him, Nay: for the LORD hath called these three kings together, to deliver them into the hand of Moab.

14 And Elisha said, [a]*As* the LORD of hosts liveth, before whom I stand, surely, were it not that I regard the presence of Jehoshaphat the king of Judah, I would not look toward thee, nor see thee.

15 But now bring me [a]a [1]minstrel. And it came to pass, when the minstrel [b]played, that [c]the hand of the LORD came upon him.

16 And he said, Thus saith the LORD, [a]Make this valley full of [1]ditches.

17 For thus saith the LORD, Ye shall not see wind, neither shall ye see rain; yet that valley shall be filled with water, that ye may drink, both ye, and your cattle, and your beasts.

18 And this is *but* a light thing in the sight of the LORD: he will deliver the Moabites also into your hand.

19 And ye shall [1]smite every [2]fenced city, and every choice city, and shall [3]fell every good tree, and [4]stop all wells of water, and [5]mar every good piece of land with stones.

20 And it came to pass in the morning, when [a]the meat offering was offered, that, behold, there came water by the way of Edom, and the country was filled with water.

21 And when all the Moabites heard that the kings were come up to fight against them, they [1]gathered all that were able to put on armour, [2]and upward, and stood in the border.

22 And they rose up early in the morning, and the sun shone upon the water, and the Moabites saw the water on the other side *as* red as blood:

23 And they said, This *is* blood: the kings [1]are surely slain, and they have [2]smitten one another: now therefore, Moab, to the spoil.

24 And when they came to the camp of Israel, the Israelites rose up and smote the Moabites, so that they fled before them: but they went forward [1]smiting the Moabites, even in *their* country.

25 And they [1]beat down the cities, and on every good piece of land [2]cast every man his stone, and filled it; and they [3]stopped all the wells of water, and [4]felled all the good trees: only in [a]Kir-haraseth [5]left they the stones thereof; howbeit the slingers [6]went about *it,* and [7]smote it.

26 And when the king of Moab saw that the battle was too [1]sore for him, he took with him seven hundred men that drew swords, to break through *even* unto the king of Edom: but they could not.

27 Then [a]he took his eldest son that should have reigned in his stead, and offered him *for* a burnt offering upon the wall. And there was great [1]indignation against Israel: [b]and they departed from him, and returned to *their own* land.

## CHAPTER 4

Now there cried a certain woman of the wives of [a]the sons of the prophets unto Elisha, saying, Thy servant my husband is dead; and thou knowest that thy servant did fear the LORD: and the creditor is

3:2 [a] 1 Kin. 16:31, 32 [1] *sacred pillar*
3:3 [a] 1 Kin. 12:28–32 [1] *persisted in*
3:4 [a] 2 Sam. 8:2 [b] Is. 16:1, 2 [1] *sheep breeder* [2] *regularly paid to*
3:5 [a] 2 Kin. 1:1
3:6 [1] *mustered*
3:7 [a] 1 Kin. 22:4
3:9 [1] *marched on that roundabout route*
3:11 [a] 1 Kin. 22:7 [b] 1 Kin. 19:21; [John 13:4, 5, 13, 14] [1] Was the personal servant
3:12 [a] 2 Kin. 2:25
3:13 [a] [Ezek. 14:3] [b] Judg. 10:14; Ruth 1:15 [c] 1 Kin. 22:6–11 [d] 1 Kin. 18:19
3:14 [a] 1 Kin. 17:1; 2 Kin. 5:16
3:15 [a] 1 Sam. 10:5 [b] 1 Sam. 16:16, 23; 1 Chr. 25:1 [c] Ezek. 1:3; 3:14, 22; 8:1 [1] *musician*
3:16 [a] Jer. 14:3 [1] *water canals*
3:19 [1] *attack* [2] *fortified* [3] *cut down* [4] *stop up every spring* [5] *ruin*
3:20 [a] Ex. 29:39, 40
3:21 [1] *summoned* [2] *and older*
3:23 [1] *have surely struck swords* [2] *killed*
3:24 [1] *killing*
3:25 [a] Is. 16:7, 11; Jer. 48:31, 36 [1] *destroyed* [2] *every man threw* [3] *stopped up all the springs* [4] *cut down* [5] *they left intact* [6] *surrounded* [7] *attacked*
3:26 [1] *intense*
3:27 [a] [Deut. 18:10; Amos 2:1; Mic. 6:7] [b] 2 Kin. 8:20 [1] *wrath*
4:1 [a] 1 Kin. 20:35; 2 Kin. 2:3

come [b]to take unto him my two sons to be [l]bondmen.

2 And Elisha said unto her, What shall I do for thee? tell me, what hast thou in the house? And she said, Thine handmaid hath not any thing in the house, save a pot of oil.

3 Then he said, Go, borrow thee vessels abroad of all thy neighbours, *even* empty vessels; [a]borrow[l] not a few.

4 And when thou art come in, thou shalt shut the door upon thee and upon thy sons, and shalt pour out into all those vessels, and thou shalt set aside that which is full.

5 So she went from him, and shut the door upon her and upon her sons, who brought *the vessels* to her; and she poured out.

6 And it came to pass, when the vessels were full, that she said unto her son, Bring me yet a vessel. And he said unto her, *There is* not a vessel more. And the oil [l]stayed.

7 Then she came and told the man of God. And he said, Go, sell the oil, and pay thy debt, and live thou and thy children of the rest.

8 And it fell on a day, that Elisha passed to [a]Shunem, where *was* a [l]great woman; and she [2]constrained him [3]to eat bread. And *so* it was, *that* as oft as he passed by, he turned in [4]thither to eat bread.

9 And she said unto her husband, Behold now, I perceive that this *is* an holy man of God, which passeth by us [l]continually.

10 Let us make [l]a little chamber, I pray thee, on the wall; and let us set for him there a bed, and a table, and a stool, and a candlestick: and it shall be, when he cometh to us, that he shall turn in thither.

11 And it fell on a day, that he came thither, and he turned into the chamber, and lay there.

12 And he said to [a]Gehazi his servant, Call this Shunammite. And when he had called her, she stood before him.

13 And he said unto him, Say now unto her, Behold, thou hast been [l]careful for us with all this care; what *is* to be done for thee? wouldest thou be spoken for to the king, or to the captain of the host? And she answered, I dwell among mine own people.

14 And he said, What then *is* to be done for her? And Gehazi answered, Verily she hath no child, and her husband is old.

15 And he said, Call her. And when he had called her, she stood in the door.

16 And he said, About this season, [l]according to the time of life, thou

shalt embrace a son. And she said, Nay, my lord, *thou* man of God, [a]do not lie unto thine handmaid.

17 And the woman conceived, and bare a son at that season that Elisha had said unto her, according to the time of life.

18 And when the child was grown, it fell on a day, that he went out to his father to the reapers.

19 And he said unto his father, My head, my head. And he said to a lad, Carry him to his mother.

20 And when he had taken him, and brought him to his mother, he sat on her knees till noon, and *then* died.

21 And she went up, and laid him on the bed of the man of God, and shut *the door* upon him, and went out.

22 And she called unto her husband, and said, Send me, I pray thee, one of the young men, and one of the asses, that I may run to the man of God, and come again.

23 And he said, Wherefore wilt thou go to him to day? *it is* neither [a]new moon, nor sabbath. And she said, [l]*It shall be* well.

24 Then she saddled an ass, and said to her servant, Drive, and go forward; [l]slack not *thy* riding for me, except I bid thee.

25 So she went and came unto the man of God [a]to mount Carmel. And it came to pass, when the man of God saw her afar off, that he said to Gehazi his servant, Behold, *yonder is* that Shunammite:

26 Run now, I pray thee, to meet her, and say unto her, *Is it* well with thee? *is it* well with thy husband? *is it* well with the child? And she answered, *It is* well.

27 And when she came to the man of God to the hill, she caught him by the feet: but Gehazi came near to thrust her away. And the man of God said, Let her alone; for her soul *is* [l]vexed within her: and the LORD hath hid *it* from me, and hath not told me.

28 Then she said, Did I desire a son of my lord? [a]did I not say, Do not deceive me?

29 Then he said to Gehazi, [a]Gird[l] up thy loins, and take my staff in thine hand, and go thy way: if thou meet any man, [b]salute him not; and if any salute thee, answer him not again: and [c]lay my staff upon the face of the child.

30 And the mother of the child said, [a]*As* the LORD liveth, and *as* thy soul liveth, I will not [b]leave thee. And he arose, and followed her.

31 And Gehazi passed on before them, and laid the staff upon the face of the child; but *there was* neither voice, nor hearing. Wherefore

---

4:1 [b] [Lev. 25:39–41, 48]; 1 Sam. 22:2; Neh. 5:2–5; Matt. 18:25  [l] *slaves*

4:3 [a] 2 Kin. 3:16  [l] *do not gather just a few*

4:6 [l] *ceased*

4:8 [a] Josh. 19:18  [l] *notable*  [2] Lit. *laid hold on him*  [3] *to eat food*  [4] *there*

4:9 [l] *regularly*

4:10 [l] *a small walled upper chamber*

4:12 [a] 2 Kin. 4:29–31; 5:20–27; 8:4, 5

4:13 [l] *concerned*

4:16 [l] *about this time next year*

[a] 2 Kin. 4:28

4:23 [a] Num. 10:10; 28:11; 1 Chr. 23:31  [l] It is *well*

4:24 [l] *do not slacken the pace*

4:25 [a] 2 Kin. 2:25

4:27 [l] *in deep distress*

4:28 [a] 2 Kin. 4:16

4:29 [a] 1 Kin. 18:46; 2 Kin. 9:1  [b] Luke 10:4

[c] Ex. 7:19; 14:16; 2 Kin. 2:8, 14; Acts 19:12  [l] *Get yourself ready. The skirt of the robe was tucked in the belt to gain freedom of movement.*

4:30 [a] 2 Kin. 2:2  [b] 2 Kin. 2:4

he went again to meet him, and told him, saying, The child is [a]not awaked.

32 And when Elisha was come into the house, behold, the child was dead, *and* laid upon his bed.

33 He [a]went in therefore, and shut the door upon them twain, [b]and prayed unto the LORD.

34 And he went up, and [1]lay upon the child, and put his mouth upon his mouth, and his eyes upon his eyes, and his hands upon his hands: and [a]he stretched himself upon the child; and the flesh of the child waxed warm.

35 Then he returned, and walked in the house to and fro; and went up, [a]and stretched himself upon him: and [b]the child sneezed seven times, and the child opened his eyes.

36 And he called Gehazi, and said, Call this Shunammite. So he called her. And when she was come in unto him, he said, [1]Take up thy son.

37 Then she went in, and fell at his feet, and bowed herself to the ground, and [a]took up her son, and went out.

38 And Elisha came again to [a]Gilgal: and *there was* a [b]dearth[1] in the land; and the sons of the prophets *were* [c]sitting before him: and he said unto his servant, Set on the great pot, and seethe pottage for the sons of the prophets.

39 And one went out into the field to gather herbs, and found a wild vine, and gathered thereof wild gourds his lap full, and came and shred *them* into the pot of pottage: for they knew *them* not.

40 So they poured out for the men to eat. And it came to pass, as they were eating of the pottage, that they cried out, and said, O *thou* man of God, *there is* [a]death in the pot. And they could not eat *thereof.*

41 But he said, Then bring meal. And [a]he cast *it* into the pot; and he said, Pour out for the people, that they may eat. And there was [1]no harm in the pot.

42 And there came a man from [a]Baal-shalisha, [b]and brought the man of God bread of the firstfruits, twenty loaves of barley, and full ears of [1]corn in the [2]husk thereof. And he said, Give unto the people, that they may eat.

43 And his servitor said, [a]What, should I set this before an hundred men? He said again, Give the people, that they may eat: for thus saith the LORD, [b]They shall eat, and shall leave *thereof.*

44 So he set *it* before them, and they did eat, [a]and left *thereof,* according to the word of the LORD.

4:31 [a] John 11:11
4:33 [2] 2 Kin. 4:4; [Matt. 6:6]; Luke 8:51 [b] 1 Kin. 17:20
4:34 [a] 1 Kin. 17:21-23; Acts 20:10 [1] he stretched himself out on
4:35 [a] 1 Kin. 17:21 [b] 2 Kin. 8:1, 5
4:36 [1] Pick up
4:37 [a] 1 Kin. 17:23; [Heb. 11:35]
4:38 [a] 2 Kin. 2:1 [b] 2 Kin. 8:1 [c] Luke 10:39; Acts 22:3 [1] famine
4:40 [a] Ex. 10:17
4:41 [a] Ex. 15:25; 2 Kin. 2:21 [1] nothing harmful
4:42 [a] 1 Sam. 9:4 [b] 1 Sam. 9:7; [1 Cor. 9:11; Gal. 6:6] [1] grain [2] knapsack
4:43 [a] Luke 9:13; John 6:9 [b] Luke 9:17; John 6:11
4:44 [a] Matt. 14:20; 15:37; John 6:13

5:1 [a] Luke 4:27 [b] Ex. 11:3 [1] victory
5:2 [a] 2 Kin. 6:23; 13:20 [1] in bands [2] served, lit. was before
5:3 [1] heal
5:4 [1] Naaman
5:5 [a] 1 Sam. 9:8; 2 Kin. 8:8, 9
5:7 [a] [Gen. 30:2; Deut. 32:39; 1 Sam. 2:6] [1] tore
5:10 [a] 2 Kin. 4:41; John 9:7
5:11 [1] wave [2] heal
5:12 [1] So with Kt., LXX, Vg.; Qr., Syr., Tg. Amanah
5:13 [a] 1 Sam. 28:23

## CHAPTER 5

Now [a]Naaman, captain of the host of the king of Syria, was [b]a great man with his master, and honourable, because by him the LORD had given [1]deliverance unto Syria: he was also a mighty man in valour, *but he was* a leper.

2 And the Syrians had gone out [a]by[1] companies, and had brought away captive out of the land of Israel a little maid; and she [2]waited on Naaman's wife.

3 And she said unto her mistress, Would God my lord *were* with the prophet that *is* in Samaria! for he would [1]recover him of his leprosy.

4 And [1]one went in, and told his lord, saying, Thus and thus said the maid that *is* of the land of Israel.

5 And the king of Syria said, Go to, go, and I will send a letter unto the king of Israel. And he departed, and [a]took with him ten talents of silver, and six thousand *pieces* of gold, and ten changes of raiment.

6 And he brought the letter to the king of Israel, saying, Now when this letter is come unto thee, behold, I have *therewith* sent Naaman my servant to thee, that thou mayest recover him of his leprosy.

7 And it came to pass, when the king of Israel had read the letter, that he [1]rent his clothes, and said, *Am* I [a]God, to kill and to make alive, that this man doth send unto me to recover a man of his leprosy? wherefore consider, I pray you, and see how he seeketh a quarrel against me.

8 And it was *so,* when Elisha the man of God had heard that the king of Israel had rent his clothes, that he sent to the king, saying, Wherefore hast thou rent thy clothes? let him come now to me, and he shall know that there is a prophet in Israel.

9 So Naaman came with his horses and with his chariot, and stood at the door of the house of Elisha.

10 And Elisha sent a messenger unto him, saying, Go and [a]wash in Jordan seven times, and thy flesh shall come again to thee, and thou shalt be clean.

11 But Naaman was wroth, and went away, and said, Behold, I thought, He will surely come out to me, and stand, and call on the name of the LORD his God, and [1]strike his hand over the place, and [2]recover the leper.

12 *Are not* [1]Abana and Pharpar, rivers of Damascus, better than all the waters of Israel? may I not wash in them, and be clean? So he turned and went away in a rage.

13 And his [a]servants came near, and spake unto him, and said, My father, *if* the prophet had bid thee do

*some* great thing, wouldest thou not have done *it?* how much rather then, when he saith to thee, Wash, and be clean?

14 Then went he down, and dipped himself seven times in Jordan, according to the saying of the man of God: and his ªflesh came again like unto the flesh of a little child, and ᵇhe was clean.

15 And he returned to the man of God, he and all his company, and came, and stood before him: and he said, Behold, now I know that *there is* ªno God in all the earth, but in Israel: now therefore, I pray thee, take ᵇa ¹blessing of thy servant.

16 But he said, ªAs the LORD liveth, before whom I stand, ᵇI will receive none. And he urged him to take *it;* but he refused.

17 And Naaman said, Shall there not then, I pray thee, be given to thy servant two mules' burden of earth? for thy servant will henceforth offer neither burnt offering nor sacrifice unto other gods, but unto the LORD.

18 In this thing the LORD pardon thy servant, *that* when my master goeth into the house of Rimmon to worship there, and ªhe leaneth on my hand, and I bow myself in the house of Rimmon: when I bow down myself in the house of Rimmon, the LORD pardon thy servant in this thing.

19 And he said unto him, Go in peace. So he departed from him a little way.

20 But ªGehazi, the servant of Elisha the man of God, said, Behold, my master hath spared Naaman this Syrian, in not receiving at his hands that which he brought: but, *as* the LORD liveth, I will run after him, and take somewhat of him.

21 So Gehazi followed after Naaman. And when Naaman saw *him* running after him, he lighted down from the chariot to meet him, and said, *Is* all well?

22 And he said, All *is* ªwell. My master hath sent me, saying, Behold, even now there be come to me from mount Ephraim two young men of the sons of the prophets: give them, I pray thee, a talent of silver, and two changes of garments.

23 And Naaman said, Be content, take two talents. And he urged him, and bound two talents of silver in two bags, with two changes of garments, and laid *them* upon two of his servants; and they bare *them* before him.

24 And when he came to the ¹tower, he took *them* from their hand, and ²bestowed *them* in the house: and he let the men go, and they departed.

5:14 ª 2 Kin. 5:10; Job 33:25 ᵇ Luke 4:27; 5:13
5:15 ª Dan. 2:47; 3:29; 6:26, 27 ᵇ Gen. 33:11 ¹ *gift*
5:16 ª 2 Kin. 3:14 ᵇ Gen. 14:22, 23; 2 Kin. 5:20, 26; [Matt. 10:8]; Acts 8:18, 20
5:18 ª 2 Kin. 7:2, 17
5:20 ª 2 Kin. 4:12; 8:4, 5
5:22 ª 2 Kin. 4:26
5:24 ¹ Lit. *the hill* ² *stored them away*
5:25 ¹ *nowhere*
5:26 ª [Eccl. 3:1, 6] ¹ *Did not my heart go*
5:27 ª [1 Tim. 6:10] ᵇ Ex. 4:6; Num. 12:10; 2 Kin. 15:5
6:1 ª 2 Kin. 4:38 ¹ *small*
6:3 ª 2 Kin. 5:23
6:5 ª [Ex. 22:14] ¹ Lit. *iron*
6:6 ª Ex. 15:25; 2 Kin. 2:21; 4:41
6:8 ª 2 Kin. 8:28, 29
6:10 ¹ *he was watchful* ² *not just once or twice*

25 But he went in, and stood before his master. And Elisha said unto him, Whence *comest thou,* Gehazi? And he said, Thy servant went ¹no whither.

26 And he said unto him, ¹Went not mine heart *with thee,* when the man turned again from his chariot to meet thee? *Is it* a ªtime to receive money, and to receive garments, and oliveyards, and vineyards, and sheep, and oxen, and menservants, and maidservants?

27 The leprosy therefore of Naaman ªshall cleave unto thee, and unto thy seed for ever. And he went out from his presence ᵇa leper *as white* as snow.

## CHAPTER 6

AND ªthe sons of the prophets said unto Elisha, Behold now, the place where we dwell with thee is too ¹strait for us.

2 Let us go, we pray thee, unto Jordan, and take thence every man a beam, and let us make us a place there, where we may dwell. And he answered, Go ye.

3 And one said, Be ªcontent, I pray thee, and go with thy servants. And he answered, I will go.

4 So he went with them. And when they came to Jordan, they cut down wood.

5 But as one was felling a beam, the ¹axe head fell into the water: and he cried, and said, Alas, master! for it was ªborrowed.

6 And the man of God said, Where fell it? And he shewed him the place. And ªhe cut down a stick, and cast *it* in thither; and the iron did swim.

7 Therefore said he, Take *it* up to thee. And he put out his hand, and took it.

8 Then the ªking of Syria warred against Israel, and took counsel with his servants, saying, In such and such a place *shall be* my camp.

9 And the man of God sent unto the king of Israel, saying, Beware that thou pass not such a place; for thither the Syrians are come down.

10 And the king of Israel sent to the place which the man of God told him and warned him of, and ¹saved himself there, ²not once nor twice.

11 Therefore the heart of the king of Syria was sore troubled for this thing; and he called his servants, and said unto them, Will ye not shew me which of us *is* for the king of Israel?

12 And one of his servants said, None, my lord, O king: but Elisha, the prophet that *is* in Israel, telleth the king of Israel the words that thou speakest in thy bedchamber.

13 And he said, Go and spy where he *is,* that I may send and fetch him.

And it was told him, saying, Behold, he is in ªDothan.

14 Therefore sent he thither horses, and chariots, and a ¹great host: and they came by night, and compassed the city about.

15 And when the servant of the man of God was risen early, and gone forth, behold, an host compassed the city both with horses and chariots. And his servant said unto him, Alas, my master! how shall we do?

16 And he answered, ªFear not: for ᵇthey that *be* with us *are* more than they that *be* with them.

17 And Elisha prayed, and said, LORD, I pray thee, open his eyes, that he may see. And the LORD ªopened the eyes of the young man; and he saw: and, behold, the mountain *was* full of ᵇhorses and chariots of fire round about Elisha.

18 And when ¹they came down to him, Elisha prayed unto the LORD, and said, ²Smite this people, I pray thee, with blindness. And ªhe smote them with blindness according to the word of Elisha.

19 And Elisha said unto them, This *is* not the way, neither *is* this the city: follow me, and I will bring you to the man whom ye seek. But he led them to Samaria.

20 And it came to pass, when they were come into Samaria, that Elisha said, LORD, open the eyes of these *men,* that they may see. And the LORD opened their eyes, and they saw; and, behold, *they were* in the midst of Samaria.

21 And the king of Israel said unto Elisha, when he saw them, My ªfather, shall I ¹smite *them?* shall I smite *them?*

22 And he answered, Thou shalt not smite *them:* wouldest thou smite those whom thou hast taken captive with thy sword and with thy bow? ªset bread and water before them, that they may eat and drink, and go to their master.

23 And he prepared great provision for them: and when they had eaten and drunk, he sent them away, and they went to their master. So ªthe bands of Syria came no more into the land of Israel.

24 And it came to pass after this, that ªBen-hadad king of Syria gathered all his host, and went up, and besieged Samaria.

25 And there was a great ªfamine in Samaria: and, behold, they besieged it, until an ass's head was *sold* for ¹fourscore *pieces* of silver, and ²the fourth part of a cab of dove's dung for five *pieces* of silver.

26 And as the king of Israel was passing by upon the wall, there cried

6:13 ª Gen. 37:17
6:14 ¹ *great army*
6:16 ª Ex. 14:13; 1 Kin. 17:13 ᵇ 2 Chr. 32:7; Ps. 55:18; [Rom. 8:31]
6:17 ª Num. 22:31; Luke 24:31 ᵇ 2 Kin. 2:11; Ps. 34:7; 68:17; Zech. 1:8; 6:1-7
6:18 ª Gen. 19:11; Acts 13:11 ¹ The Syrians ² *Strike*
6:21 ª 2 Kin. 2:12; 5:13; 8:9 ¹ *kill*
6:22 ª [Rom. 12:20]
6:23 ª 2 Kin. 5:2; 6:8, 9
6:24 ª 1 Kin. 20:1
6:25 ª 2 Kin. 4:38; 8:1 ¹ *eighty* ² *a fourth of a kab of dove droppings*

6:27 ¹ *from the threshingfloor*
6:28 ¹ *What is troubling you?*
6:29 ª Lev. 26:27-29; Deut. 28:52-57; Lam. 4:10
6:30 ª 1 Kin. 21:27 ¹ *tore* ² *underneath*
6:31 ª Ruth 1:17; 1 Kin. 19:2
6:32 ª Ezek. 8:1; 14:1; 20:1 ᵇ Luke 13:32 ᶜ 1 Kin. 18:4, 13, 14; 21:10, 13 ¹ *Lit. he*
6:33 ª Job 2:9 ¹ Jehoram ² *calamity is from*
7:1 ª 2 Kin. 7:18, 19 ¹ Heb. *seah,* a third of an ephah
7:2 ª 2 Kin. 5:18; 7:17, 19, 20 ᵇ Gen. 7:11; Mal. 3:10
7:3 ª [Lev. 13:45, 46; Num. 5:2-4; 12:10-14] ¹ *entrance of*
7:4 ª 2 Kin. 6:24 ¹ *surrender*

a woman unto him, saying, Help, my lord, O king.

27 And he said, If the LORD do not help thee, whence shall I help thee? ¹out of the barnfloor, or out of the winepress?

28 And the king said unto her, ¹What aileth thee? And she answered, This woman said unto me, Give thy son, that we may eat him to day, and we will eat my son to morrow.

29 So ªwe boiled my son, and did eat him: and I said unto her on the next day, Give thy son, that we may eat him: and she hath hid her son.

30 And it came to pass, when the king heard the words of the woman, that he ªrent¹ his clothes; and he passed by upon the wall, and the people looked, and, behold, *he had* sackcloth ²within upon his flesh.

31 Then he said, ªGod do so and more also to me, if the head of Elisha the son of Shaphat shall stand on him this day.

32 But Elisha sat in his house, and ªthe elders sat with him; and ¹*the king* sent a man from before him: but ere the messenger came to him, he said to the elders, ᵇSee ye how this son of ᶜa murderer hath sent to take away mine head? look, when the messenger cometh, shut the door, and hold him fast at the door: *is* not the sound of his master's feet behind him?

33 And while ¹he yet talked with them, behold, the messenger came down unto him: and he said, Behold, this ²evil *is* of the LORD; ªwhat should I wait for the LORD any longer?

## CHAPTER 7

THEN Elisha said, Hear ye the word of the LORD; Thus saith the LORD, ªTo morrow about this time *shall* a ¹measure of fine flour *be sold* for a shekel, and two ¹measures of barley for a shekel, in the gate of Samaria.

2 ªThen a lord on whose hand the king leaned answered the man of God, and said, Behold, ᵇ*if* the LORD would make windows in heaven, might this thing be? And he said, Behold, thou shalt see *it* with thine eyes, but shalt not eat thereof.

3 And there were four leprous men ªat the ¹entering in of the gate: and they said one to another, Why sit we here until we die?

4 If we say, We will enter into the city, then the famine *is* in the city, and we shall die there: and if we sit still here, we die also. Now therefore come, and let us ¹fall unto the ªhost of the Syrians: if they save us alive, we shall live; and if they kill us, we shall but die.

5 And they rose up in the twilight, to go unto the camp of the Syrians:

and when they were come to the uttermost part of the camp of Syria, behold, *there was* no man there.

6 For the Lord had made the host of the Syrians [a]to hear a noise of chariots, and a noise of horses, *even* the noise of a great host: and they said one to another, Lo, the king of Israel hath hired against us [b]the kings of the Hittites, and the kings of the Egyptians, to come upon us.

7 Wherefore they [a]arose and fled in the twilight, and left their tents, and their horses, and their asses, even the camp as it *was,* and fled for their life.

8 And when these lepers came to the uttermost part of the camp, they went into one tent, and did eat and drink, and carried thence silver, and gold, and raiment, and went and hid *it;* and came again, and entered into another tent, and carried thence *also,* and went and hid *it.*

9 Then they said one to another, [1]We do not well: this day *is* a day of good tidings, and we hold our peace: if we [2]tarry till the morning light, some [3]mischief will come upon us: now therefore come, that we may go and tell the king's household.

10 So they came and called unto the [1]porter of the city: and they told them, saying, We came to the camp of the Syrians, and, behold, *there was* no man there, neither voice of man, but horses tied, and asses tied, and the tents as they *were.*

11 And he called the porters; and they told *it* to the king's house within.

12 And the king arose in the night, and said unto his servants, I will now shew you what the Syrians have done to us. They know that we *be* [a]hungry; therefore are they gone out of the camp to [1]hide themselves in the field, saying, When they come out of the city, we shall catch them alive, and get into the city.

13 And one of his servants answered and said, Let *some* take, I pray thee, five of the horses that remain, which are left in the city, (behold, they *are* as all the multitude of Israel that are left in it: behold, *I say,* they *are* even as all the multitude of the Israelites that are consumed:) and let us send and see.

14 They took therefore two chariot horses; and the king sent after the host of the Syrians, saying, Go and see.

15 And they went after them unto Jordan: and, lo, all the way *was* full of garments and vessels, which the Syrians had cast away in their haste. And the messengers returned, and told the king.

16 And the people went out, and [1]spoiled the tents of the Syrians. So

a measure of fine flour was *sold* for a shekel, and two measures of barley for a shekel, [a]according to the word of the LORD.

17 And the king appointed the lord on whose hand he leaned to have the charge of the gate: and the people [1]trode upon him in the gate, and he died, [a]as the man of God had said, who spake when the king came down to him.

18 And it came to pass as the man of God had spoken to the king, saying, [a]Two measures of barley for a shekel, and a measure of fine flour for a shekel, shall be to morrow about this time in the gate of Samaria:

19 And that lord answered the man of God, and said, Now, behold, *if* the LORD should make windows in heaven, might such a thing be? And he said, Behold, thou shalt see it with thine eyes, but shalt not eat thereof.

20 And so it fell out unto him: for the people trode upon him in the gate, and he died.

## CHAPTER 8

THEN spake Elisha unto the woman, [a]whose son he had restored to life, saying, Arise, and go thou and thine household, and [1]sojourn wheresoever thou canst sojourn: for the LORD [b]hath called for a [c]famine; and it shall also come upon the land seven years.

2 And the woman arose, and did after the saying of the man of God: and she went with her household, and sojourned in the land of the Philistines seven years.

3 And it came to pass at the seven years' end, that the woman returned out of the land of the Philistines: and she went forth to [1]cry unto the king for her house and for her land.

4 And the king talked with [a]Gehazi the servant of the man of God, saying, Tell me, I pray thee, all the great things that Elisha hath done.

5 And it came to pass, as he was telling the king how he had [a]restored a dead body to life, that, behold, the woman, whose son he had restored to life, cried to the king for her house and for her land. And Gehazi said, My lord, O king, this *is* the woman, and this *is* her son, whom Elisha restored to life.

6 And when the king asked the woman, she told him. So the king appointed unto her a certain officer, saying, Restore all that *was* hers, and all the fruits of the field since the day that she left the land, even until now.

7 And Elisha came to Damascus; and [a]Ben-hadad the king of Syria was sick; and it was told him, saying, The man of God is come hither.

8 And the king said unto [a]Hazael, [b]Take a present in thine hand, and

### Cross-references (center column)

7:6 [a] 2 Sam. 5:24; 2 Kin. 19:7; Job 15:21 [b] 1 Kin. 10:29
7:7 [a] Ps. 48:4–6; [Prov. 28:1]
7:9 [1] We are not doing right [2] wait [3] punishment or calamity
7:10 [1] gatekeeper
7:12 [a] 2 Kin. 6:24–29 [1] hide themselves in ambush
7:16 [1] plundered

a 2 Kin. 7:1
7:17 [a] 2 Kin. 6:32; 7:2 [1] trampled him
7:18 [a] 2 Kin. 7:1
8:1 [a] 2 Kin. 4:18, 31–35 [b] Ps. 105:16; Hag. 1:11 [c] 2 Sam. 21:1; 1 Kin. 18:2; 2 Kin. 4:38; 6:25 [1] dwell temporarily
8:3 [1] make an appeal
8:4 [a] 2 Kin. 4:12; 5:20–27
8:5 [a] 2 Kin. 4:35
8:7 [a] 2 Kin. 6:24
8:8 [a] 1 Kin. 19:15 [b] 1 Sam. 9:7; 1 Kin. 14:3; 2 Kin. 5:5

go, meet the man of God, and ᶜenquire of the LORD by him, saying, Shall I recover of this disease?

9 So ᵃHazael went to meet him, and took a present with him, even of every good thing of Damascus, forty camels' burden, and came and stood before him, and said, Thy son Benhadad king of Syria hath sent me to thee, saying, Shall I recover of this disease?

10 And Elisha said unto him, Go, say unto him, Thou mayest certainly recover: howbeit the LORD hath shewed me that ᵃhe shall surely die.

11 And he ¹settled his countenance stedfastly, until he was ashamed: and the man of God ᵃwept.

12 And Hazael said, Why weepeth my lord? And he answered, Because I know ᵃthe evil that thou wilt do unto the children of Israel: their strong holds wilt thou set on fire, and their young men wilt thou slay with the sword, and ᵇwilt dash their children, and rip up their women with child.

13 And Hazael said, But what, ᵃis thy servant a dog, that he should do this great thing? And Elisha answered, ᵇThe LORD hath shewed me that thou ʃhalt be king over Syria.

14 So he departed from Elisha, and came to his master; who said to him, What said Elisha to thee? And he answered, He told me that thou shouldest surely recover.

15 And it came to pass on the morrow, that he took a thick cloth, and dipped it in water, and spread it on his face, so that he died: and Hazael reigned in his stead.

16 And ᵃin the fifth year of Joram the son of Ahab king of Israel, Jehoshaphat being then king of Judah, ᵇJehoram the son of Jehoshaphat king of Judah ¹began to reign.

17 ᵃThirty and two years old was he when he began to reign; and he reigned eight years in Jerusalem.

18 And he walked in the way of the kings of Israel, as did the house of Ahab: for ᵃthe daughter of Ahab was his wife: and he did evil in the sight of the LORD.

19 Yet the LORD would not destroy Judah for David his servant's sake, ᵃas he promised him to give him alway a ¹light, and to his children.

20 In his days ᵃEdom revolted from under the hand of Judah, ᵇand made a king over themselves.

21 So Joram went over to Zair, and all the chariots with him: and he rose by night, and smote the Edomites which compassed him about, and the captains of the chariots: and the people fled into their tents.

22 Yet Edom ¹revolted from under the hand of Judah unto this day.

ᵃThen Libnah revolted at the same time.

23 And the rest of the acts of ¹Joram, and all that he did, are they not written in the book of the chronicles of the kings of Judah?

24 And Joram ¹slept with his fathers, and was buried with his fathers in the city of David: and ᵃAhaziah² his son reigned in his stead.

25 In the twelfth year of Joram the son of Ahab king of Israel did Ahaziah the son of Jehoram king of Judah begin to reign.

26 ᵃTwo and twenty years old was Ahaziah when he began to reign; and he reigned one year in Jerusalem. And his mother's name was Athaliah, the ¹daughter of Omri king of Israel.

27 ᵃAnd he walked in the way of the house of Ahab, and did evil in the sight of the LORD, as did the house of Ahab: for he was the son in law of the house of Ahab.

28 And he went ᵃwith Joram the son of Ahab to the war against Hazael king of Syria in ᵇRamoth-gilead; and the Syrians wounded Joram.

29 And ᵃking Joram went back to be healed in Jezreel of the wounds which the Syrians had ¹given him at ²Ramah, when he fought against Hazael king of Syria. ᵇAnd Ahaziah the son of Jehoram king of Judah went down to see Joram the son of Ahab in Jezreel, because he was sick.

## CHAPTER 9

AND Elisha the prophet called one of ᵃthe children of the prophets, and said unto him, ᵇGird¹ up thy loins, and take this box of oil in thine hand, ᶜand go to Ramoth-gilead:

2 And when thou comest thither, ¹look out there Jehu the son of Jehoshaphat the son of Nimshi, and go in, and make him arise up from among ᵃhis brethren, and carry him to an ²inner chamber;

3 Then ᵃtake the box of oil, and pour it on his head, and say, Thus saith the LORD, I have anointed thee king over Israel. Then open the door, and flee, and ¹tarry not.

4 So the young man, even the young man the prophet, went to Ramoth-gilead.

5 And when he came, behold, the captains of the host were sitting; and he said, I have an errand to thee, O captain. And Jehu said, Unto which of all us? And he said, To thee, O captain.

6 And he arose, and went into the house; and he poured the oil on his head, and said unto him, ᵃThus saith the LORD God of Israel, I have anointed thee king over the people of the LORD, even over Israel.

### Cross references (center column)

8:8 ᶜ 2 Kin. 1:2
8:9 ᵃ 1 Kin. 19:15
8:10 ᵃ 2 Kin. 8:15
8:11 ᵃ Luke 19:41
¹ fixed his gaze
8:12 ᵃ 2 Kin. 10:32; 12:17; 13:3, 7; Amos 1:3, 4
ᵇ 2 Kin. 15:16; Hos. 13:16; Amos 1:13; Nah. 3:10
8:13 ᵃ 1 Sam. 17:43; 2 Sam. 9:8
ᵇ 1 Kin. 19:15
8:16 ᵃ 2 Kin. 1:17; 3:1 ᵇ 2 Chr. 21:3
¹ As coregent with his father
8:17 ᵃ 2 Chr. 21:5–10
8:18 ᵃ 2 Kin. 8:26, 27
8:19 ᵃ 2 Sam. 7:13; 1 Kin. 11:36; 15:4; 2 Chr. 21:7 ¹ lamp
8:20 ᵃ Gen. 27:40; 2 Chr. 21:8–10
ᵇ 1 Kin. 22:47
8:22 ¹ has been in revolt

a Josh. 21:13; 2 Kin. 19:8; 2 Chr. 21:10
8:23 ¹ Jehoram, 2 Kin. 8:16
8:24 ᵃ 2 Chr. 22:1, 7 ¹ rested in death ² Azariah, 2 Chr. 22:6; Jehoahaz, 2 Chr. 21:17
8:26 ᵃ 2 Chr. 22:2 ¹ granddaughter
8:27 ᵃ 2 Chr. 22:3, 4
8:28 ᵃ 2 Chr. 22:5 ᵇ 1 Kin. 22:3, 29
8:29 ᵃ 2 Kin. 9:15 ᵇ 2 Kin. 9:16; 2 Chr. 22:6, 7 ¹ inflicted ² Ramoth, 2 Kin. 8:28
9:1 ᵃ 1 Kin. 20:35 ᵇ 2 Kin. 4:29; Jer. 1:17 ᶜ 2 Kin. 8:28, 29 ¹ Get yourself ready
9:2 ᵃ 2 Kin. 9:5, 11 ¹ look there for ² inner room
9:3 ᵃ 1 Kin. 19:16 ¹ do not delay
9:6 ᵃ 1 Sam. 2:7, 8; 1 Kin. 19:16; 2 Kin. 9:3; 2 Chr. 22:7

7 And thou shalt ¹smite the house of Ahab thy master, that I may ªavenge the blood of my servants the prophets, and the blood of all the servants of the LORD, ᵇat the hand of Jezebel.

8 For the whole house of Ahab shall perish: and ªI will cut off from Ahab ᵇhim¹ that pisseth against the wall, and ᶜhim that is shut up and left in Israel:

9 And I will make the house of Ahab like the house of ªJeroboam the son of Nebat, and like the house of ᵇBaasha the son of Ahijah:

10 ªAnd the dogs shall eat Jezebel in the ¹portion of Jezreel, and *there shall be* none to bury *her.* And he opened the door, and fled.

11 Then Jehu came forth to the servants of his lord: and *one* said unto him, *Is* all well? ¹wherefore came ªthis mad *fellow* to thee? And he said unto them, Ye know the man, and his ²communication.

12 And they said, *It is* ¹false; tell us now. And he said, Thus and thus spake he to me, saying, Thus saith the LORD, I have anointed thee king over Israel.

13 Then they ¹hasted, and ªtook every man his garment, and put *it* ²under him on the top of the stairs, and blew with trumpets, saying, Jehu is king.

14 So Jehu the son of Jehoshaphat the son of Nimshi conspired against ªJoram. (Now ¹Joram had kept Ramoth-gilead, he and all Israel, because of Hazael king of Syria.

15 But ªking ¹Joram was returned to be healed in Jezreel of the wounds which the Syrians had given him, when he fought with Hazael king of Syria.) And Jehu said, If ²it be your minds, *then* let none go forth *nor* escape out of the city to go to tell *it* in Jezreel.

16 So Jehu rode in a chariot, and went to Jezreel; for Joram lay there. ªAnd Ahaziah king of Judah was come down to see Joram.

17 And there stood a watchman on the tower in Jezreel, and he spied the company of Jehu as he came, and said, I see a company. And Joram said, Take an horseman, and send to meet them, and let him say, ¹*Is it* peace?

18 So there went one on horseback to meet him, and said, Thus saith the king, *Is it* peace? And Jehu said, What hast thou to do with peace? ¹turn thee behind me. And the watchman told, saying, The messenger came to them, but he ²cometh not again.

19 Then he sent out a second on horseback, which came to them, and said, Thus saith the king, *Is it* peace?

And Jehu answered, What hast thou to do with peace? turn thee behind me.

20 And the watchman told, saying, He came even unto them, and cometh not again: and the driving *is* like the driving of Jehu the son of Nimshi; for he driveth furiously.

21 And Joram said, ¹Make ready. And his chariot was made ready. And ªJoram king of Israel and Ahaziah king of Judah went out, each in his chariot, and they went out against Jehu, and ²met him ᵇin the portion of Naboth the Jezreelite.

22 And it came to pass, when Joram saw Jehu, that he said, *Is it* peace, Jehu? And he answered, What peace, so long as the ¹whoredoms of thy mother Jezebel and her witchcrafts *are so* many?

23 And Joram turned his hands, and fled, and said to Ahaziah, *There is* treachery, O Ahaziah.

24 And Jehu ¹drew a bow with his full strength, and smote Jehoram between his arms, and the arrow went out at his heart, and he ²sunk down in his chariot.

25 Then said *Jehu* to Bidkar his captain, Take up, *and* cast him in the portion of the field of Naboth the Jezreelite: for remember how that, when I and thou rode together after Ahab his father, ªthe LORD laid this ᵇburden upon him;

26 Surely I have seen yesterday the blood of Naboth, and the blood of his sons, saith the LORD; ªand I will ¹requite thee in this ²plat, saith the LORD. Now therefore take *and* cast him into the plat *of ground,* according to the word of the LORD.

27 But when Ahaziah the king of Judah saw *this,* he fled by the way of ¹the garden house. And Jehu followed after him, and said, ²Smite him also in the chariot. *And they did so* at the going up to Gur, which *is* by Ibleam. And he fled to ªMegiddo, and died there.

28 And his servants carried him in a chariot to Jerusalem, and buried him in his sepulchre with his fathers in the city of David.

29 And in the eleventh year of Joram the son of Ahab began Ahaziah to reign over Judah.

30 And when Jehu was come to Jezreel, Jezebel heard *of it;* ªand she ¹painted her face, and ²tired her head, and looked out at a window.

31 And as Jehu entered in at the gate, she said, ªHad¹ Zimri peace, ²who slew his master?

32 And he lifted up his face to the window, and said, Who *is* on my side? who? And there looked out to him two *or* three eunuchs.

9:7 ª [Deut. 32:35, 41] ᵇ 1 Kin. 18:4; 21:15 ¹ *strike down*

9:8 ª 1 Kin. 14:10; 21:21; 2 Kin. 10:17 ᵇ 1 Sam. 25:22 ᶜ Deut. 32:36; 2 Kin. 14:26 ¹ *all the males*

9:9 ª 1 Kin. 14:10; 15:29; 21:22 ᵇ 1 Kin. 16:3, 11

9:10 ª 1 Kin. 21:23; 2 Kin. 9:35, 36 ¹ *vicinity*

9:11 ª Jer. 29:26; Hos. 9:7; Mark 3:21; John 10:20; Acts 26:24; [1 Cor. 4:10] ¹ *why did this madman come* ² *babble*

9:12 ¹ *a lie*

9:13 ª Matt. 21:7, 8; Mark 11:7, 8 ¹ *hastened* ² *under his feet*

9:14 ª 2 Kin. 8:28

9:15 ª 2 Kin. 8:29 ¹ *Jehoram,* 2 Kin. 9:24 ² *you be so minded*

9:16 ª 2 Kin. 8:29

9:17 ¹ *Are you peaceful?*

9:18 ¹ *turn around and follow me* ² *is not coming back*

9:21 ª 1 Kin. 19:17; 2 Chr. 22:7 ᵇ 1 Kin. 21:1–14 ¹ *Harness up* ² Lit. *found*

9:22 ¹ *harlotries*

9:24 ¹ Lit. *filled his hand with* ² *sank*

9:25 ª 1 Kin. 21:19, 24–29 ᵇ Is. 13:1

9:26 ª 1 Kin. 21:13, 19 ¹ *repay* ² *property*

9:27 ª 2 Chr. 22:7, 9 ¹ Or *Beth-haggan* ² *Shoot*

9:30 ª [Jer. 4:30]; Ezek. 23:40 ¹ Lit. *made up her eyes with paint* ² *adorned*

9:31 ª 1 Kin. 16:9–20; 2 Kin. 9:18–22 ¹ *Is it peace, Zimri* ² *murderer of*

33 And he said, Throw her down. So they threw her down: and *some* of her blood was sprinkled on the wall, and on the horses: and he trode her under foot.

34 And when he was come in, he did eat and drink, and said, Go, see now this cursed *woman,* and bury her: for [a]she *is* a king's daughter.

35 And they went to bury her: but they found no more of her than the skull, and the feet, and the palms of *her* hands.

36 Wherefore they came again, and told him. And he said, This *is* the word of the LORD, which he spake by his servant Elijah the Tishbite, saying, [a]In the portion of Jezreel shall dogs eat the flesh of Jezebel:

37 And the carcase of Jezebel shall be [a]as dung upon the face of the field in the portion of Jezreel; *so* that they shall not say, This *is* Jezebel.

### CHAPTER 10

A ND Ahab had seventy sons in Samaria. And Jehu wrote letters, and sent to Samaria, unto the rulers of Jezreel, to the elders, and to [1]them that brought up Ahab's *children,* saying,

2 Now as soon as this letter cometh to you, seeing your master's sons *are* with you, and *there are* with you chariots and horses, a [1]fenced city also, and armour;

3 [1]Look even out the best and [2]meetest of your master's sons, and set *him* on his father's throne, and fight for your master's house.

4 But they were exceedingly afraid, and said, Behold, [a]two kings [1]stood not before him: how then shall we stand?

5 And he that *was* over the house, and he that *was* over the city, the elders also, and the bringers up *of the children,* sent to Jehu, saying, We *are* thy servants, and will do all that thou shalt bid us; we will not make any king: do thou *that which is* good in thine eyes.

6 Then he wrote a letter the second time to them, saying, If ye [1]be mine, and *if* ye will hearken unto my voice, take ye the heads of the men your master's sons, and come to me to Jezreel by to morrow this time. Now the king's sons, *being* seventy persons, *were* with the great men of the city, which brought them up.

7 And it came to pass, when the letter came to them, that they took the king's sons, and [a]slew[1] seventy persons, and put their heads in baskets, and sent him *them* to Jezreel.

8 And there came a messenger, and told him, saying, They have brought the heads of the king's sons. And he

said, Lay ye them in two heaps at the entering in of the gate until the morning.

9 And it came to pass in the morning, that he went out, and stood, and said to all the people, Ye *be* righteous: behold, [a]I conspired against my master, and slew him: but who slew all these?

10 Know now that there shall [a]fall unto the earth nothing of the word of the LORD, which the LORD spake concerning the house of Ahab: for the LORD hath done *that* which he spake [b]by his servant Elijah.

11 So Jehu slew all that remained of the house of Ahab in Jezreel, and all his great men, and his [1]kinsfolks, and his priests, until he left him none remaining.

12 And he arose and departed, and [1]came to Samaria. *And* as he *was* at [2]the shearing house [3]in the way,

13 [a]Jehu met with the brethren of Ahaziah king of Judah, and said, Who *are* ye? And they answered, We *are* the brethren of Ahaziah; and we go down [1]to salute the children of the king and the children of the queen.

14 And he said, Take them alive. And they took them alive, and [a]slew them at the pit of the shearing house, *even* two and forty men; neither left he any of them.

15 And when he was departed thence, he [1]lighted on [a]Jehonadab the son of [b]Rechab *coming* to meet him: and he saluted him, and said to him, Is thine heart right, as my heart *is* with thy heart? And Jehonadab answered, It is. If it be, [c]give *me* thine hand. And he gave *him* his hand; and he took him up to him into the chariot.

16 And he said, Come with me, and see my [a]zeal for the LORD. So they made him ride in his chariot.

17 And when he came to Samaria, [a]he slew all that remained unto Ahab in Samaria, till he had destroyed him, according to the saying of the LORD, [b]which he spake to Elijah.

18 And Jehu gathered all the people together, and said unto them, [a]Ahab served Baal a little; *but* Jehu shall serve him much.

19 Now therefore call unto me all the [a]prophets of Baal, all his servants, and all his priests; let none be [1]wanting: for I have a great sacrifice *to do* to Baal; whosoever shall be [1]wanting, he shall not live. But Jehu did *it* [2]in subtilty, to the intent that he might destroy the worshippers of Baal.

20 And Jehu said, [1]Proclaim a solemn assembly for Baal. And they proclaimed *it.*

21 And Jehu sent through all Israel: and all the worshippers of Baal came, so that there was not a man left that

### Cross references (center column)

9:34 [a] [Ex. 22:28]; 1 Kin. 16:31
9:36 [a] 1 Kin. 21:23
9:37 [a] Ps. 83:10
10:1 [1] *the guardians of*
10:2 [1] *fortified*
10:3 [1] *Choose* [2] *most upright*
10:4 [a] 2 Kin. 9:24, 27 [1] *could not stand up to*
10:6 [1] *are for me*
10:7 [a] Judg. 9:5; 1 Kin. 21:21; 2 Kin. 11:1 [1] *slaughtered*

10:9 [a] 2 Kin. 9:14–24
10:10 [a] 1 Sam. 3:19; 1 Kin. 8:56; Jer. 44:28 [b] 1 Kin. 21:17–24, 29
10:11 [1] *close acquaintances*
10:12 [1] *went* [2] *Or Beth-eked of the Shepherds* [3] *on*
10:13 [a] 2 Chr. 22:8 [1] *to greet*
10:14 [a] 2 Chr. 22:8
10:15 [a] Jer. 35:6 [b] 1 Chr. 2:55 [c] Ezra 10:19; Ezek. 17:18 [1] *met or found*
10:16 [a] 1 Kin. 19:10
10:17 [a] 2 Kin. 9:8; 2 Chr. 22:8 [b] 1 Kin. 21:21, 29
10:18 [a] 1 Kin. 16:31, 32
10:19 [a] 1 Kin. 18:19; 22:6 [1] *missing* [2] *acted deceptively*
10:20 [1] *Lit. Consecrate an assembly of restraint*

came not. And they came into the house of Baal; and the [a]house of Baal was full from one end to another.

22 And he said unto him that *was* [1]over the vestry, Bring forth vestments for all the worshippers of Baal. And he brought them forth vestments.

23 And Jehu went, and Jehonadab the son of Rechab, into the house of Baal, and said unto the worshippers of Baal, Search, and look that there be here with you none of the servants of the LORD, but the worshippers of Baal only.

24 And when they went in to offer sacrifices and burnt offerings, Jehu appointed fourscore men without, and said, *If* any of the men whom I have brought into your hands escape, *he that letteth him go,* [a]his life *shall be* for the life of him.

25 And it came to pass, as soon as he had made an end of offering the burnt offering, that Jehu said to the guard and to the captains, Go in, *and* slay them; let none come forth. And they [1]smote them with the edge of the sword; and the guard and the captains cast *them* out, and went to the [2]city of the house of Baal.

26 And they brought forth the [a]images[1] out of the house of Baal, and burned them.

27 And they brake down the image of Baal, and brake down the house of Baal, and [a]made it a [1]draught house unto this day.

28 Thus Jehu destroyed Baal out of Israel.

29 Howbeit *from* the sins of Jeroboam the son of Nebat, who made Israel to sin, Jehu departed not from after them, *to wit,* [a]the golden calves that *were* in Beth-el, and that *were* in Dan.

30 And the LORD [a]said unto Jehu, Because thou hast done well in executing *that which is* right in mine eyes, *and* hast done unto the house of Ahab according to all that *was* in mine heart, [b]thy children of the fourth *generation* shall sit on the throne of Israel.

31 But Jehu [1]took no heed to walk in the law of the LORD God of Israel with all his heart: for he departed not from [a]the sins of Jeroboam, which made Israel to sin.

32 In those days the LORD began to [1]cut Israel short: and [a]Hazael smote them in all the coasts of Israel;

33 From Jordan eastward, all the land of Gilead, the Gadites, and the Reubenites, and the Manassites, from [a]Aroer, which *is* by the river Arnon, even [b]Gilead and Bashan.

34 Now the rest of the acts of Jehu, and all that he did, and all his might,

*are* they not written in the book of the chronicles of the kings of Israel?

35 And Jehu [1]slept with his fathers: and they buried him in Samaria. And [a]Jehoahaz his son reigned in his stead.

36 And the time that Jehu reigned over Israel in Samaria *was* twenty and eight years.

## CHAPTER 11

AND when [a]Athaliah [b]the mother of Ahaziah saw that her son was [c]dead, she arose and destroyed all the [1]seed royal.

2 But [1]Jehosheba, the daughter of king Joram, sister of [a]Ahaziah, took [2]Joash the son of Ahaziah, and stole him from among the king's sons *which were* slain; and they hid him, *even* him and his nurse, in the [3]bedchamber from Athaliah, so that he was not slain.

3 And he was with her hid in the house of the LORD six years. And Athaliah did reign over the land.

4 And [a]the seventh year Jehoiada sent and [1]fetched the [2]rulers over hundreds, with the captains and the [3]guard, and brought them to him into the house of the LORD, and made a covenant with them, and took an oath of them in the house of the LORD, and shewed them the king's son.

5 And he commanded them, saying, This *is* the thing that ye shall do; A third part of you that [1]enter in [a]on the sabbath shall even be [2]keepers of the watch of the king's house;

6 And a third part *shall be* at the gate of Sur; and a third part at the gate behind the guard: so shall ye keep the watch of the house, that it be not broken down.

7 And two [1]parts of all you that go forth on the sabbath, even they shall keep the watch of the house of the LORD [2]about the king.

8 And ye shall [1]compass the king round about, every man with his weapons in his hand: and he that cometh within the [2]ranges, let him be [3]slain: and be ye with the king as he goeth out and as he cometh in.

9 [a]And the captains over the hundreds did according to all *things* that Jehoiada the priest commanded: and they took every man his men that were to come in on the sabbath, with them that should go out on the sabbath, and came to Jehoiada the priest.

10 And to the captains over hundreds did the priest give king David's spears and shields, [a]that *were* in the temple of the LORD.

11 And the guard stood, every man with his weapons in his hand, round

### Center column references

10:21 [a]1 Kin. 16:32; 2 Kin. 11:18
10:22 [1]*in charge of the wardrobe*
10:24 [a]1 Kin. 20:39
10:25 [1]*killed* [2]*inner room of the temple*
10:26 [a][Deut. 7:5, 25]; 1 Kin. 14:23; 2 Kin. 3:2 [1]*sacred pillars*
10:27 [a]Ezra 6:11; Dan. 2:5; 3:29 [1]*refuse house or dump*
10:29 [a]1 Kin. 12:28–30; 13:33, 34
10:30 [a]2 Kin. 9:6, 7 [b]2 Kin. 13:1, 10; 14:23; 15:8, 12
10:31 [a]1 Kin. 14:16 [1]*was not careful*
10:32 [a]1 Kin. 19:17; 2 Kin. 8:12; 13:22 [1]*cut off portions of Israel*
10:33 [a]Deut. 2:36 [b]Amos 1:3–5
10:35 [a]2 Kin. 13:1 [1]*rested in death with*
11:1 [a]2 Chr. 22:10 [b]2 Kin. 8:26 [c]2 Kin. 9:27 [1]*royal heirs*
11:2 [a]2 Kin. 8:25 [1]*Or Jehoshabeath,* 2 Chr. 22:11 [2]*Jehoash,* 2 Kin. 11:21 [3]*bedroom*
11:4 [a]2 Kin. 12:2; 2 Chr. 23:1 [1]*brought* [2]*captains of the hundreds of* [3]*escorts*
11:5 [a]1 Chr. 9:25 [1]*come on duty* [2]*keeping watch over*
11:7 [1]*companies* [2]*for the king*
11:8 [1]*surround* [2]*within range* [3]*put to death*
11:9 [a]2 Chr. 23:8
11:10 [a]2 Sam. 8:7; 1 Chr. 18:7

about the king, from the right ¹corner of the temple to the left corner of the temple, *along* by the altar and the temple.

12 And he brought forth the king's son, and put the crown upon him, and *gave him* the ªtestimony; and they made him king, and anointed him; and they clapped their hands, and said, ᵇGod¹ save the king.

13 ªAnd when Athaliah heard the noise of the guard *and* of the people, she came to the people into the temple of the LORD.

14 And when she looked, behold, the king stood by ªa pillar, as the manner *was,* and the princes and the trumpeters by the king, and all the people of the land rejoiced, and blew with trumpets: and Athaliah ¹rent her clothes, and cried, Treason, Treason.

15 But Jehoiada the priest commanded the captains of the hundreds, the officers of the host, and said unto them, ¹Have her forth ²without the ranges: and him that followeth her kill with the sword. For the priest had said, Let her not be slain in the house of the LORD.

16 And they laid hands on her; and she went by the way by the which the horses came into the king's house: and there was she slain.

17 ªAnd Jehoiada ᵇmade a covenant between the LORD and the king and the people, that they should be the LORD's people; ᶜbetween the king also and the people.

18 And all the people of the land went into the ªhouse of Baal, and ¹brake it down; his altars and his images ᵇbrake they in pieces thoroughly, and ᶜslew Mattan the priest of Baal before the altars. And ᵈthe priest appointed ²officers over the house of the LORD.

19 And he took the rulers over hundreds, and the captains, and the guard, and all the people of the land; and they brought down the king from the house of the LORD, and came by the way of the gate of the guard to the king's house. And he sat on the throne of the kings.

20 And all the people of the land rejoiced, and the city was in quiet: and they slew Athaliah with the sword *beside* the king's house.

21 ªSeven years old *was* Jehoash when he began to reign.

## CHAPTER 12

IN the seventh year of Jehu ªJehoash¹ began to reign; and forty years reigned he in Jerusalem. And his mother's name *was* Zibiah of Beer-sheba.

2 And Jehoash did *that which was* right in the sight of the LORD all his

11:11 ¹ *side,* lit. *shoulder*
11:12 ª Ex. 25:16; 31:18 ᵇ 1 Sam. 10:24 ¹ *Long live the king*
11:13 ª 2 Kin. 8:26; 2 Chr. 23:12
11:14 ª 2 Kin. 23:3; 2 Chr. 34:31 ¹ *tore*
11:15 ¹ *Take her outside* ² *under guard,* lit. *between ranks*
11:17 ª 2 Chr. 23:16 ᵇ Josh. 24:24, 25; 2 Chr. 15:12–15 ᶜ 2 Sam. 5:3
11:18 ª 2 Kin. 10:26, 27 ᵇ [Deut. 12:3] ᶜ 1 Kin. 18:40; 2 Kin. 10:11 ᵈ 2 Chr. 23:18 ¹ *tore it* ² Lit. *offices*
11:21 ª 2 Chr. 24:1–14
12:1 ª 2 Chr. 24:1 ¹ *Joash,* 2 Kin. 11:2

12:2 ª 2 Kin. 11:4
12:3 ª 1 Kin. 15:14; 22:43; 2 Kin. 14:4; 15:35 ¹ *Places for pagan worship*
12:4 ª 2 Kin. 22:4 ᵇ Ex. 30:13–16 ᶜ Lev. 27:2–28 ᵈ Ex. 35:5; 1 Chr. 29:3–9 ¹ *dedicated gifts* ² *census money,* lit. *money coming over* ³ *assessed,* Lev. 27:2 ⁴ *any man's heart prompts him to bring*
12:5 ¹ *from his constituency* ² *damages*
12:6 ª 2 Chr. 24:5
12:7 ª 2 Chr. 24:6 ¹ *take no more money from your constituency*
12:9 ª 2 Chr. 23:1; 24:8 ᵇ Mark 12:41; Luke 21:1 ¹ *guarded at the door*
12:10 ª 2 Sam. 8:17; 2 Kin. 19:2; 22:3, 4, 12 ¹ *secretary* ² *tied up in bags* ³ *counted*
12:11 ¹ Lit. *weighed out* ² *paid*
12:12 ª 2 Kin. 22:5, 6 ¹ *was paid out*
12:13 ª 2 Chr. 24:14

days wherein ªJehoiada the priest instructed him.

3 But ªthe ¹high places were not taken away: the people still sacrificed and burnt incense in the high places.

4 And Jehoash said to the priests, ªAll the money of the ¹dedicated things that is brought into the house of the LORD, *even* ᵇthe ²money of every one that passeth *the account,* ᶜthe money that every man is ³set at, *and* all the money that ᵈcometh⁴ into any man's heart to bring into the house of the LORD,

5 Let the priests take *it* to them, every man ¹of his acquaintance: and let them repair the ²breaches of the house, wheresoever any breach shall be found.

6 But it was *so, that* in the three and twentieth year of king Jehoash ªthe priests had not repaired the breaches of the house.

7 ªThen king Jehoash called for Jehoiada the priest, and the *other* priests, and said unto them, Why repair ye not the breaches of the house? now therefore ¹receive no *more* money of your acquaintance, but deliver it for the breaches of the house.

8 And the priests consented to receive no *more* money of the people, neither to repair the breaches of the house.

9 But Jehoiada the priest took ªa chest, and bored a hole in the lid of it, and set it beside the altar, on the right side as one cometh into the house of the LORD: and the priests that ¹kept the door put ᵇtherein all the money *that was* brought into the house of the LORD.

10 And it was *so,* when they saw that *there was* much money in the chest, that the king's ªscribe¹ and the high priest came up, and they ²put up in bags, and ³told the money that was found in the house of the LORD.

11 And they gave the money, being ¹told, into the hands of them that did the work, that had the oversight of the house of the LORD: and they ²laid it out to the carpenters and builders, that wrought upon the house of the LORD,

12 And to masons, and hewers of stone, and to buy timber and hewed stone to ªrepair the breaches of the house of the LORD, and for all that was ¹laid out for the house to repair *it.*

13 Howbeit ªthere were not made for the house of the LORD bowls of silver, snuffers, basons, trumpets, any vessels of gold, or vessels of silver, of the money *that was* brought into the house of the LORD:

14 But they gave that to the workmen, and repaired therewith the house of the LORD.

**15** Moreover [a]they [1]reckoned not with the men, into whose hand they delivered the money to be bestowed on workmen: for they dealt faithfully.

**16** [a]The trespass money and sin money was not brought into the house of the LORD: [b]it was the priests'.

**17** Then [a]Hazael king of Syria went up, and fought against Gath, and took it: and [b]Hazael set his face to [1]go up to Jerusalem.

**18** And Jehoash king of Judah [a]took all the hallowed things that Jehoshaphat, and Jehoram, and Ahaziah, his fathers, kings of Judah, had dedicated, and his own hallowed things, and all the gold *that was* found in the treasures of the house of the LORD, and in the king's house, and sent *it* to Hazael king of Syria: and he went away from Jerusalem.

**19** And the rest of the acts of [1]Joash, and all that he did, *are* they not written in the book of the chronicles of the kings of Judah?

**20** And [a]his servants arose, and made a conspiracy, and slew Joash in the house of Millo, which goeth down to Silla.

**21** For [1]Jozachar the son of Shimeath, and Jehozabad the son of [2]Shomer, his servants, [3]smote him, and he died; and they buried him with his fathers in the city of David: and [a]Amaziah his son reigned in his stead.

## CHAPTER 13

IN the three and twentieth year of [a]Joash[1] the son of Ahaziah king of Judah [b]Jehoahaz the son of Jehu began to reign over Israel in Samaria, *and reigned* seventeen years.

**2** And he did *that which was* evil in the sight of the LORD, and followed the [a]sins of Jeroboam the son of Nebat, which made Israel to sin; he [1]departed not therefrom.

**3** And [a]the anger of the LORD was [1]kindled against Israel, and he [2]delivered them into the hand of [b]Hazael king of Syria, and into the hand of [c]Ben-hadad the son of Hazael, all *their* days.

**4** And Jehoahaz [a]besought the LORD, and the LORD hearkened unto him: for [b]he saw the oppression of Israel, because the king of Syria oppressed them.

**5** ([a]And the LORD gave Israel a saviour, so that they went out from under the hand of the Syrians: and the children of Israel dwelt in their tents, as beforetime.

**6** Nevertheless they departed not from the sins of the house of Jeroboam, who made Israel sin, *but* walked therein: [a]and there remained the grove also in Samaria.)

**7** Neither did he leave of the peo-ple to Jehoahaz but fifty horsemen, and ten chariots, and ten thousand footmen; for the king of Syria had destroyed them, [a]and had made them [b]like the dust by threshing.

**8** Now the rest of the acts of Jehoahaz, and all that he did, and his might, *are* they not written in the book of the chronicles of the kings of Israel?

**9** And Jehoahaz [1]slept with his fathers; and they buried him in Samaria: and [2]Joash his son reigned in his stead.

**10** In the thirty and seventh year of Joash king of Judah began Jehoash the son of Jehoahaz to reign over Israel in Samaria, *and reigned* sixteen years.

**11** And he did *that which was* evil in the sight of the LORD; he departed not from all the sins of Jeroboam the son of Nebat, who made Israel sin: *but* he walked therein.

**12** [a]And the rest of the acts of Joash, and [b]all that he did, and [c]his might wherewith he fought against Amaziah king of Judah, *are* they not written in the book of the chronicles of the kings of Israel?

**13** And Joash [a]slept[1] with his fathers; and Jeroboam sat upon his throne: and Joash was buried in Samaria with the kings of Israel.

**14** Now Elisha was fallen sick of his sickness whereof he died. And Joash the king of Israel came down unto him, and wept over his face, and said, O my father, my father, [a]the chariot of Israel, and the horsemen thereof.

**15** And Elisha said unto him, Take bow and arrows. And he took unto him bow and arrows.

**16** And he said to the king of Israel, Put thine hand upon the bow. And he put his hand *upon it:* and Elisha put his hands upon the king's hands.

**17** And he said, Open the window eastward. And he opened *it.* Then Elisha said, Shoot. And he shot. And he said, The arrow of the LORD's deliverance, and the arrow of deliverance from Syria: for thou shalt [1]smite the Syrians in [a]Aphek, till thou have [2]consumed *them.*

**18** And he said, Take the arrows. And he took *them.* And he said unto the king of Israel, [1]Smite upon the ground. And he smote thrice, and [2]stayed.

**19** And the man of God was wroth with him, and said, Thou shouldest have smitten five or six times; then hadst thou [1]smitten Syria till thou hadst [2]consumed *it:* [a]whereas now thou shalt smite Syria *but* thrice.

**20** And Elisha [1]died, and they buried him. And the [a]bands of the Moabites invaded the land at the coming in of the year.

---

*Center column references:*

12:15 [a] 2 Kin. 22:7; [1 Cor. 4:2]; 2 Cor. 8:20 [1] *did not require an accounting from*
12:16 [a] [Lev. 5:15, 18] [b] [Lev. 7:7; Num. 18:9]
12:17 [a] 2 Kin. 8:12 [b] 2 Chr. 24:23 [1] *advance upon*
12:18 [a] 1 Kin. 15:18; 2 Kin. 16:8; 18:15, 16
12:19 [1] *Jehoash,* 2 Kin. 12:1
12:20 [a] 2 Kin. 14:5; 2 Chr. 24:25
12:21 [a] 2 Chr. 24:27 [1] *Zabad,* 2 Chr. 24:26 [2] *Shimrith,* 2 Chr. 24:26 [3] *struck*
13:1 [a] 2 Kin. 12:1 [b] 2 Kin. 10:35 [1] *Jehoash,* 2 Kin. 12:1
13:2 [a] 1 Kin. 12:26–33 [1] *did not turn from them*
13:3 [a] Judg. 2:14 [b] 2 Kin. 8:12 [c] Amos 1:4 [1] *aroused* [2] Lit. *gave*
13:4 [a] [Ps. 78:34] [b] [Ex. 3:7, 9; Judg. 2:18]; 2 Kin. 14:26
13:5 [a] 2 Kin. 13:25; 14:25, 27; Neh. 9:27
13:6 [a] 1 Kin. 16:33
13:7 [a] 2 Kin. 10:32 [b] [Amos 1:3]
13:9 [1] *rested in death* [2] *Jehoash,* 2 Kin. 13:10
13:12 [a] 2 Kin. 14:8–15 [b] 2 Kin. 13:14–19, 25 [c] 2 Kin. 14:9; 2 Chr. 25:17–25
13:13 [a] 2 Kin. 14:16 [1] *rested in death*
13:14 [a] 2 Kin. 2:12
13:17 [a] 1 Kin. 20:26 [1] *strike* [2] *destroyed*
13:18 [1] *Strike* [2] *stopped*
13:19 [a] 2 Kin. 13:25 [1] *struck* [2] *destroyed*
13:20 [a] 2 Kin. 3:5; 24:2 [1] *Having prophesied at least 55 years*

21 And it came to pass, as they were burying a man, that, behold, they spied a band *of men;* and they cast the man into the sepulchre of Elisha: and when the man was let down, and touched the bones of Elisha, he revived, and stood up on his feet.

22 But [a]Hazael king of Syria oppressed Israel all the days of Jehoahaz.

23 And the LORD was [a]gracious unto them, and had compassion on them, and [b]had[1] respect unto them, [c]because of his covenant with Abraham, Isaac, and Jacob, and would not destroy them, neither cast he them from his presence as yet.

24 So Hazael king of Syria died; and Ben-hadad his son reigned in his stead.

25 And [1]Jehoash the son of Jehoahaz [2]took again out of the hand of Ben-hadad the son of Hazael the cities, which he had taken out of the hand of Jehoahaz his father by war. [a]Three times did Joash beat him, and recovered the cities of Israel.

## CHAPTER 14

IN [a]the second year of Joash son of Jehoahaz king of Israel reigned [b]Amaziah the son of Joash king of Judah.

2 He was twenty and five years old when he began to reign, and reigned twenty and nine years in Jerusalem. And his mother's name *was* Jehoaddan of Jerusalem.

3 And he did *that which was* right in the sight of the LORD, yet not like David his father: he did according to all things [a]as Joash his father did.

4 [a]Howbeit the [1]high places were not taken away: as yet the people did sacrifice and burnt incense on the high places.

5 And it came to pass, as soon as the kingdom was [1]confirmed in his hand, that he slew his servants [a]which had slain the king his father.

6 But the children of the murderers he slew not: according unto that which is written in the book of the law of Moses, wherein the LORD commanded, saying, [a]The fathers shall not be put to death for the children, nor the children be put to death for the fathers; but every man shall be put to death for his own sin.

7 [a]He slew of Edom in [b]the valley of salt ten thousand, and took [1] *Selah* by war, [c]and called the name of it Joktheel unto this day.

8 [a]Then Amaziah sent messengers to [1]Jehoash, the son of Jehoahaz son of Jehu, king of Israel, saying, Come, let us [2]look one another in the face.

9 And Jehoash the king of Israel sent to Amaziah king of Judah, saying, [a]The thistle that *was* in Lebanon

sent to the [b]cedar that *was* in Lebanon, saying, Give thy daughter to my son to wife: and there passed by a wild beast that *was* in Lebanon, and trode down the thistle.

10 Thou hast indeed smitten Edom, and [a]thine heart hath [1]lifted thee up: [2]glory *of this,* and tarry at home: for why shouldest thou meddle [3]to *thy* hurt, that thou shouldest fall, *even* thou, and Judah with thee?

11 But Amaziah would not hear. Therefore Jehoash king of Israel went up; and he and Amaziah king of Judah [1]looked one another in the face at [a]Beth-shemesh, which *belongeth* to Judah.

12 And Judah was [1]put to the worse before Israel; and they fled every man to their tents.

13 And Jehoash king of Israel took Amaziah king of Judah, the son of Jehoash the son of Ahaziah, at Bethshemesh, and came to Jerusalem, and brake down the wall of Jerusalem from [a]the gate of Ephraim unto [b]the corner gate, [1]four hundred cubits.

14 And he took all [a]the gold and silver, and all the vessels that were found in the house of the LORD, and in the treasures of the king's house, and hostages, and returned to Samaria.

15 [a]Now the rest of the acts of Jehoash which he did, and his might, and how he fought with Amaziah king of Judah, *are* they not written in the book of the chronicles of the kings of Israel?

16 And Jehoash [1]slept with his fathers, and was buried in Samaria with the kings of Israel; and Jeroboam his son reigned in his stead.

17 [a]And Amaziah the son of Joash king of Judah lived after the death of Jehoash son of Jehoahaz king of Israel fifteen years.

18 And the rest of the acts of Amaziah, *are* they not written in the book of the chronicles of the kings of Judah?

19 Now [a]they made a conspiracy against him in Jerusalem: and he fled to [b]Lachish; but they sent after him to Lachish, and slew him there.

20 And they brought him on horses: and he was buried at Jerusalem with his fathers in the city of David.

21 And all the people of Judah took [a]Azariah,[1] which *was* sixteen years old, and made him king instead of his father Amaziah.

22 He built [a]Elath,[1] and restored it to Judah, after that [2]the king slept with his fathers.

23 In the fifteenth year of Amaziah the son of Joash king of Judah Jeroboam the son of Joash king of Israel

### Center column references

13:22 [a] 2 Kin. 8:12, 13

13:23 [a] 2 Kin. 14:27 [b] [Ex. 2:24, 25] [c] Gen. 13:16, 17; 17:2–7; Ex. 32:13 [1] *regarded them*

13:25 [a] 2 Kin. 13:18, 19 [1] *Joash,* 2 Kin. 13:9 [2] *recaptured*

14:1 [a] 2 Kin. 13:10 [b] 2 Chr. 25:1, 2

14:3 [a] 2 Kin. 12:2

14:4 [a] 2 Kin. 12:3 [1] *Places for pagan worship*

14:5 [a] 2 Kin. 12:20 [1] *established*

14:6 [a] Deut. 24:16; [Jer. 31:30; Ezek. 18:4, 20]

14:7 [a] 2 Chr. 25:5–16 [b] 2 Sam. 8:13; 1 Chr. 18:12; Ps. 60:title [c] Josh. 15:38 [1] *Lit. The Rock;* the city of Petra

14:8 [a] 2 Chr. 25:17, 18 [1] *Joash,* 2 Kin. 13:9 [2] *face one another*

14:9 [a] Judg. 9:8–15

14:10 [a] Deut. 8:14; 2 Chr. 32:25; [Ezek. 28:2, 5, 17; Hab. 2:4] [1] *made you proud* [2] *glory in your success* [3] *with trouble*

14:11 [a] Josh. 19:38; 21:16 [1] *faced one another*

14:12 [1] *defeated by*

14:13 [a] Neh. 8:16; 12:39 [b] Jer. 31:38; Zech. 14:10 [1] 600 feet

14:14 [a] 1 Kin. 7:51; 2 Kin. 12:18; 16:8

14:15 [a] 2 Kin. 13:12, 13

14:16 [1] *rested in death*

14:17 [a] 2 Chr. 25:25–28

14:19 [a] 2 Chr. 25:27 [b] Josh. 10:31

14:21 [a] 2 Kin. 15:13; 2 Chr. 26:1 [1] *Uzziah,* 2 Chr. 26:1ff; Is. 6:1

14:22 [a] 1 Kin. 9:26; 2 Kin. 16:6; 2 Chr. 8:17 [1] *Heb. Eloth* [2] *Amaziah rested in death*

[b] 1 Kin. 4:33

began to reign in Samaria, *and reigned* forty and one years.

24 And he did *that which was* evil in the sight of the LORD: he departed not from all the [a]sins of Jeroboam the son of Nebat, who made Israel to sin.

25 He [a]restored the [1]coast of Israel [b]from the entering of Hamath unto [c]the [2]sea of the plain, according to the word of the LORD God of Israel, which he spake by the hand of his servant [d]Jonah, the son of Amittai, the prophet, which *was* of [e]Gath-hepher.

26 For the LORD [a]saw the affliction of Israel, *that it was* very bitter: for [b]there was not any [1]shut up, nor any left, nor any helper for Israel.

27 [a]And the LORD said not that he would blot out the name of Israel from under heaven: but he saved them by the hand of Jeroboam the son of Joash.

28 Now the rest of the acts of Jeroboam, and all that he did, and his might, how he warred, and how he [1]recovered [a]Damascus, and Hamath, [b]*which belonged* to Judah, for Israel, *are* they not written in the book of the chronicles of the kings of Israel?

29 And Jeroboam [1]slept with his fathers, *even* with the kings of Israel; and [a]Zachariah his son reigned in his stead.

## CHAPTER 15

IN the twenty and seventh year of Jeroboam king of Israel [a]began [b]Azariah son of Amaziah king of Judah to reign.

2 Sixteen years old was he when he began to reign, and he reigned two and fifty years in Jerusalem. And his mother's name *was* Jecholiah of Jerusalem.

3 And he did *that which was* right in the sight of the LORD, according to all that his father Amaziah had done;

4 [a]Save[1] that the [2]high places were not removed: the people sacrificed and burnt incense still on the high places.

5 And the LORD [a]smote[1] the king, so that he was a leper unto the day of his [b]death, and [c]dwelt in a [2]several house. And Jotham the king's son *was* over the [3]house, judging the people of the land.

6 And the rest of the acts of Azariah, and all that he did, *are* they not written in the book of the chronicles of the kings of Judah?

7 So Azariah [1]slept with his fathers; and [a]they buried him with his fathers in the city of David: and Jotham his son reigned in his stead.

8 In the thirty and eighth year of Azariah king of Judah did [a]Zachariah

the son of Jeroboam reign over Israel in Samaria six months.

9 And he did *that which was* evil in the sight of the LORD, [a]as his fathers had done: he departed not from the sins of Jeroboam the son of Nebat, who made Israel to sin.

10 And Shallum the son of Jabesh conspired against him, and [a]smote[1] him [2]before the people, and slew him, and reigned in his stead.

11 And the rest of the acts of Zachariah, behold, they *are* written in the book of the chronicles of the kings of Israel.

12 This *was* the [a]word of the LORD which he spake unto Jehu, saying, Thy sons shall sit on the throne of Israel unto the fourth *generation*. And so it came to pass.

13 Shallum the son of Jabesh began to reign in the nine and thirtieth year of [1]Uzziah king of Judah; and he reigned a full month in Samaria.

14 For Menahem the son of Gadi went up from [a]Tirzah, and came to Samaria, and [1]smote Shallum the son of Jabesh in Samaria, and slew him, and reigned in his stead.

15 And the rest of the acts of Shallum, and his conspiracy which he [1]made, behold, they *are* written in the book of the chronicles of the kings of Israel.

16 Then Menahem smote [a]Tiphsah, and all that *were* therein, and the [1]coasts thereof from Tirzah: because they [2]opened not *to him*, therefore he smote *it*; *and* all [b]the women therein that were with child he ripped up.

17 In the nine and thirtieth year of Azariah king of Judah began Menahem the son of Gadi to reign over Israel, *and reigned* ten years in Samaria.

18 And he did *that which was* evil in the sight of the LORD: he departed not all his days from the sins of Jeroboam the son of Nebat, who made Israel to sin.

19 *And* [a]Pul[1] the king of Assyria came against the land: and Menahem gave Pul a thousand talents of silver, that [2]his hand might be with him to [b]confirm[3] the kingdom in his hand.

20 And Menahem [a]exacted[1] the money of Israel, *even* of all the mighty men of wealth, of each man fifty shekels of silver, to give to the king of Assyria. So the king of Assyria turned back, and stayed not there in the land.

21 And the rest of the acts of Menahem, and all that he did, *are* they not written in the book of the chronicles of the kings of Israel?

22 And Menahem [1]slept with his fathers; and Pekahiah his son reigned in his stead.

23 In the fiftieth year of Azariah king of Judah Pekahiah the son of

14:24 [a]1 Kin. 12:26–33

14:25 [a]2 Kin. 10:32; 13:5, 25 [b]Num. 13:21; [c]1 Kin. 8:65 [d]Deut. 3:17 [d]Jon. 1:1; Matt. 12:39, 40 [e]Josh. 19:13 [1]*border* [2]*Sea of the Arabah, the Dead Sea*

14:26 [a]Ex. 3:7; 2 Kin. 13:4; Ps. 106:44 [b]Deut. 32:36 [1]*whether bond or free*

14:27 [a][2 Kin. 13:5, 23]

14:28 [a]1 Kin. 11:24 [b]2 Sam. 8:6; 1 Kin. 11:24; 2 Chr. 8:3 [1]*recaptured*

14:29 [a]2 Kin. 15:8 [1]*rested in death*

15:1 [a]2 Kin. 15:13, 30 [b]2 Kin. 14:21; 2 Chr. 26:1, 3, 4

15:4 [a]2 Kin. 12:3; 14:4; 15:35 [1]*Except* [2]*Places for pagan worship*

15:5 [a]2 Chr. 26:19–23; Ps. 78:31 [b]Is. 6:1 [c][Lev. 13:46]; Num. 12:14 [1]*struck* [2]*separate* [3]*royal house*

15:7 [a]2 Chr. 26:23 [1]*rested in death*

15:8 [a]2 Kin. 14:29

15:9 [a]2 Kin. 14:24

15:10 [a]Amos 7:9 [1]*struck* [2]*in front of*

15:12 [a]2 Kin. 10:30

15:13 [1]*Azariah*, 2 Kin. 14:21

15:14 [a]1 Kin. 14:17; Song 6:4 [1]*Lit. struck*

15:15 [1]*conspired*

15:16 [a]1 Kin. 4:24 [b]2 Kin. 8:12; Hos. 13:16 [1]*its territory* [2]*did not open it*

15:19 [a]1 Chr. 5:26; Is 66:19; Hos. 8:9 [b]2 Kin. 14:5 [1]*Tiglath-pileser III*, 2 Kin. 15:29 [2]*his support* [3]*strengthen*

15:20 [a]2 Kin. 23:35 [1]*took*

15:22 [1]*rested in death*

Menahem began to reign over Israel in Samaria, *and reigned* two years.

24 And he did *that which was* evil in the sight of the LORD: he departed not from the sins of Jeroboam the son of Nebat, who made Israel to sin.

25 But Pekah the son of Remaliah, a captain of his, conspired against him, and [1]smote him in Samaria, in the [a]palace[2] of the king's house, with Argob and Arieh, and with him fifty men of the Gileadites: and he killed him, and reigned in his [3]room.

26 And the rest of the acts of Pekahiah, and all that he did, behold, they *are* written in the book of the chronicles of the kings of Israel.

27 In the two and fiftieth year of Azariah king of Judah [a]Pekah the son of Remaliah began to reign over Israel in Samaria, *and reigned* twenty years.

28 And he did *that which was* evil in the sight of the LORD: he departed not from the sins of Jeroboam the son of Nebat, who made Israel to sin.

29 In the days of Pekah king of Israel [a]came [1]Tiglath-pileser king of Assyria, and took [b]Ijon, and Abel-beth-maachah, and Janoah, and Kedesh, and Hazor, and Gilead, and Galilee, all the land of Naphtali, and [c]carried them captive to Assyria.

30 And Hoshea the son of Elah made a conspiracy against Pekah the son of Remaliah, and [1]smote him, and slew him, and [a]reigned in his stead, in the twentieth year of Jotham the son of Uzziah.

31 And the rest of the acts of Pekah, and all that he did, behold, they *are* written in the book of the chronicles of the kings of Israel.

32 In the second year of Pekah the son of Remaliah king of Israel began [a]Jotham the son of Uzziah king of Judah to reign.

33 Five and twenty years old was he when he began to reign, and he reigned sixteen years in Jerusalem. And his mother's name *was* [1]Jerusha, the daughter of Zadok.

34 And he did *that which was* right in the sight of the LORD: he did [a]according to all that his father Uzziah had done.

35 [a]Howbeit the [1]high places were not removed: the people sacrificed and burned incense still in the high places. [b]He built the [2]higher gate of the house of the LORD.

36 Now the rest of the acts of Jotham, and all that he did, *are* they not written in the book of the chronicles of the kings of Judah?

37 In those days the LORD began to send against Judah [a]Rezin the king of Syria, and [b]Pekah the son of Remaliah.

15:25 [a]1 Kin. 16:18
[1] *killed* [2] *citadel*
[3] *place*

15:27 [a]2 Chr. 28:6; Is. 7:1

15:29 [a]2 Kin. 16:7, 10; 1 Chr. 5:26 [b]1 Kin. 15:20 [c]2 Kin. 17:6 [1]*Pul,* 2 Kin. 15:19

15:30 [a]2 Kin. 17:1; [Hos. 10:3, 7, 15] [1]*struck and killed him*

15:32 [a]2 Chr. 27:1

15:33 [1]*Jerushah,* 2 Chr. 27:1

15:34 [a]2 Kin. 15:3, 4; 2 Chr. 26:4, 5

15:35 [a]2 Kin. 15:4 [b]2 Chr. 23:20; 27:3 [1]*Places for pagan worship* [2]*upper*

15:37 [a]2 Kin. 16:5–9; Is. 7:1–17 [b]2 Kin. 15:26, 27

15:38 [1]*rested in death*

16:3 [a][Lev. 18:21]; 2 Kin. 17:17; 2 Chr. 28:3; Ps. 106:37, 38; Is. 1:1 [b][Deut. 12:31]; 2 Kin. 21:2, 11

16:4 [a]2 Kin. 15:34, 35 [b][Deut. 12:2]; 1 Kin. 14:23

16:5 [a]2 Kin. 15:37; Is. 7:1, 4 [1]*attacked*

16:6 [a]2 Kin. 14:22; 2 Chr. 26:2 [1]*captured* [2]*men of Judah* [3]Lit. *Large Tree;* sing. of *Eloth* [4]Qr., LXX, Tg., Vg. *Edomites*

16:7 [a]2 Kin. 15:29; 1 Chr. 5:26; 2 Chr. 28:20 [1]*Pul,* 2 Kin. 15:19

16:8 [a]2 Kin. 12:17, 18; 2 Chr. 28:21

16:9 [a]2 Kin. 14:28 [b]Amos 1:5 [c]Is. 22:6; Amos 9:7

16:10 [1]*design*

16:11 [a]Is. 8:2 [1]*before*

16:12 [a]2 Chr. 26:16, 19 [1]*made offerings on it*

38 And Jotham [1]slept with his fathers, and was buried with his fathers in the city of David his father: and Ahaz his son reigned in his stead.

## CHAPTER 16

IN the seventeenth year of Pekah the son of Remaliah Ahaz the son of Jotham king of Judah began to reign.

2 Twenty years old *was* Ahaz when he began to reign, and reigned sixteen years in Jerusalem, and did not *that which was* right in the sight of the LORD his God, like David his father.

3 But he walked in the way of the kings of Israel, yea, [a]and made his son to pass through the fire, according to the [b]abominations of the heathen, whom the LORD cast out from before the children of Israel.

4 And he sacrificed and burnt incense in the [a]high places, and [b]on the hills, and under every green tree.

5 [a]Then Rezin king of Syria and Pekah son of Remaliah king of Israel [1]came up to Jerusalem to war: and they besieged Ahaz, but could not overcome *him.*

6 At that time Rezin king of Syria [a]recovered[1] Elath to Syria, and drave the [2]Jews from [3]Elath: and the [4]Syrians came to Elath, and dwelt there unto this day.

7 So Ahaz sent messengers to [a]Tiglath-pileser[1] king of Assyria, saying, I *am* thy servant and thy son: come up, and save me out of the hand of the king of Syria, and out of the hand of the king of Israel, which rise up against me.

8 And Ahaz [a]took the silver and gold that was found in the house of the LORD, and in the treasures of the king's house, and sent *it for* a present to the king of Assyria.

9 And the king of Assyria hearkened unto him: for the king of Assyria went up against [a]Damascus, and [b]took it, and carried *the people of* it captive to [c]Kir, and slew Rezin.

10 And king Ahaz went to Damascus to meet Tiglath-pileser king of Assyria, and saw an altar that *was* at Damascus: and king Ahaz sent to Urijah the priest the [1]fashion of the altar, and the pattern of it, according to all the workmanship thereof.

11 And [a]Urijah the priest built an altar according to all that king Ahaz had sent from Damascus: so Urijah the priest made *it* [1]against king Ahaz came from Damascus.

12 And when the king was come from Damascus, the king saw the altar: and [a]the king approached to the altar, and [1]offered thereon.

13 And he burnt his burnt offering and his meat offering, and poured his drink offering, and sprinkled the

blood of his peace offerings, upon the altar.

14 And he brought also [a]the brasen altar, which *was* before the LORD, from the forefront of the 'house, from between the altar and the house of the LORD, and put it on the north side of the altar.

15 And king Ahaz commanded Urijah the priest, saying, Upon the great altar burn [a]the morning burnt offering, and the evening meat offering, and the king's burnt sacrifice, and his meat offering, with the burnt offering of all the people of the land, and their meat offering, and their drink offerings; and sprinkle upon it all the blood of the burnt offering, and all the blood of the sacrifice: and the brasen altar shall be for me to 'enquire *by.*

16 Thus did Urijah the priest, according to all that king Ahaz commanded.

17 [a]And king Ahaz cut off [b]the borders of the bases, and removed the laver from off them; and took down [c]the 'sea from off the brasen oxen that *were* under it, and put it upon a pavement of stones.

18 And the 'covert for the sabbath that they had built in the house, and the king's entry without, [2]turned he from the house of the LORD [3]for the king of Assyria.

19 Now the rest of the acts of Ahaz which he did, *are* they not written in the book of the chronicles of the kings of Judah?

20 And Ahaz slept with his fathers, and [a]was buried with his fathers in the city of David: and Hezekiah his son reigned in his stead.

## CHAPTER 17

IN the twelfth year of Ahaz king of Judah began [a]Hoshea the son of Elah to reign in Samaria over Israel nine years.

2 And he did *that which was* evil in the sight of the LORD, but not as the kings of Israel that were before him.

3 Against him came up [a]Shalmaneser king of Assyria; and Hoshea [b]became his 'servant, and [2]gave him presents.

4 And the king of Assyria found conspiracy in Hoshea: for he had sent messengers to So king of Egypt, and brought 'no present to the king of Assyria, as *he had done* year by year: therefore the king of Assyria shut him up, and bound him in prison.

5 Then [a]the king of Assyria came up throughout all the land, and went up to Samaria, and besieged it three years.

6 [a]In the ninth year of Hoshea the king of Assyria took Samaria, and [b]carried Israel away into Assyria,

16:14 [a] Ex. 27:1, 2; 40:6, 29; 2 Chr. 4:1 ' *temple*
16:15 [a] Ex. 29:39–41 ' *make inquiry*
16:17 [a] 2 Chr. 28:24 [b] 1 Kin. 7:27–29 [c] 1 Kin. 7:23–25 ' *bason*
16:18 ' *covered pavilion* [2] *removed* [3] *on account of*
16:20 [a] 2 Chr. 28:27
17:1 [a] 2 Kin. 15:30
17:3 [a] 2 Kin. 18:9–12 [b] 2 Kin. 24:1 ' *vassal* [2] *paid him tribute money*
17:4 ' *tribute*
17:5 [a] Hos. 13:16
17:6 [a] Hos. 1:4; 13:16 [b] [Deut. 28:36, 64; 29:27, 28]

[c] 1 Chr. 5:26
17:7 [a] [Josh. 23:16] [b] Judg. 6:10
17:8 [a] [Lev. 18:3]
17:9 [a] 2 Kin. 18:8 ' Places for pagan worship [2] *fortified*
17:10 [a] Is. 57:5 [b] [Ex. 34:12–14] [c] [Deut. 12:2] ' *sacred pillars* [2] *wooden images*
17:12 [a] [Ex. 20:3–5] [b] [Deut. 4:19]
17:13 [a] Neh. 9:29, 30 [b] 1 Sam. 9:9 [c] [Jer. 18:11; 25:5; 35:15]
17:14 [a] [Acts 7:51] [b] Deut. 9:23 ' *stiffened*
17:15 [a] Jer. 44:3 [b] Deut. 29:25 [c] Deut. 32:21 [d] [Rom. 1:21–23] [e] [Deut. 12:30, 31] ' *idols, and became idolaters*
17:16 [a] 1 Kin. 12:28 [b] [1 Kin. 14:15] [c] [Deut. 4:19] [d] 1 Kin. 16:31; 22:53 ' *wooden image*
17:17 [a] 2 Kin. 16:3 [b] [Deut. 18:10–12]
17:18 [c] 1 Kin. 21:20
17:18 [a] 1 Kin. 11:13, 32

[c]and placed them in Halah and in Habor *by* the river of Gozan, and in the cities of the Medes.

7 For [a]so it was, that the children of Israel had sinned against the LORD their God, which had brought them up out of the land of Egypt, from under the hand of Pharaoh king of Egypt, and had [b]feared other gods,

8 And [a]walked in the statutes of the heathen, whom the LORD cast out from before the children of Israel, and of the kings of Israel, which they had made.

9 And the children of Israel did secretly *those* things that *were* not right against the LORD their God, and they built them 'high places in all their cities, [a]from the tower of the watchmen to the [2]fenced city.

10 [a]And they set them up 'images and [b]groves[2] [c]in every high hill, and under every green tree:

11 And there they burnt incense in all the high places, as *did* the heathen whom the LORD carried away before them; and wrought wicked things to provoke the LORD to anger:

12 For they served idols, [a]whereof the LORD had said unto them, [b]Ye shall not do this thing.

13 Yet the LORD testified against Israel, and against Judah, by all the [a]prophets, *and by* all [b]the seers, saying, [c]Turn ye from your evil ways, and keep my commandments *and* my statutes, according to all the law which I commanded your fathers, and which I sent to you by my servants the prophets.

14 Notwithstanding they would not hear, but [a]hardened' their necks, like to the neck of their fathers, that [b]did not believe in the LORD their God.

15 And they [a]rejected his statutes, [b]and his covenant that he made with their fathers, and his testimonies which he testified against them; and they followed [c]vanity,' and [d]became vain, and went after the heathen that *were* round about them, *concerning* whom the LORD had charged them, that they should [e]not do like them.

16 And they left all the commandments of the LORD their God, and [a]made them molten images, *even* two calves, [b]and made a 'grove, and worshipped all the [c]host of heaven, [d]and served Baal.

17 [a]And they caused their sons and their daughters to pass through the fire, and [b]used divination and enchantments, and [c]sold themselves to do evil in the sight of the LORD, to provoke him to anger.

18 Therefore the LORD was very angry with Israel, and removed them out of his sight: there was none left [a]but the tribe of Judah only.

19 Also [a]Judah kept not the commandments of the LORD their God, but walked in the statutes of Israel which they made.

20 And the LORD rejected all the seed of Israel, and afflicted them, and [a]delivered them into the hand of [1]spoilers, until he had cast them out of his [b]sight.

21 For [a]he [1]rent Israel from the house of David; and [b]they made Jeroboam the son of Nebat king: and Jeroboam drave Israel from following the LORD, and made them sin a great sin.

22 For the children of Israel walked in all the sins of Jeroboam which he did; they departed not from them;

23 Until the LORD removed Israel out of his sight, [a]as he had said by all his servants the prophets. [b]So was Israel carried away out of their own land to Assyria unto this day.

24 [a]And the king of Assyria brought *men* from Babylon, and from Cuthah, and from [b]Ava, and from Hamath, and from Sepharvaim, and placed *them* in the cities of Samaria instead of the children of Israel: and they possessed Samaria, and dwelt in the cities thereof.

25 And *so* it was at the beginning of their dwelling there, *that* they feared not the LORD: therefore the LORD sent lions among them, which slew *some* of them.

26 Wherefore they spake to the king of Assyria, saying, The nations which thou hast removed, and placed in the cities of Samaria, know not the [1]manner of the God of the land: therefore he hath sent lions among them, and, behold, they slay them, because they know not the manner of the God of the land.

27 Then the king of Assyria commanded, saying, Carry thither one of the priests whom ye brought from thence; and let them go and dwell there, and let him teach them the manner of the God of the land.

28 Then one of the priests whom they had carried away from Samaria came and dwelt in Beth-el, and taught them how they should fear the LORD.

29 Howbeit every nation made gods of their own, and put *them* [a]in the houses of the high places which the Samaritans had made, every nation in their cities wherein they dwelt.

30 And the men of [a]Babylon made Succoth-benoth, and the men of Cuth made Nergal, and the men of Hamath made Ashima,

31 [a]And the Avites made Nibhaz and Tartak, and the Sepharvites [b]burnt their children in fire to Adrammelech and Anammelech, the gods of Sepharvaim.

17:19 [a] Jer. 3:8
17:20 [a] 2 Kin. 13:3; 15:29 [b] 2 Kin. 24:20 [1] *plunderers*
17:21 [a] 1 Kin. 11:11, 31 [b] 1 Kin. 12:20, 28 [1] *tore away*
17:23 [a] 1 Kin. 14:16 [b] 2 Kin. 17:6
17:24 [a] Ezra 4:2, 10 [b] 2 Kin. 18:34
17:26 [1] *rituals*
17:29 [a] 1 Kin. 12:31; 13:32
17:30 [a] 2 Kin. 17:24
17:31 [a] Ezra 4:9 [b] [Lev. 18:21; Deut. 12:31]
17:32 [a] 1 Kin. 12:31; 13:33 [1] Places for pagan worship
17:33 [a] Zeph. 1:5 [1] *from among whom they were carried away*
17:34 [a] Gen. 32:28; 35:10
17:35 [a] Judg. 6:10 [b] [Ex. 20:5]
17:36 [a] Ex. 14:15–30 [b] Ex. 6:6; 9:15 [c] [Deut. 10:20] [1] *hold in awesome reverence*
17:37 [a] Deut. 5:32 [1] *be careful to observe*
17:38 [a] Deut. 4:23; 6:12 [1] *reverence*
17:39 [1] *hold in awesome reverence*
17:41 [a] 2 Kin. 17:32, 33
18:1 [a] 2 Kin. 17:1 [b] 2 Chr. 28:27; 29:1
18:2 [a] Is. 38:5 [1] *Abijah,* 2 Chr. 29:1ff
18:4 [a] 2 Chr. 31:1 [b] Num. 21:5–9 [1] Places for pagan worship [2] *sacred pillars* [3] *wooden images* [4] Lit. *A Bronze Thing*
18:5 [a] 2 Kin. 19:10; [Job 13:15; Ps. 13:5] [b] 2 Kin. 23:25

32 So they feared the LORD, [a]and made unto themselves of the lowest of them priests of the high places, which sacrificed for them in the houses of the [1]high places.

33 [a]They feared the LORD, and served their own gods, after the manner of the nations [1]whom they carried away from thence.

34 Unto this day they do after the former manners: they fear not the LORD, neither do they after their statutes, or after their ordinances, or after the law and commandment which the LORD commanded the children of Jacob, [a]whom he named Israel;

35 With whom the LORD had made a covenant, and charged them, saying, [a]Ye shall not fear other gods, nor [b]bow yourselves to them, nor serve them, nor sacrifice to them:

36 But the LORD, who [a]brought you up out of the land of Egypt with great power and [b]a stretched out arm, [c]him shall ye [1]fear, and him shall ye worship, and to him shall ye do sacrifice.

37 And the statutes, and the ordinances, and the law, and the commandment, which he wrote for you, [a]ye shall [1]observe to do for evermore; and ye shall not fear other gods.

38 And the covenant that I have made with you [a]ye shall not forget; neither shall ye [1]fear other gods.

39 But the LORD your God ye shall [1]fear; and he shall deliver you out of the hand of all your enemies.

40 Howbeit they did not hearken, but they did after their former manner.

41 [a]So these nations feared the LORD, and served their graven images, both their children, and their children's children: as did their fathers, so do they unto this day.

## CHAPTER 18

Now it came to pass in the third year of [a]Hoshea son of Elah king of Israel, *that* [b]Hezekiah the son of Ahaz king of Judah began to reign.

2 Twenty and five years old was he when he began to reign; and he reigned twenty and nine years in Jerusalem. His mother's name also *was* [a]Abi,[1] the daughter of Zachariah.

3 And he did *that which was* right in the sight of the LORD, according to all that David his father did.

4 [a]He removed the [1]high places, and brake the [2]images, and cut down the [3]groves, and brake in pieces the [b]brasen serpent that Moses had made: for unto those days the children of Israel did burn incense to it: and he called it [4]Nehushtan.

5 He [a]trusted in the LORD God of Israel; [b]so that after him was none like

him among all the kings of Judah, nor *any* that were before him.

6 For he [a]clave[1] to the LORD, *and* departed not from following him, but kept his commandments, which the LORD commanded Moses.

7 And the LORD [a]was with him; *and* he [b]prospered whithersoever he went forth: and he [c]rebelled against the king of Assyria, and served him not.

8 [a]He [1]smote the Philistines, *even* unto Gaza, and the borders thereof, [b]from the tower of the watchmen to the [2]fenced city.

9 And [a]it came to pass in the fourth year of king Hezekiah, which *was* the seventh year of Hoshea son of Elah king of Israel, *that* Shalmaneser king of Assyria came up against Samaria, and besieged it.

10 And at the end of three years they took it: *even* in the sixth year of Hezekiah, that *is* [a]the ninth year of Hoshea king of Israel, Samaria was taken.

11 [a]And the king of Assyria did carry away Israel unto Assyria, and put them [b]in Halah and in Habor *by* the river of Gozan, and in the cities of the Medes:

12 Because they obeyed [a]not the voice of the LORD their God, but transgressed his covenant, *and* all that Moses the servant of the LORD commanded, and would not hear *them,* nor do *them.*

13 Now [a]in the fourteenth year of king Hezekiah did [1]Sennacherib king of Assyria come up against all the [2]fenced cities of Judah, and took them.

14 And Hezekiah king of Judah sent to the king of Assyria to Lachish, saying, I have [1]offended; [2]return from me: [3]that which thou puttest on me will I bear. And the king of Assyria appointed unto Hezekiah king of Judah three hundred talents of silver and thirty talents of gold.

15 And Hezekiah [a]gave *him* all the silver that was found in the house of the LORD, and in the treasures of the king's house.

16 At that time did Hezekiah cut off *the gold from* the doors of the temple of the LORD, and *from* the pillars which Hezekiah king of Judah had overlaid, and gave [1]it to the king of Assyria.

17 And the king of Assyria sent [1]Tartan and [2]Rabsaris and [3]Rab-shakeh from Lachish to king Hezekiah with a great host against Jerusalem. And they went up and came to Jerusalem. And when they were come up, they came and stood by the [a]conduit of the upper pool, [b]which *is* in the highway of the fuller's field.

18 And when they had called to the king, there came out to them [a]Eliakim the son of Hilkiah, which *was* over the household, and Shebna the [1]scribe, and Joah the son of Asaph the recorder.

19 And Rab-shakeh said unto them, Speak ye now to Hezekiah, Thus saith the great king, the king of Assyria, [a]What confidence *is* this wherein thou trustest?

20 Thou [1]sayest, (but *they are but* [2]vain words,) *I have* counsel and strength for the war. Now on whom dost thou trust, that thou rebellest against me?

21 [a]Now, behold, thou trustest upon the staff of this bruised reed, *even* upon Egypt, on which if a man lean, it will go into his hand, and pierce it: so *is* Pharaoh king of Egypt unto all that trust on him.

22 But if ye say unto me, We trust in the LORD our God: *is* not that he, [a]whose [1]high places and whose altars Hezekiah hath taken away, and hath said to Judah and Jerusalem, Ye shall worship before this altar in Jerusalem?

23 Now therefore, I pray thee, give pledges to my lord the king of Assyria, and I will deliver thee two thousand horses, if thou be able on thy part to set riders upon them.

24 How then wilt thou turn away the face of one captain of the least of my master's servants, and put thy trust on Egypt for chariots and for horsemen?

25 Am I now come up without the LORD against this place to destroy it? The LORD said to me, Go up against this land, and destroy it.

26 [a]Then said Eliakim the son of Hilkiah, and Shebna, and Joah, unto Rab-shakeh, Speak, I pray thee, to thy servants in the [b]Syrian[1] language; for we understand *it:* and talk not with us in the [2]Jews' language [3]in the ears of the people that *are* on the wall.

27 But Rab-shakeh said unto them, Hath my master sent me to thy master, and to thee, to speak these words? *hath* he not *sent me* to the men which sit on the wall, that they may [1]eat their own dung, and drink their own piss with you?

28 Then Rab-shakeh stood and cried with a loud voice in the [1]Jews' language, and spake, saying, Hear the word of the great king, the king of Assyria:

29 Thus saith the king, [a]Let not Hezekiah deceive you: for he shall not be able to deliver you out of his hand:

30 Neither let Hezekiah make you trust in the LORD, saying, The LORD

## Cross references

18:6 [a] Deut. 10:20; Josh. 23:8 [1] held fast

18:7 [a] [2 Chr. 15:2] [b] Gen. 39:2, 3; 1 Sam. 18:5, 14; Ps. 60:12 [c] 2 Kin. 16:7

18:8 [a] 1 Chr. 4:41; 2 Chr. 28:18; Is. 14:29 [b] 2 Kin. 17:9 [1] defeated [2] fortified

18:9 [a] 2 Kin. 17:3

18:10 [a] 2 Kin. 17:6

18:11 [a] 2 Kin. 17:6; Hos. 1:4; Amos 4:2 [b] 1 Chr. 5:26

18:12 [a] 2 Kin. 17:7–18

18:13 [a] 2 Chr. 32:1; Is. 36:1–39:8 [1] Heb. Sanherib [2] fortified

18:14 [1] done wrong [2] turn away [3] whatever you impose on

18:15 [a] 1 Kin. 15:18, 19; 2 Kin. 12:18; 16:8

18:16 [1] Lit. them

18:17 [a] 2 Kin. 20:20 [b] Is. 7:3 [1] A title, probably Commander-in-Chief [2] A title, probably Chief Officer [3] A title, probably Chief of Staff or Governor

18:18 [a] 2 Kin. 19:2; Is. 22:20 [1] secretary

18:19 [a] 2 Chr. 32:10; [Ps. 118:8, 9]

18:20 [1] say [2] words of the lips

18:21 [a] Is. 30:2–7; Ezek. 29:6, 7

18:22 [a] 2 Kin. 18:4; 2 Chr. 31:1; 32:12 [1] Places for pagan worship

18:26 [a] Is. 36:11–39:8 [b] Ezra 4:7; Dan. 2:4 [1] Lit. Aramaic [2] Hebrew [3] in the hearing

18:27 [1] eat and drink their own waste

18:28 [1] Hebrew

18:29 [a] 2 Chr. 32:15

will surely deliver us, and this city shall not be delivered into the hand of the king of Assyria.

31 Hearken not to Hezekiah: for thus saith the king of Assyria, Make an agreement with me [1]by a present, and come out to me, and *then* eat ye every man of his own [a]vine, and every one of his fig tree, and drink ye every one the waters of his cistern:

32 Until I come and take you away to a land like your own land, [a]a land of [1]corn and wine, a land of bread and vineyards, a land of oil olive and of honey, that ye may live, and not die: and hearken not unto Hezekiah, [2]when he persuadeth you, saying, The LORD will deliver us.

33 [a]Hath any of the gods of the nations delivered at all his land out of the hand of the king of Assyria?

34 Where *are* the gods of [a]Hamath, and of Arpad? where *are* the gods of Sepharvaim, Hena, and [b]Ivah? have they delivered Samaria out of mine hand?

35 Who *are* they among all the gods of the countries, that have delivered their country out of mine hand, [a]that the LORD should deliver Jerusalem out of mine hand?

36 But the people held their peace, and answered him not a word: for the king's commandment was, saying, Answer him not.

37 Then came Eliakim the son of Hilkiah, which *was* over the household, and Shebna the scribe, and Joah the son of Asaph the recorder, to Hezekiah [a]with *their* clothes [1]rent, and told him the words of Rab-shakeh.

## CHAPTER 19

AND [a]it came to pass, when king Hezekiah heard *it,* that he [1]rent his clothes, and covered himself with [b]sackcloth, and went into the house of the LORD.

2 And he sent Eliakim, which *was* over the household, and Shebna the scribe, and the elders of the priests, covered with sackcloth, to Isaiah the prophet the son of Amoz.

3 And they said unto him, Thus saith Hezekiah, This day *is* a day of trouble, and of rebuke, and of blasphemy: for the children are come to the birth, and *there is* not strength to [1]bring forth.

4 [a]It may be the LORD thy God will hear all the words of Rab-shakeh, whom the king of Assyria his master hath sent to [b]reproach the living God; and will [c]reprove the words which the LORD thy God hath heard: wherefore lift up *thy* prayer for the remnant that are left.

5 So the servants of king Hezekiah came to Isaiah.

6 [a]And Isaiah said unto them, Thus shall ye say to your master, Thus saith the LORD, Be not [b]afraid of the words which thou hast heard, with which the [c]servants of the king of Assyria have blasphemed me.

7 Behold, I will send [a]a [1]blast upon him, and he shall hear a rumour, and shall return to his own land; and I will cause him to fall by the sword in his own land.

8 So Rab-shakeh returned, and found the king of Assyria warring against Libnah: for he had heard that he was departed [a]from Lachish.

9 And [a]when he heard say of Tirhakah king of Ethiopia, Behold, he is come out to fight against thee: he sent messengers again unto Hezekiah, saying,

10 Thus shall ye speak to Hezekiah king of Judah, saying, Let not thy God [a]in whom thou trustest deceive thee, saying, Jerusalem shall not be delivered into the hand of the king of Assyria.

11 Behold, thou hast heard what the kings of Assyria have done to all lands, by destroying them utterly: and shalt thou be delivered?

12 [a]Have the gods of the nations delivered them which my fathers have destroyed; *as* Gozan, and Haran, and Rezeph, and the children of [b]Eden which *were* in Thelasar?

13 [a]Where *is* the king of Hamath, and the king of Arpad, and the king of the city of Sepharvaim, of Hena, and Ivah?

14 [a]And Hezekiah received the letter of the hand of the messengers, and read it: and Hezekiah went up into the house of the LORD, and spread it before the LORD.

15 And Hezekiah prayed before the LORD, and said, O LORD God of Israel, [a]which dwellest *between* the cherubims, [b]thou art the God, *even* thou alone, of all the kingdoms of the earth; thou hast made heaven and earth.

16 LORD, [a]bow down thine ear, and hear: [b]open, LORD, thine eyes, and see: and hear the words of Sennacherib, [c]which hath sent him to reproach the living God.

17 Of a truth, LORD, the kings of Assyria have destroyed the nations and their lands,

18 And have cast their gods into the fire: for they *were* [a]no gods, but [b]the work of men's hands, wood and stone: therefore they have destroyed them.

19 Now therefore, O LORD our God, I beseech thee, save thou us out of his hand, [a]that all the kingdoms of the earth may [b]know that thou *art* the LORD God, *even* thou only.

20 Then Isaiah the son of Amoz sent to Hezekiah, saying, Thus saith the LORD God of Israel, <sup>a</sup>*That* which thou hast prayed to me against Sennacherib king of Assyria <sup>b</sup>I have heard.

21 This *is* the word that the LORD hath spoken concerning him; The virgin <sup>a</sup>the daughter of Zion hath despised thee, *and* laughed thee to scorn; the daughter of Jerusalem <sup>b</sup>hath shaken her head <sup>1</sup>at thee.

22 Whom hast thou reproached and blasphemed? and against whom hast thou exalted *thy* voice, and lifted up thine eyes on high? *even* against <sup>a</sup>the Holy *One* of Israel.

23 <sup>a</sup>By thy messengers thou hast reproached the Lord, and hast said, <sup>b</sup>With the multitude of my chariots I am come up to the height of the mountains, to the sides of Lebanon, and will cut down the tall cedar trees thereof, *and* the choice <sup>1</sup>fir trees thereof: and I will enter into the lodgings of his borders, *and into* <sup>2</sup>the forest of his Carmel.

24 I have digged and drunk strange waters, and with the sole of my feet have I <sup>a</sup>dried up all the <sup>1</sup>rivers of besieged places.

25 Hast thou not heard long ago *how* <sup>a</sup>I have done it, *and* of ancient times that I have formed it? now have I brought it to pass, that <sup>b</sup>thou shouldest be to lay waste <sup>1</sup>fenced cities *into* ruinous heaps.

26 Therefore their inhabitants were of <sup>1</sup>small power, they were dismayed and confounded; they were *as* the grass of the field, and *as* the green herb, *as* <sup>a</sup>the grass on the house tops, and *as* corn blasted before it be grown up.

27 But <sup>a</sup>I know thy abode, and thy going out, and thy coming in, and thy rage against me.

28 Because thy rage against me and thy tumult is come up into mine ears, therefore <sup>a</sup>I will put my hook in thy nose, and my bridle in thy lips, and I will turn thee back <sup>b</sup>by the way by which thou camest.

29 And this *shall be* a <sup>a</sup>sign unto thee, Ye shall eat this year such things as grow <sup>1</sup>of themselves, and in the second year that which springeth of the same; and in the third year sow ye, and reap, and plant vineyards, and eat the fruits thereof.

30 <sup>a</sup>And the remnant that is escaped of the house of Judah shall yet again take root downward, and bear fruit upward.

31 For out of Jerusalem shall go forth a remnant, and they that escape out of mount Zion: <sup>a</sup>the zeal of the LORD *of hosts* shall do this.

32 Therefore thus saith the LORD concerning the king of Assyria, He shall <sup>a</sup>not come into this city, nor shoot an arrow there, nor come before it with shield, nor cast a <sup>1</sup>bank against it.

33 By the way that he came, by the same shall he return, and shall not come into this city, saith the LORD.

34 For <sup>a</sup>I will <sup>b</sup>defend this city, to save it, for mine own sake, and <sup>c</sup>for my servant David's sake.

35 And <sup>a</sup>it came to pass that night, that the angel of the LORD went out, and <sup>1</sup>smote in the camp of the Assyrians an hundred fourscore and five thousand: and when <sup>2</sup>they arose early in the morning, behold, <sup>3</sup>they *were* all dead corpses.

36 So Sennacherib king of Assyria departed, and went and returned, and dwelt at <sup>a</sup>Nineveh.

37 And it came to pass, as he was worshipping in the house of Nisroch his god, that <sup>a</sup>Adrammelech and Sharezer his sons <sup>b</sup>smote<sup>1</sup> him with the sword: and they escaped into the land of <sup>2</sup>Armenia. And <sup>c</sup>Esar-haddon his son reigned in his stead.

## CHAPTER 20

IN <sup>a</sup>those days was Hezekiah sick unto death. And the prophet Isaiah the son of Amoz came to him, and said unto him, Thus saith the LORD, Set thine house in order; for thou shalt die, and not live.

2 Then he turned his face to the wall, and prayed unto the LORD, saying,

3 I beseech thee, O LORD, <sup>a</sup>remember now how I have walked before thee in truth and with a perfect heart, and have done *that which is* good in thy sight. And Hezekiah wept <sup>1</sup>sore.

4 And it came to pass, afore Isaiah was gone out into the middle court, that the word of the LORD came to him, saying,

5 Turn again, and tell Hezekiah <sup>a</sup>the captain of my people, Thus saith the LORD, the God of David thy father, <sup>b</sup>I have heard thy prayer, I have seen <sup>c</sup>thy tears: behold, I will heal thee: on the third day thou shalt go up unto the house of the LORD.

6 And I will add unto thy days fifteen years; and I will deliver thee and this city out of the hand of the king of Assyria; and <sup>a</sup>I will defend this city for mine own sake, and for my servant David's sake.

7 And <sup>a</sup>Isaiah said, Take a lump of figs. And they took and laid *it* on the boil, and he recovered.

8 And Hezekiah said unto Isaiah, <sup>a</sup>What *shall be* the sign that the LORD will heal me, and that I shall go up into the house of the LORD the third day?

9 And Isaiah said, <sup>a</sup>This sign shalt thou have of the LORD, that the LORD

### Center reference column

19:20 <sup>a</sup> Is. 37:21
<sup>b</sup> 2 Kin. 20:5; Ps. 65:2

19:21 <sup>a</sup> Jer. 14:17; Lam. 2:13 <sup>b</sup> Ps. 22:7, 8 <sup>1</sup> *behind your back*

19:22 <sup>a</sup> Jer. 51:5

19:23 <sup>a</sup> 2 Kin. 18:17 <sup>b</sup> Ps. 20:7 <sup>1</sup> *cypress* <sup>2</sup> *its fruitful forest*

19:24 <sup>a</sup> Is. 19:6 <sup>1</sup> *brooks of defence*

19:25 <sup>a</sup> [Is. 45:7] <sup>b</sup> Is. 10:5, 6 <sup>1</sup> *fortified*

19:26 <sup>a</sup> Ps. 129:6 <sup>1</sup> *little strength*

19:27 <sup>a</sup> Ps. 139:1–3; Is. 37:28

19:28 <sup>a</sup> Job 41:2; Ezek. 29:4; 38:4; Amos 4:2 <sup>b</sup> 2 Kin. 19:33, 36

19:29 <sup>a</sup> Ex. 3:12; 1 Sam. 2:34; 2 Kin. 20:8, 9; Is. 7:11–14; Luke 2:12 <sup>1</sup> *without cultivation*

19:30 <sup>a</sup> 2 Kin. 19:4; 2 Chr. 32:22, 23

19:31 <sup>a</sup> 2 Kin. 25:26; Is. 9:7

19:32 <sup>a</sup> Is. 8:7–10 <sup>1</sup> *siege mound*

19:34 <sup>a</sup> 2 Kin. 20:6; 2 Chr. 32:21 <sup>b</sup> Is. 31:5 <sup>c</sup> 1 Kin. 11:12, 13

19:35 <sup>a</sup> Ex. 12:29; Is. 10:12–19; 37:36; Hos. 1:7 <sup>1</sup> *killed* <sup>2</sup> *The Israelites* <sup>3</sup> *The Assyrians*

19:36 <sup>a</sup> Gen. 10:11

19:37 <sup>a</sup> 2 Kin. 17:31 <sup>b</sup> 2 Kin. 19:7; 2 Chr. 32:21 <sup>c</sup> Ezra 4:2 <sup>1</sup> *struck him down* <sup>2</sup> *Heb. Ararat*

20:1 <sup>a</sup> 2 Kin. 18:13; 2 Chr. 32:24; Is. 38:1–22

20:3 <sup>a</sup> 2 Kin. 18:3–6; Neh. 13:22 <sup>1</sup> *bitterly*

20:5 <sup>a</sup> 1 Sam. 9:16; 10:1 <sup>b</sup> 2 Kin. 19:20; Ps. 65:2 <sup>c</sup> Ps. 39:12; 56:8

20:6 <sup>a</sup> 2 Kin. 19:34; 2 Chr. 32:21

20:7 <sup>a</sup> Is. 38:21

20:8 <sup>a</sup> Judg. 6:17, 37, 39; Is. 7:11, 14; 38:22

20:9 <sup>a</sup> Num. 23:19; Is. 38:7, 8

will do the thing that he hath spoken: shall the shadow go forward ten degrees, or go back ten degrees?

10 And Hezekiah answered, It is [1]a light thing for the shadow to go down [2]ten degrees: nay, but let the shadow return backward ten degrees.

11 And Isaiah the prophet cried unto the LORD: and [a]he brought the shadow ten degrees backward, by which it had gone down in the [1]dial of Ahaz.

12 [a]At that time [1]Berodach-baladan, the son of Baladan, king of Babylon, sent letters and a present unto Hezekiah: for he had heard that Hezekiah had been sick.

13 And [a]Hezekiah hearkened unto them, and shewed them all the house of his [1]precious things, the silver, and the gold, and the spices, and the precious ointment, and *all* the house of his armour, and all that was found in his treasures: there was nothing in his house, nor in all his dominion, that Hezekiah shewed them not.

14 Then came Isaiah the prophet unto king Hezekiah, and said unto him, What said these men? and from whence came they unto thee? And Hezekiah said, They are come from a far country, *even* from Babylon.

15 And he said, What have they seen in thine house? And Hezekiah answered, [a]All *the things* that *are* in mine house have they seen: there is nothing among my treasures that I have not shewed them.

16 And Isaiah said unto Hezekiah, Hear the word of the LORD.

17 Behold, the days come, that all that *is* in thine house, and that which thy fathers have laid up in store unto this day, [a]shall be carried into Babylon: nothing shall be left, saith the LORD.

18 And of thy sons that shall [1]issue from thee, which thou shalt beget, [a]shall they take away; [b]and [2]they shall be [c]eunuchs in the palace of the king of Babylon.

19 Then said Hezekiah unto Isaiah, [a]Good *is* the word of the LORD which thou hast spoken. And he said, [1]*Is it* not *good*, if peace and truth be in my days?

20 [a]And the rest of the acts of Hezekiah, and all his might, and how he [b]made a [c]pool, and a [1]conduit, and [d]brought water into the city, *are* they not written in the book of the chronicles of the kings of Judah?

21 And [a]Hezekiah [1]slept with his fathers: and Manasseh his son reigned in his stead.

## CHAPTER 21

**M**ANASSEH [a]*was* twelve years old when he began to reign, and

reigned fifty and five years in Jerusalem. And his mother's name *was* Hephzi-bah.

2 And he did *that which was* evil in the sight of the LORD, [a]after the abominations of the heathen, whom the LORD cast out before the children of Israel.

3 For he built up again the [1]high places [a]which Hezekiah his father had destroyed; and he reared up altars for Baal, and made a [2]grove, [b]as did Ahab king of Israel; and [c]worshipped all [3]the host of heaven, and served them.

4 And [a]he built altars in the house of the LORD, of which the LORD said, [b]In Jerusalem will I put my name.

5 And he built altars for all the host of heaven in the [a]two courts of the house of the LORD.

6 [a]And he made his son pass through the fire, and [1]observed [b]times, and [2]used enchantments, and dealt with [3]familiar spirits and wizards: he wrought much wickedness in the sight of the LORD, to provoke *him* to anger.

7 And he set [1]a graven image of the grove that he had made in the [2]house, of which the LORD said to David, and to Solomon his son, [a]In this house, and in Jerusalem, which I have chosen out of all tribes of Israel, will I put my name for ever:

8 [a]Neither will I make the feet of Israel move any more out of the land which I gave their fathers; only if they will observe to do according to all that I have commanded them, and according to all the law that my servant Moses commanded them.

9 But they hearkened not: and Manasseh [a]seduced them to do more evil than did the nations whom the LORD destroyed before the children of Israel.

10 And the LORD spake [a]by his servants the prophets, saying,

11 [a]Because Manasseh king of Judah hath done these abominations, [b]*and* hath done wickedly above all that the [c]Amorites did, which *were* before him, and [d]hath made Judah also to sin with his idols:

12 Therefore thus saith the LORD God of Israel, Behold, I *am* bringing *such* [1]evil upon Jerusalem and Judah, that whosoever heareth of it, both [a]his ears shall tingle.

13 And I will stretch over Jerusalem [a]the line of Samaria, and the [1]plummet of the house of Ahab: and [b]I will wipe Jerusalem as *a man* wipeth a dish, wiping *it*, and turning *it* upside down.

14 And I will forsake the [a]remnant of mine inheritance, and deliver them into the hand of their enemies;

---

**Center column references:**

20:10 [1] *an easy*
[2] Lit. *steps*

20:11 [a] Josh. 10:12–14; Is. 38:8
[1] *sundial*

20:12 [a] 2 Kin. 8:8, 9; 2 Chr. 32:31; Is. 39:1–8
[1] *Merodach-baladan,* Is. 39:1

20:13 [a] 2 Kin. 16:9; 2 Chr. 32:27, 31
[1] *treasures*

20:15 [a] 2 Kin. 20:13

20:17 [a] Jer. 27:21, 22; 52:17

20:18 [a] 2 Kin. 24:12 [b] Dan. 1:3–7 [c] Dan. 1:11, 18 [1] *be born from*
[2] Fulfilled in 2 Kin. 24:14

20:19 [a] 1 Sam. 3:18
[1] *Will there not be peace and truth at least in my days?*

20:20 [a] 2 Chr. 32:32 [b] Neh. 3:16 [c] Is. 7:3 [d] 2 Chr. 32:3, 30 [1] *tunnel or aqueduct*

20:21 [a] 2 Chr. 32:33 [1] *rested in death*

21:1 [a] 2 Chr. 33:1–9

21:2 [a] 2 Kin. 16:3

21:3 [a] 2 Kin. 18:4, 22 [b] 1 Kin. 16:31–33 [c] [Deut. 4:19; 17:2–5] [1] *Places for pagan worship* [2] *wooden image* [3] The gods of the Assyrians

21:4 [a] Jer. 7:30; 32:34 [b] 1 Kin. 11:13

21:5 [a] 1 Kin. 6:36; 7:12

21:6 [a] [Lev. 18:21; 20:2] [b] [Deut. 18:10–14] [1] *practised soothsaying* [2] *witchcraft* [3] *mediums and spiritists*

21:7 [a] 1 Kin. 8:29; 9:3 [1] *a carved image of Asherah, a Canaanite goddess* [2] *Temple*

21:8 [a] 2 Sam. 7:10

21:9 [a] [Prov. 29:12]

21:10 [a] 2 Kin. 17:13

21:11 [a] 2 Kin. 23:26, 27; 24:3, 4 [b] 1 Kin. 21:26 [c] Gen. 15:16 [d] 2 Kin. 21:9

21:12 [a] Jer. 19:3 [1] *calamity*

21:13 [a] Amos 7:7, 8 [b] 2 Kin. 22:16–19; 25:4–11 [1] *A carpenter's measure*

21:14 [a] Jer. 6:9

and they shall become a prey and a 'spoil to all their enemies;

15 Because they have done *that which was* evil in my sight, and have provoked me to anger, since the day their fathers came forth out of Egypt, even unto this day.

16 ªMoreover Manasseh shed innocent blood very much, till he had filled Jerusalem from one end to another; beside his sin wherewith he made Judah to sin, in doing *that which was* evil in the sight of the LORD.

17 Now ªthe rest of the acts of ᵇManasseh, and all that he did, and his sin that he sinned, *are* they not written in the book of the chronicles of the kings of Judah?

18 And ªManasseh 'slept with his fathers, and was buried in the garden of his own house, in the garden of Uzza: and Amon his son reigned in his stead.

19 ªAmon *was* twenty and two years old when he 'began to reign, and he reigned two years in Jerusalem. And his mother's name *was* Meshullemeth, the daughter of Haruz of Jotbah.

20 And he did *that which was* evil in the sight of the LORD, ªas his father Manasseh did.

21 And he walked in all the way that his father walked in, and served the idols that his father served, and worshipped them:

22 And he ªforsook the LORD God of his fathers, and walked not in the way of the LORD.

23 ªAnd the servants of Amon ᵇconspired against him, and slew the king in his own house.

24 And the people of the land ªslew all them that had conspired against king Amon; and the people of the land made Josiah his son king in his stead.

25 Now the rest of the acts of Amon which he did, *are* they not written in the book of the chronicles of the kings of Judah?

26 And he was buried in his sepulchre in the garden of Uzza: and Josiah his son reigned in his stead.

## CHAPTER 22

Josiah ªwas eight years old when he began to reign, and he reigned thirty and one years in Jerusalem. And his mother's name *was* Jedidah, the daughter of Adaiah of 'Boscath.

2 And he did *that which was* right in the sight of the LORD, and walked in all the way of David his father, and ªturned not aside to the right hand or to the left.

3 ªAnd it came to pass in the eighteenth year of king Josiah, *that* the king sent Shaphan the son of Azaliah,

the son of Meshullam, the scribe, to the house of the LORD, saying,

4 Go up to Hilkiah the high priest, that he may 'sum the silver which is ªbrought into the house of the LORD, which ᵇthe keepers of the door have gathered of the people:

5 And let them ªdeliver it into the hand of the doers of the work, that have the oversight of the house of the LORD: and let them give it to the doers of the work which *is* in the house of the LORD, to repair the breaches of the house,

6 Unto carpenters, and builders, and masons, and to buy timber and hewn stone to repair the house.

7 Howbeit ªthere was no 'reckoning made with them of the money that was delivered into their hand, because they dealt faithfully.

8 And Hilkiah the high priest said unto Shaphan the scribe, ªI have found the book of the law in the house of the LORD. And Hilkiah gave the book to Shaphan, and he read it.

9 And Shaphan the scribe came to the king, and brought the king word again, and said, Thy servants have 'gathered the money that was found in the house, and have delivered it into the hand of them that do the work, that have the oversight of the house of the LORD.

10 And Shaphan the scribe shewed the king, saying, Hilkiah the priest hath delivered me a book. And Shaphan read it before the king.

11 And it came to pass, when the king had heard the words of the book of the law, that he 'rent his clothes.

12 And the king commanded Hilkiah the priest, and ªAhikam the son of Shaphan, and 'Achbor the son of Michaiah, and Shaphan the scribe, and ²Asahiah a servant of the king's, saying,

13 Go ye, enquire of the LORD for me, and for the people, and for all Judah, concerning the words of this book that is found: for great *is* ªthe wrath of the LORD that is kindled against us, because our fathers have not hearkened unto the words of this book, to do according unto all that which is written concerning us.

14 So Hilkiah the priest, and Ahikam, and Achbor, and Shaphan, and 'Asahiah, went unto Huldah the prophetess, the wife of Shallum the son of ªTikvah, the son of Harhas, keeper of the wardrobe; (now she dwelt in Jerusalem ²in the college;) and they ³communed with her.

15 And she said unto them, Thus saith the LORD God of Israel, Tell the man that sent you to me,

16 Thus saith the LORD, Behold, ªI will bring 'evil upon this place, and

21:14 ¹ plunder
21:16 ª 2 Kin. 24:4
21:17 ª 2 Chr. 33:11–19 ᵇ 2 Kin. 20:21
21:18 ª 2 Chr. 33:20 ¹ rested in death
21:19 ª 2 Chr. 33:21–23 ¹ became king
21:20 ª 2 Kin. 21:2–6, 11, 16
21:22 ª Judg. 2:12, 13; 1 Kin. 11:33; 1 Chr. 28:9
21:23 ª 1 Chr. 3:14; 2 Chr. 33:24, 25; Matt. 1:10 ᵇ 2 Kin. 12:20; 14:19
21:24 ª 2 Kin. 14:5
22:1 ª 1 Kin. 13:2; 2 Chr. 34:1 ¹ Bozkath, Josh. 15:39
22:2 ª Deut. 5:32; Josh. 1:7
22:3 ª 2 Chr. 34:8

22:4 ª 2 Kin. 12:4 ᵇ 2 Kin. 12:9, 10 ¹ count
22:5 ª 2 Kin. 12:11–14
22:7 ª 2 Kin. 12:15; [1 Cor. 4:2] ¹ accounting
22:8 ª Deut. 31:24–26; 2 Chr. 34:14
22:9 ¹ poured out
22:11 ¹ tore
22:12 ª 2 Kin. 25:22; Jer. 26:24 ¹ Abdon the son of Micah, 2 Chr. 34:20 ² Asaiah, 2 Chr. 34:20
22:13 ª [Deut. 29:23–28; 31:17, 18]
22:14 ª 2 Chr. 34:22 ¹ Asaiah, 2 Chr. 34:20 ² in the second quarter ³ spoke
22:16 ª Deut. 29:27; [Dan. 9:11–14] ¹ calamity

upon the inhabitants thereof, *even* all the words of the book which the king of Judah hath read:

17 ªBecause they have forsaken me, and have burned incense unto other gods, that they might provoke me to anger with all the works of their hands; therefore my wrath shall be kindled against this place, and shall not be quenched.

18 But to ªthe king of Judah which sent you to enquire of the LORD, thus shall ye say to him, Thus saith the LORD God of Israel, *As touching* the words which thou hast heard;

19 Because thine ªheart was tender, and thou hast ᵇhumbled thyself before the LORD, when thou heardest what I spake against this place, and against the inhabitants thereof, that they should become ᶜa desolation and ᵈa curse, and hast ¹rent thy clothes, and wept before me; I also have heard *thee*, saith the LORD.

20 Behold therefore, I ¹will gather thee unto thy fathers, and thou ªshalt ²be gathered into thy grave in peace; and thine eyes shall not see all the evil which I will bring upon this place. And they brought the king word again.

### CHAPTER 23

AND ªthe king sent, and they gathered unto him all the elders of Judah and of Jerusalem.

2 And the king went up into the house of the LORD, and all the men of Judah and all the inhabitants of Jerusalem with him, and the priests, and the prophets, and all the people, both small and great: and he ªread in their ears all the words of the book of the covenant ᵇwhich was found in the house of the LORD.

3 And the king ªstood by a pillar, and made a ᵇcovenant before the LORD, to walk after the LORD, and to keep his commandments and his testimonies and his statutes with all *their* heart and all *their* soul, to perform the words of this covenant that were written in this book. And all the people ¹stood to the covenant.

4 And the king commanded Hilkiah the high priest, and the ªpriests of the second order, and the keepers of the door, to bring ᵇforth out of the temple of the LORD all the vessels that were made for Baal, and for ¹the grove, and for all the ²host of heaven: and he burned them ³without Jerusalem in the fields of Kidron, and carried the ashes of them unto Beth-el.

5 And he ¹put down the idolatrous priests, whom the kings of Judah had ordained to burn incense in the high places in the cities of Judah, and in the places round about Jerusalem;

*Center column notes:*

22:17 ª Deut. 29:25–27; 2 Kin. 21:22
22:18 ª 2 Chr. 34:26
22:19 ª [Ps. 51:17] ᵇ 1 Kin. 21:29 ᶜ Lev. 26:31, 32 ᵈ Jer. 26:6; 44:22 ¹ torn
22:20 ª [Is. 57:1, 2] ¹ Cause you to join your ancestors in death ² Die a natural death
23:1 ª 2 Chr. 34:29, 30
23:2 ª Deut. 31:10–13 ᵇ 2 Kin. 22:8
23:3 ª 2 Kin. 11:14 ᵇ 2 Kin. 11:17 ¹ took their stand for
23:4 ª 2 Kin. 25:18 ᵇ 2 Kin. 21:3–7 ¹ Heb. Asherah, a Canaanite goddess ² The gods of the Assyrians ³ outside
23:5 ¹ removed

23:6 ª 2 Kin. 21:7 ᵇ Ex. 32:20 ᶜ 2 Chr. 34:4 ¹ Heb. Asherah, a Canaanite goddess ² outside ³ ground it to ashes
23:7 ª 1 Kin. 14:24; 15:12 ᵇ Ezek. 16:16 ᶜ Ex. 38:8
23:8 ª Josh. 21:17
23:9 ª [Ezek. 44:10–14] ᵇ 1 Sam. 2:36
23:10 ª Is. 30:33 ᵇ Josh. 15:8 ᶜ [Lev. 18:21] ᵈ 2 Kin. 21:6 ¹ sons
23:11 ¹ dedicated ² officer
23:12 ª Jer. 19:13 ᵇ 2 Kin. 21:5 ¹ broke down ² pulverized them
23:13 ª 1 Kin. 11:5–7 ¹ Places for pagan worship ² South of the Mount of Olives
23:14 ¹ [Ex. 23:24] ¹ sacred pillars ² Places for pagan worship
23:15 ª 1 Kin. 12:28–33 ¹ Place for pagan worship

*Center column note (ch 23 opening):*
ª 2 Kin. 21:3 ² constellations of the zodiac

them also that burned incense unto Baal, to the sun, and to the moon, and to the planets, and to ªall the ²host of heaven.

6 And he brought out the ªgrove¹ from the house of the LORD, ²without Jerusalem, unto the brook Kidron, and burned it at the brook Kidron, and ³stamped *it* small to ᵇpowder, and cast the powder thereof upon ᶜthe graves of the children of the people.

7 And he brake down the houses ªof the sodomites, that *were* by the house of the LORD, ᵇwhere the ᶜwomen wove hangings for the grove.

8 And he brought all the priests out of the cities of Judah, and defiled the high places where the priests had burned incense, from ªGeba to Beer-sheba, and brake down the high places of the gates that *were* in the entering in of the gate of Joshua the governor of the city, which *were* on a man's left hand at the gate of the city.

9 ªNevertheless the priests of the high places came not up to the altar of the LORD in Jerusalem, ᵇbut they did eat of the unleavened bread among their brethren.

10 And he defiled ªTopheth, which *is* in ᵇthe valley of the ¹children of Hinnom, ᶜthat no man might make his son or his daughter to ᵈpass through the fire to Molech.

11 And he took away the horses that the kings of Judah had ¹given to the sun, at the entering in of the house of the LORD, by the chamber of Nathan-melech the ²chamberlain, which *was* in the suburbs, and burned the chariots of the sun with fire.

12 And the altars that *were* ªon the top of the upper chamber of Ahaz, which the kings of Judah had made, and the altars which ᵇManasseh had made in the two courts of the house of the LORD, did the king ¹beat down, and ²brake *them* down from thence, and cast the dust of them into the brook Kidron.

13 And the ¹high places that *were* before Jerusalem, which *were* ²on the right hand of the mount of corruption, which ªSolomon the king of Israel had builded for Ashtoreth the abomination of the Zidonians, and for Chemosh the abomination of the Moabites, and for Milcom the abomination of the children of Ammon, did the king defile.

14 And he ªbrake in pieces the ¹images, and cut down the ²groves, and filled their places with the bones of men.

15 Moreover the altar that *was* at Beth-el, *and* the ¹high place ªwhich Jeroboam the son of Nebat, who made Israel to sin, had made, both

that altar and the high place he brake down, and burned the high place, *and* stamped *it* small to powder, and burned the grove.

16 And as Josiah turned himself, he spied the sepulchres that *were* there in the mount, and sent, and took the bones out of the sepulchres, and burned *them* upon the altar, and ¹polluted it, according to the ªword of the LORD which the man of God proclaimed, who proclaimed these words.

17 Then he said, What ¹title *is* that that I see? And the men of the city told him, *It is* ªthe sepulchre of the man of God, which came from Judah, and proclaimed these things that thou hast done against the altar of Beth-el.

18 And he said, Let him alone; let no man move his bones. So they let his bones alone, with the bones of ªthe prophet that came out of Samaria.

19 And all the ¹houses also of the ²high places that *were* ªin the cities of Samaria, which the kings of Israel had made to provoke *the LORD* to anger, Josiah took away, and did to them according to all the acts that he had done in Beth-el.

20 And ªhe ᵇslew all the priests of the ¹high places that *were* there upon the ²altars, and ᶜburned men's bones upon them, and returned to Jerusalem.

21 And the king commanded all the people, saying, ªKeep the passover unto the LORD your God, ᵇas *it is* written in the book of this covenant.

22 Surely ªthere was not ¹holden such a passover from the days of the judges that judged Israel, nor in all the days of the kings of Israel, nor of the kings of Judah;

23 But in the eighteenth year of king Josiah, *wherein* this passover was holden to the LORD in Jerusalem.

24 Moreover the ¹*workers with* familiar spirits, and ²the wizards, and the ³images, and the idols, and all the abominations that were spied in the land of Judah and in Jerusalem, did Josiah put away, that he might perform the words of ªthe law which were written in the book ᵇthat Hilkiah the priest found in the house of the LORD.

25 ªAnd like unto him was there no king before him, that turned to the LORD with all his heart, and with all his soul, and with all his might, according to all the law of Moses; neither after him arose there *any* like him.

26 Notwithstanding the LORD turned not from the fierceness of his great wrath, wherewith his anger

23:16 ª 1 Kin. 13:2
¹ *defiled*

23:17 ª 1 Kin. 13:1,
30, 31 ¹ *gravestone*

23:18 ª 1 Kin. 13:11, 31

23:19 ª 2 Chr. 34:6, 7 ¹ *temples* ² *pagan shrines*

23:20 ª 1 Kin. 13:2 ᵇ [Ex. 22:20]; 1 Kin. 18:40; 2 Kin. 10:25; 11:18 ᶜ 2 Chr. 34:5 ¹ *shrines* ² *Places for pagan worship*

23:21 ª Num. 9:5; Josh. 5:10; 2 Chr. 35:1 ᵇ Ex. 12:3; Lev. 23:5; Num. 9:2; Deut. 16:2–8

23:22 ª 2 Chr. 35:18, 19 ¹ *held*

23:24 ª [Lev. 19:31; 20:27]; Deut. 18:11 ᵇ 2 Kin. 22:8 ¹ *those who consulted mediums* ² *spiritists* ³ *household gods*

23:25 ª 2 Kin. 18:5

23:26 ª 2 Kin. 21:11, 12; 24:3, 4; Jer. 15:4

23:27 ª 2 Kin. 17:18, 20; 18:11; 21:13 ᵇ 1 Kin. 8:29; 9:3; 2 Kin. 21:4, 7

23:29 ª 2 Chr. 35:20; Jer. 2:16; 46:2 ᵇ Judg. 5:19; Zech. 12:11 ᶜ 2 Kin. 14:8 ¹ *to the aid of* ² Pharaoh-nechoh ³ *encountered him*

23:30 ª 2 Chr. 35:24; 2 Kin. 22:20 ᵇ 2 Chr. 36:1–4

23:31 ª 1 Chr. 3:15; Jer. 22:11 ᵇ 2 Kin. 24:18

23:33 ª 2 Kin. 25:6; Jer. 52:27 ¹ *prison*

23:34 ª 2 Chr. 36:4 ᵇ 2 Kin. 24:17; Dan. 1:7 ᶜ Matt. 1:11 ᵈ Jer. 22:11, 12; Ezek. 19:3, 4 ¹ Pharaoh-nechoh *took* ² Jehoahaz *died*

23:35 ª 2 Kin. 23:33

23:36 ª 2 Chr. 36:5; Jer. 22:18, 19; 26:1

24:1 ª 2 Chr. 36:6; Jer. 25:1, 9; Dan. 1:1 ᵇ 2 Kin. 20:14

was kindled against Judah, ªbecause of all the provocations that Manasseh had provoked him withal.

27 And the LORD said, I will remove Judah also out of my sight, as ªI have removed Israel, and will cast off this city Jerusalem which I have chosen, and the house of which I said, ᵇMy name shall be there.

28 Now the rest of the acts of Josiah, and all that he did, *are* they not written in the book of the chronicles of the kings of Judah?

29 ªIn his days Pharaoh-nechoh king of Egypt went ¹up against the king of Assyria to the river Euphrates: and king Josiah went against him; and ²he slew him at ᵇMegiddo, when he ᶜhad³ seen him.

30 ªAnd his servants carried him in a chariot dead from Megiddo, and brought him to Jerusalem, and buried him in his own sepulchre. And ᵇthe people of the land took Jehoahaz the son of Josiah, and anointed him, and made him king in his father's stead.

31 ªJehoahaz *was* twenty and three years old when he began to reign; and he reigned three months in Jerusalem. And his mother's name *was* ᵇHamutal, the daughter of Jeremiah of Libnah.

32 And he did *that which was* evil in the sight of the LORD, according to all that his fathers had done.

33 And Pharaoh-nechoh put him in ¹bands ªat Riblah in the land of Hamath, that he might not reign in Jerusalem; and put the land to a tribute of an hundred talents of silver, and a talent of gold.

34 And ªPharaoh-nechoh made Eliakim the son of Josiah king in the room of Josiah his father, and ᵇturned his name to ᶜJehoiakim, and ¹took Jehoahaz away: ᵈand he came to Egypt, and ²died there.

35 And Jehoiakim gave ªthe silver and the gold to Pharaoh; but he taxed the land to give the money according to the commandment of Pharaoh: he exacted the silver and the gold of the people of the land, of every one according to his taxation, to give *it* unto Pharaoh-nechoh.

36 ªJehoiakim *was* twenty and five years old when he began to reign; and he reigned eleven years in Jerusalem. And his mother's name *was* Zebudah, the daughter of Pedaiah of Rumah.

37 And he did *that which was* evil in the sight of the LORD, according to all that his fathers had done.

## CHAPTER 24

IN ªhis days Nebuchadnezzar king of ᵇBabylon came up, and Jehoiakim

became his servant three years: then he turned and rebelled against him.

2 [a]And the LORD sent against him [1]bands of the Chaldees, and bands of the Syrians, and bands of the Moabites, and bands of the children of Ammon, and sent them against Judah to destroy it, [b]according to the word of the LORD, which he spake by his servants the prophets.

3 Surely at the commandment of the LORD came *this* upon Judah, to remove *them* out of his sight, [a]for the sins of Manasseh, according to all that he did;

4 [a]And also for the innocent blood that he shed: for he filled Jerusalem with innocent blood; which the LORD would not pardon.

5 Now the rest of the acts of Jehoiakim, and all that he did, *are* they not written in the book of the chronicles of the kings of Judah?

6 [a]So Jehoiakim slept with his fathers: and Jehoiachin his son reigned in his stead.

7 And [a]the king of Egypt came not again any more out of his land: for [b]the king of Babylon had taken from the river of Egypt unto the river Euphrates all that pertained to the king of Egypt.

8 [a]Jehoiachin[1] *was* eighteen years old when he began to reign, and he reigned in Jerusalem three months. And his mother's name *was* Nehushta, the daughter of Elnathan of Jerusalem.

9 And he did *that which was* evil in the sight of the LORD, according to all that his father had done.

10 [a]At that time the servants of Nebuchadnezzar king of Babylon came up against Jerusalem, and the city [1]was besieged.

11 And Nebuchadnezzar king of Babylon came against the city, and his servants did besiege it.

12 [a]And Jehoiachin the king of Judah went out to the king of Babylon, he, and his mother, and his servants, and his princes, and his officers: and the king of Babylon took him [b]in the eighth year of his reign.

13 [a]And he carried out thence all the treasures of the house of the LORD, and the treasures of the king's house, and [b]cut in pieces all the vessels of gold which Solomon king of Israel had made in the temple of the LORD, [c]as the LORD had said.

14 And [a]he [1]carried away all Jerusalem, and all the princes, and all the mighty men of valour, [b]*even* ten thousand captives, and [c]all the craftsmen and smiths: none remained, save [d]the poorest sort of the people of the land.

15 And [a]he carried away Jehoiachin to Babylon, and the king's mother, and the king's wives, and his officers, and the mighty of the land, *those* carried he into captivity from Jerusalem to Babylon.

16 And [a]all the men of might, *even* seven thousand, and craftsmen and smiths a thousand, all *that were* strong *and* [1]apt for war, even them the king of Babylon brought captive to Babylon.

17 And [a]the king of Babylon made Mattaniah [b]his [1]father's brother king in his stead, and [c]changed his name to Zedekiah.

18 [a]Zedekiah *was* twenty and one years old when he began to reign, and he reigned eleven years in Jerusalem. And his mother's name *was* [b]Hamutal, the daughter of Jeremiah of Libnah.

19 [a]And he did *that which was* evil in the sight of the LORD, according to all that Jehoiakim had done.

20 For [1]through the anger of the LORD it came to pass in Jerusalem and Judah, until he had cast them out from his presence, [a]that Zedekiah rebelled against the king of Babylon.

## CHAPTER 25

AND it came to pass [a]in the ninth year of his reign, in the tenth month, in the tenth *day* of the month, *that* Nebuchadnezzar king of Babylon came, he, and all his host, against Jerusalem, and [1]pitched against it; and they built [2]forts against it round about.

2 And the city was besieged unto the eleventh year of king Zedekiah.

3 And on the ninth *day* of the [a]*fourth* month the famine prevailed in the city, and there was no bread for the people of the land.

4 And [a]the city was [1]broken up, and all the men of war *fled* by night by the way of the gate between two walls, which *is* by the king's garden: (now the Chaldees *were* against the city round about:) and [b]*the king* went the way toward the [2]plain.

5 And the army of the Chaldees pursued after the king, and overtook him in the plains of Jericho: and all his army were scattered from him.

6 So they took the king, and brought him up to the king of Babylon [a]to Riblah; and they [1]gave judgment upon him.

7 And they slew the sons of Zedekiah before his eyes, and [a]put[1] out the eyes of Zedekiah, and bound him with fetters of brass, and carried him to Babylon.

8 And in the fifth month, [a]on the seventh *day* of the month, which *is* [b]the nineteenth year of king Nebuchadnezzar king of Babylon, [c]came Nebuzar-adan, captain of the guard,

24:2 [a] Jer. 25:9; 32:28; 35:11; Ezek. 19:8 [b] 2 Kin. 20:17; 21:12–14; 23:27 [1] *troops*
24:3 [a] 2 Kin. 21:2, 11; 23:26
24:4 [a] 2 Kin. 21:16
24:6 [a] 2 Chr. 36:6, 8; Jer. 22:18, 19
24:7 [a] Jer. 37:5–7 [b] Jer. 46:2
24:8 [a] 1 Chr. 3:16; 2 Chr. 36:9 [1] *Jeconiah,* 1 Chr. 3:16; Jer. 24:1; and *Coniah,* Jer. 22:24, 28
24:10 [a] Dan. 1:1 [1] Lit. *came under siege*
24:12 [a] Jer. 22:24–30; 24:1; 29:1, 2; Ezek. 17:12 [b] 2 Chr. 36:10
24:13 [a] 2 Kin. 20:17; Is. 39:6 [b] Dan. 5:2, 3 [c] Jer. 20:5
24:14 [a] Is. 3:2, 3; Jer. 24:1 [b] 2 Kin. 24:16; Jer. 52:28 [c] 1 Sam. 13:19 [d] 2 Kin. 25:12 [1] *carried away into captivity*
24:15 [a] 2 Chr. 36:10; Esth. 2:6; Jer. 22:24–28; Ezek. 17:12
24:16 [a] Jer. 52:28 [1] *fit*
24:17 [a] Jer. 37:1 [b] 1 Chr. 3:15; 2 Chr. 36:10 [c] 2 Chr. 36:4 [1] Jehoiachin's uncle
24:18 [a] 2 Chr. 36:11; Jer. 52:1 [b] 2 Kin. 23:31
24:19 [a] 2 Chr. 36:12
24:20 [a] 2 Chr. 36:13; Ezek. 17:15 [1] *because of*
25:1 [a] 2 Chr. 36:17; Jer. 6:6; 34:2; Ezek. 4:2; 24:1, 2; Hab. 1:6 [1] *encamped* [2] *siege wall*
25:3 [a] 2 Kin. 6:24, 25; Is. 3:1; Jer. 39:2; Lam. 4:9, 10
25:4 [a] Jer. 39:2 [b] Jer. 39:4–7; Ezek. 12:12 [1] *broken through* [2] Heb. *Arabah,* the Jordan Valley
25:6 [a] 2 Kin. 23:33; Jer. 52:9 [1] *pronounced*
25:7 [a] Jer. 39:7; Ezek. 17:16 [1] *blinded*
25:8 [a] Jer. 52:12 [b] 2 Kin. 24:12 [c] Jer. 39:9

a servant of the king of Babylon, unto Jerusalem:

9 ᵃAnd he burnt the house of the LORD, ᵇand the king's house, and all the houses of Jerusalem, and every great *man's* house ᶜburnt he with fire.

10 And all the army of the Chaldees, that *were with* the captain of the guard, ᵃbrake down the walls of Jerusalem round about.

11 ᵃNow the rest of the people *that were* left in the city, and the ¹fugitives that fell away to the king of Babylon, with the remnant of the multitude, did Nebuzar-adan the captain of the guard carry away.

12 But the captain of the guard ᵃleft of the poor of the land *to be* vinedressers and husbandmen.

13 And ᵃthe ᵇpillars of brass that *were* in the house of the LORD, and ᶜthe bases, and ᵈthe brasen sea that *was* in the house of the LORD, did the Chaldees break in pieces, and ᵉcarried the brass of them to Babylon.

14 And ᵃthe pots, and the shovels, and the snuffers, and the spoons, and all the vessels of brass wherewith they ministered, took they away.

15 And the firepans, and the bowls, ¹*and* such things as *were* of gold, *in* gold, and of silver, *in* silver, the captain of the guard took away.

16 The two pillars, one sea, and the bases which Solomon had made for the house of the LORD; ᵃthe brass of all these vessels was ¹without weight.

17 ᵃThe height of the one pillar *was* ¹eighteen cubits, and the chapiter upon it *was* brass: and the height of the chapiter three cubits; and the wreathen work, and pomegranates upon the chapiter round about, all of brass: and like unto these had the second pillar with wreathen work.

18 ᵃAnd the captain of the guard took ᵇSeraiah the chief priest, and ᶜZephaniah the second priest, and the three ¹keepers of the door:

19 And out of the city he took an officer that was set over the men of war, and ᵃfive men of them that were ¹in the king's presence, which were found in the city, and the ²principal scribe of the host, which mustered the people of the land, and threescore men of the people of the land *that were* found in the city:

20 And Nebuzar-adan captain of the guard took these, and brought them to the king of Babylon to Riblah:

21 And the king of Babylon smote them, and slew them at Riblah in the land of Hamath. ᵃSo Judah was carried away out of their land.

22 ᵃAnd *as for* the people that remained in the land of Judah, whom Nebuchadnezzar king of Babylon had left, even over them he made Gedaliah the son of ᵇAhikam, the son of Shaphan, ruler.

23 And when all the ᵃcaptains of the armies, they and their men, heard that the king of Babylon had made Gedaliah governor, there came to Gedaliah to Mizpah, even Ishmael the son of Nethaniah, and Johanan the son of Careah, and Seraiah the son of Tanhumeth the Netophathite, and ¹Jaazaniah the son of a Maachathite, they and their men.

24 And Gedaliah sware to them, and to their men, and said unto them, Fear not to be the servants of the Chaldees: dwell in the land, and serve the king of Babylon; and it shall be well with you.

25 But ᵃit came to pass in the seventh month, that Ishmael the son of Nethaniah, the son of Elishama, of the seed royal, came, and ten men with him, and ¹smote Gedaliah, that he died, and the Jews and the Chaldees that were with him at Mizpah.

26 And all the people, both small and great, and the captains of the armies, arose, ᵃand came to Egypt: for they were afraid of the Chaldees.

27 ᵃAnd it came to pass in the seven and thirtieth year of the captivity of Jehoiachin king of Judah, in the twelfth month, on the seven and twentieth *day* of the month, *that* ¹Evil-merodach king of Babylon in the year that he began to reign ᵇdid ²lift up the head of Jehoiachin king of Judah out of prison;

28 And he spake kindly to him, and set his throne above the throne of the kings that *were* with him in Babylon;

29 And changed his prison garments: and he did ᵃeat ᵇbread continually before him all the days of his life.

30 And his ¹allowance *was* a ²continual allowance given him of the king, a daily rate for every day, all the days of his life.

## Cross references

25:9 ᵃ 2 Kin. 25:13; 2 Chr. 36:19; Ps. 79:1; Jer. 7:14 ᵇ Jer. 39:8 ᶜ Jer. 17:27

25:10 ᵃ 2 Kin. 14:13; Neh. 1:3

25:11 ᵃ Is. 1:9; Jer. 5:19; 39:9 ¹ defectors who had deserted

25:12 ᵃ 2 Kin. 24:14; Jer. 39:10; 40:7; 52:16

25:13 ᵃ Jer. 52:17 ᵇ 1 Kin. 7:15 ᶜ 1 Kin. 7:27 ᵈ 1 Kin. 7:23 ᵉ 2 Kin. 20:17; Jer. 27:19–22

25:14 ᵃ Ex. 27:3; 1 Kin. 7:45

25:15 ¹ things made of solid gold and solid silver

25:16 ᵃ 1 Kin. 7:47 ¹ beyond measure

25:17 ᵃ 1 Kin. 7:15–22; Jer. 52:21 ¹ About 27 feet

25:18 ᵃ Jer. 39:9–13; 52:12–16, 24 ᵇ 1 Chr. 6:14; Ezra 7:1 ᶜ Jer. 21:1; 29:25, 29 ¹ doorkeepers

25:19 ᵃ Esth. 1:14; Jer. 52:25 ¹ the king's close associates ² scribe of the captain of the army

25:21 ᵃ Lev. 26:33; Deut. 28:36, 64; 2 Kin. 23:27

25:22 ᵃ 2 Kin. 22:12 ᵇ Is. 1:9; Jer. 40:5

25:23 ᵃ Jer. 40:7–9 ¹ Jezaniah, Jer. 40:8

25:25 ᵃ Jer. 41:1–3 ¹ struck

25:26 ᵃ 2 Kin. 19:31; Jer. 43:4–7

25:27 ᵃ 2 Kin. 24:12, 15; Jer. 52:31–34 ᵇ Gen. 40:13, 20 ¹ Lit. The Man of Marduk ² released

25:29 ᵃ 2 Sam. 9:7 ¹ food

25:30 ¹ provisions ² regular ration

# THE FIRST BOOK OF THE
# CHRONICLES

The books of First and Second Chronicles cover the same period of Jewish history described in Second Samuel through Second Kings, but the perspective is different. These books are no mere repetition of the same material, but rather form a divine editorial on the history of God's people. While Second Samuel and First and Second Kings give a political history of Israel and Judah, First and Second Chronicles present a religious history of the Davidic dynasty of Judah. The former are written from a prophetic and moral viewpoint, and the latter from a priestly and spiritual perspective. The Book of First Chronicles begins with the royal line of David and then traces the spiritual significance of David's righteous reign.

The books of First and Second Chronicles were originally one continuous work in the Hebrew. The title was *Dibere Hayyamim*, meaning "The Words [accounts, events] of the Days." The equivalent meaning today would be "The Events of the Times." Chronicles was divided into two parts in the third-century B.C. Greek translation of the Hebrew Bible (the Septuagint). At that time it was given the name *Paraleipomenon*, "Of Things Omitted," referring to the things omitted from Samuel and Kings. Some copies add the phrase, *Basileon Iouda*, "Concerning the Kings of Judah." The first book of Chronicles was called *Paraleipomenon Primus*, "The First Book of Things Omitted." The name "Chronicles" comes from Jerome in his Latin Vulgate Bible (A.D. 385–405): *Chronicorum Liber*. He meant his title in the sense of the "Chronicles of the Whole of Sacred History."

## CHAPTER 1

ADAM,[a] [b]Sheth,[1] Enosh,

2 [1]Kenan, [a]Mahalaleel, Jered,

3 [1]Henoch, Methuselah, Lamech,

4 [a]Noah, Shem, Ham, and Japheth.

5 [a]The sons of Japheth; Gomer, and Magog, and Madai, and Javan, and Tubal, and Meshech, and Tiras.

6 And the sons of Gomer; Ashchenaz, and Riphath, and Togarmah.

7 And the sons of Javan; Elishah, and [1]Tarshish, Kittim, and Dodanim.

8 [a]The sons of Ham; Cush, and Mizraim, Put, and Canaan.

9 And the sons of Cush; Seba, and Havilah, and [1]Sabta, and [2]Raamah, and Sabtecha. And the sons of Raamah; Sheba, and Dedan.

10 And Cush [a]begat Nimrod: he began to be [1]mighty upon the earth.

11 And Mizraim begat Ludim, and Anamim, and Lehabim, and Naphtuhim,

12 And Pathrusim, and Casluhim, (of whom came the Philistines,) and [a]Caphthorim.

13 And [a]Canaan begat Zidon his firstborn, and Heth,

14 The Jebusite also, and the Amorite, and the Girgashite,

15 And the Hivite, and the Arkite, and the Sinite,

16 And the Arvadite, and the Zemarite, and the Hamathite.

17 The sons of [a]Shem; Elam, and Asshur, and [b]Arphaxad, and Lud, and Aram, and Uz, and Hul, and Gether, and [1]Meshech.

18 And Arphaxad begat Shelah, and Shelah begat Eber.

19 And unto Eber were born two sons: the name of the one *was* [1]Peleg; because in his days the [2]earth was divided: and his brother's name *was* Joktan.

20 And [a]Joktan begat Almodad, and Sheleph, and Hazarmaveth, and Jerah,

21 Hadoram also, and Uzal, and Diklah,

22 And [1]Ebal, and Abimael, and Sheba,

23 And Ophir, and Havilah, and Jobab. All these *were* the sons of Joktan.

24 [a]Shem, Arphaxad, Shelah,

25 [a]Eber, Peleg, Reu,

26 Serug, Nahor, Terah,

27 [a]Abram; the same *is* Abraham.

28 [a]The sons of Abraham; [b]Isaac, and [c]Ishmael.

29 These *are* their generations: The [a]firstborn of Ishmael, Nebaioth; then Kedar, and Adbeel, and Mibsam,

30 Mishma, and Dumah, Massa, [1]Hadad, and Tema,

31 Jetur, Naphish, and Kedemah. These are the sons of Ishmael.

32 Now [a]the sons of Keturah, Abraham's concubine: she bare Zimran, and Jokshan, and Medan, and Midian, and Ishbak, and Shuah. And the sons of Jokshan; Sheba, and Dedan.

33 And the sons of Midian; Ephah, and Epher, and Henoch, and Abida, and Eldaah. All these *are* the sons of Keturah.

34 And [a]Abraham begat Isaac. [b]The sons of Isaac; Esau and Israel.

---

1:1 [a] Gen. 1:27; 2:7; 5:1, 2, 5  [b] Gen. 4:25, 26; 5:3–9  [1] *Seth*, Gen. 4:25
1:2 [a] Luke 3:37  [1] *Cainan*, Gen. 5:9
1:3 [1] *Enoch*, Gen. 4:17
1:4 [a] Gen. 5:28–10:1
1:5 [a] Gen. 10:2–4
1:7 [1] Heb. *Tarshishah*
1:8 [a] Gen. 10:6
1:9 [1] *Sabtah*, Gen. 10:7  [2] Heb. *Raama*
1:10 [a] Gen. 10:8–10, 13  [1] *a mighty one*
1:12 [a] Deut. 2:23
1:13 [a] Gen. 9:18, 25–27; 10:15
1:17 [a] Gen. 10:22–29; 11:10  [b] Luke 3:36  [1] *Mash*, Gen. 10:23
1:19 [1] Lit. *Division*  [2] *land*
1:20 [a] Gen. 10:26
1:22 [1] *Obal*, Gen. 10:28
1:24 [a] Gen. 11:10–26; Luke 3:34–36
1:25 [a] Gen. 11:15
1:27 [a] Gen. 17:5
1:28 [a] Gen. 21:2, 3  [b] Gen. 21:2  [c] Gen. 16:11, 15
1:29 [a] Gen. 25:13–16
1:30 [1] *Hadar*, Gen. 25:15
1:32 [d] Gen. 25:1–4  1:34 [a] Gen. 21:2  [b] Gen. 25:9, 25, 26, 29; 32:28

362

35 The sons of ªEsau; Eliphaz, Reuel, and Jeush, and Jaalam, and Korah.

36 The sons of Eliphaz; Teman, and Omar, ¹Zephi, and Gatam, Kenaz, and ªTimna, and Amalek.

37 The sons of Reuel; Nahath, Zerah, Shammah, and Mizzah.

38 And ªthe sons of Seir; Lotan, and Shobal, and Zibeon, and Anah, and Dishon, and Ezar, and Dishan.

39 And the sons of Lotan; Hori, and ¹Homam: and Timna *was* Lotan's sister.

40 The sons of Shobal; ¹Alian, and Manahath, and Ebal, ²Shephi, and Onam. And the sons of Zibeon; ³Aiah, and Anah.

41 The sons of Anah; ªDishon. And the sons of Dishon; ¹Amram, and Eshban, and Ithran, and Cheran.

42 The sons of Ezer; Bilhan, and Zavan, *and* ¹Jakan. The sons of Dishan; Uz, and Aran.

43 Now these *are* the ªkings that reigned in the land of Edom before *any* king reigned over the children of Israel; Bela the son of Beor: and the name of his city *was* Dinhabah.

44 And when Bela was dead, Jobab the son of Zerah of Bozrah reigned in his stead.

45 And when Jobab was dead, Husham of the land of the Temanites reigned in his ¹stead.

46 And when Husham was dead, Hadad the son of Bedad, which ¹smote Midian in the field of Moab, reigned in his stead: and the name of his city *was* Avith.

47 And when Hadad was dead, Samlah of Masrekah reigned in his stead.

48 ªAnd when Samlah was dead, Shaul of Rehoboth by the river reigned in his stead.

49 And when Shaul was dead, Baalhanan the son of Achbor reigned in his stead.

50 And when Baal-hanan was dead, ¹Hadad reigned in his stead: and the name of his city *was* ²Pai; and his wife's name *was* Mehetabel, the daughter of Matred, the daughter of Mezahab.

51 Hadad died also. And the dukes of Edom were; duke Timnah, duke ¹Aliah, duke Jetheth,

52 Duke Aholibamah, duke Elah, duke Pinon,

53 Duke Kenaz, duke Teman, duke Mibzar,

54 Duke Magdiel, duke Iram. These *are* the dukes of Edom.

## CHAPTER 2

THESE *are* the ªsons of ¹Israel; ᵇReuben, Simeon, Levi, and Judah, Issachar, and Zebulun,

2 Dan, Joseph, and Benjamin, Naphtali, Gad, and Asher.

3 The sons of ªJudah; Er, and Onan, and Shelah: *which* three were born unto him of the daughter of ᵇShua the Canaanitess. And ᶜEr, the firstborn of Judah, was evil in the sight of the LORD; and he slew him.

4 And ªTamar his daughter in law ᵇbare him Pharez and Zerah. All the sons of Judah *were* five.

5 The sons of ªPharez; Hezron, and Hamul.

6 And the sons of Zerah; ¹Zimri, ªand Ethan, and Heman, and Calcol, and ²Dara: five of them in all.

7 And the sons of ªCarmi; ¹Achar, the troubler of Israel, who transgressed in the thing ᵇaccursed.²

8 And the sons of Ethan; Azariah.

9 The sons also of Hezron, that were born unto him; Jerahmeel, and ¹Ram, and ²Chelubai.

10 And Ram ªbegat Amminadab; and Amminadab begat Nahshon, ᵇprince of the children of Judah;

11 And Nahshon begat ¹Salma, and Salma begat Boaz,

12 And Boaz begat Obed, and Obed begat Jesse,

13 ªAnd Jesse begat his firstborn Eliab, and Abinadab the second, and ¹Shimma the third,

14 Nethaneel the fourth, Raddai the fifth,

15 Ozem the sixth, David the ªseventh:

16 Whose sisters *were* Zeruiah, and Abigail. ªAnd the sons of Zeruiah; Abishai, and Joab, and Asahel, three.

17 And Abigail bare Amasa: and the father of Amasa *was* ¹Jether the Ishmeelite.

18 And Caleb the son of Hezron begat *children* of Azubah *his* wife, and of Jerioth: her sons *are* these; Jesher, and Shobab, and Ardon.

19 And when Azubah was dead, Caleb ¹took unto him ªEphrath,² which bare him Hur.

20 And Hur begat Uri, and Uri begat ªBezaleel.

21 And afterward Hezron went in to the daughter of ªMachir the father of Gilead, whom he married when he *was* threescore years old; and she bare him Segub.

22 And Segub begat ªJair, who had three and twenty cities in the land of Gilead.

23 ªAnd he took Geshur, and Aram, with the towns of Jair, from them, with Kenath, and the towns thereof, *even* threescore cities. All these *belonged to* the sons of Machir the father of Gilead.

24 And after that Hezron was dead in Caleb-ephratah, then Abiah Hezron's wife bare him ªAshur the father of Tekoa.

1:35 ª Gen. 36:10–19
1:36 ª Gen. 36:12 ¹ Zepho, Gen. 36:11
1:38 ª Gen. 36:20–28
1:39 ¹ Hemam, Gen. 36:22
1:40 ¹ Alvan, Gen. 36:23 ² Shepho, Gen. 36:23 ³ Ajah, Gen. 36:24
1:41 ª Gen. 36:25 ¹ Hemdan, Gen. 36:26
1:42 ¹ Akan, Gen. 36:27
1:43 ª Gen. 36:31–43
1:45 ¹ place
1:46 ¹ attacked
1:48 ª Gen. 36:37
1:50 ¹ Hadar, Gen. 36:39 ² Pau, Gen. 36:39
1:51 ¹ Alvah, Gen. 36:40
2:1 ª Gen. 29:32–35; 35:23, 26; 46:8–27 ᵇ Gen. 29:32; 35:22 ¹ Jacob, Gen. 32:28
2:3 ª Gen. 38:3–5; 46:12; Num. 26:19 ᵇ Gen. 38:2 ᶜ Gen. 38:7
2:4 ª Gen. 38:6 ᵇ Matt. 1:3
2:5 ª Gen. 46:12; Ruth 4:18
2:6 ª 1 Kin. 4:31 ¹ Zabdi, Josh. 7:1 ² Darda, 1 Kin. 4:31
2:7 ª 1 Chr. 4:1 ᵇ Josh. 6:18 ¹ Achan, Josh. 7:1 ² banned
2:9 ¹ Aram, Matt. 1:3, 4 ² Caleb, 1 Chr. 2:18, 42
2:10 ª Ruth 4:19–22; Matt. 1:4 ᵇ Num. 1:7; 2:3
2:11 ¹ Salmon, Ruth 4:21; Luke 3:32
2:13 ª 1 Sam. 16:6 ¹ Shammah, 1 Sam. 16:9
2:15 ª 1 Sam. 16:10, 11; 17:12
2:16 ª 2 Sam. 2:18
2:17 ¹ Ithra an Israelite, 2 Sam. 17:25
2:19 ª 1 Chr. 2:50 ¹ married ² Ephrath, 1 Chr. 2:50
2:20 ª Ex. 31:2; 38:22
2:21 ª Num. 27:1; Judg. 5:14; 1 Chr. 7:14
2:22 ª Judg. 10:3  2:23 ª Num. 32:41; Deut. 3:14; Josh. 13:30  2:24 ª 1 Chr. 4:5

25 And the sons of Jerahmeel the firstborn of Hezron were, Ram the firstborn, and Bunah, and Oren, and Ozem, *and* Ahijah.

26 Jerahmeel had also another wife, whose name *was* Atarah; she *was* the mother of Onam.

27 And the sons of Ram the firstborn of Jerahmeel were, Maaz, and Jamin, and Eker.

28 And the sons of Onam were, Shammai, and Jada. And the sons of Shammai; Nadab, and Abishur.

29 And the name of the wife of Abishur *was* Abihail, and she bare him Ahban, and Molid.

30 And the sons of Nadab; Seled, and Appaim: but Seled died without children.

31 And the sons of Appaim; Ishi. And the sons of Ishi; Sheshan. And [a]the children of Sheshan; Ahlai.

32 And the sons of Jada the brother of Shammai; Jether, and Jonathan: and Jether died without children.

33 And the sons of Jonathan; Peleth, and Zaza. These were the sons of Jerahmeel.

34 Now Sheshan had no sons, but daughters. And Sheshan had a servant, an Egyptian, whose name *was* Jarha.

35 And Sheshan gave his daughter to Jarha his servant to wife; and she bare him Attai.

36 And Attai begat Nathan, and Nathan begat [a]Zabad,

37 And Zabad begat Ephlal, and Ephlal begat [a]Obed,

38 And Obed begat Jehu, and Jehu begat Azariah,

39 And Azariah begat Helez, and Helez begat Eleasah,

40 And Eleasah begat Sisamai, and Sisamai begat Shallum,

41 And Shallum begat Jekamiah, and Jekamiah begat Elishama.

42 Now the sons of Caleb the brother of Jerahmeel *were*, Mesha his firstborn, which *was* the father of Ziph; and the sons of Mareshah the father of Hebron.

43 And the sons of Hebron; Korah, and Tappuah, and Rekem, and Shema.

44 And Shema begat Raham, the father of Jorkoam: and Rekem begat Shammai.

45 And the son of Shammai *was* Maon: and Maon *was* the father of Beth-zur.

46 And Ephah, Caleb's concubine, bare Haran, and Moza, and Gazez: and Haran begat Gazez.

47 And the sons of Jahdai; Regem, and Jotham, and Gesham, and Pelet, and Ephah, and Shaaph.

48 Maachah, Caleb's concubine, bare Sheber, and Tirhanah.

49 She bare also Shaaph the father of Madmannah, Sheva the father of Machbenah, and the father of Gibea: and the daughter of Caleb *was* [a]Achsa.

50 And These were the sons of Caleb the son of [a]Hur, the firstborn of [1]Ephratah; Shobal the father of [b]Kirjathjearim,

51 Salma the father of Beth-lehem, Hareph the father of Beth-gader.

52 And Shobal the father of Kirjathjearim had sons; [1]Haroeh, *and* half of the [2]Manahethites.

53 And the families of Kirjathjearim; the Ithrites, and the Puhites, and the Shumathites, and the Mishraites; of them came the Zareathites, and the Eshtaulites.

54 The sons of Salma; Beth-lehem, and the Netophathites, [1]Ataroth, the house of Joab, and half of the Manahethites, the Zorites.

55 And the families of the scribes which dwelt at Jabez; the Tirathites, the Shimeathites, *and* Suchathites. These *are* the [a]Kenites that came of Hemath, the father of the house of [b]Rechab.

## CHAPTER 3

Now these were the sons of David, which were born unto him in Hebron; the firstborn [a]Amnon, of [b]Ahinoam the [c]Jezreelitess; the second [1]Daniel, of [d]Abigail the Carmelitess:

2 The third, [a]Absalom the son of Maachah the daughter of Talmai king of Geshur: the fourth, [b]Adonijah the son of Haggith:

3 The fifth, Shephatiah of Abital: the sixth, Ithream by [a]Eglah his wife.

4 *These* six were born unto him in Hebron; and [a]there he reigned seven years and six months: and [b]in Jerusalem he reigned thirty and three years.

5 [a]And these were born unto him in Jerusalem; [1]Shimea, and Shobab, and Nathan, and [b]Solomon, four, of [2]Bath-shua the daughter of [3]Ammiel:

6 Ibhar also, and [1]Elishama, and [2]Eliphelet,

7 And Nogah, and Nepheg, and Japhia,

8 And Elishama, and [1]Eliada, and Eliphelet, [a]nine.

9 *These were* all the sons of David, beside the sons of the concubines, and [a]Tamar their sister.

10 And Solomon's son *was* [a]Rehoboam, [1]Abia his son, Asa his son, Jehoshaphat his son,

11 [1]Joram his son, [2]Ahaziah his son, [3]Joash his son,

12 Amaziah his son, [1]Azariah his son, Jotham his son,

13 Ahaz his son, Hezekiah his son, Manasseh his son,

14 Amon his son, Josiah his son.

---

**Center reference column:**

2:31 [a] 1 Chr. 2:34, 35
2:36 [a] 1 Chr. 11:41
2:37 [a] 2 Chr. 23:1

2:49 [a] Josh. 15:17
2:50 [a] 1 Chr. 4:4
[b] Josh. 9:17; 18:14
[1] Ephrath, 1 Chr. 2:19
2:52 [1] Reaiah, 1 Chr. 4:2 [2] Heb. Manuhoth
2:54 [1] Or Atrothbethjoab
2:55 [a] Judg. 1:16
[b] Jer. 35:2
3:1 [a] 2 Sam. 3:2–5
[b] 1 Sam. 25:43
[c] Josh. 15:56
[d] 1 Sam. 25:39–42
[1] Chileab, 2 Sam. 3:3
3:2 [a] 2 Sam. 13:37; 15:1 [b] 1 Kin. 1:5
3:3 [a] 2 Sam. 3:5
3:4 [a] 2 Sam. 2:11
[b] 2 Sam. 5:5
3:5 [a] 1 Chr. 14:4–7
[b] 2 Sam. 12:24, 25
[1] Shammua, 1 Chr. 14:4 and 2 Sam. 5:14 [2] Bathsheba, 2 Sam. 11:3
[3] Eliam, 2 Sam. 11:3
3:6 [1] Elishua, 1 Chr. 14:5 and 2 Sam. 5:15 [2] Elpalet, 1 Chr. 14:5
3:8 [a] 2 Sam. 5:14–16 [1] Beeliada, 1 Chr. 14:7
3:9 [a] 2 Sam. 13:1
3:10 [a] 1 Kin. 11:43
[1] Abijam, 1 Kin. 15:1
3:11 [1] Jehoram, 2 Kin. 1:17; 8:16 [2] Jehoahaz, 2 Chr. 21:17 [3] Jehoash, 2 Kin. 12:1
3:12 [1] Uzziah, Is. 6:1

15 And the sons of Josiah *were,* the firstborn Johanan, the second [1]Jehoiakim, the third [2]Zedekiah, the fourth Shallum.

16 And the sons of [a]Jehoiakim: [1]Jeconiah his son, [2]Zedekiah his son.

17 And the sons of [1]Jeconiah; [2]Assir, [3]Salathiel [a]his son,

18 Malchiram also, and Pedaiah, and Shenazar, Jecamiah, Hoshama, and Nedabiah.

19 And the sons of Pedaiah *were,* Zerubbabel, and Shimei: and the sons of Zerubbabel; Meshullam, and Hananiah, and Shelomith their sister:

20 And Hashubah, and Ohel, and Berechiah, and Hasadiah, Jushab-hesed, five.

21 And the sons of Hananiah; Pelatiah, and Jesaiah: the sons of Rephaiah, the sons of Arnan, the sons of Obadiah, the sons of Shechaniah.

22 And the sons of Shechaniah; Shemaiah: and the sons of Shemaiah; [a]Hattush, and Igeal, and Bariah, and Neariah, and Shaphat, six.

23 And the sons of Neariah; Elioenai, and Hezekiah, and Azrikam, three.

24 And the sons of Elioenai *were,* Hodaiah, and Eliashib, and Pelaiah, and Akkub, and Johanan, and Dalaiah, and Anani, seven.

## CHAPTER 4

THE sons of Judah; [a]Pharez, Hezron, and [1]Carmi, and Hur, and Shobal.

2 And [1]Reaiah the son of Shobal begat Jahath; and Jahath begat Ahumai, and Lahad. These *are* the families of the Zorathites.

3 And these *were of* the father of Etam; Jezreel, and Ishma, and Idbash: and the name of their sister *was* Hazelelponi.

4 And Penuel the father of Gedor, and Ezer the father of Hushah. These *are* the sons of [a]Hur, the firstborn of Ephratah, the father of Beth-lehem.

5 And [a]Ashur the father of Tekoa had two wives, Helah and Naarah.

6 And Naarah bare him Ahuzam, and Hepher, and Temeni, and Haahashtari. These *were* the sons of Naarah.

7 And the sons of Helah *were,* Zereth, and Jezoar, and Ethnan.

8 And Coz begat Anub, and Zobebah, and the families of Aharhel the son of Harum.

9 And Jabez was [a]more honourable than his brethren: and his mother called his name [1]Jabez, saying, Because I bare him with sorrow.

10 And Jabez called on the God of Israel, saying, Oh that thou wouldest bless me indeed, and enlarge my

[center column references]
3:15 [1] *Eliakim,* 2 Kin. 23:34
[2] *Mattaniah,* 2 Kin. 24:17
3:16 [a] Matt. 1:11 [1] *Jehoiachin,* 2 Kin. 24:8 or *Coniah, Jer.* 22:24
[2] *Mattaniah,* 2 Kin. 24:17
3:17 [a] Matt. 1:12 [1] *Jehoiachin,* 2 Kin. 24:8 or *Coniah, Jer.* 22:24 [2] *Or the captive or prisoner* [3] *Shealtiel, Ezra* 3:2
3:22 [a] Ezra 8:2
4:1 [a] Gen. 38:29; 46:12 [1] *Chelubai,* 1 Chr. 2:9 or *Caleb,* 1 Chr. 2:18
4:2 [1] *Haroeh,* 1 Chr. 2:52
4:4 [a] 1 Chr. 2:50
4:5 [a] 1 Chr. 2:24
4:9 [a] Gen. 34:19 [1] Lit. *He Will Cause Pain, Sorrowful*
4:10 [1] *border* [2] *cause pain*
4:11 [a] Gen. 38:1–5
4:12 [1] Lit. *City of Nahash*
4:13 [a] Josh. 15:17; Judg. 3:9, 11
4:14 [a] Neh. 11:35 [1] Lit. *Valley of Craftsmen;* Heb. *Ge Harashim*
4:15 [a] Josh. 14:6, 14; 15:13, 17; 1 Chr. 6:56 [1] *Or Uknaz*
4:17 [1] *Mered's wife*
4:18 [1] Lit. *the Judean*
4:19 [a] 2 Kin. 25:23
4:21 [a] Gen. 38:11, 14 [b] Gen. 38:1–5; 46:12 [1] *the linen workers*
4:22 [1] *ancient records*
4:24 [a] Num. 26:12–14 [1] *Jemuel, Gen.* 46:10 [2] *Jachin, Num.* 26:12 [3] *Zohar, Gen.* 46:10; Ex. 6:15
4:27 [a] Num. 2:9

[1]coast, and that thine hand might be with me, and that thou wouldest keep *me* from evil, that it may not [2]grieve me! And God granted him that which he requested.

11 And Chelub the brother of [a]Shuah begat Mehir, which *was* the father of Eshton.

12 And Eshton begat Beth-rapha, and Paseah, and Tehinnah the father of [1]Ir-nahash. These *are* the men of Rechah.

13 And the sons of Kenaz; [a]Othniel, and Seraiah: and the sons of Othniel; Hathath.

14 And Meonothai begat Ophrah: and Seraiah begat Joab, the father of [a]the [1]valley of Charashim; for they were craftsmen.

15 And the sons of [a]Caleb the son of Jephunneh; Iru, Elah, and Naam: and the sons of Elah, even [1]Kenaz.

16 And the sons of Jehaleleel; Ziph, and Ziphah, Tiria, and Asareel.

17 And the sons of Ezra *were,* Jether, and Mered, and Epher, and Jalon: and [1]she bare Miriam, and Shammai, and Ishbah the father of Eshtemoa.

18 And his wife [1]Jehudijah bare Jered the father of Gedor, and Heber the father of Socho, and Jekuthiel the father of Zanoah. And these *are* the sons of Bithiah the daughter of Pharaoh, which Mered took.

19 And the sons of *his* wife Hodiah the sister of Naham, the father of Keilah the Garmite, and Eshtemoa the [a]Maachathite.

20 And the sons of Shimon *were,* Amnon, and Rinnah, Ben-hanan, and Tilon. And the sons of Ishi *were,* Zoheth, and Ben-zoheth.

21 The sons of [a]Shelah [b]the son of Judah *were,* Er the father of Lecah, and Laadah the father of Mareshah, and the families of the house of [1]them that wrought fine linen, of the house of Ashbea,

22 And Jokim, and the men of Chozeba, and Joash, and Saraph, who had the dominion in Moab, and Jashubilehem. And *these are* [1]ancient things.

23 These *were* the potters, and those that dwelt among plants and hedges: there they dwelt with the king for his work.

24 The [a]sons of Simeon *were,* [1]Nemuel, and Jamin, [2]Jarib, [3]Zerah, *and* Shaul:

25 Shallum his son, Mibsam his son, Mishma his son.

26 And the sons of Mishma; Hamuel his son, Zacchur his son, Shimei his son.

27 And Shimei had sixteen sons and six daughters; but his brethren had not many children, [a]neither did all their family multiply, like to the children of Judah.

28 And they dwelt at Beer-sheba, and Moladah, and Hazar-shual,

29 And at ¹Bilhah, and at Ezem, and at ²Tolad,

30 And at Bethuel, and at Hormah, and at Ziklag,

31 And at Beth-marcaboth, and ¹Hazar-susim, and at Beth-birei, and at Shaaraim. These *were* their cities unto the reign of David.

32 And their villages *were*, ¹Etam, and Ain, Rimmon, and Tochen, and Ashan, five cities:

33 And all their villages that *were* round about the same cities, unto ¹Baal. These *were* their ²habitations, and their genealogy.

34 And Meshobab, and Jamlech, and Joshah the son of Amaziah,

35 And Joel, and Jehu the son of Josibiah, the son of Seraiah, the son of Asiel,

36 And Elioenai, and Jaakobah, and Jeshohaiah, and Asaiah, and Adiel, and Jesimiel, and Benaiah,

37 And Ziza the son of Shiphi, the son of Allon, the son of Jedaiah, the son of Shimri, the son of Shemaiah;

38 These mentioned by *their* names *were* ¹princes in their families: and the house of their fathers increased greatly.

39 And they went to the entrance of Gedor, *even* unto the east side of the valley, to seek pasture for their flocks.

40 And they found fat pasture and good, and the land *was* wide, and quiet, and peaceable; for ¹*they* of Ham had dwelt there of old.

41 And these written by name came in the days of Hezekiah king of Judah, and ªsmote¹ their tents, and the habitations that were found there, and ᵇdestroyed them utterly unto this day, and dwelt in their rooms: because *there was* pasture there for their flocks.

42 And *some* of them, *even* of the sons of Simeon, five hundred men, went to mount Seir, having for their captains Pelatiah, and Neariah, and Rephaiah, and Uzziel, the sons of Ishi.

43 And they ¹smote ªthe rest of the Amalekites that were escaped, and dwelt there unto this day.

### CHAPTER 5

Now the sons of Reuben the first-born of Israel, (for ªhe *was* the firstborn; but, forasmuch as he ᵇdefiled his father's bed, ᶜhis birthright was given unto the sons of Joseph the son of Israel: and the genealogy is not to be reckoned after the birthright.

2 For ªJudah prevailed above his brethren, and of him *came* the ᵇchief¹ ruler; but ²the birthright *was* Joseph's:)

4:29 ¹ *Balah,* Josh. 19:3 ² *Eltolad,* Josh. 19:4
4:31 ¹ *Hazarsusah,* Josh. 19:5
4:32 ¹ *Ether,* Josh. 19:7
4:33 ¹ *Baalathbeer,* Josh. 19:8 ² *places of dwelling*
4:38 ¹ *leaders*
4:40 ¹ *the Hamites*
4:41 ª 2 Kin. 18:8 ᵇ 2 Kin. 19:11 ¹ *attacked*
4:43 ª Ex. 17:14; 1 Sam. 15:8; 30:17 ¹ *defeated*
5:1 ª Gen. 29:32; 49:3 ᵇ Gen. 35:22; 49:4 ᶜ Gen. 48:15, 22
5:2 ª Gen. 49:8, 10; Ps. 60:7; 108:8 ᵇ Mic. 5:2; Matt. 2:6 ¹ *a leader* ² *the rights of the firstborn*
5:3 ª Gen. 46:9; Ex. 6:14; Num. 26:5
5:6 ª 2 Kin. 18:11 ¹ *Tiglath-pileser,* 2 Kin. 15:29
5:7 ª 1 Chr. 5:17
5:8 ª Num. 32:34; Josh. 12:2; 13:15, 16
5:9 ª Josh. 22:8, 9 ¹ *as far as the beginning of* ² *had increased*
5:10 ª Gen. 25:12 ¹ *land east of*
5:11 ª Num. 26:15–18 ᵇ Josh. 13:11, 24–28 ᶜ Deut. 3:10
5:16 ª 1 Chr. 27:29; Song 2:1; Is. 35:2; 65:10 ¹ *The Gadites* ² *open lands of* ³ *within*
5:17 ª 2 Kin. 15:5, 32 ᵇ 2 Kin. 14:16, 28
5:19 ª Gen. 25:15; 1 Chr. 1:31
5:20 ª [1 Chr. 5:22]

3 The sons, *I say*, of ªReuben the firstborn of Israel *were*, Hanoch, and Pallu, Hezron, and Carmi.

4 The sons of Joel; Shemaiah his son, Gog his son, Shimei his son,

5 Micah his son, Reaia his son, Baal his son,

6 Beerah his son, whom ¹Tilgath-pilneser king of Assyria ªcarried away *captive:* he *was* prince of the Reubenites.

7 And his brethren by their families, ªwhen the genealogy of their generations was reckoned, *were* the chief, Jeiel, and Zechariah,

8 And Bela the son of Azaz, the son of Shema, the son of Joel, who dwelt in ªAroer, even unto Nebo and Baal-meon:

9 And eastward he inhabited ¹unto the entering in of the wilderness from the river Euphrates: because their cattle ²were multiplied ªin the land of Gilead.

10 And in the days of Saul they made war ªwith the Hagarites, who fell by their hand: and they dwelt in their tents throughout all the ¹east *land* of Gilead.

11 And the ªchildren of Gad dwelt over against them, in the land of ᵇBashan unto ᶜSalcah:

12 Joel the chief, and Shapham the next, and Jaanai, and Shaphat in Bashan.

13 And their brethren of the house of their father's *were,* Michael, and Meshullam, and Sheba, and Jorai, and Jachan, and Zia, and Heber, seven.

14 These *are* the children of Abihail the son of Huri, the son of Jaroah, the son of Gilead, the son of Michael, the son of Jeshishai, the son of Jahdo, the son of Buz;

15 Ahi the son of Abdiel, the son of Guni, chief of the house of their fathers.

16 And ¹they dwelt in Gilead in Bashan, and in her towns, and in all the ²suburbs of ªSharon, ³upon their borders.

17 All these were reckoned by genealogies in the days of ªJotham king of Judah, and in the days of ᵇJeroboam king of Israel.

18 The sons of Reuben, and the Gadites, and half the tribe of Manasseh, of valiant men, men able to bear buckler and sword, and to shoot with bow, and skilful in war, *were* four and forty thousand seven hundred and three-score, that went out to the war.

19 And they made war with the Hagarites, with ªJetur, and Nephish, and Nodab.

20 And ªthey were helped against them, and the Hagarites were delivered into their hand, and all that *were*

with them: for they ᵇcried to God in the battle, and he ¹was intreated of them; because they ᶜput their trust in him.

21 And they took away their cattle; of their camels fifty thousand, and of sheep two hundred and fifty thousand, and of asses two thousand, and of men an hundred thousand.

22 For there fell down many slain, because the war ᵃ*was* of God. And they dwelt in their ¹steads until ᵇthe captivity.

23 And the children of the half tribe of Manasseh dwelt in the land: they increased from Bashan unto Baal-hermon and ᵃSenir, and unto mount Hermon.

24 And these *were* the heads of the house of their fathers, even Epher, and Ishi, and Eliel, and Azriel, and Jeremiah, and Hodaviah, and Jahdiel, mighty men of valour, famous men, *and* heads of the house of their fathers.

25 And they transgressed against the God of their fathers, and ¹went a ᵃwhoring after the gods of the people of the land, whom God destroyed before them.

26 And the God of Israel stirred up the spirit of ᵃPul king of Assyria, and the spirit of ᵇTilgath-pilneser¹ king of Assyria, and he carried them away, even the Reubenites, and the Gadites, and the half tribe of Manasseh, and brought them unto ᶜHalah, and Habor, and Hara, and to the river Gozan, unto this day.

### CHAPTER 6

THE sons of Levi; ᵃGershon,¹ Kohath, and Merari.

2 And the sons of Kohath; Amram, ᵃIzhar, and Hebron, and Uzziel.

3 And the children of Amram; Aaron, and Moses, and Miriam. The sons also of Aaron; ᵃNadab, and Abihu, Eleazar, and Ithamar.

4 Eleazar begat Phinehas, Phinehas begat Abishua,

5 And Abishua begat Bukki, and Bukki begat Uzzi,

6 And Uzzi begat Zerahiah, and Zerahiah begat Meraioth,

7 Meraioth begat Amariah, and Amariah begat Ahitub,

8 And ᵃAhitub begat ᵇZadok, and Zadok begat Ahimaaz,

9 And Ahimaaz begat Azariah, and Azariah begat Johanan,

10 And Johanan begat Azariah, (he *it is* ᵃthat ¹executed the priest's office in the ᵇtemple² that Solomon built in Jerusalem:)

11 And ᵃAzariah begat ᵇAmariah, and Amariah begat Ahitub,

12 And Ahitub begat Zadok, and Zadok begat ¹Shallum,

13 And Shallum begat Hilkiah, and Hilkiah begat Azariah,

14 And Azariah begat ᵃSeraiah, and Seraiah begat Jehozadak,

15 And Jehozadak went *into captivity*, ᵃwhen the LORD carried away Judah and Jerusalem by the hand of Nebuchadnezzar.

16 The sons of Levi; ᵃGershom,¹ Kohath, and Merari.

17 And these *be* the names of the sons of Gershom; Libni, and Shimei.

18 And the sons of Kohath *were*, Amram, and Izhar, and Hebron, and Uzziel.

19 The sons of Merari; Mahli, and Mushi. And these *are* the families of the Levites according to their fathers.

20 Of Gershom; Libni his son, Jahath his son, ᵃZimmah his son,

21 ¹Joah his son, ²Iddo his son, Zerah his son, ³Jeaterai his son.

22 The sons of Kohath; ¹Amminadab his son, ᵃKorah his son, Assir his son,

23 Elkanah his son, and Ebiasaph his son, and Assir his son,

24 Tahath his son, Uriel his son, Uzziah his son, and Shaul his son.

25 And the sons of Elkanah; ᵃAmasai, and Ahimoth.

26 *As for* Elkanah: the sons of Elkanah; ¹Zophai his son, and ²Nahath his son,

27 ¹Eliab his son, Jeroham his son, Elkanah his son.

28 And the sons of Samuel; ¹the firstborn ²Vashni, and Abiah.

29 The sons of Merari; Mahli, Libni his son, Shimei his son, Uzza his son,

30 Shimea his son, Haggiah his son, Asaiah his son.

31 And these *are* ᵃthey whom David ¹set over the service of song in the house of the LORD, ²after that the ᵇark had rest.

32 And they ministered before the dwelling place of the tabernacle of the congregation with singing, until Solomon had built the house of the LORD in Jerusalem: and *then* they ¹waited on their office according to their order.

33 And these *are* they that ¹waited with their children. Of the sons of the ᵃKohathites: Heman a singer, the son of Joel, the son of Shemuel,

34 The son of Elkanah, the son of Jeroham, the son of ¹Eliel, the son of ²Toah,

35 The son of ¹Zuph, the son of Elkanah, the son of Mahath, the son of Amasai,

36 The son of Elkanah, the son of Joel, the son of Azariah, the son of Zephaniah,

37 The son of Tahath, the son of Assir, the son of ᵃEbiasaph, the son of Korah,

5:20 ᵇ 2 Chr. 14:11–13  ᶜ Ps. 9:10; 20:7, 8; 22:4, 5 ¹ *heeded their prayers*

5:22 ᵃ [Josh. 23:10; 2 Chr. 32:8; Rom. 8:31] ᵇ 2 Kin. 15:29; 17:6 ¹ *places*

5:23 ᵃ Deut. 3:9

5:25 ᵃ 2 Kin. 17:7 ¹ *played the harlot after*

5:26 ᵃ 2 Kin. 15:19 ᵇ 2 Kin. 15:29 ᶜ 2 Kin. 17:6; 18:11 ¹ *Tiglath-pileser*, 2 Kin. 15:29

6:1 ᵃ Gen. 46:11; Ex. 6:16; Num. 26:57; 1 Chr. 23:6 ¹ *Gershom*, 1 Chr. 6:16

6:2 ᵃ 1 Chr. 6:18, 22

6:3 ᵃ Lev. 10:1, 2

6:8 ᵃ 2 Sam. 8:17 ᵇ 2 Sam. 15:27

6:10 ᵃ 2 Chr. 26:17, 18 ᵇ 1 Kin. 6:1; 2 Chr. 3:1 ¹ *ministered as priest* ² Lit. *house*

6:11 ᵃ Ezra 7:3 ᵇ 2 Chr. 19:11

6:12 ¹ *Meshullam*, 1 Chr. 9:11

6:14 ᵃ 2 Kin. 25:18–21; Neh. 11:11

6:15 ᵃ 2 Kin. 25:21

6:16 ᵃ Gen. 46:11; Ex. 6:16 ¹ *Gershon*, 1 Chr. 6:1

6:20 ᵃ 1 Chr. 6:42

6:21 ¹ *Ethan*, 1 Chr. 6:42 ² *Adaiah*, 1 Chr. 6:41 ³ *Ethni*, 1 Chr. 6:41

6:22 ᵃ Num. 16:1 ¹ *Izhar*, 1 Chr. 6:2, 18

6:25 ᵃ 1 Chr. 6:35, 36

6:26 ¹ *Zuph*, 1 Chr. 6:35; 1 Sam. 1:1 ² *Toah*, 1 Chr. 6:34

6:27 ¹ *Eliel*, 1 Chr. 6:34

6:28 ¹ LXX, Syr., Arab. *Joel*; 1 Chr. 6:33; 1 Sam. 8:2 ² Lit. *the second*

6:31 ᵃ 1 Chr. 15:16–22, 27; 16:4–6 ᵇ 2 Sam. 6:17; 1 Kin. 8:4; 1 Chr. 15:25–16:1 ¹ *appointed over* ² *after the ark came to rest*

6:32 ¹ *served in*

6:33 ᵃ Num. 26:57 ¹ *ministered with their sons*

6:34 ¹ *Elihu*, 1 Sam. 1:1

² *Tohu*, 1 Sam. 1:1   6:35 ¹ *Zophai*, 1 Chr.
6:37 ᵃ Ex. 6:24

38 The son of Izhar, the son of Kohath, the son of Levi, the son of Israel.

39 And his brother [a]Asaph, who stood on his right hand, *even* Asaph the son of Berachiah, the son of Shimea,

40 The son of Michael, the son of Baaseiah, the son of Malchiah,

41 The son of [a]Ethni, the son of Zerah, the son of Adaiah,

42 The son of Ethan, the son of Zimmah, the son of Shimei,

43 The son of Jahath, the son of Gershom, the son of Levi.

44 And their brethren the sons of Merari *stood* on the left hand: [1]Ethan the son of [2]Kishi, the son of Abdi, the son of Malluch,

45 The son of Hashabiah, the son of Amaziah, the son of Hilkiah,

46 The son of Amzi, the son of Bani, the son of Shamer,

47 The son of Mahli, the son of Mushi, the son of Merari, the son of Levi.

48 Their brethren also the Levites *were* appointed unto all [a]manner of service of the tabernacle of the house of God.

49 [a]But Aaron and his sons offered [b]upon the altar of the burnt offering, and [c]on the altar of incense, *and* were appointed for all the work of the *place* most holy, and to make an atonement for Israel, according to all that Moses the servant of God had commanded.

50 And these *are* the [a]sons of Aaron; Eleazar his son, Phinehas his son, Abishua his son,

51 Bukki his son, Uzzi his son, Zerahiah his son,

52 Meraioth his son, Amariah his son, Ahitub his son,

53 Zadok his son, Ahimaaz his son.

54 [a]Now these *are* their dwelling places throughout their castles in their [1]coasts, of the sons of Aaron, of the families of the Kohathites: for theirs was the lot.

55 [a]And they gave them Hebron in the land of Judah, and the suburbs thereof round about it.

56 [a]But the fields of the city, and the villages thereof, they gave to Caleb the son of Jephunneh.

57 And [a]to the sons of Aaron they gave the cities of Judah, *namely,* Hebron, *the city* of refuge, and Libnah with her suburbs, and Jattir, and Eshtemoa, with their suburbs,

58 And [1]Hilen with her suburbs, Debir with her suburbs,

59 And [1]Ashan with her suburbs, and Beth-shemesh with her suburbs:

60 And out of the tribe of Benjamin; Geba with her suburbs, and Alemeth with her suburbs, and Anathoth with

her suburbs. All their cities throughout their families *were* thirteen cities.

61 And unto the sons of Kohath, [a]which *were* left of the family of that tribe, *were cities given* out of the half tribe, *namely, out of* the half *tribe* of Manasseh, [b]by lot, ten cities.

62 And to the sons of Gershom throughout their families out of the tribe of Issachar, and out of the tribe of Asher, and out of the tribe of Naphtali, and out of the tribe of Manasseh in Bashan, thirteen cities.

63 Unto the sons of Merari *were given* by lot, throughout their families, out of the tribe of Reuben, and out of the tribe of Gad, and out of the tribe of Zebulun, [a]twelve cities.

64 And the children of Israel gave to the Levites *these* cities with their [1]suburbs.

65 And they gave by lot out of the tribe of the children of Judah, and out of the tribe of the children of Simeon, and out of the tribe of the children of Benjamin, these cities, which are called by *their* names.

66 And [a]*the residue* of the families of the sons of Kohath had cities of their [1]coasts out of the tribe of Ephraim.

67 [a]And they gave unto them, *of* the cities of refuge, Shechem in mount Ephraim with her suburbs; *they gave* also Gezer with her suburbs,

68 And [a]Jokmeam with her suburbs, and Beth-horon with her suburbs,

69 And Aijalon with her suburbs, and Gath-rimmon with her suburbs:

70 And out of the half tribe of Manasseh; Aner with her suburbs, and Bileam with her suburbs, for the family of the remnant of the sons of Kohath.

71 Unto the sons of Gershom *were given* out of the family of the half tribe of Manasseh, Golan in Bashan with her suburbs, and [1]Ashtaroth with her suburbs:

72 And out of the tribe of Issachar; [1]Kedesh with her suburbs, Daberath with her suburbs,

73 And Ramoth with her suburbs, and Anem with her suburbs:

74 And out of the tribe of Asher; Mashal with her suburbs, and Abdon with her suburbs,

75 And Hukok with her suburbs, and Rehob with her suburbs:

76 And out of the tribe of Naphtali; Kedesh in Galilee with her suburbs, and Hammon with her suburbs, and Kirjathaim with her suburbs.

77 Unto the rest of the children of Merari *were given* out of the tribe of Zebulun, [1]Rimmon with her suburbs, Tabor with her suburbs:

78 And on the other side Jordan by Jericho, on the east side of Jordan,

6:39 [a] 2 Chr. 5:12
6:41 [a] 1 Chr. 6:21
6:44 [1] *Jeduthun*, 1 Chr. 9:16; 25:1, 3, 6; 2 Chr. 35:15; Ps. 62:title [2] *Kushaiah*, 1 Chr. 15:17
6:48 [a] 1 Chr. 9:14–34
6:49 [a] Ex. 28:1; [Num. 18:1–8] [b] Lev. 1:8, 9 [c] Ex. 30:7
6:50 [a] 1 Chr. 6:4–8; Ezra 7:5
6:54 [1] Josh. 21 [1] *borders, territories*
6:55 [a] Josh. 14:13; 21:11, 12
6:56 [a] Josh. 14:13; 15:13
6:57 [a] Josh. 21:13, 19
6:58 [1] *Holon*, Josh. 21:15
6:59 [1] *Ain*, Josh. 21:16
6:60 [1] *Almon*, Josh. 21:18

6:61 [a] 1 Chr. 6:66–70 [b] Josh. 21:5
6:63 [a] Josh. 21:7, 34–40
6:64 [1] *open lands*
6:66 [a] 1 Chr.
6:61 [1] *borders, territories*
6:67 [a] Josh. 21:21
6:68 [a] Josh. 21:22
6:71 [1] *Beesh-terah*, Josh. 21:27
6:72 [1] *Kishon*, Josh. 21:28
6:77 [1] Heb. *Rimmono*, alternate of *Rimmon*; 1 Chr. 4:32

*were given them* out of the tribe of Reuben, Bezer in the wilderness with her suburbs, and Jahzah with her suburbs,

79 Kedemoth also with her suburbs, and Mephaath with her suburbs:

80 And out of the tribe of Gad; Ramoth in Gilead with her suburbs, and Mahanaim with her suburbs,

81 And Heshbon with her suburbs, and Jazer with her suburbs.

## CHAPTER 7

Now the sons of Issachar *were*, aTola, and ¹Puah, ²Jashub, and Shimrom, four.

2 And the sons of Tola; Uzzi, and Rephaiah, and Jeriel, and Jahmai, and Jibsam, and Shemuel, heads of their father's house, *to wit*, of Tola: they were ¹valiant men of might in their generations; awhose number *was* in the days of David two and twenty thousand and six hundred.

3 And the sons of Uzzi; Izrahiah: and the sons of Izrahiah; Michael, and Obadiah, and Joel, Ishiah, five: all of them chief men.

4 And with them, by their generations, after the house of their fathers, *were* bands of soldiers for war, six and thirty thousand *men:* for they had many wives and sons.

5 And their brethren among all the families of Issachar *were* ¹valiant men of might, reckoned in all by their genealogies fourscore and seven thousand.

6 *The sons* of aBenjamin; Bela, and Becher, and Jediael, three.

7 And the sons of Bela; Ezbon, and Uzzi, and Uzziel, and Jerimoth, and Iri, five; heads of the house of *their* fathers, mighty men of valour; and were reckoned by their genealogies twenty and two thousand and thirty and four.

8 And the sons of Becher; Zemira, and Joash, and Eliezer, and Elioenai, and Omri, and Jerimoth, and Abiah, and Anathoth, and Alameth. All these *are* the sons of Becher.

9 And the number of them, after their genealogy by their generations, heads of the house of their fathers, mighty men of valour, *was* twenty thousand and two hundred.

10 The sons also of Jediael; Bilhan: and the sons of Bilhan; Jeush, and Benjamin, and Ehud, and Chenaanah, and Zethan, and Tharshish, and Ahishahar.

11 All these the sons of Jediael, by the heads of their fathers, mighty men of valour, *were* seventeen thousand and two hundred *soldiers,* fit to go out for war *and* battle.

12 ¹Shuppim also, and ²Huppim, the children of ³Ir, *and* Hushim, the sons of ⁴Aher.

13 The asons of Naphtali; ¹Jahziel, and Guni, and Jezer, and ²Shallum, the sons of Bilhah.

14 The asons of Manasseh; ¹Ashriel, whom she bare: (*but* his concubine the Aramitess bare bMachir the father of Gilead:

15 And Machir took to wife *the sister* of ¹Huppim and ²Shuppim, ³whose sister's name *was* Maachah;) and the name of the second *was* aZelophehad: and Zelophehad had daughters.

16 And Maachah the wife of Machir bare a son, and she called his name Peresh; and the name of his brother *was* Sheresh; and his sons *were* Ulam and Rakem.

17 And the sons of Ulam; aBedan. These *were* the sons of Gilead, the son of Machir, the son of Manasseh.

18 And his sister Hammoleketh bare Ishod, and ¹Abiezer, and Mahalah.

19 And the sons of Shemidah were, Ahian, and Shechem, and Likhi, and Aniam.

20 And athe sons of Ephraim; Shuthelah, and Bered his son, and Tahath his son, and Eladah his son, and Tahath his son,

21 And Zabad his son, and Shuthelah his son, and Ezer, and Elead, whom the men of Gath *that were* born in *that* land slew, because they came down to take away their cattle.

22 And Ephraim their father mourned many days, and his brethren came to comfort him.

23 And when he went in to his wife, she conceived, and bare a son, and he called his name ¹Beriah, because ²it went evil with his house.

24 (And his daughter *was* Sherah, who built aBeth-horon the nether, and the upper, and Uzzen-sherah.)

25 And Rephah *was* his son, also Resheph, and Telah his son, and Tahan his son,

26 Laadan his son, Ammihud his son, aElishama his son,

27 ¹Non his son, aJehoshuah his son.

28 And their apossessions and habitations *were,* Beth-el and the towns thereof, and eastward ¹Naaran, and westward Gezer, with the towns thereof; Shechem also and the towns thereof, unto ²Gaza and the towns thereof:

29 And by the borders of the children of aManasseh, Beth-shean and her towns, Taanach and her towns, bMegiddo and her towns, Dor and her towns. In these dwelt the children of Joseph the son of Israel.

30 aThe sons of Asher; Imnah, and Isuah, and Ishuai, and Beriah, and Serah their sister.

31 And the sons of Beriah; Heber, and Malchiel, who *is* the father of ¹Birzavith.

---

7:1 a Num. 26:23–25 ¹ *Phuvah*, Gen. 46:13 ² *Job*, Gen. 46:13

7:2 a 2 Sam. 24:1–9; 1 Chr. 27:1 ¹ *mighty men of valour*

7:5 ¹ *mighty men of valour*

7:6 a Gen. 46:21; Num. 26:38–41; 1 Chr. 8:1

7:12 ¹ *Shupham*, Num. 26:39 ² *Hupham*, Num. 26:39 ³ *Iri*, 1 Chr. 7:7 ⁴ *Ahiram*, Num. 26:38

7:13 a Num. 26:48–50 ¹ *Jahzeel*, Gen. 46:24 ² *Shillem*, Gen. 46:24

7:14 a Num. 26:29–34 b 1 Chr. 2:21 ¹ *The son of Gilead*, Num. 26:30–33

7:15 a Num. 26:30–33; 27:1 ¹ *Hupham*, Num. 26:39 ² *Shupham*, Num. 26:39 ³ *whose name*

7:17 a 1 Sam. 12:11

7:18 ¹ *Jeezer*, Num. 26:30

7:20 a Num. 26:35–37

7:23 ¹ Lit. *In Tragedy* ² *tragedy had come upon*

7:24 a Josh. 16:3, 5; 2 Chr. 8:5

7:26 a Num. 10:22

7:27 a Ex. 17:9, 14; 24:13; 33:11 ¹ *Nun*, Josh. 1:1

7:28 a Josh. 16:1–10 ¹ *Naarath*, Josh. 16:7 ² *Or Ayyah*

7:29 a Gen. 41:51; Josh. 17:7 b Josh. 17:11

7:30 a Gen. 46:17; Num. 26:44–47

7:31 ¹ *Or Birzaith or Birzoth*

32 And Heber begat Japhlet, and ¹Shomer, and ²Hotham, and Shua their sister.

33 And the sons of Japhlet; Pasach, and Bimhal, and Ashvath. These *are* the children of Japhlet.

34 And the sons of ªShamer; Ahi, and Rohgah, Jehubbah, and Aram.

35 And the sons of his brother Helem; Zophah, and Imna, and Shelesh, and Amal.

36 The sons of Zophah; Suah, and Harnepher, and Shual, and Beri, and Imrah,

37 Bezer, and Hod, and Shamma, and Shilshah, and ¹Ithran, and Beera.

38 And the sons of Jether; Jephunneh, and Pispah, and Ara.

39 And the sons of Ulla; Arah, and Haniel, and Rezia.

40 All these *were* the children of Asher, heads of *their* father's house, choice *and* mighty men of valour, chief of the princes. And the number throughout the genealogy of them that were apt to the war *and* to battle *was* twenty and six thousand men.

### CHAPTER 8

Now Benjamin begat ªBela his firstborn, Ashbel the second, and ¹Aharah the third,

2 Nohah the fourth, and Rapha the fifth.

3 And the sons of Bela were, ¹Addar, and Gera, and Abihud,

4 And Abishua, and Naaman, and Ahoah,

5 And Gera, and ¹Shephuphan, and Huram.

6 And these *are* the sons of Ehud: these are the heads of the fathers of the inhabitants of ªGeba, and they removed them to ᵇManahath:

7 And Naaman, and Ahiah, and Gera, he removed them, and begat Uzza, and Ahihud.

8 And Shaharaim begat *children* in the country of Moab, after he had sent them away; Hushim and Baara *were* his wives.

9 And he begat of Hodesh his wife, Jobab, and Zibia, and Mesha, and Malcham,

10 And Jeuz, and Shachia, and Mirma. These *were* his sons, heads of the fathers.

11 And of Hushim he begat Abitub, and Elpaal.

12 The sons of Elpaal; Eber, and Misham, and Shamed, who built Ono, and Lod, with the towns thereof:

13 Beriah also, and ªShema, who *were* heads of the fathers of the inhabitants of Aijalon, who drove away the inhabitants of Gath:

14 And Ahio, Shashak, and Jeremoth,

15 And Zebadiah, and Arad, and Ader,

16 And Michael, and Ispah, and Joha, the sons of Beriah;

17 And Zebadiah, and Meshullam, and Hezeki, and Heber,

18 Ishmerai also, and Jezliah, and Jobab, the sons of Elpaal;

19 And Jakim, and Zichri, and Zabdi,

20 And Elienai, and Zilthai, and Eliel,

21 And Adaiah, and Beraiah, and Shimrath, the sons of ¹Shimhi;

22 And Ishpan, and Heber, and Eliel,

23 And Abdon, and Zichri, and Hanan,

24 And Hananiah, and Elam, and Antothijah,

25 And Iphedeiah, and Penuel, the sons of Shashak;

26 And Shamsherai, and Shehariah, and Athaliah,

27 And Jaresiah, and Eliah, and Zichri, the sons of Jeroham.

28 These *were* heads of the fathers, by their generations, chief *men*. These dwelt in Jerusalem.

29 And at Gibeon dwelt the ¹father of Gibeon; whose ªwife's name *was* Maachah:

30 And his firstborn son Abdon, and Zur, and Kish, and Baal, and Nadab,

31 And Gedor, and Ahio, and ¹Zacher.

32 And Mikloth begat ¹Shimeah. And these also dwelt with their ²brethren in Jerusalem, ³over against them.

33 And ªNer¹ begat Kish, and Kish begat Saul, and Saul begat Jonathan, and Malchi-shua, and ²Abinadab, and ³Esh-baal.

34 And the son of Jonathan *was* ¹Merib-baal; and Merib-baal begat ªMicah.

35 And the sons of Micah *were,* Pithon, and Melech, and ¹Tarea, and Ahaz.

36 And Ahaz begat ¹Jehoadah; and Jehoadah begat Alemeth, and Azmaveth, and Zimri; and Zimri begat Moza,

37 And Moza begat Binea: ¹Rapha *was* his son, Eleasah his son, Azel his son:

38 And Azel had six sons, whose names *are* these, Azrikam, Bocheru, and Ishmael, and Sheariah, and Obadiah, and Hanan. All these *were* the sons of Azel.

39 And the sons of Eshek his brother *were,* Ulam his firstborn, Jehush the second, and Eliphelet the third.

40 And the sons of Ulam *were* mighty men of valour, archers, and had many sons, and sons' sons, an

---

*Center column cross-references:*

7:32 ¹ *Shemer,* 1 Chr. 7:34
² *Helem,* 1 Chr. 7:35
7:34 ª 1 Chr. 7:32
7:37 ¹ *Jether,* 1 Chr. 7:38
8:1 ª Gen. 46:21; Num. 26:38; 1 Chr. 7:6 ¹ *Ahiram,* Num. 26:38
8:3 ¹ *Ard,* Num. 26:40
8:5 ¹ *Shupham,* Num. 26:39 or *Shuppim,* 1 Chr. 7:12
8:6 ª 1 Chr. 6:60 ᵇ 1 Chr. 2:52
8:13 ª 1 Chr. 8:21

8:21 ¹ *Shema,* 1 Chr. 8:13
8:29 ª 1 Chr. 9:35–38 ¹ *Jehiel*
8:31 ¹ *Zechariah,* 1 Chr. 9:37
8:32 ¹ *Shimeam,* 1 Chr. 9:38 ² *relatives* ³ *opposite*
8:33 ª 1 Sam. 14:51 ¹ The son of Gibeon ² *Ishui,* 1 Sam. 14:49 ³ *Ish-bosheth,* 2 Sam. 2:8
8:34 ª 2 Sam. 9:12 ¹ *Mephibosheth,* 2 Sam. 4:4
8:35 ¹ *Tahrea,* 1 Chr. 9:41
8:36 ¹ *Jarah,* 1 Chr. 9:42, Heb. *Jehoaddah*
8:37 ¹ *Rephaiah,* 1 Chr. 9:43

hundred and fifty. All these *are* of the sons of Benjamin.

## CHAPTER 9

So [a]all Israel [1]were reckoned by genealogies; and, behold, they *were* written in the book of the kings of Israel and Judah, *who* were carried away to Babylon for their [2]transgression.

2 [a]Now the first inhabitants that *dwelt* in their possessions in their cities *were,* the Israelites, the priests, Levites, and [b]the Nethinims.

3 And in [a]Jerusalem dwelt of the children of Judah, and of the children of Benjamin, and of the children of Ephraim, and Manasseh;

4 Uthai the son of Ammihud, the son of Omri, the son of Imri, the son of Bani, of the children of Pharez the son of Judah.

5 And of the Shilonites; Asaiah the firstborn, and his sons.

6 And of the sons of Zerah; Jeuel, and their brethren, six hundred and ninety.

7 And of the sons of Benjamin; Sallu the son of Meshullam, the son of Hodaviah, the son of Hasenuah,

8 And Ibneiah the son of Jeroham, and Elah the son of Uzzi, the son of Michri, and Meshullam the son of Shephathiah, the son of Reuel, the son of Ibnijah;

9 And their brethren, according to their generations, nine hundred and fifty and six. All these men *were* chief of the fathers in the house of their fathers.

10 [a]And of the priests; Jedaiah, and Jehoiarib, and Jachin,

11 And [1]Azariah the son of Hilkiah, the son of Meshullam, the son of Zadok, the son of Meraioth, the son of Ahitub, the [a]ruler of the house of God;

12 And Adaiah the son of Jeroham, the son of Pashur, the son of Malchijah, and Maasiai the son of Adiel, the son of Jahzerah, the son of Meshullam, the son of Meshillemith, the son of Immer;

13 And their brethren, heads of the house of their fathers, a thousand and seven hundred and threescore; [1]very able men for the work of the service of the house of God.

14 And of the Levites; Shemaiah the son of Hasshub, the son of Azrikam, the son of Hashabiah, of the sons of Merari;

15 And Bakbakkar, Heresh, and Galal, and Mattaniah the son of Micah, the son of [a]Zichri, the son of Asaph;

16 And [a]Obadiah the son of [b]Shemaiah, the son of Galal, the son of Jeduthun, and Berechiah the son of Asa, that dwelt in the villages of the Netophathites.

17 And the porters *were,* Shallum, and Akkub, and Talmon, and Ahiman, and their brethren: Shallum *was* the chief;

18 Who hitherto *waited* in the king's gate eastward: they *were* porters in the companies of the children of Levi.

19 And Shallum the son of Kore, the son of Ebiasaph, the son of Korah, and his brethren, of the house of his father, the Korahites, *were* [1]over the work of the service, keepers of the [2]gates of the tabernacle: and their fathers, *being* over the host of the LORD, *were* keepers of the [3]entry.

20 And [a]Phinehas the son of Eleazar was the ruler over them in time past, *and* the LORD *was* with him.

21 *And* [a]Zechariah the son of Meshelemiah *was* [1]porter of the door of the tabernacle of the congregation.

22 All these *which were* chosen to be [1]porters in the gates *were* two hundred and twelve. [a]These were reckoned by their genealogy in their villages, whom David and Samuel [b]the seer [2]did ordain in their [3]set office.

23 So they and their children *had* the oversight of the gates of the house of the LORD, *namely,* the house of the tabernacle, by wards.

24 In four quarters were the [1]porters, toward the east, west, north, and south.

25 And their brethren, *which were* in their villages, *were* to come [a]after seven days from time to time with them.

26 For these Levites, the four chief [1]porters, were in *their* [2]set office, and were over the chambers and treasuries of the house of God.

27 And they lodged round about the house of God, because the [a]charge[1] *was* upon them, and the opening thereof every morning *pertained* to them.

28 And *certain* of them had the charge of the ministering vessels, that they should bring them in and out [1]by tale.

29 *Some* of them also *were* appointed to oversee the [1]vessels, and all the [2]instruments of the sanctuary, and the [a]fine flour, and the wine, and the oil, and the frankincense, and the spices.

30 And *some* of the sons of the priests made [a]the ointment of the spices.

31 And Mattithiah, *one* of the Levites, who *was* the firstborn of Shallum the Korahite, had the [1]set office [a]over the things that were [2]made in the pans.

32 And *other* of their brethren, of the sons of the Kohathites, [a]were

9:1 [a] Ezra 2:59
[1] *were recorded or enrolled* [2] *unfaithfulness*
9:2 [a] Ezra 2:70; Neh. 7:73 [b] Ezra 2:43; 8:20
9:3 [a] Neh. 11:1, 2
9:10 [a] Neh. 11:10–14
9:11 [a] 2 Chr. 31:13; Jer. 20:1 [1] *Seraiah,* Neh. 11:11
9:13 [1] Lit. *mighty men of strength*
9:15 [a] Neh. 11:17
9:16 [a] Neh. 11:17 [b] Neh. 11:17

9:19 [1] *in charge of* [2] Lit. *thresholds* [3] *entrance*
9:20 [a] Num. 25:6–13; 31:6
9:21 [a] 1 Chr. 26:2, 14 [1] *gatekeeper*
9:22 [a] 1 Chr. 26:1, 2 [b] 1 Sam. 9:9 [1] *gatekeepers* [2] *had appointed* [3] *trusted*
9:24 [1] *gatekeepers*
9:25 [a] 2 Kin. 11:4–7; 2 Chr. 23:8
9:26 [1] *gatekeepers* [2] *trusted*
9:27 [a] 1 Chr. 23:30–32 [1] *watch was committed to*
9:28 [1] *by count*
9:29 [a] 1 Chr. 23:29 [1] *furnishings* [2] *implements*
9:30 [a] Ex. 30:22–25
9:31 [a] Lev. 2:5; 6:21 [1] *trusted office* [2] *baked*
9:32 [a] Lev. 24:5–8

over the shewbread, to prepare *it* every sabbath.

33 And these *are* ªthe singers, chief of the fathers of the Levites, *who remaining* in the chambers *were* ¹free: for they were employed in *that* work day and night.

34 These chief fathers of the Levites *were* chief throughout their generations; these dwelt at Jerusalem.

35 And in Gibeon dwelt the father of Gibeon, Jehiel, whose wife's name *was* ªMaachah:

36 And his firstborn son Abdon, then Zur, and Kish, and Baal, and Ner, and Nadab,

37 And Gedor, and Ahio, and ¹Zechariah, and Mikloth.

38 And Mikloth begat ¹Shimeam. And they also dwelt with their brethren at Jerusalem, over against their brethren.

39 ªAnd Ner begat Kish; and Kish begat Saul; and Saul begat Jonathan, and Malchi-shua, and Abinadab, and Esh-baal.

40 And the son of Jonathan *was* Merib-baal: and Merib-baal begat Micah.

41 And the sons of Micah *were*, Pithon, and Melech, and ¹Tahrea, ªand *Ahaz*.

42 And Ahaz begat ¹Jarah; and Jarah begat Alemeth, and Azmaveth, and Zimri; and Zimri begat Moza;

43 And Moza begat Binea; and ¹Rephaiah his son, Eleasah his son, Azel his son.

44 And Azel had six sons, whose names *are* these, Azrikam, Bocheru, and Ishmael, and Sheariah, and Obadiah, and Hanan: these *were* the sons of Azel.

## CHAPTER 10

Now ªthe Philistines fought against Israel; and the men of Israel fled from before the Philistines, and fell down slain in mount Gilboa.

2 And the Philistines followed hard after Saul, and after his sons; and the Philistines slew Jonathan, and ¹Abinadab, and Malchi-shua, the sons of Saul.

3 And the battle ¹went sore against Saul, and the archers hit him, and he was wounded of the archers.

4 Then said Saul to his armourbearer, Draw thy sword, and thrust me through therewith; lest these uncircumcised come and abuse me. But his armourbearer would not; for he was ¹sore afraid. So Saul took a sword, and fell upon it.

5 And when his armourbearer saw that Saul was dead, he fell likewise on the sword, and died.

6 So Saul died, and his three sons, and all his house died together.

9:33 ª 1 Chr. 6:31;
25:1 ¹ Free from
other duties
9:35 ª 1 Chr.
8:29–32
9:37 ¹ Zacher,
1 Chr. 8:31
9:38 ¹ Shimeah,
1 Chr. 8:32
9:39 ª 1 Chr.
8:33–38
9:41 ª 1 Chr. 8:35
¹ Tarea, 1 Chr. 8:35
9:42 ¹ Jehoadah,
1 Chr. 8:36
9:43 ¹ Rapha,
1 Chr. 8:37
10:1 ª 1 Sam. 31:1, 2
10:2 ¹ Ishui, 1 Sam.
14:49
10:3 ¹ became
intense against
10:4 ¹ greatly

10:8 ¹ plunder
10:10 ª 1 Sam.
31:10 ¹ Temple
10:12 ª 1 Sam.
14:52 ᵇ 2 Sam.
21:12
10:13 ª 1 Sam.
13:13, 14; 15:22–26
ᵇ [Lev. 19:31;
20:6]; 1 Sam. 28:7
¹ Lit. transgressed
² consulting
a medium for
guidance
10:14 ª 1 Sam.
15:28; 2 Sam. 3:9,
10; 5:3; 1 Chr.
12:23
11:1 ª 2 Sam. 5:1
11:2 ª 1 Sam.
16:1–3; Ps. 78:70–
72  ᵇ 2 Sam. 7:7
¹ shepherd
11:3 ª 2 Sam. 5:3
ᵇ 1 Sam. 16:1, 4,
12, 13  ¹ Lit. by the
hand of Samuel
11:4 ª 2 Sam.
5:6  ᵇ Josh. 15:8,
63; Judg. 1:21;
19:10, 11
11:6 ¹ attacks  ² Lit.
head  ³ became

7 And when all the men of Israel that *were* in the valley saw that they fled, and that Saul and his sons were dead, then they forsook their cities, and fled: and the Philistines came and dwelt in them.

8 And it came to pass on the morrow, when the Philistines came to ¹strip the slain, that they found Saul and his sons fallen in mount Gilboa.

9 And when they had stripped him, they took his head, and his armour, and sent into the land of the Philistines round about, to carry tidings unto their idols, and to the people.

10 ªAnd they put his armour in the ¹house of their gods, and fastened his head in the temple of Dagon.

11 And when all Jabesh-gilead heard all that the Philistines had done to Saul,

12 They arose, all the ªvaliant men, and took away the body of Saul, and the bodies of his sons, and brought them to ᵇJabesh, and buried their bones under the oak in Jabesh, and fasted seven days.

13 So Saul died for his transgression which he ¹committed against the LORD, ªeven against the word of the LORD, which he kept not, and also for ²asking *counsel of one that had* a familiar spirit, ᵇto enquire *of it;*

14 And enquired not of the LORD: therefore he slew him, and ªturned the kingdom unto David the son of Jesse.

## CHAPTER 11

Then ªall Israel gathered themselves to David unto Hebron, saying, Behold, we *are* thy bone and thy flesh.

2 And moreover in time past, even when Saul was king, thou *wast* he that leddest out and broughtest in Israel: and the LORD thy ªGod said unto thee, Thou shalt ᵇfeed¹ my people Israel, and thou shalt be ruler over my people Israel.

3 Therefore came all the elders of Israel to the king to Hebron; and David made a covenant with them in Hebron before the LORD; and ªthey anointed David king over Israel, according to the word of the LORD ¹by ᵇSamuel.

4 And David and all Israel ªwent to Jerusalem, which *is* Jebus; ᵇwhere the Jebusites *were*, the inhabitants of the land.

5 And the inhabitants of Jebus said to David, Thou shalt not come hither. Nevertheless David took the castle of Zion, which *is* the city of David.

6 And David said, Whosoever ¹smiteth the Jebusites first shall be ²chief and captain. So Joab the son of Zeruiah went first up, and ³was chief.

**7** And David dwelt in the [1]castle; therefore they called it [2]the city of David.

**8** And he built the city round about, even from Millo round about: and Joab [1]repaired the rest of the city.

**9** So David [a]waxed[1] greater and greater: for the LORD of hosts *was* with [b]him.

**10** [a]These also *are* the chief of the mighty men whom David had, who strengthened themselves with him in his kingdom, *and* with all Israel, to make him king, according to [b]the word of the LORD concerning Israel.

**11** And this *is* the number of the mighty men whom David had; [a]Jashobeam, [1]an Hachmonite, [b]chief of the captains: he lifted up his spear against three hundred slain *by him* at one time.

**12** And after him *was* Eleazar the son of [a]Dodo, the Ahohite, who *was* one of the three mighties.

**13** He was with David at [1]Pasdammim, and there the Philistines were gathered together to battle, where was a [2]parcel of ground full of barley; and the people fled from before the Philistines.

**14** And they [1]set themselves in the midst of *that* parcel, and delivered it, and slew the Philistines; and the LORD saved *them* by a great deliverance.

**15** Now three of the thirty captains [a]went down to the rock to David, into the cave of Adullam; and the host of the Philistines encamped [b]in the valley of [1]Rephaim.

**16** And David *was* then in the [1]hold, and the Philistines' garrison *was* then at Beth-lehem.

**17** And David longed, and said, Oh that one would give me drink of the water of the well of Beth-lehem, that *is* at the gate!

**18** And the three brake through the host of the Philistines, and drew water out of the well of Beth-lehem, that *was* by the gate, and took *it*, and brought *it* to David: but David would not drink *of* it, but poured it out to the LORD,

**19** And said, My God forbid it me, that I should do this thing: shall I drink the blood of these men that have put their lives in jeopardy? for with *the jeopardy of* their lives they brought it. Therefore he would not drink it. These things did these three mightiest.

**20** [a]And Abishai the brother of Joab, he was chief of the three: for lifting up his spear against three hundred, he slew *them*, and had a name among the three.

**21** [a]Of the three, he [1]was more honourable than the two; for he was their captain: howbeit he attained not to the *first* three.

**22** Benaiah the son of Jehoiada, the son of a valiant man of Kabzeel, who [1]had done many acts; [a]he slew two lionlike men of Moab: also he went down and slew a lion in a pit in a snowy day.

**23** And he slew an Egyptian, a man of *great* stature, five cubits high; and in the Egyptian's hand *was* a spear like a weaver's beam; and he went down to him with a staff, and plucked the spear out of the Egyptian's hand, and slew him with his own spear.

**24** These *things* did Benaiah the son of Jehoiada, and had the name among the three mighties.

**25** Behold, he [1]was honourable among the thirty, but attained not to the *first* three: and David set him over his guard.

**26** Also the [1]valiant men of the armies *were*, [a]Asahel the brother of Joab, Elhanan the son of Dodo of Beth-lehem,

**27** [1]Shammoth the Harorite, [a]Helez the [2]Pelonite,

**28** [a]Ira the son of Ikkesh the Tekoite, [b]Abiezer the Antothite,

**29** [1]Sibbecai the Hushathite, [2]Ilai the Ahohite,

**30** [a]Maharai the Netophathite, [1]Heled the son of Baanah the Netophathite,

**31** [1]Ithai the son of Ribai of Gibeah, *that pertained* to the children of Benjamin, [a]Benaiah the Pirathonite,

**32** [1]Hurai of the brooks of Gaash, [2]Abiel the Arbathite,

**33** Azmaveth the [1]Baharumite, Eliahba the Shaalbonite,

**34** The sons of [1]Hashem the Gizonite, Jonathan the son of Shage the Harorite,

**35** Ahiam the son of [1]Sacar the Harorite, [2]Eliphal the son of [3]Ur,

**36** Hepher the Mecherathite, Ahijah the Pelonite,

**37** [1]Hezro the Carmelite, [2]Naarai the son of Ezbai,

**38** Joel the brother of Nathan, Mibhar the son of [1]Haggeri,

**39** Zelek the Ammonite, Naharai the Berothite, the armourbearer of Joab the son of Zeruiah,

**40** Ira the Ithrite, Gareb the Ithrite,

**41** [a]Uriah the Hittite, [1]Zabad the son of Ahlai,

**42** Adina the son of Shiza the Reubenite, a captain of the Reubenites, and thirty with him,

**43** Hanan the son of Maachah, and Joshaphat the Mithnite,

**44** Uzzia the Ashterathite, Shama and Jehiel the sons of Hothan the Aroerite,

**45** Jediael the [1]son of Shimri, and Joha his brother, the Tizite,

---

**11:7** [1] *strong hold*  [2] *Zion,* 2 Sam. 5:7
**11:8** [1] Lit. *revived*
**11:9** [a] 2 Sam. 3:1  [b] 1 Sam. 16:18  [1] *went on and became great*
**11:10** [a] 2 Sam. 23:8  [b] 1 Sam. 16:1, 12
**11:11** [a] 1 Chr. 27:2  [b] 1 Chr. 12:18  [1] *Or the son of a Hachmonite*
**11:12** [a] 1 Chr. 27:4
**11:13** [1] *Ephesdammim,* 1 Sam. 17:1  [2] *piece or plot*
**11:14** [1] *stationed*
**11:15** [a] 2 Sam. 23:13  [b] 2 Sam. 5:18; 1 Chr. 14:9  [1] Lit. *Giants*
**11:16** [1] *stronghold*
**11:20** [a] 2 Sam. 23:18; 1 Chr. 18:12
**11:21** [a] 2 Sam. 23:19  [1] *was more honoured*
**11:22** [a] 2 Sam. 23:20  [1] *was great in deeds*
**11:25** [1] *was honoured*
**11:26** [a] 2 Sam. 23:24  [1] *mighty warriors*
**11:27** [a] 2 Sam. 23:26; 1 Chr. 27:10  [1] *Shammah the Harodite,* 2 Sam. 23:25  [2] *Paltite,* 2 Sam. 23:26
**11:28** [a] 1 Chr. 27:9  [b] 1 Chr. 27:12
**11:29** [1] *Mebunnai,* 2 Sam. 23:27  [2] *Zalmon,* 2 Sam. 23:28
**11:30** [a] 1 Chr. 27:13  [1] *Heleb,* 2 Sam. 23:29 or *Heldai,* 1 Chr. 27:15
**11:31** [a] 1 Chr. 27:14  [1] *Ittai,* 2 Sam. 23:29
**11:32** [1] *Hiddai,* 2 Sam. 23:30  [2] *Abi-albon,* 2 Sam. 23:31
**11:33** [1] *Barhumite,* 2 Sam. 23:31
**11:34** [1] *Jashen,* 2 Sam. 23:32
**11:35** [1] *Sharar,* 2 Sam. 23:33  [2] *Eliphelet,* 2 Sam. 23:34  [3] *Ahasbai,* 2 Sam. 23:34
**11:37** [1] *Hezrai,* 2 Sam. 23:35
**11:38** [1] Heb. *Hagri*
**11:41** [a] 2 Sam. 23:39  [1] The last 16 are not listed in 2 Sam. 23.
**11:45** [1] Or *Shimrite*

373

46 Eliel the Mahavite, and Jeribai, and Joshaviah, the sons of Elnaam, and Ithmah the Moabite,

47 Eliel, and Obed, and Jasiel the Mesobaite.

## CHAPTER 12

Now ªthese *are* they that came to David to ᵇZiklag, while he ¹yet kept himself close because of Saul the son of Kish: and they *were* among the mighty men, helpers of the war.

2 *They were* armed with bows, and could use both the right hand and ªthe left in *hurling* stones and *shooting* arrows out of a bow, *even* of Saul's brethren of Benjamin.

3 The chief *was* Ahiezer, then Joash, the sons of ¹Shemaah the Gibeathite; and Jeziel, and Pelet, the sons of Azmaveth; and Berachah, and Jehu the Antothite,

4 And Ismaiah the Gibeonite, a mighty man among the thirty, and over the thirty; and Jeremiah, and Jahaziel, and Johanan, and Josabad the Gederathite,

5 Eluzai, and Jerimoth, and Bealiah, and Shemariah, and Shephatiah the Haruphite,

6 Elkanah, and Jesiah, and Azareel, and Joezer, and Jashobeam, the Korhites,

7 And Joelah, and Zebadiah, the sons of Jeroham of Gedor.

8 And of the Gadites there ¹separated themselves unto David into the ²hold to the wilderness men of might, *and* ³men of war *fit* for the battle, that could handle shield and buckler, whose faces *were like* the faces of lions, and *were* ªas swift as the ⁴roes upon the mountains;

9 Ezer the first, Obadiah the second, Eliab the third,

10 Mishmannah the fourth, Jeremiah the fifth,

11 Attai the sixth, Eliel the seventh,

12 Johanan the eighth, Elzabad the ninth,

13 Jeremiah the tenth, Machbanai the eleventh.

14 These *were* of the sons of Gad, captains of the host: one of the least *was* over an hundred, and the greatest over a ªthousand.

15 These *are* they that went over Jordan in the first month, when it had overflown all his ªbanks; and they put to flight all *them* of the valleys, *both* toward the east, and toward the west.

16 And there came of the children of Benjamin and Judah to the ¹hold unto David.

17 And David went out ¹to meet them, and answered and said unto them, If ye be come peaceably unto me to help me, mine heart shall be

### Marginal notes

12:1 ª 1 Sam.
27:2 ᵇ 1 Sam.
27:6 ¹ *was still a fugitive from*

12:2 ª Judg. 3:15; 20:16

12:3 ¹ *Or Hasmaah*

12:8 ª 2 Sam. 2:18
¹ *joined* ² *strong hold* ³ *warriors trained for battle* 4 *gazelles*

12:14 ª 1 Sam. 18:13

12:15 ª Josh. 3:15; 4:18, 19

12:16 ¹ *strong hold*

12:17 ¹ Lit. *before them*

² *united with*
³ Lit. *violence*

12:18 ª 2 Sam. 17:25 ¹ Lit. *the spirit clothed*

12:19 ª 1 Sam. 29:2
ᵇ 1 Sam. 29:4
¹ *after counsel* ² *defect* ³ *and endanger our heads*

12:20 ¹ *those of Manasseh defected to him*

12:21 ª 1 Sam. 30:1, 9, 10

12:22 ª Gen. 32:2; Josh. 5:13–15
¹ *army*

12:23 ª 2 Sam. 2:1–4 ᵇ 1 Chr. 11:1 ᶜ 1 Chr. 10:14 ᵈ 1 Sam. 16:1–4
¹ *divisions*

12:24 ¹ *equipped*

12:28 ª 2 Sam. 8:17; 1 Chr. 6:8, 53

12:29 ª 2 Sam. 2:8, 9 ¹ *kinsmen* ² *remained loyal to*

12:30 ¹ Lit. *men of names*

12:31 ¹ *designated*

2knit unto you: but if *ye be come* to betray me to mine enemies, seeing *there is* no ³wrong in mine hands, the God of our fathers look *thereon*, and rebuke *it*.

18 Then ¹the spirit came upon ªAmasai, *who was* chief of the captains, *and he said*, Thine are we, David, and on thy side, thou son of Jesse: peace, peace *be* unto thee, and peace *be* to thine helpers; for thy God helpeth thee. Then David received them, and made them captains of the band.

19 And there fell *some* of Manasseh to David, ªwhen he came with the Philistines against Saul to battle: but they helped them not: for the lords of the Philistines ¹upon advisement sent him away, saying, ᵇHe will ²fall to his master Saul ³to *the jeopardy of* our heads.

20 As he went to Ziklag, ¹there fell to him of Manasseh, Adnah, and Jozabad, and Jediael, and Michael, and Jozabad, and Elihu, and Zilthai, captains of the thousands that *were* of Manasseh.

21 And they helped David against ªthe band *of the rovers:* for they *were* all mighty men of valour, and were captains in the host.

22 For at *that* time day by day there came to David to help him, until *it was* a great ¹host, ªlike the host of God.

23 And these *are* the numbers of the ¹bands *that were* ready armed to the war, *and* ªcame to David to ᵇHebron, to ᶜturn the kingdom of Saul to him, ᵈaccording to the word of the LORD.

24 The children of Judah that bare shield and spear *were* six thousand and eight hundred, ¹ready armed to the war.

25 Of the children of Simeon, mighty men of valour for the war, seven thousand and one hundred.

26 Of the children of Levi four thousand and six hundred.

27 And Jehoiada *was* the leader of the Aaronites, and with him *were* three thousand and seven hundred;

28 And ªZadok, a young man mighty of valour, and of his father's house twenty and two captains.

29 And of the children of Benjamin, the ¹kindred of Saul, three thousand: for hitherto ªthe greatest part of them had ²kept the ward of the house of Saul.

30 And of the children of Ephraim twenty thousand and eight hundred, mighty men of valour, ¹famous throughout the house of their fathers.

31 And of the half tribe of Manasseh eighteen thousand, which were ¹expressed by name, to come and make David king.

32 And of the children of Issachar, ªwhich *were men* that had understanding of the times, to know what Israel ought to do; the heads of them *were* two hundred; and all their brethren *were* at their commandment.

33 Of Zebulun, such as went forth to battle, expert in war, with all instruments of war, fifty thousand, which could keep rank: *they were* ¹not of ªdouble heart.

34 And of Naphtali a thousand captains, and with them with shield and spear thirty and seven thousand.

35 And of the Danites expert in war twenty and eight thousand and six hundred.

36 And of Asher, such as went forth to battle, ¹expert in war, forty thousand.

37 And on the other side of Jordan, of the Reubenites, and the Gadites, and of the half tribe of Manasseh, with all manner of instruments of war for the battle, an hundred and twenty thousand.

38 All these men of war, that could keep rank, came with a ¹perfect heart to Hebron, to make David king over all Israel: and all the rest also of Israel *were* of ªone ²heart to make David king.

39 And there they were with David three days, eating and drinking: for their brethren had prepared for them.

40 Moreover they that were nigh them, *even* unto Issachar and Zebulun and Naphtali, brought bread on asses, and on camels, and on mules, and on oxen, *and* meat, meal, cakes of figs, and bunches of raisins, and wine, and oil, and oxen, and sheep abundantly: for *there was* joy in Israel.

### CHAPTER 13

ND David consulted with the ªcaptains of thousands and hundreds, *and* with every leader.

2 And David said unto all the congregation of Israel, *If it seem* good unto you, and *that it be* of the LORD our God, let us send abroad unto our brethren every where, ¹that are ªleft in all the land of Israel, and with them *also* to the priests and Levites *which are* in their cities *and* suburbs, that they may gather themselves unto us:

3 And let us bring again the ark of our God to us: ªfor we enquired not at it in the days of Saul.

4 And all the congregation said that they would do so: for the thing was right in the eyes of all the people.

5 So ªDavid gathered all Israel together, from ᵇShihor of Egypt even unto the entering of Hemath, to

12:32 ª Esth. 1:13
12:33 ª Ps. 12:2;
[James 1:8]
¹ stouthearted
12:36 ¹ able
to keep battle
formation
12:38 ª 2 Chr.
30:12 ¹ loyal
² mind
13:1 ª 1 Chr. 11:15;
12:34
13:2 ª 1 Sam. 31:1;
Is. 37:4 ¹ who
remain
13:3 ª 1 Sam. 7:1, 2
13:5 ª 1 Sam. 7:5
ᵇ Josh. 13:3

c 1 Sam. 6:21; 7:1, 2
13:6 ª Josh. 15:9,
60 ᵇ Ex. 25:22;
1 Sam. 4:4; 2 Kin.
19:15 ¹ Baale of
Judah, 2 Sam. 6:2
13:7 ª Num.
4:15; 1 Sam. 6:7
ᵇ 1 Sam. 7:1 ¹ Lit.
caused the ark
to ride
13:8 ª 2 Sam. 6:5
¹ Played musick
² songs
13:9 ¹ Nachon,
2 Sam. 6:6 ² let
it fall
13:10 ª [Num.
4:15]; 1 Chr. 15:13,
15 ᵇ Lev. 10:2
¹ aroused ² struck
13:11 ¹ became
angry ² Lit. Out-
break of Uzza
13:13 ¹ would not
move
13:14 ª 2 Sam. 6:11
ᵇ [Gen. 30:27];
1 Chr. 26:4–8
14:1 ª 2 Sam. 5:11;
1 Kin. 5:1
14:2 ª Num.
24:7 ¹ was highly
exalted
14:4 ª 1 Chr.
3:5–8 ¹ Shimea,
1 Chr. 3:5
14:5 ¹ Elishua,
1 Chr. 3:6 ² Eliph-
elet, 1 Chr. 3:6
14:7 ¹ Eliada,
1 Chr. 3:8; 2 Sam.
5:16
14:8 ª 2 Sam.
5:17–21 ¹ search
for

bring the ark of God ᶜfrom Kirjath-jearim.

6 And David went up, and all Israel, to ªBaalah,¹ *that is,* to Kirjath-jearim, which *belonged* to Judah, to bring up thence the ark of God the LORD, ᵇthat dwelleth *between* the cherubims, whose name is called *on it.*

7 And they ¹carried the ark of God ªin a new cart ᵇout of the house of Abinadab: and Uzza and Ahio drave the cart.

8 ªAnd David and all Israel ¹played before God with all *their* might, and with ²singing, and with harps, and with psalteries, and with timbrels, and with cymbals, and with trumpets.

9 And when they came unto the threshingfloor of ¹Chidon, Uzza put forth his hand to hold the ark; for the oxen ²stumbled.

10 And the anger of the LORD was ¹kindled against Uzza, and he ²smote him, ªbecause he put his hand to the ark: and there he ᵇdied before God.

11 And David ¹was displeased, because the LORD had made a breach upon Uzza: wherefore that place is called ²Perez-uzza to this day.

12 And David was afraid of God that day, saying, How shall I bring the ark of God *home* to me?

13 So David ¹brought not the ark *home* to himself to the city of David, but carried it aside into the house of Obed-edom the Gittite.

14 ªAnd the ark of God remained with the family of Obed-edom in his house three months. And the LORD blessed ᵇthe house of Obed-edom, and all that he had.

### CHAPTER 14

OW ªHiram king of Tyre sent messengers to David, and timber of cedars, with masons and carpenters, to build him an house.

2 And David perceived that the LORD had confirmed him king over Israel, for his kingdom ¹was ªlifted up on high, because of his people Israel.

3 And David took more wives at Jerusalem: and David begat more sons and daughters.

4 Now ªthese *are* the names of *his* children which he had in Jerusalem; ¹Shammua, and Shobab, Nathan, and Solomon,

5 And Ibhar, and ¹Elishua, and ²Elpalet,

6 And Nogah, and Nepheg, and Japhia,

7 And Elishama, and ¹Beeliada, and Eliphalet.

8 And when the Philistines heard that ªDavid was anointed king over all Israel, all the Philistines went up to ¹seek David. And David heard *of it,* and went out against them.

9 And the Philistines came and ¹spread themselves ᵃin the valley of ²Rephaim.

10 And David ᵃenquired of God, saying, Shall I go up against the Philistines? and wilt thou deliver them into mine hand? And the LORD said unto him, Go up; for I will deliver them into thine hand.

11 So they came up to Baal-perazim; and David ¹smote them there. Then David said, God hath ²broken in upon mine enemies by mine hand like ³the breaking forth of waters: therefore they called the name of that place ⁴Baal-perazim.

12 And when they had left their gods there, David gave a commandment, and they were burned with fire.

13 ᵃAnd the Philistines yet again ¹spread themselves abroad in the valley.

14 Therefore David enquired again of God; and God said unto him, Go not up after them; turn away from them, ᵃand come upon them ¹over against the mulberry trees.

15 And it shall be, when thou shalt hear a sound of going in the tops of the mulberry trees, *that* then thou shalt go out to battle: for God is gone forth before thee to ¹smite the host of the Philistines.

16 David therefore did as God commanded him: and they ¹smote the host of the Philistines from ²Gibeon even to Gazer.

17 And ᵃthe fame of David went out into all lands; and the LORD ᵇbrought the fear of him upon all nations.

## CHAPTER 15

AND *David* made him houses in the city of David, and prepared a place for the ark of God, ᵃand pitched for it a tent.

2 Then David said, ¹None ought to carry the ᵃark of God but the Levites: for ᵇthem hath the LORD chosen to carry the ark of God, and to minister unto him for ever.

3 And David ᵃgathered all Israel together to Jerusalem, to bring up the ark of the LORD unto his place, which he had prepared for it.

4 And David assembled the children of Aaron, and the Levites:

5 Of the sons of Kohath; Uriel the chief, and his ¹brethren an hundred and twenty:

6 Of the sons of Merari; Asaiah the chief, and his brethren two hundred and twenty:

7 Of the sons of Gershom; Joel the chief, and his brethren an hundred and thirty:

8 Of the sons of ᵃElizaphan; Shemaiah the chief, and his brethren two hundred:

9 Of the sons of ᵃHebron; Eliel the chief, and his brethren fourscore:

10 Of the sons of Uzziel; Amminadab the chief, and his brethren an hundred and twelve.

11 And David called for ᵃZadok and ᵇAbiathar the priests, and for the Levites, for Uriel, Asaiah, and Joel, Shemaiah, and Eliel, and Amminadab,

12 And said unto them, *Ye are* the chief of the fathers of the Levites: ¹sanctify yourselves, *both* ye and your brethren, that ye may bring up the ark of the LORD God of Israel unto *the place that* I have prepared for it.

13 For ᵃbecause ye *did it* not at the first, ᵇthe LORD our God ¹made a breach upon us, for that we sought him not ²after the due order.

14 So the priests and the Levites ¹sanctified themselves to bring up the ark of the LORD God of Israel.

15 And the children of the Levites bare the ark of God upon their shoulders ¹with the staves thereon, as ᵃMoses commanded according to the word of the LORD.

16 And David spake to the chief of the Levites to appoint their brethren *to be* the singers with instruments of musick, psalteries and harps and cymbals, sounding, by lifting up the voice with joy.

17 So the Levites appointed ᵃHeman the son of Joel; and of his brethren, ᵇAsaph the son of Berechiah; and of the sons of Merari their brethren, ᶜEthan the son of Kushaiah;

18 And with them their brethren of the second *degree,* Zechariah, Ben, and Jaaziel, and Shemiramoth, and Jehiel, and Unni, Eliab, and Benaiah, and Maaseiah, and Mattithiah, and Elipheleh, and Mikneiah, and Obed-edom, and Jeiel, the porters.

19 So the singers, Heman, Asaph, and Ethan, *were appointed* to sound with cymbals of brass;

20 And Zechariah, and ¹Aziel, and Shemiramoth, and Jehiel, and Unni, and Eliab, and Maaseiah, and Benaiah, with ²psalteries on ᵃAlamoth;

21 And Mattithiah, and Elipheleh, and Mikneiah, and Obed-edom, and Jeiel, and Azaziah, with harps on the ᵃSheminith ¹to excel.

22 And Chenaniah, chief of the Levites, *was* for song: he instructed about the song, because he *was* skilful.

23 And Berechiah and Elkanah *were* doorkeepers for the ark.

24 And Shebaniah, and Jehoshaphat, and Nethaneel, and Amasai, and Zechariah, and Benaiah, and Eliezer, the priests, ᵃdid blow with the trumpets before the ark of God: and ᵇObed-edom and Jehiah *were* doorkeepers for the ark.

### Cross references (center column)

14:9 ᵃ Josh. 17:15; 18:16; 1 Chr. 11:15; 14:13 ¹ *made a raid* ² Lit. *Giants*
14:10 ᵃ 1 Sam. 23:2, 4; 30:8; 2 Sam. 2:1; 5:19, 23; 21:1
14:11 ¹ *defeated* ² *broken through* ³ *breaking through* ⁴ Lit. *Master of Breakthroughs*
14:13 ᵃ 2 Sam. 5:22–25 ¹ *made a raid*
14:14 ᵃ 2 Sam. 5:23 ¹ *in front of the*
14:15 ¹ *strike*
14:16 ¹ *defeated* ² *Geba,* 2 Sam. 5:25
14:17 ᵃ Josh. 6:27; 2 Chr. 26:8 ᵇ [Ex. 15:14–16; Deut. 2:25; 11:25]; 2 Chr. 20:29
15:1 ᵃ 1 Chr. 16:1
15:2 ᵃ [Num. 4:15]; 2 Sam. 6:1–11 ᵇ Num. 4:2–15; Deut. 10:8; 31:9 ¹ *None may carry*
15:3 ᵃ Ex. 40:20, 21; 2 Sam. 6:12; 1 Kin. 8:1; 1 Chr. 13:5
15:5 ¹ *kinsmen*
15:8 ᵃ Ex. 6:22
15:9 ᵃ Ex. 6:18
15:11 ᵃ 2 Sam. 8:17; 15:24–29, 35, 36; 18:19, 22, 27; 19:11; 20:25; 1 Chr. 12:28 ᵇ 1 Sam. 22:20–23; 23:6; 30:7; 1 Kin. 2:22, 26, 27; Mark 2:6
15:12 ¹ *consecrate*
15:13 ᵃ 2 Sam. 6:3 ᵇ 1 Chr. 13:7–11 ¹ *broke out against us* ² *regarding the ordinance*
15:14 ¹ *consecrated*
15:15 ᵃ Ex. 25:14; Num. 4:15; 7:9 ¹ *by its poles*
15:17 ᵃ 1 Chr. 6:33; 25:1 ᵇ 1 Chr. 6:39 ᶜ 1 Chr. 6:44
15:20 ᵃ Ps. 46:title ¹ *Jaaziel,* 1 Chr. 15:18 ² *strings*
15:21 ᵃ Ps. 6:title ¹ *to lead*
15:24 ᵃ [Num. 10:8]; Ps. 81:3 ᵇ 1 Chr. 13:13, 14

25 So ᵃDavid, and the elders of Israel, and the captains over thousands, went to bring up the ark of the covenant of the LORD out of the house of Obed-edom with joy.

26 And it came to pass, when God helped the Levites that bare the ark of the covenant of the LORD, that they offered seven bullocks and seven rams.

27 And David *was* clothed with a robe of fine ᵃlinen, and all the Levites that bare the ark, and the singers, and Chenaniah the master of the song with the singers: David also *had* upon him an ephod of linen.

28 ᵃThus all Israel brought up the ark of the covenant of the LORD with shouting, and with sound of the cornet, and with trumpets, and with cymbals, making a noise with psalteries and harps.

29 And it came to pass, ᵃ*as* the ark of the covenant of the LORD came to the city of David, that Michal the daughter of Saul looking out at a window saw king David ¹dancing and playing: and she despised him in her heart.

## CHAPTER 16

So ᵃthey brought the ark of God, and set it in the midst of the tent that David had ¹pitched for it: and they offered burnt sacrifices and peace offerings before God.

2 And when David had ¹made an end of offering the burnt offerings and the peace offerings, ᵃhe blessed the people in the name of the LORD.

3 And he ¹dealt to every one of Israel, both man and woman, to every one a loaf of bread, and a good piece of flesh, and a ²flagon *of wine*.

4 And he appointed *certain* of the Levites to minister before the ark of the LORD, and to ᵃrecord, and to thank and praise the LORD God of Israel:

5 Asaph the chief, and next to him Zechariah, ᵃJeiel, and Shemiramoth, and Jehiel, and Mattithiah, and Eliab, and Benaiah, and Obed-edom: and Jeiel with ¹psalteries and with harps; but Asaph made a sound with cymbals;

6 Benaiah also and Jahaziel the priests with trumpets continually before the ark of the covenant of God.

7 Then on that day ᵃDavid delivered ᵇfirst *this psalm* to thank the LORD into the hand of Asaph and his brethren.

8 ᵃGive thanks unto the LORD, call upon his name, make known his deeds among the people.

9 Sing unto him, sing psalms unto him, talk ye of all his wondrous works.

10 Glory ye in his holy name: let the heart of them rejoice that seek the LORD.

11 Seek the LORD and his strength, seek his face continually.

12 Remember his marvellous works that he hath done, his wonders, and the judgments of his mouth;

13 O ye seed of Israel his servant, ye children of Jacob, his chosen ones.

14 He *is* the LORD our God; his ᵃjudgments *are* in all the earth.

15 Be ye mindful always of his covenant; the word *which* he commanded to a thousand generations;

16 *Even of the* ᵃcovenant which he made with Abraham, and of his oath unto Isaac;

17 And hath ᵃconfirmed the same to ᵇJacob for a law, *and* to Israel *for* an everlasting covenant,

18 Saying, Unto thee will I give the land of Canaan, the ¹lot of your inheritance;

19 When ye were but few, ᵃeven a few, and strangers in it.

20 And *when* they went from nation to nation, and from *one* kingdom to another people;

21 He suffered no man to do them wrong: yea, he ᵃreproved kings for their sakes,

22 *Saying,* ᵃTouch not mine anointed, and do my prophets no harm.

23 ᵃSing unto the LORD, all the earth; shew forth from day to day his salvation.

24 Declare his glory among the heathen; his marvellous works among all nations.

25 For great *is* the LORD, and greatly to be praised: he also *is* to be ¹feared above all gods.

26 For all the gods ᵃof the people *are* ¹idols: but the LORD made the heavens.

27 Glory and honour *are* in his presence; strength and gladness *are* in his place.

28 Give unto the LORD, ye kindreds of the people, give unto the LORD glory and strength.

29 Give unto the LORD the glory *due* unto his name: bring an offering, and come before him: worship the LORD in the beauty of holiness.

30 ¹Fear before him, all the earth: the world also shall be stable, that it be not moved.

31 Let the heavens be glad, and let the earth rejoice: and let *men* say among the nations, The LORD reigneth.

32 Let the sea roar, and the fulness thereof: let the fields rejoice, and all that *is* therein.

33 Then shall the ᵃtrees of the wood sing out at the presence of the LORD,

## Cross references

15:25 ᵃ 2 Sam. 6:12, 13; 1 Kin. 8:1
15:27 ᵃ 1 Sam. 2:18, 28
15:28 ᵃ Num. 23:21; Josh. 6:20; 1 Chr. 13:8; Zech. 4:7; 1 Thess. 4:16
15:29 ᵃ 1 Sam. 18:20, 27; 19:11–17; 2 Sam. 3:13, 14; 6:16, 20–23
¹ whirling
16:1 ᵃ 2 Sam. 6:17; 1 Chr. 15:1
¹ erected
16:2 ᵃ 1 Kin. 8:14
¹ finished
16:3 ¹ distributed
² Or cake of raisins
16:4 ᵃ Ps. 38:title; 70:title
16:5 ᵃ 1 Chr. 15:18 ¹ stringed instruments
16:7 ᵃ 2 Sam. 22:1; 23:1 ᵇ Ps. 105:1–15
16:8 ᵃ 1 Chr. 17:19, 20; Ps. 105:1–15
16:14 ᵃ Ps. 48:10; [Is. 26:9]
16:16 ᵃ Gen. 17:2; 26:3; 28:13; 35:11
16:17 ᵃ Gen. 35:11, 12 ᵇ Gen. 28:10–15
16:18 ¹ allotment
16:19 ᵃ Gen. 34:30; Deut. 7:7
16:21 ᵃ Gen. 12:17; 20:3; Ex. 7:15–18
16:22 ᵃ Gen. 20:7; Ps. 105:15
16:23 ᵃ Ps. 96:1–13
16:25 ¹ held in reverential awe
16:26 ᵃ Lev. 19:4; [1 Cor. 8:5, 6] ¹ worthless things
16:30 ¹ Tremble
16:33 ᵃ Is. 55:12, 13

because he [b]cometh to judge the earth.

34 [a]O give thanks unto the LORD; for *he is* good; for his mercy *endureth* for ever.

35 [a]And say ye, Save us, O God of our salvation, and gather us together, and deliver us from the heathen, that we may give thanks to thy holy name, *and* [1]glory in thy praise.

36 [a]Blessed *be* the LORD God of Israel for ever and ever. And all [b]the people said, Amen, and praised the LORD.

37 So he left there before the ark of the covenant of the LORD [a]Asaph and his brethren, to minister before the ark continually, as every day's work [b]required:

38 And [a]Obed-edom with their brethren, threescore and eight; Obed-edom also the son of Jeduthun and Hosah *to be* porters:

39 And Zadok the priest, and his brethren the priests, [a]before the tabernacle of the LORD [b]in the [1]high place that *was* at Gibeon,

40 To offer burnt offerings unto the LORD upon the altar of the burnt offering continually [a]morning and evening, and *to do* according to all that is written in the law of the LORD, which he commanded Israel;

41 And with them Heman and Jeduthun, and the rest that were chosen, who were [1]expressed by name, to give thanks to the LORD, [a]because his mercy *endureth* for ever;

42 And with them Heman and Jeduthun with trumpets and cymbals for those that should make a sound, and with musical instruments of God. And the sons of Jeduthun *were* [1]porters.

43 [a]And all the people departed every man to his house: and David returned to bless his house.

## CHAPTER 17

Now [a]it came to pass, as David sat in his house, that David said to Nathan the prophet, Lo, I dwell in an house of cedars, but the ark of the covenant of the LORD *remaineth* under curtains.

2 Then Nathan said unto David, Do all that *is* in thine heart; for God *is* with thee.

3 And it came to pass the same night, that the word of God came to Nathan, saying,

4 Go and tell David my servant, Thus saith the LORD, Thou shalt [a]not build me an house to dwell in:

5 For I have not dwelt in an house since the day that I brought up Israel unto this day; but have gone from tent to tent, and from *one* tabernacle *to another.*

6 Wheresoever I have walked with all Israel, spake I a word to any of the judges of Israel, whom I commanded to feed my people, saying, Why have ye not built me an house of cedars?

7 Now therefore thus shalt thou say unto my servant David, Thus saith the LORD of hosts, I took thee [a]from the [1]sheepcote, *even* from following the sheep, that thou shouldest be ruler over my people Israel:

8 And I have been with thee whithersoever thou hast walked, and have [1]cut off all thine enemies from before thee, and have [2]made thee a name like the name of the great men that *are* in the earth.

9 Also I will [1]ordain a place for my people Israel, and will [a]plant them, and they shall dwell in their place, and shall be moved no more; neither shall the children of wickedness [2]waste them any more, as at the beginning,

10 And since the time that I commanded judges *to be* over my people Israel. Moreover I will subdue all thine enemies. Furthermore I tell thee that the LORD will build thee an house.

11 And it shall come to pass, when thy days be [a]expired[1] that thou must go *to* [2]*be* with thy fathers, that I will raise up thy [b]seed after thee, which shall be of thy sons; and I will establish his kingdom.

12 [a]He shall build me an house, and I will stablish his throne for ever.

13 [a]I will be his father, and he shall be my son: and I will not take my mercy away from him, [b]as I took *it* from *him* that was before thee:

14 But [a]I will [1]settle him in mine house and in my kingdom for ever: and his throne shall be established for evermore.

15 According to all these words, and according to all this vision, so did Nathan speak unto David.

16 [a]And David the king came and sat before the LORD, and said, Who *am* I, O LORD God, and what *is* mine house, that thou hast brought me [1]hitherto?

17 And *yet* this was a small thing in thine eyes, O God; for thou hast *also* spoken of thy servant's house for a great while to come, and hast regarded me according to the estate of a man of high degree, O LORD God.

18 What can David *speak* more to thee for the honour of thy servant? for thou knowest thy servant.

19 O LORD, for thy servant's sake, and according to thine own heart, hast thou done all this greatness, in making known all *these* great things.

20 O LORD, *there is* none like thee, neither *is there any* God beside thee,

16:33 [b] [Joel 3:1–14]; Zech. 14:1–14; [Matt. 25:31–46]
16:34 [a] 2 Chr. 5:13; 7:3; Ezra 3:11; Ps. 106:1; 107:1; 118:1; 136:1; Jer. 33:11
16:35 [a] Ps. 106:47, 48 [1] *triumph*
16:36 [a] 1 Kin. 8:15, 56; Ps. 72:18 [b] Deut. 27:15; Neh. 8:6
16:37 [a] 1 Chr. 16:4, 5 [b] 2 Chr. 8:14; Ezra 3:4
16:38 [a] 1 Chr. 13:14
16:39 [a] 1 Chr. 21:29; 2 Chr. 1:3 [b] 1 Kin. 3:4 [1] Places for pagan worship
16:40 [a] [Ex. 29:38–42; Num. 28:3, 4]
16:41 [a] 1 Chr. 25:1–6; 2 Chr. 5:13; 7:3; Ezra 3:11; Jer. 33:11 [1] *designated*
16:42 [1] *gatekeepers*
16:43 [a] 2 Sam. 6:18–20
17:1 [a] 2 Sam. 7:1; 1 Chr. 14:1
17:4 [a] [1 Chr. 28:2, 3]
17:7 [a] 1 Sam. 16:11–13 [1] *sheepfold*
17:8 [1] *destroyed* [2] *given you prestige*
17:9 [a] [Deut. 30:1–9; Jer. 16:14–16; 23:5–8; 24:6; Ezek. 37:21–27]; Amos 9:14 [1] *appoint* [2] *oppress*
17:11 [a] 1 Kin. 2:10; 1 Chr. 29:28 [b] 1 Kin. 5:5; 6:12; 8:19–21; [1 Chr. 22:9–13; 28:20]; Matt. 1:6; Luke 3:31 [1] *fulfilled* [2] *rest in death with your ancestors*
17:12 [a] 1 Kin. 6:38; 2 Chr. 6:2; [Ps. 89:20–37]
17:13 [a] 2 Sam. 7:14, 15; Matt. 3:17; Mark 1:11; Luke 3:22; 2 Cor. 6:18; Heb. 1:5 [b] [1 Sam. 15:23–28]; 1 Chr. 10:14
17:14 [a] Ps. 89:3, 4; Matt. 19:28; 25:31; [Luke 1:31–33] [1] *establish*
17:16 [a] 2 Sam. 7:18 [1] *this far*

according to all that we have heard with our ears.

21 ªAnd what one nation in the earth *is* like thy people Israel, whom God went to redeem *to be* his own people, to make thee a name ¹of greatness and terribleness, by driving out nations from before thy people, whom thou hast redeemed out of Egypt?

22 For thy people Israel didst thou make thine own people for ever; and thou, LORD, becamest their God.

23 Therefore now, LORD, let the thing that thou hast spoken concerning thy servant and concerning his house be established for ever, and do as thou hast said.

24 Let it even be established, that thy name may be magnified for ever, saying, The LORD of hosts *is* the God of Israel, *even* a God to Israel: and *let* the house of David thy servant *be* established before thee.

25 For thou, O my God, ¹hast told thy servant that thou wilt build him an house: therefore thy servant hath found *in his heart* to pray before thee.

26 And now, LORD, ¹thou art God, and hast promised this goodness unto thy servant:

27 Now therefore ¹let it please thee to bless the house of thy servant, that it may be before thee for ever: for thou blessest, O LORD, and *it shall be* blessed for ever.

## CHAPTER 18

Now after this ªit came to pass, that David ¹smote the Philistines, and subdued them, and took Gath and her towns out of the hand of the Philistines.

2 And he ¹smote ªMoab; and the Moabites became David's ᵇservants, *and* brought gifts.

3 And ªDavid ¹smote ²Hadarezer king of Zobah unto Hamath, as he went to stablish his dominion by the river Euphrates.

4 And David took from him a thousand chariots, and ¹seven thousand horsemen, and twenty thousand footmen: David also ²houghed all the chariot *horses,* but reserved of them an hundred chariots.

5 And when the ªSyrians of ¹Damascus came to help Hadarezer king of Zobah, David slew of the Syrians two and twenty thousand men.

6 Then David put *garrisons* in Syria-damascus; and the Syrians became David's servants, *and* brought gifts. Thus the LORD preserved David ¹whithersoever he went.

7 And David took the shields of gold that were on the servants of Hadarezer, and brought them to Jerusalem.

8 Likewise from ¹Tibhath, and from ²Chun, cities of ³Hadarezer, brought David very much ªbrass, wherewith ᵇSolomon made the ⁴brasen sea, and the pillars, and the vessels of brass.

9 Now when ¹Tou king of Hamath heard how David had ²smitten all the host of Hadarezer king of Zobah;

10 He sent ¹Hadoram his son to king David, to ²enquire of his welfare, and to ³congratulate him, because he had fought against Hadarezer, and ⁴smitten him; (for Hadarezer had war with Tou;) and *with him* all manner of ªvessels of gold and silver and brass.

11 Them also king David dedicated unto the LORD, with the silver and the gold that he brought from all *these* nations; from Edom, and from Moab, and from the ªchildren of Ammon, and from the ᵇPhilistines, and from ᶜAmalek.

12 Moreover ªAbishai the son of Zeruiah slew of the ¹Edomites in the valley of salt ᵇeighteen thousand.

13 ªAnd he put garrisons in Edom; and all the Edomites became David's servants. Thus the LORD preserved David ¹whithersoever he went.

14 So David reigned over all Israel, and ¹executed judgment and justice among all his people.

15 And Joab the son of Zeruiah *was* over the host; and Jehoshaphat the son of Ahilud, recorder.

16 And Zadok the son of Ahitub, and ¹Abimelech the son of Abiathar, *were* the priests; and ²Shavsha was scribe;

17 ªAnd Benaiah the son of Jehoiada *was* over the Cherethites and the Pelethites; and the sons of David *were* ¹chief about the king.

## CHAPTER 19

Now ªit came to pass after this, that Nahash the king of the children of Ammon died, and his son reigned in his stead.

2 And David said, I will shew kindness unto Hanun the son of Nahash, because his father shewed kindness to me. And David sent messengers to comfort him concerning his father. So the servants of David came into the land of the children of Ammon to Hanun, to comfort him.

3 But the princes of the children of Ammon said to Hanun, ¹Thinkest thou that David doth honour thy father, that he hath sent comforters unto thee? are not his servants come unto thee for to search, and to overthrow, and to spy out the land?

4 Wherefore Hanun took David's servants, and shaved them, and cut off their garments ¹in the midst hard by their ªbuttocks, and sent them away.

17:21 ª [Deut. 4:6–8, 33–38]; Ps. 147:20 ¹ *by great and awesome deeds*

17:25 ¹ Lit. *have uncovered the ear of*

17:26 ¹ *you alone are*

17:27 ¹ *you have been pleased to*

18:1 ª 2 Sam. 8:1– 18 ¹ *attacked*

18:2 ² 2 Sam. 8:2; Zeph. 2:9 ᵇ Ps. 60:8 ¹ *defeated*

18:3 ² 2 Sam. 8:3 ¹ *defeated* ² *Hadadezer,* 2 Sam. 8:3

18:4 ¹ *seven hundred,* 2 Sam. 8:4 ² *hamstrung, crippled*

18:5 ² 2 Sam. 8:5, 6; 1 Kin. 11:23–25 ¹ Heb. *Darmeseq*

18:6 ¹ *wherever*

18:8 ª 2 Sam. 8:8 ᵇ 1 Kin. 7:15, 23; 2 Chr. 4:12, 15, 16 ¹ *Betah,* 2 Sam. 8:8 ² *Berothai,* 2 Sam. 8:8 ³ *Hadadezer,* 2 Sam. 8:3 ⁴ *bronze sea* (the great laver or bason)

18:9 ¹ *Toi,* 2 Sam. 8:9 ² *defeated*

18:10 ª 2 Sam. 8:10–12 ¹ *Joram,* 2 Sam. 8:10 ² *greet him* ³ *bless* ⁴ *defeated*

18:11 ª 2 Sam. 10:12 ᵇ 2 Sam. 5:17–25 ᶜ 2 Sam. 1:1

18:12 ª 2 Sam. 23:18; 1 Chr. 2:16 ᵇ 2 Sam. 8:13 ¹ *Syrians,* 2 Sam. 8:13

18:13 ª Gen. 27:29–40; Num. 24:18; 2 Sam. 8:14 ¹ *wherever*

18:14 ¹ *administered*

18:16 ¹ *Ahimelech,* 2 Sam. 8:17 ² *Seraiah,* 2 Sam. 8:17 or *Shisha,* 1 Kin. 4:3

18:17 ª 2 Sam. 8:18 ¹ Lit. *heads at the hand of the king*

19:1 ª 1 Sam. 11:1; 2 Sam. 10:1–19

19:3 ¹ Lit. *In your eyes is David honouring your father because*

19:4 ª Is. 20:4 ¹ Lit. *in half at the buttocks*

5 Then there went *certain,* and told David how the men were served. And he sent to meet them: for the men were greatly ashamed. And the king said, Tarry at Jericho until your beards be grown, and *then* return.

6 And when the children of Ammon saw that they had made themselves [1]odious to David, Hanun and the children of Ammon sent a thousand talents of silver to hire them chariots and horsemen out of [2]Mesopotamia, and out of Syria-maachah, [a]and out of [3]Zobah.

7 So they hired thirty and two thousand chariots, and the king of Maachah and his people; who came and [1]pitched before Medeba. And the children of Ammon gathered themselves together from their cities, and came to battle.

8 And when David heard *of it,* he sent Joab, and all the host of the mighty men.

9 And the children of Ammon came out, and [1]put the battle in array before the gate of the city: and the kings that were come *were* by themselves in the field.

10 Now when Joab saw that the battle was set against him before and behind, he [1]chose out of all the choice of Israel, and put *them* in array against the Syrians.

11 And the rest of the people he delivered unto the hand of Abishai his brother, and they set *themselves* in array against the children of Ammon.

12 And he said, If the Syrians be too strong for me, then thou shalt help me: but if the children of Ammon be too strong for thee, then I will help thee.

13 Be of good courage, and let us [1]behave ourselves valiantly for our people, and for the cities of our God: and let the LORD do *that which is* good in his sight.

14 So Joab and the people that *were* with him drew nigh before the Syrians unto the battle; and they fled before him.

15 And when the children of Ammon saw that the Syrians were fled, they likewise fled before Abishai his brother, and entered into the city. Then Joab came to Jerusalem.

16 And when the Syrians saw that they [1]were put to the worse before Israel, they sent messengers, and drew forth the Syrians that *were* beyond the [2]river: and [3]Shophach the captain of the host of Hadarezer *went* before them.

17 And it was told David; and he gathered all Israel, and passed over Jordan, and came upon them, and set *the battle* in array against them. So when David had [1]put the battle in

19:6 [a] 1 Chr. 18:5, 9
[1] *repulsive* [2] Heb.
*Aram-naharaim*
[3] *Zoba,* 2 Sam.
10:6
19:7 [1] *encamped*
19:9 [1] *put themselves in battle array*
19:10 [1] *chose some of*
19:13 [1] *be strong for*
19:16 [1] *had been defeated by*
[2] *The Euphrates*
[3] *Shobach,* 2 Sam.
10:16 or *Zoba,* 2 Sam. 10:6
19:17 [1] *set up in battle array*

19:18 [1] *seven hundred,* 2 Sam.
10:18 [2] *horsemen,* 2 Sam. 10:18
19:19 [1] *defeated by*
20:1 [a] 2 Sam. 11:1
[b] 2 Sam. 11:2–
12:25 [c] 2 Sam. 12:26 [1] Lit. *at the return of the year (in the spring)*
[2] *stayed*
20:2 [a] 2 Sam. 12:30, 31 [1] *plunder*
20:3 [1] MT *put them to work with*
20:4 [a] 2 Sam. 21:18 [b] 1 Chr. 11:29
[1] *Gob,* 2 Sam. 21:18 [2] *Saph,* 2 Sam. 21:18 [3] Heb. *haraphah*
20:5 [a] 1 Sam. 17:7; 1 Chr. 11:23 [1] *Jaare-oregim,* 2 Sam. 21:19
20:6 [a] 1 Sam. 5:8; 2 Sam. 21:20 [1] Lit. *born to* [2] Heb. *haraphah*
20:7 [1] *Shammah,* 1 Sam. 16:9
21:1 [a] 2 Sam. 24:1– 25; Job 1:6 [1] Lit. *moved* [2] *take a census of*

array against the Syrians, they fought with him.

18 But the Syrians fled before Israel; and David slew of the Syrians [1]seven thousand *men which fought in* chariots, and forty thousand [2]footmen, and killed Shophach the captain of the host.

19 And when the servants of Hadarezer saw that they were [1]put to the worse before Israel, they made peace with David, and became his servants: neither would the Syrians help the children of Ammon any more.

## CHAPTER 20

AND [a]it came to pass, that [1]after the year was expired, at the time that kings go out *to battle,* Joab led forth the power of the army, and wasted the country of the children of Ammon, and came and besieged Rabbah. But [b]David [2]tarried at Jerusalem. And [c]Joab smote Rabbah, and destroyed it.

2 And David [a]took the crown of their king from off his head, and found it to weigh a talent of gold, and *there were* precious stones in it; and it was set upon David's head: and he brought also exceeding much [1]spoil out of the city.

3 And he brought out the people that *were* in it, and [1]cut *them* with saws, and with harrows of iron, and with axes. Even so dealt David with all the cities of the children of Ammon. And David and all the people returned to Jerusalem.

4 And it came to pass after this, [a]that there arose war at [1]Gezer with the Philistines; at which time [b]Sibbechai the Hushathite slew [2]Sippai, *that was* of the children of [3]the giant: and they were subdued.

5 And there was war again with the Philistines; and Elhanan the son of [1]Jair slew Lahmi the brother of Goliath the Gittite, whose spear staff *was* like a weaver's [a]beam.

6 And yet again [a]there was war at Gath, where was a man of *great* stature, whose fingers and toes *were* four and twenty, six *on each hand,* and six *on each foot:* and he also was [1]the son of [2]the giant.

7 But when he defied Israel, Jonathan the son of [1]Shimea David's brother slew him.

8 These were born unto the giant in Gath; and they fell by the hand of David, and by the hand of his servants.

## CHAPTER 21

AND [a]Satan stood up against Israel, and [1]provoked David to [2]number Israel.

2 And David said to Joab and to the rulers of the people, Go, number Israel

from Beer-sheba even to Dan; [a]and bring the number of them to me, that I may know *it.*

3 And Joab answered, The LORD make his people an hundred times so many more as they *be:* but, my lord the king, *are* they not all my lord's servants? why then doth my lord require this thing? why will he be a cause of [1]trespass to Israel?

4 Nevertheless the king's word prevailed against Joab. Wherefore Joab departed, and went throughout all Israel, and came to Jerusalem.

5 And Joab gave the sum of the number of the people unto David. And all *they of* Israel were a thousand thousand and an hundred thousand men that drew sword: and Judah *was* four hundred threescore and ten thousand men that drew sword.

6 [a]But Levi and Benjamin counted he not among them: for the king's [1]word was abominable to Joab.

7 And [1]God was displeased with this thing; therefore he [2]smote Israel.

8 And David said unto God, [a]I have sinned greatly, because I have done this thing: [b]but now, I beseech thee, [1]do away the iniquity of thy servant; for I have done very foolishly.

9 And the LORD spake unto Gad, David's [a]seer, saying,

10 Go and tell David, [a]saying, Thus saith the LORD, I offer thee three *things:* choose thee one of them, that I may do *it* unto thee.

11 So Gad came to David, and said unto him, Thus saith the LORD, Choose thee

12 [a]Either [1]three years' famine; or three months to be destroyed before thy foes, while that the sword of thine enemies overtaketh *thee;* or else three days the sword of the LORD, even the pestilence, in the land, and the angel of the LORD destroying throughout all the [2]coasts of Israel. Now therefore [3]advise thyself what word I shall bring again to him that sent me.

13 And David said unto Gad, I am in a great [1]strait: let me fall now into the hand of the LORD; for very great *are* his [a]mercies: but let me not fall into the hand of man.

14 So the LORD sent [a]pestilence upon Israel: and there fell of Israel seventy thousand men.

15 And God sent an [a]angel unto Jerusalem to destroy it: and as he was destroying, the LORD beheld, and [b]he [1]repented him of the evil, and said to the angel that destroyed, It is enough, stay now thine hand. And the angel of the LORD stood by the [c]threshingfloor of [2]Ornan the Jebusite.

16 And David lifted up his eyes, and [a]saw the angel of the LORD stand

between the earth and the heaven, having a drawn sword in his hand stretched out over Jerusalem. Then David and the elders of *Israel, who were* clothed in sackcloth, fell upon their faces.

17 And David said unto God, *Is it* not I *that* commanded the people to be numbered? even I it is that have sinned and done evil indeed; but *as for* these [a]sheep, what have they done? let thine hand, I pray thee, O LORD my God, be on me, and on my father's house; but not on thy people, that they should be plagued.

18 Then the [a]angel of the LORD commanded Gad to say to David, that David should go up, and set up an altar unto the LORD in the threshingfloor of Ornan the Jebusite.

19 And David went up at the saying of Gad, which he spake in the name of the LORD.

20 And Ornan turned back, and saw the angel; and his four sons with him hid themselves. Now Ornan was threshing wheat.

21 And as David came to Ornan, Ornan looked and saw David, and went out of the threshingfloor, and bowed himself to David with *his* face to the ground.

22 Then David said to Ornan, [1]Grant me the place of *this* threshingfloor, that I may build an altar therein unto the LORD: thou shalt grant it me for the full price: that the plague may be [2]stayed from the people.

23 And Ornan said unto David, Take *it* to thee, and let my lord the king do *that which is* good in his eyes: lo, I give *thee* the oxen *also* for burnt offerings, and the threshing instruments for wood, and the wheat for the [1]meat offering; I give it all.

24 And king David said to Ornan, Nay; but I will verily buy it for the full price: for I will not take *that* which *is* thine for the LORD, nor offer burnt offerings without cost.

25 So [a]David gave to Ornan for the place six hundred shekels of gold by weight.

26 And David built there an altar unto the LORD, and offered burnt offerings and peace offerings, and called upon the LORD; and [a]he answered him from heaven by fire upon the altar of burnt offering.

27 And the LORD commanded the angel; and he put up his sword again into the sheath thereof.

28 At that time when David saw that the LORD had answered him in the threshingfloor of Ornan the Jebusite, then he sacrificed there.

29 [a]For the tabernacle of the LORD, which Moses made in the wilderness, and the altar of the burnt offering,

---

**Center column references:**

21:2 [a] 1 Chr. 27:23, 24
21:3 [1] *guilt*
21:6 [a] 1 Chr. 27:24 [1] *command*
21:7 [1] Lit. *it was evil in the eyes of God* [2] *struck*
21:8 [a] 2 Sam. 24:10 [b] 2 Sam. 12:13 [1] *take away*
21:9 [a] 1 Sam. 9:9; 2 Kin. 17:13; 1 Chr. 29:29; 2 Chr. 16:7, 10; Is. 30:9, 10; Amos 7:12, 13
21:10 [a] 2 Sam. 24:12–14
21:12 [a] 2 Sam. 24:13 [1] *seven,* 2 Sam. 24:13 [2] *territory* [3] *consider what answer I should take back*
21:13 [a] Ps. 51:1; 130:4, 7 [1] *distress*
21:14 [a] 1 Chr. 27:24
21:15 [a] 2 Sam. 24:16 [b] Gen. 6:6 [c] 2 Chr. 3:1 [1] *relented of the disaster* [2] *Araunah,* 2 Sam. 24:16
21:16 [a] Josh. 5:13; 2 Chr. 3:1
21:17 [a] 2 Sam. 7:8; Ps. 74:1
21:18 [a] 1 Chr. 21:11, 12; 2 Chr. 3:1
21:22 [1] Lit. *Give* [2] *withdrawn*
21:23 [1] *meal* or *grain*
21:25 [a] 2 Sam. 24:24
21:26 [a] Lev. 9:24; Judg. 6:21; 1 Kin. 18:36–38; 2 Chr. 3:1; 7:1
21:29 [a] 1 Kin. 3:4; 2 Chr. 1:3

*were* at that season in the high place at [b]Gibeon.

30 But David could not go before it to enquire of God: for he was afraid because of the sword of the angel of the LORD.

## CHAPTER 22

THEN David said, [a]This *is* the house of the LORD God, and this *is* the altar of the burnt offering for Israel.

2 And David commanded to gather together the [a]strangers that *were* in the land of Israel; and he set masons to [b]hew wrought stones to build the house of God.

3 And David prepared iron in abundance for the nails for the doors of the gates, and for the joinings; and brass in abundance [a]without[1] weight;

4 Also cedar trees in abundance: for the [a]Zidonians and they of Tyre brought much cedar wood to David.

5 And David said, [a]Solomon my son *is* young and tender, and the house *that is* to be builded for the LORD *must be* exceeding magnifical, of fame and of glory throughout all countries: I will *therefore* now make preparation for it. So David prepared abundantly before his death.

6 Then he called for Solomon his son, and [1]charged him to build an house for the LORD God of Israel.

7 And David said to Solomon, My son, as for me, [a]it was in my mind to build an house [b]unto the name of the LORD my God:

8 But the word of the LORD came to me, saying, [a]Thou hast shed blood abundantly, and hast made great wars: thou shalt not build an house unto my name, because thou hast shed much blood upon the earth in my sight.

9 [a]Behold, a son shall be born to thee, who shall be a man of rest; and I will give him [b]rest from all his enemies round about: for his name shall be [1]Solomon, and I will give peace and quietness unto Israel in his days.

10 [a]He shall build an house for my name; and [b]he shall be my son, and I *will be* his father; and I will establish the throne of his kingdom over Israel for ever.

11 Now, my son, [a]the LORD be with thee; and prosper thou, and build the house of the LORD thy God, as he hath said of thee.

12 Only the LORD [a]give thee wisdom and understanding, and give thee charge concerning Israel, that thou mayest keep the law of the LORD thy God.

13 [a]Then shalt thou prosper, if thou takest heed to fulfil the statutes and judgments which the LORD [1]charged Moses with concerning Israel: [b]be

strong, and of good courage; dread not, nor be dismayed.

14 Now, behold, [1]in my trouble I have prepared for the house of the LORD an hundred thousand talents of gold, and a thousand thousand talents of silver; and of brass and iron [a]without weight; for it is in abundance: timber also and stone have I prepared; and thou mayest add thereto.

15 Moreover *there are* workmen with thee in abundance, [1]hewers and workers of stone and timber, and all manner of cunning men for every manner of work.

16 Of the gold, the silver, and the brass, and the iron, *there is* no number. Arise *therefore*, and be doing, and [a]the LORD be with thee.

17 David also commanded all the [a]princes of Israel to help Solomon his son, *saying,*

18 *Is* not the LORD your God with you? [a]and hath he *not* given you rest on every side? for he hath given the inhabitants of the land into [1]mine hand; and the land is subdued before the LORD, and before his people.

19 Now set your heart and your soul to seek the LORD your God; arise therefore, and build ye the sanctuary of the LORD God, to [a]bring the ark of the covenant of the LORD, and the holy vessels of God, into the house that is to be built [b]to the name of the LORD.

## CHAPTER 23

SO when David was old and full of days, he made [a]Solomon his son king over Israel.

2 And he gathered together all the princes of Israel, with the priests and the Levites.

3 Now the Levites were numbered from the age of [a]thirty years and upward: and their number by their polls, man by man, was thirty and eight thousand.

4 Of which, twenty and four thousand *were* [1]to [a]set forward the work of the house of the LORD; and six thousand *were* [b]officers and judges:

5 Moreover four thousand *were* [1]porters; and four thousand [a]praised the LORD with the instruments [b]which I made, *said David,* to praise *therewith.*

6 And [a]David divided them into [1]courses among the sons of Levi, *namely,* Gershon, Kohath, and Merari.

7 Of the [a]Gershonites *were,* [1]Laadan, and Shimei.

8 The sons of Laadan; the chief *was* Jehiel, and Zetham, and Joel, three.

9 The sons of Shimei; Shelomith, and Haziel, and Haran, three. These

---

Center column cross-references:

21:29 [b] 1 Chr. 16:39

22:1 [a] Deut. 12:5; 2 Sam. 24:18; 1 Chr. 21:18, 19, 26, 28; 2 Chr. 3:1

22:2 [a] 1 Kin. 9:20, 21; 2 Chr. 2:17, 18
[b] 1 Kin. 5:17, 18

22:3 [a] 1 Kin. 7:47; 1 Chr. 22:14 [1] *beyond measure*

22:4 [a] 1 Kin. 5:6–10

22:5 [a] 1 Kin. 3:7; 1 Chr. 29:1, 2

22:6 [1] *commanded*

22:7 [a] 2 Sam. 7:1, 2; 1 Kin. 8:17; 1 Chr. 17:1; 28:2
[b] Deut. 12:5, 11

22:8 [a] 2 Sam. 7:5–13; 1 Kin. 5:3; 1 Chr. 28:3

22:9 [a] 1 Chr. 28:5
[b] 1 Kin. 4:20, 25; 5:4 [1] Lit. *Peaceful*

22:10 [a] 2 Sam. 7:13; 1 Kin. 5:5; 6:38; 1 Chr. 17:12, 13; 28:6; 2 Chr. 6:2
[b] Heb. 1:5

22:11 [a] 1 Chr. 22:16

22:12 [a] 1 Kin. 3:9–12; 2 Chr. 1:10

22:13 [a] [Josh. 1:7, 8]; 1 Chr. 28:7
[b] [Deut. 31:7, 8; Josh. 1:6, 7, 9; 1 Chr. 28:20]
[1] *commanded*

22:14 [a] 1 Chr. 22:3 [1] *I have taken trouble to prepare*

22:15 [1] *woodsmen and stonecutters*

22:16 [a] 1 Chr. 22:11

22:17 [a] 1 Chr. 28:1–6

22:18 [a] Deut. 12:10; Josh. 22:4; 2 Sam. 7:1; [1 Kin. 5:4; 8:56] [1] *my control*

22:19 [a] 1 Kin. 8:1–11; 2 Chr. 5:2–14
[b] 1 Kin. 5:3

23:1 [a] 1 Kin. 1:33–40; 1 Chr. 28:4, 5

23:3 [a] Num. 4:1–3

23:4 [a] 2 Chr. 2:2, 18; Ezra 3:8, 9
[b] Deut. 16:18–20 [1] *to look after*

23:5 [a] 1 Chr. 15:16
[b] 2 Chr. 29:25–27 [1] *gatekeepers*

23:6 [a] Ex. 6:16; Num. 26:57; 2 Chr. 8:14 [1] *divisions or groups*

23:7 [a] 1 Chr. 26:21 [1] *Libni, Ex. 6:17*

*were* the chief of the fathers of Laadan.

10 And the sons of Shimei *were,* Jahath, ¹Zina, and Jeush, and Beriah. These four *were* the sons of Shimei.

11 And Jahath was the chief, and Zizah the second: but Jeush and Beriah had not many sons; therefore they were ¹in one reckoning, according to *their* father's house.

12 ªThe sons of Kohath; Amram, Izhar, Hebron, and Uzziel, four.

13 The sons of ªAmram; Aaron and Moses: and ᵇAaron was ¹separated, that he should ²sanctify the most holy things, he and his sons for ever, ᶜto burn incense before the LORD, ᵈto minister unto him, and ᵉto bless in his name for ever.

14 Now *concerning* Moses the man of God, ªhis sons were named of the tribe of Levi.

15 ªThe sons of Moses *were,* ¹Gershom, and Eliezer.

16 Of the sons of Gershom, ªShebuel¹ *was* the chief.

17 And the ¹sons of Eliezer *were,* ªRehabiah ²the chief. And Eliezer had none other sons; but the sons of Rehabiah were very many.

18 Of the sons of Izhar; ªShelomith the chief.

19 ªOf the sons of Hebron; Jeriah the first, Amariah the second, Jahaziel the third, and Jekameam the fourth.

20 Of the sons of Uzziel; Micah the first, and Jesiah the second.

21 ªThe sons of Merari; Mahli, and Mushi. The sons of Mahli; Eleazar, and ᵇKish.

22 And Eleazar died, and ªhad no sons, but daughters: and their ¹brethren the sons of Kish ᵇtook them.

23 ªThe sons of Mushi; Mahli, and Eder, and Jeremoth, three.

24 These *were* the sons of ªLevi after the house of their fathers; *even* the chief of the fathers, as they were counted by number of names ¹by their polls, that did the work for the service of the house of the LORD, from the age of ᵇtwenty years and upward.

25 For David said, The LORD God of Israel ªhath given rest unto his people, that they may dwell in Jerusalem for ever:

26 And also unto the Levites; they shall no *more* ªcarry the tabernacle, nor any vessels of it for the service thereof.

27 For by the ªlast words of David the Levites *were* numbered from twenty years old and above:

28 Because ¹their office *was* to wait on the sons of Aaron for the service of the house of the LORD, in the courts, and in the chambers, and in the purifying of all holy things, and

the work of the service of the house of God;

29 Both for ªthe shewbread, and for ᵇthe fine flour for ¹meat offering, and for ᶜthe unleavened cakes, and for ᵈ*that which is baked in* the pan, and for that which is fried, and for all manner of ᵉmeasure and size;

30 And to stand every morning to thank and praise the LORD, and likewise at ¹even;

31 And to offer all burnt sacrifices unto the LORD ªin the sabbaths, in the new moons, and on the ᵇset¹ feasts, by number, according to the order commanded unto them, ²continually before the LORD:

32 And that they should ªkeep¹ the ᵇcharge of the tabernacle of the congregation, and the charge of the holy *place,* and ᶜthe charge of the sons of Aaron their brethren, in the service of the house of the LORD.

## CHAPTER 24

Now *these are* the divisions of the sons of Aaron. ªThe sons of Aaron; Nadab, and Abihu, Eleazar, and Ithamar.

2 But ªNadab and Abihu died before their father, and had no children: therefore Eleazar and Ithamar ¹executed the priest's office.

3 And David distributed them, both Zadok of the sons of Eleazar, and ªAhimelech of the sons of Ithamar, according to their offices in their service.

4 And there were more chief men found of the sons of Eleazar than of the sons of Ithamar; and *thus* were they divided. Among the sons of Eleazar *there were* sixteen chief men of the house of *their* fathers, and eight among the sons of Ithamar according to the house of their fathers.

5 Thus were they divided by lot, one sort with another; for the governors of the sanctuary, and governors *of the house* of God, were of the sons of Eleazar, and of the sons of Ithamar.

6 And Shemaiah the son of Nethaneel the scribe, *one* of the Levites, wrote them before the king, and the princes, and Zadok the priest, and Ahimelech the son of Abiathar, and *before* the chief of the fathers of the priests and Levites: one principal household being taken for Eleazar, and *one* taken for Ithamar.

7 Now the first lot came forth to Jehoiarib, the second to Jedaiah,

8 The third to Harim, the fourth to Seorim,

9 The fifth to Malchijah, the sixth to Mijamin,

10 The seventh to Hakkoz, the eighth to ªAbijah,

11 The ninth to Jeshuah, the tenth to Shecaniah,

23:10 ¹ LXX, Vg. Zizah, 1 Chr. 23:11

23:11 ¹ *assigned as one father's*

23:12 ª Ex. 6:18

23:13 ª Ex. 6:20 ᵇ Ex. 28:1; Heb. 5:4 ᶜ Ex. 30:7; 1 Sam. 2:28 ᵈ [Deut. 21:5] ᵉ Num. 6:23 ¹ *set apart* ² *consecrate*

23:14 ª 1 Chr. 26:20–24

23:15 ª Ex. 18:3, 4 ¹ *Gershon,* Ex. 6:16

23:16 ª 1 Chr. 26:24 ¹ *Shubael,* 1 Chr. 24:20

23:17 ª 1 Chr. 26:25 ¹ *son of Eliezer was* ² *the first*

23:18 ª 1 Chr. 24:22

23:19 ª 1 Chr. 24:23

23:21 ª 1 Chr. 24:26 ᵇ 1 Chr. 24:29

23:22 ª 1 Chr. 24:28 ᵇ Num. 36:6 ¹ *kinsmen*

23:23 ª 1 Chr. 24:30

23:24 ª Num. 10:17, 21 ᵇ Num. 1:3; Ezra 3:8 ¹ *individually*

23:25 ª 1 Chr. 22:18

23:26 ª Num. 4:5, 15; 7:9; Deut. 10:8

23:27 ª 2 Sam. 23:1

23:28 ¹ *their duty was to help*

23:29 ª Ex. 25:30 ᵇ Lev. 6:20 ᶜ Lev. 2:1, 4 ᵈ Lev. 2:5, 7 ᵉ Lev. 19:35 ¹ *meal or grain*

23:30 ¹ *evening*

23:31 ª Num. 10:10 ᵇ Lev. 23:2–4 ¹ *appointed feasts* ² *regularly*

23:32 ª 2 Chr. 13:10, 11 ᵇ [Num. 1:53]; 1 Chr. 9:27 ᶜ Num. 3:6–9, 38 ¹ *attend to the needs of*

24:1 ª Lev. 10:1–6; Num. 26:60, 61; 1 Chr. 6:3

24:2 ª Num. 3:1–4; 26:61 ¹ *ministered as priests*

24:3 ª 1 Chr. 18:16

24:10 ª Neh. 12:4, 17; Luke 1:5

12 The eleventh to Eliashib, the twelfth to Jakim,

13 The thirteenth to Huppah, the fourteenth to Jeshebeab,

14 The fifteenth to Bilgah, the sixteenth to Immer,

15 The seventeenth to Hezir, the eighteenth to ¹Aphses,

16 The nineteenth to Pethahiah, the twentieth to Jehezekel,

17 The one and twentieth to Jachin, the two and twentieth to Gamul,

18 The three and twentieth to Delaiah, the four and twentieth to Maaziah.

19 These *were* the ¹orderings of them in their service ᵃto come into the house of the LORD, according to their manner, under Aaron their father, as the LORD God of Israel had commanded him.

20 And the rest of the sons of Levi *were these:* Of the sons of Amram; ¹Shubael: of the sons of Shubael; Jehdeiah.

21 Concerning ᵃRehabiah: of the sons of Rehabiah, the first *was* Isshiah.

22 Of the Izharites; ¹Shelomoth: of the sons of Shelomoth; Jahath.

23 And the sons *of* ᵃHebron; Jeriah *the first,* Amariah the second, Jahaziel the third, Jekameam the fourth.

24 *Of* the sons of Uzziel; Michah: of the sons of Michah; Shamir.

25 The brother of Michah *was* Isshiah: of the sons of Isshiah; Zechariah.

26 ᵃThe sons of Merari *were* Mahli and Mushi: the sons of Jaaziah; Beno.

27 The sons of Merari by Jaaziah; Beno, and Shoham, and Zaccur, and Ibri.

28 Of Mahli *came* Eleazar, ᵃwho had no sons.

29 Concerning Kish: the son of Kish *was* Jerahmeel.

30 ᵃThe sons also of Mushi; Mahli, and Eder, and Jerimoth. These *were* the sons of the Levites after the house of their fathers.

31 These likewise cast lots over against their brethren the sons of Aaron in the presence of David the king, and Zadok, and Ahimelech, and the chief of the fathers of the priests and Levites, even the principal fathers over against their younger brethren.

## CHAPTER 25

MOREOVER David and the captains of the host ¹separated to the service of the sons of ᵃAsaph, and of Heman, and of Jeduthun, who should prophesy with harps, with psalteries, and with cymbals: and the number of the workmen according to their service was:

*(marginal references)*
24:15 ¹ MT Happizzez
24:19 ᵃ 1 Chr. 9:25 ¹ schedules
24:20 ¹ Shebuel, 1 Chr. 23:16
24:21 ᵃ 1 Chr. 23:17
24:22 ¹ Shelomith, 1 Chr. 23:18
24:23 ᵃ 1 Chr. 23:19; 26:31
24:26 ᵃ Ex. 6:19; 1 Chr. 23:21
24:28 ᵃ 1 Chr. 23:22
24:30 ᵃ 1 Chr. 23:23
25:1 ¹ 1 Chr. 6:30, 33, 39, 44; 2 Chr. 5:12 ¹ set apart
25:2 ¹ Jesharelah, 1 Chr. 25:14 ² Lit. at the hands of
25:3 ᵃ 1 Chr. 16:41, 42 ¹ Izri, 1 Chr. 25:11 ² Shimei appears in one Heb. ms. and several LXX mss. completing the six.
25:4 ¹ Azareel, 1 Chr. 25:18 ² Shubael, 1 Chr. 25:20 ³ Jeremoth, 1 Chr. 25:22
25:5 ᵃ 1 Chr. 16:42 ¹ To increase his power or influence
25:6 ᵃ 1 Chr. 15:16 ᵇ 1 Chr. 15:19; 25:2
25:7 ᵃ 1 Chr. 23:5
25:8 ᵃ 2 Chr. 23:13
25:11 ¹ Zeri, 1 Chr. 25:3
25:14 ¹ Asarelah, 1 Chr. 25:2
25:18 ¹ Uzziel, 1 Chr. 25:4
25:20 ¹ Shebuel, 1 Chr. 25:4

2 Of the sons of Asaph; Zaccur, and Joseph, and Nethaniah, and ¹Asarelah, the sons of Asaph under the hands of Asaph, which prophesied ²according to the order of the king.

3 Of ᵃJeduthun: the sons of Jeduthun; Gedaliah, and ¹Zeri, and Jeshaiah, Hashabiah, and Mattithiah, ²six, under the hands of their father Jeduthun, who prophesied with a harp, to give thanks and to praise the LORD.

4 Of Heman: the sons of Heman; Bukkiah, Mattaniah, ¹Uzziel, ²Shebuel, and ³Jerimoth, Hananiah, Hanani, Eliathah, Giddalti, and Romamtiezer, Joshbekashah, Mallothi, Hothir, *and* Mahazioth:

5 All these *were* the sons of Heman the king's seer in the words of God, ¹to lift up the ᵃhorn. And God gave to Heman fourteen sons and three daughters.

6 All these *were* under the hands of their father for song *in* the house of the LORD, with cymbals, psalteries, and ᵃharps, for the service of the house of God, ᵇaccording to the king's order to Asaph, Jeduthun, and Heman.

7 So the ᵃnumber of them, with their brethren that were instructed in the songs of the LORD, *even* all that were cunning, was two hundred fourscore and eight.

8 And they cast lots, ward against *ward,* as well the small as the great, ᵃthe teacher as the scholar.

9 Now the first lot came forth for Asaph to Joseph: the second to Gedaliah, who with his brethren and sons *were* twelve:

10 The third to Zaccur, *he,* his sons, and his brethren, *were* twelve:

11 The fourth to ¹Izri, *he,* his sons, and his brethren, *were* twelve:

12 The fifth to Nethaniah, *he,* his sons, and his brethren, *were* twelve:

13 The sixth to Bukkiah, *he,* his sons, and his brethren, *were* twelve:

14 The seventh to ¹Jesharelah, *he,* his sons, and his brethren, *were* twelve:

15 The eighth to Jeshaiah, *he,* his sons, and his brethren, *were* twelve:

16 The ninth to Mattaniah, *he,* his sons, and his brethren, *were* twelve:

17 The tenth to Shimei, *he,* his sons, and his brethren, *were* twelve:

18 The eleventh to ¹Azareel, *he,* his sons, and his brethren, *were* twelve:

19 The twelfth to Hashabiah, *he,* his sons, and his brethren, *were* twelve:

20 The thirteenth to ¹Shubael, *he,* his sons, and his brethren, *were* twelve:

21 The fourteenth to Mattithiah, *he,* his sons, and his brethren, *were* twelve:

22 The fifteenth to ¹Jeremoth, *he,* his sons, and his brethren, *were* twelve:

23 The sixteenth to Hananiah, *he,* his sons, and his brethren, *were* twelve:

24 The seventeenth to Joshbekashah, *he,* his sons, and his brethren, *were* twelve:

25 The eighteenth to Hanani, *he,* his sons, and his brethren, *were* twelve:

26 The nineteenth to Mallothi, *he,* his sons, and his brethren, *were* twelve:

27 The twentieth to Eliathah, *he,* his sons, and his brethren, *were* twelve:

28 The one and twentieth to Hothir, *he,* his sons, and his brethren, *were* twelve:

29 The two and twentieth to Giddalti, *he,* his sons, and his brethren, *were* twelve:

30 The three and twentieth to Mahazioth, *he,* his sons, and his brethren, *were* twelve:

31 The four and twentieth to Romamti-ezer, *he,* his sons, and his brethren, *were* twelve.

## CHAPTER 26

CONCERNING the divisions of the ¹porters: Of the Korhites *was* ²Meshelemiah the son of ªKore, of the sons of ³Asaph.

2 And the sons of Meshelemiah *were,* ªZechariah the firstborn, Jediael the second, Zebadiah the third, Jathniel the fourth,

3 Elam the fifth, Jehohanan the sixth, Elioenai the seventh.

4 Moreover the sons of ªObededom *were,* Shemaiah the firstborn, Jehozabad the second, Joah the third, and Sacar the fourth, and Nethaneel the fifth,

5 Ammiel the sixth, Issachar the seventh, Peulthai the eighth: for God blessed him.

6 Also unto Shemaiah his son were sons born, that ruled throughout the house of their father: for they *were* mighty men of valour.

7 The sons of Shemaiah; Othni, and Rephael, and Obed, Elzabad, whose brethren *were* strong men, Elihu, and Semachiah.

8 All these of the sons of Obededom: they and their sons and their brethren, ªable men for strength for the service, *were* threescore and two of Obed-edom.

9 And Meshelemiah had sons and brethren, strong men, eighteen.

10 Also ªHosah, of the children of Merari, had sons; Simri the chief, (for *though* he was not the firstborn, yet his father made him the chief;)

11 Hilkiah the second, Tebaliah the third, Zechariah the fourth: all the sons and brethren of Hosah *were* thirteen.

12 Among these *were* the divisions of the ¹porters, *even* among the chief men, *having* wards one against another, to minister in the house of the LORD.

13 And they ªcast lots, ¹as well the small as the great, according to the house of their fathers, for every gate.

14 And the lot eastward fell to ¹Shelemiah. Then for Zechariah his son, a wise counsellor, they cast lots; and his lot came out northward.

15 To Obed-edom southward; and to his sons ¹the house of Asuppim.

16 To Shuppim and Hosah *the lot came forth* westward, with the gate Shallecheth, by the causeway of the going ªup, ¹ward against ward.

17 Eastward *were* six Levites, northward four a day, southward four a day, and toward ¹Asuppim two *and* two.

18 At ¹Parbar westward, four at the ²causeway, *and* two at ¹Parbar.

19 These *are* the divisions of the ¹porters among the sons of Kore, and among the sons of Merari.

20 And of the Levites, Ahijah *was* ªover the treasures of the house of God, and over the treasures of the ᵇdedicated¹ things.

21 *As concerning* the sons of ¹Laadan; the sons of the Gershonite Laadan, chief fathers, *even* of Laadan the Gershonite, *were* ²Jehieli.

22 The sons of Jehieli; Zetham, and Joel his brother, *which were* over the treasures of the house of the LORD.

23 Of the ªAmramites, *and* the Izharites, the Hebronites, *and* the Uzzielites:

24 And ªShebuel the son of Gershom, the son of Moses, *was* ruler of the treasures.

25 And his brethren by Eliezer; Rehabiah his son, and Jeshaiah his son, and Joram his son, and Zichri his son, and ªShelomith his son.

26 Which Shelomith and his brethren *were* over all the treasures of the dedicated things, ªwhich David the king, and the chief fathers, the captains over thousands and hundreds, and the captains of the host, had dedicated.

27 Out of ¹the spoils won in battles did they dedicate to maintain the house of the LORD.

28 And all that Samuel ªthe seer, and Saul the son of Kish, and Abner the son of Ner, and Joab the son of Zeruiah, had dedicated; *and* whosoever had dedicated any thing, *it was* under the hand of Shelomith, and of his brethren.

29 Of the Izharites, Chenaniah and his sons *were* ¹for the ªoutward business over Israel, for ᵇofficers and judges.

### Cross-references (center column)

25:22 ¹ *Jerimoth,* 1 Chr. 25:4

26:1 ª Ps. 42:title ¹ *gatekeepers* ² *Shelemiah,* 1 Chr. 26:14 ³ *Ebiasaph,* 1 Chr. 6:37; 9:19

26:2 ª 1 Chr. 9:21

26:4 ª 1 Chr. 15:18, 21

26:8 ª 1 Chr. 9:13

26:10 ª,1 Chr. 16:38

26:12 ¹ *gatekeepers*

26:13 ª 1 Chr. 24:5, 31; 25:8 ¹ *the small as well as the great*

26:14 ¹ *Meshelemiah,* 1 Chr. 26:1

26:15 ¹ Or *the storehouse*

26:16 ª 1 Kin. 10:5; 2 Chr. 9:4 ¹ *watchman opposite watchman*

26:17 ¹ Lit. *The Storehouse*

26:18 ¹ Possibly a court or colonnade extending west from the temple ² *highway*

26:19 ¹ *gatekeepers*

26:20 ª 1 Chr. 9:26 ᵇ 2 Sam. 8:11; 1 Chr. 26:22, 24, 26; 28:12; Ezra 2:69 ¹ *holy things*

26:21 ¹ *Libni,* 1 Chr. 6:17 ² *Jehiel,* 1 Chr. 23:8; 29:8

26:23 ¹ Ex. 6:18; Num. 3:19

26:24 ª 1 Chr. 23:16

26:25 ª 1 Chr. 23:18

26:26 ª 2 Sam. 8:11

26:27 ¹ *some of the plunder*

26:28 ª 1 Sam. 9:9

26:29 ª Neh. 11:16 ᵇ 1 Chr. 23:4 ¹ *assigned duties over Israel outside of Jerusalem as officials*

30 *And* of the Hebronites, [a]Hashabiah and his brethren, men of valour, a thousand and seven hundred, [1]*were* officers among them of Israel on this side Jordan westward in all the business of the LORD, and in the service of the king.

31 Among the Hebronites *was* [a]Jerijah the chief, *even* among the Hebronites, according to the generations of his fathers. In the fortieth year of the reign of David they were sought for, and there were found among them mighty men of valour [b]at Jazer of Gilead.

32 And his brethren, men of valour, *were* two thousand and seven hundred chief fathers, whom king David made rulers over the Reubenites, the Gadites, and the half tribe of Manasseh, for every matter pertaining to God, and [a]affairs of the king.

## CHAPTER 27

Now the children of Israel after their number, *to wit*, the [1]chief fathers and captains of thousands and hundreds, and their officers that served the king in any matter of the [2]courses, which came in and went out month by month throughout all the months of the year, of every course *were* twenty and four thousand.

2 Over the first [1]course for the first month *was* [a]Jashobeam the son of Zabdiel: and in his course *were* twenty and four thousand.

3 Of the children of [1]Perez *was* the chief of all the captains of the host for the first month.

4 And over the course of the second month *was* [1]Dodai an Ahohite, and of his course *was* Mikloth also the ruler: in his course likewise *were* twenty and four thousand.

5 The third captain of the host for the third month *was* [a]Benaiah the son of Jehoiada, a chief priest: and in his [1]course *were* twenty and four thousand.

6 This *is that* Benaiah, *who was* [a]mighty *among* the thirty, and above the thirty: and in his course *was* Ammizabad his son.

7 The fourth *captain* for the fourth month *was* [a]Asahel the brother of Joab, and Zebadiah his son after him: and in his [1]course *were* twenty and four thousand.

8 The fifth captain for the fifth month *was* [1]Shamhuth the Izrahite: and in his course *were* twenty and four thousand.

9 The sixth *captain* for the sixth month *was* [a]Ira the son of Ikkesh the Tekoite: and in his course *were* twenty and four thousand.

10 The seventh *captain* for the seventh month *was* [a]Helez the Pelonite,

of the children of Ephraim: and in his [1]course *were* twenty and four thousand.

11 The eighth *captain* for the eighth month *was* [a]Sibbecai the Hushathite, of the Zarhites: and in his course *were* twenty and four thousand.

12 The ninth *captain* for the ninth month *was* [a]Abiezer the Anetothite, of the Benjamites: and in his [1]course *were* twenty and four thousand.

13 The tenth *captain* for the tenth month *was* [a]Maharai the Netophathite, of the Zarhites: and in his course *were* twenty and four thousand.

14 The eleventh *captain* for the eleventh month *was* [a]Benaiah the Pirathonite, of the children of Ephraim: and in his [1]course *were* twenty and four thousand.

15 The twelfth *captain* for the twelfth month *was* [1]Heldai the Netophathite, of Othniel: and in his course *were* twenty and four thousand.

16 Furthermore over the tribes of Israel: the ruler of the Reubenites *was* Eliezer the son of Zichri: of the Simeonites, Shephatiah the son of Maachah:

17 Of the Levites, [a]Hashabiah the son of Kemuel: of the Aaronites, Zadok:

18 Of Judah, [a]Elihu, *one* of the brethren of David: of Issachar, Omri the son of Michael:

19 Of Zebulun, Ishmaiah the son of Obadiah: of Naphtali, Jerimoth the son of Azriel:

20 Of the children of Ephraim, Hoshea the son of Azaziah: of the half tribe of Manasseh, Joel the son of Pedaiah:

21 Of the half *tribe* of Manasseh in Gilead, Iddo the son of Zechariah: of Benjamin, Jaasiel the son of Abner:

22 Of Dan, Azareel the son of Jeroham. These *were* the princes of the tribes of Israel.

23 But David took not the number of them from twenty years old and under: because [a]the LORD had said he would increase Israel like to the [b]stars of the heavens.

24 Joab the son of Zeruiah began [1]to number, but he finished not, because [a]there fell wrath for it against Israel; neither was the number [2]put in the account of the chronicles of king David.

25 And over the king's treasures *was* Azmaveth the son of Adiel: and over the storehouses in the fields, in the cities, and in the villages, and in the castles, *was* Jehonathan the son of Uzziah:

26 And over them that did the work of the field for tillage of the ground *was* Ezri the son of Chelub:

26:30 [a] 1 Chr. 27:17 [1] *had the oversight of Israel*
26:31 [a] 1 Chr. 23:19 [b] Josh. 21:39
26:32 [a] 2 Chr. 19:11
27:1 [1] *heads of fathers' houses* [2] *military divisions*
27:2 [a] 1 Chr. 11:11 [1] *division*
27:3 [1] *Pharez, Gen. 38:29*
27:4 [1] *Dodo, 2 Sam. 23:9*
27:5 [a] 1 Chr. 18:17 [1] *division*
27:6 [a] 2 Sam. 23:20–23
27:7 [a] 2 Sam. 23:24; 1 Chr. 11:26 [1] *division*
27:8 [1] *Shammoth, 1 Chr. 11:27 or Shammah, 2 Sam. 23:11*
27:9 [a] 1 Chr. 11:28
27:10 [a] 1 Chr. 11:27
[1] *division*
27:11 [a] 2 Sam. 21:18; 1 Chr. 11:29; 20:4
27:12 [a] 1 Chr. 11:28 [1] *division*
27:13 [a] 2 Sam. 23:28; 1 Chr. 11:30
27:14 [a] 1 Chr. 11:31 [1] *division*
27:15 [1] *Heled, 1 Chr. 11:30 or Heleb, 2 Sam. 23:29*
27:17 [a] 1 Chr. 26:30
27:18 [a] 1 Sam. 16:6
27:23 [a] [Deut. 6:3] [b] Gen. 15:5; 22:17; 26:4; Ex. 32:13; Deut. 1:10
27:24 [a] 2 Sam. 24:12–15; 1 Chr. 21:1–7 [1] *a census* [2] *recorded*

27 And over the vineyards *was* Shimei the Ramathite: over the ¹increase of the vineyards for the wine cellars *was* Zabdi the Shiphmite:

28 And over the olive trees and the sycomore trees that *were* in the low plains *was* Baal-hanan the Gederite: and over the cellars of oil *was* Joash:

29 And over the herds that fed in Sharon *was* Shitrai the Sharonite: and over the herds *that were* in the valleys *was* Shaphat the son of Adlai:

30 Over the camels also *was* Obil the Ishmaelite: and over the asses *was* Jehdeiah the Meronothite:

31 And over the flocks *was* Jaziz the ᵃHagerite. All these *were* the rulers of the ¹substance which *was* king David's.

32 Also ¹Jonathan David's uncle was a counsellor, a wise man, and a ²scribe: and Jehiel the ³son of Hachmoni *was* with the king's sons:

33 And ᵃAhithophel *was* the king's counsellor: and ᵇHushai the Archite *was* the king's companion:

34 And after Ahithophel *was* Jehoiada the son of Benaiah, and ᵃAbiathar: and the general of the king's army *was* ᵇJoab.

## CHAPTER 28

A ND David assembled all ᵃthe princes of Israel, the princes of the tribes, and ᵇthe captains of the ¹companies that ministered to the king by course, and the captains over the thousands, and captains over the hundreds, and ᶜthe stewards over all the substance and ²possession of the king, and of his sons, with the ³officers, and with ᵈthe mighty men, and with all the valiant men, unto Jerusalem.

2 Then David the king stood up upon his feet, and said, Hear me, my brethren, and my people: *As for me,* ᵃI *had* in mine heart to build an house of rest for the ark of the covenant of the LORD, and for ᵇthe footstool of our God, and had made ready for the building:

3 But God said unto me, ᵃThou shalt not build an house for my name, because thou ¹hast *been* a man of war, and hast shed ᵇblood.

4 Howbeit the LORD God of Israel ᵃchose me before all the house of my father to be king over Israel for ever: for he hath chosen ᵇJudah *to be* the ruler; and of the house of Judah, ᶜthe house of my father; and ᵈamong the sons of my father he ¹liked me to make *me* king over all Israel:

5 ᵃAnd of all my sons, (for the LORD hath given me many sons,) ᵇhe hath chosen Solomon my son to sit upon the throne of the kingdom of the LORD over Israel.

6 And he said unto me, ᵃSolomon thy son, he shall build my house and my courts: for I have chosen him *to be* my son, and I will be his father.

7 Moreover I will establish his kingdom for ever, ᵃif he be ¹constant to do my commandments and my judgments, as at this day.

8 Now therefore in the sight of all Israel the congregation of the LORD, and in the audience of our God, keep and seek for all the commandments of the LORD your God: that ye may possess this good land, and leave *it* for an inheritance for your children after you for ever.

9 And thou, Solomon my son, ᵃknow thou the God of thy father, and serve him ᵇwith a perfect heart and with a willing mind: for ᶜthe LORD searcheth all hearts, and understandeth all the imaginations of the thoughts: ᵈif thou seek him, he will be found of thee; but if thou forsake him, he will ᵉcast thee off for ever.

10 Take heed now; ᵃfor the LORD hath chosen thee to build an house for the sanctuary: be strong, and do *it.*

11 Then David gave to Solomon his son ᵃthe ¹pattern of the porch, and of the houses thereof, and of the treasuries thereof, and of the upper chambers thereof, and of the inner parlours thereof, and of the place of the mercy seat,

12 And the ᵃpattern of all that he had by the spirit, of the courts of the house of the LORD, and of all the chambers round about, ᵇof the treasuries of the house of God, and of the treasuries of the dedicated things:

13 Also for the courses of the priests and the ᵃLevites, and for all the work of the service of the house of the LORD, and for all the vessels of service in the house of the LORD.

14 *He gave* of gold by weight for *things* of gold, for all instruments of all manner of service; *silver also* for all instruments of silver by weight, for all instruments of every kind of service:

15 Even the weight for the ᵃcandlesticks of gold, and for their lamps of gold, by weight for every candlestick, and for the lamps thereof: and for the candlesticks of silver by weight, *both* for the candlestick, and *also* for the lamps thereof, according to the use of every candlestick.

16 And by weight *he gave* gold for the tables of shewbread, for every ᵃtable; and *likewise* silver for the tables of silver:

17 Also pure gold for the fleshhooks, and the bowls, and the cups: and for the golden basons *he gave gold* by weight for every bason; and

### Center column references

27:27 ¹ *produce*
27:31 ᵃ 1 Chr. 5:10 ¹ *property*
27:32 ¹ Or *Jehonathan* ² *secretary* ³ Or *Hachmonite*
27:33 ᵃ 2 Sam. 15:12 ᵇ 2 Sam. 15:32–37
27:34 ᵃ 1 Kin. 1:7 ᵇ 1 Chr. 11:6
28:1 ᵃ 1 Chr. 27:16 ᵇ 1 Chr. 27:1, 2 ᶜ 1 Chr. 27:25 ᵈ 2 Sam. 23:8–39; 1 Chr. 11:10–47 ¹ *divisions who served the king, the captains over thousands* ² *livestock* ³ *officials*
28:2 ᵃ 2 Sam. 7:2 ᵇ Ps. 99:5; 132:7; [Is. 66:1]
28:3 ᵃ 2 Sam. 7:5, 13; 1 Kin. 5:3 ᵇ [1 Chr. 17:4; 22:8]
28:4 ᵃ 1 Sam. 16:6–13 ᵇ Gen. 49:8–10; 1 Chr. 5:2; Ps. 60:7 ᶜ 1 Sam. 16:1 ᵈ 1 Sam. 13:14; 16:12, 13; Acts 13:22 ¹ *was pleased with me*
28:5 ᵃ 1 Chr. 3:1–9; 14:3–7; 23:1 ᵇ 1 Chr. 22:9; 29:1
28:6 ᵃ 2 Sam. 7:13, 14; 1 Kin. 6:38; 1 Chr. 22:9, 10; 2 Chr. 1:9; 6:2
28:7 ᵃ 1 Chr. 22:13 ¹ *steadfast to observe*
28:9 ᵃ [1 Sam. 12:24]; Jer. 9:24; Hos. 4:1; [John 17:3] ᵇ 2 Kin. 20:3 ᶜ [1 Sam. 16:7; 1 Kin. 8:39; 1 Chr. 29:17]; Jer. 11:20; 17:10; 20:12; Rev. 2:23 ᵈ 2 Chr. 15:2; [Jer. 29:13] ᵉ Deut. 31:17
28:10 ᵃ 1 Chr. 22:13; 28:6
28:11 ᵃ 1 Kin. 6:3; 1 Chr. 28:19 ¹ *plan*
28:12 ᵃ Ex. 25:40; Heb. 8:5 ᵇ 1 Chr. 26:20, 28
28:13 ᵃ 1 Chr. 23:6
28:15 ᵃ Ex. 25:31–39; 1 Kin. 7:49
28:16 ᵃ 1 Kin. 7:48

*likewise silver* by weight for every bason of silver:

18 And for the [a]altar of incense refined gold by weight; and gold for the pattern of the chariot of the [b]cherubims, that spread out *their wings*, and covered the ark of the covenant of the LORD.

19 All *this, said David,* [a]the LORD made me understand in writing by *his* hand upon me, *even* all the [1]works of this pattern.

20 And David said to Solomon his son, [a]Be strong and of good courage, and do *it*: fear not, nor be dismayed: for the LORD God, *even* my God, *will be* with thee; [b]he will not fail thee, nor forsake thee, until thou hast finished all the work for the service of the house of the LORD.

21 And, behold, [a]the courses of the priests and the Levites, *even they shall be with thee* for all the service of the house of God: and *there shall be* with thee for all manner of workmanship [b]every willing skilful man, for any manner of service: also the princes and all the people *will be* wholly at thy commandment.

## CHAPTER 29

FURTHERMORE David the king said unto all the congregation, Solomon my son, whom alone God hath [a]chosen, *is yet* [b]young and [1]tender, and the work *is* great: for the [2]palace *is* not for man, but for the LORD God.

2 Now I have prepared with all my might for the house of my God the gold for *things to be made* of gold, and the silver for *things* of silver, and the brass for *things* of brass, the iron for *things* of iron, and wood for *things* of wood; [a]onyx stones, and *stones* to be set, glistering stones, and of divers colours, and all manner of precious stones, and marble stones in abundance.

3 Moreover, because I have set my affection to the house of my God, I have of mine own [1]proper good, of gold and silver, *which* I have given to the house of my God, over and above all that I have prepared for the holy house,

4 *Even* three thousand talents of gold, of the gold of [a]Ophir, and seven thousand talents of refined silver, to overlay the walls of the houses *withal*:

5 The gold for *things* of gold, and the silver for *things* of silver, and for all manner of work *to be made* by the hands of artificers. And who *then* is [a]willing to [1]consecrate his service this day unto the LORD?

6 Then [a]the chief of the fathers and princes of the tribes of Israel, and the captains of thousands and

of hundreds, with [b]the rulers of the king's work, [c]offered willingly,

7 And gave for the service of the house of God of gold five thousand talents and ten thousand drams, and of silver ten thousand talents, and of brass eighteen thousand talents, and one hundred thousand talents of iron.

8 And they with whom *precious* stones were found gave *them* to the treasure of the house of the LORD, by the hand of [a]Jehiel[1] the Gershonite.

9 Then the people rejoiced, for that they offered willingly, because with [1]perfect heart they [a]offered willingly to the LORD: and David the king also rejoiced with great joy.

10 Wherefore David blessed the LORD before all the congregation: and David said, Blessed *be* thou, LORD God of Israel our father, for ever and ever.

11 [a]Thine, O LORD, *is* the greatness, and the power, and the glory, and the victory, and the majesty: for all *that is* in the heaven and in the earth *is thine*; thine *is* the kingdom, O LORD, and thou art exalted as head above all.

12 [a]Both riches and honour *come* of thee, and thou reignest over all; and in thine hand *is* power and might; and in thine hand *it is* to make great, and to give strength unto all.

13 Now therefore, our God, we thank thee, and praise thy glorious name.

14 But who *am* I, and what *is* my people, that we should be able to offer so willingly after this sort? for all things *come* of thee, and [1]of thine own have we given thee.

15 For [a]we *are* strangers before thee, and [1]sojourners, as *were* all our fathers: [b]our days on the earth *are* as a shadow, and *there is* [2]none abiding.

16 O LORD our God, all this store that we have prepared to build thee an house for thine holy name *cometh* of thine hand, and *is* all thine own.

17 I know also, my God, that thou [a]triest[1] the heart, and [b]hast pleasure in uprightness. As for me, in the uprightness of mine heart I have willingly offered all these things: and now have I seen with joy thy people, which are present here, to offer willingly unto thee.

18 O LORD God of Abraham, Isaac, and of Israel, our fathers, keep this for ever in the imagination of the thoughts of the heart of thy people, and [1]prepare their heart unto thee:

19 And [a]give unto Solomon my son a [1]perfect heart, to keep thy commandments, thy testimonies, and thy statutes, and to do all *these things,* and to build the [2]palace, *for* the which [b]I have made provision.

20 And David said to all the congregation, Now bless the LORD your God. And all the congregation blessed the LORD God of their fathers, and bowed down their heads, and worshipped the LORD, and the king.

21 And they sacrificed sacrifices unto the LORD, and offered burnt offerings unto the LORD, on the morrow after that day, *even* a thousand bullocks, a thousand rams, *and* a thousand lambs, with their drink offerings, and ªsacrifices in abundance for all Israel:

22 And did eat and drink before the LORD on that day with great gladness. And they made Solomon the son of David king the second time, and ªanointed *him* unto the LORD *to be* the chief governor, and Zadok *to be* priest.

23 Then Solomon sat on the throne of the LORD as king instead of David his father, and prospered; and all Israel obeyed him.

24 And all the princes, and the mighty men, and all the sons likewise of king David, ªsubmitted[1] themselves unto Solomon the king.

25 And the LORD magnified Solomon exceedingly in the sight of all Israel, and ªbestowed upon him *such* royal majesty as had not been on any king before him in Israel.

26 Thus David the son of Jesse reigned over all Israel.

27 ªAnd the time that he reigned over Israel *was* forty years; ᵇseven years reigned he in Hebron, and thirty and three *years* reigned he in Jerusalem.

28 And he ªdied in a good old age, ᵇfull of days, riches, and honour: and Solomon his son reigned in his [1]stead.

29 Now the [1]acts of David the king, first and last, behold, they *are* written in the book of Samuel the seer, and in the book of Nathan the prophet, and in the book of Gad the seer,

30 With all his reign and his might, ªand the times that went over him, and over Israel, and over all the kingdoms of the countries.

**Cross references (center column):**

29:21 ª 1 Kin. 8:62, 63

29:22 ª 1 Kin. 1:32–35, 39; 1 Chr. 23:1

29:24 ª Eccl. 8:2
[1] Lit. *gave the hand*

29:25 ª 1 Kin. 3:13; 2 Chr. 1:12; Eccl. 2:9

29:27 ª 2 Sam. 5:4; 1 Kin. 2:11
ᵇ 2 Sam. 5:5

29:28 ª Gen. 25:8 ᵇ 1 Chr. 23:1
[1] *place*

29:29 [1] Lit. *words*

29:30 ª Dan. 2:21; 4:23, 25

# THE SECOND BOOK OF THE
# CHRONICLES

The Book of Second Chronicles parallels First and Second Kings but virtually ignores the northern kingdom of Israel because of its false worship and refusal to acknowledge the temple in Jerusalem. Chronicles focuses on those kings who pattern their lives and reigns after the life and reign of godly King David. It gives extended treatment to such zealous reformers as Asa, Jehoshaphat, Joash, Hezekiah, and Josiah.

The temple and temple worship, central throughout the book, befit a nation whose worship of God is central to its very survival. The book begins with Solomon's glorious temple and concludes with Cyrus's edict to rebuild the temple more than four hundred years later.

## CHAPTER 1

AND ᵃSolomon the son of David was strengthened in his kingdom, and ᵇthe LORD his God *was* with him, and ᶜmagnified¹ him exceedingly.

2 Then Solomon spake unto all Israel, to ᵃthe captains of thousands and of hundreds, and to the judges, and to every ¹governor in all Israel, the ²chief of the fathers.

3 So Solomon, and all the congregation with him, went to the ¹high place that *was* at ᵃGibeon; for there was the ²tabernacle of the congregation of God, which Moses the servant of the LORD had ᵇmade in the wilderness.

4 ᵃBut the ark of God had David brought up from Kirjath-jearim to *the place which* David had prepared for it: for he had pitched a tent for it at Jerusalem.

5 Moreover ᵃthe brasen altar, that ᵇBezaleel the son of Uri, the son of Hur, had made, ¹he put before the tabernacle of the LORD: and Solomon and the congregation sought ²unto it.

6 And Solomon went up thither to the brasen altar before the LORD, which *was* at the tabernacle of the congregation, and ᵃoffered a thousand burnt offerings upon it.

7 ᵃIn that night did God appear unto Solomon, and said unto him, Ask what I shall give thee.

8 And Solomon said unto God, Thou hast shewed great ᵃmercy unto David my father, and hast made me ᵇto¹ reign in his stead.

9 Now, O LORD God, let thy promise unto David my father be established: ᵃfor thou hast made me king over a people ¹like the ᵇdust of the earth in multitude.

10 ᵃGive me now wisdom and knowledge, that I may ᵇgo out and come in before this people: for who can judge this thy people, *that is so* great?

11 ᵃAnd God said to Solomon, Because this was in thine heart, and thou hast not asked riches, wealth, or honour, nor the life of thine enemies, neither yet hast asked long life; but hast asked wisdom and knowledge for thyself, that thou mayest judge my people, over whom I have made thee king:

12 Wisdom and knowledge *is* granted unto thee; and I will give thee riches, and wealth, and honour, such as ᵃnone of the kings have had that *have been* before thee, neither shall there any after thee have the like.

13 Then Solomon came *from his journey* to the ¹high place that *was* at Gibeon to Jerusalem, from before the tabernacle of the congregation, and reigned over Israel.

14 ᵃAnd Solomon gathered chariots and horsemen: and he had a thousand and four hundred chariots, and twelve thousand horsemen, which he placed in the chariot cities, and with the king at Jerusalem.

15 ᵃAnd the king made silver and gold at Jerusalem *as plenteous* as stones, and cedar trees made he as the sycomore trees that *are* in the vale for abundance.

16 ᵃAnd Solomon had horses brought out of Egypt, and ¹linen yarn: the king's merchants ²received the linen yarn at a price.

17 And they ¹fetched up, and brought forth out of Egypt a chariot for six hundred *shekels* of silver, and an horse for an hundred and fifty: and so brought they out *horses* for all the kings of the Hittites, and for the kings of Syria, ²by their means.

## CHAPTER 2

AND Solomon ᵃdetermined to build an ¹house for the name of the LORD, and an ²house for his kingdom.

2 And ᵃSolomon ¹told out threescore and ten thousand men to bear

---

1:1 ᵃ 1 Kin. 2:46
ᵇ Gen. 39:2 ᶜ 1 Chr. 29:25 ¹ *exalted*
1:2 ᵃ 1 Chr. 27:1–34 ¹ *leader* ² *heads of the fathers' houses*
1:3 ᵃ 1 Kin. 3:4 ᵇ Ex. 25–27; 35:4–36:38 ¹ *Place for worship* ² *tent of meeting*
1:4 ᵃ 2 Sam. 6:2–17
1:5 ᵃ Ex. 27:1, 2; 38:1, 2 ᵇ Ex. 31:2 ¹ *was there* ² *him there*
1:6 ᵃ 1 Kin. 3:4
1:7 ᵃ 1 Kin. 3:5–14; 9:2
1:8 ᵃ Ps. 18:50 ᵇ 1 Chr. 28:5 ¹ *be king in his place*
1:9 ᵃ 2 Sam. 7:8–16; 1 Kin. 3:7, 8 ᵇ Gen. 13:16; Num. 23:10 ¹ *as numerous as the dust of the earth*
1:10 ᵃ 1 Kin. 3:9 ᵇ Num. 27:17; Deut. 31:2
1:11 ᵃ 1 Kin. 3:11–13
1:12 ᵃ 1 Kin. 10:23; 1 Chr. 29:25; 2 Chr. 9:22; Eccl. 2:9
1:13 ¹ *Place for worship*
1:14 ᵃ 1 Kin. 10:26; 2 Chr. 9:25
1:15 ᵃ 1 Kin. 10:27; 2 Chr. 9:27; Job 22:24
1:16 ᵃ 1 Kin. 10:28; 22:36; 2 Chr. 9:28 ¹ Heb. *Keveh* ² *bought them in Keveh at the prevailing price*
1:17 ¹ *acquired* ² *by their agents,* lit. *by their hands*
2:1 ᵃ 1 Kin. 5:5 ¹ *temple* ² *royal house*
2:2 ᵃ 1 Kin. 5:15, 16; 2 Chr. 2:18 ¹ *selected*

burdens, and fourscore thousand to ²hew in the mountain, and three thousand and six hundred to oversee them.

3 And Solomon sent to ¹Huram the king of Tyre, saying, ªAs thou didst deal with David my father, and didst send him cedars to build him an house to dwell therein, *even so deal with me.*

4 Behold, ªI build an house to the name of the LORD my God, to dedicate *it* to him, *and* ᵇto burn before him ¹sweet incense, and for ᶜthe continual shewbread, and for ᵈthe burnt offerings morning and evening, on the ᵉsabbaths, and on the new moons, and on the ²solemn feasts of the LORD our God. This *is an ordinance* for ever to Israel.

5 And the house which I build ¹*is* great: for ªgreat *is* our God above all gods.

6 ªBut who is able to build him an house, seeing the heaven and heaven of heavens cannot contain him? who *am* I then, that I should build him an house, save only to burn sacrifice before him?

7 Send me now therefore a man ¹cunning to work in gold, and in silver, and in ²brass, and in iron, and in purple, and crimson, and blue, and that ³can skill to grave with the ¹cunning men that *are* with me in Judah and in Jerusalem, ªwhom David my father did provide.

8 ªSend me also cedar trees, ¹fir trees, and algum trees, out of Lebanon: for I know that thy servants ²can skill to cut timber in Lebanon; and, behold, my servants *shall be* with thy servants,

9 Even to prepare me timber in abundance: for the ¹house which I am about to build *shall be* ²wonderful great.

10 ªAnd, behold, I will give to thy servants, the hewers that cut timber, twenty thousand ¹measures of ²beaten wheat, and twenty thousand measures of barley, and twenty thousand baths of wine, and twenty thousand baths of oil.

11 Then ¹Huram the king of Tyre answered in writing, which he sent to Solomon, ªBecause the LORD hath loved his people, he hath made thee king over them.

12 Huram said moreover, ªBlessed *be* the LORD God of Israel, ᵇthat made heaven and earth, who hath given to David the king a wise son, ¹endued with prudence and understanding, that might build an house for the LORD, and an ²house for his kingdom.

13 And now I have sent a ¹cunning man, ²endued with understanding, of ³Huram my ⁴father's,

14 ªThe son of a woman of the daughters of Dan, and his father *was* a man of Tyre, skilful to work in gold, and in silver, in ¹brass, in iron, in stone, and in timber, in purple, in blue, and in fine linen, and in crimson; also to ²grave any manner of graving, and to ³find out every device which shall be put to him, with thy ⁴cunning men, and with the cunning men of my lord David thy father.

15 Now therefore the wheat, and the barley, the oil, and the wine, which ªmy lord hath spoken of, let him send unto his servants:

16 ªAnd we will cut wood out of Lebanon, as much as thou shalt need: and we will bring it to thee in ¹floats by sea to ²Joppa; and thou shalt carry it up to Jerusalem.

17 ªAnd Solomon numbered all the strangers that *were* in the land of Israel, after the numbering wherewith ᵇDavid his father had numbered them; and they were found an hundred and fifty thousand and three thousand and six hundred.

18 And he set ªthreescore and ten thousand of them *to be* bearers of burdens, and fourscore thousand *to be* ¹hewers in the mountain, and three thousand and six hundred overseers to set the people a work.

## CHAPTER 3

THEN ªSolomon began to build the house of the LORD at ᵇJerusalem in mount Moriah, where the LORD appeared unto David his father, in the place that David had prepared in the threshingfloor of ᶜOrnan¹ the Jebusite.

2 And he began to build in the second *day* of the second month, in the fourth year of his reign.

3 Now these *are the things wherein* Solomon was instructed for the building of the house of God. The length by cubits after the first measure ªwas threescore cubits, and the breadth twenty cubits.

4 And the ªporch that *was* in the front *of the* ¹house, the length *of it was* according to the breadth of the house, twenty cubits, and the height *was* an hundred and twenty: and he overlaid it within with pure gold.

5 And ªthe greater ¹house he ᵇcieled² with fir tree, which he overlaid with fine gold, and set thereon palm trees and chains.

6 And he ¹garnished the house with precious stones for beauty: and the gold *was* gold of Parvaim.

7 He overlaid also the house, the beams, the posts, and the walls thereof, and the doors thereof, with gold; and ¹graved cherubims on the walls.

### Center column references

2:2 ² *quarry stone*
2:3 ª 1 Chr. 14:1 ¹ *Hiram,* 1 Kin. 5:1
2:4 ª 2 Chr. 2:1 ᵇ Ex. 30:7 ᶜ Ex. 25:30; Lev. 24:8 ᵈ Ex. 29:38–42 ᵉ Num. 28:3, 9–11 ¹ Lit. *incense of spices* ² *appointed*
2:5 ª Ps. 135:5; [1 Cor. 8:5, 6] ¹ *will be*
2:6 ª 1 Kin. 8:27; 2 Chr. 6:18; Is. 66:1
2:7 ª 1 Chr. 22:15 ¹ *skilful* ² *bronze* ³ *has skill to engrave*
2:8 ª 1 Kin. 5:6 ¹ *cypress* ² *have the skill*
2:9 ¹ *temple* ² Lit. *great and wonderful*
2:10 ª 1 Kin. 5:11 ¹ Heb. *kor* ² *ground*
2:11 ª 1 Kin. 10:9; 2 Chr. 9:8 ¹ *Hiram,* 1 Chr. 14:1
2:12 ª 1 Kin. 5:7 ᵇ Gen. 1; 2; Acts 4:24; 14:15; Rev. 10:6 ¹ Lit. *knowing prudence and understanding* ² *royal house for himself*
2:13 ¹ *skilful* ² *endowed* ³ *Hiram,* 1 Kin. 7:13 ⁴ *master craftsman*
2:14 ª 1 Kin. 7:13, 14 ¹ *bronze* ² *make any engraving* ³ *accomplish any plan* ⁴ *skilful*
2:15 ª 2 Chr. 2:10
2:16 ª 1 Kin. 5:8, 9 ¹ *rafts* ² Heb. *Japho*
2:17 ª 1 Kin. 5:13; 2 Chr. 8:7, 8 ᵇ 1 Chr. 22:2
2:18 ª 2 Chr. 2:2 ¹ *stonecutters*
3:1 ª 1 Kin. 6:1 ᵇ Gen. 22:2–14 ᶜ 1 Chr. 21:18; 22:1 ¹ *Araunah,* 2 Sam. 24:16
3:3 ª 1 Kin. 6:2
3:4 ª 1 Kin. 6:3 ¹ *sanctuary,* the main room of the temple, *the holy place,* 1 Kin. 6:3
3:5 ª 1 Kin. 6:17 ᵇ 1 Kin. 6:15 ¹ *room* ² *panelled with cypress*
3:6 ¹ *decorated*
3:7 ¹ *carved*

8 And he made the [a]most holy [1]house, the length whereof *was* according to the breadth of the house, twenty cubits, and the breadth thereof twenty cubits: and he overlaid it with fine gold, *amounting* to six hundred talents.

9 And the weight of the nails *was* fifty shekels of gold. And he overlaid the upper [a]chambers[1] with gold.

10 [a]And in the most holy [1]house he made two cherubims [2]of image work, and overlaid them with gold.

11 And the wings of the cherubims *were* twenty cubits long: one wing *of the one cherub was* five cubits, reaching to the wall of the house: and the other wing *was likewise* five cubits, reaching to the wing of the other cherub.

12 And *one* wing of the other cherub *was* five cubits, reaching to the wall of the house: and the other wing *was* five cubits *also*, joining to the wing of the other cherub.

13 The wings of these cherubims spread themselves forth twenty cubits: and they stood on their feet, and their faces *were* inward.

14 And he made the [a]vail *of* blue, and purple, and crimson, and fine linen, and wrought cherubims thereon.

15 Also he made before the [1]house [a]two pillars of [2]thirty and five cubits [9]high, and the [4]chapiter that *was* on the top of each of them *was* five cubits.

16 And he made chains, as in the [1]oracle, and put *them* on the [2]heads of the pillars; and made [a]an hundred pomegranates, and put *them* on the chains.

17 And he [a]reared up the pillars before the temple, one on the right hand, and the other on the left; and called the name of that on the right hand [1]Jachin, and the name of that on the left [2]Boaz.

## CHAPTER 4

MOREOVER he made [a]an altar of brass, twenty cubits the length thereof, and twenty cubits the breadth thereof, and ten cubits the height thereof.

2 [a]Also he made a molten sea of ten cubits from brim to brim, round in compass, and five cubits the height thereof; and a line of thirty cubits [1]did compass it round about.

3 [a]And under it *was* the [1]similitude of oxen, which did compass it round about: ten in a cubit, compassing the sea round about. Two rows of oxen *were* cast, when it was cast.

4 It stood upon twelve [a]oxen, three looking toward the north, and three looking toward the west, and three looking toward the south, and

three looking toward the east: and the [1]sea *was set* above upon them, and all their hinder parts *were* inward.

5 And the thickness of it *was* an handbreadth, and the brim of it like the work of the brim of a cup, with flowers of lilies; *and* it received and held [a]three thousand baths.

6 He made also [a]ten lavers, and put five on the right hand, and five on the left, to wash in them: such things as they offered for the burnt offering they washed in them; but the [1]sea *was* for the [b]priests to wash in.

7 [a]And he made ten [1]candlesticks of gold [b]according to their form, and set *them* in the temple, five on the right hand, and five on the left.

8 [a]He made also ten tables, and placed *them* in the temple, five on the right side, and five on the left. And he made an hundred [b]basons[1] of gold.

9 Furthermore [a]he made the court of the priests, and the [b]great court, and doors for the court, and overlaid the doors of them with [1]brass.

10 And [a]he set the [1]sea on the right side of the east end, over against the south.

11 And [a]Huram[1] made the pots, and the shovels, and the [2]basons. And Huram finished the work that he was to make for king Solomon for the house of God;

12 To wit, the two pillars, and [a]the [1]pommels, and the chapiters *which were* on the top of the two pillars, and the two wreaths to cover the two [1]pommels of the chapiters which *were* on the top of the pillars;

13 And [a]four hundred pomegranates on the two wreaths; two rows of pomegranates on each wreath, to cover the two [1]pommels of the chapiters which *were* upon the pillars.

14 He made also [a]bases,[1] and lavers made he upon the bases;

15 One [1]sea, and twelve oxen under it.

16 The pots also, and the shovels, and the [1]fleshhooks, and all their instruments, did [a]Huram[2] his father make to king Solomon for the house of the LORD of bright brass.

17 In the plain of Jordan did the king cast them, in the clay ground between Succoth and [1]Zeredathah.

18 [a]Thus Solomon made all these vessels in great abundance: for the weight of the [1]brass could not be [2]found out.

19 And [a]Solomon made all the vessels that *were for* the house of God, the golden altar also, and the tables whereon [b]the shewbread *was set*;

20 Moreover the [1]candlesticks with their lamps, that they should burn [a]after the manner before the oracle, of pure gold;

---

*Cross-references (center column):*

3:8 [a] Ex. 26:33 [1] place
3:9 [a] 1 Chr. 28:11 [1] rooms
3:10 [a] 1 Kin. 6:23–28 [1] place [2] fashioned by carving
3:14 [a] Ex. 26:31
3:15 [a] 1 Kin. 7:15–20 [1] temple [2] eighteen, 1 Kin. 7:15; 2 Kin. 25:17 [3] Lit. long [4] capital
3:16 [a] 1 Kin. 7:20 [1] inner sanctuary [2] Lit. tops
3:17 [a] 1 Kin. 7:21 [1] Lit. He Shall Establish [2] Lit. In Him Is Strength
4:1 [a] Ex. 27:1, 2
4:2 [a] 1 Kin. 7:23–26 [1] measured its circumference
4:3 [a] 1 Kin. 7:24–26 [1] likeness
4:4 [a] 1 Kin. 7:25

[1] Great bason
4:5 [a] 1 Kin. 7:26
4:6 [a] 1 Kin. 7:38, 40 [b] Ex. 30:19–21 [1] Great bason
4:7 [a] 1 Kin. 7:49 [b] Ex. 25:31; 1 Chr. 28:12, 19 [1] lampstands
4:8 [a] 1 Kin. 7:48 [b] 1 Chr. 28:17 [1] bowls
4:9 [a] 1 Kin. 6:36 [b] 2 Kin. 21:5 [1] bronze
4:10 [a] 1 Kin. 7:39 [1] Great bason
4:11 [a] 1 Kin. 7:40–51 [1] Hiram, 1 Kin. 7:13 [2] bowls
4:12 [a] 1 Kin. 7:41 [1] bowl-shaped capitals on the top
4:13 [a] 1 Kin. 7:20 [1] bowl-shaped capitals on the top
4:14 [a] 1 Kin. 7:27, 43 [1] carts
4:15 [1] Great bason
4:16 [a] 1 Kin. 7:45; 2 Chr. 2:13 [1] forks [2] Hiram his master craftsman
4:17 [1] Zarthan, 1 Kin. 7:46
4:18 [a] 1 Kin. 7:47 [1] bronze [2] determined
4:19 [a] 1 Kin. 7:48–50 [b] Ex. 25:30
4:20 [a] Ex. 27:20, 21 [1] lampstands

21 And <sup>a</sup>the flowers, and the lamps, and the tongs, *made he of* gold, *and* that ¹perfect gold;

22 And the snuffers, and the ¹basons, and the spoons, and the censers, *of* pure gold: and the entry of the ²house, the inner doors thereof for the most holy *place,* and the doors of the house of the temple, *were of* gold.

### CHAPTER 5

THUS <sup>a</sup>all the work that Solomon made for the house of the LORD was finished: and Solomon brought in *all* the things that David his father had dedicated; and the silver, and the gold, and all the instruments, put he among the treasures of the house of God.

2 <sup>a</sup>Then Solomon assembled the elders of Israel, and all the heads of the tribes, the chief of the fathers of the children of Israel, unto Jerusalem, to bring up the ark of the covenant of the LORD <sup>b</sup>out of the city of David, which *is* Zion.

3 <sup>a</sup>Wherefore all the men of Israel assembled themselves unto the king <sup>b</sup>in the feast which *was* in the seventh month.

4 And all the elders of Israel came; and the <sup>a</sup>Levites took up the ark.

5 And they brought up the ark, and the tabernacle of the congregation, and all the holy vessels that *were* in the tabernacle, these did the priests *and* the Levites bring up.

6 Also king Solomon, and all the congregation of Israel that were assembled unto him before the ark, sacrificed sheep and oxen, which could not be ¹told nor numbered for multitude.

7 And the priests brought in the ark of the covenant of the LORD unto his place, to the <sup>a</sup>oracle¹ of the house, into the most holy *place, even* under the wings of the cherubims:

8 For the cherubims spread forth *their* wings over the place of the ark, and the cherubims covered the ark and the staves thereof above.

9 And ¹they drew out the <sup>a</sup>staves *of the ark,* that the ends of the staves were seen from the ark before the oracle; but they were not seen ²without. And ³there it is unto this day.

10 *There was* nothing in the ark ¹save the two tables which <sup>a</sup>put *therein* at Horeb, ²when the LORD made *a covenant* with the children of Israel, when they came out of Egypt.

11 And it came to pass, when the priests were come out of the holy *place:* (for all the priests *that were* present ¹were sanctified, *and* did not *then* wait by <sup>a</sup>course:

12 <sup>a</sup>Also the Levites *which were* the singers, all of them of Asaph, of

Heman, of Jeduthun, with their sons and their brethren, *being* arrayed in white linen, having cymbals and ¹psalteries and harps, stood at the east end of the altar, <sup>b</sup>and with them an hundred and twenty priests sounding with trumpets:)

13 It came even to pass, as the trumpeters and singers *were* as one, to make one sound to be heard in praising and thanking the LORD; and when they lifted up *their* voice with the trumpets and cymbals and instruments of musick, and praised the LORD, *saying,* <sup>a</sup>For *he is* good; for his mercy *endureth* for ever: that *then* the house was filled with a cloud, *even* the house of the LORD;

14 So that the priests could not ¹stand to minister by reason of the cloud: <sup>a</sup>for the glory of the LORD had filled the house of God.

### CHAPTER 6

THEN <sup>a</sup>said Solomon, The LORD hath said that he would dwell in ¹the <sup>b</sup>thick darkness.

2 But I have built an house of habitation for thee, and a <sup>a</sup>place for thy dwelling for ever.

3 And the king turned his face, and <sup>a</sup>blessed the whole congregation of Israel: and all the congregation of Israel stood.

4 And he said, Blessed *be* the LORD God of Israel, who hath with his hands fulfilled *that* which he spake with his mouth to my father David, <sup>a</sup>saying,

5 Since the day that I brought forth my people out of the land of Egypt I chose no city among all the tribes of Israel to build an house in, that my name might be there; neither chose I any man to be a ruler over my people Israel:

6 <sup>a</sup>But I have chosen Jerusalem, that my name might be there; and <sup>b</sup>have chosen David to be over my people Israel.

7 Now <sup>a</sup>it was in the heart of David my father to build an house for the name of the LORD God of Israel.

8 But the LORD said to David my father, Forasmuch as it was in thine heart to build an house for my name, thou didst well in that it was in thine heart:

9 Notwithstanding thou shalt not build the house; but thy son which shall come forth out of thy loins, he shall build the house for my <sup>a</sup>name.

10 The LORD therefore hath performed his word that he hath spoken: for I am risen up in the ¹room of David my father, and am <sup>a</sup>set on the throne of Israel, as the LORD promised, and have built the house for the name of the LORD God of Israel.

11 And in it have I put the ark, ᵃwherein *is* the covenant of the LORD, that he made with the children of Israel.

12 ᵃAnd ¹he stood before the altar of the LORD in the presence of all the congregation of Israel, and spread forth his hands:

13 For Solomon had made a ¹brasen scaffold, of five cubits long, and five cubits broad, and three cubits high, and had set it in the midst of the court: and upon it he stood, and kneeled down upon his knees before all the congregation of Israel, and spread forth his hands toward heaven,

14 And said, O LORD God of Israel, ᵃthere *is* no God like thee in the heaven, nor in the earth; which keepest ᵇcovenant, and *shewest* mercy unto thy servants, that walk before thee with all their hearts:

15 ᵃThou which hast kept with thy servant David my father that which thou hast promised him; and spakest with thy mouth, and hast fulfilled *it* with thine hand, as *it is* this day.

16 Now therefore, O LORD God of Israel, keep with thy servant David my father that which thou hast promised him, saying, ᵃThere shall not fail thee a man in my sight to sit upon the throne of Israel; ᵇyet so that thy children take heed to their way to walk in my law, as thou hast walked before me.

17 Now then, O LORD God of Israel, let thy word ¹be verified, which thou hast spoken unto thy servant David.

18 But will God ¹in very deed dwell with men on the earth? ᵃbehold, heaven and the heaven of heavens cannot contain thee; how much less this ²house which I have built!

19 Have ¹respect therefore to the prayer of thy servant, and to his supplication, O LORD my God, to hearken unto the cry and the prayer which thy servant prayeth before thee:

20 That thine eyes may be ᵃopen upon this house day and night, upon the place whereof thou hast said that thou wouldest put thy name there; to hearken unto the prayer which thy servant prayeth ᵇtoward this place.

21 Hearken therefore unto the supplications of thy servant, and of thy people Israel, which they shall ¹make toward this place: hear thou from thy dwelling place, *even* from heaven; and when thou hearest, ᵃforgive.

22 If a man sin against his neighbour, and ¹an ᵃoath be laid upon him to make him swear, and ²the oath come before thine altar in this house;

23 Then hear thou from heaven, and do, and judge thy servants, by ¹requiting the wicked, by recompensing his way upon his own head; and

6:11 ᵃ 2 Chr. 5:7–10

6:12 ᵃ 1 Kin. 8:22; 2 Chr. 7:7–9 ¹ Solomon

6:13 ¹ *bronze platform*

6:14 ᵃ [Ex. 15:11; Deut. 4:39] ᵇ [Deut. 7:9]

6:15 ᵃ 1 Chr. 22:9, 10

6:16 ᵃ 2 Sam. 7:12, 16; 1 Kin. 2:4; 6:12; 2 Chr. 7:18 ᵇ Ps. 132:12

6:17 ¹ *come true*

6:18 ᵃ [2 Chr. 2:6; Is. 66:1; Acts 7:49] ¹ *indeed* ² *temple*

6:19 ¹ *regard*

6:20 ᵃ 2 Chr. 7:15 ᵇ Ps. 5:7; Dan. 6:10

6:21 ᵃ [Is. 43:25; 44:22; Mic. 7:18] ¹ *pray*

6:22 ᵃ Ex. 22:8–11 ¹ *he be forced to take an oath* ² *comes and takes an oath before*

6:23 ¹ *bringing retribution on*

ᵃ [Job 34:11]

6:24 ᵃ 2 Kin. 21:14, 15 ¹ *are defeated*

6:26 ᵃ Deut. 28:23, 24; 1 Kin. 17:1

6:28 ᵃ 2 Chr. 20:9 ᵇ [Mic. 6:13] ¹ *famine* ² *blight* ³ *grasshoppers* ⁴ *plague*

6:29 ¹ *burden* ² *toward*

6:30 ᵃ [1 Chr. 28:9; Prov. 21:2; 24:12] ᵇ [1 Sam. 16:7]

6:31 ¹ *hold you in reverential awe*

6:32 ᵃ John 12:20; Acts 8:27 ¹ *foreigner*

6:33 ¹ Lit. *your name is called upon this house*

by justifying the righteous, by giving him according to his ᵃrighteousness.

24 And if thy people Israel ¹be put to the worse before the ᵃenemy, because they have sinned against thee; and shall return and confess thy name, and pray and make supplication before thee in this house;

25 Then hear thou from the heavens, and forgive the sin of thy people Israel, and bring them again unto the land which thou gavest to them and to their fathers.

26 When the ᵃheaven is shut up, and there is no rain, because they have sinned against thee; *yet* if they pray toward this place, and confess thy name, and turn from their sin, when thou dost afflict them;

27 Then hear thou from heaven, and forgive the sin of thy servants, and of thy people Israel, when thou hast taught them the good way, wherein they should walk; and send rain upon thy land, which thou hast given unto thy people for an inheritance.

28 If there ᵃbe ¹dearth in the land, if there be pestilence, if there be ²blasting, or mildew, locusts, or ³caterpillers; if their enemies besiege them in the cities of their land; whatsoever ⁴sore or whatsoever ᵇsickness *there be:*

29 *Then* what prayer *or* what supplication soever shall be made of any man, or of all thy people Israel, when every one shall know his own ¹sore and his own grief, and shall spread forth his hands ²in this house:

30 Then hear thou from heaven thy dwelling place, and forgive, and render unto every man according unto all his ways, whose heart thou knowest; (for thou only ᵃknowest the ᵇhearts of the children of men:)

31 That they may ¹fear thee, to walk in thy ways, so long as they live in the land which thou gavest unto our fathers.

32 Moreover concerning the ¹stranger, ᵃwhich is not of thy people Israel, but is come from a far country for thy great name's sake, and thy mighty hand, and thy stretched out arm; if they come and pray in this house;

33 Then hear thou from the heavens, *even* from thy dwelling place, and do according to all that the stranger calleth to thee for; that all people of the earth may know thy name, and fear thee, as *doth* thy people Israel, and may know that ¹this house which I have built is called by thy name.

34 If thy people go out to war against their enemies by the way that thou shalt send them, and they pray unto thee toward this city which

thou hast chosen, and the house which I have built for thy name;

35 Then hear thou from the heavens their prayer and their supplication, and maintain their cause.

36 If they sin against thee, (for *there is* [a]no man which sinneth not,) and thou be angry with them, and deliver them over before *their* enemies, and they carry them away [b]captives unto a land far off or near;

37 Yet *if* they [1]bethink themselves in the land whither they are carried captive, and [2]turn and pray unto thee in the land of their captivity, saying, We have sinned, we have done amiss, and have dealt wickedly;

38 If they return to thee with all their heart and with all their soul in the land of their captivity, whither they have carried them captives, and pray toward their land, which thou gavest unto their fathers, and *toward* the [a]city which thou hast chosen, and toward the house which I have built for thy name:

39 Then hear thou from the heavens, *even* from thy dwelling place, their prayer and their supplications, and maintain their cause, and forgive thy people which have sinned against thee.

40 Now, my God, let, I beseech thee, thine eyes be [a]open, and *let* thine ears *be* [1]attent unto the prayer *that is made* in this place.

41 Now [a]therefore arise, O LORD God, into thy [b]resting place, thou, and the ark of thy strength: let thy priests, O LORD God, be clothed with salvation, and let thy saints [c]rejoice in goodness.

42 O LORD God, turn not away the face of thine anointed: [a]remember the mercies of David thy servant.

### CHAPTER 7

Now [a]when Solomon had made an end of praying, the [b]fire came down from heaven, and consumed the burnt offering and the sacrifices; and [c]the glory of the LORD filled the [1]house.

2 [a]And the priests could not enter into the house of the LORD, because the glory of the LORD had filled the LORD's house.

3 And when all the children of Israel saw how the fire came down, and the glory of the LORD upon the house, they bowed themselves with their faces to the ground upon the pavement, and worshipped, and praised the LORD, [a]*saying,* For *he is* good; [b]for his mercy *endureth* for ever.

4 [a]Then the king and all the people offered sacrifices before the LORD.

5 And king Solomon offered a sacrifice of twenty and two thousand oxen,

and an hundred and twenty thousand sheep: so the king and all the people dedicated the house of God.

6 [a]And the priests [1]waited on their offices: the Levites also with instruments of musick of the LORD, which David the king had made to praise the LORD, because his mercy *endureth* for ever, when David [2]praised by their ministry; and [b]the priests sounded trumpets before them, and all Israel stood.

7 Moreover [a]Solomon [1]hallowed the middle of the court that *was* before the house of the LORD: for there he offered burnt offerings, and the fat of the peace offerings, because the brasen altar which Solomon had made was not able to receive the burnt offerings, and the [2]meat offerings, and the fat.

8 [a]Also at the same time Solomon kept the feast seven days, and all Israel with him, a very great congregation, [b]from the [1]entering in of Hamath unto [c]the[2] river of Egypt.

9 And in the eighth day they made a [a]solemn assembly: for they kept the dedication of the altar seven days, and the feast seven days.

10 And [a]on the three and twentieth day of the seventh month he sent the people away into their tents, glad and merry in heart for the goodness that the LORD had [1]shewed unto David, and to Solomon, and to Israel his people.

11 Thus [a]Solomon finished the house of the LORD, and the king's house: and all that came into Solomon's heart to make in the house of the LORD, and in his own house, he [1]prosperously effected.

12 And the LORD [a]appeared to Solomon by night, and said unto him, I have heard thy prayer, [b]and have chosen this [c]place to myself for an house of sacrifice.

13 [a]If I shut up heaven that there be no rain, or if I command the locusts to devour the land, or if I send pestilence among my people;

14 If my people, which are [a]called by my name, shall [b]humble themselves, and pray, and seek my face, and turn from their wicked ways; [c]then will I hear from heaven, and will forgive their sin, and will heal their land.

15 Now [a]mine eyes shall be open, and mine ears [1]attent unto the prayer *that is made* in this place.

16 For now have [a]I chosen and [1]sanctified this house, that my name may be there for ever: and [2]mine eyes and [3]mine heart shall be there perpetually.

17 [a]And as for thee, if thou wilt walk before me, as David thy father walked,

6:36 [a] Prov. 20:9; Eccl. 7:20; [Rom. 3:9, 19; 5:12; Gal. 3:10]; James 3:2; 1 John 1:8 [b] Deut. 28:63–68

6:37 [1] come to themselves, lit. return to their hearts [2] repent

6:38 [a] Dan. 6:10

6:40 [a] 2 Chr. 6:20 [1] attentive

6:41 [a] Ps. 132:8–10, 16 [b] 1 Chr. 28:2 [c] Neh. 9:25

6:42 [a] 2 Sam. 7:15; Ps. 89:49; 132:1, 8–10; Is. 55:3

7:1 [a] 1 Kin. 8:54 [b] Lev. 9:24; Judg. 6:21; 1 Kin. 18:38; 1 Chr. 21:26 [c] 1 Kin. 8:10, 11 [1] temple

7:2 [a] 2 Chr. 5:14

7:3 [a] 2 Chr. 5:13; Ps. 106:1; 136:1 [b] 1 Chr. 16:41; 2 Chr. 20:21

7:4 [a] 1 Kin. 8:62, 63

7:6 [a] 1 Chr. 15:16 [b] 2 Chr. 5:12 [1] attended to their services [2] offered praise by their hand

7:7 [a] 1 Kin. 8:64–66; 9:3 [1] consecrated [2] grain or meal

7:8 [a] 1 Kin. 8:65 [b] 1 Kin. 4:21, 24; 2 Kin. 14:25 [c] Josh. 13:3 [1] entrance of [2] The Shihor, 1 Chr. 13:5

7:9 [a] Lev. 23:36

7:10 [a] 1 Kin. 8:66 [1] done

7:11 [a] 1 Kin. 9:1 [1] successfully accomplished

7:12 [a] 1 Kin. 3:5; 11:9 [b] Deut. 12:5, 11 [c] 2 Chr. 6:20

7:13 [a] Deut. 28:23, 24; 1 Kin. 17:1; 2 Chr. 6:26–28

7:14 [a] Deut. 28:10; [Is. 43:7] [b] 2 Chr. 12:6, 7; [James 4:10] [c] 2 Chr. 6:27, 30

7:15 [a] 2 Chr. 6:20, 40 [1] attentive

7:16 [a] 1 Kin. 9:3; 2 Chr. 6:6 [1] set apart [2] My attention [3] My concern

7:17 [a] 1 Kin. 9:4

and do according to all that I have commanded thee, and shalt observe my statutes and my judgments;

18 Then will I stablish the throne of thy kingdom, according as I have covenanted with David thy father, saying, [a]There shall not fail thee a man *to be* ruler in Israel.

19 [a]But if ye turn away, and forsake my statutes and my commandments, which I have set before you, and shall go and serve other gods, and worship them;

20 [a]Then will I pluck [1]them up by the roots out of my land which I have given them; and this house, which I have [2]sanctified for my name, will I cast out of my sight, and will make it *to be* a proverb and a [b]byword among all nations.

21 And [a]this [1]house, which [2]is high, shall be an [b]astonishment to every one that passeth by it; so that he shall say, [c]Why hath the LORD done thus unto this land, and unto this [1]house?

22 And it shall be answered, Because they forsook the LORD God of their fathers, which brought them forth out of the land of Egypt, and [1]laid hold on other gods, and worshipped them, and served them: therefore hath he brought all this [2]evil upon them.

## CHAPTER 8

AND [a]it came to pass at the end of [b]twenty years, wherein Solomon had built the house of the LORD, and his own house,

2 That the cities which [1]Huram had restored to Solomon, Solomon built them, and caused the children of Israel to dwell there.

3 And Solomon went to Hamathzobah, and [1]prevailed against it.

4 [a]And he built Tadmor in the wilderness, and all the [1]store cities, which he built in [b]Hamath.

5 Also he built Beth-horon the upper, and [a]Beth-horon the [1]nether, [2]fenced cities, with walls, gates, and bars;

6 And Baalath, and all the store cities that Solomon had, and all the chariot cities, and the cities of the horsemen, and all that Solomon [a]desired to build in Jerusalem, and in Lebanon, and throughout all the land of his dominion.

7 [a]*As for* all the people *that were* left of the Hittites, and the Amorites, and the Perizzites, and the Hivites, and the Jebusites, which *were* not of Israel,

8 *But* of their children, who were left after them in the land, whom the children of Israel [1]consumed not, them did Solomon make to pay tribute until this day.

9 But of the children of Israel did Solomon make no [1]servants for his work; but they *were* men of war, and chief of his captains, and captains of his chariots and horsemen.

10 And these *were* the chief of king Solomon's officers, *even* [a]two hundred and fifty, that bare rule over the people.

11 And Solomon [a]brought up the daughter of Pharaoh out of the city of David unto the house that he had built for her: for he said, My wife shall not dwell in the house of David king of Israel, because *the places are* holy, whereunto the ark of the LORD hath come.

12 Then Solomon offered burnt offerings unto the LORD on the altar of the LORD, which he had built before the porch,

13 Even after a certain rate [a]every day, offering according to the commandment of Moses, on the sabbaths, and on the new moons, and on the [1]solemn [b]feasts, [c]three times in the year, *even* in the feast of unleavened bread, and in the feast of weeks, and in the feast of tabernacles.

14 And he appointed, according to the [1]order of David his father, the [a]courses[2] of the priests to their service, and [b]the Levites [3]to their charges, to praise and minister before the priests, as the duty of every day required: the [c]porters[4] also by their courses at every gate: for so had David the man of God commanded.

15 And they departed not from the commandment of the king unto the priests and Levites concerning any matter, or concerning the [a]treasures.

16 Now all the work of Solomon was [1]prepared unto the day of the foundation of the house of the LORD, and until it was finished. *So* the house of the LORD was [2]perfected.

17 Then went Solomon to [a]Eziongeber, and to [1]Eloth, at the sea side in the land of Edom.

18 [a]And [1]Huram sent him by the hands of his servants ships, and servants that had knowledge of the sea; and they went with the servants of Solomon to [b]Ophir, and [2]took thence four hundred and fifty talents of gold, and brought *them* to king Solomon.

## CHAPTER 9

AND [a]when the queen of Sheba heard of the fame of Solomon, she came to [1]prove Solomon with hard questions at Jerusalem, with a very great company, and camels that bare spices, and gold in abundance, and precious stones: and when she was come to Solomon, she communed with him of all that was in her heart.

### Cross references

7:18 [a] 2 Sam. 7:12–16; 1 Kin. 2:4; 2 Chr. 6:16
7:19 [a] Lev. 26:14, 33; [Deut. 28:15, 36]
7:20 [a] Deut. 28:63–68; 2 Kin. 25:1–7 [b] Ps. 44:14 [1] Israel [2] set apart
7:21 [a] 2 Kin. 25:9 [b] 2 Chr. 29:8 [c] [Deut. 29:24, 25; Jer. 22:8, 9] [1] temple [2] is exalted
7:22 [1] embraced [2] calamity
8:1 [a] 1 Kin. 9:10–14 [b] 1 Kin. 6:38–7:1
8:2 [1] Hiram, 1 Kin. 7:13
8:3 [1] seized it
8:4 [a] 1 Kin. 9:17, 18 [b] 1 Chr. 18:3, 9 [1] storage
8:5 [a] 1 Chr. 7:24 [1] lower [2] fortified
8:6 [a] 2 Chr. 7:11
8:7 [a] Gen. 15:18–21; 1 Kin. 9:20
8:8 [1] destroyed
8:9 [1] slaves
8:10 [a] 1 Kin. 9:23
8:11 [a] 1 Kin. 3:1; 7:8; 9:24; 11:1
8:13 [a] Ex. 29:38–42; Num. 28:3, 9, 11, 26; 29:1 [b] Ex. 23:14–17; 34:22, 23; Deut. 16:16 [c] Lev. 23:1–44 [1] appointed
8:14 [a] 1 Chr. 24:3 [b] 1 Chr. 25:1 [c] 1 Chr. 9:17; 26:1 [1] ordinance [2] divisions [3] for their duties [4] gatekeepers
8:15 [a] 1 Chr. 26:20–28
8:16 [1] wellordered from the day [2] completed
8:17 [a] 1 Kin. 9:26; 2 Chr. 20:36 [1] Elath, 2 Kin. 14:22
8:18 [a] 1 Kin. 9:27; 2 Chr. 9:10, 13 [b] 1 Chr. 29:4 [1] Hiram, 1 Kin. 7:13 [2] acquired from there
9:1 [a] 1 Kin. 10:1; Ps. 72:10; [Matt. 12:42; Luke 11:31] [1] test

2 And Solomon [1]told her all her questions: and there was nothing hid from Solomon which he [2]told her not.

3 And when the queen of Sheba had seen the wisdom of Solomon, and the house that he had built,

4 And the [1]meat of his table, and the [2]sitting of his servants, and the attendance of his ministers, and their apparel; his [a]cupbearers also, and their apparel; and his [3]ascent by which he went up into the house of the LORD; there was no more spirit in her.

5 And she said to the king, *It was* a true report which I heard in mine own land of thine [1]acts, and of thy wisdom:

6 Howbeit I believed not their words, until I came, and mine eyes had seen *it:* and, behold, the one half of the greatness of thy wisdom was not told me: *for* thou exceedest the fame that I heard.

7 Happy *are* thy men, and happy *are* these thy servants, which stand continually before thee, and hear thy wisdom.

8 Blessed be the LORD thy God, which delighted in thee to set thee on his throne, *to be* king for the LORD thy God: because thy God [a]loved Israel, to establish them for ever, therefore made he thee king over them, to do [1]judgment and justice.

9 And she gave the king an hundred and twenty talents of gold, and of spices great abundance, and precious stones: neither was there any such spice as the queen of Sheba gave king Solomon.

10 And the servants also of [1]Huram, and the servants of Solomon, [a]which brought gold from Ophir, brought [2]algum trees and precious stones.

11 And the king made *of* the [1]algum trees terraces to the house of the LORD, and to the king's palace, and harps and psalteries for singers: and there were none such seen before in the land of Judah.

12 And king Solomon gave to the queen of Sheba all her desire, whatsoever she asked, beside *that* which she had brought unto the king. So she turned, and went away to her own land, she and her servants.

13 [a]Now the weight of gold that came to Solomon in one year was six hundred and threescore and six talents of gold;

14 Beside *that which* [1]chapmen and merchants brought. And all the kings of Arabia and governors of the country brought gold and silver to Solomon.

15 And king Solomon made two hundred [1]targets *of* beaten gold: six

hundred *shekels* of beaten gold went to one [1]target.

16 And three hundred shields *made he of* beaten gold: three hundred *shekels* of gold went to one shield. And the king put them in the [a]house of the forest of Lebanon.

17 Moreover the king made a great throne of ivory, and overlaid it with pure gold.

18 And *there were* six steps to the throne, with a footstool of gold, *which were* fastened to the throne, and [1]stays on each side of the sitting place, and two lions standing by the stays:

19 And twelve lions stood there on the one side and on the other upon the six steps. There was not the like made in any kingdom.

20 And all the drinking vessels of king Solomon *were of* gold, and all the vessels of the house of the forest of Lebanon *were of* pure gold: none *were of* silver; it was [1]*not* any thing accounted of in the days of Solomon.

21 For the king's ships went to [a]Tarshish with the servants of [1]Huram: every three years once came the [2]ships of Tarshish bringing gold, and silver, ivory, and apes, and [3]peacocks.

22 And king Solomon [1]passed all the kings of the earth in riches and wisdom.

23 And all the kings of the earth sought the presence of Solomon, to hear his wisdom, that God had put in his heart.

24 And they brought every man his present, vessels of silver, and vessels of gold, and raiment, [a]harness,[1] and spices, horses, and mules, [2]a rate year by year.

25 And Solomon [a]had four thousand stalls for horses and chariots, and twelve thousand horsemen; whom he bestowed in the chariot cities, and with the king at Jerusalem.

26 [a]And he reigned over all the kings [b]from [1]the river even unto the land of the Philistines, and to the border of Egypt.

27 [a]And the king made silver in Jerusalem as stones, and cedar trees made he as the sycomore trees that *are* in the low plains in [b]abundance.

28 [a]And they brought unto Solomon horses out of Egypt, and out of all lands.

29 [a]Now the rest of the acts of Solomon, first and last, *are* they not written in the book of Nathan the prophet, and in the prophecy of [b]Ahijah the Shilonite, and in the visions of [c]Iddo the seer against Jeroboam the son of Nebat?

30 [a]And Solomon reigned in Jerusalem over all Israel forty years.

31 And Solomon [1]slept with his fathers, and he was buried in the city of

### Center reference column

9:2 [1] *answered* [2] *could not explain to her*
9:4 [a] Neh. 1:11 [1] *food* [2] *seating* [3] *entryway*
9:5 [1] *words*
9:8 [a] Deut. 7:8; 2 Chr. 2:11; [Ps. 44:3] [1] *justice and righteousness*
9:10 [a] 2 Chr. 8:18 [1] *Hiram,* 1 Kin. 10:11 [2] *almug,* 1 Kin. 10:11, 12
9:11 [1] *almug,* 1 Kin. 10:11, 12
9:13 [a] 1 Kin. 10:14–29
9:14 [1] *traders*
9:15 [1] *large shields*
[1] *large shields*
9:16 [a] 1 Kin. 7:2
9:18 [1] *armrests*
9:20 [1] *accounted as nothing*
9:21 [a] 2 Chr. 20:36, 37; Ps. 72:10 [1] *Hiram,* 1 Kin. 10:22 [2] *merchant ships, deep-sea vessels* [3] Or *monkeys*
9:22 [1] *surpassed*
9:24 [a] 1 Kin. 20:11 [1] *armour* [2] *at a set rate*
9:25 [a] Deut. 17:16; 1 Kin. 4:26; 10:26; 2 Chr. 1:14; Is. 2:7
9:26 [a] 1 Kin. 4:21 [b] Gen. 15:18; Ps. 72:8 [1] The Euphrates
9:27 [a] 1 Kin. 10:27 [b] 2 Chr. 1:15–17
9:28 [a] 1 Kin. 10:28; 2 Chr. 1:16
9:29 [a] 1 Kin. 11:41 [b] 1 Kin. 11:29 [c] 2 Chr. 12:15; 13:22
9:30 [a] 1 Kin. 4:21; 11:42, 43; 1 Chr. 29:28
9:31 [1] *rested in death with*

David his father: and Rehoboam his son reigned in his ²stead.

## CHAPTER 10

AND ᵃRehoboam went to Shechem: for to Shechem were all Israel come to make him king.

2 And it came to pass, when Jeroboam the son of Nebat, who *was* in Egypt, ᵃwhither he had fled from the presence of Solomon the king, heard *it,* that Jeroboam returned out of Egypt.

3 And they sent and called him. So Jeroboam and all Israel came and spake to Rehoboam, saying,

4 Thy father made our yoke grievous: now therefore ease thou somewhat the ¹grievous servitude of thy father, and his heavy yoke that he put upon us, and we will serve thee.

5 And he said unto them, Come again unto me after three days. And the people departed.

6 And king Rehoboam ¹took counsel with the old men that had stood before Solomon his father while he yet lived, saying, What counsel give ye *me* to return answer to this people?

7 And they spake unto him, saying, If thou be kind to this people, and please them, and speak good words to them, they will be thy servants for ever.

8 ᵃBut he forsook the counsel which the old men gave him, and took counsel with the young men that were brought up with him, that stood before him.

9 And he said unto them, What advice give ye that we may return answer to this people, which have spoken to me, saying, Ease somewhat the yoke that thy father did put upon us?

10 And the young men that were brought up with him spake unto him, saying, Thus shalt thou answer the people that spake unto thee, saying, Thy father made our yoke heavy, but make thou *it* somewhat lighter for us; thus shalt thou say unto them, My little *finger* shall be thicker than my father's ¹loins.

11 For whereas my father put a heavy yoke upon you, I will ¹put more to your yoke: my father chastised you with whips, but I *will chastise you* with ²scorpions.

12 So ᵃJeroboam and all the people came to Rehoboam on the third day, as the king bade, saying, Come again to me on the third day.

13 And the king answered them roughly; and king Rehoboam forsook the counsel of the old men,

14 And answered them after the advice of the young men, saying, My

### Marginal notes (center column)

9:31 ² *place*
10:1 ᵃ 1 Kin. 12:1–20
10:2 ᵃ 1 Kin. 11:40
10:4 ¹ *burdensome service*
10:6 ¹ *consulted with the elders*
10:8 ᵃ 1 Kin. 12:8–11
10:10 ¹ *waist*
10:11 ¹ *add to* ² Possibly a barbed scourge
10:12 ᵃ 1 Kin. 12:12–14

10:15 ᵃ Judg. 14:4; 1 Chr. 5:22; 2 Chr. 11:4; 22:7 ᵇ 1 Kin. 11:29–39 ¹ *did not listen to* ² *turn of affairs*
10:18 ¹ *in charge of revenue* ² *hastened*
10:19 ᵃ 1 Kin. 12:19
11:1 ᵃ 1 Kin. 12:21–24 ¹ *assembled from*
11:2 ᵃ 1 Chr. 12:5; 2 Chr. 12:15
11:4 ¹ *from me*
11:7 ¹ *Sochoh,* 1 Kin. 4:10
11:10 ¹ *fortified*
11:11 ¹ *food*

### (right column continues)

father made your yoke heavy, but I will add thereto: my father chastised you with whips, but I *will chastise you* with scorpions.

15 So the king ¹hearkened not unto the people: ᵃfor the ²cause was of God, that the LORD might perform his ᵇword, which he spake by the hand of Ahijah the Shilonite to Jeroboam the son of Nebat.

16 And when all Israel *saw* that the king would not hearken unto them, the people answered the king, saying, What portion have we in David? and *we have* none inheritance in the son of Jesse: every man to your tents, O Israel: *and* now, David, see to thine own house. So all Israel went to their tents.

17 But *as for* the children of Israel that dwelt in the cities of Judah, Rehoboam reigned over them.

18 Then king Rehoboam sent Hadoram that *was* ¹over the tribute; and the children of Israel stoned him with stones, that he died. But king Rehoboam ²made speed to get him up to *his* chariot, to flee to Jerusalem.

19 ᵃAnd Israel rebelled against the house of David unto this day.

## CHAPTER 11

AND ᵃwhen Rehoboam was come to Jerusalem, he ¹gathered of the house of Judah and Benjamin an hundred and fourscore thousand chosen *men,* which were warriors, to fight against Israel, that he might bring the kingdom again to Rehoboam.

2 But the word of the LORD came ᵃto Shemaiah the man of God, saying,

3 Speak unto Rehoboam the son of Solomon, king of Judah, and to all Israel in Judah and Benjamin, saying,

4 Thus saith the LORD, Ye shall not go up, nor fight against your brethren: return every man to his house: for this thing is ¹done of me. And they obeyed the words of the LORD, and returned from going against Jeroboam.

5 And Rehoboam dwelt in Jerusalem, and built cities for defence in Judah.

6 He built even Beth-lehem, and Etam, and Tekoa,

7 And Beth-zur, and ¹Shoco, and Adullam,

8 And Gath, and Mareshah, and Ziph,

9 And Adoraim, and Lachish, and Azekah,

10 And Zorah, and Aijalon, and Hebron, which *are* in Judah and in Benjamin ¹fenced cities.

11 And he fortified the strong holds, and put captains in them, and store of ¹victual, and of oil and wine.

12 And in [1]every several city *he put* shields and spears, and made them exceeding strong, having Judah and Benjamin on his side.

13 And the priests and the Levites that *were* in all Israel [1]resorted to him out of all their [2]coasts.

14 For the Levites left [a]their [1]suburbs and their possession, and came to Judah and Jerusalem: for [b]Jeroboam and his sons had cast them off from [2]executing the priest's office unto the LORD;

15 [a]And he [1]ordained him priests for the [2]high places, and for [b]the [3]devils, and for [c]the [4]calves which he had made.

16 [a]And after [1]them out of all the tribes of Israel such as set their hearts to seek the LORD God of Israel [b]came to Jerusalem, to sacrifice unto the LORD God of their fathers.

17 So they [a]strengthened the kingdom of Judah, and made Rehoboam the son of Solomon strong, three years: for three years they walked in the way of David and Solomon.

18 And Rehoboam took him Mahalath the daughter of Jerimoth the son of David to wife, *and* Abihail the daughter of [a]Eliab the son of Jesse;

19 Which bare him children; Jeush, and Shamariah, and Zaham.

20 And after her he took [a]Maachah the [1]daughter of [b]Absalom; which bare him [c]Abijah, and Attai, and Ziza, and Shelomith.

21 And Rehoboam loved Maachah the [1]daughter of Absalom above all his [a]wives and his concubines: (for he took eighteen wives, and threescore concubines; and begat twenty and eight sons, and threescore daughters.)

22 And Rehoboam [a]made [b]Abijah the son of Maachah the chief, *to be* ruler among his brethren: for *he thought* to make him king.

23 And he dealt wisely, and [1]dispersed of all his children throughout all the countries of Judah and Benjamin, unto every [a]fenced[2] city: and he gave them victual in abundance. And he [3]desired many wives.

### CHAPTER 12

AND [a]it came to pass, when Rehoboam had established the kingdom, and had strengthened himself, [b]he forsook the law of the LORD, and all Israel with him.

2 [a]And it came to pass, *that* in the fifth year of king Rehoboam Shishak king of Egypt came up against Jerusalem, because they had transgressed against the LORD,

3 With twelve hundred chariots, and threescore thousand horsemen: and the people *were* without number that came with him out of Egypt;

11:12 [1] *each and every*
11:13 [1] *took their stand with* [2] *territories*
11:14 [a] Num. 35:2–5 [b] 1 Kin. 12:28–33; 2 Chr. 13:9 [1] *common lands* [2] *serving as priests*
11:15 [a] 1 Kin. 12:31; 13:33; 14:9; [Hos. 13:2] [b] [Lev. 17:7; 1 Cor. 10:20] [c] 1 Kin. 12:28 [1] *appointed for himself* [2] *Places for worship* [3] *demons* [4] *calf idols*
11:16 [a] 2 Chr. 14:7 [b] 2 Chr. 15:9, 10; 30:11, 18 [1] *The Levites*
11:17 [a] 2 Chr. 12:1, 13
11:18 [a] 1 Sam. 16:6
11:20 [a] 2 Chr. 13:2 [b] 1 Kin. 15:2 [c] 1 Kin. 14:31 [1] *granddaughter*
11:21 [a] Deut. 17:17 [1] *granddaughter*
11:22 [a] Deut. 21:15–17 [b] 2 Chr. 13:1
11:23 [a] 2 Chr. 11:5 [1] *distributed* [2] *fortified* [3] *sought*
12:1 [a] 2 Chr. 11:17 [b] 1 Kin. 14:22–24
12:2 [a] 1 Kin. 11:40; 14:25

12:3 [a] 2 Chr. 16:8; Nah. 3:9
12:4 [1] *fortified*
12:5 [a] 2 Chr. 11:2
12:6 [a] [James 4:10] [b] Ex. 9:27; [Dan. 9:14]
12:7 [a] 1 Kin. 21:28, 29
12:8 [a] Is. 26:13 [b] [Deut. 28:47, 48] [1] *distinguish my service from the service*
12:9 [a] 1 Kin. 14:25, 26 [b] 1 Kin. 10:16, 17; 2 Chr. 9:15, 16
12:10 [a] 1 Kin. 14:27
12:13 [a] 1 Kin.
14:21 [b] 2 Chr. 6:6 [c] 1 Kin. 11:1, 5
12:14 [1] *It was not his basic purpose*
12:15 [a] 2 Chr. 9:29; 13:22 [b] 1 Kin. 14:30
12:16 [1] *rested in death with*

[a]the Lubims, the Sukkiims, and the Ethiopians.

4 And he took the [1]fenced cities which *pertained* to Judah, and came to Jerusalem.

5 Then came [a]Shemaiah the prophet to Rehoboam, and *to* the princes of Judah, that were gathered together to Jerusalem because of Shishak, and said unto them, Thus saith the LORD, Ye have forsaken me, and therefore have I also left you in the hand of Shishak.

6 Whereupon the princes of Israel and the king [a]humbled themselves; and they said, [b]The LORD *is* righteous.

7 And when the LORD saw that they humbled themselves, [a]the word of the LORD came to Shemaiah, saying, They have humbled themselves; *therefore* I will not destroy them, but I will grant them some deliverance; and my wrath shall not be poured out upon Jerusalem by the hand of Shishak.

8 Nevertheless [a]they shall be his servants; that they may [1]know [b]my service, and the service of the kingdoms of the countries.

9 [a]So Shishak king of Egypt came up against Jerusalem, and took away the treasures of the house of the LORD, and the treasures of the king's house; he took all: he carried away also the shields of gold which Solomon had [b]made.

10 Instead of which king Rehoboam made shields of brass, and committed *them* [a]to the hands of the chief of the guard, that kept the entrance of the king's house.

11 And when the king entered into the house of the LORD, the guard came and fetched them, and brought them again into the guard chamber.

12 And when he humbled himself, the wrath of the LORD turned from him, that he would not destroy *him* altogether: and also in Judah things went well.

13 So king Rehoboam strengthened himself in Jerusalem, and reigned: for [a]Rehoboam *was* one and forty years old when he began to reign, and he reigned seventeen years in Jerusalem, [b]the city which the LORD had chosen out of all the tribes of Israel, to put his name there. And his mother's name *was* Naamah an [c]Ammonitess.

14 And he did evil, because [1]he prepared not his heart to seek the LORD.

15 Now the acts of Rehoboam, first and last, *are* they not written in the book of Shemaiah the prophet, [a]and of Iddo the seer concerning genealogies? [b]And *there were* wars between Rehoboam and Jeroboam continually.

16 And Rehoboam [1]slept with his fathers, and was buried in the city of

David: and [a]Abijah[2] his son reigned in his stead.

## CHAPTER 13

Now [a]in the eighteenth year of king Jeroboam began Abijah to reign over [b]Judah.

2 He reigned three years in Jerusalem. His mother's name also *was* [1]Michaiah the daughter of Uriel of Gibeah. And there was war between Abijah and Jeroboam.

3 And Abijah set the battle in [1]array with an army of valiant men of war, *even* four hundred thousand chosen men: Jeroboam also set the battle in array against him with eight hundred thousand chosen men, *being* mighty men of valour.

4 And Abijah stood up upon mount [a]Zemaraim, which *is* in mount Ephraim, and said, Hear me, thou Jeroboam, and all Israel;

5 Ought ye not to know that the LORD God of Israel [a]gave the kingdom over Israel to David for ever, *even* to him and to his sons [b]by a covenant of salt?

6 Yet Jeroboam the son of Nebat, the servant of Solomon the son of David, is risen up, and hath [a]rebelled against his lord.

7 And there are gathered unto him [a]vain[1] men, the [2]children of Belial, and have strengthened themselves against Rehoboam the son of Solomon, when Rehoboam was [b]young and [3]tenderhearted, and could not withstand them.

8 And now ye think to withstand the kingdom of the LORD in the hand of the sons of David; and ye *be* a great multitude, and *there are* with you golden calves, which Jeroboam [a]made you for gods.

9 [a]Have ye not cast out the priests of the LORD, the sons of Aaron, and the Levites, and have made you priests after the manner of the nations of *other* lands? [b]so that whosoever cometh to consecrate himself with a young bullock and seven rams, *the same* may be a priest of [c]them *that are* no gods.

10 But as for us, the LORD *is* our [a]God, and we have not forsaken him; and the priests, which minister unto the LORD, *are* the sons of Aaron, and the Levites [1]wait upon *their* business:

11 [a]And they burn unto the LORD every morning and every evening burnt sacrifices and sweet incense: the [b]shewbread also *set they in order* upon the pure table; and the [1]candlestick of gold with the lamps thereof, [c]to burn every evening: for we keep the [2]charge of the LORD our God; but ye have forsaken him.

12 And, behold, God himself *is* with us for *our* [a]captain,[1] [b]and his priests with sounding trumpets to cry alarm against you. O children of Israel, fight ye not against the LORD God of your fathers; for ye shall not prosper.

13 But Jeroboam caused an ambushment to come about behind them: so they were before Judah, and the ambushment *was* behind them.

14 And when Judah looked back, behold, the battle *was* before and behind: and they [a]cried unto the LORD, and the priests sounded with the trumpets.

15 Then the men of Judah gave a shout: and as the men of Judah shouted, it came to pass, that God [a]smote Jeroboam and all Israel before Abijah and Judah.

16 And the children of Israel fled before Judah: and God delivered them into their hand.

17 And Abijah and his people [1]slew them with a great slaughter: so there fell down slain of Israel five hundred thousand chosen men.

18 Thus the children of Israel were [1]brought under at that time, and the children of Judah prevailed, [a]because they relied upon the LORD God of their fathers.

19 And Abijah pursued after Jeroboam, and took cities from him, Beth-el with the towns thereof, and Jeshanah with the towns thereof, and [1]Ephrain with the towns thereof.

20 Neither did Jeroboam recover strength again in the days of Abijah: and the LORD [a]struck him, and [b]he died.

21 But Abijah waxed mighty, and married fourteen wives, and begat twenty and two sons, and sixteen daughters.

22 And the rest of the acts of Abijah, and his ways, and his sayings, *are* written in [a]the [1]story of the prophet Iddo.

## CHAPTER 14

So Abijah slept with his fathers, and they buried him in the city of David: and [a]Asa his son reigned in his stead. In his days the land was quiet ten years.

2 And Asa did *that which was* good and right in the eyes of the LORD his God:

3 For he took away the altars of the strange *gods,* and [a]the [1]high places, and [b]brake down the [2]images, [c]and cut down the [3]groves:

4 And commanded Judah to [a]seek the LORD God of their fathers, and to [1]do the law and the commandment.

5 Also he took away out of all the cities of Judah the [1]high places and

---

**Cross-references (center column):**

12:16 [a] 2 Chr. 11:20–22 [2] *Abijam,* 1 Kin. 14:31
13:1 [a] 1 Kin. 15:1 [b] 1 Kin. 12:17
13:2 [1] *Maachah,* 2 Chr. 11:20, 21; 1 Kin. 15:2
13:3 [1] *order*
13:4 [a] Josh. 18:22
13:5 [a] 2 Sam. 7:8–16 [b] Lev. 2:13; Num. 18:19
13:6 [a] 1 Kin. 11:28; 12:20
13:7 [a] Judg. 9:4 [b] 2 Chr. 12:13 [1] *worthless* [2] *reprobates* [3] *inexperienced*
13:8 [a] 1 Kin. 12:28; 14:9; 2 Chr. 11:15; [Hos. 8:4–6]
13:9 [a] 2 Chr. 11:13–15 [b] Ex. 29:29–33 [c] Jer. 2:11; 5:7
13:10 [a] Josh. 24:15 [1] *attend to their duties*
13:11 [a] Ex. 29:38; 2 Chr. 2:4 [b] Ex. 25:30; Lev. 24:5–9 [c] Ex. 27:20, 21; Lev. 24:2, [3] *lampstand* [2] *command*
13:12 [a] Josh. 5:13–15; [Heb. 2:10] [b] [Num. 10:8–10] [1] Lit. *head*
13:14 [a] Josh. 24:7; 2 Chr. 6:34, 35; 14:11
13:15 [a] 1 Kin. 14:14; 2 Chr. 14:12
13:17 [1] Lit. *struck*
13:18 [a] 1 Chr. 5:20; 2 Chr. 14:11; [Ps. 22:5] [1] *subdued*
13:19 [1] *Ephron,* Josh. 15:9
13:20 [a] 1 Sam. 2:6; 25:38; Acts 12:23 [b] 1 Kin. 14:20
13:22 [a] 2 Chr. 9:29 [1] *annals,* Heb. *midrash*
14:1 [a] 1 Kin. 15:8
14:3 [a] 1 Kin. 15:14; 2 Chr. 15:17 [b] [Ex. 34:13] [c] 1 Kin. 11:7 [1] Places for pagan worship [2] *sacred pillars* [3] *wooden images*
14:4 [a] [2 Chr. 7:14] [1] *observe*
14:5 [1] Places for pagan worship

the [2]images: and the kingdom was quiet [3]before him.

6 And he built [1]fenced cities in Judah: for the land had rest, and he had no war in those years; because the LORD had given him [a]rest.

7 Therefore he said unto Judah, Let us build these cities, and make about *them* walls, and towers, gates, and bars, *while* the land *is* yet before us; because we have sought the LORD our God, we have sought *him,* and he hath given us rest on every side. So they built and prospered.

8 And Asa had an army *of men* that bare [1]targets and spears, out of Judah three hundred thousand; and out of Benjamin, that bare shields and drew [a]bows, two hundred and fourscore thousand: all these *were* mighty men of [b]valour.

9 [a]And there came out against them Zerah the Ethiopian with an host of a thousand thousand, and three hundred chariots; and came unto [b]Mareshah.

10 Then Asa went out against him, and they set the battle in array in the valley of Zephathah at Mareshah.

11 And Asa [a]cried unto the LORD his God, and said, LORD, *it is* [b]nothing with thee to help, whether with many, or with them that have no power: help us, O LORD our God; for we rest on thee, and [c]in thy name we go against this multitude. O LORD, thou *art* our God; let not man prevail against thee.

12 So the LORD [a]smote[1] the Ethiopians before Asa, and before Judah; and the Ethiopians fled.

13 And Asa and the people that *were* with him pursued them unto [a]Gerar: and the Ethiopians were overthrown, that they could not recover themselves; for they were [1]destroyed before the LORD, and before his host; and they carried away very much [2]spoil.

14 And they [1]smote all the cities round about Gerar; for [a]the fear of the LORD came upon them: and they [2]spoiled all the cities; for there was exceeding much [3]spoil in them.

15 They [1]smote also the [2]tents of cattle, and carried away sheep and camels in abundance, and returned to Jerusalem.

## CHAPTER 15

A ND [a]the Spirit of God came upon Azariah the son of Oded:

2 And he went out [1]to meet Asa, and said unto him, Hear ye me, Asa, and all Judah and Benjamin; [a]The LORD *is* with you, while ye be with him; and [b]if ye seek him, he will be found of you; but [c]if ye forsake him, he will forsake you.

3 Now [a]for a long season Israel *hath been* without the true God, and without a [b]teaching priest, and without [c]law.

4 But [a]when they in their trouble did turn unto the LORD God of Israel, and sought him, he was found of them.

5 And in those times *there was* no peace to him that went out, nor to him that came in, but great [1]vexations *were* upon all the inhabitants of the countries.

6 [a]And nation was destroyed [1]of nation, and city of city: for God did [2]vex them with all adversity.

7 Be ye strong therefore, and let not your hands be weak: for your work shall be rewarded.

8 And when Asa heard these words, and the prophecy of Oded the prophet, he took courage, and put away the abominable idols out of all the land of Judah and Benjamin, and out of the cities [a]which he had taken from mount Ephraim, and [1]renewed the altar of the LORD, that *was* before the porch of the LORD.

9 And he gathered all Judah and Benjamin, and [a]the strangers with them out of Ephraim and Manasseh, and out of Simeon: for they [1]fell to him out of Israel in abundance, when they saw that the LORD his God *was* with him.

10 So they gathered themselves together at Jerusalem in the third month, in the fifteenth year of the reign of Asa.

11 [a]And they offered unto the LORD [1]the same time, of the [2]spoil *which* they had brought, seven hundred oxen and seven thousand sheep.

12 And they [a]entered into a covenant to seek the LORD God of their fathers with all their heart and with all their soul;

13 [a]That whosoever would not seek the LORD God of Israel [b]should be put to death, whether small or great, whether man or woman.

14 And they [1]sware unto the LORD with a loud voice, and with shouting, and with trumpets, and with [2]cornets.

15 And all Judah rejoiced at the oath: for they had sworn with all their heart, and [a]sought him with their whole desire; and he was found of them: and the LORD gave them [b]rest round about.

16 And also *concerning* [a]Maachah the [1]mother of Asa the king, he removed her from *being* queen, because she had made an [2]idol in a grove: and Asa cut down her idol, and [3]stamped *it,* and burnt *it* at the brook Kidron.

17 But [a]the [1]high places were not taken away out of Israel: nevertheless the heart of Asa was [2]perfect all his days.

### Center column notes

14:5 [2] *incense altars* [3] *under*

14:6 [a] 2 Chr. 15:15 [1] *fortified*

14:8 [a] 1 Chr. 12:2 [b] 2 Chr. 13:3 [1] *large shields*

14:9 [a] 2 Chr. 12:2, 3; 16:8 [b] Josh. 15:44

14:11 [a] Ex. 14:10; 2 Chr. 13:14; [Ps. 22:5] [b] [1 Sam. 14:6] [c] 1 Sam. 17:45; [Prov. 18:10]

14:12 [a] 2 Chr. 13:15 [1] Lit. *struck*

14:13 [a] Gen. 10:19; 20:1 [1] *broken* [2] *plunder*

14:14 [a] Gen. 35:5; Deut. 11:25; Josh. 2:9; 2 Chr. 17:10 [1] *defeated* [2] *plundered* [3] *plunder*

14:15 [1] *attacked* [2] *livestock enclosures*

15:1 [a] Num. 24:2; Judg. 3:10; 2 Chr. 20:14; 24:20

15:2 [a] [James 4:8] [b] [1 Chr. 28:9]; 2 Chr. 14:4; 33:12, 13; [Jer. 29:13; Matt. 7:7] [c] 2 Chr. 24:20 [1] Lit. *before*

15:3 [a] Hos. 3:4 [b] 2 Kin. 12:2 [c] Lev. 10:11; 2 Chr. 17:8, 9

15:4 [a] [Deut. 4:29]

15:5 [1] *turmoil*

15:6 [a] Matt. 24:7 [1] *by* [2] *trouble*

15:8 [a] 2 Chr. 13:19 [1] *restored*

15:9 [a] 2 Chr. 11:16 [1] *came over*

15:11 [a] 2 Chr. 14:13–15 [1] Lit. *in that day* [2] *plunder*

15:12 [a] 2 Kin. 23:3; 2 Chr. 23:16; 34:31; Neh. 10:29

15:13 [a] Ex. 22:20 [b] Deut. 13:5–15

15:14 [1] *took an oath before* [2] *rams' horns*

15:15 [a] 2 Chr. 15:2 [b] 2 Chr. 14:7

15:16 [a] 1 Kin. 15:2, 10, 13 [1] *grandmother* [2] *obscene image of Asherah, a Canaanite deity* [3] *crushed*

15:17 [a] 1 Kin. 15:14; 2 Chr. 14:3, 5 [1] *Places for pagan worship* [2] *loyal*

18 And he brought into the house of God the things that his father had dedicated, and that he himself had dedicated, silver, and gold, and vessels.

19 And there was no *more* war unto the five and thirtieth year of the reign of Asa.

## CHAPTER 16

IN the six and thirtieth year of the reign of Asa [a]Baasha king of Israel came up against Judah, and built Ramah, [b]to the intent that he might let none go out or come in to Asa king of Judah.

2 Then Asa brought out silver and gold out of the treasures of the house of the LORD and of the king's house, and sent to Ben-hadad king of Syria, that dwelt at Damascus, saying,

3 *There is* a [1]league between me and thee, as *there was* between my father and thy father: behold, I have sent thee silver and gold; go, break thy league with Baasha king of Israel, that he may [2]depart from me.

4 And Ben-hadad hearkened unto king Asa, and sent the captains of his armies against the cities of Israel; and they smote Ijon, and Dan, and Abel-maim, and all the store cities of Naphtali.

5 And it came to pass, when Baasha heard *it, that* he left off building of Ramah, and let his work cease.

6 Then Asa the king took all Judah; and they carried away the stones of Ramah, and the timber thereof, wherewith Baasha was building; and he built therewith Geba and Mizpah.

7 And at that time [a]Hanani the seer came to Asa king of Judah, and said unto him, [b]Because thou hast relied on the king of Syria, and not relied on the LORD thy God, therefore is the [1]host of the king of Syria escaped out of thine hand.

8 Were not [a]the Ethiopians and [b]the Lubims a huge host, with very many chariots and horsemen? yet, because thou didst rely on the LORD, he delivered them into thine [c]hand.

9 [a]For the eyes of the LORD run to and fro throughout the whole earth, to shew himself strong in the behalf of *them* whose heart *is* [1]perfect toward him. Herein [b]thou hast done foolishly: therefore from henceforth [c]thou shalt have wars.

10 Then Asa was wroth with the seer, and [a]put him in a prison house; for *he was* in a rage with him because of this *thing*. And Asa oppressed *some* of the people the same time.

11 [a]And, behold, the acts of Asa, first and last, lo, they *are* written in the book of the kings of Judah and Israel.

12 And Asa in the thirty and ninth year of his reign was diseased in his feet, until his disease *was* exceeding great: yet in his disease he [a]sought not to the LORD, but to the physicians.

13 [a]And Asa [1]slept with his fathers, and died in the one and fortieth year of his reign.

14 And they buried him in his own [1]sepulchres, which he had [2]made for himself in the city of David, and laid him in the bed which was filled [a]with sweet odours and divers kinds *of spices* prepared by the apothecaries' art: and they made [b]a very great burning for him.

## CHAPTER 17

AND [a]Jehoshaphat his son reigned in his [1]stead, and strengthened himself against Israel.

2 And he placed [1]forces in all the [2]fenced cities of Judah, and set garrisons in the land of [a]Judah, and in the cities of Ephraim, [b]which Asa his father had taken.

3 And the LORD was with Jehoshaphat, because he walked in the first ways of his father David, and sought not unto Baalim;

4 But sought to the *LORD* God of his father, and walked in his commandments, and not [1]after [a]the doings of Israel.

5 Therefore the LORD stablished the kingdom in his hand; and all Judah [a]brought[1] to Jehoshaphat presents; [b]and he had riches and honour in abundance.

6 And his heart was lifted up in the ways of the LORD: moreover [a]he took away the [1]high places and [2]groves out of Judah.

7 Also in the third year of his reign he sent to his princes, *even* to Benhail, and to Obadiah, and to Zechariah, and to Nethaneel, and to Michaiah, [a]to teach in the cities of Judah.

8 And with them *he sent* Levites, *even* Shemaiah, and Nethaniah, and Zebadiah, and Asahel, and Shemiramoth, and Jehonathan, and Adonijah, and Tobijah, and Tob-adonijah, Levites; and with them Elishama and Jehoram, priests.

9 [a]And they taught in Judah, and *had* the book of the law of the LORD with them, and went about throughout all the cities of Judah, and taught the people.

10 And [a]the fear of the LORD fell upon all the kingdoms of the lands that *were* round about Judah, so that they made no war against Jehoshaphat.

11 Also *some* of the Philistines [a]brought Jehoshaphat presents, and tribute silver; and the Arabians

### Center cross-reference column

16:1 [a] 1 Kin. 15:17–22 [b] 2 Chr. 15:9
16:3 [1] *treaty* [2] *withdraw*
16:7 [a] 1 Kin. 16:1; 2 Chr. 19:2 [b] 2 Chr. 32:8–10; Ps. 118:9; [Is. 31:1; Jer. 17:5] [1] *army*
16:8 [a] 2 Chr. 14:9 [b] 2 Chr. 12:3 [c] 2 Chr. 13:16, 18
16:9 [a] Job 34:21; [Prov. 5:21; 15:3; Jer. 16:17; 32:19]; Zech. 4:10 [b] 1 Sam. 13:13 [c] 1 Kin. 15:32 [1] *at peace with* or *loyal to*
16:10 [a] 2 Chr. 18:26; Jer. 20:2; Matt. 14:3
16:11 [a] 1 Kin. 15:23, 24; 2 Chr. 14:2
16:12 [a] [Jer. 17:5]
16:13 [a] 1 Kin. 15:24 [1] *rested in death with*
16:14 [a] Gen. 50:2; Mark 16:1; John 19:39, 40 [b] 2 Chr. 21:19; Jer. 34:5 [1] *tomb* [2] Lit. *dug*
17:1 [a] 1 Kin. 15:24; 2 Chr. 20:31 [1] *place*
17:2 [a] 2 Chr. 11:5 [b] 2 Chr. 15:8 [1] *troops* [2] *fortified*
17:4 [a] 1 Kin. 12:28 [1] *according to the acts*
17:5 [a] 1 Sam. 10:27; 1 Kin. 10:25 [b] 2 Chr. 18:1 [1] Lit. *gave*
17:6 [a] 1 Kin. 22:43; 2 Chr. 15:17; 19:3; 20:33 [1] *Places for pagan worship* [2] *wooden images*
17:7 [a] 2 Chr. 15:3; 35:3
17:9 [a] Deut. 6:4–9; 2 Chr. 35:3; Neh. 8:3, 7
17:10 [a] Gen. 35:5; 2 Chr. 14:14
17:11 [a] 2 Sam. 8:2; 2 Chr. 9:14; 26:8

brought him flocks, seven thousand and seven hundred rams, and seven thousand and seven hundred he goats.

12 And Jehoshaphat [1]waxed great exceedingly; and he built in Judah [2]castles, and cities of store.

13 And he had much business in the cities of Judah: and the men of war, mighty men of valour, *were* in Jerusalem.

14 And these *are* the numbers of them according to the house of their fathers: Of Judah, the captains of thousands; Adnah the chief, and with him mighty men of valour three hundred thousand.

15 And next to him *was* Jehohanan the captain, and with him two hundred and fourscore thousand.

16 And next him *was* Amasiah the son of Zichri, [a]who willingly offered himself unto the LORD; and with him two hundred thousand mighty men of valour.

17 And of Benjamin; Eliada a mighty man of valour, and with him armed men with bow and shield two hundred thousand.

18 And next him *was* Jehozabad, and with him an hundred and fourscore thousand ready prepared for the war.

19 These waited on the king, beside [a]*those* whom the king put in the [1]fenced cities throughout all Judah.

## CHAPTER 18

Now Jehoshaphat [a]had riches and honour in abundance, and [b]joined[1] affinity with [c]Ahab.

2 [a]And after *certain* years he went down to Samaria. And Ahab killed sheep and oxen for him in abundance, and for the people that *he had* with him, and persuaded him to go up *with him* to Ramoth-gilead.

3 And Ahab king of Israel said unto Jehoshaphat king of Judah, Wilt thou go with me [1]to Ramoth-gilead? And he answered him, I *am* as thou *art*, and my people as thy people; and *we will be* with thee in the war.

4 And Jehoshaphat said unto the king of Israel, [a]Enquire, I pray thee, at the word of the LORD to day.

5 Therefore the king of Israel gathered together of prophets four hundred men, and said unto them, Shall we go to Ramoth-gilead to battle, or shall I [1]forbear? And they said, Go up; for God will deliver *it* into the king's hand.

6 But Jehoshaphat said, *Is there* not here a prophet of the LORD [1]besides, that we might enquire of [a]him?

7 And the king of Israel said unto Jehoshaphat, *There is* yet one man, by whom we may enquire of the

17:12 [1] *became increasingly powerful* [2] *fortresses*

17:16 [a] Judg. 5:2, 9; 1 Chr. 29:9

17:19 [a] 2 Chr. 17:2 [1] *fortified*

18:1 [a] 2 Chr. 17:5 [b] 1 Kin. 22:44; 2 Kin. 8:18 [c] 1 Kin. 22:40 [1] *by marriage he allied himself with*

18:2 [a] [Ex. 23:2]; 1 Kin. 22:2

18:3 [1] *Against*

18:4 [a] 1 Sam. 23:2, 4, 9; 2 Sam. 2:1

18:5 [1] *refrain*

18:6 [a] 2 Kin. 3:11 [1] Lit. *still*

18:9 [1] *each* [2] *a threshingfloor at the entrance*

18:10 [a] Zech. 1:18–21 [1] *destroyed*

18:13 [a] Num. 22:18–20, 35; 23:12, 26; 1 Kin. 22:14

18:15 [1] *make you swear*

18:16 [a] [Jer. 23:1–8; 31:10] [b] Num. 27:17; 1 Kin. 22:17; [Ezek. 34:5–8]; Matt. 9:36; Mark 6:34

18:18 [a] Is. 6:1–5; Dan. 7:9, 10 [1] Micaiah

18:20 [a] Job 1:6; 2 Thess. 2:9

LORD: but I hate him; for he never prophesied good unto me, but always evil: the same *is* Micaiah the son of Imla. And Jehoshaphat said, Let not the king say so.

8 And the king of Israel called for one *of his* officers, and said, Fetch quickly Micaiah the son of Imla.

9 And the king of Israel and Jehoshaphat king of Judah sat [1]either of them on his throne, clothed in *their* robes, and they sat in [2a] void place at the entering in of the gate of Samaria; and all the prophets prophesied before them.

10 And Zedekiah the son of Chenaanah had made him [a]horns of iron, and said, Thus saith the LORD, With these thou shalt push Syria until they be [1]consumed.

11 And all the prophets prophesied so, saying, Go up to Ramoth-gilead, and prosper: for the LORD shall deliver *it* into the hand of the king.

12 And the messenger that went to call Micaiah spake to him, saying, Behold, the words of the prophets *declare* good to the king with one assent; let thy word therefore, I pray thee, be like one of theirs, and speak thou good.

13 And Micaiah said, *As* the LORD liveth, [a]even what my God saith, that will I speak.

14 And when he was come to the king, the king said unto him, Micaiah, shall we go to Ramoth-gilead to battle, or shall I forbear? And he said, Go ye up, and prosper, and they shall be delivered into your hand.

15 And the king said to him, How many times shall I [1]adjure thee that thou say nothing but the truth to me in the name of the LORD?

16 Then he said, I did see all Israel [a]scattered upon the mountains, as sheep that have no [b]shepherd: and the LORD said, These have no master; let them return *therefore* every man to his house in peace.

17 And the king of Israel said to Jehoshaphat, Did I not tell thee *that* he would not prophesy good unto me, but evil?

18 Again [1]he said, Therefore hear the word of the LORD; I saw the LORD sitting upon his [a]throne, and all the host of heaven standing on his right hand and *on* his left.

19 And the LORD said, Who shall entice Ahab king of Israel, that he may go up and fall at Ramoth-gilead? And one spake saying after this manner, and another saying after that manner.

20 Then there came out a [a]spirit, and stood before the LORD, and said, I will entice him. And the LORD said unto him, Wherewith?

21 And he said, I will go out, and be a lying spirit in the mouth of all his prophets. And *the* LORD said, Thou shalt entice *him,* and thou shalt also prevail: go out, and do *even* so.

22 Now therefore, behold, [a]the LORD hath put a lying spirit in the mouth of these thy prophets, and the LORD hath [1]spoken evil against thee.

23 Then Zedekiah the son of Chenaanah came near, and [a]smote[1] Micaiah upon the cheek, and said, Which way went the Spirit of the LORD from me to speak unto thee?

24 And Micaiah said, Behold, thou shalt see on that day when thou shalt go into an inner chamber to hide thyself.

25 Then the king of Israel said, Take ye Micaiah, and carry him back to Amon the governor of the city, and to Joash the king's son;

26 And say, Thus saith the king, [a]Put this *fellow* in the prison, and feed him with bread of affliction and with water of affliction, until I return in peace.

27 And Micaiah said, If thou certainly return in peace, *then* hath not the LORD spoken by [a]me. And he said, Hearken, all ye people.

28 So the king of Israel and Jehoshaphat the king of Judah went up to Ramoth-gilead.

29 And the king of Israel said unto Jehoshaphat, I will [a]disguise myself, and will go to the battle; but put thou on thy robes. So the king of Israel disguised himself; and they went to the battle.

30 Now the king of Syria had commanded the captains of the chariots that *were* with him, saying, Fight ye not with small or great, save only with the king of Israel.

31 And it came to pass, when the captains of the chariots saw Jehoshaphat, that they said, It *is* the king of Israel. Therefore they [1]compassed about him to fight: but Jehoshaphat [a]cried out, and the LORD helped him; and God moved them *to depart* from him.

32 For it came to pass, that, when the captains of the chariots perceived that it was not the king of Israel, they turned back again from pursuing him.

33 And a *certain* man drew a bow [1]at a venture, and [2]smote the king of Israel [3]between the joints of the harness: therefore he said to his chariot man, Turn thine hand, that thou mayest carry me out of the host; for I am wounded.

34 And the battle increased that day: howbeit the king of Israel stayed *himself* up in *his* chariot against the Syrians until the even: and about the time of the sun going down he died.

### Cross References (center column)

18:22 [a] Job 12:16, 17; Is. 19:12–14; Ezek. 14:9 [1] declared disaster
18:23 [a] Jer. 20:2; Mark 14:65; Acts 23:2 [1] struck
18:26 [a] 2 Chr. 16:10
18:27 [a] Deut. 18:22
18:29 [a] 2 Chr. 35:22
18:31 [a] 2 Chr. 13:14, 15 [1] surrounded
18:33 [1] at random [2] struck [3] between the scale armour and the breastplate

19:1 [1] safety
19:2 [a] 1 Sam. 9:9; 1 Kin. 16:1; 2 Chr. 20:34 [b] Ps. 139:21 [c] 2 Chr. 32:25
19:3 [a] 2 Chr. 17:4, 6 [b] 2 Chr. 30:19 [1] wooden images
19:4 [a] Deut. 15:8–13
19:5 [a] [Deut. 16:18–20] [1] fortified
19:6 [a] [Lev. 19:15; Deut. 1:17]; Ps. 58:1 [b] Ps. 82:1; [Eccl. 5:8] [1] Lit. in the matter of judgment
19:7 [a] [Gen. 18:25; Deut. 32:4]; Rom. 9:17 [b] [Deut. 10:17, 18; Job 34:19]; Acts 10:34; Rom. 2:11; Gal. 2:6; [Eph. 6:9; Col. 3:25] [1] partiality [2] bribes
19:8 [a] Deut. 16:18; 2 Chr. 17:8 [1] appoint
19:9 [a] [2 Sam. 23:3] [1] loyal
19:10 [a] Deut. 17:8 [b] Num. 16:46 [c] [Ezek. 3:18] [1] whether of bloodshed [2] or offences against law [3] be guilty
19:11 [a] Ezra 7:3 [b] 1 Chr. 26:30 [c] [2 Chr. 15:2; 20:17]
20:1 [a] 1 Chr. 18:2 [b] 1 Chr. 19:15 [c] 2 Chr. 26:7

## CHAPTER 19

AND Jehoshaphat the king of Judah returned to his house in [1]peace to Jerusalem.

2 And Jehu the son of Hanani [a]the seer went out to meet him, and said to king Jehoshaphat, Shouldest thou help the ungodly, and [b]love them that hate the LORD? therefore *is* [c]wrath upon thee from before the LORD.

3 Nevertheless there are [a]good things found in thee, in that thou hast taken away the [1]groves out of the land, and hast [b]prepared thine heart to seek God.

4 And Jehoshaphat dwelt at Jerusalem: and he went out again through the people from Beer-sheba to mount Ephraim, and brought them back unto the LORD God of their [a]fathers.

5 And he set [a]judges in the land throughout all the [1]fenced cities of Judah, city by city,

6 And said to the judges, Take heed what ye do: for [a]ye judge not for man, but for the LORD, [b]who *is* with you [1]in the judgment.

7 Wherefore now let the fear of the LORD be upon you; take heed and do *it:* for [a]*there is* no iniquity with the LORD our God, nor [b]respect[1] of persons, nor taking of [2]gifts.

8 Moreover in Jerusalem did Jehoshaphat [a]set[1] of the Levites, and *of* the priests, and of the chief of the fathers of Israel, for the judgment of the LORD, and for controversies, when they returned to Jerusalem.

9 And he charged them, saying, Thus shall ye do [a]in the fear of the LORD, faithfully, and with a [1]perfect heart.

10 [a]And what cause soever shall come to you of your brethren that dwell in their cities, [1]between blood and blood, [2]between law and commandment, statutes and judgments, ye shall even warn them that they trespass not against the LORD, and so [b]wrath come upon [c]you, and upon your brethren: this do, and ye shall not [3]trespass.

11 And, behold, [a]Amariah the chief priest *is* over you [b]in all matters of the LORD; and Zebadiah the son of Ishmael, the ruler of the house of Judah, for all the king's matters: also the Levites *shall be* officers before you. Deal courageously, and the LORD shall be [c]with the good.

## CHAPTER 20

IT came to pass after this also, *that* the children of [a]Moab, and the children of [b]Ammon, and with them *other* beside the [c]Ammonites, came against Jehoshaphat to battle.

2 Then there came some that told Jehoshaphat, saying, There cometh

a great multitude against thee from beyond the sea on this side Syria; and, behold, they *be* ᵃin Hazazon-tamar, which is ᵇEn-gedi.

3 And Jehoshaphat feared, and set ¹himself to ᵃseek the LORD, and ᵇproclaimed a fast throughout all Judah.

4 And Judah gathered themselves together, to ask ᵃ*help* of the LORD: even out of all the cities of Judah they came to seek the LORD.

5 And Jehoshaphat stood in the congregation of Judah and Jerusalem, in the house of the LORD, before the new court,

6 And said, O LORD God of our fathers, *art* not thou ᵃGod in heaven? and ᵇrulest *not* thou over all the kingdoms of the ¹heathen? and ᶜin thine hand *is there not* power and might, so that none is able to withstand thee?

7 *Art* not thou ᵃour God, *who* ᵇdidst drive out the inhabitants of this land before thy people Israel, and gavest it to the seed of Abraham ᶜthy friend for ever?

8 And they dwelt therein, and have built thee a sanctuary therein for thy name, saying,

9 ᵃIf, *when* evil cometh upon us, *as* the sword, judgment, or pestilence, or famine, we stand before this house, and in thy presence, (for thy ᵇname *is* in this house,) and cry unto thee in our affliction, then thou wilt hear and help.

10 And now, behold, the children of Ammon and Moab and mount Seir, whom thou ᵃwouldest not let Israel invade, when they came out of the land of Egypt, but ᵇthey turned from them, and destroyed them not;

11 Behold, *I say, how* they reward us, ᵃto come to cast us out of thy possession, which thou hast given us to inherit.

12 O our God, wilt thou not ᵃjudge them? for we have no might against this great company that cometh against us; neither know we what to do: but ᵇour eyes *are* upon thee.

13 And all Judah stood before the LORD, with their little ones, their wives, and their children.

14 Then upon Jahaziel the son of Zechariah, the son of Benaiah, the son of Jeiel, the son of Mattaniah, a Levite of the sons of Asaph, ᵃcame the Spirit of the LORD in the midst of the congregation;

15 And he said, Hearken ye, all Judah, and ye inhabitants of Jerusalem, and thou king Jehoshaphat, Thus saith the LORD unto you, ᵃBe not afraid nor dismayed by reason of this great multitude; ᵇfor the battle *is* not yours, but God's.

16 To morrow go ye down against them: behold, they come up by the

¹cliff of Ziz; and ye shall find them at the end of the ²brook, before the wilderness of Jeruel.

17 ᵃYe shall not *need* to fight in this *battle:* ¹set yourselves, stand ye *still,* and see the salvation of the LORD with you, O Judah and Jerusalem: fear not, nor be dismayed; to morrow go out against them: ᵇfor the LORD *will be* with you.

18 And Jehoshaphat ᵃbowed his head with *his* face to the ground: and all Judah and the inhabitants of Jerusalem fell before the LORD, worshipping the LORD.

19 And the Levites, of the children of the Kohathites, and of the children of the Korhites, stood up to praise the LORD God of Israel with a loud voice on high.

20 And they rose early in the morning, and went forth into the wilderness of Tekoa: and as they went forth, Jehoshaphat stood and said, Hear me, O Judah, and ye inhabitants of Jerusalem; ᵃBelieve in the LORD your God, so shall ye be established; believe his prophets, so shall ye prosper.

21 And when he had consulted with the people, he appointed singers unto the LORD, ᵃand that should praise the beauty of holiness, as they went out before the army, and to say, ᵇPraise the LORD; ᶜfor his mercy *endureth* for ever.

22 And when they began to sing and to praise, ᵃthe LORD set ambushments against the children of Ammon, Moab, and mount Seir, which were come against Judah; and they were ¹smitten.

23 For the children of Ammon and Moab stood up against the inhabitants of mount Seir, utterly to slay and destroy *them:* and when they ¹had made an end of the inhabitants of Seir, ᵃevery one helped to destroy another.

24 And when Judah came toward the watch tower in the wilderness, ¹they looked unto the multitude, and, behold, they *were* dead bodies fallen to the earth, and none escaped.

25 And when Jehoshaphat and his people came to take away the ¹spoil of them, they found among them in abundance both riches with the ²dead bodies, and precious jewels, which they stripped off for themselves, more than they could carry away: and they were three days in gathering of the spoil, it was so much.

26 And on the fourth day they assembled themselves in the valley of ¹Berachah; for there they blessed the LORD: therefore the name of the same place was called, The valley of Berachah, unto this day.

20:2 ᵃ Gen. 14:7
ᵇ Josh. 15:62
20:3 ᵃ 2 Chr. 19:3
ᵇ 1 Sam. 7:6; Ezra 8:21; Jer. 36:9; Jon. 3:5 ¹ Lit. *his face*
20:4 ᵃ 2 Chr. 14:11
20:6 ᵃ Deut. 4:39; Josh. 2:11; [1 Kin. 8:23]; Matt. 6:9
ᵇ Ps. 22:28; 47:2, 8; Dan. 4:17, 25, 32 ᶜ 1 Chr. 29:12; 2 Chr. 25:8; Ps. 62:11; Matt. 6:13 ¹ *nations*
20:7 ᵃ Gen. 13:14–17; 17:7; Ex. 6:7
ᵇ Ps. 44:2 ᶜ Is. 41:8; James 2:23
20:9 ᵃ 1 Kin. 8:33, 37; 2 Chr. 6:28–30
ᵇ 2 Chr. 6:20
20:10 ᵃ Deut. 2:4, 9, 19 ᵇ Num. 20:21
20:11 ᵃ Ps. 83:1–18
20:12 ᵃ Judg. 11:27; [1 Sam. 3:13]
ᵇ Ps. 25:15; 121:1, 2; 123:1, 2; 141:8
20:14 ᵃ Num. 11:25, 26; 24:2; 2 Chr. 15:1; 24:20
20:15 ᵃ Ex. 14:13, 14; [Deut. 1:29, 30; 31:6, 8]; 2 Chr. 32:7 ᵇ 1 Sam. 17:47; Zech. 14:3

20:16 ¹ *ascent* ² *wadi or streambed*
20:17 ᵃ Ex. 14:13, 14 ᵇ Num. 14:9; [2 Chr. 15:2; 32:8] ¹ *position*
20:18 ᵃ Ex. 4:31; 2 Chr. 7:3; 29:28
20:20 ᵃ Is. 7:9
20:21 ᵃ 1 Chr. 16:29; Ps. 29:2; 90:17; 96:9; 110:3
ᵇ 1 Chr. 16:34; Ps. 106:1; 136:1 ᶜ 1 Chr. 16:41; 2 Chr. 5:13
20:22 ᵃ Judg. 7:22; 1 Sam. 14:20 ¹ *defeated*
20:23 ᵃ Judg. 7:22; 1 Sam. 14:20 ¹ Lit. *had finished with*
20:24 ¹ *there were their dead*
20:25 ¹ *plunder* ² A few mss., Lat. and Vg. *garments;* LXX *armour*
20:26 ¹ Lit. *Blessing*

27 Then they returned, every man of Judah and Jerusalem, and Jehoshaphat in the forefront of them, to go again to Jerusalem with joy; for the LORD had ªmade them to rejoice over their enemies.

28 And they came to Jerusalem with ¹psalteries and harps and trumpets unto the house of the LORD.

29 And ªthe ¹fear of God was on all the kingdoms of *those* countries, when they had heard that the LORD fought against the enemies of Israel.

30 So the realm of Jehoshaphat was quiet: for his ªGod gave him rest round about.

31 ªAnd Jehoshaphat reigned over Judah: *he was* thirty and five years old when he began to reign, and he reigned twenty and five years in Jerusalem. And his mother's name *was* Azubah the daughter of Shilhi.

32 And he walked in the way of ªAsa his father, and departed not from it, doing *that which was* right in the sight of the LORD.

33 Howbeit ªthe ¹high places were not taken away: for as yet the people had not ᵇprepared² their hearts unto the God of their fathers.

34 Now the rest of the acts of Jehoshaphat, first and last, behold, they *are* written in the book of Jehu the son of Hanani, ªwho *is* mentioned in the book of the kings of Israel.

35 And after this ªdid Jehoshaphat king of Judah join himself with Ahaziah king of Israel, ᵇwho did very ᶜwickedly:

36 And he joined himself with him ªto make ships to go to Tarshish: and they made the ships in Ezion-gaber.

37 Then Eliezer the son of Dodavah of Mareshah prophesied against Jehoshaphat, saying, Because thou hast joined thyself with Ahaziah, the LORD hath broken thy works. ªAnd the ships were broken, that they were not able to go ᵇto Tarshish.

## CHAPTER 21

Now ªJehoshaphat ¹slept with his fathers, and was buried with his fathers in the city of David. And Jehoram his son reigned in his stead.

2 And he had brethren the sons of Jehoshaphat, Azariah, and Jehiel, and Zechariah, and Azariah, and Michael, and Shephatiah: all these *were* the sons of Jehoshaphat king of Israel.

3 And their father gave them great gifts of silver, and of gold, and of precious things, with ¹fenced cities in Judah: but the kingdom gave he to Jehoram; because he *was* the firstborn.

4 Now when Jehoram was ¹risen up to the kingdom of his father, he strengthened himself, and ²slew all

20:27 ª Neh. 12:43
20:28 ¹ *stringed instruments*
20:29 ª 2 Chr. 14:14; 17:10 ¹ *awesome reverence*
20:30 ª 1 Kin. 22:41–43; 2 Chr. 14:6, 7; 15:15; Job 34:29
20:31 ª [1 Kin. 22:41–43]
20:32 ª 2 Chr. 14:2
20:33 ª 2 Chr. 15:17; 17:6 ᵇ 2 Chr. 12:14; 19:3 ¹ *Places for pagan worship* ² *directed*
20:34 ª 1 Kin. 16:1, 7
20:35 ª 2 Chr. 18:1 ᵇ 1 Kin. 22:48–53 ᶜ [2 Chr. 19:2]
20:36 ª 1 Kin. 9:26; 10:22
20:37 ª 1 Kin. 22:48 ᵇ 2 Chr. 9:21
21:1 ª 1 Kin. 22:50 ¹ *rested in death with*
21:3 ¹ *fortified*
21:4 ¹ *established* ² *killed all his brothers*

21:5 ª 2 Kin. 8:17–22
21:6 ª 2 Chr. 18:1 ¹ *as a wife*
21:7 ª 2 Sam. 7:8–17 ᵇ 1 Kin. 11:36; 2 Kin. 8:19; Ps. 132:11 ¹ *lamp*
21:8 ª 2 Kin. 8:20; 14:7, 10; 2 Chr. 25:14, 19
21:9 ¹ *surrounded him,*
21:10 ¹ *Rule or authority*
21:11 ª [Lev. 20:5] ¹ *Places for pagan worship* ² *led Judah astray*
21:13 ª 2 Chr.
21:11 ᵇ [Ex. 34:15]; Deut. 31:16
ᶜ 1 Kin. 16:31–33; 2 Kin. 9:22 ¹ *play the harlot like the harlotry* ᵈ 1 Kin. 2:32; 2 Chr. 21:4
21:15 ª 2 Chr. 21:18, 19
21:16 ª 2 Chr. 33:11; [Jer. 51:11] ᵇ 1 Kin. 11:14, 23 ᶜ 2 Chr. 17:11
21:17 ª 2 Chr. 24:7 ¹ *invaded it* ² *possessions* 3 *Ahaziah,* 2 Chr. 22:1

his brethren with the sword, and *divers* also of the princes of Israel.

5 ªJehoram *was* thirty and two years old when he began to reign, and he reigned eight years in Jerusalem.

6 And he walked in the way of the kings of Israel, like as did the house of Ahab: for he had the daughter of ªAhab ¹to wife: and he wrought *that which was* evil in the eyes of the LORD.

7 Howbeit the LORD would not destroy the house of David, because of the ªcovenant that he had made with David, and as he promised to give a ¹light to him and to his ᵇsons for ever.

8 ªIn his days the Edomites revolted from under the dominion of Judah, and made themselves a king.

9 Then Jehoram went forth with his princes, and all his chariots with him: and he rose up by night, and smote the Edomites which ¹compassed him in, and the captains of the chariots.

10 So the Edomites revolted from under the ¹hand of Judah unto this day. The same time *also* did Libnah revolt from under his hand; because he had forsaken the LORD God of his fathers.

11 Moreover he made ¹high places in the mountains of Judah, and caused the inhabitants of Jerusalem to ªcommit fornication, and ²compelled Judah *thereto.*

12 And there came a writing to him from Elijah the prophet, saying, Thus saith the LORD God of David thy father, Because thou hast not walked in the ways of Jehoshaphat thy father, nor in the ways of Asa king of Judah,

13 But hast walked in the way of the kings of Israel, and hast ªmade Judah and the inhabitants of Jerusalem to ᵇgo¹ a whoring, like to the ᶜwhoredoms of the house of Ahab, and also hast ᵈslain thy brethren of thy father's house, *which were* better than thyself:

14 Behold, with a great plague will the LORD smite thy people, and thy children, and thy wives, and all thy goods:

15 And thou *shalt have* great sickness by ªdisease of thy bowels, until thy bowels fall out by reason of the sickness day by day.

16 Moreover the ªLORD ᵇstirred up against Jehoram the spirit of the Philistines, and of the ᶜArabians, that *were* near the Ethiopians:

17 And they came up into Judah, and ¹brake into it, and carried away all the ²substance that was found in the king's house, and ªhis sons also, and his wives; so that there was never a son left him, save 3Jehoahaz, the youngest of his sons.

18 And after all this the LORD ¹smote him ᵃin his bowels with an incurable disease.

19 And it came to pass, that in process of time, after the end of two years, his bowels fell out by reason of his sickness: so he died ¹of sore diseases. And his people made no ²burning for him, like ᵃthe burning of his fathers.

20 Thirty and two years old was he when he began to reign, and he reigned in Jerusalem eight years, and departed ¹without being desired. Howbeit they buried him in the city of David, but not in the ²sepulchres of the kings.

## CHAPTER 22

AND the inhabitants of Jerusalem made ᵃAhaziah his youngest son king in his stead: for the band of men that came with the ᵇArabians to the camp had slain all the ᶜeldest. So Ahaziah the son of Jehoram king of Judah reigned.

2 ¹Forty and two years old *was* Ahaziah when he began to reign, and he reigned one year in Jerusalem. His mother's name also *was* ᵃAthaliah the ²daughter of Omri.

3 He also walked in the ways of the house of Ahab: for his mother was his counsellor to do wickedly.

4 Wherefore he did evil in the sight of the LORD like the house of Ahab: for they were his counsellors after the death of his father to his destruction.

5 He walked also after their counsel, and went with ¹Jehoram the son of Ahab king of Israel to war against Hazael king of Syria at Ramothgilead: and the Syrians smote Joram.

6 ᵃAnd he returned to be healed in Jezreel because of the wounds which were given him at Ramah, when he fought with Hazael king of Syria. And ¹Azariah the son of Jehoram king of Judah went down to see Jehoram the son of Ahab at Jezreel, because he was sick.

7 And the ¹destruction of Ahaziah ᵃwas of God by coming to Joram: for when he was come, he ᵇwent out with Jehoram against Jehu the son of Nimshi, ᶜwhom the LORD had anointed to ²cut off the house of Ahab.

8 And it came to pass, that, when Jehu was ᵃexecuting judgment upon the house of Ahab, and ᵇfound the princes of Judah, and the sons of the brethren of Ahaziah, that ministered to Ahaziah, he slew them.

9 ᵃAnd he sought Ahaziah: and they caught him, (for he was hid in Samaria,) and brought him to Jehu: and when they had slain him, they buried

him: Because, said they, he *is* the son of ᵇJehoshaphat, who ᶜsought the LORD with all his heart. So the house of Ahaziah had ¹no power to keep still the kingdom.

10 ᵃBut when Athaliah the mother of Ahaziah saw that her son was dead, she arose and destroyed all the ¹seed royal of the house of Judah.

11 But ¹Jehoshabeath, the daughter of the king, took ᵃJoash the son of Ahaziah, and ²stole him from among the king's sons that were ³slain, and put him and his nurse in a bedchamber. So Jehoshabeath, the daughter of king Jehoram, the wife of Jehoiada the priest, (for she was the sister of Ahaziah,) hid him from Athaliah, so that she slew him not.

12 And he was with them hid in the house of God six years: and Athaliah reigned over the land.

## CHAPTER 23

AND ᵃin the seventh year ᵇJehoiada strengthened himself, and took the captains of hundreds, Azariah the son of Jeroham, and Ishmael the son of Jehohanan, and Azariah the son of ᶜObed, and Maaseiah the son of Adaiah, and Elishaphat the son of Zichri, into covenant with him.

2 And they went about in Judah, and gathered the Levites out of all the cities of Judah, and the ᵃchief of the fathers of Israel, and they came to Jerusalem.

3 And all the congregation made a covenant with the king in the house of God. And he said unto them, Behold, the king's son shall reign, as the LORD hath ᵃsaid of the sons of David.

4 This *is* the thing that ye shall do; A third part of you ᵃentering on the sabbath, of the priests and of the Levites, *shall be* ¹porters of the doors;

5 And a third part *shall be* at the king's house; and a third part at the gate of the foundation: and all the people *shall be* in the courts of the house of the LORD.

6 But let none come into the house of the LORD, save the priests, and ᵃthey that minister of the Levites; they shall go in, for they *are* holy: but all the people shall keep the watch of the LORD.

7 And the Levites shall ¹compass the king round about, every man with his weapons in his hand; and whosoever *else* cometh into the house, he shall be put to death: but be ye with the king when he cometh in, and when he goeth out.

8 So the Levites and all Judah did according to all things that Jehoiada the priest had commanded, and took every man his men that were to come in on the sabbath, with them that

21:18 ᵃ 2 Chr. 13:20; 21:15; Acts 12:23 ¹ *struck*

21:19 ᵃ 2 Chr. 16:14 ¹ *in great pain* ² *burning of spices*

21:20 ¹ *to the sorrow of no one* ² *tombs*

22:1 ᵃ 2 Chr. 21:17; 22:6 ᵇ 2 Chr. 21:16 ᶜ 2 Chr. 21:17

22:2 ᵃ 2 Chr. 21:6 ¹ *twenty-two*, 2 Kin. 8:26 ² *granddaughter*

22:5 ¹ *Joram*, 2 Kin. 8:28; 2 Chr. 22:7

22:6 ᵃ 2 Kin. 9:15 ¹ *Ahaziah*, 2 Kin. 8:29

22:7 ᵃ Judg. 14:4; 1 Kin. 12:15; 2 Chr. 10:15 ᵇ 2 Kin. 9:21–24 ᶜ 2 Kin. 9:6, 7 ¹ Lit. *crushing* ² *destroy*

22:8 ᵃ 2 Kin. 9:22–24 ᵇ 2 Kin. 10:10–14; Hos. 1:4

22:9 ᵃ [2 Kin. 9:27]

b ¹ Kin. 15:24 ᶜ 2 Chr. 17:4; 20:3, 4 ¹ *no one to assume power over the kingdom*

22:10 ᵃ 2 Kin. 11:1–3 ¹ *royal heirs*

22:11 ᵃ 2 Kin. 12:18 ¹ *Jehosheba*, 2 Kin. 11:2 ² *stole him away from* ³ *being murdered*

23:1 ᵃ 2 Kin. 11:4 ᵇ 2 Kin. 12:2 ᶜ 1 Chr. 2:37, 38

23:2 ᵃ Ezra 1:5

23:3 ᵃ 2 Sam. 7:12; 1 Kin. 2:4; 9:5; 2 Chr. 6:16; 7:18; 21:7

23:4 ᵃ 1 Chr. 9:25 ¹ *keeping watch*

23:6 ᵃ 1 Chr. 23:28–32

23:7 ¹ *surround the king on all sides*

were to go *out* on the sabbath: for Jehoiada the priest dismissed not [a]the courses.

9 Moreover Jehoiada the priest delivered to the captains of hundreds spears, and [1]bucklers, and [a]shields, that *had been* king David's, which *were* in the house of God.

10 And he set all the people, every man having his weapon in his hand, from the right side of the temple to the left side of the temple, along by the altar and the temple, by the king round about.

11 Then they brought out the king's son, and put upon him the crown, and [a]gave him the [1]testimony, and made him king. And Jehoiada and his sons anointed him, and said, [2]God save the king.

12 Now when [a]Athaliah heard the noise of the people running and praising the king, she came to the people into the house of the LORD:

13 And she looked, and, behold, the king stood at his pillar at the entering in, and the princes and the trumpets by the king: and all the people of the land rejoiced, and sounded with trumpets, also the singers with instruments of musick, and [a]such as [1]taught to sing praise. Then Athaliah [2]rent her clothes, and said, [b]Treason, Treason.

14 Then Jehoiada the priest brought out the captains of hundreds that were set over the host, and said unto them, [1]Have her forth of the ranges: and whoso followeth her, let him be slain with the sword. For the priest said, Slay her not in the house of the LORD.

15 So they laid hands on her; and when she was come to the entering [a]of the horse gate by the king's house, they slew her there.

16 And Jehoiada made a [a]covenant between him, and between all the people, and between the king, that they should be the LORD's people.

17 Then all the people went to the [1]house of Baal, and brake it down, and brake his altars and his images in pieces, and [a]slew Mattan the priest of Baal before the altars.

18 Also Jehoiada appointed the offices of the house of the LORD by the hand of the priests the Levites, whom David had [a]distributed in the house of the LORD, to offer the burnt offerings of the LORD, as *it is* written in the [b]law of Moses, with rejoicing and with singing, *as it was ordained* by David.

19 And he set the [a]porters[1] at the gates of the house of the LORD, that none *which was* unclean in any thing should enter in.

20 [a]And he took the captains of hundreds, and the nobles, and the

governors of the people, and all the people of the land, and brought down the king from the house of the LORD: and they came through the [1]high gate into the king's house, and set the king upon the throne of the kingdom.

21 And all the people of the land rejoiced: and the city was quiet, after that they had slain Athaliah with the sword.

## CHAPTER 24

JOASH [a]*was* seven years old when he began to reign, and he reigned forty years in Jerusalem. His mother's name also *was* Zibiah of Beersheba.

2 And Joash [a]did *that which was* right in the sight of the LORD all the days of Jehoiada the priest.

3 And Jehoiada took for him two wives; and he begat sons and daughters.

4 And it came to pass after this, *that* Joash [1]was minded to repair the house of the LORD.

5 And he gathered together the priests and the Levites, and said to them, Go out unto the cities of Judah, and [a]gather of all Israel money to repair the house of your God from year to year, and see that ye [1]hasten the matter. Howbeit the Levites hastened *it* not.

6 [a]And the king called for Jehoiada the chief, and said unto him, Why hast thou not required of the Levites to bring in out of Judah and out of Jerusalem the collection, *according to the commandment* of [b]Moses the servant of the LORD, and of the congregation of Israel, for the [c]tabernacle of witness?

7 For [a]the sons of Athaliah, that wicked woman, had [1]broken up the house of God; and also all the [b]dedicated things of the house of the LORD did they [2]bestow upon Baalim.

8 And at the king's commandment [a]they made a chest, and set it [1]without at the gate of the house of the LORD.

9 And they made a proclamation through Judah and Jerusalem, to bring in to the LORD [a]the collection *that* Moses the servant of God *laid* upon Israel in the wilderness.

10 And all the princes and all the people rejoiced, and brought in, and cast into the chest, until [1]they had made an end.

11 Now it came to pass, that at what time the chest was brought unto the king's office by the hand of the Levites, and [a]when they saw that *there was* much money, the king's scribe and the high priest's officer came and emptied the chest, and took it, and

23:8 [a] 1 Chr. 24:1–31

23:9 [a] 2 Sam. 8:7
[1] *large shields and small shields*

23:11 [a] Deut. 17:18
[1] The Law, Ex. 25:16, 21 [2] *Long live*

23:12 [a] 2 Chr. 22:10

23:13 [a] 1 Chr. 25:8
[b] 2 Kin. 9:23 [1] *led in* [2] *tore*

23:14 [1] *Take her outside under guard*

23:15 [a] Neh. 3:28; Jer. 31:40

23:16 [a] Josh. 24:24, 25; 2 Chr. 15:12–15

23:17 [a] Deut. 13:6–9; 1 Kin. 18:40 [1] *temple*

23:18 [a] 1 Chr. 23:6, 30, 31; 24:1
[b] Num. 28:2

23:19 [a] 1 Chr. 26:1–19 [1] *gate-keepers*

23:20 [a] 1 Kin. 9:22; 2 Kin. 11:19

[1] *Upper Gate*
24:1 [a] 2 Kin. 11:21; 12:1–15

24:2 [a] 2 Chr. 26:4, 5

24:4 [1] *set his heart on repairing*

24:5 [a] 2 Kin. 12:4 [1] *do the matter quickly*

24:6 [a] 2 Kin. 12:7
[b] Ex. 30:12–16
[c] Num. 1:50; Acts 7:44

24:7 [a] 2 Chr. 21:17 [b] 2 Kin. 12:4 [1] Lit. *broken into* [2] *give to*

24:8 [a] 2 Kin. 12:9 [1] *outside*

24:9 [a] 2 Chr. 24:6

24:10 [1] *all had given*

24:11 [a] 2 Kin. 12:10

carried it to his place again. Thus they did day by day, and gathered money in abundance.

12 And the king and Jehoiada gave it to such as did the work of the service of the house of the LORD, and hired masons and carpenters to [a]repair the house of the LORD, and also such as wrought iron and brass to mend the house of the LORD.

13 So the workmen wrought, and the work was [1]perfected by them, and they set the house of God [2]in his state, and strengthened it.

14 And when they had finished *it,* they brought the rest of the money before the king and Jehoiada, [a]whereof were made vessels for the house of the LORD, *even* vessels to minister, and to offer *withal,* and spoons, and vessels of gold and silver. And they offered burnt offerings in the house of the LORD continually all the days of Jehoiada.

15 But Jehoiada waxed old, and was full of days when he died; an hundred and thirty years old *was he* when he died.

16 And they buried him in the city of David among the kings, because he had done good in Israel, both toward God, and toward his house.

17 Now after the death of Jehoiada came the princes of Judah, and [1]made obeisance to the king. Then the king hearkened unto them.

18 And they left the house of the LORD God of their fathers, and served [a]groves[1] and idols: and [b]wrath came upon Judah and Jerusalem for this their trespass.

19 Yet he [a]sent prophets to them, to bring them again unto the LORD; and they testified against them: but they would not give ear.

20 And the Spirit of God [1]came upon [a]Zechariah the son of Jehoiada the priest, which stood above the people, and said unto them, Thus saith God, [b]Why transgress ye the commandments of the LORD, that ye cannot prosper? [c]because ye have forsaken the LORD, he hath also forsaken you.

21 And they conspired against him, and [a]stoned him with stones at the commandment of the king in the court of the house of the LORD.

22 Thus Joash the king remembered not the kindness which Jehoiada his [1]father had done to him, but slew his son. And when he died, he said, The LORD look upon *it,* and [a]require[2] *it.*

23 And it came to pass at the end of the year, *that* [a]the host of Syria came up against him: and they came to Judah and Jerusalem, and destroyed all the princes of the people from among the people, and sent all the

24:12 [a] 2 Chr. 30:12
24:13 [1] completed [2] in its original condition
24:14 [a] 2 Kin. 12:13
24:17 [1] bowed down
24:18 [a] 1 Kin. 14:23 [b] [Ex. 34:12–14]; Judg. 5:8; 2 Chr. 19:2; 28:13; 29:8; 32:25 [1] wooden images
24:19 [a] 2 Kin. 17:13; 21:10–15; 2 Chr. 36:15, 16; Jer. 7:25, 26; 25:4
24:20 [a] Judg. 6:34; Matt. 23:35 [b] Num. 14:41; [Prov. 28:13] [c] [2 Chr. 15:2] [1] Lit. clothed
24:21 [a] [Neh. 9:26]; Matt. 23:35; Acts 7:58, 59
24:22 [a] [Gen. 9:5] [1] Foster father [2] repay
24:23 [a] 2 Kin. 12:17; Is. 7:2

[1] plunder
24:24 [a] Lev. 26:8; [Deut. 32:30]; Is. 30:17 [b] Lev. 26:25; [Deut. 28:25] [c] 2 Chr. 22:8; Is. 10:5
24:25 [a] 2 Kin. 12:20, 21; 2 Chr. 25:3 [1] severely wounded [2] LXX, Vg. son
24:26 [1] Jozachar, 2 Kin. 12:21 [2] Shomer, 2 Kin. 12:21
24:27 [a] 2 Kin. 12:18 [1] many oracles about him [b] 2 Kin. 12:21 [2] annals or commentary
25:1 [a] 2 Kin. 14:1–6
25:2 [a] 2 Kin. 14:4; 2 Chr. 25:14 [1] loyal
25:3 [a] 2 Kin. 14:5; 2 Chr. 24:25 [1] murdered his father the king
25:4 [a] Deut. 24:16; 2 Kin. 14:6; Jer. 31:30; [Ezek. 18:20]
25:5 [a] Num. 1:3
25:7 [a] 2 Chr. 11:2

[1]spoil of them unto the king of Damascus.

24 For the army of the Syrians [a]came with a small company of men, and the LORD [b]delivered a very great host into their hand, because they had forsaken the LORD God of their fathers. So they [c]executed judgment against Joash.

25 And when they were departed from him, (for they left him [1]in great diseases,) [a]his own servants conspired against him for the blood of the [2]sons of Jehoiada the priest, and slew him on his bed, and he died: and they buried him in the city of David, but they buried him not in the sepulchres of the kings.

26 And these are they that conspired against him; [1]Zabad the son of Shimeath an Ammonitess, and Jehozabad the son of [2]Shimrith a Moabitess.

27 Now *concerning* his sons, and the [1]greatness of [a]the burdens *laid* upon him, and the repairing of the house of God, behold, they *are* written in the [2]story of the book of the kings. [b]And Amaziah his son reigned in his stead.

## CHAPTER 25

AMAZIAH [a]*was* twenty and five years old *when* he began to reign, and he reigned twenty and nine years in Jerusalem. And his mother's name *was* Jehoaddan of Jerusalem.

2 And he did *that which was* right in the sight of the LORD, [a]but not with a [1]perfect heart.

3 [a]Now it came to pass, when the kingdom was established to him, that he slew his servants that had [1]killed the king his father.

4 But he slew not their children, but *did* as *it is* written in the law in the book of Moses, where the LORD commanded, saying, [a]The fathers shall not die for the children, neither shall the children die for the fathers, but every man shall die for his own sin.

5 Moreover Amaziah gathered Judah together, and made them captains over thousands, and captains over hundreds, according to the houses of *their* fathers, throughout all Judah and Benjamin: and he numbered them [a]from twenty years old and above, and found them three hundred thousand choice *men, able* to go forth to war, that could handle spear and shield.

6 He hired also an hundred thousand mighty men of valour out of Israel for an hundred talents of silver.

7 But there came a [a]man of God to him, saying, O king, let not the army of Israel go with thee; for the LORD

*is* not with Israel, *to wit, with* all the children of Ephraim.

8 But if thou wilt go, do *it*, be strong for the battle: God shall make thee fall before the enemy: for God hath ªpower to help, and to cast down.

9 And Amaziah said to the man of God, But what shall we do for the hundred talents which I have given to the ¹army of Israel? And the man of God answered, ªThe LORD is able to give thee much more than this.

10 Then Amaziah separated them, *to wit*, the army that was come to him out of Ephraim, to go home again: wherefore their anger was greatly kindled against Judah, and they returned home in great anger.

11 And Amaziah strengthened himself, and led forth his people, and went to ªthe valley of salt, and smote of the children of Seir ten thousand.

12 And *other* ten thousand *left* alive did the children of Judah carry away captive, and brought them unto the top of the rock, and cast them down from the top of the rock, that they all were ¹broken in pieces.

13 But the soldiers of the army which Amaziah sent back, that they should not go with him to battle, fell upon the cities of Judah, from Samaria even unto Beth-horon, and smote three thousand of them, and took much ¹spoil.

14 Now it came to pass, after that Amaziah was come from the slaughter of the Edomites, that ªhe brought the gods of the children of Seir, and set them up *to be* ᵇhis gods, and bowed down himself before them, and burned incense unto them.

15 Wherefore the anger of the LORD was kindled against Amaziah, and he sent unto him a prophet, which said unto him, Why hast thou sought after ªthe gods of the people, which ᵇcould not deliver their own people out of thine hand?

16 And it came to pass, as he talked with him, that *the king* said unto him, ¹Art thou made of the king's counsel? ²forbear; why shouldest thou be ³smitten? Then the prophet forbare, and said, I know that God hath ªdetermined to destroy thee, because thou hast done this, and hast not hearkened unto my ⁴counsel.

17 Then ªAmaziah king of Judah took advice, and sent to ¹Joash, the son of Jehoahaz, the son of Jehu, king of Israel, saying, Come, let us ²see one another in the face.

18 And Joash king of Israel sent to Amaziah king of Judah, saying, The thistle that *was* in Lebanon sent to the cedar that *was* in Lebanon, saying, Give thy daughter to my son to wife: and there passed by a wild beast

that *was* in Lebanon, and ¹trode down the thistle.

19 Thou sayest, Lo, thou hast ¹smitten the Edomites; and thine heart lifteth thee up to ªboast: abide now at home; why shouldest thou meddle ²to *thine* hurt, that thou shouldest fall, *even* thou, and Judah with thee?

20 But Amaziah would not hear; for ªit *came* of God, that he might deliver them into the hand *of their enemies*, because they ᵇsought after the gods of Edom.

21 So Joash the king of Israel went up; and they ¹saw one another in the face, *both* he and Amaziah king of Judah, at ªBeth-shemesh, which *belongeth* to Judah.

22 And Judah was ¹put to the worse before Israel, and they fled every man to his tent.

23 And Joash the king of Israel took Amaziah king of Judah, the son of Joash, the son of ªJehoahaz, at Beth-shemesh, and brought him to Jerusalem, and brake down the wall of Jerusalem from the gate of Ephraim to the corner gate, four hundred cubits.

24 And *he took* all the gold and the silver, and all the vessels that were found in the house of God with ªObed-edom, and the treasures of the king's house, the hostages also, and returned to Samaria.

25 ªAnd Amaziah the son of Joash king of Judah lived after the death of Joash son of Jehoahaz king of Israel fifteen years.

26 Now the rest of the acts of Amaziah, first and last, behold, *are* they not written in the book of the kings of Judah and Israel?

27 Now after the time that Amaziah did turn away from following the LORD they made a conspiracy against him in Jerusalem; and he fled to Lachish: but they sent to Lachish after him, and slew him there.

28 And they brought him upon horses, and buried him with his fathers in the city of ¹Judah.

## CHAPTER 26

THEN all the people of Judah took ¹Uzziah, who *was* sixteen years old, and made him king in the room of his father Amaziah.

2 He built ¹Eloth, and restored it to Judah, after that the king slept with his fathers.

3 Sixteen years old *was* Uzziah when he began to reign, and he reigned fifty and two years in Jerusalem. His mother's name also *was* Jecoliah of Jerusalem.

4 And he did *that which was* ªright in the sight of the LORD, according to all that his father Amaziah did.

### Center column references

25:8 ª 2 Chr. 14:11; 20:6
25:9 ª [Deut. 8:18]; Prov. 10:22 ¹ troops
25:11 ª 2 Kin. 14:7
25:12 ¹ *dashed in pieces*
25:13 ¹ *plunder*
25:14 ª 2 Chr. 28:23 ᵇ [Ex. 20:3, 5]
25:15 ª [Ps. 96:5] ᵇ 2 Chr. 25:11
25:16 ª [1 Sam. 2:25] ¹ *Have we made you the king's* ² *cease* ³ *destroyed* ⁴ *advice*
25:17 ª 2 Kin. 14:8–14 ¹ *Jehoash*, 2 Kin. 14:8 ² *face each other in battle*
25:18 ¹ *trampled*
25:19 ª 2 Chr. 26:16; 32:25; [Prov. 16:18] ¹ *defeated* ² *with trouble*
25:20 ª 1 Kin. 12:15; 2 Chr. 22:7 ᵇ 2 Chr. 25:14
25:21 ª Josh. 19:38 ¹ *faced each other in battle*
25:22 ¹ *defeated by Israel*
25:23 ª 2 Chr. 21:17; 22:1, 6
25:24 ª 1 Chr. 26:15
25:25 ª 2 Kin. 14:17–22
25:28 ¹ *David*
26:1 ¹ *Azariah*, 2 Kin. 14:21
26:2 ¹ *Elath*, 2 Kin. 14:22
26:4 ª 2 Chr. 24:2

5 And ᵃhe sought God in the days of Zechariah, who ᵇhad understanding in the ¹visions of God: and as long as he sought the LORD, God made him to ᶜprosper.

6 And he went forth and ᵃwarred against the Philistines, and brake down the wall of Gath, and the wall of Jabneh, and the wall of Ashdod, and built cities ¹about Ashdod, and among the Philistines.

7 And God helped him against ᵃthe Philistines, and against the Arabians that dwelt in Gur-baal, and the ¹Mehunims.

8 And the Ammonites ᵃgave ¹gifts to Uzziah: and his name spread abroad *even* to the entering in of Egypt; for he strengthened *himself* exceedingly.

9 Moreover Uzziah built towers in Jerusalem at the ᵃcorner gate, and at the valley gate, and at the turning *of the wall,* and fortified them.

10 Also he built towers in the desert, and digged many wells: for he had much ¹cattle, both in the low country, and in the plains: ²husbandmen *also,* and vine dressers in the mountains, and in ³Carmel: for he loved ⁴husbandry.

11 Moreover Uzziah had an host of fighting men, that went out to war by ¹bands, according to the number of their account by the hand of Jeiel the scribe and Maaseiah the ruler, under the hand of Hananiah, *one* of the king's captains.

12 The whole number of the chief of the fathers of the mighty men of valour *were* two thousand and six hundred.

13 And under their hand *was* an army, three hundred thousand and seven thousand and five hundred, that made war with mighty power, to help the king against the enemy.

14 And Uzziah prepared for them throughout all the host shields, and spears, and helmets, and ¹habergeons, and bows, and slings *to cast* stones.

15 And he made in Jerusalem engines, invented by ᵃcunning¹ men, to be on the towers and upon the bulwarks, to shoot arrows and great stones withal. And his name spread far abroad; for he was marvellously helped, till he was strong.

16 But ᵃwhen he was strong, his heart was ᵇlifted up to *his* destruction: for he transgressed against the LORD his God, and ᶜwent into the temple of the LORD to burn incense upon the altar of incense.

17 And ᵃAzariah the priest went in after him, and with him fourscore priests of the LORD, *that were* valiant men:

18 And they withstood Uzziah the king, and said unto him, *It* ᵃapper-

*taineth* not unto thee, Uzziah, to burn incense unto the LORD, but to the ᵇpriests the sons of Aaron, that are consecrated to burn incense: go out of the sanctuary; for thou hast trespassed; neither *shall it be* for thine honour from the LORD God.

19 Then Uzziah was wroth, and *had* a censer in his hand to burn incense: and while he was wroth with the priests, ᵃthe leprosy even rose up in his forehead before the priests in the house of the LORD, from beside the incense altar.

20 And Azariah the chief priest, and all the priests, looked upon him, and, behold, he *was* leprous in his forehead, and they thrust him out from thence; yea, himself ᵃhasted¹ also to go out, because the LORD had ²smitten him.

21 ᵃAnd Uzziah the king was a leper unto the day of his death, and dwelt in ¹a ᵇseveral house, *being* a leper; for he was cut off from the house of the LORD: and Jotham his son *was* over the king's house, judging the people of the land.

22 Now the rest of the acts of Uzziah, first and last, did ᵃIsaiah the prophet, the son of Amoz, write.

23 ᵃSo Uzziah ¹slept with his fathers, and they buried him with his fathers in the field of the burial which *belonged* to the kings; for they said, He *is* a leper: and Jotham his son reigned in his stead.

## CHAPTER 27

JOTHAM ᵃ*was* twenty and five years old when he began to reign, and he reigned sixteen years in Jerusalem. His mother's name also *was* ¹Jerushah, the daughter of Zadok.

2 And he did *that which was* right in the sight of the LORD, according to all that his father Uzziah did: howbeit he entered not into the temple of the LORD. And ᵃthe people did yet corruptly.

3 He built the ¹high gate of the house of the LORD, and on the wall of ᵃOphel he built much.

4 Moreover he built cities in the mountains of Judah, and in the forests he built ¹castles and towers.

5 He fought also with the king of the ᵃAmmonites, and prevailed against them. And the children of Ammon gave him the same year an hundred talents of silver, and ten thousand measures of wheat, and ten thousand of barley. ¹So much did the children of Ammon pay unto him, both the second year, and the third.

6 So Jotham became mighty, ᵃbecause he prepared his ways before the LORD his God.

26:5 ᵃ 2 Chr. 24:2 ᵇ Gen. 41:15; Dan. 1:17; 10:1 ᶜ [2 Chr. 15:2; 20:20; 31:21] ¹ Heb. mss., LXX, Syr., Tg., and Arab. *fear*

26:6 ᵃ Is. 14:29 ¹ *around, near*

26:7 ᵃ 2 Chr. 21:16 ¹ *Meunites*

26:8 ᵃ 2 Sam. 8:2; 2 Chr. 17:11 ¹ *tribute*

26:9 ᵃ 2 Kin. 14:13; 2 Chr. 25:23; Neh. 3:13, 19, 32; Zech. 14:10

26:10 ¹ *livestock* ² *farmers* ³ Or *fertile fields* ⁴ *the soil*

26:11 ¹ *companies*

26:14 ¹ *body armour*

26:15 ᵃ Ex. 39:3, 8 ¹ *skilful*

26:16 ᵃ [Deut. 32:15] ᵇ Deut. 8:14; 2 Chr. 25:19 ᶜ 1 Kin. 13:1–4; 2 Kin. 16:12, 13

26:17 ᵃ 1 Chr. 6:10

26:18 ᵃ [Num. 3:10; 16:39, 40; 18:7]

26:19 ᵃ Lev. 13:42; Num. 12:10; 2 Kin. 5:25–27

26:20 ᵃ Esth. 6:12 ¹ *hurried* ² *struck*

26:21 ᵃ 2 Kin. 15:5 ᵇ [Lev. 13:46; Num. 5:2] ¹ *an isolated*

26:22 ᵃ 2 Kin. 20:1; 2 Chr. 32:20, 32; Is. 1:1

26:23 ᵃ 2 Kin. 15:7; 2 Chr. 21:20; 28:27; Is. 6:1 ¹ *rested in death with his ancestors*

27:1 ᵃ 2 Kin. 15:32–35 ¹ *Jerusha,* 2 Kin. 15:33

27:2 ᵃ 2 Kin. 15:35; Ezek. 20:44; 30:13

27:3 ᵃ 2 Chr. 33:14; Neh. 3:26 ¹ *Upper Gate*

27:4 ¹ *fortresses*

27:5 ᵃ 2 Chr. 26:8 ¹ *The same amount*

27:6 ᵃ 2 Chr. 26:5

ᵇ Ex. 30:7, 8; Heb. 7:14

7 Now the rest of the acts of Jotham, and all his wars, and his ways, lo, they *are* written in the book of the kings of Israel and Judah.

8 He was five and twenty years old when he began to reign, and reigned sixteen years in Jerusalem.

9 ªAnd Jotham ¹slept with his fathers, and they buried him in the city of David: and ᵇAhaz his son reigned in his stead.

## CHAPTER 28

Aᴴᴬᶻ ªwas twenty years old when he began to reign, and he reigned sixteen years in Jerusalem: but he did not *that which was* right in the sight of the LORD, like David his father:

2 For he walked in the ways of the kings of Israel, and made also ªmolten images for ᵇBaalim.

3 Moreover he burnt incense in ªthe valley of the son of Hinnom, and burnt ᵇhis children in the ᶜfire, after the abominations of the heathen whom the LORD ᵈcast out before the children of Israel.

4 He sacrificed also and burnt incense in the ¹high places, and on the hills, and under every green tree.

5 Wherefore ªthe LORD his God delivered him into the hand of the king of Syria; and they ᵇsmote¹ him, and carried away a great multitude of them captives, and brought *them* to Damascus. And he was also delivered into the hand of the king of Israel, who ²smote him with a great slaughter.

6 For ªPekah the son of Remaliah slew in Judah an hundred and twenty thousand in one day, *which were* all valiant men; ᵇbecause they had forsaken the LORD God of their fathers.

7 And Zichri, a mighty man of Ephraim, slew Maaseiah the king's son, and Azrikam the governor of the house, and Elkanah *that was* ¹next to the king.

8 And the children of Israel carried away captive of their ªbrethren two hundred thousand, women, sons, and daughters, and took also away much ¹spoil from them, and brought the spoil to Samaria.

9 But a ªprophet of the LORD was there, whose name *was* Oded: and he went out before the host that came to Samaria, and said unto them, Behold, ᵇbecause the LORD God of your fathers was ¹wroth with Judah, he hath delivered them into your hand, and ye have slain them in a rage *that* ᶜreacheth up unto heaven.

10 And now ye purpose to ¹keep under the children of Judah and Jerusalem for ªbondmen² and ³bondwomen unto you: *but* ⁴are there not with you, even with you, sins against the LORD your God?

11 Now hear me therefore, and deliver the captives again, which ye have taken captive of your brethren: ªfor the fierce wrath of the LORD is upon you.

12 Then certain of the heads of the children of Ephraim, Azariah the son of Johanan, Berechiah the son of Meshillemoth, and Jehizkiah the son of Shallum, and Amasa the son of Hadlai, stood up against them that came from the war,

13 And said unto them, Ye shall not bring in the captives hither: for whereas we have offended against the LORD *already,* ye intend to add *more* to our sins and to our trespass: for our sins are great, and *there is* fierce wrath against Israel.

14 So the armed men left the captives and the ¹spoil before the princes and all the congregation.

15 And the men ªwhich were ¹expressed by name rose up, and took the captives, and with the ²spoil clothed all that were naked among them, and arrayed them, and ³shod them, and ᵇgave them to eat and to drink, and anointed them, and carried all the feeble of them upon asses, and brought them to Jericho, ᶜthe city of palm trees, to their brethren: then they returned to Samaria.

16 ªAt that time did king Ahaz send unto the kings of Assyria to help him.

17 For again the ªEdomites had come and ¹smitten Judah, and carried away captives.

18 ªThe Philistines also had invaded the cities of the low country, and of the south of Judah, and had taken Beth-shemesh, and Ajalon, and Gederoth, and Shocho with the villages thereof, and Timnah with the villages thereof, Gimzo also and the villages thereof: and they dwelt there.

19 For the LORD ¹brought Judah low because of Ahaz king of ªIsrael; for he ᵇmade Judah naked, and transgressed ²sore against the LORD.

20 And ªTilgath-pilneser¹ king of Assyria came unto him, and distressed him, but ²strengthened him not.

21 For Ahaz took away a ¹portion *out* of the house of the LORD, and *out* of the house of the king, and of the princes, and gave *it* unto the king of Assyria: but he helped him not.

22 And in the time of his distress did he trespass yet more against the LORD: this *is that* king Ahaz.

23 For ªhe sacrificed unto the gods of Damascus, which ¹smote him: and he said, Because the gods of the kings of Syria help them, *therefore* will I sacrifice to them, that ᵇthey may help me. But they were the ruin of him, and of all Israel.

### Cross-references

27:9 ª 2 Kin. 15:38
ᵇ Is. 1:1; Hos. 1:1; Mic. 1:1 ¹ *rested in death with his ancestors*

28:1 ª 2 Kin. 16:2–4

28:2 ª Ex. 34:17; Lev. 19:4 ᵇ Judg. 2:11

28:3 ª Josh. 15:8 ᵇ 2 Kin. 23:10 ᶜ [Lev. 18:21]; 2 Kin. 16:3; 2 Chr. 33:6 ᵈ [Lev. 18:24–30]

28:4 ¹ *Places for pagan worship*

28:5 ª [Is. 10:5] ᵇ 2 Kin. 16:5, 6; [2 Chr. 24:24]; Is. 7:1, 17 ¹ *defeated* ² Lit. *struck*

28:6 ª 2 Kin. 15:27 ᵇ [2 Chr. 29:8]

28:7 ¹ *the second to*

28:8 ª Deut. 28:25, 41; 2 Chr. 11:4 ¹ *plunder*

28:9 ª 2 Chr. 25:15 ᵇ Ps. 69:26; [Is. 10:5; 47:6]; Ezek. 25:12, 15; 26:2; Obad. 10; [Zech. 1:15] ᶜ Ezra 9:6; Rev. 18:5 ¹ *angry*

28:10 ª [Lev. 25:39, 42, 43, 46] ¹ *force* ² *male slaves* ³ *female slaves* ⁴ *are you not also guilty before the LORD*

28:11 ᵈ Ps. 78:49; James 2:13

28:14 ¹ *plunder*

28:15 ª 2 Chr. 28:19 ᵇ [Prov. 25:21, 22; Luke 6:27; Rom. 12:20] ᶜ Deut. 34:3; Judg. 1:16 ¹ *designated* ² *plunder* ³ *gave them sandals*

28:16 ª 2 Kin. 16:7

28:17 ª 2 Chr. 21:10; Obad. 10–14 ¹ *attacked*

28:18 ª 2 Chr. 21:16, 17; Ezek. 16:27, 57

28:19 ª 2 Kin. 16:2; 2 Chr. 21:2 ᵇ Ex. 32:25 ¹ *humbled Judah* ² *greatly*

28:20 ª 2 Kin. 15:29; 16:7–9; 1 Chr. 5:26 ¹ Or *Tiglath-pileser,* 2 Kin. 15:29 ² *did not assist him*

28:21 ¹ *portion of the treasures from*

28:23 ª 2 Chr. 25:14 ᵇ Jer. 44:17, 18 ¹ *defeated*

24 And Ahaz gathered together the vessels of the house of God, and cut in pieces the vessels of the house of God, ᵃand shut up the doors of the house of the LORD, and he made him altars in every corner of Jerusalem.

25 And in every ¹several city of Judah he made ²high places to burn incense unto other gods, and provoked to anger the LORD God of his fathers.

26 ᵃNow the rest of his acts and of all his ways, first and last, behold, they *are* written in the book of the kings of Judah and Israel.

27 And Ahaz ¹slept with his fathers, and they buried him in the city, *even* in Jerusalem: but they brought him ᵃnot into the sepulchres of the kings of Israel: and Hezekiah his son reigned in his stead.

## CHAPTER 29

HEZEKIAH ᵃbegan to reign *when he was* five and twenty years old, and he reigned nine and twenty years in Jerusalem. And his mother's name *was* ¹Abijah, the daughter ᵇof Zechariah.

2 And he did *that which was* right in the sight of the LORD, according to all that David his father had done.

3 He in the first year of his reign, in the first month, ᵃopened the doors of the house of the LORD, and repaired them.

4 And he brought in the priests and the Levites, and gathered them together into the east ¹street,

5 And said unto them, Hear me, ye Levites, ¹sanctify now yourselves, and ᵃsanctify the house of the LORD God of your fathers, and carry forth the ²filthiness out of the holy *place*.

6 For our fathers have trespassed, and done *that which was* evil in the eyes of the LORD our God, and have forsaken him, and have ᵃturned away their faces from the ¹habitation of the LORD, and turned *their* backs.

7 ᵃAlso they have shut up the doors of the porch, and put out the lamps, and have not burned incense nor offered burnt offerings in the holy *place* unto the God of Israel.

8 Wherefore the ᵃwrath of the LORD was upon Judah and Jerusalem, and he hath ᵇdelivered them to trouble, to astonishment, and to ᶜhissing,¹ as ye see with your ᵈeyes.

9 For, lo, ᵃour fathers have fallen by the sword, and our sons and our daughters and our wives *are* in captivity for this.

10 Now *it is* in mine heart to make ᵃa covenant with the LORD God of Israel, that his fierce wrath may turn away from us.

11 My sons, be not now negligent: for the LORD hath ᵃchosen you to stand before him, to serve him, and that ye should minister unto him, and burn incense.

12 Then the Levites arose, ᵃMahath the son of Amasai, and Joel the son of Azariah, of the sons of the ᵇKohathites: and of the sons of Merari, Kish the son of Abdi, and Azariah the son of Jehalelel: and of the Gershonites; Joah the son of Zimmah, and Eden the son of Joah:

13 And of the sons of Elizaphan; Shimri, and Jeiel: and of the sons of Asaph; Zechariah, and Mattaniah:

14 And of the sons of Heman; Jehiel, and Shimei: and of the sons of Jeduthun; Shemaiah, and Uzziel.

15 And they gathered their brethren, and ᵃsanctified¹ themselves, and came, according to the commandment of the king, ²by the words of the LORD, ᵇto cleanse the house of the LORD.

16 And the priests went into the inner part of the house of the LORD, to cleanse *it*, and brought out all the ¹uncleanness that they found in the temple of the LORD into the court of the house of the LORD. And the Levites took *it*, to carry *it* out abroad into the brook ᵃKidron.

17 Now they began on the first *day* of the first month to ¹sanctify, and on the eighth day of the month came they to the porch of the LORD: so they sanctified the house of the LORD in eight days; and in the sixteenth day of the first month they made an end.

18 Then they went in to Hezekiah the king, and said, We have cleansed all the house of the LORD, and the altar of burnt offering, with all the vessels thereof, and the shewbread table, with all the vessels thereof.

19 Moreover all the vessels, which king Ahaz in his reign did ᵃcast ¹away in his transgression, have we prepared and ²sanctified, and, behold, they *are* before the altar of the LORD.

20 Then Hezekiah the king rose early, and gathered the rulers of the city, and went up to the house of the LORD.

21 And they brought seven bullocks, and seven rams, and seven lambs, and seven he goats, for a ᵃsin offering for the kingdom, and for the sanctuary, and for Judah. And he commanded the priests the sons of Aaron to offer *them* on the altar of the LORD.

22 So they killed the bullocks, and the priests received the blood, and ᵃsprinkled *it* on the altar: likewise, when they had killed the rams, they sprinkled the blood upon the altar: they killed also the lambs, and they sprinkled the blood upon the altar.

23 And they brought forth the he goats *for* the sin offering before the

king and the congregation; and they laid their [a]hands upon them:

24 And the priests killed them, and they [1]made reconciliation with their blood upon the altar, [a]to make an atonement for all Israel: for the king commanded *that* the burnt offering and the sin offering *should be made* for all Israel.

25 [a]And he set the Levites in the house of the LORD with cymbals, with [1]psalteries, and with harps, [b]according to the commandment of David, and of [c]Gad the king's seer, and Nathan the prophet: [d]for *so was* the commandment of the LORD by his prophets.

26 And the Levites stood with the instruments [a]of David, and the priests with [b]the trumpets.

27 And Hezekiah commanded to offer the burnt offering upon the altar. And when the burnt offering began, [a]the song of the LORD began *also* with the trumpets, and with the instruments *ordained* by David king of Israel.

28 And all the congregation worshipped, and the singers sang, and the trumpeters sounded: *and all this continued* until the burnt offering was finished.

29 And when they had made an end of offering, [a]the king and all that were present with him bowed themselves, and worshipped.

30 Moreover Hezekiah the king and the princes commanded the Levites to sing praise unto the LORD with the words of David, and of Asaph the seer. And they sang praises with gladness, and they bowed their heads and worshipped.

31 Then Hezekiah answered and said, Now ye have consecrated yourselves unto the LORD, come near and bring sacrifices and [a]thank offerings into the house of the LORD. And the congregation brought in sacrifices and thank offerings; and as many as were of a [b]free heart burnt offerings.

32 And the number of the burnt offerings, which the congregation brought, was threescore and ten bullocks, an hundred rams, *and* two hundred lambs: all these *were* for a burnt offering to the LORD.

33 And the consecrated things *were* six hundred oxen and three thousand sheep.

34 But the priests were too few, so that they could not [1]flay all the burnt offerings: wherefore [a]their brethren the Levites did help them, till the work was ended, and until the *other* priests had [2]sanctified themselves: [b]for the Levites *were* more [c]upright[3] in heart to [d]sanctify themselves than the priests.

35 And also the burnt offerings *were* in abundance, with [a]the fat of the peace offerings, and [b]the drink offerings for *every* burnt offering. So the service of the house of the LORD was set in order.

36 And Hezekiah rejoiced, and all the people, that God had prepared the people: for the thing was *done* suddenly.

## CHAPTER 30

AND Hezekiah sent to all Israel and Judah, and wrote letters also to Ephraim and Manasseh, that they should come to the house of the LORD at Jerusalem, to keep the passover unto the LORD God of Israel.

2 For the king had taken counsel, and his princes, and all the congregation in Jerusalem, to keep the passover in the second [a]month.

3 For they could not keep it [a]at that time, [b]because [1]the priests had not sanctified themselves sufficiently, neither had the people gathered themselves together to Jerusalem.

4 And the thing pleased the king and all the congregation.

5 So they established a decree to make proclamation throughout all Israel, from Beer-sheba even to Dan, that they should come to keep the passover unto the LORD God of Israel at Jerusalem: for they had not done *it* of a long *time in such sort* as it was written.

6 So the [a]posts[1] went with the letters from the king and his princes throughout all Israel and Judah, and according to the commandment of the king, saying, Ye children of Israel, [b]turn again unto the LORD God of Abraham, Isaac, and Israel, and he will return to the remnant of you, that are escaped out of the hand of [c]the kings of [d]Assyria.

7 And be not ye [a]like your fathers, and like your brethren, which trespassed against the LORD God of their fathers, *who* therefore [b]gave them up to [c]desolation, as ye see.

8 Now be ye not [a]stiffnecked,[1] as your fathers *were*, *but* yield yourselves unto the LORD, and enter into his sanctuary, which he hath sanctified for ever: and serve the LORD your God, [b]that the fierceness of his wrath may turn away from you.

9 For if ye turn again unto the LORD, your brethren and your children *shall find* [a]compassion before them that lead them captive, so that they shall come again into this land: for the LORD your God *is* [b]gracious and merciful, and will not turn away *his* face from you, if ye [c]return unto him.

10 So the [1]posts passed from city to city through the country of Ephraim

---

**Cross references (center column):**

29:23 [a] Lev. 4:15; 24; 8:14

29:24 [a] Lev. 14:20 [1] *presented their blood on the altar as a sin offering, to make*

29:25 [a] 1 Chr. 16:4; 25:6 [b] 1 Chr. 23:5; 25:1; 2 Chr. 8:14 [c] 2 Sam. 24:11 [d] 2 Chr. 30:12 [1] *stringed instruments*

29:26 [a] 1 Chr. 23:5; Amos 6:5 [b] Num. 10:8, 10; 1 Chr. 15:24; 16:6; 2 Chr. 5:12

29:27 [a] 2 Chr. 23:18

29:29 [a] 2 Chr. 20:18

29:31 [a] Lev. 7:12 [b] Ex. 35:5, 22

29:34 [a] 2 Chr. 35:11 [b] 2 Chr. 30:3 [c] Ps. 7:10 [d] 2 Chr. 29:5 [1] *skin* [2] *consecrated* [3] *diligent*

29:35 [a] Lev. 3:16 [b] Num. 15:5–10

30:2 [a] Num. 9:10, 11; 2 Chr. 30:13, 15

30:3 [a] Ex. 12:6, 18 [b] 2 Chr. 29:17, 34 [1] *a sufficient number of priests had not consecrated themselves*

30:6 [a] Esth. 8:14; Job 9:25; Jer. 51:31 [b] [Jer. 4:1; Joel 2:13] [c] 2 Kin. 15:19, 29 [d] 2 Chr. 28:20 [1] *runners*

30:7 [a] Ezek. 20:18 [b] Is. 1:9 [c] 2 Chr. 29:8

30:8 [a] Ex. 32:9; Deut. 10:16; Acts 7:51 [b] 2 Chr. 29:10 [1] *rebellious*

30:9 [a] Ps. 106:46 [b] [Ex. 34:6; Mic. 7:18] [c] [Is. 55:7]

30:10 [1] *runners*

and Manasseh even unto Zebulun: but [a]they laughed them to scorn, and mocked them.

11 Nevertheless [a]divers of Asher and Manasseh and of Zebulun humbled themselves, and came to Jerusalem.

12 Also in Judah [a]the hand of God was to give them [1]one heart to do the commandment of the king and of the princes, [b]by the word of the LORD.

13 And there assembled at Jerusalem much people to keep the feast of [a]unleavened bread in the second month, a very great congregation.

14 And they arose and took away the [a]altars that *were* in Jerusalem, and all the altars for incense took they away, and cast *them* into the brook [b]Kidron.

15 Then they [1]killed the passover on the fourteenth *day* of the second month: and the priests and the Levites were [a]ashamed, and [2]sanctified themselves, and brought in the burnt offerings into the house of the LORD.

16 And they stood in their [a]place [1]after their manner, according to the law of Moses the man of God: the priests sprinkled the blood, *which they received* of the hand of the Levites.

17 For *there were* many in the congregation that [1]were not sanctified: [a]therefore the Levites had the charge of the killing of the passovers for every one *that was* not clean, to sanctify *them* unto the LORD.

18 For a multitude of the people, *even* [a]many of Ephraim, and Manasseh, Issachar, and Zebulun, had not [1]cleansed themselves, [b]yet did they eat the passover otherwise than it was written. But Hezekiah prayed for them, saying, The good LORD pardon every one

19 *That* [a]prepareth his heart to seek God, the LORD God of his fathers, though *he be* not *cleansed* according to the purification of the sanctuary.

20 And the LORD hearkened to Hezekiah, and healed the people.

21 And the children of Israel that were present at Jerusalem kept [a]the feast of unleavened bread seven days with great gladness: and the Levites and the priests praised the LORD day by day, *singing* with loud instruments unto the LORD.

22 And Hezekiah [1]spake comfortably unto all the Levites [a]that taught the good knowledge of the LORD: and they did eat throughout the feast seven days, offering peace offerings, and [b]making confession to the LORD God of their fathers.

23 And the whole assembly [1]took counsel to keep [a]other seven days: and they kept *other* seven days with gladness.

24 For Hezekiah king of Judah [a]did give to the congregation a thousand bullocks and seven thousand sheep; and the princes gave to the congregation a thousand bullocks and ten thousand sheep: and a great number of priests [b]sanctified[1] themselves.

25 And all the congregation of Judah, with the priests and the Levites, and all the congregation that came out of Israel, and the [1]strangers [a]that came out of the land of Israel, and that dwelt in Judah, rejoiced.

26 So there was great joy in Jerusalem: for since the time of [a]Solomon the son of David king of Israel *there was* not the like in Jerusalem.

27 Then the priests the Levites arose and [a]blessed the people: and their voice was heard, and their prayer came *up* to [b]his holy dwelling place, *even* unto heaven.

## CHAPTER 31

Now when all this was finished, all Israel that were present went out to the cities of Judah, and [a]brake the [1]images in pieces, and cut down the [2]groves, and threw down the [3]high places and the altars out of all Judah and Benjamin, in Ephraim also and Manasseh, until they had utterly destroyed them all. Then all the children of Israel returned, every man to his possession, into their own cities.

2 And Hezekiah appointed [a]the [1]courses of the priests and the Levites after their courses, every man according to his service, the priests and Levites [b]for burnt offerings and for peace offerings, to minister, and to give thanks, and to praise in the gates of the [2]tents of the LORD.

3 [1]*He appointed* also the king's portion of his [a]substance for the burnt offerings, *to wit*, for the morning and evening burnt offerings, and the burnt offerings for the sabbaths, and for the new moons, and for the set feasts, as *it is* written in the [b]law of the LORD.

4 Moreover he commanded the people that dwelt in Jerusalem to give the [a]portion[1] of the priests and the Levites, that they might [2]be encouraged in [b]the law of the LORD.

5 And as soon as the commandment came abroad, the children of Israel brought in abundance [a]the firstfruits of corn, wine, and oil, and honey, and of all the increase of the field; and the [b]tithe of all *things* brought they in abundantly.

6 And *concerning* the children of Israel and Judah, that dwelt in the cities of Judah, they also brought in the tithe of oxen and sheep, and the [a]tithe of holy things which were consecrated unto the LORD their God, and laid *them* by heaps.

### Center column references

30:10 [a] 2 Chr. 36:16

30:11 [a] 2 Chr. 11:16; 30:18, 21

30:12 [a] [2 Cor. 3:5; Phil. 2:13; Heb. 13:20, 21] [b] 2 Chr. 29:25 [1] *singleness of heart*

30:13 [a] Lev. 23:6; Num. 9:11

30:14 [a] 2 Chr. 28:24 [b] 2 Chr. 29:16

30:15 [a] 2 Chr. 29:34 [1] *slaughtered the passover lamb* [2] *consecrated*

30:16 [a] 2 Chr. 35:10, 15 [1] *according to their custom*

30:17 [a] 2 Chr. 29:34 [1] *had not consecrated themselves*

30:18 [a] 2 Chr. 30:1, 11, 25 [b] Ex. 12:43–49; [Num. 9:10] [1] *purified*

30:19 [a] 2 Chr. 19:3

30:21 [a] Ex. 12:15; 13:6; 1 Kin. 8:65

30:22 [a] [Deut. 33:10]; 2 Chr. 17:9; 35:3 [b] Ezra 10:11 [1] *gave encouragement*

30:23 [a] 1 Kin. 8:65; 2 Chr. 35:17, 18 [1] *agreed*

30:24 [a] 2 Chr. 35:7, 8 [b] 2 Chr. 29:34 [1] *consecrated*

30:25 [a] 2 Chr. 30:11, 18 [1] *sojourners*

30:26 [a] 2 Chr. 7:8–10

30:27 [a] Num. 6:23 [b] Deut. 26:15; Ps. 68:5

31:1 [a] 2 Kin. 18:4 [1] *sacred pillars* [2] *wooden images* [3] Places for pagan worship

31:2 [a] 1 Chr. 23:6; 24:1 [b] 1 Chr. 23:30, 31 [1] *divisions* [2] Temple, lit. *camps*

31:3 [a] 2 Chr. 35:7 [b] Num. 28:1–29:40 [1] *The king appointed a portion of his possessions for*

31:4 [a] Num. 18:8; 2 Kin. 12:16; Neh. 13:10; Ezek. 44:29 [b] Mal. 2:7 [1] *portion due to* [2] *devote themselves to*

31:5 [a] Ex. 22:29; Neh. 13:12 [b] [Lev. 27:30]; Deut. 14:28; 26:12, 13

31:6 [a] [Lev. 27:30]; Deut. 14:28

7 In the third month they began to ¹lay the foundation of the heaps, and finished *them* in the seventh month.

8 And when Hezekiah and the princes came and saw the heaps, they blessed the LORD, and his people Israel.

9 Then Hezekiah questioned with the priests and the Levites concerning the heaps.

10 And Azariah the chief priest of the ᵃhouse of Zadok answered him, and said, ᵇSince *the people* began to bring the offerings into the house of the LORD, we have had enough to eat, and have left plenty: for the LORD hath blessed his people; and that which is left *is* this great ᶜstore.¹

11 Then Hezekiah commanded to prepare ᵃchambers¹ in the house of the LORD; and they prepared *them,*

12 And brought in the offerings and the tithes and the dedicated *things* faithfully: ᵃover which Cononiah the Levite *was* ruler, and Shimei his brother *was* the next.

13 And Jehiel, and Azaziah, and Nahath, and Asahel, and Jerimoth, and Jozabad, and Eliel, and Ismachiah, and Mahath, and Benaiah, *were* overseers under the hand of Cononiah and Shimei his brother, at the commandment of Hezekiah the king, and Azariah the ᵃruler of the house of God.

14 And Kore the son of Imnah the Levite, the ¹porter toward the east, *was* over the ᵃfreewill offerings of God, to distribute the ²oblations of the LORD, and the most holy things.

15 And next him *were* ᵃEden, and Miniamin, and Jeshua, and Shemaiah, Amariah, and Shecaniah, in ᵇthe cities of the priests, ¹in *their* ᶜset office, to give to their brethren by courses, as well to the great as to the small:

16 Beside their genealogy of males, from three years old and upward, *even* unto every one that entereth into the house of the LORD, his daily portion for ¹their service in their charges according to their ²courses;

17 Both to the genealogy of the priests by the house of their fathers, and the Levites ᵃfrom twenty years old and upward, ¹in their charges by their courses;

18 And to the genealogy of all their little ones, their wives, and their sons, and their daughters, through all the congregation: for in their ¹set office they ²sanctified themselves in holiness:

19 Also of the sons of Aaron the priests, *which were* in ᵃthe fields of the ¹suburbs of their cities, in every ²several city, the men that were ᵇexpressed by name, to give portions to

all the males among the priests, and to all that were reckoned by genealogies among the Levites.

20 And thus did Hezekiah throughout all Judah, and ᵃwrought *that which was* good and right and truth before the LORD his God.

21 And in every work that he began in the service of the house of God, and in the law, and in the commandments, to seek his God, he did *it* with all his heart, and ᵃprospered.

## CHAPTER 32

AFTER ᵃthese things, and ¹the establishment thereof, Sennacherib king of Assyria came, and entered into Judah, and encamped against the ²fenced cities, and thought to win them for himself.

2 And when Hezekiah saw that Sennacherib was come, and that he was purposed to fight against Jerusalem,

3 He took counsel with his princes and his mighty men to stop the waters of the ¹fountains which *were* ²without the city: and they did help him.

4 So there was gathered much people together, who stopped all the ᵃfountains,¹ and the brook that ran through the midst of the land, saying, Why should the kings of Assyria come, and find much water?

5 Also ᵃhe strengthened himself, ᵇand built up all the wall that was broken, and raised *it* up to the towers, and another wall ¹without, and repaired ᶜMillo *in* the city of David, and made ²darts and shields in abundance.

6 And he set captains of war over the people, and gathered them together to him in the street of the gate of the city, and spake ᵃcomfortably¹ to them, saying,

7 ᵃBe strong and courageous, ᵇbe not afraid nor dismayed for the king of Assyria, nor for all the multitude that *is* with him: for ᶜ*there be* more with us than with him:

8 With him *is* an ᵃarm of flesh; but ᵇwith us *is* the LORD our God to help us, and to fight our battles. And the people ¹rested themselves upon the words of Hezekiah king of Judah.

9 ᵃAfter this did Sennacherib king of Assyria send his servants to Jerusalem, (but he *himself laid siege* against Lachish, and all his ¹power with him,) unto Hezekiah king of Judah, and unto all Judah that *were* at Jerusalem, saying,

10 ᵃThus saith Sennacherib king of Assyria, Whereon do ye trust, that ye abide in the siege in Jerusalem?

11 Doth not Hezekiah persuade you to give over yourselves to die by famine and by thirst, saying, ᵃThe LORD

---

**31:7** ¹ *lay them in heaps*

**31:10** ᵃ 1 Chr. 6:8, 9 ᵇ [Mal. 3:10] ᶜ Ex. 36:5 ¹ *abundance*

**31:11** ᵃ 1 Kin. 6:5–8 ¹ *storerooms*

**31:12** ᵃ 2 Chr. 35:9; Neh. 13:13

**31:13** ᵃ 1 Chr. 9:11; Jer. 20:1

**31:14** ᵃ Deut. 23:23; 2 Chr. 35:8 ¹ *keeper* ² *offerings*

**31:15** ᵃ 2 Chr. 29:12 ᵇ Josh. 21:1–3, 9 ᶜ 1 Chr. 9:26 ¹ *faithful assistants*

**31:16** ¹ *the work of their service* ² *divisions*

**31:17** ᵃ 1 Chr. 23:24, 27 ¹ *according to their duties*

**31:18** ¹ *faithfulness* ² *consecrated*

**31:19** ᵃ Lev. 25:34; Num. 35:1–4 ᵇ 2 Chr. 31:12–15 ¹ *common lands* ² *single*

**31:20** ᵃ 2 Kin. 20:3; 22:2

**31:21** ᵃ 2 Chr. 26:5; 32:30; Ps. 1:3

**32:1** ᵃ 2 Kin. 18:13– 19:37; Is. 36:1– 37:38 ¹ *deeds of faithfulness* ² *fortified*

**32:3** ¹ *springs* ² *outside*

**32:4** ᵃ 2 Kin. 20:20 ¹ *springs*

**32:5** ᵃ Is. 22:9, 10 ᵇ 2 Kin. 25:4; 2 Chr. 25:23 ᶜ 2 Sam. 5:9; 1 Kin. 9:15, 24; 11:27; 2 Kin. 12:20; 1 Chr. 11:8 ¹ *outside* ² *weapons or javelins*

**32:6** ᵃ 2 Chr. 30:22; Is. 40:2 ¹ *encouragingly*

**32:7** ᵃ [Deut. 31:6] ᵇ 2 Chr. 20:15 ᶜ 2 Kin. 6:16; [Rom. 8:31]

**32:8** ᵃ [Jer. 17:5; 1 John 4:4] ᵇ Ex. 14:13; [1 Sam. 17:45–47]; 2 Chr. 13:12; 20:17; [Rom. 8:31] ¹ *were strengthened*

**32:9** ᵃ 2 Kin. 18:17 ¹ *forces*

**32:10** ᵃ 2 Kin. 18:19

**32:11** ᵃ 2 Kin. 18:30

our God shall deliver us out of the hand of the king of Assyria?

12 [a]Hath not the same Hezekiah taken away his [1]high places and his altars, and commanded Judah and Jerusalem, saying, Ye shall worship before one altar, and burn incense upon [b]it?

13 Know ye not what I and my fathers have done unto all the people of *other* lands? [a]were the gods of the nations of those lands any ways able to deliver their lands out of mine hand?

14 Who *was there* among all the gods of those nations that my fathers utterly destroyed, that could deliver his people out of mine hand, that your God should be able to deliver you out of mine [a]hand?

15 Now therefore [a]let not Hezekiah deceive you, nor persuade you on this manner, neither yet believe him: for no god of any nation or kingdom was able to deliver his people out of mine hand, and out of the hand of my fathers: how much less shall your God deliver you out of mine hand?

16 And his servants spake yet *more* against the LORD God, and against his servant Hezekiah.

17 He wrote also letters to [1]rail on the LORD God of Israel, and to speak against him, saying, [a]As the gods of the nations of *other* lands have not delivered their people out of mine hand, so shall not the God of Hezekiah deliver his people out of mine [b]hand.

18 [a]Then they cried with a loud voice in the [1]Jews' speech unto the people of Jerusalem that *were* on the wall, to [2]affright them, and to trouble them; that they might take the city.

19 And they spake against the God of Jerusalem, as against the gods of the people of the earth, *which were* [a]the work of the hands of man.

20 [a]And for this *cause* Hezekiah the king, and [b]the prophet Isaiah the son of Amoz, prayed and cried to heaven.

21 [a]And the LORD sent an angel, which cut off all the mighty men of valour, and the leaders and captains in the camp of the king of Assyria. So he returned with [b]shame of face to his own land. And when he was come into the house of his god, [1]they that came forth of his own bowels slew him there with the sword.

22 Thus the LORD saved Hezekiah and the inhabitants of Jerusalem from the hand of Sennacherib the king of Assyria, and from the hand of all *other,* and guided them on every side.

23 And many brought gifts unto the LORD to Jerusalem, and [a]presents[1] to Hezekiah king of Judah: so that he

32:12 [a] 2 Kin. 18:22 [b] 2 Chr. 31:1, 2 [1] Places for pagan worship
32:13 [a] 2 Kin. 18:33–35
32:14 [a] [Is. 10:5–12]
32:15 [a] 2 Kin. 18:29
32:17 [a] 2 Kin. 19:9; [1 Cor. 8:5, 6] [1] *revile* [b] 2 Kin. 19:12
32:18 [a] 2 Kin. 18:28 [1] *Judean language,* Hebrew [2] *frighten*
32:19 [a] [Ps. 96:5; 115:4–8]
32:20 [a] 2 Kin. 19:15 [b] 2 Kin. 19:2
32:21 [a] Zech. 14:3 [b] Ps. 44:7 [1] his own children
32:23 [a] 2 Sam. 8:10 [1] Lit. *precious things*

was [b]magnified[2] in the sight of all nations from thenceforth.

24 [a]In those days Hezekiah was sick to the death, and prayed unto the LORD: and he spake unto him, and he gave him a sign.

25 But Hezekiah [a]rendered[1] not again according to the benefit *done* unto him; for [b]his heart was lifted up: [c]therefore there was wrath upon him, and upon Judah and Jerusalem.

26 [a]Notwithstanding Hezekiah humbled himself for the pride of his heart, *both* he and the inhabitants of Jerusalem, so that the wrath of the LORD came not upon them [b]in the days of Hezekiah.

27 And Hezekiah had exceeding much riches and honour: and he made himself treasuries for silver, and for gold, and for precious stones, and for spices, and for shields, and for all manner of [1]pleasant jewels;

28 Storehouses also for the increase of corn, and wine, and oil; and stalls for all manner of beasts, and [1]cotes for flocks.

29 Moreover he provided him cities, and possessions of flocks and herds in abundance: for [a]God had given him [1]substance very much.

30 [a]This same Hezekiah also stopped the upper watercourse of Gihon, and brought it [1]straight down to the west side of the city of David. And Hezekiah [b]prospered in all his works.

31 Howbeit in *the business of* the ambassadors of the princes of Babylon, who [a]sent unto him to enquire of the wonder that was *done* in the land, God left him, to [b]try[1] him, that he might know all *that was* in his heart.

32 Now the rest of the acts of Hezekiah, and his goodness, behold, they *are* written in [a]the vision of Isaiah the prophet, the son of Amoz, *and* in the [b]book of the kings of Judah and Israel.

33 And [a]Hezekiah [1]slept with his fathers, and they buried him in the [2]chiefest of the sepulchres of the sons of David: and all Judah and the inhabitants of Jerusalem did him [b]honour at his death. And Manasseh his son reigned in his stead.

## CHAPTER 33

MANASSEH [a]*was* twelve years old when he began to reign, and he reigned fifty and five years in Jerusalem:

2 But did *that which was* evil in the sight of the LORD, like unto the [a]abominations of the heathen, whom the LORD had cast out before the children of Israel.

3 For he built again the [1]high places which Hezekiah his father had [a]broken down, and he reared up altars for

[b] 2 Chr. 1:1 [2] *exalted*
32:24 [a] Is. 38:1–8
32:25 [a] Ps. 116:12 [b] [Hab. 2:4] [c] 2 Chr. 24:18 [1] *did not repay*
32:26 [a] Jer. 26:18, 19 [b] 2 Kin. 20:19
32:27 [1] *desirable articles*
32:28 [1] *sheepfolds*
32:29 [a] 1 Chr. 29:12 [1] *very much property*
32:30 [a] Is. 22:9–11 [b] 2 Chr. 31:21 [1] *By tunnel*
32:31 [a] Is. 39:1 [b] [Deut. 8:2, 16] [1] *test*
32:32 [a] Is. 36–39 [b] 2 Kin. 18–20
32:33 [a] 2 Kin. 20:21 [b] Prov. 10:7 [1] *rested in death with* [2] *upper tombs*
33:1 [a] 2 Kin. 21:1–9
33:2 [a] 2 Chr. 28:3
33:3 [a] 2 Kin. 18:4 [1] Places for pagan worship

Baalim, and [b]made [2]groves, and worshipped [c]all [3]the host of heaven, and served them.

4 Also he built altars in the house of the LORD, whereof the LORD had said, [a]In Jerusalem shall my name be for ever.

5 And he built altars for all the host of heaven [a]in the two courts of the house of the LORD.

6 [a]And he caused his children to pass through the fire in the valley of the son of Hinnom: also he [1]observed times, and used [b]enchantments,[2] and used [3]witchcraft, and [c]dealt[4] with a familiar spirit, and with [5]wizards: he wrought much evil in the sight of the LORD, to provoke him to anger.

7 And [a]he set a carved image, the idol which he had made, in the [1]house of God, of which God had said to David and to Solomon his son, In [b]this house, and in Jerusalem, which I have chosen before all the tribes of Israel, will I put my name for ever:

8 [a]Neither will I any more remove the foot of Israel from out of the land which I have appointed for your fathers; so that they will take heed to do all that I have commanded them, according to the whole law and the statutes and the ordinances by the hand of Moses.

9 So Manasseh made Judah and the inhabitants of Jerusalem to err, *and* to do worse than the heathen, whom the LORD had destroyed before the children of Israel.

10 And the LORD spake to Manasseh, and to his people: but they would not [1]hearken.

11 [a]Wherefore the LORD brought upon them the captains of the host of the king of Assyria, which took Manasseh [1]among the thorns, and [b]bound him with [2]fetters, and carried him to Babylon.

12 And when he was in affliction, he besought the LORD his God, and [a]humbled himself greatly before the God of his fathers,

13 And prayed unto him: and he was [a]intreated of him, and heard his supplication, and brought him again to Jerusalem into his kingdom. Then Manasseh [b]knew that the LORD he *was* God.

14 Now after this he built a wall [1]without the city of David, on the west side of [a]Gihon, in the valley, even to the entering in at the fish gate, and compassed [b]about Ophel, and raised it up a very great height, and put captains of war in all the [2]fenced cities of Judah.

15 And he took away [a]the [1]strange gods, and the idol out of the house of the LORD, and all the altars that he had built in the mount of the house

33:3 [b] Deut.
16:21 [c] Deut. 17:3
[2] *wooden images*
[3] The gods of the Assyrians
33:4 [a] 2 Chr. 6:6; 7:16
33:5 [a] 2 Chr. 4:9
33:6 [a] [Lev. 18:21] [b] Deut. 18:11 [c] 2 Kin. 21:6 [1] *practised soothsaying* [2] *witchcraft* [3] *sorcery* [4] *consulted mediums* [5] *spiritists*
33:7 [a] 2 Chr. 25:14 [b] Ps. 132:14 [1] *Temple*
33:8 [a] 2 Sam. 7:10
33:10 [1] *obey*
33:11 [a] Deut. 28:36 [b] 2 Chr. 36:6; Job 36:8; Ps. 107:10, 11 [1] *With nose hooks* [2] *bronze chains*
33:12 [a] 2 Chr. 7:14; 32:26; [1 Pet. 5:6]
33:13 [a] 1 Chr. 5:20; Ezra 8:23 [b] 1 Kin. 20:13; Ps. 9:16; Dan. 4:25
33:14 [a] 1 Kin. 1:33 [b] 2 Chr. 27:3 [1] *outside* [2] *fortified*
33:15 [a] 2 Chr. 33:3, 5, 7 [1] *foreign*
33:16 [a] Lev. 7:12
33:17 [a] 2 Chr. 32:12 [1] *Places for pagan worship*
33:18 [a] 1 Sam. 9:9 [1] *Lit. words*
33:19 [1] *Places for pagan worship* [2] *wooden images* [3] *carved* [4] MT *Hozai*
33:20 [a] 1 Kin. 1:21; 2 Kin. 21:18 [1] *rested in death with his ancestors*
33:21 [a] 2 Kin. 21:19–24; 1 Chr. 3:14
33:23 [a] 2 Chr. 33:12, 19
33:24 [a] 2 Kin. 21:23, 24; 2 Chr. 24:25 [b] 2 Chr. 25:27
34:1 [a] 2 Kin. 22:1, 2; Jer. 1:2; 3:6
34:2 [1] *did not turn aside*
34:3 [a] Eccl. 12:1 [b] 2 Chr. 15:2; [Prov. 8:17] [c] 1 Kin. 13:2 [d] 2 Chr. 33:17–19, 22 [1] *Places for pagan worship* [2] *wooden images*
34:4 [a] Lev. 26:30; 2 Kin. 23:4

of the LORD, and in Jerusalem, and cast *them* out of the city.

16 And he repaired the altar of the LORD, and sacrificed thereon peace offerings and [a]thank offerings, and commanded Judah to serve the LORD God of Israel.

17 [a]Nevertheless the people did sacrifice still in the [1]high places, *yet* unto the LORD their God only.

18 Now the rest of the acts of Manasseh, and his prayer unto his God, and the words of [a]the seers that spake to him in the name of the LORD God of Israel, behold, they *are written* in the [1]book of the kings of Israel.

19 His prayer also, and *how God* was intreated of him, and all his sin, and his trespass, and the places wherein he built [1]high places, and set up [2]groves and [3]graven images, before he was humbled: behold, they *are* written among the sayings of [4]the seers.

20 [a]So Manasseh [1]slept with his fathers, and they buried him in his own house: and Amon his son reigned in his stead.

21 [a]Amon *was* two and twenty years old when he began to reign, and reigned two years in Jerusalem.

22 But he did *that which was* evil in the sight of the LORD, as did Manasseh his father: for Amon sacrificed unto all the carved images which Manasseh his father had made, and served them;

23 And humbled not himself before the LORD, [a]as Manasseh his father had humbled himself; but Amon trespassed more and more.

24 [a]And his servants conspired against him, and [b]slew him in his own house.

25 But the people of the land slew all them that had conspired against king Amon; and the people of the land made Josiah his son king in his stead.

## CHAPTER 34

JOSIAH [a]*was* eight years old when he began to reign, and he reigned in Jerusalem one and thirty years.

2 And he did *that which was* right in the sight of the LORD, and walked in the ways of David his father, and [1]declined *neither* to the right hand, nor to the left.

3 For in the eighth year of his reign, while he was yet [a]young, he began to [b]seek after the God of David his father: and in the twelfth year he began [c]to purge Judah and Jerusalem [d]from the [1]high places, and the [2]groves, and the carved images, and the molten images.

4 [a]And they brake down the altars of Baalim in his presence; and the

[1]images, that *were* on high above them, he cut down; and the [2]groves, and the carved images, and the molten images, he brake in pieces, and made dust *of them*, [b]and strowed *it* upon the graves of them that had sacrificed unto them.

5 And he [a]burnt the bones of the priests upon their [b]altars, and cleansed Judah and Jerusalem.

6 And *so did he* in the cities of Manasseh, and Ephraim, and Simeon, even unto Naphtali, with their [1]mattocks round about.

7 And when he had broken down the altars and the [1]groves, and had [a]beaten the [2]graven images into powder, and cut down all the [3]idols throughout all the land of Israel, he returned to Jerusalem.

8 Now [a]in the eighteenth year of his reign, when he had purged the land, and the [1]house, he sent [b]Shaphan the son of Azaliah, and Maaseiah the [c]governor of the city, and Joah the son of Joahaz the recorder, to repair the house of the LORD his God.

9 And when they came to Hilkiah the high priest, they delivered [a]the money that was brought into the house of God, which the Levites that kept the doors had gathered of the hand of Manasseh and Ephraim, and of all the [b]remnant of Israel, and of all Judah and Benjamin; and they returned to Jerusalem.

10 And they put *it* in the hand of the workmen that had the oversight of the house of the LORD, and they gave it to the workmen that wrought in the house of the LORD, to repair and [1]amend the house:

11 Even to the [1]artificers and builders gave they *it,* to buy hewn stone, and timber for [2]couplings, and to floor the houses which the kings of Judah had destroyed.

12 And the men did the work faithfully: and the overseers of them *were* Jahath and Obadiah, the Levites, of the sons of Merari; and Zechariah and Meshullam, of the sons of the Kohathites, to set *it* forward; and *other of* the Levites, all that [1]could skill of instruments of musick.

13 Also *they were* [a]over the bearers of burdens, and *were* overseers of all that wrought the work in any manner of service: [b]and of the Levites *there were* scribes, and officers, and porters.

14 And when they brought out the money that was brought into the house of the LORD, Hilkiah the priest [a]found a book of the law of the LORD *given* by Moses.

15 And Hilkiah answered and said to Shaphan the scribe, I have found the book of the law in the house of

the LORD. And Hilkiah delivered the [a]book to Shaphan.

16 And Shaphan carried the book to the king, and brought the king word back again, saying, All that was committed to thy servants, they do *it.*

17 And they have [1]gathered together the money that was found in the house of the LORD, and have delivered it into the hand of the overseers, and to the hand of the workmen.

18 Then Shaphan the scribe told the king, saying, Hilkiah the priest hath given me a book. And Shaphan read it before the king.

19 And it came to pass, when the king had heard the words of the law, that he [1]rent his clothes.

20 And the king commanded Hilkiah, and [a]Ahikam the son of Shaphan, and [1]Abdon the son of Micah, and Shaphan the scribe, and Asaiah a servant of the king's, saying,

21 Go, enquire of the LORD for me, and for them that are left in Israel and in Judah, concerning the words of the book that is found: for great *is* the wrath of the LORD that is poured out upon us, because our fathers have not [a]kept the word of the LORD, to do after all that is written in this book.

22 And Hilkiah, and *they* that the king *had appointed,* went to Huldah the prophetess, the wife of Shallum the son of [1]Tikvath, the son of [2]Hasrah, keeper of the wardrobe; (now she dwelt in Jerusalem in the [3]college:) and they spake to her to that *effect.*

23 And she answered them, Thus saith the LORD God of Israel, Tell ye the man that sent you to me,

24 Thus saith the LORD, Behold, I will [a]bring [1]evil upon this place, and upon the inhabitants thereof, *even* all the curses that are written in the [b]book which they have read before the king of Judah:

25 Because they have forsaken me, and have burned incense unto other gods, that they might provoke me to anger with all the works of their hands; therefore my wrath shall be poured out upon this place, and shall not be quenched.

26 And as for the king of Judah, who sent you to enquire of the LORD, so shall ye say unto him, Thus saith the LORD God of Israel *concerning* the words which thou hast heard;

27 Because thine heart was tender, and thou didst humble thyself before God, when thou heardest his words against this place, and against the inhabitants thereof, and humbledst thyself before me, and [1]didst rend thy clothes, and weep before me; I have even heard *thee* also, saith the [a]LORD.

### Cross-references (center column)

34:4 [b] 2 Kin. 23:6
[1] *incense altars*
[2] *wooden images*

34:5 [a] 1 Kin. 13:2
[b] 2 Kin. 23:20

34:6 [1] *axes,* lit. *swords*

34:7 [a] Deut. 9:21
[1] *wooden images*
[2] *carved* [3] *incense altars*

34:8 [a] 2 Kin. 22:3–20 [b] 2 Kin. 25:22 [c] 2 Chr. 18:25 [1] *Temple*

34:9 [a] 2 Kin. 12:4
[b] 2 Chr. 30:6

34:10 [1] *restore*

34:11 [1] *craftsmen*
[2] *beams*

34:12 [1] *were skilful with*

34:13 [a] 2 Chr. 8:10
[b] 1 Chr. 23:4, 5

34:14 [a] 2 Kin. 22:8

34:15 [a] Deut. 31:24, 26

34:17 [1] Lit. *poured out*

34:19 [1] *tore*

34:20 [a] Jer. 26:24
[1] *Achbor the son of Michaiah,* 2 Kin. 22:12

34:21 [a] 2 Kin. 17:15–19

34:22 [1] *Tikvah,* 2 Kin. 22:14
[2] *Harhas,* 2 Kin. 22:14 [3] *second quarter*

34:24 [a] 2 Chr. 36:14–20 [b] Deut. 28:15–68 [1] *calamity*

34:27 [a] 2 Kin. 22:19; 2 Chr. 12:7; 30:6; 33:12, 13 [1] *tore*

28 Behold, I will gather thee to thy fathers, and thou shalt be gathered to thy grave in peace, neither shall thine eyes see all the [1]evil that I will bring upon this place, and upon the inhabitants of the same. So they brought the king word again.

29 [a]Then the king sent and gathered together all the elders of Judah and Jerusalem.

30 And the king went up into the house of the LORD, and all the men of Judah, and the inhabitants of Jerusalem, and the priests, and the Levites, and all the people, great and small: and he [a]read in their ears all the words of the book of the covenant that was found in the house of the LORD.

31 And the king [a]stood in [b]his place, and made a [c]covenant before the LORD, to walk after the LORD, and to keep his commandments, and his testimonies, and his statutes, with all his heart, and with all his soul, to perform the words of the covenant which are written in this book.

32 And he caused all that were present in Jerusalem and Benjamin to [1]stand *to it.* And the inhabitants of Jerusalem did according to the covenant of God, the God of their fathers.

33 And Josiah took away all the [a]abominations out of all the countries that *pertained* to the children of Israel, and made all that were present in Israel to serve, *even* to serve the LORD their God. [b]*And* all his days they departed not from following the LORD, the God of their fathers.

## CHAPTER 35

MOREOVER [a]Josiah kept a passover unto the LORD in Jerusalem: and they killed the passover on the [b]fourteenth *day* of the first month.

2 And he set the priests in their [a]charges,[1] and [b]encouraged them to the service of the house of the LORD,

3 And said unto the Levites [a]that taught all Israel, which were holy unto the LORD, [b]Put the holy ark [c]in the [1]house which Solomon the son of David king of Israel did build; [d]*it shall* not *be* a burden upon *your* shoulders: serve now the LORD your God, and his people Israel,

4 And prepare *yourselves* [a]by the [1]houses of your fathers, after your [2]courses, according to the [b]writing of David king of Israel, and according to the [c]writing of Solomon his son.

5 And [a]stand in the holy *place* according to the divisions of the families of the fathers of your brethren the people, and *after* the division of the families of the Levites.

6 So kill the passover, and [a]sanctify[1] yourselves, and prepare your brethren, that *they* may do according to the word of the LORD by the hand of Moses.

7 And Josiah [a]gave to the people, of the flock, lambs and kids, all for the passover offerings, for all that were present, to the number of thirty thousand, and three thousand bullocks: these *were* of the king's [b]substance.[1]

8 And his [a]princes gave willingly unto the people, to the priests, and to the Levites: Hilkiah and Zechariah and Jehiel, rulers of the house of God, gave unto the priests for the passover offerings two thousand and six hundred *small cattle,* and three hundred oxen.

9 [a]Conaniah also, and Shemaiah and Nethaneel, his brethren, and Hashabiah and Jeiel and Jozabad, chief of the Levites, gave unto the Levites for passover offerings five thousand *small cattle,* and five hundred oxen.

10 So the service was prepared, and the priests [a]stood in their place, and the [b]Levites in their courses, according to the king's commandment.

11 And they killed the passover, and the priests [a]sprinkled *the blood* from their hands, and the Levites [b]flayed[1] *them.*

12 And they removed the burnt offerings, that they might give according to the divisions of the families of the people, to offer unto the LORD, as *it is* written [a]in the book of Moses. And so *did they* with the oxen.

13 And they [a]roasted the passover with fire according to the [1]ordinance: but the *other* holy *offerings* [b]sod[2] they in pots, and in caldrons, and in pans, and divided *them* speedily among all the people.

14 And afterward they made ready for themselves, and for the priests: because the priests the sons of Aaron *were busied* in offering of burnt offerings and the fat until night; therefore the Levites prepared for themselves, and for the priests the sons of Aaron.

15 And the singers the sons of Asaph *were* in their place, according to the [a]commandment of David, and Asaph, and Heman, and Jeduthun the king's seer; and the [1]porters [b]*waited* at every gate; they might not depart from their service; for their brethren the Levites prepared for them.

16 So all the service of the LORD was prepared the same day, to keep the passover, and to offer burnt offerings upon the altar of the LORD, according to the commandment of king Josiah.

---

**Cross-references (center column):**

34:28 [1] *calamity*
34:29 [a] 2 Kin. 23:1-3
34:30 [a] Neh. 8:1-3
34:31 [a] 2 Chr. 6:13　[b] 2 Kin. 11:14; 23:3; 2 Chr. 30:16　[c] 2 Chr. 23:16; 29:10
34:32 [1] *take their stand*
34:33 [a] 1 Kin. 11:5; 2 Chr. 33:2　[b] Jer. 3:10
35:1 [a] 2 Kin. 23:21, 22　[b] Ex. 12:6; Num. 9:3; Ezra 6:19
35:2 [a] 2 Chr. 23:18; Ezra 6:18　[b] 2 Chr. 29:5-15　[1] *duties*
35:3 [a] Deut. 33:10; 2 Chr. 17:8, 9; Neh. 8:7　[b] 2 Chr. 34:14　[c] Ex. 40:21; 2 Chr. 5:7　[d] 1 Chr. 23:26　[1] *Temple*
35:4 [a] 1 Chr. 9:10-13　[b] 1 Chr. 23-26　[c] 2 Chr. 8:14　[1] *households*　[2] *divisions*
35:5 [a] Ps. 134:1

35:6 [a] 2 Chr. 29:5, 15　[1] *consecrate*
35:7 [a] 2 Chr. 30:24　[b] 2 Chr. 31:3　[1] *possessions*
35:8 [a] Num. 7:2
35:9 [a] 2 Chr. 31:12
35:10 [a] Ezra 6:18; Heb. 9:6　[b] 2 Chr. 5:12; 7:6; 8:14, 15; 13:10; 29:25-34
35:11 [a] Ex. 12:22; 2 Chr. 29:22　[b] 2 Chr. 29:34　[1] *skinned*
35:12 [a] Lev. 3:3; Ezra 6:18
35:13 [a] Ex. 12:8, 9; Deut. 16:7　[b] 1 Sam. 2:13-15　[1] *law*　[2] *boiled*
35:15 [a] 1 Chr. 25:1-6　[b] 1 Chr. 9:17, 18　[1] *gatekeepers*

17 And the children of Israel that were present kept the passover at that time, and the feast of ªunleavened bread seven days.

18 And ªthere was no passover like to that kept in Israel from the days of Samuel the prophet; neither did all the kings of Israel keep such a passover as Josiah kept, and the priests, and the Levites, and all Judah and Israel that were present, and the inhabitants of Jerusalem.

19 In the eighteenth year of the reign of Josiah was this passover kept.

20 ªAfter all this, when Josiah had prepared the temple, Necho king of Egypt came up to fight against ᵇCharchemish by Euphrates: and Josiah went out against him.

21 But he sent ambassadors to him, saying, What have I to do with thee, thou king of Judah? *I come* up against thee this day, but against ¹the house wherewith I have war: for God commanded me to make haste: forbear thee from *meddling with* God, who *is* with me, that he destroy thee not.

22 Nevertheless Josiah would not turn his face from him, but ªdisguised himself, that he might fight with him, and hearkened not unto the words of Necho from the mouth of God, and came to fight in the valley of Megiddo.

23 And the archers shot at king Josiah; and the king said to his servants, ¹Have me away; for I am ²sore wounded.

24 ªHis servants therefore took him out of that chariot, and put him in the second chariot that he had; and they brought him to Jerusalem, and he died, and was buried in *one of* the sepulchres of his fathers. And ᵇall Judah and Jerusalem mourned for Josiah.

25 And Jeremiah ªlamented for ᵇJosiah: and ᶜall the singing men and the singing women spake of Josiah in their lamentations to this day, ᵈand made them an ordinance in Israel: and, behold, they *are* written in the lamentations.

26 Now the rest of the acts of Josiah, and his goodness, according to *that which was* written in the law of the LORD,

27 And his deeds, first and last, behold, they *are* written in the book of the kings of Israel and Judah.

## CHAPTER 36

THEN ªthe people of the land took Jehoahaz the son of Josiah, and made him king in his father's stead in Jerusalem.

2 ¹Jehoahaz *was* twenty and three years old when he began to reign, and he reigned three months in Jerusalem.

3 And the king of Egypt ¹put him down at Jerusalem, and ²condemned the land in an hundred talents of silver and a talent of gold.

4 And the king of Egypt made Eliakim his brother king over Judah and Jerusalem, and turned his name to Jehoiakim. And Necho took ¹Jehoahaz his brother, and carried him to Egypt.

5 ªJehoiakim *was* twenty and five years old when he began to reign, and he reigned eleven years in Jerusalem: and he did *that which was* ᵇevil in the sight of the LORD his God.

6 ªAgainst him came up Nebuchadnezzar king of Babylon, and bound him in ¹fetters, to ᵇcarry him to Babylon.

7 ªNebuchadnezzar also carried of the vessels of the house of the LORD to Babylon, and put them in his temple at Babylon.

8 Now the rest of the acts of Jehoiakim, and his abominations which he did, and that which was found in him, behold, they *are* written in the book of the kings of Israel and Judah: and ¹Jehoiachin his son reigned in his stead.

9 ªJehoiachin *was* ¹eight years old when he began to reign, and he reigned three months and ten days in Jerusalem: and he did *that which was* evil in the sight of the LORD.

10 And when the year was expired, ªking Nebuchadnezzar sent, and brought him to Babylon, ᵇwith the goodly vessels of the house of the LORD, and made ᶜZedekiah¹ his ²brother king over Judah and Jerusalem.

11 ªZedekiah *was* one and twenty years old when he began to reign, and reigned eleven years in Jerusalem.

12 And he did *that which was* evil in the sight of the LORD his God, *and* humbled ªnot himself before Jeremiah the prophet *speaking* from the mouth of the LORD.

13 And he also ªrebelled against king Nebuchadnezzar, who had made him ¹swear by God: but he ᵇstiffened his neck, and hardened his heart from turning unto the LORD God of Israel.

14 Moreover all the chief of the priests, and the people, transgressed very much after all the abominations of the heathen; and polluted the house of the LORD which he had hallowed in Jerusalem.

15 ªAnd the LORD God of their fathers sent to them by his messengers, rising up ¹betimes, and sending; because he had compassion on his people, and on his dwelling place:

16 But ªthey mocked the messengers of God, and ᵇdespised his words,

### Cross references (center column)

35:17 ¹ Ex. 12:15; 13:6; 2 Chr. 30:21
35:18 ª 2 Kin. 23:22, 23
35:20 ª 2 Kin. 23:29 ᵇ Is. 10:9; Jer. 46:2
35:21 ¹ The kingdom
35:22 ª 1 Kin. 22:30; 2 Chr. 18:29
35:23 ¹ *Take* ² *severely*
35:24 ª 2 Kin. 23:30 ᵇ 1 Kin. 14:18; Zech. 12:11
35:25 ª Lam. 4:20 ᵇ Jer. 22:10, 11 ᶜ Matt. 9:23 ᵈ Jer. 22:20
36:1 ª 2 Kin. 23:30–34
36:2 ¹ MT *Joahaz*

36:3 ¹ *deposed him* ² *imposed on*
36:4 ¹ MT *Joahaz*
36:5 ª 2 Kin. 23:36, 37; 1 Chr. 3:15 ᵇ [Jer. 22:13–19]
36:6 ª 2 Kin. 24:1; Hab. 1:6 ᵇ [Deut. 29:22–29]; 2 Chr. 33:11; Jer. 36:30 ¹ *bronze chains*
36:7 ª 2 Kin. 24:13; Dan. 1:1, 2
36:8 ¹ *Jeconiah*, Jer. 27:20
36:9 ª 2 Kin. 24:8–17 ¹ *eighteen*, 2 Kin. 24:8
36:10 ª 2 Kin. 24:10–17 ᵇ Dan. 1:1, 2 ᶜ Jer. 37:1 ¹ *Mattaniah*, 2 Kin. 24:17 ² *father's brother*, 2 Kin. 24:17
36:11 ª 2 Kin. 24:18–20; Jer. 52:1
36:12 ª Jer. 21:3–7; 44:10
36:13 ª Jer. 52:3; Ezek. 17:15 ᵇ 2 Kin. 17:14; [2 Chr. 30:8] ¹ *swear an oath*
36:15 ª Jer. 7:13; 25:3, 4 ¹ *early*
36:16 ª 2 Chr. 30:10; Jer. 5:12, 13 ᵇ [Prov. 1:24–32]

and ^cmisused his prophets, until the ^dwrath of the LORD arose against his people, till *there was* no remedy.

17 ^aTherefore he brought upon them the king of the Chaldees, who ^bslew their young men with the sword in the house of their sanctuary, and had no compassion upon young man or maiden, old man, or him that stooped for age: he gave *them* all into his hand.

18 ^aAnd all the vessels of the house of God, great and small, and the treasures of the house of the LORD, and the treasures of the king, and of his princes; all *these* he brought to Babylon.

19 ^aAnd they burnt the house of God, and brake down the wall of Jerusalem, and burnt all the palaces thereof with fire, and destroyed all the goodly vessels thereof.

20 And ^athem that had escaped from the sword carried he away to Babylon; ^bwhere they were servants

36:16 ^c Jer. 38:6; Matt. 23:34
^d 2 Chr. 34:25; Ps. 79:5
36:17 ^a Num. 33:56; Deut. 4:26; 28:49; 2 Kin. 25:1; Ezra 9:7; Is. 3:8
^b Ps. 74:20
36:18 ^a 2 Kin. 25:13–15; 2 Chr. 36:7, 10
36:19 ^a 2 Kin. 25:9; Ps. 79:1, 7; Is. 1:7, 8; Jer. 52:13
36:20 ^a 2 Kin. 25:11; Jer. 5:19; Mic. 4:10 ^b Jer. 17:4; 27:7
36:21 ^a Jer. 25:9–12; 27:6–8; 29:10
^b Lev. 26:34–43; Dan. 9:2 ^c Lev. 25:4, 5
36:22 ^a Ezra 1:1–3
^b Jer. 29:10 ^c Is. 44:28; 45:1
36:23 ^a Ezra 1:2, 3
^1 Temple

to him and his sons until the reign of the kingdom of Persia:

21 To fulfil the word of the LORD by the mouth of ^aJeremiah, until the land ^bhad enjoyed her sabbaths: *for* as long as she lay desolate ^cshe kept sabbath, to fulfil threescore and ten years.

22 ^aNow in the first year of Cyrus king of Persia, that the word of the LORD *spoken* by the mouth of ^bJeremiah might be accomplished, the LORD stirred up the spirit of ^cCyrus king of Persia, that he made a proclamation throughout all his kingdom, and *put it* also in writing, saying,

23 ^aThus saith Cyrus king of Persia, All the kingdoms of the earth hath the LORD God of heaven given me; and he hath charged me to build him an ^1house in Jerusalem, which *is* in Judah. Who *is there* among you of all his people? The LORD his God *be* with him, and let him go up.

# THE BOOK OF
# EZRA

**E**zra continues the Old Testament narrative of Second Chronicles by showing how God fulfills His promise to return His people to the Land of Promise after seventy years of exile. Israel's "second exodus," this one from Babylon, is less impressive than the return from Egypt because only a remnant chooses to leave Babylon.

Ezra relates the story of two returns from Babylon—the first led by Zerubbabel to rebuild the temple (1–6), and the second under the leadership of Ezra to rebuild the spiritual condition of the people (7–10). Sandwiched between these two accounts is a gap of nearly six decades, during which Esther lives and rules as queen in Persia.

Ezra is the Aramaic form of the Hebrew word *ezer*, "help," and perhaps means "Yahweh helps." Ezra and Nehemiah were originally bound together as one book because Chronicles, Ezra, and Nehemiah were viewed as one continuous history. The Septuagint, a Greek-language version of the Old Testament translated in the third century B.C., calls Ezra–Nehemiah, *Esdras Deuteron*, "Second Esdras." First Esdras is the name of the apocryphal book of Esdras. The Latin title is *Liber Primus Esdrae*, "First Book of Ezra." In the Latin Bible, Ezra is called First Ezra and Nehemiah is called Second Ezra.

## CHAPTER 1

**N**ow in the first year of Cyrus king of Persia, that the word of the LORD ᵃby the mouth of Jeremiah might be fulfilled, the LORD stirred up the spirit of Cyrus king of Persia, ᵇthat he made a proclamation throughout all his kingdom, and *put it* also in writing, saying,

2 Thus saith Cyrus king of Persia, The LORD God of heaven hath given me all the kingdoms of the earth; and he hath ᵃcharged me to build him an ¹house at Jerusalem, which *is* in Judah.

3 Who *is there* among you of all his people? his God be with him, and let him go up to Jerusalem, which *is* in Judah, and build the house of the LORD God of Israel, (ᵃhe *is* the God,) which *is* in Jerusalem.

4 And whosoever remaineth in any place where he sojourneth, let the men of his place help him with silver, and with gold, and with goods, and with beasts, beside the freewill offering for the house of God that *is* in Jerusalem.

5 Then rose up the chief of the fathers of Judah and Benjamin, and the priests, and the Levites, with all *them* whose spirit ᵃGod had ¹raised, to go up to build the house of the LORD which *is* in Jerusalem.

6 And all they that *were* about them ¹strengthened their hands with vessels of silver, with gold, with goods, and with beasts, and with precious things, beside all *that* was ᵃwillingly offered.

7 ᵃAlso Cyrus the king brought forth the vessels of the house of the

1:1 ᵃ 2 Chr. 36:22, 23; Jer. 25:12; 29:10 ᵇ Ezra 5:13, 14; Is. 44:28–45:13
1:2 ᵃ Is. 44:28; 45:1, 13 ¹ Temple
1:3 ᵃ 1 Kin. 8:23; 18:39; Is. 37:16; Dan. 6:26
1:5 ᵃ [Phil. 2:13] ¹ stirred up
1:6 ᵃ Ezra 2:68 ¹ encouraged them with
1:7 ᵃ Ezra 5:14; 6:5; Dan. 1:2; 5:2, 3
1:8 ᵃ Ezra 5:14, 16 ¹ counted
1:9 ¹ platters
1:11 ¹ the captives who were brought up
2:1 ᵃ Neh. 7:6–73; Jer. 32:15; 50:5; Ezek. 14:22 ᵇ 2 Kin. 24:14–16; 25:11; 2 Chr. 36:20
2:2 ¹ Azariah, Neh. 7:7 ² Raamiah, Neh. 7:7 ³ Mispereth, Neh. 7:7 ⁴ Nehum, Neh. 7:7

LORD, ᵇwhich Nebuchadnezzar had brought forth out of Jerusalem, and had put them in the ¹house of his gods;

8 Even those did Cyrus king of Persia bring forth by the hand of Mithredath the treasurer, and ¹numbered them unto ᵃSheshbazzar, the prince of Judah.

9 And this *is* the number of them: thirty chargers of gold, a thousand ¹chargers of silver, nine and twenty knives,

10 Thirty basons of gold, silver basons of a second *sort* four hundred and ten, *and* other vessels a thousand.

11 All the vessels of gold and of silver *were* five thousand and four hundred. All *these* did Sheshbazzar bring up with ¹*them of* the captivity that were brought up from Babylon unto Jerusalem.

## CHAPTER 2

**N**ow ᵃthese *are* the children of the province that went up out of the captivity, of those which had been carried away, ᵇwhom Nebuchadnezzar the king of Babylon had carried away unto Babylon, and came again unto Jerusalem and Judah, every one unto his city;

2 Which came with Zerubbabel: Jeshua, Nehemiah, ¹Seraiah, ²Reelaiah, Mordecai, Bilshan, ³Mizpar, Bigvai, ⁴Rehum, Baanah. The number of the men of the people of Israel:

3 The children of Parosh, two thousand an hundred seventy and two.

4 The children of Shephatiah, three hundred seventy and two.

5 The children of Arah, ªseven hundred seventy and five.

6 The children of ªPahath-moab, of the children of Jeshua *and* Joab, two thousand eight hundred and twelve.

7 The children of Elam, a thousand two hundred fifty and four.

8 The children of Zattu, nine hundred forty and five.

9 The children of Zaccai, seven hundred and threescore.

10 The children of ¹Bani, six hundred forty and two.

11 The children of Bebai, six hundred twenty and three.

12 The children of Azgad, a thousand two hundred twenty and two.

13 The children of Adonikam, six hundred sixty and six.

14 The children of Bigvai, two thousand fifty and six.

15 The children of Adin, four hundred fifty and four.

16 The children of Ater of Hezekiah, ninety and eight.

17 The children of Bezai, three hundred twenty and three.

18 The children of ¹Jorah, an hundred and twelve.

19 The children of Hashum, two hundred twenty and three.

20 The children of ¹Gibbar, ninety and five.

21 The children of Beth-lehem, an hundred twenty and three.

22 The men of Netophah, fifty and six.

23 The men of Anathoth, an hundred twenty and eight.

24 The children of ¹Azmaveth, forty and two.

25 The children of ¹Kirjath-arim, Chephirah, and Beeroth, seven hundred and forty and three.

26 The children of Ramah and Gaba, six hundred twenty and one.

27 The men of Michmas, an hundred twenty and two.

28 The men of Beth-el and Ai, two hundred twenty and three.

29 The children of Nebo, fifty and two.

30 The children of Magbish, an hundred fifty and six.

31 The children of the other ªElam, a thousand two hundred fifty and four.

32 The children of Harim, three hundred and twenty.

33 The children of Lod, Hadid, and Ono, seven hundred twenty and five.

34 The children of Jericho, three hundred forty and five.

35 The children of Senaah, three thousand and six hundred and thirty.

36 The priests: the children of ªJedaiah, of the house of Jeshua, nine hundred seventy and three.

37 The children of ªImmer, a thousand fifty and two.

38 The children of ªPashur, a thousand two hundred forty and seven.

39 The children of ªHarim, a thousand and seventeen.

40 The Levites: the children of Jeshua and Kadmiel, of the children of ¹Hodaviah, seventy and four.

41 The singers: the children of Asaph, an hundred twenty and eight.

42 The children of the ¹porters: the children of Shallum, the children of Ater, the children of Talmon, the children of Akkub, the children of Hatita, the children of Shobai, *in* all an hundred thirty and nine.

43 ªThe Nethinims: the children of Ziha, the children of Hasupha, the children of Tabbaoth,

44 The children of Keros, the children of ¹Siaha, the children of Padon,

45 The children of Lebanah, the children of Hagabah, the children of Akkub,

46 The children of Hagab, the children of Shalmai, the children of Hanan,

47 The children of Giddel, the children of Gahar, the children of Reaiah,

48 The children of Rezin, the children of Nekoda, the children of Gazzam,

49 The children of Uzza, the children of Paseah, the children of Besai,

50 The children of Asnah, the children of Mehunim, the children of ¹Nephusim,

51 The children of Bakbuk, the children of Hakupha, the children of Harhur,

52 The children of ¹Bazluth, the children of Mehida, the children of Harsha,

53 The children of Barkos, the children of Sisera, the children of Thamah,

54 The children of Neziah, the children of Hatipha.

55 The children of ªSolomon's servants: the children of Sotai, the children of ᵇSophereth, the children of ¹Peruda,

56 The children of Jaalah, the children of Darkon, the children of Giddel,

57 The children of Shephatiah, the children of Hattil, the children of Pochereth of Zebaim, the children of ¹Ami.

58 All the ªNethinims, and the children of ᵇSolomon's servants, *were* three hundred ninety and two.

59 And these *were* they which went up from Tel-melah, Tel-harsa, Cherub, ¹Addan, *and* Immer: but they could not ²shew their father's house, and their ³seed, whether they *were* of Israel:

60 The children of Delaiah, the children of Tobiah, the children of Nekoda, six hundred fifty and two.

61 And of the children of the priests: the children of [a]Habaiah, the children of [1]Koz, the children of [b]Barzillai; which took a wife of the daughters of Barzillai the Gileadite, and was called after their name:

62 These sought their register *among* those that were reckoned by genealogy, but they were not found: [a]therefore were they, as [1]polluted, [2]put from the priesthood.

63 And the [1]Tirshatha said unto them, that they [a]should not eat of the most holy things, till there stood up a priest with [b]Urim and with Thummim.

64 [a]The whole congregation together *was* forty and two thousand three hundred *and* threescore,

65 Beside their servants and their maids, of whom *there were* seven thousand three hundred thirty and seven: and *there were* among them two hundred singing men and singing women.

66 Their horses *were* seven hundred thirty and six; their mules, two hundred forty and five;

67 Their camels, four hundred thirty and five; *their* asses, six thousand seven hundred and twenty.

68 [a]And *some* of the chief of the fathers, when they came to the house of the LORD which *is* at Jerusalem, offered freely for the house of God to set it up in his place:

69 They gave after their ability unto the [a]treasure of the work threescore and one thousand drams of gold, and five thousand pound of silver, and one hundred priests' garments.

70 [a]So the priests, and the Levites, and *some* of the people, and the singers, and the [1]porters, and the Nethinims, dwelt in their cities, and all Israel in their cities.

## CHAPTER 3

A ND when the [a]seventh month was come, and the children of Israel *were* in the cities, the people gathered themselves together as one man to Jerusalem.

2 Then stood up [1]Jeshua the son of [a]Jozadak, and his brethren the priests, and [b]Zerubbabel the son of [c]Shealtiel, and his brethren, and builded the altar of the God of Israel, to offer burnt offerings thereon, as *it is* [d]written in the law of Moses the man of God.

3 And they set the altar upon [1]his bases; for fear *was* upon them because of the people of those countries: and they offered burnt offerings thereon unto the LORD, *even* [a]burnt offerings morning and evening.

4 [a]They kept also the feast of tabernacles, [b]as *it is* written, and [c]offered

the daily burnt offerings [1]by number, according to the custom, as the duty of every day required;

5 And afterward *offered* the [a]continual burnt offering, both of the new moons, and of all the set feasts of the LORD that were consecrated, and of every one that willingly offered a freewill offering unto the LORD.

6 From the first day of the seventh month began they to offer burnt offerings unto the LORD. But the foundation of the temple of the LORD was not *yet* laid.

7 They gave money also unto the masons, and to the carpenters; and [a]meat, and drink, and oil, unto them of Zidon, and to them of Tyre, to bring cedar trees from Lebanon to the sea of [b]Joppa, [c]according to the grant that they had of Cyrus king of Persia.

8 Now in the second year of their coming unto the house of God at Jerusalem, in the second month, began [a]Zerubbabel the son of Shealtiel, and Jeshua the son of Jozadak, and the remnant of their brethren the priests and the Levites, and all they that were come out of the captivity unto Jerusalem; [b]and appointed the Levites, from twenty years old and upward, to [1]set forward the work of the house of the LORD.

9 Then stood Jeshua *with* his sons and his brethren, Kadmiel and his sons, the sons of [1]Judah, [2]together, to set forward the workmen in the house of God: the sons of Henadad, *with* their sons and their brethren the Levites.

10 And when the builders laid the foundation of the temple of the LORD, [a]they[1] set the priests in their apparel with trumpets, and the Levites the sons of Asaph with cymbals, to praise the LORD, after the [b]ordinance[2] of David king of Israel.

11 [a]And they sang [1]together by course in praising and giving thanks unto the LORD; [b]because *he is* good, [c]for his mercy *endureth* for ever toward Israel. And all the people shouted with a great shout, when they praised the LORD, because the foundation of the house of the LORD was laid.

12 But many of the priests and Levites and [a]chief of the fathers, *who were* ancient men, that had seen the first house, when the foundation of this house was laid before their eyes, wept with a loud voice; and many shouted aloud for joy:

13 So that the people could not discern the noise of the shout of joy from the noise of the weeping of the people: for the people shouted with a loud shout, and the noise was heard afar off.

---

*Center column references:*

2:61 [a] Neh. 7:63
[b] 2 Sam. 17:27;
1 Kin. 2:7 [1] Or
*Hakkoz*

2:62 [a] Num.
3:10 [1] *defiled*
[2] *excluded*

2:63 [a] Lev. 22:2,
10, 15, 16 [b] Ex.
28:30; Num. 27:21
[1] Lit. *governor*

2:64 [a] Neh. 7:66;
Is. 10:22

2:68 [a] Ezra 1:6;
3:5; Neh. 7:70

2:69 [a] 1 Chr.
26:20; Ezra
8:25–35

2:70 [a] Ezra 6:16,
17; Neh. 7:73
[1] *gatekeepers*

3:1 [a] Neh. 7:73;
8:1, 2

3:2 [a] 1 Chr. 6:14,
15; Ezra 4:3; Neh.
12:1, 8; Hag. 1:1;
2:2 [b] Ezra 2:2;
4:2, 3; 5:2 [c] 1 Chr.
3:17 [d] Deut.
12:5, 6 [1] *Joshua*,
Hag. 1:1

3:3 [a] Num. 28:3
[1] *its foundations*

3:4 [a] Lev. 23:33–
43; Neh. 8:14–18;
Zech. 14:16 [b] Ex.
23:16 [c] Num.
29:12, 13

[1] *in number
required by
ordinance for
each day*

3:5 [a] Ex. 29:38;
Num. 28:3, 11, 19,
26; Ezra 1:4; 2:68;
7:15, 16; 8:28

3:7 [a] 1 Kin. 5:6, 9;
2 Chr. 2:10; Acts
12:20 [b] 2 Chr.
2:16; Acts 9:36
[c] Ezra 1:2; 6:3

3:8 [a] Ezra 3:2; 4:3
[b] 1 Chr. 23:4, 24
[1] *oversee*

3:9 [1] *Hodaviah*,
Ezra 2:40 [2] *as
one*

3:10 [a] 1 Chr. 16:5,
6 [b] 1 Chr. 6:31;
16:4; 25:1 [1] *the
priests stood*
[2] Lit. *hands*

3:11 [a] Ex. 15:21;
2 Chr. 7:3; Neh.
12:24 [b] 1 Chr.
16:34; Ps. 136:1
[c] 1 Chr. 16:41; Jer.
33:11 [1] *responsively, praising*

3:12 [a] Ezra 2:68

## CHAPTER 4

Now when ᵃthe ¹adversaries of Judah and Benjamin heard that the children of the captivity builded the temple unto the LORD God of Israel;

2 Then they came to Zerubbabel, and to the chief of the fathers, and said unto them, Let us build with you: for we seek your God, as ye *do;* and we do sacrifice unto him ᵃsince the days of Esar-haddon king of Assur, which brought us up hither.

3 But Zerubbabel, and Jeshua, and the rest of the chief of the fathers of Israel, said unto them, ᵃYe have nothing to do with us to build an ¹house unto our God; but we ourselves together will build unto the LORD God of Israel, as ᵇking Cyrus the king of Persia hath commanded us.

4 Then ᵃthe people of the land ¹weakened the hands of the people of Judah, and troubled them in building,

5 And hired counsellors against them, to frustrate their purpose, all the days of Cyrus king of Persia, even until the reign of ᵃDarius king of Persia.

6 And in the reign of Ahasuerus, in the beginning of his reign, wrote they *unto him* an accusation against the inhabitants of Judah and Jerusalem.

7 And in the days of ᵃArtaxerxes wrote ¹Bishlam, Mithredath, Tabeel, and the rest of their companions, unto Artaxerxes king of Persia; and the writing of the letter *was* written in the ᵇSyrian tongue, and interpreted in the Syrian tongue.

8 ¹Rehum the chancellor and Shimshai the ²scribe wrote a letter against Jerusalem to Artaxerxes the king in this sort:

9 Then *wrote* Rehum the chancellor, and Shimshai the scribe, and the rest of their companions; ᵃthe Dinaites, the Apharsathchites, the Tarpelites, the Apharsites, the Archevites, the Babylonians, the Susanchites, the Dehavites, *and* the Elamites,

10 ᵃAnd the rest of the nations whom the great and noble Asnapper brought over, and ¹set in the cities of Samaria, and the rest *that are* on this side ²the river, ᵇand ³at such a time.

11 This *is* the copy of the letter that they sent unto him, *even* unto Artaxerxes the king; Thy servants the men on this side the river, and at such a time.

12 Be it known unto the king, that the Jews which came up from thee to us are come unto Jerusalem, building the ᵃrebellious and the bad city, and have set up the ᵇwalls *thereof,* and joined the foundations.

13 Be it known now unto the king, that, if this city be builded, and the walls set up *again, then* will they not pay ᵃtoll, tribute, and custom, and *so* thou shalt endamage the revenue of the kings.

14 Now because we ¹have maintenance from *the king's* palace, and it was not ²meet for us to see the king's dishonour, therefore have we sent and ³certified the king;

15 That search may be made in the book of the records of thy fathers: so shalt thou find in the book of the records, and know that this city *is* a rebellious city, and hurtful unto kings and provinces, and that they have moved sedition within the same of old time: for which cause was this city destroyed.

16 We certify the king that, if this city be builded *again,* and the walls thereof set up, by this means thou shalt have ¹no portion on this side the river.

17 *Then* sent the king an answer unto Rehum the chancellor, and *to* Shimshai the scribe, and *to* the rest of their companions that dwell in Samaria, and *unto* the rest beyond the river, Peace, and ¹at such a time.

18 The letter which ye sent unto us hath been plainly read before me.

19 And ¹I commanded, and search hath been made, and it is found that this city of old time hath made insurrection against kings, and *that* rebellion and sedition have been made therein.

20 There have been mighty kings also over Jerusalem, which have ᵃruled over all *countries* ᵇbeyond the river; and toll, tribute, and custom, was paid unto them.

21 ¹Give ye now commandment to cause these men to cease, and that this city be not builded, until *another* commandment shall be given from me.

22 Take heed now that ye fail not to do this: why should damage grow to the hurt of the kings?

23 Now when the copy of king Artaxerxes' letter *was* read before Rehum, and Shimshai the scribe, and their companions, they went up in haste to Jerusalem unto the Jews, and made them to cease by force ¹and power.

24 Then ceased the work of the house of God which *is* at Jerusalem. So it ceased unto the second year of the reign of Darius king of Persia.

## CHAPTER 5

THEN the prophets, ᵃHaggai the prophet, and ᵇZechariah the son of Iddo, prophesied unto the Jews that *were* in Judah and Jerusalem in the name of the God of Israel, *even* unto them.

---

**4:1** ᵃ Ezra 4:7–9
¹ *enemies*

**4:2** ᵃ 2 Kin. 17:24; 19:37; Ezra 4:10

**4:3** ᵃ Neh. 2:20
ᵇ Ezra 1:1–4
¹ *Temple*

**4:4** ᵃ Ezra 3:3 ¹ *tried to discourage*

**4:5** ᵃ Ezra 5:5; 6:1

**4:7** ᵃ Ezra 7:1, 7, 21
ᵇ 2 Kin. 18:26 ¹ *Or in peace*

**4:8** ¹ The original language of Ezra 4:8 through 6:18 is Aramaic.
² *secretary*

**4:9** ᵃ 2 Kin. 17:30, 31

**4:10** ᵃ 2 Kin. 17:24; Ezra 4:1
ᵇ Ezra 4:11, 17; 7:12
¹ *settled* ² The Euphrates ³ *so forth*

**4:12** ᵃ 2 Chr. 36:13
ᵇ Ezra 5:3, 9

**4:13** ᵃ Ezra 4:20; 7:24

**4:14** ¹ *receive support* ² *proper* ³ *informed*

**4:16** ¹ *no dominion*

**4:17** ¹ *so forth*

**4:19** ¹ Lit. *by me a decree has been put forth*

**4:20** ᵃ 1 Kin. 4:21; 1 Chr. 18:3; Ps. 72:8 ᵇ Gen. 15:18; Josh. 1:4

**4:21** ¹ *Now put forth a decree*

**4:23** ¹ *of arms*

**5:1** ᵃ Hag. 1:1
ᵇ Zech. 1:1

2 Then rose up [a]Zerubbabel the son of Shealtiel, and Jeshua the son of Jozadak, and began to build the house of God which *is* at Jerusalem: and [b]with them *were* the prophets of God helping them.

3 At the same time came to them [a]Tatnai, governor on this side [1]the river, and Shethar-boznai, and their companions, and said thus unto them, [b]Who hath commanded you to build this [2]house, and to [3]make up this wall?

4 [a]Then said we unto them after this manner, What are the names of the men that [1]make this building?

5 But [a]the eye of their God was upon the elders of the Jews, that they could not cause them to cease, till the matter came to Darius: and then they returned [b]answer by letter concerning this *matter.*

6 The copy of the letter that Tatnai, governor on this side the river, and Shethar-boznai, [a]and his companions the Apharsachites, which *were* on this side the river, sent unto Darius the king:

7 They sent a letter unto him, wherein was written thus; Unto Darius the king, all peace.

8 Be it known unto the king, that we went into the province of Judea, to the [1]house of the great God, which is builded with [2]great stones, and timber is laid in the walls, and this work goeth fast on, and prospereth in their hands.

9 Then asked we those elders, *and* said unto them thus, [a]Who commanded you to build this house, and to make up these walls?

10 We asked their names also, to [1]certify thee, that we might write the names of the men that *were* the chief of them.

11 And thus they returned us answer, saying, We are the servants of the God of heaven and earth, and build the [1]house that was builded these many years ago, which a great king of Israel builded [a]and set up.

12 But [a]after that our fathers had provoked the God of heaven unto wrath, he gave them into the hand of [b]Nebuchadnezzar the king of Babylon, the Chaldean, who destroyed this house, and [c]carried the people away into Babylon.

13 But in the first year of [a]Cyrus the king of Babylon *the same* king Cyrus made a decree to build this [1]house of God.

14 And [a]the vessels also of gold and silver of the house of God, which Nebuchadnezzar took out of the temple that *was* in Jerusalem, and brought them into the temple of Babylon, those did Cyrus the king take out of the temple of Babylon, and they were delivered unto *one,* [b]whose name *was* Sheshbazzar, whom he had made governor;

15 And said unto him, Take these vessels, go, carry them into the [1]temple that *is* in Jerusalem, and let the house of God be builded in his place.

16 Then came the same Sheshbazzar, *and* [a]laid the foundation of the [1]house of God which *is* in Jerusalem: and since that time even until now hath it been in building, and [b]*yet* it is not finished.

17 Now therefore, if *it seem* good to the king, [a]let there be search made in the king's treasure house, which *is* there at Babylon, whether it be *so,* that a decree was made of Cyrus the king to build this house of God at Jerusalem, and let the king send his pleasure to us concerning this matter.

## CHAPTER 6

THEN Darius the king made a decree, [a]and search was made in the [1]house of the rolls, where the treasures were laid up in Babylon.

2 And there was found at [1]Achmetha, in the palace that *is* in the province of the [a]Medes, a roll, and therein *was* a record thus written:

3 In the first year of Cyrus the king *the same* Cyrus the king made a [a]decree *concerning* the house of God at Jerusalem, Let the [1]house be builded, the place where they offered sacrifices, and let the foundations thereof be strongly laid; the height thereof threescore cubits, *and* the breadth thereof threescore cubits;

4 [a]*With* three rows of great stones, and a row of new timber: and let the [b]expenses be given out of the king's [1]house:

5 And also let [a]the golden and silver vessels of the house of God, which Nebuchadnezzar took forth out of the temple which *is* at Jerusalem, and brought unto Babylon, be restored, and brought again unto the temple which *is* at Jerusalem, *every one* to his place, and place *them* in the house of God.

6 [a]Now *therefore,* Tatnai, governor beyond the river, Shethar-boznai, and your companions the Apharsachites, which *are* beyond the river, be ye far from thence:

7 Let the work of this house of God alone; let the governor of the Jews and the elders of the Jews build this house of God in his place.

8 Moreover I make a decree what ye shall do to the elders of these Jews for the building of this [1]house of God: that of the king's goods, *even* of the tribute beyond the river, forthwith

5:2 [a] Ezra 3:2; Hag. 1:12 [b] Ezra 6:14; Hag. 2:4
5:3 [a] Ezra 5:6; 6:6 [b] Ezra 1:3; 5:9 [1] The Euphrates [2] Temple [3] *finish this wall*
5:4 [a] Ezra 5:10 [1] *were constructing*
5:5 [a] 2 Chr. 16:9; Ezra 7:6, 28; Ps. 33:18 [b] Ezra 6:6
5:6 [a] Ezra 4:7–10
5:8 [1] Temple [2] Stones too heavy to be carried, lit. *stones of rolling*
5:9 [a] Ezra 5:3, 4
5:10 [1] *inform*
5:11 [a] 1 Kin. 6:1, 38 [1] Temple
5:12 [a] 2 Chr. 34:25; 36:16, 17 [b] 2 Kin. 24:2; 25:8–11; 2 Chr. 36:17; Jer. 52:12–15 [c] Jer. 13:19
5:13 [a] Ezra 1:1 [1] Temple
5:14 [a] Ezra 1:7, 8; 6:5; Dan. 5:2 [b] Hag. 1:14; 2:2, 21
5:15 [1] *temple site*
5:16 [a] Ezra 3:8–10; Hag. 2:18 [b] Ezra 6:15 [1] Temple
5:17 [a] Ezra 6:1, 2
6:1 [a] Ezra 5:17 [1] *archives*
6:2 [a] 2 Kin. 17:6 [1] Probably *Ecbatana*, the ancient capital of Media
6:3 [a] Ezra 1:1; 5:13 [1] Temple
6:4 [a] 1 Kin. 6:36 [b] Ezra 3:7 [1] *treasury*
6:5 [a] Ezra 1:7, 8; 5:14
6:6 [a] Ezra 5:3, 6
6:8 [1] Temple

expenses be given unto these men, that they be not hindered.

9 And that which they have need of, both young bullocks, and rams, and lambs, for the burnt offerings of the God of heaven, wheat, salt, wine, and oil, according to the appointment of the priests which *are* at Jerusalem, let it be given them day by day without fail:

10 ªThat they may offer sacrifices of sweet savours unto the God of heaven, and pray for the life of the king, and of his sons.

11 Also I have made a decree, that whosoever shall alter this word, let timber be pulled down from his house, and being set up, let him be hanged thereon; ªand let his house be made a dunghill for this.

12 And the God that hath caused his ªname to dwell there destroy all kings and people, that shall put to their hand to alter *and* to destroy this ¹house of God which *is* at Jerusalem. I Darius have made a decree; let it be done with speed.

13 Then Tatnai, governor on this side the river, Shethar-boznai, and their companions, according to that which Darius the king had sent, so they did speedily.

14 ªAnd the elders of the Jews builded, and they prospered through the prophesying of Haggai the prophet and Zechariah the son *of* Iddo. And they builded, and finished *it,* according to the commandment of the God of Israel, and according to the commandment of ᵇCyrus, and ᶜDarius, and ᵈArtaxerxes king of Persia.

15 And this house was finished on the third day of the month Adar, which was in the sixth year of the reign of Darius the king.

16 And the children of Israel, the priests, and the Levites, and the rest of the ¹children of the captivity, kept ªthe dedication of this house of God with joy,

17 And ªoffered at the dedication of this ¹house of God an hundred bullocks, two hundred rams, four hundred lambs; and for a sin offering for all Israel, twelve he goats, according to the number of the tribes of Israel.

18 And they set the priests in their ªdivisions, and the Levites in their ᵇcourses,¹ for the service of God, which *is* at Jerusalem; ᶜas it is written in the book of Moses.

19¹ And the children of the captivity kept the passover ªupon the fourteenth *day* of the first month.

20 For the priests and the Levites were ªpurified together, all of them *were* pure, and ᵇkilled the passover for all the children of the captivity,

6:10 ª Ezra 7:23; [Jer. 29:7; 1 Tim. 2:1, 2]
6:11 ª Dan. 2:5; 3:29
6:12 ª Deut. 12:5, 11; 1 Kin. 9:3 ¹ Temple
6:14 ª Ezra 5:1, 2 ᵇ Ezra 1:1; 5:13; 6:3 ᶜ Ezra 4:24; 6:12 ᵈ Ezra 7:1, 11; Neh. 2:1
6:16 ª 1 Kin. 8:63; 2 Chr. 7:5 ¹ descendants
6:17 ª Ezra 8:35 ¹ Temple
6:18 ª 1 Chr. 24:1; 2 Chr. 35:5 ᵇ 1 Chr. 23:6 ᶜ Num. 3:6; 8:9 ¹ divisions
6:19 ª Ex. 12:6 ¹ The Hebrew language continues from Ezra 6:19 through 7:11.
6:20 ª 2 Chr. 29:34; 30:15 ᵇ 2 Chr. 35:11

6:21 ª Ezra 9:11 ¹ uncleanness
6:22 ª Ex. 12:15; 13:6, 7; 2 Chr. 30:21; 35:17 ᵇ Ezra 7:27; [Prov. 21:1] ᶜ 2 Kin. 23:29; 2 Chr. 33:11; Ezra 1:1; 6:1
7:1 ª Neh. 2:1 ᵇ 1 Chr. 6:14 ᶜ Jer. 52:24 ᵈ 2 Chr. 35:8
7:6 ª Ezra 7:11, 12, 21 ᵇ Ezra 7:9, 28; 8:22 ¹ skilled
7:7 ª Ezra 8:1–14 ᵇ Ezra 8:15 ᶜ Ezra 2:43; 8:20
7:9 ª Ezra 7:6; Neh. 2:8, 18
7:10 ª Ps. 119:45 ᵇ Deut. 33:10; Ezra 7:6, 25; Neh. 8:1–8; [Mal. 2:7] ¹ Study
7:12 ª Ezek. 26:7; Dan. 2:37 ᵇ Ezra 4:10 ¹ The original language of Ezra 7:12 through 7:26 is Aramaic. ² so forth

and for their brethren the priests, and for themselves.

21 And the children of Israel, which were come again out of captivity, and all such as had separated themselves unto them from the ªfilthiness¹ of the heathen of the land, to seek the LORD God of Israel, did eat,

22 And kept the ªfeast of unleavened bread seven days with joy: for the LORD had made them joyful, and ᵇturned the heart ᶜof the king of Assyria unto them, to strengthen their hands in the work of the house of God, the God of Israel.

## CHAPTER 7

Now after these things, in the reign of ªArtaxerxes king of Persia, Ezra the ᵇson of Seraiah, ᶜthe son of Azariah, the son of ᵈHilkiah,

2 The son of Shallum, the son of Zadok, the son of Ahitub,

3 The son of Amariah, the son of Azariah, the son of Meraioth,

4 The son of Zerahiah, the son of Uzzi, the son of Bukki,

5 The son of Abishua, the son of Phinehas, the son of Eleazar, the son of Aaron the chief priest:

6 This Ezra went up from Babylon; and he *was* ªa ¹ready scribe in the law of Moses, which the LORD God of Israel had given: and the king granted him all his request, ᵇaccording to the hand of the LORD his God upon him.

7 ªAnd there went up *some* of the children of Israel, and of the priests, and ᵇthe Levites, and the singers, and the porters, and ᶜthe Nethinims, unto Jerusalem, in the seventh year of Artaxerxes the king.

8 And he came to Jerusalem in the fifth month, which *was* in the seventh year of the king.

9 For upon the first *day* of the first month began he to go up from Babylon, and on the first *day* of the fifth month came he to Jerusalem, ªaccording to the good hand of his God upon him.

10 For Ezra had prepared his heart to ªseek¹ the law of the LORD, and to do *it,* and to ᵇteach in Israel statutes and judgments.

11 Now this *is* the copy of the letter that the king Artaxerxes gave unto Ezra the priest, the scribe, *even* a scribe of the words of the commandments of the LORD, and of his statutes to Israel.

12 ¹Artaxerxes, ªking of kings, unto Ezra the priest, a scribe of the law of the God of heaven, perfect *peace,* ᵇand ²at such a time.

13 I make a decree, that all they of the people of Israel, and *of* his priests and Levites, in my realm, which are

minded of their own freewill to go up to Jerusalem, go with thee.

14 Forasmuch as thou art sent [1]of the king, and of his [a]seven counsellors, to enquire concerning Judah and Jerusalem, according to the law of thy God which *is* in thine hand;

15 And to carry the silver and gold, which the king and his counsellors have freely offered unto the God of Israel, [a]whose habitation *is* in Jerusalem,

16 [a]And all the silver and gold that thou canst find in all the province of Babylon, with the freewill offering of the people, and of the priests, [b]offering willingly for the [1]house of their God which *is* in Jerusalem:

17 That thou mayest buy speedily with this money bullocks, rams, lambs, with their [a]meat offerings and their drink offerings, and [b]offer them upon the altar of the house of your God which *is* in Jerusalem.

18 And whatsoever shall seem good to thee, and to thy brethren, to do with the rest of the silver and the gold, that do after the will of your God.

19 The vessels also that are given thee for the service of the house of thy God, *those* deliver thou before the God of Jerusalem.

20 And whatsoever more shall be needful for the house of thy God, which thou shalt have occasion to bestow, bestow *it* out of the king's treasure house.

21 And I, *even* I Artaxerxes the king, do make a decree to all the treasurers which *are* beyond the river, that whatsoever Ezra the priest, the scribe of the law of the God of heaven, shall require of you, it be done speedily,

22 Unto an hundred talents of silver, and to an hundred [1]measures of wheat, and to an hundred baths of wine, and to an hundred baths of oil, and salt without prescribing *how much.*

23 Whatsoever is [1]commanded by the God of heaven, let it be diligently done for the [2]house of the God of heaven: for why should there be wrath against the realm of the king and his sons?

24 Also we certify you, that touching any of the priests and Levites, singers, [1]porters, Nethinims, or ministers of this house of God, it shall not be lawful to impose toll, tribute, or custom, upon them.

25 And thou, Ezra, after the wisdom of thy God, that *is* in thine hand, [a]set magistrates and judges, which may judge all the people that *are* beyond the river, all such as know the laws of thy God; and [b]teach ye them that know *them* not.

26 And whosoever will not do the law of thy God, and the law of the king, let judgment be executed speedily upon him, whether *it be* unto death, or [1]to banishment, or to confiscation of goods, or to imprisonment.

27 [a]Blessed[1] *be* the LORD God of our fathers, [b]which hath put *such a thing* as this in the king's heart, to beautify the house of the LORD which *is* in Jerusalem:

28 And [a]hath extended mercy unto me before the king, and his counsellors, and before all the king's mighty princes. And I was strengthened as [b]the hand of the LORD my God *was* upon me, and I gathered together out of Israel chief men to go up with me.

## CHAPTER 8

THESE *are* now the chief of their fathers, and *this is* the genealogy of them that went up with me from Babylon, in the reign of Artaxerxes the king.

2 Of the sons of Phinehas; Gershom: of the sons of Ithamar; Daniel: of the sons of David; [a]Hattush.

3 Of the sons of Shechaniah, of the sons of [a]Pharosh; Zechariah: and with him were reckoned by genealogy of the males an hundred and fifty.

4 Of the sons of [a]Pahath-moab; Elihoenai the son of Zerahiah, and with him two hundred males.

5 Of the sons of Shechaniah; the son of Jahaziel, and with him three hundred males.

6 Of the sons also of Adin; Ebed the son of Jonathan, and with him fifty males.

7 And of the sons of Elam; Jeshaiah the son of Athaliah, and with him seventy males.

8 And of the sons of Shephatiah; Zebadiah the son of Michael, and with him fourscore males.

9 Of the sons of Joab; Obadiah the son of Jehiel, and with him two hundred and eighteen males.

10 And of the sons of Shelomith; the son of Josiphiah, and with him an hundred and threescore males.

11 And of the sons of [a]Bebai; Zechariah the son of Bebai, and with him twenty and eight males.

12 And of the sons of Azgad; Johanan [1]the son of Hakkatan, and with him an hundred and ten males.

13 And of the last sons of Adonikam, whose names *are* these, Eliphelet, Jeiel, and Shemaiah, and with them threescore males.

14 Of the sons also of Bigvai; Uthai, and [1]Zabbud, and with them seventy males.

15 And I gathered them together to the river that runneth to Ahava; and

7:14 [a] Esth. 1:14
[1] Lit. *from before the king*

7:15 [a] 2 Chr. 6:2; Ezra 6:12; Ps. 135:21

7:16 [a] Ezra 8:25
[b] 1 Chr. 29:6, 9
[1] Temple

7:17 [a] Num. 15:4–13 [b] Deut. 12:5–11

7:22 [1] Lit. *kor*

7:23 [1] Lit. *from the decree of*
[2] Temple

7:24 [1] *gatekeepers*

7:25 [a] Ex. 18:21, 22; Deut. 16:18
[b] 2 Chr. 17:7; Ezra 7:10; [Mal. 2:7; Col. 1:28]

7:26 [1] Lit. *rooting out*

7:27 [a] 1 Chr. 29:10
[b] Ezra 6:22; [Prov. 21:1] [1] The original language is Hebrew from Ezra 7:27.

7:28 [a] Ezra 9:9
[b] Ezra 5:5; 7:6, 9; 8:18

8:2 [a] 1 Chr. 3:22; Ezra 2:68

8:3 [a] Ezra 2:3

8:4 [a] Ezra 10:30

8:11 [a] Ezra 10:28

8:12 [1] Or *the youngest son*

8:14 [1] Or *Zakkur*

there [1]abode we in tents three days: and I [2]viewed the people, and the priests, and found there none of the [a]sons of Levi.

16 Then sent I for Eliezer, for Ariel, for Shemaiah, and for Elnathan, and for Jarib, and for Elnathan, and for Nathan, and for Zechariah, and for [a]Meshullam, chief men; also for Joiarib, and for Elnathan, men of understanding.

17 And I sent them with commandment unto Iddo the chief at the place Casiphia, and [1]I told them what they should say unto Iddo, *and* to his brethren the Nethinims, at the place Casiphia, that they should bring unto us ministers for the house of our God.

18 And by the good hand of our God upon us they [a]brought us a man of understanding, of the sons of Mahli, the son of Levi, the son of Israel; and Sherebiah, with his sons and his brethren, eighteen;

19 And [a]Hashabiah, and with him Jeshaiah of the sons of Merari, his brethren and their sons, twenty;

20 [a]Also of the Nethinims, whom David and the princes had appointed for the service of the Levites, two hundred and twenty Nethinims: all of them were [1]expressed by name.

21 Then I [a]proclaimed a fast there, at the river of Ahava, that we might [b]afflict[1] ourselves before our God, to seek of him a [c]right way for us, and for our little ones, and for all our substance.

22 For [a]I was ashamed to require of the king a band of soldiers and horsemen to help us against the enemy in the way: because we had spoken unto the king, saying, [b]The hand of our God *is* upon all them for [c]good that seek him; but his power and his wrath *is* [d]against all them that [e]forsake him.

23 So we fasted and besought our God for this: and he was [a]intreated of us.

24 Then I separated twelve of the chief of the priests, Sherebiah, Hashabiah, and ten of their brethren with them,

25 And weighed unto them [a]the silver, and the gold, and the vessels, *even* the offering of the house of our God, which the king, and his counsellors, and his lords, and all Israel *there* present, had offered:

26 I even weighed unto their hand six hundred and fifty talents of silver, and silver vessels an hundred talents, *and* of gold an hundred talents;

27 Also twenty basons of gold, [1]of a thousand drams; and two vessels of [2]fine copper, precious as gold.

28 And I said unto them, Ye *are* [a]holy[1] unto the LORD; the vessels *are*

[b]holy also; and the silver and the gold *are* a freewill offering unto the LORD God of your fathers.

29 Watch ye, and keep *them,* until ye weigh *them* before the chief of the priests and the Levites, and [a]chief of the fathers of Israel, at Jerusalem, in the chambers of the house of the LORD.

30 So took the priests and the Levites the weight of the silver, and the gold, and the vessels, to bring *them* to Jerusalem unto the house of our God.

31 Then we departed from the river of Ahava on the twelfth *day* of the first month, to go unto Jerusalem: and [a]the hand of our God was upon us, and he delivered us from the hand of the enemy, and [1]of such as lay in [2]wait by the way.

32 And we [a]came to Jerusalem, and abode there three days.

33 Now on the fourth day was the silver and the gold and the vessels [a]weighed in the house of our God by the hand of Meremoth the son of Uriah the priest; and with him *was* Eleazar the son of Phinehas; and with them *was* [b]Jozabad the son of Jeshua, and Noadiah the son of Binnui, Levites;

34 By number *and* by weight of every one: and all the weight was written at that time.

35 *Also* the children of those that had been [a]carried away, which were come out of the captivity, [b]offered burnt offerings unto the God of Israel, twelve bullocks for all Israel, ninety and six rams, seventy and seven lambs, twelve he goats *for* a sin offering: all *this was* a burnt offering unto the LORD.

36 And they delivered the king's [a]commissions unto the king's lieutenants, and to the governors on this side the river: and they [1]furthered the people, and the [2]house of God.

## CHAPTER 9

Now when these things were done, the princes came to me, saying, The people of Israel, and the priests, and the Levites, have not [a]separated themselves from the people of the lands, [b]*doing* according to their abominations, *even* of the Canaanites, the Hittites, the Perizzites, the Jebusites, the Ammonites, the Moabites, the Egyptians, and the Amorites.

2 For they have [a]taken of their daughters for themselves, and for their sons: so that the [b]holy seed have [c]mingled themselves with the people of *those* lands: yea, the hand of the princes and rulers hath been chief in this [1]trespass.

8:15 [a] Ezra 7:7;
8:2 [1] *camped*
[2] *looked among*
8:16 [a] Ezra 10:15
8:17 [1] Lit. *I put words in their mouths to say*
8:18 [a] 2 Chr. 30:22; Neh. 8:7
8:19 [a] Neh. 12:24
8:20 [a] Ezra 2:43; 7:7 [1] *designated*
8:21 [a] 1 Sam. 7:6; 2 Chr. 20:3 [b] Lev. 16:29; 23:29; Is. 58:3, 5 [c] Ps. 5:8 [1] *humble*
8:22 [a] 1 Cor. 9:15 [b] Ezra 7:6, 9, 28 [c] [Ps. 33:18, 19; 34:15, 22; Rom. 8:28] [d] [Ps. 34:16] [e] [2 Chr. 15:2]
8:23 [a] [1 Chr. 5:20]; 2 Chr. 33:13; Is. 19:22
8:25 [a] Ezra 7:15, 16
8:27 [1] *worth a thousand drachmas* [2] *fine polished bronze*
8:28 [a] Lev. 21:6–9; Deut. 33:8 [1] *consecrated*

8:29 [a] Ezra 4:3
8:31 [a] Ezra 7:6, 9, 28 [1] *from ambush* [2] *along the road*
8:32 [a] Neh. 2:11
8:33 [a] Ezra 8:26, 30 [b] Neh. 11:16
8:35 [a] Ezra 2:1 [b] Ezra 6:17
8:36 [a] Ezra 7:21–24 [1] *gave support to* [2] Temple
9:1 [a] Ezra 6:21; Neh. 9:2 [b] Deut. 12:30, 31
9:2 [a] Ex. 34:16; [Deut. 7:3]; Ezra 10:2; Neh. 13:23 [b] Ex. 22:31; [Deut. 7:6] [c] [2 Cor. 6:14] [1] *unfaithfulness*

[b] Lev. 22:2, 3; Num. 4:4, 15, 19, 20

3 And when I heard this thing, [a]I [1]rent my garment and my mantle, and plucked off the hair of my head and of my beard, and sat down [b]astonied.

4 Then were assembled unto me every one that [a]trembled at the words of the God of Israel, because of the transgression of those that had been carried away; and I sat astonied until the [b]evening sacrifice.

5 And at the evening sacrifice I arose up from my [1]heaviness; and having [2]rent my garment and my mantle, I fell upon my knees, and [a]spread out my hands unto the LORD my God,

6 And said, O my God, I am [a]ashamed and blush to lift up my face to thee, my God: for [b]our iniquities are increased over *our* head, and our [1]trespass is [c]grown up unto the heavens.

7 Since the days of our fathers *have* [a]we *been* in a great trespass unto this day; and for our iniquities [b]have we, our kings, *and* our priests, been delivered into the hand of the kings of the lands, to the [c]sword, to captivity, and to [1]a spoil, and to [d]confusion[2] of face, as *it is* this day.

8 And now for a little [1]space grace hath been *shewed* from the LORD our God, to leave us a remnant to escape, and to give us a [2]nail in his holy place, that our God may [a]lighten our eyes, and give us a little reviving in our bondage.

9 [a]For we *were* [1]bondmen; [b]yet our God hath not forsaken us in our bondage, but [c]hath extended mercy unto us in the sight of the kings of Persia, to give us a reviving, to set up the house of our God, and to repair the [2]desolations thereof, and to give us [d]a wall in Judah and in Jerusalem.

10 And now, O our God, what shall we say after this? for we have forsaken thy commandments,

11 Which thou hast commanded by thy servants the prophets, saying, The land, unto which ye go to possess it, is an unclean land with the [a]filthiness of the people of the lands, with their abominations, which have filled it from one end to another with their [1]uncleanness.

12 Now therefore [a]give not your daughters unto their sons, neither take their daughters unto your sons, [b]nor seek their peace or their wealth for ever: that ye may be strong, and eat the good of the land, and [c]leave *it* for an inheritance to your children for ever.

13 And after all that is come upon us for our evil deeds, and for our great [1]trespass, seeing that thou our God [a]hast punished us less than our

iniquities *deserve,* and hast given us *such* deliverance as this;

14 Should we [a]again break thy commandments, and [b]join in [1]affinity with the people of these abominations? wouldest not thou be [c]angry with us till thou hadst [2]consumed *us,* so that *there should be* no remnant nor escaping?

15 O LORD God of Israel, [a]thou *art* righteous: for we remain yet escaped, as *it is* this day: [b]behold, we *are* before thee [c]in our trespasses: for we cannot stand before thee because of this.

## CHAPTER 10

Now [a]when Ezra had prayed, and when he had confessed, weeping and casting himself down [b]before the house of God, there assembled unto him out of Israel a very great congregation of men and women and children: for the people wept very [c]sore[1].

2 And Shechaniah the son of Jehiel, *one* of the sons of Elam, answered and said unto Ezra, We have [a]trespassed[1] against our God, and have taken strange wives of the people of the land: yet now there is hope in Israel concerning this thing.

3 Now therefore let us make [a]a covenant with our God to put away all the wives, and such as are born of them, according to the counsel of my lord, and of those that [b]tremble at [c]the commandment of our God; and let it be done according to the [d]law.

4 Arise; for *this* matter *belongeth* unto thee: we also *will be* with thee: [a]be of good courage, and do *it.*

5 Then arose Ezra, and made the chief priests, the Levites, and all Israel, [a]to [1]swear that they should do according to this word. And they sware.

6 Then Ezra rose up from before the house of God, and went into the chamber of Johanan the son of Eliashib: and *when* he came thither, he [a]did eat no bread, nor drink water: for he mourned because of the [1]transgression of them that had been carried away.

7 And they made proclamation throughout Judah and Jerusalem unto all the children of the captivity, that they should gather themselves together unto Jerusalem;

8 And that whosoever would not come within three days, according to the counsel of the princes and the elders, all his [1]substance should be [2]forfeited, and himself separated from the congregation of those that had been carried away.

9 Then all the men of Judah and Benjamin gathered themselves together unto Jerusalem within three

### Cross references (center column)

9:3 [a] Job 1:20
[b] Ps. 143:4  [1] *tore*

9:4 [a] Ezra 10:3; Is. 66:2  [b] Ex. 29:39

9:5 [a] Ex. 9:29
[1] *fasting*  [2] *torn*

9:6 [a] Dan. 9:7, 8
[b] Ps. 38:4  [c] 2 Chr. 28:9; [Ezra 9:13, 15]; Rev. 18:5
[1] *guilt*

9:7 [a] 2 Chr. 36:14–17; Ps. 106:6; Dan. 9:5, 6  [b] Deut. 28:36; Neh. 9:30  [c] Deut. 32:25  [d] Dan. 9:7, 8  [1] *plunder*  [2] *humiliation,* lit. *shame of faces*

9:8 [a] Ps. 34:5
[1] *while*  [2] *peg*

9:9 [a] Neh. 9:36; Esth. 7:4  [b] Neh. 9:17; Ps. 136:23  [c] Ezra 7:28  [d] Is. 5:2  [1] *slaves*  [2] *ruins*

9:11 [a] Ezra 6:21
[1] *impurity*

9:12 [a] [Ex. 23:32; 34:15, 16; Deut. 7:3, 4]; Ezra 9:2  [b] Deut. 23:6  [c] [Prov. 13:22; 20:7]

9:13 [a] [Ps. 103:10]
[1] *guilt*

9:14 [a] [John 5:14; 2 Pet. 2:20]  [b] Neh. 13:23  [c] Deut. 9:8  [1] *marriage*  [2] *destroyed*

9:15 [a] Neh. 9:33; Dan. 9:14  [b] [Rom. 3:19]  [c] 1 Cor. 15:17

10:1 [a] Dan. 9:4, 20  [b] 2 Chr. 20:9  [c] Neh. 8:1–9  [1] *bitterly*

10:2 [a] Ezra 10:10, 13, 14, 17, 18; Neh. 13:23–27  [1] *been unfaithful to*

10:3 [a] 2 Chr. 34:31
[b] Ezra 9:4  [c] Deut. 7:2, 3  [d] Deut. 24:1, 2

10:4 [a] 1 Chr. 28:10

10:5 [a] Ezra 10:12, 19; Neh. 5:12; 13:25  [1] *swear an oath*

10:6 [a] Deut. 9:18
[1] *guilt*

10:8 [1] *property*  [2] *confiscated*

days. It *was* the ninth month, on the twentieth *day* of the month; and [a]all the people sat in the street of the house of God, trembling because of *this* matter, and for the great rain.

10 And Ezra the priest stood up, and said unto them, Ye have [1]transgressed, and [2]have taken strange wives, to increase the trespass of Israel.

11 Now therefore [a]make confession unto the LORD God of your fathers, and do his [1]pleasure: and [b]separate yourselves from the people of the land, and from the strange wives.

12 Then all the congregation answered and said with a loud voice, As thou hast said, so must we do.

13 But the people *are* many, and *it is* a time of much rain, and we are not able to stand [1]without, neither *is this* a work of one day or two: for we are many that have transgressed in this thing.

14 Let now our rulers of all the congregation stand, and let all them which have taken strange wives in our cities come at appointed times, and with them the elders of every city, and the judges thereof, until [a]the fierce wrath of our God for this matter be turned from us.

15 Only Jonathan the son of Asahel and Jahaziah the son of Tikvah [1]were employed about this *matter:* and [a]Meshullam and Shabbethai the Levite [2]helped them.

16 And the children of the captivity did so. And Ezra the priest, *with* certain [a]chief of the fathers, after the house of their fathers, and all of them by *their* names, were separated, and sat down in the first day of the tenth month to examine the matter.

17 And they made an end with all the men that had taken strange wives by the first day of the first month.

18 And among the sons of the priests there were found that had taken strange wives: *namely,* of the sons of [a]Jeshua the son of Jozadak, and his brethren; Maaseiah, and Eliezer, and Jarib, and Gedaliah.

19 And they [a]gave [1]their hands that they would put away their wives; and *being* [b]guilty, *they offered* a ram of the flock for their [c]trespass.

20 And of the sons of Immer; Hanani, and Zebadiah.

21 And of the sons of Harim; Maaseiah, and Elijah, and Shemaiah, and Jehiel, and Uzziah.

22 And of the sons of Pashur; Elioenai, Maaseiah, Ishmael, Nethaneel, Jozabad, and Elasah.

23 Also of the Levites; Jozabad, and Shimei, and Kelaiah, (the same *is* Kelita,) Pethahiah, Judah, and Eliezer.

24 Of the singers also; Eliashib: and of the [1]porters; Shallum, and Telem, and Uri.

25 Moreover of Israel: of the [a]sons of Parosh; Ramiah, and Jeziah, and Malchiah, and Miamin, and Eleazar, and Malchijah, and Benaiah.

26 And of the sons of Elam; Mattaniah, Zechariah, and Jehiel, and Abdi, and Jeremoth, and Eliah.

27 And of the sons of Zattu; Elioenai, Eliashib, Mattaniah, and Jeremoth, and Zabad, and Aziza.

28 Of the [a]sons also of Bebai; Jehohanan, Hananiah, Zabbai, *and* Athlai.

29 And of the sons of Bani; Meshullam, Malluch, and Adaiah, Jashub, and Sheal, and [1]Ramoth.

30 And of the [a]sons of Pahathmoab; Adna, and Chelal, Benaiah, Maaseiah, Mattaniah, Bezaleel, and Binnui, and Manasseh.

31 And *of* the sons of Harim; Eliezer, Ishijah, Malchiah, Shemaiah, Shimeon,

32 Benjamin, Malluch, *and* Shemariah.

33 Of the sons of Hashum; Mattenai, Mattathah, Zabad, Eliphelet, Jeremai, Manasseh, *and* Shimei.

34 Of the sons of Bani; Maadai, Amram, and Uel,

35 Benaiah, Bedeiah, [1]Chelluh,

36 Vaniah, Meremoth, Eliashib,

37 Mattaniah, Mattenai, and [1]Jaasau,

38 And Bani, and Binnui, Shimei,

39 And Shelemiah, and Nathan, and Adaiah,

40 Machnadebai, Shashai, Sharai,

41 Azareel, and Shelemiah, Shemariah,

42 Shallum, Amariah, *and* Joseph.

43 Of the sons of Nebo; Jeiel, Mattithiah, Zabad, Zebina, [1]Jadau, and Joel, Benaiah.

44 All these had taken strange wives: and *some* of them had wives by whom they had children.

### Center reference column

10:9 [a] 1 Sam. 12:18; Ezra 9:4; 10:3

10:10 [1] *acted unfaithfully* [2] *have taken pagan wives*

10:11 [a] [Lev. 26:40–42]; Josh. 7:19; [Prov. 28:13] [b] Ezra 10:3 [1] *will*

10:13 [1] *outside*

10:14 [a] 2 Kin. 23:26; 2 Chr. 28:11–13; 29:10; 30:8

10:15 [a] Ezra 8:16; Neh. 3:4 [1] *opposed this* [2] *gave them support*

10:16 [a] Ezra 4:3

10:18 [a] Ezra 5:2; Hag. 1:1, 12; 2:4; Zech. 3:1; 6:11

10:19 [a] 2 Kin. 10:15 [b] Lev. 6:4, 6 [c] Lev. 5:6, 15 [1] *their promise*

10:24 [1] *gatekeepers*

10:25 [a] Ezra 2:3; 8:3; Neh. 7:8

10:28 [a] Ezra 8:11

10:29 [1] Or *Jeremoth*

10:30 [a] Ezra 8:4

10:35 [1] Or *Cheluhi*

10:37 [1] Or *Jaasu*

10:43 [1] Or *Jaddu*

# THE BOOK OF
# NEHEMIAH

Nehemiah, contemporary of Ezra and cupbearer to the king in the Persian palace, leads the third and last return to Jerusalem after the Babylonian exile. His concern for the welfare of Jerusalem and its inhabitants prompts him to take bold action. Granted permission to return to his homeland, Nehemiah challenges his countrymen to arise and rebuild the shattered wall of Jerusalem. In spite of opposition from without and abuse from within, the task is completed in only fifty-two days, a feat even the enemies of Israel must attribute to God's enabling. By contrast, the task of reviving and reforming the people of God within the rebuilt wall demands years of Nehemiah's godly life and leadership.

The Hebrew for Nehemiah is *Nehemyah*, "Comfort of Yahweh." The book is named after its chief character, whose name appears in the opening verse. The combined book of Ezra–Nehemiah is given the Greek title *Esdras Deuteron*, "Second Esdras" in the Septuagint, a third-century B.C. Greek-language translation of the Hebrew Old Testament. The Latin title of Nehemiah is *Liber Secundus Esdrae*, "Second Book of Ezra" (Ezra was the first). At this point, it is considered a separate book from Ezra, and is later called *Liber Nehemiae*, "Book of Nehemiah."

## CHAPTER 1

THE words of ªNehemiah the son of Hachaliah. And it came to pass in the month ¹Chisleu, in the ᵇtwentieth year, as I was in ᶜShushan² the ³palace,

2 That ªHanani, one of my brethren, came, he and *certain* men of Judah; and I asked them concerning the Jews that had escaped, which were left of the captivity, and concerning Jerusalem.

3 And they said unto me, The remnant that are left of the captivity there in the ªprovince *are* in great ¹affliction and ᵇreproach: ᶜthe wall of Jerusalem also ᵈ*is* broken down, and the gates thereof are burned with fire.

4 And it came to pass, when I heard these words, that I sat down and wept, and mourned *certain* days, and fasted, and prayed before the God of heaven,

5 And said, I beseech thee, ªO LORD God of heaven, the great and ᵇterrible¹ God, ᶜthat keepeth covenant and mercy for them that love ²him and ³observe ⁴his commandments;

6 Let thine ear now be attentive, and ªthine eyes open, that thou mayest hear the prayer of thy servant, which I pray before thee now, day and night, for the children of Israel thy servants, and ᵇconfess the sins of the children of Israel, which we have sinned against thee: both I and my father's house have sinned.

7 ªWe have ¹dealt very corruptly against thee, and ᵇnot kept the commandments, nor the statutes, nor the ²judgments, which thou commandedst thy servant Moses.

8 Remember, I beseech thee, the word that thou commandedst thy servant Moses, saying, ªIf ye ¹transgress, I will scatter you abroad among the nations:

9 ªBut *if* ye turn unto me, and keep my commandments, and do them; ᵇthough there were of you cast out unto the uttermost part of the heaven, *yet* will I gather them from thence, and will bring them unto the place that I have chosen ¹to set my name there.

10 ªNow these *are* thy servants and thy people, whom thou hast redeemed by thy great power, and by thy strong hand.

11 O Lord, I beseech thee, ªlet now thine ear be attentive to the prayer of thy servant, and to the prayer of thy servants, who ᵇdesire to fear thy name: and prosper, I pray thee, thy servant this day, and grant him mercy in the sight of this man. For I was the king's ᶜcupbearer.

## CHAPTER 2

AND it came to pass in the month Nisan, in the twentieth year of ªArtaxerxes¹ the king, *that* wine *was* before him: and ᵇI took up the wine, and gave *it* unto the king. Now I had not been ²*beforetime* sad in his presence.

2 Wherefore the king said unto me, Why *is* thy ¹countenance sad, seeing thou *art* not sick? this *is* nothing *else* but ªsorrow of heart. Then I was very ²sore afraid,

3 And said unto the king, ªLet the king live for ever: why should not my ¹countenance be sad, when ᵇthe city,

1:1 ª Neh. 10:1
ᵇ Neh. 2:1 ᶜ Esth.
1:1, 2, 5 ¹ Or
*Chislev* ² Or *Susa*
³ *citadel*
1:2 ª Neh. 7:2
1:3 ª Neh. 7:6
ᵇ Neh. 2:17 ᶜ Neh.
2:17 ᵈ 2 Kin. 25:10
¹ *distress*
1:5 ª Dan. 9:4
ᵇ Neh. 4:14 ᶜ [Ex.
20:6; 34:6, 7]
¹ *awesome* ² *you*
³ *keep* ⁴ *your*
1:6 ª 2 Chr. 6:40
ᵇ Dan. 9:20
1:7 ª Dan. 9:5
ᵇ Deut. 28:15
¹ *acted* ² *ordinances*

1:8 ª Lev. 26:33
¹ *are unfaithful*
1:9 ª [Deut.
4:29–31; 30:2–5]
ᵇ Deut. 30:4 ¹ *as
a dwelling for my
name*
1:10 ª Deut. 9:29
1:11 ª Neh. 1:6 ᵇ Is.
26:8 ᶜ Neh. 2:1
2:1 ª Ezra 7:1
ᵇ Neh. 1:11 ¹ Artaxerxes Longimanus ² *previously*
2:2 ª Prov. 15:13
¹ *face* ² *dreadfully*
2:3 ª Dan.
2:4; 5:10; 6:6,
21 ᵇ 2 Chr.
36:19 ¹ *face*

the place of my fathers' sepulchres, *lieth* waste, and the gates thereof are ²consumed with ᶜfire?

4 Then the king said unto me, For what dost thou make request? So I ᵃprayed to the God of heaven.

5 And I said unto the king, If it please the king, and if thy servant have found favour in thy sight, that thou wouldest send me unto Judah, unto the city of my fathers' sepulchres, that I may build it.

6 And the king said unto me, (the queen also sitting by him,) For how long shall thy journey be? and when wilt thou return? So it pleased the king to send me; and I set him ᵃa time.

7 Moreover I said unto the king, If it please the king, let letters be given me to the ᵃgovernors beyond the river, that they may ¹convey me over till I come into Judah;

8 And a letter unto Asaph the keeper of the king's forest, that he may give me timber to make beams for the gates of the ¹palace which *appertained* ᵃto the ²house, and for the wall of the city, and for the house that I shall enter into. And the king granted me, ᵇaccording to the good hand of my God upon me.

9 Then I came to the governors beyond the river, and gave them the king's letters. Now the king had sent captains of the army and horsemen with me.

10 When ᵃSanballat the Horonite, and Tobiah the servant, the Ammonite, heard *of it,* it grieved them exceedingly that there was come a man to seek the welfare of the children of Israel.

11 So I ᵃcame to Jerusalem, and was there three days.

12 And I arose in the night, I and some few men with me; neither told I *any* man what my God had put in my heart to do at Jerusalem: neither *was there any* beast with me, save the beast that I rode upon.

13 And I went out by night ᵃby the ¹gate of the valley, even before the ²dragon well, and to the ³dung port, and ⁴viewed the walls of Jerusalem, which were ᵇbroken down, and the gates thereof were ⁵consumed with fire.

14 Then I went on to the ᵃgate of the fountain, and to the ᵇking's pool: but *there was* no place for the beast *that was* under me to pass.

15 Then went I up in the night by the ᵃbrook,¹ and ²viewed the wall, and turned back, and entered by the ³gate of the valley, and *so* returned.

16 And the ¹rulers knew not whither I went, or what I did; neither had I as yet told *it* to the Jews, nor to

the priests, nor to the nobles, nor to the rulers, nor to the rest that did the work.

17 Then said I unto them, Ye see the distress that we *are* in, how Jerusalem *lieth* ¹waste, and the gates thereof are burned with fire: come, and let us build up the wall of Jerusalem, that we be no more ᵃa reproach.

18 Then I told them of ᵃthe hand of my God which was good upon me; as also the king's words that he had spoken unto me. And they said, Let us rise up and build. So they ᵇstrengthened¹ their hands for *this* good *work.*

19 But when Sanballat the Horonite, and Tobiah the servant, the Ammonite, and Geshem the Arabian, heard *it,* they laughed us to scorn, and despised us, and said, What *is* this thing that ye do? ᵃwill ye rebel against the king?

20 Then answered I them, and said unto them, The God of heaven, he will prosper us; therefore we his servants will arise and build: ᵃbut ye have no ¹portion, nor right, nor memorial, in Jerusalem.

## CHAPTER 3

THEN ᵃEliashib the high priest rose up with his brethren the priests, ᵇand they builded the sheep gate; they ¹sanctified it, and set up the doors of it; ᶜeven unto the tower of ²Meah they sanctified it, unto the tower of ᵈHananeel.

2 And next unto ¹him builded ᵃthe men of Jericho. And next to them builded Zaccur the son of Imri.

3 ᵃBut the fish gate did the sons of Hassenaah build, who *also* laid the beams thereof, and ᵇset up the doors thereof, the locks thereof, and the bars thereof.

4 And next unto them repaired ᵃMeremoth the son of Urijah, the son of ¹Koz. And next unto them repaired ᵇMeshullam the son of Berechiah, the son of Meshezabeel. And next unto them repaired Zadok the son of Baana.

5 And next unto them the Tekoites repaired; but their nobles ¹put not their necks to ᵃthe work of their Lord.

6 Moreover ᵃthe old gate repaired Jehoiada the son of Paseah, and Meshullam the son of Besodeiah; they laid the beams thereof, and set up the doors thereof, and the locks thereof, and the bars thereof.

7 And next unto them repaired Melatiah the Gibeonite, and Jadon the Meronothite, the ᵃmen of Gibeon, and of Mizpah, unto ¹the ᵇthrone of the governor ²on this side the river.

8 Next unto him repaired Uzziel the son of Harhaiah, of the goldsmiths. Next unto him also repaired Hananiah

### Center reference column

2:3 ᶜ Neh. 1:3
² *burned*

2:4 ᵃ Neh. 1:4

2:6 ᵃ Neh. 5:14;
13:6

2:7 ᵃ Ezra 7:21;
8:36 ¹ *allow me
to pass through*

2:8 ᵃ Neh. 3:7
ᵇ Ezra 5:5; 7:6,
9, 28; Neh. 2:18
¹ *citadel* ² *Temple*

2:10 ᵃ Neh.
2:19; 4:1

2:11 ᵃ Ezra 8:32

2:13 ᵃ 2 Chr. 26:9;
Neh. 3:13 ᵇ Neh.
1:3; 2:17 ¹ *valley
gate* ² *serpent*
³ *refuse gate*
⁴ *examined*
⁵ *burned*

2:14 ᵃ Neh. 3:15
ᵇ 2 Kin. 20:20

2:15 ᵃ 2 Sam.
15:23; Jer. 31:40
¹ *torrent valley*
² *examined* ³ *valley gate*

2:16 ¹ *officials*

2:17 ᵃ Neh. 1:3; Ps.
44:13; 79:4; Jer.
24:9; Ezek. 5:14,
15; 22:4 ¹ *desolate*

2:18 ᵃ Neh. 2:8
ᵇ 2 Sam. 2:7 ¹ *set
their hands to*

2:19 ᵃ Neh. 6:6

2:20 ᵃ Ezra
4:3; Neh. 6:16
¹ *heritage*

3:1 ᵃ Neh. 3:20;
12:10; 13:4, 7,
28 ᵇ John 5:2
ᶜ Neh. 12:39 ᵈ Jer.
31:38; Zech. 14:10
¹ *consecrated*
² *Or Hammeah,*
lit. *the tower of
the hundred,*
Neh. 12:39

3:2 ᵃ Ezra 2:34;
Neh. 7:36
¹ *Eliashib*

3:3 ᵃ 2 Chr. 33:14;
Neh. 12:39; Zeph.
1:10 ᵇ Neh. 6:1; 7:1

3:4 ᵃ Ezra 8:33
ᵇ Ezra 10:15 ¹ *Or
Hakkoz*

3:5 ᵃ [Judg. 5:23]
¹ *did not put their
shoulders to*

3:6 ᵃ Neh. 12:39

3:7 ᵃ Neh. 7:25
ᵇ Ezra 8:36;
Neh. 2:7–9 ¹ *the
residence* ² Lit.
*beyond the river,
west of the
Euphrates*

the son of *one of* the [1]apothecaries,
and they [2]fortified Jerusalem unto the
[a]broad wall.

9 And next unto them repaired Rephaiah the son of Hur, the ruler of the
half part of Jerusalem.

10 And next unto them repaired
Jedaiah the son of Harumaph, even
over against his house. And next
unto him repaired Hattush the son of
Hashabniah.

11 Malchijah the son of Harim, and
Hashub the son of Pahath-moab,
repaired [1]the other piece, [a]and the
tower of the furnaces.

12 And next unto him repaired
Shallum the son of [1]Halohesh, the
ruler of the half part of Jerusalem, he
and his daughters.

13 [a]The valley gate repaired Hanun,
and the inhabitants of Zanoah; they
built it, and set up the doors thereof,
the locks thereof, and the bars
thereof, and a thousand cubits on the
wall unto [b]the dung gate.

14 But the dung gate repaired Malchiah the son of Rechab, the ruler
of part of [a]Beth-haccerem; he built
it, and set up the doors thereof, the
locks thereof, and the bars thereof.

15 But [a]the gate of the fountain repaired Shallun the son of Col-hozeh,
the ruler of part of Mizpah; he built it,
and covered it, and set up the doors
thereof, the locks thereof, and the
bars thereof, and the wall of the pool
of [b]Siloah[1] by the [c]king's garden, and
unto the stairs that go down from the
city of David.

16 After him repaired Nehemiah
the son of Azbuk, the ruler of the half
part of Beth-zur, unto *the place* over
against the [1]sepulchres of David, and
to the [a]pool that was made, and unto
the house of the [2]mighty.

17 After him repaired the Levites,
Rehum the son of Bani. Next unto
him repaired Hashabiah, the ruler of
the half part of Keilah, in his part.

18 After him repaired their brethren, Bavai the son of Henadad, the
ruler of the half part of Keilah.

19 And next to him repaired Ezer
the son of Jeshua, the ruler of Mizpah, another piece over against
the [1]going up to the armoury at the
[a]turning[2] *of the wall.*

20 After him Baruch the son of
[1]Zabbai earnestly repaired the other
piece, from the [2]turning *of the wall*
unto the door of the house of Eliashib
the high priest.

21 After him repaired Meremoth
the son of Urijah the son of [1]Koz another piece, from the door of the
house of Eliashib even to the end of
the house of Eliashib.

22 And after him repaired the
priests, the men of the plain.

23 After him repaired Benjamin and
[1]Hashub [2]over against their house.
After him repaired Azariah the son of
Maaseiah the son of Ananiah by his
house.

24 After him repaired [a]Binnui the
son of Henadad another piece, from
the house of Azariah unto [b]the [1]turn-
ing *of the wall,* even unto the corner.

25 Palal the son of Uzai, [1]over
against the turning *of the wall,* and
the tower which [2]lieth out from the
king's [3]high house, that *was* by the
[a]court of the prison. After him Pedaiah the son of Parosh.

26 Moreover [a]the Nethinims [1]dwelt
in [b]Ophel, unto *the place* [2]over
against [c]the water gate toward the
east, and the tower that [3]lieth out.

27 After them the Tekoites repaired
another piece, over against the great
[1]tower that lieth out, even unto the
wall of Ophel.

28 From above the [a]horse gate repaired the priests, every one [1]over
against his house.

29 After them repaired Zadok the
son of Immer [1]over against his house.
After him repaired also Shemaiah the
son of Shechaniah, the keeper of the
east gate.

30 After him repaired Hananiah
the son of Shelemiah, and Hanun the
sixth son of Zalaph, another piece. After him repaired Meshullam the son of
Berechiah [1]over against his chamber.

31 After him repaired Malchiah [1]the
goldsmith's son unto the place of the
Nethinims, and of the merchants,
over against the gate [2]Miphkad, and
to the [3]going up of the corner.

32 And between the [1]going up of the
corner unto the [a]sheep gate repaired
the goldsmiths and the merchants.

## CHAPTER 4

BUT it came to pass, [a]that when
Sanballat heard that we builded
the wall, he was [1]wroth, and took
great indignation, and mocked the
Jews.

2 And he spake before his brethren
and the army of Samaria, and said,
What do these feeble Jews? will they
fortify themselves? will they sacrifice? will they [1]make an end in a day?
will they revive the stones out of
the heaps of the rubbish which are
burned?

3 Now [a]Tobiah the Ammonite *was*
by him, and he said, Even that which
they build, if a fox go up, he shall
even break down their stone wall.

4 [a]Hear, O our God; for we are despised: and [b]turn their reproach
upon their own head, and give them
for [1]a prey in the land of captivity:

5 And [a]cover not their iniquity, and
let not their sin be blotted out from

**Center column references:**

3:8 [a] Neh. 12:38
[1] *perfumers* [2] *re-
stored Jerusalem
as far as*

3:11 [a] Neh. 12:38
[1] *another section*

3:12 [1] *Hallohesh,*
Neh. 10:24

3:13 [a] Neh. 2:13, 15
[b] Neh. 2:13

3:14 [a] Jer. 6:1

3:15 [a] Neh. 2:14
[b] Is. 8:6; John 9:7
[c] 2 Kin. 25:4 [1] *Or
Shelah*

3:16 [a] 2 Kin.
20:20; Is. 7:3;
22:11 [1] *tombs*
[2] *mighty warriors*

3:19 [a] 2 Chr. 26:9
[1] *ascent* [2] *buttress*

3:20 [1] A few Heb.
mss., Vg., Syr.
*Zaccai* [2] *buttress*

3:21 [1] *Or Hakkoz*

3:23 [1] *Or Hash-
shub* [2] *in front of*

3:24 [a] Ezra
8:33 [b] Neh. 3:19
[1] *buttress*

3:25 [a] Jer. 32:2;
33:1; 37:21 [1] *op-
posite* [2] *projects
from* [3] *upper*

3:26 [a] Ezra 2:43;
Neh. 11:21 [b] 2 Chr.
27:3 [c] Neh. 8:1, 3;
12:37 [1] *who dwelt
in Ophel repaired
unto* [2] *opposite*
[3] *projects out*

3:27 [1] *projecting
tower*

3:28 [a] 2 Kin. 11:16;
2 Chr. 23:15; Jer.
31:40 [1] *in front of*

3:29 [1] *in front of*

3:30 [1] *in front of
his dwelling*

3:31 [1] *one of the
goldsmiths* [2] Lit.
*of inspection or
recruiting* [3] *upper
room of*

3:32 [a] Neh. 3:1;
12:39 [1] *upper
room*

4:1 [a] Neh. 2:10, 19
[1] *furious*

4:2 [1] *complete it*

4:3 [a] Neh. 2:10, 19

4:4 [a] Ps. 123:3, 4
[b] Ps. 79:12; Prov.
3:34 [1] *plunder*

4:5 [a] Ps. 69:27,
28; 109:14, 15; Jer.
18:23

before thee: for they have provoked *thee* to anger before the builders.

6 So built we the wall; and all the wall was joined together unto the half thereof: for the people had a mind to work.

7 But it came to pass, *that* [a]when Sanballat, and Tobiah, and [b]the Arabians, and the Ammonites, and the Ashdodites, heard that the walls of Jerusalem were [1]made up, *and* that the [2]breaches began to be stopped, then they were very [3]wroth,

8 And [a]conspired all of them together to come *and* to fight against Jerusalem, and to [1]hinder it.

9 Nevertheless [a]we made our prayer unto our God, and set a watch against them day and night, because of them.

10 And Judah said, The strength of the bearers of burdens is [1]decayed, and *there is* much rubbish; so that we are not able to build the wall.

11 And our adversaries said, They shall not know, neither see, till we come in the midst among them, and slay them, and cause the work to cease.

12 And it came to pass, that when the Jews which dwelt by them came, they said unto us ten times, [1]From all places whence ye shall return unto us *they will be upon you.*

13 Therefore [1]set I in the lower places behind the wall, *and* [2]on the higher places, I even set the people after their families with their swords, their spears, and their bows.

14 And I looked, and rose up, and said unto the nobles, and to the rulers, and to the rest of the people, [a]Be not ye afraid of them: remember the Lord, *which is* [b]great and [1]terrible, and [c]fight for your brethren, your sons, and your daughters, your wives, and your houses.

15 And it came to pass, when our enemies heard that it was known unto us, [a]and God had brought their counsel to nought, that we returned all of us to the wall, every one unto his work.

16 And it came to pass from that time forth, *that* the half of my servants [1]wrought in the work, and the other half of them held both the spears, the shields, and the bows, and [2]the habergeons; and the rulers [3]*were* behind all the house of Judah.

17 They which builded on the wall, and they that bare burdens, [1]with those that laded, *every one* with one of his hands wrought in the work, and with the other *hand* held a weapon.

18 For the builders, every one had his sword girded by his side, and *so* builded. And he that sounded the trumpet *was* by me.

19 And I said unto the nobles, and to the rulers, and to the rest of the people, The work *is* great and [1]large, and we are separated upon the wall, one far from another.

20 In what place *therefore* ye hear the sound of the trumpet, [1]resort ye thither unto us: [a]our God shall fight for us.

21 So we laboured in the work: and half of them held the spears from the rising of the morning till the stars appeared.

22 Likewise at the same time said I unto the people, Let every one with his servant lodge within Jerusalem, that in the night they may be a guard to us, and labour on the day.

23 So neither I, nor my brethren, nor my servants, nor the men of the guard which followed me, none of us put off our clothes, [1]*saving that* every one put them off for washing.

## CHAPTER 5

AND there was a great [a]cry[1] of the people and of their wives against their [b]brethren the Jews.

2 For there were that said, We, our sons, and our daughters, *are* many: therefore we take up [1]corn *for them,* that we may eat, and live.

3 *Some* also there were that said, We have mortgaged our lands, vineyards, and houses, that we might buy [1]corn, because of the [2]dearth.

4 There were also that said, We have borrowed money for the king's [1]tribute, *and that upon* our lands and vineyards.

5 Yet now [a]our flesh *is* as the flesh of our brethren, our children as their children: and, lo, we [b]bring into [1]bondage our sons and our daughters to be servants, and *some* of our daughters are brought unto bondage *already:* neither *is it* in our power *to redeem them;* for other men have our lands and vineyards.

6 And I was very angry when I heard their cry and these words.

7 [1]Then I consulted with myself, and I rebuked the nobles, and the rulers, and said unto them, [a]Ye [2]exact usury, every one of his brother. And I [3]set a great assembly against them.

8 And I said unto them, We [1]after our ability have [a]redeemed our brethren the Jews, which were sold unto the heathen; and will ye even sell your brethren? or shall they be sold unto us? Then [2]held they their peace, and found nothing *to answer.*

9 Also I said, [1]It *is* not good that ye do: ought ye not to walk [a]in the fear of our God [b]because of the reproach of the heathen our enemies?

10 I likewise, *and* my brethren, and my servants, [1]might exact of them

4:7 [a] Neh. 4:1 [b] Neh. 2:19 [1] *were being restored* [2] *gaps were beginning to be closed* [3] *angry*
4:8 [a] Ps. 83:3–5 [1] *create confusion*
4:9 [a] [Ps. 50:15]
4:10 [1] *failing*
4:12 [1] *From whatever place you shall turn they will come upon us*
4:13 [1] *I positioned men* [2] *at the open places*
4:14 [a] [Num. 14:9]; Deut. 1:29 [b] [Deut. 10:17] [c] 2 Sam. 10:12 [1] *awesome*
4:15 [a] Job 5:12
4:16 [1] *worked on the construction* [2] *wore the armour* [3] *Supported*
4:17 [1] *loaded themselves so that*
4:19 [1] *extensive*
4:20 [a] Ex. 14:14, 25; Deut. 1:30; 3:22; 20:4; Josh. 23:10; 2 Chr. 20:29 [1] *rally there*
4:23 [1] *except*
5:1 [a] Lev. 25:35–37; Neh. 5:7, 8 [b] Deut. 15:7 [1] *outcry*
5:2 [1] *grain*
5:3 [1] *grain* [2] *famine*
5:4 [1] *tax on our lands*
5:5 [a] Is. 58:7 [b] Ex. 21:7; [Lev. 25:39] [1] *slavery*
5:7 [a] [Ex. 22:25; Lev. 25:36; Deut. 23:19, 20]; Ezek. 22:12 [1] *After serious thought* [2] *charge excessive interest* [3] *held*
5:8 [a] Lev. 25:48 [1] *according to* [2] *they were silenced*
5:9 [a] Lev. 25:36 [b] 2 Sam. 12:14; Rom. 2:24; [1 Pet. 2:12] [1] *What you are doing is not good*
5:10 [1] *am lending them*

money and [2]corn: I pray you, let us leave off this [3]usury.

11 Restore, I pray you, to them, even this day, their lands, their vineyards, their [1]oliveyards, and their houses, also the hundredth *part* of the money, and of the [2]corn, the wine, and the oil, that ye [3]exact of them.

12 Then said they, We will restore *them,* and will require nothing of them; so will we do as thou sayest. Then I called the priests, [a]and took an oath of them, that they should do according to this promise.

13 Also [a]I shook [1]my lap, and said, So God shake out every man from his house, and from his [2]labour, that performeth not this promise, even thus be he shaken out, and emptied. And all the congregation said, Amen, and praised the LORD. [b]And the people did according to this promise.

14 Moreover from the time that I was appointed to be their governor in the land of Judah, from the twentieth year [a]even unto the two and thirtieth year of Artaxerxes the king, *that is,* twelve years, I and my brethren have not [b]eaten the [1]bread of the governor.

15 But the former governors that *had been* before me were chargeable unto the people, and had taken of them bread and wine, beside forty shekels of silver; yea, even their servants bare rule over the people: but [a]so did not I, because of the [b]fear of God.

16 Yea, also I continued in the [a]work of this wall, neither bought we any land: and all my servants *were* gathered thither unto the work.

17 Moreover *there were* [a]at my table an hundred and fifty of the Jews and rulers, beside those that came unto us from among the heathen that *are* about us.

18 Now *that* [a]which was prepared *for me* daily *was* one ox *and* six choice sheep; also fowls were prepared for me, and once in ten days [1]store of all sorts of wine: yet for all this [b]required[2] not I the bread of the governor, because the bondage was heavy upon this people.

19 [a]Think upon me, my God, for good, *according* to all that I have done for this people.

## CHAPTER 6

Now it came to pass, [a]when Sanballat, and Tobiah, and [1]Geshem the Arabian, and the rest of our enemies, heard that I had [2]builded the wall, and *that* there was no [3]breach left therein; ([b]though at that time I had not set up the doors upon the gates;)

2 That Sanballat and [1]Geshem [a]sent unto me, saying, Come, let us meet together in *some one of* [2]the villages in the plain of [b]Ono. But they [c]thought to do me [3]mischief.

3 And I sent messengers unto them, saying, I *am* doing a great work, so that I cannot come down: why should the work cease, whilst I leave it, and come down to you?

4 Yet they sent unto me four times after this sort; and I answered them after the same manner.

5 Then sent Sanballat his servant unto me in like manner the fifth time with an open letter in his hand;

6 Wherein *was* written, It is reported among the heathen, and [1]Gashmu saith *it, that* thou and the Jews [2]think to rebel: for which cause thou buildest the wall, [a]that thou mayest be their king, according to these [3]words.

7 And thou hast also appointed prophets to preach of thee at Jerusalem, saying, *There is* a king in Judah: and now shall it be reported to the king according to these words. Come now therefore, and let us take counsel together.

8 Then I sent unto him, saying, There are no such things done as thou sayest, but thou [1]feignest them out of thine own heart.

9 For they all [1]made us afraid, saying, Their hands shall be weakened from the work, that it be not done. Now therefore, *O God,* strengthen my hands.

10 Afterward I came unto the house of Shemaiah the son of Delaiah the son of Mehetabeel, who *was* [1]shut up; and he said, Let us meet together in the house of God, within the temple, and let us shut the doors of the temple: for they [2]will come to slay thee; yea, in the night will they come to slay thee.

11 And I said, Should such a man as I flee? and who *is there,* that, *being* as I *am,* would go into the temple to save his life? I will not go in.

12 And, lo, I perceived that God had not sent him; but that [a]he pronounced this prophecy against me: for Tobiah and Sanballat had hired him.

13 Therefore *was* he hired, that I should be afraid, and do so, and sin, and *that* they might have *matter* for an evil report, that they might reproach me.

14 [a]My God, think thou upon Tobiah and Sanballat according to these their works, and on the [b]prophetess Noadiah, and the rest of the prophets, that would have put me in fear.

15 So the wall was finished in the twenty and fifth *day* of *the month* Elul, in fifty and two days.

---

*Center column references:*

5:10 [2] *grain* [3] *excessive interest*
5:11 [1] *olive groves* [2] *grain* [3] *have charged*
5:12 [a] Ezra 10:5; Jer. 34:8, 9
5:13 [a] Matt. 10:14; Acts 13:51; 18:6 [b] 2 Kin. 23:3 [1] *the fold of my garment* [2] *property*
5:14 [a] Neh. 2:1; 13:6 [b] [1 Cor. 9:4–15] [1] *provision*
5:15 [a] 2 Cor. 11:9; 12:13 [b] Neh. 5:9
5:16 [a] Neh. 4:1; 6:1
5:17 [a] 2 Sam. 9:7; 1 Kin. 18:19
5:18 [a] 1 Kin. 4:22 [b] Neh. 5:14, 15 [1] *an abundance of all kinds* [2] *I did not demand the food*
5:19 [a] 2 Kin. 20:3; Neh. 13:14, 22, 31
6:1 [a] Neh. 2:10, 19; 4:1, 7; 13:28 [b] Neh. 3:1, 3 [1] *Gashmu,* Neh. 6:6 [2] *rebuilt* [3] *break*

6:2 [a] Prov. 26:24, 25 [b] 1 Chr. 8:12; Neh. 11:35 [c] Ps. 37:12, 32 [1] *Gashmu,* Neh. 6:6 [2] Heb. *kephirim,* an unknown place [3] *harm*
6:6 [a] Neh. 2:19 [1] *Geshem,* Neh. 2:19; 6:1, 2 [2] *are planning* [3] *rumours*
6:8 [1] *invent*
6:9 [1] *attempted to make*
6:10 [1] *confined* [2] *are coming*
6:12 [a] Ezek. 13:22
6:14 [a] Neh. 13:29 [b] Ezek. 13:17

---

16 And it came to pass, that [a]when all our enemies heard *thereof,* and all the heathen that *were* about us saw *these things,* they were much cast down in their own eyes: for [b]they perceived that this work was [1]wrought of our God.

17 Moreover in those days the nobles of Judah sent many letters unto Tobiah, and *the letters* of Tobiah came unto them.

18 For *there were* many in Judah sworn unto him, because he *was* the [a]son in law of Shechaniah the son of Arah; and his son Johanan had taken the daughter of [b]Meshullam the son of Berechiah.

19 Also they reported his good deeds before me, and uttered my [1]words to him. *And* Tobiah sent letters to put me in fear.

## CHAPTER 7

Now it came to pass, when the wall was built, and I had [a]set up the doors, and the [1]porters and the singers and the Levites were appointed,

2 That I gave my brother [a]Hanani, and Hananiah the ruler [b]of the [1]palace, charge over Jerusalem: for he *was* a faithful man, and [c]feared God above many.

3 And I said unto them, Let not the gates of Jerusalem be opened until the sun be hot; and while they [1]stand by, let them shut the doors, and bar *them:* and appoint [2]watches of the inhabitants of Jerusalem, every one [3]in his watch, and every one [4]*to be* over against his house.

4 Now the city *was* [1]large and great: but the people *were* [a]few therein, and the houses *were* not [2]builded.

5 And my God put into mine heart to gather together the nobles, and the rulers, and the people, that they might be [1]reckoned by genealogy. And I found a register of the genealogy of them which came up at the first, and found written therein,

6 [a]These *are* the children of the province, that went up out of the captivity, of those that had been carried away, whom Nebuchadnezzar the king of Babylon had carried away, and came again to Jerusalem and to Judah, every one unto his city;

7 Who came with [a]Zerubbabel, Jeshua, Nehemiah, [1]Azariah, Raamiah, Nahamani, Mordecai, Bilshan, [2]Mispereth, Bigvai, Nehum, Baanah. The number, *I say,* of the men of the people of Israel *was this;*

8 The children of Parosh, two thousand an hundred seventy and two.

9 The children of Shephatiah, three hundred seventy and two.

10 The children of Arah, six hundred fifty and two.

11 The children of Pahath-moab, of the children of Jeshua and Joab, two thousand and eight hundred *and* eighteen.

12 The children of Elam, a thousand two hundred fifty and four.

13 The children of Zattu, eight hundred forty and five.

14 The children of Zaccai, seven hundred and threescore.

15 The children of [1]Binnui, six hundred forty and eight.

16 The children of Bebai, six hundred twenty and eight.

17 The children of Azgad, two thousand three hundred twenty and two.

18 The children of Adonikam, six hundred threescore and seven.

19 The children of Bigvai, two thousand threescore and seven.

20 The children of Adin, six hundred fifty and five.

21 The children of Ater of Hezekiah, ninety and eight.

22 The children of Hashum, three hundred twenty and eight.

23 The children of Bezai, three hundred twenty and four.

24 The children of [1]Hariph, an hundred and twelve.

25 The children of [1]Gibeon, ninety and five.

26 The men of Beth-lehem and Netophah, an hundred fourscore and eight.

27 The men of Anathoth, an hundred twenty and eight.

28 The men of [1]Beth-azmaveth, forty and two.

29 The men of [1]Kirjath-jearim, Chephirah, and Beeroth, seven hundred forty and three.

30 The men of Ramah and Gaba, six hundred twenty and one.

31 The men of Michmas, an hundred and twenty and two.

32 The men of Beth-el and Ai, an hundred twenty and three.

33 The men of the other Nebo, fifty and two.

34 The children of the other [a]Elam, a thousand two hundred fifty and four.

35 The children of Harim, three hundred and twenty.

36 The children of Jericho, three hundred forty and five.

37 The children of Lod, Hadid, and Ono, seven hundred twenty and one.

38 The children of Senaah, three thousand nine hundred and thirty.

39 The priests: the children of [a]Jedaiah, of the house of Jeshua, nine hundred seventy and three.

40 The children of [a]Immer, a thousand fifty and two.

41 The children of [a]Pashur, a thousand two hundred forty and seven.

42 The children of [a]Harim, a thousand and seventeen.

6:16 [a] Neh. 2:10, 20; 4:1, 7; 6:1   [b] Ps. 126:2   [1] *accomplished*

6:18 [a] Neh. 13:4, 28   [b] Ezra 10:15; Neh. 3:4

6:19 [1] *matters*

7:1 [a] Neh. 6:1, 15   [1] *gatekeepers*

7:2 [a] Neh. 1:2   [b] Neh. 2:8; 10:23   [c] Ex. 18:21   [1] *citadel*

7:3 [1] *stand guard*   [2] *guards from among*   [3] *at his watch station*   [4] *in front of his own*

7:4 [a] Deut. 4:27   [1] *broad, spacious*   [2] *rebuilt*

7:5 [1] *registered*

7:6 [a] Ezra 2:1–70

7:7 [a] Ezra 5:2; Neh. 12:1, 47; Matt. 1:12, 13   [1] *Seraiah, Ezra 2:2*   [2] *Mizpar, Ezra 2:2*

7:15 [1] *Bani, Ezra 2:10*

7:24 [1] *Jorah, Ezra 2:18*

7:25 [1] *Gibbar, Ezra 2:20*

7:28 [1] *Azmaveth, Ezra 2:24*

7:29 [1] *Kirjath-arim, Ezra 2:25*

7:34 [a] Neh. 7:12

7:39 [a] 1 Chr. 24:7

7:40 [a] 1 Chr. 9:12

7:41 [a] 1 Chr. 9:12; 24:9

7:42 [a] 1 Chr. 24:8

43 The Levites: the children of Jeshua, of Kadmiel, *and* of the children of [1]Hodevah, seventy and four.

44 The singers: the children of Asaph, an hundred forty and eight.

45 The [1]porters: the children of Shallum, the children of Ater, the children of Talmon, the children of Akkub, the children of Hatita, the children of Shobai, an hundred thirty and eight.

46 The Nethinims: the children of Ziha, the children of Hashupha, the children of Tabbaoth,

47 The children of Keros, the children of [1]Sia, the children of Padon,

48 The children of [1]Lebana, the children of [2]Hagaba, the children of [3]Shalmai,

49 The children of Hanan, the children of Giddel, the children of Gahar,

50 The children of Reaiah, the children of Rezin, the children of Nekoda,

51 The children of Gazzam, the children of Uzza, the children of Phaseah,

52 The children of Besai, the children of Meunim, the children of [1]Nephishesim,

53 The children of Bakbuk, the children of Hakupha, the children of Harhur,

54 The children of [1]Bazlith, the children of Mehida, the children of Harsha,

55 The children of Barkos, the children of Sisera, the children of Tamah,

56 The children of Neziah, the children of Hatipha.

57 The children of Solomon's servants: the children of Sotai, the children of Sophereth, the children of [1]Perida,

58 The children of Jaala, the children of Darkon, the children of Giddel,

59 The children of Shephatiah, the children of Hattil, the children of Pochereth of Zebaim, the children of [1]Amon.

60 All the Nethinims, and the children of Solomon's servants, *were* three hundred ninety and two.

61 And these *were* they which went up *also* from Tel-melah, Tel-haresha, Cherub, [1]Addon, and Immer: but they [2]could not shew their father's house, nor their [3]seed, whether they *were* of Israel.

62 The children of Delaiah, the children of Tobiah, the children of Nekoda, six hundred forty and two.

63 And of the priests: the children of Habaiah, the children of Koz, the children of Barzillai, which took *one* of the daughters of Barzillai the Gileadite to wife, and was called after their name.

64 These sought their register *among* those that were reckoned by genealogy, but it was not found: therefore

were they, as [1]polluted, put from the priesthood.

65 And the [1]Tirshatha said unto them, that they should not eat of the most holy things, till there stood up a priest with Urim and Thummim.

66 The whole congregation together *was* forty and two thousand three hundred and threescore,

67 Beside their manservants and their maidservants, of whom *there were* seven thousand three hundred thirty and seven: and they had two hundred forty and five singing men and singing women.

68 Their horses, seven hundred thirty and six: their mules, two hundred forty and five:

69 *Their* camels, four hundred thirty and five: six thousand seven hundred and twenty asses.

70 And some of the [1]chief of the fathers gave unto the work. [a]The [2]Tirshatha gave to the [3]treasure a thousand [4]drams of gold, fifty basons, five hundred and thirty priests' garments.

71 And *some* of the [1]chief of the fathers gave to the [2]treasure of the work [a]twenty thousand [3]drams of gold, and two thousand and two hundred [4]pound of silver.

72 And *that* which the rest of the people gave *was* twenty thousand [1]drams of gold, and two thousand [2]pound of silver, and threescore and seven priests' garments.

73 So the priests, and the Levites, and the [1]porters, and the singers, and *some* of the people, and the Nethinims, and all Israel, dwelt in their cities; [a]and when the seventh month came, the children of Israel *were* in their cities.

## CHAPTER 8

AND all [a]the people gathered themselves together as one man into the [1]street that *was* [b]before the water gate; and they spake unto Ezra the [c]scribe to bring the book of the law of Moses, which the LORD had commanded to Israel.

2 And Ezra the priest brought [a]the law before the congregation both of men and women, and all that could hear with understanding, [b]upon the first day of the seventh month.

3 And he [a]read therein before the [1]street that *was* before the water gate [2]from the morning until midday, before the men and the women, and those that could understand; and the ears of all the people *were attentive* unto the book of the law.

4 And Ezra the scribe stood upon a [1]pulpit of wood, which they had made for the purpose; and beside him stood Mattithiah, and Shema,

7:43 [1] *Hodaviah,* Ezra 2:40 or *Judah,* Ezra 3:9

7:45 [1] *gatekeepers*

7:47 [1] *Siaha,* Ezra 2:44

7:48 [1] *Lebanah,* Ezra 2:45 [2] *Hagabah,* Ezra 2:45 [3] Heb. *Salmai*

7:52 [1] *Nephusim,* Ezra 2:50

7:54 [1] *Bazluth,* Ezra 2:52

7:57 [1] *Peruda,* Ezra 2:55

7:59 [1] *Ami,* Ezra 2:57

7:61 [1] *Addan,* Ezra 2:59 [2] *could not identify their genealogies* [3] *lineage*

7:64 [1] *defiled and excluded from*

7:65 [1] Lit. *governor*

7:70 [a] Neh. 8:9 [1] *heads of the fathers' houses* [2] Lit. *governor* [3] *treasury* [4] *drachmas*

7:71 [a] Ezra 2:69 [1] *heads of the fathers' houses* [2] *treasury* [3] *drachmas* [4] *minas*

7:72 [1] *drachmas* [2] *minas*

7:73 [a] Ezra 3:1 [1] *gatekeepers*

8:1 [a] Ezra 3:1 [b] Neh. 3:26 [c] Ezra 7:6 [1] *plaza*

8:2 [a] [Deut. 31:11, 12]; Neh. 8:9 [b] Lev. 23:24; Num. 29:1–6

8:3 [a] Deut. 31:9–11; 2 Kin. 23:2 [1] *plaza* [2] Lit. *from the light*

8:4 [1] *platform*

439

and Anaiah, and Urijah, and Hilkiah, and Maaseiah, on his right hand; and on his left hand, Pedaiah, and Mishael, and Malchiah, and Hashum, and Hashbadana, Zechariah, *and* Meshullam.

5 And Ezra opened the book in the sight of all the people; (for he was above all the people;) and when he opened it, all the people ªstood up:

6 And Ezra blessed the LORD, the great God. And all the people ªanswered, Amen, Amen, with ᵇlifting up their hands: and they ᶜbowed their heads, and worshipped the LORD with *their* faces to the ground.

7 Also Jeshua, and Bani, and Sherebiah, Jamin, Akkub, Shabbethai, Hodijah, Maaseiah, Kelita, Azariah, Jozabad, Hanan, Pelaiah, and the Levites, ªcaused the people to understand the law: and the people ᵇstood in their place.

8 So they read in the book in the law of God distinctly, and ¹gave the sense, and caused *them* to understand the reading.

9 ªAnd Nehemiah, which *is* the ¹Tirshatha, and Ezra the priest the scribe, and the Levites that taught the people, said unto all the people, ᵇThis day *is* holy unto the LORD your God; ᶜmourn not, nor weep. For all the people wept, when they heard the words of the law.

10 Then he said unto them, Go your way, eat the fat, and drink the sweet, ªand send portions unto them for whom nothing is prepared: for *this* day *is* holy unto our Lord: neither be ye sorry; for the joy of the LORD is your strength.

11 So the Levites stilled all the people, saying, ¹Hold your peace, for the day *is* holy; neither be ye grieved.

12 And all the people went their way to eat, and to drink, and to ªsend portions, and to make great ¹mirth, because they had ᵇunderstood the words that were declared unto them.

13 And on the second day were gathered together the ¹chief of the fathers of all the people, the priests, and the Levites, unto Ezra the scribe, even to understand the words of the law.

14 And they found written in the law which the LORD had commanded by Moses, that the children of Israel should dwell in ªbooths¹ in the feast of the seventh month:

15 And ªthat they should publish and proclaim in all their cities, and ᵇin Jerusalem, saying, Go forth unto the mount, and ᶜfetch olive branches, and pine branches, and myrtle branches, and palm branches, and branches of thick trees, to make booths, as *it is* written.

16 So the people went forth, and brought *them*, and made themselves booths, every one upon the ªroof of his house, and in their courts, and in the courts of the house of God, and in the street of the ᵇwater gate, ᶜand in the ¹street of the gate of Ephraim.

17 And all the congregation of them that were come again out of the captivity made booths, and sat under the ¹booths: for since the days of Jeshua the son of Nun unto that day had not the children of Israel done so. And there was very ªgreat gladness.

18 Also ªday by day, from the first day unto the last day, he read in the book of the law of God. And they kept the feast ᵇseven days; and on the ᶜeighth day *was* ¹a solemn assembly, according unto the ²manner.

## CHAPTER 9

Now in the twenty and fourth day of ªthis month the children of Israel were assembled with fasting, and with sackclothes, ᵇand ¹earth upon them.

2 And ªthe seed of Israel separated themselves from all ¹strangers, and stood and ᵇconfessed their sins, and the iniquities of their fathers.

3 And they stood up in their place, and ªread in the book of the law of the LORD their God *one* fourth part of the day; and *another* fourth part they confessed, and worshipped the LORD their God.

4 Then stood up upon the ¹stairs, of the Levites, Jeshua, and Bani, Kadmiel, Shebaniah, Bunni, Sherebiah, Bani, *and* Chenani, and cried with a loud voice unto the LORD their God.

5 Then the Levites, Jeshua, and Kadmiel, Bani, Hashabniah, Sherebiah, Hodijah, Shebaniah, *and* Pethahiah, said, Stand up *and* bless the LORD your God for ever and ever: and blessed be ªthy glorious name, which is exalted above all blessing and praise.

6 ªThou, *even* thou, *art* LORD alone; ᵇthou hast made heaven, ᶜthe heaven of heavens, with ᵈall their host, the earth, and all *things* that *are* therein, the seas, and all that *is* therein, and thou ᵉpreservest them all; and the host of heaven worshippeth thee.

7 Thou *art* the LORD the God, who didst choose ªAbram, and broughtest him forth out of Ur of the Chaldees, and gavest him the name of ᵇAbraham;

8 And foundest his heart ªfaithful before thee, and madest a ᵇcovenant with him to give the land of the Canaanites, the Hittites, the Amorites, and the Perizzites, and the Jebusites, and the Girgashites, to give *it, I say,* to his seed, and ᶜhast performed thy words; for thou *art* righteous:

### Cross References

8:5 ª Judg. 3:20; 1 Kin. 8:12–14
8:6 ª Neh. 5:13; [1 Cor. 14:16] ᵇ Ps. 28:2; Lam. 3:41; 1 Tim. 2:8 ᶜ Ex. 4:31; 12:27; 2 Chr. 20:18
8:7 ª Lev. 10:11; Deut. 33:10; 2 Chr. 17:7; [Mal. 2:7] ᵇ Neh. 9:3
8:8 ¹ expounded the meaning
8:9 ª Ezra 2:63; Neh. 7:65, 70; 10:1 ᵇ Lev. 23:24; Num. 29:1 ᶜ Deut. 16:14; Eccl. 3:4 ¹ Lit. governor
8:10 ª [Deut. 26:11–13]; Esth. 9:19, 22; Rev. 11:10
8:11 ¹ Be still
8:12 ª Neh. 8:10 ᵇ Neh. 8:7, 8 ¹ rejoicing
8:13 ¹ heads of the fathers' houses
8:14 ª Lev. 23:34, 40, 42; Deut. 16:13 ¹ Temporary shelters
8:15 ª Lev. 23:4 ᵇ Deut. 16:16 ᶜ Lev. 23:40
8:16 ª Deut. 22:8 ᵇ Neh. 12:37 ᶜ 2 Kin. 14:13; Neh. 12:39 ¹ plaza
8:17 ª 2 Chr. 30:21 ¹ Temporary shelters
8:18 ª Deut. 31:11 ᵇ Lev. 23:36 ᶜ Num. 29:35 ¹ Lit. an assembly of restraint ² prescribed manner
9:1 ª Neh. 8:2 ᵇ 1 Sam. 4:12 ¹ dust on their heads
9:2 ª Neh. 13:3, 30 ᵇ Neh. 1:6 ¹ foreigners
9:3 ª Neh. 8:7, 8
9:4 ¹ Lit. ascent
9:5 ª 1 Chr. 29:13
9:6 ª 2 Kin. 19:15, 19 ᵇ Rev. 14:7 ᶜ [Deut. 10:14] ᵈ Gen. 2:1 ᵉ [Ps. 36:6]
9:7 ª Gen. 11:31 ᵇ Gen. 17:5
9:8 ª Gen. 15:6; 22:1–3 ᵇ Gen. 15:18 ᶜ Josh. 23:14

9 [a]And didst see the affliction of our fathers in Egypt, and [b]heardest their cry by the Red sea;

10 And [a]shewedst signs and wonders upon Pharaoh, and on all his servants, and on all the people of his land: for thou knewest that they [b]dealt [1]proudly against them. So didst thou [c]get[2] thee a name, as *it is* this day.

11 [a]And thou didst divide the sea before them, so that they went through the midst of the sea on the dry land; and their persecutors thou threwest into the deeps, [b]as a stone into the mighty waters.

12 Moreover thou [a]leddest them in the day by a cloudy pillar; and in the night by a pillar of fire, to give them light in the way wherein they should go.

13 [a]Thou camest down also upon mount Sinai, and spakest with them from heaven, and gavest them [b]right[1] judgments, and true laws, good statutes and commandments:

14 And madest known unto them thy [a]holy sabbath, and commandedst them precepts, statutes, and laws, by the hand of Moses thy servant:

15 And [a]gavest them bread from heaven for their hunger, and [b]broughtest forth water for them out of the rock for their thirst, and promisedst them that they should [c]go in to possess the land [1]which thou hadst sworn to give them.

16 [a]But they and our fathers [1]dealt proudly, and [b]hardened[2] their necks, and [3]hearkened not to thy commandments,

17 And refused to obey, [a]neither were mindful of thy wonders that thou didst among them; but hardened their necks, and in their rebellion appointed [b]a captain to return to their bondage: but thou *art* a God ready to pardon, [c]gracious and merciful, slow to anger, and of great kindness, and forsookest them not.

18 Yea, [a]when they had made them a molten calf, and said, This *is* thy God that brought thee up out of Egypt, and had [1]wrought great provocations;

19 Yet thou in thy [a]manifold mercies forsookest them not in the wilderness: the [b]pillar of the cloud departed not from them by day, to lead them in the way; neither the pillar of fire by night, to shew them light, and the way wherein they should go.

20 Thou gavest also thy [a]good spirit to instruct them, and withheldest not thy [b]manna from their mouth, and gavest them [c]water for their thirst.

21 Yea, [a]forty years didst thou sustain them in the wilderness, *so that* they lacked nothing; their [b]clothes [1]waxed not old, and their feet swelled not.

22 Moreover thou gavest them kingdoms and nations, and didst divide them into [1]corners: so they possessed the land of [a]Sihon, and the land of the king of Heshbon, and the land of Og king of Bashan.

23 [a]Their children also multipliedst thou as the stars of heaven, and broughtest them into the land, concerning which thou hadst promised to their fathers, that they should go in to possess *it*.

24 So [a]the children went in and possessed the land, and [b]thou subduedst before them the inhabitants of the land, the Canaanites, and gavest them into their hands, with their kings, and the people of the land, that they might do with them as they would.

25 And they took strong cities, and a [a]fat[1] land, and possessed [b]houses full of all goods, [2]wells digged, vineyards, and [3]oliveyards, and fruit trees in abundance: so they did eat, and were filled, and [c]became fat, and delighted themselves in thy great [d]goodness.

26 Nevertheless they [a]were disobedient, and rebelled against thee, and [b]cast thy law behind their backs, and slew thy [c]prophets which [1]testified against them to turn them to thee, and they wrought great provocations.

27 [a]Therefore thou deliveredst them into the hand of their enemies, who [1]vexed them: and in the time of their trouble, when they cried unto thee, thou [b]heardest *them* from heaven; and according to thy manifold mercies [c]thou gavest them [2]saviours, who saved them out of the hand of their enemies.

28 But after they had rest, [a]they did evil again before thee: therefore leftest thou them in the hand of their enemies, so that they had the dominion over them: yet when they returned, and cried unto thee, thou heardest *them* from heaven; and [b]many times didst thou [1]deliver them according to thy mercies;

29 And testifiedst against them, that thou mightest bring them again unto thy law: yet they [1]dealt proudly, and [2]hearkened not unto thy commandments, but sinned against thy judgments, ([a]which if a man do, he shall live in them;) and [3]withdrew the shoulder, and [4]hardened their neck, and would not hear.

30 Yet many years [1]didst thou forbear them, and [2]testifiedst [a]against them by thy spirit [b]in thy prophets: yet would they not [3]give ear: [c]therefore gavest

---

9:9 [a] Ex. 2:25; 3:7 [b] Ex. 14:10
9:10 [a] Ex. 7–14 [b] Ex. 18:11 [c] Jer. 32:20 [1] *presumptuously* or *insolently* [2] *make yourself*
9:11 [a] Ex. 14:20–28 [b] Ex. 15:1, 5
9:12 [a] Ex. 13:21, 22
9:13 [a] Ex. 20:1–18 [b] [Rom. 7:12] [1] *just ordinances*
9:14 [a] Gen. 2:3
9:15 [a] Ex. 16:14–17 [b] Ex. 17:6 [c] Deut. 1:8 [1] Lit. *which you have raised up your hand to give*
9:16 [a] Ps. 106:6 [b] Deut. 1:26–33; 31:27 [1] *acted presumptuously* or *insolently* [2] Lit. *stiffened their necks, became stubborn* [3] *did not heed*
9:17 [a] Ps. 78:11, 42–45 [b] Num. 14:4 [c] Joel 2:13
9:18 [a] Ex. 32:4–8, 31 [1] *worked*
9:19 [a] Ps. 106:45 [b] 1 Cor. 10:1
9:20 [a] Num. 11:17 [b] Ex. 16:14–16 [c] Ex. 17:6
9:21 [a] Deut. 2:7 [b] Deut. 8:4; 29:5 [1] *did not wear out*
9:22 [a] Num. 21:21–35 [1] *districts*
9:23 [a] Gen. 15:5; 22:17; Heb. 11:12
9:24 [a] Josh. 1:2–4 [b] Josh. 18:1; [Ps. 44:2, 3]
9:25 [a] Num. 13:27 [b] Deut. 6:11; Josh. 24:13 [c] [Deut. 32:15] [d] Hos. 3:5 [1] *rich* [2] *cisterns* [3] *olive groves*
9:26 [a] Judg. 2:11 [b] 1 Kin. 14:9; Ps. 50:17 [c] 1 Kin. 18:4; 19:10; Matt. 23:37; Acts 7:52 [1] *warned* or *admonished*
9:27 [a] Judg. 2:14; Ps. 106:41 [b] Ps. 106:44 [c] Judg. 2:18 [1] *oppressed* [2] *deliverers*
9:28 [a] Judg. 3:12 [b] Ps. 106:43 [1] *rescued*
9:29 [a] Lev. 18:5; Rom. 10:5; [Gal. 3:12] [1] *acted presumptuously* [2] *did not heed* [3] *turned a stubborn shoulder*

4 *became stubborn, lit. stiffened their necks*
9:30 [a] 2 Kin. 17:13–18; 2 Chr. 36:11–20; Jer. 7:25 [b] [Acts 7:51]; 1 Pet. 1:11 [c] Is. 5:5 [1] *you had patience with* [2] *admonished* or *warned* [3] *listen*

thou them into the hand of the people of the lands.

31 Nevertheless [1]for thy great mercies' sake [a]thou didst not utterly consume them, nor forsake them; for thou *art* a gracious and merciful God.

32 Now therefore, our God, the great, the [a]mighty, and the [1]terrible God, who keepest covenant and mercy, let not all the [2]trouble seem little before thee, that hath come upon us, on our kings, on our princes, and on our priests, and on our prophets, and on our fathers, and on all thy people, [b]since the time of the kings of Assyria unto this day.

33 Howbeit [a]thou *art* just in all that is brought upon us; for thou hast done [1]right, but [b]we have done wickedly:

34 Neither have our kings, our princes, our priests, nor our fathers, kept thy law, nor hearkened unto thy commandments and thy testimonies, wherewith thou didst testify against them.

35 For they have [a]not served thee in their kingdom, and in thy great goodness that thou gavest them, and in the large and [1]fat land which thou gavest before them, neither turned they from their wicked works.

36 Behold, [a]we *are* servants this day, and *for* the land that thou gavest unto our fathers to eat the fruit thereof and the good thereof, behold, we *are* servants in it:

37 And [a]it yieldeth much increase unto the kings whom thou hast set over us because of our sins: also they have [b]dominion over our bodies, and over our cattle, at their pleasure, and we *are* in great distress.

38 And because of all this we [a]make a sure *covenant,* and write *it;* and our princes, Levites, *and* priests, [b]seal *unto it.*

## CHAPTER 10

Now those that [1]sealed *were,* Nehemiah, the [2]Tirshatha, [a]the son of Hachaliah, and Zidkijah,

2 [a]Seraiah, Azariah, Jeremiah,

3 Pashur, Amariah, Malchijah,

4 Hattush, Shebaniah, Malluch,

5 Harim, Meremoth, Obadiah,

6 Daniel, Ginnethon, Baruch,

7 Meshullam, Abijah, Mijamin,

8 Maaziah, Bilgai, Shemaiah: these *were* the priests.

9 And the Levites: both Jeshua the son of Azaniah, Binnui of the sons of Henadad, Kadmiel;

10 And their brethren, Shebaniah, Hodijah, Kelita, Pelaiah, Hanan,

11 Micha, Rehob, Hashabiah,

12 Zaccur, Sherebiah, Shebaniah,

13 Hodijah, Bani, Beninu.

14 The chief of the people; [a]Parosh, Pahath-moab, Elam, Zatthu, Bani,

15 Bunni, Azgad, Bebai,

16 Adonijah, Bigvai, Adin,

17 Ater, Hizkijah, Azzur,

18 Hodijah, Hashum, Bezai,

19 Hariph, Anathoth, Nebai,

20 Magpiash, Meshullam, Hezir,

21 Meshezabeel, Zadok, Jaddua,

22 Pelatiah, Hanan, Anaiah,

23 Hoshea, Hananiah, Hashub,

24 Hallohesh, Pileha, Shobek,

25 Rehum, Hashabnah, Maaseiah,

26 And Ahijah, Hanan, Anan,

27 Malluch, Harim, Baanah.

28 [a]And the rest of the people, the priests, the Levites, the [1]porters, the singers, the Nethinims, [b]and all they that had separated themselves from the people of the lands unto the law of God, their wives, their sons, and their daughters, every one having knowledge, and having understanding;

29 They [1]clave to their brethren, their nobles, [a]and entered into a curse, and into an oath, [b]to walk in God's law, which was given by Moses the servant of God, and to observe and do all the commandments of the LORD our Lord, and his [2]judgments and his statutes;

30 And that we would not [1]give [a]our daughters unto the people of the land, nor take their daughters for our sons:

31 [a]And *if* the people of the land bring [1]ware or any [2]victuals on the sabbath day to sell, *that* we would not buy it of them on the sabbath, or on the holy day: and *that* we would [3]leave the [b]seventh year, and the [c]exaction[4] of every debt.

32 Also we made ordinances for us, to charge ourselves yearly with the third [a]part of a shekel for the service of the house of our God;

33 For [a]the shewbread, and for the [b]continual [1]meat offering, and for the continual burnt offering, of the sabbaths, of the new moons, for the set feasts, and for the holy *things,* and for the sin offerings to make an atonement for Israel, and *for* all the work of the house of our God.

34 And we cast the lots among the priests, the Levites, and the people, [a]for the wood offering, to bring *it* into the house of our God, after the houses of our fathers, at times appointed year by year, to burn upon the altar of the LORD our God, [b]as *it is* written in the law:

35 And [a]to bring the firstfruits of our [1]ground, and the firstfruits of all fruit of all trees, year by year, unto the house of the LORD:

36 Also the [a]firstborn of our sons, and of our cattle, as *it is* written in the law, and the firstlings of our herds and of our flocks, to bring to the

### Cross-references (center column)

9:31 [a] Jer. 4:27; [Rom. 11:2–5] [1] *in thy great mercy thou*

9:32 [a] [Ex. 34:6, 7] [b] 2 Kin. 15:19; 17:3–6; Ezra 4:2, 10 [1] *awesome* [2] *hardship* or *weariness*

9:33 [a] Ps. 119:137; [Dan. 9:14] [b] Ps. 106:6; [Dan. 9:5, 6, 8] [1] *faithfully*

9:35 [a] Deut. 28:47 [1] *rich*

9:36 [a] Deut. 28:48; Ezra 9:9

9:37 [a] Deut. 28:33, 51 [b] Deut. 28:48

9:38 [a] 2 Kin. 23:3; 2 Chr. 29:10; Ezra 10:3 [b] Neh. 10:1

10:1 [a] Neh. 1:1 [1] *placed their seal on the document* [2] Lit. *governor*

10:2 [a] Neh. 12:1–21

10:14 [a] Ezra 2:3

10:28 [a] Ezra 2:36–43 [b] Ezra 9:1; Neh. 13:3 [1] *gatekeepers*

10:29 [a] Deut. 29:12; Neh. 5:12; Ps. 119:106 [b] 2 Kin. 23:3; 2 Chr. 34:31 [1] *joined with* [2] *ordinances*

10:30 [a] Ex. 34:16; Deut. 7:3; [Ezra 9:12] [1] *give as wives*

10:31 [a] Ex. 20:10; Lev. 23:3; Deut. 5:12 [b] Ex. 23:10, 11; Lev. 25:4; Jer. 34:14 [c] [Deut. 15:1, 2]; Neh. 5:12 [1] *merchandise* [2] *grain* [3] *forego the produce of the* [4] *collection*

10:32 [a] Ex. 30:11–16; 38:25, 26; 2 Chr. 24:6, 9; Matt. 17:24

10:33 [a] Lev. 24:5; 2 Chr. 2:4 [b] Num. 28; 29 [1] *grain or meal*

10:34 [a] Neh. 13:31; [Is. 40:16] [b] Lev. 6:12

10:35 [a] Ex. 23:19; 34:26; Lev. 19:23; Num. 18:12; Deut. 26:1, 2 [1] *land*

10:36 [a] Ex. 13:2, 12, 13; Lev. 27:26, 27; Num. 18:15, 16

house of our God, unto the priests that minister in the house of our God:

37 ªAnd *that* we should bring the firstfruits of our dough, and our offerings, and the fruit of all manner of trees, of wine and of oil, unto the priests, to the ¹chambers of the ²house of our God; and ᵇthe tithes of our ³ground unto the Levites, that the same Levites might have the tithes in all the ⁴cities of our tillage.

38 And the priest the son of Aaron shall be with the Levites, ªwhen the Levites take tithes: and the Levites shall bring up the tithe of the tithes unto the ¹house of our God, to ᵇthe ²chambers, into the treasure house.

39 For the children of Israel and the children of Levi ªshall bring the offering of the ¹corn, of the new wine, and the oil, unto the ²chambers, where *are* the vessels of the sanctuary, and the priests that minister, and the ³porters, ᵇand the singers: and we will not ᶜforsake the ⁴house of our God.

## CHAPTER 11

A ND the rulers of the people dwelt at Jerusalem: the rest of the people also cast lots, to bring one of ten to dwell in Jerusalem ªthe holy city, and nine parts *to dwell* in *other* cities.

2 And the people blessed all the men, that ªwillingly offered themselves to dwell at Jerusalem.

3 ªNow these *are* the chief of the province that dwelt in Jerusalem: but in the cities of Judah dwelt every one in his possession in their cities, *to wit*, Israel, the priests, and the Levites, and ᵇthe Nethinims, and the ᶜchildren of Solomon's servants.

4 And ªat Jerusalem dwelt *certain* of the children of Judah, and of the children of Benjamin. Of the children of Judah; Athaiah the son of Uzziah, the son of Zechariah, the son of Amariah, the son of Shephatiah, the son of Mahalaleel, of the children of ᵇPerez;

5 And Maaseiah the son of Baruch, the son of Col-hozeh, the son of Hazaiah, the son of Adaiah, the son of Joiarib, the son of Zechariah, the son of Shiloni.

6 All the sons of Perez that dwelt at Jerusalem *were* four hundred threescore and eight valiant men.

7 And these *are* the sons of Benjamin; Sallu the son of Meshullam, the son of Joed, the son of Pedaiah, the son of Kolaiah, the son of Maaseiah, the son of Ithiel, the son of Jesaiah.

8 And after him Gabbai, Sallai, nine hundred twenty and eight.

9 And Joel the son of Zichri *was* their overseer: and Judah the son of ¹Senuah *was* second over the city.

10 ªOf the priests: Jedaiah the son of Joiarib, Jachin.

11 Seraiah the son of Hilkiah, the son of Meshullam, the son of Zadok, the son of Meraioth, the son of Ahitub, *was* the ruler of the house of God.

12 And their brethren that did the work of the house *were* eight hundred twenty and two: and Adaiah the son of Jeroham, the son of Pelaliah, the son of Amzi, the son of Zechariah, the son of Pashur, the son of Malchiah,

13 And his brethren, chief of the fathers, two hundred forty and two: and Amashai the son of Azareel, the son of Ahasai, the son of Meshillemoth, the son of Immer,

14 And their brethren, ¹mighty men of valour, an hundred twenty and eight: and their overseer *was* Zabdiel, the son of *one* ²*of* the great men.

15 Also of the Levites: Shemaiah the son of Hashub, the son of Azrikam, the son of Hashabiah, the son of Bunni;

16 And ªShabbethai and ᵇJozabad, of the chief of the Levites, ¹*had* the oversight of ᶜthe ²outward business of the ³house of God.

17 And Mattaniah the son of ¹Micha, the son of Zabdi, the son of Asaph, *was* the ²principal to begin the thanksgiving in prayer: and Bakbukiah the second among his brethren, and Abda the son of Shammua, the son of Galal, the son of Jeduthun.

18 All the Levites in ªthe holy city *were* two hundred fourscore and four.

19 Moreover the ¹porters, Akkub, Talmon, and their brethren that kept the gates, *were* an hundred seventy and two.

20 And the residue of Israel, of the priests, *and* the Levites, *were* in all the cities of Judah, every one in his inheritance.

21 ªBut the Nethinims dwelt in Ophel: and Ziha and Gispa *were* over the Nethinims.

22 The overseer also of the Levites at Jerusalem *was* Uzzi the son of Bani, the son of Hashabiah, the son of Mattaniah, the son of Micha. Of the sons of Asaph, the singers *were* over the ¹business of the ²house of God.

23 For ª*it was* the king's commandment concerning them, that ¹a certain portion should be for the singers, due for every day.

24 And Pethahiah the son of Meshezabeel, of the children of ªZerah the son of Judah, *was* ᵇat¹ the king's hand in all matters concerning the people.

25 And for the villages, with their fields, *some* of the children of Judah dwelt at ªKirjath-arba, and *in* the villages thereof, and at Dibon, and *in*

### Center reference column

10:37 ª Lev. 23:17; Num. 15:19; 18:12; Deut. 18:4; 26:2
ᵇ Lev. 27:30; Num. 18:21; Mal. 3:10 ¹ *storerooms* ² Temple ³ *land* ⁴ *farming villages*
10:38 ª Num. 18:26 ᵇ 1 Chr. 9:26; 2 Chr. 31:11 ¹ Temple ² *rooms of the storehouse*
10:39 ª Deut. 12:6, 11; 2 Chr. 31:12; Neh. 13:12 ᵇ Neh. 13:10, 11 ᶜ [Heb. 10:25] ¹ *grain* ² *storerooms* ³ *gatekeepers* ⁴ Temple
11:1 ª Neh. 10:18; Matt. 4:5; 5:35; 27:53
11:2 ª Judg. 5:9; 2 Chr. 17:16
11:3 ª 1 Chr. 9:2, 3 ᵇ Ezra 2:43 ᶜ Ezra 2:55
11:4 ª 1 Chr. 9:3 ᵇ Gen. 38:29
11:9 ¹ Or *Hassenuah*

11:10 ª 1 Chr. 9:10
11:14 ¹ *mighty warriors* ² Heb. *haggedolim*
11:16 ª Ezra 10:15 ᵇ Ezra 8:33 ᶜ 1 Chr. 26:29 ¹ *had authority over* ² *outside* ³ Temple
11:17 ¹ Or *Michah* ² *leader who began*
11:18 ª Neh. 11:1
11:19 ¹ *gatekeepers*
11:21 ª 2 Chr. 27:3; Neh. 3:26
11:22 ¹ *service* ² Temple
11:23 ª Ezra 6:8, 9; 7:20 ¹ *a fixed share*
11:24 ª Gen. 38:30 ᵇ 1 Chr. 18:17 ¹ *the king's deputy*
11:25 ª Josh. 14:15

the villages thereof, and at Jekabzeel, and *in* the villages thereof,

26 And at Jeshua, and at Moladah, and at Beth-phelet,

27 And at Hazar-shual, and at Beer-sheba, and *in* the villages thereof,

28 And at Ziklag, and at Mekonah, and in the villages thereof,

29 And at En-rimmon, and at Za-reah, and at Jarmuth,

30 Zanoah, Adullam, and *in* their villages, at Lachish, and the fields thereof, at Azekah, and *in* the villages thereof. And they dwelt from Beer-sheba unto the valley of Hinnom.

31 The children also of Benjamin from Geba *dwelt* at Michmash, and Aija, and Beth-el, and *in* their villages,

32 *And* at Anathoth, Nob, Ananiah,

33 Hazor, Ramah, Gittaim,

34 Hadid, Zeboim, Neballat,

35 Lod, and Ono, ᵃthe valley of craftsmen.

36 And of the Levites *were* divisions *in* Judah, *and* in Benjamin.

## CHAPTER 12

Now these *are* the ᵃpriests and the Levites that went up with ᵇZe-rubbabel the son of Shealtiel, and Jeshua: ᶜSeraiah, Jeremiah, Ezra,

2 Amariah, ¹Malluch, Hattush,

3 ¹Shechaniah, ²Rehum, ³Mere-moth,

4 Iddo, ¹Ginnetho, ⁸Abijah,

5 ¹Miamin, ²Maadiah, Bilgah,

6 Shemaiah, and Joiarib, Jedaiah,

7 ¹Sallu, Amok, Hilkiah, Jedaiah. These *were* the chief of the priests and of their brethren in the days of ᵃJeshua.

8 Moreover the Levites: Jeshua, Binnui, Kadmiel, Sherebiah, Judah,¹ *and* Mattaniah, ᵃ*which was* over the thanksgiving, he and his brethren.

9 Also Bakbukiah and Unni, their brethren, *were* over against them in the watches.

10 And Jeshua begat Joiakim, Joiakim also begat Eliashib, and Eliashib begat Joiada,

11 And Joiada begat Jonathan, and Jonathan begat Jaddua.

12 And in the days of Joiakim were priests, the ᵃchief¹ of the fathers: of Seraiah, Meraiah; of Jeremiah, Han-aniah;

13 Of Ezra, Meshullam; of Amariah, Jehohanan;

14 Of ¹Melicu, Jonathan; of ²Sheba-niah, Joseph;

15 Of ¹Harim, Adna; of ²Meraioth, Helkai;

16 Of Iddo, Zechariah; of Gin-nethon, Meshullam;

17 Of Abijah, Zichri; of ¹Miniamin, of ²Moadiah, Piltai;

18 Of Bilgah, Shammua; of She-maiah, Jehonathan;

19 And of Joiarib, Mattenai; of Je-daiah, Uzzi;

20 Of ¹Sallai, Kallai; of Amok, Eber;

21 Of Hilkiah, Hashabiah; of Je-daiah, Nethaneel.

22 The Levites in the days of Eliashib, Joiada, and Johanan, and Jaddua, *were* ᵃrecorded ¹chief of the fathers: also the priests, to the reign of Darius the Persian.

23 The sons of Levi, the ¹chief of the fathers, *were* written in the book of the ᵃchronicles, even until the days of Johanan the son of Eliashib.

24 And the ¹chief of the Levites: Hashabiah, Sherebiah, and Jeshua the son of Kadmiel, with their breth-ren ²over against them, to ᵃpraise *and* to give thanks, ᵇaccording to the commandment of David the man of God, ᶜward³ over against ward.

25 Mattaniah, and Bakbukiah, Oba-diah, Meshullam, Talmon, Akkub, *were* ¹porters keeping the ward at the ²thresholds of the gates.

26 These *were* in the days of Joiakim the son of Jeshua, the son of ¹Jozadak, and in the days of Nehe-miah ᵃthe governor, and of Ezra the priest, ᵇthe scribe.

27 And at ᵃthe dedication of the wall of Jerusalem they sought the Levites out of all their places, to bring them to Jerusalem, to keep the dedication with gladness, ᵇboth with thanksgiv-ings, and with singing, *with* cymbals, ¹psalteries, and with harps.

28 And the sons of the singers gath-ered themselves together, both out of the plain country round about Jeru-salem, and from the ᵃvillages of Ne-tophathi;

29 Also from the house of Gil-gal, and out of the fields of Geba and Azmaveth: for the singers had builded them villages round about Jerusalem.

30 And the priests and the Levites ᵃpurified themselves, and purified the people, and the gates, and the wall.

31 Then I brought up the princes of Judah upon the wall, and appointed two ¹great *companies of them that gave* thanks, *whereof* ᵃone went on the right hand upon the wall ᵇtoward the dung gate:

32 And after them went Hoshaiah, and half of the princes of Judah,

33 And Azariah, Ezra, and Meshul-lam,

34 Judah, and Benjamin, and She-maiah, and Jeremiah,

35 And *certain* of the priests' sons ᵃwith trumpets; *namely,* Zechariah the son of Jonathan, the son of She-maiah, the son of Mattaniah, the son of Michaiah, the son of Zaccur, the son of Asaph:

### Center column notes

11:35 ᵃ 1 Chr. 4:14

12:1 ᵃ Ezra 2:1, 2; 7:7 ᵇ Neh. 7:7; Matt. 1:12, 13 ᶜ Neh. 10:2–8

12:2 ¹ *Melicu,* Neh. 12:14

12:3 ¹ *Sheba-niah,* Neh. 12:14 ² *Harim,* Neh. 12:15 ³ *Meraioth,* Neh. 12:15

12:4 ᵃ Luke 1:5 ¹ *Ginnethon,* Neh. 12:16

12:5 ¹ *Miniamin,* Neh. 12:17 ² *Moa-diah,* Neh. 12:17

12:7 ᵃ Ezra 3:2; Hag. 1:1; Zech. 3:1 ¹ *Sallai,* Neh. 12:20

12:8 ᵃ Neh. 11:17 ¹ *who read the thanksgiving psalms*

12:12 ᵃ Neh. 7:70, 71; 8:13; 11:13 ¹ *heads of the fathers' houses*

12:14 ¹ *Mal-luch,* Neh. 12:2 ² *Shechaniah,* Neh. 12:3

12:15 ¹ *Rehum,* Neh. 12:3 ² *Mere-moth,* Neh. 12:3

12:17 ¹ *Miamin,* Neh. 12:5 ² *Maa-diah,* Neh. 12:5

12:20 ¹ *Sallu,* Neh. 12:7

12:22 ᵃ 1 Chr. 24:6 ¹ *heads of the fathers' houses*

12:23 ᵃ 1 Chr. 9:14–22 ¹ *heads of the fathers' houses*

12:24 ᵃ Neh. 11:17 ᵇ Ezra 3:11 ᶜ 1 Chr. 23–26 ¹ *heads* ² *across from* ³ *group alternat-ing with group*

12:25 ¹ *gatekeep-ers* ² *storerooms*

12:26 ᵃ Neh. 8:9 ᵇ Ezra 7:6, ¹¹ ¹ *Jehozadak,* 1 Chr. 6:14

12:27 ᵃ Deut. 20:5; Neh. 7:1; Ps. 30:title ᵇ 1 Chr. 25:6; 2 Chr. 5:13; 7:6 ¹ *stringed instruments*

12:28 ᵃ 1 Chr. 9:16

12:30 ᵃ Ezra 6:20; Neh. 13:22, 30

12:31 ᵃ Neh. 12:38 ᵇ Neh. 2:13; 3:13 ¹ *Lit. large thanks-giving choirs*

12:35 ᵃ Num. 10:2, 8

36 And his brethren, Shemaiah, and Azarael, Milalai, Gilalai, Maai, Nethaneel, and Judah, Hanani, with ᵃthe musical ᵇinstruments of David the man of God, and Ezra the scribe before them.

37 ᵃAnd at the fountain gate, which was ¹over against them, they went up by ᵇthe stairs of the ᶜcity of David, ²at the going up of the wall, above the house of David, even unto ᵈthe water gate eastward.

38 ᵃAnd the other *company of them that gave* thanks went over against *them,* and I after them, and the half of the people upon the wall, from beyond ᵇthe tower of the furnaces even unto ᶜthe broad wall;

39 ᵃAnd from above the gate of Ephraim, and above ᵇthe old gate, and above ᶜthe fish gate, ᵈand the tower of Hananeel, and the tower of ¹Meah, even unto ᵉthe sheep gate: and they stood still in ᶠthe prison gate.

40 So stood the two *companies of them that gave* thanks in the house of God, and I, and the half of the rulers with me:

41 And the priests; Eliakim, Maaseiah, ¹Miniamin, Michaiah, Elioenai, Zechariah, *and* Hananiah, with trumpets;

42 And Maaseiah, and Shemaiah, and Eleazar, and Uzzi, and Jehohanan, and Malchijah, and Elam, and Ezer. And the singers sang loud, with Jezrahiah *their* overseer.

43 Also that day they offered great sacrifices, and rejoiced: for God had made them rejoice with great joy: the wives also and the children rejoiced: so that the joy of Jerusalem was heard even ᵃafar off.

44 ᵃAnd at that time were some appointed over the ¹chambers for the treasures, for the offerings, for the firstfruits, and for the ᵇtithes, to gather into them out of the fields of the cities the ²portions of the law for the priests and Levites: for Judah rejoiced for the priests and for the Levites that ³waited.

45 And both the singers and the ¹porters kept the ²ward of their God, and the ward of the purification, ᵃaccording to the commandment of David, *and* of Solomon his son.

46 For in the days of David ᵃand Asaph of old *there were* ¹chief of the singers, and songs of praise and thanksgiving unto God.

47 And all Israel in the days of Zerubbabel, and in the days ¹of Nehemiah, gave the portions of the singers and the porters, ᵃevery day his portion: ᵇand they ²sanctified *holy things* unto the Levites; ᶜand the Levites sanctified *them* unto the children of Aaron.

## CHAPTER 13

ON that day ᵃthey read in the book of Moses in the audience of the people; and therein was found written, ᵇthat the Ammonite and the Moabite should not come into the congregation of God for ever;

2 Because they met not the children of Israel with bread and with water, but ᵃhired Balaam against them, that he should curse them: ᵇhowbeit our God turned the curse into a blessing.

3 Now it came to pass, when they had heard the law, ᵃthat they separated from Israel all the mixed multitude.

4 And before this, ᵃEliashib the priest, having the oversight of the ¹chamber of the house of our God, *was* allied unto ᵇTobiah:

5 And he had prepared for him a great ¹chamber, ᵃwhere aforetime they laid the ²meat offerings, the frankincense, and the vessels, and the tithes of the ³corn, the new wine, and the oil, ᵇwhich was commanded *to be given* to the Levites, and the singers, and the ⁴porters; and the offerings of the priests.

6 But in all this *time* was not I at Jerusalem: ᵃfor in the two and thirtieth year of Artaxerxes king of Babylon ¹came I unto the king, and after certain days ²obtained I leave of the king:

7 And I came to Jerusalem, and understood of the evil that Eliashib did for Tobiah, in ᵃpreparing him a chamber in the courts of the ¹house of God.

8 And it grieved me ¹sore: therefore I cast forth all the household stuff of Tobiah out of the chamber.

9 Then I commanded, and they ᵃcleansed the ¹chambers: and thither brought I again the vessels of the house of God, with the ²meat offering and the frankincense.

10 And I perceived that the portions of the Levites had ᵃnot been given *them:* for the Levites and the singers, that did the work, were fled every one to ᵇhis field.

11 Then ᵃcontended I with the rulers, and said, ᵇWhy is the house of God forsaken? And I gathered them together, and set them in their place.

12 ᵃThen brought all Judah the tithe of the ¹corn and the new wine and the oil unto the ²treasuries.

13 ᵃAnd I ¹made treasurers over the ²treasuries, Shelemiah the priest, and Zadok the scribe, and of the Levites, Pedaiah: and next to them *was* Hanan the son of Zaccur, the son of Mattaniah: for they were ³counted ᵇfaithful, and their ⁴office *was* to distribute unto their brethren.

12:36 ᵃ 1 Chr. 23:5
ᵇ 2 Chr. 29:26, 27
12:37 ᵃ Neh. 2:14;
3:15  ᵇ Neh. 3:15
ᶜ 2 Sam. 5:7–9
ᵈ Neh. 3:26; 8:1, 3,
16 ¹ *opposite* ² *on the stairway*
12:38 ᵃ Neh.
12:31 ᵇ Neh. 3:11
ᶜ Neh. 3:8
12:39 ᵃ 2 Kin. 14:13;
Neh. 8:16  ᵇ Neh.
3:6  ᶜ Neh. 3:3
ᵈ Neh. 3:1  ᵉ Neh.
3:32  ᶠ Jer. 32:2
¹ *Or Hammeah, the tower of the hundred*
12:41 ¹ *Miamin,* Neh. 12:5
12:43 ᵃ Ezra 3:13
12:44 ᵃ 2 Chr. 31:11, 12; Neh. 13:5, 12, 13
ᵇ Neh. 10:37–39
¹ *rooms of the storehouse* ² *portions specified by* ³ Lit. *stood*
12:45 ᵃ 1 Chr. 25; 26 ¹ *gatekeepers* ² *watch*
12:46 ᵃ 1 Chr. 25:1; 2 Chr. 29:30 ¹ *heads*
12:47 ᵃ Neh. 11:23 ᵇ Num. 18:21, 24 ᶜ Num. 18:26 ¹ *for* ² *set apart*
13:1 ᵃ [Deut. 31:11, 12]; 2 Kin. 23:2; Neh. 8:3, 8; 9:3; Is. 34:16 ᵇ Deut. 23:3, 4
13:2 ᵃ Num. 22:5; Josh. 24:9, 10 ᵇ Num. 23:11; 24:10; Deut. 23:5
13:3 ᵃ Neh. 9:2; 10:28
13:4 ᵃ Neh. 12:10 ᵇ Neh. 2:10; 4:3; 6:1 ¹ *storerooms*
13:5 ᵃ Neh. 12:44 ᵇ Num. 18:21, 24 ¹ *storerooms* ² *meal or grain* ³ *grain* ⁴ *gatekeepers*
13:6 ᵃ Neh. 5:14–16 ¹ *returned* ² *asked*
13:7 ᵃ Neh. 13:1, 5 ¹ *Temple*
13:8 ¹ *bitterly*
13:9 ᵃ 2 Chr. 29:5, 15, 16 ¹ *rooms* ² *grain or meal*
13:10 ᵃ Neh. 10:37; Mal. 3:8 ᵇ Num. 35:2
13:11 ᵃ Neh. 13:17, 25 ᵇ Neh. 10:39
13:12 ᵃ Neh. 10:38; 12:44 ¹ *grain* ² *storehouses*
13:13 ᵃ 2 Chr. 31:12 ᵇ 1 Cor. 4:2 ¹ *appointed* ² *storehouses* ³ *considered* ⁴ *duty*

14 [a]Remember me, O my God, concerning this, and wipe not out my good deeds that I have done for the house of my God, and for the [1]offices thereof.

15 In those days saw I in Judah *some* treading wine presses [a]on the sabbath, and bringing in sheaves, and [1]lading asses; as also wine, grapes, and figs, and all *manner of* burdens, [b]which they brought into Jerusalem on the sabbath day: and I [2]testified *against them* in the day wherein they sold [3]victuals.

16 There dwelt men of Tyre also therein, which brought fish, and all manner of [1]ware, and sold on the sabbath unto the children of Judah, and in Jerusalem.

17 Then I contended with the nobles of Judah, and said unto them, What evil thing *is* this that ye do, and profane the sabbath day?

18 [a]Did not your fathers thus, and did not our God bring all this [1]evil upon us, and upon this city? yet ye bring more wrath upon Israel by profaning the sabbath.

19 And it came to pass, that when the gates of Jerusalem [a]began to be dark before the sabbath, I commanded that the gates should be shut, and charged that they should not be opened till after the sabbath: [b]and *some* of my servants set I at the gates, *that* there should no burden be brought in on the sabbath day.

20 So the merchants and sellers of all kind of [1]ware [2]lodged [3]without Jerusalem once or twice.

21 Then I [1]testified against them, and said unto them, Why [2]lodge ye [3]about the wall? if ye do *so* again, I will lay hands on you. From that time forth came they no *more* on the sabbath.

22 And I commanded the Levites that [a]they should cleanse themselves, and *that* they should come

13:14 [a] Neh. 5:19;
13:22, 31 [1] *services*
13:15 [a] [Ex.
20:10] [b] Neh.
10:31; [Jer. 17:21]
[1] *loading donkeys*
[2] *warned* [3] *provisions*
13:16 [1] *merchandise*
13:18 [a] Ezra
9:13; [Jer. 17:21]
[1] *disaster*
13:19 [a] Lev. 23:32
[b] Jer. 17:21, 22
13:20 [1] *merchandise* [2] *spent the night* [3] *outside*
13:21 [1] *warned*
[2] *spend the night*
[3] Lit. *before*
13:22 [a] Neh. 12:30

[1] *guard* [2] *set apart*
13:23 [a] Ezra 9:2
[b] Neh. 4:7
13:25 [a] Prov. 28:4
[b] Neh. 10:29, 30
[1] *announced a curse on* [2] *struck*
13:26 [a] 1 Kin. 11:1,
2 [b] 2 Sam. 12:24,
25 [c] 1 Kin. 11:4–8
[1] *foreign, pagan*
13:27 [a] [Ezra 10:2]
[1] *foreign, pagan*
13:28 [a] Neh. 12:10,
12 [b] Neh. 4:1, 7;
6:1, 2
13:29 [a] Neh. 6:14
[b] Mal. 2:4, 11, 12
13:30 [a] Neh. 10:30
[b] Neh. 12:1 [1] *duties to* [2] *service*
13:31 [a] Neh. 10:34
[b] Neh. 13:14, 22

*and* [1]keep the gates, to [2]sanctify the sabbath day. Remember me, O my God, *concerning* this also, and spare me according to the greatness of thy mercy.

23 In those days also saw I Jews *that* [a]had married wives of [b]Ashdod, of Ammon, *and* of Moab:

24 And their children spake half in the speech of Ashdod, and could not speak in the Jews' language, but according to the language of each people.

25 And I [a]contended with them, and [1]cursed them, and [2]smote certain of them, and plucked off their hair, and made them [b]swear by God, *saying,* Ye shall not give your daughters unto their sons, nor take their daughters unto your sons, or for yourselves.

26 [a]Did not Solomon king of Israel sin by these things? yet among many nations was there no king like him, [b]who was beloved of his God, and God made him king over all Israel: [c]nevertheless even him did [1]outlandish women cause to sin.

27 Shall we then hearken unto you to do all this great evil, to [a]transgress against our God in marrying [1]strange wives?

28 And *one* of the sons [a]of Joiada, the son of Eliashib the high priest, *was* son in law to [b]Sanballat the Horonite: therefore I chased him from me.

29 [a]Remember them, O my God, because they have defiled the priesthood, and [b]the covenant of the priesthood, and of the Levites.

30 [a]Thus cleansed I them from all strangers, and [b]appointed the [1]wards of the priests and the Levites, every one in his [2]business;

31 And for [a]the wood offering, at times appointed, and for the firstfruits. [b]Remember me, O my God, for good.

# THE BOOK OF
# ESTHER

God's hand of providence and protection on behalf of His people is evident throughout the Book of Esther, though His name does not appear once. Haman's plot brings grave danger to the Jews and is countered by the courage of beautiful Esther and the counsel of her wise cousin Mordecai, resulting in a great deliverance. The Feast of Purim becomes an annual reminder of God's faithfulness on behalf of His people.

Esther's Hebrew name was *Hadassah*, "Myrtle" (2:7), but her Persian name *Ester* was derived from the Persian word for "Star" (*Stara*). The Greek title for this book is *Esther*, and the Latin title is *Hester*.

## CHAPTER 1

Now it came to pass in the days of [a]Ahasuerus,[1] (this *is* Ahasuerus that reigned, [b]from India even unto Ethiopia, [c]*over* an hundred and seven and twenty provinces:)

2 *That* in those days, when the king Ahasuerus [a]sat on the throne of his kingdom, which *was* in [b]Shushan[1] the [2]palace,

3 In the third year of his reign, he [a]made a feast unto all his princes and his servants; the power of Persia and Media, the nobles and princes of the provinces, *being* before him:

4 When he shewed the riches of his glorious kingdom and the honour of his excellent majesty many days, *even* an hundred and fourscore days.

5 And when these days were [1]expired, the king made a feast unto all the people that were present in [2]Shushan the [3]palace, both unto great and small, seven days, in the court of the garden of the king's palace;

6 *Where were* white, green, and blue, [1]*hangings,* fastened with cords of fine linen and purple to silver rings and pillars of marble: [a]the beds *were of* gold and silver, upon a pavement of red, and blue, and white, and black, marble.

7 And they gave *them* drink in vessels of gold, (the vessels being diverse one from another,) and royal wine in abundance, [a]according to the [1]state of the king.

8 [1]And the drinking *was* according to the law; none did compel: for so the king had [2]appointed to all the officers of his house, that they should do according to every man's pleasure.

9 Also Vashti the queen made a feast for the women *in* the royal house which *belonged* to king Ahasuerus.

10 On the seventh day, when the heart of the king was merry with wine, he commanded Mehuman, Biztha, [a]Harbona, Bigtha, and Abagtha,

Zethar, and Carcas, the seven [1]chamberlains that served in the presence of Ahasuerus the king,

11 To bring Vashti the queen before the king with the crown royal, to shew the people and the princes her beauty: for she *was* [1]fair to look on.

12 But the queen Vashti refused to come at the king's commandment by *his* chamberlains: therefore was the king [1]very wroth, and his anger burned in him.

13 Then the king said to the [a]wise men, [b]which knew the times, (for so *was* the king's manner toward all that knew law and judgment:

14 And the next unto him *was* Carshena, Shethar, Admatha, Tarshish, Meres, Marsena, *and* Memucan, the [a]seven princes of Persia and Media, [b]which [1]saw the king's face, *and* which [2]sat the first in the kingdom;)

15 What shall we do unto the queen Vashti according to law, because she hath not performed the commandment of the king Ahasuerus by the chamberlains?

16 And Memucan answered before the king and the princes, Vashti the queen hath not done wrong to the king only, but also to all the princes, and to all the people that *are* in all the provinces of the king Ahasuerus.

17 For *this* [1]deed of the queen shall come abroad unto all women, so that they shall [a]despise their husbands in their eyes, when it shall be reported, The king Ahasuerus commanded Vashti the queen to be brought in before him, but she came not.

18 *Likewise* shall the ladies of Persia and Media say this day unto all the king's princes, which have heard of the deed of the queen. Thus *shall there arise* too much contempt and wrath.

19 If it please the king, [1]let there go a royal commandment from him, and let it be written among the laws of the Persians and the Medes, that it [2]be [a]not altered, That Vashti come no

1:1 [a] Ezra 4:6
[b] Esth. 8:9 [c] Dan.
6:1 [1] Generally
identified with
Xerxes I (485–
464 B.C.)
1:2 [a] 1 Kin. 1:46
[b] Neh. 1:1 [1] Or
Susa [2] *citadel*
1:3 [a] Gen. 40:20
1:5 [1] *completed*
[2] Or Susa
[3] *citadel*
1:6 [a] Amos 2:8;
6:4 [1] *Linen curtains*
1:7 [a] Esth. 2:18
[1] *generosity*
1:8 [1] *In accordance with the law, the drinking was not compulsory* [2] *ordered*
1:10 [a] Esth. 7:9

[1] *eunuchs*
1:11 [1] *lovely to behold*
1:12 [1] *furious*
1:13 [a] Jer. 10:7;
Dan. 2:12; Matt.
2:1 [b] 1 Chr. 12:32
1:14 [a] Ezra 7:14
[b] 2 Kin. 25:19;
[Matt. 18:10]
[1] *had access to the king* [2] *ranked highest*
1:17 [a] [Eph. 5:33]
[1] *behaviour*
1:19 [a] Esth. 8:8;
Dan. 6:8 [1] *let a royal decree go forth* [2] Lit. *pass not away*

more before king Ahasuerus; and let the king give her royal [3]estate unto another that is better than she.

20 And when the king's decree which he shall make shall be published throughout all his empire, (for it is great,) all the wives shall [a]give to their husbands honour, both to great and small.

21 And the saying pleased the king and the princes; and the king did according to the word of Memucan:

22 For he sent letters into all the king's provinces, [a]into every province according to the writing thereof, and to every people after their language, that every man should [b]bear rule in his own house, and [1]that *it* should be published according to the language of every people.

## CHAPTER 2

AFTER these things, when the wrath of king Ahasuerus [1]was appeased, he remembered Vashti, and [a]what she had done, and what was decreed against her.

2 Then said the king's servants that ministered unto him, Let there be fair young virgins sought for the king:

3 And let the king appoint officers in all the provinces of his kingdom, that they may gather together all the fair young virgins unto [1]Shushan the [2]palace, to the house of the women, unto the custody of [3]Hege the king's [4]chamberlain, [5]keeper of the women; and let their [6]things for purification be given *them:*

4 And let the maiden which pleaseth the king be queen instead of Vashti. And the thing pleased the king; and he did so.

5 *Now* in [1]Shushan the palace there was a certain Jew, whose name *was* Mordecai, the son of Jair, the son of Shimei, the son of [a]Kish, a Benjamite;

6 [a]Who[1] had been carried away from Jerusalem with the captivity which had been carried away with [2]Jeconiah king of Judah, whom Nebuchadnezzar the king of Babylon had carried away.

7 And [1]he brought up Hadassah, that *is,* Esther, [a]his uncle's daughter: for she had neither father nor mother, and the maid *was* [2]fair and beautiful; whom Mordecai, when her father and mother were dead, took for his own daughter.

8 So it came to pass, when the king's commandment and his decree was heard, and when many maidens were [a]gathered together unto [1]Shushan the [2]palace, to the custody of Hegai, that Esther was brought also unto the king's house, to the custody of Hegai, [3]keeper of the women.

9 And the maiden pleased him, and she obtained kindness of him; and he speedily gave her her [a]things[1] for purification, with [2]such things as belonged to her, and seven maidens, *which were* [3]meet to be given her, out of the king's house: and [4]he preferred her and her maids unto the best *place* of the house of the women.

10 [a]Esther had not [1]shewed her people nor her kindred: for Mordecai had charged her that she should not shew *it.*

11 And Mordecai walked every day before the court of the women's house, to know how Esther did, and what should become of her.

12 Now when every maid's turn was come to go in to king Ahasuerus, after that she had been twelve months, according to the manner of the women, (for so were the days of their purifications accomplished, *to wit,* six months with oil of myrrh, and six months with sweet odours, and with *other* [1]things for the purifying of the women;)

13 Then thus came *every* maiden unto the king; whatsoever she desired was given her to go with her out of the house of the women unto the king's house.

14 In the evening she went, and on the morrow she returned into the second house of the women, to the custody of Shaashgaz, the king's [1]chamberlain, which kept the concubines: she came in unto the king no more, except the king delighted in her, and [2]that she were called by name.

15 Now when the turn of Esther, [a]the daughter of Abihail the uncle of Mordecai, who had taken her for his daughter, was come to go in unto the king, she [1]required nothing but what Hegai the king's chamberlain, the keeper of the women, [2]appointed. And Esther [b]obtained favour in the sight of all them that looked upon her.

16 So Esther was taken unto king Ahasuerus into his [1]house royal in the tenth month, which *is* the month Tebeth, in the seventh year of his reign.

17 And the king loved Esther above all the women, and she obtained grace and favour in his sight more than all the virgins; so that he set the royal [a]crown upon her head, and made her queen instead of Vashti.

18 Then the king [a]made a great feast unto all his princes and his servants, *even* Esther's feast; and he [1]made a release to the provinces, and gave gifts, [2]according to the state of the king.

19 And when the virgins were gathered together the second time, then Mordecai sat in the king's gate.

20 [a]Esther had not *yet* [1]shewed her kindred nor her people; as Mordecai had charged her: for Esther did the commandment of Mordecai, like as when she was brought up with him.

21 In those days, while Mordecai sat in the king's gate, two of the king's [1]chamberlains, [2]Bigthan and Teresh, of those which kept the door, were [3]wroth, and sought to lay hand on the king Ahasuerus.

22 And the thing was known to Mordecai, [a]who told *it* unto Esther the queen; and Esther certified the king *thereof* in Mordecai's name.

23 And when [1]inquisition was made of the matter, it was found out; therefore they were both hanged on a tree: and it was written in [a]the book of the chronicles before the king.

## CHAPTER 3

AFTER these things did king Ahasuerus promote Haman the son of Hammedatha the [a]Agagite, and [b]advanced him, and [1]set his seat above all the princes that *were* with him.

2 And all the king's servants, that *were* [a]in the king's gate, bowed, and [1]reverenced Haman: for the king had so commanded concerning him. But Mordecai [b]bowed not, nor did *him* reverence.

3 Then the king's servants, which *were* in the king's gate, said unto Mordecai, Why transgressest thou the [a]king's commandment?

4 Now it came to pass, when they spake daily unto him, and he hearkened not unto them, that they told Haman, to see whether Mordecai's [1]matters would stand: for [2]he had told them that he *was* a Jew.

5 And when Haman saw that Mordecai [a]bowed not, nor did him reverence, then was Haman [b]full of wrath.

6 And he [1]thought scorn to lay hands on Mordecai alone; for they had [2]shewed him the people of Mordecai: wherefore Haman [a]sought to destroy all the Jews that *were* throughout the whole kingdom of Ahasuerus, *even* the people of Mordecai.

7 In the first month, that *is*, the month Nisan, in the twelfth year of king Ahasuerus, [a]they cast Pur, that *is*, the lot, before Haman [1]from day to day, and from month to month, *to* the twelfth *month*, that *is*, the month Adar.

8 And Haman said unto king Ahasuerus, There is a certain people scattered abroad and dispersed among the people in all the provinces of thy kingdom; and [a]their laws *are* [1]diverse from all people; neither keep they the king's laws: therefore it is not for the king's profit to [2]suffer them.

9 If it please the king, let it be written that they may be destroyed: and I will pay ten thousand talents of silver to the hands of those that have the charge of the business, to bring *it* into the king's treasuries.

10 And the king [a]took [b]his [1]ring from his hand, and gave it unto Haman the son of Hammedatha the Agagite, the Jews' [c]enemy.

11 And the king said unto Haman, The silver *is* given to thee, the people also, to do with them as it seemeth good to thee.

12 [a]Then were the king's scribes called on the thirteenth day of the first month, and there was written according to all that Haman had commanded unto the king's [1]lieutenants, and to the governors that *were* over every province, and to the rulers of every people of every province [b]according to the writing thereof, and *to* every people after their language; [c]in the name of king Ahasuerus was it written, and sealed with the king's [2]ring.

13 And the letters were [a]sent by [1]posts into all the king's provinces, to destroy, to kill, and to [2]cause to perish, all Jews, both young and old, little children and women, [b]in one day, *even* upon the thirteenth *day* of the twelfth month, which *is* the month Adar, and [c]to [3]take the spoil of them for a prey.

14 [a]The copy of the writing [1]for a commandment to be given in every province was published unto all people, that they should be ready against that day.

15 The [1]posts went out, being hastened by the king's commandment, and the decree was given in [2]Shushan the [3]palace. And the king and Haman sat down to drink; but [a]the city Shushan was [4]perplexed.

## CHAPTER 4

WHEN Mordecai perceived all that was done, Mordecai [a]rent[1] his clothes, and put on sackcloth [b]with ashes, and went out into the midst of the city, and [c]cried with a loud and a bitter cry;

2 And came even before the king's gate: for none *might* enter into the king's gate clothed with sackcloth.

3 And in every province, whithersoever the king's commandment and his decree came, *there was* great mourning among the Jews, and fasting, and weeping, and wailing; and many lay in sackcloth and ashes.

4 So Esther's maids and her [1]chamberlains came and told *it* her. Then was the queen [2]exceedingly grieved; and she sent raiment to clothe Mordecai, and to take away his sackcloth from him: but he received *it* not.

---

2:20 [a] Esth. 2:10; [Prov. 22:6] [1] *revealed the identity of*
2:21 [1] *eunuchs* [2] Or *Bigthana,* Esth. 6:2 [3] *furious*
2:22 [a] Esth. 6:1, 2
2:23 [a] Esth. 6:1 [1] *inquiry*
3:1 [a] Num. 24:7; 1 Sam. 15:8 [b] Esth. 5:11 [1] *set his rank*
3:2 [a] Esth. 2:19, 21; 5:9 [b] Esth. 3:5; Ps. 15:4 [1] *paid homage to*
3:3 [a] Esth. 3:2
3:4 [1] *words* [2] *Mordecai*
3:5 [a] Esth. 3:2; 5:9 [b] Dan. 3:19
3:6 [a] Ps. 83:4; [Rev. 12:1–17] [1] *disdained* [2] *revealed to him the identity of*
3:7 [a] Esth. 9:24–26 [1] *to determine the day and the month*
3:8 [a] Ezra 4:12–15; Acts 16:20, 21 [1] *different from all other people's* [2] *let them remain*
3:10 [a] Gen. 41:42 [b] Esth. 8:2, 8 [c] Esth. 7:6 [1] *signet ring*
3:12 [a] Esth. 8:9 [b] Esth. 1:22 [c] 1 Kin. 21:8; Esth. 8:8–10 [1] *satraps* [2] *signet ring*
3:13 [a] 2 Chr. 30:6; Esth. 8:10, 14 [b] Esth. 8:12 [c] Esth. 8:11; 9:10 [1] *couriers* [2] *annihilate* [3] *plunder their possessions*
3:14 [a] Esth. 8:13, 14 [1] *as law*
3:15 [a] Esth. 8:15; [Prov. 29:2] [1] *couriers* [2] Or *Susa* [3] *citadel* [4] *in confusion*
4:1 [a] 2 Sam. 1:11; Esth. 3:8–10; Jon. 3:5, 6 [b] Josh. 7:6; Ezek. 27:30 [c] Gen. 27:34 [1] *tore*
4:4 [1] *eunuchs* [2] *deeply distressed*

5 Then called Esther for Hatach, *one* of the king's [1]chamberlains, whom he had appointed to attend upon her, and gave him a commandment to Mordecai, to know what it *was,* and why it *was.*

6 So Hatach went forth to Mordecai unto the street of the city, which *was* before the king's gate.

7 And Mordecai told him of all that had happened unto him, and of [a]the sum of the money that Haman had promised to pay to the king's treasuries for the Jews, to destroy them.

8 Also he gave him [a]the copy of the writing of the decree that was given at [1]Shushan to destroy them, to shew *it* unto Esther, and to declare *it* unto her, and to charge her that she should go in unto the king, to make supplication unto him, and to [2]make request before him for her people.

9 And Hatach came and told Esther the words of Mordecai.

10 Again Esther spake unto Hatach, and gave him commandment unto Mordecai;

11 All the king's servants, and the people of the king's provinces, do know, that whosoever, whether man or woman, shall come unto the king into [a]the inner court, who is not called, [b]there is one law of his to put *him* to death, except such [c]to whom the king shall hold out the golden sceptre, that he may live: but I have not been [d]called to come in unto the king these thirty days.

12 And they told to Mordecai Esther's words.

13 Then Mordecai commanded to answer Esther, Think not with thyself that thou shalt escape in the king's house, more than all the Jews.

14 For if thou [1]altogether holdest thy peace at this time, *then* shall there [2]enlargement and deliverance arise to the Jews from another place; but thou and thy father's house shall be destroyed: and who knoweth whether thou art come to the kingdom for *such* a time as this?

15 Then Esther [1]bade *them* return Mordecai *this answer,*

16 Go, gather together all the Jews that are present in [1]Shushan, and fast ye for me, and neither eat nor drink [a]three days, night or day: I also and my maidens will fast likewise; and so will I go in unto the king, which *is* not according to the law: [b]and if I perish, I perish.

17 So Mordecai went his way, and did according to all that Esther had commanded him.

## CHAPTER 5

Now it came to pass [a]on the third day, that Esther put on *her* royal apparel, and stood in [b]the inner court of the king's house, [1]over against the king's house: and the king sat upon his royal throne in the royal house, [1]over against the gate of the house.

2 And it was so, when the king saw Esther the queen standing in the court, *that* [a]she obtained favour in his sight: and [b]the king held out to Esther the golden sceptre that *was* in his hand. So Esther drew near, and touched the top of the sceptre.

3 Then said the king unto her, What wilt thou, queen Esther? and what *is* thy request? [a]it shall be even given thee to the half of the kingdom.

4 And Esther answered, If *it seem* good unto the king, let the king and Haman come this day unto the banquet that I have prepared for him.

5 Then the king said, [1]Cause Haman to make haste, that he may do as Esther hath said. So the king and Haman came to the banquet that Esther had prepared.

6 [a]And the king said unto Esther at the banquet of wine, [b]What *is* thy petition? and it shall be granted thee: and what *is* thy request? even to the half of the kingdom it shall be performed.

7 Then answered Esther, and said, My petition and my request *is;*

8 If I have found favour in the sight of the king, and if it please the king to grant my petition, and [1]to perform my request, let the king and Haman come to the [a]banquet that I shall prepare for them, and I will do to morrow as the king hath said.

9 Then went Haman forth that day [a]joyful and with a glad heart: but when Haman saw Mordecai in the king's gate, [b]that he stood not up, [1]nor moved for him, he was full of indignation against Mordecai.

10 Nevertheless Haman [a]refrained himself: and when he came home, he sent and called for his friends, and Zeresh his wife.

11 And Haman told them of the glory of his riches, and [a]the multitude of his children, and all *the things* wherein the king had promoted him, and how he had [b]advanced him above the princes and servants of the king.

12 Haman said moreover, Yea, Esther the queen did let no man come in with the king unto the banquet that she had prepared but myself; and to morrow am I invited unto her also with the king.

13 Yet all this availeth me nothing, so long as I see Mordecai the Jew sitting at the king's gate.

14 Then said Zeresh his wife and all his friends unto him, Let a [a]gallows[1] be made of [2]fifty cubits high, and

---

4:5 [1] eunuchs
4:7 [a] Esth. 3:9
4:8 [a] Esth. 3:14, 15 [1] Or *Susa* [2] *plead*
4:11 [a] Esth. 5:1; 6:4 [b] Dan. 2:9 [c] Esth. 5:2; 8:4 [d] Esth. 2:14
4:14 [1] *remain completely silent* [2] *relief*
4:15 [1] *ordered them to*
4:16 [a] Esth. 5:1 [b] Gen. 43:14 [1] Or *Susa*
5:1 [a] Esth. 4:16

[b] Esth. 4:11; 6:4 [1] *across from*
5:2 [a] [Prov. 21:1] [b] Esth. 4:11; 8:4
5:3 [a] Esth. 7:2; Mark 6:23
5:5 [1] *Bring Haman quickly*
5:6 [a] Esth. 7:2 [b] Esth. 9:12
5:8 [a] Esth. 6:14 [1] *to fulfil*
5:9 [a] [Job 20:5; Luke 6:25] [b] Esth. 3:5 [1] *trembled before him*
5:10 [a] 2 Sam. 13:22
5:11 [a] Esth. 9:7–10 [b] Esth. 3:1
5:14 [a] Esth. 7:9 [1] Lit. *tree or wood* [2] About 75 feet

to morrow [b]speak thou unto the king that Mordecai may be hanged thereon: then go thou in merrily with the king unto the banquet. And the thing pleased Haman; and he caused [c]the gallows to be made.

## CHAPTER 6

O[N] that night [1]could not the king sleep, and he commanded to bring [a]the book of records of the chronicles; and they were read before the king.

2 And it was found written, that Mordecai had told of [1]Bigthana and Teresh, two of the king's [2]chamberlains, the keepers of the door, who sought to lay hand on the king Ahasuerus.

3 And the king said, What honour and dignity hath been done to Mordecai for this? Then said the king's servants that ministered unto him, [1]There is nothing done for him.

4 And the king said, Who *is* in the court? Now Haman was come into [a]the outward court of the king's house, [b]to speak unto the king to hang Mordecai on the gallows that he had prepared for him.

5 And the king's servants said unto him, Behold, Haman standeth in the court. And the king said, Let him come in.

6 So Haman came in. And the king said unto him, What shall be done unto the man whom the king delighteth to honour? Now Haman thought in his heart, To whom would the king delight to do honour more than to [a]myself?

7 And Haman answered the king, For the man whom the king delighteth to honour,

8 Let the royal [1]apparel be brought which the king [2]*useth* to wear, and [a]the horse that the king rideth upon, and the [3]crown royal which is set upon [4]his head:

9 And let this [1]apparel and horse be delivered to the hand of one of the king's most noble princes, that they may array the man *withal* whom the king delighteth to honour, and [2]bring him on horseback through the street of the city, [a]and proclaim before him, Thus shall it be done to the man whom the king delighteth to honour.

10 Then the king said to Haman, Make haste, *and* take the apparel and the horse, as thou hast said, and do even so to Mordecai the Jew, that sitteth at the king's gate: [1]let nothing fail of all that thou hast spoken.

11 Then took Haman the apparel and the horse, and arrayed Mordecai, and brought him on horseback through the street of the city, and proclaimed before him, Thus shall

it be done unto the man whom the king delighteth to honour.

12 And Mordecai came again to the king's gate. But Haman [a]hasted[1] to his house mourning, [b]and having his head covered.

13 And Haman told Zeresh his wife and all his friends every *thing* that had befallen him. Then said his wise men and Zeresh his wife unto him, If Mordecai *be* of the seed of the Jews, before whom thou hast begun to fall, thou shalt not prevail against [a]him, but shalt surely fall before him.

14 And while they *were* yet talking with him, came the king's [1]chamberlains, and hasted to bring Haman unto [a]the banquet that Esther had prepared.

## CHAPTER 7

S[O] the king and Haman came to banquet with Esther the queen.

2 And the king said again unto Esther on the second day [a]at the banquet of wine, What *is* thy petition, queen Esther? and it shall be granted thee: and what *is* thy request? and it shall be performed, *even* to the half of the kingdom.

3 Then Esther the queen answered and said, If I have found favour in thy sight, O king, and if it please the king, let my life be given me at my petition, and my people at my request:

4 For we are [a]sold, I and my people, to be destroyed, to be slain, and to [1]perish. But if we had been sold for [b]bondmen and bondwomen, I [2]had held my tongue, although the enemy could [3]not countervail the king's damage.

5 Then the king Ahasuerus answered and said unto Esther the queen, Who is he, and where is he, [1]that durst presume in his heart to do so?

6 And Esther said, The adversary and [a]enemy *is* this wicked Haman. Then Haman [1]was afraid before the king and the queen.

7 And the king arising from the banquet of wine in his wrath *went* into the palace garden: and Haman stood up [1]to make request for his life to Esther the queen; for he saw that there was evil determined against him by the king.

8 Then the king returned out of the palace garden into the place of the banquet of wine; and Haman was fallen upon [a]the bed whereon Esther *was*. Then said the king, Will he [1]force the queen also [2]before me in the house? As the word went out of the king's mouth, they [b]covered Haman's face.

9 And [a]Harbonah, one of the [1]chamberlains, said before the king, Behold

### Center column marginal notes

5:14 [b] Esth. 6:4
[c] Esth. 7:10
6:1 [a] Esth. 2:23;
10:2 [1] Lit. *the king's sleep fled away*
6:2 [1] *Bigthan,* Esth. 2:21 [2] *eunuchs*
6:3 [1] *Nothing has been done*
6:4 [a] Esth. 5:1
[b] Esth. 5:14
6:6 [a] [Prov. 16:18; 18:12]
6:8 [a] 1 Kin. 1:33 [1] *robe* [2] *has worn* [3] *royal crest* [4] *its*
6:9 [a] Gen. 41:43 [1] *robe* [2] *parade him*
6:10 [1] *leave nothing undone*

6:12 [a] 2 Chr. 26:20 [b] 2 Sam. 15:30; Jer. 14:3, 4 [1] *hastened*
6:13 [a] [Gen. 12:3]; Zech. 2:8
6:14 [a] Esth. 5:8 [1] *eunuchs*
7:2 [a] Esth. 5:6
7:4 [a] Esth. 3:9; 4:7 [b] Deut. 28:68 [1] *be annihilated* [2] *would have* [3] *compensate*
7:5 [1] *who dares to*
7:6 [a] Esth. 3:10 [1] *was terrified*
7:7 [1] *pleading*
7:8 [a] Esth. 1:6 [1] *assault* [2] Lit. *with me*
7:9 [a] Esth. 1:10 [1] *eunuchs*

also, [b]the [2]gallows fifty cubits high, which Haman had made for Mordecai, who had spoken [c]good for the king, standeth in the house of Haman. Then the king said, Hang him thereon.

10 So [a]they [b]hanged Haman on the gallows that he had prepared for Mordecai. Then [1]was the king's wrath pacified.

## CHAPTER 8

O[N] that day did the king Ahasuerus give the house of Haman the Jews' [a]enemy unto Esther the queen. And Mordecai came before the king; for Esther had told [b]what he *was* unto her.

2 And the king took off [a]his [1]ring, which he had taken from Haman, and gave it unto Mordecai. And Esther set Mordecai over the house of Haman.

3 And Esther spake yet again before the king, and fell down at his feet, [1]and besought him with tears to [2]put away the mischief of Haman the Agagite, and his [3]device that he had devised against the Jews.

4 Then [a]the king held out the golden sceptre toward Esther. So Esther arose, and stood before the king,

5 And said, If it please the king, and if I have found favour in his sight, and the thing *seem* right before the king, and I *be* pleasing in his eyes, let it be written to [1]reverse the [a]letters devised by Haman the son of Hammedatha the Agagite, which he wrote to [2]destroy the Jews which *are* in all the king's provinces:

6 For how can I endure to see [a]the evil that shall come unto my people? or how can I endure to see the destruction of my kindred?

7 Then the king Ahasuerus said unto Esther the queen and to Mordecai the Jew, Behold, [a]I have given Esther the house of Haman, and him they have hanged upon the gallows, because he laid his hand upon the Jews.

8 Write ye also for the Jews, [1]as it liketh you, in the king's name, and seal *it* with the king's [2]ring: for the writing which is written in the king's name, and sealed with the king's ring, [a]may no man [3]reverse.

9 [a]Then were the king's scribes called at that time in the third month, that *is*, the month Sivan, on the three and twentieth *day* thereof; and it was written according to all that Mordecai commanded unto the Jews, and to the [1]lieutenants, and the [2]deputies and rulers of the provinces which *are* [b]from India unto Ethiopia, an hundred twenty and seven provinces, unto every province [c]according to the writing thereof, and unto every people after their language, and to the

Jews according to their writing, and according to their language.

10 [a]And he wrote in the king Ahasuerus' name, and sealed *it* with the king's [1]ring, and sent letters by [2]posts on horseback, *and* riders on [3]mules, camels, *and* young dromedaries:

11 Wherein the king granted the Jews which *were* in every city to [a]gather themselves together, and to stand for their life, to [b]destroy, to slay, and to cause to perish, all the power of the people and province that would assault them, *both* little ones and women, and *to* [1]take the spoil of them for a prey,

12 [a]Upon one day in all the provinces of king Ahasuerus, *namely*, upon the thirteenth *day* of the twelfth month, which *is* the month Adar.

13 [a]The copy of the writing for a commandment to be given in every province *was* published unto all people, and that the Jews should be ready against that day to avenge themselves on their enemies.

14 *So* the [1]posts that rode upon mules *and* camels went out, being hastened and pressed on by the king's commandment. And the decree was given at [2]Shushan the [3]palace.

15 And Mordecai went out from the presence of the king in royal apparel of [1]blue and white, and with a great crown of gold, and with a garment of fine linen and purple: and [a]the city of [2]Shushan rejoiced and was glad.

16 The Jews had [a]light, and gladness, and joy, and honour.

17 And in every province, and in every city, whithersoever the king's commandment and his decree came, the Jews had joy and gladness, a feast [a]and a [1]good day. And many of the people of the land [b]became Jews; for [c]the fear of the Jews fell upon them.

## CHAPTER 9

N[OW][a] in the twelfth month, that *is*, the month Adar, on the thirteenth day of the same, [b]when the king's commandment and his decree drew near to be put in execution, in the day that the enemies of the Jews hoped to have power over them, (though it was turned to the contrary, that the Jews [c]had[1] rule over them that hated them;)

2 The Jews [a]gathered themselves together in their cities throughout all the provinces of the king Ahasuerus, to lay hand on such as [b]sought their hurt: and no man could withstand them; for [c]the fear of them fell upon all people.

3 And all the rulers of the provinces, and the [1]lieutenants, and the [2]deputies, and [3]officers of the king, helped the Jews; because the fear of Mordecai fell upon them.

---

7:9 [b] Esth. 5:14; [Ps. 7:16; Prov. 11:5, 6] [c] Esth. 6:2 [2] Lit. *tree or wood*

7:10 [a] [Ps. 7:16; 94:23; Prov. 11:5, 6] [b] Ps. 37:35, 36; Dan. 6:24 [1] *the king's wrath subsided*

8:1 [a] Esth. 7:6 [b] Esth. 2:7, 15

8:2 [a] Esth. 3:10 [1] *signet ring*

8:3 [1] Lit. *and she wept, and implored him* [2] *counteract the evil plot* [3] *scheme*

8:4 [a] Esth. 4:11; 5:2

8:5 [a] Esth. 3:13 [1] *revoke* [2] *annihilate*

8:6 [a] Neh. 2:3; Esth. 7:4; 9:1

8:7 [a] Esth. 8:1; Prov. 13:22

8:8 [a] Esth. 1:19; Dan. 6:8, 12, 15 [1] *as you please* [2] *signet ring* [3] *revoke*

8:9 [a] Esth. 3:12 [b] Esth. 1:1 [c] Esth. 1:22; 3:12 [1] *satraps* [2] *governors*

8:10 [a] 1 Kin. 21:8; Esth. 3:12, 13 [1] *signet ring* [2] *couriers* [3] *royal horses bred from swift steeds*

8:11 [a] Esth. 9:2 [b] Esth. 9:10, 15, 16 [1] *plunder their possessions*

8:12 [a] Esth. 3:13; 9:1

8:13 [a] Esth. 3:14, 15

8:14 [1] *couriers* [2] Or *Susa* [3] *citadel*

8:15 [a] Esth. 3:15; Prov. 29:2 [1] *violet* [2] Or *Susa*

8:16 [a] Ps. 97:11; 112:4

8:17 [a] 1 Sam. 25:8; Esth. 9:19 [b] Ps. 18:43 [c] Gen. 35:5; Ex. 15:16; Deut. 2:25; 11:25; 1 Chr. 14:17; Esth. 9:2 [1] *holiday*

9:1 [a] Esth. 8:12 [b] Esth. 3:13 [c] 2 Sam. 22:41 [1] *overpowered*

9:2 [a] Esth. 8:11; 9:15–18 [b] Ps. 71:13, 14 [c] Esth. 8:17

9:3 [1] *satraps* [2] *governors* [3] *those who were doing the king's work*

4 For Mordecai *was* great in the king's house, and his fame went out throughout all the provinces: for this man Mordecai [a]waxed[1] greater and greater.

5 Thus the Jews smote all their enemies with the stroke of the sword, and slaughter, and destruction, and did [1]what they would unto those that hated them.

6 And in [a]Shushan[1] the [2]palace the Jews slew and destroyed five hundred men.

7 And Parshandatha, and Dalphon, and Aspatha,

8 And Poratha, and Adalia, and Aridatha,

9 And Parmashta, and Arisai, and Aridai, and Vajezatha,

10 [a]The ten sons of Haman the son of Hammedatha, the enemy of the Jews, slew they; [b]but on the [1]spoil laid they not their hand.

11 On that day the number of those that were slain in [1]Shushan the palace [2]was brought before the king.

12 And the king said unto Esther the queen, The Jews have slain and destroyed five hundred men in [1]Shushan the [2]palace, and the ten sons of Haman; what have they done in the rest of the king's provinces? now [a]what *is* thy petition? and it shall be granted thee: or what *is* thy request further? and it shall be done.

13 Then said Esther, If it please the king, let it be granted to the Jews which *are* in [1]Shushan to do to morrow also [a]according unto this day's decree, and let Haman's ten sons [b]be hanged upon the gallows.

14 And the king commanded it so to be done: and the decree was given at Shushan; and they hanged Haman's ten sons.

15 For the Jews that *were* in [1]Shushan [a]gathered themselves together on the fourteenth day also of the month Adar, and slew three hundred men at Shushan; [b]but on the [2]prey they laid not their hand.

16 But the other Jews that *were* in the king's provinces [a]gathered themselves together, and stood for their lives, and had rest from their enemies, and slew of their foes seventy and five thousand, [b]but they laid not their hands on the [1]prey,

17 On the thirteenth day of the month Adar; and on the fourteenth day of the same rested they, and made it a day of feasting and gladness.

18 But the Jews that *were* at [1]Shushan assembled together [a]on the thirteenth *day* thereof, and on the fourteenth thereof; and on the fifteenth *day* of the same they rested, and made it a day of feasting and gladness.

19 Therefore the Jews of the villages, that dwelt in the unwalled towns, made the fourteenth day of the month Adar [a]*a day of* gladness and feasting, [b]and a good day, and of [c]sending [1]portions one to another.

20 And Mordecai wrote these things, and sent letters unto all the Jews that *were* in all the provinces of the king Ahasuerus, *both* nigh and far,

21 To stablish *this* among them, that they should keep the fourteenth day of the month Adar, and the fifteenth day of the same, yearly,

22 As the days wherein the Jews rested from their enemies, and the month which was turned unto them from sorrow to joy, and from mourning into a [1]good day: that they should make them days of feasting and joy, and of [a]sending [2]portions one to another, and gifts to the [b]poor.

23 And the Jews undertook to do as they had begun, and as Mordecai had written unto them;

24 Because Haman the son of Hammedatha, the Agagite, the enemy of all the Jews, [a]had [1]devised against the Jews to [2]destroy them, and had cast Pur, that *is,* the lot, to consume them, and to destroy them;

25 But [a]when *Esther* came before the king, he commanded by letters that his wicked [1]device, which he devised against the Jews, should [b]return upon his own head, and that he and [2]his sons should be hanged on the gallows.

26 Wherefore they called these days Purim after the name of [1]Pur. Therefore for all the words of [a]this letter, and *of that* which they had seen concerning this matter, and which had come unto them,

27 The Jews [1]ordained, and took upon them, and upon their seed, and upon all such as [a]joined themselves unto them, so as it should not fail, that they would keep these two days according to their writing, and according to their *appointed* time every year;

28 And *that* these days *should be* remembered and kept throughout every generation, every family, every province, and every city; and *that* these days of Purim should not fail from among the Jews, nor the memorial of them perish from their seed.

29 Then Esther the queen, [a]the daughter of Abihail, and Mordecai the Jew, wrote with all authority, to confirm this [b]second letter of Purim.

30 And [1]he sent the letters unto all the Jews, to [a]the hundred twenty and seven provinces of the kingdom of Ahasuerus, *with* words of peace and truth,

31 To confirm these days of Purim in their times *appointed,* according

---

9:4 [a] 2 Sam. 3:1; 1 Chr. 11:9; [Prov. 4:18] [1] *became increasingly prominent*
9:5 [1] *what they pleased*
9:6 [a] Esth. 1:2; 3:15; 4:16 [1] *Or Susa* [2] *citadel*
9:10 [a] Esth. 5:11; 9:7–10; Job 18:19; 27:13–15; Ps. 21:10 [b] Esth. 8:11 [1] *plunder*
9:11 [1] *Or Susa* [2] Lit. *came*
9:12 [a] Esth. 5:6; 7:2 [1] *Or Susa* [2] *citadel*
9:13 [a] Esth. 8:11; 9:15 [b] 2 Sam. 21:6, 9 [1] *Or Susa*
9:15 [a] Esth. 8:11; 9:2 [b] Esth. 9:10 [1] *Or Susa* [2] *plunder*
9:16 [a] Esth. 9:2 [b] Esth. 8:11 [1] *plunder*
9:18 [a] Esth. 9:11, 15 [1] *Or Susa*

9:19 [a] Deut. 16:11, 14 [b] Esth. 8:16, 17 [c] Neh. 8:10, 12; Esth. 9:22 [1] *presents*
9:22 [a] Neh. 8:10; Esth. 9:19 [b] [Deut. 15:7–11]; Job 29:16 [1] *holiday* [2] *presents*
9:24 [a] Esth. 3:6, 7; 9:26 [1] *plotted* [2] *annihilate*
9:25 [a] Esth. 7:4–10; 8:3; 9:13, 14 [b] Esth. 7:10 [1] *plot* [2] *Haman's*
9:26 [a] Esth. 9:20 [1] Lit. *Lot*
9:27 [a] Esth. 8:17; [Is. 56:3, 6]; Zech. 2:11 [1] *established and imposed on themselves*
9:29 [a] Esth. 2:15 [b] Esth. 8:10; 9:20, 21
9:30 [a] Esth. 1:1 [1] *Mordecai*

as Mordecai the Jew and Esther the queen had enjoined them, and as they had decreed for themselves and for their seed, the matters of ªthe fastings and their cry.

32 And the decree of Esther confirmed these matters of Purim; and it was written in the book.

## CHAPTER 10

AND the king Ahasuerus laid a tribute upon the land, and *upon* ªthe isles of the sea.

9:31 ª Esth. 4:3, 16
10:1 ª Is. 11:11;
24:15

10:2 ª Esth. 8:15;
9:4  b Esth. 6:1
¹ Lit. *made him
great*
10:3 ª Gen. 41:40,
43, 44  b Neh.
2:10

2 And all the acts of his power and of his might, and the declaration of the greatness of Mordecai, ªwhereunto the king ¹advanced him, *are* they not written in the book of ᵇchronicles of the kings of Media and Persia?

3 For Mordecai the Jew *was* ªnext unto king Ahasuerus, and great among the Jews, and accepted of the multitude of his brethren, ᵇseeking the wealth of his people, and speaking peace to all his seed.

# THE BOOK OF
# JOB

Job is perhaps the earliest book of the Bible. Set in the period of the patriarchs (Abraham, Isaac, Jacob, and Joseph), it tells the story of a man who loses everything—his wealth, his family, his health—and wrestles with the question, Why?

The book begins with a heavenly debate between God and Satan, moves through three cycles of earthly debates between Job and his friends, and concludes with a dramatic "divine diagnosis" of Job's problem. In the end, Job acknowledges the sovereignty of God in his life and receives back more than he had before his trials.

*Iyyob* is the Hebrew title for this book, and the name has two possible meanings. If derived from the Hebrew word for "Persecution," it means "Persecuted One." It is more likely that it comes from the Arabic word meaning "To Come Back" or "Repent." If so, it may be defined "Repentant One." Both meanings apply to the book. The Greek title is *Iob*, and the Latin title is *Iob*.

## CHAPTER 1

THERE was a man ªin the land of Uz, whose name *was* ᵇJob; and that man was ᶜperfect¹ and upright, and one that ᵈfeared God, and ²eschewed evil.

2 And there were born unto him seven sons and three daughters.

3 His ¹substance also was seven thousand sheep, and three thousand camels, and five hundred yoke of oxen, and five hundred ²she asses, and a very great household; so that this man was the greatest of all the ³men of the east.

4 And his sons went and feasted *in their* houses, every one his day; and sent and called for their three sisters to eat and to drink with them.

5 And it was so, when the days of *their* feasting were gone about, that Job sent and ¹sanctified them, and rose up early in the morning, ªand offered burnt offerings *according* to the number of them all: for Job said, It may be that my sons have sinned, and ᵇcursed² God in their hearts. Thus did Job ³continually.

6 Now ªthere was a day when the sons of God came to present themselves before the LORD, and ¹Satan came also among them.

7 And the LORD said unto Satan, Whence comest thou? Then Satan answered the LORD, and said, From ªgoing to and fro in the earth, and from walking up and down in it.

8 And the LORD said unto Satan, ¹Hast thou considered my servant Job, that *there is* none like him in the earth, a ²perfect and an upright man, one that feareth God, and ³escheweth evil?

9 Then Satan answered the LORD, and said, Doth Job fear God for ¹nought?

10 ªHast not thou made an ¹hedge about him, and about his house, and about all that he hath on every side? ᵇthou hast blessed the work of his hands, and his ²substance is increased in the land.

11 ªBut ¹put forth thine hand now, and touch all that he hath, and he will ᵇcurse² thee to thy face.

12 And the LORD said unto Satan, Behold, all that he hath *is* in thy ¹power; only upon ²himself put not forth thine hand. So Satan went forth from the presence of the LORD.

13 And there was a day ªwhen his sons and his daughters *were* eating and drinking wine in their eldest brother's house:

14 And there came a messenger unto Job, and said, The oxen were plowing, and the asses feeding beside them:

15 And the Sabeans ¹fell *upon them*, and took them away; yea, they have slain the servants with the edge of the sword; and I only am escaped alone to tell thee.

16 While he *was* yet speaking, there came also another, and said, The fire of God is fallen from heaven, and hath burned up the sheep, and the servants, and ¹consumed them; and I only am escaped alone to tell thee.

17 While he *was* yet speaking, there came also another, and said, The Chaldeans ¹made out three bands, and ²fell upon the camels, and have carried them away, yea, and slain the servants with the edge of the sword; and I only am escaped alone to tell thee.

18 While he *was* yet speaking, there came also another, and said, ªThy sons and thy daughters *were* eating and drinking wine in their eldest brother's house:

---

1:1 ª 1 Chr. 1:17
ᵇ Ezek. 14:14,
20 ᶜ Gen. 6:9;
17:1 ᵈ [Prov.
16:6] ¹ *blameless*
² *shunned*
1:3 ¹ *possessions*
² *female donkeys*
³ Lit. *sons*
1:5 ª [Job 42:8]
ᵇ 1 Kin. 21:10, 13
¹ *set them apart,
consecrated them*
² Lit. *blessed*, but
in an evil sense
³ *regularly*
1:6 ª Job 2:1 ¹ The
adversary
1:7 ª [1 Pet. 5:8]
1:8 ¹ Lit. *Have you
set your heart
on* ² *blameless*
³ *shuns*
1:9 ¹ *nothing*

1:10 ª Ps. 34:7
ᵇ [Prov. 10:22]
¹ *hedge of protection* ² *possessions*
1:11 ª Job 2:5; 19:21
ᵇ Is. 8:21 ¹ *stretch*
² Lit. *bless*, but in
an evil sense
1:12 ¹ Lit. *hand*
² *his person*
1:13 ª [Eccl. 9:12]
1:15 ¹ *attacked*
1:16 ¹ *destroyed*
1:17 ¹ *formed*
² *raided*
1:18 ª Job 1:4, 13

---

19 And, behold, there came a great wind ¹from the wilderness, and ²smote the four corners of the house, and it fell upon the young men, and they are dead; and I only am escaped alone to tell thee.

20 Then Job arose, ªand ¹rent his ²mantle, and shaved his head, and ᵇfell down upon the ground, and worshipped,

21 And said, ªNaked came I out of my mother's womb, and naked shall I return thither: the LORD ᵇgave, and the LORD hath ᶜtaken away; ᵈblessed be the name of the LORD.

22 ªIn all this Job sinned not, nor charged God ¹foolishly.

## CHAPTER 2

AGAIN ªthere was a day when the sons of God came to present themselves before the LORD, and Satan came also among them to present himself before the LORD.

2 And the LORD said unto Satan, From whence comest thou? And ªSatan answered the LORD, and said, From going to and fro in the earth, and from walking up and down in it.

3 And the LORD said unto Satan, Hast thou considered my servant Job, that *there is* none like him in the earth, ªa ¹perfect and an upright man, one that feareth God, and ²escheweth evil? and still he ᵇholdeth fast his integrity, although thou ¹movedst me against him, ᶜto destroy him without cause.

4 And Satan answered the LORD, and said, Skin for skin, yea, all that a man hath will he give for his life.

5 ªBut ¹put forth thine hand now, and touch his ᵇbone and his flesh, and he will curse thee to thy face.

6 ªAnd the LORD said unto Satan, Behold, he *is* in thine hand; but save his life.

7 So went Satan forth from the presence of the LORD, and ¹smote Job with sore boils ªfrom the sole of his foot unto his crown.

8 And he took him a potsherd to scrape himself withal; ªand he sat down among the ashes.

9 Then said his wife unto him, Dost thou still retain thine integrity? ¹curse God, and die.

10 But he said unto her, Thou speakest as one of the foolish women speaketh. What? ªshall we ¹receive good at the hand of God, and shall we not ²receive evil? ᵇIn all this did not Job ᶜsin with his lips.

11 Now when Job's three friends heard of all this evil that was come upon him, they came every one from his own place; Eliphaz the ªTemanite, and Bildad the ᵇShuhite, and Zophar the Naamathite: for they had made

---

1:19 ¹ MT *from across* ² *struck*

1:20 ª Gen. 37:29, 34 ᵇ [1 Pet. 5:6] ¹ *tore* ² *robe*

1:21 ª [Eccl. 5:15] ᵇ [James 1:17] ᶜ Gen. 31:16 ᵈ Eph. 5:20

1:22 ª Job 2:10 ¹ *accused with wrong*

2:1 ª Job 1:6–8

2:2 ª Job 1:7

2:3 ª Job 1:1, 8 ᵇ Job 27:5, 6 ᶜ Job 9:17 ¹ *blameless* ² *shuns* ³ *incited*

2:5 ª Job 1:11 ᵇ Job 19:20 ¹ *stretch*

2:6 ª Job 1:12

2:7 ª Is. 1:6 ¹ *struck*

2:8 ª Ezek. 27:30

2:9 ¹ Lit. *bless*, but in an evil sense

2:10 ª Job 1:21, 22 ᵇ Job 1:22 ᶜ Ps. 39:1 ¹ *accept* ² *accept calamity*

2:11 ª Gen. 36:11 ᵇ Gen. 25:2 ᶜ Rom. 12:15

2:12 ª Neh. 9:1 ¹ *did not recognize him* ˣ *each one tore his robe*

2:13 ª Gen. 50:10

3:2 ¹ Lit. *answered*

3:3 ª Jer. 20:14–18 ¹ *male*

3:4 ¹ *may God above not seek it*

3:5 ª Jer. 13:16 ¹ *claim it* ² *settle*

3:6 ¹ *be included in*

3:7 ¹ *barren*

3:8 ª Jer. 9:17 ¹ *arouse* ² Lit. *Leviathan*, a large sea creature of unknown identity

3:9 ¹ Lit. *the eyelids of the dawn*

3:11 ª Job 10:18, 19 ¹ *expire, perish*

3:12 ª Gen. 30:3 ¹ *receive*

3:13 ¹ *would*

3:14 ª Job 15:28; Is. 58:12 ¹ *ruins*

3:16 ª Ps. 58:8 ¹ *why was I not hidden like a stillborn child*

3:17 ª Job 17:16 ¹ Lit. *wearied of strength*

3:18 ª Job 39:7

3:20 ª Jer. 20:18 ᵇ 2 Kin. 4:27

---

an appointment together to come ᶜto mourn with him and to comfort him.

12 And when they lifted up their eyes afar off, and ¹knew him not, they lifted up their voice, and wept; and ²they rent every one his mantle, and ªsprinkled dust upon their heads toward heaven.

13 So they sat down with him upon the ground ªseven days and seven nights, and none spake a word unto him: for they saw that *his* grief was very great.

## CHAPTER 3

AFTER this opened Job his mouth, and cursed his day.

2 And Job ¹spake, and said,

3 ªLet the day perish wherein I was born, and the night *in which* it was said, There is a ¹man child conceived.

4 Let that day be darkness; ¹let not God regard it from above, neither let the light shine upon it.

5 Let darkness and ªthe shadow of death ¹stain it; let a cloud ²dwell upon it; let the blackness of the day terrify it.

6 *As for* that night, let darkness seize upon it; let it not ¹be joined unto the days of the year, let it not come into the number of the months.

7 Lo, let that night be ¹solitary, let no joyful voice come therein.

8 Let them curse it that curse the day, ªwho are ready to ¹raise up ²their mourning.

9 Let the stars of the twilight thereof be dark; let it look for light, but *have* none; neither let it see ¹the dawning of the day:

10 Because it shut not up the doors of my *mother's* womb, nor hid sorrow from mine eyes.

11 ªWhy died I not from the womb? *why* did I *not* ¹give up the ghost when I came out of the belly?

12 ªWhy did the knees ¹prevent me? or why the breasts that I should suck?

13 For now ¹should I have lain still and been quiet, I ¹should have slept: then had I been at rest,

14 With kings and counsellors of the earth, which ªbuilt ¹desolate places for themselves;

15 Or with princes that had gold, who filled their houses with silver:

16 Or ªas¹ an hidden untimely birth I had not been; as infants *which* never saw light.

17 There the wicked cease *from* troubling; and there the ¹weary be at ªrest.

18 *There* the prisoners rest together; ªthey hear not the voice of the oppressor.

19 The small and great are there; and the servant *is* free from his master.

20 ªWherefore is light given to him that is in misery, and life unto the ᵇbitter in soul;

21 Which [a]long[1] for death, but it *cometh* not; and dig for it more than [b]for hid treasures?

22 Which rejoice exceedingly, *and* are glad, when they can find the [a]grave?

23 *Why is light given* to a man whose way is hid, [a]and whom God hath hedged in?

24 For my sighing cometh before [1]I eat, and my roarings are poured out like the waters.

25 For the thing which I greatly [a]feared is come upon me, and that which I was afraid of is come unto me.

26 I was not in safety, neither had I rest, neither was I quiet; yet trouble came.

## CHAPTER 4

THEN Eliphaz the Temanite answered and said,

2 *If* we [1]assay to commune with thee, wilt thou be grieved? but who can withhold himself from speaking?

3 Behold, thou hast instructed many, and thou [a]hast strengthened the weak hands.

4 Thy words have [1]upholden him that was falling, and thou [a]hast strengthened the [2]feeble knees.

5 But now it is come upon thee, and thou faintest; it toucheth thee, and thou art troubled.

6 *Is* not *this* [a]thy[1] fear, [b]thy confidence, thy hope, and the [2]uprightness of thy ways?

7 Remember, I pray thee, [a]who *ever* perished, being innocent? or where were the righteous cut off?

8 Even as I have seen, [a]they that plow iniquity, and sow wickedness, reap the same.

9 By the blast of God they perish, and by the breath of his [1]nostrils are they consumed.

10 The roaring of the lion, and the voice of the fierce lion, and [a]the teeth of the young lions, are broken.

11 [a]The old lion perisheth for lack of prey, and the stout lion's whelps are scattered abroad.

12 Now a thing was secretly brought to me, and mine ear received a little thereof.

13 [a]In thoughts from the visions of the night, when deep sleep falleth on men,

14 Fear came upon me, and [a]trembling, which made all my bones to shake.

15 Then a spirit passed before my face; the hair of my flesh stood up:

16 It stood still, but I could not discern [1]the form thereof: [2]an image *was* before mine eyes, *there was* silence, and I heard a voice, *saying,*

17 Shall mortal man be more just than God? shall a man be more pure than his maker?

18 Behold, he [a]put no trust in his servants; and his angels he charged with [1]folly:

19 How much less *in* them that dwell in houses of clay, whose foundation *is* in the dust, *which* are crushed before the moth?

20 [a]They are [1]destroyed from morning to evening: they perish for ever without [2]any regarding *it.*

21 Doth not their excellency *which is* in them go away? they die, even without wisdom.

## CHAPTER 5

CALL now, if there be any that will answer thee; and to which of the [1]saints wilt thou turn?

2 For wrath killeth the foolish man, and envy slayeth the [1]silly one.

3 [a]I have seen the foolish taking root: but suddenly I cursed his [1]habitation.

4 His children are [a]far from safety, and they are crushed in the gate, [b]neither *is there* any to deliver *them.*

5 Whose harvest the hungry eateth up, and taketh it even out of the thorns, and the robber swalloweth up their [1]substance.

6 Although affliction cometh not forth of the dust, neither doth trouble spring out of the ground;

7 Yet man is [a]born unto [1]trouble, as the sparks fly upward.

8 [1]I would seek unto God, and unto God would I commit my cause:

9 Which doeth great things and unsearchable; marvellous things without number:

10 [a]Who giveth rain upon the earth, and sendeth waters upon the fields:

11 [a]To set up on high those that be low; that those which mourn may be exalted to safety.

12 [a]He [1]disappointeth the devices of the crafty, so that their hands cannot perform *their* [2]enterprise.

13 He taketh the [a]wise in their own craftiness: and the counsel of the [1]froward is carried headlong.

14 They meet with darkness in the daytime, and grope in the noonday as in the night.

15 But [a]he saveth the poor from the sword, from their mouth, and from the hand of the mighty.

16 [a]So the poor hath hope, and [1]iniquity stoppeth her mouth.

17 [a]Behold, happy *is* the man whom God correcteth: therefore despise not thou the chastening of the Almighty:

18 [a]For he maketh sore, and bindeth up: he woundeth, and his hands make whole.

### Cross-references (center column)

3:21 [a] Rev. 9:6 [b] Prov. 2:4 [1] Lit. *wait*
3:22 [a] Job 7:15, 16
3:23 [a] Job 19:8; Ps. 88:8; Lam. 3:7
3:24 [1] Lit. *my bread*
3:25 [a] [Job 9:28; 30:15]
4:2 [1] *attempts a word*
4:3 [a] Is. 35:3
4:4 [a] Is. 35:3 [1] *upheld him who was stumbling* [2] Lit. *bending*
4:6 [a] Job 1:1 [b] Prov. 3:26 [1] Fear of God [2] *integrity*
4:7 [a] [Job 8:20; 36:6, 7; Ps. 37:25]
4:8 [a] [Job 15:31, 35; Prov. 22:8; Hos. 10:13; Gal. 6:7]
4:9 [1] *anger*
4:10 [a] Job 5:15; Ps. 58:6
4:11 [a] Job 29:17; Ps. 34:10
4:13 [a] Job 33:15
4:14 [a] Hab. 3:16
4:16 [1] *its appearance* [2] *a form*

4:18 [a] Job 15:15 [1] *error*
4:20 [a] Ps. 90:5, 6 [1] Lit. *broken in pieces* [2] *anyone*
5:1 [1] Lit. *holy ones*
5:2 [1] *simple*
5:3 [a] [Ps. 37:35, 36]; Jer. 12:1–3 [1] *abode*
5:4 [a] Ps. 119:155 [b] Ps. 109:12
5:5 [1] *wealth*
5:7 [a] Job 14:1 [1] *distress or toil*
5:8 [1] *But as for me I would*
5:10 [a] [Job 36:27–29; 37:6–11; 38:26]
5:11 [a] Ps. 113:7
5:12 [a] Neh.
4:15 [1] *frustrates* [2] *plans*
5:13 [a] [1 Cor. 3:19] [1] *wily comes quickly on themselves*
5:15 [a] Ps. 35:10
5:16 [a] 1 Sam. 2:8 [1] *injustice*
5:17 [a] Ps. 94:12
5:18 [a] [1 Sam. 2:6, 7]

19 [a]He shall deliver thee in six troubles: yea, in seven [b]there shall no evil touch thee.

20 [a]In famine he shall redeem thee from death: and in war from the [1]power of the sword.

21 [a]Thou shalt be hid from the scourge of the tongue: neither shalt thou be afraid of destruction when it cometh.

22 At destruction and famine thou shalt laugh: [a]neither shalt thou be afraid of the [b]beasts of the earth.

23 [a]For thou shalt [1]be in league with the stones of the field: and the beasts of the field shall be at peace with thee.

24 And thou shalt know that [1]thy tabernacle *shall be* in peace; and thou shalt visit thy habitation, and [2]shalt not sin.

25 Thou shalt know also that [a]thy [1]seed *shall be* great, and thine offspring [b]as the grass of the earth.

26 [a]Thou shalt come to *thy* grave in a full age, like as a shock of corn cometh in in his season.

27 Lo this, we have [a]searched it, so it *is;* hear it, and know thou *it* [1]for thy good.

### CHAPTER 6

B UT Job answered and said,

2 Oh that my grief were throughly weighed, and my calamity [1]laid in the balances together!

3 For now it would be heavier than the sand of the sea: therefore my words [1]are swallowed up.

4 [a]For the arrows of the Almighty *are* within me, the poison whereof drinketh up my spirit: [b]the terrors of God do set themselves in array [c]against me.

5 Doth the [a]wild ass bray when he hath grass? or loweth the ox over his fodder?

6 Can that which is [1]unsavoury be eaten without salt? or is there *any* taste in the white of an egg?

7 The things *that* my soul refused to touch *are* as [1]my sorrowful meat.

8 Oh that I might have my request; and that God would grant *me* the thing that I long for!

9 Even that it would please God to destroy me; that he would let loose his hand, and [a]cut me off!

10 Then should I yet have comfort; [1]yea, I would harden myself in sorrow: let him not spare; for [a]I have not concealed the words of [b]the Holy One.

11 What *is* my strength, that I should hope? and what *is* mine end, that I should prolong my life?

12 *Is* my strength the strength of stones? or *is* my flesh of brass?

13 *Is* not my help in me? and is wisdom driven quite from me?

14 [a]To him that is [1]afflicted [2]pity *should be shewed* from his friend; but he forsaketh the fear of the Almighty.

15 [a]My brethren have dealt deceitfully as a brook, and [b]as the stream of brooks they pass away;

16 Which are blackish by reason of the ice, *and* wherein the snow is hid:

17 What time they [1]wax warm, they [2]vanish: when it is hot, they are consumed out of their place.

18 The paths of their way are turned aside; they go to nothing, and perish.

19 The [1]troops of [a]Tema looked, the [2]companies of [b]Sheba waited for them.

20 They were [a]confounded[1] because they [2]had hoped; they came thither, and were [3]ashamed.

21 For now [a]ye are nothing; ye see *my* casting down, and [b]are afraid.

22 Did I [1]say, Bring unto me? or, [2]Give a reward for me of your substance?

23 Or, Deliver me from the enemy's hand? or, Redeem me from the hand of the [1]mighty?

24 Teach me, and I will hold my tongue: and cause me to understand wherein I have erred.

25 How [1]forcible are right words! but what doth your arguing [2]reprove?

26 Do ye [1]imagine to reprove words, and the speeches of one that is desperate, *which are* as wind?

27 Yea, ye overwhelm the fatherless, and ye [a]dig[1] *a pit* for your friend.

28 Now therefore [1]be content, look upon me; for [2]*it is* evident unto you if I lie.

29 [a]Return, I pray you, [1]let it not be iniquity; yea, return again, my [b]righteousness [2]*is* in it.

30 Is there [1]iniquity in my tongue? cannot my [2]taste discern [3]perverse things?

### CHAPTER 7

I s *there* not [a]an[1] appointed time to man upon earth? *are not* his days also like the days of an hireling?

2 As a servant [1]earnestly desireth the shadow, and as an hireling [2]looketh for *the reward of* his work:

3 So [1]am I made to possess [a]months of vanity, and [2]wearisome nights are appointed to me.

4 [a]When I lie down, I say, When shall I arise, and the night be gone? and I am full of tossings to and fro unto the dawning of the day.

5 My flesh is [a]clothed[1] with worms

---

5:19 [a] Ps. 34:19;
91:3 [b] Ps. 91:10
5:20 [a] Ps. 33:19,
20; 37:19 [1] Lit.
hand
5:21 [a] Ps. 31:20
5:22 [a] Ezek. 34:25
[b] Hos. 2:18
5:23 [a] Ps. 91:12
[1] have a covenant
with
5:24 [1] your tent
[2] find nothing
amiss
5:25 [a] Ps. 112:2
[b] Ps. 72:16 [1] de-
scendants will be
many
5:26 [a] [Prov. 9:11;
10:27]
5:27 [a] Ps. 111:2
[1] Lit. for yourself
6:2 [1] laid with it in
the balances!
6:3 [1] have been
rash
6:4 [a] Ps. 38:2
[b] Ps. 88:15, 16
[c] Job 30:15
6:5 [a] Job 39:5–8
6:6 [1] flavourless
6:7 [1] loathsome
food to me
6:9 [a] Job 7:16;
9:21; 10:1
6:10 [a] Acts
20:20 [b] [Is.
57:15] [1] though in
anguish I would
exult
6:14 [a] [Prov.
17:17] [1] despairing
[2] kindness
6:15 [a] Ps. 38:11
[b] Jer. 15:18
6:17 [1] become
[2] cease to flow
6:19 [a] Gen. 25:15
[b] 1 Kin. 10:1 [1] car-
avans [2] travellers
6:20 [a] Jer. 14:3
[1] disappointed
[2] were confident
[3] confused
6:21 [a] Job 13:4
[b] Ps. 38:11
6:22 [1] ever say
[2] Offer a bribe
6:23 [1] oppressors
6:25 [1] forceful
[2] prove
6:26 [1] intend to
reprove my words
6:27 [a] Ps. 57:6
[1] undermine
6:28 [1] be pleased
to [2] I will never lie
to your face
6:29 [a] Job 17:10
[b] Job 27:5, 6; 34:5
[1] let there be no
injustice [2] still
stands
6:30 [1] injustice
[2] palate
[3] unsavoury

7:1 [a] [Job 14:5, 13, 14] [1] a time of hard service
7:2 [1] longs for the shade, lit. pants [2] eagerly looks
for his wages 7:3 [a] [Job 15:31] [1] I have been allotted
months of futility [2] nights of misery 7:4 [a] Deut.
28:67 7:5 [a] Is. 14:11 [1] caked

and clods of dust; my skin is [2]broken, and [3]become loathsome.

6 [a]My days are swifter than a weaver's shuttle, and are spent without hope.

7 O remember that [a]my life *is* wind: mine eye shall no more see good.

8 [a]The eye of him that hath seen me shall see me no *more:* thine eyes *are* upon me, and [1]I *am* not.

9 *As* the cloud is consumed and vanisheth away: so [a]he that goeth down to the grave shall come up no *more.*

10 He shall return no more to his house, [a]neither shall his place know him any more.

11 Therefore I will [a]not [1]refrain my mouth; I will speak in the anguish of my spirit; I will [b]complain in the bitterness of my soul.

12 *Am* I a sea, or a [1]whale, that thou settest a watch over me?

13 [a]When I say, My bed shall comfort me, my couch shall ease my complaint;

14 Then thou scarest me with dreams, and terrifiest me through visions:

15 So that my soul chooseth strangling, *and* death rather than my [1]life.

16 [a]I loathe *it;* I would not live alway: [b]let me alone; for [c]my days *are* [1]vanity.

17 [a]What *is* man, that thou shouldest magnify him? and that thou shouldest set thine heart upon him?

18 And *that* thou shouldest [1]visit him every morning, *and* try him every moment?

19 How long wilt thou not depart from me, nor let me alone till I swallow down my spittle?

20 [1]I have sinned; what [2]shall I do unto thee, [a]O thou [3]preserver of men? why [b]hast thou set me as [4]a mark against thee, so that I am a burden [5]to myself?

21 And why dost thou not pardon my transgression, and take away mine iniquity? for now shall I [1]sleep in the dust; and thou shalt seek me in the morning, but I *shall* [2]not *be.*

## CHAPTER 8

THEN answered Bildad the Shuhite, and said,

2 How long wilt thou speak these *things?* and *how long shall* the words of thy mouth *be like* a strong wind?

3 [a]Doth God [1]pervert judgment? or doth the Almighty pervert justice?

4 If [a]thy children have sinned against him, and he have cast them away [1]for their transgression;

5 [a]If thou wouldest seek unto God [1]betimes, and make thy supplication to the Almighty;

6 If thou *wert* pure and upright; surely now he would [1]awake for thee,

and make the habitation of thy righteousness prosperous.

7 Though thy beginning was small, yet thy latter end should greatly [a]increase.

8 [a]For enquire, I pray thee, of the former age, and [1]prepare thyself to the search of their fathers:

9 (For [a]we *are but of* yesterday, and know nothing, because our days upon earth *are* a shadow:)

10 Shall not they teach thee, *and* tell thee, and utter words out of their heart?

11 Can the [1]rush grow up without [2]mire? can the [3]flag grow without water?

12 [a]Whilst it *is* yet in his greenness, *and* not cut down, it withereth before any *other* herb.

13 So *are* the paths of all that [a]forget God; and the [b]hypocrite's hope shall perish:

14 Whose hope shall be cut off, and whose trust *shall be* a spider's [1]web.

15 [a]He shall lean upon his house, but it shall not stand: he shall hold it fast, but it shall not endure.

16 He *is* green before the sun, and his branch shooteth forth in his garden.

17 His roots are wrapped about the [1]heap, *and* seeth the place of stones.

18 [a]If he destroy him from his place, then *it* shall deny him, *saying,* I have not seen thee.

19 Behold, this *is* the joy of his way, and [a]out of the earth shall others grow.

20 Behold, [a]God will not [1]cast away a [2]perfect *man,* neither will he [3]help the evil doers:

21 Till he fill thy mouth with laughing, and thy lips with [1]rejoicing.

22 They that hate thee shall be [a]clothed with shame; and the dwelling place of the wicked [1]shall come to nought.

## CHAPTER 9

THEN Job answered and said,

2 I know *it is* so of a truth: but how [1]should [a]man be [b]just with God?

3 [1]If he will contend with him, he cannot answer him [2]one of a thousand.

4 [a]*He is* wise in heart, and mighty in strength: who hath hardened[1] *himself* against him, and hath prospered?

5 Which removeth the mountains, and they know not: which overturneth them in his anger.

6 Which [a]shaketh the earth out of her place, and the [b]pillars thereof tremble.

### Cross references (center column)

7:5 [2] *cracked* [3] *breaks out afresh*
7:6 [a] Job 9:25; 16:22; 17:11
7:7 [a] Ps. 78:39; 89:47
7:8 [a] Job 8:18; 20:9 [1] *I will no longer be*
7:9 [a] 2 Sam. 12:23
7:10 [a] Ps. 103:16
7:11 [a] Ps. 39:1, 9 [b] 1 Sam. 1:10 [1] *restrain*
7:12 [1] Lit. *sea monster*
7:13 [a] Job 9:27
7:15 [1] Lit. *bones*
7:16 [a] Job 10:1 [b] Job 14:6 [c] Ps. 62:9 [1] *a breath or vapour*
7:17 [a] Ps. 8:4; 144:3
7:18 [1] *seek him or examine him*
7:20 [a] Ps. 36:6 [b] Ps. 21:12 [1] *Have I sinned* [2] *have I done* [3] *watcher* [4] *your target* [5] LXX *to you*
7:21 [1] *lie down* [2] *no longer*
8:3 [a] [Deut. 32:4] [1] *subvert*
8:4 [a] Job 1:5, 18, 19 [1] Lit. *in the hand of their*
8:5 [a] [Job 5:17–27; 11:13] [1] *earnestly*
8:6 [1] *arise*
8:7 [a] Job 42:12
8:8 [a] Deut. 4:32; 32:7 [1] *consider the things discovered by their fathers*
8:9 [a] Gen. 47:9
8:11 [1] *papyrus* [2] *marsh* [3] *reeds*
8:12 [a] Ps. 129:6
8:13 [a] Ps. 9:17 [b] Job 11:20; 18:14; 27:8
8:14 [1] Lit. *house*
8:15 [a] Job 8:22; 27:18
8:17 [1] *rock heap,* 8:18
8:18 [a] Job 7:10
8:19 [a] Ps. 113:7
8:20 [a] Job 4:7 [1] *reject* [2] *blameless.* [3] *uphold*
8:21 [1] Lit. *shouts of joy*
8:22 [a] Ps. 35:26; 109:29 [1] *come to nothing*
9:2 [a] [Job 4:17; 15:14–16] [b] [Hab. 2:4] [1] *can a man be righteous before God?*

### Footnotes (bottom)

9:3 [1] *If one wished to argue* [2] *one time out of*
9:4 [a] Job 36:5 [1] *God* 9:6 [a] Heb. 12:26 [b] Job 26:11

7 Which commandeth the sun, and it riseth not; and sealeth up the stars.

8 [a]Which alone spreadeth out the heavens, and [1]treadeth upon the [2]waves of the sea.

9 [a]Which maketh [1]Arcturus, Orion, and Pleiades, and the chambers of the south.

10 [a]Which doeth great things past finding out; yea, and wonders without number.

11 [a]Lo, he goeth by me, and I see *him* not: he passeth on also, but I perceive him not.

12 [a]Behold, he taketh away, who can [1]hinder him? who will say unto him, What doest thou?

13 *If* God will not withdraw his anger, [a]the [1]proud helpers do [2]stoop under him.

14 How much less [1]shall I answer him, *and* choose out my words *to reason* with him?

15 [a]Whom, though I were righteous, *yet* [1]would I not answer, *but* I would make supplication to my judge.

16 If I had called, and he had answered me; *yet* would I not believe that he had hearkened unto my voice.

17 For he breaketh me with a tempest, and multiplieth my wounds [a]without cause.

18 He will not suffer me to take my breath, but filleth me with bitterness.

19 If I *speak* of strength, lo, *he is* strong: and if of [1]judgment, who shall set me a time *to plead?*

20 [1]If I justify myself, mine own mouth [2]shall condemn me: *if I say,* I *am* perfect, it shall also prove me perverse.

21 [1]*Though* I *were* perfect, *yet* [2]would I not know my soul: [3]I would despise my life.

22 This *is* one *thing,* therefore I said it, [a]He destroyeth the [1]perfect and the wicked.

23 If the scourge slay suddenly, he will laugh at the [1]trial of the innocent.

24 The earth *is* given into the hand of the wicked: he covereth the faces of the judges thereof; if not, [1]where, *and* who *is* he?

25 Now [a]my days are swifter than a [1]post: they flee away, they see no good.

26 They are passed away as the [1]swift ships: [a]as the eagle [2]*that* hasteth to the prey.

27 [a]If I say, I will forget my complaint, I will leave off my [1]heaviness, and [2]comfort *myself:*

28 [a]I am afraid of all my sorrows, I know that thou [b]wilt not hold me innocent.

29 *If* I [1]be wicked, why then labour I in vain?

30 [a]If I wash myself with snow water, and [1]make my hands never so clean;

31 Yet shalt thou plunge me in the [1]ditch, and mine own clothes shall [2]abhor me.

32 For [a]*he is* not a man, as I *am, that* I should answer him, *and* we should come together in [1]judgment.

33 [a]Neither is there any [1]daysman betwixt us, *that* might lay his hand upon us both.

34 [a]Let him take his rod away from me, and let not [1]his fear terrify me:

35 *Then* would I speak, and not fear him; but *it is* not so with me.

## CHAPTER 10

MY [a]soul [1]is weary of my life; I will [2]leave my complaint upon myself; [b]I will speak in the bitterness of my soul.

2 I will say unto God, Do not condemn me; shew me wherefore thou contendest with me.

3 *Is it* good unto thee that thou shouldest oppress, that thou shouldest despise the work of thine hands, and [1]shine upon the counsel of the wicked?

4 Hast thou eyes of flesh? or [a]seest thou as man seeth?

5 *Are* thy days as the days of [1]man? *are* thy years as [2]man's days,

6 That thou enquirest after mine iniquity, and searchest after my sin?

7 Thou knowest that I am not wicked; and *there is* none that can deliver out of thine hand.

8 [a]Thine hands have made me and fashioned me together round about; yet thou dost [b]destroy me.

9 Remember, I beseech thee, [a]that thou hast made me as the clay; and wilt thou bring me into dust again?

10 [a]Hast thou not poured me out as milk, and curdled me like cheese?

11 Thou hast clothed me with skin and flesh, and hast [1]fenced me with bones and sinews.

12 Thou hast granted me life and favour, and thy [1]visitation hath preserved my spirit.

13 And these *things* hast thou hid in thine heart: I know that this *is* with thee.

14 If I sin, then [a]thou markest me, and thou wilt not acquit me from mine iniquity.

15 If I be wicked, [a]woe unto me; [b]and *if* I be righteous, *yet* [1]will I not lift up my head. *I am* full of [2]confusion; therefore [c]see thou mine affliction;

16 [1]For it increaseth. [a]Thou huntest me as a fierce lion: and again thou shewest thyself marvellous upon me.

17 Thou renewest thy witnesses against me, and increasest thine indignation upon me; changes and war *are* against me.

9:8 [a] Ps. 104:2, 3
[1] *walks* [2] *heights*
9:9 [a] Amos 5:8
[1] Or *The Great Bear*
9:10 [a] Job 5:9
9:11 [a] [Job 23:8, 9; 35:14]
9:12 [a] [Is. 45:9]
[1] *turn him back?*
9:13 [a] Job 26:12
[1] *allies of the proud* [2] *lie prostrate beneath*
9:14 [1] *can I*
9:15 [a] Job 10:15; 23:1–7 [1] *could*
9:17 [a] Job 2:3
9:19 [1] *justice*
9:20 [1] *Though I were righteous* [2] *would condemn*
9:21 [1] *I am blameless* [2] *I do not know* [3] *I despise*
9:22 [a] Ezek. 21:3
[1] *blameless*
9:23 [1] *plight*
9:24 [1] *who else could it be?*
9:25 [a] Job 7:6, 7
[1] *runner*
9:26 [a] Hab. 1:8
[1] Lit. *ships of reeds* [2] *swooping on its prey*
9:27 [a] Job 7:13
[1] *sad face* [2] *wear a smile*
9:28 [a] Ps. 119:120
[b] Ex. 20:7
9:29 [1] *shall be condemned*
9:30 [a] [Jer. 2:22]
[1] *cleanse my hands with soap*
9:31 [1] *pit* [2] *loathe*
9:32 [a] [Is. 45:9]
[1] *court*
9:33 [a] [1 Sam. 2:25] [1] *mediator*
9:34 [a] Job 13:20, 21 [1] *dread of him*
10:1 [a] Job 7:16 [b] Job 7:11
[1] *loathes* [2] *give free course to my complaint*
10:3 [1] *look favourably*
10:4 [a] [1 Sam. 16:7]
10:5 [1] *a mortal man* [2] *the days of a mighty man*
10:8 [a] Ps. 119:73
[b] [Job 9:22]
10:9 [a] Gen. 2:7
10:10 [a] [Ps. 139:14–16]
10:11 [1] *knit me together*
10:12 [1] *care*
10:14 [a] Ps. 139:1
10:15 [a] Is. 3:11

[b] [Job 9:12, 15] [c] Ps. 25:18 [1] *I cannot* [2] *disgrace*
10:16 [a] Is. 38:13 [1] *If my head is exalted*

18 ᵃWherefore then hast thou brought me forth out of the womb? Oh that I had given up the ghost, and no eye had seen me!

19 I should have been as though I had not been; I should have been carried from the womb to the grave.

20 ᵃ*Are* not my days few? cease *then, and* ᵇlet me alone, that I may take comfort a little,

21 Before I go *whence* I shall not return, ᵃ*even* to the land of darkness ᵇand the shadow of death;

22 A land of darkness, as darkness *itself; and* of the shadow of death, without any order, and *where* the light *is* as darkness.

## CHAPTER 11

THEN answered Zophar the Naamathite, and said,

2 Should not the multitude of words be answered? and should ¹a man full of talk be ²justified?

3 Should thy ¹lies make men ²hold their peace? and when thou mockest, shall no man ³make thee ashamed?

4 For ᵃthou hast said, My doctrine *is* pure, and I am clean in thine eyes.

5 But oh that God would speak, and open his lips against thee;

6 And that he would shew thee the secrets of wisdom, that *they are* double to that which is! Know therefore that ᵃGod ¹exacteth of thee *less* than thine iniquity *deserveth.*

7 ᵃCanst thou ᵇby searching find out God? canst thou find out the Almighty unto perfection?

8 *It is* as high as heaven; what canst thou do? deeper than ¹hell; what canst thou know?

9 The measure thereof *is* longer than the earth, and broader than the sea.

10 ᵃIf he ¹cut off, and ²shut up, or gather together, then who can ³hinder him?

11 For ᵃhe knoweth ¹vain men: he seeth wickedness also; will he not then consider *it?*

12 For ᵃvain¹ man would be wise, ²though man be born *like* a wild ass's colt.

13 If thou ᵃprepare thine heart, and ᵇstretch out thine hands toward him;

14 If iniquity *be* in thine hand, put it far away, and ᵃlet not wickedness dwell in thy ¹tabernacles.

15 ᵃFor then shalt thou lift up thy face without spot; yea, thou shalt be stedfast, and shalt not fear:

16 Because thou shalt ᵃforget *thy* misery, *and* remember *it* as waters *that* pass away:

17 And *thine* ¹age ᵃshall be ²clearer than the noonday; thou shalt shine forth, thou shalt be as the morning.

18 And thou shalt be secure, because there is hope; yea, thou shalt

10:18 ᵃ Job 3:11–13
10:20 ᵃ Ps. 39:5
ᵇ Job 7:16, 19
10:21 ᵃ Ps. 88:12
ᵇ Ps. 23:4
11:2 ¹ Lit. *a man of lips* ² *vindicated*
11:3 ¹ *empty talk* ² *be silent* ³ *rebuke thee*
11:4 ᵃ Job 6:30
11:6 ᵃ [Ezra 9:13] ¹ Lit. *forgets some of your iniquity for you*
11:7 ᵃ [Eccl. 3:11] ¹ *search out the deep things of God?*
11:8 ¹ Heb. *Sheol*
11:10 ᵃ [Rev. 3:7] ¹ *passes by* ² *imprisons* ³ *restrain*
11:11 ᵃ [Ps. 10:14] ¹ *deceitful*
11:12 ᵃ Rom. 1:22 ¹ *empty-headed* ² *when a wild donkey's colt is born a man*
11:13 ᵃ [1 Sam. 7:3] ᵇ Ps. 88:9
11:14 ᵃ Ps. 101:3 ¹ *tents*
11:15 ᵃ Ps. 119:6
11:16 ᵃ Is. 65:16
11:17 ᵃ Is. 58:8, 10 ¹ *life* ² *brighter*
11:18 ᵃ Lev. 26:5, 6
11:19 ¹ *would court your favour*
11:20 ᵃ Deut. 28:65 ᵇ [Prov. 11:7] ¹ Lit. *the breathing out of life*
12:3 ᵃ Job 13:2 ¹ Lit. *a heart*
12:4 ᵃ Job 21:3 ᵇ Ps. 91:15 ¹ *by his friends*
12:5 ᵃ Prov. 14:2
12:6 ᵃ [Job 9:24; 21:6–16] ¹ *tents*
12:10 ᵃ [Acts 17:28] ᵇ Job 27:3; 33:4 ¹ *life* ² Lit. *all flesh of man*
12:11 ¹ *test* ² *palate* ³ *food*
12:12 ¹ *aged* ² *Long life*
12:13 ᵃ Job 9:4; 36:5 ¹ *God*
12:14 ᵃ Job 11:10 ¹ *imprisons* ² *no release*
12:15 ᵃ [1 Kin. 8:35, 36] ᵇ Gen. 7:11–24
12:17 ¹ *plundered*
12:18 ¹ *waist with a belt*

dig *about thee, and* ᵃthou shalt take thy rest in safety.

19 Also thou shalt lie down, and none shall make *thee* afraid; yea, many ¹shall make suit unto thee.

20 But ᵃthe eyes of the wicked shall fail, and they shall not escape, and ᵇtheir hope *shall be* ¹*as* the giving up of the ghost.

## CHAPTER 12

AND Job answered and said,

2 No doubt but ye *are* the people, and wisdom shall die with you.

3 But I have ¹understanding as well as you; I *am* not ᵃinferior to you: yea, who knoweth not such things as these?

4 ᵃI am *as* one mocked ¹of his neighbour, who ᵇcalleth upon God, and he answereth him: the just upright *man is* laughed to scorn.

5 ᵃHe that is ready to slip with *his* feet *is as* a lamp despised in the thought of him that is at ease.

6 ᵃThe ¹tabernacles of robbers prosper, and they that provoke God are secure; into whose hand God bringeth *abundantly.*

7 But ask now the beasts, and they shall teach thee; and the fowls of the air, and they shall tell thee:

8 Or speak to the earth, and it shall teach thee: and the fishes of the sea shall declare unto thee.

9 Who knoweth not in all these that the hand of the LORD hath wrought this?

10 ᵃIn whose hand *is* the ¹soul of every living thing, and the ᵇbreath of ²all mankind.

11 Doth not the ear ¹try words? and the ²mouth taste his ³meat?

12 With the ¹ancient *is* wisdom; and in ²length of days understanding.

13 With ¹him *is* ᵃwisdom and strength, he hath counsel and understanding.

14 Behold, ᵃhe breaketh down, and it cannot be built again: he ¹shutteth up a man, and there can be ²no opening.

15 Behold, he ᵃwithholdeth the waters, and they dry up: also he ᵇsendeth them out, and they overturn the earth.

16 With him *is* strength and wisdom: the deceived and the deceiver *are* his.

17 He leadeth counsellors away ¹spoiled, and maketh the judges fools.

18 He looseth the bond of kings, and girdeth their ¹loins with a girdle.

19 He leadeth ¹princes away ²spoiled, and overthroweth the mighty.

12:19 ¹ Lit. *priests,* but not in a technical sense ² *plundered*

461

20 ᵃHe ¹removeth away the speech of the trusty, and taketh away the ²understanding of the aged.

21 ᵃHe poureth contempt upon princes, and ¹weakeneth the strength of the mighty.

22 He ᵃdiscovereth deep things out of darkness, and bringeth out to light the shadow of death.

23 ᵃHe ¹increaseth the nations, and destroyeth them: he ²enlargeth the nations, and ³straiteneth them *again.*

24 He taketh away the ¹heart of the chief of the people of the earth, and ᵃcauseth them to wander in a wilderness *where there is* no way.

25 ᵃThey grope in the dark without light, and he maketh them to ᵇstagger like *a* drunken *man.*

## CHAPTER 13

Lo, mine eye hath seen all *this,* mine ear hath heard and understood it.

2 ᵃWhat ye know, *the same* do I know also: I *am* not inferior unto you.

3 ᵃSurely I would speak to the Almighty, and I desire to reason with God.

4 But ye *are* forgers of lies, ᵃye *are* all physicians of no value.

5 ᵃO that ye would altogether ¹hold your peace! and it ²should be your wisdom.

6 Hear now my reasoning, and hearken to the pleadings of my lips.

7 ᵃWill ye speak ¹wickedly for God? and talk deceitfully for him?

8 Will ye ¹accept his person? will ye contend for God?

9 ¹Is it good that he should search you out? or as one man mocketh another, do ye *so* mock him?

10 He will surely ¹reprove you, if ye do secretly accept persons.

11 Shall not his ¹excellency make you afraid? and his dread fall upon you?

12 Your ¹remembrances *are* like unto ashes, your ²bodies to bodies of clay.

13 ¹Hold your peace, let me alone, that I may speak, and let come on me what *will.*

14 Wherefore ᵃdo I take my flesh in my teeth, and put my life in mine hand?

15 ᵃThough he slay me, yet will I trust in him: ᵇbut I will ¹maintain mine own ways before him.

16 He also *shall be* my salvation: for an ᵃhypocrite shall not come before him.

17 Hear diligently my speech, and my declaration with your ears.

18 Behold now, I have ¹ordered *my* cause; I know that I shall be ᵃjustified.²

19 ᵃWho *is* he *that* will ¹plead with me? for now, if I hold my tongue, I shall ²give up the ghost.

20 ᵃOnly do not two *things* unto me: then will I not hide myself from thee.

21 ᵃWithdraw thine hand far from me: and let not thy dread make me afraid.

22 Then call thou, and I will ᵃanswer: or let me speak, and answer thou me.

23 How many *are* mine iniquities and sins? make me to know my transgression and my sin.

24 ᵃWherefore hidest thou thy face, and ᵇholdest¹ me for thine enemy?

25 ᵃWilt thou break a leaf driven to and fro? and wilt thou pursue the dry stubble?

26 For thou writest bitter things against me, and ᵃmakest me ¹to possess the iniquities of my youth.

27 ᵃThou puttest my feet also in the stocks, and ¹lookest narrowly unto all my paths; thou ²settest a print upon the ³heels of my feet.

28 And he, as a rotten thing, ¹consumeth, as a garment that is moth eaten.

## CHAPTER 14

Man *that is* born of a woman *is* of few days, and ᵃfull of ¹trouble.

2 ᵃHe cometh forth like a flower, and ¹is cut down: he fleeth also as a shadow, and continueth not.

3 And dost ᵃthou open thine eyes upon ¹such an one, and ᵇbringest me into judgment with thee?

4 Who ᵃcan bring a clean *thing* out of an unclean? not one.

5 ᵃSeeing his days *are* determined, the number of his months *are* with thee, thou hast appointed his bounds that he cannot pass;

6 ᵃTurn¹ from him, that he may rest, till he ²shall ³accomplish, ᵇas an ⁴hireling, his day.

7 For there is hope of a tree, if it be cut down, that it will sprout again, and that the tender branch thereof will not cease.

8 Though the root thereof ¹wax old in the earth, and the ²stock thereof die in the ground;

9 *Yet* through the scent of water it will bud, and bring forth boughs like a plant.

10 But man dieth, and ¹wasteth away: yea, man ²giveth up the ghost, and where *is* ᵃhe?

11 *As* the waters ¹fail from the sea, and the flood decayeth and drieth up:

### Cross-references
12:20 ᵃ Job 32:9 ¹ *deprives the trusted ones of speech* ² *discernment*
12:21 ᵃ Ps. 107:40 ¹ *disarms the mighty*
12:22 ᵃ [1 Cor. 4:5]
12:23 ᵃ Is. 9:3; 26:15 ¹ *makes great* ² *Lit. spreads out* ³ *guides*
12:24 ᵃ Ps. 107:4 ¹ *understanding*
12:25 ᵃ Job 5:14; 15:30; 18:18 ᵇ Ps. 107:27
13:2 ᵃ Job 12:3
13:3 ᵃ Job 23:3; 31:35
13:4 ᵃ Job 6:21
13:5 ᵃ Prov. 17:28 ¹ *keep silent* ² *would*
13:7 ᵃ Job 27:4; 36:4 ¹ *unrighteously*
13:8 ¹ *show partiality for him*
13:9 ¹ *Will it be well when he searches*
13:10 ¹ *rebuke*
13:11 ¹ Lit. *exaltation*
13:12 ¹ *platitudes are proverbs of ashes* ² *defences are defences of*
13:13 ¹ *Be silent*
13:14 ᵃ Job 18:4
13:15 ᵃ Ps. 23:4 ᵇ Job 27:5 ¹ *defend my ways*
13:16 ᵃ Job 8:13
13:18 ᵃ [Rom. 8:34] ¹ *prepared my case* ² *vindicated*
13:19 ᵃ Is. 50:8 ¹ *contend* ² *perish*
13:20 ᵃ Job 9:34
13:21 ᵃ Ps. 39:10
13:22 ᵃ Job 9:16; 14:15
13:24 ᵃ [Deut. 32:20] ᵇ Lam. 2:5 ¹ *hold me as*
13:25 ᵃ Is. 42:3
13:26 ᵃ Job 20:11 ¹ *inherit*
13:27 ᵃ Job 33:11 ¹ *watch carefully* ² *set a limit, lit. inscribe a print* ³ *soles, lit. roots*
13:28 ¹ *decays*
14:1 ᵃ Eccl. 2:23 ¹ *turmoil*
14:2 ᵃ Job 8:9 ¹ *fades away*
14:3 ᵃ Ps. 8:4; 144:3 ᵇ [Ps. 143:2]

¹ LXX, Vg., Syr. *him*  14:4  ᵃ [Ps. 51:2, 5, 10]  14:5 ᵃ Job 7:1; 21:21  14:6 ᵃ Ps. 39:13  ᵇ Job 7:1 ¹ *look away* ² Lit. *cease* ³ *finishes* ⁴ *hired man*  14:8 ¹ *grows* ² *stump*  14:10 ᵃ Job 10:21, 22 ¹ *is laid away* ² *breathes his last*  14:11 ¹ *disappear*

12 So man lieth down, and riseth not: [a]till the heavens *be* no more, they shall not awake, nor be raised out of their sleep.

13 O that thou wouldest hide me in the grave, that thou wouldest [1]keep me secret, until thy wrath be past, that thou wouldest appoint me a set time, and remember me!

14 If a man die, shall he live *again?* all the days of my [1]appointed time [a]will I wait, till my change come.

15 [a]Thou shalt call, and I will answer thee: thou wilt have a desire to the work of thine hands.

16 [a]For now thou numberest my steps: dost thou not watch over my sin?

17 [a]My transgression *is* sealed up in a bag, and thou [1]sewest up mine iniquity.

18 And surely the mountain [1]falling cometh to nought, and the rock is removed out of his place.

19 The waters [1]wear the stones: thou washest away the things which grow *out* of the dust of the earth; and thou destroyest the hope of man.

20 Thou prevailest for ever against him, and he passeth: thou changest his countenance, and sendest him away.

21 His sons come to honour, and [a]he knoweth *it* not; and they are brought low, but he perceiveth *it* not of them.

22 But his flesh upon him shall have pain, and his soul within him shall mourn.

## CHAPTER 15

T HEN answered [a]Eliphaz the Temanite, and said,

2 Should a wise man [1]utter vain knowledge, and fill [2]his belly with the east wind?

3 Should he reason with unprofitable talk? or with speeches wherewith he can do no good?

4 Yea, thou castest off fear, and restrainest [1]prayer before God.

5 For [1]thy mouth uttereth thine iniquity, and thou choosest the tongue of the crafty.

6 [a]Thine own mouth condemneth thee, and not I: yea, thine own lips testify against thee.

7 *Art* thou the first man *that* was born? [a]or wast thou made before the hills?

8 [a]Hast thou heard the [1]secret of God? and dost thou [2]restrain wisdom to thyself?

9 [a]What knowest thou, that we know not? *what* understandest thou, which *is* not in us?

10 [a]With us *are* both the grayheaded and very aged men, much elder than thy father.

11 *Are* the consolations of God [1]small with thee? is there any [2]secret thing with thee?

12 Why doth thine heart carry thee away? and [1]what do thy eyes wink at,

13 That thou turnest thy spirit against God, and lettest *such* words go out of thy mouth?

14 [a]What *is* man, that he should be clean? and *he which is* born of a woman, that he should be righteous?

15 [a]Behold, [1]he putteth no trust in his saints; yea, the heavens are not clean in his sight.

16 [a]How much more abominable and filthy *is* man, [b]which drinketh iniquity like water?

17 I will [1]shew thee, hear me; and that *which* I have seen I will declare;

18 Which wise men have told [a]from their fathers, and have not hid *it:*

19 Unto whom alone the [1]earth was given, and [a]no [2]stranger passed among them.

20 The wicked man [1]travaileth with pain all *his* days, [a]and the number of years is hidden to the oppressor.

21 A [1]dreadful sound *is* in his ears: [a]in prosperity the destroyer shall come upon him.

22 He believeth not that he shall [a]return out of darkness, and [1]he is waited for of the sword.

23 He [a]wandereth abroad for bread, *saying,* Where *is it?* he knoweth [b]that the day of darkness is ready at his hand.

24 Trouble and anguish shall make him afraid; they shall [1]prevail against him, as a king ready to the [2]battle.

25 For he stretcheth out his hand against God, and [1]strengtheneth himself against the Almighty.

26 He [1]runneth upon him, *even* on *his* neck, upon the thick bosses of his bucklers:

27 [a]Because he covereth his face with his fatness, and maketh [1]collops of fat on *his* flanks.

28 And he dwelleth in desolate cities, *and* in houses which no man inhabiteth, which are ready to become [1]heaps.

29 He shall not be rich, neither shall his [1]substance [a]continue, neither shall [2]he prolong the perfection thereof upon the earth.

30 He shall not depart out of darkness; the flame shall dry up his branches, and [a]by the breath of his mouth shall he go away.

31 Let not him that is deceived [a]trust in [1]vanity: for vanity shall be his [2]recompence.

32 It shall be accomplished [a]before his time, and his branch shall not be green.

### Cross-references (center column)

14:12 [a] [Is. 51:6; 65:17; 66:22]
14:13 [1] *conceal me*
14:14 [a] Job 13:15 [1] *hard service*
14:15 [a] Job 13:22
14:16 [a] Prov. 5:21
14:17 [a] Deut. 32:32–34 [1] Lit. *plaster over (cover over)*
14:18 [1] *falls and crumbles away*
14:19 [1] *wear away stones*
14:21 [a] Eccl. 9:5
15:1 [a] Job 4:1
15:2 [1] *answer with empty knowledge* [2] *himself*
15:4 [1] *meditation or complaint*
15:5 [1] *your iniquity teaches your mouth*
15:6 [a] [Luke 19:22]
15:7 [a] Prov. 8:25
15:8 [a] Rom. 11:34 [1] *secret counsel* [2] *limit*
15:9 [a] Job 12:3; 13:2
15:10 [a] Job 8:8–10; 12:12; 32:6, 7
15:11 [1] *too small* [2] *Or gently spoken word*
15:12 [1] *Or why do your eyes flash*
15:14 [a] Prov. 20:9
15:15 [a] Job 4:18; 25:5 [1] *God*
15:16 [a] Ps. 14:3; 53:3 [b] Prov. 19:28
15:17 [1] *tell*
15:18 [a] Job 8:8; 20:4
15:19 [a] Joel 3:17 [1] *land* [2] *alien*
15:20 [a] Ps. 90:12 [1] *writhes*
15:21 [a] 1 Thess. 5:3 [1] *sound of dreadful or terrifying things*
15:22 [a] Job 14:10–12 [1] *he watches for*
15:23 [a] Ps. 59:15; 109:10 [b] Job 18:12
15:24 [1] *overpower* [2] *attack*
15:25 [1] *acts defiantly*
15:26 [1] *runs stubbornly against him with a thick, strong, embossed shield*
15:27 [a] Ps. 17:10; 73:7; 119:70 [1] *his waist heavy with fat*
15:28 [1] *ruins*

15:29 [a] Job 20:28; 27:16, 17 [1] *wealth* [2] *his possessions overspread the earth* 15:30 [a] Job 4:9 15:31 [a] Is. 59:4 [1] *futile things* [2] *reward* 15:32 [a] Job 22:16

33 He shall shake off his unripe grape as the vine, and shall cast off his flower as the olive.

34 For the congregation of hypocrites *shall be* ¹desolate, and fire shall consume the ²tabernacles of bribery.

35 ªThey conceive ¹mischief, and bring forth ²vanity, and their ³belly prepareth deceit.

## CHAPTER 16

THEN Job answered and said,
  2 I have heard many such things: ªmiserable¹ comforters *are* ye all.

3 Shall ¹vain words have an end? or what ²emboldeneth thee that thou answerest?

4 I also could speak as ye *do:* if your soul were in my soul's stead, I could heap up words against you, and ªshake mine head at you.

5 *But* I would strengthen you with my mouth, and the ¹moving of my lips should ²assuage *your grief.*

6 Though I speak, my grief is not ¹assuaged: and *though* I ²forbear, what ³am I eased?

7 But now he hath made me ªweary: thou ᵇhast made desolate all my company.

8 And thou hast filled me with wrinkles, *which* is a ªwitness *against me:* and my leanness rising up in me beareth witness to my face.

9 ªHe teareth *me* in his wrath, who hateth me: he gnasheth upon me with his teeth; ᵇmine ¹enemy sharpeneth his eyes upon me.

10 ¹They have ªgaped upon me with their mouth; they ᵇhave smitten me upon the cheek reproachfully; they have gathered themselves together against me.

11 God ªhath delivered me to the ungodly, and turned me over into the hands of the wicked.

12 I was at ease, but he hath ¹broken me ªasunder: he hath also taken *me* by my neck, and shaken me to pieces, and ᵇset me up for his ²mark.

13 His archers ¹compass me round about, he ²cleaveth my reins asunder, and doth not ³spare; he poureth out my gall upon the ground.

14 He breaketh me with ¹breach upon breach, he runneth upon me like a ²giant.

15 I have sewed sackcloth upon my skin, and ªdefiled¹ my horn in the dust.

16 My face is ¹foul with weeping, and on my eyelids *is* the shadow of death;

17 ¹Not for *any* injustice in mine hands: also my prayer *is* pure.

18 O earth, cover not thou my blood, and ªlet my cry have no ¹place.

19 Also now, behold, ªmy witness *is* in heaven, and my record *is* on high.

20 My friends scorn me: *but* mine eye poureth out *tears* unto God.

21 ªO that one might plead for a man with God, as a man *pleadeth* for his ¹neighbour!

22 When a few years are ¹come, then I shall ªgo the way *whence* I shall not return.

## CHAPTER 17

MY ¹breath is corrupt, my days are ²extinct, ªthe graves *are ready* for me.

2 *Are there* not mockers with me? and doth not mine eye ¹continue in their ªprovocation?

3 Lay down now, put me in a ¹surety with thee; who *is* he *that* ªwill ²strike hands with me?

4 For thou hast hid their heart from ªunderstanding: therefore shalt thou not exalt *them.*

5 He that speaketh flattery to *his* friends, even the eyes of his children shall ªfail.

6 He hath made me also ªa byword of the people; and ¹aforetime I was as a tabret.

7 ªMine eye also is dim by reason of sorrow, and all my members *are* as a shadow.

8 Upright *men* shall be astonied at this, and the innocent shall stir up himself against the hypocrite.

9 The righteous also shall hold on his ªway, and he that hath ᵇclean hands shall be stronger and stronger.

10 But as for you all, ªdo¹ ye return, and come now: for I cannot find *one* wise *man* among you.

11 ªMy days are past, my purposes are broken off, *even* the ¹thoughts of my heart.

12 They change the night into day: ¹the light *is* short because of darkness.

13 ¹If I wait, the grave *is* mine house: I have made my bed in the darkness.

14 I have said to corruption, Thou *art* my father: to the worm, *Thou art* my mother, and my sister.

15 And where *is* now my ªhope? as for my hope, who shall see it?

16 They shall go down ªto the bars of ¹the pit, when *our* ᵇrest together *is* in the dust.

## CHAPTER 18

THEN answered ªBildad the Shuhite, and said,

2 How long *will it be ere* ye make an end of words? ¹mark, and afterwards we will speak.

---

15:34 ¹ *barren*
² *tents*
15:35 ª Is. 59:4
¹ *trouble* ² *futility*
³ *womb*
16:2 ª Job 13:4;
21:34 ¹ *troublesome*
16:3 ¹ *empty words,* lit. *words of wind* ² *provokes*
16:4 ª Ps. 22:7; 109:25
16:5 ¹ *comfort from* ² *relieve*
16:6 ¹ *relieved* ² *remain silent* ³ *ease do I get*
16:7 ª Job 7:3
ᵇ Job 16:20; 19:13–15
16:8 ª Job 10:17
16:9 ª Hos. 6:1
ᵇ Job 13:24; 33:10 ¹ *adversary sharpens his gaze on*
16:10 ª Ps. 22:13; 35:21 ᵇ Lam. 3:30
¹ *Men*
16:11 ª Job 1:15, 17
16:12 ª Job 9:17 ᵇ Job 7:20
¹ *shattered me* ² *target*
16:13 ¹ *surround* ² *pierces my heart,* lit. *splits my kidneys* ³ *pity*
16:14 ¹ *wound* ² MT *warrior*
16:15 ª Ps. 7:5
¹ *laid my head*
16:16 ¹ *flushed from*
16:17 ¹ *Although no violence is in*
16:18 ª [Ps. 66:18]
¹ *burial place*
16:19 ª Rom. 1:9
16:21 ª Job 31:35
¹ *friend*
16:22 ª Eccl. 12:5
¹ *finished*
17:1 ª Ps. 88:3, 4
¹ *spirit is broken* ² *extinguished*
17:2 ª Job 12:4; 17:6; 30:1, 9; 34:7
¹ *dwell,* lit. *lodge*
17:3 ª Prov. 6:1;
17:18; 22:26
¹ *pledge* ² *shake*
17:4 ª Job 12:20; 32:9
17:5 ª Job 11:20
17:6 ª Job 30:9
¹ *I have become one in whose face they spit*
17:7 ª Ps. 6:7; 31:9
17:9 ª Prov. 4:18
ᵇ Ps. 24:4
17:10 ª Job 6:29
¹ *please, come back again*
17:11 ª Job 7:6 ¹ *desires* 17:12 ¹ *the light is near in the face of darkness* 17:13 ¹ *If I wait for the grave as* 17:15 ª Job 7:6; 13:15; 14:19; 19:10 17:16 ª Jon. 2:6 ᵇ Job 3:17–19; 21:33 ¹ Heb. *Sheol* 18:1 ª Job 8:1 18:2 ¹ *gain understanding*

3 Wherefore are we counted [a]as beasts, *and* [1]reputed vile in your sight?

4 [a]He teareth [1]himself in his anger: shall the earth be forsaken for thee? and shall the rock be removed out of his place?

5 Yea, [a]the light of the wicked shall be put out, and the spark of his fire shall not shine.

6 The light shall be dark in his [1]tabernacle, [a]and his [2]candle shall be put out [3]with him.

7 The steps of his strength shall be [1]straitened, and [a]his own counsel shall cast him down.

8 For [a]he is cast into a net by his own feet, and he walketh upon a snare.

9 The [1]gin shall take *him* by the heel, *and* [a]the[2] robber shall prevail against him.

10 [1]The snare *is* laid for him in the ground, and a trap for him in the way.

11 [a]Terrors shall make him afraid on every side, and shall drive him to his feet.

12 His strength shall be hungerbitten, and [a]destruction *shall be* ready at his side.

13 It shall devour [1]the strength of his skin: *even* the firstborn of death shall devour his [2]strength.

14 [a]His[1] confidence shall be rooted out of his tabernacle, and [2]it shall bring him to the king of terrors.

15 [1]It shall dwell in his tabernacle, [2]because *it is* none of his: brimstone shall be scattered upon his habitation.

16 [a]His roots shall be dried up beneath, and above shall his branch be cut off.

17 [a]His[1] remembrance shall perish from the earth, and he shall have no name [2]in the street.

18 [1]He shall be driven from light into darkness, and chased out of the world.

19 [a]He shall neither have son nor [1]nephew among his people, nor any remaining in his dwellings.

20 [1]They that come after *him* shall be astonied [a]at his day, as [2]they that went before [3]were affrighted.

21 Surely such *are* the dwellings of the wicked, and this *is* the place *of him that* [a]knoweth not God.

### CHAPTER 19

THEN Job answered and said,

2 How long will ye [1]vex my soul, and break me in pieces with words?

3 These ten times have ye [1]reproached me: ye are not ashamed *that* ye [2]make yourselves strange to me.

4 And be it indeed *that* I have erred, mine error remaineth with myself.

5 If indeed ye will [a]magnify *yourselves* against me, and plead against me my [1]reproach:

6 Know now that [a]God hath [1]overthrown me, and hath [2]compassed me with his net.

7 Behold, I cry out [1]of wrong, but I am not heard: I cry aloud, but *there is* no [2]judgment.

8 [a]He hath [1]fenced up my way that I cannot pass, and he hath set darkness in my paths.

9 [a]He hath stripped me of my glory, and taken the crown *from* my head.

10 He [1]hath destroyed me on every side, and I am gone: and mine [a]hope hath he [2]removed like a tree.

11 He hath also kindled his wrath against me, and [a]he counteth me unto him as *one of* his enemies.

12 His troops come together, and raise up their way against me, and encamp round about my [1]tabernacle.

13 [a]He hath [1]put my brethren far from me, and mine acquaintance are [2]verily estranged from me.

14 My kinsfolk have failed, and my [1]familiar friends have forgotten me.

15 They that dwell in mine house, and my maids, count me for a stranger: I am an alien in their sight.

16 I called my servant, and he gave *me* no answer; I intreated him with my mouth.

17 My breath is [1]strange to my wife, though I intreated for the children's *sake* of mine own body.

18 Yea, [a]young children despised me; I arose, and they spake against me.

19 [a]All my [1]inward friends abhorred me: and they whom I loved are turned against me.

20 [a]My bone [1]cleaveth to my skin and to my flesh, and I am escaped with the skin of my teeth.

21 Have pity upon me, have pity upon me, O ye my friends; for the hand of God hath touched me.

22 Why do ye [a]persecute me as God, and are not satisfied with my flesh?

23 Oh that my words were now written! oh that they were printed in a book!

24 That they were graven with an iron pen and lead in the rock for ever!

25 For I know *that* my [1]redeemer liveth, and *that* he shall stand [2]at the latter *day* upon the earth:

26 And *though* after my skin *worms* destroy this *body,* yet [a]in my flesh shall I see God:

27 Whom I shall see for myself, and mine eyes shall behold, and not another; [1]*though* my reins be consumed within me.

18:3 [a] Ps. 73:22
[1] *regarded as stupid*
18:4 [a] Job 13:14
[1] Lit. *his soul*
18:5 [a] Prov. 13:9; 20:20; 24:20
18:6 [a] Job 21:17
[1] *tent* [2] *lamp*
[3] *beside him*
18:7 [a] Job 5:12, 13; 15:6 [1] *shortened*
18:8 [a] Job 22:10
18:9 [a] Job 5:5
[1] *net* [2] *a snare*
18:10 [1] *A noose is hidden for him*
18:11 [a] Jer. 6:25
18:12 [a] Job 15:23
18:13 [1] *patches of* [2] *limbs or parts*
18:14 [a] Job 11:20
[1] *He shall be rooted from the security of his tent* [2] *they parade him before*
18:15 [1] *They* [2] *who are none of his*
18:16 [a] Job 29:19
18:17 [a] [Ps. 34:16]
[1] *The memory of him* [2] *among the renown or distinguished,* lit. *before the outside*
18:18 [1] *Or They drive him*
18:19 [a] Is. 14:22
[1] *posterity*
18:20 [a] Ps. 37:13
[1] *Those in the west shall* [2] *those in the east* [3] Lit. *were seized with horror*
18:21 [a] Jer. 9:3
19:2 [1] *torment*
19:3 [1] *shamed or disgraced* [2] *deal harshly with me*
19:5 [a] Ps. 35:26; 38:16; 55:12, 13
[1] *humiliation*
19:6 [a] Job 16:11
[1] *wronged* [2] *surrounded*
19:7 [1] *concerning violence* [2] *justice*
19:8 [a] Job 3:23
[1] *walled off my way*
19:9 [a] Ps. 89:44
19:10 [a] Job 17:14, 16 [1] *breaks me down on* [2] *uprooted*
19:11 [a] Job 13:24; 33:10
19:12 [1] *tent*
19:13 [a] Ps. 31:11; 38:11; 69:8; 88:8, 18 [1] *removed my brothers* [2] *completely*
19:14 [1] *close* 19:17 [1] *repulsive* 19:18 [a] 2 Kin. 2:23
19:19 [a] Ps. 38:11; 55:12, 13 [1] *close* 19:20 [a] Ps. 102:5
[1] *clings* 19:22 [a] Ps. 69:26 19:25 [1] Lit. *kinsman* [2] *at last* 19:26 [a] [Ps. 17:15] 19:27 [1] *how my heart yearns*

28 But ye should say, Why persecute we him, seeing the root of the matter is found in me?

29 Be ye afraid of the sword: for wrath *bringeth* the punishments of the sword, that ye may know *there is* a judgment.

## CHAPTER 20

THEN answered ªZophar the Naamathite, and said,

2 Therefore do my ¹thoughts cause me to answer, ²and for *this* I make haste.

3 I have heard the ¹check of my reproach, and the spirit of my understanding causeth me to answer.

4 Knowest thou *not* this of ªold, since man was placed upon earth,

5 ªThat the triumphing of the wicked *is* short, and the joy of the hypocrite *but* for a ᵇmoment?

6 ªThough his excellency mount up to the heavens, and his head reach unto the clouds;

7 *Yet* he shall perish for ever like his own ¹dung: they which have seen him shall say, Where *is* he?

8 He shall fly away ªas a dream, and shall not be found: yea, he ᵇshall be chased away as a vision of the night.

9 The eye also *which* saw him shall *see him* no more; neither shall his place any more behold him.

10 His children shall seek ¹to please the poor, and his hands shall restore their goods.

11 His bones are full¹ *of* ªthe sin of his youth, ᵇwhich shall lie down with him in the dust.

12 Though wickedness be sweet in his mouth, *though* he hide it under his tongue;

13 *Though* he spare it, and forsake it not; but keep it still ¹within his mouth:

14 *Yet* his ¹meat in his bowels ²is turned, *it* ³*is* the gall of asps within him.

15 He hath swallowed down riches, and he shall vomit them up again: God shall cast them out of his belly.

16 He shall suck the poison of ¹asps: the viper's tongue shall slay him.

17 He shall not see ªthe ¹rivers, the ²floods, the brooks of honey and butter.

18 That which he laboured for shall he restore, and shall not swallow *it* down: ¹according to *his* substance *shall* the restitution *be,* and he shall not rejoice *therein.*

19 Because he hath oppressed *and* hath forsaken the poor; *because* he hath violently ¹taken away an house which he builded not;

20 ªSurely he shall not ¹feel quietness ²in his belly, he shall not save ³of that which he desired.

20:1 ª Job 11:1
20:2 ¹ *anxious thoughts*
² *because of the turmoil within me*
20:3 ¹ *reproof of my insulting correction*
20:4 ª Job 8:8; 15:10
20:5 ª Ps. 37:35, 36  ᵇ [Job 8:13; 13:16; 15:34; 27:8]
20:6 ª Is. 14:13, 14
20:7 ¹ *refuse*
20:8 ª Ps. 73:20; 90:5  ᵇ Job 18:18; 27:21–23
20:10 ¹ *the favour of*
20:11 ª Job 13:26  ᵇ Job 21:26
¹ *youthful vigour*
20:13 ¹ Lit. *in his palate*
20:14 ¹ *food in his stomach* ² *turns sour* ³ *becomes cobra venom*
20:16 ¹ *cobras*
20:17 ª Jer. 17:8
¹ *streams* ² *rivers flowing with honey and cream*
20:18 ¹ *from the proceeds of his business, he will have no enjoyment*
20:19 ¹ *seized*
20:20 ª Eccl. 5:13–15  ¹ Lit. *know* ² *in his heart* ³ *anything which*
20:21 ¹ *food* ² *his prosperity will not endure*
20:22 ¹ *his self-sufficiency* ² *distress* ³ Or *wretched or sufferer*
20:24 ª Amos 5:19  ¹ *bronze*
20:25 ª Job 16:13  ᵇ Job 18:11, 14
¹ *Gallbladder*
20:26 ª Ps. 21:9
¹ *Total* ² *reserved for his treasures* ³ *an unfanned fire* ⁴ *tent*
20:28 ª Job 20:15; 21:30
20:29 ª Job 27:13; 31:2, 3
21:2 ¹ *comfort*
21:3 ª Job 16:10
¹ *Bear with me*
21:4 ¹ *impatient*
21:5 ª Judg. 18:19
¹ *Look at me*
21:7 ª [Jer. 12:1]
21:8 ¹ *descendants are*

21 There shall none of his ¹meat be left; therefore ²shall no man look for his goods.

22 In ¹the fulness of his sufficiency he shall be in ²straits: every hand of the ³wicked shall come upon him.

23 *When* he is about to fill his belly, *God* shall cast the fury of his wrath upon him, and shall rain *it* upon him while he is eating.

24 ªHe shall flee from the iron weapon, *and* the bow of ¹steel shall strike him through.

25 It is drawn, and cometh out of the body; yea, ªthe glittering sword cometh out of his ¹gall: ᵇterrors *are* upon him.

26 ¹All darkness *shall be* ²hid in his secret places: ªa ³fire not blown shall consume him; it shall go ill with him that is left in his ⁴tabernacle.

27 The heaven shall reveal his iniquity; and the earth shall rise up against him.

28 The increase of his house shall depart, *and his goods* shall flow away in the day of his ªwrath.

29 ªThis *is* the portion of a wicked man from God, and the heritage appointed unto him by God.

## CHAPTER 21

BUT Job answered and said,
2 Hear diligently my speech, and let this be your ¹consolations.

3 ¹Suffer me that I may speak; and after that I have spoken, ªmock on.

4 As for me, *is* my complaint to man? and if *it were so,* why should not my spirit be ¹troubled?

5 ¹Mark me, and be astonished, ªand lay *your* hand upon *your* mouth.

6 Even when I remember I am afraid, and trembling taketh hold on my flesh.

7 ªWherefore do the wicked live, become old, yea, are mighty in power?

8 Their ¹seed is established in their sight with them, and their offspring before their eyes.

9 Their houses *are* safe from fear, ªneither *is* the rod of ¹God upon them.

10 Their bull ¹gendereth, and faileth not; their cow calveth, ²and ªcasteth not her calf.

11 They send forth their little ones like a flock, and their children dance.

12 They ¹take the timbrel and harp, and rejoice at the sound of the ²organ.

13 They ªspend their days in wealth, and ¹in a moment go down to the ²grave.

14 ªTherefore they say unto God, Depart from us; for we desire not the knowledge of thy ways.

21:9 ª Ps. 73:5  ¹ God's chastisement  21:10 ª Ex. 23:26
¹ *breeds* ² *without miscarriage*  21:12 ¹ *sing to the tambourine* ² *flute*  21:13 ª Job 21:23; 36:11  ¹ Without lingering illness  ² Heb. *Sheol*  21:14 ª Job 22:17

15 <sup></sup>What *is* the Almighty, that we should serve him? and <sup></sup>what profit should we have, if we pray unto him?

16 Lo, <sup>1</sup>their good *is* not in their hand: <sup></sup>the counsel of the wicked is far from me.

17 How oft is the <sup>1</sup>candle of the wicked put out! and *how oft* cometh their destruction upon them! *God* <sup></sup>distributeth sorrows in his anger.

18 <sup></sup>They are as stubble before the wind, and as chaff that the storm <sup>1</sup>carrieth away.

19 God <sup>1</sup>layeth up his iniquity <sup></sup>for his children: he rewardeth him, and he shall know *it*.

20 His eyes shall see his destruction, and <sup></sup>he shall drink of the wrath of the Almighty.

21 For what <sup>1</sup>pleasure *hath* he in his house after him, when the number of his months is cut off in the midst?

22 <sup></sup>Shall *any* teach God knowledge? seeing he judgeth those that are high.

23 One dieth in his full strength, being wholly at ease and <sup>1</sup>quiet.

24 His <sup>1</sup>breasts are full of milk, and <sup>2</sup>his bones are moistened with marrow.

25 And another dieth in the bitterness of his soul, and never eateth with pleasure.

26 They shall <sup></sup>lie down alike in the dust, and the worms shall cover them.

27 Behold, I know your thoughts, and the <sup>1</sup>devices *which* ye wrongfully imagine against me.

28 For ye say, Where *is* the house of the prince? and <sup>1</sup>where *are* the dwelling places of the wicked?

29 Have ye not asked them that <sup>1</sup>go by the way? and do ye not know their <sup>2</sup>tokens,

30 <sup></sup>That the wicked is reserved to the day of destruction? they shall be brought forth to the day of wrath.

31 Who shall declare his way to his face? and who shall repay him *what* he hath done?

32 Yet shall he be brought to the grave, and <sup>1</sup>shall remain in the tomb.

33 The clods of the valley shall be sweet unto him, and <sup></sup>every man shall <sup>1</sup>draw after him, as *there are* innumerable before him.

34 How then comfort ye me <sup>1</sup>in vain, seeing in your answers there remaineth <sup>2</sup>falsehood?

## CHAPTER 22

THEN <sup></sup>Eliphaz the Temanite answered and said,

2 <sup></sup>Can a man be profitable unto God, <sup>1</sup>as he that is wise may be profitable unto himself?

3 *Is it* any pleasure to the Almighty, that thou art righteous? or *is it* gain *to him,* that thou makest thy ways <sup>1</sup>perfect?

4 Will he reprove thee <sup>1</sup>for fear of thee? will he enter with thee into judgment?

5 *Is* not thy wickedness great? and thine iniquities <sup>1</sup>infinite?

6 For thou hast <sup></sup>taken a pledge from thy brother for nought, and stripped the naked of their clothing.

7 Thou hast not given water to the weary to drink, and thou <sup></sup>hast withholden bread from the hungry.

8 But *as for* the <sup>1</sup>mighty man, he <sup>2</sup>had the earth; and the honourable man dwelt in it.

9 Thou hast sent widows away empty, and the <sup>1</sup>arms of the fatherless have been <sup>2</sup>broken.

10 Therefore snares *are* round about thee, and sudden fear troubleth thee;

11 Or darkness, *that* thou canst not see; and abundance of <sup></sup>waters cover thee.

12 *Is* not God in the height of heaven? and behold the <sup>1</sup>height of the stars, how high they are!

13 And thou sayest, <sup></sup>How<sup>1</sup> doth God know? can he judge through the <sup>2</sup>dark cloud?

14 <sup></sup>Thick clouds *are* a covering to him, that he seeth not; and he walketh in the circuit of heaven.

15 <sup>1</sup>Hast thou marked the old way which wicked men have trodden?

16 Which <sup></sup>were cut down out of time, whose foundation was <sup>1</sup>overflown with a flood:

17 <sup></sup>Which said unto God, Depart from us: and what can the Almighty do <sup>1</sup>for them?

18 Yet he filled their houses with good *things:* but the counsel of the wicked is far from me.

19 <sup></sup>The righteous see *it,* and are glad: and the innocent laugh them to scorn.

20 Whereas our <sup>1</sup>substance is not cut down, but the remnant of them the fire consumeth.

21 Acquaint now thyself with <sup>1</sup>him, and <sup></sup>be at peace: thereby good shall come unto thee.

22 Receive, I pray thee, <sup>1</sup>the <sup></sup>law from his mouth, and <sup></sup>lay up his words in thine heart.

23 If thou return to the Almighty, thou shalt be built up, thou shalt put away iniquity far from thy <sup>1</sup>tabernacles.

24 Then shalt thou <sup></sup>lay up gold <sup>1</sup>as dust, and the *gold* of Ophir as the stones of the brooks.

25 Yea, the Almighty shall be thy <sup>1</sup>defence, and thou shalt have plenty of silver.

21:15 <sup></sup> Ex. 5:2 <sup></sup> Mal. 3:14
21:16 <sup></sup> Prov. 1:10 <sup>1</sup> *their prosperity*
21:17 <sup></sup> [Luke 12:46] <sup>1</sup> *lamp*
21:18 <sup></sup> Ps. 1:4; 35:5 <sup>1</sup> Lit. *steals away*
21:19 <sup></sup> [Ex. 20:5] <sup>1</sup> *stores up a man's iniquity*
21:20 <sup></sup> Is. 51:17
21:21 <sup>1</sup> *does he care about his household*
21:22 <sup></sup> [Is. 40:13; 45:9]
21:23 <sup>1</sup> *secure*
21:24 <sup>1</sup> LXX, Vg. *bowels*; Syr. *sides* <sup>2</sup> *the marrow of his bones is moist*
21:26 <sup></sup> Eccl. 9:2
21:27 <sup>1</sup> *schemes*
21:28 <sup>1</sup> MT *where is the tent, the dwelling places*
21:29 <sup>1</sup> *travel the road* <sup>2</sup> *signs*
21:30 <sup></sup> [Prov. 16:4]
21:32 <sup>1</sup> *a vigil shall be kept over*
21:33 <sup></sup> Heb. 9:27 <sup>1</sup> *follow*
21:34 <sup>1</sup> *with empty words* <sup>2</sup> *faithlessness*
22:1 <sup></sup> Job 4:1; 15:1; 42:9
22:2 <sup></sup> [Luke 17:10] <sup>1</sup> *though*
22:3 <sup>1</sup> *blameless*
22:4 <sup>1</sup> *because of your fear of him*
22:5 <sup>1</sup> *without end*
22:6 <sup></sup> [Ex. 22:26, 27]
22:7 <sup></sup> Deut. 15:7
22:8 <sup>1</sup> Lit. *man of arm* <sup>2</sup> *possessed the land*
22:9 <sup>1</sup> *strength* <sup>2</sup> *crushed*
22:11 <sup></sup> Ps. 69:1, 2; 124:5
22:12 <sup>1</sup> *highest stars*
22:13 <sup></sup> Ps. 73:11 <sup>1</sup> *What* <sup>2</sup> *thick darkness*
22:14 <sup></sup> Ps. 139:11, 12
22:15 <sup>1</sup> *Will you keep to the*
22:16 <sup></sup> Job 14:19; 15:32 <sup>1</sup> *washed away*
22:17 <sup></sup> Job 21:14, 15 <sup>1</sup> *to them?*; LXX, Syr. *to us?*
22:19 <sup></sup> Ps. 52:6; 58:10; 107:42
22:20 <sup>1</sup> MT *adversary is*  22:21 <sup></sup> Is. 27:5 <sup>1</sup> *God*
22:22 <sup></sup> Prov. 2:6 <sup></sup> [Ps. 119:11] <sup>1</sup> *instruction*
22:23 <sup>1</sup> *tents*  22:24 <sup></sup> 2 Chr. 1:15 <sup>1</sup> *in the dust*
22:25 <sup>1</sup> MT *gold*

26 For then shalt thou have thy ᵃdelight in the Almighty, and shalt lift up thy face unto God.

27 ᵃThou shalt make thy prayer unto him, and he shall hear thee, and thou shalt pay thy vows.

28 Thou shalt also decree a thing, and it shall be established unto thee: and the light shall shine upon thy ways.

29 When *men* are cast down, then thou shalt say, *There is* ¹lifting up; and ᵃhe shall save the humble person.

30 He shall deliver ¹the island of the innocent: and it is delivered by the pureness of thine hands.

## CHAPTER 23

THEN Job answered and said,

2 Even to day *is* my ᵃcomplaint bitter: my stroke is heavier than my groaning.

3 ᵃOh that I knew where I might find him! *that* I might come *even* to his seat!

4 I would order *my* cause before him, and fill my mouth with arguments.

5 I would know the words *which* he would answer me, and understand what he would say unto me.

6 ᵃWill he ¹plead against me with *his* great power? No; but he would ²put *strength* in me.

7 There the ¹righteous might dispute with him; so should I be delivered for ever from my judge.

8 ᵃBehold, I go forward, but he *is* not *there;* and backward, but I cannot perceive him:

9 On the left hand, where he doth work, ¹but I cannot behold *him;* he ²hideth himself on the right hand, ³that I cannot see *him:*

10 But ᵃhe knoweth the way that I take: *when* ᵇhe hath tried me, I shall come forth as gold.

11 ᵃMy foot hath ¹held his steps, his way have I kept, and not declined.

12 Neither have I gone back from the ᵃcommandment of his lips; ᵇI ¹have esteemed the words of his mouth more than my ²necessary *food.*

13 But he *is* ¹in one *mind,* and who can ²turn him? and *what* ᵃhis soul desireth, even *that* he doeth.

14 For he performeth the thing that *is* ᵃappointed for me: and many such *things are* with him.

15 Therefore am I troubled at his presence: when I consider, I am afraid of him:

16 For God ᵃmaketh my heart ¹soft, and the Almighty troubleth me:

17 Because I was not ᵃcut off ¹before the darkness, *neither* hath he ²covered the darkness from my face.

## CHAPTER 24

WHY, seeing ᵃtimes are not hidden from the Almighty, do they that know him not see his ᵇdays?

2 *Some* remove the ᵃlandmarks; they violently take away flocks, and feed *thereof.*

3 They drive away the ¹ass of the fatherless, they ᵃtake the widow's ox for a pledge.

4 They ¹turn the needy out of the ²way: the ᵃpoor of the ³earth hide themselves together.

5 Behold, *as* wild ¹asses in the desert, go they forth to their work; rising betimes for a prey: the wilderness *yieldeth* food for them *and* for *their* children.

6 They ¹reap *every one* his corn in the field: and they ²gather the vintage of the wicked.

7 They ᵃcause¹ the naked to lodge without clothing, that *they have* no covering in the cold.

8 They are wet with the showers of the mountains, and ᵃembrace¹ the rock for want of a shelter.

9 They pluck the fatherless from the breast, and take a pledge of the poor.

10 They cause *him* to go naked without ᵃclothing, and they take away the sheaf *from* the hungry;

11 *Which* make oil within their walls, *and* tread *their* winepresses, and suffer thirst.

12 Men groan from out of the city, and the soul of the wounded crieth out: yet God ¹layeth not folly *to them.*

13 They are of those that rebel against the light; they know not the ways thereof, nor abide in the paths thereof.

14 ᵃThe murderer rising with the light killeth the poor and needy, and in the night is as a thief.

15 ᵃThe eye also of the adulterer waiteth for the twilight, ᵇsaying, No eye shall see me: and ¹disguiseth *his* face.

16 In the dark they ¹dig through houses, *which* they had marked for themselves in the daytime: ᵃthey know not the light.

17 For the morning *is* to them even as the shadow of death: if *one* ¹know them, *they are in* the terrors of the shadow of death.

18 ¹He *is* swift as the waters; their portion is cursed in the earth: ²he beholdeth not the way of the vineyards.

19 Drought and heat ¹consume the snow waters: *so doth* the ²grave *those which* have sinned.

20 The womb shall forget him; the worm shall feed sweetly on him; ᵃhe

shall be no more remembered; and wickedness shall be broken as a tree.

21 He ¹evil entreateth the barren *that* beareth not: and doeth not good to the widow.

22 ¹He draweth also the mighty with his power: he riseth up, and no *man* is sure of life.

23 ¹*Though* it be given him *to be* in safety, whereon he resteth; yet ªhis² eyes *are* upon their ways.

24 They are exalted for a little while, ¹but are gone and brought low; they are ²taken out of the way as all *other*, and cut off as the ³tops of the ears of corn.

25 And if *it be* not *so* now, who will ¹make me a liar, and make my speech ²nothing worth?

## CHAPTER 25

THEN answered ªBildad the Shuhite, and said,

2 Dominion and fear *are* with him, he maketh peace in his high places.

3 ¹Is there any number of his armies? and upon whom doth not ªhis light arise?

4 ªHow then can man be ¹justified with God? or how can he be ᵇclean *that is* born of a woman?

5 Behold even to the moon, and it shineth not; yea, the stars are not pure in his ªsight.

6 How much less man, *that is* ªa ¹worm? and the son of man, *which is* a worm?

## CHAPTER 26

BUT Job answered and said,
2 How hast thou helped *him that is* without power? *how* savest thou the arm *that hath* no strength?

3 How hast thou counselled *him that hath* no wisdom? and *how* hast thou plentifully declared the ¹thing as it is?

4 To whom hast thou uttered words? and whose spirit came from thee?

5 Dead *things* ¹are formed from under the waters, and the inhabitants thereof.

6 ªHell¹ *is* naked before him, and destruction hath no covering.

7 ªHe stretcheth out the north over the empty place, *and* hangeth the earth upon nothing.

8 ªHe bindeth up the waters in his thick clouds; and the cloud ¹is not rent under them.

9 He ¹holdeth back the face of his throne, *and* spreadeth his cloud upon it.

10 ªHe hath ¹compassed the waters ²with bounds, until the day and night come to an end.

11 The pillars of heaven tremble and are ¹astonished at his reproof.

### Center column notes

24:21 ¹ preys upon
24:22 ¹ God
24:23 ª [Prov. 15:3] ¹ He gives them security, and they rely on it ² God's
24:24 ¹ then ² Lit. gathered up ³ heads of grain
24:25 ¹ prove ² worth nothing
25:1 ª Job 8:1; 18:1
25:3 ª James 1:17 ¹ Can his armies be counted?
25:4 ª Job 4:17; 15:14 ᵇ [Job 14:4] ¹ righteous before
25:5 ª Job 15:15
25:6 ª Ps. 22:6 ¹ a maggot
26:3 ¹ sound advice
26:5 ¹ tremble
26:6 ª Prov. 15:11 ¹ Heb. Sheol
26:7 ª Job 9:8
26:8 ª Prov. 30:4 ¹ does not burst
26:9 ¹ covers
26:10 ª Prov. 8:29 ¹ drawn on the face of the waters ² a circular boundary; horizon
26:11 ¹ amazed
26:12 ª Is. 51:15 ¹ stirs up ² breaks up ³ Or the storm, Heb. rahab
26:13 ª Ps. 33:6 ᵇ Is. 27:1 ¹ adorned ² fleeing
26:14 ¹ mere edges ² whisper
27:1 ¹ discourse
27:2 ª Job 34:5 ¹ justice ² Lit. made my soul bitter
27:3 ¹ As long as ² breath of
27:5 ª Job 2:9; 13:15 ¹ Far be it from me ² say you are right ³ put away
27:6 ª Job 2:3; 33:9 ᵇ Acts 24:16 ¹ reprove
27:8 ª Matt. 16:26
27:9 ª Jer. 14:12
27:10 ª Job 22:26, 27
27:11 ¹ about
27:12 ¹ do you behave with complete nonsense
27:13 ª Job 20:29
27:14 ª Deut. 28:41

12 ªHe ¹divideth the sea with his power, and by his understanding he ²smiteth through ³the proud.

13 ªBy his spirit he hath ¹garnished the heavens; his hand hath formed ᵇthe ²crooked serpent.

14 Lo, these *are* ¹parts of his ways: but how little a ²portion is heard of him? but the thunder of his power who can understand?

## CHAPTER 27

MOREOVER Job continued his ¹parable, and said,

2 *As* God liveth, ªwho hath taken away my ¹judgment; and the Almighty, *who* hath ²vexed my soul;

3 ¹All the while my breath *is* in me, and the ²spirit of God *is* in my nostrils;

4 My lips shall not speak wickedness, nor my tongue utter deceit.

5 ¹God forbid that I should ²justify you: till I die ªI will not ³remove mine integrity from me.

6 My righteousness I ªhold fast, and will not let it go: ᵇmy heart shall not ¹reproach *me* so long as I live.

7 Let mine enemy be as the wicked, and he that riseth up against me as the unrighteous.

8 ªFor what *is* the hope of the hypocrite, though he hath gained, when God taketh away his soul?

9 ªWill God hear his cry when trouble cometh upon him?

10 ªWill he delight himself in the Almighty? will he always call upon God?

11 I will teach you ¹by the hand of God: *that* which *is* with the Almighty will I not conceal.

12 Behold, all ye yourselves have seen *it;* why then ¹are ye thus altogether vain?

13 ªThis *is* the portion of a wicked man with God, and the heritage of oppressors, *which* they shall receive of the Almighty.

14 ªIf his children be multiplied, *it is* for the sword: and his offspring shall not be satisfied with bread.

15 Those that ¹remain of him shall be buried in death: and ªhis² widows shall not weep.

16 Though he heap up silver as the dust, and prepare raiment as the clay;

17 He may prepare *it,* but ªthe just shall put *it* on, and the innocent shall divide the silver.

18 He buildeth his house as a moth, and ªas a ¹booth *that* the ²keeper maketh.

19 The rich man shall lie down, but he shall not be gathered: he openeth his eyes, and he *is* ªnot.

27:15 ª Ps. 78:64 ¹ survive him ² their   27:17 ª Prov. 28:8   27:18 ª Is. 1:8 ¹ Temporary shelter ² watchman
27:19 ª Job 7:8, 21; 20:7

20 ᵃTerrors ¹take hold on him as waters, a tempest stealeth him away in the night.

21 The east wind carrieth him away, and he ¹departeth: and as a storm hurleth him out of his place.

22 For ¹God shall cast upon him, and not ᵃspare: he ²would fain flee out of his hand.

23 *Men* shall clap their hands at him, and shall hiss him out of his place.

## CHAPTER 28

SURELY there is ¹a vein for the silver, and a place for gold *where* they ²fine *it.*

2 Iron is taken out of the ¹earth, and ²brass *is* molten *out of* the stone.

3 He setteth an end to darkness, and searcheth out ¹all perfection: the stones of darkness, and the shadow of death.

4 The flood breaketh out from the inhabitant; *even the waters* forgotten of the foot: they are dried up, they are gone away from men.

5 *As for* the earth, out of it cometh bread: and ¹under it is turned up as it were fire.

6 The stones of it *are* the place of sapphires: and it hath ¹dust of gold.

7 *There is* a path which no fowl knoweth, and which the vulture's eye hath not seen:

8 The ¹lion's whelps have not trodden it, nor the fierce lion passed by it.

9 He putteth forth his hand upon the ¹rock; he overturneth the mountains ²by the roots.

10 He cutteth out ¹rivers among the rocks; and his eye seeth every precious thing.

11 He ¹bindeth the floods from overflowing; and *the thing that is* hid bringeth he forth to light.

12 ᵃBut where shall wisdom be found? and where *is* the place of understanding?

13 Man knoweth not the ᵃprice¹ thereof; neither is it found in the land of the living.

14 ᵃThe ¹depth saith, It *is* not in me: and the sea saith, *It is* not with me.

15 It ᵃcannot be gotten for ¹gold, neither shall silver be weighed *for* the price thereof.

16 It cannot be valued with the gold of Ophir, with the precious onyx, or the sapphire.

17 The ᵃgold and the crystal cannot equal it: and the exchange of it *shall not be for* ¹jewels of fine gold.

18 No mention shall be made of ¹coral, or of ²pearls: for the price of wisdom *is* above ᵃrubies.

19 The topaz of Ethiopia shall not equal it, neither shall it be valued with pure ᵃgold.

---

20 ᵃWhence then cometh wisdom? and where *is* the place of understanding?

21 Seeing it is hid from the eyes of all living, and ¹kept close from the fowls of ²the air.

22 ᵃDestruction¹ and death say, We have heard the ²fame thereof with our ears.

23 God understandeth the way thereof, and he knoweth the place thereof.

24 For he looketh to the ends of the earth, *and* ᵃseeth under the whole heaven;

25 ᵃTo make the weight for the winds; and he weigheth the waters by measure.

26 When he ᵃmade¹ a decree for the rain, and a way for the lightning of the ²thunder:

27 Then did he see ¹it, and declare it; he prepared it, yea, and searched it out.

28 And unto man he said, Behold, ᵃthe fear of the Lord, that *is* wisdom; and to depart from evil *is* understanding.

## CHAPTER 29

MOREOVER Job continued his ¹parable, and said,

2 Oh that I were as *in* months ᵃpast, as *in* the days *when* God ᵇpreserved¹ me;

3 ᵃWhen his ¹candle shined upon my head, *and when* by his light I walked *through* darkness;

4 As I was in the days of my youth, when ᵃthe ¹secret of God *was* upon my ²tabernacle;

5 When the Almighty *was* yet with me, *when* my children *were* about me;

6 ¹When ᵃI washed my steps with ²butter, and ᵇthe rock poured me out rivers of oil;

7 When I went out to the gate through the city, *when* I ¹prepared my seat in the street!

8 The young men saw me, and hid themselves: and the aged arose, *and* stood up.

9 The princes refrained talking, and ᵃlaid *their* hand on their mouth.

10 The ¹nobles held their peace, and their ᵃtongue ²cleaved to the roof of their mouth.

11 When the ear heard *me,* then it blessed me; and when the eye saw *me,* it gave ¹witness to me:

12 Because ᵃI delivered the poor that cried, and the fatherless, and *him that had* none to help him.

13 The blessing of him that was ready to perish came upon me: and I

---

27:20 ᵃ Job 18:11
¹ *overtake him like a flood*
27:21 ¹ *is gone*
27:22 ᵃ Jer. 13:14
¹ Lit. *it will hurl against him*
² *desperately flees from its power*
28:1 ¹ *a mine*
² *refine*
28:2 ¹ Lit. *dust*
² *copper is smelted from ore*
28:3 ¹ *every recess*
28:5 ¹ *underneath*
28:6 ¹ *gold dust*
28:8 ¹ *the proud or great lions,* lit. *sons of pride*
28:9 ¹ *flint* ² *At the base*
28:10 ¹ *channels through*
28:11 ¹ *dams up*
28:12 ᵃ Eccl. 7:24
28:13 ᵃ Prov. 3:15
¹ *value*
28:14 ᵃ Job 28:22
¹ *deep*
28:15 ᵃ Prov. 3:13–15; 8:10, 11, 19 ¹ Or *pure gold*
28:17 ᵃ Prov. 8:10; 16:16 ¹ *vessels*
28:18 ᵃ Prov. 3:15; 8:11 ¹ Heb. *ramoth* ² *quartz or crystal*
28:19 ᵃ Prov. 8:19
28:20 ᵃ Job 28:12
28:21 ¹ *concealed* ² *heaven*
28:22 ᵃ Job 28:14
¹ Heb. *Abaddon* ² *report of it*
28:24 ᵃ [Prov. 15:3]
28:25 ᵃ Ps. 135:7
28:26 ᵃ Job 37:3; 38:25 ¹ *set a limit* ² *thunderbolt*
28:27 ¹ *Wisdom*
28:28 ᵃ [Prov. 1:7; 9:10]
29:1 ¹ *discourse*
29:2 ᵃ Job 1:1–5 ᵇ Job 1:10 ¹ *watched over*
29:3 ᵃ Job 18:6 ¹ *lamp*
29:4 ᵃ [Ps. 25:14] ¹ *intimate counsel* ² *tent*
29:6 ᵃ Deut. 32:14; Job 20:17 ᵇ Ps. 81:16 ¹ *My steps were bathed* ² MT *wrath;* ancient vss. and a few Heb. mss. *cream,* Job 20:17
29:7 ¹ *took my seat in the plaza*
29:9 ᵃ Job 21:5 29:10 ᵃ Ps. 137:6 ¹ *voice of the nobles was hushed* ² *stuck* 29:11 ¹ *approval of* 29:12 ᵃ [Ps. 72:12]

caused the widow's heart to sing for joy.

14 ᵃI put on righteousness, and it clothed me: my ¹judgment *was* as a robe and a diadem.

15 I was ᵃeyes to the blind, and feet *was* I to the lame.

16 I *was* a father to the poor: and the ¹cause *which* I knew not I ²searched out.

17 And I brake ᵃthe ¹jaws of the wicked, and plucked the ²spoil out of his teeth.

18 Then I said, ᵃI shall die in my nest, and I shall multiply *my* days as the sand.

19 ᵃMy root *was* spread out ᵇby the waters, and the dew lay all night upon my branch.

20 My glory *was* fresh in me, and my ᵃbow was renewed in my hand.

21 Unto me *men* gave ear, and waited, and kept silence at my counsel.

22 After my words they spake not again; and my speech dropped upon them.

23 And they waited for me as for the rain; and they opened their mouth wide *as* for ᵃthe ¹latter rain.

24 *If* I laughed on them, they believed *it* not; and the light of my countenance they cast not down.

25 I chose out their way, and sat chief, and dwelt as a king in the army, as one *that* comforteth the mourners.

## CHAPTER 30

B UT now *they that are* ¹younger than I have me in derision, whose fathers I would have disdained to have set with the dogs of my flock.

2 Yea, whereto *might* the strength of their hands *profit* me, in whom ¹old age was perished?

3 For want and famine *they were* ¹solitary; fleeing into the wilderness in former time desolate and waste.

4 Who cut up ¹mallows by the bushes, and juniper roots *for* their ²meat.

5 They were driven forth from among *men,* (they ¹cried after them as *after* a thief;)

6 To dwell in the ¹cliffs of the ²valleys, *in* ³caves of the earth, and *in* the rocks.

7 Among the bushes they brayed; under the nettles they were gathered together.

8 *They were* ¹children of fools, yea, ²children of base men: they were ³viler than the earth.

9 ᵃAnd now am I their song, yea, I am their byword.

10 They abhor me, they flee far from me, and ¹spare not ᵃto spit in my face.

11 Because he ᵃhath loosed my ¹cord, and afflicted me, they have also ²let loose the bridle before me.

12 Upon *my* right *hand* rise the ¹youth; they push away my feet, and ᵃthey raise up against me the ways of their destruction.

13 They ¹mar my path, they ²set forward my calamity, they have no helper.

14 They came *upon me* as ¹a wide breaking in *of waters:* ²in the desolation they rolled themselves *upon me.*

15 Terrors are turned upon me: they pursue my ¹soul as the wind: and my ²welfare passeth away as a cloud.

16 ᵃAnd now my soul is ᵇpoured out ¹upon me; the days of affliction have taken hold upon me.

17 My bones are pierced in me in the night season: and my ¹sinews take no rest.

18 By the great force *of my disease* is my garment ¹changed: it bindeth me about as the collar of my coat.

19 He hath cast me into the mire, and I am become like dust and ashes.

20 I ᵃcry unto thee, and thou dost not ¹hear me: I stand up, and thou regardest me *not.*

21 Thou art become cruel to me: with thy strong hand thou ᵃopposest thyself against me.

22 Thou liftest me up to the wind; thou causest me to ride *upon it,* and ¹dissolvest my substance.

23 For I know *that* thou wilt bring me *to* death, and *to* the house ᵃappointed for all living.

24 Howbeit he will not stretch out *his* hand ¹to the grave, though they cry in his destruction.

25 ᵃDid not I weep for him that was in trouble? was *not* my soul grieved for the poor?

26 ᵃWhen I looked for good, then evil came *unto me:* and when I waited for light, there came darkness.

27 ¹My bowels boiled, and rested not: the days of affliction ²prevented me.

28 ᵃI went mourning without the sun: I stood up, *and* I cried in the congregation.

29 ᵃI am a brother to ¹dragons, and a companion to ²owls.

30 ᵃMy skin ¹is black upon me, and ᵇmy bones are burned with ²heat.

31 My harp also is *turned* to mourning, and my ¹organ into the voice of them that weep.

## CHAPTER 31

I MADE a covenant with mine eyes; why then should I ¹think upon a ᵃmaid?²

2 For what ᵃportion of God *is there* from above? and *what* inheritance of the Almighty from on high?

29:14 ᵃ [Is. 59:17; 61:10] ¹ *justice was as a robe and a turban*
29:15 ᵃ Num. 10:31
29:16 ᵃ Prov. 29:7 ¹ *case* ² *investigated*
29:17 ᵃ Prov. 30:14 ¹ *fangs* ² *prey or victim*
29:18 ᵃ Ps. 30:6
29:19 ᵃ Job 18:16 ᵇ Ps. 1:3
29:20 ᵃ Gen. 49:24
29:23 ᵃ [Zech. 10:1] ¹ *spring*
30:1 ¹ Lit. *of fewer days*
30:2 ¹ *vigour has perished*
30:3 ¹ *gaunt*
30:4 ¹ A plant of the salty marshes ² *food*
30:5 ¹ *shouted at*
30:6 ¹ *clefts* ² *wadis* ³ Lit. *holes*
30:8 ¹ Lit. *sons* ² *vile men* ³ *scourged from*
30:9 ᵃ Job 17:6
30:10 ᵃ Is. 50:6 ¹ *do not hesitate*
30:11 ᵃ Job 12:18 ¹ *his bowstring* ² *cast off restraint*
30:12 ᵃ Job 19:12 ¹ *rabble*
30:13 ¹ *break up* ² *promote*
30:14 ¹ *broad breakers* ² *under the ruinous storm*
30:15 ¹ *honour* ² *prosperity*
30:16 ᵃ Ps. 42:4 ᵇ Ps. 22:14 ¹ *because of my plight*
30:17 ¹ *gnawing pains*
30:18 ¹ *disfigured*
30:20 ᵃ Job 19:7 ¹ Lit. *answer*
30:21 ᵃ Job 10:3; 16:9, 14; 19:6, 22
30:22 ¹ *spoil my success*
30:23 ᵃ [Heb. 9:27]
30:24 ¹ *against a heap of ruins*
30:25 ᵃ Ps. 35:13, 14
30:26 ᵃ Jer. 8:15
30:27 ¹ *My heart is in turmoil* ² *confront*
30:28 ᵃ Ps. 38:6; 42:9; 43:2
30:29 ᵃ Mic. 1:8 ¹ *jackals* ² Or *ostriches*
30:30 ᵃ Ps. 119:83 ᵇ Ps. 102:3 ¹ *grows black* ² *fever*
30:31 ¹ *flute*  31:1 ᵃ [Matt. 5:28] ¹ *look intently* or *gaze* ² *virgin* or *young woman*  31:2 ᵃ Job 20:29

3 *Is* not destruction to the wicked? and a ¹strange *punishment* to the workers of iniquity?

4 ªDoth not he see my ways, and count all my steps?

5 If I have walked with ¹vanity, or if my foot hath hasted to deceit;

6 ¹Let me be weighed in an even balance, that God may know mine ªintegrity.

7 If my step hath turned out of the way, and ªmine heart walked after mine eyes, and if ¹any blot hath cleaved to mine hands;

8 *Then* ªlet me sow, and let another eat; yea, let my ¹offspring be ²rooted out.

9 If mine heart have been ¹deceived by a woman, or *if* I have laid wait at my neighbour's door;

10 *Then* let my wife grind unto ªanother, and let others bow down upon her.

11 For this *is* an heinous crime; yea, ªit *is* an iniquity *to be punished by* the judges.

12 For it *is* a fire *that* consumeth to destruction, and would root out all mine increase.

13 If I did ªdespise the cause of my manservant or of my maidservant, when they ¹contended with me;

14 What then shall I do when ªGod riseth up? and when he ¹visiteth, what shall I answer him?

15 ªDid not he that made me in the womb make him? and did not one fashion us in the womb?

16 If I have withheld the poor from *their* desire, or have caused the eyes of the widow to ªfail;

17 Or have eaten my morsel myself alone, and the fatherless hath not eaten thereof;

18 (For from my youth he was brought up with me, as *with* a father, and I have guided ¹her from my mother's womb;)

19 If I have seen any perish for want of clothing, or any poor without covering;

20 If his ¹loins have not ªblessed me, and *if* he were *not* warmed with the fleece of my sheep;

21 If I have lifted up my hand ªagainst the fatherless, when I saw my help in the gate:

22 *Then* let mine arm fall from my shoulder blade, and mine arm be broken from the ¹bone.

23 For ªdestruction *from* God *was* a terror to me, and by reason of his ¹highness I could not endure.

24 ªIf I have made gold my hope, or have said to the fine gold, Thou *art* my confidence;

25 ªIf I rejoiced because my wealth *was* great, and because mine hand had gotten much;

26 ªIf I beheld the ¹sun when it shined, or the moon walking *in* brightness;

27 And my heart hath been secretly enticed, or my mouth hath kissed my hand:

28 This also *were* an iniquity *to be punished by* the judge: for I should have denied the God *that is* above.

29 ªIf I rejoiced at the destruction of him that hated me, or lifted up myself when evil found him:

30 ªNeither have I ¹suffered my mouth to sin by ²wishing a curse to his ³soul.

31 If the men of my tabernacle said not, ¹Oh that we had of his flesh! we cannot be satisfied.

32 ªThe stranger did not lodge in the street: *but* I opened my doors to the traveller.

33 If I covered my transgressions ªas¹ Adam, by hiding mine iniquity in my bosom:

34 Did I fear a great ªmultitude, or did the contempt of families terrify me, that I kept silence, *and* went not out of the door?

35 ªOh that one would hear me! ¹behold, my desire *is, that* the Almighty would answer me, and ᵇ*that* mine ²adversary had written a book.

36 Surely I would take it upon my shoulder, *and* bind it *as* a crown to me.

37 I would declare unto him the number of my steps; as a prince would I go near unto him.

38 If my land cry against me, or that the furrows likewise thereof ¹complain;

39 If ªI have eaten ¹the fruits thereof without money, or ᵇhave caused the owners thereof to lose their life:

40 Let ªthistles grow instead of wheat, and ¹cockle instead of barley. The words of Job are ended.

## CHAPTER 32

So these three men ceased to answer Job, because he *was* ªrighteous in his own eyes.

2 Then was kindled the wrath of Elihu the son of Barachel the ªBuzite, of the kindred of Ram: against Job was his wrath kindled, because he ᵇjustified himself rather than God.

3 Also against his three friends was his wrath kindled, because they had found no answer, and *yet* had condemned Job.

4 Now Elihu had waited ¹till Job had spoken, because they *were* ²elder than he.

5 When Elihu saw that *there was* no answer in the mouth of *these* three men, then his wrath was kindled.

6 And Elihu the son of Barachel the Buzite answered and said, I *am* ªyoung, and ye *are* very old; where-

fore I was afraid, and 'durst not shew you mine opinion.

7 I said, 'Days should speak, and multitude of years should teach wisdom.

8 But *there is* a spirit in man: and [a]the 'inspiration of the Almighty giveth them understanding.

9 [a]Great[1] men are not *always* wise: neither do the aged [2]understand judgment.

10 Therefore I said, Hearken to me; I also will shew mine opinion.

11 Behold, I waited for your words; I gave ear to your 'reasons, whilst ye [2]searched out what to say.

12 Yea, I 'attended unto you, and, behold, *there was* none of you that convinced Job, *or* that answered his words:

13 [a]Lest ye should say, We have found out wisdom: God 'thrusteth him down, not man.

14 Now he hath not directed *his* words against me: neither will I answer him with your speeches.

15 They were amazed, they answered no more: 'they left off speaking.

16 When I had waited, (for they spake not, but stood still, *and* answered no more;)

17 *I said,* I will answer also my part, I also will shew mine opinion.

18 For I am full of 'matter, the spirit within me constraineth me.

19 Behold, my 'belly *is as* wine *which* hath no [2]vent; it is ready to burst like new [3]bottles.

20 I will speak, that I may 'be refreshed: I will open my lips and answer.

21 Let me not, I pray you, 'accept any man's person, neither let me give flattering titles unto man.

22 For I know not to give flattering titles; *in so doing* my maker would soon take me [a]away.

## CHAPTER 33

WHEREFORE, Job, I pray thee, hear my speeches, and hearken to all my words.

2 Behold, now I have opened my mouth, my tongue hath spoken in my mouth.

3 My words *shall be of* the uprightness of my heart: and my lips shall utter knowledge 'clearly.

4 [a]The spirit of God hath made me, and the breath of the Almighty hath given me life.

5 If thou canst answer me, set *thy words* in order before me, stand up.

6 [a]Behold, I *am* 'according to thy wish in God's stead: I also am formed out of the clay.

7 [a]Behold, 'my terror shall not make thee afraid, neither shall my hand be heavy upon thee.

8 Surely thou hast spoken 'in mine hearing, and I have heard the voice of *thy* words, *saying,*

9 [a]I am clean without transgression, I *am* innocent; neither *is there* iniquity in me.

10 Behold, he findeth occasions against me, [a]he counteth me for his enemy,

11 [a]He putteth my feet in the stocks, he 'marketh all my paths.

12 Behold, *in* this thou art not 'just: I will answer thee, that God is greater than man.

13 Why dost thou [a]strive' against him? for he giveth not account of any of his matters.

14 [a]For God speaketh once, yea twice, *yet man* perceiveth it not.

15 [a]In a dream, in a vision of the night, when deep sleep falleth upon men, in slumberings upon the bed;

16 [a]Then he openeth the ears of men, and sealeth their instruction,

17 That he may 'withdraw man *from his* purpose, and hide pride from man.

18 He keepeth back his soul from the pit, and his life from 'perishing by the sword.

19 'He is chastened also with pain upon his [a]bed, and the multitude of his bones with strong *pain:*

20 [a]So that his life abhorreth [b]bread, and his soul 'dainty meat.

21 His flesh is 'consumed away, that it cannot be seen; and his bones *that* were not seen stick out.

22 Yea, his soul draweth near unto the 'grave, and his life to the destroyers.

23 If there be a messenger with him, 'an interpreter, one among a thousand, to shew unto man his uprightness:

24 Then he is gracious unto him, and saith, Deliver him from going down to the pit: I have found 'a ransom.

25 His flesh shall be 'fresher than a child's: he shall return to the days of his youth:

26 He shall pray unto God, and he will be 'favourable unto him: and he shall see his face with joy: for he will [2]render unto man his righteousness.

27 'He looketh upon men, and *if any* [a]say, I have sinned, and perverted *that which was* right, and it [b]profited me not;

28 He will [a]deliver' his soul from going into the pit, and his life shall see the light.

29 Lo, all these *things* worketh God 'oftentimes with man,

30 [a]To bring back his soul from the pit, to be enlightened with the light of the living.

---

32:6 [1] *dared*

32:7 [1] *Age*

32:8 [a] 1 Kin. 3:12; 4:29; [Job 35:11; 38:36; Prov. 2:6; Eccl. 2:26; Dan. 1:17; 2:21; Matt. 11:25; James 1:5] [1] *breath*

32:9 [a] [1 Cor. 1:26] [1] Or *Men of many years* [2] *always understand*

32:11 [1] *reasonings* [2] *pondered*

32:12 [1] *paid close attention to*

32:13 [a] [Jer. 9:23]; 1 Cor. 1:29] [1] *will vanquish him*

32:15 [1] *words escape them*

32:18 [1] *words*

32:19 [1] *bosom* [2] *opening* [3] *wineskins*

32:20 [1] *be relieved*

32:21 [1] *show partiality to anyone*

32:22 [a] Job 27:8

33:3 [1] *purely*

33:4 [a] [Gen. 2:7]; Job 32:8

33:6 [a] Job 4:19 [1] Lit. *as your mouth before God*

33:7 [a] Job 9:34 [1] *fear of me*

33:8 [1] Lit. *in my ears*

33:9 [a] Job 10:7

33:10 [a] Job 13:24; 16:9

33:11 [a] Job 13:27; 19:8 [1] *watches*

33:12 [1] *right*

33:13 [a] Job 40:2; [Is. 45:9] [1] *complain*

33:14 [a] Job 33:29; 40:5; Ps. 62:11

33:15 [a] [Num. 12:6]

33:16 [a] [Job 36:10, 15]

33:17 [1] *turn man from his deed*

33:18 [1] Lit. *passing*

33:19 [a] Job 30:17 [1] *Man*

33:20 [a] Ps. 107:18 [b] Job 3:24; 6:7 [1] *succulent or desirable food*

33:21 [1] *wastes away from sight*

33:22 [1] Lit. *pit*

33:23 [1] *a mediator*

33:24 [1] *an atonement*

33:25 [1] *young as*

33:26 [1] *delight in him* [2] *restore*

33:27 [a] [Luke 15:21] [b] [Rom. 6:21]

[1] *He shall look upon men, and say* 33:28 [a] Is. 38:17 [1] Kt. *redeem my soul* 33:29 [1] Lit. *twice or three times with man* 33:30 [a] Ps. 56:13

31 Mark well, O Job, hearken unto me: hold thy peace, and I will speak.

32 If thou hast any thing to say, answer me: speak, for I desire to justify thee.

33 If not, ᵃhearken unto me: ¹hold thy peace, and I shall teach thee wisdom.

## CHAPTER 34

Furthermore Elihu answered and said,

2 Hear my words, O ye wise *men;* and give ear unto me, ye that have knowledge.

3 ᵃFor the ear ¹trieth words, as the ²mouth tasteth meat.

4 Let us choose to us ¹judgment: let us know among ourselves what *is* good.

5 For Job hath said, ᵃI am righteous: and ᵇGod hath taken away ¹my judgment.

6 ᵃShould I lie ¹against my right? my ²wound *is* incurable without transgression.

7 What man *is* like Job, ᵃ*who* drinketh up ¹scorning like water?

8 Which goeth in company with the workers of iniquity, and walketh with wicked men.

9 For ᵃhe hath said, It profiteth a man nothing that he should delight himself with God.

10 Therefore hearken unto me, ye ¹men of understanding: ᵃfar be it from God, *that he should do* wickedness; and *from* the Almighty, *that he should commit* iniquity.

11 ᵃFor the work of a man shall he ¹render unto him, and cause every man to find according to *his* ways.

12 Yea, surely God will not do wickedly, neither will the Almighty ᵃpervert judgment.

13 Who hath given him a charge over the earth? or who hath ¹disposed the whole world?

14 If he set his heart upon man, *if* he ᵃgather unto himself his spirit and his breath;

15 ᵃAll flesh shall perish together, and man shall turn again unto dust.

16 If now *thou hast* understanding, hear this: hearken to the voice of my words.

17 ᵃShall even he that hateth ¹right govern? and wilt thou ᵇcondemn him that is most just?

18 ᵃ*Is it fit* to say to a king, *Thou art* ¹wicked? *and* to princes, *Ye are* ²ungodly?

19 ¹*How much less to him* that ᵃaccepteth not the persons of princes, nor regardeth the rich more than the poor? for ᵇthey all *are* the work of his hands.

20 In a moment shall they die, and the people shall be troubled ᵃat mid-

33:33 ᵃ Ps. 34:11
¹ keep silent

34:3 ᵃ Job 6:30;
12:11 ¹ tests ² palate tastes food

34:4 ¹ justice

34:5 ᵃ Job 13:18;
33:9 ᵇ Job 27:2
¹ my justice

34:6 ᵃ Job 6:4;
9:17 ¹ concerning
² Lit. arrow

34:7 ᵃ Job 15:16
¹ derision

34:9 ᵃ Mal. 3:14

34:10 ᵃ Job 8:3;
36:23 ¹ Lit. O men of heart

34:11 ᵃ Ps. 62:12
¹ repay him

34:12 ᵃ Job 8:3

34:13 ¹ appointed him over

34:14 ᵃ Ps. 104:29

34:15 ᵃ [Gen. 3:19]

34:17 ᵃ 2 Sam.
23:3 ᵇ Job 40:8
¹ justice rule

34:18 ᵃ Ex. 22:28
¹ worthless
² wicked

34:19 ᵃ [Deut.
10:17] ᵇ Job 31:15
¹ Yet he is not partial to princes

34:20 ᵃ Ex. 12:29

34:21 ᵃ Job 31:4

34:22 ᵃ [Amos 9:2, 3]

34:23 ¹ need not further consider a man ² go before God in judgment

34:24 ᵃ [Dan. 2:21] ¹ without inquiry ² place

34:25 ¹ overthrows ² crushed

34:27 ᵃ 1 Sam. 15:11 ᵇ Is. 5:12

34:28 ᵃ Job 35:9 ᵇ [Ex. 22:23]

34:29 ¹ alone

34:31 ¹ For has anyone said to God

34:33 ¹ terms

34:34 ¹ Lit. of heart

34:35 ᵃ Job 35:16; 38:2

34:36 ¹ utmost ² Like those of

34:37 ᵃ Job 7:11; 10:1 ¹ boasts himself

35:3 ᵃ Job 21:15; 34:9 ¹ more than if I had sinned

35:4 ᵃ Job 34:8

35:5 ᵃ [Job 22:12]

night, and pass away: and the mighty shall be taken away without hand.

21 ᵃFor his eyes *are* upon the ways of man, and he seeth all his goings.

22 ᵃ*There is* no darkness, nor shadow of death, where the workers of iniquity may hide themselves.

23 For he ¹will not lay upon man more *than right;* that he should ²enter into judgment with God.

24 ᵃHe shall break in pieces mighty men ¹without number, and set others in their ²stead.

25 Therefore he knoweth their works, and he ¹overturneth *them* in the night, so that they are ²destroyed.

26 He striketh them as wicked men in the open sight of others;

27 Because they ᵃturned back from him, and ᵇwould not consider any of his ways:

28 So that they ᵃcause the cry of the poor to come unto him, and he ᵇheareth the cry of the afflicted.

29 When he giveth quietness, who then can make trouble? and when he hideth *his* face, who then can behold him? whether *it be done* against a nation, or against a man ¹only:

30 That the hypocrite reign not, lest the people be ensnared.

31 ¹Surely it is meet to be said unto God, I have borne *chastisement,* I will not offend *any more:*

32 *That which* I see not teach thou me: if I have done iniquity, I will do no more.

33 *Should it be* according to thy ¹mind? he will recompense it, whether thou refuse, or whether thou choose; and not I: therefore speak what thou knowest.

34 Let men ¹of understanding tell me, and let a wise man hearken unto me.

35 ᵃJob hath spoken without knowledge, and his words *were* without wisdom.

36 My desire *is that* Job may be tried unto the ¹end because of *his* answers ²for wicked men.

37 For he addeth ᵃrebellion unto his sin, he ¹clappeth *his hands* among us, and multiplieth his words against God.

## CHAPTER 35

Elihu spake moreover, and said,

2 Thinkest thou this to be right, *that* thou saidst, My righteousness *is* more than God's?

3 For ᵃthou saidst, What advantage will it be unto thee? *and,* What profit shall I have, ¹*if I be cleansed* from my sin?

4 I will answer thee, and ᵃthy companions with thee.

5 ᵃLook unto the heavens, and see; and behold the clouds *which* are higher than thou.

6 If thou sinnest, what [1]doest thou [a]against him? or *if* thy transgressions be multiplied, what doest thou unto him?

7 [a]If thou be righteous, what givest thou him? or what receiveth he of thine hand?

8 Thy wickedness *may hurt* a man as thou *art;* and thy righteousness *may profit* the son of man.

9 [a]By reason of the multitude of oppressions [1]they make *the oppressed* to cry: they cry out by reason of the arm of the mighty.

10 But none saith, [a]Where *is* God my maker, [b]who giveth songs in the night;

11 Who [a]teacheth us more than the beasts of the earth, and maketh us wiser than the fowls of heaven?

12 [a]There they cry, but none giveth answer, because of the pride of evil men.

13 [a]Surely God will not [1]hear vanity, neither will the Almighty regard it.

14 [a]Although thou sayest thou [1]shalt not see him, *yet* [2]judgment *is* before him; therefore [b]trust[3] thou in him.

15 But now, because [1]*it is* not *so,* he hath [a]visited in his anger; yet he knoweth *it* not in great extremity:

16 [a]Therefore doth Job open his mouth in vain; he multiplieth words without knowledge.

## CHAPTER 36

ELIHU also proceeded, and said,
2 [1]Suffer me a little, and I will shew thee that [2]*I have* yet to speak on God's behalf.

3 I will fetch my knowledge from afar, and will ascribe righteousness to my Maker.

4 For truly my words *shall* not *be* false: he that is perfect in knowledge *is* with thee.

5 Behold, God *is* mighty, and despiseth not *any:* [a]he *is* mighty in strength *and* wisdom.

6 He preserveth not the life of the wicked: but giveth [1]right to the [a]poor.

7 [a]He withdraweth not his eyes from the righteous: but [b]with kings *are they* on the throne; yea, he doth establish them for ever, and they are exalted.

8 And [a]if *they be* bound in [1]fetters, *and* [2]be holden in cords of affliction;

9 Then he [1]sheweth them their work, and their transgressions that they have [2]exceeded.

10 [a]He openeth also their ear to discipline, and commandeth that they return from iniquity.

11 If they obey and serve *him,* they shall [a]spend their days in prosperity, and their years in pleasures.

12 But if they obey not, they shall perish by the sword, and they shall die [1]without [a]knowledge.

13 But the hypocrites in heart [a]heap[1] up wrath: they cry not when he bindeth them.

14 [a]They die in youth, and their life *is* among the [1]unclean.

15 He delivereth the poor in his affliction, and openeth their ears [1]in oppression.

16 Even so would he have removed thee out of [1]the strait [2]*into* a broad place, where *there is* no [2]straitness; and [b]that which should be set on thy table *should be* full of [c]fatness.[3]

17 But thou [1]hast fulfilled the judgment of the [a]wicked: judgment and justice take hold *on thee.*

18 Because *there is* wrath, *beware* lest he take thee away with *his* stroke: then [a]a great ransom cannot deliver thee.

19 [a]Will he esteem thy riches? *no,* not gold, nor all the forces of strength.

20 Desire not the night, when people are cut off in their place.

21 Take heed, [a]regard[1] not iniquity: for [b]this hast thou chosen rather than affliction.

22 Behold, God exalteth by his power: who teacheth like him?

23 [a]Who hath [1]enjoined him his way? or who can say, Thou hast [2]wrought [b]iniquity?

24 Remember that thou [a]magnify his work, which men [1]behold.

25 Every man may see it; man may behold *it* afar off.

26 Behold, God *is* great, and we [a]know *him* not, [b]neither can the number of his years be searched out.

27 For he [a]maketh[1] small the drops of water: [2]they pour down rain according to the vapour thereof:

28 [a]Which the clouds do drop *and* distil upon man abundantly.

29 Also can *any* understand the spreadings of the clouds, *or* the [1]noise of his tabernacle?

30 Behold, he [a]spreadeth his light upon it, and covereth the bottom of the sea.

31 For [a]by them judgeth he the people; he [b]giveth meat in abundance.

32 [a]With[1] clouds he covereth the light; and commandeth it [2]*not to shine* by *the cloud* that cometh betwixt.

33 [a]The[1] noise thereof sheweth concerning it, the cattle also concerning [2]the vapour.

## CHAPTER 37

AT this also my heart trembleth, and [1]is moved out of his place.

### Center column notes

35:6 [a] [Jer. 7:19] [1] *do you accomplish*

35:7 [a] Prov. 9:12

35:9 [a] Job 34:28 [1] *they cry out*

35:10 [a] Is. 51:13 [b] Acts 16:25

35:11 [a] Ps. 94:12

35:12 [a] Prov. 1:28

35:13 [a] [Is. 1:15] [1] *listen to an empty cry*

35:14 [a] Job 9:11 [b] [Ps. 37:5, 6] [1] *do not* [2] *justice* [3] *you must wait for*

35:15 [a] Ps. 89:32 [1] *he has not punished in his anger, nor taken much notice of folly*

35:16 [a] Job 34:35; 38:2

36:2 [1] *Bear with me* [2] *there are yet words to speak*

36:5 [a] Job 12:13, 16; 37:23

36:6 [a] Job 5:15 [1] *justice to the oppressed*

36:7 [a] [Ps. 33:18; 34:15] [b] Ps. 113:8

36:8 [a] Ps. 107:10 [1] *chains* [2] *are held in cords*

36:9 [1] Lit. *declares* to [2] *acted defiantly*

36:10 [a] Job 33:16; 36:15

36:11 [a] [Is. 1:19, 20]

36:12 [a] Job 4:21 [1] MT *as one without knowledge*

36:13 [a] [Rom. 2:5] [1] *store up*

36:14 [a] Ps. 55:23 [1] *perverted*, lit. *holy ones, those practising sodomy and prostitution in religious rituals*

36:15 [1] *by*

36:16 [a] Ps. 18:19; 31:8; 118:5 [b] Ps. 23:5 [c] Ps. 36:8 [1] *dire distress* [2] *restriction* [3] *richness*

36:17 [a] Job 22:5, 10, 11 [1] *are filled with the judgment due*

36:18 [a] Ps. 49:7

36:19 [a] [Prov. 11:4]

36:21 [a] [Ps. 31:6; 66:18] [b] [Heb. 11:25] [1] *do not turn to*

36:23 [a] Job 34:13; [Is. 40:13, 14] [b] Job 8:3 [1] *assigned him* [2] *done wrong*

36:24 [a] [Rev. 15:3] [1] *have sung about*  36:26 [a] [1 Cor. 13:12] [b] Heb. 1:12  36:27 [a] Ps. 147:8 [1] Lit. *draws up the drops of water* [2] *they distil as rain from mist* 36:28 [a] [Prov. 3:20]  36:29 [1] *thunder from his canopy* 36:30 [a] Job 37:3  36:31 [a] [Acts 14:17] [b] Ps. 104:14, 15 36:32 [a] Ps. 147:8 [1] *He covers his hands with lightning* [2] *to strike the mark*  36:33 [a] 1 Kin. 18:41 [1] *His thunder* [2] *the rising storm*  37:1 [1] *leaps from*

2 Hear attentively the ¹noise of his voice, and the ²sound *that* goeth out of his mouth.

3 He directeth it under the whole heaven, and his ¹lightning unto the ends of the earth.

4 After it ªa voice roareth: he thundereth with ¹the voice of his excellency; and he will not ²stay them when his voice is heard.

5 God thundereth marvellously with his voice; ªgreat things doeth he, which we cannot comprehend.

6 For ªhe saith to the snow, Be thou *on* the earth; likewise to the ¹small rain, and to the great rain of his strength.

7 He sealeth up the hand of every man; ªthat ᵇall men may know his work.

8 Then the beasts ªgo into dens, and remain in their places.

9 Out of the ¹south cometh the whirlwind: and cold out of the ²north.

10 ªBy the breath of God ¹frost is given: and the breadth of the waters is ²straitened.

11 Also ¹by watering he wearieth the thick cloud: he scattereth his bright cloud:

12 And it is turned round about by his ¹counsels: that they may ªdo whatsoever he commandeth them upon the face of the ²world in the earth.

13 ªHe causeth it to come, whether for ¹correction, or ᵇfor his land, or ᶜfor mercy.

14 Hearken unto this, O Job: stand still, and ªconsider the wondrous works of God.

15 Dost thou know when God ¹disposed them, and caused the light of his cloud to shine?

16 ªDost thou know the balancings of the clouds, the wondrous works of ᵇhim which is perfect in knowledge?

17 How thy garments *are* warm, when he quieteth the earth by the south *wind?*

18 Hast thou with him ªspread out the ᵇsky, *which is* strong, *and* as a ¹molten looking glass?

19 Teach us what we shall say unto him; *for* we cannot ¹order *our speech* by reason of darkness.

20 Shall it be told him that I speak? if a man speak, surely he shall be swallowed up.

21 And now *men* ¹see not the bright light which *is* in the ²clouds: ³but the wind passeth, and cleanseth them.

22 ¹Fair weather cometh out of the north: with God *is* ²terrible majesty.

23 *Touching* the Almighty, ªwe cannot find him out: ᵇ*he is* excellent in power, and in judgment, and in ¹plenty of justice: he will not ²afflict.

24 Men do therefore ªfear him: he

respecteth not any *that are* ᵇwise of heart.

## CHAPTER 38

THEN the LORD answered Job ªout of the whirlwind, and said,

2 ªWho *is* this that darkeneth counsel by ᵇwords without knowledge?

3 ªGird¹ up now thy loins like a man; for I will ²demand of thee, and answer thou me.

4 ªWhere wast thou when I laid the foundations of the earth? declare, if thou hast understanding.

5 Who hath ¹laid the measures thereof, if thou knowest? or who hath stretched the ²line upon it?

6 Whereupon are the foundations thereof fastened? or who laid the corner stone thereof;

7 When the morning stars sang together, and all ªthe sons of God shouted for joy?

8 ªOr *who* shut up the sea with doors, when it brake forth, *as if* it had issued out of the womb?

9 When I made the cloud the garment thereof, and thick darkness a swaddlingband for it,

10 And ªbrake¹ up for it my decreed *place*, and set bars and doors,

11 And said, Hitherto shalt thou come, but no further: and here shall thy proud waves ªbe¹ stayed?

12 Hast thou ªcommanded the morning since thy days; *and* caused the ¹dayspring to know his place;

13 That it might take hold of the ends of the earth, that ªthe wicked might be shaken out of it?

14 It ¹is turned as clay *to* the seal; and they ²stand as a garment.

15 And from the wicked their ªlight is ¹withholden, and ᵇthe ²high arm shall be broken.

16 Hast thou ªentered into the springs of the sea? or hast thou walked in the search of the depth?

17 Have ªthe gates of death been ¹opened unto thee? or hast thou seen the doors of the shadow of death?

18 Hast thou perceived the breadth of the earth? declare if thou knowest it all.

19 Where *is* the way *where* light dwelleth? and *as for* darkness, where *is* the place thereof,

20 That thou shouldest take it to the ¹bound thereof, and that thou shouldest know the paths *to* the house thereof?

21 Knowest thou *it,* because thou wast then born? or *because* the number of thy days *is* great?

37:2 ¹ *thunder* ² *rumbling that comes*

37:3 ¹ *light*

37:4 ª Ps. 29:3 ¹ *his majestic voice.* ² *restrain*

37:5 ª Job 5:9; 9:10; 36:26

37:6 ª Ps. 147:16, 17 ¹ Lit. *shower of rain*

37:7 ª Ps. 109:27 ᵇ Ps. 19:3, 4

37:8 ª Ps. 104:21, 22

37:9 ¹ *chamber of the south* ² *scattering winds of the north*

37:10 ª Ps. 147:17, 18 ¹ *ice* ² *frozen*

37:11 ¹ *with moisture he loads*

37:12 ª Job 36:32 ¹ *guidance* ² *whole earth*

37:13 ª Ex. 9:18, 23 ᵇ Job 38:26, 27 ᶜ 1 Kin. 18:41–46 ¹ Lit. *a rod*

37:14 ª Ps. 111:2

37:15 ¹ Lit. *placed them*

37:16 ª Job 36:29 ᵇ Job 36:4

37:18 ª [Is. 44:24] ᵇ Ps. 104:2 ¹ *cast metal mirror*

37:19 ¹ *prepare anything because of*

37:21 ¹ *cannot look at* ² *skies* ³ *when the wind has passed and cleared them*

37:22 ¹ *In golden splendour he comes* ² *awesome*

37:23 ª [1 Tim. 6:16] ᵇ [Job 9:4; 36:5] ¹ *abundant justice* ² *oppress*

37:24 ª [Matt. 10:28] ᵇ [Matt. 11:25]

38:1 ª Ex. 19:16

38:2 ª Job 34:35; 42:3 ᵇ 1 Tim. 1:7

38:3 ª Job 40:7 ¹ *Prepare yourself* ² *question me*

38:4 ª Ps. 104:5

38:5 ¹ *determined its measurements* ² *measuring line*

38:7 ª Job 1:6

38:8 ª Gen. 1:9

38:10 ª Job 26:10 ¹ *I fixed my limit for it*

38:11 ª [Ps. 89:9; 93:4] ¹ *must stop*

38:12 ª [Ps. 74:16;

14:8:5] ¹ *dawn*    38:13 ª Ps. 104:35    38:14 ¹ *takes on form like clay under a seal* ² *stand out*    38:15 ª Job 18:5 ᵇ Ps. 10:15; 37:17 ¹ *withheld* ² *uplifted*    38:16 ª [Ps. 77:19]    38:17 ª Ps. 9:13 ¹ *revealed*    38:20 ¹ *its territory*

22 Hast thou entered into [a]the [1]treasures of the snow? or hast thou seen the treasures of the hail,

23 [a]Which I have reserved against the time of trouble, against the day of battle and war?

24 By what way is the light [1]parted, [2]*which* scattereth the east wind upon the earth?

25 Who [a]hath divided a watercourse for the overflowing of waters, or a way for the [1]lightning of thunder;

26 To cause it to rain on the earth, *where* no man *is; on* the wilderness, wherein *there is* no man;

27 [a]To satisfy the desolate and waste *ground;* and to cause the bud of the tender herb to spring forth?

28 [a]Hath the rain a father? or who hath begotten the drops of dew?

29 Out of whose womb came the ice? and the [a]hoary frost of heaven, who [1]hath gendered it?

30 The waters [1]are hid as *with* a stone, and the [2]face of the deep is [a]frozen.[3]

31 Canst thou bind the [1]sweet influences of [a]Pleiades,[2] or loose the [3]bands of Orion?

32 Canst thou bring forth [1]Mazzaroth in his season? or canst thou guide [2]Arcturus with his sons?

33 Knowest thou [a]the ordinances of heaven? canst thou set the dominion thereof in the earth?

34 Canst thou lift up thy voice to the clouds, that abundance of waters may cover thee?

35 Canst thou send lightnings, that they may go, and say unto thee, Here we *are?*

36 [a]Who hath put wisdom in the [1]inward parts? or who hath given understanding to the heart?

37 Who can number the clouds in wisdom? or who can [1]stay the bottles of heaven,

38 When the dust [1]groweth into hardness, and the clods [2]cleave fast together?

39 [a]Wilt thou hunt the prey for the lion? or fill the appetite of the young lions,

40 When they [1]couch in *their* dens, *and* [2]abide in the covert to lie in wait?

41 [a]Who provideth for the raven his food? when his young ones cry unto God, they wander for lack of [1]meat.

## CHAPTER 39

K NOWEST thou the time when the wild [a]goats[1] of the rock bring forth? *or* canst thou mark when [b]the [2]hinds do calve?

2 Canst thou number the months *that* they fulfil? or knowest thou the time when they bring forth?

3 They bow themselves, they bring

---

38:22 [a] Ps. 135:7
[1] *treasury*

38:23 [a] Is. 30:30

38:24 [1] Lit. *divided,* possibly meaning *diffused* or *diffracted* [2] or *the east wind scattered*

38:25 [a] Job 28:26
[1] *thunderbolt*

38:27 [a] Ps. 104:13, 14; 107:35

38:28 [a] Job 36:27, 28

38:29 [a] Ps. 147:16, 17 [1] *gives it birth*

38:30 [a] [Job 37:10] [1] *harden like stone* [2] *surface* [3] Lit. *imprisoned*

38:31 [a] Amos 5:8 [1] *cluster of* [2] Or *The Seven Stars* [3] *belt*

38:32 [1] Lit. *Constellations* [2] Or *The Great Bear*

38:33 [a] Jer. 31:35, 36

38:36 [a] [Ps. 51:6]
[1] *mind*

38:37 [1] *pour out*

38:38 [1] *hardens into clumps* [2] *cling*

38:39 [a] Ps. 104:21

38:40 [1] *crouch* [2] *lurk in their lairs*

38:41 [a] [Matt. 6:26] [1] *food*

39:1 [a] Ps. 104:18 [b] Ps. 29:9 [1] *mountain goats bear young* [2] *deer*

39:3 [1] *offspring,* lit. *pangs*

39:4 [1] *healthy* [2] *grow strong* [3] *grain*

39:5 [1] *onager,* a species of wild donkey

39:6 [a] Jer. 2:24 [1] Lit. *salt*

39:7 [1] *tumult* [2] *heeds* [3] *shouts*

39:8 [a] Gen. 1:29

39:9 [a] Num. 23:22 [1] *wild ox* [2] *manger*

39:10 [1] *wild ox* [2] *ropes*

39:12 [1] *grain* [2] *threshingfloor*

39:13 [1] *The wings of the ostrich wave proudly, but are her wings and pinions like the kindly stork's?*

39:15 [1] Lit. *trample*

39:16 [a] Lam. 4:3

---

forth their young ones, they cast out their [1]sorrows.

4 Their young ones are [1]in good liking, they [2]grow up with [3]corn; they go forth, and return not unto them.

5 Who hath sent out the wild ass free? or who hath loosed the bands of the [1]wild ass?

6 [a]Whose house I have made the wilderness, and the [1]barren land his dwellings.

7 He scorneth the [1]multitude of the city, neither [2]regardeth he the [3]crying of the driver.

8 The range of the mountains *is* his pasture, and he searcheth after [a]every green thing.

9 Will the [a]unicorn[1] be willing to serve thee, or abide by thy [2]crib?

10 Canst thou bind the [1]unicorn with [2]his band in the furrow? or will he harrow the valleys after thee?

11 Wilt thou trust him, because his strength *is* great? or wilt thou leave thy labour to him?

12 Wilt thou believe him, that he will bring home thy [1]seed, and gather *it into* thy [2]barn?

13 [1]*Gavest thou* the goodly wings unto the peacocks? or wings and feathers unto the ostrich?

14 Which leaveth her eggs in the earth, and warmeth them in dust,

15 And forgetteth that the foot may crush them, or that the wild beast may [1]break them.

16 She [1]*is* [a]hardened against her young ones, as though *they were* not hers: her labour is in vain without [2]fear;

17 Because God hath deprived her of wisdom, neither hath he [a]imparted to her understanding.

18 What time she lifteth up herself on high, she scorneth the horse and his rider.

19 Hast thou given the horse strength? hast thou clothed his neck with [1]thunder?

20 Canst thou make him [1]afraid as a [2]grasshopper? the [3]glory of his nostrils *is* terrible.

21 He paweth in the valley, and rejoiceth in *his* strength: [a]he [1]goeth on to meet the armed men.

22 He mocketh at fear, and is not affrighted; neither turneth he back from the sword.

23 The quiver rattleth against him, the glittering spear and the [1]shield.

24 He [1]swalloweth the ground with fierceness and rage: neither [2]believeth he that *it is* the sound of the trumpet.

---

[1] *treats her young harshly* [2] *concern*   39:17 [a] Job 35:11   39:19 [1] *a mane*   39:20 [1] *spring in fear* [2] *locust* [3] *majesty of his snorting is terrifying*   39:21 [a] Jer. 8:6 [1] *gallops into the clash of arms*   39:23 [1] *javelin* 39:24 [1] *devours the distance* [2] *does he stand firm because the trumpet has sounded*

25 He saith among the trumpets, Ha, ha; and he smelleth the battle afar off, the thunder of the captains, and the shouting.

26 Doth the hawk fly by thy wisdom, *and* stretch her wings toward the south?

27 Doth the [a]eagle mount up at thy command, and [b]make her nest on high?

28 She dwelleth and abideth on the rock, upon the crag of the rock, and the strong place.

29 From thence she [1]seeketh the prey, *and* her eyes behold afar off.

30 Her young ones also suck up blood: and [a]where the slain *are,* there *is* she.

## CHAPTER 40

MOREOVER the LORD [a]answered Job, and said,

2 Shall he that [a]contendeth with the Almighty instruct *him?* he that [b]reproveth[1] God, let him answer it.

3 Then Job answered the LORD, and said,

4 [a]Behold, I am vile; what shall I answer thee? [b]I will lay mine hand upon my mouth.

5 Once have I spoken; but I will not answer: yea, twice; but I will proceed no further.

6 [a]Then answered the LORD unto Job out of the whirlwind, and said,

7 [a]Gird[1] up thy loins now like a man: [b]I will demand of thee, and declare thou unto me.

8 [a]Wilt thou also [1]disannul my judgment? wilt thou condemn me, that thou mayest be righteous?

9 Hast thou an arm like God? or canst thou thunder with [a]a voice like him?

10 [a]Deck[1] thyself now *with* majesty and excellency; and array thyself with glory and beauty.

11 Cast abroad the rage of thy wrath: and behold every one *that is* proud, and [1]abase him.

12 Look on every one *that is* [a]proud, *and* bring him low; and tread down the wicked in their place.

13 Hide them in the dust together; *and* bind their faces in secret.

14 Then will I also confess unto thee that thine own right hand can save thee.

15 Behold now [1]behemoth, which I made with thee; he eateth grass as an ox.

16 Lo now, his strength *is* in his loins, and his force *is* in [1]the navel of his belly.

17 He moveth his tail like a cedar: the sinews of his [1]stones are [2]wrapped together.

18 His bones *are as* strong pieces of [1]brass; his bones *are* like bars of iron.

39:27 [a] Prov. 30:18, 19 [b] Jer. 49:16
39:29 [1] spies out
39:30 [a] Matt. 24:28
40:1 [a] Job 38:1
40:2 [a] Job 9:3; 10:2; 33:13 [b] Job 13:3; 23:4 [1] rebukes
40:4 [a] Ezra 9:6 [b] Job 29:9
40:6 [a] Job 38:1
40:7 [a] Job 38:3 [b] Job 42:4 [1] Prepare yourself
40:8 [a] [Rom. 3:4] [1] nullify
40:9 [a] [Ps. 29:3, 4]
40:10 [a] Ps. 93:1; 104:1 [1] Adorn
40:11 [1] humble
40:12 [a] Dan. 4:37
40:15 [1] A large animal, exact identity unknown
40:16 [1] stomach muscles
40:17 [1] thighs [2] tightly knit
40:18 [1] bronze
40:19 [a] Job 26:14
40:20 [a] Ps. 104:14
40:21 [1] lotus [2] marsh
40:22 [1] lotus [2] surround
40:23 [1] The river may rage yet he is not disturbed [2] he is confident though Jordan gush into his mouth.
40:24 [1] Though he takes it in his eyes, or one pierces his nose with a snare.
41:1 [a] Is. 27:1 [1] A large sea creature, exact identity unknown
41:2 [a] 1 Kin. 19:38; Is. 37:29 [1] reed [2] hook
41:6 [1] bargain over him [2] divide
41:7 [1] harpoons
41:9 [1] overcoming him is futile
41:11 [a] [Rom. 11:35] [b] Ex. 19:5; [Deut. 10:14; Job 9:5–10; 26:6–14]; Ps. 24:1; 50:12; 1 Cor. 10:26, 28 [1] preceded
41:12 [1] Lit. keep silent concerning [2] limbs [3] graceful proportions
41:13 [1] remove his outer coat
41:15 [1] Lit. shields
41:17 [1] separated

19 He *is* the chief of the [a]ways of God: he that made him can make his sword to approach *unto him.*

20 Surely the mountains [a]bring him forth food, where all the beasts of the field play.

21 He lieth under the [1]shady trees, in the covert of the reed, and [2]fens.

22 The [1]shady trees cover him *with* their shadow; the willows of the brook [2]compass him about.

23 Behold, [1]he drinketh up a river, *and* hasteth not: [2]he trusteth that he can draw up Jordan into his mouth.

24 [1]He taketh it with his eyes: *his* nose pierceth through snares.

## CHAPTER 41

CANST thou draw out [a]leviathan[1] with an hook? or his tongue with a cord *which* thou lettest down?

2 Canst thou [a]put an [1]hook into his nose? or bore his jaw through with a [2]thorn?

3 Will he make many supplications unto thee? will he speak soft *words* unto thee?

4 Will he make a covenant with thee? wilt thou take him for a servant for ever?

5 Wilt thou play with him as *with* a bird? or wilt thou bind him for thy maidens?

6 Shall the companions [1]make a banquet of him? shall they [2]part him among the merchants?

7 Canst thou fill his skin with [1]barbed irons? or his head with fish spears?

8 Lay thine hand upon him, remember the battle, do no more.

9 Behold, the hope of [1]him is in vain: shall not *one* be cast down even at the sight of him?

10 None *is so* fierce that dare stir him up: who then is able to stand before me?

11 [a]Who hath [1]prevented me, that I should repay *him?* [b]*whatsoever is* under the whole heaven is mine.

12 I will not [1]conceal his [2]parts, nor his power, nor his [3]comely proportion.

13 Who can [1]discover the face of his garment? *or* who can come *to him* with his double bridle?

14 Who can open the doors of his face? his teeth *are* terrible round about.

15 *His* [1]scales *are his* pride, shut up together *as with* a close seal.

16 One is so near to another, that no air can come between them.

17 They are joined one to another, they stick together, that they cannot be [1]sundered.

18 By his neesings a light doth shine, and his eyes *are* like the eyelids of the morning.

19 Out of his mouth go burning lamps, *and* sparks of fire leap out.

20 Out of his nostrils goeth smoke, as *out* of a ¹seething pot or ²caldron.

21 His breath kindleth coals, and a flame goeth out of his mouth.

22 In his neck remaineth strength, and ¹sorrow is turned into joy before him.

23 The ¹flakes of his flesh are joined together: they are firm in themselves; they cannot be moved.

24 His heart is as firm as a stone; yea, as hard as a piece of the ¹nether *millstone.*

25 When he raiseth up himself, the mighty are afraid: by reason of breakings they ¹purify themselves.

26 The sword of him that ¹layeth at him cannot hold: the spear, the dart, nor the ²habergeon.

27 He esteemeth iron as straw, *and* brass as rotten wood.

28 The arrow cannot make him flee: slingstones are turned with him into stubble.

29 Darts are counted as ¹stubble: he laugheth at the shaking of a spear.

30 ¹Sharp stones *are* under him: he spreadeth sharp pointed things upon the mire.

31 He maketh the deep to boil like a pot: he maketh the sea like a pot of ointment.

32 He maketh a path to shine after him; *one* would think the deep ¹*to be* hoary.

33 Upon earth there is not his like, who is made without fear.

34 He beholdeth all high *things:* he *is* a king over all the children of pride.

### CHAPTER 42

THEN Job answered the LORD, and said,

2 I know that thou ᵃcanst do every *thing,* and *that* ¹no thought can be withholden from thee.

3 ᵃWho *is* he that hideth counsel without knowledge? therefore have I uttered that I understood not; ᵇthings too wonderful for me, which I knew not.

4 Hear, I beseech thee, and I will speak: ᵃI will ¹demand of thee, and declare thou unto me.

5 I have ᵃheard of thee by the hearing of the ear: but now mine eye seeth thee.

---

**Marginal notes (center column):**

41:20 ¹ *boiling* ² *burning rushes*

41:22 ¹ *despair dances before him*

41:23 ¹ *folds*

41:24 ¹ *lower*

41:25 ¹ *are beside themselves*

41:26 ¹ *reaches him cannot avail* ² *Or javelin*

41:29 ¹ *straw*

41:30 ¹ *His undersides are sharp like potsherds*

41:32 ¹ *had white hair*

42:2 ᵃ Gen. 18:14; [Matt. 19:26; Mark 10:27; 14:36; Luke 18:27] ¹ *no purpose of yours can be withheld*

42:3 ᵃ Job 38:2 ᵇ Ps. 40:5; 131:1; 139:6

42:4 ᵃ Job 38:3; 40:7 ¹ *question thee*

42:5 ᵃ Job 26:14; [Rom. 10:17]

42:6 ᵃ Ezra 9:6; Job 40:4 ¹ *despise*

42:8 ᵃ Num. 23:1 ᵇ [Matt. 5:24] ᶜ Gen. 20:17; [James 5:15, 16; 1 John 5:16] ¹ *Lit. his face*

42:9 ¹ *Lit. lifted up the face of Job*

42:10 ᵃ Deut. 30:3; Ps. 14:7; 85:1–3; 126:1 ᵇ Is. 40:2 ¹ *restored* ² *losses*

42:11 ᵃ Job 19:13 ¹ *adversity* ² *silver*

42:12 ᵃ Job 1:10; 8:7; James 5:11 ᵇ Job 1:3 ¹ *female donkeys*

42:13 ᵃ Job 1:2

42:14 ¹ Heb. *Jemimah,* lit. *Handsome as the Day* ² *Cassia,* a fragrance ³ *Lit. The Horn of Colour*

42:16 ᵃ Job 5:26; Prov. 3:16

42:17 ᵃ Gen. 15:15; 25:8; Job 5:26

---

6 Wherefore I ᵃabhor¹ *myself,* and repent in dust and ashes.

7 And it was *so,* that after the LORD had spoken these words unto Job, the LORD said to Eliphaz the Temanite, My wrath is kindled against thee, and against thy two friends: for ye have not spoken of me *the thing that is* right, as my servant Job *hath.*

8 Therefore take unto you now ᵃseven bullocks and seven rams, and ᵇgo to my servant Job, and offer up for yourselves a burnt offering; and my servant Job shall ᶜpray for you: for ¹him will I accept: lest I deal with you *after your* folly, in that ye have not spoken of me *the thing which is* right, like my servant Job.

9 So Eliphaz the Temanite and Bildad the Shuhite *and* Zophar the Naamathite went, and did according as the LORD commanded them: the LORD also ¹accepted Job.

10 ᵃAnd the LORD ¹turned the ²captivity of Job, when he prayed for his friends: also the LORD gave Job ᵇtwice as much as he had before.

11 Then came there unto him ᵃall his brethren, and all his sisters, and all they that had been of his acquaintance before, and did eat bread with him in his house: and they bemoaned him, and comforted him over all the ¹evil that the LORD had brought upon him: every man also gave him a piece of ²money, and every one an earring of gold.

12 So the LORD blessed ᵃthe latter end of Job more than his beginning: for he had ᵇfourteen thousand sheep, and six thousand camels, and a thousand yoke of oxen, and a thousand ¹she asses.

13 ᵃHe had also seven sons and three daughters.

14 And he called the name of the first, ¹Jemima; and the name of the second, ²Kezia; and the name of the third, ³Keren-happuch.

15 And in all the land were no women found *so* fair as the daughters of Job: and their father gave them inheritance among their brethren.

16 After this ᵃlived Job an hundred and forty years, and saw his sons, and his sons' sons, *even* four generations.

17 So Job died, *being* old and ᵃfull of days.

# THE BOOK OF
# PSALMS

The Book of Psalms is the largest and perhaps most widely used book in the Bible. It explores the full range of human experience in a very personal and practical way. Its 150 "songs" run from the Creation through the patriarchal, theocratic, monarchical, exilic, and postexilic periods. The tremendous breadth of subject matter in the Psalms includes diverse topics, such as jubilation, war, peace, worship, judgment, messianic prophecy, praise, and lament. The Psalms were set to the accompaniment of stringed instruments and served as the temple hymnbook and devotional guide for the Jewish people.

The Book of Psalms was gradually collected and originally unnamed, perhaps due to the great variety of material. It came to be known as *Sepher Tehillim*—"Book of Praises"—because almost every psalm contains some note of praise to God. The Septuagint uses the Greek word *Psalmoi* as its title for this book, meaning "Poems Sung to the Accompaniment of Musical Instruments." It also calls it the *Psalterium* ("A Collection of Songs"), and this word is the basis for the term *Psalter*. The Latin title is *Liber Psalmorum*, "Book of Psalms."

## BOOK I: Psalms 1–41

### PSALM 1

BLESSED [a]*is* the man that walketh not in the counsel of the [1]ungodly, nor standeth in the way of sinners, [b]nor sitteth in the seat of the scornful.

2 But [a]his delight *is* in the law of the LORD; [b]and in his law doth he [1]meditate day and night.

3 And he shall be like a tree [a]planted by the [1]rivers of water, that bringeth forth his fruit in his season; his leaf also shall not wither; and whatsoever he doeth shall [b]prosper.

4 The ungodly *are* not so: but *are* [a]like the chaff which the wind driveth away.

5 Therefore the ungodly shall not stand in the judgment, nor sinners in the congregation of the righteous.

6 For [a]the LORD knoweth the way of the righteous: but the way of the ungodly shall perish.

### PSALM 2

WHY [a]do the [1]heathen [2]rage, and the people [3]imagine a [4]vain thing?

2 The kings of the earth set themselves, and the [a]rulers take counsel together, against the LORD, and against his [b]anointed,[1] *saying,*

3 [a]Let us break their bands asunder, and cast away their cords from us.

4 He that sitteth in the heavens [a]shall laugh: the Lord shall have them in derision.

5 Then shall he speak unto them in his wrath, and [1]vex them in his [2]sore displeasure.

6 Yet have I [1]set my king [2]upon my holy hill of Zion.

---

1:1 [a] Prov. 4:14
[b] Jer. 15:17
[1] *wicked*
1:2 [a] Ps. 119:14, 16, 35 [b] [Josh. 1:8] [1] *ponder by talking to oneself*
1:3 [a] Jer. 17:8 [b] Gen. 39:2, 3, 23 [1] *channels*
1:4 [a] Job 21:18
1:6 [a] Ps. 37:18
2:1 [a] Acts 4:25, 26 [1] *Gentiles* [2] *throng tumultuously or restlessly* [3] *plot,* lit. *meditate* [4] *empty or worthless*
2:2 [a] [Mark 3:6; 11:18] [b] [John 1:41] [1] *Messiah,* Christ
2:3 [a] Luke 19:14
2:4 [a] Ps. 37:13
2:5 [1] *distress* [2] *deep*
2:6 [1] Lit. *installed* [2] Lit. *upon Zion, the hill of my holiness*
2:7 [a] [Heb. 1:5; 5:5] [1] *Or decree of the LORD: he said to me*
2:8 [1] *nations or Gentiles*
2:9 [a] Ps. 89:23; 110:5, 6
2:12 [a] [Rev. 6:16, 17] [b] [Ps. 5:11; 34:22] [1] *An act of homage and submission*
3:title [a] 2 Sam. 15:13–17
3:3 [a] Ps. 5:12; 28:7 [b] Ps. 9:13; 27:6 [1] *around* [2] *one who lifts up*
3:4 [a] Ps. 4:3; 34:4 [b] Ps. 2:6; 15:1;

---

7 I will declare the [1]decree: the LORD hath said unto me, [a]Thou *art* my Son; this day have I begotten thee.

8 Ask of me, and I shall give *thee* the [1]heathen *for* thine inheritance, and the uttermost parts of the earth *for* thy possession.

9 [a]Thou shalt break them with a rod of iron; thou shalt dash them in pieces like a potter's vessel.

10 Be wise now therefore, O ye kings: be instructed, ye judges of the earth.

11 Serve the LORD with fear, and rejoice with trembling.

12 [1]Kiss the Son, lest he be angry, and ye perish *from* the way, when [a]his wrath is kindled but a little. [b]Blessed *are* all they that put their trust in him.

### PSALM 3

A Psalm of David, [a]when he fled from Absalom his son.

LORD, how are they increased that [1]trouble me! many *are* they that rise up against me.

2 Many *there be* which say of my soul, *There is* no help for him in God. *Selah.*

3 But thou, O LORD, *art* [a]a shield [1]for me; my glory, and [b]the [2]lifter up of mine head.

4 I cried unto the LORD with my voice, and [a]he heard me out of his [b]holy [1]hill. *Selah.*

5 [a]I laid me down and slept; I awaked; for the LORD sustained me.

6 [a]I will not be afraid of ten thousands of people, that have set *themselves* against me round about.

7 Arise, O LORD; save me, O my God: [a]for thou hast [1]smitten all mine

---

43:3 [1] *mountain* 3:5 [a] Lev. 26:6 ; 3:6 [a] Ps. 93:4; 27:3
3:7 [a] Job 16:10 [1] *struck*

enemies *upon* the cheek bone; thou hast broken the teeth of the ungodly.

8 [a]Salvation *belongeth* unto the LORD: thy blessing *is* upon thy people.     *Selah.*

## PSALM 4

To the [1]chief Musician on Neginoth, A Psalm of David.

HEAR me when I call, O God of my righteousness: thou hast [1]enlarged me *when I was* in distress; [2]have mercy upon me, and hear my prayer.

2 O ye sons of men, how long *will ye turn* my glory into shame? *how long* will ye love [1]vanity, *and* seek after [2]leasing?     *Selah.*

3 But know that [a]the LORD hath set apart him that is godly for himself: the LORD will hear when I call unto him.

4 [a]Stand[1] in awe, and sin not: [b]commune with your own heart upon your bed, and be still.    *Selah.*

5 Offer [a]the sacrifices of righteousness, and [b]put your trust in the LORD.

6 *There be* many that say, Who will shew us *any* good? [a]LORD, lift thou up the light of thy countenance upon us.

7 Thou hast put [a]gladness in my heart, more than in the time *that* their [1]corn and their wine increased.

8 [a]I will both lay me down in peace, and sleep: [b]for thou, LORD, only makest me dwell in safety.

## PSALM 5

To the chief Musician upon Nehiloth, A Psalm of David.

GIVE [a]ear to my words, O LORD, consider my [1]meditation.

2 Hearken unto the voice of my cry, my King, and my God: for unto thee will I pray.

3 My voice shalt thou hear in the morning, O LORD; [a]in the morning will I direct *my prayer* unto thee, and will look up.

4 For thou *art* not a God that hath pleasure in wickedness: neither shall evil [1]dwell with thee.

5 The [a]foolish[1] shall not [b]stand in thy sight: thou hatest all workers of iniquity.

6 Thou shalt destroy them that speak [1]leasing: the LORD will abhor the [a]bloody[2] and deceitful man.

7 But as for me, I will come *into* thy house in the multitude of thy mercy: *and* in thy fear will I worship toward [1]thy holy temple.

8 [a]Lead me, O LORD, in thy righteousness because of mine enemies; make thy way straight before my face.

9 For *there is* no [1]faithfulness in their mouth; their inward part *is*

[2]very wickedness; [a]their throat *is* [3]an open sepulchre; they flatter with their tongue.

10 [1]Destroy thou them, O God; let them fall by their own counsels; cast them out in the multitude of their transgressions; for they have rebelled against thee.

11 But let all those that put their trust in thee rejoice: let them ever shout for joy, because [1]thou defendest them: let them also that love thy name be joyful in thee.

12 For thou, LORD, wilt bless the righteous; with favour wilt thou [1]compass him as *with* a shield.

## PSALM 6

To the chief Musician on Neginoth [a]upon [1]Sheminith, A Psalm of David.

O LORD, [a]rebuke me not in thine anger, neither chasten me in thy hot displeasure.

2 Have mercy upon me, O LORD; for I *am* weak: O LORD, [a]heal me; for my bones are [1]vexed.

3 My soul is also [1]sore [a]vexed: but thou, O LORD, how long?

4 Return, O LORD, deliver my soul: oh save me for thy [1]mercies' sake.

5 [a]For in death *there is* no remembrance of thee: in the grave who shall give thee thanks?

6 I am weary with my groaning; [1]all the night make I my bed to swim; I [2]water my couch with my tears.

7 [a]Mine eye [1]is consumed because of grief; it [2]waxeth old because of all mine enemies.

8 [a]Depart from me, all ye workers of iniquity; for the LORD hath [b]heard the voice of my weeping.

9 The LORD hath heard my supplication; the LORD will receive my prayer.

10 Let all mine enemies be ashamed and [1]sore vexed: let them return *and* be ashamed suddenly.

## PSALM 7

[a]Shiggaion[1] of David, which he sang unto the LORD, [b]concerning the words of Cush the Benjamite.

O LORD my God, in thee do I put my trust: [a]save me from all them that persecute me, and deliver me:

2 [a]Lest he tear my soul like a lion, [b]rending[1] *it* in pieces, while *there is* none to deliver.

3 O LORD my God, [a]if I have done this; if there be [b]iniquity in my hands;

4 If I have rewarded evil unto him that was at peace with me; (yea, [a]I have delivered him that without cause is mine enemy:)

5 Let the enemy persecute my soul, and take *it;* yea, let him tread down my life upon the earth, and lay mine honour in the dust.    *Selah.*

### Center column references

3:8 [a] [Is. 43:11]
4:title [1] *choir director*
4:1 [1] *relieved* [2] *be gracious to me*
4:2 [1] *worthlessness* [2] *falsehood*
4:3 [a] [2 Tim. 2:19]
4:4 [a] [Eph. 4:26] [b] Ps. 77:6 [1] Lit. *Tremble* or *Be agitated*
4:5 [a] Deut. 33:19 [b] Ps. 37:3, 5; 62:8
4:6 [a] Num. 6:26
4:7 [a] Is. 9:3 [1] *grain*
4:8 [a] Ps. 3:5 [b] [Lev. 25:18]
5:1 [a] Ps. 4:1 [1] Lit. *groaning*
5:3 [a] Ps. 55:17; 88:13
5:4 [1] Lit. *sojourn*
5:5 [a] [Hab. 1:13] [b] Ps. 1:5 [1] *boastful*
5:6 [a] Ps. 55:23 [1] *falsehood* [2] *bloodthirsty*
5:7 [1] Lit. *the temple of your holiness*
5:8 [a] Ps. 25:4, 5; 27:11; 31:3
5:9 [a] Rom. 3:13 [1] *uprightness* [2] *destruction* [3] *an open tomb*
5:10 [1] *Pronounce them guilty*
5:11 [1] *thou protectest,* lit. *thou coverest*
5:12 [1] *surround*
6:title [a] Ps. 12:title [1] *an eight-stringed harp*
6:1 [a] Ps. 38:1; 118:18
6:2 [a] [Hos. 6:1] [1] *troubled*
6:3 [a] Ps. 88:3 [1] *greatly troubled*
6:4 [1] *lovingkindnesses*
6:5 [a] [Eccl. 9:10]
6:6 [1] Or *every night* [2] *drench*
6:7 [a] Job 17:7 [1] *has wasted away* [2] *grows*
6:8 [a] [Matt. 25:41] [b] Ps. 3:4; 28:6
6:10 [1] *greatly troubled*
7:title [a] Hab. 3:1 [b] 2 Sam. 16 [1] *Meditation* or *Song*
7:1 [a] Ps. 31:15
7:2 [a] Is. 38:13 [b] Ps. 50:22 [1] *tearing me*
7:3 [a] 2 Sam. 16:7 [1] Sam. 24:11
7:4 [a] 1 Sam. 24:7; 26:9

6 Arise, O LORD, in thine anger, [a]lift up thyself because of the rage of mine enemies: and [b]awake for me *to* the judgment *that* thou hast commanded.

7 So shall the congregation of the people [1]compass thee about: for their sakes therefore return thou on high.

8 The LORD shall judge the people: [a]judge me, O LORD, [b]according to my righteousness, and according to mine integrity *that is* in me.

9 Oh let the wickedness of the wicked come to an end; but establish the just: [a]for the righteous God [1]trieth the hearts and [2]reins.

10 My defence *is* of God, which saveth the [a]upright in heart.

11 [1]God judgeth the righteous, and God is angry *with the wicked* every day.

12 If he turn not, he will [a]whet[1] his sword; he hath bent his bow, and made it ready.

13 He hath also prepared for him the instruments of death; he [1]ordaineth his arrows [2]against the persecutors.

14 [a]Behold, he travaileth with iniquity, and hath conceived [1]mischief, and brought forth falsehood.

15 He [1]made a pit, and [2]digged it, [a]and is fallen into the ditch *which* he made.

16 [a]His [1]mischief shall return upon his own head, and his violent dealing shall come down upon [2]his own pate.

17 I will praise the LORD according to his righteousness: and will sing praise to the name of the LORD most high.

## PSALM 8

To the chief Musician [1]upon Gittith, A Psalm of David.

O LORD, our Lord, how [a]excellent *is* thy name in all the earth! who [b]hast set thy glory above the heavens.

2 [a]Out of the mouth of babes and [1]sucklings hast thou [2]ordained strength because of thine enemies, that thou mightest [3]still [b]the enemy and the avenger.

3 When I [a]consider thy heavens, the work of thy fingers, the moon and the stars, which thou hast ordained;

4 [a]What is man, that thou art mindful of him? and the son of man, that thou [b]visitest[1] him?

5 For thou hast made him a little lower than the angels, and hast crowned him with glory and honour.

6 [a]Thou madest him to have dominion over the works of thy hands; [b]thou hast put all *things* under his feet:

7 All sheep and oxen, yea, and the beasts of the field;

8 The fowl of the air, and the fish of the sea, *and whatsoever* passeth through the paths of the seas.

9 [a]O LORD our Lord, how excellent *is* thy name in all the earth!

## PSALM 9

To the chief Musician, upon [1]Muthlabben, A Psalm of David.

I WILL praise *thee,* O LORD, with my whole heart; I will [1]shew forth all thy marvellous works.

2 I will be glad and [a]rejoice in thee: I will sing praise to thy name, O [b]thou most High.

3 When mine enemies are turned back, they shall fall and perish at thy presence.

4 For thou hast maintained my right and my cause; [1]thou satest in the throne judging [2]right.

5 Thou hast rebuked the [1]heathen, thou hast destroyed the wicked, thou hast [a]put[2] out their name for ever and ever.

6 O thou enemy, destructions are [1]come to a perpetual end: and thou hast destroyed cities; their memorial is [a]perished with them.

7 [a]But the LORD shall endure for ever: he hath prepared his throne for judgment.

8 And [a]he shall judge the world in righteousness, he shall minister judgment to the people in uprightness.

9 The LORD also will be a [a]refuge[1] for the oppressed, a refuge in times of trouble.

10 And they that [a]know thy name will put their trust in thee: for thou, LORD, hast not forsaken them that seek thee.

11 Sing praises to the LORD, which dwelleth in Zion: [a]declare among the people his [1]doings.

12 [a]When he [1]maketh inquisition for blood, he remembereth them: he forgetteth not the cry of the [2]humble.

13 Have mercy upon me, O LORD; consider my trouble *which I suffer* of them that hate me, thou that liftest me up from the gates of death:

14 That I may shew forth all thy praise in the gates of [1]the daughter of Zion: I will [a]rejoice in thy salvation.

15 [a]The [1]heathen are sunk down in the pit *that* they made: in the net which they hid is their own foot [2]taken.

16 The LORD is [a]known *by* the judgment *which* he executeth: the wicked is snared in the work of his own hands. [b]Higgaion.[1]          *Selah.*

17 The wicked shall be turned into hell, *and* all the [1]nations [a]that forget God.

7:6 [a] Ps. 94:2  [b] Ps. 35:23; 44:23
7:7 [1] surround
7:8 [a] Ps. 26:1; 35:24; 43:1  [b] Ps. 18:20; 35:24
7:9 [a] [1 Sam. 16:7]  [1] tests  [2] inner man or minds, lit. kidneys
7:10 [a] Ps. 97:10, 11; 125:4
7:11 [1] God is a just judge
7:12 [a] Deut. 32:41  [1] sharpen
7:13 [1] makes  [2] into fiery shafts
7:14 [a] Is. 59:4  [1] trouble
7:15 [a] [Job 4:8]  [1] Lit. has dug  [2] dug it out
7:16 [a] Esth. 9:25  [1] trouble  [2] The crown of his own head
8:title [1] on the instrument of Gath
8:1 [a] Ps. 148:13  [b] Ps. 113:4
8:2 [a] [1 Cor. 1:27]  [b] Ps. 44:16  [1] infants  [2] established  [3] silence
8:3 [a] Ps. 111:2
8:4 [a] Job 7:17, 18  [b] [Job 10:12]  [1] pay attention to or care for
8:6 [a] [Gen. 1:26, 28]  [b] [Heb. 2:8]
8:9 [a] Ps. 8:1
9:title [1] The tune of "Death of the Son"
9:1 [1] tell of
9:2 [a] Ps. 5:11; 104:34  [b] [Ps. 83:18; 92:1]
9:4 [1] you sat  [2] in righteousness
9:5 [a] Prov. 10:7  [1] Gentiles or nations  [2] blotted
9:6 [a] [Ps. 34:16]  [1] finished forever
9:7 [a] Heb. 1:11
9:8 [a] [Ps. 96:13; 98:9]
9:9 [a] Ps. 32:7; 46:1; 91:2  [1] stronghold, lit. secure height
9:10 [a] Ps. 91:14
9:11 [a] Ps. 66:16; 107:22  [1] deeds
9:12 [a] [Ps. 72:14]  [1] avenges blood  [2] afflicted
9:14 [a] Ps. 13:5; 20:5; 35:9  [1] Jerusalem
9:15 [a] Ps. 7:15, 16  [1] nations or Gentiles  [2] caught
9:16 [a] Ex. 7:5  [b] Ps. 92:3  [1] Meditation or Song
9:17 [a] Job 8:13  [1] Gentiles

18 [a]For the needy shall not alway be forgotten: [b]the expectation of the poor shall *not* perish for ever.

19 Arise, O LORD; let not man prevail: let the [1]heathen be judged in thy sight.

20 Put them in fear, O LORD: *that* the nations may know themselves *to be but* men. **Selah.**

## PSALM 10

Why standest thou afar off, O LORD? *why* hidest thou *thyself* in times of trouble?

2 The wicked in *his* pride [1]doth persecute the poor: [a]let them be taken in the [2]devices that they have [3]imagined.

3 For the wicked [a]boasteth of his heart's desire, and [b]blesseth the [1]covetous, [2]*whom* the LORD abhorreth.

4 The wicked, through the pride of his countenance, will not seek *after God:* [1]God *is* not in all his [a]thoughts.

5 His ways are always [1]grievous; thy judgments *are* far above out of his sight: *as for* all his enemies, he [2]puffeth at them.

6 [a]He hath said in his heart, I shall not be moved: for [b]*I shall* never *be* in [1]adversity.

7 [a]His mouth is full of cursing and [b]deceit and [1]fraud: under his tongue *is* [2]mischief and [3]vanity.

8 He sitteth in the lurking places of the villages: in the secret places doth he murder the innocent: his eyes are [1]privily set against the poor.

9 He lieth in wait secretly as a lion in his den: he lieth in wait to catch the poor: he doth catch the poor, when he draweth him into his net.

10 He croucheth, *and* [1]humbleth himself, that the poor may fall by his [2]strong ones.

11 He hath said in his heart, God hath forgotten: he hideth his face; he will never see *it.*

12 Arise, O LORD; O God, [a]lift up thine hand: forget not the [b]humble.

13 Wherefore doth the wicked [1]contemn God? he hath said in his heart, Thou wilt not require [2]*it.*

14 Thou hast [a]seen *it;* for thou beholdest [1]mischief and [2]spite, to [3]requite *it* with thy hand: the poor [b]committeth[4] himself unto thee; [c]thou art the helper of the fatherless.

15 Break thou the arm of the wicked and the evil *man:* seek out his wickedness *till* thou find none.

16 [a]The LORD *is* King for ever and ever: the [1]heathen are perished out of his land.

17 LORD, thou hast heard the desire of the humble: thou wilt prepare their heart, thou wilt cause thine ear to hear:

18 To [1]judge the fatherless and the oppressed, that the man of the earth may no more [2]oppress.

---

9:18 [a] Ps. 9:12; 12:5 [b] Prov. 23:18
9:19 [1] *nations or Gentiles*
10:2 [a] Ps. 7:16; 9:16 [1] Lit. *hotly pursues* [2] *plots* [3] *devised*
10:3 [a] Ps. 49:6; 94:3, 4 [1] *greedy* [2] *and renounces the LORD*
28:4 [1] *greedy* [2] *and renounces the LORD*
10:4 [a] Ps. 14:1; 36:1 [1] Or *All his thoughts are, There is no God*
10:5 [1] *prosperous,* lit. *strong* [2] *blasts or sneers at*
10:6 [a] [Eccl. 8:11] [b] Rev. 18:7 [1] *trouble*
10:7 [a] [Rom. 3:14] [b] Ps. 55:10, 11 [1] *oppression* [2] *trouble* [3] *iniquity*
10:8 [1] *secretly*
10:10 [1] *bows down* [2] Or *strength*
10:12 [a] Mic. 5:9 [b] Ps. 9:12
10:13 [1] *renounce* [2] An *account*
10:14 [a] [Ps. 11:4] [b] [2 Tim. 1:12] [c] Ps. 68:5 [1] *trouble* [2] *grief* [3] *repay* [4] Entrusts, lit. *leaves*
10:16 [a] Ps. 29:10 [1] *nations or Gentiles*
10:18 [1] *vindicate* [2] *terrify*
11:1 [a] Ps. 56:11
11:2 [a] Ps. 64:3, 4 [1] *secretly,* lit. *in darkness*
11:3 [a] Ps. 82:5; 87:1; 119:152
11:4 [a] [Is. 66:1] [b] [Ps. 33:18; 34:15, 16] [1] *test*
11:5 [a] Gen. 22:1 [1] *tests*
11:6 [a] Ps. 75:8 [1] *burning coals* [2] *a burning wind* [3] *Their portion to partake of*
11:7 [a] Ps. 33:5; 45:7 [1] Or *the upright beholds his countenance*
12:title [a] Ps. 6:title [1] *the eight-stringed harp*
12:1 [a] [Is. 57:1] [1] *Save* [2] *disappear*
12:2 [a] Ps. 10:7; 41:6 [1] *idly or falsely* [2] With an inconsistent mind

---

## PSALM 11

To the chief Musician,
*A Psalm* of David.

In [a]the LORD put I my trust: how say ye to my soul, Flee *as* a bird to your mountain?

2 For, lo, [a]the wicked bend *their* bow, they make ready their arrow upon the string, that they may [1]privily shoot at the upright in heart.

3 [a]If the foundations be destroyed, what can the righteous do?

4 The LORD *is* in his holy temple, the LORD's [a]throne *is* in heaven: [b]his eyes behold, his eyelids [1]try, the children of men.

5 The LORD [a]trieth[1] the righteous: but the wicked and him that loveth violence his soul hateth.

6 Upon the wicked he shall rain [1]snares, fire and brimstone, and [2]an horrible tempest: [a]*this shall be* [3]the portion of their cup.

7 For the righteous LORD [a]loveth righteousness; [1]his countenance doth behold the upright.

## PSALM 12

To the chief Musician [a]upon [1]Sheminith, A Psalm of David.

Help,[1] LORD; for the godly man [a]ceaseth; for the faithful [2]fail from among the children of men.

2 [a]They speak [1]vanity every one with his neighbour: *with* flattering lips *and* [2]with a double heart do they speak.

3 The LORD shall [1]cut off all flattering lips, *and* the tongue that speaketh [2]proud things:

4 Who have said, With our tongue will we prevail; our lips *are* our own: who *is* lord over us?

5 For the oppression of the poor, for the sighing of the needy, now will I arise, saith the LORD; I will set *him* in [1]safety *from him that* puffeth at him.

6 The words of the LORD *are* [a]pure words: *as* silver tried in a furnace of earth, purified seven times.

7 Thou shalt keep them, O LORD, thou shalt preserve them from this generation for ever.

8 The wicked walk on every side, when the vilest men are exalted.

## PSALM 13

To the [1]chief Musician,
A Psalm of David.

How long wilt thou forget me, O LORD? for ever? [a]how long wilt thou hide thy face from me?

2 How long shall I take counsel in my soul, *having* sorrow in my heart

---

12:3 [1] *destroy* [2] *great*    12:5 [1] *the safety for which he yearns*    12:6 [a] 2 Sam. 22:31; Ps. 18:30; 119:140
13:title [1] *choir director*    13:1 [a] Job 13:24

daily? how long shall mine enemy be exalted over me?

3 Consider *and* hear me, O LORD my God: [a]lighten[1] mine eyes, [b]lest I sleep the *sleep of* death;

4 Lest mine enemy say, I have prevailed against him; *and* those that trouble me rejoice when I am moved.

5 But I have trusted in thy [1]mercy; my heart shall rejoice in thy salvation.

6 I will sing unto the LORD, because he hath dealt bountifully with me.

## PSALM 14

To the chief Musician,
*A Psalm* of David.

THE [a]fool hath said in his heart, *There is* no God. They are corrupt, they have done abominable works, *there* is none that doeth good.

2 [a]The LORD looked down from heaven upon the children of men, to see if there were any that did understand, *and* seek God.

3 [a]They are all gone aside, they are *all* together become [1]filthy: *there is* none that doeth good, no, not one.

4 Have all the workers of iniquity no knowledge? who eat up my people *as* they eat bread, and [a]call not upon the LORD.

5 There were they in great fear: for God *is* in the generation of the righteous.

6 Ye have shamed the counsel of the poor, because the LORD *is* his [a]refuge.

7 [a]Oh[1] that the salvation of Israel *were come* out of Zion! [b]when the LORD bringeth back [2]the captivity of his people, Jacob shall rejoice, *and* Israel shall be glad.

## PSALM 15

A Psalm of David.

LORD, [a]who shall [1]abide in thy tabernacle? who shall dwell in thy holy hill?

2 He that walketh uprightly, and worketh righteousness, and speaketh the [a]truth in his heart.

3 *He that* [a]backbiteth not with his tongue, nor doeth evil to his neighbour, [b]nor [1]taketh up a reproach against his neighbour.

4 [a]In whose eyes a vile person is [1]contemned; but he honoureth them that fear the LORD. *He that* [b]sweareth to *his own* hurt, and changeth not.

5 *He that* putteth not out his money to usury, nor taketh reward against the innocent. He that doeth these *things* [a]shall never be moved.

## PSALM 16

[a]Michtam[1] of David.

PRESERVE[1] me, O God: for in thee do I put my trust.

2 *O my soul,* thou hast said unto the LORD, Thou *art* my Lord: [a]my goodness [1]*extendeth* not to thee;

3 *But* to the saints that *are* in the earth, [1]and *to* the excellent, in [a]whom *is* all my delight.

4 Their sorrows shall be multiplied *that* hasten *after* another *god:* their drink offerings of [a]blood will I not offer, [b]nor take up their names into my lips.

5 The LORD *is* the portion of mine inheritance and of my cup: thou [1]maintainest my lot.

6 The lines are fallen unto me in pleasant *places;* yea, I have a goodly [1]heritage.

7 I will bless the LORD, who hath given me counsel: my [1]reins also instruct me in the night seasons.

8 [a]I have set the LORD always before me: because *he is* at my right hand, I shall not be moved.

9 Therefore my heart is glad, and my glory rejoiceth: my flesh also shall [1]rest in hope.

10 [a]For thou wilt not leave my soul in [1]hell; neither wilt thou [2]suffer thine Holy One to see corruption.

11 Thou wilt shew me the [a]path of life: in thy presence *is* fulness of joy; at thy right hand *there are* pleasures for evermore.

## PSALM 17

A Prayer of David.

HEAR [1]the right, O LORD, attend unto my cry, give ear unto my prayer, *that goeth* not out of [2]feigned lips.

2 Let my [1]sentence come forth from thy presence; let thine eyes behold the things that are [2]equal.

3 Thou hast [1]proved mine heart; thou hast [2]visited *me* in the night; [a]thou hast [3]tried me, *and* shalt find [4]nothing; I am purposed *that* my mouth shall not [b]transgress.

4 Concerning the works of men, by the word of thy lips I have kept *me from* the paths of the destroyer.

5 [a]Hold[1] up my goings in thy paths, *that* my footsteps slip not.

6 [a]I have called upon thee, for thou wilt hear me, O God: incline thine ear unto me, *and hear* my speech.

7 Shew thy marvellous lovingkindness, O thou that [1]savest by thy right hand them which put their trust *in thee* from those that rise up *against them.*

8 Keep me as the [1]apple of the eye, hide me under the shadow of thy wings,

9 From the wicked that oppress me, *from* my deadly enemies, *who* [1]compass me about.

10 They [1]are inclosed in their own

### Cross References

13:3 [a] Ezra 9:8
[b] Jer. 51:39
[1] enlighten

13:5 [1] *loving-kindness*

14:1 [a] Ps. 10:4; 53:1
14:2 [a] Ps. 33:13, 14; 102:19
14:3 [a] Rom. 3:12
[1] corrupt
14:4 [a] Is. 64:7
14:6 [a] Ps. 9:9; 40:17; 46:1; 142:5
14:7 [a] Ps. 53:6
[b] Job 42:10 [1] Lit. Who will give out of Zion the salvation of Israel? [2] Or his captive people
15:1 [a] Ps. 24:3–5
[1] sojourn
15:2 [a] [Eph. 4:25]
15:3 [a] [Lev. 19:16–18] [b] Ex. 23:1
[1] receives
15:4 [a] Esth. 3:2 [b] Lev. 5:4
[1] despised
15:5 [a] 2 Pet. 1:10
16:title [a] Ps. 56–60 [1] Contemplation
16:1 [1] Watch over
16:2 [a] Job 35:7
[1] is nothing apart from thee
16:3 [a] Ps. 119:63
[1] they are the excellent
16:4 [a] Ps. 106:37, 38 [b] [Ex. 23:13]
16:5 [1] Lit. uphold
16:6 [1] inheritance
16:7 [1] heart, lit. kidneys
16:8 [a] [Acts 2:25–28]
16:9 [1] Or dwell securely
16:10 [a] Ps. 49:15; 86:13 [1] Or Sheol, the abode of the dead [2] allow
16:11 [a] [Matt. 7:14]
17:1 [1] a just cause [2] deceitful
17:2 [1] vindication [2] upright
17:3 [a] Job 23:10 [b] Ps. 39:1 [1] tested [2] searched me out [3] tested [4] Nothing evil
17:5 [a] Ps. 44:18; 119:133 [1] Uphold my steps
17:6 [a] Ps. 86:7; 116:2
17:7 [1] delivers
17:8 [1] pupil
17:9 [1] surround me
17:10 [1] have closed up their fat hearts

[a]fat: with their mouth they [b]speak proudly.

11 They have now [1]compassed us in our steps: they have set their eyes [2]bowing down to the earth;

12 Like as a lion *that* is [1]greedy of his prey, and as it were a young lion lurking in secret places.

13 Arise, O LORD, [1]disappoint him, cast him down: deliver my soul from the wicked, [2]*which is* thy sword:

14 From men [1]*which are* thy hand, O LORD, from men of the world, *which have* their portion in *this* life, and whose belly thou fillest with thy [2]hid *treasure:* they are [3]full of children, and leave the rest of their *substance* to their babes.

15 As for me, [a]I will behold thy face in righteousness: [b]I shall be satisfied, when I [c]awake, with thy likeness.

## PSALM 18

To the chief Musician, *A Psalm* of David, [a]the servant of the LORD, who spake unto the LORD the words of [b]this song in the day *that* the LORD delivered him from the hand of all his enemies, and from the hand of Saul: And he said,

I [a]WILL love thee, O LORD, my strength.

2 The LORD *is* my rock, and my fortress, and my deliverer; my God, [1]my strength, [a]in whom I will trust; my [2]buckler, and the [3]horn of my salvation, *and* my [4]high tower.

3 I will call upon the LORD, [a]*who is worthy* to be praised: so shall I be saved from mine enemies.

4 [a]The [1]sorrows of death [2]compassed me, and the floods of [3]ungodly men made me afraid.

5 The [1]sorrows of hell compassed me about: the snares of death [2]prevented me.

6 In my distress I called upon the LORD, and cried unto my God: he heard my voice [1]out of his temple, and my cry came before him, *even* into his ears.

7 [a]Then the earth shook and trembled; the foundations also of the hills [1]moved and were shaken, because he was [2]wroth.

8 There went up a smoke out of his nostrils, and fire out of his mouth devoured: coals were kindled by it.

9 [a]He bowed the heavens also, and came down: and darkness *was* under his feet.

10 [a]And he rode upon a cherub, and did fly: yea, [b]he did fly upon the wings of the wind.

11 He made darkness his secret place; [a]his pavilion round about him *were* dark waters *and* thick clouds of the skies.

12 [a]At the brightness *that was* before him his thick clouds passed, hail *stones* and coals of fire.

13 The LORD also thundered in the heavens, and the [1]Highest gave [a]his voice; hail *stones* and coals of fire.

14 [a]Yea, he sent out his arrows, and scattered them; and he shot out lightnings, and [1]discomfited them.

15 Then the channels of waters were seen, and the foundations of the world were [1]discovered at thy rebuke, O LORD, at the blast of the breath of thy nostrils.

16 [a]He sent from above, he took me, he drew me out of many waters.

17 He delivered me from my strong enemy, and from them which hated me: for they were too strong for me.

18 They [1]prevented me in the day of my calamity: but the LORD was my [2]stay.

19 [a]He brought me forth also into [1]a large place; he delivered me, because he delighted in me.

20 [a]The LORD rewarded me according to my righteousness; according to the cleanness of my hands hath he recompensed me.

21 For I have kept the ways of the LORD, and have not wickedly departed from my God.

22 For all his judgments *were* before me, and I did not put away his statutes from me.

23 I was also upright [1]before him, and I kept myself from mine iniquity.

24 [a]Therefore hath the LORD recompensed me according to my righteousness, according to the cleanness of my hands in his eyesight.

25 [a]With the merciful thou wilt shew thyself merciful; with an upright man thou wilt shew thyself upright;

26 With the pure thou wilt shew thyself pure; and [a]with the [1]froward thou wilt shew thyself [2]froward.

27 For thou wilt save the afflicted people; but wilt bring down [a]high[1] looks.

28 [a]For thou wilt light my [1]candle: the LORD my God will enlighten my darkness.

29 For by thee I [1]have run through a troop; and by my God [2]have I leaped over a wall.

30 *As for* God, [a]his way *is* perfect: [b]the word of the LORD is [1]tried: he *is* a [2]buckler [c]to all those that trust in him.

31 [a]For who *is* God [1]save the LORD? or who *is* a rock save our God?

32 *It is* God that [a]girdeth me with strength, and maketh my way perfect.

33 [a]He maketh my feet [1]like hinds' *feet,* and [b]setteth me upon my high places.

17:10 [a] Ezek. 16:49 [b] [1 Sam. 2:3]
17:11 [1] surrounded [2] crouching down
17:12 [1] eager to tear
17:13 [1] confront [2] with thy sword
17:14 [1] with thy hand [2] hidden [3] satisfied with
17:15 [a] [1 John 3:2] [b] Ps. 4:6, 7; 16:11 [c] [Is. 26:19]
18:title [a] Ps. 36:title [b] 2 Sam. 22
18:1 [a] Ps. 144:1
18:2 [a] Heb. 2:13 [1] Lit. *my rock* [2] shield [3] Strength [4] stronghold
18:3 [a] Rev. 5:12
18:4 [a] Ps. 116:3 [1] pangs [2] encompass [3] ungodliness, lit. Belial
18:5 [1] Lit. cords of Sheol [2] confronted
18:6 [1] from
18:7 [a] Acts 4:31 [1] quaked [2] angry
18:9 [a] Ps. 144:5
18:10 [a] Ps. 80:1; 99:1 [b] [Ps. 104:3]
18:11 [a] Ps. 97:2
18:12 [a] Ps. 97:3; 140:10
18:13 [a] [Ps. 29:3–9; 104:7] [1] Most High
18:14 [a] Ps. 144:6 [1] vanquished
18:15 [1] uncovered
18:16 [a] Ps. 144:7
18:18 [1] confronted [2] support
18:19 [a] Ps. 4:1; 31:8; 118:5 [1] a broad
18:20 [a] 1 Sam. 24:19
18:23 [1] with
18:24 [a] 1 Sam. 26:23
18:25 [a] [1 Kin. 8:32]
18:26 [a] [Lev. 26:23–28] [1] devious [2] shrewd
18:27 [a] [Ps. 101:5] [1] haughty
18:28 [a] Job 18:6 [1] lamp
18:29 [1] Or can run against [2] Or I can leap
18:30 [a] Rev. 15:3 [b] Ps. 12:6; 119:140 [c] [Ps. 17:7] [1] proven [2] shield
18:31 [a] [1 Sam. 2:2] [1] except
18:32 [a] [Ps. 91:2]  18:33 [a] Hab. 3:19 [b] Deut. 32:13; 33:29 [1] like the feet of deer

34 [a]He teacheth my hands to war, so that a [b]bow of steel is broken by mine arms.

35 Thou hast also given me the shield of thy salvation: and thy right hand hath [1]holden me up, and thy gentleness hath made me great.

36 Thou hast enlarged my [1]steps under me, [a]that my feet did not slip.

37 I have pursued mine enemies, and overtaken them: neither did I turn again till they were [1]consumed.

38 I have wounded them that they were not able to rise: they are fallen under my feet.

39 For thou hast girded me with strength unto the battle: thou hast [1]subdued under me those that rose up against me.

40 Thou hast also given me the necks of mine enemies; that I might destroy them that hate me.

41 They cried, but *there was* none to save *them:* [a]*even* unto the LORD, but he answered them not.

42 Then did I beat them [1]small as the dust before the wind: I did [a]cast them out as the dirt in the streets.

43 Thou hast delivered me from the strivings of the people; *and* [a]thou hast made me the head of the [1]heathen: [b]a people *whom* I have not known shall serve me.

44 As soon as they hear of me, they shall obey me: the [1]strangers shall [2]submit themselves unto me.

45 [a]The [1]strangers shall fade away, and be afraid out of their [2]close places.

46 The LORD liveth; and blessed *be* my rock; and let the God of my salvation be exalted.

47 *It is* God that avengeth me, [a]and subdueth the people under me.

48 He delivereth me from mine enemies: yea, [a]thou liftest me up above those that rise up against me: thou hast delivered me from the violent man.

49 [a]Therefore will I give thanks unto thee, O LORD, among the [1]heathen, and sing praises unto thy name.

50 [a]Great deliverance giveth he to his king; and sheweth mercy to his anointed, to David, and to his [1]seed for evermore.

## PSALM 19

To the chief Musician,
A Psalm of David.

THE [a]heavens declare the glory of God; and the [b]firmament[1] sheweth [2]his handywork.

2 Day unto day uttereth speech, and night unto night [1]sheweth knowledge.

3 *There is* no speech nor language, *where* their voice is not heard.

18:34 [a] Ps. 144:1
[1] *bow of bronze can be bent*
18:35 [1] *held*
18:36 [a] Prov. 4:12
[1] *path*
18:37 [1] *destroyed*
18:39 [1] Lit. *caused to bow*
18:41 [a] Job 27:9
18:42 [a] Zech. 10:5
[1] *as fine as*
18:43 [a] 2 Sam. 8
[b] Is. 52:15 [1] *nations* or *Gentiles*
18:44 [1] *foreigners*
[2] *feign submission*
18:45 [a] Mic. 7:17 [1] *foreigners*
[2] *hideouts*
18:47 [a] Ps. 47:3
18:48 [a] Ps. 27:6; 59:1
18:49 [a] Rom. 15:9 [1] *Gentiles* or *nations*
18:50 [a] Ps. 21:1; 144:10 [1] *descendants*
19:1 [a] Is. 40:22; [Rom. 1:19, 20]
[b] Gen. 1:6, 7 [1] *expanse* of heaven
[2] *the work of his hands*
19:2 [1] *reveals*

19:4 [a] Rom. 10:18
[1] *measuring line*
[2] *tent*
19:5 [a] Eccl. 1:5
19:6 [1] *rising*
19:7 [a] Ps. 111:7; [Rom. 7:12] [b] Ps. 119:130 [1] *restoring*
19:10 [a] Ps. 119:72, 127; Prov. 8:10, 11, 19 [1] Lit. *the drippings of the honeycomb*
19:12 [a] [Ps. 51:1, 2]
19:13 [a] Num. 15:30
[b] Ps. 119:133; [Rom. 6:12–14]
[1] *much or great*
19:14 [a] Ps. 51:15
[b] Ps. 31:5; Is. 47:4
[1] Lit. *my rock*
20:1 [1] May the LORD answer thee
[2] Lit. *set thee on high*
20:4 [a] Ps. 21:2
[1] *heart's desire*
[2] *purpose*
20:6 [1] *Messiah,* commissioned one [2] *answer*
20:7 [a] Deut. 20:1; Ps. 33:16, 17; Prov. 21:31; Is. 31:1

4 [a]Their [1]line is gone out through all the earth, and their words to the end of the world. In them hath he set a [2]tabernacle for the sun,

5 Which *is* as a bridegroom coming out of his chamber, [a]*and* rejoiceth as a strong man to run a race.

6 His [1]going forth *is* from the end of the heaven, and his circuit unto the ends of it: and there is nothing hid from the heat thereof.

7 [a]The law of the LORD *is* perfect, [1]converting the soul: the testimony of the LORD *is* sure, making [b]wise the simple.

8 The statutes of the LORD *are* right, rejoicing the heart: the commandment of the LORD *is* pure, enlightening the eyes.

9 The fear of the LORD *is* clean, enduring for ever: the judgments of the LORD *are* true *and* righteous altogether.

10 More to be desired *are they* than [a]gold, yea, than much fine gold: sweeter also than honey and [1]the honeycomb.

11 Moreover by them is thy servant warned: *and* in keeping of them *there is* great reward.

12 Who can understand *his* errors? [a]cleanse thou me from secret *faults.*

13 Keep back thy servant also from [a]presumptuous *sins;* let them not have [b]dominion over me: then shall I be upright, and I shall be innocent from [1]the great transgression.

14 [a]Let the words of my mouth, and the meditation of my heart, be acceptable in thy sight, O LORD, [1]my strength, and my [b]redeemer.

## PSALM 20

To the chief Musician,
A Psalm of David.

THE[1] LORD hear thee in the day of trouble; the name of the God of Jacob [2]defend thee;

2 Send thee help from the sanctuary, and strengthen thee out of Zion;

3 Remember all thy offerings, and accept thy burnt sacrifice;　　*Selah.*

4 Grant thee according to thine [1]own heart, and [a]fulfil all thy [2]counsel.

5 We will rejoice in thy salvation, and in the name of our God we will set up *our* banners: the LORD fulfil all thy petitions.

6 Now know I that the LORD saveth his [1]anointed; he will [2]hear him from his holy heaven with the saving strength of his right hand.

7 Some *trust* in chariots, and some in [a]horses: but we will remember the name of the LORD our God.

8 They are brought down and fallen: but we are risen, and stand upright.

9 Save, LORD: let the king hear us when we call.

## PSALM 21

To the chief Musician,
A Psalm of David.

THE king shall joy in thy strength, O LORD; and in thy salvation how greatly shall he rejoice!

2 Thou hast given him his heart's desire, and hast not ¹withholden the ᵃrequest of his lips.          *Selah.*

3 For ¹thou preventest him with the blessings of goodness: thou settest a crown of pure gold on his head.

4 ᵃHe asked life of thee, *and* thou gavest *it* him, *even* length of days for ever and ever.

5 His glory *is* great in thy salvation: honour and majesty hast thou laid upon him.

6 For thou hast made him most blessed for ever: ᵃthou hast made him ¹exceeding glad with thy ²countenance.

7 For the king trusteth in the LORD, and through the mercy of the most High he shall not be ¹moved.

8 Thine hand shall find out all thine enemies: thy right hand shall find out those that hate thee.

9 Thou shalt make them as a fiery oven in the time of thine anger: the LORD shall swallow them up in his wrath, and the fire shall devour them.

10 Their ¹fruit shalt thou destroy from the earth, and their ²seed from among the children of men.

11 For they intended evil against thee: they ¹imagined a mischievous device, *which* they are not able *to* ᵃperform.

12 Therefore shalt thou make them turn their back, *when* thou shalt make ready *thine arrows* upon thy strings against the face of them.

13 Be thou exalted, LORD, in thine own strength: *so* will we sing and praise thy power.

## PSALM 22

To the chief Musician upon ¹Aijeleth Shahar, A Psalm of David.

MY ᵃGod, my God, why hast thou forsaken me? *why art thou so* far from helping me, *and from* the words of my ¹roaring?

2 O my God, I cry in the daytime, but thou hearest not; and in the night season, and am not silent.

3 But thou *art* holy, *O thou* that inhabitest the ᵃpraises of Israel.

4 Our fathers trusted in thee: they trusted, and thou didst deliver them.

5 They cried unto thee, and were delivered: ᵃthey trusted in thee, and were not ¹confounded.

6 But I am ᵃa worm, and no man; ᵇa reproach of men, and despised of the people.

7 ᵃAll they that see me laugh me to scorn: they ¹shoot out the lip, they shake the head, *saying,*

8 ᵃHe¹ trusted on the LORD ²*that* he would deliver him: ᵇlet him deliver him, seeing he delighted in him.

9 ᵃBut thou *art* he that took me out of the womb: thou ¹didst make me hope *when I was* upon my mother's breasts.

10 I was cast upon thee from the womb: ᵃthou *art* my God from my mother's belly.

11 Be not far from me; for trouble *is* near; for *there is* none to help.

12 ᵃMany bulls have ¹compassed me: strong *bulls* of ᵇBashan have ²beset me round.

13 ᵃThey ¹gaped upon me *with* their mouths, *as* a ²ravening and a roaring lion.

14 I am poured out like water, ᵃand all my bones are out of joint: my heart is like wax; it is melted ¹in the midst of my bowels.

15 ᵃMy strength is dried up like a potsherd; and ᵇmy tongue ¹cleaveth to my jaws; and thou hast brought me into the dust of death.

16 For dogs have ¹compassed me: the assembly of the wicked have inclosed me: ᵃthey pierced my hands and my feet.

17 I ¹may tell all my bones: ᵃthey look *and* stare upon me.

18 ᵃThey ¹part my garments among them, and cast lots ²upon my vesture.

19 But be not thou far from me, O LORD: O my strength, haste thee to help me.

20 Deliver my soul from the sword; ᵃmy ¹darling from the power of the dog.

21 ᵃSave me from the lion's mouth: ᵇfor¹ thou hast heard me from the horns of the unicorns.

22 ᵃI will declare thy name unto ᵇmy brethren: in the midst of the congregation will I praise thee.

23 ᵃYe that fear the LORD, praise him; all ye the ¹seed of Jacob, glorify him; and ²fear him, all ye the seed of Israel.

24 For he hath not despised nor abhorred the affliction of the afflicted; neither hath he hid his face from him; but ᵃwhen he cried unto him, he heard.

25 ᵃMy praise *shall be* of thee in the great congregation: ᵇI will pay my vows before them that fear him.

26 The meek shall eat and be satisfied: they shall praise the LORD that seek him: your heart shall live for ever.

### Center column notes

21:2 ᵃ 2 Sam. 7:26–29 ¹ *withheld*

21:3 ¹ *thee meeteth*

21:4 ᵃ Ps. 61:5, 6; 133:3

21:6 ᵇ Ps. 16:11; 45:7 ¹ Lit. *joyful with gladness* ² *presence*

21:7 ¹ *shaken*

21:10 ¹ *offspring* ² *descendants*

21:11 ᵃ Ps. 2:1–4 ¹ *devised a plot*

22:title ¹ *the deer of the morning*

22:1 ᵃ Mark 15:34 ¹ *groaning*

22:3 ᵃ Deut. 10:21

22:5 ᵃ Is. 49:23 ¹ *ashamed*

22:6 ᵃ Is. 41:14 ᵇ [Is. 53:3]

22:7 ᵃ Matt. 27:39 ¹ Show contempt with their mouth

22:8 ᵃ Matt. 27:43 ᵇ Ps. 91:14 ¹ Lit. *He rolled himself on the LORD* ² Lit. *let him rescue him*

22:9 ᵃ [Ps. 71:5, 6] ¹ *caused me to trust*

22:10 ᵃ [Is. 46:3; 49:1]

22:12 ᵃ Ps. 22:21; 68:30 ᵇ Deut. 32:14 ¹ *surrounded* ² *encircled me*

22:13 ᵃ Job 16:10 ¹ Lit. *opened their mouths at me* ² *raging* or *tearing*

22:14 ᵃ Dan. 5:6 ¹ *within me*

22:15 ᵃ Prov. 17:22 ᵇ John 19:28 ¹ *clings*

22:16 ᵃ Matt. 27:35 ¹ *surrounded*

22:17 ᵃ Luke 23:27, 35 ¹ *can count*

22:18 ᵃ Matt. 27:35 ¹ *divide* ² *for my clothing*

22:20 ᵃ Ps. 35:17 ¹ *precious life*

22:21 ᵃ 2 Tim. 4:17 ᵇ Is. 34:7 ¹ *and from the horns of the wild oxen! You have answered me.*

22:22 ᵃ Heb. 2:12 ᵇ [Rom. 8:29]

22:23 ᵃ Ps. 135:19, 20 ¹ *descendants* ² Hold him in awesome reverence

22:24 ᵃ Heb. 5:7

22:25 ᵃ Ps. 35:18; 40:9, 10 ᵇ Eccl. 5:4

27 All the ends of the world shall remember and turn unto the LORD: and all the kindreds of the nations shall worship before thee.

28 ªFor the kingdom *is* the LORD's: and he *is* the governor among the nations.

29 ªAll *they that* ¹*be* fat upon earth shall eat and worship: ᵇall they that go down to ²the dust shall bow before him: and none can ³keep alive his own soul.

30 A ¹seed shall serve him; it shall be ²accounted to the Lord for a generation.

31 They shall come, and shall declare his righteousness unto a people that shall be born, that he hath done *this.*

## PSALM 23

A Psalm of David.

THE LORD *is* ªmy shepherd; ᵇI shall not ¹want.

2 ªHe maketh me to lie down in ¹green pastures: ᵇhe leadeth me beside the ²still waters.

3 He restoreth my soul: ªhe leadeth me in the paths of righteousness for his name's sake.

4 Yea, though I walk through the valley of ªthe shadow of death, ᵇI will fear no evil: ᶜfor thou *art* with me; thy rod and thy staff they comfort me.

5 Thou ªpreparest a table before me in the presence of mine enemies: thou ᵇanointest my head with oil; my cup runneth over.

6 Surely goodness and ¹mercy shall follow me all the days of my life: and I will dwell in the house of the LORD for ever.

## PSALM 24

A Psalm of David.

THE ªearth *is* the LORD's, and the fulness thereof; the world, and they that dwell therein.

2 For he hath ªfounded it upon the seas, and established it upon the ¹floods.

3 ªWho shall ascend into the hill of the LORD? or who shall stand in his holy place?

4 He that hath ªclean hands, and ᵇa pure heart; who hath not lifted up his soul ¹unto vanity, nor ᶜsworn deceitfully.

5 He shall receive the blessing from the LORD, and righteousness from the God of his salvation.

6 This *is* the generation of them that ªseek him, that seek thy face, O Jacob. *Selah.*

7 ªLift up your heads, O ye gates; and be ye lift up, ye everlasting doors; ᵇand the King of glory shall come in.

8 Who *is* this King of glory? The

LORD strong and mighty, the LORD mighty in ªbattle.

9 Lift up your heads, O ye gates; even lift *them* up, ye everlasting doors; and the King of glory shall come in.

10 Who is this King of glory? The LORD of hosts, he *is* the King of glory. *Selah.*

## PSALM 25

*A Psalm* of David.

UNTO ªthee, O LORD, do I lift up my soul.

2 O my God, I ªtrust in thee: let me not be ashamed, ᵇlet not mine enemies triumph over me.

3 Yea, let none that ¹wait on thee be ashamed: let them be ashamed which ²transgress without cause.

4 ªShew me thy ways, O LORD; teach me thy paths.

5 Lead me in thy truth, and teach me: for thou *art* the God of my salvation; on thee do I wait all the day.

6 Remember, O LORD, ªthy tender mercies and thy lovingkindnesses; for they *have been* ever of old.

7 Remember not ªthe sins of my youth, nor my transgressions: ᵇaccording to thy mercy remember thou me for thy goodness' sake, O LORD.

8 Good and upright *is* the LORD: therefore will he teach sinners in the way.

9 The ¹meek will he guide in ²judgment: and the meek will he teach his way.

10 All the paths of the LORD *are* mercy and truth unto such as keep his covenant and his testimonies.

11 ªFor thy name's sake, O LORD, pardon mine iniquity; for it *is* great.

12 What man *is* he that feareth the LORD? ªhim shall he teach in the way *that* he shall choose.

13 ªHis soul shall dwell ¹at ease; and ᵇhis² seed shall inherit the earth.

14 ªThe secret of the LORD *is* with them that fear him; and he will ¹shew them his covenant.

15 ªMine eyes *are* ever toward the LORD; for he shall ¹pluck my feet out of the net.

16 ªTurn thee unto me, and have mercy upon me; for I *am* ¹desolate and afflicted.

17 The troubles of my heart are enlarged: *O* bring thou me out of my distresses.

18 ªLook upon mine affliction and my pain; and forgive all my sins.

19 Consider mine enemies; for they are many; and they hate me with ¹cruel hatred.

20 O keep my soul, and deliver me: let me not be ashamed; for I put my trust in thee.

22:28 ª Matt. 6:13

22:29 ª Ps. 17:10; 45:12 ᵇ [Is. 26:19] ¹ *prosper* ² Death ³ *keep himself alive*

22:30 ¹ *posterity* ² *recounted of the* LORD *to the next generation*

23:1 ª [Is. 40:11] ᵇ [Phil. 4:19] ¹ *lack*

23:2 ª Ezek. 34:14 ᵇ [Rev. 7:17] ¹ Lit. *pastures of tender green grass* ² Lit. *waters of rest*

23:3 ª Ps. 5:8; 31:3

23:4 ª Job 3:5; 10:21, 22; 24:17 ᵇ [Ps. 3:6; 27:1] ᶜ [Is. 43:2]

23:5 ª Ps. 104:15 ᵇ Ps. 92:10

23:6 ¹ *lovingkindness*

24:1 ª 1 Cor. 10:26, 28

24:2 ª Ps. 89:11 ¹ Lit. *rivers*

24:3 ª Ps. 15:1–5

24:4 ª [Job 17:9] ᵇ [Matt. 5:8] ᶜ Ps. 15:4 ¹ *to an idol*

24:6 ª Ps. 27:4, 8

24:7 ª Is. 26:2 ᵇ Ps. 29:2, 9; 97:6

24:8 ª Rev. 19:13–16

25:1 ª Ps. 86:4; 143:8

25:2 ª Ps. 34:8 ᵇ Ps. 13:4; 41:11

25:3 ¹ *Wait in faith on* ² *deal treacherously*

25:4 ª Ex. 33:13

25:6 ª Ps. 103:17; 106:1

25:7 ª [Jer. 3:25] ᵇ Ps. 51:1

25:9 ¹ *humble* ² *justice*

25:11 ª Ps. 31:3; 79:9; 109:21; 143:11

25:12 ª [Ps. 25:8; 37:23]

25:13 ª [Prov. 19:23] ᵇ Matt. 5:5 ¹ Lit. *in goodness* ² *his descendants*

25:14 ª [John 7:17] ¹ Lit. *cause them to know*

25:15 ª [Ps. 123:2; 141:8] ¹ Lit. *bring out*

25:16 ª Ps. 69:16 ¹ *lonely*

25:18 ª 2 Sam. 16:12

25:19 ¹ *violent*

21 Let integrity and uprightness preserve me; for I [1]wait on thee.

22 [a]Redeem Israel, O God, out of all his troubles.

## PSALM 26

*A Psalm* of David.

JUDGE[1] [a]me, O LORD; for I have [b]walked in mine integrity: [c]I have trusted also in the LORD; *therefore* I shall not [2]slide.

2 [a]Examine me, O LORD, and [1]prove me; [2]try my reins and my heart.

3 For thy lovingkindness *is* before mine eyes: and [a]I have walked in thy truth.

4 I have not [a]sat with [1]vain persons, neither will I go in with [2]dissemblers.

5 I have [a]hated the congregation of evildoers; and will not sit with the wicked.

6 I will wash mine hands in innocency: so will I [1]compass thine altar, O LORD:

7 That I may [1]publish with the voice of thanksgiving, and tell of all thy wondrous works.

8 LORD, [a]I have loved the habitation of thy house, and the place where thine [1]honour dwelleth.

9 [a]Gather[1] not my soul with sinners, nor my life with [2]bloody men:

10 In whose hands *is* [1]mischief, and their right hand is full of [a]bribes.

11 But as for me, I will walk in mine integrity: redeem me, and be merciful unto me.

12 [a]My foot standeth in an even place: in the congregations will I bless the LORD.

## PSALM 27

*A Psalm* of David.

THE LORD *is* my [a]light and my salvation; whom shall I fear? the [b]LORD *is* the strength of my life; of whom shall I be afraid?

2 When the wicked, *even* mine enemies and my foes, came upon me to [a]eat[1] up my flesh, they stumbled and fell.

3 [a]Though an host should encamp against me, my heart shall not fear: though war should rise against me, in this *will* I *be* confident.

4 [a]One *thing* have I desired of the LORD, that will I seek after; that I may [b]dwell in the house of the LORD all the days of my life, to behold the [1]beauty of the LORD, and to enquire in his temple.

5 For [a]in the time of trouble he shall hide me in his pavilion: in the secret of his tabernacle shall he hide me; he shall [b]set me up upon a rock.

6 And now shall [a]mine head be [1]lifted up above mine enemies round about me: therefore will I offer in his tabernacle sacrifices of joy; I will sing, yea, I will sing praises unto the LORD.

7 Hear, O LORD, *when* I cry with my voice: have mercy also upon me, and answer me.

8 [1]*When thou saidst,* Seek ye my face; my heart said unto thee, Thy face, LORD, will I seek.

9 [a]Hide not thy face *far* from me; [1]put not thy servant away in anger: thou hast been my help; leave me not, neither forsake me, O God of my salvation.

10 [a]When my father and my mother forsake me, then the LORD will [1]take me up.

11 [a]Teach me thy way, O LORD, and lead me in a [1]plain path, because of mine enemies.

12 Deliver me not over unto the will of mine enemies: for [a]false witnesses are risen up against me, and such as breathe out [1]cruelty.

13 *I had fainted,* unless I had believed to see the goodness of the LORD [a]in the land of the living.

14 [a]Wait[1] on the LORD: be of good courage, and he shall strengthen thine heart: wait, I say, on the LORD.

## PSALM 28

*A Psalm* of David.

UNTO thee will I cry, O LORD my rock; [a]be not silent to me: [b]lest, *if* thou be silent to me, I become like them that go down into the pit.

2 Hear the voice of my supplications, when I cry unto thee, [a]when I lift up my hands [b]toward thy holy [1]oracle.

3 [1]Draw me not away with the wicked, and with the workers of iniquity, [a]which speak peace to their neighbours, but [2]mischief *is* in their hearts.

4 [a]Give them according to their deeds, and according to the wickedness of their endeavours: give them [1]after the work of their hands; render to them [2]their desert.

5 Because [a]they regard not the works of the LORD, nor the operation of his hands, he shall destroy them, and not build them up.

6 Blessed *be* the LORD, because he hath heard the voice of my supplications.

7 The LORD *is* [a]my strength and my shield; my heart [b]trusted in him, and I am helped: therefore my heart greatly rejoiceth; and with my song will I praise him.

8 The LORD *is* their strength, and he *is* the [a]saving strength of his [1]anointed.

9 Save thy people, and bless [a]thine inheritance: [1]feed them also, [b]and lift them up for ever.

25:21 [1] *Wait in faith on*
25:22 [a] [Ps. 130:8]
26:1 [a] Ps. 7:8 [b] 2 Kin. 20:3 [c] [Ps. 13:5; 28:7] [1] *Vindicate* [2] *slip*
26:2 [a] Ps. 17:3; 139:23 [1] *try* [2] *test my mind*
26:3 [a] 2 Kin. 20:3
26:4 [a] Ps. 1:1 [1] *idolatrous* [2] *hypocrites*
26:5 [a] Ps. 31:6; 139:21
26:6 [1] *go about*
26:7 [1] *proclaim*
26:8 [a] Ps. 27:4; 84:1–4, 10 [1] *glory*
26:9 [a] Ps. 28:3 [1] *Do not take away* [2] *bloodthirsty*
26:10 [a] 1 Sam. 8:3 [1] *a sinister scheme*
26:12 [a] Ps. 40:2
27:1 [a] [Mic. 7:8] [b] Ps. 62:7; 118:14
27:2 [a] Ps. 14:4 [1] *devour*
27:3 [a] Ps. 3:6
27:4 [a] Ps. 26:8; 65:4 [b] Luke 2:37 [1] *delightfulness*
27:5 [a] Ps. 31:20; 91:1 [b] Ps. 40:2
27:6 [a] Ps. 3:3 [1] *lifted up in honour*
27:8 [1] *Or My heart said, Let my face seek your face*
27:9 [a] Ps. 69:17; 143:7 [1] *turn*
27:10 [a] Is. 49:15 [1] *take care of me*
27:11 [a] Ps. 25:4; 86:11; 119:33 [1] *smooth*
27:12 [a] Ps. 35:11 [1] *violence*
27:13 [a] Ezek. 26:20
27:14 [a] Is. 25:9 [1] *Wait in faith*
28:1 [a] Ps. 35:22; 39:12; 83:1 [b] Ps. 88:4; 143:7
28:2 [a] Ps. 5:7 [b] Ps. 138:2 [1] *sanctuary*
28:3 [a] Ps. 12:2; 55:21; 62:4 [1] *Drag* [2] *evil*
28:4 [a] [Rev. 18:6; 22:12] [1] *according to* [2] *what they deserve*
28:5 [a] Is. 5:12
28:7 [a] Ps. 18:2; 59:17 [b] Ps. 13:5; 112:7
28:8 [a] Ps. 20:6 [1] *Messiah, commissioned one*
28:9 [a] [Deut. 9:29; 32:9] [b] Deut. 1:31 [1] *shepherd*

## PSALM 29

### A Psalm of David.

GIVE <sup>a</sup>unto the LORD, O ye mighty, give unto the LORD glory and strength.

2 <sup>1</sup>Give unto the LORD the glory <sup>2</sup>due unto his name; worship the LORD in <sup>a</sup>the <sup>3</sup>beauty of holiness.

3 The voice of the LORD *is* upon the waters: <sup>a</sup>the God of glory thundereth: the LORD *is* upon many waters.

4 The voice of the LORD *is* powerful; the voice of the LORD *is* full of majesty.

5 The voice of the LORD <sup>1</sup>breaketh <sup>a</sup>the cedars; yea, the LORD <sup>1</sup>breaketh the cedars of Lebanon.

6 <sup>a</sup>He maketh them also to skip like a calf; Lebanon and <sup>b</sup>Sirion like a young <sup>1</sup>unicorn.

7 The voice of the LORD <sup>1</sup>divideth the flames of fire.

8 The voice of the LORD shaketh the wilderness; the LORD shaketh the wilderness of <sup>a</sup>Kadesh.

9 The voice of the LORD <sup>1</sup>maketh the <sup>a</sup>hinds to calve, and <sup>2</sup>discovereth the forests: and in his temple doth every one speak of *his* glory.

10 The <sup>a</sup>LORD <sup>1</sup>sitteth upon the flood; yea, <sup>b</sup>the LORD sitteth King for ever.

11 <sup>a</sup>The LORD will give strength unto his people; the LORD will bless his people with peace.

## PSALM 30

### A Psalm *and* Song <sup>a</sup>at the dedication of the house of David.

I WILL extol thee, O LORD; for thou hast <sup>a</sup>lifted me up, and hast not made my foes to <sup>b</sup>rejoice over me.

2 O LORD my God, I cried unto thee, and thou hast <sup>a</sup>healed me.

3 O LORD, <sup>a</sup>thou hast brought up my soul from the <sup>1</sup>grave: thou hast kept me alive, that I should not go down to the <sup>2</sup>pit.

4 <sup>a</sup>Sing unto the LORD, O ye saints of his, and give thanks at the remembrance of his <sup>1</sup>holiness.

5 For <sup>a</sup>his anger *endureth but* a moment; <sup>b</sup>in his favour *is* life: weeping may endure for a night, but <sup>1</sup>joy *cometh* in the morning.

6 And in my prosperity I said, I shall never be moved.

7 LORD, by thy favour thou hast made my mountain to stand strong: <sup>a</sup>thou didst hide thy face, *and* I was troubled.

8 I cried to thee, O LORD; and unto the LORD I made supplication.

9 What profit *is there* in my blood, when I go down to the <sup>1</sup>pit? <sup>a</sup>Shall the dust praise thee? shall it declare thy truth?

10 Hear, O LORD, and have mercy upon me: LORD, be thou my helper.

29:1 <sup>a</sup> 1 Chr. 16:28, 29
29:2 <sup>a</sup> 2 Chr. 20:21 <sup>1</sup> *Ascribe* <sup>2</sup> Lit. *of his name* <sup>3</sup> *majesty*
29:3 <sup>a</sup> [Job 37:4, 5]
29:5 <sup>a</sup> Is. 2:13; 14:8 <sup>1</sup> *splinters*
29:6 <sup>a</sup> Ps. 114:4 <sup>b</sup> Deut. 3:9 <sup>1</sup> *wild ox*
29:7 <sup>1</sup> *stirs or divides,* lit. *hews out*
29:8 <sup>a</sup> Num. 13:26
29:9 <sup>a</sup> Job 39:1 <sup>1</sup> *makes the deer give birth* <sup>2</sup> *strips the forests bare*
29:10 <sup>a</sup> Gen. 6:17 <sup>b</sup> Ps. 10:16 <sup>1</sup> *sat enthroned at*
29:11 <sup>a</sup> Ps. 28:8; 68:35
30:title <sup>a</sup> Deut. 20:5
30:1 <sup>a</sup> Ps. 28:9 <sup>b</sup> Ps. 25:2
30:2 <sup>a</sup> Ps. 6:2; 103:3
30:3 <sup>a</sup> Ps. 86:13 <sup>1</sup> Or *Sheol,* the place of the dead <sup>2</sup> *grave*
30:4 <sup>a</sup> Ps. 97:12 <sup>1</sup> Or *his holy name*
30:5 <sup>a</sup> Ps. 103:9 <sup>b</sup> Ps. 63:3 <sup>1</sup> *a shout of joy*
30:7 <sup>a</sup> [Ps. 104:29; 143:7]
30:9 <sup>a</sup> [Ps. 6:5] <sup>1</sup> *grave*
30:11 <sup>a</sup> Jer. 31:4
30:12 <sup>1</sup> *my soul*
31:1 <sup>a</sup> Ps. 22:5
31:2 <sup>a</sup> Ps. 17:6; 71:2; 86:1; 102:2 <sup>1</sup> *rock of refuge* <sup>2</sup> Lit. *fortresses*
31:3 <sup>a</sup> [Ps. 18:2] <sup>b</sup> Ps. 23:3; 25:11
31:4 <sup>1</sup> *secretly*
31:5 <sup>a</sup> Luke 23:46 <sup>b</sup> [Deut. 32:4]
31:6 <sup>a</sup> Jon. 2:8 <sup>1</sup> *vain idols*
31:7 <sup>a</sup> [John 10:27]
31:8 <sup>a</sup> [Deut. 32:30] <sup>b</sup> [Ps. 4:1; 18:19] <sup>1</sup> *given me over* <sup>2</sup> *wide place*
31:9 <sup>a</sup> Ps. 6:7 <sup>1</sup> *wastes away* <sup>2</sup> *body*
31:10 <sup>1</sup> *waste away*
31:11 <sup>a</sup> [Is. 53:4] <sup>b</sup> Job 19:13 <sup>c</sup> Ps. 64:8 <sup>1</sup> *a despised thing* <sup>2</sup> *outside*
31:12 <sup>a</sup> Ps. 88:4, 5
31:13 <sup>a</sup> Jer. 20:10 <sup>b</sup> Lam. 2:22 <sup>c</sup> Matt. 27:1 <sup>1</sup> *schemed*

11 <sup>a</sup>Thou hast turned for me my mourning into dancing: thou hast put off my sackcloth, and girded me with gladness;

12 To the end that <sup>1</sup>*my* glory may sing praise to thee, and not be silent. O LORD my God, I will give thanks unto thee for ever.

## PSALM 31

### To the chief Musician, A Psalm of David.

IN <sup>a</sup>thee, O LORD, do I put my trust; let me never be ashamed: deliver me in thy righteousness.

2 <sup>a</sup>Bow down thine ear to me; deliver me speedily: be thou my <sup>1</sup>strong rock, for an house of <sup>2</sup>defence to save me.

3 <sup>a</sup>For thou *art* my rock and my fortress; therefore <sup>b</sup>for thy name's sake lead me, and guide me.

4 Pull me out of the net that they have laid <sup>1</sup>privily for me: for thou *art* my strength.

5 <sup>a</sup>Into thine hand I commit my spirit: thou hast redeemed me, O LORD God of <sup>b</sup>truth.

6 I have hated them <sup>a</sup>that regard <sup>1</sup>lying vanities: but I trust in the LORD.

7 I will be glad and rejoice in thy mercy: for thou hast considered my trouble; thou hast <sup>a</sup>known my soul in adversities;

8 And hast not <sup>a</sup>shut<sup>1</sup> me up into the hand of the enemy: <sup>b</sup>thou hast set my feet in a <sup>2</sup>large room.

9 Have mercy upon me, O LORD, for I am in trouble: <sup>a</sup>mine eye is <sup>1</sup>consumed with grief, *yea,* my soul and my <sup>2</sup>belly.

10 For my life is spent with grief, and my years with sighing: my strength faileth because of mine iniquity, and my bones <sup>1</sup>are consumed.

11 <sup>a</sup>I was <sup>1</sup>a reproach among all mine enemies, but <sup>b</sup>especially among my neighbours, and a fear to mine acquaintance: <sup>c</sup>they that did see me <sup>2</sup>without fled from me.

12 <sup>a</sup>I am forgotten as a dead man out of mind: I am like a broken vessel.

13 <sup>a</sup>For I have heard the slander of many: <sup>b</sup>fear *was* on every side: while they <sup>c</sup>took counsel together against me, they <sup>1</sup>devised to take away my life.

14 But I trusted in thee, O LORD: I said, Thou *art* my God.

15 My times *are* in thy <sup>a</sup>hand: deliver me from the hand of mine enemies, and from them that persecute me.

16 <sup>a</sup>Make thy face to shine upon thy servant: save me for thy mercies' sake.

31:15 <sup>a</sup> [Job 14:5; 24:1]   31:16 <sup>a</sup> Ps. 4:6; 80:3

17 [a]Let me not be ashamed, O LORD; for I have called upon thee: let the wicked be ashamed, *and* [b]let them be silent in the [1]grave.

18 [a]Let the lying lips be put to silence; which [b]speak [1]grievous things proudly and contemptuously against the righteous.

19 [a]*Oh* how great *is* thy goodness, which thou hast laid up for them that fear thee; *which* thou hast wrought for them that trust in thee before the sons of men!

20 [a]Thou shalt hide them in [1]the secret of thy presence from the [2]pride of man: [b]thou shalt keep them secretly in a [3]pavilion from the strife of tongues.

21 Blessed *be* the LORD: for [a]he hath shewed me his marvellous kindness in a strong city.

22 For I said in my haste, I am cut off from before thine eyes: nevertheless thou heardest the voice of my supplications when I cried unto thee.

23 O love the LORD, all ye his saints: *for* the LORD preserveth the faithful, and [1]plentifully rewardeth the proud doer.

24 [a]Be of good courage, and he shall strengthen your heart, all ye that hope in the LORD.

## PSALM 32

*A Psalm* of David, [1]Maschil.

**B**LESSED *is he whose* [a]transgression *is* forgiven, *whose* sin *is* covered.

2 Blessed *is* the man unto whom the LORD [a]imputeth [1]not iniquity, and [b]in whose spirit *there is* no [2]guile.

3 When I kept silence, my bones [1]waxed old through my [2]roaring all the day long.

4 For day and night thy [a]hand was heavy upon me: [1]my moisture is turned into the drought of summer. *Selah.*

5 I acknowledged my sin unto thee, and mine iniquity have I not hid. [a]I said, I will confess my transgressions unto the LORD; and thou forgavest the iniquity of my sin. *Selah.*

6 [a]For this shall every one that is godly [b]pray unto thee in a time when thou mayest be found: surely in the floods of great waters they shall not come nigh unto him.

7 [a]Thou *art* my hiding place; thou shalt preserve me from trouble; thou shalt [1]compass me about with [b]songs of deliverance. *Selah.*

8 I will instruct thee and teach thee in the way which thou shalt go: I will guide thee with mine eye.

9 Be ye not as the [a]horse, *or* as the mule, *which* have no understanding: whose mouth must be held in with

---

31:17 [a] Ps. 25:2, 20
[b] Ps. 94:17; 115:17
[1] Or *Sheol*

31:18 [a] Ps. 109:2; 120:2 [b] Ps. 94:4
[1] *insolent*

31:19 [a] [Rom. 2:4; 11:22]

31:20 [a] [Ps. 27:5; 32:7] [b] Job 5:21
[1] *the secret place*
[2] *plots* [3] *shelter*

31:21 [a] [Ps. 17:7]

31:23 [1] *fully repays*

31:24 [a] [Ps. 27:14]

32:title [1] *Contemplation*

32:1 [a] [Ps. 85:2; 103:3]

32:2 [a] [2 Cor. 5:19] [b] John 1:47
[1] *does not charge his account with*
[2] *deceit*

32:3 [1] *grew*
[2] *groaning*

32:4 [a] 1 Sam. 5:6
[1] *my vitality*

32:5 [a] [Prov. 28:13]

32:6 [a] [1 Tim. 1:16]
[b] Is. 55:6

32:7 [a] Ps. 9:9
[b] Ex. 15:1 [1] *surround*

32:9 [a] Prov. 26:3

32:10 [a] [Rom. 2:9] [b] Prov. 16:20
[1] *surround*

32:11 [a] Ps. 64:10; 68:3; 97:12

33:1 [a] Ps. 32:11; 97:12 [1] *beautiful*

33:3 [1] *shout of joy*

33:5 [1] *justice*
[2] *lovingkindness*

33:6 [a] [Heb. 11:3]
[b] Gen. 2:1 [c] [Job 26:13]

33:7 [a] Job 26:10; 38:8 [1] *deep*

33:9 [a] Gen. 1:3

33:10 [a] Is. 8:10; 19:3 [1] *nations or Gentiles* [2] *plans*

33:11 [a] [Job 23:13]

33:12 [a] [Ex. 19:5]

33:13 [a] Job 28:24

33:15 [a] [Jer. 32:19]
[1] *individually*
[2] *understands*

33:16 [a] Ps. 44:6; 60:11

33:17 [a] [Prov. 21:31] [1] *false hope*

33:18 [a] [Job 36:7]

33:19 [a] Job 5:20

---

bit and bridle, lest they come near unto thee.

10 [a]Many sorrows *shall be* to the wicked: but [b]he that trusteth in the LORD, mercy shall [1]compass him about.

11 [a]Be glad in the LORD, and rejoice, ye righteous: and shout for joy, all *ye that are* upright in heart.

## PSALM 33

**R**EJOICE [a]in the LORD, O ye righteous: *for* praise is [1]comely for the upright.

2 Praise the LORD with harp: sing unto him with the psaltery *and* an instrument of ten strings.

3 Sing unto him a new song; play skilfully with a [1]loud noise.

4 For the word of the LORD *is* right; and all his works *are done* in truth.

5 He loveth righteousness and [1]judgment: the earth is full of the [2]goodness of the LORD.

6 [a]By the word of the LORD were the heavens made; and all the [b]host of them [c]by the breath of his mouth.

7 [a]He gathereth the waters of the sea together as an heap: he layeth up the [1]depth in storehouses.

8 Let all the earth fear the LORD: let all the inhabitants of the world stand in awe of him.

9 For [a]he spake, and it was *done;* he commanded, and it stood fast.

10 [a]The LORD bringeth the counsel of the [1]heathen to nought: he maketh the [2]devices of the people of none effect.

11 [a]The counsel of the LORD standeth for ever, the thoughts of his heart to all generations.

12 Blessed *is* the nation whose God *is* the LORD; *and* the people *whom* he hath [a]chosen for his own inheritance.

13 [a]The LORD looketh from heaven; he beholdeth all the sons of men.

14 From the place of his habitation he looketh upon all the inhabitants of the earth.

15 He fashioneth their hearts [1]alike; [a]he [2]considereth all their works.

16 [a]There is no king saved by the multitude of an host: a mighty man is not delivered by much strength.

17 [a]An horse *is* a [1]vain thing for safety: neither shall he deliver *any* by his great strength.

18 [a]Behold, the eye of the LORD *is* upon them that fear him, upon them that hope in his mercy;

19 To deliver their soul from death, and [a]to keep them alive in famine.

20 Our soul waiteth for the LORD: he *is* our help and our shield.

21 For our heart shall rejoice in him, because we have trusted in his holy name.

22 Let thy mercy, O LORD, be upon us, according as we hope in thee.

## PSALM 34

*A Psalm* of David, when he changed his behaviour before Abimelech; who drove him away, and he departed.

I WILL [a]bless the LORD at all times: his praise *shall* continually *be* in my mouth.

2 My soul shall make her boast in the LORD: the humble shall hear *thereof,* and be glad.

3 O magnify the LORD with me, and let us exalt his name together.

4 I [a]sought the LORD, and he heard me, and delivered me from all my fears.

5 They looked unto him, and were [1]lightened: and their faces were not ashamed.

6 This poor man cried, and the LORD heard *him,* and saved him out of all his troubles.

7 [a]The angel of the LORD [b]encampeth round about them that fear him, and delivereth them.

8 O [a]taste and see that the LORD *is* good: [b]blessed *is* the man *that* trusteth in him.

9 O fear the LORD, ye his saints: for *there is* no [1]want to them that fear him.

10 The young lions do lack, and suffer hunger: [a]but they that seek the LORD shall not [1]want any good *thing.*

11 Come, ye children, hearken unto me: [a]I will teach you the fear of the LORD.

12 [a]What man *is he that* desireth life, *and* loveth *many* days, that he may see good?

13 Keep thy tongue from evil, and thy lips from speaking [a]guile.[1]

14 [a]Depart from evil, and do good; [b]seek peace, and pursue it.

15 [a]The eyes of the LORD *are* upon the righteous, and his ears *are open* unto their cry.

16 [a]The face of the LORD *is* against them that do evil, [b]to [1]cut off the remembrance of them from the earth.

17 *The righteous* cry, and [a]the LORD heareth, and delivereth them out of all their troubles.

18 [a]The LORD *is* nigh [b]unto them that are of a broken heart; and saveth such as be [1]of a contrite spirit.

19 [a]Many *are* the afflictions of the righteous: [b]but the LORD delivereth him out of them all.

20 He keepeth all his bones: [a]not one of them is broken.

21 [a]Evil shall slay the wicked: and they that hate the righteous shall be [1]desolate.

22 The LORD [a]redeemeth the soul of

34:1 [a] [Eph. 5:20]
34:4 [a] [Matt. 7:7]
34:5 [1] *radiant*
34:7 [a] Dan. 6:22
  [b] 2 Kin. 6:17
34:8 [a] 1 Pet. 2:3
  [b] Ps. 2:12
34:9 [1] *lack*
34:10 [a] [Ps. 84:11]
  [1] *lack*
34:11 [a] Ps. 32:8
34:12 [a] 1 Pet. 3:10–12]
34:13 [a] [Eph. 4:25]
  [1] *deceit*
34:14 [a] Ps. 37:27
  [b] [Rom. 14:19]
34:15 [a] Job 36:7
34:16 [a] Lev. 17:10
  [b] [Prov. 10:7]
  [1] *destroy*
34:17 [a] Ps. 34:6; 145:19
34:18 [a] [Ps. 145:18]
  [b] [Is. 57:15]
  [1] *crushed in spirit*
34:19 [a] Prov. 24:16
  [b] Ps. 34:4, 6, 17
34:20 [a] John 19:33, 36
34:21 [a] Ps. 94:23; 140:11 [1] *condemned or held guilty*
34:22 [a] 1 Kin. 1:29

35:1 [1] *contend*
35:2 [1] A small shield
35:3 [1] *stop those who chase*
35:4 [a] Ps. 40:14, 15; 70:2, 3 [b] Ps. 129:5 [1] *brought to dishonour and* [2] *life* [3] *plot*
35:5 [a] Job 21:18
35:6 [a] Ps. 73:18 [1] *pursue*
35:7 [a] Ps. 9:15 [1] *life*
35:8 [a] [1 Thess. 5:3] [1] *unexpectedly*
35:10 [a] Ps. 51:8 [b] [Ex. 15:11] [1] *plunders*
35:11 [1] *Fierce* [2] *ask me things*
35:12 [a] John 10:32 [1] *sorrow*
35:13 [a] Job 30:25 [1] *heart*
35:14 [1] *in mourning*
35:15 [1] Lit. *limping or stumbling* [2] *attackers*
35:16 [1] *ungodly*
35:17 [a] [Hab. 1:13] [1] *my precious life*
35:18 [1] *a mighty*

his servants: and none of them that trust in him shall be desolate.

## PSALM 35

*A Psalm* of David.

PLEAD *my cause,* O LORD, with them that [1]strive with me: fight against them that fight against me.

2 Take hold of shield and [1]buckler, and stand up for mine help.

3 Draw out also the spear, and [1]stop *the way* against them that persecute me: say unto my soul, I *am* thy salvation.

4 [a]Let them be [1]confounded and put to shame that seek after my [2]soul: let them be [b]turned back and brought to confusion that [3]devise my hurt.

5 [a]Let them be as chaff before the wind: and let the angel of the LORD chase *them.*

6 Let their way be [a]dark and slippery: and let the angel of the LORD [1]persecute them.

7 For without cause have they [a]hid for me their net *in* a pit, *which* without cause they have digged for my [1]soul.

8 Let [a]destruction come upon him [1]at unawares; and let his net that he hath hid catch himself: into that very destruction let him fall.

9 And my soul shall be joyful in the LORD: it shall rejoice in his salvation.

10 [a]All my bones shall say, LORD, [b]who *is* like unto thee, which deliverest the poor from him that is too strong for him, yea, the poor and the needy from him that [1]spoileth him?

11 [1]False witnesses did rise up; they [2]laid to my charge *things* that I knew not.

12 [a]They rewarded me evil for good *to* the [1]spoiling of my soul.

13 But as for me, [a]when they were sick, my clothing *was* sackcloth: I humbled my soul with fasting; and my prayer returned into mine own [1]bosom.

14 I behaved myself as though *he had been* my friend *or* brother: I bowed down [1]heavily, as one that mourneth *for his* mother.

15 But in mine [1]adversity they rejoiced, and gathered themselves together: *yea,* the [2]abjects gathered themselves together against me, and I knew *it* not; they did tear *me,* and ceased not:

16 With [1]hypocritical mockers in feasts, they gnashed upon me with their teeth.

17 Lord, how long wilt thou [a]look on? rescue my soul from their destructions, [1]my darling from the lions.

18 I will give thee thanks in the great congregation: I will praise thee among [1]much people.

19 [a]Let not them that are [1]mine enemies wrongfully rejoice over me:
*neither* let them wink with the eye
that hate me without a cause.
20 For they speak not peace: but
they devise deceitful matters against
*them that are* quiet in the land.
21 Yea, they opened their mouth
wide against me, *and* said, Aha, aha,
our eye hath seen *it*.
22 *This* thou hast seen, O LORD:
keep not silence: O Lord, be not far
from me.
23 Stir up thyself, and awake to my
[1]judgment, *even* unto my cause, my
God and my Lord.
24 [1]Judge me, O LORD my God, according to thy righteousness; and let
them not rejoice over me.
25 Let them not say in their hearts,
Ah, so would we have it: let them not
say, We have swallowed him up.
26 Let them be ashamed and
brought to [1]confusion together that
rejoice at mine hurt: let them be
[a]clothed with shame and dishonour
that magnify *themselves* against me.
27 [a]Let them shout for joy, and be
glad, that favour my righteous cause:
yea, let them say continually, Let the
LORD be magnified, which hath pleasure in the prosperity of his servant.
28 And my tongue shall speak of
thy righteousness *and* of thy praise
all the day long.

## PSALM 36

To the chief Musician, *A Psalm* of
David, the servant of the LORD.

THE[1] transgression of the wicked
saith within my heart, [a]*that there
is* no fear of God before his eyes.
2 For he flattereth himself in his
own eyes, [1]until his iniquity be found
[2]to be hateful.
3 The words of his mouth *are* [1]iniq-
uity and deceit: [a]he hath [2]left off to be
wise, *and* to do good.
4 [a]He [1]deviseth mischief upon his
bed; he setteth himself [b]in a way *that
is* not good; he [2]abhorreth not [c]evil.
5 Thy [1]mercy, O LORD, *is* in the heavens; *and* thy faithfulness *reacheth*
unto the clouds.
6 Thy righteousness *is* like the
[1]great mountains; [a]thy judgments
*are* a great [2]deep: O LORD, thou pre-
servest man and beast.
7 How [1]excellent *is* thy lovingkindness, O God! therefore the children
of men [a]put their trust under the
shadow of thy wings.
8 [a]They shall be abundantly satisfied with the [1]fatness of thy house;
and thou shalt make them drink of
[b]the river of thy pleasures.
9 [a]For with thee *is* the fountain of
life: [b]in thy light shall we see light.
10 O continue thy lovingkindness
unto them that know thee; and thy
righteousness to the upright in heart.
11 Let not the foot of pride come
against me, and let not the hand of
the wicked [1]remove me.
12 There are the workers of iniquity
fallen: they are cast down, and shall
not be able to rise.

## PSALM 37

*A Psalm* of David.

FRET[a] not thyself because of evildoers, neither be thou envious
against the workers of iniquity.
2 For they shall soon be cut down
[a]like the grass, and wither as the
green herb.
3 Trust in the LORD, and do good;
*so* shalt thou dwell in the land, and
[1]verily thou shalt be fed.
4 [a]Delight thyself also in the LORD;
and he shall give thee the desires of
thine [b]heart.
5 [a]Commit[1] thy way unto the LORD;
trust also in him; and he shall bring *it*
to pass.
6 [a]And he shall bring forth thy righteousness as the light, and thy [1]judg-
ment as the noonday.
7 Rest in the LORD, [a]and wait patiently for him: fret not thyself because of him who [b]prospereth in his
way, because of the man who bringeth wicked [1]devices to pass.
8 [a]Cease from anger, and forsake
wrath: [b]fret not thyself [1]in any wise
to do evil.
9 For evildoers shall be [1]cut off: but
those that wait upon the LORD, they
shall [a]inherit the earth.
10 For [a]yet a little while, and the
wicked *shall* not *be*: yea, [b]thou shalt
diligently [1]consider his place, and it
*shall* not *be*.
11 [a]But the meek shall inherit the
earth; and shall delight themselves
in the abundance of peace.
12 The wicked plotteth against the
just, [a]and gnasheth upon him with
his teeth.
13 [a]The Lord shall laugh at him: for
he seeth that [b]his day is coming.
14 The wicked have drawn out the
sword, and have bent their bow, to
cast down the poor and needy, *and*
to slay such as be of upright [1]conver-
sation.
15 Their sword shall enter into their
own heart, and their bows shall be
broken.
16 [a]A little that a righteous man
hath *is* better than the riches of many
wicked.
17 For the arms of the wicked shall
be broken: but the LORD upholdeth
the righteous.
18 The LORD knoweth the days of

35:19 [a] Ps. 69:4; 109:3 [1] *wrongfully my enemies*
35:23 [1] *vindication*
35:24 [1] *Vindicate*
35:26 [a] Ps. 109:29 [1] *mutual confusion*
35:27 [a] Rom. 12:15
36:1 [a] Rom. 3:18 [1] *An oracle within my heart of the transgression of the wicked*
36:2 [1] *when* [2] *and when he hates*
36:3 [a] Jer. 4:22 [1] *wickedness* [2] *ceased being wise*
36:4 [a] Prov. 4:16 [b] Is. 65:2 [c] [Rom. 12:9] [1] *plots wickedness* [2] *despises*
36:5 [1] *lovingkindness*
36:6 [a] [Rom. 11:33] [1] Lit. *mountains of God* [2] *ocean*
36:7 [a] Ps. 17:8; 57:1; 91:4 [1] *precious*
36:8 [a] Ps. 63:5; 65:4 [b] Rev. 22:1 [1] *fulness*
36:9 [a] [Jer. 2:13] [b] [1 Pet. 2:9]
36:11 [1] *drive me away*
37:1 [a] Ps. 73:3
37:2 [a] Ps. 90:5, 6; 92:7
37:3 [1] *feed on his faithfulness*
37:4 [a] Is. 58:14 [b] Ps. 21:2; 145:19
37:5 [a] [Ps. 55:22] [1] Lit. *Roll off onto*
37:6 [a] Job 11:17 [1] *justice*
37:7 [a] [Lam. 3:26] [b] [Ps. 73:3–12] [1] *schemes*
37:8 [a] [Eph. 4:26] [b] Ps. 73:3 [1] *it only causes harm*
37:9 [a] [Is. 57:13; 60:21] [1] *destroyed*
37:10 [a] [Heb. 10:36] [b] Job 7:10 [1] *look diligently for*
37:11 [a] [Matt. 5:5]
37:12 [a] Ps. 35:16
37:13 [a] Ps. 2:4; 59:8 [b] 1 Sam. 26:10
37:14 [1] *conduct*
37:16 [a] Prov. 15:16; 16:8

the upright: and their inheritance shall be for ever.

19 They shall not be ashamed in the evil time: and in the days of famine they shall be satisfied.

20 But the wicked shall perish, and the enemies of the LORD *shall be* as the ¹fat of lambs: they shall ²consume; into smoke shall they consume away.

21 The wicked borroweth, and ¹payeth not again: but ᵃthe righteous sheweth mercy, and giveth.

22 ᵃFor *such as be* blessed of him shall inherit the ¹earth; and *they that be* cursed of him shall be ²cut off.

23 ᵃThe steps of a *good* man are ¹ordered by the LORD: and he delighteth in his way.

24 ᵃThough he fall, he shall not be utterly cast down: for the LORD upholdeth *him with* his hand.

25 I have been young, and *now* am old; yet have I not seen the righteous forsaken, nor his ¹seed begging bread.

26 ᵃ*He is* ¹ever merciful, and lendeth; and his ²seed *is* blessed.

27 Depart from evil, and do good; and dwell for evermore.

28 For the LORD loveth ¹judgment, and forsaketh not his saints; they are preserved for ever: but the seed of the wicked shall be cut off.

29 ᵃThe righteous shall inherit the land, and dwell therein for ever.

30 ᵃThe mouth of the righteous speaketh wisdom, and his tongue talketh of ¹judgment.

31 The law of his God *is* in his heart; none of his steps shall ¹slide.

32 The wicked ᵃwatcheth the righteous, and seeketh to slay him.

33 The LORD ᵃwill not leave him in his hand, nor condemn him when he is judged.

34 ᵃWait on the LORD, and keep his way, and he shall exalt thee to inherit the land: when the wicked are cut off, thou shalt see *it.*

35 I have seen the wicked in great power, and spreading himself like a ¹green bay tree.

36 Yet he passed away, and, lo, he *was* not: yea, I sought him, but he could not be found.

37 Mark the ¹perfect *man,* and behold the upright: for the end of *that* man *is* peace.

38 ᵃBut the transgressors shall be destroyed together: the end of the wicked shall be cut off.

39 But the salvation of the righteous *is* of the LORD: *he is* their strength ᵃin the time of trouble.

40 And ᵃthe LORD shall help them, and deliver them: he shall deliver them from the wicked, and save them, ᵇbecause they trust in him.

37:20 ¹ *splendour of the meadows* ² *vanish*

37:21 ª Ps. 112:5, 9 ¹ *does not repay*

37:22 ª [Prov. 3:33] ¹ *land* ² *destroyed*

37:23 ª [1 Sam. 2:9] ¹ *established*

37:24 ª Prov. 24:16

37:25 ¹ *descendants*

37:26 ª [Deut. 15:8] ¹ Lit. *merciful all the day* ² *descendants*

37:28 ¹ *justice*

37:29 ª Prov. 2:21

37:30 ª [Matt. 12:35] ¹ *justice*

37:31 ¹ *slip*

37:32 ª Ps. 10:8; 17:11

37:33 ª Ps. 31:8; [2 Pet. 2:9]

37:34 ª Ps. 27:14; 37:9

37:35 ¹ *native green tree*

37:37 ¹ *blameless*

37:38 ª [Ps. 1:4–6; 37:20, 28]

37:39 ª Ps. 9:9; 37:19

37:40 ª Ps. 22:4; Is. 31:5; Dan. 3:17; 6:23 ᵇ 1 Chr. 5:20; Ps. 34:22

38:title ª Ps. 70:title

38:1 ª Ps. 6:1

38:2 ¹ *pierce me deeply* ² *down*

38:3 ¹ *health,* lit. *peace*

38:5 ¹ *are foul and festering*

38:6 ¹ Lit. *bent down*

38:7 ¹ *inflammation*

38:8 ¹ *severely* ² *groaned* ³ *turmoil*

38:9 ¹ *sighing*

38:11 ª Ps. 31:11; 88:18 ¹ *loved ones* ² *my plague* ³ *neighbours*

38:12 ¹ *speak of destruction,* ² *plan deception*

38:14 ¹ *responses*

38:15 ª [Ps. 39:7] ¹ *I wait for thee, O LORD* ² *answer*

38:17 ª Ps. 51:3 ¹ *to fall*

38:18 ª Ps. 32:5 ᵇ [2 Cor. 7:9, 10] ¹ *be in anguish over*

38:19 ¹ *vigorous*

38:20 ª Ps. 35:12

## PSALM 38

A Psalm of David, ªto bring to remembrance.

O LORD ªrebuke me not in thy wrath: neither chasten me in thy hot displeasure.

2 For thine arrows ¹stick fast in me, and thy hand presseth me ²sore.

3 *There is* no soundness in my flesh because of thine anger; neither *is there any* ¹rest in my bones because of my sin.

4 For mine iniquities are gone over mine head: as an heavy burden they are too heavy for me.

5 My wounds ¹stink *and* are corrupt because of my foolishness.

6 I am ¹troubled; I am bowed down greatly; I go mourning all the day long.

7 For my loins are filled with ¹a loathsome *disease:* and *there is* no soundness in my flesh.

8 I am feeble and ¹sore broken: I have ²roared by reason of the ³disquietness of my heart.

9 Lord, all my desire *is* before thee; and my ¹groaning is not hid from thee.

10 My heart panteth, my strength faileth me: as for the light of mine eyes, it also is gone from me.

11 My ¹lovers and my friends ªstand aloof from ²my sore; and my ³kinsmen stand afar off.

12 They also that seek after my life lay snares *for me:* and they that seek my hurt ¹speak mischievous things, and ²imagine deceits all the day long.

13 But I, as a deaf *man,* heard not; and *I was* as a dumb man *that* openeth not his mouth.

14 Thus I was as a man that heareth not, and in whose mouth *are* no ¹reproofs.

15 For ¹in thee, O LORD, ªdo I hope: thou wilt ²hear, O Lord my God.

16 For I said, *Hear me,* lest *otherwise* they should rejoice over me: when my foot slippeth, they magnify *themselves* against me.

17 ªFor I *am* ready ¹to halt, and my sorrow *is* continually before me.

18 For I will ªdeclare mine iniquity; I will ¹be ᵇsorry for my sin.

19 But mine enemies *are* ¹lively, *and* they are strong: and they that hate me wrongfully are multiplied.

20 They also ªthat render evil for good are mine adversaries; because I follow *the thing that* good *is.*

21 Forsake me not, O LORD: O my God, ªbe not far from me.

22 Make haste to help me, O Lord my salvation.

38:21 ª Ps. 22:19; 35:22

## PSALM 39

To the chief Musician, *even*
to Jeduthun, A Psalm of David.

I SAID, I will take heed to my ways,
that I sin not with my ªtongue: I
will ¹keep my mouth with a bridle,
while the wicked is before me.

2 ªI was ¹dumb with silence, I held
my peace, *even* from good; and my
sorrow was stirred.

3 My heart was hot within me,
while I was ¹musing the fire burned:
*then* spake I with my tongue,

4 LORD, ªmake me to know mine
end, and the measure of my days,
what it *is; that* I may know how frail
I *am.*

5 Behold, thou hast made my days
*as* an handbreadth; and mine age *is*
as nothing before thee: verily every
man at his best state *is* altogether
ªvanity.¹ *Selah.*

6 Surely every man walketh ¹in a
vain shew: surely they ²are disquieted in vain: he heapeth up *riches,* and
knoweth not who shall gather them.

7 And now, Lord, what wait I for?
my ªhope *is* in thee.

8 Deliver me from all my transgressions: make me not ªthe reproach of
the foolish.

9 ªI was ¹dumb, I opened not my
mouth; because ᵇthou didst *it.*

10 ªRemove thy ¹stroke away from
me: I am consumed by the blow of
thine hand.

11 When thou with rebukes dost
correct man for iniquity, thou makest his beauty ªto ¹consume away like
a moth: surely every man *is* ²vanity.
*Selah.*

12 Hear my prayer, O LORD, and
give ear unto my cry; hold not thy
peace at my tears: for I *am* a stranger
with thee, *and* a sojourner, ªas all my
fathers *were.*

13 ªO¹ spare me, that I may recover
strength, before I go hence, and ᵇbe
no more.

## PSALM 40

To the chief Musician,
A Psalm of David.

I ªWAITED patiently for the LORD;
and he inclined unto me, and heard
my cry.

2 He brought me up also out of an
horrible pit, out of ªthe miry clay, and
ᵇset my feet upon a rock, *and* established my ¹goings.

3 ªAnd he hath put a new song in
my mouth, *even* praise unto our God:
many shall see *it,* and fear, and shall
trust in the LORD.

4 ªBlessed *is* that man that maketh
the LORD his trust, and respecteth
not the proud, nor such as turn aside
to lies.

---

39:1 ª Job 2:10; Ps.
34:13; [James 3:5–
12] ¹ *restrain*

39:2 ª Ps. 38:13
¹ *mute*

39:3 ¹ *meditating*

39:4 ª Ps. 90:12;
119:84

39:5 ª Ps. 62:9;
[Eccl. 6:12]
¹ *vapour*

39:6 ¹ *as a
shadow* ² *make
an uproar for
nothing*

39:7 ª Ps. 38:15

39:8 ª Ps. 44:13;
79:4; 119:22

39:9 ª Ps. 39:2
ᵇ 2 Sam. 16:10;
Job 2:10 ¹ *mute*

39:10 ª Job 9:34;
13:21 ¹ *plague*

39:11 ª Job 13:28
¹ *melt away*
² *vapour*

39:12 ª Gen. 47:9

39:13 ª Job 7:19;
10:20, 21; 14:6
ᵇ [Job 14:10]
¹ *Remove your
gaze from me*

40:1 ª Ps. 25:5;
27:14; 37:7

40:2 ª Ps. 69:2, 14
ᵇ Ps. 27:5 ¹ *steps*

40:3 ª Ps. 32:7;
33:3

40:4 ª Ps. 34:8;
84:12

40:5 ª Job
9:10 ᵇ [Is. 55:8]
¹ *recounted*

40:6 ª [Heb.
10:5–9]

40:7 ¹ *scroll*

40:8 ª [John 4:34;
6:38] ᵇ [Jer. 31:33]

40:9 ª Ps. 22:22,
25 ᵇ Ps. 119:13
¹ *proclaimed the
good news of
righteousness*
² *restrained*

40:10 ª Acts
20:20, 27

40:11 ª Ps. 61:7

40:12 ª Ps. 38:4;
65:3 ¹ *surrounded*
² *overtaken me*

40:13 ª Ps. 70:1

40:14 ª Ps.
35:4, 26; 70:2;
71:13 ¹ *mutually
confounded* ² *life*
³ *be disgraced*

40:15 ª Ps.
73:19 ¹ *appalled
because of their
shame*

40:16 ª Ps. 70:4
ᵇ Ps. 35:27

40:17 ª Ps. 70:5;
86:1; 109:22
ᵇ 1 Pet. 5:7
¹ *do not delay*

---

5 ªMany, O LORD my God, *are* thy
wonderful works *which* thou hast
done, ᵇand thy thoughts *which are*
to us-ward: they cannot be ¹reckoned
up in order unto thee: *if* I would declare and speak *of them,* they are
more than can be numbered.

6 ªSacrifice and offering thou didst
not desire; mine ears hast thou
opened: burnt offering and sin offering hast thou not required.

7 Then said I, Lo, I come: in the ¹vol-
ume of the book *it is* written of me,

8 ªI delight to do thy will, O my
God: yea, thy law *is* ᵇwithin my heart.

9 ªI have ¹preached righteousness
in the great congregation: lo, ᵇI have
not ²refrained my lips, O LORD, thou
knowest.

10 ªI have not hid thy righteousness
within my heart; I have declared thy
faithfulness and thy salvation: I have
not concealed thy lovingkindness and
thy truth from the great congregation.

11 Withhold not thou thy tender
mercies from me, O LORD: ªlet thy
lovingkindness and thy truth continually preserve me.

12 For innumerable evils have ¹compassed me about: ªmine iniquities
have ²taken hold upon me, so that I
am not able to look up; they are more
than the hairs of mine head: therefore
my heart faileth me.

13 ªBe pleased, O LORD, to deliver
me: O LORD, make haste to help me.

14 ªLet them be ashamed and ¹confounded together that seek after my
²soul to destroy it; let them be driven
backward and ³put to shame that
wish me evil.

15 Let them be ªdesolate¹ for a reward of their shame that say unto
me, Aha, aha.

16 ªLet all those that seek thee rejoice and be glad in thee: let such as
love thy salvation ᵇsay continually,
The LORD be magnified.

17 ªBut I *am* poor and needy; ᵇyet
the Lord thinketh upon me: thou *art*
my help and my deliverer; ¹make no
tarrying, O my God.

## PSALM 41

To the chief Musician,
A Psalm of David.

B LESSED *is* he that considereth the
¹poor: the LORD will deliver him in
time of trouble.

2 The LORD will preserve him,
and keep him alive; *and* he shall be
blessed upon the earth: ªand thou
wilt not deliver him unto the will of
his enemies.

3 The LORD will strengthen him
upon ¹the bed of languishing: thou
wilt ²make all his bed in his sickness.

---

41:1 ¹ *helpless or powerless* 41:2 ª Ps. 27:12 41:3 ¹ *his
bed of illness* ² *restore him in his sickbed*

4 I said, LORD, be merciful unto me: [a]heal my soul; for I have sinned against thee.

5 Mine enemies speak evil of me, When shall he die, and his name perish?

6 And if he come to see *me*, he speaketh [1]vanity: his heart gathereth iniquity to itself; *when* he goeth abroad, he telleth *it*.

7 All that hate me whisper together against me: against me do they [1]devise my hurt.

8 [1]An evil disease, *say they*, [2]cleaveth fast unto him: and *now* that he [3]lieth he shall rise up no more.

9 [a]Yea, mine own familiar friend, in whom I trusted, [b]which did eat of my bread, hath [1]lifted up *his* heel against me.

10 But thou, O LORD, be merciful unto me, and raise me up, that I may [1]requite them.

11 By this I know that thou [1]favourest me, because mine enemy doth not triumph over me.

12 And as for me, thou upholdest me in mine integrity, and [a]settest me before thy face for ever.

13 [a]Blessed *be* the LORD God of Israel from everlasting, and to everlasting. Amen, and Amen.

# BOOK II: Psalms 42–72

## PSALM 42

To the chief Musician, [1]Maschil, for the sons of Korah.

As the [1]hart panteth after the water brooks, so panteth my soul after thee, O God.

2 [a]My soul thirsteth for God, for the [b]living God: when shall I come and appear before God?

3 [a]My tears have been my [1]meat day and night, while they continually say unto me, [b]Where *is* thy God?

4 When I remember these *things*, [a]I pour out my soul in me: for I had gone with the multitude, [b]I went with them to the house of God, with the voice of joy and praise, with a multitude that kept [1]holyday.

5 [a]Why art thou [1]cast down, O my soul? and *why* art thou disquieted in me? [b]hope thou in God: for I shall yet praise him *for* the help of his [2]countenance.

6 O my God, my soul is cast down within me: therefore will I remember thee from the land of Jordan, and of the Hermonites, from [1]the hill Mizar.

7 Deep calleth unto deep at the noise of thy [1]waterspouts: [a]all thy waves and thy billows are gone over me.

8 *Yet* the LORD will [a]command his

lovingkindness in the daytime, and [b]in the night his song *shall be* with me, *and* my prayer unto the God of my life.

9 I will say unto God my rock, [a]Why hast thou forgotten me? why go I mourning because of the oppression of the enemy?

10 *As* with [1]a sword in my bones, mine enemies [2]reproach me; [a]while they say [3]daily unto me, Where *is* thy God?

11 [a]Why art thou cast down, O my soul? and why art thou disquieted within me? hope thou in God: for I shall yet praise him, *who is* the [1]health of my countenance, and my God.

## PSALM 43

JUDGE[1] [a]me, O God, and [b]plead my cause against an ungodly nation: O deliver me from the deceitful and unjust man.

2 For thou *art* the God of my strength: why dost thou cast me off? [a]why go I mourning because of the oppression of the enemy?

3 [a]O send out thy light and thy truth: let them lead me; let them bring me unto [b]thy holy hill, and to thy [1]tabernacles.

4 Then will I go unto the altar of God, unto God my exceeding joy: yea, upon the harp will I praise thee, O God my God.

5 [a]Why art thou cast down, O my soul? and why art thou disquieted within me? hope in God: for I shall yet praise him, *who is* [1]the health of my countenance, and my God.

## PSALM 44

To the chief Musician for the sons of Korah, [a]Maschil.[1]

WE have heard with our ears, O God, [a]our fathers have told us, *what* work thou didst in their days, in the times of old.

2 *How* [a]thou didst drive out the [1]heathen with thy hand, and plantedst them; *how* thou didst afflict the people, and cast them out.

3 For [a]they got not the land in possession by their own sword, neither did their own arm save them: but thy right hand, and thine arm, and the light of thy [1]countenance, [b]because thou hadst a favour unto them.

4 [a]Thou art my King, O God: command deliverances for Jacob.

5 Through thee [a]will we push down our enemies: through thy name will we [1]tread them under that rise up against us.

6 For [a]I will not trust in my bow, neither shall my sword save me.

7 But thou hast saved us from our enemies, and hast put them to shame that hated us.

8 [a]In God we boast all the day long,
and praise thy name for ever. *Selah.*
9 But [a]thou hast cast off, and put
us to shame; and goest not forth with
our armies.
10 Thou makest us to [a]turn back
from the enemy: and they which hate
us [1]spoil for themselves.
11 [a]Thou hast [1]given us like sheep
*appointed* for [2]meat; and hast [b]scat-
tered us among the heathen.
12 [a]Thou sellest thy people for
nought, and [1]dost not increase *thy*
*wealth* by their price.
13 [a]Thou makest us a reproach to
our neighbours, a scorn and a derision to them that are round about us.
14 [a]Thou makest us a byword
among the heathen, [b]a shaking of the
head among the people.
15 My [1]confusion *is* continually before me, and the shame of my face
hath covered me,
16 For the voice of him that reproacheth and [1]blasphemeth; [a]by
reason of the enemy and avenger.
17 [a]All this is come upon us; yet
have we not forgotten thee, neither
have we dealt falsely in thy covenant.
18 Our heart is not turned back,
[a]neither have our steps [1]declined
from thy way;
19 Though thou hast sore broken us
in [a]the place of [1]dragons, and covered
us [b]with the shadow of death.
20 If we have forgotten the name of
our God, or [a]stretched[1] out our hands
to a [2]strange god;
21 [a]Shall not God search this out? for
he knoweth the secrets of the heart.
22 [a]Yea, for thy sake are we killed
all the day long; we are counted as
sheep for the slaughter.
23 [a]Awake, why sleepest thou,
O Lord? arise, cast *us* not off for ever.
24 [a]Wherefore hidest thou thy face,
*and* forgettest our affliction and our
oppression?
25 For [a]our soul is bowed down to
the dust: our belly cleaveth unto the
[1]earth.
26 Arise for our help, and redeem
us for thy mercies' sake.

## PSALM 45

To the chief Musician [a]upon[1]
Shoshannim, for the sons of Korah,
[2]Maschil, A Song of loves.

MY heart is [1]inditing a good matter: I speak of [2]the things which
I have made touching the king: my
tongue *is* the pen of a [3]ready writer.
2 Thou art fairer than the children
of men: [a]grace is poured into thy lips:
therefore God hath blessed thee for
ever.
3 [1]Gird thy [a]sword upon *thy* thigh,
[b]O *most* mighty, with thy [c]glory and
thy majesty.

44:8 [a] Ps. 34:2
44:9 [a] Ps. 60:1
44:10 [a] Lev. 26:17 [1] *have taken plunder*
44:11 [a] Rom. 8:36 [b] Deut. 4:27; 28:64 [1] *given us up* [2] *food*
44:12 [a] Is. 52:3, 4 [1] *are not enriched*
44:13 [a] Deut. 28:37
44:14 [a] Jer. 24:9 [b] Job 16:4
44:15 [1] *dishonour*
44:16 [a] Ps. 8:2 [1] *reviles*
44:17 [a] Dan. 9:13
44:18 [a] Job 23:11 [1] *departed*
44:19 [a] Is. 34:13 [b] [Ps. 23:4] [1] *jackals*
44:20 [a] [Deut. 6:14] [1] Worshipped [2] *foreign*
44:21 [a] [Ps. 139:1, 2]
44:22 [a] Rom. 8:36
44:23 [a] Ps. 7:6
44:24 [a] Job 13:24
44:25 [a] Ps. 119:25 [1] *ground*
45:title [a] Ps. 69:title [1] *Set to "The Lilies," of* [2] *Contemplation*
45:1 [1] *overflowing with a* [2] *my works to the king:* [3] *skilful*
45:2 [a] Luke 4:22
45:3 [a] [Heb. 4:12] [b] [Is. 9:6] [c] Jude 25 [1] *Belt on*
45:4 [a] Rev. 6:2 [1] *humility* [2] *awesome*
45:6 [a] [Ps. 93:2] [b] [Num. 24:17] [1] *sceptre of righteousness*
45:7 [a] Ps. 2:2 [b] Ps. 21:6 [1] *companions*
45:8 [a] Song 1:12, 13
45:9 [a] Song 6:8 [b] 1 Kin. 2:19
45:10 [a] Deut. 21:13
45:11 [a] [Is. 54:5]
45:12 [a] Is. 49:23 [1] *seek*
45:13 [1] *woven with gold*
45:14 [a] Song 1:4 [1] *robes of many colours*
45:16 [a] [1 Pet. 2:9]
45:17 [a] Mal. 1:11
46:title [a] 1 Chr. 15:20 [1] *of*
46:1 [a] Ps. 62:7, 8 [b] [Deut. 4:7] [1] *an abundantly available help*

4 [a]And in thy majesty ride prosper-
ously because of truth and [1]meekness
*and* righteousness; and thy right
hand shall teach thee [2]terrible things.
5 Thine arrows *are* sharp in the
heart of the king's enemies; *whereby*
the people fall under thee.
6 [a]Thy throne, O God, *is* for ever and
ever: the [b]sceptre of thy kingdom *is* a
[1]right sceptre.
7 Thou lovest righteousness, and
hatest wickedness: therefore God,
thy God, hath [a]anointed thee with the
oil of [b]gladness above thy [1]fellows.
8 All thy garments [a]*smell* of myrrh,
and aloes, *and* cassia, out of the ivory
palaces, whereby they have made
thee glad.
9 [a]Kings' daughters *were* among
thy honourable women: [b]upon thy
right hand did stand the queen in
gold of Ophir.
10 Hearken, O daughter, and consider, and incline thine ear; [a]forget
also thine own people, and thy father's house;
11 So shall the king greatly desire
thy beauty: [a]for he *is* thy Lord; and
worship thou him.
12 And the daughter of Tyre *shall*
*be there* with a gift; *even* [a]the rich
among the people shall [1]intreat thy
favour.
13 The king's daughter *is* all glorious
within: her clothing *is* [1]of wrought
gold.
14 [a]She shall be brought unto the
king in [1]raiment of needlework: the
virgins her companions that follow
her shall be brought unto thee.
15 With gladness and rejoicing
shall they be brought: they shall enter into the king's palace.
16 Instead of thy fathers shall be
thy children, [a]whom thou mayest
make princes in all the earth.
17 [a]I will make thy name to be remembered in all generations: therefore shall the people praise thee for
ever and ever.

## PSALM 46

To the chief Musician [1]for the sons
of Korah, A Song [a]upon Alamoth.

GOD *is* our [a]refuge and strength, [b]a[1]
very present help in trouble.
2 Therefore will not we fear, though
the earth be removed, and though
the mountains be carried into [1]the
midst of the sea;
3 [a]*Though* the waters thereof roar
*and* be troubled, *though* the mountains shake with the swelling thereof.
*Selah.*
4 *There is* a [a]river, the streams
whereof shall make glad the [b]city of

46:2 [1] Lit. *the heart of* 46:3 [a] [Ps. 93:3, 4]
46:4 [a] [Ezek. 47:1–12] [b] Is. 60:14

God, the holy *place* of the [1]tabernacles of the most High.

5 God *is* [a]in the midst of her; she shall not be [1]moved: God shall help her, [2]*and that* right early.

6 [a]The heathen raged, the kingdoms were moved: he uttered his voice, the earth melted.

7 The [a]LORD of hosts *is* with us; the God of Jacob *is* our refuge.   *Selah.*

8 Come, behold the works of the LORD, what desolations he hath made in the earth.

9 [a]He maketh wars to cease unto the end of the earth; [b]he breaketh the bow, and cutteth the spear in sunder; [c]he burneth the chariot in the fire.

10 Be still, and know that I *am* God: [a]I will be exalted among the heathen, I will be exalted in the earth.

11 The LORD of hosts *is* with us; the God of Jacob *is* our refuge.   *Selah.*

## PSALM 47

To the chief Musician,
A Psalm [1]for the sons of Korah.

O CLAP your hands, all ye people; shout unto God with the voice of triumph.

2 For the LORD most high *is* [1]terrible; *he is* a great [a]King over all the earth.

3 [a]He shall subdue the people under us, and the nations under our feet.

4 He shall choose our [a]inheritance for us, the excellency of Jacob whom he loved.   *Selah.*

5 [a]God is [1]gone up with a shout, the LORD with the sound of a trumpet.

6 Sing praises to God, sing praises: sing praises unto our King, sing praises.

7 [a]For God *is* the King of all the earth: [b]sing ye praises with understanding.

8 [a]God reigneth over the [1]heathen: God [b]sitteth upon the throne of his [c]holiness.

9 The princes of the people are gathered together, [a]*even* the people of the God of Abraham: [b]for the shields of the earth *belong* unto God: he is greatly exalted.

## PSALM 48

A Song *and* Psalm [1]for the sons of Korah.

G REAT *is* the LORD, and greatly to be praised in the [a]city of our God, *in* the mountain of his holiness.

2 [a]Beautiful [1]for situation, the joy of the whole earth, *is* mount Zion, *on* the sides of the north, the city of the great King.

3 God is known in her palaces for a refuge.

4 For, lo, [a]the kings were assembled, they passed by together.

---

5 They saw *it, and* so they marvelled; they were troubled, *and* hasted away.

6 Fear [a]took hold upon them there, *and* pain, as of a woman in [1]travail.

7 Thou breakest the [a]ships of Tarshish with an east wind.

8 As we have heard, so have we seen in the city of the LORD of hosts, in the city of our God: God will [a]establish it for ever.   *Selah.*

9 We have thought of [a]thy lovingkindness, O God, in the midst of thy temple.

10 According to [a]thy name, O God, so *is* thy praise unto the ends of the earth: thy right hand is full of righteousness.

11 Let mount Zion rejoice, let the daughters of Judah be glad, because of thy judgments.

12 Walk about Zion, and go round about her: [1]tell the towers thereof.

13 Mark ye well her bulwarks, consider her palaces; that ye may [a]tell *it* to the generation following.

14 For this God *is* our God for ever and ever: [a]he will be our guide *even* unto death.

## PSALM 49

To the chief Musician,
A Psalm [1]for the sons of Korah.

H EAR this, all *ye* people; give ear, all *ye* inhabitants of the world:

2 Both low and high, rich and poor, together.

3 My mouth shall speak of wisdom; and the meditation of my heart *shall be* of understanding.

4 I will incline mine ear to a [1]parable: I will open my [2]dark saying upon the harp.

5 Wherefore should I fear in the days of evil, *when* the iniquity of my heels shall [1]compass me about?

6 They that [a]trust in their wealth, and boast themselves in the multitude of their riches;

7 None *of them* can by any means redeem his brother, nor [a]give to God a ransom for him:

8 (For [a]the redemption of their soul *is* [1]precious, and it ceaseth for ever:)

9 That he should still live for ever, *and* [a]not see [1]corruption.

10 For he seeth *that* wise men die, likewise the fool and the [1]brutish person perish, and leave their wealth to others.

11 Their inward thought *is, that* their houses *shall continue* for ever, *and* their dwelling places to all generations; they [a]call *their* lands after their own names.

12 Nevertheless man *being* in honour [1]abideth not: he is like the beasts *that* perish.

46:4 [1] *dwelling places*
46:5 [a] [Zeph. 3:15]
[1] *shaken* [2] *at the break of dawn*
46:6 [a] Ps. 2:1, 2
46:7 [a] Num. 14:9
46:9 [a] Is. 2:4 [b] Ps. 76:3 [c] Ezek. 39:9
46:10 [a] [Is. 2:11, 17]
47:title [1] *of*
47:2 [a] Deut. 7:21; Neh. 1:5; Ps. 76:12 [1] *awesome*
47:3 [a] Ps. 18:47
47:4 [a] [1 Pet. 1:4]
47:5 [a] Ps. 68:24, 25 [1] *ascended*
47:7 [a] Zech. 14:9 [b] 1 Cor. 14:15
47:8 [a] 1 Chr. 16:31 [b] Ps. 97:2 [c] Ps. 48:1 [1] *nations or Gentiles*
47:9 [a] [Rom. 4:11, 12] [b] [Ps. 89:18]
48:title [1] *of*
48:1 [a] Ps. 46:4; 87:3; Matt. 5:35
48:2 [a] Ps. 50:2 [1] *in elevation or height*
48:4 [a] 2 Sam. 10:6, 14

48:6 [a] Ex. 15:15 [1] *childbirth*
48:7 [a] 1 Kin. 10:22; Ezek. 27:25
48:8 [a] [Ps. 87:5; Is. 2:2]; Mic. 4:1
48:9 [a] Ps. 26:3
48:10 [a] [Deut. 28:58]; Josh. 7:9; Mal. 1:11
48:12 [1] *count*
48:13 [a] [Ps. 78:5-7]
48:14 [a] Is. 58:11
49:title [1] *of*
49:4 [1] *proverb* [2] *riddle*
49:5 [1] *surround*
49:6 [a] Job 31:24; Ps. 52:7; [Prov. 11:28; Mark 10:24]
49:7 [a] Job 36:18, 19
49:8 [a] [Matt. 16:26] [1] *costly*
49:9 [a] Ps. 89:48 [1] *the pit*
49:10 [1] *senseless*
49:11 [a] Gen. 4:17; Deut. 3:14
49:12 [1] *does not endure*

13 This [1]their way *is* their [a]folly: [2]yet their posterity approve their sayings. *Selah.*

14 Like sheep they are laid in the grave; death shall feed on them; and [a]the upright shall have dominion over them in the morning; [b]and their beauty shall [1]consume in the [2]grave from their dwelling.

15 But God [a]will redeem my soul from the power of [1]the grave: for he shall [b]receive me. *Selah.*

16 Be not thou afraid when one is made rich, when the glory of his house is increased;

17 For when he dieth he shall carry nothing away: his glory shall not descend after him.

18 Though while he lived [a]he blessed [1]his soul: and *men* will praise thee, when thou doest well to thyself.

19 He shall go to the generation of his fathers; they shall never see [a]light.[1]

20 Man *that is* in honour, and understandeth not, [a]is like the beasts *that* perish.

## PSALM 50

A Psalm of Asaph.

THE [a]mighty God, *even* the LORD, hath spoken, and called the earth from the rising of the sun unto the going down thereof.

2 Out of Zion, the perfection of beauty, [a]God hath shined.

3 Our God shall come, and shall not keep silence: [a]a fire shall devour before him, and it shall be very tempestuous round about him.

4 [a]He shall call to the heavens from above, and to the earth, that he may judge his people.

5 Gather [a]my saints together unto me; [b]those that have [1]made a covenant with me by sacrifice.

6 And the [a]heavens shall declare his righteousness: for [b]God *is* judge himself. *Selah.*

7 Hear, O my people, and I will speak; O Israel, and I will testify against thee: [a]I *am* God, *even* thy God.

8 [a]I will not [1]reprove thee [b]for thy sacrifices or thy burnt offerings, *to have been* continually before me.

9 [a]I will take no [1]bullock out of thy house, *nor* he goats out of thy folds.

10 For every beast of the forest *is* mine, *and* the cattle upon a thousand hills.

11 I know all the [1]fowls of the mountains: and the wild beasts of the field *are* mine.

12 If I were hungry, I would not tell thee: [a]for the world *is* mine, and the fulness thereof.

13 [a]Will I eat the flesh of bulls, or drink the blood of goats?

14 [a]Offer unto God thanksgiving; and [b]pay thy vows unto the most High:

15 And [a]call upon me in the day of trouble: I will deliver thee, and thou shalt glorify me.

16 But unto the wicked God saith, What hast thou to do to declare my statutes, or *that* thou shouldest take my covenant in thy mouth?

17 [a]Seeing thou hatest instruction, and castest my words behind thee.

18 When thou sawest a thief, then thou [a]consentedst with him, and hast been [b]partaker with adulterers.

19 Thou givest thy mouth to evil, and [a]thy tongue frameth deceit.

20 Thou sittest *and* speakest against thy brother; thou slanderest thine own mother's son.

21 These *things* hast thou done, and I kept silence; [a]thou thoughtest that I was altogether *such an one* as thyself: *but* I will [1]reprove thee, and [b]set *them* in order before thine eyes.

22 Now consider this, ye that [a]forget God, lest I tear *you* in pieces, and *there be* none to deliver.

23 Whoso offereth praise glorifieth me: and [a]to him that ordereth *his* [1]conversation *aright* will I shew the salvation of God.

## PSALM 51

To the chief Musician, A Psalm of David, [a]when Nathan the prophet came unto him, after he had gone in to Bath-sheba.

HAVE mercy upon me, O God, according to thy lovingkindness: according unto the multitude of thy tender mercies [a]blot out my transgressions.

2 [a]Wash me thoroughly from mine iniquity, and cleanse me from my sin.

3 For I acknowledge my transgressions: and my sin *is* ever before me.

4 [a]Against thee, thee only, have I sinned, and done *this* evil [b]in thy sight: [c]that thou mightest [1]be justified when thou speakest, *and* be [2]clear when thou judgest.

5 [a]Behold, I was [1]shapen in iniquity; and in sin did my mother conceive me.

6 Behold, thou desirest truth in the inward parts: and in the hidden *part* thou shalt make me to know wisdom.

7 [a]Purge me with hyssop, and I shall be clean: wash me, and I shall be [b]whiter than snow.

8 Make me to hear joy and gladness; *that* the bones *which* thou hast broken [a]may rejoice.

9 Hide thy face from my sins, and blot out all mine iniquities.

49:13 [a] [Luke 12:20] [1] *the way of those who are foolish* [2] *and of their*
49:14 [a] Ps. 47:3; [Dan. 7:18; 1 Cor. 6:2; Rev. 2:26] [b] Job 4:21 [1] *be consumed* [2] Or *Sheol*
49:15 [a] [Hos. 13:4]; Mark 16:6, 7; Acts 2:31, 32 [b] Ps. 73:24 [1] Or *Sheol*
49:18 [a] Deut. 29:19; Luke 12:19 [1] *himself*
49:19 [a] Job 33:30 [1] The light of life
49:20 [a] Eccl. 3:19
50:1 [a] Is. 9:6
50:2 [a] Deut. 33:2; Ps. 80:1
50:3 [a] Lev. 10:2; Num. 16:35; [Ps. 97:3]
50:4 [a] Deut. 4:26; 31:28; 32:1; Is. 1:2
50:5 [a] Deut. 33:3 [b] Ex. 24:7 [1] Lit. *cut a covenant*
50:6 [a] [Ps. 97:6] [b] Ps. 75:7
50:7 [a] Ex. 20:2
50:8 [a] Jer. 7:22 [b] Is. 1:11; [Hos. 6:6] [1] *rebuke*
50:9 [a] Ps. 69:31 [1] *bull*
50:11 [1] *birds*
50:12 [a] Ex. 19:5; [Deut. 10:14; Job 41:11]; 1 Cor. 10:26
50:13 [a] [Ps. 51:15–17]
50:14 [a] Hos. 14:2; Heb. 13:15 [b] Num. 30:2; Deut. 23:21
50:15 [a] Job 22:27; [Zech. 13:9]
50:17 [a] Neh. 9:26; Rom. 2:21
50:18 [a] [Rom. 1:32] [b] 1 Tim. 5:22
50:19 [a] Ps. 52:2
50:21 [a] [Rom. 2:4] [b] [Ps. 90:8] [1] *rebuke*
50:22 [a] [Job 8:13]
50:23 [a] Gal. 6:16 [1] *conduct*
51:title [a] 2 Sam. 12:1
51:1 [a] [Is. 43:25; 44:22; Acts 3:19; Col. 2:14]
51:2 [a] Jer. 33:8; Ezek. 36:33; [Heb. 9:14; 1 John 1:7, 9]
51:4 [a] 2 Sam. 12:13 [b] [Luke 5:21] [c] Rom. 3:4 [1] *be found just* [2] *blameless*
51:5 [a] [Job 14:4; Ps. 58:3; John 3:6; Rom. 5:12] [1] *brought forth*
51:7 [a] Ex. 12:22; Lev. 14:4; Num. 19:18; Heb. 9:19 [b] [Is. 1:18]
51:8 [a] [Matt. 5:4]

10 <sup>a</sup>Create in me a clean heart, O God; and renew a <sup>1</sup>right spirit within me.

11 Cast me not away from thy presence; and take not thy <sup>a</sup>holy spirit from me.

12 Restore unto me the joy of thy salvation; and uphold me *with thy* <sup>a</sup>free<sup>1</sup> spirit.

13 *Then* will I teach transgressors thy ways; and sinners shall be converted unto thee.

14 Deliver me from bloodguiltiness, O God, thou God of my salvation: *and* my tongue shall sing aloud of thy righteousness.

15 O Lord, open thou my lips; and my mouth shall shew forth thy praise.

16 For <sup>a</sup>thou desirest not sacrifice; else would I give *it:* thou delightest not in burnt offering.

17 <sup>a</sup>The sacrifices of God *are* a broken spirit: a broken and a contrite heart, O God, thou wilt not despise.

18 Do good in thy good pleasure unto Zion: build thou the walls of Jerusalem.

19 Then shalt thou be pleased with <sup>a</sup>the sacrifices of righteousness, with burnt offering and whole burnt offering: then shall they offer bullocks upon thine altar.

## PSALM 52

To the chief Musician, <sup>1</sup>Maschil, *A Psalm* of David, <sup>a</sup>when Doeg the Edomite came and <sup>b</sup>told Saul, and said unto him, David is come to the house of Ahimelech.

WHY boastest thou thyself <sup>1</sup>in mischief, O mighty man? the <sup>2</sup>goodness of God *endureth* continually.

2 The tongue <sup>1</sup>deviseth mischiefs; like a sharp razor, working deceitfully.

3 Thou lovest evil more than good; *and* lying rather than to speak righteousness. *Selah.*

4 Thou lovest all devouring words, O *thou* deceitful tongue.

5 God shall likewise destroy thee for ever, he shall take thee away, and pluck thee out of *thy* dwelling place, and root thee out of the land of the living. *Selah.*

6 The righteous also shall see, and fear, and shall laugh at him:

7 Lo, *this is* the man *that* made not God his strength; but trusted in the abundance of his riches, *and* strengthened himself in his <sup>1</sup>wickedness.

8 But I *am* <sup>a</sup>like a green olive tree in the house of God: I trust in the mercy of God for ever and ever.

9 I will praise thee for ever, because thou hast done *it:* and I will wait on thy name; for *it is* good before thy saints.

---

51:10 <sup>a</sup> [Ezek. 18:31; Eph. 2:10]
<sup>1</sup> steadfast
51:11 <sup>a</sup> [Luke 11:13]
51:12 <sup>a</sup> [2 Cor. 3:17]
<sup>1</sup> generous
51:16 <sup>a</sup> [1 Sam. 15:22]; Ps. 50:8–14; [Mic. 6:6–8]
51:17 <sup>a</sup> Ps. 34:18; [Is. 57:15]; 66:2
51:19 <sup>a</sup> Ps. 4:5
52:title <sup>a</sup> 1 Sam. 22:9 <sup>b</sup> Ezek. 22:9
<sup>1</sup> Contemplation
52:1 <sup>1</sup> in evil <sup>2</sup> lovingkindness
52:2 <sup>1</sup> plans destruction
52:7 <sup>1</sup> destruction
52:8 <sup>a</sup> Jer. 11:16

53:title <sup>1</sup> Contemplation
53:1 <sup>a</sup> Ps. 10:4 <sup>b</sup> Rom. 3:10–12
53:2 <sup>a</sup> [2 Chr. 15:2]
53:3 <sup>1</sup> turned aside <sup>2</sup> corrupt
53:4 <sup>a</sup> Jer. 4:22
53:5 <sup>a</sup> Lev. 26:17, 36; Prov. 28:1
53:6 <sup>a</sup> Ps. 14:7
<sup>1</sup> his captive people
54:title <sup>a</sup> 1 Sam. 23:19 <sup>1</sup> With stringed instruments <sup>2</sup> Contemplation
54:3 <sup>1</sup> life
54:4 <sup>1</sup> sustain
54:5 <sup>1</sup> destroy them <sup>2</sup> Or faithfulness
54:7 <sup>a</sup> Ps. 59:10
55:title <sup>1</sup> With stringed instruments <sup>2</sup> Contemplation
55:2 <sup>a</sup> Is. 38:14; 59:11; Ezek. 7:16
<sup>1</sup> wander <sup>2</sup> moan noisily

---

## PSALM 53

To the chief Musician upon Mahalath, <sup>1</sup>Maschil, *A Psalm* of David.

THE <sup>a</sup>fool hath said in his heart, *There is* no God. Corrupt are they, and have done abominable iniquity: <sup>b</sup>*there is* none that doeth good.

2 God looked down from heaven upon the children of men, to see if there were *any* that did understand, that did <sup>a</sup>seek God.

3 Every one of them <sup>1</sup>is gone back: they are altogether become <sup>2</sup>filthy; *there is* none that doeth good, no, not one.

4 Have the workers of iniquity <sup>a</sup>no knowledge? who eat up my people *as* they eat bread: they have not called upon God.

5 <sup>a</sup>There were they in great fear, *where* no fear was: for God hath scattered the bones of him that encampeth *against* thee: thou hast put *them* to shame, because God hath despised them.

6 <sup>a</sup>Oh that the salvation of Israel *were come* out of Zion! When God bringeth back <sup>1</sup>the captivity of his people, Jacob shall rejoice, *and* Israel shall be glad.

## PSALM 54

To the chief Musician, <sup>1</sup>on Neginoth, <sup>2</sup>Maschil, *A Psalm* of David, <sup>a</sup>when the Ziphims came and said to Saul, Doth not David hide himself with us?

SAVE me, O God, by thy name, and judge me by thy strength.

2 Hear my prayer, O God; give ear to the words of my mouth.

3 For strangers are risen up against me, and oppressors seek after my <sup>1</sup>soul: they have not set God before them. *Selah.*

4 Behold, God *is* mine helper: the Lord *is* with them that <sup>1</sup>uphold my soul.

5 He shall reward evil unto mine enemies: <sup>1</sup>cut them off in thy <sup>2</sup>truth.

6 I will freely sacrifice unto thee: I will praise thy name, O LORD; for *it is* good.

7 For he hath delivered me out of all trouble: <sup>a</sup>and mine eye hath seen *his desire* upon mine enemies.

## PSALM 55

To the chief Musician, <sup>1</sup>on Neginoth, <sup>2</sup>Maschil, *A Psalm* of David.

GIVE ear to my prayer, O God; and hide not thyself from my supplication.

2 Attend unto me, and hear me: I <sup>a</sup>mourn<sup>1</sup> in my complaint, and <sup>2</sup>make a noise;

3 Because of the voice of the enemy, because of the oppression of

the wicked: [a]for they [1]cast iniquity upon me, and in wrath they hate me.

4 [a]My heart is [1]sore pained within me: and the terrors of death are fallen upon me.

5 Fearfulness and trembling are come upon me, and horror hath overwhelmed me.

6 And I said, Oh that I had wings like a dove! *for then* would I fly away, and be at rest.

7 Lo, *then* would I wander far off, *and* remain in the wilderness.    *Selah.*

8 I would hasten my escape from the windy storm *and* tempest.

9 Destroy, O Lord, *and* divide their [1]tongues: for I have seen [a]violence and strife in the city.

10 Day and night they go about it upon the walls thereof: [a]mischief[1] also and sorrow *are* in the midst of it.

11 [1]Wickedness *is* in the midst thereof: [a]deceit and guile depart not from her streets.

12 [a]For *it was* not an enemy *that* reproached me; then I could [1]have borne *it:* neither *was it* he that hated me *that* did [b]magnify *himself* against me; then I would have hid myself from him:

13 But *it was* thou, a man mine equal, [a]my [1]guide, and mine acquaintance.

14 We took sweet counsel together, *and* [a]walked unto the house of God in [1]company.

15 Let death seize upon them, *and* let them [a]go down [1]quick into [2]hell: for wickedness *is* in their dwellings, *and* among them.

16 As for me, I will call upon God; and the LORD shall save me.

17 [a]Evening, and morning, and at noon, will I pray, and cry aloud: and he shall hear my voice.

18 He hath delivered my soul in peace from the battle *that was* against me: for [a]there were many [1]with me.

19 God shall hear, and afflict them, [a]even he that abideth of old.    *Selah.* Because they [1]have no changes, therefore they fear not God.

20 He hath [a]put forth his hands against such as [b]be at peace with him: he hath broken his [1]covenant.

21 [a]*The words* of his mouth were smoother than butter, but war *was* in his heart: his words were softer than oil, yet *were* they drawn swords.

22 [a]Cast thy burden upon the LORD, and [b]he shall sustain thee: he shall never [1]suffer the righteous to be [2]moved.

23 But thou, O God, shalt bring them down into the pit of destruction: [a]bloody[1] and deceitful men [b]shall not live out half their days; but I will trust in thee.

55:3 [a] 2 Sam. 16:7, 8 [1] *bring down trouble*
55:4 [a] Ps. 116:3 [1] *severely*
55:9 [a] Jer. 6:7 [1] *speech, counsel*
55:10 [a] Ps. 10:7 [1] *iniquity and trouble*
55:11 [a] Ps. 10:7 [1] *Destruction*
55:12 [a] Ps. 41:9 [b] Ps. 35:26; 38:16 [1] *bear it:*
55:13 [a] 2 Sam. 15:12 [1] *companion*
55:14 [a] Ps. 42:4 [1] *the throng*
55:15 [a] Num. 16:30, 33 [1] *Or alive* [2] *Or Sheol*
55:17 [a] Dan. 6:10
55:18 [a] 2 Chr. 32:7, 8 [1] *against*
55:19 [a] [Deut. 33:27] [1] *do not change*
55:20 [a] Acts 12:1 [b] Ps. 7:4 [1] *treaty*
55:21 [a] Ps. 28:3; 57:4
55:22 [a] [Ps. 37:5] [b] Ps. 37:24 [1] *permit* [2] *shaken*
55:23 [a] Ps. 5:6 [b] Prov. 10:27 [1] *bloodthirsty*
56:title [a] 1 Sam. 21:11 [1] *Set to "The Silent Dove in Distant Lands"* [2] *Contemplation of David*
56:1 [a] Ps. 57:1
56:2 [a] Ps. 57:3 [1] *hound me*
56:4 [a] Ps. 118:6
56:5 [1] *All day they twist*
56:6 [1] *lie in wait for my life*
56:8 [a] [Mal. 3:16] [1] *count or take account*
56:9 [a] [Rom. 8:31]
56:12 [1] *are binding upon*
56:13 [a] Ps. 116:8, 9 [b] Job 33:30
57:title [a] 1 Sam. 22:1 [1] *Set to "Do Not Destroy"* [2] *Contemplation*
57:1 [a] Ps. 17:8; 63:7 [b] Is. 26:20 [1] *passed by*
57:2 [a] [Ps. 138:8]
57:3 [a] Ps. 144:5, 7 [b] Ps. 43:3 [1] *snaps at me or hounds me*
57:4 [a] Prov. 30:14
57:5 [a] Ps. 108:5
57:6 [a] Ps. 9:15

## PSALM 56

To the chief Musician [1]upon Jonath-elem-rechokim, [2]Michtam of David, when the [a]Philistines took him in Gath.

**B**E [a]merciful unto me, O God: for man would swallow me up; he fighting daily oppresseth me.

2 Mine enemies would daily [a]swallow[1] *me* up: for *they be* many that fight against me, O thou most High.

3 What time I am afraid, I will trust in thee.

4 In God I will praise his word, In God I have put my trust; [a]I will not fear what flesh can do unto me.

5 [1]Every day they wrest my words: all their thoughts *are* against me for evil.

6 They gather themselves together, they hide themselves, they mark my steps, when they [1]wait for my soul.

7 Shall they escape by iniquity? in *thine* anger cast down the people, O God.

8 Thou [1]tellest my wanderings: put thou my tears into thy bottle: [a]*are they* not in thy book?

9 When I cry *unto thee*, then shall mine enemies turn back: this I know; for [a]God *is* for me.

10 In God will I praise *his* word: in the LORD will I praise *his* word.

11 In God have I put my trust: I will not be afraid what man can do unto me.

12 Thy vows *are* [1]upon me, O God: I will render praises unto thee.

13 [a]For thou hast delivered my soul from death: *wilt* not *thou deliver* my feet from falling, that I may walk before God in the [b]light of the living?

## PSALM 57

To the chief Musician, [1]Altaschith, [2]Michtam of David, [a]when he fled from Saul in the cave.

**B**E merciful unto me, O God, be merciful unto me: for my soul trusteth in thee: [a]yea, in the shadow of thy wings will I make my refuge, [b]until *these* calamities be [1]overpast.

2 I will cry unto God most high; unto God [a]that performeth *all things* for me.

3 [a]He shall send from heaven, and save me *from* the reproach of him that [1]would swallow me up. *Selah.* God [b]shall send forth his mercy and his truth.

4 My soul *is* among lions: *and* I lie *even among* them that are set on fire, *even* the sons of men, [a]whose teeth *are* spears and arrows, and their tongue a sharp sword.

5 [a]Be thou exalted, O God, above the heavens; *let* thy glory *be* above all the earth.

6 [a]They have prepared a net for my

steps; my soul is bowed down: they have digged a pit before me, into the midst whereof they are fallen *themselves.* *Selah.*

7 ᵃMy heart is ¹fixed, O God, my heart is fixed: I will sing and give praise.

8 Awake up, ᵃmy glory; awake, ¹psaltery and harp: I *myself* will ²awake early.

9 ᵃI will praise thee, O Lord, among the people: I will sing unto thee among the ¹nations.

10 ᵃFor thy mercy *is* great unto the heavens, and thy truth unto the clouds.

11 ᵃBe thou exalted, O God, above the heavens: *let* thy glory *be* above all the earth.

## PSALM 58

To the chief Musician, ¹Altaschith, ²Michtam of David.

Dᵒ ye indeed speak righteousness, ¹O congregation? do ye judge uprightly, O ye sons of men?

2 Yea, in heart ye work wickedness; ye weigh the violence of your hands in the earth.

3 ᵃThe wicked are estranged from the womb: they go astray as soon as they be born, speaking lies.

4 ᵃTheir poison *is* like the poison of a serpent: *they are* like the deaf ¹adder *that* stoppeth her ear;

5 Which will not ᵃhearken to the voice of charmers, charming ¹never so wisely.

6 ᵃBreak¹ their teeth, O God, in their mouth: break out the great teeth of the young lions, O LORD.

7 ᵃLet them ¹melt away as waters *which* run continually: *when* he bendeth *his bow to shoot* his arrows, let them be as cut in pieces.

8 As a snail *which* melteth, let *every one of them* pass away: ᵃ*like* the ¹untimely birth of a woman, *that* they may not see the sun.

9 Before your ᵃpots can feel the ¹thorns, he shall take them away ᵇas with a whirlwind, ²both living, and in *his* wrath.

10 The righteous shall rejoice when he seeth the ᵃvengeance: ᵇhe shall wash his feet in the blood of the wicked.

11 ᵃSo that a man shall say, Verily *there is* a reward for the righteous: verily he is a God that ᵇjudgeth in the earth.

## PSALM 59

To the chief Musician, ¹Altaschith, ²Michtam of David; ᵃwhen Saul sent, and they watched the house to kill him.

Dᴇʟɪᴠᴇʀ me from mine enemies, O my God: ¹defend me from them that rise up against me.

2 Deliver me from the workers of iniquity, and save me from ¹bloody men.

3 For, lo, they lie in wait for my ¹soul: ᵃthe mighty are gathered against me; not *for* my transgression, nor *for* my sin, O LORD.

4 They run and prepare themselves ¹without *my* fault: ᵃawake to help me, and behold.

5 Thou therefore, O LORD God of hosts, the God of Israel, awake to ¹visit all the ²heathen: be not merciful to any wicked transgressors. *Selah.*

6 ᵃThey return at evening: they ¹make a noise like a dog, and go round about the city.

7 Behold, they belch out with their mouth: ᵃswords *are* in their lips: for ᵇwho, *say they,* doth hear?

8 But ᵃthou, O LORD, shalt laugh at them; thou shalt have all the ¹heathen in derision.

9 *Because of* his strength will I wait upon thee: ᵃfor God *is* my ¹defence.

10 The God of my mercy shall ᵃprevent¹ me: God shall let ᵇme see *my desire* upon mine enemies.

11 Slay them not, lest my people forget: scatter them by thy power; and bring them down, O Lord our shield.

12 ᵃ*For* the sin of their mouth *and* the words of their lips let them even be taken in their pride: and for cursing and lying *which* they speak.

13 ᵃConsume *them* in wrath, consume *them,* that they *may* not *be:* and ᵇlet them know that God ruleth in Jacob unto the ends of the earth. *Selah.*

14 And ᵃat evening let them return; *and* let them make a noise like a dog, and go round about the city.

15 Let them ᵃwander up and down for ¹meat, and ²grudge if they be not satisfied.

16 But I will sing of thy power; yea, I will sing aloud of thy mercy in the morning: for thou hast been my defence and refuge in the day of my trouble.

17 Unto thee, ᵃO my strength, will I sing: for God *is* my defence, *and* the God of my mercy.

## PSALM 60

To the chief Musician ᵃupon ¹Shushaneduth, ²Michtam of David, to teach; ᵇwhen he strove with ³Aram-naharaim and with ⁴Aram-zobah, when Joab returned, and smote of Edom in the valley of salt twelve thousand.

O GOD, ᵃthou hast cast us off, thou hast ¹scattered us, thou hast been displeased; O ²turn thyself to us again.

2 Thou hast made the earth to tremble; thou hast broken it: ᵃheal the breaches thereof; for it shaketh.

## Cross-references

57:7 ᵃ Ps. 108:1–5 ¹ steadfast
57:8 ᵃ Ps. 16:9 ¹ lute ² awaken the dawn
57:9 ᵃ Ps. 108:3 ¹ Gentiles
57:10 ᵃ Ps. 103:11
57:11 ᵃ Ps. 57:5
58:title ¹ Set to "Do Not Destroy" ² Contemplation
58:1 ¹ ye silent ones
58:3 ᵃ [Is. 48:8]
58:4 ᵃ Eccl. 10:11 ¹ cobra
58:5 ᵃ Jer. 8:17 ¹ ever so skilfully
58:6 ᵃ Job 4:10 ¹ Break away
58:7 ᵃ Josh. 2:11; 7:5 ¹ flow
58:8 ᵃ Job 3:16 ¹ stillborn child of
58:9 ᵃ Eccl. 7:6 ᵇ Prov. 10:25 ¹ burning *thorns* ² as in his living and burning wrath
58:10 ᵃ Jer. 11:20 ᵇ Ps. 68:23
58:11 ᵃ Ps. 92:15 ᵇ Ps. 50:6; 75:7
59:title ᵃ 1 Sam. 19:11 ¹ Set to "Do Not Destroy" ² Contemplation
59:1 ¹ Lit. *set me on high*
59:2 ¹ *bloodthirsty*
59:3 ᵃ Ps. 56:6 ¹ life
59:4 ᵃ Ps. 35:23 ¹ apart from any fault of mine
59:5 ¹ punish ² nations or Gentiles
59:6 ᵃ Ps. 59:14 ¹ growl
59:7 ᵃ Prov. 12:18 ᵇ Ps. 10:11
59:8 ᵃ Prov. 1:26 ¹ nations or Gentiles
59:9 ᵃ [Ps. 62:2] ¹ Lit. stronghold
59:10 ᵃ Ps. 21:3 ᵇ Ps. 54:7 ¹ meet
59:12 ᵃ Prov. 12:13
59:13 ᵃ Ps. 104:35 ᵇ Ps. 83:18
59:14 ᵃ Ps. 59:6
59:15 ᵃ Job 15:23 ¹ food ² howl
59:17 ᵃ Ps. 18:1
60:title ᵃ Ps. 80 ᵇ 2 Sam. 8:3, 13 ¹ Set to "Lily of the Testimony" ² Contemplation ³ Mesopotamia ⁴ Syria of Zobah
60:1 ᵃ Ps. 44:9 ¹ broken ² restore us again
60:2 ᵃ [2 Chr. 7:14]

3 [a]Thou hast shewed thy people hard things: [b]thou hast made us to drink the wine of [1]astonishment.

4 [a]Thou hast given a banner to them that [f]fear thee, that it may be displayed because of the truth. *Selah.*

5 [a]That thy beloved may be delivered; save *with* thy right hand, and hear me.

6 God hath [a]spoken in his holiness; I will rejoice, I will [b]divide [c]Shechem, and [1]mete out [d]the valley of Succoth.

7 Gilead *is* mine, and Manasseh *is* mine; [a]Ephraim also *is* the [1]strength of mine head; [b]Judah *is* my lawgiver;

8 [a]Moab *is* my washpot; [b]over Edom will I cast out my shoe: [c]Philistia, triumph thou because of me.

9 Who will bring me *into* the strong city? who will lead me into Edom?

10 *Wilt* not thou, O God, [a]*which* hadst cast us off? and *thou,* O God, *which* didst [b]not go out with our armies?

11 Give us help from trouble: [a]for vain *is* the help of man.

12 Through God [a]we shall do valiantly: for he *it is that* shall tread down our enemies.

## PSALM 61

To the chief Musician upon [1]Neginah, *A Psalm* of David.

**H**EAR my cry, O God; attend unto my prayer.

2 From the end of the earth will I cry unto thee, when my heart is overwhelmed: lead me to the rock *that* is higher than I.

3 For thou hast been a shelter for me, *and* [a]a strong tower from the enemy.

4 I will abide in thy [1]tabernacle for ever: [a]I will trust in the [2]covert of thy wings. *Selah.*

5 For thou, O God, hast heard my vows: thou hast given *me* the heritage of those that fear thy name.

6 Thou wilt prolong the king's life: *and* his years as many generations.

7 He shall abide before God for ever: O prepare mercy [a]and truth, *which* may [1]preserve him.

8 So will I sing praise unto thy name for ever, that I may daily perform my vows.

## PSALM 62

To the chief Musician, to [a]Jeduthun, A Psalm of David.

**T**RULY [a]my soul [1]waiteth upon God: from him *cometh* my salvation.

2 He only *is* my rock and my salvation; *he is* my [1]defence; I shall not be greatly [2]moved.

3 How long will ye [1]imagine mischief against a man? ye shall be slain

60:3 [a] Ps. 71:20
[b] Jer. 25:15 [1] *staggering*

60:4 [a] Ps. 20:5
[1] Have a reverential awe for thee

60:5 [a] Ps. 108:6–13

60:6 [a] Ps. 89:35
[b] Josh. 1:6 [c] Gen. 12:6 [d] Josh. 13:27
[1] *measure out*

60:7 [a] Deut. 33:17
[b] [Gen. 49:10]
[1] *helmet*

60:8 [a] 2 Sam. 8:2 [b] 2 Sam. 8:14
[c] 2 Sam. 8:1

60:10 [a] Ps. 108:11
[b] Josh. 7:12

60:11 [a] Ps. 118:8; 146:3

60:12 [a] Num. 24:18

61:title [1] *a stringed instrument*

61:3 [a] Prov. 18:10

61:4 [a] Ps. 91:4
[1] *tent* [2] *shelter*

61:7 [a] Ps. 40:11
[1] Lit. *guard* or *keep*

62:title [a] 1 Chr. 25:1

62:1 [a] Ps. 33:20
[1] *waits silently*

62:2 [a] Ps. 55:22
[1] *strong tower*
[2] *shaken*

62:3 [a] Is. 30:13
[1] *attack a man*
[2] *leaning*

62:4 [a] Ps. 28:3
[1] *high position*

62:5 [1] *wait silently*
[2] *hope*

62:6 [1] *shaken*

62:7 [a] [Jer. 3:23]

62:8 [a] 1 Sam. 1:15

62:9 [a] Is. 40:17 [1] *a vapour* [2] *weighed*

62:10 [a] [Luke 12:15] [1] *do not vainly hope in*

62:12 [a] [Matt. 16:27] [1] *rewardeth*

63:title [a] 1 Sam. 22:5

63:1 [a] Ps. 42:2

63:2 [a] Ps. 27:4
[1] *so I have looked for thee*

63:3 [a] Ps. 138:2

63:4 [a] Ps. 28:2; 143:6

63:5 [1] The best, lit. *fat* [2] Abundance

63:6 [a] Ps. 42:8

63:8 [1] *close behind thee*

63:10 [1] Lit. *They shall pour him out by the hand of the sword* [2] A prey [3] *jackals*

all of you: [a]as a [2]bowing wall *shall ye be, and as* a tottering fence.

4 They only consult to cast *him* down from his [1]excellency: they [a]delight in lies: they bless with their mouth, but they curse inwardly. *Selah.*

5 My soul, [1]wait thou only upon God; for my [2]expectation *is* from him.

6 He only *is* my rock and my salvation: *he is* my defence; I shall not be [1]moved.

7 [a]In God *is* my salvation and my glory: the rock of my strength, *and* my refuge, *is* in God.

8 Trust in him at all times; ye people, [a]pour out your heart before him: God *is* a refuge for us. *Selah.*

9 [a]Surely men of low degree *are* [1]vanity, *and* men of high degree *are* a lie: to be [2]laid in the balance, they *are* altogether *lighter* than vanity.

10 Trust not in oppression, and [1]become not vain in robbery: [a]if riches increase, set not your heart *upon them.*

11 God hath spoken once; twice have I heard this; that power *belongeth* unto God.

12 Also unto thee, O Lord, *belongeth* mercy: for [a]thou [1]renderest to every man according to his work.

## PSALM 63

A Psalm of David, [a]when he was in the wilderness of Judah.

**O** GOD, thou *art* my God; early will I seek thee: [a]my soul thirsteth for thee, my flesh longeth for thee in a dry and thirsty land, where no water is;

2 To see [a]thy power and thy glory, [1]so *as* I have seen thee in the sanctuary.

3 [a]Because thy lovingkindness *is* better than life, my lips shall praise thee.

4 Thus will I bless thee while I live: I will [a]lift up my hands in thy name.

5 My soul shall be satisfied as *with* [1]marrow and [2]fatness; and my mouth shall praise *thee* with joyful lips:

6 When [a]I remember thee upon my bed, *and* meditate on thee in the *night* watches.

7 Because thou hast been my help, therefore in the shadow of thy wings will I rejoice.

8 My soul followeth [1]hard after thee: thy right hand upholdeth me.

9 But those *that* seek my soul, to destroy *it,* shall go into the lower parts of the earth.

10 [1]They shall fall by the sword: they shall be [2]a portion for [3]foxes.

11 But the king shall rejoice in God; [a]every one that sweareth by him shall

63:11 [a] Deut. 6:13; [Is. 45:23; 65:16]

glory: but the mouth of them that speak lies shall be stopped.

## PSALM 64

To the chief Musician,
A Psalm of David.

HEAR my voice, O God, in my [1]prayer: preserve my life from fear of the enemy.

2 Hide me from the secret counsel of the wicked; from the [1]insurrection of the workers of iniquity:

3 Who [1]whet their tongue like a sword, [a]*and* bend *their bows to shoot* their arrows, *even* bitter words:

4 That they may shoot in secret at the [1]perfect: suddenly do they shoot at him, and fear not.

5 They encourage themselves *in* an evil matter: they [1]commune of laying snares [2]privily; [a]they say, Who shall see them?

6 They [1]search out iniquities; they [2]accomplish a diligent search: both the inward *thought* of every one *of them,* and the heart, *is* deep.

7 But God shall shoot at them *with* an arrow; suddenly shall they be wounded.

8 So they shall [1]make their own tongue to fall upon themselves: [a]all that see them shall flee away.

9 And all men shall fear, and shall [a]declare the work of God; for they shall wisely consider of his doing.

10 [a]The righteous shall be glad in the LORD, and shall trust in him; and all the upright in heart shall glory.

## PSALM 65

To the chief Musician,
A Psalm *and* Song of David.

PRAISE waiteth for thee, O God, in Sion: and unto thee shall the [1]vow be performed.

2 O thou that hearest prayer, [a]unto thee shall all flesh come.

3 Iniquities prevail against me: *as for* our transgressions, thou shalt [a]purge[1] them away.

4 [a]Blessed *is the* man *whom* thou [b]choosest, and causest to approach *unto thee, that* he may dwell in thy courts: [c]we shall be satisfied with the goodness of thy house, *even* of thy holy temple.

5 *By* [1]terrible things in righteousness wilt thou answer us, O God of our salvation; *who art* the confidence of all the ends of the earth, and of them that are afar off *upon* the sea:

6 Which by his strength [1]setteth fast the mountains; [a]*being* girded with power:

7 [a]Which stilleth the noise of the seas, the noise of their waves, [b]and the tumult of the people.

8 They also that dwell in the utter-

---

64:1 [1] *meditation or complaint*
64:2 [1] *tumult*
64:3 [a] Ps. 58:7 [1] *sharpen*
64:4 [1] *blameless*
64:5 [a] Ps. 10:11; 59:7 [1] *talk* [2] *secretly*
64:6 [1] *devise* [2] *have perfected a shrewd scheme*
64:8 [a] Ps. 31:11 [1] *stumble over their own tongue*
64:9 [a] Jer. 50:28; 51:10
64:10 [a] Job 22:19; Ps. 32:11
65:1 [1] A promised deed
65:2 [a] [Is. 66:23]
65:3 [a] Ps. 51:2; 79:9; Is. 6:7; [Heb. 9:14; 1 John 1:7, 9] [1] *provide atonement*
65:4 [a] Ps. 33:12 [b] Ps. 4:3 [c] Ps. 36:8
65:5 [1] *awesome*
65:6 [a] Ps. 93:1 [1] *established*
65:7 [a] Matt. 8:26 [b] Is. 17:12, 13

65:8 [1] *signs* [2] *shout for joy*
65:9 [a] [Deut. 11:12]; Jer. 5:24 [b] Ps. 46:4; 104:13; 147:8 [1] *give attention to* [2] *grain*
65:10 [1] *growth*
65:11 [1] *abundance*
65:13 [a] Is. 44:23; 55:12 [1] *grain*
66:1 [a] Ps. 100:1 [1] *shout* [2] *the earth*
66:3 [a] Ps. 65:5 [b] Ps. 18:44 [1] *awesome*
66:4 [a] Ps. 117:1; Zech. 14:16
66:5 [1] *awesome*
66:6 [a] Ex. 14:21 [b] Josh. 3:14–16 [1] *river*
66:9 [1] *among the living* [2] *slip*
66:10 [a] Ps. 17:3 [b] [1 Pet. 1:7] [1] *tested* [2] *refined us*
66:11 [a] Lam. 1:13
66:12 [a] Is. 51:23 [b] Is. 43:2 [1] *an abundant*
66:13 [a] Ps. 100:4; 116:14, 17–19 [b] [Eccl. 5:4] [1] *Promised deeds*

---

most parts are afraid at thy [1]tokens: thou makest the outgoings of the morning and evening to [2]rejoice.

9 Thou [1]visitest the earth, and [a]waterest it: thou greatly enrichest it [b]with the river of God, *which* is full of water: thou preparest them [2]corn, when thou hast so provided for it.

10 Thou waterest the ridges thereof abundantly: thou settlest the furrows thereof: thou makest it soft with showers: thou blessest the [1]springing thereof.

11 Thou crownest the year with thy goodness; and thy paths drop [1]fatness.

12 They drop *upon* the pastures of the wilderness: and the little hills rejoice on every side.

13 The pastures are clothed with flocks; [a]the valleys also are covered over with [1]corn; they shout for joy, they also sing.

## PSALM 66

To the chief Musician,
A Song *or* Psalm.

MAKE [a]a joyful [1]noise unto God, all [2]ye lands:

2 Sing forth the honour of his name: make his praise glorious.

3 Say unto God, How [a]terrible[1] *art thou in* thy works! [b]through the greatness of thy power shall thine enemies submit themselves unto thee.

4 [a]All the earth shall worship thee, and shall sing unto thee; they shall sing *to* thy name. *Selah.*

5 Come and see the works of God: *he is* [1]terrible *in his* doing toward the children of men.

6 [a]He turned the sea into dry *land:* [b]they went through the [1]flood on foot: there did we rejoice in him.

7 He ruleth by his power for ever; his eyes behold the nations: let not the rebellious exalt themselves. *Selah.*

8 O bless our God, ye people, and make the voice of his praise to be heard:

9 Which holdeth our soul [1]in life, and suffereth not our feet to [2]be moved.

10 For [a]thou, O God, hast [1]proved us: [b]thou hast [2]tried us, as silver is tried.

11 [a]Thou broughtest us into the net; thou laidst affliction upon our loins.

12 [a]Thou hast caused men to ride over our heads; [b]we went through fire and through water: but thou broughtest us out into [1]a wealthy *place.*

13 [a]I will go into thy house with burnt offerings: [b]I will pay thee my [1]vows,

14 Which my lips have uttered, and my mouth hath spoken, when I was in trouble.

15 I will offer unto thee burnt sacrifices of fatlings, with the incense of rams; I will offer bullocks with goats. *Selah.*

16 Come *and* hear, all ye that fear God, and I will declare what he hath done for my soul.

17 I cried unto him with my mouth, and he was [1]extolled with my tongue.

18 [a]If I regard iniquity in my heart, the Lord will not hear *me:*

19 *But* verily God [a]hath heard *me;* he hath attended to the voice of my prayer.

20 Blessed *be* God, which hath not turned away my prayer, nor his mercy from me.

## PSALM 67

To the chief Musician, [1]on Neginoth, A Psalm *or* Song.

GOD be merciful unto us, and bless us; *and* [a]cause his face to shine upon us; *Selah.*

2 That [a]thy way may be known upon earth, [b]thy [1]saving health among all nations.

3 Let the people praise thee, O God; let all the people praise thee.

4 O let the nations be glad and sing for joy: for [a]thou shalt judge the people righteously, and govern the nations upon earth. *Selah.*

5 Let the people praise thee, O God; let all the people praise thee.

6 [a]*Then* shall the earth [1]yield her increase; *and* God, *even* our own God, shall bless us.

7 God shall bless us; and all the ends of the earth shall fear him.

## PSALM 68

To the chief Musician, A Psalm *or* Song of David.

LET [a]God arise, let his enemies be scattered: let them also that hate him flee before him.

2 [a]As smoke is driven away, *so* drive *them* away: [b]as wax melteth before the fire, *so* let the wicked perish at the presence of God.

3 But [a]let the righteous be glad; let them rejoice before God: yea, let them exceedingly rejoice.

4 Sing unto God, sing praises to his name: [a]extol[1] him that rideth upon the [2]heavens [b]by his name [3]JAH, and rejoice before him.

5 [a]A father of the fatherless, and a [1]judge of the widows, *is* God in his holy habitation.

6 [a]God setteth the [1]solitary in families: [b]he bringeth out those which are bound with [2]chains: but [c]the rebellious dwell in a dry *land.*

7 O God, [a]when thou wentest forth before thy people, when thou didst march through the wilderness; *Selah:*

66:17 [1] *praised*
66:18 [a] Is. 1:15
66:19 [a] Ps. 116:1, 2
67:title [1] *on stringed instruments*
67:1 [a] Num. 6:25
67:2 [a] Acts 18:25 [b] Titus 2:11 [1] *salvation among*
67:4 [a] [Ps. 96:10, 13; 98:9]
67:6 [a] Lev. 26:4 [1] *give her produce*
68:1 [a] Num. 10:35
68:2 [a] [Is. 9:18] [b] Mic. 1:4
68:3 [a] Ps. 32:11
68:4 [a] Deut. 33:26 [b] [Ex. 6:3] [1] *praise* [2] MT *deserts;* Tg. *heavens* [3] Lit. LORD, a shortened Heb. form
68:5 [a] [Ps. 10:14, 18; 146:9] [1] *defender*
68:6 [a] Ps. 107:4–7 [b] Acts 12:6 [c] Ps. 107:34 [1] *lonely* [2] *prosperity*
68:7 [a] Ex. 13:21
68:8 [1] *dropped rain*
68:9 [a] Deut. 11:11
68:10 [a] Deut. 26:5
68:11 [1] *host* [2] *proclaimed*
68:12 [a] Josh. 10:16 [1] Lit. *flee, they flee* [2] *remained* [3] *plunder*
68:13 [a] Ps. 81:6 [b] Ps. 105:37 [1] *sheepfolds* or *saddlebags*
68:14 [a] Josh. 10:10 [1] Or *Zalmon*
68:15 [1] *mountain* [2] *a mountain of peaks is the mountain*
68:16 [a] [Deut. 12:5] [1] Lit. *do you stare with envy* [2] *mountain of many peaks* [3] *mountain*
68:17 [a] Deut. 33:2 [1] *thousands*
68:18 [a] Eph. 4:8 [b] Judg. 5:12 [c] Acts 2:4, 33; 10:44–46 [d] [1 Tim. 1:13] [e] Ps. 78:60 [1] *among*
68:20 [a] [Deut. 32:39] [1] *escapes*
68:21 [a] Hab. 3:13 [b] Ps. 55:23
68:22 [a] Num. 21:33; Deut. 30:1–9; Amos 9:1–3 [b] Ex. 14:22
68:23 [a] Ps. 58:10 [b] 1 Kin. 21:19; Jer. 15:3 [1] *crush them in blood* [2] *may have their portion*

8 The earth shook, the heavens also [1]dropped at the presence of God: *even* Sinai itself *was moved* at the presence of God, the God of Israel.

9 [a]Thou, O God, didst send a plentiful rain, whereby thou didst confirm thine inheritance, when it was weary.

10 Thy congregation hath dwelt therein: [a]thou, O God, hast prepared of thy goodness for the poor.

11 The Lord gave the word: great *was* the [1]company of those that [2]published *it.*

12 [a]Kings of armies [1]did flee apace: and she that [2]tarried at home divided the [3]spoil.

13 [a]Though ye have lien among the [1]pots, [b]*yet shall ye be as* the wings of a dove covered with silver, and her feathers with yellow gold.

14 [a]When the Almighty scattered kings in it, it was *white* as snow in [1]Salmon.

15 The [1]hill of God *is as* the [1]hill of Bashan; [2]an high hill *as* the hill of Bashan.

16 Why [1]leap ye, ye [2]high hills? [a]*this is* the [3]hill *which* God desireth to dwell in; yea, the LORD will dwell *in it* for ever.

17 [a]The chariots of God *are* twenty thousand, *even* thousands of [1]angels: the Lord *is* among them, *as in* Sinai, in the holy *place.*

18 [a]Thou hast ascended on high, [b]thou hast led captivity captive: [c]thou hast received gifts [1]for men; yea, *for* [d]the rebellious also, [e]that the LORD God might dwell *among them.*

19 Blessed *be* the Lord, *who* daily loadeth us *with benefits, even* the God of our salvation. *Selah.*

20 *He that is* our God *is* the God of salvation; and [a]unto GOD the Lord *belong* the [1]issues from death.

21 But [a]God shall wound the head of his enemies, [b]and the hairy scalp of such an one as goeth on still in his trespasses.

22 The Lord said, I will bring [a]again from Bashan, I will bring *my people* again [b]from the depths of the sea:

23 [a]That thy foot may [1]be dipped in the blood of *thine* enemies, [b]*and* the tongue of thy dogs [2]in the same.

24 They have seen thy [1]goings, O God; *even* the goings of my God, my King, in the sanctuary.

25 [a]The singers went before, the players on instruments *followed* after; among *them were* the damsels playing with timbrels.

26 Bless ye God in the congregations, *even* the Lord, from [a]the fountain of Israel.

27 [1]There *is* [a]little Benjamin *with*

68:24 [1] *procession*  68:25 [a] 1 Chr. 13:8  68:26 [a] Deut. 33:28; Is. 48:1  68:27 [a] Judg. 5:14; 1 Sam. 9:21 [1] *Little Benjamin, their leader, is there*

their ruler, the princes of Judah *and* their [2]council, the princes of Zebulun, *and* the princes of Naphtali.

28 Thy God hath [a]commanded thy strength: strengthen, O God, that which thou hast wrought for us.

29 Because of thy temple at Jerusalem [a]shall kings bring presents unto thee.

30 Rebuke the [1]company of spearmen, [a]the [2]multitude of the bulls, with the calves of the people, *till every one* [b]submit himself with pieces of silver: scatter thou the people *that* delight in war.

31 [a]Princes shall come out of Egypt; [b]Ethiopia shall [1]soon [c]stretch out her hands unto God.

32 Sing unto God, ye [a]kingdoms of the earth; O sing praises unto the Lord; *Selah*:

33 To him [a]that rideth upon the heavens of heavens, *which were* of old; lo, he doth send out his voice, *and that* a [b]mighty voice.

34 [a]Ascribe ye strength unto God: his excellency *is* over Israel, and his strength *is* in the clouds.

35 O God, [a]*thou art* [1]terrible out of thy holy places: the God of Israel *is* he that giveth strength and power unto *his* people. Blessed *be* God.

## PSALM 69

To the chief Musician [1]upon Shoshannim, *A Psalm* of David.

**S**AVE me, O God; for [a]the waters are come in unto *my* [1]soul.

2 [a]I sink in deep mire, where *there is* no standing: I am come into deep waters, where the floods overflow me.

3 [a]I am weary of my crying: my throat is dried: [b]mine eyes fail while I wait for my God.

4 They that [a]hate me without a cause are more than the hairs of mine head: they that would destroy me, *being* mine enemies wrongfully, are mighty: then I restored *that* which I [1]took not away.

5 O God, thou knowest my foolishness; and my sins are not hid from thee.

6 Let not them that [1]wait on thee, O Lord GOD of hosts, be ashamed [2]for my sake: let not those that seek thee be [3]confounded for my sake, O God of Israel.

7 Because for thy sake I have borne reproach; shame hath covered my face.

8 [a]I am become a stranger unto my brethren, and an alien unto my mother's children.

9 [a]For the zeal [1]of thine house hath eaten me up; [b]and the reproaches of them that reproached thee are fallen upon me.

### Center column references

68:27 [2] *company* or *throng*
68:28 [a] Ps. 42:8; Is. 26:12
68:29 [a] 1 Kin. 10:10, 25; 2 Chr. 32:23; Ps. 45:12; 72:10; Is. 18:7
68:30 [a] Ps. 22:12 [b] 2 Sam. 8:2 [1] Lit. *beasts of the reeds* [2] *herd*
68:31 [a] Is. 19:19–23 [b] Is. 45:14; Zeph. 3:10 [c] Ps. 44:20 [1] *quickly*
68:32 [a] [Ps. 67:3, 4]
68:33 [a] Deut. 33:26; Ps. 18:10 [b] Ps. 46:6; Is. 30:30
68:34 [a] Ps. 29:1
68:35 [a] Ps. 76:12 [1] *awesome*
69:title [1] *Set to "The Lilies"*
69:1 [a] Job 22:11; Jon. 2:5 [1] *Neck*
69:2 [a] Ps. 40:2
69:3 [a] Ps. 6:6 [b] Deut. 28:32; Ps. 119:82, 123; Is. 38:14
69:4 [a] Ps. 35:19; John 15:25 [1] *did not steal*
69:6 [1] *Wait in faith for* [2] *because of me* [3] *disgraced*
69:8 [a] Is. 53:3; Mark 3:21; Luke 8:19; John 7:3–5
69:9 [a] John 2:17 [b] Rom. 15:3 [1] *for*
69:10 [1] *became*
69:11 [1] A symbol of sorrow [2] *byword*
69:12 [a] Job 30:9 [1] Sit as judges
69:17 [1] *quickly*
69:19 [a] Ps. 22:6, 7; Heb. 12:2
69:20 [a] Is. 63:5 [b] Job 16:2 [1] Lit. *sickness*
69:21 [a] Matt. 27:34, 48 [1] *food*
69:22 [a] Rom. 11:9, 10 [1] *well-being*
69:23 [a] Is. 6:9, 10
69:24 [a] [1 Thess. 2:16]
69:25 [a] Matt. 23:38
69:26 [a] [Is. 53:4] [1] *struck*
69:27 [a] [Rom. 1:28] [b] [Is. 26:10]
69:28 [a] [Ex. 32:32] [b] Ezek. 13:9

10 When I wept, *and chastened* my soul with fasting, that [1]was to my reproach.

11 I made [1]sackcloth also my garment; and I became a [2]proverb to them.

12 They that [1]sit in the gate speak against me; and I *was* the song of the [a]drunkards.

13 But as for me, my prayer *is* unto thee, O LORD, *in* an acceptable time: O God, in the multitude of thy mercy hear me, in the truth of thy salvation.

14 Deliver me out of the mire, and let me not sink: let me be delivered from them that hate me, and out of the deep waters.

15 Let not the waterflood overflow me, neither let the deep swallow me up, and let not the pit shut her mouth upon me.

16 Hear me, O LORD; for thy lovingkindness *is* good: turn unto me according to the multitude of thy tender mercies.

17 And hide not thy face from thy servant; for I am in trouble: hear me [1]speedily.

18 Draw nigh unto my soul, *and* redeem it: deliver me because of mine enemies.

19 Thou hast known [a]my reproach, and my shame, and my dishonour: mine adversaries *are* all before thee.

20 Reproach hath broken my heart; and I am full of [1]heaviness: and [a]I looked *for some* to take pity, but *there was* none; and for [b]comforters, but I found none.

21 They gave me also gall for my [1]meat; [a]and in my thirst they gave me vinegar to drink.

22 [a]Let their table become a snare before them: and *that which should have been* for *their* [1]welfare, *let it become* a trap.

23 [a]Let their eyes be darkened, that they see not; and make their loins continually to shake.

24 [a]Pour out thine indignation upon them, and let thy wrathful anger take hold of them.

25 [a]Let their habitation be desolate; *and* let none dwell in their tents.

26 For they persecute [a]*him* whom thou hast [1]smitten; and they talk to the grief of those whom thou hast wounded.

27 [a]Add iniquity unto their iniquity: [b]and let them not come into thy righteousness.

28 Let them [a]be blotted out of the book of the living, [b]and not be written with the righteous.

29 But I *am* poor and sorrowful: let thy salvation, O God, set me up on high.

30 [a]I will praise the name of God with a song, and will magnify him with thanksgiving.

31 [a]*This* also shall please the LORD better than an ox *or* bullock that hath horns and hoofs.

32 [a]The humble shall see *this, and* be glad: and [b]your heart shall live that seek God.

33 For the LORD heareth the poor, and despiseth not [a]his prisoners.

34 [a]Let the heaven and earth praise him, the seas, [b]and every thing that moveth therein.

35 [a]For God will save Zion, and will build the cities of Judah: that they may dwell there, and have it in possession.

36 [a]The [1]seed also of his servants shall inherit it: and they that love his name shall dwell therein.

## PSALM 70

To the chief Musician, *A Psalm* of David, [a]to bring to remembrance.

**M**AKE haste, [a]O God, to deliver me; make haste to help me, O LORD.

2 [a]Let them be [1]ashamed and confounded that seek after my [2]soul: let them be turned backward, and put to confusion, that desire my hurt.

3 [a]Let them be turned back for a reward of their shame that say, [1]Aha, aha.

4 Let all those that seek thee rejoice and be glad in thee: and let such as love thy salvation say continually, Let God be magnified.

5 [a]But I *am* poor and needy: [b]make haste unto me, O God: thou *art* my help and my deliverer; O LORD, [1]make no tarrying.

## PSALM 71

**I**N [a]thee, O LORD, do I put my trust: let me never be put to [1]confusion.

2 [a]Deliver me in thy righteousness, and cause me to escape: [b]incline thine ear unto me, and save me.

3 [a]Be thou [1]my strong habitation, whereunto I may continually resort: thou hast given [b]commandment to save me; for thou *art* my rock and my fortress.

4 [a]Deliver me, O my God, out of the hand of the wicked, out of the hand of the unrighteous and cruel man.

5 For thou *art* [a]my hope, O Lord GOD: *thou art* my trust from my youth.

6 [a]By thee have I been [1]holden up from the womb: thou art he that took me out of my mother's [2]bowels: my praise *shall be* continually of thee.

7 [a]I am as a wonder unto many; but thou *art* my strong refuge.

8 Let [a]my mouth be filled *with* thy praise *and with* thy [1]honour all the day.

9 Cast me not off in the time of old age; forsake me not when my strength faileth.

10 For mine enemies speak against me; and they that [1]lay wait for my soul [a]take counsel together,

11 Saying, God hath forsaken him: [1]persecute and take him; for *there is* none to deliver *him.*

12 [a]O God, be not far from me: O my God, [b]make haste for my help.

13 Let them be [1]confounded *and* consumed that are adversaries to my soul; let them be covered *with* reproach and dishonour that seek my hurt.

14 But I will hope continually, and will yet praise thee more and more.

15 My mouth shall [1]shew forth thy righteousness *and* thy salvation all the day; for I know not the [2]numbers *thereof.*

16 I will go in the strength of the Lord GOD: I will make mention of thy righteousness, *even* of thine only.

17 O God, thou hast taught me from my [a]youth: and hitherto have I declared thy wondrous works.

18 Now also [a]when I am old and greyheaded, O God, forsake me not; until I have [1]shewed thy strength unto *this* generation, *and* thy power to every one *that* is to come.

19 [a]Thy righteousness also, O God, *is* [1]very high, who hast done great things: [b]O God, who *is* like unto thee!

20 [a]*Thou,* which hast shewed me great and [1]sore troubles, [b]shalt [2]quicken me again, and shalt bring me up again from the depths of the earth.

21 Thou shalt increase my greatness, and comfort me on every side.

22 I will also praise thee [a]with the [1]psaltery, *even* thy [2]truth, O my God: unto thee will I sing with the harp, O thou [b]Holy One of Israel.

23 My lips shall greatly rejoice when I sing unto thee; and [a]my soul, which thou hast redeemed.

24 My tongue also shall talk of thy righteousness all the day long: for they are confounded, for they are brought unto shame, that seek my hurt.

## PSALM 72

*A Psalm* [a]for[1] Solomon.

**G**IVE the king thy judgments, O God, and thy righteousness unto the king's son.

2 [a]He shall judge thy people with righteousness, and thy poor with [1]judgment.

3 [a]The mountains shall bring peace to the people, and the little hills, by righteousness.

4 [a]He shall [1]judge the poor of the people, he shall save the children of

---

69:30 [a] [Ps. 28:7]
69:31 [a] Ps. 50:13, 14, 23; 51:16
69:32 [a] Ps. 34:2
[b] Ps. 22:26
69:33 [a] Eph. 3:1
69:34 [a] Ps. 96:11
[b] Is. 55:12
69:35 [a] Is. 44:26
69:36 [a] Ps. 102:28
[1] *descendants*
70:title [a] Ps. 38:title
70:1 [a] Ps. 40:13–17
70:2 [a] Ps. 35:4, 26
[1] *disgraced* [2] *life*
70:3 [a] Ps. 40:15
[1] An expression of scorn
70:5 [a] Ps. 72:12, 13
[b] Ps. 141:1 [1] *do not delay*
71:1 [a] Ps. 25:2, 3
[1] *shame*
71:2 [a] Ps. 31:1
[b] Ps. 17:6
71:3 [a] Ps. 31:2, 3
[b] Ps. 44:4 [1] Lit. *a rock of*
71:4 [a] Ps. 140:1, 3
71:5 [a] Jer. 14:8; 17:7, 13, 17; 50:7
71:6 [a] Ps. 22:9, 10 [1] *upheld from birth* [2] *womb*
71:7 [a] Is. 8:18
71:8 [a] Ps. 35:28
[1] *glory*

71:10 [a] 2 Sam. 17:1
[1] Lit. *watch for my life*
71:11 [1] *pursue*
71:12 [a] Ps. 35:22
[b] Ps. 70:1
71:13 [1] *ashamed*
71:15 [1] *proclaim*
[2] *limits*
71:17 [a] Deut. 4:5; 6:7
71:18 [a] [Is. 46:4]
[1] *declared*
71:19 [a] Ps. 57:10
[b] Ps. 35:10 [1] Lit. *to the height of heaven*
71:20 [a] Ps. 60:3
[b] Hos. 6:1, 2
[1] *severe* [2] *revive*
71:22 [a] Ps. 92:1–3
[b] 2 Kin. 19:22
[1] *lute* or *lyre*
[2] *faithfulness*
71:23 [a] Ps. 103:4
72:title [a] Ps. 127:title [1] *of*
72:2 [a] [Is. 9:7; 11:2–5; 32:1]
[1] *justice*
72:3 [a] Ps. 85:10
72:4 [a] Is. 11:4
[1] *bring justice to*

the needy, and shall [2]break in pieces the oppressor.

5 They shall fear thee [a]as long as the sun and moon endure, throughout all generations.

6 [a]He shall come down like rain upon the mown grass: as showers *that* water the earth.

7 In his days shall the righteous flourish; [a]and abundance of peace [1]so long as the moon endureth.

8 [a]He shall have dominion also from sea to sea, and from the river unto the ends of the earth.

9 [a]They that dwell in the wilderness shall bow before him; [b]and his enemies shall lick the dust.

10 [a]The kings of Tarshish and of the isles shall bring presents: the kings of Sheba and Seba shall offer gifts.

11 [a]Yea, all kings shall fall down before him: all nations shall serve him.

12 For he [a]shall deliver the needy when he crieth; the poor also, and *him* that hath no helper.

13 He shall spare the poor and needy, and shall save the souls of the needy.

14 He shall redeem their [1]soul from [2]deceit and violence: and [a]precious shall their blood be in his sight.

15 And he shall live, and to him shall be given of the gold of [a]Sheba: prayer also shall be made for him continually; *and* daily shall he be praised.

16 There shall be [1]an handful of corn in the earth upon the top of the mountains; the fruit thereof shall shake like Lebanon: [a]and *they* of the city shall flourish like grass of the earth.

17 [a]His name shall endure for ever: his name shall be continued as long as the sun: and [b]*men* shall be blessed in him: [c]all nations shall call him blessed.

18 [a]Blessed *be* the LORD God, the God of Israel, [b]who only doeth wondrous things.

19 And [a]blessed *be* his glorious name for ever: [b]and let the whole earth be filled *with* his glory; Amen, and Amen.

20 The prayers of David the son of Jesse are ended.

## BOOK III: Psalms 73–89

### PSALM 73

A Psalm of [a]Asaph.

T RULY God *is* good to Israel, *even* to such as are of a [1]clean heart.

2 But as for me, my [1]feet were almost gone; my steps had well nigh [a]slipped.

---

*Cross references (center column):*

72:4 [2] *crush*
72:5 [a] Ps. 72:7, 17; 89:36
72:6 [a] Hos. 6:3
72:7 [a] Is. 2:4 [1] Lit. *until the moon is no more*
72:8 [a] Ex. 23:31
72:9 [a] Is. 23:13 [b] Is. 49:23
72:10 [a] 2 Chr. 9:21
72:11 [a] Is. 49:23
72:12 [a] Job 29:12
72:14 [a] [Ps. 116:15] [1] *life* [2] *oppression*
72:15 [a] Is. 60:6
72:16 [a] 1 Kin. 4:20 [1] *an abundance of grain*
72:17 [a] [Ps. 89:36] [b] [Gen. 12:3] [c] Luke 1:48
72:18 [a] 1 Chr. 29:10 [b] Ex. 15:11
72:19 [a] [Neh. 9:5] [b] Num. 14:21
73:title [a] Ps. 50:title
73:1 [1] *pure*
73:2 [a] Job 12:5 [1] *feet had almost stumbled*
73:3 [a] Ps. 37:1, 7 [b] Job 21:5–16 [1] *boastful*
73:4 [1] *pangs or pain*
73:5 [a] Job 21:9
73:6 [a] Ps. 109:18 [1] *serves as a necklace*
73:7 [a] Jer. 5:28 [1] *bulge with abundance*
73:8 [a] Ps. 53:1 [b] 2 Pet. 2:18 [1] *scoff* [2] *Proudly*
73:9 [a] Rev. 13:6
73:10 [a] [Ps. 75:8] [1] *drained by them*
73:11 [a] Job 22:13
73:12 [1] *are always at ease*
73:13 [a] Job 21:15; 35:3 [1] *kept my heart pure in vain*
73:15 [1] *would have been untrue to the*
73:16 [1] *understand* [2] *troublesome in my eyes*
73:17 [a] [Ps. 37:38; 55:23]
73:18 [a] Ps. 35:6
73:21 [1] *pierced in my mind*
73:22 [a] Ps. 92:6
73:23 [1] *held*
73:24 [a] Ps. 32:8; 48:14
73:25 [a] [Phil. 3:8]
73:26 [a] Ps. 84:2 [b] Ps. 16:5 [1] Lit. *rock*

---

3 [a]For I was envious at the [1]foolish, *when* I saw the prosperity of the [b]wicked.

4 For *there are* no [1]bands in their death: but their strength *is* firm.

5 [a]They *are* not in trouble *as other* men; neither are they plagued like *other* men.

6 Therefore pride [1]compasseth them about as a chain; violence covereth them [a]*as* a garment.

7 [a]Their eyes [1]stand out with fatness: they have more than heart could wish.

8 [a]They [1]are corrupt, and speak wickedly *concerning* oppression: they [b]speak [2]loftily.

9 They set their mouth [a]against the heavens, and their tongue walketh through the earth.

10 Therefore his people return hither: [a]and waters of a full *cup* are [1]wrung out to them.

11 And they say, [a]How doth God know? and is there knowledge in the most High?

12 Behold, these *are* the ungodly, who [1]prosper in the world; they increase *in* riches.

13 Verily I have [1]cleansed my heart in [a]vain, and washed my hands in innocency.

14 For all the day long have I been plagued, and chastened every morning.

15 If I say, I will speak thus; behold, I [1]should offend *against* the generation of thy children.

16 When I thought to [1]know this, it *was* too [2]painful for me;

17 Until I went into the sanctuary of God; *then* understood I their [a]end.

18 Surely [a]thou didst set them in slippery places: thou castedst them down into destruction.

19 How are they *brought* into desolation, as in a moment! they are utterly consumed with terrors.

20 As a dream when *one* awaketh; *so,* O Lord, when thou awakest, thou shalt despise their image.

21 Thus my heart was grieved, and I was [1]pricked in my reins.

22 [a]So foolish *was* I, and ignorant: I was *as* a beast before thee.

23 Nevertheless I *am* continually with thee: thou hast [1]holden *me* by my right hand.

24 [a]Thou shalt guide me with thy counsel, and afterward receive me *to* glory.

25 [a]Whom have I in heaven *but* thee? and *there is* none upon earth *that* I desire beside thee.

26 [a]My flesh and my heart faileth: *but* God *is* the [1]strength of my heart, and my [b]portion for ever.

27 For, lo, [a]they that are far from thee shall perish: thou hast destroyed all them [1]that go a whoring from thee.

28 But *it is* good for me to [a]draw near to God: I have put my trust in the Lord GOD, that I may [b]declare all thy works.

## PSALM 74

### [1]Maschil of Asaph.

O GOD, why hast thou cast *us* off for ever? *why* doth thine anger smoke against the sheep of thy pasture?

2 Remember thy congregation, *which* thou hast purchased of old; [1]the rod of thine inheritance, *which* thou hast redeemed; this mount Zion, wherein thou hast dwelt.

3 Lift up thy feet unto the perpetual desolations; *even* all *that* the enemy hath done wickedly in the sanctuary.

4 [a]Thine enemies roar in the midst of thy [1]congregations; [b]they set up their [2]ensigns *for* signs.

5 *A man* was famous according as he had lifted up axes upon the thick trees.

6 But now they break down the carved work thereof at once with axes and hammers.

7 They have [1]cast fire into thy sanctuary, they have defiled *by casting down* the dwelling place of thy name to the ground.

8 [a]They said in their hearts, Let us [1]destroy them together: they have burned up all the [2]synagogues of God in the land.

9 We see not our signs: [a]*there is* [1]no more any prophet: neither *is there* among us any that knoweth how long.

10 O God, how long shall the adversary [1]reproach? shall the enemy blaspheme thy name for ever?

11 [a]Why withdrawest thou thy hand, even thy right hand? [1]pluck *it* out of thy bosom.

12 For [a]God *is* my King of old, working salvation in the midst of the earth.

13 [a]Thou didst divide the sea by thy strength: thou brakest the heads of the [1]dragons in the waters.

14 Thou brakest the heads of [1]leviathan in pieces, *and* gavest him *to be* [2]meat to the people inhabiting the wilderness.

15 [a]Thou didst [1]cleave the fountain and the flood: [b]thou driedst up mighty rivers.

16 The day *is* thine, the night also *is* [a]thine: [b]thou hast prepared the light and the sun.

17 Thou hast [a]set all the borders of the earth: [b]thou hast made summer and winter.

73:27 [a] [Ps. 119:155] [1] Who are unfaithful to thee

73:28 [a] [Heb. 10:22] [b] 2 Cor. 4:13

74:title [1] Contemplation

74:2 [1] the tribe

74:4 [a] Lam. 2:7 [b] Num. 2:2 [1] meeting places [2] banners

74:7 [1] burned, lit. set on fire

74:8 [a] Ps. 83:4 [1] oppress them altogether [2] meeting places

74:9 [a] Amos 8:11 [1] no longer any

74:10 [1] revile

74:11 [a] Lam. 2:3 [1] Take it out of thy bosom and destroy them.

74:12 [a] Ps. 44:4

74:13 [a] Ex. 14:21 [1] sea monsters or serpents

74:14 [1] A large sea creature of unknown identity [2] food

74:15 [a] Ex. 17:5, 6 [b] Josh. 2:10; 3:13 [1] break open

74:16 [a] Job 38:12 [b] Gen. 1:14–18

74:17 [a] Acts 17:26 [b] Gen. 8:22

74:19 [1] life [2] wild beasts

74:20 [a] Lev. 26:44, 45 [1] hiding places [2] homes [3] violence

74:22 [1] reviles or taunts

75:title [a] Ps. 57:title [1] Set to "Do Not Destroy"

75:2 [1] choose the appointed or proper time

75:3 [1] firmly set up

75:4 [a] [1 Sam. 2:3] [1] boastful [2] boastfully [3] Raise the head proudly like a horned animal

75:5 [1] In insolent pride

75:6 [1] exaltation

75:7 [a] Ps. 50:6 [b] 1 Sam. 2:7; Ps. 147:6; Dan. 2:21 [1] exalts

75:8 [a] Job 21:20; Ps. 60:3; Jer. 25:15; Rev. 14:10; 16:19 [1] fully mixed [2] drain it

75:10 [a] Ps. 101:8; Jer. 48:25

18 Remember this, *that* the enemy hath reproached, O LORD, and *that* the foolish people have blasphemed thy name.

19 O deliver not the [1]soul of thy turtledove unto the [2]multitude *of the wicked:* forget not the congregation of thy poor for ever.

20 [a]Have respect unto the covenant: for [1]the dark places of the earth are full of the [2]habitations of [3]cruelty.

21 O let not the oppressed return ashamed: let the poor and needy praise thy name.

22 Arise, O God, plead thine own cause: remember how the foolish man [1]reproacheth thee daily.

23 Forget not the voice of thine enemies: the tumult of those that rise up against thee increaseth continually.

## PSALM 75

### To the chief Musician, [a]Altaschith,[1] A Psalm *or* Song of Asaph.

U NTO thee, O God, do we give thanks, *unto thee* do we give thanks: for *that* thy name is near thy wondrous works declare.

2 When I shall [1]receive the congregation I will judge uprightly.

3 The earth and all the inhabitants thereof are dissolved: I [1]bear up the pillars of it. *Selah.*

4 I said unto the [1]fools, Deal not [2]foolishly: and to the wicked, [a]Lift[3] not up the horn:

5 Lift not up your horn on high: speak *not* [1]with a stiff neck.

6 For [1]promotion *cometh* neither from the east, nor from the west, nor from the south.

7 But [a]God *is* the judge: [b]he putteth down one, and [1]setteth up another.

8 For [a]in the hand of the LORD *there is* a cup, and the wine is red; it is [1]full of mixture; and he poureth out of the same: but the dregs thereof, all the wicked of the earth shall [2]wring *them* out, *and* drink *them.*

9 But I will declare for ever; I will sing praises to the God of Jacob.

10 [a]All the [1]horns of the wicked also will I [2]cut off; *but* [b]the horns of the righteous shall be [c]exalted.

## PSALM 76

### To the chief Musician [1]on Neginoth, A Psalm *or* Song of Asaph.

I N [a]Judah *is* God known: his name *is* great in Israel.

2 In [1]Salem also is his tabernacle, and his dwelling place in Zion.

3 There brake he the arrows of the bow, the shield, and the sword, and the battle. *Selah.*

[b] Ps. 89:17; 148:14 [c] 1 Sam. 2:1 [1] Strength [2] destroy
76:title [1] on stringed instruments 76:1 [a] Ps. 48:1, 3
76:2 [1] Jerusalem

4 Thou *art* more glorious *and* excellent [a]than the mountains of prey.

5 [a]The stouthearted are [1]spoiled, [b]they have [2]slept their sleep: and none of the men of might have [3]found their hands.

6 [a]At thy rebuke, O God of Jacob, both the chariot and horse are cast into a dead sleep.

7 Thou, *even* thou, *art* to be feared: and [a]who may stand in thy sight when once thou art angry?

8 [a]Thou didst cause judgment to be heard from heaven; [b]the earth feared, and was still,

9 When God [a]arose to judgment, to save all the meek of the earth. *Selah.*

10 [a]Surely the wrath of man shall praise thee: the remainder of wrath shalt thou restrain.

11 [a]Vow, and pay unto the LORD your God: [b]let all that be round about him bring presents unto him that ought to be feared.

12 He shall cut off the spirit of princes: [a]*he is* [1]terrible to the kings of the earth.

## PSALM 77

To the chief Musician, [a]to Jeduthun, A Psalm of Asaph.

I CRIED unto God with my voice, *even* unto God with my voice; and he gave ear unto me.

2 In the day of my trouble I sought the Lord: [1]my sore ran in the night, and ceased not: my soul refused to be comforted.

3 I remembered God, and was troubled: I complained, and my spirit was overwhelmed. *Selah.*

4 Thou [1]holdest mine eyes waking: I am so troubled that I cannot speak.

5 I have considered the days of old, the years of ancient times.

6 I call to remembrance my song in the night: I commune with mine own heart: and my spirit [1]made diligent search.

7 Will the Lord cast off for ever? and will he be favourable no more?

8 Is his mercy [1]clean gone for ever? doth *his* [a]promise fail [2]for evermore?

9 Hath God forgotten to be gracious? hath he in anger shut up his tender mercies? *Selah.*

10 And I said, This *is* my [1]infirmity: *but I will remember* the years of the right hand of the most High.

11 I will remember the works of the LORD: surely I will remember thy wonders of old.

12 I will meditate also of all thy work, and talk of thy doings.

13 Thy way, O God, *is* in [1]the [a]sanctuary: who *is* so great a God as *our* God?

76:4 [a] Ezek. 38:12
76:5 [a] Is. 10:12; 46:12　[b] Ps. 13:3
[1] *plundered*
[2] *sunk into their sleep* [3] *found the use of their hands*
76:6 [a] Ex. 15:1–21; Ezek. 39:20; Nah. 2:13; Zech. 12:4
76:7 [a] [Ezra 9:15; Nah. 1:6; Mal. 3:2; Rev. 6:17]
76:8 [a] Ex. 19:9 [b] 1 Chr. 16:30; 2 Chr. 20:29
76:9 [a] [Ps. 9:7–9]
76:10 [a] Ex. 9:16; Rom. 9:17
76:11 [a] [Eccl. 5:4–6] [b] 2 Chr. 32:22, 23
76:12 [a] Ps. 68:35
[1] *awesome*
77:title [a] Ps. 39:title
77:2 [1] *my hand was stretched out in the night*
77:4 [1] *hold my eyelids open*
77:6 [1] *pondered diligently*
77:8 [a] [2 Pet. 2:8, 9] [1] *ceased completely* [2] Lit. *unto generation and generation*
77:10 [1] *anguish*
77:13 [a] Ps. 73:17 [1] Or *holiness*

14 Thou *art* the God that doest wonders: thou hast declared thy strength among the people.

15 Thou hast with *thine* arm redeemed thy people, the sons of Jacob and Joseph. *Selah.*

16 The waters saw thee, O God, the waters saw thee; they were [a]afraid: the depths also [1]were troubled.

17 The clouds poured out water: the skies sent out a sound: thine arrows also went abroad.

18 The voice of thy thunder *was* in the [1]heaven: the lightnings lightened the world: the earth trembled and shook.

19 Thy way *is* in the sea, and thy path in the great waters, and thy footsteps are not known.

20 Thou leddest thy people like a flock by the hand of Moses and Aaron.

## PSALM 78

[a]Maschil[1] of Asaph.

G IVE[1] ear, O my people, *to* my law: incline your ears to the words of my mouth.

2 I will open my mouth in a [a]parable: I will [1]utter dark sayings of old:

3 Which we have heard and known, and our fathers have told us.

4 [a]We will not hide *them* from their children, [b]shewing to the generation to come the praises of the LORD, and his strength, and his wonderful works that he hath done.

5 For [a]he established a testimony in Jacob, and appointed a law in Israel, which he commanded our fathers, that [b]they should make them known to their children:

6 [a]That the generation to come might know *them, even* the children *which* should be born; *who* should arise and declare *them* to their children:

7 That they might set their hope in God, and not forget the works of God, but keep his commandments:

8 And [a]might not be as their fathers, [b]a stubborn and rebellious generation; [c]*that* [1]set not their heart aright, and whose spirit was not stedfast with God.

9 The children of Ephraim, *being* armed, *and* [1]carrying bows, turned back in the day of battle.

10 [a]They kept not the covenant of God, and refused to walk in his law;

11 And [a]forgat his works, and his wonders that he had shewed them.

12 [a]Marvellous things did he in the sight of their fathers, in the land of Egypt, [b]*in* the field of Zoan.

13 [a]He divided the sea, and caused them to pass through; and [b]he made the waters to stand as an heap.

77:16 [a] Ex. 14:21; Hab. 3:8, 10
[1] *trembled*
77:18 [1] *whirlwind*
78:title [a] Ps. 74:title [1] *Contemplation*
78:1 [1] *Listen*
78:2 [a] Matt. 13:34, 35 [1] *speak obscure sayings or riddles*
78:4 [a] Deut. 4:9; 6:7 [b] Ex. 13:8, 14
78:5 [a] Ps. 147:19 [b] Deut. 4:9; 11:19
78:6 [a] Ps. 102:18
78:8 [a] 2 Kin. 17:14 [b] Ex. 32:9 [c] Ps. 78:37 [1] Lit. *did not prepare its heart*
78:9 [1] Lit. *bow shooters*
78:10 [a] 2 Kin. 17:15
78:11 [a] Ps. 106:13
78:12 [a] Ex. 7–12 [b] Num. 13:22
78:13 [a] Ex. 14:21 [b] Ex. 15:8

14 ᵃIn the daytime also he led them with a cloud, and all the night with a light of fire.

15 ᵃHe ¹clave the rocks in the wilderness, and gave *them* drink as *out of* the great depths.

16 He brought ᵃstreams also out of the rock, and caused waters to run down like rivers.

17 And they sinned yet more against him ¹by ᵃprovoking the most High in the wilderness.

18 And ᵃthey ¹tempted God in their heart by asking ²meat for their lust.

19 ᵃYea, they spake against God; they said, Can God ¹furnish a table in the wilderness?

20 ᵃBehold, he smote the rock, that the waters gushed out, and the streams overflowed; can he give bread also? can he provide flesh for his people?

21 Therefore the LORD heard *this*, and ᵃwas ¹wroth: so a fire was kindled against Jacob, and anger also came up against Israel;

22 Because they ᵃbelieved not in God, and trusted not in his salvation:

23 Though he had commanded the clouds from above, ᵃand opened the doors of heaven,

24 ᵃAnd had rained down manna upon them to eat, and had given them of the ¹corn of ᵇheaven.

25 Man did eat angels' food: he sent them ¹meat to the full.

26 ᵃHe caused an east wind to blow in the heaven: and by his power he brought in the south wind.

27 He rained flesh also upon them as dust, and feathered fowls like as the sand of the sea:

28 And he let *it* fall in the midst of their camp, round about their ¹habitations.

29 ᵃSo they did eat, and were well filled: for he gave them their own desire;

30 They were not ¹estranged from their ²lust. But ᵃwhile their meat *was* yet in their mouths,

31 The wrath of God came upon them, and slew the ¹fattest of them, and smote down the ²chosen *men* of Israel.

32 For all this ᵃthey sinned still, and ᵇbelieved not for his wondrous works.

33 ᵃTherefore their days did he consume in ¹vanity, and their years in ²trouble.

34 ᵃWhen he slew them, then they sought him: and they returned and ¹enquired early after God.

35 And they remembered that ᵃGod *was* their rock, and the high God ᵇtheir redeemer.

36 Nevertheless they did ᵃflatter him with their mouth, and they lied unto him with their tongues.

37 For their heart was not ¹right with him, neither were they ²stedfast in his covenant.

38 ᵃBut he, *being* full of ᵇcompassion, forgave *their* iniquity, and destroyed *them* not: yea, many a time ᶜturned he his anger away, and ᵈdid not stir up all his wrath.

39 For ᵃhe remembered ᵇthat they *were but* flesh; ᶜa wind that passeth away, and cometh not again.

40 How oft did they ᵃprovoke¹ him in the wilderness, *and* grieve him in the desert!

41 Yea, ᵃthey turned back and tempted God, and limited the Holy One of Israel.

42 They remembered not ¹his hand, *nor* the day when he delivered them from the enemy.

43 How he had wrought his signs in Egypt, and his wonders in the field of Zoan:

44 ᵃAnd had turned their rivers into blood; and their ¹floods, that they could not drink.

45 ᵃHe sent divers sorts of flies among them, which devoured them; and ᵇfrogs, which destroyed them.

46 He gave also their ¹increase unto the caterpiller, and their labour unto the ᵃlocust.

47 ᵃHe destroyed their vines with hail, and their sycomore trees with frost.

48 He gave up their ᵃcattle also to the hail, and their flocks to ¹hot thunderbolts.

49 He cast upon them the fierceness of his anger, wrath, and indignation, and trouble, by sending evil angels *among them.*

50 He ¹made a way to his anger; he spared not their soul from death, but gave their ²life over to the ³pestilence;

51 And smote all the ᵃfirstborn in Egypt; ¹the chief of *their* strength in the tabernacles of Ham:

52 But ᵃmade his own people to go forth like sheep, and guided them in the wilderness like a flock.

53 And he ᵃled them on safely, so that they feared not: but the sea ᵇoverwhelmed their enemies.

54 And he brought them to the border of his ᵃsanctuary, *even to* this mountain, ᵇ*which* his right hand had purchased.

55 ᵃHe cast out the heathen also before them, and ᵇdivided them an inheritance by ¹line, and made the tribes of Israel to dwell in their tents.

56 ᵃYet they tempted and provoked the most high God, and kept not his testimonies:

---

78:14 ᵃ Ex. 13:21
78:15 ᵃ Num. 20:11 ¹ *split*
78:16 ᵃ Num. 20:8, 10, 11
78:17 ᵃ Heb. 3:16 ¹ *by rebelling against*
78:18 ᵃ Ex. 16:2 ¹ *tested* ² *for food according to their desires*
78:19 ᵃ Num. 11:4; 20:3; 21:5 ¹ *prepare*
78:20 ᵃ Num. 20:11
78:21 ᵃ Num. 11:1 ¹ *furious*
78:22 ᵃ [Heb. 3:18]
78:23 ᵃ [Mal. 3:10]
78:24 ᵃ Ex. 16:4 ᵇ John 6:31 ¹ *bread,* lit. *grain*
78:25 ¹ *food to satiation*
78:26 ᵃ Num. 11:31
78:28 ¹ *dwellings*
78:29 ᵃ Num. 11:19, 20
78:30 ᵃ Num. 11:33 ¹ *deprived* ² *craving*
78:31 ¹ *stoutest* ² *choice*
78:32 ᵃ Num. 14:16, 17 ᵇ Num. 14:11
78:33 ᵃ Num. 14:29, 35 ¹ *futility* ² *sudden terror*
78:34 ᵃ [Hos. 5:15] ¹ *sought diligently*
78:35 ᵃ [Deut. 32:4, 15] ᵇ Is. 41:14; 44:6; 63:9
78:36 ᵃ Ezek. 33:31
78:37 ¹ *steadfast* ² *faithful*
78:38 ᵃ [Num. 14:18–20] ᵇ Ex. 34:6 ᶜ [Is. 48:9] ᵈ 1 Kin. 21:29
78:39 ᵃ Job 10:9 ᵇ John 3:6 ᶜ [Job 7:7, 16]
78:40 ᵃ Heb. 3:16 ¹ *rebel against*
78:41 ᵃ Num. 14:22
78:42 ¹ *His delivering power*
78:44 ᵃ Ex. 7:20 ¹ *streams*
78:45 ᵃ Ex. 8:24 ᵇ Ex. 8:6
78:46 ¹ *crops* ᵃ Ex. 10:14
78:47 ᵃ Ex. 9:23–25
78:48 ᵃ Ex. 9:19 ¹ *fiery bolts of lightning*
78:50 ¹ *levelled a path for* ² Or *beasts* ³ *plague*
78:51 ᵃ Ex. 12:29, 30

¹ *the first of* 78:52 ᵃ Ps. 77:20   78:53 ᵃ Ex. 14:19, 20 ᵇ Ex. 14:27, 28   78:54 ᵃ Ex. 15:17 ᵇ Ps. 44:3   78:55 ᵃ Ps. 44:2 ᵇ Josh. 13:7; 19:51; 23:4 ¹ Surveyed measurement, lit. *measuring cord*   78:56 ᵃ Judg. 2:11–13

57 But ᵃturned back, and dealt unfaithfully like their fathers: they were turned aside ᵇlike a deceitful bow.

58 ᵃFor they provoked him to anger with their ᵇhigh places, and moved him to jealousy with their graven images.

59 When God heard *this,* he was ¹wroth, and greatly abhorred Israel:

60 ᵃSo that he forsook the tabernacle of Shiloh, the tent *which* he placed among men;

61 ᵃAnd delivered his strength into captivity, and his glory into the enemy's hand.

62 ᵃHe gave his people over also unto the sword; and was ¹wroth with his inheritance.

63 The fire consumed their young men; and ᵃtheir maidens were not given to marriage.

64 ᵃTheir priests fell by the sword; and ᵇtheir widows made no lamentation.

65 Then the Lord awaked as one out of sleep, *and* ᵃlike a mighty man that shouteth by reason of wine.

66 And ᵃhe smote his enemies in the hinder parts: he put them to a perpetual reproach.

67 Moreover he refused the tabernacle of Joseph, and chose not the tribe of Ephraim:

68 But chose the tribe of Judah, the mount Zion ᵃwhich he loved.

69 And he built his ᵃsanctuary like high *palaces,* like the earth which he hath established for ever.

70 ᵃHe chose David also his servant, and took him from the sheepfolds:

71 From following ᵃthe ewes great with young he brought him ᵇto feed Jacob his people, and Israel his inheritance.

72 So he fed them according to the ᵃintegrity of his heart; and guided them by the skilfulness of his hands.

### PSALM 79

#### A Psalm of Asaph.

O GOD, the ¹heathen are come into ᵃthine inheritance; thy holy temple have they defiled; ᵇthey have laid Jerusalem ²on heaps.

2 ᵃThe dead bodies of thy servants have they given *to be* ¹meat unto the fowls of the heaven, the flesh of thy saints unto the beasts of the earth.

3 Their blood have they shed like water round about Jerusalem; and *there was* none to bury *them.*

4 We are become a reproach to our ᵃneighbours, a scorn and derision to them that are round about us.

5 ᵃHow long, LORD? wilt thou be angry for ever? shall thy ᵇjealousy burn like fire?

6 ᵃPour out thy wrath upon the ¹heathen that have ᵇnot known thee, and upon the kingdoms that have ᶜnot called upon thy name.

7 For they have devoured Jacob, and laid waste his dwelling place.

8 ᵃO remember not against us ¹former iniquities: let thy tender mercies speedily ²prevent us: for we are brought very low.

9 Help us, O God of our salvation, for the glory of thy name: and deliver us, and ¹purge away our sins, ᵃfor thy name's sake.

10 ᵃWherefore should the ¹heathen say, Where *is* their God? let him be known among the heathen in our sight *by* the ²revenging of the blood of thy servants *which is* shed.

11 Let ᵃthe ¹sighing of the prisoner come before thee; according to the greatness of ²thy power preserve thou those that are appointed to die;

12 And ¹render unto our neighbours ᵃsevenfold into their bosom ᵇtheir reproach, wherewith they have reproached thee, O Lord.

13 So ᵃwe thy people and sheep of thy pasture will give thee thanks for ever: ᵇwe will shew forth thy praise to all generations.

### PSALM 80

#### To the chief Musician ᵃupon¹ Shoshannim-²Eduth, A Psalm of Asaph.

G IVE ear, O Shepherd of Israel, ᵃthou that leadest Joseph ᵇlike a flock; thou that dwellest *between* the cherubims, ᶜshine forth.

2 Before ᵃEphraim and Benjamin and Manasseh stir up thy strength, and come *and* save us.

3 ᵃTurn¹ us again, O God, ᵇand cause thy face to shine; and we shall be saved.

4 O LORD God of hosts, ᵃhow long wilt thou be angry against the prayer of thy people?

5 ᵃThou feedest them with the bread of tears; and givest them tears to drink in great measure.

6 Thou makest us a strife unto our neighbours: and our enemies laugh among themselves.

7 ¹Turn us again, O God of hosts, and cause thy face to shine; and we shall be saved.

8 Thou hast brought ᵃa vine out of Egypt: ᵇthou hast cast out the ¹heathen, and planted it.

9 Thou preparedst *room* before it, and didst cause it to take deep root, and it filled the land.

10 The hills were covered with the shadow of it, and the ᵃboughs thereof *were like* ¹the goodly cedars.

11 She sent out her boughs unto ¹the sea, and her branches unto ²the river.

78:57 ᵃ Ezek. 20:27, 28 ᵇ Hos. 7:16
78:58 ᵃ Judg. 2:12 ᵇ Deut. 12:2
78:59 ¹ furious
78:60 ᵃ 1 Sam. 4:11
78:61 ᵃ Judg. 18:30
78:62 ᵃ 1 Sam. 4:10 ¹ furious
78:63 ᵃ Jer. 7:34; 16:9; 25:10
78:64 ᵃ 1 Sam. 4:17; 22:18 ᵇ Job 27:15; Ezek. 24:23
78:65 ᵃ Is. 42:13
78:66 ᵃ 1 Sam. 5:6
78:68 ᵃ [Ps. 87:2]
78:69 ᵃ 1 Kin. 6:1–38
78:70 ᵃ 1 Sam. 16:11, 12
78:71 ᵃ [Is. 40:11] ᵇ 2 Sam. 5:2
78:72 ᵃ 1 Kin. 9:4
79:1 ᵃ Ps. 74:2 ᵇ Mic. 3:12 ¹ nations or Gentiles ² in ruins
79:2 ᵃ Jer. 7:33; 19:7; 34:20 ¹ food
79:4 ᵃ Ps. 44:13
79:5 ᵃ Ps. 74:1, 9 ᵇ [Zeph. 3:8]
79:6 ᵃ Jer. 10:25 ᵇ Is. 45:4, 5 ᶜ Ps. 53:4 ¹ nations or Gentiles
79:8 ᵃ Is. 64:9 ¹ Or the iniquities of them that were before us ² meet
79:9 ᵃ Jer. 14:7, 21 ¹ provide atonement for
79:10 ᵃ Ps. 42:10 ¹ nations or Gentiles ² avenging
79:11 ᵃ Ps. 102:20 ¹ groaning ² Lit. thy arm
79:12 ᵃ Gen. 4:15 ᵇ Ps. 74:10, 18, 22 ¹ return
79:13 ᵃ Ps. 74:1; 95:7 ᵇ Is. 43:21
80:title ᵃ Ps. 45:title ¹ Set to "The Lilies" ² a testimony of Asaph, a Psalm
80:1 ᵃ [Ex. 25:20–22] ᵇ Ps. 77:20 ᶜ Deut. 33:2
80:2 ᵃ Ps. 78:9, 67
80:3 ᵃ Lam. 5:21 ¹ Restore us
80:4 ᵃ Ps. 79:5
80:5 ᵃ Is. 30:20
80:7 ¹ Restore us
80:8 ᵃ [Is. 5:1, 7] ᵇ Ps. 44:2 ¹ nations or Gentiles
80:10 ᵃ Lev. 23:40 ¹ Lit. cedars of God
80:11 ¹ The Mediterranean ² The Euphrates

12 Why hast thou *then* ᵃbroken down her ¹hedges, so that all they which pass by the way do pluck ²her?

13 The boar out of the wood doth waste it, and the wild beast of the field doth devour it.

14 Return, we beseech thee, O God of hosts: ᵃlook down from heaven, and behold, and visit this vine;

15 And the vineyard which thy right hand hath planted, and the branch *that* thou madest strong ᵃfor thyself.

16 *It is* burned with fire, *it is* cut down: ᵃthey perish at the rebuke of thy ¹countenance.

17 ᵃLet thy hand be upon the man of thy right hand, upon the son of man *whom* thou madest strong for thyself.

18 So will not we go back from thee: ¹quicken us, and we will call upon thy name.

19 ¹Turn us again, O LORD God of hosts, cause thy face to shine; and we shall be saved.

## PSALM 81

### To the chief Musician ᵃupon¹ Gittith, *A Psalm* of Asaph.

Sing aloud unto God our strength: make a joyful ¹noise unto the God of Jacob.

2 ¹Take a psalm, and ²bring hither the timbrel, the pleasant harp with the ³psaltery.

3 Blow up the trumpet ¹in the new moon, in the time appointed, on our solemn feast day.

4 For ᵃthis *was* a statute for Israel, *and* a law of the God of Jacob.

5 This he ordained in Joseph *for* a testimony, when he went out through the land of Egypt: ᵃ*where* I heard a language *that* I understood not.

6 I removed his shoulder from the burden: his hands were delivered from the ¹pots.

7 ᵃThou calledst in trouble, and I delivered thee; ᵇI answered thee in the secret place of thunder: I ᶜproved thee at the waters of ¹Meribah.     *Selah.*

8 ᵃHear, O my people, and I will ¹testify unto thee: O Israel, if thou wilt ²hearken unto me;

9 There shall no ᵃstrange¹ god be in thee; neither shalt thou worship any strange god.

10 ᵃI *am* the LORD thy God, which brought thee out of the land of Egypt: ᵇopen thy mouth wide, and I will fill it.

11 But my people would not ¹hearken to my voice; and Israel ²would ᵃnone of me.

12 ᵃSo I gave them up unto their own hearts' ¹lust: *and* they walked in their own counsels.

13 ᵃOh that my people had hearkened unto me, *and* Israel had walked in my ways!

14 I should soon have subdued their enemies, and turned my hand against their adversaries.

15 ᵃThe haters of the LORD ¹should have submitted themselves unto him: but their ²time should have endured for ever.

16 He should ᵃhave fed them also with the finest of the wheat: and with honey ᵇout of the rock should I have satisfied thee.

## PSALM 82

### A Psalm of Asaph.

God ᵃstandeth¹ in the congregation of the ²mighty; he judgeth among ᵇthe ³gods.

2 How long will ye judge unjustly, and ᵃaccept¹ the persons of the wicked?     *Selah.*

3 ¹Defend the poor and fatherless: do justice to the afflicted and ᵃneedy.

4 Deliver the poor and needy: ¹rid *them* out of the hand of the wicked.

5 They know not, neither will they understand; they walk on in darkness: all the ᵃfoundations of the earth are ¹out of course.

6 I have said, ᵃYe *are* ¹gods; and all of you *are* children of the most High.

7 But ye shall die like men, and fall like one of the princes.

8 Arise, O God, judge the earth: ᵃfor thou shalt inherit all nations.

## PSALM 83

### A Song *or* Psalm of Asaph.

Keep ᵃnot thou silence, O God: hold not thy peace, and be not still, O God.

2 For, lo, ᵃthine enemies make a ¹tumult: and they that hate thee have ²lifted up the head.

3 They have taken crafty counsel against thy people, and consulted ᵃagainst thy ¹hidden ones.

4 They have said, Come, and ᵃlet us cut them off from *being* a nation; that the name of Israel may be no more in remembrance.

5 For they have consulted together with one ¹consent: they are confederate against thee:

6 ᵃThe ¹tabernacles of Edom, and the Ishmaelites; of Moab, and the ²Hagarenes;

7 Gebal, and Ammon, and Amalek; the Philistines with the inhabitants of Tyre;

8 Assur also is joined with them: they have holpen the children of Lot.     *Selah.*

---

80:12 ᵃ Is. 5:5
¹ walls or fences
² her fruit

80:14 ᵃ Is. 63:15

80:15 ᵃ [Is. 49:5]

80:16 ᵃ [Ps. 39:11]
¹ presence

80:17 ᵃ Ps. 89:21

80:18 ¹ revive

80:19 ¹ Restore

81:title ᵃ Ps.
8:title ¹ On an instrument of Gath

81:1 ¹ shout

81:2 ¹ Raise a song ² strike
³ lute or lyre

81:3 ¹ at the time of the new moon

81:4 ᵃ Num. 10:10

81:5 ᵃ Ps. 114:1

81:6 ¹ baskets

81:7 ᵃ Ex. 2:23; 14:10 ᵇ Ex. 19:19; 20:18 ᶜ Ex. 17:6, 7 ¹ Lit. Strife or Contention

81:8 ᵃ [Ps. 50:7]
¹ admonish
² listen

81:9 ᵃ [Is. 43:12]
¹ foreign

81:10 ᵃ Ex. 20:2
ᵇ Ps. 103:5

81:11 ᵃ Deut. 32:15
¹ heed ² would have

81:12 ᵃ [Acts 7:42]
¹ stubbornness

81:13 ᵃ [Is. 48:18]

81:15 ᵃ Rom. 1:30
¹ would pretend submission to him
² fate would

81:16 ᵃ Deut. 32:14
ᵇ Job 29:6

82:1 ᵃ [2 Chr. 19:6] ᵇ Ps. 82:6
¹ takes his stand
² Heb. El, lit. God
³ mighty ones or judges, Heb. Elohim, lit. God

82:2 ᵃ [Deut. 1:17]
¹ show partiality to

82:3 ᵃ [Deut. 24:17] ¹ Vindicate

82:4 ¹ free

82:5 ᵃ Ps. 11:3
¹ unstable

82:6 ᵃ John 10:34
¹ mighty ones or judges, Heb. Elohim, lit. God

82:8 ᵃ [Rev. 11:15]

83:1 ᵃ Ps. 28:1

83:2 ᵃ Ps. 81:15
¹ uproar ² Exalted themselves

83:3 ᵃ [Ps. 27:5]
¹ sheltered ones

83:4 ᵃ Jer. 11:19; 31:36

83:5 ¹ Lit. heart   83:6 ᵃ 2 Chr. 20:1, 10, 11 ¹ tents ² Hagrites

9 Do unto them as *unto* the [a]Midianites; as *to* [b]Sisera, as *to* Jabin, at the brook of Kison:

10 *Which* perished at En-dor: [a]they became *as* [1]dung for the earth.

11 Make their nobles like Oreb, and like [a]Zeeb: yea, all their princes as [b]Zebah, and as Zalmunna:

12 Who said, Let us take to ourselves the [1]houses of God in possession.

13 [a]O my God, make them like [1]a wheel; [b]as the stubble before the wind.

14 As the fire burneth a wood, and as the flame [a]setteth the mountains on fire;

15 So [1]persecute them with thy tempest, and make them afraid with thy storm.

16 Fill their faces with shame; that they may seek thy name, O LORD.

17 Let them be [1]confounded and troubled for ever; yea, let them be put to shame, and perish:

18 [a]That *men* may know that thou, whose [b]name alone *is* [1]JEHOVAH, *art* [c]the most high over all the earth.

## PSALM 84

To the chief Musician [a]upon[1] Gittith, A Psalm for the [2]sons of Korah.

Ow [a]amiable[1] are *thy* tabernacles, O LORD of hosts!

2 [a]My soul longeth, yea, even fainteth for the courts of the LORD: my heart and my flesh crieth out for the living God.

3 Yea, the sparrow hath found an house, and the swallow a nest for herself, where she may lay her young, *even* thine altars, O LORD of hosts, my King, and my God.

4 Blessed *are* they that dwell in thy [a]house: they will be still praising thee. *Selah.*

5 Blessed *is* the man whose strength *is* in thee; in whose heart *are* the ways *of them.*

6 *Who* passing through the valley [a]of [1]Baca make it a [2]well; the rain also [3]filleth the pools.

7 They go [a]from strength to strength, *every one of them* [1]in Zion [b]appeareth before God.

8 O LORD God of hosts, hear my prayer: give ear, O God of Jacob. *Selah.*

9 Behold, [a]O God our shield, and look upon the face of thine [1]anointed.

10 For a day in thy courts *is* better than a thousand. I had rather [1]be a doorkeeper in the house of my God, than to dwell in the tents of wickedness.

11 For the LORD God *is* [a]a sun and [b]shield: the LORD will give grace and glory: [c]no good *thing* will he withhold from them that walk uprightly.

83:9 [a] Judg. 7:22
[b] Judg. 4:15–24; 5:20, 21
83:10 [a] Zeph. 1:17
[1] refuse on
83:11 [a] Judg. 7:25
[b] Judg. 8:12–21
83:12 [1] pastures
83:13 [a] Is. 17:13
[b] Ps. 35:5 [1] the whirling dust
83:14 [a] Deut. 32:22
83:15 [1] pursue
83:17 [1] ashamed and dismayed
83:18 [a] Ps. 59:13
[b] Ex. 6:3 [c] [Ps. 92:8] [1] Lit. LORD
84:title [a] Ps. 8:title [1] On an instrument of Gath [2] of
84:1 [a] Ps. 27:4; 46:1, 5 [1] lovely are your dwellings
84:2 [a] Ps. 42:1, 2
84:4 [a] [Ps. 65:4]
84:6 [a] 2 Sam. 5:22–25 [1] Lit. Weeping [2] spring [3] Or covers it with blessings
84:7 [a] Prov. 4:18
[b] Deut. 16:16 [1] appears before God in Zion
84:9 [a] Gen. 15:1 [1] Messiah, commissioned one
84:10 [1] Lit. stand at the threshold in
84:11 [a] Is. 60:19, 20 [b] Gen. 15:1 [c] Ps. 34:9, 10
84:12 [a] [Ps. 2:12; 40:4]
85:title [a] Ps. 42:title [1] of
85:1 [a] Joel 3:1 [1] shown favour
85:4 [a] Ps. 80:3, 7 [1] Restore
85:5 [a] Ps. 79:5 [1] prolong
85:6 [a] Hab. 3:2
85:8 [1] foolishness
85:9 [a] Is. 46:13
[b] Hag. 2:7; Zech. 2:5; [John 1:14]
85:10 [a] Ps. 72:3; [Is. 32:17]; Luke 2:14
85:12 [a] [Ps. 84:11; James 1:17]
85:13 [1] make his footsteps into a way
86:2 [1] life
86:3 [1] all day long
86:4 [a] Ps. 25:1; 143:8 [1] Make glad

12 O LORD of hosts, [a]blessed *is* the man that trusteth in thee.

## PSALM 85

To the chief Musician,
A Psalm [a]for[1] the sons of Korah.

ORD, thou hast [1]been favourable unto thy land: thou hast [a]brought back the captivity of Jacob.

2 Thou hast forgiven the iniquity of thy people, thou hast covered all their sin. *Selah.*

3 Thou hast taken away all thy wrath: thou hast turned *thyself* from the fierceness of thine anger.

4 [a]Turn[1] us, O God of our salvation, and cause thine anger toward us to cease.

5 [a]Wilt thou be angry with us for ever? wilt thou [1]draw out thine anger to all generations?

6 Wilt thou not [a]revive us again: that thy people may rejoice in thee?

7 Shew us thy mercy, O LORD, and grant us thy salvation.

8 I will hear what God the LORD will speak: for he will speak peace unto his people, and to his saints: but let them not turn again to [1]folly.

9 Surely [a]his salvation *is* nigh them that fear him; [b]that glory may dwell in our land.

10 Mercy and truth are met together; [a]righteousness and peace have kissed *each other.*

11 Truth shall spring out of the earth; and righteousness shall look down from heaven.

12 [a]Yea, the LORD shall give *that which is* good; and our land shall yield her increase.

13 Righteousness shall go before him; and shall [1]set *us* in the way of his steps.

## PSALM 86

A Prayer of David.

OW down thine ear, O LORD, hear me: for I *am* poor and needy.

2 Preserve my [1]soul; for I *am* holy: O thou my God, save thy servant that trusteth in thee.

3 Be merciful unto me, O Lord: for I cry unto thee [1]daily.

4 [1]Rejoice the soul of thy servant: [a]for unto thee, O Lord, do I lift up my soul.

5 For [a]thou, Lord, *art* good, and ready to forgive; and plenteous in mercy unto all them that call upon thee.

6 Give ear, O LORD, unto my prayer; and attend to the voice of my supplications.

7 In the day of my trouble I will call upon thee: for thou wilt answer me.

86:5 [a] Ps. 130:7; 145:9; [Joel 2:13]

8 [a]Among the gods *there is* none
like unto thee, O Lord; neither *are*
*there any works* like unto thy works.
9 All nations whom thou hast made
shall come and worship before thee,
O Lord; and shall glorify thy name.
10 For thou *art* great, and [a]doest
wondrous things: [b]thou *art* God alone.
11 [a]Teach me thy way, O LORD; I
will walk in thy truth: [1]unite my heart
to [2]fear thy name.
12 I will praise thee, O Lord my
God, with all my heart: and I will glorify thy name for evermore.
13 For great *is* thy mercy toward
me: and thou hast delivered my soul
from the [1]lowest [2]hell.
14 O God, the proud are risen
against me, and [1]the assemblies of violent *men* have sought after my soul;
and have not set thee before them.
15 But [a]thou, O Lord, *art* a God full
of compassion, and gracious, longsuffering, and plenteous in mercy
and truth.
16 O turn unto me, and have mercy
upon me; give thy strength unto thy
servant, and save the son of thine
handmaid.
17 Shew me [1]a token for good; that
they which hate me may see *it*, and
be ashamed: because thou, LORD,
hast holpen me, and comforted me.

## PSALM 87

A Psalm *or* Song [1]for the sons of Korah.

HIS foundation *is* in the holy
mountains.
2 [a]The LORD loveth the gates of
Zion more than all the dwellings of
Jacob.
3 [a]Glorious things are spoken of
thee, O city of God. *Selah.*
4 I will make mention of [1]Rahab
and Babylon to them that know me:
behold Philistia, and Tyre, with Ethiopia; this *man* was born there.
5 And of Zion it shall be said, This
and that man was born in her: and
the highest himself shall establish
her.
6 The LORD shall count, when he
[a]writeth[1] up the people, *that* this
*man* was born there. *Selah.*
7 [1]As well the singers as the players
on instruments *shall be there:* all my
springs *are* in thee.

## PSALM 88

A Song *or* Psalm [1]for the sons of
Korah, to the chief Musician [2]upon
Mahalath Leannoth, [3]Maschil
of [a]Heman the Ezrahite.

O LORD [a]God of my salvation, I
have [1]cried day *and* night before
thee:
2 Let my prayer come before thee:
[1]incline thine ear unto my cry;

86:8 [a] [Ex. 15:11]; 2 Sam. 7:22; 1 Kin. 8:23; Ps. 89:6; Jer. 10:6
86:10 [a] [Ex. 15:11] [b] Deut. 6:4; Is. 37:16; Mark 12:29; 1 Cor. 8:4
86:11 [a] Ps. 27:11; 143:8 [1] Give me singleness of heart [2] Have reverential awe for
86:13 [1] *depths of* [2] Or *Sheol*
86:14 [1] *mobs*
86:15 [a] Ex. 34:6; [Ps. 86:5]
86:17 [1] *a sign*
87:title [1] *of*
87:2 [a] Ps. 78:67, 68
87:3 [a] Is. 60:1
87:4 [1] Egypt
87:6 [a] Is. 4:3 [1] *registers*
87:7 [1] *Both the singers and the players*
88:title [a] 1 Kin. 4:31; 1 Chr. 2:6 [1] *of* [2] *Set to* [3] *Contemplation*
88:1 [a] Ps. 27:9; [Luke 18:7] [1] *cried out*
88:2 [1] Listen to
88:3 [a] Ps. 107:18 [1] *near* [2] Or *Sheol*
88:4 [a] [Ps. 28:1] [b] Ps. 31:12 [1] Are dying
88:5 [1] *Adrift*
88:7 [a] Ps. 42:7 [1] *heavy*
88:8 [a] Job 19:13, 19 [b] Lam. 3:7 [1] *taken away my friends*
88:9 [a] Ps. 86:3 [1] *wastes away*
88:10 [1] *work wonders for* [2] Spirits of the dead
88:13 [1] *come before*
88:15 [1] *distraught*
88:16 [1] *destroyed me*
88:17 [1] *all day long* [2] *engulfed me altogether*
88:18 [a] Ps. 31:11; 38:11 [1] *Loved one*
89:title [a] 1 Kin. 4:31 [1] *Contemplation*
89:2 [a] [Ps. 119:89, 90] [1] *Lovingkindness*
89:3 [a] 1 Kin. 8:16 [b] 2 Sam. 7:11
89:4 [a] [Luke 1:33]
89:5 [a] [Ps. 19:1]

3 For my soul is full of troubles: and
my life [a]draweth [1]nigh unto the [2]grave.
4 I am counted with them that [a]go[1]
down into the pit: [b]I am as a man
*that hath* no strength:
5 [1]Free among the dead, like the
slain that lie in the grave, whom thou
rememberest no more: and they are
cut off from thy hand.
6 Thou hast laid me in the lowest
pit, in darkness, in the deeps.
7 Thy wrath lieth [1]hard upon me,
and thou hast afflicted *me* with all
[a]thy waves. *Selah.*
8 [a]Thou hast [1]put away mine acquaintance far from me; thou hast
made me an abomination unto
them: [b]*I am* shut up, and I cannot
come forth.
9 Mine eye [1]mourneth by reason of
affliction: [a]LORD, I have called daily
upon thee, I have stretched out my
hands unto thee.
10 Wilt thou [1]shew wonders to the
dead? shall the [2]dead arise *and* praise
thee? *Selah.*
11 Shall thy lovingkindness be declared in the grave? *or* thy faithfulness in destruction?
12 Shall thy wonders be known in
the dark? and thy righteousness in
the land of forgetfulness?
13 But unto thee have I cried,
O LORD; and in the morning shall my
prayer [1]prevent thee.
14 LORD, why castest thou off
my soul? *why* hidest thou thy face
from me?
15 I *am* afflicted and ready to die
from *my* youth up: *while* I suffer thy
terrors I am [1]distracted.
16 Thy fierce wrath goeth over me;
thy terrors have [1]cut me off.
17 They came round about me
[1]daily like water; they [2]compassed
me about together.
18 [a]Lover[1] and friend hast thou put
far from me, *and* mine acquaintance
into darkness.

## PSALM 89

[1]Maschil of [a]Ethan the Ezrahite.

I WILL sing of the mercies of the
LORD for ever: with my mouth will
I make known thy faithfulness to all
generations.
2 For I have said, [1]Mercy shall be
built up for ever: [a]thy faithfulness
shalt thou establish in the very heavens.
3 [a]I have made a covenant with my
chosen, I have [b]sworn unto David my
servant,
4 Thy seed will I establish for ever,
and build up thy throne [a]to all generations. *Selah.*
5 And [a]the heavens shall praise thy
wonders, O LORD: thy faithfulness
also in the congregation of the saints.

6 [a]For who in the heaven can be compared unto the LORD? *who* among the sons of the mighty can be likened unto the LORD?

7 [a]God is greatly to be feared in the assembly of the saints, and to be [1]had in reverence of all *them that are* about him.

8 O LORD God of hosts, who *is* a strong LORD like unto thee? or to thy faithfulness round about thee?

9 [a]Thou rulest the raging of the sea: when the waves thereof arise, thou stillest them.

10 [a]Thou hast broken [1]Rahab in pieces, as one that is slain; thou hast scattered thine enemies with thy strong arm.

11 [a]The heavens *are* thine, the earth also *is* thine: *as for* the world and the fulness thereof, thou hast founded them.

12 The north and the south thou hast created them: [a]Tabor and [b]Hermon shall rejoice in thy name.

13 Thou hast a mighty arm: strong is thy hand, *and* high is thy right hand.

14 [1]Justice and judgment *are* the [2]habitation of thy throne: [3]mercy and truth shall go before thy face.

15 Blessed *is* the people that know the [a]joyful sound: they shall walk, O LORD, in the light of thy countenance.

16 In thy name shall they rejoice all the day: and in thy righteousness shall they be exalted.

17 For thou *art* the glory of their strength: and in thy favour [1]our horn shall be [a]exalted.

18 For [1]the LORD *is* our defence; and the Holy One of Israel *is* our king.

19 Then thou spakest in vision to thy [1]holy one, and saidst, I have [2]laid help upon *one that is* mighty; I have exalted *one* [a]chosen out of the people.

20 [a]I have found David my servant; with my holy oil have I anointed him:

21 [a]With whom my hand shall be established: mine arm also shall strengthen him.

22 The enemy shall not [1]exact upon him; nor the son of wickedness afflict him.

23 And I will beat down his foes before his face, and plague them that hate him.

24 But my faithfulness and my [1]mercy *shall be* with him: and in my name shall his horn be exalted.

25 I will [a]set his hand also in the sea, and his right hand in the rivers.

26 He shall cry unto me, Thou *art* [a]my father, my God, and [b]the rock of my salvation.

27 Also I will make him [a]*my* firstborn, [b]higher than the kings of the earth.

28 [a]My mercy will I keep for him for evermore, and my covenant shall stand fast with him.

29 His seed also will I make *to endure* for ever, [a]and his throne [b]as the days of heaven.

30 [a]If his children [b]forsake my law, and walk not in my judgments;

31 If they [1]break my statutes, and [2]keep not my commandments;

32 Then will I [1]visit their transgression with the rod, and their iniquity with stripes.

33 [a]Nevertheless my lovingkindness will I not [1]utterly take from him, nor suffer my faithfulness [2]to fail.

34 My covenant will I not break, nor [a]alter[1] the thing that is gone out of my lips.

35 Once have I sworn [a]by my holiness that I will not lie unto David.

36 [a]His seed shall endure for ever, and his throne [b]as the sun before me.

37 It shall be established for ever as the moon, and *as* a faithful witness in [1]heaven. *Selah.*

38 But thou hast [a]cast off and [b]abhorred,[1] thou hast been [2]wroth with thine [3]anointed.

39 Thou hast [1]made void the covenant of thy servant: [a]thou hast [2]profaned his crown *by casting it* to the ground.

40 Thou hast broken down all his hedges; thou hast brought his [1]strong holds to ruin.

41 All that pass by the way [a]spoil[1] him: he is a reproach to his neighbours.

42 Thou [1]hast set up the right hand of his adversaries; thou hast made all his enemies to rejoice.

43 Thou hast also turned the edge of his sword, and hast not [1]made him to stand in the battle.

44 Thou hast made his [1]glory to cease, and cast his throne down to the ground.

45 The days of his youth hast thou shortened: thou hast covered him with shame. *Selah.*

46 How long, LORD? wilt thou hide thyself for ever? shall thy wrath burn like fire?

47 Remember how short my time [a]is: [1]wherefore hast thou made all men in [b]vain?

48 What man *is he that* liveth, and shall not [1]see [a]death? shall he deliver his soul from the [2]hand of [3]the grave? *Selah.*

49 Lord, where *are* thy former lovingkindnesses, *which* thou [a]swarest unto David [b]in thy truth?

---

89:6 [a] Ps. 86:8; 113:5

89:7 [a] Ps. 76:7, 11 [1] held

89:9 [a] Ps. 65:7; 93:3, 4; 107:29

89:10 [a] Ps. 87:4 [1] Egypt

89:11 [a] [Gen. 1:1]

89:12 [a] Josh. 19:22 [b] Josh. 11:17; 12:1

89:14 [1] *Righteousness and justice* [2] foundation [3] lovingkindness

89:15 [a] Ps. 98:6

89:17 [a] Ps. 75:10; 92:10; 132:17 [1] Our strength

89:18 [1] Or *our shield belongs to the LORD*

89:19 [a] 1 Kin. 11:34 [1] MT, LXX, Vg. *holy ones;* many Heb. mss. *holy one* [2] *given help to*

89:20 [a] 1 Sam. 13:14; 16:1–12

89:21 [a] Ps. 80:17

89:22 [1] *outwit* or *deceive*

89:24 [1] *lovingkindness*

89:25 [a] Ps. 72:8

89:26 [a] [1 Chr. 22:10] [b] 2 Sam. 22:47

89:27 [a] [Col. 1:15, 18] [b] Rev. 19:16

89:28 [a] Is. 55:3

89:29 [a] Jer. 33:17 [b] Deut. 11:21

89:30 [a] [2 Sam. 7:14] [b] Ps. 119:53

89:31 [1] *profane* [2] *obey*

89:32 [1] *attend to*

89:33 [a] 2 Sam. 7:14, 15 [1] Lit. *break off* [2] *to be false*

89:34 [a] Jer. 33:20–22 [1] *change the word*

89:35 [a] Amos 4:2

89:36 [a] [Luke 1:33] [b] Ps. 72:17

89:37 [1] *the sky*

89:38 [a] [1 Chr. 28:9] [b] Deut. 32:19 [1] *rejected* [2] *furious* [3] *Messiah,* commissioned one

89:39 [a] Lam. 5:16 [1] *renounced* [2] *defiled*

89:40 [1] *fortresses*

89:41 [a] Ps. 80:12 [1] *plunder*

89:42 [1] *hast exalted*

89:43 [1] *sustained him* 89:44 [1] *splendour* or *brightness* 89:47 [a] Ps. 90:9 [b] Ps. 62:9 [1] *for what futility hast thou made all men?* 89:48 [a] [Eccl. 3:19] [1] *experience death* [2] *power of* [3] Or *Sheol* 89:49 [a] [2 Sam. 7:15] [b] Ps. 54:5

50 Remember, Lord, the reproach of thy servants; [a]*how* I do bear in my bosom *the reproach of* all the mighty people;

51 [a]Wherewith thine enemies have reproached, O LORD; wherewith they have reproached the footsteps of thine [1]anointed.

52 [a]Blessed *be* the LORD for evermore. Amen, and Amen.

# BOOK IV: Psalms 90–106

## PSALM 90

A Prayer [a]of Moses the man of God.

LORD, [a]thou hast been our [1]dwelling place in all generations.

2 [a]Before the mountains were brought forth, or ever thou [1]hadst formed the earth and the world, even from everlasting to everlasting, thou *art* God.

3 Thou turnest man to destruction; and sayest, [a]Return, ye children of men.

4 [a]For a thousand years in thy sight *are but* as yesterday when it is past, and *as* a watch in the night.

5 Thou carriest them away as with a flood; [a]they are *as* a sleep: in the morning [b]*they are* like grass *which* groweth up.

6 In the morning it flourisheth, and groweth up; in the evening it is cut down, and withereth.

7 For we are consumed by thine anger, and by thy wrath are we [1]troubled.

8 [a]Thou hast set our iniquities before thee, our [b]secret *sins* in the light of thy countenance.

9 For all our days are passed away in thy wrath: we spend our years as a [1]tale *that is told.*

10 The days of our [1]years *are* threescore years and ten; and if by reason of strength *they be* fourscore years, yet *is* our [2]strength labour and sorrow; for it is soon cut off, and we fly away.

11 Who knoweth the power of thine anger? even according to thy fear, *so is* thy wrath.

12 [a]So teach *us* to number our days, that we may [1]apply *our* hearts unto wisdom.

13 Return, O LORD, how long? and [1]let it [a]repent thee concerning thy servants.

14 O satisfy us early with thy mercy; [a]that we may rejoice and be glad all our days.

15 Make us glad according to the days *wherein* thou hast afflicted us, *and* the years *wherein* we have seen evil.

16 Let [a]thy work appear unto thy servants, and thy glory unto their children.

17 [a]And let the beauty of the LORD our God be upon us: and [b]establish thou the work of our hands upon us; yea, the work of our hands establish thou it.

## PSALM 91

HE [a]that dwelleth in the secret place of the most High shall abide [b]under the shadow of the Almighty.

2 [a]I will say of the LORD, *He is* my refuge and my fortress: my God; in him will I trust.

3 Surely [a]he shall deliver thee from the snare of the [1]fowler, *and* from the [2]noisome pestilence.

4 [a]He shall cover thee with his feathers, and under his wings shalt thou [1]trust: his truth *shall be thy* shield and [2]buckler.

5 [a]Thou shalt not be afraid [1]for the terror by night; *nor* for the arrow *that* flieth by day;

6 *Nor* for the pestilence *that* walketh in darkness; *nor* for the destruction *that* [1]wasteth at noonday.

7 A thousand shall fall at thy side, and ten thousand at thy right hand; *but* it shall not come nigh thee.

8 Only [a]with thine eyes shalt thou behold and see the reward of the wicked.

9 Because thou hast made the LORD, *which is* [a]my refuge, *even* the most High, [b]thy [1]habitation;

10 [a]There shall no evil befall thee, neither shall any plague come nigh thy dwelling.

11 [a]For he shall give his angels charge over thee, to keep thee in all thy ways.

12 They shall [1]bear thee up in *their* hands, [a]lest thou [2]dash thy foot against a stone.

13 Thou shalt tread upon the lion and [1]adder: the young lion and the [2]dragon shalt thou trample under feet.

14 Because he hath set his love upon me, therefore will I deliver him: I will set him on high, because he hath [a]known my name.

15 He shall [a]call upon me, and I will answer him: I *will be* [b]with him in trouble; I will deliver him, and honour him.

16 With [1]long life will I satisfy him, and shew him my salvation.

## PSALM 92

A Psalm *or* Song for the sabbath day.

IT is a [a]good *thing* to give thanks unto the LORD, and to sing praises unto thy name, O most High:

---

**Center column references:**

89:50 [a] Ps. 69:9, 19
89:51 [a] Ps. 74:10, 18, 22 [1] *Messiah, commissioned one*
89:52 [a] Ps. 41:13
90:title [a] Deut. 33:1
90:1 [a] [Ezek. 11:16] [1] LXX, [Tg.], Vg. *refuge*
90:2 [a] [Prov. 8:25, 26] [1] Lit. *gave birth to*
90:3 [a] Gen. 3:19
90:4 [a] 2 Pet. 3:8
90:5 [a] Ps. 73:20 [b] Is. 40:6
90:7 [1] Lit. *terrified*
90:8 [a] Ps. 50:21 [b] Ps. 19:12
90:9 [1] *sigh.*
90:10 [1] *lives are seventy years* [2] *boast only labour*
90:12 [a] Ps. 39:4 [1] *gain a heart of wisdom*
90:13 [a] Deut. 32:36 [1] *have compassion on*
90:14 [a] Ps. 85:6
90:16 [a] Hab. 3:2
90:17 [a] Ps. 27:4 [b] Is. 26:12
91:1 [a] Ps. 27:5; 31:20; 32:7 [b] Ps. 17:8
91:2 [a] Ps. 142:5
91:3 [a] Ps. 124:7 [1] Trapper of birds [2] *perilous or deadly*
91:4 [a] Ps. 17:8 [1] *take refuge* [2] A *small shield*
91:5 [a] [Job 5:19] [1] *of*
91:6 [1] *lays waste*
91:8 [a] Mal. 1:5
91:9 [a] Ps. 91:2 [b] Ps. 90:1 [1] *dwelling place*
91:10 [a] [Prov. 12:21]
91:11 [a] [Heb. 1:14]
91:12 [a] Matt. 4:6 [1] *lift* [2] *strike*
91:13 [1] *cobra* [2] *serpent*
91:14 [a] [Ps. 9:10]
91:15 [a] Ps. 50:15 [b] Is. 43:2
91:16 [1] Lit. *length of days*
92:1 [a] Ps. 147:1

2 To [a]shew[1] forth thy lovingkindness in the morning, and thy faithfulness every night,

3 [a]Upon an instrument of ten strings, and upon the [1]psaltery; upon the harp with a [2]solemn sound.

4 For thou, LORD, hast made me glad through thy work: I will triumph in the works of thy hands.

5 [a]O LORD, how great are thy works! *and* [b]thy thoughts are very deep.

6 [a]A [1]brutish man knoweth not; neither doth a fool understand this.

7 When [a]the wicked [1]spring as the grass, and when all the workers of iniquity do flourish; *it is* that they shall be destroyed for ever:

8 [a]But thou, LORD, *art most* high for evermore.

9 For, lo, thine enemies, O LORD, for, lo, thine enemies shall perish; all the workers of iniquity shall [d]be scattered.

10 But [a]my[1] horn shalt thou exalt like *the horn of* an [2]unicorn: I shall be [b]anointed with fresh oil.

11 [a]Mine eye also shall see *my desire* on mine enemies, *and* mine ears shall hear *my desire* of the wicked that rise up against me.

12 [a]The righteous shall flourish like the palm tree: he shall grow like a cedar in Lebanon.

13 Those that be planted in the house of the LORD shall flourish in the courts of our God.

14 They shall still bring forth fruit in old age; they shall be [1]fat and [2]flourishing;

15 To shew that the LORD *is* upright: [a]*he is* my rock, and [b]*there is* no unrighteousness in him.

## PSALM 93

T HE [a]LORD reigneth, he is clothed with majesty; the LORD is clothed with strength, [b]*wherewith* he hath girded himself: the world also is stablished, that it cannot be [1]moved.

2 [a]Thy throne *is* established of old: thou *art* from everlasting.

3 The floods have [1]lifted up, O LORD, the floods have lifted up their voice; the floods lift up their waves.

4 [a]The LORD on high *is* mightier than the noise of many waters, *yea, than* the mighty waves of the sea.

5 Thy testimonies are very sure: holiness [1]becometh thine house, O LORD, for ever.

## PSALM 94

O LORD God, [a]to whom vengeance belongeth; O God, to whom vengeance belongeth, [1]shew thyself.

2 [1]Lift up thyself, thou [a]judge of the earth: [2]render a reward to the proud.

3 LORD, [a]how long shall the wicked, how long shall the wicked triumph?

4 *How long* shall they [a]utter *and* speak [1]hard things? *and* all the workers of iniquity boast themselves?

5 They break in pieces thy people, O LORD, and afflict thine heritage.

6 They slay the widow and the stranger, and murder the fatherless.

7 [a]Yet they say, The LORD shall not see, neither shall the God of Jacob [1]regard *it*.

8 Understand, ye [1]brutish among the people: and *ye* fools, when will ye be wise?

9 [a]He that planted the ear, shall he not hear? he that formed the eye, shall he not see?

10 He that [1]chastiseth the [2]heathen, shall he not correct? he that teacheth man knowledge, *shall not he know?*

11 The LORD [a]knoweth the thoughts of man, that they *are* [1]vanity.

12 Blessed *is* the man whom thou [a]chastenest,[1] O LORD, and teachest him out of thy law;

13 That thou mayest give him [1]rest from the days of adversity, until the pit be digged for the wicked.

14 For the LORD will not [1]cast off his people, neither will he forsake his inheritance.

15 But judgment shall return unto righteousness: and all the upright in heart shall follow it.

16 Who will rise up for me against the evildoers? *or* who will stand up for me against the workers of iniquity?

17 Unless the LORD *had been* my help, my soul [1]had almost dwelt in silence.

18 When I said, My foot slippeth; thy mercy, O LORD, held me up.

19 In the multitude of my [1]thoughts within me thy comforts delight my soul.

20 Shall [a]the throne of iniquity have fellowship with thee, which [1]frameth mischief by a law?

21 They gather themselves together against the [1]soul of the righteous, and condemn the [a]innocent blood.

22 But the LORD is my defence; and my God *is* the rock of my refuge.

23 And he shall bring upon them their own iniquity, and shall cut them off in their own wickedness; *yea,* the LORD our God shall [1]cut them off.

## PSALM 95

O COME, let us sing unto the LORD: let us [1]make a joyful noise to the rock of our salvation.

2 Let us come before his presence with thanksgiving, and [1]make a joyful noise unto him with [a]psalms.[2]

3 For [a]the LORD *is* a great God, and a great King above all gods.

4 [1]In his hand *are* the deep places of the earth: [2]the strength of the hills *is* his also.

92:2 [a] Ps. 89:1
[1] declare
92:3 [a] 1 Chr. 23:5 [1] lute or lyre [2] harmonious or melodic
92:5 [a] Ps. 40:5 [b] [Is. 28:29]
92:6 [a] Ps. 73:22 [1] senseless
92:7 [a] Job 12:6 [1] spring up or sprout
92:8 [a] [Ps. 83:18]
92:9 [a] Ps. 68:1
92:10 [a] Ps. 89:17 [b] Ps. 23:5 [1] My strength [2] wild ox
92:11 [a] Ps. 54:7
92:12 [a] Ps. 52:8
92:14 [1] plump [2] green
92:15 [a] [Deut. 32:4] [b] [Rom. 9:14]
93:1 [a] Ps. 96:10 [b] Ps. 65:6 [1] shaken
93:2 [a] Ps. 45:6
93:3 [1] raised up
93:4 [a] Ps. 65:7
93:5 [1] adorns
94:1 [a] [Nah. 1:2] [1] shine forth
94:2 [a] [Gen. 18:25] [1] Rise up [2] repay with punishment
94:3 [a] [Job 20:5]
94:4 [a] Ps. 31:18 [1] insolent
94:7 [a] Ps. 10:11 [1] pay attention to
94:8 [1] senseless
94:9 [a] [Ex. 4:11]
94:10 [1] instructs or disciplines [2] nations or Gentiles
94:11 [a] 1 Cor. 3:20 [1] futile
94:12 [a] [Heb. 12:5, 6] [1] instructeth
94:13 [1] relief
94:14 [1] abandon
94:17 [1] would soon have
94:19 [1] anxious thoughts
94:20 [a] Amos 6:3 [1] devises
94:21 [a] [Ex. 23:7] [1] life
94:23 [1] destroy them
95:1 [1] shout joyfully
95:2 [a] James 5:13 [1] shout joyfully [2] songs
95:3 [a] [Ps. 96:4]
95:4 [1] In his possession [2] the heights

5 <sup>a</sup>The sea *is* his, and he made it: and his hands formed the dry *land*.

6 O come, let us worship and bow down: let <sup>a</sup>us kneel before the LORD our maker.

7 For he *is* our God; and <sup>a</sup>we *are* the people of his pasture, and the sheep <sup>1</sup>of his hand. <sup>b</sup>To day if ye will hear his voice,

8 Harden not your heart, as in the <sup>1</sup>provocation, *and* <sup>a</sup>as *in* the day of <sup>2</sup>temptation in the wilderness:

9 When <sup>a</sup>your fathers <sup>1</sup>tempted me, proved me, and <sup>b</sup>saw my work.

10 <sup>a</sup>Forty years long <sup>1</sup>was I grieved with *this* generation, and said, It is a people that <sup>2</sup>do err in their heart, and they have not known my ways:

11 Unto whom <sup>a</sup>I sware in my wrath that they should not enter into my rest.

## PSALM 96

O <sup>a</sup>SING unto the LORD a new song: sing unto the LORD, all the earth.

2 Sing unto the LORD, bless his name; <sup>1</sup>shew forth his salvation from day to day.

3 Declare his glory among the <sup>1</sup>heathen, his wonders among all people.

4 For <sup>a</sup>the LORD *is* great, and <sup>b</sup>greatly to be praised: <sup>c</sup>he *is* to be feared above all gods.

5 For <sup>a</sup>all the gods of the nations *are* idols: <sup>b</sup>but the LORD made the heavens.

6 Honour and majesty *are* before him: strength and <sup>a</sup>beauty *are* in his sanctuary.

7 <sup>a</sup>Give<sup>1</sup> unto the LORD, O ye kindreds of the people, give unto the LORD glory and strength.

8 <sup>1</sup>Give unto the LORD the glory *due unto* his name: bring an offering, and come into his courts.

9 O worship the LORD <sup>a</sup>in the beauty of holiness: <sup>1</sup>fear before him, all the earth.

10 Say among the <sup>1</sup>heathen *that* <sup>a</sup>the LORD reigneth: the world also <sup>2</sup>shall be established that it shall not be <sup>3</sup>moved: <sup>b</sup>he shall judge the people righteously.

11 <sup>a</sup>Let the heavens rejoice, and let the earth be glad; <sup>b</sup>let the sea roar, and the <sup>1</sup>fulness thereof.

12 Let the field be joyful, and all that *is* therein: then shall all the trees of the wood rejoice

13 Before the LORD: for he cometh, for he cometh to judge the earth: <sup>a</sup>he shall judge the world with righteousness, and the people with his truth.

## PSALM 97

T HE LORD <sup>a</sup>reigneth; let the earth rejoice; let the multitude of <sup>1</sup>isles be glad *thereof*.

---

95:5 <sup>a</sup> Gen. 1:9, 10
95:6 <sup>a</sup> [Phil. 2:10]
95:7 <sup>a</sup> Ps. 79:13
<sup>b</sup> Heb. 3:7–11, 15; 4:7 <sup>1</sup> Under his care
95:8 <sup>a</sup> Ex. 17:2–7 <sup>1</sup> rebellion, Heb. Meribah <sup>2</sup> trial or testing, Heb. Massah
95:9 <sup>a</sup> Ps. 78:18 <sup>b</sup> Num. 14:22 <sup>1</sup> tried
95:10 <sup>a</sup> Heb. 3:10, 17 <sup>1</sup> I was disgusted with <sup>2</sup> Lit. go astray
95:11 <sup>a</sup> Heb. 4:3, 5
96:1 <sup>a</sup> 1 Chr. 16:23–33
96:2 <sup>1</sup> proclaim the good news of his salvation
96:3 <sup>1</sup> nations or Gentiles
96:4 <sup>a</sup> Ps. 145:3 <sup>b</sup> Ps. 18:3 <sup>c</sup> Ps. 95:3
96:5 <sup>a</sup> [Jer. 10:11] <sup>b</sup> Is. 42:5
96:6 <sup>a</sup> Ps. 29:2
96:7 <sup>a</sup> Ps. 29:1, 2 <sup>1</sup> Ascribe
96:8 <sup>1</sup> Ascribe
96:9 <sup>a</sup> Ps. 29:2 <sup>1</sup> tremble
96:10 <sup>a</sup> Ps. 93:1; 97:1 <sup>b</sup> Ps. 67:4 <sup>1</sup> nations or Gentiles <sup>2</sup> is firmly established <sup>3</sup> shaken
96:11 <sup>a</sup> Ps. 69:34 <sup>b</sup> Ps. 98:7 <sup>1</sup> all that is in it
96:13 <sup>a</sup> [Rev. 19:11]
97:1 <sup>a</sup> [Ps. 96:10] <sup>1</sup> Or coastlands
97:2 <sup>a</sup> Ps. 18:11 <sup>b</sup> [Ps. 89:14] <sup>1</sup> foundation
97:3 <sup>a</sup> Ps. 18:8
97:4 <sup>a</sup> Ex. 19:18
97:5 <sup>a</sup> Mic. 1:4 <sup>1</sup> mountains
97:6 <sup>a</sup> Ps. 19:1
97:7 <sup>a</sup> [Ex. 20:4] <sup>b</sup> [Heb. 1:6] <sup>1</sup> Let all be put to shame who
97:9 <sup>a</sup> Ps. 83:18 <sup>b</sup> Ex. 18:11
97:10 <sup>a</sup> [Ps. 34:14] <sup>b</sup> Prov. 2:8 <sup>c</sup> Ps. 37:40
97:11 <sup>a</sup> Job 22:28
97:12 <sup>a</sup> Ps. 33:1 <sup>b</sup> Ps. 30:4 <sup>1</sup> Or for the memory <sup>2</sup> Or his holy name
98:1 <sup>a</sup> Is. 42:10 <sup>b</sup> Ex. 15:11
98:2 <sup>a</sup> Is. 52:10 <sup>b</sup> Is. 62:2 <sup>1</sup> revealed

---

2 <sup>a</sup>Clouds and darkness *are* round about him: <sup>b</sup>righteousness and judgment *are* the <sup>1</sup>habitation of his throne.

3 <sup>a</sup>A fire goeth before him, and burneth up his enemies round about.

4 <sup>a</sup>His lightnings enlightened the world: the earth saw, and trembled.

5 <sup>a</sup>The <sup>1</sup>hills melted like wax at the presence of the LORD, at the presence of the Lord of the whole earth.

6 <sup>a</sup>The heavens declare his righteousness, and all the people see his glory.

7 <sup>a</sup>Confounded<sup>1</sup> be all they that serve graven images, that boast themselves of idols: <sup>b</sup>worship him, all *ye* gods.

8 Zion heard, and was glad; and the daughters of Judah rejoiced because of thy judgments, O LORD.

9 For thou, LORD, *art* <sup>a</sup>high above all the earth: <sup>b</sup>thou art exalted far above all gods.

10 Ye that love the LORD, <sup>a</sup>hate evil: <sup>b</sup>he preserveth the souls of his saints; <sup>c</sup>he delivereth them out of the hand of the wicked.

11 <sup>a</sup>Light is sown for the righteous, and gladness for the upright in heart.

12 <sup>a</sup>Rejoice in the LORD, ye righteous; <sup>b</sup>and give thanks <sup>1</sup>at the remembrance of <sup>2</sup>his holiness.

## PSALM 98

### A Psalm.

O <sup>a</sup>SING unto the LORD a new song; for he hath <sup>b</sup>done marvellous things: his right hand, and his holy arm, hath gotten him the victory.

2 <sup>a</sup>The LORD hath made known his salvation: <sup>b</sup>his righteousness hath he <sup>1</sup>openly shewed in the sight of the <sup>2</sup>heathen.

3 He hath remembered his <sup>1</sup>mercy and his <sup>2</sup>truth toward the house of Israel: <sup>a</sup>all the ends of the earth have seen the salvation of our God.

4 <sup>1</sup>Make a joyful noise unto the LORD, all the earth: <sup>2</sup>make a loud noise, and rejoice, and sing praise.

5 Sing unto the LORD with the harp; with the harp, and the <sup>1</sup>voice of a psalm.

6 With trumpets and sound of cornet <sup>1</sup>make a joyful noise before the LORD, the King.

7 Let the sea roar, and the fulness thereof; the world, and they that dwell therein.

8 Let the <sup>1</sup>floods clap *their* hands: let the hills be joyful together

9 Before the LORD; <sup>a</sup>for he cometh to judge the earth: with righteousness shall he judge the world, and the people <sup>1</sup>with equity.

---

<sup>2</sup> nations or Gentiles  98:3 <sup>a</sup> Luke 3:6  <sup>1</sup> lovingkindness <sup>2</sup> faithfulness  98:4 <sup>1</sup> Shout joyfully  <sup>2</sup> break forth in song  98:5 <sup>1</sup> sound of a song  98:6 <sup>1</sup> shout joyfully  98:8 <sup>1</sup> rivers  98:9 <sup>a</sup> [Ps. 96:10, 13]  <sup>1</sup> in uprightness

## PSALM 99

T HE LORD reigneth; let the people tremble: [a]he sitteth *between* the cherubims; let the earth [1]be moved.

2 The LORD *is* great in Zion; and he *is* high above all the people.

3 Let them praise thy great and [1]terrible name; *for* [2]it *is* holy.

4 The king's strength also loveth judgment; thou dost establish [1]equity, thou executest judgment and righteousness in Jacob.

5 Exalt ye the LORD our God, and worship at his footstool; *for* he *is* holy.

6 Moses and Aaron among his priests, and Samuel among them that [a]call upon his name; they called upon the LORD, and he answered them.

7 He spake unto them in the cloudy pillar: they kept his testimonies, and the [1]ordinance *that* he gave them.

8 Thou answeredst them, O LORD our God: thou wast a God that forgavest them, though thou tookest vengeance [1]of their inventions.

9 Exalt the LORD our God, and worship at his holy hill; for the LORD our God *is* holy.

## PSALM 100

[a]A Psalm of [1]praise.

M AKE[1] [a]a joyful noise unto the LORD, [2]all ye lands.

2 Serve the LORD with gladness: come before his presence with singing.

3 Know ye that the LORD he *is* God: [a]*it is* he *that* hath made us, [1]and not we ourselves; [b]*we are* his people, and the sheep of his pasture.

4 [a]Enter into his gates with thanksgiving, *and* into his courts with praise: be thankful unto him, *and* bless his name.

5 For the LORD *is* good; [a]his mercy *is* everlasting; and his truth *endureth* to all generations.

## PSALM 101

A Psalm of David.

I WILL sing of [1]mercy and [2]judgment: unto thee, O LORD, will I [3]sing.

2 I will behave myself wisely in a perfect way. O when wilt thou come unto me? I will [a]walk within my house with a [1]perfect heart.

3 I will set no [1]wicked thing before mine eyes: [a]I hate the work of them [b]that turn aside; *it* shall not [2]cleave to me.

4 A [1]froward heart shall depart from me: I will not [a]know a [2]wicked *person.*

5 Whoso [1]privily slandereth his neighbour, him will I [2]cut off: [a]him

---

99:1 [a] Ex. 25:22
[1] be shaken
99:3 [1] awesome
[2] he
99:4 [1] uprightness
99:6 [a] 1 Sam. 7:9; 12:18
99:7 [1] statute
99:8 [1] on their evil deeds
100:title [a] Ps. 145:title [1] thanksgiving
100:1 [a] Ps. 95:1
[1] Shout joyfully
[2] Lit. all the earth
100:3 [a] [Eph. 2:10]
[b] Ezek. 34:30, 31
[1] Some mss. and his we are
100:4 [a] Ps. 66:13; 116:17–19
100:5 [a] Ps. 136:1
101:1 [1] lovingkindness [2] justice
[3] sing praises
101:2 [a] 1 Kin. 11:4
[1] blameless
101:3 [a] Ps. 97:10
[b] Josh. 23:6
[1] worthless, Heb. Belial [2] cling
101:4 [a] [Ps. 119:115]
[1] perverse [2] wickedness
101:5 [a] Prov. 6:17 [1] secretly
[2] destroy

[3] endure
101:6 [1] blameless
101:7 [1] continue, lit. be established
101:8 [a] Jer. 21:12
[b] Ps. 48:2, 8
[1] Lit. workers of iniquity
102:title [a] Ps. 61:2
102:2 [a] Ps. 27:9; 69:17
102:3 [a] James 4:14 [1] Lit. finished in
102:4 [1] stricken
102:5 [1] cling
[2] flesh
102:8 [1] deride me
102:10 [1] exalted
102:15 [a] 1 Kin. 8:43 [1] nations or Gentiles
102:16 [a] [Is. 60:1, 2]
102:17 [a] Neh. 1:6
102:18 [a] [Rom. 15:4] [b] Ps. 22:31

---

that hath an high look and a proud heart will not I [3]suffer.

6 Mine eyes *shall be* upon the faithful of the land, that they may dwell with me: he that walketh in a [1]perfect way, he shall serve me.

7 He that worketh deceit shall not dwell within my house: he that telleth lies shall not [1]tarry in my sight.

8 I will [a]early destroy all the wicked of the land; that I may cut off all [1]wicked doers [b]from the city of the LORD.

## PSALM 102

A Prayer of the afflicted, [a]when he is overwhelmed, and poureth out his complaint before the LORD.

H EAR my prayer, O LORD, and let my cry come unto thee.

2 [a]Hide not thy face from me in the day *when* I am in trouble; incline thine ear unto me: in the day *when* I call answer me speedily.

3 For my days are [a]consumed[1] like smoke, and my bones are burned as an hearth.

4 My heart is [1]smitten, and withered like grass; so that I forget to eat my bread.

5 By reason of the voice of my groaning my bones [1]cleave to my [2]skin.

6 I am like a pelican of the wilderness: I am like an owl of the desert.

7 I watch, and am as a sparrow alone upon the house top.

8 Mine enemies reproach me all the day; *and* they that [1]are mad against me are sworn against me.

9 For I have eaten ashes like bread, and mingled my drink with weeping,

10 Because of thine indignation and thy wrath: for thou hast [1]lifted me up, and cast me down.

11 My days *are* like a shadow that declineth; and I am withered like grass.

12 But thou, O LORD, shalt endure for ever; and thy remembrance unto all generations.

13 Thou shalt arise, *and* have mercy upon Zion: for the time to favour her, yea, the set time, is come.

14 For thy servants take pleasure in her stones, and favour the dust thereof.

15 So the [1]heathen shall [a]fear the name of the LORD, and all the kings of the earth thy glory.

16 When the LORD shall build up Zion, [a]he shall appear in his glory.

17 [a]He will regard the prayer of the destitute, and not despise their prayer.

18 This shall be [a]written for the generation to come: and [b]the people which shall be created shall praise the LORD.

19 For he ªlooked down from the height of his sanctuary; from heaven did the LORD behold the earth;

20 ªTo hear the groaning of the prisoner; to loose those that are appointed to death;

21 To ªdeclare the name of the LORD in Zion, and his praise in Jerusalem;

22 ªWhen the people are gathered together, and the kingdoms, to serve the LORD.

23 He weakened my strength in the way; he ªshortened my days.

24 ªI said, O my God, take me not away in the midst of my days: ᵇthy years *are* throughout all generations.

25 ªOf old hast thou laid the foundation of the earth: and the heavens *are* the work of thy hands.

26 ªThey shall perish, but thou shalt ¹endure: yea, all of them shall ²wax old like a garment; as a ³vesture shalt thou change them, and they shall be changed:

27 But ªthou *art* the same, and thy years shall have no end.

28 ªThe children of thy servants shall continue, and their ¹seed shall be established before thee.

## PSALM 103

*A Psalm* of David.

BLESS ªthe LORD, O my soul: and all that is within me, *bless* his holy name.

2 Bless the LORD, O my soul, and forget not all his benefits:

3 ªWho forgiveth all thine iniquities; who ᵇhealeth all thy diseases;

4 Who redeemeth thy life from destruction; ªwho crowneth thee with lovingkindness and tender mercies;

5 Who satisfieth thy mouth with good *things; so that* ªthy youth is renewed like the eagle's.

6 The LORD executeth righteousness and judgment for all that are oppressed.

7 ªHe made known his ways unto Moses, his acts unto the children of Israel.

8 ªThe LORD *is* merciful and gracious, slow to anger, and ¹plenteous in ²mercy.

9 ªHe will not always ¹chide: neither will he keep *his anger* for ever.

10 ªHe hath not dealt with us after our sins; nor rewarded us according to our iniquities.

11 For as the heaven is high above the earth, *so* great is his ¹mercy toward them that fear him.

12 As far as the east is from the west, *so* far hath he ªremoved our transgressions from us.

13 ªLike as a father pitieth *his* children, *so* the LORD pitieth them that fear him.

102:19 ª Deut. 26:15
102:20 ª Ps. 79:11
102:21 ª Ps. 22:22
102:22 ª [Is. 2:2, 3; 49:22, 23; 60:3]
102:23 ª Job 21:21
102:24 ª Is. 38:10
ᵇ [Ps. 90:2]
102:25 ª [Heb. 1:10–12]
102:26 ª Is. 34:4; 51:6 ¹ *continue* ² *grow* ³ *cloak*
102:27 ª [Mal. 3:6]
102:28 ª Ps. 69:36 ¹ *descendants*
103:1 ª Ps. 104:1, 35
103:3 ª Ps. 130:8
ᵇ [Ex. 15:26]
103:4 ª [Ps. 5:12]
103:5 ª [Is. 40:31]
103:7 ª Ps. 147:19
103:8 ª [Ex. 34:6, 7] ¹ *abounding* ² *lovingkindness*
103:9 ª [Ps. 30:5] ¹ *strive*
103:10 ª [Ezra 9:13]
103:11 ¹ *lovingkindness*
103:12 ª [Is. 38:17; 43:25]
103:13 ª Mal. 3:17
103:14 ¹ Understands our constitution
103:15 ª 1 Pet. 1:24
103:16 ª [Is. 40:7]
ᵇ Job 7:10 ¹ Lit. *it is not* ² *not remember it*
103:17 ¹ *lovingkindness*
103:18 ª [Deut. 7:9]
103:19 ª [Dan. 4:17, 25]
103:20 ª Ps. 148:2
ᵇ [Matt. 6:10]
103:21 ª [Heb. 1:14] ¹ *servants*
104:1 ª Ps. 103:1
104:3 ª [Amos 9:6] ¹ *upper chambers*
104:4 ¹ *servants*
104:5 ¹ Lit. *He has founded the earth upon her bases* ² *shake*
104:6 ª Gen. 1:6
104:8 ¹ *The mountains rise up; the valleys sink down*
104:9 ª [Jer. 5:22]
ᵇ Gen. 9:11–15 ¹ *boundary*
104:11 ¹ *donkeys*
104:13 ª Ps. 147:8
ᵇ Jer. 10:13 ¹ *upper chambers*

14 For he ¹knoweth our frame; he remembereth that we *are* dust.

15 *As for* man, ªhis days *are* as grass: as a flower of the field, so he flourisheth.

16 ªFor the wind passeth over it, and ¹it is gone; and ᵇthe place thereof shall ²know it no more.

17 But the ¹mercy of the LORD *is* from everlasting to everlasting upon them that fear him, and his righteousness unto children's children;

18 ªTo such as keep his covenant, and to those that remember his commandments to do them.

19 The LORD hath prepared his throne in the heavens; and ªhis kingdom ruleth over all.

20 ªBless the LORD, ye his angels, that excel in strength, that ᵇdo his commandments, hearkening unto the voice of his word.

21 Bless ye the LORD, all *ye* his hosts; ª*ye* ¹ministers of his, that do his pleasure.

22 Bless the LORD, all his works in all places of his dominion: bless the LORD, O my soul.

## PSALM 104

BLESS ªthe LORD, O my soul. O LORD my God, thou art very great; thou art clothed with honour and majesty.

2 Who coverest *thyself* with light as *with* a garment: who stretchest out the heavens like a curtain:

3 ªWho layeth the beams of his ¹chambers in the waters: who maketh the clouds his chariot: who walketh upon the wings of the wind:

4 Who maketh his angels spirits; his ¹ministers a flaming fire:

5 ¹*Who* laid the foundations of the earth, *that* it should not ²be removed for ever.

6 Thou ªcoveredst it with the deep as *with* a garment: the waters stood above the mountains.

7 At thy rebuke they fled; at the voice of thy thunder they hasted away.

8 ¹They go up by the mountains; they go down by the valleys unto the place which thou hast founded for them.

9 Thou hast ªset a ¹bound that they may not pass over; ᵇthat they turn not again to cover the earth.

10 He sendeth the springs into the valleys, *which* run among the hills.

11 They give drink to every beast of the field: the wild ¹asses quench their thirst.

12 By them shall the fowls of the heaven have their habitation, *which* sing among the branches.

13 ªHe watereth the hills from his ¹chambers: the earth is satisfied with ᵇthe fruit of thy works.

14 ᵃHe causeth the grass to grow for the cattle, and ¹herb for the service of man: that he may bring forth ᵇfood out of the earth;

15 And ᵃwine *that* maketh glad the heart of man, *and* oil to make *his* face to shine, and bread *which* strengtheneth man's heart.

16 The trees of the LORD are full *of sap;* the cedars of Lebanon, which he hath planted;

17 Where the birds make their nests: *as for* the stork, the fir trees *are* her house.

18 The high hills *are* a refuge for the wild goats; *and* the ¹rocks for the ᵃconies.²

19 ᵃHe appointed the moon for seasons: the ᵇsun knoweth his going down.

20 ᵃThou makest darkness, and it is night: wherein all the beasts of the forest do creep *forth.*

21 ᵃThe young lions roar after their prey, and seek their meat from God.

22 The sun ariseth, they gather themselves together, and lay them down in their dens.

23 Man goeth forth unto ᵃhis work and to his labour until the evening.

24 ᵃO LORD, how manifold are thy works! in wisdom hast thou made them all: the earth is full of thy ᵇriches.¹

25 *So is* this great and wide sea, wherein *are* ¹things creeping innumerable, both small and great ²beasts.

26 There go the ships: *there is* that ᵃleviathan,¹ *whom* thou hast ²made to play therein.

27 ᵃThese wait all upon thee; that thou mayest give *them* their meat in due season.

28 ¹*That* thou givest them they gather: thou openest thine hand, they are filled with good.

29 Thou hidest thy face, they are troubled: ᵃthou takest away their breath, they die, and return to their dust.

30 ᵃThou sendest forth thy spirit, they are created: and thou renewest the face of the earth.

31 The glory of the LORD shall endure for ever: the LORD ᵃshall rejoice in his works.

32 He looketh on the earth, and it ᵃtrembleth: ᵇhe toucheth the hills, and they smoke.

33 ᵃI will sing unto the LORD as long as I live: I will sing praise to my God while I have my being.

34 My ᵃmeditation of him shall be sweet: I will be glad in the LORD.

35 Let ᵃthe sinners be consumed out of the earth, and let the wicked be no more. Bless thou the LORD, O my soul. ¹Praise ye the LORD.

## Center reference column

104:14 ᵃ Gen. 1:29 ᵇ Job 28:5 ¹ *vegetation*
104:15 ᵃ Judg. 9:13
104:18 ᵃ Lev. 11:5 ¹ *cliffs* ² *rock badgers*
104:19 ᵃ Gen. 1:14 ᵇ Ps. 19:6
104:20 ᵃ [Is. 45:7]
104:21 ᵃ Job 38:39
104:23 ᵃ Gen. 3:19
104:24 ᵃ Prov. 3:19 ᵇ Ps. 65:9 ¹ *possessions*
104:25 ¹ *teeming things* ² *living creatures*
104:26 ᵃ Job 41:1 ¹ A large sea creature of unknown identity ² Lit. *formed*
104:27 ᵃ Ps. 136:25
104:28 ¹ *What*
104:29 ᵃ Job 34:15
104:30 ᵃ Is. 32:15
104:31 ᵃ Gen. 1:31
104:32 ᵃ Hab. 3:10 ᵇ Ps. 144:5
104:33 ᵃ Ps. 63:4
104:34 ᵃ Ps. 19:14
104:35 ᵃ Ps. 37:38 ¹ Heb. *Hallelujah*
105:1 ᵃ Is. 12:4 ᵇ Ps. 145:12
105:2 ᵃ Ps. 119:27
105:4 ᵃ Ps. 27:8
105:5 ᵃ Ps. 77:11
105:7 ᵃ [Is. 26:9]
105:8 ᵃ Luke 1:72
105:9 ᵃ Gen. 17:2
105:11 ᵃ Gen. 13:15; 15:18 ¹ *the allotment*
105:12 ᵃ [Deut. 7:7] ᵇ Heb. 11:9
105:14 ᵃ Gen. 35:5 ᵇ Gen. 12:17 ¹ *permitted* ² *rebuked*
105:15 ¹ *anointed ones*
105:16 ᵃ Gen. 41:54 ᵇ Lev. 26:26 ¹ *destroyed* ² *provision*
105:17 ᵃ [Gen. 45:5] ᵇ Gen. 37:28, 36 ¹ *as a slave*
105:18 ᵃ Gen. 40:15 ¹ Lit. *his soul came into iron*
105:19 ᵃ Gen. 39:11–21; 41:25, 42, 43 ¹ *came to pass* ² *tested*
105:20 ᵃ Gen. 41:14
105:21 ᵃ Gen. 41:40–44

## God's Glory Endures Forever (right column)

### PSALM 105

O ᵃGIVE thanks unto the LORD; call upon his name: ᵇmake known his deeds among the people.

2 Sing unto him, sing psalms unto him: ᵃtalk ye of all his wondrous works.

3 Glory ye in his holy name: let the heart of them rejoice that seek the LORD.

4 Seek the LORD, and his strength: ᵃseek his face evermore.

5 ᵃRemember his marvellous works that he hath done; his wonders, and the judgments of his mouth;

6 O ye seed of Abraham his servant, ye children of Jacob his chosen.

7 He *is* the LORD our God: ᵃhis judgments *are* in all the earth.

8 He hath ᵃremembered his covenant for ever, the word *which* he commanded to a thousand generations.

9 ᵃWhich *covenant* he made with Abraham, and his oath unto Isaac;

10 And confirmed the same unto Jacob for a law, *and* to Israel *for* an everlasting covenant:

11 Saying, ᵃUnto thee will I give the land of Canaan, ¹the lot of your inheritance:

12 ᵃWhen they were *but* a few men in number; yea, very few, ᵇand strangers in it.

13 When they went from one nation to another, from *one* kingdom to another people;

14 ᵃHe ¹suffered no man to do them wrong: yea, ᵇhe ²reproved kings for their sakes;

15 *Saying,* Touch not mine ¹anointed, and do my prophets no harm.

16 Moreover ᵃhe called for a famine upon the land: he ¹brake the whole ᵇstaff² of bread.

17 ᵃHe sent a man before them, *even* Joseph, *who* ᵇwas sold ¹for a servant:

18 ᵃWhose feet they hurt with fetters: ¹he was laid in iron:

19 Until the time that his word ¹came: ᵃthe word of the LORD ²tried him.

20 ᵃThe king sent and loosed him; *even* the ruler of the people, and let him go free.

21 ᵃHe made him lord of his house, and ruler of all his ¹substance:

22 To ¹bind his princes at his pleasure; and teach his ²senators wisdom.

23 ᵃIsrael also came into Egypt; and Jacob sojourned ᵇin the land of Ham.

24 And ᵃhe increased his people greatly; and made them stronger than their enemies.

¹ *possessions*　105:22 ¹ Bind as prisoners ² *elders*
105:23 ᵃ Gen. 46:6 ᵇ Ps. 78:51　105:24 ᵃ Ex. 1:7, 9

25 ᵃHe turned their heart to hate his people, to deal ¹subtilly with his servants.

26 ᵃHe sent Moses his servant; *and* Aaron whom he had chosen.

27 They ᵃshewed¹ his signs among them, and wonders in the land of Ham.

28 He sent darkness, and made it dark; and they rebelled not against his word.

29 ᵃHe turned their waters into blood, and slew their fish.

30 ᵃTheir land brought forth frogs in abundance, in the chambers of their kings.

31 ᵃHe spake, and there came divers sorts of flies, *and* lice in all their ¹coasts.

32 ᵃHe gave them hail for rain, *and* flaming fire in their land.

33 ᵃHe ¹smote their vines also and their fig trees; and ²brake the trees of their ³coasts.

34 ᵃHe spake, and the locusts came, and ¹caterpillers, and that without number,

35 And did eat up all the ¹herbs in their land, and devoured the fruit of their ground.

36 ᵃHe ¹smote also all the firstborn in their land, ᵇthe ²chief of all their strength.

37 ᵃHe brought them forth also with silver and gold: and *there was* not one feeble *person* among their tribes.

38 ᵃEgypt was glad when they departed: for the fear of them fell upon them.

39 ᵃHe spread a cloud for a covering; and fire to give light in the night.

40 ᵃ*The people* asked, and he brought quails, and ᵇsatisfied them with the bread of heaven.

41 ᵃHe opened the rock, and the waters gushed out; they ran in the dry places *like* a river.

42 For he remembered ᵃhis holy promise, *and* Abraham his servant.

43 And he brought forth his people with joy, *and* his chosen with ¹gladness:

44 ᵃAnd gave them the lands of the ¹heathen: and they inherited the labour of the people;

45 ᵃThat they might observe his statutes, and keep his laws. ¹Praise ye the LORD.

## PSALM 106

P RAISE¹ ye the LORD. ᵃO give thanks unto the LORD; for *he is* good: for his mercy *endureth* for ever.

2 Who can ¹utter the mighty acts of the LORD? *who* can shew forth all his praise?

3 Blessed *are* they that keep ¹judgment, *and* he that ᵃdoeth righteousness at ᵇall times.

4 ᵃRemember me, O LORD, with the favour *that thou bearest unto* thy people: O visit me with thy salvation;

5 That I may see the good of thy chosen, that I may rejoice in the gladness of thy nation, that I may glory with ¹thine inheritance.

6 ᵃWe have sinned with our fathers, we have committed iniquity, we have done wickedly.

7 Our fathers understood not thy wonders in Egypt; they remembered not the multitude of thy ¹mercies; ᵃbut provoked *him* at the sea, *even* at the Red sea.

8 Nevertheless he saved them for his name's sake, ᵃthat he might make his mighty power to be known.

9 ᵃHe rebuked the Red sea also, and it was dried up: so ᵇhe led them through the depths, as through the wilderness.

10 And he ᵃsaved them from the hand of him that hated *them,* and redeemed them from the hand of the enemy.

11 ᵃAnd the waters covered their enemies: there was not one of them left.

12 ᵃThen believed they his words; they sang his praise.

13 ᵃThey¹ soon forgat his works; they waited not for his counsel:

14 ᵃBut lusted exceedingly in the wilderness, and tempted God in the desert.

15 ᵃAnd he gave them their request; but ᵇsent leanness into their soul.

16 ᵃThey envied Moses also in the camp, *and* Aaron the saint of the LORD.

17 ᵃThe earth opened and swallowed up Dathan and covered the ¹company of Abiram.

18 ᵃAnd a fire was kindled in their company; the flame burned up the wicked.

19 ᵃThey made a calf in Horeb, and worshipped the ¹molten image.

20 Thus ᵃthey changed their glory into the ¹similitude of an ox that eateth grass.

21 They forgat God their saviour, which had done great things in Egypt;

22 Wondrous works in the land of Ham, *and* ¹terrible things by the Red sea.

23 ᵃTherefore he said that he would destroy them, had not Moses his chosen ᵇstood before him in the breach, to turn away his wrath, lest he should destroy *them.*

24 Yea, they despised ᵃthe pleasant land, they ᵇbelieved not his word:

---

105:25 ᵃ Ex. 1:8–10; 4:21 ¹ *craftily*
105:26 ᵃ Ex. 3:10; 4:12–15
105:27 ᵃ Ps. 78:43 ¹ *performed his signs*
105:29 ᵃ Ex. 7:20, 21
105:30 ᵃ Ex. 8:6
105:31 ᵃ Ex. 8:16, 17 ¹ *territory*
105:32 ᵃ Ex. 9:23–25
105:33 ᵃ Ps. 78:47 ¹ *struck* ² *splintered* ³ *territory*
105:34 ᵃ Ex. 10:4 ¹ *young locusts*
105:35 ¹ *vegetation*
105:36 ᵃ Ex. 12:29; 13:15 ᵇ Gen. 49:3 ¹ *struck down* ² Lit. *firstfruits*
105:37 ᵃ Ex. 12:35, 36
105:38 ᵃ Ex. 12:33
105:39 ᵃ Ex. 13:21
105:40 ᵃ Ex. 16:12 ᵇ Ps. 78:24
105:41 ᵃ Ex. 17:6
105:42 ᵃ Gen. 15:13, 14
105:43 ¹ *a joyful shout*
105:44 ᵃ Josh. 11:16–23; 13:7 ¹ *Gentiles* or *nations*
105:45 ᵃ [Deut. 4:1, 40] ¹ Heb. *Hallelujah*
106:1 ᵃ 1 Chr. 16:34, 41 ¹ Heb. *Hallelujah*
106:2 ¹ *express*
106:3 ᵃ Ps. 15:2 ᵇ [Gal. 6:9] ¹ *justice*
106:4 ᵃ Ps. 119:132
106:5 ¹ The people of thy inheritance
106:6 ᵃ [Dan. 9:5]
106:7 ᵃ Ex. 14:11, 12 ¹ *lovingkindnesses*
106:8 ᵃ Ex. 9:16
106:9 ᵃ Ex. 14:21 ᵇ Is. 63:11–13
106:10 ᵃ Ex. 14:30
106:11 ᵃ Ex. 14:27, 28; 15:5
106:12 ᵃ Ex. 15:1–21
106:13 ᵃ Ex. 15:24; 16:2; 17:2 ¹ Lit. They hurried, they forgot
106:14 ᵃ 1 Cor. 10:6
106:15 ᵃ Num. 11:31 ᵇ Is. 10:16
106:16 ᵃ Num. 16:1–3
106:17 ᵃ Deut. 11:6

¹ *faction*  106:18 ᵃ Num. 16:35, 46  106:19 ᵃ Ex. 32:1–4 ¹ *moulded*  106:20 ᵃ Rom. 1:23 ¹ *image*  106:22 ¹ *awesome*  106:23 ᵃ Ex. 32:10 ᵇ Ezek. 22:30  106:24 ᵃ Deut. 8:7 ᵇ [Heb. 3:18, 19]

25 aBut murmured in their tents, *and* hearkened not unto the voice of the LORD.

26 aTherefore he [1]lifted up his hand against them, bto [2]overthrow them in the wilderness:

27 aTo [1]overthrow their seed also among the nations, and to scatter them in the lands.

28 aThey joined themselves also unto Baal-peor, and ate the sacrifices [1]of the dead.

29 Thus they provoked *him* to anger with their [1]inventions: and the plague brake in upon them.

30 aThen stood up Phinehas, and [1]executed judgment: and *so* the plague was [2]stayed.

31 And that was counted unto him afor righteousness unto all generations for evermore.

32 aThey angered *him* also at the waters of strife, bso that it went ill with Moses [1]for their sakes:

33 aBecause they provoked his spirit, so that he spake [1]unadvisedly with his lips.

34 aThey did not destroy the nations, bconcerning whom the LORD commanded them:

35 aBut were mingled among the [1]heathen, and learned their works.

36 And athey served their idols: bwhich were a snare unto them.

37 Yea, [1]they sacrificed their sons and their daughters unto bdevils,[1]

38 And shed innocent blood, *even* the blood of their sons and of their daughters, whom they sacrificed unto the idols of Canaan: and athe land was polluted with blood.

39 Thus were they adefiled[1] with their own works, and bwent[2] a whoring [3]with their own inventions.

40 Therefore awas the wrath of the LORD kindled against his people, insomuch that he abhorred bhis own inheritance.

41 And ahe gave them into the hand of the [1]heathen; and they that hated them ruled over them.

42 Their enemies also oppressed them, and they were brought into subjection under their hand.

43 aMany times did he deliver them; but they [1]provoked *him* with their counsel, and were brought low for their iniquity.

44 Nevertheless he regarded their affliction, when ahe heard their cry:

45 aAnd he remembered for them his covenant, and brepented[1] caccording to the multitude of his [2]mercies.

46 aHe made them also to be pitied of all those that carried them captives.

47 aSave us, O LORD our God, and gather us from among the [1]heathen,

to give thanks unto thy holy name, *and* to triumph in thy praise.

48 aBlessed *be* the LORD God of Israel from everlasting to everlasting: and let all the people say, Amen. [1]Praise ye the LORD.

# BOOK V: Psalms 107–150

## PSALM 107

O aGIVE thanks unto the LORD, for *he is* good: for his [1]mercy *endureth* for ever.

2 Let the redeemed of the LORD say *so*, whom he hath redeemed from the hand of the enemy;

3 And agathered them out of the lands, from the east, and from the west, from the north, and from the south.

4 They wandered in athe wilderness in a [1]solitary way; they found no city to dwell in.

5 Hungry and thirsty, their soul fainted in them.

6 aThen they cried unto the LORD in their trouble, *and* he delivered them out of their distresses.

7 And he led them forth by the aright way, that they might go to a city of habitation.

8 aOh that *men* would praise the LORD *for* his [1]goodness, and *for* his wonderful works to the children of men!

9 For ahe satisfieth the longing soul, and filleth the hungry soul with goodness.

10 Such as asit in darkness and in the shadow of death, *being* bbound[1] in affliction and iron;

11 Because they arebelled against the words of God, and [1]contemned bthe counsel of the most High:

12 Therefore he brought down their heart with labour; they fell down, and *there was* anone to help.

13 Then they cried unto the LORD in their trouble, *and* he saved them out of their distresses.

14 aHe brought them out of darkness and the shadow of death, and [1]brake their bands in sunder.

15 Oh that *men* would praise the LORD *for* his [1]goodness, and *for* his wonderful works to the children of men!

16 For he hath abroken the gates of [1]brass, and cut the bars of iron in sunder.

17 Fools abecause of their transgression, and because of their iniquities, are afflicted.

---

106:25 a Num. 14:2, 27

106:26 a Ezek. 20:15, 16   b Num. 14:28–30.  [1]Took an oath  [2]*make them fall*

106:27 a Lev. 26:33  [1]*make their descendants fall also*

106:28 a Hos. 9:10  [1]*offered to the dead*

106:29 [1]*deeds*

106:30 a Num. 25:7, 8  [1]*intervened*  [2]*stopped*

106:31 a Num. 25:11–13

106:32 a Num. 20:3–13  b Deut. 1:37; 3:26  [1]*on account of them*

106:33 a Num. 20:3, 10  [1]*rashly*

106:34 a Judg. 1:21  b [Deut. 7:2, 16]

106:35 a Judg. 3:5, 6  [1]*Gentiles*

106:36 a Judg. 2:12  b Deut. 7:16

106:37 a 2 Kin. 16:3; 17:17  b [Lev. 17:7]  [1]*demons*

106:38 a [Num. 35:33]

106:39 a Ezek. 20:18  b [Lev. 17:7]  [1]*unclean by*  [2]*played the harlot, were unfaithful*  [3]*by their own deeds*

106:40 a Judg. 2:14  b [Deut. 9:29; 32:9]

106:41 a Judg. 2:14  [1]*Gentiles or nations*

106:43 a Judg. 2:16  [1]*rebelled against him*

106:44 a Judg. 3:9; 6:7; 10:10

106:45 a [Lev. 26:41, 42]  b Judg. 2:18  c Ps. 69:16  [1]*relented*  [2]*lovingkindnesses*

106:46 a Ezra 9:9

106:47 a 1 Chr. 16:35, 36  [1]*Gentiles or nations*

106:48 a Ps. 41:13  [1]Heb. *Hallelujah*

107:1 a Ps. 106:1  [1]*lovingkindness*

107:3 a Is. 43:5, 6

107:4 a [Deut. 2:7; 32:10]  [1]*desolate*

107:6 a Ps. 50:15

107:7 a Ezra 8:21

107:8 a Ps. 107:15, 21  [1]*lovingkindness*

107:9 a [Ps. 34:10]

107:10 a [Luke 1:79]  b Job 36:8  [1]*prisoners*  107:11 a Lam. 3:42  b [Ps. 73:24]  [1]*despised*  107:12 a Ps. 22:11  107:14 a Ps. 68:6  [1]*broke their chains in pieces*  107:15 [1]*lovingkindness*  107:16 a Is. 45:1, 2  [1]*bronze*  107:17 a Lam. 3:39

18 ᵃTheir soul abhorreth all manner of meat; and they ᵇdraw near unto the gates of death.

19 Then they cry unto the LORD in their trouble, *and* he saveth them out of their distresses.

20 ᵃHe sent his word, and ᵇhealed them, and ᶜdelivered *them* from their destructions.

21 Oh that *men* would ¹praise the LORD *for* his ²goodness, and *for* his wonderful works to the children of men!

22 And ᵃlet them sacrifice the sacrifices of thanksgiving, and ᵇdeclare his works with ¹rejoicing.

23 They that go down to the sea in ships, that do business in great waters;

24 These see the works of the LORD, and his wonders in the deep.

25 For he commandeth, and ᵃraiseth the stormy wind, which lifteth up the waves thereof.

26 They mount up to the heaven, they go down again to the depths: ᵃtheir soul is melted because of trouble.

27 They reel to and fro, and stagger like a drunken man, and ¹are at their wit's end.

28 Then they cry unto the LORD in their trouble, and he bringeth them out of their distresses.

29 ᵃHe maketh the storm a calm, so that the waves thereof are still.

30 Then are they glad because they be quiet; so he bringeth them unto their desired haven.

31 ᵃOh that *men* would ¹praise the LORD *for* his ²goodness, and *for* his wonderful works to the children of men!

32 Let them exalt him also ᵃin the congregation of the people, and praise him in the assembly of the elders.

33 He ᵃturneth rivers into a wilderness, and the watersprings into dry ground;

34 A ᵃfruitful land into ¹barrenness, for the wickedness of them that dwell therein.

35 ᵃHe turneth the wilderness into ¹a standing water, and dry ground into watersprings.

36 And there he maketh the hungry to dwell, that they may prepare a city for habitation;

37 And sow the fields, and plant vineyards, which may yield fruits of increase.

38 ᵃHe blesseth them also, so that they are multiplied greatly; and suffereth not their cattle to ᵇdecrease.

39 Again, they are ᵃminished¹ and brought low through oppression, affliction, and sorrow.

40 ᵃHe poureth contempt upon princes, and causeth them to wander

in the ¹wilderness, *where there is* no way.

41 ᵃYet setteth he the poor on high ¹from affliction, and ᵇmaketh *him* families like a flock.

42 ᵃThe righteous shall see *it,* and rejoice: and all ᵇiniquity shall stop her mouth.

43 ᵃWhoso *is* wise, and will observe these *things,* even they shall understand the lovingkindness of the LORD.

## PSALM 108

A Song *or* Psalm of David.

O ᵃGOD, my heart is ¹fixed; I will sing and give praise, even with my glory.

2 ᵃAwake, ¹psaltery and harp: I *myself* will ²awake early.

3 I will praise thee, O LORD, among the people: and I will sing praises unto thee among the nations.

4 For thy ¹mercy *is* great above the ²heavens: and thy truth *reacheth* unto the clouds.

5 ᵃBe thou exalted, O God, above the heavens: and thy glory above all the earth;

6 ᵃThat thy beloved may be delivered: save *with* thy right hand, and answer me.

7 God hath spoken in his holiness; I will rejoice, I will divide Shechem, and ¹mete out the valley of Succoth.

8 Gilead *is* mine; Manasseh *is* mine; Ephraim also *is* the ¹strength of mine head; ᵃJudah *is* my lawgiver;

9 Moab *is* my washpot; over Edom will I cast out my shoe; over Philistia will I triumph.

10 ᵃWho will bring me into the strong city? who will lead me into Edom?

11 *Wilt* not *thou,* O God, *who* hast cast us off? and wilt not thou, O God, go forth with our hosts?

12 Give us help from trouble: for vain *is* the help of man.

13 ᵃThrough God we shall do valiantly: for he *it is that* shall tread down our enemies.

## PSALM 109

To the chief Musician,
A Psalm of David.

H OLD ᵃnot thy peace, O God of my praise;

2 For the mouth of the wicked and the mouth of the deceitful are opened against me: they have spoken against me with a ᵃlying tongue.

3 They ¹compassed me about also with words of hatred; and fought against me ᵃwithout a cause.

4 ¹For my love they are my adversaries: but I *give myself unto* prayer.

5 And ᵃthey have rewarded me evil for good, and hatred for my love.

*Center column references:*

107:18 ᵃ Job 33:20
ᵇ Job 33:22
107:20 ᵃ Matt. 8:8
ᵇ Ps. 30:2 ᶜ Job 33:28, 30
107:21 ¹ *give thanks* ² *lovingkindness*
107:22 ᵃ Lev. 7:12
ᵇ Ps. 9:11 ¹ *joyful singing*
107:25 ᵃ Jon. 1:4
107:26 ᵃ Ps. 22:14
107:27 ¹ Lit. *all their wisdom is swallowed up*
107:29 ᵃ Ps. 89:9
107:31 ᵃ Ps. 107:8, 15, 21 ¹ *give thanks to* ² *lovingkindness*
107:32 ᵃ Ps. 22:22, 25
107:33 ᵃ 1 Kin. 17:1, 7
107:34 ᵃ Gen. 13:10 ¹ Lit. *a salty waste*
107:35 ᵃ Ps. 114:8 ¹ *pools of water*
107:38 ᵃ Gen. 12:2; 17:16, 20 ᵇ [Deut. 7:14]
107:39 ᵃ 2 Kin. 10:32 ¹ *diminished*
107:40 ᵃ Job 12:21, 24
¹ Or *void place*
107:41 ᵃ 1 Sam. 2:8
ᵇ Ps. 78:52 ¹ *far from*
107:42 ᵃ Job 5:15, 16 ᵇ [Rom. 3:19]
107:43 ᵃ Jer. 9:12
108:1 ᵃ Ps. 57:7–11 ¹ *steadfast*
108:2 ᵃ Ps. 57:8–11 ¹ *lute or lyre* ² *awaken the dawn*
108:4 ¹ *lovingkindness* ² *skies*
108:5 ᵃ Ps. 57:5, 11
108:6 ᵃ Ps. 60:5–12
108:7 ¹ *measure*
108:8 ᵃ [Gen. 49:10] ¹ *helmet*
108:10 ᵃ Ps. 60:9
108:13 ᵃ Ps. 60:12
109:1 ᵃ Ps. 83:1
109:2 ᵃ Ps. 27:12
109:3 ᵃ John 15:25 ¹ *surrounded me*
109:4 ¹ *In return for*
109:5 ᵃ Ps. 35:7, 12; 38:20

6 Set thou a wicked man over him: and let ᵃSatan¹ stand at his right hand.

7 When he shall be judged, let him ᵇbe condemned: and ᵃlet his prayer become sin.

8 Let his days be ᵃfew; *and* ᵇlet another take his office.

9 ᵃLet his children be fatherless, and his wife a widow.

10 Let his children ¹be continually vagabonds, and beg: let them seek *their bread* also out of their desolate places.

11 ᵃLet the ¹extortioner catch all that he hath; and let the strangers ²spoil his labour.

12 Let there be none to extend mercy unto him: neither let there be any to favour his fatherless children.

13 ᵃLet his ¹posterity be cut off; *and* in the generation following let their ᵇname be blotted out.

14 ᵃLet the iniquity of his fathers be remembered with the LORD; and let not the sin of his mother ᵇbe blotted out.

15 Let them be before the LORD continually, that he may ᵃcut¹ off the memory of them from the earth.

16 Because that he remembered not to shew mercy, but persecuted the poor and needy man, that he might even slay the ᵃbroken in heart.

17 ᵃAs he loved cursing, so let it come unto him: as he delighted not in blessing, so let it be far from him.

18 As he clothed himself with cursing like as with his garment, so let it ᵃcome into his ᵇbowels like water, and like oil into his bones.

19 Let it be unto him as the garment *which* covereth him, and for a ¹girdle wherewith he is girded continually.

20 *Let* this *be* the reward of mine ¹adversaries from the LORD, and of them that speak evil against my ²soul.

21 But do thou for me, O GOD the Lord, for thy name's sake: because thy ¹mercy *is* good, deliver thou me.

22 For I *am* poor and needy, and my heart is wounded within me.

23 I am gone ᵃlike the shadow when it ¹declineth: I am ²tossed up and down as the locust.

24 My ᵃknees are weak through fasting; and my flesh faileth of fatness.

25 I became also ᵃa reproach unto them: *when* they looked upon me ᵇthey shaked their heads.

26 Help me, O LORD my God: O save me according to thy mercy:

27 ᵃThat they may know that this *is* thy hand; *that* thou, LORD, hast done it.

28 ᵃLet them curse, but bless thou: when they arise, let them be ashamed; but let ᵇthy servant rejoice.

29 ᵃLet mine adversaries be clothed with shame, and let them cover themselves with their own confusion, as with a mantle.

30 I will greatly praise the LORD with my mouth; yea, ᵃI will praise him among the multitude.

31 For ᵃhe shall stand at the right hand of the poor, to save *him* from those ¹that condemn his soul.

## PSALM 110

### A Psalm of David.

THE ᵃLORD said unto my Lord, Sit thou at my right hand, until I make thine enemies thy ᵇfootstool.

2 The LORD shall send the rod of thy strength ᵃout of Zion: ᵇrule thou in the midst of thine enemies.

3 ᵃThy people *shall be* ¹willing in the day of thy power, ᵇin the beauties of holiness from the womb of the morning: thou hast the dew of thy youth.

4 The LORD hath sworn, and ᵃwill not ¹repent, Thou *art* a ᵇpriest for ever ²after the order of ᶜMelchizedek.

5 The Lord ᵃat thy right hand shall ¹strike through kings ᵇin the day of his wrath.

6 He shall judge among the ¹heathen, he shall fill *the places* with the dead bodies; ᵃhe shall ²wound the heads over many countries.

7 He shall drink of the brook in the way: ᵃtherefore shall he lift up the head.

## PSALM 111

PRAISE¹ ye the LORD. ᵃI will praise the LORD with *my* whole heart, in the assembly of the upright, and *in* the congregation.

2 ᵃThe works of the LORD *are* great, ᵇsought¹ out of all them that have pleasure therein.

3 His work *is* ᵃhonourable and glorious: and his righteousness endureth for ever.

4 He hath made his wonderful works to be remembered: ᵃthe LORD *is* gracious and full of compassion.

5 He hath given ¹meat unto them that fear him: he will ever be mindful of his covenant.

6 He hath shewed his people the power of his works, that he may give them the ¹heritage of the heathen.

7 The works of his hands *are* ᵃverity¹ and judgment; all his commandments *are* sure.

8 ᵃThey stand fast for ever and ever, *and are* ᵇdone in truth and uprightness.

9 ᵃHe sent redemption unto his people: he hath commanded his

109:6 ᵃ Zech. 3:1 ¹ *an accuser,* Heb. *Satan*

109:7 ᵃ [Prov. 28:9] ¹ *be found guilty*

109:8 ᵃ [Ps. 55:23] ᵇ Acts 1:20

109:9 ᵃ Ex. 22:24

109:10 ¹ *wander continuously*

109:11 ᵃ Job 5:5; 18:9 ¹ *creditor* seize ² *plunder*

109:13 ᵃ Job 18:19 ᵇ Prov. 10:7 ¹ *descendants be destroyed*

109:14 ᵃ [Ex. 20:5] ᵇ Neh. 4:5

109:15 ᵃ Job 18:17 ¹ *destroy*

109:16 ᵃ [Ps. 34:18]

109:17 ᵃ Prov. 14:14

109:18 ᵃ Num. 5:22 ¹ *body*

109:19 ¹ *belt*

109:20 ¹ *accusers* ² *person*

109:21 ¹ *lovingkindness*

109:23 ᵃ Ps. 102:11 ¹ *lengthens* ² *shaken off like*

109:24 ᵃ Heb. 12:12

109:25 ᵃ Ps. 22:7 ᵇ Matt. 27:39

109:27 ᵃ Job 37:7

109:28 ᵃ 2 Sam. 6:11, 12 ᵇ Is. 65:14

109:29 ᵃ Ps. 35:26

109:30 ᵃ Ps. 35:18; 111:1

109:31 ᵃ Ps. 16:8] ¹ Lit. *judging his soul*

110:1 ᵃ Matt. 22:44 ᵇ [1 Cor. 15:25]

110:2 ᵃ [Rom. 11:26, 27] ᵇ [Dan. 7:13, 14]

110:3 ᵃ Judg. 5:2 ᵇ Ps. 96:9 ¹ *volunteers*

110:4 ᵃ [Num. 23:19] ᵇ [Zech. 6:13] ᶜ [Heb. 5:6, 10; 6:20] ¹ *relent* ² *according to*

110:5 ᵃ [Ps. 16:8] ᵇ Ps. 2:5, 12 ¹ Lit. *break kings in pieces*

110:6 ᵃ Ps. 68:21 ¹ *nations or Gentiles* ² Lit. *break in pieces the leaders*

110:7 ᵃ [Is. 53:12]

111:1 ᵃ Ps. 35:18 ¹ Heb. *Hallelujah*

111:2 ᵃ Ps. 92:5 ᵇ Ps. 143:5 ¹ *studied by*

111:3 ᵃ Ps. 145:4, 5

111:4 ᵃ [Ps. 86:5]

111:5 ¹ *food, lit. prey*  111:6 ¹ *inheritance of the nations*
111:7 ᵃ [Rev. 15:3] ¹ *truth*  111:8 ᵃ Is. 40:8 ᵇ [Rev. 15:3]
111:9 ᵃ Luke 1:68

covenant for ever: [b]holy and reverend *is* his name.

10 [a]The[1] fear of the LORD *is* the beginning of wisdom: a good understanding have all they that do *his commandments:* his praise endureth for ever.

## PSALM 112

PRAISE[1] ye the LORD. Blessed *is* the man *that* feareth the LORD, *that* [a]delighteth greatly in his commandments.

2 [a]His seed shall be mighty upon earth: the generation of the upright shall be blessed.

3 [a]Wealth and riches *shall be* in his house: and his righteousness [1]endureth for ever.

4 [a]Unto the upright there ariseth light in the darkness: *he is* gracious, and full of compassion, and righteous.

5 [a]A good man [1]sheweth favour, and lendeth: he will guide his affairs [b]with [2]discretion.

6 Surely he shall not be [1]moved for ever: [a]the righteous shall be in everlasting remembrance.

7 [a]He shall not be afraid of evil tidings: his heart is [1]fixed, trusting in the LORD.

8 His [a]heart *is* established, [b]he shall not be afraid, until he [c]see *his desire* upon his enemies.

9 He hath [1]dispersed, he hath given to the poor; his righteousness endureth for ever; his [2]horn shall be exalted with honour.

10 The wicked shall see *it,* and be grieved; he shall gnash with his teeth, and melt away: the desire of the wicked shall perish.

## PSALM 113

PRAISE[1] ye the LORD. [a]Praise, O ye servants of the LORD, praise the name of the LORD.

2 [a]Blessed be the name of the LORD from this time forth and for evermore.

3 [a]From the rising of the sun unto the going down of the same the LORD's name *is* to be praised.

4 The LORD *is* [a]high above all nations, *and* [b]his glory above the heavens.

5 [a]Who *is* like unto the LORD our God, who dwelleth on high,

6 [a]Who humbleth *himself* to behold *the things that are* in heaven, and in the earth!

7 [a]He raiseth up the poor out of the dust, *and* lifteth the [b]needy out of [1]the dunghill;

8 That he may [a]set *him* with princes, *even* with the princes of his people.

---

111:9 [b] Luke 1:49
111:10 [a] Eccl. 12:13
[1] An awe-filled reverence toward the Lord
112:1 [a] Ps. 128:1
[1] Heb. *Hallelujah*
112:2 [a] [Ps. 102:28]
112:3 [a] [Matt. 6:33] [1] *stands*
112:4 [a] Job 11:17
112:5 [a] [Luke 6:35]
[b] [Eph. 5:15] [1] *is gracious* [2] Lit. *justice*
112:6 [a] Prov. 10:7
[1] *shaken*
112:7 [a] [Prov. 1:33]
[1] *steadfast*
112:8 [a] Heb. 13:9
[b] Prov. 1:33; 3:24
[c] Ps. 59:10
112:9 [1] *distributed abroad*
[2] Strength
113:1 [a] Ps. 135:1
[1] Heb. *Hallelujah*
113:2 [a] [Dan. 2:20]
113:3 [a] Is. 59:19
113:4 [a] Ps. 97:9;
99:2 [b] [Ps. 8:1]
113:5 [a] [Is. 57:15]
113:6 [a] [Ps. 11:4]
113:7 [a] 1 Sam. 2:8
[b] Ps. 72:12 [1] *the ash heap*
113:8 [a] [Job 36:7]

113:9 [a] 1 Sam. 2:5 [1] *causes* [2] *childless* [3] *dwell in a home*
114:1 [a] Ex. 12:51;
13:3 [b] Ps. 81:5
[1] *having a foreign*
114:2 [a] Ex. 6:7;
19:6; 25:8; 29:45, 46
114:3 [a] Ex. 14:21
[b] Josh. 3:13–16
[1] *turned back*
114:4 [a] Ps. 29:6
114:5 [a] Hab. 3:8
[1] *fled* [2] *turned back*
114:8 [a] Ex. 17:6
[1] *pool of*
115:1 [a] [Is. 48:11]
[1] *lovingkindness*
115:2 [a] Ps. 42:3, 10 [1] *Gentiles or nations*
115:3 [a] [1 Chr. 16:26]
115:4 [a] Jer. 10:3
115:8 [a] Is. 44:9–11
115:9 [a] Ps. 118:2, 3
[b] Ps. 33:20
115:12 [1] *has remembered us*
115:13 [a] Ps. 128:1, 4
115:14 [1] *give you increase*

---

9 [a]He [1]maketh the [2]barren woman to [3]keep house, *and to be* a joyful mother of children. Praise ye the LORD.

## PSALM 114

WHEN [a]Israel went out of Egypt, the house of Jacob [b]from a people [1]of strange language;

2 [a]Judah was his sanctuary, *and* Israel his dominion.

3 [a]The sea saw *it,* and fled: [b]Jordan [1]was driven back.

4 [a]The mountains skipped like rams, *and* the little hills like lambs.

5 [a]What *ailed* thee, O thou sea, that thou [1]fleddest? thou Jordan, *that* thou [2]wast driven back?

6 Ye mountains, *that* ye skipped like rams; *and* ye little hills, like lambs?

7 Tremble, thou earth, at the presence of the Lord, at the presence of the God of Jacob;

8 [a]Which turned the rock *into* a [1]standing water, the flint into a fountain of waters.

## PSALM 115

NOT [a]unto us, O LORD, not unto us, but unto thy name give glory, for thy [1]mercy, *and* for thy truth's sake.

2 Wherefore should the [1]heathen say, [a]Where *is* now their God?

3 [a]But our God *is* in the heavens: he hath done whatsoever he hath pleased.

4 [a]Their idols *are* silver and gold, the work of men's hands.

5 They have mouths, but they speak not: eyes have they, but they see not:

6 They have ears, but they hear not: noses have they, but they smell not:

7 They have hands, but they handle not: feet have they, but they walk not: neither speak they through their throat.

8 [a]They that make them are like unto them; *so is* every one that trusteth in them.

9 [a]O Israel, trust thou in the LORD: [b]he *is* their help and their shield.

10 O house of Aaron, trust in the LORD: he *is* their help and their shield.

11 Ye that fear the LORD, trust in the LORD: he *is* their help and their shield.

12 The LORD [1]hath been mindful of us: he will bless *us;* he will bless the house of Israel; he will bless the house of Aaron.

13 [a]He will bless them that fear the LORD, *both* small and great.

14 The LORD shall [1]increase you more and more, you and your children.

15 Ye *are* ᵃblessed of the LORD ᵇwhich made heaven and earth.

16 The heaven, *even* the heavens, *are* the LORD's: but the earth hath he given to the children of men.

17 ᵃThe dead praise not the LORD, neither any that go down into ¹silence.

18 ᵃBut we will bless the LORD from this time forth and for evermore. Praise the LORD.

## PSALM 116

I ᵃLOVE the LORD, because he hath heard my voice *and* my supplications.

2 Because he ¹hath inclined his ear unto me, therefore will I call upon *him* as long as I live.

3 ᵃThe sorrows of death ¹compassed me, and the ²pains of ³hell ⁴gat hold upon me: I found trouble and sorrow.

4 Then called I upon the name of the LORD; O LORD, I beseech thee, deliver my soul.

5 ᵃGracious *is* the LORD, and ᵇrighteous; yea, our God *is* merciful.

6 The LORD preserveth the simple: I was brought low, and he ¹helped me.

7 Return unto thy ᵃrest, O my soul; for ᵇthe LORD hath dealt bountifully with thee.

8 ᵃFor thou hast delivered my soul from death, mine eyes from tears, *and* my feet from falling.

9 I will walk before the LORD ᵃin the land of the living.

10 ᵃI believed, therefore have I spoken: I was greatly afflicted:

11 ᵃI said in my haste, ᵇAll men *are* liars.

12 What shall I render unto the LORD *for* all his benefits toward me?

13 I will take the cup of salvation, and call upon the name of the LORD.

14 ᵃI will pay my vows unto the LORD now in the presence of all his people.

15 ᵃPrecious in the sight of the LORD *is* the death of his saints.

16 O LORD, truly ᵃI *am* thy servant; I *am* thy servant, *and* ᵇthe son of thine ¹handmaid: thou hast loosed my bonds.

17 I will offer to thee ᵃthe sacrifice of thanksgiving, and will call upon the name of the LORD.

18 I will pay my vows unto the LORD now in the presence of all his people,

19 In the ᵃcourts of the LORD's house, in the midst of thee, O Jerusalem. ¹Praise ye the LORD.

## PSALM 117

O ᵃPRAISE the LORD, all ye ¹nations: ²praise him, all ye people.

2 For his ¹merciful kindness is great toward us: and ᵃthe truth of the LORD *endureth* for ever. Praise ye the LORD.

## PSALM 118

O ᵃGIVE thanks unto the LORD; for *he is* good: ᵇbecause his ¹mercy *endureth* for ever.

2 ᵃLet Israel now say, that his mercy *endureth* for ever.

3 Let the house of Aaron now say, that his mercy *endureth* for ever.

4 Let them now that fear the LORD say, that his ¹mercy *endureth* for ever.

5 ᵃI called upon the LORD in distress: the LORD answered me, *and* ᵇset *me* in a ¹large place.

6 ᵃThe LORD *is* on my side; I will not fear: what can man do unto me?

7 ᵃThe LORD taketh my part with them that help me: therefore shall ᵇI see *my desire* upon them that hate me.

8 ᵃIt¹ *is* better to trust in the LORD than to put confidence in man.

9 ᵃIt *is* better to trust in the LORD than to put confidence in princes.

10 All nations ¹compassed me about: but in the name of the LORD will I destroy them.

11 They ᵃcompassed¹ me about; yea, they compassed me about: but in the name of the LORD I will destroy them.

12 They ¹compassed me about ᵃlike bees; they are quenched ᵇas the fire of thorns: for in the name of the LORD I will destroy them.

13 Thou hast ¹thrust sore at me that I might fall: but the LORD helped me.

14 ᵃThe LORD *is* my strength and song, and is become my salvation.

15 The voice of rejoicing and salvation *is* in the ¹tabernacles of the righteous: the right hand of the LORD doeth valiantly.

16 ᵃThe right hand of the LORD is exalted: the right hand of the LORD doeth valiantly.

17 ᵃI shall not die, but live, and ᵇdeclare the works of the LORD.

18 The LORD hath ᵃchastened¹ me sore: but he hath not given me over unto death.

19 ᵃOpen to me the gates of righteousness: I will go into them, *and* I will praise the LORD:

20 ᵃThis gate of the LORD, ᵇinto which the righteous shall enter.

21 I will praise thee: for thou hast ᵃheard¹ me, and art become my salvation.

22 ᵃThe stone *which* the builders ¹refused is become the ²head *stone* of the corner.

23 This is ¹the LORD's doing; it *is* marvellous in our eyes.

115:15 ᵃ [Gen. 14:19] ᵇ Gen. 1:1
115:17 ᵃ [Is. 38:18] ¹ The place of the dead
115:18 ᵃ Dan. 2:20
116:1 ᵃ Ps. 18:1
116:2 ¹ *hath listened to me*
116:3 ᵃ Ps. 18:4–6 ¹ surrounded ² distress ³ Or Sheol ⁴ *laid hold, lit. found me*
116:5 ᵃ [Ps. 103:8] ᵇ [Ezra 9:15]
116:6 ¹ Lit. *saved*
116:7 ᵃ [Jer. 6:16] ᵇ Ps. 13:6
116:8 ᵃ Ps. 56:13
116:9 ᵃ Ps. 27:13
116:10 ᵃ 2 Cor. 4:13
116:11 ᵃ Ps. 31:22 ᵇ Rom. 3:4
116:14 ᵃ Ps. 116:18
116:15 ᵃ Ps. 72:14
116:16 ᵃ Ps. 119:125; 143:12 ᵇ Ps. 86:16 ¹ *maidservant*
116:17 ᵃ Lev. 7:12
116:19 ᵃ Ps. 96:8 ¹ Heb. *Hallelujah*
117:1 ᵃ Rom. 15:11 ¹ Gentiles ² *glorify*
117:2 ᵃ [Ps. 100:5] ¹ *lovingkindness*
118:1 ᵃ 1 Chr. 16:8, 34 ᵇ [Ps. 136:1–26] ¹ *loving-kindness*
118:2 ᵃ [Ps. 115:9]
118:4 ¹ *loving-kindness*
118:5 ᵃ Ps. 120:1 ᵇ Ps. 18:19 ¹ *broad*
118:6 ᵃ Ps. 27:1; 56:9
118:7 ᵃ Ps. 54:4 ᵇ Ps. 59:10
118:8 ᵃ Ps. 40:4 ¹ The middle verse of the Bible
118:9 ᵃ Ps. 146:3
118:10 ¹ *surrounded*
118:11 ᵃ Ps. 88:17 ¹ surrounded
118:12 ᵃ Deut. 1:44 ᵇ Nah. 1:10 ¹ surrounded
118:13 ¹ *pushed at me violently*
118:14 ᵃ Is. 12:2
118:15 ¹ tents
118:16 ᵃ Ex. 15:6
118:17 ᵃ Hab. 1:12 ᵇ Ps. 73:28
118:18 ᵃ 2 Cor. 6:9 ¹ *disciplined me severely*
118:19 ᵃ Is. 26:2
118:20 ᵃ Ps. 24:7 ᵇ Is. 35:8
118:21 ᵃ Ps. 116:1 ¹ Lit. *answered* 118:22 ᵃ Matt. 21:42 ¹ *rejected* ² *chief corner stone* 118:23 ¹ Lit. *from the LORD*

24 This *is* the day *which* the LORD hath made; we will rejoice and be glad in it.

25 Save now, I beseech thee, O LORD: O LORD, I beseech thee, send now prosperity.

26 ªBlessed *be* he that cometh in the name of the LORD: we have blessed you out of the house of the LORD.

27 God *is* the LORD, ¹which hath shewed us ªlight: bind the sacrifice with cords, *even* unto the horns of the altar.

28 Thou *art* my God, and I will praise thee: ªthou *art* my God, I will exalt thee.

29 O give thanks unto the LORD; for *he is* good: for his mercy *endureth* for ever.

## PSALM 119

### א ALEPH

**B**LESSED *are* the ¹undefiled in the way, ªwho walk in the law of the LORD.

2 Blessed *are* they that keep his testimonies, *and that* seek him with the ªwhole heart.

3 ªThey also do no iniquity: they walk in his ways.

4 Thou hast commanded *us* to keep thy precepts diligently.

5 O that my ways were directed to keep thy statutes!

6 ªThen shall I not be ashamed, when I ¹have respect unto all thy commandments.

7 I will praise thee with uprightness of heart, when I shall have learned thy righteous judgments.

8 I will keep thy statutes: O forsake me not utterly.

### ב BETH

9 Wherewithal shall a young man cleanse his way? by taking heed *thereto* according to thy word.

10 With my whole heart have I ªsought thee: O let me not wander from thy commandments.

11 ªThy word have I hid in mine heart, that I might not sin against thee.

12 Blessed *art* thou, O LORD: teach me thy statutes.

13 With my lips have I ªdeclared all the judgments of thy mouth.

14 I have rejoiced in the way of thy testimonies, as *much as* in all riches.

15 I will meditate in thy precepts, and ¹have respect unto thy ways.

16 I will ªdelight myself in thy statutes: I will not forget thy word.

### ג GIMEL

17 ªDeal bountifully with thy servant, *that* I may live, and keep thy word.

---

118:26 ª Mark 11:9
118:27 ª [1 Pet. 2:9]
  ¹ *and he hath given us light*
118:28 ª Is. 25:1
119:1 ª Ps. 128:1
  ¹ *blameless*
119:2 ª Deut. 6:5; 10:12; 11:13; 13:3
119:3 ª [1 John 3:9; 5:18]
119:6 ª Job 22:26
  ¹ *look into*
119:10 ª 2 Chr. 15:15
119:11 ª Ps. 37:31; Luke 2:19
119:13 ª Ps. 34:11
119:15 ¹ *contemplate*
119:16 ª Ps. 1:2
119:17 ª Ps. 116:7

119:19 ª Gen. 47:9; Lev. 25:23; 1 Chr. 29:15; Ps. 39:12; Heb. 11:13
119:20 ª Ps. 42:1, 2; 63:1; 84:2 ¹ *is crushed with*
119:21 ¹ *stray*
119:22 ª Ps. 39:8
119:25 ª Ps. 44:25 ᵇ Ps. 143:11
  ¹ *clings to* ² *revive*
119:26 ª Ps. 25:4; 27:11; 86:11 ¹ Lit. *answered*
119:27 ª Ps. 145:5, 6 ¹ *meditate on*
119:28 ª Ps. 107:26
  ¹ *weeps* ² *grief*
119:31 ¹ *cling to*
119:32 ª 1 Kin. 4:29; Is. 60:5; 2 Cor. 6:11, 13
119:33 ª [Matt. 10:22; Rev. 2:26]
119:34 ª [Prov. 2:6; James 1:5]
119:36 ª Ezek. 33:31; [Mark 7:20–23]; Luke 12:15; [Heb. 13:5]
  ¹ *Cause me to long for*
119:37 ª Is. 33:15
  ᵇ Prov. 23:5
  ¹ *looking at worthless things* ² *revive*
119:38 ª 2 Sam. 7:25 ¹ *Establish* ² *fearing you*
119:40 ¹ *revive*
119:41 ¹ *lovingkindness*

---

18 Open thou mine eyes, that I may behold wondrous things out of thy law.

19 ªI *am* a stranger in the earth: hide not thy commandments from me.

20 ªMy soul ¹breaketh for the longing *that it hath* unto thy judgments at all times.

21 Thou hast rebuked the proud *that are* cursed, which ¹do err from thy commandments.

22 ªRemove from me reproach and contempt; for I have kept thy testimonies.

23 Princes also did sit *and* speak against me: *but* thy servant did meditate in thy statutes.

24 Thy testimonies also *are* my delight *and* my counsellors.

### ד DALETH

25 ªMy soul ¹cleaveth unto the dust: ᵇquicken² thou me according to thy word.

26 I have declared my ways, and thou ¹heardest me: ªteach me thy statutes.

27 Make me to understand the way of thy precepts: so ªshall I ¹talk of thy wondrous works.

28 ªMy soul ¹melteth for ²heaviness: strengthen thou me according unto thy word.

29 Remove from me the way of lying: and grant me thy law graciously.

30 I have chosen the way of truth: thy judgments have I laid *before me*.

31 I ¹have stuck unto thy testimonies: O LORD, put me not to shame.

32 I will run the way of thy commandments, when thou shalt ªenlarge my heart.

### ה HE

33 ªTeach me, O LORD, the way of thy statutes; and I shall keep it *unto* the end.

34 ªGive me understanding, and I shall keep thy law; yea, I shall observe it with *my* whole heart.

35 Make me to go in the path of thy commandments; for therein do I delight.

36 ¹Incline my heart unto thy testimonies, and not to ªcovetousness.

37 ªTurn away mine eyes from ᵇbeholding¹ vanity; *and* ²quicken thou me in thy way.

38 ªStablish¹ thy word unto thy servant, who *is devoted* to ²thy fear.

39 Turn away my reproach which I fear: for thy judgments *are* good.

40 Behold, I have longed after thy precepts: ¹quicken me in thy righteousness.

### ו VAU

41 Let thy ¹mercies come also unto me, O LORD, *even* thy salvation, according to thy word.

42 So shall I have [1]wherewith to answer him that reproacheth me: for I trust in thy word.

43 And take not the word of truth utterly out of my mouth; for I have hoped in thy judgments.

44 So shall I keep thy law continually for ever and ever.

45 And I will walk [1]at [a]liberty: for I seek thy precepts.

46 [a]I will speak of thy testimonies also before kings, and will not be ashamed.

47 And I will delight myself in thy commandments, which I have loved.

48 My hands also will I lift up unto thy commandments, which I have loved; and I will meditate in thy statutes.

### [1] ZAIN

49 Remember the word unto thy servant, upon which thou hast caused me to hope.

50 This *is* my [a]comfort in my affliction: for thy word hath [1]quickened me.

51 The proud have had me greatly in derision: *yet* have I not [1]declined from thy law.

52 I remembered thy judgments of old, O LORD; and have comforted myself.

53 [a]Horror[1] hath taken hold upon me because of the wicked that forsake thy law.

54 Thy statutes have been my songs in the house of my pilgrimage.

55 I have remembered thy name, O LORD, in the night, and have kept thy law.

56 This I had, because I kept thy precepts.

### ⊓ CHETH

57 [a]*Thou art* my portion, O LORD: I have said that I would keep thy words.

58 I intreated thy favour with *my* whole heart: be merciful unto me according to thy word.

59 I [a]thought on my ways, and turned my feet unto thy testimonies.

60 I made haste, and delayed not to keep thy commandments.

61 The [1]bands of the wicked have [2]robbed me: *but* I have not forgotten thy law.

62 [2][a]At midnight I will rise to give thanks unto thee because of thy righteous judgments.

63 I *am* a companion of all *them* that fear thee, and of them that keep thy precepts.

64 [a]The earth, O LORD, is full of thy [1]mercy: teach me thy statutes.

### ♍ TETH

65 Thou hast dealt well with thy servant, O LORD, according unto thy word.

66 Teach me good judgment and [a]knowledge: for I have believed thy commandments.

67 Before I was [a]afflicted I went astray: but now have I kept thy word.

68 Thou *art* [a]good, and doest good; teach me thy statutes.

69 The proud have [a]forged[1] a lie against me: *but* I will keep thy precepts with *my* whole heart.

70 [a]Their heart is [1]as fat as grease; *but* I delight in thy law.

71 *It is* good for me that I have been afflicted; that I might learn thy statutes.

72 [a]The law of thy mouth *is* better unto me than thousands of gold and silver.

### ' JOD

73 [a]Thy hands have made me and fashioned me: give me understanding, that I may learn thy commandments.

74 [a]They that fear thee will be glad when they see me; because I have hoped in thy word.

75 I know, O LORD, [a]that thy judgments *are* [1]right, and *that* thou in faithfulness hast afflicted me.

76 Let, I pray thee, thy merciful kindness be for my comfort, according to thy word unto thy servant.

77 Let thy tender mercies come unto me, that I may live: for thy law *is* my delight.

78 Let the proud [a]be ashamed; for they [1]dealt perversely with me without a cause: *but* I will meditate in thy precepts.

79 Let those that fear thee turn unto me, and those that have known thy testimonies.

80 Let my heart be [1]sound in thy statutes; that I be not ashamed.

### ⊃ CAPH

81 [a]My soul fainteth for thy salvation: *but* I hope in thy word.

82 Mine eyes fail for thy word, saying, When wilt thou comfort me?

83 For [a]I am become like a [1]bottle in the smoke; *yet* do I not forget thy statutes.

84 [a]How many *are* the days of thy servant? [b]when wilt thou execute judgment on them that persecute me?

85 [a]The proud have [1]digged pits for me, which *are* not [2]after thy law.

86 All thy commandments *are* faithful: they persecute me [a]wrongfully; help thou me.

87 They had almost [1]consumed me upon earth; but I forsook not thy precepts.

88 [1]Quicken me after thy lovingkindness; so shall I keep the testimony of thy mouth.

## ל LAMED

89 [a]For ever, O LORD, thy word [1]is settled in heaven.

90 Thy faithfulness *is* unto all generations: thou hast established the earth, and it [1]abideth.

91 They continue this day according to [a]thine ordinances: for all *are* thy servants.

92 Unless thy law *had been* my delights, I should then have perished in mine affliction.

93 I will never forget thy precepts: for with them thou hast [1]quickened me.

94 I *am* thine, save me; for I have sought thy precepts.

95 The wicked have waited for me to destroy me: *but* I will [1]consider thy testimonies.

96 [a]I have seen an end of all perfection: *but* thy commandment *is* exceeding broad.

## מ MEM

97 O how love I thy law! [a]it *is* my meditation all the day.

98 Thou through thy commandments hast made me [a]wiser than mine enemies: for they *are* ever with me.

99 I have more understanding than all my teachers: [a]for thy testimonies *are* my meditation.

100 [a]I understand more than the [1]ancients, because I keep thy precepts.

101 I have [1]refrained my feet from every evil way, that I might keep thy word.

102 I have not departed from thy judgments: for thou hast taught me.

103 [a]How sweet are thy words unto my taste! *yea, sweeter* than honey to my mouth!

104 Through thy precepts I get understanding: therefore I hate every false way.

## נ NUN

105 [a]Thy word *is* a lamp unto my feet, and a light unto my path.

106 [a]I have sworn, and I will [1]perform *it,* that I will keep thy righteous judgments.

107 I am afflicted very much: [1]quicken me, O LORD, according unto thy word.

108 Accept, I beseech thee, [a]the freewill offerings of my mouth, O LORD, and teach me thy judgments.

109 [a]My [1]soul *is* continually [2]in my hand: yet do I not forget thy law.

110 [a]The wicked have laid a snare for me: yet I [1]erred not from thy precepts.

111 [a]Thy testimonies have I taken as [1]an heritage for ever: for they *are* the rejoicing of my heart.

119:89 [a] Ps. 89:2; Is. 40:8; Matt. 24:35; [1 Pet. 1:25]
[1] Lit. *stands firm*

119:90 [1] Lit. *stands*

119:91 [a] Jer. 33:25

119:93 [1] *given me life*

119:95 [1] *give attention to*

119:96 [a] Matt. 5:18

119:97 [a] Ps. 1:2

119:98 [a] Deut. 4:6

119:99 [a] [2 Tim. 3:15]

119:100 [a] [Job 32:7–9] [1] *aged*

119:101 [1] *restrained*

119:103 [a] Ps. 19:10; Prov. 8:11

119:105 [a] Prov. 6:23

119:106 [a] Neh. 10:29 [1] *confirm*

119:107 [1] *revive*

119:108 [a] Hos. 14:2; Heb. 13:15

119:109 [a] Job 13:14 [1] *life* [2] *In danger*

119:110 [a] Ps. 140:5 [1] *strayed*

119:111 [a] Deut. 33:4 [1] *an inheritance*

119:113 [1] *the double-minded*

119:114 [a] [Ps. 32:7]

119:115 [a] Matt. 7:23

119:116 [a] [Rom. 5:5; 9:33; 10:11]

119:117 [1] *Uphold me* [2] *observe your statutes*

119:118 [1] *rejected* [2] *stray*

119:119 [a] Ezek. 22:18, 19 [1] *destroy,* lit. *cause to cease* [2] *slag or refuse*

119:120 [a] Hab. 3:16

119:122 [a] Heb. 7:22 [1] *security*

119:123 [1] *from seeking for* [2] *thy righteous word*

119:124 [1] *lovingkindness*

119:125 [a] Ps. 116:16

119:126 [1] *regarded thy law as void*

119:127 [a] Ps. 19:10

119:130 [a] Prov. 6:23 [b] [Ps. 19:7]

119:131 [a] Ps. 42:1

119:132 [a] Ps. 106:4 [b] [2 Thess. 1:6] [1] *thy custom is toward those*

119:133 [a] Ps. 17:5 [b] [Rom. 6:12] [1] *Direct*

119:134 [a] Luke 1:74 [1] *Redeem*

112 I have inclined mine heart to perform thy statutes alway, *even* unto the end.

## ס SAMECH

113 I hate [1]*vain* thoughts: but thy law do I love.

114 [a]Thou *art* my hiding place and my shield: I hope in thy word.

115 [a]Depart from me, ye evildoers: for I will keep the commandments of my God.

116 Uphold me according unto thy word, that I may live: and let me not [a]be ashamed of my hope.

117 [1]Hold thou me up, and I shall be safe: and I will [2]have respect unto thy statutes continually.

118 Thou hast [1]trodden down all them that [2]err from thy statutes: for their deceit *is* falsehood.

119 Thou [1]puttest away all the wicked of the earth [a]like [2]dross: therefore I love thy testimonies.

120 [a]My flesh trembleth for fear of thee; and I am afraid of thy judgments.

## ע AIN

121 I have done judgment and justice: leave me not to mine oppressors.

122 Be [a]surety[1] for thy servant for good: let not the proud oppress me.

123 Mine eyes fail [1]for thy salvation, and for [2]the word of thy righteousness.

124 Deal with thy servant according unto thy [1]mercy, and teach me thy statutes.

125 [a]I *am* thy servant; give me understanding, that I may know thy testimonies.

126 *It is* time for *thee,* LORD, to work: *for* they have [1]made void thy law.

127 [a]Therefore I love thy commandments above gold; yea, above fine gold.

128 Therefore I esteem all *thy* precepts *concerning* all *things to be* right; *and* I hate every false way.

## פ PE

129 Thy testimonies *are* wonderful: therefore doth my soul keep them.

130 The entrance of thy words giveth light; [a]it giveth understanding unto the [b]simple.

131 I opened my mouth, and [a]panted: for I longed for thy commandments.

132 [a]Look thou upon me, and be merciful unto me, [b]as [1]thou usest to do unto those that love thy name.

133 [a]Order[1] my steps in thy word: and [b]let not any iniquity have dominion over me.

134 [a]Deliver[1] me from the oppression of man: so will I keep thy precepts.

135 ᵃMake thy face to shine upon thy servant; and teach me thy statutes.

136 ᵃRivers of waters run down mine eyes, because ¹they keep not thy law.

### צ TZADDI

137 ᵃRighteous *art* thou, O LORD, and upright *are* thy judgments.

138 ᵃThy testimonies *that* thou hast commanded *are* righteous and very faithful.

139 ᵃMy zeal hath ¹consumed me, because mine enemies have forgotten thy words.

140 ᵃThy word *is* very ¹pure: therefore thy servant loveth it.

141 I *am* small and despised: *yet* do not I forget thy precepts.

142 Thy righteousness *is* an everlasting righteousness, and thy law *is* ᵃthe truth.

143 Trouble and anguish have ¹taken hold on me: *yet* thy commandments *are* my delights.

144 The righteousness of thy testimonies *is* everlasting: give me understanding, and I shall live.

### ק KOPH

145 I cried with *my* whole heart; hear me, O LORD: I will keep thy statutes.

146 I cried unto thee; save me, and I shall keep thy testimonies.

147 ᵃI ¹prevented the dawning of the morning, and ²cried: I hoped in thy word.

148 ᵃMine eyes ¹prevent the *night* watches, that I might meditate in thy word.

149 Hear my voice according unto thy lovingkindness: O LORD, ¹quicken me according to thy ²judgment.

150 They draw nigh that follow after mischief: they are far from thy law.

151 Thou *art* ᵃnear, O LORD; and all thy commandments *are* truth.

152 Concerning thy testimonies, I have known of old that thou hast founded them ᵃfor ever.

### ר RESH

153 ᵃConsider mine affliction, and deliver me: for I do not forget thy law.

154 ᵃPlead my cause, and deliver me: ¹quicken me according to thy word.

155 Salvation *is* far from the wicked: for they seek not thy statutes.

156 Great *are* thy tender mercies, O LORD: quicken me according to thy judgments.

157 Many *are* my persecutors and mine enemies; *yet* do I not ᵃdecline¹ from thy testimonies.

158 I beheld the transgressors, and ¹was ᵃgrieved; because they kept not thy word.

---

119:135 ᵃ Ps. 4:6
119:136 ᵃ Jer. 9:1, 18; 14:17 ¹ Men
119:137 ¹ Neh. 9:33
119:138 ᵃ [Ps. 19:7–9]
119:139 ᵃ John 2:17 ¹ put an end to
119:140 ᵃ Ps. 12:6 ¹ Lit. refined or tried
119:142 ᵃ [John 17:17]
119:143 ¹ Lit. found
119:147 ᵃ Ps. 5:3 ¹ rose before ² cried for help
119:148 ᵃ Ps. 63:1, 6 ¹ are awake through
119:149 ¹ revive ² justice
119:151 ᵃ [Ps. 145:18]
119:152 ᵃ Luke 21:33
119:153 ᵃ Lam. 5:1
119:154 ᵃ 1 Sam. 24:15 ¹ revive
119:157 ᵃ Ps. 44:18 ¹ turn away
119:158 ᵃ Ezek. 9:4 ¹ am disgusted
119:159 ¹ revive
119:160 ¹ in its entirety
119:161 ᵃ 1 Sam. 24:11; 26:18
119:162 ¹ treasure
119:165 ᵃ Prov. 3:2; [Is. 26:3; 32:17] ¹ causes them to stumble
119:166 ᵃ Gen. 49:18
119:168 ᵃ Job 24:23; Prov. 5:21
119:169 ᵃ Ps. 119:27, 144
119:170 ¹ Prayer of supplication
119:171 ᵃ Ps. 119:7
119:173 ᵃ Josh. 24:22; Luke 10:42
119:174 ᵃ Ps.
119:166 ᵇ Ps. 119:16, 24
119:176 ᵃ [Is. 53:6]; Jer. 50:6; Matt. 18:12; Luke 15:4; [1 Pet. 2:25]
120:1 ᵃ Jon. 2:2
120:3 ¹ deceitful
120:4 ¹ warrior ² the broom tree
120:5 ᵃ Gen. 10:2; 1 Chr. 1:5; Ezek. 27:13; 38:2, 3; 39:1 ᵇ Gen. 25:13; Is. 21:16; 60:7; Jer. 2:10; 49:28; Ezek. 27:21
120:6 ¹ dwelt too long

---

159 Consider how I love thy precepts: ¹quicken me, O LORD, according to thy lovingkindness.

160 Thy word *is* true ¹*from* the beginning: and every one of thy righteous judgments *endureth* for ever.

### ש SCHIN

161 ᵃPrinces have persecuted me without a cause: but my heart standeth in awe of thy word.

162 I rejoice at thy word, as one that findeth great ¹spoil.

163 I hate and abhor lying: *but* thy law do I love.

164 Seven times a day do I praise thee because of thy righteous judgments.

165 ᵃGreat peace have they which love thy law: and nothing ¹shall offend them.

166 ᵃLORD, I have hoped for thy salvation, and done thy commandments.

167 My soul hath kept thy testimonies; and I love them exceedingly.

168 I have kept thy precepts and thy testimonies: ᵃfor all my ways *are* before thee.

### ת TAU

169 Let my cry come near before thee, O LORD: ᵃgive me understanding according to thy word.

170 Let my ¹supplication come before thee: deliver me according to thy word.

171 ᵃMy lips shall utter praise, when thou hast taught me thy statutes.

172 My tongue shall speak of thy word: for all thy commandments *are* righteousness.

173 Let thine hand help me; for ᵃI have chosen thy precepts.

174 ᵃI have longed for thy salvation, O LORD; and ᵇthy law *is* my delight.

175 Let my soul live, and it shall praise thee; and let thy judgments help me.

176 ᵃI have gone astray like a lost sheep; seek thy servant; for I do not forget thy commandments.

## PSALM 120

### A Song of degrees.

IN ᵃmy distress I cried unto the LORD, and he heard me.

2 Deliver my soul, O LORD, from lying lips, *and* from a deceitful tongue.

3 What shall be given unto thee? or what shall be done unto thee, ¹thou false tongue?

4 Sharp arrows of the ¹mighty, with coals of ²juniper.

5 Woe is me, that I sojourn in ᵃMesech, ᵇ*that* I dwell in the tents of Kedar!

6 My soul hath ¹long dwelt with him that hateth peace.

7 I *am for* peace: but when I speak, they *are* for war.

## PSALM 121
### A Song of degrees.

I [a]WILL lift up mine eyes unto the [1]hills, from whence cometh my help.

2 [a]My help *cometh* from the LORD, which made heaven and earth.

3 [a]He will not suffer thy foot to [1]be moved: [b]he that keepeth thee will not slumber.

4 Behold, he that keepeth Israel shall neither slumber nor sleep.

5 The LORD *is* thy [1]keeper: the LORD *is* [a]thy shade [b]upon thy right hand.

6 [a]The sun shall not smite thee by day, nor the moon by night.

7 The LORD shall [1]preserve thee from all evil: he shall [a]preserve thy soul.

8 The LORD shall [a]preserve[1] thy going out and thy coming in from this time forth, and even for evermore.

## PSALM 122
### A Song of degrees of David.

I WAS glad when they said unto me, [a]Let us go into the house of the LORD.

2 Our feet shall stand within thy gates, O Jerusalem.

3 Jerusalem is builded as a city that is [a]compact together:

4 [a]Whither the tribes go up, the tribes of the LORD, [1]unto [b]the testimony of Israel, to give thanks unto the name of the LORD.

5 [a]For there are set thrones of judgment, the thrones of the house of David.

6 [a]Pray for the peace of Jerusalem: they shall prosper that love thee.

7 Peace be within thy walls, *and* prosperity within thy palaces.

8 For my brethren and companions' sakes, I will now say, Peace *be* within thee.

9 Because of the house of the LORD our God I will [a]seek thy good.

## PSALM 123
### A Song of degrees.

U NTO thee [a]lift I up mine eyes, O thou [b]that dwellest in the heavens.

2 Behold, as the eyes of servants *look* unto the hand of their masters, *and* as the eyes of a [1]maiden unto the hand of her mistress; [a]so our eyes [2]*wait* upon the LORD our God, until that he have mercy upon us.

3 Have mercy upon us, O LORD, have mercy upon us: for we are exceedingly filled with contempt.

4 Our soul is exceedingly filled with

121:1 [a] [Jer. 3:23] [1] *mountains*
121:2 [a] [Ps. 124:8]
121:3 [a] 1 Sam. 2:9; Prov. 3:23, 26 [b] [Ps. 127:1; Prov. 24:19]; Is. 27:3 [1] *slip*
121:5 [a] Is. 25:4 [b] Ps. 16:8 [1] *protector*
121:6 [a] Ps. 91:5; Is. 49:10; Jon. 4:8; Rev. 7:16
121:7 [a] Ps. 41:2 [1] Lit. *keep*
121:8 [a] Deut. 28:6; [Prov. 2:8; 3:6] [1] Lit. *keep*
122:1 [a] [Is. 2:3]; Mic. 4:2]; Zech. 8:21
122:3 [a] 2 Sam. 5:9
122:4 [a] Ex. 23:17; Deut. 16:16 [b] Ex. 16:34 [1] Or *as a testimony to*
122:5 [a] Deut. 17:8; 2 Chr. 19:8
122:6 [a] Ps. 51:18
122:9 [a] Neh. 2:10
123:1 [a] Ps. 121:1; 141:8 [b] Ps. 2:4; 11:4; 115:3
123:2 [a] Ps. 25:15 [1] *maid* [2] Look

124:1 [a] [Rom. 8:31] [b] Ps. 129:1
124:3 [a] Prov. 1:12 [1] *alive*
124:4 [1] *would have* [2] *swept over*
124:5 [1] *would have swept over*
124:7 [a] Ps. 91:3 [b] Prov. 6:5 [1] Trapper of birds
124:8 [a] [Ps. 121:2] [b] Gen. 1:1
125:1 [1] *moved*
125:2 [1] *surround*
125:3 [a] Prov. 22:8 [1] *sceptre of wickedness* [2] *land allotted to* [3] *reach*
125:5 [a] Prov. 2:15 [b] [Gal. 6:16]
126:1 [a] Hos. 6:11 [b] Acts 12:9 [1] Brought back those of the captivity
126:2 [a] Job 8:21 [1] *nations* or *Gentiles*
126:4 [1] *Bring back our captives*
126:5 [a] Jer. 31:9
126:6 [a] Is. 61:3 [1] *to and fro* [2] Lit. *a bag of seed for sowing* [3] *shouts of joy*

the scorning of those that are at ease, *and* with the contempt of the proud.

## PSALM 124
### A Song of degrees of David.

I F *it had* not *been* the LORD who was on our [a]side, [b]now may Israel say;

2 If *it had not been* the LORD who was on our side, when men rose up against us:

3 Then they had [a]swallowed us up [1]quick, when their wrath was kindled against us:

4 Then the waters [1]had overwhelmed us, the stream had [2]gone over our soul:

5 Then the proud waters [1]had gone over our soul.

6 Blessed *be* the LORD, who hath not given us *as* a prey to their teeth.

7 [a]Our soul is escaped [b]as a bird out of the snare of the [1]fowlers: the snare is broken, and we are escaped.

8 [a]Our help *is* in the name of the LORD, [b]who made heaven and earth.

## PSALM 125
### A Song of degrees.

T HEY that trust in the LORD *shall be* as mount Zion, *which* cannot be [1]removed, *but* abideth for ever.

2 *As* the mountains [1]*are* round about Jerusalem, so the LORD *is* round about his people from henceforth even for ever.

3 For [a]the [1]rod of the wicked shall not rest upon the [2]lot of the righteous; lest the righteous [3]put forth their hands unto iniquity.

4 Do good, O LORD, unto *those that be* good, and to *them that are* upright in their hearts.

5 As for such as turn aside unto their [a]crooked ways, the LORD shall lead them forth with the workers of iniquity: *but* [b]peace *shall be* upon Israel.

## PSALM 126
### A Song of degrees.

W HEN [a]the LORD [1]turned again the captivity of Zion, [b]we were like them that dream.

2 Then [a]was our mouth filled with laughter, and our tongue with singing: then said they among the [1]heathen, The LORD hath done great things for them.

3 The LORD hath done great things for us; *whereof* we are glad.

4 [1]Turn again our captivity, O LORD, as the streams in the south.

5 [a]They that sow in tears shall reap in joy.

6 He that goeth [1]forth and weepeth, bearing [2]precious seed, shall doubtless come again with [a]rejoicing,[3] bringing his sheaves *with him.*

## PSALM 127

A Song of degrees [1]for Solomon.

Except the LORD build the house, they labour in vain that build it: except [a]the LORD [1]keep the city, the watchman [2]waketh *but* in vain.

2 *It is* vain for you to rise up early, to sit up late, to [a]eat the bread of sorrows: *for* so he giveth his beloved sleep.

3 Lo, [a]children *are* an heritage of the LORD: *and* [b]the fruit of the womb *is his* [c]reward.

4 As arrows *are* in the hand of a [1]mighty man; so *are* children of the youth.

5 [a]Happy *is* the man that hath his quiver full of them: [b]they shall not be ashamed, but they shall speak with the enemies in the gate.

## PSALM 128

A Song of degrees.

Blessed [a]*is* every one that feareth the LORD; that walketh in his ways.

2 [a]For thou shalt eat the [1]labour of thine hands: happy *shalt* thou *be,* and *it shall be* [b]well with thee.

3 Thy wife *shall be* [a]as a fruitful vine [1]by the sides of thine house: thy [b]children [c]like olive plants round about thy table.

4 Behold, that thus shall the man be blessed that feareth the LORD.

5 [a]The LORD shall bless thee out of Zion: and thou shalt see the good of Jerusalem all the days of thy life.

6 Yea, thou shalt [a]see thy children's children, *and* [b]peace upon Israel.

## PSALM 129

A Song of degrees.

Many a time have they [a]afflicted[1] me from [b]my youth, [c]may Israel now say:

2 Many a time have they afflicted me from my youth: yet they have not prevailed against me.

3 The plowers plowed upon my back: they made long their furrows.

4 The LORD *is* righteous: he hath [1]cut asunder the cords of the wicked.

5 Let them all be [1]confounded and turned back that hate Zion.

6 Let them be as [a]the grass *upon* the housetops, which withereth afore it groweth up:

7 Wherewith the [1]mower filleth not his hand; nor he that bindeth sheaves his [2]bosom.

8 Neither do they which go by say, [a]The blessing of the LORD *be* upon you: we bless you in the name of the LORD.

### Cross references

127:title [1] *of*
127:1 [a] [Ps. 121:3–5] [1] *guards* [2] *stays awake in vain*
127:2 [a] [Gen. 3:17, 19]
127:3 [a] [Josh. 24:3, 4] [b] Deut. 7:13; 28:4 [c] [Ps. 113:9]
127:4 [1] *warrior*
127:5 [a] Ps. 128:2, 3 [b] Prov. 27:11
128:1 [a] Ps. 119:1
128:2 [a] Is. 3:10 [b] Deut. 4:40 [1] *Fruit of the labour*
128:3 [a] Ezek. 19:10 [b] Ps. 127:3–5 [c] Ps. 52:8; 144:12 [1] *in the heart of*
128:5 [a] Ps. 134:3
128:6 [a] Job 42:16 [b] Ps. 125:5
129:1 [a] [Jer. 1:19; 15:20] [b] Ezek. 23:3; [c] Ps. 124:1 [1] *persecuted*
129:4 [1] *cut in pieces*
129:5 [1] *put to shame*
129:6 [a] Ps. 37:2
129:7 [1] *reaper* [2] *armsful*
129:8 [a] Ruth 2:4
130:1 [a] Lam. 3:55
130:3 [a] [Ps. 143:2] [b] [Nah. 1:6] [1] *take note of*
130:4 [a] [Ex. 34:7] [b] [1 Kin. 8:39, 40] [1] *Reverenced with awe*
130:5 [a] [Ps. 27:14] [b] Ps. 119:81
130:6 [a] Ps. 119:147
130:7 [a] Ps. 131:3 [b] [Is. 55:7] [1] *lovingkindness* [2] *abundant*
130:8 [a] [Ps. 103:3, 4]
131:1 [a] [Rom. 12:16] [1] *Proud* [2] *Conceited* [3] *concern* [4] *difficult or profound*
131:2 [a] [Matt. 18:3] [1] *calmed*
131:3 [a] [Ps. 130:7]
132:2 [a] Ps. 65:1 [b] Gen. 49:24
132:3 [1] *chamber*
132:4 [a] Prov. 6:4
132:5 [a] Acts 7:46 [1] *dwelling place*
132:6 [a] 1 Sam. 17:12 [b] 1 Sam. 7:1 [c] 1 Chr. 13:5 [1] *Or Jaar*
132:7 [a] Ps. 5:7; 99:5 [1] *dwelling places*
132:8 [a] Num. 10:35 [b] Ps. 78:61
132:9 [a] Job 29:14
132:10 [1] *Messiah, commissioned one* 132:11 [a] [Ps. 89:3, 4, 35; 110:4]

## PSALM 130

A Song of degrees.

Out [a]of the depths have I cried unto thee, O LORD.

2 Lord, hear my voice: let thine ears be attentive to the voice of my supplications.

3 [a]If thou, LORD, shouldst [1]mark iniquities, O Lord, who shall [b]stand?

4 But *there is* [a]forgiveness with thee, that [b]thou mayest be [1]feared.

5 [a]I wait for the LORD, my soul doth wait, and [b]in his word do I hope.

6 [a]My soul *waiteth* for the Lord more than they that watch for the morning: *I say, more than* they that watch for the morning.

7 [a]Let Israel hope in the LORD: for [b]with the LORD *there is* [1]mercy, and with him *is* [2]plenteous redemption.

8 And [a]he shall redeem Israel from all his iniquities.

## PSALM 131

A Song of degrees of David.

Lord, my heart is not [1]haughty, nor mine eyes [2]lofty: [a]neither do I [3]exercise myself in great matters, or in things too [4]high for me.

2 Surely I have [1]behaved and quieted myself, [a]as a child that is weaned of his mother: my soul *is* even as a weaned child.

3 [a]Let Israel hope in the LORD from henceforth and for ever.

## PSALM 132

A Song of degrees.

Lord, remember David, *and* all his afflictions:

2 How he sware unto the LORD, [a]*and* vowed unto [b]the mighty *God* of Jacob;

3 Surely I will not come into the [1]tabernacle of my house, nor go up into my bed;

4 I will [a]not give sleep to mine eyes, *or* slumber to mine eyelids,

5 Until I [a]find out a place for the LORD, an [1]habitation for the mighty *God* of Jacob.

6 Lo, we heard of it [a]at Ephratah: [b]we found it [c]in the fields of [1]the wood.

7 We will go into his [1]tabernacles: [a]we will worship at his footstool.

8 [a]Arise, O LORD, into thy rest; thou, and [b]the ark of thy strength.

9 Let thy priests [a]be clothed with righteousness; and let thy saints shout for joy.

10 For thy servant David's sake turn not away the face of thine [1]anointed.

11 [a]The LORD hath sworn *in* truth unto David; he will not turn from

it; [b]Of [1]the fruit of thy body will I set upon thy throne.

12 If thy children will keep my covenant and my testimony that I shall teach them, their children also shall sit upon thy throne for evermore.

13 [a]For the LORD hath chosen Zion; he hath desired *it* for his [1]habitation.

14 [a]This *is* my [1]rest for ever: here will I dwell; for I have desired it.

15 [a]I will abundantly bless her [1]provision: I will satisfy her poor with bread.

16 [a]I will also clothe her priests with salvation: [b]and her saints shall shout aloud for joy.

17 [a]There will I make the [1]horn of David to [2]bud: [b]I have [3]ordained a lamp for mine anointed.

18 His enemies will I [a]clothe with shame: but upon himself shall his crown flourish.

## PSALM 133

A Song of degrees of David.

**B**EHOLD, how good and how pleasant *it is* for [a]brethren to dwell together in unity!

2 *It is* like the precious [1]ointment upon the head, that ran down upon the beard, *even* Aaron's beard: that went down to the [2]skirts of his garments;

3 As the dew of [a]Hermon, *and as the dew* that descended upon the mountains of Zion: for [b]there the LORD commanded the blessing, *even* life for evermore.

## PSALM 134

A Song of degrees.

**B**EHOLD, bless ye the LORD, all *ye* servants of the LORD, which by night stand in the house of the LORD.

2 [a]Lift up your hands *in* the sanctuary, and bless the LORD.

3 The LORD that made heaven and earth bless thee out of Zion.

## PSALM 135

**P**RAISE ye the LORD. Praise ye the name of the LORD; [a]praise *him*, O ye servants of the LORD.

2 [a]Ye that stand in the house of the LORD, in [b]the courts of the house of our God,

3 Praise the LORD; for [a]the LORD *is* good: sing praises unto his name; [b]for *it is* pleasant.

4 For [a]the LORD hath chosen Jacob unto himself, *and* Israel for his [1]peculiar treasure.

5 For I know that [a]the LORD *is* great, and *that* our Lord *is* above all gods.

6 [a]Whatsoever the LORD pleased, *that* did he in heaven, and in earth, in the seas, and all deep places.

### Marginal references

132:11 [b] 2 Sam. 7:12 [1] *the offspring*
132:13 [a] [Ps. 48:1, 2] [1] *dwelling place*
132:14 [a] Ps. 68:16 [1] *resting place*
132:15 [a] Ps. 147:14 [1] *supply of food*
132:16 [a] 2 Chr. 6:41 [b] 1 Sam. 4:5
132:17 [a] Ezek. 29:21 [b] 1 Kin. 11:36; 15:4 [1] Government [2] *grow* [3] *prepared*
132:18 [a] Ps. 35:26
133:1 [a] Gen. 13:8
133:2 [1] *oil* [2] *edge*
133:3 [a] Deut. 4:48 [b] Lev. 25:21
134:2 [a] [1 Tim. 2:8]
135:1 [a] Ps. 113:1
135:2 [a] Luke 2:37 [b] Ps. 116:19
135:3 [a] [Ps. 119:68] [b] Ps. 147:1
135:4 [a] [Ex. 19:5] [1] *special*
135:5 [a] Ps. 95:3; 97:9
135:6 [a] Ps. 115:3
135:7 [a] Jer. 10:13 [b] Job 28:25, 26; 38:24–28 [c] Jer. 51:16 [1] *Water vapour*
135:8 [a] Ex. 12:12 [1] Lit. *struck down*
135:9 [a] Ex. 7:10 [b] Ps. 136:15 [1] *signs*
135:10 [a] Num. 21:24 [1] *defeated,* lit. *struck*
135:11 [a] Josh. 12:7–24
135:12 [a] Ps. 78:55; 136:21, 22 [1] *inheritance*
135:13 [a] [Ex. 3:15]
135:14 [a] Deut. 32:36 [1] *have compassion on his servants*
135:15 [a] [Ps. 115:4–8]
135:19 [a] [Ps. 115:9]
135:21 [a] Ps. 134:3
136:1 [a] Ps. 106:1 [b] 1 Chr. 16:34 [1] *lovingkindness*
136:2 [a] [Deut. 10:17]
136:4 [a] Ps. 72:18
136:5 [a] Jer. 51:15
136:6 [a] Jer. 10:12
136:7 [a] Gen. 1:14–18
136:8 [a] Gen. 1:16

7 [a]He causeth the [1]vapours to ascend from the ends of the earth; [b]he maketh lightnings for the rain; he bringeth the wind out of his [c]treasuries.

8 [a]Who [1]smote the firstborn of Egypt, both of man and beast.

9 [a]*Who* sent [1]tokens and wonders into the midst of thee, O Egypt, [b]upon Pharaoh, and upon all his servants.

10 [a]Who [1]smote great nations, and slew mighty kings;

11 Sihon king of the Amorites, and Og king of Bashan, and [a]all the kingdoms of Canaan:

12 [a]And gave their land *for* an [1]heritage, an heritage unto Israel his people.

13 [a]Thy name, O LORD, *endureth* for ever; *and* thy memorial, O LORD, throughout all generations.

14 [a]For the LORD will judge his people, and he will [1]repent himself concerning his servants.

15 [a]The idols of the heathen *are* silver and gold, the work of men's hands.

16 They have mouths, but they speak not; eyes have they, but they see not;

17 They have ears, but they hear not; neither is there *any* breath in their mouths.

18 They that make them are like unto them: *so is* every one that trusteth in them.

19 [a]Bless the LORD, O house of Israel: bless the LORD, O house of Aaron:

20 Bless the LORD, O house of Levi: ye that fear the LORD, bless the LORD.

21 Blessed be the LORD [a]out of Zion, which dwelleth at Jerusalem. Praise ye the LORD.

## PSALM 136

**O** [a]GIVE thanks unto the LORD; for he is good: [b]for his [1]mercy *endureth* for ever.

2 O give thanks unto [a]the God of gods: for his mercy *endureth* for ever.

3 O give thanks to the Lord of lords: for his mercy *endureth* for ever.

4 To him [a]who alone doeth great wonders: for his mercy *endureth* for ever.

5 [a]To him that by wisdom made the heavens: for his mercy *endureth* for ever.

6 [a]To him that stretched out the earth above the waters: for his mercy *endureth* for ever.

7 [a]To him that made great lights: for his mercy *endureth* for ever:

8 [a]The sun to rule by day: for his mercy *endureth* for ever:

9 The moon and stars to rule by night: for his mercy *endureth* for ever.

10 <sup>a</sup>To him that <sup>1</sup>smote Egypt in their firstborn: for his mercy *endureth* for ever:

11 <sup>a</sup>And brought out Israel from among them: for his mercy *endureth* for ever:

12 <sup>a</sup>With a strong hand, and with <sup>1</sup>a stretched out arm: for his mercy *endureth* for ever.

13 <sup>a</sup>To him which divided the Red sea into parts: for his mercy *endureth* for ever:

14 And made Israel to pass through the midst of it: for his mercy *endureth* for ever:

15 <sup>a</sup>But overthrew Pharaoh and his host in the Red sea: for his mercy *endureth* for ever:

16 <sup>a</sup>To him which led his people through the wilderness: for his mercy *endureth* for ever.

17 <sup>a</sup>To him which <sup>1</sup>smote great kings: for his mercy *endureth* for ever:

18 <sup>a</sup>And slew famous kings: for his mercy *endureth* for ever:

19 <sup>a</sup>Sihon king of the Amorites: for his mercy *endureth* for ever:

20 <sup>a</sup>And Og the king of Bashan: for his mercy *endureth* for ever:

21 <sup>a</sup>And gave their land for an <sup>1</sup>heritage: for his mercy *endureth* for ever:

22 *Even* an heritage unto Israel his servant: for his mercy *endureth* for ever.

23 Who <sup>a</sup>remembered us in our <sup>1</sup>low estate: for his mercy *endureth* for ever:

24 And hath <sup>a</sup>redeemed<sup>1</sup> us from our enemies: for his mercy *endureth* for ever.

25 <sup>a</sup>Who giveth food to all flesh: for his mercy *endureth* for ever.

26 O give thanks unto the God of heaven: for his mercy *endureth* for ever.

## PSALM 137

B Y the rivers of Babylon, there we sat down, yea, we wept, when we remembered Zion.

2 We hanged our harps upon the willows in the midst thereof.

3 For there they that carried us away captive <sup>1</sup>required of us a song; and they that <sup>a</sup>wasted<sup>2</sup> us *required of us* mirth, *saying,* Sing us *one* of the songs of Zion.

4 How shall we sing the LORD's song in a <sup>1</sup>strange land?

5 If I forget thee, O Jerusalem, let my right hand forget *her* <sup>1</sup>cunning.

6 If I do not remember thee, let my <sup>a</sup>tongue <sup>1</sup>cleave to the roof of my mouth; if I prefer not Jerusalem above my chief joy.

7 Remember, O LORD, <sup>a</sup>the children of Edom in the day of Jerusalem; who said, <sup>1</sup>Rase *it,* rase *it, even* to the foundation thereof.

136:10 <sup>a</sup> Ex. 12:29
<sup>1</sup> struck
136:11 <sup>a</sup> Ex. 12:51;
13:3, 16
136:12 <sup>a</sup> Ex. 6:6
<sup>1</sup> an outstretched
arm, mighty
power
136:13 <sup>a</sup> Ex. 14:21
136:15 <sup>a</sup> Ex. 14:27
136:16 <sup>a</sup> Ex. 13:18;
15:22
136:17 <sup>a</sup> Ps.
135:10–12 <sup>1</sup> struck
down
136:18 <sup>a</sup> Deut.
29:7
136:19 <sup>a</sup> Num.
21:21
136:20 <sup>a</sup> Num.
21:33
136:21 <sup>a</sup> Josh. 12:1
<sup>1</sup> inheritance
136:23 <sup>a</sup> Gen. 8:1
<sup>1</sup> lowly state
136:24 <sup>a</sup> Ps. 44:7
<sup>1</sup> rescued
136:25 <sup>a</sup> Ps.
104:27; 145:15
137:3 <sup>a</sup> Ps. 79:1
<sup>1</sup> demanded
<sup>2</sup> plundered
137:4 <sup>1</sup> foreign
137:5 <sup>1</sup> Skill
137:6 <sup>a</sup> Ezek. 3:26
<sup>1</sup> cling
137:7 <sup>a</sup> Jer. 49:7
22 <sup>1</sup> Lit. *Make
it bare*
137:8 <sup>a</sup> Is. 13:1–6;
47:1 <sup>b</sup> Jer. 50:15
137:9 <sup>a</sup> Is. 13:16
138:1 <sup>a</sup> Ps. 119:46
138:2 <sup>a</sup> Ps. 28:2
<sup>b</sup> 1 Kin. 8:29 <sup>c</sup> Is.
42:21
138:3 <sup>1</sup> made me
bold
138:4 <sup>a</sup> Ps. 102:15
138:5 <sup>1</sup> of
138:6 <sup>a</sup> [Ps. 113:4–
7] <sup>b</sup> [James 4:6]
<sup>1</sup> regards
138:7 <sup>a</sup> [Ps.
23:3, 4]
138:8 <sup>a</sup> Ps. 57:2
<sup>b</sup> Job 10:3, 8
<sup>1</sup> complete
139:1 <sup>a</sup> Ps. 17:3
139:2 <sup>a</sup> 2 Kin.
19:27 <sup>b</sup> Matt. 9:4
139:3 <sup>a</sup> Job
14:16; 31:4
<sup>1</sup> comprehendeth,
lit. winnow
139:4 <sup>a</sup> [Heb. 4:13]
139:5 <sup>1</sup> enclosed
or hedged
139:6 <sup>a</sup> Job 42:3
139:7 <sup>a</sup> [Jer. 23:24]
<sup>1</sup> can
139:8 <sup>a</sup> [Amos
9:2–4] <sup>b</sup> [Job
26:6] <sup>1</sup> Or Sheol

8 O daughter of Babylon, <sup>a</sup>who art to be destroyed; happy *shall he be,* <sup>b</sup>that rewardeth thee as thou hast served us.

9 Happy *shall he be,* that taketh and <sup>a</sup>dasheth thy little ones against the stones.

## PSALM 138

*A Psalm* of David.

I WILL praise thee with my whole heart: <sup>a</sup>before the gods will I sing praise unto thee.

2 <sup>a</sup>I will worship <sup>b</sup>toward thy holy temple, and praise thy name for thy lovingkindness and for thy truth: for thou hast <sup>c</sup>magnified thy word above all thy name.

3 In the day when I cried thou answeredst me, *and* <sup>1</sup>strengthenedst me *with* strength in my soul.

4 <sup>a</sup>All the kings of the earth shall praise thee, O LORD, when they hear the words of thy mouth.

5 Yea, they shall sing <sup>1</sup>in the ways of the LORD: for great *is* the glory of the LORD.

6 <sup>a</sup>Though the LORD *be* high, yet <sup>b</sup>hath<sup>1</sup> he respect unto the lowly: but the proud he knoweth afar off.

7 <sup>a</sup>Though I walk in the midst of trouble, thou wilt revive me: thou shalt stretch forth thine hand against the wrath of mine enemies, and thy right hand shall save me.

8 <sup>a</sup>The LORD will <sup>1</sup>perfect *that which* concerneth me: thy mercy, O LORD, *endureth* for ever: <sup>b</sup>forsake not the works of thine own hands.

## PSALM 139

To the chief Musician,
A Psalm of David.

O LORD, <sup>a</sup>thou hast searched me, and known *me.*

2 <sup>a</sup>Thou knowest my downsitting and mine uprising, thou <sup>b</sup>understandest my thought afar off.

3 <sup>a</sup>Thou <sup>1</sup>compassest my path and my lying down, and art acquainted *with* all my ways.

4 For *there is* not a word in my tongue, *but,* lo, O LORD, <sup>a</sup>thou knowest it altogether.

5 Thou hast <sup>1</sup>beset me behind and before, and laid thine hand upon me.

6 <sup>a</sup>*Such* knowledge *is* too wonderful for me; it is high, I cannot *attain* unto it.

7 <sup>a</sup>Whither <sup>1</sup>shall I go from thy spirit? or whither <sup>1</sup>shall I flee from thy presence?

8 <sup>a</sup>If I ascend up into heaven, thou *art* there: <sup>b</sup>if I make my bed in <sup>1</sup>hell, behold, thou *art there.*

9 *If* I take the wings of the morning, *and* dwell in the uttermost parts of the sea;

10 Even there shall thy hand lead me, and thy right hand shall hold me.

11 If I say, Surely the darkness shall ¹cover me; even the night shall be light about me.

12 Yea, ᵃthe darkness ¹hideth not from thee; but the night shineth as the day: the darkness and the light *are* both alike *to thee.*

13 For thou hast ¹possessed my reins: thou hast ²covered me in my mother's womb.

14 I will praise thee; for I am fearfully *and* wonderfully made: marvellous *are* thy works; and *that* my soul knoweth ¹right well.

15 ᵃMy ¹substance was not hid from thee, when I was made in secret, *and* ²curiously wrought in the lowest parts of the earth.

16 Thine eyes did see my substance, yet being ¹unperfect; and in thy book all *my members* were written, ²*which* in continuance were fashioned, when *as yet there was* none of them.

17 ᵃHow precious also are thy thoughts unto me, O God! how great is the sum of them!

18 *If* I should count them, they are more in number than the sand: when I awake, I am still with thee.

19 Surely thou wilt ᵃslay the wicked, O God: ᵇdepart from me therefore, ye ¹bloody men.

20 For they ᵃspeak against thee wickedly, *and* thine enemies take *thy name* in vain.

21 ᵃDo not I hate them, O LORD, that hate thee? and ¹am not I grieved with those that rise up against thee?

22 I hate them with ¹perfect hatred: I count them mine enemies.

23 ᵃSearch me, O God, and know my heart: try me, and know my ¹thoughts:

24 And see if *there be any* wicked way in me, and ᵃlead me in the way everlasting.

## PSALM 140

To the chief Musician,
A Psalm of David.

**D**ELIVER me, O LORD, from the evil man: preserve me from the violent man;

2 Which ¹imagine mischiefs in *their* heart; ᵃcontinually are they gathered together *for* war.

3 They have sharpened their tongues like a serpent; ᵃadders'¹ poison *is* under their lips. *Selah.*

4 ᵃKeep me, O LORD, from the hands of the wicked; preserve me from the violent man; who have purposed to ¹overthrow my goings.

5 The proud have ¹hid a ᵃsnare for me, and cords; they have spread a net by the wayside; they have set ²gins for me. *Selah.*

139:11 ¹ MT *fall on me*
139:12 ᵃ Job 26:6; 34:22 ¹ Lit. *is not dark to thee*
139:13 ¹ *formed my inward parts* ² *weaved*
139:14 ¹ *very well*
139:15 ᵃ Job 10:8, 9 ¹ *frame, lit. bones* ² *skilfully*
139:16 ¹ *unformed* ² *the days fashioned for me*
139:17 ᵃ [Ps. 40:5]
139:19 ᵃ [Is. 11:4] ᵇ Ps. 119:115 ¹ *bloodthirsty*
139:20 ᵃ Jude 15
139:21 ᵃ 2 Chr. 19:2 ¹ *do I not loathe those*
139:22 ¹ *complete*
139:23 ᵃ Job 31:6 ¹ *anxious thoughts*
139:24 ᵃ Ps. 5:8; 143:10
140:2 ᵃ Ps. 56:6 ¹ *plan evil things*
140:3 ᵃ Ps. 58:4 ¹ *asps'*
140:4 ᵃ Ps. 71:4 ¹ *make my steps stumble*
140:5 ᵃ Jer. 18:22 ¹ *hidden a trap* ² *snares or traps*
140:7 ¹ *provided a shelter for*
140:8 ᵃ Deut. 32:27 ¹ *scheme* ² *be exalted*
140:9 ¹ *surround* ² *evil*
140:10 ᵃ Ps. 11:6
140:11 ¹ *a slanderer* ² *Or let evil hunt*
140:12 ᵃ 1 Kin. 8:45 ¹ *justice for*
141:2 ᵃ [Rev. 5:8; 8:3, 4] ᵇ [1 Tim. 2:8] ᶜ Ex. 29:39, 41
141:3 ᵃ [Prov. 13:3; 21:23] ¹ *guard* ² *keep watch over the door*
141:4 ᵃ Prov. 23:6 ¹ *Let not my heart incline* ² *delicacies*
141:5 ᵃ [Prov. 9:8] ¹ *let not my head refuse it* ² *against their wicked deeds*
141:6 ¹ *by the sides of the cliff*
141:7 ¹ *plows and breaks up the earth*
141:8 ᵃ Ps. 25:15
141:9 ᵃ Ps. 119:110 ¹ *traps*
141:10 ᵃ Ps. 35:8 ¹ *while I escape safely*

6 I said unto the LORD, Thou *art* my God: hear the voice of my supplications, O LORD.

7 O GOD the Lord, the strength of my salvation, thou hast ¹covered my head in the day of battle.

8 Grant not, O LORD, the desires of the wicked: further not his wicked ¹device; ᵃ*lest* they ²exalt themselves. *Selah.*

9 *As for* the head of those that ¹compass me about, let the ²mischief of their own lips cover them.

10 ᵃLet burning coals fall upon them: let them be cast into the fire; into deep pits, that they rise not up again.

11 Let not ¹an evil speaker be established in the earth: ²evil shall hunt the violent man to overthrow *him.*

12 I know that the LORD will ᵃmaintain the cause of the afflicted, *and* ¹the right of the poor.

13 Surely the righteous shall give thanks unto thy name: the upright shall dwell in thy presence.

## PSALM 141

A Psalm of David.

**L**ORD, I cry unto thee: make haste unto me; give ear unto my voice, when I cry unto thee.

2 Let my prayer be set forth before thee ᵃ*as* incense; *and* ᵇthe lifting up of my hands *as* ᶜthe evening sacrifice.

3 Set a ¹watch, O LORD, before my ᵃmouth; ²keep the door of my lips.

4 ¹Incline not my heart to *any* evil thing, to practise wicked works with men that work iniquity: ᵃand let me not eat of their ²dainties.

5 ᵃLet the righteous smite me; *it shall be* a kindness: and let him reprove me; *it shall be* an excellent oil, ¹which shall not break my head: for yet my prayer also *shall be* ²in their calamities.

6 When their judges are overthrown ¹in stony places, they shall hear my words; for they are sweet.

7 Our bones are scattered at the grave's mouth, as when one ¹cutteth and cleaveth *wood* upon the earth.

8 But ᵃmine eyes *are* unto thee, O GOD the Lord: in thee is my trust; leave not my soul destitute.

9 Keep me from ᵃthe snares *which* they have laid for me, and the ¹gins of the workers of iniquity.

10 ᵃLet the wicked fall into their own nets, ¹whilst that I withal escape.

## PSALM 142

ᵃMaschil¹ of David; A Prayer ᵇwhen he was in the cave.

**I** CRIED unto the LORD with my voice; with my voice unto the LORD did I make my supplication.

142:title ᵃ Ps. 32:title ᵇ 1 Sam. 22:1 ¹ *Contemplation*

2 I poured out my complaint before him; I ¹shewed before him my trouble.

3 When my spirit ¹was ᵃoverwhelmed within me, then thou knewest my path. In the way wherein I walked have they ²privily ᵇlaid a snare for me.

4 ¹I looked on *my* right hand, and beheld, but *there was* no man that would ²know me: refuge failed me; no man cared for my soul.

5 I cried unto thee, O LORD: I said, Thou *art* my refuge *and* my portion in the land of the living.

6 ¹Attend unto my cry; for I am brought very low: deliver me from my persecutors; for they are stronger than I.

7 Bring my soul out of prison, that I may ᵃpraise thy name: the righteous shall ¹compass me about; for thou shalt deal bountifully with me.

## PSALM 143

### A Psalm of David.

HEAR my prayer, O LORD, give ear to my supplications: in thy faithfulness answer me, *and* in thy righteousness.

2 And enter not into judgment with thy servant: ᵃfor in thy sight shall no man living be ¹justified.

3 For the enemy hath persecuted my soul; he hath ¹smitten my life down to the ground; he hath made me to dwell in ²darkness, as those that have been long dead.

4 ᵃTherefore is my spirit overwhelmed within me; my heart within me is desolate.

5 ᵃI remember the days of old; I meditate on all thy works; I ¹muse on the work of thy hands.

6 I stretch forth my hands unto thee: ᵃmy soul *thirsteth* after thee, as a thirsty land.     *Selah.*

7 ¹Hear me speedily, O LORD: my spirit faileth: hide not thy face from me, ᵃlest I ²be like unto them that go down into the pit.

8 Cause me to hear thy lovingkindness ᵃin the morning; for in thee do I trust: ᵇcause me to know the way wherein I should walk; for I ᶜlift up my soul unto thee.

9 Deliver me, O LORD, from mine enemies: ¹I flee unto thee to hide me.

10 ᵃTeach me to do thy will; for thou *art* my God: ᵇthy spirit *is* good; lead me into ᶜthe land of uprightness.

11 ᵃQuicken¹ me, O LORD, for thy name's sake: for thy righteousness' sake bring my soul out of trouble.

12 And of thy mercy ᵃcut¹ off mine enemies, and destroy all them that afflict my soul: for I *am* thy servant.

142:2 ¹ declared
142:3 ᵃ Ps. 77:3
  ᵇ Ps. 141:9 ¹ Lit. fainted ² secretly
142:4 ¹ Look on the right hand, and see ² acknowledge
142:6 ¹ Give heed
142:7 ᵃ Ps. 34:1, 2 ¹ surround
143:2 ᵃ [Gal. 2:16] ¹ righteous
143:3 ¹ crushed ² dark places
143:4 ᵃ Ps. 77:3
143:5 ᵃ Ps. 77:5, 10, 11 ¹ ponder
143:6 ᵃ Ps. 63:1
143:7 ᵃ Ps. 28:1 ¹ Answer ² become
143:8 ᵃ Ps. 46:5 ᵇ Ps. 5:8 ᶜ Ps. 25:1
143:9 ¹ MT Unto thee I take cover.
143:10 ᵃ Ps. 25:4, 5 ᵇ Neh. 9:20 ᶜ Is. 26:10
143:11 ᵃ Ps. 119:25 ¹ Revive
143:12 ᵃ Ps. 54:5 ¹ put an end to
144:1 ᵃ 2 Sam. 22:35 ¹ Lit. rock ² battle
144:2 ¹ lovingkindness ² take refuge
144:3 ᵃ Heb. 2:6 ¹ think
144:4 ᵃ Ps. 39:11 ᵇ Job 8:9; 14:2 ¹ a breath
144:5 ᵃ Ps. 18:9 ᵇ Ps. 104:32
144:6 ᵃ Ps. 18:13, 14
144:7 ¹ Stretch out ² rescue ³ foreigners
144:8 ᵃ Ps. 12:2 ¹ empty words
144:9 ᵃ Ps. 33:2, 3; 40:3 ¹ harp
144:10 ᵃ Ps. 18:50 ¹ deliverance to his kings ² deadly
144:11 ¹ Rescue ² foreigners ³ empty words
144:12 ᵃ Ps. 128:3 ¹ pillars, sculptured in palace style
144:13 ¹ barns ² produce ³ fields
144:14 ¹ well laden ² no breach ³ outcry
144:15 ᵃ [Ps. 33:12] ¹ state
145:title ᵃ Ps. 100:title
145:1 ¹ praise
145:3 ᵃ [Ps. 147:5] ᵇ [Rom. 11:33] ¹ Beyond our understanding

## PSALM 144

### A Psalm of David.

BLESSED *be* the LORD my ¹strength, ᵃwhich teacheth my hands to war, *and* my fingers to ²fight:

2 My ¹goodness, and my fortress; my high tower, and my deliverer; my shield, and *he* in whom I ²trust; who subdueth my people under me.

3 ᵃLORD, what *is* man, that thou takest knowledge of him! *or* the son of man, that thou ¹makest account of him!

4 ᵃMan is like ¹to vanity: ᵇhis days *are* as a shadow that passeth away.

5 ᵃBow thy heavens, O LORD, and come down: ᵇtouch the mountains, and they shall smoke.

6 ᵃCast forth lightning, and scatter them: shoot out thine arrows, and destroy them.

7 ¹Send thine hand from above; ²rid me, and deliver me out of great waters, from the hand of ³strange children;

8 Whose mouth ᵃspeaketh ¹vanity, and their right hand *is* a right hand of falsehood.

9 I will ᵃsing a new song unto thee, O God: upon a ¹psaltery *and* an instrument of ten strings will I sing praises unto thee.

10 ᵃ*It is he* that giveth ¹salvation unto kings: who delivereth David his servant from the ²hurtful sword.

11 ¹Rid me, and deliver me from the hand of ²strange children, whose mouth speaketh ³vanity, and their right hand *is* a right hand of falsehood:

12 That our sons *may be* ᵃas plants grown up in their youth; *that* our daughters *may be* as corner ¹stones, polished *after* the similitude of a palace:

13 *That* our ¹garners *may be* full, affording all manner of ²store: *that our* sheep may bring forth thousands and ten thousands in our ³streets:

14 *That* our oxen *may be* ¹strong to labour; *that there be* ²no breaking in, nor going out; that *there be* no ³complaining in our streets.

15 ᵃHappy *is that* people, that is in such a ¹case: *yea,* happy *is that* people, whose God *is* the LORD.

## PSALM 145

### David's ᵃ*Psalm* of praise.

I WILL ¹extol thee, my God, O king; and I will bless thy name for ever and ever.

2 Every day will I bless thee; and I will praise thy name for ever and ever.

3 ᵃGreat *is* the LORD, and greatly to be praised; and ᵇhis greatness *is* ¹unsearchable.

4 [a]One generation shall praise thy works to another, and shall declare thy mighty acts.

5 I will [1]speak of the glorious [2]honour of thy majesty, and of thy wondrous works.

6 And *men* shall speak of the might of thy [1]terrible acts: and I will declare thy greatness.

7 They shall [1]abundantly utter the memory of thy great goodness, and shall sing of thy righteousness.

8 [a]The LORD *is* gracious, and full of compassion; slow to anger, and of great mercy.

9 [a]The LORD *is* good to all: and his tender mercies *are* over all his works.

10 [a]All thy works shall praise thee, O LORD; and thy saints shall bless thee.

11 They shall speak of the glory of thy kingdom, and talk of thy power;

12 To make known to the sons of men his mighty acts, and the glorious majesty of his kingdom.

13 [a]Thy kingdom *is* an everlasting kingdom, and thy dominion *endureth* throughout all generations.

14 The LORD upholdeth all that fall, and [a]raiseth up all *those that be* bowed down.

15 [a]The eyes of all [1]wait upon thee; and [b]thou givest them their [2]meat in due season.

16 Thou openest thine hand, [a]and satisfiest the desire of every living thing.

17 The LORD *is* righteous in all his ways, and [1]holy in all his works.

18 [a]The LORD *is* nigh unto all them that call upon him, to all that call upon him [b]in truth.

19 He will fulfil the desire of them that fear him: he also will hear their cry, and will save them.

20 [a]The LORD preserveth all them that love him: but all the wicked will he destroy.

21 My mouth shall speak the praise of the LORD: and let all flesh bless his holy name for ever and ever.

## PSALM 146

**P**RAISE[1] ye the LORD. [a]Praise the LORD, O my soul.

2 [a]While I live will I praise the LORD: I will sing praises unto my God while I have any being.

3 [a]Put not your trust in princes, *nor* in [1]the son of man, in whom *there is* no [2]help.

4 [a]His [1]breath goeth forth, he returneth to his earth; in that very day [b]his thoughts perish.

5 [a]Happy *is he* that *hath* the God of Jacob for his help, whose hope *is* in the LORD his God:

6 [a]Which made heaven, and earth, the sea, and all that therein *is:* which keepeth truth for ever:

7 [a]Which executeth [1]judgment for the oppressed: [b]which giveth food to the hungry. [c]The LORD [2]looseth the prisoners:

8 [a]The LORD openeth *the eyes of* the blind: [b]the LORD raiseth them that are bowed down: the LORD loveth the righteous:

9 [a]The LORD [1]preserveth the strangers; he relieveth the fatherless and widow: [b]but the way of the wicked he [2]turneth upside down.

10 [a]The LORD shall reign for ever, *even* thy God, O Zion, unto all generations. Praise ye the LORD.

## PSALM 147

**P**RAISE[1] ye the LORD: for [a]*it is* good to sing praises unto our God; [b]for *it is* pleasant; *and* [c]praise is [2]comely.

2 The LORD doth [a]build up Jerusalem: [b]he gathereth together the outcasts of Israel.

3 [a]He healeth the broken in heart, and bindeth up their [1]wounds.

4 [a]He [1]telleth the number of the stars; he calleth them all by *their* names.

5 [a]Great *is* our Lord, and of [b]great power: [c]his understanding *is* [1]infinite.

6 [a]The LORD lifteth up the [1]meek: he casteth the wicked down to the ground.

7 Sing unto the LORD with thanksgiving; sing praise upon the harp unto our God:

8 [a]Who covereth the heaven with clouds, who prepareth rain for the earth, who maketh grass to grow upon the mountains.

9 [a]He giveth to the beast his food, *and* [b]to the young ravens which cry.

10 [a]He delighteth not in the strength of the horse: he taketh not pleasure in the legs of a man.

11 The LORD taketh pleasure in them that fear him, in those that hope in his [1]mercy.

12 Praise the LORD, O Jerusalem; praise thy God, O Zion.

13 For he hath strengthened the bars of thy gates; he hath blessed thy children within thee.

14 [a]He maketh peace *in* thy borders, *and* [b]filleth thee with the [1]finest of the wheat.

15 [a]He sendeth forth his commandment *upon* earth: his word runneth very swiftly.

16 [a]He giveth snow like wool: he scattereth the hoarfrost like ashes.

17 He casteth forth his ice [1]like morsels: who can stand before his cold?

18 [a]He sendeth out his word, and melteth them: he causeth his wind to blow, *and* the waters flow.

---

145:4 [a] Is. 38:19
145:5 [1] *meditate* [2] *splendour*
145:6 [1] *awesome*
145:7 [1] *eagerly utter,* lit. *bubble forth*
145:8 [a] [Num. 14:18]
145:9 [a] Nah. 1:7
145:10 [a] Ps. 19:1
145:13 [a] [1 Tim. 1:17]
145:14 [a] Ps. 146:8
145:15 [a] Ps. 104:27 [b] Ps. 136:25 [1] *look expectantly to you* [2] *food*
145:16 [a] Ps. 104:21, 28
145:17 [1] *gracious*
145:18 [a] [Deut. 4:7] [b] [John 4:24]
145:20 [a] [Ps. 31:23]
146:1 [a] Ps. 103:1 [1] Heb. *Hallelujah*
146:2 [a] Ps. 104:33
146:3 [a] [Is. 2:22] [1] *a son of man,* a human being [2] *salvation*
146:4 [a] [Eccl. 12:7] [b] [1 Cor. 2:6] [1] *spirit departs*
146:5 [a] Jer. 17:7
146:6 [a] Rev. 14:7
146:7 [a] Ps. 103:6 [b] Ps. 107:9 [c] Ps. 107:10 [1] *justice* [2] *gives freedom to*
146:8 [a] Matt. 9:30 [b] Luke 13:13
146:9 [a] Deut. 10:18 [b] Ps. 147:6 [1] *watches over* [2] Lit. *makes crooked*
146:10 [a] Ex. 15:18
147:1 [a] Ps. 92:1 [b] Ps. 135:3 [c] Ps. 33:1 [1] Heb. *Hallelujah* [2] *beautiful*
147:2 [a] Ps. 102:16 [b] Deut. 30:3
147:3 [a] [Ps. 51:17] [1] Lit. *sorrows*
147:4 [a] Is. 40:26 [1] *counts*
147:5 [a] Ps. 48:1 [b] Nah. 1:3 [c] Is. 40:28 [1] Lit. *innumerable*
147:6 [a] Ps. 146:8, 9 [1] *humble*
147:8 [a] Job 38:26
147:9 [a] Job 38:41 [b] [Matt. 6:26]
147:10 [a] Ps. 33:16, 17
147:11 [1] *loving-kindness*
147:14 [a] Is. 54:13; 60:17, 18 [b] Ps. 132:15

[1] Lit. *fat* 147:15 [a] [Ps. 107:20] 147:16 [a] Job 37:6 147:17 [1] *as fragments* of food 147:18 [a] Job 37:10

19 ªHe sheweth his word unto Jacob, ᵇhis statutes and his judgments unto Israel.

20 ªHe hath not dealt so with any nation: and *as for his* judgments, they have not known them. ¹Praise ye the LORD.

## PSALM 148

P RAISE¹ ye the LORD. Praise ye the LORD from the heavens: praise him in the heights.

2 Praise ye him, all his angels: praise ye him, all his hosts.

3 Praise ye him, sun and moon: praise him, all ye stars of light.

4 Praise him, ªye heavens of heavens, and ᵇye waters that *be* above the heavens.

5 Let them praise the name of the LORD: for ªhe commanded, and they were created.

6 ªHe hath also ¹stablished them for ever and ever: he hath made a decree which shall not pass.

7 Praise the LORD from the earth, ªye ¹dragons, and all deeps:

8 Fire, and hail; snow, and vapours; stormy wind fulfilling his word:

9 ªMountains, and all hills; fruitful trees, and all cedars:

10 Beasts, and all cattle; creeping things, and flying fowl:

11 Kings of the earth, and all people; princes, and all judges of the earth:

12 Both young men, and maidens; old men, and children:

13 Let them praise the name of the LORD: for his ªname alone is ¹excellent; his glory *is* above the earth and heaven.

14 He also ªexalteth the ¹horn of his people, the praise of ᵇall his saints; *even* of the children of Israel, ᶜa people near unto him. ²Praise ye the LORD.

147:19 ª Deut. 33:4  ᵇ Mal. 4:4
147:20 ª Deut. 4:32–34; [Rom. 3:1, 2]  ¹ Heb. *Hallelujah*
148:1 ¹ Heb. *Hallelujah*
148:4 ª 1 Kin. 8:27  ᵇ Gen. 1:7
148:5 ª Gen. 1:1, 6
148:6 ª Ps. 89:37  ¹ *established*
148:7 ª Is. 43:20  ¹ *sea creatures*
148:9 ª Is. 44:23; 49:13
148:13 ª Ps. 8:1  ¹ *exalted*
148:14 ª Ps. 75:10  ᵇ Ps. 149:9  ᶜ Eph. 2:17  ¹ *Strength* or *dominion*  ² Heb. *Hallelujah*
149:1 ª Ps. 33:3  ¹ Heb. *Hallelujah*
149:2 ª Zech. 9:9  ¹ *their maker*
149:3 ª Ps. 81:2
149:4 ª Ps. 35:27  ᵇ Ps. 132:16  ¹ *humble*
149:5 ª Job 35:10
149:6 ª Heb. 4:12
149:7 ¹ *nations* or *Gentiles*
149:9 ª Deut. 7:1, 2  ᵇ 1 Cor. 6:2  ¹ Heb. *Hallelujah*
150:1 ª Ps. 145:5, 6  ¹ Heb. *Hallelujah*  ² *his mighty firmament* or *expanse*
150:2 ª Deut. 3:24
150:3 ¹ *cornet*  ² *lute* or *lyre*
150:6 ¹ Heb. *Hallelujah*

## PSALM 149

P RAISE¹ ye the LORD. ªSing unto the LORD a new song, *and* his praise in the congregation of saints.

2 Let Israel rejoice in ¹him that made him: let the children of Zion be joyful in their ªKing.

3 ªLet them praise his name in the dance: let them sing praises unto him with the timbrel and harp.

4 For ªthe LORD taketh pleasure in his people: ᵇhe will beautify the ¹meek with salvation.

5 Let the saints be joyful in glory: let them ªsing aloud upon their beds.

6 *Let* the high praises of God *be* in their mouth, and ªa two-edged sword in their hand;

7 To execute vengeance upon the ¹heathen, *and* punishments upon the people;

8 To bind their kings with chains, and their nobles with fetters of iron;

9 ªTo execute upon them the judgment written: ᵇthis honour have all his saints. ¹Praise ye the LORD.

## PSALM 150

P RAISE¹ ªye the LORD. Praise God in his sanctuary: praise him in ²the firmament of his power.

2 Praise him for his mighty acts: praise him according to his excellent ªgreatness.

3 Praise him with the sound of the ¹trumpet: praise him with the ²psaltery and harp.

4 Praise him with the timbrel and dance: praise him with stringed instruments and organs.

5 Praise him upon the loud cymbals: praise him upon the high sounding cymbals.

6 Let every thing that hath breath praise the LORD. ¹Praise ye the LORD.

# THE BOOK OF
# PROVERBS

The key word in Proverbs is *wisdom*, "the ability to live life skillfully." A godly life in an ungodly world, however, is no simple assignment. Proverbs provides God's detailed instructions for His people to deal successfully with the practical affairs of everyday life: how to relate to God, parents, children, neighbors, and government. Solomon, the principal author, uses a combination of poetry, parables, pithy questions, short stories, and wise maxims to give in strikingly memorable form the common sense and divine perspective necessary to handle life's issues.

Because Solomon, the pinnacle of Israel's wise men, was the principal contributor, the Hebrew title of this book is *Mishle Shelomoh*, "Proverbs of Solomon" (1:1). The Greek title is *Paroimiai Salomontos*, "Proverbs of Solomon." The Latin title *Liber Proverbiorum*, "Book of Proverbs," combines the words *pro* "for" and *verba* "words" to describe the way the proverbs concentrate many words into a few. The rabbinical writings called Proverbs *Sepher Hokhmah*, "Book of Wisdom."

## CHAPTER 1

THE aproverbs of Solomon the son of David, king of Israel;

2 To know wisdom and instruction; to [1]perceive the words of understanding;

3 To receive the instruction of wisdom, justice, and judgment, and equity;

4 To give [1]subtilty to the asimple, to the young man knowledge and discretion.

5 aA wise *man* will hear, and will increase learning; and a man of understanding shall [1]attain unto wise counsels:

6 To understand a proverb, and [1]the interpretation; the words of the wise, and their adark [2]sayings.

7 aThe [1]fear of the LORD *is* the [2]beginning of knowledge: *but* fools despise wisdom and instruction.

8 aMy son, hear the instruction of thy father, and forsake not the law of thy mother:

9 For they *shall be* an ornament of agrace unto thy head, and chains about thy neck.

10 My son, if sinners entice thee, aconsent thou not.

11 If they say, Come with us, let us alay wait [1]for blood, let us lurk [2]privily for the innocent without cause:

12 Let us swallow them up alive as [1]the grave; and whole, aas those that go down into the pit:

13 We shall find all precious [1]substance, we shall fill our houses with [2]spoil:

14 Cast in thy lot among us; let us all have one purse:

15 My son, awalk not thou in the way with them; brefrain[1] thy foot from their path:

16 aFor their feet run to evil, and make haste to shed blood.

1:1 a 1 Kin. 4:32
1:2 [1] understand or *discern*
1:4 a Prov. 9:4 [1] *prudence*
1:5 a Prov. 9:9 [1] *acquire*
1:6 a Ps. 78:2 [1] *an enigma* [2] *riddles*
1:7 a Job 28:28 [1] *reverential awe* [2] Principal beginning
1:8 a Prov. 4:1
1:9 a Prov. 3:22
1:10 a Gen. 39:7–10
1:11 a Jer. 5:26 [1] To shed blood [2] *secretly*
1:12 a Ps. 28:1 [1] Heb. Sheol
1:13 [1] Lit. *wealth* [2] *plunder*
1:15 a Ps. 1:1 b Ps. 119:101 [1] *keep*
1:16 a [Is. 59:7]
1:17 [1] *futility* [2] Lit. *lord of the wing*
1:18 [1] *secretly*
1:19 a [1 Tim. 6:10]
1:20 a [John 7:37] [1] *calls aloud in the street* [2] *raises* [3] *plazas*
1:21 [1] Lit. *concourses*
1:22 [1] *naive* [2] *naivete*
1:23 a Joel 2:28
1:24 a Jer. 7:13
1:25 a Luke 7:30 [1] *disdained* [2] *would have*
1:26 a Ps. 2:4 [1] *terror*
1:27 a [Prov. 10:24, 25] [1] *terror* [2] *a storm*

17 Surely in [1]vain the net is spread in the sight of any [2]bird.

18 And they lay wait for their *own* blood; they lurk [1]privily for their *own* lives.

19 aSo *are* the ways of every one that is greedy of gain; *which* taketh away the life of the owners thereof.

20 aWisdom [1]crieth without; she [2]uttereth her voice in the [3]streets:

21 She crieth in the chief [1]place of concourse, in the openings of the gates: in the city she uttereth her words, *saying*,

22 How long, ye [1]simple ones, will ye love [2]simplicity? and the scorners delight in their scorning, and fools hate knowledge?

23 Turn you at my reproof: behold, aI will pour out my spirit unto you, I will make known my words unto you.

24 aBecause I have called, and ye refused; I have stretched out my hand, and no man regarded;

25 But ye ahave [1]set at nought all my counsel, and [2]would none of my reproof:

26 aI also will laugh at your calamity; I will mock when your [1]fear cometh;

27 When ayour [1]fear cometh as [2]desolation, and your destruction cometh as a whirlwind; when distress and anguish cometh upon you.

28 aThen shall they call upon me, but I will not answer; they shall seek me [1]early, but they shall not find me:

29 For that they ahated knowledge, and did not bchoose the fear of the LORD:

30 aThey [1]would none of my counsel: they despised all my reproof.

31 Therefore ashall they eat of the fruit of their own way, and be filled with their own devices.

1:28 a Is. 1:15 [1] *diligently*  1:29 a Job 21:14 b Ps. 119:173
1:30 a Ps. 81:11 [1] *would have*  1:31 a Job 4:8

**32** For ¹the turning away of the simple shall slay them, and the ²prosperity of fools shall destroy them.

**33** But whoso hearkeneth unto me shall dwell ᵃsafely, and ᵇshall be ¹quiet from fear of evil.

## CHAPTER 2

**M**Y son, if thou wilt receive my words, and ᵃhide¹ my commandments with thee;

**2** So that thou incline thine ear unto wisdom, *and* apply thine heart to understanding;

**3** Yea, if thou criest after ¹knowledge, *and* liftest up thy voice for understanding;

**4** ᵃIf thou seekest her as silver, and searchest for her as *for* hid treasures;

**5** ᵃThen shalt thou understand the ¹fear of the LORD, and find the knowledge of God.

**6** ᵃFor the LORD giveth wisdom: out of his mouth *cometh* knowledge and understanding.

**7** He ¹layeth up sound wisdom for the righteous: ᵃ*he is* a ²buckler to them that walk uprightly.

**8** He ¹keepeth the paths of judgment, and ᵃpreserveth the way of his saints.

**9** Then shalt thou understand righteousness, and ¹judgment, and equity; *yea,* every good path.

**10** When wisdom entereth into thine heart, and knowledge is pleasant unto thy soul;

**11** Discretion shall preserve thee, ᵃunderstanding shall keep thee:

**12** To deliver thee from the way of the evil *man,* from the man that speaketh ¹froward things;

**13** Who leave the paths of uprightness, to ᵃwalk in the ways of darkness;

**14** ᵃWho rejoice to do evil, *and* delight in the ¹frowardness of the wicked;

**15** ᵃWhose ways *are* crooked, and *they* ¹froward in their paths:

**16** To deliver thee from ᵃthe ¹strange woman, ᵇ*even* from the ²stranger *which* flattereth with her words;

**17** Which forsaketh the ¹guide of her youth, and forgetteth the covenant of her God.

**18** For ᵃher house ¹inclineth unto death, and her paths unto the dead.

**19** None that go unto her return again, neither ¹take they hold of the paths of life.

**20** That thou mayest walk in the way of ¹good *men,* and keep the paths of ²the righteous.

**21** For the upright shall dwell in the ᵃland, and the ¹perfect shall remain in it.

**22** But the wicked shall be ¹cut off from the ²earth, and the transgressors shall be rooted out of it.

1:32 ¹ *the waywardness* ² *complacency*
1:33 ᵃ Prov. 3:24–26  ᵇ Ps. 112:7 ¹ *secure or at ease*
2:1 ᵃ [Prov. 4:21] ¹ *treasure*
2:3 ¹ *discernment*
2:4 ᵃ [Prov. 3:14]
2:5 ᵃ [James 1:5, 6] ¹ *reverential awe*
2:6 ᵃ 1 Kin. 3:9, 12
2:7 ᵃ [Ps. 84:11] ¹ *stores up* ² *shield*
2:8 ᵃ [1 Sam. 2:9] ¹ *guards the paths of justice*
2:9 ¹ *justice*
2:11 ᵃ Prov. 4:6; 6:22
2:12 ¹ *perverse*
2:13 ᵃ [John 3:19, 20]
2:14 ᵃ [Rom. 1:32] ¹ *perversity*
2:15 ᵃ Ps. 125:5 ¹ *devious*
2:16 ᵃ Prov. 5:20; 6:24; 7:5  ᵇ Prov. 5:3 ¹ *immoral* ² *seductress*
2:17 ¹ *companion*
2:18 ᵃ Prov. 7:27 ¹ *sinks down*
2:19 ¹ *do they regain*
2:20 ¹ *goodness* ² *righteousness*
2:21 ᵃ Ps. 37:3 ¹ *blameless*
2:22 ¹ *destroyed* ² *land*
3:1 ᵃ Deut. 8:1
3:2 ᵃ Ps. 119:165
3:3 ᵃ Prov. 6:21  ᵇ [2 Cor. 3:3] ¹ *lovingkindness*
3:4 ᵃ Rom. 14:18 ¹ *high esteem*
3:5 ᵃ [Ps. 37:3, 5]  ᵇ [Jer. 9:23, 24]
3:6 ᵃ [1 Chr. 28:9] ¹ *Or make smooth or straight*
3:7 ᵃ Rom. 12:16
3:8 ᵃ Job 21:24 ¹ *Body* ² *strength,* lit. *refreshment*
3:9 ᵃ Ex. 22:29 ¹ *possessions*
3:10 ᵃ Deut. 28:8 ¹ *vats*
3:11 ¹ Job 5:17 ¹ *detest*
3:12 ᵃ Deut. 8:5
3:13 ᵃ Prov. 8:32, 34, 35
3:14 ᵃ Job 28:13 ¹ Lit. *gain* ² *profit*
3:15 ᵃ Matt. 13:44

## CHAPTER 3

**M**Y son, forget not my law; ᵃbut let thine heart keep my commandments:

**2** For length of days, and long life, and ᵃpeace, shall they add to thee.

**3** Let not ¹mercy and truth forsake thee: ᵃbind them about thy neck; ᵇwrite them upon the table of thine heart:

**4** ᵃSo shalt thou find favour and ¹good understanding in the sight of God and man.

**5** ᵃTrust in the LORD with all thine heart; ᵇand lean not unto thine own understanding.

**6** ᵃIn all thy ways acknowledge him, and he shall ¹direct thy paths.

**7** Be not wise in thine own ᵃeyes: fear the LORD, and depart from evil.

**8** It shall be health to thy ¹navel, and ᵃmarrow² to thy bones.

**9** ᵃHonour the LORD with thy ¹substance, and with the firstfruits of all thine increase:

**10** ᵃSo shall thy barns be filled with plenty, and thy ¹presses shall burst out with new wine.

**11** ᵃMy son, despise not the chastening of the LORD; neither ¹be weary of his correction:

**12** For whom the LORD loveth he correcteth; ᵃeven as a father the son *in whom* he delighteth.

**13** ᵃHappy *is* the man *that* findeth wisdom, and the man *that* getteth understanding.

**14** ᵃFor the ¹merchandise of it *is* better than the ²merchandise of silver, and the gain thereof than fine gold.

**15** She *is* more precious than rubies: and ᵃall the things thou canst desire are not to be compared unto her.

**16** ᵃLength of days *is* in her right hand; *and* in her left hand riches and honour.

**17** ᵃHer ways *are* ways of pleasantness, and all her paths *are* peace.

**18** She *is* ᵃa tree of life to them that lay hold upon her: and happy *is every one* that ¹retaineth her.

**19** ᵃThe LORD by wisdom hath founded the earth; by understanding hath he established the heavens.

**20** By his knowledge the ¹depths are ᵃbroken up, and the clouds drop down the dew.

**21** My son, let not them depart from thine eyes: keep sound wisdom and discretion:

**22** So shall they be life unto thy soul, and ¹grace to thy neck.

**23** ᵃThen shalt thou walk in thy way safely, and thy foot shall not stumble.

3:16 ᵃ [1 Tim. 4:8]    3:17 ᵃ [Matt. 11:29]    3:18 ᵃ Gen. 2:9 ¹ *holds her fast*    3:19 ᵃ Ps. 104:24    3:20 ᵃ Gen. 7:11 ¹ *deeps*    3:22 ¹ *favour*    3:23 ᵃ Prov. 10:9

24 When thou liest down, thou shalt not be afraid: yea, thou shalt lie down, and thy sleep shall be sweet.

25 ᵃBe not afraid of sudden ¹fear, neither of the ²desolation of the wicked, when it cometh.

26 For the LORD shall be thy confidence, and shall keep thy foot from being ¹taken.

27 ᵃWithhold not good from ¹them to whom it is due, when it is in the power of thine hand to do *it*.

28 ᵃSay not unto thy neighbour, Go, and come again, and to morrow I will give; when thou hast it by thee.

29 Devise not evil against thy neighbour, seeing he dwelleth ¹securely by thee.

30 ᵃStrive not with a man without cause, if he have done thee no harm.

31 ᵃEnvy thou not the oppressor, and choose none of his ways.

32 For the ¹froward *is* abomination to the LORD: ᵃbut his ²secret *is* with the righteous.

33 ᵃThe curse of the LORD *is* in the house of the wicked: but ᵇhe blesseth the ¹habitation of the just.

34 ᵃSurely he scorneth the scorners: but he giveth grace unto the ¹lowly.

35 The wise shall inherit glory: but shame shall be ¹the promotion of fools.

### CHAPTER 4

HEAR, ᵃye children, the instruction of a father, and attend to know understanding.

2 For I give you good doctrine, forsake ye not my law.

3 For I was my father's son, ᵃtender and only *beloved* in the sight of my mother.

4 ᵃHe taught me also, and said unto me, Let thine heart retain my words: ᵇkeep my commandments, and live.

5 ᵃGet wisdom, get understanding: forget *it* not; neither ¹decline from the words of my mouth.

6 Forsake her not, and she shall preserve thee: ᵃlove her, and she shall keep thee.

7 ¹Wisdom *is* the principal thing; *therefore* get wisdom: and with all thy getting get understanding.

8 ᵃExalt her, and she shall promote thee: she shall bring thee to honour, when thou dost embrace her.

9 She shall ¹give to thine head ᵃan ornament of grace: a crown of glory shall she deliver to thee.

10 Hear, O my son, and receive my sayings; ᵃand the years of thy life shall be many.

11 I have ᵃtaught thee in the way of wisdom; I have led thee in right paths.

12 When thou goest, ᵃthy steps shall not be ¹straitened; ᵇand when

3:25 ᵃ Ps. 91:5
¹ terror ² trouble from

3:26 ¹ caught

3:27 ᵃ Rom. 13:7
¹ Lit. *its owners*

3:28 ᵃ Lev. 19:13

3:29 ¹ in safety with

3:30 ᵃ [Rom. 12:18]

3:31 ᵃ Ps. 37:1

3:32 ᵃ Ps. 25:14
¹ perverse person ² secret council

3:33 ᵃ Lev. 26:14, 16; Deut. 11:28; Zech. 5:3, 4; Mal. 2:2 ᵇ Job 8:6; Ps. 1:3 ¹ dwelling

3:34 ᵃ James 4:6; 1 Pet. 5:5 ¹ humble

3:35 ¹ the legacy

4:1 ᵃ Ps. 34:11; Prov. 1:8

4:3 ᵃ 1 Chr. 29:1

4:4 ᵃ 1 Chr. 28:9; Eph. 6:4 ᵇ Prov. 7:2

4:5 ᵃ Prov. 2:2, 3
¹ turn away

4:6 ᵃ 2 Thess. 2:10

4:7 ᵃ Prov. 3:13, 14; Matt. 13:44

4:8 ᵃ 1 Sam. 2:30

4:9 ᵃ Prov. 3:22
¹ place on

4:10 ᵃ Prov. 3:2

4:11 ᵃ 1 Sam. 12:23

4:12 ᵃ Job 18:7; Ps. 18:36 ᵇ [Ps. 91:11]; Prov. 3:23
¹ hindered

4:13 ¹ firm

4:14 ᵃ Ps. 1:1; Prov. 1:15

4:15 ¹ do not travel on it

4:16 ᵃ Ps. 36:4; Mic. 2:1 ¹ unless ² evil ³ Lit. *their sleep is robbed*

4:18 ᵃ Is. 26:7; Matt. 5:14, 45; Phil. 2:15 ᵇ 2 Sam. 23:4 ¹ Lit. *bright light* ² *ever brighter*

4:19 ᵃ 1 Sam. 2:9; [Job 18:5, 6]; Prov. 2:13; [Is. 59:9, 10; Jer. 23:12]; John 12:35

4:23 ᵃ [Matt. 12:34; 15:18, 19; Mark 7:21; Luke 6:45]

4:24 ¹ deceitful

4:26 ᵃ Prov. 5:21; Heb. 12:13

5:1 ¹ pay attention to ² incline

5:2 ᵃ Mal. 2:7
¹ preserve

5:3 ᵃ Prov. 2:16 ᵇ Ps. 55:21 ¹ an

thou runnest, thou shalt not stumble.

13 Take ¹fast hold of instruction; let *her* not go: keep her; for she *is* thy life.

14 ᵃEnter not into the path of the wicked, and go not in the way of evil *men*.

15 Avoid it, ¹pass not by it, turn from it, and pass away.

16 ᵃFor they sleep not, ¹except they have done ²mischief; and ³their sleep is taken away, unless they cause *some* to fall.

17 For they eat the bread of wickedness, and drink the wine of violence.

18 ᵃBut the path of the just ᵇ*is* as the ¹shining light, that shineth ²more and more unto the perfect day.

19 ᵃThe way of the wicked *is* as darkness: they know not at what they stumble.

20 My son, attend to my words; incline thine ear unto my sayings.

21 Let them not depart from thine eyes; keep them in the midst of thine heart.

22 For they *are* life unto those that find them, and health to all their flesh.

23 Keep thy heart with all diligence; for out of it *are* the issues of ᵃlife.

24 Put away from thee a ¹froward mouth, and perverse lips put far from thee.

25 Let thine eyes look right on, and let thine eyelids look straight before thee.

26 Ponder the path of thy ᵃfeet, and let all thy ways be established.

27 Turn not to the right hand nor to the left: remove thy foot from evil.

### CHAPTER 5

MY son, ¹attend unto my wisdom, *and* ²bow thine ear to my understanding:

2 That thou mayest ¹regard discretion, and *that* thy lips ᵃmay keep knowledge.

3 ᵃFor the lips of ¹a strange woman ²drop *as* an honeycomb, and her mouth *is* ᵇsmoother than oil:

4 But ¹her end is bitter as wormwood, sharp as a twoedged sword.

5 Her feet go down to death; ᵃher steps take hold on ¹hell.

6 Lest thou shouldest ponder the path of ¹life, her ways are ²moveable, *that* thou canst not know *them*.

7 Hear me now therefore, O ye children, and depart not from the words of my mouth.

8 Remove thy way far from her, and come not nigh the door of her house:

9 Lest thou give thine ¹honour unto others, and thy years unto the ²cruel:

immoral ² drip honey   5:4 ¹ *in the end she is bitter*
5:5 ᵃ Prov. 7:27 ¹ Heb. *Sheol*   5:6 ¹ *her life* ² *unstable*
5:9 ¹ *vigour* ² *cruel one*

10 Lest [1]strangers be filled with thy [2]wealth; and thy labours *be* in the house of a [3]stranger;

11 And thou mourn at the last, when thy flesh and thy body are consumed,

12 And say, How have I hated instruction, and my heart despised reproof;

13 And have not obeyed the voice of my teachers, nor inclined mine ear to them that instructed me!

14 I was [1]almost in all evil in the midst of the congregation and assembly.

15 Drink waters out of thine own cistern, and running waters out of thine own well.

16 [1]Let thy fountains be dispersed abroad, *and* [2]rivers of waters in the streets.

17 Let them be only thine own, and not strangers' with thee.

18 Let thy fountain be blessed: and rejoice with [a]the wife of thy youth.

19 [a]Let her be *as* the loving [1]hind and [2]pleasant roe; let her breasts satisfy thee at all times; and be thou [3]ravished always with her love.

20 And why wilt thou, my son, be [1]ravished with [a]a [2]strange woman, and embrace the bosom of a [3]stranger?

21 [a]For the ways of man *are* before the eyes of the LORD, and he [1]pondereth all his goings.

22 [a]His own iniquities shall [1]take the wicked himself, and he shall be [2]holden with the cords of his sins.

23 [a]He shall die [1]without instruction; and in the greatness of his folly he shall go astray.

## CHAPTER 6

MY son, [a]if thou be [1]surety for thy friend, *if* thou hast [2]stricken thy hand with a stranger,

2 Thou art snared with the words of thy mouth, thou art taken with the words of thy mouth.

3 Do this now, my son, and deliver thyself, when thou art come into the hand of thy friend; go, humble thyself, and [1]make sure thy friend.

4 [a]Give not sleep to thine eyes, nor slumber to thine eyelids.

5 Deliver thyself as a [1]roe from the hand *of the hunter,* and as a bird from the hand of the [2]fowler.

6 [a]Go to the ant, thou sluggard; consider her ways, and be wise:

7 Which having no [1]guide, overseer, or ruler,

8 Provideth her [1]meat in the summer, *and* gathereth her food in the harvest.

9 [a]How long wilt thou [1]sleep, O sluggard? when wilt thou arise out of thy sleep?

10 *Yet* a little sleep, a little slumber, a little folding of the hands to sleep:

11 [a]So shall thy poverty come as [1]one that travelleth, and thy [2]want as an armed man.

12 A [1]naughty person, a wicked man, walketh with a [2]froward mouth.

13 [a]He winketh with his eyes, he [1]speaketh with his feet, he [2]teacheth with his fingers;

14 [1]Frowardness *is* in his heart, [a]he deviseth [2]mischief continually; [b]he soweth discord.

15 Therefore shall his calamity come [a]suddenly; suddenly shall he [b]be broken [c]without remedy.

16 These six *things* doth the LORD hate: yea, seven *are* an abomination unto [1]him:

17 [a][1] proud look, [b]a lying tongue, and [c]hands that shed innocent blood,

18 [a]An heart that [1]deviseth wicked imaginations, [b]feet that be swift in running to [2]mischief,

19 [a]A false witness *that* speaketh lies, and he that [b]soweth discord among brethren.

20 [a]My son, keep thy father's commandment, and forsake not the law of thy mother:

21 [a]Bind them continually upon thine heart, *and* tie them about thy neck.

22 [a]When thou goest, it shall lead thee; when thou sleepest, [b]it shall keep thee; and *when* thou awakest, it shall talk with thee.

23 [a]For the commandment *is* a lamp; and the law *is* light; and reproofs of instruction *are* the way of life:

24 [a]To keep thee from the evil woman, from the flattery of the tongue of a [1]strange woman.

25 [a]Lust not after her beauty in thine heart; neither let her [1]take thee with her eyelids.

26 For [a]by means of a [1]whorish woman *a man is* [2]brought to a piece of bread: [b]and the [3]adulteress will [c]hunt[4] for the precious life.

27 Can a man take fire in his bosom, and his clothes not be burned?

28 Can one go upon hot coals, and his feet not be burned?

29 So he that goeth in to his neighbour's wife; whosoever toucheth her shall not be innocent.

30 *Men* do not despise a thief, if he steal to satisfy his soul when he is [1]hungry;

31 But *if* he be found, [a]he shall restore sevenfold; he shall give all the substance of his house.

32 *But* whoso committeth adultery with a woman [a]lacketh understand-

5:10 [1] *aliens* [2] Lit. *strength* [3] *foreigner*
5:14 [1] *on the verge of total ruin*
5:16 [1] *Should* [2] *channels*
5:18 [a] Mal. 2:14
5:19 [a] Song 2:9 [1] *deer* [2] *graceful doe* [3] *enraptured, lit. be intoxicated*
5:20 [a] Prov. 2:16 [1] *enraptured* [2] *an immoral* [3] *seductress, lit. foreigner*
5:21 [a] Hos. 7:2 [1] *observes*
5:22 [a] Num. 32:23 [1] *entrap* [2] *caught*
5:23 [a] Job 4:21 [1] *for lack of*
6:1 [a] Prov. 11:15 [1] *a guaranty or collateral* [2] Lit. *struck hands in pledge for*
6:3 [1] *plead with*
6:4 [a] Ps. 132:4
6:5 [1] *gazelle* [2] *One who catches birds in a trap or snare*
6:6 [a] Job 12:7
6:7 [1] Lit. *leader*
6:8 [1] Lit. *grain or bread*
6:9 [a] Prov. 24:33, 34 [1] Lit. *lie down*
6:11 [a] Prov. 10:4 [1] *a prowler* [2] *need*
6:12 [1] *worthless man,* lit. *man of Belial* [2] *perverse*
6:13 [a] Job 15:12 [1] *signals with or shuffles* [2] *points*
6:14 [a] Mic. 2:1 [b] Prov. 6:19 [1] *Perversity* [2] *evil*
6:15 [a] Is. 30:13 [b] Jer. 19:11 [c] 2 Chr. 36:16
6:16 [1] Lit. *his soul*
6:17 [a] Ps. 101:5 [b] Ps. 120:2 [c] Is. 1:15 [1] Lit. *Haughty eyes*
6:18 [a] Gen. 6:5 [b] Is. 59:7 [1] *devises wicked plans* [2] *evil*
6:19 [a] Ps. 27:12 [b] Prov. 6:14
6:20 [a] Eph. 6:1
6:21 [a] Prov. 3:3
6:22 [a] [Prov. 3:23] [b] Prov. 2:11
6:23 [a] Ps. 19:8
6:24 [a] Prov. 2:16 [1] *seductress*
6:25 [a] Matt. 5:28 [1] *allure*
6:26 [a] Prov.
29:3 [b] Gen. 39:14 [c] Ezek. 13:18 [1] *harlot* [2] *reduced to a crust of bread* [3] *Another man's wife, lit. a man's wife* [4] *prey upon his precious life* 6:30 [1] *starving*
6:31 [a] Ex. 22:1–4 6:32 [a] Prov. 7:7

ing: he *that* doeth it destroyeth his own soul.

33 A wound and dishonour shall he get; and his reproach shall not be wiped away.

34 For ªjealousy *is* ¹the rage of a man: therefore he will not spare in the day of vengeance.

35 He will ¹not regard any ransom; neither will he ²rest content, though thou givest many gifts.

## CHAPTER 7

M Y son, keep my words, and ªlay¹ up my commandments with thee.

2 ¹Keep my commandments, and live; ᵇand my law as the apple of thine eye.

3 ªBind them upon thy fingers, write them upon the table of thine heart.

4 Say unto wisdom, Thou *art* my sister; and call understanding *thy* ¹kinswoman:

5 ªThat they may keep thee from the ¹strange woman, from the ²stranger *which* flattereth with her words.

6 For at the window of my house I looked through my ¹casement,

7 And beheld among the simple ones, I discerned among ¹the youths, a young man ªvoid² of understanding,

8 Passing through the street near her corner; and he went the way to her house,

9 ªIn the twilight, in the evening, in the black and dark night:

10 And, behold, there met him a woman *with* the attire of an harlot, and ¹subtil of heart.

11 ª(She *is* loud and ¹stubborn; ᵇher feet abide not in her house:

12 Now *is* *she* without, now in the streets, and ¹lieth in wait at every corner.)

13 So she caught him, and kissed him, *and* with ¹an impudent face said unto him,

14 *I have* peace offerings with me; this day have I payed my vows.

15 Therefore came I forth to meet thee, diligently to seek thy face, and I have found thee.

16 I have decked my bed with coverings of tapestry, with ¹carved *works*, with ªfine linen of Egypt.

17 I have perfumed my bed with myrrh, aloes, and cinnamon.

18 Come, let us take our fill of love until the morning: let us ¹solace ourselves with loves.

19 For ¹the goodman *is* not at home, he is gone a long journey:

20 He hath taken a bag of money with him, *and* will come home ¹at the day appointed.

21 ¹With ªher much fair speech she caused him to yield, ᵇwith the flattering of her lips she ²forced him.

22 He goeth after her ¹straightway, as an ox goeth to the slaughter, or ²as a fool to the correction of the ³stocks;

23 Till a ¹dart strike through his liver; ªas a bird hasteth to the snare, and knoweth not that it ²*is* for his life.

24 Hearken unto me now therefore, O ye children, and attend to the words of my mouth.

25 Let not thine heart ¹decline to her ways, go not astray in her paths.

26 For she hath cast down many wounded: yea, ªmany strong *men* have been slain by her.

27 ªHer house *is* the way to ¹hell, going down to the chambers of death.

## CHAPTER 8

D OTH not ªwisdom ¹cry? and understanding put forth her voice?

2 She ¹standeth in the top of ²high places, ³by the way in the places of the paths.

3 She ¹crieth at the gates, at the entry of the city, at the ²coming in at the doors.

4 Unto you, O men, I call; and my voice *is* to the sons of man.

5 O ye simple, understand ¹wisdom: and, ye fools, be ye of an understanding heart.

6 Hear; for I will speak of ªexcellent things; and the opening of my lips *shall be* right things.

7 For my mouth shall speak truth; and wickedness *is* an abomination to my lips.

8 All the words of my mouth *are* in righteousness; *there is* nothing ¹froward or perverse in them.

9 They *are* all plain to him that understandeth, and right to them that find knowledge.

10 Receive my instruction, and not silver; and knowledge rather than choice gold.

11 ªFor wisdom *is* better than rubies; and all the things that may be desired are not to be compared to it.

12 I wisdom dwell with prudence, and find out knowledge ¹of witty inventions.

13 ªThe fear of the LORD *is* to hate evil: ᵇpride, and arrogancy, and the evil way, and ᶜthe ¹froward mouth, do I hate.

14 Counsel *is* mine, and sound wisdom: I *am* understanding; ªI have strength.

15 ªBy me kings reign, and princes decree justice.

16 By me princes rule, and nobles, *even* all the judges of ¹the earth.

---

**Cross-references (center column):**

6:34 ª Song 8:6
¹ *a husband's fury*

6:35 ¹ *accept no recompence* ² *be appeased*

7:1 ª Prov. 2:1
¹ *treasure*

7:2 ª Lev. 18:5
ᵇ Deut. 32:10

7:3 ª Deut. 6:8

7:4 ¹ *near kin*

7:5 ª Prov. 2:16;
5:3 ¹ *immoral* ² *seductress*

7:6 ¹ *lattice*

7:7 ª [Prov. 6:32;
9:4, 16] ¹ Lit. *the sons* ² *devoid*

7:9 ª Job 24:15

7:10 ¹ *crafty*

7:11 ª Prov.
9:13 ᵇ Titus 2:5
¹ *rebellious*

7:12 ¹ *lurking*

7:13 ¹ *a defiant or shameless*

7:16 ª Is. 19:9 ¹ *coloured coverings of Egyptian linen*

7:18 ¹ *delight*

7:19 ¹ *my husband*

7:20 ¹ *at the new or full moon*

7:21 ª Prov. 5:3
ᵇ Ps. 12:2 ¹ *By her enticing speech* ² *seduced*

7:22 ¹ *immediately* ² LXX, Tg., Syr. *as a dog to bonds;* Vg. *as a lamb ... to bonds* ³ *chains*

7:23 ª Eccl. 9:12
¹ *arrow* ² *Would take*

7:25 ¹ *turn aside*

7:26 ª Neh. 13:26

7:27 ª Prov. 2:18;
5:5; 9:18 ¹ Or *Sheol*

8:1 ª Prov. 1:20, 21;
9:3 ¹ *cry out*

8:2 ¹ *takes her stand on* ² *high hills, lit. heights* ³ *beside the way, where the paths meet*

8:3 ¹ *cries out* ² *entrance of*

8:5 ¹ *prudence*

8:6 ª Prov. 22:20

8:8 ¹ *crooked*

8:11 ª Job 28:15

8:12 ¹ *and discretion*

8:13 ª Prov. 3:7;
16:6 ᵇ [Prov. 6:17, 18] ᶜ Prov. 4:24 ¹ *perverse*

8:14 ª Eccl. 7:19;
9:16

8:15 ª Rom. 13:1

8:16 ¹ MT, Tg., Vg., Syr. *righteousness;* LXX, Bg., many mss. *earth*

17 ªI love them that love me; and ᵇthose that seek me ¹early shall find me.

18 ªRiches and honour *are* with me; yea, ¹durable riches and righteousness.

19 My fruit *is* better than gold, yea, than fine gold; and my revenue than choice silver.

20 I ¹lead in the way of righteousness, in the midst of the paths of ²judgment:

21 That I may cause those that love me to inherit ¹substance; and I will fill their treasures.

22 ªThe LORD possessed me in the beginning of his way, before his works of old.

23 ªI was set up from everlasting, from the beginning, or ever the earth was.

24 When *there were* no depths, I was brought forth; when *there were* no fountains abounding with water.

25 ªBefore the mountains were settled, before the hills was I brought forth:

26 While as yet he had not made the earth, nor the ¹fields, nor the ²highest part of the dust of the world.

27 When he prepared the heavens, I *was* there: when he ¹set a compass upon the face of the ²depth:

28 When he established the clouds above: when he strengthened the fountains of the deep:

29 ªWhen he gave to the sea ¹his decree, that the waters should not ²pass his commandment: when ᵇhe appointed the foundations of the earth:

30 ªThen I was by him, *as* ¹one brought up *with him:* ᵇand I was daily *his* delight, rejoicing always before him;

31 Rejoicing in the habitable part of his earth; and ªmy delights *were* with the sons of men.

32 Now therefore hearken unto me, O ye children: for ªblessed *are they that* keep my ways.

33 Hear instruction, and be wise, and ¹refuse it not.

34 ªBlessed *is* the man that heareth me, watching daily at my gates, waiting at the posts of my doors.

35 For whoso findeth me findeth life, and shall ªobtain favour of the LORD.

36 But he that sinneth against me ªwrongeth his own soul: all they that hate me love death.

### CHAPTER 9

Wisdom hath ªbuilded her house, she hath hewn out her seven pillars:

2 ªShe hath ¹killed her beasts; ᵇshe hath ²mingled her wine; she hath also ³furnished her table.

3 She hath sent forth her maidens: she ¹crieth upon the highest places of the city,

4 ªWhoso *is* simple, let him turn in hither: *as for* him that ¹wanteth understanding, she saith to him,

5 ªCome, eat of my bread, and drink of the wine *which* I have ¹mingled.

6 Forsake ¹the foolish, and live; and go in the way of understanding.

7 He that reproveth a ¹scorner getteth to himself shame: and he that rebuketh a wicked *man* ²getteth himself a blot.

8 ªReprove not a ¹scorner, lest he hate thee: ᵇrebuke a wise man, and he will love thee.

9 Give *instruction* to a wise *man,* and he will be yet wiser: teach a just *man,* ªand he will increase in learning.

10 ªThe fear of the LORD *is* the beginning of wisdom: and the knowledge of the ¹holy *is* understanding.

11 ªFor by me thy days shall be multiplied, and the ¹years of thy life shall be increased.

12 ªIf thou be wise, thou shalt be wise for thyself: but *if* thou scornest, thou alone shalt bear *it.*

13 ªA foolish woman *is* ¹clamorous: *she is* simple, and knoweth nothing.

14 For she sitteth at the door of her house, on a seat ªin the high places of the city,

15 To call ¹passengers who go right on their ways:

16 ªWhoso *is* ¹simple, let him turn in hither: and *as for* him that wanteth understanding, she saith to him,

17 ªStolen waters are sweet, and bread *eaten* in secret is pleasant.

18 But he knoweth not that ªthe dead *are* there; *and that* her guests *are* in the depths of ¹hell.

### CHAPTER 10

The proverbs of ªSolomon. ᵇA wise son maketh a glad father: but a foolish son *is* the ¹heaviness of his mother.

2 ªTreasures of wickedness profit nothing: ᵇbut righteousness delivereth from death.

3 ªThe LORD will not suffer the soul of the righteous to famish: but he casteth away the ¹substance of the wicked.

4 ªHe becometh poor that dealeth *with* a ¹slack hand: but ᵇthe hand of the diligent maketh rich.

5 He that gathereth in ªsummer *is* a wise son: *but* he that sleepeth in harvest *is* ᵇa son that causeth shame.

6 Blessings *are* upon the head of the ¹just: but violence covereth the mouth of the wicked.

8:17 ª [John 14:21] ᵇ James 1:5 ¹ diligently
8:18 ª Prov. 3:16 ¹ enduring
8:20 ¹ walk ² justice
8:21 ¹ wealth
8:22 ª Prov. 3:19
8:23 ª [Ps. 2:6]
8:25 ª Job 15:7, 8
8:26 ¹ outer places ² Lit. beginning of the dust
8:27 ¹ drew a circle ² deep
8:29 ª Gen. 1:9, 10 ᵇ Job 28:4, 6 ¹ its limit ² transgress
8:30 ª [John 1:1–3, 18] ᵇ [Matt. 3:17] ¹ MT a master craftsman; a Jewish trad. one brought up
8:31 ª Ps. 16:3
8:32 ª Luke 11:28
8:33 ¹ do not disdain it
8:34 ª Prov. 3:13, 18
8:35 ª [John 17:3]
8:36 ª Prov. 20:2
9:1 ª [Matt. 16:18]
9:2 ª Matt. 22:4 ᵇ Prov. 23:30 ¹ slaughtered her meat ² mixed ³ Lit. set her table in order
9:3 ¹ cries out
9:4 ª Ps. 19:7 ¹ lacks
9:5 ª Is. 55:1 ¹ mixed
9:6 ¹ foolishness
9:7 ¹ scoffer ² only harms himself
9:8 ª Matt. 7:6 ᵇ Ps. 141:5 ¹ scoffer
9:9 ª [Matt. 13:12]
9:10 ª Job 28:28 ¹ Holy One
9:11 ª Prov. 3:2, 16 ¹ years of life will be added to you
9:12 ª Job 35:6, 7
9:13 ª Prov. 7:11 ¹ boisterous
9:14 ª Prov. 9:3
9:15 ¹ to those who pass by
9:16 ª Prov. 7:7, 8 ¹ naive
9:17 ª Prov. 20:17
9:18 ª Prov. 2:18; 7:27 ¹ Heb. Sheol
10:1 ª Prov. 1:1; 25:1 ᵇ Prov. 15:20; 17:21, 25; 19:13; 29:3, 15 ¹ grief
10:2 ª [Luke 12:19, 20] ᵇ Dan. 4:27 10:3 ª Ps. 34:9, 10; 37:25 ¹ desire 10:4 ª Prov. 19:15 ᵇ Prov. 12:24; 13:4; 21:5 ¹ negligent 10:5 ª Prov. 6:8 ᵇ Prov. 19:26 10:6 ¹ righteous

7 [a]The memory of the [1]just *is* blessed: but the name of the wicked shall rot.

8 The wise in heart will receive commandments: [a]but a [1]prating fool shall [2]fall.

9 [a]He that walketh uprightly walketh [1]surely: but he that perverteth his ways shall be known.

10 He that winketh with the eye causeth [1]sorrow: but a [2]prating fool shall fall.

11 The mouth of a righteous *man is* a well of life: but violence covereth the mouth of the wicked.

12 Hatred stirreth up strifes: but [a]love covereth all sins.

13 In the lips of him that hath understanding wisdom is found: but [a]a rod *is* for the back of him that is [1]void of understanding.

14 Wise *men* lay up knowledge: but [a]the mouth of the foolish *is* near destruction.

15 The [a]rich man's wealth *is* his strong city: the destruction of the poor *is* their poverty.

16 The labour of the righteous [1]*tendeth* to [a]life: the [2]fruit of the wicked to sin.

17 He *is in* the way of life that keepeth instruction: but he that refuseth reproof [1]erreth.

18 He that [a]hideth hatred *with* lying lips, and [b]he that uttereth a slander, *is* a fool.

19 [a]In the multitude of words there wanteth not sin: but [b]he that [1]refraineth his lips *is* wise.

20 The tongue of the just *is as* choice silver: the heart of the wicked *is* little worth.

21 The lips of the righteous feed many: but fools die for [1]want of [2]wisdom.

22 [a]The blessing of the LORD, it maketh rich, and he addeth no sorrow with it.

23 [a]*It is* as sport to a fool to do [1]mischief: but a man of understanding hath wisdom.

24 [a]The fear of the wicked, it shall come upon him: but [b]the desire of the righteous shall be granted.

25 As the whirlwind passeth, [a]so *is* the wicked no *more:* but [b]the righteous *is* an everlasting foundation.

26 As vinegar to the teeth, and as smoke to the eyes, so *is* the sluggard to them that send him.

27 [a]The fear of the LORD prolongeth days: but [b]the years of the wicked shall be shortened.

28 The hope of the righteous *shall be* gladness: but the [a]expectation of the wicked shall perish.

29 The way of the LORD *is* strength to the upright: but [a]destruction *shall be* to the workers of iniquity.

30 [a]The righteous shall never be removed: but the wicked shall not inhabit the [1]earth.

31 [a]The mouth of the just bringeth forth wisdom: but the [1]froward tongue shall be cut out.

32 The lips of the righteous know what is acceptable: but the mouth of the wicked *speaketh* [1]frowardness.

## CHAPTER 11

A[a]FALSE[1] balance *is* abomination to the LORD: but [2]a just weight *is* his delight.

2 *When* pride cometh, then cometh [a]shame: but with the [1]lowly *is* wisdom.

3 The integrity of the upright shall guide [a]them: but the [1]perverseness of [2]transgressors shall destroy them.

4 [a]Riches profit not in the day of wrath: but [b]righteousness delivereth from death.

5 The righteousness of the [1]perfect shall [2]direct his way: but the wicked shall fall by his own [a]wickedness.

6 The righteousness of the upright shall deliver them: but transgressors shall be taken in *their own* [1]naughtiness.

7 When a wicked man dieth, *his* expectation shall [a]perish: and the hope of unjust *men* perisheth.

8 [a]The righteous is delivered out of trouble, and the [1]wicked cometh in his stead.

9 An hypocrite with *his* mouth destroyeth his neighbour: but through knowledge shall the [1]just be delivered.

10 [a]When it goeth well with the righteous, the city rejoiceth: and when the wicked perish, *there is* shouting.

11 By the blessing of the upright the city is [a]exalted: but it is overthrown by the mouth of the wicked.

12 He [1]that is void of wisdom despiseth his neighbour: but a man of understanding holdeth his peace.

13 [a]A talebearer revealeth secrets: but he that is of a faithful spirit [b]concealeth the matter.

14 [a]Where no counsel *is,* the people fall: but in the multitude of counsellors *there is* safety.

15 He that is [a]surety[1] for a stranger shall [2]smart *for it:* and he that hateth [3]suretiship is [4]sure.

16 A gracious woman retaineth honour: [1]and strong *men* retain riches.

17 [a]The merciful man doeth good to his own soul: but *he that is* cruel troubleth his own flesh.

18 The wicked worketh a deceitful work: but [a]to him that soweth righteousness *shall be* a sure reward.

10:7 [a] Eccl. 8:10
[1] *righteous*
10:8 [a] Prov. 10:10
[1] *babbling fool*, lit. *foolish of lips*
[2] *be ruined*, lit. *be thrust down*
10:9 [a] [Ps. 23:4]
[1] *securely*
10:10 [1] *trouble*
[2] *babbling*
10:12 [a] [1 Cor. 13:4–7]
10:13 [a] Prov. 26:3
[1] *devoid*
10:14 [a] Prov. 18:7
10:15 [a] Job 31:24
10:16 [a] Prov. 6:23
[1] *leads* [2] *wages*
10:17 [1] *goes astray*
10:18 [a] Prov. 26:24
[b] Ps. 15:3; 101:5
10:19 [a] Eccl. 5:3
[b] [James 1:19; 3:2]
[1] *restrains*
10:21 [1] *lack* [2] Lit. *heart*
10:22 [a] Gen. 24:35; 26:12
10:23 [a] Prov. 2:14; 15:21 [1] *evil*
10:24 [a] Job 15:21
[b] Ps. 145:19
10:25 [a] Ps. 37:9, 10
[b] Ps. 15:5
10:27 [a] Prov. 9:11
[b] Job 15:32
10:28 [a] Job 8:13
10:29 [a] Ps. 1:6
10:30 [a] Ps. 37:22
[1] *land*
10:31 [a] Ps. 37:30
[1] *perverse*
10:32 [1] *perversity*
11:1 [a] Lev. 19:35, 36 [1] *deceptive balance* [2] Lit. *a perfect stone*
11:2 [a] Prov. 16:18; 18:12; 29:23
[1] *humble*
11:3 [a] Prov. 13:6
[1] *deceit* [2] *unfaithful*
11:4 [a] Ezek. 7:19
[b] Gen. 7:1
11:5 [a] Prov. 5:22
[1] *blameless*
[2] Lit. *make his way smooth or straight*
11:6 [1] *lust*
11:7 [a] Prov. 10:28
11:8 [a] Prov. 21:18
[1] *it comes to the wicked instead*
11:9 [1] *righteous*
11:10 [a] Prov. 28:12
11:11 [a] Prov. 14:34
11:12 [1] *who lacks wisdom*
11:13 [a] Lev. 19:16
[b] Prov. 19:11
11:14 [a] 1 Kin. 12:1
11:15 [a] Prov. 6:1, 2 [1] *a guaranty* [2] *suffer* [3] *those pledging guaranty,* lit. *those who strike hands* [4] *secure*
11:16 [1] *but ruthless men*  11:17 [a] [Matt. 5:7; 25:34–36]
11:18 [a] Hos. 10:12

**19** As righteousness [1]*tendeth* to [a]life: so he that pursueth evil *pursueth it* to his own [b]death.

**20** They that are of [1]a froward heart *are* abomination to the LORD: but *such as are* upright in *their* way *are* his delight.

**21** [a]*Though* [1]hand *join* in hand, the wicked shall not be unpunished: but [b]the [2]seed of the righteous shall be delivered.

**22** *As* a [1]jewel of gold in a swine's snout, *so is* a [2]fair woman [3]which is without discretion.

**23** The desire of the righteous *is* only good: *but* the expectation of the wicked [a]*is* wrath.

**24** There is that [a]scattereth, and yet increaseth; and *there is* that withholdeth more than is [1]meet, but *it* [2]tendeth to poverty.

**25** [a]The [1]liberal soul shall be made [2]fat: [b]and he that watereth shall be watered also himself.

**26** [a]He that withholdeth corn, the people shall curse him: but [b]blessing *shall be* upon the head of him that selleth *it.*

**27** He that diligently seeketh good [1]procureth favour: but [a]he that seeketh [2]mischief, it shall come unto him.

**28** [a]He that trusteth in his riches shall fall: but [b]the righteous shall flourish [1]as a branch.

**29** He that troubleth his own house [a]shall inherit the wind: and the fool *shall be* [b]servant to the wise of heart.

**30** The fruit of the righteous *is* a tree of life; and [a]he that [1]winneth souls *is* wise.

**31** [a]Behold, the righteous shall be [1]recompensed in the earth: much more the wicked and the sinner.

## CHAPTER 12

**W**HOSO loveth instruction loveth knowledge: but he that hateth reproof *is* [1]brutish.

**2** A good *man* obtaineth favour of the LORD: but a man of wicked [1]devices will he condemn.

**3** A man shall not be [1]established by wickedness: but the [a]root of the righteous shall not be moved.

**4** [a]A[1] virtuous woman *is* a crown to her husband: but she that maketh ashamed *is* [b]as rottenness in his bones.

**5** The thoughts of the righteous *are* right: *but* the counsels of the wicked *are* deceit.

**6** [a]The words of the wicked *are* to lie in wait for blood: [b]but the mouth of the upright shall deliver them.

**7** [a]The wicked are overthrown, and *are* [1]not: but the house of the righteous shall stand.

**8** A man shall be [1]commended according to his wisdom: [a]but he that is of a perverse heart shall be despised.

**9** [a]*He that is* [1]despised, and hath a servant, *is* better than he that honoureth himself, and lacketh bread.

**10** [a]A righteous *man* regardeth the life of his beast: but the tender mercies of the wicked *are* cruel.

**11** [a]He that [1]tilleth his land shall be satisfied with [b]bread: but he that followeth [2]vain *persons* [c]*is* [3]void of [4]understanding.

**12** The wicked [1]desireth the net of evil *men:* but the root of the righteous yieldeth *fruit.*

**13** The wicked *is* [1]snared by the transgression of *his* lips: [b]but the just shall come out of trouble.

**14** [a]A man shall be satisfied with good by the fruit of *his* mouth: [b]and the recompence of a man's hands shall be rendered unto him.

**15** [a]The way of a fool *is* right in his own eyes: but he that hearkeneth unto counsel *is* wise.

**16** [a]A fool's wrath *is* [1]presently known: but a prudent *man* covereth shame.

**17** [a]*He that* speaketh truth [1]sheweth forth righteousness: but a false witness deceit.

**18** [a]There is [1]that speaketh like the piercings of a sword: but the tongue of the wise [2]*is* health.

**19** The [1]lip of truth shall be established for ever: [a]but a lying tongue *is* but for a moment.

**20** Deceit *is* in the heart of them that [1]imagine evil: but to the counsellors of peace *is* joy.

**21** There shall no [a]evil[1] happen to the [2]just: but the wicked shall be filled with [3]mischief.

**22** [a]Lying lips *are* abomination to the LORD: but they that deal [1]truly *are* his delight.

**23** [a]A prudent man concealeth knowledge: but the heart of fools proclaimeth foolishness.

**24** [a]The hand of the diligent [1]shall bear rule: but the [2]slothful shall be [3]under tribute.

**25** [a]Heaviness[1] in the heart of man [2]maketh it stoop: but [b]a good word maketh it glad.

**26** The righteous [1]*is* more excellent than his neighbour: [2]but the way of the wicked [3]seduceth them.

**27** The slothful *man* roasteth not that which he took in hunting: but the substance of a diligent man *is* precious.

**28** In the way of righteousness *is* life; and *in* the pathway *thereof there is* no death.

11:19 [a] Prov. 10:16;
12:28 [b] [Rom.
6:23] [1] leads
11:20 [1] a perverse
11:21 [a] Prov.
16:5 [b] Ps. 112:2
[1] they join forces
[2] posterity
11:22 [1] ring
[2] beautiful [3] Lit.
who lacks taste
11:23 [a] Rom. 2:8, 9
11:24 [a] Ps. 112:9
[1] right [2] leads
11:25 [a] [2 Cor. 9:6,
7] [b] [Matt. 5:7]
[1] generous [2] rich
11:26 [a] Amos 8:5,
6 [b] Job 29:13
11:27 [a] Esth.
7:10 [1] Lit. seeks
[2] trouble
11:28 [a] Job 31:24
[b] Ps. 1:3 [1] like
foliage
11:29 [a] Eccl. 5:16
[b] Prov. 14:19
11:30 [a] [Dan. 12:3]
[1] Lit. takes
11:31 [a] Jer. 25:29
[1] rewarded
12:1 [1] stupid
12:2 [1] intentions
12:3 [a] [Prov. 10:25]
[1] made secure
12:4 [a] 1 Cor. 11:7
[b] Prov. 14:30 [1] An
excellent wife,
lit. A woman of
valour
12:6 [a] Prov. 1:11, 18
[b] Prov. 14:3
12:7 [a] Matt. 7:24–
27 [1] no more
12:8 [a] 1 Sam. 25:17
[1] praised
12:9 [a] Prov. 13:7
[1] lightly esteemed
12:10 [a] Deut. 25:4
12:11 [a] Gen. 3:19
[b] Prov. 28:19
[c] Prov. 6:32
[1] works or culti-
vates [2] worthless
things [3] devoid
[4] Lit. heart
12:12 [1] covet the
catch
12:13 [a] Prov. 18:7
[b] [2 Pet. 2:9]
[1] ensnared
12:14 [a] Prov. 13:2;
15:23; 18:20 [b] [Is.
3:10, 11]
12:15 [a] Luke 18:11
12:16 [a] Prov. 11:13;
29:11 [1] known at
once
12:17 [a] Prov. 14:5
[1] declares
12:18 [a] Ps. 57:4
[1] one who [2] Pro-
motes
12:19 [a] Prov. 19:9
[1] truthful lip
12:20 [1] devise

12:21 [a] 1 Pet. 3:13 [1] grave trouble [2] righteous [3] trouble
12:22 [a] Rev. 22:15 [1] truthfully   12:23 [a] Prov. 13:16
12:24 [a] Prov. 10:4 [1] shall rule [2] lazy [3] put to forced labour   12:25 [a] Prov. 15:13 [b] Is. 50:4 [1] Anxiety [2] causes
depression   12:26 [1] should choose his friends carefully
[2] for [3] leads them astray

## CHAPTER 13

A WISE son *heareth* his father's instruction: [a]but a [1]scorner [2]heareth not rebuke.

2 [a]A man shall eat good by the fruit of *his* mouth: but the soul of the [1]transgressors *shall* [2]*eat* violence.

3 [a]He that [1]keepeth his mouth [2]keepeth his life: *but* he that openeth wide his lips shall have destruction.

4 [a]The soul of the [1]sluggard desireth, and *hath* nothing: but the soul of the diligent shall be made [2]fat.

5 A righteous *man* hateth lying: but a wicked *man* is loathsome, and cometh to shame.

6 [a]Righteousness keepeth *him* [1]*that is* upright in the way: but wickedness overthroweth the sinner.

7 [a]There is [1]that maketh himself rich, yet *hath* nothing: *there is* [1]that maketh himself poor, yet *hath* great riches.

8 The ransom of a man's life *are* his riches: but the poor heareth not rebuke.

9 The light of the righteous rejoiceth: [a]but the lamp of the wicked shall be put out.

10 [1]Only by pride cometh [a]contention: but with the well advised *is* wisdom.

11 [a]Wealth *gotten* by [1]vanity shall be diminished: but he that gathereth by labour shall increase.

12 Hope deferred maketh the heart sick: but [a]*when* the desire cometh, *it is* a tree of life.

13 Whoso [a]despiseth the word shall be destroyed: but he that feareth the commandment shall be rewarded.

14 [a]The law of the wise *is* a fountain of life, to [1]depart from [b]the snares of death.

15 Good understanding [1]giveth [a]favour: but the way of [2]transgressors *is* hard.

16 [a]Every prudent *man* [1]dealeth with knowledge: but a fool layeth open *his* folly.

17 A wicked messenger falleth into [1]mischief: but [a]a faithful ambassador [2]*is* health.

18 Poverty and shame *shall be to* him that [1]refuseth instruction: but [a]he that regardeth reproof shall be honoured.

19 The desire accomplished is sweet to the soul: but *it is* abomination to fools to depart from evil.

20 He that walketh with wise *men* shall be wise: but a companion of fools shall be destroyed.

21 [a]Evil pursueth sinners: but to the righteous good shall be repayed.

22 A good *man* leaveth an inheritance to his children's children: and [a]the wealth of the sinner *is* [1]laid up for the just.

23 [a]Much food *is in* the [1]tillage of the poor: but there is [2]*that is* destroyed for want of [3]judgment.

24 [a]He that spareth his rod hateth his son: but he that loveth him chasteneth him [1]betimes.

25 [a]The righteous eateth to the satisfying of his soul: but the belly of the wicked shall want.

## CHAPTER 14

E VERY wise woman buildeth her house: but the foolish [1]plucketh it down with her hands.

2 He that walketh in his uprightness feareth the LORD: [a]but *he that is* perverse in his ways despiseth him.

3 In the mouth of the foolish *is* a rod of pride: [a]but the lips of the wise shall preserve them.

4 Where no oxen *are,* the [1]crib *is* clean: but much increase *is* by the strength of the ox.

5 A [a]faithful witness will not lie: but a false witness will utter [b]lies.

6 A [1]scorner seeketh wisdom, and *findeth it* not: but [a]knowledge *is* easy unto him that understandeth.

7 Go from the presence of a foolish man, when thou perceivest not *in him* the lips of [a]knowledge.

8 The wisdom of the prudent *is* to understand his way: but the folly of fools *is* deceit.

9 [a]Fools [1]make a mock at sin: but among the righteous *there is* favour.

10 The heart knoweth his own bitterness; and a stranger doth not [1]intermeddle with his joy.

11 [a]The house of the wicked shall be overthrown: but the [1]tabernacle of the upright shall flourish.

12 [a]There is a way which seemeth right unto a man, but [b]the end thereof *are* the ways of [c]death.

13 Even in laughter the heart is sorrowful; and [a]the end of that mirth *is* [1]heaviness.

14 The backslider in heart shall be [a]filled with his own ways: and a good man *shall be satisfied* [1]from [b]himself.

15 The [1]simple believeth every word: but the prudent *man* [2]looketh well to his going.

16 [a]A wise *man* feareth, and departeth from evil: but the fool rageth, and is [1]confident.

17 *He that is* [1]soon angry dealeth foolishly: and a man of wicked [2]devices is hated.

18 The simple inherit folly: but the prudent are crowned with knowledge.

19 The evil bow before the good; and the wicked at the gates of the righteous.

### Cross References (center column)

13:1 [a] Is. 28:14, 15
[1] *scoffer* [2] *does not listen or heed*
13:2 [a] Prov. 12:14
[1] Lit. *unfaithful*
[2] *feed on*
13:3 [a] Prov. 21:23 [1] *guards*
[2] *preserves*
13:4 [a] Prov. 10:4
[1] *lazy* [2] *rich*
13:6 [a] Prov. 11:3, 5,
6 [1] *whose way is blameless*
13:7 [a] [Prov. 11:24;
12:9] [1] *one who*
13:9 [a] Prov. 24:20
13:10 [a] Prov. 10:12
[1] *By pride comes nothing but contention*
13:11 [a] Prov. 10:2;
20:21 [1] *dishonesty*
13:12 [a] Prov. 13:19
13:13 [a] Num. 15:31
13:14 [a] Prov. 6:22; 10:11; 14:27
[b] 2 Sam. 22:6
[1] *turn one away from*
13:15 [a] Prov. 3:4
[1] *gains* [2] Lit. *unfaithful*
13:16 [a] Prov. 12:23
[1] *acts*
13:17 [a] Prov. 25:13
[1] *trouble* [2] *Brings*
13:18 [a] Prov. 15:5, 31, 32 [1] *disdains,* lit. *ignores*
13:21 [a] Prov. 32:10
13:22 [a] [Eccl. 2:26]
[1] *stored up*
13:23 [a] Prov. 12:11
[1] Lit. *fallow or untilled ground*
[2] Lit. *what is swept away*
[3] *justice*
13:24 [a] Prov. 19:18
[1] *promptly*
13:25 [a] Ps. 34:10
14:1 [1] *pulls*
14:2 [a] [Rom. 2:4]
14:3 [a] Prov. 12:6
14:4 [1] *feed trough*
14:5 [a] Rev. 1:5;
3:14 [b] Prov. 6:19; 12:17
14:6 [a] Prov. 8:9;
17:24 [1] *scoffer*
14:7 [a] Prov. 23:9
14:9 [a] Prov. 10:23
[1] *mock at guilt*
14:10 [1] *share*
14:11 [a] Job 8:15
[1] *tent*
14:12 [a] Prov. 16:25 [b] Rom. 6:21
[c] Prov. 12:15
14:13 [a] Eccl. 2:1, 2
[1] *grief*
14:14 [a] Prov. 1:31;
12:15 [b] Prov. 13:2;
18:20 [1] Lit. *from*

*above himself* 14:15 [1] *naive* [2] *considers carefully* 14:16 [a] Prov. 22:3 [1] *self-confident* 14:17 [1] *quick-tempered* [2] *intentions*

20 [a]The poor is hated even [1]of his own neighbour: but [2]the rich *hath* many [b]friends.

21 He that despiseth his neighbour sinneth: [a]but he that hath mercy on the poor, happy *is* he.

22 Do they not [1]err that devise evil? but mercy and truth *shall be* to them that devise good.

23 In all labour there is profit: but [1]the talk of the lips *tendeth* only to [2]penury.

24 The crown of the wise *is* their riches: *but* the foolishness of fools *is* folly.

25 A true witness [1]delivereth [a]souls: but a deceitful *witness* speaketh lies.

26 In the fear of the LORD *is* strong confidence: and his children shall have a place of refuge.

27 [a]The fear of the LORD *is* a fountain of life, [1]to depart from the snares of death.

28 In the multitude of people *is* the king's honour: but in the [1]want of people *is* the destruction of the prince.

29 [a]*He that is* slow to wrath *is* of great understanding: but *he that is* [1]hasty of spirit exalteth folly.

30 A sound heart *is* the life of the flesh: but [a]envy [b]the rottenness of the bones.

31 [a]He that oppresseth the poor reproacheth [b]his Maker: but he that honoureth him hath mercy on the [1]poor.

32 The wicked is driven away in his wickedness: but [a]the righteous hath [1]hope in his death.

33 Wisdom resteth in the heart of him that hath understanding: but [a]*that which is* in the midst of fools is made known.

34 Righteousness exalteth a [a]nation: but sin *is* a [1]reproach to any people.

35 [a]The king's favour *is* toward a wise servant: but his wrath is *against* him that causeth shame.

### CHAPTER 15

A [a]SOFT answer turneth away wrath: but [b]grievous[1] words stir up anger.

2 The tongue of the wise useth knowledge aright: [a]but the mouth of fools poureth out foolishness.

3 [a]The eyes of the LORD *are* in every place, beholding the evil and the good.

4 A [1]wholesome tongue *is* a tree of life: but perverseness therein [2]*is* a breach in the spirit.

5 [a]A fool despiseth his father's instruction: [b]but he that [1]regardeth reproof is prudent.

6 In the house of the righteous *is* much treasure: but in the revenues of the wicked is trouble.

7 The lips of the wise [1]disperse knowledge: but the heart of the foolish *doeth* not so.

8 [a]The sacrifice of the wicked *is* an abomination to the LORD: but the prayer of the upright *is* his delight.

9 The way of the wicked *is* an abomination unto the LORD: but he loveth him that [a]followeth after righteousness.

10 [1]Correction *is* [a]grievous unto him that forsaketh the way: *and* [b]he that hateth reproof shall die.

11 [a]Hell[1] and [2]destruction *are* before the LORD: how much more then [b]the hearts of the children of men?

12 [a]A [1]scorner loveth not one that reproveth him: neither will he go unto the wise.

13 [a]A merry heart maketh a cheerful [1]countenance: but [b]by sorrow of the heart the spirit is broken.

14 The heart of him that hath understanding seeketh knowledge: but the mouth of fools feedeth on foolishness.

15 All the days of the afflicted *are* evil: [a]but he that is of a merry heart *hath* a continual feast.

16 [a]Better *is* little with the fear of the LORD than great treasure and trouble therewith.

17 [a]Better *is* a dinner of [1]herbs where love is, than a [2]stalled ox and hatred therewith.

18 [a]A wrathful man stirreth up strife: but *he that is* slow to anger appeaseth [1]strife.

19 [a]The way of the [1]slothful *man is* as an hedge of thorns: but the way of the righteous *is* [2]made plain.

20 [a]A wise son maketh a glad father: but a foolish man despiseth his mother.

21 [a]Folly *is* joy to *him that is* destitute of [1]wisdom: [b]but a man of understanding walketh uprightly.

22 [a]Without counsel [1]purposes are disappointed: but in the multitude of counsellors they are established.

23 A man hath joy by the answer of his mouth: and [a]a word *spoken* [1]in due season, how good *is it!*

24 [a]The way of life [1]*is* above to the wise, that he may [b]depart from [2]hell beneath.

25 [a]The LORD will destroy the house of the proud: but [b]he will establish the [1]border of the widow.

26 [a]The thoughts of the wicked *are* an abomination to the LORD: [b]but *the words* of the pure *are* pleasant words.

27 [a]He that is greedy of gain troubleth his own house; but he that hateth [1]gifts shall live.

---

14:20 [a] Prov. 19:7 [b] Prov. 19:4 [1] *by* [2] Lit. *the lovers of the rich are many*
14:21 [a] Ps. 112:9
14:22 [1] *go astray*
14:23 [1] *idle chatter* [2] *poverty*
14:25 [a] [Ezek. 3:18–21] [1] *saves lives*
14:27 [a] Prov. 13:14 [1] *to turn one away from*
14:28 [1] *lack*
14:29 [a] James 1:19 [1] *impulsive,* lit. *short of spirit*
14:30 [a] Ps. 112:10 [b] Prov. 12:4
14:31 [a] Matt. 25:40 [b] [Prov. 22:2] [1] Lit. *needy*
14:32 [a] Job 13:15 [1] *refuge*
14:33 [a] Prov. 12:16
14:34 [a] Prov. 11:11 [1] *shame* or *disgrace*
14:35 [a] Matt. 24:45–47
15:1 [a] Prov. 25:15 [b] 1 Sam. 25:10 [1] *harsh*
15:2 [a] Prov. 12:23
15:3 [a] Job 34:21
15:4 [1] Lit. *healing* [2] *breaks the spirit*
15:5 [a] Prov. 10:1 [b] Prov. 13:18 [1] Lit. *keeps*
15:7 [1] *spread*
15:8 [a] Is. 1:11
15:9 [a] Prov. 21:21
15:10 [a] 1 Kin. 22:8 [b] Prov. 5:12 [1] *Harsh correction is for him*
15:11 [a] Job 26:6 [b] 2 Chr. 6:30 [1] Or *Sheol* [2] Heb. *Abaddon*
15:12 [a] Amos 5:10 [1] *scoffer*
15:13 [a] Prov. 12:25 [b] Prov. 17:22 [1] *face*
15:15 [a] Prov. 17:22
15:16 [a] Ps. 37:16
15:17 [a] Prov. 17:1 [1] *vegetables* [2] *fatted calf*
15:18 [a] Prov. 26:21 [1] *contention*
15:19 [a] Prov. 22:5 [1] *lazy* [2] *a highway*
15:20 [a] Prov. 10:1
15:21 [a] Prov. 10:23 [b] Eph. 5:15 [1] *discernment,* lit. *heart*
15:22 [a] Prov. 11:14 [1] *plans go awry*
15:23 [a] Prov. 25:11 [1] Lit. *in its time*
15:24 [a] Phil. 3:20 [b] Prov. 14:16 [1] *leads upward* [2] Or *Sheol*   15:25 [a] Prov. 12:7 [b] Ps. 68:5, 6 [1] *boundary*
15:26 [a] Prov. 6:16, 18 [b] Ps. 37:30   15:27 [a] Is. 5:8 [1] *bribes*

28 The heart of the righteous [a]studieth[1] to answer: but the mouth of the wicked poureth out evil things.

29 [a]The LORD *is* far from the wicked: but [b]he heareth the prayer of the righteous.

30 The light of the eyes rejoiceth the heart: *and* a good report maketh the bones [1]fat.

31 The ear that heareth the reproof of life abideth among the wise.

32 He that [1]refuseth instruction despiseth his own soul: but he that [2]heareth reproof getteth understanding.

33 [a]The fear of the LORD *is* the instruction of wisdom; and [b]before honour *is* humility.

### CHAPTER 16

THE [a]preparations[1] of the heart [2]in man, [b]and the answer of the tongue, *is* from the LORD.

2 All the ways of a man *are* clean in his own [a]eyes; but the LORD weigheth the spirits.

3 [a]Commit[1] thy works unto the LORD, and thy thoughts shall be established.

4 The [a]LORD hath made all *things* for himself: [b]yea, even the wicked for the day of [1]evil.

5 [a]Every one *that is* proud in heart *is* an abomination to the LORD: *though* hand *join* in hand, he shall not be unpunished.

6 [a]By mercy and truth [1]iniquity is purged: and [b]by the fear of the LORD *men* depart from evil.

7 When a man's ways please the LORD, he maketh even his enemies to be at peace with him.

8 [a]Better *is* a little with righteousness than great revenues without [1]right.

9 [a]A man's heart [1]deviseth his way: [b]but the LORD directeth his steps.

10 A [1]divine sentence *is* in the lips of the king: his mouth [2]transgresseth not in judgment.

11 [a]A just weight and balance *are* the LORD'S: all the weights of the bag *are* his [1]work.

12 *It is* an abomination to kings to commit wickedness: for [a]the throne is established by righteousness.

13 [a]Righteous lips *are* the delight of kings; and they love him that speaketh right.

14 The wrath of a king *is as* messengers of death: but a wise man will [a]pacify[1] it.

15 In the light of the king's countenance *is* life; and his favour *is* as a [a]cloud of the latter rain.

16 [a]How much better *is it* to get wisdom than gold! and to get understanding rather to be chosen than silver!

17 The highway of the upright *is* to depart from evil: he that keepeth his way preserveth his soul.

18 Pride *goeth* before destruction, and an haughty spirit before [a]a fall.

19 Better *it is to be* of an humble spirit with the lowly, than to divide the [1]spoil with the proud.

20 He that [1]handleth a matter wisely shall find good: and whoso [a]trusteth in the LORD, happy *is* he.

21 The wise in heart shall be called prudent: and the sweetness of the lips increaseth learning.

22 Understanding *is* a wellspring of life unto him that hath it: but the instruction of fools *is* folly.

23 The heart of the wise teacheth his mouth, and addeth learning to his lips.

24 Pleasant words *are as* an honeycomb, sweet to the soul, and health to the bones.

25 There is a way that seemeth right unto a man, but the end thereof *are* the ways of [a]death.

26 He that laboureth laboureth for himself; for [1]his mouth craveth it of [a]him.

27 [1]An ungodly man diggeth up evil: and in his lips *there is* as a burning [a]fire.

28 A [1]froward man soweth strife: and [a]a whisperer separateth [2]chief friends.

29 A violent man enticeth his neighbour, and leadeth him into the way *that is* not good.

30 He [1]shutteth his eyes to devise [2]froward things: [3]moving his lips he bringeth evil to pass.

31 [a]The [1]hoary head *is* a crown of glory, *if* it be found in the way of righteousness.

32 [a]*He that is* slow to anger *is* better than the mighty; and he that ruleth his spirit than he that taketh a city.

33 The lot is cast into the lap; but the whole [1]disposing thereof *is* of the LORD.

### CHAPTER 17

BETTER *is* [a]a dry morsel, and quietness therewith, than an house full of [1]sacrifices *with* strife.

2 A wise servant shall have rule over [a]a son that causeth shame, and shall have part of the inheritance among the brethren.

3 The [1]fining pot *is* for silver, and the furnace for gold: [a]but the LORD trieth the hearts.

4 A wicked doer giveth heed to false lips; *and* a liar giveth ear to a [1]naughty tongue.

5 [a]Whoso mocketh the poor reproacheth his Maker: *and* he that is glad at calamities shall not be unpunished.

15:28 [a] 1 Pet. 3:15
[1] *studies how to*
15:29 [a] Ps. 10:1; 34:16 [b] Ps. 145:18
15:30 [1] *healthy*
15:32 [1] *disdains or ignores* [2] *heeds*
15:33 [a] Prov. 1:7 [b] Prov. 18:12
16:1 [a] Jer. 10:23 [b] Matt. 10:19
[1] *plans* [2] *belong to man*
16:2 [a] Prov. 21:2
16:3 [a] Ps. 37:5 [1] Lit. *Roll on the LORD your works*
16:4 [a] Is. 43:7 [b] [Rom. 9:22] [1] *doom*
16:5 [a] Prov. 6:17; 8:13
16:6 [a] Dan. 4:27 [b] Prov. 8:13; 14:16 [1] *atonement is provided for iniquity*
16:8 [a] Ps. 37:16 [1] *justice*
16:9 [a] Prov. 19:21 [b] Jer. 10:23 [1] *plans*
16:10 [1] Lit. *divination* [2] *must not transgress*
16:11 [a] Lev. 19:36 [1] *concern*
16:12 [a] Prov. 25:5
16:13 [a] Prov. 14:35
16:14 [a] Prov. 25:15 [1] *appease*
16:15 [a] Zech. 10:1
16:16 [a] Prov. 8:10, 11, 19
16:18 [1] *stumbling*
16:19 [1] *plunder*
16:20 [a] Ps. 34:8 [1] *wisely heeds the word*
16:25 [a] Prov. 14:12
16:26 [a] [Eccl. 6:7] [1] *his hungry mouth drives him on*
16:27 [a] [James 3:6] [1] Lit. *A man of Belial*
16:28 [a] Prov. 17:9 [1] *perverse* [2] *the best of friends*
16:30 [1] *winks* [2] *perverse* [3] *pursing, lit. compressing*
16:31 [a] Prov. 20:29 [1] *silvery*
16:32 [a] Prov. 14:29; 19:11
16:33 [1] *decision*
17:1 [a] Prov. 15:17 [1] *Or sacrificial meals or feasting*
17:2 [a] Prov. 10:5
17:3 [a] Jer. 17:10 [1] *refining*
17:4 [1] Lit. *destructive*
17:5 [a] Prov. 14:31 [b] Job 31:29

6 [a]Children's children *are* the crown of old men; and the glory of children *are* their fathers.

7 Excellent speech becometh not a fool: much less do lying lips a prince.

8 A gift *is as* a precious stone in the eyes of him that hath it: whithersoever [1]it turneth, [1]it prospereth.

9 [a]He that covereth a transgression seeketh love; but [b]he that repeateth a matter separateth [1]*very* friends.

10 A [a]reproof [1]entereth more into a wise man than an hundred [2]stripes into a fool.

11 An evil *man* seeketh only rebellion: therefore a cruel messenger shall be sent against him.

12 [1]Let [a]a bear robbed of her whelps meet a man, rather than a fool in his folly.

13 Whoso [a]rewardeth evil for good, evil shall not depart from his house.

14 The beginning of strife *is* [1]as when one letteth out water: therefore [a]leave[2] off contention, before it be meddled with.

15 [a]He that justifieth the wicked, and he that condemneth the just, even they both *are* abomination to the LORD.

16 Wherefore *is there* a price in the hand of a fool to get wisdom, seeing *he hath* no heart [1]*to it?*

17 [a]A friend loveth at all times, and a brother is born for adversity.

18 [a]A man [1]void of [2]understanding [3]striketh hands, *and* becometh [4]surety in the presence of his friend.

19 He loveth transgression that loveth strife: *and* [a]he that exalteth his gate seeketh destruction.

20 He that hath a [1]froward heart findeth no good: and he that hath [a]a perverse tongue falleth into [2]mischief.

21 He that begetteth a [1]fool *doeth it* to his sorrow: and the father of a fool hath no joy.

22 A [a]merry heart doeth good *like* a medicine: but a broken spirit drieth the bones.

23 A wicked *man* taketh a [1]gift out of the bosom to pervert the ways of judgment.

24 [a]Wisdom *is* before him that hath understanding; but the eyes of a fool *are* in the ends of the earth.

25 A [a]foolish son *is* a grief to his father, and bitterness to her that bare him.

26 Also to punish the [1]just *is* not good, *nor* to strike princes [2]for equity.

27 [a]He that hath knowledge spareth his words: *and* a man of understanding is of an [1]excellent spirit.

28 [a]Even a fool, when he [1]holdeth his peace, is counted wise: *and* he that shutteth his lips *is esteemed* a man of understanding.

17:6 [a] [Ps. 127:3; 128:3]
17:8 [a] *he*
17:9 [a] [Prov. 10:12]
[b] Prov. 16:28 [1] The best of
17:10 [a] [Mic. 7:9]
[1] *is more effective to* [2] *blows*
17:12 [a] Hos. 13:8
[1] *Let a man meet a bear robbed of her cubs*
17:13 [a] Ps. 109:4, 5
17:14 [a] [Prov. 20:3]
[1] *like releasing water* [2] *stop contention before a quarrel starts*
17:15 [a] Ex. 23:7
17:16 [1] For it
17:17 [a] Ruth 1:16
17:18 [a] Prov. 6:1
[1] *devoid* [2] Lit. *heart* [3] Shakes hands in pledge [4] *a guaranty for his friend*
17:19 [a] Prov. 16:18
17:20 [a] James 3:8 [1] *deceitful* or *crooked* [2] *evil*
17:21 [1] *scoffer*
17:22 [a] Prov. 12:25; 15:13, 15
17:23 [1] *bribe*
17:24 [a] Eccl. 2:14
17:25 [a] Prov. 10:1; 15:20; 19:13
17:26 [1] *righteous* [2] *for their uprightness*
17:27 [a] James 1:19 [1] *calm*
17:28 [a] Job 13:5 [1] *keeps silent, is considered wise*
18:1 [1] *A man who isolates himself seeks his own desire; he rages against all wise judgment.*
18:2 [a] Eccl. 10:3 [1] *express itself*
18:3 [1] *with dishonour reproach*
18:4 [a] Prov. 10:11 [b] [James 3:17]
18:5 [a] Prov. 17:15 [1] *to show partiality to*
18:6 [1] *blows*
18:7 [a] Prov. 10:14 [b] Eccl. 10:12
18:8 [a] James 12:18 [1] *gossip* or *slanderer* [2] *tasty morsels,* Jewish trad. *wounds* [3] Lit. *chambers of the belly*
18:9 [1] *destroyer*
18:10 [a] 2 Sam. 22:2, 3, 33 [1] Lit. *set on high*

## CHAPTER 18

THROUGH[1] desire a man, having separated himself, seeketh *and* intermeddleth with all wisdom.

2 A fool hath no delight in understanding, but that his heart may [1]discover [a]itself.

3 When the wicked cometh, *then* cometh also contempt, and [1]with ignominy reproach.

4 [a]The words of a man's mouth *are as* deep waters, [b]*and* the wellspring of wisdom *as* a flowing brook.

5 *It is* not good [1]to accept the person of the wicked, to overthrow the righteous in [a]judgment.

6 A fool's lips enter into contention, and his mouth calleth for [1]strokes.

7 [a]A fool's mouth *is* his destruction, and his lips *are* the snare of his [b]soul.

8 [a]The words of a [1]talebearer *are* as [2]wounds, and they go down into the [3]innermost parts of the belly.

9 He also that is slothful in his work is brother to him that is a great [1]waster.

10 The name of the LORD *is* a strong [a]tower: the righteous runneth into it, and is [1]safe.

11 The rich man's wealth *is* his strong city, and as an high wall in his own [1]conceit.

12 [a]Before destruction the heart of man is haughty, and before honour *is* humility.

13 He that answereth a matter before he heareth *it,* it *is* folly and shame unto him.

14 The spirit of a man will [1]sustain his infirmity; but a [2]wounded spirit who can bear?

15 The heart of the prudent getteth knowledge; and the ear of the wise seeketh knowledge.

16 [a]A man's gift maketh room for him, and bringeth him before great men.

17 *He that is* [1]first in his own cause *seemeth* just; but his neighbour cometh and [2]searcheth him.

18 [a]The [a]lot causeth contentions to cease, and [2]parteth between the mighty.

19 A brother offended *is harder to be won* than a strong city: and *their* contentions *are* like the bars of a castle.

20 [a]A man's belly shall be satisfied with the fruit of his mouth; *and* with the [1]increase of his lips shall he be filled.

21 [a]Death and life *are* in the power of the tongue: and they that love it shall eat the fruit thereof.

18:11 [1] *esteem*　18:12 [a] Prov. 15:33; 16:18　18:14 [1] *sustain him in sickness* [2] *broken*　18:16 [a] Gen. 32:20, 21　18:17 [1] *first to plead* [2] *examines*　18:18 [a] [Prov. 16:33] [1] *Casting lots* [2] *keeps apart*　18:20 [a] Prov. 12:14; 14:14 [1] *produce*　18:21 [a] Matt. 12:37

22 [a]*Whoso* findeth a wife findeth a
good *thing,* and obtaineth favour of
the LORD.
23 The poor useth intreaties; but
the rich answereth [a]roughly.
24 A man *that hath* friends [1]must
shew himself friendly: [a]and there is
a friend *that* sticketh closer than a
brother.

## CHAPTER 19

BETTER [a]*is* the poor that walketh in
his integrity, than *he that is* perverse in his lips, and is a fool.
2 Also, *that* the soul *be* without
knowledge, *it is* not good; and he that
hasteth with *his* feet sinneth.
3 The foolishness of man [1]pervert-
eth his way: and his heart fretteth
against the LORD.
4 [a]Wealth maketh many friends;
but the poor is separated from his
[1]neighbour.
5 A [a]false witness shall not be unpunished, and *he that* speaketh lies
shall not escape.
6 Many will intreat the favour of
the prince: and every man *is* a friend
to him that giveth gifts.
7 [a]All the brethren of the poor do
hate him: how much more do his
friends go [b]far from him? he pursueth *them with* words, *yet* [1]they *are*
wanting *to him.*
8 He that getteth [1]wisdom loveth
his own soul: he that keepeth understanding [a]shall find good.
9 A false witness shall not be unpunished, and *he that* speaketh lies
shall perish.
10[1] Delight is not [2]seemly for a fool;
much less [a]for a servant to have rule
over princes.
11 [a]The discretion of a man [1]defer-
reth his anger; [b]and *it is* his glory to
[2]pass over a transgression.
12 [a]The king's wrath *is* as the roaring of a lion; but his favour *is* [b]as dew
upon the grass.
13 [a]A foolish son *is* the [1]calamity of
his father: [b]and the contentions of a
wife *are* a [2]continual dropping.
14 [a]House and riches *are* the inheritance [1]of fathers: and [b]a prudent
wife *is* from the LORD.
15 [a]Slothfulness[1] casteth into a
deep sleep; and an idle soul shall
[b]suffer hunger.
16 [a]He that keepeth the commandment keepeth his own soul; *but* he
that [1]despiseth his ways shall die.
17 [a]He that hath pity upon the poor
lendeth unto the LORD; and that which
he hath given will he pay him again.
18 [a]Chasten thy son while there is
hope, and [1]let not thy soul spare [2]for
his crying.
19 A man of great wrath shall suffer
punishment: for if thou deliver *him,*
yet thou must do it again.
20 Hear counsel, and receive instruction, that thou mayest be wise
[a]in thy latter [1]end.
21 *There are* many [1]devices in a
man's heart; [a]nevertheless the counsel of the LORD, that shall stand.
22 The desire of a man *is* his kindness: and a poor man *is* better than a
liar.
23 [a]The fear of the LORD *tendeth* to
life: and *he that hath it* shall abide satisfied; he shall not be visited with evil.
24 [a]A [1]slothful *man* hideth his hand
in *his* [2]bosom, and will not so much
as bring it to his mouth again.
25 Smite a scorner, and the simple [a]will beware: and [b]reprove one
that hath understanding, *and* he will
understand knowledge.
26 He that [1]wasteth *his* father, *and*
chaseth away *his* mother, *is* [a]a son
that causeth shame, and bringeth reproach.
27 Cease, my son, to hear the instruction [1]*that causeth* to err from
the words of knowledge.
28[1] An ungodly witness scorneth
[2]judgment: and [a]the mouth of the
wicked [3]devoureth iniquity.
29 Judgments are prepared for
[1]scorners, [a]and [2]stripes for the back
of fools.

## CHAPTER 20

WINE [a]*is* a mocker, [1]strong drink
*is* [2]raging: and whosoever is deceived thereby is not wise.
2 The [1]fear of a king *is* as the roaring
of a lion: *whoso* provoketh him to anger sinneth *against* his own [2]soul.
3 [a]*It is* [1]an honour for a man to
cease from strife: but every fool [2]will
be meddling.
4 [a]The sluggard will not plow [1]by
reason of the cold; [b]*therefore* shall he
beg in harvest, and *have* nothing.
5 Counsel in the heart of man *is*
*like* deep water; but a man of understanding will draw it out.
6 Most men will proclaim every
one his own goodness: but a faithful
man who can find?
7 [a]The just *man* walketh in his integrity: [b]his children *are* blessed after him.
8 A king that sitteth in the throne
of judgment scattereth away all evil
with his eyes.
9 [a]Who can say, I have made my
heart clean, I am pure from my sin?
10 [a]Divers[1] weights, *and* divers
measures, both of them *are* alike
abomination to the LORD.

18:22 [a] [Prov. 12:4; 19:14]
18:23 [a] James 2:3, 6
18:24 [a] Prov. 17:17 [1] Or *may come to ruin: but*
19:1 [a] Prov. 28:6
19:3 [1] *twists*
19:4 [a] Prov. 14:20 [1] *friend*
19:5 [a] Ex. 23:1
19:7 [a] Prov. 14:20 [b] Ps. 38:11 [1] *they abandon him,* lit. *they are not*
19:8 [a] Prov. 16:20 [1] Lit. *heart*
19:10 [a] Prov. 30:21, 22 [1] *Luxury* [2] *fitting*
19:11 [a] James 1:19 [b] Eph. 4:32 [1] *makes him slow to anger* [2] *overlook*
19:12 [a] Prov. 16:14 [b] Hos. 14:5
19:13 [a] Prov. 10:1 [b] Prov. 21:9, 19 [1] *ruin* [2] An unending irritation
19:14 [a] 2 Cor. 12:14 [b] Prov. 18:22 [1] *from*
19:15 [a] Prov. 6:9 [b] Prov. 10:4 [1] *Laziness*
19:16 [a] Luke 10:28; 11:28 [1] *is careless of*
19:17 [a] [2 Cor. 9:6–8]
19:18 [a] Prov. 13:24 [1] *do not set your heart* [2] Lit. *to put him to death* (on his destruction); Jewish trad. *on his crying*
19:20 [a] Ps. 37:37 [1] *days*
19:21 [a] Heb. 6:17 [1] *plans*
19:23 [a] [1 Tim. 4:8]
19:24 [a] Prov. 15:19 [1] *lazy* [2] MT *bowl;* LXX, Syr. *bosom;* Vg., Tg. *armpit*
19:25 [a] Deut. 13:11 [b] Prov. 9:8
19:26 [a] Prov. 17:2 [1] *assaults or mistreats*
19:27 [1] *and you will go astray from*
19:28 [a] Job 15:16 [1] Heb. *Belial,* a disreputable [2] *justice* [3] *swallows*
19:29 [a] Prov. 26:3 [1] *scoffers* [2] *beatings*
20:1 [a] Gen. 9:21 [1] *intoxicating drink* [2] *arouses brawling* 20:2 [1] Lit. *wrath or terror, produced by the king's wrath* [2] *life* 20:3 [a] Prov. 17:14 [1] *honourable* [2] *can start a quarrel* 20:4 [a] Prov. 10:4 [b] Prov. 19:15 [1] *because of winter* 20:7 [a] 2 Cor. 1:12 [b] Ps. 37:26 20:9 [a] [1 Kin. 8:46] 20:10 [a] Deut. 25:13 [1] *Differing weights,* lit. *A stone and a stone*

11 Even a child is [a]known by his doings, whether his work *be* pure, and whether *it be* right.

12 [a]The hearing ear, and the seeing eye, the LORD hath made even both of them.

13 [a]Love not sleep, lest thou come to poverty; open thine eyes, *and* thou shalt be satisfied with bread.

14 [1]*It is* naught, *it is* naught, saith the buyer: but when he is gone his way, then he boasteth.

15 There is gold, and a multitude of rubies: but [a]the lips of knowledge *are* a precious jewel.

16 [a]Take his garment that is [1]surety *for* a stranger: and [2]take a pledge of him for a [3]strange woman.

17 [a]Bread [1]of deceit *is* sweet to a man; but afterwards his mouth shall be filled with gravel.

18 [a]*Every* purpose is established by counsel: [b]and with good advice make war.

19 [a]He that goeth about *as* a talebearer revealeth secrets: therefore [1]meddle not with him [b]that flattereth with his lips.

20 [a]Whoso curseth his father or his mother, [b]his lamp shall be put out in [1]obscure darkness.

21 [a]An inheritance *may be* gotten hastily at the beginning; [b]but the end thereof shall not be blessed.

22 [a]Say not thou, I will [1]recompense evil; *but* [b]wait on the LORD, and he shall save thee.

23 [1]Divers weights *are* an abomination unto the LORD; and [2]a false balance *is* not good.

24 Man's [1]goings *are* of the LORD; how can a man then understand his own way?

25 *It is* a snare to the man [1]*who* devoureth *that which is* [2]holy, and after vows to [3]make enquiry.

26 [a]A wise king [1]scattereth the wicked, and bringeth the [2]wheel over them.

27 [a]The spirit of man *is* the [1]candle of the LORD, searching all the [2]inward parts of the belly.

28 [a]Mercy and truth preserve the king: and his throne is upholden by mercy.

29 The glory of young men *is* their strength: and [a]the beauty of old men *is* the grey head.

30 [1]The blueness of a wound cleanseth away evil: so *do* stripes the [2]inward parts of the belly.

## CHAPTER 21

THE king's heart *is* in the hand of the LORD, *as* the [1]rivers of water: he turneth it whithersoever he [2]will.

2 [a]Every way of a man *is* right in his own eyes: [b]but the LORD [1]pondereth the hearts.

3 [a]To do [1]justice and judgment *is* more acceptable to the LORD than sacrifice.

4 [a]An high look, and a proud heart, *and* the [1]plowing of the wicked, *is* sin.

5 [a]The [1]thoughts of the diligent [2]*tend* only to plenteousness; but of every one *that is* hasty [3]only to want.

6 [a]The getting of treasures by a lying tongue *is* a vanity tossed to and fro of them that seek death.

7 The [1]robbery of the wicked shall [2]destroy them; because they refuse to do [3]judgment.

8 The way of [1]man *is* froward and strange: but *as for* the pure, his work *is* right.

9 *It is* better to dwell in a corner of the housetop, than with [a]a [1]brawling woman in a wide house.

10 [a]The soul of the wicked desireth evil: his neighbour findeth no favour in his eyes.

11 When the [1]scorner is punished, the simple is made wise: and when the [a]wise is instructed, he receiveth knowledge.

12 The righteous [1]*man* wisely considereth the house of the wicked: [2]*but God* overthroweth the wicked for *their* wickedness.

13 [a]Whoso stoppeth his ears at the cry of the poor, he also shall cry himself, but shall not be heard.

14 A gift in secret pacifieth anger: and a [1]reward [2]in the bosom strong wrath.

15 *It is* joy to the just to do judgment: but destruction *shall be* to the workers of iniquity.

16 The man that wandereth out of the way of understanding shall remain in the congregation of the [a]dead.

17 He that loveth pleasure *shall be* a poor man: he that loveth wine and oil shall not be rich.

18 The wicked *shall be* a ransom for the righteous, and the [1]transgressor for the upright.

19 *It is* better to dwell [1]in the wilderness, than with a contentious and an angry woman.

20 [a]*There is* treasure to be desired and oil in the dwelling of the wise; but a foolish man [1]spendeth it up.

21 [a]He that followeth after righteousness and mercy findeth life, righteousness, and honour.

22 A [a]wise *man* [1]scaleth the city of the mighty, and casteth down the [2]strength of the confidence thereof.

23 [a]Whoso keepeth his mouth and his tongue keepeth his soul from troubles.

---

20:11 [a] Matt. 7:16
20:12 [a] Ex. 4:11
20:13 [a] Rom. 12:11
20:14 [1] *It is good for nothing*, lit. *Evil, evil*
20:15 [a] [Prov. 3:13–15]
20:16 [a] Prov. 22:26 [1] *guaranty* [2] *hold it as a* [3] *seductress*
20:17 [a] Prov. 9:17 [1] *gained by*
20:18 [a] Prov. 24:6 [b] Luke 14:31
20:19 [a] Prov. 11:13 [b] Rom. 16:18 [1] *associate not with*
20:20 [a] Matt. 15:4 [b] Job 18:5, 6 [1] *deep*
20:21 [a] Prov. 28:20 [b] Hab. 2:6
20:22 [a] [Rom. 12:17–19] [b] 2 Sam. 16:12 [1] *repay*
20:23 [1] *Differing weights*, lit. *A stone and a stone* [2] Lit. *balances of deceit*
20:24 [1] *steps*
20:25 [1] *to devote rashly* something as holy [2] *consecrated* [3] *reconsider his vows*
20:26 [a] Ps. 101:8 [1] *sifts out* [2] *threshing wheel*
20:27 [a] 1 Cor. 2:11 [1] *lamp* [2] Lit. *chambers of the belly*
20:28 [a] Prov. 21:21
20:29 [a] Prov. 16:31
20:30 [1] *Blows that wound* [2] Lit. *chambers of the belly*
21:1 [1] *channels* [2] *wishes*
21:2 [a] Prov. 16:2 [b] Prov. 24:12 [1] Lit. *weighs*
21:3 [a] 1 Sam. 15:22 [1] *righteousness and justice*
21:4 [a] Prov. 6:17 [1] Or *lamp*
21:5 [a] Prov. 10:4 [1] *plans* [2] *lead surely* [3] *surely to poverty*
21:6 [a] 2 Pet. 2:3
21:7 [1] *violence* [2] Lit. *drag them away* [3] *justice*
21:8 [1] *a guilty man is perverse*
21:9 [a] Prov. 19:13 [1] *contentious*
21:10 [a] James 4:5
21:11 [a] Prov. 19:25 [1] *scoffer*

21:12 [1] *one* (God) [2] *overthrowing*  21:13 [a] [Matt. 7:2; 18:30–34]  21:14 [1] *bribe* [2] *behind the back*  21:16 [a] Ps. 49:14  21:18 [1] *unfaithful*  21:19 [1] Lit. *in the land of the desert*  21:20 [a] Ps. 112:3 [1] *squanders it*  21:21 [a] Matt. 5:6  21:22 [a] Prov. 24:5 [1] *climbs over the walls of* [2] *trusted strong hold*  21:23 [a] [James 3:2]

24 Proud *and* haughty scorner *is* his name, who ¹dealeth in proud wrath.

25 The ᵃdesire of the ¹slothful killeth him; for his hands refuse to labour.

26 He coveteth greedily all the day long: but the righteous ᵃgiveth and spareth not.

27 ᵃThe sacrifice of the wicked *is* abomination: how much more, *when* he bringeth it with a wicked ¹mind?

28 A false witness shall perish: but the man that heareth speaketh ¹constantly.

29 A wicked man hardeneth his face: but *as for* the upright, he ¹directeth his way.

30 ᵃ*There is* no wisdom nor understanding nor counsel against the LORD.

31 The horse *is* prepared against the day of battle: but ᵃsafety¹ *is* of the LORD.

## CHAPTER 22

A ᵃ*GOOD* name *is* rather to be chosen than great riches, *and* loving favour rather than silver and gold.

2 The ᵃrich and poor ¹meet together: the ᵇLORD *is* the maker of them all.

3 A prudent *man* foreseeth the evil, and hideth himself: but the simple pass on, and are ᵃpunished.

4 By humility *and* the fear of the LORD *are* riches, and honour, and life.

5 Thorns *and* snares *are* in the way of the ¹froward: he that ²doth keep his soul shall be far from them.

6 ᵃTrain up a child in the way he should go: ¹and when he is old, he will not depart from it.

7 The ᵃrich ruleth over the poor, and the borrower *is* servant to the lender.

8 He that soweth iniquity shall reap ᵃvanity:¹ and the rod of his ²anger shall fail.

9 ᵃHe that hath a ¹bountiful eye shall be ᵇblessed; for he giveth of his bread to the poor.

10 ᵃCast out the scorner, and contention shall go out; yea, strife and reproach shall cease.

11 ᵃHe that loveth pureness of heart, ¹*for* the grace of his lips the king *shall be* his friend.

12 The eyes of the LORD preserve knowledge, and he overthroweth the words of the ¹transgressor.

13 ᵃThe slothful *man* saith, There is a lion without, I shall be slain in the streets.

14 ᵃThe mouth of ¹strange women *is* a deep pit: ᵇhe that is abhorred of the LORD shall fall therein.

15 Foolishness *is* bound in the heart of a child; *but* ᵃthe rod of correction shall drive it far from him.

16 He that oppresseth the poor to increase his *riches, and* he that giveth to the rich, *shall* surely *come* to ¹want.

---

21:24 ¹ *acts in arrogant pride*

21:25 ᵃ Prov. 13:4 ¹ *lazy*

21:26 ᵃ [Prov. 22:9]

21:27 ᵃ Jer. 6:20 ¹ *intent*

21:28 ¹ *endlessly*

21:29 ¹ *establishes; LXX, Qr. understands*

21:30 ᵃ [Jer. 9:23, 24]

21:31 ᵃ Ps. 3:8 ¹ *deliverance*

22:1 ᵃ Eccl. 7:1

22:2 ᵃ Prov. 29:13 ᵇ Job 31:15 ¹ *have this in common*

22:3 ᵃ Prov. 27:12

22:5 ¹ *perverse* ² *guards*

22:6 ᵃ Eph. 6:4 ¹ Lit. *even*

22:7 ᵃ James 2:6

22:8 ᵃ Job 4:8 ¹ *trouble* ² *wrath shall perish*

22:9 ᵃ 2 Cor. 9:6 ᵇ Prov. 19:17 ¹ *generous, lit. good eye*

22:10 ᵃ Ps. 101:5

22:11 ᵃ Ps. 101:6 ¹ *and has grace on his lips*

22:12 ¹ *faithless*

22:13 ᵃ Prov. 26:13

22:14 ᵃ Prov. 2:16; 5:3; 7:5 ᵇ Eccl. 7:26 ¹ *an immoral woman*

22:15 ᵃ Prov. 13:24; 23:13, 14

22:16 ¹ *poverty*

22:18 ¹ *fixed upon*

22:21 ᵃ Luke 1:3, 4 ᵇ 1 Pet. 3:15 ¹ Or *send you*

22:22 ᵃ Ex. 23:6

22:23 ᵃ 1 Sam. 24:12 ¹ *plunder* ² *plundered*

22:24 ᵃ Prov. 29:22

22:26 ᵃ Prov. 11:15 ¹ Shakes hands in a pledge ² *collateral*

22:27 ¹ *with which to pay*

22:28 ᵃ Deut. 19:14; 27:17 ¹ *boundary*

22:29 ¹ *excel in his work* ² *obscure or unknown*

23:3 ¹ *delicacies* ² *food*

23:4 ᵃ [1 Tim. 6:9, 10] ᵇ Rom. 12:16 ¹ *Do not overwork* ² *because of*

23:5 ¹ Lit. *Will you*

---

17 Bow down thine ear, and hear the words of the wise, and apply thine heart unto my knowledge.

18 For *it is* a pleasant thing if thou keep them within thee; they shall withal be ¹fitted in thy lips.

19 That thy trust may be in the LORD, I have made known to thee this day, even to thee.

20 Have not I written to thee excellent things in counsels and knowledge,

21 ᵃThat I might make thee know the certainty of the words of truth; ᵇthat thou mightest answer the words of truth to them that ¹send unto thee?

22 Rob not the ᵃpoor, because he *is* poor: neither oppress the afflicted in the gate:

23 ᵃFor the LORD will plead their cause, and ¹spoil the soul of those that ²spoiled them.

24 Make no friendship with an angry man; and with a ᵃfurious man thou shalt not go:

25 Lest thou learn his ways, and get a snare to thy soul.

26 ᵃBe not thou *one* of them that ¹strike hands, *or* of them that ²sureties for debts.

27 If thou hast nothing ¹to pay, why should he take away thy bed from under thee?

28 ᵃRemove not the ancient ¹landmark, which thy fathers have set.

29 Seest thou a man ¹diligent in his business? he shall stand before kings; he shall not stand before ²mean *men*.

## CHAPTER 23

W HEN thou sittest to eat with a ruler, consider diligently what *is* before thee:

2 And put a knife to thy throat, if thou *be* a man given to appetite.

3 Be not desirous of his ¹dainties: for they *are* deceitful ²meat.

4 ᵃLabour¹ not to be rich: ᵇcease ²from thine own wisdom.

5 ¹Wilt thou set thine eyes upon that which is not? for *riches* certainly make themselves wings; they fly away as an eagle toward heaven.

6 Eat thou not the bread of *him that* ¹hath ᵃan evil eye, neither desire thou his ²dainty meats:

7 For as he thinketh in his heart, so *is* he: Eat and drink, ᵃsaith he to thee; but his heart *is* not with thee.

8 The morsel *which* thou hast eaten shalt thou vomit up, and lose thy ¹sweet words.

9 ᵃSpeak not in the ears of a fool: for he will despise the wisdom of thy words.

---

*cause your eyes to fly on it, and it is not* 23:6 ᵃ Deut. 15:9 ¹ *is a miser,* ² *delicacies* 23:7 ᵃ Prov. 12:2 23:8 ¹ *pleasant* 23:9 ᵃ Matt. 7:6

10 Remove not the old ¹landmark; and enter not into the fields of the fatherless:

11 ªFor their redeemer *is* mighty; he shall plead their cause ¹with thee.

12 Apply thine heart unto instruction, and thine ears to the words of knowledge.

13 ªWithhold not correction from the child: for *if* thou beatest him with the rod, he shall not die.

14 Thou shalt beat him with the rod, and shalt deliver his soul from ¹hell.

15 My son, if thine heart be wise, ¹my heart shall rejoice, even mine.

16 Yea, my ¹reins shall rejoice, when thy lips speak right things.

17 ªLet not thine heart envy sinners: but ᵇ*be thou* in the fear of the LORD all the day long.

18 ªFor surely there is ¹an end; and thine ²expectation shall not be cut off.

19 Hear thou, my son, and be wise, and guide thine heart in the way.

20 ªBe not among winebibbers; among ¹riotous eaters of flesh:

21 For the drunkard and the glutton shall come to poverty: and drowsiness shall clothe *a man* with rags.

22 ªHearken unto thy father that begat thee, and despise not thy mother when she is old.

23 ªBuy the truth, and sell *it* not; *also* wisdom, and instruction, and understanding.

24 ªThe father of the righteous shall greatly rejoice: and he that begetteth a wise *child* shall ¹have joy of him.

25 Thy father and thy mother shall be glad, and she that bare thee shall rejoice.

26 My son, give me thine heart, and let thine eyes observe my ways.

27 ªFor a ¹whore *is* a deep ²ditch; and a ³strange woman *is* a narrow pit.

28 ªShe also lieth in wait as *for a* ¹prey, and increaseth the ²transgressors among men.

29 ªWho hath woe? who hath sorrow? who hath contentions? who hath ¹babbling? who hath wounds without cause? who ᵇhath redness of eyes?

30 ªThey that ¹tarry long at the wine; they that go to seek ᵇmixed wine.

31 Look not thou upon the wine when it is red, when it ¹giveth his colour in the cup, *when* it ²moveth itself aright.

32 At the last it biteth like a serpent, and stingeth like ¹an adder.

33 Thine eyes shall behold ¹strange women, and thine heart shall utter perverse things.

34 Yea, thou shalt be as he that lieth down ¹in the midst of the sea, or as he that lieth upon the top of a mast.

---

23:10 ¹ *boundary*
23:11 ª Prov. 22:23 ¹ *against*
23:13 ª Prov. 13:24
23:14 ¹ Heb. *Sheol*
23:15 ¹ *indeed my own heart shall rejoice*
23:16 ¹ *inmost being*
23:17 ª Ps. 37:1 ᵇ Prov. 28:14
23:18 ª [Ps. 37:37] ¹ *a hereafter* ² *hope*
23:20 ª Is. 5:22 ¹ *gluttonous eaters of meat*
23:22 ª Prov. 1:8
23:23 ª [Matt. 13:44]
23:24 ª Prov. 10:1 ¹ *delight in*
23:27 ª Prov. 22:14 ¹ *harlot* ² *pit* ³ *seductress*
23:28 ª Prov. 7:12 ¹ *victim* ² *unfaithful*
23:29 ª Is. 5:11, 22 ᵇ Gen. 49:12 ¹ *complaints*
23:30 ª [Eph. 5:18] ᵇ Ps. 75:8 ¹ *linger*
23:31 ¹ *sparkles in the cup* ² Lit. *goes smoothly*
23:32 ¹ *a viper*
23:33 ¹ *strange things*
23:34 ¹ Lit. *in the heart of the sea*
23:35 ª Jer. 5:3 ᵇ Eph. 4:19 ¹ *hurt* ² *Another drink*
24:1 ª Ps. 1:1; 37:1 ¹ *of*
24:2 ¹ *devises violence* ² *trouble*
24:5 ª Prov. 21:22
24:6 ª Luke 14:31 ¹ *wage your own*
24:7 ª Ps. 10:5 ¹ *lofty*
24:8 ª Rom. 1:30 ¹ *plots* ² *schemer,* lit. *master of evil plots*
24:9 ¹ *planning*
24:10 ª Heb. 12:3
24:11 ª Ps. 82:4 ¹ *Deliver those who are drawn toward death, and hold back those stumbling to the slaughter.*
24:12 ª Prov. 21:2 ᵇ Ps. 62:12 ¹ *weighs*
24:13 ª Song 5:1
24:14 ª Ps. 19:10; 58:11 ¹ *future,* lit. *hereafter* ² *hope*
24:15 ¹ *Do not lie in wait* ² Lit. *assault*

---

35 ªThey have stricken me, *shalt thou say, and* I was not ¹sick; they have beaten me, *and* I felt *it* not: when shall ᵇI awake? I will seek ²it yet again.

## CHAPTER 24

B E not thou ªenvious ¹against evil men, neither desire to be with them.

2 For their heart ¹studieth destruction, and their lips talk of ²mischief.

3 Through wisdom is an house builded; and by understanding it is established:

4 And by knowledge shall the chambers be filled with all precious and pleasant riches.

5 ªA wise man *is* strong; yea, a man of knowledge increaseth strength.

6 ªFor by wise counsel thou shalt ¹make thy war: and in multitude of counsellors *there is* safety.

7 ªWisdom *is* too ¹high for a fool: he openeth not his mouth in the gate.

8 He that ªdeviseth¹ to do evil shall be called a ²mischievous person.

9 The ¹thought of foolishness *is* sin: and the scorner *is* an abomination to men.

10 *If* thou ªfaint in the day of adversity, thy strength *is* small.

11 ªIf¹ thou forbear to deliver *them that are* drawn unto death, and *those that are* ready to be slain;

12 If thou sayest, Behold, we knew it not; doth not ªhe that ¹pondereth the heart consider *it?* and he that keepeth thy soul, doth *not* he know *it?* and shall *not* he render to *every* man ᵇaccording to his works?

13 My son, ªeat thou honey, because *it is* good; and the honeycomb, *which is* sweet to thy taste:

14 ªSo *shall* the knowledge of wisdom *be* unto thy soul: when thou hast found *it,* then there shall be a ¹reward, and thy ²expectation shall not be cut off.

15 ¹Lay not wait, O wicked *man,* against the dwelling of the righteous; ²spoil not his resting place:

16 ªFor a just *man* falleth seven times, and riseth up again: ᵇbut the wicked shall ¹fall into mischief.

17 ªRejoice not when thine enemy falleth, and let not thine heart be glad when he stumbleth:

18 Lest the LORD see *it,* and ¹it displease him, and he turn away his wrath from him.

19 ªFret not thyself because of evil *men,* neither be thou envious at the wicked;

20 For there shall be no reward to the evil *man;* ¹the candle of the wicked shall be put out.

---

24:16 ª [Mic. 7:8] ᵇ Esth. 7:10 ¹ *stumble into calamity*
24:17 ª Obad. 12   24:18 ¹ Lit. *it be evil in his eyes*
24:19 ª Ps. 37:1   24:20 ¹ *the lamp*

21 My son, [a]fear thou the LORD and the king: *and* [1]meddle not with them that are given to change:

22 For their calamity shall rise suddenly; and who knoweth the ruin [1]of them both?

23 These *things* also *belong* to the wise. [a]*It is* not good to [1]have respect of persons in judgment.

24 [a]He that saith unto the wicked, Thou *art* righteous; him shall the people curse, nations shall abhor him:

25 But to them that rebuke [1]*him* shall be [a]delight, and a good blessing shall come upon them.

26 *Every man* shall kiss *his* lips that giveth a right answer.

27 [a]Prepare thy [1]work without, and make it fit for thyself in the field; and afterwards build thine house.

28 [a]Be not a witness against thy neighbour without cause; [1]and deceive *not* with thy lips.

29 [a]Say not, I will do so to him as he hath done to me: I will render to the man according to his work.

30 I went by the field of the slothful, and by the vineyard of the man void of understanding;

31 And, lo, [a]it was all grown over with thorns, *and* nettles had covered [1]the face thereof, and the stone wall thereof was broken down.

32 Then I saw, *and* considered *it* well: I looked upon *it, and* received instruction.

33 [a]*Yet* a little sleep, a little slumber, a little folding of the hands to [1]sleep:

34 [a]So shall thy poverty come *as* [1]one that travelleth; and thy want as [2]an armed man.

## CHAPTER 25

THESE[a] *are* also proverbs of Solomon, which the men of Hezekiah king of Judah copied out.

2 [a]*It is* the glory of God to conceal a thing: but the honour of kings *is* to search out a matter.

3 The heaven for height, and the earth for depth, and the heart of kings *is* unsearchable.

4 [a]Take away the dross from the silver, and there shall come forth a vessel for the [1]finer.

5 Take away the wicked *from* before the king, and his throne shall be established in [a]righteousness.

6 [1]Put not forth thyself in the presence of the king, and stand not in the place of great *men*:

7 [a]For better *it is* that it be said unto thee, Come up hither; than that thou shouldest be put lower in the presence of the prince whom thine eyes have seen.

8 [a]Go not forth hastily to [1]strive, lest *thou know not* what to do in the

24:21 [a] [1 Pet. 2:17]
[1] *do not associate with*
24:22 [1] *both of them can bring*
24:23 [a] Lev. 19:15
[1] *show partiality,* lit. *recognize faces*
24:24 [a] Is. 5:23
24:25 [a] Prov. 28:23 [1] *the wicked*
24:27 [a] Prov. 27:23–27 [1] *outside work*
24:28 [a] Eph. 4:25 [1] LXX, Vg.; MT *and deceive with thy lips*
24:29 [a] [Prov. 20:22]
24:31 [a] Gen. 3:18 [1] *its surface*
24:33 [a] Prov. 6:9, 10 [1] *rest*
24:34 [a] Prov. 6:9–11 [1] *a prowler* [2] Lit. *a man with a shield*
25:1 [a] 1 Kin. 4:32
25:2 [a] Deut. 29:29
25:4 [a] 2 Tim. 2:21 [1] *refiner*
25:5 [a] Prov. 16:12; 20:8
25:6 [1] *Do not honour thyself*
25:7 [a] Luke 14:7–11
25:8 [a] Matt. 5:25 [1] *bring a lawsuit*
25:9 [a] [Matt. 18:15] [1] *Plead your case* [2] *do not disclose the secret*
25:10 [1] *the evil report concerning you does not pass away*
25:11 [a] Prov. 15:23 [1] *spoken at the right time* [2] *in settings*
25:13 [a] Prov. 13:17
25:14 [a] Prov. 20:6 [b] Jude 12 [1] *falsely of giving*
25:15 [a] Prov. 15:1 [1] *gentle*
25:16 [1] *eat only as much*
25:17 [1] *Let your foot seldom be in thy*
25:18 [a] Ps. 57:4 [1] *club*
25:19 [1] *bad*
25:20 [a] Dan. 6:18 [1] *soda*
25:21 [a] Rom. 12:20
25:22 [a] 2 Sam. 16:12
25:23 [a] Ps. 101:5 [1] *brings*

end thereof, when thy neighbour hath put thee to shame.

9 [a]Debate[1] thy cause with thy neighbour *himself;* and [2]discover not a secret to another:

10 Lest he that heareth *it* put thee to shame, and [1]thine infamy turn not away.

11 A word [1]fitly [a]spoken *is like* apples of gold [2]in pictures of silver.

12 *As* an earring of gold, and an ornament of fine gold, *so is* a wise reprover upon an obedient ear.

13 [a]As the cold of snow in the time of harvest, *so is* a faithful messenger to them that send him: for he refresheth the soul of his masters.

14 [a]Whoso boasteth [1]himself of a false gift *is like* [b]clouds and wind without rain.

15 [a]By long forbearing is a prince persuaded, and a [1]soft tongue breaketh the bone.

16 Hast thou found honey? [1]eat so much as is sufficient for thee, lest thou be filled therewith, and vomit it.

17 [1]Withdraw thy foot from thy neighbour's house; lest he be weary of thee, and *so* hate thee.

18 [a]A man that beareth false witness against his neighbour *is* a [1]maul, and a sword, and a sharp arrow.

19 Confidence in an unfaithful man in time of trouble *is like* a [1]broken tooth, and a foot out of joint.

20 *As* he that taketh away a garment in cold weather, *and as* vinegar upon [1]nitre, so *is* he that [a]singeth songs to an heavy heart.

21 [a]If thine enemy be hungry, give him bread to eat; and if he be thirsty, give him water to drink:

22 For thou shalt heap coals of fire upon his head, [a]and the LORD shall reward thee.

23 The north wind [1]driveth away rain: so *doth* [2]an angry countenance [a]a backbiting tongue.

24 [a]*It is* better to dwell in the corner of the housetop, than [1]with a brawling woman and in a wide house.

25 *As* cold waters to a [1]thirsty soul, so *is* [a]good news from a far country.

26 A righteous man [1]falling down before the wicked *is as* a [2]troubled fountain, and a [3]corrupt spring.

27 *It is* not good to eat much honey: so *for men* [a]to [1]search their own glory *is not* glory.

28 [a]He that *hath* no rule over his own spirit *is like* a city *that is* broken down, *and* without walls.

forth [2] *a backbiting tongue an angry countenance* 25:24 [a] Prov. 19:13 [1] *in a house shared with a contentious woman* 25:25 [a] Prov. 15:30 [1] *weary* 25:26 [1] *who falters* [2] *murky spring* [3] *polluted well* 25:27 [a] Prov. 27:2 [1] *seek* 25:28 [a] Prov. 16:32

## CHAPTER 26

A s snow in summer, [a]and as rain in harvest, so honour is not [1]seemly for a fool.

2 [1]As the bird by wandering, as the [2]swallow by flying, so [a]the curse [3]causeless shall not [4]come.

3 [a]A whip for the horse, a bridle for the [1]ass, and a rod for the fool's back.

4 Answer not a fool according to his folly, lest thou also be like unto him.

5 [a]Answer a fool according to his folly, lest he be wise in his own [1]conceit.

6 He that sendeth a message by the hand of a fool cutteth off the feet, *and* drinketh [1]damage.

7 The legs of the lame [1]are not equal: so *is* a parable in the mouth of fools.

8 As he that bindeth a stone in a sling, so *is* he that giveth honour to a fool.

9 *As* a thorn goeth up into the hand of a drunkard, so *is* a [1]parable in the mouth of fools.

10 [1]The great *God* that formed all *things* both rewardeth the fool, and rewardeth transgressors.

11 [a]As a dog returneth to his vomit, [b]so a fool [1]returneth to his folly.

12 [a]Seest thou a man wise in his own [1]conceit? *there is* more hope of a fool than of him.

13 The slothful *man* saith, *There is* a lion in the way; a [1]lion *is* in the [2]streets.

14 *As* the door turneth upon his hinges, so *doth* the slothful upon his bed.

15 The [a]slothful [1]hideth his hand in *his* [2]bosom; it [3]grieveth him to bring it again to his mouth.

16 The sluggard *is* wiser in his own [1]conceit than seven men that can [2]render a reason.

17 He that passeth by, *and* meddleth with strife *belonging* not to him, *is like* one that taketh a dog by the ears.

18 As a mad *man* who casteth firebrands, arrows, and death,

19 So *is* the man *that* deceiveth his neighbour, and saith, [a]Am not I [1]in sport?

20 Where no wood is, *there* the fire goeth out: so where *there is* no [1]talebearer, the strife ceaseth.

21 [a]As [1]coals *are* to burning coals, and wood to fire; so *is* a contentious man to kindle strife.

22 The words of a talebearer *are* as [1]wounds, and they go down into the [2]innermost parts of the belly.

23 [1]Burning lips and a wicked heart *are like* [2]a potsherd covered with silver dross.

24 He that hateth [1]dissembleth with his lips, and layeth up deceit within him;

25 [a]When [1]he speaketh fair, believe him not: for *there are* seven abominations in his heart.

26 *Whose* hatred is covered by deceit, his wickedness shall be shewed before the *whole* congregation.

27 [a]Whoso diggeth a pit shall fall therein: and he that rolleth a stone, it will [1]return upon him.

28 A lying tongue hateth *those that are* [1]afflicted by it; and a flattering mouth worketh [a]ruin.

## CHAPTER 27

B OAST [a]not thyself of to morrow; for thou knowest not what a day may bring forth.

2 [a]Let another man praise thee, and not thine own mouth; a stranger, and not thine own lips.

3 A stone *is* heavy, and the sand weighty; but a fool's wrath *is* heavier than them both.

4 Wrath *is* cruel, and anger *is* [1]outrageous; but [a]who *is* able to stand before [2]envy?

5 [a]Open rebuke *is* better than [1]secret love.

6 Faithful *are* the wounds of a friend; but the kisses of an enemy *are* [a]deceitful.

7 The full soul [1]loatheth an honeycomb; but to the hungry soul every bitter thing is sweet.

8 As a bird that wandereth from her nest, so *is* a man that wandereth from his place.

9 Ointment and perfume [1]rejoice the heart: so *doth* the sweetness of a man's friend by [2]hearty counsel.

10 Thine own friend, and thy father's friend, forsake not; neither go into thy brother's house in the day of thy calamity: for [a]better *is* a neighbour *that is* near than a brother far off.

11 My son, be wise, and make my heart glad, [a]that I may answer him that reproacheth me.

12 A prudent *man* foreseeth the evil, *and* hideth himself; *but* the simple pass on, *and* are [a]punished.

13 Take his garment that is [1]surety for a stranger, and [2]take a pledge of him for a strange woman.

14 He that blesseth his friend with a loud voice, rising early in the morning, it shall be counted a curse to him.

15 A [a]continual dropping in a very rainy day and a contentious woman are alike.

16 Whosoever [1]hideth her hideth the wind, and [2]the ointment of his right hand, *which* bewrayeth *itself.*

17 Iron sharpeneth iron; so a man sharpeneth the countenance of his friend.

---

26:1 [a] 1 Sam. 12:17
[1] *fitting*

26:2 [a] Deut. 23:5
[1] *Like a flitting sparrow* [2] *flying swallow* [3] *without cause* [4] *alight*

26:3 [a] Ps. 32:9
[1] *donkey*

26:5 [a] Matt. 16:1–4
[1] Lit. *eyes*

26:6 [1] *violence*

26:7 [1] *hang limp*

26:9 [1] *proverb*

26:10 [1] Heb. is difficult; ancient and modern translations differ greatly.

26:11 [a] 2 Pet. 2:22 [b] Ex. 8:15
[1] *repeats his*

26:12 [a] [Rev. 3:17]
[1] Lit. *eyes*

26:13 [1] *fierce lion* [2] *plaza* or *square*

26:15 [a] Prov. 19:24
[1] *buries* [2] MT *bowl;* LXX, Syr. *bosom;* Vg., Tg. *armpit* [3] *wearies*

26:16 [1] Lit. *eyes* [2] *answer sensibly*

26:19 [a] Eph. 5:4
[1] *joking*

26:20 [1] *gossip,* lit. *whisperer*

26:21 [a] Prov. 15:18
[1] *charcoal*

26:22 [1] *tasty morsels;* Jewish trad. *wounds* [2] Lit. *chambers of the belly*

26:23 [1] *Fervent* [2] *earthenware*

26:24 [1] *disguises it*

26:25 [a] Ps. 28:3
[1] Lit. *his voice is gracious*

26:27 [a] Ps. 7:15
[1] *roll back on*

26:28 [a] Prov. 29:5
[1] *crushed*

27:1 [a] James 4:13–16

27:2 [a] Prov. 25:27

27:4 [a] 1 John 3:12 [1] *a torrent* [2] *jealousy*

27:5 [a] [Prov. 28:23] [1] *concealed*

27:6 [a] Matt. 26:49

27:7 [1] *tramples*

27:9 [1] *delight* [2] Lit. *counsel of the soul*

27:10 [a] Prov. 17:17; 18:24

27:11 [a] Prov. 10:1; 23:15–26

27:12 [a] Prov. 22:3

27:13 [1] *guaranty*

or *collateral* [2] *hold it in pledge* when *he is surety for a seductress* 27:15 [a] Prov. 19:13 27:16 [1] *restrains* [2] *grasps oil with his right hand*

18 [a]Whoso [1]keepeth the fig tree shall eat the fruit thereof: so he that waiteth on his master shall be honoured.

19 As in water face [1]answereth to face, so the heart of man [2]to man.

20 [a]Hell[1] and [2]destruction are never full; so [b]the eyes of man are never satisfied.

21 [a]As the [1]fining pot for silver, and the furnace for gold; [2]so *is* a man to his praise.

22 [a]Though thou shouldest [1]bray a fool in a mortar [2]among wheat with a pestle, *yet* will not his foolishness depart from him.

23 Be thou diligent to know the state of thy [a]flocks, *and* [1]look well to thy herds.

24 For riches *are* not for ever: and doth the crown *endure* to every generation?

25 [a]The hay [1]appeareth, and the tender grass sheweth itself, and herbs of the mountains are gathered.

26 The lambs *are* for thy clothing, and the goats *are* the price of the field.

27 And *thou shalt have* goats' milk enough for thy food, for the food of thy household, and *for* the [1]maintenance for thy maidens.

## CHAPTER 28

THE [a]wicked flee when no man pursueth: but the righteous are bold as a lion.

2 For the transgression of a land many *are* the princes thereof: but by a man of understanding *and* knowledge [1]the state *thereof* shall be prolonged.

3 [a]A poor man that oppresseth the poor *is like* a sweeping rain [1]which leaveth no food.

4 [a]They that forsake the law praise the wicked: [b]but such as keep the law contend with them.

5 [a]Evil men understand not [1]judgment: but [b]they that seek the LORD understand all *things*.

6 Better *is* the poor that walketh in his [1]uprightness, than *he that is* perverse *in his* ways, though he *be* rich.

7 Whoso keepeth the law *is* a [1]wise son: but he that is a companion of [2]riotous *men* shameth his father.

8 He that by usury and [1]unjust gain increaseth his [2]substance, he shall gather it for him that will pity the poor.

9 He that turneth away his ear from hearing the law, [a]even his prayer *shall be* abomination.

10 [a]Whoso causeth the [1]righteous to go astray in an evil way, he shall fall himself into his own pit: [b]but the upright shall [2]have good *things* in possession.

11 The rich man *is* wise in his own [1]conceit; but the poor that hath understanding searcheth him out.

12 When righteous *men* do rejoice, *there is* great [a]glory: but when the wicked rise, a man is [1]hidden.

13 [a]He that covereth his sins shall not prosper: but whoso confesseth and forsaketh *them* shall have mercy.

14 Happy *is* the man [1]that feareth alway: but he that hardeneth his heart shall fall into [2]mischief.

15 [a]As a roaring lion, and a [1]ranging bear; [b]so *is* a wicked ruler over the poor people.

16 The prince that [1]wanteth understanding *is* also a great [a]oppressor: *but* he that hateth covetousness shall prolong *his* days.

17 [a]A man that [1]doeth violence to the blood of *any* person shall flee to the pit; let no man [2]stay him.

18 Whoso walketh uprightly shall be [1]saved: but *he that is* perverse *in his* ways shall fall at once.

19 [a]He that tilleth his land shall have plenty of bread: but he that followeth after [1]vain *persons* shall have poverty enough.

20 A faithful man shall abound with blessings: [a]but he that maketh haste to be rich shall not [1]be innocent.

21 [a]To [1]have respect of persons *is* not good: [b]for for a piece of bread *that* man will transgress.

22 He that hasteth to be rich *hath* an evil eye, and considereth not that [a]poverty shall come upon him.

23 [a]He that rebuketh a man afterwards shall find more favour than he that flattereth with the tongue.

24 Whoso robbeth his father or his mother, and saith, *It is* no transgression; the same [a]is the companion of a destroyer.

25 [a]He that is of a proud heart stirreth up strife: [b]but he that putteth his trust in the LORD shall be [1]made fat.

26 He that [a]trusteth in his own heart is a fool: but whoso walketh wisely, he shall be delivered.

27 [a]He that giveth unto the poor shall not lack: but he that hideth his eyes shall have many a curse.

28 When the wicked rise, [a]men hide themselves: but when they perish, the righteous increase.

## CHAPTER 29

HE,[a] that being often reproved hardeneth *his* neck, shall suddenly be destroyed, and that without remedy.

2 When the righteous are [1]in authority, the [a]people rejoice: but when the wicked beareth rule, [b]the people [2]mourn.

3 Whoso loveth wisdom [1]rejoiceth his father: but he that keepeth com-

---

**27:18** [a] [1 Cor. 3:8; 9:7–13] [1] *protects*
**27:19** [1] *reflects* [2] *reveals the man*
**27:20** [a] Hab. 2:5 [b] Eccl. 1:8; 4:8 [1] Or *Sheol* [2] Heb. *Abaddon*
**27:21** [a] Prov. 17:3 [1] *refining* [2] *and a man is tested by what others say to his praise*
**27:22** [a] Jer. 5:3 [1] *grind* [2] *along with crushed grain*
**27:23** [a] Prov. 24:27 [1] *attend to*
**27:25** [a] Ps. 104:14 [1] *is removed*
**27:27** [1] *nourishment of your maidservants*
**28:1** [a] Ps. 53:5
**28:2** [1] Lit. *it*
**28:3** [a] Matt. 18:28 [1] Lit. *and there is no bread*
**28:4** [a] Ps. 49:18 [b] 1 Kin. 18:18
**28:5** [a] Ps. 92:6 [b] John 17:17 [1] *justice*
**28:6** [1] *integrity*
**28:7** [1] *discerning* [2] *gluttons*
**28:8** [1] *extortion* [2] *possessions*
**28:9** [a] Prov. 15:8
**28:10** [a] Prov. 26:27 [b] [Matt. 6:33] [1] Lit. *upright* [2] *inherit good things*
**28:11** [1] *eyes*
**28:12** [a] Prov. 11:10; 29:2 [1] Lit. *will be sought*
**28:13** [a] Ps. 32:3–5
**28:14** [1] *who is always reverent* [2] *calamity*
**28:15** [a] 1 Pet. 5:8 [b] Matt. 2:16 [1] *charging*
**28:16** [a] Eccl. 10:16 [1] *lacks*
**28:17** [a] Gen. 9:6 [1] *is burdened with bloodshed shall flee* [2] *help*
**28:18** [1] *delivered*
**28:19** [a] Prov. 12:11; 20:13 [1] *empty things, frivolous things*
**28:20** [a] 1 Tim. 6:9 [1] *go unpunished*
**28:21** [a] Prov. 18:5 [b] Ezek. 13:19 [1] *show partiality, lit. regard faces*
**28:22** [a] Prov. 21:5
**28:23** [a] Prov. 27:5, 6
**28:24** [a] Prov. 18:9
**28:25** [a] Prov. 13:10 [b] 1 Tim. 6:6 [1] *prospered*
**28:26** [a] Prov. 3:5   **28:27** [a] Deut. 15:7   **28:28** [a] Job 24:4   **29:1** [a] 2 Chr. 36:16   **29:2** [a] Prov. 28:12 [b] Esth. 4:3 [1] *increased* [2] *groan*   **29:3** [1] *makes his father rejoice*

pany with harlots [2]spendeth *his* substance.

4 The king by [1]judgment establisheth the land: but he that receiveth [2]gifts overthroweth it.

5 A man that [a]flattereth his neighbour spreadeth a net for his feet.

6 [1]In the transgression of an evil man *there is* a snare: but the righteous doth sing and rejoice.

7 The righteous [a]considereth the cause of the poor: *but* the wicked [1]regardeth not to know *it.*

8 Scornful men [1]bring a city into a [a]snare: but wise *men* turn away wrath.

9 *If* a wise man contendeth with a foolish man, [a]whether [1]he rage or laugh, *there is* no rest.

10 [a]The bloodthirsty hate the upright: but the just seek his [1]soul.

11 A fool [1]uttereth all his [a]mind: but a wise *man* [2]keepeth it in till afterwards.

12 If a ruler hearken to lies, all his servants *are* wicked.

13 The poor and [1]the deceitful man [2]meet together: [a]the Lᴏʀᴅ [3]lighteneth both their eyes.

14 The king that [1]faithfully judgeth the [a]poor, his throne shall be established for ever.

15 The rod and reproof give [a]wisdom: but a child left *to himself* bringeth his mother to shame.

16 When the wicked are multiplied, transgression increaseth: but the righteous shall see their [a]fall.

17 Correct thy son, and he shall give thee rest; yea, he shall give delight unto thy soul.

18 [a]Where *there is* no [1]vision, the people [2]perish: but [b]he that keepeth the law, happy *is* he.

19 A servant will not be corrected by [1]words: for though he understand he will not [2]answer.

20 Seest thou a man *that is* hasty in his words? [a]*there is* more hope of a fool than of him.

21 He that [1]delicately bringeth up his servant from [2]a child shall have him become *his* son at the [3]length.

22 [a]An angry man stirreth up strife, and a furious man aboundeth in transgression.

23 [a]A man's pride shall bring him low: but honour shall [1]uphold the humble in spirit.

24 Whoso is partner with a thief hateth his own [1]soul: [a]he heareth [2]cursing, and bewrayeth *it* not.

25 [a]The fear of man bringeth a snare: but whoso putteth his trust in the Lᴏʀᴅ shall be [1]safe.

26 [a]Many seek the ruler's [1]favour; but [2]*every* man's judgment *cometh* from the Lᴏʀᴅ.

27 An unjust man *is* an abomination to the just: and *he that is* upright

## Center column notes

29:3 [2] *wastes his wealth*

29:4 [1] *justice* [2] *bribes*

29:5 [a] Prov. 26:28

29:6 [1] *By transgression an evil man is snared*

29:7 [a] Job

29:16 [1] *does not understand such knowledge*

29:8 [a] Prov. 11:11 [1] *inflame a city*

29:9 [a] Matt. 11:17 [1] *The fool*

29:10 [a] 1 John 3:12 [1] *well-being*

29:11 [a] Prov. 14:33 [1] *vents all his feelings* [2] *holds it back*

29:13 [a] [Matt. 5:45] [1] *the oppressor* [2] *have this in common* [3] *gives light to the eyes of both*

29:14 [a] Is. 11:4 [1] *judges the poor with truth*

29:15 [a] Prov. 22:15

29:16 [a] Ps. 37:34

29:18 [a] 1 Sam. 3:1 [b] John 13:17 [1] *prophetic vision or revelation* [2] *cast off restraint*

29:19 [1] *mere words* [2] *respond*

29:20 [a] Prov. 26:12

29:21 [1] *pampers* [2] *childhood* [3] *end*

29:22 [a] Prov. 26:21

29:23 [a] Is. 66:2 [1] *Or the humble in spirit will retain honour*

29:24 [a] Lev. 5:1 [1] *life* [2] *an oath but tells nothing*

29:25 [a] Gen. 12:12; 20:2 [1] *secure, lit. set on high*

29:26 [a] Ps. 20:9 [1] Lit. *face* [2] *justice for man*

30:2 [a] Ps. 73:22 [1] *stupid*

30:3 [a] [Prov. 9:10] [1] *Holy One*

30:4 [a] [John 3:13] [b] Job 38:4 [1] *know it*

30:5 [a] Ps. 12:6; 19:8; 119:140 [b] Ps. 18:30; 84:11; 115:9–11 [1] *tried, found pure*

30:6 [a] Deut. 4:2; 12:32

30:7 [1] *requested* [2] *deprive me not*

30:8 [a] Matt. 6:11 [1] *falsehood*

in the way *is* abomination to the wicked.

## CHAPTER 30

Tʜᴇ words of Agur the son of Jakeh, *even* the prophecy: the man spake unto Ithiel, even unto Ithiel and Ucal,

2 [a]Surely I *am* more [1]brutish than *any* man, and have not the understanding of a man.

3 I neither learned wisdom, nor have the [a]knowledge of the [1]holy.

4 [a]Who hath ascended up into heaven, or descended? [b]who hath gathered the wind in his fists? who hath bound the waters in a garment? who hath established all the ends of the earth? what *is* his name, and what *is* his son's name, if thou [1]canst tell?

5 [a]Every word of God *is* [1]pure: [b]he *is* a shield unto them that put their trust in him.

6 [a]Add thou not unto his words, lest he reprove thee, and thou be found a liar.

7 Two *things* have I [1]required of thee; [2]deny me *them* not before I die:

8 Remove far from me [1]vanity and lies: give me neither poverty nor riches; [a]feed me with food [2]convenient for me:

9 [a]Lest I be full, and deny *thee,* and say, Who *is* the Lᴏʀᴅ? or lest I be poor, and steal, and [1]take the name of my God *in vain.*

10 [1]Accuse not a servant unto his master, lest he curse thee, and thou be found guilty.

11 *There is* a generation *that* curseth their [a]father, and doth not bless their mother.

12 *There is* a generation [a]*that are* pure in their own eyes, and *yet* is not washed from their filthiness.

13 *There is* a generation, O how [a]lofty are their eyes! and their eyelids are [1]lifted up.

14 [a]*There is* a generation, whose teeth *are as* swords, and their jaw teeth *as* knives, [b]to devour the poor from off the earth, and the needy from *among* men.

15 The [1]horseleach hath two daughters, *crying,* Give, Give. There are three *things that* are never satisfied, *yea,* four *things* say not, *It is* enough:

16 [a]The grave; and the barren womb; the earth *that* is not filled with water; and the fire *that* saith not, *It is* enough.

17 [a]The eye *that* mocketh at *his* father, and [1]despiseth to obey *his* mother, the ravens of the valley shall pick it out, and the young eagles shall eat it.

[2] *you prescribe*   30:9 [a] Deut. 8:12–14   [1] *profane the name of my God*   30:10 [1] *Do not malign*   30:11 [a] Ex. 21:17   30:12 [a] Luke 18:11   30:13 [a] Prov. 6:17   [1] *lifted up in arrogance*   30:14 [a] Job 29:17   [b] Amos 8:4   30:15 [1] *leech*   30:16 [a] Prov. 27:20   30:17 [a] Gen. 9:22   [1] *scorns obedience to*

18 There be three *things which* are too wonderful for me, yea, four which I know not:

19 The way of an eagle in the air; the way of a serpent upon a rock; the way of a ship in the ¹midst of the sea; and the way of a man with a ²maid.

20 Such *is* the way of an adulterous woman; she eateth, and wipeth her mouth, and saith, I have done no wickedness.

21 For three *things* the earth is disquieted, and for four *which* it cannot bear:

22 ªFor a servant when he reigneth; and a fool when he is filled with ¹meat;

23 For an ¹odious *woman* when she is married; and an handmaid that is heir to her mistress.

24 There be four *things which are* little upon the earth, but they *are* exceeding wise:

25 ªThe ants *are* a people not strong, yet they prepare their ¹meat in the summer;

26 ªThe ¹conies *are but* a feeble folk, yet make they their houses in the rocks;

27 The locusts have no king, yet go they forth all of them ¹by bands;

28 The ¹spider taketh hold with her hands, and is in kings' palaces.

29 There be three *things* which ¹go well, yea, four are ²comely in going:

30 A lion *which is* ¹strongest among beasts, and turneth not away for any;

31 A ¹greyhound; an he goat also; and a king, ²against whom *there is* no rising up.

32 If thou hast done foolishly in ¹lifting up thyself, or if thou hast ²thought evil, ªlay thine hand upon thy mouth.

33 Surely the churning of milk bringeth forth butter, and the wringing of the nose bringeth forth blood: so the forcing of wrath bringeth forth strife.

## CHAPTER 31

THE words of king Lemuel, the prophecy that his mother taught him.

2 What, my son? and what, the son of my womb? and what, ªthe son of my vows?

3 ªGive not thy strength unto women, nor thy ways ᵇto that which destroyeth kings.

4 ªIt is not for kings, O Lemuel, *it is* not for kings to drink wine; nor for princes strong drink:

5 ªLest they drink, and forget the law, and pervert the ¹judgment of any of the ²afflicted.

6 ªGive strong drink unto him that is ready to perish, and wine unto those that be ¹of heavy hearts.

30:19 ¹ Lit. *heart*
² *virgin*
30:22 ª Prov. 19:10
¹ *food*
30:23 ¹ *hateful*, lit. *hated*
30:25 ª Prov. 6:6
¹ *food*
30:26 ¹ Ps. 104:18
¹ *rock badger* or *hyrax*
30:27 ¹ *in ranks*
30:28 ¹ Or *lizard*
30:29 ¹ *are majestic in pace*
² *stately in walk*
30:30 ¹ *mighty*
30:31 ¹ Or perhaps *strutting rooster;* exact identity unknown ² MT *whose troops are with him;* Jewish trad. *against whom there is no uprising*
30:32 ª Mic. 7:16 ¹ *exalting* ² *devised*
31:2 ª Is. 49:15
31:3 ª Prov. 5:9 ᵇ Deut. 17:17; 1 Kin. 11:1; Neh. 13:26; Prov. 7:26; Hos. 4:11
31:4 ª Eccl. 10:17
31:5 ª Hos. 4:11 ¹ *justice* ² Lit. *sons of affliction*
31:6 ª Ps. 104:15 ¹ *bitter of heart*
31:8 ª Job 29:15, 16; Ps. 82 ¹ *speechless* ² Lit. *sons of passing away*
31:9 ª Lev. 19:15; Deut. 1:16 ᵇ Job 29:12; Is. 1:17; Jer. 22:16
31:10 ª Ruth 3:11; Prov. 12:4; 19:14 ¹ Lit. *wife of valour* ² *worth*
31:11 ¹ *lack of gain*
31:15 ª Prov. 20:13; Rom. 12:11 ᵇ Luke 12:42 ¹ *food*, lit. *prey* ² *maidservants*
31:16 ¹ *earnings*
31:18 ¹ *lamp*
31:20 ª Deut. 15:11; Job 31:16–20; Prov. 22:9; Rom. 12:13; Eph. 4:28; Heb. 13:16 ¹ *extends*
31:22 ¹ *fine linen*
31:23 ª Prov. 12:4
31:24 ¹ *linen garments* ² Them ³ *sashes*
31:29 ¹ *well*
31:30 ¹ *Charm*

7 Let him drink, and forget his poverty, and remember his misery no more.

8 ªOpen thy mouth for the ¹dumb in the cause of all such as are ²appointed to destruction.

9 Open thy mouth, ªjudge righteously, and ᵇplead the cause of the poor and needy.

10 ªWho can find a ¹virtuous woman? for her ²price *is* far above rubies.

11 The heart of her husband doth safely trust in her, so that he shall have no ¹need of spoil.

12 She will do him good and not evil all the days of her life.

13 She seeketh wool, and flax, and worketh willingly with her hands.

14 She is like the merchants' ships; she bringeth her food from afar.

15 ªShe riseth also while it is yet night, and ᵇgiveth ¹meat to her household, and a portion to her ²maidens.

16 She considereth a field, and buyeth it: with the ¹fruit of her hands she planteth a vineyard.

17 She girdeth her loins with strength, and strengtheneth her arms.

18 She perceiveth that her merchandise *is* good: her ¹candle goeth not out by night.

19 She layeth her hands to the spindle, and her hands hold the distaff.

20 ªShe ¹stretcheth out her hand to the poor; yea, she reacheth forth her hands to the needy.

21 She is not afraid of the snow for her household: for all her household *are* clothed with scarlet.

22 She maketh herself coverings of tapestry; her clothing *is* ¹silk and purple.

23 ªHer husband is known in the gates, when he sitteth among the elders of the land.

24 She maketh ¹fine linen, and selleth ²*it;* and delivereth ³girdles unto the merchant.

25 Strength and honour *are* her clothing; and she shall rejoice in time to come.

26 She openeth her mouth with wisdom; and in her tongue *is* the law of kindness.

27 She looketh well to the ways of her household, and eateth not the bread of idleness.

28 Her children arise up, and call her blessed; her husband *also,* and he praiseth her.

29 Many daughters have done ¹virtuously, but thou excellest them all.

30 ¹Favour *is* deceitful, and beauty *is* vain: *but* a woman *that* feareth the LORD, she shall be praised.

31 Give her of the fruit of her hands; and let her own works praise her in the gates.

# THE BOOK OF
# ECCLESIASTES

The key word in Ecclesiastes is *vanity*, "the futile emptiness of trying to be happy apart from God." The Preacher (traditionally taken to be Solomon—1:1, 12—the wisest, richest, most influential king in Israel's history) looks at life "under the sun" (1:9) and, from the human perspective, declares it all to be empty. Power, popularity, prestige, pleasure—nothing can fill the God-shaped void in man's life but God Himself! But once seen from God's perspective, life takes on meaning and purpose, causing Solomon to exclaim, "Eat . . . drink . . . rejoice . . . do good . . . live joyfully . . . fear God . . . keep his commandments!" Skepticism and despair melt away when life is viewed as a daily gift from God.

The Hebrew title *Qoheleth* is a rare term, found only in Ecclesiastes (1:1, 2, 12; 7:27; 12:8–10). It comes from the word *qahal*, "to convoke an assembly, to assemble." Thus, it means "One Who Addresses an Assembly," "A Preacher." The Septuagint used the Greek word *Ekklesiastes* as its title for this book. Derived from the word *ekklesia*, "assembly," "congregation," "church," it simply means "Preacher." The Latin *Ecclesiastes* means "Speaker Before an Assembly."

## CHAPTER 1

THE words of the Preacher, the son of David, ªking in Jerusalem.

2 ªVanity¹ of vanities, saith the Preacher, vanity of vanities; ᵇall *is* vanity.

3 ªWhat profit hath a man ¹of all his labour which he ²taketh under the sun?

4 *One* generation passeth away, and *another* generation cometh: ªbut the earth abideth for ever.

5 ªThe sun also ariseth, and the sun goeth down, and ¹hasteth to his place where he arose.

6 ªThe wind goeth toward the south, and turneth about unto the north; it whirleth about continually, and the wind returneth again according to his circuits.

7 ªAll the rivers run into the sea; yet the sea *is* not full; unto the place from whence the rivers come, thither they ¹return again.

8 All things *are* ¹full of labour; man cannot ²utter *it:* ªthe eye is not satisfied with seeing, nor the ear filled with hearing.

9 ªThe thing that hath been, it *is that* which shall be; and that which is done *is* that which shall be done: and *there is* no new *thing* under the sun.

10 Is there *any* thing whereof it may be said, See, this *is* new? it hath been already ¹of old time, which was before us.

11 *There is* ªno remembrance of former *things;* neither shall there be *any* remembrance of *things* that are to come with *those* that shall come after.

12 I the Preacher was king over Israel in Jerusalem.

13 And I ¹gave my heart to seek and ªsearch out by wisdom concerning all

1:1 ª Prov. 1:1
1:2 ª Ps. 39:5, 6; 62:9; 144:4 ᵇ [Rom. 8:20, 21] ¹ *Futility of futilities*
1:3 ª Eccl. 2:22; 3:9 ¹ *from* ² *toils or labours*
1:4 ª Ps. 104:5; 119:90
1:5 ª Ps. 19:4–6 ¹ *Is eager for, lit. panting*
1:6 ª John 3:8
1:7 ª [Jer. 5:22] ¹ *return to go again*
1:8 ª Prov. 27:20 ¹ *wearisome* ² *express*
1:9 ª Eccl. 3:15
1:10 ¹ *in ancient times*
1:11 ª Eccl. 2:16
1:13 ª [Eccl. 7:25; 8:16, 17] ᵇ Eccl. 3:10 ¹ *set* ² *grievous task* ³ *Or afflicted*
1:14 ¹ *a grasping for the wind*
1:15 ª Eccl. 7:13 ¹ *lacking*
1:16 ª 1 Kin. 3:12, 13 ¹ *greatness* ² *understood great wisdom*
1:17 ª Eccl. 2:3, 12; 7:23, 25 ¹ *set* ² *a grasping for the wind*
1:18 ª Eccl. 12:12
2:1 ª Luke 12:19 ᵇ [Eccl. 7:4; 8:15] ᶜ Eccl. 1:2 ¹ *test* ² *gladness* ³ *futility*
2:2 ¹ *does it accomplish*

*things* that are done under heaven: ᵇthis ²sore travail hath God given to the sons of man to be ³exercised therewith.

14 I have seen all the works that are done under the sun; and, behold, all *is* vanity and ¹vexation of spirit.

15 ªThat which is crooked cannot be made straight: and that which is ¹wanting cannot be numbered.

16 I communed with mine own heart, saying, Lo, I am come to ¹great estate, and have gotten ªmore wisdom than all *they* that have been before me in Jerusalem: yea, my heart had ²great experience of wisdom and knowledge.

17 ªAnd I ¹gave my heart to know wisdom, and to know madness and folly: I perceived that this also is ²vexation of spirit.

18 For ªin much wisdom *is* much grief: and he that increaseth knowledge increaseth sorrow.

## CHAPTER 2

I ªSAID in mine heart, Go to now, I will ¹prove thee with ᵇmirth,² therefore enjoy pleasure: and, behold, ᶜthis also *is* ³vanity.

2 I said of laughter, *It is* mad: and of mirth, What ¹doeth it?

3 ªI sought in mine heart ¹to give myself unto wine, yet ²acquainting mine heart with wisdom; and ³to lay hold on folly, till I might see what *was* that ᵇgood for the sons of men, which they should do under the heaven all the days of their life.

4 I made me great works; I builded me ªhouses; I planted me vineyards:

2:3 ª Eccl. 1:17 ᵇ [Eccl. 3:12, 13; 5:18; 6:12] ¹ *how to gratify my flesh with, lit. to drag my flesh with* ² *guiding* ³ *how to*   2:4 ª 1 Kin. 7:1–12

5 I made me gardens and orchards, and I planted trees in them of all *kind of* fruits:

6 I made me pools of water, to ¹water therewith the ²wood that bringeth forth trees:

7 I got *me* ¹servants and maidens, and had ²servants born in my house; also I had great possessions of ³great and small cattle above all that were in Jerusalem before me:

8 ªI gathered me also silver and gold, and the ¹peculiar treasure of kings and of the provinces: I ²gat me men singers and women singers, and the delights of the sons of men, *as* ³musical instruments, and that of all sorts.

9 ªSo I was great, and ¹increased ᵇmore than all that were before me in Jerusalem: also my wisdom remained with me.

10 And whatsoever mine eyes desired I kept not from them, I withheld not my heart from any ¹joy; for my heart rejoiced in all my labour: and ªthis was my ²portion of all my labour.

11 Then I looked on all the works that my hands had wrought, and on the labour that I had ¹laboured to do: and, behold, all *was* ªvanity² and ³vexation of spirit, and *there was* no profit under the sun.

12 And I turned myself to behold wisdom, ªand madness, and folly: for what *can* the man *do* that cometh after the king? *even* that which hath been already ᵇdone.

13 Then I saw that wisdom ªexcelleth folly, as far as light excelleth darkness.

14 ªThe wise man's eyes *are* in his head; but the fool walketh in darkness: and I myself perceived also that ᵇone event happeneth to them all.

15 Then said I in my heart, As it happeneth to the fool, so it happeneth even to me; and why was I then more wise? Then I said in my heart, that this also *is* ¹vanity.

16 For *there is* ªno remembrance of the wise more than of the fool for ever; seeing that which now *is* in the days to come shall all be forgotten. And how dieth the wise *man?* as the fool.

17 Therefore I hated life; because the work that is wrought under the sun *is* grievous unto me: for all *is* ¹vanity and ²vexation of spirit.

18 Yea, I hated all my labour which I had ¹taken under the sun: because ªI should leave it unto the man that shall be after me.

19 And who knoweth whether he shall be a wise *man* or a fool? yet shall he have rule over all my labour wherein I have laboured, and

wherein I have shewed myself wise under the sun. This *is* also vanity.

20 Therefore I went about to cause my heart to despair of all the labour which I ¹took under the sun.

21 For there is a man whose labour *is* ¹in wisdom, and in knowledge, and ²in equity; yet to a man that hath not laboured therein shall he leave it *for* ³his portion. This also *is* vanity and a great evil.

22 ªFor what hath man of all his labour, and of the ¹vexation of his heart, wherein he hath laboured under the sun?

23 For all his days *are* ªsorrows, and his ¹travail grief; yea, his heart taketh not rest ²in the night. This is also ³vanity.

24 ªThere is nothing better for a man, *than* that he should eat and drink, and *that* ¹he should make his soul enjoy good in his labour. This also I saw, that it *was* from the hand of God.

25 For who can eat, or who else can ¹hasten *hereunto,* ²more than I?

26 For *God* giveth to a man ¹that *is* good in his sight ªwisdom, and knowledge, and joy: but to the sinner he giveth ²travail, to gather and to heap up, that ᵇhe may give to *him that is* good before God. This also *is* ³vanity and ⁴vexation of spirit.

## CHAPTER 3

To every *thing there is* a season, and a ªtime to every purpose under the heaven:

2 A time ¹to be born, and ªa time to die; a time to plant, and a time to pluck up *that which is* planted;

3 A time to kill, and a time to heal; a time to break down, and a time to build up;

4 A time to ªweep, and a time to laugh; a time to mourn, and a time to dance;

5 A time to cast away stones, and a time to gather stones together; ªa time to embrace, and a time to refrain from embracing;

6 A time to ¹get, and a time to lose; a time to keep, and a time to cast away;

7 A time to ¹rend, and a time to ²sew; ªa time to keep silence, and a time to ᵇspeak;

8 A time to love, and a time to ªhate; a time of war, and a time of peace.

9 ªWhat profit hath he that worketh in that wherein he laboureth?

10 ªI have seen the ¹travail, which God hath given to the sons of men ²to be exercised in it.

11 He hath made every *thing* beautiful in his time: also he hath set ¹the world in their heart, ²so that ªno man

### Center column notes

2:6 ¹ *irrigate* ² Or *grove of growing trees*

2:7 ¹ *male and female servants* ² Lit. *sons of my house* ³ *herds and flocks more than*

2:8 ª 1 Kin. 9:28; 10:10, 14, 21 ¹ *special* ² *acquired* ³ Exact meaning unknown

2:9 ª Eccl. 1:16 ᵇ 2 Chr. 9:22 ¹ *excelled*

2:10 ª Eccl. 3:22; 5:18; 9:9 ¹ *pleasure* ² *reward from*

2:11 ª Eccl. 1:3, 14 ¹ *toiled* ² *futility* ³ *a grasping for the wind*

2:12 ª Eccl. 1:17; 7:25 ᵇ Eccl. 1:9

2:13 ª Eccl. 7:11, 12, 19; 9:18; 10:10

2:14 ª Prov. 17:24 ᵇ Ps. 49:10

2:15 ¹ *futility*

2:16 ª Eccl. 1:11; 4:16

2:17 ¹ *futility* ² *a grasping for the wind*

2:18 ª Ps. 49:10 ¹ *toiled*

2:20 ¹ *toiled*

2:21 ¹ *with* ² *with skill* ³ *heritage*

2:22 ª Eccl. 1:3; 3:9 ¹ *striving*

2:23 ª Job 5:7; 14:1 ¹ *task grievous* ² *even in* ³ *futility*

2:24 ª Eccl. 3:12, 13, 22 ¹ *his soul should enjoy good*

2:25 ¹ *have enjoyment* ² Some Heb. mss., LXX, Syr., Jerome *without him*

2:26 ª Prov. 2:6 ᵇ Prov. 28:8 ¹ *who* ² *the task of gathering and collecting* ³ *futility* ⁴ *a grasping for the wind*

3:1 ª Eccl. 3:17; 8:6

3:2 ª Heb. 9:27 ¹ Lit. *to bear*

3:4 ª Rom. 12:15

3:5 ª Joel 2:16

3:6 ¹ *gain*

3:7 ª Amos 5:13 ᵇ Prov. 25:11 ¹ *tear apart* ² *sew together*

3:8 ª Luke 14:26

3:9 ª Eccl. 1:3

3:10 ª Eccl. 1:13 ¹ *task or endeavour* ² *with which to be occupied*

3:11 ª Rom. 11:33 ¹ *eternity* ² *except*

can find out the work that God ³maketh from the beginning to the end.

12 I know that *there is* ¹no ᵃgood in them, but for *a* man to rejoice, and to do good in his life.

13 And also ᵃthat every man should eat and drink, and enjoy the good of all his labour, it *is* the gift of God.

14 I know that, whatsoever God doeth, it shall be for ever: ᵃnothing can be ¹put to it, nor any thing taken from it: and God doeth *it,* that *men* should fear before him.

15 ᵃThat which hath been is now; and that which is to be hath already been; and God requireth ¹that which is past.

16 And moreover ᵃI saw under the sun ¹the place of judgment, *that* wickedness *was* there; and the place of righteousness, *that* ²iniquity *was* there.

17 I said in mine heart, ᵃGod shall judge the righteous and the wicked: for *there is* a time there for every ¹purpose and for every work.

18 I said in mine heart concerning the estate of the sons of men, that God might ¹manifest them, and that they might see that they themselves are ²beasts.

19 ᵃFor that which ¹befalleth the sons of men befalleth beasts; even one thing befalleth them: as the one dieth, so dieth the other; yea, they have all one breath; so that a man hath no ²preeminence above a beast: for all *is* vanity.

20 All go unto one place; ᵃall are of the dust, and all turn to dust again.

21 ᵃWho¹ knoweth the spirit of man that goeth upward, and the spirit of the beast that goeth downward to the earth?

22 ᵃWherefore I perceive that *there is* nothing better, than that a man should rejoice in his own works; for ᵇthat *is* his ¹portion: ᶜfor who shall bring him to see what shall be after him?

## CHAPTER 4

So I returned, and considered all the ᵃoppressions that are done under the sun: and behold the tears of *such as were* oppressed, and they had no comforter; and ¹on the side of their oppressors *there was* power; but they had no comforter.

2 ᵃWherefore I praised the dead which are already dead more than the living which are yet alive.

3 ᵃYea, better *is he* than both they, which hath not yet been, who hath not seen the evil work that is done under the sun.

4 Again, I ¹considered all travail, and every ²right work, that for this a man is envied ³of his neighbour. This *is* also vanity and ⁴vexation of spirit.

3:11 ¹ does
3:12 ᵃ Eccl. 2:3, 24
¹ nothing better for them
3:13 ᵃ Eccl. 2:24
3:14 ᵃ James 1:17
¹ added
3:15 ᵃ Eccl. 1:9
¹ an account of what is past
3:16 ᵃ Eccl. 5:8
¹ in the place of justice there was wickedness
² wickedness
3:17 ᵃ [Rom. 2:6–10] ¹ matter in which one delights and
3:18 ¹ test ² like beasts
3:19 ᵃ [Eccl. 2:16]
¹ happens to
² advantage
3:20 ᵃ Gen. 3:19
3:21 ᵃ Eccl. 12:7
¹ LXX, Vg., Syr., Tg. Who knows whether the spirit of the sons of men goes upward, and whether the spirit of the beast goes
3:22 ᵃ Eccl. 2:24;
5:18 ᵇ Eccl. 2:10
ᶜ Eccl. 6:12; 8:7
¹ heritage

4:1 ᵃ Eccl. 3:16; 5:8
¹ Lit. at the hand
4:2 ᵃ Job 3:17, 18
4:3 ᵃ Job 3:11–22
4:4 ¹ saw all the toil ² skilful ³ by
⁴ a grasping for the wind
4:5 ᵃ Prov. 6:10;
24:33 ¹ consumes
4:6 ᵃ Prov. 15:16,
17; 16:8 ¹ toil ² a grasping for the wind
4:7 ¹ futility
4:8 ᵃ [1 John 2:16]
ᵇ Ps. 39:6 ᶜ Eccl. 2:18–21 ¹ companion ² Lit. son
³ deprive ⁴ futility
⁵ grievous toil, lit. evil task
4:10 ¹ companion
4:12 ¹ though one may be overpowered by another
4:13 ¹ youth
² longer
4:14 ¹ even though the youth was born poor in his kingdom
4:15 ¹ youth
4:16 ¹ futility ² a grasping for the wind
5:1 ᵃ Ex. 3:5
ᵇ [1 Sam. 15:22]
¹ Walk prudently,

5 ᵃThe fool foldeth his hands together, and ¹eateth his own flesh.

6 ᵃBetter *is* an handful *with* quietness, than both the hands full *with* ¹travail and ²vexation of spirit.

7 Then I returned, and I saw ¹vanity under the sun.

8 There is one *alone,* and *there is* not a ¹second; yea, he hath neither ²child nor brother: yet *is there* no end of all his labour; neither is his ᵃeye satisfied with riches; ᵇneither *saith he,* For whom do I labour, and ³bereave my soul ᶜof good? This *is* also ⁴vanity, yea, it *is* a ⁵sore travail.

9 Two *are* better than one; because they have a good reward for their labour.

10 For if they fall, the one will lift up his ¹fellow: but woe to him *that is* alone when he falleth; for *he hath* not another to help him up.

11 Again, if two lie together, then they have heat: but how can one be warm *alone?*

12 And ¹if one prevail against him, two shall withstand him; and a threefold cord is not quickly broken.

13 Better *is* a poor and a wise ¹child than an old and foolish king, who will no ²more be admonished.

14 For out of prison he cometh to reign; ¹whereas also *he that is* born in his kingdom becometh poor.

15 I considered all the living which walk under the sun, with the second ¹child that shall stand up in his stead.

16 *There is* no end of all the people, *even* of all that have been before them: they also that come after shall not rejoice in him. Surely this also *is* ¹vanity and ²vexation of spirit.

## CHAPTER 5

Keep¹ ᵃthy foot when thou goest to the house of God, and ²be more ready to hear, ᵇthan to give the sacrifice of fools: for they consider not that they do evil.

2 Be not ᵃrash with thy mouth, and let not thine heart be hasty to utter *any* thing before God: for God *is* in heaven, and thou upon earth: therefore let thy words ᵇbe few.

3 For a dream cometh through the multitude of ¹business; and ᵃa fool's voice *is known* by multitude of words.

4 ᵃWhen thou vowest a vow unto God, ¹defer not to ᵇpay it; for *he hath* no pleasure in fools: pay that which thou hast vowed.

5 ᵃBetter *is it* that thou shouldest not vow, than that thou shouldest vow and not pay.

lit. Guard thy feet  ² draw near to hear, rather than
5:2 ᵃ Prov. 20:25  ᵇ Matt. 6:7   5:3 ᵃ Prov. 10:19  ¹ effort or activity  5:4 ᵃ Num. 30:2  ᵇ Ps. 66:13, 14  ¹ delay
5:5 ᵃ Acts 5:4

6 ¹Suffer not thy ᵃmouth to cause thy flesh to sin; ᵇneither say thou before the ²angel, that it *was* an error: wherefore should God be angry at thy ³voice, and destroy the work of thine hands?

7 For in the multitude of dreams and many words ¹*there are* also *divers* vanities: but ᵃfear thou God.

8 If thou ᵃseest the oppression of the poor, and violent ¹perverting of judgment and justice in a province, marvel not at the matter: for ᵇhe² *that is* higher than the highest regardeth; and *there be* higher than they.

9 Moreover the profit of the earth is for all: the king *himself* is served by the field.

10 He that loveth silver shall not be satisfied with silver; nor he that loveth abundance with increase: this *is* also ¹vanity.

11 When goods increase, they are increased that eat them: and what good *is there* to the owners thereof, saving the beholding *of them* with their eyes?

12 The sleep of a labouring man *is* sweet, whether he eat little or much: but the abundance of the rich will not ¹suffer him to sleep.

13 ᵃThere is a ¹sore evil *which* I have seen under the sun, *namely,* riches kept for the owners thereof to their hurt.

14 But those riches perish by ¹evil travail: and he begetteth a son, and *there is* nothing in his hand.

15 ᵃAs he came forth of his mother's womb, naked shall he return to go as he came, and shall take nothing of his labour, which he may carry away in his hand.

16 And this also *is* a ¹sore evil, *that* in all points as he came, so shall he go: and ᵃwhat profit hath he ᵇthat hath laboured for the wind?

17 All his days also ᵃhe eateth in darkness, and *he hath* much sorrow and wrath with his sickness.

18 Behold *that* which I have seen: ᵃ*it is* good and ¹comely *for one* to eat and to drink, and to enjoy the good of all his labour ²that he taketh under the sun all the days of his life, which God giveth him: ᵇfor it *is* his ³portion.

19 ᵃEvery man also to whom God hath given riches and wealth, and hath given him power to eat thereof, and to ¹take his portion, and to rejoice in his labour; this *is* the ᵇgift of God.

20 For he shall not much remember the days of his life; because God ¹answereth *him* in the joy of his heart.

## CHAPTER 6

THEREᵃ is an evil which I have seen under the sun, and it *is* common among men:

2 A man to whom God hath given riches, wealth, and honour, ᵃso that he ¹wanteth nothing for ²his soul of all that he desireth, ᵇyet God giveth him not power to eat thereof, but a stranger eateth it: this *is* ³vanity, and it *is* an evil ⁴disease.

3 If a man beget an hundred *children,* and live many years, so that the days of his years be many, and his soul be not ¹filled with good, and ᵃalso *that* he have no burial; I say, *that* ᵇan² untimely birth *is* better than he.

4 For he cometh in with ¹vanity, and departeth in darkness, and his name shall be covered with darkness.

5 Moreover he hath not seen the sun, nor known *any thing:* this hath more rest than the other.

6 Yea, though he live a thousand years twice ¹*told,* yet hath he seen no good: do not all go to one ᵃplace?

7 ᵃAll the labour of man *is* for his mouth, and yet ¹the appetite is not ²filled.

8 For what hath the wise more than the fool? what hath the poor, that knoweth ¹to walk before the living?

9 Better *is* ¹the ᵃsight of the eyes ²than the wandering of the desire: this *is* also vanity and ³vexation of spirit.

10 That which hath been is named ᵃalready, and it is known that it *is* man: ᵇneither¹ may he contend with him that is mightier than he.

11 Seeing there be many things that increase vanity, what *is* man the better?

12 For who knoweth what *is* good for man in *this* life, ¹all the days of his ²vain life which he spendeth as ᵃa shadow? for ᵇwho can tell a man what shall ³be after him under the sun?

## CHAPTER 7

AᵃGOOD name *is* better than precious ointment; and the day of death than the day of one's ᵇbirth.

2 *It is* better to go to the house of mourning, than to go to the house of feasting: for that *is* the end of all men; and the living will ¹lay *it* to his ᵃheart.

3 ¹Sorrow *is* better than laughter: ᵃfor by the sadness of the countenance the heart is made ²better.

4 The heart of the wise *is* in the house of mourning; but the heart of fools *is* in the house of mirth.

5 ᵃ*It is* better to hear the rebuke of the wise, than for a man to hear the song of fools.

6 ᵃFor as the ¹crackling of thorns under a pot, so *is* the laughter of the fool: this also *is* vanity.

7 Surely oppression maketh a wise man ¹mad; ªand a ²gift ³destroyeth the heart.

8 Better *is* the end of a thing than the beginning thereof: *and* ªthe patient in spirit *is* better than the proud in spirit.

9 ªBe not hasty in thy spirit to be angry: for anger resteth in the bosom of fools.

10 Say not thou, What is *the cause* that the former days were better than these? for thou dost not enquire wisely concerning this.

11 Wisdom *is* good with an inheritance: and *by it there is* profit ªto them that see the sun.

12 For wisdom *is* ¹a ªdefence, *and* money *is* a defence: but the ²excellency of knowledge *is, that* wisdom giveth ᵇlife to them that have it.

13 Consider the work of God: for ªwho can make *that* straight, which he hath made crooked?

14 ªIn the day of prosperity be joyful, but in the day of adversity consider: God ¹also hath set the one over against the other, to the end that man should find ²nothing after him.

15 All *things* have I seen in ¹the days of my vanity: ªthere is a just *man* that perisheth in his righteousness, and there is a wicked *man* that prolongeth *his life* in his wickedness.

16 ªBe not ¹righteous over much; ᵇneither make thyself ²over wise: why shouldest thou destroy thyself?

17 Be not ¹over much wicked, neither be thou foolish: ªwhy shouldest thou die before thy time?

18 *It is* good that thou shouldest ¹take hold of this; yea, also from this withdraw not thine hand: for he that ªfeareth God shall ²come forth of them all.

19 ªWisdom strengtheneth the wise more than ten ¹mighty *men* which are in the city.

20 ªFor *there is* not a just man upon earth, that doeth good, and sinneth not.

21 Also ¹take no heed unto all words that are spoken; lest thou hear thy servant curse thee:

22 For oftentimes also thine own heart knoweth that thou thyself likewise hast cursed others.

23 All this have I ¹proved by wisdom: ªI said, I will be wise; but it *was* far from me.

24 ªThat which is far off, and ᵇexceeding deep, who can find it out?

25 ªI applied mine heart to know, and to search, and to seek out wisdom, and the reason *of things,* and to know the wickedness of folly, even of foolishness *and* madness:

26 ªAnd I find more bitter than death the woman, whose heart *is*

7:7 ª Ex. 23:8
¹ *a fool* ² *bribe*
³ *corrupts*

7:8 ª Prov. 14:29

7:9 ª James 1:19

7:11 ª Eccl. 11:7

7:12 ª Eccl. 9:18
ᵇ Prov. 3:18 ¹ *A protective shade,* lit. *a shadow* ² *advantage*

7:13 ª Job 12:14

7:14 ª Deut. 28:47 ¹ *surely has appointed the one as well as the other* ² *nothing that will happen after him*

7:15 ª Eccl. 8:12–14 ¹ *my days of futility*

7:16 ª Prov. 25:16 ᵇ Rom. 12:3 ¹ *overly righteous* ² *overly*

7:17 ª Job 15:32 ¹ *overly*

7:18 ª Eccl. 3:14; 5:7; 8:12, 13 ¹ *grasp this* ² *escape them all*

7:19 ª Prov. 21:22 ¹ *rulers*

7:20 ª 1 John 1:8

7:21 ¹ *do not take to heart*

7:23 ª Rom. 1:22 ¹ *tested*

7:24 ª 1 Tim. 6:16 ᵇ Rom. 11:33

7:25 ª Eccl. 1:17

7:26 ª Prov. 5:3, 4 ¹ *fetters or chains* ² Lit. *the good one before God*

7:27 ª Eccl. 1:1, 2 ¹ *adding one thing to another* ² *reason*

7:28 ª Job 33:23 ¹ *one wise man*

7:29 ª Gen. 1:27 ᵇ Gen. 3:6, 7 ¹ *schemes*

8:1 ª Acts 6:15 ᵇ Deut. 28:50 ¹ *sternness,* lit. *strength*

8:2 ª 1 Chr. 29:24 ¹ *for the sake of the oath*

8:3 ª Eccl. 10:4 ¹ *presence* ² *do not take your stand for*

8:4 ª Job 34:18

8:5 ¹ *shall experience nothing harmful* ² Lit. *knows*

8:6 ª Eccl. 3:1, 17 ¹ *matter in which one delights*

8:7 ª Eccl. 6:12

8:8 ª Ps. 49:6, 7 ᵇ Deut. 20:5–8

snares and nets, *and* her hands *as* ¹bands: ²whoso pleaseth God shall escape from her; but the sinner shall be taken by her.

27 Behold, this have I found, saith ªthe preacher, ¹counting one by one, to find out the ²account:

28 Which yet my soul seeketh, but I find not: ªone¹ man among a thousand have I found; but a woman among all those have I not found.

29 Lo, this only have I found, ªthat God hath made man upright; but ᵇthey have sought out many ¹inventions.

## CHAPTER 8

WHO *is* as the wise *man?* and who knoweth the interpretation of a thing? ªa man's wisdom maketh his face to shine, and ᵇthe ¹boldness of his face shall be changed.

2 I *counsel thee* to keep the king's commandment, ªand¹ *that* in regard of the oath of God.

3 ªBe not hasty to go out of his ¹sight: ²stand not in an evil thing; for he doeth whatsoever pleaseth him.

4 Where the word of a king *is, there is* power: and ªwho may say unto him, What doest thou?

5 Whoso keepeth the commandment ¹shall feel no evil thing: and a wise man's heart ²discerneth both time and judgment.

6 Because ªto every ¹purpose there is time and judgment, therefore the misery of man *is* great upon him.

7 ªFor he knoweth not that which shall be: for who can tell him when it shall be?

8 ªThere is no man that hath power over the spirit to retain the spirit; neither *hath he* power in the day of death: and *there is* ᵇno discharge in *that* war; neither shall wickedness deliver those that are given to it.

9 All this have I seen, and applied my heart unto every work that is done under the sun: *there is* a time wherein one man ruleth over another to his own hurt.

10 And so I saw the wicked buried, who had come and gone from the place of ¹the holy, and they were ªforgotten in the city where they had so done: this *is* also vanity.

11 ªBecause sentence against an evil work is not executed speedily, therefore the heart of the sons of men is fully set in them to do evil.

12 ªThough a sinner do evil an hundred times, and his *days* be prolonged, yet surely I know that ᵇit shall be well with them that fear God, which fear before him:

8:10 ª Eccl. 2:16; 9:5 ¹ *holiness*　8:11 ª Is. 26:10
8:12 ª Is. 65:20 ᵇ [Is. 3:10]

13 But it shall not be well with the wicked, neither shall he prolong *his* days, *which are* as a shadow; because he feareth not before God.

14 There is a vanity which is done upon the earth; that there be just *men,* unto whom it ªhappeneth according to the work of the wicked; again, there be wicked *men,* to whom it happeneth according to the work of the ᵇrighteous: I said that this also *is* vanity.

15 ªThen I commended ¹mirth, because a man hath no better thing under the sun, than to eat, and to drink, and to be merry: for that shall abide with him of his labour the days of his life, which God giveth him under the sun.

16 When I applied mine heart to know wisdom, and to see the business that is done upon the earth: (for also *there is that* neither day nor night seeth sleep with his eyes:)

17 Then I beheld all the work of God, that ªa man cannot find out the work that is done under the sun: because though a man labour to seek *it* out, yet he shall not find *it;* yea farther; though a wise *man* ¹think to know *it,* yet shall he not be able to find *it.*

### CHAPTER 9

For all this I ¹considered in my heart even to declare all this, ªthat the righteous, and the wise, and their works, *are* in the hand of God: no man knoweth either love or hatred *by* ²all *that* is before them.

2 ªAll *things* ¹come alike to all: *there is* one event to the righteous, and to the wicked; to the good and to the clean, and to the unclean; to him that sacrificeth, and to him that sacrificeth not: as *is* the good, so *is* the sinner; *and* he that ²sweareth, as *he* that feareth an oath.

3 This *is* an evil among all *things* that are done under the sun, that *there is* one event unto all: yea, also the heart of the sons of men is full of evil, and madness *is* in their heart while they live, and after that *they* go to the dead.

4 For to him that is joined to all the living there is hope: for a living dog is better than a dead lion.

5 For the living know that they shall die: but ªthe dead know not any thing, neither have they any more a reward; for ᵇthe memory of them is forgotten.

6 Also their love, and their hatred, and their envy, is now perished; neither have they any more a ¹portion for ever in any *thing* that is done under the sun.

7 Go thy way, ªeat thy bread with joy, and drink thy wine with a merry

heart; for God now accepteth thy works.

8 Let thy garments be always white; and let thy head lack no ¹ointment.

9 ¹Live joyfully with the wife whom thou lovest all the days of ²the life of thy vanity, which he hath given thee under the sun, all the days of thy vanity: ªfor that *is* thy portion in *this* life, and in thy labour which thou ³takest under the sun.

10 ªWhatsoever thy hand findeth to do, do *it* with thy ᵇmight; for *there is* no work, nor device, nor knowledge, nor wisdom, in the grave, whither thou goest.

11 I returned, ªand saw under the sun, that the race *is* not to the swift, nor the battle to the strong, neither yet bread to the wise, nor yet riches to men of understanding, nor yet favour to men of skill; but time and ᵇchance happeneth to them all.

12 For ªman also knoweth not his time: as the fishes that are taken in an ¹evil net, and as the birds that are caught in the snare; so *are* the sons of men ᵇsnared in an evil time, when it falleth suddenly upon them.

13 This wisdom have I seen also under the sun, and it *seemed* great unto me:

14 ªThere *was* a little city, and few men within it; and there came a great king against it, and besieged it, and built great ¹bulwarks against it:

15 Now there was found in it a poor wise man, and he by his wisdom delivered the city; yet no man remembered that same poor man.

16 Then said I, Wisdom *is* better than ªstrength: nevertheless ᵇthe poor man's wisdom *is* despised, and his words are not heard.

17 The words of wise *men* ¹are heard in quiet more than the cry of him that ruleth among fools.

18 Wisdom *is* better than weapons of war: but ªone sinner destroyeth much good.

### CHAPTER 10

Dead¹ flies ²cause the ointment of the ³apothecary to send forth a ⁴stinking savour: *so doth* a little folly ⁵him that is in reputation for wisdom *and* honour.

2 A wise man's heart *is* at his right hand; but a fool's heart at his left.

3 Yea also, when he that is a fool walketh ¹by the way, ²his wisdom faileth *him,* ªand he ³saith to every one *that* he *is* a fool.

4 If the spirit of the ruler rise up against thee, ªleave not thy ¹place; for ᵇyielding² pacifieth great offences.

5 There is an evil *which* I have seen under the sun, as an error *which* proceedeth from the ruler:

---

Center reference column:

8:14 ª Ps. 73:14
ᵇ Eccl. 2:14; 7:15;
9:1–3
8:15 ª Eccl. 2:24
¹ *joy*
8:17 ª Job 5:9;
Ps. 73:16; Eccl.
3:11; Rom. 11:33
¹ *attempts*
9:1 ª Deut. 33:3;
Job 12:10; Eccl.
8:14 ¹ Lit. *took*
² *anything*
9:2 ª Gen. 3:17–19;
Job 21:7; Ps. 73:3,
12, 13; Mal. 3:15
¹ Happen ² *takes
an oath*
9:5 ª Job 14:21; Is.
63:16 ᵇ Job 7:8–
10; Eccl. 1:11; 2:16;
8:10; Is. 26:14
9:6 ¹ *share in all
that is done*
9:7 ª Eccl. 8:15
9:8 ¹ *oil*
9:9 ª Eccl. 2:10
¹ Lit. *See* or *Enjoy
life* ² *thy empty
life* ³ *performest*
9:10 ª [Col. 3:17]
ᵇ Rom. 12:11; Col.
3:23
9:11 ª Jer. 9:23;
Amos 2:14, 15
ᵇ 1 Sam. 6:9
9:12 ª Eccl. 8:7
ᵇ Prov. 29:6;
Luke 12:20, 39;
17:26; 1 Thess. 5:3
¹ *cruel*
9:14 ª 2 Sam.
20:16–22 ¹ MT
*snares* or *siege-
works;* LXX, Syr.,
Vg. *bulwarks*
9:16 ª Eccl. 7:12, 19
ᵇ Mark 6:2, 3
9:17 ¹ spoken
*quietly* should be
*heard rather than
the shout*
9:18 ª Josh. 7:1–
26; 2 Kin. 21:2–17
10:1 ¹ Lit. *Flies of
death* ² MT *pu-
trefy and cause;*
Vg., Tg. omit *pu-
trefy* ³ *perfumer*
⁴ *foul odour* ⁵ *to
one respected for
wisdom*
10:3 ª Prov. 13:16;
18:2 ¹ *along* ² *he
lacks wisdom*
³ *shows*
10:4 ª Eccl.
8:3 ᵇ 1 Sam.
25:24–33; Prov.
25:15 ¹ *post*
² *composure*

6 ᵃFolly is set in ¹great dignity, and the rich sit ²in low place.

7 I have seen servants ᵃupon horses, and princes walking as servants upon the ¹earth.

8 ᵃHe that diggeth a pit shall fall into it; and whoso ¹breaketh an hedge, a serpent ²shall bite him.

9 Whoso ¹removeth stones shall be hurt therewith; *and* he that ²cleaveth wood shall be endangered thereby.

10 If the ¹iron be blunt, and he ²do not whet the edge, then must he put to more strength: but wisdom *is* ³profitable to direct.

11 Surely the serpent will bite ᵃwithout¹ enchantment; and a babbler is no better.

12 ᵃThe words of a wise man's mouth *are* gracious; but ᵇthe lips of a fool will swallow up himself.

13 The beginning of the words of his mouth *is* foolishness: and the end of his talk *is* ¹mischievous madness.

14 ᵃA fool also ¹is full of words: ²a man cannot tell what shall be; and ᵇwhat shall be after him, who can tell him?

15 The labour of the foolish wearieth every one of them, because he knoweth not how to go to the city.

16 ᵃWoe to thee, O land, when thy king *is* a child, and thy princes ¹eat in the morning!

17 Blessed *art* thou, O land, when thy king *is* the son of nobles, and thy ᵃprinces ¹eat in due season, for strength, and not for drunkenness!

18 By ¹much slothfulness the building decayeth; and ᵃthrough idleness of the hands the house ²droppeth through.

19 A feast is made for laughter, and ᵃwine ¹maketh merry: but money answereth all *things*.

20 ᵃCurse not the king, no not in thy thought; and curse not the rich in thy bedchamber: for a bird of the air shall carry the voice, and that which hath wings shall tell the matter.

## CHAPTER 11

CAST thy bread ᵃupon the waters: ᵇfor thou shalt find it after many days.

2 ᵃGive a portion ᵇto seven, and also to eight; ᶜfor thou knowest not what evil shall be upon the earth.

3 If the clouds be full of rain, they empty *themselves* upon the earth: and if the tree fall toward the south, or toward the north, in the place where the tree falleth, there it shall be.

4 He that observeth the wind shall not sow; and he that regardeth the clouds shall not reap.

5 As ᵃthou knowest not what *is* the way of the ¹spirit, ᵇnor how the bones do grow in the womb of her that is with child: even so thou knowest not the works of God who maketh all.

6 In the morning sow thy seed, and in the evening withhold not thine hand: for thou knowest not ¹whether shall prosper, either this or that, or whether they both *shall be* alike good.

7 Truly the light *is* sweet, and a pleasant *thing it is* for the eyes ᵃto behold the sun:

8 But if a man live many years, *and* ᵃrejoice in them all; yet let him ᵇremember the days of darkness; for they shall be many. All that cometh *is* ¹vanity.

9 Rejoice, O young man, in thy youth; and let thy heart cheer thee in the days of thy youth, ᵃand walk in the ¹ways of thine heart, and ²in the sight of thine eyes: but know thou, that for all these *things* ᵇGod will bring thee into judgment.

10 Therefore remove ¹sorrow from thy heart, and ᵃput away evil from thy flesh: ᵇfor childhood and ²youth *are* vanity.

## CHAPTER 12

REMEMBERᵃ now thy Creator in the days of thy youth, ¹while the evil days come not, nor the years draw nigh, ᵇwhen thou shalt say, I have no pleasure in them;

2 While the sun, or the light, or the moon, or the stars, be not darkened, nor the clouds return after the rain:

3 In the day when the keepers of the house shall tremble, and the strong men shall ¹bow themselves, and the grinders ²cease because they are few, and those that look out of the windows ³be darkened,

4 And the doors shall be shut in the streets, when the sound of the grinding is low, and he shall rise up at the voice of the bird, and all ᵃthe daughters of musick shall be brought low;

5 Also *when* they shall be afraid of *that which is* high, and ¹fears *shall be* in the way, and the almond tree shall ²flourish, and the grasshopper shall be a burden, and desire shall fail: because man goeth to ᵃhis ³long home, and ᵇthe mourners go about the streets:

6 Or ever the silver cord be loosed, or the golden bowl be broken, or the pitcher be ¹broken at the fountain, or the wheel broken at the cistern.

7 ᵃThen shall the dust return to the earth as it was: ᵇand the spirit shall return unto God ᶜwho gave it.

8 ᵃVanity of vanities, saith the preacher; all *is* vanity.

9 And moreover, because the preacher was wise, he still taught the people knowledge; yea, he ¹gave good heed, and sought out, *and* ᵃset² in order many proverbs.

10 The preacher sought to find out ¹acceptable words: and *that which was* written *was* upright, *even* words of truth.

11 The words of the wise *are* as goads, and as nails fastened *by* the masters of ¹assemblies, *which* are given from one shepherd.

12 And further, by these, my son, be admonished: of making many books

12:10 ¹ Lit. *delightful*
12:11 ¹ *collections*

12:12 ª Eccl. 1:18
12:13 ª [Deut. 6:2; 10:12]; Mic. 6:8
12:14 ª Eccl. 11:9; Matt. 12:36; [Acts 17:30, 31; Rom. 2:16; 1 Cor. 4:5; 2 Cor. 5:10]

*there is* no end; and ªmuch study *is* a weariness of the flesh.

13 Let us hear the conclusion of the whole matter: ªFear God, and keep his commandments: for this *is* the whole *duty* of man.

14 For ªGod shall bring every work into judgment, with every secret thing, whether *it be* good, or whether *it be* evil.

# THE
# SONG OF SOLOMON

The Song of Solomon is a love song written by Solomon and abounding in metaphors and oriental imagery. Historically, it depicts the wooing and wedding of a shepherdess by King Solomon, and the joys and heartaches of wedded love.

Allegorically, it pictures Israel as God's betrothed bride (Hos. 2:19, 20), and the church as the bride of Christ. As human life finds its highest fulfillment in the love of man and woman, so spiritual life finds its highest fulfillment in the love of God for His people and Christ for His church.

The book reads like scenes in a drama with three main speakers: the bride (Shulamite), the king (Solomon), and a chorus (daughters of Jerusalem).

The Hebrew title *Shir Hashirim* comes from 1:1, "The song of songs." This is in the superlative and speaks of Solomon's most exquisite song. The Greek title *Asma Asmaton* and the Latin *Canticum Canticorum* also mean "Song of Songs" or "The Best Song." The name *Canticles* ("Songs") is derived from the Latin title. Because Solomon is mentioned in 1:1, the book is also known as the Song of Solomon.

## CHAPTER 1

THE [a]song of songs, which *is* Solomon's.

2 Let him kiss me with the kisses of his mouth: [a]for thy love *is* better than wine.

3 Because of the [1]savour of thy good ointments thy name *is* as ointment poured forth, therefore do the virgins love thee.

4 [a]Draw[1] me, [b]we will run after thee: the king [c]hath brought me into his chambers: we will be glad and rejoice in thee, we will remember thy love more than wine: [2]the upright love thee.

5 I *am* [1]black, but [2]comely, O ye daughters of Jerusalem, as the tents of Kedar, as the curtains of Solomon.

6 Look not upon me, because I *am* [1]black, because the sun hath [3]looked upon me: my mother's [3]children were angry with me; they made me the keeper of the vineyards; *but* mine own [a]vineyard have I not kept.

7 Tell me, O thou whom my soul loveth, where thou [1]feedest, where thou makest *thy flock* to rest at noon: for why should I be as one [2]that turneth aside by the flocks of thy companions?

8 If thou know not, [a]O thou fairest among women, [1]go thy way forth by the footsteps of the flock, and feed thy [2]kids beside the shepherds' tents.

9 I have compared thee, [a]O my love, [b]to [1]a company of horses in Pharaoh's chariots.

10 [a]Thy cheeks are [1]comely with [2]rows of *jewels,* thy neck with chains *of gold.*

11 We will make thee [1]borders of gold with studs of silver.

12 While the king *sitteth* at his table, my [1]spikenard sendeth forth [2]the smell thereof.

13 A bundle of myrrh *is* my wellbeloved unto me; he shall lie all night [1]betwixt my breasts.

14 My beloved *is* unto me *as* a cluster of [1]camphire in the vineyards of En-gedi.

15 [a]Behold, thou *art* fair, [1]my love; behold, thou *art* fair; thou *hast* doves' eyes.

16 Behold, thou *art* [a]fair,[1] my beloved, yea, pleasant: also our [2]bed *is* green.

17 The beams of our house *are* cedar, *and* our rafters of fir.

## CHAPTER 2

I AM the rose of Sharon, *and* the lily of the valleys.

2 As the lily among thorns, so *is* my love among the daughters.

3 As the apple tree among the trees of the wood, so *is* my beloved among the sons. I sat down under his [1]shadow with great delight, and [a]his fruit *was* sweet to my taste.

4 He brought me to the [1]banqueting house, and his banner over me *was* love.

5 [1]Stay me with flagons, [2]comfort me with apples: for I *am* [3]sick of love.

6 [a]His left hand *is* under my head, and his right hand doth embrace me.

7 [a]I[1] charge you, O ye daughters of Jerusalem, by the [2]roes, and by the [3]hinds of the field, that ye stir not up, nor awake *my* love, till he please.

8 The voice of my beloved! behold, he cometh leaping upon the mountains, skipping upon the hills.

9 [a]My beloved is like a [1]roe or a

1:1 [a] 1 Kin. 4:32
1:2 [a] Song 4:10
1:3 [1] fragrance
1:4 [a] Hos. 11:4 [b] Phil. 3:12–14 [c] Ps. 45:14, 15 [1] Lead me away [2] rightly do they love you
1:5 [1] dark [2] lovely
1:6 [a] Song 8:11, 12 [1] dark [2] tanned me [3] sons
1:7 [1] feedest your flock [2] who veils herself
1:8 [a] Song 5:9 [1] follow in the footsteps [2] little goats
1:9 [a] Song 2:2, 10, 13; 4:1, 7 [b] 2 Chr. 1:16 [1] my filly among Pharaoh's
1:10 [a] Ezek. 16:11 [1] lovely [2] ornaments
1:11 [1] ornaments
1:12 [1] perfume [2] its fragrance
1:13 [1] between
1:14 [1] henna blooms
1:15 [a] Song 4:1; 5:12 [1] my companion or my friend
1:16 [a] Song 5:10–16 [1] handsome [2] couch
2:3 [a] Rev. 22:1, 2 [1] shade
2:4 [1] Lit. house of wine
2:5 [1] Sustain me with cakes of raisins [2] refresh [3] lovesick
2:6 [a] Song 8:3
2:7 [a] Song 3:5; 8:4 [1] I adjure you [b] gazelles [3] does
2:9 [a] Song 2:17 [1] gazelle

young [2]hart: behold, he standeth behind our wall, he looketh forth at the windows, [3]shewing himself through the lattice.

10 My beloved spake, and said unto me, Rise up, my love, my fair one, and come away.

11 For, lo, the winter is past, the rain is over *and* gone;

12 The flowers appear on the earth; the time of the singing *of birds* is come, and the voice of the [1]turtle is heard in our land;

13 The fig tree putteth forth her green figs, and the vines *with* the tender grape give a *good* smell. Arise, my love, my fair one, and come away.

14 O my [a]dove, *that art* in the clefts of the rock, in the secret *places* of the [1]stairs, let me see thy [2]countenance, [b]let me hear thy voice; for sweet *is* thy voice, and thy [3]countenance *is* comely.

15 [1]Take us [a]the foxes, the little foxes, that spoil the vines: for our vines *have* tender grapes.

16 [a]My beloved *is* mine, and I *am* his: he [1]feedeth among the lilies.

17 [a]Until the day break, and the shadows flee away, turn, my beloved, and be thou [b]like a [1]roe or a young [2]hart upon the mountains of [3]Bether.

### CHAPTER 3

BY [a]night on my bed I sought him whom my soul loveth: I sought him, but I found him not.

2 I will rise now, and go about the city in the streets, and in the [1]broad ways I will seek him whom my soul loveth: I sought him, but I found him not.

3 [a]The watchmen that go about the city found me: *to whom I said,* Saw ye him whom my soul loveth?

4 *It was* but a little that I passed from them, but I found him whom my soul loveth: I held him, and would not let him go, until I had brought him into my [a]mother's house, and into the [1]chamber of her that conceived me.

5 [a]I[1] charge you, O ye daughters of Jerusalem, by the [2]roes, and by the [3]hinds of the field, that ye stir not up, nor awake *my* love, till he please.

6 [a]Who *is* this that cometh out of the wilderness like pillars of smoke, perfumed with myrrh and frankincense, with all [1]powders of the merchant?

7 Behold [1]his bed, which *is* Solomon's; threescore valiant men *are* about it, of the valiant of Israel.

8 They all hold swords, *being* expert in war: every man *hath* his sword upon his thigh because of fear in the night.

9 King Solomon made himself [1]a chariot of the wood of Lebanon.

10 He made the pillars thereof *of* silver, the [1]bottom thereof *of* gold, the [2]covering of it *of* purple, the [3]midst thereof being paved *with* love, [4]for the daughters of Jerusalem.

11 Go forth, O ye daughters of Zion, and behold king Solomon with the crown wherewith his mother crowned him in the day of his [1]espousals, and in the day of the gladness of his heart.

### CHAPTER 4

BEHOLD, [a]thou *art* fair, my love; behold, thou *art* fair; thou *hast* doves' eyes [1]within thy locks: thy hair *is* as a [b]flock of goats, that [2]appear from mount Gilead.

2 [a]Thy teeth *are* like a flock *of sheep that are even* shorn, which came up from the washing; whereof every one bear twins, and none *is* [1]barren among them.

3 Thy lips *are* like a thread of scarlet, and thy [1]speech *is* comely: [a]thy temples *are* like a piece of a pomegranate [2]within thy locks.

4 [a]Thy neck *is* like the tower of David builded [b]for an armoury, whereon there hang a thousand [1]bucklers, all shields of mighty men.

5 [a]Thy two breasts *are* like two [1]young roes [2]that are twins, which feed among the lilies.

6 [a]Until the day break, and the shadows flee away, I will get me to the mountain of myrrh, and to the hill of frankincense.

7 [a]Thou *art* all fair, my love; *there is* no spot in thee.

8 Come with me from Lebanon, *my* spouse, with me from Lebanon: look from the top of Amana, from the top of [1]Shenir [a]and Hermon, from the lions' dens, from the mountains of the leopards.

9 Thou hast [1]ravished my heart, my sister, *my* spouse; thou hast ravished my heart with [2]one of thine eyes, with one [3]chain of thy neck.

10 How fair is thy love, my sister, *my* spouse! [a]how much better is thy love than wine! and the [1]smell of thine [2]ointments than all spices!

11 Thy lips, O *my* spouse, [1]drop *as* the honeycomb: [a]honey and milk *are* under thy tongue; and the [2]smell of thy garments *is* [b]like the [2]smell of Lebanon.

12 A garden [1]inclosed *is* my sister, *my* spouse; a spring shut up, a fountain sealed.

13 Thy plants *are* an orchard of pomegranates, with pleasant fruits; [1]camphire, with spikenard,

14 Spikenard and saffron; calamus and cinnamon, with all trees of frankincense; myrrh and aloes, with all the chief spices:

15 A fountain of gardens, a well of [a]living waters, and streams from Lebanon.

16 Awake, O north wind; and come, thou south; blow upon my garden, *that* the spices thereof may flow out. [a]Let my beloved come into his garden, and eat his pleasant [b]fruits.

## CHAPTER 5

I [a]AM come into my garden, my [b]sister, *my* spouse: I have gathered my myrrh with my spice; [c]I have eaten my honeycomb with my honey; I have drunk my wine with my milk: eat, O [d]friends; drink, yea, drink abundantly, O beloved.

2 I sleep, but my heart waketh: *it is* the voice of my beloved [a]that knocketh, *saying,* Open to me, my sister, my love, my dove, my [1]undefiled: for my head is [2]filled with dew, *and* my [3]locks with the drops of the night.

3 I have put off my coat; how shall I put it on? I have washed my feet; how shall I [1]defile them?

4 My beloved put in his hand by the [1]hole *of the door,* and my [2]bowels were moved for him.

5 I rose up to open to my beloved; and my hands [1]dropped *with* myrrh, and my fingers *with* [2]sweet smelling myrrh, upon the handles of the lock.

6 I opened to my beloved; but my beloved had withdrawn himself, *and* was gone: [1]my soul failed when he spake: [a]I sought him, but I could not find him; I called him, but he gave me no answer.

7 [a]The watchmen that went about the city found me, they [1]smote me, they wounded me; the keepers of the walls took away my veil from me.

8 I charge you, O daughters of Jerusalem, if ye find my beloved, that ye tell him, that I am [1]sick of love.

9 What *is* thy beloved more than *another* beloved, [a]O thou fairest among women? what *is* thy beloved more than *another* beloved, that thou dost so [1]charge us?

10 My beloved *is* white and ruddy, the [1]chiefest among ten thousand.

11 His head *is as* the most fine gold, his locks *are* [1]bushy, *and* black as a raven.

12 [a]His eyes *are as the eyes* of doves by the rivers of waters, washed with milk, *and* [1]fitly set.

13 His cheeks *are as* a bed of spices, *as* [1]sweet flowers: his lips *like* lilies, [2]dropping sweet smelling myrrh.

14 His hands *are as* gold [1]rings set with the beryl: his [2]belly *is as* bright ivory overlaid *with* sapphires.

15 His legs *are as* pillars of marble, set upon [1]sockets of fine gold: his countenance *is* as Lebanon, excellent as the cedars.

16 His mouth *is* most sweet: yea, he *is* altogether lovely. This *is* my beloved, and this *is* my friend, O daughters of Jerusalem.

## CHAPTER 6

WHITHER is thy beloved gone, [a]O thou fairest among women? whither is thy beloved turned aside? that we may seek him with thee.

2 My beloved is gone down into his [a]garden, to the beds of spices, to [1]feed in the gardens, and to gather lilies.

3 [a]I *am* my beloved's, and my beloved *is* mine: he [1]feedeth among the lilies.

4 Thou *art* beautiful, O my love, as Tirzah, [1]comely as Jerusalem, [2]terrible as *an army* with banners.

5 Turn away thine eyes from me, for they have [1]overcome me: thy hair *is* [a]as a flock of goats [2]that appear from Gilead.

6 [a]Thy teeth *are* as a flock of sheep which go up from the washing, whereof every one beareth twins, and *there is* not one [b]barren among them.

7 [a]As a piece of a pomegranate *are* thy temples [1]within thy locks.

8 There are threescore queens, and fourscore concubines, and [a]virgins without number.

9 My dove, my [a]undefiled[1] is *but* one; she *is* the *only* one of her mother, she *is* the choice *one* of her that bare her. The daughters saw her, and blessed her; *yea,* the queens and the concubines, and they praised her.

10 Who *is* she *that* looketh forth as the morning, fair as the moon, clear as the sun, [a]*and* [1]terrible as *an army* with banners?

11 I went down into the garden of nuts to see the fruits of the valley, *and* [a]to see whether the vine [1]flourished, *and* the pomegranates [2]budded.

12 [1]Or ever I was aware, my soul made me *like* the chariots of [2]Amminadib.

13 Return, return, O [1]Shulamite; return, return, that we may look upon thee. What will ye see in the Shulamite? As it were [2]the company of [3]two armies.

## CHAPTER 7

HOW beautiful are thy feet [1]with shoes, [a]O prince's daughter! the joints of thy thighs *are* like jewels, the work of the hands of a cunning workman.

2 Thy navel *is like* a round goblet, *which* [1]wanteth not liquor: thy belly *is like* an heap of wheat set about with lilies.

3 [a]Thy two breasts *are* like two [1]young roes *that are* [2]twins.

### Cross references (center column)

4:15 [a] Zech. 14:8; John 4:10; 7:38
4:16 [a] Song 5:1 [b] Song 7:13
5:1 [a] Song 4:16 [b] Song 4:9 [c] Song 4:11 [d] Luke 15:7, 10; John 3:29
5:2 [a] Rev. 3:20 [1] perfect one [2] covered [3] hair
5:3 [1] dirty
5:4 [1] latch or opening [2] heart yearned for him
5:5 [1] dripped [2] liquid myrrh
5:6 [a] Song 3:1 [1] my heart went out to him when
5:7 [a] Song 3:3 [1] struck
5:8 [1] lovesick
5:9 [a] Song 1:8; 6:1 [1] adjure
5:10 [1] distinguished
5:11 [1] wavy
5:12 [a] Song 1:15; 4:1 [1] sitting in a setting
5:13 [1] banks of scented herbs [2] dripping liquid myrrh
5:14 [1] rods [2] body
5:15 [1] bases
6:1 [a] Song 1:8; 5:9
6:2 [a] Song 4:16; 5:1 [1] feed his flock
6:3 [a] Song 2:16; 7:10 [1] feeds his flock
6:4 [1] lovely [2] awesome
6:5 [a] Song 4:1 [1] overwhelmed [2] going down from
6:6 [a] Song 4:2 [1] bereaved
6:7 [a] Song 4:3 [1] behind your veil
6:8 [a] Song 1:3
6:9 [a] Song 2:14; 5:2 [1] perfect one
6:10 [a] Song 6:4 [1] awesome
6:11 [a] Song 7:12 [1] had budded [2] bloomed
6:12 [1] Before I was even aware [2] Lit. My Noble People
6:13 [1] A Palestinian young woman [2] the dance [3] Heb. Mahanaim, lit. the double camp
7:1 [a] Ps. 45:13 [1] in sandals
7:2 [1] lacks no mixed wine
7:3 [a] Song 4:5 [1] fawns [2] twins of a gazelle

4 <sup>a</sup>Thy neck *is* as a tower of ivory; thine eyes *like* the <sup>1</sup>fishpools in Heshbon, by the gate of Bath-rabbim: thy nose *is* as the tower of Lebanon which looketh toward Damascus.

5 Thine head upon thee *is* like <sup>1</sup>Carmel, and the hair of thine head like purple; the king *is* <sup>2</sup>held in the galleries.

6 How fair and how pleasant art thou, O love, for delights!

7 This thy stature is like to a palm tree, and thy breasts to clusters *of grapes.*

8 I said, I will go up to the palm tree, I will take hold of the boughs thereof: now also thy breasts shall be as clusters of the vine, and the <sup>1</sup>smell of thy nose like apples;

9 And the roof of thy mouth like the best wine for my beloved, that goeth *down* <sup>1</sup>sweetly, <sup>2</sup>causing the lips of those that are asleep to speak.

10 <sup>a</sup>I *am* my beloved's, and <sup>b</sup>his desire *is* toward me.

11 Come, my beloved, let us go forth into the field; let us lodge in the villages.

12 Let us get up early to the vineyards; let us <sup>a</sup>see if the vine <sup>1</sup>flourish, *whether* the <sup>2</sup>tender grape appear, *and* the pomegranates bud forth: there will I give thee my loves.

13 The <sup>a</sup>mandrakes give a <sup>1</sup>smell, and at our gates <sup>b</sup>*are* all manner of pleasant *fruits,* new and old, *which* I have laid up for thee, O my beloved.

## CHAPTER 8

O THAT thou *wert* as my brother, that <sup>1</sup>sucked the breasts of my mother! *when* I should find thee <sup>2</sup>without, I would kiss thee; yea, I should not be despised.

2 I would lead thee, *and* bring thee into my mother's <sup>a</sup>house, *who* would instruct me: I would cause thee to drink of <sup>b</sup>spiced wine of the juice of my pomegranate.

---

7:4 <sup>a</sup> Song 4:4
<sup>1</sup> *pools*

7:5 <sup>1</sup> Mount
Carmel <sup>2</sup> *held captive by thy tresses*

7:8 <sup>1</sup> *fragrance of thy breath*

7:9 <sup>1</sup> *smoothly*
<sup>2</sup> *moving gently or gliding over the lips of those that sleep*

7:10 <sup>a</sup> Song 2:16;
6:3 <sup>b</sup> Ps. 45:11

7:12 <sup>a</sup> Song 6:11
<sup>1</sup> *has budded*
<sup>2</sup> *grape blossoms are open*

7:13 <sup>a</sup> Gen. 30:14
<sup>b</sup> Song 2:3; 4:13,
16; Matt. 13:52
<sup>1</sup> *fragrance*

8:1 <sup>1</sup> *nursed*
<sup>2</sup> *outside*

8:2 <sup>a</sup> Song 3:4
<sup>b</sup> Prov. 9:2

8:3 <sup>a</sup> Song 2:6

8:4 <sup>a</sup> Song 2:7; 3:5

8:5 <sup>a</sup> Song 3:6
<sup>1</sup> *awakened*

8:6 <sup>a</sup> Is. 49:16; Jer.
22:24; Hag. 2:23
<sup>b</sup> Prov. 6:34, 35
<sup>1</sup> *severe,* lit. *hard*
<sup>2</sup> *flames*

8:7 <sup>a</sup> Prov. 6:35
<sup>1</sup> *wealth* <sup>2</sup> *despised*

8:8 <sup>a</sup> Ezek. 23:33

8:9 <sup>1</sup> *battlement*

8:10 <sup>1</sup> Lit. *peace*

8:11 <sup>a</sup> Matt. 21:33

8:13 <sup>a</sup> Song 2:14

8:14 <sup>a</sup> Rev. 22:17,
20 <sup>b</sup> Song 2:7, 9,
17 <sup>1</sup> *Hurry,* lit. *Flee*
<sup>2</sup> *gazelle* <sup>3</sup> *stag*

---

3 <sup>a</sup>His left hand *should be* under my head, and his right hand should embrace me.

4 <sup>a</sup>I charge you, O daughters of Jerusalem, that ye stir not up, nor awake *my* love, until he please.

5 <sup>a</sup>Who *is* this that cometh up from the wilderness, leaning upon her beloved? I <sup>1</sup>raised thee up under the apple tree: there thy mother brought thee forth: there she brought thee forth *that* bare thee.

6 <sup>a</sup>Set me as a seal upon thine heart, as a seal upon thine arm: for love *is* strong as death; <sup>b</sup>jealousy *is* <sup>1</sup>cruel as the grave: the <sup>2</sup>coals thereof *are* coals of fire, *which hath* a most vehement flame.

7 Many waters cannot quench love, neither can the floods drown it: <sup>a</sup>if a man would give all the <sup>1</sup>substance of his house for love, it would utterly be <sup>2</sup>contemned.

8 <sup>a</sup>We have a little sister, and she hath no breasts: what shall we do for our sister in the day when she shall be spoken for?

9 If she *be* a wall, we will build upon her a <sup>1</sup>palace of silver: and if she *be* a door, we will inclose her with boards of cedar.

10 I *am* a wall, and my breasts like towers: then was I in his eyes as one that found <sup>1</sup>favour.

11 Solomon had a vineyard at Baal-hamon; <sup>a</sup>he let out the vineyard unto keepers; every one for the fruit thereof was to bring a thousand *pieces* of silver.

12 My vineyard, which *is* mine, *is* before me: thou, O Solomon, *must have* a thousand, and those that keep the fruit thereof two hundred.

13 Thou that dwellest in the gardens, the companions hearken to thy voice: <sup>a</sup>cause me to hear *it.*

14 <sup>a</sup>Make<sup>1</sup> haste, my beloved, and <sup>b</sup>be thou like to a <sup>2</sup>roe or to a young <sup>3</sup>hart upon the mountains of spices.

# THE BOOK OF THE PROPHET

# ISAIAH

Isaiah is like a miniature Bible. The first thirty-nine chapters (like the thirty-nine books of the Old Testament) are filled with judgment upon immoral and idolatrous men. Judah has sinned; the surrounding nations have sinned; the whole earth has sinned. Judgment must come, for God cannot allow such blatant sin to go unpunished forever. But the final twenty-seven chapters (like the twenty-seven books of the New Testament) declare a message of hope. The Messiah is coming as a Savior and a Sovereign to bear a cross and to wear a crown.

Isaiah's prophetic ministry, spanning the reigns of four kings of Judah, covers at least forty years. *Yesha'yahu* and its shortened form *Yeshaiah* mean "Yahweh Is Salvation." This name is an excellent summary of the contents of the book. The Greek form in the Septuagint is *Hesaias*, and the Latin form is *Esaias* or *Isaias*.

## CHAPTER 1

THE ªvision of Isaiah the son of Amoz, which he saw concerning Judah and Jerusalem in the ᵇdays of Uzziah, Jotham, Ahaz, *and* Hezekiah, kings of Judah.

2 ªHear, O heavens, and give ear, O earth: for the LORD hath spoken, I have nourished and brought up children, and they have rebelled against me.

3 ªThe ox knoweth his owner, and the ass his master's ¹crib: *but* Israel ᵇdoth not ²know, my people doth not consider.

4 Ah sinful nation, a people ¹laden with iniquity, ªa seed of evildoers, children that are corrupters: they have forsaken the LORD, they have provoked the Holy One of Israel unto anger, they are ²gone away backward.

5 ªWhy should ye be stricken any more? ye will revolt more and more: the whole head is sick, and the whole heart faint.

6 From the sole of the foot even unto the head *there is* no soundness in it; *but* wounds, and bruises, and putrifying sores: they have not been closed, neither bound up, neither ¹mollified with ointment.

7 ªYour country *is* desolate, your cities *are* burned with fire: your land, strangers devour it in your presence, and *it is* desolate, as overthrown by strangers.

8 And ¹the daughter of Zion is left ªas a ²cottage in a vineyard, as a ³lodge in a garden of cucumbers, ᵇas a besieged city.

9 ªExcept the LORD of hosts had left unto us a very small remnant, we should have been as ᵇSodom, *and* we should have been like unto Gomorrah.

10 Hear the word of the LORD, ye rulers ªof Sodom; give ear unto the law of our God, ye people of Gomorrah.

11 To what purpose *is* the multitude of your ªsacrifices unto me? saith the LORD: I am full of the burnt offerings of rams, and the fat of fed beasts; and I delight not in the blood of bullocks, or of lambs, or of he goats.

12 When ye come ªto appear before me, who hath required this at your hand, to ¹tread my courts?

13 Bring no more ªvain¹ oblations; incense is an abomination unto me; the new moons and sabbaths, ᵇthe calling of assemblies, I cannot ⁹away with; *it is* iniquity, even the solemn meeting.

14 Your ªnew moons and your ᵇappointed feasts my soul hateth: they are a trouble unto me; I am weary to bear *them*.

15 And ªwhen ye ¹spread forth your hands, I will hide mine eyes from you: ᵇyea, when ye make many prayers, I will not hear: your hands are full of ²blood.

16 ªWash you, make you clean; put away the evil of your doings from before mine eyes; ᵇcease to do evil;

17 Learn to do well; seek ¹judgment, ²relieve the ³oppressed, ⁴judge the fatherless, plead for the widow.

18 Come now, and let us ªreason together, saith the LORD: though your sins be as scarlet, ᵇthey shall be as white as snow; though they be red like crimson, they shall be as wool.

19 If ye be willing and obedient, ye shall eat the good of the land:

20 But if ye refuse and rebel, ye shall be devoured with the sword: ªfor the mouth of the LORD hath spoken *it*.

21 ªHow is the faithful city become ¹an harlot! it was full of ²judgment; righteousness lodged in it; but now ᵇmurderers.

22 ªThy silver is become dross, thy wine mixed with water:

---

1:1 ª Num. 12:6
ᵇ 2 Chr. 26–32

1:2 ª Jer. 2:12

1:3 ª Jer. 8:7 ᵇ Jer. 9:3, 6 ¹ *manger or feed trough* ² *understand*

1:4 ª Matt. 3:7 ¹ *weighed down,* lit. *heavy* ² *turned*

1:5 ª Jer. 5:3

1:6 ¹ *soothed*

1:7 ª Deut. 28:51, 52

1:8 ª Job 27:18 ᵇ Jer. 4:17 ¹ *Jerusalem* ² *booth or shelter* ³ *hut*

1:9 ª Lam. 3:22 ᵇ Gen. 19:24

1:10 ª Deut. 32:32

1:11 ª [1 Sam. 15:22]

1:12 ª Ex. 23:17 ¹ *trample*

1:13 ª Matt. 15:9 ᵇ Joel 1:14 ¹ *futile sacrifices* ² *endure*

1:14 ª Num. 28:11 ᵇ Lam. 2:6

1:15 ª Prov. 1:28 ᵇ Mic. 3:4 ¹ *Pray* ² *bloodshed*

1:16 ª Jer. 4:14 ᵇ Rom. 12:9

1:17 ¹ *justice* ² *reprove* ³ MT *oppressor;* some ancient vss. *oppressed* ⁴ *vindicate or defend*

1:18 ª Is. 43:26 ᵇ Ps. 51:7

1:20 ª [Titus 1:2]

1:21 ª Jer. 2:20 ᵇ Mic. 3:1–3 ¹ Unfaithful ² *justice*

1:22 ª Jer. 6:28

23 <sup>a</sup>Thy princes *are* rebellious, and <sup>b</sup>companions of thieves: <sup>c</sup>every one loveth <sup>1</sup>gifts, and followeth after rewards: they <sup>d</sup>judge<sup>2</sup> not the fatherless, neither doth the cause of the widow come unto them.

24 Therefore saith the Lord, the LORD of hosts, the mighty One of Israel, Ah, <sup>a</sup>I will <sup>1</sup>ease me of mine adversaries, and avenge me of mine enemies:

25 And I will turn my hand upon thee, and <sup>a</sup>purely<sup>1</sup> purge away thy dross, and take away all thy <sup>2</sup>tin:

26 And I will restore thy judges <sup>a</sup>as at the first, and thy counsellors as at the beginning: afterward <sup>b</sup>thou shalt be called, The city of righteousness, the faithful city.

27 Zion shall be redeemed with <sup>1</sup>judgment, and her <sup>2</sup>converts with righteousness.

28 And the <sup>a</sup>destruction of the transgressors and of the sinners *shall be* together, and they that forsake the LORD shall be consumed.

29 For they shall be ashamed of the <sup>1</sup>oaks which ye have desired, and ye shall be <sup>2</sup>confounded for the gardens that ye have chosen.

30 For ye shall be as <sup>1</sup>an oak whose leaf fadeth, and as a garden that hath no water.

31 <sup>a</sup>And the strong shall be as <sup>1</sup>tow, and <sup>2</sup>the maker of it as a spark, and they shall both burn together, and none shall <sup>b</sup>quench *them*.

## CHAPTER 2

THE word that Isaiah the son of Amoz saw concerning Judah and Jerusalem.

2 And <sup>a</sup>it shall come to pass <sup>b</sup>in the last days, <sup>c</sup>*that* the mountain of the LORD's house shall be established in the top of the mountains, and shall be exalted above the hills; and all nations shall flow unto it.

3 And many people shall go and say, <sup>a</sup>Come ye, and let us go up to the mountain of the LORD, to the house of the God of Jacob; and he will teach us of his ways, and we will walk in his paths: <sup>b</sup>for out of Zion shall go forth the law, and the word of the LORD from Jerusalem.

4 And he shall judge among the nations, and shall rebuke many people: and they shall beat their swords into plowshares, and their spears into <sup>1</sup>pruninghooks: nation shall not lift up sword against nation, neither shall they learn war any more.

5 O house of Jacob, come ye, and let us <sup>a</sup>walk in the light of the LORD.

6 Therefore thou hast forsaken thy people the house of Jacob, because they <sup>1</sup>be replenished <sup>a</sup>from the east, and <sup>b</sup>*are* soothsayers like the Philis-

tines, <sup>c</sup>and they <sup>2</sup>please themselves in the children of strangers.

7 <sup>a</sup>Their land also is full of silver and gold, neither *is there any* end of their treasures; their land is also full of horses, neither *is there any* end of their chariots:

8 <sup>a</sup>Their land also is full of idols; they worship the work of their own hands, that which their own fingers have made:

9 And the <sup>1</sup>mean man boweth down, and <sup>2</sup>the great man humbleth himself: therefore forgive them not.

10 <sup>a</sup>Enter into the rock, and hide thee in the dust, <sup>1</sup>for fear of the LORD, and for the glory of his majesty.

11 The <sup>1</sup>lofty looks of man shall be <sup>a</sup>humbled, and the haughtiness of men shall be bowed down, and the LORD alone shall be exalted <sup>b</sup>in that day.

12 For the day of the LORD of hosts *shall be* upon every *one that is* proud and lofty, and upon every *one that is* lifted up; and he shall be brought low:

13 And upon all <sup>a</sup>the cedars of Lebanon, *that are* high and lifted up, and upon all the oaks of Bashan,

14 And <sup>a</sup>upon all the high mountains, and upon all the hills *that are* lifted up,

15 And upon every high tower, and upon every <sup>1</sup>fenced wall,

16 <sup>a</sup>And upon all the ships of Tarshish, and upon all <sup>1</sup>pleasant pictures.

17 And the <sup>1</sup>loftiness of man shall be bowed down, and the haughtiness of men shall be made low: and the LORD alone shall be exalted in that day.

18 And the idols <sup>1</sup>he shall utterly abolish.

19 And they shall go into the <sup>a</sup>holes of the rocks, and into the caves of the <sup>1</sup>earth, <sup>b</sup>for<sup>2</sup> fear of the LORD, and for the glory of his majesty, when he ariseth <sup>c</sup>to<sup>3</sup> shake terribly the earth.

20 In that day a man shall <sup>1</sup>cast his idols of silver, and his idols of gold, which they made *each one* for himself to worship, to the moles and to the bats;

21 To go into the clefts of the rocks, and into the <sup>1</sup>tops of the ragged rocks, <sup>2</sup>for fear of the LORD, and for the glory of his majesty, when he ariseth <sup>3</sup>to shake terribly the earth.

22 <sup>a</sup>Cease ye from man, whose <sup>b</sup>breath *is* in his nostrils: for <sup>1</sup>wherein is he to be accounted of?

## CHAPTER 3

FOR, behold, the Lord, the LORD of hosts, <sup>a</sup>doth take away from Jerusalem and from Judah <sup>b</sup>the <sup>1</sup>stay and

1:23 <sup>a</sup> Hos. 9:15
<sup>b</sup> Prov. 29:24
<sup>c</sup> Jer. 22:17  <sup>d</sup> Jer. 5:28  <sup>1</sup> *bribes*
<sup>2</sup> *defend* or *vindicate*
1:24 <sup>a</sup> Deut. 28:63
<sup>1</sup> *be relieved of*
1:25 <sup>a</sup> Mal. 3:3
<sup>1</sup> *thoroughly cleanse* or *refine with lye*  <sup>2</sup> *alloy*
1:26 <sup>a</sup> Jer. 33:7–11
<sup>b</sup> Zech. 8:3
1:27 <sup>1</sup> *justice*
<sup>2</sup> *penitents*, lit. *returners*
1:28 <sup>a</sup> [2 Thess. 1:8, 9]
1:29 <sup>1</sup> *terebinth trees*, sites of pagan worship
<sup>2</sup> *ashamed*
1:30 <sup>1</sup> *a terebinth tree*
1:31 <sup>a</sup> Ezek. 32:21
<sup>b</sup> Mark 9:43
<sup>1</sup> *tinder*  <sup>2</sup> *the work of it*
2:2 <sup>a</sup> Mic. 4:1
<sup>b</sup> Gen. 49:1  <sup>c</sup> Ps. 68:15
2:3 <sup>a</sup> Jer. 50:5
<sup>b</sup> Luke 24:47
2:4 <sup>1</sup> *pruning knives*
2:5 <sup>a</sup> Eph. 5:8
2:6 <sup>a</sup> Num. 23:7
<sup>b</sup> Deut. 18:14  <sup>c</sup> Ps. 106:35  <sup>1</sup> *are filled with eastern ways*
<sup>2</sup> *clap (shake) hands to make bargains with the children of foreigners*
2:7 <sup>a</sup> Deut. 17:16
2:8 <sup>a</sup> Jer. 2:28
2:9 <sup>1</sup> *people*
<sup>2</sup> *each man*
2:10 <sup>a</sup> Rev. 6:15, 16  <sup>1</sup> *from the terror of*
2:11 <sup>a</sup> Prov. 16:5  <sup>b</sup> Hos. 2:16
<sup>1</sup> *proud*
2:13 <sup>a</sup> Zech. 11:1, 2
2:14 <sup>a</sup> Is. 30:25
2:15 <sup>1</sup> *fortified*
2:16 <sup>a</sup> 1 Kin. 10:22
<sup>1</sup> *beautiful sloops*
2:17 <sup>1</sup> *pride*
2:18 <sup>1</sup> *vanish*
2:19 <sup>a</sup> Hos. 10:8
<sup>b</sup> [2 Thess. 1:9]
<sup>c</sup> Hag. 2:6, 7  <sup>1</sup> Lit. *dust*  <sup>2</sup> *from the terror*  <sup>3</sup> Lit. *to make the earth tremble*
2:20 <sup>1</sup> *cast away*
2:21 <sup>1</sup> *crags*
<sup>2</sup> *from the terror*
<sup>3</sup> Lit. *to make the earth tremble*
2:22 <sup>a</sup> Jer. 17:5
<sup>b</sup> Job 27:3  <sup>1</sup> *why should he be esteemed*  3:1 <sup>a</sup> Jer. 37:21  <sup>b</sup> Lev. 26:26
<sup>1</sup> *stock and the store, every support*

the staff, the whole ²stay of bread, and the whole ²stay of water,

2 ªThe mighty man, and the man of war, the judge, and the prophet, and the ¹prudent, and the ²ancient,

3 The captain of fifty, and the ¹honourable man, and the counsellor, and the ²cunning artificer, and the ³eloquent orator.

4 And I will give ªchildren¹ *to be* their princes, and ²babes shall rule over them.

5 And the people shall be oppressed, every one by another, and every one by his neighbour: the child shall ¹behave himself proudly against the ancient, and the ²base against the honourable.

6 When a man shall take hold of his brother of the house of his father, *saying,* Thou hast clothing, be thou our ruler, and *let* this ruin *be* under thy hand:

7 In that day shall he ¹swear, saying, I ²will not be an healer; for in my house *is* neither bread nor clothing: make me not a ruler of the people.

8 For ªJerusalem ¹is ruined, and Judah is fallen: because their tongue and their doings *are* against the LORD, to ²provoke the eyes of his glory.

9 The ¹shew of their countenance doth witness against them; and they declare their sin as ªSodom, they hide *it* not. Woe unto their soul! for they have ²rewarded evil unto themselves.

10 Say ye to the righteous, ªthat *it shall be* well *with him:* ᵇfor they shall eat the fruit of their doings.

11 Woe unto the wicked! ª*it shall be* ill *with him:* for the reward of his hands shall be ¹given him.

12 *As for* my people, children *are* their oppressors, and women rule over them. O my people, ªthey which lead thee ¹cause *thee* to err, and destroy the way of thy paths.

13 The LORD standeth up ªto ¹plead, and standeth to judge the people.

14 The LORD will enter into judgment with the ¹ancients of his people, and the princes thereof: for ye have ²eaten up ªthe vineyard; the ³spoil of the poor *is* in your houses.

15 What mean ye ¹*that* ye ªbeat my people to pieces, and ²grind the faces of the poor? saith the Lord GOD of hosts.

16 Moreover the LORD saith, Because the daughters of Zion are ¹haughty, and walk with ²stretched forth necks and ³wanton eyes, walking and ⁴mincing *as* they go, and making a ⁵tinkling with their feet:

17 Therefore the Lord will smite ªa scab the crown of the head of the daughters of Zion, and the LORD will ᵇdiscover¹ their secret parts.

18 In that day the Lord will take away the ¹bravery of *their* tinkling ornaments *about their feet,* and *their* ²cauls, and *their* ªround³ tires like the moon,

19 The ¹chains, and the bracelets, and the ²mufflers,

20 The ¹bonnets, and the ornaments of the legs, and the headbands, and the ²tablets, and the ³earrings,

21 The rings, and nose jewels,

22 The ¹changeable suits of apparel, and the mantles, and the ²wimples, and the ³crisping pins,

23 The ¹glasses, and the fine linen, and the ²hoods, and the ³vails.

24 And it shall come to pass, *that* instead of sweet smell there shall be stink; and instead of a ¹girdle a ²rent; and instead of well set hair ªbaldness; and instead of a ³stomacher a girding of sackcloth; *and* ⁴burning instead of beauty.

25 Thy men shall fall by the sword, and thy ¹mighty in the war.

26 ªAnd her gates shall lament and mourn; and she *being* desolate ᵇshall sit upon the ground.

## CHAPTER 4

AND ªin that day seven women shall take hold of one man, saying, We will ᵇeat our own bread, and wear our own apparel: only let us be called by thy name, to take away ᶜour reproach.

2 In that day shall ªthe branch of the LORD be beautiful and glorious, and the fruit of the earth *shall be* excellent and ¹comely for them that ²are escaped of Israel.

3 And it shall come to pass, *that* he that *is* left in Zion, and *he that* remaineth in Jerusalem, ªshall be called holy, *even* every one that is ᵇwritten¹ among the living in Jerusalem:

4 When ªthe LORD shall have washed away the filth of the daughters of Zion, and shall have purged the ¹blood of Jerusalem from the midst thereof by the spirit of judgment, and by the spirit of burning.

5 And the LORD will create upon every dwelling place of mount Zion, and upon her assemblies, ªa cloud and smoke by day, and ᵇthe shining of a flaming fire by night: for ¹upon all the glory *shall be* a ²defence.

6 And there shall be a tabernacle for a ¹shadow in the daytime from the heat, and ªfor a place of refuge, and for a ²covert from storm and from rain.

## CHAPTER 5

Now will I sing to my wellbeloved a song of my beloved ªtouching

---

*Center column notes:*

3:1 ² supply
3:2 ª 2 Kin. 24:14
¹ diviner ² elder
3:3 ¹ Eminent in appearance ² skilful artisan ³ expert enchanter
3:4 ª Eccl. 10:16
¹ boys ² Or capricious ones
3:5 ¹ be insolent against the aged ² despised
3:7 ¹ protest ² cannot cure your ills
3:8 ª Mic.
3:12 ¹ Lit. has stumbled ² rebel against
3:9 ª Gen. 13:13
¹ look on their faces ² brought
3:10 ª [Eccl. 8:12]
ᵇ Ps. 128:2
3:11 ª [Ps. 11:6]
¹ done to him
3:12 ª Is. 9:16
¹ lead thee astray
3:13 ª Mic. 6:2
¹ contend
3:14 ª Matt. 21:33 ¹ elders or aged ² burned ³ plunder
3:15 ª Mic. 3:2, 3 ¹ by crushing ² grinding
3:16 ¹ proud ² outstretched necks, heads held high ³ seductive ⁴ tripping or skipping ⁵ jingling
3:17 ª Deut. 28:27 ᵇ Jer. 13:22
¹ uncover
3:18 ª Judg. 8:21, 26 ¹ finery, jingling anklets ² scarves or headbands ³ crescents
3:19 ¹ pendants ² veils
3:20 ¹ headdresses ² perfume boxes ³ charms or amulets
3:22 ¹ festal apparel ² outer garments ³ purses
3:23 ¹ mirrors ² turbans ³ robes
3:24 ª Is. 22:12 ¹ sash ² rope ³ rich robe ⁴ a branding scar
3:25 ¹ Lit. strength
3:26 ª Jer. 14:2 ᵇ Lam. 2:10
4:1 ª Is. 2:11, 17 ᵇ 2 Thess. 3:12 ᶜ Luke 1:25
4:2 ª [Jer. 23:5] ¹ appealing

---

² have survived   4:3 ª Is. 60:21   ᵇ Phil. 4:3   ¹ recorded   4:4 ª Mal. 3:2, 3   ¹ bloodshed   4:5 ª Ex. 13:21, 22   ᵇ Zech. 2:5   ¹ over   ² covering   4:6 ª Is. 25:4   ¹ shade   ² shelter   5:1 ª Matt. 21:33

his vineyard. My wellbeloved hath a vineyard in a very fruitful hill:

2 And he [1]fenced it, and [2]gathered out the stones thereof, and planted it with the choicest vine, and built a tower in the midst of it, and also [3]made a winepress therein: [a]and he looked that it should bring forth grapes, and it brought forth wild grapes.

3 And now, O inhabitants of Jerusalem, and men of Judah, [a]judge, I pray you, betwixt me and my vineyard.

4 What could have been done more to my vineyard, that I have not done in [a]it? wherefore, when I looked that it should bring forth grapes, brought it forth wild grapes?

5 And now I [1]go to; I will tell you what I will do to my vineyard: [a]I will take away the hedge thereof, and it shall be [2]eaten up; *and* break down the wall thereof, and it shall be [3]trodden down:

6 And I will lay it [a]waste: it shall not be pruned, nor digged; but there shall come up briers and [b]thorns: I will also command the clouds that they rain no rain upon it.

7 For the vineyard of the LORD of hosts *is* the house of Israel, and the men of Judah his pleasant plant: and he looked for [1]judgment, but behold oppression; for righteousness, but behold a cry.

8 Woe unto them that [1]join [a]house to house, *that* [2]lay field to field, till *there be* no place, that they may [3]be placed alone in the midst of the [4]earth!

9 [a]In mine ears *said* the LORD of hosts, Of a truth many houses shall be desolate, *even* great and [1]fair, without inhabitant.

10 Yea, ten acres of vineyard shall yield one [a]bath,[1] and the seed of an [2]homer shall yield an ephah.

11 [a]Woe unto them that rise up early in the morning, *that* they may [1]follow strong drink; that continue until night, *till* wine inflame them!

12 And [a]the harp, and the [1]viol, the [2]tabret, and [3]pipe, and wine, are in their feasts: but [b]they regard not the work of the LORD, neither consider the operation of his hands.

13 [a]Therefore my people are gone into captivity, because *they have* no [b]knowledge: and their honourable men *are* famished, and their multitude dried up with thirst.

14 Therefore [a]hell hath enlarged herself, and opened her mouth without measure: and their glory, and their multitude, and their pomp, and he that rejoiceth, shall descend into it.

15 And [a]the [1]mean man shall be brought down, and [2]the mighty man

shall be humbled, and the eyes of the lofty shall be humbled:

16 But the LORD of hosts shall be [a]exalted in judgment, and God that is holy shall be [1]sanctified in righteousness.

17 Then shall the lambs feed [1]after their manner, and [2]the waste places of [a]the [3]fat ones shall strangers eat.

18 Woe unto them that [1]draw iniquity with cords of [2]vanity, and sin as it were with a cart rope:

19 [a]That say, Let him make speed, *and* hasten his [1]work, that we may see *it:* and let the counsel of the Holy One of Israel draw nigh and come, that we may know *it!*

20 Woe unto them that call evil good, and good evil; that put darkness for light, and light for darkness; that put bitter for sweet, and sweet for bitter!

21 Woe unto *them that are* [a]wise in their own eyes, and prudent in their own sight!

22 Woe unto *them that are* mighty to drink wine, and men of strength to mingle strong drink:

23 Which [a]justify the wicked for [1]reward, and take away the righteousness of the righteous from him!

24 Therefore [a]as [1]the fire devoureth the stubble, and the flame consumeth the chaff, *so* [b]their root shall be as rottenness, and their blossom shall go up as dust: because they have cast away the law of the LORD of hosts, and despised the word of the Holy One of Israel.

25 [a]Therefore is the anger of the LORD kindled against his people, and he hath stretched forth his hand against them, and hath [1]smitten them: and [b]the hills did tremble, and their carcases [2]*were* torn in the midst of the streets. [c]For all this his anger is not turned away, but his hand *is* stretched out still.

26 [a]And he will lift up [1]an ensign to the nations from far, and will [b]hiss[2] unto them from [c]the end of the earth: and, behold, [d]they shall come with speed swiftly:

27 None shall be weary nor stumble among them; none shall slumber nor sleep; neither [a]shall the [1]girdle of their loins be loosed, nor the [2]latchet of their shoes be broken:

28 [a]Whose arrows *are* sharp, and all their bows bent, their horses' hoofs shall be counted like flint, and their wheels like a whirlwind:

29 Their roaring *shall* be like a lion, they shall roar like young lions: yea, they shall roar, and lay hold of the prey, and shall carry *it* away safe, and none shall deliver *it.*

30 And in that day they shall roar against them like the roaring of the

5:2 [a] Deut. 32:6 [1] *dug it up* [2] *cleared* [3] Lit. *hewed out*

5:3 [a] [Rom. 3:4]

5:4 [a] 2 Chr. 36:15, 16

5:5 [a] Ps. 80:12; 89:40, 41 [1] *come* [2] *burned* or *consumed* [3] *trampled down*

5:6 [a] 2 Chr. 36:19–21 [b] Is. 7:19–25

5:7 [1] *justice*

5:8 [a] Mic. 2:2 [1] *Accumulate houses* [2] *Accumulate fields* [3] *dwell* [4] *land*

5:9 [a] Is. 22:14 [1] *beautiful ones*

5:10 [a] Ezek. 45:11 [1] 1 bath = 1/10 homer [2] 1 homer = 1/10 ephah

5:11 [a] Prov. 23:29, 30 [1] *pursue intoxicating drink*

5:12 [a] Amos 6:5 [b] Job 34:27 [1] *strings* [2] *tambourine* [3] *flute*

5:13 [a] 2 Kin. 24:14–16 [b] Hos. 4:6

5:14 [1] Or *Sheol*

5:15 [a] Is. 2:9, 11 [1] *people* [2] *each man*

5:16 [a] Is. 2:11 [1] *hallowed*

5:17 [a] Is. 10:16 [1] *in their pasture* [2] *in the* [3] *Rich ones,* lit. *fatlings*

5:18 [1] *drag* [2] *falsehood* or *emptiness*

5:19 [a] Jer. 17:15 [1] *work* of judgment

5:21 [a] Rom. 1:22; 12:16

5:23 [a] Prov. 17:15 [1] *a bribe*

5:24 [a] Ex. 15:7 [b] Job 18:16 [1] Lit. *the tongue of fire*

5:25 [a] 2 Kin. 22:13, 17 [b] Jer. 4:24 [c] Is. 9:12, 17 [1] *stricken* [2] *were as refuse*

5:26 [a] Is. 11:10, 12 [b] Is. 7:18 [c] Mal. 1:11 [d] Joel 2:7 [1] *a banner* [2] *whistle*

5:27 [a] Dan. 5:6 [1] *belt on* [2] *strap of their sandals*

5:28 [a] Jer. 5:16

sea: and if *one* [a]look unto the land, behold darkness *and* [1]sorrow, and the light is darkened [2]in the heavens thereof.

## CHAPTER 6

IN the year that [a]king Uzziah died I [b]saw also the Lord sitting upon a throne, high and lifted up, and [1]his train filled the temple.

2 Above it stood the seraphims: each one had six wings; with [1]twain he covered his face, and [a]with twain he covered his feet, and with twain he did fly.

3 And one cried unto another, and said, [a]Holy, holy, holy, *is* the LORD of hosts: [b]the whole earth *is* full of his glory.

4 And the posts of the door [1]moved at the voice of him that [2]cried, and the house was filled with smoke.

5 Then said I, Woe *is* me! for I am [1]undone; because I *am* a man of [a]unclean lips, and I dwell in the midst of a people of unclean lips: for mine eyes have seen the King, the LORD of hosts.

6 Then flew one of the seraphims unto me, having a live coal in his hand, *which* he had taken with the tongs from off [a]the altar:

7 And he [a]laid *it* upon my mouth, and said, Lo, this hath touched thy lips; and thine iniquity is taken away, and thy sin [1]purged.

8 Also I heard the voice of the Lord, saying, Whom shall I send, and who will go for [a]us? Then said I, Here *am* I; send me.

9 And he said, Go, and [a]tell this people, [1]Hear ye indeed, but understand not; and [2]see ye indeed, but perceive not.

10 Make [a]the heart of this people [1]fat, and make their ears heavy, and shut their eyes; [b]lest they see with their eyes, and hear with their ears, and understand with their heart, and convert, and be healed.

11 Then said I, Lord, how long? And he answered, [a]Until the cities be wasted without inhabitant, and the houses without man, and the land be utterly desolate,

12 [a]And the LORD have removed men far away, and *there be* [1]a great forsaking in the midst of the land.

13 But yet in it *shall be* a tenth, and *it* shall return, and shall be [1]eaten: as a [2]teil tree, and as an oak, whose [3]substance *is* in them, when they cast their *leaves: so* [a]the holy seed *shall be* [4]the substance thereof.

## CHAPTER 7

AND it came to pass in the days of [a]Ahaz the son of Jotham, the son of Uzziah, king of Judah, *that* Rezin

---

*Center column notes:*

5:30 [a] Is. 8:22
[1] distress   [2] by the clouds

6:1 [a] 2 Kin. 15:7
[b] John 12:41   [1] the train of his robe

6:2 [a] Ezek. 1:11
[1] two

6:3 [a] Rev. 4:8
[b] Num. 14:21

6:4 [1] were shaken
[2] cried out

6:5 [a] Ex. 6:12, 30
[1] destroyed

6:6 [a] Rev. 8:3

6:7 [a] Jer. 1:9
[1] atoned for or covered

6:8 [a] Gen. 1:26

6:9 [a] Matt. 13:14   [1] Keep on listening   [2] keep on seeing

6:10 [a] Ps. 119:70
[b] Jer. 5:21   [1] dull, lit. fat

6:11 [a] Mic. 3:12

6:12 [a] 2 Kin. 25:21
[1] many forsaken places

6:13 [a] Ezra 9:2
[1] for consuming
[2] terebinth tree
[3] stump remains when it is cut down   [4] its stump

7:1 [a] 2 Chr. 28

[b] 2 Kin. 16:5, 9
[1] conquer it

7:2 [1] has encamped in or has deployed its forces in   [2] shaken

7:3 [1] Lit. A Remnant Shall Return
[2] aqueduct

7:4 [a] Is. 30:15   [1] Be careful   [2] be calm
[3] stubs

7:5 [1] plotted evil

7:6 [1] trouble
[2] gap in its wall

7:7 [a] Is. 8:10

7:8 [a] 2 Sam. 8:6
[1] Lit. shattered

7:9 [a] 2 Chr. 20:20

7:11 [a] Matt. 12:38
[1] Lit. make the request deep or make it high above

7:12 [1] test

7:14 [a] Matt. 1:23
[b] [Is. 9:6]   [c] Is. 8:8, 10   [1] Lit. God With Us

7:15 [1] Curds

7:16 [a] Is. 8:4
[b] 2 Kin. 15:30
[1] dread

7:17 [a] 2 Chr. 28:19, 20   [1] Kin. 12:16

7:18 [a] Is. 5:26
[1] whistle

---

the king of Syria, and Pekah the son of Remaliah, king of Israel, went up toward Jerusalem to war against [b]it, but could not [1]prevail against it.

2 And it was told the house of David, saying, Syria [1]is confederate with Ephraim. And his heart was [2]moved, and the heart of his people, as the trees of the wood are moved with the wind.

3 Then said the LORD unto Isaiah, Go forth now to meet Ahaz, thou, and [1]Shear-jashub thy son, at the end of the [2]conduit of the upper pool in the highway of the fuller's field;

4 And say unto him, [1]Take heed, and [2]be [a]quiet; fear not, neither be fainthearted for the two [3]tails of these smoking firebrands, for the fierce anger of Rezin with Syria, and of the son of Remaliah.

5 Because Syria, Ephraim, and the son of Remaliah, have [1]taken evil counsel against thee, saying,

6 Let us go up against Judah, and [1]vex it, and let us make a [2]breach therein for us, and set a king in the midst of it, *even* the son of Tabeal:

7 Thus saith the Lord GOD, [a]It shall not stand, neither shall it come to pass.

8 [a]For the head of Syria *is* Damascus, and the head of Damascus *is* Rezin; and within threescore and five years shall Ephraim be [1]broken, that it be not a people.

9 And the head of Ephraim *is* Samaria, and the head of Samaria *is* Remaliah's son. [a]If ye will not believe, surely ye shall not be established.

10 Moreover the LORD spake again unto Ahaz, saying,

11 [a]Ask thee a sign of the LORD thy God; [1]ask it either in the depth, or in the height above.

12 But Ahaz said, I will not ask, neither will I [1]tempt the LORD.

13 And he said, Hear ye now, O house of David; *Is it* a small thing for you to weary men, but will ye weary my God also?

14 Therefore the Lord himself shall give you a sign; [a]Behold, a virgin shall conceive, and bear [b]a son, and shall call his name [c]Immanuel.[1]

15 [1]Butter and honey shall he eat, that he may know to refuse the evil, and choose the good.

16 [a]For before the child shall know to refuse the evil, and choose the good, the land that thou [1]abhorrest shall be forsaken of [b]both her kings.

17 [a]The LORD shall bring upon thee, and upon thy people, and upon thy father's house, days that have not come, from the day that [b]Ephraim departed from Judah; *even* the king of Assyria.

18 And it shall come to pass in that day, *that* the LORD [a]shall [1]hiss for the

fly that *is* in the uttermost part of the rivers of Egypt, and for the bee that *is* in the land of Assyria.

19 And they shall come, and shall rest all of them in the desolate valleys, and in ªthe ¹holes of the rocks, and upon all thorns, and ²upon all bushes.

20 In the same day shall the Lord shave with a ªrazor that is ᵇhired, *namely,* by them beyond ¹the river, by the king of Assyria, the head, and the hair of the ²feet: and it shall also ³consume the beard.

21 And it shall come to pass in that day, *that* a man shall ¹nourish a young cow, and two sheep;

22 And it shall come to pass, ¹for the abundance of milk *that* they shall give he shall eat ²butter: for butter and honey shall every one eat that is left in the land.

23 And it shall come to pass in that day, *that* every place ¹shall be, where there were a thousand vines ²at a thousand silverlings, ªit shall *even* be for briers and thorns.

24 With arrows and with bows shall *men* come thither; because all the land shall become briers and thorns.

25 And *on* all hills that ¹shall be digged with the mattock, there shall not come thither the fear of briers and thorns: but it shall be for the sending forth of oxen, and for the treading of ²lesser cattle.

## CHAPTER 8

MOREOVER the Lord said unto me, Take thee a great roll, and ªwrite in it with a man's pen concerning ¹Maher-shalal-hash-baz.

2 And I took unto me faithful witnesses to record, ªUriah the priest, and Zechariah the son of Jeberechiah.

3 And I went unto the prophetess; and she conceived, and bare a son. Then said the Lord to me, Call his name Maher-shalal-hash-baz.

4 ªFor before the child shall have knowledge to cry, My father, and my mother, ᵇthe riches of Damascus and the ¹spoil of Samaria shall be taken away before the king of Assyria.

5 The Lord spake also unto me again, saying,

6 Forasmuch as this people refuseth the waters of ªShiloah that go softly, and rejoice ᵇin Rezin and Remaliah's son;

7 Now therefore, behold, the Lord bringeth up upon them the waters of ¹the river, strong and ²many, *even* the king of Assyria, and all his glory: and he shall come up over all his channels, and go over all his banks:

8 And he shall pass through Judah; he shall overflow and go over, ªhe

7:19 ª Jer. 16:16
¹ clefts ² in all pastures
7:20 ª 2 Kin. 16:7
ᵇ Is. 10:5, 15 ¹ The Euphrates ² legs ³ remove
7:21 ¹ keep alive
7:22 ¹ from ² curds
7:23 ª Is. 5:6
¹ where there could be ² worth a thousand shekels of silver
7:25 ¹ could be ² sheep
8:1 ª Hab. 2:2
¹ Lit. Speed the Spoil, Hasten the Booty
8:2 ª 2 Kin. 16:10
8:4 ª 2 Kin. 17:6; Is. 7:16 ᵇ 2 Kin. 15:29 ¹ plunder
8:6 ª John 9:7 ᵇ Is. 7:1, 2
8:7 ¹ The Euphrates ² great or mighty
8:8 ª Is. 30:28
ᵇ Is. 7:14 ¹ Lit. God With Us
8:9 ª Joel 3:9 ¹ Be shattered ² be broken ³ but
8:10 ª Is. 7:7 ᵇ Is. 7:14 ᶜ Rom. 8:31 ¹ Heb. Immanuel
8:11 ¹ Mighty power
8:12 ¹ conspiracy ² Lit. in dread
8:13 ¹ Hallow
8:14 ª Ezek. 11:16 ᵇ Luke 2:34; 20:17 ¹ holy abode ² stumbling over ³ trap
8:15 ª Matt. 21:44 ¹ captured
8:17 ª Is. 54:8 ᵇ Hab. 2:3
8:18 ª Heb. 2:13 ᵇ Ps. 71:7
8:19 ª 1 Sam. 28:8 ᵇ Is. 29:4 ᶜ Ps. 106:28 ¹ are mediums ² whisper ³ than the dead in behalf of the living
8:20 ª Luke 16:29 ᵇ Mic. 3:6 ¹ Or they have no dawn
8:21 ª Rev. 16:11 ¹ hard-pressed ² be enraged ³ curse by
8:22 ¹ gloom
9:1 ª Is. 8:22 ᵇ 2 Kin. 15:29 ¹ gloom ² upon her who is distressed, as when ³ esteemed

shall reach *even* to the neck; and the stretching out of his wings shall fill the breadth of thy land, O ᵇImmanuel.¹

9 ªAssociate¹ yourselves, O ye people, and ²ye shall be broken in pieces; and give ear, all ye of far countries: gird yourselves, ²and ye shall be broken in pieces; gird yourselves, ³and ye shall be broken in pieces.

10 ªTake counsel together, and it shall come to nought; speak the word, ᵇand it shall not stand: ᶜfor ¹God *is* with us.

11 For the Lord spake thus to me with ¹a strong hand, and instructed me that I should not walk in the way of this people, saying,

12 Say ye not, A ¹confederacy, to all *them to* whom this people shall say, A confederacy; neither fear ye their fear, nor be ²afraid.

13 ¹Sanctify the Lord of hosts himself; and *let* him *be* your fear, and *let* him *be* your dread.

14 And ªhe shall be for a ¹sanctuary; but for ᵇa stone of stumbling and for a rock of ²offence to both the houses of Israel, for a ³gin and for a snare to the inhabitants of Jerusalem.

15 And many among them shall ªstumble, and fall, and be broken, and be snared, and be ¹taken.

16 Bind up the testimony, seal the law among my disciples.

17 And I will wait upon the Lord, that ªhideth his face from the house of Jacob, and I ᵇwill look for him.

18 ªBehold, I and the children whom the Lord hath given me ᵇare for signs and for wonders in Israel from the Lord of hosts, which dwelleth in mount Zion.

19 And when they shall say unto you, ªSeek unto them that ¹have familiar spirits, and unto wizards ᵇthat ²peep, and that mutter: should not a people seek unto their God? ³for the living ᶜto the dead?

20 ªTo the law and to the testimony: if they speak not according to this word,¹ *it is* because ᵇ*there is* no light in them.

21 And they shall pass through it, ¹hardly bestead and hungry: and it shall come to pass, that when they shall be hungry, they shall ²fret themselves, and ªcurse³ their king and their God, and look upward.

22 And they shall look unto the earth; and behold trouble and darkness, ¹dimness of anguish; and *they shall be* driven to darkness.

## CHAPTER 9

NEVERTHELESS ªthe ¹dimness *shall* not *be* ²such as *was* in her vexation, when at the ᵇfirst he lightly ³afflicted the land of Zebulun and the

land of Naphtali, and [c]afterward [4]did more grievously afflict *her by* the way of the sea, beyond Jordan, in Galilee of the [5]nations.

2 [a]The people that walked in darkness have seen a great light: they that dwell in the land of the shadow of death, upon them hath the light shined.

3 Thou hast multiplied the nation, *and* [1]not increased the joy: they joy before thee according to the joy in harvest, *and as* men rejoice [a]when they divide the [2]spoil.

4 For thou hast broken the yoke of his burden, and the staff of his shoulder, the rod of his oppressor, as in the day of [a]Midian.

5 For every [1]battle of the warrior [2]*is* with confused noise, and garments rolled in blood; [a]but[3] *this* shall be with burning *and* fuel [4]of fire.

6 [a]For unto us a child is born, unto us a [b]son is given: and [c]the government shall be upon his shoulder: and his name shall be called [d]Wonderful, Counsellor, [e]The mighty God, The everlasting Father, [f]The Prince of Peace.

7 Of the increase of *his* government and peace [a]*there shall be* no end, upon the throne of David, and upon his kingdom, to order it, and to establish it with judgment and with justice from henceforth even for ever. The [b]zeal of the LORD of hosts will perform this.

8 The Lord sent a word [1]into [a]Jacob, and it hath [1]lighted upon Israel.

9 And all the people shall know, *even* Ephraim and the inhabitant of Samaria, that say in the pride and [1]stoutness of heart,

10 The bricks are fallen down, but we will build with hewn stones: the sycomores are cut down, but we will [1]change *them into* cedars.

11 Therefore the LORD shall set up the adversaries of Rezin against him, and [1]join his enemies together;

12 The Syrians before, and the Philistines behind; and they shall devour Israel with open mouth. For all this his anger is not turned away, but his hand *is* [1]stretched out still.

13 For the people turneth not unto him that [1]smiteth them, neither do they seek the LORD of hosts.

14 Therefore the LORD will cut off from Israel head and tail, [1]branch and [2]rush, [a]in one day.

15 The [1]ancient and honourable, he *is* the head; and the prophet that teacheth lies, he *is* the tail.

16 For [a]the leaders of this people cause *them* to err; and *they that are* led of them *are* destroyed.

17 Therefore the Lord [a]shall have no joy in their young men, neither shall have mercy on their father-

less and widows: for every one *is* an hypocrite and an evildoer, and every mouth speaketh [1]folly. [b]For all this his anger is not turned away, but his hand *is* [2]stretched out still.

18 For wickedness [a]burneth as the fire: it shall devour the briers and thorns, and shall kindle in the thickets of the forest, and they shall mount up *like* [1]the lifting up of smoke.

19 Through the wrath of the LORD of hosts is [a]the land [1]darkened, and the people shall be [2]as the fuel of the fire: [b]no man shall spare his brother.

20 And he shall [1]snatch on the right hand, and be hungry; and he shall eat on the left hand, [a]and they shall not be satisfied: [b]they shall eat every man the flesh of his own arm:

21 [1]Manasseh, Ephraim; and Ephraim, Manasseh: *and* they together *shall be* [a]against Judah. [b]For all this his anger is not turned away, but his hand *is* [2]stretched out still.

## CHAPTER 10

WOE unto them that [a]decree unrighteous decrees, and that write [1]grievousness *which* they have prescribed;

2 To [1]turn aside the needy [2]from judgment, and to take away [3]the right from the poor of my people, that widows may be their prey, and *that* they may rob the fatherless!

3 And [a]what will ye do in [b]the day of [1]visitation, and in the desolation *which* shall come from [c]far? to whom will ye flee for help? and where will ye leave your glory?

4 Without me they shall bow down [1]under the [a]prisoners, and they shall fall [1]under the slain. [b]For all this his anger is not turned away, but his hand *is* [2]stretched out still.

5 [1]O Assyrian, [a]the rod of mine anger, and the staff in their hand is mine indignation.

6 I will send him against [a]an[1] hypocritical nation, and against the people of my wrath will I [b]give him a charge, to [2]take the spoil, and to take the prey, and to tread them down like the mire of the streets.

7 [a]Howbeit he meaneth not so, neither doth his heart think so; but *it is* in his heart to destroy and cut off nations not a few.

8 [a]For he saith, *Are* not my princes [1]altogether kings?

9 *Is* not [a]Calno [b]as Carchemish? *is* not Hamath as Arpad? *is* not Samaria [c]as Damascus?

10 As my hand hath found the kingdoms of the idols, and whose graven images did excel them of Jerusalem and of Samaria;

---

9:1 [c] Matt. 4:13–16
[4] Or *he shall glorify the way*
[5] *Gentiles*
9:2 [a] Matt. 4:16
9:3 [a] Judg. 5:30
[1] Qr. *increased*
[2] *plunder*
9:4 [a] Judg. 7:22
9:5 [a] Is. 66:15
[1] *sandal or boot*
[2] *from the noisy battle* [3] *shall be used for burning*
[4] *for*
9:6 [a] [Luke 2:11]
[b] [John 3:16]
[c] [Matt. 28:18]
[d] Judg. 13:18
[e] Titus 2:13 [f] Eph. 2:14
9:7 [a] Dan. 2:44
[b] Is. 37:32
9:8 [a] Gen. 32:28
[1] *against* [2] *fallen*
9:9 [1] *arrogance*
9:10 [1] *replace them with cedars*
9:11 [1] *spur his enemies on*
9:12 [1] *stretched out in judgment*
9:13 [1] *strikes*
9:14 [a] Rev. 18:8
[1] *palm branch*
[2] *bulrush*
9:15 [1] *elder*
9:16 [a] Is. 3:12
9:17 [a] Ps. 147:10 [b] Is. 5:25
[1] *foolishness*
[2] *stretched out in judgment*
9:18 [a] Mal. 4:1
[1] *rising*
9:19 [a] Is. 8:22
[b] Mic. 7:2, 6
[1] *burned up* [2] *as fuel for*
9:20 [a] Lev. 26:26
[b] Jer. 19:9 [1] *slice off or tear*
9:21 [a] 2 Chr. 28:6, 8 [b] Is. 9:12, 17
[1] *Manasseh shall devour Ephraim*
[2] *stretched out in judgment*
10:1 [a] Ps. 58:2
[1] *misfortune*
10:2 [1] *deprive*
[2] *justice* [3] *what is right*
10:3 [a] Job 31:14
[b] Hos. 9:7 [c] Is. 5:26 [1] *punishment*
10:4 [a] Is. 24:22
[b] Is. 5:25 [1] *among*
[2] *stretched out in judgment*
10:5 [a] Jer. 51:20
[1] *Woe to Assyria*
10:6 [a] Is. 9:17
[b] Jer. 34:22 [1] *an ungodly* [2] *seize the plunder*
10:7 [a] Gen. 50:20   10:8 [a] 2 Kin. 19:10 [1] *all*
10:9 [a] Amos 6:2 [b] 2 Chr. 35:20 [c] 2 Kin. 16:9

11 Shall I not, as I have done unto Samaria and her idols, so do to Jerusalem and her idols?

12 Wherefore it shall come to pass, *that* when the Lord hath [1]performed his whole work [a]upon mount Zion and on Jerusalem, [b]I will punish the fruit of the [2]stout heart of the king of Assyria, and the glory of his [3]high looks.

13 [a]For he saith, By the strength of my hand I have done *it,* and by my wisdom; for I am prudent: and I have removed the [1]bounds of the people, and have robbed their treasures, and I have put down the inhabitants like a [2]valiant *man:*

14 And [a]my hand hath found as a nest the riches of the people: and as one gathereth eggs *that are* left, have I gathered all the earth; and there was none that moved the wing, or opened the mouth, or peeped.

15 Shall [a]the axe boast itself against him that [1]heweth therewith? *or* shall the saw magnify itself against him that [2]shaketh it? as if the rod should [3]shake *itself* against them that lift it up, *or* as if the staff should lift up *itself, as if it were* no wood.

16 Therefore shall the Lord, the [1]Lord of hosts, send among his fat ones leanness; and under his glory he shall kindle a burning like the burning of a fire.

17 And the light of Israel shall be for a fire, and his Holy One for a flame: [a]and it shall burn and devour his thorns and his briers in one day;

18 And shall consume the glory of his forest, and of [a]his fruitful field, both soul and body: and they shall be as when a standardbearer fainteth.

19 And the rest of the trees of his forest shall be few, that a child may write them.

20 And it shall come to pass in that day, *that* the remnant of Israel, and such as are escaped of the house of Jacob, [a]shall no more again [1]stay upon him that [2]smote them; but shall [1]stay upon the LORD, the Holy One of Israel, in truth.

21 The remnant shall return, *even* the remnant of Jacob, unto the [a]mighty God.

22 [a]For though thy people Israel be as the sand of the sea, [b]*yet* a remnant of them shall return: the [1]consumption decreed shall overflow with righteousness.

23 [a]For the Lord GOD of hosts shall make a [1]consumption, even determined, in the midst of all the land.

24 Therefore thus saith the Lord GOD of hosts, O my people that dwellest in Zion, [a]be not afraid of the Assyrian: he shall [1]smite thee with a rod, and shall lift up his staff against thee, after the manner of [b]Egypt.

25 For yet a very little while, [a]and the indignation shall cease, [1]and mine anger in their destruction.

26 And the LORD of hosts shall stir up [a]a scourge for him according to the slaughter of [b]Midian at the rock of Oreb: and [c]*as* his rod *was* upon the sea, so shall he lift it up after the manner of Egypt.

27 And it shall come to pass in that day, *that* his burden shall be taken away from off thy shoulder, and his yoke from off thy neck, and the yoke shall be destroyed because of [a]the [1]anointing.

28 He is come to Aiath, he is passed to Migron; at Michmash he hath laid up his [1]carriages:

29 They are gone [1]over [a]the passage: they have taken up their lodging at Geba; Ramah is afraid; [b]Gibeah of Saul is fled.

30 Lift up thy voice, O daughter [a]of Gallim: cause it to be heard unto [b]Laish, O poor Anathoth.

31 [a]Madmenah [1]is removed; the inhabitants of Gebim [2]gather themselves to flee.

32 As yet shall he remain [a]at Nob that day: he shall [b]shake his [1]hand *against* the mount of [c]the daughter of Zion, the hill of Jerusalem.

33 Behold, the Lord, the LORD of hosts, shall [1]lop the bough with terror: and [a]the high ones of stature *shall be* hewn down, and the haughty shall be humbled.

34 And he shall cut down the thickets of the forest with iron, and Lebanon shall fall by a mighty one.

## CHAPTER 11

AND [a]there shall come forth a [1]rod out of the [2]stem of [b]Jesse, and [c]a Branch shall [3]grow out of his roots:

2 [a]And the spirit of the LORD shall rest upon him, the spirit of wisdom and understanding, the spirit of counsel and might, the spirit of knowledge and of the fear of the LORD;

3 And [1]shall make him of quick understanding in the fear of the LORD: and he shall not judge [2]after the sight of his eyes, neither [3]reprove after the hearing of his ears:

4 But [a]with righteousness shall he judge the poor, and [1]reprove with equity for the meek of the earth: and he shall [b]smite[2] the earth with the rod of his mouth, and with the breath of his lips shall he slay the wicked.

5 And righteousness shall be the [1]girdle of his loins, and faithfulness the [2]girdle of his reins.

6 [a]The wolf also shall dwell with the lamb, and the leopard shall lie down with the kid; and the calf and the young lion and the fatling together; and a little child shall lead them.

7 And the cow and the bear shall [1]feed; their young ones shall lie down together: and the lion shall eat straw like the ox.

8 And the [1]sucking child shall play on the hole of the [2]asp, and the weaned child shall put his hand [3]on the cockatrice' den.

9 [a]They shall not hurt nor destroy in all my holy mountain: for [b]the earth shall be full of the knowledge of the LORD, as the waters cover the sea.

10 [a]And in that day [b]there shall be a root of Jesse, which shall stand for [1]an [c]ensign of the people; [2]to it shall the [d]Gentiles seek: and his [3]rest shall be glorious.

11 And it shall come to pass in that day, *that* the Lord shall set his hand again the second time to recover the remnant of his people, which shall be left, [a]from Assyria, and from Egypt, and from Pathros, and from Cush, and from Elam, and from Shinar, and from Hamath, and from the [1]islands of the sea.

12 And he shall set up [1]an ensign for the nations, and shall assemble the outcasts of Israel, and gather together [a]the dispersed of Judah from the [2]four corners of the earth.

13 [a]The envy also of Ephraim shall depart, and the adversaries of Judah shall be cut off: Ephraim shall not envy Judah, and Judah shall not [1]vex Ephraim.

14 But they shall fly upon the shoulders of the Philistines toward the west; they shall [1]spoil them of the east together: [a]they shall lay their hand upon Edom and Moab; and the children of Ammon shall obey them.

15 And the LORD [a]shall utterly destroy the tongue of the Egyptian sea; and with his mighty wind shall he shake his [1]hand over [2]the river, and shall [3]smite it in the seven streams, and make *men* [4]go over dryshod.

16 And [a]there shall be an highway for the remnant of his people, which shall be left, from Assyria; [b]like as it was to Israel in the day that he came up out of the land of Egypt.

## CHAPTER 12

AND [a]in that day thou shalt say, O LORD, I will praise thee: though thou wast angry with me, thine anger is turned away, and thou comfortedst me.

2 Behold, God *is* my salvation; I will trust, and not be afraid: [a]for [1]the [b]LORD JEHOVAH *is* my strength and *my* song; he also is become my salvation.

3 Therefore with joy shall ye draw [a]water out of the wells of salvation.

4 And in that day shall ye say, [a]Praise the LORD, call upon his name,

[b]declare his [1]doings among the people, make mention that his [c]name is exalted.

5 [a]Sing unto the LORD; for he hath done excellent things: this *is* known in all the earth.

6 [a]Cry out and shout, thou inhabitant of Zion: for great *is* [b]the Holy One of Israel in the midst of thee.

## CHAPTER 13

THE [a]burden[1] of Babylon, which Isaiah the son of Amoz did see.

2 [a]Lift ye up a banner [b]upon the high mountain, [1]exalt the voice unto them, [c]shake[2] the hand, that they may go into the gates of the nobles.

3 I have commanded my [1]sanctified ones, I have also called [a]my mighty ones for mine anger, *even* them that [b]rejoice in my [2]highness.

4 The [a]noise of a multitude in the mountains, like as of [1]a great people; a tumultuous noise of the kingdoms of nations gathered together: the LORD of hosts mustereth the host of the battle.

5 They come from a far country, from the end of heaven, *even* the [a]LORD, and the weapons of his indignation, to destroy the whole [b]land.

6 Howl ye; [a]for the day of the LORD *is* at hand; [b]it shall come as a destruction from the Almighty.

7 Therefore shall all hands [1]be faint, and every man's heart shall melt:

8 And they shall be afraid: [a]pangs[1] and sorrows shall take hold of them; they shall be in pain as a woman [2]that travaileth: they shall be amazed one at another; their faces *shall be as* flames.

9 Behold, [a]the day of the LORD cometh, cruel both with wrath and fierce anger, to lay the land desolate: and he shall destroy [b]the sinners thereof out of it.

10 For the stars of heaven and the constellations thereof shall not give their light: the sun shall be [a]darkened in his going forth, and the moon shall not cause her light to shine.

11 And I will [a]punish the world for *their* evil, and the wicked for their iniquity; [b]and I will cause the arrogancy of the proud to cease, and will lay low the haughtiness of the [1]terrible.

12 I will make a man more [1]precious than fine gold; even a man than the golden wedge of Ophir.

13 [a]Therefore I will shake the heavens, and the earth shall remove out of her place, in the wrath of the LORD of hosts, and in [b]the day of his fierce anger.

14 And it shall be as the [1]chased roe, and as a sheep that no man [2]taketh up: [a]they shall every man turn to his own people, and flee every one into his own land.

---

11:7 [1] *graze*
11:8 [1] *nursing* [2] *cobra* [3] *in the viper's*
11:9 [a] Job 5:23 [b] Hab. 2:14
11:10 [a] Is. 2:11 [b] Rom. 15:12 [c] Is. 27:12, 13 [d] Rom. 15:10 [1] *a banner to* [2] *to him* [3] *resting place*
11:11 [a] Zech. 10:10 [1] *coastlands*
11:12 [a] John 7:35 [1] *a banner* [2] Lit. *four wings*
11:13 [a] Jer. 3:18 [1] *harass*
11:14 [a] Dan. 11:41 [1] *plunder*
11:15 [a] Zech. 10:10, 11 [1] *fist* [2] The Euphrates [3] *strike* [4] *cross over in dry sandals*
11:16 [a] Is. 19:23 [b] Ex. 14:29
12:1 [a] Is. 2:11
12:2 [a] Ps. 83:18 [b] Ex. 15:2 [1] Heb. YAH
12:3 [a] [John 4:10, 14; 7:37, 38]
12:4 [a] 1 Chr. 16:8

[b] Ps. 145:4–6 [c] Ps. 34:3 [1] *deeds*
12:5 [a] Ex. 15:1
12:6 [a] Zeph. 3:14, 15 [b] Ps. 89:18
13:1 [a] Jer. 50; 51 [1] *oracle* or *prophecy against*
13:2 [a] Is. 18:3 [b] Jer. 51:25 [c] Is. 10:32 [1] *raise your* [2] *wave your*
13:3 [a] Joel 3:11 [b] Ps. 149:2 [1] *set apart* or *consecrated* [2] *exaltation*
13:4 [a] Is. 17:12 [1] *many*
13:5 [a] Is. 42:13 [b] Is. 24:1; 34:2
13:6 [a] Zeph. 1:7 [b] Joel 1:15
13:7 [1] *fall limp*
13:8 [a] Ps. 48:6 [1] *sharp pains* [2] *in childbirth*
13:9 [a] Mal. 4:1 [b] Prov. 2:22
13:10 [a] Joel 2:31
13:11 [a] Is. 26:21 [b] [Is. 2:17] [1] Or *tyrants*
13:12 [1] *rare*
13:13 [a] Hag. 2:6 [b] Lam. 1:12
13:14 [a] Jer. 50:16; 51:9 [1] *hunted gazelle* [2] *gathers*

15 Every one that is found shall be thrust through; and every one that is [1]joined *unto them* shall fall by the sword.

16 Their children also shall be [a]dashed to pieces before their eyes; their houses shall be [1]spoiled, and their wives [b]ravished.

17 [a]Behold, I will stir up the Medes against them, which shall not [1]regard silver; and *as for* gold, they shall not delight in it.

18 *Their* bows also shall dash the young men to pieces; and they shall have no pity on the fruit of the womb; their eye shall not spare children.

19 [a]And Babylon, the glory of kingdoms, the beauty of the Chaldees' excellency, shall be as when God overthrew [b]Sodom and Gomorrah.

20 [a]It shall never be inhabited, neither shall it be dwelt in from generation to generation: neither shall the Arabian pitch tent there; neither shall the shepherds make their fold there.

21 [a]But wild beasts of the desert shall lie there; and their houses shall be full of [1]doleful creatures; and [2]owls shall dwell there, and [3]satyrs shall dance there.

22 And the [1]wild beasts of the islands shall cry in their [2]desolate houses, and [3]dragons in *their* pleasant palaces: [a]and her time *is* near to come, and her days shall not be prolonged.

## CHAPTER 14

For the LORD [a]will have mercy on Jacob, and [b]will yet choose Israel, and set them in their own land: [c]and the strangers shall be joined with them, and they shall [1]cleave to the house of Jacob.

2 And the people shall take them, [a]and bring them to their place: and the house of Israel shall possess them in the land of the LORD for servants and handmaids: and they shall take them captives, whose captives they were; [b]and they shall rule over their oppressors.

3 And it shall come to pass in the day that the LORD shall give thee rest from thy sorrow, and from thy fear, and from the hard bondage wherein thou wast made to serve,

4 That thou [a]shalt take up this proverb against the king of Babylon, and say, How hath the oppressor ceased! the [b]golden[1] city ceased!

5 The LORD hath broken [a]the staff of the wicked, *and* the sceptre of the rulers.

6 He who [1]smote the people in wrath with a continual stroke, he that ruled the nations in anger, is persecuted, *and* none hindereth.

7 The whole earth is at rest, *and* is quiet: they break forth into singing.

8 [a]Yea, the [1]fir trees rejoice at thee, *and* the cedars of Lebanon, *saying,* Since thou art laid down, no [2]feller is come up against us.

9 [a]Hell[1] from beneath is [2]moved for thee to meet *thee* at thy coming: it stirreth up the dead for thee, *even* all the chief ones of the earth; it hath raised up from their thrones all the kings of the nations.

10 All they shall [a]speak and say unto thee, Art thou also become weak as we? art thou become like unto us?

11 Thy pomp is brought down to [1]the grave, *and* the noise of thy [2]viols: the [3]worm is spread under thee, and the worms cover thee.

12 [a]How art thou fallen from heaven, O [1]Lucifer, son of the morning! *how* art thou cut down to the ground, which didst weaken the nations!

13 For thou hast said in thine heart, [a]I will ascend into heaven, [b]I will exalt my throne above the stars of God: I will sit also upon the [c]mount of the congregation, [d]in the [1]sides of the north:

14 I will ascend above the heights of the clouds; [a]I will be like the most High.

15 Yet thou [a]shalt be brought down to [1]hell, to the [2]sides of the pit.

16 They that see thee shall [1]narrowly look upon thee, *and* consider thee, *saying, Is* this the man that made the earth to tremble, that did shake kingdoms;

17 *That* made the world as a wilderness, and destroyed the cities thereof; *that* [1]opened not the house of his prisoners?

18 All the kings of the nations, *even* all of them, lie in glory, every one in his own house.

19 But thou art cast out of thy grave like an [1]abominable branch, *and as* the [2]raiment of those that are slain, [3]thrust through with a sword, that go down to the stones of the pit; as a carcase trodden under feet.

20 Thou shalt not be joined with them in burial, because thou hast destroyed thy land, *and* slain thy people: [a]the seed of evildoers shall never be [1]renowned.

21 Prepare slaughter for his children [a]for[1] the iniquity of their fathers; that they do not rise, nor possess the land, nor fill the face of the world with cities.

22 For I will rise up against them, saith the LORD of hosts, and cut off from Babylon [a]the name, and [b]remnant, [c]and [1]son, and [2]nephew, saith the LORD.

23 [a]I will also make it a possession for the [1]bittern, and [2]pools of water:

13:15 [1] *captured*
13:16 [a] Nah. 3:10 [b] Zech. 14:2 [1] *plundered*
13:17 [a] Dan. 5:28, 31 [1] *esteem*
13:19 [a] Is. 14:4 [b] Gen. 19:24
13:20 [a] Jer. 50:3
13:21 [a] Is. 34:11–15 [1] *owls* [2] *ostriches* [3] *wild goats*
13:22 [a] Jer. 51:33 [1] *hyenas* [2] *citadels* [3] *jackals*
14:1 [a] Ps. 102:13 [b] Zech. 1:17; 2:12 [c] Is. 60:4, 5, 10 [1] *cling*
14:2 [a] Is. 49:22; 60:9; 66:20 [b] Is. 60:14
14:4 [a] Hab. 2:6 [b] Rev. 18:16 [1] Or *insolent*
14:5 [a] Ps. 125:3
14:6 [1] *struck*
14:8 [a] Ezek. 31:16 [1] *cypress* [2] *woodsman*
14:9 [a] Ezek. 32:21 [1] Or *Sheol* [2] *excited about thee*
14:10 [a] Ezek. 32:21
14:11 [1] Or *Sheol* [2] *harps or lutes* [3] *maggots*
14:12 [a] Is. 34:4 [1] Lit. *Day Star*
14:13 [a] Ezek. 28:2 [b] Dan. 8:10 [c] Ezek. 28:14 [d] Ps. 48:2 [1] *farthest sides*
14:14 [a] 2 Thess. 2:4
14:15 [a] Matt. 11:23 [1] Or *Sheol* [2] *lowest depths,* lit. *recesses*
14:16 [1] *gaze at*
14:17 [1] Would not release
14:19 [1] *despised* [2] *garment* [3] *pierced*
14:20 [a] Ps. 21:10; 109:13 [1] *named*
14:21 [a] Ex. 20:5 [1] *because of*
14:22 [a] Prov. 10:7 [b] 1 Kin. 14:10 [c] Job 18:19 [1] *offspring* [2] *posterity*
14:23 [a] Zeph. 2:14 [1] *porcupine* [2] *marshes*

and I will sweep it with the [3]besom of destruction, saith the LORD of hosts.

24 The LORD of hosts hath sworn, saying, Surely as I have thought, so shall it come to pass; and as I have purposed, *so* shall it [a]stand:

25 That I will break the [a]Assyrian in my land, and upon my mountains tread him under foot: then shall [b]his yoke depart from off them, and his burden depart from off their shoulders.

26 This *is* the [a]purpose that is purposed upon the whole earth: and this *is* the hand that is stretched out upon all the nations.

27 For the LORD of hosts hath [a]purposed, and who shall disannul *it?* and his hand *is* stretched out, and who shall turn it back?

28 In the year that [a]king Ahaz died was this [b]burden.

29 Rejoice not [1]thou, whole Palestina, [a]because the rod of him that [2]smote thee is broken: for out of the serpent's root shall come forth [3]a cockatrice, [b]and his fruit *shall be* a fiery flying serpent.

30 And the firstborn of the poor shall feed, and the needy shall lie down in safety: and I will kill thy root with famine, and he shall slay thy remnant.

31 Howl, O gate; cry, O city; [1]thou, whole Palestina, *art* [2]dissolved: for there shall come from the north a smoke, and none *shall be* alone in his appointed times.

32 What shall *one* then answer the messengers of the nation? That [a]the LORD hath founded Zion, and [b]the poor of his people shall [1]trust in it.

### CHAPTER 15

THE [a]burden[1] of Moab. Because in the night [b]Ar of [c]Moab is laid waste, *and* [2]brought to silence; because in the night Kir of Moab is laid waste, *and* [2]brought to silence;

2 He is gone up to [1]Bajith, and to Dibon, [2]the high places, to weep: Moab shall howl over Nebo, and over Medeba: [a]on all their heads *shall be* baldness, *and* every beard cut off.

3 In their streets they shall gird themselves with sackcloth: on the tops of their houses, and in their streets, every one shall howl, [a]weeping abundantly.

4 And Heshbon shall cry, and Elealeh: their voice shall be heard *even* unto [a]Jahaz: therefore the armed soldiers of Moab shall cry out; his life shall be grievous unto him.

5 [a]My heart shall cry out for Moab; his fugitives *shall flee* unto Zoar, [1]an heifer of three years old: for [b]by the [2]mounting up of Luhith with weeping shall they [3]go it up; for in the way

of Horonaim they shall raise up a cry of destruction.

6 For the waters [a]of Nimrim shall be desolate: for the hay is withered away, the grass faileth, there is no green thing.

7 Therefore the abundance they have gotten, and that which they have laid up, shall they carry away to the brook of the willows.

8 For the cry is gone round about the borders of Moab; the howling thereof unto Eglaim, and the howling thereof unto Beer-elim.

9 For the waters of Dimon shall be full of blood: for I will bring more upon Dimon, [a]lions upon him that escapeth of Moab, and upon the remnant of the land.

### CHAPTER 16

SEND [a]ye the lamb to the ruler of the land [b]from [1]Sela to the wilderness, unto the mount of the daughter of Zion.

2 For it shall be, *that,* as a [a]wandering bird cast out of the nest, *so* the daughters of Moab shall be at the fords of [b]Arnon.

3 Take counsel, execute judgment; make thy shadow as the night in the midst of the noonday; hide the outcasts; [1]bewray not him that wandereth.

4 Let mine outcasts dwell with thee, Moab; be thou a [1]covert to them from the face of the [2]spoiler: for the extortioner is at an end, the [3]spoiler ceaseth, the oppressors are consumed out of the land.

5 And in mercy [a]shall the throne be established: and he shall sit upon it in truth in the tabernacle of David, [b]judging, and seeking [1]judgment, and [2]hasting [c]righteousness.

6 We have heard of the [a]pride of Moab; *he is* very proud: *even* of his haughtiness, and his pride, and his wrath: [b]*but* his [1]lies *shall* not *be* so.

7 Therefore shall Moab [a]howl for Moab, every one shall howl: for the foundations [b]of Kir-hareseth shall ye mourn; surely *they are* stricken.

8 For [a]the fields of Heshbon languish, *and* [b]the vine of Sibmah: the lords of the heathen have broken down the [1]principal plants thereof, they are come *even* unto Jazer, they wandered *through* the wilderness: her branches are stretched out, they are gone over the [c]sea.

9 Therefore I will bewail with the weeping of Jazer the vine of Sibmah: I will [1]water thee with my tears, [a]O Heshbon, and Elealeh: for the [2]shouting for thy summer fruits and [3]for thy harvest is fallen.

10 And [a]gladness is taken away, and joy out of the plentiful field; and in

the vineyards there shall be no singing, neither shall there be shouting: the treaders shall tread out no wine in *their* presses; I have made *their* vintage shouting to cease.

11 Wherefore [a]my [1]bowels shall [2]sound like an harp for Moab, and [3]mine inward parts for [4]Kir-haresh.

12 And it shall come to pass, when it is seen that Moab is weary on [a]the high place, that he shall come to his sanctuary to pray; but he shall not prevail.

13 This *is* the word that the LORD hath spoken concerning Moab since that time.

14 But now the LORD hath spoken, saying, Within three years, [a]as the years of an hireling, and the glory of Moab shall be [1]contemned, with all that great multitude; and the remnant *shall be* very small *and* feeble.

## CHAPTER 17

THE [a]burden[1] of Damascus. Behold, Damascus [2]is taken away from *being* a city, and it shall be a ruinous heap.

2 The cities of [a]Aroer *are* forsaken: they shall be for flocks, which shall lie down, and [b]none shall make *them* afraid.

3 [a]The fortress also shall cease from Ephraim, and the kingdom from Damascus, and the remnant of Syria: they shall be as the glory of the children of Israel, saith the LORD of hosts.

4 And in that day it shall come to pass, *that* the glory of Jacob shall [1]be made thin, and [a]the fatness of his flesh shall [2]wax lean.

5 [a]And it shall be as when the harvestman gathereth the [1]corn, and reapeth the ears with his arm; and it shall be as he that gathereth ears in the valley of Rephaim.

6 [a]Yet gleaning grapes shall be left in it, as the shaking of an olive tree, two *or* three [1]berries in the top of the uppermost bough, four *or* five in the outmost fruitful branches thereof, saith the LORD God of Israel.

7 At that day shall a man [a]look to his Maker, and his eyes shall [1]have respect to the Holy One of Israel.

8 And he shall not look to the altars, the work of his hands, neither shall respect *that* which his [a]fingers have made, either the [1]groves, or the [2]images.

9 In that day shall his strong cities be as a forsaken bough, and an uppermost branch, which they left because of the children of Israel: and there shall be desolation.

10 Because thou hast forgotten [a]the God of thy salvation, and hast not been mindful of the rock of thy

[1]strength, therefore shalt thou plant pleasant plants, and shalt [2]set it with strange slips:

11 In the day shalt thou make thy plant to grow, and in the morning shalt thou make thy seed to flourish: *but* the harvest *shall be* a heap in the day of grief and of desperate sorrow.

12 Woe to the multitude of many people, *which* make a noise [a]like the noise of the seas; and to the rushing of nations, *that* make a rushing like the rushing of mighty waters!

13 The nations shall rush like the rushing of many waters: but *God* shall [a]rebuke them, and they shall flee far off, and [b]shall be chased as the chaff of the mountains before the wind, and like a rolling thing before the whirlwind.

14 And behold at eveningtide trouble; *and* before the morning [1]he *is* not. This *is* the portion of them that [2]spoil us, and the lot of them that rob us.

## CHAPTER 18

WOE [a]to the land [1]shadowing with wings, which *is* beyond the rivers of [2]Ethiopia:

2 That sendeth ambassadors by the sea, even in vessels of [1]bulrushes upon the waters, *saying,* Go, ye swift messengers, to a nation [2]scattered and peeled, to a people terrible from their beginning hitherto; a nation [3]meted out and trodden down, whose land the rivers [4]have spoiled!

3 All ye inhabitants of the world, and dwellers on the earth, see ye, [a]when he lifteth up [1]an ensign on the mountains; and when he bloweth a trumpet, hear ye.

4 For so the LORD said unto me, I will take my rest, and I will [1]consider in my dwelling place like a clear heat [2]upon herbs, *and* like a cloud of dew in the heat of harvest.

5 For [1]afore the harvest, when the bud is perfect, and the sour grape is ripening in the flower, he shall both cut off the sprigs with [2]pruning hooks, and take away *and* cut down the branches.

6 They shall be left together unto the [1]fowls of the mountains, and to the beasts of the earth: and the [1]fowls shall summer upon them, and all the beasts of the earth shall winter upon them.

7 In that time [a]shall [1]the present be brought unto the LORD of hosts of a people [2]scattered and peeled, and from a people terrible from their beginning hitherto; a nation [3]meted out and trodden under foot, whose land the rivers [4]have spoiled, to the place of the name of the LORD of hosts, the mount Zion.

16:11 [a] Jer. 48:36
[1] heart, lit. belly
[2] resound [3] my inner being [4] Or Kir-heres

16:12 [a] Is. 15:2

16:14 [a] Is. 21:16
[1] despised

17:1 [a] Zech. 9:1 [1] oracle or prophecy against [2] will cease

17:2 [a] Num. 32:34 [b] Jer. 7:33

17:3 [a] Is. 7:16; 8:4

17:4 [a] Is. 10:16
[1] wane [2] grow

17:5 [a] Jer. 51:33
[1] grain

17:6 [a] Is. 24:13
[1] olives

17:7 [a] Mic. 7:7
[1] look to

17:8 [a] Is. 2:8; 31:7
[1] Or Asherim; wooden images of Asherah, a Canaanite goddess [2] incense altars

17:10 [a] Ps. 68:19

[1] stronghold
[2] set out foreign seedlings

17:12 [a] Jer. 6:23

17:13 [a] Ps. 9:5 [b] Hos. 13:3

17:14 [1] he is no more [2] plunder

18:1 [a] Zeph. 2:12; 3:10 [1] shadowed with buzzing wings [2] Heb. Cush

18:2 [1] reeds [2] tall and smooth of skin [3] powerful and treading [4] divide

18:3 [a] Is. 5:26 [1] a banner

18:4 [1] look from [2] in sunshine

18:5 [1] before [2] pruning knives

18:6 [1] birds of prey

18:7 [a] Zeph. 3:10 [1] a gift [2] tall and smooth of skin [3] powerful and treading down [4] divide

## CHAPTER 19

THE [a]burden[1] of Egypt. Behold, the LORD [b]rideth upon a swift cloud, and shall come into Egypt: and [c]the idols of Egypt shall [2]be moved at his presence, and the heart of Egypt shall melt in the midst of it.

2 And I will [a]set the Egyptians against the Egyptians: and they shall fight every one against his brother, and every one against his neighbour; city against city, *and* kingdom against kingdom.

3 And the spirit of Egypt shall fail in the midst thereof: and I will destroy the counsel thereof: and they shall [a]seek[1] to the idols, and to the charmers, and to [2]them that have familiar spirits, and to the wizards.

4 And the Egyptians will I give over [a]into the hand of a cruel [1]lord; and a fierce king shall rule over them, saith the Lord, the LORD of hosts.

5 [a]And the waters shall fail from the sea, and the river shall be wasted and dried up.

6 And [1]they shall turn the rivers far away; *and* the brooks [a]of defence shall be emptied and dried up: the reeds and [2]flags shall wither.

7 The [1]paper reeds by the [2]brooks, by the mouth of the brooks, and every thing sown by the brooks, shall wither, be driven away, and be no *more.*

8 The fishers also shall mourn, and all they that cast [1]angle into the brooks shall lament, and they that spread nets upon the waters shall languish.

9 Moreover they that work in [a]fine flax, and they that weave [1]networks, shall be [2]confounded.

10 And [1]they shall be broken in the purposes thereof, all that make [2]sluices *and* ponds for fish.

11 Surely the princes of [a]Zoan *are* fools, the counsel of the wise counsellors of Pharaoh is become [1]brutish: [b]how say ye unto Pharaoh, I *am* the son of the wise, the son of ancient kings?

12 [a]Where *are* they? where *are* thy wise *men?* and let them tell thee now, and let them know what the LORD of hosts hath [b]purposed upon Egypt.

13 The princes of Zoan are become fools, [a]the princes of [1]Noph are deceived; they have also [2]seduced Egypt, *even they that are* the [3]stay of the tribes thereof.

14 The LORD hath mingled [a]a perverse spirit in the midst thereof: and they have caused Egypt to err in every work thereof, as a drunken *man* staggereth in his vomit.

15 Neither shall be *any* work for Egypt, which [a]the head or tail, branch or [1]rush, may do.

16 In that day shall Egypt [a]be like unto women: and it shall be afraid and fear because of the [1]shaking of the hand of the LORD of hosts, [b]which he [2]shaketh over it.

17 And the land of Judah shall be a terror unto Egypt, every one that maketh mention thereof shall be afraid in himself, because of the counsel of the LORD of hosts, which he hath [a]determined against it.

18 In that day shall five cities in the land of Egypt [a]speak the language of Canaan, and [b]swear to the LORD of hosts; one shall be called, The city of destruction.

19 In that day [a]shall there be an altar to the LORD in the midst of the land of Egypt, and a pillar at the border thereof to the [b]LORD.

20 And [a]it shall be for a sign and for a witness unto the LORD of hosts in the land of Egypt: for they shall cry unto the LORD because of the oppressors, and he shall send them a [b]saviour, and a [1]great one, and he shall deliver them.

21 And the LORD shall be known to Egypt, and the Egyptians shall [a]know the LORD in that day, and [b]shall [1]do sacrifice and oblation; yea, they shall vow a vow unto the LORD, and perform *it.*

22 And the LORD shall [1]smite Egypt: he shall smite and [a]heal *it:* and they shall return *even* to the LORD, and he shall be intreated of them, and shall heal them.

23 In that day [a]shall there be a highway out of Egypt to Assyria, and the Assyrian shall come into Egypt, and the Egyptian into Assyria, and the Egyptians shall [b]serve with the Assyrians.

24 In that day shall Israel be the third with Egypt and with Assyria, *even* a blessing in the midst of the land:

25 Whom the LORD of hosts shall bless, saying, Blessed *be* Egypt my people, and Assyria [a]the work of my hands, and Israel mine inheritance.

## CHAPTER 20

IN the year that [a]Tartan[1] came unto Ashdod, (when Sargon the king of Assyria sent him,) and fought against Ashdod, and took it;

2 At the same time spake the LORD by Isaiah the son of Amoz, saying, Go and [1]loose [a]the sackcloth from off thy loins, and put off thy [2]shoe from thy foot. And he did so, [b]walking naked and barefoot.

3 And the LORD said, Like as my servant Isaiah hath walked naked and barefoot three years [a]for a sign and wonder upon Egypt and upon Ethiopia;

### Center reference column

19:1 [a] Joel 3:19
[b] Ps. 18:10; 104:3
[c] Jer. 43:12 [1] *oracle or prophecy against* [2] Lit. *tremble*
19:2 [a] Judg. 7:22
19:3 [a] Is. 8:19; 47:12 [1] *consult* [2] *the mediums*
19:4 [a] Ezek. 29:19 [1] *master*
19:5 [a] Jer. 51:36
19:6 [a] 2 Kin. 19:24 [1] *the rivers will turn foul* [2] *rushes*
19:7 [1] *papyrus* [2] *The Nile, lit. river*
19:8 [1] *hooks*
19:9 [a] Prov. 7:16 [1] *fine fabric* [2] *ashamed*
19:10 [1] *its foundations shall be* [2] *wages shall be troubled of soul*
19:11 [a] Num. 13:22 [b] 1 Kin. 4:29, 30 [1] *foolish*
19:12 [a] 1 Cor. 1:20 [b] Ps. 33:11
19:13 [a] Jer. 2:16 [1] *Ancient Memphis* [2] *led Egypt astray* [3] *cornerstone or mainstay*
19:14 [a] Is. 29:10
19:15 [a] Is. 9:14–16 [1] *bulrush*

19:16 [a] Nah. 3:13 [b] Is. 11:15 [1] *waving* [2] *waves*
19:17 [a] Dan. 4:35
19:18 [a] Zeph. 3:9 [b] Is. 45:23
19:19 [a] Ex. 24:4 [b] Ps. 68:31
19:20 [a] Josh. 4:20; 22:27 [b] Is. 43:11 [1] *mighty*
19:21 [a] [Is. 2:3, 4; 11:9] [b] Mal. 1:11 [1] *make sacrifice and offering*
19:22 [a] Deut. 32:39 [1] *strike*
19:23 [a] Is. 11:16; 35:8; 49:11; 62:10 [b] Is. 27:13
19:25 [a] Is. 29:23
20:1 [a] 2 Kin. 18:17 [1] *Or the Commander-in-Chief*
20:2 [a] Zech. 13:4 [b] 1 Sam. 19:24 [1] *remove* [2] *sandal*
20:3 [a] Is. 8:18

4 So shall the [a]king of Assyria lead away the Egyptians prisoners, and the Ethiopians captives, young and old, naked and barefoot, [b]even with *their* buttocks uncovered, to the shame of Egypt.

5 [a]And they shall be afraid and ashamed of Ethiopia their expectation, and of Egypt their glory.

6 And the inhabitant of this [1]isle shall say in that day, Behold, such *is* our expectation, whither we flee for [a]help to be delivered from the king of Assyria: and how shall we escape?

## CHAPTER 21

THE [1]burden of the desert of the sea. As [a]whirlwinds in the south pass through; *so* it cometh from the desert, from a terrible land.

2 A [1]grievous vision is declared unto me; [a]the treacherous dealer dealeth treacherously, and the [2]spoiler spoileth. [b]Go up, O Elam: besiege, O Media; all the sighing thereof have I made to cease.

3 Therefore [a]are my loins filled with pain: [b]pangs[1] have taken hold upon me, as the pangs of a woman [2]that travaileth: I was [3]bowed down at the hearing *of it;* I was dismayed at the seeing *of it.*

4 My heart [1]panted, fearfulness [2]affrighted me: [a]the night of my [3]pleasure hath he turned into fear unto me.

5 [a]Prepare the table, [1]watch in the watchtower, eat, drink: arise, ye princes, *and* anoint the shield.

6 For thus hath the Lord said unto me, Go, set a watchman, let him declare what he seeth.

7 And he saw a chariot *with* a couple of horsemen, a chariot of [1]asses, *and* a chariot of camels; and he hearkened diligently with [2]much heed:

8 [1]And he cried, A lion: My lord, I stand continually upon the [a]watchtower in the daytime, and I [2]am set in my ward whole nights:

9 And, behold, here cometh a chariot of men, *with* a couple of horsemen. And he answered and said, [a]Babylon is fallen, is fallen; and [b]all the graven images of her gods he hath broken unto the ground.

10 [a]O my threshing, and the [1]corn of my floor: that which I have heard of the LORD of hosts, the God of Israel, have I declared unto you.

11 [a]The [1]burden of Dumah. He calleth to me out of [b]Seir, Watchman, what of the night? Watchman, what of the night?

12 The watchman said, The morning cometh, and also the night: if ye will enquire, enquire ye: return, come.

13 [a]The [1]burden upon Arabia. In the forest in Arabia shall ye lodge, O ye travelling companies [b]of [2]Dedanim.

14 The inhabitants of the land of Tema brought water to him that was thirsty, they [1]prevented with their bread him that fled.

15 For they fled from the swords, from the drawn sword, and from the bent bow, and from the grievousness of war.

16 For thus hath the Lord said unto me, Within a year, [a]according to the years of an hireling, and all the glory of [b]Kedar shall fail:

17 And the residue of the number of archers, the mighty men of the children of Kedar, shall be diminished: for the LORD God of Israel hath spoken *it.*

## CHAPTER 22

THE [1]burden of the valley of vision. What aileth thee now, that thou art wholly gone up to the housetops?

2 Thou that art full of [1]stirs, a tumultuous city, [a]a joyous city: thy slain *men are* not slain with the sword, nor dead in battle.

3 All thy rulers are fled together, they are [1]bound by the archers: all that are found in thee are bound together, *which* have fled from far.

4 Therefore said I, Look away from me; [a]I will weep bitterly, labour not to comfort me, because of the [1]spoiling of the daughter of my people.

5 [a]For *it is* a day of trouble, and of treading down, and of [1]perplexity [b]by the Lord GOD of hosts in the valley of vision, breaking down the walls, and of crying to the mountains.

6 [a]And Elam bare the quiver with chariots of men *and* horsemen, and [b]Kir uncovered the shield.

7 And it shall come to pass, *that* thy choicest valleys shall be full of chariots, and the horsemen shall set themselves in array at the gate.

8 [a]And he [1]discovered the covering of Judah, and thou didst look in that day to the armour [b]of the house of the forest.

9 [a]Ye have seen also the [1]breaches of the city of David, that they are many: and ye gathered together the waters of the lower pool.

10 And ye have numbered the houses of Jerusalem, and the houses have ye broken down to fortify the wall.

11 [a]Ye made also a [1]ditch between the two walls for the water of the old [b]pool: but ye have not looked unto the maker thereof, neither had respect unto him that fashioned it long ago.

12 And in that day did the Lord GOD of hosts [a]call to weeping, and to mourning, and [b]to baldness, and to girding with sackcloth:

13 And behold joy and gladness, slaying oxen, and killing sheep, eating

### Center column references

20:4 [a] Is. 19:4
[b] Jer. 13:22
20:5 [a] 2 Kin. 18:21
20:6 [a] Is. 30:5, 7
[1] territory
21:1 [a] Zech. 9:14 [1] *oracle or prophecy against the wilderness*
21:2 [a] Is. 33:1
[b] Jer. 49:34
[1] *distressing*
[2] *plunderer plundereth*
21:3 [a] Is. 15:5; 16:11
[b] Is. 13:8 [1] *sharp pains* [2] *in childbirth* [3] *distressed*
21:4 [a] Deut. 28:67 [1] *wavered* [2] *frightened* [3] *longing*
21:5 [a] Dan. 5:5
[1] *set a watchman*
21:7 [1] *donkeys* [2] *great care*
21:8 [a] Hab. 2:1
[1] DSS *Then the observer cried, My lord!* [2] *have sat at my post every night*
21:9 [a] Jer. 51:8
[b] Is. 46:1
21:10 [a] Jer. 51:33
[1] *grain*
21:11 [a] Gen. 25:14 [b] Gen. 32:3 [1] *prophecy against*
21:13 [a] Jer. 25:24; 49:28 [b] 1 Chr. 1:9, 32 [1] *prophecy against* [2] *Dedanites*

21:14 [1] *met*
21:16 [a] Is. 16:14
[b] Ps. 120:5
22:1 [1] *oracle or prophecy against*
22:2 [a] Is. 32:13
[1] *noise*
22:3 [1] *captured*
22:4 [a] Jer. 4:19
[1] *plundering*
22:5 [a] Is. 37:3
[b] Lam. 1:5; 2:2
[1] *confusion*
22:6 [a] Jer. 49:35
[b] Is. 15:1
22:8 [a] 2 Kin. 18:15, 16 [b] 1 Kin. 7:2; 10:17 [1] *removed the protection*
22:9 [a] 2 Kin. 20:20 [1] *damage to*
22:11 [a] Neh. 3:16
[b] 2 Chr. 32:3, 4
[1] *reservoir*
22:12 [a] Joel 1:13;
2:17 [b] Mic. 1:16

flesh, and [a]drinking wine: [b]let us eat and drink; for to morrow we shall die.

14 [a]And it was revealed in mine ears by the LORD of hosts, Surely this iniquity [b]shall not be purged from you till ye die, saith the Lord GOD of hosts.

15 Thus saith the Lord GOD of hosts, Go, get thee unto this [1]treasurer, *even* unto [a]Shebna, which *is* over the house, *and say,*

16 What hast thou here? and whom hast thou here, that thou hast hewed thee out a sepulchre here, *as* he [a]that heweth him out a sepulchre on high, *and* that [1]graveth an habitation for himself in a rock?

17 Behold, the LORD will [1]carry thee away with a mighty captivity, [a]and will surely [2]cover thee.

18 He will surely violently turn and toss thee *like* a ball into a large country: there shalt thou die, and there the [a]chariots of thy glory *shall be* the shame of thy lord's house.

19 And I will drive thee from thy [1]station, and from thy [2]state shall he pull thee down.

20 And it shall come to pass in that day, that I will call my servant [a]Eliakim the son of Hilkiah:

21 And I will clothe him with thy robe, and strengthen him with thy [1]girdle, and I will commit thy [2]government into his hand: and he shall be a father to the inhabitants of Jerusalem, and to the house of Judah.

22 And the key of the house of David will I lay upon his [a]shoulder; so he shall [b]open, and none shall shut; and he shall shut, and none shall open.

23 And I will fasten him *as* [a]a [1]nail in a sure place; and he shall be for a glorious throne to his father's house.

24 And they shall hang upon him all the glory of his father's house, the offspring and the issue, all vessels of small quantity, from the vessels of cups, even to all the vessels of [1]flagons.

25 In that day, saith the LORD of hosts, shall the [1]nail that is fastened in the sure place be removed, and be cut down, and fall; and the burden that *was* upon it shall be cut off: for the LORD hath spoken *it.*

## CHAPTER 23

THE [a]burden[1] of Tyre. Howl, ye ships of Tarshish; for it is laid waste, so that there is no house, no [2]entering in: from the land of [3]Chittim it is revealed to them.

2 Be still, ye inhabitants of the [1]isle; thou whom the merchants of [2]Zidon, that pass over the sea, have [3]replenished.

3 And by great waters the [1]seed of Sihor, the harvest of [2]the river, *is* her

revenue; and [a]she is a [3]mart of nations.

4 Be thou ashamed, O [1]Zidon: for the sea hath spoken, *even* the strength of the sea, saying, I travail not, nor bring forth children, neither do I [2]nourish up young men, *nor* bring up virgins.

5 [a]As at the report concerning Egypt, *so* shall they be sorely pained at the report of Tyre.

6 Pass ye over to Tarshish; howl, ye inhabitants of the [1]isle.

7 *Is* this your [a]joyous *city,* whose antiquity *is* of ancient days? her own feet shall carry her afar off to sojourn.

8 Who hath taken this counsel against Tyre, [a]the crowning *city,* whose merchants *are* princes, whose [1]traffickers *are* the honourable of the earth?

9 The LORD of hosts hath [a]purposed it, [1]to stain the [b]pride of all glory, *and* to bring into contempt all the honourable of the earth.

10 Pass through thy land as [1]a river, O daughter of Tarshish: *there is* no more [2]strength.

11 He stretched out his hand over the sea, he shook the kingdoms: the LORD hath given a commandment [a]against [1]the merchant *city,* to destroy the strong holds thereof.

12 And he said, Thou shalt no more rejoice, O thou oppressed virgin, daughter of [1]Zidon: arise, [a]pass over to [2]Chittim; there also shalt thou have no rest.

13 Behold the land of the [a]Chaldeans; this people was not, *till* the Assyrian founded it for [b]them[1] that dwell in the wilderness: they set up the towers thereof, they raised up the palaces thereof; *and* he brought it to ruin.

14 [a]Howl, ye ships of Tarshish: for your strength is laid waste.

15 And it shall come to pass in that day, that Tyre shall be forgotten seventy years, according to the days of one king: after the end of seventy years [1]shall Tyre sing as an harlot.

16 Take an harp, go about the city, thou harlot that hast been forgotten; make sweet melody, sing many songs, that thou mayest be remembered.

17 And it shall come to pass after the end of seventy years, that the LORD will visit Tyre, and she shall [1]turn to her hire, and [a]shall commit fornication with all the kingdoms of the world upon the face of the earth.

18 And her [1]merchandise and her hire [a]shall be [2]holiness to the LORD: it shall not be treasured nor laid up; for her merchandise shall be for them that dwell before the LORD, to eat sufficiently, and for [3]durable clothing.

### Center column references

22:13 [a] Luke 17:26–29 [b] 1 Cor. 15:32
22:14 [a] Is. 5:9 [b] Ezek. 24:13
22:15 [1] steward
22:16 [a] Matt. 27:60 [1] *carves a tomb*
22:17 [a] Esth. 7:8 [1] *throw you away violently, O mighty man* [2] *seize*
22:18 [a] Is. 2:7
22:19 [1] *office* [2] *position*
22:20 [a] 2 Kin. 18:18
22:21 [1] *belt* [2] *responsibility*
22:22 [a] Is. 9:6 [b] Job 12:14; Rev. 3:7
22:23 [a] Ezra 9:8 [1] *peg*
22:24 [1] *pitchers*
22:25 [1] *peg*
23:1 [a] Zech. 9:2, 4 [1] *prophecy against* [2] *harbour* [3] Heb. *Kittim, western lands, especially Cyprus*
23:2 [1] *coastland* [2] Or *Sidon* [3] *filled*
23:3 [a] Ezek. 27:3–23 [1] *grain* [2] The Nile [3] *marketplace*
23:4 [1] Or *Sidon* [2] *rear*
23:5 [a] Is. 19:16
23:6 [1] *coastland*
23:7 [a] Is. 22:2; 32:13
23:8 [a] Ezek. 28:2, 12 [1] *traders*
23:9 [a] Is. 14:26 [b] Dan. 4:37 [1] *to dishonour*
23:10 [1] The Nile [2] *restraint, lit. belt*
23:11 [a] Zech. 9:2–4 [1] *Canaan*
23:12 [a] Rev. 18:22 [1] Or *Sidon* [2] *Cyprus*
23:13 [a] Is. 47:1 [b] Ps. 72:9 [1] *wild beasts of the desert*
23:14 [a] Ezek. 27:25–30
23:15 [1] *it shall be with Tyre as in the song of the harlot*
23:17 [a] Rev. 17:2 [1] *return*
23:18 [a] Zech. 14:20, 21 [1] *gain* [2] *set apart for* [3] *fine or choice*

## CHAPTER 24

BEHOLD, the LORD maketh the earth empty, and maketh it waste, and [1]turneth it upside down, and scattereth abroad the inhabitants thereof.

2 And it shall be, as with the people, so with the [a]priest; as with the servant, so with his master; as with the maid, so with her mistress; [b]as with the buyer, so with the seller; as with the lender, so with the borrower; as with the [1]taker of usury, so with the [2]giver of usury to him.

3 The land shall be utterly emptied, and utterly [1]spoiled: for the LORD hath spoken this word.

4 The earth mourneth *and* fadeth away, the world languisheth *and* fadeth away, the [a]haughty[1] people of the earth do languish.

5 [a]The earth also is defiled under the inhabitants thereof; because they have [b]transgressed the laws, changed the ordinance, broken the [c]everlasting covenant.

6 Therefore hath [a]the curse devoured the earth, and they that dwell therein are [1]desolate: therefore the inhabitants of the earth are [b]burned, and few men left.

7 [a]The new wine [1]mourneth, the vine languisheth, all the merryhearted do sigh.

8 The mirth [a]of [1]tabrets ceaseth, the noise of them that rejoice endeth, the joy of the harp ceaseth.

9 They shall not drink wine with a song; strong drink shall be bitter to them that drink it.

10 The city of confusion is broken down: every house is shut up, that no man may come in.

11 *There is* a crying for wine in the streets; all joy is darkened, the mirth of the land is gone.

12 In the city is left desolation, and the gate is [1]smitten with destruction.

13 When thus it shall be in the midst of the land among the people, [a]*there shall be* as the shaking of an olive tree, *and* as the gleaning grapes when the vintage is done.

14 They shall lift up their voice, they shall sing for the majesty of the LORD, they shall cry aloud from the sea.

15 Wherefore [a]glorify ye the LORD in the [1]fires, *even* [b]the name of the LORD God of Israel in the [2]isles of the sea.

16 From the uttermost part of the earth have we heard songs, *even* glory to the righteous. But I said, My [1]leanness, my leanness, woe unto me! [a]the treacherous dealers have dealt treacherously; yea, the treacherous dealers have dealt very treacherously.

17 [a]Fear, and the pit, and the snare, *are* upon thee, O inhabitant of the earth.

18 And it shall come to pass, *that* he who fleeth from the noise of the fear shall fall into the pit; and he that cometh up out of the midst of the pit shall be [1]taken in the snare: for [a]the windows from on high are open, and [b]the foundations of the earth do shake.

19 [a]The earth is [1]utterly broken down, the earth is [2]clean dissolved, the earth is [3]moved exceedingly.

20 The earth shall [a]reel to and fro like a drunkard, and shall [2]be removed like a cottage; and the transgression thereof shall be heavy upon it; and it shall fall, and not rise again.

21 And it shall come to pass in that day, *that* the LORD shall punish the host of the high ones *that are* on high, [a]and the kings of the earth upon the earth.

22 And they shall be gathered together, *as* prisoners are gathered in the pit, and shall be shut up in the prison, and after many days shall they be [1]visited.

23 Then the [a]moon shall be [1]confounded, and the sun ashamed, when the LORD of hosts shall [b]reign in [c]mount Zion, and in Jerusalem, and before his [2]ancients gloriously.

## CHAPTER 25

O LORD, thou *art* my God; [a]I will exalt thee, I will praise thy name; [b]for thou hast done wonderful [c]*things; thy* counsels of old *are* faithfulness *and* truth.

2 For thou hast made [a]of a city [1]an heap; *of a* [2]defenced city a ruin: a palace of strangers to be no city; it shall never be [3]built.

3 Therefore shall the strong people [a]glorify thee, the city of the [1]terrible nations shall fear thee.

4 For thou hast been a strength to the poor, a strength to the needy in his distress, [a]a refuge from the storm, a shadow from the heat, when the blast of the terrible ones *is* as a storm *against* the wall.

5 Thou shalt bring down the noise of strangers, as the heat in a dry place; *even* the heat with the shadow of a cloud: the [1]branch of the terrible ones shall be [2]brought low.

6 And in [a]this mountain shall [b]the LORD of hosts make unto [c]all people a feast of [1]fat things, a feast of [2]wines on the lees, of fat things full of marrow, of wines on the lees well refined.

7 And he will [1]destroy in this mountain the face of the covering cast over all people, and [a]the vail that is spread over all nations.

8 He will [a]swallow up death [1]in victory; and the Lord GOD will [b]wipe away tears from off all faces; and the rebuke of his people shall he take

---

**Cross-references (center column):**

24:1 [1] *distorts its surface*
24:2 [a] Hos. 4:9 [b] Ezek. 7:12, 13 [1] *creditor* [2] *debtor*
24:3 [1] *plundered*
24:4 [a] Is. 25:11 [1] *proud*
24:5 [a] Num. 35:33 [b] Is. 59:12 [c] 1 Chr. 16:14–19
24:6 [a] Mal. 4:6 [b] Is. 9:19 [1] *Or held guilty*
24:7 [a] Joel 1:10, 12 [1] *fails*
24:8 [a] Ezek. 26:13 [1] *tambourines*
24:12 [1] *stricken*
24:13 [a] [Is. 17:5, 6; 27:12]
24:15 [a] Is. 25:3 [b] Mal. 1:11 [1] *dawning light* [2] *coastlands*
24:16 [a] Jer. 3:20; 5:11 [1] *poverty*
24:17 [a] Jer. 48:43
24:18 [a] Gen. 7:11 [b] Ps. 18:7; 46:2 [1] *caught*
24:19 [a] Jer. 4:23 [1] *violently* [2] *split open* [3] *shaken*
24:20 [a] Is. 19:14; 24:1; 28:7 [1] *stagger* [2] *totter like a hut*
24:21 [a] Ps. 76:12
24:22 [1] *punished*
24:23 [a] Is. 13:10; 60:19 [b] Rev. 19:4, 6 [c] [Heb. 12:22] [1] *disgraced or ashamed* [2] *elders*
25:1 [a] Ex. 15:2 [b] Ps. 98:1 [c] Num. 23:19
25:2 [a] Jer. 51:37 [1] *a ruin* [2] *fortified* [3] *rebuilt*
25:3 [a] Is. 24:15 [1] *ruthless*
25:4 [a] Is. 4:6
25:5 [1] *song* [2] *diminished*
25:6 [a] [Is. 2:2–4; 56:7] [b] Prov. 9:2 [c] [Dan. 7:14] [1] *choice pieces* [2] *wines matured on the sediment*
25:7 [a] [Eph. 4:18] [1] *Lit. swallow*
25:8 [a] [Hos. 13:14] [b] Rev. 7:17; 21:4 [1] *forever*

away from off all the earth: for the LORD hath spoken *it.*

9 And it shall be said in that day, Lo, this *is* our God; ªwe have waited for him, and he will save us: this *is* the LORD; we have waited for him, ᵇwe will be glad and rejoice in his salvation.

10 For in this mountain shall the hand of the LORD rest, and ªMoab shall be ¹trodden down under him, even as straw is trodden down for the dunghill.

11 And he shall spread forth his hands in the midst of them, as he that swimmeth spreadeth forth *his hands* to swim: and he shall bring down their ªpride together with the ¹spoils of their hands.

12 And the ªfortress of the high fort of thy walls shall he bring down, lay low, *and* bring to the ground, *even* to the dust.

## CHAPTER 26

IN ªthat day shall this song be sung in the land of Judah; We have a strong city; ᵇsalvation will *God* appoint *for* walls and bulwarks.

2 ªOpen ye the gates, that the righteous nation which keepeth the truth may enter in.

3 Thou wilt keep *him* in perfect ªpeace, *whose* mind *is* ¹stayed *on thee:* because he trusteth in thee.

4 Trust ye in the LORD for ever: ªfor in ¹the LORD JEHOVAH *is* ²everlasting strength:

5 For he ¹bringeth down them that dwell on high; ªthe lofty city, he layeth it low; he layeth it low, *even* to the ground; he bringeth it *even* to the dust.

6 The foot shall ¹tread it down, *even* the feet of the poor, *and* the steps of the needy.

7 The way of the just *is* uprightness: ªthou, most upright, dost ¹weigh the path of the just.

8 Yea, ªin the way of thy judgments, O LORD, have we ᵇwaited for thee; the desire of *our* soul *is* to thy name, and to the remembrance of thee.

9 ªWith my soul have I desired thee in the night; yea, with my spirit within me will I seek thee early: for when thy judgments *are* in the earth, the inhabitants of the world will learn righteousness.

10 ªLet ¹favour be shewed to the wicked, *yet* will he not learn righteousness: in ᵇthe land of uprightness will he deal unjustly, and will not behold the majesty of the LORD.

11 LORD, *when* thy hand is lifted up, ªthey will not see: *but* they shall see, and be ashamed for ¹*their* envy at the people; yea, the fire of thine enemies shall devour them.

12 LORD, thou wilt ¹ordain peace for us: for thou also hast wrought all our works in us.

13 O LORD our God, ªother lords beside thee have had dominion over us: *but* by thee only will we make mention of thy name.

14 *They are* dead, they shall not live; *they are* deceased, they shall not rise: therefore hast thou ¹visited and destroyed them, and made all their memory to ªperish.

15 Thou hast ªincreased the nation, O LORD, thou hast increased the nation: thou art glorified: thou ¹hadst removed *it* far *unto* all the ends of the earth.

16 LORD, ªin trouble have they visited thee, they ¹poured out a prayer *when* thy chastening *was* upon them.

17 Like as ªa woman with child, *that* draweth near the time of her delivery, is in pain, *and* crieth out in her ¹pangs; so have we been in thy sight, O LORD.

18 We have been with child, we have been in pain, we have as it were ¹brought forth wind; we have not wrought any deliverance in the earth; neither have ªthe inhabitants of the world fallen.

19 ªThy dead *men* shall live, *together with* my dead body shall they arise. ᵇAwake and sing, ye that dwell in dust: for thy dew *is as* the dew of herbs, and the earth shall cast out the dead.

20 Come, my people, ªenter thou into thy chambers, and shut thy doors about thee: hide thyself as it were ᵇfor a little moment, until the indignation be overpast.

21 For, behold, the LORD ªcometh out of his place to punish the inhabitants of the earth for their iniquity: the earth also shall disclose her blood, and shall no more cover her slain.

## CHAPTER 27

IN that day the LORD with his ¹sore and great and strong sword shall punish ²leviathan the ³piercing serpent, ªeven leviathan that ⁴crooked serpent; and he shall slay ᵇthe ⁵dragon that *is* in the sea.

2 In that day ªsing ye unto her, ᵇA vineyard of red wine.

3 ªI the LORD do keep it; I will water it every moment: lest *any* hurt it, I will keep it night and day.

4 Fury *is* not in me: who would set ªthe briers *and* thorns against me in battle? I would go through them, I would burn them together.

5 Or let him take hold ªof my strength, *that* he may ᵇmake peace with me; *and* he shall make peace with me.

---

25:9 ª Gen. 49:18
ᵇ Ps. 20:5
25:10 ª Amos 2:1–3
¹ trampled
25:11 ª Is. 24:4;
26:5 ¹ trickery
25:12 ª Is. 26:5
26:1 ª Is. 2:11; 12:1
ᵇ Is. 60:18
26:2 ª Ps. 118:19,
20
26:3 ª Is. 57:19
¹ sustained by
26:4 ª Is. 12:2;
45:17 ¹ Heb. YAH
² Or Rock of Ages
26:5 ª Is. 25:11, 12
¹ bringeth low
26:6 ¹ trample
26:7 ª Ps. 37:23
¹ Or make level
26:8 ª Is. 64:5
ᵇ Is. 25:9; 33:2
26:9 ª Ps. 63:6
26:10 ª [Rom.
2:4] ᵇ Ps. 143:10
¹ grace
26:11 ª Is. 5:12
¹ thy zeal for

26:12 ¹ establish
26:13 ª 2 Chr. 12:8
26:14 ª Eccl. 9:5
¹ punished
26:15 ª Is. 9:3
¹ have expanded all the borders of the land
26:16 ª Hos. 5:15
¹ Or whispered
26:17 ª [John 16:21] ¹ sharp pains
26:18 ª Ps. 17:14
¹ given birth to
26:19 ª [Ezek. 37:1–14] ᵇ [Dan. 12:2]
26:20 ª Ex. 12:22, 23 ᵇ [Ps. 30:5]
26:21 ª Mic. 1:3
27:1 ª Ps. 74:13, 14
ᵇ Is. 51:9 ¹ severe
² A large sea creature, identity unknown ³ fleeing ⁴ twisted ⁵ A large reptile
27:2 ª Is. 5:1
ᵇ Is. 5:7
27:3 ª Is. 31:5
27:4 ª 2 Sam. 23:6
27:5 ª Is. 45:4
ᵇ Job 22:21

6 He shall cause them that come [1]of Jacob [a]to take root: Israel shall blossom and bud, and fill the face of the world with fruit.

7 [a]Hath he smitten [1]him, as he smote those that smote him? *or is* he slain according to the slaughter of them that are slain by him?

8 [a]In measure, [1]when it shooteth forth, thou [2]wilt debate with it: [b]he [3]stayeth his rough wind in the day of the east wind.

9 By this therefore shall the iniquity of Jacob be [1]purged; and this *is* all the fruit to take away his sin; when he maketh all the stones of the altar as chalkstones that are beaten in sunder, [2]the groves and [3]images shall not stand up.

10 Yet the [1]defenced city *shall be* [a]desolate, *and* the habitation forsaken, and left like a wilderness: there shall the calf feed, and there shall he lie down, and consume the branches thereof.

11 When the boughs thereof are withered, they shall be broken off: the women come, *and* set them on fire: for [a]it *is* a people of no understanding: therefore he that made them will [b]not have mercy on them, and [c]he that formed them will shew them no favour.

12 And it shall come to pass in that day, *that* the LORD shall [1]beat off from the channel of [2]the river unto the [3]stream of Egypt, and ye shall be [a]gathered one by one, O ye children of Israel.

13 [a]And it shall come to pass in that day, [b]*that* the great trumpet shall be blown, and they shall come which were ready to perish in the land of Assyria, and the outcasts in the land of [c]Egypt, and shall [d]worship the LORD in the holy mount at Jerusalem.

## CHAPTER 28

WOE to the crown of pride, to the drunkards of Ephraim, whose glorious beauty *is* a fading flower, which *are* [1]on the head of the [2]fat valleys of them that are overcome with wine!

2 Behold, the Lord hath a mighty and strong one, [a]*which* as a tempest of hail *and* a destroying storm, as a flood of mighty waters overflowing, shall [1]cast down to the earth with the hand.

3 The crown of pride, the drunkards of Ephraim, shall be [1]trodden under feet:

4 And the glorious beauty, which *is* [1]on the head of the [2]fat valley, shall be a fading flower, *and* as the [3]hasty fruit before the summer; which *when* he that looketh upon it seeth, while it is yet in his hand he eateth it up.

27:6 [a] Is. 37:31
[1] *to take root in Jacob*
27:7 [a] Is. 10:12, 17; 30:30–33 [1] Israel
27:8 [a] Job 23:6
[b] [Ps. 78:38] [1] *by sending it away* [2] *didst contend* [3] *removes it by*
27:9 [1] *covered* [2] Or *Asherim, wooden images of Canaanite deities* [3] *incense altars*
27:10 [a] Is. 5:6, 17; 32:14 [1] *fortified*
27:11 [a] Deut. 32:28 [b] Is. 9:17 [c] Deut. 32:18
27:12 [a] [Is. 11:11; 56:8] [1] *thresh from* [2] The Euphrates [3] *brook*
27:13 [a] Is. 2:11 [b] Rev. 11:15 [c] Is. 19:21, 22 [d] Zech. 14:16
28:1 [a] *at* [2] *verdant*
28:2 [a] Ezek. 13:11 [1] *cast* them
28:3 [1] *trampled*
28:4 [1] *at* [2] *verdant* [3] *firstfruit*

5 In that day shall the LORD of hosts be for a crown of glory, and for a diadem of beauty, unto the residue of his people,

6 And for a spirit of [1]judgment to him that sitteth in judgment, and for strength to them that [2]turn the battle [3]to the gate.

7 But they also [a]have erred through wine, and through [1]strong drink are out of the way; [b]the priest and the prophet have erred through strong drink, they are swallowed up of wine, they are out of the way through strong drink; they err in vision, they stumble *in* judgment.

8 For all tables are full of vomit *and* filthiness, *so that there is* no place *clean.*

9 [a]Whom shall he teach knowledge? and whom shall he make to understand [1]doctrine? *them that are* [2]weaned from the milk, *and* [3]drawn from the breasts.

10 [a]For precept *must be* upon precept, precept upon precept; line upon line, line upon line; here a little, *and* there a little:

11 For with [a]stammering lips and another tongue will he speak to this people.

12 To whom he said, This *is* the [a]rest *wherewith* ye may cause the weary to rest; and this *is* the refreshing: yet they would not hear.

13 But the word of the LORD was unto them precept upon precept, precept upon precept; line upon line, line upon line; here a little, *and* there a little; that they might go, and fall backward, and be broken, and snared, and taken.

14 Wherefore hear the word of the LORD, ye scornful men, that rule this people which *is* in Jerusalem.

15 Because ye have said, We have made a covenant with death, and with [1]hell are we at agreement; when the overflowing scourge shall pass through, it shall not come unto us: [a]for we have made lies our refuge, and under falsehood have we hid ourselves:

16 Therefore thus saith the Lord GOD, Behold, I lay in Zion for a foundation [a]a stone, a tried stone, a precious corner *stone,* a sure foundation: he that believeth shall not make haste.

17 [1]Judgment also will I [2]lay to the line, and righteousness [3]to the plummet: and the hail shall sweep away the refuge of lies, and the waters shall overflow the hiding place.

18 And your covenant with death shall be disannulled, and your agreement with [1]hell shall not stand; when the overflowing scourge shall pass through, then ye shall be [2]trodden down by it.

28:6 [1] *justice* [2] *turn back* [3] *at*
28:7 [a] Hos. 4:11 [b] Is. 56:10, 12 [1] *intoxicating drink*
28:9 [a] Jer. 6:10 [1] *the message* [2] *just weaned* [3] *just drawn*
28:10 [a] [2 Chr. 36:15]
28:11 [a] 1 Cor. 14:21
28:12 [a] Is. 30:15
28:15 [a] Is. 9:15 [1] Or *Sheol*
28:16 [a] Matt. 21:42
28:17 [1] *Justice* [2] *make the measuring line* [3] *to be*
28:18 [1] Or *Sheol* [2] *trampled*

19 ¹From the time that it goeth forth it shall take you: for morning by morning shall it pass over, by day and by night: and it shall be a ²vexation only *to* understand the report.

20 For the bed is shorter than that *a man* can stretch himself *on it:* and the covering narrower than that he can wrap himself *in it.*

21 For the LORD shall rise up as *in* mount ªPerazim, he shall be wroth as *in* the valley of ᵇGibeon, that he may do his work, ᶜhis ¹strange work; and bring to pass his act, his ²strange act.

22 Now therefore be ye not mockers, lest your ¹bands be made strong: for I have heard from the Lord GOD of hosts ªa ²consumption, even determined upon the whole earth.

23 Give ye ear, and hear my voice; hearken, and hear my speech.

24 Doth the plowman plow all day to sow? doth he ¹open and break the clods of his ground?

25 When he hath ¹made plain the face thereof, doth he not ²cast abroad the fitches, and scatter the cummin, and ³cast in the principal wheat and the ⁴appointed barley and the ⁵rie in their place?

26 For his God doth instruct him to discretion, *and* doth teach him.

27 For the ¹fitches are not threshed with a threshing ²instrument, neither is a cart wheel ³turned about upon the cummin; but the fitches are beaten out with a staff, and the cummin with a rod.

28 Bread ¹*corn* is bruised; because he will not ever be threshing it, nor break *it with* the wheel of his cart, nor ²bruise it *with* his horsemen.

29 This also cometh forth from the LORD of hosts, ª*which* is wonderful in counsel, *and* excellent in ¹working.

## CHAPTER 29

WOE to ¹Ariel, ªto Ariel, the city ᵇ*where* David dwelt! add ye year to year; let ²them kill sacrifices.

2 Yet I will distress Ariel, and there shall be heaviness and sorrow: and it shall be unto me as Ariel.

3 And I will camp against thee round about, and will lay siege against thee with a ¹mount, and I will raise ²forts against thee.

4 And thou shalt be brought down, *and* shalt speak out of the ground, and thy speech shall be low out of the dust, and thy voice shall be, as ¹of one that hath a familiar spirit, ªout of the ground, and thy speech shall whisper out of the dust.

5 Moreover the multitude of thy ªstrangers¹ shall be like ²small dust, and the multitude of the terrible ones *shall be* ᵇas chaff that passeth

away: yea, it shall be ᶜat an instant suddenly.

6 ªThou shalt be ¹visited of the LORD of hosts with thunder, and with ᵇearthquake, and great noise, with storm and tempest, and the flame of devouring fire.

7 ªAnd the multitude of all the nations that fight against ¹Ariel, even all that fight against her and her ²munition, and that distress her, shall be ᵇas a dream of a night vision.

8 ªIt shall even be as when an hungry *man* dreameth, and, behold, he eateth; but he awaketh, and his soul is empty: or as when a thirsty man dreameth, and, behold, he drinketh; but he awaketh, and, behold, *he* is faint, and his soul ¹hath appetite: so shall the multitude of all the nations be, that fight against mount Zion.

9 ¹Stay yourselves, and wonder; ²cry ye out, and cry: ªthey are drunken, ᵇbut not with wine; they stagger, but not with strong drink.

10 For ªthe LORD hath poured out upon you the spirit of deep sleep, and hath ᵇclosed your eyes: ¹the prophets and your ²rulers, ᶜthe seers hath he covered.

11 And the ¹vision of all is become unto you as the words of a ²book ªthat is sealed, which *men* deliver to one that is learned, saying, Read this, I pray thee: ᵇand he saith, I cannot; for it *is* sealed:

12 And the book is delivered to him that ¹is not learned, saying, Read this, I pray thee: and he saith, I am not learned.

13 Wherefore the Lord said, ªForasmuch as this people draw near *me* with their mouth, and ᵇwith their lips do honour me, but have removed their heart far from me, and their fear toward me is taught by the precept of men:

14 ªTherefore, behold, I will ¹proceed to do a marvellous work among this people, *even* a marvellous work and a wonder: ᵇfor the wisdom of their wise *men* shall perish, and the understanding of their prudent *men* shall be hid.

15 ªWoe unto them that seek deep to hide their counsel from the LORD, and their works are in the dark, and ᵇthey say, Who seeth us? and who knoweth us?

16 Surely ¹your turning of things upside down shall be esteemed as the potter's clay: for shall the ²work say of him that made it, He made me not? or shall the thing ²framed say of him that framed it, He had no understanding?

17 *Is* it not yet a very little while, and ªLebanon shall be turned into a fruitful field, and the fruitful field shall be esteemed as a forest?

**Center column references:**

28:19 ¹ *As often as* ² *terror just*

28:21 ª 2 Sam. 5:20 ᵇ Josh. 10:10, 12 ᶜ [Lam. 3:33] ¹ *awesome* ² *unusual*

28:22 ª Is. 10:22 ¹ *bonds* ² *destruction*

28:24 ¹ *keep turning*

28:25 ¹ *levelled* ² *sow the black cummin* ³ *plant in rows* ⁴ *barley in the appointed place* ⁵ *spelt*

28:27 ¹ *black cummin is* ² *sledge* ³ *rolled*

28:28 ¹ *flour must be ground* ² *crush*

28:29 ª Ps. 92:5 ¹ *guidance*

29:1 ª Ezek. 24:6, 9 ᵇ 2 Sam. 5:9 ¹ *Jerusalem, lit. Lion of God* ² *feasts come around*

29:3 ¹ *mound* ² *siegeworks*

29:4 ª Is. 8:19 ¹ *a medium's*

29:5 ª Is. 25:5 ᵇ Job 21:18 ᶜ Is. 30:13; 47:11 ¹ *foes* ² *fine*

29:6 ª Is. 28:2; 30:30 ᵇ Rev. 16:18, 19 ¹ *punished by*

29:7 ª Mic. 4:11, 12 ᵇ Job 20:8 ¹ *Jerusalem* ² *fortress*

29:8 ª Ps. 73:20 ¹ *still craves*

29:9 ª Is. 28:7, 8 ᵇ Is. 51:21 ¹ *Pause* ² *blind yourselves and be blind*

29:10 ª Rom. 11:8 ᵇ Ps. 69:23 ᶜ Is. 44:18 ¹ *namely, the prophets* ² Lit. *heads*

29:11 ª Is. 8:16 ᵇ Dan. 12:4, 9 ¹ *whole vision* ² *scroll*

29:12 ¹ Lit. *does not know books*

29:13 ª Ezek. 33:31 ᵇ Col. 2:22

29:14 ª Hab. 1:5 ᵇ Jer. 49:7 ¹ *again do*

29:15 ª Is. 30:1 ᵇ Ps. 10:11; 94:7

29:16 ª Is. 45:9 ¹ *you have things turned around! Shall the potter be esteemed like the clay* ² *formed*

29:17 ª Is. 32:15

18 And ᵃin that day shall the deaf hear the words of the book, and the eyes of the blind shall see out of obscurity, and out of darkness.

19 ᵃThe meek also shall increase *their* joy in the LORD, and ᵇthe poor among men shall rejoice in the Holy One of Israel.

20 For the ¹terrible one is brought to nought, and ᵃthe scorner is consumed, and all that ᵇwatch² for iniquity are cut off:

21 That make a man an offender for a word, and ᵃlay a snare for him that reproveth in the gate, and turn aside the just ᵇfor a thing of nought.

22 Therefore thus saith the LORD, ᵃwho redeemed Abraham, concerning the house of Jacob, Jacob shall not now be ᵇashamed, neither shall his face now ¹wax pale.

23 But when he seeth his children, ᵃthe work of mine hands, in the midst of him, they shall ¹sanctify my name, and sanctify the Holy One of Jacob, and shall fear the God of Israel.

24 They also ᵃthat erred in spirit shall ¹come to understanding, and they that murmured shall learn doctrine.

## CHAPTER 30

WOE to the rebellious children, saith the LORD, ᵃthat take counsel, but not of me; and that ¹cover with a covering, but not of my spirit, ᵇthat they may add sin to sin:

2 That walk to go down into Egypt, and ᵇhave not ¹asked at my mouth; to strengthen themselves in the strength of Pharaoh, and to trust in the shadow of Egypt!

3 ᵃTherefore shall the strength of Pharaoh be your shame, and the trust in the shadow of Egypt *your* ¹confusion.

4 For his princes were at ᵃZoan, and his ambassadors came to Hanes.

5 ᵃThey were all ashamed of a people *that* could not profit them, nor be an help nor profit, but a shame, and also a reproach.

6 ᵃThe ¹burden of the beasts of the south: into the land of trouble and anguish, from whence *come* the ²young and old lion, ᵇthe viper and fiery flying serpent, they will carry their riches upon the shoulders of young ³asses, and their treasures upon the ⁴bunches of camels, to a people *that* shall not profit *them*.

7 ᵃFor the Egyptians shall help in vain, and to no purpose: therefore have I ¹cried concerning this, ²Their strength *is* to sit still.

8 Now go, ᵃwrite it before them ¹in a table, and note it ²in a book, that it may be for the time to come for ever and ever:

29:18 ᵃ Is. 35:5
29:19 ᵃ [Is. 11:4; 61:1] ᵇ [James 2:5]
29:20 ᵃ Is. 28:14 ᵇ Mic. 2:1 ¹ *terrifying* ² *Lie in wait*
29:21 ᵃ Amos 5:10, 12 ᵇ Prov. 28:21
29:22 ᵃ Josh. 24:3 ᵇ Is. 45:17 ¹ *grow*
29:23 ᵃ [Is. 45:11; 49:20–26] ¹ *hallow*
29:24 ᵃ Is. 28:7 ¹ *know understanding*
30:1 ᵃ Is. 29:15 ᵇ Deut. 29:19 ¹ *devise plans,* lit. *weave a web*
30:2 ᵃ Is. 31:1 ᵇ Josh. 9:14 ¹ *asked my advice*
30:3 ᵃ Is. 20:5 ¹ *humiliation*
30:4 ᵃ Is. 19:11
30:5 ᵃ Jer. 2:36
30:6 ᵃ Is. 57:9 ᵇ Deut. 8:15 ¹ *oracle* or *prophecy against* ² *lioness and lion* ³ *donkeys* ⁴ *humps*
30:7 ᵃ Jer. 37:7 ¹ *Or called her* ² *Rahab-hemshebeth,* lit. *Rahab Sits Idle*
30:8 ᵃ Hab. 2:2 ¹ *on a tablet* ² *on a scroll*
30:9 ᵃ Is. 1:2, 4; 65:2
30:10 ᵃ Jer. 11:21 ᵇ 1 Kin. 22:8, 13 ¹ *Or rely*
30:12 ᵃ Is. 5:24 ¹ *Or rely*
30:13 ᵃ Ps. 62:3, 4 ᵇ Is. 29:5 ¹ *a bulge*
30:14 ᵃ Jer. 19:11 ¹ *among its fragments* ² *a shard* ³ *cistern*
30:15 ᵃ Is. 7:4; 28:12 ᵇ Matt. 23:37
30:17 ᵃ Josh. 23:10 ¹ *threat* ² *a pole* ³ *a banner*
30:18 ᵃ Is. 33:2 ᵇ Jer. 17:7 ᶜ Is. 26:8 ¹ *justice*
30:19 ᵃ Is. 65:9 ᵇ Is. 25:8 ᶜ Is. 65:24
30:20 ᵃ 1 Kin. 22:27 ᵇ Amos 8:11
30:21 ᵃ Josh. 1:7
30:22 ᵃ Is. 2:20; 31:7

9 That ᵃthis *is* a rebellious people, lying children, children *that* will not hear the law of the LORD:

10 ᵃWhich say to the seers, See not; and to the prophets, Prophesy not unto us right things, ᵇspeak unto us smooth things, prophesy deceits:

11 Get you out of the way, turn aside out of the path, cause the Holy One of Israel to cease from before us.

12 Wherefore thus saith the Holy One of Israel, Because ye ᵃdespise this word, and trust in oppression and perverseness, and ¹stay thereon:

13 Therefore this iniquity shall be to you ᵃas a breach ready to fall, ¹swelling out in a high wall, whose breaking ᵇcometh suddenly at an instant.

14 And ᵃhe shall break it as the breaking of the potters' vessel that is broken in pieces; he shall not spare: so that there shall not be found ¹in the bursting of it ²a sherd to take fire from the hearth, or to take water *withal* out of the ³pit.

15 For thus saith the Lord GOD, the Holy One of Israel; ᵃIn returning and rest shall ye be saved; in quietness and in confidence shall be your strength: ᵇand ye would not.

16 But ye said, No; for we will flee upon horses; therefore shall ye flee: and, We will ride upon the swift; therefore shall they that pursue you be swift.

17 ᵃOne thousand *shall flee* at the ¹rebuke of one; at the rebuke of five shall ye flee: till ye be left as ²a beacon upon the top of a mountain, and as ³an ensign on an hill.

18 And therefore will the LORD wait, that he may be ᵃgracious unto you, and therefore will he be exalted, that he may have mercy upon you: for the LORD *is* a God of ¹judgment: ᵇblessed *are* all they that ᶜwait for him.

19 For the people ᵃshall dwell in Zion at Jerusalem: thou shalt ᵇweep no more: he will be very gracious unto thee at the voice of thy cry; when he shall hear it, he will ᶜanswer thee.

20 And *though* the Lord give you ᵃthe bread of adversity, and the water of affliction, yet shall not ᵇthy teachers be removed into a corner any more, but thine eyes shall see thy teachers:

21 And thine ears shall hear a word behind thee, saying, This *is* the way, walk ye in it, when ye ᵃturn to the right hand, and when ye turn to the left.

22 ᵃYe shall defile also the covering of thy graven images of silver, and the ornament of thy molten images of gold: thou shalt cast them away as

[1]a menstruous cloth; [b]thou shalt say unto it, Get thee hence.

23 [a]Then shall he give the rain [1]of thy seed, that thou shalt sow the ground withal; and bread of the increase of the earth, and it shall be [2]fat and plenteous: in that day shall thy cattle feed in large pastures.

24 The oxen likewise and the young [1]asses that ear the ground shall eat [2]clean provender, which hath been winnowed with the shovel and with the fan.

25 And there shall be [a]upon every high mountain, and upon every high hill, rivers *and* streams of waters in the day of the [b]great slaughter, when the towers fall.

26 Moreover [a]the light of the moon shall be as the light of the sun, and the light of the sun shall be sevenfold, as the light of seven days, in the day that the LORD bindeth up the [1]breach of his people, and healeth the stroke of their wound.

27 Behold, the name of the LORD cometh from far, burning *with* his anger, and the burden *thereof is* heavy: his lips are full of indignation, and his tongue as a devouring fire:

28 And [a]his breath, as an overflowing stream, [b]shall reach to the midst of the neck, to sift the nations with the sieve of [1]vanity: and *there shall be* [c]a bridle in the jaws of the people, causing *them* to err.

29 Ye shall have a song, as in the night *when* a holy [1]solemnity is kept; and gladness of heart, as when one goeth with a pipe to come into [a]the mountain of the LORD, to [2]the mighty One of Israel.

30 [a]And the LORD shall cause his glorious voice to be heard, and shall shew the [1]lighting down of his arm, with the indignation of *his* anger, and *with* the flame of a devouring fire, *with* scattering, and tempest, [b]and hailstones.

31 For [a]through the voice of the LORD shall the Assyrian be [1]beaten down, [b]*which* smote with a rod.

32 And *in* every place where the [1]grounded staff shall pass, which the LORD shall lay upon him, *it* shall be with [2]tabrets and harps: and in battles of [a]shaking[3] will he fight with it.

33 [a]For Tophet *is* ordained of old; yea, for the king it is prepared; he hath made *it* deep *and* large: the pile thereof *is* fire and much wood; the breath of the LORD, like a stream of brimstone, doth kindle it.

### CHAPTER 31

WOE to them [a]that go down to Egypt for help; and [b]stay[1] on horses, and trust in chariots, because *they are* many; and in horsemen, because they are very strong; but they look not unto the Holy One of Israel, [c]neither seek the LORD!

2 Yet he also *is* wise, and will bring [1]evil, and [a]will not [2]call back his words: but will arise against the house of the evildoers, and against the help of them that work iniquity.

3 Now the Egyptians *are* men, and not God; and their horses flesh, and not spirit. When the LORD shall stretch out his hand, both he that helpeth shall fall, and he that is [1]holpen shall fall down, and they all shall [2]fail [a]together.

4 For thus hath the LORD spoken unto me, [a]Like as the lion and the young lion roaring on his prey, when a multitude of shepherds is called forth against him, *he* will not be afraid of their voice, nor [1]abase himself for the noise of them: so shall the LORD of hosts come down to fight for mount Zion, and for the hill thereof.

5 [a]As birds flying, so will the LORD of hosts defend Jerusalem; defending also he will deliver *it; and* passing over he will preserve *it.*

6 [1]Turn ye unto *him from* whom the children of Israel have [a]deeply revolted.

7 For in that day every man shall [a]cast away his idols of silver, and his idols of gold, which your own hands have made unto you *for* [b]a sin.

8 Then shall the Assyrian [a]fall with the sword, not of [1]a mighty man; and the sword, not of [2]a mean man, shall [b]devour him: but he shall flee from the sword, and his young men shall [3]be discomfited.

9 [a]And he shall pass over to his strong hold for fear, and his princes shall be afraid of the [1]ensign, saith the LORD, whose fire *is* in Zion, and his furnace in Jerusalem.

### CHAPTER 32

BEHOLD, [a]a king shall reign in righteousness, and princes shall rule [1]in judgment.

2 And a man shall be as an hiding place from the wind, and [a]a [1]covert from the tempest; as rivers of water in a dry place, as the shadow of a great rock in a weary land.

3 And [a]the eyes of them that see shall not be dim, and the ears of them that hear shall hearken.

4 The heart also of the rash shall [a]understand knowledge, and the tongue of the stammerers shall be ready to speak plainly.

5 The [1]vile person shall be no more called [2]liberal, nor the [3]churl said *to be* bountiful.

6 For the [1]vile person will speak [2]villany, and his heart will work [a]iniquity, to practise [3]hypocrisy, and to utter error against the LORD, to make

---

**Center reference column:**

30:22 [b] Hos. 14:8 [1] *an unclean thing*

30:23 [a] [Matt. 6:33]; 1 Tim. 6:8 [1] *for* [2] *rich*

30:24 [1] *donkeys that work* [2] *cured fodder*

30:25 [a] Is. 2:14, 15 [b] Is. 2:10–21; 34:2

30:26 [a] [Is. 60:19, 20; Rev. 21:23; 22:5] [1] *bruise*

30:28 [a] Is. 11:4; 2 Thess. 2:8 [b] Is. 8:8 [c] 2 Kin. 19:28; Is. 37:29 [1] *futility*

30:29 [a] [Is. 2:3] [1] *feast* [2] Lit. *the Rock*

30:30 [a] Is. 29:6 [b] Is. 28:2 [1] *descent*

30:31 [a] Is. 14:25; 37:36 [b] Is. 10:5, 24 [1] *crushed*

30:32 [a] Is. 11:15 [1] *staff of punishment* [2] *tambourines* [3] *brandishing*

30:33 [a] 2 Kin. 23:10; Jer. 7:31

31:1 [a] Is. 30:1, 2 [b] Deut. 17:16; Ps. 20:7; Is. 2:7; 30:16 [c] Is. 9:13; Dan. 9:13; Amos 5:4–8 [1] *rely*

31:2 [a] Num. 23:19; Jer. 44:29 [1] *disaster* [2] *retract*

31:3 [a] Is. 20:6 [1] *helped* [2] *perish*

31:4 [a] Num. 24:9; Hos. 11:10; Amos 3:8 [1] *be disturbed by*

31:5 [a] Deut. 32:11; Ps. 91:4

31:6 [a] Hos. 9:9 [1] *Return*

31:7 [a] Is. 2:20; 30:22 [b] 1 Kin. 12:30

31:8 [a] 2 Kin. 19:35, 36 [b] Is. 37:36 [1] *man* [2] *mankind* [3] *become forced labour*

31:9 [a] Is. 37:37 [1] *banner*

32:1 [a] Ps. 45:1 [1] *with justice*

32:2 [a] Is. 4:6 [1] *shelter*

32:3 [a] Is. 29:18; 35:5

32:4 [a] Is. 29:24

32:5 [1] *foolish* [2] *generous or noble* [3] *miser*

32:6 [a] Prov. 24:7–9 [1] *foolish* [2] *foolishness* [3] *ungodliness*

---

4empty the soul of the hungry, and he will cause the drink of the thirsty to fail.

7 The ¹instruments also of the ²churl *are* evil: he deviseth wicked ³devices to destroy the poor with ªlying words, even when the needy speaketh right.

8 But the ¹liberal deviseth ²liberal things; and by liberal things shall he stand.

9 Rise up, ye women ªthat are at ease; hear my voice, ye ¹careless daughters; give ear unto my speech.

10 ¹Many days and years shall ye be troubled, ye ²careless women: for the vintage shall fail, the gathering shall not come.

11 Tremble, ye women that are at ease; be troubled, ye ¹careless ones: strip you, and make you bare, and gird *sackcloth* upon *your* loins.

12 They shall ¹lament for the teats, for the pleasant fields, for the fruitful vine.

13 ªUpon the land of my people shall come up thorns *and* briers; yea, upon all the ¹houses of joy *in* ᵇthe joyous city:

14 ªBecause the palaces shall be forsaken; the multitude of the city shall be left; the forts and towers shall be for ¹dens for ever, a joy of wild asses, a pasture of flocks;

15 Until ªthe spirit be poured upon us from on high, and ᵇthe wilderness be a fruitful field, and the fruitful field be counted for a forest.

16 Then judgment shall dwell in the wilderness, and righteousness remain in the fruitful field.

17 ªAnd the work of righteousness shall be peace; and the effect of righteousness quietness and assurance for ever.

18 And my people shall dwell in a peaceable habitation, and in ¹sure dwellings, and in quiet ªresting places;

19 ªWhen it shall hail, coming down ᵇon the forest; and the city shall be ¹low in a low place.

20 Blessed *are* ye that sow beside all waters, that send forth *thither* the feet of ªthe ox and the ass.

## CHAPTER 33

WOE to thee ªthat ¹spoilest, and thou *wast* not ²spoiled; and dealest treacherously, and they dealt not treacherously with thee! ᵇwhen thou shalt cease to ³spoil, thou shalt be ᶜspoiled;² *and* when thou shalt make an end to deal treacherously, they shall deal treacherously with thee.

2 O LORD, be gracious unto us; ªwe have waited for thee: be thou their arm every morning, our salvation also in the time of trouble.

32:6 ⁴ *unsatisfied*
32:7 ª Jer. 5:26–28
¹ *schemes*
² *schemer* ³ *plans*
32:8 ¹ *generous* or *noble* ² *generous things*
32:9 ª Amos 6:1
¹ *complacent*
32:10 ¹ *In a year and some days*
² *complacent*
32:11 ¹ *complacent*
32:12 ¹ *mourn upon their breasts*
32:13 ª Hos. 9:6
ᵇ Is. 22:2 ¹ *happy homes*
32:14 ª Is. 27:10
¹ *lairs*
32:15 ª [Joel 2:28]
ᵇ Is. 29:17
32:17 ª James 3:18
32:18 ª [Zech. 2:5; 3:10] ¹ *secure*
32:19 ª Is. 30:30
ᵇ Zech. 11:2
¹ *brought low in humiliation*
32:20 ª Is. 30:23, 24
33:1 ª Hab. 2:8
ᵇ Rev. 13:10 ᶜ Is. 10:12; 14:25;
31:8 ¹ *plunderest*
² *plundered*
³ *plunder*
33:2 ª Is. 25:9; 26:8

33:3 ª Is. 17:13
33:4 ¹ *plunder*
33:5 ª Ps. 97:9
¹ *justice*
33:7 ª 2 Kin. 18:18, 37 ¹ *outside*
33:8 ª Judg. 5:6
ᵇ 2 Kin. 18:13–17
33:9 ª Is. 24:4
¹ *shrivelled*
33:10 ª Ps. 12:5
33:11 ª [Ps. 7:14]
33:12 ª Is. 9:18
33:13 ª Is. 49:1
33:14 ª Heb. 12:29
33:15 ª Ps. 15:2; 24:3, 4 ᵇ Ps. 119:37 ¹ *refusing bribes* ² *bloodshed*
33:16 ¹ *fortress*
33:17 ª Ps. 27:4
33:18 ª 1 Cor. 1:20
¹ *on terror* ² *he who weighs*
33:19 ª 2 Kin. 19:32 ᵇ Jer. 5:15
¹ *obscure speech, beyond perception* ² *Unintelligible language*
33:20 ª Ps. 48:12
¹ *solemn feasts*

3 At the noise of the tumult the people ªfled; at the lifting up of thyself the nations were scattered.

4 And your ¹spoil shall be gathered *like* the gathering of the caterpiller: as the running to and fro of locusts shall he run upon them.

5 ªThe LORD is exalted; for he dwelleth on high: he hath filled Zion with ¹judgment and righteousness.

6 And wisdom and knowledge shall be the stability of thy times, *and* strength of salvation: the fear of the LORD *is* his treasure.

7 Behold, their valiant ones shall cry ¹without: ªthe ambassadors of peace shall weep bitterly.

8 ªThe highways lie waste, the wayfaring man ceaseth: ᵇhe hath broken the covenant, he hath despised the cities, he regardeth no man.

9 ªThe earth mourneth *and* languisheth: Lebanon is ashamed *and* ¹hewn down: Sharon is like a wilderness; and Bashan and Carmel shake off *their* fruits.

10 ªNow will I rise, saith the LORD; now will I be exalted; now will I lift up myself.

11 ªYe shall conceive chaff, ye shall bring forth stubble: your breath, *as* fire, shall devour you.

12 And the people shall be *as* the burnings of lime: ªas thorns cut up shall they be burned in the fire.

13 Hear, ªye *that are* far off, what I have done; and, ye *that are* near, acknowledge my might.

14 The sinners in Zion are afraid; fearfulness hath surprised the hypocrites. Who among us shall dwell with the devouring ªfire? who among us shall dwell with everlasting burnings?

15 He that ªwalketh righteously, and speaketh uprightly; he that despiseth the gain of oppressions, that shaketh his hands ¹from holding of bribes, that stoppeth his ears from hearing of ²blood, and ᵇshutteth his eyes from seeing evil;

16 He shall dwell on high: his place of defence *shall be* the ¹munitions of rocks: bread shall be given him; his waters *shall be* sure.

17 Thine eyes shall see the king in his ªbeauty: they shall behold the land that is very far off.

18 Thine heart shall meditate ¹terror. ªWhere *is* the scribe? where *is* ²the receiver? where *is* he that counted the towers?

19 ªThou shalt not see a fierce people, ᵇa people of ¹a deeper speech than thou canst perceive; of a ²stammering tongue, *that thou canst* not understand.

20 ªLook upon Zion, the city of our ¹solemnities: thine eyes shall see

[b]Jerusalem a quiet habitation, a tabernacle *that* shall not be taken down; [c]not one of [d]the stakes thereof shall ever be removed, neither shall any of the cords thereof be broken.

21 But there the glorious LORD *will be* unto us a place of broad rivers *and* streams; wherein shall go no [1]galley with oars, neither shall [2]gallant ship pass thereby.

22 For the LORD *is* our [a]judge, the LORD *is* our [b]lawgiver, [c]the LORD *is* our king; he will save us.

23 Thy tacklings are loosed; they could not well strengthen their mast, they could not spread the sail: then is the prey of a great [1]spoil divided; the lame take the prey.

24 And the inhabitant shall not say, I am sick: [a]the people that dwell therein *shall be* forgiven *their* iniquity.

## CHAPTER 34

COME[a] near, ye nations, to hear; and hearken, ye people: [b]let the earth hear, and all that is therein; the world, and all things that come forth of it.

2 For the indignation of the LORD *is* upon all nations, and *his* fury upon all their armies: he hath utterly destroyed them, he hath delivered them to the [a]slaughter.

3 Their slain also shall be cast out, and [a]their stink shall come up out of their carcases, and the mountains shall be melted with their blood.

4 And [a]all the host of heaven shall be dissolved, and the heavens shall be rolled together as a scroll: [b]and all their host shall fall down, as the leaf falleth off from the vine, and as a [c]falling *fig* from the fig tree.

5 For [a]my sword shall be bathed in heaven: behold, it [b]shall come down upon [1]Idumea, and upon the people of my curse, to judgment.

6 The [a]sword of the LORD is filled with blood, it is made [1]fat with fatness, *and* with the blood of lambs and goats, with the fat of the kidneys of rams: for [b]the LORD hath a sacrifice in Bozrah, and a great slaughter in the land of [2]Idumea.

7 And the [1]unicorns shall come down with them, and the bullocks with the bulls; and their land shall be soaked with blood, and their dust [2]made fat with fatness.

8 For *it is* the day of the LORD's [a]vengeance, *and* the year of recompences for the [1]controversy of Zion.

9 [a]And the streams thereof shall be turned into pitch, and the dust thereof into brimstone, and the land thereof shall become burning pitch.

10 It shall not be quenched night nor day; [a]the smoke thereof shall go up for ever: [b]from generation to generation it shall lie waste; none shall pass through it for ever and ever.

11 [a]But the [1]cormorant and the [2]bittern shall possess it; the owl also and the raven shall dwell in it: and [b]he shall stretch out upon it the line of confusion, and the stones of emptiness.

12 They shall call the nobles thereof to the kingdom, but none *shall be* there, and all her princes shall be nothing.

13 And [a]thorns shall come up in her palaces, nettles and brambles in the fortresses thereof: and [b]it shall be an habitation of [1]dragons, *and* a court for [2]owls.

14 The wild beasts of the desert shall also meet with the [1]wild beasts of the island, and the [2]satyr shall cry to his fellow; the [3]screech owl also shall rest there, and find for herself a place of rest.

15 There shall the [1]great owl make her nest, and lay, and hatch, and gather under her shadow: there shall the [2]vultures also be gathered, every one with her mate.

16 Seek ye out of [a]the book of the LORD, and read: no one of these shall fail, none shall want her mate: for my mouth it hath commanded, and his spirit it hath gathered them.

17 And he hath cast the lot for them, and his hand hath divided it unto them [1]by line: they shall possess it for ever, from generation to generation shall they dwell therein.

## CHAPTER 35

THE [a]wilderness and the [1]solitary place shall be glad for them; and the [b]desert shall rejoice, and blossom as the rose.

2 [a]It shall blossom abundantly, and rejoice even with joy and singing: the glory of Lebanon shall be given unto it, the excellency of Carmel and Sharon, they shall see the [b]glory of the LORD, *and* the excellency of our God.

3 [a]Strengthen ye the [1]weak hands, and [2]confirm the feeble knees.

4 Say to them *that are* of a fearful heart, Be strong, fear not: behold, your God will come *with* [a]vengeance, *even* God *with* a recompence; he will come and [b]save you.

5 Then the [a]eyes of the blind shall be opened, and [b]the ears of the deaf shall be unstopped.

6 Then shall the [a]lame *man* leap as [1]an hart, and the [b]tongue of the [2]dumb sing: for in the wilderness shall [c]waters break out, and streams in the desert.

7 And the parched ground shall become a pool, and the thirsty land

### Cross references

33:20 [b] Ps. 46:5; 125:1 [c] Is. 37:33 [d] Is. 54:2
33:21 [1] *ship* [2] *majestic*
33:22 [a] [Acts 10:42] [b] James 4:12 [c] Ps. 89:18
33:23 [1] *plunder*
33:24 [a] Is. 40:2
34:1 [a] Ps. 49:1 [b] Deut. 32:1
34:2 [a] Is. 13:5
34:3 [a] Joel 2:20
34:4 [a] Is. 13:13 [b] Is. 14:12 [c] Rev. 6:12–14
34:5 [a] Jer. 46:10 [b] Mal. 1:4 [1] *Edom*
34:6 [a] Is. 66:16 [b] Zeph. 1:7 [1] *overflowing* [2] *Edom*
34:7 [1] *wild oxen* [2] *saturated*
34:8 [a] Is. 63:4 [1] *cause*
34:9 [a] Deut. 29:23
34:10 [a] Rev. 14:11; 18:18; 19:3
[b] Mal. 1:3, 4
34:11 [a] Zeph. 2:14 [b] Lam. 2:8 [1] *owl or pelican* [2] *porcupine or hedgehog*
34:13 [a] Is. 32:13 [b] Is. 13:21 [1] *jackals* [2] *ostriches*
34:14 [1] *jackals* [2] *wild goat* [3] *night monster or creature*
34:15 [1] *arrow snake* [2] *hawks*
34:16 [a] [Mal. 3:16]
34:17 [1] *with a measuring line*
35:1 [a] Is. 32:15; 55:12 [b] Is. 41:19; 51:3 [1] *desert*
35:2 [a] Is. 32:15 [b] Is. 40:5
35:3 [a] Heb. 12:12 [1] Lit. *sinking* [2] *make firm*
35:4 [a] Is. 34:8 [b] Is. 33:22
35:5 [a] Is. 29:18 [b] [Matt. 11:5]
35:6 [a] Acts 8:7 [b] Is. 32:4 [c] [John 7:38] [1] *a deer* [2] *mute*

springs of water: in [a]the habitation of [1]dragons, where each lay, *shall be* grass with reeds and rushes.

8 And an [a]highway shall be there, and a [1]way, and it shall be called The way of holiness; [b]the unclean shall not pass over it; but it *shall be* for those: [2]the wayfaring men, though fools, shall not [3]err *therein.*

9 [a]No lion shall be there, nor *any* ravenous beast shall go up thereon, it shall not be found there; but the redeemed shall walk *there:*

10 And the [a]ransomed of the LORD shall return, and come to Zion with songs and everlasting joy upon their heads: they shall obtain joy and gladness, and [b]sorrow and sighing shall flee away.

## CHAPTER 36

Now [a]it came to pass in the fourteenth year of king Hezekiah, *that* Sennacherib king of Assyria came up against all the [1]defenced cities of Judah, and took them.

2 And the king of Assyria sent [1]Rabshakeh from Lachish to Jerusalem unto king Hezekiah with a great army. And he stood by the [2]conduit of the upper pool in the highway of the fuller's field.

3 Then came forth unto him [a]Eliakim, Hilkiah's son, which was over the house, and [b]Shebna the scribe, and Joah, Asaph's son, the recorder.

4 [a]And Rabshakeh said unto them, Say ye now to Hezekiah, Thus saith the great king, the king of Assyria, What confidence *is* this wherein thou trustest?

5 I say, *sayest thou,* (but *they are but* [1]vain words) *I have* counsel and strength for war: now on whom dost thou trust, that thou rebellest against me?

6 Lo, thou trustest in the [a]staff of this broken reed, on Egypt; whereon if a man lean, it will go into his hand, and pierce it: so *is* Pharaoh king of Egypt to all that [b]trust in him.

7 But if thou say to me, We trust in the LORD our God: *is it* not he, whose high places and whose altars Hezekiah hath taken away, and said to Judah and to Jerusalem, Ye shall worship before this altar?

8 Now therefore give pledges, I pray thee, to my master the king of Assyria, and I will give thee two thousand horses, if thou be able on thy part to set riders upon them.

9 How then wilt thou turn away the face of one captain of the least of my master's servants, and put thy trust on Egypt for chariots and for horsemen?

10 And am I now come up without the LORD against this land to destroy it? the LORD said unto me, Go up against this land, and destroy it.

11 Then said Eliakim and Shebna and Joah unto Rabshakeh, Speak, I pray thee, unto thy servants in the [1]Syrian language; for we understand *it:* and speak not to us in [2]the Jews' language, in the [3]ears of the people that *are* on the wall.

12 But Rabshakeh said, Hath my master sent me to thy master and to thee to speak these words? *hath he* not *sent me* to the men that sit upon the wall, [1]that they may eat their own dung, and drink their own piss with you?

13 Then Rabshakeh stood, and cried with a loud voice in the Jews' language, and said, Hear ye the words of the great king, the king of Assyria.

14 Thus saith the king, Let not Hezekiah deceive you: for he shall not be able to deliver you.

15 Neither let Hezekiah make you trust in the LORD, saying, The LORD will surely deliver us: this city shall not be delivered into the hand of the king of Assyria.

16 Hearken not to Hezekiah: for thus saith the king of Assyria, Make [1]*an agreement* with me *by* a [2]present, and come out to me: [a]and eat ye every one of his vine, and every one of his fig tree, and drink ye every one the waters of his own cistern;

17 Until I come and take you away to a land like your own land, a land of [1]corn and wine, a land of bread and vineyards.

18 *Beware* lest Hezekiah persuade you, saying, The LORD will deliver us. Hath any of the [a]gods of the nations delivered his land out of the hand of the king of Assyria?

19 Where *are* the gods of Hamath and [1]Arphad? where *are* the gods of Sepharvaim? and have they delivered [a]Samaria out of my hand?

20 Who *are they* among all the gods of these lands, that have delivered their land out of my hand, that the LORD should deliver Jerusalem out of my hand?

21 But they [1]held their peace, and answered him not a word: for the king's commandment was, saying, Answer him not.

22 Then came Eliakim, the son of Hilkiah, that *was* over the household, and Shebna the scribe, and Joah, the son of Asaph, the recorder, to Hezekiah with *their* clothes [1]rent, and told him the words of Rabshakeh.

## CHAPTER 37

And [a]it came to pass, when king Hezekiah heard *it,* that he [1]rent his clothes, and covered himself with

35:7 [a] Is. 34:13 [1] *jackals*
35:8 [a] Is. 19:23 [1] *road* [b] Is. 52:1; Joel 3:17; [Matt. 7:13, 14]; 1 Pet. 1:15, 16; Rev. 21:27 [2] *they who walk the road* [3] *go* astray
35:9 [a] Lev. 26:6; [Is. 11:7, 9]; Ezek. 34:25
35:10 [a] Is. 51:11 [b] Is. 25:8; 30:19; 65:19; [Rev. 7:17; 21:4]
36:1 [a] 2 Kin. 18:13, 17; 2 Chr. 32:1 [1] *fortified*
36:2 [1] A title, probably *Chief of Staff* or *Governor* [2] *aqueduct*
36:3 [a] Is. 22:20 [b] Is. 22:15
36:4 [a] 2 Kin. 18:19
36:5 [1] *empty*
36:6 [a] Ezek. 29:6 [b] Ps. 146:3; Is. 30:3, 5, 7
36:11 [1] Lit. *Aramaic* [2] *Hebrew,* lit. *Judean* [3] *hearing*
36:12 [1] *who will eat and drink their own waste with you*
36:16 [a] 1 Kin. 4:25; Mic. 4:4; Zech. 3:10 [1] Peace [2] *gift*
36:17 [1] *grain and new wine*
36:18 [a] 2 Kin. 19:12; Is. 37:12
36:19 [a] 2 Kin. 17:6 [1] Or *Arpad*
36:21 [1] *were silent*
36:22 [1] *torn*
37:1 [a] 2 Kin. 19:1–37; Is. 37:1–38 [1] *tore*

sackcloth, and went into the house of the LORD.

2 And he sent Eliakim, who *was* over the household, and Shebna the scribe, and the elders of the priests covered with sackcloth, unto Isaiah the prophet the son of Amoz.

3 And they said unto him, Thus saith Hezekiah, This day *is* a day of [a]trouble, and of rebuke, and of [1]blasphemy: for the children are come to the birth, and *there is* not strength to bring forth.

4 It may be the LORD thy God will hear the words of [1]Rabshakeh, whom the king of Assyria his master hath sent to [a]reproach the living God, and will [2]reprove the words which the LORD thy God hath heard: wherefore lift up *thy* prayer for the remnant that is left.

5 So the servants of king Hezekiah came to Isaiah.

6 And Isaiah said unto them, Thus shall ye say unto your master, Thus saith the LORD, Be not afraid of the words that thou hast heard, wherewith the servants of the king of Assyria have blasphemed me.

7 Behold, I will send a [1]blast upon him, and he shall hear a rumour, and return to his own land; and I will cause him to fall by the sword in his own land.

8 So Rabshakeh returned, and found the king of Assyria warring against Libnah: for he had heard that he was departed from Lachish.

9 And he heard say concerning Tirhakah king of Ethiopia, He is come forth to make war with thee. And when he heard *it,* he sent messengers to Hezekiah, saying,

10 Thus shall ye speak to Hezekiah king of Judah, saying, Let not thy God, in whom thou trustest, deceive thee, saying, Jerusalem shall not be given into the hand of the king of Assyria.

11 Behold, thou hast heard what the kings of Assyria have done to all lands by destroying them utterly; and shalt thou be delivered?

12 Have the [a]gods of the nations delivered them which my fathers have destroyed, *as* Gozan, and Haran, and Rezeph, and the children of Eden which *were* in Telassar?

13 Where *is* the king of [a]Hamath, and the king of [1]Arphad, and the king of the city of Sepharvaim, Hena, and Ivah?

14 And Hezekiah received the letter from the hand of the messengers, and read it: and Hezekiah went up unto the house of the LORD, and spread it before the LORD.

15 And Hezekiah prayed unto the LORD, saying,

16 O LORD of hosts, God of Israel, that dwellest *between* the cherubims, thou *art* the God, *even* thou [a]alone, of all the kingdoms of the earth: thou hast made heaven and earth.

17 [a]Incline thine ear, O LORD, and hear; open thine eyes, O LORD, and see: and [b]hear all the words of Sennacherib, which hath sent to reproach the living God.

18 Of a truth, LORD, the kings of Assyria have laid waste all the nations, and their [a]countries,

19 And have cast their gods into the fire: for they *were* [a]no gods, but the work of men's hands, wood and stone: therefore they have destroyed them.

20 Now therefore, O LORD our God, [a]save us from his hand, that all the kingdoms of the earth may [b]know that thou *art* the LORD, *even* thou only.

21 Then Isaiah the son of Amoz sent unto Hezekiah, saying, Thus saith the LORD God of Israel, Whereas thou hast prayed to me against Sennacherib king of Assyria:

22 This *is* the word which the LORD hath spoken concerning him; The virgin, the daughter of Zion, hath despised thee, *and* [1]laughed thee to scorn; the daughter of Jerusalem hath shaken her head at thee.

23 Whom hast thou reproached and blasphemed? and against whom hast thou [1]exalted *thy* voice, and lifted up thine eyes on high? *even* against the Holy One of Israel.

24 By thy servants hast thou reproached the Lord, and hast said, By the multitude of my chariots am I come up to the height of the mountains, to the sides of Lebanon; and I will cut down the tall cedars thereof, *and* the choice [1]fir trees thereof: and I will enter into [2]the height of his border, *and* [3]the forest of his Carmel.

25 I have digged, and drunk water; and with the sole of my feet have I dried up all the [1]rivers of [2]the besieged places.

26 Hast thou not heard [a]long ago, *how* I have done it; *and* of ancient times, that I have formed it? now have I brought it to pass, that thou shouldest be [1]to lay waste defenced cities *into* [2]ruinous heaps.

27 Therefore their inhabitants [1]*were* of small power, they were dismayed and confounded: they were *as* the grass of the field, and *as* the green herb, *as* the grass on the housetops, and *as* [2]*corn* blasted before it be grown up.

28 But I know thy [1]abode, and thy going out, and thy coming in, and thy rage against me.

29 Because thy rage against me, and thy tumult, is come up into mine

37:3 [a] Is. 22:5; 26:16; 33:2 [1] *contempt*
37:4 [a] Is. 36:15, 18, 20 [1] A title, probably *Chief of Staff* or *Governor* [2] *rebuke*
37:7 [1] *spirit*
37:12 [a] Is. 36:18, 19
37:13 [a] Is. 49:23 [1] Or *Arpad*
37:16 [a] Is. 43:10, 11
37:17 [a] 2 Chr. 6:40; Ps. 17:6; Dan. 9:18 [b] Ps. 74:22
37:18 [a] 2 Kin. 15:29; 16:9; 17:6, 24; 1 Chr. 5:26
37:19 [a] Is. 40:19, 20
37:20 [a] Is. 33:22 [b] Ps. 83:18
37:22 [1] *mocked thee*
37:23 [1] *raised*
37:24 [1] *cypress* [2] *its farthest height* [3] *to its fruitful forest*
37:25 [1] *brooks* [2] *defence* or perhaps *Egypt*
37:26 [a] Is. 25:1; 40:21; 45:21 [1] *for crushing fortified cities* [2] *heaps of ruins*
37:27 [1] had *little* [2] grain *blighted*
37:28 [1] *dwelling place*

ears, therefore [a]will I put my hook in thy nose, and my bridle in thy lips, and I will [b]turn thee back by the way by which thou camest.

30 And this *shall be* a sign unto thee, Ye shall eat *this* year such as groweth of itself; and the second year that which springeth of the same: and in the third year sow ye, and reap, and plant vineyards, and eat the fruit thereof.

31 And the remnant that is escaped of the house of Judah shall again take root downward, and bear fruit upward:

32 For out of Jerusalem shall go forth a remnant, and they that escape out of mount Zion: the [a]zeal of the LORD of hosts shall do this.

33 Therefore thus saith the LORD concerning the king of Assyria, He shall not come into this city, nor shoot an arrow there, nor come before it with shields, nor [1]cast a bank against it.

34 By the way that he came, by the same shall he return, and shall not come into this city, saith the LORD.

35 For I will [a]defend this city to save it for mine own sake, and for my servant [b]David's sake.

36 Then the [a]angel of the LORD went forth, and [1]smote in the camp of the Assyrians a hundred and fourscore and five thousand: and when [2]they arose early in the morning, behold, [3]they *were* all dead corpses.

37 So Sennacherib king of Assyria departed, and went and returned, and dwelt at Nineveh.

38 And it came to pass, as he was worshipping in the house of Nisroch his god, that Adrammelech and Sharezer his sons [1]smote him with the sword; and they escaped into the land of [2]Armenia: and [a]Esar-haddon his son reigned in his stead.

## CHAPTER 38

IN [a]those days was Hezekiah sick [1]unto death. And Isaiah the prophet the son of Amoz came unto him, and said unto him, Thus saith the LORD, [b]Set thine house in order: for thou shalt die, and not live.

2 Then Hezekiah turned his face toward the wall, and prayed unto the LORD,

3 And said, [a]Remember now, O LORD, I beseech thee, how I have walked before thee in truth and with a [1]perfect heart, and have done *that which is* good in thy [b]sight. And Hezekiah wept [2]sore.

4 Then came the word of the LORD to Isaiah, saying,

5 Go, and say to Hezekiah, Thus saith the LORD, the God of David thy father, I have heard thy prayer, I have

seen thy tears: behold, I will add unto thy days fifteen years.

6 And I will deliver thee and this city out of the hand of the king of Assyria: and [a]I will defend this city.

7 And this *shall be* [a]a sign unto thee from the LORD, that the LORD will do this thing that he hath spoken;

8 Behold, I will bring again the shadow [1]of the degrees, which [2]is gone down in the sun dial of Ahaz, ten degrees backward. So the sun returned ten degrees, [3]by which degrees it was gone down.

9 The writing of Hezekiah king of Judah, when he had been sick, and was recovered of his sickness:

10 I said in the [1]cutting off of my days, I shall go to the gates of [2]the grave: I am deprived of the [3]residue of my years.

11 I said, I shall not see [1]the LORD, *even* the LORD, [a]in the land of the living: I shall behold man no more with the inhabitants of the world.

12 [a]Mine[1] age is departed, and is removed from me as a shepherd's tent: I have cut off like a weaver my life: he [2]will cut me off [3]with pining sickness: from day *even* to night wilt thou make an end of me.

13 I reckoned till morning, *that,* as a lion, so will he break all my bones: from day *even* to night wilt thou make an end of me.

14 Like a crane *or* a swallow, so did I chatter: [a]I did mourn as a dove: mine eyes fail *with looking* upward: O [1]LORD, I am oppressed; undertake for me.

15 What shall I say? he hath both spoken unto me, and himself hath done *it:* I shall [1]go softly all my years [a]in the bitterness of my soul.

16 O Lord, by these *things men* live, and in all these *things is* the life of my spirit: so wilt thou recover me, and make me to live.

17 Behold, [1]for peace I had great bitterness: but thou hast in love to my soul *delivered it* from the pit of corruption: for thou hast cast all my sins behind thy back.

18 For [a]the[1] grave cannot praise thee, death can *not* celebrate thee: they that go down into the pit cannot hope for thy truth.

19 The living, the living, he shall praise thee, as I *do* this day: [a]the father to the children shall make known thy truth.

20 The LORD *was ready* to save me: therefore we will sing my songs to the stringed instruments all the days of our life in the house of the LORD.

21 For [a]Isaiah had said, Let them take a lump of figs, and [1]lay *it* for a plaister upon the boil, and he shall recover.

### Cross references

37:29 [a] 2 Kin. 19:35–37; 2 Chr. 32:21; Is. 30:28; Ezek. 38:4 [b] Ezek. 38:4; 39:2

37:32 [a] 2 Kin. 19:31; Is. 9:7; 59:17; Joel 2:18; Zech. 1:14

37:33 [1] *build a siege mound*

37:35 [a] 2 Kin. 20:6; Is. 31:5; 38:6 [b] 1 Kin. 11:13

37:36 [a] 2 Kin. 19:35; Is. 10:12, 33, 34 [1] *killed,* lit. *struck* [2] *the people arose* [3] *there they were, all dead corpses*

37:38 [a] Ezra 4:2 [1] *struck him down* [2] *Ararat*

38:1 [a] 2 Kin. 20:1–6, 9–11; 2 Chr. 32:24; Is. 38:1–8 [b] 2 Sam. 17:23 [1] *and near death*

38:3 [a] Neh. 13:14 [b] 2 Kin. 18:5, 6; Ps. 26:3 [1] *loyal or whole* [2] *bitterly*

38:6 [a] 2 Kin. 19:35–37; 2 Chr. 32:21; Is. 31:5; 37:35

38:7 [a] Judg. 6:17, 21, 36–40; 2 Kin. 20:8; Is. 7:11

38:8 [1] *on the sundial* [2] *has gone down with the sun on the sundial* [3] *on the dial by which it had gone*

38:10 [1] *middle* [2] Or *Sheol* [3] *remainder*

38:11 [a] Ps. 27:13; 116:9 [1] Heb. *YAH, YAH*

38:12 [a] Job 7:6 [1] *My life span* [2] *cuts* [3] *from the loom*

38:14 [a] Is. 59:11; Ezek. 7:16; Nah. 2:7 [1] MT, DSS *Lord*

38:15 [a] Job 7:11; 10:1; Is. 38:17 [1] *walk carefully*

38:17 [1] *for my own peace*

38:18 [a] Ps. 6:5; 30:9; 88:11; 115:17; [Eccl. 9:10] [1] Or *Sheol*

38:19 [a] Deut. 4:9; 6:7; Ps. 78:3, 4

38:21 [a] 2 Kin. 20:7 [1] *apply* it *as a poultice*

22 [a]Hezekiah also had said, What *is* the sign that I shall go up to the house of the LORD?

## CHAPTER 39

AT [a]that time [1]Merodach-baladan, the son of Baladan, king of Babylon, sent letters and a present to Hezekiah: for he had heard that he had been sick, and was recovered.

2 [a]And Hezekiah was glad of them, and shewed them the house of his [1]precious things, the silver, and the gold, and the spices, and the precious ointment, and all [2]the house of his armour, and all that was found in his treasures: there was nothing in his house, nor in all his dominion, that Hezekiah shewed them not.

3 Then came Isaiah the prophet unto king Hezekiah, and said unto him, What said these men? and from whence came they unto thee? And Hezekiah said, They are come from a [a]far country unto me, *even* from Babylon.

4 Then said he, What have they seen in thine house? And Hezekiah answered, All that *is* in mine house have they seen: there is nothing among my treasures that I have not shewed them.

5 Then said Isaiah to Hezekiah, Hear the word of the LORD of hosts:

6 Behold, the days come, [a]that all that *is* in thine house, and *that* which thy fathers have laid up in store until this day, shall be carried to Babylon: nothing shall be left, saith the LORD.

7 And of thy [a]sons that shall [1]issue from thee, which thou shalt beget, shall they take away; and they shall be eunuchs in the palace of the king of Babylon.

8 Then said Hezekiah to Isaiah, [a]Good[1] *is* the word of the LORD which thou hast spoken. He said moreover, [2]For there shall be peace and truth in my days.

## CHAPTER 40

COMFORT ye, comfort ye my people, saith your God.

2 Speak ye [1]comfortably to Jerusalem, and cry unto her, that her warfare is [2]accomplished, that her iniquity is pardoned: [a]for she hath received of the LORD's hand double for all her sins.

3 [a]The voice of him that crieth in the wilderness, [b]Prepare ye the way of the LORD, [c]make straight in the desert a highway for our God.

4 Every valley shall be [1]exalted, and every mountain and hill shall be made low: [a]and the crooked shall be made straight, and the rough places [2]plain:

5 And the [a]glory of the LORD shall be revealed, and all flesh shall see *it* together: for the mouth of the LORD hath spoken *it.*

6 The voice said, [1]Cry. And he said, What shall I cry? [a]All flesh *is* grass, and all the [2]goodliness thereof *is* as the flower of the field:

7 The grass withereth, the flower fadeth: because the [1]spirit of the LORD bloweth upon it: surely the people *is* grass.

8 The grass withereth, the flower fadeth: but [a]the word of our God shall stand for ever.

9 O Zion, that bringest good tidings, get thee up into the high mountain; O Jerusalem, that bringest good tidings, lift up thy voice with strength; lift *it* up, be not afraid; say unto the cities of Judah, Behold your God!

10 Behold, the Lord GOD will come [1]with strong *hand,* and [a]his arm shall rule for him: behold, [b]his reward *is* with him, and his [2]work before him.

11 He shall [a]feed his flock like a shepherd: he shall gather the lambs with his arm, and carry *them* in his bosom, *and* shall gently lead those that are with young.

12 [a]Who hath measured the waters in the hollow of his hand, and [1]meted out heaven with [2]the span, and [3]comprehended the dust of the earth in a measure, and weighed the mountains in scales, and the hills in a balance?

13 [a]Who hath directed the Spirit of the LORD, or *being* his counsellor hath taught him?

14 With whom took he counsel, and *who* instructed him, and [a]taught him in the path of [1]judgment, and taught him knowledge, and shewed to him the way of understanding?

15 Behold, the nations *are* as a drop [1]of a bucket, and are counted as the [2]small dust of the balance: behold, he [3]taketh up the isles as a very little thing.

16 And Lebanon *is* not sufficient to burn, nor the beasts thereof sufficient for a burnt offering.

17 All nations before him *are* as [a]nothing; and [b]they are counted to him less than nothing, and [1]vanity.

18 To whom then will ye [a]liken God? or what likeness will ye compare unto him?

19 [a]The workman [1]melteth a graven image, and the goldsmith spreadeth it over with gold, and [2]casteth silver chains.

20 He that *is* so impoverished that he hath [1]no oblation chooseth a tree *that* will not rot; he seeketh unto him a [2]cunning workman [a]to prepare a graven image, *that* shall not [3]be moved.

21 [a]Have ye not known? have ye not heard? hath it not been told you from

38:22 [a] 2 Kin. 20:8
39:1 [a] 2 Kin. 20:12–19 [1] Or *Berodach-baladan,* 2 Kin. 20:12
39:2 [a] 2 Chr. 32:25, 31 [1] *treasures* [2] *his armoury*
39:3 [a] Deut. 28:49
39:6 [a] Jer. 20:5
39:7 [a] Dan. 1:1–7 [1] *descend*
39:8 [a] 1 Sam. 3:18 [1] Just [2] *At least there will be*
40:2 [a] Is. 61:7 [1] *comfort,* lit. *on the heart of* [2] *ended*
40:3 [a] Matt. 3:3 [b] [Mal. 3:1; 4:5, 6] [c] Ps. 68:4
40:4 [a] Is. 45:2 [1] *lifted up* [2] *smooth*
40:5 [a] Is. 35:2
40:6 [a] Job 14:2 [1] *Cry out* [2] *loveliness*
40:7 [1] *breath*
40:8 [a] [John 12:34]
40:10 [a] Is. 59:16, 18 [b] Is. 62:11 [1] *in strength* [2] *wage*
40:11 [a] [John 10:11, 14–16]
40:12 [a] Prov. 30:4 [1] *measured* [2] A span = ½ cubit, 9 inches [3] *calculated*
40:13 [a] [1 Cor. 2:16]
40:14 [a] Job 36:22, 23 [1] *justice*
40:15 [1] *in* [2] *fine dust on* [3] *lifteth*
40:17 [a] Dan. 4:35 [b] Ps. 62:9 [1] *worthless*
40:18 [a] Is. 46:5
40:19 [a] Is. 41:7; 44:10 [1] *moulds* [2] *the silversmith casts*
40:20 [a] Is. 41:7; 46:7 [1] *no such offering* [2] *skilful* [3] *totter*
40:21 [a] Rom. 1:19

the beginning? have ye not understood from the foundations of the earth?

22 *It is* he that sitteth ¹upon the circle of the earth, and the inhabitants thereof *are* as grasshoppers; that ᵃstretcheth out the heavens as a curtain, and spreadeth them out as a ᵇtent to dwell in:

23 That ¹bringeth the ᵃprinces to nothing; he maketh the judges of the earth ²as vanity.

24 Yea, they shall ¹not be planted; yea, they shall ¹not be sown: yea, their stock shall ¹not take root in the earth: and he shall also blow upon them, and they shall wither, and the whirlwind shall take them away as stubble.

25 ᵃTo whom then will ye liken me, or shall I be equal? saith the Holy One.

26 Lift up your eyes on high, and behold who hath created these *things,* that bringeth out their host by number: ᵃhe calleth them all by names by the greatness of his might, for that *he is* strong in power; not one ¹faileth.

27 ᵃWhy sayest thou, O Jacob, and speakest, O Israel, My way is hid from the LORD, and my ¹judgment is passed over from my God?

28 Hast thou not known? hast thou not heard, *that* the everlasting God, the LORD, the Creator of the ends of the earth, fainteth not, neither is weary? ᵃ*there is* no searching of his understanding.

29 He giveth power to the ¹faint; and to *them that have* no might he increaseth strength.

30 Even the youths shall faint and be weary, and the young men shall utterly fall:

31 But they that ᵃwait upon the LORD ᵇshall renew *their* strength; they shall mount up with wings as eagles; they shall run, and not be weary; *and* they shall walk, and not faint.

## CHAPTER 41

KEEPᵃ silence before me, O ¹islands; and let the people renew *their* strength: let them come near; then let them speak: let us ᵇcome near together to judgment.

2 Who raised up ¹the righteous *man* ᵃfrom the east, ²called him to his foot, ᵇgave the nations before him, and made *him* rule over kings? he gave *them* as the dust to his sword, *and* as driven stubble to his bow.

3 He pursued them, *and* passed ¹safely; *even* by the way *that* he had not gone with his feet.

4 ᵃWho hath wrought and done *it,* calling the generations from the beginning? I the LORD, the ᵇfirst, and with the last; I *am* ᶜhe.

---

40:22 ᵃ Jer. 10:12
ᵇ Ps. 19:4 ¹ *above*
40:23 ᵃ Ps. 107:40 ¹ *reduces* ² *useless*
40:24 ¹ *scarcely*
40:25 ᵃ Is. 40:18
40:26 ᵃ Ps. 147:4 ¹ *is missing*
40:27 ᵃ Is. 54:7, 8 ¹ *just claim*
40:28 ᵃ Rom. 11:33
40:29 ¹ *weak*
40:31 ᵃ Is. 30:15; 49:23 ᵇ Ps. 103:5
41:1 ᵃ Zech. 2:13 ᵇ Is. 1:18 ¹ *coastlands*
41:2 ᵃ Is. 46:11 ᵇ Is. 45:1, 13 ¹ Or *one* ² Or *who in righteousness raised him to his feet*
41:3 ¹ Lit. *in peace*
41:4 ᵃ Is. 41:26 ᵇ Rev. 1:8, 17; 22:13 ᶜ Is. 43:10; 44:6

41:5 ¹ *coastlands*
41:6 ᵃ Is. 40:19 ¹ Lit. *Be strong*
41:7 ᵃ Is. 44:13 ᵇ Is. 40:19 ᶜ Is. 40:20 ¹ *craftsman* ² *refiner* ³ *inspired him that struck* ⁴ Or *Of the soldering, it is good* ⁵ *pegs* ⁶ *totter*
41:8 ᵃ Deut. 7:6; 10:15 ᵇ James 2:23
41:9 ¹ MT *farthest regions*
41:10 ᵃ Is. 41:13, 14; 43:5 ᵇ [Deut. 31:6]
41:11 ᵃ Zech. 12:3 ¹ *disgraced*
41:12 ¹ *as nothing*
41:14 ᵃ Job 25:6
41:15 ᵃ Mic. 4:13
41:16 ᵃ Jer. 51:2 ᵇ Is. 45:25 ¹ *winnow*
41:17 ᵃ Rom. 11:2
41:18 ᵃ Is. 35:6, 7; 43:19; 44:3 ᵇ Ps. 107:35 ¹ *bare heights*
41:19 ᵃ Is. 35:1 ¹ *acacia* ² *cypress*

---

5 The ¹isles saw *it,* and feared; the ends of the earth were afraid, drew near, and came.

6 ᵃThey helped every one his neighbour; and *every one* said to his brother, ¹Be of good courage.

7 ᵃSo the ¹carpenter encouraged the ᵇgoldsmith,² *and* he that smootheth *with* the hammer ³him that smote the anvil, saying, ⁴It *is* ready for the sodering: and he fastened it with ⁵nails, ᶜ*that* it should not ⁶be moved.

8 But thou, Israel, *art* my servant, Jacob whom I have ᵃchosen, the seed of Abraham my ᵇfriend.

9 *Thou* whom I have taken from the ends of the earth, and called thee from the ¹chief men thereof, and said unto thee, Thou *art* my servant; I have chosen thee, and not cast thee away.

10 ᵃFear thou not; ᵇfor I *am* with thee: be not dismayed; for I *am* thy God: I will strengthen thee; yea, I will help thee; yea, I will uphold thee with the right hand of my righteousness.

11 Behold, all they that were incensed against thee shall be ᵃashamed and ¹confounded: they shall be as nothing; and they that strive with thee shall perish.

12 Thou shalt seek them, and shalt not find them, *even* them that contended with thee: they that war against thee shall be as nothing, and ¹as a thing of nought.

13 For I the LORD thy God will hold thy right hand, saying unto thee, Fear not; I will help thee.

14 Fear not, thou ᵃworm Jacob, *and* ye men of Israel; I will help thee, saith the LORD, and thy redeemer, the Holy One of Israel.

15 Behold, ᵃI will make thee a new sharp threshing instrument having teeth: thou shalt thresh the mountains, and beat *them* small, and shalt make the hills as chaff.

16 Thou shalt ᵃfan¹ them, and the wind shall carry them away, and the whirlwind shall scatter them: and thou shalt rejoice in the LORD, *and* ᵇshalt glory in the Holy One of Israel.

17 *When* the poor and needy seek water, and *there is* none, *and* their tongue faileth for thirst, I the LORD will hear them, *I* the God of Israel will not ᵃforsake them.

18 I will open ᵃrivers in ¹high places, and fountains in the midst of the valleys: I will make the ᵇwilderness a pool of water, and the dry land springs of water.

19 I will plant in the wilderness the cedar, the ¹shittah tree, and the myrtle, and the oil tree; I will set in the ᵃdesert the ²fir tree, *and* the pine, and the box tree together:

20 [a]That they may see, and know, and consider, and understand together, that the hand of the LORD hath done this, and the Holy One of Israel hath created it.

21 Produce your [1]cause, saith the LORD; bring forth your strong *reasons,* saith the [a]King of Jacob.

22 [a]Let them bring *them* forth, and shew us what shall happen: let them shew the [b]former things, what they *be,* that we may consider them, and know the latter end of them; or declare us things for to come.

23 [a]Shew the things that are to come hereafter, that we may know that ye *are* gods: yea, [b]do good, or do evil, that we may be dismayed, and behold *it* together.

24 Behold, [a]ye *are* [1]of nothing, and your work [2]of nought: an abomination *is he that* chooseth you.

25 I have raised up *one* from the north, and he shall come: from the [1]rising of the sun [a]shall he call upon my name: [b]and he shall come upon princes as *upon* morter, and as the potter treadeth clay.

26 [a]Who hath declared from the beginning, that we may know? and beforetime, that we may say, *He is* righteous? yea, *there is* none that sheweth, yea, *there is* none that declareth, yea, *there is* none that heareth your words.

27 [a]The first [b]*shall say* to Zion, Behold, behold them: and I will give to Jerusalem one that bringeth good tidings.

28 [a]For I beheld, and *there was* no man; even among them, and *there was* no counsellor, that, when I asked of them, could answer a word.

29 [a]Behold, they *are* all [1]vanity; their works *are* nothing: their molten images *are* wind and confusion.

## CHAPTER 42

BEHOLD [a]my servant, whom I uphold; [1]mine elect, *in whom* my soul [b]delighteth; [c]I have put my spirit upon him: he shall bring forth [2]judgment to the Gentiles.

2 He shall not [1]cry, nor [2]lift up, nor cause his voice to be heard in the street.

3 A bruised reed shall he not break, and the [1]smoking flax shall he not [2]quench: he shall bring forth [3]judgment unto truth.

4 He shall not fail nor be discouraged, till he have set [1]judgment in the earth: [a]and the [2]isles shall wait for his law.

5 Thus saith God the LORD, [a]he that created the heavens, and stretched them out; he that spread forth the earth, and that which cometh out of it; [b]he that giveth breath unto the people upon it, and spirit to them that walk therein:

6 [a]I the LORD have called thee in righteousness, and will hold thine hand, and will keep thee, [b]and give thee for a covenant [1]of the people, for [c]a light of the Gentiles;

7 [a]To open the blind eyes, to [b]bring out the prisoners from the prison, *and* them that sit in [c]darkness out of the prison house.

8 I *am* the LORD: that *is* my name: and my [a]glory will I not give to another, neither my praise to graven images.

9 Behold, the former things are come to pass, and new things do I declare: before they spring forth I tell you of them.

10 [a]Sing unto the LORD a new song, *and* his praise from the end of the earth, [b]ye that go down to the sea, and all that is therein; the [1]isles, and the inhabitants thereof.

11 Let the wilderness and the cities thereof lift up *their voice,* the villages *that* Kedar doth inhabit: let the inhabitants of [1]the rock sing, let them shout from the top of the mountains.

12 Let them give glory unto the LORD, and declare his praise in the [1]islands.

13 The LORD shall go forth as a mighty man, he shall stir up [1]jealousy like a man of war: he shall [2]cry, [a]yea, [3]roar; he shall prevail against his enemies.

14 I have long time holden my peace; I have been still, *and* [1]refrained myself: *now* will I cry like a [2]travailing woman; I will [3]destroy and [4]devour at once.

15 I will make waste mountains and hills, and dry up all their [1]herbs; and I will make the rivers [2]islands, and I will dry up the pools.

16 And I will bring the blind by a way *that* they knew not; I will lead them in paths *that* they have not known: I will make darkness light before them, and crooked [1]things straight. These things will I do unto them, and not forsake them.

17 They shall be [a]turned back, they shall be greatly ashamed, that trust in graven images, that say to the molten images, Ye *are* our gods.

18 Hear, ye deaf; and look, ye blind, that ye may see.

19 [a]Who *is* blind, but my servant? or deaf, as my messenger *that* I sent? who *is* blind as *he that is* perfect, and blind as the LORD's servant?

20 Seeing many things, [a]but thou observest not; opening the ears, but he heareth not.

21 The LORD is well pleased for his righteousness' sake; he will magnify the law, and make *it* honourable.

41:20 [a] Job 12:9
41:21 [a] Is. 43:15 [1] *case*
41:22 [a] Is. 45:21 [b] Is. 43:9
41:23 [a] [John 13:19] [b] Jer. 10:5
41:24 [a] [1 Cor. 8:4] [1] *nothing* [2] *is nothing*
41:25 [a] Ezra 1:2 [b] Is. 41:2 [1] East
41:26 [a] Is. 43:9
41:27 [a] Is. 41:4 [b] Is. 40:9
41:28 [a] Is. 63:5
41:29 [a] Is. 41:24 [1] *worthless*
42:1 [a] [Phil. 2:7] [b] Matt. 3:17; 17:5 [c] [Is. 11:2] [1] *my chosen one* [2] *justice*
42:2 [1] *cry out* [2] *raise* his voice
42:3 [1] *dimly burning* [2] *extinguish* [3] *justice for*
42:4 [a] [Gen. 49:10] [1] *justice* [2] *coastlands*
42:5 [a] Zech. 12:1 [b] Acts 17:25
42:6 [a] Is. 43:1 [b] Is. 49:8 [c] Luke 2:32 [1] *to*
42:7 [a] Is. 35:5 [b] Luke 4:18 [c] Is. 9:2
42:8 [a] Is. 48:11
42:10 [a] Ps. 33:3; 40:3; 98:1 [b] Ps. 107:23 [1] *coastlands*
42:11 [1] Heb. *Sela*
42:12 [1] *coastlands*
42:13 [a] Is. 31:4 [1] his *zeal* [2] *cry out* [3] *shout aloud*
42:14 [1] *restrained* [2] *woman in labour* [3] *pant* [4] *gasp*
42:15 [1] *vegetation* [2] *coastlands*
42:16 [1] *places*
42:17 [a] Ps. 97:7
42:19 [a] [John 9:39, 41]
42:20 [a] Rom. 2:21

22 But this *is* a people robbed and ¹spoiled; *they are* all of them ²snared in holes, and they are hid in prison houses: they are for a prey, and none delivereth; for ³a spoil, and none saith, Restore.

23 Who among you will give ear to this? *who* will hearken and hear for the time to come?

24 Who gave Jacob for ¹a spoil, and Israel to the robbers? did not the LORD, he against whom we have sinned? ²for they would not walk in his ways, neither were they obedient unto his law.

25 Therefore he hath poured upon him the fury of his anger, and the strength of battle: ²and it hath set him on fire round about, ᵇyet he knew not; and it burned him, yet he ¹laid *it* not to ᶜheart.

## CHAPTER 43

BUT now thus saith the LORD that created thee, O Jacob, and he that formed thee, O Israel, Fear not: ²for I have redeemed thee, ᵇI have called *thee* by thy name; thou *art* mine.

2 ²When thou passest through the waters, ᵇI *will be* with thee; and through the rivers, they shall not overflow thee: when thou ᶜwalkest through the fire, thou shalt not be burned; neither shall the flame ¹kindle upon thee.

3 For I *am* the LORD thy God, the Holy One of Israel, thy Saviour: ²I gave Egypt *for* thy ransom, Ethiopia and Seba ¹for thee.

4 Since thou wast precious in my sight, thou hast been ¹honourable, and I have ²loved thee: therefore will I give men for thee, and people for thy life.

5 ²Fear not: for I *am* with thee: I will bring thy seed from the east, and ᵇgather thee from the west;

6 I will say to the ²north, ¹Give up; and to the south, ²Keep not back: bring my sons from far, and my daughters from the ends of the earth;

7 *Even* every one that is ²called by my name: for ᵇI have created him for my glory, I have formed him; yea, I have made him.

8 ²Bring forth the blind people that have eyes, and the ᵇdeaf that have ears.

9 Let all the nations be gathered together, and let the people be assembled: ²who among them can declare this, and shew us former things? let them bring forth their witnesses, that they may be justified: or let them hear, and say, *It is* truth.

10 ²Ye *are* my witnesses, saith the LORD, ᵇand my servant whom I have chosen: that ye may know and ᶜbelieve me, and understand that I

*am* he: before me there was no God formed, neither shall there be after me.

11 I, *even* I, ²*am* the LORD; and beside me *there is* no saviour.

12 I have declared, and have saved, and I have ¹shewed, when *there was* no ²strange² *god* among you: ᵇtherefore ye *are* my witnesses, saith the LORD, that I *am* God.

13 ²Yea, before the day *was* I *am* he; and *there is* none that can deliver out of my hand: I will work, and who shall ᵇlet¹ it?

14 Thus saith the LORD, your redeemer, the Holy One of Israel; For your sake I have sent to Babylon, and ¹have brought down all their nobles, and the Chaldeans, ²whose cry *is* in the ships.

15 I *am* the LORD, your Holy One, the creator of Israel, your ²King.

16 Thus saith the LORD, which ²maketh a way in the sea, and a ᵇpath in the mighty waters;

17 Which ²bringeth forth the chariot and horse, the army and the power; they shall lie down together, they shall not rise: they are ¹extinct, they are quenched as tow.

18 ²Remember ye not the former things, neither consider the things of old.

19 Behold, I will do a ²new thing; now it shall spring forth; shall ye not know it? ᵇI will even make a way in the wilderness, *and* rivers in the desert.

20 The beast of the field shall honour me, the ¹dragons and the ²owls: because ²I give waters in the wilderness, *and* rivers in the desert, to give drink to my people, my chosen.

21 ²This people have I formed for myself; they shall ¹shew forth my ᵇpraise.

22 But thou hast not called upon me, O Jacob; but thou ²hast been weary of me, O Israel.

23 ²Thou hast not brought me the ¹small cattle of thy burnt offerings; neither hast thou honoured me with thy sacrifices. I have not caused thee to serve with ²an offering, nor wearied thee with incense.

24 Thou hast bought me no sweet cane with money, neither hast thou ¹filled me with the fat of thy sacrifices: but thou hast ²made me to serve with thy sins, thou hast ²wearied me with thine iniquities.

25 I, *even* I, *am* he that ²blotteth out thy transgressions ᵇfor mine own sake, ᶜand will not remember thy sins.

26 Put me in remembrance: let us ¹plead together: declare ²thou, that thou mayest be justified.

27 Thy first father hath sinned, and thy ¹teachers have transgressed against me.

### Center cross-reference column

42:22 ¹ plundered
² Or trapped in caves ³ plunder
42:24 ª Is. 65:2
¹ plunder
42:25 ª 2 Kin. 25:9 ᵇ Hos. 7:9
ᶜ Is. 29:13 ¹ took
43:1 ª Is. 43:5; 44:6
ᵇ Is. 42:6; 45:4
43:2 ª [Ps. 66:12; 91:3] ᵇ [Deut. 31:6] ᶜ Dan. 3:25
¹ scorch
43:3 ª [Prov. 11:8; 21:18] ¹ in thy place
43:4 ª Is. 63:9
¹ honoured
43:5 ª Is. 41:10; 44:2 ᵇ Is. 54:7
43:6 ª Is. 49:12
¹ Give them up
² Keep them not
43:7 ª James 2:7
ᵇ [2 Cor. 5:17]
43:8 ª Ezek. 12:2
ᵇ Is. 29:18
43:9 ª Is. 41:21, 22, 26
43:10 ª Is. 44:8
ᵇ Is. 55:4 ᶜ Is. 41:4; 44:6
43:11 ª Hos. 13:4
43:12 ª Deut. 32:16 ᵇ Is. 44:8
¹ proclaimed
² foreign
43:13 ª Ps. 90:2 ᵇ Job 9:12
¹ reverse
43:14 ¹ have brought them all down as fugitives
² who rejoice in their
43:15 ª Is. 41:20, 21
43:16 ª Ex. 14:16, 21, 22 ᵇ Josh. 3:13
43:17 ª Ex. 14:4–9, 25 ¹ extinguished
43:18 ª Jer. 16:14
43:19 ª [2 Cor. 5:17] ᵇ Ex. 17:6
43:20 ª Is. 48:21
¹ jackals ² ostriches
43:21 ª Ps. 102:18 ᵇ Jer. 13:11
¹ declare
43:22 ª Mal. 1:13; 3:14
43:23 ª Amos 5:25 ¹ sheep for ² grain offerings
43:24 ª Is. 1:14; 7:13 ¹ satisfied me ² burdened me with
43:25 ª Jer. 50:20 ᵇ Ezek. 36:22 ᶜ Is. 1:18
43:26 ¹ contend ² thy case
43:27 ¹ mediators, lit. interpreters

28 Therefore I have profaned the princes of the sanctuary, [a]and have given Jacob to the curse, and Israel to reproaches.

## CHAPTER 44

YET now hear, O Jacob my servant; and Israel, whom I have chosen:

2 Thus saith the LORD that made thee, and formed thee from the womb, *which* will help thee; Fear not, O Jacob, my servant; and thou, Jesurun, whom I have chosen.

3 For I will pour water upon him that is thirsty, and floods upon the dry ground: I will pour my spirit upon thy seed, and my blessing upon thine offspring:

4 And they shall spring up *as* among the grass, as willows by the water courses.

5 One shall say, I *am* the LORD's; and another shall call *himself* by the name of Jacob; and another shall [1]subscribe *with* his hand unto the LORD, and surname *himself* by the name of Israel.

6 Thus saith the LORD the King of Israel, and his redeemer the LORD of hosts; [a]I *am* the first, and I *am* the last; and beside me *there is* no God.

7 And [a]who, as I, [1]shall call, and shall declare it, and set it in order for me, since I appointed the ancient people? and the things that are coming, and shall come, let them shew unto them.

8 Fear ye not, neither be afraid: [a]have not I told thee from that time, and have declared *it?* [b]ye *are* even my witnesses. Is there a God beside me? yea, [c]*there is* [1]no God; I know not *any.*

9 [a]They that make a graven image *are* all of them [1]vanity; and their [2]delectable things shall not profit; and they *are* their own witnesses; [b]they see not, nor know; that they may be ashamed.

10 Who hath formed a god, or [1]molten a graven image [a]*that* is profitable for nothing?

11 Behold, all his [1]fellows shall be [a]ashamed: and the workmen, they *are* [2]of men: let them all be gathered together, let them stand up; *yet* they shall fear, *and* they shall be ashamed together.

12 [a]The [1]smith with the tongs both worketh in the coals, and fashioneth it with hammers, and worketh it with the strength of his arms: yea, he is hungry, and his strength faileth: he drinketh no water, and is faint.

13 The [1]carpenter stretcheth out *his* rule; he marketh it out with [2]a line; he [3]fitteth it with planes, and he marketh it out with the compass, and maketh it after the figure of a man,

according to the beauty of a man; that it may remain in the house.

14 He heweth him down cedars, and taketh the cypress and the oak, which he [1]strengtheneth for himself among the trees of the forest: he planteth [2]an ash, and the rain doth nourish *it.*

15 Then shall it be for a man to burn: for he will take thereof, and warm himself; yea, he kindleth *it,* and baketh bread; yea, he maketh a god, and worshippeth *it;* he maketh it a graven image, and falleth down thereto.

16 He burneth [1]part thereof in the fire; with [1]part thereof he eateth flesh; he roasteth roast, and is satisfied: yea, he warmeth *himself,* and saith, Aha, I am warm, I have seen the fire:

17 And the residue thereof he maketh a god, *even* his graven image: he falleth down unto it, and worshippeth *it,* and prayeth unto it, and saith, Deliver me; for thou *art* my god.

18 [a]They have not known nor understood: for [b]he hath shut their eyes, that they cannot see; *and* their hearts, that they cannot [c]understand.

19 And none [a]considereth in his heart, neither *is there* knowledge nor understanding to say, I have burned [1]part of it in the fire; yea, also I have baked bread upon the coals thereof; I have roasted flesh, and eaten *it:* and shall I make the residue thereof an abomination? shall I fall down to [2]the stock of a tree?

20 He feedeth on ashes: [a]a deceived heart hath turned him aside, that he cannot deliver his soul, nor say, *Is there* not a [b]lie in my right hand?

21 Remember these, O Jacob and Israel; for thou *art* my servant: I have formed thee; thou *art* my servant: O Israel, thou shalt not be [a]forgotten [1]of me.

22 [a]I have blotted out, as a thick cloud, thy transgressions, and, as a cloud, thy sins: return unto me; for [b]I have redeemed thee.

23 [a]Sing, O ye heavens; for the LORD hath done *it:* shout, ye lower parts of the earth: break forth into singing, ye mountains, O forest, and every tree therein: for the LORD hath redeemed Jacob, and [b]glorified himself in Israel.

24 Thus saith the LORD, [a]thy redeemer, and [b]he that formed thee from the womb, I *am* the LORD that maketh all *things;* [c]that stretcheth [1]forth the heavens [2]alone; that spreadeth abroad the earth by myself;

25 That [a]frustrateth the [1]tokens [b]of the liars, and [2]maketh diviners mad; [c]that turneth wise *men* backward, [c]and maketh their knowledge foolish;

### Cross references

44:28 [a] Dan. 9:11
44:5 [1] *write* with *his hand, the* LORD's
44:6 [a] Is. 41:4
44:7 [a] Is. 41:4, 22, 26 [1] *Or can proclaim it? Then let him declare it*
44:8 [a] Is. 41:22 [b] Is. 43:10, 12 [c] 1 Sam. 2:2 [1] *no other Rock*
44:9 [a] Is. 41:24 [b] Ps. 115:4 [1] *useless* [2] *precious*
44:10 [a] Hab. 2:18 [1] *moulded*
44:11 [a] Ps. 97:7 [1] *companions* [2] *mere men*
44:12 [a] Jer. 10:3–5 [1] *blacksmith*
44:13 [1] *craftsman* [2] *chalk* [3] *fashions it with a plane*
44:14 [1] *secures* [2] *a pine*
44:16 [1] *half*
44:18 [a] Is. 45:20 [b] Is. 6:9, 10; 29:10 [c] Jer. 10:14
44:19 [a] Is. 46:8 [1] *half* [2] *a block of wood*
44:20 [a] 2 Thess. 2:11 [b] Rom. 1:25
44:21 [a] Is. 49:15 [1] *by*
44:22 [a] Is. 43:25 [b] 1 Cor. 6:20
44:23 [a] Ps. 69:34 [b] Is. 49:3; 60:21
44:24 [a] Is. 43:14 [b] Is. 43:1 [c] Job 9:8 [1] *out* [2] *all alone*
44:25 [a] Is. 47:13 [b] Jer. 50:36 [c] 1 Cor. 1:20, 27 [1] *signs of the babblers* [2] *drives*

26 [a]That confirmeth the word of his servant, and performeth the counsel of his messengers; that saith to Jerusalem, Thou shalt be inhabited; and to the cities of Judah, Ye shall be built, and I will raise up the [1]decayed places thereof:

27 [a]That saith to the deep, Be dry, and I will dry up thy rivers:

28 That saith of [a]Cyrus, *He is* my shepherd, and shall perform all my pleasure: even saying to Jerusalem, [b]Thou shalt be built; and to the temple, Thy foundation shall be laid.

## CHAPTER 45

THUS saith the LORD to his anointed, to [a]Cyrus, whose [b]right hand I have [1]holden, [c]to subdue nations before him; and I will [d]loose the [2]loins of kings, to open before him the [3]two leaved gates; and the gates shall not be shut;

2 I will go before thee, [a]and make the crooked places straight: [b]I will break in pieces the gates of [1]brass, and cut in sunder the bars of iron:

3 And I will give thee the treasures of darkness, and hidden riches of secret places, [a]that thou mayest know that I, the LORD, which [b]call *thee* by thy name, *am* the God of Israel.

4 For [a]Jacob my servant's sake, and Israel mine elect, I have even called thee by thy name: I have surnamed thee, though thou hast not known me.

5 I [a]*am* the LORD, and [b]*there is* none else, *there is* no God beside me: [c]I girded thee, though thou hast not known me:

6 [a]That they may [b]know from the rising of the sun, and [1]from the west, that *there is* none beside me. I *am* the LORD, and *there is* none else.

7 I form the light, and create darkness: I make peace, and [a]create [1]evil: I the LORD do all these *things*.

8 [a]Drop[1] down, ye heavens, from above, and let the skies pour down righteousness: let the earth open, and let them bring forth salvation, and let righteousness spring up together; I the LORD have created it.

9 Woe unto him that striveth with [a]his Maker! *Let* the potsherd *strive* with the potsherds of the earth. [b]Shall the clay say to him that fashioneth it, What makest thou? or [1]thy work, He hath no hands?

10 Woe unto him that saith unto *his* father, What begettest thou? or to the woman, What hast thou brought forth?

11 Thus saith the LORD, the Holy One of Israel, and his Maker, [a]Ask me of things to come concerning [b]my sons, and concerning [c]the work of my hands command ye me.

44:26 [a] Zech. 1:6
[1] Lit. *waste*
44:27 [a] Jer. 50:38; 51:36
44:28 [a] Ezra 1:1
[b] Ezra 6:7
45:1 [a] Is. 44:28
[b] Is. 41:13 [c] Dan. 5:30 [d] Job 12:21
[1] *held* [2] *armour*
[3] *double doors*
45:2 [a] Is. 40:4
[b] Ps. 107:16
[1] *bronze*
45:3 [a] Is. 41:23
[b] Ex. 33:12
45:4 [a] Is. 44:1
45:5 [a] Deut. 4:35; 32:39 [b] Is. 45:14, 18 [c] Ps. 18:32
45:6 [a] Mal. 1:11
[b] [Is. 11:9; 52:10]
[1] *to its setting*
45:7 [a] Amos 3:6
[1] *calamity*
45:8 [a] Ps. 85:11
[1] *Rain down*
45:9 [a] Is. 64:8
[1] *shall thy work* say [b] Jer. 18:6
45:11 [a] Is. 8:19
[b] Jer. 31:9 [c] Is. 29:23; 60:21; 64:8

45:12 [a] Is. 42:5
[b] Gen. 1:26
[c] Gen. 2:1
45:13 [a] Is. 41:2
[b] 2 Chr. 36:22
[c] [Rom. 3:24] [1] Or *make all his ways straight*
45:14 [a] Zech. 8:22, 23 [b] Ps. 149:8
[c] 1 Cor. 14:25 [d] Is. 45:5
45:15 [a] Ps. 44:24
45:16 [a] Is. 44:11
[1] *disgraced*
45:17 [a] Is. 26:4
[b] Is. 51:6 [c] Is. 29:22 [1] *by* [2] *disgraced*
45:18 [a] Is. 42:5
[b] Ps. 115:16 [c] Is. 45:5 [1] *empty or a waste*
45:19 [a] Deut. 30:11
[b] Ps. 19:8
45:20 [a] Is. 44:9; 46:7 [1] *have escaped from* [2] *carry about*
45:21 [a] Is. 41:22; 43:9 [b] Is. 44:8
45:22 [a] Ps. 22:27; 65:5 [1] *Turn*
45:23 [a] [Heb. 6:13] [b] Rom. 14:11 [c] Deut. 6:13 [1] *take an oath*
45:24 [a] [1 Cor. 1:30] [b] Is. 41:11
[1] *He shall say to me, only* [2] *angry*
45:25 [a] Is. 45:17
[b] 1 Cor. 1:31

12 [a]I have made the earth, and [b]created man upon it: I, *even* my hands, have stretched out the heavens, and [c]all their host have I commanded.

13 [a]I have raised him up in righteousness, and I will [1]direct all his ways: he shall [b]build my city, and he shall let go my captives, [c]not for price nor reward, saith the LORD of hosts.

14 Thus saith the LORD, [a]The labour of Egypt, and merchandise of Ethiopia and of the Sabeans, men of stature, shall come over unto thee, and they shall be thine: they shall come after thee; [b]in chains they shall come over, and they shall fall down unto thee, they shall make supplication unto thee, *saying,* [c]Surely God *is* in thee; and *there is* none else, [d]*there is* no God.

15 Verily thou *art* a God [a]that hidest thyself, O God of Israel, the Saviour.

16 They shall be [a]ashamed, and also [1]confounded, all of them: they shall go to confusion together *that are* makers of idols.

17 [a]*But* Israel shall be saved [1]in the LORD with an [b]everlasting salvation: ye shall not be ashamed nor [c]confounded[2] world without end.

18 For thus saith the LORD [a]that created the heavens; God himself that formed the earth and made it; he hath established it, he created it not [1]in vain, he formed it to be [b]inhabited: [c]I *am* the LORD; and *there is* none else.

19 I have not spoken in [a]secret, in a dark place of the earth: I said not unto the seed of Jacob, Seek ye me in vain: [b]I the LORD speak righteousness, I declare things that are right.

20 Assemble yourselves and come; draw near together, ye *that* [1]*are* escaped of the nations: [a]they have no knowledge that [2]set up the wood of their graven image, and pray unto a god *that* cannot save.

21 Tell ye, and bring *them* near; yea, let them take counsel together: [a]who hath declared this from ancient time? *who* hath told it from that time? *have* not I the LORD? [b]and *there* is no God else beside me; a just God and a Saviour; *there is* none beside me.

22 [1]Look unto me, and be ye saved, [a]all the ends of the earth: for I *am* God, and *there is* none else.

23 [a]I have sworn by myself, the word is gone out of my mouth *in* righteousness, and shall not return, That unto me every [b]knee shall bow, [c]every tongue shall [1]swear.

24 [1]Surely, shall *one* say, in the LORD have I [a]righteousness and strength: *even* to him shall *men* come; and [b]all that are [2]incensed against him shall be ashamed.

25 [a]In the LORD shall all the seed of Israel be justified, and [b]shall glory.

## CHAPTER 46

**B**EL [a]boweth down, Nebo stoopeth, their idols were upon the beasts, and upon the cattle: your carriages *were* heavy loaden; [b]*they are* a burden to the weary *beast.*

2 They stoop, they bow down together; they could not deliver the burden, [a]but themselves are gone into captivity.

3 Hearken unto me, O house of Jacob, and all the remnant of the house of Israel, [a]which are [1]borne *by me* from [2]the belly, which are carried from the womb:

4 And *even* to *your* old age [a]I *am* he; and *even* to [1]hoar hairs [b]will I carry *you:* I have made, and I will bear; even I will carry, and will deliver *you.*

5 [a]To whom will ye liken me, and make *me* equal, and compare me, that we may be like?

6 [a]They lavish gold out of the bag, and weigh silver in the balance, *and* hire a [b]goldsmith; and he maketh it a god: they [1]fall down, yea, they worship.

7 [a]They bear him upon the shoulder, they carry him, and set him in his place, and he standeth; from his place shall he not [1]remove: yea, [b]one shall cry unto him, yet can he not answer, nor save him out of his trouble.

8 Remember this, and [1]shew yourselves men: [a]bring *it* again to mind, O ye transgressors.

9 [a]Remember the former things of old: for I *am* God, and [b]*there is* none else; *I* am God, and *there is* none like me,

10 [a]Declaring the end from the beginning, and from ancient times *the things* that are not *yet* done, saying, [b]My counsel shall stand, and I will do all my pleasure:

11 Calling a ravenous bird [a]from the east, the man [b]that executeth my counsel from a far country: yea, [c]I have spoken *it,* I will also bring it to pass; I have purposed *it,* I will also do it.

12 Hearken unto me, ye [a]stouthearted,[1] [b]that *are* far from righteousness:

13 [a]I bring near my righteousness; it shall not be far off, and my salvation [b]shall not [1]tarry: and I will place [c]salvation in Zion for Israel my glory.

## CHAPTER 47

**C**OME [a]down, and [b]sit in the dust, O virgin daughter of [c]Babylon, sit on the ground: *there is* no throne, O daughter of the Chaldeans: for thou shalt no more be called tender and [1]delicate.

2 [a]Take the millstones, and grind meal: [1]uncover thy locks, [2]make bare

the leg, uncover the thigh, pass over the rivers.

3 [a]Thy nakedness shall be uncovered, yea, thy shame shall be seen: [b]I will take vengeance, and I will not [1]meet *thee as* a man.

4 *As for* [a]our redeemer, the LORD of hosts *is* his name, the Holy One of Israel.

5 Sit thou [a]silent, and get thee into darkness, O daughter of the Chaldeans: [b]for thou shalt no more be called, [1]the lady of kingdoms.

6 [a]I was [1]wroth with my people, [b]I have [2]polluted mine inheritance, and given them into thine hand: thou didst shew them no mercy; [c]upon the [3]ancient hast thou very heavily laid thy yoke.

7 And thou saidst, I shall be [a]a lady for ever: *so* that thou didst not [b]lay these *things* to thy heart, [c]neither didst remember the latter end of it.

8 Therefore hear now this, *thou that art* given to pleasures, that dwellest [1]carelessly, that sayest in thine heart, I *am,* and none else beside me; I shall not sit *as* a widow, neither shall I know the loss of children:

9 But these two *things* shall come to thee [a]in a moment in one day, the loss of children, and widowhood: they shall come upon thee in their [1]perfection for the multitude of thy sorceries, *and* for the great abundance of thine enchantments.

10 For thou hast trusted in thy wickedness: thou hast said, None [a]seeth me. Thy wisdom and thy knowledge, it hath [1]perverted thee; and thou hast said in thine heart, I *am,* and none else beside me.

11 Therefore shall evil come upon thee; thou shalt not know from [1]whence it riseth: and [2]mischief shall fall upon thee; thou shalt not be able to [3]put it off: and [a]desolation shall come upon thee [b]suddenly, *which* thou shalt not know.

12 Stand now with thine enchantments, and with the multitude of thy sorceries, wherein thou hast laboured from thy youth; if so be thou shalt be able to profit, if so be thou mayest prevail.

13 [a]Thou art wearied in the multitude of thy counsels. Let now [b]the [1]astrologers, the stargazers, [2]the monthly prognosticators, stand up, and save thee from *these things* that shall come upon thee.

14 Behold, they shall be [a]as stubble; the fire shall [b]burn them; they shall not deliver themselves from the power of the flame: *there shall* not *be* a coal to warm at, *nor* fire to sit before it.

15 Thus shall they be unto thee with whom thou hast laboured, *even*

### Cross references

46:1 [a] Jer. 50:2 [b] Jer. 10:5

46:2 [a] Jer. 48:7

46:3 [a] Ps. 71:6 [1] upheld [2] birth

46:4 [a] Mal. 3:6 [b] Ps. 48:14 [1] gray hairs

46:5 [a] Is. 40:18, 25

46:6 [a] Is. 40:19; 41:6 [b] Is. 44:12 [1] prostrate themselves

46:7 [a] Jer. 10:5 [b] Is. 45:20 [1] move

46:8 [a] Is. 44:19 [1] be men, take courage

46:9 [a] Deut. 32:7 [b] Is. 45:5, 21

46:10 [a] Is. 45:21; 48:3 [b] Ps. 33:11

46:11 [a] Is. 41:2, 25 [b] Is. 44:28 [c] Num. 23:19

46:12 [a] Ps. 76:5 [b] [Rom. 10:3] [1] stubbornminded

46:13 [a] [Rom. 1:17] [b] Hab. 2:3 [c] Is. 62:11 [1] linger or delay

47:1 [a] Jer. 48:18 [b] Is. 3:26 [c] Jer. 25:12; 50:1–51:64 [1] pampered

47:2 [a] Ex. 11:5 [1] remove thy veil [2] take off the skirt

47:3 [a] Is. 3:17; 20:4 [b] [Rom. 12:19] [1] arbitrate with a man

47:4 [a] Jer. 50:34

47:5 [a] 1 Sam. 2:9 [b] [Dan. 2:37]

47:6 [a] 2 Sam. 24:14 [b] Is. 43:28 [c] Deut. 28:49, 50 [1] angry [2] profaned [3] elderly

47:7 [a] Rev. 18:7 [b] Is. 42:25; 46:8 [c] Deut. 32:29

47:8 [1] securely

47:9 [a] 1 Thess. 5:3 [1] fulness

47:10 [a] Is. 29:15 [1] led thee astray

47:11 [a] 1 Thess. 5:3 [b] Is. 29:5 [1] where it arises [2] trouble [3] Lit. cover it

47:13 [a] Is. 57:10 [b] Dan. 2:2, 10 [1] Lit. viewers of the heavens [2] Lit. those giving knowledge for new moons

47:14 [a] Nah. 1:10 [b] Jer. 51:58

ᵃthy merchants, from thy youth: they shall wander every one to his ¹quarter; none shall save thee.

## CHAPTER 48

Hᴇᴀʀ ye this, O house of Jacob, which are called by the name of Israel, and are come forth out of the ¹waters of Judah, which swear by the name of the Lᴏʀᴅ, and make mention of the God of Israel, *but* ᵃnot in truth, nor in righteousness.

2 For they call themselves ᵃofᶦ the holy city, and ᵇstay² themselves upon the God of Israel; The Lᴏʀᴅ of hosts *is* his name.

3 I have ᵃdeclared the former things from the beginning; and they went forth out of my mouth, and I ¹shewed them; I did *them* suddenly, ᵇand they came to pass.

4 Because I knew that thou *art* obstinate, and ᵃthy neck *is* an iron sinew, and thy brow ᵇbrass;

5 I have even from the beginning declared *it* to thee; before it came to pass I ¹shewed *it* thee: lest thou shouldest say, Mine idol hath done them, and my graven image, and my molten image, hath commanded them.

6 Thou hast heard, see all this; and will not ye declare *it?* I have ¹shewed thee new things from this time, even hidden things, and thou didst not know them.

7 They are created now, and not from the beginning; ¹even before the day when thou heardest them not; lest thou shouldest say, Behold, I knew them.

8 Yea, thou heardest not; yea, thou knewest not; yea, from ¹that time *that* thine ear was not opened: for I knew that thou wouldest deal very treacherously, and wast called ᵃa transgressor from the womb.

9 ᵃFor my name's sake ᵇwill I ¹defer mine anger, and for my praise will I ²refrain for thee, that I ³cut thee not off.

10 Behold, ᵃI have refined thee, but not ¹with silver; I have ²chosen thee in the ᵇfurnace of affliction.

11 For mine own sake, *even* for mine own sake, will I do *it:* for ᵃhow should *my name* be ¹polluted? and ᵇI will not give my glory unto another.

12 Hearken unto me, O Jacob and Israel, my called; I *am* he; ᵃI *am* the ᵇfirst, I also *am* the last.

13 ᵃMine hand also hath laid the foundation of the earth, and my right hand hath ¹spanned the heavens: *when* ᵇI call unto them, they stand up together.

14 All ye, assemble yourselves, and hear; which among them hath declared these *things?* ᵃThe Lᴏʀᴅ hath

47:15 ᵃ Rev. 18:11
¹ *own side or way*

48:1 ᵃ Jer. 4:2; 5:2
¹ *wellsprings*

48:2 ᵃ Is. 52:1;
64:10 ᵇ Mic. 3:11
¹ *after* ² *lean*

48:3 ᵃ Is. 44:7,
8; 46:10 ᵇ Josh.
21:45 ¹ *caused
them to hear it*

48:4 ᵃ Deut. 31:27
¹ *bronze*

48:5 ¹ *proclaimed*

48:6 ¹ *made you
hear*

48:7 ¹ *and before
this day thou*

48:8 ᵃ Ps. 58:3
¹ *long ago thine
ear*

48:9 ᵃ Ezek. 20:9,
14, 22, 44 ᵇ Ps.
78:38 ¹ *delay* ² *re-
strain* ³ *destroy
thee not*

48:10 ᵃ Ps. 66:10
ᵇ Deut. 4:20 ¹ *as*
² *tested*

48:11 ᵃ Ezek.
20:9 ᵇ Is. 42:8
¹ *profaned*

48:12 ᵃ Deut.
32:39 ᵇ [Rev.
22:13]

48:13 ᵃ Ps. 102:25
ᵇ Is. 40:26
¹ *stretched out*

48:14 ᵃ Is. 45:1
ᵇ Is. 44:28;
47:1–15

48:15 ᵃ Is. 45:1, 2

48:16 ᵃ Is. 45:19
ᵇ Zech. 2:8, 9, 11
¹ *Or has sent me
and his Spirit*

48:17 ᵃ Is. 43:14
ᵇ Ps. 32:8

48:18 ᵃ Ps. 81:13
ᵇ Ps. 119:165
¹ *heeded*

48:19 ᵃ Gen. 22:17
¹ *body,* ² *grains
of sand*

48:20 ᵃ Zech. 2:6,
7 ᵇ [Ex. 19:4–6]
¹ *from*

48:21 ᵃ [Is. 41:17,
18] ᵇ Ex. 17:6
¹ *split*

48:22 ᵃ [Is. 57:21]

49:1 ᵃ Is. 41:1
ᵇ Jer. 1:5 ¹ *coast-
lands* ² *body,* lit.
*inward parts*

49:2 ᵃ Rev. 1:16;
2:12 ᵇ Is. 51:16
ᶜ Ps. 45:5

49:3 ᵃ [Zech. 3:8]
ᵇ Is. 44:23

49:4 ᵃ [Ezek. 3:19]
¹ *my reward*

49:5 ᵃ Matt. 23:37
¹ *So that* ² DSS,
LXX, Qr. *gathered
to him;* Kt. *not
gathered*

loved him: ᵇhe will do his pleasure on Babylon, and his arm *shall be on* the Chaldeans.

15 I, *even* I, have spoken; yea, ᵃI have called him: I have brought him, and he shall make his way prosperous.

16 Come ye near unto me, hear ye this; ᵃI have not spoken in secret from the beginning; from the time that it was, there *am* I: and now ᵇthe Lord Gᴏᴅ, ¹and his Spirit, hath sent me.

17 Thus saith ᵃthe Lᴏʀᴅ, thy Redeemer, the Holy One of Israel; I *am* the Lᴏʀᴅ thy God which teacheth thee to profit, ᵇwhich leadeth thee by the way *that* thou shouldest go.

18 ᵃO that thou hadst ¹hearkened to my commandments! ᵇthen had thy peace been as a river, and thy righteousness as the waves of the sea:

19 ᵃThy seed also had been as the sand, and the offspring of thy ¹bowels like the ²gravel thereof; his name should not have been cut off nor destroyed from before me.

20 ᵃGo ye forth ¹of Babylon, flee ye from the Chaldeans, with a voice of singing declare ye, tell this, utter it *even* to the end of the earth; say ye, The Lᴏʀᴅ hath ᵇredeemed his servant Jacob.

21 And they ᵃthirsted not *when* he led them through the deserts: he ᵇcaused the waters to flow out of the rock for them: he ¹clave the rock also, and the waters gushed out.

22 ᵃ*There is* no peace, saith the Lᴏʀᴅ, unto the wicked.

## CHAPTER 49

Lɪsᴛᴇɴ, ᵃO ¹isles, unto me; and hearken, ye people, from far; ᵇThe Lᴏʀᴅ hath called me from the womb; from the ²bowels of my mother hath he made mention of my name.

2 And he hath made ᵃmy mouth like a sharp sword; ᵇin the shadow of his hand hath he hid me, and made me ᶜa polished shaft; in his quiver hath he hid me;

3 And said unto me, ᵃThou *art* my servant, O Israel, ᵇin whom I will be glorified.

4 ᵃThen I said, I have laboured in vain, I have spent my strength for nought, and in vain: *yet* surely my judgment *is* with the Lᴏʀᴅ, and ¹my work with my God.

5 And now, saith the Lᴏʀᴅ that formed me from the womb *to be* his servant, to bring Jacob again to him, ¹Though Israel ᵇbe ²not gathered, yet shall I be glorious in the eyes of the Lᴏʀᴅ, and my God shall be my strength.

6 And he said, It is a light thing that thou shouldest be my servant

to raise up the tribes of Jacob, and to restore the preserved of Israel: I will also give thee for a [a]light to the Gentiles, that thou mayest be my salvation unto the [1]end of the earth.

7 Thus saith the LORD, the Redeemer of Israel, *and* [1]his Holy One, [a]to [2]him whom man despiseth, to him whom the nation abhorreth, to a servant of rulers, [b]Kings shall see and arise, princes also shall worship, because of the LORD that is faithful, *and* the Holy One of Israel, and he [3]shall choose thee.

8 Thus saith the LORD, In [1]an [a]acceptable time have I heard thee, and in a day of salvation have I helped thee: and I will preserve thee, [b]and give thee for a covenant of the people, to [2]establish the earth, to cause to inherit the desolate heritages;

9 That thou mayest say [a]to the prisoners, Go forth; to them that *are* in darkness, Shew yourselves. They shall feed [1]in the ways, and their pastures *shall be* in all [2]high places.

10 They shall not [a]hunger nor thirst; [b]neither shall the heat nor sun [1]smite them: for he that hath mercy on them [c]shall lead them, even by the springs of water shall he guide them.

11 [a]And I will make all my mountains a [1]way, and my highways shall be exalted.

12 Behold, [a]these shall come from far: and, lo, these from the north and from the west; and these from the land of Sinim.

13 [a]Sing, O heavens; and be joyful, O earth; and break forth into singing, O mountains: for the LORD hath comforted his people, and will have mercy upon his afflicted.

14 [a]But Zion said, The LORD hath forsaken me, and my Lord hath forgotten me.

15 [a]Can a woman forget her [1]sucking child, [2]that she should not have compassion on the son of her womb? yea, they may forget, [b]yet will I not forget thee.

16 Behold, [a]I have [1]graven thee upon the palms of *my* hands; thy walls *are* continually before me.

17 Thy [1]children shall make haste; thy destroyers and they that made thee waste shall go [2]forth of thee.

18 [1]Lift up thine eyes round about, and behold: all these gather themselves together, *and* come to thee. As I live, saith the LORD, thou shalt surely clothe thee with them all, [b]as with an ornament, and bind them *on thee*, as a bride *doeth*.

19 For thy waste and thy desolate places, and the land of thy destruction, [a]shall even now be too [1]narrow by reason of the inhabitants, and

49:6 [a] [Luke 2:32]
[1] ends
49:7 [a] [Ps. 22:6; Is. 53:3; Matt. 26:67; 27:41]; Mark 15:29; Luke 23:35 [b] [Is. 52:15]
[1] *its* [2] Lit. *the despised of soul*
[3] *has chosen*
49:8 [a] Ps. 69:13; 2 Cor. 6:2 [b] Is. 42:6 [1] *a favourable* [2] *restore*
49:9 [a] Is. 61:1; Zech. 9:12; Luke 4:18 [1] *along the roads* [2] *desolate heights*
49:10 [a] Is. 33:16; 48:21; Rev. 7:16 [b] Ps. 121:6 [c] Ps. 23:2; Is. 40:11; 48:17 [1] *strike*
49:11 [a] Is. 40:4 [1] *road*
49:12 [a] Is. 43:5, 6
49:13 [a] Is. 44:23
49:14 [a] Is. 40:27
49:15 [a] Ps. 103:13; Mal. 3:17 [b] Rom. 11:29 [1] *nursing* [2] *and not have*
49:16 [a] Ex. 13:9; Song 8:6; Hag. 2:23 [1] *inscribed*
49:17 [1] Lit. *sons* [2] *away from*
49:18 [a] Is. 60:1; John 4:35 [b] Prov. 17:6
49:19 [a] Is. 54:1, 2; Zech. 10:10 [1] *small for the*
49:20 [a] Is. 60:4 [b] [Matt. 3:9; Rom. 11:11] [1] *small* [2] *give me a place*
49:21 [1] *these for me* [2] *wandering*
49:22 [a] Is. 60:4 [1] *Make an oath* [2] *nations* [3] *banner* [4] Lit. *bosom*
49:23 [a] Ps. 72:11; Is. 52:15 [b] Ps. 72:9; Mic. 7:17 [c] Ps. 34:22; [Rom. 5:5] [1] *foster fathers*
49:24 [a] Matt. 12:29; Luke 11:21, 22 [1] *the captives of the righteous*
49:26 [a] Is. 9:20 [b] Rev. 14:20 [c] Ps. 9:16; Is. 60:16
50:1 [a] Deut. 24:1; Jer. 3:8 [b] Deut. 32:30; 2 Kin. 4:1; Neh. 5:5 [c] Is. 52:3 [1] *certificate*
50:2 [a] Ps. 106:9; Nah. 1:4
50:3 [a] Ex. 10:21 [b] Is. 13:10; Rev. 6:12
50:4 [a] Ex. 4:11

they that swallowed thee up shall be far away.

20 [a]The children which thou shalt have, [b]after thou hast lost the other, shall say again in thine ears, The place *is* too [1]strait for me: [2]give place to me that I may dwell.

21 Then shalt thou say in thine heart, Who hath begotten [1]me these, seeing I have lost my children, and am desolate, a captive, and [2]removing to and fro? and who hath brought up these? Behold, I was left alone; these, where *had* they *been?*

22 [a]Thus saith the Lord GOD, Behold, I will [1]lift up mine hand to the [2]Gentiles, and set up my [3]standard to the people: and they shall bring thy sons in *their* [4]arms, and thy daughters shall be carried upon *their* shoulders.

23 [a]And kings shall be thy [1]nursing fathers, and their queens thy nursing mothers: they shall bow down to thee with *their* face toward the earth, and [b]lick up the dust of thy feet; and thou shalt know that I *am* the LORD: [c]for they shall not be ashamed that wait for me.

24 [a]Shall the prey be taken from the mighty, or [1]the lawful captive delivered?

25 But thus saith the LORD, Even the captives of the mighty shall be taken away, and the prey of the terrible shall be delivered: for I will contend with him that contendeth with thee, and I will save thy children.

26 And I will [a]feed them that oppress thee with their own flesh; and they shall be drunken with their own [b]blood, as with sweet wine: and all flesh [c]shall know that I the LORD *am* thy Saviour and thy Redeemer, the mighty One of Jacob.

## CHAPTER 50

Thus saith the LORD, Where *is* [a]the [1]bill of your mother's divorcement, whom I have put away? or which of my [b]creditors *is it* to whom I have sold you? Behold, for your iniquities [c]have ye sold yourselves, and for your transgressions is your mother put away.

2 Wherefore, when I came, *was there* no man? when I called, *was there* none to answer? Is my hand shortened at all, that it cannot redeem? or have I no power to deliver? behold, at my [a]rebuke I dry up the sea, I make the rivers a wilderness: their fish stinketh, because *there is* no water, and dieth for thirst.

3 [a]I clothe the heavens with blackness, [b]and I make sackcloth their covering.

4 [a]The Lord GOD hath given me the tongue of the learned, that I should

know how to speak a word in season to *him that is* ᵇweary: he wakeneth morning by morning, he wakeneth mine ear to hear as the learned.

5 The Lord God ᵃhath opened mine ear, and I was not ᵇrebellious, neither turned away back.

6 ᵃI gave my back to ¹the smiters, and ᵇmy cheeks to them that plucked off the ²hair: I hid not my face from shame and ᶜspitting.

7 For the Lord God will help me; therefore shall I not be ᶜconfounded: therefore have ᵃI set my face like a flint, and I know that I shall not be ashamed.

8 ᵃ*He is* near that justifieth me; who will contend with me? let us stand together: who *is* ¹mine adversary? let him come near to me.

9 Behold, the Lord God will help me; who *is* he *that* shall condemn me? ᵃlo, they all shall ¹wax old as a garment; ᵇthe moth shall eat them up.

10 Who *is* among you that feareth the Lord, that obeyeth the voice of his servant, that ᵃwalketh *in* darkness, and hath no light? ᵇlet him trust in the name of the Lord, and ¹stay upon his God.

11 Behold, all ye that kindle a fire, that ¹compass *yourselves* about with sparks: walk in the light of your fire, and in the sparks *that* ye have kindled. ᵃThis shall ye have of mine hand; ye shall lie down ᵇin ²sorrow.

## CHAPTER 51

HᴇARKEN to me, ᵃye that ¹follow after righteousness, ye that seek the Lord: look unto the rock *whence* ye are hewn, and to the hole of the pit *whence* ye are digged.

2 ᵃLook unto Abraham your father, and unto Sarah *that* bare you: ᵇfor I called him alone, and ᶜblessed him, and increased him.

3 For the Lord shall ᵃcomfort Zion: he will comfort all her waste places; and he will make her wilderness like Eden, and her desert ᵇlike the garden of the Lord; joy and gladness shall be found therein, thanksgiving, and the voice of melody.

4 Hearken unto me, my people; and give ear unto me, O my nation: ᵃfor a law shall ¹proceed from me, and I will make my ²judgment to rest ᵇfor a light of the people.

5 ᵃMy righteousness *is* near; my salvation is gone forth, ᵇand mine arms shall judge the people; ᶜthe ¹isles shall wait upon me, and ᵈon mine arm shall they trust.

6 ᵃLift up your eyes to the heavens, and look upon the earth beneath: for ᵇthe heavens shall vanish away like smoke, ᶜand the earth shall ¹wax old

### Center column references

50:4 ᵇ Matt. 11:28
50:5 ᵃ Ps. 40:6
ᵇ Matt. 26:39
50:6 ᵃ Matt. 27:26
ᵇ Matt. 26:67;
27:30 ᶜ Lam. 3:30
¹ *those who struck me* ² *beard*
50:7 ᵃ Ezek. 3:8, 9
¹ *disgraced*
50:8 ᵃ [Rom. 8:32–34] ¹ Lit. *master of my judgment*
50:9 ᵃ Job 13:28
ᵇ Is. 51:6, 8 ¹ *grow*
50:10 ᵃ Ps. 23:4
ᵇ 2 Chr. 20:20
¹ *rely*
50:11 ᵃ [John 9:39] ᵇ Ps. 16:4 ¹ *encircle* ² *torment*
51:1 ᵃ [Rom. 9:30–32] ¹ *pursue*
51:2 ᵃ Heb. 11:11
ᵇ Gen. 12:1 ᶜ Gen. 24:35
51:3 ᵃ Is. 40:1; 52:9
ᵇ Gen. 13:10
51:4 ᵃ Is. 2:3 ᵇ Is. 42:6 ¹ *go forth* ² *justice*
51:5 ᵃ Is. 46:13
ᵇ Ps. 67:4 ᶜ Is. 60:9 ᵈ [Rom. 1:16] ¹ *coastlands*
51:6 ᵃ Is. 40:26
ᵇ Matt. 24:35 ᶜ Is. 24:19, 20; 50:9 ¹ *grow*

ᵈ Is. 45:17
² *broken*
51:7 ᵃ Ps. 37:31
ᵇ [Matt. 5:11, 12; 10:28]
51:8 ᵃ Is. 50:9
51:9 ᵃ Ps. 44:23
ᵇ Ps. 93:1 ᶜ Ps. 44:1 ᵈ Job 26:12
ᵉ Ps. 87:4 ᶠ Ps. 74:13 ¹ *days of old* ² *serpent*
51:10 ᵃ Ex. 14:21
¹ *the one* ² *redeemed*
51:11 ᵃ Is. 35:10
¹ *sighing*
51:12 ᵃ 2 Cor. 1:3
ᵇ Ps. 118:6 ᶜ Is. 40:6, 7 ¹ *mortal man*
51:13 ᵃ Is. 17:10
ᵇ Ps. 104:2 ᶜ Job 20:7 ¹ Or *when preparing to*
51:14 ᵃ Zech. 9:11
51:15 ᵃ Job 26:12
51:16 ᵃ Deut. 18:18
ᵇ Is. 49:2 ᶜ Is. 65:17 ¹ *establish*
51:17 ᵃ Is. 52:1
ᵇ Job 21:20
¹ *drained it out*
51:19 ᵃ Is. 47:9

like a garment, and they that dwell therein shall die in like manner: but my salvation shall be ᵈfor ever, and my righteousness shall not be ²abolished.

7 Hearken unto me, ye that know righteousness, the people ᵃin whose heart *is* my law; ᵇfear ye not the reproach of men, neither be ye afraid of their revilings.

8 For ᵃthe moth shall eat them up like a garment, and the worm shall eat them like wool: but my righteousness shall be for ever, and my salvation from generation to generation.

9 ᵃAwake, awake, ᵇput on strength, O arm of the Lord; awake, ᶜas in the ¹ancient days, in the generations of old. ᵈ*Art* thou not it that hath cut ᵉRahab, *and* wounded the ᶠdragon?²

10 *Art* thou not ¹it which hath ᵃdried the sea, the waters of the great deep; that hath made the depths of the sea a way for the ²ransomed to pass over?

11 Therefore ᵃthe redeemed of the Lord shall return, and come with singing unto Zion; and everlasting joy *shall be* upon their head: they shall obtain gladness and joy; *and* sorrow and ¹mourning shall flee away.

12 I, *even* I, *am* he ᵃthat comforteth you: who *art* thou, that thou shouldest be afraid ᵇof a ¹man *that* shall die, and of the son of man *which* shall be made ᶜ*as* grass;

13 And ᵃforgettest the Lord thy maker, ᵇthat hath stretched forth the heavens, and laid the foundations of the earth; and hast feared continually every day because of the fury of the oppressor, ¹as if he were ready to destroy? ᶜand where *is* the fury of the oppressor?

14 The captive exile hasteneth that he may be loosed, ᵃand that he should not die in the pit, nor that his bread should fail.

15 But I *am* the Lord thy God, that ᵃdivided the sea, whose waves roared: The Lord of hosts *is* his name.

16 And ᵃI have put my words in thy mouth, and ᵇI have covered thee in the shadow of mine hand, ᶜthat I may ¹plant the heavens, and lay the foundations of the earth, and say unto Zion, Thou *art* my people.

17 ᵃAwake, awake, stand up, O Jerusalem, which ᵇhast drunk at the hand of the Lord the cup of his fury; thou hast drunken the dregs of the cup of trembling, *and* ¹wrung *them* out.

18 *There is* none to guide her among all the sons *whom* she hath brought forth; neither *is there any* that taketh her by the hand of all the sons *that* she hath brought up.

19 ᵃThese two *things* are come unto thee; who shall be sorry for thee?

desolation, and destruction, and the famine, and the sword: [b]by whom shall I comfort thee?

20 [a]Thy sons have fainted, they lie at the head of all the streets, as [1]a wild bull in a net: they are full of the fury of the LORD, the rebuke of thy God.

21 Therefore hear now this, thou afflicted, and drunken, [a]but not with wine:

22 Thus saith thy Lord the LORD, and thy God *that* [a]pleadeth the cause of his people, Behold, I have taken out of thine hand the cup of trembling, *even* the dregs of the cup of my fury; thou shalt no more drink it again:

23 [a]But I will put it into the hand of them that afflict thee; which have said to thy soul, Bow down, that we may [1]go over: and thou hast laid thy body as the ground, and as the street, to them that [2]went over.

## CHAPTER 52

AWAKE, awake; put on thy strength, O Zion; put on thy beautiful garments, O Jerusalem, the holy city: for henceforth there shall no more come into thee the uncircumcised [a]and the unclean.

2 [a]Shake thyself from the dust; arise, *and* sit down, O Jerusalem: [b]loose thyself from the bands of thy neck, O captive daughter of Zion.

3 For thus saith the LORD, [a]Ye have sold yourselves for [1]nought; and ye shall be redeemed [b]without money.

4 For thus saith the Lord GOD, My people went down aforetime into [a]Egypt to sojourn there; and the Assyrian oppressed them without cause.

5 Now therefore, what have I here, saith the LORD, that my people is taken away for nought? they that rule over them make them to howl, saith the LORD; and my name continually every day *is* [a]blasphemed.

6 Therefore my people shall know my name: therefore *they shall know* in that day that I *am* he that doth speak: behold, *it is* I.

7 [a]How beautiful upon the mountains are the feet of him that bringeth [1]good tidings, that [2]publisheth peace; that bringeth [1]good tidings of [3]good, that [2]publisheth salvation; that saith unto Zion, [b]Thy God reigneth!

8 Thy watchmen shall lift up the voice; with the voice together shall they sing: for they shall see eye to eye, when the LORD shall bring [1]again Zion.

9 Break forth into joy, sing together, ye waste places of Jerusalem: for the LORD hath comforted his people, he hath redeemed Jerusalem.

10 [a]The LORD hath [1]made bare his holy arm in the eyes of [b]all the na-

tions; and all the ends of the earth shall see the salvation of our God.

11 [a]Depart ye, depart ye, go ye out from thence, touch no unclean *thing*; go ye out of the midst of her; [b]be ye clean, that bear the vessels of the LORD.

12 For [a]ye shall not go out with haste, nor go by flight: [b]for the LORD will go before you; [c]and the God of Israel *will be* your [1]rereward.

13 Behold, [a]my servant shall [1]deal prudently, [b]he shall be exalted and [2]extolled, and be very high.

14 As many were astonied at thee; his [a]visage[1] was so marred more than any man, and his form more than the sons of men:

15 [a]So shall he [1]sprinkle many nations; the kings shall shut their mouths at him: for *that* [b]which had not been told them shall they see; and *that* which they had not heard shall they consider.

## CHAPTER 53

WHO [a]hath believed our report? and to whom is [1]the arm of the LORD revealed?

2 For he shall grow up before him as a tender plant, and as a root out of a dry ground: he hath [1]no form nor [2]comeliness; and when we shall see him, *there is* no [3]beauty that we should desire him.

3 [a]He is despised and [1]rejected of men; a man of [2]sorrows, and [b]acquainted with [3]grief: and we hid as it were *our* faces from him; he was despised, and [c]we esteemed him not.

4 Surely [a]he hath borne our [1]griefs, and carried our [2]sorrows: yet we did [3]esteem him stricken, [4]smitten of God, and afflicted.

5 But he *was* [a]wounded[1] for our transgressions, *he was* [2]bruised for our iniquities: the chastisement of our peace *was* upon him; and with his [b]stripes[3] we are healed.

6 All we like sheep have gone astray; we have turned every one to his own way; and the LORD [1]hath laid on him the iniquity of us all.

7 He was oppressed, and he was afflicted, yet [a]he opened not his mouth: [b]he [1]is brought as a lamb to the slaughter, and as a sheep before her shearers is dumb, so he openeth not his mouth.

8 He was [a]taken [1]from prison and from judgment: and who shall [2]declare his generation? for [b]he was cut off out of the land of the living: for the transgression of my people was he stricken.

9 [a]And he made his grave with the wicked, and with the rich in his death; because he had done no violence, neither *was any* [b]deceit in his mouth.

51:19 [b] Amos 7:2
51:20 [a] Lam. 2:11
[1] an antelope
51:21 [a] Lam. 3:15
51:22 [a] Jer. 50:34
51:23 [a] Zech. 12:2
[1] walk over you
[2] walk
52:1 [a] [Rev. 21:2–27]
52:2 [a] Is. 3:26
[b] Zech. 2:7
52:3 [a] Ps. 44:12 [b] Is. 45:13
[1] nothing
52:4 [a] Gen. 46:6
52:5 [a] Ezek. 36:20, 23
52:7 [a] Rom. 10:15
[b] Ps. 93:1 [1] good news [2] proclaims [3] good things
52:8 [1] back
52:10 [a] Ps. 98:1–3 [b] Luke 3:6 [1] Revealed his power
52:11 [a] Is. 48:20 [b] Lev. 22:2
52:12 [a] Ex. 12:11, 33 [b] Mic. 2:13 [c] Ex. 14:19, 20 [1] rear guard
52:13 [a] Is. 42:1 [b] Phil. 2:9 [1] prosper [2] Lit. lifted up
52:14 [a] Ps. 22:6, 7 [1] appearance
52:15 [a] Ezek. 36:25 [b] Rom. 15:21 [1] Or startle
53:1 [a] John 12:38 [1] The power
53:2 [1] no stately form [2] splendour [3] Lit. appearance
53:3 [a] Ps. 22:6 [b] [Heb. 4:15] [c] [John 1:10, 11] [1] Or forsaken by [2] Lit. pains [3] Lit. sickness
53:4 [a] [Matt. 8:17] [1] Lit. sicknesses [2] Lit. pains [3] reckon [4] struck down by
53:5 [a] [Rom. 4:25] [b] [1 Pet. 2:24, 25] [1] Or pierced through [2] crushed [3] Blows that cut in
53:6 [1] Lit. has caused the iniquity of us all to land on him
53:7 [a] Matt. 26:63; 27:12–14 [b] Acts 8:32, 33 [1] was led
53:8 [a] Luke 23:1–25 [b] [Dan. 9:26] [1] out of oppression [2] consider it among his generation
53:9 [a] Matt. 27:57–60 [b] 1 Pet. 2:22

10 Yet it pleased the LORD to ¹bruise him; he hath put *him* to grief: when thou shalt make his soul ªan offering for sin, he shall see *his* seed, he shall prolong *his* days, and the pleasure of the LORD shall prosper in his hand.

11 He shall see of the ¹travail of his soul, *and* shall be satisfied: by his knowledge shall ªmy righteous ᵇservant ᶜjustify many; for he shall bear their iniquities.

12 ªTherefore will I divide him *a portion* with the great, ᵇand he shall divide the ¹spoil with the strong; because he hath ᶜpoured out his soul unto death: and he was ᵈnumbered with the transgressors; and he bare the sin of many, and ᵉmade intercession for the transgressors.

## CHAPTER 54

SING, O ªbarren, thou *that* didst not bear; break forth into singing, and cry aloud, thou *that* didst not travail with child: for more *are* the children of the desolate than the children of the married wife, saith the LORD.

2 ªEnlarge the place of thy tent, and let them stretch forth the curtains of ¹thine habitations: spare not, lengthen thy cords, and strengthen thy stakes;

3 For thou shalt ¹break forth on the right hand and on the left; and thy seed shall ªinherit the Gentiles, and make the desolate cities to be inhabited.

4 ªFear not; for thou shalt not be ashamed: neither be thou ¹confounded; for thou shalt not be put to shame: for thou shalt forget the shame of thy youth, and shalt not remember the reproach of thy widowhood any more.

5 ªFor thy Maker *is* thine husband; the LORD of hosts *is* his name; and thy Redeemer the Holy One of Israel; ᵇThe God of the whole earth shall he be called.

6 For the LORD ªhath called thee as a woman forsaken and grieved in spirit, and a wife of youth, when thou wast refused, saith thy God.

7 ªFor a small moment have I forsaken thee; but with great mercies will ᵇI gather thee.

8 In a little wrath I hid my face from thee for a moment; ªbut with everlasting ¹kindness will I have mercy on thee, saith the LORD thy Redeemer.

9 For this *is as* the waters of ªNoah unto me: for *as* I have sworn that the waters of Noah should no more go over the earth; so have I sworn that I would not be ¹wroth with ᵇthee, nor rebuke thee.

10 For ªthe mountains shall depart, and the hills be removed; ᵇbut my kindness shall not depart from

thee, neither shall the covenant of my peace be removed, saith the LORD that hath mercy on thee.

11 O thou afflicted, tossed with tempest, *and* not comforted, behold, I will lay thy stones with ªfair¹ colours, and lay thy foundations with sapphires.

12 And I will make thy ¹windows of agates, and thy gates of ²carbuncles, and all thy borders of ³pleasant stones.

13 And all thy children *shall be* ªtaught of the LORD; and ᵇgreat *shall be* the peace of thy children.

14 In righteousness shalt thou be established: thou shalt be far from oppression; for thou shalt not fear: and from terror; for it shall not come near thee.

15 Behold, they shall surely gather together, *but* not by me: whosoever shall gather together against thee shall ªfall for thy sake.

16 Behold, I have created the smith that bloweth the coals in the fire, and that bringeth forth an ¹instrument for his work; and I have created the ²waster to destroy.

17 No weapon that is formed against thee shall ªprosper; and every tongue *that* shall rise against thee in judgment thou shalt condemn. This *is* the heritage of the servants of the LORD, ᵇand their righteousness *is* ¹of me, saith the LORD.

## CHAPTER 55

HO, ªevery one that thirsteth, come ye to the waters, and he that hath no money; ᵇcome ye, buy, and eat; yea, come, buy wine and milk without money and without price.

2 Wherefore do ye spend money for *that which is* not bread? and your labour for *that which* satisfieth not? hearken diligently unto me, and eat ye *that which is* good, and let your soul delight itself in ¹fatness.

3 Incline your ear, and ªcome unto me: hear, and your soul shall live; ᵇand I will make an everlasting covenant with you, *even* the ᶜsure mercies of David.

4 Behold, I have given him *for* ªa witness to the people, ᵇa leader and commander to the people.

5 ªBehold, thou shalt call a nation *that* thou knowest not, ᵇand nations *that* knew not thee shall run unto thee because of the LORD thy God, and for the Holy One of Israel; ᶜfor he hath glorified thee.

6 ªSeek ye the LORD while he may be ᵇfound, call ye upon him while he is near:

7 ªLet the wicked forsake his way, and the unrighteous man ᵇhis thoughts: and let him return unto

### Cross references

53:10 ª [2 Cor. 5:21] ¹ *crush*
53:11 ª [1 John 2:1] ᵇ Is. 42:1 ᶜ [Rom. 5:15–18] ¹ *distress*
53:12 ª Ps. 2:8 ᵇ Col. 2:15 ᶜ Is. 50:6 ᵈ Matt. 27:38 ᵉ Luke 23:34 ¹ *plunder*
54:1 ª Gal. 4:27
54:2 ª Is. 49:19, 20 ¹ *thy dwellings*
54:3 ª Is. 14:2; 49:22, 23; 60:9 ¹ *expand*
54:4 ª Is. 41:10 ¹ *disgraced*
54:5 ª Jer. 3:14 ᵇ Zech. 14:9
54:6 ª Is. 62:4
54:7 ª Is. 26:20; 60:10 ᵇ [Is. 43:5; 56:8]
54:8 ª Jer. 31:3 ¹ *lovingkindness*
54:9 ª Gen. 8:21; 9:11 ᵇ Ezek. 39:29 ¹ *angry*
54:10 ª Is. 51:6 ᵇ Ps. 89:33, 34
54:11 ª Rev. 21:18, 19 ¹ *colourful gems* or *antimony*
54:12 ¹ *pinnacles of rubies* ² *crystal* ³ *precious*
54:13 ª [John 6:45] ᵇ Ps. 119:165
54:15 ª Is. 41:11–16
54:16 ¹ Or *weapon* ² *destroyer*
54:17 ª Is. 17:12–14; 29:8 ᵇ Is. 45:24, 25; 54:14 ¹ *from*
55:1 ª [John 4:14; 7:37] ᵇ [Rev. 3:18]
55:2 ¹ *abundance*
55:3 ª Matt. 11:28 ᵇ Jer. 32:40 ᶜ 2 Sam. 7:8
55:4 ª [Rev. 1:5] ᵇ [Dan. 9:25]
55:5 ª Eph. 2:11, 12 ᵇ Is. 60:5 ᶜ Is. 60:9
55:6 ª [Heb. 3:13] ᵇ Ps. 32:6
55:7 ª Is. 1:16 ᵇ Zech. 8:17

the LORD, <sup>c</sup>and he will have mercy upon him; and to our God, for he will abundantly pardon.

8 <sup>a</sup>For my thoughts *are* not your thoughts, neither *are* your ways my ways, saith the LORD.

9 <sup>a</sup>For *as* the heavens are higher than the earth, so are my ways higher than your ways, and my thoughts than your thoughts.

10 For <sup>a</sup>as the rain cometh down, and the snow from heaven, and returneth not thither, but watereth the earth, and maketh it bring forth and bud, that it may give seed to the sower, and bread to the eater:

11 <sup>a</sup>So shall my word be that goeth forth out of my mouth: it shall not return unto me <sup>1</sup>void, but it shall accomplish that which I please, and it shall <sup>b</sup>prosper *in the thing* whereto I sent it.

12 <sup>a</sup>For ye shall go out with joy, and be led forth with peace: the mountains and the hills shall <sup>b</sup>break forth before you into singing, and <sup>c</sup>all the trees of the field shall clap *their* hands.

13 <sup>a</sup>Instead of <sup>b</sup>the thorn shall come up the <sup>1</sup>fir tree, and instead of the brier shall come up the myrtle tree: and it shall be to the LORD <sup>c</sup>for a name, for an everlasting sign *that* shall not be cut off.

## CHAPTER 56

THUS saith the LORD, Keep ye <sup>1</sup>judgment, and do <sup>2</sup>justice: <sup>a</sup>for my salvation *is* <sup>3</sup>near to come, and my righteousness to be revealed.

2 Blessed *is* the man *that* doeth this, and the son of man *that* layeth hold on it; <sup>a</sup>that keepeth <sup>1</sup>the sabbath from polluting it, and keepeth his hand from doing any evil.

3 Neither let <sup>a</sup>the son of the <sup>1</sup>stranger, that hath joined himself to the LORD, speak, saying, The LORD hath utterly separated me from his people: neither let the <sup>b</sup>eunuch say, Behold, I *am* a dry tree.

4 For thus saith the LORD unto the eunuchs that keep my sabbaths, and choose *the things* that please me, and <sup>1</sup>take hold of my covenant;

5 Even unto them will I give in <sup>a</sup>mine house and within my walls a place <sup>b</sup>and a name better than of sons and of daughters: I will give them an everlasting name, that shall not be cut off.

6 Also the sons of the <sup>1</sup>stranger, that join themselves to the LORD, to serve him, and to love the name of the LORD, to be his servants, every one that keepeth <sup>2</sup>the sabbath from polluting it, and <sup>3</sup>taketh hold of my covenant;

7 Even them will I <sup>a</sup>bring to my holy mountain, and make them joyful in my <sup>b</sup>house of prayer: <sup>c</sup>their

---

55:7 <sup>c</sup> Jer. 3:12
55:8 <sup>a</sup> 2 Sam. 7:19
55:9 <sup>a</sup> Ps. 103:11
55:10 <sup>a</sup> Deut. 32:2
55:11 <sup>a</sup> Is. 45:23
<sup>b</sup> Is. 46:9–11
<sup>1</sup> empty, without fruit
55:12 <sup>a</sup> Is. 35:10
<sup>b</sup> Ps. 98:8 <sup>c</sup> 1 Chr. 16:33
55:13 <sup>a</sup> Is. 41:19
<sup>b</sup> Mic. 7:4 <sup>c</sup> Jer. 13:11 <sup>1</sup> cypress
56:1 <sup>a</sup> Matt. 3:2; 4:17 <sup>1</sup> justice
<sup>2</sup> righteousness
<sup>3</sup> about
56:2 <sup>a</sup> Is. 58:13
<sup>1</sup> from defiling the sabbath
56:3 <sup>a</sup> [Eph. 2:12–19] <sup>b</sup> Acts 8:27
<sup>1</sup> foreigner
56:4 <sup>1</sup> hold fast to
56:5 <sup>a</sup> 1 Tim. 3:15
<sup>b</sup> [1 John 3:1, 2]
56:6 <sup>1</sup> foreigner
<sup>2</sup> from defiling the sabbath <sup>3</sup> holds fast to
56:7 <sup>a</sup> [Is. 2:2, 3; 60:11] <sup>b</sup> Mark 11:17
<sup>c</sup> [Rom. 12:1] <sup>d</sup> Is. 60:7 <sup>e</sup> Matt. 21:13
<sup>f</sup> [Mal. 1:11]
56:8 <sup>a</sup> Is. 11:12; 27:12; 54:7
<sup>b</sup> [John 10:16]
56:9 <sup>a</sup> Jer. 12:9
56:10 <sup>a</sup> Matt. 15:14
<sup>b</sup> Phil. 3:2 <sup>1</sup> mute
<sup>2</sup> dreaming
56:11 <sup>a</sup> [Mic. 3:5, 11] <sup>b</sup> Ezek. 34:2–10 <sup>1</sup> Lit. never know satisfaction
<sup>2</sup> Lit. from his end
56:12 <sup>a</sup> Is. 28:7
<sup>b</sup> Luke 12:19
<sup>c</sup> 2 Pet. 3:4
57:1 <sup>a</sup> Ps. 12:1
<sup>b</sup> 1 Kin. 14:13
<sup>1</sup> takes <sup>2</sup> presence of evil
57:2 <sup>a</sup> 2 Chr. 16:14
57:3 <sup>a</sup> Matt. 16:4
<sup>1</sup> harlot
57:4 <sup>1</sup> ridicule?
<sup>2</sup> stick
57:5 <sup>a</sup> 2 Kin. 16:4 <sup>b</sup> Jer. 7:31
<sup>1</sup> Inflaming <sup>2</sup> with gods <sup>3</sup> clefts
57:6 <sup>a</sup> Jer. 3:9
<sup>b</sup> Jer. 5:9, 29; 9:9
<sup>1</sup> grain or meal
57:7 <sup>a</sup> Ezek. 16:16
<sup>b</sup> Ezek. 23:41
57:8 <sup>a</sup> Ezek. 16:26 <sup>1</sup> uncovered
<sup>2</sup> have gone up to them <sup>3</sup> Lit. cut
<sup>4</sup> their hand
57:9 <sup>a</sup> Hos. 7:11
<sup>b</sup> Ezek. 23:16, 40
<sup>1</sup> Or Sheol

---

burnt offerings and their sacrifices *shall be* <sup>d</sup>accepted upon mine altar; for <sup>e</sup>mine house shall be called an house of prayer <sup>f</sup>for all people.

8 The Lord GOD <sup>a</sup>which gathereth the outcasts of Israel saith, <sup>b</sup>Yet will I gather *others* to him, beside those that are gathered unto him.

9 <sup>a</sup>All ye beasts of the field, come to devour, *yea,* all ye beasts in the forest.

10 His watchmen *are* <sup>a</sup>blind: they are all ignorant, <sup>b</sup>they *are* all <sup>1</sup>dumb dogs, they cannot bark; <sup>2</sup>sleeping, lying down, loving to slumber.

11 Yea, *they are* <sup>a</sup>greedy dogs *which* <sup>b</sup>can<sup>1</sup> never have enough, and they *are* shepherds *that* cannot understand: they all look to their own way, every one for his gain, from <sup>2</sup>his quarter.

12 Come ye, *say they,* I will fetch wine, and we will fill ourselves with strong <sup>a</sup>drink; <sup>b</sup>and to morrow shall be <sup>c</sup>as this day, *and* much more abundant.

## CHAPTER 57

THE righteous perisheth, and no man <sup>1</sup>layeth *it* to heart: and <sup>a</sup>merciful men *are* taken away, <sup>b</sup>none considering that the righteous is taken away from the <sup>2</sup>evil *to come.*

2 He shall enter into peace: they shall rest in <sup>a</sup>their beds, *each one* walking *in* his uprightness.

3 But draw near hither, <sup>a</sup>ye sons of the sorceress, the seed of the adulterer and the <sup>1</sup>whore.

4 Against whom do ye <sup>1</sup>sport yourselves? against whom make ye a wide mouth, *and* <sup>2</sup>draw out the tongue? *are* ye not children of transgression, a seed of falsehood,

5 <sup>1</sup>Enflaming yourselves <sup>2</sup>with idols <sup>a</sup>under every green tree, <sup>b</sup>slaying the children in the valleys under the <sup>3</sup>clifts of the rocks?

6 Among the smooth <sup>a</sup>*stones* of the stream *is* thy portion; they, they *are* thy lot: even to them hast thou poured a drink offering, thou hast offered a <sup>1</sup>meat offering. Should I receive comfort in <sup>b</sup>these?

7 <sup>a</sup>Upon a lofty and high mountain hast thou set <sup>b</sup>thy bed: even thither wentest thou up to offer sacrifice.

8 Behind the doors also and the posts hast thou set up thy remembrance: for thou hast <sup>1</sup>discovered *thyself to another* than me, and <sup>2</sup>art gone up; thou hast enlarged thy bed, and <sup>3</sup>made thee *a covenant* with them; <sup>a</sup>thou lovedst their bed where thou sawest <sup>4</sup>*it.*

9 And <sup>a</sup>thou wentest to the king with ointment, and didst increase thy perfumes, and didst send thy <sup>b</sup>messengers far off, and didst debase *thyself even* unto <sup>1</sup>hell.

10 Thou art wearied in the ¹greatness of thy way; ᵃyet saidst thou not, There is no hope: thou hast found ²the life of thine hand; therefore thou wast not grieved.

11 And ᵃof whom hast thou been afraid or feared, that thou hast lied, and hast not remembered me, nor laid *it* to thy heart? ᵇhave not I ¹held my peace even of old, and thou fearest me not?

12 I will declare thy righteousness, and thy works; for they shall not profit thee.

13 When thou ¹criest, let thy ²companies deliver thee; but the wind shall carry them all away; ³vanity shall take *them:* but he that putteth his trust in me shall possess the land, and shall inherit my holy mountain;

14 And shall say, ᵃCast¹ ye up, cast ye up, prepare the way, take up the stumblingblock out of the way of my people.

15 For thus saith the high and lofty One that inhabiteth eternity, ᵃwhose name *is* Holy; ᵇI dwell in the high and holy *place,* ᶜwith him also *that is* of a contrite and humble spirit, ᵈto revive the spirit of the humble, and to revive the heart of the contrite ones.

16 ᵃFor I will not contend for ever, neither will I be always ¹wroth: for the spirit should fail before me, and the souls ᵇwhich I have made.

17 For the iniquity of ᵃhis covetousness was I ¹wroth, and ²smote him: ᵇI hid me, and was ¹wroth, ᶜand he went on ³frowardly in the way of his heart.

18 I have seen his ways, and ᵃwill heal him: I will lead him also, and restore comforts unto him and to ᵇhis mourners.

19 I create ᵃthe fruit of the lips; Peace, peace ᵇto *him that is* far off, and to *him that is* near, saith the LORD; and I will heal him.

20 ᵃBut the wicked *are* like the troubled sea, when it cannot rest, whose waters cast up mire and dirt.

21 ᵃ*There is* no peace, saith my God, to the wicked.

## CHAPTER 58

CRY aloud, ¹spare not, lift up thy voice like a trumpet, and ᵃshew² my people their transgression, and the house of Jacob their sins.

2 Yet they seek me daily, and delight to know my ways, as a nation that did righteousness, and forsook not the ordinance of their God: they ask of me the ordinances of justice; they take delight in approaching to God.

3 ᵃWherefore have we fasted, *say they,* and thou seest not? *wherefore* have we ᵇafflicted our soul, and thou

takest no knowledge? Behold, in the day of your fast ye find pleasure, and ¹exact all your ²labours.

4 ᵃBehold, ye fast for strife and debate, and to ¹smite with the fist of wickedness: ye shall not fast as *ye do this* day, to make your voice to be heard on high.

5 Is it ᵃsuch a fast that I have chosen? ᵇa day for a man to afflict his soul? *is it* to bow down his head as a bulrush, and ᶜto spread sackcloth and ashes *under him?* wilt thou call this a fast, and an acceptable day to the LORD?

6 *Is* not this the fast that I have chosen? to ᵃloose the bands of wickedness, ᵇto undo the ¹heavy burdens, and ᶜto let the oppressed go free, and that ye break every yoke?

7 *Is it* not ᵃto ¹deal thy bread to the hungry, and that thou bring the poor that are ²cast out to thy house? ᵇwhen thou seest the naked, that thou cover him; and that thou hide not thyself from ᶜthine own flesh?

8 ᵃThen shall thy light break forth as the morning, and thine ¹health shall spring forth speedily: and thy righteousness shall go before thee; ᵇthe glory of the LORD shall be thy ²rereward.

9 Then shalt thou call, and the LORD shall answer; thou shalt cry, and he shall say, Here I *am.* If thou take away from the midst of thee the yoke, the ¹putting forth of the finger, and ᵃspeaking ²vanity;

10 And *if* thou ¹draw out thy soul to the hungry, and satisfy the afflicted soul; then shall thy light rise in ²obscurity, and thy ³darkness *be* as the noon day:

11 And the LORD shall guide thee continually, and satisfy thy soul in ¹drought, and ²make fat thy bones: and thou shalt be like a watered garden, and like a spring of water, whose waters fail not.

12 And *they that shall be* of thee ᵃshall build the old waste places: thou shalt raise up the foundations of many generations; and thou shalt be called, The repairer of the breach, The restorer of ¹paths to dwell in.

13 If ᵃthou turn away thy foot from the sabbath, *from* doing thy pleasure on my holy day; and call the sabbath a delight, the holy of the LORD, honourable; and shalt honour him, not doing thine own ways, nor finding thine own pleasure, nor speaking *thine own* words:

14 ᵃThen shalt thou delight thyself in the LORD; and I will cause thee to ᵇride upon the high ¹places of the earth, and feed thee with the heritage of Jacob thy father: ᶜfor the mouth of the LORD hath spoken *it.*

*Center reference column:*

57:10 ᵃ Jer. 2:25; 18:12 ¹ *length of your road* ² Strength

57:11 ᵃ Is. 51:12, 13 ᵇ Ps. 50:21 ¹ *remained silent*

57:13 ¹ *cry out* ² *collection* of idols ³ *a breath*

57:14 ᵃ Is. 40:3; 62:10 ¹ *Heap up*

57:15 ᵃ Job 6:10 ᵇ Zech. 2:13 ᶜ Ps. 34:18; 51:17 ᵈ Is. 61:1–3

57:16 ᵃ [Mic. 7:18] ᵇ Num. 16:22 ¹ *angry*

57:17 ᵃ Jer. 6:13 ᵇ Is. 8:17; 45:15; 59:2 ᶜ Is. 9:13 ¹ *angry* ² *struck* ³ *backsliding* or *turning back*

57:18 ᵃ Jer. 3:22 ᵇ Is. 61:2

57:19 ᵃ Heb. 13:15 ᵇ Eph. 2:17

57:20 ᵃ Job 15:20

57:21 ᵃ Is. 48:22

58:1 ᵃ Mic. 3:8 ¹ *do not hold back* ² *tell*

58:3 ᵃ Mal. 3:13–18 ᵇ Lev. 16:29; 23:27

¹ *exploit* ² *labourers*

58:4 ᵃ 1 Kin. 21:9 ¹ *strike*

58:5 ᵃ Zech. 7:5 ᵇ Lev. 16:29 ᶜ Esth. 4:3

58:6 ᵃ Luke 4:18, 19 ᵇ Neh. 5:10–12 ᶜ Jer. 34:9 ¹ Lit. *bonds of the yoke*

58:7 ᵃ Ezek. 18:7 ᵇ Job 31:19–22 ᶜ Neh. 5:5 ¹ *share* ² Lit. *wandering*

58:8 ᵃ Job 11:17 ᵇ Ex. 14:19 ¹ *healing* ² *rear guard*

58:9 ᵃ Ps. 12:2 ¹ *pointing of* ² *wickedness*

58:10 ¹ *extend* ² *darkness* ³ Or *gloom*

58:11 ¹ Lit. *dry places* ² *strengthen*

58:12 ᵃ Is. 61:4 ¹ *streets*

58:13 ᵃ Is. 56:2, 4, 6

58:14 ᵃ Job 22:26 ᵇ Deut. 32:13; 33:29 ᶜ Is. 1:20; 40:5 ¹ *hills*

## CHAPTER 59

**B**EHOLD, the LORD's hand is not [a]shortened, that it cannot save; neither his ear heavy, that it cannot hear:

2 But your iniquities have separated between you and your God, and your sins have hid *his* face from you, that he will [a]not hear.

3 For [a]your hands are defiled with [1]blood, and your fingers with iniquity; your lips have spoken lies, your tongue hath muttered perverseness.

4 None calleth for justice, nor *any* pleadeth for truth: they trust in [a]vanity,[1] and speak lies; [b]they conceive [2]mischief, and bring forth iniquity.

5 They hatch [1]cockatrice' eggs, and weave the spider's web: he that eateth of their eggs dieth, and that which is crushed [2]breaketh out into a viper.

6 [a]Their webs shall not become garments, neither shall they cover themselves with their works: their works *are* works of iniquity, and the act of violence *is* in their hands.

7 [a]Their feet run to evil, and they make haste to shed [b]innocent blood: [c]their thoughts *are* thoughts of iniquity; wasting and [d]destruction *are* in their paths.

8 The way of [a]peace they know not; and *there is* no [1]judgment in their [2]goings: [b]they have made them crooked paths: whosoever goeth therein shall not know peace.

9 Therefore is [1]judgment far from us, neither doth [2]justice overtake us: [a]we wait for light, but behold [3]obscurity; for brightness, *but* we walk in [4]darkness.

10 [a]We grope for the wall like the blind, and we grope as if *we had* no eyes: we stumble at noon day as [1]in the night; *we are* in desolate places as dead *men*.

11 We [1]roar all like bears, and [a]mourn[2] sore like doves: we look for [3]judgment, but *there is* none; for salvation, *but* it is far off from us.

12 For our [a]transgressions are multiplied before thee, and our sins testify against us: for our transgressions *are* with us; and *as for* our iniquities, we know them;

13 In transgressing and lying against the LORD, and departing away from our God, speaking oppression and revolt, conceiving and uttering [a]from the heart words of falsehood.

14 And [1]judgment is turned away backward, and [2]justice standeth afar off: for truth is fallen in the street, and [3]equity cannot enter.

15 Yea, truth faileth; and he *that* departeth from evil maketh himself a [a]prey: and the LORD saw *it*, and it

[1]displeased him that *there was* no [2]judgment.

16 [a]And he saw that *there was* no man, and [b]wondered that *there was* no intercessor: [c]therefore his arm brought salvation unto him; and his righteousness, it sustained him.

17 [a]For he put on righteousness as a breastplate, and an helmet of salvation upon his head; and he put on the garments of vengeance *for* clothing, and was clad with zeal as a cloke.

18 [a]According to *their* deeds, accordingly he will repay, fury to his adversaries, recompence to his enemies; to the [1]islands he will [2]repay recompence.

19 [a]So shall they fear the name of the LORD from the west, and his glory from the rising of the sun. When the enemy shall come in [b]like a flood, the Spirit of the LORD shall lift up a [1]standard against him.

20 And [a]the Redeemer shall come to Zion, and unto them that turn from transgression in Jacob, saith the LORD.

21 [a]As for me, this *is* my covenant with them, saith the LORD; My spirit that *is* upon thee, and my words which I have put in thy mouth, shall not depart out of thy mouth, nor out of the mouth of thy seed, nor out of the mouth of thy seed's seed, saith the LORD, from henceforth and for ever.

## CHAPTER 60

**A**RISE, [a]shine; for thy light is come, and [b]the glory of the LORD is risen upon thee.

2 For, behold, the darkness shall cover the earth, and gross darkness the people: but the LORD shall arise upon thee, and his glory shall be seen upon thee.

3 And the [a]Gentiles shall come to thy light, and kings to the brightness of thy rising.

4 [a]Lift up thine eyes round about, and see: all they gather themselves together, [b]they come to thee: thy sons shall come from far, and thy daughters shall be nursed at *thy* side.

5 Then thou shalt see, and [1]flow together, and thine heart shall [2]fear, and be enlarged; because [a]the abundance of the sea shall be converted unto thee, the [3]forces of the [4]Gentiles shall come unto thee.

6 The multitude of camels shall cover [1]thee, the dromedaries of Midian and [a]Ephah; all they from [b]Sheba shall come: they shall bring [c]gold and incense; and they shall [2]shew forth the praises of the LORD.

7 All the flocks of [a]Kedar shall be gathered together unto thee, the rams of Nebaioth shall minister unto

### Cross references

59:1 [a] Num. 11:23
59:2 [a] Is. 1:15
59:3 [a] Ezek. 7:23 [1] *bloodshed*
59:4 [a] Is. 30:12; Jer. 7:4 [b] Job 15:35; Ps. 7:14; Is. 33:11 [1] *empty words* [2] *trouble or evil*
59:5 [1] *vipers'* [2] *hatches out*
59:6 [a] Job 8:14
59:7 [a] Prov. 1:16; Rom. 3:15 [b] Prov. 6:17 [c] Is. 55:7 [d] Rom. 3:16, 17
59:8 [a] Is. 57:20, 21 [b] Ps. 125:5; Prov. 2:15 [1] *justice* [2] *tracks*
59:9 [a] Jer. 8:15 [1] *justice* [2] *righteousness* [3] *darkness* [4] *gloom or blackness*
59:10 [a] Deut. 28:29; Job 5:14; Amos 8:9 [1] *at twilight*
59:11 [a] Is. 38:14; Ezek. 7:16 [1] *growl* [2] *moan sadly* [3] *justice*
59:12 [a] Is. 24:5; 58:1
59:13 [a] Matt. 12:34
59:14 [1] *justice* [2] *righteousness* [3] *uprightness*
59:15 [a] Is. 5:23; 10:2; 29:21; 32:7 [1] Lit. *was evil in his eyes* [2] *justice*
59:16 [a] Is. 41:28; 63:5; 64:7; Ezek. 22:30 [b] Mark 6:6 [c] Ps. 98:1; Is. 63:5
59:17 [a] Eph. 6:14, 17; 1 Thess. 5:8
59:18 [a] Is. 63:6; Rom. 2:6 [1] *coastlands* [2] *fully repay*
59:19 [a] Ps. 113:3; Mal. 1:11 [b] Rev. 12:15 [1] *banner*
59:20 [a] Rom. 11:26
59:21 [a] [Heb. 8:10; 10:16]
60:1 [a] Eph. 5:14 [b] Mal. 4:2
60:3 [a] Is. 49:6, 23; Rev. 21:24
60:4 [a] Is. 49:18 [b] Is. 49:20–22
60:5 [a] [Rom. 11:25–27] [1] *become radiant* [2] *swell with joy* [3] *wealth* [4] *nations*
60:6 [a] Gen. 25:4 [b] Gen. 25:3; Ps. 72:10 [c] Is. 61:6; Matt. 2:11 [1] *thy land* [2] *proclaim*
60:7 [a] Gen. 25:13

thee: they shall come up with [b]acceptance on mine altar, and [c]I will glorify the house of my glory.

8 Who *are* these *that* fly as a cloud, and as the doves to their [1]windows?

9 [a]Surely the [1]isles shall wait for me, and the ships of Tarshish first, [b]to bring thy sons from far, [c]their silver and their gold with them, unto the name of the LORD thy God, and to the Holy One of Israel, [d]because he hath glorified thee.

10 And [a]the sons of [1]strangers shall build up thy walls, [b]and their kings shall minister unto thee: for [c]in my wrath I [2]smote thee, [d]but in my favour have I had mercy on thee.

11 Therefore thy gates [a]shall be open continually; they shall not be shut day nor night; that *men* may bring unto thee the [1]forces of the Gentiles, and *that* their kings *may be* [2]brought.

12 [a]For the nation and kingdom that will not serve thee shall perish; yea, *those* nations shall be utterly [1]wasted.

13 [a]The glory of Lebanon shall come unto thee, the [1]fir tree, the pine tree, and the [2]box together, to beautify the place of my sanctuary; and I will make [b]the place of my feet glorious.

14 The sons also of them that afflicted thee shall come [a]bending[1] unto thee; and all they that despised thee shall [b]bow themselves down at the soles of thy feet; and they shall call thee, The city of the LORD, [c]The Zion of the Holy One of Israel.

15 Whereas thou hast been forsaken and hated, so that no man went through *thee,* I will make thee an eternal excellency, a joy of many generations.

16 Thou shalt also suck the milk of the Gentiles, [a]and shalt suck the breast of kings: and thou shalt know that [b]I the LORD *am* thy Saviour and thy Redeemer, the mighty One of Jacob.

17 [1]For brass I will bring gold, and for iron I will bring silver, and for wood [2]brass, and for stones iron: I will also make thy officers peace, and [3]thine exactors righteousness.

18 Violence shall no [1]more be heard in thy land, [2]wasting nor destruction within thy borders; but thou shalt call [a]thy walls Salvation, and thy gates Praise.

19 The [a]sun shall be no more thy light by day; neither for brightness shall the moon give light unto thee: but the LORD shall be unto thee an everlasting light, and [b]thy God thy glory.

20 [a]Thy sun shall no more go down; neither shall thy moon withdraw itself: for the LORD shall be thine everlasting light, and the days of thy mourning shall be ended.

60:7 [b] Is. 56:7 [c] Is. 60:13; Hag. 2:7, 9
60:8 [1] *roosts*
60:9 [a] Ps. 72:10 [b] [Gal. 4:26] [c] Jer. 3:17 [d] Is. 55:5 [1] *coastlands*
60:10 [a] Zech. 6:15 [b] Rev. 21:24 [c] Is. 57:17 [d] Is. 54:7, 8 [1] *foreigners* [2] *struck*
60:11 [a] Rev. 21:25, 26 [1] *wealth* [2] *led in procession*
60:12 [a] Zech. 14:17 [1] *ruined*
60:13 [a] Is. 35:2 [b] 1 Chr. 28:2 [1] *cypress* [2] *box tree*
60:14 [a] Is. 45:14 [b] Rev. 3:9 [c] [Heb. 12:22] [1] *bowing*
60:16 [a] Is. 49:23 [b] Is. 43:3
60:17 [1] *Instead of bronze* [2] *bronze* [3] *your magistrates*
60:18 [a] Is. 26:1 [1] *longer* [2] *devastation*
60:19 [a] Rev. 21:23; 22:5 [b] Zech. 2:5
60:20 [a] Amos 8:9

60:21 [a] Rev. 21:27 [b] Ps. 37:11 [c] Is. 61:3 [d] [Eph. 2:10]
60:22 [a] Matt. 13:31, 32 [1] *its*
61:1 [a] Luke 4:18, 19 [b] Luke 7:22 [c] Ps. 147:3 [d] Is. 42:7 [1] *poor* [2] *to heal*
61:2 [a] Lev. 25:9 [b] Is. 34:8 [c] Matt. 5:4
61:3 [a] Ps. 30:11 [b] Is. 60:21 [c] [John 15:8] [1] *console*
61:4 [a] Ezek. 36:33 [1] *ruins* [2] *ruined*
61:5 [a] [Eph. 2:12]
61:6 [a] Ex. 19:6 [b] Is. 60:5, 11 [1] *Servants*
61:7 [a] Zech. 9:12 [1] *double honour*
61:8 [a] Ps. 11:7 [b] Is. 1:11, 13 [c] Is. 55:3 [1] *justice* [2] *Or in* [3] *Lit. cut*
61:9 [a] Is. 65:23
61:10 [a] Hab. 3:18 [b] Ps. 132:9, 16 [c] Is. 49:18

21 [a]Thy people also *shall be* all righteous: [b]they shall inherit the land for ever, [c]the branch of my planting, [d]the work of my hands, that I may be glorified.

22 [a]A little one shall become a thousand, and a small one a strong nation: I the LORD will hasten it in [1]his time.

## CHAPTER 61

THE [a]Spirit of the Lord GOD *is* upon me; because the LORD [b]hath anointed me to preach good tidings unto the [1]meek; he hath sent me [c]to[2] bind up the brokenhearted, to proclaim [d]liberty to the captives, and the opening of the prison to *them that are* bound;

2 [a]To proclaim the acceptable year of the LORD, and [b]the day of vengeance of our God; [c]to comfort all that mourn;

3 To [1]appoint unto them that mourn in Zion, [a]to give unto them beauty for ashes, the oil of joy for mourning, the garment of praise for the spirit of heaviness; that they might be called trees of righteousness, [b]the planting of the LORD, [c]that he might be glorified.

4 And they shall [a]build the old [1]wastes, they shall raise up the former desolations, and they shall repair the [2]waste cities, the desolations of many generations.

5 And [a]strangers shall stand and feed your flocks, and the sons of the alien *shall be* your plowmen and your vinedressers.

6 [a]But ye shall be named the Priests of the LORD: *men* shall call you the [1]Ministers of our God: [b]ye shall eat the riches of the Gentiles, and in their glory shall ye boast yourselves.

7 [a]For your shame *ye shall have* [1]double; and *for* confusion they shall rejoice in their portion: therefore in their land they shall possess the double: everlasting joy shall be unto them.

8 For [a]I the LORD love [1]judgment, [b]I hate robbery [2]for burnt offering; and I will direct their work in truth, [c]and I will [3]make an everlasting covenant with them.

9 And their seed shall be known among the Gentiles, and their offspring among the people: all that see them shall acknowledge them, [a]that they *are* the seed *which* the LORD hath blessed.

10 [a]I will greatly rejoice in the LORD, my soul shall be joyful in my God; for [b]he hath clothed me with the garments of salvation, he hath covered me with the robe of righteousness, [c]as a bridegroom decketh *himself* with ornaments, and as a bride adorneth *herself* with her jewels.

11 For as the earth bringeth forth her bud, and as the garden causeth the things that are sown in it to spring forth; so the Lord GOD will cause ªrighteousness and ᵇpraise to spring forth before all the nations.

## CHAPTER 62

FOR Zion's sake will I not ¹hold my peace, and for Jerusalem's sake I will not rest, until the righteousness thereof go forth as brightness, and the salvation thereof as a lamp *that* burneth.

2 ªAnd the Gentiles shall see thy righteousness, and all ᵇkings thy glory: ᶜand thou shalt be called by a new name, which the mouth of the LORD shall name.

3 Thou shalt also be ªa crown of glory in the hand of the LORD, and a royal diadem in the hand of thy God.

4 ªThou shalt no more be termed ᵇForsaken;¹ neither shall thy land any more be termed ᶜDesolate:² but thou shalt be called ³Hephzi-bah, and thy land ⁴Beulah: for the LORD delighteth in thee, and thy land shall be married.

5 For *as* a young man marrieth a virgin, *so* shall thy sons marry thee: and *as* the bridegroom rejoiceth over the bride, ªso shall thy God rejoice over thee.

6 ªI have set watchmen upon thy walls, O Jerusalem, *which* shall never ¹hold their peace day nor night: ye that ²make mention of the LORD, keep not silence,

7 And give him no rest, till he establish, and till he make Jerusalem ªa praise in the earth.

8 The LORD hath sworn by his right hand, and by the arm of his strength, Surely I will no more ªgive thy ¹corn *to be* meat for thine enemies; and the sons of the ²stranger shall not drink thy wine, for the which thou hast laboured:

9 But they that have gathered it shall eat it, and praise the LORD; and they that have brought it together shall drink it ªin ¹the courts of my holiness.

10 Go through, go through the gates; ªprepare ye the way of the people; ¹cast up, cast up the highway; ²gather out the stones; ᵇlift up a ³standard for the people.

11 Behold, the LORD hath proclaimed unto the end of the world, ªSay ye to the daughter of Zion, Behold, thy salvation cometh; behold, his ᵇreward *is* with him, and his ¹work before him.

12 And they shall call them, The holy people, The redeemed of the LORD: and thou shalt be called, Sought out, A city not forsaken.

---

61:11 ª Ps. 72:3;
85:11 ᵇ Is. 60:18;
62:7
62:1 ¹ *keep silent*
62:2 ª Is. 60:3
ᵇ Ps. 102:15, 16;
138:4, 5; 148:11,
13 ᶜ Is. 62:4, 12;
65:15
62:3 ª Zech. 9:16
62:4 ª Hos. 1:10
ᵇ Is. 49:14; 54:6,
7 ᶜ Is. 54:1 ¹ Heb.
*Azubah* ² Heb.
*Shemamah* ³ Lit.
*My Delight Is in
Her* ⁴ Lit. *Married*
62:5 ª Is. 65:19
62:6 ª Ezek. 3:17;
33:7 ¹ *keep silent*
² *remember*
62:7 ª Zeph.
3:19, 20
62:8 ª Deut. 28:31,
33 ¹ *grain to be
food* ² *foreigner*
62:9 ª Deut. 12:12;
14:23, 26 ¹ *my
holy courts*
62:10 ª Is. 40:3;
57:14 ᵇ Is. 11:12
¹ *build up* ² *remove* ³ *banner*
62:11 ª Zech. 9:9
ᵇ [Rev. 22:12]
¹ *recompense*

63:2 ª [Rev. 19:13,
15] ¹ *winepress*
63:3 ª Rev. 14:19,
20; 19:15
63:4 ª Is. 34:8;
35:4; 61:2
63:5 ª Is. 41:28;
59:16 ᵇ [John
16:32] ᶜ Ps. 98:1
63:9 ª Judg. 10:16
ᵇ Ex. 14:19 ᶜ Deut.
7:7 ᵈ Ex. 19:4
¹ Kt., LXX, Syr. *not
afflicted*
63:10 ª Ex. 15:24
ᵇ Ps. 78:40 ᶜ Ex.
23:21 ¹ *grieved*
63:11 ª Ps. 106:44,
45 ᵇ Ex. 14:30
ᶜ Num. 11:17, 25,
29 ¹ Many mss.;
MT, Vg. *shepherds*
63:12 ª Ex. 15:6
ᵇ Ex. 14:21, 22
63:13 ª Ps. 106:9
63:14 ª 2 Sam.
7:23

---

## CHAPTER 63

WHO *is* this that cometh from Edom, with dyed garments from Bozrah? this *that is* glorious in his apparel, travelling in the greatness of his strength? I that speak in righteousness, mighty to save.

2 Wherefore ªart thou red in thine apparel, and thy garments like him that treadeth in the ¹winefat?

3 I have ªtrodden the winepress alone; and of the people *there was* none with me: for I will tread them in mine anger, and trample them in my fury; and their blood shall be sprinkled upon my garments, and I will stain all my raiment.

4 For the ªday of vengeance *is* in mine heart, and the year of my redeemed is come.

5 ªAnd I looked, and ᵇthere was none to help; and I wondered that *there was* none to uphold: therefore mine own ᶜarm brought salvation unto me; and my fury, it upheld me.

6 And I will tread down the people in mine anger, and make them drunk in my fury, and I will bring down their strength to the earth.

7 I will mention the lovingkindnesses of the LORD, *and* the praises of the LORD, according to all that the LORD hath bestowed on us, and the great goodness toward the house of Israel, which he hath bestowed on them according to his mercies, and according to the multitude of his lovingkindnesses.

8 For he said, Surely they *are* my people, children *that* will not lie: so he was their Saviour.

9 ªIn all their affliction he was ¹afflicted, ᵇand the angel of his presence saved them: ᶜin his love and in his pity he redeemed them; and ᵈhe bare them, and carried them all the days of old.

10 But they ªrebelled, and ᵇvexed¹ his holy Spirit: ᶜtherefore he was turned to be their enemy, *and* he fought against them.

11 Then he ªremembered the days of old, Moses, *and* his people, *saying,* Where *is* he that ᵇbrought them up out of the sea with the ¹shepherd of his flock? ᶜwhere *is* he that put his holy Spirit within him?

12 That led *them* by the right hand of Moses ªwith his glorious arm, ᵇdividing the water before them, to make himself an everlasting name?

13 ªThat led them through the deep, as an horse in the wilderness, *that* they should not stumble?

14 As a beast goeth down into the valley, the Spirit of the LORD caused him to rest: so didst thou lead thy people, ªto make thyself a glorious name.

15 [a]Look down from heaven, and behold [b]from [1]the habitation of thy holiness and of thy glory: where *is* thy zeal and thy strength, the [2]sounding [c]of thy bowels and of thy mercies toward me? are they restrained?

16 [a]Doubtless thou *art* our father, though Abraham [b]be ignorant of us, and Israel acknowledge us not: thou, O LORD, *art* our father, our redeemer; thy name *is* from everlasting.

17 O LORD, why hast thou [a]made us to [1]err from thy ways, *and* hardened our heart from thy fear? Return for thy servants' sake, the tribes of thine inheritance.

18 [a]The people of thy holiness have possessed *it* but a little while: [b]our adversaries have trodden down thy sanctuary.

19 We [1]are *thine:* thou never barest rule over them; they were [2]not called by thy name.

## CHAPTER 64

O H that thou wouldest [1]rend the heavens, that thou wouldest come down, that the mountains might [2]flow down at thy [a]presence,

2 As *when* the [1]melting fire burneth, the fire causeth the waters to boil, to make thy name known to thine adversaries, *that* the nations may tremble at thy presence!

3 When [a]thou didst [1]terrible things *which* we looked not for, thou camest down, the mountains [2]flowed down at thy presence.

4 For since the beginning of the world [a]*men* have not heard, nor perceived by the ear, neither hath the eye seen, [1]O God, beside thee, [2]*what* he hath prepared for him that waiteth for him.

5 Thou meetest him that rejoiceth and worketh righteousness, *those that* remember thee in thy ways: behold, thou art [1]wroth; for we have sinned: [a]in [2]those is continuance, and we [3]shall be saved.

6 But we are all as an unclean *thing,* and all [a]our righteousnesses *are* as [1]filthy rags; and we all do [b]fade as a leaf; and our iniquities, like the wind, have taken us away.

7 And *there is* none that calleth upon thy name, that stirreth up himself to take hold of thee: for thou hast hid thy face from us, and hast [1]consumed us, because of our iniquities.

8 But now, O LORD, thou *art* our father; we *are* the clay, and thou our [a]potter; and we all *are* the work of thy hand.

9 Be not [1]wroth very sore, O LORD, neither remember iniquity for ever: behold, see, we beseech thee, we *are* all thy people.

10 Thy holy cities are a wilderness,

63:15 [a] Deut. 26:15
[b] Ps. 33:14  [c] Jer. 31:20  [1] *your holy and glorious habitation*  [2] *yearning of your heart*
63:16 [a] Deut. 32:6
[b] Job 14:21
63:17 [a] John 12:40
[1] *stray*
63:18 [a] Deut. 7:6
[b] Ps. 74:3–7
63:19 [1] *have become like those of old*  [2] *never*
64:1 [a] Mic. 1:3,
4  [1] *tear open*  [2] *shake*
64:2 [1] *fire burns brushwood*
64:3 [a] Ex. 34:10
[1] *awesome*  [2] *shook*
64:4 [a] Ps. 31:19
[1] *any God besides*  [2] *who acts for him*
64:5 [a] Mal. 3:6
[1] *angry*  [2] *these ways*  [3] *need to be*
64:6 [a] [Phil. 3:9]
[b] Ps. 90:5, 6  [1] Lit. *a filthy garment*
64:7 [1] Lit. *caused us to melt*
64:8 [a] Is. 29:16; 45:9
64:9 [1] *furious*
64:11 [a] Ezek. 24:21
[1] *temple*  [2] *have become a ruin*
64:12 [a] Is. 42:14
[b] Ps. 83:1  [1] *keep silent*  [2] *severely*
65:1 [a] Rom. 9:24;
10:20  [b] Is. 63:19
65:2 [a] Rom. 10:21
[b] Is. 1:2, 23  [c] Is. 42:24
65:3 [a] Deut. 32:21
[b] Is. 1:29
65:4 [a] Deut. 18:11
[b] Is. 66:17  [1] *sit*  [2] *tombs*  [3] Unclean meats
65:5 [a] Matt. 9:11
[1] *Cause my wrath to smoke*
65:6 [a] Deut. 32:34
[b] Ps. 50:3  [c] Ps. 79:12
65:7 [a] Ex. 20:5
[b] Ezek. 18:6
[c] Ezek. 20:27, 28
65:8 [a] Joel 2:14
[b] Is. 1:9
65:9 [a] Matt. 24:22
65:10 [a] Is. 33:9
[b] Josh. 7:24  [c] Is. 55:6
65:11 [a] Is. 56:7
[b] Ezek. 23:41
[1] Heb. *Gad,* lit. *Troop* or *Fortune,* a pagan deity
[2] Heb. *Meni,*

Zion is a wilderness, Jerusalem a desolation.

11 Our holy and our beautiful [1]house, where our fathers praised thee, is burned up with fire: and all [a]our pleasant things [2]are laid waste.

12 [a]Wilt thou refrain thyself for these *things,* O LORD? [b]wilt thou [1]hold thy peace, and afflict us very [2]sore?

## CHAPTER 65

I [a]AM sought of *them that* asked not *for me;* I am found of *them that* sought me not: I said, Behold me, behold me, unto a nation *that* [b]was not called by my name.

2 [a]I have spread out my hands all the day unto a [b]rebellious people, which [c]walketh in a way *that was* not good, after their own thoughts;

3 A people [a]that provoketh me to anger continually to my face; [b]that sacrificeth in gardens, and burneth incense upon altars of brick;

4 [a]Which [1]remain among the graves, and lodge in the [2]monuments, [b]which eat swine's flesh, and broth of [3]abominable *things is in* their vessels;

5 [a]Which say, Stand by thyself, come not near to me; for I am holier than thou. These [1]*are* a smoke in my nose, a fire that burneth all the day.

6 Behold, [a]*it is* written before me: [b]I will not keep silence, [c]but will recompense, even recompense into their bosom,

7 Your iniquities, and [a]the iniquities of your fathers together, saith the LORD, [b]which have burned incense upon the mountains, [c]and blasphemed me upon the hills: therefore will I measure their former work into their bosom.

8 Thus saith the LORD, As the new wine is found in the cluster, and *one* saith, Destroy it not; for [a]a blessing *is* in it: so will I do for my servants' sakes, that I may not destroy them [b]all.

9 And I will bring forth a seed out of Jacob, and out of Judah an inheritor of my mountains: and mine [a]elect shall inherit it, and my servants shall dwell there.

10 And [a]Sharon shall be a fold of flocks, and [b]the valley of Achor a place for the herds to lie down in, for my people that have [c]sought me.

11 But ye *are* they that forsake the LORD, that forget [a]my holy mountain, that prepare [b]a table for [1]that troop, and that furnish the drink offering unto [2]that number.

12 Therefore will I number you [1]to the sword, and ye shall all bow down to the slaughter: [a]because when I called, ye did not answer; when I

lit. *Number* or *Destiny,* a pagan deity   65:12 [a] Prov. 1:24  [1] *for*

spake, ye did not hear; but did evil before mine eyes, and did choose *that* wherein I delighted not.

13 Therefore thus saith the Lord God, Behold, my servants shall eat, but ye shall be hungry: behold, my servants shall drink, but ye shall be thirsty: behold, my servants shall rejoice, but ye shall be ashamed:

14 Behold, my servants shall sing for joy of heart, but ye shall cry for sorrow of heart, and ªshall ¹howl for ²vexation of spirit.

15 And ye shall leave your name ªfor a curse unto ᵇmy chosen: for the Lord God shall slay thee, and ᶜcall his servants by another name:

16 ªThat he who blesseth himself in the earth shall bless himself in the God of truth; and ᵇhe that sweareth in the earth shall swear by the God of truth; because the former troubles are forgotten, and because they are hid from mine eyes.

17 For, behold, I create ªnew heavens and a new earth: and the former shall not be remembered, nor ¹come into mind.

18 But be ye glad and rejoice for ever *in that* which I create: for, behold, I create Jerusalem a rejoicing, and her people a joy.

19 And ªI will rejoice in Jerusalem, and joy in my people: and the ᵇvoice of weeping shall be no more heard in her, nor the voice of crying.

20 There shall be no more thence an infant ¹of days, nor an old man that hath not filled his days: for the child shall die an hundred years old; ªbut the sinner *being* an hundred years old shall be accursed.

21 ªAnd they shall build houses, and inhabit *them;* and they shall plant vineyards, and eat the fruit of them.

22 They shall not build, and another inhabit; they shall not plant, and ªanother eat: for ᵇas the days of a tree *are* the days of my people, and ᶜmine elect shall long enjoy the work of their hands.

23 They shall not labour ¹in vain, ªnor ²bring forth for trouble; for ᵇthey *are* the seed of the blessed of the Lord, and their offspring with them.

24 And it shall come to pass, that ªbefore they call, I will answer; and while they are yet speaking, I will ᵇhear.

25 The ªwolf and the lamb shall feed together, and the lion shall eat straw like the ¹bullock: ᵇand dust *shall be* the serpent's ²meat. They shall not hurt nor destroy in all my holy mountain, saith the Lord.

## CHAPTER 66

THUS saith the Lord, ªThe heaven *is* my throne, and the earth *is* my

65:14 ª Matt. 8:12
¹ wail ² grief of spirit
65:15 ª Jer. 29:22
ᵇ Is. 65:9, 22
ᶜ [Acts 11:26]
65:16 ª Jer. 4:2
ᵇ Zeph. 1:5
65:17 ª Rev. 21:1
¹ Lit. come upon the heart
65:19 ª Is. 62:4, 5
ᵇ Rev. 7:17; 21:4
65:20 ª Eccl. 8:12, 13 ¹ Live but a few days
65:21 ª Amos 9:14
65:22 ª Is. 62:8, 9 ᵇ Ps. 92:12 ᶜ Is. 65:9, 15
65:23 ª Hos. 9:12 ᵇ Is. 61:9 ¹ futilely ² bring forth children for
65:24 ª Is. 58:9 ᵇ Dan. 9:20–23
65:25 ª Is. 11:6–9 ᵇ Gen. 3:14 ¹ ox ² food
66:1 ª 1 Kin. 8:27

66:2 ª [Is. 57:15; 61:1] ᵇ Ps. 34:18; 51:17 ¹ exist
66:3 ª [Is. 1:10–17; 58:1–7] ᵇ Deut. 23:18 ¹ a bull ² broke ³ a grain offering
66:4 ª Is. 65:12
66:5 ª Is. 60:15 ᵇ Is. 5:19 ᶜ [Titus 2:13] ¹ that we may see your joy
66:6 ¹ sound ² fully repays
66:7 ¹ gave birth
66:8 ¹ give birth
66:9 ¹ time of birth ² delivery
66:11 ¹ feed ² consolation of her bosom ³ drink deeply
66:12 ª Is. 48:18; 60:5 ᵇ Is. 60:16 ᶜ Is. 49:22; 60:4 ¹ nurse or feed
66:13 ª Is. 51:3
66:14 ª Ezek. 37:1

footstool: where *is* the house that ye build unto me? and where *is* the place of my rest?

2 For all those *things* hath mine hand made, and all those *things* ¹have been, saith the Lord: ªbut to this *man* will I look, ᵇeven to *him that is* poor and of a contrite spirit, and trembleth at my word.

3 ªHe that killeth ¹an ox *is as if* he slew a man; he that sacrificeth a lamb, *as if* he ᵇcut² off a dog's neck; he that offereth ³an oblation, *as if he offered* swine's blood; he that burneth incense, *as if* he blessed an idol. Yea, they have chosen their own ways, and their soul delighteth in their abominations.

4 I also will choose their delusions, and will bring their fears upon them; ªbecause when I called, none did answer; when I spake, they did not hear: but they did evil before mine eyes, and chose *that* in which I delighted not.

5 Hear the word of the Lord, ye that tremble at his word; Your brethren that ªhated you, that cast you out for my name's sake, said, ᵇLet the Lord be glorified: ¹but ᶜhe shall appear to your joy, and they shall be ashamed.

6 A ¹voice of noise from the city, a voice from the temple, a voice of the Lord that ²rendereth recompence to his enemies.

7 Before she travailed, she ¹brought forth; before her pain came, she was delivered of a man child.

8 Who hath heard such a thing? who hath seen such things? Shall the earth be made to ¹bring forth in one day? *or* shall a nation be born at once? for as soon as Zion travailed, she brought forth her children.

9 Shall I bring to the ¹birth, and not cause ²to bring forth? saith the Lord: shall I cause to bring forth, and shut *the womb?* saith thy God.

10 Rejoice ye with Jerusalem, and be glad with her, all ye that love her: rejoice for joy with her, all ye that mourn for her:

11 That ye may ¹suck, and be satisfied with the ²breasts of her consolations; that ye may ³milk out, and be delighted with the abundance of her glory.

12 For thus saith the Lord, Behold, ªI will extend peace to her like a river, and the glory of the Gentiles like a flowing stream: then shall ye ᵇsuck,¹ ye shall be ᶜborne upon *her* sides, and be dandled upon *her* knees.

13 As one whom his mother comforteth, so will I ªcomfort you; and ye shall be comforted in Jerusalem.

14 And when ye see *this,* your heart shall rejoice, and ªyour bones shall

flourish like ¹an herb: and the hand of the LORD shall be known ²toward his servants, and *his* indignation ²toward his enemies.

15 ªFor, behold, the LORD will come with fire, and with his chariots like a whirlwind, to render his anger with fury, and his rebuke with flames of fire.

16 For by fire and by ªhis sword will the LORD ¹plead with all flesh: and the slain of the LORD shall be ᵇmany.

17 ªThey that sanctify themselves, and purify themselves ¹in the gardens behind one *tree* in the midst, eating swine's flesh, and the abomination, and the mouse, shall ²be consumed together, saith the LORD.

18 For I *know* their works and their ªthoughts: it shall come, that I will ᵇgather all nations and tongues; and they shall come, and see my glory.

19 ªAnd I will set a sign among them, and I will send those that escape of them unto the nations, *to* Tarshish, Pul, and Lud, that draw the bow, *to* Tubal, and Javan, *to* the ¹isles afar off, that have not heard my fame, neither have seen my glory; ᵇand

they shall declare my glory among the Gentiles.

20 And they shall ªbring all your brethren ᵇ*for* an offering unto the LORD out of all nations upon horses, and in chariots, and in litters, and upon mules, and upon ¹swift beasts, to my holy mountain Jerusalem, saith the LORD, as the children of Israel bring an offering in a clean vessel into the house of the LORD.

21 And I will also take ¹of them for ªpriests *and* for Levites, saith the LORD.

22 For as ªthe new heavens and the new earth, which I will make, shall remain before me, saith the LORD, so shall your seed and your name remain.

23 And ªit shall come to pass, *that* from one new moon to another, and from one sabbath to another, ᵇshall all flesh come to worship before me, saith the LORD.

24 And they shall go forth, and look upon the carcases of the men that have transgressed against me: for their ªworm shall not die, neither shall their fire be quenched; and they shall be an abhorring unto all flesh.

## Cross references

66:14 ¹ *grass* ² *to*
66:15 ª Is. 9:5
66:16 ª Is. 27:1
    ᵇ Is. 34:6 ¹ *judge all*
66:17 ª Is. 65:3–8
    ¹ *to go to the gardens after an idol in the midst*
    ² *come to an end together*
66:18 ª Is. 59:7
    ᵇ Is. 45:22–25; Jer. 3:17
66:19 ª Luke 2:34 ᵇ Mal. 1:11
    ¹ *coastlands*
66:20 ª Is. 49:22
    ᵇ Is. 18:7; [Rom. 15:16] ¹ *camels*
66:21 ª Ex. 19:6; Is. 61:6; 1 Pet. 2:9; Rev. 1:6 ¹ *some of them*
66:22 ª Is. 65:17; Heb. 12:26, 27; 2 Pet. 3:13; Rev. 21:1
66:23 ª Zech. 14:16 ᵇ Zech. 14:17–21
66:24 ª Is. 14:11; Mark 9:44, 46, 48

# THE BOOK OF THE PROPHET
# JEREMIAH

The Book of Jeremiah is the prophecy of a man divinely called in his youth from the priest-city of Anathoth. A heartbroken prophet with a heartbreaking message, Jeremiah labors far more than forty years proclaiming a message of doom to the stiff-necked people of Judah. Despised and persecuted by his countrymen, Jeremiah bathes his harsh prophecies in tears of compassion. His broken heart causes him to write a broken book, which is difficult to arrange chronologically or topically. But through his sermons and signs he faithfully declares that surrender to God's will is the only way to escape calamity.

*Yirmeyahu* or *Yirmeyah* literally means "Yahweh Throws," perhaps in the sense of laying a foundation. It may effectively mean "Yahweh Establishes, Appoints, or Sends." The Greek form of the Hebrew name in the Septuagint is *Hieremias*, and the Latin form is *Jeremias*.

## CHAPTER 1

THE words of Jeremiah the son of Hilkiah, of the priests that *were* [a]in Anathoth in the land of Benjamin:

2 To whom the word of the LORD came in the days of [a]Josiah the son of Amon king of Judah, [b]in the thirteenth year of his reign.

3 It came also in the days of [a]Jehoiakim the son of Josiah king of Judah, [b]unto the end of the eleventh year of Zedekiah the son of Josiah king of Judah, [c]unto the carrying away of Jerusalem captive [d]in the fifth month.

4 Then the word of the LORD came unto me, saying,

5 Before I [a]formed thee in the [1]belly [b]I knew thee; and before thou camest forth out of the womb I [c]sanctified[2] thee, *and* I [3]ordained thee a prophet unto the nations.

6 Then said I, [a]Ah, Lord GOD! behold, I cannot speak: for I *am* a [1]child.

7 But the LORD said unto me, Say not, I *am* a child: for thou shalt go to all that I shall send thee, and [a]whatsoever I command thee thou shalt speak.

8 [a]Be not afraid of their faces: for [b]I *am* with thee to deliver thee, saith the LORD.

9 Then the LORD put forth his hand, and [a]touched my mouth. And the LORD said unto me, Behold, I have [b]put my words in thy mouth.

10 [a]See, I have this day set thee over the nations and over the kingdoms, to [b]root out, and to [1]pull down, and to destroy, and to throw down, to build, and to plant.

11 Moreover the word of the LORD came unto me, saying, Jeremiah, what seest thou? And I said, I see a [1]rod of an almond tree.

12 Then said the LORD unto me, Thou hast well seen: for I [1]will hasten my word to perform it.

13 And the word of the LORD came unto me the second time, saying, What seest thou? And I said, I see [a]a [1]seething pot; and the face thereof *is* [2]toward the north.

14 Then the LORD said unto me, Out of the [a]north [1]an evil shall break forth upon all the inhabitants of the land.

15 For, lo, I will [a]call all the families of the kingdoms of the north, saith the LORD; and they shall come, and they shall [b]set every one his throne at the entering of the gates of Jerusalem, and against all the walls thereof round about, and against all the cities of Judah.

16 And I will utter my judgments against them [1]touching all their wickedness, [a]who have forsaken me, and have burned [b]incense unto other gods, and worshipped the works of their own [c]hands.

17 Thou therefore [a]gird[1] up thy loins, and arise, and speak unto them all that I command thee: [b]be not dismayed at their faces, lest I [2]confound thee before them.

18 For, behold, I have made thee this day [a]a [1]defenced city, and an iron pillar, and brasen walls against the whole land, against the kings of Judah, against the princes thereof, against the priests thereof, and against the people of the land.

19 And they shall fight against thee; but they shall not prevail against thee; for I *am* with thee, saith the LORD, to deliver thee.

## CHAPTER 2

MOREOVER the word of the LORD came to me, saying,

2 Go and cry in the ears of Jerusalem, saying, Thus saith the LORD; I remember thee, the kindness of thy [a]youth, the love of [1]thine espousals, [b]when thou wentest after me in the wilderness, in a land *that was* not sown.

### Cross-references and notes (center column)

1:1 [a] Josh. 21:18
1:2 [a] 2 Kin. 21:24 [b] Jer. 25:3
1:3 [a] 2 Kin. 23:34 [b] Jer. 39:2 [c] Jer. 52:12 [d] 2 Kin. 25:8
1:5 [a] Is. 49:1, 5 [b] Ex. 33:12 [c] [Luke 1:15] [1] *womb* [2] *set thee apart* [3] *appointed*
1:6 [a] Ex. 4:10; 6:12, 30 [1] *youth*
1:7 [a] Num. 22:20, 38
1:8 [a] Ezek. 2:6; 3:9 [b] Ex. 3:12
1:9 [a] Is. 6:7 [b] Is. 51:16
1:10 [a] 1 Kin. 19:17 [b] [2 Cor. 10:4, 5] [1] *tear down*
1:11 [1] *branch*
1:12 [1] *am watching over*
1:13 [a] Ezek. 11:3; 24:3 [1] *boiling* [2] *away from*
1:14 [a] Jer. 6:1 [1] *a calamity*
1:15 [a] Jer. 6:22; 25:9 [b] Jer. 39:3
1:16 [a] Deut. 28:20 [b] Jer. 7:9 [c] Is. 37:19 [1] *regarding*
1:17 [a] Job 38:3 [b] Ezek. 2:6 [1] *prepare thyself* [2] *dismay*
1:18 [a] Is. 50:7 [1] *fortified*
2:2 [a] Ezek. 16:8 [b] Deut. 2:7 [1] *thy betrothals*

3 ᵃIsrael *was* holiness unto the LORD, *and* ᵇthe firstfruits of his increase: ᶜall that devour him shall offend; ¹evil shall ᵈcome upon them, saith the LORD.

4 Hear ye the word of the LORD, O house of Jacob, and all the families of the house of Israel:

5 Thus saith the LORD, ᵃWhat ¹iniquity have your fathers found in me, that they are gone far from me, ᵇand have ²walked after vanity, and are become vain?

6 Neither said they, Where *is* the LORD that ᵃbrought us up out of the land of Egypt, that led us through ᵇthe wilderness, through a land of deserts and of pits, through a land of drought, and of the shadow of death, through a land that no man passed through, and where no man dwelt?

7 And I brought you into ᵃa plentiful country, to eat the fruit thereof and the goodness thereof; but when ye entered, ye ᵇdefiled my land, and made mine heritage an abomination.

8 The priests said not, Where *is* the LORD? and they that handle the ᵃlaw knew me not: the ᵇpastors also transgressed against me, ᵇand the prophets prophesied by Baal, and walked after *things that* do not profit.

9 Wherefore ᵃI will yet ¹plead with you, saith the LORD, and with your children's children will I ¹plead.

10 For pass over the isles of ¹Chittim, and see; and send unto ²Kedar, and consider diligently, and see if there be such a ᵃthing.

11 ᵃHath a nation changed *their* gods, which *are* ᵇyet no gods? ᶜbut my people have changed their glory for *that which* doth not profit.

12 Be astonished, O ye heavens, at this, and be horribly afraid, be ye very desolate, saith the LORD.

13 For my people have committed two evils; they have forsaken me the ᵃfountain of living waters, *and* hewed them out cisterns, broken cisterns, that can hold no water.

14 *Is* Israel ᵃa servant? *is* he a homeborn *slave?* why is he ¹spoiled?

15 ᵃThe young lions roared upon him, *and* yelled, and they made his land waste: his cities are burned without inhabitant.

16 Also the children of ¹Noph and ᵃTahapanes have ²broken the crown of thy head.

17 ᵃHast thou not procured this unto thyself, in that thou hast forsaken the LORD thy God, when ᵇhe led thee by the way?

18 And now ¹what hast thou to do ᵃin the way of Egypt, to drink the waters of ᵇSihor? or ¹what hast thou to do in the way of ᶜAssyria, to drink the waters of ²the river?

19 Thine own wickedness shall ᵃcorrect thee, and thy backslidings shall reprove thee: know therefore and see that *it is* an evil *thing* and bitter, that thou hast forsaken the LORD thy God, and that ¹my fear *is* not in thee, saith the Lord GOD of hosts.

20 For of old time I have ᵃbroken thy yoke, *and* burst thy ¹bands; and ᵇthou saidst, I will not ²transgress; when ᶜupon every high hill and under every green tree ³thou wanderest, ᵈplaying the harlot.

21 Yet I had ᵃplanted thee a noble vine, wholly a right seed: how then art thou turned into ᵇthe degenerate plant of a strange vine unto me?

22 For though thou wash thee with ¹nitre, and take thee much soap, *yet* thine iniquity is ᵃmarked² before me, saith the Lord GOD.

23 ᵃHow canst thou say, I am not ¹polluted, I have not gone after ²Baalim? see thy way in the valley, know what thou hast done: *thou art* a swift dromedary ³traversing her ways;

24 A wild ¹ass used to the wilderness, *that* ²snuffeth up the wind ³at her pleasure; in her ⁴occasion who can turn her away? all they that seek her will not weary themselves; in her month they shall find her.

25 Withhold thy foot from being unshod, and thy throat from thirst: but thou saidst, ᵃThere is no hope: no; for I have loved ᵇstrangers,¹ and after them will I go.

26 As the thief is ashamed when he is ¹found, so is the house of Israel ashamed; they, their kings, their princes, and their priests, and their ᵃprophets,

27 Saying to a ¹stock, Thou *art* my father; and to a ᵃstone, Thou hast ²brought me forth: for they have turned *their* back unto me, and not *their* face: but in the time of their ᵇtrouble they will say, Arise, and save us.

28 But ᵃwhere *are* thy gods that thou hast made thee? let them arise, if they ᵇcan save thee in the time of thy ¹trouble: for ᶜ*according to* the number of thy cities are thy gods, O Judah.

29 Wherefore will ye plead with me? ye all have transgressed against me, saith the LORD.

30 In vain have I ᵃsmitten¹ your children; they ᵇreceived no correction: your own sword hath ᶜdevoured your prophets, like a destroying lion.

31 O generation, see ye the word of the LORD. Have I been a wilderness unto Israel? a land of darkness? wherefore say my people, We ¹are lords; ᵃwe will come no more unto thee?

32 Can a ¹maid forget her ornaments, *or* a bride her attire? yet my

---

**Cross references**

2:3 ᵃ [Ex. 19:5, 6] ᵇ Rev. 14:4 ᶜ Jer. 12:14 ᵈ Is. 41:11 ¹ disaster
2:5 ᵃ Is. 5:4 ᵇ 2 Kin. 17:15 ¹ injustice ² followed idols
2:6 ᵃ Is. 63:11 ᵇ Deut. 8:15; 32:10
2:7 ᵃ Num. 13:27 ᵇ Num. 35:33
2:8 ᵃ Rom. 2:20 ᵇ Jer. 23:13 ¹ rulers, lit. shepherds
2:9 ᵃ Mic. 6:2 ¹ contend
2:10 ᵃ Jer. 18:13 ¹ Heb. Kittim, Cyprus, the western cultures ² In the northern Arabian desert, the eastern cultures
2:11 ᵃ Mic. 4:5 ᵇ Is. 37:19 ᶜ Rom. 1:23
2:13 ᵃ Ps. 36:9
2:14 ᵃ [Ex. 4:22] ¹ plundered
2:15 ᵃ Is. 1:7
2:16 ᵃ Jer. 43:7–9 ¹ Memphis of ancient Egypt ² shaved, lit. grazed
2:17 ᵃ Jer. 4:18 ᵇ Deut. 32:10
2:18 ᵃ Is. 30:1–3 ᵇ Josh. 13:3 ᶜ Hos. 5:13 ¹ why take the road to ² The Euphrates
2:19 ᵃ Jer. 4:18 ¹ dread of me
2:20 ᵃ Lev. 26:13 ᵇ Judg. 10:16 ᶜ Deut. 12:2 ᵈ Ex. 34:15 ¹ bonds ² Kt. serve ³ thou layest down
2:21 ᵃ Ex. 15:17 ᵇ Is. 5:4
2:22 ᵃ Job 14:16, 17 ¹ lye ² stained
2:23 ᵃ Prov. 30:12 ¹ defiled ² Baals ³ breaking loose in
2:24 ¹ donkey ² sniffs at ³ in her desire ⁴ time of mating
2:25 ᵃ Jer. 18:12 ᵇ Jer. 3:13 ¹ aliens
2:26 ᵃ Is. 28:7 ¹ found out
2:27 ᵃ Jer. 3:9 ᵇ Is. 26:16 ¹ tree ² begotten me
2:28 ᵃ Judg. 10:14 ᵇ Is. 45:20 ᶜ Jer. 11:13 ¹ calamity
2:30 ᵃ Is. 9:13 ᵇ Jer. 5:3; 7:28 ¹ chastened
2:31 ᵃ Deut. 32:15 ¹ have dominion or roam
2:32 ¹ virgin

people [a]have forgotten me days without number.

33 Why [1]trimmest thou thy way to seek love? therefore hast thou also taught the wicked ones thy ways.

34 Also in thy skirts is found [a]the blood of the souls of the poor innocents: I have not found it by secret search, but [1]upon all these.

35 [a]Yet thou sayest, Because I am innocent, surely his anger shall turn from me. Behold, [b]I will plead with thee, [c]because thou sayest, I have not sinned.

36 [a]Why gaddest thou about so much to change thy way? [b]thou also shalt be ashamed of Egypt, [c]as thou wast ashamed of Assyria.

37 Yea, thou shalt go forth from him, and thine hands upon [a]thine head: for the LORD hath rejected thy [1]confidences, and thou shalt [b]not prosper in them.

## CHAPTER 3

THEY say, If a man [1]put away his wife, and she go from him, and become another man's, [a]shall he return unto her again? [2]shall not that [b]land be greatly polluted? but thou hast [c]played the harlot with many lovers; [d]yet return again to me, saith the LORD.

2 Lift up thine eyes unto [a]the high places, and see where thou hast not been [1]lien with. [b]In the ways hast thou sat for them, as the Arabian in the wilderness; [c]and thou hast polluted the land with thy whoredoms and with thy wickedness.

3 Therefore the [a]showers have been withholden, and there hath been no latter rain; and thou hadst a [b]whore's[1] forehead, thou refusedst to be ashamed.

4 Wilt thou not from this time cry unto me, My father, thou *art* [a]the guide of [b]my youth?

5 [a]Will he [1]reserve *his anger* for ever? will he keep *it* to the end? Behold, thou hast spoken and done evil things as thou [2]couldest.

6 The LORD said also unto me in the days of Josiah the king, Hast thou seen *that* which [a]backsliding Israel hath done? she is [b]gone up upon every high mountain and under every green tree, and there hath played the harlot.

7 [a]And I said after she had done all these *things,* Turn thou unto me. But she returned not. And her treacherous [b]sister Judah saw *it.*

8 And I saw, when [a]for all the causes whereby backsliding Israel committed adultery I had [b]put her away, and given her a [1]bill of divorce; [c]yet her treacherous sister Judah feared not, but went and played the harlot also.

9 And it came to pass through the [1]lightness of her whoredom, that she [a]defiled the land, and committed adultery with [b]stones and with stocks.

10 And yet for all this her treacherous sister Judah hath not turned unto me [a]with her whole heart, but [1]feignedly, saith the LORD.

11 And the LORD said unto me, [a]The backsliding Israel hath [1]justified herself more than treacherous Judah.

12 Go and proclaim these words toward [a]the north, and say, Return, thou backsliding Israel, saith the LORD; *and* I will not cause mine anger to fall upon you: for I *am* [b]merciful, saith the LORD, *and* I will not [1]keep *anger* for ever.

13 [a]Only acknowledge thine iniquity, that thou hast transgressed against the LORD thy God, and hast [b]scattered thy [1]ways to the [c]strangers [d]under every green tree, and ye have not obeyed my voice, saith the LORD.

14 Turn, O backsliding children, saith the LORD; [a]for I am married unto you: and I will take you [b]one of a city, and two of a family, and I will bring you to [c]Zion:

15 And I will give you [a]pastors[1] according to mine heart, which shall [b]feed you with knowledge and understanding.

16 And it shall come to pass, when ye be multiplied and [a]increased in the land, in those days, saith the LORD, they shall say no more, The ark of the covenant of the LORD: [b]neither shall it come to mind: neither shall they remember it; neither shall they visit *it;* neither shall [1]*that* be done any more.

17 At that time they shall call Jerusalem the throne of the LORD; and all the nations shall be gathered unto it, [a]to the name of the LORD, to Jerusalem: neither shall they [b]walk any more after the [1]imagination of their evil heart.

18 In those days [a]the house of Judah shall walk with the house of Israel, and they shall come together out of the land of [b]the north to [c]the land that I have given for an inheritance unto your fathers.

19 But I said, How shall I put thee among the children, and give thee [a]a pleasant land, [1]a goodly heritage of the hosts of nations? and I said, Thou shalt call me, [b]My father; and shalt not turn away from me.

20 Surely *as* a wife treacherously departeth from her [1]husband, so [a]have ye dealt treacherously with me, O house of Israel, saith the LORD.

21 A voice was heard upon [a]the [1]high places, weeping *and* supplications of the children of Israel: for

### Center reference column

2:32 [a] Ps. 106:21
2:33 [1] *dost thou beautify*
2:34 [a] Ps. 106:38
   [1] *plainly on all*
2:35 [a] Jer. 2:23, 29
   [b] Jer. 2:9 [c] [Prov. 28:13]
2:36 [a] Hos. 5:13;
   12:1 [b] Is. 30:3
   [c] 2 Chr. 28:16
2:37 [a] 2 Sam. 13:19
   [b] Jer. 37:7–10
   [1] *trusted allies*
3:1 [a] Deut. 24:1–4
   [b] Jer. 2:7 [c] Ezek. 16:26 [d] [Zech. 1:3]
   [1] *divorce* [2] *would not*
3:2 [a] Deut. 12:2
   [b] Prov. 23:28 [c] Jer. 2:7 [1] *Kt. violated*
3:3 [a] Lev. 26:19
   [b] Zeph. 3:5
   [1] *harlot's*
3:4 [a] Prov. 2:17
   [b] Jer. 2:2
3:5 [a] [Is. 57:16]
   [1] *remain angry*
   [2] *wast able*
3:6 [a] Jer. 7:24
   [b] Jer. 2:20
3:7 [a] 2 Kin. 17:13
   [b] Ezek. 16:47, 48
3:8 [a] Ezek. 23:9 [b] 2 Kin. 17:6 [c] Ezek. 23:11
   [1] *certificate*
3:9 [a] Jer. 2:7 [b] Jer. 2:27 [1] *casualness*
3:10 [a] Jer. 12:2 [1] *in pretense*
3:11 [a] Ezek. 16:51, 52 [1] *shown herself more righteous than*
3:12 [a] 2 Kin. 17:6 [b] Ps. 86:15
   [1] *remain angry*
3:13 [a] Deut. 30:1, 2 [b] Ezek. 16:15 [c] Jer. 2:25 [d] Deut. 12:2 [1] *favours to foreign deities*
3:14 [a] Hos. 2:19, 20 [b] Jer. 31:6 [c] [Rom. 11:5]
3:15 [a] Eph. 4:11 [b] Acts 20:28 [1] *rulers,* lit. *shepherds*
3:16 [a] Is. 49:19 [b] Is. 65:17 [1] *it be made anymore*
3:17 [a] Is. 60:9 [b] Deut. 29:19; Jer. 7:24 [1] *stubbornness*
3:18 [a] Is. 11:13 [b] Jer. 31:8 [c] Amos 9:15
3:19 [a] Ps. 106:24 [b] Is. 63:16 [1] *a beautiful*
3:20 [a] Is. 48:8 [1] Lit. *companion*
3:21 [a] Ps. 15:2 [1] *bare heights*

they have perverted their way, *and* they have forgotten the LORD their God.

22 Return, ye backsliding children, *and* I will <sup>a</sup>heal your backslidings. Behold, we come unto thee; for thou *art* the LORD our God.

23 <sup>a</sup>Truly in vain *is salvation hoped for* from the hills, *and from* the multitude of mountains: <sup>b</sup>truly in the LORD our God *is* the salvation of Israel.

24 <sup>a</sup>For shame hath devoured the labour of our fathers from our youth; their flocks and their herds, their sons and their daughters.

25 We lie down in our shame, and our ¹confusion covereth us: <sup>a</sup>for we have sinned against the LORD our God, we and our fathers, from our youth even unto this day, and <sup>b</sup>have not obeyed the voice of the LORD our God.

## CHAPTER 4

IF thou wilt return, O Israel, saith the LORD, <sup>a</sup>return unto me: and if thou wilt put away thine abominations out of my sight, then shalt thou not ¹remove.

2 <sup>a</sup>And thou shalt swear, The LORD liveth, <sup>b</sup>in truth, in ¹judgment, and in righteousness; <sup>c</sup>and the nations shall bless themselves in him, and in him shall they <sup>d</sup>glory.

3 For thus saith the LORD to the men of Judah and Jerusalem, <sup>a</sup>Break up your ¹fallow ground, and <sup>b</sup>sow not among thorns.

4 <sup>a</sup>Circumcise yourselves to the LORD, and take away the foreskins of your heart, ye men of Judah and inhabitants of Jerusalem: lest my fury come forth like fire, and burn that none can quench *it,* because of the evil of your doings.

5 Declare ye in Judah, and ¹publish in Jerusalem; and say, <sup>a</sup>Blow ye the trumpet in the land: cry, gather together, and say, <sup>b</sup>Assemble yourselves, and let us go into the ²defenced cities.

6 Set up the ¹standard toward Zion: ²retire, ³stay not: for I will bring ⁴evil from the <sup>a</sup>north, and a great destruction.

7 <sup>a</sup>The lion is come up from his thicket, and <sup>b</sup>the destroyer of the Gentiles is on his way; he is gone forth from his place <sup>c</sup>to make thy land desolate; *and* thy cities shall be laid waste, without an inhabitant.

8 For this <sup>a</sup>gird you with sackcloth, lament and howl: for the fierce anger of the LORD is not turned back from us.

9 And it shall come to pass at that day, saith the LORD, *that* the heart of the king shall perish, and the heart

of the princes; and the priests shall be astonished, and the prophets shall wonder.

10 Then said I, Ah, Lord GOD! <sup>a</sup>surely thou hast greatly deceived this people and Jerusalem, <sup>b</sup>saying, Ye shall have peace; whereas the sword reacheth unto the soul.

11 At that time shall it be said to this people and to Jerusalem, <sup>a</sup>A dry wind of the ¹high places in the wilderness toward the daughter of my people, not to fan, nor to cleanse,

12 *Even* ¹a full wind from those *places* shall come unto me: now also <sup>a</sup>will I ²give sentence against them.

13 Behold, he shall come up as clouds, and <sup>a</sup>his chariots *shall be* as a whirlwind: <sup>b</sup>his horses are swifter than eagles. Woe unto us! for we are ¹spoiled.

14 O Jerusalem, <sup>a</sup>wash thine heart from wickedness, that thou mayest be saved. How long shall thy ¹vain thoughts lodge within thee?

15 For a voice declareth <sup>a</sup>from Dan, and ¹publisheth affliction from mount Ephraim.

16 Make ye mention to the nations; behold, ¹publish against Jerusalem, *that* watchers come from a <sup>a</sup>far country, and give out their voice against the cities of Judah.

17 <sup>a</sup>As keepers of a field, are they against her round about; because she hath been rebellious against me, saith the LORD.

18 <sup>a</sup>Thy way and thy doings have procured these *things* unto thee; this *is* thy wickedness, because it is bitter, because it reacheth unto ¹thine heart.

19 My <sup>a</sup>bowels, my ¹bowels! I am pained at my very heart; my heart maketh a noise in me; I cannot hold my peace, because thou hast heard, O my soul, the sound of the trumpet, the alarm of war.

20 <sup>a</sup>Destruction upon destruction is cried; for the whole land is ¹spoiled: suddenly are <sup>b</sup>my tents ¹spoiled, *and* my curtains in a moment.

21 How long shall I see the ¹standard, *and* hear the sound of the trumpet?

22 For my people *is* foolish, they have not known me; they *are* ¹sottish children, and they have ²none understanding: <sup>a</sup>they *are* wise to do evil, but to do good they have no knowledge.

23 <sup>a</sup>I beheld the earth, and, lo, *it was* <sup>b</sup>without form, and void; and the heavens, and they *had* no light.

24 <sup>a</sup>I beheld the mountains, and, lo, they trembled, and all the hills moved ¹lightly.

25 I beheld, and, lo, *there was* no man, and <sup>a</sup>all the birds of the heavens were fled.

### Center reference column

3:22 <sup>a</sup> Hos. 6:1; 14:4
3:23 <sup>a</sup> Ps. 121:1, 2 <sup>b</sup> Ps. 3:8
3:24 <sup>a</sup> Hos. 9:10
3:25 <sup>a</sup> Ezra 9:6, 7 <sup>b</sup> Jer. 22:21 ¹ *disgrace*
4:1 <sup>a</sup> Joel 2:12 ¹ *be shaken or moved*
4:2 <sup>a</sup> Deut. 10:20 <sup>b</sup> Zech. 8:8 <sup>c</sup> [Gen. 22:18] <sup>d</sup> 1 Cor. 1:31 ¹ *justice*
4:3 <sup>a</sup> Hos. 10:12 <sup>b</sup> Matt. 13:7 ¹ *untilled*
4:4 <sup>a</sup> Deut. 10:16; 30:6
4:5 <sup>a</sup> Hos. 8:1 <sup>b</sup> Jer. 8:14 ¹ *proclaim* ² *fortified*
4:6 <sup>a</sup> Jer. 1:13–15; 6:1, 22; 50:17 ¹ *banner* ² *take refuge* ³ *delay* ⁴ *disaster*
4:7 <sup>a</sup> Dan. 7:4 <sup>b</sup> Jer. 25:9 <sup>c</sup> Is. 1:7; 6:11
4:8 <sup>a</sup> Is. 22:12

4:10 <sup>a</sup> Ezek. 14:9 <sup>b</sup> Jer. 5:12; 14:13
4:11 <sup>a</sup> Hos. 13:15 ¹ *bare heights*
4:12 <sup>a</sup> Jer. 1:16 ¹ *a wind too strong for these* ² *speak judgment*
4:13 <sup>a</sup> Is. 5:28 <sup>b</sup> Deut. 28:49 ¹ *plundered*
4:14 <sup>a</sup> James 4:8 ¹ *wicked*
4:15 <sup>a</sup> Jer. 8:16; 50:17 ¹ *proclaims wickedness*
4:16 <sup>a</sup> Is. 39:3 ¹ *proclaim*
4:17 <sup>a</sup> 2 Kin. 25:1, 4
4:18 <sup>a</sup> Is. 50:1
4:19 <sup>a</sup> Is. 15:5; 16:11; 21:3; 22:4 ¹ *inner parts, soul*
4:20 <sup>a</sup> Ezek. 7:26 <sup>b</sup> Jer. 10:20 ¹ *plundered*
4:21 ¹ *banner*
4:22 <sup>a</sup> Rom. 16:19 ¹ *stupid or silly* ² *no*
4:23 <sup>a</sup> Is. 24:19 <sup>b</sup> Gen. 1:2
4:24 <sup>a</sup> Ezek. 38:20 ¹ *back and forth*
4:25 <sup>a</sup> Zeph. 1:3

26 I beheld, and, lo, the fruitful place *was* a ªwilderness, and all the cities thereof were broken down at the presence of the LORD, *and* by his fierce anger.

27 For thus hath the LORD said, The whole land shall be desolate; ªyet will I not make a full end.

28 For this ªshall the earth mourn, and ᵇthe heavens above be black: because I have spoken *it,* I have ᶜpurposed *it,* and ᵈwill not ¹repent, neither will I turn back from it.

29 The whole city shall flee for the noise of the horsemen and bowmen; they shall go into thickets, and climb up upon the rocks: every city *shall be* forsaken, and not a man dwell therein.

30 And *when* thou *art* ¹spoiled, what wilt thou do? Though thou clothest thyself with crimson, though thou ²deckest thee with ornaments of gold, ªthough thou ³rentest thy face with painting, in vain shalt thou make thyself fair; ᵇ*thy* lovers will despise thee, they will seek thy life.

31 For I have heard a voice as of a woman in ¹travail, *and* the anguish as of her that bringeth forth her first child, the voice of the daughter of Zion, *that* bewaileth herself, *that* ªspreadeth her hands, *saying,* Woe *is* me now! for my soul is ²wearied because of murderers.

## CHAPTER 5

RUN ye to and fro through the streets of Jerusalem, and see now, and know, and seek in the ¹broad places thereof, ªif ye can find a man, ᵇif there be *any* that executeth ²judgment, that seeketh the truth; ᶜand I will pardon it.

2 And ªthough they say, ᵇThe LORD liveth; surely they ᶜswear falsely.

3 O LORD, *are* not ªthine eyes upon the truth? thou hast ᵇstricken them, but they have not grieved; thou hast consumed them, *but* ᶜthey have refused to receive correction: they have made their faces harder than a rock; they have refused to return.

4 Therefore I said, Surely these *are* poor; they are foolish: for ªthey know not the way of the LORD, *nor* the judgment of their God.

5 I will get me unto the great men, and will speak unto them; for ªthey have known the way of the LORD, *and* the judgment of their God: but these have altogether ᵇbroken the yoke, *and* burst the bonds.

6 Wherefore ªa lion out of the forest shall slay them, ᵇ*and* a wolf of the ¹evenings shall ²spoil them, ᶜa leopard shall watch over their cities: every one that goeth out thence shall be torn in pieces: because their

transgressions are many, *and* their backslidings are increased.

7 How shall I pardon thee for this? thy children have forsaken me, and ªsworn by ᵇ*them that are* no gods: ᶜwhen I had fed them to the full, they then committed adultery, and assembled themselves by troops in the harlots' houses.

8 ªThey were *as* ¹fed horses in the morning: every one neighed after his neighbour's wife.

9 Shall I not ¹visit for these *things?* saith the LORD: and shall not my soul be ªavenged on such a nation as this?

10 Go ye up upon her walls, and destroy; but ¹make not a ªfull end: take away her ²battlements; for they *are* not the LORD's.

11 For ªthe house of Israel and the house of Judah have dealt very treacherously against me, saith the LORD.

12 ªThey have ¹belied the LORD, and said, ᵇ*It is* not he; neither shall evil come upon us; ᶜneither shall we see sword nor famine:

13 And the prophets shall become wind, and the word *is* not in them: thus shall it be done unto them.

14 Wherefore thus saith the LORD God of hosts, Because ye speak this word, ªbehold, I will make my words in thy mouth fire, and this people wood, and it shall devour them.

15 Lo, I will bring a ªnation upon you ᵇfrom far, O house of Israel, saith the LORD: it *is* a mighty nation, it *is* an ancient nation, a nation whose language thou knowest not, neither understandest what they say.

16 Their quiver *is* as an open sepulchre, they *are* all mighty men.

17 And they shall eat up thine ªharvest, and thy bread, *which* thy sons and thy daughters should eat: they shall eat up thy flocks and thine herds: they shall eat up thy vines and thy fig trees: they shall ¹impoverish thy ²fenced cities, wherein thou trustedst, with the sword.

18 Nevertheless in those days, saith the LORD, I ªwill not ¹make a full end with you.

19 And it shall come to pass, when ye shall say, ªWherefore doeth the LORD our God all these *things* unto us? then shalt thou answer them, Like as ye have ᵇforsaken me, and served strange gods in your land, so ᶜshall ye serve strangers in a land *that is* not yours.

20 Declare this in the house of Jacob, and ¹publish it in Judah, saying,

21 Hear now this, O ªfoolish people, and without ¹understanding; which have eyes, and see not; which have ears, and hear not:

22 ªFear ye not me? saith the LORD: will ye not tremble at my presence,

---

**Cross-references (center column):**

4:26 ª Jer. 9:10
4:27 ª Jer. 5:10, 18; 30:11; 46:28
4:28 ª Hos. 4:3
ᵇ Is. 5:30; 50:3
ᶜ [Dan. 4:35]
ᵈ [Num. 23:19]
¹ *relent*

4:30 ª 2 Kin. 9:30 ᵇ Jer. 22:20, 22 ¹ *plundered* ² *adorn* ³ *enlarge your eyes with paint*

4:31 ª Lam. 1:17 ¹ *childbirth* ² *faint*

5:1 ª Ezek. 22:30 ᵇ Gen. 18:23–32 ᶜ Gen. 18:26 ¹ *open* ² *justice*

5:2 ª Titus 1:16 ᵇ Jer. 4:2 ᶜ Jer. 7:9

5:3 ª [2 Chr. 16:9] ᵇ Is. 1:5; 9:13 ᶜ Zeph. 3:2

5:4 ª Jer. 8:7

5:5 ª Mic. 3:1 ᵇ Ps. 2:3

5:6 ª Jer. 4:7 ᵇ Zeph. 3:3 ᶜ Hos. 13:7 ¹ *deserts* ² *destroy*

5:7 ª Zeph. 1:5 ᵇ Deut. 32:21 ᶜ Deut. 32:15

5:8 ª Ezek. 22:11 ¹ *well-fed lusty stallions*

5:9 ª Jer. 9:9 ¹ *punish them*

5:10 ª Jer. 4:27 ¹ *do not completely destroy* ² *branches*

5:11 ª Jer. 3:6, 7, 20

5:12 ª 2 Chr. 36:16 ᵇ Jer. 23:17 ᶜ Jer. 14:13 ¹ *lied about*

5:14 ª Jer. 1:9; 23:29

5:15 ª Deut. 28:49 ᵇ Jer. 4:16

5:17 ª Lev. 26:16 ¹ *destroy* ² *fortified*

5:18 ª Jer. 30:11 ¹ *completely destroy*

5:19 ª Deut. 29:24–29 ᵇ Jer. 1:16; 2:13 ᶜ Deut. 28:48

5:20 ¹ *proclaim*

5:21 ª Matt. 13:14 ¹ Lit. *heart*

5:22 ª [Rev. 15:4]

which have placed the sand *for* the
[b]bound of the sea by a perpetual decree, that it cannot pass it: and though
the waves thereof toss [1]themselves,
yet can they not prevail; though they
roar, yet can they not pass over it?

23 But this people hath a revolting
and a rebellious heart; they are revolted and [1]gone.

24 Neither say they in their heart,
Let us now fear the LORD our God,
[a]that giveth rain, both the [b]former
and the latter, in his season: [c]he reserveth unto us the appointed weeks
of the harvest.

25 [a]Your iniquities have turned
away these *things,* and your sins have
withholden good *things* from you.

26 For among my people are found
wicked *men:* they [a]lay[1] wait, as he
that setteth snares; they set a trap,
they catch men.

27 As a cage is full of birds, so *are*
their houses full of deceit: therefore
they are become great, and [1]waxen
rich.

28 They [1]are waxen [a]fat, they [2]shine:
yea, they [3]overpass the deeds of the
wicked: they [4]judge not [b]the cause,
the cause of the fatherless, [c]yet they
prosper; and the right of the needy
do they not [5]judge.

29 [a]Shall I not [1]visit for these *things?*
saith the LORD: shall not my soul be
avenged on such a nation as this?

30 [1]A wonderful and [a]horrible thing
is committed in the land;

31 The prophets prophesy [1]falsely,
and the priests [1]bear rule by their
[2]means; and my people [b]love *to have*
*it* so: and what will ye do in the end
thereof?

## CHAPTER 6

O YE children of Benjamin, gather
yourselves to flee out of the
midst of Jerusalem, and blow the
trumpet in Tekoa, and set up a [1]sign
of fire in [a]Beth-haccerem: [b]for [2]evil
appeareth out of the north, and great
destruction.

2 I have likened the daughter of
Zion to a [1]comely and delicate *woman.*

3 The [a]shepherds with their flocks
shall come unto her; they shall pitch
*their* tents against her round about;
they shall [1]feed every one in his place.

4 [a]Prepare ye war against her;
arise, and let us go up [b]at noon. Woe
unto us! for the day goeth away,
for the shadows of the evening are
[1]stretched out.

5 Arise, and let us go by night, and
let us destroy her palaces.

6 For thus hath the LORD of hosts
said, Hew ye down trees, and [1]cast a
mount against Jerusalem: this *is* the
city to be [2]visited; she *is* [3]wholly oppression in the midst of her.

7 [a]As a fountain [1]casteth out her
waters, so she [1]casteth out her wickedness: [b]violence and [2]spoil is heard
in her; before me continually *is* [3]grief
and wounds.

8 Be thou instructed, O Jerusalem,
lest [a]my soul depart from thee; lest I
make thee desolate, a land not inhabited.

9 Thus saith the LORD of hosts,
They shall throughly glean the remnant of Israel as a vine: turn back
thine hand as a grapegatherer into
the [1]baskets.

10 To whom shall I speak, and give
warning, that they may hear? behold,
their [a]ear *is* uncircumcised, and they
cannot hearken: behold, [b]the word
of the LORD is unto them a reproach;
they have no delight in it.

11 Therefore I am full of the fury of
the LORD; [a]I am weary with holding
in: I will pour it out [b]upon the children [1]abroad, and upon the assembly
of young men together: for even the
husband with the wife shall be taken,
the aged with *him that is* full of days.

12 And [a]their houses shall be
turned [1]unto others, *with their* fields
and wives together: for I will stretch
out my hand upon the inhabitants of
the land, saith the LORD.

13 For from the least of them even
unto the greatest of them every one
*is* given to [a]covetousness; and from
the prophet even unto the [b]priest every one dealeth falsely.

14 They have [a]healed also the
[1]hurt *of the daughter* of my people
[2]slightly, [b]saying, Peace, peace; when
*there is* no peace.

15 Were they [a]ashamed when they
had committed abomination? nay,
they were not at all ashamed, neither [1]could they blush: therefore they
shall fall among them that fall: at the
time *that* I [a]visit them they shall be
cast down, saith the LORD.

16 Thus saith the LORD, Stand ye
in the ways, and see, and ask for the
[a]old paths, where *is* the good way,
and walk therein, and ye shall find
[b]rest for your souls. But they said, We
will not walk *therein.*

17 Also I set [a]watchmen over you,
*saying,* [b]Hearken to the sound of the
trumpet. But they said, We will not
hearken.

18 Therefore hear, ye nations, and
know, O congregation, what *is* among
them.

19 [a]Hear, O earth: behold, I will
bring [b]evil[1] upon this people, *even*
[c]the fruit of their thoughts, because
they have not hearkened unto my
words, nor to my law, but rejected it.

20 [a]To what purpose cometh there
to me [1]incense [b]from Sheba, and the
[c]sweet cane from a far country? [d]your

### Center reference column

5:22 [b] Job 26:10
[1] *to and fro*
5:23 [1] *departed*
5:24 [a] Acts
14:17 [b] Joel 2:23
[c] [Gen. 8:22]
5:25 [a] Jer. 3:3
5:26 [a] Hab. 1:15
[1] *lie in wait*
5:27 [1] *grown*
5:28 [a] Deut.
32:15 [b] Zech. 7:10
[c] Job 12:6 [1] *have*
*grown* [2] *are sleek*
[3] *surpass* [4] *plead*
[5] *defend*
5:29 [a] Mal. 3:5
[1] *punish*
5:30 [a] Hos. 6:10
[1] *An astonishing*
5:31 [a] Ezek. 13:6
[b] Mic. 2:11 [1] *rule*
[2] *own power*
6:1 [a] Neh. 3:14
[b] Jer. 4:6 [1] *signal-*
*fire* [2] *disaster*
6:2 [1] *lovely*
6:3 [a] 2 Kin. 25:1–4
[1] *pasture*
6:4 [a] Joel
3:9 [b] Jer. 15:8
[1] *lengthening*
6:6 [1] *build a*
*mound* [2] *pun-*
*ished* [3] *full of*

6:7 [a] Is. 57:20
[b] Ps. 55:9 [1] *wells*
*up with* [2] *plun-*
*dering* [3] *sickness*
6:8 [a] Hos. 9:12
6:9 [1] *branches*
6:10 [a] [Acts 7:51]
[b] Jer. 8:9; 20:8
6:11 [a] Jer. 20:9
[b] Jer. 9:21 [1] *in the*
*street*
6:12 [a] Deut. 28:30
[1] *over to*
6:13 [a] Is. 56:11; Jer.
8:10; 22:17 [b] Jer.
5:31; 23:11
6:14 [a] Jer. 8:11–15
[b] Jer. 4:10; 23:17
[1] Lit. *crushing*
[2] Superficially
6:15 [a] Jer. 3:3; 8:12
[1] *did they know*
*how to* [2] *punish*
6:16 [a] Jer. 18:15
[b] Matt. 11:29
6:17 [a] Hab. 2:1
[b] Deut. 4:1
6:19 [a] Is. 1:2 [b] Jer.
19:3, 15 [c] Prov.
1:31 [1] *calamity*
6:20 [a] Mic. 6:6,
7 [b] Is. 60:6 [c] Is.
43:24 [d] Jer. 7:21–
23 [1] *frankincense*

burnt offerings *are* not acceptable, nor your sacrifices sweet unto me.

21 Therefore thus saith the LORD, Behold, I will lay stumblingblocks before this people, and the fathers and the sons together shall fall upon them; the neighbour and his friend shall perish.

22 Thus saith the LORD, Behold, a people cometh from the ªnorth country, and a great nation shall be raised from the ¹sides of the earth.

23 They shall lay hold on bow and spear; they *are* cruel, and have no mercy; their voice ªroareth like the sea; and they ride upon horses, set in array as men for war against thee, O daughter of Zion.

24 We have heard the ¹fame thereof: our hands ²wax feeble: ªanguish hath taken hold of us, *and* pain, as of a woman in ³travail.

25 Go not forth into the field, nor walk by the way; for the sword of the enemy *and* fear *is* on every side.

26 O daughter of my people, ªgird *thee* with sackcloth, ᵇand wallow thyself in ashes: ᶜmake thee mourning, *as for* an only son, most bitter lamentation: for the ¹spoiler shall suddenly come upon us.

27 I have set thee *for* ¹a tower *and* ªa fortress among my people, that thou mayest know and ²try their way.

28 ªThey *are* all ¹grievous revolters, ᵇwalking with slanders: *they are* ᶜbrass² and iron; they *are* all corrupters.

29 The bellows ¹are burned, the lead is consumed of the fire; the ²founder melteth in vain: for the wicked are not ³plucked away.

30 Reprobate¹ silver shall *men* call them, because the LORD hath rejected them.

### CHAPTER 7

T HE word that came to Jeremiah from the LORD, saying,

2 ªStand in the gate of ¹the LORD's house, and proclaim there this word, and say, Hear the word of the LORD, all *ye of* Judah, that enter in at these gates to worship the LORD.

3 Thus saith the LORD of hosts, the God of Israel, ªAmend your ways and your doings, and I will cause you to dwell in this place.

4 ªTrust ye not in lying words, saying, The temple of the LORD, The temple of the LORD, The temple of the LORD, *are* these.

5 For if ye throughly amend your ways and your doings; if ye throughly ªexecute ¹judgment between a man and his neighbour;

6 *If* ye oppress not the stranger, the fatherless, and the widow, and shed not innocent blood in this place,

6:22 ª Jer. 1:15;
10:22; 50:41–43
¹ *farthest parts*

6:23 ª Is. 5:30

6:24 ª Jer. 4:31;
13:21; 49:24 ¹ *report of it* ² *grow*
³ *childbirth*

6:26 ª Jer.
4:8 ᵇ Mic. 1:10
ᶜ [Zech. 12:10]
¹ *plunderer*

6:27 ª Jer. 1:18
¹ *an assayer* ² *test*

6:28 ª Jer. 5:23
ᵇ Jer. 9:4 ᶜ Ezek.
22:18 ¹ *stubborn rebels* ² *bronze*

6:29 ¹ *blow fiercely* ² *smelter refines* ³ *drawn off*

6:30 ª Is. 1:22
¹ *Rejected*

7:2 ª Jer. 17:19;
26:2 ¹ The temple

7:3 ª Jer. 4:1; 18:11;
26:13

7:4 ª Mic. 3:11

7:5 ª Jer. 21:12;
22:3 ¹ *justice*

7:6 ª Deut. 6:14, 15

7:7 ª Deut. 4:40
ᵇ Jer. 3:18

7:8 ª Jer. 5:31;
14:13, 14

7:9 ª 1 Kin. 18:21
ᵇ Ex. 20:3

7:10 ª Ezek. 23:39
ᵇ Jer. 7:11, 14;
32:34; 34:15

7:11 ª Is. 56:7
ᵇ Matt. 21:13

7:12 ª Josh. 18:1
ᵇ Deut. 12:11
ᶜ 1 Sam. 4:10

7:13 ª 2 Chr. 36:15
ᵇ Prov. 1:24

7:14 ª 1 Sam.
4:10, 11

7:15 ª 2 Kin. 17:23
ᵇ Ps. 78:67

7:16 ª Ex. 32:10;
Jer. 11:14 ᵇ Jer.
15:1

7:18 ª Jer. 44:17
ᵇ Jer. 19:13

7:19 ª Deut.
32:16, 21

7:21 ª Jer. 6:20
¹ *Add*

7:22 ª [Hos. 6:6]

ªneither walk after other gods to your hurt:

7 ªThen will I cause you to dwell in this place, in ᵇthe land that I gave to your fathers, for ever and ever.

8 Behold, ye trust in ªlying words, that cannot profit.

9 ªWill ye steal, murder, and commit adultery, and swear falsely, and burn incense unto Baal, and ᵇwalk after other gods whom ye know not;

10 ªAnd come and stand before me in this house, ᵇwhich is called by my name, and say, We are delivered to do all these abominations?

11 Is ªthis house, which is called by my name, become a ᵇden of robbers in your eyes? Behold, even I have seen *it,* saith the LORD.

12 But go ye now unto ªmy place which *was* in Shiloh, ᵇwhere I set my name at the first, and see ᶜwhat I did to it for the wickedness of my people Israel.

13 And now, because ye have done all these works, saith the LORD, and I spake unto you, ªrising up early and speaking, but ye heard not; and I ᵇcalled you, but ye answered not;

14 Therefore will I do unto *this* house, which is called by my name, wherein ye trust, and unto the place which I gave to you and to your fathers, as I have done to ªShiloh.

15 And I will cast you out of my sight, ªas I have cast out all your brethren, ᵇ*even* the whole seed of Ephraim.

16 Therefore ªpray not thou for this people, neither lift up cry nor prayer for them, neither make intercession to me: ᵇfor I will not hear thee.

17 Seest thou not what they do in the cities of Judah and in the streets of Jerusalem?

18 ªThe children gather wood, and the fathers kindle the fire, and the women knead *their* dough, to make cakes to the queen of heaven, and to ᵇpour out drink offerings unto other gods, that they may provoke me to anger.

19 ªDo they provoke me to anger? saith the LORD: *do they* not *provoke* themselves to the confusion of their own faces?

20 Therefore thus saith the Lord GOD; Behold, mine anger and my fury shall be poured out upon this place, upon man, and upon beast, and upon the trees of the field, and upon the fruit of the ground; and it shall burn, and shall not be quenched.

21 Thus saith the LORD of hosts, the God of Israel; ªPut¹ your burnt offerings unto your sacrifices, and eat flesh.

22 ªFor I spake not unto your fathers, nor commanded them in the

day that I brought them out of the land of Egypt, concerning burnt offerings or sacrifices:

23 But this thing commanded I them, saying, [a]Obey my voice, and [b]I will be your God, and ye shall be my people: and walk ye in all the ways that I have commanded you, that it may be well unto you.

24 [a]But they hearkened not, nor inclined their ear, but [b]walked in the counsels *and* in the [1]imagination of their evil heart, and [c]went[2] backward, and not forward.

25 Since the day that your fathers came forth out of the land of Egypt unto this day I have even [a]sent unto you all my servants the prophets, daily rising up early and sending *them:*

26 [a]Yet they hearkened not unto me, nor inclined their ear, but [b]hardened[1] their neck: [c]they did worse than their fathers.

27 Therefore [a]thou shalt speak all these words unto them; but they will not hearken to thee: thou shalt also call unto them; but they will not answer thee.

28 But thou shalt say unto them, This *is* a nation that obeyeth not the voice of the LORD their God, [a]nor receiveth [1]correction: [b]truth is perished, and is cut off from their mouth.

29 [a]Cut off thine hair, *O Jerusalem,* and cast *it* away, and take up a lamentation on [1]high places; for the LORD hath rejected and forsaken the generation of his wrath.

30 For the children of Judah have done evil in my sight, saith the LORD: [a]they have set their abominations in the house which is called by my name, to [1]pollute it.

31 And they have built the [a]high[1] places of Tophet, which *is* in the valley of the son of Hinnom, to [b]burn their sons and their daughters in the fire; [c]which I commanded *them* not, neither came it into my heart.

32 Therefore, behold, [a]the days come, saith the LORD, that it shall no more be called Tophet, nor the valley of the son of Hinnom, but the valley of slaughter: [b]for they shall bury in Tophet, till there be no place.

33 And the [a]carcases of this people shall be meat for the fowls of the heaven, and for the beasts of the earth; and none shall [1]fray *them* away.

34 Then will I cause to [a]cease from the cities of Judah, and from the streets of Jerusalem, the voice of mirth, and the voice of gladness, the voice of the bridegroom, and the voice of the bride: for [b]the land shall be desolate.

## CHAPTER 8

[A]T that time, saith the LORD, they shall bring out the bones of the kings of Judah, and the bones of his princes, and the bones of the priests, and the bones of the prophets, and the bones of the inhabitants of Jerusalem, out of their graves:

2 And they shall spread them before the sun, and the moon, and all the host of heaven, whom they have loved, and whom they have served, and after whom they have walked, and whom they have sought, and [a]whom they have worshipped: they shall not be gathered, [b]nor be buried; they shall be [1]for dung upon the face of the earth.

3 And [a]death shall be chosen rather than life by all the [1]residue of them that remain of this evil family, which remain in all the places whither I have driven them, saith the LORD of hosts.

4 Moreover thou shalt say unto them, Thus saith the LORD; Shall they fall, and not arise? shall he turn away, and not return?

5 Why *then* is this people of Jerusalem [a]slidden back by a perpetual backsliding? [b]they hold fast [1]deceit, [c]they refuse to return.

6 [a]I hearkened and heard, *but* they spake not aright: [b]no man repented him of his wickedness, saying, What have I done? every one turned to [1]his course, as the horse rusheth into the battle.

7 Yea, [a]the stork in the heaven knoweth her appointed times; and the [1]turtle and [2]the crane and the swallow observe the time of their coming; but [b]my people know not the judgment of the LORD.

8 How [1]do ye say, We *are* wise, [a]and the law of the LORD *is* with us? Lo, [2]certainly in vain made he *it;* the pen of the scribes *is* in vain.

9 [a]The wise *men* are ashamed, they are dismayed and taken: lo, they have rejected the word of the LORD; and [b]what wisdom *is* in them?

10 Therefore [a]will I give their wives unto others, *and* their fields to them that shall inherit *them:* for every one from the least even unto the greatest is given to [b]covetousness, from the prophet even unto the priest every one dealeth falsely.

11 For they have [a]healed the hurt of the daughter of my people [1]slightly, saying, [b]Peace, peace; when *there is* no peace.

12 Were they [a]ashamed when they had committed abomination? nay, they were not at all ashamed, neither [1]could they blush: therefore shall they fall among them that fall: in the time of their [2]visitation they shall be cast down, saith the LORD.

---

### Cross-references (center column)

7:23 [a] Deut. 6:3
[b] [Ex. 19:5, 6]
7:24 [a] Ps. 81:11
[b] Deut. 29:19
[c] Jer. 32:33  [1] *stubbornness*  [2] Lit. *were*
7:25 [a] 2 Chr. 36:15
7:26 [a] Jer. 11:8
[b] Neh. 9:17  [c] Jer. 16:12  [1] *stiffened*
7:27 [a] Ezek. 2:7
7:28 [a] Jer. 5:3
[b] Jer. 9:3  [1] *instruction*
7:29 [a] Mic. 1:16
[1] *the bare heights*
7:30 [a] Dan. 9:27; 11:31  [1] *defile*
7:31 [a] 2 Kin. 23:10  [b] Ps. 106:38  [c] Deut. 17:3  [1] A sacred place for pagan worship
7:32 [a] Jer. 19:6  [b] 2 Kin. 23:10
7:33 [a] Jer. 9:22; 19:11  [1] *frighten*
7:34 [a] Is. 24:7, 8  [b] Lev. 26:33

8:2 [a] 2 Kin. 23:5  [b] Jer. 22:19  [1] *like refuse*
8:3 [a] Rev. 9:6  [1] *remnant*
8:5 [a] Jer. 7:24  [b] Jer. 9:6  [c] Jer. 5:3  [1] *to deceit*
8:6 [a] Ps. 14:2  [b] Mic. 7:2  [1] *his own*
8:7 [a] Song 2:12  [b] Jer. 5:4; 9:3  [1] *turtledove*  [2] *the swift*
8:8 [a] Rom. 2:17  [1] *can*  [2] *the false pen of the scribe certainly works falsehood.*
8:9 [a] Jer. 6:15  [b] Jer. 4:22
8:10 [a] Deut. 28:30  [b] Is. 56:11; 57:17
8:11 [a] Jer. 6:14  [b] Ezek. 13:10  [1] Superficially
8:12 [a] Jer. 3:3; 6:15  [1] *did they know how to*  [2] *punishment*

13 I will surely ¹consume them, saith the LORD: *there shall be* no grapes ᵃon the vine, nor figs on the ᵇfig tree, and the leaf shall fade; and *the things that* I have given them shall ᶜpass away from them.

14 Why do we sit still? ᵃassemble yourselves, and let us enter into the ¹defenced cities, and let us be silent there: for the LORD our God hath put us to silence, and given us ᵇwater² of gall to drink, because we have sinned against the LORD.

15 We ᵃlooked for peace, but no good *came; and* for a time of health, and behold trouble!

16 The snorting of his horses was heard from ᵃDan: the whole land trembled at the sound of the neighing of his ᵇstrong ones; for they are come, and have devoured the land, and all that is in it; the city, and those that dwell therein.

17 For, behold, I will send serpents, ¹cockatrices, among you, which *will* not *be* ᵃcharmed, and they shall bite you, saith the LORD.

18 *When* I would comfort myself against sorrow, my heart *is* faint in me.

19 Behold the voice of the cry of the daughter of my people because of them that dwell in ᵃa far country: *Is* not the LORD in Zion? *is* not her king in her? Why have they provoked me to anger with their graven images, *and* with ¹strange vanities?

20 The harvest is past, the summer is ended, and we are not saved.

21 ᵃFor the hurt of the daughter of my people am I hurt; I am ᵇblack;¹ astonishment hath taken hold on me.

22 *Is there* no ᵃbalm in Gilead; *is there* no physician there? why then is not the health of the daughter of my people ¹recovered?

## CHAPTER 9

OH ᵃthat my head were waters, and mine eyes a fountain of tears, that I might weep day and night for the slain of the daughter of my people!

2 Oh that I had in the wilderness a lodging place of wayfaring men; that I might leave my people, and go from them! for ᵃthey *be* all adulterers, an assembly of treacherous men.

3 And ᵃthey bend their tongues *like* their bow *for* lies: but they are not valiant for the truth upon the earth; for they proceed from ᵇevil to evil, and they ᶜknow not me, saith the LORD.

4 ᵃTake ye heed every one of his ¹neighbour, and trust ye not in any brother: for every brother will utterly supplant, and every ¹neighbour ᵇwill walk with slanders.

5 And they will ᵃdeceive every one his neighbour, and will not speak the truth: they have taught their tongue to speak lies, *and* weary themselves to commit iniquity.

6 Thine habitation *is* in the midst of deceit; through deceit they refuse to know me, saith the LORD.

7 Therefore thus saith the LORD of hosts, Behold, ᵃI will ¹melt them, and ²try them; ᵇfor how shall I do for the daughter of my people?

8 Their tongue *is as* an arrow shot out; it speaketh ᵃdeceit: *one* speaketh ᵇpeaceably to his neighbour with his mouth, but ¹in heart he layeth his wait.

9 ᵃShall I not ¹visit them for these *things?* saith the LORD: shall not my soul be avenged on such a nation as this?

10 For the mountains will I take up a weeping and wailing, and ᵃfor the ¹habitations of the wilderness a lamentation, because they are burned up, so that none can pass through *them;* neither can *men* hear the voice of the cattle; ᵇboth the fowl of the heavens and the beast are fled; they are gone.

11 And I will make Jerusalem ᵃheaps,¹ *and* ᵇa den of ²dragons; and I will make the cities of Judah desolate, without an inhabitant.

12 ᵃWho *is* the wise man, that may understand this? and *who is he* to whom the mouth of the LORD hath spoken, that he may declare it, for what the land perisheth *and* is burned up like a wilderness, that none passeth through?

13 And the LORD saith, Because they have forsaken my law which I set before them, and have ᵃnot obeyed my voice, neither walked therein;

14 But have ᵃwalked after the ¹imagination of their own heart, and after Baalim, ᵇwhich their fathers taught them:

15 Therefore thus saith the LORD of hosts, the God of Israel; Behold, I will ᵃfeed them, *even* this people, ᵇwith wormwood, and give them ¹water of gall to drink.

16 I will ᵃscatter them also among the ¹heathen, whom neither they nor their fathers have known: ᵇand I will send a sword after them, till I have consumed them.

17 Thus saith the LORD of hosts, Consider ye, and call for ᵃthe mourning women, that they may come; and send for ¹cunning *women,* that they may come:

18 And let them make haste, and take up a wailing for us, that ᵃour eyes may run down with tears, and our eyelids gush out with waters.

19 For a voice of wailing is heard out of Zion, How are we ¹spoiled! we

### Center column references

8:13 ᵃ Joel 1:17
ᵇ Matt. 21:19
ᶜ Deut. 28:39, 40
¹ Or *take them away*
8:14 ᵃ Jer.
4:5 ᵇ Jer. 9:15
¹ *fortified* ² *Bitter or poisonous water*
8:15 ᵃ Jer. 14:19
8:16 ᵃ Jer. 4:15
ᵇ Jer. 47:3
8:17 ᵃ Ps. 58:4, 5
¹ *vipers*
8:19 ᵃ Is. 39:3
¹ *foreign idols*
8:21 ᵃ Jer.
9:1 ᵇ Joel 2:6
¹ *mourning*
8:22 ᵃ Jer. 46:11
¹ *restored*
9:1 ᵃ Is. 22:4
9:2 ᵃ Jer. 5:7, 8; 23:10
9:3 ᵃ Ps. 64:3
ᵇ Jer. 4:22; 13:23
ᶜ 1 Sam. 2:12
9:4 ᵃ Mic. 7:5, 6 ᵇ Jer. 6:28
¹ *friend*

9:5 ᵃ Is. 59:4
9:7 ᵃ Is. 1:25
ᵇ Hos. 11:8 ¹ *refine* ² *test*
9:8 ᵃ Ps. 12:2 ᵇ Ps. 55:21 ¹ *inwardly he sets his ambush*
9:9 ᵃ Jer. 5:9, 29
¹ *punish*
9:10 ᵃ Hos. 4:3
ᵇ Jer. 4:25 ¹ Or *pastures,* Jer. 12:4; 23:10
9:11 ᵃ Is. 25:2 ᵇ Is. 13:22; 34:13 ¹ *a heap of ruins* ² *jackals*
9:12 ᵃ Hos. 14:9
9:13 ᵃ Jer. 3:25; 7:24
9:14 ᵃ Jer. 7:24; 11:8 ᵇ Gal. 1:14
¹ *stubbornness*
9:15 ᵃ Ps. 80:5
ᵇ Lam. 3:15 ¹ *Bitter or poisonous water*
9:16 ᵃ Lev. 26:33
ᵇ Ezek. 5:2
¹ *Gentiles*
9:17 ᵃ 2 Chr. 35:25
¹ *skilful wailing women*
9:18 ᵃ Jer. 9:1; 14:17
9:19 ¹ *plundered*

are greatly [2]confounded, because we have forsaken the land, because [a]our[3] dwellings have cast *us* out.

20 Yet hear the word of the LORD, O ye women, and let your ear receive the word of his mouth, and teach your daughters wailing, and every one her neighbour lamentation.

21 For death is come up into our windows, *and* is entered into our palaces, to [1]cut off [a]the children from without, *and* the young men from the streets.

22 Speak, Thus saith the LORD, Even the carcases of men shall fall [a]as dung upon the open field, and as the handful after the harvestman, and none shall gather *them.*

23 Thus saith the LORD, [a]Let not the wise *man* glory in his wisdom, neither let the mighty *man* glory in his [b]might, let not the rich *man* glory in his riches:

24 But [a]let him that glorieth glory in this, that he understandeth and knoweth me, that I *am* the LORD which exercise lovingkindness, [1]judgment, and righteousness, in the earth: [b]for in these *things* I delight, saith the LORD.

25 Behold, the days come, saith the LORD, that [a]I will punish all *them which are* circumcised with the uncircumcised;

26 Egypt, and Judah, and Edom, and the children of Ammon, and Moab, and all *that are* in the [a]utmost corners, that dwell in the wilderness: for all *these* nations *are* uncircumcised, and all the house of Israel *are* [b]uncircumcised in the heart.

## CHAPTER 10

HEAR ye the word which the LORD speaketh unto you, O house of Israel:

2 Thus saith the LORD, [a]Learn not the way of the [1]heathen, and be not dismayed at the signs of heaven; for the [1]heathen are dismayed at them.

3 For the customs of the people *are* [1]vain: for [a]one cutteth a tree out of the forest, the work of the hands of the workman, with the axe.

4 They [1]deck it with silver and with gold; they [a]fasten it with nails and with hammers, that it move not.

5 They *are* upright as the palm tree, [a]but speak not: they must needs be [b]borne, because they cannot go. Be not afraid of them; for [c]they cannot do evil, neither also *is it* in them to do good.

6 Forasmuch as *there is* none [a]like unto thee, O LORD; thou *art* great, and thy name *is* great in might.

7 [a]Who would not fear thee, O King of nations? for to thee [1]doth it appertain: forasmuch as [b]among all

the wise *men* of the nations, and in all their kingdoms, *there is* none like unto thee.

8 But they are altogether [a]brutish[1] and foolish: the [2]stock *is* [3]a doctrine of vanities.

9 Silver [1]spread into plates is brought from Tarshish, and [a]gold from Uphaz, the work of the [2]workman, and of the hands of the [3]founder: blue and purple *is* their clothing: they *are* all [b]the work of [4]cunning *men.*

10 But the LORD *is* the true God, he *is* [a]the living God, and an [b]everlasting king: at his wrath the earth shall tremble, and the nations shall not be able to abide his indignation.

11 Thus shall ye say unto them, [a]The gods that have not made the heavens and the earth, *even* [b]they shall perish from the earth, and from under these heavens.

12 He [a]hath made the earth by his power, he hath [b]established the world by his wisdom, and [c]hath stretched out the heavens by his discretion.

13 [a]When he uttereth his voice, *there is* a multitude of waters in the heavens, and [b]he causeth the vapours to ascend from the ends of the earth; he maketh lightnings with rain, and bringeth forth the wind out of his treasures.

14 [a]Every man is [b]brutish[1] in *his* knowledge; [c]every [2]founder is confounded by the graven image: [d]for his molten image *is* falsehood, and *there is* no breath in them.

15 They *are* [1]vanity, *and* the work of errors: in the time of their [2]visitation they shall perish.

16 [a]The portion of Jacob *is* not like them: for he *is* the [1]former of all *things;* and [b]Israel *is* the [2]rod of his inheritance: [c]The LORD of hosts *is* his name.

17 [a]Gather up thy wares out of the land, O inhabitant [1]of the fortress.

18 For thus saith the LORD, Behold, I will [a]sling[1] out the inhabitants of the land at this [2]once, and will distress them, [b]that they may find *it so.*

19 [a]Woe is me for my hurt! my wound is grievous: but I said, [b]Truly this *is* a grief, and [c]I must bear it.

20 [a]My tabernacle is [1]spoiled, and all my cords are broken: my children are gone forth of me, and they *are* [b]not: *there is* none to stretch forth my tent any more, and to set up my curtains.

21 For the [1]pastors are become [2]brutish, and have not sought the LORD: therefore they shall not prosper, and all their flocks shall be [a]scattered.

22 Behold, the noise of the [1]bruit is come, and a great commotion out of

### Center reference column

9:19 [a] Lev. 18:28
[2] ashamed
[3] Or they have cast down our dwellings
9:21 [a] Jer. 6:11; 18:21 [1] kill
9:22 [a] Jer. 8:1, 2
9:23 [a] [Eccl. 9:11]
[b] Ps. 33:16–18
9:24 [a] 1 Cor. 1:31 [b] Mic. 7:18
[1] justice
9:25 [a] [Rom. 2:28, 29]
9:26 [a] Jer. 25:23
[b] [Rom. 2:28]
10:2 [a] [Lev. 18:3; 20:23] [1] Gentiles
10:3 [a] Is. 40:19; 45:20 [1] futile
10:4 [a] Is. 41:7
[1] decorate
10:5 [a] Ps. 115:5
[b] Ps. 115:7 [c] Is. 41:23, 24
10:6 [a] Ex. 15:11
10:7 [a] Rev. 15:4
[b] Ps. 89:6 [1] it is fitting
10:8 [a] Hab. 2:18
[1] dull-hearted
[2] wooden idol
[3] worthless teaching
10:9 [a] Dan. 10:5 [b] Ps. 115:4
[1] beaten [2] craftsman [3] metalsmith
[4] skilful
10:10 [a] 1 Tim. 6:17
[b] Ps. 10:16
10:11 [a] Ps. 96:5
[b] Zeph. 2:11
10:12 [a] Jer. 51:15
[b] Ps. 93:1 [c] Job 9:8
10:13 [a] Job 38:34
[b] Ps. 135:7
10:14 [a] Jer. 51:17
[b] Prov. 30:2
[c] Is. 42:17; 44:11
[d] Hab. 2:18 [1] dull-hearted, without
[2] metalsmith is shamed
10:15 [1] futile
[2] punishment
10:16 [a] Lam. 3:24
[b] Deut. 32:9 [c] Is. 47:4 [1] maker
[2] tribe
10:17 [a] Jer. 6:1
[1] under siege
10:18 [a] 1 Sam. 25:29 [b] Ezek. 6:10
[1] throw [2] time
10:19 [a] Jer. 8:21
[b] Ps. 77:10 [c] Mic. 7:9
10:20 [a] Jer. 4:20 [b] Jer. 31:15
[1] plundered
10:21 [a] Jer. 23:2
[1] shepherds [2] dull-hearted
10:22 [1] report

the [a]north country, to make the cities of Judah desolate, *and* a [b]den of [2]dragons.

23 O LORD, I know that the [a]way of man *is* not in himself: *it is* not in man that walketh to direct his steps.

24 O LORD, [a]correct me, but with [1]judgment; not in thine anger, lest thou bring me to nothing.

25 [a]Pour out thy fury upon the [1]heathen [b]that know thee not, and upon the families that call not on thy name: for they have eaten up Jacob, and [c]devoured him, and consumed him, and have made his habitation desolate.

## CHAPTER 11

THE word that came to Jeremiah from the LORD, saying,

2 Hear ye the words of this covenant, and speak unto the men of Judah, and to the inhabitants of Jerusalem;

3 And say thou unto them, Thus saith the LORD God of Israel; [a]Cursed *be* the man that obeyeth not the words of this covenant,

4 Which I commanded your fathers in the day *that* I brought them forth out of the land of Egypt, [a]from the iron furnace, saying, [b]Obey my voice, and do them, according to all which I command you: so shall ye be my people, and I will be your God:

5 That I may [1]perform the [a]oath which I have sworn unto your fathers, to give them [b]a land flowing with milk and honey, as *it is* this day. Then answered I, and said, [2]So be it, O LORD.

6 Then the LORD said unto me, Proclaim all these words in the cities of Judah, and in the streets of Jerusalem, saying, Hear ye the words of this covenant, [a]and do them.

7 For I earnestly [1]protested unto your fathers in the day *that* I brought them up out of the land of Egypt, *even* unto this day, [a]rising early and [2]protesting, saying, Obey my voice.

8 [a]Yet they obeyed not, nor inclined their ear, but [b]walked every one in the [1]imagination of their evil heart: therefore I will bring upon them all the words of this covenant, which I commanded *them* to do; but they did *them* not.

9 And the LORD said unto me, [a]A conspiracy is found among the men of Judah, and among the inhabitants of Jerusalem.

10 They are turned back to [a]the iniquities of their forefathers, which refused to hear my words; and they went after other gods to serve them: the house of Israel and the house of Judah have broken my covenant which I made with their fathers.

11 Therefore thus saith the LORD, Behold, I will bring [1]evil upon them, which they shall not be able to [2]escape; and [a]though they shall cry unto me, I will not hearken unto them.

12 Then shall the cities of Judah and inhabitants of Jerusalem go, and [a]cry[1] unto the gods unto whom they offer incense: but they shall not save them at all in the time of their trouble.

13 For *according to* the number of thy [a]cities were thy gods, O Judah; and *according to* the number of the streets of Jerusalem have ye set up altars to *that* shameful thing, *even* altars to burn incense unto Baal.

14 Therefore [a]pray not thou for this people, neither lift up a cry or prayer for them: for I will not hear *them* in the time that they cry unto me for their trouble.

15 [a]What hath my beloved to do in mine house, *seeing* she hath [b]wrought[1] lewdness with many, and [c]the holy flesh is passed from thee? when thou doest evil, then thou [d]rejoicest.

16 The LORD called thy name, [a]A green olive tree, [1]fair, *and* of [2]goodly fruit: with the noise of a great tumult he hath kindled fire upon it, and the branches of it are broken.

17 For the LORD of hosts, [a]that planted thee, hath pronounced [1]evil against thee, for the evil of the house of Israel and of the house of Judah, which they have done against themselves to provoke me to anger in offering incense unto Baal.

18 And the LORD hath given me knowledge *of it,* and I know *it:* then thou shewedst me their doings.

19 But I *was* like a [1]lamb *or* an ox *that* is brought to the slaughter; and I knew not that they had devised [2]devices against me, *saying,* Let us destroy the tree with the fruit thereof, [a]and let us cut him off from [b]the land of the living, that his name may be no more remembered.

20 But, O LORD of hosts, that judgest righteously, that [a]triest[1] the [2]reins and the heart, let me see thy [b]vengeance on them: for unto thee have I revealed my cause.

21 Therefore thus saith the LORD [1]of the men of [a]Anathoth, that seek thy life, saying, [b]Prophesy not in the name of the LORD, that thou die not by our hand:

22 Therefore thus saith the LORD of hosts, Behold, I will punish them: the young men shall die by the sword; their sons and their daughters shall [a]die by famine:

23 And there shall be no remnant of them: for I will bring [1]evil upon the men of Anathoth, *even* [a]the year of their [2]visitation.

### Cross References (center column)

10:22 [a] Jer. 5:15 [b] Jer. 9:11 [2] jackals
10:23 [a] Prov. 16:1; 20:24
10:24 [a] Jer. 30:11 [1] justice
10:25 [a] Ps. 79:6, 7 [b] Job 18:21 [c] Jer. 8:16 [1] Gentiles
11:3 [a] Deut. 27:26
11:4 [a] Deut. 4:20 [b] Lev. 26:3
11:5 [a] Ps. 105:9 [b] Ex. 3:8 [1] establish [2] Heb. Amen
11:6 [a] [Rom. 2:13]
11:7 [a] Jer. 35:15 [1] exhorted [2] exhorting
11:8 [a] Jer. 7:26 [b] Jer. 13:10 [1] stubbornness
11:9 [a] Ezek. 22:25
11:10 [a] Ezek. 20:18
11:11 [a] Prov. 1:28 [1] calamity [2] Lit. go out
11:12 [a] Deut. 32:37 [1] cry out to
11:13 [a] Jer. 2:28
11:14 [a] Ex. 32:10
11:15 [a] Ps. 50:16 [b] Ezek. 16:25 [c] [Titus 1:15] [d] Prov. 2:14 [1] done lewd things
11:16 [a] Ps. 52:8 [1] lovely [2] good
11:17 [a] Is. 5:2 [1] doom
11:19 [a] Ps. 83:4 [b] Ps. 27:13 [1] docile lamb brought [2] schemes
11:20 [a] Ps. 7:9 [b] Jer. 15:15 [1] tests [2] mind, lit. kidneys
11:21 [a] Jer. 1:1; 12:5, 6 [b] Mic. 2:6 [1] concerning
11:22 [a] Jer. 9:21
11:23 [a] Jer. 23:12 [1] disaster [2] punishment

## CHAPTER 12

RIGHTEOUS [a]*art* thou, O LORD, when I plead with thee: yet let me talk with thee of *thy* judgments: [b]Wherefore doth the way of the wicked prosper? *wherefore* are all they happy that deal very treacherously?

2 Thou hast planted them, yea, they have taken root: they grow, yea, they bring forth fruit: [a]thou *art* near in their mouth, and far from their [1]reins.

3 But thou, O LORD, [a]knowest me: thou hast seen me, and [b]tried[1] mine heart toward thee: pull them out like sheep for the slaughter, and prepare them for [c]the day of slaughter.

4 How long shall [a]the land mourn, and the herbs of every field wither, [b]for the wickedness of them that dwell therein? [c]the beasts are consumed, and the birds; because they said, He shall not see our [1]last end.

5 If thou hast run with the footmen, and they have wearied thee, then how canst thou contend with horses? and *if* in the land of peace, *wherein* thou trustedst, *they wearied thee,* then how wilt thou do in [a]the swelling of Jordan?

6 For even [a]thy brethren, and the house of thy father, even they have dealt treacherously with thee; yea, they have called [1]a multitude after thee: [b]believe them not, though they speak [2]fair words unto thee.

7 I have forsaken mine house, I have left mine heritage; I have given the dearly beloved of my soul into the hand of her enemies.

8 Mine heritage is unto me as a lion in the forest; it crieth out against me: therefore have I [a]hated it.

9 Mine heritage *is* unto me *as* a speckled [1]bird, the [2]birds round about *are* against her; come ye, assemble all the beasts of the field, [a]come[3] to devour.

10 Many [a]pastors[1] have destroyed [b]my vineyard, they have [c]trodden my portion under foot, they have made my [2]pleasant portion a desolate wilderness.

11 They have made it [a]desolate, *and being* desolate it mourneth unto me; the whole land is made desolate, because [b]no man [1]layeth *it* to heart.

12 The [1]spoilers are come upon all [2]high places through the wilderness: for the sword of the LORD shall devour from the *one* end of the land even to the *other* end of the land: no flesh shall have peace.

13 [a]They have sown wheat, but shall reap thorns: they have [1]put themselves to pain, *but* shall not profit: and they shall be ashamed of your [2]revenues because of the fierce anger of the LORD.

14 Thus saith the LORD against all mine evil neighbours, that [a]touch the inheritance which I have caused my people Israel to inherit; Behold, I will [b]pluck them out of their land, and pluck out the house of Judah from among them.

15 [a]And it shall come to pass, after that I have plucked them out I will return, and have compassion on them, [b]and will bring them again, every man to his heritage, and every man to his land.

16 And it shall come to pass, if they will diligently learn the ways of my people, [a]to swear by my name, [1]The LORD liveth; as they taught my people to swear by Baal; then shall they be [b]built[2] in the midst of my people.

17 But if they will not [a]obey, I will utterly pluck up and destroy that nation, saith the LORD.

## CHAPTER 13

THUS saith the LORD unto me, Go and get thee a linen [1]girdle, and put it [2]upon thy loins, and put it not in water.

2 So I got a [1]girdle according to the word of the LORD, and put *it* [2]on my loins.

3 And the word of the LORD came unto me the second time, saying,

4 Take the [1]girdle that thou hast got, which *is* upon thy loins, and arise, go to [2]Euphrates, and hide it there in a hole of the rock.

5 So I went, and hid it by Euphrates, as the LORD commanded me.

6 And it came to pass after many days, that the LORD said unto me, Arise, go to Euphrates, and take the [1]girdle from thence, which I commanded thee to hide there.

7 Then I went to Euphrates, and digged, and took the [1]girdle from the place where I had hid it: and, behold, the girdle was [2]marred, it was profitable for nothing.

8 Then the word of the LORD came unto me, saying,

9 Thus saith the LORD, After this manner [a]will I [1]mar the pride of Judah, and the great [b]pride of Jerusalem.

10 This evil people, which [a]refuse to hear my words, which [b]walk in the [1]imagination of their heart, and walk after other gods, to serve them, and to worship them, shall even be as this [2]girdle, which is good for nothing.

11 For as the [1]girdle cleaveth to the loins of a man, so have I caused to [2]cleave unto me the whole house of Israel and the whole house of Judah, saith the LORD; that [a]they might be unto me for a people, and [b]for [3]a name, and for a praise, and for a [c]glory: but they would [d]not hear.

12:1 [a] Ps. 51:14 [b] Mal. 3:15
12:2 [a] Matt. 15:8 [1] Most secret parts, lit. *kidneys*
12:3 [a] Ps. 17:3 [b] Jer. 11:20 [c] James 5:5 [1] *tested*
12:4 [a] Hos. 4:3 [b] Ps. 107:34 [c] Jer. 9:10 [1] *final*
12:5 [a] Josh. 3:15
12:6 [a] Jer. 9:4, 5 [b] Prov. 26:25 [1] Or *abundantly* [2] *smooth*, lit. *good*
12:8 [a] Hos. 9:15
12:9 [a] Lev. 26:22 [1] *vulture* [2] *vultures* [3] *bring them*
12:10 [a] Jer. 6:3; 23:1 [b] Is. 5:1–7 [c] Is. 63:18 [1] *rulers*, lit. *shepherds* [2] *desired portion of land*
12:11 [a] Jer. 10:22; 22:6 [b] Is. 42:25 [1] *takes*
12:12 [1] *plunderers* [2] *bare heights*
12:13 [a] Hag. 1:6 [1] Or *strained themselves,* [2] *harvest*
12:14 [a] Zech. 2:8 [b] Deut. 30:3
12:15 [a] Ezek. 28:25 [b] Amos 9:14
12:16 [a] [Jer. 4:2] [b] [1 Pet. 2:5] [1] *As the* [2] *established*
12:17 [a] Is. 60:12
13:1 [1] *sash* or *waistband* [2] *around your waist*
13:2 [1] *sash* [2] *around my waist*
13:4 [1] *sash* [2] Heb. *Perath*
13:6 [1] *sash*
13:7 [1] *sash* [2] *ruined*
13:9 [a] Lev. 26:19 [b] Zeph. 3:11 [1] *ruin*
13:10 [a] Jer. 16:12 [b] Jer. 7:24; 16:12 [1] *stubbornness* [2] *sash*
13:11 [a] [Ex. 19:5, 6] [b] Jer. 33:9 [c] Is. 43:21 [d] Jer. 7:13, 24, 26 [1] *sash clings to the waist* [2] *cling* [3] *renown*

12 Therefore thou shalt speak unto them this word; Thus saith the LORD God of Israel, Every bottle shall be filled with wine: and they shall say unto thee, Do we not certainly know that every bottle shall be filled with wine?

13 Then shalt thou say unto them, Thus saith the LORD, Behold, I will fill all the inhabitants of this land, even the kings that sit upon David's throne, and the priests, and the prophets, and all the inhabitants of Jerusalem, [a]with drunkenness.

14 And [a]I will dash them one against another, even the fathers and the sons together, saith the LORD: I will not pity, nor spare, nor have mercy, but destroy them.

15 Hear ye, and give ear; be not proud: for the LORD hath spoken.

16 [a]Give glory to the LORD your God, before he cause [b]darkness, and before your feet stumble upon the dark mountains, and, while ye [c]look for light, he turn it into [d]the shadow of death, _and_ make _it_ gross darkness.

17 But if ye will not hear it, my soul shall [a]weep in secret places for _your_ pride; and mine eye shall weep sore, and run down with tears, because the LORD's flock is carried away captive.

18 Say unto [a]the king and to the [1]queen, Humble yourselves, sit down: for your [2]principalities shall come down, _even_ the crown of your glory.

19 The cities of the south shall be shut up, and none shall open _them:_ Judah shall be carried away captive all of it, it shall be wholly carried away captive.

20 Lift up your eyes, and behold them that come from the [a]north: where _is_ the flock _that_ was given thee, thy beautiful flock?

21 What wilt thou say when he shall punish thee? for thou hast taught them _to be_ captains, _and_ as chief over thee: shall not [a]sorrows[1] take thee, as a woman in [2]travail?

22 And if thou say in thine heart, [a]Wherefore[1] come these things upon me? For the greatness of thine iniquity are [b]thy skirts [2]discovered, _and_ thy heels [3]made bare.

23 Can the Ethiopian change his skin, or the leopard his spots? _then_ may ye also do good, that are accustomed to do evil.

24 Therefore will I [a]scatter them [b]as the stubble that passeth away by the wind of the wilderness.

25 [a]This _is_ thy lot, the portion of thy measures from me, saith the LORD; because thou hast forgotten me, and trusted in [b]falsehood.

26 Therefore [a]will I [1]discover thy skirts upon thy face, that thy shame may appear.

27 I have seen thine adulteries, and thy [a]neighings,[1] the lewdness of thy [2]whoredom, _and_ thine abominations [b]on the hills in the fields. Woe unto thee, O Jerusalem! wilt thou not be made clean? when _shall it_ once _be?_

## CHAPTER 14

THE word of the LORD that came to Jeremiah concerning the [1]dearth.

2 Judah mourneth, and [a]the gates thereof languish; they [1]are [b]black unto the ground; and [c]the cry of Jerusalem is gone up.

3 And their nobles have sent their [1]little ones to the waters: they came to the [2]pits, _and_ found no water; they returned with their vessels empty; they were [a]ashamed and confounded, [b]and covered their heads.

4 Because the ground is [1]chapt, for there was [a]no rain in the earth, the plowmen were ashamed, they covered their heads.

5 Yea, the [1]hind also calved in the field, and [2]forsook _it,_ because there was no grass.

6 And [a]the wild [1]asses did stand in the [2]high places, they snuffed up the wind like [3]dragons; their eyes did fail, because _there was_ no grass.

7 O LORD, though our iniquities testify against us, do thou _it_ [a]for thy name's sake: for our backslidings are many; we have sinned against thee.

8 [a]O the hope of Israel, the saviour thereof in time of trouble, why shouldest thou be as a stranger in the land, and as a wayfaring man _that_ turneth aside to tarry for a night?

9 Why shouldest thou be as a man astonied, as a mighty man [a]_that_ cannot save? yet thou, O LORD, [b]_art_ in the midst of us, and we are called by thy name; leave us not.

10 Thus saith the LORD unto this people, [a]Thus have they loved to wander, they have not [1]refrained their feet, therefore the LORD doth not accept them; [b]he will now remember their iniquity, and [2]visit their sins.

11 Then said the LORD unto me, [a]Pray not for this people for _their_ good.

12 [a]When they fast, I will not hear their cry; and [b]when they offer burnt offering and [1]an oblation, I will not accept them: but [c]I will consume them by the sword, and by the famine, and by the pestilence.

13 [a]Then said I, Ah, Lord GOD! behold, the prophets say unto them, Ye shall not see the sword, neither shall ye have famine; but I will give you [1]assured [b]peace in this place.

14 Then the LORD said unto me, [a]The prophets prophesy lies in my name: [b]I sent them not, neither have I commanded them, neither spake unto them: they prophesy unto you

Cross-references:
13:13 [a] Is. 51:17; 63:6
13:14 [a] Jer. 19:9–11
13:16 [a] Josh. 7:19 [b] Amos 8:9 [c] Is. 59:9 [d] Ps. 44:19
13:17 [a] Jer. 9:1; 14:17
13:18 [a] Jer. 22:26 [1] queen mother [2] rule shall collapse
13:20 [a] Jer. 10:22; 46:20
13:21 [a] Jer. 6:24 [1] pangs seize [2] childbirth
13:22 [a] Jer. 16:10 [b] Is. 47:2 [1] Why [2] uncovered [3] Lit. suffer violence
13:24 [a] Jer. 9:16 [b] Hos. 13:3
13:25 [a] Job 20:29 [b] Jer. 10:14
13:26 [a] Lam. 1:8 [1] uncover
13:27 [a] Jer. 5:7, 8 [b] Is. 65:7; Ezek. 6:13 [1] lustful neighings [2] harlotry
14:1 [1] droughts
14:2 [a] Is. 3:26 [b] Jer. 8:21 [c] 1 Sam. 5:12 [1] mourn for the land
14:3 [a] Ps. 40:14 [b] 2 Sam. 15:30 [1] lads [2] cisterns
14:4 [a] Jer. 3:3 [1] parched, lit. shattered
14:5 [1] deer [2] abandoned
14:6 [a] Jer. 2:24 [1] donkeys [2] bare heights [3] jackals
14:7 [a] Ps. 25:11
14:8 [a] Jer. 17:13
14:9 [a] Is. 59:1 [b] Ex. 29:45
14:10 [a] Jer. 2:23–25 [b] Hos. 8:13 [1] restrained [2] punish
14:11 [a] Ex. 32:10
14:12 [a] Ezek. 8:18 [b] Jer. 6:20 [c] Jer. 9:16 [1] grain offering
14:13 [a] Jer. 4:10 [b] Jer. 8:11; 23:17 [1] Lit. true
14:14 [a] Jer. 27:10 [b] Jer. 29:8, 9

a false vision and ¹divination, and a ²thing of nought, and the ᶜdeceit of their heart.

15 Therefore thus saith the LORD concerning the prophets that prophesy in my name, and I sent them not, ᵃyet they say, Sword and famine shall not be in this land; By sword and famine shall those prophets be consumed.

16 And the people to whom they prophesy shall be cast out in the streets of Jerusalem because of the famine and the sword; ᵃand they shall have none to bury them, them, their wives, nor their sons, nor their daughters: for I will pour their wickedness upon them.

17 Therefore thou shalt say this word unto them; ᵃLet mine eyes run down with tears night and day, and let them not cease: ᵇfor the virgin daughter of my people is broken with a ¹great breach, with a very ²grievous blow.

18 If I go forth into ᵃthe field, then behold the slain with the sword! and if I enter into the city, then behold them that are sick with famine! yea, both the prophet and the ᵇpriest go about into a land that they know not.

19 ᵃHast thou utterly rejected Judah? hath thy soul lothed Zion? why hast thou smitten us, and ᵇthere is no healing for us? ᶜwe looked for peace, and there is no good; and for the time of healing, and behold trouble!

20 We acknowledge, O LORD, our wickedness, and the iniquity of our ᵃfathers: for ᵇwe have sinned against thee.

21 Do not abhor us, for thy name's sake, do not disgrace the throne of thy glory: ᵃremember, break not thy covenant with us.

22 ᵃAre there any among ᵇthe ¹vanities of the Gentiles that can cause ᶜrain? or can the heavens give showers? ᵈart not thou he, O LORD our God? therefore we will wait upon thee: for thou hast made all these things.

## CHAPTER 15

THEN said the LORD unto me, ᵃThough ᵇMoses and ᶜSamuel stood before me, yet my mind could not ¹be toward this people: cast them out of my sight, and let them go forth.

2 And it shall come to pass, if they say unto thee, Whither shall we go forth? then thou shalt tell them, Thus saith the LORD; ᵃSuch as are for death, to death; and such as are for the sword, to the sword; and such as are for the famine, to the famine; and such as are for the ᵇcaptivity, to the captivity.

3 And I will ᵃappoint over them four ¹kinds, saith the LORD: the sword to slay, and the dogs to ²tear, and ᵇthe

**Reference column:**

14:14 ᶜ Jer. 23:16 ¹ Pagan fortune-telling ² worthless thing
14:15 ᵃ Ezek. 14:10
14:16 ᵃ Ps. 79:2, 3
14:17 ᵃ Jer. 9:1; 13:17 ᵇ Jer. 8:21 ¹ mighty stroke ² severe
14:18 ᵃ Ezek. 7:15 ᵇ Jer. 23:11
14:19 ᵃ Lam. 5:22 ᵇ Jer. 15:18 ᶜ Jer. 8:15
14:20 ᵃ Jer. 3:25 ᵇ Dan. 9:8
14:21 ᵃ Ps. 106:45
14:22 ᵃ Zech. 10:1 ᵇ Deut. 32:21 ᶜ Jer. 5:24 ᵈ Ps. 135:7 ¹ idols
15:1 ᵃ Ezek. 14:14 ᵇ Ex. 32:11–14 ᶜ 1 Sam. 7:9 ¹ be favourable
15:2 ᵃ Zech. 11:9 ᵇ Jer. 9:16; 16:13
15:3 ᵃ Ezek. 14:21 ᵇ Jer. 7:33 ¹ forms of destruction ² drag off

fowls of the heaven, and the beasts of the earth, to devour and destroy.

4 And I will ¹cause them to be ᵃremoved into all kingdoms of the earth, because of ᵇManasseh the son of Hezekiah king of Judah, for that which he did in Jerusalem.

5 For who shall have pity upon thee, O Jerusalem? or who shall bemoan thee? or who shall go aside to ask how thou doest?

6 ᵃThou hast forsaken me, saith the LORD, thou art ᵇgone backward: therefore will I stretch out my hand against thee, and destroy thee; ᶜI am weary with ¹repenting.

7 And I will ¹fan them with a ²fan in the gates of the land; I will ᵃbereave them of children, I will destroy my people, since they ᵇreturn not from their ways.

8 Their widows are increased to me above the sand of the seas: I have brought upon them against the mother of the young men a ¹spoiler at noonday: I have caused him to fall upon it ᵃsuddenly, and ²terrors upon the city.

9 ᵃShe that hath borne seven languisheth: she hath ¹given up the ghost; ᵇher sun is gone down while it was yet day: she hath been ashamed and confounded: and the ²residue of them will I deliver to the sword before their enemies, saith the LORD.

10 ᵃWoe is me, my mother, that thou hast borne me a man of strife and a man of contention to the whole ¹earth! I have neither lent ²on usury, nor men have lent to me ²on usury; yet every one of them doth curse me.

11 The LORD said, Verily it shall be well with thy remnant; verily I will cause ᵃthe enemy to ¹intreat thee well in the time of ²evil and in the time of affliction.

12 ¹Shall iron break the northern iron and the ²steel?

13 Thy substance and thy treasures will I give ¹to the ᵃspoil without price, and that for all thy sins, even in all thy ²borders.

14 And I will make thee to ¹pass with thine enemies ᵃinto a land which thou knowest not: for a ᵇfire is kindled in mine anger, which shall burn upon you.

15 O LORD, ᵃthou knowest: remember me, and ¹visit me, and ᵇrevenge² me of my persecutors; take me not away in thy longsuffering: know that ᶜfor thy sake I have suffered rebuke.

16 Thy words were found, and I did ᵃeat them; and ᵇthy word was unto me the joy and rejoicing of mine heart: for I am called by thy name, O LORD God of hosts.

17 ᵃI sat not in the assembly of the mockers, nor rejoiced; I sat alone

**Reference column (right):**

15:4 ᵃ Deut. 28:25 ᵇ 2 Kin. 24:3, 4 ¹ hand them over to trouble
15:6 ᵃ Jer. 2:13 ᵇ Jer. 7:24 ᶜ Jer. 20:16 ¹ relenting
15:7 ᵃ Jer. 18:21 ᵇ Is. 9:13 ¹ winnow ² winnowing fan
15:8 ᵃ Is. 29:5 ¹ plunderer ² anguish and terror
15:9 ᵃ 1 Sam. 2:5 ᵇ Amos 8:9 ¹ breathed her last ² remnant
15:10 ᵃ Job 3:1 ¹ land ² for interest
15:11 ᵃ Jer. 40:4, 5 ¹ intercede with thee ² adversity
15:12 ¹ Can any-one break iron ² bronze
15:13 ᵃ Ps. 44:12 ¹ as plunder ² territories
15:14 ᵃ Jer. 16:13 ᵇ Deut. 32:22 ¹ pass over
15:15 ᵃ Jer. 12:3 ᵇ Jer. 20:12 ᶜ Ps. 69:7–9 ¹ take notice of ² take vengeance for me on
15:16 ᵃ Ezek. 3:1, 3 ᵇ [Job 23:12]
15:17 ᵃ Ps. 26:4, 5

because of thy hand: for thou hast filled me with indignation.

18 Why is my [a]pain perpetual, and my wound incurable, *which* refuseth to be healed? wilt thou be altogether unto me [b]as [1]a liar, *and as* waters *that* [2]fail?

19 Therefore thus saith the LORD, [a]If thou return, then will I bring thee again, *and* thou shalt [b]stand before me: and if thou [c]take forth the precious from the vile, thou shalt be as my mouth: let them return unto thee; but return not thou unto them.

20 And I will make thee unto this people a [1]fenced brasen [a]wall: and they shall fight against thee, but [b]they shall not prevail against thee: for I *am* with thee to save thee and to deliver thee, saith the LORD.

21 And I will deliver thee out of the hand of the wicked, and I will redeem thee out of the [1]hand of the terrible.

## CHAPTER 16

THE word of the LORD came also unto me, saying,

2 Thou shalt not take thee a wife, neither shalt thou have sons or daughters in this place.

3 For thus saith the LORD concerning the sons and concerning the daughters that are born in this place, and concerning their mothers that bare them, and concerning their fathers that begat them in this land;

4 They shall die of [a]grievous deaths; they shall not be [b]lamented; neither shall they be [c]buried; *but* they shall be [d]as [1]dung upon the face of the earth: and they shall be consumed by the sword, and by famine; and their [e]carcases shall be meat for the fowls of heaven, and for the beasts of the earth.

5 For thus saith the LORD, [a]Enter not into the house of mourning, neither go to lament nor bemoan them: for I have taken away my peace from this people, saith the LORD, *even* lovingkindness and mercies.

6 Both the great and the small shall die in this land: they shall not be buried, [a]neither shall *men* lament for them, nor [b]cut[1] themselves, nor [c]make[1] themselves bald for them:

7 Neither shall *men* [1]tear *themselves* for them in mourning, to comfort them for the dead; neither shall *men* give them the cup of consolation to [a]drink for their father or for their mother.

8 Thou shalt not also go into the house of feasting, to sit with them to eat and to drink.

9 For thus saith the LORD of hosts, the God of Israel; Behold, [a]I will cause to cease out of this place in your eyes, and in your days, the voice of [1]mirth,

and the voice of gladness, the voice of the bridegroom, and the voice of the bride.

10 And it shall come to pass, when thou shalt shew this people all these words, and they shall say unto thee, [a]Wherefore hath the LORD pronounced all this great [1]evil against us? or what *is* our iniquity? or what *is* our sin that we have committed against the LORD our God?

11 Then shalt thou say unto them, [a]Because your fathers have forsaken me, saith the LORD, and have walked after other gods, and have served them, and have worshipped them, and have forsaken me, and have not kept my law;

12 And ye have done [a]worse than your fathers; for, behold, [b]ye walk every one after the [1]imagination of his evil heart, that they may not hearken unto me:

13 [a]Therefore will I cast you out of this land [b]into a land that ye know not, *neither* ye nor your fathers; and there shall ye serve other gods day and night; where I will not shew you favour.

14 Therefore, behold, the [a]days come, saith the LORD, that it shall no more be said, The LORD liveth, that brought up the children of Israel out of the land of Egypt;

15 But, The LORD liveth, that brought up the children of Israel from the land of the [a]north, and from all the lands whither he had driven them: and [b]I will bring them again into their land that I gave unto their fathers.

16 Behold, I will send for many [a]fishers,[1] saith the LORD, and they shall fish them; and after will I send for many hunters, and they shall hunt them from every mountain, and from every hill, and out of the holes of the rocks.

17 For mine [a]eyes *are* upon all their ways: they are not hid from my face, neither is their iniquity hid from mine eyes.

18 And first I will [1]recompense their iniquity and their sin [a]double; because [b]they have defiled my land, they have filled mine inheritance with the carcases of their detestable and abominable [2]things.

19 O LORD, [a]my strength, and my fortress, and [b]my refuge in the day of affliction, the Gentiles shall come unto thee from the ends of the earth, and shall say, Surely our fathers have inherited lies, [1]vanity, and *things* [c]wherein *there is* no profit.

20 Shall a man make gods unto himself, and [a]they *are* no gods?

21 Therefore, behold, I will this once cause them to know, I will cause them to know mine hand and

### Center reference column

15:18 [a] Jer. 10:19;
30:15 [b] Job 6:15
[1] *an unreliable
stream* [2] *Or cannot be trusted*

15:19 [a] Zech. 3:7
[b] Jer. 15:1 [c] Ezek. 22:26; 44:23

15:20 [a] Ezek. 3:9 [b] Jer. 1:8, 19; 20:11; 37:21; 38:13; 39:11, 12 [1] *fortified bronze*

15:21 [1] *grip*

16:4 [a] Jer. 15:2
[b] Jer. 22:18; 25:33
[c] Jer. 14:16; 19:11
[d] Ps. 83:10 [e] Ps. 79:2 [1] *refuse*

16:5 [a] Ezek. 24:17, 22, 23

16:6 [a] Jer. 22:18
[b] Deut. 14:1 [c] Is. 22:12 [1] *Pagan signs of grief*

16:7 [a] Prov. 31:6
[1] *break bread*

16:9 [a] Rev. 18:23
[1] *rejoicing*

16:10 [a] Deut. 29:24 [1] *disaster*

16:11 [a] Jer. 22:9

16:12 [a] Jer. 7:26
[b] Jer. 3:17; 18:12
[1] *stubbornness*

16:13 [a] Deut. 4:26; 28:36, 63 [b] Jer. 15:14

16:14 [a] Jer. 23:7, 8

16:15 [a] Jer. 3:18
[b] Jer. 24:6; 30:3; 32:37

16:16 [a] Amos 4:2
[1] *fishermen*

16:17 [a] Heb. 4:13

16:18 [a] Jer. 17:18
[b] [Ezek. 43:7]
[1] *repay* [2] *idols*

16:19 [a] Ps. 18:1,
2 [b] Jer. 17:17 [c] Is. 44:10 [1] *worthlessness*

16:20 [a] Gal. 4:8

## CHAPTER 17

THE sin of Judah *is* [a]written with a [b]pen of iron, *and* with the point of a diamond: *it is* [c]graven[1] upon the [2]table of their heart, and upon the horns of your altars;

2 Whilst their children remember their altars and their [a]groves[1] by the green trees upon the high hills.

3 O my mountain in the field, I will give thy substance *and* all thy treasures [1]to the spoil, *and* thy high places for sin, throughout all thy borders.

4 And thou, even thyself, shalt [1]discontinue from thine heritage that I gave thee; and I will cause thee to serve thine enemies in [a]the land which thou knowest not: for [b]ye have kindled a fire in mine anger, *which* shall burn for ever.

5 Thus saith the LORD; [a]Cursed *be* the man that trusteth in [1]man, and maketh [b]flesh his arm, and whose heart departeth from the LORD.

6 For he shall be [a]like [1]the heath in the desert, and [b]shall not see when good cometh; but shall inhabit the parched places in the wilderness, [c]*in* a salt land and not inhabited.

7 [a]Blessed *is* the man that trusteth in the LORD, and whose hope the LORD is.

8 For he shall be [a]as a tree planted by the waters, and *that* spreadeth out her roots by the river, and shall not [1]see when heat cometh, but her leaf shall be green; and shall not be [2]careful in the year of drought, neither shall cease from yielding fruit.

9 The [a]heart *is* deceitful above all *things*, and [1]desperately wicked: who can know it?

10 I the LORD [a]search the heart, *I* [1]try the [2]reins, [b]even to give every man according to his ways, *and* according to the fruit of his [3]doings.

11 *As* the partridge sitteth *on eggs*, and hatcheth *them* not; *so* he that getteth riches, and not by right, [a]shall leave them in the midst of his days, and at his end shall be [b]a fool.

12 A glorious high throne from the beginning *is* the place of our sanctuary.

13 O LORD, [a]the hope of Israel, [b]all that forsake thee shall be ashamed, *and* they that depart from me shall be [c]written in the earth, because they have forsaken the LORD, the [d]fountain of living waters.

14 Heal me, O LORD, and I shall be healed; save me, and I shall be saved: for [a]thou *art* my praise.

15 Behold, they say unto me, [a]Where *is* the word of the LORD? let it come now.

16 As for me, [a]I have not [1]hastened from *being* a [2]pastor to follow thee: neither have I desired the woeful day; thou knowest: that which came out of my lips was *right* before thee.

17 Be not a terror unto me: [a]thou *art* my hope in the day of [1]evil.

18 [a]Let them be [1]confounded that persecute me, but [b]let not me be [2]confounded: let them be dismayed, but let not me be dismayed: bring upon them the day of [3]evil, and [c]destroy[4] them with double destruction.

19 Thus said the LORD unto me; Go and stand in the gate of the children of the people, whereby the kings of Judah come in, and by the which they go out, and in all the gates of Jerusalem;

20 And say unto them, [a]Hear ye the word of the LORD, ye kings of Judah, and all Judah, and all the inhabitants of Jerusalem, that enter in by these gates:

21 Thus saith the LORD; [a]Take heed to yourselves, and bear no burden on the sabbath day, nor bring *it* in by the gates of Jerusalem;

22 Neither carry forth a burden out of your houses on the sabbath day, neither do ye any work, but hallow ye the sabbath day, as I [a]commanded your fathers.

23 [a]But they obeyed not, neither inclined their ear, but [1]made their neck stiff, that they might not hear, nor receive instruction.

24 And it shall come to pass, [a]if ye diligently hearken unto me, saith the LORD, to bring in no burden through the gates of this city on the [b]sabbath day, but hallow the sabbath day, to do no work therein;

25 [a]Then shall there enter into the gates of this city kings and princes sitting upon the throne of David, riding in chariots and on horses, they, and their princes, the men of Judah, and the inhabitants of Jerusalem: and this city shall remain for ever.

26 And they shall come from the cities of Judah, and from [a]the places about Jerusalem, and from the land of Benjamin, and from [b]the [1]plain, and from the mountains, and from [c]the [2]south, bringing burnt offerings, and sacrifices, and [3]meat offerings, and incense, and bringing [d]sacrifices of praise, unto the house of the LORD.

27 But if ye will not hearken unto me to hallow the sabbath day, and not to bear a burden, [1]even entering in at the gates of Jerusalem on the sabbath day; then [a]will I kindle a fire in the gates thereof, [b]and it shall devour the palaces of Jerusalem, and it shall not be [c]quenched.

### Cross References

16:21 [a] Amos 5:8
[1] Heb. YHWH, Jehovah

17:1 [a] Jer. 2:22
[b] Job 19:24
[c] 2 Cor. 3:3 [1] engraved [2] tablet

17:2 [a] Judg. 3:7
[1] Heb. Asherim, wooden images

17:3 [1] as plunder

17:4 [a] Jer. 16:13
[b] Jer. 15:14 [1] let go of

17:5 [a] Is. 30:1, 2; 31:1 [b] Is. 31:3
[1] Strength

17:6 [a] Jer. 48:6
[b] Job 20:17
[c] Deut. 29:23 [1] a shrub

17:7 [a] [Is. 30:18]

17:8 [a] [Ps. 1:3]
[1] MT fear; Qr., Tg. see [2] anxious

17:9 [a] [Eccl. 9:3]
[1] Or incurably sick

17:10 [a] Rev. 2:23 [b] Rom. 2:6
[1] test [2] mind, lit. kidneys, the most secret parts [3] deeds

17:11 [a] Ps. 55:23
[b] Luke 12:20

17:13 [a] Jer. 14:8
[b] [Is. 1:28] [c] Luke 10:20 [d] Jer. 2:13

17:14 [a] Deut. 10:21

17:15 [a] Is. 5:19

17:16 [a] Jer. 1:4–12
[1] hurried away [2] Lit. shepherd

17:17 [a] Jer. 16:19
[1] doom

17:18 [a] Ps. 35:4; 70:2 [b] Ps. 25:2
[c] Jer. 11:20
[1] ashamed [2] put to shame [3] doom [4] Lit. crush

17:20 [a] Jer. 19:3, 4

17:21 [a] Neh. 13:19

17:22 [a] Ex. 20:8; 31:13

17:23 [a] Jer. 7:24, 26 [1] Were stubborn

17:24 [a] Jer. 11:4; 26:3 [b] Ex. 16:23–30; 20:8–10

17:25 [a] Jer. 22:4

17:26 [a] Jer. 33:13 [b] Zech. 7:7
[c] Judg. 1:9 [d] Ps. 107:22; 116:17
[1] Heb. shephelah, lowland [2] Heb. Negev [3] grain or meal

17:27 [a] Lam. 4:11
[b] 2 Kin. 25:9
[c] Jer. 7:20 [1] when

## CHAPTER 18

THE word which came to Jeremiah from the LORD, saying,

2 Arise, and go down to the potter's house, and there I will cause thee to hear my words.

3 Then I went down to the potter's house, and, behold, he wrought a work on the ¹wheels.

4 And the vessel that he ¹made of clay was ²marred in the hand of the potter: so he made it again another vessel, as seemed good to the potter to make *it*.

5 Then the word of the LORD came to me, saying,

6 O house of Israel, ªcannot I do with you as this potter? saith the LORD. Behold, ᵇas the clay *is* in the potter's hand, so *are* ye in mine hand, O house of Israel.

7 *At what* instant I shall speak concerning a nation, and concerning a kingdom, to ªpluck up, and to pull down, and to destroy *it;*

8 ªIf that nation, against whom I have pronounced, turn from their evil, ᵇI will ¹repent of the evil that I thought to do unto them.

9 And *at what* instant I shall speak concerning a nation, and concerning a kingdom, to build and to plant *it;*

10 If it do evil in my sight, that it obey not my voice, then I will ¹repent of the good, wherewith I said I would benefit them.

11 Now therefore go to, speak to the men of Judah, and to the inhabitants of Jerusalem, saying, Thus saith the LORD; Behold, I ¹frame evil against you, and devise a ²device against you: ªreturn ye now every one from his evil way, and make your ways and your doings ᵇgood.

12 And they said, ªThere is no hope: but we will walk ¹after our own devices, and we will every one do the ᵇimagination² of his evil heart.

13 Therefore thus saith the LORD; ªAsk ye now among the ¹heathen, who hath heard such things: the virgin of Israel hath done ᵇa very horrible thing.

14 Will *a man* ¹leave the snow of Lebanon *which cometh* from the rock of the field? *or* shall the cold flowing waters that come from another place be forsaken?

15 Because my people hath forgotten ªme, they have burned incense to ¹vanity, and they have caused them to stumble in their ways *from* the ᵇancient paths, to walk in paths, ²*in* a way not cast up;

16 To make their land ªdesolate, *and* a perpetual ᵇhissing; every one that passeth thereby shall be astonished, and ¹wag his head.

17 ªI will scatter them ᵇas with an east wind before the enemy; ᶜI will shew them ¹the back, and not ¹the face, in the day of their calamity.

18 Then said they, ªCome, and let us devise ¹devices against Jeremiah; ᵇfor the law shall not perish from the priest, nor counsel from the wise, nor the word from the prophet. Come, and let us ²smite him with the tongue, and let us not give heed to any of his words.

19 Give heed to me, O LORD, and ¹hearken to the voice of them that contend with me.

20 ªShall evil be ¹recompensed for good? for they have ᵇdigged a pit for my ²soul. Remember that I ᶜstood before thee to speak good ³for them, *and,* to turn away thy wrath from them.

21 Therefore ªdeliver up their children to the famine, and pour out their *blood* by the force of the sword; and let their wives be ᵇbereaved of their children, and *be* widows; and let their men be put to death; *let* their young men *be* slain by the sword in battle.

22 Let a cry be heard from their houses, when thou shalt bring a troop suddenly upon them: for they have digged a pit to take me, and hid snares for my feet.

23 Yet, LORD, thou knowest all their counsel against me to slay *me:* ªforgive¹ not their iniquity, neither blot out their sin from thy sight, but let them be overthrown before thee; deal *thus* with them in the time of thine ᵇanger.

## CHAPTER 19

THUS saith the LORD, Go and get a potter's earthen bottle, and *take* of the ¹ancients of the people, and of the ¹ancients of the priests;

2 And go forth unto ªthe valley of the son of Hinnom, which *is* by the entry of the ¹east gate, and proclaim there the words that I shall tell thee,

3 ªAnd say, Hear ye the word of the LORD, O kings of Judah, and inhabitants of Jerusalem; Thus saith the LORD of hosts, the God of Israel; Behold, I will bring ¹evil upon this place, the which whosoever heareth, his ears shall ᵇtingle.

4 Because they ªhave forsaken me, and have ¹estranged this place, and have burned incense in it unto other gods, whom neither they nor their fathers have known, nor the kings of Judah, and have filled this place with ᵇthe blood of innocents;

5 ªThey have built also the ¹high places of Baal, to burn their sons with fire *for* burnt offerings unto Baal, ᵇwhich I commanded not, nor spake *it,* neither came *it* into my mind:

---

18:3 ¹ Potter's wheel
18:4 ¹ *was making* ² ruined
18:6 ª Rom. 9:20, 21 ᵇ Is. 64:8
18:7 ª Jer. 1:10
18:8 ª [Ezek. 18:21; 33:11] ᵇ Jer. 26:3 ¹ *relent concerning the disaster*
18:10 ¹ *relent*
18:11 ª 2 Kin. 17:13 ᵇ Jer. 7:3–7 ¹ *am fashioning a disaster* ² *plan*
18:12 ª Jer. 2:25 ᵇ Jer. 3:17; 23:17 ¹ *according to our own plans* ² *stubbornness*
18:13 ª Jer. 2:10, 11 ᵇ Jer. 5:30 ¹ *Gentiles*
18:14 ¹ *forsake*
18:15 ª Jer. 2:13, 32 ᵇ Jer. 6:16 ¹ *worthless idols* ² *and not on a highway*
18:16 ª Jer. 19:8 ᵇ 1 Kin. 9:8 ¹ *shake*
18:17 ª Jer. 13:24 ᵇ Ps. 48:7

ᶜ Jer. 2:27 ¹ My
18:18 ª Jer. 11:19 ᵇ Lev. 10:11 ¹ *plans* ² *attack*
18:19 ¹ *listen*
18:20 ª Ps. 109:4 ᵇ Jer. 5:26 ᶜ Jer. 14:7–15:1 ¹ *repaid* ² *life* ³ *concerning*
18:21 ª Ps. 109:9– 20 ᵇ Jer. 15:7, 8
18:23 ª Ps. 35:14; 109:14 ᵇ Jer. 7:20 ¹ *do not atone for*
19:1 ¹ *elders*
19:2 ª Josh. 15:8 ¹ *Potsherd Gate*
19:3 ª Jer. 17:20 ᵇ 1 Sam. 3:11 ¹ *a catastrophe*
19:4 ª Is. 65:11 ᵇ 2 Kin. 21:12 ¹ *made this an alien place*
19:5 ª Jer. 7:31; 32:35 ᵇ Lev. 18:21 ¹ *sacred places for pagan worship*

6 Therefore, behold, the days come, saith the LORD, that this place shall no more be called Tophet, nor ªThe valley of the son of Hinnom, but The valley of slaughter.

7 And I will make void the counsel of Judah and Jerusalem in this place; ªand I will cause them to fall by the sword before their enemies, and by the hands of them that seek their lives: and their ᵇcarcases will I give to be meat for the fowls of the heaven, and for the beasts of the earth.

8 And I will make this city ªdesolate, and ¹an hissing; every one that passeth thereby shall be astonished and hiss because of all the plagues thereof.

9 And I will cause them to eat the ªflesh of their sons and the flesh of their daughters, and they shall eat every one the flesh of his friend in the siege and ¹straitness, wherewith their enemies, and they that seek their lives, shall ²straiten them.

10 ªThen shalt thou break the bottle in the sight of the men that go with thee,

11 And shalt say unto them, Thus saith the LORD of hosts; ªEven so will I break this people and this city, as *one* breaketh a potter's vessel, that cannot be ¹made whole again: and they shall ᵇbury *them* in Tophet, till *there be* no place to bury.

12 Thus will I do unto this place, saith the LORD, and to the inhabitants thereof, and *even* make this city as Tophet:

13 And the houses of Jerusalem, and the houses of the kings of Judah, shall be defiled ªas the place of Tophet, because of all the houses upon whose ᵇroofs they have burned incense unto all the host of heaven, and ᶜhave poured out drink offerings unto other gods.

14 Then came Jeremiah from Tophet, whither the LORD had sent him to prophesy; and he stood in ªthe court of the LORD's house; and said to all the people,

15 Thus saith the LORD of hosts, the God of Israel; Behold, I will bring upon this city and upon all her towns all the ¹evil that I have pronounced against it, because ªthey have ²hardened their necks, that they might not hear my words.

## CHAPTER 20

Now ªPashur the son of ᵇImmer the priest, who *was* also chief governor in the house of the LORD, heard that Jeremiah prophesied these things.

2 Then Pashur ¹smote Jeremiah the prophet, and put him in the stocks

---

19:6 ª Josh. 15:8
19:7 ª Lev. 26:17
ᵇ Ps. 79:2
19:8 ª Jer. 18:16;
49:13; 50:13 ¹ *an object of*
19:9 ª Lev. 26:29
¹ *desperation* ² *drive them to despair*
19:10 ª Jer. 51:63, 64
19:11 ª Is. 30:14
ᵇ Jer. 7:32 ¹ *restored*
19:13 ª 2 Kin. 23:10 ᵇ Zeph. 1:5
ᶜ Jer. 7:18
19:14 ª 2 Chr. 20:5
19:15 ª Neh. 9:17, 29 ¹ *doom* ² *stiffened*
20:1 ª Ezra 2:37, 38 ᵇ 1 Chr. 24:14
20:2 ¹ *struck*

ª Jer. 37:13
20:3 ¹ Lit. *Fear on Every Side*
20:4 ª Jer. 21:4–10
20:5 ª 2 Kin. 20:17
ᵇ Is. 39:6 ¹ *wealth* ² *produce* ³ *plunder* ⁴ *seize*
20:6 ª Jer. 14:13–15
20:7 ª Jer. 1:6, 7 ᵇ Lam. 3:14 ¹ *induced* ² *persuaded* ³ Lit. *a laughingstock*
20:8 ª Jer. 6:7 ¹ *plunder*
20:9 ª Ps. 39:3 ᵇ Job 32:18 ¹ *of holding back* ² Endure it
20:10 ª Ps. 31:13 ᵇ Ps. 41:9; 55:13, 14 ¹ *mocking or slander* ² *acquaintances* ³ *stumbling* ⁴ *Perhaps*
20:11 ª Jer. 1:18, 19 ᵇ Jer. 15:20; 17:18 ᶜ Jer. 23:40 ¹ *awesome*
20:12 ª [Jer. 11:20; 17:10] ¹ *tests* ² *mind*, lit. *kidneys* ³ *pled*
20:13 ª Ps. 35:9, 10; 109:30, 31 ¹ *life*

---

that *were* in the high ªgate of Benjamin, which *was* by the house of the LORD.

3 And it came to pass on the morrow, that Pashur brought forth Jeremiah out of the stocks. Then said Jeremiah unto him, The LORD hath not called thy name Pashur, but ¹Magor-missabib.

4 For thus saith the LORD, Behold, I will make thee a terror to thyself, and to all thy friends: and they shall fall by the sword of their enemies, and thine eyes shall behold *it:* and I will ªgive all Judah into the hand of the king of Babylon, and he shall carry them captive into Babylon, and shall slay them with the sword.

5 Moreover I ªwill deliver all the ¹strength of this city, and all the ²labours thereof, and all the precious things thereof, and all the treasures of the kings of Judah will I give into the hand of their enemies, which shall ³spoil them, and ⁴take them, and ᵇcarry them to Babylon.

6 And thou, Pashur, and all that dwell in thine house shall go into captivity: and thou shalt come to Babylon, and there thou shalt die, and shalt be buried there, thou, and all thy friends, to whom thou hast ªprophesied lies.

7 O LORD, thou hast ¹deceived me, and I was ²deceived: ªthou art stronger than I, and hast prevailed: ᵇI am ³in derision daily, every one mocketh me.

8 For since I spake, I cried out, ªI cried violence and ¹spoil; because the word of the LORD was made a reproach unto me, and a derision, daily.

9 Then I said, I will not make mention of him, nor speak any more in his name. But *his word* was in mine heart as a ªburning fire shut up in my bones, and I was weary ¹with forbearing, and ᵇI could not ²stay.

10 ªFor I heard the ¹defaming of many, fear on every side. Report, *say they,* and we will report it. ᵇAll my ²familiars watched for my ³halting, *saying,* ⁴Peradventure he will be enticed, and we shall prevail against him, and we shall take our revenge on him.

11 But the LORD *is* ªwith me as a mighty ¹terrible one: therefore my persecutors shall stumble, and they shall not ᵇprevail: they shall be greatly ashamed; for they shall not prosper: *their* ᶜeverlasting confusion shall never be forgotten.

12 But, O LORD of hosts, that ªtriest¹ the righteous, *and* seest the ²reins and the heart, ᵇlet me see thy vengeance on them: for unto thee have I ³opened my cause.

13 Sing unto the LORD, praise ye the LORD: for ªhe hath delivered the ¹soul of the poor from the hand of evildoers.

14 [a]Cursed *be* the day wherein I was born: let not the day wherein my mother bare me be blessed.

15 Cursed *be* the man who brought [1]tidings to my father, saying, A [2]man child is born unto thee; making him very glad.

16 And let that man be as the cities which the LORD [a]overthrew, and [1]repented not: and let him [b]hear the cry in the morning, and the shouting at noontide;

17 [a]Because he slew me not from the womb; or that my mother might have been my grave, and her womb *to be* always great *with me.*

18 [a]Wherefore came I forth out of the womb to [b]see [1]labour and sorrow, that my days should be consumed with shame?

## CHAPTER 21

THE word which came unto Jeremiah from the LORD, when [a]king Zedekiah sent unto him [b]Pashur the son of Melchiah, and [c]Zephaniah the son of Maaseiah the priest, saying,

2 [a]Enquire, I pray thee, of the LORD for us; for [1]Nebuchadrezzar king of Babylon maketh war against us; if so be that the LORD will deal with us according to all his wondrous works, that [2]he may go up from us.

3 Then said Jeremiah unto them, Thus shall ye say to Zedekiah:

4 Thus saith the LORD God of Israel; Behold, I will turn back the weapons of war that *are* in your hands, wherewith ye fight against the king of Babylon, and *against* [1]the Chaldeans, which besiege you [2]without the walls, and [a]I will assemble them into the midst of this city.

5 And I [a]myself will fight against you with an [b]outstretched hand and with a strong arm, even in anger, and in fury, and in great wrath.

6 And I will smite the inhabitants of this city, both man and beast: they shall die of a great pestilence.

7 And afterward, saith the LORD, [a]I will deliver Zedekiah king of Judah, and his servants, and the people, and such as are left in this city from the pestilence, from the sword, and from the famine, into the hand of Nebuchadrezzar king of Babylon, and into the hand of their enemies, and into the hand of those that seek their life: and he shall [1]smite them with the edge of the sword; [b]he shall not spare them, neither have pity, nor have mercy.

8 And unto this people thou shalt say, Thus saith the LORD; Behold, [a]I set before you the way of life, and the way of death.

9 He that [a]abideth[1] in this city shall die by the sword, and by the famine,

and by the pestilence: but he that goeth out, and [2]falleth to the Chaldeans that besiege you, he shall [b]live, and his life shall be unto him [3]for a prey.

10 For I have [a]set my face against this city for [1]evil, and not for good, saith the LORD: [b]it shall be given into the hand of the king of Babylon, and he shall [c]burn it with fire.

11 And touching the house of the king of Judah, *say,* Hear ye the word of the LORD;

12 O house of David, thus saith the LORD; [a]Execute[1] judgment [b]in the morning, and deliver *him that is* [2]spoiled out of the hand of the oppressor, lest my fury go out like fire, and burn that none can quench *it,* because of the evil of your doings.

13 Behold, [a]I *am* against thee, O [1]inhabitant of the valley, *and* rock of the plain, saith the LORD; which say, [b]Who shall come down against us? or who shall enter into our habitations?

14 But I will punish you according to the [a]fruit of your [1]doings, saith the LORD: and I will kindle a fire in the forest thereof, and [b]it shall devour all things round about it.

## CHAPTER 22

THUS saith the LORD; Go down to the house of the king of Judah, and speak there this word,

2 And say, [a]Hear the word of the LORD, O king of Judah, that sittest upon the throne of David, thou, and thy servants, and thy people that enter in by these gates:

3 Thus saith the LORD; [a]Execute[1] ye judgment and righteousness, and deliver the [2]spoiled out of the hand of the oppressor: and do no wrong, do no violence to the stranger, the [b]fatherless, nor the widow, neither shed innocent blood in this place.

4 For if ye do this thing indeed, [a]then shall there enter in by the gates of this house kings sitting upon the throne of David, riding in chariots and on horses, he, and his servants, and his people.

5 But if ye will not [1]hear these words, [a]I swear by myself, saith the LORD, that this house shall become a desolation.

6 For thus saith the LORD unto the king's house of Judah; Thou *art* [a]Gilead unto me, *and* the head of Lebanon: *yet* surely I will make thee a wilderness, *and* cities *which* are not inhabited.

7 And I will prepare destroyers against thee, every one with his weapons: and they shall cut down [a]thy choice cedars, [b]and cast *them* into the fire.

### Center column references

20:14 [a] Job 3:3
20:15 [1] *the news*
[2] *male*
20:16 [a] Gen. 19:25 [b] Jer. 18:22
[1] *relented*
20:17 [a] Job 3:10, 11
20:18 [a] Job 3:20
[b] Lam. 3:1 [1] *toil*
21:1 [a] 2 Kin. 24:17, 18 [b] Jer. 38:1
[c] 2 Kin. 25:18
21:2 [a] Jer. 37:3, 7
[1] Or *Nebuchadnezzar, Jer.* 27:6
[2] The king
21:4 [a] Is. 13:4
[1] The Babylonians
[2] *outside*
21:5 [a] Is. 63:10
[b] Ex. 6:6
21:7 [a] Jer. 37:17; 39:5; 52:9
[b] 2 Chr. 36:17
[1] *strike*
21:8 [a] Deut. 30:15, 19
21:9 [a] Jer. 38:2
[1] *remains*

[b] Jer. 39:18
[2] *surrenders* [3] *as a prize*
21:10 [a] Amos 9:4
[b] Jer. 38:3 [c] Jer. 34:2, 22; 37:10
[1] *disaster*
21:12 [a] Zech. 7:9 [b] Ps. 101:8
[1] *Dispense justice*
[2] *plundered*
21:13 [a] [Ezek. 13:8] [b] Jer. 49:4
[1] *dweller*
21:14 [a] Is. 3:10, 11; [b] 2 Chr. 36:19
[1] *deeds*
22:2 [a] Jer. 17:20
22:3 [a] Jer. 21:12 [b] Jer. 7:6
[1] *Dispense justice*
[2] *plundered*
22:4 [a] Jer. 17:25
22:5 [a] Heb. 6:13, 17 [1] *Obey*
22:6 [a] Song 4:1
22:7 [a] Is. 37:24
[b] Jer. 21:14

8 And many nations shall pass by this city, and they shall say every man to his neighbour, ªWherefore hath the LORD done thus unto this great city?

9 Then they shall answer, ªBecause they have forsaken the covenant of the LORD their God, and worshipped other gods, and served them.

10 Weep ye not for ªthe dead, neither bemoan him: *but* weep ¹sore for him ᵇthat goeth away: for he shall return no more, nor see his native country.

11 For thus saith the LORD touching ªShallum¹ the son of Josiah king of Judah, which reigned instead of Josiah his father, ᵇwhich went forth out of this place; He shall not return thither any more:

12 But he shall die in the place whither they have led him captive, and shall see this land no more.

13 ªWoe unto him that buildeth his house by unrighteousness, and his ¹chambers by ²wrong; ᵇ*that* useth his neighbour's service without wages, and giveth him not for his work;

14 That saith, I will build me a wide house and large ¹chambers, and cutteth him out windows; and ²*it is* cieled with cedar, and ³painted with vermilion.

15 Shalt thou reign, because thou ¹closest *thyself* in cedar? did not thy father eat and drink, and do ²judgment and justice, *and* then ª*it was* well with him?

16 He ¹judged the cause of the poor and needy; then *it was* well *with him: was* not this to know me? saith the LORD.

17 ªBut thine eyes and thine heart *are* not but for thy covetousness, and for to shed innocent blood, and for oppression, and for violence, to do *it.*

18 Therefore thus saith the LORD concerning Jehoiakim the son of Josiah king of Judah; ªThey shall not lament for him, *saying,* ᵇAh my brother! or, Ah sister! they shall not lament for him, *saying,* Ah lord! or, Ah his glory!

19 ªHe shall be buried with the burial of an ass, ¹drawn and cast forth beyond the gates of Jerusalem.

20 Go up to Lebanon, and cry; and lift up thy voice in Bashan, and cry from ¹the passages: for all thy lovers are destroyed.

21 I spake unto thee in thy prosperity; *but* thou saidst, I will not hear. ªThis *hath been* thy manner from thy youth, that thou obeyedst not my voice.

22 The wind shall eat up all ªthy ¹pastors, and thy lovers shall go into captivity: surely then shalt thou be ashamed and ²confounded for all thy wickedness.

23 O inhabitant of Lebanon, that makest thy nest in the cedars, how gracious shalt thou be when pangs come upon thee, ªthe pain as of a woman in ¹travail!

24 *As* I live, saith the LORD, ªthough ¹Coniah the son of Jehoiakim king of Judah ᵇwere the ²signet upon my right hand, yet would I pluck thee thence;

25 ªAnd I will give thee into the hand of them that seek thy life, and into the hand *of them* whose face thou fearest, even into the hand of Nebuchadrezzar king of Babylon, and into the hand of ¹the Chaldeans.

26 ªAnd I will cast thee out, and thy mother that bare thee, into another country, where ye were not born; and there shall ye die.

27 But to the land whereunto they desire to return, thither shall they not return.

28 *Is* this man Coniah a despised broken idol? *is he* ªa vessel wherein *is* no pleasure? wherefore are they cast out, he and his seed, and are cast into a land which they know not?

29 ªO earth, earth, earth, hear the word of the LORD.

30 Thus saith the LORD, Write ye this man ªchildless, a man *that* shall not prosper in his days: for ᵇno man of his seed shall prosper, sitting upon the throne of David, and ruling any more in Judah.

## CHAPTER 23

WOE ªbe unto the ¹pastors that destroy and scatter the sheep of my pasture! saith the LORD.

2 Therefore thus saith the LORD God of Israel against the ¹pastors that feed my people; Ye have scattered my flock, and driven them away, and have not ²visited them: ªbehold, I will ³visit upon you the evil of your doings, saith the LORD.

3 And ªI will gather the remnant of my flock out of all countries whither I have driven them, and will bring them again to their folds; and they shall be fruitful and increase.

4 And I will set up ªshepherds over them which shall feed them: and they shall fear no more, nor be dismayed, neither shall they be lacking, saith the LORD.

5 Behold, ªthe days come, saith the LORD, that I will raise unto David a righteous Branch, and a King shall reign and ¹prosper, ᵇand shall execute ²judgment and justice in the ³earth.

6 ªIn his days Judah shall be saved, and Israel ᵇshall dwell safely: and ᶜthis *is* his name whereby he shall be called, ¹THE LORD OUR RIGHTEOUSNESS.

### Center column notes

22:8 ª Deut. 29:24–26

22:9 ª 2 Chr. 34:25

22:10 ª 2 Kin.
22:20 ᵇ Jer. 14:17;
22:11 ¹ *bitterly*

22:11 ª 1 Chr. 3:15
ᵇ 2 Kin. 23:34 ¹ Or *Jehoahaz*

22:13 ª 2 Kin. 23:35 ᵇ James 5:4 ¹ *upper chambers* ² *injustice*

22:14 ¹ *upper chambers* ² *panel it with* ³ *paint it*

22:15 ª Ps. 128:2
¹ *enclose* ² *justice and* righteousness

22:16 ¹ Defended

22:17 ª Ezek. 19:6

22:18 ª Jer. 16:4, 6
ᵇ 1 Kin. 13:30

22:19 ª Jer. 36:30
¹ *dragged*

22:20 ¹ *Abarim*

22:21 ª Jer. 3:24, 25; 32:30

22:22 ª Jer. 23:1 ¹ *rulers,* lit. *shepherds* ² *humiliated*

22:23 ª Jer. 6:24
¹ *childbirth*

22:24 ª 2 Kin. 24:6, 8 ᵇ Hag. 2:23 ¹ Or *Jeconiah* or *Jehoiachin* ² *signet ring*

22:25 ª Jer. 34:20
¹ The Babylonians

22:26 ª 2 Kin. 24:15

22:28 ª Hos. 8:8

22:29 ª Deut. 32:1

22:30 ª Matt. 1:12
ᵇ Jer. 36:30

23:1 ª Jer. 10:21
¹ Lit. *shepherds*

23:2 ª Ex. 32:34
¹ Lit. *shepherds*
² *attended to*
³ *attend to you for*

23:3 ª Jer. 32:37

23:4 ª Jer. 3:15

23:5 ª Jer. 33:14
ᵇ Ps. 72:2 ¹ *act wisely* ² *justice and* righteousness ³ *land*

23:6 ª Zech. 14:11 ᵇ Jer. 32:37
ᶜ [1 Cor. 1:30]
¹ Heb. *YHWH Tsidkenu*

7 Therefore, behold, ªthe days come, saith the LORD, that they shall no more say, The LORD liveth, which brought up the children of Israel out of the land of Egypt;

8 But, The LORD liveth, which brought up and which led the seed of the house of Israel out of the north country, ªand from all countries whither I had driven them; and they shall dwell in their own ᵇland.

9 Mine heart within me is broken because of the prophets; ªall my bones shake; I am like a drunken man, and like a man whom wine hath overcome, because of the LORD, and because of ¹the words of his holiness.

10 For ªthe land is full of adulterers; for ᵇbecause of ¹swearing the land mourneth; ᶜthe pleasant places of the wilderness are dried up, and their ²course is evil, and their ³force is not right.

11 For ªboth prophet and priest are profane; yea, ᵇin my house have I found their wickedness, saith the LORD.

12 ªWherefore their way shall be unto them as slippery *ways* in the darkness: they shall be driven on, and fall therein: for I ᵇwill bring ¹evil upon them, *even* the year of their ²visitation, saith the LORD.

13 And I have seen ¹folly in the prophets of Samaria; ªthey prophesied ²in Baal, and ᵇcaused my people Israel to err.

14 I have seen also in the prophets of Jerusalem an horrible thing: ªthey commit adultery, and walk in lies: they ᵇstrengthen also the hands of evildoers, that none doth ¹return from his wickedness: they are all of them unto me as ᶜSodom, and the inhabitants thereof as Gomorrah.

15 Therefore thus saith the LORD of hosts concerning the prophets; Behold, I will feed them with ªwormwood, and make them drink the ¹water of gall: for from the prophets of Jerusalem is ²profaneness gone forth into all the land.

16 Thus saith the LORD of hosts, ¹Hearken not unto the words of the prophets that prophesy unto you: they make you ²vain: ªthey speak a vision of their own heart, *and* not out of the mouth of the LORD.

17 They say ¹still unto them that despise me, The LORD hath said, ªYe shall have peace; and they say unto every one that ᵇwalketh after the ²imagination of his own heart, ᶜNo evil shall come upon you.

18 For ªwho hath stood in the counsel of the LORD, and hath perceived and heard his word? who hath marked his word, and heard *it*?

19 Behold, a ªwhirlwind of the LORD

is gone forth in fury, even a ¹grievous whirlwind: it shall fall grievously upon the head of the wicked.

20 The ªanger of the LORD shall not ¹return, until he have executed, and till he have performed the thoughts of his heart: ᵇin the latter days ye shall ²consider it perfectly.

21 ªI have not sent these prophets, yet they ran: I have not spoken to them, yet they prophesied.

22 But if they had stood in my counsel, and had caused my people to hear my words, then they should have ªturned them from their evil way, and from the evil of their doings.

23 *Am* I a God at hand, saith the LORD, and not a God afar off?

24 Can any ªhide himself in secret places that I shall not see him? saith the LORD. ᵇDo not I fill heaven and earth? saith the LORD.

25 I have heard what the prophets said, that prophesy lies in my name, saying, I have dreamed, I have dreamed.

26 How long shall *this* be in the heart of the prophets that prophesy lies? yea, *they are* prophets of the deceit of their own heart;

27 Which think to cause my people to forget my name by their dreams which they tell every man to his neighbour, ªas their fathers have forgotten my name for Baal.

28 The prophet that hath a dream, let him tell a dream; and he that hath my word, let him speak my word faithfully. What *is* the chaff to the wheat? saith the LORD.

29 *Is* not my word like as a ªfire? saith the LORD; and like a hammer *that* breaketh the rock in pieces?

30 Therefore, behold, ªI *am* against the prophets, saith the LORD, that steal my words every one from his neighbour.

31 Behold, I *am* ªagainst the prophets, saith the LORD, that use their tongues, and say, He saith.

32 Behold, I *am* against them that prophesy false dreams, saith the LORD, and do tell them, and cause my people to err by their ªlies, and by ᵇtheir ¹lightness; yet I sent them not, nor commanded them: therefore they shall not ᶜprofit this people at all, saith the LORD.

33 And when this people, or the prophet, or a priest, shall ask thee, saying, What *is* ªthe ¹burden of the LORD? thou shalt then say unto them, What ¹burden? I will even forsake you, saith the LORD.

34 And *as for* the prophet, and the priest, and the people, that shall say, The ¹burden of the LORD, I will even ²punish that man and his house.

## Cross References

23:7 ª Jer. 16:14
23:8 ª Is. 43:5, 6　ᵇ Gen. 12:7
23:9 ª Hab. 3:16　¹ *his holy words*
23:10 ª Jer. 9:2　ᵇ Hos. 4:2　ᶜ Jer. 9:10　¹ *a curse*　² *course of life is*　³ *might*
23:11 ª Zeph. 3:4　ᵇ Jer. 7:30; 32:34
23:12 ª [Prov. 4:19]　ᵇ Jer. 11:23　¹ *disaster*　² *punishment*
23:13 ª Jer. 2:8　ᵇ Is. 9:16　¹ Lit. *unsavouriness*　² *by*
23:14 ª Jer. 29:23　ᵇ Ezek. 13:22, 23　ᶜ Is. 1:9, 10　¹ *turn back from*
23:15 ª Jer. 9:15　¹ *bitter or poisonous water*　² *ungodliness*
23:16 ª Jer. 14:14; Ezek. 13:3, 6　¹ *Do not listen*　² *worthless*
23:17 ª Jer. 8:11; Ezek. 13:10; Zech. 10:2　ᵇ Deut. 29:19; Jer. 3:17　ᶜ Jer. 5:12; Amos 9:10; Mic. 3:11　¹ *continually*　² *stubbornness*
23:18 ª Job 15:8, 9; [Jer. 23:22]; 1 Cor. 2:16]
23:19 ª Jer. 25:32; 30:23; Amos 1:14
¹ *violent*
23:20 ª 2 Kin. 23:26, 27; Jer. 30:24　ᵇ Gen. 49:1　¹ *turn back*　² *understand*
23:21 ª Jer. 14:14; 23:32; 27:15
23:22 ª Jer. 25:5
23:24 ª [Ps. 139:7]; Amos 9:2, 3　ᵇ [i Kin. 8:27]; Ps. 139:7
23:27 ª Judg. 3:7
23:29 ª Jer. 5:14
23:30 ª Deut. 18:20; Ps. 34:16; Jer. 14:14, 15; Ezek. 13:8, 9
23:31 ª Ezek. 13:9
23:32 ª Jer. 20:6; 27:10; Lam. 2:14; 3:37　ᵇ Zeph. 3:4　ᶜ Jer. 7:8; Lam. 2:14　¹ *recklessness*
23:33 ª Is. 13:1; Nah. 1:1; Hab. 1:1; Zech. 9:1; Mal. 1:1　¹ *oracle or prophecy*
23:34 ¹ *oracle*　² *attend to*

35 Thus shall ye say every one to his neighbour, and every one to his brother, What hath the LORD answered? and, What hath the LORD spoken?

36 And the [1]burden of the LORD shall ye mention no more: for every man's word shall be his [1]burden; for ye have [a]perverted the words of the living God, of the LORD of hosts our God.

37 Thus shalt thou say to the prophet, What hath the LORD answered thee? and, What hath the LORD spoken?

38 But since ye say, The [1]burden of the LORD; therefore thus saith the LORD; Because ye say this word, The [1]burden of the LORD, and I have sent unto you, saying, Ye shall not say, The [1]burden of the LORD;

39 Therefore, behold, I, even I, [a]will utterly forget you, and I will forsake you, and the city that I gave you and your fathers, *and cast you* out of my presence:

40 And I will bring [a]an everlasting reproach upon you, and a perpetual [b]shame, which shall not be forgotten.

## CHAPTER 24

THE [a]LORD shewed me, and, behold, two baskets of figs *were* set before the temple of the LORD, after that Nebuchadrezzar [b]king of Babylon had carried away captive [c]Jeconiah[1] the son of Jehoiakim king of Judah, and the princes of Judah, with the [2]carpenters and smiths, from Jerusalem, and had brought them to Babylon.

2 One basket *had* very good figs, *even* like the figs *that are* first ripe: and the other basket *had* very [1]naughty figs, which could not be eaten, they were so [a]bad.

3 Then said the LORD unto me, What seest thou, Jeremiah? And I said, Figs; the good figs, very good; and the [1]evil, very [1]evil, that cannot be eaten, they are so [1]evil.

4 Again the word of the LORD came unto me, saying,

5 Thus saith the LORD, the God of Israel; Like these good figs, so will I [1]acknowledge them that are carried away captive of Judah, whom I have sent out of this place into the land of the Chaldeans for *their* good.

6 For I will set mine eyes upon them for good, and [a]I will bring them again to this land: and [b]I will build them, and not pull *them* down; and I will plant them, and not pluck *them* up.

7 And I will give them [a]an heart to know me, that I *am* the LORD: and they shall be [b]my people, and I will be their God: for they shall return unto me [c]with their whole heart.

8 And as the [1]evil [a]figs, which cannot be eaten, they are so [1]evil; surely thus saith the LORD, So will I give Zedekiah the king of Judah, and his princes, and the [b]residue of Jerusalem, that remain in this land, and [c]them that dwell in the land of Egypt:

9 And I will deliver them [1]to [a]be removed into all the kingdoms of the earth for *their* [2]hurt, [b]*to be* a reproach and a [3]proverb, a taunt and a curse, in all places whither I shall drive them.

10 And I will send the sword, the famine, and the pestilence, among them, till they be [1]consumed from off the land that I gave unto them and to their fathers.

## CHAPTER 25

THE word that came to Jeremiah concerning all the people of Judah [a]in the fourth year of [b]Jehoiakim the son of Josiah king of Judah, that *was* the first year of Nebuchadrezzar king of Babylon;

2 The which Jeremiah the prophet spake unto all the people of Judah, and to all the inhabitants of Jerusalem, saying,

3 [a]From the thirteenth year of Josiah the son of Amon king of Judah, even unto this day, that *is* the three and twentieth year, the word of the LORD hath come unto me, and I have spoken unto you, rising early and speaking; [b]but ye have not [1]hearkened.

4 And the LORD hath sent unto you all his servants the prophets, [a]rising early and sending *them;* but ye have not [1]hearkened, nor inclined your ear to hear.

5 They said, [a]Turn[1] ye again now every one from his evil way, and from the evil of your doings, and dwell in the land that the LORD hath given unto you and to your fathers for ever and ever:

6 And go not after other gods to serve them, and to worship them, and provoke me not to anger with the works of your hands; and I will do you no [1]hurt.

7 Yet ye have not [1]hearkened unto me, saith the LORD; that ye might [a]provoke me to anger with the works of your hands to your own [2]hurt.

8 Therefore thus saith the LORD of hosts; Because ye have not heard my words,

9 Behold, I will send and take [a]all the families of the north, saith the LORD, and Nebuchadrezzar the king of Babylon, [b]my servant, and will bring them against this land, and against the inhabitants thereof, and against all these nations round about, and will utterly destroy them, and [c]make them an astonishment, and an hissing, and perpetual desolations.

### Center column references

23:36 [a] Deut. 4:2
[1] *oracle*
23:38 [1] *oracle* or *prophecy*
23:39 [a] Hos. 4:6
23:40 [a] Jer. 20:11; Ezek. 5:14, 15
[b] Mic. 3:5–7
24:1 [a] Amos 7:1, 4; 8:1 [b] 2 Kin. 24:12–16; 2 Chr. 36:10
[c] Jer. 22:24–28; 29:2 [1] Or *Coniah* or *Jehoiachin*
[2] *craftsmen*
24:2 [a] Is. 5:4, 7; Jer. 29:17 [1] *bad*
24:3 [1] *bad*
24:5 [1] *regard*
24:6 [a] Jer. 12:15; 29:10 [b] Jer. 32:41; 33:7; 42:10
24:7 [a] [Deut. 30:6] [b] Jer. 30:22; 31:33; 32:38
[c] Jer. 29:13

24:8 [a] Jer. 29:17
[b] Jer. 39:9 [c] Jer. 44:1, 26–30 [1] *bad*
24:9 [a] Deut. 28:25, 37 [b] Ps. 44:13, 14 [1] *to trouble* [2] *harm*
[3] *byword*
24:10 [1] *destroyed*
25:1 [a] Jer. 36:1
[b] 2 Kin. 24:1, 2
25:3 [a] Jer. 1:2
[b] Jer. 7:13; 11:7, 8, 10 [1] *listened*
25:4 [a] Jer. 7:13; 25 [1] *listened*
25:5 [a] Jer. 18:11 [1] *Repent now*
25:6 [1] *harm*
25:7 [a] Deut. 32:21 [1] *listened* [2] *harm*
25:9 [a] Jer. 1:15 [b] Is. 45:1 [c] Jer. 18:16 [1]

10 Moreover I will ¹take from them the ªvoice of mirth, and the voice of gladness, the voice of the bridegroom, and the voice of the bride, ᵇthe sound of the millstones, and the light of the ²candle.

11 And this whole land shall be a desolation, *and* an astonishment; and these nations shall serve the king of Babylon seventy ªyears.

12 And it shall come to pass, ªwhen¹ seventy years are accomplished, *that* I will punish the king of Babylon, and that nation, saith the LORD, for their iniquity, and the land of the Chaldeans, ᵇand will make it perpetual desolations.

13 And I will bring upon that land all my words which I have pronounced against it, *even* all that is written in this book, which Jeremiah hath prophesied against all the nations.

14 ªFor many nations ᵇand great kings shall ᶜserve¹ themselves of them also: ᵈand I will recompense them according to their deeds, and according to the works of their own hands.

15 For thus saith the LORD God of Israel unto me; Take the ªwine cup of this ¹fury at my hand, and cause all the nations, to whom I send thee, to drink it.

16 And ªthey shall drink, and ¹be moved, and ²be mad, because of the sword that I will send among them.

17 Then took I the cup at the LORD's hand, and made all the nations to drink, unto whom the LORD had sent me:

18 *To wit,* Jerusalem, and the cities of Judah, and the kings thereof, and the princes thereof, to make them ªa desolation, an astonishment, an hissing, and ᵇa curse; as *it is* this day;

19 Pharaoh king of Egypt, and his servants, and his princes, and all his people;

20 And all the ¹mingled people, and all the kings of ªthe land of Uz, and all the kings of the land of the ᵇPhilistines, and Ashkelon, and ²Azzah, and Ekron, and ᶜthe remnant of Ashdod,

21 ªEdom, and Moab, and the children of Ammon,

22 And all the kings of ªTyrus,¹ and all the kings of ²Zidon, and the kings of the ³isles which *are* beyond the ᵇsea,

23 ªDedan, and Tema, and Buz, and all *that are* in the utmost corners,

24 And all the kings of Arabia, and all the kings of the ªmingled people that dwell in the desert,

25 And all the kings of Zimri, and all the kings of ªElam, and all the kings of the ᵇMedes,

26 ªAnd all the kings of the north, far and near, one with another, and all the kingdoms of the world, which *are* upon the face of the earth: and

the king of ¹Sheshach shall drink after them.

27 Therefore thou shalt say unto them, Thus saith the LORD of hosts, the God of Israel; ªDrink ye, and ᵇbe drunken, and ¹spue, and fall, and rise no more, because of the sword which I will send among you.

28 And it shall be, if they refuse to take the cup at thine hand to drink, then shalt thou say unto them, Thus saith the LORD of hosts; Ye shall certainly drink.

29 For, lo, ªI begin to bring ¹evil on the city ᵇwhich is called by my name, and should ye be utterly unpunished? Ye shall not be unpunished: for ᶜI will call for a sword upon all the inhabitants of the earth, saith the LORD of hosts.

30 Therefore prophesy thou against them all these words, and say unto them, The LORD shall ªroar from on high, and utter his voice from ᵇhis holy habitation; he shall mightily roar upon ᶜhis ¹habitation; he shall give ᵈa shout, as they that tread *the grapes,* against all the inhabitants of the earth.

31 A noise shall come *even* to the ends of the earth; for the LORD hath ªa controversy with the nations, ᵇhe will ¹plead with all flesh; he will give them *that are* wicked to the sword, saith the LORD.

32 Thus saith the LORD of hosts, Behold, ¹evil shall go forth from nation to nation, and ªa great whirlwind shall be raised up from the ²coasts of the earth.

33 ªAnd the slain of the LORD shall be at that day from *one* end of the earth even unto the *other* end of the earth: they shall not be ᵇlamented, ᶜneither gathered, nor buried; they shall be ¹dung upon the ground.

34 ªHowl,¹ ye shepherds, and cry; and wallow yourselves *in the ashes,* ye ²principal of the flock: for the days of your slaughter and of your dispersions are accomplished; and ye shall fall like a ³pleasant vessel.

35 And the shepherds shall have no ¹way to flee, nor the principal of the flock to escape.

36 A voice of the cry of the shepherds, and an ¹howling of the ²principal of the flock, *shall be heard:* for the LORD hath ³spoiled their pasture.

37 And the ¹peaceable habitations are cut down because of the fierce anger of the LORD.

38 He hath ¹forsaken his covert, as the lion: for their land is desolate because of the fierceness of the oppressor, and because of his fierce anger.

## CHAPTER 26

IN the beginning of the reign of Jehoiakim the son of Josiah king

### Center column references

25:10 ª Rev. 18:23
ᵇ Eccl. 12:4 ¹ Lit. *cause to perish*
² *lamp*

25:11 ª Jer. 29:10

25:12 ª Ezra 1:1
ᵇ Is. 13:20 ¹ Beginning circa 605 B.C. (2 Kin. 24:1) and ending circa 536 B.C. (Ezra 1:1)

25:14 ª Jer. 50:9; 51:27, 28 ᵇ Jer. 51:27 ᶜ Jer. 27:7 ᵈ Jer. 50:29; 51:6, 24 ¹ *be served by them*

25:15 ª Rev. 14:10 ¹ *wrath*

25:16 ª Nah. 3:11 ¹ *stagger* ² *go*

25:18 ª Jer. 25:9, 11 ᵇ Jer. 24:9

25:20 ª Job 1:1 ᵇ Jer. 47:1–7 ᶜ Is. 20:1 ¹ *mixed multitude* ² Or *Gaza*

25:21 ª Jer. 49:7

25:22 ª Jer. 47:4 ᵇ Jer. 49:23 ¹ Or *Tyre* ² Or *Sidon* ³ *coastlands*

25:23 ª Jer. 49:7, 8

25:24 ª Ezek. 30:5

25:25 ª Jer. 49:34 ᵇ Jer. 51:11, 28

25:26 ª Jer. 50:9

¹ A code word for *Babylon,* Jer. 51:41

25:27 ª Hab. 2:16 ᵇ Is. 63:6 ¹ *vomit*

25:29 ª Ezek. 9:6 ᵇ Dan. 9:18 ᶜ Ezek. 38:21 ¹ *calamity*

25:30 ª Amos 1:2 ᵇ Ps. 11:4 ᶜ 1 Kin. 9:3 ᵈ Is. 16:9 ¹ *fold*

25:31 ª Mic. 6:2 ᵇ Is. 66:16 ¹ *plead his case*

25:32 ª Jer. 23:19; 30:23 ¹ *disaster* ² *farthest parts*

25:33 ª Is. 34:2, 3; 66:16 ᵇ Jer. 16:4, 6 ᶜ Ps. 79:3 ¹ *refuse*

25:34 ª Jer. 4:8; 6:26 ¹ *Wail* ² *leaders* ³ *precious*

25:35 ¹ Or *refuge*

25:36 ¹ *wailing in distress* ² *leaders* ³ *plundered*

25:37 ¹ *peaceful*

25:38 ¹ *left his lair*

of Judah came this word from the LORD, saying,

2 Thus saith the LORD; Stand in ᵃthe court of ¹the LORD's house, and speak unto all the cities of Judah, which come to worship in the LORD's house, ᵇall the words that I command thee to speak unto them; ᶜdiminish not a word:

3 ᵃIf so be they will ¹hearken, and turn every man from his evil way, that I may ᵇrepent² me of the evil, which I purpose to do unto them because of the evil of their doings.

4 And thou shalt say unto them, Thus saith the LORD; ᵃIf ye will not ¹hearken to me, to walk in my law, which I have set before you,

5 To ¹hearken to the words of my servants the prophets, ᵃwhom I sent unto you, both rising up early, and sending *them*, but ye have not hearkened;

6 Then will I make this house like ᵃShiloh, and will make this city ᵇa curse to all the nations of the earth.

7 So the priests and the prophets and all the people heard Jeremiah speaking these words in the house of the LORD.

8 Now it came to pass, when Jeremiah had made an end of speaking all that the LORD had commanded *him* to speak unto all the people, that the priests and the prophets and all the people ¹took him, saying, Thou shalt surely die.

9 Why hast thou prophesied in the name of the LORD, saying, This house shall be like Shiloh, and this city shall be ᵃdesolate without an inhabitant? And all the people were gathered against Jeremiah in ¹the house of the LORD.

10 When the princes of Judah heard these things, then they came up from the king's house unto the house of the LORD, and sat down in the ¹entry of the new gate of the LORD's *house*.

11 Then spake the priests and the prophets unto the princes and to all the people, saying, ¹This man *is* worthy to ᵃdie; for he hath prophesied against this city, as ye have heard with your ears.

12 Then spake Jeremiah unto all the princes and to all the people, saying, The LORD sent me to prophesy against this house and against this city all the words that ye have heard.

13 Therefore now ᵃamend your ways and your doings, and obey the voice of the LORD your God; and the LORD will ¹repent him of the evil that he hath pronounced against you.

14 As for me, behold, ᵃI *am* in your hand: do with me as seemeth good and ¹meet unto you.

15 But know ye for certain, that if ye

put me to death, ye shall surely bring innocent blood upon yourselves, and upon this city, and upon the inhabitants thereof: for of a truth the LORD hath sent me unto you to speak all these words in your ¹ears.

16 Then said the princes and all the people unto the priests and to the prophets; This man *is* not worthy to die: for he hath spoken to us in the name of the LORD our God.

17 ᵃThen rose up certain of the elders of the land, and spake to all the assembly of the people, saying,

18 ᵃMicah the Morasthite prophesied in the days of Hezekiah king of Judah, and spake to all the people of Judah, saying, Thus saith the LORD of hosts; ᵇZion shall be plowed *like* a field, and Jerusalem shall become ᶜheaps,¹ and the mountain of ²the house as the ³high places of a forest.

19 Did Hezekiah king of Judah and all Judah put him at all to death? ᵃdid he not fear the LORD, and ᵇbesought¹ the LORD, and the LORD ᶜrepented² him of the evil which he had pronounced against them? ᵈThus³ might we procure great evil against our souls.

20 And there was also a man that prophesied in the name of the LORD, Urijah the son of Shemaiah of Kirjathjearim, who prophesied against this city and against this land according to all the words of Jeremiah:

21 And when Jehoiakim the king, with all his mighty men, and all the princes, heard his words, the king sought to put him to death: but when Urijah heard it, he was afraid, and fled, and went into Egypt;

22 And Jehoiakim the king sent men into Egypt, *namely,* Elnathan the son of Achbor, and *certain* men with him into Egypt.

23 And they fetched forth Urijah out of Egypt, and brought him unto Jehoiakim the king; who slew him with the sword, and cast his dead body into the graves of the ¹common people.

24 Nevertheless ᵃthe hand of Ahikam the son of Shaphan was with Jeremiah, that they should not give him into the hand of the people to put him to death.

## CHAPTER 27

IN the beginning of the reign of ¹Jehoiakim the son of Josiah ᵃking of Judah came this word unto Jeremiah from the LORD, saying,

2 Thus saith the LORD to me; Make thee bonds and yokes, ᵃand put them upon thy neck,

3 And send them to the king of Edom, and to the king of Moab, and to the king of the Ammonites, and to the king of ¹Tyrus, and to the king of

### Cross references (center column)

26:2 ᵃ Jer. 19:14
ᵇ Matt. 28:20
ᶜ Acts 20:27 ¹ The temple
26:3 ᵃ Jer. 36:3–7
ᵇ Jer. 18:8 ¹ *listen*
² *relent of the calamity*
26:4 ᵃ Lev. 26:14, 15 ¹ *listen*
26:5 ᵃ Jer. 25:4; 29:19 ¹ *listen*
26:6 ᵃ 1 Sam. 4:10, 11 ᵇ Is. 65:15
26:8 ¹ *seized*
26:9 ᵃ Jer. 9:11 ¹ The temple
26:10 ¹ *entrance*
26:11 ᵃ Jer. 38:4 ¹ Lit. *A judgment of death to this man*
26:13 ᵃ Jer. 7:3; [Joel 2:13]; Jon. 3:8 ¹ *relent of the doom*
26:14 ᵃ Jer. 38:5 ¹ *right*

26:15 ¹ *hearing*
26:17 ᵃ Acts 5:34
26:18 ᵃ Mic. 1:1 ᵇ Mic. 3:12; ᶜ Neh. 4:2; Ps. 79:1; Jer. 9:11 ¹ *ruinous heaps* ² The temple ³ *bare heights*
26:19 ᵃ 2 Chr. 32:26; Is. 37:1, 4, 15–20 ᵇ 2 Kin. 20:1–19 ᶜ Ex. 32:14; 2 Sam. 24:16; Jer. 18:8 ᵈ [Acts 5:39] ¹ *seek the LORD's favour* ² *relented of the doom* ³ *But we are doing great evil against ourselves*
26:23 ¹ Lit. *the sons of the people*
26:24 ᵃ 2 Kin. 22:12–14; Jer. 39:14; 40:5–7
27:1 ᵃ Jer. 27:3, 12, 20; 28:1 ¹ A few mss. *Zedekiah*, Jer. 27:3, 12; 28:1
27:2 ᵃ Jer. 28:10, 12; Ezek. 4:1; 12:3; 24:3
27:3 ¹ Or *Tyre*

²Zidon, by the hand of the messengers which come to Jerusalem unto Zedekiah king of Judah;

4 And command them to ¹say unto their masters, Thus saith the LORD of hosts, the God of Israel; Thus shall ye say unto your masters;

5 ªI have made the earth, the man and the beast that *are* upon the ground, by my great power and by my outstretched arm, and ᵇhave given it unto whom it seemed ¹meet unto me.

6 ªAnd now have I given all these lands into the hand of Nebuchadnezzar the king of Babylon, ᵇmy servant; and ᶜthe beasts of the field have I given him also to serve him.

7 ªAnd all nations shall serve him, and his son, and his son's son, ᵇuntil the very time of his land come: ᶜand then many nations and great kings shall ¹serve themselves of him.

8 And it shall come to pass, *that* the nation and kingdom which will not serve the same Nebuchadnezzar the king of Babylon, and that will not put their neck under the yoke of the king of Babylon, that nation will I punish, saith the LORD, with the sword, and with the famine, and with the pestilence, until I have consumed them by his hand.

9 Therefore hearken not ye to your prophets, nor to your diviners, nor to your ¹dreamers, nor to your ²enchanters, nor to your sorcerers, which speak unto you, saying, Ye shall not serve the king of Babylon:

10 For they prophesy a ªlie unto you, to remove you far from your land; and that I should drive you out, and ye should perish.

11 But the nations that bring their neck under the yoke of the king of Babylon, and serve him, those will I let remain still in their own land, saith the LORD; and they shall till it, and dwell therein.

12 I spake also to ªZedekiah king of Judah according to all these words, saying, Bring your necks under the yoke of the king of Babylon, and serve him and his people, and live.

13 ªWhy will ye die, thou and thy people, by the sword, by the famine, and by the pestilence, as the LORD hath spoken against the nation that will not serve the king of Babylon?

14 Therefore ªhearken¹ not unto the words of the prophets that speak unto you, saying, Ye shall not serve the king of Babylon: for they prophesy ᵇa lie unto you.

15 For I have ªnot sent them, saith the LORD, yet they prophesy a lie in my name; that I might drive you out, and that ye might perish, ye, and the prophets that prophesy unto you.

16 Also I spake to the priests and to all this people, saying, Thus saith the LORD; ¹Hearken not to the words of your prophets that prophesy unto you, saying, Behold, ªthe vessels of the LORD's house shall now shortly be brought again from Babylon: for they prophesy a lie unto you.

17 ¹Hearken not unto them; serve the king of Babylon, and live: wherefore should this city be laid waste?

18 But if they *be* prophets, and if the word of the LORD be with them, let them now make intercession to the LORD of hosts, that the vessels which are left in the house of the LORD, and *in* the house of the king of Judah, and at Jerusalem, go not to Babylon.

19 For thus saith the LORD of hosts ªconcerning the pillars, and concerning the sea, and concerning the ¹bases, and concerning the ²residue of the vessels that remain in this city,

20 Which Nebuchadnezzar king of Babylon took not, when he carried away ªcaptive Jeconiah the son of Jehoiakim king of Judah from Jerusalem to Babylon, and all the nobles of Judah and Jerusalem;

21 Yea, thus saith the LORD of hosts, the God of Israel, concerning the ªvessels that remain *in* the house of the LORD, and *in* the house of the king of Judah and of Jerusalem;

22 They shall be ªcarried to Babylon, and there shall they be until the day that I ᵇvisit¹ them, saith the LORD; then ᶜwill I bring them up, and restore them to this place.

## CHAPTER 28

AND ªit came to pass the same year, in the beginning of the reign of Zedekiah king of Judah, in the ᵇfourth year, *and* in the fifth month, *that* Hananiah the son of ᶜAzur the prophet, which *was* of Gibeon, spake unto me in the house of the LORD, in the presence of the priests and of all the people, saying,

2 Thus speaketh the LORD of hosts, the God of Israel, saying, I have broken ªthe yoke of the king of Babylon.

3 ªWithin two full years will I bring again into this place all the vessels of the LORD's house, that Nebuchadnezzar king of Babylon ᵇtook away from this place, and carried them to Babylon:

4 And I will bring again to this place ¹Jeconiah the son of Jehoiakim king of Judah, with all the ²captives of Judah, that went into Babylon, saith the LORD: for I will break the yoke of the king of Babylon.

5 Then the prophet Jeremiah said unto the prophet Hananiah in the presence of the priests, and in the

### Center column cross-references

27:3 ² Or *Sidon*
27:4 ¹ Or go to *their masters, saying*
27:5 ª Ps. 115:15; 146:6; Is. 45:12
ᵇ Deut. 9:29; Ps. 115:16; Jer. 32:17; Dan. 4:17, 25, 32
¹ *proper to*
27:6 ª Jer. 28:14
ᵇ Jer. 25:9; 43:10; Ezek. 29:18, 20
ᶜ Jer. 28:14; Dan. 2:38
27:7 ª 2 Chr. 36:20
ᵇ Jer. 25:12; 50:27; [Dan. 5:26]; Zech. 2:8, 9 ᶜ Jer. 25:14
¹ *make him serve them*
27:9 ¹ Lit. *dreams*
² *soothsayers*
27:10 ª Jer. 23:16, 32; 28:15
27:12 ª Jer. 28:1; 38:17
27:13 ª [Prov. 8:36]; Jer. 27:8; 38:23; [Ezek. 18:31]
27:14 ª Jer. 23:16
ᵇ Jer. 14:14; 23:21; 29:8, 9; Ezek. 13:22 ¹ *do not listen*
27:15 ª Jer. 23:21; 29:9

27:16 ª 2 Kin. 24:13; 2 Chr. 36:7, 10; Jer. 28:3; Dan. 1:2 ¹ *Do not listen*
27:17 ¹ *Do not listen*
27:19 ª 1 Kin. 7:15; 2 Kin. 25:13–17; Jer. 52:17, 20, 21 ¹ *carts* ² *remainder*
27:20 ª 2 Kin. 24:14, 15; 2 Chr. 36:10, 18; Jer. 24:1
27:21 ª Jer. 20:5
27:22 ª 2 Kin. 25:13; 2 Chr. 36:18
ᵇ 2 Chr. 36:21; Jer. 29:10; 32:5
ᶜ Ezra 1:7; 7:19
¹ *attend to*
28:1 ª Jer. 27:1
ᵇ Jer. 51:59
ᶜ Ezek. 11:1
28:2 ª Jer. 27:12
28:3 ª Jer. 27:16
ᵇ 2 Kin. 24:13; Dan. 1:2
28:4 ¹ Or *Coniah* or *Jehoiachin*
² *exiles*

presence of all the people that stood in the house of the LORD,

6 Even the prophet Jeremiah said, [a]Amen: the LORD do so: the LORD perform thy words which thou hast prophesied, to bring again the vessels of the LORD's house, and all that is carried away captive, from Babylon into this place.

7 Nevertheless hear thou now this word that I speak in thine ears, and in the ears of all the people;

8 The prophets that have been before me and before thee of old prophesied both against many countries, and against great kingdoms, of war, and of evil, and of pestilence.

9 [a]The prophet which prophesieth of [b]peace, when the word of the prophet shall come to pass, *then* shall the prophet be known, that the LORD hath truly sent him.

10 Then Hananiah the prophet took the [a]yoke from off the prophet Jeremiah's neck, and brake it.

11 And Hananiah spake in the presence of all the people, saying, Thus saith the LORD; Even so will I break the yoke of Nebuchadnezzar king of Babylon [a]from the neck of all nations within the space of two full years. And the prophet Jeremiah went his way.

12 Then the word of the LORD came unto Jeremiah *the prophet,* after that Hananiah the prophet had broken the yoke from off the neck of the prophet Jeremiah, saying,

13 Go and tell Hananiah, saying, Thus saith the LORD; Thou hast broken the yokes of wood; but thou [1]shalt make for them yokes of iron.

14 For thus saith the LORD of hosts, the God of Israel; [a]I have put a yoke of iron upon the neck of all these nations, that they may serve Nebuchadnezzar king of Babylon; and they shall serve him: and [b]I have given him the beasts of the field also.

15 Then said the prophet Jeremiah unto Hananiah the prophet, Hear now, Hananiah; The LORD hath not sent thee; but [a]thou makest this people to trust in a [b]lie.

16 Therefore thus saith the LORD; Behold, I will cast thee from off the face of the earth: this year thou shalt [a]die, because thou hast taught [b]rebellion against the LORD.

17 So Hananiah the prophet died the same year in the seventh month.

## CHAPTER 29

Now these *are* the words of the letter that Jeremiah the prophet sent from Jerusalem unto the [1]residue of the elders which were [a]carried away captives, and to the priests, and to the prophets, and to all the people whom Nebuchadnezzar had

carried away captive from Jerusalem to Babylon;

2 (After that [a]Jeconiah[1] the king, and the [b]queen,[2] and the [3]eunuchs, the princes of Judah and Jerusalem, and the carpenters, and the smiths, were departed from Jerusalem;)

3 By the hand of Elasah the son of [a]Shaphan, and Gemariah the son of Hilkiah, (whom Zedekiah king of Judah sent unto Babylon to Nebuchadnezzar king of Babylon) saying,

4 Thus saith the LORD of hosts, the God of Israel, unto all that are carried away captives, whom I have caused to be carried away from Jerusalem unto Babylon;

5 Build ye houses, and dwell *in* them; and plant gardens, and eat the fruit of them;

6 Take ye wives, and beget sons and daughters; and take wives for your sons, and give your daughters to husbands, that they may bear sons and daughters; that ye may be increased there, and not diminished.

7 And seek the peace of the city whither I have caused you to be carried away captives, [a]and pray unto the LORD for it: for in the peace thereof shall ye have peace.

8 For thus saith the LORD of hosts, the God of Israel; Let not your prophets and your diviners, that *be* in the midst of you, [a]deceive you, neither hearken to your dreams which ye cause to be dreamed.

9 For they prophesy [a]falsely unto you in my name: I have not sent them, saith the LORD.

10 For thus saith the LORD, That after [a]seventy years be accomplished at Babylon I will visit you, and perform my good word toward you, in causing you to [b]return to this place.

11 For I know the thoughts that I think toward you, saith the LORD, thoughts of peace, and not of [1]evil, to give you [2]an expected end.

12 Then shall ye [a]call upon me, and ye shall go and pray unto me, and I will [b]hearken[1] unto you.

13 And [a]ye shall seek me, and find *me,* when ye shall search for me [b]with all your heart.

14 And [a]I will be found of you, saith the LORD: and I will [1]turn away your captivity, and [b]I will gather you from all the nations, and from all the places whither I have driven you, saith the LORD; and I will bring you again into the place whence I caused you to be carried away captive.

15 Because ye have said, The LORD hath [1]raised us up prophets in Babylon;

16 [a]*Know* that thus saith the LORD of the king that sitteth upon the throne of David, and of all the people

### Cross References

28:6 [a]1 Kin. 1:36; Ps. 41:13; Jer. 11:5
28:9 [a]Deut. 18:22 [b]Jer. 23:17; Ezek. 13:10, 16
28:10 [a]Jer. 27:2
28:11 [a]Jer. 27:7
28:13 [1]*hast made in their place*
28:14 [a]Deut. 28:48; Jer. 27:7, 8 [b]Jer. 27:6
28:15 [a]Jer. 20:6; 29:31; Lam. 2:14; Ezek. 13:22; Zech. 13:3 [b]Jer. 27:10; 29:9
28:16 [a]Jer. 20:6 [b]Deut. 13:5; Jer. 29:32
29:1 [a]Jer. 27:20 [1]*remainder*

29:2 [a]2 Kin. 24:12–16; 2 Chr. 36:9, 10; Jer. 22:24–28 [b]2 Kin. 24:12, 15; Jer. 13:18 [1]Or *Jehoiachin* [2]*queen mother* [3]Or *officers*
29:3 [a]2 Chr. 34:8
29:7 [a]Ezra 6:10; Neh. 1:4–11; Dan. 9:16; 1 Tim. 2:2
29:8 [a]Jer. 14:14; 23:21; 27:14, 15; Eph. 5:6
29:9 [a]Jer. 28:15; 37:19
29:10 [a]2 Chr. 36:21–23; Ezra 1:1–4; Jer. 25:12; 27:22; Dan. 9:2; Zech. 7:5 [b][Jer. 24:6, 7]; Zeph. 2:7
29:11 [1]*calamity* [2]*a future and a hope*
29:12 [a]Ps. 50:15; Jer. 33:3; Dan. 9:3 [b]Ps. 145:19 [1]*listen*
29:13 [a]Lev. 26:39–42; Deut. 30:1–3 [b]1 Chr. 22:19; 2 Chr. 22:9; Jer. 24:7
29:14 [a][Deut. 4:7]; Ps. 32:6; 46:1; [Is. 55:6, 7]; Jer. 24:7 [b]Is. 43:5, 6; Jer. 23:8; 32:37 [1]*bring you back from*
29:15 [1]*raised up prophets for us*
29:16 [a]Jer. 38:2, 3, 17–23

that dwelleth in this city, *and* of your brethren that are not gone forth with you into captivity;

17 Thus saith the LORD of hosts; Behold, I will send upon them the sword, the famine, and the pestilence, and will make them like [a]vile[1] figs, that cannot be eaten, they are so [2]evil.

18 And I will [1]persecute them with the sword, with the famine, and with the pestilence, and [a]will deliver them to [2]be removed to all the kingdoms of the earth, to be [b]a curse, and an astonishment, and an hissing, and a reproach, among all the nations whither I have driven them:

19 Because they have not hearkened to my words, saith the LORD, which [a]I sent unto them by my servants the prophets, rising up early and sending *them;* but ye would not hear, saith the LORD.

20 Hear ye therefore the word of the LORD, all ye of the captivity, whom I have sent from Jerusalem to Babylon:

21 Thus saith the LORD of hosts, the God of Israel, of Ahab the son of Kolaiah, and of Zedekiah the son of Maaseiah, which prophesy a [a]lie unto you in my name; Behold, I will deliver them into the hand of Nebuchadrezzar king of Babylon; and he shall slay them before your eyes;

22 [a]And of them shall be taken up a curse by all the captivity of Judah which *are* in Babylon, saying, The LORD make thee like Zedekiah and like Ahab, [b]whom the king of Babylon roasted in the fire;

23 Because [a]they have [1]committed villany in Israel, and have committed adultery with their neighbours' wives, and have spoken lying words in my name, which I have not commanded them; even I [b]know, and *am* a witness, saith the LORD.

24 *Thus* shalt thou also speak to Shemaiah the Nehelamite, saying,

25 Thus speaketh the LORD of hosts, the God of Israel, saying, Because thou hast sent letters in thy name unto all the people that *are* at Jerusalem, [a]and to Zephaniah the son of Maaseiah the priest, and to all the priests, saying,

26 The LORD hath made thee priest in the stead of Jehoiada the priest, that [1]ye should be [a]officers in the house of the LORD, [2]for every man *that is* [b]mad,[3] and [4]maketh himself a prophet, that thou shouldest [c]put him in prison, and in the stocks.

27 Now therefore why hast thou not reproved Jeremiah of Anathoth, which maketh himself a prophet to you?

28 For therefore he sent unto us *in* Babylon, saying, This *captivity is*

29:17 [a] Jer. 24:3,
8–10 [1] *rotten*
[2] *bad*

29:18 [a] Deut.
28:25; 2 Chr. 29:8;
Jer. 15:4; 24:9;
34:17; Ezek. 12:15
[b] Jer. 26:6; 42:18
[1] *pursue* [2] *trouble
among*

29:19 [a] Jer. 25:4;
26:5; 35:15

29:21 [a] Jer. 14:14,
15; Lam. 2:14;
2 Pet. 2:1

29:22 [a] Gen.
48:20; Is. 65:15
[b] Dan. 3:6, 21

29:23 [a] Jer. 23:14
[b] [Prov. 5:21;
Jer. 16:17]; Mal.
3:5; [Heb. 4:13]
[1] *done disgraceful
things*

29:25 [a] 2 Kin.
25:18; Jer. 21:1

29:26 [a] Jer. 20:1
[b] 2 Kin. 9:11; Hos.
9:7; Mark 3:21;
John 10:20; Acts
26:24; [2 Cor.
5:13] [c] Jer. 20:1, 2;
Acts 16:24 [1] *there
should be* [2] *over*
[3] *demented*
[4] *considers*

29:31 [a] Jer. 28:15
[b] Ezek. 13:8–16,
22, 23

29:32 [a] Jer. 28:16

30:3 [a] Ps. 53:6;
Jer. 29:14; 30:18;
32:44; Ezek.
39:25; Amos 9:14;
Zeph. 3:20 [b] Jer.
16:15; Ezek. 20:42;
36:24 [1] *back from
captivity my*

30:5 [1] *dread*

30:6 [a] Jer. 4:31;
6:24 [1] Lit. *male
can give birth*
[2] *childbirth*

30:7 [a] [Is. 2:12];
Hos. 1:11; Joel 2:11;
Amos 5:18; Zeph.
1:14 [b] Lam. 1:12;
Dan. 9:12; 12:1

30:8 [1] *enslave
them*

30:9 [a] Is. 55:3;
Ezek. 34:23;
37:24; Hos. 3:5
[b] [Luke 1:69]; Acts
2:30; 13:23]

30:10 [a] Is. 41:13;
43:5; 44:2; Jer.
46:27, 28 [b] Jer.
3:18

long: build ye houses, and dwell *in them;* and plant gardens, and eat the fruit of them.

29 And Zephaniah the priest read this letter in the ears of Jeremiah the prophet.

30 Then came the word of the LORD unto Jeremiah, saying,

31 Send to all them of the captivity, saying, Thus saith the LORD concerning Shemaiah the Nehelamite; Because that Shemaiah hath prophesied unto you, [a]and I sent him not, and he caused you to trust in a [b]lie:

32 Therefore thus saith the LORD; Behold, I will punish Shemaiah the Nehelamite, and his seed: he shall not have a man to dwell among this people; neither shall he behold the good that I will do for my people, saith the LORD; [a]because he hath taught rebellion against the LORD.

## CHAPTER 30

THE word that came to Jeremiah from the LORD, saying,

2 Thus speaketh the LORD God of Israel, saying, Write thee all the words that I have spoken unto thee in a book.

3 For, lo, the days come, saith the LORD, that [a]I will bring [1]again the captivity of my people Israel and Judah, saith the LORD: [b]and I will cause them to return to the land that I gave to their fathers, and they shall possess it.

4 And these *are* the words that the LORD spake concerning Israel and concerning Judah.

5 For thus saith the LORD; We have heard a voice of trembling, of [1]fear, and not of peace.

6 Ask ye now, and see whether a [1]man doth travail with child? wherefore do I see every man with his hands on his loins, [a]as a woman in [2]travail, and all faces are turned into paleness?

7 [a]Alas! for that day *is* great, [b]so that none *is* like it: it *is* even the time of Jacob's trouble; but he shall be saved out of it.

8 For it shall come to pass in that day, saith the LORD of hosts, *that* I will break his yoke from off thy neck, and will burst thy bonds, and strangers shall no more [1]serve themselves of him:

9 But they shall serve the LORD their God, and [a]David their king, whom I will [b]raise up unto them.

10 Therefore [a]fear thou not, O my servant Jacob, saith the LORD; neither be dismayed, O Israel: for, lo, I will save thee from afar, and thy seed [b]from the land of their captivity; and Jacob shall return, and shall be in rest, and be quiet, and none shall make *him* afraid.

11 For I *am* with ªthee, saith the LORD, to save thee: ᵇthough I make a full end of all nations whither I have scattered thee, ᶜyet will I not make a full end of thee: but I will correct thee ᵈin ¹measure, and will not leave thee altogether unpunished.

12 For thus saith the LORD, ªThy bruise *is* incurable, *and* thy wound *is* grievous.

13 *There is* none to plead thy cause, that thou mayest be bound up: ªthou hast no healing medicines.

14 ªAll thy lovers have forgotten thee; they seek thee not; for I have wounded thee with the wound ᵇof an enemy, with the chastisement ᶜof a cruel one, for the multitude of thine iniquity; ᵈ*because* thy sins were increased.

15 Why ªcriest thou for thine affliction? thy sorrow *is* incurable for the multitude of thine iniquity: *because* thy sins were increased, I have done these things unto thee.

16 Therefore all they that devour thee ªshall be devoured; and all thine adversaries, every one of them, shall go into ᵇcaptivity; and they that ¹spoil thee shall ²be a ᶜspoil, and all that prey upon thee will I give for a ᵈprey.

17 ªFor I will restore health unto thee, and I will heal thee of thy wounds, saith the LORD; because they called thee an Outcast, *saying,* This *is* Zion, whom no man seeketh after.

18 Thus saith the LORD; Behold, I will bring ¹again the captivity of Jacob's tents, and ªhave mercy on his dwellingplaces; and the city shall be builded upon her own ²heap, and the palace shall remain ³after the manner thereof.

19 And ªout of them shall proceed thanksgiving and the voice of them that make merry: ᵇand I will multiply them, and they shall not be few; I will also glorify them, and they shall not be small.

20 Their children also shall be ªas aforetime, and their congregation shall be established before me, and I will punish all that oppress them.

21 And their nobles shall be of themselves, ªand their governor shall proceed from the midst of them; and I will ᵇcause him to draw near, and he shall approach unto me: for who *is* this that ¹engaged his heart to approach unto me? saith the LORD.

22 And ye shall be ªmy people, and I will be your God.

23 Behold, the ªwhirlwind of the LORD goeth forth with fury, a ¹continuing whirlwind: it shall fall ²with pain upon the head of the wicked.

24 The fierce anger of the LORD shall not return, until he have done

---

30:11 ª [Is. 43:2–5]
ᵇ Amos 9:8　ᶜ Jer.
4:27; 46:27, 28
ᵈ Ps. 6:1; Is. 27:8;
Jer. 10:24; 46:28
¹ *justice*
30:12 ª 2 Chr.
36:16; Jer. 15:18
30:13 ª Jer. 8:22
30:14 ª Jer. 22:20,
22; Lam. 1:2
ᵇ Job 13:24; 16:9;
19:11 ᶜ Job 30:21
ᵈ Jer. 5:6
30:15 ª Jer. 15:18
30:16 ª Ex. 23:22;
Is. 41:11; Jer. 10:25
ᵇ Is. 14:2; Joel 3:8
ᶜ Is. 33:1; Ezek.
39:10 ᵈ Jer. 2:3
¹ *plunder* ² *become plunder*
30:17 ª Ex. 15:26;
Ps. 107:20; Is.
30:26; Jer. 33:6
30:18 ª Ps. 102:13
¹ *back* ² *ruins*
³ *according to*
30:19 ª Is. 51:11
ᵇ Zech. 10:8
30:20 ª Is. 1:26
30:21 ª Gen. 49:10
ᵇ Num. 16:5
¹ *pledged*
30:22 ª Ezek.
36:28
30:23 ª Jer. 23:19,
20; 25:32 ¹ Or
*sweeping* ² *violently on*

30:24 ª Gen. 49:1
31:1 ª Jer. 30:24
ᵇ Jer. 30:22
31:2 ª Num. 10:33
31:3 ª Mal. 1:2
ᵇ Rom. 11:28
ᶜ Hos. 11:4 ¹ Lit.
*from afar*
31:4 ª Jer. 33:7
ᵇ Judg. 11:34
¹ *tambourines*
31:5 ª Amos 9:14
¹ *ordinary food*
31:6 ª [Mic. 4:2]
31:7 ª Is. 12:5, 6
¹ *proclaim*
31:8 ª Jer. 3:12,
18; 23:8 ᵇ Ezek.
20:34, 41; 34:13
¹ *ends* ² *is in labour*
31:9 ª [Jer. 50:4]
ᵇ Is. 35:8; 43:19;
49:10, 11 ᶜ Ex.
4:22
31:10 ª Is. 40:11
¹ *coastlands*
31:11 ª Is. 44:23;
48:20 ᵇ Is. 49:24
31:12 ª Ezek. 17:23
ᵇ Hos. 3:5 ᶜ Is.
58:11 ᵈ Is. 35:10;
65:19 ¹ *new wine*
² *well-watered*

---

*it,* and until he have performed the intents of his heart: ªin the latter days ye shall consider it.

## CHAPTER 31

AT ªthe same time, saith the LORD, ᵇwill I be the God of all the families of Israel, and they shall be my people.

2 Thus saith the LORD, The people *which were* left of the sword found grace in the wilderness; *even* Israel, when ªI went to cause him to rest.

3 The LORD hath appeared ¹of old unto me, *saying,* Yea, ªI have loved thee with ᵇan everlasting love: therefore with lovingkindness have I ᶜdrawn thee.

4 Again ªI will build thee, and thou shalt be built, O virgin of Israel: thou shalt again be adorned with thy ᵇtabrets,¹ and shalt go forth in the dances of them that make merry.

5 ªThou shalt yet plant vines upon the mountains of Samaria: the planters shall plant, and shall eat *them* as ¹common things.

6 For there shall be a day, *that* the watchmen upon the mount Ephraim shall cry, ªArise ye, and let us go up to Zion unto the LORD our God.

7 For thus saith the LORD; ªSing with gladness for Jacob, and shout among the chief of the nations: ¹publish ye, praise ye, and say, O LORD, save thy people, the remnant of Israel.

8 Behold, I will bring them ªfrom the north country, and ᵇgather them from the ¹coasts of the earth, *and* with them the blind and the lame, the woman with child and her that ²travaileth with child together: a great company shall return thither.

9 ªThey shall come with weeping, and with supplications will I lead them: I will cause them to walk ᵇby the rivers of waters in a straight way, wherein they shall not stumble: for I am a father to Israel, and Ephraim *is* my ᶜfirstborn.

10 Hear the word of the LORD, O ye nations, and declare *it* in the ¹isles afar off, and say, He that scattered Israel ªwill gather him, and keep him, as a shepherd *doth* his flock.

11 For ªthe LORD hath redeemed Jacob, and ransomed him ᵇfrom the hand of *him that was* stronger than he.

12 Therefore they shall come and sing in ªthe height of Zion, and shall flow together to ᵇthe goodness of the LORD, for wheat, and for ¹wine, and for oil, and for the young of the flock and of the herd: and their soul shall be as a ᶜwatered² garden; ᵈand they shall not sorrow any more at all.

13 Then shall the virgin rejoice in the dance, both young men and old

together: for I will turn their mourning into joy, and will comfort them, and make them rejoice from their sorrow.

14 And I will ¹satiate the soul of the priests with ²fatness, and my people shall be satisfied with my goodness, saith the LORD.

15 Thus saith the LORD; ᵃA voice was heard in ᵇRamah, lamentation, *and* bitter ᶜweeping; Rahel weeping for her children refused to be comforted for her children, because ᵈthey *were* not.

16 Thus saith the LORD; Refrain thy voice from ᵃweeping, and thine eyes from tears: for thy work shall be rewarded, saith the LORD; and they shall come again from the land of the enemy.

17 And there is ᵃhope in ¹thine end, saith the LORD, that thy children shall come again to their own border.

18 I have surely heard Ephraim bemoaning himself *thus;* Thou hast ᵃchastised me, and I was chastised, as ¹a bullock unaccustomed *to the yoke:* ᵇturn² thou me, and I shall ³be turned; for thou *art* the LORD my God.

19 Surely ᵃafter that I was turned, I repented; and after that I was instructed, I ¹smote upon *my* thigh: I was ᵇashamed, yea, even ²confounded, because I did bear the reproach of my youth.

20 *Is* Ephraim my dear son? *is he* a pleasant child? for since I spake against him still: ᵃtherefore my ¹bowels are troubled for him; ᵇI will surely have mercy upon him, saith the LORD.

21 Set thee up ¹waymarks, make thee ²high heaps: ᵃset thine heart toward the highway, *even* the way which thou wentest: turn again, O virgin of Israel, ³turn again to these thy cities.

22 How long wilt thou ᵃgo about, O thou ᵇbacksliding daughter? for the LORD hath created a new thing in the earth, A woman shall ¹compass a man.

23 Thus saith the LORD of hosts, the God of Israel; ¹As yet they shall use this speech in the land of Judah and in the cities thereof, when I shall bring again their captivity; ᵃThe LORD bless thee, O habitation of justice, *and* ᵇmountain of holiness.

24 And there shall dwell in Judah itself, and ᵃin all the cities thereof together, ¹husbandmen, and they *that* go forth with flocks.

25 For I have ¹satiated the weary soul, and I have replenished every sorrowful soul.

26 Upon this I awaked, and beheld; and my sleep was ᵃsweet unto me.

27 Behold, the days come, saith the LORD, that ᵃI will sow the house of Israel and the house of Judah with the seed of man, and with the seed of beast.

28 And it shall come to pass, *that* like as I have ᵃwatched over them, ᵇto pluck up, and to break down, and to throw down, and to destroy, and to afflict; so will I watch over them, ᶜto build, and to plant, saith the LORD.

29 ᵃIn those days they shall say no more, The fathers have eaten a sour grape, and the children's teeth are set on edge.

30 ᵃBut every one shall die for his own iniquity: every man that eateth the sour grape, his teeth shall be set on edge.

31 Behold, the ᵃdays come, saith the LORD, that I will make a new covenant with the house of Israel, and with the house of Judah:

32 Not according to the covenant that I made with their fathers in the day *that* ᵃI took them by the hand to bring them out of the land of Egypt; which my covenant they brake, although I was an husband unto them, saith the LORD:

33 ᵃBut this *shall be* the covenant that I will make with the house of Israel; After those days, saith the LORD, ᵇI will put my law in their ¹inward parts, and write it in their hearts; ᶜand will be their God, and they shall be my people.

34 And they shall teach no more every man his neighbour, and every man his brother, saying, Know the LORD: for ᵃthey shall all know me, from the least of them unto the greatest of them, saith the LORD: for ᵇI will forgive their iniquity, and I will remember their sin no more.

35 Thus saith the LORD, ᵃwhich giveth the sun for a light by day, *and* the ordinances of the moon and of the stars for a light by night, which ¹divideth ᵇthe sea ²when the waves thereof roar; ᶜThe LORD of hosts *is* his name:

36 ᵃIf those ordinances depart from before me, saith the LORD, *then* the seed of Israel also shall cease from being a nation before me for ever.

37 Thus saith the LORD; ᵃIf heaven above can be measured, and the foundations of the earth searched out beneath, I will also ᵇcast off all the seed of Israel for all that they have done, saith the LORD.

38 Behold, the days come, saith the LORD, that the city shall be built to the LORD ᵃfrom the tower of Hananeel unto the gate of the corner.

39 And ᵃthe measuring line shall yet go forth over against it upon the hill Gareb, and shall ¹compass about to Goath.

---

**Center column references:**

31:14 ¹ *fill* ² *abundance*

31:15 ᵃ Matt. 2:17, 18 ᵇ Josh. 18:25 ᶜ Gen. 37:35 ᵈ Jer. 10:20

31:16 ᵃ [Is. 25:8; 30:19]

31:17 ᵃ Jer. 29:11 ¹ *thy future*

31:18 ᵃ Ps. 94:12 ᵇ Lam. 5:21 ¹ *an untrained bull* ² *restore* ³ *return*

31:19 ᵃ Deut. 30:2 ᵇ Ezek. 36:31 ¹ *struck myself on the* ² *humiliated*

31:20 ᵃ Is. 63:15 ᵇ [Hos. 14:4] ¹ *heart,* lit. *inward parts*

31:21 ᵃ Jer. 50:5 ¹ *signposts* ² *landmarks* ³ Or *return*

31:22 ᵃ Jer. 2:18, 23, 36 ᵇ Jer. 3:6, 8, 11, 12, 14, 22 ¹ *encompass*

31:23 ᵃ Is. 1:26 ᵇ [Zech. 8:3] ¹ *Again*

31:24 ᵃ Jer. 33:12 ¹ *farmers*

31:25 ¹ *satisfied*

31:26 ᵃ Prov. 3:24

31:27 ᵃ Ezek. 36:9–11

31:28 ᵃ Jer. 44:27 ᵇ Jer. 1:10; 18:7 ᶜ Jer. 24:6

31:29 ᵃ Ezek. 18:2, 3

31:30 ᵃ [Gal. 6:5, 7]

31:31 ᵃ Heb. 8:8–12; 10:16, 17

31:32 ᵃ Deut. 1:31

31:33 ᵃ Jer. 32:40 ᵇ Ps. 40:8 ᶜ Jer. 24:7; 30:22; 32:38 ¹ *Mind*

31:34 ᵃ [John 6:45] ᵇ [Rom. 11:27]

31:35 ᵃ Gen. 1:14–18 ᵇ Is. 51:15 ᶜ Jer. 10:16 ¹ *disturbs* ² *and*

31:36 ᵃ Ps. 148:6

31:37 ᵃ Jer. 33:22 ᵇ [Rom. 11:2–5, 26, 27]

31:38 ᵃ Zech. 14:10

31:39 ᵃ Zech. 2:1, ¹ *turn toward*

40 And the whole valley of the dead bodies, and of the ashes, and all the fields unto the brook of Kidron, ᵃunto the corner of the horse gate toward the east, ᵇ*shall be* holy unto the LORD; it shall not be plucked up, nor thrown down any more for ever.

## CHAPTER 32

THE word that came to Jeremiah from the LORD ᵃin the tenth year of Zedekiah king of Judah, which *was* the eighteenth year of ¹Nebuchadrezzar.

2 For then the king of Babylon's army besieged Jerusalem: and Jeremiah the prophet was ¹shut up ᵃin the court of the prison, which *was* in the king of Judah's house.

3 For Zedekiah king of Judah had shut him up, saying, Wherefore dost thou ᵃprophesy, and say, Thus saith the LORD, ᵇBehold, I will give this city into the hand of the king of Babylon, and he shall take it;

4 And Zedekiah king of Judah ᵃshall not escape out of the hand of the Chaldeans, but shall surely be delivered into the hand of the king of Babylon, and shall speak with him ¹mouth to mouth, and ²his eyes shall behold his ᵇeyes;

5 And he shall ᵃlead Zedekiah to Babylon, and there shall he be ᵇuntil I visit him, saith the LORD: ᶜthough ye fight with the Chaldeans, ye shall not ¹prosper.

6 And Jeremiah said, The word of the LORD came unto me, saying,

7 Behold, Hanameel the son of Shallum thine uncle shall come unto thee, saying, Buy thee my field that *is* in Anathoth: for the ᵃright of redemption *is* thine to buy *it.*

8 So Hanameel mine uncle's son came to me in the court of the prison according to the word of the LORD, and said unto me, Buy my field, I pray thee, that *is* in Anathoth, which *is* in the country of Benjamin: for the right of inheritance *is* thine, and the redemption *is* thine; buy *it* for thyself. Then I knew that this *was* the word of the LORD.

9 And I bought the field of Hanameel my uncle's son, that *was* in Anathoth, and ᵃweighed him the money, *even* seventeen shekels of silver.

10 And I ¹subscribed the evidence, and sealed *it,* and took witnesses, and weighed *him* the money in the balances.

11 So I took the ¹evidence of the purchase, *both* that which was sealed *according* to the law and custom, and that which was open:

12 And I gave the ¹evidence of the purchase unto ᵃBaruch the son of Neriah, the son of Maaseiah, in the

sight of Hanameel mine uncle's *son,* and in the presence of the ᵇwitnesses that ²subscribed the book of the purchase, before all the Jews that sat in the court of the prison.

13 And I charged ᵃBaruch before them, saying,

14 Thus saith the LORD of hosts, the God of Israel; Take these ¹evidences, this ²evidence of the purchase, both which is sealed, and this ²evidence which is open; and put them in an earthen vessel, that they may ³continue many days.

15 For thus saith the LORD of hosts, the God of Israel; Houses and fields and vineyards shall be ᵃpossessed again in this land.

16 Now when I had delivered the ¹evidence of the purchase unto Baruch the son of Neriah, I prayed unto the LORD, saying,

17 Ah Lord GOD! behold, ᵃthou hast made the heaven and the earth by thy great power and stretched out arm, *and* ᵇthere is nothing ¹too hard for thee:

18 Thou shewest ᵃlovingkindness unto thousands, and ¹recompensest the iniquity of the fathers into the bosom of their children after them: the Great, ᵇthe Mighty God, ᶜthe LORD of hosts, *is* his name,

19 ᵃGreat in counsel, and mighty in ¹work: for thine ᵇeyes *are* open upon all the ways of the sons of men: ᶜto give every one according to his ways, and according to the fruit of his doings:

20 Which hast set signs and wonders in the land of Egypt, *even* unto this day, and in Israel, and among *other* men; and hast made thee ᵃa name, as at this day;

21 And ᵃhast brought forth thy people Israel out of the land of Egypt with signs, and with wonders, and with a strong hand, and with a stretched out arm, and with great terror;

22 And hast given them this land, which thou didst swear to their fathers to give them, ᵃa land flowing with milk and honey;

23 And they came in, and possessed it; but ᵃthey obeyed not thy voice, neither walked in thy law; they have done nothing of all that thou commandedst them to do: therefore thou hast caused all this ¹evil to come upon them:

24 Behold the ¹mounts, they are come unto the city to take it; and the city is given into the hand of the Chaldeans, that fight against it, because of ᵃthe sword, and of the famine, and of the pestilence: and what thou hast spoken is come to pass; and, behold, thou seest *it.*

### Cross-references

31:40 ᵃ Neh. 3:28
ᵇ [Joel 3:17]

32:1 ᵃ Jer. 39:1, 2
¹ Or Nebuchadnezzar

32:2 ᵃ Jer. 33:1; 37:21; 39:14
¹ imprisoned

32:3 ᵃ Jer. 26:8, 9
ᵇ Jer. 21:3–7; 34:2

32:4 ᵃ Jer. 34:3; 38:18, 23; 39:5; 52:9 ᵇ Jer. 39:5
¹ face to face
² see him eye to eye

32:5 ᵃ Ezek. 12:12, 13 ᵇ Jer. 27:22
ᶜ Jer. 21:4; 33:5
¹ succeed

32:7 ᵃ Lev. 25:24, 25, 32; Ruth 4:4

32:9 ᵃ Gen. 23:16; Zech. 11:12

32:10 ¹ signed the deed

32:11 ¹ deed of

32:12 ᵃ Jer. 36:4
¹ deed

ᵇ Is. 8:2  ² signed the deed of

32:13 ᵃ Jer. 36:4

32:14 ¹ deeds
² deed ³ last

32:15 ᵃ Ezra 2:1; [Jer. 31:5, 12, 14]; Amos 9:14, 15; Zech. 3:10

32:16 ¹ deed

32:17 ᵃ 2 Kin. 19:15; Ps. 102:25; Is. 40:26–29; Jer. 27:5 ᵇ Gen. 18:14; Jer. 32:27; Zech. 8:6; Matt. 19:26; Mark 10:27; Luke 18:27 ¹ too difficult

32:18 ᵃ Ex. 20:6; 34:7; Deut. 5:9, 10 ᵇ Ps. 50:11; [Is. 9:6]; Jer. 20:11
ᶜ Jer. 10:16 ¹ repay

32:19 ᵃ Is. 28:29 ᵇ Job 34:21; Ps. 33:13; Prov. 5:21; Jer. 16:17 ᶜ Ps. 62:12; Jer. 17:10; [Matt. 16:27; John 5:29] ¹ deed

32:20 ᵃ Ex. 9:16; 1 Chr. 17:21; Is. 63:12; Jer. 13:11; Dan. 9:15

32:21 ᵃ Ex. 6:6; 2 Sam. 7:23; 1 Chr. 17:21; Ps. 136:11, 12

32:22 ᵃ Ex. 3:8, 17; Deut. 1:8; Ps. 105:9–11; Jer. 11:5

32:23 ᵃ [Neh. 9:26]; Jer. 11:8; [Dan. 9:10–14]
¹ calamity

32:24 ᵃ Jer. 14:12; Ezek. 14:21 ¹ siege mounds

25 And thou hast said unto me, O Lord GOD, Buy thee the field for money, and take witnesses; for the city is given into the hand of the Chaldeans.

26 Then came the word of the LORD unto Jeremiah, saying,

27 Behold, I *am* the LORD, the [a]God of all flesh: is there any thing too hard for me?

28 Therefore thus saith the LORD; Behold, I will give this city into the hand of the Chaldeans, and into the hand of [1]Nebuchadrezzar king of Babylon, and he shall take it:

29 And the Chaldeans, that fight against this city, shall come and [a]set fire on this city, and burn it with the houses, [b]upon whose roofs they have offered incense unto Baal, and poured out drink offerings unto other gods, to provoke me to anger.

30 For the children of Israel and the children of Judah [a]have only done evil before me from their youth: for the children of Israel have only provoked me to anger with the work of their hands, saith the LORD.

31 For this city hath been to me *as* a provocation of mine anger and of my fury from the day that they built it even unto this day; [a]that I should remove it from before my face,

32 Because of all the evil of the children of Israel and of the children of Judah, which they have done to provoke me to anger, [a]they, their kings, their princes, their priests, and [b]their prophets, and the men of Judah, and the inhabitants of Jerusalem.

33 And they have turned unto me the [a]back, and not the face: though I taught them, [b]rising up early and teaching *them,* yet they have not [1]hearkened to receive instruction.

34 But they [a]set their abominations in [1]the house, which is called by my name, to defile it.

35 And they built the [1]high places of Baal, which *are* in the valley of the son of Hinnom, to [a]cause their sons and their daughters to pass through *the fire* unto [b]Molech; [c]which I commanded them not, neither came it into my mind, that they should do this abomination, to cause Judah to sin.

36 And now therefore thus saith the LORD, the God of Israel, concerning this city, whereof ye say, It shall be delivered into the hand of the king of Babylon by the sword, and by the famine, and by the pestilence;

37 Behold, I will [a]gather them out of all countries, whither I have driven them in mine anger, and in my fury, and in great wrath; and I will bring them again unto this place, and I will cause them [b]to dwell safely:

32:27 [a] [Num. 16:22]

32:28 [1] Or Nebuchadnezzar

32:29 [a] 2 Chr. 36:19; Jer. 21:10; 37:8, 10; 52:13 [b] Jer. 19:13

32:30 [a] Deut. 9:7–12; Is. 63:10; Jer. 2:7; 3:25; 7:22–26; Ezek. 20:28

32:31 [a] 2 Kin. 23:27; 24:3; Jer. 27:10

32:32 [a] Dan. 9:8 [b] Jer. 23:14

32:33 [a] Jer. 2:27; 7:24 [b] Jer. 7:13 [1] *listened*

32:34 [a] Jer. 7:10–12, 30; 23:11 [1] The temple

32:35 [a] Jer. 7:31; 19:5 [b] Lev. 18:21 [c] Jer. 7:31 [1] *sacred places* of pagan worship

32:37 [a] Deut. 30:3 [b] Jer. 33:16

32:38 [a] [Jer. 24:7; 30:22; 31:33]

32:39 [a] [Ezek. 11:19] [1] *have reverential awe toward*

32:40 [a] Is. 55:3 [b] [Jer. 31:33]

32:41 [a] Deut. 30:9 [b] Amos 9:15 [1] *truly*

32:42 [a] Jer. 31:28 [1] *calamity*

32:43 [a] Jer. 33:10

32:44 [a] Jer. 17:26 [b] Jer. 33:7, 11 [1] *sign deeds* [2] Heb. *shephelah, lowland* [3] Heb. *Negev*

33:1 [a] Jer. 32:2, 3 [1] *imprisoned*

33:2 [a] Is. 37:26 [b] Ex. 15:3 [1] Heb. YHWH, Jehovah

33:3 [a] Jer. 29:12 [1] *inaccessible*

33:4 [a] Is. 22:10 [1] *were pulled down* to fortify *against* [2] *siege mounds*

33:5 [a] 2 Kin. 23:14 [1] *their places*

33:6 [a] Jer. 30:17 [1] *healing* [2] *heal*

33:7 [a] Jer. 30:3; 32:44 [b] Is. 1:26 [1] *captives* [2] *those places*

33:8 [a] Zech. 13:1

38 And they shall be [a]my people, and I will be their God:

39 And I will [a]give them one heart, and one way, that they may [1]fear me for ever, for the good of them, and of their children after them:

40 And [a]I will make an everlasting covenant with them, that I will not turn away from them, to do them good; but [b]I will put my fear in their hearts, that they shall not depart from me.

41 Yea, [a]I will rejoice over them to do them good, and [b]I will plant them in this land [1]assuredly with my whole heart and with my whole soul.

42 For thus saith the LORD; [a]Like as I have brought all this great [1]evil upon this people, so will I bring upon them all the good that I have promised them.

43 And fields shall be bought in this land, [a]whereof ye say, It *is* desolate without man or beast; it is given into the hand of the Chaldeans.

44 Men shall buy fields for money, and [1]subscribe evidences, and seal *them,* and take witnesses in [a]the land of Benjamin, and in the places about Jerusalem, and in the cities of Judah, and in the cities of the mountains, and in the cities of the [2]valley, and in the cities of the [3]south: for [b]I will cause their captivity to return, saith the LORD.

## CHAPTER 33

MOREOVER the word of the LORD came unto Jeremiah the second time, while he was yet [a]shut[1] up in the court of the prison, saying,

2 Thus saith the LORD the [a]maker thereof, the LORD that formed it, to establish it; [b]the[1] LORD *is* his name;

3 [a]Call unto me, and I will answer thee, and shew thee great and [1]mighty things, which thou knowest not.

4 For thus saith the LORD, the God of Israel, concerning the houses of this city, and concerning the houses of the kings of Judah, which [1]are thrown down by [a]the [2]mounts, and by the sword;

5 They come to fight with the Chaldeans, but *it is* to [a]fill [1]them with the dead bodies of men, whom I have slain in mine anger and in my fury, and for all whose wickedness I have hid my face from this city.

6 Behold, [a]I will bring it health and [1]cure, and I will [2]cure them, and will reveal unto them the abundance of peace and truth.

7 And [a]I will cause the [1]captivity of Judah and the captivity of Israel to return, and will build [2]them, [b]as at the first.

8 And I will [a]cleanse them from all their iniquity, whereby they have

sinned against me; and I will pardon all their iniquities, whereby they
have sinned, and whereby they have
transgressed against me.
9 [a]And it shall be to me a name of
joy, a praise and an honour before all
the nations of the earth, which shall
hear all the good that I do unto them:
and they shall [b]fear and tremble for
all the goodness and for all the prosperity that I [1]procure unto it.
10 Thus saith the LORD; Again there
shall be heard in this place, [a]which
ye say *shall be* desolate without man
and without beast, *even* in the cities
of Judah, and in the streets of Jerusalem, that are desolate, without man,
and without inhabitant, and without
beast,
11 The [a]voice of joy, and the voice
of gladness, the voice of the bridegroom, and the voice of the bride, the
voice of them that shall say, [b]Praise
the LORD of hosts: for the LORD *is*
good; for his mercy *endureth* for ever:
*and* of them that shall bring [c]the sacrifice of praise into the house of the
LORD. For I will cause [1]to return the
captivity of the land, as at the first,
saith the LORD.
12 Thus saith the LORD of hosts;
[a]Again in this place, which is desolate
without man and without beast, and
in all the cities thereof, shall be an
habitation of shepherds causing *their*
flocks to lie down.
13 [a]In the cities of the mountains,
in the cities of the [1]vale, and in the
cities of the [2]south, and in the land
of Benjamin, and in the places about
Jerusalem, and in the cities of Judah,
shall the flocks [b]pass again under the
hands of him that [3]telleth *them,* saith
the LORD.
14 [a]Behold, the days come, saith
the LORD, that [b]I will perform that
good thing which I have promised
unto the house of Israel and to the
house of Judah.
15 In those days, and at that time,
will I cause the [a]Branch of righteousness to grow up unto David; and he
shall execute [1]judgment and righteousness in the [2]land.
16 In those days shall Judah be
saved, and Jerusalem shall dwell
safely: and this *is the name* wherewith she shall be called, [1]The LORD
our righteousness.
17 For thus saith the LORD; David
shall never [a]want[1] a man to sit upon
the throne of the house of Israel;
18 Neither shall the [a]priests the Levites [1]want a man before me to [b]offer
burnt offerings, and to [2]kindle meat
offerings, and to do sacrifice continually.
19 And the word of the LORD came
unto Jeremiah, saying,
20 Thus saith the LORD; If ye can
break my covenant of the day, and
my covenant of the night, and that
there should not be day and night in
their season;
21 *Then* may also [a]my covenant be
broken with David my servant, that
he should not have a son to reign
upon his throne; and with the Levites the priests, my ministers.
22 As [a]the host of heaven cannot be
numbered, neither the sand of the
sea measured: so will I [b]multiply the
seed of David my servant, and the
[c]Levites that minister unto me.
23 Moreover the word of the LORD
came to Jeremiah, saying,
24 Considerest thou not what this
people have spoken, saying, The two
families which the LORD hath chosen, he hath even cast them off? thus
they have [a]despised my people, that
they should be no more a nation before them.
25 Thus saith the LORD; If [a]my covenant *be* not with day and night, *and*
*if* I have not [b]appointed the ordinances of heaven and earth;
26 [a]Then will I [b]cast away the seed
of Jacob, and David my servant, *so*
that I will not take *any* of his seed *to*
*be* rulers over the seed of Abraham,
Isaac, and Jacob: for I will cause their
[1]captivity to return, and have mercy
on them.

## CHAPTER 34

THE word which came unto Jeremiah from the LORD, [a]when Nebuchadnezzar king of Babylon, and
all his army, and [b]all the kingdoms
of the earth of his dominion, and all
the people, fought against Jerusalem, and against all the cities thereof,
saying,
2 Thus saith the LORD, the God of
Israel; Go and [a]speak to Zedekiah
king of Judah, and tell him, Thus saith
the LORD; Behold, [b]I will give this city
into the hand of the king of Babylon,
and he shall burn it with fire:
3 And [a]thou shalt not escape out
of his hand, but shalt surely be
taken, and delivered into his hand;
and thine eyes shall behold the eyes
of the king of Babylon, and he shall
speak with thee [b]mouth[1] to mouth,
and thou shalt go to Babylon.
4 Yet hear the word of the LORD,
O Zedekiah king of Judah; Thus saith
the LORD of thee, Thou shalt not die
by the sword:
5 *But* thou shalt die in peace: and
with [a]the [1]burnings of thy fathers, the
former kings which were before thee,
[b]so shall they burn [2]*odours* for thee;
and [c]they will lament thee, *saying,*
Ah lord! for I have pronounced the
word, saith the LORD.

33:9 [a] Is. 62:7 [b] Is. 60:5 [1] *provide for*
33:10 [a] Jer. 32:43
33:11 [a] Rev. 18:23 [b] Is. 12:4 [c] Lev. 7:12 [1] *the captives of the land to return*
33:12 [a] Is. 65:10
33:13 [a] Jer. 17:26; 32:44 [b] Lev. 27:33 [1] Heb. *shephelah, lowland* [2] Heb. *Negev* [3] *counts*
33:14 [a] Jer. 23:5; 31:27, 31 [b] Jer. 29:10; 32:42
33:15 [a] Jer. 23:5 [1] *justice* [2] *earth*
33:16 [1] Heb. *YHWH Tsidkenu*
33:17 [a] 2 Sam. 7:16 [1] *lack*
33:18 [a] Ezek. 44:15 [b] [1 Pet. 2:5, 9] [1] *lack* [2] *burn grain or meal*
33:21 [a] 2 Sam. 23:5; Ps. 89:34
33:22 [a] Gen. 15:5; 22:17 [b] Jer. 30:19 [c] Is. 66:21
33:24 [a] Esth. 3:6–8
33:25 [a] Gen. 8:22 [b] Ps. 74:16; 104:19
33:26 [a] Jer. 31:37 [b] Rom. 11:1, 2 [1] *captives*
34:1 [a] 2 Kin. 25:1 [b] Jer. 1:15; 25:9
34:2 [a] 2 Chr. 36:11, 12 [b] Jer. 21:10; 32:3, 28
34:3 [a] 2 Kin. 25:4, 5 [b] Jer. 32:4; 39:5, 6 [1] *face to face*
34:5 [a] 2 Chr. 16:14; 21:19 [b] Dan. 2:46 [c] Jer. 22:18 [1] *ceremonies* [2] *incense*

6 Then Jeremiah the prophet spake all these words unto Zedekiah king of Judah in Jerusalem.

7 When the king of Babylon's army fought against Jerusalem, and against all the cities of Judah that were left, against Lachish, and against Azekah: for ᵃthese¹ defenced cities remained of the cities of Judah.

8 *This is* the word that came unto Jeremiah from the LORD, after that the king Zedekiah had made a covenant with all the people which *were* at Jerusalem, to proclaim ᵃliberty unto them;

9 ᵃThat every man should ¹let his manservant, and every man his maidservant, *being* an Hebrew or an Hebrewess, go free; ᵇthat none should ²serve himself of them, *to wit,* of a Jew his brother.

10 Now when all the princes, and all the people, which had entered into the covenant, heard that every one should let his manservant, and every one his maidservant, go free, that none should ¹serve themselves of them any more, then they obeyed, and let *them* go.

11 But afterward they ¹turned, and caused the servants and the handmaids, whom they had let go free, to return, and brought them into subjection for servants and for handmaids.

12 Therefore the word of the LORD came to Jeremiah from the LORD, saying,

13 Thus saith the LORD, the God of Israel; I made a ᵃcovenant with your fathers in the day that I brought them forth out of the land of Egypt, out of the house of bondmen, saying,

14 At the end of ᵃseven years let ye go every man his ¹brother an Hebrew, which hath ²been sold unto thee; and when he hath served thee six years, thou shalt let him go free from thee: but your fathers ³hearkened not unto me, neither inclined their ear.

15 And ¹ye were now turned, and ²had done right in my sight, in proclaiming liberty every man to his neighbour; and ye had ᵃmade a covenant before me ᵇin the house which is called by my name:

16 But ye ¹turned and ᵃpolluted² my name, and caused every man his servant, and every man his handmaid, whom he had set at liberty at their pleasure, to return, and brought them into subjection, to be unto you for servants and for handmaids.

17 Therefore thus saith the LORD; Ye have not hearkened unto me, in proclaiming liberty, every one to his brother, and every man to his neighbour: ᵃbehold, I proclaim a liberty for you, saith the LORD, ᵇto the sword,

34:7 ᵃ 2 Kin. 18:13;
19:8 ¹ only these
fortified

34:8 ᵃ Ex. 21:2

34:9 ᵃ Neh. 5:11
ᵇ Lev. 25:39–46
¹ set free ² keep a
Jewish brother in
bondage

34:10 ¹ keep them
in bondage

34:11 ¹ changed
their minds

34:13 ᵃ Ex. 24:3, 7,
8; Deut. 5:2, 3, 27;
Jer. 31:32

34:14 ᵃ Ex. 21:2;
23:10; Deut.
15:12; 1 Kin. 9:22
¹ Hebrew brother
² Or sold himself
³ did not obey

34:15 ᵃ 2 Kin.
23:3; Neh. 10:29
ᵇ Jer. 7:10 ¹ Lit.
today ye turned
² did

34:16 ᵃ Ex. 20:7;
Lev. 19:12 ¹ turned
around ² pro-
faned

34:17 ᵃ Lev. 26:34,
35; Esth. 7:10;
Dan. 6:24; [Matt.
7:2; Gal. 6:7];
James 2:13 ᵇ Jer.
32:24, 36

to the pestilence, and to the famine; and I will ¹make you to be ᶜremoved into all the kingdoms of the earth.

18 And I will give the men that have transgressed my covenant, which have not performed the words of the covenant which they had ¹made before me, when ᵃthey cut the calf in ²twain, and passed between the parts thereof,

19 The princes of Judah, and the princes of Jerusalem, the ¹eunuchs, and the priests, and all the people of the land, which passed between the parts of the calf;

20 I will even ᵃgive them into the hand of their enemies, and into the hand of them that seek their life: and their ᵇdead bodies shall be for meat unto the fowls of the heaven, and to the beasts of the earth.

21 And Zedekiah king of Judah and his princes will I give into the hand of their enemies, and into the hand of them that seek their life, and into the hand of the king of Babylon's army, ᵃwhich are gone up from you.

22 ᵃBehold, I will command, saith the LORD, and cause them to return to this city; and they shall fight against it, ᵇand take it, and burn it with fire: and ᶜI will make the cities of Judah a desolation without an inhabitant.

ᶜ Deut. 28:25, 64;
Jer. 29:18 ¹ deliver
you to trouble
into

34:18 ᵃ Gen. 15:10,
17 ¹ Lit. cut ² two

34:19 ¹ Or officers

34:20 ᵃ 2 Kin.
25:19–21; Jer.
22:25 ᵇ Deut.
28:26; 1 Sam.
17:44, 46; 1 Kin.
14:11; 16:4; Ps.
79:2; Jer. 7:33;
16:4; 19:7

34:21 ᵃ Jer. 37:5–
11; 39:4–7

34:22 ᵃ Jer. 37:8,
10 ᵇ Jer. 38:3;
39:1, 2, 8; 52:7, 13
ᶜ Jer. 9:11; 44:2, 6

35:2 ᵃ 2 Sam. 4:2;
2 Kin. 10:15; 1 Chr.
2:55 ᵇ 1 Kin. 6:5,
8; 1 Chr. 9:26, 33
¹ The temple

35:4 ᵃ 2 Kin. 12:9;
25:18; 1 Chr. 9:18,
19 ¹ Lit. threshold

35:5 ¹ bowls

35:6 ᵃ 2 Kin. 10:15,
23 ᵇ Lev. 10:9;
Num. 6:2–4;
Judg. 13:7, 14;
Prov. 31:4; Ezek.
44:21; Luke 1:15

## CHAPTER 35

THE word which came unto Jeremiah from the LORD in the days of Jehoiakim the son of Josiah king of Judah, saying,

2 Go unto the house of the ᵃRechabites, and speak unto them, and bring them into ¹the house of the LORD, into one of ᵇthe chambers, and give them wine to drink.

3 Then I took Jaazaniah the son of Jeremiah, the son of Habaziniah, and his brethren, and all his sons, and the whole house of the Rechabites;

4 And I brought them into the house of the LORD, into the chamber of the sons of Hanan, the son of Igdaliah, a man of God, which *was* by the chamber of the princes, which *was* above the chamber of Maaseiah the son of Shallum, ᵃthe keeper of the ¹door:

5 And I set before the sons of the house of the Rechabites ¹pots full of wine, and cups, and I said unto them, Drink ye wine.

6 But they said, We will drink no wine: for ᵃJonadab the son of Rechab our father commanded us, saying, Ye shall drink ᵇno wine, *neither* ye, nor your sons for ever:

7 Neither shall ye build house, nor sow seed, nor plant vineyard, nor have *any:* but all your days ye shall

dwell in tents; [a]that ye may live many days in the land where ye [1]*be* strangers.

8 Thus have we [a]obeyed the voice of Jonadab the son of Rechab our father in all that he hath charged us, to drink no wine all our days, we, our wives, our sons, nor our daughters;

9 Nor to build houses for us to dwell in: neither have we vineyard, nor field, nor seed:

10 But we have dwelt in tents, and have obeyed, and done according to all that Jonadab our father commanded us.

11 But it came to pass, when [1]Nebuchadrezzar king of Babylon came up into the land, that we said, Come, and let us [a]go to Jerusalem for fear of the army of the Chaldeans, and for fear of the army of the Syrians: so we dwell at Jerusalem.

12 Then came the word of the LORD unto Jeremiah, saying,

13 Thus saith the LORD of hosts, the God of Israel; Go and tell the men of Judah and the inhabitants of Jerusalem, Will ye not [a]receive instruction to [1]hearken to my words? saith the LORD.

14 The words of Jonadab the son of Rechab, that he commanded his sons not to drink wine, are performed; for unto this day they drink none, but obey their father's commandment: [a]notwithstanding I have spoken unto you, [b]rising early and speaking; but ye [1]hearkened not unto me.

15 I have sent also unto you all my [a]servants the prophets, rising up early and sending *them,* saying, [b]Return[1] ye now every man from his evil way, and amend your doings, and go not after other gods to serve them, and ye shall [c]dwell in the land which I have given to you and to your fathers: but ye have not inclined your ear, nor hearkened unto me.

16 Because the sons of Jonadab the son of Rechab have performed the commandment of their [a]father, which he commanded them; but this people hath not hearkened unto me:

17 Therefore thus saith the LORD God of hosts, the God of Israel; Behold, I will bring upon Judah and upon all the inhabitants of Jerusalem all the [1]evil that I have pronounced against them: [a]because I have spoken unto them, but they have not heard; and I have called unto them, but they have not answered.

18 And Jeremiah said unto the house of the Rechabites, Thus saith the LORD of hosts, the God of Israel; Because ye have obeyed the commandment of Jonadab your father, and kept all his precepts, and done according unto all that he hath commanded you:

19 Therefore thus saith the LORD of hosts, the God of Israel; Jonadab the son of Rechab shall not [1]want a man to [a]stand before me for ever.

## CHAPTER 36

AND it came to pass in the [a]fourth year of Jehoiakim the son of Josiah king of Judah, *that* this word came unto Jeremiah from the LORD, saying,

2 Take thee a [a]roll[1] of a book, and [b]write therein all the words that I have spoken unto thee against Israel, and against Judah, and against [c]all the nations, from the day I spake unto thee, from the days of [d]Josiah, even unto this day.

3 It [a]may be that the house of Judah will hear all the [1]evil which I purpose to do unto them; that they may [b]return[2] every man from his evil way; that I may forgive their iniquity and their sin.

4 Then Jeremiah [a]called Baruch the son of Neriah: and [b]Baruch wrote from the mouth of Jeremiah all the words of the LORD, which he had spoken unto him, upon a [1]roll of a book.

5 And Jeremiah commanded Baruch, saying, I *am* [1]shut up; I cannot go into [2]the house of the LORD:

6 Therefore go thou, and read [1]in the roll, which thou hast written from my mouth, the words of the LORD in the ears of the people in the LORD's house upon [a]the fasting day: and also thou shalt read them in the ears of all Judah that come out of their cities.

7 It may be they will present their supplication before the LORD, and will [1]return every one from his evil way: for great *is* the anger and the fury that the LORD hath pronounced against this people.

8 And Baruch the son of Neriah did according to all that Jeremiah the prophet commanded him, reading in the book the words of the LORD in the LORD's house.

9 And it came to pass in the fifth year of Jehoiakim the son of Josiah king of Judah, in the ninth month, *that* they proclaimed a fast before the LORD to all the people in Jerusalem, and to all the people that came from the cities of Judah unto Jerusalem.

10 Then read Baruch in the book the words of Jeremiah in the house of the LORD, in the chamber of Gemariah the son of Shaphan the scribe, in the [1]higher court, at the [a]entry[2] of the new gate of the LORD's house, in the [3]ears of all the people.

11 When Michaiah the son of Gemariah, the son of Shaphan, had heard out of the book all the words of the LORD,

35:7 [a] Ex. 20:12; Eph. 6:2, 3 [1] *are sojourners*

35:8 [a] [Prov. 1:8, 9; 4:1, 2, 10; 6:20; Eph. 6:1; Col. 3:20]

35:11 [a] Jer. 4:5–7; 8:14 [1] Or *Nebuchadnezzar*

35:13 [a] [Is. 28:9–12]; Jer. 6:10; 17:23; 32:33 [1] *listen*

35:14 [a] 2 Chr. 36:15 [b] Jer. 7:13; 25:3 [1] *listened*

35:15 [a] Jer. 26:4, 5; 29:19 [b] [Is. 1:16, 17]; Jer. 18:11; 25:5, 6; [Ezek. 18:30–32]; Acts 26:20 [c] Jer. 7:7; 25:5, 6 [1] *Turn*

35:16 [a] [Heb. 12:9]

35:17 [a] Prov. 1:24; Is. 65:12; 66:4; Jer. 7:13 [1] *doom*

35:19 [a] [Ex. 20:12]; Jer. 15:19; [Luke 21:36; Eph. 6:2, 3] [1] *lack*

36:1 [a] 2 Kin. 24:1; 2 Chr. 36:5–7; Jer. 25:1, 3; 45:1; Dan. 1:1

36:2 [a] Is. 8:1; Ezek. 2:9; Zech. 5:1 [b] Jer. 30:2; Hab. 2:2 [c] Jer. 25:15 [d] Jer. 25:3 [1] *scroll*

36:3 [a] Jer. 26:3; Ezek. 12:3 [b] [Deut. 30:2, 8; 1 Sam. 7:3]; Is. 55:7; Jer. 18:8; Jon. 3:8 [1] *adversities* [2] *turn*

36:4 [a] Jer. 32:12 [b] Jer. 45:1 [1] *scroll*

36:5 [1] *confined* [2] The temple

36:6 [a] Lev. 16:29; 23:27–32; Acts 27:9 [1] *from the scroll*

36:7 [1] *turn*

36:10 [a] Jer. 26:10 [1] *upper* [2] *entrance* [3] *hearing*

12 Then he went down into the king's house, into the scribe's chamber: and, lo, all the princes sat there, *even* ªElishama the scribe, and Delaiah the son of Shemaiah, and ᵇElnathan the son of Achbor, and Gemariah the son of Shaphan, and Zedekiah the son of Hananiah, and all the princes.

13 Then Michaiah declared unto them all the words that he had heard, when Baruch read the book in the ¹ears of the people.

14 Therefore all the princes sent Jehudi the son of Nethaniah, the son of Shelemiah, the son of Cushi, unto Baruch, saying, Take in thine hand the ¹roll wherein thou hast read in the ²ears of the people, and come. So Baruch the son of Neriah took the ¹roll in his hand, and came unto them.

15 And they said unto him, Sit down now, and read it in our ears. So Baruch read *it* in their ears.

16 Now it came to pass, when they had heard all the words, they ¹were afraid both one and other, and said unto Baruch, We will surely tell the king of all these words.

17 And they asked Baruch, saying, Tell us now, How didst thou write all these words ¹at his mouth?

18 Then Baruch answered them, He pronounced all these words unto me with his mouth, and I wrote *them* with ink in the book.

19 Then said the princes unto Baruch, Go, hide thee, thou and Jeremiah; and let no man know where ye be.

20 And they went in to the king into the court, but they ¹laid up the roll in the chamber of Elishama the scribe, and told all the words in the ²ears of the king.

21 So the king sent Jehudi to ¹fetch the roll: and he took it out of Elishama the scribe's chamber. And Jehudi read it in the ears of the king, and in the ears of all the princes which stood beside the king.

22 Now the king sat in ªthe winterhouse in the ninth month: and *there was a fire* on the hearth burning before him.

23 And it came to pass, *that* when Jehudi had read three or four leaves, he cut it with the ¹penknife, and cast *it* into the fire that *was* on the hearth, until all the ²roll *was* consumed in the fire that *was* on the hearth.

24 Yet they were ªnot afraid, nor ᵇrent¹ their garments, *neither* the king, nor any of his servants that heard all these words.

25 Nevertheless Elnathan and Delaiah and Gemariah had made intercession to the king that he would not burn the ¹roll: but he would not ²hear them.

26 But the king commanded Jerahmeel the son of ¹Hammelech, and Seraiah the son of Azriel, and Shelemiah the son of Abdeel, to take Baruch the scribe and Jeremiah the prophet: but the LORD hid them.

27 Then the word of the LORD came to Jeremiah, after that the king had burned the ¹roll, and the words which Baruch wrote at the mouth of Jeremiah, saying,

28 Take thee again another ¹roll, and write in it all the former words that were in the first roll, which Jehoiakim the king of Judah hath burned.

29 And thou shalt say to Jehoiakim king of Judah, Thus saith the LORD; Thou hast burned this ¹roll, saying, ªWhy hast thou written therein, saying, The king of Babylon shall certainly come and destroy this land, and shall cause to ᵇcease from thence man and beast?

30 Therefore thus saith the LORD of Jehoiakim king of Judah; ªHe shall have none to sit upon the throne of David: and his dead body shall be ᵇcast out in the day to the heat, and in the night to the frost.

31 And I will punish him and his ¹seed and his servants for their iniquity; and I will bring upon them, and upon the inhabitants of Jerusalem, and upon the men of Judah, all the ²evil that I have pronounced against them; but they hearkened not.

32 Then took Jeremiah another ¹roll, and gave it to Baruch the scribe, the son of Neriah; who wrote therein from the mouth of Jeremiah all the words of the book which Jehoiakim king of Judah had burned in the fire: and there were added besides unto them many ²like words.

## CHAPTER 37

A ND king ªZedekiah the son of Josiah reigned instead of ¹Coniah the son of Jehoiakim, whom Nebuchadrezzar king of Babylon made king in the land of Judah.

2 ªBut neither he, nor his servants, nor the people of the land, ¹did hearken unto the words of the LORD, which he spake by the prophet Jeremiah.

3 And Zedekiah the king sent Jehucal the son of Shelemiah and ªZephaniah the son of Maaseiah the priest to the prophet Jeremiah, saying, ᵇPray now unto the LORD our God for us.

4 Now Jeremiah came in and went out among the people: for they had not put him into prison.

5 Then ªPharaoh's army was come forth out of Egypt: and when the Chaldeans that besieged Jerusalem heard ¹tidings of them, they departed from Jerusalem.

---

36:12 ª Jer. 41:1
ᵇ Jer. 26:22

36:13 ¹ *hearing*

36:14 ¹ *scroll*
² *hearing*

36:16 ¹ *looked in fear from one to another*

36:17 ¹ Lit. *from*

36:20 ¹ *stored the scroll* ² *hearing*

36:21 ¹ *bring the scroll*

36:22 ª Judg. 3:20; Amos 3:15

36:23 ¹ *scribe's knife* ² *scroll*

36:24 ¹ [Ps. 36:1]; Jer. 36:16 ᵇ Gen. 37:29, 34; 2 Sam. 1:11; 1 Kin. 21:27; 2 Kin. 19:1, 2; 22:11; Is. 36:22; 37:1; Jon. 3:6 ¹ *tore*

36:25 ¹ *scroll* ² *listen to*

36:26 ¹ Lit. *the king*

36:27 ¹ *scroll*

36:28 ¹ *scroll*

36:29 ª Jer. 32:3 ᵇ Jer. 25:9–11; 26:9 ¹ *scroll*

36:30 ª Jer. 22:30 ᵇ Jer. 22:19

36:31 ¹ *descendants* ² *doom*

36:32 ¹ *scroll* ² *similar*

37:1 ª 2 Kin. 24:17; 1 Chr. 3:15; 2 Chr. 36:10; Jer. 22:24 ¹ Or *Jehoiachin*

37:2 ª 2 Kin. 24:19, 20; 2 Chr. 36:12–16; [Prov. 29:12] ¹ *gave heed*

37:3 ª Jer. 21:1, 2; 29:25; 52:24 ᵇ 1 Kin. 13:6; Jer. 42:2; Acts 8:24

37:5 ª 2 Kin. 24:7; Jer. 37:7; Ezek. 17:15 ¹ *news*

6 Then came the word of the LORD unto the prophet Jeremiah, saying,

7 Thus saith the LORD, the God of Israel; Thus shall ye say to the king of Judah, [a]that sent you unto me to enquire of me; Behold, Pharaoh's army, which is come forth to help you, shall return to Egypt into their own land.

8 [a]And the Chaldeans shall come again, and fight against this city, and take it, and burn it with fire.

9 Thus saith the LORD; Deceive not yourselves, saying, The Chaldeans shall surely depart from us: for they shall not depart.

10 [a]For though ye had [1]smitten the whole army of the Chaldeans that fight against you, and there remained *but* wounded men among them, *yet* should they rise up every man in his tent, and burn this city with fire.

11 And it came to pass, that when the army of the Chaldeans [1]was broken up from Jerusalem for fear of Pharaoh's army,

12 Then Jeremiah went forth out of Jerusalem to go into the land of Benjamin, to [1]separate himself thence in the midst of the people.

13 And when he was in the gate of Benjamin, a captain of the ward *was* there, whose name *was* Irijah, the son of Shelemiah, the son of Hananiah; and he [1]took Jeremiah the prophet, saying, Thou [2]fallest away to the Chaldeans.

14 Then said Jeremiah, *It is* [1]false; I [2]fall not away to the Chaldeans. But he [3]hearkened not to him: so Irijah took Jeremiah, and brought him to the princes.

15 Wherefore the princes were [1]wroth with Jeremiah, and [2]smote him, [a]and put him in prison in the [b]house of Jonathan the scribe: for they had made that the prison.

16 When Jeremiah was entered into [a]the dungeon, and into the [1]cabins, and Jeremiah had remained there many days;

17 Then Zedekiah the king sent, and took him out: and the king asked him secretly in his house, and said, Is there *any* word from the LORD? And Jeremiah said, There is: for, said he, thou shalt be [a]delivered into the hand of the king of Babylon.

18 Moreover Jeremiah said unto king Zedekiah, What have I offended against thee, or against thy servants, or against this people, that ye have put me in prison?

19 Where *are* now your prophets which prophesied unto you, saying, The king of Babylon shall not come against you, nor against this land?

20 Therefore hear now, I pray thee, O my lord the king: let my [1]supplication, I pray thee, be accepted before thee; that thou cause me not to return to the house of Jonathan the scribe, lest I die there.

21 Then Zedekiah the king commanded that they should commit Jeremiah [a]into the court of the prison, and that they should give him daily a piece of bread out of the bakers' street, [b]until all the bread in the city [1]were spent. Thus Jeremiah remained in the court of the prison.

## CHAPTER 38

THEN Shephatiah the son of Mattan, and Gedaliah the son of Pashur, and [a]Jucal[1] the son of Shelemiah, and [c]Pashur the son of Malchiah, [c]heard the words that Jeremiah had spoken unto all the people, saying,

2 Thus saith the LORD, [a]He that remaineth in this city shall die by the sword, by the famine, and by the pestilence: but he that goeth forth to the Chaldeans shall live; for he shall have his life [1]for a prey, and shall live.

3 Thus saith the LORD, [a]This city shall surely be [b]given into the hand of the king of Babylon's army, which shall take it.

4 Therefore the princes said unto the king, We beseech thee, [a]let this man be put to death: for thus he [1]weakeneth the hands of the men of war that remain in this city, and the hands of all the people, in speaking such words unto them: for this man seeketh not the [2]welfare of this people, but the [3]hurt.

5 Then Zedekiah the king said, Behold, he *is* in your hand: for the king *is* not *he that* can do *any* thing against you.

6 [a]Then took they Jeremiah, and cast him into the dungeon of Malchiah the son of [1]Hammelech, that *was* in the court of the prison: and they let down Jeremiah with [2]cords. And in the dungeon *there was* no water, but mire: so Jeremiah sunk in the mire.

7 [a]Now when Ebed-melech the Ethiopian, one of the [1]eunuchs which was in the king's house, heard that they had put Jeremiah in the dungeon; the king then sitting in the gate of Benjamin;

8 Ebed-melech went forth out of the king's house, and spake to the king, saying,

9 My lord the king, these men have done evil in all that they have done to Jeremiah the prophet, whom they have cast into the dungeon; and he is [1]like to die for hunger in the place where he is: for *there is* [a]no more bread in the city.

10 Then the king commanded Ebed-melech the Ethiopian, saying,

---

37:7 [a] Is. 36:6; Jer. 21:2; Ezek. 17:17
37:8 [a] 2 Chr. 36:19; Jer. 34:22
37:10 [a] Lev. 26:36–38; Is. 30:17; Jer. 21:4, 5 [1] *defeated*
37:11 [1] *left* the siege of
37:12 [1] *claim his property there among*
37:13 [1] *seized* [2] *are defecting*
37:14 [1] *a lie* [2] *am not defecting* [3] *did not listen*
37:15 [a] Jer. 20:2; [Matt. 21:35] [b] Gen. 39:20; 2 Chr. 16:10; 18:26; Jer. 38:26; Acts 5:18 [1] *angry* [2] *struck*
37:16 [a] Jer. 38:6 [1] *cells*
37:17 [a] 2 Kin. 25:4–7; Jer. 21:7; Ezek. 12:12, 13; 17:19–21
37:20 [1] *petition*

37:21 [a] Jer. 32:2; 38:13, 28 [b] 2 Kin. 25:3; Jer. 38:9; 52:6 [1] *was gone*
38:1 [a] Jer. 37:3 [b] Jer. 21:1 [c] Jer. 21:8 [1] *Jehucal,* Jer. 37:3
38:2 [a] Jer. 21:9 [1] *as a prize*
38:3 [a] Jer. 21:10; 32:3 [b] Jer. 34:2
38:4 [a] Jer. 26:11 [1] *Is discouraging* [2] *good* [3] *harm*
38:6 [a] Jer. 37:21; Lam. 3:55 [1] *Lit. the king* [2] *ropes*
38:7 [a] Jer. 39:16 [1] *officers*
38:9 [a] Jer. 37:21 [1] *likely*

Take from hence thirty men with thee, and ¹take up Jeremiah the prophet out of the dungeon, before he die.

11 So Ebed-melech took the men with him, and went into the house of the king under the treasury, and took thence old ¹cast clouts and old rotten rags, and let them down by ²cords into the dungeon to Jeremiah.

12 And Ebed-melech the Ethiopian said unto Jeremiah, Put now *these* old ¹cast clouts and rotten rags under thine ²armholes under the ³cords. And Jeremiah did so.

13 So they drew up Jeremiah with ¹cords, and took him up out of the dungeon: and Jeremiah remained ᵃin the court of the prison.

14 Then Zedekiah the king sent, and took Jeremiah the prophet unto him into the third entry that *is* in ¹the house of the LORD: and the king said unto Jeremiah, I will ᵃask thee a thing; hide nothing from me.

15 Then Jeremiah said unto Zedekiah, If I declare *it* unto thee, wilt thou not surely put me to death? and if I give thee counsel, ¹wilt thou not hearken unto me?

16 So Zedekiah the king sware secretly unto Jeremiah, saying, *As* the LORD liveth, ᵃthat made ¹us this soul, I will not put thee to death, neither will I give thee into the hand of these men that seek thy life.

17 Then said Jeremiah unto Zedekiah, Thus saith the LORD, the God of hosts, the God of Israel; If thou wilt assuredly ᵃgo¹ forth ᵇunto the king of Babylon's princes, then thy soul shall live, and this city shall not be burned with fire; and thou shalt live, and thine house:

18 But if thou wilt not ¹go forth to the king of Babylon's princes, then shall this city be given into the hand of the Chaldeans, and they shall burn it with fire, and ᵃthou shalt not escape out of their hand.

19 And Zedekiah the king said unto Jeremiah, I am afraid of the Jews that ¹are ᵃfallen to the Chaldeans, lest they deliver me into their hand, and they ᵇmock² me.

20 But Jeremiah said, They shall not deliver *thee*. Obey, I beseech thee, the voice of the LORD, which I speak unto thee: so it shall be ᵃwell unto thee, and thy soul shall live.

21 But if thou refuse to go forth, this *is* the word that the LORD hath shewed me:

22 And, behold, all the ᵃwomen that are left in the king of Judah's house *shall be* ¹brought forth to the king of Babylon's princes, and those *women* shall say, ²Thy friends have ¹set thee on, and have prevailed against thee:

38:10 ¹ *lift*
38:11 ¹ *clothes* ² *ropes*
38:12 ¹ *clothes* ² *armpits* ³ *ropes*
38:13 ᵃ Neh. 3:25; Jer. 37:21; Acts 23:35; 24:27; 28:16, 30 ¹ *ropes*
38:14 ᵃ Jer. 21:1, 2; 37:17 ¹ *The temple*
38:15 ¹ *you will not listen to*
38:16 ᵃ Num. 16:22; Is. 57:16; Zech. 12:1; [Acts 17:25, 28] ¹ *our very souls*
38:17 ᵃ 2 Kin. 24:12 ᵇ Jer. 39:3 ¹ *surrender*
38:18 ᵃ Jer. 32:4; 34:3 ¹ *surrender*
38:19 ᵃ Jer. 39:9 ᵇ 1 Sam. 31:4 ¹ *have defected* ² *abuse*
38:20 ᵃ Jer. 40:9
38:22 ᵃ Jer. 8:10 ¹ *surrendered to* ² *Your close friends,* lit. *The men of your peace* ³ *set upon you or misled you*
4 *Have deserted you*
38:23 ᵃ Jer. 39:6; 41:10 ᵇ Jer. 39:5 ¹ *surrender*
38:26 ᵃ Jer. 37:20 ᵇ Jer. 37:15 ¹ *request*
38:27 ¹ *ceased* ² *conversation had not been heard*
38:28 ᵃ [Ps. 23:4]; Jer. 37:21; 39:14
39:1 ᵃ 2 Kin. 25:1-12; Jer. 52:4; Ezek. 24:1, 2
39:2 ᵃ Jer. 1:3 ¹ *penetrated,* lit. *breached*
39:3 ᵃ Jer. 1:15; 38:17
39:4 ᵃ 2 Kin. 25:4; Is. 30:16; Jer. 52:7; Amos 2:14 ¹ *between* ² Or *the Arabah,* the Jordan Valley
39:5 ᵃ Jer. 21:7; 32:4; 38:18, 23 ᵇ 2 Kin. 23:33; Jer. 52:9, 26, 27 ¹ *pronounced*

thy feet are sunk in the mire, *and* they ⁴are turned away back.

23 So they shall ¹bring out all thy wives and ᵃthy children to the Chaldeans: and ᵇthou shalt not escape out of their hand, but shalt be taken by the hand of the king of Babylon: and thou shalt cause this city to be burned with fire.

24 Then said Zedekiah unto Jeremiah, Let no man know of these words, and thou shalt not die.

25 But if the princes hear that I have talked with thee, and they come unto thee, and say unto thee, Declare unto us now what thou hast said unto the king, hide it not from us, and we will not put thee to death; also what the king said unto thee:

26 Then thou shalt say unto them, ᵃI presented my ¹supplication before the king, that he would not cause me to return ᵇto Jonathan's house, to die there.

27 Then came all the princes unto Jeremiah, and asked him: and he told them according to all these words that the king had commanded. So they ¹left off speaking with him; for the ²matter was not perceived.

28 So ᵃJeremiah abode in the court of the prison until the day that Jerusalem was taken: and he was *there* when Jerusalem was taken.

## CHAPTER 39

IN the ᵃninth year of Zedekiah king of Judah, in the tenth month, came Nebuchadrezzar king of Babylon and all his army against Jerusalem, and they besieged it.

2 *And* in the ᵃeleventh year of Zedekiah, in the fourth month, the ninth *day* of the month, the city was ¹broken up.

3 ᵃAnd all the princes of the king of Babylon came in, and sat in the middle gate, *even* Nergal-sharezer, Samgar-nebo, Sarsechim, Rab-saris, Nergal-sharezer, Rab-mag, with all the residue of the princes of the king of Babylon.

4 ᵃAnd it came to pass, *that* when Zedekiah the king of Judah saw them, and all the men of war, then they fled, and went forth out of the city by night, by the way of the king's garden, by the gate ¹betwixt the two walls: and he went out the way of ²the plain.

5 But the Chaldeans' army pursued after them, and ᵃovertook Zedekiah in the plains of Jericho: and when they had taken him, they brought him up to Nebuchadnezzar king of Babylon to ᵇRiblah in the land of Hamath, where he ¹gave judgment upon him.

6 Then the king of Babylon slew the sons of Zedekiah in Riblah before his

[a]eyes: also the king of Babylon slew all the [b]nobles of Judah.

7 Moreover [a]he [1]put out Zedekiah's eyes, and bound him with [2]chains, to carry him to Babylon.

8 [a]And the Chaldeans burned the king's house, and the houses of the people, with [b]fire, and brake down the [c]walls of Jerusalem.

9 [a]Then Nebuzar-adan the captain of the guard carried away captive into Babylon the remnant of the people that remained in the city, and those that fell away, that [b]fell[1] to him, with the rest of the people that remained.

10 But Nebuzar-adan the captain of the guard left [1]of the [a]poor of the people, which had nothing, in the land of Judah, and gave them vineyards and fields [2]at the same time.

11 Now Nebuchadrezzar king of Babylon gave charge concerning Jeremiah to Nebuzar-adan the captain of the guard, saying,

12 Take him, and [1]look well to him, and do him no [a]harm; but do unto him [2]even as he shall say unto thee.

13 So Nebuzar-adan the captain of the guard sent, and Nebushasban, Rab-saris, and Nergal-sharezer, Rab-mag, and all the king of Babylon's [1]princes;

14 Even they sent, [a]and took Jeremiah out of the court of the prison, and committed him [b]unto Gedaliah the son of [c]Ahikam the son of Shaphan, that he should carry him home: so he dwelt among the people.

15 Now the word of the LORD came unto Jeremiah, while he was shut up in the court of the prison, saying,

16 Go and speak to [a]Ebed-melech the Ethiopian, saying, Thus saith the LORD of hosts, the God of Israel; Behold, [b]I will bring my words upon this city for [1]evil, and not for good; and they shall be *accomplished* in that day before thee.

17 But I will deliver thee in that day, saith the LORD: and thou shalt not be given into the hand of the men of whom thou *art* afraid.

18 For I will surely deliver thee, and thou shalt not fall by the sword, but [a]thy life shall be [1]for a prey unto thee: [b]because thou hast put thy trust in me, saith the LORD.

## CHAPTER 40

THE word that came to Jeremiah from the LORD, [a]after that Nebuzar-adan the captain of the guard had let him go from Ramah, when he had taken him being bound in chains among all that were carried away captive of Jerusalem and Judah, which were carried away captive unto Babylon.

---

**39:6** [a] Deut. 28:34
[b] Jer. 34:19–21

**39:7** [2] 2 Kin. 25:7; Jer. 52:11; Ezek. 12:13 [1] *blinded Zedekiah*
[2] *bronze fetters*

**39:8** [a] 2 Kin. 25:9; Jer. 38:18; 52:13 [b] Jer. 21:10
[c] 2 Kin. 25:10; Neh. 1:3; Jer. 52:14

**39:9** [a] 2 Kin. 25:8, 11, 12, 20 [b] Jer. 38:19 [1] *defected to him*

**39:10** [a] Jer. 40:7
[1] *the poor people*
[2] Lit. *on that day*

**39:12** [a] Jer. 1:18, 19; 15:20, 21 [1] *look after* [2] *just*

**39:13** [1] *chief officers*

**39:14** [a] Jer. 38:28 [b] Jer. 40:5
[c] 2 Kin. 22:12, 14; 2 Chr. 34:20; Jer. 26:24

**39:16** [a] Jer. 38:7, 12 [b] Jer. 21:10; [Dan. 9:12; Zech. 1:6]
[1] *adversity*

**39:18** [a] Jer. 21:9; 45:5 [b] 1 Chr. 5:20; Ps. 37:40; [Jer. 17:7, 8] [1] *as a prize*

**40:1** [a] Jer. 39:9, 11

**40:2** [a] Jer. 50:7
[1] *doom*

**40:3** [a] Deut. 29:24, 25; Jer. 50:7; Dan. 9:11; [Rom. 2:5]

**40:4** [a] Jer. 39:12 [b] Gen. 20:15 [1] *Or are* [2] *look after* [3] *remain here*

**40:5** [a] Jer. 39:14 [b] 2 Kin. 25:22; Jer. 41:10 [1] *rations* [2] *gift*

**40:6** [a] Jer. 39:14 [b] Judg. 20:1; 1 Sam. 7:5; 2 Chr. 16:6

**40:7** [a] 2 Kin. 25:23, 24 [b] Jer. 39:10 [1] *armies* [2] *poorest*

**40:8** [a] Jer. 41:11–10 [b] Jer. 41:11; 43:2 [c] Jer. 42:1 [d] Deut. 3:14; Josh. 12:5; 2 Sam. 10:6 [1] *Jaazaniah*, 2 Kin. 25:23

**40:9** [a] Jer. 27:11; 38:17–20 [1] *took an oath before them and their*

---

2 And the captain of the guard took Jeremiah, and [a]said unto him, The LORD thy God hath pronounced this [1]evil upon this place.

3 Now the LORD hath brought *it,* and done according as he hath said: [a]because ye have sinned against the LORD, and have not obeyed his voice, therefore this thing is come upon you.

4 And now, behold, I loose thee this day from the chains which [1]*were* upon thine hand. [a]If it seem good unto thee to come with me into Babylon, come; and I will [2]look well unto thee: but if it seem ill unto thee to come with me into Babylon, [3]forbear: behold, [b]all the land *is* before thee: whither it seemeth good and convenient for thee to go, thither go.

5 Now while he was not yet gone back, *he said,* Go back also to [a]Gedaliah the son of Ahikam the son of Shaphan, [b]whom the king of Babylon hath made governor over the cities of Judah, and dwell with him among the people; or go wheresoever it seemeth convenient unto thee to go. So the captain of the guard gave him [1]victuals and a [2]reward, and let him go.

6 [a]Then went Jeremiah unto Gedaliah the son of Ahikam to [b]Mizpah; and dwelt with him among the people that were left in the land.

7 [a]Now when all the captains of the [1]forces which *were* in the fields, *even* they and their men, heard that the king of Babylon had made Gedaliah the son of Ahikam governor in the land, and had committed unto him men, and women, and children, and of [b]the [2]poor of the land, of them that were not carried away captive to Babylon;

8 Then they came to Gedaliah to Mizpah, [a]even Ishmael the son of Nethaniah, and [b]Johanan and Jonathan the sons of Kareah, and Seraiah the son of Tanhumeth, and the sons of Ephai the Netophathite, and [c]Jezaniah[1] the son of a [d]Maachathite, they and their men.

9 And Gedaliah the son of Ahikam the son of Shaphan [1]sware unto them and to their men, saying, Fear not to serve the Chaldeans: dwell in the land, and serve the king of Babylon, and it shall be [a]well with you.

10 As for me, behold, I will dwell at Mizpah, to serve the Chaldeans, which will come unto us: but ye, gather ye wine, and summer fruits, and oil, and put *them* in your vessels, and dwell in your cities that ye have taken.

11 Likewise when all the Jews that *were* in Moab, and among the Ammonites, and in Edom, and that *were*

in all the countries, heard that the king of Babylon had left a remnant of Judah, and that he had set over them Gedaliah the son of Ahikam the son of Shaphan;

12 Even all the Jews [a]returned out of all places whither they were driven, and came to the land of Judah, to Gedaliah, unto Mizpah, and gathered wine and summer fruits [1]very much.

13 Moreover Johanan the son of Kareah, and all the captains of the forces that *were* in the fields, came to Gedaliah to Mizpah,

14 And said unto him, [1]Dost thou certainly know that [a]Baalis the king of the Ammonites hath sent Ishmael the son of Nethaniah to [2]slay thee? But Gedaliah the son of Ahikam believed them not.

15 Then Johanan the son of Kareah spake to Gedaliah in Mizpah secretly, saying, Let me go, I pray thee, and I will [1]slay Ishmael the son of Nethaniah, and no man shall know *it:* wherefore should he [2]slay thee, that all the Jews which are gathered unto thee should be scattered, and the [a]remnant in Judah perish?

16 But Gedaliah the son of Ahikam said unto Johanan the son of Kareah, Thou shalt not do this thing: for thou speakest falsely of Ishmael.

## CHAPTER 41

Now it came to pass in the seventh month, [a]*that* Ishmael the son of Nethaniah the son of Elishama, of the [1]seed royal, and the [2]princes of the king, even ten men with him, came unto Gedaliah the son of Ahikam to [b]Mizpah; and there they did eat bread together in Mizpah.

2 Then arose Ishmael the son of Nethaniah, and the ten men that were with him, and [a]smote[1] Gedaliah the son of [b]Ahikam the son of Shaphan with the sword, and [2]slew him, whom the king of Babylon had made [c]governor over the land.

3 Ishmael also [1]slew all the Jews that were with him, *even* with Gedaliah, at Mizpah, and the Chaldeans that were found there, *and* the men of war.

4 And it came to pass the second day after he had slain Gedaliah, and no man knew *it,*

5 That there came certain from Shechem, from Shiloh, and from Samaria, *even* fourscore men, [a]having their beards shaven, and their clothes [1]rent, and having cut themselves, with offerings and incense in their hand, to bring *them* to [b]the house of the LORD.

6 And Ishmael the son of Nethaniah went forth from Mizpah to meet

---

40:12 [a] Jer. 43:5
[1] *in abundance*

40:14 [a] Jer. 41:10
[1] Or *Certainly you know* [2] *murder*

40:15 [a] Jer. 42:2
[1] *kill* [2] *murder*

41:1 [a] 2 Kin. 25:25
[b] Jer. 40:6, 10
[1] *royal family*
[2] *chief officers*

41:2 [a] 2 Sam. 3:27;
20:9, 10; 2 Kin.
25:25; Ps. 41:9;
109:5; John 13:18
[b] Jer. 26:24 [c] Jer.
40:5 [1] *struck down* [2] *killed*

41:3 [1] *struck down*

41:5 [a] Lev. 19:27,
28; Deut. 14:1; Is.
15:2 [b] 1 Sam. 1:7;
2 Kin. 25:9; Neh.
10:34, 35 [1] *torn*

41:6 [1] *as he went along*

41:7 [a] Ps. 55:23; Is.
59:7; Ezek. 22:27;
33:24, 26 [1] *killed*

41:8 [1] *Do not kill us* [2] *desisted*

41:9 [a] 1 Kin.
15:22; 2 Chr. 16:6
[1] *cistern*

41:10 [a] Jer. 40:11,
12 [b] Jer. 43:6
[c] Jer. 40:7 [d] Jer.
40:14 [1] *rest*

41:11 [a] Jer. 40:7,
8, 13–16

41:12 [a] 2 Sam. 2:13
[1] *pool that is*

41:14 [1] *turned around and came back*

41:16 [a] Jer. 40:11,
12; 43:4–7

41:17 [a] 2 Sam.
19:37, 38

---

them, weeping [1]all along as he went: and it came to pass, as he met them, he said unto them, Come to Gedaliah the son of Ahikam.

7 And it was *so,* when they came into the midst of the city, that Ishmael the son of Nethaniah [a]slew[1] them, *and* cast *them* into the midst of the pit, he, and the men that *were* with him.

8 But ten men were found among them that said unto Ishmael, [1]Slay us not: for we have treasures in the field, of wheat, and of barley, and of oil, and of honey. So he [2]forbare, and slew them not among their brethren.

9 Now the [1]pit wherein Ishmael had cast all the dead bodies of the men, whom he had slain because of Gedaliah, *was* it [a]which Asa the king had made for fear of Baasha king of Israel: *and* Ishmael the son of Nethaniah filled it with *them that were* slain.

10 Then Ishmael carried away captive all the [a]residue[1] of the people that *were* in Mizpah, [b]*even* the king's daughters, and all the people that remained in Mizpah, [c]whom Nebuzaradan the captain of the guard had committed to Gedaliah the son of Ahikam: and Ishmael the son of Nethaniah carried them away captive, and departed to go over to [d]the Ammonites.

11 But when [a]Johanan the son of Kareah, and all the captains of the forces that *were* with him, heard of all the evil that Ishmael the son of Nethaniah had done,

12 Then they took all the men, and went to fight with Ishmael the son of Nethaniah, and found him by [a]the great [1]waters that *are* in Gibeon.

13 Now it came to pass, *that* when all the people which *were* with Ishmael saw Johanan the son of Kareah, and all the captains of the forces that *were* with him, then they were glad.

14 So all the people that Ishmael had carried away captive from Mizpah [1]cast about and returned, and went unto Johanan the son of Kareah.

15 But Ishmael the son of Nethaniah escaped from Johanan with eight men, and went to the Ammonites.

16 Then took Johanan the son of Kareah, and all the captains of the forces that *were* with him, all the [a]remnant of the people whom he had recovered from Ishmael the son of Nethaniah, from Mizpah, after *that* he had slain Gedaliah the son of Ahikam, *even* mighty men of war, and the women, and the children, and the eunuchs, whom he had brought again from Gibeon:

17 And they departed, and dwelt in the habitation of [a]Chimham, which

is by Bethlehem, to go to enter into
[b]Egypt,

18 Because of the Chaldeans: for
they were afraid of them, because
Ishmael the son of Nethaniah had
[1]slain Gedaliah the son of Ahikam,
[a]whom the king of Babylon made
governor in the land.

## CHAPTER 42

THEN all the captains of the forces,
[a]and Johanan the son of Kareah,
and Jezaniah the son of Hoshaiah,
and all the people from the least even
unto the greatest, came near,

2 And said unto Jeremiah the
prophet, Let, we [a]beseech thee, our
supplication be accepted before thee,
and [b]pray for us unto the LORD thy
God, *even* for all this remnant; (for we
are left *but* [1]thine
eyes do behold us:)

3 That the LORD thy God may shew
us [a]the way wherein we [1]may walk,
and the thing that we [1]may do.

4 Then Jeremiah the prophet said
unto them, I have heard *you;* behold,
I will pray unto the LORD your God
according to your words; and it shall
come to pass, *that* [a]whatsoever thing
the LORD shall answer you, I will declare *it* unto you; I will [b]keep nothing
back from you.

5 Then they said to Jeremiah, [a]The
LORD be a true and faithful witness
between us, if we do not even according to all things for the which the
LORD thy God shall send thee to us.

6 Whether *it be* [1]good, or whether *it
be* [2]evil, we will [a]obey the voice of the
LORD our God, to whom we send thee;
[b]that it may be well with us, when we
obey the voice of the LORD our God.

7 And it came to pass after ten
days, that the word of the LORD came
unto Jeremiah.

8 Then called he Johanan the son
of Kareah, and all the captains of the
forces which *were* with him, and all
the people from the least even to the
greatest,

9 And said unto them, Thus saith
the LORD, the God of Israel, unto
whom ye sent me to present your
[1]supplication before him;

10 If ye will still abide in this land,
then [a]will I build you, and not pull
*you* down, and I will plant you, and
not pluck *you* up: for I [b]repent[1] me of
the evil that I have [2]done unto you.

11 Be not afraid of the king of Babylon, of whom ye are afraid; be not
afraid of him, saith the LORD: [a]for I
*am* with you to save you, and to deliver you from his hand.

12 And [a]I will shew mercies unto
you, that he may have mercy upon
you, and cause you to return to your
own land.

41:17 [b] Jer. 43:7
41:18 [1] *murdered*
[a] Jer. 40:5
42:1 [a] Jer. 40:8,
13; 41:11
42:2 [a] Jer. 15:11
[b] Is. 37:4 [c] Lev.
26:22 [1] *thou
canst see*
42:3 [a] Ezra 8:21
[1] *should*
42:4 [a] 1 Kin. 22:14
[b] 1 Sam. 3:17, 18
42:5 [a] Gen. 31:50
42:6 [a] Ex. 24:7
[b] Jer. 7:23 [1] *pleas-
ing* [2] *displeasing*
42:9 [1] *petition*
42:10 [a] Jer. 24:6;
31:28; 33:7 [b] [Jer.
18:8] [1] *relent
concerning the di-
saster* [2] *brought
upon*
42:11 [a] Rom. 8:31
42:12 [a] Ps. 106:46

42:13 [a] Jer. 44:16
[1] *disobeying*
42:14 [a] Jer. 41:17;
43:7 [1] *for*
42:15 [a] Deut. 17:16
[b] Luke 9:51 [1] *Or
surely*
42:16 [a] Ezek. 11:8
[1] *closely*
42:17 [a] Jer.
44:14, 28
42:18 [a] Jer. 7:20
[b] Is. 65:15 [1] *oath*
42:19 [a] Deut. 17:16
[1] *warned*
42:20 [1] *were
hypocrites in your
hearts,* lit. *used
deceit against
your souls*
42:21 [a] Is. 30:1–7
42:22 [a] Ezek. 6:11
43:1 [a] Jer. 42:9–18
43:2 [a] Jer. 42:1

13 But if [a]ye say, We will not dwell
in this land, [1]neither obey the voice of
the LORD your God,

14 Saying, No; but we will go into
the land of [a]Egypt, where we shall
see no war, nor hear the sound of the
trumpet, nor have hunger [1]of bread;
and there will we dwell:

15 And now therefore hear the
word of the LORD, ye remnant of Judah; Thus saith the LORD of hosts, the
God of Israel; If ye [a]wholly[1] set [b]your
faces to enter into Egypt, and go to
sojourn there;

16 Then it shall come to pass, *that*
the [a]sword, which ye feared, shall
overtake you there in the land of
Egypt, and the famine, whereof ye
were afraid, shall follow [1]close after
you there in Egypt; and there ye shall
die.

17 So shall it be with all the men
that set their faces to go into Egypt
to sojourn there; they shall die by
the sword, by the famine, and by the
pestilence: and [a]none of them shall
remain or escape from the evil that I
will bring upon them.

18 For thus saith the LORD of hosts,
the God of Israel; As mine anger and
my fury hath been [a]poured forth
upon the inhabitants of Jerusalem;
so shall my fury be poured forth upon
you, when ye shall enter into Egypt:
and [b]ye shall be an [1]execration, and
an astonishment, and a curse, and a
reproach; and ye shall see this place
no more.

19 The LORD hath said concerning
you, O ye remnant of Judah; [a]Go ye
not into Egypt: know certainly that I
have [1]admonished you this day.

20 For ye [1]dissembled in your
hearts, when ye sent me unto the
LORD your God, saying, Pray for us
unto the LORD our God; and according unto all that the LORD our God
shall say, so declare unto us, and we
will do *it.*

21 And *now* I have this day declared
*it* to you; but ye have [a]not obeyed the
voice of the LORD your God, nor any
*thing* for the which he hath sent me
unto you.

22 Now therefore know certainly
that [a]ye shall die by the sword, by the
famine, and by the pestilence, in the
place whither ye desire to go *and* to
sojourn.

## CHAPTER 43

AND it came to pass, *that* when
Jeremiah had made an end of
speaking unto all the people all the
[a]words of the LORD their God, for
which the LORD their God had sent
him to them, *even* all these words,

2 [a]Then spake Azariah the son of
Hoshaiah, and Johanan the son of

Kareah, and all the proud men, saying unto Jeremiah, Thou speakest falsely: the LORD our God hath not sent thee to say, Go not into Egypt to sojourn there:

3 But ªBaruch the son of Neriah ¹setteth thee on against us, for to deliver us into the hand of the Chaldeans, that they might put us to death, and carry us away captives into Babylon.

4 So Johanan the son of Kareah, and all the captains of the forces, and all the people, obeyed ªnot the voice of the LORD, to ¹dwell in the land of Judah.

5 But Johanan the son of Kareah, and all the captains of the forces, took ªall the remnant of Judah, that were returned from all nations, whither they had been driven, to dwell in the land of Judah;

6 *Even* men, and women, and children, ªand the king's daughters, ᵇand every person that Nebuzar-adan the captain of the guard had left with Gedaliah the son of Ahikam the son of Shaphan, and Jeremiah the prophet, and Baruch the son of Neriah.

7 ªSo they came into the land of Egypt: for they obeyed not the voice of the LORD: thus came they *even* to ᵇTahpanhes.

8 Then came the ªword of the LORD unto Jeremiah in Tahpanhes, saying,

9 Take great stones in thine hand, and hide them in the ¹clay in the brickkiln, which *is* at the entry of Pharaoh's house in Tahpanhes, in the sight of the men of Judah;

10 And say unto them, Thus saith the LORD of hosts, the God of Israel; Behold, I will send and ¹take ²Nebuchadrezzar the king of Babylon, ªmy servant, and will set his throne upon these stones that I have hid; and he shall spread his royal pavilion over them.

11 ªAnd when he cometh, he shall ¹smite the land of Egypt, *and deliver* ᵇsuch *as are* for death to death; and such *as are* for captivity to captivity; and such *as are* for the sword to the sword.

12 And I will kindle a fire in the houses of ªthe gods of Egypt; and he shall burn them, and carry them away captives: and he shall array himself with the land of Egypt, as a shepherd putteth on his garment; and he shall go forth from thence in peace.

13 He shall break also the ¹images of ²Beth-shemesh, that *is* in the land of Egypt; and the houses of the gods of the Egyptians shall he burn with fire.

### CHAPTER 44

THE word that came to Jeremiah concerning all the Jews which

dwell in the land of Egypt, which dwell at ªMigdol, and at ᵇTahpanhes, and at ᶜNoph,¹ and in the country of ᵈPathros, saying,

2 Thus saith the LORD of hosts, the God of Israel; Ye have seen all the ¹evil that I have brought upon Jerusalem, and upon all the cities of Judah; and, behold, this day they *are* ªa desolation, and no man dwelleth therein.

3 Because of their wickedness which they have committed to provoke me to anger, in that they went ªto burn incense, *and* to ᵇserve other gods, whom they knew not, *neither* they, ye, nor your fathers.

4 Howbeit ªI sent unto you all my servants the prophets, rising early and sending *them*, saying, Oh, do not this abominable thing that I hate.

5 But they ¹hearkened not, nor inclined their ear to turn from their wickedness, to burn no incense unto other gods.

6 Wherefore my fury and mine anger was poured forth, and was kindled in the cities of Judah and in the streets of Jerusalem; and they ¹are wasted *and* desolate, as at this day.

7 Therefore now thus saith the LORD, the God of hosts, the God of Israel; Wherefore commit ye *this* great evil ªagainst your souls, to cut off from you man and woman, child and suckling, out of Judah, to leave you none to remain;

8 In that ye ªprovoke me unto wrath with the works of your hands, burning incense unto other gods in the land of Egypt, whither ye be gone to dwell, that ye might cut yourselves off, and that ye might be ᵇa curse and a reproach among all the nations of the earth?

9 Have ye forgotten the wickedness of your fathers, and the wickedness of the kings of Judah, and the wickedness of their wives, and your own wickedness, and the wickedness of your wives, which they have committed in the land of Judah, and in the streets of Jerusalem?

10 They are not ªhumbled¹ *even* unto this day, neither have they ᵇfeared, nor walked in my law, nor in my statutes, that I set before you and before your fathers.

11 Therefore thus saith the LORD of hosts, the God of Israel; Behold, ªI will set my face against you for ¹evil, and to ²cut off all Judah.

12 And I will take the remnant of Judah, that have set their faces to go into the land of Egypt to sojourn there, and ªthey shall all be consumed, *and* fall in the land of Egypt; they shall *even* be consumed by the sword *and* by the famine: they shall die, from the least even unto the

---

*Cross-reference column:*

43:3 ª Jer. 36:4; 45:1 ¹ Or *incited thee against*

43:4 ª 2 Kin. 25:26 ¹ *remain*

43:5 ª Jer. 40:11, 12

43:6 ª Jer. 41:10 ᵇ Jer. 39:10; 40:7

43:7 ª Jer. 42:19 ᵇ Jer. 2:16; 44:1

43:8 ª Jer. 44:1–30

43:9 ¹ Or *mortar*

43:10 ª Jer. 25:9; 27:6; Ezek. 29:18, 20 ¹ *bring* ² Or *Nebuchadnezzar*

43:11 ª Is. 19:1–25; Jer. 25:15–19; 44:13; 46:1, 2, 13–26; Ezek. 29:19, 20 ᵇ Jer. 15:2; Zech. 11:9 ¹ *strike*

43:12 ª Ex. 12:12; Is. 19:1; Jer. 46:25; Ezek. 30:13

43:13 ¹ *sacred pillars* ² Lit. *House of the Sun*, ancient On, later called Heliopolis

44:1 ª Ex. 14:2; Jer. 46:14 ᵇ Jer. 43:7; Ezek. 30:18 ᶜ Is. 19:13; Jer. 2:16; 46:14; Ezek. 30:13, 16; Hos. 9:6 ᵈ Is. 11:11; Ezek. 29:14; 30:14 ¹ Ancient Memphis

44:2 ª Is. 6:11; Jer. 4:7; 9:11; 34:22; Mic. 3:12 ¹ *calamity*

44:3 ª Jer. 19:4 ᵇ Deut. 13:6; 32:17

44:4 ª 2 Chr. 36:15; Jer. 7:25; 25:4; 26:5; 29:19; Zech. 7:7

44:5 ¹ *did not listen*

44:6 ¹ *became a ruin*

44:7 ª Num. 16:38; Jer. 7:19; [Ezek. 33:11]; Hab. 2:10

44:8 ª 2 Kin. 17:15–17; Jer. 25:6, 7; 44:3; 1 Cor. 10:21, 22 ᵇ 1 Kin. 9:7, 8; 2 Chr. 7:20; Jer. 42:18

44:10 ª 2 Chr. 36:12; Jer. 6:15; 8:12; Dan. 5:22 ᵇ [Prov. 28:14] ¹ *contrite*

44:11 ª Lev. 17:10; 20:5, 6; Jer. 21:10; Amos 9:4 ¹ *catastrophe* ² *destroy*

44:12 ª Jer. 42:15–17, 22

greatest, by the sword and by the famine: and ᵇthey shall be an ¹execration, *and* an astonishment, and a curse, and a reproach.

13 ªFor I will punish them that dwell in the land of Egypt, as I have punished Jerusalem, by the sword, by the famine, and by the pestilence:

14 So that none of the remnant of Judah, which are gone into the land of Egypt to sojourn there, shall escape or ¹remain, that they should return into the land of Judah, to the which they ²have a ªdesire to return to dwell there: for ᵇnone shall return but such as shall escape.

15 Then all the men which knew that their wives had burned incense unto other gods, and all the women that stood by, a great multitude, even all the people that dwelt in the land of Egypt, in Pathros, answered Jeremiah, saying,

16 *As for* the word that thou hast spoken unto us in the name of the LORD, ªwe will not ¹hearken unto thee.

17 But we will certainly do ªwhatsoever thing goeth forth out of our own mouth, to burn incense unto the ᵇqueen of heaven, and to pour out drink offerings unto her, as we have done, we, and our fathers, our kings, and our princes, in the cities of Judah, and in the streets of Jerusalem: for *then* had we plenty of ¹victuals, and were ²well, and saw no ³evil.

18 But since we ¹left off to burn incense to the queen of heaven, and to pour out drink offerings unto her, we have ²wanted all *things,* and have been consumed by the sword and by the famine.

19 ªAnd¹ when we burned incense to the queen of heaven, and poured out drink offerings unto her, did we make her cakes to worship her, and pour out drink offerings unto her, without our ²men?

20 Then Jeremiah said unto all the people, to the men, and to the women, and to all the people which had given him *that* answer, saying,

21 The incense that ye burned in the cities of Judah, and in the streets of Jerusalem, ye, and your fathers, your kings, and your princes, and the people of the land, did not the LORD remember them, and came it *not* into his mind?

22 So that the LORD could no longer bear, because of the evil of your doings, *and* because of the abominations which ye have committed; therefore is your land a desolation, and an astonishment, and a curse, without an inhabitant, ªas at this day.

23 Because ye have burned incense, and because ye have sinned against the LORD, and have not obeyed the

voice of the LORD, nor walked in his law, nor in his statutes, nor in his testimonies; ªtherefore this ¹evil is happened unto you, as at this day.

24 Moreover Jeremiah said unto all the people, and to all the women, Hear the word of the LORD, all Judah that *are* in the land of Egypt:

25 Thus saith the LORD of hosts, the God of Israel, saying; Ye and your wives have both spoken with your mouths, and fulfilled with your hand, saying, We will surely perform our vows that we have vowed, to burn incense to the queen of heaven, and to pour out drink offerings unto her: ye will surely accomplish your vows, and surely perform your vows.

26 Therefore hear ye the word of the LORD, all Judah that dwell in the land of Egypt; Behold, ªI have sworn by my ᵇgreat name, saith the LORD, that ᶜmy name shall no more be named in the mouth of any man of Judah in all the land of Egypt, saying, The Lord GOD liveth.

27 Behold, I will watch over them for ¹evil, and not for good: and all the men of Judah that *are* in the land of Egypt ªshall be consumed by the sword and by the famine, until there be an end of them.

28 Yet ªa small number that escape the sword shall return out of the land of Egypt into the land of Judah, and all the remnant of Judah, that are gone into the land of Egypt to sojourn there, shall know whose words shall stand, mine, or theirs.

29 And this *shall be* a sign unto you, saith the LORD, that I will punish you in this place, that ye may know that my words shall surely ªstand against you for ¹evil:

30 Thus saith the LORD; Behold, ªI will give Pharaoh-hophra king of Egypt into the hand of his enemies, and into the hand of them that seek his life; as I gave ᵇZedekiah king of Judah into the hand of Nebuchadrezzar king of Babylon, his enemy, and that sought his life.

## CHAPTER 45

THE ªword that Jeremiah the prophet spake unto ᵇBaruch the son of Neriah, when he had written these words in a book at the mouth of Jeremiah, in the ᶜfourth year of Jehoiakim the son of Josiah king of Judah, saying,

2 Thus saith the LORD, the God of Israel, unto thee, O Baruch;

3 Thou didst say, Woe is me now! for the LORD hath added grief to my sorrow; I ªfainted in my sighing, and I find no rest.

4 Thus shalt thou say unto him, The LORD saith thus; Behold, ª*that* which

### Center reference column

44:12 ᵇ Is. 65:15; Jer. 42:18 ¹ *oath*
44:13 ª Jer. 43:11
44:14 ª Jer. 22:26, 27 ᵇ [Is. 4:2; 10:20]; Jer. 44:28; [Rom. 9:27] ¹ *survive* ² Lit. *lift up their soul*
44:16 ª Jer. 6:16 ¹ *listen*
44:17 ª Num. 30:12; Deut. 23:23; Judg. 11:36 ᵇ 2 Kin. 17:16; Jer. 7:18 ¹ *food* ² *well-off* ³ *trouble*
44:18 ¹ *stopped burning* ² *lacked everything*
44:19 ª Jer. 7:18 ¹ *And* the women said ² *husbands'* permission
44:22 ª Jer. 25:11, 18, 38
44:23 ª 1 Kin. 9:9; Neh. 13:18; Jer.
44:2; Dan. 9:11, 12 ¹ *calamity*
44:26 ª Gen. 22:16; Deut. 32:40, 41; Jer. 22:5; Amos 6:8; Heb. 6:13 ᵇ Jer. 10:6 ᶜ Neh. 9:5; Ps. 50:16; Ezek. 20:39
44:27 ª Jer. 1:10; 31:28; Ezek. 7:6 ¹ *adversity*
44:28 ª Is. 10:19; 27:12, 13
44:29 ª [Ps. 33:11] ¹ *adversity*
44:30 ª Jer. 46:25, 26; Ezek. 29:3; 30:21 ᵇ 2 Kin. 25:4–7; Jer. 39:5
45:1 ª Jer. 36:1, 4, 32 ᵇ Jer. 32:12, 16; 43:3 ᶜ Jer. 25:1; 36:1; 46:2
45:3 ª Ps. 6:6; 69:3; [2 Cor. 4:1, 16; Gal. 6:9]
45:4 ª Is. 5:5; Jer. 1:10; 11:17; 18:7–10; 31:28

I have built will I break down, and that which I have planted I will pluck up, even this whole land.

5 And seekest thou great things for thyself? seek *them* not: for, behold, [a]I will bring [1]evil upon all flesh, saith the LORD: but thy [b]life will I give unto thee [2]for a prey in all places whither thou goest.

## CHAPTER 46

THE word of the LORD which came to Jeremiah the prophet against [a]the [1]Gentiles;

2 Against [a]Egypt, [b]against the army of Pharaoh-necho king of Egypt, which was by the river Euphrates in Carchemish, which [1]Nebuchadrezzar king of Babylon [c]smote[2] in the [d]fourth year of Jehoiakim the son of Josiah king of Judah.

3 [1]Order ye the [2]buckler and shield, and draw near to battle.

4 Harness the horses; and get up, ye horsemen, and stand forth with *your* helmets; [1]furbish the spears, *and* [a]put on the [2]brigandines.

5 Wherefore have I seen them dismayed *and* turned away back? and their mighty ones are beaten down, and [1]are fled apace, and look not back: *for* [a]fear *was* [2]round about, saith the LORD.

6 Let not the swift flee away, nor the mighty man escape; they shall [a]stumble, and fall toward the north by the river Euphrates.

7 Who *is* this *that* cometh up [a]as a flood, whose waters are moved as the rivers?

8 Egypt riseth up like a flood, and *his* waters are moved like the rivers; and he saith, I will go up, *and* will cover the earth; I will destroy the city and the inhabitants thereof.

9 Come up, ye horses; and rage, ye chariots; and let the mighty men come forth; [1]the Ethiopians and [2]the Libyans, that handle the shield; and the Lydians, [a]that handle *and* bend the bow.

10 For this *is* [a]the day of the Lord GOD of hosts, a day of vengeance, that he may avenge [1]of his adversaries: and [b]the sword shall devour, and it shall be [2]satiate and made drunk with their blood: for the Lord GOD of hosts [c]hath a sacrifice in the north country by the river Euphrates.

11 [a]Go up into Gilead, and take balm, [b]O virgin, the daughter of Egypt: in vain shalt thou use many medicines; *for* [c]thou shalt not be cured.

12 The nations have heard of thy [a]shame, and thy cry hath filled the land: for the mighty man hath stumbled against the mighty, *and* they are fallen both together.

45:5 [a] Jer. 25:26
[b] Jer. 21:9; 38:2;
39:18 [1] *adversity*
[2] *as a prize*

46:1 [a] Jer. 25:15
[1] *nations*

46:2 [a] Jer. 25:17–
19 [b] 2 Kin. 23:33–
35 [c] 2 Chr. 35:20
[d] Jer. 45:1 [1] Or
*Nebuchadnezzar*
[2] *defeated*

46:3 [1] *Set in order*
[2] A small shield

46:4 [a] Jer. 51:11, 12
[1] *polish* [2] *armour*

46:5 [a] Jer. 49:29
[1] *have speedily
fled* [2] *all around*

46:6 [a] Dan. 11:19

46:7 [a] Jer. 47:2

46:9 [a] Is. 66:19
[1] Heb. *Cush*
[2] Heb. *Put*

46:10 [a] Joel 1:15
[b] Deut. 32:42
[c] Is. 34:6 [1] *on*
[2] *satisfied*

46:11 [a] Jer. 8:22
[b] Is. 47:1 [c] Ezek.
30:21

46:12 [a] Jer. 2:36

46:13 [a] Is. 19:1
[1] Or *Nebuchadnezzar* [2] *strike*

46:14 [a] Jer.
44:1 [b] Ezek.
30:18 [1] Ancient
Memphis [2] *all around*

46:16 [a] Lev. 26:36,
37 [b] Jer. 51:9
[1] *back*

46:18 [a] Jer. 48:15

46:19 [a] Jer. 48:18
[b] Is. 20:4 [1] *prepare* [2] Ancient
Memphis

46:20 [a] Hos. 10:11
[b] Jer. 1:14 [1] *pretty*

46:21 [a] [Ps. 37:13]
[1] *mercenaries*
[2] Lit. *young bulls
of the stall*

46:22 [a] [Is. 29:4]
[1] *noise* [2] *those
who chop*

46:23 [a] Is. 10:34
[b] Judg. 6:5; 7:12
[1] *more numerous*

46:24 [a] Jer. 1:15
[1] *ashamed*

46:25 [a] Ezek.
30:14–16 [b] Jer.
43:12, 13 [c] Is.
30:1–5; 31:1–3
[1] Heb. *Amon, a
sun god* [2] Ancient Thebes

46:26 [a] Ezek. 32:11
[b] Ezek. 29:8–14
[1] Or *Nebuchadnezzar*

46:27 [a] Is. 41:13,
14; 43:5; 44:2
[b] Is. 11:11

13 The word that the LORD spake to Jeremiah the prophet, how [1]Nebuchadrezzar king of Babylon should come *and* [a]smite[2] the land of Egypt.

14 Declare ye in Egypt, and publish in [a]Migdol, and publish in [1]Noph and in [b]Tahpanhes: say ye, Stand fast, and prepare thee; for the sword shall devour [2]round about thee.

15 Why are thy valiant *men* swept away? they stood not, because the LORD did drive them.

16 He made many to fall, yea, [a]one fell upon another: and they said, Arise, and [b]let us go [1]again to our own people, and to the land of our nativity, from the oppressing sword.

17 They did cry there, Pharaoh king of Egypt *is but* a noise; he hath passed the time appointed.

18 *As* I live, saith the King, [a]whose name *is* the LORD of hosts, Surely as Tabor *is* among the mountains, and as Carmel by the sea, *so* shall he come.

19 O [a]thou daughter dwelling in Egypt, [1]furnish thyself [b]to go into captivity: for [2]Noph shall be waste and desolate without an inhabitant.

20 Egypt *is like* a very [1]fair [a]heifer, *but* destruction cometh; it cometh [b]out of the north.

21 Also her [1]hired men *are* in the midst of her like [2]fatted bullocks; for they also are turned back, *and* are fled away together: they did not stand, because [a]the day of their calamity was come upon them, *and* the time of their visitation.

22 [a]The [1]voice thereof shall go like a serpent; for they shall march with an army, and come against her with axes, as [2]hewers of wood.

23 They shall [a]cut down her forest, saith the LORD, though it cannot be searched; because they are [1]more than [b]the grasshoppers, and *are* innumerable.

24 The daughter of Egypt shall be [1]confounded; she shall be delivered into the hand of [a]the people of the north.

25 The LORD of hosts, the God of Israel, saith; Behold, I will punish [1]the multitude of [a]No,[2] and Pharaoh, and Egypt, [b]with their gods, and their kings; even Pharaoh, and *all* them that [c]trust in him:

26 [a]And I will deliver them into the hand of those that seek their lives, and into the hand of [1]Nebuchadrezzar king of Babylon, and into the hand of his servants: and [b]afterward it shall be inhabited, as in the days of old, saith the LORD.

27 [a]But fear not thou, O my servant Jacob, and be not dismayed, O Israel: for, behold, I will [b]save thee from afar off, and thy seed from the land

of their captivity; and Jacob shall return, and be in rest and at ease, and none shall make *him* afraid.

28 Fear thou not, O Jacob my servant, saith the LORD: for I *am* with thee; for I will make a full end of all the nations whither I have driven thee: but I will not make ªa full end of thee, but ᵇcorrect thee ¹in measure; yet will I not leave thee wholly unpunished.

## CHAPTER 47

THE word of the LORD that came to Jeremiah the prophet ªagainst the Philistines, ᵇbefore that Pharaoh smote Gaza.

2 Thus saith the LORD; Behold, ªwaters rise up ᵇout of the north, and shall be an overflowing flood, and shall overflow the land, and all that is therein; the city, and them that dwell therein: then the men shall cry, and all the inhabitants of the land shall ¹howl.

3 At the ªnoise of the stamping of the hoofs of his strong *horses,* at the rushing of his chariots, *and* at the rumbling of his wheels, the fathers shall not look back ¹to *their* children for ²feebleness of hands;

4 Because of the day that cometh to ¹spoil all the ªPhilistines, *and* to cut off from ᵇTyrus and Zidon every helper that remaineth: for the LORD will ¹spoil the Philistines, ᶜthe remnant of the country of ᵈCaphtor.²

5 ªBaldness is come upon Gaza; ᵇAshkelon is cut off *with* the remnant of their valley: how long wilt thou cut thyself?

6 O thou ªsword of the LORD, how long *will it be* ere thou be quiet? put up thyself into thy scabbard, rest, and be still.

7 How can ¹it be quiet, seeing the LORD hath ªgiven it a charge against Ashkelon, and against the sea shore? there hath he ᵇappointed it.

## CHAPTER 48

AGAINST ªMoab thus saith the LORD of hosts, the God of Israel; Woe unto ᵇNebo! for it is ¹spoiled: ᶜKiriathaim is ²confounded *and* taken: ³Misgab is ²confounded and dismayed.

2 ª*There shall be* no more praise of Moab: in ᵇHeshbon they have devised evil against it; come, and let us cut it off from *being* a nation. Also thou shalt ¹be cut down, O ᶜMadmen;² the sword shall pursue thee.

3 A voice of crying *shall be* from ªHoronaim, ¹spoiling and great destruction.

4 Moab is destroyed; her little ones have caused a cry to be heard.

5 ªFor in the ¹going up of Luhith ²continual weeping shall go up; for

---

46:28 ª Amos 9:8,
9 ᵇ Jer. 30:11 ¹ *as is right*
47:1 ª Zeph. 2:4, 5
ᵇ Amos 1:6
47:2 ª Is. 8:7, 8
ᵇ Jer. 1:14 ¹ *wail*
47:3 ª Jer. 8:16
¹ *for* ² Lack of courage
47:4 ª Is. 14:29–31 ᵇ Jer. 25:22 ᶜ Ezek. 25:16 ᵈ Gen. 10:14 ¹ *plunder* ² Cappadocia in Asia Minor
47:5 ª Mic. 1:16
ᵇ Jer. 25:20
47:6 ª Ezek. 21:3–5
47:7 ª Ezek. 14:17
ᵇ Mic. 6:9 ¹ Lit. *you*
48:1 ª Is. 15:1–16:14; 25:10 ᵇ Is. 15:2 ᶜ Num. 32:37 ¹ *plundered* ² *shamed* ³ Or *the high stronghold*
48:2 ª Is. 16:14
ᵇ Jer. 49:3 ᶜ Is. 10:31 ¹ *be silenced* ² A city of Moab
48:3 ª Is. 15:5
¹ *plundering*
48:5 ª Is. 15:5
¹ *ascent* ² *they ascend with continual weeping* ³ *descent*
48:6 ª Jer. 17:6
¹ *juniper* or *Aroer,* a city of Moab
48:7 ª Jer. 9:23
ᵇ Jer. 48:7 ᶜ Jer. 49:3
48:8 ª Jer. 6:26
¹ *plunderer*
48:9 ª Ps. 55:6
48:10 ª 1 Sam. 15:3
48:11 ª Zeph. 1:12
¹ *dregs*
48:12 ¹ *wineworkers,* lit. *pourers* ² *pour him off*
48:13 ª 1 Kin. 11:7 ᵇ Hos. 10:6
ᶜ 1 Kin. 12:29; 13:32–34
48:14 ª Is. 16:6
48:15 ª Jer. 50:27
ᵇ Jer. 46:18; 51:57
¹ *plundered*
48:16 ¹ *at hand*
48:17 ª Is. 9:4; 14:4, 5 ¹ *around*
48:18 ª Is. 47:1 ᵇ Is. 15:2 ¹ *plunderer*
48:19 ª Deut. 2:36
ᵇ 1 Sam. 4:13, 14, 16
¹ *watch*
48:20 ª Is. 16:7
ᵇ Num. 21:13
¹ *shamed* ² *wail* ³ *plundered*
48:21 ¹ Or *Jahzah*

---

in the ³going down of Horonaim the enemies have heard a cry of destruction.

6 Flee, save your lives, and be like the ªheath¹ in the wilderness.

7 For because thou hast trusted in thy works and in thy ªtreasures, thou shalt also be taken: and ᵇChemosh shall go forth into captivity *with* his ᶜpriests and his princes together.

8 And ªthe ¹spoiler shall come upon every city, and no city shall escape: the valley also shall perish, and the plain shall be destroyed, as the LORD hath spoken.

9 ªGive wings unto Moab, that it may flee and get away: for the cities thereof shall be desolate, without any to dwell therein.

10 ªCursed *be* he that doeth the work of the LORD deceitfully, and cursed *be* he that keepeth back his sword from blood.

11 Moab hath been at ease from his youth, and he ªhath settled on his ¹lees, and hath not been emptied from vessel to vessel, neither hath he gone into captivity: therefore his taste remained in him, and his scent is not changed.

12 Therefore, behold, the days come, saith the LORD, that I will send unto him ¹wanderers, that shall ²cause him to wander, and shall empty his vessels, and break their bottles.

13 And Moab shall be ashamed of ªChemosh, as the house of Israel ᵇwas ashamed of ᶜBeth-el their confidence.

14 How say ye, ªWe *are* mighty and strong men for the war?

15 Moab is ¹spoiled, and gone up *out of* her cities, and his chosen young men are ªgone down to the slaughter, saith ᵇthe King, whose name *is* the LORD of hosts.

16 The calamity of Moab *is* near ¹to come, and his affliction hasteth fast.

17 All ye that are ¹about him, bemoan him; and all ye that know his name, say, ªHow is the strong staff broken, *and* the beautiful rod!

18 ªThou daughter that dost inhabit ᵇDibon, come down from *thy* glory, and sit in thirst; for the ¹spoiler of Moab shall come upon thee, *and* he shall destroy thy strong holds.

19 O inhabitant of ªAroer, ᵇstand by the way, and ¹espy; ask him that fleeth, and her that escapeth, *and* say, What is done?

20 Moab is ¹confounded; for it is broken down: ªhowl² and cry; tell ye it in ᵇArnon, that Moab is ³spoiled,

21 And judgment is come upon the plain country; upon Holon, and upon ¹Jahazah, and upon Mephaath,

22 And upon Dibon, and upon Nebo, and upon Beth-diblathaim,

23 And upon Kiriathaim, and upon Beth-gamul, and upon Beth-meon,

24 And upon ᵃKerioth, and upon Bozrah, and upon all the cities of the land of Moab, far or near.

25 ᵃThe ¹horn of Moab is cut off, and his ᵇarm is broken, saith the LORD.

26 ᵃMake ye him drunken: for he magnified *himself* against the LORD: Moab also shall wallow in his vomit, and he also shall be in derision.

27 For ᵃwas not Israel a derision unto thee? ᵇwas he found among thieves? for since thou spakest of him, thou ¹skippedst for ᶜjoy.

28 O ye that dwell in Moab, leave the cities, and ᵃdwell in the rock, and be like ᵇthe dove *that* maketh her nest in the sides of the ¹hole's mouth.

29 We have heard the ᵃpride of Moab, (he is exceeding proud) his loftiness, and his arrogancy, and his ᵇpride, and the haughtiness of his heart.

30 I know his wrath, saith the LORD; but *it shall* not *be* so; ᵃhis lies ¹shall not so effect *it*.

31 Therefore ᵃwill I ¹howl for Moab, and I will cry out for all Moab; *mine heart* shall mourn for the men of Kir-heres.

32 ᵃO vine of Sibmah, I will weep for thee with the weeping of ᵇJazer: thy plants are gone over the sea, they reach *even* to the sea of Jazer: the ¹spoiler is fallen upon thy summer fruits and upon thy vintage.

33 And ᵃjoy and gladness is taken from the plentiful field, and from the land of Moab; and I have caused wine to ¹fail from the winepresses: none shall tread with shouting; *their* shouting *shall* ²*be* no shouting.

34 ᵃFrom the cry of Heshbon *even* unto ᵇElealeh, *and even* unto Jahaz, have they uttered their voice, ᶜfrom Zoar *even* unto Horonaim, ¹*as* an heifer of three years old: for the waters also of Nimrim shall be desolate.

35 Moreover I will cause to cease in Moab, saith the LORD, ᵃhim that offereth in the ¹high places, and him that burneth incense to his gods.

36 Therefore ᵃmine heart shall ¹sound for Moab like ²pipes, and mine heart shall ¹sound like ²pipes for the men of Kir-heres: because ᵇthe riches *that* he hath gotten are perished.

37 For ᵃevery head *shall be* bald, and every beard clipped: upon all the hands *shall be* ¹cuttings, and ᵇupon the loins sackcloth.

38 *There shall be* lamentation generally upon all the ᵃhousetops of Moab, and in the streets thereof: for I have ᵇbroken Moab like a vessel wherein *is* no pleasure, saith the LORD.

39 They shall ¹howl, *saying*, How is it broken down! how hath Moab turned the back with shame! so shall Moab be a derision and a dismaying to all them about him.

40 For thus saith the LORD; Behold, ᵃhe shall fly as an eagle, and shall ᵇspread his wings over Moab.

41 Kerioth is taken, and the strong holds are surprised, and ᵃthe mighty men's hearts in Moab at that day shall be as the heart of a woman in her ¹pangs.

42 And Moab shall be destroyed ᵃfrom *being* a people, because he hath magnified *himself* against the LORD.

43 ᵃFear, and the pit, and the snare, *shall be* upon thee, O inhabitant of Moab, saith the LORD.

44 He that fleeth from the fear shall fall into the pit; and he that getteth up out of the pit shall be ¹taken in the ᵃsnare: for ᵇI will bring upon it, *even* upon Moab, the year of their ²visitation, saith the LORD.

45 They that fled stood under the shadow of Heshbon because of ¹the force: but ᵃa fire shall come forth out of Heshbon, and a flame from the midst of ᵇSihon, and ᶜshall devour the ²corner of Moab, and the crown of the head of the ³tumultuous ones.

46 ᵃWoe be unto thee, O Moab! the people of Chemosh perisheth: for thy sons are taken captives, and thy daughters captives.

47 Yet will I bring again the ¹captivity of Moab ᵃin the latter days, saith the LORD. Thus far *is* the judgment of Moab.

## CHAPTER 49

CONCERNING ᵃthe Ammonites, thus saith the LORD; Hath Israel no sons? hath he no heir? why *then* doth ¹their king inherit ᵇGad, and his people dwell in his cities?

2 ᵃTherefore, behold, the days come, saith the LORD, that I will cause an alarm of war to be heard in ᵇRabbah of the Ammonites; and it shall be a desolate ¹heap, and her ²daughters shall be burned with fire: then shall Israel be heir unto them that were his heirs, saith the LORD.

3 ¹Howl, O ᵃHeshbon, for Ai is spoiled: cry, ye daughters of Rabbah, ᵇgird you with sackcloth; lament, and run to and fro by the hedges; for ²their king shall go into captivity, *and* his ᶜpriests and his princes together.

4 Wherefore ᵃgloriest thou in the valleys, ¹thy flowing valley, O ᵇbacksliding daughter? that trusted in her ᶜtreasures, ᵈ*saying*, Who shall come unto me?

5 Behold, I will bring a fear upon thee, saith the Lord GOD of hosts, from all those that ¹be about thee;

---

48:24 ᵃ Amos 2:2
48:25 ᵃ Ps. 75:10
ᵇ Ezek. 30:21
¹ Strength
48:26 ᵃ Jer. 25:15
48:27 ᵃ Zeph. 2:8
ᵇ Jer. 2:26 ᶜ Lam. 2:15 ¹ *shake your head in scorn*
48:28 ᵃ Ps. 55:6, 7 ᵇ Song 2:14 ¹ *cave's*
48:29 ᵃ Is. 16:6
ᵇ Jer. 49:16
48:30 ᵃ Jer. 50:36
¹ *have made nothing right*
48:31 ᵃ Is. 15:5; 16:7, 11 ¹ *wail*
48:32 ᵃ Is. 16:8, 9 ᵇ Num. 21:32 ¹ *plunderer*
48:33 ᵃ Joel 1:12 ¹ *cease* ² *not be shouts of joy*
48:34 ᵃ Is. 15:4–6 ᵇ Num. 32:3, 37 ᶜ Is. 15:5, 6 ¹ Or *The Third Eglath, an unknown city,* Is. 15:5
48:35 ᵃ Is. 15:2; 16:12 ¹ *sacred places* for pagan worship
48:36 ᵃ Is. 15:5; 16:11 ᵇ Is. 15:7 ¹ *wail* ² *flutes*
48:37 ᵃ Is. 15:2, 3 ᵇ Gen. 37:34 ¹ *cuts*
48:38 ᵃ Is. 15:3 ᵇ Jer. 22:28
48:39 ¹ *wail*
48:40 ᵃ Deut. 28:49 ᵇ Is. 8:8
48:41 ᵃ Is. 13:8; 21:3 ¹ *birth pangs*
48:42 ᵃ Ps. 83:4
48:43 ᵃ Is. 24:17, 18
48:44 ᵃ Is. 24:18 ᵇ Jer. 11:23 ¹ *caught* ² *punishment*
48:45 ᵃ Num. 21:28, 29 ᵇ Ps. 135:11 ᶜ Num. 24:17 ¹ *exhaustion* ² *brow* ³ *sons of tumult*
48:46 ᵃ Num. 21:29
48:47 ᵃ Jer. 49:6, 39 ¹ *captives*
49:1 ᵃ Ezek. 21:28–32; 25:1–7 ᵇ Amos 1:13–15 ¹ Heb. *Malcam,* or *Milcom,* an Ammonite god, 1 Kin. 11:5, 33
49:2 ᵃ Amos 1:13–15 ᵇ Ezek. 25:5 ¹ *mound* ² *villages*
49:3 ᵃ Jer. 48:2

ᵇ Is. 32:11 ᶜ Jer. 48:7 ¹ *Wail* ² Heb. *Malcam,* Jer. 49:1 49:4 ᵃ Jer. 9:23 ᵇ Jer. 3:14 ᶜ Jer. 48:7 ᵈ Jer. 21:13 ¹ *your valley is flowing away* 49:5 ¹ *are around*

and ye shall be driven out every man right forth; and none shall gather up him that wandereth.

6 And [a]afterward I will bring again the captivity of the children of Ammon, saith the LORD.

7 [a]Concerning Edom, thus saith the LORD of hosts; [b]*Is* wisdom no more in Teman? [c]is counsel perished from the prudent? is their wisdom [d]vanished?

8 Flee ye, turn back, dwell [1]deep, O inhabitants of [a]Dedan; for I will bring the calamity of Esau upon him, the time *that* I will [2]visit him.

9 If [a]grapegatherers come to thee, would they not leave *some* gleaning grapes? if thieves by night, they will destroy till they have enough.

10 [a]But I have made Esau bare, I have uncovered his secret places, and he shall not be able to hide himself: his [1]seed is spoiled, and his brethren, and his neighbours, and [b]he *is* [2]not.

11 Leave thy fatherless children, I will preserve *them* alive; and let thy widows trust in me.

12 For thus saith the LORD; Behold, [a]they whose judgment *was* not to drink of the cup have assuredly drunken; and *art* thou he *that* shall altogether go unpunished? thou shalt not go unpunished, but thou shalt surely drink *of it.*

13 For [a]I have sworn by myself, saith the LORD, that [b]Bozrah shall become a desolation, a reproach, a [1]waste, and a curse; and all the cities thereof shall be perpetual [2]wastes.

14 I have heard a [a]rumour[1] from the LORD, and an ambassador is sent unto the [2]heathen, *saying,* Gather ye together, and come against her, and rise up to the battle.

15 For, lo, I will make thee small among the [1]heathen, *and* despised among men.

16 Thy [1]terribleness hath deceived thee, *and* the [a]pride of thine heart, O thou that dwellest in the clefts of the rock, that holdest the height of the hill: [b]though thou shouldest make thy [c]nest as high as the eagle, [d]I will bring thee down from thence, saith the LORD.

17 Also Edom shall be [1]a desolation: [a]every one that goeth by it shall be astonished, and shall hiss at all the plagues thereof.

18 [a]As in the overthrow of Sodom and Gomorrah and the neighbour *cities* thereof, saith the LORD, no man shall abide there, neither shall a son of man dwell in it.

19 [a]Behold, he shall come up like a lion from [b]the [1]swelling of Jordan against the habitation of the strong: but I will suddenly make him run away from her: and who *is* a chosen

49:6 [a] Jer. 48:47
49:7 [a] Ezek. 25:12–14; 35:1–15 [b] Gen. 36:11 [c] Is. 19:11 [d] Jer. 8:9
49:8 [a] Jer. 25:23 [1] *in the depths* [2] *punish*
49:9 [a] Obad. 5, 6
49:10 [b] Mal. 1:3 [b] Is. 17:14 [1] *descendants are plundered* [2] *no more*
49:12 [a] Jer. 25:29
49:13 [a] Amos 6:8 [b] Is. 34:6; 63:1 [1] *ruin* [2] *ruins*
49:14 [a] Obad. 1–4 [1] *message* [2] *nations*
49:15 [1] *nations*
49:16 [a] Jer. 48:29 [b] Obad. 3, 4 [c] Job 39:27 [d] Amos 9:2 [1] *fierceness*
49:17 [a] Jer. 18:16; 49:13; 50:13 [1] *an astonishment*
49:18 [a] Deut. 29:23
49:19 [a] Jer. 50:44 [b] Jer. 12:5 [1] Or *thicket*

[c] Ex. 15:11 [d] Job 41:10 [2] *arraign me in court*
49:20 [a] Jer. 50:45 [1] *drag*
49:21 [a] Jer. 50:46 [1] *shakes*
49:22 [a] Jer. 48:40, 41 [1] *birth pangs*
49:23 [a] Amos 1:3, 5 [b] Jer. 39:5 [c] [Is. 57:20] [1] *ashamed* [2] *bad news* [3] *anxiety*
49:24 [a] Is. 13:8 [1] *has grown* [2] *childbirth*
49:25 [a] Jer. 33:9 [1] *Why* [2] *deserted*
49:26 [a] Jer. 50:30 [1] *silenced*
49:27 [a] Amos 1:4
49:28 [a] Ezek. 27:21 [b] Judg. 6:3 [1] Or *Nebuchadnezzar* [2] *strike* [3] *devastate*
49:29 [a] Ps. 120:5 [b] Jer. 46:5
49:30 [1] *in the depths* [2] *plan*
49:31 [a] Ezek. 38:11 [b] Num. 23:9 [1] *securely*
49:32 [a] Ezek. 5:10 [1] *for* [2] *for plunder* [3] *cut off the corners of their hair*

*man, that* I may appoint over her? for [c]who *is* like me? and who will [2]appoint me the time? and [d]who *is* that shepherd that will stand before me?

20 [a]Therefore hear the counsel of the LORD, that he hath taken against Edom; and his purposes, that he hath purposed against the inhabitants of Teman: Surely the least of the flock shall [1]draw them out: surely he shall make their habitations desolate with them.

21 [a]The earth [1]is moved at the noise of their fall, at the cry the noise thereof was heard in the Red sea.

22 Behold, [a]he shall come up and fly as the eagle, and spread his wings over Bozrah: and at that day shall the heart of the mighty men of Edom be as the heart of a woman in her [1]pangs.

23 [a]Concerning Damascus. [b]Hamath is [1]confounded, and Arpad: for they have heard [2]evil tidings: they are fainthearted; [c]*there is* [3]sorrow on the sea; it cannot be quiet.

24 Damascus [1]is waxed feeble, *and* turneth herself to flee, and fear hath seized on her: [a]anguish and sorrows have taken her, as a woman in [2]travail.

25 [1]How is [a]the city of praise not [2]left, the city of my joy!

26 [a]Therefore her young men shall fall in her streets, and all the men of war shall be [1]cut off in that day, saith the LORD of hosts.

27 And I will kindle a [a]fire in the wall of Damascus, and it shall consume the palaces of Ben-hadad.

28 [a]Concerning Kedar, and concerning the kingdoms of Hazor, which [1]Nebuchadrezzar king of Babylon shall [2]smite, thus saith the LORD; Arise ye, go up to Kedar, and [3]spoil [b]the men of the east.

29 Their [a]tents and their flocks shall they take away: they shall take to themselves their curtains, and all their vessels, and their camels; and they shall cry unto them, [b]Fear *is* on every side.

30 Flee, get you far off, dwell [1]deep, O ye inhabitants of Hazor, saith the LORD; for Nebuchadrezzar king of Babylon hath taken counsel against you, and hath conceived a [2]purpose against you.

31 Arise, get you up unto [a]the wealthy nation, that dwelleth [1]without care, saith the LORD, which have neither gates nor bars, *which* [b]dwell alone.

32 And their camels shall be [1]a booty, and the multitude of their cattle [2]a spoil: and I will [a]scatter into all winds them *that* [3]*are* in the utmost corners; and I will bring their calamity from all sides thereof, saith the LORD.

33 And Hazor ªshall be a dwelling for ¹dragons, *and* a desolation for ever: there shall no man abide there, nor *any* son of man dwell in it.

34 The word of the LORD that came to Jeremiah the prophet against ªElam in the ᵇbeginning of the reign of Zedekiah king of Judah, saying,

35 Thus saith the LORD of hosts; Behold, I will break ªthe ¹bow of Elam, the chief of their might.

36 And upon Elam will I bring the four winds from the four quarters of heaven, and will scatter them toward all those winds; and there shall be no nation whither the outcasts of Elam shall not come.

37 For I will cause Elam to be dismayed before their enemies, and before them that seek their life: and I will bring ¹evil upon them, *even* my fierce anger, saith the LORD; ªand I will send the sword after them, till I have consumed them:

38 And I will ªset my throne in Elam, and will destroy from thence the king and the princes, saith the LORD.

39 But it shall come to pass ªin the latter days, *that* I will bring again the captivity of Elam, saith the LORD.

## CHAPTER 50

THE word that the LORD spake ªagainst Babylon *and* against the land of the Chaldeans by Jeremiah the prophet.

2 Declare ye among the nations, and ¹publish, and ²set up a standard; ¹publish, *and* conceal not: say, Babylon is ªtaken, ᵇBel³ is confounded, ⁴Merodach is broken in pieces; ᶜher idols are ⁵confounded, her images are broken in pieces.

3 ªFor out of the north there cometh up ᵇa nation against her, which shall make her land ¹desolate, and none shall dwell therein: they shall ²remove, they shall depart, both man and beast.

4 In those days, and in that time, saith the LORD, the children of Israel shall come, ªthey and the children of Judah together, ᵇgoing¹ and weeping: they shall ²go, ᶜand seek the LORD their God.

5 They shall ask the way to Zion with their faces thitherward, *saying,* Come, and let us join ourselves to the LORD in ªa perpetual covenant *that* shall not be forgotten.

6 My people hath been ªlost sheep: their shepherds have ¹caused them to go ªstray, they have turned them away *on* ᶜthe mountains: they have gone from mountain to hill, they have forgotten their restingplace.

7 All that found them have ªdevoured them: and ᵇtheir adversaries said, ᶜWe offend not, because they

have sinned against the LORD, ᵈthe habitation of justice, even the LORD, ᵉthe hope of their fathers.

8 ªRemove¹ out of the midst of Babylon, and go forth out of the land of the Chaldeans, and be as the ²he goats before the flocks.

9 ªFor, lo, I will raise and cause to come up against Babylon an assembly of great nations from the north country: and they shall set themselves in array against her; from thence she shall be ¹taken: their arrows *shall be* as of ²a mighty expert man; ᵇnone shall return in vain.

10 And Chaldea shall ¹be a spoil: ªall that ²spoil her shall be satisfied, saith the LORD.

11 ªBecause ye were glad, because ye rejoiced, O ye destroyers of mine heritage, because ye are grown fat ᵇas the heifer ¹at grass, and ²bellow as bulls;

12 Your mother shall be ¹sore confounded; she that bare you shall be ashamed: behold, the ²hindermost of the nations *shall be* a ªwilderness, a dry land, and a desert.

13 Because of the wrath of the LORD it shall not be inhabited, ªbut it shall be wholly desolate: ᵇevery one that goeth by Babylon shall be ¹astonished, and hiss at all her plagues.

14 ªPut yourselves in array against Babylon round about: all ye that bend the bow, shoot at her, spare no arrows: for she hath sinned against the LORD.

15 Shout against her round about: she hath ªgiven her hand: her foundations are fallen, ᵇher walls are thrown down: for ᶜit *is* the vengeance of the LORD: take vengeance upon her; as she hath done, do unto her.

16 Cut off the sower from Babylon, and him that handleth the sickle in the time of harvest: for fear of the oppressing sword ªthey shall turn every one to his people, and they shall flee every one to his own land.

17 Israel *is* a ªscattered sheep; ᵇthe lions have driven *him* away: first ᶜthe king of Assyria hath devoured him; and last this ᵈNebuchadrezzar¹ king of Babylon hath broken his bones.

18 Therefore thus saith the LORD of hosts, the God of Israel; Behold, I will punish the king of Babylon and his land, as I have punished the king of ªAssyria.

19 ªAnd I will bring Israel again to his habitation, and he shall feed on Carmel and Bashan, and his soul shall be satisfied upon mount Ephraim and Gilead.

20 In those days, and in that time, saith the LORD, ªthe iniquity of Israel shall be sought for, and *there shall be* none; and the sins of Judah, and they

### Center column references

49:33 ª Mal. 1:3
¹ jackals

49:34 ª Jer. 25:25
ᵇ 2 Kin. 24:17, 18

49:35 ª Is. 22:6
¹ Power

49:37 ª Jer. 9:16
¹ disaster

49:38 ª Jer. 43:10

49:39 ª Jer. 48:47

50:1 ª Is. 13:1; 47:1

50:2 ª Is. 21:9 ᵇ Is. 46:1 ᶜ Jer. 43:12, 13 ¹ proclaim ² lift up a banner ³ A Babylonian god ⁴ Or Marduk, a Babylonian god ⁵ humiliated

50:3 ª Jer. 51:48
ᵇ Is. 13:17, 18, 20
¹ a horror ² Or wander

50:4 ª Hos. 1:11
ᵇ Ezra 3:12, 13
ᶜ Hos. 3:5 ¹ with continual weeping ² come

50:5 ª Jer. 31:31

50:6 ª Is. 53:6
ᵇ Jer. 23:1 ᶜ [Jer. 2:20; 3:6, 23] ¹ led

50:7 ª Ps. 79:7
ᵇ Zech. 11:5 ᶜ Jer. 2:3

ᵈ [Ps. 90:1; 91:1]
ᵉ Ps. 22:4

50:8 ª Is. 48:20
¹ Move ² rams

50:9 ª Jer. 15:14;
51:27 ᵇ 2 Sam. 1:22 ¹ captured ² an expert warrior

50:10 ª [Rev. 17:16]
¹ become plunder
² plunder

50:11 ª Is. 47:6
ᵇ Hos. 10:11
¹ threshing grain
² Or neigh like stallions

50:12 ª Jer. 51:43
¹ deeply ashamed
² least

50:13 ª Jer. 25:12 ᵇ Jer. 49:17
¹ horrified

50:14 ª Jer. 51:2

50:15 ª Lam. 5:6
ᵇ Jer. 51:58 ᶜ Jer. 51:6, 11

50:16 ª Is. 13:14

50:17 ª 2 Kin. 24:10, 14 ᵇ Jer. 2:15 ᶜ 2 Kin. 15:29; 17:6; 18:9–13 ᵈ 2 Kin. 24:10–14; 25:1–7 ¹ Or Nebuchadnezzar

50:18 ª Ezek. 31:3, 11, 12

50:19 ª Is. 65:10

50:20 ª [Jer. 31:34]

shall not be found: for I will pardon them [b]whom I [1]reserve.

21 Go up against the land of [1]Merathaim, *even* against it, and against the inhabitants of [a]Pekod:[2] [3]waste and utterly destroy after them, saith the LORD, and do [b]according to all that I have commanded thee.

22 [a]A sound of battle *is* in the land, and of great destruction.

23 How is [a]the hammer of the whole earth cut [1]asunder and broken! how is Babylon become a desolation among the nations!

24 I have laid a snare for thee, and thou art [1]also [a]taken, O Babylon, and thou wast not aware: thou art found, and also caught, because thou hast [b]striven against the LORD.

25 The LORD hath opened his armoury, and hath brought forth [a]the weapons of his indignation: for this *is* the work of the Lord GOD of hosts in the land of the Chaldeans.

26 Come against her from the utmost border, open her storehouses: cast her up as [1]heaps, and destroy her utterly: let nothing of her be left.

27 Slay all her [a]bullocks; let them go down to the slaughter: woe unto them! for their day is come, the time of [b]their [1]visitation.

28 The voice of them that flee and escape out of the land of Babylon, [a]to declare in Zion the vengeance of the LORD our God, the vengeance of his temple.

29 Call together the archers against Babylon: all ye that bend the bow, camp against it round about; let none thereof escape: [a]recompense[1] her according to her work; according to all that she hath done, do unto her: [b]for she hath been proud against the LORD, against the Holy One of Israel.

30 [a]Therefore shall her young men fall in the streets, and all her men of war shall be cut off in that day, saith the LORD.

31 Behold, I *am* against thee, O *thou* most proud, saith the Lord GOD of hosts: for thy day is come, the time *that* I will [1]visit thee.

32 And the most [a]proud shall stumble and fall, and none shall raise him up: and [b]I will kindle a fire in his cities, and it shall devour all round about him.

33 Thus saith the LORD of hosts; The children of Israel and the children of Judah *were* oppressed together: and all that took them captives held them fast; they refused to let them go.

34 [a]Their Redeemer *is* strong; [b]the LORD of hosts *is* his name: he shall throughly plead their [c]cause,[1] that he may give rest to the land, and disquiet the inhabitants of Babylon.

35 A sword *is* [1]upon the Chaldeans,

saith the LORD, and upon the inhabitants of Babylon, and [a]upon her princes, and upon [b]her wise *men*.

36 A sword *is* [a]upon[1] the liars; and they shall [2]dote: a sword *is* upon her mighty men; and they shall be dismayed.

37 A sword *is* upon their horses, and upon their chariots, and upon all [a]the [1]mingled people that *are* in the midst of her; and [b]they shall become as women: a sword *is* upon her treasures; and they shall be robbed.

38 [a]A drought *is* upon her waters; and they shall be dried up: for it *is* the land of graven images, and they are [1]mad upon *their* idols.

39 [a]Therefore the [1]wild beasts of the desert with the [1]wild beasts of the islands shall dwell *there,* and the [2]owls shall dwell therein: [b]and it shall be no more inhabited for ever; neither shall it be dwelt in from generation to generation.

40 [a]As God overthrew Sodom and Gomorrah and the neighbour *cities* thereof, saith the LORD; *so* shall no man abide there, neither shall any son of man [b]dwell therein.

41 [a]Behold, a people shall come from the north, and a great nation, and many kings shall be raised up from the [1]coasts of the earth.

42 [a]They shall hold the bow and the lance: [b]they *are* cruel, and will not shew mercy: [c]their voice shall roar like the sea, and they shall ride upon horses, *every one* put in array, like a man to the battle, against thee, O daughter of Babylon.

43 The king of Babylon hath [a]heard the report of them, and his hands [1]waxed feeble: anguish took hold of him, *and* pangs as of a woman in [b]travail.[2]

44 [a]Behold, he shall come up like a lion from the [1]swelling of Jordan unto the habitation of the strong: but I will make them suddenly run away from her: and who *is* a chosen *man,* that I may appoint over her? for who *is* like me? and who will [2]appoint me the time? and [b]who *is* that shepherd that will stand before me?

45 Therefore hear ye [a]the counsel of the LORD, that he hath taken against Babylon; and his [b]purposes, that he hath purposed against the land of the Chaldeans: [c]Surely the least of the flock shall draw them out: surely he shall make *their* habitation desolate with them.

46 [a]At the noise of the taking of Babylon the earth [1]is moved, and the cry is heard among the nations.

## CHAPTER 51

**T**HUS saith the LORD; Behold, I will raise up against [a]Babylon, and

---

50:20 [b] Is. 1:9
[1] *preserve*

50:21 [a] Ezek. 23:23 [b] 2 Sam. 16:11 [1] Lit. *Two Rebels* [2] Lit. *Visitation* [3] *devastate* or *slay*

50:22 [a] Jer. 51:54

50:23 [a] Jer. 51:20–24 [1] *apart*

50:24 [a] Dan. 5:30 [b] [Is. 45:9] [1] *indeed trapped*

50:25 [a] Is. 13:5

50:26 [1] *ruinous heaps*

50:27 [a] Is. 34:7 [b] Jer. 48:44 [1] *punishment*

50:28 [a] Jer. 51:10

50:29 [a] Jer. 51:56 [b] [Is. 47:10] [1] *repay*

50:30 [a] Jer. 49:26; 51:4

50:31 [1] *punish*

50:32 [a] Mal. 4:1 [b] Jer. 21:14

50:34 [a] Rev. 18:8 [b] Is. 47:4 [c] Jer. 32:18; 51:19–22 [1] *case*

50:35 [1] *against*

---

[a] Dan. 5:30 [b] Is. 47:13

50:36 [a] Is. 44:25 [1] *against the soothsayers* [2] *be fools*

50:37 [a] Jer. 25:20 [b] Jer. 51:30 [1] *mixed*

50:38 [a] Rev. 16:12 [1] *insane with*

50:39 [a] Rev. 18:2 [b] Is. 13:20 [1] *jackals shall* [2] *ostriches*

50:40 [a] Is. 13:19 [b] Is. 13:20

50:41 [a] Jer. 6:22; 25:14; 51:27 [1] *ends*

50:42 [a] Jer. 6:23 [b] Is. 13:18 [c] Is. 5:30

50:43 [a] Jer. 51:31 [b] Jer. 6:24 [1] *grow* [2] *childbirth*

50:44 [a] Jer. 49:19–21 [b] Job 41:10 [1] Or *thicket* [2] *arraign*

50:45 [a] Jer. 51:10, 11 [b] Jer. 51:29 [c] Jer. 49:19, 20

50:46 [a] Rev. 18:9 [1] *trembles*

51:1 [a] Is. 47:1

---

against them that dwell in 1the midst of them that rise up against me, ba destroying wind;

2 And will send unto Babylon afanners,1 that shall 2fan her, and shall empty her land: bfor in the day of trouble they shall be against her 3round about.

3 Against *him that* bendeth alet the archer bend his bow, and against *him that* lifteth himself up in his 1brigandine: and spare ye not her young men; bdestroy ye utterly all her 2host.

4 Thus the slain shall fall in the land of the Chaldeans, aand *they that are* thrust through in her streets.

5 For Israel *hath* anot *been* forsaken, nor Judah 1of his God, 1of the LORD of hosts; though their land was filled with sin against the Holy One of Israel.

6 aFlee out of the midst of Babylon, and deliver every man his 1soul: be not cut off in her iniquity; for bthis *is* the time of the LORD's vengeance; che will render unto her a recompence.

7 aBabylon *hath been* a golden cup in the LORD's hand, that made all the earth drunken: bthe nations have drunken of her wine; therefore the nations care 1mad.

8 Babylon is suddenly afallen and destroyed: bhowl1 for her; ctake balm for her pain, 2if so be she may be healed.

9 We would have healed Babylon, but she is not healed: forsake her, and alet us go every one into his own country: bfor her judgment reacheth unto heaven, and is lifted up *even* to the skies.

10 The LORD hath abrought forth our righteousness: come, and let us bdeclare in Zion the work of the LORD our God.

11 aMake1 bright the arrows; gather the shields: bthe LORD hath raised up the spirit of the kings of the Medes: cfor his 2device *is* against Babylon, to destroy it; because it *is* dthe vengeance of the LORD, the vengeance 3of his temple.

12 aSet up the 1standard upon the walls of Babylon, make the watch strong, set up the watchmen, prepare the ambushes: for the LORD hath both devised and done that which he spake against the inhabitants of Babylon.

13 aO thou that dwellest upon many waters, abundant in treasures, thine end is come, *and* the measure of thy covetousness.

14 aThe LORD of hosts hath sworn by himself, *saying,* Surely I will fill thee with men, bas with 1caterpillers; and they shall lift cup a shout against thee.

15 aHe hath made the earth by his

51:1 b Jer. 4:11
1 Heb. *Leb-kamai,* a code word for Chaldea, Babylonia
51:2 a Jer. 15:7
b Jer. 50:14 1 *winnowers* 2 *winnow* 3 *all around*
51:3 a Jer. 50:14, 29 b Jer. 50:21
1 *armour* 2 *army*
51:4 a Jer. 49:26; 50:30, 37
51:5 a [Jer. 33:24–26; 46:28] 1 *by*
51:6 a Rev. 18:4
b Jer. 50:15 c Jer. 25:14 1 *life*
51:7 a Rev. 17:4
b Rev. 14:8 c Jer. 25:16 1 *deranged*
51:8 a Is. 21:9
b Rev. 18:9, 11, 19
c Jer. 46:11 1 *wail* 2 *perhaps she*
51:9 a Is. 13:14
b Rev. 18:5
51:10 a Ps. 37:6
b Jer. 50:28
51:11 a Jer. 46:4, 9 b Is. 13:17 c Jer. 50:45 d Jer. 50:28
1 *Sharpen* or *Purify* 2 *plan* 3 *for*
51:12 a Nah. 2:1; 3:14 1 *banner*
51:13 a Rev. 17:1, 15
51:14 a Jer. 49:13
b Nah. 3:15 c Jer. 50:15 1 *locusts*
51:15 a Gen. 1:1, 6

power, he hath established the world by his wisdom, and bhath stretched out the heaven by his understanding.

16 When he uttereth *his* voice, *there is* a multitude of waters in the heavens; and ahe causeth the vapours to ascend from the ends of the earth: he maketh lightnings with rain, and bringeth forth the wind out of his treasures.

17 aEvery man is 1brutish by *his* knowledge; every 2founder is confounded by the graven image: bfor his molten image *is* falsehood, and *there is* no breath in them.

18 They *are* 1vanity, the work of errors: in the time of their 2visitation they shall perish.

19 The portion of Jacob *is* not like them; for he *is* the 1former of all things: and *Israel is* the 2rod of his inheritance: the LORD of hosts *is* his name.

20 aThou *art* my battle axe *and* weapons of war: for with thee will I break in pieces the nations, and with thee will I destroy kingdoms;

21 And with thee will I break in pieces the horse and his rider; and with thee will I break in pieces the chariot and his rider;

22 With thee also will I break in pieces man and woman; and with thee will I break in pieces aold and young; and with thee will I break in pieces the young man and the maid;

23 I will also break in pieces with thee the shepherd and his flock; and with thee will I break in pieces the husbandman and his yoke of oxen; and with thee will I break in pieces 1captains and rulers.

24 aAnd I will 1render unto Babylon and to all the inhabitants of Chaldea all their evil that they have done in Zion in your sight, saith the LORD.

25 Behold, I *am* against thee, aO destroying 1mountain, saith the LORD, which destroyest all the earth: and I will stretch out mine hand 2upon thee, and roll thee down from the rocks, band will make thee a burnt mountain.

26 And they shall not take of thee a stone for a corner, nor a stone for foundations; abut thou shalt be desolate for ever, saith the LORD.

27 aSet ye up a 1standard in the land, blow the trumpet among the nations, bprepare the nations against her, call together against her cthe kingdoms of Ararat, Minni, and Ashchenaz; appoint a captain against her; cause the horses to come up as the 2rough caterpillers.

28 Prepare against her the nations with the kings of the Medes, the 1captains thereof, and all the rulers

b Job 9:8
51:16 a Ps. 135:7
51:17 a Jer. 10:14
b Jer. 50:2 1 *dull-hearted, without* 2 *metalsmith is shamed*
51:18 1 *futile* 2 *punishment*
51:19 1 *maker* 2 *tribe*
51:20 a Is. 10:5, 15
51:22 a 2 Chr. 36:17
51:23 1 *governors*
51:24 a Jer. 50:15, 29 1 *repay*
51:25 a Zech. 4:7
b Rev. 8:8 1 *Power* 2 *against*
51:26 a Jer. 50:26, 40
51:27 a Is. 13:2
b Jer. 25:14 c Jer. 50:41, 42 1 *banner* 2 *bristling locusts*
51:28 1 *governors*

thereof, and all the land of his dominion.

29 And the land shall tremble and sorrow: for every [a]purpose of the LORD shall be performed against Babylon, [b]to make the land of Babylon a desolation without an inhabitant.

30 The mighty men of Babylon have [1]forborn to fight, they have remained in *their* [2]holds: their might hath failed; [a]they became as women: they have burned her dwellingplaces; [b]her bars are broken.

31 [a]One [1]post shall run to meet another, and one messenger to meet another, to shew the king of Babylon that his city is taken [2]at *one* end,

32 And that [a]the passages are stopped, and the reeds they have burned with fire, and the men of war are [1]affrighted.

33 For thus saith the LORD of hosts, the God of Israel; The daughter of Babylon *is* [a]like a threshingfloor, [b]*it* *is* time to thresh her: yet a little while, [c]and the time of her harvest shall come.

34 Nebuchadrezzar the king of Babylon hath [a]devoured me, he hath crushed me, he hath made me an [b]empty vessel, he hath swallowed me up like a dragon, he hath filled his belly with my [1]delicates, he hath cast me out.

35 The violence done to me and to my flesh *be* upon Babylon, shall the inhabitant of Zion say; and my blood upon the inhabitants of Chaldea, shall Jerusalem say.

36 Therefore thus saith the LORD; Behold, [a]I will plead thy cause, and take vengeance for thee; [b]and I will dry up her sea, and make her springs dry.

37 [a]And Babylon shall become [1]heaps, a dwellingplace for [2]dragons, [b]an astonishment, and an hissing, without an inhabitant.

38 They shall roar together like lions: they shall [1]yell as lions' whelps.

39 In their [1]heat I will make their feasts, and [a]I will make them drunken, that they may rejoice, and sleep a perpetual sleep, and not wake, saith the LORD.

40 I will bring them down like lambs to the slaughter, like rams with [1]he goats.

41 How is [a]Sheshach[1] taken! and how is [b]the praise of the whole earth [2]surprised! how is Babylon become [3]an astonishment among the nations!

42 [a]The sea is come up upon Babylon: she is covered with the multitude of the waves thereof.

43 [a]Her cities are a desolation, a dry land, and a wilderness, a land

wherein [b]no man dwelleth, neither doth *any* son of man pass thereby.

44 And I will punish [a]Bel[1] in Babylon, and I will bring forth out of his mouth that which he hath swallowed up: and the nations shall not flow together any more unto him: yea, [b]the wall of Babylon shall fall.

45 [a]My people, go ye out of the midst of her, and deliver ye every man [1]his soul from the fierce anger of the LORD.

46 And lest your heart faint, and ye fear [a]for the rumour that shall be heard in the land; a rumour shall both come *one* year, and after that in *another* year *shall come* a rumour, and violence in the land, ruler against ruler.

47 Therefore, behold, the days come, that I will [1]do judgment upon the graven images of Babylon: and her whole land shall be [2]confounded, and all her slain shall fall in the midst of her.

48 Then [a]the heaven and the earth, and all that *is* therein, shall [1]sing for Babylon: [b]for the [2]spoilers shall come unto her from the north, saith the LORD.

49 As Babylon *hath caused* the slain of Israel to fall, so at Babylon shall fall the slain of all the earth.

50 [a]Ye that have escaped the sword, go away, stand not still: [b]remember the LORD afar off, and let Jerusalem come into your mind.

51 [a]We are [1]confounded, because we have heard reproach: shame hath covered our faces: for strangers [b]are come into the [2]sanctuaries of the LORD's house.

52 Wherefore, behold, the days come, saith the LORD, that I will [1]do judgment upon her graven images: and through all her land the wounded shall groan.

53 [a]Though Babylon should [1]mount up to heaven, and though she should fortify the height of her strength, *yet* from me shall [2]spoilers come unto her, saith the LORD.

54 [a]A sound of a cry *cometh* from Babylon, and great destruction from the land of the Chaldeans:

55 Because the LORD hath [1]spoiled Babylon, and [2]destroyed out of her the great voice; when her waves do roar like great waters, a noise of their voice is uttered:

56 Because the [1]spoiler is come upon her, *even* upon Babylon, and her mighty men are taken, every one of their bows is broken: [a]for the LORD God of recompences shall surely [2]requite.

57 And I will make drunk her princes, and her [a]wise *men*, her [1]captains, and her rulers, and her mighty

**Cross-references:**

51:29 [a] Jer. 50:45 [b] Jer. 50:13; 51:26, 43

51:30 [a] Is. 19:16 [b] Lam. 2:9 [1] ceased fighting [2] strong holds

51:31 [a] Jer. 50:24 [1] runner [2] on all sides

51:32 [a] Jer. 50:38 [1] terrified

51:33 [a] Is. 21:10 [b] Hab. 3:12 [c] Rev. 14:15 [1] When it is

51:34 [a] Jer. 50:17 [b] Is. 24:1–3 [1] delicacies

51:36 [a] Jer. 50:34 [b] Jer. 50:38

51:37 [a] Is. 13:22 [b] Jer. 25:9, 11 [1] a heap of ruins [2] jackals

51:38 [1] growl

51:39 [a] Jer. 51:57 [1] excitement

51:40 [1] male

51:41 [a] Jer. 25:26 [b] Is. 13:19 [1] A code word for Babylon, Jer. 25:26 [2] seized [3] desolate

51:42 [a] Is. 8:7, 8

51:43 [a] Jer. 50:39, 40

51:43 [b] Is. 13:20

51:44 [a] Jer. 50:2 [b] Jer. 50:15 [1] A Babylonian god

51:45 [a] [Rev. 18:4] [1] himself

51:46 [a] 2 Kin. 19:7

51:47 [1] bring [2] ashamed

51:48 [a] Is. 44:23; 48:20; 49:13 [b] Jer. 50:3, 41 [1] sing joyously [2] plunderers

51:50 [a] Jer. 44:28 [b] [Deut. 4:29–31]

51:51 [a] Ps. 44:15; 79:4 [b] Lam. 1:10 [1] ashamed [2] holy places

51:52 [1] bring

51:53 [a] Amos 9:2 [1] ascend [2] plunderers

51:54 [a] Jer. 50:22

51:55 [1] plundered [2] silenced her

51:56 [a] Jer. 50:29 [1] plunderer [2] repay

51:57 [a] Jer. 50:35 [1] governors

men: and they shall sleep a perpetual sleep, and not wake, saith [b]the King, whose name *is* the LORD of hosts.

58 Thus saith the LORD of hosts; The broad walls of Babylon shall be utterly [a]broken,[1] and her high gates shall be burned with fire; and [b]the people shall labour in vain, and the [2]folk in the fire, and they shall be weary.

59 The word which Jeremiah the prophet commanded Seraiah the son of [a]Neriah, the son of Maaseiah, when he went with Zedekiah the king of Judah into Babylon in the fourth year of his reign. And *this* Seraiah *was* a [1]quiet prince.

60 So Jeremiah [a]wrote in a book all the evil that should come upon Babylon, *even* all these words that are written against Babylon.

61 And Jeremiah said to Seraiah, When thou comest to Babylon, and shalt see, and shalt read all these words;

62 Then shalt thou say, O LORD, thou hast spoken against this place, to cut it off, that [a]none shall remain in it, neither man nor beast, but that it shall be desolate for ever.

63 And it shall be, when thou hast made an end of reading this book, [a]*that* thou shalt bind a stone to it, and cast it into the midst of Euphrates:

64 And thou shalt say, Thus shall Babylon sink, and shall not rise from the evil that I will bring upon her: and they shall be weary. Thus far *are* the words of Jeremiah.

### CHAPTER 52

ZEDEKIAH *was* [a]one and twenty years old when he began to reign, and he reigned eleven years in Jerusalem. And his mother's name *was* Hamutal the daughter of Jeremiah of [b]Libnah.

2 And he did *that which was* evil in the eyes of the LORD, according to all that Jehoiakim had done.

3 For through the anger of the LORD it came to pass in Jerusalem and Judah, till he had cast them out from his presence, that Zedekiah [a]rebelled against the king of Babylon.

4 And it came to pass in the [a]ninth year of his reign, in the tenth month, in the tenth *day* of the month, *that* Nebuchadrezzar king of Babylon came, he and all his army, against Jerusalem, and [1]pitched against it, and built [2]forts against it round about.

5 So the city was besieged unto the eleventh year of king Zedekiah.

6 And in the fourth month, in the ninth *day* of the month, the famine was [1]sore in the city, so that there was no [2]bread for the people of the land.

7 Then the [1]city was broken up, and

all the men of war fled, and went forth out of the city by night by the way of the gate between the two walls, which *was* by the king's garden; (now the Chaldeans *were* [2]by the city round about:) and they went by the way of the [3]plain.

8 But the army of the Chaldeans pursued after the king, and overtook Zedekiah in the plains of Jericho; and all his army was scattered from him.

9 [a]Then they took the king, and carried him up unto the king of Babylon to Riblah in the land of Hamath; where he [1]gave judgment upon him.

10 [a]And the king of Babylon slew the sons of Zedekiah before his eyes: he slew also all the princes of Judah in Riblah.

11 Then he [a]put[1] out the eyes of Zedekiah; and the king of Babylon bound him in [2]chains, and carried him to Babylon, and put him in prison till the day of his death.

12 [a]Now in the fifth month, in the tenth *day* of the month, [b]which *was* the nineteenth year of Nebuchadrezzar king of Babylon, [c]came Nebuzaradan, captain of the guard, *which* served the king of Babylon, into Jerusalem,

13 And burned the house of the LORD, and the king's house; and all the houses of Jerusalem, and all the houses of the great *men*, burned he with fire:

14 And all the army of the Chaldeans, that *were* with the captain of the guard, brake down all the walls of Jerusalem round about.

15 [a]Then Nebuzar-adan the captain of the guard carried away captive *certain* of the poor of the people, and the [1]residue of the people that remained in the city, and those that fell away, that [2]fell to the king of Babylon, and the rest of the [3]multitude.

16 But Nebuzar-adan the captain of the guard left *certain* of the poor of the land for vinedressers and for [1]husbandmen.

17 [a]Also the [b]pillars of [1]brass that *were* in the house of the LORD, and the [2]bases, and the brasen sea that *was* in the house of the LORD, the Chaldeans [3]brake, and carried all the [1]brass of them to Babylon.

18 [a]The [1]caldrons also, and the shovels, and the snuffers, and the [2]bowls, and the spoons, and all the [3]vessels of brass wherewith they ministered, took they away.

19 And the basons, and the [1]firepans, and the bowls, and the [2]caldrons, and the [3]candlesticks, and the spoons, and the cups; *that* which *was* of [4]gold *in* gold, and *that* which *was* of [5]silver *in* silver, took the captain of the guard away.

---

**Marginal references:**

51:57 [b] Jer. 46:18; 48:15

51:58 [a] Jer. 50:15 [b] Hab. 2:13 [1] Lit. laid bare [2] Lit. nations because of

51:59 [a] Jer. 32:12 [1] quartermaster

51:60 [a] Is. 30:8; Jer. 36:2

51:62 [a] Is. 13:20; 14:22, 23; Jer. 50:3, 39

51:63 [a] Jer. 19:10, 11; Rev. 18:21

52:1 [a] 2 Kin. 24:18; 2 Chr. 36:11 [b] Josh. 10:29; 2 Kin. 8:22; Is. 37:8

52:3 [a] 2 Chr. 36:13

52:4 [a] 2 Kin. 25:1; Jer. 39:1; Ezek. 24:1, 2; Zech. 8:19 [1] encamped [2] siege walls

52:6 [1] severe [2] food

52:7 [1] city wall was broken through

[2] near [3] Heb. Arabah, Jordan Valley

52:9 [a] 2 Kin. 25:6; Jer. 32:4; 39:5 [1] pronounced

52:10 [a] Ezek. 12:13

52:11 [a] Ezek. 12:13 [1] blinded [2] bronze fetters

52:12 [a] 2 Kin. 25:8–21 [b] Jer. 52:29 [c] Jer. 39:9

52:15 [a] Jer. 39:9 [1] rest [2] defected [3] craftsmen

52:16 [1] farmers

52:17 [a] Jer. 27:19 [b] 1 Kin. 7:15, 23, 27, 50 [1] bronze [2] stands or carts [3] broke in pieces

52:18 [a] Ex. 27:3; 1 Kin. 7:40, 45; 2 Kin. 25:14 [1] pots [2] basons [3] bronze utensils

52:19 [1] censers [2] pots [3] lampstands [4] solid gold [5] solid silver

---

20 The two pillars, one sea, and twelve brasen bulls that *were* [1]under the [2]bases, which king Solomon had made in the house of the LORD: [a]the brass of all these vessels was [3]without weight.

21 And *concerning* the [a]pillars, the height of one pillar *was* eighteen [1]cubits; and a [2]fillet of twelve cubits did compass it; and the thickness thereof *was* [3]four fingers: *it was* hollow.

22 And a [1]chapiter of brass *was* upon it; and the height of one chapiter *was* five cubits, with network and pomegranates upon the chapiters round about, all *of* [2]brass. The second pillar also and the pomegranates *were* like unto these.

23 And there were ninety and six pomegranates on a side; *and* [a]all the pomegranates upon the network *were* an hundred round about.

24 And [a]the captain of the guard took Seraiah the chief priest, [b]and Zephaniah the second priest, and the three keepers of the door:

25 He took also out of the city [1]an eunuch, which had the charge of the men of war; and seven men of them that were [2]near the king's person, which were found in the city; and the principal scribe of the host, who mustered the people of the land; and threescore men of the people of the land, that were found in the midst of the city.

26 So Nebuzar-adan the captain of the guard took them, and brought them to the king of Babylon to Riblah.

27 And the king of Babylon [1]smote them, and put them to death in Riblah in the land of Hamath. Thus Judah was carried away captive out of his own land.

28 [a]This *is* the people whom Nebuchadrezzar carried away captive: [b]in the seventh year [c]three thousand Jews and three and twenty;

29 [a]In the eighteenth year of [1]Nebuchadrezzar he carried away captive from Jerusalem eight hundred thirty and two persons:

30 In the three and twentieth year of Nebuchadrezzar Nebuzar-adan the captain of the guard carried away captive of the Jews seven hundred forty and five persons: all the persons *were* four thousand and six hundred.

31 [a]And it came to pass in the seven and thirtieth year of the captivity of Jehoiachin king of Judah, in the twelfth month, in the five and twentieth *day* of the month, *that* [1]Evil-merodach king of Babylon in the *first* year of his reign [b]lifted[2] up the head of Jehoiachin king of Judah, and brought him forth out of prison,

32 And spake kindly unto him, and set his throne above the throne of the kings that *were* with him in Babylon,

33 And [1]changed his prison garments: [a]and he did continually eat bread before [2]him all the days of his life.

34 And *for* his [1]diet, there was a [2]continual diet given him of the king of Babylon, every day a portion until the day of his death, all the days of his life.

---

52:20 [a] 1 Kin. 7:47; 2 Kin. 25:16  [1] *under it*,  [2] *stands or carts*  [3] *beyond measure*

52:21 [a] 1 Kin. 7:15; 2 Kin. 25:17; 2 Chr. 3:15  [1] *A cubit = about 18 inches*  [2] *measuring line*  [3] *About 3 inches*

52:22 [1] *capital of bronze*  [2] *bronze*

52:23 [a] 1 Kin. 7:20

52:24 [a] 2 Kin. 25:18; 1 Chr. 6:14; Ezra 7:1  [b] Jer. 21:1; 29:25

52:25 [1] *an officer*  [2] *close associates of the king*

52:27 [1] *struck*

52:28 [a] 2 Kin. 24:2  [b] 2 Kin. 24:12  [c] 2 Kin. 24:14

52:29 [a] 2 Kin. 25:11; Jer. 39:9  [1] *Or Nebuchadnezzar*

52:31 [a] 2 Kin. 25:27–30  [b] Gen. 40:13, 20; Ps. 3:3; 27:6  [1] *Or Awil-marduk*  [2] *Showed favor to*

52:33 [a] 2 Sam. 9:7, 13; 1 Kin. 2:7  [1] *Jehoiachin changed*  [2] *The king*

52:34 [1] *provisions*  [2] *regular ration*

# THE
# LAMENTATIONS
## OF JEREMIAH

Lamentations describes the funeral of a city. It is a tearstained portrait of the once proud Jerusalem, now reduced to rubble by the invading Babylonian hordes. In a five-poem dirge, Jeremiah exposes his emotions. A death has occurred; Jerusalem lies barren.

Jeremiah writes his lament in acrostic or alphabetical fashion. Beginning each chapter with the first letter *A* (aleph) he progresses verse by verse through the Hebrew alphabet, literally weeping from *A* to *Z*. And then, in the midst of this terrible holocaust, Jeremiah triumphantly cries out, "Great *is* thy faithfulness" (3:23). In the face of death and destruction, with life seemingly coming apart, Jeremiah turns tragedy into a triumph of faith. God has never failed him in the past. God has promised to remain faithful in the future. In the light of the God he knows and loves, Jeremiah finds hope and comfort.

The Hebrew title of this book comes from the first word of chapters 1, 2, and 4: *Ekah*, "Ah, how!" Another Hebrew word *Ginoth* ("Elegies" or "Lamentations") has also been used as the title because it better represents the contents of the book. The Greek title *Threnoi* means "Dirges" or "Laments," and the Latin title *Threni* ("Tears" or "Lamentations") was derived from this word. The subtitle in Jerome's Vulgate reads: "*Id est lamentationes Jeremiae prophetae*," and this became the basis for the English title "The Lamentations of Jeremiah."

## CHAPTER 1

How [1]doth the city sit solitary, *that was* full of people! [a]how [2]is she become as a widow! she *that was* great among the nations, *and* [b]princess among the provinces, *how* is she become [3]tributary!

2 She [a]weepeth sore in the [b]night, and her tears *are* on her cheeks: among all her lovers she hath none to comfort *her:* all her friends have dealt treacherously with her, they are become her enemies.

3 [a]Judah is gone into captivity [1]because of affliction, and because of great servitude: [b]she dwelleth among the [2]heathen, she findeth no [c]rest: all her persecutors overtook her [3]between the straits.

4 The [1]ways of Zion do mourn, because none come to the [2]solemn feasts: all her gates are [a]desolate: her priests sigh, her virgins are afflicted, and she *is* in bitterness.

5 Her adversaries [a]are [1]the chief, her enemies prosper; for the LORD hath afflicted her [b]for the multitude of her transgressions: her [c]children are gone into captivity before the enemy.

6 And from the daughter of Zion all her beauty is departed: her princes are become like [1]harts *that* find no pasture, and they [2]are gone without strength before the pursuer.

7 Jerusalem [a]remembered in the days of her affliction and of her miseries all her pleasant things that she had in the days of old, when her people fell into the hand of the enemy,

1:1 [a] Is. 47:7–9
[b] Ezra 4:20
[1] lonely the city sits [2] she is like [3] a slave, lit. forced labour
1:2 [a] Jer. 13:17
[b] Job 7:3
1:3 [a] Jer. 52:27
[b] Lam. 2:9
[c] Deut. 28:65
[1] under affliction and hard [2] nations or Gentiles [3] in narrow straits
1:4 [a] Is. 27:10
[1] roads to [2] appointed
1:5 [a] Deut. 28:43
[b] Dan. 9:7, 16
[c] Jer. 52:28 [1] her masters
1:6 [1] deer [2] flee
1:7 [a] Ps. 137:1 [1] MT destruction
1:8 [a] [1 Kin. 8:46]
[b] Ezek. 16:37
[1] wickedly [2] MT has become vile [3] away
1:9 [a] Is. 47:7 [1] considers [2] destiny [3] had a spectacular fall
1:10 [a] Jer. 51:51
[b] Deut. 23:3 [1] desirable [2] Gentiles [3] holy place, the temple
1:11 [a] Jer. 38:9; 52:6 [1] desirable things [2] food to restore life [3] despised
1:12 [a] Dan. 9:12

and none did help her: the adversaries saw her, *and* did mock at her [1]sabbaths.

8 [a]Jerusalem hath [1]grievously sinned; therefore she [2]is removed: all that honoured her despise her, because [b]they have seen her nakedness: yea, she sigheth, and turneth [3]backward.

9 Her filthiness *is* in her skirts; she [a]remembereth[1] not her [2]last end; therefore she [3]came down wonderfully: she had no comforter. O LORD, behold my affliction: for the enemy hath magnified *himself.*

10 The adversary hath spread out his hand upon all her [1]pleasant things: for she hath seen *that* [a]the [2]heathen entered into her [3]sanctuary, whom thou didst command *that* [b]they should not enter into thy congregation.

11 All her people sigh, [a]they seek bread; they have given their [1]pleasant things for [2]meat to relieve the soul: see, O LORD, and consider; for I am [3]become vile.

12 *Is it* nothing to you, all ye that pass [1]by? behold, and see [a]if there be any [2]sorrow like unto my [2]sorrow, which is [3]done unto me, wherewith the LORD hath afflicted *me* in the day of his fierce anger.

13 From above hath he sent fire into my bones, and it [1]prevaileth against them: he hath [a]spread a net for my feet, he hath turned me back:

[1] this way [2] suffering [3] brought on    1:13 [a] Ezek. 12:13; 17:20 [1] overpowered

672

he hath made me desolate *and* faint all the day.

14 ᵃThe yoke of my transgressions is bound by his hand: they are ¹wreathed, *and* come up upon my neck: he hath made my strength ²to fall, the Lord hath delivered me into *their* hands, *from whom* I am not able to ³rise up.

15 The Lord hath ¹trodden under foot all my mighty *men* in the midst of me: he hath called an assembly against me to crush my young men: ᵃthe Lord hath ¹trodden the virgin, the daughter of Judah, *as* in a winepress.

16 For these *things* I weep; mine eye, ᵃmine eye runneth down with ¹water, because the comforter that should ²relieve my soul is far from me: my children are desolate, because the enemy prevailed.

17 ᵃZion ¹spreadeth forth her hands, *and there is* none to comfort her: the LORD hath commanded concerning Jacob, *that* his adversaries *should be* ᵇround about him: Jerusalem is ²as a menstruous woman among them.

18 The LORD is ᵃrighteous; for I have ᵇrebelled against his ¹commandment: hear, I pray you, all people, and behold my ²sorrow: my virgins and my young men are gone into captivity.

19 I called for my lovers, *but* they deceived me: my priests and mine elders ¹gave up the ghost in the city, while they sought ²their meat to relieve their souls.

20 Behold, O LORD; for I *am* in distress: my ᵃbowels¹ are troubled; mine heart is ²turned within me; for I have grievously rebelled: ᵇabroad³ the sword bereaveth, at home *there is* as death.

21 They have heard that I sigh: *there is* none to comfort me: all mine enemies have heard of my trouble; they are ᵃglad that thou hast done *it:* ¹thou wilt bring ᵇthe day *that* thou hast ²called, and they shall be like unto me.

22 ᵃLet all their wickedness come before thee; and do unto them, as thou hast done unto me for all my transgressions: for my sighs *are* many, and my heart *is* faint.

## CHAPTER 2

How hath the Lord covered the daughter of Zion with a ᵃcloud in his anger, ᵇ*and* cast down from heaven unto the earth ᶜthe beauty of Israel, and remembered not ᵈhis footstool in the day of his anger!

2 The Lord hath swallowed up all the habitations of Jacob, and hath ᵃnot pitied: he hath thrown down in his wrath the strong holds of the daughter of Judah; he hath brought *them* down to the ground: ᵇhe hath

---

1:14 ᵃ Deut. 28:48
¹ woven together
² fail ³ withstand
1:15 ᵃ [Rev. 14:19]
¹ trampled
1:16 ᵃ Eccl. 4:1
¹ Tears ² restore my life
1:17 ᵃ Jer. 4:31
ᵇ 2 Kin. 24:2–4
¹ Prays ² an unclean thing
1:18 ᵃ Dan. 9:7, 14 ᵇ 1 Sam. 12:14, 15 ¹ Lit. mouth
² suffering
1:19 ¹ breathed their last ² food to restore their life
1:20 ᵃ Is. 16:11
ᵇ Ezek. 7:15 ¹ soul, lit. inward parts
² overturned
³ outside
1:21 ᵃ Ps. 35:15
ᵇ [Jer. 46] ¹ bring on ² proclaimed
1:22 ᵃ Ps. 109:15; 137:7, 8
2:1 ᵃ [Lam. 3:44]
ᵇ Matt. 11:23
ᶜ 2 Sam. 1:19 ᵈ Ps. 99:5
2:2 ᵃ Lam. 3:43
ᵇ Ps. 89:39, 40

¹ defiled
2:3 ᵃ Ps. 74:11
ᵇ Ps. 89:46
¹ Strength ² withdrawn
2:4 ᵃ Is. 63:10
ᵇ Ezek. 24:25 ¹ Or eye; on the tent
2:5 ᵃ Jer. 30:14
ᵇ Jer. 52:13
2:6 ᵃ Ps. 80:12; 89:40 ᵇ Is. 1:8
ᶜ Is. 43:28 ¹ done violence to his booth or tent
² spurned
2:7 ᵃ Ezek. 24:21
ᵇ Ps. 74:3–8 ¹ rejected ² spurned
³ delivered
2:8 ᵃ Jer. 52:14
ᵇ [Is. 34:11] ¹ determined
2:9 ᵃ Jer. 51:30
ᵇ Deut. 28:36
ᶜ 2 Chr. 15:3 ᵈ Ps. 74:9 ¹ nations
² Prophetic revelation
2:10 ᵃ Is. 3:26
ᵇ Job 2:12 ᶜ Is. 15:3 ¹ A sign of mourning ² bow
2:11 ᵃ Lam. 3:48
ᵇ Job 16:13 ᶜ Lam. 4:4 ¹ soul, lit. inward parts ² Bile
³ infants faint
2:12 ¹ grain ² faint
³ life
2:13 ᵃ Lam. 1:12
¹ How shall I admonish you

---

¹polluted the kingdom and the princes thereof.

3 He hath cut off in *his* fierce anger all the ¹horn of Israel: ᵃhe hath ²drawn back his right hand from before the enemy, ᵇand he burned against Jacob like a flaming fire, *which* devoureth round about.

4 ᵃHe hath bent his bow like an enemy: he stood with his right hand as an adversary, and slew ᵇall *that were* pleasant to the ¹eye in the tabernacle of the daughter of Zion: he poured out his fury like fire.

5 ᵃThe Lord was as an enemy: he hath swallowed up Israel, he hath swallowed up all her palaces: ᵇhe hath destroyed his strong holds, and hath increased in the daughter of Judah mourning and lamentation.

6 And he hath ¹violently ᵃtaken away his tabernacle, ᵇas *if it were of* a garden: he hath destroyed his places of the assembly: the LORD hath caused the solemn feasts and sabbaths to be forgotten in Zion, and hath ᶜdespised² in the indignation of his anger the king and the priest.

7 The Lord hath ¹cast off his altar, he hath ᵃabhorred² his sanctuary, he hath ³given up into the hand of the enemy the walls of her palaces; ᵇthey have made a noise in the house of the LORD, as in the day of a solemn feast.

8 The LORD hath ¹purposed to destroy the ᵃwall of the daughter of Zion: ᵇhe hath stretched out a line, he hath not withdrawn his hand from destroying: therefore he made the rampart and the wall to lament; they languished together.

9 Her gates are sunk into the ground; he hath destroyed and ᵃbroken her bars: ᵇher king and her princes *are* among the ¹Gentiles: ᶜthe law *is* no *more;* her ᵈprophets also find no ²vision from the LORD.

10 The elders of the daughter of Zion ᵃsit upon the ground, *and* keep silence: they have ᵇcast¹ up dust upon their heads; they have ᶜgirded themselves with sackcloth: the virgins of Jerusalem ²hang down their heads to the ground.

11 ᵃMine eyes do fail with tears, my ᵇbowels are troubled, ᵇmy ²liver is poured upon the earth, for the destruction of the daughter of my people; because ᶜthe children and the ³sucklings swoon in the streets of the city.

12 They say to their mothers, Where *is* ¹corn and wine? when they ²swooned as the wounded in the streets of the city, when their ³soul was poured out into their mothers' bosom.

13 ¹What thing shall I take to ᵃwitness for thee? what thing shall I liken to thee, O daughter of Jerusalem?

what shall I [2]equal to thee, that I may comfort thee, O virgin daughter of Zion? for thy [3]breach *is* great like the sea: who can heal thee?

14 Thy [a]prophets have seen [1]vain and [2]foolish things for thee: and they have not [b]discovered[3] thine iniquity, to turn away thy captivity; but have seen for thee [4]false [c]burdens and causes of banishment.

15 All that pass [1]by [a]clap *their* hands at thee; they hiss [b]and [2]wag their head at the daughter of Jerusalem, *saying, Is* this the city that *men* call [c]The perfection of beauty, The joy of the whole earth?

16 [a]All thine enemies have opened their mouth against thee: they hiss and gnash the teeth: they say, [b]We have swallowed *her* up: certainly this *is* the [c]day that we looked for; we have found, [d]we have seen *it.*

17 The LORD hath done *that* which he had [a]devised;[1] he hath fulfilled his word that he had commanded in the days of old: he hath thrown down, and hath not pitied: and he hath caused *thine* enemy to [b]rejoice over thee, he hath [2]set up the horn of thine adversaries.

18 Their heart cried unto the Lord, O wall of the daughter of Zion, [a]let tears run down like a river day and night: give thyself no [1]rest; let not the [2]apple of thine eye [3]cease.

19 Arise, [a]cry out in the night: in the beginning of the watches [b]pour out thine heart like water before the face of the Lord: lift up thy hands toward him for the life of thy young children, that faint for hunger [c]in the top of every street.

20 Behold, O LORD, and consider to whom thou hast done this. [a]Shall the women eat their [1]fruit, *and* children [2]of a span long? shall the priest and the prophet be slain in the sanctuary of the Lord?

21 [a]The young and the old lie on the ground in the streets: my virgins and my young men are fallen by the [b]sword; thou hast slain *them* in the day of thine anger; thou hast killed, *and* not pitied.

22 Thou hast called as [1]in a solemn day [a]my terrors round about, so that in the day of the LORD's anger none escaped nor [2]remained: [b]those that I have [3]swaddled and brought up hath mine enemy [c]consumed.

## CHAPTER 3

I AM the man *that* hath seen affliction by the rod of his wrath.

2 He hath led me, and [1]brought *me into* darkness, but not *into* light.

3 Surely against me is he turned; he turneth his hand *against me* all the day.

4 [a]My flesh and my skin hath he made old; he hath [b]broken my bones.

5 He hath [1]builded against me, and [2]compassed *me* with [3]gall and [4]travail.

6 [a]He hath set me in dark places, as *they that be* dead of old.

7 [a]He hath [1]hedged me about, that I cannot get out: he hath made my chain heavy.

8 Also [a]when I cry and shout, he shutteth out my prayer.

9 He hath [1]inclosed my ways with hewn stone, he hath made my paths crooked.

10 [a]He *was* unto me *as* a bear lying in wait, *and as* a lion in [1]secret places.

11 He hath turned aside my ways, and [a]pulled[1] me in pieces: he hath made me desolate.

12 He hath bent his bow, and [a]set me as a [1]mark for the arrow.

13 He hath caused [a]the arrows of his quiver to enter into my [1]reins.

14 I was a [a]derision[1] to all my people; *and* [b]their [2]song all the day.

15 [a]He hath filled me with bitterness, he hath made me drunken with wormwood.

16 He hath also broken my teeth [a]with gravel stones, he hath [1]covered me with ashes.

17 And thou hast removed my soul far off from peace: I forgat [1]prosperity.

18 [a]And I said, My strength and my hope is perished from the LORD:

19 [1]Remembering mine affliction and my misery, [a]the wormwood and the [2]gall.

20 My soul hath *them* still in remembrance, and is [1]humbled in me.

21 This I recall to my mind, therefore have I [a]hope.

22 [a]*It is of* the LORD's mercies that we are not consumed, because his compassions fail [b]not.

23 *They are* new [a]every morning: great *is* thy faithfulness.

24 The LORD *is* my [a]portion, saith my soul; therefore will I [b]hope in him.

25 The LORD *is* good unto them that [a]wait for him, to the soul *that* seeketh him.

26 *It is* good that *a man* should both [a]hope [b]and quietly wait for the salvation of the LORD.

27 [a]*It is* good for a man that he bear the yoke in his youth.

28 [a]He[1] sitteth alone and keepeth silence, because [2]he hath [3]borne *it* upon him.

29 [a]He[1] putteth his mouth in the dust; if so be there may be hope.

### Center column notes

2:13 [2] *compare* [3] *breakage is as broad as*

2:14 [a] Jer. 2:8; 23:25–29; 29:8, 9; 37:19   [b] Is. 58:1   [c] Jer. 23:33–36 [1] *false* [2] *deceptive visions* [3] *uncovered* [4] *false and misleading prophecies*

2:15 [a] Ezek. 25:6 [b] Ps. 44:14; [c] [Ps. 48:2; 50:2] [1] Lit. *by this way* [2] *shake*

2:16 [a] Job 16:9, 10 [b] Ps. 56:2; 124:3 [c] Lam. 1:21 [d] Ps. 35:21

2:17 [a] Lev. 26:16 [b] Ps. 38:16 [1] *purposed* [2] *exalted*

2:18 [a] Jer. 14:17 [1] *relief* [2] Lit. *daughter* [3] *rest*

2:19 [a] Ps. 119:147 [b] Ps. 42:4; 62:8 [c] Is. 51:20

2:20 [a] Lev. 26:29 [1] *offspring* [2] Vg.; MT *they have cuddled*

2:21 [a] 2 Chr. 36:17 [b] Jer. 18:21

2:22 [a] Ps. 31:13 [b] Hos. 9:12 [c] Jer. 16:2–4; 44:7 [1] *to a feast day* [2] *survived* [3] *borne*

3:2 [1] *made me walk* in

3:4 [a] Job 16:8 [b] Ps. 51:8

3:5 [1] *besieged* [2] *surrounded* [3] *bitterness* [4] *hardship* or *woe*

3:6 [a] [Ps. 88:5, 6; 143:3]

3:7 [a] Hos. 2:6 [1] *walled me in*

3:8 [a] Job 30:20 [1] *blocked*

3:10 [a] Is. 38:13 [1] *Ambush*

3:11 [a] Hos. 6:1 [1] *torn*

3:12 [a] Job 7:20; 16:12 [1] *target*

3:13 [a] Job 6:4 [1] *loins,* lit. *kidneys*

3:14 [a] Jer. 20:7 [b] Job 30:9 [1] *laughingstock* [2] *taunting song*

3:15 [a] Jer. 9:15

3:16 [a] [Prov. 20:17] [1] Lit. *bent me down in*

3:17 [1] Lit. *good*

3:18 [a] Ps. 31:22

3:19 [a] Jer. 9:15 [1] *Remember* [2] *bitterness*

3:20 [1] Lit. *is bowed down*

3:21 [a] Ps. 130:7   3:22 [a] [Mal. 3:6] [b] Ps. 78:38   3:23 [a] Is. 33:2   3:24 [a] Ps. 16:5; 73:26; 119:57 [b] Mic. 7:7   3:25 [a] Is. 30:18   3:26 [a] [Rom. 4:16–18] [b] Ps. 37:7   3:27 [a] Ps. 94:12   3:28 [a] Jer. 15:17 [1] *Let him sit* [2] God [3] *laid*   3:29 [a] Job 42:6 [1] *Let him put*

30 [a]He[1] giveth *his* cheek to him that [2]smiteth him: he is filled full with reproach.

31 [a]For the Lord will not cast off for ever:

32 But though he cause grief, yet will he have compassion according to the multitude of his mercies.

33 For [a]he doth not afflict [1]willingly nor grieve the children of men.

34 To crush under his feet all the prisoners of the earth,

35 To turn aside the [1]right of a man before the face of the most High,

36 To subvert a man in his cause, [a]the Lord approveth not.

37 Who *is* he [a]that saith, and it cometh to pass, *when* the Lord commandeth *it* not?

38 [1]Out of the mouth of the most High proceedeth [2]not [a]evil and [3]good?

39 [a]Wherefore[1] doth a living man complain, [b]a man for the punishment of his sins?

40 Let us search and [1]try our ways, and turn again to the LORD.

41 [a]Let us lift up our heart with *our* hands unto God in the heavens.

42 [a]We have transgressed and have rebelled: thou hast not pardoned.

43 Thou hast covered with anger, and [1]persecuted us: thou hast slain, thou hast not pitied.

44 Thou hast covered thyself with a cloud, that *our* prayer should not pass through.

45 Thou hast made us *as* the [a]offscouring[1] and refuse in the midst of the people.

46 [a]All our enemies have opened their mouths against us.

47 [a]Fear and a snare is come upon us, [b]desolation and destruction.

48 [a]Mine eye runneth down with rivers of water for the destruction of the daughter of my people.

49 [a]Mine eye trickleth down, and ceaseth not, without [1]any intermission,

50 Till the LORD [a]look down, and behold from heaven.

51 Mine eye [1]affecteth mine heart because of all the daughters of my city.

52 Mine enemies [1]chased me sore, like a bird, [a]without cause.

53 They have [1]cut off my life [a]in the [2]dungeon, and [b]cast [3]a stone upon me.

54 [a]Waters flowed over mine head; *then* [b]I said, I am cut off.

55 [a]I called upon thy name, O LORD, out of the [1]low [b]dungeon.

56 [a]Thou hast heard my voice: hide not thine ear at my [1]breathing, at my cry.

57 Thou [a]drewest near in the day *that* I called upon thee: thou saidst, [b]Fear not.

58 O Lord, thou hast [a]pleaded the causes of my soul; [b]thou hast redeemed my life.

59 O LORD, thou hast seen [1]my wrong: [a]judge thou my cause.

60 Thou hast seen all their vengeance *and* all their [a]imaginations[1] against me.

61 Thou hast heard their reproach, O LORD, *and* all their [1]imaginations against me;

62 The lips of those that rose up against me, and their [1]device against me all the day.

63 Behold their [a]sitting down, and their rising up; I *am* their [1]musick.

64 [a]Render unto them a recompence, O LORD, according to the work of their hands.

65 Give them [1]sorrow of heart, thy curse unto them.

66 [1]Persecute and destroy them in anger [a]from under the [b]heavens of the LORD.

## CHAPTER 4

How [1]is the gold become dim! *how* [2]is the most fine gold changed! the stones of the sanctuary are [3]poured out in the top of every street.

2 The precious sons of Zion, [1]comparable to fine gold, how are they [2]esteemed [a]as earthen pitchers, the work of the hands of the potter!

3 Even the [1]sea monsters [2]draw out the breast, they [3]give suck to their young ones: the daughter of my people *is become* cruel, [a]like the ostriches in the wilderness.

4 The tongue of the [1]sucking child cleaveth to the roof of his mouth for thirst: [a]the young children ask bread, *and* no man breaketh *it* unto them.

5 They that [1]did feed delicately are desolate in the streets: they that were brought up in [2]scarlet [a]embrace [3]dunghills.

6 For the punishment of the iniquity of the daughter of my people is greater than the punishment of the [a]sin of Sodom, that was [b]overthrown as in a moment, and no hands [1]stayed on her.

7 Her [1]Nazarites were purer than snow, they were whiter than milk, they were more ruddy in body than rubies, their polishing *was* of sapphire:

8 Their [1]visage is blacker than [2]a coal; they are not known in the streets: [a]their skin [3]cleaveth to their bones; it is withered, it is become like a stick.

9 *They that be* slain with the sword are [1]better than *they that be* slain with

3:30 [a] Is. 50:6
[1] *Let him give*
[2] *strikes*
3:31 [a] Ps. 77:7;
94:14
3:33 [a] [Ezek. 33:11]
[1] *with delight*, lit.
*from his heart*
3:35 [1] *justice* due
3:36 [a] [Hab. 1:13]
3:37 [a] [Ps. 33:9–11]
3:38 [a] Job 2:10
[1] *Is* it *not from*
[2] *woe* [3] *well-being*
3:39 [a] Prov. 19:3
[b] Mic. 7:9 [1] *How can*
3:40 [1] *examine*
3:41 [a] Ps. 86:4
3:42 [a] Dan. 9:5
3:43 [1] *pursued*
3:45 [a] 1 Cor. 4:13
[1] *outcast*
3:46 [a] Lam. 2:16
3:47 [a] Is. 24:17, 18
[b] Is. 51:19
3:48 [a] Jer. 4:19;
14:17
3:49 [a] Jer. 14:17
[1] *interruption*
3:50 [a] Is. 63:15
3:51 [1] *brings suffering to*
3:52 [a] Ps. 35:7,
19, [1] *hunted me down*
3:53 [a] Jer. 37:16
[b] Dan. 6:17 [1] MT
*silenced* [2] *pit*
[3] *stones*
3:54 [a] Ps. 69:2
[b] Is. 38:10
3:55 [a] Ps. 130:1
[b] Jer. 38:6–13
[1] *lowest pit*
3:56 [a] Ps. 3:4
[1] *sighing*
3:57 [a] James 4:8
[b] Is. 41:10, 14
3:58 [a] Jer. 51:36
[b] Ps. 71:23
3:59 [a] Ps. 9:4
[1] *how I am wronged*
3:60 [a] Jer. 11:19
[1] *schemes*
3:61 [1] *schemes*
3:62 [1] *whispering*
3:63 [a] Ps. 139:2
[1] *taunting song*
3:64 [a] Ps. 28:4
3:65 [1] MT *a veiled*,
a Jewish trad.
*sorrow of*
3:66 [a] Deut. 25:19
[b] Ps. 8:3 [1] *Pursue*
4:1 [1] *the gold has* [2] *changed is* [3] *scattered*
4:2 [a] Is. 30:14
[1] Lit. *weighed against* [2] *reckoned*
4:3 [a] Job 39:14–17 [1] *jackals* [2] *present their* [3] *nurse*
4:4 [a] Ps. 22:15 [1] *infant clings*  4:5 [a] Job 24:8 [1] *ate delicacies* [2] *purple* [3] *ash heaps*  4:6 [a] Ezek. 16:48
[b] Gen. 19:25 [1] *helped*  4:7 [1] Or *nobles*  4:8 [a] Ps. 102:5
[1] *appearance* [2] *soot* [3] *clings*  4:9 [1] *better off*

hunger: for these [a]pine[2] away, stricken through for *want* of the fruits of the [b]field.

10 The hands of the [a]pitiful[1] women have [2]sodden their [b]own children: they were their [c]meat[3] in the destruction of the daughter of my people.

11 The LORD hath accomplished his fury; [a]he hath poured out his fierce anger, and [b]hath kindled a fire in Zion, and it hath devoured the foundations thereof.

12 The kings of the earth, and all the inhabitants of the world, would not have believed that the adversary and the enemy [1]should have [a]entered into the gates of Jerusalem.

13 [a]For the sins of her prophets, *and* the iniquities of her priests, [b]that have shed the blood of the just in the midst of her,

14 They have wandered *as* blind *men* in the streets, [a]they have [1]polluted themselves with blood, [b]so that men could not touch their garments.

15 They cried unto them, Depart ye; *it is* [a]unclean; depart, depart, touch not: when they fled away and wandered, they said among the [1]heathen, They shall no more sojourn *there*.

16 The [1]anger of the LORD hath [2]divided them; he will no more regard them: [a]they[3] respected not the persons of the priests, they favoured not the elders.

17 As for us, [a]our eyes [1]as yet failed for our vain help: in our watching we have watched for a nation *that* could not save *us*.

18 [a]They [1]hunt our steps, that we cannot [2]go in our streets: [b]our end is near, our days are fulfilled; for our end is come.

19 Our [1]persecutors are [a]swifter than the eagles of the heaven: they pursued us upon the mountains, they laid wait for us in the wilderness.

20 The [a]breath of our nostrils, the anointed of the LORD, [b]was [1]taken in their pits, of whom we said, Under his shadow we shall live among the [2]heathen.

21 Rejoice and be glad, O daughter of [a]Edom, that dwellest in the land of Uz; [b]the cup also shall pass through unto thee: thou shalt be drunken, and shalt make thyself naked.

22 [a]The punishment of thine iniquity [1]is accomplished, O daughter of Zion; he will no more carry thee away into captivity: [b]he will [2]visit thine iniquity, O daughter of Edom; he will [3]discover thy sins.

---

4:9 [a] Lev. 26:39
[b] Jer. 16:4  [2] Lit. *flow away*
4:10 [a] Lam. 2:20
[b] Is. 49:15  [c] Deut. 28:57  [1] compassionate  [2] boiled  [3] food
4:11 [a] Jer. 7:20
[b] Deut. 32:22
4:12 [a] Jer. 21:13
[1] could
4:13 [a] Jer. 5:31
[b] Matt. 23:31
4:14 [a] Jer. 2:34
[b] Num. 19:16  [1] defiled
4:15 [a] Lev. 13:45, 46  [1] nations
4:16 [a] Lam. 5:12
[1] face  [2] scattered  [3] The people
4:17 [a] 2 Kin. 24:7
[1] failed watching vainly for our
4:18 [a] 2 Kin. 25:4
[b] Ezek. 7:2, 3, 6  [1] tracked  [2] walk
4:19 [a] Deut. 28:49  [1] pursuers
4:20 [a] Gen. 2:7  [b] Jer. 52:9  [1] caught  [2] nations
4:21 [a] Ps. 83:3–6  [b] Jer. 25:15
4:22 [a] [Is. 40:2]  [b] Ps. 137:7  [1] has been completed  [2] punish  [3] uncover
5:1 [a] Ps. 89:50
[b] Lam. 2:15
5:2 [a] Ps. 79:1  [1] turned over to
5:3 [a] Jer. 15:8; 18:21
5:4 [1] must pay for the water we drink
5:5 [a] Jer. 28:14  [1] pursuers are at our necks
5:6 [a] Gen. 24:2  [b] Hos. 9:3; 12:1  [c] Hos. 5:13
5:7 [a] Jer. 31:29
5:9 [1] get  [2] at the risk of our lives, lit. *with our soul*
5:10 [1] hot  [2] fever of
5:11 [a] Zech. 14:2
5:12 [1] respected
5:13 [a] Judg. 16:21  [1] Young men ground at the millstones  [2] staggered under loads of

---

## CHAPTER 5

REMEMBER, [a]O LORD, what is come upon us: consider, and behold [b]our reproach.

2 [a]Our inheritance is [1]turned to strangers, our houses to aliens.

3 We are orphans and fatherless, our mothers *are* as [a]widows.

4 We [1]have drunken our water for money; our wood is sold unto us.

5 [a]Our [1]necks *are* under persecution: we labour, *and* have no rest.

6 [a]We have given the hand [b]*to* the Egyptians, *and to* the [c]Assyrians, to be satisfied with bread.

7 [a]Our fathers have sinned, *and are* not; and we have borne their iniquities.

8 Servants have ruled over us: *there is* none that doth deliver *us* out of their hand.

9 We [1]gat our bread [2]with *the peril of* our lives because of the sword of the wilderness.

10 Our skin was [1]black like an oven because of the [2]terrible famine.

11 They [a]ravished the women in Zion, *and* the maids in the cities of Judah.

12 Princes are hanged up by their hand: the faces of elders were not [1]honoured.

13 [1]They took the young men to [a]grind, and the children [9]fell under the wood.

14 The elders have ceased from the gate, the young men from their [a]musick.

15 The joy of our heart is ceased; our dance is turned into [a]mourning.

16 [a]The [1]crown is fallen *from* our head: woe unto us, that we have sinned!

17 For this our heart is faint; [a]for these *things* our eyes are dim.

18 Because of the mountain of Zion, which is [a]desolate, the foxes walk upon it.

19 Thou, O LORD, [a]remainest for ever; [b]thy throne from generation to generation.

20 [a]Wherefore dost thou forget us for ever, *and* forsake us so long time?

21 [a]Turn thou us [1]unto thee, O LORD, and we shall be turned; renew our days as of old.

22 [1]But thou hast utterly rejected us; thou art very [2]wroth against us.

---

5:14 [a] Jer. 7:34  5:15 [a] Amos 8:10  5:16 [a] Ps. 89:39  [1] Or *crown of our head has fallen*  5:17 [a] Ps. 6:7  5:18 [a] Is. 27:10  5:19 [a] Ps. 9:7  [b] Ps. 45:6  5:20 [a] Ps. 13:1; 44:24  5:21 [a] Jer. 31:18  [1] *back to*  5:22 [1] *Unless*  [2] *angry*

# THE BOOK OF THE PROPHET
# EZEKIEL

Ezekiel, a priest and a prophet, ministers during the darkest days of Judah's history: the seventy-year period of Babylonian captivity. Carried to Babylon before the final assault on Jerusalem, Ezekiel uses prophecies, parables, signs, and symbols to dramatize God's message to His exiled people. Though they are like dry bones in the sun, God will reassemble them and breathe life into the nation once again. Present judgment will be followed by future glory so that "ye shall know that I *am* the LORD" (6:7).

The Hebrew name *Yehezke'l* means "God Strengthens" or "Strengthened by God." Ezekiel is indeed strengthened by God for the prophetic ministry to which he is called (3:8, 9). The name occurs twice in this book and nowhere else in the Old Testament. The Greek form in the Septuagint is *Iezekiel* and the Latin form in the Vulgate is *Ezechiel*.

## CHAPTER 1

Now it came to pass in the thirtieth year, in the fourth *month,* in the fifth *day* of the month, as I *was* among the ¹captives ᵃby the river of Chebar, *that* ᵇthe heavens were opened, and I saw ᶜvisions of God.

2 In the fifth *day* of the month, which *was* the fifth year of king Jehoiachin's captivity,

3 The word of the LORD came expressly unto Ezekiel the priest, the son of Buzi, in the land of the ¹Chaldeans by the river Chebar; and ᵃthe hand of the LORD was there upon him.

4 And I looked, and, behold, ᵃa whirlwind came ᵇout of the north, a great cloud, ¹and a fire infolding itself, and a brightness *was* about it, and ²out of the midst thereof as the colour of amber, out of the midst of the fire.

5 ᵃAlso out of the midst thereof *came* the likeness of four living creatures. And ᵇthis *was* their appearance; they had ᶜthe likeness of a man.

6 And every one had four faces, and every one had four wings.

7 And their ¹feet *were* straight feet; and the sole of their feet *was* like the sole of a calf's foot: and they sparkled ᵃlike the colour of burnished brass.

8 ᵃAnd *they had* the hands of a man under their wings on their four sides; and they four had their faces and their wings.

9 Their wings ¹*were* joined one to another; they turned not when they went; they went every one straight ᵃforward.

10 As for ᵃthe likeness of their faces, they four ᵇhad the face of a man, ᶜand the face of a lion, on the right side: ᵈand they four had the face of an ox on the left side; ᵉthey four also had the face of an eagle.

11 Thus *were* their faces: and their wings *were* ¹stretched upward; two

*wings* of every one ²*were* joined to another, and ᵃtwo covered their bodies.

12 And ᵃthey went every one straight forward: whither the spirit ¹was to go, they went; *and* they ²turned not when they went.

13 As for the likeness of the living creatures, their appearance *was* like burning coals of fire, ᵃ*and* like the appearance of ¹lamps: ²it went up and down among the living creatures; and the fire was bright, and out of the fire went forth lightning.

14 And the living creatures ran ¹and returned ᵃas the appearance of a flash of lightning.

15 Now as I beheld the living creatures, behold ᵃone wheel ¹upon the earth by ²the living creatures, with his four faces.

16 ᵃThe appearance of the wheels and their work *was* ᵇlike unto the colour of a beryl: and they four had one likeness: and their appearance and their work *was* as it were a wheel in the middle of a wheel.

17 When they went, they went ¹upon their four sides: *and* they ²turned not when they went.

18 As for their ¹rings, they were so high that they were ²dreadful; and their ¹rings *were* ᵃfull of eyes round about them four.

19 And ᵃwhen the living creatures went, the wheels went ¹by them: and when the living creatures were lifted up from the earth, the wheels were lifted up.

20 Whithersoever the spirit ¹was to go, they went, ²thither *was their* spirit to go; and the wheels were lifted up ³over against them: ᵃfor the spirit of the living creature *was* in the wheels.

21 When those went, *these* went; and when those stood, *these* stood; and when those were lifted up from

### Cross references (center column)

1:1 ᵃ Ezek. 3:15, 23; 10:15 ᵇ Rev. 4:1; 19:11 ᶜ Ezek. 8:3
¹ exiles

1:3 ᵃ Ezek. 3:14, 22
¹ Or *Babylonians*

1:4 ᵃ Jer. 23:19; 25:32 ᵇ Jer. 1:14
¹ with raging fire engulfing
² radiating out

1:5 ᵃ Rev. 4:6–8 ᵇ Ezek. 10:8 ᶜ Ezek. 10:14

1:7 ᵃ Dan. 10:6
¹ legs

1:8 ᵃ Ezek. 10:8, 21

1:9 ᵃ Ezek. 1:12; 10:20–22
¹ touched

1:10 ᵃ Rev. 4:7 ᵇ Num. 2:10 ᶜ Num. 2:3 ᵈ Num. 2:18 ᵉ Num. 2:25

1:11 ᵃ Is. 6:2
¹ spread out above ² touched

1:12 ᵃ Ezek. 10:11, 22 ¹ wanted ² turned not aside

1:13 ᵃ Rev. 4:5
¹ torches ² it was going back and forth

1:14 ᵃ [Matt. 24:27] ¹ back and forth

1:15 ᵃ Ezek. 10:9
¹ was on ² each living creature

1:16 ᵃ Ezek. 10:9, 10 ᵇ Dan. 10:6

1:17 ¹ any of their four directions ² turned not aside

1:18 ᵃ Ezek. 10:12
¹ rims ² awesome

1:19 ᵃ Ezek. 10:16, 17 ¹ beside

1:20 ᵃ Ezek. 10:17 ¹ wanted ² because there the spirit went ³ together with

677

the earth, the wheels were lifted up [1]over against them: for the spirit of the living creature *was* in the wheels.

22 [a]And the likeness of the [1]firmament [2]upon the heads of the living creature *was* as the colour of [3]the terrible [b]crystal, stretched forth over their heads [c]above.

23 And under the firmament *were* their wings [1]straight, the one toward the other: every one had two, which covered on this side, and every one had two, which covered on that side, their bodies.

24 [a]And when they went, I heard the noise of their wings, [b]like the noise of [1]great waters, as [c]the voice of the Almighty, the [2]voice of speech, as the noise of an [3]host: when they [4]stood, they let down their wings.

25 And there was a voice from the firmament that *was* over their heads, when they stood, *and* had let down their wings.

26 [a]And above the [1]firmament that *was* over their heads *was* the likeness of a throne, [b]as the appearance of a sapphire stone: and upon the likeness of the throne *was* the likeness as the appearance of a man [2]above upon [c]it.

27 [a]And I saw as the colour of amber, as the appearance of fire round about within it, from the appearance of his [1]loins even upward, and from the appearance of his [1]loins even downward, I saw as it were the appearance of fire, and it had brightness round about.

28 [a]As the appearance of [1]the bow that is in the cloud in the day of rain, so *was* the appearance of the brightness round about. [b]This *was* the appearance of the likeness of the glory of the LORD. And when I saw *it,* [c]I fell upon my face, and I heard a voice of one that spake.

## CHAPTER 2

AND he said unto me, Son of man, [a]stand upon thy feet, and I will speak unto thee.

2 And [a]the spirit entered into me when he spake unto me, and set me upon my feet, that I heard him that spake unto me.

3 And he said unto me, Son of man, I send thee to the children of Israel, to a rebellious nation that hath [a]rebelled against me: [b]they and their fathers have transgressed against me, *even* unto this very day.

4 [a]For *they are* [1]impudent children and stiffhearted. I do send thee unto them; and thou shalt say unto them, Thus saith the Lord GOD.

5 [a]And they, whether they will hear, or whether they will [1]forbear, (for they *are* a [b]rebellious house,) yet

1:21 [1] *together with them*
1:22 [a] Ezek. 10:1 [b] Rev. 4:6 [c] Ezek. 10:1 [1] *expanse* [2] *above* [3] *an awesome*
1:23 [1] *spread out straight*
1:24 [a] Ezek. 3:13; 10:5 [b] Rev. 1:15 [c] Job 37:4, 5 [1] *many* [2] *sound of a tumult* [3] *army* [4] *stood still*
1:26 [a] Ezek. 10:1 [b] Ex. 24:10, 16 [c] Ezek. 8:2 [1] *expanse* [2] *high above it*
1:27 [a] Ezek. 8:2 [1] *waist and*
1:28 [a] Rev. 4:3; 10:1 [b] Ezek. 3:23; 8:4 [c] Dan. 8:17 [1] *a rainbow*
2:1 [a] Dan. 10:11
2:2 [a] Ezek. 3:24
2:3 [a] Ezek. 5:6; 20:8, 13, 18 [b] Jer. 3:25
2:4 [a] Ezek. 3:7 [1] Lit. *stiff-faced and hardhearted sons*
2:5 [a] Ezek. 3:11, 26, 27 [b] Ezek. 3:26 [1] *refuse*

[c] Ezek. 33:33
2:6 [a] Jer. 1:8, 17 [b] Mic. 7:4 [c] [1 Pet. 3:14] [d] Ezek. 3:9, 26, 27
2:7 [a] Jer. 1:7, 17 [1] *refuse*
2:8 [a] Rev. 10:9
2:9 [a] [Ezek. 8:3] [b] Ezek. 3:1 [1] *stretched out to me* [2] *scroll*
3:1 [a] Ezek. 2:8, 9 [1] *scroll*
3:3 [a] Rev. 10:9 [b] Ps. 19:10; 119:103 [1] *feed thy belly* [2] *stomach* [3] *scroll*
3:5 [1] *unfamiliar*
3:6 [a] Matt. 11:21
3:7 [a] John 15:20, 21 [b] Ezek. 2:4 [1] Lit. *strong of forehead*
3:9 [a] Mic. 3:8 [b] Jer. 1:8, 17 [1] *adamant stone*

[c]shall know that there hath been a prophet among them.

6 And thou, son of man, [a]be not afraid of them, neither be afraid of their words, though [b]briers and thorns *be* with thee, and thou dost dwell among scorpions: [c]be not afraid of their words, nor be dismayed at their looks, [d]though they *be* a rebellious house.

7 [a]And thou shalt speak my words unto them, whether they will hear, or whether they will [1]forbear: for they *are* most rebellious.

8 But thou, son of man, hear what I say unto thee; Be not thou rebellious like that rebellious house: open thy mouth, and [a]eat that I give thee.

9 And when I looked, behold, [a]an hand *was* [1]sent unto me; and, lo, [b]a [2]roll of a book *was* therein;

10 And he spread it before me; and it *was* written within and without: and *there was* written therein lamentations, and mourning, and woe.

## CHAPTER 3

MOREOVER he said unto me, Son of man, eat that thou findest; [a]eat this [1]roll, and go speak unto the house of Israel.

2 So I opened my mouth, and he caused me to eat that roll.

3 And he said unto me, Son of man, [1]cause thy belly to eat, and fill thy [2]bowels with this [3]roll that I give thee. Then did I [a]eat *it;* and it was in my mouth [b]as honey for sweetness.

4 And he said unto me, Son of man, go, get thee unto the house of Israel, and speak with my words unto them.

5 For thou *art* not sent to a people of [1]a strange speech and of an hard language, *but* to the house of Israel;

6 Not to many people of a strange speech and of an hard language, whose words thou canst not understand. Surely, [a]had I sent thee to them, they would have hearkened unto thee.

7 But the house of Israel will not hearken unto thee; [a]for they will not hearken unto me: [b]for all the house of Israel *are* [1]impudent and hardhearted.

8 Behold, I have made thy face strong against their faces, and thy forehead strong against their foreheads.

9 [a]As an [1]adamant harder than flint have I made thy forehead: [b]fear them not, neither be dismayed at their looks, though they *be* a rebellious house.

10 Moreover he said unto me, Son of man, all my words that I shall speak unto thee receive in thine heart, and hear with thine ears.

11 And go, get thee to them of the captivity, unto the children of thy

people, and speak unto them, and tell them, <sup>a</sup>Thus saith the Lord GOD; whether they will hear, or whether they will <sup>1</sup>forbear.

12 Then <sup>a</sup>the spirit took me up, and I heard behind me a voice of a great <sup>1</sup>rushing, *saying,* Blessed *be* the <sup>b</sup>glory of the LORD from his place.

13 *I heard* also the <sup>a</sup>noise of the wings of the living creatures that touched one another, and the noise of the wheels over against them, and a noise of a great <sup>1</sup>rushing.

14 So the spirit lifted me up, and took me away, and I went in bitterness, in the <sup>1</sup>heat of my spirit; but <sup>a</sup>the hand of the LORD was strong upon me.

15 Then I came to them of the captivity at Tel-abib, that dwelt by the river of Chebar, and <sup>a</sup>I sat where they sat, and remained there astonished among them seven days.

16 And it <sup>a</sup>came to pass at the end of seven days, that the word of the LORD came unto me, saying,

17 <sup>a</sup>Son of man, I have made thee <sup>b</sup>a watchman unto the house of Israel: therefore hear the word at my mouth, and give them <sup>c</sup>warning from me.

18 When I say unto the wicked, Thou shalt surely die; and thou givest him not warning, nor speakest to warn the wicked from his wicked way, to save his life; the same wicked *man* <sup>a</sup>shall die in his iniquity; but his blood will I require at thine hand.

19 Yet if thou warn the wicked, and he turn not from his wickedness, nor from his wicked way, he shall die in his iniquity; <sup>a</sup>but thou hast delivered thy soul.

20 Again, When a <sup>a</sup>righteous *man* doth turn from his righteousness, and commit iniquity, and I lay a stumblingblock before him, he shall die: because thou hast not given him warning, he shall die in his sin, and his righteousness which he hath done shall not be remembered; but his blood will I require at thine hand.

21 Nevertheless if thou warn the righteous *man,* that the righteous sin not, and he doth not sin, he shall surely live, because he <sup>1</sup>is warned; also thou hast delivered thy soul.

22 <sup>a</sup>And the hand of the LORD was there upon me; and he said unto me, Arise, go forth <sup>b</sup>into the plain, and I will there talk with thee.

23 Then I arose, and went forth into the plain: and, behold, <sup>a</sup>the glory of the LORD stood there, as the glory which I <sup>b</sup>saw by the river of Chebar: <sup>c</sup>and I fell on my face.

24 Then <sup>a</sup>the spirit entered into me, and set me upon my feet, and spake with me, and said unto me, Go, shut thyself within thine house.

3:11 <sup>a</sup> Ezek. 2:5, 7
<sup>1</sup> refuse
3:12 <sup>a</sup> Ezek. 8:3;
1 Kin. 18:12; Acts
8:39 <sup>b</sup> Ezek. 1:28;
8:4 <sup>1</sup> tumult
3:13 <sup>a</sup> Ezek. 1:24;
10:5 <sup>1</sup> tumult
3:14 <sup>a</sup> 2 Kin. 3:15;
Ezek. 1:3; 8:1 <sup>1</sup> Or
anger
3:15 <sup>a</sup> Job 2:13;
Ps. 137:1
3:16 <sup>a</sup> Jer. 42:7
3:17 <sup>a</sup> Ezek. 33:7–9
<sup>b</sup> Is. 52:8; 56:10;
Jer. 6:17 <sup>c</sup> [Lev.
19:17; Prov. 14:25];
Is. 58:1
3:18 <sup>a</sup> Ezek. 33:6;
[John 8:21, 24]
3:19 <sup>a</sup> Is. 49:4, 5;
Ezek. 14:14, 20;
Acts 18:6; 20:26;
1 Tim. 4:16
3:20 <sup>a</sup> Ps. 125:5;
Ezek. 18:24; 33:18;
Zeph. 1:6
3:21 <sup>1</sup> took
warning
3:22 <sup>a</sup> Ezek. 1:3
<sup>b</sup> Ezek. 8:4
3:23 <sup>a</sup> Ezek. 1:28;
Acts 7:55 <sup>b</sup> Ezek.
1:1 <sup>c</sup> Ezek. 1:28
3:24 <sup>a</sup> Ezek. 2:2

3:25 <sup>a</sup> Ezek. 4:8
<sup>1</sup> ropes
3:26 <sup>a</sup> Ezek.
24:27; Luke 1:20,
22 <sup>b</sup> Hos. 4:17;
Amos 8:11 <sup>c</sup> Ezek.
2:5–7 <sup>1</sup> cling
<sup>2</sup> mute <sup>3</sup> one who
rebukes
3:27 <sup>a</sup> Ex. 4:11,
12; Ezek. 24:27;
33:22 <sup>b</sup> Ezek. 3:11
<sup>1</sup> refuses

4:1 <sup>1</sup> clay tablet
4:2 <sup>a</sup> Jer. 6:6;
Ezek. 21:22
<sup>b</sup> 2 Kin. 25:1
<sup>1</sup> siege wall
<sup>2</sup> heap up a
mound
4:3 <sup>a</sup> Jer. 39:1, 2;
Ezek. 5:2 <sup>b</sup> Ezek.
12:6, 11; 24:24, 27
<sup>1</sup> plate
4:5 <sup>a</sup> Num. 14:34
4:6 <sup>1</sup> a day for
each year
4:8 <sup>a</sup> Ezek. 3:25
<sup>1</sup> constrain thee
4:9 <sup>1</sup> spelt
4:10 <sup>1</sup> food

25 But thou, O son of man, behold, <sup>a</sup>they shall put <sup>1</sup>bands upon thee, and shall bind thee with them, and thou shalt not go out among them:

26 And <sup>a</sup>I will make thy tongue <sup>1</sup>cleave to the roof of thy mouth, that thou shalt be <sup>2</sup>dumb, and shalt <sup>b</sup>not be to them <sup>3</sup>a reprover: <sup>c</sup>for they *are* a rebellious house.

27 <sup>a</sup>But when I speak with thee, I will open thy mouth, and thou shalt say unto them, <sup>b</sup>Thus saith the Lord GOD; He that heareth, let him hear; and he that <sup>1</sup>forbeareth, let him forbear: for they *are* a rebellious house.

## CHAPTER 4

THOU also, son of man, take thee a <sup>1</sup>tile, and lay it before thee, and pourtray upon it the city, *even* Jerusalem:

2 And <sup>a</sup>lay siege against it, and build a <sup>b</sup>fort<sup>1</sup> against it, and <sup>2</sup>cast a mount against it; set the camp also against it, and set *battering* rams against it round about.

3 Moreover take thou unto thee an iron <sup>1</sup>pan, and set it *for* a wall of iron between thee and the city: and set thy face against it, and it shall be <sup>a</sup>besieged, and thou shalt lay siege against it. <sup>b</sup>This *shall be* a sign to the house of Israel.

4 Lie thou also upon thy left side, and lay the iniquity of the house of Israel upon it: *according* to the number of the days that thou shalt lie upon it thou shalt bear their iniquity.

5 For I have laid upon thee the years of their iniquity, according to the number of the days, three hundred and ninety days: <sup>a</sup>so shalt thou bear the iniquity of the house of Israel.

6 And when thou hast accomplished them, lie again on thy right side, and thou shalt bear the iniquity of the house of Judah forty days: I have appointed thee <sup>1</sup>each day for a year.

7 Therefore thou shalt set thy face toward the siege of Jerusalem, and thine arm *shall be* uncovered, and thou shalt prophesy against it.

8 <sup>a</sup>And, behold, I will <sup>1</sup>lay bands upon thee, and thou shalt not turn thee from one side to another, till thou hast ended the days of thy siege.

9 Take thou also unto thee wheat, and barley, and beans, and lentiles, and millet, and <sup>1</sup>fitches, and put them in one vessel, and make thee bread thereof, *according* to the number of the days that thou shalt lie upon thy side, three hundred and ninety days shalt thou eat thereof.

10 And thy <sup>1</sup>meat which thou shalt eat *shall be* by weight, twenty shekels a day: from time to time shalt thou eat it.

11 Thou shalt drink also water by measure, the sixth part of an hin: from time to time shalt thou drink.

12 And thou shalt eat it *as* barley cakes, and thou shalt bake it with [1]dung that cometh out of man, in their sight.

13 And the LORD said, Even thus [a]shall the children of Israel eat their defiled bread among the Gentiles, whither I will drive them.

14 Then said I, [a]Ah Lord GOD! behold, [1]my soul hath not been polluted: for from my youth up even till now have I not eaten of [b]that which dieth of itself, or is [2]torn in pieces; neither came there [c]abominable[3] flesh into my mouth.

15 Then he said unto me, Lo, I have given thee cow's dung for [1]man's dung, and thou shalt prepare thy bread [2]therewith.

16 Moreover he said unto me, Son of man, behold, I will [1]break the [a]staff of bread in Jerusalem: and they shall [b]eat bread by weight, and with [2]care; and they shall [c]drink water by measure, and with [3]astonishment:

17 That they may [1]want bread and water, and be [2]astonied one with another, and [a]consume[3] away for their iniquity.

## CHAPTER 5

AND thou, son of man, take thee a sharp [1]knife, [2]take thee a barber's razor, [a]and cause *it* to pass upon thine head and upon thy beard: then take thee balances to weigh, and divide the *hair.*

2 [a]Thou shalt burn with fire a third part in the midst of [b]the city, when [c]the days of the siege are fulfilled: and thou shalt take a third part, *and* [1]smite about it with a knife: and a third part thou shalt scatter in the wind; and I will draw out a sword after [d]them.

3 [a]Thou shalt also take thereof a few in number, and bind them in thy [1]skirts.

4 Then take [1]of them again, and [a]cast them into the midst of the fire, and burn them in the fire; *for* thereof shall a fire come forth into all the house of Israel.

5 Thus saith the Lord GOD; This is Jerusalem: I have set it in the midst of the nations and countries *that are* round about her.

6 And she hath [1]changed my judgments [2]into wickedness more than the nations, and my statutes more than the countries that *are* round about her: for they have refused my judgments and my statutes, they have not walked in them.

7 Therefore thus saith the Lord GOD; Because ye [1]multiplied more than the nations that *are* round about you, *and* have not walked in my statutes, [a]neither have kept my judgments, neither have done according to the judgments of the nations that *are* round about you;

8 Therefore thus saith the Lord GOD; Behold, I, even I, *am* against thee, and will execute judgments in the midst of thee in the sight of the nations.

9 [a]And I will do in thee that which I have not done, and whereunto I will not do any more the like, because of all thine abominations.

10 Therefore the fathers [a]shall eat the sons in the midst of thee, and the sons shall eat their fathers; and I will execute judgments in thee, and the whole remnant of thee will I [b]scatter into all the winds.

11 Wherefore, *as* I live, saith the Lord GOD; Surely, because thou hast [a]defiled my sanctuary with all thy [b]detestable things, and with all thine abominations, therefore will I also diminish *thee;* [c]neither shall mine eye spare, neither will I have any pity.

12 [a]A third part of thee shall die with the pestilence, and with famine shall they be consumed in the midst of thee: and a third part shall fall by the sword round about thee; and [b]I will scatter a third part into all the winds, and I will draw out a sword after [c]them.

13 Thus shall mine anger [a]be [1]accomplished, and I will [b]cause my fury to rest upon them, [c]and I will be [2]comforted: [d]and they shall know that I the LORD have spoken *it* in my zeal, when I have [1]accomplished my fury in them.

14 Moreover [a]I will make thee [1]waste, and a reproach among the nations that *are* round about thee, in the sight of all that pass by.

15 So it shall be a [a]reproach and a taunt, [1]an [b]instruction and an astonishment unto the nations that *are* round about thee, when I shall execute judgments in thee in anger and in fury and in [c]furious rebukes. I the LORD have spoken *it.*

16 When I shall [a]send upon them the [1]evil arrows of famine, which shall be for *their* destruction, *and* which I will send to destroy you: and I will increase the famine upon you, and will break your [b]staff[2] of bread:

17 So will I send upon you famine and [a]evil[1] beasts, and they shall bereave thee; and [b]pestilence and blood shall pass through thee; and I will bring the sword upon thee. I the LORD have spoken *it.*

## CHAPTER 6

AND the word of the LORD came unto me, saying,

4:12 [1] *human waste as fuel*
4:13 [a] Hos. 9:3
4:14 [a] Acts 10:14 [b] Lev. 17:15; 22:8 [c] Deut. 14:3 [1] *I have never defiled myself* [2] *torn by beasts* [3] *unclean*
4:15 [1] *human waste* [2] *over it*
4:16 [a] Is. 3:1 [b] Ezek. 4:10, 11; 12:19 [c] Ezek. 4:11 [1] *cut off the supply* [2] *anxiety* [3] *dread*
4:17 [a] Lev. 26:39 [1] *lack* [2] *dismayed* [3] *waste*
5:1 [a] Is. 7:20 [1] *sword* [2] *take it as*
5:2 [a] Ezek. 5:12 [b] Ezek. 4:1 [c] Ezek. 4:8, 9 [d] Lev. 26:25 [1] *strike all around it*
5:3 [a] Jer. 40:6; 52:16 [1] garment
5:4 [a] Jer. 41:1, 2; 44:14 [1] *some of*
5:6 [1] *rebelled against* [2] *by doing wickedness*
5:7 [1] *multiplied* disobedience
[a] Jer. 2:10, 11
5:9 [a] [Amos 3:2]
5:10 [a] Jer. 19:9 [b] Zech. 2:6; 7:14
5:11 [a] [Jer. 7:9–11] [b] Ezek. 11:21 [c] Ezek. 7:4, 9; 8:18; 9:10
5:12 [a] Ezek. 6:12 [b] Jer. 9:16 [c] Jer. 43:10, 11; 44:27
5:13 [a] Lam. 4:11 [b] Ezek. 21:17 [c] Is. 1:24 [d] Ezek. 36:6; 38:19 [1] *spent* [2] *avenged*
5:14 [a] Lev. 26:31 [1] *a ruin*
5:15 [a] Jer. 24:9 [b] [Is. 26:9] [c] Ezek. 5:8; 25:17 [1] *a lesson*
5:16 [a] Deut. 32:23 [b] Lev. 26:26 [1] *terrible* [2] *supply*
5:17 [a] Lev. 26:22 [b] Ezek. 38:22 [1] *wild*

2 Son of man, [a]set thy face toward the [b]mountains of Israel, and prophesy against them,

3 And say, Ye mountains of Israel, hear the word of the Lord GOD; Thus saith the Lord GOD to the mountains, and to the hills, to the [1]rivers, and to the valleys; Behold, I, *even* I, will bring a sword upon you, and [a]I will destroy your [2]high places.

4 And your altars shall be desolate, and your [1]images shall be broken: and [a]I will cast down your slain *men* before your idols.

5 And I will lay the dead carcases of the children of Israel before their idols; and I will scatter your bones round about your altars.

6 In all your dwellingplaces the cities shall be laid [1]waste, and the [2]high places shall be desolate; that your altars may be laid [1]waste and made desolate, and your idols may be broken and [3]cease, and your [4]images may be cut down, and your works may be abolished.

7 And the slain shall fall in the midst of you, and [a]ye shall know that I *am* the LORD.

8 [a]Yet will I leave a remnant, that ye may have *some* that shall escape the sword among the nations, when ye shall be [b]scattered through the countries.

9 And they that escape of you shall [a]remember me among the nations whither they shall be carried captives, because [b]I am [1]broken with their [2]whorish heart, which hath departed from me, and [c]with their eyes, which [3]go a whoring after their idols: and [d]they shall lothe themselves for the evils which they have committed in all their abominations.

10 And they shall know that I *am* the LORD, *and that* I have not said in vain that I would [1]do this evil unto them.

11 Thus saith the Lord GOD; [1]Smite [a]with thine hand, and stamp with thy foot, and say, Alas for all the evil abominations of the house of Israel! [b]for they shall fall by the sword, by the famine, and by the pestilence.

12 He that is far off shall die of the pestilence; and he that is near shall fall by the sword; and he that remaineth and is besieged shall die by the famine: [a]thus will I [1]accomplish my fury upon them.

13 Then shall ye know that I *am* the LORD, when their slain *men* shall be among their idols round about their altars, [a]upon every high hill, [b]in all the tops of the mountains, and [c]under every green tree, and under every thick oak, the place where they did offer sweet [1]savour to all their idols.

14 So will I [a]stretch out my hand

---

upon them, and make the land desolate, yea, more desolate than the wilderness toward [b]Diblath, in all their habitations: and they shall know that I *am* the LORD.

## CHAPTER 7

MOREOVER the word of the LORD came unto me, saying,

2 Also, thou son of man, thus saith the Lord GOD unto the land of Israel; [a]An end, the end is come upon the four corners of the land.

3 Now *is* the end *come* upon thee, and I will send mine anger upon thee, and will judge thee [a]according to thy ways, and will [1]recompense upon thee all thine abominations.

4 And [a]mine eye shall not spare thee, neither will I have pity: but I will recompense thy ways upon thee, and thine abominations shall be in the midst of thee: [b]and ye shall know that I *am* the LORD.

5 Thus saith the Lord GOD; [1]An evil, an only [a]evil, behold, [2]is come.

6 An end is come, the end is come: it [1]watcheth for thee; behold, it is come.

7 [a]The[1] morning is come unto thee, O thou that dwellest in the land: [b]the time is come, the day of trouble *is* near, and not [2]the sounding again of the mountains.

8 Now will I shortly [a]pour out my fury upon thee, and [1]accomplish mine anger upon thee: and I will judge thee according to thy ways, and will recompense thee for all thine abominations.

9 And mine eye shall not spare, neither will I have pity: I will [1]recompense thee according to thy ways and thine abominations *that* are in the midst of thee; and ye shall know that I *am* the LORD that [2]smiteth.

10 Behold the day, behold, it is come: [a]the[1] morning is gone forth; the rod hath blossomed, pride hath budded.

11 [a]Violence is risen up into a rod of wickedness: none of them *shall remain*, nor of their multitude, nor of any of [1]theirs: [b]neither *shall there be* wailing for them.

12 The time is come, the day draweth near: let not the buyer [a]rejoice, nor the seller [b]mourn: for wrath *is* upon all the multitude thereof.

13 For the seller shall not return to that which is sold, although they were yet alive: for the vision [1]*is* touching the whole multitude thereof, *which* shall not [2]return; neither shall any strengthen himself [3]in the iniquity of his life.

14 They have blown the trumpet, even to make all ready; but none goeth to the battle: for my wrath *is* upon all the multitude thereof.

---

6:2 [a] Ezek. 20:46; 21:2; 25:2  [b] Ezek. 36:1

6:3 [a] Lev. 26:30
[1] *ravines* [2] *sacred places* for pagan worship

6:4 [a] Lev. 26:30
[1] *incense altars*

6:6 [1] *in ruins* [2] *sacred places* for pagan worship
[3] *ended* [4] *incense altars*

6:7 [a] Ezek. 7:4, 9

6:8 [a] Jer. 44:28
[b] Ezek. 5:12

6:9 [a] [Deut. 4:29]  [b] Ps. 78:40
[c] Ezek. 20:7, 24
[d] Ezek. 20:43;
36:31 [1] *crushed by* [2] *adulterous*
[3] *played the harlot*

6:10 [1] *bring this calamity*

6:11 [a] Ezek. 21:14
[b] Ezek. 5:12
[1] *Strike, Pound*

6:12 [a] Ezek. 5:13
[1] *spend*

6:13 [a] Jer. 2:20;
3:6  [b] Hos. 4:13
[c] Is. 57:5 [1] *incense*

6:14 [a] Is. 5:25

[b] Num. 33:46
7:2 [a] Amos 8:2, 10
7:3 [a] [Rom. 2:6]
[1] *repay you for*
7:4 [a] Ezek. 5:11
[b] Ezek. 12:20

7:5 [a] 2 Kin. 21:12,
13 [1] *A disaster, a singular disaster*
[2] *it has come*
7:6 [1] *has dawned*
7:7 [a] Ezek. 7:10
[b] Zeph. 1:14, 15
[1] *Or Doom* [2] *of rejoicing in the mountains*
7:8 [a] Ezek. 20:8,
21 [1] *spend*
7:9 [1] *repay*, lit. *give* [2] *strikes*
7:10 [a] Ezek. 7:7
[1] *Or doom*
7:11 [a] Jer. 6:7
[b] Jer. 16:5, 6 [1] *Or their wealth*
7:12 [a] Prov. 20:14
[b] Is. 24:2

7:13 [1] *concerns*
[2] *turn back* [3] *who lives in iniquity*

---

15 ᵃThe sword *is* ¹without, and the pestilence and the famine within: he that *is* in the field shall die with the sword; and he that *is* in the city, famine and pestilence shall devour him.

16 But they that ᵃescape¹ of them shall escape, and shall be on the mountains like doves of the valleys, all of them mourning, every one for his iniquity.

17 All ᵃhands shall be feeble, and all knees shall be weak *as* water.

18 They shall also ᵃgird *themselves* with sackcloth, and horror shall cover them; and shame *shall be* upon all faces, and baldness upon all their heads.

19 They shall cast their silver in the streets, and their gold shall be ¹removed: their ᵃsilver and their gold shall not be able to deliver them in the day of the wrath of the LORD: they shall not satisfy their souls, neither fill their ²bowels: because it ³is the stumblingblock of their iniquity.

20 As for the beauty of his ornament, he set it in majesty: ᵃbut they made the images of their abominations *and* of their detestable things therein: therefore have I ¹set it far from them.

21 And I will give it into the hands of the strangers for ¹a ᵃprey, and to the wicked of the earth for a spoil; and they shall ²pollute it.

22 My face will I turn also from them, and they shall ¹pollute my secret *place:* for the robbers shall enter into it, and defile it.

23 Make a chain: for ᵃthe land is full of bloody crimes, and the city is full of violence.

24 Wherefore I will bring the ᵃworst of the ¹heathen, and they shall possess their houses: I will also make the pomp of the strong to cease; and their holy places shall be ᵇdefiled.

25 ¹Destruction cometh; and they shall seek peace, and *there shall be* none.

26 ᵃMischief¹ shall come upon mischief, and rumour shall be upon rumour; ᵇthen shall they seek a ²vision of the prophet; but the law shall perish from the priest, and counsel from the ³ancients.

27 The king shall mourn, and the prince shall be clothed with desolation, and the hands of the people of the land shall be troubled: I will do unto them ¹after their way, and according to ²their deserts will I judge them; and they shall know that I *am* the LORD.

## CHAPTER 8

AND it came to pass in the sixth year, in the sixth *month,* in the fifth *day* of the month, *as* I sat in

7:15 ᵃ Jer. 14:18
¹ outside
7:16 ᵃ Ezek. 6:8;
14:22 ¹ survive
7:17 ᵃ Is. 13:7
7:18 ᵃ Amos 8:10
7:19 ᵃ Zeph.
1:18 ¹ like refuse
² stomachs
³ became
7:20 ᵃ Jer. 7:30
¹ made it like
refuse to them
7:21 ᵃ 2 Kin. 24:13
¹ plunder ² defile
7:22 ¹ defile
7:23 ᵃ 2 Kin. 21:16
7:24 ᵃ Ezek. 21:31;
28:7 ᵇ Ezek. 24:21
¹ Gentiles
7:25 ¹ Lit. Anguish
7:26 ᵃ Jer. 4:20
ᵇ Ps. 74:9 ¹ Disaster ² Prophetic
revelation
³ elders
7:27 ¹ according
to ² what they
deserve

8:1 ᵃ Ezek. 14:1;
20:1; 33:31 ᵇ Ezek.
1:3; 3:22
8:2 ᵃ Ezek. 1:26,
27 ᵇ Ezek. 1:4, 27
¹ waist and
8:3 ᵃ Dan. 5:5
ᵇ Ezek. 3:14
ᶜ Ezek. 11:1, 24;
40:2 ᵈ Ezek. 5:11
ᵉ Deut. 32:16,
21 ¹ hair ² idol
³ provokes the
LORD to
8:4 ᵃ Ezek. 3:12;
9:3 ᵇ Ezek. 1:28;
3:22, 23 ¹ like the
vision
8:5 ¹ entrance
8:6 ᵃ 2 Kin. 23:4, 5
8:10 ᵃ Ex. 20:4
ᵇ Rom. 1:23 ¹ Or
carved
8:11 ᵃ Num. 11:16,
25 ¹ elders
8:12 ᵃ Ezek. 9:9
¹ elders ² room of
his idols ³ land

mine house, and ᵃthe elders of Judah sat before me, that ᵇthe hand of the Lord GOD fell there upon me.

2 ᵃThen I beheld, and lo a likeness as the appearance of fire: from the appearance of his ¹loins even downward, fire; and from his ¹loins even upward, as the appearance of brightness, ᵇas the colour of amber.

3 And he ᵃput forth the form of an hand, and took me by a lock of mine ¹head; and ᵇthe spirit lifted me up between the earth and the heaven, and ᶜbrought me in the visions of God to Jerusalem, to the door of the inner gate that looketh toward the north; ᵈwhere *was* the seat of the ²image of jealousy, which ᵉprovoketh³ to jealousy.

4 And, behold, the ᵃglory of the God of Israel *was* there, ¹according to the vision that I ᵇsaw in the plain.

5 Then said he unto me, Son of man, lift up thine eyes now the way toward the north. So I lifted up mine eyes the way toward the north, and behold northward at the gate of the altar this image of jealousy in the ¹entry.

6 He said furthermore unto me, Son of man, seest thou what they do? *even* the great ᵃabominations that the house of Israel committeth here, that I should go far off from my sanctuary? but turn thee yet again, *and* thou shalt see greater abominations.

7 And he brought me to the door of the court; and when I looked, behold a hole in the wall.

8 Then said he unto me, Son of man, dig now in the wall: and when I had digged in the wall, behold a door.

9 And he said unto me, Go in, and behold the wicked abominations that they do here.

10 So I went in and saw; and behold every ᵃform of ᵇcreeping things, and abominable beasts, and all the idols of the house of Israel, ¹pourtrayed upon the wall round about.

11 And there stood before them ᵃseventy men of the ¹ancients of the house of Israel, and in the midst of them stood Jaazaniah the son of Shaphan, with every man his censer in his hand; and a thick cloud of incense went up.

12 Then said he unto me, Son of man, hast thou seen what the ¹ancients of the house of Israel do in the dark, every man in the ²chambers of his imagery? for they say, ᵃThe LORD seeth us not; the LORD hath forsaken the ³earth.

13 He said also unto me, Turn thee yet again, *and* thou shalt see greater abominations that they do.

14 Then he brought me to the door of the gate of the LORD's house which

*was* toward the north; and, behold, there sat women weeping for ¹Tammuz.

15 Then said he unto me, Hast thou seen *this,* O son of man? turn thee yet again, *and* thou shalt see greater abominations than these.

16 And he brought me into the inner court of the LORD's house, and, behold, at the door of the temple of the LORD, ᵃbetween the porch and the altar, ᵇ*were* about five and twenty men, ᶜwith their backs toward the temple of the LORD, and their faces toward the east; and they worshipped ᵈthe sun toward the east.

17 Then he said unto me, Hast thou seen *this,* O son of man? Is it a ¹light thing to the house of Judah that they commit the abominations which they commit here? for they have ᵃfilled the land with violence, and have returned to provoke me to anger: and, lo, they put the branch to their nose.

18 ᵃTherefore will I also deal in fury: mine ᵇeye shall not spare, neither will I have pity: and though they ᶜcry in mine ears with a loud voice, *yet* will I not hear them.

## CHAPTER 9

H E cried also in mine ¹ears with a loud voice, saying, ²Cause them that have charge over the city to draw near, even every man *with* his ³destroying weapon in his hand.

2 And, behold, six men came from the way of the ¹higher gate, which ²lieth toward the north, and every man ³a slaughter weapon in his hand; ᵃand one man among them *was* clothed with linen, with a writer's inkhorn ⁴by his side: and they went in, and stood beside the brasen altar.

3 And ᵃthe glory of the God of Israel was gone up from the cherub, whereupon he was, to the threshold of ¹the house. And he called to the man clothed with linen, which *had* the writer's inkhorn by his side;

4 And the LORD said unto him, Go through the midst of the city, through the midst of Jerusalem, and ¹set ᵃa mark upon the foreheads of the men ᵇthat sigh and that cry ²for all the abominations that be done in the midst thereof.

5 And to the others he said in ¹mine hearing, Go ye after him through the city, and ᵃsmite:² ᵇlet not your eye spare, neither have ye pity:

6 ᵃSlay ¹utterly old *and* young, both maids, and little children, and women: but ᵇcome not near any man upon whom *is* the mark; and ᶜbegin at my ²sanctuary. ᵈThen they began at the ³ancient men which *were* before the ⁴house.

7 And he said unto them, Defile the ¹house, and fill the courts with the slain: go ye forth. And they went forth, and slew in the city.

8 And it came to pass, while they were slaying them, and I was ¹left, that I ᵃfell upon my face, and cried, and said, ᵇAh Lord GOD! wilt thou destroy all the ²residue of Israel in thy pouring out of thy fury upon Jerusalem?

9 Then said he unto me, The iniquity of the house of Israel and Judah *is* exceeding great, and ᵃthe land is full of ¹blood, and the city full of perverseness: for they say, ᵇThe LORD hath forsaken the ²earth, and ᶜthe LORD seeth not.

10 And as for me also, mine ᵃeye shall not spare, neither will I have pity, *but* ᵇI will ¹recompense their way upon their head.

11 And, behold, the man clothed with linen, which *had* the inkhorn by his side, reported the matter, saying, I have done as thou hast commanded me.

## CHAPTER 10

T HEN I looked, and, behold, in the ᵃfirmament¹ that was above the head of the cherubims there appeared over them ²as it were a sapphire stone, as the appearance of the likeness of a throne.

2 ᵃAnd he spake unto the man clothed with linen, and said, Go in between the wheels, *even* under the cherub, and fill thine hand with ᵇcoals of fire from between the cherubims, and ᶜscatter *them* over the city. And he went in in my sight.

3 Now the cherubims stood on the ¹right side of ²the house, when the man went in; and the ᵃcloud filled the inner court.

4 ᵃThen the glory of the LORD went up from the cherub, *and stood* over the threshold of ¹the house; and ᵇthe¹ house was filled with the cloud, and the court was full of the brightness of the LORD's ᶜglory.

5 And the ᵃsound of the cherubims' wings was heard *even* to the outer court, as ᵇthe voice of the Almighty God when he speaketh.

6 And it came to pass, *that* when he had commanded the man clothed with linen, saying, Take fire from between the wheels, from between the cherubims; then he went in, and stood beside the wheels.

7 And *one* cherub stretched forth his hand from between the cherubims unto the fire that *was* between the cherubims, and took *thereof,* and put *it* into the hands of *him that was* clothed with linen: who took *it,* and went out.

8:14 ¹ A Sumerian fertility god similar to the Greek god Adonis
8:16 ᵃ Joel 2:17
ᵇ Ezek. 11:1 ᶜ Jer. 2:27; 32:33
ᵈ Deut. 4:19
8:17 ᵃ Ezek. 9:9
¹ trivial
8:18 ᵃ Ezek. 5:13; 16:42; 24:13
ᵇ Ezek. 5:11; 7:4, 9; 9:5, 10 ᶜ Mic. 3:4
9:1 ¹ hearing ² Let
³ deadly
9:2 ᵃ Lev. 16:4
¹ upper ² faces
³ with his battle axe ⁴ Lit. upon his loins
9:3 ᵃ Ezek. 3:23; 8:4; 10:4, 18; 11:22, 23 ¹ The temple
9:4 ᵃ Rev. 7:2, 3; 9:4; 14:1 ᵇ Jer. 13:17 ¹ put ² over
9:5 ᵃ Ezek. 7:9
ᵇ Ezek. 5:11 ¹ Lit. my ears ² kill
9:6 ᵃ 2 Chr. 36:17
ᵇ Rev. 9:4 ᶜ Jer. 25:29 ᵈ Ezek. 8:11, 12, 16 ¹ Lit. to destruction ² The temple ³ elders ⁴ temple

9:7 ¹ temple
9:8 ᵃ Josh. 7:6
ᵇ Ezek. 11:13 ¹ left alone ² remnant
9:9 ᵃ 2 Kin. 21:16
ᵇ Ezek. 8:12 ᶜ Is. 29:15 ¹ bloodshed ² land
9:10 ᵃ Ezek. 5:11; 7:4; 8:18 ᵇ Ezek. 11:21 ¹ repay their deeds
10:1 ᵃ Ezek. 1:22, 26 ¹ expanse ² something like
10:2 ᵃ Dan. 10:5
ᵇ Ezek. 1:13 ᶜ Rev. 8:5
10:3 ¹ South ² The temple ᵃ 1 Kin. 8:10, 11
10:4 ᵃ Ezek. 1:28
ᵇ 1 Kin. 8:10; Ezek. 43:5 ᶜ Ezek. 11:22, 23 ¹ The temple
10:5 ᵃ [Job 40:9]; Ezek. 1:24; [Rev. 10:3] ᵇ [Ps. 29:3]

8 [a]And[1] there appeared in the cherubims the form of a man's hand under their wings.

9 [a]And when I looked, behold the four wheels by the cherubims, one wheel by one cherub, and another wheel by [1]another cherub: and the appearance of the wheels *was* as the colour of a [b]beryl stone.

10 And *as for* their appearances, they four [1]had one likeness, as if a wheel had been in the [2]midst of a wheel.

11 [a]When they went, they went [1]upon their four sides; they [2]turned not as they went, but to the place whither the head looked they followed it; they [2]turned not as they went.

12 And their whole body, and their backs, and their hands, and their wings, and the wheels, *were* [a]full of eyes round about, *even* the wheels that they four had.

13 As for the wheels, [1]it was cried unto them in my hearing, O wheel.

14 [a]And every one had four faces: the first face *was* the face of a cherub, and the second face *was* the face of a man, and the third the face of a lion, and the fourth the face of an eagle.

15 And the cherubims were lifted up. This *is* [a]the living creature that I saw by the river of Chebar.

16 [a]And when the cherubims went, the wheels went [1]by them: and when the cherubims lifted up their wings to mount up from the earth, the same wheels also turned not from beside them.

17 [a]When they stood, *these* stood; and when they were lifted up, *these* lifted up themselves *also:* for the spirit of the living creature *was* in them.

18 Then [a]the glory of the LORD [b]departed from off the threshold of the house, and stood over the cherubims.

19 And [a]the cherubims lifted up their wings, and mounted up from the earth in my sight: when they went out, the wheels also *were* beside them, and *every one* stood at the door of the [b]east gate of the LORD's house; and the glory of the God of Israel *was* over them above.

20 [a]This *is* the living creature that I saw under the God of Israel [b]by the river of Chebar; and I knew that they *were* the cherubims.

21 [a]Every one had four faces apiece, and every one four wings; and the likeness of the hands of a man *was* under their wings.

22 And [a]the likeness of their faces *was* the same faces which I saw by the river of Chebar, their appearances and [1]themselves: [b]they went every one straight forward.

10:8 [a] Ezek. 1:8;
10:21 [1] The cherubim appeared to have the form
10:9 [a] Ezek. 1:15
[b] Ezek. 1:16 [1] each other
10:10 [1] looked alike [2] middle
10:11 [a] Ezek. 1:17
[1] toward any of
[2] did not turn aside
10:12 [a] Rev. 4:6, 8
10:13 [1] they were called in my hearing, whirling wheels
10:14 [a] 1 Kin. 7:29, 36; Ezek. 1:6, 10, 11; Rev. 4:7
10:15 [a] Ezek. 1:3, 5
10:16 [a] Ezek. 1:19
[1] beside
10:17 [a] Ezek. 1:12, 20, 21
10:18 [a] Ezek. 10:4
[b] Hos. 9:12
10:19 [a] Ezek. 11:22
[b] Ezek. 11:1
10:20 [a] Ezek. 1:22
[b] Ezek. 1:1
10:21 [a] Ezek. 1:6, 8; 10:14; 41:18, 19
10:22 [a] Ezek. 1:10
[b] Ezek. 1:9, 12
[1] their persons

11:1 [a] Ezek. 3:12, 14 [b] Ezek. 10:19
[c] Ezek. 8:16
11:2 [1] iniquity
[2] Advice
11:3 [a] Ezek. 12:22, 27; 2 Pet. 3:4
[b] Jer. 1:13; Ezek. 11:7, 11; 24:3, 6
[1] The time is not near to build
[2] Pot [3] meat
11:5 [a] Ezek. 2:2; 3:24 [b] [Jer. 16:17; 17:10]
11:6 [a] Is. 1:15; Ezek. 7:23; 22:2–6, 9, 12, 27
11:7 [a] Ezek. 24:3, 6; Mic. 3:2, 3
[b] 2 Kin. 25:18–22; Jer. 52:24–27; Ezek. 11:9
11:8 [a] Jer. 42:16
11:9 [a] Ezek. 5:8
11:10 [a] Jer. 39:6; 52:10 [b] 2 Kin. 14:25 [c] Ps. 9:16
11:11 [a] Ezek. 11:3, 7
11:12 [a] Deut. 12:30, 31 [1] customs [2] Gentiles
11:13 [a] Acts 5:5
[b] Ezek. 9:8
11:15 [1] relatives

## CHAPTER 11

MOREOVER [a]the spirit lifted me up, and brought me unto [b]the east gate of the LORD's house, which looketh eastward: and behold [c]at the door of the gate five and twenty men; among whom I saw Jaazaniah the son of Azur, and Pelatiah the son of Benaiah, princes of the people.

2 Then said he unto me, Son of man, these *are* the men that devise [1]mischief, and give wicked [2]counsel in this city:

3 Which say, [1]*It is* not [a]near; let us build houses: [b]this *city is* the [2]caldron, and we *be* the [3]flesh.

4 Therefore prophesy against them, prophesy, O son of man.

5 And [a]the Spirit of the LORD fell upon me, and said unto me, Speak; Thus saith the LORD; Thus have ye said, O house of Israel: for [b]I know the things that come into your mind, *every one of* them.

6 [a]Ye have multiplied your slain in this city, and ye have filled the streets thereof with the slain.

7 Therefore thus saith the Lord GOD; [a]Your slain whom ye have laid in the midst of it, they *are* the flesh, and this *city is* the caldron: [b]but I will bring you forth out of the midst of it.

8 Ye have [a]feared the sword; and I will bring a sword upon you, saith the Lord GOD.

9 And I will bring you out of the midst thereof, and deliver you into the hands of strangers, and [a]will execute judgments among you.

10 [a]Ye shall fall by the sword; I will judge you in [b]the border of Israel; [c]and ye shall know that I *am* the LORD.

11 [a]This *city* shall not be your caldron, neither shall ye be the flesh in the midst thereof; *but* I will judge you in the border of Israel:

12 And ye shall know that I *am* the LORD: for ye have not walked in my statutes, neither executed my judgments, but [a]have done after the [1]manners of the [2]heathen that *are* round about you.

13 And it came to pass, when I prophesied, that [a]Pelatiah the son of Benaiah died. Then [b]fell I down upon my face, and cried with a loud voice, and said, Ah Lord GOD! wilt thou make a full end of the remnant of Israel?

14 Again the word of the LORD came unto me, saying,

15 Son of man, thy brethren, *even* thy [1]brethren, the men of thy kindred, and all the house of Israel wholly, *are* they unto whom the inhabitants of Jerusalem have said, Get you far from the LORD: unto us is this land given in possession.

16 Therefore say, Thus saith the Lord GOD; Although I have cast them far off among the [1]heathen, and although I have scattered them among the countries, [a]yet will I be to them as a little [2]sanctuary in the countries where they shall come.

17 Therefore say, Thus saith the Lord GOD; [a]I will even gather you from the people, and assemble you out of the countries where ye have been scattered, and I will give you the land of Israel.

18 And they shall come thither, and they shall take away all the [a]detestable things thereof and all the abominations thereof from thence.

19 And [a]I will give them one heart, and I will put [b]a new spirit within [1]you; and I will take [c]the stony heart out of their flesh, and will give them an heart of flesh:

20 [a]That they may walk in my statutes, and keep mine [1]ordinances, and do them: [b]and they shall be my people, and I will be their God.

21 But *as for them* whose heart walketh after the heart of their detestable things and their abominations, [a]I will [1]recompense their way upon their own heads, saith the Lord GOD.

22 Then did the cherubims [a]lift up their wings, and the wheels beside them; and the glory of the God of Israel *was* [1]over them above.

23 And [a]the glory of the LORD went up from the midst of the city, and stood [b]upon the mountain [c]which *is* on the east side of the city.

24 Afterwards [a]the spirit took me up, and brought me in a vision by the Spirit of God into [1]Chaldea, to them of the captivity. So the vision that I had seen went up from me.

25 Then I spake unto them of the captivity all the things that the LORD had shewed me.

## CHAPTER 12

THE word of the LORD also came unto me, saying,

2 Son of man, thou dwellest in the midst of [a]a rebellious house, which [b]have eyes to see, and see not; they have ears to hear, and hear not: [c]for they *are* a rebellious house.

3 Therefore, thou son of man, prepare [1]thee stuff for removing, and [2]remove by day in their sight; and thou shalt remove from thy place to another place in their sight: it may be they will consider, though they *be* a rebellious house.

4 Then shalt thou bring forth thy [1]stuff by day in their sight, as [1]stuff [2]for removing: and thou shalt go forth at [3]even in their sight, as they that go forth into captivity.

5 Dig thou through the wall in their sight, and carry out thereby.

6 In their sight shalt thou bear *it* upon *thy* shoulders, *and* carry *it* forth in the twilight: thou shalt cover thy face, that thou see not the ground: [a]for I have set thee *for* a sign unto the house of Israel.

7 And I did so as I was commanded: I brought forth my [1]stuff by day, as stuff for captivity, and [2]in the even I digged through the wall with mine hand; I brought *it* forth in the twilight, *and* I bare *it* upon *my* shoulder in their sight.

8 And in the morning came the word of the LORD unto me, saying,

9 Son of man, hath not the house of Israel, [a]the rebellious house, said unto thee, [b]What doest thou?

10 Say thou unto them, Thus saith the Lord GOD; This [a]burden[1] *concerneth* the prince in Jerusalem, and all the house of Israel that *are* among them.

11 Say, [a]I *am* your sign: like as I have done, so shall it be done unto them: [b]they shall [1]remove *and* go into captivity.

12 And [a]the prince that *is* among them shall [1]bear upon *his* shoulder in the twilight, and shall go forth: they shall dig through the wall to carry out thereby: he shall cover his face, that he see not the ground with *his* eyes.

13 My [a]net also will I spread [1]upon him, and he shall be [2]taken in my snare: and [b]I will bring him to Babylon *to* the land of the Chaldeans; yet shall he not see it, though he shall die there.

14 And [a]I will scatter toward every wind all that *are* about him to help him, and all his [1]bands; and [b]I will draw out the sword after them.

15 [a]And they shall know that I *am* the LORD, when I shall scatter them among the nations, and disperse them [1]in the countries.

16 [a]But I will leave a few men of them from the sword, from the famine, and from the pestilence; that they may declare all their abominations among the [1]heathen whither they come; and they shall know that I *am* the LORD.

17 Moreover the word of the LORD came to me, saying,

18 Son of man, [a]eat thy bread with [1]quaking, and drink thy water with trembling and with [2]carefulness;

19 And say unto the people of the land, Thus saith the Lord GOD [1]of the inhabitants of Jerusalem, *and* of the land of Israel; They shall eat their bread with [2]carefulness, and drink their water with [3]astonishment, that her land may [a]be [4]desolate from all that is therein, [b]because of the violence of all them that dwell therein.

### Center column references

11:16 [a] Is. 8:14
[1] *Gentiles* [2] *holy place*
11:17 [a] Jer. 3:12, 18; 24:5
11:18 [a] Ezek. 37:23
11:19 [a] Jer. 32:39
[b] Ezek. 18:31
[c] Zech. 7:12 [1] LXX, many Heb. mss. *them*
11:20 [a] Ps. 105:45
[b] Jer. 24:7 [1] *judgments*
11:21 [a] Ezek. 9:10
[1] *repay their deeds*
11:22 [a] Ezek. 1:19
[1] *high above them*
11:23 [a] Ezek. 8:4; 9:3 [b] Zech. 14:4
[c] Ezek. 43:2
11:24 [a] Ezek. 8:3
[1] *Or Babylon*
12:2 [a] Ezek. 2:3, 6–8 [b] Jer. 5:21
[c] Ezek. 2:5
12:3 [1] *thy belongings for captivity*
[2] *go into captivity*
12:4 [1] *belongings*
[2] *for captivity*
[3] *evening*

12:6 [a] Ezek. 4:3; 24:24
12:7 [1] *belongings*
[2] *at evening*
12:9 [a] Ezek. 2:5
[b] Ezek. 17:12; 24:19
12:10 [a] Mal. 1:1 [1] *oracle or prophecy*
12:11 [a] Ezek. 12:6
[b] 2 Kin. 25:4, 5, 7
[1] *be carried away*
12:12 [a] Jer. 39:4; 52:7 [1] *bear his belongings*
12:13 [a] Jer. 52:9
[b] Jer. 52:11 [1] *over*
[2] *caught*
12:14 [a] Ezek. 5:10
[b] Ezek. 5:2, 12
[1] *troops*
12:15 [a] Ezek. 6:7, 14; 12:16, 20
[1] *throughout*
12:16 [a] Ezek. 6:8–10 [1] *Gentiles*
12:18 [a] Ezek. 4:16 [1] *shaking*
[2] *anxiety*
12:19 [a] Zech. 7:14 [b] Ps. 107:34
[1] *concerning*
[2] *anxiety* [3] *dread*
[4] *emptied*

20 And the cities that are inhabited
shall be laid waste, and the land shall
be desolate; and ye shall know that I
*am* the LORD.
21 And the word of the LORD came
unto me, saying,
22 Son of man, what *is* that proverb *that* ye have in the land of Israel,
saying, [a]The days are prolonged, and
every vision faileth?
23 Tell them therefore, Thus saith
the Lord GOD; I will make this proverb to cease, and they shall no more
use it as a proverb in Israel; but say
unto them, [a]The days are at hand,
and the [1]effect of every vision.
24 For [a]there shall be no more any
[b]vain[1] vision nor flattering divination
within the house of Israel.
25 For I *am* the LORD: I will speak,
and [a]the word that I shall speak shall
come to pass; it shall be no more
[1]prolonged: for in your days, O rebellious house, will I say the word, and
will [b]perform it, saith the Lord GOD.
26 Again the word of the LORD
came to me, saying,
27 [a]Son of man, behold, *they of* the
house of Israel say, The vision that he
seeth *is* [b]for many days [1]*to come,* and
he prophesieth of the times *that are*
far off.
28 [a]Therefore say unto them, Thus
saith the Lord GOD; There shall none
of my words be [1]prolonged any more,
but the word which I have spoken
[b]shall be done, saith the Lord GOD.

## CHAPTER 13

AND the word of the LORD came
unto me, saying,
2 Son of man, prophesy [a]against
the prophets of Israel that prophesy,
and say thou unto [b]them that prophesy out of their own [c]hearts,[1] Hear ye
the word of the LORD;
3 Thus saith the Lord GOD; Woe
unto the foolish prophets, that follow
their own spirit, and have seen [1]noth-
ing!
4 O Israel, thy prophets are [a]like the
foxes in the deserts.
5 Ye [a]have not gone up into the
[1]gaps, neither [2]made up the hedge
for the house of Israel to stand in the
battle in the day of the LORD.
6 [a]They have seen [1]vanity and lying
divination, saying, The LORD saith:
and the LORD hath [b]not sent them:
[2]and they have made *others* to hope
that they would confirm the word.
7 Have ye not seen a [1]vain vision,
and have ye not spoken [2]a lying divination, whereas ye say, The LORD
saith *it;* albeit I have not spoken?
8 Therefore thus saith the Lord
GOD; Because ye have spoken vanity,
and [1]seen lies, therefore, behold, I *am*
against you, saith the Lord GOD.
9 And mine hand shall be [a]upon[1]
the prophets that see [2]vanity, and
that [b]divine lies: they shall not be in
the assembly of my people, [c]neither
shall they be written in the [3]writing of
the house of Israel, [d]neither shall they
enter into the land of Israel; [e]and ye
shall know that I *am* the Lord GOD.
10 Because, even because they have
seduced my people, saying, [a]Peace;
and *there was* no peace; and one built
up a wall, and, lo, others [b]daubed[1] it
with [2]untempered *morter:*
11 Say unto them which [1]daub *it*
with untempered *morter,* that it shall
fall: [a]there shall be [2]an overflowing
shower; and ye, O great hailstones,
shall fall; and a stormy wind shall
[3]rend *it.*
12 Lo, when the wall is fallen,
shall it not be said unto you, Where
*is* the [1]daubing wherewith ye have
[2]daubed *it?*
13 Therefore thus saith the Lord
GOD; I will [1]even rend *it* with a stormy
wind in my fury; and there shall be
[2]an overflowing shower in mine anger, and great hailstones in *my* fury
to consume *it.*
14 So will I break down the wall
that ye have [1]daubed with untempered *morter,* and bring it down to
the ground, so that the foundation
thereof shall be discovered, and it
shall fall, and ye shall be consumed in
the midst thereof: [a]and ye shall know
that I *am* the LORD.
15 Thus will I accomplish my wrath
upon the wall, and upon them that
have [1]daubed it with untempered
*morter,* and will say unto you, The
wall *is* no *more,* neither they that
[1]daubed it;
16 *To wit,* the prophets of Israel
which prophesy concerning Jerusalem, and which [a]see visions of peace
for her, and *there is* no peace, saith
the Lord GOD.
17 Likewise, thou son of man, [a]set
thy face against the daughters of
thy people, [b]which prophesy out of
their own [1]heart; and prophesy thou
against them,
18 And say, Thus saith the Lord
GOD; Woe to the *women* that sew [1]pil-
lows to all armholes, and make [2]ker-
chiefs upon the head of every stature
to hunt souls! Will ye [a]hunt the souls
of my people, and will ye [3]save the
souls alive *that come* unto you?
19 And will ye [1]pollute me among my
people [a]for handfuls of barley and for
pieces of bread, [2]to slay the souls that
should not die, and [3]to save the souls
alive that should not live, by your lying
to my people that hear *your* lies?
20 Wherefore thus saith the Lord
GOD; Behold, I *am* against your [1]pil-
lows, wherewith ye there hunt the

12:22 [a] Ezek. 11:3; 12:27
12:23 [a] Zeph. 1:14 [1] *fulfillment*
12:24 [a] Ezek. 13:6 [b] Lam. 2:14 [1] *false*
12:25 [a] [Luke 21:33] [b] [Is. 14:24] [1] *postponed*
12:27 [a] Ezek. 12:22 [b] Dan. 10:14 [1] From now
12:28 [a] Ezek. 12:23, 25 [b] Jer. 4:7 [1] *postponed*
13:2 [a] Ezek. 22:25–28 [b] Ezek. 13:17 [c] Jer. 14:14; 23:16, 26 [1] Inspiration
13:3 [1] No vision
13:4 [a] Song 2:15
13:5 [a] Ps. 106:23 [1] *breaches* [2] *built up a wall*
13:6 [a] Ezek. 22:28 [b] Jer. 27:8–15 [1] *futility and false* [2] *yet they hope that* their word *may come true*
13:7 [1] *futile* [2] *false*
13:8 [1] *envisioned*
13:9 [a] Jer. 23:30 [b] Jer. 20:3–6 [c] Ezra 2:59, 62 [d] Jer. 20:3–6 [e] Ezek. 11:10, 12 [1] *against* [2] *futility* [3] *record*
13:10 [a] Jer. 6:14; 8:11 [b] Ezek. 22:28 [1] *plastered* [2] *mud-plaster* or *whitewash*
13:11 [a] Ezek. 38:22 [1] *plaster* [2] *a flooding rain* [3] *tear* it *down*
13:12 [1] *mortar* or *plaster* [2] *plastered*
13:13 [1] *cause a stormy wind to break forth in* [2] *a flooding rain*
13:14 [1] *plastered* [a] Ezek. 13:9, 21, 23; 14:8
13:15 [1] *plastered*
13:16 [a] Jer. 6:14; 8:11; 28:9
13:17 [a] Ezek. 20:46; 21:2 [b] Ezek. 13:2 [1] Inspiration
13:18 [a] [2 Pet. 2:14] [1] magic *charms on their sleeves* [2] *veils* [3] *keep yourselves alive*
13:19 [a] Mic. 3:5 [1] *profane* [2] *killing people* [3] *keeping people alive*
13:20 [1] magic *charms*

souls [2]to make *them* fly, and I will
tear them from your arms, and will
let the souls go, *even* the souls that
ye hunt [2]to make *them* fly.
21 Your [1]kerchiefs also will I [2]tear,
and deliver my people out of your
hand, and they shall be no more in
your hand to be hunted; [a]and ye shall
know that I *am* the LORD.
22 Because with [a]lies ye have made
the heart of the righteous sad, whom
I have not made sad; and [b]strength-
ened the hands of the wicked, that
he should not return from his wicked
way, [1]by promising him life:
23 Therefore [a]ye shall [1]see no more
vanity, nor [2]divine divinations: for I
will deliver my people out of your
hand: and ye shall know that I *am* the
LORD.

## CHAPTER 14

THEN [a]came certain of the elders of
Israel unto me, and sat before me.
2 And the word of the LORD came
unto me, saying,
3 Son of man, these men have set
up their idols in their heart, and put
[a]the[1] stumblingblock of their iniquity
before their face: [b]should I be enquired of at all by them?
4 Therefore speak unto them, and
say unto them, Thus saith the Lord
GOD; Every man of the house of Israel
that setteth up his idols in his heart,
and putteth the stumblingblock of
his iniquity before his face, and cometh to the prophet; I the LORD will
answer him that cometh according
to the multitude of his idols;
5 That I may [1]take the house of Israel in their own heart, because they
are all estranged from me through
their idols.
6 Therefore say unto the house of
Israel, Thus saith the Lord GOD; Repent, and [1]turn *yourselves* from your
idols; and [a]turn away your faces from
all your abominations.
7 For every one of the house of
Israel, or of the stranger that sojourneth in Israel, which separateth
himself from me, and setteth up his
idols in his heart, and putteth the
stumblingblock of his iniquity before
his face, and cometh to a prophet to
enquire of him concerning me; I the
LORD will answer him by myself:
8 And [a]I will set my face against
that man, and will make him a [b]sign
and a proverb, and I will cut him off
from the midst of my people; [c]and ye
shall know that I *am* the LORD.
9 And if the prophet be [1]deceived
[2]when he hath spoken a thing, I the
LORD [a]have [1]deceived that prophet,
and I will stretch out my hand [3]upon
him, and will destroy him from the
midst of my people Israel.
10 And they shall bear the punishment of their iniquity: the punishment of the prophet shall be even as
the punishment of him that [1]seeketh
*unto him;*
11 That the house of Israel may
[a]go no more astray from me, neither
be [1]polluted any more with all their
transgressions; [b]but that they may
be my people, and I may be their God,
saith the Lord GOD.
12 The word of the LORD came
again to me, saying,
13 Son of man, when the land sinneth against me by [1]trespassing
grievously, then will I stretch out
mine hand upon it, and will break the
[a]staff[2] of the bread thereof, and will
send famine upon it, and will cut off
man and beast from it:
14 [a]Though these three men, Noah,
Daniel, and Job, were in it, they
[1]should deliver *but* their own souls
[b]by their righteousness, saith the
Lord GOD.
15 If I cause [a]noisome[1] beasts to
pass through the land, and they
[2]spoil it, [3]so that it be desolate, that
no man may pass through because of
the beasts:
16 [a]*Though* these three men *were*
[1]in it, *as* I live, saith the Lord GOD,
they [2]shall deliver neither sons nor
daughters; they only [2]shall be delivered, but the land shall be [b]desolate.
17 Or *if* [a]I bring a sword upon that
land, and say, Sword, go through the
land; so that I [b]cut off man and beast
from it:
18 [a]Though these three men *were* in
it, *as* I live, saith the Lord GOD, they
[1]shall deliver neither sons nor daughters, but they only [1]shall be delivered
themselves.
19 Or *if* I send [a]a pestilence into that
land, and [b]pour out my fury upon it
in blood, to cut off from it man and
beast:
20 [a]Though Noah, Daniel, and Job,
*were* in it, *as* I live, saith the Lord GOD,
they [1]shall deliver neither son nor
daughter; they [1]shall *but* deliver their
own souls by their righteousness.
21 For thus saith the Lord GOD; How
much more when [a]I send my four
[1]sore judgments upon Jerusalem, the
sword, and the famine, and the [2]noi-
some beast, and the pestilence, to cut
off from it man and beast?
22 [a]Yet, behold, therein shall be
left a remnant that shall be [b]brought
forth, *both* sons and daughters: behold, they shall come forth unto
you, and [c]ye shall see their way and
their doings: and ye shall be comforted concerning the [1]evil that I
have brought upon Jerusalem, *even*
concerning all that I have brought
upon it.

13:20 [2] *like birds*
13:21 [a] Ezek. 13:9 [1] *veils* [2] *tear off*
13:22 [a] Jer. 28:15 [b] Jer. 23:14 [1] *to save his life*
13:23 [a] Mic. 3:5, 6 [1] *no longer see futility* [2] *practise*
14:1 [a] Ezek. 8:1; 20:1; 33:31
14:3 [a] Ezek. 7:19 [b] Ezek. 20:3, 31 [1] *that which causes them to stumble into iniquity*
14:5 [1] *take hold of the heart of the house of Israel*
14:6 [a] Is. 2:20; 30:22; 55:6, 7 [1] *turn away from*
14:8 [a] Jer. 44:11 [b] Num. 26:10 [c] Ezek. 6:7; 13:14
14:9 [a] 2 Thess. 2:11 [1] *induced* [2] *to speak* [3] *against*
14:10 [1] *inquired of*
14:11 [a] 2 Pet. 2:15 [b] Ezek. 11:20; 37:27 [1] *profaned*
14:13 [a] Is. 3:1 [1] *persistent unfaithfulness* [2] *supply*
14:14 [a] Jer. 15:1 [b] [Prov. 11:4] [1] *would deliver* only
14:15 [a] Lev. 26:22 [1] *wild* [2] *empty,* lit. *bereave it* of children [3] *and make it so desolate*
14:16 [a] Ezek. 14:14, 18, 20 [b] Ezek. 15:8; 33:28, 29 [1] Lit. *in the midst of it* [2] *would*
14:17 [a] Lev. 26:25 [b] Zeph. 1:3
14:18 [a] Ezek. 14:14 [1] *would*
14:19 [a] 2 Sam. 24:15 [b] Ezek. 7:8
14:20 [a] Ezek. 14:14 [1] *would*
14:21 [a] Ezek. 5:17; 33:27 [1] *severe* [2] *wild*
14:22 [a] Ezek. 12:16; 36:20 [b] Ezek. 6:8 [c] Ezek. 20:43 [1] *disaster*

23 And they shall comfort you, when ye see their ways and their doings: and ye shall know that I have not done [a]without cause all that I have done in it, saith the Lord GOD.

## CHAPTER 15

AND the word of the LORD came unto me, saying,

2 Son of man, [1]What is the vine tree more than any tree, *or than* a branch which is among the trees of the forest?

3 Shall wood be taken thereof to [1]do any work? or [2]will *men* take a pin of it to hang any vessel thereon?

4 Behold, [a]it is cast into the fire for fuel; the fire devoureth both the ends of it, and the midst of it is burned. Is it [1]meet for *any* work?

5 Behold, when it was whole, [1]it was meet for no work: how much less shall it be [2]meet yet for *any* work, when the fire hath devoured it, and it is burned?

6 Therefore thus saith the Lord GOD; As the [1]vine tree among the trees of the forest, which I have given to the fire for fuel, so will I give the inhabitants of Jerusalem.

7 And [a]I will set my face against them; [b]they shall go out from *one* fire, and *another* fire shall devour them; [c]and ye shall know that I *am* the LORD, when I set my face against them.

8 And I will make the land desolate, because they have [1]committed a trespass, saith the Lord GOD.

## CHAPTER 16

AGAIN the word of the LORD came unto me, saying,

2 Son of man, [a]cause Jerusalem to know her abominations,

3 And say, Thus saith the Lord GOD unto Jerusalem; Thy [1]birth [a]and thy nativity *is* of the land of Canaan; [b]thy father *was* an Amorite, and thy mother an Hittite.

4 And *as for* thy [1]nativity, [a]in the day thou wast born thy [2]navel was not cut, neither wast thou washed in water to [3]supple *thee;* thou wast not [4]salted at all, nor [5]swaddled at all.

5 None eye pitied thee, to do any of these unto thee, to have compassion upon thee; but thou wast cast out in the open field, [1]to the lothing of thy person, in the day that thou wast born.

6 And when I passed by thee, and saw thee [1]polluted in thine own blood, I said unto thee *when thou wast* in thy blood, Live; yea, I said unto thee *when thou wast* in thy blood, Live.

7 [a]I have caused thee to [1]multiply as the [2]bud of the field, and thou

14:23 [a] Jer. 22:8, 9
15:2 [1] *How is the wood of the vine better than any other wood, the vine branch which*
15:3 [1] *make any object* [2] *can men make a peg*
15:4 [a] [John 15:6] [1] *useful*
15:5 [1] *no object could be made from it* [2] *useful*
15:6 [1] *wood of the vine*
15:7 [a] Ezek. 14:8 [b] Is. 24:18 [c] Ezek. 7:4
15:8 [1] *persisted in unfaithfulness*
16:2 [a] Ezek. 20:4; 22:2
16:3 [a] Ezek. 21:30 [b] Ezek. 16:45 [1] *origin and your birth are from*
16:4 [a] Hos. 2:3 [1] *birth* [2] *navel cord* [3] *cleanse* [4] *rubbed with salt* [5] *swathed in swaddling clothes*
16:5 [1] *when thou thyself wast loathed*
16:6 [1] *struggling*
16:7 [a] Ex. 1:7 [1] *thrive* [2] *plant* [3] *hast grown* [4] *are mature* [5] *Became very beautiful*
16:8 [a] Ruth 3:9 [b] Gen. 22:16–18 [c] Ex. 24:6–8 [d] [Ex. 19:5] [1] *wing* [2] *swore an oath*
16:10 [1] *cloth* [2] *dolphin or dugong*
16:11 [a] Gen. 24:22, 47 [b] Prov. 1:9
16:12 [1] *ring in thy nose*
16:13 [a] Deut. 32:13, 14 [b] Ps. 48:2 [1] *cloth* [2] *succeed to royalty*
16:14 [a] Lam. 2:15 [1] *nations or Gentiles* [2] *splendour*
16:15 [a] Mic. 3:11 [b] Is. 1:21; 57:8 [1] *fame* [2] *harlotry*
16:16 [a] Ezek. 7:20 [1] *some of* [2] *adorned* [3] *sacred places for pagan worship*
16:17 [1] *beautiful jewelry* [2] *male images* [3] *play the harlot*
16:19 [a] Hos. 2:8 [1] *food* [2] *as sweet incense*
16:20 [a] Jer. 7:31 [1] *harlotry*

3hast increased and [4]waxen great, and thou [5]art come to excellent ornaments: *thy* breasts are fashioned, and thine hair is grown, whereas thou *wast* naked and bare.

8 Now when I passed by thee, and looked upon thee, behold, thy time *was* the time of love; [a]and I spread my [1]skirt over thee, and covered thy nakedness: yea, I [b]sware[2] unto thee, and entered into a [c]covenant with thee, saith the Lord GOD, and [d]thou becamest mine.

9 Then washed I thee with water; yea, I throughly washed away thy blood from thee, and I anointed thee with oil.

10 I clothed thee also with broidered [1]work, and shod thee with [2]badgers' skin, and I girded thee about with fine linen, and I covered thee with silk.

11 I decked thee also with ornaments, and I [a]put bracelets upon thy hands, [b]and a chain on thy neck.

12 And I put a [1]jewel on thy forehead, and earrings in thine ears, and a beautiful crown upon thine head.

13 Thus wast thou decked with gold and silver; and thy raiment *was* of fine linen, and silk, and broidered [1]work; [a]thou didst eat fine flour, and honey, and oil: and thou wast exceeding [b]beautiful, and thou didst [2]prosper into a kingdom.

14 And [a]thy renown went forth among the [1]heathen for thy beauty: for it *was* perfect through my [2]comeliness, which I had put upon thee, saith the Lord GOD.

15 [a]But thou didst trust in thine own beauty, [b]and playedst the harlot because of thy [1]renown, and pouredst out thy [2]fornications on every one that passed by; his it was.

16 [a]And [1]of thy garments thou didst take, and [2]deckedst thy [3]high places with divers colours, and playedst the harlot thereupon: *the like things* shall not come, neither shall it be so.

17 Thou hast also taken thy [1]fair jewels of my gold and of my silver, which I had given thee, and madest to thyself [2]images of men, and didst [3]commit whoredom with them,

18 And tookest thy broidered garments, and coveredst them: and thou hast set mine oil and mine incense before them.

19 [a]My [1]meat also which I gave thee, fine flour, and oil, and honey, *wherewith* I fed thee, thou hast even set it before them [2]for a sweet savour: and *thus* it was, saith the Lord GOD.

20 [a]Moreover thou hast taken thy sons and thy daughters, whom thou hast borne unto me, and these hast thou sacrificed unto them to be devoured. *Is this* of thy [1]whoredoms a small matter,

21 That thou hast slain my children, and ¹delivered them to cause them to pass through *the* ᵃ*fire* for them?

22 And in all thine abominations and thy ¹whoredoms thou hast not remembered the days of thy ᵃyouth, ᵇwhen thou wast naked and bare, *and* wast ²polluted in thy blood.

23 And it came to pass after all thy wickedness, (woe, woe unto thee! saith the Lord GOD;)

24 *That* ᵃthou hast also built unto thee ¹an eminent place, and ᵇhast made thee an ²high place in every street.

25 Thou hast built thy high place ᵃat every head of the ¹way, and hast made thy beauty to be abhorred, and hast ²opened thy feet to every one that passed by, and multiplied thy ³whoredoms.

26 Thou hast also committed ¹fornication with ᵃthe Egyptians thy ²neighbours, great of flesh; and hast increased thy ³whoredoms, to ᵇprovoke me to anger.

27 Behold, therefore I have stretched out my hand ¹over thee, and have diminished thine ²ordinary *food,* and delivered thee unto the will of them that hate thee, ᵃthe daughters of the Philistines, which are ashamed of thy lewd ³way.

28 Thou hast played the ¹whore also with the ᵃAssyrians, because thou wast unsatiable; yea, thou hast played the harlot with them, and yet couldest not be satisfied.

29 Thou hast moreover multiplied thy ¹fornication ²in the land of Canaan ᵃunto Chaldea; and yet thou wast not satisfied herewith.

30 How ¹weak is thine heart, saith the Lord GOD, seeing thou doest all these *things,* the work of ²an imperious whorish woman;

31 In that ᵃthou buildest thine ¹eminent place in the head of every ²way, and makest thine high place in every street; and hast not been as an harlot, in that thou scornest ᵇhire;

32 *But as* a wife that committeth adultery, *which* taketh strangers instead of her husband!

33 They ¹give gifts to all ²whores: but ᵃthou givest thy gifts to all thy lovers, and ³hirest them, that they may come unto thee on every side for thy ⁴whoredom.

34 And the ¹contrary is in thee from *other* women in thy ²whoredoms, whereas none ³followeth thee to ⁴commit whoredoms: and in that thou givest ⁵a reward, and no reward is given unto thee, therefore thou art ¹contrary.

35 Wherefore, O harlot, hear the word of the LORD:

36 Thus saith the Lord GOD; Because thy filthiness was poured out, and thy nakedness ¹discovered through thy ²whoredoms with thy lovers, and with all ³the idols of thy abominations, and by ᵃthe blood of thy children, which thou didst give unto them;

37 Behold, therefore ᵃI will gather all thy lovers, with whom thou hast taken pleasure, and all *them* that thou hast loved, with all *them* that thou hast hated; I will even gather them round about against thee, and will ¹discover thy nakedness unto them, that they may see all thy nakedness.

38 And I will judge thee, as ᵃwomen that ¹break wedlock and ᵇshed blood are judged; and I will ²give thee blood in fury and jealousy.

39 And I will also give thee into their hand, and they shall throw down ᵃthine ¹eminent place, and shall break down thy ²high places: ᵇthey shall strip thee also of thy clothes, and shall take thy ³fair jewels, and leave thee naked and bare.

40 ᵃThey shall also bring up ¹a company against thee, ᵇand they shall stone thee with stones, and thrust thee through with their swords.

41 And they shall ᵃburn thine houses with fire, and ᵇexecute judgments upon thee in the sight of many women: and I will cause thee to ᶜcease from playing the harlot, and thou also shalt ¹give no hire any more.

42 So ᵃwill I make my fury toward thee to rest, and my jealousy shall depart from thee, and I will be quiet, and will be no more angry.

43 Because ᵃthou hast not remembered the days of thy youth, but hast ¹fretted me in all these *things;* behold, therefore ᵇI also will recompense thy ²way upon *thine* head, saith the Lord GOD: and thou shalt not commit this lewdness ³above all thine abominations.

44 Behold, every one that useth proverbs shall use *this* proverb against thee, saying, As *is* the mother, *so is* her daughter.

45 Thou *art* thy mother's daughter, that ¹lotheth her husband and her children; and thou *art* the ᵃsister of thy sisters, which lothed their husbands and their children: ᵇyour mother *was* an Hittite, and your father an Amorite.

46 And thine elder sister is Samaria, she and her daughters that dwell ¹at thy left hand: and ᵃthy younger sister, that dwelleth ²at thy right hand, *is* Sodom and her daughters.

---

16:21 ᵃ Jer. 19:5
¹ offered

16:22 ᵃ Jer. 2:2
ᵇ Ezek. 16:4–6
¹ acts of harlotry
² struggling

16:24 ᵃ Jer. 11:13
ᵇ Jer. 2:20; 3:2 ¹ a
shrine ² sacred
place for pagan
worship

16:25 ᵃ Prov. 9:14
¹ road ² offered
yourself ³ acts of
harlotry

16:26 ᵃ Ezek.
16:26; 20:7, 8
ᵇ Deut. 31:20
¹ harlotry ² very
fleshly neighbours
³ acts of harlotry

16:27 ᵃ Ezek. 16:57
¹ against ² Allowance of food
³ behaviour

16:28 ᵃ Jer. 2:18,
36 ¹ harlot

16:29 ᵃ Ezek.
23:14–17 ¹ acts of
harlotry ² as far
as the land of the
trader

16:30 ¹ degenerate ² a brazen
harlot

16:31 ᵃ Ezek.
16:24, 39 ᵇ Is.
52:3 ¹ shrine
² street

16:33 ᵃ Hos.
8:9, 10 ¹ make
payments ² harlots ³ Or bribe
⁴ harlotry

16:34 ¹ opposite
² harlotry ³ solicited ⁴ be a harlot
⁵ payment

16:36 ᵃ Jer. 2:34
¹ uncovered
² harlotry ³ thy
abominable idols

16:37 ᵃ Lam. 1:8
¹ uncover

16:38 ᵃ Lev.
20:10 ᵇ Gen. 9:6
¹ commit adultery
or ² bring blood
upon you

16:39 ᵃ Ezek.
16:24, 31 ᵇ Hos.
2:3 ¹ shrines ² sacred places for
pagan worship
³ beautiful

16:40 ᵃ Ezek.
23:45–47 ᵇ John
8:5, 7 ¹ an
assembly

16:41 ᵃ Deut. 13:16
ᵇ Ezek. 5:8; 23:10,
48 ᶜ Ezek. 23:27
¹ no longer hire
lovers

16:42 ᵃ Ezek. 5:13;
21:17

16:43 ᵃ Ps. 78:42
ᵇ Ezek. 9:10; 11:21;
22:31 ¹ agitated
me with ² deeds

³ in addition to   16:45 ᵃ Ezek. 23:2–4 ᵇ Ezek. 16:3
¹ Or despised   16:46 ᵃ Is. 1:10 ¹ to the north of you
² to the south of you

47 Yet hast thou not walked after their ways, nor done after their abominations: but, as *if that were* [1]a very little *thing,* [a]thou wast corrupted more than they in all thy ways.

48 *As* I live, saith the Lord GOD, [a]Sodom thy sister hath not done, she nor her daughters, as thou hast done, thou and thy daughters.

49 Behold, this was the iniquity of thy sister Sodom, pride, [a]fulness of [1]bread, and abundance of idleness was in her and in her daughters, neither did she strengthen the hand of the poor and needy.

50 And they were haughty, and [a]committed abomination before me: therefore [b]I took them away as I saw good.

51 Neither hath Samaria committed [a]half of thy sins; but thou hast multiplied thine abominations more than they, and [b]hast justified thy sisters in all thine abominations which thou hast done.

52 Thou also, which hast judged thy sisters, bear thine own shame for thy sins that thou hast committed more abominable than [1]they: they are more righteous than thou: yea, be thou [2]confounded also, and bear thy shame, in that thou hast justified thy sisters.

53 [a]When I shall bring again their [1]captivity, the captivity of Sodom and her daughters, and the captivity of Samaria and her daughters, then *will I bring again* [b]the [2]captivity of thy captives in the midst of them:

54 That thou mayest bear thine own shame, and mayest be [1]confounded in all that thou hast done, in that thou art [a]a comfort unto them.

55 When thy sisters, Sodom and her daughters, shall return to their former [1]estate, and Samaria and her daughters shall return to their former estate, then thou and thy daughters shall return to your former estate.

56 For thy sister Sodom was not mentioned by thy mouth in the day of thy pride,

57 Before thy wickedness was [1]discovered, as at the time of *thy* [a]reproach of the daughters of [2]Syria, and all *that are* round about her, [b]the daughters of the Philistines, which despise thee round about.

58 [a]Thou hast [1]borne thy lewdness and thine abominations, saith the LORD.

59 For thus saith the Lord GOD; I will even deal with thee as thou hast done, which hast [a]despised [b]the oath in breaking the covenant.

60 Nevertheless I will [a]remember my covenant with thee in the days of thy youth, and I will establish unto thee [b]an everlasting covenant.

61 Then [a]thou shalt remember thy ways, and be ashamed, when thou shalt receive thy sisters, thine elder and thy younger: and I will give them unto thee for [b]daughters, [c]but not [1]by thy covenant.

62 [a]And I will establish my covenant with thee; and thou shalt know that I *am* the LORD:

63 That thou mayest [a]remember, and be [1]confounded, [b]and never open thy mouth any more because of thy shame, when I [2]am pacified toward thee for all that thou hast done, saith the Lord GOD.

## CHAPTER 17

AND the word of the LORD came unto me, saying,

2 Son of man, put forth a riddle, and speak a [a]parable unto the house of Israel;

3 And say, Thus saith the Lord GOD; [a]A great eagle with great wings, [1]longwinged, full of feathers, which had [2]divers colours, came unto Lebanon, and [b]took the highest branch of the cedar:

4 He cropped off [1]the top of his young twigs, and carried it into a land of [2]traffick; he set it in a city of merchants.

5 He took also [1]of the seed of the land, and planted it in [a]a [2]fruitful field; he placed *it* by [3]great waters, *and* set it [b]*as* a willow tree.

6 And it grew, and became a spreading vine [a]of low stature, whose branches turned toward him, and the roots thereof were under him: so it became a vine, and brought forth branches, and shot forth sprigs.

7 There was also another great eagle with great wings and many feathers: and, behold, [a]this vine did bend her roots toward him, and shot forth her branches toward him, that he might water it by the furrows [1]of her plantation.

8 It was planted in a good [1]soil by [2]great waters, that it might bring forth branches, and that it might bear fruit, that it might be a [3]goodly vine.

9 Say thou, Thus saith the Lord GOD; Shall it [1]prosper? [a]shall he not pull up the roots thereof, and cut off the fruit thereof, that it wither? [2]it shall wither in all the leaves of her spring, even without great power or many people to pluck it up by the roots thereof.

10 Yea, behold, *being* planted, shall it [1]prosper? [a]shall it not utterly wither, when the east wind toucheth it? it shall wither in the furrows where it grew.

11 Moreover the word of the LORD came unto me, saying,

12 Say now to [a]the rebellious house, Know ye not what these *things mean?*

### Center column references

16:47 [a] Ezek. 5:6, 7
[1] too little
16:48 [a] Matt. 10:15; 11:24
16:49 [a] Gen. 13:10
[1] food
16:50 [a] Gen. 13:13; 18:20; 19:5 [b] Gen. 19:24
16:51 [a] Ezek. 23:11 [b] Jer. 3:8–11
16:52 [1] theirs [2] disgraced
16:53 [a] Is. 1:9 [b] Jer. 20:16 [1] captives [2] captives of thy captivity among
16:54 [a] Ezek. 14:22 [1] disgraced
16:55 [1] state
16:57 [a] 2 Kin. 16:5 [b] Ezek. 16:27 [1] uncovered [2] Heb. Aram
16:58 [a] Ezek. 23:49 [1] borne the penalty of
16:59 [a] Ezek. 17:13 [b] Deut. 29:12
16:60 [a] Ps. 106:45 [b] Is. 55:3

16:61 [a] Ezek. 20:43; 36:31 [b] [Gal. 4:26] [c] Jer. 31:31 [1] because of
16:62 [a] Hos. 2:19, 20
16:63 [a] Ezek. 36:31, 32 [b] [Rom. 3:19] [1] ashamed [2] provide thee an atonement
17:2 [a] Ezek. 20:49; 24:3
17:3 [a] Ezek. 17:12 [b] 2 Kin. 24:12 [1] long pinions [2] various
17:4 [1] its topmost young twig [2] trade
17:5 [a] Deut. 8:7–9 [b] Is. 44:4 [1] some of [2] fertile [3] abundant
17:6 [a] Ezek. 17:14
17:7 [a] Ezek. 17:15 [1] where it had been planted
17:8 [1] Lit. field [2] many [3] majestic
17:9 [a] 2 Kin. 25:7 [1] thrive [2] all of its spring leaves will wither
17:10 [a] Hos. 13:15 [1] thrive
17:12 [a] Ezek. 2:3–5; 12:9

tell *them*, Behold, [b]the king of Babylon is come to Jerusalem, and hath taken the king thereof, and the princes thereof, and led them with him to Babylon:

13 [a]And hath taken of the king's [1]seed, and made a [2]covenant with him, [b]and hath [3]taken an oath of him: he hath also taken the mighty of the land:

14 That the kingdom might be [a]base,[1] that it might not lift itself up, *but* that by keeping of his [2]covenant it might stand.

15 But [a]he rebelled against him in sending his ambassadors into Egypt, [b]that they might give him horses and much people. [c]Shall he prosper? shall he escape that doeth such *things*? or shall he break the [1]covenant, and be delivered?

16 *As* I live, saith the Lord GOD, surely [a]in the place *where* the king *dwelleth* that made him king, whose oath he despised, and whose covenant he brake, *even* with him in the midst of Babylon he shall die.

17 [a]Neither shall Pharaoh with *his* mighty army and great company [1]make for him in the war, [b]by casting up [2]mounts, and building [3]forts, to cut off many persons:

18 Seeing he despised the oath by breaking the [1]covenant, when, lo, he [2]had [a]given his hand, and [3]hath done all these *things,* he shall not escape.

19 Therefore thus saith the Lord GOD; *As* I live, surely mine oath that he hath despised, and my covenant that he hath broken, even it will I recompense upon his own head.

20 And I will [a]spread my net upon him, and he shall be taken in my snare, and I will bring him to Babylon, and [b]will plead with him there for his [1]trespass that he hath trespassed against me.

21 And [a]all his fugitives with all his [1]bands shall fall by the sword, and they that remain shall be [b]scattered toward all winds: and ye shall know that I the LORD have spoken *it*.

22 Thus saith the Lord GOD; I will also take of the highest [a]branch of the high cedar, and will set *it;* I will crop off from the top of his young twigs [b]a tender one, and will [c]plant *it* upon an high mountain and [1]eminent:

23 [a]In[1] the mountain of the height of Israel will I plant it: and it shall bring forth boughs, and bear fruit, and be a [2]goodly cedar: and [b]under it shall dwell all fowl of every wing; in the shadow of the branches thereof shall they dwell.

24 And all the trees of the field shall know that I the LORD [a]have brought down the high tree, have exalted the low tree, have dried up the green

tree, and have made the dry tree to flourish: [b]I the LORD have spoken and have done *it*.

## CHAPTER 18

THE word of the LORD came unto me again, saying,

2 What mean ye, that ye use this proverb concerning the land of Israel, saying, The [a]fathers have eaten sour grapes, and the children's teeth are set on edge?

3 *As* I live, saith the Lord GOD, ye shall not have *occasion* any more to use this proverb in Israel.

4 Behold, all souls are [a]mine; as the soul of the father, so also the soul of the son is mine: [b]the soul that sinneth, it shall die.

5 But if a man be just, and do that which is lawful and right,

6 [a]*And* hath not eaten [1]upon the mountains, neither hath lifted up his eyes to the idols of the house of Israel, neither hath [b]defiled his neighbour's wife, [c]neither hath come near to a menstruous woman,

7 And hath not [a]oppressed any, *but* hath restored to the debtor his [b]pledge, hath [1]spoiled none by violence, hath [c]given his bread to the hungry, and hath covered the naked with a [d]garment;

8 He *that* hath not [1]given forth upon [a]usury,[2] neither hath taken any increase, *that* hath withdrawn his hand from iniquity, [b]hath executed true [3]judgment between man and man,

9 Hath walked in my statutes, and hath kept my judgments, to deal [1]truly; he *is* just, he shall surely [a]live, saith the Lord GOD.

10 If he beget a son *that is* a robber, [a]a shedder of blood, and *that* doeth the like to *any* one of these *things,*

11 And that doeth not any of those *duties,* but even hath eaten [1]upon the mountains, and defiled his neighbour's wife,

12 Hath oppressed the poor and needy, hath [1]spoiled by violence, hath not restored the pledge, and hath lifted up his eyes to the idols, hath [a]committed abomination,

13 Hath [1]given forth upon [2]usury, and hath taken increase: shall he then live? he shall not live: he hath done [3]all these abominations; he shall surely die; [a]his blood shall be upon him.

14 Now, lo, *if* he beget a son, that seeth all his father's sins which he hath done, and considereth, and doeth not such like,

15 [a]*That* hath not eaten [1]upon the mountains, neither hath lifted up his eyes to the idols of the house of Israel, hath not defiled his neighbour's wife,

### Center column references

17:12 [b] 2 Kin. 24:11–16

17:13 [a] 2 Kin. 24:17  [b] 2 Chr. 36:13  [1] *offspring*  [2] *treaty*  [3] *put him under oath*

17:14 [a] Ezek. 29:14  [1] *abased*  [2] *treaty*

17:15 [a] 2 Kin. 24:20  [b] Deut.
17:16 [c] Ezek. 17:9  [1] *treaty*

17:16 [a] Ezek. 12:13

17:17 [a] Jer. 37:7  [b] Jer. 52:4  [1] *do anything*  [2] *siege mounds*  [3] Or *siege walls*

17:18 [a] 1 Chr. 29:24  [1] *treaty*  [2] Had promised  [3] *still did*

17:20 [a] Ezek. 12:13  [b] Ezek. 20:36  [1] *treason*

17:21 [a] Ezek. 12:14  [b] Ezek. 12:15; 22:15  [1] *troops*

17:22 [a] [Zech. 3:8]  [b] Is. 53:2  [c] [Ps. 2:6]  [1] *prominent*

17:23 [a] [Is. 2:2, 3]  [b] Dan. 4:12  [1] *On the high mountain*  [2] *majestic*

17:24 [a] Amos 9:11

[b] Ezek. 22:14
18:2 [a] Lam. 5:7
18:4 [a] Num. 16:22; 27:16  [b] [Rom. 6:23]

18:6 [a] Ezek. 22:9  [b] Lev. 18:20; 20:10  [c] Lev. 18:19; 20:18  [1] *At the mountain shrines*

18:7 [a] Ex. 22:21  [b] Deut. 24:12  [1] *robbed*  [c] Deut. 15:7, 11  [d] Is. 58:7

18:8 [a] Ex. 22:25  [b] Zech. 8:16  [1] *loaned money on*  [2] *interest*  [3] *justice*

18:9 [a] Amos 5:4  [1] *faithfully*

18:10 [a] Num. 35:31
18:11 [1] At the mountain shrines
18:12 [a] Ezek. 8:6, 17  [1] *robbed*

18:13 [a] Lev. 20:9, 11–13, 16, 27  [1] *loaned* money on  [2] *interest*  [3] *any of*

18:15 [a] Ezek. 18:6  [1] At the mountain shrines

16 Neither hath oppressed any, hath not withholden the pledge, neither hath ¹spoiled by violence, *but* hath given his bread to the hungry, and hath covered the naked with a garment,

17 *That* hath ¹taken off his hand from the poor, *that* hath not received usury nor increase, hath executed my judgments, hath walked in my statutes; he shall not die for the iniquity of his father, he shall surely live.

18 *As for* his father, because he cruelly oppressed, ¹spoiled his brother by violence, and did *that* which *is* not good among his people, lo, even ªhe shall die ²in his iniquity.

19 Yet say ye, Why? ªdoth not the son bear the ¹iniquity of the father? When the son hath done that which is lawful and right, *and* hath kept all my statutes, and hath done them, he shall surely live.

20 ªThe soul that sinneth, it shall die. ᵇThe son shall not bear the ¹iniquity of the father, neither shall the father bear the ¹iniquity of the son: ᶜthe righteousness of the righteous shall be upon him, ᵈand the wickedness of the wicked shall be upon him.

21 But ªif the wicked will turn from all his sins that he hath committed, and keep all my statutes, and do that which is lawful and right, he shall surely live, he shall not die.

22 ªAll his transgressions that he hath committed, they shall not be ¹mentioned unto him: in his righteousness that he hath done he shall ᵇlive.

23 ªHave I any pleasure at all that the wicked should die? saith the Lord GOD: *and* not that he should return from his ways, and live?

24 But ªwhen the righteous turneth away from his righteousness, and committeth iniquity, *and* doeth according to all the abominations that the wicked *man* doeth, shall he live? ᵇAll his righteousness that he hath done shall not be mentioned: ¹in his trespass that he ²hath trespassed, and in his sin that he hath sinned, in them shall he die.

25 Yet ye say, ²The way of the Lord is not ¹equal. Hear now, O house of Israel; Is not my way ¹equal? are not your ways ²unequal?

26 ªWhen a righteous *man* turneth away from his righteousness, and committeth iniquity, and dieth in them; for his iniquity that he hath done shall he die.

27 Again, ªwhen the wicked *man* turneth away from his wickedness that he hath committed, and doeth that which is lawful and right, he shall ¹save his soul alive.

28 Because he ªconsidereth, and turneth away from all his transgressions that he hath committed, he shall surely live, he shall not die.

29 ªYet saith the house of Israel, The way of the Lord is not ¹equal. O house of Israel, are not my ways ¹equal? are not your ways ²unequal?

30 ªTherefore I will judge you, O house of Israel, every one according to his ways, saith the Lord GOD. ᵇRepent, and turn *yourselves* from all your transgressions; so iniquity shall not be your ruin.

31 ªCast away from you all your transgressions, whereby ye have transgressed; and make you a ᵇnew heart and a new spirit: for why will ye die, O house of Israel?

32 For ªI have no pleasure in the death of him that dieth, saith the Lord GOD: wherefore turn *yourselves*, and ᵇlive ye.

## CHAPTER 19

MOREOVER ªtake thou up a lamentation for the princes of Israel,

2 And say, What *is* thy mother? A lioness: she lay down among lions, she nourished her ¹whelps among young lions.

3 And she brought up one of her ¹whelps: ªit became a young lion, and it learned to catch the prey; it devoured men.

4 The nations also heard of him; he was ¹taken in their pit, and they brought him with chains unto the land of ªEgypt.

5 Now when she saw that she had waited, *and* her hope was lost, then she took ªanother of her ¹whelps, *and* made him a young lion.

6 ªAnd he went up and down among the lions, ᵇhe became a young lion, and learned to catch the prey, *and* devoured men.

7 And he knew ¹their desolate palaces, and he laid waste their cities; and the land was desolate, and the fulness thereof, by the noise of his roaring.

8 ªThen the nations set against him on every side from the provinces, and spread their net over him: ᵇhe was ¹taken in their pit.

9 ªAnd they put him in ¹ward in chains, and brought him to the king of Babylon: they brought him ²into holds, that his voice should no more be heard upon ᵇthe mountains of Israel.

10 Thy mother *is* ªlike a vine in thy ¹blood, planted by the waters: she was ᵇfruitful and full of branches by reason of many waters.

11 And she had strong ¹rods for the sceptres of them that bare rule, and her ªstature ²was exalted among the

thick branches, and she [3]appeared in her height [4]with the multitude of her branches.

12 But she was [a]plucked up in fury, she was cast down to the ground, and the [b]east wind dried up her fruit: her strong [1]rods were broken and withered; the fire consumed them.

13 And now she *is* planted in the wilderness, in a dry and thirsty ground.

14 [a]And fire is gone out of a rod of her branches, *which* hath devoured her fruit, so that she hath no strong [1]rod *to be* a sceptre to rule. [b]This *is* a lamentation, and [2]shall be for a lamentation.

## CHAPTER 20

AND it came to pass in the seventh year, in the fifth *month,* the tenth *day* of the month, *that* [a]certain of the elders of Israel came to enquire of the LORD, and sat before me.

2 Then came the word of the LORD unto me, saying,

3 Son of man, speak unto the elders of Israel, and say unto them, Thus saith the Lord GOD; Are ye come to enquire of me? *As* I live, saith the Lord GOD, [a]I will not be enquired of by you.

4 Wilt thou judge them, son of man, wilt thou judge *them?* [a]cause them to know the abominations of their fathers.

5 And say unto them, Thus saith the Lord GOD; In the day when [a]I chose Israel, and [1]lifted up mine hand unto the seed of the house of Jacob, and made myself [b]known unto them in the land of Egypt, when I lifted up mine hand unto them, saying, [c]I *am* the LORD your God;

6 In the day *that* I [1]lifted up mine hand unto them, [a]to bring them forth of the land of Egypt into a land that I had [2]espied for them, [b]flowing with milk and honey, which *is* [c]the glory of all lands:

7 Then said I unto them, [a]Cast ye away every man [b]the abominations [1]of his eyes, and defile not yourselves with [c]the idols of Egypt: I *am* the LORD your God.

8 But they rebelled against me, and would not [1]hearken unto me: they did not every man cast away the abominations [2]of their eyes, neither did they forsake the idols of Egypt: then I said, I will [a]pour out my fury upon them, to accomplish my anger against them in the midst of the land of Egypt.

9 [a]But I [1]wrought for my name's sake, that it should not be [2]polluted before the [3]heathen, among whom they *were,* in whose sight I made myself [b]known unto them, in bringing them forth out of the land of Egypt.

10 Wherefore I [a]caused them to go forth out of the land of Egypt, and brought them into the wilderness.

11 [a]And I gave them my statutes, and [1]shewed them my judgments, [b]which *if* a man do, he shall even live in them.

12 Moreover also I gave them my [a]sabbaths, to be a sign between me and them, that they might know that I *am* the LORD that sanctify them.

13 But the house of Israel [a]rebelled against me in the wilderness: they walked not in my statutes, and they [b]despised my judgments, [c]which *if* a man do, he shall even live in them; and my sabbaths they greatly [d]polluted:[1] then I said, I would pour out my fury upon them in the [e]wilderness, to consume them.

14 [a]But I [1]wrought for my name's sake, that it should not be [2]polluted before the [3]heathen, in whose sight I brought them out.

15 Yet also [a]I [1]lifted up my hand unto them in the wilderness, that I would not bring them into the land which I had given *them,* [b]flowing with milk and honey, which *is* [c]the glory of all lands;

16 [a]Because they despised my judgments, and walked not in my statutes, but [1]polluted my sabbaths: for [b]their heart went after their idols.

17 [a]Nevertheless mine eye spared them from destroying them, neither did I make an end of them in the wilderness.

18 But I said unto their children in the wilderness, Walk ye not in the statutes of your fathers, neither observe their judgments, nor defile yourselves with their idols:

19 I *am* the LORD your God; [a]walk in my statutes, and keep my judgments, and do them;

20 [a]And hallow my sabbaths; and they shall be a sign between me and you, that ye may know that I *am* the LORD your God.

21 Notwithstanding [a]the children rebelled against me: they walked not in my statutes, neither kept my judgments to do them, [b]which *if* a man do, he shall even live in them; they [1]polluted my sabbaths: then I said, I would pour out my fury upon them, to accomplish my anger against them in the wilderness.

22 Nevertheless I [1]withdrew mine [1]hand, and wrought for my name's sake, that it should not be [2]polluted in the sight of the [3]heathen, in whose sight I brought them forth.

23 I [1]lifted up mine hand unto them also in the wilderness, that [a]I would scatter them among the [2]heathen, and disperse them through the countries;

### Center reference column

19:11 [3] *was seen* [4] *amid the dense foliage*

19:12 [a] Jer. 31:27, 28 [b] Hos. 13:5 [1] *branches*

19:14 [a] Judg. 9:15 [b] Lam. 2:5 [1] *branch* [2] *has become a*

20:1 [a] Ezek. 8:1, 11, 12; 14:1

20:3 [a] Ezek. 7:26; 14:3

20:4 [a] Ezek. 16:2; 22:2

20:5 [a] Ex. 6:6–8 [b] Deut. 4:34 [c] Ex. 20:2 [1] *Took an oath*

20:6 [a] Jer. 32:22 [b] Ex. 3:8 [c] Jer. 11:5; 32:22 [1] *Took an oath* [2] *searched out*

20:7 [a] Ezek. 18:31 [b] 2 Chr. 15:8 [c] Lev. 18:3 [1] *which are before*

20:8 [a] Ezek. 7:8 [1] *obey* [2] *before*

20:9 [a] Num. 14:13 [b] Josh. 2:10; 9:9, 10 [1] *acted* [2] *profaned* [3] *Gentiles*

20:10 [a] Ex. 13:18

20:11 [a] Neh. 9:13 [b] Lev. 18:5 [1] Lit. *made known to*

20:12 [a] Deut. 5:12

20:13 [a] Num. 14:22 [b] Prov. 1:25 [c] Lev. 18:5 [d] Ex. 16:27 [e] Num. 14:29 [1] *defiled*

20:14 [a] Ezek. 20:9, 20 [1] *acted* [2] *profaned* [3] *Gentiles*

20:15 [a] Num. 14:28 [b] Ex. 3:8 [1] *Took an oath* [c] Ezek. 20:6

20:16 [a] Ezek. 20:13, 24 [b] Amos 5:25 [1] *profaned*

20:17 [a] [Ps. 78:38]

20:19 [a] Deut. 5:32

20:20 [a] Jer. 17:22

20:21 [a] Num. 25:1 [b] Lev. 18:5 [1] *profaned*

20:22 [1] *hand of judgment* [2] *profaned* [3] *Gentiles*

20:23 [a] Lev. 26:33 [1] *Took an oath* [2] *Gentiles*

24 ᵃBecause they had not executed my judgments, but had despised my statutes, and had ¹polluted my sabbaths, and ᵇtheir eyes were after their fathers' idols.

25 Wherefore ᵃI gave them also statutes *that were* not good, and judgments whereby they ¹should not live;

26 And I ¹polluted them in their ²own gifts, in that they caused to pass ᵃthrough *the fire* all ³that openeth the womb, that I might make them desolate, to the end that they ᵇmight know that I *am* the LORD.

27 Therefore, son of man, speak unto the house of Israel, and say unto them, Thus saith the Lord GOD; Yet in this your fathers have ᵃblasphemed me, in that they have ¹committed a trespass against me.

28 *For* when I had brought them into the land, *for* the which I ¹lifted up mine hand to give it to them, then ᵃthey saw every high hill, and all the thick trees, and they offered there their sacrifices, and there they presented the provocation of their offering: there also they made their ᵇsweet² savour, and poured out there their drink offerings.

29 Then I said unto them, What *is* the ¹high place whereunto ye go? And the name thereof is called ²Bamah unto this day.

30 Wherefore say unto the house of Israel, Thus saith the Lord GOD; Are ye ¹polluted after the manner of your ᵃfathers? and commit ye ²whoredom after their ᵇabominations?

31 For when ye offer ᵃyour gifts, when ye make your sons to pass through the fire, ye ¹pollute yourselves with all your idols, even unto this day: and shall I be enquired of by you, O house of Israel? *As* I live, saith the Lord GOD, I will ᵇnot be enquired of by you.

32 And that ᵃwhich cometh into your mind shall not be at all, that ye say, We will be as the ¹heathen, as the families of the countries, to serve wood and stone.

33 As I live, saith the Lord GOD, surely with a mighty hand, and ᵃwith a stretched out arm, and with fury poured out, will I rule over you:

34 And I will bring you out from the people, and will gather you out of the countries wherein ye are scattered, with a mighty hand, and with a stretched out arm, and with fury poured out.

35 And I will bring you into the wilderness of the people, and there ᵃwill I plead with you face to face.

36 ᵃLike as I pleaded with your fathers in the wilderness of the land of Egypt, so will I ¹plead with you, saith the Lord GOD.

37 And I will cause you to ᵃpass under the rod, and I will bring you into the bond of the ᵇcovenant:

38 And ᵃI will purge out from among you the rebels, and them that transgress against me: I will bring them forth out of the country where they sojourn, and ᵇthey shall not enter into the land of Israel: and ye shall know that I *am* the LORD.

39 As for you, O house of Israel, thus saith the Lord GOD; ᵃGo ye, serve ye every one his idols, and hereafter *also*, if ye will not hearken unto me: ᵇbut ¹pollute ye my holy name no more with your gifts, and with your idols.

40 For ᵃin mine holy mountain, in the mountain of the height of Israel, saith the Lord GOD, there shall ᵇall the house of Israel, all of them in the land, serve me: there ᶜwill I accept them, and there will I require your offerings, and the firstfruits of your ¹oblations, with all your holy things.

41 I will accept you ¹with your ᵃsweet² savour, when I bring you out from the people, and gather you out of the countries wherein ye have been scattered; and I will be ³sanctified in you before the ⁴heathen.

42 ᵃAnd ye shall know that I *am* the LORD, ᵇwhen I shall bring you into the land of Israel, into the country *for* the which I ¹lifted up mine hand to give it to your fathers.

43 And ᵃthere shall ye remember your ways, and all your doings, wherein ye have been defiled; and ᵇye shall ¹lothe yourselves in your own sight for all your evils that ye have committed.

44 ᵃAnd ye shall know that I *am* the LORD, when I have ¹wrought with you ᵇfor my name's sake, not according to your wicked ways, nor according to your corrupt doings, O ye house of Israel, saith the Lord GOD.

45 Moreover the word of the LORD came unto me, saying,

46 ᵃSon of man, set thy face toward the south, and ¹drop *thy word* toward the south, and prophesy against the ²forest of the ³south field;

47 And say to the forest of the south, Hear the word of the LORD; Thus saith the Lord GOD; Behold, ᵃI will kindle a fire in thee, and it shall devour ᵇevery green tree in thee, and every dry tree: the ¹flaming flame shall not be quenched, and all faces ᶜfrom the south to the north shall be ²burned therein.

48 And all flesh shall see that I the LORD have kindled it: it shall not be quenched.

49 Then said I, Ah Lord GOD! they say of me, Doth he not speak ᵃparables?

---

20:24 ᵃ Ezek. 20:13, 16 ᵇ Ezek. 6:9 ¹ *profaned*

20:25 ᵃ Rom. 1:24 ¹ *could*

20:26 ᵃ Jer. 32:35 ᵇ Ezek. 6:7; 20:12, 20 ¹ *pronounced them unclean because of* ² *ritual gifts* ³ *their firstborn*

20:27 ᵃ Rom. 2:24 ¹ *been unfaithful to me*

20:28 ᵃ Ezek. 6:13 ᵇ Ezek. 16:19 ¹ *Took an oath* ² *soothing aroma*

20:29 ¹ *sacred place* for pagan worship ² Lit. *High Place*

20:30 ᵃ Judg. 2:19 ᵇ Jer. 7:26; 16:12 ¹ *defiled* ² *harlotry*

20:31 ᵃ Ezek. 16:20; 20:26 ᵇ Ezek. 20:3 ¹ *defile*

20:32 ᵃ Ezek. 11:5 ¹ *Gentiles*

20:33 ᵃ Jer. 21:5

20:35 ᵃ Jer. 2:9, 35; Ezek. 17:20

20:36 ᵃ Num. 14:21–23, 28 ¹ *plead my case*

20:37 ᵃ Lev. 27:32 ᵇ Ps. 89:30–34

20:38 ᵃ Ezek. 34:17 ᵇ Jer. 44:14

20:39 ᵃ Amos 4:4 ᵇ Is. 1:13–15 ¹ *profane*

20:40 ᵃ Is. 2:2, 3 ᵇ Ezek. 37:22 ᶜ Zech. 8:20–22 ¹ *offerings*

20:41 ᵃ Phil. 4:18 ¹ *as a* ² *soothing aroma* ³ *hallowed* ⁴ *Gentiles*

20:42 ᵃ Ezek. 36:23; 38:23 ᵇ Ezek. 11:17; 34:13; 36:24 ¹ *Took an oath*

20:43 ᵃ Ezek. 16:61 ᵇ Lev. 26:39 ¹ *despise*

20:44 ᵃ Ezek. 24:24 ᵇ Ezek. 36:22 ¹ *dealt*

20:46 ᵃ Ezek. 21:2 ¹ *preach against* ² *forest land* ³ Heb. *Negev*

20:47 ᵃ Jer. 21:14 ᵇ Luke 23:31 ᶜ Ezek. 21:4 ¹ *blazing* ² *scorched by it*

20:49 ᵃ Ezek. 12:9; 17:2

## CHAPTER 21

AND the word of the LORD came unto me, saying,

2 [a]Son of man, set thy face toward Jerusalem, and [b]drop[1] *thy word* toward the holy places, and prophesy against the land of Israel,

3 And say to the land of Israel, Thus saith the LORD; Behold, I *am* [a]against thee, and will draw forth my sword out of his sheath, and will cut off from thee [b]the righteous and the wicked.

4 Seeing then that I will cut off from thee the righteous and the wicked, therefore shall my sword go forth out of his sheath against all flesh [a]from the south to the north:

5 That all flesh may know that I the LORD have drawn forth my sword out of his sheath: it [a]shall not return any more.

6 [a]Sigh therefore, thou son of man, with [1]the breaking of *thy* loins; and with bitterness sigh before their eyes.

7 And it shall be, when they say unto thee, Wherefore sighest thou? that thou shalt answer, [1]For the tidings; because it cometh: and every heart shall melt, and [a]all hands shall be feeble, and every spirit shall faint, and all knees shall be weak *as* water: behold, it cometh, and shall be brought to pass, saith the Lord GOD.

8 Again the word of the LORD came unto me, saying,

9 Son of man, prophesy, and say, Thus saith the LORD; Say, [a]A sword, a sword is sharpened, and also [1]furbished:

10 It is sharpened to make a [1]sore slaughter; it is [2]furbished that it may [3]glitter: should we then make mirth? it [4]contemneth the rod of my son, *as* [5]every tree.

11 And he hath given it to be [1]furbished, that it may be handled: this sword is sharpened, and it is [1]furbished, to give it into the hand of [a]the slayer.

12 Cry and [1]howl, son of man: for it shall be upon my people, it *shall be* upon all the princes of Israel: [2]terrors by reason of the sword shall be upon my people: [a]smite[3] therefore upon *thy* thigh.

13 Because *it is* [a]a [1]trial, and what if *the sword* [2]contemn even the rod? [b]it[3] shall be no *more,* saith the Lord GOD.

14 Thou therefore, son of man, prophesy, and [a]smite[1] *thine* hands together, and let the sword [2]be doubled the third time, the sword of the slain: it *is* the sword [3]of the great *men that are* slain, which entereth into their [b]privy[4] chambers.

15 I have set the point of the sword against all their gates, that *their* heart may [1]faint, and [2]*their* ruins be

multiplied: ah! [a]*it is* made bright, *it is* [3]wrapped up for the slaughter.

16 [a]Go[1] thee one way or other, *either* on the right hand, *or* on the left, whithersoever thy [2]face *is* set.

17 I will also [a]smite[1] mine hands together, and [b]I will cause my fury to rest: I the LORD have said *it.*

18 The word of the LORD came unto me again, saying,

19 Also, thou son of man, appoint thee two ways, [1]that the sword of the king of Babylon [2]may come: both twain shall come forth out of one land: and [3]choose thou a place, choose *it* at the head of the way to the city.

20 Appoint a way, that the sword may come to [a]Rabbath of the Ammonites, and to Judah [1]in Jerusalem the defenced.

21 For the king of Babylon stood at the parting of the way, at the head of the two ways, to use divination: he [1]made *his* arrows bright, he consulted with [2]images, he looked in the liver.

22 At his right hand was the divination for Jerusalem, to [1]appoint captains, to [2]open the mouth in the slaughter, to [a]lift up the voice with shouting, [b]to appoint *battering* rams against the gates, to [3]cast a mount, *and* to build a [4]fort.

23 And it shall be unto them as a false divination in their sight, to them that [a]have sworn oaths: but he will call to remembrance the iniquity, that they may be taken.

24 Therefore thus saith the Lord GOD; Because ye have made your iniquity to be remembered, in that your transgressions are [1]discovered, so that in all your doings your sins do appear; because, *I say,* that ye are come to remembrance, ye shall be taken with the hand.

25 And thou, [a]profane wicked prince of Israel, [b]whose day is come, when iniquity *shall have* an end,

26 Thus saith the Lord GOD; Remove the [1]diadem, and take off the crown: [2]this *shall* not *be* the same: [a]exalt *him that is* low, and abase *him that is* [3]high.

27 I will [1]overturn, [2]overturn, overturn, it: [a]and it shall be no [3]*more,* until he come whose right it is; and I will give it [b]*him.*

28 And thou, son of man, prophesy and say, Thus saith the Lord GOD [a]concerning the Ammonites, and concerning their reproach; even say thou, The sword, the sword *is* drawn: for the slaughter *it is* [1]furbished, [2]to consume because of the glittering:

### Center reference column

21:2 [a] Ezek. 20:46
[b] Amos 7:16
[1] *preach*

21:3 [a] Ezek. 5:8
[b] Job 9:22

21:4 [a] Ezek. 20:47

21:5 [a] [Is. 45:23; 55:11]

21:6 [a] Is. 22:4 [1] A *breaking heart*

21:7 [a] Ezek. 7:17
[1] *Because of the news*

21:9 [a] Deut. 32:41
[1] *polished*

21:10 [1] *dreadful*
[2] *polished* [3] *flash*
[4] *despises the sceptre* [5] *all wood*

21:11 [a] Ezek. 21:19
[1] *polished*

21:12 [a] Jer. 31:19
[1] *wail* [2] *including*
[3] *strike*

21:13 [a] Job
9:23 [b] Ezek.
21:27 [1] *testing*
[2] *despises even the sceptre* [3] The *sceptre*

21:14 [a] Num.
24:10 [b] 1 Kin.
20:30 [1] *strike*
[2] *do double damage* [3] *that slays great men* [4] *private*

21:15 [a] Ezek. 21:10,
28 [1] *melt* [2] *many may stumble*
[3] *grasped*

21:16 [a] Ezek.
14:17 [1] *Sharpen yourself, thrust right, set yourself, thrust left* [2] *edge is ordered*

21:17 [a] Ezek. 22:13
[b] Ezek. 5:13; 16:42;
24:13 [1] *strike*

21:19 [1] *for* [2] *to go*
[3] *make a sign, put it at the head*

21:20 [a] Jer. 49:2
[1] *into fortified Jerusalem*

21:21 [1] *shook the arrows* [2] Heb. *teraphim*

21:22 [a] Jer. 51:14
[b] Ezek. 4:2 [1] *set up battering rams* [2] *call for a slaughter* [3] *heap up a siege mound* [4] *siege wall*

21:23 [a] Ezek.
17:16, 18

21:24 [1] *uncovered*

21:25 [a] Jer. 52:2
[b] Ezek. 21:29

21:26 [a] Luke 1:52
[1] *turban* [2] *nothing shall remain* [3] *exalted*

21:27 [a] [Luke
1:32, 33]

[b] [Jer. 23:5, 6] [1] *make it overthrown* [2] *overthrown* [3] *longer*    21:28 [a] Ezek. 25:1–7 [1] *polished* [2] *to consume to flash*

29 Whiles they ᵃsee ¹vanity unto thee, whiles they divine a lie unto thee, to bring thee upon the necks of *them that are* slain, of the wicked, ᵇwhose day is come, when their iniquity *shall have* an end.

30 ᵃShall I cause *it* to return into his sheath? ᵇI will judge thee in the place where thou wast created, ᶜin the land of thy ¹nativity.

31 And I will ᵃpour out mine indignation upon thee, I will ᵇblow against thee in the fire of my wrath, and deliver thee into the hand of ¹brutish men, *and* skilful to ᶜdestroy.

32 Thou shalt be for fuel to the fire; thy blood shall be in the midst of the land; ᵃthou shalt be no *more* remembered: for I the LORD have spoken *it*.

## CHAPTER 22

Moreover the word of the LORD came unto me, saying,

2 Now, thou son of man, ᵃwilt thou judge, wilt thou judge ᵇthe bloody city? yea, thou shalt shew her all her abominations.

3 Then say thou, Thus saith the Lord GOD, The city sheddeth ᵃblood in the midst of it, that her time may come, and maketh idols against herself to defile herself.

4 Thou art become guilty ¹in thy blood that thou hast ᵃshed; and hast defiled thyself in thine idols which thou hast made; and thou hast caused thy days to draw near, and art come *even* unto thy years: ᵇtherefore have I made thee a reproach unto the ²heathen, and a ³mocking to all countries.

5 *Those that be* near, and *those that be* far from thee, shall mock thee, *which art* ¹infamous *and* ²much vexed.

6 Behold, ᵃthe princes of Israel, every one ¹were in thee to their power to shed blood.

7 In thee have they ᵃset¹ light by father and mother: in the midst of thee have they ᵇdealt by oppression with the stranger: in thee have they ²vexed the ³fatherless and the widow.

8 Thou hast despised mine holy things, and hast ᵃprofaned my sabbaths.

9 In thee are ᵃmen that ¹carry tales to shed blood: ᵇand in thee ²they eat upon the mountains: in the midst of thee they commit lewdness.

10 In thee have they ᵃdiscovered¹ their fathers' nakedness: in thee have they ²humbled her that was ᵇset apart ³for pollution.

11 And one hath committed abomination ᵃwith his neighbour's wife; and another ᵇhath lewdly defiled his daughter in law; and another in thee hath ¹humbled his sister, his father's ᶜdaughter.

---

12 In thee ᵃhave they taken ¹gifts to shed blood; ᵇthou hast taken usury and increase, and thou hast ²greedily gained of thy neighbours by extortion, and ᶜhast forgotten me, saith the Lord GOD.

13 Behold, therefore I have ᵃsmitten¹ mine hand at thy dishonest gain which thou hast made, and at thy ²blood which hath been in the midst of thee.

14 ᵃCan thine heart endure, or can thine hands be strong, in the days that I shall deal with thee? ᵇI the LORD have spoken *it*, and will do *it*.

15 And ᵃI will scatter thee among the ¹heathen, and disperse thee in the countries, and ᵇwill ²consume thy filthiness out of thee.

16 And thou shalt ¹take thine inheritance in thyself in the sight of the heathen, and ᵃthou shalt know that I *am* the LORD.

17 And the word of the LORD came unto me, saying,

18 Son of man, ᵃthe house of Israel is to me become dross: all they *are* ¹brass, and tin, and iron, and lead, in the midst of the ᵇfurnace; they are *even* the dross of silver.

19 Therefore thus saith the Lord GOD; Because ye are all become dross, behold, therefore I will gather you into the midst of Jerusalem.

20 *As* they gather silver, and ¹brass, and iron, and lead, and tin, into the midst of the furnace, to blow the fire upon it, to ᵃmelt *it;* so will I gather *you* in mine anger and in my fury, and I will leave *you there,* and melt you.

21 Yea, I will gather you, and blow upon you in the fire of my wrath, and ye shall be melted in the midst thereof.

22 As silver is melted in the midst of the furnace, so shall ye be melted in the midst thereof; and ye shall know that I the LORD have ᵃpoured out my fury upon you.

23 And the word of the LORD came unto me, saying,

24 Son of man, say unto her, Thou *art* the land that is ᵃnot cleansed, nor rained upon in the day of indignation.

25 ᵃThere is a conspiracy of her prophets in the midst thereof, like a roaring lion ¹ravening the prey; they ᵇhave devoured ²souls; they have taken the treasure and precious things; ᶜthey have made her many widows in the midst thereof.

26 ᵃHer priests have ¹violated my law, and have ᵇprofaned mine holy things: they have ²put no ᶜdifference

---

21:29 ᵃ Ezek. 12:24; 13:6–9; 22:28 ᵇ Job 18:20 ¹ vain visions for thee
21:30 ᵃ Jer. 47:6, 7 ᵇ Gen. 15:14 ᶜ Ezek. 16:3 ¹ Or origin
21:31 ᵃ Ezek. 7:8 ᵇ Ezek. 22:20, 21 ᶜ Hab. 1:6–10 ¹ brutal
21:32 ᵃ Ezek. 25:10
22:2 ᵃ Ezek. 20:4 ᵇ Nah. 3:1
22:3 ᵃ Ezek. 24:6, 7
22:4 ᵃ 2 Kin. 21:16 ᵇ Deut. 28:37 ¹ by ² Gentiles ³ mockery
22:5 ¹ Lit. defiled of name ² full of tumult
22:6 ᵃ Is. 1:23 ¹ has used his power to shed blood in thee
22:7 ᵃ Lev. 20:9 ᵇ Ex. 22:22 ¹ made light of ² mistreated ³ Lit. orphan
22:8 ᵃ Lev. 19:30
22:9 ᵃ Lev. 19:16 ᵇ Ezek. 18:6, 11 ¹ slander to cause bloodshed ² are they who
22:10 ᵃ Lev. 18:7, 8 ᵇ Lev. 18:19; 20:18 ¹ uncovered ² violated women who are ³ during their impurity
22:11 ᵃ Ezek. 18:11 ᵇ Lev. 18:15 ᶜ Lev. 18:9 ¹ violated
22:12 ᵃ Ex. 23:8 ᵇ Ex. 22:25 ᶜ Ezek. 23:35 ¹ bribes ² profited from
22:13 ᵃ Ezek. 21:17 ¹ struck ² bloodshed
22:14 ᵃ Ezek. 21:7 ᵇ Ezek. 17:24
22:15 ᵃ Deut. 4:27 ᵇ Ezek. 23:27, 48 ¹ nations ² remove
22:16 ᵃ Ps. 9:16 ¹ defile thyself in the sight of the nations
22:18 ᵃ Is. 1:22 ᵇ Prov. 17:3 ¹ bronze
22:20 ᵃ Is. 1:25 ¹ bronze
22:22 ᵃ Ezek. 20:8, 33
22:24 ᵃ Ezek. 24:13
22:25 ᵃ Hos. 6:9 ᵇ Matt. 23:14

ᶜ Mic. 3:11 ¹ tearing ² lives   22:26 ᵃ Mal. 2:8
ᵇ 1 Sam. 2:29 ᶜ Lev. 10:10 ¹ done violence to ² not distinguished

between the holy and ³profane, neither have they shewed *difference* between the unclean and the clean, and have hid their eyes from my sabbaths, and I am profaned among them.

27 Her ªprinces in the midst thereof *are* like wolves ¹ravening the prey, to shed blood, *and* to destroy ²souls, to get dishonest gain.

28 And ªher prophets have ¹daubed them with untempered *morter*, ᵇseeing ²vanity, and divining ᶜlies unto them, saying, Thus saith the Lord GOD, when the LORD hath not spoken.

29 The people of the land have used oppression, and exercised robbery, and have ¹vexed the poor and needy: yea, they have ªoppressed the stranger wrongfully.

30 ªAnd I sought for a man among them, that should ᵇmake up ¹the hedge, and ᶜstand in the gap before me for the land, that I should not destroy it: but I found none.

31 Therefore have I ªpoured out mine indignation upon them; I have consumed them with the fire of my wrath: ᵇtheir ¹own way have I recompensed upon their heads, saith the Lord GOD.

## CHAPTER 23

THE word of the LORD came again unto me, saying,

2 Son of man, there were ªtwo women, the daughters of one mother:

3 And ªthey committed ¹whoredoms in Egypt; they committed ¹whoredoms in ᵇtheir youth: there were their breasts ²pressed, and there they bruised ³the teats of their virginity.

4 And the names of them *were* ¹Aholah the elder, and ²Aholibah ªher sister: and ᵇthey were mine, and they bare sons and daughters. Thus *were* their names; Samaria *is* ¹Aholah, and Jerusalem ²Aholibah.

5 And Aholah played the harlot when she was mine; and she ¹doted on her lovers, on ªthe Assyrians *her* neighbours,

6 *Which were* clothed with ¹blue, captains and rulers, all of them desirable young men, horsemen riding upon horses.

7 Thus she committed her ¹whoredoms with them, with all them *that were* the ²chosen men of Assyria, and with all ³on whom she doted: with all their idols she defiled herself.

8 Neither left she her ¹whoredoms brought ªfrom Egypt: for in her youth they lay with her, and they ²bruised the breasts of her virginity, and poured their ³whoredom upon her.

9 Wherefore I have delivered her into the hand of her lovers, into the hand of the ªAssyrians, upon whom she ¹doted.

10 These ¹discovered her nakedness: they took her sons and her daughters, and slew her with the sword: and she became ²famous among women; for they had executed judgment upon her.

11 And ªwhen her sister ¹Aholibah saw *this*, ᵇshe was more corrupt in her inordinate love than she, and in her ²whoredoms more than her sister in *her* ²whoredoms.

12 She ¹doted upon the ªAssyrians *her* neighbours, ᵇcaptains and rulers clothed most gorgeously, horsemen riding upon horses, all of them desirable young men.

13 Then I saw that she was defiled, *that* they *took* both one way,

14 And *that* she increased her ¹whoredoms: for when she saw men pourtrayed upon the wall, the images of the ªChaldeans pourtrayed with vermilion,

15 Girded with ¹girdles upon their ²loins, ³exceeding in dyed attire upon their heads, all of them princes to look to, after the manner of the Babylonians of Chaldea, the land of their nativity:

16 ªAnd as soon as she saw them with her eyes, she ¹doted upon them, and sent ᵇmessengers unto them into Chaldea.

17 And the ¹Babylonians came to her into the bed of love, and they defiled her with their ²whoredom, and she was ³polluted with them, and ªher⁴ mind was alienated from them.

18 So she ¹discovered her whoredoms, and ²discovered her nakedness: then ªmy³ mind was ᵇalienated from her, like as my mind was alienated from her sister.

19 Yet she multiplied her ¹whoredoms, in calling to remembrance the days of her youth, ªwherein she had played the harlot in the land of Egypt.

20 For she ¹doted upon their ²paramours, whose flesh *is as* the flesh of ³asses, and whose issue *is like* the issue of horses.

21 Thus thou calledst to remembrance the lewdness of thy youth, ¹in bruising thy teats by the ªEgyptians for the paps of thy youth.

22 Therefore, O ¹Aholibah, thus saith the Lord GOD; ªBehold, I will raise up thy lovers against thee, from whom ²thy mind is alienated, and I will bring them against thee on every side;

23 The Babylonians, and all the Chaldeans, ªPekod, and Shoa, and Koa, *and* ᵇall the Assyrians with them: all of them desirable young men, ¹captains and rulers, ²great lords and renowned, all of them riding upon horses.

---

22:26 ³ *unholy*

22:27 ª Is. 1:23
¹ *tearing* ² *lives*

22:28 ª Ezek.
13:10  ᵇ Ezek. 13:6,
7  ᶜ Jer. 23:25–32
¹ *plastered* ² *false
visions*

22:29 ª Ex. 23:9
¹ *mistreated*

22:30 ª Jer. 5:1
ᵇ Ezek. 13:5  ᶜ Ps.
106:23  ¹ *a wall*

22:31 ª Ezek.
22:22  ᵇ Ezek. 9:10
¹ *deeds*

23:2 ª Ezek.
16:44–46

23:3 ª Lev. 17:7
ᵇ Ezek. 16:22
¹ *harlotry* ² *embraced* ³ *their
virgin bosom*

23:4 ª Jer. 3:6,7
ᵇ Ezek. 16:8, 20
¹ Or Oholah, lit.
*Her Own Tabernacle* ² Or Oholibah,
*My Tabernacle Is
in Her*

23:5 ª Hos. 5:13;
8:9, 10  ¹ *lusted for*

23:6 ¹ *purple*

23:7 ¹ *harlotry*
² *choice* ³ *for
whom she lusted*

23:8 ª Ezek. 23:3,
19  ¹ *harlotry*
² *pressed her
virgin bosom*
³ *immorality*

23:9 ª 2 Kin. 17:3
¹ *lusted*

23:10 ¹ *uncovered*
² *a byword*

23:11 ª Jer. 3:8
ᵇ Jer. 3:8–11
¹ Or Oholibah
² *harlotry*

23:12 ª 2 Kin. 16:7,
8  ᵇ Ezek. 23:6, 23
¹ *lusted for*

23:14 ª Ezek. 8:10;
16:29  ¹ *harlotry*

23:15 ¹ *belts*
² *waists* ³ *with
flowing turbans
upon*

23:16 ª 2 Kin. 24:1
ᵇ Is. 57:9  ¹ *lusted
for*

23:17 ª Ezek. 23:22,
28  ¹ Lit. *sons of
Babel* ² *immorality* ³ *defiled* ⁴ *she
alienated herself*

23:18 ª Jer.
6:8  ᵇ Jer. 12:8
¹ *revealed her
harlotry* ² *uncovered* ³ *I alienated
myself*

23:19 ª Ezek. 23:2
¹ *harlotry*

23:20 ¹ *lusted
for* ² *illicit lovers*
³ *donkeys*

23:21 ª Ezek. 16:26

¹ *when the Egyptians pressed thy bosom of thy
youthful breasts*  23:22 ª Ezek. 16:37–41; 23:28
¹ Or Oholibah ² *thou hast alienated thyself*
23:23 ª Jer. 50:21 ᵇ Ezek. 23:12 ¹ *governors* ² *captains*

24 And they shall come against thee with chariots, wagons, and [1]wheels, and with [2]an assembly of people, *which* shall set against thee [3]buckler and shield and helmet round about: and I will [4]set judgment [5]before them, and they shall judge thee according to their judgments.

25 And I will set my [a]jealousy against thee, and they shall deal furiously with thee: they shall [1]take away thy nose and thine ears; and thy remnant shall fall by the sword: they shall take thy sons and thy daughters; and thy [2]residue shall be devoured by the fire.

26 [a]They shall also strip thee out of thy clothes, and take away thy [1]fair jewels.

27 Thus [a]will I make thy lewdness to cease from thee, and thy [b]whoredom[1] *brought* from the land of Egypt: so that thou shalt not lift up thine eyes unto them, nor remember Egypt any more.

28 For thus saith the Lord GOD; Behold, I will deliver thee into the hand *of them* [a]whom thou hatest, into the hand *of them* [b]from whom thy mind is alienated:

29 [a]And they shall deal with thee hatefully, and shall take away all [1]thy labour, and [b]shall leave thee naked and bare: and the nakedness of thy [2]whoredoms shall be [3]discovered, both thy lewdness and thy [2]whoredoms.

30 I will do these *things* unto thee, because thou hast [a]gone [1]a whoring after the [2]heathen, *and* because thou art [3]polluted with their idols.

31 Thou hast walked in the way of thy sister; therefore will I give her [a]cup into thine hand.

32 Thus saith the Lord GOD; Thou shalt drink of thy sister's cup deep and [1]large: [a]thou shalt be laughed to scorn and [2]had in derision; it containeth much.

33 Thou shalt be filled with drunkenness and sorrow, with the cup of [1]astonishment and desolation, with the cup of thy sister Samaria.

34 Thou shalt [a]even drink it and [1]suck it out, and thou shalt break the [2]sherds thereof, and [3]pluck off thine own breasts: for I have spoken *it*, saith the Lord GOD.

35 Therefore thus saith the Lord GOD; Because thou [a]hast forgotten me, and [b]cast me behind thy back, therefore bear thou also thy lewdness and thy [1]whoredoms.

36 The LORD said moreover unto me; Son of man, wilt thou [a]judge Aholah and Aholibah? yea, [b]declare unto them their abominations;

37 That they have committed adultery, and [a]blood *is* in their hands, and

---

23:24 [1] *warhorses* [2] *a horde* [3] A large shield [4] *delegate* [5] *to*

23:25 [a] Ex. 34:14 [1] *remove* [2] *remnant*

23:26 [a] Is. 3:18–23 [1] *beautiful*

23:27 [a] Ezek. 16:41; 22:15 [b] Ezek. 23:3, 19 [1] *harlotry*

23:28 [a] Ezek. 16:37–41 [b] Ezek. 23:17

23:29 [a] Deut. 28:48 [b] Ezek. 16:39 [1] *thou hast laboured for* [2] *harlotry* [3] *uncovered*

23:30 [a] Ezek. 6:9 [1] *as a harlot* [2] *Gentiles* [3] *defiled*

23:31 [a] Jer. 7:14; 15; 25:15

23:32 [a] Ezek. 22:4, 5 [1] *wide* [2] *held*

23:33 [1] *horror*

23:34 [a] Is. 51:17 [1] *drain it* [2] *fragments* [3] *tear at*

23:35 [a] Jer. 3:21 [b] 1 Kin. 14:9 [1] *harlotry*

23:36 [a] Ezek. 20:4; 99:9 [b] Is. 58:1

23:37 [a] Ezek. 16:38

[b] Ezek. 16:20, 21, 36, 45; 20:26, 31

23:38 [1] 2 Kin. 21:4, 7 [b] Ezek. 22:8

23:39 [a] 2 Kin. 21:2–8

23:40 [a] Is. 57:9 [b] Ruth 3:3 [c] Jer. 4:30 [1] *adorned*

23:41 [a] Is. 57:7 [b] Prov. 7:17 [1] *glorious couch*

23:42 [1] *carefree multitude* [2] Or *drunkards* [3] *wrists*

23:43 [1] *harlotry*

23:45 [a] Ezek. 16:38 [b] Ezek. 23:37

23:46 [a] Ezek. 16:40 [1] *plundered*

23:47 [a] Ezek. 16:40 [b] Ezek. 24:21 [1] *execute*, lit. *cut down*

23:48 [a] Ezek. 22:15 [b] Deut. 13:11 [1] *practise*

23:49 [a] Ezek. 23:35 [b] Ezek. 20:38, 42, 44; 25:5 [1] *your idolatrous sins*

---

with their idols have they committed adultery, and have also caused their sons, [b]whom they bare unto me, to pass for them through *the fire,* to devour *them.*

38 Moreover this they have done unto me: they have [a]defiled my sanctuary in the same day, and [b]have profaned my sabbaths.

39 For when they had slain their children to their idols, then they came the same day into my sanctuary to profane it; and, lo, [a]thus have they done in the midst of mine house.

40 And furthermore, that ye have sent for men to come from far, [a]unto whom a messenger *was* sent; and, lo, they came: for whom thou didst [b]wash thyself, [c]paintedst thy eyes, and [1]deckedst thyself with ornaments,

41 And satest upon a [1]stately [a]bed, and a table prepared before it, [b]whereupon thou hast set mine incense and mine oil.

42 And a voice of a [1]multitude being at ease *was* with her: and with the men of the common sort *were* brought [2]Sabeans from the wilderness, which put bracelets upon their [3]hands, and beautiful crowns upon their heads.

43 Then said I unto *her that was* old in adulteries, Will they now commit [1]whoredoms with her, and she *with them?*

44 Yet they went in unto her, as they go in unto a woman that playeth the harlot: so went they in unto Aholah and unto Aholibah, the lewd women.

45 And the righteous men, they shall [a]judge them after the manner of adulteresses, and after the manner of women that shed blood; because they *are* adulteresses, and [b]blood *is* in their hands.

46 For thus saith the Lord GOD; [a]I will bring up a company upon them, and will give them to be removed and [1]spoiled.

47 [a]And the company shall stone them with stones, and [1]dispatch them with their swords; [b]they shall slay their sons and their daughters, and burn up their houses with fire.

48 Thus [a]will I cause lewdness to cease out of the land, [b]that all women may be taught not to [1]do after your lewdness.

49 And they shall recompense your lewdness upon you, and ye shall [a]bear [1]the sins of your idols: [b]and ye shall know that I *am* the Lord GOD.

## CHAPTER 24

AGAIN in the ninth year, in the tenth month, in the tenth *day* of the month, the word of the LORD came unto me, saying,

2 Son of man, write thee the name of the day, *even* of this same day: the king of Babylon [1]set himself against Jerusalem [a]this same day.

3 [a]And utter a parable unto the rebellious house, and say unto them, Thus saith the Lord GOD; [b]Set on a pot, set *it* on, and also pour water into it:

4 Gather the [1]pieces thereof into it, *even* every good piece, the thigh, and the shoulder; fill *it* with the choice [2]bones.

5 Take the choice of the flock, and burn also the bones under it, *and* make it boil well, and let them [1]seethe the [2]bones of it therein.

6 Wherefore thus saith the Lord GOD; Woe to [a]the bloody city, to the pot whose scum *is* therein, and whose scum is not gone out of it! bring it out piece by piece; let no [b]lot fall upon it.

7 For her blood is in the midst of her; she set it upon the top of a rock; [a]she poured it not upon the ground, to cover it with dust;

8 That it might cause fury to come up to take vengeance; [a]I have set her blood upon the top of a rock, that it should not be covered.

9 Therefore thus saith the Lord GOD; [a]Woe to the bloody city! I will even make the pile for fire great.

10 Heap on wood, kindle the fire, [1]consume the flesh, and [2]spice it well, and let the bones be burned.

11 Then set it empty upon the coals thereof, that the [1]brass of it may be hot, and may burn, and *that* [a]the filthiness of it may be [2]molten in it, *that* the scum of it may be consumed.

12 She hath wearied *herself* with lies, and her great scum went not forth out of her: her scum *shall be* in the fire.

13 In thy [a]filthiness *is* lewdness: because I have purged thee, and thou wast not purged, thou shalt [b]not be purged from thy filthiness any more, [c]till I have caused my fury to rest upon thee.

14 [a]I the LORD have spoken *it:* [b]it shall come to pass, and I will do *it;* I will not go back, [c]neither will I spare, neither will I [1]repent; according to thy ways, and according to thy doings, shall they judge thee, saith the Lord GOD.

15 Also the word of the LORD came unto me, saying,

16 Son of man, behold, I take away from thee the desire of thine eyes with a stroke: yet [a]neither shalt thou mourn nor weep, neither shall thy tears run down.

17 [1]Forbear to cry, [a]make no mourning for the dead, [b]bind the [2]tire of thine head upon thee, and [c]put on

thy [3]shoes upon thy feet, and [d]cover not *thy* [4]lips, and eat not [5]the bread of men.

18 So I spake unto the people in the morning: and at [1]even my wife died; and I did in the morning as I was commanded.

19 And the people said unto me, [a]Wilt thou not tell us what these *things are* to us, that thou doest *so?*

20 Then I answered them, The word of the LORD came unto me, saying,

21 Speak unto the house of Israel, Thus saith the Lord GOD; Behold, [a]I will profane my sanctuary, the [1]excellency of your [2]strength, the desire of your eyes, and that which your soul [3]pitieth; [b]and your sons and your daughters whom ye have left shall fall by the sword.

22 And ye shall do as I have done: [a]ye shall not cover *your* [1]lips, nor eat [2]the bread of men.

23 And your [1]tires *shall be* upon your heads, and your [2]shoes upon your feet: [a]ye shall not mourn nor weep; but [b]ye shall pine away for your iniquities, and mourn one toward another.

24 Thus [a]Ezekiel is unto you a sign: according to all that he hath done shall ye do: [b]and when this cometh, [c]ye shall know that I *am* the Lord GOD.

25 Also, thou son of man, *shall it* not *be* in the day when I take from them [a]their [1]strength, the joy of their glory, the desire of their eyes, and [2]that whereupon they set their minds, their sons and their daughters,

26 *That* [a]he that escapeth in that day shall come unto thee, to cause *thee* to hear *it* with *thine* ears?

27 [a]In that day shall thy mouth be opened to him which is escaped, and thou shalt speak, and be no more [1]dumb: and thou shalt be a sign unto them; and they shall know that I *am* the LORD.

## CHAPTER 25

THE word of the LORD came again unto me, saying,

2 Son of man, [a]set thy face [b]against the Ammonites, and prophesy against them;

3 And say unto the Ammonites, Hear the word of the Lord GOD; Thus saith the Lord GOD; [a]Because thou saidst, Aha, against my sanctuary, when it was profaned; and against the land of Israel, when it was desolate; and against the house of Judah, when they went into captivity;

4 Behold, therefore I will deliver thee to the [1]men of the east for a possession, and they shall set their [2]palaces in thee, and make their dwellings in thee: they shall eat thy fruit, and they shall drink thy milk.

---

24:2 [a] 2 Kin. 25:1
[1] *laid his siege*

24:3 [a] Ezek. 17:12
[b] Jer. 1:13

24:4 [1] *pieces* of meat [2] *Portions*

24:5 [1] *cook*
[2] *Portions*

24:6 [a] Ezek. 22:2, 3, 27 [b] Nah. 3:10

24:7 [a] Lev. 17:13

24:8 [a] [Matt. 7:2]

24:9 [a] Hab. 2:12

24:10 [1] *cook the meat well* [2] *mix in the spices*

24:11 [a] Ezek. 22:15
[1] *bronze* [2] *melted*

24:13 [a] Ezek. 23:36–48 [b] Jer. 6:28–30 [c] Ezek. 5:13; 8:18; 16:42

24:14 [a] [1 Sam. 15:29] [b] Is. 55:11 [c] Ezek. 5:11
[1] *relent*

24:16 [a] Jer. 16:5

24:17 [a] Jer. 16:5
[b] Lev. 10:6; 21:10
[c] 2 Sam. 15:30
[1] *Groan silently*
[2] *turban*

[d] Mic. 3:7 [3] *sandals* [4] Lit. *moustache* [5] *man's bread of sorrow*

24:18 [1] *evening*

24:19 [a] Ezek. 12:9; 37:18

24:21 [a] Jer. 7:14
[b] Ezek. 23:25, 47 [1] Lit. *pride*
[2] *power* [3] To have compassion for

24:22 [a] Jer. 16:6, 7 [1] Lit. *moustache*
[2] *man's bread* of sorrow

24:23 [a] Job 27:15
[b] Lev. 26:39 [1] *turbans* [2] *sandals*

24:24 [a] Is. 20:3
[b] Jer. 17:15 [c] Ezek. 6:7; 25:5

24:25 [a] Ezek.
24:21 [1] *stronghold*
[2] Lit. *the lifting up of their souls*

24:26 [a] Ezek. 33:21

24:27 [a] Ezek. 3:26; 33:22 [1] *mute*

25:2 [a] Ezek. 35:2
[b] Jer. 49:1

25:3 [a] Ezek. 26:2

25:4 [1] Lit. *sons of the east*
[2] *encampments among*

5 And I will make [a]Rabbah [b]a stable for camels, and the Ammonites a [1]couching place for flocks: [c]and ye shall know that I *am* the LORD.

6 For thus saith the Lord GOD; Because thou [a]hast clapped *thine* hands, and stamped with the feet, and [b]rejoiced in heart with all thy [1]despite against the land of Israel;

7 Behold, therefore I will [a]stretch out mine hand upon thee, and will deliver thee [1]for a spoil to the [2]heathen; and I will cut thee off from the people, and I will cause thee to perish out of the countries: I will destroy thee; and thou shalt know that I *am* the LORD.

8 Thus saith the Lord GOD; Because that [a]Moab and [b]Seir do say, Behold, the house of Judah *is* like unto all the [1]heathen;

9 Therefore, behold, I will [1]open the side of Moab [2]from the cities, [2]from his cities *which are* on his frontiers, the glory of the country, Beth-jeshimoth, Baal-meon, and [a]Kiriathaim,

10 [a]Unto the men of the east with the Ammonites, and will give them in possession, that the Ammonites [b]may not be remembered among the nations.

11 And I will execute judgments upon Moab; and they shall know that I *am* the LORD.

12 Thus saith the Lord GOD; [a]Because that Edom hath dealt against the house of Judah by taking vengeance, and hath greatly offended, [1]and revenged himself upon them;

13 Therefore thus saith the Lord GOD; I will also stretch out mine hand upon Edom, and will cut off man and beast from it; and I will make it desolate from Teman; [1]and they of Dedan shall fall by the sword.

14 And [a]I will lay my vengeance upon Edom by the hand of my people Israel: and they shall do in Edom according to mine anger and according to my fury; and they shall know my vengeance, saith the Lord GOD.

15 Thus saith the Lord GOD; [a]Because [b]the Philistines have dealt [1]by revenge, and have taken vengeance with a [2]despiteful heart, to destroy *it* [3]for the old hatred;

16 Therefore thus saith the Lord GOD; Behold, [a]I will stretch out mine hand upon the Philistines, and I will cut off the [b]Cherethims, [c]and destroy the remnant of the sea coast.

17 And I will [a]execute great vengeance upon them with furious rebukes; [b]and they shall know that I *am* the LORD, when I shall lay my vengeance upon them.

## CHAPTER 26

A ND it came to pass in the eleventh year, in the first *day* of the

month, *that* the word of the LORD came unto me, saying,

2 Son of man, [a]because that [1]Tyrus hath said against Jerusalem, [b]Aha, she is broken *that was* the [2]gates of the people: she is [3]turned unto me: I shall be [4]replenished, *now* she is laid waste:

3 Therefore thus saith the Lord GOD; Behold, I *am* against thee, O Tyrus, and will cause many nations to come up against thee, as the sea causeth his waves to come up.

4 And they shall destroy the walls of [1]Tyrus, and break down her towers: I will also scrape her dust from her, and [a]make her like the top of a rock.

5 It shall be *a place for* the spreading of nets [a]in the midst of the sea: for I have spoken *it*, saith the Lord GOD: and it shall become a [1]spoil to the nations.

6 And her daughters which *are* in the field shall be slain by the sword; [a]and they shall know that I *am* the LORD.

7 For thus saith the Lord GOD; Behold, I will bring upon Tyrus [a]Nebuchadrezzar[1] king of Babylon, [b]a king of kings, from the north, with horses, and with chariots, and with horsemen, and [2]companies, and much people.

8 He shall slay with the sword thy daughters in the field: and he shall [a]make[1] a fort against thee, and [2]cast a mount against thee, and lift up [3]the buckler against thee.

9 And he shall set [1]engines of war against thy walls, and with his axes he shall break down thy towers.

10 By reason of the abundance of his horses their dust shall cover thee: thy walls shall shake at the noise of the horsemen, and of the [1]wheels, and of the chariots, when he shall enter into thy gates, as men enter into a city [2]wherein is made a breach.

11 With the hoofs of his [a]horses shall he [1]tread down all thy streets: he shall slay thy people by the sword, and thy strong [2]garrisons shall go down to the ground.

12 And they shall [1]make a spoil of thy riches, and [2]make a prey of thy merchandise: and they shall break down thy walls, and destroy thy pleasant houses: and they shall lay thy stones and thy timber and thy dust in the [a]midst of the water.

13 [a]And I will cause the [1]noise of [b]thy songs to cease; and the sound of thy harps shall be no more heard.

14 And [a]I will make thee like the top of a rock: thou shalt be *a place* to spread nets upon; thou shalt be built no more: for I the LORD have spoken *it*, saith the Lord GOD.

---

**Center column references:**

25:5 [a] Ezek. 21:20
[b] Is. 17:2 [c] Ezek. 24:24 [1] *resting place*
25:6 [a] Job 27:23
[b] Ezek. 36:5 [1] *disdain*
25:7 [a] Ezek. 35:3 [1] *plunder* [2] *nations*
25:8 [a] Amos 2:1, 2 [b] Ezek. 35:2, 5 [1] *nations*
25:9 [a] Jer. 48:23 [1] *clear the territory* [2] *of*
25:10 [a] Ezek. 25:4 [b] Ezek. 21:32
25:12 [a] Obad. 10–14 [1] *by avenging*
25:13 [1] *Or even to Dedan they shall fall*
25:14 [1] Is. 11:14
25:15 [a] Jer. 25:20 [b] 2 Chr. 28:18 [1] *vengefully* [2] *spiteful* [3] *because of*
25:16 [a] Zeph. 2:4 [b] 1 Sam. 30:14 [c] Jer. 47:4 [1] *Cherethites*
25:17 [a] Ezek. 5:15 [b] Ps. 9:16

26:2 [a] Jer. 25:22 [b] Ezek. 25:3 [1] *Or Tyre* [2] *gateway of* [3] *turned over to* [4] *filled*
26:4 [a] Ezek. 26:14 [1] *Or Tyre*
26:5 [a] Ezek. 27:32 [1] *plunder*
26:6 [a] Ezek. 25:5
26:7 [a] Jer. 27:3–6 [b] Dan. 2:37, 47 [1] *Or Nebuchadnezzar* [2] *an army with many*
26:8 [a] Ezek. 21:22 [1] *heap up a siege mound* [2] *build a wall* [3] *A large shield*
26:9 [1] *battering rams*
26:10 [1] *wagons* [2] *that has been breached*
26:11 [a] Hab. 1:8 [1] *trample* [2] *pillars*
26:12 [a] Ezek. 27:27, 32 [1] *plunder* [2] *pillage*
26:13 [a] Is. 14:11; 24:8 [b] Rev. 18:22 [1] *sound*
26:14 [a] Ezek. 26:4, 5

15 Thus saith the Lord GOD to Tyrus; Shall not the [1]isles [a]shake at the sound of thy fall, when the wounded cry, when the slaughter is made in the midst of thee?

16 Then all the [a]princes of the sea shall [b]come down from their thrones, and lay away their robes, and put off their broidered garments: they shall clothe themselves with trembling; [c]they shall sit upon the ground, and [d]shall tremble at *every* moment, and [e]be astonished at thee.

17 And they shall take up a [a]lamentation for thee, and say to thee, How [1]art thou destroyed, *that wast* inhabited of seafaring men, the renowned city, which wast [b]strong in the sea, she and her inhabitants, which cause their terror *to be* on all [2]that haunt it!

18 Now shall [a]the [1]isles tremble in the day of thy fall; yea, the [1]isles that *are* in the sea shall be troubled at thy departure.

19 For thus saith the Lord GOD; When I shall make thee a desolate city, like the cities that are not inhabited; when I shall bring up the deep upon thee, and great waters shall cover thee;

20 When I shall bring thee down [a]with them that descend into the pit, with the people of old time, and shall set thee in the low parts of the earth, in places desolate [1]of old, with them that go down to the pit, that thou be not inhabited; and I shall set glory [b]in the land of the living;

21 [a]I will make thee a terror, and thou *shalt be* no *more:* [b]though thou be sought for, yet shalt thou never be found again, saith the Lord GOD.

## CHAPTER 27

THE word of the LORD came again unto me, saying,

2 Now, thou son of man, [a]take up a lamentation for [1]Tyrus;

3 And say unto Tyrus, [a]O thou that [1]art situate at the [2]entry of the sea, *which art* [b]a merchant of the people for many [3]isles, Thus saith the Lord GOD; O Tyrus, thou hast said, [c]I *am* of perfect beauty.

4 Thy borders *are* in the midst of the seas, thy builders have perfected thy beauty.

5 They have [1]made all thy [2]*ship* boards of fir trees of [a]Senir: they have taken cedars from Lebanon to make masts for thee.

6 *Of* the [a]oaks of Bashan have they made thine oars; the company of the Ashurites have [1]made thy benches *of* ivory, *brought* out of [b]the isles of [2]Chittim.

7 Fine linen with broidered work from Egypt was that which thou spreadest forth to be thy sail; blue

and purple from the [1]isles of Elishah was that which covered thee.

8 The inhabitants of Zidon and Arvad were thy [1]mariners: thy wise *men,* O Tyrus, *that* were in thee, were thy pilots.

9 The [1]ancients of [a]Gebal and the wise *men* thereof were in thee [2]thy calkers: all the ships of the sea with their mariners were in thee to [3]occupy thy merchandise.

10 They of Persia and of [1]Lud and of [2]Phut were in thine army, thy men of war: they hanged the shield and helmet in thee; they set forth thy [3]comeliness.

11 The men of Arvad with thine army *were* upon thy walls round about, and the [1]Gammadims were in thy towers: they hanged their shields upon thy walls round about; they have made [a]thy beauty perfect.

12 [a]Tarshish *was* thy merchant by reason of the multitude of all *kind of* riches; with silver, iron, tin, and lead, they traded [1]in thy fairs.

13 [a]Javan, Tubal, and Meshech, they *were* thy merchants: they traded [b]the [1]persons of men and vessels of [2]brass [3]in thy market.

14 They of the house of [a]Togarmah traded [1]in thy fairs with horses and [2]horsemen and mules.

15 The men of [a]Dedan *were* thy merchants; many isles *were* the [1]merchandise of thine hand: they brought thee *for* a [2]present [3]horns of ivory and ebony.

16 Syria *was* thy merchant by reason of the multitude of the [1]wares of thy making: they [2]occupied in thy fairs with emeralds, purple, and broidered work, and fine linen, and coral, and [3]agate.

17 Judah, and the land of Israel, they *were* thy merchants: they traded [1]in thy market wheat of [a]Minnith, and [2]Pannag, and honey, and oil, and [b]balm.

18 Damascus *was* thy merchant in the multitude of the wares of thy making, for the multitude of all riches; in the wine of Helbon, and white wool.

19 Dan also and Javan [1]going to and fro [2]occupied in thy fairs: [3]bright iron, cassia, and [4]calamus, were [5]in thy market.

20 [a]Dedan *was* thy merchant in [1]precious clothes for chariots.

21 Arabia, and all the princes of [a]Kedar, they [1]occupied with thee in lambs, and rams, and goats: in these *were they* thy merchants.

22 The merchants of [a]Sheba and Raamah, they *were* thy merchants: they [1]occupied in thy fairs with chief of all spices, and with [2]all precious stones, and gold.

23 ªHaran, and Canneh, and Eden, the merchants of ᵇSheba, ¹Asshur, *and* Chilmad, *were* thy merchants.

24 These *were* thy merchants in ¹all sorts *of things*, in ²blue clothes, and broidered work, and in chests of ³rich apparel, bound with ⁴cords, and made of cedar, among thy merchandise.

25 ªThe ships of Tarshish ¹did sing of thee in thy market: and thou ²wast replenished, and made very glorious ᵇin the midst of the seas.

26 Thy ¹rowers have brought thee into ²great waters: ªthe east wind hath broken thee in the midst of the seas.

27 Thy ªriches, and thy ¹fairs, thy merchandise, thy mariners, and thy pilots, thy ²calkers, and the ³occupiers of thy merchandise, and all thy men of war, that *are* in thee, and in all thy company which *is* in the midst of thee, shall fall into the midst of the seas in the day of thy ruin.

28 The ªsuburbs¹ shall shake at the sound of the cry of thy pilots.

29 And ªall that handle the oar, the mariners, *and* all the pilots of the sea, shall come down from their ships, they shall stand upon the ¹land;

30 And shall cause their voice to be heard ¹against thee, and shall cry bitterly, and shall ªcast up dust upon their heads, they ᵇshall wallow themselves in the ashes:

31 And they shall ªmake themselves utterly bald for thee, and gird them with sackcloth, and they shall weep for thee with bitterness of heart *and* bitter wailing.

32 And in their wailing they shall ªtake up a lamentation for thee, and lament over thee, *saying*, ᵇWhat *city is* like Tyrus, like the destroyed in the midst of the sea?

33 ªWhen thy wares went forth ¹out of the seas, thou filledst many people; thou didst enrich the kings of the earth with the multitude of thy riches and of thy merchandise.

34 In the time *when* ªthou shalt be broken by the seas in the depths of the waters ᵇthy merchandise and all thy company in the midst of thee shall fall.

35 ªAll the inhabitants of the isles shall be astonished at thee, and their kings shall be sore afraid, they shall be troubled in *their* countenance.

36 The merchants among the people ªshall hiss at thee; ᵇthou shalt be a ¹terror, and never *shalt be* any ᶜmore.

## CHAPTER 28

THE word of the LORD came again unto me, saying,

2 Son of man, say unto the prince

---

27:23 ª 2 Kin.
19:12 ᵇ Gen. 25:3
¹ Assyria

27:24 ¹ choice
things ² purple
³ multicoloured
⁴ strong twined
cords in your
marketplace

27:25 ª Is. 2:16
ᵇ Ezek. 27:4
¹ were carriers of
your merchandise
² were filled

27:26 ª Ps. 48:7
¹ oarsmen ² many

27:27 ª [Prov. 11:4]
¹ wares ² caulkers
³ dealers in

27:28 ª Ezek. 26:15
¹ common-lands
or pasturelands

27:29 ª Rev. 18:17
¹ shore

27:30 ª Rev.
18:19 ᵇ Jer. 6:26
¹ because of

27:31 ª Ezek. 29:18

27:32 ª Ezek. 26:17
ᵇ Rev. 18:18

27:33 ª Rev. 18:19
¹ by sea

27:34 ª Ezek.
26:19 ᵇ Ezek.
27:27

27:35 ª Ezek.
26:15, 16

27:36 ª Jer. 18:16
ᵇ Ezek. 26:2 ¹ Ps.
37:10, 36 ¹ horror

28:2 ª Jer. 49:16
ᵇ Ezek. 28:9
ᶜ Ezek. 27:3, 4
ᵈ Is. 31:3 ¹ Proud
² a god ³ gods

28:3 ª Dan. 1:20;
2:20–23, 28;
5:11, 12

28:4 ª Zech. 9:1–3

28:5 ª Ps. 62:10
¹ in trade

28:6 ¹ a god

28:7 ª Ezek. 26:7
ᵇ Ezek. 7:24; 21:31;
30:11 ¹ most terrible ² splendour

28:8 ª Is. 14:15

28:9 ª Ezek. 28:2
¹ a god

28:10 ª Ezek.
31:18; 32:19, 21,
25, 27

28:12 ª Ezek. 27:2
ᵇ Ezek. 27:3; 28:3
¹ were the seal of
perfection

28:13 ª Ezek. 31:8,
9; 36:35 ᵇ Ezek.
26:13 ¹ ruby ² turquoise ³ timbrels

28:14 ª Ex. 25:20
ᵇ Ezek. 20:40

28:15 ª [Is. 14:19]

28:16 ¹ trading

---

of Tyrus, Thus saith the Lord GOD; Because thine heart *is* ªlifted¹ up, and ᵇthou hast said, I *am* ²a God, I sit *in* the seat of ³God, ᶜin the midst of the seas; ᵈyet thou *art* a man, and not ²God, though thou set thine heart as the heart of ²God:

3 Behold, ªthou *art* wiser than Daniel; there is no secret that they can hide from thee:

4 With thy wisdom and with thine understanding thou hast gotten thee ªriches, and hast gotten gold and silver into thy treasures:

5 ªBy thy great wisdom ¹*and* by thy traffick hast thou increased thy riches, and thine heart is lifted up because of thy riches:

6 Therefore thus saith the Lord GOD; Because thou hast set thine heart as the heart of ¹God;

7 Behold, therefore I will bring ªstrangers upon thee, ᵇthe ¹terrible of the nations: and they shall draw their swords against the beauty of thy wisdom, and they shall defile thy ²brightness.

8 They shall bring thee down to the ªpit, and thou shalt die the deaths of *them that are* slain in the midst of the seas.

9 Wilt thou yet ªsay before him that slayeth thee, I *am* ¹God? but thou *shalt be* a man, and no God, in the hand of him that slayeth thee.

10 Thou shalt die the deaths of ªthe uncircumcised by the hand of strangers: for I have spoken *it*, saith the Lord GOD.

11 Moreover the word of the LORD came unto me, saying,

12 Son of man, ªtake up a lamentation upon the king of Tyrus, and say unto him, Thus saith the Lord GOD; ᵇThou ¹sealest up the sum, full of wisdom, and perfect in beauty.

13 Thou hast been in ªEden the garden of God; every precious stone *was* thy covering, the ¹sardius, topaz, and the diamond, the beryl, the onyx, and the jasper, the sapphire, the emerald, and the ²carbuncle, and gold: the workmanship of ᵇthy ³tabrets and of thy pipes was prepared in thee in the day that thou wast created.

14 Thou *art* the anointed ªcherub that covereth; and I have set thee *so:* thou wast upon ᵇthe holy mountain of God; thou hast walked up and down in the midst of the stones of fire.

15 Thou *wast* perfect in thy ways from the day that thou wast created, till ªiniquity was found in thee.

16 By the multitude of thy ¹merchandise they have filled the midst of thee with violence, and thou hast sinned: therefore I will cast thee as profane out of the mountain of God:

and I will destroy thee, [a]O covering cherub, from the midst of the stones of fire.

17 [a]Thine heart was [1]lifted up because of thy beauty, thou hast corrupted thy wisdom by reason of thy [2]brightness: I will cast thee to the ground, I will lay thee before kings, that they may behold thee.

18 Thou hast defiled thy sanctuaries by the multitude of thine iniquities, by the iniquity of thy [1]traffick; therefore will I bring forth a fire from the midst of thee, it shall devour thee, and I will [2]bring thee to ashes upon the earth in the sight of all them that behold thee.

19 All they that know thee among the people shall be astonished at thee: [a]thou shalt be a [1]terror, and never [shalt] thou [be] any [b]more.

20 Again the word of the LORD came unto me, saying,

21 Son of man, [a]set thy face [b]against[1] [2]Zidon, and prophesy against it,

22 And say, Thus saith the Lord GOD; [a]Behold, I [am] against thee, O Zidon; and I will be glorified in the midst of thee: and [b]they shall know that I [am] the LORD, when I shall have executed judgments in her, and shall be [c]sanctified[1] in her.

23 [a]For I will send into her pestilence, and blood into her streets; and the wounded shall be judged in the midst of her by the sword upon her on every side; and they shall know that I [am] the LORD.

24 And there shall be no more [a]a pricking brier unto the house of Israel, nor [any] [1]grieving thorn of all [that are] round about them, that [b]despised them; and they shall know that I [am] the Lord GOD.

25 Thus saith the Lord GOD; When I shall have [a]gathered the house of Israel from the people among whom they are scattered, and shall be [b]sanctified[1] in them in the sight of the [2]heathen, then shall they dwell in their land that I have given to my servant Jacob.

26 And they shall [a]dwell [1]safely therein, and shall [b]build houses, and [c]plant vineyards; yea, they shall dwell [1]with confidence, when I have executed judgments upon all those that despise them round about them; and they shall know that I [am] the LORD their God.

## CHAPTER 29

IN the tenth year, in the tenth [month,] in the twelfth [day] of the month, the word of the LORD came unto me, saying,

2 Son of man, [a]set thy face against Pharaoh king of Egypt, and prophesy against him, and [b]against all Egypt:

3 Speak, and say, Thus saith the Lord GOD; [a]Behold, I [am] against thee, Pharaoh king of Egypt, the great [b]dragon[1] that lieth in the midst of his rivers, [c]which hath said, [2]My river [is] mine own, and I have made [it] for myself.

4 But [a]I will put hooks in thy jaws, and I will cause the fish of thy rivers to stick unto thy scales, and I will bring thee up out of the midst of thy rivers, and all the fish of thy rivers shall stick unto thy scales.

5 And I will leave thee [thrown] into the wilderness, thee and all the fish of thy rivers: thou shalt fall upon the open [a]fields; [b]thou shalt not be [1]brought together, nor gathered: [c]I have given thee for [2]meat to the beasts of the field and to the fowls of the heaven.

6 And all the inhabitants of Egypt shall know that I [am] the LORD, because they have been a [a]staff of reed to the house of Israel.

7 [a]When they took hold of thee by thy hand, thou didst break, and [1]rend all their shoulder: and when they leaned upon thee, thou brakest, and madest all their loins [2]to be at a stand.

8 Therefore thus saith the Lord GOD; Behold, I will bring [a]a sword upon thee, and cut off man and beast [1]out of thee.

9 And the land of Egypt shall be [a]desolate and waste; and they shall know that I [am] the LORD: because he hath said, The river [is] mine, and I have made [it.]

10 Behold, therefore I [am] against thee, and against thy rivers, [a]and I will make the land of Egypt utterly waste [and] desolate, [b]from [1]the tower [2]of Syene even unto the border of Ethiopia.

11 [a]No foot of man shall pass through it, nor foot of beast shall pass through it, neither shall it be inhabited forty years.

12 [a]And I will make the land of Egypt desolate in the midst of the countries [that are] desolate, and her cities among the cities [that are] laid waste shall be desolate forty years: and I will [b]scatter the Egyptians among the nations, and will disperse them through the countries.

13 Yet thus saith the Lord GOD; At the [a]end of forty years will I gather the Egyptians from the people whither they were scattered:

14 And I will bring again the [1]captivity of Egypt, and will cause them to return [into] the land of Pathros, into the land of their [2]habitation; and they shall be there a [a]base[3] kingdom.

15 It shall be the [1]basest of the kingdoms; neither shall it exalt itself any

more above the nations: for I will diminish them, that they shall no more rule over the nations.

16 And it shall be no more [a]the confidence of the house of Israel, [1]which bringeth *their* iniquity to remembrance, when they [2]shall look after them: but they shall know that I *am* the Lord GOD.

17 And it came to pass in the seven and twentieth year, in the first *month,* in the first *day* of the month, the word of the LORD came unto me, saying,

18 Son of man, [a]Nebuchadrezzar[1] king of Babylon caused his army to [2]serve a great service against [3]Tyrus: every head *was* made [b]bald, and every shoulder *was* [4]peeled: yet had he no wages, nor his army, [5]for Tyrus, for the [6]service that he had served against it:

19 Therefore thus saith the Lord GOD; Behold, I will give the land of Egypt unto [a]Nebuchadrezzar king of Babylon; and he shall take her [1]multitude, and [2]take her spoil, and [3]take her prey; and it shall be the wages for his army.

20 I have given him the land of Egypt *for* his labour wherewith he [a]served against it, because they wrought for me, saith the Lord GOD.

21 In that day [a]will I cause the [1]horn of the house of Israel to bud forth, and I will give thee [b]the opening of the mouth in the midst of them; and they shall know that I *am* the LORD.

### CHAPTER 30

THE word of the LORD came again unto me, saying,

2 Son of man, prophesy and say, Thus saith the Lord GOD; [a]Howl[1] ye, Woe [2]worth the day!

3 For [a]the day *is* near, even the day of the LORD *is* near, a cloudy day; it shall be the time of the [1]heathen.

4 And the sword shall come upon Egypt, and great [1]pain shall be in [2]Ethiopia, when the slain shall fall in Egypt, and they [a]shall take away her [3]multitude, and [b]her foundations shall be broken down.

5 [1]Ethiopia, and [2]Libya, and [3]Lydia, and [a]all the mingled people, and Chub, and the men of the land that is in league, shall fall with them by the sword.

6 Thus saith the LORD; They also that uphold Egypt shall fall; and the pride of her power shall come down: [a]from [1]the tower of Syene shall they fall in it by the sword, saith the Lord GOD.

7 [a]And they shall be desolate in the midst of the countries *that are* desolate, and her cities shall be in the midst of the cities *that are* [1]wasted.

8 And they shall know that I *am* the LORD, when I have set a fire in Egypt, and *when* all her helpers shall be destroyed.

9 In that day [a]shall messengers go forth from me in ships to make the [1]careless Ethiopians afraid, and great [2]pain shall come upon them, as in the day of Egypt: for, lo, it cometh.

10 Thus saith the Lord GOD; [a]I will also make the multitude of Egypt to cease by the hand of [1]Nebuchadrezzar king of Babylon.

11 He and his people with him, [a]the [1]terrible of the nations, shall be brought to destroy the land: and they shall draw their swords against Egypt, and fill the land with the slain.

12 And [a]I will make the rivers dry, and [b]sell the land into the hand of the wicked: and I will make the land [1]waste, and all that is therein, by the hand of strangers: I the LORD have spoken *it.*

13 Thus saith the Lord GOD; I will also [a]destroy the idols, and I will cause *their* images to cease out of [1]Noph; [b]and there shall be no more a prince of the land of Egypt: [c]and I will put a fear in the land of Egypt.

14 And I will make [a]Pathros desolate, and will set fire in [b]Zoan,[1] [c]and will execute judgments in [2]No.

15 And I will pour my fury upon [1]Sin, the strength of Egypt; and [a]I will [2]cut off the multitude of [3]No.

16 And I will [a]set fire in Egypt: [1]Sin shall have great [2]pain, and [3]No shall be [4]rent asunder, and [5]Noph *shall have* distresses daily.

17 The young men of [1]Aven and of Pi-beseth shall fall by the sword: and these *cities* shall go into captivity.

18 [a]At [1]Tehaphnehes also the day shall be darkened, when I shall break there the yokes of Egypt: and the [2]pomp of her strength shall cease in her: as for her, a cloud shall cover her, and her daughters shall go into captivity.

19 Thus will I [a]execute judgments in Egypt: and they shall know that I *am* the LORD.

20 And it came to pass in the eleventh year, in the first *month,* in the seventh *day* of the month, *that* the word of the LORD came unto me, saying,

21 Son of man, I have [a]broken the arm of Pharaoh king of Egypt; and, lo, [b]it shall not be bound up to be healed, [1]to put a roller to bind it, to make it strong to hold the sword.

22 Therefore thus saith the Lord GOD; Behold, I *am* [a]against Pharaoh king of Egypt, and will [b]break his arms, the strong, and that which was broken; and I will cause the sword to fall out of his hand.

29:16 [a] Is. 30:2, 3; 36:4, 6 [1] *but shall* [2] *turned to follow them*

29:18 [a] Jer. 25:9; 27:6 [b] Ezek. 27:31 [1] Or *Nebuchadnezzar* [2] *labour strenuously* [3] Tyre [4] *rubbed raw* [5] *from* [6] *labour he had expended*

29:19 [a] Jer. 43:10–13 [1] *wealth* [2] *carry off her plunder* [3] *pillage her booty*

29:20 [a] Jer. 25:9

29:21 [a] Ps. 92:10; 132:17 [b] Ezek. 24:27 [1] *Strength*

30:2 [a] Is. 13:6; 15:2 [1] *Wail* [2] *to*

30:3 [a] Joel 2:1 [1] *Gentiles*

30:4 [a] Ezek. 29:19 [b] Jer. 50:15 [1] *anguish* [2] Heb. *Cush* [3] *wealth*

30:5 [a] Jer. 25:20, 24 [1] Heb. *Cush* [2] Heb. *Put* [3] Heb. *Lud*

30:6 [a] Ezek. 29:10 [1] *Migdol to*

30:7 [a] Ezek. 29:12 [1] *laid waste*

30:9 [a] Is. 18:1, 2 [1] *secure* [2] *anguish*

30:10 [a] Ezek. 29:19 [1] Or *Nebuchadnezzar*

30:11 [a] Ezek. 28:7; 31:12 [1] *most terrible*

30:12 [a] Is. 19:5, 6 [b] Is. 19:4 [1] *desolate*

30:13 [a] Is. 19:1 [b] Zech. 10:11 [c] Is. 19:16 [1] *Ancient Memphis*

30:14 [a] Ezek. 29:14 [b] Ps. 78:12, 43 [c] Nah. 3:8–10 [1] Or *Tanis* [2] Ancient Thebes

30:15 [a] Jer. 46:25 [1] Ancient Pelusium [2] *destroy* [3] Ancient Thebes

30:16 [a] Ezek. 30:8 [1] Pelusium [2] *anguish* [3] Thebes [4] *torn open* [5] Memphis

30:17 [1] Ancient On, Heliopolis

30:18 [a] Jer. 2:16 [1] Tahpanhes, Jer. 43:7 [2] *pride*

30:19 [a] [Ps. 9:16]

30:21 [a] Jer. 48:25 [b] Jer. 46:11 [1] *nor a splint put on*

30:22 [a] Jer. 46:25 [b] Ps. 37:17

23 ᵃAnd I will scatter the Egyptians among the nations, and will disperse them through the countries.

24 And I will strengthen the arms of the king of Babylon, and put my sword in his hand: but I will break Pharaoh's arms, and he shall groan before him with the groanings of a ¹deadly wounded *man.*

25 But I will strengthen the arms of the king of Babylon, and the arms of Pharaoh shall fall down; and ᵃthey shall know that I *am* the LORD, when I shall put my sword into the hand of the king of Babylon, and he shall stretch it out upon the land of Egypt.

26 ᵃAnd I will scatter the Egyptians among the nations, and disperse them among the countries; and they shall know that I *am* the LORD.

## CHAPTER 31

A ND it came to pass in the ᵃeleventh year, in the third *month,* in the first *day* of the month, *that* the word of the LORD came unto me, saying,

2 Son of man, speak unto Pharaoh king of Egypt, and to his multitude; ᵃWhom art thou like in thy greatness?

3 ᵃBehold, the Assyrian *was* a cedar in Lebanon with ¹fair branches, and with ²a shadowing shroud, and of an high stature; and his top was among the thick boughs.

4 ᵃThe waters made ¹him great, the ²deep set him up on high with her rivers running round about ³his plants, and sent out her ⁴little rivers unto all the trees of the field.

5 Therefore ᵃhis height was exalted above all the trees of the field, and his boughs were multiplied, and his branches became long because of the multitude of waters, ¹when he shot forth.

6 All the ᵃfowls¹ of heaven made their nests in his boughs, and under his branches did all the beasts of the field bring forth their young, and under his shadow dwelt all great nations.

7 Thus was he ¹fair in his greatness, in the length of his branches: for his root ²was by great waters.

8 The cedars in the ᵃgarden of God could not hide him: the fir trees were not like his boughs, and the ¹chesnut trees were not like his branches; nor any tree in the garden of God was like unto him in his beauty.

9 I have made him ¹fair by the multitude of his branches: so that all the trees of Eden, that *were* in the garden of God, envied him.

10 Therefore thus saith the Lord GOD; Because thou hast ¹lifted up thyself in height, and he hath shot up his top among the thick boughs, and ᵃhis heart is ²lifted up in his height;

11 I have therefore delivered him into the hand of the ᵃmighty one of the ¹heathen; he shall surely deal with him: I have driven him out for his wickedness.

12 And strangers, ᵃthe ¹terrible of the nations, have cut him ²off, and have left him: ᵇupon the mountains and in all the valleys his branches are fallen, and his boughs are ᶜbroken by all the rivers of the land; and all the people of the earth are gone down from his shadow, and have left him.

13 ᵃUpon his ruin shall all the fowls of the heaven remain, and all the beasts of the field shall ¹be upon his branches:

14 To the end that none of all the trees by the waters exalt themselves for their height, neither shoot up their top among the thick boughs, ¹neither their trees stand up in their height, all that drink water: for ᵃthey are all delivered unto death, ᵇto the ²nether parts of the earth, in the midst of the children of men, with them that go down to the pit.

15 Thus saith the Lord GOD; In the day when he ᵃwent down to ¹the grave I caused a mourning: I covered the deep for him, and I restrained the ²floods thereof, and the great waters were ³stayed: and I caused Lebanon to mourn for him, and all the trees of the field ⁴fainted for him.

16 I made the nations to ᵃshake at the sound of his fall, when I ᵇcast him down to ¹hell with them that descend into the pit: and ᶜall the trees of Eden, the choice and best of Lebanon, all that drink water, ᵈshall be comforted in the ²nether parts of the earth.

17 They also went down into hell with him unto *them that be* slain with the sword; and *they that were* his arm, *that* ᵃdwelt under his shadow in the midst of the ¹heathen.

18 ᵃTo whom art thou thus like in glory and in greatness among the trees of Eden? yet shalt thou be brought down with the trees of Eden unto the ¹nether parts of the earth: ᵇthou shalt lie in the midst of the uncircumcised with *them that be* slain by the sword. This is Pharaoh and all his multitude, saith the Lord GOD.

## CHAPTER 32

A ND it came to pass in the twelfth year, in the ᵃtwelfth month, in the first *day* of the month, *that* the word of the LORD came unto me, saying,

2 Son of man, ᵃtake up a lamentation for Pharaoh king of Egypt, and say unto him, ᵇThou art like a young lion of the nations, ᶜand thou *art* as a ¹whale in the seas: and thou ᵈcamest² forth with thy rivers, and troubledst

---

30:23 ᵃ Ezek. 29:12; 30:17, 18, 26
30:24 ¹ mortally
30:25 ᵃ Ps. 9:16
30:26 ᵃ Ezek. 29:12
31:1 ᵃ Ezek. 30:20; 32:1
31:2 ᵃ Ezek. 31:18
31:3 ᵃ Dan. 4:10, 20–23 ¹ beautiful ² forest shade
31:4 ᵃ Jer. 51:36 ¹ *it grow* ² underground waters gave it height ³ its planting place ⁴ rivulets
31:5 ᵃ Dan. 4:11 ¹ as it sent them out
31:6 ᵃ Dan. 4:12, 21 ¹ birds
31:7 ¹ beautiful ² reached to
31:8 ᵃ Gen. 2:8, 9; 13:10 ¹ Or plane trees, Heb. armon
31:9 ¹ beautiful
31:10 ᵃ Dan. 5:20 ¹ increased ² Proud

31:11 ᵃ Ezek. 30:10 ¹ nations
31:12 ᵃ Ezek. 28:7; 30:11; 32:12 ᵇ Ezek. 32:5; 35:8 ᶜ Ezek. 30:24, 25 ¹ most terrible ² down
31:13 ᵃ Is. 18:6 ¹ come to
31:14 ᵃ Ps. 82:7 ᵇ Ezek. 32:18 ¹ that no tree which drinks water may ever be high enough to reach up to them ² depths
31:15 ᵃ Ezek. 32:22, 23 ¹ Or Sheol, hell ² rivers ³ held back ⁴ wilted
31:16 ᵃ Ezek. 26:15 ᵇ Is. 14:15 ᶜ Is. 14:8 ᵈ Ezek. 32:31 ¹ Or Sheol ² depths
31:17 ᵃ Lam. 4:20 ¹ nations
31:18 ᵃ Ezek. 32:19 ᵇ Ezek. 28:10; 32:19, 21 ¹ depths
32:1 ᵃ Ezek. 31:1; 33:21
32:2 ᵃ Ezek. 27:2 ᵇ Ezek. 19:2–6 ᶜ Ezek. 29:3 ᵈ Jer. 46:7, 8 ¹ monster ² burst

---

the waters with thy feet, and ᵉfouledst their rivers.

3 Thus saith the Lord GOD; I will therefore ᵃspread out my net over thee with a company of many people; and they shall ¹bring thee up in my net.

4 Then ᵃwill I leave thee upon the land, I will cast thee forth upon the open field, and ᵇwill cause all the fowls of the heaven to ¹remain upon thee, and I will fill the beasts of the whole earth with thee.

5 And I will lay thy ¹flesh ᵃupon the mountains, and fill the valleys with thy height.

6 I will also water ¹with thy blood the land wherein thou swimmest, *even* to the mountains; and the rivers shall be full of thee.

7 And when I shall ¹put thee out, ᵃI will cover the heaven, and make the stars thereof dark; I will cover the sun with a cloud, and the moon shall not give her light.

8 All the bright lights of heaven will I make dark over thee, and set darkness upon thy land, saith the Lord GOD.

9 I will also ¹vex the hearts of many people, when I shall bring thy destruction among the nations, into the countries which thou hast not known.

10 Yea, I will make many people ¹amazed at thee, and their kings shall be horribly afraid for thee, when I shall brandish my sword before them; and ᵃthey shall tremble at *every* moment, every man for his own life, in the day of thy fall.

11 ᵃFor thus saith the Lord GOD; The sword of the king of Babylon shall come upon thee.

12 By the swords of the mighty will I cause thy multitude to fall, ᵃthe ¹terrible of the nations, all of them: and ᵇthey shall ²spoil the pomp of Egypt, and all the multitude thereof shall be destroyed.

13 I will destroy also all the beasts thereof from beside the great waters; ᵃneither shall the foot of man ¹trouble them any more, nor the hoofs of beasts ¹trouble them.

14 Then will I make their waters ¹deep, and cause their rivers to run like oil, saith the Lord GOD.

15 When I shall make the land of Egypt desolate, and the country shall be destitute of that whereof it was full, when I shall smite all them that dwell therein, ᵃthen shall they know that I *am* the LORD.

16 This *is* the ᵃlamentation wherewith they shall lament her: the daughters of the nations shall lament her: they shall lament for her, *even* for Egypt, and for all her multitude, saith the Lord GOD.

17 It came to pass also in the twelfth year, in the fifteenth *day* of the month, ᵃ*that* the word of the LORD came unto me, saying,

18 Son of man, wail for the multitude of Egypt, and ᵃcast them down, *even* her, and the daughters of the famous nations, unto the ¹nether parts of the earth, with them that go down into the pit.

19 ᵃWhom dost thou ¹pass in beauty? ᵇgo down, and be thou laid with the uncircumcised.

20 They shall fall in the midst of *them that are* slain by the sword: she is delivered to the sword: ᵃdraw her and all her multitudes.

21 ᵃThe strong among the mighty shall speak to him out of the midst of hell with them that help him: they are ᵇgone down, they ¹lie uncircumcised, slain by the sword.

22 ᵃAsshur¹ *is* there and all her company: his graves *are* about him: all of them slain, fallen by the sword:

23 ᵃWhose graves are set in the ¹sides of the pit, and her company is round about her grave: all of them slain, fallen by the sword, which ᵇcaused terror in the land of the living.

24 There *is* ᵃElam and all her multitude round about her grave, all of them slain, fallen by the sword, which are ᵇgone down uncircumcised into the ¹nether parts of the earth, ᶜwhich caused their terror in the land of the living; yet have they borne their shame with them that go down to the pit.

25 They have set her a ᵃbed in the midst of the slain with all her multitude: her graves *are* round about him: all of them uncircumcised, slain by the sword: though their terror was caused in the land of the living, yet have they borne their shame with them that go down to the pit: he is put in the midst of *them that be* slain.

26 There *is* ᵃMeshech, Tubal, and all her multitude: her graves *are* round about him: all of them ᵇuncircumcised, slain by the sword, though they caused their terror in the land of the living.

27 ᵃAnd they shall not lie with the mighty *that are* fallen of the uncircumcised, which are gone down to hell with their weapons of war: and they have laid their swords under their heads, but their iniquities shall be upon their bones, though *they were* the terror of the mighty in the land of the living.

28 Yea, thou shalt be broken in the midst of the uncircumcised, and shalt lie with *them that are* slain with the sword.

29 There *is* ᵃEdom, her kings, and all her princes, which ¹with their might

---

**Cross-references (center column):**

32:2 ᵉ Ezek. 34:18

32:3 ᵃ Ezek. 12:13; 17:20 ¹ *draw*

32:4 ᵃ Ezek. 29:5 ᵇ Is. 18:6; Ezek. 31:13 ¹ Lit. *dwell*

32:5 ᵃ Ezek. 31:12 ¹ *carcase*

32:6 ¹ Or *the land with the flow of your blood, even to*

32:7 ᵃ Rev. 6:12, 13; 8:12 ¹ *put out thy light*

32:9 ¹ *trouble*

32:10 ᵃ Ezek. 26:16 ¹ *astonished*

32:11 ᵃ Jer. 46:26

32:12 ᵃ Ezek. 28:7; 30:11; 31:12 ᵇ Ezek. 29:19 ¹ *most terrible* ² *plunder*

32:13 ᵃ Ezek. 29:11 ¹ *muddy*

32:14 ¹ *settle* or *become clear*

32:15 ¹ Ps. 9:16

32:16 ᵃ Ezek. 26:17

32:17 ᵃ Ezek. 32:1; 33:21

32:18 ᵃ Ezek. 26:20; 31:14 ¹ *depths*

32:19 ᵃ Ezek. 31:2, 18 ᵇ Ezek. 28:10 ¹ *surpass*

32:20 ᵃ Ps. 28:3

32:21 ᵃ Is. 1:31; 14:9, 10 ᵇ Ezek. 32:19, 25 ¹ *lie with the*

32:22 ᵃ Ezek. 31:3, 16 ¹ *Assyria*

32:23 ᵃ Is. 14:15 ᵇ Ezek. 32:24–27, 32 ¹ *recesses*

32:24 ᵃ Gen. 10:22; 14:1; Is. 11:11; Jer. 25:25; 49:34–39 ᵇ Ezek. 32:21 ᶜ Ezek. 32:23 ¹ *lower*

32:25 ᵃ Ps. 139:8

32:26 ᵃ Gen. 10:2; Ezek. 27:13; 38:2, 3; 39:1 ᵇ Ezek. 32:19

32:27 ᵃ Is. 14:18, 19

32:29 ᵃ Is. 34:5, 6; Jer. 9:25, 26; 49:7–22; Ezek. 25:12–14 ¹ *despite*

are laid [2]by *them that were* slain by the sword: they shall lie with the uncircumcised, and with them that go down to the pit.

30 [a]There *be* the princes of the north, all of them, and all the [b]Zidonians,[1] which are gone down with the slain; [2]with their terror they are ashamed of their might; and they lie uncircumcised with *them that be* slain by the sword, and bear their shame with them that go down to the pit.

31 Pharaoh shall see them, and shall be [a]comforted over all his multitude, *even* Pharaoh and all his army slain by the sword, saith the Lord GOD.

32 For I have caused my terror in the land of the living: and he shall be laid in the midst of the uncircumcised with *them that are* slain with the sword, *even* Pharaoh and all his multitude, saith the Lord GOD.

## CHAPTER 33

AGAIN the word of the LORD came unto me, saying,

2 Son of man, speak to [a]the children of thy people, and say unto them, [b]When I bring the sword upon a land, if the people of the land take a man of their [1]coasts, and set him for their [c]watchman:

3 If when he seeth the sword come upon the land, he blow the trumpet, and warn the people;

4 Then whosoever heareth the sound of the trumpet, and taketh [a]not warning; if the sword come, and take him away, [b]his blood shall be upon his own head.

5 He heard the sound of the trumpet, and took not warning; his blood shall be upon him. But he that taketh warning shall [1]deliver his soul.

6 But if the watchman see the sword come, and blow not the trumpet, and the people be not warned; if the sword come, and take *any* person from among them, [a]he is taken away in his iniquity; but his blood will I require at the watchman's hand.

7 [a]So thou, O son of man, I have set thee a watchman unto the house of Israel; therefore thou shalt hear the word at my mouth, and warn them from me.

8 When I say unto the wicked, O wicked *man,* thou shalt surely die; if thou dost not speak to warn the wicked from his way, that wicked *man* shall die in his iniquity; but his blood will I require at thine hand.

9 Nevertheless, if thou warn the wicked of his way to turn from it; if he do not turn from his way, he shall die in his iniquity; but thou hast [1]delivered thy soul.

10 Therefore, O thou son of man, speak unto the house of Israel; Thus ye speak, saying, If our transgressions and our sins *be* upon us, and we [a]pine[1] away in them, [b]how should we then live?

11 Say unto them, *As* I live, saith the Lord GOD, [a]I have no pleasure in the death of the wicked; but that the wicked [b]turn from his way and live: turn ye, turn ye from your evil ways; for [c]why will ye die, O house of Israel?

12 Therefore, thou son of man, say unto the children of thy people, The [a]righteousness of the righteous shall not deliver him in the day of his transgression: as for the wickedness of the wicked, [b]he shall not fall thereby in the day that he turneth from his wickedness; neither shall the righteous be able to live for his *righteousness* in the day that he sinneth.

13 When I shall say to the righteous, *that* he shall surely live; [a]if he trust to his own righteousness, and commit iniquity, all his righteousnesses shall not be remembered; but for his iniquity that he hath committed, he shall die for it.

14 Again, [a]when I say unto the wicked, Thou shalt surely die; if he turn from his sin, and do that which is lawful and right;

15 *If* the wicked [a]restore the pledge, [b]give[1] again that he had robbed, walk in [c]the statutes of life, without committing iniquity; he shall surely live, he shall not die.

16 [a]None of his sins that he hath committed shall be [1]mentioned unto him: he hath done that which is lawful and right; he shall surely live.

17 [a]Yet the children of thy people say, The way of the Lord is not [1]equal: but as for them, their way is not [1]equal.

18 [a]When the righteous turneth from his righteousness, and committeth iniquity, he shall even die thereby.

19 But if the wicked turn from his wickedness, and do that which is lawful and right, he shall live thereby.

20 Yet ye say, [a]The way of the Lord is not [1]equal. O ye house of Israel, I will judge you every one [2]after his ways.

21 And it came to pass in the twelfth year [a]of our captivity, in the tenth *month,* in the fifth *day* of the month, [b]*that* one that had escaped out of Jerusalem came unto me, saying, [c]The city [1]is smitten.

22 Now [a]the hand of the LORD was upon me in the evening, [1]afore he that was escaped came; and had [b]opened my mouth, until he came to me in the morning; and my mouth was opened, and I was [2]no more dumb.

23 Then the word of the LORD came unto me, saying,

---

### Center reference column

32:29 [2] *beside*

32:30 [a] Jer. 1:15; 25:26; Ezek. 38:6, 15; 39:2　[b] Jer. 25:22; Ezek. 28:21–23　[1] Or *Sidonians* [2] *in shame at the terror which they caused by their might*

32:31 [a] Ezek. 14:22; 31:16

33:2 [a] Ezek. 3:11 [b] Ezek. 14:17 [c] 2 Sam. 18:24, 25; 2 Kin. 9:17; Hos. 9:8　[1] *territory*

33:4 [a] 2 Chr. 25:16; Jer. 6:17; Zech. 1:4　[b] Ezek. 18:13; 35:9; [Acts 18:6]

33:5 [1] *save his life*

33:6 [a] Ezek. 33:8

33:7 [a] Is. 62:6; Ezek. 3:17–21

33:9 [1] Or *saved thy life*

33:10 [a] Lev. 26:39; Ezek. 24:23　[b] Is. 49:14; Ezek. 37:11 [1] Or *waste away*

33:11 [a] [2 Sam. 14:14; Lam. 3:33]; Ezek. 18:23, 32; Hos. 11:8; [2 Pet. 3:9]　[b] Ezek. 18:21, 30; [Hos. 14:1, 4; Acts 3:19]　[c] [Is. 55:6, 7]; Jer. 3:22; Ezek. 18:30, 31; Hos. 14:1; [Acts 3:19]

33:12 [a] Ezek. 3:20; 18:24, 26　[b] [2 Chr. 7:14]; Ezek. 18:21; 33:19

33:13 [a] Ezek. 3:20; 18:24

33:14 [a] Ezek. 3:18, 19; 18:27

33:15 [a] Ezek. 18:7 [b] Lev. 6:2, 4, 5 [c] Ezek. 20:11, 13, 21 [1] *give back what he*

33:16 [a] [Is. 1:18; 43:25] [1] *remembered against*

33:17 [a] Ezek. 18:25, 29 [1] *fair*

33:18 [a] Ezek. 18:26

33:20 [a] Ezek. 18:25, 29 [1] *fair* [2] *according to*

33:21 [a] Ezek. 1:2 [b] Ezek. 24:26 [c] 2 Kin. 25:4 [1] *has been captured*

33:22 [a] Ezek. 1:3; 8:1; 37:1　[b] Ezek. 24:27 [1] *before* [2] *no longer mute*

24 Son of man, [a]they that inhabit
those [b]wastes[1] of the land of Israel
speak, saying, [c]Abraham was one,
and he inherited the land: [d]but we
*are* many; the land is given us for [e]in-
heritance.[2]
25 Wherefore say unto them, Thus
saith the Lord GOD; [a]Ye [1]eat with the
blood, and [b]lift up your eyes toward
your idols, and [c]shed blood: and shall
ye possess the [d]land?
26 Ye [1]stand upon your sword, ye
work abomination, and ye [a]defile
every one his neighbour's wife: and
shall ye possess the land?
27 Say thou thus unto them, Thus
saith the Lord GOD; *As* I live, surely
[a]they that *are* in the [1]wastes shall fall
by the sword, and him that *is* in the
open field [b]will I give to the beasts to
be devoured, and they that *be* in the
forts and [c]in the caves shall die of the
pestilence.
28 [a]For I will [1]lay the land most desolate, and the [b]pomp[2] of her strength
shall cease; and [c]the mountains of Israel shall be desolate, that none shall
pass through.
29 Then shall they know that I *am*
the LORD, when I have laid the land
most desolate because of all their
abominations which they have committed.
30 Also, thou son of man, the children of thy people still are talking
[1]against thee by the walls and in the
doors of the houses, and [a]speak one
to another, every one to his brother,
saying, Come, I pray you, and hear
what is the word that cometh forth
from the LORD.
31 And [a]they come unto thee [1]as the
people cometh, and they [b]sit before
thee *as* my people, and they [c]hear thy
words, but they will not do them: [d]for
with their mouth they shew much
love, *but* [e]their heart goeth after their
covetousness.
32 And, lo, thou *art* unto them as
a very lovely song of one that hath
a pleasant voice, and can play well
on an instrument: for they hear thy
words, but they do them [a]not.
33 [a]And when this cometh to pass,
(lo, it will come,) then [b]shall they
know that a prophet hath been among
them.

## CHAPTER 34

AND the word of the LORD came
unto me, saying,
2 Son of man, prophesy against the
shepherds of Israel, prophesy, and
say unto them, Thus saith the Lord
GOD unto the shepherds; [a]Woe *be* to
the shepherds of Israel that do feed
themselves! should not the shepherds feed the flocks?
3 [a]Ye eat the fat, and ye clothe you
with the wool, ye [b]kill them that are
[1]fed: *but* ye feed not the flock.
4 [a]The [1]diseased have ye not
strengthened, neither have ye healed
that which was sick, neither have ye
bound up *that which was* broken,
neither have ye brought again that
which was driven away, neither have
ye [b]sought that which was lost; but
with [c]force and with [2]cruelty have ye
ruled them.
5 [a]And they were [b]scattered, because *there is* no shepherd: [c]and they
became [1]meat to all the beasts of the
field, when they were scattered.
6 My sheep [a]wandered through all
the mountains, and upon every high
hill: yea, my flock was scattered upon
all the face of the earth, and none did
search or seek *after them.*
7 Therefore, ye shepherds, hear the
word of the LORD;
8 *As* I live, saith the Lord GOD,
surely because my flock became a
prey, and my flock [a]became [1]meat to
every beast of the field, because *there
was* no shepherd, neither did my
shepherds search for my flock, [b]but
the shepherds fed themselves, and
fed not my flock;
9 Therefore, O ye shepherds, hear
the word of the LORD;
10 Thus saith the Lord GOD; Behold,
I *am* [a]against the shepherds; and [b]I
will require my flock at their hand,
and cause them to cease from feeding the [1]flock; neither shall the shepherds [c]feed themselves any more;
for I will [d]deliver my flock from their
mouth, that they may not be [2]meat
for them.
11 For thus saith the Lord GOD; Behold, I, *even* I, will both search my
sheep, and seek them out.
12 As a [a]shepherd seeketh out his
flock in the day that he is among his
sheep *that are* scattered; so will I
seek out my sheep, and will deliver
them out of all places where they
have been scattered in [b]the cloudy
and dark day.
13 And [a]I will bring them out from
the people, and gather them from
the countries, and will bring them to
their own land, and feed them upon
the mountains of Israel by the [1]rivers,
and in all the inhabited places of the
country.
14 [a]I will feed them in a good pasture, and upon the high mountains
of Israel shall their fold be: [b]there
shall they lie in a good fold, and *in* a
[1]fat pasture shall they feed upon the
mountains of Israel.
15 I will feed my flock, and I will
cause them to lie down, saith the
Lord GOD.
16 [a]I will seek that which was lost,
and bring again that which was driven

33:24 [a] Ezek. 34:2 [b] Ezek. 36:4 [c] Is. 51:2 [d] [Matt. 3:9] [e] Ezek. 11:15 [1] *ruins* [2] *a possession*
33:25 [a] Lev. 3:17; 7:26; 17:10–14; 19:26 [b] Ezek. 18:6 [c] Ezek. 22:6, 9 [d] Deut. 29:28 [1] *eat meat*
33:26 [a] Ezek. 18:6; 22:11 [1] *rely*
33:27 [a] Ezek. 33:24 [b] Ezek. 39:4 [c] 1 Sam. 13:6 [1] *ruins*
33:28 [a] Jer. 44:2, 6, 22 [b] Ezek. 7:24; 24:21 [c] Ezek. 6:2, 3, 6 [1] *make* [2] *pride*
33:30 [a] Is. 29:13 [1] *about*
33:31 [a] Ezek. 14:1 [b] Ezek. 8:1 [c] Is. 58:2 [d] Ps. 78:36, 37 [e] [Matt. 13:22] [1] *as people do*
33:32 [a] [Matt. 7:21–28]
33:33 [a] 1 Sam. 3:20 [b] Ezek. 2:5
34:2 [a] Zech. 11:17
34:3 [a] Zech. 11:16 [b] Ezek. 33:25, 26 [1] *fatlings*
34:4 [a] Zech. 11:16 [b] Luke 15:4 [c] [1 Pet. 5:3] [1] *weak* [2] *harshness*
34:5 [a] Ezek. 33:21 [b] Matt. 9:36 [c] Is. 56:9 [1] *food for*
34:6 [a] 1 Pet. 2:25
34:8 [a] Ezek. 34:5, 6 [b] Ezek. 34:2, 10 [1] *food for*
34:10 [a] Jer. 21:13; 52:24–27 [b] Heb. 13:17 [c] Ezek. 34:2, 8 [d] Ezek. 13:23 [1] *sheep* [2] *food*
34:12 [a] Jer. 31:10 [b] Ezek. 30:3
34:13 [a] Jer. 23:3 [1] *streams*
34:14 [a] [John 10:9] [b] Jer. 33:12 [1] *rich*
34:16 [a] Mic. 4:6

away, and will bind up *that which*
*was* broken, and will strengthen that
which was sick: but I will destroy [b]the
fat and the strong; I will feed them
[c]with [1]judgment.
17 And *as for* you, O my flock, thus
saith the Lord GOD; [a]Behold, I judge
between [1]cattle and cattle, between
the rams and the [2]he goats.
18 *Seemeth it* a small thing unto
you to have eaten up the good pasture, but ye must [1]tread down with
your feet the [2]residue of your pastures? and to have drunk of the deep
waters, but ye must foul the residue
with your feet?
19 And *as for* my flock, they eat that
which ye have [1]trodden with your
feet; and they drink that which ye
have fouled with your feet.
20 Therefore thus saith the Lord
GOD unto them; [a]Behold, I, *even* I,
will judge between the fat [1]cattle and
between the lean [1]cattle.
21 Because ye have [1]thrust with
side and with shoulder, and [2]pushed
all the [3]diseased with your horns, till
ye have scattered them abroad;
22 Therefore will I save my flock,
and they shall no more be a prey; and
I will judge between [1]cattle and cattle.
23 And I will set up one [a]shepherd
over them, and he shall feed them,
[b]*even* my servant David; he shall feed
them, and he shall be their shepherd.
24 And [a]I the LORD will be their
God, and my servant David [b]a prince
among them; I the LORD have spoken *it*.
25 And [a]I will make with them a
covenant of peace, and [b]will cause
the [1]evil beasts to cease out of the
land: and they [c]shall dwell safely
in the wilderness, and sleep in the
woods.
26 And I will make them and the
places round about [a]my hill [b]a blessing; and I will [c]cause the shower to
come down in his season; there shall
be [d]showers of blessing.
27 And [a]the tree of the field shall
yield her fruit, and the earth shall
yield her increase, and they shall be
safe in their land, and shall know that
I *am* the LORD, when I have [b]broken
the bands of their yoke, and delivered
them out of the hand of those that
[c]served[1] themselves of them.
28 And they shall no more be a
prey [1]to the heathen, neither shall
the beast of the land devour them;
but [a]they shall dwell safely, and none
shall make *them* afraid.
29 And I will raise up for them a
[a]plant[1] of renown, and they shall [b]be
no more [2]consumed with hunger in
the land, [c]neither bear the shame of
the [3]heathen any more.

34:16 [b] Is. 10:16 [c] Jer. 10:24 [1] *justice*
34:17 [a] [Matt. 25:32] [1] *sheep and sheep* [2] *male*
34:18 [1] *trample* [2] *remainder*
34:19 [1] *trampled*
34:20 [a] Ezek. 34:17 [1] *sheep*
34:21 [1] *pushed* [2] *butted* [3] *weak*
34:22 [1] *sheep and sheep*
34:23 [a] [Is. 40:11] [b] Jer. 30:9
34:24 [a] Ex. 29:45 [b] Ezek. 37:24, 25
34:25 [a] Ezek. 37:26 [b] Is. 11:6–9 [c] Jer. 23:6 [1] *wild*
34:26 [a] Is. 56:7 [b] Zech. 8:13 [c] Lev. 26:4 [d] Ps. 68:9
34:27 [a] Is. 4:2 [b] Jer. 2:20 [c] Jer. 25:14 [1] *enslaved them.*
34:28 [a] Jer. 30:10 [1] *for the nations*
34:29 [a] [Is. 11:1] [b] Ezek. 36:29 [c] Ezek. 36:3, 6, 15 [1] *garden*, lit. *planting place* [2] Lit. *gathered by famine* [3] *Gentiles*
34:30 [a] Ezek. 34:24 [b] Ezek. 14:11; 36:28
34:31 [a] Ps. 100:3
35:2 [a] Ezek. 25:12–14 [b] Amos 1:11
35:3 [a] Ezek. 6:14 [1] *a desolation and a waste*
35:5 [a] Ezek. 25:12 [b] Ps. 137:7 [1] *an ancient*, lit. *an everlasting* [2] *power* [3] had come to *an end*
35:6 [a] Is. 63:1–6 [b] Ps. 109:17 [1] *since* [2] Or *bloodshed*
35:7 [a] Judg. 5:6 [1] *leaves*
35:8 [1] *ravines*
35:9 [a] Jer. 49:13 [b] Ezek. 36:11 [1] Lit. *desolated forever* [2] *be inhabited*
35:10 [a] Ps. 83:4–12 [b] [Ps. 48:1–3; 132:13, 14] [1] *although*
35:11 [a] [James 2:13] [1] *showed in*
35:12 [a] Ps. 9:16 [b] Zeph. 2:8 [c] Is. 52:5
35:13 [a] [1 Sam. 2:3] [b] Ezek. 36:3 [1] Lit. *made yourself great*
35:14 [a] Is. 65:13, 14
35:15 [a] Obad. 12, 15

30 Thus shall they know that [a]I the
LORD their God *am* with them, and
*that* they, *even* the house of Israel,
*are* [b]my people, saith the Lord GOD.
31 And ye my [a]flock, the flock of my
pasture, *are* men, *and* I *am* your God,
saith the Lord GOD.

## CHAPTER 35

MOREOVER the word of the LORD
came unto me, saying,
2 Son of man, set thy face against
[a]mount Seir, and [b]prophesy against it,
3 And say unto it, Thus saith the
Lord GOD; Behold, O mount Seir, I
*am* against thee, and [a]I will stretch
out mine hand against thee, and I
will make thee [1]most desolate.
4 I will lay thy cities waste, and
thou shalt be desolate, and thou shalt
know that I *am* the LORD.
5 [a]Because thou hast had [1]a perpetual hatred, and hast shed *the blood of*
the children of Israel by the [2]force of
the sword in the time of their calamity, [b]in the time *that their* iniquity
[3]*had* an end:
6 Therefore, *as* I live, saith the Lord
GOD, I will prepare thee unto [a]blood,
and blood shall pursue thee: [b]sith[1]
thou hast not hated [2]blood, even
blood shall pursue thee.
7 Thus will I make mount Seir most
desolate, and cut off from it [a]him that
[1]passeth out and him that returneth.
8 And I will fill his mountains with
his slain *men:* in thy hills, and in thy
valleys, and in all thy [1]rivers, shall
they fall that are slain with the sword.
9 [a]I will make thee [1]perpetual desolations, and thy cities shall not [2]re-
turn: [b]and ye shall know that I *am*
the LORD.
10 Because thou hast said, These
two nations and these two countries
shall be mine, and we will [a]possess it;
[1]whereas [b]the LORD was there:
11 Therefore, *as* I live, saith the
Lord GOD, I will even do [a]according
to thine anger, and according to thine
envy which thou hast [1]used out of thy
hatred against them; and I will make
myself known among them, when I
have judged thee.
12 [a]And thou shalt know that I *am*
the LORD, *and that* I have [b]heard all
thy [c]blasphemies which thou hast
spoken against the mountains of Israel, saying, They are laid desolate,
they are given us to consume.
13 Thus [a]with your mouth ye have
[1]boasted against me, and have multiplied your [b]words against me: I have
heard *them*.
14 Thus saith the Lord GOD; [a]When
the whole earth rejoiceth, I will make
thee desolate.
15 [a]As thou didst rejoice at the
inheritance of the house of Israel,

because it was desolate, [b]so will I do unto thee: thou shalt be desolate, O mount Seir, and all [1]Idumea, *even* all of it: and they shall know that I *am* the LORD.

## CHAPTER 36

ALSO, thou son of man, prophesy unto the [a]mountains of Israel, and say, Ye mountains of Israel, hear the word of the LORD:

2 Thus saith the Lord GOD; Because [a]the enemy hath said against you, Aha, [b]even the ancient [1]high places [c]are ours in possession:

3 Therefore prophesy and say, Thus saith the Lord GOD; Because they have made *you* desolate, and swallowed you up on every side, that ye might be a possession unto the [1]residue of the heathen, [a]and ye are taken up in the lips of [b]talkers, and *are* [2]an infamy of the people:

4 Therefore, ye mountains of Israel, hear the word of the Lord GOD; Thus saith the Lord GOD to the mountains, and to the hills, to the [1]rivers, and to the valleys, to the desolate wastes, and to the cities that are forsaken, which [a]became [2]a prey and [b]derision[3] to the [4]residue of the heathen that *are* round about;

5 Therefore thus saith the Lord GOD; [a]Surely in [1]the fire of my jealousy have I spoken against the [2]residue of the heathen, and against all [3]Idumea, [b]which have [4]appointed my land into their possession with [5]the joy of all *their* heart, with [6]despiteful minds, to cast it out for a prey.

6 Prophesy therefore concerning the land of Israel, and say unto the mountains, and to the hills, to the rivers, and to the valleys, Thus saith the Lord GOD; Behold, I have spoken in my jealousy and in my fury, because ye have [a]borne the shame of the [1]heathen:

7 Therefore thus saith the Lord GOD; I have [a]lifted[1] up mine hand, Surely the [2]heathen that *are* about you, they shall [b]bear [3]their shame.

8 But ye, O mountains of Israel, ye shall shoot forth your branches, and yield your fruit to my people of Israel; for they are [1]at hand to come.

9 For, behold, I *am* for you, and I will turn unto you, and ye shall be tilled and sown:

10 And I will multiply men upon you, all the house of Israel, *even* all of it: and the cities shall be inhabited, and [a]the [1]wastes shall be builded:

11 And [a]I will multiply upon you man and beast; and they shall increase and bring fruit: and I will [1]settle you after your old estates, and will do [b]better *unto you* than at your

### Cross References

35:15 [b] Lam. 4:21
[1] Heb. *Edom*
36:1 [a] Ezek. 6:2, 3
36:2 [a] Ezek. 25:3;
26:2 [b] Deut.
32:13 [c] Ezek.
35:10 [1] *heights*
36:3 [a] Deut.
28:37 [b] Ezek.
35:13 [1] *rest of the nations* [2] *slandered by*
36:4 [a] Ezek. 34:8,
28 [b] Ps. 79:4
[1] *ravines* [2] *plunder* [3] *mockery* [4] *rest of the nations*
36:5 [a] Deut. 4:24
[b] Ezek. 35:10,
12 [1] *my burning jealousy* [2] *rest of the nations* [3] *Edom* [4] *given* [5] *wholehearted joy* [6] *spiteful*
36:6 [a] Ps. 74:10;
123:3, 4 [1] *nations*
36:7 [a] Ezek. 20:5
[b] Jer. 25:9, 15, 29
[1] Taken an oath [2] *nations* [3] *their own*
36:8 [1] *about to*
36:10 [a] Amos
9:14 [1] *ruins*
36:11 [a] Jer. 31:27;
33:12 [b] Is. 51:3
[c] Ezek. 35:9; 37:6,
13 [1] *make you inhabited as in former times*
36:12 [a] Obad. 17
[b] Jer. 15:7 [1] Their children
36:13 [a] Num.
13:32 [1] You are a land which
36:15 [a] Ezek.
34:29 [1] *the taunts of the nations* [2] *stumble*
36:17 [a] Jer.
2:7 [b] Lev. 15:19
[1] *woman in her customary impurity*
36:18 [a] Ezek.
16:36, 38; 23:37
[1] *defiled*
36:19 [a] Deut.
28:64 [b] [Rom.
2:6] [1] *nations*
36:20 [a] Rom.
2:24 [1] *nations*
36:21 [a] Ezek.
20:9, 14 [1] *concern* [2] *nations*
36:22 [a] Ps. 106:8
[1] *nations*
36:23 [a] Ezek.
20:41; 28:22 [1] *nations* [2] *hallowed*
36:24 [a] Ezek.
34:13; 37:21
[1] *nations*
36:25 [a] Heb. 9:13,
19; 10:22 [b] Jer.
33:8

beginnings: [c]and ye shall know that I *am* the LORD.

12 Yea, I will cause men to walk upon you, *even* my people Israel; [a]and they shall possess thee, and thou shalt be their inheritance, and thou shalt no more henceforth [b]bereave them of [1]men.

13 Thus saith the Lord GOD; Because they say unto you, [a]Thou[1] *land* devourest up men, and hast bereaved thy nations;

14 Therefore thou shalt devour men no more, neither bereave thy nations any more, saith the Lord GOD.

15 [a]Neither will I cause *men* to hear in thee [1]the shame of the heathen any more, neither shalt thou bear the reproach of the people any more, neither shalt thou cause thy nations to [2]fall any more, saith the Lord GOD.

16 Moreover the word of the LORD came unto me, saying,

17 Son of man, when the house of Israel dwelt in their own land, [a]they defiled it by their own way and by their doings: their way was before me as [b]the uncleanness of a [1]removed woman.

18 Wherefore I poured my fury upon them [a]for the blood that they had shed upon the land, and for their idols *wherewith* they had [1]polluted it:

19 And I [a]scattered them among the [1]heathen, and they were dispersed through the countries: [b]according to their way and according to their doings I judged them.

20 And when they entered unto the [1]heathen, whither they went, they [a]profaned my holy name, when they said to them, These *are* the people of the LORD, and are gone forth out of his land.

21 But I had [1]pity [a]for mine holy name, which the house of Israel had profaned among the [2]heathen, whither they went.

22 Therefore say unto the house of Israel, Thus saith the Lord GOD; I do not *this* for your sakes, O house of Israel, [a]but for mine holy name's sake, which ye have profaned among the [1]heathen, whither ye went.

23 And I will sanctify my great name, which was profaned among the [1]heathen, which ye have profaned in the midst of them; and the [1]heathen shall know that I *am* the LORD, saith the Lord GOD, when I shall be [a]sanctified[2] in you before their eyes.

24 For [a]I will take you from among the [1]heathen, and gather you out of all countries, and will bring you into your own land.

25 [a]Then will I sprinkle clean water upon you, and ye shall be clean: [b]from all your filthiness, and from all your idols, will I cleanse you.

26 A ᵃnew heart also will I give you, and a new spirit will I put within you: and I will take away the stony heart out of your flesh, and I will give you an heart of flesh.

27 And I will put my ᵃspirit within you, and cause you to walk in my statutes, and ye shall keep my judgments, and do *them*.

28 ᵃAnd ye shall dwell in the land that I gave to your fathers; ᵇand ye shall be my people, and I will be your God.

29 I will also ᵃsave you from all your uncleannesses: and ᵇI will call for the ¹corn, and will increase it, and ᶜlay no famine upon you.

30 ᵃAnd I will multiply the fruit of the tree, and the increase of the field, that ye shall receive no more reproach of famine among the ¹heathen.

31 Then ᵃshall ye remember your own evil ways, and your doings that *were* not good, and ᵇshall lothe yourselves in your own sight for your iniquities and for your abominations.

32 ᵃNot for your sakes do I *this*, saith the Lord GOD, be it known unto you: be ashamed and confounded for your own ways, O house of Israel.

33 Thus saith the Lord GOD; In the day that I shall have cleansed you from all your iniquities I will also cause *you* to dwell in the cities, ᵃand the ¹wastes shall be builded.

34 And the desolate land shall be tilled, whereas it lay desolate in the sight of all that passed by.

35 And they shall say, This land that was desolate is become like the garden of ᵃEden; and the waste and desolate and ruined cities *are become* ¹fenced, *and* are inhabited.

36 Then the ¹heathen that are left round about you shall know that I the LORD ²build the ruined *places, and* plant that that was desolate: ᵃI the LORD have spoken *it,* and I will do *it.*

37 Thus saith the Lord GOD; ᵃI will ¹yet *for* this be enquired of by the house of Israel, to do *it* for them; I will ᵇincrease them with men like a flock.

38 As ¹the holy flock, as the flock of Jerusalem in her ²solemn feasts; so shall the ³waste cities be filled with flocks of men: and they shall know that I *am* the LORD.

## CHAPTER 37

THE ᵃhand of the LORD was upon me, and carried me out ᵇin the spirit of the LORD, and set me down in the midst of the valley which *was* full of bones.

2 And caused me to pass by them round about: and, behold, *there were*

---

*Reference column:*

36:26 ᵃ Ezek. 11:19
36:27 ᵃ Ezek. 11:19; 37:14
36:28 ᵃ Ezek. 28:25; 37:25  ᵇ Jer. 30:22
36:29 ᵃ [Rom. 11:26]  ᵇ Ps. 105:16  ᶜ Ezek. 34:27, 29  ¹ grain
36:30 ᵃ Ezek. 34:27  ¹ nations
36:31 ᵃ Ezek. 16:61, 63  ᵇ Ezek. 6:9; 20:43
36:32 ᵃ Deut. 9:5
36:33 ᵃ Ezek. 36:10  ¹ ruins
36:35 ᵃ Joel 2:3  ¹ fortified
36:36 ᵃ Ezek. 17:24; 22:14; 37:14  ¹ nations  ² rebuilt
36:37 ᵃ Ezek. 14:3; 20:3, 31  ᵇ Ezek. 36:10  ¹ also let the house of Israel inquire of me
36:38 ¹ a flock for holy sacrifices  ² appointed feasts  ³ ruined
37:1 ᵃ Ezek. 1:3  ᵇ Ezek. 3:14; 8:3; 11:24

37:3 ᵃ [1 Sam. 2:6]
37:5 ᵃ Ps. 104:29, 30  ¹ spirit
37:6 ᵃ Joel 2:27; 3:17  ¹ put  ² spirit
37:7 ¹ suddenly a rattling
37:8 ¹ over  ² spirit
37:9 ᵃ [Ps. 104:30]  ¹ Breath of life
37:10 ᵃ Rev. 11:11  ¹ Breath of life
37:11 ᵃ Ezek. 36:10  ᵇ Ps. 141:7  ¹ ourselves are cut off
37:12 ᵃ Is. 26:19; 66:14  ᵇ Ezek. 36:24
37:14 ᵃ Ezek. 36:27
37:16 ᵃ Num. 17:2, 3  ᵇ 2 Chr. 11:12, 13, 16; 15:9; 30:11, 18
37:17 ᵃ Hos. 1:11

---

very many in the open valley; and, lo, *they were* very dry.

3 And he said unto me, Son of man, can these bones live? And I answered, O Lord GOD, ᵃthou knowest.

4 Again he said unto me, Prophesy upon these bones, and say unto them, O ye dry bones, hear the word of the LORD.

5 Thus saith the Lord GOD unto these bones; Behold, I will ᵃcause ᵇbreath to enter into you, and ye shall live:

6 And I will ¹lay sinews upon you, and will bring up flesh upon you, and cover you with skin, and put ²breath in you, and ye shall live; ᵃand ye shall know that I *am* the LORD.

7 So I prophesied as I was commanded: and as I prophesied, there was a noise, and ¹behold a shaking, and the bones came together, bone to his bone.

8 And when I beheld, lo, the sinews and the flesh came up upon them, and the skin covered them ¹above: but *there was* no ²breath in them.

9 Then said he unto me, Prophesy unto the ¹wind, prophesy, son of man, and say to the wind, Thus saith the Lord GOD; ᵃCome from the four winds, O ¹breath, and breathe upon these slain, that they may live.

10 So I prophesied as he commanded me, ᵃand the ¹breath came into them, and they lived, and stood up upon their feet, an exceeding great army.

11 Then he said unto me, Son of man, these bones are the ᵃwhole house of Israel: behold, they say, ᵇOur bones are dried, and our hope is lost: we ¹are cut off for our parts.

12 Therefore prophesy and say unto them, Thus saith the Lord GOD; Behold, ᵃO my people, I will open your graves, and cause you to come up out of your graves, and ᵇbring you into the land of Israel.

13 And ye shall know that I *am* the LORD, when I have opened your graves, O my people, and brought you up out of your graves,

14 And ᵃshall put my spirit in you, and ye shall live, and I shall place you in your own land: then shall ye know that I the LORD have spoken *it,* and performed *it,* saith the LORD.

15 The word of the LORD came again unto me, saying,

16 Moreover, thou son of man, ᵃtake thee one stick, and write upon it, For Judah, and for ᵇthe children of Israel his companions: then take another stick, and write upon it, For Joseph, the stick of Ephraim, and *for* all the house of Israel his companions:

17 And ᵃjoin them one to another

into one stick; and they shall become one in thine hand.

18 And when the children of thy people shall speak unto thee, saying, [a]Wilt thou not shew us what thou *meanest* by these?

19 [a]Say unto them, Thus saith the Lord GOD; Behold, I will take [b]the stick of Joseph, which *is* in the hand of Ephraim, and the tribes of Israel his [1]fellows, and will put them with him, *even* with the stick of Judah, and make them one stick, and they shall be one in mine hand.

20 And the sticks whereon thou writest shall be in thine hand [a]before their eyes.

21 And say unto them, Thus saith the Lord GOD; Behold, [a]I will take the children of Israel from among the [1]heathen, whither they be gone, and will gather them on every side, and bring them into their own land:

22 And [a]I will make them one nation in the land upon the mountains of Israel; and [b]one king shall be king to them all: and they shall be no more two nations, neither shall they be divided into two kingdoms any more at all:

23 [a]Neither shall they defile themselves any more with their idols, nor with their detestable things, nor with any of their transgressions: but [b]I will save them out of all their dwellingplaces, wherein they have sinned, and will cleanse them: so shall they be my people, and I will be their God.

24 And [a]David my servant *shall be* king over them; and [b]they all shall have one shepherd: [c]they shall also walk in my judgments, and observe my statutes, and do them.

25 [a]And they shall dwell in the land that I have given unto Jacob my servant, wherein your fathers have dwelt; and they shall dwell therein, *even* they, and their children, and their children's children [b]for ever: and [c]my servant David *shall be* their prince for ever.

26 Moreover I will [1]make [a]a covenant of peace with them; it shall be an everlasting covenant with them: and I will [2]place them, and [b]multiply them, and will set my [c]sanctuary in the midst of them for evermore.

27 [a]My [1]tabernacle also shall be with them: yea, I will be [b]their God, and they shall be my people.

28 And [a]the heathen shall know that I the LORD do [b]sanctify Israel, when my sanctuary shall be in the midst of them for evermore.

## CHAPTER 38

AND the word of the LORD came unto me, saying,

2 [a]Son of man, [b]set thy face against [c]Gog, the land of [d]Magog, the [1]chief prince of [e]Meshech and Tubal, and prophesy against him,

3 And say, Thus saith the Lord GOD; Behold, I *am* against thee, O Gog, the [1]chief prince of Meshech and Tubal:

4 And [a]I will turn thee [b]back, and put hooks into thy jaws, and I will [b]bring thee forth, and all thine army, horses and horsemen, [c]all of them [2]clothed with all sorts *of armour, even* a great company *with* [3]bucklers and shields, all of them handling swords:

5 Persia, [1]Ethiopia, and [2]Libya with them; all of them with shield and helmet:

6 [a]Gomer, and all his [1]bands; the house of [b]Togarmah of the [2]north quarters, and all his [1]bands: *and* many people with thee.

7 [a]Be thou prepared, and prepare for thyself, thou, and all thy company that are [1]assembled unto thee, and be thou a guard unto them.

8 [a]After many days [b]thou shalt be visited: in the latter years thou shalt come into the land *that is* brought back from the sword, [c]and is gathered out of many people, [a]against [d]the mountains of Israel, which have [2]been always waste: but it is brought forth out of the nations, and they shall [e]dwell safely all of them.

9 [1]Thou shalt ascend and come [a]like a storm, thou shalt be [b]like a cloud to cover the land, thou, and all thy [1]bands, and many people with thee.

10 Thus saith the Lord GOD; It shall also come to pass, *that* [1]at the same time [2]shall things come into thy mind, and thou shalt [3]think an evil thought:

11 And thou shalt say, I will go up to the land of [a]unwalled villages; I will [b]go to them that are at rest, [c]that dwell [1]safely, all of them dwelling without walls, and having neither bars nor gates,

12 To take [1]a spoil, and to take [2]a prey; to turn thine hand upon the desolate places *that are now* inhabited, [a]and upon the people *that are* gathered out of the nations, which have gotten [3]cattle and goods, that dwell in the midst of the land.

13 [a]Sheba, and [b]Dedan, and the merchants [c]of Tarshish, with all [d]the young lions thereof, shall say unto thee, Art thou come to take [1]a spoil? hast thou gathered [2]thy company to take a prey? to carry away silver and gold, to take away [3]cattle and goods, to take a great [1]spoil?

14 Therefore, son of man, prophesy and say unto Gog, Thus saith the Lord GOD; [a]In that day when my people of Israel [b]dwelleth safely, shalt thou not know *it?*

## Cross-references (center column)

37:18 [a] Ezek. 12:9; 24:19
37:19 [a] Zech. 10:6 [b] Ezek. 37:16, 17 [1] *companions*
37:20 [a] Ezek. 12:3
37:21 [a] Ezek. 36:24 [1] *nations*
37:22 [a] Jer. 3:18 [b] Ezek. 34:23
37:23 [a] Ezek. 36:25 [b] Ezek. 36:28, 29
37:24 [a] Is. 40:11 [b] [John 10:16] [c] Ezek. 36:27
37:25 [a] Ezek. 36:28 [b] Is. 60:21 [c] John 12:34
37:26 [a] Is. 55:3 [b] Ezek. 36:10 [c] [2 Cor. 6:16] [1] Lit. *cut* [2] *establish*
37:27 [a] [John 1:14] [b] Ezek. 11:20 [1] *dwelling place*
37:28 [a] Ezek. 36:23 [b] Ezek. 20:12

38:2 [a] Ezek. 39:1 [b] Ezek. 35:2, 3
[c] Rev. 20:8 [d] Gen. 10:2 [e] Ezek. 32:26 [1] *prince of Rosh*
38:3 [1] *prince of Rosh*
38:4 [a] 2 Kin. 19:28 [b] Is. 43:17 [c] Ezek. 23:12 [1] *around* [2] *splendidly clothed,* [3] A large shield
38:5 [1] Heb. *Cush* [2] Heb. *Put*
38:6 [a] Gen. 10:2 [b] Ezek. 27:14 [1] *troops* [2] *far north*
38:7 [a] Is. 8:9, 10 [1] *gathered about*
38:8 [a] Is. 24:22 [b] Is. 29:6 [c] Ezek. 34:13 [d] Ezek. 36:1, 4 [e] Ezek. 34:25; 39:26 [1] *on* [2] *long been desolate*
38:9 [a] Is. 28:2 [b] Jer. 4:13 [1] *troops*
38:10 [1] *on that day* [2] *thoughts will arise in* [3] *devise an evil plan*
38:11 [a] Zech. 2:4 [b] Jer. 49:31 [c] Ezek. 38:8 [1] *securely*
38:12 [a] Ezek. 38:8 [1] *plunder* [2] *booty* [3] *livestock*
38:13 [a] Ezek. 27:22 [b] Ezek. 27:15, 20 [c] Ezek. 27:12 [d] Ezek. 19:3, 5 [1] *plunder* [2] *thine army to take booty* [3] *livestock*
38:14 [a] Is. 4:1 [b] Ezek. 38:8, 11

15 ᵃAnd thou shalt come from thy place out of the ᴵnorth parts, thou, and many people with thee, all of them riding upon horses, a great company, and a mighty army:

16 And thou shalt come up against my people of Israel, as a cloud to cover the land; it shall be in the latter days, and I will bring thee against my land, that the ᴵheathen may ᵃknow me, when I shall be ᵇsanctified² in thee, O Gog, before their eyes.

17 Thus saith the Lord GOD; *Art* thou he of whom I have spoken in old time by my servants the prophets of Israel, which prophesied in those days *many* years that I would bring thee against them?

18 And it shall come to pass at the same time when Gog shall come against the land of Israel, saith the Lord GOD, *that* my fury shall ᴵcome up in my face.

19 For ᵃin my jealousy ᵇ*and* in the fire of my wrath have I spoken, ᶜSurely in that day there shall be a great ᴵshaking in the land of Israel;

20 So that ᵃthe fishes of the sea, and the fowls of the heaven, and the beasts of the field, and all creeping things that creep upon the earth, and all the men that *are* upon the face of the earth, shall shake at my presence, ᵇand the mountains shall be thrown down, and the steep places shall fall, and every wall shall fall to the ground.

21 And I will ᵃcall for ᵇa sword against him throughout all my mountains, saith the Lord GOD: ᶜevery man's sword shall be against his brother.

22 And I will ᵃplead¹ against him with ᵇpestilence and with ²blood; and ᶜI will rain upon him, and upon his ³bands, and upon the many ⁴people that *are* with him, an ⁵overflowing rain, and ᵈgreat hailstones, fire, and brimstone.

23 Thus will I magnify myself, and ᵃsanctify myself; ᵇand I will be known in the eyes of many nations, and they shall know that I *am* the LORD.

## CHAPTER 39

THEREFORE, ᵃthou son of man, prophesy against Gog, and say, Thus saith the Lord GOD; Behold, I *am* against thee, O Gog, ᴵthe chief prince of Meshech and Tubal:

2 And I will ᵃturn thee ᴵback, and ²leave but the sixth part of thee, ᵇand will cause thee to come up from the ³north parts, and will bring thee upon the mountains of Israel:

3 And I will ᴵsmite thy bow out of thy left hand, and will cause thine arrows to fall out of thy right hand.

4 ᵃThou shalt ᴵfall upon the mountains of Israel, thou, and all thy ²bands,

and the ³people that *is* with thee: ᵇI will give thee unto the ⁴ravenous birds of every sort, and *to* the beasts of the field to be devoured.

5 Thou shalt ᴵfall upon the open field: for I have spoken *it,* saith the Lord GOD.

6 ᵃAnd I will send a fire on Magog, and among them that dwell ᴵcarelessly in ᵇthe ²isles: and they shall know that I *am* the LORD.

7 ᵃSo will I make my holy name known in the midst of my people Israel; and I will not *let them* ᵇpollute¹ my holy name any more: ᶜand the ²heathen shall know that I *am* the LORD, the Holy One in Israel.

8 ᵃBehold, it is ᴵcome, and it ²is done, saith the Lord GOD; this *is* the day ᵇwhereof I have spoken.

9 And they that dwell in the cities of Israel shall go forth, and shall set on fire and burn the weapons, both the shields and the ᴵbucklers, the bows and the arrows, and the ²handstaves, and the spears, and they shall ³burn them with fire seven years:

10 So that they shall take no wood out of the field, neither cut down *any* out of the forests; for they shall burn the weapons with fire: ᵃand they shall ᴵspoil those that ²spoiled them, and ³rob those that robbed them, saith the Lord GOD.

11 And it shall come to pass in that day, *that* I will give unto Gog a ᴵplace there of graves in Israel, the valley of ²the passengers on the east of the sea: and it shall stop the *noses* of ²the passengers: and there shall they bury Gog and all his multitude: and they shall call *it* The valley of ³Hamon-gog.

12 And seven months shall the house of Israel be burying of them, ᵃthat they may cleanse the land.

13 Yea, all the people of the land shall bury *them;* and it shall ᴵbe to them a ᵃrenown the day that ᵇI shall be glorified, saith the Lord GOD.

14 And they shall ᴵsever out men ²of continual employment, ³passing through the land to bury with the ⁴passengers ⁵those that remain upon the face of the earth, ᵃto cleanse it: after the end of seven months shall they search.

15 And the ᴵpassengers *that* pass through the land, when *any* seeth a man's bone, then shall he ²set up a sign by it, till the buriers have buried it in the valley of Hamon-gog.

16 And also the name of the city *shall be* ᴵHamonah. Thus shall they ᵃcleanse the land.

17 And, thou son of man, thus saith the Lord GOD; ᵃSpeak unto every feathered fowl, and to every beast of

### Center references

38:15 ᵃ Ezek. 39:2
¹ *far north*

38:16 ᵃ Ezek. 35:11 ᵇ Ezek. 28:22 ¹ *nations* ² *hallowed*

38:18 ¹ *show*

38:19 ᵃ Ezek. 36:5, 6 ᵇ Ps. 89:46 ᶜ Rev. 16:8 ¹ *earthquake*

38:20 ᵃ Hos. 4:3 ᵇ Jer. 4:24

38:21 ᵃ Ps. 105:16 ᵇ Ezek. 14:17 ᶜ 1 Sam. 14:20

38:22 ᵃ Is. 66:16 ᵇ Ezek. 5:17 ᶜ Ps. 11:6 ᵈ Rev. 16:21 ¹ *bring judgment to him* ² *bloodshed* ³ *troops* ⁴ *peoples* ⁵ *flooding*

38:23 ᵃ Ezek. 36:23 ᵇ Ezek. 37:28; 38:16

39:1 ᵃ Ezek. 38:2, 3 ¹ *prince of Rosh*

39:2 ᵃ Ezek. 38:8 ᵇ Ezek. 38:15 ¹ *around* ² *Or lead you on, and will cause* ³ *far north*

39:3 ¹ *knock*

39:4 ᵃ Ezek. 38:4, 21 ᵇ Ezek. 33:27 ¹ *Be slain* ² *troops* ³ *peoples* ⁴ *birds of prey*

39:5 ¹ *Be slain*

39:6 ᵃ Amos 1:4, 7, 10 ᵇ Ps. 72:10 ¹ *securely* ² *coastlands*

39:7 ᵃ Ezek. 39:25 ᵇ Lev. 18:21 ᶜ Ezek. 38:16 ¹ *profane* ² *nations*

39:8 ᵃ Rev. 16:17; 21:6 ᵇ Ezek. 38:17 ¹ *coming* ² *shall be done*

39:9 ¹ *Large shields* ² *javelins* ³ *make fires with them*

39:10 ᵃ Is. 14:2; 33:1 ¹ *plunder* ² *plundered* ³ *pillage*

39:11 ¹ *burial place there* ² *those who pass by* ³ Lit. *The Multitude of Gog*

39:12 ᵃ Deut. 21:23

39:13 ᵃ Zeph. 3:19, 20 ᵇ Ezek. 28:22 ¹ *give them renown*

39:14 ᵃ Ezek. 39:12 ¹ *set apart* ² *for regular* ³ *to pass* ⁴ *those passing through* ⁵ *those bodies*

39:15 ¹ Lit. *ones passing through*

² *build a marker*  39:16 ᵃ Ezek. 39:12  ¹ Lit. *The Multitude*  39:17 ᵃ Rev. 19:17, 18

the field, ᵇAssemble yourselves, and come; gather yourselves on every side to my ᶜsacrifice¹ that I do sacrifice for you, *even* a great sacrifice ᵈupon the mountains of Israel, that ye may eat flesh, and drink blood.

18 ᵃYe shall eat the flesh of the mighty, and drink the blood of the princes of the earth, of rams, of lambs, and of goats, of bullocks, all of them ᵇfatlings of Bashan.

19 And ye shall eat fat till ye be full, and drink blood till ye be drunken, of my ¹sacrifice which I have sacrificed for you.

20 ᵃThus ye shall be filled at my table with horses and ¹chariots, ᵇwith mighty men, and with all men of war, saith the Lord GOD.

21 ᵃAnd I will set my glory among the ¹heathen, and all the ¹heathen shall see my judgment that I have executed, and ᵇmy hand that I have laid upon them.

22 ᵃSo the house of Israel shall know that I *am* the LORD their God from that day and forward.

23 ᵃAnd the ¹heathen shall know that the house of Israel went into captivity for their iniquity: because they ²trespassed against me, therefore ᵇhid I my face from them, and ᶜgave them into the hand of their enemies: so fell they all by the sword.

24 ᵃAccording to their uncleanness and according to their transgressions have I done unto them, and hid my face from them.

25 Therefore thus saith the Lord GOD; ᵃNow will I ¹bring again the captivity of Jacob, and have mercy upon the ᵇwhole house of Israel, and will be jealous for my holy name;

26 ᵃAfter that they have borne their shame, and all their ¹trespasses whereby they have ²trespassed against me, when they ᵇdwelt safely in their land, and none made *them* afraid.

27 ᵃWhen I have brought them again from the ¹people, and gathered them out of their enemies' lands, and ᵇam ²sanctified in them in the sight of many nations;

28 ᵃThen shall they know that I *am* the LORD their God, which caused them to be led into captivity among the ¹heathen: but I have gathered them unto their own land, and have left none of them any more ²there.

29 ᵃNeither will I hide my face any more from them: for I have ᵇpoured out my spirit upon the house of Israel, saith the Lord GOD.

## CHAPTER 40

IN the five and twentieth year of our captivity, in the beginning of the year, in the tenth *day* of the month,

in the fourteenth year after that ᵃthe city was ¹smitten, in the selfsame day ᵇthe hand of the LORD was upon me, and brought me thither.

2 ᵃIn the visions of God brought he me into the land of Israel, and ᵇset me upon a very high mountain, ¹by which *was* as the frame of a city on the south.

3 And he brought me thither, and, behold, *there was* a man, whose appearance *was* ᵃlike the appearance of ¹brass, ᵇwith a line of flax in his hand, ᶜand a measuring ²reed; and he stood in the gate.

4 And the man said unto me, ᵃSon of man, behold with thine eyes, and hear with thine ears, and ¹set thine heart upon all that I shall shew thee; for ²to the intent that I might shew *them* unto thee *art* thou brought hither: ᵇdeclare all that thou seest to the house of Israel.

5 And behold ᵃa wall on the outside of the ¹house round about, and in the man's hand a measuring ²reed of six cubits *long* by the cubit and an hand breadth: so he measured the breadth of the ³building, ⁴one reed; and the height, one reed.

6 Then came he unto the gate which ¹looketh toward the ᵃeast, and went up the stairs thereof, and measured the threshold of the gate, *which was* one reed broad; and the other threshold *of the gate, which was* one reed broad.

7 And *every* ¹little chamber *was* one reed long, and one reed broad; and between the ²little chambers *were* five cubits; and the threshold of the gate by the ³porch of the gate within *was* one reed.

8 He measured also the porch of the ¹gate within, one reed.

9 Then measured he the porch of the gate, eight cubits; and the posts thereof, two cubits; and the porch of the gate *was* ¹inward.

10 And the little chambers of the ¹gate eastward *were* three on this side, and three on that side; they three *were* of one ²measure: and the posts had one measure on this side and on that side.

11 And he measured the breadth of the entry of the gate, ten cubits; *and* the length of the gate, thirteen cubits.

12 The ¹space also before the ²little chambers *was* one cubit *on this side,* and the space *was* one cubit on that side: and the ²little chambers *were* six cubits on this side, and six cubits on that side.

13 He measured then the gate from the roof of *one* ¹little chamber to the

roof of another: the breadth *was* five and twenty cubits, door against door.

14 He [1]made also posts of threescore cubits, even unto the post of the court round about the gate.

15 And from the [1]face of the gate of the entrance unto the [1]face of the [2]porch of the inner gate *were* fifty cubits.

16 And *there were* [a]narrow[1] windows to the [2]little chambers, and to their posts within the gate round about, and likewise to the [3]arches: and windows *were* round about [4]inward: and upon *each* post *were* [b]palm trees.

17 Then brought he me into [a]the outward court, and, lo, *there were* [b]chambers, and a pavement made for the court round about: [c]thirty chambers [1]*were* upon the pavement.

18 And the pavement by the side of the gates [1]over against the length of the gates *was* the lower pavement.

19 Then he measured the breadth from the forefront of the lower gate unto the forefront of the inner court [1]without, an hundred cubits eastward and northward.

20 And the gate of the outward court that [1]looked toward the north, he measured the length thereof, and the breadth thereof.

21 And the [1]little chambers thereof *were* three on this side and three on that side; and the posts thereof and the [2]arches thereof were after the measure of the first gate: the length thereof *was* fifty cubits, and the breadth five and twenty cubits.

22 And their windows, and their arches, and their palm trees, *were* after the measure of the gate that looketh toward the east; and they went up unto it by seven steps; and the arches thereof *were* before them.

23 And the gate of the inner court *was* [1]over against the gate toward the north, [2]and toward the east; and he measured from gate to gate an hundred cubits.

24 After that he brought me toward the south, and behold a gate [1]toward the south: and he measured the posts thereof and the arches thereof according to these measures.

25 And *there were* windows in it and in the arches thereof round about, like those windows: the length *was* fifty cubits, and the breadth five and twenty cubits.

26 And *there were* seven steps to go up to it, and the arches thereof *were* before them: and it had palm trees, one on this side, and another on that side, upon the posts thereof.

27 And *there was* a gate in the inner court [1]toward the south: and he measured from gate to gate toward the south an hundred cubits.

28 And he brought me to the inner court by the south gate: and he measured the south gate according to these measures;

29 And the [1]little chambers thereof, and the posts thereof, and the arches thereof, according to these measures: and *there were* windows in it and in the arches thereof round about: *it was* fifty cubits long, and five and twenty cubits broad.

30 And the arches round about *were* [a]five and twenty cubits long, and five cubits [1]broad.

31 And the arches thereof [1]*were* toward the utter court; and palm trees *were* upon the posts thereof: and the going up to it *had* eight steps.

32 And he brought me into the inner court [1]toward the east: and he measured the gate according to these measures.

33 And the [1]little chambers thereof, and the posts thereof, and the arches thereof, *were* according to these measures: and *there were* windows therein and in the arches thereof round about: *it was* fifty cubits long, and five and twenty cubits broad.

34 And the arches thereof [1]*were* toward the outward court; and palm trees *were* upon the posts thereof, on this side, and on that side: and the going up to it *had* eight steps.

35 And he brought me to the north gate, and measured *it* according to these measures;

36 The [1]little chambers thereof, the posts thereof, and the arches thereof, and the windows to it round about: the length *was* fifty cubits, and the breadth five and twenty cubits.

37 And the posts thereof [1]*were* toward the utter court; and palm trees *were* upon the posts thereof, on this side, and on that side: and the going up to it *had* eight steps.

38 And [1]the chambers and [2]the entries thereof *were* by the posts of the gates, where they [a]washed the burnt offering.

39 And in the [1]porch of the gate *were* two tables on this side, and two tables on that side, to slay thereon the burnt offering and [a]the sin offering and [b]the trespass offering.

40 And at the [1]side without, as one goeth up to the entry of the north gate, *were* two tables; and on the other side, which *was* at the [2]porch of the gate, *were* two tables.

41 Four tables *were* on this side, and four tables on that side, by the side of the gate; eight tables, whereupon they slew *their sacrifices.*

42 And the four tables *were* of hewn stone for the burnt offering, of a cubit and an half long, and a cubit and an half broad, and one cubit high:

---

**Center reference column:**

40:14 [1] *measured*

40:15 [1] *front*
[2] *vestibule*

40:16 [a] 1 Kin. 6:4; Ezek. 41:16, 26 [b] 1 Kin. 6:29, 32, 35; 2 Chr. 3:5; Ezek. 40:22, 26, 31, 34, 37; 41:18–20, 25, 26 [1] *narrowing, shuttered* [2] *gate* [3] Or *vestibules* [4] *on the inside*

40:17 [a] Ezek. 10:5; 42:11; 46:21; Rev. 11:2 [b] 1 Kin. 6:5; 2 Chr. 31:11; Ezek. 40:38 [c] Ezek. 45:5 [1] *faced*

40:18 [1] *corresponding to*

40:19 [1] *exterior*

40:20 [1] *faced*

40:21 [1] *gate* [2] Or *vestibules*

40:23 [1] *opposite* [2] *just as the eastern gate*

40:24 [1] *facing*

40:27 [1] *facing*

40:29 [1] *gate chambers*

40:30 [a] Ezek. 40:21, 25, 33, 36 [1] *wide*

40:31 [1] *faced*

40:32 [1] *facing*

40:33 [1] *gate*

40:34 [1] *faced*

40:36 [1] *gate*

40:37 [1] *faced*

40:38 [a] 2 Chr. 4:6 [1] *a chamber* [2] *its entrance was*

40:39 [a] Lev. 4:2, 3 [b] Lev. 5:6; 6:6; 7:1 [1] *vestibule*

40:40 [1] *outer side* [2] *vestibule*

whereupon also they laid the instruments wherewith they [1]slew the burnt offering and the sacrifice.

43 And within *were* hooks, an [1]hand broad, fastened round about: and upon the tables *was* the flesh of the offering.

44 And [1]without the inner gate *were* the chambers of [a]the singers in the inner court, which *was* at the side of the north gate; and their [2]prospect *was* toward the south: one at the side of the east gate *having* the [2]prospect toward the north.

45 And he said unto me, This chamber, whose [1]prospect *is* toward the south, *is* for the priests, [a]the[2] keepers of the charge of the house.

46 And the chamber [1]whose prospect *is* toward the north *is* for the priests, [a]the[2] keepers of the charge of the altar: these *are* the sons of [b]Zadok among the sons of Levi, which come near to the LORD to minister unto him.

47 So he measured the court, an hundred cubits long, and an hundred cubits broad, foursquare; and the altar *that was* before the [1]house.

48 And he brought me to the [a]porch[1] of the [2]house, and measured *each* post of the [1]porch, five cubits on this side, and five cubits on that side: and the breadth of the gate *was* three cubits on this side, and three cubits on that side.

49 [a]The length of the [1]porch *was* twenty cubits, and the breadth eleven cubits; and *he brought me* by the steps whereby they went up to it: and *there were* [b]pillars by the posts, one on this side, and another on that side.

## CHAPTER 41

AFTERWARD he [a]brought me to the [1]temple, and measured the posts, six cubits broad on the one side, and six cubits broad on the other side, *which was* the breadth of the tabernacle.

2 And the breadth of the [1]door *was* ten cubits; and the sides of the door *were* five cubits on the one side, and five cubits on the other side: and he measured the length thereof, forty cubits: and the breadth, twenty cubits.

3 Then went he [1]inward, and measured the post of the door, two cubits; and the door, six cubits; and the breadth of the door, seven cubits.

4 So [a]he measured the length thereof, twenty cubits; and the breadth, twenty cubits, before the [1]temple: and he said unto me, This *is* the most holy *place*.

5 After he measured the wall of [1]the house, six cubits; and the breadth of *every* side chamber, four cubits, round about [1]the house on every side.

6 [a]And the side chambers *were* [1]three, one over another, and thirty [2]in order; and they [3]entered into the wall which *was* of the house for the side chambers round about, that they might [4]have hold, but they had [b]not hold in the wall of the [5]house.

7 [1]And [a]*there was* an enlarging, and a winding about still upward to the side chambers: for the winding about of the house went still upward round about the house: therefore the breadth of the house [2]was *still* upward, [3]and so increased *from* the lowest *chamber* to the highest [4]by the midst.

8 I saw also the height of the house round about: the foundations of the side chambers *were* [a]a full [1]reed of six great cubits.

9 The thickness of the wall, which *was* for the side chamber [1]without, *was* five cubits: and *that* which *was* left [2]*was* the place of the side chambers [3]that *were* within.

10 And between the chambers *was* the [1]wideness of twenty cubits round about the house on every side.

11 And the doors of the side chambers [1]were toward *the place that was* left, one door toward the north, and another door toward the south: and the breadth of the [2]place that was left *was* five cubits round about.

12 Now the building that *was* before the [1]separate place at the end toward the west *was* seventy cubits broad; and the wall of the building *was* five cubits thick round about, and the length thereof ninety cubits.

13 So he measured [1]the house, an [a]hundred cubits long; and the [2]separate place, and the building, with the walls thereof, an hundred cubits long;

14 Also the [1]breadth of the face of the house, and of the [2]separate place toward the east, an hundred cubits.

15 And he measured the length of the building [1]over against the [2]separate place which *was* behind it, and the [a]galleries thereof on the one side and on the other side, an hundred cubits, with the inner [3]temple, and the porches of the court;

16 The door posts, and [a]the [1]narrow windows, and the galleries round about on their three stories, over against the door, [2]cieled with [b]wood round about, and from the ground up to the windows, and the windows *were* covered;

17 To that above the door, even unto the inner [1]house, and [2]without, and by

### Cross-references (center column)

40:42 [1] slaughtered

40:43 [1] handbreadth wide

40:44 [a] 1 Chr. 6:31, 32; 16:41–43; 25:1–7 [1] outside [2] face

40:45 [a] Lev. 8:35; Num. 3:27, 28, 32, 38; 18:5; 1 Chr. 9:23; 2 Chr. 13:11; Ps. 134:1 [1] face [2] who have charge

40:46 [a] Lev. 6:12, 13; Num. 18:5; Ezek. 44:15 [b] 1 Kin. 2:35; Ezek. 43:19; 44:15, 16 [1] which faces [2] who have charge

40:47 [1] Temple

40:48 [a] 1 Kin. 6:3; 2 Chr. 3:4 [1] vestibule [2] Temple

40:49 [a] 1 Kin. 6:3 [b] 1 Kin. 7:15–22; 2 Chr. 3:17; Jer. 52:17–23; [Rev. 3:12] [1] vestibule

41:1 [a] Ezek. 40:2, 3, 17 [1] sanctuary, the Holy Place

41:2 [1] entryway

41:3 [1] inside

41:4 [a] 1 Kin. 6:20; 2 Chr. 3:8 [1] sanctuary

41:5 [1] The temple

41:6 [a] 1 Kin. 6:5–10 [b] 1 Kin. 6:6, 10 [1] in three stories [2] in each story [3] rested on ledges [4] be supported but not be fastened to [5] The temple

41:7 [a] 1 Kin. 6:8 [1] As one went up from story to story, the side chambers became wider all around, because their supporting ledges in the wall of the temple ascended like steps: [2] increased [3] as one went up [4] by way of the middle one

41:8 [a] Ezek. 40:5 [1] rod

41:9 [1] outside [2] by [3] of the temple

41:10 [1] width

41:11 [1] opened onto the terrace [2] terrace

41:12 [1] separating courtyard

41:13 [a] Ezek. 40:47 [1] The temple [2] separating courtyard

41:14 [1] width [2] separating courtyard    41:15 [a] Ezek. 42:3, 5 [1] facing [2] separating courtyard [3] Or sanctuary    41:16 [a] Ezek. 40:16, 25 [b] 1 Kin. 6:15 [1] shuttered or bevelled window frames [2] were panelled

41:17 [1] room, the Holy of Holies [2] outside

all the wall round about within and without, by measure.

18 And *it was* made [a]with cherubims and [b]palm trees, so that a palm tree *was* between a cherub and a cherub; and *every* cherub had two faces;

19 [a]So that the face of a man *was* toward the palm tree on the one side, and the face of a young lion toward the palm tree on the other side: *it was* made through all the house round about.

20 From the ground unto above the door *were* cherubims and palm trees made, and *on* the wall of the [1]temple.

21 The [a]posts[1] of the temple *were* squared, *and* the face of the sanctuary; the appearance *of the one* as the appearance *of the other.*

22 [a]The altar of wood *was* three cubits high, and the length thereof two cubits; and the corners thereof, and the length thereof, and the [1]walls thereof, *were* of wood: and he said unto me, This *is* [b]the table that *is* [c]before the LORD.

23 [a]And the temple and the sanctuary had two doors.

24 And the doors had two [a]leaves[1] *apiece,* two [2]turning leaves; two *leaves* for the one door, and two leaves for the other *door.*

25 And *there were* [1]made on them, on the doors of the temple, cherubims and palm trees, like as *were* [1]made upon the walls; and *there* [2]were thick planks upon the [3]face of the temple [4]without.

26 And *there were* [a]narrow[1] windows and palm trees on the one side and on the other side, on the sides of the [2]porch, and *upon* the side chambers of [3]the house, and [4]thick planks.

## CHAPTER 42

THEN he [a]brought me forth into the utter court, the way toward the [b]north: and he brought me into [c]the chamber that *was* [1]over against the [2]separate place, and which *was* [3]before the building toward the north.

2 [1]Before the length of an hundred cubits *was* the north door, and the breadth *was* fifty cubits.

3 [1]Over against the twenty *cubits* which *were* for the inner court, and [1]over against the [a]pavement which *was* for the utter court, *was* [b]gallery against gallery in three *stories.*

4 And [1]before the chambers *was* a walk of ten cubits breadth [2]inward, a [3]way of one cubit; and their doors [4]toward the north.

5 Now the upper chambers *were* shorter: for the galleries [1]were higher than these, than the lower, and than the middlemost of the building.

6 For they *were* in three *stories,* but had not pillars as the pillars of the

courts: therefore *the* [1]building was [2]straitened more than the lowest and the [3]middlemost from the ground.

7 And the wall that *was* [1]without [2]over against the chambers, toward the utter court [3]on the forepart of the chambers, the length thereof *was* fifty cubits.

8 For the length of the chambers that *were* [1]in the utter court *was* fifty cubits: and, lo, [2]before the temple *were* an [a]hundred cubits.

9 And from [1]under these chambers *was* the [2]entry on the east side, as one goeth into them from the utter court.

10 [1]The chambers *were* in the thickness of the wall of the court toward the east, [2]over against the [3]separate place, and [2]over against the building.

11 And [a]the [1]way before them *was* like the appearance of the chambers which *were* toward the north, as long as they, *and* as broad as they: and all their [2]goings out *were* both according to their [3]fashions, and according to their doors.

12 And [1]according to the doors of the chambers that *were* [2]toward the south *was* a door in [3]the head of the way, *even* the way directly before the wall toward the east, as one entereth into them.

13 Then said he unto me, The north chambers *and* the south chambers, which *are* before [1]the separate place, they *be* holy chambers, where the priests that approach unto the LORD [a]shall eat the most holy [2]things: there shall they lay the most holy [2]things, and [b]the [3]meat offering, and the sin offering, and the trespass offering; for the place *is* holy.

14 [a]When the priests enter therein, then shall they not go out of the holy *place* into the utter court, but there they shall lay their garments wherein they minister; for they *are* holy; and shall put on other garments, and shall approach *to those things* which *are* for the people.

15 Now when he had made an end of measuring the inner [1]house, he brought me forth toward the gate [2]whose prospect *is* toward the [a]east, and measured it round about.

16 He measured the east side with the measuring [1]reed, [2]five hundred reeds, with the measuring reed round about.

17 He measured the north side, five hundred reeds, with the measuring reed round about.

18 He measured the south side, five hundred reeds, with the measuring reed.

19 He turned about to the west side, *and* measured five hundred reeds with the measuring reed.

20 He measured it by the four sides: [a]it had a wall round about, [b]five hundred *reeds* long, and five hundred broad, to make a separation between the [1]sanctuary and the [2]profane place.

## CHAPTER 43

AFTERWARD he brought me to the gate, *even* the gate [a]that looketh toward the east:

2 [a]And, behold, the glory of the God of Israel came from the way of the east: and [b]his voice *was* like a [1]noise of many waters: [c]and the earth shined with his glory.

3 And *it was* [a]according to the appearance of the vision which I saw, *even* according to the vision that I saw when [1]I came [b]to destroy the city: and the visions *were* like the vision that I saw [c]by the river Chebar; and I fell upon my face.

4 [a]And the glory of the LORD came into [1]the house by the way of the gate [2]whose prospect *is* toward the east.

5 [a]So the spirit [1]took me up, and brought me into the inner court; and, behold, [b]the glory of the LORD filled the house.

6 And I heard *him* speaking unto me out of [1]the house; and [a]the[2] man stood by me.

7 And he said unto me, Son of man, [a]the place of my throne, and [b]the place of the soles of my feet, [c]where I will dwell in the midst of the children of Israel for ever, and my holy name, shall the house of Israel [d]no more defile, *neither* they, nor their kings, by their [1]whoredom, nor by [e]the carcases of their kings in their high places.

8 [a]In their setting of their threshold by my thresholds, and their [1]post by my posts, [2]and the wall between me and them, they have even defiled my holy name by their abominations that they have committed: wherefore I have consumed them in mine anger.

9 Now let them put away their [1]whoredom, and the carcases of their kings, far from me, and I will dwell in the midst of them for ever.

10 Thou son of man, [a]shew[1] the house to the house of Israel, that they may be ashamed of their iniquities: and let them measure the pattern.

11 And if they be ashamed of all that they have done, [1]shew them the [2]form of the house, and the [3]fashion thereof, and the [4]goings out thereof, and the [5]comings in thereof, and all the forms thereof, and all the [a]ordinances thereof, and all the forms thereof, and all the laws thereof: and write *it* in their sight, that they may

keep the whole form thereof, and all the ordinances thereof, and [b]do them.

12 This *is* the law of [1]the house; Upon [a]the top of the mountain the whole [2]limit thereof round about *shall be* most holy. Behold, this *is* the law of [1]the house.

13 And these *are* the measures of the [a]altar [1]after the cubits: [b]The cubit *is* a cubit and an hand breadth; even the [2]bottom *shall be* a cubit, and the breadth a cubit, and the [3]border thereof by the edge thereof round about *shall be* [4]a span: and this *shall be* the [5]higher place of the altar.

14 And from the [1]bottom *upon* the ground *even* to the lower [2]settle *shall be* two cubits, and the breadth one cubit; and from the lesser [2]settle *even* to the greater [2]settle *shall be* four cubits, and the breadth *one* cubit.

15 So the [1]altar *shall be* four cubits; and from the [1]altar and upward *shall be* four [a]horns.

16 And the [1]altar *shall be* twelve cubits long, twelve broad, [a]square in the four squares thereof.

17 And the [1]settle *shall be* fourteen cubits long and fourteen broad in the four [2]squares thereof; and the [3]border about it *shall be* half a cubit; and the [4]bottom thereof *shall be* a cubit about; and [a]his stairs shall [5]look toward the east.

18 And he said unto me, Son of man, thus saith the Lord GOD; These *are* the ordinances of the altar in the day when they shall make it, to offer [a]burnt offerings thereon, and to [b]sprinkle blood thereon.

19 And thou shalt give to [a]the priests the Levites that be of the seed of [b]Zadok, which approach unto me, to minister unto me, saith the Lord GOD, [c]a young bullock for a sin offering.

20 And thou shalt take of the blood thereof, and put *it* on the four horns of it, and on the four corners of the [1]settle, and upon the [2]border round about: thus shalt thou cleanse and [3]purge it.

21 Thou shalt take the bullock also of the sin offering, and he [a]shall burn it in the appointed place of [1]the house, [b]without[2] the sanctuary.

22 And on the second day thou shalt offer a kid of the goats without blemish for a sin offering; and they shall cleanse the altar, as they did cleanse *it* with the bullock.

23 When thou hast made an end of cleansing *it,* thou shalt offer a young bullock without blemish, and a ram out of the flock without blemish.

24 And thou shalt offer them before the LORD, [a]and the priests shall cast salt upon them, and they shall offer

42:20 [a] Ezek. 40:5
[b] Ezek. 45:2 [1] *holy areas* [2] *common*

43:1 [a] Ezek. 10:19; 46:1

43:2 [a] Ezek. 11:23
[b] Rev. 1:15; 14:2
[c] Rev. 18:1 [1] *sound*

43:3 [a] Ezek. 1:4–28 [b] Jer. 1:10
[c] Ezek. 1:28; 3:23
[1] *Some mss. he*

43:4 [a] Ezek. 10:19; 11:23 [1] *The temple* [2] *which faces*

43:5 [a] Ezek. 3:12, 14; 8:3 [b] 1 Kin. 8:10, 11 [1] *lifted*

43:6 [a] Ezek. 1:26; 40:3 [1] *The temple* [2] *a*

43:7 [a] Ps. 99:1
[b] 1 Chr. 28:2
[c] Joel 3:17 [d] Ezek. 39:7 [e] Lev. 26:30
[1] *harlotry, unfaithful conduct*

43:8 [a] Ezek. 8:3; 23:39; 44:7
[1] *doorpost* [2] *with only a wall*

43:9 [1] *harlotry*

43:10 [a] Ezek. 40:4
[1] *describe the temple*

43:11 [a] Ezek. 44:5
[1] *make known to* [2] *design* [3] *arrangement* [4] *exits* [5] *entries*

[b] Ezek. 11:20

43:12 [a] Ezek. 40:2
[1] *The temple* [2] *area surrounding it*

43:13 [a] Ex. 27:1–8
[b] Ezek. 41:8 [1] *in cubits* [2] *base* [3] *rim* [4] *one-half cubit* [5] *height*

43:14 [1] *base* [2] *ledge*

43:15 [a] Ex. 27:2
[1] *altar hearth*

43:16 [a] Ex. 27:1
[1] *altar hearth*

43:17 [a] Ex. 20:26
[1] *ledge* [2] *sides* [3] *rim* [4] *base* [5] *face*

43:18 [a] Ex. 40:29
[b] Lev. 1:5, 11

43:19 [a] Ezek. 40:46 [b] Lev. 8:14
[c] Ezek. 44:15, 16

43:20 [1] *ledge* [2] *rim* [3] *make atonement for it*

43:21 [a] Ex. 29:14
[b] Heb. 13:11 [1] *The temple* [2] *outside*

43:24 [a] Lev. 2:13

them up *for* a burnt offering unto the LORD.

25 [a]Seven days shalt thou prepare every day a goat *for* a sin offering: they shall also prepare a young bullock, and a ram out of the flock, without blemish.

26 Seven days shall they [1]purge the altar and purify it; and they shall [2]consecrate themselves.

27 [a]And when these days are expired, it shall be, *that* upon the eighth day, and *so* forward, the priests shall make your burnt offerings upon the altar, and your peace offerings; and I will [b]accept you, saith the Lord GOD.

## CHAPTER 44

THEN he brought me back the way of the [1]gate of the outward sanctuary [a]which looketh toward the east; and it *was* shut.

2 Then said the LORD unto me; This gate shall be shut, it shall not be opened, and no man shall enter in by it; [a]because the LORD, the God of Israel, hath entered in by it, therefore it shall be shut.

3 *It is* for the [a]prince; the prince, he shall sit in it to [b]eat bread before the LORD; he shall enter by the way of the [1]porch of *that* gate, and shall go out by the way of the same.

4 Then brought he me the way of the north gate [1]before the house: and I looked, and, [a]behold, the glory of the LORD filled the house of the LORD: [b]and I fell upon my face.

5 And the LORD said unto me, [a]Son of man, mark well, and behold with thine eyes, and hear with thine ears all that I say unto thee concerning all the [b]ordinances of the house of the LORD, and all the laws thereof; and mark well [1]the entering in of the house, [2]with every going forth of the sanctuary.

6 And thou shalt say to the [a]rebellious, *even* to the house of Israel, Thus saith the Lord GOD; O ye house of Israel, [b]let[1] it suffice you of all your abominations,

7 [a]In that ye have brought *into my sanctuary* [b]strangers,[1] [c]uncircumcised in heart, and uncircumcised in flesh, to be in my sanctuary, to [2]pollute it, *even* my house, when ye offer [d]my [3]bread, [e]the fat and the blood, and they have broken my covenant because of all your abominations.

8 And ye have not [a]kept the charge of mine holy things: but ye have set keepers of my charge in my sanctuary for yourselves.

9 Thus saith the Lord GOD; [a]No [1]stranger, uncircumcised in heart, nor uncircumcised in flesh, shall enter into my sanctuary, of any [1]stranger that *is* among the children of Israel.

10 [a]And the Levites that are gone away far from me, when Israel went astray, which went astray away from me after their idols; they shall even bear their iniquity.

11 Yet they shall be ministers in my sanctuary, [a]*having* charge at the gates of the house, and ministering to the house: [b]they shall slay the burnt offering and the sacrifice for the people, and [c]they shall stand before them to minister unto them.

12 Because they ministered unto them before their idols, and [a]caused[1] the house of Israel to fall into iniquity; therefore have I [b]lifted up mine hand against them, saith the Lord GOD, and they shall bear their iniquity.

13 [a]And they shall not come near unto me, to [1]do the office of a priest unto me, nor to come near to any of my holy things, [2]in the most holy *place:* but they shall [b]bear their shame, and their abominations which they have committed.

14 But I will make them [a]keepers of the charge of the house, for all the [1]service thereof, and for all that shall be done therein.

15 [a]But the priests the Levites, [b]the sons of Zadok, that kept the charge of my sanctuary [c]when the children of Israel went astray from me, they shall come near to me to minister unto me, and they [d]shall stand before me to offer unto me [e]the fat and the blood, saith the Lord GOD:

16 They shall [a]enter into my sanctuary, and they shall come near to [b]my table, to minister unto me, and they shall keep my charge.

17 And it shall come to pass, *that* when they enter in at the gates of the inner court, [a]they shall be clothed with linen garments; and no wool shall come upon them, whiles they minister in the gates of the inner court, and [1]within.

18 [a]They shall have linen [1]bonnets upon their heads, and shall have linen [2]breeches upon their loins; they shall not [3]gird *themselves* with any thing that causeth sweat.

19 And when they go forth into the utter court, *even* into the utter court to the people, [a]they shall [1]put off their garments wherein they ministered, and lay them in the holy chambers, and they shall put on other garments; and they shall [b]not sanctify the people with their garments.

20 [a]Neither shall they shave their heads, nor [1]suffer their locks to grow [b]long; they shall [2]only poll their heads.

21 [a]Neither shall any priest drink wine, when they enter into the inner court.

43:25 [a] Ex. 29:35
43:26 [1] *make atonement for* [2] Or *consecrate it,* lit. *fill his hands*
43:27 [a] Lev. 9:1–4 [b] Ezek. 20:40, 41
44:1 [a] Ezek. 43:1 [1] *outer gate of the sanctuary*
44:2 [a] Ezek. 43:2–4
44:3 [a] Gen. 31:54 [b] Ezek. 46:2, 8 [1] *vestibule*
44:4 [a] Ezek. 3:23; 43:5 [b] Ezek. 1:28; 43:3 [1] *to the front of the temple*
44:5 [a] Ezek. 40:4 [b] Ezek. 43:10, 11 [1] *who may enter the temple* [2] *and all who go out*
44:6 [a] Ezek. 2:5 [b] 1 Pet. 4:3 [1] *let us have no more of*
44:7 [a] Acts 21:28 [b] Lev. 22:25 [c] Lev. 26:41 [d] Lev. 21:17 [e] Lev. 3:16 [1] *foreigners* [2] *defile* [3] *food*
44:8 [a] Lev. 22:2
44:9 [a] Ezek. 44:7 [1] *foreigner*

44:10 [a] 2 Kin. 23:8
44:11 [a] 1 Chr. 26:1–19 [b] 2 Chr. 29:34; 30:17 [c] Num. 16:9
44:12 [a] Is. 9:16 [b] Ps. 106:26 [1] Lit. *became a stumbling block of iniquity to the house of Israel*
44:13 [a] 2 Kin. 23:9 [b] Ezek. 32:30 [1] *minister as* [2] *nor into*
44:14 [a] Num. 18:4 [1] *work*
44:15 [a] Ezek. 40:46 [b] [1 Sam. 2:35] [c] Ezek. 44:10 [d] Deut. 10:8 [e] Ezek. 44:7
44:16 [a] Num. 18:5, 7, 8 [b] Ezek. 41:22
44:17 [a] Ex. 28:39–43; 39:27–29 [1] *within the house*
44:18 [a] Ex. 28:40; 39:28 [1] *turbans* [2] *trousers* [3] *clothe*
44:19 [a] Ezek. 42:14 [b] Lev. 6:27 [1] *take off*
44:20 [a] Lev. 21:5 [b] Num. 6:5 [1] *let their hair* [2] *keep their heads well trimmed*
44:21 [a] Lev. 10:9

22 Neither shall they take for their wives a <sup>a</sup>widow, nor her that is <sup>1</sup>put away: but they shall take maidens of the <sup>2</sup>seed of the house of Israel, or a widow <sup>3</sup>that had a priest before.

23 And <sup>a</sup>they shall teach my people *the difference* between the holy and <sup>1</sup>profane, and cause them to <sup>b</sup>discern between the unclean and the clean.

24 And <sup>a</sup>in controversy they shall stand <sup>1</sup>in judgment; *and* they shall judge it according to my judgments: and they shall keep my laws and my statutes in all mine <sup>2</sup>assemblies; <sup>b</sup>and they shall hallow my sabbaths.

25 And they shall come <sup>1</sup>at no dead person to defile themselves: but for father, or for mother, or for son, or for daughter, for brother, or for sister that hath had no husband, they may defile themselves.

26 And <sup>a</sup>after he is cleansed, they shall <sup>1</sup>reckon unto him seven days.

27 And in the day that he goeth into the sanctuary, <sup>a</sup>unto the inner court, to minister in the sanctuary, <sup>b</sup>he shall offer his sin offering, saith the Lord GOD.

28 And it shall be unto them for an inheritance: I <sup>a</sup>am their inheritance: and ye shall give them no <sup>b</sup>possession in Israel: I *am* their possession.

29 <sup>a</sup>They shall eat the <sup>1</sup>meat offering, and the sin offering, and the trespass offering; and <sup>b</sup>every <sup>2</sup>dedicated thing in Israel shall be theirs.

30 And the <sup>a</sup>first<sup>1</sup> of all the firstfruits of all *things,* and every <sup>2</sup>oblation of all, of every *sort* of your oblations, shall be the priest's: ye <sup>b</sup>shall also give unto the priest the first of your <sup>3</sup>dough, <sup>c</sup>that he may cause the blessing to rest in thine house.

31 The priests shall not eat of any thing that <sup>1</sup>is a <sup>a</sup>dead of itself, or <sup>2</sup>torn, whether it be fowl or beast.

## CHAPTER 45

MOREOVER, when ye shall <sup>a</sup>divide by lot the land for inheritance, ye shall <sup>b</sup>offer <sup>1</sup>an oblation unto the LORD, an holy portion of the land: the length *shall be* the length of five and twenty thousand <sup>2</sup>reeds, and the breadth *shall be* ten thousand. This *shall be* holy <sup>3</sup>in all the borders thereof round about.

2 Of this there shall be for the sanctuary <sup>a</sup>five hundred *in length,* with five hundred *in breadth,* square round about; and fifty cubits round about for <sup>1</sup>the suburbs thereof.

3 And of this measure shalt thou measure the length of five and twenty thousand, and the breadth of ten thousand: <sup>a</sup>and in it shall be the sanctuary and the most holy *place.*

4 <sup>a</sup>The holy *portion* of the land shall be for the priests the ministers of the

44:22 <sup>a</sup> Lev. 21:7, 13, 14 <sup>1</sup> *divorced* <sup>2</sup> *descendants* 3 *of a priest*
44:23 <sup>a</sup> Mal. 2:6–8 <sup>b</sup> Lev. 20:25 <sup>1</sup> *unholy*
44:24 <sup>a</sup> Deut. 17:8, 9 <sup>b</sup> Ezek. 22:26 <sup>1</sup> *as judges* <sup>2</sup> *appointed meetings*
44:25 <sup>1</sup> *near*
44:26 <sup>a</sup> Num. 6:10; 19:11, 13–19 <sup>1</sup> *count*
44:27 <sup>a</sup> Ezek. 44:17 <sup>b</sup> Lev. 5:3, 6
44:28 <sup>a</sup> Num. 18:20 <sup>b</sup> Ezek. 45:4
44:29 <sup>a</sup> Lev. 7:6 <sup>b</sup> Lev. 27:21, 28 <sup>1</sup> *grain or meal* <sup>2</sup> *devoted*
44:30 <sup>a</sup> Num. 3:13; 18:12 <sup>b</sup> Neh. 10:37 <sup>c</sup> [Mal. 3:10] <sup>1</sup> *best* <sup>2</sup> *sacrifice* 3 *ground meal*
44:31 <sup>a</sup> Lev. 22:8 <sup>1</sup> *died naturally* <sup>2</sup> *was torn by wild beasts*
45:1 <sup>a</sup> Ezek. 47:22 <sup>b</sup> Ezek. 48:8, 9 <sup>1</sup> *a district* <sup>2</sup> *Or cubits* 3 *throughout its territory*
45:2 <sup>a</sup> Ezek. 42:20 <sup>1</sup> *an open space*
45:3 <sup>a</sup> Ezek. 48:10
45:4 <sup>a</sup> Ezek. 48:10, 11
45:5 <sup>a</sup> Ezek. 48:13 <sup>b</sup> Ezek. 40:17 <sup>1</sup> *The temple*
45:6 <sup>a</sup> Ezek. 48:15 <sup>1</sup> *adjacent to the district*
45:7 <sup>a</sup> Ezek. 48:21 <sup>1</sup> *holy district* <sup>2</sup> *bordering on* 3 *alongside* 4 *tribal portions*
45:8 <sup>a</sup> [Is. 11:3–5]; Jer. 22:17; Ezek. 22:27
45:9 <sup>a</sup> Ezek. 44:6 <sup>b</sup> Jer. 22:3; Zech. 8:16 <sup>1</sup> *Enough* <sup>2</sup> *plundering* 3 *justice and righteousness* 4 *stop dispossessing*
45:10 <sup>a</sup> Lev. 19:36; Deut. 25:15; Prov. 16:11; Amos 8:4–6; Mic. 6:10, 11
45:11 <sup>1</sup> *according to*
45:12 <sup>a</sup> Ex. 30:13; Lev. 27:25; Num. 3:47 <sup>1</sup> *mina*
45:13 <sup>1</sup> *offering*
45:14 <sup>1</sup> *Or kor*
45:15 <sup>a</sup> Lev. 1:4; 6:30 <sup>1</sup> *rich* <sup>2</sup> *grain or meal* 3 *atonement*
45:16 <sup>1</sup> *offering*

sanctuary, which shall come near to minister unto the LORD: and it shall be a place for their houses, and an holy place for the sanctuary.

5 <sup>a</sup>And the five and twenty thousand of length, and the ten thousand of breadth, shall also the Levites, the ministers of <sup>1</sup>the house, have for themselves, for a possession for <sup>b</sup>twenty chambers.

6 <sup>a</sup>And ye shall appoint the possession of the city five thousand broad, and five and twenty thousand long, <sup>1</sup>over against the oblation of the holy *portion:* it shall be for the whole house of Israel.

7 <sup>a</sup>And *a portion shall be* for the prince on the one side and on the other side of the <sup>1</sup>oblation of the holy *portion,* and of the possession of the city, <sup>2</sup>before the <sup>1</sup>oblation of the holy *portion,* and <sup>2</sup>before the possession of the city, from the west side westward, and from the east side eastward: and the length *shall be* <sup>3</sup>over against one of the <sup>4</sup>portions, from the west border unto the east border.

8 In the land shall be his possession in Israel: and <sup>a</sup>my princes shall no more oppress my people; and *the rest of* the land shall they give to the house of Israel according to their tribes.

9 Thus saith the Lord GOD; <sup>a</sup>Let<sup>1</sup> it suffice you, O princes of Israel: <sup>b</sup>remove violence and <sup>2</sup>spoil, and execute <sup>3</sup>judgment and justice, <sup>4</sup>take away your exactions from my people, saith the Lord GOD.

10 Ye shall have just <sup>a</sup>balances, and a just ephah, and a just bath.

11 The ephah and the bath shall be of one measure, that the bath may contain the tenth part of an homer, and the ephah the tenth part of an homer: the measure thereof shall be <sup>1</sup>after the homer.

12 And the <sup>a</sup>shekel *shall be* twenty gerahs: twenty shekels, five and twenty shekels, fifteen shekels, shall be your <sup>1</sup>maneh.

13 This *is* the <sup>1</sup>oblation that ye shall offer; the sixth part of an ephah of an homer of wheat, and ye shall give the sixth part of an ephah of an homer of barley:

14 Concerning the ordinance of oil, the bath of oil, *ye shall offer* the tenth part of a bath out of the <sup>1</sup>cor, *which is* an homer of ten baths; for ten baths *are* an homer:

15 And one lamb out of the flock, out of two hundred, out of the <sup>1</sup>fat pastures of Israel; for a <sup>2</sup>meat offering, and for a burnt offering, and for peace offerings, <sup>a</sup>to make <sup>3</sup>reconciliation for them, saith the Lord GOD.

16 All the people of the land shall give this <sup>1</sup>oblation for the prince in Israel.

17 And it shall be the [a]prince's part *to give* burnt offerings, and [1]meat offerings, and drink offerings, in the feasts, and in the new moons, and in the sabbaths, in all [2]solemnities of the house of Israel: he shall prepare the sin offering, and the [1]meat offering, and the burnt offering, and the peace offerings, to make [3]reconciliation for the house of Israel.

18 Thus saith the Lord GOD; In the first *month,* in the first *day* of the month, thou shalt take a young bullock without blemish, and [a]cleanse the sanctuary:

19 [a]And the priest shall take of the blood of the sin offering, and put *it* upon the [1]posts of [2]the house, and upon the four corners of the [3]settle of the altar, and upon the posts of the gate of the inner court.

20 And so thou shalt do the seventh *day* of the month, [a]for every one that [1]erreth, [2]and for *him that is* simple: so shall ye [3]reconcile the house.

21 [a]In the first *month,* in the fourteenth day of the month, ye shall have the passover, a feast of seven days; unleavened bread shall be eaten.

22 And upon that day shall the prince prepare for himself and for all the people of the land [a]a bullock *for* a sin offering.

23 And [a]seven days of the feast he shall prepare a burnt offering to the LORD, seven bullocks and seven rams without blemish daily the seven days; [b]and a kid of the goats daily *for* a sin offering.

24 [a]And he shall prepare a [1]meat offering of an ephah for [2]a bullock, and an ephah for [2]a ram, and an hin of oil for [2]an ephah.

25 In the seventh *month,* in the fifteenth day of the month, shall he do the like in the [a]feast of the seven days, according to the sin offering, according to the burnt offering, and according to the [1]meat offering, and according to the oil.

## CHAPTER 46

THUS saith the Lord GOD; The gate of the inner court that [1]looketh toward the east shall be shut the six [a]working days; but on the sabbath it shall be opened, and in the day of the new moon it shall be opened.

2 [a]And the prince shall enter by the way of the [1]porch of *that* gate [2]without, and shall stand by the post of the gate, and the priests shall prepare his burnt offering and his peace offerings, and he shall worship at the threshold of the gate: then he shall go forth; but the gate shall not be shut until the evening.

3 Likewise the people of the land shall worship at the door of this gate

before the LORD in the sabbaths and in the new moons.

4 And the burnt offering that [a]the prince shall offer unto the LORD in the [b]sabbath day *shall be* six lambs without blemish, and a ram without blemish.

5 [a]And the meat offering *shall be* an ephah for a ram, and the [1]meat offering for the lambs [2]as he shall be able to give, and an hin of oil [3]to an ephah.

6 And in the day of the new moon *it shall be* a young bullock without blemish, and six lambs, and a ram: they shall be without blemish.

7 And he shall prepare a [1]meat offering, an ephah for a bullock, and an ephah for a ram, and for the lambs [2]according as his hand shall attain unto, and an hin of oil [3]to an ephah.

8 [a]And when the prince shall enter, he shall go in by the way of the [1]porch of *that* gate, and he shall go forth by [2]the way thereof.

9 But when the people of the land [a]shall come before the LORD in the [1]solemn feasts, he that entereth in by the way of the north [b]gate to worship shall go out by the way of the south gate; and he that entereth by the way of the south gate shall go forth by the way of the north gate: he shall not return by the way of the gate whereby he came in, but shall go forth [2]over against it.

10 And the prince in the midst of them, when they go in, shall go in; and when they go forth, shall go forth.

11 And in the [1]feasts and in the [2]solemnities [a]the [3]meat offering shall be an ephah to a bullock, and an ephah to a ram, and to the lambs as he [4]is able to give, and an hin of oil [5]to an ephah.

12 Now when the prince shall prepare a voluntary burnt offering or peace offerings voluntarily unto the LORD, [a]*one* shall then open him the gate that [1]looketh toward the east, and he shall prepare his burnt offering and his peace offerings, as he did on the sabbath day: then he shall go forth; and after his going forth *one* shall shut the gate.

13 [a]Thou shalt daily prepare a burnt offering unto the LORD of a lamb of the first year without blemish: thou shalt prepare it [1]every morning.

14 And thou shalt prepare a [1]meat offering [2]for it every morning, the sixth part of an ephah, and the third part of an hin of oil, to [3]temper with the fine flour; a [1]meat offering [4]continually by a perpetual [5]ordinance unto the LORD.

15 Thus shall they prepare the lamb, and the [1]meat offering, and the oil, every morning *for* a [a]continual[2] burnt offering.

45:17 [a] Ezek. 46:4–12 [1] *grain or meal* [2] *appointed feasts* [3] *atonement*
45:18 [a] Lev. 16:16, 33; Ezek. 43:22, 26
45:19 [a] Lev. 16:18–20; Ezek. 43:20 [1] *doorposts* [2] The temple [3] *ledge*
45:20 [a] Lev. 4:27; Ps. 19:12 [1] *sinned unintentionally* [2] *or in ignorance* [3] *make atonement for*
45:21 [a] Ex. 12:18; Lev. 23:5, 6; Num. 9:2, 3; 28:16, 17; Deut. 16:1
45:22 [a] Lev. 4:14
45:23 [a] Lev. 23:8 [b] Num. 28:15, 22, 30; 29:5, 11, 16, 19
45:24 [a] Num. 28:12–15; Ezek. 46:5, 7 [1] *grain or meal* [2] *each*
45:25 [a] Lev. 23:34; Num. 29:12; Deut. 16:13; 2 Chr. 5:3; 7:8, 10 [1] *grain or meal*
46:1 [a] Ex. 20:9 [1] *faces*
46:2 [a] Ezek. 44:3 [1] *vestibule* [2] *from the outside*
46:4 [a] Ezek. 45:17 [b] Num. 28:9, 10
46:5 [a] Num. 28:12; Ezek. 45:24; 46:7, 11 [1] *grain or meal* [2] Lit. *the gift of his hand* [3] *with every*
46:7 [1] *grain or meal* [2] *as much as he wants to give* [3] *with every*
46:8 [a] Ezek. 44:3; 46:2 [1] *vestibule* [2] *the same way*
46:9 [a] Ex. 23:14–17; 34:23; Deut. 16:16, 17; Ps. 84:7; Mic. 6:6 [b] Ezek. 48:31, 33 [1] *appointed* [2] *opposite*
46:11 [a] Ezek. 46:5, 7 [1] *festivals* [2] *appointed feasts* [3] *grain or meal* [4] *wants* [5] *with every*
46:12 [a] Ezek. 44:3; 46:1, 2, 8 [1] *faces*
46:13 [a] Ex. 29:38; Num. 28:3–5 [1] Lit. *morning by morning*
46:14 [1] *grain or meal* [2] *with* [3] *moisten* [4] *regularly* [5] Lit. *statute*
46:15 [a] Ex. 29:42; Num. 28:6 [1] *grain or meal* [2] *regular*

16 Thus saith the Lord GOD; If the prince give a gift unto any of his sons, the inheritance thereof shall be his sons'; it *shall be* their possession by inheritance.

17 But if he give a gift of his inheritance to one of his servants, then it shall be his to [a]the year of liberty; after it shall return to the prince: but his inheritance shall be his sons' [1]for them.

18 Moreover [a]the prince shall not take of the people's inheritance by oppression, to thrust them out of their [1]possession; *but* he shall give his sons inheritance out of his own [1]possession: that my people be not scattered every man from his [1]possession.

19 After he brought me through the entry, which *was* at the side of the gate, into the holy [a]chambers of the priests, which looked toward the north: and, behold, there *was* a place on the [1]two sides westward.

20 Then said he unto me, This *is* the place where the priests shall [a]boil the trespass offering and the sin offering, where they shall [b]bake the [1]meat offering; that they bear *them* not out into the utter court, [c]to sanctify the people.

21 Then he brought me forth into the utter court, and caused me to pass by the four corners of the court; and, behold, in every corner of the court *there was* a court.

22 In the four corners of the court *there were* [1]courts joined of forty *cubits* long and thirty broad: these four corners *were* of [2]one measure.

23 And *there was* a row of [1]*building* round about in them, round about them four, and *it was* made with [2]boiling places under the rows round about.

24 Then said he unto me, These *are* the [1]places of them that boil, where the ministers of [2]the house shall [a]boil the sacrifice of the people.

## CHAPTER 47

AFTERWARD he brought me again unto the door of [1]the house; and, behold, [a]waters [2]issued out from under the threshold of the house eastward: for the forefront of [1]the house *stood toward* the east, and the waters came down from under from the right side of the house, at the south *side* of the altar.

2 Then brought he me out of the way of the [1]gate northward, and led me [2]about the way without unto the utter gate by the way that [3]looketh [a]eastward; and, behold, there ran out waters on the right side.

3 And when [a]the man that had the line in his hand went forth eastward, he measured a thousand cubits, and

46:17 [a] Lev. 25:10
[1] *it shall become theirs*
46:18 [a] Ezek. 45:8
[1] *property*
46:19 [a] Ezek. 42:13  [1] *extreme western end*
46:20 [a] 2 Chr. 35:13  [b] Lev. 2:4, 5, 7  [c] Ezek. 44:19  [1] *grain or meal*
46:22 [1] *enclosed courts of* [2] *the same size*
46:23 [1] *building stones* [2] *cooking hearths*
46:24 [a] Ezek. 46:20  [1] *Kitchens* [2] *The temple*
47:1 [a] Ps. 46:4; Is. 30:25; 55:1; [Jer. 2:13]; Joel 3:18; Zech. 13:1; 14:8; [Rev. 22:1, 17]  [1] *The temple* [2] *flowed*
47:2 [a] Ezek. 44:1, 2  [1] *north gate* [2] *around on the outside* [3] *faces*
47:3 [a] Ezek. 40:3
47:4 [1] *waist*
47:5 [1] *cross* [2] *waters one must swim* [3] *crossed*
47:6 [1] *bank*
47:7 [a] [Is. 60:13, 21; 61:3]; Ezek. 47:12; Rev. 22:2]
47:8 [1] *flow* [2] *region* [3] Heb. *Arabah,* Jordan Valley [4] The Dead Sea [5] *when it reaches the sea*
47:10 [a] Num. 34:3; Josh. 23:4; Ezek. 48:28  [1] *fishermen* [2] *by it* [3] The Mediterranean
47:11 [1] *swamps* [2] *marshes*
47:12 [a] Ezek. 47:7; [Rev. 22:2]  [b] Job 18:16; [Ps. 1:3; Jer. 17:8]  [c] [Rev. 22:2]  [1] *food* [2] *wither* [3] *fall* [4] *every month* [5] *healing*
47:13 [a] Num. 34:1-29  [b] Gen. 48:5; 1 Chr. 5:1; Ezek. 48:4, 5
47:14 [a] Gen. 12:7; 13:15; 15:7; 17:8; 26:3; 28:13; Deut. 1:8; Ezek. 20:5, 6, 28, 42  [b] Ezek. 48:29  [1] *equally* [2] Took an oath
47:15 [a] Ezek. 48:1  [b] Num. 34:7, 8

he brought me through the waters; the waters *were* to the ancles.

4 Again he measured a thousand, and brought me through the waters; the waters *were* to the knees. Again he measured a thousand, and brought me through; the waters *were* to the [1]loins.

5 Afterward he measured a thousand; *and it was* a river that I could not [1]pass over: for the waters were risen, [2]waters to swim in, a river that could not be [3]passed over.

6 And he said unto me, Son of man, hast thou seen *this?* Then he brought me, and caused me to return to the [1]brink of the river.

7 Now when I had returned, behold, at the bank of the river *were* very many [a]trees on the one side and on the other.

8 Then said he unto me, These waters [1]issue out toward the east [2]country, and go down into the [3]desert, and go into [4]the sea: [5]*which being* brought forth into the sea, the waters shall be healed.

9 And it shall come to pass, *that* every thing that liveth, which moveth, whithersoever the rivers shall come, shall live: and there shall be a very great multitude of fish, because these waters shall come thither: for they shall be healed; and every thing shall live whither the river cometh.

10 And it shall come to pass, *that* the [1]fishers shall stand [2]upon it from En-gedi even unto En-eglaim; they shall be a *place* to spread forth nets; their fish shall be according to their kinds, as the fish [a]of [3]the great sea, exceeding many.

11 But the [1]miry places thereof and the [2]marishes thereof shall not be healed; they shall be given to salt.

12 And [a]by the river upon the bank thereof, on this side and on that side, shall grow all trees for [1]meat, [b]whose leaf shall not [2]fade, neither shall the fruit thereof [3]be consumed: it shall bring forth new fruit [4]according to his months, because their waters they issued out of the sanctuary: and the fruit thereof shall be for [1]meat, and the leaf thereof for [c]medicine.[5]

13 Thus saith the Lord GOD; This *shall be* the [a]border, whereby ye shall inherit the land according to the twelve tribes of Israel: [b]Joseph *shall have two* portions.

14 And ye shall inherit it, one [1]as well as another: *concerning* the which I [a]lifted[2] up mine hand to give it unto your [a]fathers: and this land shall [b]fall unto you for inheritance.

15 And this *shall be* the border of the land toward the north side, from the great sea, [a]the way of Hethlon, as men go to [b]Zedad;

16 ᵃHamath, ᵇBerothah, Sibraim, which *is* between the border of Damascus and the border of Hamath; Hazar-hatticon, which *is* by the coast of Hauran.

17 And the border from the sea shall be ᵃHazar-enan, the border of Damascus, and the north northward, and the border of Hamath. And *this is* the north side.

18 And the east side ye shall measure ¹from Hauran, and from Damascus, and from Gilead, and from the land of Israel *by* Jordan, from the border unto the east sea. And *this is* the east side.

19 And the south side southward, from Tamar *even* to ᵃthe waters of ¹strife *in* Kadesh, the ²river to the great sea. And *this is* ³the south side ⁴southward.

20 The west side also *shall be* the great sea from the ¹border, till a man come ²over against Hamath. This *is* the west side.

21 So shall ye ᵃdivide this land unto you according to the tribes of Israel.

22 And it shall come to pass, *that* ye shall divide it by ᵃlot for an inheritance unto you, ᵇand to the strangers that sojourn among you, which shall beget children among you: ᶜand they shall be unto you as ¹born in the country among the children of Israel; they shall have inheritance with you among the tribes of Israel.

23 And it shall come to pass, *that* in what tribe the stranger sojourneth, there shall ye give *him* his inheritance, saith the Lord GOD.

### CHAPTER 48

Now these *are* the names of the tribes. ᵃFrom the north end to the coast of the way of Hethlon, as one goeth to Hamath, Hazar-enan, the border of Damascus northward, ¹to the coast of Hamath; for these are his sides east *and* west; ²a *portion for* ᵇDan.

2 And by the border of Dan, from the east side unto the west side, a *portion for* ᵃAsher.

3 And by the border of Asher, from the east side even unto the west side, a *portion for* ᵃNaphtali.

4 And by the border of Naphtali, from the east side unto the west side, a *portion for* ᵃManasseh.

5 And by the border of Manasseh, from the east side unto the west side, a *portion for* ᵃEphraim.

6 And by the border of Ephraim, from the east side even unto the west side, a *portion for* ᵃReuben.

7 And by the border of Reuben, from the east side unto the west side, a *portion for* ᵃJudah.

47:16 ᵃ Num. 34:8
ᵇ 2 Sam. 8:8
47:17 ᵃ Num. 34:9;
Ezek. 48:1
47:18 ¹ Lit. *from between*
47:19 ᵃ Num. 20:13; Deut. 32:51;
Ps. 81:7; Ezek. 48:28 ¹ Heb.
Meribah ² *brook* ³ *toward Teman* ⁴ *to the Negev*
47:20 ¹ *southern border* ² *opposite*
47:21 ᵃ Ezek. 45:1
47:22 ᵃ Num. 26:55, 56 ᵇ [Eph. 3:6; Rev. 7:9, 10]
ᶜ [Acts 11:18; 15:9;
Gal. 3:28; Eph. 2:12–14; Col. 3:11]
¹ *native-born*

48:1 ᵃ Ezek. 47:15
ᵇ Josh. 19:40–48
¹ *in the direction of* ² Lit. *one*
48:2 ᵃ Josh. 19:24–31
48:3 ᵃ Josh. 19:32–39
48:4 ᵃ Josh. 13:29–31; 17:1–11, 17, 18
48:5 ᵃ Josh. 16:5–10; 17:8–10, 14–18
48:6 ᵃ Josh. 13:15–23
48:7 ᵃ Josh. 15:1–63; 19:9
48:8 ᵃ Ezek. 45:1–6 ᵇ [Is. 12:6; 33:20–22]; Ezek. 45:3, 4 ¹ *district which you shall set apart* ² Or *cubits*
48:9 ¹ *district*
48:10 ¹ *district*
48:11 ᵃ Ezek. 40:46; 44:15
ᵇ Ezek. 44:10, 12
¹ *consecrated*
48:12 ᵃ Ezek. 45:4
¹ *district* ² *set apart*
48:13 ᵃ Ezek. 45:5
¹ *opposite*
48:14 ᵃ Ex. 22:29;
Lev. 27:10, 28, 33;
Ezek. 44:30 ¹ *this best part*
48:15 ᵃ Ezek. 45:6 ᵇ Ezek. 42:20 ¹ *along the edge of* ² *for general use by* ³ *common-land* ⁴ *center*
48:17 ¹ *common-land*
48:18 ¹ *rest of the* ² *alongside the district* ³ *adjacent to the district* ⁴ *produce* ⁵ *the workers of*

8 And by the border of Judah, from the east side unto the west side, shall be ᵃthe ¹offering which ye shall offer of five and twenty thousand ²*reeds in* breadth, and *in* length as one of the *other* parts, from the east side unto the west side: and the ᵇsanctuary shall be in the midst of it.

9 The ¹oblation that ye shall offer unto the LORD *shall be* of five and twenty thousand in length, and of ten thousand in breadth.

10 And for them, *even* for the priests, shall be *this* holy ¹oblation; toward the north five and twenty thousand *in length,* and toward the west ten thousand in breadth, and toward the east ten thousand in breadth, and toward the south five and twenty thousand in length: and the sanctuary of the LORD shall be in the midst thereof.

11 ᵃ*It shall be* for the priests that are ¹sanctified of the sons of Zadok; which have kept my charge, which went not astray when the children of Israel went astray, ᵇas the Levites went astray.

12 And *this* ¹oblation of the land that is ²offered shall be unto them a thing most ᵃholy by the border of the Levites.

13 And ¹over against the border of the priests the ᵃLevites *shall have* five and twenty thousand in length, and ten thousand in breadth: all the length *shall be* five and twenty thousand, and the breadth ten thousand.

14 ᵃAnd they shall not sell of it, neither exchange, nor alienate ¹the firstfruits of the land: for *it is* holy unto the LORD.

15 ᵃAnd the five thousand, that are left in the breadth ¹over against the five and twenty thousand, shall be ᵇa² profane *place* for the city, for dwelling, and for ³suburbs: and the city shall be in the ⁴midst thereof.

16 And these *shall be* the measures thereof; the north side four thousand and five hundred, and the south side four thousand and five hundred, and on the east side four thousand and five hundred, and the west side four thousand and five hundred.

17 And the ¹suburbs of the city shall be toward the north two hundred and fifty, and toward the south two hundred and fifty, and toward the east two hundred and fifty, and toward the west two hundred and fifty.

18 And the ¹residue in length ²over against the oblation of the holy *portion shall be* ten thousand eastward, and ten thousand westward: and it shall be ³over against the oblation of the holy *portion;* and the ⁴increase thereof shall be for food unto ⁵them that serve the city.

19 [a]And [1]they that serve the city shall [2]serve it out of all the tribes of Israel.

20 All the [1]oblation *shall be* five and twenty thousand by five and twenty thousand: ye shall [2]offer the holy oblation foursquare, with the [3]possession of the city.

21 [a]And the [1]residue *shall be* for the prince, on the one side and on the other of the holy [2]oblation, and of the [3]possession of the city, [4]over against the five and twenty thousand of the [2]oblation toward the east border, and westward [4]over against the five and twenty thousand toward the west border, [4]over against the [5]portions [6]for the prince: and it shall be the holy [2]oblation; [b]and the sanctuary of [7]the house *shall be* in the midst thereof.

22 Moreover [1]from the possession of the Levites, and from the possession of the city, *being* in the midst of *that* which is the prince's, between the border of Judah and the border of [a]Benjamin, shall be for the prince.

23 As for the rest of the tribes, from the east side unto the west side, Benjamin *shall have* [1]a *portion.*

24 And by the border of Benjamin, from the east side unto the west side, [a]Simeon *shall have* a *portion.*

25 And by the border of Simeon, from the east side unto the west side, [a]Issachar a *portion.*

26 And by the border of Issachar, from the east side unto the west side, [a]Zebulun a *portion.*

48:19 [a] Ezek. 45:6
[1] *the workers of*
[2] *cultivate*

48:20 [1] *district*
[2] *set apart the holy district*
[3] *property*

48:21 [a] Ezek. 34:24; 45:7; 48:22
[b] Ezek. 48:8, 10
[1] *remainder* [2] *district* [3] *property*
[4] *next to* [5] *tribal portions* [6] *it shall belong to* [7] The temple

48:22 [a] Josh. 18:21-28 [1] *apart from*

48:23 [1] Lit. *one*

48:24 [a] Josh. 19:1-9

48:25 [a] Josh. 19:17-23

48:26 [a] Josh. 19:10-16

48:27 [a] Josh. 13:24-28

48:28 [a] Gen. 14:7; 2 Chr. 20:2; Ezek. 47:19 [b] Ezek. 47:10, 15, 19, 20
[1] Heb. *Meribah*
[2] *along the brook*

48:29 [a] Ezek. 47:14, 21, 22

48:30 [1] *exits*

48:31 [a] [Rev. 21:10-14]

48:33 [1] Or *cubits*

48:35 [a] Jer. 23:6; 33:16 [b] Is. 12:6; 14:32; 24:23; Jer. 3:17; 8:19; 14:9;

27 And by the border of Zebulun, from the east side unto the west side, [a]Gad a *portion.*

28 And by the border of Gad, at the south side southward, the border shall be even from Tamar *unto* [a]the waters of [1]strife *in* Kadesh, *and* [2]to the river toward the [b]great sea.

29 [a]This *is* the land which ye shall divide by lot unto the tribes of Israel for inheritance, and these *are* their portions, saith the Lord GOD.

30 And these *are* the [1]goings out of the city on the north side, four thousand and five hundred measures.

31 [a]And the gates of the city *shall be* after the names of the tribes of Israel: three gates northward; one gate of Reuben, one gate of Judah, one gate of Levi.

32 And at the east side four thousand and five hundred: and three gates; and one gate of Joseph, one gate of Benjamin, one gate of Dan.

33 And at the south side four thousand and five hundred [1]measures: and three gates; one gate of Simeon, one gate of Issachar, one gate of Zebulun.

34 At the west side four thousand and five hundred, *with* their three gates; one gate of Gad, one gate of Asher, one gate of Naphtali.

35 *It was* round about eighteen thousand [1]*measures:* [a]and the name of the city from *that* day *shall be,* [b]The[2] LORD *is* there.

Ezek. 35:10; Joel 3:21; Zech. 2:10; Rev. 21:3; 22:3 [1] Or cubits [2] Heb. YHWH *Shammah*

# THE BOOK OF
# DANIEL

**D**aniel's life and ministry bridge the entire seventy-year period of Babylonian captivity. Deported to Babylon at the age of sixteen, and handpicked for government service, Daniel becomes God's prophetic mouthpiece to the gentile and Jewish world declaring God's present and eternal purpose. Nine of the twelve chapters in his book revolve around dreams, including God-given visions involving trees, animals, beasts, and images. In both his personal adventures and prophetic visions, Daniel shows God's guidance, intervention, and power in the affairs of men.

The name *Daniye'l* or *Dani'el* means "God Is My Judge," and the book is, of course, named after the author and principal character. The Greek form *Daniel* in the Septuagint is the basis for the Latin and English titles.

## CHAPTER 1

**I**N the third year of the reign of ªJehoiakim king of Judah came Nebuchadnezzar king of Babylon unto Jerusalem, and besieged it.

2 And the Lord gave Jehoiakim king of Judah into his hand, with ªpart of the vessels of ¹the house of God: which he carried ᵇinto the land of Shinar to the house of his god; ᶜand he brought the vessels into the treasure house of his god.

3 And the king spake unto Ashpenaz the master of his eunuchs, that he should bring ªcertain of the children of Israel, and of the king's ¹seed, and of the princes;

4 ¹Children ªin whom *was* no blemish, but ²well favoured, and skilful in all wisdom, and ³cunning in knowledge, and ⁴understanding science, and such as *had* ability in them to ⁵stand in the king's palace, and ᵇwhom they might teach the ⁶learning and the tongue of the Chaldeans.

5 And the king appointed them a daily provision of the king's ¹meat, and of the wine which he drank: so ²nourishing them three years, that at the end thereof they might ªstand³ before the king.

6 Now among these were of the children of Judah, Daniel, Hananiah, Mishael, and Azariah:

7 ªUnto whom the prince of the eunuchs gave names: ᵇfor he gave unto ¹Daniel *the name* of Belteshazzar; and to Hananiah, of Shadrach; and to Mishael, of Meshach; and to Azariah, of Abed-nego.

8 But Daniel purposed in his heart that he would not defile himself ªwith the portion of the ¹king's meat, nor with the wine which he drank: therefore he requested of the prince of the eunuchs that he might not defile himself.

9 Now ªGod had brought Daniel into favour and ¹tender love with the prince of the eunuchs.

10 And the prince of the eunuchs said unto Daniel, I fear my lord the king, who hath appointed your meat and your drink: for why should he see your faces worse ¹liking than the ²children which *are* of your ³sort? then shall ye make *me* endanger my head to the king.

11 Then said Daniel to ¹Melzar, whom the prince of the eunuchs had set over Daniel, Hananiah, Mishael, and Azariah,

12 ¹Prove thy servants, I beseech thee, ten days; and let them give us ²pulse to eat, and water to drink.

13 Then let our countenances be looked upon before thee, and the countenance of the children that eat of the portion of the king's meat: and as thou seest, deal with thy servants.

14 So he consented to them in this matter, and ¹proved them ten days.

15 And at the end of ten days their countenances appeared ¹fairer and fatter in flesh than all the children which did eat the portion of the king's ²meat.

16 Thus ¹Melzar took away the portion of their ²meat, and the wine that they should drink; and gave them ³pulse.

17 As for these four ¹children, ªGod gave them ᵇknowledge and skill in all ²learning and wisdom: and Daniel had ᶜunderstanding in all visions and dreams.

18 Now at the end of the days that the king had said he ¹should bring them in, then the ²prince of the eunuchs brought them in before Nebuchadnezzar.

19 And the king ¹communed with them; and among them all was found none like Daniel, Hananiah, Mishael, and Azariah: therefore ªstood² they before the king.

20 ªAnd in all matters of wisdom *and* understanding, that the king ¹enquired of them, he found them ten times better than all the magicians

1:1 ª 2 Kin. 24:1, 2
1:2 ª Jer. 27:19, 20 ᵇ Zech. 5:11 ᶜ 2 Chr. 36:7 ¹ The temple
1:3 ª Is. 39:7 ¹ descendants
1:4 ª Lev. 24:19, 20 ᵇ Acts 7:22 ¹ Young men ² good-looking ³ possessing ⁴ quick to understand ⁵ Serve ⁶ literature, lit. writing
1:5 ª Dan. 1:19 ¹ food ² training ³ Serve
1:7 ª 2 Kin. 24:17 ᵇ Dan. 2:26; 4:8; 5:12 ¹ Lit. God Is My Judge
1:8 ª Hos. 9:3 ¹ king's delicacies
1:9 ª Gen. 39:21 ¹ sympathy
1:10 ¹ looking ² young men ³ age
1:11 ¹ Or the steward
1:12 ¹ Test ² vegetables
1:14 ¹ tested
1:15 ¹ better ² food
1:16 ¹ Or the steward ² food ³ vegetables
1:17 ª 1 Kin. 3:12, 28; 2 Chr. 1:10–12; [Luke 21:15; James 1:5–7] ᵇ Acts 7:22 ᶜ Num. 12:6; 2 Chr. 26:5; Dan. 5:11, 12, 14; 10:1 ¹ young men ² literature
1:18 ¹ would ² chief
1:19 ª Gen. 41:46; [Prov. 22:29]; Dan. 1:5 ¹ examined, lit. talked ² Served
1:20 ª 1 Kin. 10:1 ¹ questioned

*and* astrologers that *were* in all his realm.

21 [a]And Daniel continued *even* unto the first year of king Cyrus.

## CHAPTER 2

AND in the second year of the reign of Nebuchadnezzar Nebuchadnezzar dreamed dreams, [a]wherewith his spirit was troubled, and [b]his sleep [1]brake from him.

2 [a]Then the king commanded to call the magicians, and the astrologers, and the sorcerers, and the Chaldeans, for to [1]shew the king his dreams. So they came and stood before the king.

3 And the king said unto them, I have dreamed a dream, and my spirit was troubled to [1]know the dream.

4 Then spake the Chaldeans to the king in [1]Syriack, [a]O king, live for ever: tell thy servants the dream, and we will shew the interpretation.

5 The king answered and said to the Chaldeans, The [1]thing is [2]gone from me: if ye will not make known unto me the dream, with the interpretation thereof, ye shall be [a]cut in pieces, and your houses shall be made [3]a dunghill.

6 [a]But if ye [1]shew the dream, and the interpretation thereof, ye shall receive of me gifts and rewards and great honour: therefore [1]shew me the dream, and the interpretation thereof.

7 They answered again and said, Let the king tell his servants the dream, and we will [1]shew the interpretation of it.

8 The king answered and said, I know of certainty that ye would [1]gain the time, because ye see the thing is [2]gone from me.

9 But if ye will not make known unto me the dream, *there is but* one decree for you: for ye have prepared lying and corrupt words to speak before me, till the [1]time be changed: therefore tell me the dream, and I shall know that ye can [2]shew me the interpretation thereof.

10 The Chaldeans answered before the king, and said, There is not a man upon the earth that can shew the king's matter: therefore *there is* no king, lord, nor ruler, *that* asked such things at any magician, or astrologer, or Chaldean.

11 And *it is* a [1]rare thing that the king requireth, and there is [2]none other that can shew it before the king, [a]except the gods, whose dwelling is not with flesh.

12 For this cause the king was angry and very furious, and commanded to destroy all the wise *men* of Babylon.

13 And the decree went forth that the wise *men* should be slain; and

they sought [a]Daniel and his fellows to be slain.

14 Then Daniel answered with counsel and [1]wisdom to Arioch the captain of the king's guard, which was gone forth to slay the wise *men* of Babylon:

15 He answered and said to Arioch the king's captain, Why *is* the decree so [1]hasty from the king? Then Arioch made the thing known to Daniel.

16 Then Daniel went in, and desired of the king that he would give him time, and that he would [1]shew the king the interpretation.

17 Then Daniel went to his house, and made the [1]thing known to Hananiah, Mishael, and Azariah, his companions:

18 [a]That they [1]would desire mercies [2]of the God of heaven concerning this secret; that Daniel and his fellows should not [3]perish with the rest of the wise *men* of Babylon.

19 Then was the secret revealed unto Daniel [a]in a night vision. Then Daniel blessed the God of heaven.

20 Daniel answered and said, [a]Blessed be the name of God for ever and ever: [b]for wisdom and might are his:

21 And he changeth [a]the times and the seasons: [b]he removeth kings, and [1]setteth up kings: [c]he giveth wisdom unto the wise, and knowledge to them that [2]know understanding:

22 [a]He revealeth the deep and secret things: [b]he knoweth what *is* in the darkness, and [c]the light dwelleth with him.

23 I thank thee, and praise thee, O thou God of my fathers, who hast given me wisdom and might, and hast made known unto me now what we [a]desired[1] of thee: for thou hast *now* made known unto us the king's matter.

24 Therefore Daniel went in unto Arioch, whom the king had [1]ordained to destroy the wise *men* of Babylon: he went and said thus unto him; Destroy not the wise *men* of Babylon: bring me in before the king, and I will [2]shew unto the king the interpretation.

25 Then Arioch brought in Daniel before the king in haste, and said thus unto him, I have found a man [1]of the captives of Judah, that will make known unto the king the interpretation.

26 The king answered and said to Daniel, whose name *was* Belteshazzar, Art thou able to make known unto me the dream which I have seen, and the interpretation thereof?

27 Daniel answered in the presence of the king, and said, The secret which the king hath demanded cannot the

wise *men,* the astrologers, the magicians, the soothsayers, [1]shew unto the king;

28 [a]But there is a God in heaven that revealeth secrets, and [1]maketh known to the king Nebuchadnezzar [b]what shall be in the latter days. Thy dream, and the visions of thy head upon thy bed, are these;

29 As for thee, O king, thy thoughts came *into thy mind* upon thy bed, what should come to pass hereafter: [a]and he that revealeth secrets maketh known to thee what shall come to pass.

30 [a]But as for me, this secret is not revealed to me for *any* wisdom that I have more than any living, but for *their* sakes that shall make known the interpretation to the king, [b]and that thou mightest [1]know the thoughts of thy heart.

31 Thou, O king, sawest, and behold a great image. This great image, whose brightness *was* excellent, stood before thee; and the form thereof *was* [1]terrible.

32 [a]This image's head *was* of fine gold, his breast and his arms of silver, his belly and his [1]thighs of [2]brass,

33 His legs of iron, his feet part of iron and part of [1]clay.

34 [1]Thou sawest till that a stone was cut out [a]without hands, which smote the image upon his feet *that were* of iron and clay, and brake them to pieces.

35 [a]Then was the iron, the clay, the brass, the silver, and the gold, [1]broken to pieces together, and became [b]like the chaff of the summer threshingfloors; and the wind carried them away, that [c]no [2]place was found for them: and the stone that smote the image [d]became a great mountain, [e]and filled the whole earth.

36 This *is* the dream; and we will tell the interpretation thereof before the king.

37 [a]Thou, O king, *art* a king of kings: [b]for the God of heaven hath given thee a kingdom, power, and strength, and glory.

38 [a]And wheresoever the children of men dwell, the beasts of the field and the fowls of the heaven hath he given into thine hand, and hath made thee ruler over them all. [b]Thou *art* this head of gold.

39 And after thee shall arise [a]another kingdom [b]inferior to thee, and another third kingdom of [1]brass, which shall bear rule over all the earth.

40 And [a]the fourth kingdom shall be strong as iron: forasmuch as iron breaketh in pieces and [1]subdueth all *things:* and as iron that breaketh all these, shall it break in pieces and [2]bruise.

41 And whereas thou sawest the feet and toes, part of [1]potters' clay, and part of iron, the kingdom shall be divided; but there shall be in it of the strength of the iron, forasmuch as thou sawest the iron mixed with [2]miry clay.

42 And *as* the toes of the feet *were* part of iron, and part of clay, [a]so the kingdom shall be partly strong, and partly [1]broken.

43 And whereas thou sawest iron mixed with [1]miry clay, they shall mingle themselves with the seed of men: but they shall not [2]cleave one to another, even as iron is not mixed with clay.

44 And in the days of these kings [a]shall the God of heaven set up a kingdom, [b]which shall never be destroyed: and the kingdom shall not be left to other people, [c]but it shall [1]break in pieces and [2]consume all these kingdoms, and it shall stand for ever.

45 [a]Forasmuch as thou sawest that the stone was cut out of the mountain without hands, and that it brake in pieces the iron, the [1]brass, the clay, the silver, and the gold; the great God hath made known to the king what shall come to pass [2]hereafter: and the dream *is* certain, and the interpretation thereof [3]sure.

46 [a]Then the king Nebuchadnezzar fell upon his face, [1]and worshipped Daniel, and commanded that they should [2]offer an oblation [b]and [3]sweet odours unto him.

47 The king answered unto Daniel, and said, Of a truth *it is,* that [a]your God *is* a God of [b]gods, and a Lord of kings, and a revealer of secrets, seeing thou couldest reveal this secret.

48 [a]Then the king made Daniel a great man, [b]and gave him many great gifts, and made him ruler over the whole province of Babylon, and [c]chief of the governors over all the wise *men* of Babylon.

49 Then Daniel requested of the king, [a]and he set Shadrach, Meshach, and Abed-nego, over the affairs of the province of Babylon: but Daniel [b]sat [1]in the gate of the king.

## CHAPTER 3

NEBUCHADNEZZAR the king made an image of gold, whose height *was* [1]threescore cubits, *and* the breadth thereof six cubits: he set it up in the plain of Dura, in the province of Babylon.

2 Then Nebuchadnezzar the king sent to gather together the princes, the governors, and the captains, the judges, the treasurers, the counsellors, the sheriffs, and all the rulers of the provinces, to come to the dedication of the image which Nebuchadnezzar the king had set up.

### Cross-references (center column)

2:27 [1] *declare*
2:28 [a] Gen. 40:8
[b] Gen. 49:1 [1] *has made known*
2:29 [a] [Dan. 2:22, 28]
2:30 [a] Acts 3:12 [b] Dan. 2:47 [1] *understand*
2:31 [1] *awesome*
2:32 [a] Dan. 2:38, 45 [1] *loins or sides* [2] *bronze*
2:33 [1] *Or baked clay*
2:34 [a] [Zech. 4:6] [1] *You were seeing*
2:35 [a] [Rev. 16:14] [b] Hos. 13:3 [c] Ps. 37:10, 36 [d] [Is. 2:2, 3] [e] Ps. 80:9 [1] *crushed* [2] *trace*
2:37 [a] Jer. 27:6, 7 [b] Ezra 1:2
2:38 [a] Dan. 4:21, 22 [b] Dan. 2:32
2:39 [a] Dan. 5:28, 31 [b] Dan. 2:32 [1] *bronze*
2:40 [a] Dan. 7:7, 23 [1] *shatters* [2] *crush*
2:41 [1] *pottery clay* [2] *ceramic*
2:42 [a] Dan. 7:24 [1] *brittle or fragile*
2:43 [1] *ceramic* [2] *adhere*
2:44 [a] Dan. 2:28, 37 [b] Is. 9:6, 7; Ezek. 37:25; Dan. 4:3, 34; 6:26; 7:14, 27; Mic. 4:7; [Luke 1:32, 33] [c] Ps. 2:9; Is. 60:12; Dan. 2:34, 35; [1 Cor. 15:24] [1] *Or crush* [2] *Lit. put an end to*
2:45 [a] Dan. 2:35; Is. 28:16 [1] *bronze* [2] *after this* [3] *trustworthy*
2:46 [a] Dan. 3:5, 7; Acts 10:25; 14:13; Rev. 19:10; 22:8 [b] Lev. 26:31; Ezra 6:10 [1] *prostrate before* [2] *present an offering* [3] *incense*
2:47 [a] Dan. 3:28, 29; 4:34–37 [b] [Deut. 10:17]
2:48 [a] [Prov. 14:35; 21:1] [b] Dan. 2:6 [c] Dan. 4:9; 5:11
2:49 [a] Dan. 1:7; 3:12 [b] Esth. 2:19, 21; 3:2; Amos 5:15 [1] *In the king's court*
3:1 [1] *About 90 feet*

3 Then the princes, the governors, and captains, the judges, the treasurers, the counsellors, the sheriffs, and all the rulers of the provinces, were gathered together unto the dedication of the image that Nebuchadnezzar the king had set up; and they stood before the image that Nebuchadnezzar had set up.

4 Then an herald cried [1]aloud, To you it is commanded, [a]O people, nations, and languages,

5 *That* at what time ye hear the sound of the [1]cornet, flute, harp, [2]sackbut, psaltery, [3]dulcimer, and all kinds of musick, ye fall down and worship the golden image that Nebuchadnezzar the king hath set up:

6 And whoso falleth not down and worshippeth shall the same hour [a]be cast into the midst of a burning fiery furnace.

7 Therefore at that time, when all the people heard the sound of the [1]cornet, flute, harp, [2]sackbut, psaltery, [3]and all kinds of musick, all the people, the nations, and the languages, fell down *and* worshipped the golden image that Nebuchadnezzar the king had set up.

8 Wherefore at that time certain Chaldeans [a]came near, and accused the Jews.

9 They spake and said to the king Nebuchadnezzar, [a]O king, live for ever.

10 Thou, O king, hast made a decree, that every man that shall hear the sound of the [1]cornet, flute, harp, [2]sackbut, psaltery, and [3]dulcimer, and all kinds of musick, shall fall down and worship the golden image:

11 And whoso falleth not down and worshippeth, *that* he should be cast into the midst of a burning fiery furnace.

12 [a]There are certain Jews whom thou hast set over the affairs of the province of Babylon, Shadrach, Meshach, and Abed-nego; these men, O king, have [b]not[1] regarded thee: they serve not thy gods, nor worship the golden image which thou hast set up.

13 Then Nebuchadnezzar in *his* [a]rage and fury commanded to bring Shadrach, Meshach, and Abed-nego. Then they brought these men before the king.

14 Nebuchadnezzar spake and said unto them, *Is it* true, O Shadrach, Meshach, and Abed-nego, do not ye serve my gods, nor worship the golden image which I have set up?

15 Now if ye be ready that at what time ye hear the sound of the [1]cornet, flute, harp, [2]sackbut, psaltery, and [3]dulcimer, and all kinds of musick, ye fall down and worship the image which I have made; [a]*well:* but if

ye worship not, ye shall be cast the same hour into the midst of a burning fiery furnace; [b]and who *is* that God that shall deliver you out of my hands?

16 Shadrach, Meshach, and Abednego, answered and said to the king, O Nebuchadnezzar, [a]we *are* not careful to [2]answer thee in this matter.

17 If it be *so,* our [a]God whom we serve is able to [b]deliver us from the burning fiery furnace, and he will deliver *us* out of thine hand, O king.

18 But if not, be it known unto thee, O king, that we will not serve thy gods, nor [a]worship the golden image which thou hast set up.

19 Then was Nebuchadnezzar full of fury, and the [1]form of his visage was changed against Shadrach, Meshach, and Abed-nego: *therefore* he spake, and commanded that they should heat the furnace one seven times more than it was [2]wont to be heated.

20 And he commanded [1]the most mighty men that *were* in his army to bind Shadrach, Meshach, and Abednego, *and* to cast *them* into the burning fiery furnace.

21 Then these men were bound in their [1]coats, their [2]hosen, and their [3]hats, and their *other* garments, and were cast into the midst of the burning fiery furnace.

22 Therefore because the king's commandment was [1]urgent, and the furnace exceeding hot, the flame of the fire slew those men that took up Shadrach, Meshach, and Abed-nego.

23 And these three men, Shadrach, Meshach, and Abed-nego, fell down bound into the midst of the burning fiery furnace.

24 Then Nebuchadnezzar the king was astonied, and rose up in haste, *and* spake, and said unto his [1]counsellors, Did not we cast three men bound into the midst of the fire? They answered and said unto the king, True, O king.

25 He answered and said, Lo, I see four men loose, [a]walking in the midst of the fire, and they [1]have no hurt; and the form of the fourth is like [b]the[2] Son of God.

26 Then Nebuchadnezzar came near to the [1]mouth of the burning fiery furnace, *and* spake, and said, Shadrach, Meshach, and Abed-nego, ye servants of the [a]most high God, come forth, and come *hither.* Then Shadrach, Meshach, and Abed-nego, came forth of the midst of the fire.

27 And the [1]princes, [2]governors, and [3]captains, and the king's counsellors, being gathered together, saw these men, [a]upon whose bodies the fire had no power, nor was an hair of

3:4 [a] Dan. 4:1; 6:25 [1] Lit. *with strength*

3:5 [1] *horn* [2] *lyre* [3] *pipes*

3:6 [a] Jer. 29:22; Ezek. 22:18–22; Matt. 13:42, 50; Rev. 9:2; 13:15; 14:11

3:7 [1] *horn* [2] *lyre* [3] Many mss. *pipes, and*

3:8 [a] Ezra 4:12–16; Esth. 3:8, 9; Dan. 6:12, 13

3:9 [a] Dan. 2:4; 5:10; 6:6, 21

3:10 [1] *horn* [2] *lyre* [3] *pipes*

3:12 [a] Dan. 2:49 [b] Dan. 1:8; 6:12, 13 [1] *disregarded*

3:13 [a] Dan. 2:12; 3:19

3:15 [a] Ex. 32:32; Luke 13:9 [1] *horn* [2] *lyre* [3] *pipes*

3:16 [a] [Matt. 10:19] [1] *have no need* [2] Lit. *return a word to you*

3:17 [a] Job 5:19; [Ps. 27:1, 2; Is. 26:3, 4]; Jer. 1:8; 15:20, 21; Dan. 6:19–22 [b] 1 Sam. 17:37; Jer. 1:8; 15:20, 21; 42:11; Dan. 6:16, 19–22; Mic. 7:7; 2 Cor. 1:10

3:18 [a] Job 13:15

3:19 [1] *expression on his face* [2] *usually*

3:20 [1] *certain mighty men of valour*

3:21 [1] *mantles* [2] *leggings* [3] *turbans*

3:22 [1] Or *severe*

3:24 [1] *high officials*

3:25 [a] [Ps. 91:3–9]; Is. 43:2 [b] Job 1:6; 38:7; [Ps. 34:7]; Dan. 3:28 [1] *are not* [2] Or *a son of the gods*

3:26 [a] [Dan. 4:2, 3, 17, 34, 35] [1] Lit. *door*

3:27 [a] [Is. 43:2]; Heb. 11:34 [1] *satraps* [2] *administrators* [3] *governors*

their head singed, neither were their [4]coats changed, nor the smell of fire had passed on them.

28 *Then* Nebuchadnezzar spake, and said, Blessed *be* the God of Shadrach, Meshach, and Abed-nego, who hath sent his [a]angel, and delivered his servants that trusted in him, and have [1]changed the king's word, and yielded their bodies, that they might not serve nor worship any god, except their own God.

29 [a]Therefore I make a decree, That every people, nation, and language, which speak any thing amiss against the [b]God of Shadrach, Meshach, and Abed-nego, shall be [c]cut in pieces, and their houses shall be made [1]a dunghill; [d]because there is no other God that can deliver [2]after this sort.

30 *Then* the king [1]promoted Shadrach, Meshach, and Abed-nego, in the province of Babylon.

## CHAPTER 4

NEBUCHADNEZZAR the king, [a]unto all people, nations, and languages, that dwell in all the earth; Peace be multiplied unto you.

2 I thought it good to shew the signs and wonders [a]that the high God hath wrought toward me.

3 [a]How great *are* his signs! and how mighty *are* his wonders! his kingdom *is* [b]an everlasting kingdom, and his dominion *is* from generation to generation.

4 I Nebuchadnezzar was at rest in mine house, and [1]flourishing in my palace:

5 I saw a dream which made me afraid, [a]and the thoughts upon my bed and the visions of my head [b]troubled me.

6 Therefore made I a decree to bring in all the wise *men* of Babylon before me, that they might make known unto me the interpretation of the dream.

7 [a]Then came in the magicians, the astrologers, the Chaldeans, and the soothsayers: and I told the dream before them; but they did not make known unto me the interpretation thereof.

8 But at the last Daniel came in before me, [a]whose name *was* Belteshazzar, according to the name of my god, [b]and in whom *is* the [1]spirit of the holy gods: and before him I told the dream, *saying*,

9 O Belteshazzar, [a]master[1] of the magicians, because I know that the [2]spirit of the holy gods *is* in thee, and no secret troubleth thee, [3]tell me the visions of my dream that I have seen, and the interpretation thereof.

10 Thus *were* the visions of mine head in my bed; [1]I saw, and behold [a]a

tree in the midst of the earth, and the height thereof *was* great.

11 The tree grew, and was strong, and the height thereof reached unto heaven, and [1]the sight thereof to the end of all the earth:

12 The leaves thereof *were* [1]fair, and the fruit thereof [2]much, and in it *was* [3]meat for all: [a]the beasts of the field [4]had shadow under it, and the fowls of the heaven dwelt in the boughs thereof, and all flesh was fed of it.

13 I saw in the visions of my head upon my bed, and, behold, [a]a watcher and [b]an holy one came down from heaven;

14 He cried [1]aloud, and said thus, [a]Hew[2] down the tree, and cut off his branches, [3]shake off his leaves, and scatter his fruit: [b]let the beasts get away from under it, and the fowls from his branches:

15 Nevertheless leave the stump of his roots in the earth, even with a band of iron and [1]brass, in the tender grass of the field; and let it be wet with the dew of heaven, and *let* [2]his portion *be* with the beasts in the grass of the earth:

16 Let his heart be changed from man's, and let a beast's heart be given unto him; and let seven [a]times[1] pass over him.

17 This matter *is* by the decree of the watchers, and the [1]demand by the word of the holy ones: to the intent [a]that the living may know [b]that the most High ruleth in the kingdom of men, and [c]giveth it to whomsoever he will, and setteth up over it the [d]basest[2] of men.

18 This dream I king Nebuchadnezzar have seen. Now thou, O Belteshazzar, declare the interpretation thereof, [a]forasmuch as all the wise *men* of my kingdom are not able to make known unto me the interpretation: but thou *art* able; [b]for the [1]spirit of the holy gods *is* in thee.

19 Then Daniel, [a]whose name *was* Belteshazzar, was [1]astonied for one hour, and his thoughts [b]troubled him. The king spake, and said, Belteshazzar, let not the dream, or the interpretation thereof, trouble thee. Belteshazzar answered and said, My lord, [c]the[2] dream [3]*be* to them that hate thee, and the interpretation thereof [3]to thine enemies.

20 [a]The tree that thou sawest, which grew, and was strong, whose height reached unto the heaven, and [1]the sight thereof to all the earth;

21 Whose leaves *were* [1]fair, and the fruit thereof [2]much, and in it *was* [3]meat for all; under which the beasts of the field dwelt, and upon whose

### Cross-references and notes

3:27 [4] *garments affected*
3:28 [a] [Ps. 34:7, 8]; Is. 37:36; [Jer. 17:7]; Dan. 6:22, 23; Acts 5:19; 12:7 [1] *frustrated*
3:29 [a] Dan. 6:26 [b] Dan. 2:46, 47; 4:34–37 [c] Ezra 6:11; Dan. 2:5 [d] Dan. 6:27 [1] *an ash heap* [2] *like this*
3:30 [1] Lit. *caused to prosper*
4:1 [a] Ezra 4:17; Dan. 3:4; 6:25
4:2 [a] Dan. 3:26
4:3 [a] 2 Sam. 7:16; Ps. 89:35–37; Dan. 6:27; 7:13, 14; [Luke 1:31–33] [b] [Dan. 2:44; 4:34; 6:26]
4:4 [1] *prospering*
4:5 [a] Dan. 2:28, 29 [b] Dan. 2:1
4:7 [a] Dan. 2:2
4:8 [a] Dan. 1:7 [b] Is. 63:11; Dan. 2:11; 4:18; 5:11, 14 [1] *Spirit of the Holy God*
4:9 [a] Dan. 2:48; 5:11 [1] *chief* [2] *Spirit of the Holy God* [3] *explain to*
4:10 [a] Ezek. 31:3; Dan. 4:20 [1] *I was looking*
4:11 [1] *its visibility extended*
4:12 [a] Lam. 4:20 [1] *lovely* [2] *abundant* [3] *food* [4] *found shade*
4:13 [a] Dan. 4:17, 23] [b] Deut. 33:2
4:14 [a] Ezek. 31:10–14 [b] Ezek. 31:12, 13 [1] Lit. *with strength* [2] *Chop* [3] *strip*
4:15 [1] *bronze* [2] *him partake with*
4:16 [a] Dan. 11:13; 12:7 [1] Lit. *seasons, years*
4:17 [a] Ps. 9:16; 83:18 [b] Dan. 2:21; 4:25, 32; 5:21 [c] Jer. 27:5–7 [d] 1 Sam. 2:8 [1] *sentence* [2] *lowest*
4:18 [a] Gen. 41:8, 15 [b] Dan. 4:8, 9; 5:11, 14 [1] *Spirit of the Holy God*
4:19 [a] Dan. 4:8 [b] Dan. 7:15, 28; 8:27 [c] 2 Sam. 18:32 [1] *appalled for a time* [2] *if only the dream* [3] *concerned*
4:20 [a] Dan. 4:10–12 [1] *its visibility extended*
4:21 [1] *lovely* [2] *abundant* [3] *food*

branches the fowls of the heaven had their habitation:

22 [a]It *is* thou, O king, that art grown and become strong: for thy greatness is grown, and reacheth unto heaven, [b]and thy dominion to the end of the earth.

23 [a]And whereas the king saw a watcher and an holy one coming down from heaven, and saying, [1]Hew the tree down, and destroy it; yet leave the stump of the roots thereof in the earth, even with a band of iron and [2]brass, in the tender grass of the field; and let it be wet with the dew of heaven, [b]and *let* [3]his portion *be* with the beasts of the field, till seven [4]times pass over him;

24 This *is* the interpretation, O king, and this *is* the decree of the most High, which is come upon my lord the king:

25 That they shall [a]drive thee from men, and thy dwelling shall be with the beasts of the field, and they shall make thee [b]to eat grass as oxen, and they shall wet thee with the dew of heaven, and seven [1]times shall pass over thee, [c]till thou know that the most High ruleth in the kingdom of men, and [d]giveth it to whomsoever he will.

26 And whereas they commanded to leave the stump of the tree roots; thy kingdom shall be [1]sure unto thee, after that thou [2]shalt have known that [3]the [a]heavens do rule.

27 Wherefore, O king, let my counsel be acceptable unto thee, and [a]break off thy sins [1]by righteousness, and thine iniquities by shewing mercy to the poor; [b]if it may be [c]a [2]lengthening of thy tranquillity.

28 All this came upon the king Nebuchadnezzar.

29 At the end of twelve months he walked [1]in the palace of the kingdom of Babylon.

30 The king [a]spake, and said, Is not this great Babylon, that I have built for [1]the house of the kingdom by the might of my power, and for the honour of my majesty?

31 [a]While the word *was* in the king's mouth, there fell [b]a voice from heaven, *saying*, O king Nebuchadnezzar, to thee it is spoken; The kingdom [1]is departed from thee.

32 And [a]they shall drive thee from men, and thy dwelling *shall be* with the beasts of the field: they shall make thee to eat grass as oxen, and seven [1]times shall pass over thee, until thou know that the most High ruleth in the kingdom of men, and giveth it to whomsoever he will.

33 The same hour was the thing fulfilled upon Nebuchadnezzar: and he was driven from men, and did eat

grass as oxen, and his body was wet with the dew of heaven, till his hairs were grown like eagles' *feathers,* and his nails like birds' *claws.*

34 And [a]at the end of the [1]days I Nebuchadnezzar lifted up mine eyes unto heaven, and mine understanding returned unto me, and I blessed the most High, and I praised and honoured him [b]that liveth for ever, whose dominion *is* [c]an everlasting dominion, and his kingdom *is* from generation to generation:

35 And [a]all the inhabitants of the earth *are* [1]reputed as nothing: and [b]he doeth according to his will in the army of heaven, and *among* the inhabitants of the earth: and [c]none can [2]stay his hand, or say unto him, [d]What doest thou?

36 At the same time mine reason returned unto me; [a]and for the glory of my kingdom, mine honour and [1]brightness returned unto me; and my counsellors and my lords sought unto me; and I was [b]established[2] in my kingdom, and excellent majesty was [c]added unto me.

37 Now I Nebuchadnezzar [a]praise and extol and honour the King of heaven, [b]all whose works *are* truth, and his ways [1]judgment: [c]and those that walk in pride he is able to [2]abase.

## CHAPTER 5

BELSHAZZAR the king [a]made a great feast to a thousand of his lords, and drank wine before the thousand.

2 Belshazzar, whiles he tasted the wine, commanded to bring the golden and silver vessels [a]which his [1]father Nebuchadnezzar had taken out of the temple which *was* in Jerusalem; that the king, and his princes, his wives, and his concubines, might drink therein.

3 Then they brought the golden [a]vessels that were taken out of the temple of the house of God which *was* at Jerusalem; and the king, and his princes, his wives, and his concubines, drank in them.

4 They drank wine, [a]and praised the gods of gold, and of silver, of [1]brass, of iron, of wood, and of stone.

5 [a]In the same hour came forth fingers of a man's hand, and wrote [1]over against the candlestick upon the plaister of the wall of the king's palace: and the king saw the part of the hand that wrote.

6 Then the king's countenance was changed, and his thoughts troubled him, so that the joints of his [1]loins were loosed, and his [a]knees [2]smote one against another.

7 [a]The king cried [1]aloud to bring in [b]the astrologers, the Chaldeans, and

### Cross-references (center column)

4:22 [a] Dan. 2:37, 38 [b] Jer. 27:6–8

4:23 [a] Dan. 4:13–15 [b] Dan. 5:21 [1] *Chop down* [2] *bronze* [3] *him partake with* [4] Lit. *seasons, years*

4:25 [a] Dan. 4:32; 5:21 [b] Ps. 106:20 [c] Dan. 4:2; 17, 32 [d] Jer. 27:5 [1] Possibly *years*

4:26 [a] Matt. 21:25 [1] *assured* [2] *come to know* [3] *Heaven does, God*

4:27 [a] [1 Pet. 4:8] [b] [Ps. 41:1–3] [c] 1 Kin. 21:29 [1] *by being righteous* [2] *prolonging*

4:29 [1] *about*

4:30 [a] Prov. 16:18 [1] *a royal dwelling by*

4:31 [a] Luke 12:20 [b] Dan. 4:24 [1] *has been taken*

4:32 [a] [Dan. 4:25] [1] Lit. *seasons, years*

4:34 [a] Dan. 4:26 [b] Ps. 102:24–27; Dan. 6:26; 12:7; [Rev. 4:10] [c] [Ps. 10:16]; Dan. 2:44; 7:14; Mic. 4:7; [Luke 1:33] [1] *time*

4:35 [a] Ps. 39:5; Is. 40:15, 17 [b] Ps. 115:3; 135:6; Dan. 6:27 [c] Job 34:29; Is. 43:13 [d] Job 9:12; Is. 45:9; Jer. 18:6; Rom. 9:20; [1 Cor. 2:16] [1] *considered* [2] *restrain*

4:36 [a] Dan. 4:26 [b] 2 Chr. 20:20 [c] Job 42:12; [Prov. 22:4; Matt. 6:33] [1] *splendour* [2] *restored to*

4:37 [a] Dan. 2:46, 47; 3:28, 29 [b] Deut. 32:4; [Ps. 33:4]; Is. 5:16; [Rev. 15:3] [c] Ex. 18:11; Job 40:11, 12; Dan. 5:20 [1] *justice* [2] *humble*

5:1 [a] Esth. 1:3; Is. 22:12–14

5:2 [a] 2 Kin. 24:13; 25:15; Ezra 1:7–11; Jer. 52:19; Dan. 1:2 [1] Or *forefather*

5:3 [a] 2 Chr. 36:10

5:4 [a] Is. 42:8; Dan. 5:23; Rev. 9:20 [1] *bronze*

5:5 [a] Dan. 4:31 [1] *opposite the lampstand*

5:6 [a] Dan. 4:6 [1] *hips* [2] *knocked*

5:7 [a] Dan. 4:6, 7; 5:11, 15 [b] Is. 47:13 [1] Lit. *with strength*

the soothsayers. *And* the king spake, and said to the wise *men* of Babylon, Whosoever shall read this writing, and ²shew me the interpretation thereof, shall be clothed with ³scarlet, and *have* a chain of gold about his neck, ᶜand shall be the third ruler in the kingdom.

8 Then came in all the king's wise *men:* ᵃbut they could not read the writing, nor make known to the king the interpretation thereof.

9 Then was king Belshazzar greatly ᵃtroubled, and his countenance was changed in him, and his lords were ¹astonied.

10 *Now* the queen by reason of the words of the king and his lords came into the banquet house: *and* the queen spake and said, O king, live for ever: let not thy thoughts trouble thee, nor let thy countenance be changed:

11 ᵃThere is a man in thy kingdom, in whom *is* the ¹spirit of the holy gods; and in the days of thy ²father light and understanding and wisdom, like the wisdom of the gods, was found in him; whom the king Nebuchadnezzar thy ²father, the king, *I say,* thy ²father, made ³master of the magicians, astrologers, Chaldeans, *and* soothsayers;

12 Forasmuch as an excellent spirit, and knowledge, and understanding, interpreting of dreams, and ¹shewing of hard sentences, and ²dissolving of doubts, were found in the same Daniel, ᵃwhom the king named Belteshazzar: now let Daniel be called, and he will ³shew the interpretation.

13 Then was Daniel brought in before the king. *And* the king spake and said unto Daniel, *Art* thou that Daniel, which *art* of the children of the captivity of Judah, whom the king my ¹father brought out of Jewry?

14 I have even heard of thee, that ᵃthe ¹spirit of the gods *is* in thee, and *that* light and understanding and excellent wisdom is found in thee.

15 And now ᵃthe wise *men,* the astrologers, have been brought in before me, that they should read this writing, and make known unto me the interpretation thereof: but they could not ¹shew the interpretation of the thing:

16 And I have heard of thee, that thou canst ¹make interpretations, and ²dissolve doubts: ᵃnow if thou canst read the writing, and make known to me the interpretation thereof, thou shalt be clothed with ³scarlet, and *have* a chain of gold about thy neck, and shalt be the third ruler in the kingdom.

17 Then Daniel answered and said before the king, Let thy gifts be to thyself, and give thy rewards to an-

5:7 ᶜ Dan. 6:2, 3
² tell ³ purple

5:8 ᵃ Gen. 41:8;
Dan. 2:27; 4:7;
5:15

5:9 ᵃ Job 18:11;
Is. 21:2–4; Jer.
6:24; Dan. 2:1; 5:6
¹ perplexed

5:11 ᵃ Dan. 2:48;
4:8, 9, 18　¹ Spirit
of the Holy God
² Or forefather
³ chief

5:12 ᵃ Dan. 1:7; 4:8
¹ solving riddles
² explaining enig-
mas ³ declare

5:13 ¹ Or fore-
father

5:14 ᵃ Dan. 4:8, 9,
18; 5:11, 12　¹ Spirit
of God

5:15 ᵃ Dan. 5:7, 8
¹ declare

5:16 ᵃ Dan. 5:7, 29
¹ give ² explain
enigmas, lit. untie
knots ³ purple

5:18 ᵃ Dan. 2:37,
38; 4:17, 22, 25
¹ forefather

5:19 ᵃ Jer. 27:7
ᵇ Dan. 2:12, 13; 3:6

5:20 ᵃ Dan. 4:30,
37　¹ Proud ² Lit.
spirit

5:21 ᵃ Dan. 4:32,
33　ᵇ Ezek. 17:24
¹ donkeys ² rec-
ognized

5:22 ᵃ 2 Chr.
33:23; 36:12

5:23 ᵃ Dan. 5:3,
4　ᵇ Ex. 40:9　ᶜ Ps.
115:5, 6　ᵈ [Jer.
10:23]　¹ exalted
² The temple
³ bronze

5:24 ¹ Lit. palm,
fingers

5:25 ¹ Lit. a mina
(50 shekels) from
the verb "to
number" ² Lit. a
shekel from the
verb "to weigh"
³ Lit. and half-
shekels from the
verb "to divide"

5:26 ¹ each word

5:27 ᵃ Ps. 62:9

5:28 ᵃ Dan. 5:31;
9:1　ᵇ Dan. 6:28
¹ Aram. Paras,
consonant with
Peres

5:29 ᵃ Dan. 5:7, 16
¹ purple

5:30 ᵃ Jer. 51:31,
39, 57

5:31 ᵃ Dan. 2:39;
9:1　¹ Mede

other; yet I will read the writing unto the king, and make known to him the interpretation.

18 O thou king, ᵃthe most high God gave Nebuchadnezzar thy ¹father a kingdom, and majesty, and glory, and honour:

19 And for the majesty that he gave him, ᵃall people, nations, and languages, trembled and feared before him: whom he would he ᵇslew; and whom he would he kept alive; and whom he would he set up; and whom he would he put down.

20 ᵃBut when his heart was ¹lifted up, and his ²mind hardened in pride, he was deposed from his kingly throne, and they took his glory from him:

21 And he was ᵃdriven from the sons of men; and his heart was made like the beasts, and his dwelling *was* with the wild ¹asses: they fed him with grass like oxen, and his body was wet with the dew of heaven; ᵇtill he ²knew that the most high God ruled in the kingdom of men, and *that* he appointeth over it whomsoever he will.

22 And thou his son, O Belshazzar, ᵃhast not humbled thine heart, though thou knewest all this;

23 ᵃBut hast thou ¹lifted up thyself against the Lord of heaven; and they have brought the ᵇvessels of ²his house before thee, and thou, and thy lords, thy wives, and thy concubines, have drunk wine in them; and thou hast praised the gods of silver, and gold, of ³brass, iron, wood, and stone, ᶜwhich see not, nor hear, nor know: and the God in whose hand thy breath *is,* ᵈand whose *are* all thy ways, hast thou not glorified:

24 Then was the ¹part of the hand sent from him; and this writing was written.

25 And this *is* the writing that was written, ¹MENE, MENE, ²TEKEL, ³UPHARSIN.

26 This *is* the interpretation of ¹the thing: MENE; God hath numbered thy kingdom, and finished it.

27 TEKEL; ᵃThou art weighed in the balances, and art found wanting.

28 PERES; Thy kingdom is divided, and given to the ᵃMedes and ᵇPersians.¹

29 Then commanded Belshazzar, and they clothed Daniel with ¹scarlet, and *put* a chain of gold about his neck, and made a proclamation concerning him, ᵃthat he should be the third ruler in the kingdom.

30 ᵃIn that night was Belshazzar the king of the Chaldeans slain.

31 ᵃAnd Darius the ¹Median took the kingdom, *being* about threescore and two years old.

## CHAPTER 6

IT pleased Darius to set over the kingdom an hundred and twenty ¹princes, which should be over the whole kingdom;

2 And over these three ¹presidents; of whom Daniel *was* ²first: that the ³princes might give accounts unto them, and the king should have no ⁴damage.

3 Then this Daniel ¹was preferred above the ²presidents and ³princes, ᵃbecause an excellent spirit *was* in him; and the king thought to set him over the whole realm.

4 ᵃThen the ¹presidents and ²princes sought to find ³occasion against Daniel concerning the kingdom; but they could find ⁴none occasion nor fault; forasmuch as he *was* faithful, neither was there any error or fault found in him.

5 Then said these men, We shall not find any occasion against this Daniel, except we find *it* against him concerning the law of his God.

6 Then these ¹presidents and ²princes ³assembled together to the king, and said thus unto him, ᵃKing Darius, live for ever.

7 All the ¹presidents of the kingdom, the ²governors, and the ³princes, the counsellors, and the ⁴captains, have ᵃconsulted together to establish a royal statute, and to make a firm decree, that whosoever shall ⁵ask a petition of any ⁶God or man for thirty days, ⁷save of thee, O king, he shall be cast into the den of lions.

8 Now, O king, establish the decree, and sign the writing, that it ¹be not changed, according to the ᵃlaw of the Medes and Persians, which altereth not.

9 Wherefore king Darius signed the ¹writing and the decree.

10 Now when Daniel knew that the writing was signed, he went into his house; and his windows being open in his chamber ᵃtoward Jerusalem, he kneeled upon his knees ᵇthree times ¹a day, and prayed, and gave thanks before his God, as he ²did aforetime.

11 Then these men assembled, and found Daniel praying and making supplication before his God.

12 ᵃThen they came near, and spake before the king concerning the king's decree; Hast thou not signed a decree, that every man that shall ask *a petition* of any ¹God or man within thirty days, save of thee, O king, shall be cast into the den of lions? The king answered and said, The thing *is* true, ᵇaccording to the law of the Medes and Persians, which ²altereth not.

13 Then answered they and said before the king, That Daniel, ᵃwhich *is* of the ¹children of the captivity of Judah, ᵇregardeth² not thee, O king, nor the decree that thou hast signed, but maketh his petition three times a day.

14 Then the king, when he heard *these* words, ᵃwas ¹sore displeased with himself, and set *his* heart on Daniel to deliver him: and he ²laboured till the going down of the sun to deliver him.

15 Then these men ¹assembled unto the king, and said unto the king, Know, O king, that ᵃthe law of the Medes and Persians *is,* That no decree nor statute which the king establisheth may be changed.

16 Then the king commanded, and they brought Daniel, and cast *him* into the den of lions. *Now* the king spake and said unto Daniel, Thy God whom thou servest continually, he will deliver thee.

17 ᵃAnd a stone was brought, and laid upon the mouth of the den; ᵇand the king sealed it with his own ¹signet, and with the ²signet of his lords; that the purpose might not be changed concerning Daniel.

18 Then the king went to his palace, and ¹passed the night fasting: neither were ²instruments of musick brought before him: ᵃand his sleep ³went from him.

19 Then the ᵃking arose very early in the morning, and went in haste unto the den of lions.

20 And when he came to the den, he cried with a ¹lamentable voice unto Daniel: *and* the king spake and said to Daniel, O Daniel, servant of the living God, ᵃis thy God, whom thou servest continually, able to deliver thee from the lions?

21 Then said Daniel unto the king, ᵃO king, live for ever.

22 ᵃMy God hath sent his angel, and hath ᵇshut the lions' mouths, that they have not hurt me: forasmuch as before him ¹innocency was found in me; and also before thee, O king, have I done no ²hurt.

23 Then was the king exceedingly glad for him, and commanded that they should take Daniel up out of the den. So Daniel was taken up out of the den, and no manner of hurt was found upon him, ᵃbecause he believed in his God.

24 And the king commanded, ᵃand they brought those men which had accused Daniel, and they cast *them* into the den of lions, them, ᵇtheir children, and their wives; and the lions ¹had the mastery of them, and brake all their bones in pieces ²or ever they came at the bottom of the den.

25 ᵃThen king Darius wrote unto all people, nations, and languages, that

### Center column notes

6:1 ¹ *satraps*

6:2 ¹ *overseers* ² *one* ³ *satraps* ⁴ *loss*

6:3 ᵃ Dan. 5:12 ¹ *distinguished himself* ² *overseers* ³ *satraps*

6:4 ᵃ Eccl. 4:4 ¹ *overseers* ² *satraps* ³ *some charge* ⁴ *no charge*

6:6 ᵃ Neh. 2:3 ¹ *overseers* ² *satraps* ³ *stormed in*

6:7 ᵃ Ps. 59:3; 62:4; 64:2–6 ¹ *overseers* ² *administrators* ³ *satraps* ⁴ *governors* ⁵ *make* ⁶ Or *god* ⁷ *except*

6:8 ᵃ Esth. 1:19; 8:8 ¹ *cannot be*

6:9 ¹ *written decree*

6:10 ᵃ Jon. 2:4 ᵇ Ps. 55:17 ¹ *that day* ² *had been doing before this*

6:12 ᵃ Dan. 3:8–12 ¹ Or *god* ᵇ Dan. 6:8, 15 ² *cannot be changed*

6:13 ᵃ Dan. 1:6; 5:13

b Dan. 3:12 ¹ Lit. *sons* ² *shows no regard for*

6:14 ᵃ Mark 6:26 ¹ *greatly* ² *strived*

6:15 ᵃ Dan. 6:8, 12 ¹ Lit. *thronged*

6:17 ᵃ Lam. 3:53 ᵇ Matt. 27:66 ¹ *signet ring* ² *signet rings*

6:18 ᵃ Dan. 2:1 ¹ *spent* ² *musicians, exact meaning unknown* ³ *fled*

6:19 ᵃ Dan. 3:24

6:20 ᵃ Dan. 3:17 ¹ Or *pained*

6:21 ᵃ Dan. 2:4; 6:6

6:22 ᵃ Dan. 3:28 ᵇ Heb. 11:33 ¹ *innocence* ² *wrong*

6:23 ᵃ Heb. 11:33

6:24 ᵃ Deut. 19:18, 19 ᵇ Deut. 24:16 ¹ *overpowered them* ² *before they ever came to*

6:25 ᵃ Dan. 4:1

dwell in all the earth; Peace be multiplied unto you.

26 ᵃI make a decree, That in every dominion of my kingdom men ᵇtremble¹ and fear before the God of Daniel: ᶜfor he *is* the living God, and stedfast for ever, and his kingdom *that* which shall not be ᵈdestroyed, and his dominion *shall be even* unto the end.

27 He delivereth and rescueth, ᵃand he worketh signs and wonders in heaven and in earth, who hath delivered Daniel from the ¹power of the lions.

28 So this Daniel prospered in the reign of Darius, ᵃand in the reign of ᵇCyrus the Persian.

## CHAPTER 7

IN the first year of Belshazzar king of Babylon ᵃDaniel ¹had a dream and ᵇvisions of his head upon his bed: then he wrote the dream, *and* told ²the sum of the matters.

2 Daniel spake and said, I saw in my vision by night, and, behold, the four winds of the heaven strove upon the great sea.

3 And four great beasts ᵃcame up from the sea, ¹diverse one from another.

4 The first *was* ᵃlike a lion, and had eagle's wings: I beheld till the wings thereof were ¹plucked, and it was lifted up from the earth, and made stand upon ²the feet as a man, and a ᵇman's heart was given to it.

5 ᵃAnd behold another beast, a second, like to a bear, and ¹it raised up itself on one side, and *it had* three ribs in the mouth of it between the teeth of it: and they said thus unto it, Arise, devour much flesh.

6 After this I beheld, and lo another, like a leopard, which had upon the back of it four wings of a fowl; the beast had also ᵃfour heads; and dominion was given to it.

7 After this I saw in the night visions, and behold ᵃa fourth beast, dreadful and terrible, and strong exceedingly; and it had great iron teeth: it devoured and brake in pieces, and ¹stamped the residue with the feet of it: and it *was* ²diverse from all the beasts that *were* before it; ᵇand it had ten horns.

8 I considered the horns, and, behold, ᵃthere came up among them another little horn, before whom there were three of the first horns plucked up by the roots: and, behold, in this horn *were* eyes like the eyes ᵇof man, ᶜand a mouth speaking ¹great things.

9 ᵃI beheld till the thrones were ¹cast down, and ᵇthe Ancient of days did sit, ᶜwhose garment *was* white

as snow, and the hair of his head like the pure wool: his throne *was like* the fiery flame, ᵈ*and* his wheels *as* burning fire.

10 ᵃA fiery stream issued and came forth from before him: ᵇthousand thousands ministered unto him, and ten thousand times ten thousand stood before him: ᶜthe ¹judgment was set, and the books were opened.

11 I beheld then because of the ¹voice of the great words which the horn spake: ᵃI beheld *even* till the beast was slain, and his body destroyed, and given to the burning flame.

12 As concerning the rest of the beasts, they had their dominion taken away: yet their lives were prolonged for a season and time.

13 I saw in the night visions, and, behold, ᵃ*one* like the Son of man came with the clouds of heaven, and came to the Ancient of days, and they brought him near before him.

14 ᵃAnd there was given him dominion, and glory, and a kingdom, that all ᵇpeople,¹ nations, and languages, should serve him: his dominion *is* ᶜan everlasting dominion, which shall not pass away, and his kingdom *that* which shall not be destroyed.

15 I Daniel was grieved in my spirit in the midst of ¹*my* body, and the visions of my head troubled me.

16 I came near unto one of them that stood by, and asked him the truth of all this. So he told me, and ¹made me know the interpretation of the things.

17 These great beasts, which are four, *are* four ¹kings, *which* shall arise out of the earth.

18 But ᵃthe saints of the most High shall ¹take the kingdom, and possess the kingdom for ever, even for ever and ever.

19 Then I would know the truth of the fourth beast, which was ¹diverse from all the others, exceeding dreadful, whose teeth *were of* iron, and his nails *of* ²brass; *which* devoured, brake in pieces, and ³stamped the residue with his feet;

20 And of the ten horns that *were* in his head, and *of* the other which came up, and before whom three fell; even *of* that horn that had eyes, and a mouth that spake ¹very great things, whose ²look *was* ³more stout than his fellows.

21 I beheld, ᵃand the same horn made war with the saints, and prevailed against them;

22 Until the Ancient of days came, ᵃand judgment was ¹given to the saints of the most High; and the time came that the saints possessed the kingdom.

### Center column references

6:26 ᵃ Dan. 3:29 ᵇ Ps. 99:1 ᶜ Dan. 4:34; 6:20 ᵈ Dan. 2:44; 4:3; 7:14, 27 ¹ must *tremble*

6:27 ᵃ Dan. 4:2, 3 ¹ *paw*, lit. *hand*

6:28 ᵃ Dan. 1:21 ᵇ Ezra 1:1, 2

7:1 ᵃ [Amos 3:7] ᵇ [Dan. 2:28] ¹ Lit. *saw* ² Lit. *the head* (*chief*) *of the words or the main facts*

7:3 ᵃ Rev. 13:1; 17:8 ¹ *each different from the other*

7:4 ᵃ Deut. 28:49 ᵇ Dan. 4:16, 34 ¹ *plucked off* ² *two*

7:5 ᵃ Dan. 2:39 ¹ *it was raised up*

7:6 ᵃ Dan. 8:8, 22

7:7 ᵃ Dan. 2:40 ᵇ Rev. 12:3; 13:1 ¹ *trampled* ² *different*

7:8 ᵃ Dan. 8:9 ᵇ Rev. 9:7 ᶜ Rev. 13:5, 6 ¹ *pompous words*

7:9 ᵃ [Rev. 20:4] ᵇ Ps. 90:2 ᶜ Rev. 1:14 ¹ *put in place*

ᵈ Ezek. 1:15

7:10 ᵃ Is. 30:33; 66:15 ᵇ Rev. 5:11 ᶜ [Rev. 20:11–15] ¹ *court was seated*

7:11 ᵃ [Rev. 19:20; 20:10] ¹ *sound of the pompous words*

7:13 ᵃ [Matt. 24:30; 26:64]

7:14 ᵃ [John 3:35, 36] ᵇ Dan. 3:4 ᶜ Mic. 4:7 ¹ *peoples*

7:15 ¹ Lit. *its sheath*

7:16 ¹ *made known to me*

7:17 ¹ Representing *their kingdoms*

7:18 ᵃ Is. 60:12–14 ¹ *receive*

7:19 ¹ *different* ² *bronze* ³ *trampled*

7:20 ¹ *pompous words* ² *appearance* ³ *greater*

7:21 ᵃ Rev. 11:7; 13:7; 17:14

7:22 ᵃ [Rev. 1:6] ¹ *made in favour of*

23 Thus he said, The fourth beast shall be [a]the fourth kingdom upon earth, which shall be [1]diverse from all kingdoms, and shall devour the whole earth, and shall [2]tread it down, and break it in pieces.

24 [a]And the ten horns out of this kingdom *are* ten kings *that* shall arise: and another shall rise after them; and he shall be [1]diverse from the first, and he shall subdue three kings.

25 [a]And he shall speak [1]*great* words against the most High, and shall [b]wear[2] out the saints of the most High, and [c]think[3] to change times and laws: and [d]they[4] shall be given into his hand [e]until [5]a time and times and the dividing of time.

26 [a]But the [1]judgment shall sit, and they shall [b]take away his dominion, to consume and to destroy *it* [2]unto the end.

27 And the [a]kingdom and dominion, and the greatness of the kingdom under the whole heaven, shall be given to the people of the saints of the most High, [b]whose kingdom *is* an everlasting kingdom, [c]and all dominions shall serve and obey him.

28 Hitherto *is* the end of the [1]matter. As for me Daniel, [a]my [2]cogitations much troubled me, and my countenance changed in me: but I [b]kept the matter in my heart.

## CHAPTER 8

IN[1] the third year of the reign of king Belshazzar a vision appeared unto me, *even unto* me Daniel, after that which appeared unto me [a]at the first.

2 And I saw in a vision; and it came to pass, when I saw, that I *was* at [a]Shushan[1] *in* the [2]palace, which *is* in the province of Elam; and I saw in a vision, and I was by the river of Ulai.

3 Then I lifted up mine eyes, and saw, and, behold, there stood before the river a ram which had *two* horns: and the *two* horns *were* high; but one *was* [a]higher than the other, and the higher came up last.

4 I saw the ram pushing westward, and northward, and southward; so that no beasts might stand before him, neither *was there any* that could deliver out of his hand; [a]but he did according to his will, and became great.

5 And as I was considering, behold, an he goat came from the west [1]on the face of the whole earth, and touched not the ground: and the goat *had* a [2]notable [a]horn between his eyes.

6 And he came to the ram that had *two* horns, which I had seen standing before the river, and ran unto him [1]in the fury of his power.

7 And I saw him come close unto the ram, and he was moved with

[1]choler against him, and [2]smote the ram, and brake his two horns: and there was no power in the ram to stand before him, but he cast him down to the ground, and [3]stamped upon him: and there was none that could deliver the ram out of his hand.

8 Therefore the [1]he goat [2]waxed very great: and when he was strong, the great horn was broken; and for it came up [a]four [3]notable ones toward the four winds of heaven.

9 [a]And out of one of them came forth a little horn, which [1]waxed exceeding great, toward the south, and [b]toward the east, and toward the [c]pleasant[2] *land*.

10 [a]And it [1]waxed great, *even* [2]to [b]the host of heaven; and [c]it cast down *some* of the host and of the stars to the ground, and [3]stamped upon them.

11 Yea, [a]he [1]magnified *himself* [2]even to [b]the prince of the host, [c]and by him [d]the daily [3]*sacrifice* was taken away, and the place of [4]his sanctuary was cast down.

12 And [a]an host was given *him* [1]against the daily *sacrifice* by reason of transgression, and [2]it cast down [b]the truth to the ground; and [3]it [c]practised, and prospered.

13 Then I heard [a]one [1]saint speaking, and another [1]saint unto that certain [2]*saint* which spake, How long *shall be* the vision *concerning* the daily [3]*sacrifice*, and the transgression [4]of desolation, to give both the sanctuary and the host to be trodden under foot?

14 And he said unto me, Unto two thousand and three hundred [1]days; then shall the sanctuary be cleansed.

15 And it came to pass, when I, *even* I Daniel, had seen the vision, and [a]sought for the meaning, then, behold, there stood before me [b]as[1] the appearance of a man.

16 And I heard a man's voice [a]between *the banks of* Ulai, which called, and said, [b]Gabriel, make this *man* to understand the vision.

17 So he came near where I stood: and when he came, I was afraid, and [a]fell upon my face: but he said unto me, Understand, O son of man: for at the time of the end *shall* [1]*be* the vision.

18 [a]Now as he was speaking with me, I was in a deep sleep [1]on my face toward the ground: [b]but he touched me, and [2]set me upright.

19 And he said, Behold, I will [1]make thee know what shall be in the [2]last end of the indignation: [a]for at the time appointed the end *shall be*.

## Cross-references

7:23 [a] Dan. 2:40 [1] *different* [2] *trample*
7:24 [a] Rev. 13:1; 17:12 [1] *different*
7:25 [a] Rev. 13:1–6 [b] Rev. 17:6 [c] Dan. 2:21 [d] Rev. 13:7; 18:24 [e] Rev. 12:14 [1] *pompous words* [2] *persecute* [3] *intend* [4] The saints [5] A year
7:26 [a] [Dan. 2:35; 7:10, 22] [b] Rev. 19:20 [1] *court* [2] *for ever*
7:27 [a] Dan. 7:14, 18, 22 [b] [Luke 1:32, 33] [c] Is. 60:12
7:28 [a] Dan. 8:27 [b] Luke 2:19, 51 [1] *account* [2] *thoughts*
8:1 [a] Dan. 7:1 [1] Heb. resumes with this verse.
8:2 [a] Esth. 1:2; 2:8 [1] Or *Susa* [2] *citadel*
8:3 [a] Dan. 7:5
8:4 [a] Dan. 5:19
8:5 [a] Dan. 8:8, 21; 11:3 [1] *across the surface* [2] *conspicuous*
8:6 [1] *with furious*
8:7 [1] *rage* [2] *attacked* [3] *trampled*
8:8 [a] Dan. 7:6; 8:22; 11:4 [1] *male* [2] *grew* [3] *conspicuous*
8:9 [a] Dan. 11:21 [b] Dan. 11:25 [c] Ps. 48:2 [1] *grew* [2] *glorious*
8:10 [a] Dan. 11:28 [b] Is. 14:13 [c] Rev. 12:4 [1] *grew* [2] *against* [3] *trampled*
8:11 [a] Dan. 8:25; 11:36, 37 [b] Josh. 5:14 [c] Dan. 11:31; 12:11 [d] Ex. 29:38 [1] *exalted* [2] *as high as* [3] Temple sacrifices [4] The temple
8:12 [a] Dan. 11:31 [b] Is. 59:14 [c] Dan. 8:4; 11:36 [1] *to oppose* [2] *he* [3] *he did all this*
8:13 [a] Dan. 4:13, 23 [1] *holy one* [2] Holy one [3] Temple sacrifice [4] Or *making desolate*
8:14 [1] Lit. *evening-mornings*
8:15 [a] 1 Pet. 1:10 [b] Ezek. 1:26 [1] *one having*
8:16 [a] Dan. 12:6, 7

[b] Luke 1:19, 26 8:17 [a] Rev. 1:17 [1] *the vision* come to pass 8:18 [a] Luke 9:32 [b] Ezek. 2:2 [1] *with* [2] *stood* 8:19 [a] Hab. 2:3 [1] *let* [2] *latter time*

20 The ram which thou sawest having *two* horns *are* the kings of Media and Persia.

21 And the ¹rough goat *is* the ²king of ³Grecia: and the great horn that *is* between his eyes ²*is* the first king.

22 ªNow that being broken, whereas four stood up for it, four kingdoms shall ¹stand up out of the nation, but not ²in his power.

23 And in the latter time of their kingdom, when the transgressors are come to ¹the full, a king ªof fierce countenance, and understanding ²dark sentences, shall ³stand up.

24 And his power shall be mighty, ªbut not by his own power: and he shall destroy ¹wonderfully, ᵇand shall prosper, and ²practise, ᶜand shall destroy the mighty and the holy people.

25 And ªthrough his ¹policy also he shall cause ²craft to prosper in his hand; ᵇand he shall magnify *himself* in his heart, and by ³peace shall destroy many: ᶜhe shall also stand up against the Prince of princes; but he shall be ᵈbroken without ⁴hand.

26 And the vision of the evening and the morning which was told *is* true: ªwherefore ¹shut thou up the vision; for it ²*shall be* for many days.

27 ªAnd I Daniel fainted, and was sick *certain* days; afterward I rose up, and did the king's business; and I was astonished at the vision, but none understood *it*.

## CHAPTER 9

IN the first year ªof Darius the son of Ahasuerus, of the seed of the Medes, which was made king over the realm of the Chaldeans;

2 In the first year of his reign I Daniel understood by ¹books the number of the years, ²whereof the word of the LORD came to ªJeremiah the prophet, that he would accomplish seventy years in the desolations of Jerusalem.

3 ªAnd I set my face unto the Lord God, to seek by prayer and supplications, with fasting, and sackcloth, and ashes:

4 And I prayed unto the LORD my God, and made my confession, and said, O ªLord, the great and ¹dreadful God, keeping the covenant and ²mercy to them that love him, and to them that keep his commandments;

5 ªWe have sinned, and have committed iniquity, and have done wickedly, and have rebelled, even by departing from thy precepts and from thy judgments:

6 ªNeither have we hearkened unto thy servants the prophets, which spake in thy name to our kings, our princes, and our fathers, and to all the people of the land.

---

8:21 ª Dan. 11:3
¹ *shaggy male goat* ² Kingdom
³ Or *Greece*

8:22 ª Dan. 11:4
¹ *arise* ² *with*

8:23 ª Deut. 28:50
¹ *their fulness*
² *riddles* ³ *arise*

8:24 ª Rev. 17:13 ᵇ Dan. 11:36 ᶜ Dan. 7:25 ¹ *fearfully*
² *accomplish*

8:25 ª Dan. 11:21
ᵇ Dan. 8:11–13;
11:36; 12:7 ᶜ Rev. 19:19, 20 ᵈ Job 34:20 ¹ *cunning*
² *deceit* ³ *prosperity* ⁴ *human hand* or *human means*

8:26 ª Ezek. 12:27
¹ *seal thou up*
² *refers to many days* in the future

8:27 ª Dan. 7:28; 8:17

9:1 ª Dan. 1:21

9:2 ª 2 Chr. 36:21 ¹ *the books*
² *which came as the word of the LORD through*

9:3 ª Neh. 1:4

9:4 ª Ex. 20:6
¹ *awesome* ² *lovingkindness*

9:5 ª 1 Kin. 8:47, 48

9:6 ª 2 Chr. 36:15

9:7 ª Neh. 9:33
¹ *shame* ² *the unfaithfulness*
³ *committed*

9:8 ¹ *shame*

9:9 ª [Ps. 130:4, 7]

9:11 ª Is. 1:3–6
ᵇ Lev. 26:14

9:12 ª Zech. 1:6
ᵇ Lam. 1:12; 2:13
¹ *disaster*

9:13 ª Deut. 28:15–68 ᵇ Is. 9:13
¹ *disaster*

9:14 ª Jer. 31:28; 44:27 ᵇ Neh. 9:33
¹ *kept the disaster* in store

9:15 ª Neh. 1:10
ᵇ Neh. 9:10 ¹ *have made a name for yourself*

9:16 ª 1 Sam. 12:7
ᵇ Zech. 8:3 ᶜ Ex. 20:5 ᵈ Lam. 2:16
ᵉ Ps. 79:4

9:17 ª Num. 6:24–26 ᵇ [John 16:24]
ᶜ Lam. 5:18 ¹ *Be gracious* ² *The temple*

9:18 ª Is. 37:17
ᵇ Ex. 3:7 ᶜ Jer. 25:29

---

7 O Lord, ªrighteousness *belongeth* unto thee, but unto us ¹confusion of faces, as at this day; to the men of Judah, and to the inhabitants of Jerusalem, and unto all Israel, *that are* near, and *that are* far off, through all the countries whither thou hast driven them, because of ²their trespass that they have ³trespassed against thee.

8 O Lord, to us *belongeth* ¹confusion of face, to our kings, to our princes, and to our fathers, because we have sinned against thee.

9 ªTo the Lord our God *belong* mercies and forgivenesses, though we have rebelled against him;

10 Neither have we obeyed the voice of the LORD our God, to walk in his laws, which he set before us by his servants the prophets.

11 Yea, ªall Israel have transgressed thy law, even by departing, that they might not obey thy voice; therefore the curse is poured upon us, and the oath that *is* written in the ᵇlaw of Moses the servant of God, because we have sinned against him.

12 And he hath ªconfirmed his words, which he spake against us, and against our judges that judged us, by bringing upon us a great ¹evil: ᵇfor under the whole heaven hath not been done as hath been done upon Jerusalem.

13 ªAs *it is* written in the law of Moses, all this ¹evil is come upon us: ᵇyet made we not our prayer before the LORD our God, that we might turn from our iniquities, and understand thy truth.

14 Therefore hath the LORD ªwatched¹ upon the evil, and brought it upon us: for ᵇthe LORD our God *is* righteous in all his works which he doeth: for we obeyed not his voice.

15 And now, O Lord our God, ªthat hast brought thy people forth out of the land of Egypt with a mighty hand, and ¹hast gotten thee ᵇrenown, as at this day; we have sinned, we have done wickedly.

16 O Lord, ªaccording to all thy righteousness, I beseech thee, let thine anger and thy fury be turned away from thy city Jerusalem, ᵇthy holy mountain: because for our sins, ᶜand for the iniquities of our fathers, ᵈJerusalem and thy people ᵉ*are become* a reproach to all *that are* about us.

17 Now therefore, O our God, hear the prayer of thy servant, and his supplications, ªand ¹cause thy face to shine upon ²thy sanctuary ᵇthat is desolate, ᶜfor the Lord's sake.

18 ªO my God, incline thine ear, and hear; open thine eyes, ᵇand behold our desolations, and the city ᶜwhich is called by thy name: for we do not present our supplications before

thee for our righteousnesses, but for thy great mercies.

19 O Lord, hear; O Lord, forgive; O Lord, [1]hearken and do; [2]defer not, for thine own sake, O my God: for thy city and thy people are called by thy name.

20 And whiles I *was* speaking, and praying, and confessing my sin and the sin of my people Israel, and presenting my supplication before the LORD my God for the holy mountain of my God;

21 Yea, whiles I *was* speaking in prayer, even the man [a]Gabriel, whom I had seen in the vision at the beginning, [1]being caused to fly swiftly, [2]touched me about the time of the evening [3]oblation.

22 And he informed *me*, and talked with me, and said, O Daniel, I am now come forth to give thee [1]skill and understanding.

23 At the beginning of thy supplications the [1]commandment came forth, and I am come to [2]shew *thee;* for thou *art* greatly [a]beloved: therefore [b]understand[3] the matter, and [4]consider the vision.

24 [1]Seventy weeks are determined upon thy people and upon thy holy city, to finish the transgression, and to make an end of sins, [a]and to make reconciliation for iniquity, [b]and to bring in everlasting righteousness, and to seal up the vision and prophecy, [c]and to anoint the [2]most Holy.

25 Know therefore and understand, *that* from the going forth of the commandment to restore and to build Jerusalem unto [a]the Messiah [b]the Prince *shall be* seven [1]weeks, and threescore and two [1]weeks: the [2]street shall be built again, and the [3]wall, even in troublous times.

26 And after threescore and two weeks [a]shall Messiah [1]be cut off, [b]but not for himself: and [c]the people of the prince that shall come [d]shall destroy the city and the sanctuary; and the end thereof *shall be* with a flood, and unto the end of the war desolations are determined.

27 And he shall confirm [a]the[1] covenant with [b]many for one week: and in the [2]midst of the week he shall cause the sacrifice and the [3]oblation to cease, and for the overspreading of abominations he shall make *it* desolate, [c]even until the consummation, and that determined shall be poured upon the [4]desolate.

## CHAPTER 10

In the third year of Cyrus king of Persia a [1]thing was revealed unto Daniel, whose [a]name was called Belteshazzar; and the [1]thing *was* true, [2]but the time appointed *was* long:

9:19 [1] listen and act [2] delay

9:21 [a] Dan. 8:16 [1] Or being weary with weariness [2] reached [3] offering

9:22 [1] skill in

9:23 [a] Dan. 10:11, 19 [b] Matt. 24:15 [1] Lit. word [2] tell [3] give heed to [4] understand

9:24 [a] [Is. 53:10] [b] Rev. 14:6 [c] Ps. 45:7 [1] Lit. Seventy sevens [2] Holy of Holies

9:25 [a] Luke 2:1, 2; John 1:41; 4:25 [b] Is. 55:4 [1] Lit. sevens [2] Or open square [3] moat

9:26 [a] [Is. 53:8]; Matt. 27:50; Mark 9:12; 15:37; [Luke 23:46; 24:26]; John 19:30; Acts 8:32 [b] [1 Pet. 2:21] [c] Matt. 24:2; Mark 13:2; Luke 19:43, 44 [1] Suffer the death penalty

9:27 [a] Is. 42:6 [b] [Matt. 26:28] [c] Dan. 11:36 [1] Or a treaty [2] middle [3] offering [4] Or desolator

10:1 [a] Dan. 1:7 [1] message [2] Or and of great conflict:

10:3 [1] desirable food

10:4 [1] The Tigris

10:5 [a] Ezek. 9:2; 10:2 [b] Rev. 1:13; 15:6 [1] waist was

10:6 [a] [Rev. 1:15] [1] torches [2] burnished bronze [3] sound

10:7 [1] terror

10:8 [1] vigour [2] frailty

10:9 [1] sound

10:10 [a] Dan. 9:21 [1] trembling upon

10:11 [a] Dan. 9:23

10:12 [a] Rev. 1:17 [b] Dan. 9:3, 4, 22, 23; Acts 10:4 [1] humble

10:13 [a] Dan. 10:20 [b] Dan. 10:21; 12:1; Jude 9; [Rev. 12:7]

10:14 [a] Gen. 49:1; Deut. 31:29; Dan. 2:28 [b] Dan. 8:26; 10:1 [1] refers to many days to come

10:15 [a] Dan. 8:18; 10:9 [1] turned [2] speechless

and he understood the thing, and had understanding of the vision.

2 In those days I Daniel was mourning three full weeks.

3 I ate no [1]pleasant bread, neither came flesh nor wine in my mouth, neither did I anoint myself at all, till three whole weeks were fulfilled.

4 And in the four and twentieth day of the first month, as I was by the side of the great river, which *is* [1]Hiddekel;

5 Then I lifted up mine eyes, and looked, and behold a certain man clothed in [a]linen, whose [1]loins *were* [b]girded with fine gold of Uphaz:

6 His body also *was* like the beryl, and his face as the appearance of lightning, and his eyes as [1]lamps of fire, and his arms and his feet like in colour to [2]polished brass, [a]and the voice of his words like the [3]voice of a multitude.

7 And I Daniel alone saw the vision: for the men that were with me saw not the vision; but a great [1]quaking fell upon them, so that they fled to hide themselves.

8 Therefore I was left alone, and saw this great vision, and there remained no strength in me: for my [1]comeliness was turned in me into [2]corruption, and I retained no strength.

9 Yet heard I the [1]voice of his words: and when I heard the voice of his words, then was I in a deep sleep on my face, and my face toward the ground.

10 [a]And, behold, an hand touched me, which set me [1]upon my knees and *upon* the palms of my hands.

11 And he said unto me, O Daniel, [a]a man greatly beloved, understand the words that I speak unto thee, and stand upright: for unto thee am I now sent. And when he had spoken this word unto me, I stood trembling.

12 Then said he unto me, [a]Fear not, Daniel: for from the first day that thou didst set thine heart to understand, and to [1]chasten thyself before thy God, [b]thy words were heard, and I am come for thy words.

13 [a]But the prince of the kingdom of Persia withstood me one and twenty days: but, lo, [b]Michael, one of the chief princes, came to help me; and I remained there with the kings of Persia.

14 Now I am come to make thee understand what shall befall thy people [a]in the latter days: [b]for yet the vision [1]is for *many* days.

15 And when he had spoken such words unto me, [a]I [1]set my face toward the ground, and I became [2]dumb.

16 And, behold, [a]*one* [1]like the similitude of the sons of men [b]touched my lips: then I opened my mouth, and spake, and said unto him that stood

10:16 [a] Dan. 8:15 [b] Jer. 1:9; Dan. 10:10 [1] having the likeness

before me, O my lord, [2]by the vision [c]my sorrows [3]are turned upon me, and I have retained no strength.

17 For how can the servant of this my lord talk with this my lord? for as for me, straightway there remained no strength in me, neither is there breath left in me.

18 Then there came again and touched me *one* like the appearance of a man, and he strengthened me,

19 [a]And said, O man greatly beloved, [b]fear not: peace *be* unto thee, be strong, yea, be strong. And when he had spoken unto me, I was strengthened, and said, Let my lord speak; for thou hast strengthened me.

20 Then said he, Knowest thou wherefore I come unto thee? and now will I return to fight [a]with the prince of Persia: and when I am gone forth, lo, the prince of [1]Grecia shall come.

21 But I will shew thee that which is noted in the scripture of truth: and *there is* none that [1]holdeth with me in these things, [a]but Michael your prince.

## CHAPTER 11

ALSO I [a]in the first year of [b]Darius the Mede, *even* I, stood to confirm and to strengthen him.

2 And now will I shew thee the truth. Behold, there shall [1]stand up yet three kings in Persia; and the fourth shall be far richer than *they* all: and by his strength through his riches he shall stir up all against the realm of [2]Grecia.

3 And [a]a mighty king shall [1]stand up, that shall rule with great dominion, and [b]do according to his will.

4 And when he shall stand up, [a]his kingdom shall be broken, and shall be divided toward the four winds of heaven; and not to his posterity, [b]nor according to his dominion which he ruled: for his kingdom shall be plucked up, even for others beside those.

5 And the king of the south shall be strong, [1]and *one* of his princes; and he shall be strong above [2]him, and have dominion; his dominion *shall be* a great dominion.

6 And in the end of years they shall join themselves together; for the king's daughter of the south shall come to the king of the north to make an agreement: but she shall not retain the power of the [1]arm; neither shall he stand, nor his [1]arm: but she shall be given up, and they that brought her, and he that begat her, and he that strengthened her in *these* times.

7 But out of a branch of her roots shall *one* stand up [1]in his estate, which shall come with an army, and shall enter into the fortress of the king of the

north, and shall deal against them, and shall prevail:

8 And shall also carry [1]captives into Egypt their gods, with their [2]princes, *and* with their precious [3]vessels of silver and of gold; and he shall continue *more* years than the king of the north.

9 [1]So the king of the south shall come into *his* kingdom, and shall return into his own land.

10 But his sons shall [1]be stirred up, and shall assemble a multitude of great forces: and *one* shall certainly come, [a]and [2]overflow, and pass through: then shall he [3]return, and be stirred up, [b]even to his fortress.

11 And the king of the south shall be [a]moved with [1]choler, and shall come forth and fight with him, *even* with the king of the north: and he shall set forth a great multitude; but the [b]multitude shall be given into [2]his hand.

12 *And* when he hath taken away the multitude, his heart shall be [1]lifted up; and he shall cast down *many* ten thousands: but he shall not be strengthened *by it.*

13 For the king of the north shall return, and shall set forth a multitude greater than the former, and shall certainly come [1]after certain years with a great army and with much [2]riches.

14 And in those times there shall many stand up against the king of the south: also the [1]robbers of thy people shall exalt themselves [2]to establish the vision; but they shall [a]fall.

15 So the king of the north shall come, and [a]cast up a [1]mount, and take [2]the most fenced cities: and the [3]arms of the south shall not [4]withstand, neither his chosen people, neither *shall there be any* strength to withstand.

16 But he that cometh against him [a]shall do according to his own will, and [b]none shall stand before him: and he shall stand in the glorious land, [1]which by his hand shall be consumed.

17 He shall also [a]set his face to enter with the strength of his whole kingdom, and [1]upright ones with him; thus shall he do: and he shall give him the daughter of women, [2]corrupting her: but she shall not stand [3]*on his side,* [b]neither be for him.

18 After this shall he turn his face unto the [1]isles, and shall take many: but a prince for his own behalf shall cause the reproach offered by him to cease; without his own reproach he shall [2]cause *it* to turn upon him.

19 Then he shall turn his face toward the fort of his own land: but he shall [a]stumble and fall, [b]and not be found.

10:16 [c] Dan. 10:8, 9 [2] *because of* [3] *have come*

10:19 [a] Dan. 10:11 b Judg. 6:23; Is. 43:1; Dan. 10:12

10:20 [a] Dan. 10:13 [1] *Or Greece*

10:21 [a] [Rev. 12:7] [1] *upholds me against*

11:1 [a] Dan. 9:1 b Dan. 5:31

11:2 [1] *arise* [2] *Or Greece*

11:3 [a] Dan. 7:6; 8:5 b Dan. 8:4; 10:16 [1] *arise*

11:4 [a] Zech. 2:6 b Dan. 8:22

11:5 [1] *as well as* [2] *The king of the south*

11:6 [1] *authority*

11:7 [1] *in his place*

11:8 [1] *their gods captive into Egypt* [2] *Or moulded images* [3] *articles*

11:9 [1] *Or Then he (the king of the north) will come into the kingdom of the king of the south, but*

11:10 [a] Is. 8:8 b Dan. 11:7 [1] *stir up strife* [2] *overwhelm* [3] *return to his fortress and stir up strife*

11:11 [a] Prov. 16:14 b [Ps. 33:10, 16] [1] *rage* [2] *his enemy's*

11:12 [1] *Proud*

11:13 [1] *at the end of some years* [2] *equipment*

11:14 [a] Job 9:13 [1] *violent men,* lit. *sons of breakage* [2] *in fulfillment of*

11:15 [a] Ezek. 4:2; 17:17 [1] *siege mound* [2] *a fortified city* [3] *forces* [4] *stand*

11:16 [a] Dan. 8:4, 7 b Josh. 1:5 [1] *with destruction in his hand*

11:17 [a] 2 Chr. 20:3 b Dan. 9:26 [1] *Or bring equitable terms with him* [2] *to destroy it* [3] *With him*

11:18 [1] *coastlands* [2] *turn back on*

11:19 [a] Jer. 46:6 b Ps. 37:36

20 Then shall stand up in his [1]estate a raiser of taxes *in* the [2]glory of the kingdom: but within few days he shall be destroyed, neither in anger, nor in battle.

21 And in his [1]estate [a]shall [2]stand up a vile person, to whom they shall not give the honour of the kingdom: but he shall come [3]in peaceably, and [4]obtain the kingdom by [5]flatteries.

22 And with the [1]arms of a [a]flood shall they be [2]overflown from before him, and shall be broken; [b]yea, also the prince of the covenant.

23 And after the league *made* with him [a]he shall work deceitfully: for he shall come up, and shall become strong with a [1]small people.

24 He shall enter [1]peaceably even [2]upon the fattest places of the province; and he shall do *that* which his fathers have not done, nor his fathers' fathers; he shall scatter among them the [3]prey, and [4]spoil, and riches: *yea,* and he shall [5]forecast his devices against the strong holds, even for a time.

25 And he shall stir up his power and his courage against the king of the south with a great army; and the king of the south shall be stirred up to battle with a very great and mighty army; but he shall not stand: for they shall [1]forecast devices against him.

26 Yea, they that [1]feed of the portion of his [2]meat shall destroy him, and his army shall fall down [3]overflow: and many shall fall down slain.

27 And both these kings' hearts *shall be* [1]to do mischief, and they shall speak lies at [2]one table; but it shall not prosper: for yet the end *shall be* at the [a]time appointed.

28 Then shall he return into his land with great riches; and his heart *shall be* against the holy covenant; and he shall do [1]*exploits,* and return to his own land.

29 At the time appointed he shall return, and come toward the south; but it shall not be as the former, or as the latter.

30 [a]For the ships of [1]Chittim shall come against him: therefore he shall be grieved, and return, and have indignation against the holy covenant: so shall he do; he shall even return, and [2]have intelligence with them that forsake the holy covenant.

31 And [1]arms shall stand on his part, [a]and they shall [2]pollute the sanctuary [3]of strength, and shall take away the daily [4]*sacrifice,* and they shall place the abomination [5]that maketh desolate.

32 And such as do wickedly against the covenant shall he [1]corrupt by flatteries: but the people that do know

their God shall be strong, and [2]do *exploits.*

33 And they that understand among the people shall instruct many: yet they shall fall by the sword, and by flame, by captivity, and by [1]spoil, *many* days.

34 Now when they shall fall, they shall be [1]holpen with a little help: but many shall [2]cleave to them [3]with flatteries.

35 And *some* of them of understanding shall fall, [a]to [1]try them, and to purge, and to make *them* white, *even* to the time of the end: because *it is* yet for a time appointed.

36 And the king shall do according to his will; and he shall [a]exalt himself, and magnify himself above every god, and shall speak [1]marvellous things against the God of gods, and shall prosper till the indignation be accomplished: for that that is determined shall be done.

37 Neither shall he regard the [1]God of his fathers, nor the desire of women, [a]nor regard any god: for he shall magnify himself above all.

38 But in [1]his estate shall he honour [2]the God of forces: and a god whom his fathers knew not shall he honour with gold, and silver, and with precious stones, and pleasant things.

39 Thus shall he do [1]in the most strong holds with a [2]strange god, whom he shall acknowledge *and* increase with glory: and he shall cause them to rule over many, and shall divide the land for [3]gain.

40 And at the [a]time of the end shall the king of the south [1]push at him: and the king of the north shall come against him [b]like a whirlwind, with chariots, [c]and with horsemen, and with many ships; and he shall enter into the countries, and shall [2]overflow and pass over.

41 He shall enter also into the glorious land, and many *countries* shall be overthrown: but these shall escape out of his hand, [a]*even* Edom, and Moab, and the [1]chief of the children of Ammon.

42 He shall stretch forth his hand also [1]upon the countries: and the land of [a]Egypt shall not escape.

43 But he shall have power over the treasures of gold and of silver, and over all the precious things of Egypt: and the Libyans and the Ethiopians *shall* [1]*be* [a]at his steps.

44 But [1]tidings out of the east and out of the north shall trouble him: therefore he shall go forth with great fury to destroy, and [2]utterly to make away many.

45 And he shall plant the [1]tabernacles of his palace between the seas in [a]the glorious holy mountain; [b]yet he

---

**Center column references:**

11:20 [1] *place*
[2] *glorious*

11:21 [a] Dan. 7:8
[1] *place* [2] *arise*
[3] *by prosperity*
[4] *seize* [5] *intrigue*

11:22 [a] Dan. 9:26
[b] Dan. 8:10, 11
[1] *Force* [2] *swept away*

11:23 [a] Dan. 8:25
[1] *small* number of

11:24 [1] *by prosperity* [2] *into the richest* [3] *plunder* [4] *booty* [5] *devise his plans*

11:25 [1] *devise plans*

11:26 [1] *eat* [2] *food* [3] *be swept away*

11:27 [a] Hab. 2:3
[1] *bent on evil*
[2] *the same*

11:28 [1] *Damage*

11:30 [a] Jer. 2:10
[1] Heb. *Kittim,* the western lands, especially Cyprus
[2] *show regard for*

11:31 [a] Dan. 8:11–13; 12:11 [1] *Forces*
[2] *defile* [3] *fortress*
[4] Temple sacrifice [5] *of desolation*

11:32 [1] *pollute*

[2] *take action*

11:33 [1] *plundering*

11:34 [1] *helped*
[2] *join with* [3] *by intrigue*

11:35 [a] Dan. 12:10
[1] *refine*

11:36 [a] Dan. 7:8, 25 [1] *unusual*

11:37 [a] Is. 14:13
[1] *gods*

11:38 [1] *their place* [2] *a god of fortresses*

11:39 [1] *against the strongest fortresses* [2] *foreign* [3] *profit*

11:40 [a] Dan. 11:27, 35; 12:4, 9 [b] Is. 21:1 [c] Rev. 9:16
[1] *thrust* [2] *overwhelm*

11:41 [a] Is. 11:14
[1] *prominent people*

11:42 [a] Joel 3:19
[1] *against*

11:43 [a] Ex. 11:8
[1] *follow at*

11:44 [1] *news*
[2] *annihilate,* lit. *devote to destruction*

11:45 [a] Ps. 48:2
[b] Rev. 19:20
[1] *tents*

shall come to his end, and none shall help him.

## CHAPTER 12

A ND at that time shall Michael stand up, the great prince which [1]standeth for the children of thy people: [a]and there shall be a time of trouble, such as never was since there was a nation *even* to that same time: and at that time thy people [b]shall be delivered, every one that shall be found [c]written in the book.

2 And many of them that sleep in the dust of the earth shall awake, [a]some to everlasting life, and some to shame [b]*and* everlasting [1]contempt.

3 And they that be wise shall [a]shine as the brightness of the firmament; [b]and they that turn many to righteousness [c]as the stars for ever and ever.

4 But thou, O Daniel, [a]shut up the words, and seal the book, *even* to the time of the end: many shall [b]run to and fro, and knowledge shall be increased.

5 Then I Daniel looked, and, behold, there stood [1]other two, the one on this side of the bank of the river, and the other on that side of the bank [a]of the river.

6 And *one* said to the man clothed in [a]linen, which *was* [1]upon the waters

of the river, [b]How long *shall it be to* the end of these wonders?

7 And I heard the man clothed in linen, which *was* [1]upon the waters of the river, when he [a]held up his right hand and his left hand unto heaven, and sware by him [b]that liveth for ever [c]that *it shall be* for a time, times, and an half; [d]and when he [2]shall have accomplished to scatter the power of [e]the holy people, all these *things* shall be finished.

8 And I heard, but I understood not: then said I, O my Lord, what *shall be* the end of these *things?*

9 And he said, Go thy way, Daniel: for the words *are* closed up and sealed till the time of the end.

10 [a]Many shall be purified, and made white, and [1]tried; [b]but the wicked shall do wickedly: and none of the wicked shall understand; but [c]the wise shall understand.

11 And from the time *that* the daily [1]*sacrifice* shall be taken away, and the abomination [2]that maketh desolate set up, *there shall be* a thousand two hundred and ninety days.

12 Blessed *is* he that waiteth, and cometh to the thousand three hundred and five and thirty days.

13 But go thou thy way till the end *be:* [a]for thou shalt rest, [b]and [1]stand in thy lot at the end of the days.

### Cross references (center column)

12:1 [a] Jer. 30:7
[b] Rom. 11:26  [c] Ex. 32:32  [1] *stands watch over*

12:2 [a] [John 5:28, 29]  [b] [Is. 66:24]
[1] Lit. *abhorrence*

12:3 [a] Matt. 13:43
[b] [James 5:19, 20]
[c] 1 Cor. 15:41

12:4 [a] Rev. 22:10
[b] Amos 8:12

12:5 [a] Dan. 10:4
[1] *two others*

12:6 [a] Ezek. 9:2
[1] *above*

[b] Dan. 8:13; 12:8

12:7 [a] Deut. 32:40  [b] Dan. 4:34  [c] Dan. 7:25  [d] Luke 21:24  [e] Dan. 8:24  [1] *above*
[2] *has completely shattered*

12:10 [a] Zech. 13:9  [b] Is. 32:6, 7
[c] John 7:17; 8:47
[1] *refined*

12:11 [1] Temple sacrifice  [2] *of desolation*

12:13 [a] Rev. 14:13
[b] Ps. 1:5  [1] *arise to thine inheritance*

# THE BOOK OF
# HOSEA

Hosea, whose name means "Salvation," ministers to the northern kingdom of Israel (also called Ephraim, after its largest tribe). Outwardly, the nation is enjoying a time of prosperity and growth; but inwardly, moral corruption and spiritual adultery permeate the people. Hosea, instructed by God to marry a woman named Gomer, finds his domestic life to be an accurate and tragic dramatization of the unfaithfulness of God's people. During his half century of prophetic ministry, Hosea repeatedly echoes his threefold message: God abhors the sins of His people; judgment is certain; but God's loyal love stands firm.

The names Hosea, Joshua, and Jesus are all derived from the same Hebrew root word. The word *hoshea* means "salvation," but "Joshua" and "Jesus" include an additional idea: "Yahweh Is Salvation." As God's messenger, Hosea offers the possibility of salvation if only the nation will turn from idolatry back to God.

Israel's last king, Hoshea, has the same name as the prophet even though the English Bible spells them differently. Hosea in the Greek and Latin is *Osee*.

## CHAPTER 1

THE word of the LORD that came unto Hosea, the son of Beeri, in the days of aUzziah, bJotham, cAhaz, *and* dHezekiah, kings of Judah, and in the days of eJeroboam the son of Joash, king of Israel.

2 ¹The beginning of the word of the LORD by Hosea. And the LORD said to Hosea, aGo, take unto thee a wife of ²whoredoms and children of ²whoredoms: for bthe land hath committed great ²whoredom, ³*departing* from the LORD.

3 So he went and took Gomer the daughter of Diblaim; which conceived, and bare him a son.

4 And the LORD said unto him, Call his name Jezreel; for yet a little *while,* aand I will ¹avenge the blood of Jezreel upon the house of Jehu, band will ²cause to cease the kingdom of the house of Israel.

5 aAnd it shall come to pass at that day, that I will break the bow of Israel in the valley of Jezreel.

6 And she conceived again, and bare a daughter. And *God* said unto him, Call her name ¹Lo-ruhamah: afor I will no more have mercy upon the house of Israel; ²but I will utterly take them away.

7 aBut I will have mercy upon the house of Judah, and will save them by the LORD their God, and bwill not save them by bow, nor by sword, nor by battle, by horses, nor by horsemen.

8 Now when she had weaned Lo-ruhamah, she conceived, and bare a son.

9 Then said *God,* Call his name ¹Lo-ammi: for ye *are* not my people, and I will not be your *God.*

10 Yet athe number of the children of Israel shall be as the sand of the

sea, which cannot be measured nor numbered; band it shall come to pass, *that* in the place where it was said unto them, Ye *are* ¹not my cpeople, *there* it shall be said unto them, Ye *are* dthe sons of the living God.

11 aThen shall the children of Judah and the children of Israel be gathered together, and appoint themselves one head, and they shall come up out of the land: for great *shall be* the day of Jezreel.

## CHAPTER 2

SAY ye unto your brethren, ¹Ammi; and to your sisters, ²Ruhamah.

2 ¹Plead with your mother, ²plead: for ashe *is* not my wife, neither *am* I her husband: let her therefore put away her bwhoredoms³ out of her sight, and her adulteries from between her breasts;

3 Lest aI strip her naked, and ¹set her as in the day that she was bborn, and make her as a wilderness, and set her like a dry land, and slay her with cthirst.

4 And I will not have mercy upon her children; for they *be* the achildren of ¹whoredoms.

5 For their mother hath played the harlot: she that conceived them hath done shamefully: for she said, I will go after my lovers, athat give *me* my bread and my water, my wool and my ¹flax, mine oil and my drink.

6 Therefore, behold, aI will hedge up thy way with thorns, and ¹make a wall, that she shall not find her paths.

7 And she shall ¹follow after her lovers, but she shall not overtake them; and she shall seek them, but shall not find *them:* then shall she say, aI will

1:1 a Amos 1:1   b 2 Chr. 27   c 2 Chr. 28   d 2 Chr. 29:1– 32:33   e 2 Kin. 13:13; 14:23–29
1:2 a Hos. 3:1   b Jer. 2:13   ¹ *When the LORD began to speak by Hosea*   ² *harlotry*   ³ *By departing*
1:4 a 2 Kin. 10:11   b 2 Kin. 15:8–10; 17:6, 23; 18:11   ¹ Lit. *visit the blood*   ² *bring an end to*
1:5 a 2 Kin. 15:29
1:6 a 2 Kin. 17:6   ¹ Lit. *No Mercy*   ² *that I may forgive them at all*
1:7 a 2 Kin. 19:29–35   b [Zech. 4:6]
1:9 ¹ Lit. *Not My People*
1:10 a Gen. 22:17; 32:12   b 1 Pet. 2:10   c Rom. 9:26   d [John 1:12]   ¹ Heb. *Lo-ammi,* Hos. 1:9
1:11 a Is. 11:11–13
2:1 ¹ Lit. *My People,* Hos. 1:9, 10   ² Lit. *Mercy,* Hos. 1:6
2:2 a Is. 50:1   b Ezek. 16:25   ¹ *Bring charges against*   ² *bring charges*   ³ *harlotries*
2:3 a Jer. 13:22, 26   b Ezek. 16:4–7, 22   c Amos 8:11–13   ¹ *expose*
2:4 a John 8:41   ¹ *harlotry*
2:5 a Hos. 2:8, 12   ¹ *linen*
2:6 a Lam. 3:7, 9   ¹ *wall her in*   2:7 a Luke 15:17, 18   ¹ *chase*

go and return to my ᵇfirst husband; for then *was it* better with me than now.

8 For she did not ªknow that I gave her ¹corn, and ²wine, and oil, and multiplied her silver and gold, *which* they prepared for Baal.

9 Therefore will I return, and take away my ¹corn in the time thereof, and my ²wine in the season thereof, and will ³recover my wool and my ⁴flax *given* to cover her nakedness.

10 And now ªwill I ¹discover her lewdness in the sight of her lovers, and none shall deliver her out of mine hand.

11 ªI will also cause all her mirth to cease, her feast days, her new moons, and her sabbaths, and all her solemn feasts.

12 And I will destroy her vines and her fig trees, whereof she hath said, These *are* my rewards that my lovers have given me: and I will make them ¹a forest, and the beasts of the field shall eat them.

13 And I will ¹visit upon her the days of ²Baalim, wherein she burned incense to them, and she decked herself with her earrings and her jewels, and she ³went after her lovers, and forgat me, saith the LORD.

14 Therefore, behold, I will allure her, and bring her into the wilderness, and speak ¹comfortably unto her.

15 And I will give her her vineyards from thence, and ªthe valley of Achor for a door of hope: and she shall sing there, as in ᵇthe days of her youth, and ᶜas in the day when she came up out of the land of Egypt.

16 And it shall be at that day, saith the LORD, *that* thou shalt call me ¹Ishi; and shalt call me no more ²Baali.

17 For ªI will take away the names of ¹Baalim out of her mouth, and they shall no more be remembered by their name.

18 And in that day will I make a ªcovenant for them with the beasts of the field, and with the fowls of heaven, and *with* the creeping things of the ground: and ᵇI will ¹break the bow and the sword and the battle out of the earth, and will make them to ᶜlie down safely.

19 And I will betroth thee unto me for ever; yea, I will betroth thee unto me in righteousness, and in ¹judgment, and in lovingkindness, and in mercies.

20 I will even betroth thee unto me in faithfulness: and ªthou shalt know the LORD.

21 And it shall come to pass in that day, ªI will ¹hear, saith the LORD, I will ¹hear the heavens, and they shall ¹hear the earth;

2:7 ᵇ Ezek. 16:8; 23:4
2:8 ª Is. 1:3 ¹ *grain* ² *new wine*
2:9 ¹ *grain* ² *new wine* ³ *take back* ⁴ *linen*
2:10 ª Ezek. 16:37 ¹ *uncover*
2:11 ª Amos 5:21; 8:10
2:12 ¹ *a thicket*
2:13 ¹ *punish her for* ² *the Baals* ³ *chased after*
2:14 ¹ *comfort, lit. to her heart*
2:15 ª Josh. 7:26 ᵇ Ezek. 16:8–14 ᶜ Ex. 15:1
2:16 ¹ Lit. *My Husband* ² Lit. *My Master*
2:17 ª Ex. 23:13 ¹ *the Baals*
2:18 ª Job 5:23 ᵇ Is. 2:4 ᶜ Lev. 26:5 ¹ *shatter*
2:19 ¹ *justice*
2:20 ª [Jer. 31:33, 34]
2:21 ª Zech. 8:12 ¹ *answer*
2:22 ¹ *answer* ² *with grain* ³ *new wine* ⁴ Lit. *God Will Sow*
2:23 ª Jer. 31:27 ᵇ Hos. 1:6 ᶜ Hos. 1:10 ¹ *for myself* ² Heb. *lo-ruhamah* ³ Heb. *lo-ammi* ⁴ Heb. *ammi*
3:1 ª Jer. 3:20 ¹ *loved by* ² *a lover* ³ *and committing adultery* ⁴ *just like* ⁵ *pagan raisin cakes*
3:2 ¹ *for myself*
3:3 ª Deut. 21:13 ¹ *nor shall you have a man*
3:4 ª Hos. 10:3 ᵇ Ex. 28:4–12 ᶜ Judg. 17:5; 18:14, 17 ¹ *sacred pillar* ² *household idols*
3:5 ª Jer. 50:4 ᵇ Jer. 30:9 ᶜ [Is. 2:2, 3]
4:1 ª Is. 1:18 ᵇ Jer. 4:22 ¹ *charge against*
4:2 ¹ *break all restraints* ² *bloodshed follows bloodshed*
4:3 ª Amos 5:16; 8:8 ᵇ Zeph. 1:3 ¹ *waste away*
4:4 ª Deut. 17:12 ¹ *contend*
4:5 ª Jer. 15:8 ¹ *stumble*
4:6 ª Is. 5:13 ᵇ Ezek. 22:26

22 And the earth shall ¹hear ²the corn, and ³the wine, and the oil; and they shall hear ⁴Jezreel.

23 And ªI will sow her ¹unto me in the earth; ᵇand I will have mercy upon her that ²had not obtained mercy; and I ᶜwill say to *them which were* ³not my people, Thou *art* ⁴my people; and they shall say, *Thou art* my God.

## CHAPTER 3

THEN said the LORD unto me, Go yet, love a woman ¹beloved of ²*her* ªfriend, ³yet an adulteress, ⁴according to the love of the LORD toward the children of Israel, who look to other gods, and love ⁵flagons of wine.

2 So I bought her ¹to me for fifteen *pieces* of silver, and *for* an homer of barley, and an half homer of barley:

3 And I said unto her, Thou shalt ªabide for me many days; thou shalt not play the harlot, ¹and thou shalt not be for *another* man: so *will* I also *be* for thee.

4 For the children of Israel shall abide many days ªwithout a king, and without a prince, and without a sacrifice, and without ¹an image, and without an ᵇephod, and *without* ᶜteraphim:²

5 Afterward shall the children of Israel return, and ªseek the LORD their God, and ᵇDavid their king; and shall fear the LORD and his goodness in the ᶜlatter days.

## CHAPTER 4

HEAR the word of the LORD, ye children of Israel: for the LORD hath a ªcontroversy¹ with the inhabitants of the land, because *there is* no truth, nor mercy, nor ᵇknowledge of God in the land.

2 By swearing, and lying, and killing, and stealing, and committing adultery, they ¹break out, and ²blood toucheth blood.

3 Therefore ªshall the land mourn, and ᵇevery one that dwelleth therein shall ¹languish, with the beasts of the field, and with the fowls of heaven; yea, the fishes of the sea also shall be taken away.

4 Yet let no man ¹strive, nor reprove another: for thy people *are* as they ªthat ¹strive with the priest.

5 Therefore shalt thou ¹fall ªin the day, and the prophet also shall ¹fall with thee in the night, and I will destroy thy mother.

6 ªMy people are destroyed for lack of knowledge: because thou hast rejected knowledge, I will also reject thee, that thou shalt be no priest to me: ᵇseeing thou hast forgotten the law of thy God, I will also forget thy children.

7 As they were increased, so they sinned against me: [a]*therefore* will I change their glory into shame.

8 They eat up the sin of my people, and they set their [1]heart on their iniquity.

9 And there shall be, [a]like people, like priest: and I will punish them for their ways, and [1]reward them their [2]doings.

10 For [a]they shall eat, and not have enough: they shall commit [1]whoredom, and shall not increase: because they have [2]left off to take heed to the LORD.

11 Whoredom and wine and new wine [a]take away the heart.

12 My people ask counsel [1]at their [a]stocks, and their [2]staff declareth unto them: for [b]the spirit of whoredoms hath caused *them* to err, and they have gone a whoring from under their God.

13 [a]They sacrifice upon the tops of the mountains, and burn incense upon the hills, under oaks and poplars and [1]elms, because the [2]shadow thereof *is* good: [b]therefore your daughters shall commit [3]whoredom, and your [4]spouses shall commit adultery.

14 I will not punish your daughters when they commit whoredom, nor your [1]spouses when they commit adultery: for [a]themselves are separated with [3]whores, and they sacrifice with [a]harlots: therefore the people *that* doth not understand shall [4]fall.

15 Though thou, Israel, play the harlot, *yet* let not Judah offend; [a]and come not ye unto Gilgal, neither go ye up to [b]Beth-aven,[1] [c]nor [2]swear, The LORD liveth.

16 For Israel [a]slideth[1] back as a [2]backsliding heifer: now the LORD will feed them as a lamb in [3]a large place.

17 Ephraim *is* joined to idols: [a]let him alone.

18 Their drink is [1]sour: they have committed [2]whoredom continually: [a]her [3]rulers [4]*with* shame do love, Give ye.

19 [a]The wind hath bound her up in her wings, and [b]they shall be ashamed because of their sacrifices.

## CHAPTER 5

HEAR ye this, O priests; and hearken, ye house of Israel; and give ye ear, O house of the king; for [1]judgment *is* toward you, because [a]ye have been a snare on Mizpah, and a net spread upon Tabor.

2 And the revolters are [a]profound[1] to make slaughter, though I *have been* a rebuker of them all.

3 [a]I know Ephraim, and Israel is not hid from me: for now, O Ephraim,

[b]thou committest [1]whoredom, *and* Israel is defiled.

4 [1]They will not frame their doings to turn unto their God: for [a]the spirit of [2]whoredoms *is* in the midst of them, and they have not known the LORD.

5 And the [a]pride of Israel doth testify to his face: therefore shall Israel and Ephraim [1]fall in their iniquity; Judah also shall [1]fall with them.

6 [a]They shall go with their flocks and with their herds to seek the LORD; but they shall not find *him;* he hath withdrawn himself from them.

7 They have [a]dealt treacherously against the LORD: for they have begotten [1]strange children: now shall a [2]month devour them with their portions.

8 [a]Blow ye the [1]cornet in Gibeah, *and* the trumpet in Ramah: [b]cry aloud *at* [c]Beth-aven, [2]after thee, O Benjamin.

9 Ephraim shall be desolate in the day of rebuke: among the tribes of Israel have I made known that which shall surely be.

10 The princes of Judah were like them that [a]remove [1]the bound: *therefore* I will pour out my wrath upon them like water.

11 Ephraim *is* [a]oppressed *and* broken in judgment, because he willingly walked [1]after [b]the commandment.

12 Therefore *will* I *be* unto Ephraim as a moth, and to the house of Judah [a]as [1]rottenness.

13 When Ephraim saw his sickness, and Judah *saw* his [a]wound, then went Ephraim [b]to the Assyrian, and sent to king Jareb: yet could he not heal you, nor cure you of your wound.

14 For [a]I *will be* unto Ephraim as a lion, and as a young lion to the house of Judah: [b]I, *even* I, will [1]tear and go away; I will [2]take away, and none shall rescue *him.*

15 I will go *and* return to my place, till they [1]acknowledge their offence, and seek my face: in their affliction they will seek me [2]early.

## CHAPTER 6

COME,[a] and let us return unto the LORD: for [b]he hath torn, and [c]he will heal us; he hath [1]smitten, and he will [2]bind us up.

2 [a]After two days will he revive us: in the third day he will raise us up, and we shall live in his sight.

3 [a]Then shall we know, [1]*if* we follow on to know the LORD: his going forth

4:7 [a] 1 Sam. 2:30
4:8 [1] Desires
4:9 [a] Is. 24:2 [1] *repay* [2] *deeds*
4:10 [a] Lev. 26:26 [1] *harlotry* [2] *ceased obeying*
4:11 [a] Is. 5:12; 28:7
4:12 [a] Jer. 2:27 [b] Is. 44:19, 20 [1] *from their wooden idols* [2] *Diviner's rod*
4:13 [a] Is. 1:29; 57:5, 7 [b] Amos 7:17 [1] *terebinths* [2] *shade* [3] *harlotry* [4] *brides*
4:14 [a] Deut. 23:18 [1] *brides* [2] *the men themselves go apart with harlots* [3] *ritual harlots* [4] *be ruined*
4:15 [a] Hos. 9:15; 12:11 [b] 1 Kin. 12:29 [c] Amos 8:14 [1] *Beth-el, lit. House of Idolatry* [2] *swear an oath*
4:16 [a] Jer. 3:6; 7:24; 8:5 [1] *is stubborn* [2] *stubborn calf* [3] *open country*
4:17 [a] Matt. 15:14
4:18 [a] Mic. 3:11 [1] *rebellion* [2] *harlotry* [3] Lit. *shields* [4] Following a Jewish trad.; Hebrew is difficult, *dearly love dishonour*
4:19 [a] Jer. 51:1 [b] Is. 1:29
5:1 [a] Hos. 6:9 [1] *the judgment is yours*
5:2 [a] Is. 29:15 [1] *deeply involved in slaughter*
5:3 [a] Amos 3:2; 5:12 [b] Hos. 4:17 [1] *harlotry*
5:4 [a] Hos. 4:12 [1] *Their deeds will not allow them to turn* [2] *harlotry*
5:5 [a] Hos. 7:10 [1] *stumble*
5:6 [a] Prov. 1:28
5:7 [a] Jer. 3:20 [1] *pagan* [2] *New Moon*
5:8 [a] Joel 2:1 [b] Is. 10:30 [c] Josh. 7:2 [1] *ram's horn* [2] *look behind you*
5:10 [a] Deut. 19:14; 27:17 [1] *a boundary*
5:11 [a] Deut. 28:33 [b] Mic. 6:16 [1] *by man's precept*
5:12 [a] Prov. 12:4 [1] *corrosion*
5:13 [a] Jer. 30:12–15 [b] 2 Kin. 15:19  5:14 [a] Lam. 3:10 [b] Ps. 50:22 [1] *tear* them [2] *take* them  5:15 [1] *confess* [2] *diligently*  6:1 [a] Is. 1:18 [b] Deut. 32:39 [c] Jer. 30:17 [1] *stricken* [2] *bandage*  6:2 [a] [1 Cor. 15:4]  6:3 [a] Is. 54:13 [1] *let us pursue the knowledge of*

is ²prepared ᵇas the morning; and ᶜhe shall come unto us ᵈas the rain, as the latter *and* former rain unto the earth.

4 O Ephraim, what shall I do unto thee? O Judah, what shall I do unto thee? for your ¹goodness *is* as a morning cloud, and as the early dew it goeth away.

5 Therefore have I ¹hewed *them* by the prophets; I have slain them by ᵃthe words of my mouth: and ²thy judgments *are as* the light *that* goeth forth.

6 For I desired ᵃmercy,¹ and ᵇnot sacrifice; and the ᶜknowledge of God more than burnt offerings.

7 But they ¹like men have transgressed the covenant: there have they dealt treacherously against me.

8 ᵃGilead is a city of them that work iniquity, *and is* ¹polluted with blood.

9 And as ¹troops of robbers wait for a man, *so* the company of ᵃpriests ᵇmurder ²in the way by consent: for they commit ᶜlewdness.³

10 I have seen an horrible thing in the house of Israel: there *is* the ¹whoredom of Ephraim, Israel is defiled.

11 Also, O Judah, he hath set an harvest for thee, when I returned the ¹captivity of my people.

## CHAPTER 7

WHEN I would have healed Israel, then the iniquity of Ephraim was ¹discovered, and the wickedness of Samaria: for ᵃthey commit ²falsehood; and the thief cometh in, *and* the ³troop of robbers ⁴spoileth without.

2 And they ¹consider not in their hearts *that* I ᵃremember all their wickedness: now their own ²doings have ³beset them about; they are before my face.

3 They make the ᵃking glad with their wickedness, and the princes ᵇwith their lies.

4 ᵃThey *are* all adulterers, as an oven heated by the baker, *who* ceaseth from ¹raising after he hath kneaded the dough, until it be leavened.

5 In the day of our king the princes have made *him* sick with ¹bottles of ᵃwine; he stretched out his hand with scorners.

6 For they have ¹made ready their heart like an oven, whiles they lie in wait: their baker sleepeth all the night; in the morning it burneth as a flaming fire.

7 They are all hot as an oven, and have devoured their judges; all their kings are fallen: ᵃ*there is* none among them that calleth unto me.

8 Ephraim, he ᵃhath mixed himself among the ¹people; Ephraim is a cake not turned.

6:3 ᵇ 2 Sam. 23:4
ᶜ Ps. 72:6 ᵈ Job
29:23 ² *established*

6:4 ¹ *faithfulness*

6:5 ᵃ [Jer. 23:29]
¹ *hewn them in
pieces* ² *the judgments on you*

6:6 ᵃ Matt. 9:13;
12:7 ᵇ [Mic. 6:6–
8] ᶜ [John 17:3]
¹ *faithfulness*

6:7 ¹ *like Adam*

6:8 ᵃ Hos. 12:11
¹ *defiled,* lit. *foottracked*

6:9 ᵃ Hos. 5:1
ᵇ Jer. 7:9, 10
ᶜ Ezek. 22:9; 23:27
¹ *bands* ² *on the
way to Shechem*
³ *infamy*

6:10 ¹ *harlotry,
spiritual adultery*

6:11 ¹ *captives*

7:1 ᵃ Hos. 5:1 ¹ *uncovered* ² *fraud*
³ *band* ⁴ *plunders
outside*

7:2 ᵃ Jer. 14:10;
17:1 ¹ Lit. *do not
say* ² *deeds*
³ *surrounded*

7:3 ᵃ Hos. 1:1
ᵇ [Rom. 1:32]

7:4 ᵃ Jer. 9:2;
23:10 ¹ *stirring up
the fire*

7:5 ᵃ Is. 28:1, 7
¹ *fever from wine,*
lit. *the heat of
wine*

7:6 ¹ *prepared*

7:7 ᵃ Is. 64:7

7:8 ᵃ Ps. 106:35
¹ *peoples*

7:9 ᵃ Hos. 8:7

7:10 ᵃ Hos. 5:5
ᵇ Is. 9:13

7:11 ᵃ Hos. 11:11
ᵇ Is. 30:3 ᶜ Hos.
5:13; 8:9 ¹ *Sense*

7:12 ᵃ Ezek. 12:13
ᵇ Lev. 26:14
¹ *birds of the air*
² *according to
the report to their
congregation*

7:13 ᵃ Mic. 6:4

7:14 ᵃ Job 35:9,
10 ᵇ Amos 2:8
¹ *wailed* ² *grain*
³ *new wine*

7:15 ¹ *trained*
² *devise evil*

7:16 ᵃ Ps. 78:57
ᵇ Ps. 73:9 ᶜ Hos.
8:13; 9:3 ¹ *upward*

8:1 ᵃ Deut. 28:49
¹ *ram's horn*
² *rebelled*

8:2 ᵃ Ps. 78:34
ᵇ Titus 1:16

8:4 ᵃ 2 Kin.
15:23, 25

8:5 ᵃ Jer. 13:27

9 ᵃStrangers have devoured his strength, and he knoweth *it* not: yea, gray hairs are here and there upon him, yet he knoweth not.

10 And the ᵃpride of Israel testifieth to his face: and ᵇthey do not return to the LORD their God, nor seek him for all this.

11 ᵃEphraim also is like a silly dove without ¹heart: ᵇthey call to Egypt, they go to ᶜAssyria.

12 When they shall go, I will ᵃspread my net upon them; I will bring them down as the ¹fowls of the heaven; I will chastise them, ᵇas² their congregation hath heard.

13 Woe unto them! for they have fled from me: destruction unto them! because they have transgressed against me: though ᵃI have redeemed them, yet they have spoken lies against me.

14 ᵃAnd they have not cried unto me with their heart, when they ¹howled upon their beds: they assemble themselves for ²corn and ᵇwine,³ *and* they rebel against me.

15 Though I ¹have bound *and* strengthened their arms, yet do they ²imagine mischief against me.

16 They return, *but* not ¹to the most High: ᵃthey are like a deceitful bow: their princes shall fall by the sword for the ᵇrage of their tongue: this *shall be* their derision ᶜin the land of Egypt.

## CHAPTER 8

SET the ¹trumpet to thy mouth. *He shall come* ᵃas an eagle against the house of the LORD, because they have transgressed my covenant, and ²trespassed against my law.

2 ᵃIsrael shall cry unto me, My God, ᵇwe know thee.

3 Israel hath cast off *the thing that is* good: the enemy shall pursue him.

4 ᵃThey have set up kings, but not by me: they have made princes, and I knew *it* not: of their silver and their gold have they made them idols, that they may be cut off.

5 Thy ¹calf, O Samaria, ᵃhath cast *thee* off; mine anger is ³kindled against them: ᵃhow long *will it be* ere they attain to innocency?

6 For from Israel *was* it also: the ᵃworkman made it; therefore it *is* not God: but the calf of Samaria shall be broken in pieces.

7 For ᵃthey have sown the wind, and they shall reap the whirlwind: ¹it hath no stalk: ²the bud shall yield no meal: ³if so be it yield, the ᵇstrangers⁴ shall swallow it up.

¹ *golden calf image* ² *is rejected* ³ *aroused* 8:6 ᵃ Is.
40:19 8:7 ᵃ Prov. 22:8 ᵇ Hos. 7:9 ¹ *the stalk has
no bud* ² *it shall never produce meal* ³ *if it should
produce* ⁴ *aliens*

8 [a]Israel is swallowed up: now shall they be among the Gentiles [b]as a vessel wherein *is* no pleasure.

9 For they are gone up to Assyria, [a]a wild [1]ass alone by himself: Ephraim [b]hath hired lovers.

10 Yea, though they have hired among the nations, now [1]will I gather them, and they shall [1]sorrow a little [2]for the burden of [b]the king of princes.

11 Because Ephraim hath made many altars to sin, altars shall be unto him [1]to sin.

12 I have written to him [a]the great things of my law, *but* they were counted as a strange thing.

13 [a]They sacrifice flesh *for* the sacrifices of mine offerings, and eat *it;* [b]*but* the LORD accepteth them not; [c]now will he remember their iniquity, and [1]visit their sins: they shall return to Egypt.

14 [a]For Israel hath forgotten [b]his Maker, and buildeth [1]temples; and Judah hath multiplied [c]fenced[2] cities: but [d]I will send a fire upon his cities, and it shall devour the [3]palaces thereof.

## CHAPTER 9

REJOICE [a]not, O Israel, [1]for joy, as [b]other people: for thou [2]hast gone a whoring from thy God, thou hast loved [3]a [b]reward upon every [4]cornfloor.

2 The [1]floor and the winepress shall not feed them, and the new wine shall fail in her.

3 They shall not dwell in [a]the LORD's land; [b]but Ephraim shall return to Egypt, and [c]they shall eat unclean *things* in Assyria.

4 They shall not offer wine *offerings* to the LORD, [a]neither shall [1]they be pleasing unto him: their [b]sacrifices *shall be* unto them as the bread of mourners; all that eat thereof shall be [2]polluted: for their bread [3]for their soul shall not come into the house of the LORD.

5 What will ye do in the [1]solemn day, and in the day of the feast of the LORD?

6 For, lo, they are gone because of destruction: Egypt shall gather them up, Memphis shall bury them: [1]the pleasant *places* for their silver, [a]nettles shall possess them: thorns *shall be* in their [2]tabernacles.

7 The [a]days of [1]visitation are come, the days of recompence are come; Israel shall know *it:* the prophet *is a* [b]fool, [c]the spiritual man *is* [2]mad, for the [3]multitude of thine iniquity, and the great [4]hatred.

8 The [a]watchman of Ephraim *was* with my God: *but* the prophet *is a* snare of a [1]fowler in all his ways, *and* [2]hatred in the house of his God.

8:8 [a] 2 Kin. 17:6
[b] Jer. 22:28; 25:34
8:9 [a] Jer. 2:24
[b] Ezek. 16:33, 34
[1] *donkey*
8:10 [a] Ezek. 16:37;
22:20 [b] Is. 10:8
[1] *begin to diminish*
[2] *because of the oracle (proclamation)*
8:11 [1] *for sinning*
8:12 [a] [Deut. 4:6–8]
8:13 [a] Zech.
7:6 [b] Jer. 14:10
[c] Amos 8:7
[1] *punish*
8:14 [a] Deut. 32:18
[b] Is. 29:23 [c] Num.
32:17 [d] Jer. 17:27
[1] *Or palaces*
[2] *fortified* [3] *Or citadels*
9:1 [a] Is. 22:12, 13
[b] Jer. 44:17 [1] *with*
[2] *have played the harlot against*
[3] *for reward*
[4] *threshingfloor*
9:2 [1] *threshingfloor*
9:3 [a] [Lev. 25:23]
[b] Hos. 7:16; 8:13
[c] Ezek. 4:13
9:4 [a] Jer. 6:20
[b] Hos. 8:13 [1] *their sacrifices* [2] *defiled*
[3] *will be for their life, it shall not come*
9:5 [1] *appointed*
9:6 [a] Is. 5:6; 7:23
[1] *their valuables of silver* [2] *tents*
9:7 [a] Is. 10:3
[b] Lam. 2:14 [c] Mic.
2:11 [1] *punishment*
[2] *insane* [3] *greatness* [4] *enmity*
9:8 [a] Ezek. 3:17;
33:7 [1] *Trapper of birds* [2] *enmity*
9:9 [a] Hos. 10:9
[b] Judg. 19:22
[1] *punish*
9:10 [a] Jer. 2:2 [b] Is.
28:4 [c] Num. 25:3
[d] Ps. 81:12 [1] *firstfruits* [2] *in her first season* [3] *Heb. nazar, dedicated themselves* [4] *they became an abomination like the thing they loved*
9:11 [1] *no birth* [2] *no pregnancy* [3] *no conception*
9:12 [a] Deut. 31:17
9:13 [a] Ezek. 26–28
9:14 [a] Luke 23:29
9:15 [a] Hos. 4:15;
12:11 [b] Is. 1:23
[1] *rebellious*
9:16 [a] Hos. 5:11
[1] *defeated* [2] *if they bear children*
9:17 [a] [Zech. 10:6]

9 [a]They have deeply corrupted *themselves,* as in the days of [b]Gibeah: *therefore* he will remember their iniquity, he will [1]visit their sins.

10 I found Israel like grapes in the [a]wilderness; I saw your fathers as the [b]firstripe[1] in the fig tree [2]at her first time: *but* they went to [c]Baal-peor, and [3]separated themselves unto *that* shame; [d]and [4]*their* abominations were according as they loved.

11 *As for* Ephraim, their glory shall fly away like a bird, [1]from the birth, and [2]from the womb, and [3]from the conception.

12 Though they bring up their children, yet will I bereave them, *that there shall* not *be* a man *left:* yea, [a]woe also to them when I depart from them!

13 Ephraim, [a]as I saw Tyrus, *is* planted in a pleasant place: but Ephraim shall bring forth his children to the murderer.

14 Give them, O LORD: what wilt thou give? give them [a]a miscarrying womb and dry breasts.

15 All their wickedness *is* in [a]Gilgal: for there I hated them: for the wickedness of their doings I will drive them out of mine house, I will love them no more: [b]all their princes *are* [1]revolters.

16 Ephraim is [a]smitten,[1] their root is dried up, they shall bear no fruit: yea, [2]though they bring forth, yet will I slay *even* the beloved *fruit* of their womb.

17 My God will [a]cast them away, because they did not [1]hearken unto him: and they shall be [b]wanderers among the nations.

## CHAPTER 10

ISRAEL [1]*is* [a]an empty vine, he bringeth forth fruit [2]unto himself: according to the multitude of his fruit [b]he hath increased the altars; according to the goodness of his land they have [3]made goodly images.

2 Their heart is [a]divided; [1]now shall they be found [2]faulty: he shall break down their altars, he shall [3]spoil their images.

3 For now they shall say, We have no king, because we feared not the LORD; what then should a king do [1]to us?

4 They have spoken words, swearing falsely in making a covenant: [a]thus judgment springeth up as hemlock in the furrows of the field.

5 The inhabitants of Samaria shall fear because of the [a]calves[1] of Beth-

[b] Lev. 26:33 [1] *obey* 10:1 [a] Nah. 2:2 [b] Jer. 2:28 [1] *empties his vine* [2] *for* [3] *improved his sacred pillars* 10:2 [a] 1 Kin. 18:21 [1] *Divided in loyalty* [2] *guilty* [3] *ruin their sacred pillars* 10:3 [1] *for* 10:4 [a] Amos 5:7 10:5 [a] Hos. 8:5, 6; 13:2 [1] *golden calf image*

aven: for the people thereof shall mourn over it, and the priests thereof [2]*that* rejoiced on it, for the [b]glory thereof, because it is departed from it.

6 [1]It shall be also carried unto Assyria *for* a present to king [a]Jareb: Ephraim shall receive shame, and Israel shall be ashamed of his own counsel.

7 *As for* Samaria, her king is cut off as [1]the foam upon the water.

8 The [a]high places also of [1]Aven, [b]the sin of Israel, shall be destroyed: the thorn and the thistle shall come up on their altars; [c]and they shall say to the mountains, Cover us; and to the hills, Fall on us.

9 O Israel, thou hast sinned from the days of [a]Gibeah: there they stood: the [b]battle in Gibeah against the children of [1]iniquity did not [2]overtake them.

10 [1]*It is* in my desire that I should chastise them; and [a]the [2]people shall be gathered against them, when [3]they shall bind themselves [4]in their two furrows.

11 And Ephraim *is as* [a]an heifer *that is* [1]taught, *and* loveth to [2]tread out *the corn;* but I [3]passed over upon her fair neck: I will make Ephraim [4]to ride; Judah shall plow, *and* Jacob shall break his clods.

12 Sow to yourselves in righteousness, reap in [1]mercy; [a]break up your [2]fallow ground: for *it is* time to seek the LORD, till he [b]come and rain righteousness upon you.

13 [a]Ye have plowed wickedness, ye have reaped iniquity; ye have eaten the fruit of lies: because thou didst trust in thy way, in the multitude of thy mighty men.

14 Therefore shall a tumult arise among thy people, and all thy fortresses shall be [1]spoiled, as Shalman [1]spoiled Beth-arbel in the day of battle: the mother was dashed in pieces upon *her* children.

15 So shall [1]Beth-el do unto you because of your great wickedness: in a morning shall the king of Israel utterly be cut off.

### CHAPTER 11

WHEN Israel *was* [1]a child, then I loved him, and [a]called my [b]son out of Egypt.

2 *As* they called them, so they [a]went from them: they sacrificed unto [1]Baalim, and burned incense to [2]graven images.

3 [a]I taught Ephraim also to [1]go, taking them by their arms; but they knew not that [b]I healed them.

4 I drew them with [1]cords of a man, with bands of love: and [a]I was to them as they that take off the yoke on their [2]jaws, and [b]I [3]laid meat unto them.

10:5 [b] Hos. 9:11
[2] *shall shriek for*
10:6 [a] Hos. 5:13
[1] The idol
10:7 [1] *a twig on*
10:8 [a] Hos. 4:15
[b] 1 Kin. 13:34
[c] Luke 23:30 [1] *Lit. Idolatry*
10:9 [a] Hos.
9:9 [b] Judg. 20
[1] Many Heb. mss., LXX, Vg. *iniquity;* MT *unruliness*
[2] *overtame*
10:10 [a] Jer. 16:16
[1] *when it is my desire* [2] *peoples* [3] *I bind them* [4] *for their transgressions*
10:11 [a] [Mic. 4:13]
[1] *trained* [2] *thresh* [3] *crossed her fair neck* with a yoke [4] *pull a plow*
10:12 [a] Jer. 4:3 [b] Hos. 6:3
[1] *lovingkindness or faithfulness* [2] *untilled*
10:13 [a] [Prov. 22:8]
10:14 [1] *plundered*
10:15 [1] *it be done to you, O Beth-el*
11:1 [a] Matt. 2:15 [b] Ex. 4:22, 23 [1] *a youth*
11:2 [a] 2 Kin. 17:13–15 [1] *the Baals* [2] *carved*
11:3 [a] Deut. 1:31; 32:10, 11 [b] Ex. 15:26 [1] *walk*
11:4 [a] Lev. 26:13 [b] Ps. 78:25 [1] *gentle cords* [2] *neck* [3] *stooped and fed*
11:5 [1] *repent*
11:6 [1] *slash* [2] *districts*
11:7 [a] Jer. 3:6, 7; 8:5 [1] The prophets [2] *upward*
11:8 [a] Jer. 9:7 [b] Gen. 14:8; 19:24, 25 [1] *churned* [2] *sympathy* [3] *stirred*
11:9 [a] Num. 23:19 [1] *again destroy* [2] *come with terror*
11:10 [a] [Joel 3:16]
11:11 [a] Is. 11:11; 60:8 [b] Ezek. 28:25, 26; 34:27, 28 [1] *make them dwell in*
11:12 [1] *encompassed* [2] *walks or roams* [3] *with the holy one who is faithful*
12:1 [a] Job 15:2, 3 [b] 2 Kin. 17:4

5 He shall not return into the land of Egypt, but the Assyrian shall be his king, because they refused to [1]return.

6 And the sword shall [1]abide on his cities, and shall consume his [2]branches, and devour *them,* because of their own counsels.

7 And my people are bent to [a]backsliding from me: though [1]they called them [2]to the most High, none at all would exalt *him.*

8 [a]How shall I give thee up, Ephraim? *how* shall I deliver thee, Israel? how shall I make thee as [b]Admah? *how* shall I set thee as Zeboim? mine heart is [1]turned within me, my [2]repentings are [3]kindled together.

9 I will not execute the fierceness of mine anger, I will not [1]return to destroy Ephraim: [a]for I *am* God, and not man; the Holy One in the midst of thee: and I will not [2]enter into the city.

10 They shall walk after the LORD: [a]he shall roar like a lion: when he shall roar, then the children shall tremble from the west.

11 They shall tremble as a bird out of Egypt, [a]and as a dove out of the land of Assyria: [b]and I will [1]place them in their houses, saith the LORD.

12 Ephraim [1]compasseth me about with lies, and the house of Israel with deceit: but Judah yet [2]ruleth with God, and [3]is faithful with the saints.

### CHAPTER 12

EPHRAIM [a]feedeth on wind, and followeth after the east wind: he daily increaseth lies and [1]desolation; [b]and they do make a [2]covenant with the Assyrians, and [c]oil is carried into Egypt.

2 [a]The LORD hath also a [1]controversy with Judah, and will punish Jacob according to his ways; according to his doings will he recompense him.

3 He took his brother [a]by the heel in the womb, and by his strength he [b]had[1] power with God:

4 Yea, he [1]had power over the angel, and prevailed: he wept, and [2]made supplication unto him: he found him *in* [a]Beth-el, and there he spake with us;

5 Even the LORD God of hosts; the LORD *is* his [a]memorial.

6 [a]Therefore turn thou to thy God: keep [1]mercy and [2]judgment, and wait on thy God continually.

7 *He is* a [1]merchant, [a]the [2]balances of deceit *are* in his hand: he loveth to oppress.

[c] Is. 30:6 [1] *ruin* [2] *treaty* 12:2 [a] Mic. 6:2 [1] *charge against* 12:3 [a] Gen. 25:26 [b] Gen. 32:24–28 [1] *struggled* 12:4 [a] [Gen. 28:12–19; 35:9–15] [1] *struggled with* [2] *sought favour from him* 12:5 [a] Ex. 3:15 12:6 [a] Mic. 6:8 [1] *lovingkindness or faithfulness* [2] *justice* 12:7 [a] Amos 8:5 [1] Or *Canaanite* [2] *deceitful scales*

8 And Ephraim said, [a]Yet I am become rich, I have found me out [1]substance: *in* all my labours they shall find none iniquity in me that *were* sin.

9 And I *that am* the LORD thy God from the land of Egypt [a]will yet make thee to dwell in [1]tabernacles, as in the days of the solemn feast.

10 [a]I have also spoken by the prophets, and I have multiplied visions, and [1]used similitudes, [2]by the ministry of the prophets.

11 *Is there* iniquity *in* [a]Gilead? surely they are [1]vanity: they sacrifice bullocks in [b]Gilgal; yea, their altars *are* as heaps in the furrows of the fields.

12 And Jacob [a]fled into the country of Syria, and [b]Israel served for a wife, and for a wife he kept *sheep.*

13 [a]And by a prophet the LORD brought Israel out of Egypt, and by a prophet was he preserved.

14 Ephraim [a]provoked *him* to anger most bitterly: therefore shall he leave his [1]blood upon him, [b]and his reproach shall his Lord return unto him.

## CHAPTER 13

WHEN Ephraim spake trembling, he exalted himself in Israel; but when he offended in Baal, he died.

2 And now they sin more and more, and have made them molten images of their silver, *and* idols according to their own [1]understanding, all of it the work of the craftsmen: they say of them, Let the men that [2]sacrifice [3]kiss the [4]calves.

3 Therefore they shall be as the morning cloud, and as the early dew that passeth away, [a]as the chaff *that* is driven with the whirlwind out of the [1]floor, and as the smoke out of the chimney.

4 Yet [a]I *am* the LORD thy God [1]from the land of Egypt, and thou shalt know no god but me: for [b]*there is* no saviour [2]beside me.

5 [a]I did [1]know thee in the wilderness, [b]in the land of [2]great drought.

6 [a]According to their pasture, so were they filled; they were filled, and their heart was exalted; therefore have they forgotten me.

7 Therefore [a]I will be unto them as a lion: as [b]a leopard by the way will I observe *them:*

8 I will meet them [a]as a bear *that is* [1]bereaved *of her whelps,* and will [2]rend the caul of their heart, and there will I devour them like a lion: the wild beast shall tear them.

9 O Israel, [1]thou hast destroyed thyself; but in me *is* thine help.

10 [1]I will be thy king: [a]where *is any other* that may save thee in all thy cities? and thy judges of whom [b]thou saidst, Give me a king and princes?

11 [a]I gave thee a king in mine anger, and took *him* away in my wrath.

12:8 [a] Rev. 3:17
[1] *wealth*
12:9 [a] Lev. 23:42
[1] *tents*
12:10 [a] 2 Kin. 17:13
[1] *given symbols*
[2] Lit. *by the hand*
12:11 [a] Hos. 6:8  [b] Hos. 9:15
[1] *worthless*
12:12 [a] Gen. 28:5
[b] Gen. 29:20, 28
12:13 [a] Ex. 12:50, 51; 13:3
12:14 [a] Ezek. 18:10–13  [b] Dan. 11:18
[1] *bloodguilt*
13:2 [1] *skill*  [2] *offer human sacrifice*
[3] Worship with kisses  [4] *calf idols*
13:3 [a] Dan. 2:35
[1] *threshingfloor*
13:4 [a] Is. 43:11
[b] Is. 43:11; 45:21, 22  [1] *ever since*
[2] *besides*
13:5 [a] Deut. 2:7; 32:10  [b] Deut. 8:15
[1] Care for  [2] Lit. *droughts*
13:6 [a] Deut. 8:12, 14; 32:13–15
13:7 [a] Lam. 3:10
[b] Jer. 5:6
13:8 [a] 2 Sam. 17:8
[1] *deprived* of her cubs  [2] *tear open the cavity*
13:9 [1] Lit. *he* (or *it*) *destroyed you*
13:10 [a] Deut. 32:38  [b] 1 Sam. 8:5, 6  [1] LXX, Syr., Tg., Vg. *Where is your king?*
13:11 [a] 1 Sam. 8:7; 10:17–24
13:12 [a] Deut. 32:34, 35  [1] *stored up*
13:13 [a] Is. 13:8
[1] *woman in childbirth*  [2] *birth*
13:14 [a] [1 Cor. 15:54, 55]  [b] Jer. 15:6  [1] Lit. *the hand*  [2] Heb. *Sheol*  [3] LXX *where is your punishment?*  [4] LXX *where is your sting?*  [5] *pity*
13:15 [a] Jer. 4:11, 12  [1] *plunder*  [2] *treasury*  [3] *every desirable prize*
13:16 [a] 2 Kin. 8:12  [b] 2 Kin. 15:16  [1] MT *is held guilty*  [2] *open*
14:1 [a] [Joel 2:13]
14:2 [a] [Heb. 13:15]  [1] Lit. *bull calves,* LXX *fruit* (sacrifices)
14:3 [a] Hos. 7:11; 10:13; 12:1  [b] [Ps. 33:17]  [c] Ps. 10:14; 68:5  [1] Or *Assyria*

12 [a]The iniquity of Ephraim is bound up; his sin *is* [1]hid.

13 [a]The sorrows of a [1]travailing woman shall come upon him: he *is* an unwise son; for he should not stay long in *the place of* the [2]breaking forth of children.

14 I will ransom them from [1]the power of [2]the grave; I will redeem them from death: [a]O death, [3]I will be thy plagues; O grave, [4]I will be thy destruction: [b]repentance[5] shall be hid from mine eyes.

15 Though he be fruitful among *his* brethren, [a]an east wind shall come, the wind of the LORD shall come up from the wilderness, and his spring shall become dry, and his fountain shall be dried up: he shall [1]spoil the [2]treasure of [3]all pleasant vessels.

16 Samaria [1]shall become desolate; for she hath [a]rebelled against her God: they shall fall by the sword: their infants shall be dashed in pieces, and their women with child shall be [b]ripped [2]up.

## CHAPTER 14

O ISRAEL, [a]return unto the LORD thy God; for thou hast fallen by thine iniquity.

2 Take with you words, and turn to the LORD: say unto him, Take away all iniquity, and receive *us* graciously: so will we render the [a]calves[1] of our lips.

3 [1]Asshur shall [a]not save us; [b]we will not ride upon horses: neither will we say any more to the work of our hands, *Ye are* our gods: [c]for in thee the fatherless findeth mercy.

4 I will heal their [a]backsliding, I will [b]love them freely: for mine anger is turned away from him.

5 I will be as the [a]dew unto Israel: he shall [1]grow as the lily, and [2]cast forth his roots as Lebanon.

6 His branches shall [1]spread, and [a]his beauty shall be as the olive tree, and [b]his [2]smell as Lebanon.

7 [a]They that dwell under his shadow shall return; they shall revive *as* the corn, and grow as the vine: the [1]scent thereof *shall be* as the wine of Lebanon.

8 Ephraim *shall say,* What have I to do any more with idols? I have heard *him,* and observed him: I *am* like a green [1]fir tree. [a]From[2] me is thy fruit found.

9 Who *is* wise, and he shall understand these *things?* prudent, and he shall know them? for [a]the ways of the LORD *are* right, and the just shall walk in them: but the transgressors shall [1]fall therein.

14:4 [a] Jer. 14:7  [b] [Eph. 1:6]  14:5 [a] Prov. 19:12  [1] *blossom*  [2] *send forth*  14:6 [a] Ps. 52:8; 128:3  [b] Gen. 27:27  [1] Lit. *go*  [2] *aroma*  14:7 [a] Dan. 4:12  [1] Lit. *remembrance*  14:8 [a] [John 15:4]  [1] *cypress*  [2] *In me*  14:9 [a] [Prov. 10:29]  [1] *stumble*

# THE BOOK OF
# JOEL

Disaster strikes the southern kingdom of Judah without warning. An ominous black cloud descends upon the land—the dreaded locusts. In a matter of hours, every living green thing has been stripped bare. Joel, God's spokesman during the reign of Joash (835–796 B.C.), seizes this occasion to proclaim God's message. Although the locust plague has been a terrible judgment for sin, God's future judgments during the day of the Lord will make that plague pale by comparison. In that day, God will destroy His enemies, but bring unparalleled blessing to those who faithfully obey Him.

The Hebrew name *Yo'el* means "Yahweh Is God." This name is appropriate to the theme of the book, which emphasizes God's sovereign work in history. The courses of nature and nations are in His hand. The Greek equivalent is *Ioel*, and the Latin is *Joel*.

## CHAPTER 1

THE word of the LORD that came to ᵃJoel the son of Pethuel.

2 Hear this, ye ¹old men, and give ear, all ye inhabitants of the land. ᵃHath ²this been in your days, or even in the days of your fathers?

3 ᵃTell ye your children of it, and *let* your children *tell* their children, and their children another generation.

4 ᵃThat which the ¹palmerworm hath left hath the ᵇlocust² eaten; and that which the ²locust hath left hath the ³cankerworm eaten; and that which the cankerworm hath left hath the ⁴caterpiller eaten.

5 Awake, ye ᵃdrunkards, and weep; and ¹howl, all ye drinkers of wine, because of the new wine; ᵇfor it is cut off from your mouth.

6 For ᵃa nation is come up upon my land, strong, and without number, ᵇwhose teeth *are* the teeth of a lion, and he hath the ¹cheek teeth of a ²great lion.

7 He hath ᵃlaid my vine waste, and ¹barked my fig tree: he hath ²made it clean bare, and cast *it* away; the branches thereof are made white.

8 ᵃLament like a virgin girded with sackcloth for ᵇthe husband of her youth.

9 ᵃThe ¹meat offering and the drink offering is cut off from the house of the LORD; the priests, the LORD's ministers, ᵇmourn.

10 The field is ¹wasted, ᵃthe land mourneth; for the ²corn is wasted: ᵇthe new wine is dried up, the oil ³languisheth.

11 ᵃBe ye ashamed, O ye ¹husbandmen; ²howl, O ye vinedressers, for the wheat and for the barley; because the harvest of the field is perished.

12 ᵃThe vine is dried up, and the fig tree ¹languisheth; the pomegranate tree, the palm tree also, and the apple tree, *even* all the trees of the field,

are withered: because ᵇjoy is withered away from the sons of men.

13 ᵃGird yourselves, and lament, ye priests: ¹howl, ye ministers of the altar: come, lie all night in sackcloth, ye ministers of my God: for the ²meat offering and the drink offering is ³withholden from the house of your God.

14 ᵃSanctify¹ ye a fast, call ᵇa ²solemn assembly, gather the elders *and* ᶜall the inhabitants of the land *into* the house of the LORD your God, and cry unto the LORD,

15 ᵃAlas for the day! for ᵇthe day of the LORD *is* at hand, and as a destruction from the Almighty shall it come.

16 Is not the ¹meat ᵃcut off before our eyes, *yea,* ᵇjoy and gladness from the house of our God?

17 The seed ¹is rotten under their clods, the ²garners are laid desolate, the barns are broken down; for the ³corn is withered.

18 How do ᵃthe beasts groan! the herds of cattle are ¹perplexed, because they have no pasture; yea, the flocks of sheep ²are made desolate.

19 O LORD, ᵃto thee will I cry: for ᵇthe fire hath devoured the ¹pastures of the wilderness, and the flame hath burned all the trees of the field.

20 The beasts of the field ᵃcry also unto thee: for ᵇthe ¹rivers of waters are dried up, and the fire hath devoured the pastures of the wilderness.

## CHAPTER 2

BLOW ᵃye the ¹trumpet in Zion, and ᵇsound an alarm in my holy mountain: let all the inhabitants of the land tremble: for ᶜthe day of the LORD cometh, for *it is* nigh at hand;

2 ᵃA day of darkness and of gloominess, a day of clouds and of thick

---

1:1 ᵃ Acts 2:16
1:2 ᵃ Joel 2:2  ¹ *elders*  ² anything like *this*
1:3 ᵃ Ps. 78:4
1:4 ᵃ Deut. 28:38  ᵇ Is. 33:4  ¹ *chewing locust*  ² *swarming locust*  ³ *crawling locust*  ⁴ *consuming locust*
1:5 ᵃ Is. 5:11; 28:1  ᵇ Is. 32:10  ¹ *wail*
1:6 ᵃ Joel 2:2, 11, 25  ᵇ Rev. 9:8  ¹ *fangs*  ² *fierce*
1:7 ᵃ Is. 5:6  ¹ *splintered*  ² *stripped*
1:8 ᵃ Is. 22:12  ᵇ Jer. 3:4
1:9 ᵃ Joel 1:13; 2:14  ᵇ Joel 2:17  ¹ *meal or grain*
1:10 ᵃ Jer. 12:11  ᵇ Is. 24:7  ¹ *ruined*  ² *grain is ruined*  ³ *fails*
1:11 ᵃ Jer. 14:3, 4  ¹ *farmers*  ² *wail*
1:12 ᵃ Joel 1:10  ᵇ Jer. 48:33  ¹ *has withered*
1:13 ᵃ Jer. 4:8  ¹ *wail*  ² *meal or grain*  ³ *withheld*
1:14 ᵃ Joel 2:15, 16  ᵇ Lev. 23:36  ᶜ 2 Chr. 20:13  ¹ *Consecrate*  ² *sacred*
1:15 ᵃ [Jer. 30:7]  ᵇ Is. 13:6
1:16 ᵃ Is. 3:1  ᵇ Deut. 12:7  ¹ *food*
1:17 ¹ *shrivels*  ² *storehouses*  ³ *grain*
1:18 ᵃ Hos. 4:3  ¹ *restless*  ² MT *suffer punishment*
1:19 ᵃ [Ps. 50:15]  ᵇ Jer. 9:10

¹ *wilderness pastures*  1:20 ᵃ Ps. 104:21; 147:9  ᵇ 1 Kin. 17:7; 18:5  ¹ *water brooks*  2:1 ᵃ Jer. 4:5  ᵇ Num. 10:5  ᶜ [Obad. 15]  ¹ *ram's horn*  2:2 ᵃ Amos 5:18

darkness, as the morning spread upon the mountains: [b]a great people and a strong; [c]there hath not been ever the like, neither shall be any more after it, *even* to the years of many generations.

3 A fire devoureth before them; and behind them a flame burneth: the land *is* as [a]the garden of Eden before them, [b]and behind them a desolate wilderness; yea, and nothing shall escape them.

4 [a]The appearance of them *is* as the appearance of horses; and as [1]horsemen, so shall they run.

5 [a]Like the noise of chariots on the tops of mountains shall they leap, like the noise of a flame of fire that devoureth the stubble, as a strong people set in battle array.

6 Before their face the people shall be much pained: [a]all faces shall [1]gather blackness.

7 They shall run like mighty men; they shall climb the wall like men of war; and they shall march every one [1]on his ways, and they shall not break their [a]ranks:

8 Neither shall one [1]thrust another; they shall walk every one in his [2]path: and *when* they [3]fall upon the sword, they shall not be [4]wounded.

9 They shall run to and fro in the city; they shall run upon the wall, they shall climb up [1]upon the houses; they shall [a]enter in at the windows [b]like a thief.

10 [a]The earth shall quake before them; the heavens shall tremble: [b]the sun and the moon shall be dark, and the stars shall [1]withdraw their shining:

11 [a]And the LORD shall utter his voice before his army: for his camp *is* very great: [b]for *he is* strong that executeth his word: for the [c]day of the LORD *is* great and very terrible; and [d]who can [1]abide it?

12 Therefore also now, saith the LORD, [a]turn ye *even* to me with all your heart, and with fasting, and with weeping, and with mourning:

13 And [a]rend[1] your heart, and not [b]your garments, and [2]turn unto the LORD your God: for he *is* [c]gracious and merciful, slow to anger, and of great [3]kindness, and [4]repenteth him of the evil.

14 [a]Who knoweth *if* he will [1]return and repent, and leave [b]a blessing behind him; *even* [c]a [2]meat offering and a drink offering unto the LORD your God?

15 [a]Blow the [1]trumpet in Zion, [b]sanctify[2] a fast, call a [3]solemn assembly:

16 Gather the people, [a]sanctify the congregation, assemble the elders, gather the children, and [1]those that

suck the breasts: [b]let the bridegroom go forth of his chamber, and the bride out of her [2]closet.

17 Let the priests, the ministers of the LORD, weep [a]between the porch and the altar, and let them say, [b]Spare thy people, O LORD, and give not thine heritage to reproach, that the [1]heathen should rule over them: [c]wherefore should they say among the [2]people, Where *is* their God?

18 Then will the LORD [a]be [1]jealous for his land, and pity his people.

19 Yea, the LORD will answer and say unto his people, Behold, I will send you [a]corn,[1] and [2]wine, and oil, and ye shall be satisfied therewith: and I will no more make you a reproach among the heathen:

20 But [a]I will remove far off from you [b]the northern *army,* and will drive him into a land barren and desolate, with his face toward the east sea, and his [1]hinder part [c]toward the [2]utmost sea, and his stink shall come up, and his [3]ill savour shall come up, because he hath done [4]great things.

21 Fear not, O land; be glad and rejoice: for the LORD will do great things.

22 Be not afraid, ye beasts of the field: for [a]the pastures of the wilderness do spring, for the tree beareth her fruit, and the fig tree and the vine do yield their strength.

23 Be glad then, ye children of Zion, and [a]rejoice in the LORD your God: for he hath given you the [1]former rain moderately, and he [b]will cause to come down for you the rain, the former rain, and the latter rain in the first *month.*

24 And the [1]floors shall be full of wheat, and the vats shall overflow with [2]wine and oil.

25 And I will restore to you the years [a]that the [1]locust hath eaten, the [2]cankerworm, and the [3]caterpiller, and the [4]palmerworm, my great army which I sent among you.

26 And ye shall [a]eat in plenty, and be satisfied, and praise the name of the LORD your God, that hath dealt wondrously with you: and my people shall never be [b]ashamed.[1]

27 And ye shall know that I *am* [a]in the midst of Israel, and *that* [b]I *am* the LORD your God, and [1]none else: and my people shall never be ashamed.

28 [a]And it shall come to pass afterward, *that* [b]I will pour out my spirit upon all flesh; [c]and your sons and your [d]daughters shall prophesy, your old men shall dream dreams, your young men shall see visions:

---

2:2 [b] Joel 1:6; 2:11, 25  [c] Dan. 9:12; 12:1
2:3 [a] Is. 51:3 [b] Zech. 7:14
2:4 [a] Rev. 9:7 [1] Or *swift steeds*
2:5 [a] Rev. 9:9
2:6 [a] Nah. 2:10 [1] So with LXX, Tg., Vg.; MT *are drained of colour*
2:7 [a] Prov. 30:27 [1] *in formation*
2:8 [1] *push* [2] *own column* [3] *lunge between the weapons* [4] *cut off* (halted by losses)
2:9 [a] Jer. 9:21 [b] John 10:1 [1] *into*
2:10 [a] Ps. 18:7 [b] Is. 13:10; 34:4 [1] *diminish their brightness*
2:11 [a] Jer. 25:30 [b] Rev. 18:8 [c] Amos 5:18 [d] [Mal. 3:2] [1] *endure*
2:12 [a] Jer. 4:1
2:13 [a] [Ps. 34:18; 51:17] [b] Gen. 37:34 [c] [Ex. 34:6] [1] *tear* [2] *return* [3] *lovingkindness* [4] *relents from doing harm*
2:14 [a] Jer. 26:3 [b] Hag. 2:19 [c] Joel 1:9, 13 [1] *turn and relent* [2] *meal or grain*
2:15 [a] Num. 10:3 [b] Joel 1:14 [1] *ram's horn* [2] *consecrate* [3] *sacred*
2:16 [a] Ex. 19:10 [b] Ps. 19:5 [1] *the nursing babes* [2] *dressing room*
2:17 [a] Matt. 23:35 [b] Ex. 32:11, 12 [c] Ps. 42:10 [1] *nations* [2] *peoples*
2:18 [a] [Is. 60:10; 63:9, 15] [1] *zealous*
2:19 [a] [Mal. 3:10] [1] *grain* [2] *new wine*
2:20 [a] Ex. 10:19 [b] Jer. 1:14, 15 [c] Deut. 11:24 [1] *back* [2] *western* [3] *foul odour* [4] *monstrous*
2:22 [a] Joel 1:19
2:23 [a] Is. 41:16 [b] Lev. 26:4 [1] *former rain faithfully or teacher of righteousness*
2:24 [1] *threshingfloors* [2] *new wine*
2:25 [a] Joel 1:4–7; 2:2–11 [1] *swarming locust* [2] *crawling locust*
[3] *consuming locust* [4] *chewing locust*   2:26 [a] Lev. 26:5 [b] Is. 45:17 [1] *put to shame*   2:27 [a] Lev. 26:11, 12 [b] [Is. 45:5, 6] [1] *there is no other*   2:28 [a] Ezek. 39:29 [b] Zech. 12:10 [c] Is. 54:13 [d] Acts 21:9

29 And also upon [a]the[1] servants and upon [2]the handmaids in those days will I pour out my spirit.

30 And [a]I will shew wonders in the heavens and in the earth, blood, and fire, and pillars of smoke.

31 [a]The sun shall be turned into darkness, and the moon into blood, [b]before the great and the terrible day of the LORD come.

32 And it shall come to pass, *that* [a]whosoever shall call on the name of the LORD shall be [1]delivered: for [b]in mount Zion and in Jerusalem shall be [2]deliverance, as the LORD hath said, and in [c]the remnant whom the LORD shall call.

### CHAPTER 3

FOR, behold, [a]in those days, and in that time, when I shall bring again the [1]captivity of Judah and Jerusalem,

2 [a]I will also gather all nations, and will bring them down into the valley of Jehoshaphat, and [b]will [1]plead with them there for my people and *for* my heritage Israel, whom they have scattered among the nations, and [2]parted my land.

3 And they have [a]cast lots for my people; and have given a boy [1]for an harlot, and sold a girl for wine, that they might drink.

4 Yea, and what have ye to do with me, [a]O Tyre, and Zidon, and all the coasts of [1]Palestine? will ye [2]render me a recompence? and if ye [2]recompense me, swiftly *and* speedily will I return your [3]recompence upon your own head;

5 Because ye have taken my silver and my gold, and have carried into your temples my [1]goodly pleasant things:

6 The [1]children also of Judah and the [1]children of Jerusalem have ye sold unto the [2]Grecians, that ye might remove them far from their border.

7 Behold, [a]I will raise them out of the place whither ye have sold them, and will return your [1]recompence upon your own head:

8 And I will sell your sons and your daughters into the hand of the [1]children of Judah, and they shall sell them to the [a]Sabeans,[2] to a people [b]far off: for the LORD hath spoken *it.*

2:29 [a] [Gal. 3:28]
[1] my *menservants*
[2] my *maidservants*

2:30 [a] Matt. 24:29

2:31 [a] Is. 13:9, 10; 34:4 [b] [Mal. 4:1, 5, 6]

2:32 [a] Rom. 10:13 [b] Is. 46:13 [c] [Mic. 4:7] [1] *saved* [2] *salvation*

3:1 [a] Jer. 30:3 [1] *captives*

3:2 [a] Zech. 14:2 [b] Is. 66:16 [1] *enter into judgment* [2] *divided up*

3:3 [a] Nah. 3:10 [1] *in exchange for*

3:4 [a] Amos 1:6–8 [1] Or *Philistia* [2] Or *retaliate against me* [3] Or *retaliation*

3:5 [1] Lit. *precious good things*

3:6 [1] *people of* [2] *Greeks*

3:7 [a] Jer. 23:8 [1] Or *retaliation*

3:8 [a] Ezek. 23:42 [b] Jer. 6:20 [1] Or *people of* [2] Lit. *Shebaites,* Is. 60:6, Ezek. 27:22

3:9 [a] Ezek. 38:7 [1] *nations*

3:10 [a] [Is. 2:4] [b] Zech. 12:8 [1] *pruning knives*

3:11 [a] Is. 13:3 [1] *nations*

3:12 [a] Is. 2:4 [1] *nations*

3:13 [a] Rev. 14:15 [b] Jer. 51:33 [c] [Is. 63:3] [1] *winepress*

3:14 [a] Joel 2:1

3:15 [1] *grow dark* [2] *diminish their brightness*

3:16 [a] [Is. 51:5, 6] [1] *a shelter* [2] *a strong hold*

3:17 [a] Zech. 8:3 [1] *aliens*

3:18 [a] Ezek. 47:1 [1] *brooks* [2] *from* [3] *Acacias*

3:20 [1] *abide*

3:21 [a] Is. 4:4 [1] *bloodguilt*

9 [a]Proclaim ye this among the [1]Gentiles; Prepare war, wake up the mighty men, let all the men of war draw near; let them come up:

10 [a]Beat your plowshares into swords, and your [1]pruninghooks into spears: [b]let the weak say, I *am* strong.

11 Assemble yourselves, and come, all ye [1]heathen, and gather yourselves together round about: thither [1]cause [a]thy mighty ones to come down, O LORD.

12 Let the [1]heathen be wakened, and come up to the valley of Jehoshaphat: for there will I sit to [a]judge all the [1]heathen round about.

13 [a]Put ye in the sickle, for [b]the harvest is ripe: come, get you down; for the [c]press[1] is full, the fats overflow; for their wickedness *is* great.

14 Multitudes, multitudes in the valley of decision: for [a]the day of the LORD *is* near in the valley of decision.

15 The sun and the moon shall [1]be darkened, and the stars shall [2]withdraw their shining.

16 The LORD also shall roar out of Zion, and utter his voice from Jerusalem; and the heavens and the earth shall shake: [a]but the LORD *will be* [1]the hope of his people, and [2]the strength of the children of Israel.

17 So shall ye know that I *am* the LORD your God dwelling in Zion, my [a]holy mountain: then shall Jerusalem be holy, and there shall no [1]strangers pass through her any more.

18 And it shall come to pass in that day, *that* the mountains shall drop down new wine, and the hills shall flow with milk, and all the [1]rivers of Judah shall flow with waters, and a [a]fountain shall come forth [2]of the house of the LORD, and shall water the valley of [3]Shittim.

19 Egypt shall be a desolation, and Edom shall be a desolate wilderness, for the violence *against* the children of Judah, because they have shed innocent blood in their land.

20 But Judah shall [1]dwell for ever, and Jerusalem from generation to generation.

21 For I will [a]cleanse their [1]blood *that* I have not cleansed: for the LORD dwelleth in Zion.

# THE BOOK OF
# AMOS

Amos prophesies during a period of national optimism in Israel. Business is booming and boundaries are bulging. But below the surface, greed and injustice are festering. Hypocritical religious motions have replaced true worship, creating a false sense of security and a growing callousness to God's disciplining hand. Famine, drought, plagues, death, destruction—nothing can force the people to their knees.

Amos, the farmer-turned-prophet, lashes out at sin unflinchingly, trying to visualize the nearness of God's judgment and mobilize the nation to repentance. The nation, like a basket of rotting fruit, stands ripe for judgment because of its hypocrisy and spiritual indifference.

The name *Amos* is derived from the Hebrew root *amas*, "to lift a burden, to carry." Thus, his name means "Burden" or "Burden-Bearer." Amos lives up to the meaning of his name by bearing up under his divinely given burden of declaring judgment to rebellious Israel. The Greek and Latin titles are both transliterated in English as *Amos*.

## CHAPTER 1

THE words of Amos, who was among the [a]herdmen of [b]Tekoa, which he saw concerning Israel in the days of [c]Uzziah king of Judah, and in the days of [d]Jeroboam the son of Joash king of Israel, two years before the [e]earthquake.

2 And he said, The LORD will [a]roar from Zion, and utter his voice from Jerusalem; and the [1]habitations of the shepherds shall mourn, and the top of [b]Carmel shall wither.

3 Thus saith the LORD; For three transgressions of [a]Damascus, and for four, I will not turn away *the punishment* thereof; because they have [b]threshed Gilead with threshing instruments of iron:

4 [a]But I will send a fire into the house of Hazael, which shall devour the palaces of [b]Ben-hadad.

5 I will break also the [a]bar[1] of Damascus, and cut off the inhabitant from the [2]plain of Aven, and him that [3]holdeth the sceptre from [4]the house of Eden: and the people of Syria shall go into captivity unto Kir, saith the LORD.

6 Thus saith the LORD; For three transgressions of [a]Gaza, and for four, I will not turn away *the punishment* thereof; because they carried away captive the whole captivity, to deliver *them* up to Edom:

7 [a]But I will send a fire on the wall of Gaza, which shall devour the palaces thereof:

8 And I will [1]cut off the inhabitant [a]from Ashdod, and him that holdeth the sceptre from Ashkelon, and I will [b]turn mine hand against Ekron: and [c]the remnant of the Philistines shall perish, saith the Lord GOD.

9 Thus saith the LORD; For three transgressions of [a]Tyrus, and for four,

I will not turn away *the punishment* thereof; because they delivered up the whole captivity to Edom, and remembered not the [1]brotherly covenant:

10 But I will send a fire on the wall of Tyrus, which shall devour the palaces thereof.

11 Thus saith the LORD; For three transgressions of [a]Edom, and for four, I will not turn away *the punishment* thereof; because he did pursue his [b]brother with the sword, and did cast off all pity, and his anger did tear perpetually, and he kept his wrath for ever:

12 But [a]I will send a fire upon Teman, which shall devour the palaces of Bozrah.

13 Thus saith the LORD; For three transgressions of [a]the children of Ammon, and for four, I will not turn away *the punishment* thereof; because they have [1]ripped up the women with child of Gilead, that they might enlarge their [2]border:

14 But I will kindle a fire in the wall of [a]Rabbah, and it shall devour the palaces thereof, [b]with[1] shouting in the day of battle, with a tempest in the day of the whirlwind:

15 And [a]their king shall go into captivity, he and his princes together, saith the LORD.

## CHAPTER 2

THUS saith the LORD; [a]For three transgressions of Moab, and for four, I will not turn away *the punishment* thereof; because he [b]burned the bones of the king of Edom into lime:

2 But I will send a fire upon Moab, and it shall devour the palaces of [a]Kirioth:[1] and Moab shall die with tumult, with shouting, *and* with the sound of the trumpet:

1:1 [a] 2 Kin. 3:4; Amos 7:14 [b] 2 Sam. 14:2 [c] 2 Chr. 26:1–23 [d] Amos 7:10 [e] Zech. 14:5
1:2 [a] Joel 3:16 [b] 1 Sam. 25:2 [1] pastures
1:3 [a] Is. 8:4; 17:1–3 [b] 2 Kin. 10:32, 33
1:4 [a] Jer. 49:27; 51:30 [b] 2 Kin. 6:24
1:5 [a] Jer. 51:30 [1] gate bar [2] valley [3] Rules [4] Or Beth-eden
1:6 [a] Jer. 47:1, 5
1:7 [a] Jer. 47:1
1:8 [a] Zeph. 2:4 [b] Ps. 81:14 [c] Ezek. 25:16 [1] destroy
1:9 [a] Is. 23:1–18

[1] covenant of brotherhood
1:11 [a] Is. 21:11 [b] Obad. 10–12
1:12 [a] Obad. 9, 10
1:13 [a] Ezek. 25:2 [1] ripped open [2] territory
1:14 [a] Deut. 3:11 [b] Amos 2:2 [1] amid
1:15 [a] Jer. 49:3
2:1 [a] Zeph. 2:8–11 [b] 2 Kin. 3:26, 27
2:2 [a] Jer. 48:24, 41 [1] Kerioth, Jer. 48:24

3 And I will cut off [a]the judge from the midst thereof, and will slay all the princes thereof with him, saith the LORD.

4 Thus saith the LORD; For three transgressions of [a]Judah, and for four, I will not turn away *the punishment* thereof; [b]because they have despised the law of the LORD, and have not kept his commandments, and [c]their lies [1]caused them to err, [d]after the which their fathers have walked:

5 [a]But I will send a fire upon Judah, and it shall devour the palaces of Jerusalem.

6 Thus saith the LORD; For three transgressions of [a]Israel, and for four, I will not turn away *the punishment* thereof; because [b]they sold the righteous for silver, and the [c]poor for a pair of [1]shoes;

7 [1]That pant after the dust of the earth [2]on the head of the poor, and [a]turn[3] aside the way of the [4]meek: [b]and a man and his father will go in unto the *same* [5]maid, [c]to [6]profane my holy name:

8 And they lay *themselves* down upon clothes [a]laid to pledge [b]by every altar, and they drink the wine of [1]the condemned *in* the house of their god.

9 Yet [1]destroyed I the [a]Amorite before them, whose height *was* like the [b]height of the cedars, and he *was* strong as the oaks; yet I [c]destroyed his fruit from above, and his roots from beneath.

10 Also [a]I brought you up from the land of Egypt, and [b]led you forty years through the wilderness, to possess the land of the Amorite.

11 And I raised up [1]of your sons for [a]prophets, and of your young men for [b]Nazarites.[2] *Is it* not even thus, O ye children of Israel? saith the LORD.

12 But ye gave the Nazarites wine to drink; and commanded the prophets, [a]saying, Prophesy not.

13 [a]Behold, I am [1]pressed under you, as a cart is [2]pressed *that is* full of sheaves.

14 [a]Therefore the [1]flight shall perish from the swift, and the strong shall not strengthen his [2]force, [b]neither shall the mighty [3]deliver himself:

15 Neither shall he stand that handleth the bow; and *he that is* swift of foot shall not [1]deliver *himself:* neither shall he that rideth the horse [2]deliver himself.

16 And *he that is* [1]courageous among the mighty shall flee away naked in that day, saith the LORD.

## CHAPTER 3

HEAR this word that the LORD hath spoken against you, O children of Israel, against the whole family

which I brought up from the land of Egypt, saying,

2 [a]You only have I known of all the families of the earth: [b]therefore I will punish you for all your iniquities.

3 Can two walk together, except they be agreed?

4 Will a lion roar in the forest, when he hath no prey? will a young lion [1]cry out of his den, if he [2]have taken nothing?

5 Can a bird fall in a snare upon the earth, where no [1]gin *is* for him? shall [2]one take up a snare from the earth, and have [3]taken nothing at all?

6 Shall a [1]trumpet be blown in the city, and the people not be afraid? [a]shall there be [2]evil in a city, and the LORD hath not done *it?*

7 Surely the Lord GOD will do nothing, [1]but [a]he revealeth his secret unto his servants the prophets.

8 The lion hath roared, who will not fear? the Lord GOD hath spoken, [a]who can but prophesy?

9 [1]Publish in the palaces at Ashdod, and in the palaces in the land of Egypt, and say, Assemble yourselves upon the mountains of Samaria, and behold the great tumults in the midst thereof, and the [2]oppressed in the midst thereof.

10 For they [a]know not to do right, saith the LORD, who store up violence and [1]robbery in their palaces.

11 Therefore thus saith the Lord GOD; An adversary *there shall be* even round about the land; and he shall [1]bring down thy strength from thee, and thy palaces shall be [2]spoiled.

12 Thus saith the LORD; As the shepherd [1]taketh out of the mouth of the lion two legs, or a piece of an ear; so shall the children of Israel be taken out that dwell in Samaria in the corner of a bed, and [2]in Damascus *in* a couch.

13 Hear ye, and testify in the house of Jacob, saith the Lord GOD, the God of hosts,

14 That in the day that I shall [1]visit the transgressions of Israel upon him I will also [2]visit the altars of [a]Beth-el: and the horns of the altar shall be cut off, and fall to the ground.

15 And I will [1]smite [a]the winter house with [b]the summer house; and the [c]houses of ivory shall perish, and the great houses shall have an end, saith the LORD.

## CHAPTER 4

HEAR this word, ye [a]kine[1] of Bashan, that *are* in the mountain of Samaria, which oppress the [b]poor, which crush the needy, which say to their [2]masters, Bring, and let us [c]drink.

2:3 [a] Num. 24:17
2:4 [a] Hos. 12:2 [b] Lev. 26:14 [c] Jer. 16:19 [d] Ezek. 20:13, 16, 18 [1] *lead them astray*
2:5 [a] Hos. 8:14
2:6 [a] 2 Kin. 17:7-18; 18:12 [b] Is. 29:21 [c] Amos 4:1; 5:11; 8:6 [1] *sandals*
2:7 [a] Amos 5:12 [b] Ezek. 22:11 [c] Lev. 20:3 [1] *Or They trample* on [2] which is on [3] *pervert* [4] *humble* [5] *girl* [6] *defile*
2:8 [a] 1 Cor. 8:10 [b] Ex. 22:26 [1] *Or those punished by fines*
2:9 [a] Num. 21:25 [b] Ezek. 31:3 [c] [Mal. 4:1] [1] *it was I who destroyed*
2:10 [a] Ex. 12:51 [1] Deut. 2:7
2:11 [a] Num. 12:6 [b] Num. 6:2, 3 [1] *some of* [2] *Or Nazirites*
2:12 [a] Is. 30:10
2:13 [a] Is. 1:14 [1] *weighed down by or tottering under* [2] *weighed down or totters*
2:14 [a] Jer. 46:6 [b] Ps. 33:16 [1] *Or place of refuge* [2] *power* [3] Lit. *save his life or soul*
2:15 [1] *save* [2] Lit. *save his life or soul*
2:16 [1] Lit. *strong of heart*
3:2 [a] [Deut. 7:6] [b] [Rom. 2:9]
3:4 [1] Lit. *give his voice* [2] *has caught*
3:5 [1] *trap or bait* [2] *a snare spring up* [3] *caught*
3:6 [a] Is. 45:7 [1] *ram's horn* [2] *calamity*
3:7 [a] [John 15:15] [1] *unless*
3:8 [a] Acts 4:20
3:9 [1] *Proclaim* [2] *Or oppression*
3:10 [a] Jer. 4:22 [1] *Or devastation*
3:11 [1] *throw down your strongholds* [2] *plundered*
3:12 [1] *Or snatches* [2] Hebrew is uncertain; on the edge of or cover of
3:14 [a] Amos 4:4 [1] *punish Israel for their transgressions* [2] *visit destruction on*
3:15 [a] Jer. 36:22 [b] Judg. 3:20 [c] 1 Kin. 22:39 [1] *destroy*
4:1 [a] Ps. 22:12 [b] Amos 2:6 [c] Prov. 23:20 [1] *cows* [2] *husbands*

2 ᵃThe Lord GOD hath sworn by his holiness, that, lo, the days shall come upon you, that he will take you away ᵇwith hooks, and your posterity with fishhooks.

3 And ᵃye shall go out at the ¹breaches, ²every *cow at that which is* before her; and ye shall ³cast *them* into the palace, saith the LORD.

4 ᵃCome to Beth-el, and transgress; at ᵇGilgal multiply transgression; and ᶜbring your sacrifices every morning, ᵈ*and* your tithes ¹after three ²years:

5 ᵃAnd offer a sacrifice of thanksgiving with leaven, and proclaim *and* ¹publish ᵇthe free offerings: for this ²liketh you, O ye children of Israel, saith the Lord GOD.

6 And I also have given you ¹cleanness of teeth in all your cities, and ²want of bread in all your places: ᵃyet have ye not returned unto me, saith the LORD.

7 And also I have withholden the rain from you, when *there were* yet three months to the harvest: and I caused it to rain upon one city, and caused it not to rain upon another city: one piece was rained upon, and the piece whereupon it rained not withered.

8 So two *or* three cities wandered unto ¹one city, to drink water; but they were not satisfied: yet have ye not returned unto me, saith the LORD.

9 ᵃI have ¹smitten you with ²blasting and mildew: when your gardens and your vineyards and your fig trees and your olive trees increased, ᵇthe ³palmerworm devoured *them*: yet have ye not returned unto me, saith the LORD.

10 I have sent among you ¹the pestilence ᵃafter the manner of Egypt: your young men have I slain with the sword, ²and have taken away your horses; and I have made the ³stink of your camps to come up unto your nostrils: yet have ye not returned unto me, saith the LORD.

11 I have overthrown *some* of you, as God overthrew ᵃSodom and Gomorrah, and ye were as a firebrand plucked out of the burning: yet have ye not returned unto me, saith the LORD.

12 Therefore thus will I do unto thee, O Israel: *and* because I will do this unto thee, ᵃprepare to meet thy God, O Israel.

13 For, lo, he that formeth the mountains, and createth the ¹wind, ᵃand declareth unto man what *is* ²his thought, that maketh the morning darkness, ᵇand treadeth upon the high places of the earth, ᶜThe LORD, The God of hosts, *is* his name.

---

4:2 ᵃ Ps. 89:35
ᵇ Jer. 16:16
4:3 ᵃ Ezek. 12:5
¹ *breaks in the walls* ² *each one straight ahead of her* ³ *Or be cast into Harmon*
4:4 ᵃ Ezek. 20:39 ᵇ Hos. 4:15 ᶜ Num. 28:3 ᵈ Deut. 14:28
¹ *every* ² Or *days,* Deut. 14:28
4:5 ᵃ Lev. 7:13 ᵇ Lev. 22:18
¹ *announce* ² *you love*
4:6 ᵃ Jer. 5:3
¹ *Hunger* ² *lack*
4:8 ¹ *another*
4:9 ᵃ Hag. 2:17 ᵇ Joel 1:4, 7
¹ *stricken* ² *blight* ³ *locusts*
4:10 ᵃ Ps. 78:50
¹ *a plague* ² *along with your captive horses* ³ *stench*
4:11 ᵃ Is. 13:19
4:12 ᵃ Amos 4:12
4:13 ᵃ Ps. 139:2 ᵇ Mic. 1:3 ᶜ Is. 47:4 ¹ Or *spirit* ² *God's*

5:1 ᵃ Jer. 7:29; 9:10, 17
5:3 ¹ *have left*
5:4 ᵃ [Jer. 29:13] ᵇ [Is. 55:3]
5:5 ᵃ Amos 4:4 ᵇ Amos 8:14 ᶜ Hos. 4:15
¹ *nothing*
5:6 ᵃ [Is. 55:3, 6, 7]
5:7 ᵃ Amos 6:12 ¹ *justice* ² *abandon*
5:8 ᵃ Job 9:9; 38:31 ᵇ Ps. 104:20 ᶜ Job 38:34 ᵈ [Amos 4:13] ¹ The Pleiades ² *as*
5:9 ¹ *He flashes forth destruction upon* ² *stronghold* ³ *ruin comes upon*
5:10 ᵃ Is. 29:21; 66:5 ᵇ 1 Kin. 22:8
5:11 ᵃ Amos 2:6 ᵇ Mic. 6:15 ¹ *you trample* ² *grain tribute or taxes* ³ *desirable*
5:12 ᵃ Hos. 5:3 ᵇ Amos 2:6 ᶜ Is. 29:21 ¹ *many* ² *from justice at the gate*
5:13 ᵃ Amos 6:10
5:14 ᵃ Mic. 3:11
5:15 ᵃ Rom. 12:9 ᵇ Joel 2:14 ¹ *justice*

---

## CHAPTER 5

HEAR ye this word which I ᵃtake up against you, *even* a lamentation, O house of Israel.

2 The virgin of Israel is fallen; she shall no more rise: she is forsaken upon her land; *there is* none to raise her up.

3 For thus saith the Lord GOD; The city that went out *by* a thousand shall ¹leave an hundred, and that which went forth *by* an hundred shall ¹leave ten, to the house of Israel.

4 For thus saith the LORD unto the house of Israel, ᵃSeek ye me, ᵇand ye shall live:

5 But seek not ᵃBeth-el, nor enter into Gilgal, and pass not to ᵇBeer-sheba: for Gilgal shall surely go into captivity, and ᶜBeth-el shall come to ¹nought.

6 ᵃSeek the LORD, and ye shall live; lest he break out like fire in the house of Joseph, and devour *it*, and *there be* none to quench *it* in Beth-el.

7 Ye who ᵃturn ¹judgment to wormwood, and ²leave off righteousness in the earth,

8 *Seek him* that maketh ¹the ᵃseven stars and Orion, and turneth the shadow of death into the morning, ᵇand maketh the day dark ²with night: that ᶜcalleth for the waters of the sea, and poureth them out upon the face of the earth: ᵈThe LORD *is* his name:

9 ¹That strengtheneth the spoiled against the ²strong, so that ³the spoiled shall come against the fortress.

10 ᵃThey hate him that rebuketh in the gate, and they ᵇabhor him that speaketh uprightly.

11 ᵃForasmuch therefore as ¹your treading *is* upon the poor, and ye take from him ²burdens of wheat: ᵇye have built houses of hewn stone, but ye shall not dwell in them; ye have planted ³pleasant vineyards, but ye shall not drink wine of them.

12 For I ᵃknow your manifold transgressions and your ¹mighty sins: ᵇthey afflict the just, they take a bribe, and they ᶜturn aside the poor ²in the gate *from their right.*

13 Therefore ᵃthe prudent shall keep silence in that time; for it *is* an evil time.

14 Seek good, and not evil, that ye may live: and so the LORD, the God of hosts, shall be with you, ᵃas ye have spoken.

15 ᵃHate the evil, and love the good, and establish ¹judgment in the gate: ᵇit may be that the LORD God of hosts will be gracious unto the remnant of Joseph.

16 Therefore the LORD, the God of hosts, the Lord, saith thus; Wailing

*shall be* in all streets; and they shall say in all the highways, Alas! alas! and they shall call the [1]husbandman to mourning, and [a]such as are skilful of lamentation to wailing.

17 And in all vineyards *shall be* wailing: for [a]I will pass through thee, saith the LORD.

18 [a]Woe unto you that desire the day of the LORD! [1]to what end *is* it for you? [b]the day of the LORD *is* darkness, and not light.

19 [a]As if a man did flee from a lion, and a bear met him; or went into the house, and leaned his hand on the wall, and a serpent bit him.

20 *Shall* not the day of the LORD *be* darkness, and not light? even very dark, and no brightness in it?

21 [a]I hate, I despise your feast days, and [b]I will not [1]smell in your [2]solemn assemblies.

22 [a]Though ye offer me burnt offerings and your [1]meat offerings, I will not accept *them:* neither will I regard the peace offerings of your fat beasts.

23 Take thou away from me the noise of thy songs; for I will not hear the melody of thy [1]viols.

24 [a]But let [1]judgment run down as waters, and righteousness as a mighty stream.

25 [a]Have ye offered unto me sacrifices and offerings in the wilderness forty years, O house of Israel?

26 But ye have borne [1]the tabernacle [a]of your Moloch and [2]Chiun your [3]images, the star of your [4]god, which ye made to yourselves.

27 Therefore will I cause you to go into captivity [a]beyond Damascus, saith the LORD, [b]whose name *is* The God of hosts.

## CHAPTER 6

WOE [a]to them *that are* at [b]ease in Zion, and [c]trust in the mountain of Samaria, *which are* [1]named [d]chief of the nations, to whom the house of Israel came!

2 [a]Pass ye unto [b]Calneh, and see; and from thence go ye to [c]Hamath the great: then go down to Gath of the Philistines: [d]*be*[1] *they* better than these kingdoms? or their [2]border greater than your [2]border?

3 [1]Ye that [a]put far away the [b]evil[1] day, [c]and cause [d]the seat of violence to come near;

4 That lie upon beds of ivory, and [1]stretch themselves upon their couches, and eat the lambs out of the flock, and the calves out of the midst of the stall;

5 [a]That [1]chant to the sound of [2]the viol, *and* invent to themselves instruments of [b]musick, [c]like David;

6 That [a]drink wine in bowls, and anoint themselves with the [1]chief

ointments: [b]but they are not grieved for the affliction of Joseph.

7 Therefore now shall they go [a]captive with the first that go captive, and [1]the banquet of them that stretched themselves shall be removed.

8 [a]The Lord GOD hath sworn by himself, saith the LORD the God of hosts, I abhor [b]the [1]excellency of Jacob, and hate his palaces: therefore will I deliver up the city with all that is therein.

9 And it shall come to pass, if there remain ten men in one house, that they shall die.

10 And a [1]man's uncle shall take him up, and he that burneth [2]him, to bring out [2]the bones out of the house, and shall say unto him that *is* [3]by the sides of the house, *Is there* yet *any* with thee? and he shall say, No. Then shall he say, [a]Hold thy tongue: [b]for we may not make mention of the name of the LORD.

11 For, behold, [a]the LORD commandeth, [b]and he will [1]smite the great house [2]with breaches, and the little house [3]with clefts.

12[1] Shall horses run upon the rock? will *one* plow *there* with oxen? for [a]ye have turned [2]judgment into gall, and the fruit of righteousness into [3]hemlock:

13 Ye which rejoice [1]in a thing of nought, which say, Have we not taken to us [2]horns by our own strength?

14 But, behold, [a]I will raise up against you a nation, O house of Israel, saith the LORD the God of hosts; and they shall afflict you from the [b]entering[1] in of Hemath unto the [2]river of the wilderness.

## CHAPTER 7

THUS hath the Lord GOD shewed unto me; and, behold, he formed [1]grasshoppers in the beginning of the [2]shooting up of the latter growth; and, lo, *it was* the [3]latter growth after the king's mowings.

2 And it came to pass, *that* when they had made an end of eating the grass of the land, then I said, O Lord GOD, forgive, I beseech thee: [a]by[1] whom shall Jacob arise? for he *is* small.

3 [a]The LORD [1]repented for this: It shall not be, saith the LORD.

4 Thus hath the Lord GOD shewed unto me: and, behold, the Lord GOD called [1]to contend by fire, and it [2]devoured the great deep, and [3]did eat up a part.

5 Then said I, O Lord GOD, cease, I beseech thee: [a]by[1] whom shall Jacob arise? for he *is* small.

---

5:16 [a] Jer. 9:17
[1] *farmer*
5:17 [a] Ex. 12:12
5:18 [a] Is. 5:19
[b] Joel 2:2 [1] *for what good* is *it to you*
5:19 [a] Jer. 48:44
5:21 [a] Is. 1:11–16
[b] Lev. 26:31
[1] *savour* [2] *sacred*
5:22 [a] Mic. 6:6, 7
[1] *grain* or *meal*
5:23 [1] *stringed instruments*
5:24 [a] Mic. 6:8
[1] *justice*
5:25 [a] Deut. 32:17
5:26 [a] 1 Kin. 11:33 [1] LXX, Vg. *the tabernacle of Moloch;* MT *Sikkuth your king,* a pagan deity
[2] A pagan deity
[3] *idols* [4] *gods*
5:27 [a] 2 Kin. 17:6
[b] Amos 4:13
6:1 [a] Luke 6:24
[b] Zeph. 1:12 [c] Is. 31:1 [d] Ex. 19:5
[1] *notable persons in the chief nation*
6:2 [a] Jer. 2:10
[b] Is. 10:9 [c] 2 Kin. 18:34 [d] Nah. 3:8
[1] *are you better*
[2] *territory*
6:3 [a] Is. 56:12
[b] Amos 5:18
[c] Amos 5:12 [d] Ps. 94:20 [1] *Woe to you* [2] *day of doom*
6:4 [1] *sprawl*
6:5 [a] Is. 5:12
[b] Amos 5:23;
3:10 [c] 1 Chr. 23:5
[1] Lit. *improvise*
[2] *stringed instruments*
6:6 [a] Amos 2:8;
4:1 [b] Gen. 37:25
[1] *best*
6:7 [a] Amos 5:27
[1] *those who recline at banquets*
6:8 [a] Jer. 51:14
[b] Amos 8:7 [1] *pride*
6:10 [a] Amos 5:13
[b] Amos 8:3 [1] *kinsman of the dead shall pick him up* [2] The bodies [3] *inside*
6:11 [a] Is. 55:11
[b] Amos 3:15
[1] *break* [2] *into bits* [3] *into pieces*
6:12 [a] Hos. 10:4
[1] *Do* [2] *justice* [3] *wormwood*
6:13 [1] *over Lo-debar, over nothing* [2] Heb. *Karnaim,* lit. *horns,* a symbol of strength
6:14 [a] Jer. 5:15

b 1 Kin. 8:65 [1] *entrance* [2] *valley of the Arabah*
7:1 [1] *locust swarms* [2] *sprouting* [3] *late crop*   7:2 [a] Is. 51:19 [1] Oh, that Jacob might stand   7:3 [a] Jon. 3:10 [1] *relented concerning this*   7:4 [1] *for conflict* [2] *consumed* [3] *devoured the territory*   7:5 [a] Amos 7:2, 3 [1] Oh, that Jacob might stand

6 The LORD ¹repented for this: This also shall not be, saith the Lord GOD.

7 Thus he shewed me: and, behold, the Lord stood upon a wall *made* ¹by a plumbline, with a plumbline in his hand.

8 And the LORD said unto me, Amos, what seest thou? And I said, A plumbline. Then said the Lord, Behold, ªI will set a plumbline in the midst of my people Israel: ᵇI will not again pass by them any more:

9 ªAnd the ¹high places of Isaac shall be desolate, and the ²sanctuaries of Israel shall be laid waste; and ᵇI will rise against the house of Jeroboam with the sword.

10 Then Amaziah the ªpriest of ᵇBeth-el sent to ᶜJeroboam king of Israel, saying, Amos hath conspired against thee in the midst of the house of Israel: the land is not able to ¹bear all his words.

11 For thus Amos saith, Jeroboam shall die by the sword, and Israel shall surely be led away ªcaptive out of their own land.

12 Also Amaziah said unto Amos, O thou seer, go, flee thee away into the land of Judah, and there eat bread, and prophesy there:

13 But ªprophesy not again any more at Beth-el: ᵇfor it *is* the king's ¹chapel, and it *is* the ²king's court.

14 Then answered Amos, and said to Amaziah, I *was* no prophet, neither *was* I ªa prophet's son; ᵇbut I *was* an herdman, and a ¹gatherer of sycomore fruit:

15 And the LORD took me ¹as I followed the flock, and the LORD said unto me, Go, ªprophesy unto my people Israel.

16 Now therefore hear thou the word of the LORD: Thou sayest, Prophesy not against Israel, and ªdrop¹ not *thy word* against the house of Isaac.

17 ªTherefore thus saith the LORD; ᵇThy wife shall be an harlot in the city, and thy sons and thy daughters shall fall by the sword, and thy land shall be divided by ¹line; and thou shalt die in a ᶜpolluted² land: and Israel shall surely go into captivity ³forth of his land.

## CHAPTER 8

THUS hath the Lord GOD shewed unto me: and behold a basket of summer fruit.

2 And he said, Amos, what seest thou? And I said, A basket of summer fruit. Then said the LORD unto me, ªThe end is come upon my people of Israel; ᵇI will not again pass by them any more.

3 And ªthe songs of the temple shall be ¹howlings in that day, saith the Lord GOD: *there shall be* many

7:6 ¹ *relented concerning this*
7:7 ¹ *with*
7:8 ª 2 Kin. 21:13 ᵇ Mic. 7:18
7:9 ª Gen. 46:1 ᵇ 2 Kin. 15:8–10 ¹ *Places for pagan worship* ² *idolatrous sanctuaries*
7:10 ª 1 Kin. 12:31, 32; 13:33 ᵇ Amos 4:4 ᶜ 2 Kin. 14:23 ¹ *endure*
7:11 ª Amos 5:27; 6:7
7:13 ª Amos 2:12 ᵇ 1 Kin. 12:29, 32 ¹ *sanctuary*, lit. *holy place* ² *royal house*
7:14 ª 1 Kin. 20:35 ᵇ Zech. 13:5 ¹ *tender of*
7:15 ª Amos 3:8 ¹ Lit. *from behind*
7:16 ª Ezek. 21:2 ¹ *spout*, lit. *drip*
7:17 ª Jer. 28:12; 29:21, 32 ᵇ Zech. 14:2 ᶜ Hos. 9:3 ¹ *survey* line ² *defiled* ³ *from his own land*
8:2 ª Ezek. 7:2 ᵇ Amos 7:8
8:3 ª Amos 5:23 ᵇ Amos 6:9, 10 ¹ *wailing*
8:4 ¹ Or *trample on*
8:5 ª Neh. 13:15 ᵇ Mic. 6:10, 11 ᶜ Lev. 19:35, 36 ¹ *past* ² *grain* ³ *trade*, lit. *open*
8:6 ª Amos 2:6 ¹ *sandals* ² *bad wheat*
8:7 ª Amos 6:8 ᵇ Hos. 7:2; 8:13 ¹ *pride*
8:8 ª Hos. 4:3 ᵇ Amos 9:5 ¹ *completely rise, swell* ² Some Heb. mss., LXX, Syr., Tg., Vg., Amos 9:5 the *River* (The Nile); MT *the light* ³ *heave* ⁴ *subside*
8:9 ª Job 5:14 ¹ *broad daylight*
8:10 ª Ezek. 7:18 ᵇ Ezek. 27:31 ᶜ [Zech. 12:10] ¹ *every waist* ² *for*
8:11 ª Ezek. 7:26
8:12 ª Hos. 5:6
8:13 ¹ *strong young men*
8:14 ª Hos. 4:15 ᵇ Deut. 9:21 ᶜ Amos 5:5 ¹ Or *Ashima*, a Syrian goddess ² *As thy god* ³ *As the*

dead bodies in every place; ᵇthey shall cast *them* forth with silence.

4 Hear this, O ye that ¹swallow up the needy, even to make the poor of the land to fail,

5 Saying, When will the new moon be ¹gone, that we may sell ²corn? and ªthe sabbath, that we may ³set forth wheat, ᵇmaking the ephah small, and the shekel great, and falsifying the balances by ᶜdeceit?

6 That we may buy the poor for ªsilver, and the needy for a pair of ¹shoes? *yea*, and sell the ²refuse of the wheat?

7 The LORD hath sworn by ªthe ¹excellency of Jacob, Surely ᵇI will never forget any of their works.

8 ªShall not the land tremble for this, and every one mourn that dwelleth therein? and it shall ¹rise up wholly as ²a flood; and it shall ³be cast out and ⁴drowned, ᵇas *by* the flood of Egypt.

9 And it shall come to pass in that day, saith the Lord GOD, ªthat I will cause the sun to go down at noon, and I will darken the earth in ¹the clear day:

10 And I will turn your feasts into ªmourning, ᵇand all your songs into lamentation; ᶜand I will bring up sackcloth upon ¹all loins, and baldness upon every head; and I will make it as the mourning ²of an only *son*, and the end thereof as a bitter day.

11 Behold, the days come, saith the Lord GOD, that I will send a famine in the land, not a famine of bread, nor a thirst for water, but ªof hearing the words of the LORD:

12 And they shall wander from sea to sea, and from the north even to the east, they shall run to and fro to seek the word of the LORD, and shall ªnot find *it*.

13 In that day shall the fair virgins and ¹young men faint for thirst.

14 They that ªswear by ᵇthe¹ sin of Samaria, and say, ²Thy god, O Dan, liveth; and, ³The manner of ᶜBeersheba liveth; even they shall fall, and never rise up again.

## CHAPTER 9

I SAW the Lord standing ¹upon the altar: and he said, Smite the ²lintel of the door, that the ³posts may shake: and ªcut⁴ them in the head, all of them; and I will slay the last of them with the sword: ᵇhe that fleeth ⁵of them shall not flee away, and he that escapeth ⁵of them shall not be delivered.

2 ªThough they dig into ¹hell, thence shall mine hand take them; ᵇthough they climb up to heaven, thence will I bring them down:

*way of* 9:1 ª Hab. 3:13 ᵇ Amos 2:14 ¹ *by* ² *Capitals of the pillars* ³ *thresholds* ⁴ *break them* ⁵ *from*
9:2 ª Ps. 139:8 ᵇ Jer. 51:53 ¹ Heb. *Sheol*

3 And though they [a]hide themselves in the top of Carmel, I will search and take them out thence; and though they be hid from my sight in the bottom of the sea, thence will I command the serpent, and he shall bite them:

4 And though they go into captivity before their enemies, [a]thence will I command the sword, and it shall slay them: and [b]I will set mine eyes upon them for [1]evil, and not for good.

5 And the Lord GOD of hosts is he that toucheth the [1]land, and it shall [a]melt, [b]and all that dwell therein shall mourn: and it shall [2]rise up wholly like [3]a flood; and shall be drowned, as by the [4]flood of Egypt.

6 It is he that buildeth his [a]stories[1] in the heaven, and hath founded his [2]troop in the earth; he that [b]calleth for the waters of the sea, and poureth them out upon the face of the earth: [c]The LORD is his name.

7 Are ye not as [1]children of the Ethiopians unto me, O children of Israel? saith the LORD. Have not I brought up Israel out of the land of Egypt? and the [a]Philistines from [b]Caphtor,[2] and the Syrians from [c]Kir?

8 Behold, [a]the eyes of the Lord GOD are upon the sinful kingdom, and I [b]will destroy it from off the face of the earth; saving that I will not utterly destroy the house of Jacob, saith the LORD.

9 For, lo, I will command, and I will [1]sift the house of Israel among all nations, like as [2]corn is sifted in a sieve, [a]yet shall not the least [3]grain fall upon the earth.

10 All the sinners of my people shall die by the sword, [a]which say, The [1]evil shall not overtake nor [2]prevent us.

11 [a]In that day will I raise up the [1]tabernacle of David that is fallen, and [2]close up the breaches thereof; and I will raise up his ruins, and I will build it as in the days of old:

12 [a]That they may possess the remnant of [b]Edom,[1] and of all the [2]heathen, which are called by my name, saith the LORD that doeth this.

13 Behold, [a]the days come, saith the LORD, that the plowman shall overtake the reaper, and the treader of grapes him that soweth seed; [b]and the mountains shall [1]drop sweet wine, and all the hills shall [2]melt.

14 [a]And I will bring [1]again the captivity of my people of Israel, and [b]they shall build the waste cities, and inhabit them; and they shall plant vineyards, and drink the wine thereof; they shall also make gardens, and eat the fruit of them.

15 And I will plant them upon their land, and [a]they shall no more be pulled up out of their land which I have given them, saith the LORD thy God.

---

9:3 [a] Jer. 23:24
9:4 [a] Lev. 26:33
[b] Jer. 21:10; 39:16; 44:11 [1] harm
9:5 [a] Mic. 1:4
[b] Amos 8:8
[1] earth [2] completely rise, swell
[3] The Nile [4] River
9:6 [a] Ps. 104:3, 13 [b] Amos 5:8
[c] Amos 4:13; 5:27
[1] layers [2] strata
9:7 [a] Jer. 47:4
[b] Deut. 2:23
[c] Amos 1:5 [1] people of Ethiopia [2] Crete
9:8 [a] Amos 9:4
[b] Jer. 5:10; 30:11
9:9 [a] [Is. 65:8–16]
[1] shake [2] Grain [3] Lit. pebble
9:10 [a] Amos 6:3 [1] calamity [2] confront
9:11 [a] Acts 15:16–18 [1] Lit. booth, a figure of a deposed dynasty [2] repair its damages
9:12 [a] Obad. 19
[b] Num. 24:18
[1] LXX mankind [2] Gentiles
9:13 [a] Lev. 26:5
[b] Joel 3:18 [1] drip [2] flow with it
9:14 [a] Jer. 30:3, 18
[b] Is. 61:4 [1] back
9:15 [a] Ezek. 34:28; 37:25

# THE BOOK OF
# OBADIAH

A struggle that began in the womb between twin brothers, Esau and Jacob, eventuates in a struggle between their respective descendants, the Edomites and the Israelites. For the Edomites' stubborn refusal to aid Israel, first during the time of wilderness wandering (Num. 20:14–21) and later during a time of invasion, they are roundly condemned by Obadiah. This little-known prophet describes their crimes, tries their case, and pronounces their judgment: total destruction.

The Hebrew name *Obadyah* means "Worshiper of Yahweh" or "Servant of Yahweh." The Greek title in the Septuagint is *Obdiou*, and the Latin title in the Vulgate is *Abdias*.

THE vision of Obadiah. Thus saith the Lord GOD ªconcerning Edom; ᵇWe have heard a ¹rumour from the LORD, and ²an ambassador is sent among the ³heathen, Arise ye, and let us rise up against her ⁴in battle.

2 Behold, I have made thee small among the ¹heathen: thou art greatly despised.

3 The ªpride of thine heart hath deceived thee, thou that dwellest in the clefts of the rock, whose habitation *is* high; ᵇthat saith in his heart, Who shall bring me down to the ground?

4 ªThough thou exalt *thyself* ¹as the eagle, and though thou ᵇset thy nest among the stars, thence will I bring thee down, saith the LORD.

5 If ªthieves came to thee, if robbers by night, ¹(how art thou cut off!) would they not have stolen till they had enough? if the grapegatherers came to thee, ᵇwould they not leave *some* ²grapes?

6 How ¹are *the things* of Esau searched out! *how* are his hidden ²things sought up!

7 All the men of thy confederacy ¹have brought thee *even* to the border: ªthe men that were at peace with thee have deceived thee, *and* prevailed against thee; *they that eat* thy bread have laid a ²wound under thee: ᵇ*there is* none ³understanding in him.

8 ªShall I not in that day, saith the LORD, even destroy the wise *men* out of Edom, and understanding out of the mount of Esau?

9 And thy ªmighty *men,* O ᵇTeman, shall be dismayed, to the end that every one of the mount of Esau may be cut off by slaughter.

10 For *thy* ªviolence against thy brother Jacob shame shall cover thee, and ᵇthou shalt be cut off for ever.

11 In the day that thou ªstoodest on the other side, in the day that the strangers carried away captive his forces, and foreigners entered into his gates, and ᵇcast lots ¹upon Jerusalem, even thou *wast* as one of them.

12 But thou shouldest not have ªlooked¹ on the day of thy brother in the day that he became a ²stranger; neither shouldest thou have ᵇrejoiced over the children of Judah in the day of their destruction; neither shouldest thou have spoken proudly in the day of distress.

13 Thou shouldest not have entered into the gate of my people in the day of their calamity; yea, thou shouldest not have ¹looked on their affliction in the day of their calamity, nor have laid *hands* on their substance in the day of their calamity;

14 Neither shouldest thou have stood in the ¹crossway, to cut off those of his that did escape; neither shouldest thou have ²delivered up those of his that did remain in the day of distress.

15 ªFor the day of the LORD *is* near upon all the ¹heathen: ᵇas thou hast done, it shall be done unto thee: thy ²reward shall return upon thine own head.

16 ªFor as ye have drunk upon my holy mountain, *so* shall all the ¹heathen drink continually, yea, they shall drink, and they shall swallow down, and they shall be as though they had not been.

17 But upon mount Zion ªshall be ¹deliverance; and ²there shall be holiness; and the house of Jacob shall possess their possessions.

18 And the house of Jacob ªshall be a fire, and the house of Joseph a flame, and the house of Esau for stubble, and they shall kindle in them, and devour them; and there shall not be *any* ¹remaining of the house of Esau; for the LORD hath spoken *it.*

19 And *they of* the ¹south ªshall possess the mount of Esau; ᵇand *they of* the ²plain the Philistines: and they shall possess the fields of Ephraim,

1:1 ª Is. 21:11 ᵇ Jer. 49:14–16 ¹ *report* ² *a messenger* ³ *nations* ⁴ Lit. *for*
1:2 ¹ *nations*
1:3 ª Jer. 49:16 ᵇ Rev. 18:7
1:4 ª Job 20:6 ᵇ Hab. 2:9 ¹ *as high as*
1:5 ª Jer. 49:9 ᵇ Deut. 24:21 ¹ *Oh, how you are* ² *gleanings*
1:6 ¹ *Esau is* ² *treasures sought out*
1:7 ª Jer. 38:22 ᵇ Is. 19:11 ¹ *forced you* ² *Or trap for* ³ *aware of it*
1:8 ª [Job 5:12–14]
1:9 ª Ps. 76:5 ᵇ Jer. 49:7
1:10 ª Gen. 27:41 ᵇ Ezek. 35:9
1:11 ª Ps. 83:5–8

ᵇ Nah. 3:10 ¹ *for*
1:12 ª Mic. 4:11; 7:10 ᵇ [Prov. 17:5] ¹ *gazed on, gloated over* ² *captive,* lit. *foreigner*
1:13 ¹ *gazed on, gloated over*
1:14 ¹ *crossroads* ² *made captive*
1:15 ª Ezek. 30:3 ᵇ Hab. 2:8 ¹ *nations* ² *reprisal*
1:16 ª Joel 3:17 ¹ *nations*
1:17 ª Amos 9:8 ¹ *salvation* ² *it shall be holy*
1:18 ª Zech. 12:6 ¹ *survivor*
1:19 ª Is. 11:14 ᵇ Zeph. 2:7 ¹ Heb. *Negev* ² Heb. *shephelah, lowland*

and the fields of Samaria: and Benjamin *shall possess* Gilead.

20 And the ¹captivity of this host of the children of Israel *shall possess* that of the Canaanites, *even* ªunto Zarephath; and the captivity of

1:20 ª 1 Kin.
17:9 ᵇ Jer. 32:44
¹ *captives* ² Heb.
*Negev*
1:21 ª [James
5:20] ᵇ [Rev. 11:15]
¹ *deliverers*

Jerusalem, which *is* in Sepharad, ᵇshall possess the cities of the ²south.

21 And ªsaviours¹ shall come up on mount Zion to judge the mount of Esau; and the ᵇkingdom shall be the LORD's.

# THE BOOK OF
# JONAH

**N**ineveh is northeast; Tarshish is west. When God calls Jonah to preach repentance to the wicked Ninevites, the prophet knows that God's mercy may follow. He turns down the assignment and heads for Tarshish instead. But once God has dampened his spirits (by tossing him out of the boat and into the water) and has demonstrated His protection (by moving him out of the water and into the fish), Jonah realizes God is serious about His command. Nineveh must hear the word of the Lord; therefore Jonah goes. Although the preaching is a success, the preacher comes away angry and discouraged and he must learn firsthand of God's compassion for sinful men.

*Yonah* is the Hebrew word for "dove." The Septuagint hellenized this word into *Ionas*, and the Latin Vulgate used the title *Jonas*.

## CHAPTER 1

**N**ow the word of the LORD came unto ᵃJonah the son of Amittai, saying,

2 Arise, go to ᵃNineveh, that ᵇgreat city, and ¹cry against it; for ᶜtheir wickedness is come up before me.

3 But Jonah rose up to flee unto ᵇTarshish from the presence of the LORD, and went down to ᵃJoppa; and he found a ship going to Tarshish: so he paid the fare thereof, and went down into it, to go with them unto Tarshish ᶜfrom the presence of the LORD.

4 But ᵃthe LORD ¹sent out a great wind ²into the sea, and there was a mighty tempest in the sea, so that the ship was ³like to be broken.

5 Then the mariners were afraid, and cried every man unto his god, and cast forth the ¹wares that *were* in the ship into the sea, to lighten *it* ²of them. But Jonah was gone down ᵃinto the sides of the ship; and he lay, and was fast asleep.

6 So the ¹shipmaster came to him, and said unto him, What meanest thou, O sleeper? arise, ᵃcall upon thy God, ᵇif² so be that God will think upon us, that we perish not.

7 And they said every one to his fellow, Come, and let us ᵃcast lots, that we may know for whose cause this ¹evil *is* upon us. So they cast lots, and the lot fell upon Jonah.

8 Then said they unto him, ᵃTell us, we pray thee, for whose cause this ¹evil *is* upon us; What *is* thine occupation? and whence comest thou? what *is* thy country? and of what people *art* thou?

9 And he said unto them, I *am* an Hebrew; and I fear ¹the LORD, the God of heaven, ᵃwhich hath made the sea and the dry *land*.

10 Then were the men exceedingly afraid, and said unto him, Why hast thou done this? For the men knew

1:1 ᵃ 2 Kin. 14:25
1:2 ᵃ Is. 37:37
ᵇ Gen. 10:11,
12 ᶜ Gen. 18:20
¹ cry out
1:3 ᵃ Josh. 19:46
ᵇ Is. 23:1 ᶜ Gen.
4:16
1:4 ᵃ Ps. 107:25
¹ Lit. *hurled* ² on
³ *about to be*
1:5 ᵃ 1 Sam. 24:3
¹ cargo ² Lit. *from
upon them*
1:6 ᵃ Ps. 107:28
ᵇ Joel 2:14 ¹ *cap-
tain* ⁸ *perhaps
your God will
consider us*
1:7 ᵃ Josh. 7:14
¹ trouble
1:8 ᵃ Josh. 7:19
¹ trouble
1:9 ᵃ [Neh. 9:6]
¹ Heb. YHWH
1:11 ¹ *for* ² *was
growing more*
1:12 ᵃ John 11:50
¹ *Pick me up*
² *hurl me* ³ *for*
⁴ *because of me*
1:13 ᵃ [Prov.
21:30] ¹ The ship
² continued to
grow more
1:14 ᵃ Deut. 21:8
ᵇ Ps. 115:3 ¹ *do not
charge us with*
1:15 ᵃ [Ps. 89:9;
107:29] ¹ *picked
up* ² *hurled him*
1:16 ᵃ Acts 5:11
1:17 ᵃ [Matt. 12:40]
2:2 ᵃ Ps. 120:1
ᵇ Ps. 65:2
¹ *because of
my* ² *answered*
³ Heb. *Sheol*
2:3 ᵃ Ps. 88:6 ᵇ Ps.
42:7 ¹ Lit. *heart*
² *surrounded me*
2:4 ᵃ Ps. 31:22
ᵇ 1 Kin. 8:38
2:5 ᵃ Lam. 3:54
¹ *deep*

that he fled from the presence of the LORD, because he had told them.

11 Then said they unto him, What shall we do unto thee, that the sea may be calm ¹unto us? for the sea ²wrought, and was tempestuous.

12 And he said unto them, ᵃTake¹ me up, and ²cast me forth into the sea; so shall the sea be calm ³unto you: for I know that ⁴for my sake this great tempest *is* upon you.

13 Nevertheless the men rowed hard to bring ¹*it* to the land; ᵃbut they could not: for the sea ²wrought, and was tempestuous against them.

14 Wherefore they cried unto the LORD, and said, We beseech thee, O LORD, we beseech thee, let us not perish for this man's life, and ᵃlay¹ not upon us innocent blood: for thou, O LORD, ᵇhast done as it pleased thee.

15 So they ¹took up Jonah, and ²cast him forth into the sea: ᵃand the sea ceased from her raging.

16 Then the men ᵃfeared the LORD exceedingly, and offered a sacrifice unto the LORD, and made vows.

17 Now the LORD had prepared a great fish to swallow up Jonah. And ᵃJonah was in the belly of the fish three days and three nights.

## CHAPTER 2

**T**HEN Jonah prayed unto the LORD his God out of the fish's belly,

2 And said, I ᵃcried ¹by reason of mine affliction unto the LORD, ᵇand he ²heard me; out of the belly of ³hell cried I, *and* thou heardest my voice.

3 ᵃFor thou hadst cast me into the deep, in the ¹midst of the seas; and the floods ²compassed me about: ᵇall thy billows and thy waves passed over me.

4 ᵃThen I said, I am cast out of thy sight; yet I will look again ᵇtoward thy holy temple.

5 The ᵃwaters compassed me about, *even* to the soul: the ¹depth closed me

round about, the weeds were wrapped about my head.

6 I went down to the [1]bottoms of the mountains; the earth with her bars [2]*was* about me for ever: yet hast thou brought up my [a]life from [3]corruption, O LORD my God.

7 When my soul fainted within me I remembered the LORD: [a]and my prayer [1]came in unto thee, into thine holy temple.

8 They that observe [a]lying[1] vanities forsake their own [2]mercy.

9 But I will [a]sacrifice unto thee with the voice of thanksgiving; I will pay *that* that I have [b]vowed. [c]Salvation *is* of the [d]LORD.

10 And the LORD spake unto the fish, and it vomited out Jonah upon the dry *land*.

## CHAPTER 3

A[ND the word of the LORD came unto Jonah the second time, saying,

2 Arise, go unto Nineveh, that great city, and preach unto it the [1]preaching that I [2]bid thee.

3 So Jonah arose, and went unto Nineveh, according to the word of the LORD. Now Nineveh was an exceeding great city [1]of three days' journey.

4 And Jonah began to enter into the city [1]a day's journey, and [a]he [2]cried, and said, Yet forty days, and Nineveh shall be overthrown.

5 So the [a]people of Nineveh believed God, and proclaimed a fast, and put on sackcloth, from the greatest of them even to the least of them.

6 For word came unto the king of Nineveh, and he arose from his throne, and he laid his robe from him, and covered *him* with sackcloth, [a]and sat in ashes.

7 [a]And he caused *it* to be proclaimed and published through Nineveh by the decree of the king and his [1]nobles, saying, Let neither man nor beast, herd nor flock, taste any thing: let them not feed, nor drink water:

8 But let man and beast be covered with sackcloth, and cry mightily unto God: yea, [a]let them turn every one from his evil way, and from [b]the violence that *is* in their hands.

9 [a]Who can tell *if* God will turn and [1]repent, and turn away from his fierce anger, that we perish not?

2:6 [a] [Ps. 16:10]
[1] *foundations* or *bases* [2] *closed behind* [3] *the pit*
2:7 [a] Ps. 18:6
[1] *went up to*
2:8 [a] Jer. 10:8
[1] *worthless idols* [2] *lovingkindness*
2:9 [a] Hos. 14:2 [b] [Eccl. 5:4, 5] [c] Ps. 3:8 [d] [Jer. 3:23]
3:2 [1] *message* [2] *tell*
3:3 [1] Exact meaning unknown
3:4 [a] [Deut. 18:22] [1] *on the first day's* [2] *cried out*
3:5 [a] [Matt. 12:41]
3:6 [a] Job 2:8
3:7 [a] 2 Chr. 20:3 [1] Lit. *great ones*
3:8 [a] Is. 58:6 [b] Is. 59:6
3:9 [a] Joel 2:14 [1] *relent*
3:10 [a] Jer. 18:8 [1] *relented from the disaster*
4:2 [a] Jon. 1:3 [b] Joel 2:13 [1] *what I said* [2] *previously* [3] *lovingkindness* [4] *one who relents from doing harm*
4:3 [a] 1 Kin. 19:4 [b] Jon. 4:8
4:4 [1] Is it *right to be*
4:5 [1] *shelter* [2] *shade*
4:6 [1] Heb. *kikayon, a plant,* exact identity unknown [2] *shade* [3] *misery* [4] *rejoiced with great joy* [5] *over the plant*
4:7 [1] *dawned* [2] *damaged,* lit. *struck* [3] *plant*
4:8 [a] Jon. 4:3 [1] *grew faint* [2] *asked death for himself*
4:9 [1] Is it *right for you to* [2] It is *right for me to*
4:10 [1] *plant*
4:11 [a] Jon. 1:2; 3:2, 3 [b] Deut. 1:39 [1] Lit. *pity* [2] *one hundred and twenty* [3] *livestock*

10 [a]And God saw their works, that they turned from their evil way; and God [1]repented of the evil, that he had said that he would do unto them; and he did *it* not.

## CHAPTER 4

B[UT it displeased Jonah exceedingly, and he was very angry.

2 And he prayed unto the LORD, and said, I pray thee, O LORD, *was* not this [1]my saying, when I was yet in my country? Therefore I [a]fled [2]before unto Tarshish: for I knew that thou *art* a [b]gracious God, and merciful, slow to anger, and of great [3]kindness, and [4]repentest thee of the evil.

3 [a]Therefore now, O LORD, take, I beseech thee, my life from me; for [b]*it is* better for me to die than to live.

4 Then said the LORD, [1]Doest thou well to be angry?

5 So Jonah went out of the city, and sat on the east side of the city, and there made him a [1]booth, and sat under it in the [2]shadow, till he might see what would become of the city.

6 And the LORD God prepared a [1]gourd, and made *it* to come up over Jonah, that it might be a [2]shadow over his head, to deliver him from his [3]grief. So Jonah [4]was exceeding glad [5]of the gourd.

7 But God prepared a worm when the morning [1]rose the next day, and it [2]smote the [3]gourd that it withered.

8 And it came to pass, when the sun did arise, that God prepared a vehement east wind; and the sun beat upon the head of Jonah, that he [1]fainted, and [2]wished in himself to die, and said, [a]*It is* better for me to die than to live.

9 And God said to Jonah, [1]Doest thou well to be angry for the gourd? And he said, [2]I do well to be angry, *even* unto death.

10 Then said the LORD, Thou hast had pity on the [1]gourd, for the which thou hast not laboured, neither madest it grow; which came up in a night, and perished in a night:

11 And should not I [1]spare Nineveh, [a]that great city, wherein are more than [2]sixscore thousand persons [b]that cannot discern between their right hand and their left hand; and *also* much [3]cattle?

# THE BOOK OF
# MICAH

Micah, called from his rustic home to be a prophet, leaves his familiar surroundings to deliver a stern message of judgment to the princes and people of Jerusalem. Burdened by the abusive treatment of the poor by the rich and influential, the prophet turns his verbal rebukes upon any who would use their social or political power for personal gain. One-third of Micah's book exposes the sins of his countrymen; another third pictures the punishment God is about to send; and the final third holds out the hope of restoration once that discipline has ended. Through it all, God's righteous demands upon His people are clear: "to do justly, and to love mercy, and to walk humbly with thy God" (6:8).

The name *Michayahu* ("Who Is Like Yahweh?") is shortened to *Michaia*. In 7:18, Micah hints at his own name with the phrase "Who *is* a God like unto thee?" The Greek and Latin titles of this book are *Michaias* and *Micha*.

## CHAPTER 1

THE word of the LORD that came to ªMicah ¹the Morasthite in the days of ᵇJotham, Ahaz, *and* Hezekiah, kings of Judah, which he saw concerning Samaria and Jerusalem.

2 Hear, all ye people; ¹hearken, O earth, and all that therein is: and let the Lord GOD be witness against you, the Lord from ªhis holy temple.

3 For, behold, the LORD cometh forth out of his place, and will come down, and tread upon the high places of the earth.

4 And ªthe mountains shall ¹be molten under him, and the valleys shall ²be cleft, as wax before the fire, *and* as the waters *that are* poured down a steep place.

5 For the transgression of Jacob *is* all this, and for the sins of the house of Israel. What *is* the transgression of Jacob? *is it* not Samaria? and what *are* the ªhigh places of Judah? *are they* not Jerusalem?

6 Therefore I will make Samaria ªas¹ an heap of the field, *and* as ²plantings of a vineyard: and I will pour down the stones thereof into the valley, and I will ᵇdiscover³ the foundations thereof.

7 And all the ¹graven images thereof shall be beaten to pieces, and all ²the ªhires thereof shall be burned with the fire, and all the idols thereof will I lay desolate: for she gathered *it* ³of the hire of an harlot, and they shall return to the ᵇhire of an harlot.

8 Therefore I will wail and howl, I will go stripped and naked: ªI will make a wailing like the ¹dragons, and mourning as the ²owls.

9 For her wound *is* incurable; for ªit is come unto Judah; ¹he is come unto the gate of my people, *even* to Jerusalem.

10 ªDeclare ye *it* not at Gath, weep

ye not at all: in ¹the house of Aphrah roll thyself in the dust.

11 Pass ye ¹away, thou inhabitant of ²Saphir, ³having thy shame naked: the inhabitant of ⁴Zaanan ⁵came not forth in the mourning of Beth-ezel; he shall ⁶receive of you his standing.

12 For the inhabitant of ¹Maroth ²waited carefully for good: but ªevil³ came down from the LORD unto the gate of Jerusalem.

13 O thou inhabitant of ªLachish, ¹bind the chariot to the ²swift beast: she *is* the beginning of the sin to the daughter of Zion: for the transgressions of Israel were ᵇfound in thee.

14 Therefore shalt thou ªgive presents ¹to ²Moresheth-gath: the houses of ᵇAchzib³ *shall be* a lie to the kings of Israel.

15 Yet will I bring an heir unto thee, O inhabitant of ªMareshah:¹ ²he shall come unto ᵇAdullam³ the glory of Israel.

16 Make thee ªbald, and ¹poll thee for thy ᵇdelicate² children; enlarge thy baldness as the eagle; for they ³are gone into ᶜcaptivity from thee.

## CHAPTER 2

WOE to them that devise iniquity, and ¹work evil upon their beds! when the ªmorning is light, they practise it, because it is in the power of their hand.

2 And they ªcovet fields, and take *them* by violence; and houses, and ¹take *them* away: so they oppress a man and his house, even a man and his ²heritage.

3 Therefore thus saith the LORD; Behold, against this ªfamily ¹do I devise an ᵇevil, from which ye shall not

1:1 ª Jer. 26:18
ᵇ Is. 1:1 ¹ Lit.
Moresheth
1:2 ª [Ps. 11:4]
¹ listen
1:4 ª Amos 9:5
¹ melt ² split
1:5 ª Deut. 32:13;
33:29
1:6 ª 2 Kin. 19:25
ᵇ Ezek. 13:14 ¹ into
a heap of ruins in
² places for planting ³ uncover
1:7 ª Hos. 2:5
ᵇ Deut. 23:18
¹ carved ² her
pay as a harlot
³ from the pay
1:8 ª Ps. 102:6
¹ jackals ² ostriches
1:9 ª 2 Kin.
18:13 ¹ it
1:10 ª 2 Sam.
1:20 ¹ Lit. House
of Dust
1:11 ¹ by ² Lit.
Beautiful ³ in
naked shame
⁴ Lit. Going Out
⁵ Or does not go
out. Beth-ezel
mourns ⁶ take
from you his
standing place
1:12 ª Is. 59:9–11
¹ Lit. Bitterness
² Lit. was sick,
yearned ³ disaster
1:13 ª Is. 36:2
ᵇ Ezek. 23:11
¹ hitch ² swift
steeds
1:14 ª 2 Sam. 8:2
ᵇ Josh. 15:44 ¹ for
² Lit. Possession
of Gath ³ Lit. Lie
1:15 ª Josh. 15:44
ᵇ 2 Chr. 11:7 ¹ Lit.
Inheritance ² the
glory of Israel
shall come to
³ Lit. Refuge
1:16 ª Job 1:20 ᵇ Lam. 4:5 ᶜ Amos 7:11, 17 ¹ cut off your
hair ² precious ³ shall go 2:1 ª Hos. 7:6, 7 ¹ work out,
plan ² Is. 5:8 ¹ seize ⁿ inheritance 2:3 ³ Jer. 8:3
ᵇ Amos 5:13 ¹ I am devising disaster

remove your necks; neither shall ye go haughtily: for this time *is* evil.

4 In that day shall *one* take up a [1]parable against you, and [a]lament with a [2]doleful lamentation, *and* say, We be utterly [3]spoiled: he hath changed the [4]portion of my people: how hath he removed *it* from me! [5]turning away [6]he hath divided our fields.

5 Therefore thou shalt have none that shall cast a [1]cord by lot in the congregation of the LORD.

6 [1]Prophesy ye not, *say to to them that* [2]prophesy: they shall not [2]prophesy [3]to them, *that* they shall not [4]take shame.

7 O *thou that art* named the house of Jacob, is the spirit of the LORD [1]straitened? *are* these his doings? do not my words do good to him that walketh uprightly?

8 Even of late my people is risen up as an enemy: ye pull off the robe with the garment from them that pass by [1]securely as men [2]averse from war.

9 The women of my people have ye cast out from their pleasant houses; from their children have ye taken away my glory for ever.

10 Arise ye, and depart; for this *is* not *your* [a]rest: because it is [b]polluted,[1] it shall destroy *you*, even with [2]a sore destruction.

11 If a man [1]walking in the spirit and falsehood do lie, *saying,* I will [2]prophesy unto thee [3]of wine and of strong drink; he shall even be the [a]prophet[4] of this people.

12 [a]I will surely assemble, O Jacob, all of thee; I will surely gather the remnant of Israel; I will put them together [b]as the sheep of [1]Bozrah, as the flock in the midst of their [2]fold: [c]they shall make great noise by reason of the [1]multitude of men.

13 The [1]breaker is come up before them: they have broken [2]up, and have passed through the gate, and are gone out by it: and [a]their king shall pass before them, [b]and the LORD [3]on the head of them.

## CHAPTER 3

A ND I said, Hear, I pray you, O heads of Jacob, and ye [a]princes[1] of the house of Israel; [b]*Is it* not for you to know [2]judgment?

2 Who hate the good, and love the evil; who [1]pluck off their skin from off [2]them, and their flesh from off their bones;

3 Who also [a]eat the flesh of my people, and flay their skin from off them; and they break their bones, and chop them in pieces, as for the pot, and [b]as flesh within the caldron.

4 Then [a]shall they cry unto the LORD, but he will not hear them: he

---

will even hide his face from them at that time, as they have [1]behaved themselves ill in their [2]doings.

5 Thus saith the LORD [a]concerning the prophets that make my people err, [1]that [b]bite with their teeth, and cry, Peace; and [c]he that putteth [2]not into their mouths, they even prepare war against him.

6 [a]Therefore night *shall be* unto you, [1]that ye shall not have a vision; and it shall be dark unto you, [2]that ye shall not divine; and the sun shall go down [3]over the prophets, and the day shall be dark [4]over [b]them.

7 Then shall the seers be ashamed, and the diviners [1]confounded: yea, they shall all cover their [2]lips; [a]for *there is* no answer [3]of God.

8 But truly I am full of power by the spirit of the LORD, and of [1]judgment, and of might, [a]to declare unto Jacob his transgression, and to Israel his sin.

9 Hear this, I pray you, ye heads of the house of Jacob, and [1]princes of the house of Israel, that abhor [2]judgment, and pervert all equity.

10 [a]They build up Zion with [b]blood,[1] and Jerusalem with iniquity.

11 [a]The heads thereof judge for [1]reward, and [b]the priests thereof teach for [2]hire, and the prophets thereof divine for money: [c]yet will they lean upon the LORD, [3]and say, *Is* not the LORD among us? [4]none evil can come upon us.

12 Therefore shall Zion for your sake be [a]plowed *as* a field, [b]and Jerusalem shall become [1]heaps, and [c]the mountain of [2]the house as the [3]high places of the forest.

## CHAPTER 4

B UT [a]in the last days it shall come to pass, *that* the mountain of the house of the LORD shall be established [1]in the top of the mountains, and it shall be exalted above the hills; and [2]people shall flow unto it.

2 And many nations shall come, and say, Come, and let us go up to the mountain of the LORD, and to the house of the God of Jacob; and he will teach us of his ways, and we will walk in his paths: for the law shall go forth [1]of Zion, and the word of the LORD from Jerusalem.

3 And he shall judge [1]among many people, and rebuke strong nations afar off; and they shall beat their swords into [a]plowshares, and their spears into [2]pruninghooks: nation shall not lift up a sword against nation, [b]neither shall they learn war any more.

4 [a]But they shall sit every man under his vine and under his fig tree;

---

**Center column cross-references:**

2:4 [a] 2 Sam. 1:17
[1] *proverb* [2] *bitter*
[3] *destroyed* [4] *in-heritance* [5] Lit. to one turning back
[6] *he apportioned*
2:5 [1] *surveyor's line*
2:6 [1] *Do not preach, lit. Do not drip* [2] *preach, lit. drip* [3] *to you* [4] MT *return insults*
2:7 [1] *restricted*
2:8 [1] *trusting you* [2] *returning*
2:10 [a] Deut. 12:9 [b] Lev. 18:25 [1] *defiled* [2] *utter*
2:11 [a] Is. 30:10 [1] *should walk in a false spirit and speak a lie* [2] *preach, lit. drip* [3] *concerning* [4] *preacher, lit. word dropper*
2:12 [a] [Mic. 4:6,7] [b] Jer. 31:10 [c] Ezek. 33:22; 36:37 [1] Lit. *of the flock* [2] *pasture*
2:13 [a] [Hos. 3:5] [b] Is. 52:12 [1] *one who breaks open* [2] *out* [3] *at*
3:1 [a] Ezek. 22:27 [b] Jer. 5:4, 5 [1] *rulers* [2] *justice*
3:2 [1] *strip* [2] *My people*
3:3 [a] Ps. 14:4; 27:2 [b] Ezek. 11:3, 6, 7
3:4 [a] Jer. 11:11 [1] *been evil* [2] *deeds*
3:5 [a] Ezek. 13:10, 19 [b] Matt. 7:15 [c] Ezek. 13:18 [1] *When there is a bite to eat, they cry "All is well"* [2] *nothing*
3:6 [a] Is. 8:20–22; 29:10–12 [b] Is. 29:10 [1] *without vision* [2] *without divination* [3] *on* [4] *for*
3:7 [a] Amos 8:11 [1] *embarrassed* [2] Mouths [3] *from*
3:8 [a] Is. 58:1 [1] *justice*
3:9 [1] *rulers* [2] *justice*
3:10 [a] Jer. 22:13, 17 [b] Hab. 2:12 [1] *bloodshed*
3:11 [a] Is. 1:23 [b] Jer. 6:13 [c] Is. 48:2 [1] *a bribe* [2] *pay* [3] Lit. *saying* [4] *no harm*
3:12 [a] Jer. 26:18 [b] Ps. 79:1 [c] Mic. 4:1, 2 [1] *heaps of ruins* [2] The temple [3] *bare hills*
4:1 [a] Is. 2:2–4 [1] *on* [2] *peoples*   4:2 [1] *out of*
4:3 [a] Is. 2:4 [b] Ps. 72:7 [1] *between* [2] *pruning knives*
4:4 [a] Zech. 3:10

and none shall make *them* afraid: for the mouth of the LORD of hosts hath spoken *it*.

5 For all people will walk every one in the name of his god, and [a]we will walk in the name of the LORD our God for ever and ever.

6 In that day, saith the LORD, [a]will I assemble [1]her that halteth, [b]and I will gather [2]her that is driven out, and her that I have afflicted;

7 And I will make [1]her that halted [a]a remnant, and [2]her that was cast far off a strong nation: and the LORD [b]shall reign over them in mount Zion from henceforth, even for ever.

8 And thou, O tower of the flock, the strong hold of the daughter of Zion, unto thee shall it come, even the [1]first dominion; the kingdom shall come to the daughter of Jerusalem.

9 Now why dost thou cry out aloud? [a]*is there* no king [1]in thee? is thy counsellor perished? for [b]pangs have taken thee as a woman [2]in travail.

10 Be in pain, and labour to bring forth, O daughter of Zion, like a woman in [1]travail: for now shalt thou go forth out of the city, and thou shalt dwell in the field, and thou shalt go *even* to [a]Babylon; there shalt thou be delivered; there the [b]LORD shall [c]redeem thee from the hand of thine enemies.

11 [a]Now also many nations are gathered against thee, that say, Let her be defiled, and let our eye [b]look upon Zion.

12 But they know not [a]the thoughts of the LORD, neither understand they his counsel: for he shall gather them [b]as the sheaves [1]into the floor.

13 [a]Arise and [b]thresh, O daughter of Zion: for I will make thine horn iron, and I will make thy hoofs [1]brass: and thou shalt [c]beat in pieces many [2]people: [d]and I will consecrate their gain unto the LORD, and their substance unto [e]the Lord of the whole earth.

## CHAPTER 5

Now gather thyself in troops, O daughter of troops: he hath laid siege against us: they shall [1]smite[1] the judge of Israel with a rod upon the cheek.

2 But thou, [a]Beth-lehem [b]Ephratah, *though* thou be little [c]among the [d]thousands of Judah, *yet* out of thee shall he come forth unto me *that is* to be [e]ruler in Israel; [f]whose goings forth *have been* from of old, from [1]everlasting.

3 Therefore will he give them up, until the time *that* [a]she which [1]travaileth hath brought forth: then [b]the remnant of his brethren shall return unto the children of Israel.

4 And he shall stand and [a]feed[1] in the strength of the LORD, in the majesty of the name of the LORD his God; and they shall abide: for now [b]shall he be great unto the ends of the earth.

5 And this *man* [a]shall be the peace, when the Assyrian shall come into our land: and when he shall tread in our palaces, then shall we raise against him seven shepherds, and eight [1]principal men.

6 And they shall [1]waste the land of Assyria with the sword, and the land of [a]Nimrod in the entrances thereof: thus shall he [b]deliver *us* from the Assyrian, when he cometh into our land, and when he treadeth within our borders.

7 And [a]the remnant of Jacob shall be in the midst of many people [b]as a dew from the LORD, as the showers upon the grass, that [1]tarrieth not for man, nor [2]waiteth for the sons of men.

8 And the remnant of Jacob shall be among the Gentiles in the midst of many people as a [a]lion among the beasts of the forest, as a young lion among the flocks of sheep: who, if he go through, both treadeth down, and teareth in pieces, and none can deliver.

9 Thine hand shall be lifted up upon thine adversaries, and all thine enemies shall be [1]cut off.

10 And it shall come to pass in that day, saith the LORD, that I will [a]cut[1] off thy [b]horses out of the midst of thee, and I will destroy thy [c]chariots:

11 And I will cut off the cities of thy land, and throw down all thy strong holds:

12 And I will cut off [1]witchcrafts out of thine hand; and thou shalt have no *more* [a]soothsayers:

13 [a]Thy [1]graven images also will I cut off, and thy [2]standing images out of the midst of thee; and thou shalt [b]no more worship the work of thine hands.

14 And I will pluck up thy [1]groves out of the midst of thee: so will I destroy thy cities.

15 And I will [a]execute vengeance in anger and fury upon the [1]heathen, such as they have not [2]heard.

## CHAPTER 6

Hear ye now what the LORD saith; Arise, [1]contend thou before the mountains, and let the hills hear thy voice.

2 [a]Hear ye, O mountains, [b]the LORD's [1]controversy, and ye strong foundations of the earth: for [c]the LORD hath a [1]controversy with his people, and he will [2]plead with Israel.

3 O my people, [a]what have I done unto thee? and wherein have I [b]wearied thee? testify against me.

4:5 [a] Zech. 10:12
4:6 [a] Ezek. 34:16
[b] Ps. 147:2 [1] *the lame* [2] *the outcast*
4:7 [a] Mic. 2:12
[b] [Is. 9:6; 24:23] [1] *the lame* [2] *the outcast*
4:8 [1] *former*
4:9 [a] Jer. 8:19 [b] Is. 13:8 [1] *among* [2] *giving birth*
4:10 [a] Amos 5:27 [b] [Is. 45:13] [c] Ps. 18:17 [1] *birth pangs*
4:11 [a] Lam. 2:16 [b] Obad. 12
4:12 [a] [Is. 55:8, 9] [b] Is. 21:10 [1] *to the threshingfloor*
4:13 [a] Jer. 51:33 [b] Is. 41:15 [c] Dan. 2:44 [d] Is. 18:7 [e] Zech. 4:14 [1] *bronze* [2] *peoples*
5:1 [a] Lam. 3:30 [1] *strike*
5:2 [a] John 7:42 [b] Gen. 35:19; 48:7; [c] 1 Sam. 23:23 [d] Ex. 18:25 [e] [Is. 9:6] [f] Ps. 90:2 [1] Lit. *the days of eternity*
5:3 [a] Mic. 4:10 [b] Mic. 4:7; 7:18 [1] *is giving birth*
5:4 [a] [Is. 40:11; 49:9] [b] Ps. 72:8 [1] *shepherd his flock*
5:5 [a] [Is. 9:6] [1] *princely*
5:6 [a] Gen. 10:8–11 [b] Is. 14:25 [1] *devastate*
5:7 [a] Mic. 5:3 [b] Deut. 32:2 [1] *wait for no man* [2] *delay*
5:8 [a] Num. 24:9
5:9 [1] *destroyed*
5:10 [a] Zech. 9:10 [b] Deut. 17:16 [c] Is. 2:7; 22:18 [1] *destroy*
5:12 [a] Is. 2:6 [1] *sorceries*
5:13 [a] Zech. 13:2 [b] Is. 2:8 [1] *carved* [2] *sacred pillars*
5:14 [1] Heb. *Asherim,* Canaanite deities
5:15 [a] [2 Thess. 1:8] [1] *nations* [2] *obeyed*
6:1 [1] *plead your case*
6:2 [a] Ps. 50:1, 4 [b] Hos. 12:2 [c] [Is. 1:18] [1] *complaint* [2] *bring charges against*
6:3 [a] Jer. 2:5, 31 [b] Is. 43:22, 23

4 ªFor I brought thee up out of the land of Egypt, and redeemed thee out of the house of ¹servants; and I sent before thee Moses, Aaron, and Miriam.

5 O my people, remember now what ªBalak king of Moab ¹consulted, and what Balaam the son of Beor answered him from ²Shittim unto Gilgal; that ye may know ᵇthe righteousness of the LORD.

6 Wherewith shall I come before the LORD, *and* bow myself before the high God? shall I come before him with burnt offerings, with calves of a year old?

7 ªWill the LORD be pleased with thousands of rams, *or* with ten thousands of ᵇrivers of oil? ᶜshall I give my firstborn *for* my transgression, ¹the fruit of my body *for* the sin of my soul?

8 He hath ªshewed thee, O man, what *is* good; and what doth the LORD require of thee, but ᵇto do justly, and to love ¹mercy, and to walk humbly with thy God?

9 The LORD's voice crieth unto the city, and *the man of* wisdom shall see thy name: hear ye the rod, and who hath appointed it.

10 Are there yet the treasures of wickedness in the house of the wicked, and the ¹scant measure *that is* abominable?

11 Shall I count *them* pure with ªthe wicked ¹balances, and with the bag of deceitful weights?

12 For the rich men thereof are full of ªviolence, and the inhabitants thereof have spoken lies, and ᵇtheir tongue *is* deceitful in their mouth.

13 Therefore also will I ¹make *thee* sick ¹in smiting thee, ²in making *thee* desolate because of thy sins.

14 ªThou shalt eat, but not be satisfied; and ¹thy casting down *shall be* in the midst of thee; and ²thou shalt take hold, but shalt not deliver; and *that* which thou deliverest will I give up to the sword.

15 Thou shalt ªsow, but thou shalt not reap; thou shalt tread the olives, but thou shalt not anoint thee with oil; ¹and sweet wine, but shalt not drink wine.

16 For the statutes of ªOmri are ᵇkept, and all the works of the house of Ahab, and ye walk in their counsels; that I should make thee ¹a desolation, and the inhabitants thereof an hissing: therefore ye shall bear the ᶜreproach of my people.

## CHAPTER 7

WOE is me! for I am as ¹when they have gathered the summer fruits, as ªthe² grapegleanings of the vintage: *there is* no cluster to eat: ᵇmy soul desired the firstripe fruit.

2 The ªgood¹ *man* is perished out of the earth: and *there is* none upright among men: they all lie in wait for blood; ᵇthey hunt every man his brother with a net.

3 That they may do evil with both hands ¹earnestly, the prince ²asketh, and the judge *asketh* for a ªreward;³ and the great *man,* he uttereth his ⁴mischievous desire: so they ⁵wrap it up.

4 The best of them ª*is* as a brier: the most upright *is sharper* than a thorn hedge: the day of thy watchmen *and* thy ¹visitation cometh; now shall be their perplexity.

5 Trust ye ªnot in a friend, put ye not confidence in a ¹guide: ²keep the doors of thy mouth from her that lieth in thy ᵇbosom.

6 For ªthe son dishonoureth the father, the daughter riseth up against her mother, the daughter in law against her mother in law; a man's enemies *are* the men of his own house.

7 Therefore I will look unto the LORD; I will ªwait for the God of my salvation: my God will hear me.

8 ªRejoice not against me, O mine enemy: ᵇwhen I fall, I shall arise; when I sit in darkness, the LORD *shall be* a light unto me.

9 ªI will bear the indignation of the LORD, because I have sinned against him, until he plead my ᵇcause,¹ and execute ²judgment for me: he will bring me forth to the light, *and* I shall behold his righteousness.

10 Then *she that is* mine enemy shall see *it,* and ªshame shall cover her which said unto me, ᵇWhere is the LORD thy God? mine eyes shall behold her: now shall she be ¹trodden down as the mire of the streets.

11 *In* the day that thy ªwalls are to be built, *in* that day shall the ¹decree be far removed.

12 *In* that day *also* ªhe¹ shall come even to thee from Assyria, and *from* the ²fortified cities, and from the ³fortress even to the ⁴river, and from sea to sea, and *from* mountain to mountain.

13 Notwithstanding the land shall be desolate because of them that dwell therein, ªfor the fruit of their ¹doings.

14 ¹Feed thy people with thy ²rod, the flock of thine heritage, which dwell ³solitarily *in* ªthe ⁴wood, in the midst of Carmel: let them feed *in* Bashan and Gilead, as in the days of old.

15 ªAccording to the days of thy coming out of the land of Egypt will I shew unto ¹him ᵇmarvellous *things.*

16 The nations ªshall see and be ¹confounded at all their might: ᵇthey shall lay *their* hand upon *their* mouth, their ears shall be deaf.

6:4 ª [Deut. 4:20]  ¹ bondage

6:5 ª Num. 22:5, 6  ᵇ Judg. 5:11  ¹ counselled  ² Acacia Grove

6:7 ª Is. 1:11  ᵇ Job 29:6  ᶜ 2 Kin. 16:3  ¹ My own child

6:8 ª [Deut. 10:12]  ᵇ Gen. 18:19  ¹ Or lovingkindness

6:10 ¹ short

6:11 ª Hos. 12:7  ¹ scales

6:12 ª Mic. 2:1, 2  ᵇ Jer. 9:2–6, 8

6:13 ª Lev. 26:16  ¹ by striking  ² by

6:14 ª Lev. 26:26  ¹ hunger, emptiness, or humiliation  ² MT you may carry away some

6:15 ª Amos 5:11  ¹ and make

6:16 ª 1 Kin. 16:25, 26  ᵇ Hos. 5:11  ᶜ Is. 25:8  ¹ an object of horror

7:1 ª Is. 17:6  ᵇ Is. 28:4  ¹ those who gather  ² those who glean vintage grapes

7:2 ª Is. 57:1  ᵇ Hab. 1:15  ¹ faithful or loyal

7:3 ª Mic. 3:11  ¹ successfully  ² asks for gifts  ³ bribe  ⁴ evil  ⁵ scheme together

7:4 ª Ezek. 2:6  ¹ punishment

7:5 ª Jer. 9:4  ᵇ Deut. 28:56  ¹ companion  ² guard

7:6 ª Matt. 10:36

7:7 ª Is. 25:9

7:8 ª Prov. 24:17  ᵇ [Prov. 24:16]

7:9 ª Lam. 3:39, 40  ᵇ Jer. 50:34  ¹ case  ² justice

7:10 ª Ps. 35:26  ᵇ Ps. 42:3  ¹ trampled

7:11 ª [Amos 9:11]  ¹ decree go far and wide or boundary be extended

7:12 ª [Is. 11:16; 19:23–25]  ¹ The captives collectively  ² Heb. arey mazor, possibly cities of Egypt  ³ Heb. mazor, possibly Egypt  ⁴ The Euphrates

7:13 ª Jer. 21:14  ¹ deeds

7:14 ª Is. 37:24  ¹ Shepherd  ² staff alone  ⁴ wood-land  7:15 ª Ps. 68:22; 78:12  ᵇ Ex. 34:10  ¹ The captives collectively  7:16 ª Is. 26:11  ᵇ Job 21:5  ¹ ashamed of

17 They shall lick the [a]dust like a serpent, [b]they shall [1]move out of their holes like [2]worms of the earth: [c]they shall be afraid of the LORD our God, and shall fear because of thee.

18 [a]Who *is* a God like unto thee, that [b]pardoneth iniquity, and passeth [1]by the transgression of [c]the remnant of his heritage? [d]he retaineth not his anger for ever, because he delighteth *in* [e]mercy.[2]

19 He will turn again, he will have compassion upon us; he will subdue our iniquities; and thou wilt cast all [1]their sins into the depths of the sea.

20 [a]Thou wilt [1]perform the truth to Jacob, *and* the [2]mercy to Abraham, [b]which thou hast sworn unto our fathers from the days of old.

7:17 [a] [Is. 49:23] [b] Ps. 18:45 [c] Jer. 33:9 [1] *crawl* [2] *snakes,* lit. *crawlers*

7:18 [a] Ex. 15:11 [b] Ex. 34:6, 7, 9 [c] Mic. 4:7 [d] Ps. 103:8, 9, 13 [e] [Ezek. 33:11] [1] *over* [2] *lovingkindness*

7:19 [1] *Our*

7:20 [a] Luke 1:72, 73 [b] Ps. 105:9 [1] *give* [2] *lovingkindness*

# THE BOOK OF
# NAHUM

"**F**or unto whomsoever much is given, of him shall be much required" (Luke 12:48). Nineveh had been given the privilege of knowing the one true God. Under Jonah's preaching this great gentile city had repented, and God had graciously stayed His judgment. However, a hundred years later, Nahum proclaims the downfall of this same city. The Assyrians have forgotten their revival and have returned to their habits of violence, idolatry, and arrogance. As a result, Babylon will so destroy the city that no trace of it will remain—a prophecy fulfilled in painful detail.

The Hebrew word *nahum* ("comfort," "consolation") is a shortened form of Nehemiah ("Comfort of Yahweh"). The destruction of the capital city of Assyria is a message of comfort and consolation to Judah and all who live in fear of the cruelty of the Assyrians. The title of this book in the Greek and Latin Bibles is *Naoum* and *Nahum*.

## CHAPTER 1

**T**HE [1]burden [a]of[2] Nineveh. The book of the vision of Nahum the Elkoshite.

2 God *is* [a]jealous, and the LORD revengeth; the LORD [1]revengeth, and *is* furious; the LORD will take vengeance on his adversaries, and he reserveth *wrath* for his enemies.

3 The LORD *is* [a]slow to anger, and [b]great in power, and will not at all acquit *the wicked*: [c]the LORD *hath* his way in the whirlwind and in the storm, and the clouds *are* the dust of his feet.

4 [a]He rebuketh the sea, and maketh it dry, and drieth up all the rivers: [b]Bashan [1]languisheth, and Carmel, and the flower of Lebanon [1]languisheth.

5 The mountains quake at him, and the hills melt, and the earth [1]is burned at his presence, yea, the world, and all that dwell therein.

6 Who can stand before his indignation? and [a]who can [1]abide in the fierceness of his anger? his fury is poured out like fire, and the rocks are thrown down by him.

7 [a]The LORD *is* good, a strong hold in the day of trouble; and [b]he knoweth them that trust in him.

8 But with an [1]overrunning flood he will make an utter end of the place thereof, and darkness shall pursue his enemies.

9 [a]What do ye [1]imagine against the LORD? [b]he will make an utter [2]end: affliction shall not rise up the second time.

10 For while *they be* [1]folden together [a]*as* thorns, [b]and while they are drunken *as* drunkards, [c]they shall be devoured as stubble fully dry.

11 There is *one* come out of thee, that [1]imagineth evil against the LORD, a [2]wicked counsellor.

1:1 [a] Zeph. 2:13
[1] *oracle* or *prophecy* [2] *against*
1:2 [a] Ex. 20:5
[1] *avenges*
1:3 [a] Ex. 34:6, 7
[b] [Job 9:4] [c] Ps. 18:17
1:4 [a] Matt. 8:26
[b] Is. 33:9 [1] *withers*
1:5 [1] MT *heaves*
1:6 [a] [Mal. 3:2]
[1] *endure*
1:7 [a] [Jer. 33:11]
[b] 2 Tim. 2:19
1:8 [1] *overflowing*
1:9 [a] Ps. 2:1
[b] 1 Sam. 3:12
[1] *conspire* [2] *end* of it
1:10 [a] 2 Sam. 23:6
[b] Nah. 3:11 [c] Mal. 4:1 [1] *tangled*
1:11 [1] *plots* [2] *counsellor of Belial* or *worthless counsellor*
1:12 [a] [Is. 10:16–19, 33, 34] [1] Lit. *safe* or *at peace*
1:14 [a] Ezek. 32:22, 23 [b] Nah. 3:6
[1] *shall your name be perpetuated* [2] *carved* [3] *dig* [4] Lit. *contemptible*
1:15 [a] Rom. 10:15
[b] Is. 29:7, 8 [1] *news* [2] *proclaims* [3] *sacred*, lit. *appointed* [4] *one of Belial* or *worthless one*
2:1 [1] MT *scatters* [2] *guard the fortress* [3] *road* [4] *flanks*
2:2 [1] Or *will restore* [2] *ruined*
2:3 [1] *spears*, lit. *cypresses* [2] *brandished*

12 Thus saith the LORD; Though *they be* [1]quiet, and likewise many, yet thus shall they be [a]cut down, when he shall pass through. Though I have afflicted thee, I will afflict thee no more.

13 For now will I break his yoke from off thee, and will burst thy bonds in sunder.

14 And the LORD hath given a commandment concerning thee, *that* no more [1]of thy name be sown: out of the house of thy gods will I cut off the [2]graven image and the molten image: I will [3]make thy [a]grave; for thou art [b]vile.[4]

15 Behold upon the mountains the [a]feet of him that bringeth good [1]tidings, that [2]publisheth peace! O Judah, keep thy [3]solemn feasts, perform thy vows: for the [4]wicked shall no more pass through thee; he is [b]utterly cut off.

## CHAPTER 2

**H**E that [1]dasheth in pieces is come up before thy face: [2]keep the munition, watch the [3]way, make *thy* [4]loins strong, fortify *thy* power mightily.

2 For the LORD [1]hath turned away the excellency of Jacob, as the excellency of Israel: for the emptiers have emptied them out, and [2]marred their vine branches.

3 The shield of his mighty men is made red, the valiant men *are* in scarlet: the chariots *shall be* with flaming torches in the day of his preparation, and the [1]fir trees shall be [2]terribly shaken.

4 The chariots shall rage in the streets, they shall [1]justle one against another in the broad [2]ways: they shall seem like torches, they shall run like the lightnings.

2:4 [1] *jostle* [2] *roads*

5 He shall ¹recount his worthies: they shall stumble in their walk; they shall make haste to the wall thereof, and the defence shall be prepared.

6 The gates of the rivers shall be opened, and the palace shall be ¹dissolved.

7 And ¹Huzzab ²shall be led away captive, she shall be brought up, and her maids shall lead *her* as with the voice of doves, ³tabering upon their breasts.

8 But Nineveh ¹*is* of old like a pool of water: yet they shall flee away. ²Stand, stand, *shall they cry;* but none shall ³look back.

9 Take ye the ¹spoil of silver, take the spoil of ªgold: for *there is* none end of the ²store *and* glory out of all the ³pleasant furniture.

10 She is empty, and ¹void, and waste: and the heart melteth, and the knees ²smite together, and much pain *is* in ³all loins, and the faces of them all ⁴gather blackness.

11 Where *is* the dwelling of the ªlions, and the feedingplace of the young lions, where the lion, *even* the ¹old lion, walked, *and* the lion's ²whelp, and none made *them* afraid?

12 The lion did tear in pieces enough for his whelps, and ¹strangled for his lionesses, and ªfilled his ²holes with prey, and his dens with ³ravin.

13 ªBehold, I *am* against thee, saith the LORD of hosts, and I will burn ¹her chariots in the smoke, and the sword shall devour thy young lions: and I will cut off thy prey from the earth, and the voice of thy ᵇmessengers shall no more be heard.

## CHAPTER 3

WOE to the ªbloody city! it *is* all full of lies *and* robbery; the prey departeth not;

2 The noise of a whip, and the noise of the rattling of the wheels, and of the ¹pransing horses, and of the ²jumping chariots.

3 The horseman ¹lifteth up both the bright sword and the glittering spear: and *there is* a multitude of slain, and a great number of carcases; and *there* ²*is* none end of *their* corpses; they stumble upon their corpses:

4 Because of the multitude of the ¹whoredoms of the ²wellfavoured harlot, ªthe mistress of ³witchcrafts, that selleth nations through her ¹whoredoms, and families through her ³witchcrafts.

5 Behold, I *am* ªagainst thee, saith the LORD of hosts; and ᵇI will ¹discover thy skirts ²upon thy face, and I will shew the nations thy nakedness, and the kingdoms thy shame.

6 And I will cast abominable filth

2:5 ¹ *remember his majestic or mighty ones*
2:6 ¹ *melted*
2:7 ¹ Lit. *It is decreed* ² *she shall be* ³ *beating*
2:8 ¹ Was ². *Halt, halt* ³ *turn*
2:9 ª Zeph. 1:18 ¹ *plunder* ² *treasure* ³ *desirable*
2:10 ¹ *desolate* ² *shake* ³ *every side* ⁴ MT *are drained of colour*
2:11 ª Job 4:10, 11 ¹ *lioness* ² *cub*
2:12 ª Jer. 51:34 ¹ *killed* ² *caves* ³ *torn flesh*
2:13 ª Nah. 3:5 ᵇ 2 Kin. 18:17–25; 19:9–13, 23 ¹ *your*
3:1 ª Hab. 2:12
3:2 ¹ *galloping* ² *jolting*
3:3 ¹ *charge with* ² *are countless corpses*
3:4 ⁴ Is. 47:9–12 ¹ *harlotries,* spiritual unfaithfulness ² *seductive* ³ *sorceries*
3:5 ª Nah. 2:13 ᵇ Is. 47:2, 3 ¹ *lift* ² *over*
3:6 ª Nah. 1:14 ᵇ Heb. 10:33 ¹ *spectacle*
3:7 ª Rev. 18:10 ᵇ Jon. 3:3; 4:11 ᶜ Jer. 15:5
3:8 ª Amos 6:2 ᵇ Jer. 46:25 ¹ Heb. *No Amon,* ancient Thebes; Tg., Vg. *populous Alexandria* ² *situated* ³ The Nile and the surrounding canals ⁴ *like*
3:9 ª Ezek. 27:10 ¹ *boundless* ² LXX *her*
3:10 ª Hos. 13:16 ᵇ Lam. 2:19 ᶜ Joel 3:3 ¹ *head*
3:11 ª Nah. 1:10 ¹ *refuge from*
3:12 ª Rev. 6:12, 13
3:13 ª Is. 19:16 ᵇ Jer. 51:30 ¹ *gate bars*
3:14 ª Nah. 2:1
3:15 ª Joel 1:4 ¹ *locust* ² *swarming locusts*
3:16 ª Rev. 18:3, 11–19 ¹ *locust plunders*
3:17 ª Rev. 9:7 ¹ *commanders,* lit. *officials* ² *swarming locusts*

upon thee, and make thee ªvile, and will set thee as ᵇa ¹gazingstock.

7 And it shall come to pass, *that* all they that look upon thee ªshall flee from thee, and say, ᵇNineveh is laid waste: ᶜwho will bemoan her? whence shall I seek comforters for thee?

8 ªArt thou better than ¹populous ᵇNo, that was ²situate among the ³rivers, *that had* the waters round about it, whose rampart *was* the sea, *and* her wall *was* ⁴from the sea?

9 Ethiopia and Egypt *were* her strength, and *it was* ¹infinite; ªPut and Lubim were ²thy helpers.

10 Yet *was* she carried away, she went into captivity: ªher young children also were dashed in pieces ᵇat the ¹top of all the streets: and they ᶜcast lots for her honourable men, and all her great men were bound in chains.

11 Thou also shalt be ªdrunken: thou shalt be hid, thou also shalt seek ¹strength because of the enemy.

12 All thy strong holds *shall be like* ªfig trees with the firstripe figs: if they be shaken, they shall even fall into the mouth of the eater.

13 Behold, ªthy people in the midst of thee *are* women: the gates of thy land shall be set wide open unto thine enemies: the fire shall devour thy ᵇbars.¹

14 Draw thee waters for the siege, ªfortify thy strong holds: go into clay, and tread the morter, make strong the brickkiln.

15 There shall the fire devour thee; the sword shall cut thee off, it shall eat thee up like ªthe ¹cankerworm: make thyself many as the ¹cankerworm, make thyself many as the ²locusts.

16 Thou hast multiplied thy ªmerchants above the stars of heaven: the ¹cankerworm spoileth, and fleeth away.

17 ªThy ¹crowned *are* as the ²locusts, and thy captains as the great grasshoppers, which camp in the hedges in the cold day, *but* when the sun ariseth they flee away, and their place is not known where they *are.*

18 ªThy shepherds slumber, O ᵇking of Assyria: thy nobles shall ¹dwell *in the dust:* thy people is ᶜscattered upon the mountains, and no man gathereth *them.*

19 *There is* no healing of thy ¹bruise; ªthy wound is ²grievous: ᵇall that hear the ³bruit of thee shall clap the hands over thee: for upon whom hath not thy wickedness passed continually?

# THE BOOK OF
# HABAKKUK

Habakkuk ministers during the "death throes" of the nation of Judah. Although repeatedly called to repentance, the nation stubbornly refuses to change her sinful ways. Habakkuk, knowing the hardheartedness of his countrymen, asks God how long this intolerable condition can continue. God replies that the Babylonians will be His chastening rod upon the nation—an announcement that sends the prophet to his knees. He acknowledges that the just in any generation shall live by faith (2:4), not by sight. Habakkuk concludes by praising God's wisdom even though he does not fully understand God's ways.

*Habaqquq* is an unusual Hebrew name derived from the verb *habaq,* "embrace." Thus his name probably means "One Who Embraces" or "Clings." At the end of his book this name becomes appropriate because Habakkuk chooses to cling firmly to God regardless of what happens to his nation (3:16–19). The Greek title in the Septuagint is *Ambakouk,* and the Latin title in Jerome's Vulgate is *Habacuc.*

## CHAPTER 1

THE ¹burden which Habakkuk the prophet did see.

2 O LORD, how long shall I cry, ªand thou wilt not hear! *even* cry out unto thee *of* ᵇviolence, and thou wilt ᶜnot save!

3 Why dost thou shew me iniquity, and cause *me* to behold ¹grievance? for ²spoiling and violence *are* before me: and ³there are *that* raise up strife and contention.

4 Therefore the law is ¹slacked, and ²judgment doth never go forth: for the ªwicked doth ³compass about the righteous; therefore ⁴wrong judgment proceedeth.

5 ªBehold ye among the ¹heathen, and regard, and wonder marvellously: for *I* will work a work in your days, *which* ye will not believe, though it be told *you.*

6 For, lo, I ªraise up the Chaldeans, *that* bitter and ¹hasty ᵇnation, which shall march through the breadth of the land, to possess the dwellingplaces *that are* not theirs.

7 They *are* terrible and dreadful: their judgment and their dignity shall proceed ¹of themselves.

8 Their horses also are ªswifter than the leopards, and are more fierce than the evening wolves: and their horsemen shall ¹spread themselves, and their horsemen shall come from far; they shall fly as the ᵇeagle *that* hasteth to eat.

9 They shall come all for violence: their faces ¹shall sup up *as* the east wind, and they shall gather the captivity as the sand.

10 And they shall scoff at the kings, and the princes shall be a scorn unto them: they shall deride every strong hold; for they shall heap ¹dust, and take it.

11 Then shall *his* ¹mind change, and he shall ²pass over, and offend, ªimputing this his power unto his god.

12 *Art* thou not ªfrom everlasting, O LORD my God, mine Holy One? we shall not die. O LORD, thou hast ordained them for judgment; and, O ¹mighty God, ᵇthou hast ²established them for ᶜcorrection.

13 *Thou art* of purer eyes than to behold evil, and canst not look on ¹iniquity: wherefore lookest thou upon them that deal treacherously, *and* holdest thy tongue when the wicked devoureth *the man that is* more righteous than he?

14 And makest men as the fishes of the sea, as the creeping things, *that have* no ruler over them?

15 They take up all of them with ¹the angle, they catch them in their net, and gather them in their ²drag: therefore they rejoice and are glad.

16 Therefore ªthey sacrifice unto their net, and burn incense unto their ¹drag; because by them their portion *is* ²fat, and their ³meat plenteous.

17 Shall they therefore empty their net, and ¹not spare continually to slay the nations?

## CHAPTER 2

I will ªstand upon my watch, and set me upon the ¹tower, and will watch to see what he will say unto me, and what I shall answer when I am reproved.

2 And the LORD answered me, and said, ªWrite the vision, and make *it* plain ¹upon tables, that he may run that readeth it.

3 For ªthe vision *is* yet for an appointed time, but at the end it shall speak, and ᵇnot lie: though it tarry, ᶜwait for it; because it will ᵈsurely come, it will not tarry.

1:1 ¹ oracle or prophecy
1:2 ª Lam. 3:8 ᵇ Mic. 2:1, 2; 3:1–3 ᶜ [Job 21:5–16]
1:3 ¹ trouble or toil ² plundering ³ there is strife
1:4 ª Jer. 12:1 ¹ powerless ² justice ³ surround ⁴ perverse
1:5 ª Is. 29:14 ¹ nations
1:6 ª 2 Kin. 24:2 ᵇ Ezek. 7:24; 21:31 ¹ impetuous
1:7 ¹ from
1:8 ª Jer. 4:13 ᵇ Hos. 8:1 ¹ charge ahead
1:9 ¹ are like the east wind
1:10 ¹ earthen mounds
1:11 ª Dan. 5:4 ¹ Lit. spirit or wind ² transgress
1:12 ª Ps. 90:2; 93:2 ᵇ Is. 10:5–7 ᶜ Jer. 25:9 ¹ Lit. Rock ² marked
1:13 ¹ wickedness
1:15 ¹ a hook ² dragnet
1:16 ª Deut. 8:17 ¹ dragnet ² sumptuous ³ food
1:17 ¹ without pity continue to
2:1 ª Is. 21:8, 11 ¹ rampart
2:2 ª Is. 8:1 ¹ on tablets
2:3 ª Dan. 8:17, 19; 10:14 ᵇ Ezek. 12:24, 25 ᶜ [Heb. 10:37, 38] ᵈ [2 Pet. 3:9]

4 Behold, his soul *which* is [1]lifted up is not upright in him: but the [a]just shall live by his faith.

5 Yea also, because he transgresseth by wine, *he is* a proud man, neither [1]keepeth at home, who [a]enlargeth his desire as [2]hell, and *is* as death, and cannot be satisfied, but gathereth unto him all nations, and heapeth unto him all [3]people:

6 Shall not all these [a]take up a [1]parable against him, and a taunting [2]proverb against him, and say, Woe to him that increaseth *that which is* not his! how long? and to him that [3]ladeth himself with [4]thick clay!

7 Shall [1]they not rise up suddenly that shall bite thee, and awake that shall [2]vex thee, and thou shalt be for [3]booties unto them?

8 [a]Because thou hast [1]spoiled many nations, all the remnant of the people shall [2]spoil thee; because of men's [3]blood, and *for* the violence of the land, of the city, and of all that dwell therein.

9 Woe to him that coveteth [1]an evil covetousness to his house, that he may [a]set his nest on high, that he may be delivered from the power of [2]evil!

10 Thou [1]hast consulted shame to thy house by cutting off many [2]people, and hast sinned *against* thy soul.

11 For the stone shall cry out of the wall, and the beam out of the timber shall answer it.

12 Woe to him that buildeth a town with [1]blood, and stablisheth a city by iniquity!

13 Behold, *is it* not of the LORD of hosts that the people shall labour [1]in the very fire, and the people shall weary themselves [2]for very vanity?

14 For the earth shall be filled with the knowledge of the glory of the LORD, as the waters cover the sea.

15 Woe unto him that giveth his neighbour drink, that [1]puttest thy [a]bottle to *him*, and makest *him* drunken also, that thou mayest look on their nakedness!

16 Thou art filled with shame [1]for glory: drink thou also, and [2]let thy foreskin be uncovered: the cup of the LORD's right hand shall be turned [3]unto thee, and [4]shameful spewing *shall be* on thy glory.

17 For the violence [1]of Lebanon shall cover thee, and the [2]spoil of beasts, *which* made them afraid, because of men's blood, and for the violence of the land, of the city, and of all that dwell therein.

18 What profiteth the [1]graven image that the maker thereof hath graven it; the molten image, and a teacher of lies, that the maker of his work trusteth therein, to make [2]dumb idols?

19 Woe unto him that saith to the wood, Awake; to the [1]dumb stone, Arise, it shall teach! Behold, it *is* [2]laid over with gold and silver, and *there is* no breath at all in the midst of it.

20 [a]But the LORD *is* in his holy temple: let all the earth keep silence before him.

## CHAPTER 3

A PRAYER of Habakkuk the prophet [1]upon Shigionoth.

2 O LORD, I have heard thy speech, *and* was afraid: O LORD, revive thy work in the midst of the years, in the midst of the years make known; in wrath remember mercy.

3 God came from Teman, and the Holy One from mount Paran. *Selah.* His glory covered the heavens, and the earth was full of his praise.

4 And *his* brightness was as the light; he had [1]horns *coming* out of his hand: and there *was* [2]the hiding of his power.

5 Before him went the pestilence, and [1]burning coals went forth at his feet.

6 He stood, and measured the earth: he beheld, and [1]drove asunder the nations; [a]and the everlasting mountains were scattered, the perpetual hills did bow: his ways *are* everlasting.

7 I saw the tents of Cushan in affliction: *and* the curtains of the land of Midian did tremble.

8 Was the LORD displeased against the rivers? *was* thine anger against the rivers? *was* thy wrath against the sea, that thou didst ride upon thine horses *and* thy chariots of salvation?

9 Thy bow was made quite [1]naked, [2]*according* to the oaths of the tribes, *even thy* word. *Selah.* Thou [3]didst cleave the earth with rivers.

10 The mountains saw thee, *and* they trembled: the overflowing of the water passed by: the deep uttered his voice, *and* [a]lifted up his hands on high.

11 The [a]sun *and* moon stood still in their habitation: at the light of thine arrows they went, *and* at the shining of thy glittering spear.

12 Thou didst march through the land in indignation, thou didst [1]thresh the [2]heathen in anger.

13 Thou wentest forth for the salvation of thy people, *even* for salvation with thine anointed; [1]thou woundedst the head [2]out of the house of the wicked, by [3]discovering the foundation unto the neck. *Selah.*

14 Thou didst strike through with [1]his staves the head of his villages: they came out as a whirlwind to scatter me: their rejoicing *was* as [2]to devour the poor secretly.

2:4 [a] [John 3:36] [1] *proud*
2:5 [a] Is. 5:11–15 [1] *stays* [2] Heb. *Sheol* [3] *peoples*
2:6 [a] Mic. 2:4 [1] *proverb* [2] *riddle* [3] *loads* [4] MT *many pledges*
2:7 [1] *your creditors* [2] *oppress* [3] *plunder*
2:8 [a] Is. 33:1 [1] *plundered* [2] *plunder* [3] *bloodshed*
2:9 [a] Obad. 4 [1] *evil gain for* [2] *disaster*
2:10 [1] *gave shameful counsel* [2] *peoples*
2:12 [1] *bloodshed*
2:13 [1] For that of no lasting value, lit. *for what satisfies fire* [2] *in vain*
2:15 [a] Hos. 7:5 [1] *pressing*, lit. *attaching or joining*
2:16 [1] *instead of* [2] *be exposed as uncircumcised* [3] *against* [4] *utter shame*
2:17 [1] Done to [2] *plunder*
2:18 [1] *carved* [2] *mute*
2:19 [1] *silent* [2] *overlaid*
2:20 [a] Zeph. 1:7; Zech. 2:13
3:1 [1] Exact meaning unknown
3:4 [1] *rays flashing from* [2] *his power hidden*
3:5 [1] *fever followed at*
3:6 [a] Nah. 1:5 [1] *startled*
3:9 [1] *bare* [2] *oaths were sworn over your arrows* [3] *divided*
3:10 [a] Ex. 14:22
3:11 [a] Josh. 10:12–14
3:12 [1] *trample* [2] *nations*
3:13 [1] *you struck* [2] *from* [3] *laying bare from*
3:14 [1] *his own arrows* [2] *feasting on*

15 <sup>a</sup>Thou didst walk through the sea with thine horses, *through* the heap of great waters.

16 When I heard, <sup>a</sup>my <sup>1</sup>belly trembled; my lips quivered at the voice: rottenness entered into my bones, and I trembled in myself, that I might rest in the day of trouble: when he cometh up unto the people, he will invade them with his troops.

17 Although the fig tree shall not blossom, neither *shall* fruit *be* in the vines; the labour of the olive shall fail, and the fields shall yield no <sup>1</sup>meat; the flock shall be cut off from the fold, and *there shall be* no herd in the stalls:

18 Yet I will <sup>a</sup>rejoice in the LORD, I will joy in the God of my salvation.

19 <sup>1</sup>The LORD God *is* my strength, and he will make my feet like <sup>a</sup>hinds'<sup>2</sup> *feet,* and he will make me to <sup>b</sup>walk upon mine high places. To the chief singer on my stringed instruments.

**Cross references:**

3:15 <sup>a</sup> Ps. 77:19; Hab. 3:8

3:16 <sup>a</sup> Ps. 119:120 <sup>1</sup> Body

3:17 <sup>1</sup> food

3:18 <sup>a</sup> Is. 41:16; 61:10

3:19 <sup>a</sup> 2 Sam. 22:34; Ps. 18:33 <sup>b</sup> Deut. 32:13; 33:29 <sup>1</sup> Heb. YHWH Adonai <sup>2</sup> deer's

# THE BOOK OF
# ZEPHANIAH

**D**uring Judah's hectic political and religious history, reform comes from time to time. Zephaniah's forceful prophecy may be a factor in the reform that occurs during Josiah's reign—a "revival" that produces outward change, but does not fully remove the inward heart of corruption which characterizes the nation. Zephaniah hammers home his message repeatedly that the day of the Lord, Judgment Day, is coming when the malignancy of sin will be dealt with. Israel and her gentile neighbors will soon experience the crushing hand of God's wrath. But after the chastening process is complete, blessing will come in the person of the Messiah, who will be the cause for praise and singing.

*Tsephan-yah* means "Yahweh Hides" or "Yahweh Has Hidden." Zephaniah was evidently born during the latter part of the reign of King Manasseh. His name may mean that he was "hidden" from Manasseh's atrocities. The Greek and Latin title is *Sophonias*.

## CHAPTER 1

**T**HE word of the LORD which came unto Zephaniah the son of Cushi, the son of Gedaliah, the son of Amariah, the son of ¹Hizkiah, in the days of ªJosiah the son of Amon, king of Judah.

2 I will ¹utterly consume all *things* from off the land, saith the LORD.

3 ªI will ¹consume man and beast; I will ¹consume the fowls of the heaven, and the fishes of the sea, and the ²stumblingblocks with the wicked; and I will cut off man from ³off the land, saith the LORD.

4 I will also stretch out mine hand upon Judah, and upon all the inhabitants of Jerusalem; and I will cut off ¹the remnant of Baal from this place, *and* the name of ªthe ²Chemarims with the ³priests;

5 And them ªthat worship the host of heaven upon the housetops; and them that worship *and* that ¹swear by the LORD, and that swear ᵇby ²Malcham;

6 And ªthem that are turned back ¹from the LORD; and *those* that ᵇhave not sought the LORD, nor enquired ²for him.

7 ªHold¹ thy peace at the presence of the Lord GOD: ᵇfor the day of the LORD *is* at hand: for ᶜthe LORD hath prepared a sacrifice, he hath ²bid his guests.

8 And it shall come to pass in the day of the LORD's sacrifice, that I will ¹punish ªthe princes, and the king's children, and all such as are clothed with ²strange apparel.

9 In the same day also will I ¹punish all those that ªleap on the threshold, which fill their masters' houses with violence and deceit.

10 And it shall come to pass in that day, saith the LORD, *that there shall be* the noise of a ¹cry from ªthe fish

gate, and an howling from the ²second, and a great crashing from the hills.

11 ªHowl, ye inhabitants of ¹Maktesh, for all the merchant people are cut down; all they that ²bear silver are cut off.

12 And it shall come to pass at that time, *that* I will search Jerusalem with ¹candles, and ²punish the men that are ªsettled³ on their lees: ᵇthat say in their heart, The LORD will not do good, neither will he do evil.

13 Therefore their goods shall become a booty, and their houses a desolation: they shall also build houses, but not inhabit *them;* and they shall plant vineyards, but ªnot drink the wine thereof.

14 ªThe great day of the LORD *is* near, *it is* near, and ¹hasteth greatly, *even* the ²voice of the day of the LORD: the mighty man shall cry there bitterly.

15 ªThat day *is* a day of wrath, a day of trouble and distress, a day of ¹wasteness and desolation, a day of darkness and gloominess, a day of clouds and thick darkness,

16 A day of ªthe trumpet and alarm against the ¹fenced cities, and against the high towers.

17 And I will bring distress upon men, that they shall ªwalk like blind men, because they have sinned against the LORD: and their blood shall be poured out as dust, and their flesh as ¹the dung.

18 ªNeither their silver nor their gold shall be able to deliver them in the day of the LORD's wrath; but the whole land shall be devoured by the fire of his jealousy: for he shall make even a speedy ¹riddance of all them that dwell in the land.

1:1 ª 2 Kin. 22:1, 2 ¹ Hezekiah, 2 Kin. 18:1
1:2 ¹ Lit. completely make an end of
1:3 ª Hos. 4:3 ¹ Lit. make an end of ² Idols ³ Lit. the face of the ground
1:4 ª Hos. 10:5 ¹ every trace ² Lit. idolatrous priests ³ pagan priests
1:5 ª 2 Kin. 23:12 ᵇ Josh. 23:7 ¹ swear oaths ² Or Milcom, an Ammonite god; Molech, Lev. 18:21
1:6 ª Is. 1:4 ᵇ Hos. 7:7 ¹ from following ² of
1:7 ª Zech. 2:13 ᵇ Is. 13:6 ᶜ Jer. 46:10 ¹ Be silent in ² invited, lit. set apart or consecrated
1:8 ª Jer. 39:6 ¹ Lit. visit upon ² foreign
1:9 ª 1 Sam. 5:5 ¹ Lit. visit
1:10 ª 2 Chr. 33:14 ¹ mournful cry ² second quarter
1:11 ª James 5:1 ¹ Lit. Mortar, a market district of Jerusalem ² handle
1:12 ª Jer. 48:11 ᵇ Ps. 94:7 ¹ lamps ² Lit. visit ³ settled like wines on their dregs, settled in complacency
1:13 ª Deut. 28:39
1:14 ª Joel 2:1, 11 ¹ hurries ² noise
1:15 ª Is. 22:5

¹ devastation  1:16 ª Jer. 4:19 ¹ fortified  1:17 ª Deut. 28:29 ¹ refuse  1:18 ª Ezek. 7:19 ¹ end

## CHAPTER 2

GATHER[a] yourselves together, yea, gather together, O nation [1]not desired;

2 Before the decree [1]bring forth, *before* the day pass as the chaff, before the fierce anger of the LORD come upon you, before the day of the LORD's anger come upon you.

3 [a]Seek ye the LORD, [b]all ye meek of the earth, which have [1]wrought his judgment; seek righteousness, seek [2]meekness: [c]it may be ye shall be hid in the day of the LORD's anger.

4 For [a]Gaza shall be forsaken, and Ashkelon a desolation: they shall drive out Ashdod [b]at the noon day, and Ekron shall be rooted up.

5 Woe unto the inhabitants of [a]the sea coast, the nation of the Cherethites! the word of the LORD *is* against you; O [b]Canaan, the land of the Philistines, I will even destroy thee, that there shall be no inhabitant.

6 And the sea coast shall be [1]dwellings *and* [2]cottages for shepherds, [a]and folds for flocks.

7 And the coast shall be for [a]the remnant of the house of Judah; they shall [1]feed thereupon: in the houses of Ashkelon shall they lie down in the evening: for the LORD their GOD shall [b]visit[2] them, and [c]turn[3] away their captivity.

8 [a]I have heard the reproach of Moab, and [b]the revilings of the children of Ammon, whereby they have reproached my people, and [c]magnified[1] *themselves* against their border.

9 Therefore *as* I live, saith the LORD of hosts, the God of Israel, Surely [a]Moab shall be as Sodom, and [b]the children of Ammon as Gomorrah, [c]*even* [1]the breeding of [2]nettles, and saltpits, and a [3]perpetual desolation: the residue of my people shall [4]spoil them, and the remnant of my people shall possess them.

10 This shall they have [a]for their pride, because they have reproached and [1]magnified *themselves* against the people of the Lord of hosts.

11 The LORD *will be* [1]terrible unto them: for he will [2]famish all the gods of the earth; [a]and *men* shall worship him, every one from his place, *even* all [b]the [3]isles of the heathen.

12 [a]Ye Ethiopians also, ye *shall be* slain by [b]my sword.

13 And he will stretch out his hand against the north, and [a]destroy Assyria; and will make Nineveh a desolation, *and* dry like a wilderness.

14 And [1]flocks shall lie down in the midst of her, all [a]the beasts of the nations: both the [b]cormorant[2] and the bittern shall lodge [3]in the upper lintels of it; *their* voice shall sing in the windows; desolation *shall be* in the

2:1 [a] Joel 1:14; 2:16 [1] undesirable
2:2 [1] is issued
2:3 [a] Amos 5:6 [b] Ps. 76:9 [c] Amos 5:14, 15 [1] upheld his justice [2] humility
2:4 [a] Zech. 9:5 [b] Jer. 6:4
2:5 [a] Ezek. 25:15–17 [b] Josh. 13:3
2:6 [a] Is. 17:2 [1] pastures [2] Underground shelters or cisterns, lit. excavations
2:7 [a] [Mic. 5:7, 8] [b] Luke 1:68 [c] Jer. 29:14 [1] feed their flocks there [2] intervene for them [3] return their captives
2:8 [a] Jer. 48:27 [b] Ezek. 25:3 [c] Jer. 49:1 [1] made arrogant threats
2:9 [a] Is. 15:1–9 [b] Amos 1:13 [c] Deut. 29:23 [1] overrun with, lit. possessed by [2] weeds [3] permanent ruin [4] plunder
2:10 [a] Is. 16:6 [1] made arrogant threats
2:11 [a] Mal. 1:11 [b] Gen. 10:5 [1] awesome [2] reduce to nothing [3] coastlands of the nations
2:12 [a] Is. 18:1–7 [b] Ps. 17:13
2:13 [a] Is. 10:5–27; 14:24–27
2:14 [a] Is. 13:21 [b] Is. 14:23; 34:11 [c] Jer. 22:14 [1] herds [2] pelican [3] on the capitals of her pillars [4] lay bare
2:15 [a] Is. 47:8 [b] Rev. 18:7 [c] Lam. 2:15 [d] Nah. 3:19 [1] securely [2] I am it
3:1 [1] rebellious
3:3 [a] Ezek. 22:27 [b] Hab. 1:8 [1] they leave not a bone till morning
3:4 [a] Hos. 9:7 [b] Ezek. 22:26 [1] insolent [2] profaned
3:5 [a] Jer. 3:3 [1] justice [2] never fails
3:6 [1] fortresses are devastated [2] desolate
3:7 [a] Jer. 8:6 [b] Gen. 6:12 [1] correction [2] despite everything for which I punished her [3] They were

thresholds: for he shall [4]uncover the [c]cedar work.

15 This *is* the rejoicing city [a]that dwelt [1]carelessly, [b]that said in her heart, [2]I *am*, and *there is* none beside me: how is she become a desolation, a place for beasts to lie down in! every one that passeth by her [c]shall hiss, *and* [d]wag his hand.

## CHAPTER 3

WOE to her that is [1]filthy and polluted, to the oppressing city!

2 She obeyed not the voice; she received not correction; she trusted not in the LORD; she drew not near to her God.

3 [a]Her princes within her *are* roaring lions; her judges *are* [b]evening wolves; [1]they gnaw not the bones till the morrow.

4 Her [a]prophets *are* [1]light *and* treacherous persons: her priests have [2]polluted the sanctuary, they have done [b]violence to the law.

5 The just LORD *is* in the midst thereof; he will not do iniquity: every morning doth he bring his [1]judgment to light, he [2]faileth not; but [a]the unjust knoweth no shame.

6 I have cut off the nations: their [1]towers are desolate; I made their streets [2]waste, that none passeth by: their cities are destroyed, so that there is no man, that there is none inhabitant.

7 [a]I said, Surely thou wilt fear me, thou wilt receive [1]instruction; so their dwelling should not be cut off, [2]howsoever I punished them: but [3]they rose early, *and* [b]corrupted all their [4]doings.

8 Therefore [a]wait ye upon me, saith the LORD, until the day that I rise up to the prey: for my determination *is* [1]to [b]gather the nations, that I may assemble the kingdoms, to pour upon them mine indignation, *even* all my fierce anger: for all the earth [c]shall be devoured with the fire of my jealousy.

9 For then will I [1]turn to the people [a]a pure language, that they may all call upon the name of the LORD, to serve him with one [2]consent.

10 [a]From beyond the rivers of Ethiopia my [1]suppliants, *even* the daughter of my dispersed, shall bring mine offering.

11 In that day shalt thou not be ashamed for all thy [1]doings, wherein thou hast transgressed against me: for then I will take away out of the midst of thee them that [a]rejoice in thy pride, and thou shalt no more be haughty [2]because of my holy mountain.

eager [4] deeds   3:8 [a] Hab. 2:3 [b] Joel 3:2 [c] Zeph. 1:18 [1] for plunder   3:9 [a] Is. 19:18; 57:19 [1] restore [2] accord 3:10 [a] Ps. 68:31 [1] worshippers   3:11 [a] Is. 2:12; 5:15 [1] deeds [2] in my

12 I will also leave in the midst of thee ªan ¹afflicted and poor people, and they shall trust in the name of the LORD.

13 ªThe remnant of Israel ᵇshall not do iniquity, ᶜnor speak lies; neither shall a deceitful tongue be found in their mouth: for ᵈthey shall ¹feed and lie down, and none shall make *them* afraid.

14 ªSing, O daughter of Zion; shout, O Israel; be glad and rejoice with all the heart, O daughter of Jerusalem.

15 The LORD hath taken away thy judgments, he hath cast out thine enemy: ªthe king of Israel, *even* the LORD, ᵇ*is* in the midst of thee: thou shalt not ¹see ²evil any more.

16 In that day ªit shall be said to Jerusalem, Fear thou not: *and to* Zion, ᵇLet not thine hands ¹be slack.

17 The LORD thy God ªin the midst

of thee *is* mighty; he will save, ᵇhe will rejoice over thee with joy; he will ¹rest in his love, he will joy over thee with singing.

18 I will gather *them that* ªare sorrowful for the ¹solemn assembly, *who* are ²of thee, *to whom* the reproach of it *was* a burden.

19 Behold, at that time I will ¹undo all that afflict thee: and I will save ²her that ªhalteth, and gather her that was driven out; and I will ³get them praise and fame in every land where they have been put to shame.

20 At that time ªwill I bring you *again,* even in the time that I gather you: for I will make you ¹a name and a praise among all people of the earth, when I ²turn back your captivity before your eyes, saith the LORD.

3:12 ª Is. 14:32 ¹ *gentle and humble*

3:13 ª [Mic. 4:7] ᵇ Is. 60:21 ᶜ Rev. 14:5 ᵈ Ezek. 34:13–15, 28 ¹ *feed their flocks*

3:14 ª Is. 12:6

3:15 ª [John 1:49] ᵇ Ezek. 48:35 ¹ So with Heb. mss., LXX, Bg.; MT, Vg. *fear* ² *disaster*

3:16 ª Is. 35:3, 4 ᵇ Heb. 12:12 ¹ *be weak*

3:17 ª Zeph. 3:5, 15 ᵇ Is. 62:5; 65:19 ¹ *quiet you*

3:18 ª Lam. 2:6 ¹ *appointed* ² *among you*

3:19 ª [Mic. 4:6, 7] ¹ *deal with all*

² *the lame* ³ *give*   3:20 ª Is. 11:12 ¹ Fame ² *return your captives*

# THE BOOK OF
# HAGGAI

With the Babylonian exile in the past, and a newly returned group of Jews back in the land, the work of rebuilding the temple can begin. However, sixteen years after the process is begun, the people have yet to finish the project, for their personal affairs have interfered with God's business. Haggai preaches a fiery series of sermonettes designed to stir up the nation to finish the temple. He calls the builders to renewed courage in the Lord, renewed holiness of life, and renewed faith in God who controls the future.

The etymology and meaning of *Haggay* is uncertain, but it is probably derived from the Hebrew word *hag*, "festival." It may also be an abbreviated form of *haggiah*, "festival of Yahweh." Thus, Haggai's name means "Festal" or "Festive," possibly because he was born on the day of a major feast, such as Tabernacles (Haggai's second message takes place during that feast, 2:1). The title in the Septuagint is *Aggaios* and in the Vulgate it is *Aggaeus*.

## CHAPTER 1

IN ᵃthe second year of Darius the king, in the sixth month, in the first day of the month, came the word of the LORD by ᵇHaggai the prophet unto ᶜZerubbabel the son of Shealtiel, governor of Judah, and to ᵈJoshua the son of ᵉJosedech,¹ the high priest, saying,

2 Thus speaketh the LORD of hosts, saying, This people say, The time is not come, the time that the LORD's house should be built.

3 Then came the word of the LORD ᵃby Haggai the prophet, saying,

4 ᵃ*Is it* time for you, O ye, to dwell in your ¹cieled houses, and ²this house ³*lie* waste?

5 Now therefore thus saith the LORD of hosts; ᵃConsider your ways.

6 Ye have ᵃsown much, and bring in little; ye eat, but ye have not enough; ye drink, but ye are not filled with drink; ye clothe you, but there is none warm; and ᵇhe that earneth wages earneth wages *to put it* into a bag with holes.

7 Thus saith the LORD of hosts; Consider your ways.

8 Go up to the ᵃmountain, and bring wood, and build ¹the house; and I will take pleasure in it, and I will be glorified, saith the LORD.

9 ᵃYe looked for much, and, lo, *it came* to little; and when ye brought *it* home, ᵇI ¹did blow upon it. Why? saith the LORD of hosts. Because of mine house that *is* ²waste, and ye run every man unto his own house.

10 Therefore ᵃthe heaven over you ¹is stayed from dew, and the earth ²is stayed *from* her fruit.

11 And I ᵃcalled for a drought upon the land, and upon the mountains, and upon the ¹corn, and upon the new wine, and upon the oil, and upon *that* which the ground bringeth forth,

and upon men, and upon ²cattle, and ᵇupon all the labour of the hands.

12 ᵃThen Zerubbabel the son of Shealtiel, and Joshua the son of ¹Josedech, the high priest, with all the remnant of the people, obeyed the voice of the LORD their God, and the words of Haggai the prophet, as the LORD their God had sent him, and the people did fear before the LORD.

13 Then spake Haggai the LORD's messenger in the LORD's message unto the people, saying, ᵃI *am* with you, saith the LORD.

14 And ᵃthe LORD stirred up the spirit of Zerubbabel the son of Shealtiel, ᵇgovernor of Judah, and the spirit of Joshua the son of ¹Josedech, the high priest, and the spirit of all the remnant of the people; ᶜand they came and did work in the house of the LORD of hosts, their God,

15 In the four and twentieth day of the sixth month, in the second year of Darius the king.

## CHAPTER 2

IN the seventh *month*, in the one and twentieth *day* of the month, came the word of the LORD ¹by the prophet Haggai, saying,

2 Speak now to Zerubbabel the son of Shealtiel, governor of Judah, and to Joshua the son of ¹Josedech, the high priest, and to the ²residue of the people, saying,

3 ᵃWho *is* left among you that saw ¹this house in her first glory? and how do ye see it now? ᵇ*is it* not in your eyes in comparison of it as nothing?

4 Yet now ᵃbe strong, O Zerubbabel, saith the LORD; and be strong, O Joshua, son of Josedech, the high priest; and be strong, all ye people of the land, saith the LORD, and work: for I *am* with you, saith the LORD of hosts:

### Cross-references

1:1 ᵃ Ezra 4:24
ᵇ Ezra 5:1; 6:14
ᶜ Ezra 2:2 ᵈ Ezra 5:2, 3 ᵉ 1 Chr. 6:15 ¹ *Jozadak,* Ezra 3:2
1:3 ᵃ Ezra 5:1
1:4 ᵃ 2 Sam. 7:2 ¹ *panelled* ² The temple ³ *to lie in ruins*
1:5 ᵃ Lam. 3:40
1:6 ᵃ Deut. 28:38–40; Hos. 8:7; Hag. 1:9, 10; 2:16, 17 ᵇ Zech. 8:10
1:8 ᵃ Ezra 3:7 ¹ The temple
1:9 ᵃ Hag. 2:16 ᵇ Hag. 2:17 ¹ *blew it away* ² *in ruins*
1:10 ᵃ Lev. 26:19; Deut. 28:23; 1 Kin. 8:35; Joel 1:18–20 ¹ *withholds the dew* ² *withholds its fruit*
1:11 ᵃ 1 Kin. 17:1; 2 Kin. 8:1 ᵇ Hag. 2:17 ¹ *grain* ² *livestock*
1:12 ᵃ Ezra 5:2 ¹ *Jehozadak,* 1 Chr. 6:15
1:13 ᵃ [Matt. 28:20; Rom. 8:31]
1:14 ᵃ 2 Chr. 36:22; Ezra 1:1 ᵇ Hag. 2:21 ᶜ Ezra 5:2, 8; Neh. 4:6 ¹ *Jehozadak,* 1 Chr. 6:15
2:1 ¹ Lit. *by the hand of the*
2:2 ¹ *Jehozadak,* 1 Chr. 6:15 ² *remnant*
2:3 ᵃ Ezra 3:12, 13 ᵇ Zech. 4:10 ¹ The temple
2:4 ᵃ Deut. 31:23; 1 Chr. 22:13; 28:20; Zech. 8:9; Eph. 6:10

5 [a]*According to* the word that I covenanted with you when ye came out of Egypt, so [b]my spirit remaineth among you: fear ye not.

6 For thus saith the LORD of hosts; [a]Yet [1]once, it *is* a little while, and [b]I will shake the heavens, and the earth, and the sea, and the dry *land;*

7 And I will shake all nations, [a]and the [1]desire of all nations shall come: and I will fill [2]this house with [b]glory, saith the LORD of hosts.

8 The silver *is* mine, and the gold *is* mine, saith the LORD of hosts.

9 [a]The glory of [1]this latter house shall be greater than of the former, saith the LORD of hosts: and in this place will I give [b]peace, saith the LORD of hosts.

10 In the four and twentieth *day* of the ninth *month,* in the second year of Darius, came the word of the LORD by Haggai the prophet, saying,

11 Thus saith the LORD of hosts; [a]Ask now the priests *concerning* the law, saying,

12 If one bear holy flesh in the [1]skirt of his garment, and with his [1]skirt do touch bread, or [2]pottage, or wine, or oil, or any meat, shall it be holy? And the priests answered and said, No.

13 Then said Haggai, If *one that is* [a]unclean by a dead body touch any of these, shall it be unclean? And the priests answered and said, It shall be unclean.

14 Then answered Haggai, and said, [a]So *is* this people, and so *is* this nation before me, saith the LORD; and so *is* every work of their hands; and that which they offer there *is* unclean.

15 And now, I pray you, [a]consider from this day and upward, from before a stone was laid upon a stone in the temple of the LORD:

16 Since those *days* were, [a]when one came to an heap of twenty [1]*measures,* there were *but* ten: when *one* came to the pressfat for to draw out fifty [2]*vessels* out of the press, there were *but* twenty.

17 [a]I [1]smote you with [2]blasting and with mildew and with hail [b]in all the labours of your hands; [c]yet ye *turned* not to me, saith the LORD.

18 Consider now from this day and [1]upward, from the four and twentieth day of the ninth *month, even* from [a]the day that the foundation of the LORD's temple was laid, consider *it.*

19 [a]Is the seed yet in the barn? yea, as yet the vine, and the fig tree, and the pomegranate, and the olive tree, hath not brought forth: from this day will I [b]bless *you.*

20 And again the word of the LORD came unto Haggai in the four and twentieth *day* of the month, saying,

21 Speak to Zerubbabel, [a]governor of Judah, saying, [b]I will shake the heavens and the earth;

22 And [a]I will overthrow the throne of kingdoms, and I will destroy the strength of the kingdoms of the [1]heathen; and [b]I will overthrow the chariots, and those that ride in them; and the horses and their riders shall come down, every one by the sword of his brother.

23 In that day, saith the LORD of hosts, will I take thee, O Zerubbabel, my servant, the son of Shealtiel, saith the LORD, [a]and will make thee as [1]a signet: for [b]I have chosen thee, saith the LORD of hosts.

---

2:5 [a] Ex. 29:45, 46 [b] [Neh. 9:20]; Is. 63:11, 14
2:6 [a] Heb. 12:26 [b] [Joel 3:16] [1] *once more*
2:7 [a] Gen. 49:10; Mal. 3:1 [b] 1 Kin. 8:11; Is. 60:7; Zech. 2:5 [1] *Or Desire of All Nations* [2] *The temple*
2:9 [a] [John 1:14] [b] Ps. 85:8, 9; Luke 2:14; [Eph. 2:14] [1] *The temple*
2:11 [a] Lev. 10:10, 11; Deut. 33:10; Mal. 2:7
2:12 [1] *fold,* lit. *wing* [2] *stew*
2:13 [a] Lev. 22:4–6; Num. 19:11, 22
2:14 [a] [Titus 1:15]
2:15 [a] Hag. 1:5, 7; 2:18
2:16 [a] Hag. 1:6, 9; Zech. 8:10 [1] *Ephahs* [2] *Baths*
2:17 [a] Deut. 28:22; 1 Kin. 8:37; Amos 4:9 [b] Hag. 1:11 [c] Jer. 5:3; Amos 4:6–11 [1] *struck* [2] *blight*
2:18 [a] Ezra 5:1, 2, 16; Zech. 8:9 [1] *forward*
2:19 [a] Zech. 8:12 [b] Ps. 128:1–6; Jer. 31:12, 14; [Mal. 3:10]
2:21 [a] Ezra 5:2; Hag. 1:1, 14; Zech. 4:6–10 [b] Hag. 2:6, 7; [Heb. 12:26, 27]
2:22 [a] [Dan. 2:44; Rev. 19:11–21]

[b] Ps. 46:9; Ezek. 39:20; Mic. 5:10; Zech. 9:10 [1] *Gentiles* 2:23 [a] Song 8:6; Jer. 22:24 [b] Is. 42:1; 43:10 [1] *a signet* ring

# THE BOOK OF
# ZECHARIAH

For a dozen years or more, the task of rebuilding the temple has been half completed. Zechariah is commissioned by God to encourage the people in their unfinished responsibility. Rather than exhorting them to action with strong words of rebuke, Zechariah seeks to encourage them to action by reminding them of the future importance of the temple. The temple must be built, for one day the Messiah's glory will inhabit it. But future blessing is contingent upon present obedience. The people are not merely building a building; they are building the future. With that as their motivation, they can enter into the building project with wholehearted zeal, for their Messiah is coming.

*Zekar-yah* means "Yahweh Remembers" or "Yahweh Has Remembered." This theme dominates the whole book: Israel will be blessed because Yahweh remembers the covenant He made with the fathers. The Greek and Latin version of his name is *Zacharias.*

## CHAPTER 1

IN the eighth month, ᵃin the second year of Darius, came the word of the LORD ᵇunto Zechariah, the son of Berechiah, the son of ᶜIddo the prophet, saying,

2 The LORD hath been ¹sore displeased with your fathers.

3 Therefore say thou unto them, Thus saith the LORD of hosts; ¹Turn ᵃye unto me, saith the LORD of hosts, and I will ¹turn unto you, saith the LORD of hosts.

4 Be ye not as your fathers, ᵃunto whom the former prophets have ¹cried, saying, Thus saith the LORD of hosts; ᵇTurn ye now from your evil ways, and *from* your evil ²doings: but they did not hear, nor ³hearken unto me, saith the LORD.

5 Your fathers, where *are* they? and the prophets, do they live for ever?

6 But ᵃmy words and my statutes, which I commanded my servants the prophets, did they not ¹take hold of your fathers? and they returned and said, ᵇLike² as the LORD of hosts ³thought to do unto us, according to our ways, and according to our ⁴doings, so hath he dealt with us.

7 Upon the four and twentieth day of the eleventh month, which *is* the month ¹Sebat, in the second year of Darius, came the word of the LORD unto Zechariah, the son of Berechiah, the son of Iddo the prophet, saying,

8 I saw by night, and behold ᵃa man riding upon a red horse, and he stood among the myrtle trees that *were* in the ¹bottom; and behind him *were there* ᵇred horses, ²speckled, and white.

9 Then said I, O ᵃmy lord, what *are* these? And the angel that talked with me said unto me, I will shew thee what these *be.*

10 And the man that stood among the myrtle trees answered and said, ᵃThese *are they* whom the LORD hath sent to walk to and fro through the earth.

11 ᵃAnd they answered the angel of the LORD that stood among the myrtle trees, and said, We have walked to and fro through the earth, and, behold, all the earth ¹sitteth still, and is at rest.

12 Then the angel of the LORD answered and said, O LORD of hosts, ᵃhow long wilt thou not have mercy on Jerusalem and on the cities of Judah, against which thou hast had indignation ᵇthese threescore and ten years?

13 And the LORD answered the angel that talked with me *with* ᵃgood words *and* ¹comfortable words.

14 So the angel that ¹communed with me said unto me, ²Cry thou, saying, Thus saith the LORD of hosts; I am ᵃjealous³ for Jerusalem and for Zion with a great jealousy.

15 And I am very ¹sore displeased with the ²heathen *that are* at ease: for ᵃI was but a little ³displeased, ⁴and they helped forward the affliction.

16 Therefore thus saith the LORD; ᵃI am returned to Jerusalem with mercies: my ᵇhouse ᶜshall be built in it, saith the LORD of hosts, and ᵈa ¹line shall be stretched forth upon Jerusalem.

17 ¹Cry yet, saying, Thus saith the LORD of hosts; My cities ²through prosperity shall yet be spread abroad; ᵃand the LORD shall ³yet comfort Zion, and ᵇshall ³yet choose Jerusalem.

18 Then lifted I up mine eyes, and saw, and behold four ᵃhorns.

19 And I said unto the angel that talked with me, What *be* these? And he answered me, ᵃThese *are* the ¹horns which have scattered Judah, Israel, and Jerusalem.

1:1 ᵃ Zech. 7:1
ᵇ Matt. 23:35
ᶜ Neh. 12:4, 16
1:2 ¹ *very angry*
1:3 ᵃ [Mal. 3:7–10]
¹ *Return*
1:4 ᵃ 2 Chr. 36:15, 16 ᵇ Is. 31:6 ¹ *preached* ² *deeds* ³ *heed*
1:6 ᵃ [Is. 55:11]
ᵇ Lam. 1:18; 2:17
¹ *overtake* ² *Just like* ³ *determined* ⁴ *deeds*
1:7 ¹ *Shebat*
1:8 ᵃ [Rev. 6:4]
ᵇ [Zech. 6:2–7]
¹ *hollow* ² *sorrel*
1:9 ᵃ Zech. 4:4, 5, 13; 6:4
1:10 ᵃ [Heb. 1:14]
1:11 ᵃ [Ps. 103:20, 21] ¹ *is resting quietly*
1:12 ᵃ Ps. 74:10
ᵇ Jer. 25:11, 12; 29:10
1:13 ᵃ Jer. 29:10
¹ *comforting*
1:14 ᵃ Zech. 8:2
¹ *spoke* ² *Proclaim* ³ *zealous*
1:15 ᵃ Is. 47:6 ¹ *exceedingly angry* ² *nations* ³ *angry* ⁴ *but they helped with evil intent*
1:16 ᵃ [Zech. 2:10; 8:3] ᵇ Ezra 6:14, 15 ᶜ Is. 44:28 ᵈ Zech. 2:1–3 ¹ *surveyor's line*
1:17 ᵃ [Is. 40:1, 2; 51:3] ᵇ Zech. 2:12 ¹ *Proclaim again* ² Lit. *shall again overflow from prosperity* ³ *again*
1:18 ᵃ [Lam. 2:17]
1:19 ᵃ Ezra 4:1, 4, 7 ¹ *Kingdoms or powers*

20 And the LORD shewed me four [1]carpenters.

21 Then said I, What come these to do? And he spake, saying, These *are* the [a]horns which have scattered Judah, so that no man did lift up his head: but [1]these are come to [2]fray them, to cast out the horns of the [3]Gentiles, which [b]lifted up *their* horn over the land of Judah to scatter it.

## CHAPTER 2

I LIFTED up mine eyes again, and looked, and behold [a]a man with a measuring line in his hand.

2 Then said I, Whither goest thou? And he said unto me, [a]To measure Jerusalem, to see what *is* the breadth thereof, and what *is* the length thereof.

3 And, behold, the angel that talked with me went forth, and another angel went out to meet him,

4 And said unto him, Run, speak to this young man, saying, [a]Jerusalem shall be inhabited *as* towns without walls [1]for the multitude of men and cattle therein:

5 For I, saith the LORD, will be unto her [a]a wall of fire round about, [b]and will be the glory in the midst of her.

6 [1]Ho, ho, *come forth,* and flee [a]from the land of the north, saith the LORD: for I have [b]spread you abroad as the four winds of the heaven, saith the LORD.

7 [a]Deliver[1] thyself, O Zion, that dwellest *with* the daughter of Babylon.

8 For thus saith the LORD of hosts; After the glory hath he sent me unto the nations which [1]spoiled you: for he that [a]toucheth you toucheth the [2]apple of his eye.

9 For, behold, I will [a]shake mine hand [1]upon them, and they shall be a [2]spoil to their servants: and [b]ye shall know that the LORD of hosts hath sent me.

10 [a]Sing and rejoice, O daughter of Zion: for, lo, I [1]come, and I [b]will dwell in the midst of thee, saith the LORD.

11 [a]And many nations shall be joined to the LORD [b]in that day, and shall be [c]my people: and I will dwell in the midst of thee, and [d]thou shalt know that the LORD of hosts hath sent me unto thee.

12 And the LORD shall [a]inherit[1] Judah [2]his portion in the holy land, and shall choose Jerusalem again.

13 [a]Be silent, O all flesh, before the LORD: for he is [1]raised up [b]out of his holy habitation.

## CHAPTER 3

A ND he shewed me [a]Joshua the high priest standing before the angel of the LORD, and [b]Satan[1] standing at his right hand to [2]resist him.

2 And the LORD said unto Satan, [a]The LORD rebuke thee, O Satan; even the LORD that [b]hath chosen Jerusalem rebuke thee: [c]*is* not this a brand plucked out of the fire?

3 Now Joshua was clothed with [a]filthy garments, and stood before the angel.

4 And he answered and spake unto those that stood before him, saying, Take away the filthy garments from him. And unto him he said, Behold, I have caused thine iniquity to pass from thee, [a]and I will clothe thee with [1]change of raiment.

5 And I said, Let them set a [1]fair [a]mitre upon his head. So they set a fair mitre upon his head, and clothed him with garments. And the angel of the LORD stood by.

6 And the angel of the LORD [1]protested unto Joshua, saying,

7 Thus saith the LORD of hosts; If thou wilt walk in my ways, and if thou wilt [a]keep my [1]charge, then thou shalt also [b]judge my house, and shalt also keep my courts, and I will give thee places to walk among these that [c]stand [2]by.

8 Hear now, O Joshua the high priest, thou, and thy [1]fellows that sit before thee: for they *are* [a]men[2] wondered at: for, behold, I will bring forth [b]my servant the [c]BRANCH.

9 For behold the stone that I have laid before Joshua; [a]upon one stone *shall be* [b]seven eyes: behold, I will engrave the [1]graving thereof, saith the LORD of hosts, and [c]I will remove the iniquity of that land in one day.

10 [a]In that day, saith the LORD of hosts, shall ye call every man his neighbour [b]under the vine and under the fig tree.

## CHAPTER 4

A ND [a]the angel that talked with me came again, and waked me, [b]as a man that is wakened out of his sleep,

2 And said unto me, What seest thou? And I said, I have looked, and behold [a]a [1]candlestick all *of* gold, with a bowl upon the top of it, [b]and his seven lamps thereon, and seven pipes to the seven lamps, which *are* upon the top thereof:

3 [a]And two olive trees by it, one upon the right *side* of the bowl, and the other upon the left *side* thereof.

4 So I answered and spake to the angel that talked with me, saying, What *are* these, my lord?

5 Then the angel that talked with me answered and said unto me, Knowest thou not what these be? And I said, No, my lord.

6 Then he answered and spake unto me, saying, This *is* the word of the LORD unto [a]Zerubbabel, saying,

1:20 [1] *craftsmen*
1:21 [a] [Ps. 75:10]
[b] Ps. 75:4, 5 [1] The craftsmen [2] *terrify* [3] *nations*
2:1 [a] Jer. 31:39
2:2 [a] Rev. 11:1
2:4 [a] Jer. 31:27 [1] *because of*
2:5 [a] [Is. 26:1]
[b] [Is. 60:19]
2:6 [a] Is. 48:20
[b] Deut. 28:64 [1] *Up, up*
2:7 [a] Is. 48:20 [1] *Up, Zion! Escape*
2:8 [a] Deut. 32:10 [1] *plundered* [2] *pupil*
2:9 [a] Is. 19:16 [b] Zech. 4:9 [1] *against* [2] *plunder*
2:10 [a] Is. 12:6 [b] [Lev. 26:12] [1] *am coming*
2:11 [a] [Is. 2:2, 3] [b] Zech. 3:10 [c] Ex. 12:49 [d] Ezek. 33:33
2:12 [a] [Deut. 32:9] [1] *possess* [2] *as his inheritance*
2:13 [a] Hab. 2:20 [b] Ps. 68:5 [1] *aroused from*
3:1 [a] Hag. 1:1 [b] Ps. 109:6 [1] *Lit. The Adversary* [2] *oppose*
3:2 [a] [Jude 9] [b] [Rom. 8:33] [c] Amos 4:11
3:3 [a] Is. 64:6
3:4 [a] Is. 61:10 [1] *rich robes*
3:5 [a] Ex. 29:6 [1] *clean turban*
3:6 [1] *admonished*
3:7 [a] Lev. 8:35 [b] Deut. 17:9, 12 [c] Zech. 4:4 [1] *command* [2] *here*
3:8 [a] Ps. 71:7 [b] Is. 42:1 [c] Is. 11:1; 53:2 [1] *companions* [2] *a wondrous sign,* lit. *men of a sign*
3:9 [a] [Zech. 4:10] [b] Ps. 118:22 [c] Jer. 31:34; 50:20 [1] *inscription*
3:10 [a] Zech. 2:11 [b] Is. 36:16
4:1 [a] Zech. 1:9; 2:13 [b] Dan. 8:18
4:2 [a] Rev. 1:12 [b] [Rev. 4:5] [1] *lampstand*
4:3 [a] Rev. 11:3, 4
4:6 [a] Hag. 1:1

[b]Not by might, nor by power, but by my spirit, saith the LORD of hosts.

7 Who *art* thou, [a]O great [1]mountain? before Zerubbabel *thou shalt become* a plain: and he shall bring forth [b]the [2]headstone *thereof* [c]*with* shoutings, *crying,* Grace, grace unto it.

8 Moreover the word of the LORD came unto me, saying,

9 The hands of Zerubbabel [a]have laid the foundation of [1]this house; his hands [b]shall also finish it; and [c]thou shalt know that the [d]LORD of hosts hath sent me unto you.

10 For who hath despised the day of [a]small things? for [1]they shall rejoice, and shall see the plummet in the hand of Zerubbabel *with* those seven; [b]they *are* the eyes of the LORD, which [2]run to and fro through the whole earth.

11 Then answered I, and said unto him, What *are* these [a]two olive trees upon the right *side* of the [1]candlestick and upon the left *side* thereof?

12 And I answered again, and said unto him, What *be these* two olive branches [1]which through the two golden pipes empty the golden *oil* out of themselves?

13 And he answered me and said, Knowest thou not what these *be?* And I said, No, my lord.

14 Then said he, [a]These *are* the two [1]anointed ones, [b]that stand by the Lord of the whole earth.

## CHAPTER 5

THEN I turned, and lifted up mine eyes, and looked, and behold a flying [a]roll.[1]

2 And he said unto me, What seest thou? And I answered, I see a flying [1]roll; the length thereof *is* twenty cubits, and the breadth thereof ten cubits.

3 Then said he unto me, This *is* the [a]curse that goeth forth over the face of the whole earth: for every one that stealeth shall be [1]cut off *as* on this side according to it; and every one that [2]sweareth shall be cut off *as* on that side according to it.

4 I will bring [1]it forth, saith the LORD of hosts, and it shall enter into the house of the [a]thief, and into the house of [b]him that sweareth falsely by my name: and it shall remain in the midst of his house, and [c]shall consume it with the timber thereof and the stones thereof.

5 Then the angel that talked with me went forth, and said unto me, Lift up now thine eyes, and see what *is* this that goeth forth.

6 And I said, What *is* it? And he said, This *is* [1]an ephah that goeth forth. He said moreover, This *is* their resemblance through all the earth.

4:6 [b] Hos. 1:7
4:7 [a] Jer. 51:25
[b] Ps. 118:22  [c] Ezra 3:10, 11, 13  [1] Difficulty or obstacle  [2] capstone
4:9 [a] Ezra 3:8–10; 5:16  [b] Ezra 6:14, 15  [c] Zech. 2:9, 11; 6:15  [d] [Is. 43:16]  [1] The temple
4:10 [a] Hag. 2:3  [b] 2 Chr. 16:9  [1] *these seven rejoice to see the plumbline in the hand of Zerubbabel;* [2] *scan*
4:11 [a] Zech. 4:3  [1] *lampstand*
4:12 [1] *that drip into the hand (receptacle) of the gold pipes from which the golden oil drains*
4:14 [a] Rev. 11:4  [b] Zech. 3:1–7  [1] Lit. *sons of fresh oil*
5:1 [a] Ezek. 2:9  [1] *scroll*
5:2 [1] *scroll*
5:3 [a] Mal. 4:6  [1] *purged out, expelled*  [2] *swears falsely*
5:4 [a] Ex. 20:15  [b] Lev. 19:12  [c] Lev. 14:34, 35  [1] The curse
5:6 [1] *a basket, a measuring container*
5:7 [1] *lead disc or cover*  [2] *inside the basket*
5:8 [1] *thrust her down*  [2] *basket*  [3] Lit. *lead stone*
5:9 [a] Lev. 11:13, 19  [1] *basket*
5:10 [a] Zech. 5:5  [1] *carry the basket*
5:11 [a] Jer. 29:5, 28  [b] Gen. 10:10  [1] Babylon  [2] *when it is ready*  [3] *the basket will be set*
6:1 [1] *bronze*
6:2 [a] Zech. 1:8  [b] Rev. 6:5  [1] With
6:3 [1] *with*  [2] *dappled horses*  [3] *strong steeds*
6:4 [a] Zech. 5:10
6:5 [a] [Heb. 1:7, 14]  [b] Dan. 7:10  [1] *their station*
6:6 [a] Jer. 1:14  [1] With their chariot  [2] *dappled*
6:7 [a] Gen. 1:10  [1] *strong steeds*  [2] *eager to go*
6:8 [a] Eccl. 10:4  [1] *he called to me*  [2] *appeased*
6:10 [1] Receive the gift *from the captives*
6:11 [a] Ex. 29:6  [1] *an elaborate crown*  [2] it

7 And, behold, there was lifted up a [1]talent of lead: and this *is* a woman that sitteth [2]in the midst of the ephah.

8 And he said, This *is* wickedness. And he [1]cast it into the midst of the [2]ephah; and he cast the [3]weight of lead upon the mouth thereof.

9 Then lifted I up mine eyes, and looked, and, behold, there came out two women, and the wind *was* in their wings; for they had wings like the wings of a [a]stork: and they lifted up the [1]ephah between the earth and the heaven.

10 Then said I to the [a]angel that talked with me, Whither do these [1]bear the ephah?

11 And he said unto me, To [a]build it an house in [b]the land of [1]Shinar: [2]and it shall be established, [3]and set there upon her own base.

## CHAPTER 6

AND I turned, and lifted up mine eyes, and looked, and, behold, there came four chariots out from between two mountains; and the mountains *were* mountains of [1]brass.

2 [1]In the first chariot *were* [a]red horses; and [1]in the second chariot [b]black horses;

3 And [1]in the third chariot white horses; and [1]in the fourth chariot [2]grisled and [3]bay horses.

4 Then I answered [a]and said unto the angel that talked with me, What *are* these, my lord?

5 And the angel answered and said unto me, [a]These *are* the four spirits of the heavens, which go forth from [b]standing[1] before the Lord of all the earth.

6 The black horses which *are* [1]therein go forth into [a]the north country; and the white go forth after them; and the [2]grisled go forth toward the south country.

7 And the [1]bay went forth, [2]and sought to go that they might [a]walk to and fro through the earth: and he said, Get you hence, walk to and fro through the earth. So they walked to and fro through the earth.

8 Then [1]cried he upon me, and spake unto me, saying, Behold, these that go toward the north country have [2]quieted my [a]spirit in the north country.

9 And the word of the LORD came unto me, saying,

10 [1]Take of *them of* the captivity, *even* of Heldai, of Tobijah, and of Jedaiah, which are come from Babylon, and come thou the same day, and go into the house of Josiah the son of Zephaniah;

11 Then take silver and gold, and make [a]crowns,[1] and set [2]*them* upon

the head of ᵇJoshua the son of ³Josedech, the high priest;

12 And speak unto him, saying, Thus speaketh the LORD of hosts, saying, Behold ᵃthe man whose name *is* The ᵇBRANCH; and he shall ¹grow up out of his place, ᶜand he shall build the temple of the LORD:

13 Even he shall build the temple of the LORD; and he ᵃshall bear the glory, and shall sit and rule upon his throne; and ᵇhe shall be a priest upon his throne: and the counsel of peace shall be between ¹them both.

14 And the ¹crowns shall be to Helem, and to Tobijah, and to Jedaiah, and to Hen the son of Zephaniah, ᵃfor a memorial in the temple of the LORD.

15 And ᵃthey *that are* far off shall come and build in the temple of the LORD, and ye shall know that the LORD of hosts hath sent me unto you. And *this* shall come to pass, if ye will diligently obey the voice of the LORD your God.

## CHAPTER 7

AND it came to pass in the fourth year of king Darius, *that* the word of the LORD came unto Zechariah in the fourth *day* of the ninth month, *even* in ¹Chisleu;

2 When ¹they had sent unto ²the house of God ³Sherezer and Regemmelech, and their men, to pray before the LORD,

3 *And* to ᵃspeak unto the priests which *were* in the house of the LORD of hosts, and to the prophets, saying, Should I weep in ᵇthe fifth month, ¹separating myself, as I have done these so many years?

4 Then came the word of the LORD of hosts unto me, saying,

5 Speak unto all the people of the land, and to the priests, saying, When ye ᵃfasted and mourned in the fifth ᵇand seventh *month*, ᶜeven those seventy years, did ye at all fast ᵈunto me, *even* to me?

6 ᵃAnd when ye did eat, and when ye did drink, did not ye eat *for yourselves*, and drink *for yourselves?*

7 *Should ye* not ¹hear the words which the LORD hath ²cried by the ᵃformer prophets, when Jerusalem was inhabited and in prosperity, and the cities thereof round about her, when *men* inhabited ᵇthe ³south and the ⁴plain?

8 And the word of the LORD came unto Zechariah, saying,

9 Thus speaketh the LORD of hosts, saying, ᵃExecute true ¹judgment, and shew ²mercy and compassions every man to his brother:

10 And ᵃoppress not the widow, nor the fatherless, the stranger, nor the

6:11 ᵇ Hag. 1:1
³ *Jehozadak,*
1 Chr. 6:15
6:12 ᵃ John 1:45
ᵇ Zech. 3:8 ᶜ [Eph. 2:20] ¹ *branch out from*
6:13 ᵃ Is. 22:24
ᵇ Ps. 110:4 ¹ Both offices
6:14 ᵃ Ex. 12:14
¹ *elaborate crown*
6:15 ᵃ Is. 57:19
7:1 ¹ Or *Chisleu*
7:2 ¹ The people
² Heb. *Beth-el*
³ Or *Sar-ezar*
7:3 ᵃ Mal. 2:7
ᵇ Zech. 8:19 ¹ *and fast*
7:5 ᵃ [Is. 58:1–9]
ᵇ Jer. 41:1 ᶜ Zech. 1:12 ᵈ [Rom. 14:6]
7:6 ¹ 1 Chr. 29:22
7:7 ᵃ Zech. 1:4
ᵇ Jer. 17:26 ¹ Obey
² *proclaimed*
³ Heb. *Negev*
⁴ Heb. *shephelah, lowland*
7:9 ᵃ Jer. 7:28
¹ *justice* ² *loving-kindness*
7:10 ᵃ Ex. 22:22
ᵇ Mic. 2:1 ¹ *plan*
7:11 ᵃ Neh. 9:29
ᵇ Jer. 17:23 ¹ Lit. *gave a rebellious or stubborn shoulder* ² Lit. *made their ears heavy*
7:12 ᵃ Ezek. 11:19
ᵇ Neh. 9:29, 30
ᶜ Dan. 9:11, 12
¹ *flint*
7:13 ᵃ Prov. 1:24–28 ¹ *called, proclaimed*
7:14 ᵃ Deut. 4:27; 28:64
8:2 ᵃ Zech. 1:14
¹ *zealous* ² *zeal*
³ *fervour*
8:3 ᵃ Zech. 1:16
ᵇ Zech. 2:10, 11 ᶜ Is. 1:21 ᵈ [Is. 2:2, 3]
ᵉ Jer. 31:23 ¹ *will return*
8:4 ᵃ Is. 65:20
¹ *again* ² *sit*
³ *because of advanced age*
8:5 ᵃ Jer. 30:19, 20
8:6 ᵃ [Luke 1:37]
¹ *extraordinary*
8:7 ᵃ Is. 11:11 ¹ Lit. *land of the rising sun and the land of the setting sun*
8:8 ᵃ Zeph. 3:20
ᵇ [Jer. 30:22; 31:1, 33] ᶜ Jer. 4:2
¹ *bring them back*
8:9 ᵃ Hag. 2:4
ᵇ Ezra 5:1, 2; 6:14
ᶜ Hag. 2:18
8:10 ᵃ Hag. 1:6, 9
¹ *wage*

poor; ᵇand let none of you ¹imagine evil against his brother in your heart.

11 But they refused to hearken, and ᵃpulled¹ away the shoulder, and ᵇstopped² their ears, that they should not hear.

12 Yea, they made their ᵃhearts *as* ¹an adamant stone, ᵇlest they should hear the law, and the words which the LORD of hosts hath sent in his spirit by the former prophets: ᶜtherefore came a great wrath from the LORD of hosts.

13 Therefore it is come to pass, *that* as he ¹cried, and they would not hear; so ᵃthey ¹cried, and I would not hear, saith the LORD of hosts:

14 But ᵃI scattered them with a whirlwind among all the nations whom they knew not. Thus the land was desolate after them, that no man passed through nor returned: for they laid the pleasant land desolate.

## CHAPTER 8

AGAIN the word of the LORD of hosts came *to me,* saying,

2 Thus saith the LORD of hosts; ᵃI was ¹jealous for Zion with great ²jealousy, and I was ¹jealous for her with great ³fury.

3 Thus saith the LORD; I ¹am ᵃreturned unto Zion, and will ᵇdwell in the midst of Jerusalem: and ᶜJerusalem ᶜshall be called a city of truth; and ᵈthe mountain of the LORD of hosts ᵉthe holy mountain.

4 Thus saith the LORD of hosts; ᵃThere shall ¹yet old men and old women ²dwell in the streets of Jerusalem, and every man with his staff in his hand ³for very age.

5 And the streets of the city shall be ᵃfull of boys and girls playing in the streets thereof.

6 Thus saith the LORD of hosts; If it be ¹marvellous in the eyes of the remnant of this people in these days, ᵃshould it also be ¹marvellous in mine eyes? saith the LORD of hosts.

7 Thus saith the LORD of hosts; Behold, ᵃI will save my people from the ¹east country, and from the west country;

8 And I will ᵃbring¹ them, and they shall dwell in the midst of Jerusalem: ᵇand they shall be my people, and I will be their God, ᶜin truth and in righteousness.

9 Thus saith the LORD of hosts; ᵃLet your hands be strong, ye that hear in these days these words by the mouth of ᵇthe prophets, which *were* in ᶜthe day *that* the foundation of the house of the LORD of hosts was laid, that the temple might be built.

10 For before these days there was no ᵃhire¹ for man, nor any hire for beast; neither *was there any* peace

to him that went out or came in because of the [2]affliction: for I set all men every one against his neighbour.

11 [a]But now I *will* not *be* unto the [1]residue of this people as in the former days, saith the LORD of hosts.

12 [a]For [1]the seed *shall be* prosperous; the vine shall give her fruit, and [b]the ground shall give her increase, and [c]the heavens shall give their dew; and I will cause the remnant of this people to possess all these *things.*

13 And it shall come to pass, *that* as ye were [a]a curse among the [1]heathen, O house of Judah, and house of Israel; so will I save you, and [b]ye shall be a blessing: fear not, *but* let your hands be strong.

14 For thus saith the LORD of hosts; [a]As I [1]thought to punish you, when your fathers provoked me to wrath, saith the LORD of hosts, [b]and I [2]repented not:

15 So again have I [1]thought in these days to do well unto Jerusalem and to the house of Judah: fear ye not.

16 These *are* the things that ye shall [a]do; [b]Speak ye every man the truth to his neighbour; execute the judgment [1]of truth and peace in your gates:

17 [a]And let none of you [1]imagine evil in your hearts against his neighbour; and love no false oath: for all these *are things* that I hate, saith the LORD.

18 And the word of the LORD of hosts came unto me, saying,

19 Thus saith the LORD of hosts; [a]The fast of the fourth *month,* [b]and the fast of the fifth, [c]and the fast of the seventh, [d]and the fast of the tenth, shall be to the house of Judah [e]joy and gladness, and cheerful feasts; [f]therefore love the truth and peace.

20 Thus saith the LORD of hosts; *It shall* yet *come to pass,* that there shall come [1]people, and the inhabitants of many cities:

21 And the inhabitants of one *city* shall go to another, saying, [a]Let us go [1]speedily to pray before the LORD, and to seek the LORD of hosts: I will go also.

22 Yea, [a]many people and strong nations shall come to seek the LORD of hosts in Jerusalem, and to pray before the LORD.

23 Thus saith the LORD of hosts; In those days *it shall come to pass,* that ten men shall [a]take hold out of all languages of the nations, even shall [b]take hold of the [1]skirt of him that is a Jew, saying, We will go with you: for we have heard [c]*that* God *is* with you.

## CHAPTER 9

THE [1]burden of the word of the LORD [2]in the land of Hadrach, and

[a]Damascus *shall be* the [3]rest thereof: when [b]the eyes of man, as of all the tribes of Israel, *shall be* toward the LORD.

2 [1]And [a]Hamath [2]also shall border thereby; [b]Tyrus, and [c]Zidon, though [3]it be very [d]wise.

3 And Tyrus did build herself a strong hold, and heaped up silver as the dust, and fine gold as the mire of the streets.

4 Behold, [a]the Lord will cast her out, and he will smite [b]her power in the sea; and she shall be devoured with fire.

5 Ashkelon shall see *it,* and fear; Gaza also *shall see it,* and be very sorrowful, and [a]Ekron; for her expectation [1]shall be ashamed; and the king shall perish from Gaza, and Ashkelon shall not be inhabited.

6 And a [1]bastard shall dwell [a]in Ashdod, and I will cut off the pride of the [b]Philistines.

7 And I will take away his blood out of his mouth, and his abominations from between his teeth: but he that remaineth, even he, *shall be* for our God, and he shall be as a [1]governor in Judah, and Ekron as a Jebusite.

8 And [a]I will encamp about mine house because of the army, because of him that passeth by, and because of him that returneth: and no oppressor shall pass through them any more: for now have I seen with mine eyes.

9 [a]Rejoice greatly, O daughter of Zion; shout, O daughter of Jerusalem: behold, [b]thy King cometh unto thee: he *is* [1]just, and having salvation; [2]lowly, and riding upon an ass, and upon a colt the foal of an ass.

10 And I [a]will cut off the chariot from Ephraim, and the horse from Jerusalem, and the [b]battle bow shall be cut off: and he shall speak peace unto the [1]heathen: and his [c]dominion *shall be* from sea *even* to sea, and from the river *even* to the ends of the earth.

11 As for thee also, [1]by the blood of thy covenant I have sent forth thy [a]prisoners out of the pit wherein *is* no water.

12 Turn you to the strong hold, [a]ye prisoners of hope: even to day do I declare *that* I will [1]render [b]double unto thee;

13 [1]When I have bent Judah [2]for me, filled the bow with Ephraim, and raised up thy sons, O Zion, against thy sons, O Greece, and made thee as the sword of a mighty man.

14 And the LORD shall be seen over them, and [a]his arrow shall go forth as the lightning: and the Lord GOD shall blow the trumpet, and shall go [b]with whirlwinds of the south.

15 The LORD of hosts shall [a]defend them; and they shall devour, and subdue with sling stones; and they shall drink, *and* [1]make a noise as [2]through wine; and they shall be [3]filled like [4]bowls, *and* as the corners of the altar.

16 And the LORD their God shall [a]save them in that day as the flock of his people: for [b]*they shall be as* the [1]stones of a crown, [c]lifted up as [2]an ensign upon his land.

17 For [a]how great *is* [1]his goodness, and how great *is* [1]his [b]beauty! [c]corn[2] shall make the young men [3]cheerful, and new wine the maids.

### CHAPTER 10

ASK ye [a]of the LORD [b]rain [c]in the time of [1]the latter rain; *so* the LORD shall make [2]bright clouds, and give them showers of rain, to every one grass in the field.

2 For the [a]idols[1] have spoken [2]vanity, and the diviners have seen a [b]lie, and have told false dreams; they [c]comfort in vain: therefore [3]they went their way as a [d]flock, they were [4]troubled, [e]because *there was* no shepherd.

3 Mine anger was kindled against the [a]shepherds, [b]and I punished the [1]goats: for the LORD of hosts [c]hath visited his flock the house of Judah, and [d]hath made them as his [2]goodly horse in the battle.

4 Out of him [1]came forth [a]the corner, out of him [b]the [2]nail, out of him the battle bow, out of him every [3]oppressor together.

5 And they shall be as mighty *men,* which [a]tread down *their enemies* in the mire of the streets in the battle: and they shall fight, because the LORD *is* with them, and the riders on horses shall be [1]confounded.

6 And I will strengthen the house of Judah, and I will save the house of Joseph, and [a]I will bring them again to place them; for I [b]have mercy upon them: and they shall be as though I had not cast them off: for I *am* the LORD their God, and [c]will hear them.

7 And *they of* Ephraim shall be like a mighty *man,* and their [a]heart shall rejoice as through wine: yea, their children shall see *it,* and be glad; their heart shall rejoice in the LORD.

8 I will [a]hiss[1] for them, and gather them; for I have redeemed them: [b]and they shall increase as they [2]have increased.

9 And [a]I will [1]sow them among the [2]people: and they shall [b]remember me in far countries; and they shall live with their children, and [3]turn again.

10 [a]I will bring them again also out of the land of Egypt, and gather them out of Assyria; and I will bring them

into the land of Gilead and Lebanon; [b]and[1] *place* shall not be found for them.

11 [a]And he shall pass through the sea with affliction, and shall smite the waves in the sea, and all the deeps of [1]the river shall dry up: and [b]the pride of Assyria shall be brought down, and [c]the sceptre of Egypt shall depart away.

12 And I will strengthen them in the LORD; and [a]they shall walk up and down in his name, saith the LORD.

### CHAPTER 11

OPEN [a]thy doors, O Lebanon, that the fire may devour thy cedars.

2 [1]Howl, fir tree; for the [a]cedar is fallen; because the [2]mighty are spoiled: howl, O ye oaks of Bashan; [b]for [3]the forest of the vintage is come down.

3 *There is* [1]a voice of the howling of the [a]shepherds; for their glory is [2]spoiled: a voice of the roaring of young lions; for the [3]pride of Jordan is [2]spoiled.

4 Thus saith the LORD my God; Feed the flock [1]of the slaughter;

5 Whose [1]possessors slay them, and [a]hold themselves not guilty: and they that sell them [b]say, Blessed *be* the LORD; for I am rich: and their own shepherds pity them [c]not.

6 For I will no more pity the inhabitants of the land, saith the LORD: but, lo, I will deliver the men every one into his neighbour's hand, and into the hand of his king: and they shall [1]smite the land, and out of their hand I will not deliver *them.*

7 And I will feed the flock [1]of slaughter, [2]*even* you, [a]O poor of the flock. And I took unto me two [3]staves; the one I called [4]Beauty, and the other I called [5]Bands; and I fed the flock.

8 Three shepherds also I [1]cut off [a]in one month; and my soul lothed them, and their soul also abhorred me.

9 Then said I, I will not feed you: [a]that that dieth, let it die; and that that is [1]to be cut off, let it [2]be cut off; and let the rest eat every one the flesh [3]of another.

10 And I took my staff, *even* [1]Beauty, and cut it asunder, that I might break my covenant which I had made with all the people.

11 And it was broken in that day: and so [a]the poor of the flock that [1]waited upon me knew that it *was* the word of the LORD.

12 And I said unto them, [1]If ye think good, give *me* my [2]price; and if not,

9:15 [a] Zech. 12:8 [1] *roar* [2] *with* [3] *filled* with blood [4] *sacrificial basons*
9:16 [a] Jer. 31:10, 11 [b] Is. 62:3 [c] Is. 11:12 [1] *jewels* [2] *a banner over*
9:17 [a] [Ps. 31:19] [b] [Ps. 45:1–16] [c] Joel 3:18 [1] *its* [2] *grain* [3] *thrive*
10:1 [a] [Jer. 14:22] [b] [Deut. 11:13, 14] [c] [Joel 2:23] [1] *The spring rain* [2] *flashing clouds or lightnings*
10:2 [a] Jer. 10:8 [b] Jer. 27:9 [c] Job 13:4 [d] Jer. 50:6, 17 [e] Ezek. 34:5–8 [1] Heb. *teraphim* [2] *delusion or iniquity* [3] *the people wander* [4] *in trouble*
10:3 [a] Jer. 25:34–36 [b] Ezek. 34:17 [c] Luke 1:68 [d] Song 1:9 [1] Leaders, lit. *he goats* [2] *royal or majestic*
10:4 [a] Is. 28:16 [b] Is. 22:23 [1] *comes* [2] *tent peg* [3] *ruler or despot*
10:5 [a] Ps. 18:42 [1] *put to shame*
10:6 [a] Jer. 3:18 [b] Hos. 1:7 [c] Zech. 13:9
10:7 [a] Ps. 104:15
10:8 [a] Is. 5:26 [b] Ezek. 36:37 [1] *whistle* [2] *once*
10:9 [a] Hos. 2:23 [b] Deut. 30:1 [1] *scatter* [2] *peoples* [3] *they shall return*
10:10 [a] Is. 11:11 [b] Is. 49:19, 20 [1] *until no more room is found*
10:11 [a] Is. 11:15 [b] Zeph. 2:13 [c] Ezek. 30:13 [1] *The Nile*
10:12 [a] Mic. 4:5
11:1 [a] Zech. 10:10
11:2 [a] Ezek. 31:3 [b] Is. 32:19 [1] *Wail, O cypress* [2] *mighty trees are ruined* [3] *the thick forest*
11:3 [a] Jer. 25:34–36 [1] *the sound of wailing* [2] *in ruins* [3] *thicket or floodplain*
11:4 [1] *for*
11:5 [a] [Jer. 2:3]; 50:7 [b] Hos. 12:8 [1] *owners*
11:6 [1] *attack*
11:7 [a] Zeph. 3:12 [1] *for* [2] *in particular, the poor* [3] *staffs* [4] *Grace* [5] *Unity* 11:8 [a] Hos. 5:7 [1] *dismissed or destroyed* 11:9 [a] Jer. 15:2 [1] *perishing* [2] *perish* [3] *of each other* 11:10 [1] *Grace* 11:11 [a] Zeph. 3:12 [1] *watched* 11:12 [1] *If you are agreeable* [2] *wages*

3forbear. So they aweighed for my 2price thirty *pieces* of silver.

13 And the LORD said unto me, Cast it unto the apotter: 1a goodly price that I was 2prised at of them. And I took the thirty *pieces* of silver, and cast them to the potter in the house of the LORD.

14 Then I cut asunder mine other staff, *even* 1Bands, that I might break the brotherhood between Judah and Israel.

15 And the LORD said unto me, aTake unto thee yet the 1instruments of a foolish shepherd.

16 For, lo, I will raise up a shepherd in the land, *which* shall not visit those that be cut off, neither shall seek the young one, nor heal that that is broken, nor feed that that standeth still: but he shall eat the flesh of the fat, and tear their 1claws in apieces.

17 aWoe to the 1idol shepherd that leaveth the flock! the sword *shall be* 2upon his arm, and 2upon his right eye: his arm shall be 3clean dried up, and his right eye shall be utterly 4darkened.

## CHAPTER 12

THE 1burden of the word of the LORD 2for Israel, saith the LORD, awhich stretcheth forth the heavens, and layeth the foundation of the earth, and bformeth the spirit of man within him.

2 Behold, I will make Jerusalem aa cup of 1trembling unto all the people round about, when they shall be in the siege both against Judah *and* against Jerusalem.

3 aAnd in that day will I make Jerusalem ba 1burdensome stone for all 2people: all that 3burden themselves with it shall be cut in pieces, though all the people of the earth be gathered together against it.

4 In that day, saith the LORD, aI will smite every horse with 1astonishment, and his rider with madness: and I will open mine eyes upon the house of Judah, and will smite every horse of the 2people with blindness.

5 And the governors of Judah shall say in their heart, The inhabitants of Jerusalem 1*shall be* my strength in the LORD of hosts their God.

6 In that day will I make the governors of Judah alike an 1hearth of fire among the wood, and like a torch of fire in a sheaf; and they shall devour all the people round about, on the right hand and on the left: and Jerusalem shall be inhabited again in her own place, *even* in Jerusalem.

7 The LORD also shall save the tents of Judah first, that the glory of the house of David and the glory of the

11:12 a Ex. 21:32
2 wages 3 refrain

11:13 a Matt. 27:3–
10 1 that princely
price 2 valued at
by them

11:14 1 Unity

11:15 a Is. 56:11
1 implements

11:16 a Ezek. 34:1–
10 1 hooves

11:17 a Jer. 23:1
1 worthless
2 against 3 completely 4 blinded

12:1 a Is. 42:5;
44:24 b [Is. 57:16]
1 oracle or prophecy 2 against

12:2 a Is. 51:17
1 drunkenness or
reeling

12:3 a Zech. 12:4,
6, 8; 13:1 b Matt.
21:44 1 very heavy
2 peoples 3 would
heave it away

12:4 a Ezek.
38:4 1 confusion
2 peoples

12:5 1 are my
strength

12:6 a Obad. 18
1 firepan in the
woodpile

12:7 1 shall not
become greater
than that of

12:9 a Hag. 2:22

12:10 a [Joel 2:28,
29] b John 19:34,
37; 20:27 c Jer.
6:26 1 grieve
2 grieves

12:11 a [Rev. 1:7]
b 2 Kin. 23:29
1 plain 2 Megiddo

12:12 a [Matt.
24:30] b Luke
3:31 1 by itself

13:1 a [Rev. 21:6,
7] b [Heb. 9:14]
c Ezek. 36:25

13:2 a Ex. 23:13
b Jer. 23:14, 15
1 depart from

13:3 a Deut. 18:20
b Deut. 13:6–11

13:4 a [Mic. 3:6, 7]
b 2 Kin. 1:8 1 robe
of coarse hair

13:5 a Amos 7:14
1 farmer

inhabitants of Jerusalem 1do not magnify *themselves* against Judah.

8 In that day shall the LORD defend the inhabitants of Jerusalem; and he that is feeble among them at that day shall be as David; and the house of David *shall be* as God, as the angel of the LORD before them.

9 And it shall come to pass in that day, *that* I will seek to adestroy all the nations that come against Jerusalem.

10 aAnd I will pour upon the house of David, and upon the inhabitants of Jerusalem, the spirit of grace and of supplications: and they shall blook upon me whom they have pierced, and they shall mourn for him, cas one mourneth for *his* only *son,* and shall 1be in bitterness for him, as one that 2is in bitterness for *his* firstborn.

11 In that day shall there be a great amourning in Jerusalem, bas the mourning of Hadad-rimmon in the 1valley of 2Megiddon.

12 aAnd the land shall mourn, every family 1apart; the family of the house of David apart, and their wives apart; the family of the house of bNathan apart, and their wives apart;

13 The family of the house of Levi apart, and their wives apart; the family of Shimei apart, and their wives apart;

14 All the families that remain, every family apart, and their wives apart.

## CHAPTER 13

IN that aday there shall be ba fountain opened to the house of David and to the inhabitants of Jerusalem for sin and for cuncleanness.

2 And it shall come to pass in that day, saith the LORD of hosts, *that* I will acut off the names of the idols out of the land, and they shall no more be remembered: and also I will cause bthe prophets and the unclean spirit to 1pass out of the land.

3 And it shall come to pass, *that* when any shall yet prophesy, then his father and his mother that begat him shall say unto him, Thou shalt anot live; for thou speakest lies in the name of the LORD: and his father and his mother that begat him bshall thrust him through when he prophesieth.

4 And it shall come to pass in that day, *that* athe prophets shall be ashamed every one of his vision, when he hath prophesied; neither shall they wear ba 1rough garment to deceive:

5 aBut he shall say, I *am* no prophet, I *am* an 1husbandman; for man taught me to keep cattle from my youth.

6 And *one* shall say unto him, What *are* these wounds in thine hands? Then he shall answer, *Those* with which I was wounded *in* the house of my friends.

7 Awake, O sword, against [a]my shepherd, and against the man [b]*that is* my [1]fellow, saith the LORD of hosts: [c]smite[2] the shepherd, and the sheep shall be scattered: and I will turn mine hand [3]upon [d]the little ones.

8 And it shall come to pass, *that* in all the land, saith the LORD, [a]two parts therein shall be cut off *and* die; [b]but the third shall be left therein.

9 And I will bring the third part [a]through the fire, and will [b]refine them as silver is refined, and will [1]try them as gold is [2]tried: [c]they shall call on my name, and I will [3]hear them: [d]I will say, It *is* my people: and they shall say, The LORD *is* my God.

## CHAPTER 14

BEHOLD, [a]the day of the LORD cometh, and thy [1]spoil shall be divided in the midst of thee.

2 For [a]I will gather all nations against Jerusalem to battle; and the city shall be taken, and the houses [1]rifled, and the women ravished; and half of the city shall go forth into captivity, and the [2]residue of the people shall not be cut off from the city.

3 Then shall the LORD go forth, and fight against those nations, as when he fought in the day of battle.

4 And his feet shall stand in that day [a]upon the mount of Olives, which *is* before Jerusalem on the east, and the mount of Olives shall [1]cleave in the midst thereof toward the east and toward the west, [b]*and there shall be* a very great valley; and half of the mountain shall remove toward the north, and half of it toward the south.

5 And ye shall flee *to* the valley of the mountains; for the valley of the mountains shall reach unto Azal: yea, ye shall flee, like as ye fled from before the [a]earthquake in the days of Uzziah king of Judah: [b]and the LORD my God shall come, *and* [c]all the saints with [1]thee.

6 And it shall come to pass in that day, *that* [1]the light shall not be clear, [2]nor dark:

7 But it shall be one day [a]which shall be known to the LORD, not day, nor night: but it shall come to pass, *that* at [b]evening time it shall be light.

8 And it shall be in that day, *that* living [a]waters shall go out from Jerusalem; half of them toward the [1]former sea, and half of them toward the [2]hinder sea: in summer and in winter shall it be.

9 And the LORD shall be [a]king over all the earth: in that day shall there be [b]one[1] LORD, and his name one.

10 All the land shall be [1]turned as a plain from Geba to Rimmon south of Jerusalem: and [2]it shall be lifted up, and [a]inhabited in her place, from

Benjamin's gate unto the place of the first gate, unto the corner gate, [b]and *from* the tower of Hananeel unto the king's winepresses.

11 And *men* shall dwell in it, and there shall be [a]no more utter destruction; [b]but Jerusalem shall be safely inhabited.

12 And this shall be the plague wherewith the LORD will smite all the people that have fought against Jerusalem; Their flesh shall [1]consume away while they stand upon their feet, and their eyes shall consume away in their [2]holes, and their tongue shall consume away in their mouth.

13 And it shall come to pass in that day, *that* [a]a great [1]tumult from the LORD shall be among them; and they shall [2]lay hold every one on the hand of his neighbour, and [b]his hand shall rise up against the hand of his neighbour.

14 And Judah also shall fight at Jerusalem; [a]and the wealth of all the heathen round about shall be gathered together, gold, and silver, and apparel, in great abundance.

15 And [a]so shall be the plague of the horse, of the mule, of the camel, and of the [1]ass, and of all the [2]beasts that shall be in these [3]tents, [4]as this plague.

16 And it shall come to pass, *that* every one that is left of all the nations which came against Jerusalem shall even [a]go up from year to year to [b]worship the King, the LORD of hosts, and to keep [c]the feast of tabernacles.

17 [a]And it shall be, *that* whoso will not come up of *all* the families of the earth unto Jerusalem to worship the King, the LORD of hosts, even upon them shall be no rain.

18 And if the family of [a]Egypt go not up, and come not, [b]that[1] *have* no *rain;* there shall be the plague, wherewith the LORD will [2]smite the heathen that come not up to keep the feast of tabernacles.

19 This shall be the [1]punishment of Egypt, and the punishment of all nations that come not up to keep the feast of tabernacles.

20 In that day shall there be upon the bells of the horses, [a]HOLINESS UNTO THE LORD; and the [b]pots in the LORD'S house shall be like the bowls before the altar.

21 Yea, every pot in Jerusalem and in Judah shall [1]be holiness unto the LORD of hosts: and all they that sacrifice shall come and take of them, and [2]seethe therein: and in that day there shall be no more the [a]Canaanite [b]in the house of the LORD of hosts.

---

13:7 [a] Is. 40:11
[b] [John 10:30]
[c] Matt. 26:31, 56, 67 [d] Luke 12:32
[1] *companion*
[2] *strike* [3] *against*
13:8 [a] Ezek. 5:2, 4, 12 [b] [Rom. 11:5]
13:9 [a] Is. 48:10
[b] 1 Pet. 1:6 [c] Ps. 50:15 [d] Hos. 2:23
[1] *test* [2] *tested*
[3] Lit. *answer*
14:1 [a] [Is. 13:6, 9]
[1] *plunder*
14:2 [a] Zech. 12:2,
3 [1] *plundered*
[2] *remnant*
14:4 [a] Ezek. 11:23
[b] Joel 3:12 [1] *split in two*
14:5 [a] Amos 1:1
[b] Matt. 24:30, 31;
25:31 [c] Joel 3:11
[1] LXX, Tg., Vg. *him*
14:6 [1] *there will be no light*
[2] *the lights will diminish*
14:7 [a] Matt. 24:36
[b] Is. 30:26
14:8 [a] Ezek. 47:1–12 [1] *eastern, the Dead Sea*
[2] *western, the Mediterranean Sea*
14:9 [a] [Rev. 11:15]
[b] Deut. 6:4 [1] Lit. *the LORD is one,* Deut. 6:4
14:10 [a] Zech. 12:6 [1] *turned into*
[2] *Jerusalem*

[b] Jer. 31:38

14:11 [a] Jer. 31:40
[b] Jer. 23:6
14:12 [1] *decay*
[2] *sockets*
14:13 [a] 1 Sam. 14:15, 20 [b] Judg. 7:22 [1] *panic*
[2] *seize*
14:14 [a] Ezek. 39:10, 17
14:15 [a] Zech. 14:12
[1] *donkey* [2] *cattle*
[3] *camps* [4] *so shall this plague be*
14:16 [a] [Is. 2:2, 3; 60:6–9; 66:18–21]
[b] Is. 27:13 [c] Lev. 23:34–44
14:17 [a] Is. 60:12
14:18 [a] Is. 19:21
[b] Deut. 11:10
[1] *they shall have* [2] *strike the nations*
14:19 [1] Lit. *sin*
14:20 [a] Is. 23:18
[b] Ezek. 46:20
14:21 [a] Is. 35:8
[b] [Eph. 2:19–22]
[1] *be engraved holiness to the LORD of hosts* [2] *cook*

# THE BOOK OF
# MALACHI

Malachi, a prophet in the days of Nehemiah, directs his message of judgment to a people plagued with corrupt priests, wicked practices, and a false sense of security in their privileged relationship with God. Using the question-and-answer method, Malachi probes deeply into their problems of hypocrisy, infidelity, mixed marriages, divorce, false worship, and arrogance. So sinful has the nation become that God's words to the people no longer have any impact. For four hundred years after Malachi's ringing condemnations, God remains silent. Only with the coming of John the Baptist (prophesied in 3:1) does God again communicate to His people through a prophet's voice.

The meaning of the name *Mal'aki* ("My Messenger") is probably a shortened form of *Mal'akya*, "Messenger of Yahweh," and it is appropriate to the book which speaks of the coming of the "messenger of the covenant" ("messenger" is mentioned three times in 2:7; 3:1). The Septuagint used the title *Malachias* even though it also translated it "by the hand of his messenger." The Latin title is *Maleachi*.

## CHAPTER 1

THE ¹burden of the word of the LORD to Israel ²by Malachi.

2 ᵃI have loved you, saith the LORD. Yet ye say, Wherein hast thou loved us? *Was* not Esau Jacob's brother? saith the LORD: yet ᵇI loved Jacob,

3 And I hated Esau, and ᵃlaid his mountains and his heritage waste for the ¹dragons of the wilderness.

4 Whereas Edom saith, We are impoverished, but we will return and build the desolate places; thus saith the LORD of hosts, They ¹shall build, but I will ᵃthrow down; and they shall call them, The ²border of wickedness, and, The people against whom the LORD hath indignation for ever.

5 And your eyes shall see, and ye shall say, ᵃThe LORD will be magnified ¹from the border of Israel.

6 A son ᵃhonoureth *his* father, and a servant his master: ᵇif then I *be* a father, where *is* mine honour? and if I *be* a master, where *is* my ¹fear? saith the LORD of hosts unto you, O priests, that despise my name. ᶜAnd ye say, Wherein have we despised thy name?

7 Ye offer ᵃpolluted¹ bread upon mine altar; and ye say, Wherein have we ²polluted thee? In that ye say, ᵇThe table of the LORD *is* ³contemptible.

8 And ᵃif¹ ye offer the blind for sacrifice, *is it* not evil? and ¹if ye offer the lame and sick, *is it* not evil? offer it now unto thy governor; will he be pleased with thee, or ᵇaccept² thy person? saith the LORD of hosts.

9 And now, I pray you, ¹beseech God that he will be gracious unto us: ᵃthis hath been by your ²means: will he ³regard your persons? saith the LORD of hosts.

10 Who *is there* even among you that would shut the doors *for nought?*

ᵃneither do ye kindle *fire* on mine altar ¹for nought. I have no pleasure in you, saith the LORD of hosts, ᵇneither will I accept an offering at your hand.

11 For ᵃfrom the rising of the sun even unto the going down of the same my name *shall be* great ᵇamong the Gentiles; ᶜand in every place ᵈincense *shall be* offered unto my name, and a pure offering: ᵉfor my name *shall be* great among the ¹heathen, saith the LORD of hosts.

12 But ye have profaned it, in that ye say, ᵃThe table of the ¹LORD *is* ²polluted; and the fruit thereof, *even* ³his meat, *is* contemptible.

13 Ye said also, Behold, what a ᵃweariness *is it!* and ye have ¹snuffed at it, saith the LORD of hosts; and ye brought *that which was* ²torn, and the lame, and the sick; thus ye brought an offering: ᵇshould I accept this of your hand? saith the LORD.

14 But cursed *be* ᵃthe deceiver, which hath in his flock a male, and voweth, and sacrificeth unto the Lord a ᵇcorrupt¹ thing: for ᶜI *am* a great King, saith the LORD of hosts, and my name *is* ²dreadful among the ³heathen.

## CHAPTER 2

AND now, O ye ᵃpriests, this commandment *is* for you.

2 ᵃIf ye will not hear, and if ye will not ¹lay *it* to heart, to give glory unto my name, saith the LORD of hosts, I will even send a curse upon you, and I will curse your blessings: yea, I have cursed them ᵇalready, because ye do not lay *it* to heart.

3 Behold, I will ¹corrupt your seed, and spread ᵃdung² up on your faces,

---

1:1 ¹ *oracle or prophecy* ² Lit. *by the hand of*
1:2 ᵃ Deut. 4:37; 7:8; 23:5 ᵇ Rom. 9:13
1:3 ᵃ Jer. 49:18 ¹ *jackals*
1:4 ᵃ Jer. 49:16–18 ¹ *may* ² *territory*
1:5 ᵇ Ps. 35:27 ¹ *beyond*
1:6 ᵃ [Ex. 20:12] ᵇ Luke 6:46 ᶜ Mal. 2:14 ¹ *reverence*
1:7 ᵃ Deut. 15:21 ᵇ Ezek. 41:22 ¹ *defiled food* ² *defiled* ³ *to be despised*
1:8 ᵃ Lev. 22:22 ᵇ [Job 42:8] ¹ *when* ² *accept you favourably,* lit. *lift up your face*
1:9 ᵃ Hos. 13:9 ¹ *entreat God's favour* ² Lit. *hands* ³ *accept you favourably,* lit. *lift up your face*
1:10 ᵃ 1 Cor. 9:13 ᵇ Is. 1:11 ¹ Lit. *in vain*
1:11 ᵃ Is. 59:19 ᵇ Is. 60:3, 5 ᶜ 1 Tim. 2:8 ᵈ Rev. 8:3 ᵉ Is. 66:18, 19 ¹ *nations*
1:12 ᵃ Mal. 1:7 ¹ MT *Lord* ² *defiled* ³ *its food*
1:13 ᵃ Is. 43:22 ᵇ Lev. 22:20 ¹ *sneered* ² *stolen*
1:14 ᵃ Mal. 1:8 ᵇ Lev. 22:18–20 ᶜ Ps. 47:2 ¹ *blemished* ² *to be feared* ³ *nations*

2:1 ᵃ Mal. 1:6 2:2 ᵃ [Deut. 28:15] ᵇ Mal. 3:9 ¹ *take*
2:3 ᵃ Ex. 29:14 ¹ *rebuke your descendants* ² *refuse*

783

*even* the dung of your solemn feasts; and *one* shall [b]take you away [3]with it.

4 And ye shall know that I have sent this commandment unto you, that my covenant might [1]be with Levi, saith the LORD of hosts.

5 [a]My covenant was with him of life and peace; and I gave them to him [b]for[1] the fear wherewith he feared me, and was [2]afraid before my name.

6 [a]The[1] law of truth was in his mouth, and [2]iniquity was not found in his lips: he walked with me in peace and equity, and did [b]turn many away from iniquity.

7 [a]For the priest's lips should keep knowledge, and they should seek the law at his mouth: [b]for he *is* the messenger of the LORD of hosts.

8 But ye are departed out of the way; ye [a]have caused many to stumble at the law; [b]ye have corrupted the covenant of Levi, saith the LORD of hosts.

9 Therefore [a]have I also made you contemptible and base before all the people, according as ye have not kept my ways, but have been [b]partial[1] in the law.

10 [a]Have we not all one father? [b]hath not one God created us? why do we deal treacherously every man against his brother, by profaning the covenant of our fathers?

11 Judah hath dealt treacherously, and an abomination is committed in Israel and in Jerusalem; for Judah hath [a]profaned the [1]holiness of the LORD which he loved, and hath married the daughter of a strange god.

12 The LORD will cut off the man that doeth this, [1]the master and the scholar, out of the [2]tabernacles of Jacob, [a]and him that offereth an offering unto the LORD of hosts.

13 And this [1]have ye done again, covering the altar of the LORD with tears, with weeping, and with crying out, [2]insomuch that he regardeth not the offering any more, or receiveth *it* with good will at your hand.

14 Yet ye say, Wherefore? Because the LORD hath been witness between thee and [a]the wife of thy youth, against whom thou hast dealt treacherously: [b]yet *is* she thy companion, and the wife of thy covenant.

15 And [a]did not he make one? [1]Yet had he the residue of the spirit. And wherefore one? That he might seek [b]a godly [2]seed. Therefore take heed to your spirit, and let none deal treacherously against the wife of his youth.

16 For [a]the LORD, the God of Israel, saith that he hateth [1]putting away: for [2]*one* covereth violence with his garment, saith the LORD of hosts: therefore take heed to your spirit, that ye deal not treacherously.

17 [a]Ye have wearied the LORD with your words. Yet ye say, Wherein have we wearied *him?* When ye say, [b]Every one that doeth evil *is* good in the sight of the LORD, and he delighteth in them; or, Where *is* the God of [1]judgment?

## CHAPTER 3

BEHOLD, [a]I will send my messenger, and he shall [b]prepare the way before me: and the Lord, whom ye seek, shall suddenly come to his temple, [c]even the messenger of the covenant, whom ye delight in: behold, [d]he shall come, saith the LORD of hosts.

2 But who may abide [a]the day of his coming? and [b]who shall stand when he appeareth? for [c]he *is* like a refiner's fire, and like [1]fullers' soap:

3 And [a]he shall sit *as* a refiner and purifier of silver: and he shall purify the sons of Levi, and [1]purge them as gold and silver, that they may [b]offer unto the LORD an offering in righteousness.

4 Then [a]shall the offering of Judah and Jerusalem be [1]pleasant unto the LORD, as in the days of old, and as in former years.

5 And I will come near to you to judgment; and I will be a swift witness against the sorcerers, and against the adulterers, [a]and against false swearers, and against those that [b]oppress[1] the hireling in *his* wages, the [c]widow, and the fatherless, and that [2]turn aside the stranger *from his right,* [3]and fear not me, saith the LORD of hosts.

6 For I *am* the LORD, [a]I change not; [b]therefore ye sons of Jacob are not consumed.

7 Even from the days of [a]your fathers ye are gone away from mine ordinances, and have not kept *them.* [b]Return unto me, and I will return unto you, saith the LORD of hosts. [c]But ye said, [1]Wherein shall we return?

8 Will a man rob God? Yet ye have robbed me. But ye say, Wherein have we robbed thee? [a]In tithes and offerings.

9 Ye *are* cursed with a curse: for ye have robbed me, *even* this whole nation.

10 [a]Bring ye all the tithes into the [b]storehouse, that there may be [1]meat in mine house, and [2]prove me now herewith, saith the LORD of hosts, if I will not open you the [c]windows of heaven, and [d]pour you out a blessing, that *there shall* not *be room* enough *to receive* it.

11 And I will rebuke [a]the devourer for your sakes, and he shall not destroy the fruits of your ground; neither shall your vine [1]cast her fruit

### Cross-references

2:3 [b] 1 Kin. 14:10  [3] Lit. *to it*
2:4 [1] *continue*
2:5 [a] Num. 25:12  [b] Deut. 33:9  [1] that he might *fear me*  [2] *reverent*
2:6 [a] Deut. 33:10  [b] Jer. 23:22  [1] *True instruction*  [2] *injustice*
2:7 [a] Deut. 17:8–11  [b] [Gal. 4:14]
2:8 [a] Jer. 18:15  [b] Neh. 13:29
2:9 [a] 1 Sam. 2:30  [b] Deut. 1:17  [1] *shown partiality*
2:10 [a] 1 Cor. 8:6  [b] Job 31:15
2:11 [a] Ezra 9:1, 2  [1] *holy institution*
2:12 [a] Neh. 13:29  [1] MT *being awake and answering*  [2] *tents*
2:13 [1] *is the second thing you do*  [2] Or *because*
2:14 [a] Mal. 3:5  [b] Prov. 2:17
2:15 [a] Matt. 19:4, 5  [b] [1 Cor. 7:14]  [1] *Having a remnant*  [2] *offspring*
2:16 [a] [Matt. 5:31; 19:6–8]  [1] *divorce*  [x] *it covers one's garment with violence*
2:17 [a] Is. 43:22, 24  [b] Is. 5:20  [1] *justice*
3:1 [a] Matt. 11:10  [b] [Is. 40:3]  [c] Is. 63:9  [d] Hab. 2:7
3:2 [a] [Mal. 4:1]  [b] Rev. 6:17  [c] [Matt. 3:10–12]  [1] *launderers' soap*
3:3 [a] Is. 1:25  [b] [1 Pet. 2:5]  [1] *refine*
3:4 [a] Mal. 1:11  [1] *pleasing*
3:5 [a] Zech. 5:4  [b] James 5:4  [c] Ex. 22:22  [1] *exploit the wage earner*  [2] *turn away the alien*  [3] *because they do not fear me*
3:6 [a] [Rom. 11:29]  [b] [Lam. 3:22]
3:7 [a] Acts 7:51  [b] Zech. 1:3  [c] Mal. 1:6  [1] *In what way*
3:8 [a] Neh. 13:10–12
3:10 [a] Prov. 3:9, 10  [b] 1 Chr. 26:20  [c] Gen. 7:11  [d] 2 Chr. 31:10  [1] *food*  [2] *test*
3:11 [a] Amos 4:9  [1] *fail to bear fruit for you in the field*

before the time in the field, saith the LORD of hosts.

12 And all nations shall call you blessed: for ye shall be [a]a [1]delightsome land, saith the LORD of hosts.

13 [a]Your words have been [1]stout against me, saith the LORD. Yet ye say, What have we spoken so *much* against thee?

14 [a]Ye have said, It *is* vain to serve God: and what profit *is it* that we have kept his ordinance, and that we have walked [1]mournfully before the LORD of hosts?

15 And now [a]we call the proud [1]happy; yea, they that work wickedness are [2]set up; yea, *they that* [b]tempt God [3]are even delivered.

16 Then they [a]that feared the LORD [b]spake often one to another: and the LORD hearkened, and heard *it,* and [c]a book of remembrance was written before him for them that feared the LORD, and that [1]thought upon his name.

17 And [a]they shall be mine, saith the LORD of hosts, in that day when I make up my [b]jewels;[1] and [c]I will spare them, as a man spareth his own son that serveth him.

18 [a]Then shall ye return, and discern between the righteous and the

wicked, between him that serveth God and him that serveth him not.

## CHAPTER 4

FOR, behold, [a]the day cometh, that shall burn as an oven; and all [b]the proud, yea, and all that do wickedly, shall be [c]stubble: and the day that cometh shall burn them up, saith the LORD of hosts, that it shall [d]leave them neither root nor branch.

2 But unto you that [a]fear my name shall the [b]Sun of righteousness arise with healing in his wings; and ye shall go forth, and [1]grow up as calves of the stall.

3 [a]And ye shall [1]tread down the wicked; for they shall be ashes under the soles of your feet in the day that I shall do *this,* saith the LORD of hosts.

4 Remember ye the [a]law of Moses my servant, which I commanded unto him in Horeb for all Israel, *with* [b]the statutes and judgments.

5 Behold, I will send you [a]Elijah the prophet [b]before the coming of the great and dreadful day of the LORD:

6 And he shall turn the heart of the fathers to the children, and the heart of the children to their fathers, lest I come and [a]smite[1] the earth with [b]a curse.

3:12 [a] Dan. 8:9
[1] *delightful*

3:13 [a] Mal. 2:17
[1] *harsh*

3:14 [a] Job 21:14
[1] *as mourners*

3:15 [a] Ps. 73:12
[b] Ps. 95:9
[1] *blessed* [2] *raised up* [3] *go free*

3:16 [a] Ps. 66:16
[b] Heb. 3:13 [c] Ps. 56:8 [1] *meditated*

3:17 [a] Ex. 19:5 [b] Is. 62:3 [c] Ps. 103:13
[1] Lit. *special treasure*

3:18 [a] [Ps. 58:11]

4:1 [a] [2 Pet. 3:7] [b] Mal. 3:18 [c] Obad. 18 [d] Amos 2:9

4:2 [a] Mal. 3:16
[b] Luke 1:78 [1] *grow fat like stall-fed calves*

4:3 [a] Mic. 7:10
[1] *trample*

4:4 [a] Ex. 20:3
[b] Deut. 4:10

4:5 [a] [Matt. 11:14; 17:10–13] [b] Joel 2:31

4:6 [a] Zech. 14:12
[b] Zech. 5:3 [1] *strike*

# THE
# NEW TESTAMENT

# THE GOSPEL ACCORDING TO
# MATTHEW

Matthew is the gospel written by a Jew to Jews about a Jew. Matthew is the writer, his countrymen are the readers, and Jesus Christ is the subject. Matthew's design is to present Jesus as the King of the Jews, the long-awaited Messiah. Through a carefully selected series of Old Testament quotations, Matthew documents Jesus Christ's claim to be the Messiah. His genealogy, baptism, messages, and miracles all point to the same inescapable conclusion: Christ is King. Even in His death, seeming defeat is turned to victory by the Resurrection, and the message again echoes forth: the King of the Jews lives.

At an early date this gospel was given the title *Kata Matthaion,* "According to Matthew." As this title suggests, other gospel accounts were known at that time (the word "Gospel" was added later). Matthew ("Gift of the Lord") was also surnamed Levi (Mark 2:14; Luke 5:27).

## CHAPTER 1

THE book of the ᵃgeneration of Jesus Christ, ᵇthe son of David, ᶜthe son of Abraham.

2 ᵃAbraham begat Isaac; and ᵇIsaac begat Jacob; and Jacob begat ᶜJudas and his brethren;

3 And ᵃJudas begat Phares and Zara of Thamar; and ᵇPhares begat Esrom; and Esrom begat Aram;

4 And Aram begat Aminadab; and Aminadab begat Naasson; and Naasson begat Salmon;

5 And Salmon begat ᵃBooz of ¹Rachab; and Booz begat Obed of Ruth; and Obed begat Jesse;

6 And ᵃJesse begat David the king; and ᵇDavid the king begat Solomon of her *that had been the wife* of Urias;

7 And ᵃSolomon begat Roboam; and Roboam begat ᵇAbia; and Abia begat Asa;

8 And Asa begat ᵃJosaphat; and Josaphat begat Joram; and Joram begat ᵇOzias;

9 And Ozias begat Joatham; and Joatham begat ᵃAchaz; and Achaz begat Ezekias;

10 And ᵃEzekias begat Manasses; and Manasses begat Amon; and Amon begat ᵇJosias;

11 And ᵃJosias begat ¹Jechonias and his brethren, about the time they were ᵇcarried away to Babylon:

12 And after they were brought to Babylon, ᵃJechonias begat ¹Salathiel; and Salathiel begat ᵇZorobabel;

13 And Zorobabel begat Abiud; and Abiud begat Eliakim; and Eliakim begat Azor;

14 And Azor begat Sadoc; and Sadoc begat Achim; and Achim begat Eliud;

15 And Eliud begat Eleazar; and Eleazar begat Matthan; and Matthan begat Jacob;

16 And Jacob begat Joseph the husband of ᵃMary, of whom was born Jesus, who is called Christ.

17 So all the generations from Abraham to David *are* fourteen generations; and from David until the carrying away into Babylon *are* fourteen generations; and from the carrying away into Babylon unto Christ *are* fourteen generations.

18 Now the ᵃbirth of Jesus Christ was ¹on this wise: When as his mother Mary was ²espoused to Joseph, before they came together, she was found with child ᵇof the ³Holy Ghost.

19 Then Joseph her husband, being a ¹just *man,* and not willing ᵃto make her a publick example, was minded to put her away ²privily.

20 But while he thought on these things, behold, the angel of the Lord appeared unto him in a dream, saying, Joseph, thou son of David, fear not to take unto thee Mary thy wife: ᵃfor that which is ¹conceived in her is of the Holy Ghost.

21 ᵃAnd she shall bring forth a son, and thou shalt call his name ¹JESUS: for ᵇhe shall save his people from their sins.

22 Now all this was done, that it might be fulfilled which was spoken of the Lord by the prophet, saying,

23 ᵃBehold, a virgin shall be with child, and shall bring forth a son, and they shall call his name Emmanuel, which ¹being interpreted is, God with us.

24 Then Joseph being raised from sleep did as the angel of the Lord had bidden him, and took unto him his wife:

25 And ¹knew her not till she had brought forth ᵃher firstborn son: and he called his name JESUS.

## CHAPTER 2

NOW when ᵃJesus was born in Bethlehem of Judaea in the days of Herod the king, behold, there

### [Cross-reference notes]

1:1 ᵃ Luke 3:23
ᵇ John 7:42
ᶜ Gen. 12:3; 22:18
1:2 ᵃ Gen. 21:2,
12  ᵇ Gen. 25:26;
28:14  ᶜ Gen.
29:35
1:3 ᵃ Gen. 38:27;
49:10  ᵇ Ruth
4:18–22
1:5 ᵃ Ruth 2:1;
4:1–13  ¹ *Rahab,*
Josh. 2:1
1:6 ᵃ 1 Sam. 16:1
ᵇ 2 Sam. 7:12;
12:24
1:7 ᵃ 1 Chr. 3:10
ᵇ 2 Chr. 11:20
1:8 ᵃ 1 Chr. 3:10
ᵇ 2 Kin. 15:13
1:9 ᵃ 2 Kin. 15:38
1:10 ᵃ 2 Kin. 20:21
ᵇ 1 Kin. 13:2
1:11 ᵃ 1 Chr. 3:15, 16
ᵇ 2 Kin. 24:14–16
¹ *Jehoiachin,*
2 Kin. 24:6; *Coniah,* Jer. 22:24
1:12 ᵃ 1 Chr. 3:17
ᵇ Ezra 3:2  ¹ *Shealtiel,* Ezra 3:2
1:16 ᵃ Matt. 13:55

1:18 ᵃ Luke 1:27
ᵇ Luke 1:35  ¹ *as follows* ² *betrothed* ³ *Holy Spirit*
1:19 ᵃ Deut. 24:1  ¹ *upright* ² *secretly*
1:20 ᵃ Luke 1:35
¹ Lit. *begotten*
1:21 ᵃ Luke 1:31;
2:21  ᵇ John 1:29
¹ Lit. *Saviour*
1:23 ᵃ Is. 7:14  ¹ *is translated*
1:25 ᵃ Luke 2:7, 21
¹ *Kept her a virgin*
2:1 ᵃ Luke 2:4–7

came [1]wise men [b]from the east to Jerusalem,

2 Saying, [a]Where is he that is born King of the Jews? for we have seen [b]his star in the east, and are come to worship him.

3 When Herod the king had heard *these things,* he was troubled, and all Jerusalem with him.

4 And when he had gathered all [a]the chief priests and [b]scribes of the people together, [c]he demanded of them where Christ should be born.

5 And they said unto him, In Bethlehem of Judaea: for thus it is written by the prophet,

6 [a]And thou Bethlehem, *in* the land of Juda, art not the least among the princes of Juda: for out of thee shall come a [1]Governor, [b]that shall [2]rule my people Israel.

7 Then Herod, when he had [1]privily called the wise men, enquired of them diligently what time the [a]star appeared.

8 And he sent them to Bethlehem, and said, Go and search diligently for the young child; and when ye have found *him,* bring me word again, that I may come and worship him also.

9 When they had heard the king, they departed; and, lo, the star, which they saw in the east, went before them, till it came and stood over where the young child was.

10 When they saw the star, they rejoiced with exceeding great joy.

11 And when they were come into the house, they saw the young child with Mary his mother, and fell down, and worshipped him: and when they had opened their treasures, [a]they presented unto him gifts; gold, and frankincense, and myrrh.

12 And being warned of God [a]in a dream that they should not return to Herod, they departed into their own country another way.

13 And when they were departed, behold, the angel of the Lord appeareth to Joseph in a dream, saying, Arise, and take the young child and his mother, and flee into Egypt, and be thou there until I bring thee word: for Herod will seek the young child to destroy him.

14 When he arose, he took the young child and his mother by night, and departed into Egypt:

15 And was there until the death of Herod: that it might be fulfilled which was spoken of the Lord by the prophet, saying, [a]Out of Egypt have I called my son.

16 Then Herod, when he saw that he was [1]mocked of the wise men, was exceeding [2]wroth, and sent forth, and slew all the [3]children that were in Bethlehem, and in all the [4]coasts

thereof, from two years old and under, according to the time which he had diligently enquired of the wise men.

17 Then was fulfilled that which was spoken by [1]Jeremy the prophet, saying,

18 [a]In Rama was there a voice heard, lamentation, and weeping, and great mourning, Rachel weeping *for* her children, and would not be comforted, because they are not.

19 But when Herod was dead, behold, an angel of the Lord appeareth in a dream to Joseph in Egypt,

20 [a]Saying, Arise, and take the young child and his mother, and go into the land of Israel: for they are dead which [b]sought the young child's life.

21 And he arose, and took the young child and his mother, and came into the land of Israel.

22 But when he heard that Archelaus did reign in Judaea [1]in the room of his father Herod, he was afraid to go [2]thither: notwithstanding, being warned of God in a [a]dream, he turned aside [b]into the [3]parts of Galilee:

23 And he came and dwelt in a city called [a]Nazareth: that it might be fulfilled [b]which was spoken by the prophets, He shall be called a Nazarene.

## CHAPTER 3

IN those days came [a]John the Baptist, preaching [b]in the wilderness of Judaea,

2 And saying, Repent ye: for [a]the kingdom of heaven is at hand.

3 For this is he that was spoken of by the prophet Esaias, saying, [a]The voice of one crying in the wilderness, [b]Prepare ye the way of the Lord, make his paths straight.

4 And [a]the same John had his raiment of camel's hair, and a leathern [1]girdle about his [2]loins; and his [3]meat was [b]locusts and [c]wild honey.

5 [a]Then went out to him Jerusalem, and all Judaea, and all the region round about Jordan,

6 [a]And were baptized of him in Jordan, confessing their sins.

7 But when he saw many of the Pharisees and Sadducees come [1]to his baptism, he said unto them, [a]O [2]generation of vipers, who hath warned you to flee from [b]the wrath to come?

8 Bring forth therefore fruits [1]meet for repentance:

9 And think not to say within yourselves, [a]We have Abraham to *our* father: for I say unto you, that God is able of these stones to raise up children unto Abraham.

10 And now also the axe is laid unto the root of the trees: [a]therefore every tree which bringeth not forth good fruit is hewn down, and cast into the fire.

---

2:1 [b] Gen. 25:6; 1 Kin. 4:30 [1]Gr. *magoi*
2:2 [a] Luke 2:11 [b] [Num. 24:17; Is. 60:3]
2:4 [a] 2 Chr. 36:14 [b] 2 Chr. 34:13 [c] Mal. 2:7
2:6 [a] Mic. 5:2; John 7:42 [b] Gen. 49:10; [Rev. 2:27] [1]*Ruler* [2]*shepherd*
2:7 [a] Num. 24:17 [1]*secretly*
2:11 [a] Ps. 72:10; Is. 60:6
2:12 [a] [Job 33:15, 16]; Matt. 1:20
2:15 [a] Num. 24:8; Hos. 11:1
2:16 [1]*deceived* [2]*angry* [3]*male children* [4]*districts*

2:17 [1]*Jeremiah*
2:18 [a] Jer. 31:15
2:20 [a] Luke 2:39 [b] Matt. 2:16
2:22 [a] Matt. 2:12, 13, 19 [b] Matt. 3:13; Luke 2:39 [1]*instead of* [2]*there* [3]*region*
2:23 [a] Luke 1:26; 2:39; John 1:45, 46 [b] Judg. 13:5
3:1 [a] Matt. 3:1–12; Mark 1:3–8; Luke 3:2–17; John 1:6–8, 19–28 [b] Josh. 14:10
3:2 [a] Dan. 2:44; Mal. 4:6; Matt. 4:17; Mark 1:15; Luke 1:17; 10:9; 11:20; 21:31
3:3 [a] Is. 40:3; Luke 3:4; John 1:23 [b] Luke 1:76
3:4 [a] 2 Kin. 1:8; Zech. 13:4; Matt. 11:8; Mark 1:6 [b] Lev. 11:22 [c] 1 Sam. 14:25, 26 [1]*belt* [2]*waist* [3]*food*
3:5 [a] Mark 1:5
3:6 [a] Acts 19:4, 18
3:7 [a] Matt. 12:34; Luke 3:7–9 [b] [Rom. 5:9; 1 Thess. 1:10] [1]*for* [2]*brood*
3:8 [1]*worthy of*
3:9 [a] John 8:33
3:10 [a] Matt. 7:19

11 [a]I indeed baptize you with water unto repentance: but he that cometh after me is mightier than I, whose shoes I am not worthy to bear: [b]he shall baptize you with the Holy Ghost, and *with* fire:

12 [a]Whose [1]fan *is* in his hand, and he will throughly purge his [2]floor, and gather his wheat into the [3]garner; but he will [b]burn up the chaff with unquenchable fire.

13 [a]Then cometh Jesus [b]from Galilee to Jordan unto John, to be baptized of him.

14 But John forbad him, saying, I have need to be baptized of thee, and comest thou to me?

15 And Jesus answering said unto him, [1]Suffer *it to be so* now: for thus it [2]becometh us to fulfil all righteousness. Then he [3]suffered him.

16 [a]And Jesus, when he was baptized, went up straightway out of the water: and, lo, the heavens were opened unto him, and he saw [b]the Spirit of God descending like a dove, and lighting upon him:

17 [a]And lo a voice from heaven, saying, [b]This is my beloved Son, in whom I am well pleased.

## CHAPTER 4

THEN was [a]Jesus led up of [b]the Spirit into the wilderness to be tempted of the devil.

2 And when he had fasted forty days and forty nights, he was afterward [1]an hungred.

3 And when the tempter came to him, he said, If thou be the Son of God, command that these stones be made bread.

4 But he answered and said, It is written, [a]Man shall not live by bread alone, but by every word that proceedeth out of the mouth of God.

5 Then the devil taketh him up [a]into the holy city, and setteth him on a pinnacle of the temple,

6 And saith unto him, If thou be the Son of God, cast thyself down: for it is written, [a]He shall give his angels charge concerning thee: and [b]in *their* hands they shall bear thee up, lest at any time thou dash thy foot against a stone.

7 Jesus said unto him, It is written again, [a]Thou shalt not [1]tempt the Lord thy God.

8 Again, the devil taketh him up into an exceeding high mountain, and [a]sheweth him all the kingdoms of the world, and the glory of them;

9 And saith unto him, All these things will I give thee, if thou wilt fall down and worship me.

10 Then saith Jesus unto him, [1]Get thee hence, Satan: for it is written, [a]Thou shalt worship the Lord thy God, and him only shalt thou serve.

11 Then the devil [a]leaveth him, and, behold, [b]angels came and ministered unto him.

12 [a]Now when Jesus had heard that John was cast into prison, he departed into Galilee;

13 And leaving Nazareth, he came and dwelt in Capernaum, which is upon the sea coast, in the borders of Zabulon and Nephthalim:

14 That it might be fulfilled which was spoken by Esaias the prophet, saying,

15 [a]The land of Zabulon, and the land of Nephthalim, *by* the way of the sea, beyond Jordan, Galilee of the Gentiles;

16 [a]The people which sat in darkness saw great light; and to them which sat in the region and shadow of death light [1]is sprung up.

17 [a]From that time Jesus began to preach, and to say, [b]Repent: for the kingdom of heaven is [1]at hand.

18 [a]And Jesus, walking by the sea of Galilee, saw two brethren, Simon [b]called Peter, and Andrew his brother, casting a net into the sea: for they were fishers.

19 And he saith unto them, Follow me, and [a]I will make you fishers of men.

20 [a]And they straightway left *their* nets, and followed him.

21 [a]And going on from thence, he saw other two brethren, James *the son* of Zebedee, and John his brother, in a ship with Zebedee their father, mending their nets; and he called them.

22 And they immediately left the ship and their father, and followed him.

23 And Jesus went about all Galilee, [a]teaching in their synagogues, and preaching [b]the gospel of the kingdom, [c]and healing [1]all manner of sickness and [2]all manner of disease among the people.

24 And his fame went throughout all Syria: and they [a]brought unto him all sick people that were taken with [1]divers diseases and torments, and those which were possessed with [2]devils, and those which were [3]lunatick, and those that [4]had the palsy; and he healed them.

25 [a]And there followed him great multitudes of people from Galilee, and *from* [1]Decapolis, and *from* Jerusalem, and *from* Judaea, and *from* beyond Jordan.

## CHAPTER 5

AND seeing the multitudes, [a]he went up into a mountain: and when he was [1]set, his disciples came unto him:

2 And he opened his mouth, and [a]taught them, saying,

3:11 [a] Luke 3:16
[b] [Acts 2:3, 4]
3:12 [a] Mal. 3:3
[b] Matt. 13:30
[1] *winnowing fan*
[2] *threshingfloor*
[3] *barn*
3:13 [a] Mark 1:9–11
[b] Matt. 2:22
3:15 [1] *Allow* [2] *is fitting for us*
[3] *allowed*
3:16 [a] Mark 1:10
[b] John 1:32
3:17 [a] John 12:28
[b] Ps. 2:7
4:1 [a] Mark 1:12
[b] Ezek. 3:14
4:2 [1] *hungry*
4:4 [a] Deut. 8:3
4:5 [a] Neh. 11:1, 18
4:6 [a] Ps. 91:11
[b] Ps. 91:12
4:7 [a] Deut. 6:16
[1] *test*
4:8 [a] [1 John 2:15–17]
4:10 [a] Deut. 6:13; 10:20 [1] *Away with you*

4:11 [a] [James 4:7]
[b] [Heb. 1:14]
4:12 [a] John 4:43
4:15 [a] Is. 9:1, 2
4:16 [a] Luke 2:32
[1] *has dawned*
4:17 [a] Mark 1:14, 15
[b] Matt. 3:2; 10:7
[1] *near*
4:18 [a] Mark 1:16–20 [b] John 1:40–42
4:19 [a] Luke 5:10
4:20 [a] Mark 10:28
4:21 [a] Mark 1:19
4:23 [a] Matt. 9:35
[b] [Matt. 24:14]
[c] Mark 1:34 [1] Lit. *every disease*
[2] Lit. *every sickness*
4:24 [a] Luke 4:40
[1] *various* [2] *demons* [3] *epileptics*
[4] *were paralyzed*
4:25 [a] Mark 3:7, 8
[1] *The Ten Cities*
5:1 [a] Mark 3:13
[1] *seated*
5:2 [a] [Matt. 7:29]

3 [a]Blessed *are* the poor in spirit: for theirs is the kingdom of heaven.

4 [a]Blessed *are* they that mourn: for they shall be comforted.

5 [a]Blessed *are* the meek: for [b]they shall inherit the [1]earth.

6 Blessed *are* they which do [a]hunger and thirst after righteousness: [b]for they shall be filled.

7 Blessed *are* the merciful: [a]for they shall obtain mercy.

8 [a]Blessed *are* the pure in heart: for [b]they shall see God.

9 [a]Blessed *are* the peacemakers: for they shall be called the [1]children of God.

10 [a]Blessed *are* they which are persecuted for righteousness' sake: for theirs is the kingdom of heaven.

11 [a]Blessed are ye, when *men* shall revile you, and persecute *you*, and shall say all manner of [b]evil against you falsely, for my sake.

12 [a]Rejoice, and be exceeding glad: for great *is* your reward in heaven: for [b]so persecuted they the prophets which were before you.

13 Ye are the salt of the earth: [a]but if the salt have lost his [1]savour, [2]wherewith shall it be salted? it is thenceforth good for nothing, but to be cast out, and to be trodden under foot of men.

14 [a]Ye are the light of the world. A city that is set on an hill cannot be hid.

15 Neither do men [a]light a [1]candle, and put it under a [2]bushel, but on a [3]candlestick; and it giveth light unto all that are in the house.

16 Let your light so shine before men, [a]that they may see your good works, and [b]glorify your Father which is in heaven.

17 [a]Think not that I am come to destroy the law, or the prophets: I am not come to destroy, but to fulfil.

18 For verily I say unto you, [a]Till heaven and earth pass, one [1]jot or one [2]tittle shall [3]in no wise pass from the law, till all be fulfilled.

19 [a]Whosoever therefore shall break one of these least commandments, and shall teach men so, he shall be called the least in the kingdom of heaven: but whosoever shall do and teach *them,* the same shall be called great in the kingdom of heaven.

20 For I say unto you, That except your righteousness shall exceed [a]the righteousness of the scribes and Pharisees, ye shall [1]in no case enter into the kingdom of heaven.

21 Ye have heard that it was said [1]by them of old time, [a]Thou shalt not [2]kill; and whosoever shall [2]kill shall be in danger of the judgment:

22 But I say unto you, That [a]whosoever is angry with his brother without

a cause shall be in danger of the judgment: and whosoever shall say to his brother, [b]Raca,[1] shall be in danger of the council: but whosoever shall say, [2]Thou fool, shall be in danger of [3]hell fire.

23 Therefore [a]if thou bring thy gift to the altar, and there rememberest that thy brother hath [1]ought against thee;

24 [a]Leave there thy gift before the altar, and go thy way; first be reconciled to thy brother, and then come and offer thy gift.

25 [a]Agree with thine adversary quickly, [b]whiles thou art in the way with him; lest at any time the adversary deliver thee to the judge, and the judge deliver thee to the officer, and thou be cast into prison.

26 Verily I say unto thee, Thou shalt by no means come out thence, till thou hast paid the uttermost [1]farthing.

27 Ye have heard that it was said [1]by them of old time, [a]Thou shalt not commit adultery:

28 But I say unto you, That whosoever [a]looketh on a woman to lust after her hath committed adultery with her already in his heart.

29 [a]And if thy right eye [1]offend thee, [b]pluck it out, and cast *it* from thee: for it is profitable for thee that one of thy members should perish, and not *that* thy whole body should be cast into hell.

30 And if thy right hand [1]offend thee, cut it off, and cast *it* from thee: for it is profitable for thee that one of thy members should perish, and not *that* thy whole body should be cast into [2]hell.

31 It hath been said, [a]Whosoever shall [1]put away his wife, let him give her a [2]writing of divorcement:

32 But I say unto you, That [a]whosoever shall put away his wife, saving for the cause of [1]fornication, causeth her to commit adultery: and whosoever shall marry her that is divorced committeth adultery.

33 Again, ye have heard that [a]it hath been said [1]by them of old time, [b]Thou shalt not [2]forswear thyself, but [c]shalt perform unto the Lord thine oaths:

34 But I say unto you, [a]Swear not at all; neither by heaven; for it is [b]God's throne:

35 Nor by the earth; for it is his footstool: neither by Jerusalem; for it is the city of [a]the great King.

36 Neither shalt thou swear by thy head, because thou canst not make one hair white or black.

37 [a]But let your [1]communication be, Yea, yea; Nay, nay: for whatsoever is more than these cometh [2]of evil.

5:3 [a] Luke 6:20–23
5:4 [a] Rev. 21:4
5:5 [a] Ps. 37:11 [b] [Rom. 4:13] [1] *land*
5:6 [a] Luke 1:53 [b] [Is. 55:1; 65:13]
5:7 [a] Ps. 41:1
5:8 [a] Ps. 15:2; 24:4 [b] 1 Cor. 13:12
5:9 [1] Lit. *sons*
5:10 [a] 1 Pet. 3:14
5:11 [a] Luke 6:22 [b] 1 Pet. 4:14
5:12 [a] 1 Pet. 4:13, 14 [b] Acts 7:52
5:13 [a] Luke 14:34 [1] *flavour* [2] *by what*
5:14 [a] [John 8:12]
5:15 [a] Luke 8:16 [1] *lamp* [2] *basket* [3] *lampstand*
5:16 [a] 1 Pet. 2:12 [b] [John 15:8]
5:17 [a] Rom. 10:4
5:18 [a] Luke 16:17 [1] Gr. *iota,* Heb. *yod,* the smallest letter. [2] The smallest stroke in a Heb. letter [3] *by no means*
5:19 [a] [James 2:10]
5:20 [a] [Rom. 10:3] [1] *by no means*
5:21 [a] Ex. 20:13; Deut. 5:17 [1] *to* [2] *murder*
5:22 [a] [1 John 3:15] [b] [James 2:20; 3:6] [1] Lit., in Aram., *Empty head* [2] Gr. *More* [3] Gr. *gehenna*
5:23 [a] Matt. 8:4 [1] *something*
5:24 [a] [Job 42:8]
5:25 [a] Luke 12:58, 59 [b] [Is. 55:6]
5:26 [1] Gr. *kodrantes*
5:27 [a] Ex. 20:14; Deut. 5:18 [1] *to*
5:28 [a] Prov. 6:25
5:29 [a] Mark 9:43 [b] [Col. 3:5] [1] *cause you to sin*
5:30 [1] *causes you to sin* [2] Gr. *gehenna*
5:31 [a] Deut. 24:1 [1] *divorce* [2] *certificate*
5:32 [a] [Luke 16:18] [1] *sexual immorality*
5:33 [a] Matt. 23:16 [b] Lev. 19:12 [c] Deut. 23:23 [1] *to* [2] *swear falsely*
5:34 [a] James 5:12 [b] Is. 66:1
5:35 [a] Ps. 48:2   5:37 [a] [Col. 4:6] [1] *word* [2] *from the evil one*

792

**38** Ye have heard that it hath been said, ªAn eye for an eye, and a tooth for a tooth:

**39** But I say unto you, ªThat ye resist not ¹evil: ᵇbut whosoever shall ²smite thee on thy right cheek, turn to him the other also.

**40** And if any man will sue thee at the law, and take away thy ¹coat, let him have *thy* cloke also.

**41** And whosoever ªshall compel thee to go a mile, go with him ¹twain.

**42** Give to him that asketh thee, and ªfrom him that would borrow of thee turn not thou away.

**43** Ye have heard that it hath been said, ªThou shalt love thy neighbour, ᵇand hate thine enemy.

**44** But I say unto you, ªLove your enemies, bless them that curse you, ᵇdo good to them that hate you, and pray ᶜfor them which ¹despitefully use you, and persecute you;

**45** That ye may be the ¹children of your Father which is in heaven: for ªhe maketh his sun to rise on the evil and on the good, and sendeth rain on the just and on the unjust.

**46** ªFor if ye love them which love you, what reward have ye? do not even the ¹publicans the same?

**47** And if ye ¹salute your brethren only, what do ye more *than others?* do not even the ²publicans so?

**48** ªBe ye therefore perfect, even ᵇas your Father which is in heaven is perfect.

## CHAPTER 6

Tᴀᴋᴇ heed that ye do not your ¹alms before men, to be seen of them: otherwise ye have no reward ²of your Father which is in heaven.

**2** Therefore ªwhen thou doest *thine* alms, do not sound a trumpet before thee, as the hypocrites do in the synagogues and in the streets, that they may have glory of men. Verily I say unto you, They have their reward.

**3** But when thou doest alms, let not thy left hand know what thy right hand doeth:

**4** That thine ¹alms may be in secret: and thy Father which seeth in secret himself ªshall reward thee openly.

**5** And when thou prayest, thou shalt not be as the ¹hypocrites *are:* for they love to pray standing in the synagogues and in the corners of the streets, that they may be seen of men. Verily I say unto you, They have their reward.

**6** But thou, when thou prayest, ªenter into thy ¹closet, and when thou hast shut thy door, pray to thy Father which is in secret; and thy Father which seeth in secret shall reward thee openly.

**7** But when ye pray, ªuse not vain

5:38 ª Ex. 21:24;
Lev. 24:20; Deut.
19:21
5:39 ª Luke 6:29
ᵇ Is. 50:6 ¹ *an evil
person* ² *slaps*
5:40 ¹ *tunic*
5:41 ª Matt. 27:32
¹ *two*
5:42 ª Luke
6:30–34
5:43 ª Lev. 19:18
ᵇ Deut. 23:3–6
5:44 ª Luke
6:27 ᵇ [Rom.
12:20] ᶜ Acts 7:60
¹ *spitefully*
5:45 ª Job 25:3
¹ Lit. *sons*
5:46 ª Luke 6:32
¹ *tax collectors*
5:47 ¹ *greet* ² *tax
collectors*
5:48 ª [Col. 1:28;
4:12] ᵇ Eph. 5:1
6:1 ¹ *charitable
deeds* ² *from*
6:2 ª Rom. 12:8
6:4 ª Luke 14:12–
14 ¹ *charitable
deed*
6:5 ¹ *pretenders*
6:6 ª 2 Kin. 4:33
¹ *inner room*
6:7 ª Eccl. 5:2

ᵇ 1 Kin. 18:26
6:8 ª [Rom.
8:26, 27]
6:9 ª Luke 11:2–4
ᵇ [Matt. 5:9, 16]
ᶜ Mal. 1:11
6:10 ª Matt. 26:42
ᵇ Ps. 103:20
6:11 ª Prov. 30:8
6:12 ª [Matt.
18:21, 22]
6:13 ª [2 Pet. 2:9]
ᵇ John 17:15 ¹ Or
*the evil one*
6:14 ª Mark 11:25
6:15 ª Matt. 18:35
6:16 ª Is. 58:3–7
¹ *pretenders*
6:17 ª Ruth 3:3
6:19 ª Prov. 23:4
¹ *ruin*
6:20 ª Matt. 19:21
6:22 ª Luke
11:34, 35 ¹ *lamp*
² *Healthy*
6:23 ¹ *Unhealthy*
6:24 ª Luke 16:9,
11, 13 ᵇ [Gal. 1:10]
¹ *be loyal to* ² Lit.,
in Aram., *riches*
6:25 ª Luke 12:22
¹ *Do not worry
about* ² *food*
³ *clothing*
6:26 ª Luke 12:24

repetitions, as the heathen *do:* ᵇfor they think that they shall be heard for their much speaking.

**8** Be not ye therefore like unto them: for your Father ªknoweth what things ye have need of, before ye ask him.

**9** After this ªmanner therefore pray ye: ᵇOur Father which art in heaven, Hallowed be thy ᶜname.

**10** Thy kingdom come. ªThy will be done in earth, ᵇas *it is* in heaven.

**11** Give us this day our ªdaily bread.

**12** And ªforgive us our debts, as we forgive our debtors.

**13** ªAnd lead us not into temptation, but ᵇdeliver us from ¹evil: For thine is the kingdom, and the power, and the glory, for ever. Amen.

**14** ªFor if ye forgive men their trespasses, your heavenly Father will also forgive you:

**15** But ªif ye forgive not men their trespasses, neither will your Father forgive your trespasses.

**16** Moreover ªwhen ye fast, be not, as the ¹hypocrites, of a sad countenance: for they disfigure their faces, that they may appear unto men to fast. Verily I say unto you, They have their reward.

**17** But thou, when thou fastest, ªanoint thine head, and wash thy face;

**18** That thou appear not unto men to fast, but unto thy Father which is in secret: and thy Father, which seeth in secret, shall reward thee openly.

**19** ªLay not up for yourselves treasures upon earth, where moth and rust doth ¹corrupt, and where thieves break through and steal:

**20** ªBut lay up for yourselves treasures in heaven, where neither moth nor rust doth corrupt, and where thieves do not break through nor steal:

**21** For where your treasure is, there will your heart be also.

**22** ªThe ¹light of the body is the eye: if therefore thine eye be ²single, thy whole body shall be full of light.

**23** But if thine eye be ¹evil, thy whole body shall be full of darkness. If therefore the light that is in thee be darkness, how great *is* that darkness!

**24** ªNo man can serve two masters: for either he will hate the one, and love the other; or else he will ¹hold to the one, and despise the other. ᵇYe cannot serve God and ²mammon.

**25** Therefore I say unto you, ªTake¹ no thought for your life, what ye shall eat, or what ye shall drink; nor yet for your body, what ye shall put on. Is not the life more than ²meat, and the body than ³raiment?

**26** ªBehold the fowls of the air: for they sow not, neither do they reap,

nor gather into barns; yet your heavenly Father feedeth them. Are ye not
much better than they?
27 Which of you by [1]taking thought
can add one cubit unto his [2]stature?
28 And why [1]take ye thought for raiment? Consider the lilies of the field,
how they grow; they toil not, neither
do they spin:
29 And yet I say unto you, That even
Solomon in all his glory was not [1]ar-
rayed like one of these.
30 Wherefore, if God so [1]clothe the
grass of the field, which to day is, and
to morrow is cast into the oven, *shall*
*he* not much more *clothe* you, O ye of
little faith?
31 Therefore [1]take no thought, saying, What shall we eat? or, What shall
we drink? or, Wherewithal shall we
be clothed?
32 (For after all these things do the
Gentiles seek:) for your heavenly Father knoweth that ye have need of all
these things.
33 But [a]seek ye first the kingdom of
God, and his righteousness; and all
these things shall be added unto you.
34 [1]Take therefore no thought for
the morrow: for the morrow shall
take thought for the things of itself.
Sufficient unto the day *is* the [2]evil
thereof.

## CHAPTER 7

JUDGE[1] [a]not, that ye be not judged.
2 For with what [1]judgment ye
judge, ye shall be judged: [a]and with
what measure ye [2]mete, it shall be
measured to you again.
3 [a]And why beholdest thou the
[1]mote that is in thy brother's eye, but
considerest not the [2]beam that is in
thine own eye?
4 Or how wilt thou say to thy
brother, Let me pull out the [1]mote
out of thine eye; and, behold, a [2]beam
*is* in thine own eye?
5 Thou hypocrite, first cast out the
beam out of thine own eye; and then
shalt thou see clearly to cast out the
[1]mote out of thy brother's eye.
6 [a]Give not that which is holy unto
the dogs, neither cast ye your pearls
before swine, lest they trample them
under their feet, and turn again and
[1]rend you.
7 [a]Ask, and it shall be given you;
seek, and ye shall find; knock, and it
shall be opened unto you:
8 For [a]every one that asketh receiveth; and he that seeketh findeth;
and to him that knocketh it shall be
opened.
9 [a]Or what man is there of you,
whom if his son ask bread, will he
give him a stone?
10 Or if he ask a fish, will he give
him a serpent?
11 If ye then, [a]being evil, know how
to give good gifts unto your children,
how much more shall your Father
which is in heaven give good things
to them that ask him?
12 Therefore all things [a]whatsoever
ye would that men should do to you,
do ye even so to them: for [b]this is the
law and the prophets.
13 [a]Enter ye in at the [1]strait gate:
for wide *is* the gate, and broad *is* the
way, that leadeth to destruction, and
many there be which go in thereat:
14 [1]Because strait *is* the gate, and
[2]narrow *is* the way, which leadeth
unto life, and few there be that find it.
15 [a]Beware of false prophets,
[b]which come to you in sheep's clothing, but inwardly they are [1]ravening
wolves.
16 [a]Ye shall know them by their
fruits. [b]Do men gather grapes of
thorns, or figs of thistles?
17 Even so [a]every good tree bringeth forth good fruit; but a corrupt
tree bringeth forth [1]evil fruit.
18 A good tree cannot bring forth
[1]evil fruit, neither *can* a corrupt tree
bring forth good fruit.
19 [a]Every tree that bringeth not
forth good fruit is hewn down, and
cast into the fire.
20 Wherefore by their fruits ye shall
know them.
21 Not every one that saith unto
me, [a]Lord, Lord, shall enter into
the kingdom of heaven; but he that
[b]doeth the will of my Father which is
in heaven.
22 Many will say to me in that day,
Lord, Lord, have we [a]not prophesied
in thy name? and in thy name have
cast out [1]devils? and in thy name
done many [2]wonderful works?
23 And [a]then will I profess unto
them, I never knew you: [b]depart
from me, ye that work [1]iniquity.
24 Therefore [a]whosoever heareth
these sayings of mine, and doeth
them, I will liken him unto a wise
man, which built his house upon [1]a
rock:
25 And the rain descended, and the
floods came, and the winds blew, and
beat upon that house; and it fell not:
for it was founded upon [1]a rock.
26 And every one that heareth these
sayings of mine, and doeth them not,
shall be likened unto a foolish man,
which built his house upon the sand:
27 And the rain descended, and the
floods came, and the winds blew, and
beat upon that house; and it fell: and
great was the fall of it.
28 And it came to pass, when Jesus
had ended these sayings, [a]the people
were astonished at his [1]doctrine:
29 [a]For he taught them as *one* having authority, and not as the scribes.

6:27 [1] *worrying* [2] *height*
6:28 [1] *do you worry about clothing*
6:29 [1] *clothed*
6:30 [1] *clothes*
6:31 [1] *do not worry*
6:33 [a] [1 Tim. 4:8]
6:34 [1] *Therefore do not worry about tomorrow* [2] *trouble*
7:1 [a] Rom. 14:3 [1] Condemn
7:2 [a] Luke 6:38 [1] Condemnation [2] use
7:3 [a] Luke 6:41 [1] *speck* [2] *plank*
7:4 [1] *speck* [2] *plank*
7:5 [1] *speck*
7:6 [a] Prov. 9:7, 8 [1] *tear*
7:7 [a] [Mark 11:24]
7:8 [a] Prov. 8:17
7:9 [a] Luke 11:11
7:11 [a] Gen. 6:5; 8:21
7:12 [a] Luke 6:31 [b] Gal. 5:14
7:13 [a] Luke 13:24 [1] *narrow*
7:14 [1] *How narrow* [2] *difficult* or *confined*
7:15 [a] Jer. 23:16 [b] Mic. 3:5 [1] *ravenous*
7:16 [a] Matt. 7:20; 12:33 [b] Luke 6:43
7:17 [a] Jer. 11:19; Matt. 12:33 [1] *bad*
7:18 [1] *bad*
7:19 [a] Matt. 3:10; Luke 3:9; [John 15:2, 6]
7:21 [a] Hos. 8:2; Matt. 25:11; Luke 6:46; Acts 19:13 [b] Rom. 2:13; James 1:22
7:22 [a] Num. 24:4 [1] *demons* [2] *miracles*
7:23 [a] Matt. 25:12; Luke 13:25; [2 Tim. 2:19] [b] Ps. 5:5; 6:8; [Matt. 25:41]; Luke 13:27 [1] *lawlessness*
7:24 [a] Matt. 7:24–27; Luke 6:47–49 [1] *the*
7:25 [1] *the*
7:28 [a] Matt. 13:54; Mark 1:22; 6:2; Luke 4:32; John 7:46 [1] *teaching*
7:29 [a] [John 7:46]

## CHAPTER 8

WHEN he was come down from the mountain, great multitudes followed him.

2 ªAnd, behold, there came a leper and ᵇworshipped him, saying, Lord, if thou wilt, thou canst make me clean.

3 And Jesus put forth *his* hand, and touched him, saying, I will; be thou clean. And immediately his leprosy ªwas cleansed.

4 And Jesus saith unto him, ªSee thou tell no man; but go thy way, shew thyself to the priest, and offer the gift that ᵇMoses ᶜcommanded, for a testimony unto them.

5 ªAnd when Jesus was entered into Capernaum, there came unto him a ᵇcenturion, beseeching him,

6 And saying, Lord, my servant lieth at home ¹sick of the palsy, grievously tormented.

7 And Jesus saith unto him, I will come and heal him.

8 The centurion answered and said, Lord, ªI am not worthy that thou shouldest come under my roof: but ᵇspeak the word only, and my servant shall be healed.

9 For I am a man under authority, having soldiers under me: and I say to this *man*, Go, and he goeth; and to another, Come, and he cometh; and to my servant, Do this, and he doeth *it*.

10 When Jesus heard *it*, he marvelled, and said to them that followed, Verily I say unto you, I have not found so great faith, no, not in Israel.

11 And I say unto you, That ªmany shall come from the east and west, and shall sit down with Abraham, and Isaac, and Jacob, in the kingdom of heaven.

12 But ªthe ¹children of the kingdom ᵇshall be cast out into outer darkness: there shall be weeping and gnashing of teeth.

13 And Jesus said unto the centurion, Go thy way; and as thou hast believed, *so* be it done unto thee. And his servant was healed in the selfsame hour.

14 ªAnd when Jesus was come into Peter's house, he saw ᵇhis wife's mother laid, and sick of a fever.

15 And he touched her hand, and the fever left her: and she arose, and ministered unto them.

16 ªWhen the even was come, they brought unto him many that were possessed with ¹devils: and he cast out the spirits with *his* word, and healed all that were sick:

17 That it might be fulfilled which was spoken by Esaias the prophet, saying, ªHimself took our infirmities, and bare *our* sicknesses.

18 Now when Jesus saw great multitudes about him, he gave commandment to depart unto the other side.

19 ªAnd a certain scribe came, and said unto him, Master, I will follow thee whithersoever thou goest.

20 And Jesus saith unto him, The foxes have holes, and the birds of the air *have* nests; but the Son of man hath not where to lay *his* head.

21 ªAnd another of his disciples said unto him, Lord, ᵇsuffer me first to go and bury my father.

22 But Jesus said unto him, Follow me; and let the dead bury their dead.

23 And when he was entered into a ship, his disciples followed him.

24 ªAnd, behold, there arose a great tempest in the sea, insomuch that the ship was covered with the waves: but he was asleep.

25 And his disciples came to *him*, and awoke him, saying, Lord, save us: we perish.

26 And he saith unto them, Why are ye fearful, O ye of little faith? Then ªhe arose, and rebuked the winds and the sea; and there was a great calm.

27 But the men marvelled, saying, What manner of man is this, that even the winds and the sea obey him!

28 ªAnd when he was come to the other side into the country of the Gergesenes, there met him two possessed with ¹devils, coming out of the tombs, exceeding fierce, so that no man might pass by that way.

29 And, behold, they cried out, saying, What have we to do with thee, Jesus, thou Son of God? art thou come hither to torment us before the time?

30 And there was a good way off from them an herd of many swine feeding.

31 So the ¹devils besought him, saying, If thou cast us out, ²suffer us to go away into the herd of swine.

32 And he said unto them, Go. And when they were come out, they went into the herd of swine: and, behold, the whole herd of swine ran violently down a steep place into the sea, and perished in the waters.

33 And they that kept them fled, and went their ways into the city, and told every thing, and what was befallen to the ¹possessed of the devils.

34 And, behold, the whole city came out to meet Jesus: and when they saw him, ªthey ¹besought *him* that he would depart out of their ²coasts.

## CHAPTER 9

AND he entered into a ship, and passed over, ªand came into his own city.

2 ªAnd, behold, they brought to him a ¹man sick of the palsy, lying on

### Center column references

8:2 ª Matt. 8:2–4; Mark 1:40–45; Luke 5:12–14
ᵇ Matt. 2:11; 9:18; 15:25; John 9:38; Acts 10:25

8:3 ª Matt. 11:5; Luke 4:27

8:4 ª Matt. 9:30; Mark 5:43; Luke 4:41; 8:56; 9:21
ᵇ Lev. 14:3, 4, 10; Mark 1:44; Luke 5:14 ᶜ Lev. 14:4–32; Deut. 24:8

8:5 ª Luke 7:1–3 ᵇ Matt. 27:54; Acts 10:1

8:6 ¹ *paralyzed*

8:8 ª Luke 15:19, 21 ᵇ Ps. 107:20

8:11 ª [Gen. 12:3; Is. 2:2, 3; 11:10]; Mal. 1:11; Luke 13:29; [Acts 10:45; 11:18; 14:27; Rom. 15:9–13; Eph. 3:6]

8:12 ª [Matt. 21:43] ᵇ Matt. 13:42, 50; 22:13; 24:51; 25:30; Luke 13:28; 2 Pet. 2:17; Jude 13 ¹ Lit. *sons*

8:14 ª Matt. 8:14–16; Mark 1:29–31; Luke 4:38, 39 ᵇ 1 Cor. 9:5

8:16 ª Mark 1:32–34; Luke 4:40, 41 ¹ *demons*

8:17 ª Is. 53:4; 1 Pet. 2:24

8:19 ª Matt. 8:19–22; Luke 9:57, 58

8:21 ª Luke 9:59, 60 ᵇ 1 Kin. 19:20

8:24 ª Mark 4:37; Luke 8:23–25

8:26 ª Ps. 65:7; 89:9; 107:29

8:28 ª Mark 5:1–4; Luke 8:26–33 ¹ *demons*

8:31 ¹ *demons begged* ² *permit*

8:33 ¹ *demon-possessed men*

8:34 ª Deut. 5:25; 1 Kin. 17:18; Amos 7:12; Luke 5:8; Acts 16:39 ¹ *begged* ² *region*

9:1 ª Matt. 4:13; 11:23; Mark 5:21

9:2 ª Mark 2:3–12; Luke 5:18–26 ¹ *paralyzed man*

a bed: [b]and Jesus seeing their faith said unto the [2]sick of the palsy; Son, be of good cheer; thy sins be forgiven thee.

3 And, behold, certain of the scribes said within themselves, This *man* blasphemeth.

4 And Jesus [a]knowing their thoughts said, Wherefore think ye evil in your hearts?

5 For [1]whether is easier, to say, Thy sins be forgiven thee; or to say, Arise, and walk?

6 But that ye may know that the Son of man hath power on earth to forgive sins, (then saith he to the [1]sick of the palsy,) Arise, take up thy bed, and go unto thine house.

7 And he arose, and departed to his house.

8 But when the multitudes saw *it,* they [a]marvelled, and glorified God, which had given such power unto men.

9 [a]And as Jesus passed forth from thence, he saw a man, named Matthew, sitting at the [1]receipt of custom: and he saith unto him, Follow me. And he arose, and followed him.

10 [a]And it came to pass, as Jesus sat [1]at meat in the house, behold, many [2]publicans and sinners came and sat down with him and his disciples.

11 And when the Pharisees saw *it,* they said unto his disciples, Why eateth your Master with [a]publicans[1] and [b]sinners?

12 But when Jesus heard *that,* he said unto them, They that [1]be whole need not a physician, but they that are sick.

13 But go ye and learn what *that* meaneth, [a]I will have mercy, and not sacrifice: for I am not come to call the righteous, [b]but sinners to repentance.

14 Then came to him the disciples of John, saying, [a]Why do we and the Pharisees fast [1]oft, but thy disciples fast not?

15 And Jesus said unto them, Can [a]the [1]children of the bridechamber mourn, as long as the bridegroom is with them? but the days will come, when the bridegroom shall be taken from them, and [b]then shall they fast.

16 No man putteth a piece of [1]new cloth unto an old garment, for [2]that which is put in to fill it up [3]taketh from the garment, and the [4]rent is made worse.

17 Neither do men put new wine into old [1]bottles: else the bottles [2]break, and the wine runneth out, and the bottles [3]perish: but they put new wine into new bottles, and both are preserved.

18 [a]While he spake these things unto them, behold, there came a cer-

tain ruler, and worshipped him, saying, My daughter is even now dead: but come and lay thy hand upon her, and she shall live.

19 And Jesus arose, and followed him, and *so did* his [a]disciples.

20 [a]And, behold, a woman, which was diseased with [1]an issue of blood twelve years, came behind *him,* and [b]touched the hem of his garment:

21 For she said within herself, If I may but touch his garment, I shall be whole.

22 But Jesus turned him about, and when he saw her, he said, Daughter, [1]be of good comfort; [a]thy faith hath made thee whole. And the woman was made whole from that hour.

23 [a]And when Jesus came into the ruler's house, and saw [b]the [1]minstrels and the [2]people making a noise,

24 He said unto them, [a]Give place: for the maid is not dead, but sleepeth. And they laughed him to scorn.

25 But when the [1]people were put [2]forth, he went in, and [a]took her by the hand, and the maid arose.

26 And the [a]fame [1]hereof went abroad into all that land.

27 And when Jesus departed thence, [a]two blind men followed him, crying, and saying, [b]*Thou* son of David, have mercy on us.

28 And when he was come into the house, the blind men came to him: and Jesus saith unto them, Believe ye that I am able to do this? They said unto him, Yea, Lord.

29 Then touched he their eyes, saying, According to your faith be it unto you.

30 And their eyes were opened; and Jesus [1]straitly charged them, saying, [a]See *that* no man know *it.*

31 [a]But they, when they were departed, spread abroad his fame in all that [1]country.

32 [a]As they went out, behold, they brought to him a [1]dumb man possessed with a [2]devil.

33 And when the [1]devil was cast out, the [2]dumb spake: and the multitudes marvelled, saying, It was never so seen in Israel.

34 But the Pharisees said, [a]He casteth out [1]devils through the [2]prince of the devils.

35 And Jesus went about all the cities and villages, [a]teaching in their synagogues, and preaching the gospel of the kingdom, and healing every sickness and every disease among the people.

36 [a]But when he saw the multitudes, he was moved with compassion on them, because they [1]fainted, and were scattered abroad, [b]as sheep having no shepherd.

9:2 [b] Matt. 8:10
[2] paralytic
9:4 [a] Ps. 139:2;
Matt. 12:25; Mark
12:15; Luke 5:22;
6:8; 9:47; 11:17
9:5 [1] which
9:6 [1] paralytic
9:8 [a] Matt. 8:27;
John 7:15
9:9 [a] Mark 2:14;
Luke 5:27 [1] tax
office
9:10 [a] Mark 2:15;
Luke 5:29 [1] at
the table [2] tax
collectors
9:11 [a] Matt.
11:19; Mark 2:16;
Luke 5:30; 15:2
[b] [Gal. 2:15] [1] tax
collectors
9:12 [1] are well
9:13 [a] Hos. 6:6;
[Mic. 6:6–8];
Matt. 12:7 [b] Mark
2:17; Luke 5:32;
1 Tim. 1:15
9:14 [a] Mark 2:18;
Luke 5:33–35;
18:12 [1] often
9:15 [a] John 3:29
[b] Acts 13:2, 3;
14:23 [1] friends of
the bridegroom
9:16 [1] unshrunk
[2] The patch
[3] pulls away from
[4] tear
9:17 [1] wineskins
[2] burst [3] are
ruined
9:18 [a] Luke
8:41–56
9:19 [a] Matt.
10:2–4
9:20 [a] Luke 8:43
[b] Matt. 14:36; 23:5
[1] a flow
9:22 [a] Luke 7:50;
8:48; 17:19; 18:42
[1] take courage
9:23 [a] Mark 5:38
[b] 2 Chr. 35:25
[1] flute players
[2] crowd
9:24 [a] Acts 20:10
9:25 [a] Mark 1:31
[1] crowd [2] outside
[1] of this
9:26 [a] Matt. 4:24
[1] of this
9:27 [a] Matt.
20:29–34 [b] Luke
18:38, 39
9:30 [a] Matt. 8:4
[1] sternly warned
9:31 [a] Mark 7:36
[1] Lit. land
9:32 [a] Matt.
12:22, 24 [1] mute
[2] demon
9:33 [1] demon
[2] mute
9:34 [a] Luke 11:15
[1] demons [2] ruler
of demons
9:35 [a] Matt. 4:23  9:36 [a] Mark 6:34  [b] Num. 27:17
[1] were weary

37 Then saith he unto his disciples, [a]The harvest truly *is* plenteous, but the labourers *are* few;

38 [a]Pray ye therefore the Lord of the harvest, that he will send forth labourers into his harvest.

## CHAPTER 10

AND [a]when he had called unto *him* his twelve disciples, he gave them power *against* unclean spirits, to cast them out, and to heal all manner of sickness and all manner of disease.

2 Now the names of the twelve apostles are these; The first, Simon, [a]who is called Peter, and Andrew his brother; James *the son* of Zebedee, and John his brother;

3 Philip, and Bartholomew; Thomas, and Matthew the [1]publican; James *the son* of Alphaeus, and Lebbaeus, whose surname was Thaddaeus;

4 [a]Simon the Canaanite, and Judas [b]Iscariot, who also betrayed him.

5 These twelve Jesus sent forth, and commanded them, saying, [a]Go not into the way of the Gentiles, and into *any* city of [b]the Samaritans enter ye not:

6 [a]But go rather to the [b]lost sheep of the house of Israel.

7 [a]And as ye go, preach, saying, [b]The kingdom of heaven [1]is at hand.

8 Heal the sick, cleanse the lepers, raise the dead, cast out [1]devils: [a]freely ye have received, freely give.

9 [a]Provide neither gold, nor silver, nor [b]brass in your [1]purses,

10 Nor [1]scrip for *your* journey, neither two [2]coats, neither [3]shoes, nor yet [4]staves: [a]for the workman is worthy of his [5]meat.

11 [a]And into whatsoever city or town ye shall enter, enquire who in it is worthy; and there abide till ye go thence.

12 And when ye come into an house, [1]salute it.

13 [a]And if the [1]house be worthy, let your peace come upon it: [b]but if it be not worthy, let your peace return to you.

14 [a]And whosoever shall not receive you, nor hear your words, when ye depart out of that house or city, [b]shake off the dust of your feet.

15 Verily I say unto you, [a]It shall be more tolerable for the land of Sodom and Gomorrha in the day of judgment, than for that city.

16 [a]Behold, I send you forth as sheep in the midst of wolves: [b]be ye therefore wise as serpents, and [c]harmless[1] as doves.

17 But beware of men: for [a]they will deliver you up to the councils, and [b]they will scourge you in their synagogues;

18 And [a]ye shall be brought before governors and kings for my sake, for a testimony [1]against them and the Gentiles.

19 [a]But when they deliver you up, [1]take no thought how or what ye shall speak: for [b]it shall be given you in that same hour what ye shall speak.

20 [a]For it is not ye that speak, but the Spirit of your Father which speaketh in you.

21 [a]And the brother shall deliver up the brother to death, and the father the child: and the children shall rise up against *their* parents, and cause them to be put to death.

22 And [a]ye shall be hated of all *men* for my name's sake: [b]but he that endureth to the end shall be saved.

23 But [a]when they persecute you in this city, flee ye into another: for verily I say unto you, Ye shall not have [b]gone [1]over the cities of Israel, [c]till the Son of man be come.

24 [a]The disciple is not above *his* [1]master, nor the servant above his lord.

25 It is enough for the disciple that he be as his [1]master, and the servant as his lord. If [a]they have called the master of the house [2]Beelzebub, how much more *shall they call* them of his household?

26 Fear them not therefore: [a]for there is nothing [1]covered, that shall not be revealed; and hid, that shall not be known.

27 What I tell you in darkness, *that* [a]speak ye in light: and what ye hear in the ear, *that* preach ye upon the housetops.

28 [a]And fear not them which kill the body, but are not able to kill the soul: but rather [b]fear him which is able to destroy both soul and body in [1]hell.

29 Are not two [a]sparrows sold for a [1]farthing? and one of them shall not fall on the ground without your Father.

30 [a]But the very hairs of your head are all numbered.

31 Fear ye not therefore, ye are of more value than many sparrows.

32 [a]Whosoever therefore shall confess me before men, [b]him will I confess also before my Father which is in heaven.

33 [a]But whosoever shall deny me before men, him will I also deny before my Father which is in heaven.

34 [a]Think not that I am come to send peace on earth: I came not to send peace, but a sword.

35 For I am come to set a man [1]at variance [a]against his father, and the daughter against her mother, and the daughter in law against her mother in law.

### Cross references

9:37 [a] Luke 10:2
9:38 [a] 2 Thess. 3:1
10:1 [a] Luke 6:13
10:2 [a] John 1:42
10:3 [1] *tax collector*
10:4 [a] Acts 1:13 [b] John 13:2, 26
10:5 [a] Matt. 4:15 [b] John 4:9
10:6 [a] Matt. 15:24 [b] Jer. 50:6
10:7 [a] Luke 9:2 [b] Matt. 3:2 [1] *has come near*
10:8 [a] [Acts 8:18] [1] *demons*
10:9 [a] 1 Sam. 9:7 [b] Mark 6:8 [1] *money belts*
10:10 [a] 1 Tim. 5:18 [1] *bag* [2] *tunics* [3] *sandals* [4] *staffs* [5] *food*
10:11 [a] Luke 10:8
10:12 [1] *greet*
10:13 [a] Luke 10:5 [b] Ps. 35:13 [1] *household*
10:14 [a] Mark 6:11 [b] Acts 13:51
10:15 [a] Matt. 11:22, 24
10:16 [a] Luke 10:3 [b] Eph. 5:15 [c] [Phil. 2:14–16] [1] *innocent*
10:17 [a] Mark 13:9 [b] Acts 5:40; 22:19; 26:11
10:18 [a] 2 Tim. 4:16 [1] *to*
10:19 [a] Luke 12:11, 12; 21:14, 15 [b] Ex. 4:12 [1] *do not worry about*
10:20 [a] 2 Sam. 23:2
10:21 [a] Mic. 7:6
10:22 [a] Luke 21:17 [b] Mark 13:13
10:23 [a] Acts 8:1 [b] [Mark 13:10] [c] Matt. 16:28 [1] *through*
10:24 [a] John 15:20 [1] *teacher*
10:25 [a] John 8:48, 52 [1] *teacher* [2] Many mss. *Beelzebul; a* Philistine deity
10:26 [a] Mark 4:22 [1] *veiled*
10:27 [a] Acts 5:20
10:28 [a] Luke 12:4 [b] Luke 12:5 [1] Gr. *gehenna*
10:29 [a] Luke 12:6, 7 [1] Gr. *assarion,* a copper coin, 1/16 of a denarius
10:30 [a] Luke 21:18
10:32 [a] Luke 12:8 [b] [Rev. 3:5]
10:33 [a] 2 Tim. 2:12
10:34 [a] [Luke 12:49]
10:35 [a] Mic. 7:6 [1] *apart from*

36 And [a]a man's foes *shall be* they of his own household.

37 [a]He that loveth father or mother more than me is not worthy of me: and he that loveth son or daughter more than me is not worthy of me.

38 [a]And he that taketh not his cross, and followeth after me, is not worthy of me.

39 [a]He that findeth his life shall lose it: and he that loseth his life for my sake shall find it.

40 [a]He that receiveth you receiveth me, and he that receiveth me receiveth him that sent me.

41 [a]He that receiveth a prophet in the name of a prophet shall receive a prophet's reward; and he that receiveth a righteous man in the name of a righteous man shall receive a righteous man's reward.

42 [a]And whosoever shall give to drink unto one of these little ones a cup of cold *water* only in the name of a disciple, verily I say unto you, he shall in no wise lose his reward.

## CHAPTER 11

AND it came to pass, when Jesus had [1]made an end of commanding his twelve disciples, he departed thence to [a]teach and to preach in their cities.

2 [a]Now when John had heard [b]in the prison the works of Christ, he sent two of his disciples,

3 And said unto him, Art thou [a]he that should come, or do we look for another?

4 Jesus answered and said unto them, Go and [1]shew John again those things which ye do hear and see:

5 [a]The blind receive their sight, and the lame walk, the lepers are cleansed, and the deaf hear, the dead are raised up, and [b]the poor have the gospel preached to them.

6 And blessed is *he,* whosoever shall not [a]be offended [1]in me.

7 [a]And as they departed, Jesus began to say unto the multitudes concerning John, What went ye out into the wilderness to see? [b]A reed shaken with the wind?

8 But what went ye out for to see? A man clothed in soft raiment? behold, they that wear soft *clothing* are in kings' houses.

9 But what went ye out for to see? A prophet? yea, I say unto you, [a]and more than a prophet.

10 For this is *he,* of whom it is written, [a]Behold, I send my messenger before thy face, which shall prepare thy way before thee.

11 Verily I say unto you, Among them that are born of women there hath not risen a greater than John the Baptist: notwithstanding he that

is least in the kingdom of heaven is greater than he.

12 [a]And from the days of John the Baptist until now the kingdom of heaven suffereth violence, and the violent take it by force.

13 [a]For all the prophets and the law prophesied until John.

14 And if ye will receive *it,* this is [a]Elias, which was for to come.

15 [a]He that hath ears to hear, let him hear.

16 [a]But whereunto shall I liken this generation? It is like unto children sitting in the markets, and calling unto their [f]fellows,

17 And saying, We have [1]piped unto you, and ye have not danced; we have mourned unto you, and ye [2]have not lamented.

18 For John came neither eating nor drinking, and they say, He hath a [1]devil.

19 The Son of man came eating and drinking, and they say, Behold a man gluttonous, and a [1]winebibber, [a]a friend of [2]publicans and sinners. [b]But wisdom is justified [3]of her children.

20 [a]Then began he to [1]upbraid the cities wherein most of his mighty works were done, because they repented not:

21 Woe unto thee, Chorazin! woe unto thee, Bethsaida! for if the mighty works, which were done in you, had been done in Tyre and Sidon, they would have repented long ago [a]in sackcloth and ashes.

22 But I say unto you, [a]It shall be more tolerable for Tyre and Sidon at the day of judgment, than for you.

23 And thou, Capernaum, [a]which art exalted unto heaven, shalt be brought down to [1]hell: for if the mighty works, which have been done in thee, had been done in Sodom, it would have remained until this day.

24 But I say unto you, [a]That it shall be more tolerable for the land of Sodom in the day of judgment, than for thee.

25 [a]At that time Jesus answered and said, I thank thee, O Father, Lord of heaven and earth, because [b]thou hast hid these things from the wise and prudent, [c]and hast revealed them unto babes.

26 Even so, Father: for so it seemed good in thy sight.

27 [a]All things are delivered unto me of my Father: and no man knoweth the Son, but the Father; [b]neither knoweth any man the Father, [1]save the Son, and *he* to whomsoever the Son will reveal *him.*

28 Come unto [a]me, all *ye* that labour and are heavy laden, and I will give you rest.

### Cross references (center column)

10:36 [a] John 13:18
10:37 [a] Luke 14:26
10:38 [a] [Mark 8:34]
10:39 [a] John 12:25
10:40 [a] Luke 9:48
10:41 [a] 1 Kin. 17:10
10:42 [a] Mark 9:41
11:1 [a] Luke 23:5
[1] finished
11:2 [a] Luke 7:18–35
[b] Matt. 4:12; 14:3
11:3 [a] John 6:14
11:4 [1] tell John the things
11:5 [a] Is. 29:18; 35:4–6 [b] Is. 61:1
11:6 [a] [Rom. 9:32]
[1] because of
11:7 [a] Luke 7:24
[b] [Eph. 4:14]
11:9 [a] Luke 1:76; 20:6
11:10 [a] Mal. 3:1
11:12 [a] Luke 16:16
11:13 [a] Mal. 4:4–6
11:14 [a] Luke 1:17
11:15 [a] Luke 8:8
11:16 [a] Luke 7:31
[1] companions
11:17 [1] played the flute [2] Lit. did not beat your breast
11:18 [1] demon
11:19 [a] Matt. 9:10
[b] Luke 7:35 [1] wine drinker [2] tax collectors [3] by
11:20 [a] Luke 10:13–15, 18
[1] rebuke
11:21 [a] Jon. 3:6–8
11:22 [a] Matt. 10:15; 11:24
11:23 [a] Is. 14:13
[1] Gr. hades
11:24 [a] Matt. 10:15
11:25 [a] Luke 10:21, 22 [b] Ps. 8:2
[c] Matt. 16:17
11:27 [a] Matt. 28:18
[b] John 1:18; 6:46; 10:15 [1] except
11:28 [a] [John 6:35–37]

29 Take my yoke upon you, [a]and learn [1]of me; for I am [2]meek and [b]lowly in heart: [c]and ye shall find rest unto your souls.

30 [a]For my yoke *is* easy, and my burden is light.

## CHAPTER 12

A T that time [a]Jesus went on the sabbath day through the [1]corn; and his disciples were [2]an hungred, and began to [b]pluck the [3]ears of corn, and to eat.

2 But when the Pharisees saw *it,* they said unto him, Behold, thy disciples do that which is not lawful to do upon the sabbath day.

3 But he said unto them, Have ye not read [a]what David did, when he was [1]an hungred, and they that were with him;

4 How he entered into the house of God, and did eat [a]the shewbread, which was not lawful for him to eat, neither for them which were with him, [b]but only for the priests?

5 Or have ye not read in the [a]law, how that on the sabbath days the priests in the temple [1]profane the sabbath, and are blameless?

6 But I say unto you, That in this place is [a]*one* greater than the temple.

7 But if ye had known what *this* meaneth, [a]I [1]will have mercy, and not sacrifice, ye would not have condemned the guiltless.

8 For the Son of man is Lord even of the sabbath day.

9 [a]And when he was departed thence, he went into their synagogue:

10 And, behold, there was a man which had *his* hand withered. And they asked him, saying, [a]Is it lawful to heal on the sabbath days? that they might accuse him.

11 And he said unto them, What man shall there be among you, that shall have one sheep, and if it fall into a pit on the sabbath day, will he not lay hold on it, and lift *it* out?

12 How much then is a man better than a sheep? Wherefore it is lawful to do well on the sabbath days.

13 Then saith he to the man, Stretch forth thine hand. And he stretched *it* forth; and it was restored whole, like as the other.

14 Then [a]the Pharisees went out, and [1]held a council against him, how they might destroy him.

15 But when Jesus knew *it,* [a]he withdrew himself from thence: [b]and great multitudes followed him, and he healed them all;

16 And [a]charged[1] them that they should not make him known:

17 That it might be fulfilled which was spoken by Esaias the prophet, saying,

18 [a]Behold my servant, whom I have chosen; my beloved, [b]in whom my soul is well pleased: I will put my spirit upon him, and he shall [1]shew judgment to the Gentiles.

19 He shall not [1]strive, nor [2]cry; neither shall any man hear his voice in the streets.

20 A bruised reed shall he not break, and smoking flax shall he not quench, till he send forth [1]judgment unto victory.

21 And in his name shall the Gentiles trust.

22 [a]Then was brought unto him one possessed with a [1]devil, blind, and [2]dumb: and he healed him, insomuch that the blind and dumb both spake and saw.

23 And all the [1]people were amazed, and said, [2]Is not this the [a]son of David?

24 [a]But when the Pharisees heard *it,* they said, This *fellow* doth not cast out [1]devils, but by [2]Beelzebub the [3]prince of the [1]devils.

25 And Jesus [a]knew their thoughts, and said unto them, Every kingdom divided against itself is brought to desolation; and every city or house divided against itself shall not stand:

26 And if Satan cast out Satan, he is divided against himself; how shall then his kingdom stand?

27 And if I by Beelzebub cast out [1]devils, by whom do your children cast *them* out? therefore they shall be your judges.

28 But if I cast out [1]devils by the Spirit of God, then [a]the kingdom of God is come unto you.

29 [a]Or else how can one enter into a strong man's house, and [1]spoil his goods, except he first bind the strong man? and then he will [1]spoil his house.

30 He that is not with me is against me; and he that gathereth not with me scattereth abroad.

31 Wherefore I say unto you, [a]All manner of sin and blasphemy shall be forgiven unto men: [b]but the blasphemy *against* the *Holy* Ghost shall not be forgiven unto men.

32 And whosoever [a]speaketh a word against the Son of man, [b]it shall be forgiven him: but whosoever speaketh against the Holy Ghost, it shall not be forgiven him, neither in this [1]world, neither in the *world* to come.

33 Either make the tree good, and [a]his fruit good; or else make the tree [1]corrupt, and his fruit [1]corrupt: for the tree is known by *his* fruit.

34 O [a]generation[1] of vipers, how can ye, being evil, speak good things? [b]for out of the abundance of the heart the mouth speaketh.

### Cross references (center column)

11:29 [a] [Phil. 2:5]
[b] Zech. 9:9 [c] Jer. 6:16 [1] *from* [2] *gentle and humble*

11:30 [a] [1 John 5:3]

12:1 [a] Luke 6:1–5
[b] Deut. 23:25
[1] *grainfields*
[2] *hungry* [3] *heads of grain*

12:3 [a] 1 Sam. 21:6
[1] *hungry*

12:4 [a] Lev. 24:5
[b] Ex. 29:32

12:5 [a] Num. 28:9 [1] *treat as common*

12:6 [a] [Is. 66:1, 2]

12:7 [a] [Hos. 6:6]
[1] *desire mercy*

12:9 [a] Mark 3:1–6

12:10 [a] John 9:16

12:14 [a] Mark 3:6
[1] *took counsel*

12:15 [a] Mark 3:7
[b] Matt. 19:2

12:16 [a] Matt. 8:4; 9:30; 17:9
[1] *warned*

12:18 [a] Is. 42:1–4; 49:3 [b] Matt. 3:17; 17:5 [1] *declare justice*

12:19 [1] *quarrel* [2] *cry out*

12:20 [1] *justice*

12:22 [a] Luke 11:14, 15 [1] *demon* [2] *mute*

12:23 [a] Matt. 9:27; 21:9 [1] *multitudes* [2] *Could this be*

12:24 [a] Matt. 9:34 [1] *demons* [2] Philistine deity [3] *ruler*

12:25 [a] Matt. 9:4

12:27 [1] *demons*

12:28 [a] [Dan. 2:44; 7:14] [1] *demons*

12:29 [a] Is. 49:24 [1] *plunder*

12:31 [a] Mark 3:28–30 [b] Acts 7:51

12:32 [a] John 7:12, 52 [b] 1 Tim. 1:13 [1] *age*

12:33 [a] Matt. 7:16–18 [1] *bad*

12:34 [a] Matt. 3:7; 23:33 [b] Luke 6:45 [1] *brood or offspring*

35 A good man out of the good treasure of the heart bringeth forth good things: and an evil man out of the evil treasure bringeth forth evil things.

36 But I say unto you, That every idle word that men shall speak, they shall give account thereof in the day of judgment.

37 For by thy words thou shalt be justified, and by thy words thou shalt be condemned.

38 [a]Then certain of the scribes and of the Pharisees answered, saying, [1]Master, we would see a sign from thee.

39 But he answered and said unto them, An evil and [a]adulterous generation seeketh after a sign; and there shall no sign be given to it, but the sign of the prophet Jonas:

40 [a]For as Jonas was three days and three nights in the [1]whale's belly; so shall the Son of man be three days and three nights in the heart of the earth.

41 [a]The men of Nineveh shall rise in judgment with this generation, and [b]shall condemn it: [c]because they repented at the preaching of Jonas; and, behold, a greater than Jonas *is* here.

42 [a]The queen of the south shall rise up in the judgment with this generation, and shall condemn it: for she came from the uttermost parts of the earth to hear the wisdom of Solomon; and, behold, a greater than Solomon *is* here.

43 [a]When the unclean spirit is gone out of a man, [b]he [1]walketh through dry places, seeking rest, and findeth none.

44 Then he saith, I will return into my house from whence I came out; and when he is come, he findeth *it* empty, swept, and [1]garnished.

45 Then goeth he, and taketh with himself seven other spirits more wicked than himself, and they enter in and dwell there: [a]and the last *state* of that man is worse than the first. Even so shall it be also unto this wicked generation.

46 While he yet talked to the [1]people, [a]behold, *his* mother and [b]his [2]brethren stood [3]without, desiring to speak with him.

47 Then one said unto him, Behold, [a]thy mother and thy brethren stand [1]without, desiring to speak with thee.

48 But he answered and said unto him that told him, Who is my mother? and who are my brethren?

49 And he stretched forth his hand toward his disciples, and said, Behold my mother and my [a]brethren!

50 For [a]whosoever shall do the will of my Father which is in heaven, the same is my brother, and sister, and mother.

12:38 [a] Mark 8:11
[1] Lit. *Teacher*
12:39 [a] Matt. 16:4
12:40 [a] Jon. 1:17
[1] Lit. *belly of the great fish*
12:41 [a] Luke 11:32
[b] Jer. 3:11 [c] Jon. 3:5
12:42 [a] [1] Kin. 10:1–13
12:43 [a] Luke 11:24–26 [b] [1 Pet. 5:8] [1] Lit. *goes*
12:44 [1] *put in order*
12:45 [a] [2 Pet. 2:20–22]
12:46 [a] Luke 8:19–21 [b] John 2:12; 7:3, 5 [1] *multitudes* [2] *brothers* [3] *outside*
12:47 [a] Matt. 13:55, 56 [1] *outside*
12:49 [a] John 20:17
12:50 [a] John 15:14

13:1 [a] Mark 4:1–12
13:2 [a] Luke 8:4 [b] Luke 5:3
13:3 [a] Luke 8:5
13:5 [1] *immediately*
13:8 [a] Gen. 26:12
13:9 [a] Matt. 11:15
13:11 [a] Mark 4:10, 11 [1] *hidden truths*
13:12 [a] Matt. 25:29
13:14 [a] Is. 6:9, 10 [b] [John 3:36]
13:15 [a] Heb. 5:11 [b] Luke 19:42 [c] Acts 28:26, 27 [1] *grown dull* [2] *turn* [3] Most mss. *waxed*
13:16 [a] Luke 10:23, 24
13:17 [a] Heb. 11:13
13:18 [a] Mark 4:13–20

## The Sign of the Prophet

### CHAPTER 13

THE same day went Jesus out of the house, [a]and sat by the sea side.

2 [a]And great multitudes were gathered together unto him, so that [b]he went into a ship, and sat; and the whole multitude stood on the shore.

3 And he spake many things unto them in parables, saying, [a]Behold, a sower went forth to sow;

4 And when he sowed, some *seeds* fell by the way side, and the fowls came and devoured them up:

5 Some fell upon stony places, where they had not much earth: and [1]forthwith they sprung up, because they had no deepness of earth:

6 And when the sun was up, they were scorched; and because they had no root, they withered away.

7 And some fell among thorns; and the thorns sprung up, and choked them:

8 But other fell into good ground, and brought forth fruit, some [a]an hundredfold, some sixtyfold, some thirtyfold.

9 [a]Who hath ears to hear, let him hear.

10 And the disciples came, and said unto him, Why speakest thou unto them in parables?

11 He answered and said unto them, Because [a]it is given unto you to know the [1]mysteries of the kingdom of heaven, but to them it is not given.

12 [a]For whosoever hath, to him shall be given, and he shall have more abundance: but whosoever hath not, from him shall be taken away even that he hath.

13 Therefore speak I to them in parables: because they seeing see not; and hearing they hear not, neither do they understand.

14 And in them is fulfilled the prophecy of Esaias, which saith, [a]By hearing ye shall hear, and shall not understand; and seeing ye shall see, and shall not [b]perceive:

15 For this people's heart is [1]waxed gross, and *their* ears [a]are dull of hearing, and their eyes they have [b]closed; lest at any time they should see with *their* eyes, and hear with *their* ears, and should understand with *their* heart, and should [2]be converted, and I [3]should [c]heal them.

16 But [a]blessed *are* your eyes, for they see: and your ears, for they hear.

17 For verily I say unto you, [a]That many prophets and righteous *men* have desired to see *those things* which ye see, and have not seen *them;* and to hear *those things* which ye hear, and have not heard *them.*

18 [a]Hear ye therefore the parable of the sower.

**19** When any one heareth the word [a]of the kingdom, and understandeth *it* not, then cometh the wicked *one*, and [1]catcheth away that which was sown in his heart. This is he which received seed by the way side.

**20** But he that received the seed into stony places, the same is he that heareth the word, and [1]anon [a]with joy receiveth it;

**21** Yet hath he not root in himself, but [1]dureth for a while: for when [a]tribulation or persecution ariseth because of the word, [2]by and by [b]he is offended.

**22** [a]He also that received seed [b]among the thorns is he that heareth the word; and the [1]care of this world, and the deceitfulness of riches, choke the word, and he becometh unfruitful.

**23** But he that received seed into the good ground is he that heareth the word, and understandeth *it;* which also beareth [a]fruit, and [1]bringeth forth, some an hundredfold, some sixty, some thirty.

**24** Another parable put he forth unto them, saying, The kingdom of heaven is likened unto a man which sowed good seed in his field:

**25** But while men slept, his enemy came and sowed tares among the wheat, and went his way.

**26** But when the [1]blade was sprung up, and brought forth fruit, then appeared the tares also.

**27** So the servants of the householder came and said unto him, Sir, didst not thou sow good seed in thy field? from whence then hath it tares?

**28** He said unto them, An enemy hath done this. The servants said unto him, Wilt thou then that we go and gather them up?

**29** But he said, Nay; lest while ye gather up the tares, ye root up also the wheat with them.

**30** Let both grow together until the harvest: and in the time of harvest I will say to the reapers, Gather ye together first the tares, and bind them in bundles to burn them: but [a]gather the wheat into my barn.

**31** Another parable put he forth unto them, saying, [a]The kingdom of heaven is like to a grain of mustard seed, which a man took, and sowed in his field:

**32** Which indeed is the least of all seeds: but when it is grown, it is the [1]greatest among herbs, and becometh a [a]tree, so that the birds of the air come and [2]lodge in the branches thereof.

**33** [a]Another parable spake he unto them; The kingdom of heaven is like unto leaven, which a woman took, and hid in three [1]measures of meal, till the [b]whole was leavened.

**34** [a]All these things spake Jesus unto the multitude in parables; and without a parable spake he not unto them:

**35** That it might be fulfilled which was spoken by the prophet, saying, [a]I will open my mouth in parables; [b]I will utter things which have been kept secret from the foundation of the world.

**36** Then Jesus sent the multitude away, and went into the house: and his disciples came unto him, saying, Declare unto us the parable of the tares of the field.

**37** He answered and said unto them, He that soweth the good seed is the Son of man;

**38** [a]The field is the world; the good seed are the [1]children of the kingdom; but the tares are [b]the children of the wicked *one;*

**39** The enemy that sowed them is the devil; [a]the harvest is the end of the [1]world; and the reapers are the angels.

**40** As therefore the tares are gathered and burned in the fire; so shall it be in the end of this [1]world.

**41** The Son of man shall send forth his angels, [a]and they shall gather out of his kingdom all things that offend, and them which [1]do iniquity;

**42** [a]And shall cast them into a furnace of fire: [b]there shall be a wailing and gnashing of teeth.

**43** [a]Then shall the righteous shine forth as the sun in the kingdom of their Father. [b]Who hath ears to hear, let him hear.

**44** Again, the kingdom of heaven is like unto treasure hid in a field; the which when a man hath found, he hideth, and for joy thereof goeth and [a]selleth all that he hath, and [b]buyeth that field.

**45** Again, the kingdom of heaven is like unto a merchant man, seeking [1]goodly pearls:

**46** Who, when he had found [a]one pearl of great price, went and sold all that he had, and bought it.

**47** Again, the kingdom of heaven is like unto a [1]net, that was cast into the sea, and [a]gathered of every kind:

**48** Which, when it was full, they drew to shore, and sat down, and gathered the good into vessels, but cast the bad away.

**49** So shall it be at the end of the [1]world: the angels shall come forth, and [a]sever[2] the wicked from among the just,

**50** And shall cast them into the furnace of fire: there shall be wailing and gnashing of teeth.

**51** Jesus saith unto them, Have ye understood all these things? They say unto him, Yea, Lord.

---

13:19 [a] Matt. 4:23
[1] *snatches away*
13:20 [a] Is. 58:2
[1] *immediately*
13:21 [Acts 14:22] [b] Matt. 11:6
[1] *only endures*
[2] *immediately he stumbles*
13:22 [a] 1 Tim. 6:9
[b] Jer. 4:3 [1] *cares*
13:23 [a] Col. 1:6
[1] *produces*
13:26 [1] *grain*
13:30 [a] Matt. 3:12
13:31 [Is. 2:2, 3; Mic. 4:1]; Mark 4:30; Luke 13:18, 19
13:32 [a] Ps. 104:12; Ezek. 17:22–24; 31:3–9; Dan. 4:12 [1] *greater than the herbs* [2] *nest*
13:33 [a] Luke 13:20, 21 [b] [1 Cor. 5:6; Gal. 5:9] [1] Gr. *sato*

13:34 [a] Mark 4:33, 34; John 10:6; 16:25
13:35 [a] Ps. 78:2 [b] Rom. 16:25, 26; 1 Cor. 2:7; Eph. 3:9; Col. 1:26
13:38 [a] Matt. 24:14; 28:19; Mark 16:15; Luke 24:47; Rom. 10:18; Col. 1:6 [b] Gen. 3:15; John 8:44; Acts 13:10 [1] Lit. *sons*
13:39 [a] Joel 3:13; Rev. 14:15 [1] *age*
13:40 [1] *age*
13:41 [a] Matt. 18:7; 2 Pet. 2:1, 2 [1] *practise lawlessness*
13:42 [a] Matt. 3:12; Rev. 19:20; 20:10 [b] Matt. 8:12; 13:50
13:43 [a] [Dan. 12:3; 1 Cor. 15:42, 43, 58] [b] Matt. 13:9
13:44 [a] Phil. 3:7, 8 [b] [Is. 55:1; Rev. 3:18]
13:45 [1] *beautiful*
13:46 [a] Prov. 2:4; 3:14, 15; 8:10, 19
13:47 [a] Matt. 22:9, 10 [1] *dragnet*
13:49 [a] Matt. 25:32 [1] *age* [2] *separate*

---

52 Then said he unto them, Therefore every ¹scribe *which is* instructed ²unto the kingdom of heaven is like unto a man *that is* an householder, which bringeth forth out of his treasure ᵃ*things* new and old.

53 And it came to pass, *that* when Jesus had finished these parables, he departed thence.

54 ᵃAnd when he was come into his own country, he taught them in their synagogue, insomuch that they were astonished, and said, Whence hath this *man* this wisdom, and *these* mighty works?

55 ᵃIs not this the carpenter's son? is not his mother called Mary? and ᵇhis brethren, ᶜJames, and Joses, and Simon, and Judas?

56 And his sisters, are they not all with us? Whence then hath this *man* all these things?

57 And they ᵃwere offended ¹in him. But Jesus said unto them, ᵇA prophet is not without honour, ²save in his own country, and in his own house.

58 And ᵃhe did not many mighty works there because of their unbelief.

## CHAPTER 14

AT that time ᵃHerod the tetrarch heard of the fame of Jesus,

2 And said unto his servants, This is John the Baptist; he is risen from the dead; and therefore ¹mighty works do shew forth themselves in him.

3 ᵃFor Herod had laid hold on John, and bound him, and put *him* in prison for Herodias' sake, his brother Philip's wife.

4 For John said unto him, ᵃIt is not lawful for thee to have her.

5 And when he would have put him to death, he feared the multitude, ᵃbecause they counted him as a prophet.

6 But when Herod's birthday was ¹kept, the daughter of Herodias danced before them, and pleased Herod.

7 Whereupon he promised with an oath to give her whatsoever she would ask.

8 And she, being ¹before instructed of her mother, said, Give me here John Baptist's head ²in a charger.

9 And the king was sorry: nevertheless for the oath's sake, and them which sat with him ¹at meat, he commanded *it* to be given *her.*

10 And he sent, and beheaded John in the prison.

11 And his head was brought ¹in a charger, and given to the damsel: and she brought *it* to her mother.

12 And his disciples came, and took up the body, and buried it, and went and told Jesus.

13 ᵃWhen Jesus heard *of it,* he departed thence by ship into a desert place ¹apart: and when the people had heard *thereof,* they followed him on foot out of the cities.

14 And Jesus went forth, and saw a great multitude, and ᵃwas moved with compassion toward them, and he healed their sick.

15 ᵃAnd when it was evening, his disciples came to him, saying, This is a desert place, and the ¹time is now past; send the multitude away, that they may go into the villages, and buy themselves victuals.

16 But Jesus said unto them, They need not depart; give ye them to eat.

17 And they say unto him, We have here but five loaves, and two fishes.

18 He said, Bring them hither to me.

19 And he commanded the multitude to sit down on the grass, and took the five loaves, and the two fishes, and looking up to heaven, ᵃhe blessed, and brake, and gave the loaves to *his* disciples, and the disciples to the multitude.

20 And they did all eat, and were filled: and they took up of the fragments that remained twelve baskets full.

21 And they that had eaten were about five thousand men, beside women and children.

22 And straightway Jesus ¹constrained his disciples to get into a ship, and to go before him unto the other side, while he sent the multitudes away.

23 ᵃAnd when he had sent the multitudes away, he went up into a mountain ¹apart to pray: ᵇand when the evening was come, he was there alone.

24 But the ship was now in the ¹midst of the sea, tossed with waves: for the wind was contrary.

25 And in the fourth watch of the night Jesus went unto them, walking on the sea.

26 And when the disciples saw him ᵃwalking on the sea, they were troubled, saying, It is a ¹spirit; and they cried out for fear.

27 But straightway Jesus spake unto them, saying, ¹Be of good ᵃcheer; ²it is I; be not afraid.

28 And Peter answered him and said, Lord, if it be thou, bid me come unto thee on the water.

29 And he said, Come. And when Peter was come down out of the ship, he walked on the water, to go to Jesus.

30 But when he saw the wind ¹boisterous, he was afraid; and beginning to sink, he cried, saying, Lord, save me.

31 And immediately Jesus stretched forth *his* hand, and caught him, and

### Center column cross-references

13:52 ᵃ Song 7:13 · ¹ A scholar in O.T. law · ² concerning

13:54 ᵃ Ps. 22:22; Matt. 2:23; Mark 6:1; Luke 4:16; John 7:15

13:55 ᵃ Is. 49:7; Mark 6:3; [Luke 3:23]; John 6:42 · ᵇ Matt. 12:46 · ᶜ Mark 15:40

13:57 ᵃ Matt. 11:6; Mark 6:3, 4 · ᵇ Luke 4:24; John 4:44 · ¹ at · ² except

13:58 ᵃ Mark 6:5, 6; John 5:44, 46, 47

14:1 ᵃ Mark 6:14–29; Luke 9:7–9

14:2 ¹ these powers are at work

14:3 ᵃ Matt. 4:12; Mark 6:17; Luke 3:19, 20

14:4 ᵃ Lev. 18:16; 20:21

14:5 ᵃ Matt. 21:26; Luke 20:6

14:6 ¹ celebrated

14:8 ¹ prompted by · ² on a platter

14:9 ¹ at the table

14:11 ¹ on a platter

14:13 ᵃ Matt. 10:23; 12:15; Mark 6:32–44; Luke 9:10–17; John 6:1, 2 · ¹ by himself

14:14 ᵃ Matt. 9:36; Mark 6:34

14:15 ᵃ Mark 6:35; Luke 9:12 · ¹ hour is already late

14:19 ᵃ 1 Sam. 9:13; Matt. 15:36; 26:26; Mark 6:41; 8:7; 14:22; Luke 24:30; Acts 27:35; [Rom. 14:6]

14:22 ¹ compelled

14:23 ᵃ Mark 6:46; Luke 9:28; John 6:15 · ᵇ John 6:16 · ¹ by himself

14:24 ¹ middle

14:26 ᵃ Job 9:8 · ¹ ghost

14:27 ᵃ Acts 23:11; 27:22, 25, 36 · ¹ Take courage · ² Lit. I am

14:30 ¹ violent

said unto him, O thou of [a]little faith, wherefore didst thou doubt?

32 And when they were come into the ship, the wind ceased.

33 Then they that were in the ship came and worshipped him, saying, Of a truth [a]thou art the Son of God.

34 [a]And when they [1]were gone over, they came into the land of Gennesaret.

35 And when the men of that place [1]had knowledge of him, they sent out into all that country round about, and brought unto him all that were diseased;

36 And [1]besought him that they might only [a]touch the hem of his garment: and [b]as many as touched were made perfectly [2]whole.

## CHAPTER 15

THEN [a]came to Jesus scribes and Pharisees, which were of Jerusalem, saying,

2 [a]Why do thy disciples transgress the tradition of the elders? for they wash not their hands when they eat bread.

3 But he answered and said unto them, Why do ye also transgress the commandment of God by your tradition?

4 For God commanded, saying, [a]Honour thy father and mother: and, [b]He that curseth father or mother, let him [1]die the death.

5 But ye say, Whosoever shall say to *his* father or *his* mother, [a]*It is* [1]a gift, by whatsoever thou mightest be profited by me;

6 And honour not his father or his mother, *he shall be free.* Thus have ye made the commandment of God of none effect by your tradition.

7 *Ye* [a]hypocrites, well did Esaias prophesy of you, saying,

8 [a]This people draweth [1]nigh unto me with their mouth, and honoureth me with *their* lips; but their heart is far from me.

9 But in vain they do worship me, [a]teaching *for* doctrines the commandments of men.

10 [a]And he called the multitude, and said unto them, Hear, and understand:

11 [a]Not that which goeth into the mouth defileth a man; but that which cometh out of the mouth, this defileth a man.

12 Then came his disciples, and said unto him, Knowest thou that the Pharisees were offended, after they heard this saying?

13 But he answered and said, [a]Every plant, which my heavenly Father hath not planted, shall be rooted up.

14 Let them alone: [a]they be blind leaders of the blind. And if the blind

14:31 [a] Matt. 6:30; 8:26
14:33 [a] Ps. 2:7; Matt. 16:16; 26:63; Mark 1:1; Luke 4:41; John 1:49; 6:69; 11:27; Acts 8:37; Rom. 1:4
14:34 [a] Mark 6:53 [1] had crossed
14:35 [1] recognized him
14:36 [a] [Mark 5:24–34] [b] [Luke 6:19] [1] begged [2] well
15:1 [a] Mark 7:1
15:2 [a] Mark 7:5
15:4 [a] [Deut. 5:16] [b] Ex. 21:17 [1] be put to death
15:5 [a] Mark 7:11, 12 [1] Dedicated to the temple
15:7 [a] Mark 7:6
15:8 [a] Is. 29:13 [1] near
15:9 [a] [Col. 2:18–22]
15:10 [a] Mark 7:14
15:11 [a] [Acts 10:15]
15:13 [a] [John 15:2]
15:14 [a] Luke 6:39

15:15 [a] Mark 7:17 [1] Explain
15:16 [a] Matt. 16:9
15:17 [a] [1 Cor. 6:13] [1] eliminated
15:18 [a] [James 3:6]
15:19 [a] Prov. 6:14
15:21 [a] Mark 7:24–30 [1] region
15:22 [a] Matt. 1:1; 22:41, 42 [1] region [2] demon-possessed
15:23 [1] urged
15:24 [a] Matt. 10:5, 6
15:26 [a] Matt. 7:6 [1] good
15:28 [a] Luke 7:9 [1] you desire [2] well
15:29 [a] Mark 7:31–37 [b] Matt. 4:18
15:30 [a] Is. 35:5, 6 [b] Luke 7:38; 8:41; 10:39 [1] mute [2] crippled
15:31 [a] Luke 5:25, 26; 19:37, 38 [1] marvelled [2] mute [3] crippled
15:32 [a] Mark 8:1–10

lead the blind, both shall fall into the ditch.

15 [a]Then answered Peter and said unto him, [1]Declare unto us this parable.

16 And Jesus said, [a]Are ye also yet without understanding?

17 Do not ye yet understand, that [a]whatsoever entereth in at the mouth goeth into the belly, and is [1]cast out into the draught?

18 But [a]those things which proceed out of the mouth come forth from the heart; and they defile the man.

19 [a]For out of the heart proceed evil thoughts, murders, adulteries, fornications, thefts, false witness, blasphemies:

20 These are *the things* which defile a man: but to eat with unwashen hands defileth not a man.

21 [a]Then Jesus went thence, and departed into the [1]coasts of Tyre and Sidon.

22 And, behold, a woman of Canaan came out of the same [1]coasts, and cried unto him, saying, Have mercy on me, O Lord, *thou* [a]son of David; my daughter is grievously [2]vexed with a devil.

23 But he answered her not a word. And his disciples came and [1]besought him, saying, Send her away; for she crieth after us.

24 But he answered and said, [a]I am not sent but unto the lost sheep of the house of Israel.

25 Then came she and worshipped him, saying, Lord, help me.

26 But he answered and said, It is not [1]meet to take the children's bread, and to cast *it* to [a]dogs.

27 And she said, Truth, Lord: yet the dogs eat of the crumbs which fall from their masters' table.

28 Then Jesus answered and said unto her, O woman, [a]great *is* thy faith: be it unto thee even as [1]thou wilt. And her daughter was made [2]whole from that very hour.

29 [a]And Jesus departed from thence, and came nigh [b]unto the sea of Galilee; and went up into a mountain, and sat down there.

30 [a]And great multitudes came unto him, having with them *those that were* lame, blind, [1]dumb, [2]maimed, and many others, and cast them down at Jesus' [b]feet; and he healed them:

31 Insomuch that the multitude [1]wondered, when they saw the [2]dumb to speak, the [3]maimed to be whole, the lame to walk, and the blind to see: and they [a]glorified the God of Israel.

32 [a]Then Jesus called his disciples *unto him,* and said, I have compassion on the multitude, because they continue with me now three days, and have nothing to eat: and I will

not send them away ¹fasting, lest they faint in the way.

33 ªAnd his disciples say unto him, ¹Whence should we have so much bread in the wilderness, as to fill so great a multitude?

34 And Jesus saith unto them, How many loaves have ye? And they said, Seven, and a few little fishes.

35 And he commanded the multitude to sit down on the ground.

36 And ªhe took the seven loaves and the fishes, and ᵇgave thanks, and brake *them,* and gave to his disciples, and the disciples to the multitude.

37 And they did all eat, and were filled: and they took up of the ¹broken *meat* that was left seven baskets full.

38 And they that did eat were four thousand men, beside women and children.

39 ªAnd he sent away the multitude, and took ship, and came into the coasts of Magdala.

### CHAPTER 16

THE ªPharisees also with the Sadducees came, and ¹tempting ²desired him that he would shew them a sign from heaven.

2 He answered and said unto them, When it is evening, ye say, *It will be* fair weather: for the sky is red.

3 And in the morning, *It will be* foul weather to day: for the sky is red and ¹lowring. O *ye* hypocrites, ye can discern the face of the sky; but can ye not *discern* the signs of the times?

4 ªA wicked and adulterous generation seeketh after a sign; and there shall no sign be given unto it, but the sign of the prophet Jonas. And he left them, and departed.

5 And ªwhen his disciples were come to the other side, they had forgotten to take bread.

6 Then Jesus said unto them, ªTake heed and beware of the ¹leaven of the Pharisees and of the Sadducees.

7 And they reasoned among themselves, saying, *It is* because we have taken no bread.

8 *Which* when Jesus perceived, he said unto them, O ye of little faith, why reason ye among yourselves, because ye have brought no bread?

9 ªDo ye not yet understand, neither remember the five loaves of the five thousand, and how many baskets ye took up?

10 ªNeither the seven loaves of the four thousand, and how many baskets ye took up?

11 How is it that ye do not understand that I spake *it* not to you concerning bread, that ye should beware of the ¹leaven of the Pharisees and of the Sadducees?

12 Then understood they how that

---

15:32 ¹ hungry
15:33 ª 2 Kin. 4:43
¹ Where could we get
15:36 ª Matt. 14:19; 26:27
ᵇ Luke 22:19
15:37 ¹ Fragments
15:39 ª Mark 8:10
16:1 ª Mark 8:11
¹ testing ² asked
16:3 ¹ threatening
16:4 ª Matt. 12:39
16:5 ª Mark 8:14
16:6 ª Luke 12:1
¹ yeast
16:9 ª Matt. 14:15–21
16:10 ª Matt. 15:32–38
16:11 ¹ yeast

16:12 ¹ teaching
16:13 ª Luke 9:18
¹ region
16:14 ª Matt. 14:2
ᵇ Matt. 21:11
16:15 ª John 6:67
16:16 ª Acts 8:37; 9:20
16:17 ª [Eph. 2:8]
ᵇ Gal. 1:16
16:18 ª John 1:42
ᵇ [Eph. 2:20] ᶜ Is. 38:10 ¹ Gr. *Petros,* lit. *A Stone* ² Gr. *petra,* lit. *large rock*
16:19 ª Matt. 18:18
16:20 ª Luke 9:21
¹ commanded
16:21 ª Luke 9:22; 18:31; 24:46
16:22 ¹ took him aside ² God be merciful to you
16:23 ª Matt. 4:10
ᵇ [Rom. 8:7] ¹ are not mindful of
16:24 ª [2 Tim. 3:12] ᵇ [1 Pet. 2:21]
16:25 ª John 12:25
16:26 ª Luke 12:20, 21 ᵇ Ps. 49:7, 8
16:27 ª Mark 8:38 ᵇ [Dan. 7:10] ᶜ Rom. 2:6
16:28 ª Luke 9:27

---

he bade *them* not beware of the leaven of bread, but of the ¹doctrine of the Pharisees and of the Sadducees.

13 When Jesus came into the ¹coasts of Caesarea Philippi, he asked his disciples, saying, ªWhom do men say that I the Son of man am?

14 And they said, ªSome *say that thou art* John the Baptist: some, Elias; and others, Jeremias, or ᵇone of the prophets.

15 He saith unto them, But whom say ªye that I am?

16 And Simon Peter answered and said, ªThou art the Christ, the Son of the living God.

17 And Jesus answered and said unto him, Blessed art thou, Simon Bar-jona: ªfor flesh and blood hath not revealed *it* unto thee, but ᵇmy Father which is in heaven.

18 And I say also unto thee, That ªthou art ¹Peter, and ᵇupon this ²rock I will build my church; and ᶜthe gates of hell shall not prevail against it.

19 And I will give unto thee the keys of the kingdom of heaven: and ªwhatsoever thou shalt bind on earth shall be bound in heaven: and whatsoever thou shalt loose on earth shall be loosed in heaven.

20 ªThen ¹charged he his disciples that they should tell no man that he was Jesus the Christ.

21 From that time forth began Jesus ªto shew unto his disciples, how that he must go unto Jerusalem, and suffer many things of the elders and chief priests and scribes, and be killed, and be raised again the third day.

22 Then Peter ¹took him, and began to rebuke him, saying, ²Be it far from thee, Lord: this shall not be unto thee.

23 But he turned, and said unto Peter, Get thee behind me, ªSatan: ᵇthou art an offence unto me: for thou ¹savourest not the things that be of God, but those that be of men.

24 ªThen said Jesus unto his disciples, If any *man* will come after me, let him deny himself, and take up his cross, and ᵇfollow me.

25 For ªwhosoever will save his life shall lose it: and whosoever will lose his life for my sake shall find it.

26 For what is a man ªprofited, if he shall gain the whole world, and lose his own soul? or ᵇwhat shall a man give in exchange for his soul?

27 For ªthe Son of man shall come in the glory of his Father ᵇwith his angels; ᶜand then he shall reward every man according to his works.

28 Verily I say unto you, ªThere be some standing here, which shall not taste of death, till they see the Son of man coming in his kingdom.

## CHAPTER 17

AND [a]after six days Jesus taketh Peter, James, and John his brother, and bringeth them up into an high mountain [1]apart,

2 And was transfigured before them: and his face did shine as the sun, and his [1]raiment was white as the light.

3 And, behold, there appeared unto them Moses and Elias talking with him.

4 Then answered Peter, and said unto Jesus, Lord, it is good for us to be here: if thou wilt, let us make here three tabernacles; one for thee, and one for Moses, and one for Elias.

5 [a]While he yet spake, behold, a bright cloud overshadowed them: and behold a voice out of the cloud, which said, [b]This is my beloved Son, [c]in whom I am well pleased; [d]hear ye him.

6 [a]And when the disciples heard *it*, they fell on their face, and were [1]sore afraid.

7 And Jesus came and [a]touched them, and said, Arise, and be not afraid.

8 And when they had lifted up their eyes, they saw no man, [1]save Jesus only.

9 And as they came down from the mountain, Jesus [1]charged them, saying, Tell the vision to no man, until the Son of man be risen again from the dead.

10 And his disciples asked him, saying, [a]Why then say the scribes that Elias must first come?

11 And Jesus answered and said unto them, Elias truly shall first come, and [a]restore all things.

12 [a]But I say unto you, That Elias is come already, and they knew him not, but [b]have done unto him whatsoever they [1]listed. Likewise [c]shall also the Son of man suffer of them.

13 [a]Then the disciples understood that he spake unto them of John the Baptist.

14 [a]And when they were come to the multitude, there came to him a *certain* man, kneeling down to him, and saying,

15 Lord, have mercy on my son: for he is [1]lunatick, and [2]sore vexed: for ofttimes he falleth into the fire, and oft into the water.

16 And I brought him to thy disciples, and they could not cure him.

17 Then Jesus answered and said, O [1]faithless and [a]perverse generation, how long shall I be with you? how long shall I [2]suffer you? bring him hither to me.

18 And Jesus [a]rebuked the [1]devil; and he departed out of him: and the child was cured from that very hour.

19 Then came the disciples to Jesus [1]apart, and said, Why could not we cast him out?

20 And Jesus said unto them, Because of your unbelief: for verily I say unto you, [a]If ye have faith as a grain of mustard seed, ye shall say unto this mountain, Remove hence to yonder place; and it shall [1]remove; and nothing shall be impossible unto you.

21 Howbeit this kind goeth not out but by prayer and fasting.

22 [a]And while they abode in Galilee, Jesus said unto them, The Son of man shall be betrayed into the hands of men:

23 And they shall kill him, and the third day he shall be raised again. And they were exceeding [a]sorry.

24 And [a]when they were come to Capernaum, they that received [1]tribute *money* came to Peter, and said, Doth not your master pay [1]tribute?

25 He saith, Yes. And when he was come into the house, Jesus [1]prevented him, saying, What thinkest thou, Simon? of whom do the kings of the earth take custom or [2]tribute? of their own [3]children, or of [a]strangers?

26 Peter saith unto him, Of strangers. Jesus saith unto him, Then are the [1]children free.

27 Notwithstanding, lest we should offend them, go thou to the sea, and cast an hook, and take up the fish that first cometh up; and when thou hast opened his mouth, thou shalt find a [1]piece of money: that take, and give unto them for me and thee.

## CHAPTER 18

AT [a]the same time came the disciples unto Jesus, saying, Who is the greatest in the kingdom of heaven?

2 And Jesus called a little [a]child unto him, and set him in the midst of them,

3 And said, Verily I say unto you, [a]Except ye be converted, and become as little children, ye shall not enter into the kingdom of heaven.

4 [a]Whosoever therefore shall humble himself as this little child, the same is greatest in the kingdom of heaven.

5 And [a]whoso shall receive one such little child in my name receiveth me.

6 [a]But whoso shall [1]offend one of these little ones which believe in me, it were better for him that a millstone were hanged about his neck, and *that* he were drowned in the depth of the sea.

7 Woe unto the world because of [1]offences! for [a]it must needs be that offences come; but [b]woe to that man by whom the offence cometh!

### Cross references

17:1 [a] Mark 9:2–8
  [1] *by themselves*
17:2 [1] *clothes*
17:5 [a] 2 Pet. 1:17  [b] Mark 1:11
  [c] Matt. 3:17; 12:18
  [d] [Deut. 18:15, 19]
17:6 [a] 2 Pet. 1:18
  [1] *greatly*
17:7 [a] Dan. 8:18
17:8 [1] *except*
17:9 [1] *commanded*
17:10 [a] Mal. 4:5
17:11 [Mal. 4:6]
17:12 [a] Mark 9:12, 13  [b] Matt. 14:3, 10  [c] Matt. 16:21
  [1] *wished*
17:13 [a] Matt. 11:14
17:14 [a] Mark 9:14–28
17:15 [1] *epileptic,* lit. *moonstruck*  [2] *suffers greatly*
17:17 [a] Phil. 2:15
  [1] *unbelieving*  [2] *bear with*
17:18 [a] Luke 4:41
  [1] *demon*
17:19 [1] *privately*
17:20 [a] Luke 17:6
  [1] *move*
17:22 [a] Mark 8:31
17:23 [a] John 16:6; 19:30
17:24 [a] Mark 9:33
  [1] The temple tax, lit. *double drachma*
17:25 [a] [Is. 60:10–17]  [1] *anticipated*  [2] *taxes*  [3] Lit. *sons*
17:26 [1] Lit. *sons*
17:27 [1] Gr. *stater,* the exact temple tax for two
18:1 [a] Luke 9:46–48; 22:24–27
18:2 [a] Matt. 19:14
18:3 [a] Luke 18:16
18:4 [a] [Matt. 20:27; 23:11]
18:5 [a] [Matt. 10:42]
18:6 [a] Mark 9:42
  [1] *cause to sin*
18:7 [a] [1 Cor. 11:19]  [b] Matt. 26:24; 27:4, 5  [1] *enticements to sin*

8 ᵃWherefore if thy hand or thy foot ¹offend thee, cut them off, and cast *them* from thee: it is better for thee to enter into life ²halt or maimed, rather than having two hands or two feet to be cast into everlasting fire.

9 And if thine eye ¹offend thee, pluck it out, and cast *it* from thee: it is better for thee to enter into life with one eye, rather than having two eyes to be cast into ²hell fire.

10 Take heed that ye despise not one of these little ones; for I say unto you, That in heaven ᵃtheir angels do always ᵇbehold the face of my Father which is in heaven.

11 ᵃFor the Son of man is come to save that which was lost.

12 ᵃHow think ye? if a man have an hundred sheep, and one of them be gone astray, doth he not leave the ninety and nine, and goeth into the mountains, and seeketh that which is gone astray?

13 And if so be that he find it, verily I say unto you, he rejoiceth more of that *sheep,* than of the ninety and nine which went not astray.

14 Even so it is not the ᵃwill of your Father which is in heaven, that one of these little ones should perish.

15 Moreover ᵃif thy brother ¹shall trespass against thee, go and tell him his fault between thee and him alone: if he shall hear thee, ᵇthou hast gained thy brother.

16 But if he will not hear *thee, then* take with thee one or two more, that in ᵃthe mouth of two or three witnesses every word may be established.

17 And if he ¹shall neglect to hear them, tell *it* unto the church: but if he ¹neglect to hear the church, let him be unto thee as an ᵃheathen man and a ²publican.

18 Verily I say unto you, ᵃWhatsoever ye shall bind on earth shall be bound in heaven: and whatsoever ye shall loose on earth shall be loosed in heaven.

19 ᵃAgain I say unto you, That if two of you shall agree on earth as touching any thing that they shall ask, ᵇit shall be done for them of my Father which is in heaven.

20 For where two or three are gathered ᵃtogether in my name, there am I in the midst of them.

21 Then came Peter to him, and said, Lord, how oft shall my brother sin against me, and I forgive him? ᵃtill seven times?

22 Jesus saith unto him, I say not unto thee, ᵃUntil seven times: but, Until seventy times seven.

23 Therefore is the kingdom of heaven likened unto a certain king, ¹which would take account of his servants.

24 And when he had begun to ¹reckon, one was brought unto him, which owed him ten thousand talents.

25 But forasmuch as he ¹had not to pay, his lord commanded him ᵃto be sold, and his wife, and children, and all that he had, and payment to be made.

26 The servant therefore fell down, and ¹worshipped him, saying, Lord, have patience with me, and I will pay thee all.

27 Then the lord of that servant was moved with compassion, and ¹loosed him, and forgave him the debt.

28 But the same servant went out, and found one of his fellowservants, which owed him an hundred ¹pence: and he laid hands on him, and took *him* by the throat, saying, Pay me ²that thou owest.

29 And his fellowservant fell down at his feet, and ¹besought him, saying, Have patience with me, and I will pay thee all.

30 And he would not: but went and cast him into prison, till he should pay the debt.

31 So when his fellowservants saw what was done, they were very sorry, and came and told unto their lord all that was done.

32 Then his lord, after that he had called him, said unto him, O thou wicked servant, I forgave thee ᵃall that debt, because thou ¹desiredst me:

33 Shouldest not thou also have had compassion on thy fellowservant, even as I had pity on thee?

34 And his lord was ¹wroth, and delivered him to the ²tormentors, till he should pay all that was due unto him.

35 ᵃSo likewise shall my heavenly Father do also unto you, if ye from your hearts forgive not every one his brother their trespasses.

## CHAPTER 19

AND it came to pass, ᵃ*that* when Jesus had finished these sayings, he departed from Galilee, and came into the ¹coasts of Judaea beyond Jordan;

2 ᵃAnd great multitudes followed him; and he healed them there.

3 The Pharisees also came unto him, ¹tempting him, and saying unto him, Is it lawful for a man to ²put away his wife for ³every cause?

4 And he answered and said unto them, Have ye not read, that he which made *them* at the beginning ᵃmade them male and female,

5 And said, ᵃFor this cause shall a man leave father and mother, and shall ¹cleave to his wife: and ᵇthey² twain shall be one flesh?

---

18:8 ᵃ Matt. 5:29, 30 ¹ *causes you to sin* ² *lame*
18:9 ¹ *causes you to sin* ² Gr. *gehenna*
18:10 ᵃ [Heb. 1:14] ᵇ Luke 1:19
18:11 ᵃ Luke 9:56
18:12 ᵃ Luke 15:4–7
18:14 ᵃ [1 Tim. 2:4]
18:15 ᵃ Lev. 19:17 ᵇ [James 5:20] ¹ *sins*
18:16 ᵃ Deut. 17:6; 19:15
18:17 ᵃ [2 Thess. 3:6, 14] ¹ *refuses* ² *tax collector*
18:18 ᵃ [John 20:22, 23]
18:19 ᵃ [1 Cor. 1:10] ᵇ [1 John 3:22; 5:14]
18:20 ᵃ Acts 20:7
18:21 ᵃ Luke 17:4
18:22 ᵃ Col. 3:13
18:23 ¹ *who wanted to settle accounts with*
18:24 ¹ *settle accounts*
18:25 ᵃ 2 Kin. 4:1 ¹ *was not able*
18:26 ¹ *prostrated himself*
18:27 ¹ *released him*
18:28 ¹ Gr. *denarii* ² *what*
18:29 ¹ *begged*
18:32 ᵃ Luke 7:41–43 ¹ *begged*
18:34 ¹ *angry* ² *torturers*
18:35 ᵃ James 2:13
19:1 ᵃ Mark 10:1–12 ¹ *region*
19:2 ᵃ Matt. 12:15
19:3 ¹ *testing* ² *divorce* ³ *any reason*
19:4 ᵃ Gen. 1:27; 5:2
19:5 ᵃ Gen. 2:24 ᵇ [1 Cor. 6:16; 7:2] ¹ *be joined* ² *the two*

**6** Wherefore they are [1]no more twain, but one flesh. What therefore God hath joined together, let not man put asunder.

**7** They say unto him, [a]Why did Moses then command to give a [1]writing of divorcement, and to put her away?

**8** He saith unto them, Moses because of the [a]hardness of your hearts [1]suffered you to put away your [b]wives: but from the beginning it was not so.

**9** [a]And I say unto you, Whosoever shall put away his wife, except *it be* for [1]fornication, and shall marry another, committeth adultery: and whoso marrieth her which is put away doth commit adultery.

**10** His disciples [1]say unto him, [a]If the case of the man be so with *his* wife, it is not good to marry.

**11** But he said unto them, [a]All *men* cannot [1]receive this saying, [2]save *they* to whom it is given.

**12** For there are some [1]eunuchs, which were so born from *their* mother's womb: and [a]there are some eunuchs, which were made eunuchs of men: and there be eunuchs, which have made themselves eunuchs for the kingdom of heaven's sake. He that is able to receive *it,* let him receive *it.*

**13** [a]Then were there brought unto him little children, that he should put *his* hands on them, and pray: and the disciples rebuked them.

**14** But Jesus said, [1]Suffer little children, and forbid them not, to come unto me: for [a]of such is the kingdom of heaven.

**15** And he laid *his* hands on them, and departed thence.

**16** [a]And, behold, one came and said unto him, [b]Good [1]Master, what good thing shall I do, that I may have eternal life?

**17** And he said unto him, Why callest thou me good? *there is* none [a]good but one, *that is,* God: but if thou [1]wilt enter into life, [b]keep the commandments.

**18** He saith unto him, Which? Jesus said, [a]Thou shalt do no murder, Thou shalt not commit adultery, Thou shalt not steal, Thou shalt not bear false witness,

**19** [a]Honour thy father and *thy* mother: and, [b]Thou shalt love thy neighbour as thyself.

**20** The young man saith unto him, All these things have I [a]kept from my youth up: what lack I yet?

**21** Jesus said unto him, If thou [1]wilt be perfect, [a]go *and* sell that thou hast, and give to the poor, and thou shalt have treasure in heaven: and come *and* follow me.

**22** But when the young man heard

that saying, he went away sorrowful: for he had great possessions.

**23** Then said Jesus unto his disciples, Verily I say unto you, That [a]a[1] rich man shall hardly enter into the kingdom of heaven.

**24** And again I say unto you, It is easier for a camel to go through the eye of a needle, than for a rich man to enter into the kingdom of God.

**25** When his disciples heard *it,* they were exceedingly amazed, saying, Who then can be saved?

**26** But Jesus beheld *them,* and said unto them, With men this is impossible; but [a]with God all things are possible.

**27** Then answered Peter and said unto him, Behold, [a]we have forsaken all, and followed thee; what shall we have therefore?

**28** And Jesus said unto them, Verily I say unto you, That ye which have followed me, in the regeneration when the Son of man shall sit in the throne of his glory, [a]ye also shall sit upon twelve thrones, judging the twelve tribes of Israel.

**29** [a]And every one that hath forsaken houses, or brethren, or sisters, or father, or mother, or wife, or children, or [1]lands, for my name's sake, shall receive an hundredfold, and shall inherit everlasting life.

**30** [a]But many *that are* first shall be last; and the last *shall be* first.

## CHAPTER 20

FOR the kingdom of heaven is like unto a man *that is* an [1]householder, which went out early in the morning to hire labourers into his vineyard.

**2** And when he had agreed with the labourers for a [1]penny a day, he sent them into his vineyard.

**3** And he went out about the third hour, and saw others standing idle in the marketplace,

**4** And said unto them; Go ye also into the vineyard, and whatsoever is right I will give you. And they went their way.

**5** Again he went out about the sixth and ninth hour, and did likewise.

**6** And about the eleventh hour he went out, and found others standing idle, and saith unto them, Why stand ye here all the day idle?

**7** They say unto him, Because no man hath hired us. He saith unto them, Go ye also into the vineyard; and whatsoever is right, *that* shall ye receive.

**8** So when even was come, the lord of the vineyard saith unto his steward, Call the labourers, and give them *their* [1]hire, beginning from the last unto the first.

### Center column notes

**19:6** [1] *no longer two*

**19:7** [a] Deut. 24:1–4 [1] *certificate*

**19:8** [a] Heb. 3:15 [b] Mal. 2:16 [1] *permitted*

**19:9** [a] [Matt. 5:32] [1] *sexual immorality*

**19:10** [a] [Prov. 21:19] [1] *said*

**19:11** [a] [1 Cor. 7:2, 7, 9, 17] [1] *accept* [2] *except*

**19:12** [a] [1 Cor. 7:32] [1] *Emasculated men*

**19:13** [a] Luke 18:15

**19:14** [a] Matt. 18:3, 4 [1] *Allow the*

**19:16** [a] Mark 10:17–30 [b] Luke 10:25 [1] *Teacher*

**19:17** [a] Nah. 1:7 [b] Lev. 18:5 [1] *want to*

**19:18** [a] Ex. 20:13–16

**19:19** [a] Ex. 20:12–16; Deut. 5:16–20 [b] Lev. 19:18

**19:20** [a] [Phil. 3:6, 7]

**19:21** [a] Acts 2:45; 4:34, 35 [1] *want to be*

**19:23** [a] [1 Tim. 6:9] [1] *it is hard for a rich man to*

**19:26** [a] Jer. 32:17

**19:27** [a] Deut. 33:9

**19:28** [a] Luke 22:28–30

**19:29** [a] Mark 10:29, 30 [1] *Lit. fields*

**19:30** [a] Luke 13:30

**20:1** [1] *landowner*

**20:2** [1] *Gr. denarius*

**20:8** [1] *wages*

9 And when they came that *were hired* about the eleventh hour, they received every man a ¹penny.

10 But when the first came, they supposed that they should have received more; and they likewise received every man a penny.

11 And when they had received *it,* they ¹murmured against the ²goodman of the house,

12 Saying, These last have ¹wrought *but* one hour, and thou hast made them equal unto us, which have borne the burden and heat of the day.

13 But he answered one of them, and said, Friend, I do thee no wrong: didst not thou agree with me for a ¹penny?

14 Take *that* thine *is,* and go thy way: I will give unto this last, even as unto thee.

15 ᵃIs it not lawful for me to do what I will with mine own? ᵇIs thine eye evil, because I am good?

16 ᵃSo the last shall be first, and the first last: ᵇfor many be called, but few chosen.

17 ᵃAnd Jesus going up to Jerusalem took the twelve disciples apart in the way, and said unto them,

18 ᵃBehold, we go up to Jerusalem; and the Son of man shall be betrayed unto the chief priests and unto the scribes, and they shall condemn him to death,

19 ᵃAnd shall deliver him to the Gentiles to ᵇmock, and to ᶜscourge, and to ᵈcrucify *him:* and the third day he shall ᵉrise again.

20 ᵃThen came to him the mother of ᵇZebedee's children with her sons, worshipping *him,* and ¹desiring a certain thing of him.

21 And he said unto her,¹What wilt thou? She saith unto him, Grant that these my two sons ᵃmay sit, the one on thy right hand, and the other on the left, in thy kingdom.

22 But Jesus answered and said,Ye know not what ye ask. Are ye able to drink of ᵃthe cup that I shall drink of, and to be baptized with ᵇthe baptism that I am baptized with? They say unto him, We are able.

23 And he saith unto them, ᵃYe shall drink indeed of my cup, and be baptized with the baptism that I am baptized with: but to sit on my right hand, and on my left, is not mine to give, but *it shall be given to them* for whom it is prepared of my Father.

24 ᵃAnd when the ten heard *it,* they were moved with indignation against the two ¹brethren.

25 But Jesus called them *unto him,* and said,Ye know that the princes of the Gentiles ¹exercise dominion over them, and they that are great exercise authority upon them.

26 But ᵃit shall not be so among you: but ᵇwhosoever will be great among you, let him be your ¹minister;

27 ᵃAnd whosoever will be ¹chief among you, let him be your ²servant:

28 ᵃEven as the ᵇSon of man came not to be ¹ministered unto, ᶜbut to ²minister, and ᵈto give his life a ransom ᵉfor many.

29 ᵃAnd as they departed from Jericho, a great multitude followed him.

30 And, behold, ᵃtwo blind men sitting by the way side, when they heard that Jesus passed by, cried out, saying, Have mercy on us, O Lord, *thou* ᵇson of David.

31 And the multitude ᵃrebuked¹ them, because they should hold their peace: but they cried the more, saying, Have mercy on us, O Lord, *thou* son of David.

32 And Jesus stood still, and called them, and said, What will ye that I shall do unto you?

33 They say unto him, Lord, that our eyes may be opened.

34 So Jesus had ᵃcompassion *on them,* and touched their eyes: and immediately their eyes received sight, and they followed him.

## CHAPTER 21

A ND ᵃwhen they drew nigh unto Jerusalem, and were come to Bethphage, unto ᵇthe mount of Olives, then sent Jesus two disciples,

2 Saying unto them,Go into the village ¹over against you, and straightway ye shall find an ²ass tied, and a colt with her: ³loose *them,* and bring *them* unto me.

3 And if any *man* say ¹ought unto you, ye shall say, The Lord hath need of them; and straightway he will send them.

4 All this was done, that it might be fulfilled which was spoken by the prophet, saying,

5 ᵃTell ye the daughter of Sion, Behold, thy King cometh unto thee, ¹meek, and sitting upon an ²ass, and a colt the foal of an ass.

6 ᵃAnd the disciples went, and did as Jesus commanded them,

7 And brought the ¹ass, and the colt, and ᵃput on them their clothes, and they set *him* thereon.

8 And a very great multitude spread their garments in the way; ᵃothers cut down branches from the trees, and ¹strawed *them* in the ²way.

9 And the multitudes that went before, and that followed, cried, saying, ᵃHosanna to the son of David: ᵇBlessed *is* he that cometh in the name of the Lord; Hosanna in the highest.

10 ᵃAnd when he was come into Jerusalem, all the city was moved, saying, Who is this?

### Center column notes

20:9 ¹ Gr. *denarius*
20:11 ¹ *grumbled* ² *landowner*
20:12 ¹ *worked*
20:13 ¹ Gr. *denarius*
20:15 ᵃ [Rom. 9:20, 21] ᵇ Deut. 15:9
20:16 ᵃ Matt. 19:30 ᵇ Matt. 22:14
20:17 ᵃ Mark 10:32–34
20:18 ᵃ Matt. 16:21; 26:47–57
20:19 ᵃ Matt. 27:2 ᵇ Matt. 26:67, 68; 27:29, 41 ᶜ Matt. 27:26 ᵈ Acts 3:13–15 ᵉ Matt. 28:5, 6
20:20 ᵃ Mark 10:35–45 ᵇ Matt. 4:21; 10:2 ¹ *asking*
20:21 ᵃ [Matt. 19:28] ¹ *What do you wish*
20:22 ᵃ Luke 22:42 ᵇ Luke 12:50
20:23 ᵃ [Acts 12:2]
20:24 ᵃ Mark 10:41 ¹ *brothers*
20:25 ¹ *lord it over*
20:26 ᵃ [I Pet. 5:3] ᵇ Matt. 23:11 ¹ *servant*
20:27 ᵃ [Matt. 18:4] ¹ *first* ² *slave*
20:28 ᵃ John 13:4 ᵇ [Phil. 2:6, 7] ᶜ Luke 22:27 ᵈ [Is. 53:10, 11] ᵉ [Rom. 5:15, 19] ¹ *served* ² *serve*
20:29 ᵃ Mark 10:46–52
20:30 ᵃ Matt. 9:27 ᵇ [Ezek. 37:21–26]
20:31 ᵃ Matt. 19:13 ¹ *warned them that they should be quiet*
20:34 ᵃ Matt. 9:36; 14:14; 15:32; 18:27
21:1 ᵃ Luke 19:29–38 ᵇ [Zech. 14:4]
21:2 ¹ *opposite* ² *donkey* ³ *untie*
21:3 ¹ *anything*
21:5 ᵃ Zech. 9:9 ¹ *lowly* ² *donkey*
21:6 ᵃ Mark 11:4
21:7 ᵃ 2 Kin. 9:13 ¹ *donkey*
21:8 ᵃ Lev. 23:40 ¹ *spread* ² *road*
21:9 ᵃ Ps. 118:25, 26 ᵇ Matt. 23:39
21:10 ᵃ John 2:13, 15

11 And the multitude said, This is Jesus [a]the prophet of Nazareth of Galilee.

12 [a]And Jesus went into the temple of God, and [1]cast out all them that sold and bought in the temple, and [2]overthrew the tables of the [b]moneychangers, and the seats of them that sold doves,

13 And said unto them, It is written, [a]My house shall be called the house of prayer; but ye have made it a [b]den of thieves.

14 And the blind and the lame came to him in the temple; and he healed them.

15 And when the chief priests and scribes saw the wonderful things that he did, and the children crying in the temple, and saying, Hosanna to the [a]son of David; they were [1]sore displeased,

16 And said unto him, Hearest thou what these say? And Jesus saith unto them, Yea; have ye never read, [a]Out of the mouth of babes and [1]sucklings thou hast perfected praise?

17 And he left them, and [a]went out of the city into Bethany; and he lodged there.

18 [a]Now in the morning as he returned into the city, he [1]hungered.

19 [a]And when he saw a fig tree [1]in the way, he came to it, and found nothing thereon, but leaves only, and said unto it, Let no fruit grow on thee henceforward for ever.And presently the fig tree withered away.

20 [a]And when the disciples saw *it*, they marvelled, saying, How soon is the fig tree withered away!

21 Jesus answered and said unto them, Verily I say unto you, [a]If ye have faith, and [b]doubt not, ye shall not only do this *which is done* to the fig tree, [c]but also if ye shall say unto this mountain, Be thou removed, and be thou cast into the sea; it shall be done.

22 And [a]all things, whatsoever ye shall ask in prayer, believing, ye shall receive.

23 [a]And when he was come into the temple, the chief priests and the elders of the people came unto him as he was teaching, and [b]said, By what authority doest thou these things? and who gave thee this authority?

24 And Jesus answered and said unto them, I also will ask you one thing, which if ye tell me, I in like wise will tell you by what authority I do these things.

25 The [a]baptism of [b]John, whence was it? from heaven, or of men?And they reasoned with themselves, saying, If we shall say, From heaven; he will say unto us, Why did ye not then believe him?

26 But if we shall say, Of men; we [a]fear the people; [b]for all hold John [1]as a prophet.

27 And they answered Jesus, and said, We cannot tell. And he said unto them, Neither tell I you by what authority I do these things.

28 But what think ye? A *certain* man had two sons; and he came to the first, and said, Son, go work to day in my [a]vineyard.

29 He answered and said, I will not: but afterward he [1]repented, and went.

30 And he came to the second, and said likewise. And he answered and said, I *go*, sir: and went not.

31 Whether of them twain did the will of *his* father? They say unto him, The first. Jesus saith unto them, [a]Verily I say unto you, That the [1]publicans and the harlots go into the kingdom of God before you.

32 For [a]John came unto you in the way of righteousness, and ye believed him not: [b]but the publicans and the harlots believed him: and ye, when ye had seen *it*, [1]repented not afterward, that ye might believe him.

33 Hear another parable: There was a certain [1]householder, [a]which planted a vineyard, and hedged it round about, and digged a winepress in it, and built a tower, and [2]let it out to [3]husbandmen, and [b]went into a far country:

34 And when the time of the [1]fruit drew near, he sent his servants to the [2]husbandmen, that they might receive the fruits of it.

35 [a]And the husbandmen took his servants, and beat one, and killed another, and stoned another.

36 Again, he sent other servants more than the first: and they did unto them likewise.

37 But last of all he sent unto them his [a]son, saying, They will [1]reverence my son.

38 But when the [1]husbandmen saw the son, they said among themselves, [a]This is the heir; [b]come, let us kill him, and let us seize on his inheritance.

39 [a]And they caught him, and cast *him* out of the vineyard, and slew *him*.

40 When the lord therefore of the vineyard cometh, what will he do unto those husbandmen?

41 [a]They say unto him, [b]He will miserably destroy those wicked men, [c]and will [1]let out *his* vineyard unto other [2]husbandmen, which shall [3]render him the fruits in their seasons.

42 Jesus saith unto them, [a]Did ye never read in the scriptures, The stone which the builders rejected, the same is become the [1]head of the corner: this is the Lord's doing, and it is marvellous in our eyes?

---

**Center reference column:**

21:11 [a] John 6:14; 7:40; 9:17
21:12 [a] Mark 11:15–18 [b] Deut. 14:25 [1] drove [2] overturned
21:13 [a] Is. 56:7 [b] Jer. 7:11
21:15 [a] John 7:42 [1] indignant
21:16 [a] Ps. 8:2 [1] nursing infants
21:17 [a] John 11:1, 18; 12:1
21:18 [a] Mark 11:12–14, 20–24 [1] was hungry
21:19 [a] Mark 11:13 [1] by the road
21:20 [a] Mark 11:20
21:21 [a] Matt. 17:20 [b] James 1:6 [c] 1 Cor. 13:2
21:22 [a] Matt. 7:7–11
21:23 [a] Luke 20:1–8 [b] Ex. 2:14
21:25 [a] [John 1:29–34] [b] John 1:15–28

21:26 [a] Matt. 14:5; 21:46 [b] Mark 6:20 [1] to be
21:28 [a] Matt. 20:1; 21:33
21:29 [1] regretted it
21:31 [a] Luke 7:29, 37–50 [1] tax collectors
21:32 [a] Luke 3:1–12; 7:29 [b] Luke 3:12, 13 [1] relented or regretted
21:33 [a] Luke 20:9–19 [b] Matt. 25:14 [1] landowner [2] leased [3] tenant farmers
21:34 [1] vintage [2] tenant farmers
21:35 [a] [1 Thess. 2:15]
21:37 [a] [John 3:16] [1] respect
21:38 [a] [Heb. 1:2] [b] John 11:53 [1] tenant farmers
21:39 [a] [Acts 2:23]
21:41 [a] Luke 20:16 [b] [Luke 21:24] [c] Acts 13:46] [1] lease [2] tenant farmers [3] pay back
21:42 [a] Ps. 118:22, 23 [1] chief corner stone

43 Therefore say I unto you, ªThe kingdom of God shall be taken from you, and given to a nation bringing forth the fruits thereof.

44 And whosoever ªshall fall on this stone shall be broken: but on whomsoever it shall fall, ᵇit will grind him to powder.

45 And when the chief priests and Pharisees had heard his parables, they ¹perceived that he spake of them.

46 But when they sought to lay hands on him, they ªfeared the multitude, because ᵇthey ¹took him for a prophet.

### CHAPTER 22

AND Jesus answered ªand spake unto them again by parables, and said,

2 The kingdom of heaven is like unto a certain king, which made a ¹marriage for his son,

3 And sent forth his servants to call them that were bidden to the wedding: and they would not come.

4 Again, he sent forth other servants, saying, Tell them which are bidden, Behold, I have prepared my dinner: ªmy oxen and *my* ¹fatlings *are* killed, and all things *are* ready: come unto the ²marriage.

5 But they made light of *it,* and went their ways, one to his farm, another to his ¹merchandise:

6 And the ¹remnant took his servants, and ²intreated *them* ³spitefully, and slew *them.*

7 But when the king heard *thereof,* he was wroth: and he sent forth ªhis armies, and destroyed those murderers, and burned up their city.

8 Then saith he to his servants, The wedding is ready, but they which were ¹bidden were not ªworthy.

9 Go ye therefore into the highways, and as many as ye shall find, ¹bid to the marriage.

10 So those servants went out into the highways, and ªgathered together all as many as they found, both bad and good: and the wedding was ¹furnished with guests.

11 And when the king came in to see the guests, he saw there a man ªwhich had not on a wedding garment:

12 And he saith unto him, Friend, how camest thou in hither not having a wedding garment? And he was ªspeechless.

13 Then said the king to the servants, Bind him hand and foot, and take him away, and cast *him*ª into outer darkness; there shall be weeping and gnashing of teeth.

14 ªFor many are called, but few *are* chosen.

---

**Cross references (center column):**

21:43 ª [Matt. 8:12]
21:44 ª Is. 8:14, 15 ᵇ [Dan. 2:44]
21:45 ¹ *knew*
21:46 ª Matt. 21:26 ᵇ Matt. 21:11 ¹ *held him to be*
22:1 ª [Rev. 19:7–9]
22:2 ¹ *wedding feast*
22:4 ª Prov. 9:2 ¹ *fattened cattle* ² *wedding feast*
22:5 ¹ *business*
22:6 ¹ *rest* ² *treated* ³ *insolently*
22:7 ª [Dan. 9:26]
22:8 ª Matt. 10:11 ¹ *invited*
22:9 ¹ *invite*
22:10 ª Matt. 13:38, 47, 48 ¹ *filled*
22:11 ª [Col. 3:10, 12]
22:12 ª [Rom. 3:19]
22:13 ª Matt. 8:12; 25:30
22:14 ª Matt. 20:16
22:15 ª Mark 12:13–17
22:16 ª Mark 3:6; 8:15; 12:13 ¹ *Teacher* ² Lit. *look not on the face of men*
22:17 ¹ *permitted* ² *pay taxes*
22:18 ¹ *knew* ² *test*
22:19 ¹ *tax* ² Gr. *denarius*
22:20 ¹ *inscription*
22:21 ª Matt. 17:25 ᵇ [Rom. 13:1–7] ᶜ [1 Cor. 3:23; 6:19, 20; 12:27] ¹ *Pay*
22:22 ¹ *were amazed*
22:23 ª Luke 20:27–40 ᵇ Acts 23:8
22:24 ª Deut. 25:5 ¹ *Teacher* ² *offspring*
22:25 ¹ *died* ² *offspring*
22:29 ª John 20:9 ¹ *are mistaken*
22:30 ª [1 John 3:2]
22:31 ¹ *concerning*
22:32 ª Ex. 3:6, 15
22:33 ª Matt. 7:28 ¹ *teaching*
22:34 ª Mark 12:28–31

---

15 ªThen went the Pharisees, and took counsel how they might entangle him in *his* talk.

16 And they sent out unto him their disciples with the ªHerodians, saying, ¹Master, we know that thou art true, and teachest the way of God in truth, neither carest thou for any *man:* for thou ²regardest not the person of men.

17 Tell us therefore, What thinkest thou? Is it ¹lawful to ²give tribute unto Caesar, or not?

18 But Jesus ¹perceived their wickedness, and said, Why ²tempt ye me, *ye* hypocrites?

19 Shew me the ¹tribute money. And they brought unto him a ²penny.

20 And he saith unto them, Whose *is* this image and ¹superscription?

21 They say unto him, Caesar's. Then saith he unto them, ªRender¹ therefore unto Caesar the things which are ᵇCaesar's; and unto God the things that are ᶜGod's.

22 When they had heard *these words,* they ¹marvelled, and left him, and went their way.

23 ªThe same day came to him the Sadducees, ᵇwhich say that there is no resurrection, and asked him,

24 Saying, ¹Master, ªMoses said, If a man die, having no children, his brother shall marry his wife, and raise up ²seed unto his brother.

25 Now there were with us seven brethren: and the first, when he had married a wife, ¹deceased, and, having no ²issue, left his wife unto his brother:

26 Likewise the second also, and the third, unto the seventh.

27 And last of all the woman died also.

28 Therefore in the resurrection whose wife shall she be of the seven? for they all had her.

29 Jesus answered and said unto them, Ye ¹do err, ªnot knowing the scriptures, nor the power of God.

30 For in the resurrection they neither marry, nor are given in marriage, but ªare as the angels of God in heaven.

31 But ¹as touching the resurrection of the dead, have ye not read that which was spoken unto you by God, saying,

32 ªI am the God of Abraham, and the God of Isaac, and the God of Jacob? God is not the God of the dead, but of the living.

33 And when the multitude heard *this,* ªthey were astonished at his ¹doctrine.

34 ªBut when the Pharisees had heard that he had put the Sadducees to silence, they were gathered together.

35 Then one of them, *which was* ªa lawyer, asked *him a question,* ¹tempting him, and saying,

36 ¹Master, which *is* the great commandment in the law?

37 Jesus said unto him, ªThou shalt love the Lord thy God with all thy heart, and with all thy soul, and with all thy mind.

38 This is the first and great commandment.

39 And the second *is* like unto it, ªThou shalt love thy neighbour as thyself.

40 ªOn these two commandments hang all the law and the prophets.

41 ªWhile the Pharisees were gathered together, Jesus asked them,

42 Saying, What think ye of Christ? whose son is he? They say unto him, *The* ªson of David.

43 He saith unto them, How then doth David ¹in spirit call him Lord, saying,

44 ªThe LORD said unto my Lord, Sit thou on my right hand, till I make thine enemies thy footstool?

45 If David then call him Lord, how is he his son?

46 ªAnd no man was able to answer him a word, ᵇneither ¹durst any *man* from that day forth ask him any more *questions.*

## CHAPTER 23

THEN spake Jesus to the multitude, and to his disciples,

2 Saying, ªThe scribes and the Pharisees sit in Moses' seat:

3 All therefore whatsoever they bid you observe, *that* observe and do; but do not ye ¹after their works: for ªthey say, and do not.

4 ªFor they bind heavy burdens ¹and grievous to be borne, and lay *them* on men's shoulders; but they *themselves* will not move them with one of their fingers.

5 But all their works they do for to ªbe seen of men: they make broad their phylacteries, and enlarge the borders of their garments,

6 ªAnd love the ¹uppermost rooms at feasts, and the ²chief seats in the synagogues,

7 And greetings in the markets, and to be called of men, Rabbi, Rabbi.

8 ªBut be not ye called Rabbi: for one is your ¹Master, *even* Christ; and all ye are brethren.

9 And call no *man* your father upon the earth: ªfor one is your Father, which is in heaven.

10 Neither be ye called ¹masters: for one is your ²Master, *even* Christ.

11 But ªhe that is greatest among you shall be your servant.

12 ªAnd whosoever shall exalt himself shall be ¹abased; and he that shall humble himself shall be ²exalted.

13 But ªwoe unto you, scribes and Pharisees, hypocrites! for ye shut up the kingdom of heaven against men: for ye neither go in *yourselves,* neither suffer ye them that are entering to go in.

14 Woe unto you, scribes and Pharisees, hypocrites! ªfor ye devour widows' houses, and for a pretence make long prayer: therefore ye shall receive the greater ¹damnation.

15 Woe unto you, scribes and Pharisees, hypocrites! for ye ¹compass sea and land to make one proselyte, and when he is made, ye make him twofold more the child of ²hell than yourselves.

16 Woe unto you, ªye blind guides, which say, ᵇWhosoever shall swear by the temple, it is nothing; but whosoever shall swear by the gold of the temple, he is ¹a debtor!

17 *Ye* fools and blind: for whether is greater, the gold, ªor the temple that sanctifieth the gold?

18 And, Whosoever shall swear by the altar, it is nothing; but whosoever sweareth by the gift that is upon it, he is ¹guilty.

19 *Ye* fools and blind: for whether *is* greater, the gift, or ªthe altar that sanctifieth the gift?

20 Whoso therefore shall ¹swear by the altar, sweareth by it, and by all things thereon.

21 And whoso shall swear by the temple, sweareth by it, and by ªhim that dwelleth therein.

22 And he that shall swear by heaven, sweareth by ªthe throne of God, and by him that sitteth thereon.

23 Woe unto you, scribes and Pharisees, hypocrites! ªfor ye pay tithe of mint and anise and cummin, and ᵇhave ¹omitted the weightier *matters* of the law, ²judgment, mercy, and faith: these ought ye to have done, and not to leave the other undone.

24 *Ye* blind guides, which strain ¹at a gnat, and swallow a camel.

25 Woe unto you, scribes and Pharisees, hypocrites! ªfor ye make clean the outside of the cup and of the ¹platter, but within they are full of extortion and ²excess.

26 *Thou* blind Pharisee, cleanse first that *which is* within the cup and platter, that the outside of them may be clean also.

27 Woe unto you, scribes and Pharisees, hypocrites! ªfor ye are like unto ¹whited sepulchres, which indeed appear beautiful outward, but are within full of dead *men's* bones, and of all uncleanness.

28 Even so ye also outwardly appear righteous unto men, but within ye are full of hypocrisy and ¹iniquity.

29 ªWoe unto you, scribes and Pharisees, hypocrites! because ye build

---

22:35 ª Luke 7:30; 10:25; 11:45, 46, 52; 14:3 ¹ *testing*
22:36 ¹ *Teacher*
22:37 ª Deut. 6:5; 10:12; 30:6
22:39 ª [Lev. 19:18]
22:40 ª [Matt. 7:12]
22:41 ª Luke 20:41–44
22:42 ª Matt. 1:1; 21:9
22:43 ¹ *in the Spirit*
22:44 ª Ps. 110:1
22:46 ª Luke 14:6 ᵇ Mark 12:34 ¹ *dared*
23:2 ª Neh. 8:4, 8
23:3 ª [Rom. 2:19] ¹ *according to*
23:4 ª Luke 11:46 ¹ *hard to bear*
23:5 ª [Matt. 6:1–6, 16–18]
23:6 ª Luke 11:43; 20:46 ¹ *place of honour,* lit. *chief place* ² *best*
23:8 ª [James 3:1] ¹ *Leader* or *Teacher*
23:9 ª [Mal. 1:6]
23:10 ¹ *leaders* or *teachers* ² *Leader*
23:11 ª Matt. 20:26, 27
23:12 ª Luke 14:11; 18:14 ¹ *humbled* ² *lifted up*
23:13 ª Luke 11:52
23:14 ª Mark 12:40 ¹ *condemnation*
23:15 ¹ *travel* ² Gr. *gehenna*
23:16 ª Matt. 15:14; 23:24 ᵇ [Matt. 5:33, 34] ¹ *obligated to perform it*
23:17 ª Ex. 30:29
23:18 ¹ *obliged to perform it*
23:19 ª Ex. 29:37
23:20 ¹ *swears an oath*
23:21 ª 1 Kin. 8:13
23:22 ª Matt. 5:34
23:23 ª Luke 11:42; 18:12 ᵇ [Hos. 6:6] ¹ *neglected* ² *justice*
23:24 ¹ *out*
23:25 ª Luke 11:39 ¹ *dish* ² *self-indulgence*
23:27 ª Acts 23:3 ¹ *whitewashed tombs*
23:28 ¹ *lawlessness*
23:29 ª Luke 11:47, 48

---

the tombs of the prophets, and [1]garnish the sepulchres of the righteous,

30 And say, If we had been in the days of our fathers, we would not have been partakers with them in the blood of the prophets.

31 Wherefore ye be witnesses [1]unto yourselves, that [a]ye are the [2]children of them which killed the prophets.

32 [a]Fill ye up then the [1]measure of your fathers.

33 *Ye* serpents, *ye*[a] generation[1] of vipers, how can ye escape the damnation of hell?

34 [a]Wherefore, behold, I send unto you prophets, and wise men, and scribes: and [b]*some* of them ye shall kill and crucify; and [c]*some* of them shall ye scourge in your synagogues, and persecute *them* from city to city:

35 [a]That upon you may come all the righteous blood shed upon the earth, [b]from the blood of righteous Abel unto [c]the blood of Zacharias son of Barachias, whom ye slew between the temple and the altar.

36 Verily I say unto you, All these things shall come upon this generation.

37 [a]O Jerusalem, Jerusalem, *thou* that killest the prophets, [b]and stonest them which are sent unto thee, how often would [c]I have gathered thy children together, even as a hen gathereth her chickens [d]under *her* wings, and ye would not!

38 Behold, your house is left unto you desolate.

39 For I say unto you, Ye shall not see me henceforth, till ye shall say, [a]Blessed *is* he that cometh in the name of the Lord.

## CHAPTER 24

AND [a]Jesus went out, and departed from the temple: and his disciples came to *him* for to shew him the buildings of the temple.

2 And Jesus said unto them, See ye not all these things? verily I say unto you, [a]There shall not be left here one stone upon another, that shall not be thrown down.

3 And as he sat upon the mount of Olives, [a]the disciples came unto him privately, saying, [b]Tell us, when shall these things be? and what *shall be* the sign of thy coming, and of the end of the [1]world?

4 And Jesus answered and said unto them, [a]Take heed that no man deceive you.

5 For [a]many shall come in my name, saying, I am Christ; [b]and shall deceive many.

6 And ye shall hear of [a]wars and rumours of wars: see that ye be not troubled: for all *these things* must come to pass, but the end is not yet.

23:29 [1] adorn
23:31 [a] [Acts 7:51, 52] [1] against [2] Lit. sons
23:32 [a] [1 Thess. 2:16] [1] measure of guilt
23:33 [a] Matt. 3:7; 12:34 [1] brood or offspring
23:34 [a] Luke 11:49 [b] Acts 7:54–60; 22:19 [c] 2 Cor. 11:24, 25
23:35 [a] Rev. 18:24 [b] Gen. 4:8 [c] 2 Chr. 24:20, 21
23:37 [a] Luke 13:34, 35 [b] 2 Chr. 24:20, 21; 36:15, 16 [c] Deut. 32:11, 12 [d] Ps. 17:8; 91:4
23:39 [a] Ps. 118:26
24:1 [a] Mark 13:1
24:2 [a] Luke 19:44
24:3 [a] Mark 13:3 [b] [1 Thess. 5:1–3] [1] age
24:4 [a] [Col. 2:8, 18]
24:5 [a] John 5:43 [b] Matt. 24:11
24:6 [a] [Rev. 6:2–4]

24:7 [a] Hag. 2:22 [b] Rev. 6:5, 6 [1] various
24:9 [a] Matt. 10:17 [1] tribulation
24:11 [a] 2 Pet. 2:1 [b] [1 Tim. 4:1]
24:12 [a] [2 Thess. 2:3] [1] lawlessness [2] grow
24:13 [a] Matt. 10:22
24:14 [a] Matt. 4:23 [b] Rom. 10:18
24:15 [a] Mark 13:14 [b] Dan. 9:27; 11:31; 12:11 [c] Dan. 9:23
24:19 [a] Luke 23:29 [1] pregnant [2] who are nursing babies
24:21 [a] Dan. 9:26
24:22 [a] Is. 65:8, 9 [1] chosen ones'
24:23 [a] Luke 17:23
24:24 [a] [2 Thess. 2:9] [b] [2 Tim. 2:19]
24:26 [1] inner rooms
24:27 [a] Luke 17:24 [1] flashes
24:28 [a] Luke 17:37 [1] carcase

7 For [a]nation shall rise against nation, and kingdom against kingdom: and there shall be [b]famines, and pestilences, and earthquakes, in [1]divers places.

8 All these *are* the beginning of sorrows.

9 [a]Then shall they deliver you up to [1]be afflicted, and shall kill you: and ye shall be hated of all nations for my name's sake.

10 And then shall many be offended, and shall betray one another, and shall hate one another.

11 And [a]many false prophets shall rise, and [b]shall deceive many.

12 And because [1]iniquity shall abound, the love of many shall [2]wax [a]cold.

13 [a]But he that shall endure unto the end, the same shall be saved.

14 And this [a]gospel of the kingdom [b]shall be preached in all the world for a witness unto all nations; and then shall the end come.

15 [a]When ye therefore shall see the abomination of desolation, spoken of by [b]Daniel the prophet, stand in the holy place, ([c]whoso readeth, let him understand:)

16 Then let them which be in Judaea flee into the mountains:

17 Let him which is on the housetop not come down to take any thing out of his house:

18 Neither let him which is in the field return back to take his clothes.

19 And [a]woe unto them that are [1]with child, and to them [2]that give suck in those days!

20 But pray ye that your flight be not in the winter, neither on the sabbath day:

21 For [a]then shall be great tribulation, such as was not since the beginning of the world to this time, no, nor ever shall be.

22 And except those days should be shortened, there should no flesh be saved: [a]but for the [1]elect's sake those days shall be shortened.

23 [a]Then if any man shall say unto you, Lo, here *is* Christ, or there; believe *it* not.

24 For [a]there shall arise false Christs, and false prophets, and shall shew great signs and wonders; insomuch that, [b]if *it were* possible, they shall deceive the very elect.

25 Behold, I have told you before.

26 Wherefore if they shall say unto you, Behold, he is in the desert; go not forth: behold, *he is* in the [1]secret chambers; believe *it* not.

27 [a]For as the lightning cometh out of the east, and [1]shineth even unto the west; so shall also the coming of the Son of man be.

28 [a]For wheresoever the [1]carcase is,

there will the eagles be gathered together.

29 [a]Immediately after the tribulation of those days [b]shall the sun be darkened, and the moon shall not give her light, and the stars shall fall from heaven, and the powers of the heavens shall be shaken:

30 [a]And then shall appear the sign of the Son of man in heaven: [b]and then shall all the tribes of the earth mourn, and they shall see the Son of man coming in the clouds of heaven with power and great glory.

31 [a]And he shall send his angels with a great sound of a trumpet, and they shall gather together his [1]elect from the four winds, from one end of heaven to the other.

32 Now learn [a]a parable [1]of the fig tree; When his branch is yet tender, and putteth forth leaves, ye know that summer *is* nigh:

33 So likewise ye, when ye shall see all these things, know [a]that [1]it is near, *even* at the doors.

34 Verily I say unto you, [a]This generation shall not pass, till all these things be fulfilled.

35 [a]Heaven and earth shall pass away, but my words shall not pass away.

36 [a]But of that day and hour knoweth no *man*, no, not the angels of heaven, [b]but my Father only.

37 But as the days of Noe *were*, so shall also the coming of the Son of man be.

38 [a]For as in the days that were before the flood they were eating and drinking, marrying and giving in marriage, until the day that Noe entered into the ark,

39 And knew not until the flood came, and took them all away; so shall also the coming of the Son of man be.

40 [a]Then shall two be in the field; the one shall be taken, and the other left.

41 Two *women shall be* grinding at the mill; the one shall be taken, and the other left.

42 [a]Watch therefore: for ye know not what hour your Lord doth come.

43 [a]But know this, that if the [1]goodman of the house had known in what [2]watch the thief would come, he would have watched, and would not have [3]suffered his house to be broken [4]up.

44 [a]Therefore be ye also ready: for in such an hour as ye think not the Son of man cometh.

45 [a]Who then is a faithful and wise servant, whom his lord hath made ruler over his household, to give them [1]meat in due season?

46 [a]Blessed *is* that servant, whom

his lord when he cometh shall find so doing.

47 Verily I say unto you, That [a]he shall make him ruler over all his goods.

48 But and if that evil servant shall say in his heart, My lord [a]delayeth his coming;

49 And shall begin to [1]smite *his* fellowservants, and to eat and drink with the drunken;

50 The lord of that servant shall come in a day when he looketh not for *him*, and in an hour that he is [a]not aware of,

51 And shall cut him [1]asunder, and appoint *him* his portion with the hypocrites: [a]there shall be weeping and gnashing of teeth.

## CHAPTER 25

THEN shall the kingdom of heaven be likened unto ten virgins, which took their lamps, and went forth to meet [a]the bridegroom.

2 [a]And five of them were wise, and five *were* foolish.

3 They that *were* foolish took their lamps, and took no oil with them:

4 But the wise took oil in their vessels with their lamps.

5 While the bridegroom [1]tarried, [a]they all slumbered and slept.

6 And at midnight [a]there was a cry made, Behold, the bridegroom cometh; go ye out to meet him.

7 Then all those virgins arose, and [a]trimmed their lamps.

8 And the foolish said unto the wise, Give us of your oil; for our lamps are [1]gone out.

9 But the wise answered, saying, *Not so;* lest there be not enough for us and you: but go ye rather to them that sell, and buy for yourselves.

10 And while they went to buy, the bridegroom came; and they that were ready went in with him to the [1]marriage: and [a]the door was shut.

11 Afterward came also the other virgins, saying, [a]Lord, Lord, open to us.

12 But he answered and said, Verily I say unto you, [a]I know you not.

13 [a]Watch therefore, for ye [b]know neither the day nor the hour wherein the Son of man cometh.

14 [a]For *the kingdom of heaven is* [b]as a man travelling into a far country, *who* called his own servants, and delivered unto them his goods.

15 And unto one he gave five talents, to another two, and to another one; [a]to every man according to his [1]several ability; and straightway took his journey.

16 Then he that had received the five talents went and traded with the same, and made *them* other five talents.

17 And likewise he that *had received* two, he also gained other two.

18 But he that had received one went and digged in the earth, and hid his lord's money.

19 After a long time the lord of those servants cometh, and [l]reckoneth with them.

20 And so he that had received five talents came and brought other five talents, saying, Lord, thou deliveredst unto me five talents: behold, I have gained beside them five talents more.

21 His lord said unto him, Well done, *thou* good and faithful servant: thou hast been [a]faithful over a few things, [b]I will make thee ruler over many things: enter thou into [c]the joy of thy lord.

22 He also that had received two talents came and said, Lord, thou deliveredst unto me two talents: behold, I have gained two other talents beside them.

23 His lord said unto him, [a]Well done, good and faithful servant; thou hast been faithful over a few things, I will make thee ruler over many things: enter thou into the [b]joy of thy lord.

24 Then he which had received the one talent came and said, Lord, I knew thee that thou art an hard man, reaping where thou hast not sown, and gathering where thou hast not [l]strawed:

25 And I was afraid, and went and hid thy talent in the earth: lo, *there* thou hast *that is* thine.

26 His lord answered and said unto him, *Thou* [a]wicked and [l]slothful servant, thou knewest that I reap where I sowed not, and gather where I have not [2]strawed:

27 Thou oughtest therefore to have put my money to the [l]exchangers, and *then* at my coming I should have received mine own with [2]usury.

28 Take therefore the talent from him, and give *it* unto him which hath ten talents.

29 [a]For unto every one that hath [l]shall be given, and he shall have abundance: but from him that hath not shall be taken away even that which he hath.

30 And cast ye the unprofitable servant [a]into outer darkness: [b]there shall be weeping and [c]gnashing of teeth.

31 [a]When the Son of man shall come in his glory, and all the holy angels with him, then shall he sit upon the throne of his glory:

32 And [a]before him shall be gathered all nations: and [b]he shall separate them one from another, as a shepherd divideth *his* sheep from the goats:

33 And he shall set the [a]sheep on his right hand, but the goats on the left.

34 Then shall the King say unto them on his right hand, Come, ye blessed of my Father, [a]inherit the kingdom [b]prepared for you from the foundation of the world:

35 [a]For I was [l]an hungred, and ye gave me [2]meat: I was thirsty, and ye gave me drink: [b]I was a stranger, and ye took me in:

36 [a]Naked, and ye clothed me: I was sick, and ye visited me: [b]I was in prison, and ye came unto me.

37 Then shall the righteous answer him, saying, Lord, when saw we thee [l]an hungred, and fed *thee?* or thirsty, and gave *thee* drink?

38 When saw we thee a stranger, and took *thee* in? or naked, and clothed *thee?*

39 Or when saw we thee sick, or in prison, and came unto thee?

40 And the King shall answer and say unto them, Verily I say unto you, [a]Inasmuch as ye have done *it* unto one of the least of these my brethren, ye have done *it* unto me.

41 Then shall he say also unto them on the left hand, [a]Depart from me, ye cursed, [b]into everlasting fire, prepared for [c]the devil and his angels:

42 For I was [l]an hungred, and ye gave me no [2]meat: I was thirsty, and ye gave me no drink:

43 I was a stranger, and ye took me not in: naked, and ye clothed me not: sick, and in prison, and ye visited me not.

44 Then shall they also answer him, saying, Lord, when saw we thee [l]an hungred, or [2]athirst, or a stranger, or naked, or sick, or in prison, and did not minister unto thee?

45 Then shall he answer them, saying, Verily I say unto you, [a]Inasmuch as ye did *it* not to one of the least of these, ye did *it* not to me.

46 And [a]these shall go away into everlasting punishment: but the righteous into life eternal.

## CHAPTER 26

AND it came to pass, when Jesus had finished all these sayings, he said unto his disciples,

2 [a]Ye know that after two days is *the feast of* the passover, and the Son of man is betrayed to be crucified.

3 [a]Then assembled together the chief priests, and the scribes, and the elders of the people, unto the palace of the high priest, who was called Caiaphas,

4 And [a]consulted[l] that they might take Jesus by [2]subtilty, and kill *him.*

5 But they said, Not on the feast *day,* lest there be an uproar among the [a]people.

### Cross references (center column)

25:19 [l] settled accounts
25:21 [a] [Luke 16:10; 1 Cor. 4:2; 2 Tim. 4:7, 8]
[b] [Matt. 24:47; 25:34, 46; Luke 12:44; 22:29, 30; Rev. 3:21; 21:7]
[c] [2 Tim. 2:12; Heb. 12:2; 1 Pet. 1:8]
25:23 [a] Matt. 24:45, 47; 25:21
[b] [Ps. 16:11; John 15:10, 11]
25:24 [l] scattered seed
25:26 [a] Matt. 18:32; Luke 19:22
[l] lazy [2] scattered seed
25:27 [l] bankers [2] interest
25:29 [a] Matt. 13:12
[l] more shall
25:30 [a] Matt. 8:12; 22:13 [b] Matt. 7:23; 8:12; 24:51 [c] Ps. 112:10
25:31 [a] [1 Thess. 4:16]
25:32 [a] [2 Cor. 5:10] [b] Ezek. 20:38
25:33 [a] [John 10:11, 27, 28]
25:34 [a] [Rom. 8:17] [b] Mark 10:40
25:35 [a] Is. 58:7 [b] [Heb. 13:2] [l] hungry [2] food
25:36 [a] [James 2:15, 16] [b] 2 Tim. 1:16
25:37 [l] hungry
25:40 [a] Mark 9:41
25:41 [a] Matt. 7:23 [b] Matt. 13:40, 42 [c] [2 Pet. 2:4]
25:42 [l] hungry [2] food
25:44 [l] hungry [2] thirsty
25:45 [a] Prov. 14:31
25:46 [a] [Dan. 12:2]
26:2 [a] Luke 22:1, 2
26:3 [a] John 11:47
26:4 [a] Acts 4:25–28 [l] plotted [2] trickery
26:5 [a] Matt. 21:26

6 Now when Jesus was in ᵃBethany, in the house of Simon the leper,

7 There came unto him a woman having an alabaster ¹box of very ²precious ointment, and poured it on his head, as he sat *at* ³*meat.*

8 ᵃBut when his disciples saw *it,* they had indignation, saying, To what purpose *is* this waste?

9 For this ointment might have been sold for much, and given to the poor.

10 When Jesus understood *it,* he said unto them, Why trouble ye the woman? for she hath wrought a good work upon me.

11 ᵃFor ye have the poor always with you; but ᵇme ye have not always.

12 For in that she hath poured this ointment on my body, she did *it* for my ᵃburial.

13 Verily I say unto you, Wheresoever this gospel shall be preached in the whole world, *there* shall also this, that this woman hath done, be told for a memorial of her.

14 ᵃThen one of the twelve, called ᵇJudas Iscariot, went unto the chief priests,

15 And said *unto them,* ᵃWhat will ye give me, and I will deliver him unto you? And they ¹covenanted with him for thirty pieces of silver.

16 And from that time he sought opportunity to betray him.

17 ᵃNow the first *day* of the *feast of* unleavened bread the disciples came to Jesus, saying unto him, Where wilt thou that we prepare for thee to eat the passover?

18 And he said, Go into the city to such a man, and say unto him, The ¹Master saith, ᵃMy time is at hand; I will keep the passover at thy house with my disciples.

19 And the disciples did as Jesus had appointed them; and they made ready the passover.

20 ᵃNow when the ¹even was come, he sat down with the twelve.

21 And as they did eat, he said, Verily I say unto you, that one of you shall ᵃbetray me.

22 And they were exceeding sorrowful, and began every one of them to say unto him, Lord, is it I?

23 And he answered and said, ᵃHe that dippeth *his* hand with me in the dish, the same shall betray me.

24 The Son of man goeth ᵃas it is written of him: but ᵇwoe unto that man by whom the Son of man is betrayed! ᶜit had been good for that man if he had not been born.

25 Then Judas, which betrayed him, answered and said, ¹Master, is it I? He said unto him, Thou hast ²said.

26 ᵃAnd as they were eating, ᵇJesus took bread, and blessed *it,* and brake

*it,* and gave *it* to the disciples, and said, Take, eat; ᶜthis is my body.

27 And he took the cup, and gave thanks, and gave *it* to them, saying, ᵃDrink¹ ye all of it;

28 For ᵃthis is my blood ᵇof the new testament, which is shed ᶜfor many for the ¹remission of sins.

29 But ᵃI say unto you, I will not drink henceforth of this fruit of the vine, ᵇuntil that day when I drink it new with you in my Father's kingdom.

30 ᵃAnd when they had sung an hymn, they went out into the mount of Olives.

31 Then saith Jesus unto them, ᵃAll ye shall ᵇbe ¹offended because of me this night: for it is written, ᶜI will ²smite the shepherd, and the sheep of the flock shall be scattered abroad.

32 But after I am risen again, ᵃI will go before you into Galilee.

33 Peter answered and said unto him, Though all *men* shall be ¹offended because of thee, *yet* will I never be ¹offended.

34 Jesus said unto him, ᵃVerily I say unto thee, That this night, before the ¹cock crow, thou shalt deny me ²thrice.

35 Peter said unto him, Though I should die with thee, yet will I not deny thee. Likewise also said all the disciples.

36 ᵃThen cometh Jesus with them unto a place called Gethsemane, and saith unto the disciples, Sit ye here, while I go and pray ¹yonder.

37 And he took with him Peter and ᵃthe two sons of Zebedee, and began to be ¹sorrowful and ²very heavy.

38 Then saith he unto them, ᵃMy soul is exceeding sorrowful, even unto death: ¹tarry ye here, and watch with me.

39 And he went a little farther, and fell on his face, and ᵃprayed, saying, ᵇO my Father, if it be possible, ᶜlet this cup pass from me: nevertheless ᵈnot as I will, but as thou *wilt.*

40 And he cometh unto the disciples, and findeth them asleep, and saith unto Peter, What, could ye not watch with me one hour?

41 ᵃWatch and pray, that ye enter not into temptation: ᵇthe spirit indeed *is* willing, but the flesh *is* weak.

42 He went away again the second time, and prayed, saying, O my Father, if this cup may not pass away from me, ¹except I drink it, thy will be done.

43 And he came and found them asleep again: for their eyes were heavy.

44 And he left them, and went away again, and prayed the third time, saying the same words.

45 Then cometh he to his disciples, and saith unto them, ¹Sleep on now,

26:6 ᵃ Mark 14:3–9

26:7 ¹ flask ² costly fragrant oil ³ The table

26:8 ᵃ John 12:4

26:11 ᵃ [Deut. 15:11] ᵇ [John 13:33; 14:19; 16:5, 28; 17:11]

26:12 ᵃ John 19:38–42

26:14 ᵃ Mark 14:10, 11; Luke 22:3–6 ᵇ Matt. 10:4

26:15 ᵃ Zech. 11:12 ¹ counted out to him

26:17 ᵃ Ex. 12:6, 18–20

26:18 ᵃ Luke 9:51 ¹ Lit. Teacher

26:20 ᵃ Mark 14:17–21 ¹ evening

26:21 ᵃ John 6:70, 71; 13:21

26:23 ᵃ Ps. 41:9

26:24 ᵃ 1 Cor. 15:3 ᵇ Luke 17:1 ᶜ John 17:12

26:25 ¹ Gr. Rabbi ² said it

26:26 ᵃ Mark 14:22–25 ᵇ 1 Cor. 11:23–25 ᶜ [1 Pet. 2:24]

26:27 ᵃ Mark 14:23 ¹ Drink from it, all of you

26:28 ᵃ [Ex. 24:8] ᵇ Jer. 31:31 ᶜ Matt. 20:28 ¹ forgiveness

26:29 ᵃ Mark 14:25 ᵇ Acts 10:41

26:30 ᵃ Mark 14:26–31

26:31 ᵃ John 16:32 ᵇ [Matt. 11:6] ᶜ Zech. 13:7 ¹ made to stumble ² strike

26:32 ᵃ Matt. 28:7, 10, 16

26:33 ¹ made to stumble

26:34 ᵃ John 13:38 ¹ rooster crows ² three times

26:36 ᵃ Mark 14:32–35 ¹ over there

26:37 ᵃ Matt. 4:21; 17:1 ¹ grieved ² deeply distressed

26:38 ᵃ John 12:27 ¹ stay

26:39 ᵃ [Heb. 5:7–9] ᵇ John 12:27 ᶜ Matt. 20:22 ᵈ John 5:30; 6:38

26:41 ᵃ Luke 22:40, 46 ᵇ [Gal. 5:17]

26:42 ¹ unless

26:45 ¹ Are you still sleeping and resting?

and take *your* rest: behold, the hour is at hand, and the Son of man is [a]betrayed into the hands of sinners.

46 Rise, let us be going: behold, he is at hand that doth betray me.

47 And [a]while he yet spake, lo, Judas, one of the twelve, came, and with him a great multitude with swords and staves, from the chief priests and elders of the people.

48 Now he that betrayed him gave them a sign, saying, Whomsoever I shall kiss, that same is he: [1]hold him fast.

49 And forthwith he came to Jesus, and said, Hail, [1]master; [a]and kissed him.

50 And Jesus said unto him, [a]Friend, wherefore art thou come? Then came they, and laid hands on Jesus, and took him.

51 And, behold, [a]one of them which were with Jesus stretched out *his* hand, and drew his sword, and struck a servant of the high priest's, and [1]smote off his ear.

52 Then said Jesus unto him, Put up again thy sword into his place: [a]for all they that take the sword shall perish with the sword.

53 Thinkest thou that I cannot now pray to my Father, and he shall [1]presently give me [a]more than twelve legions of angels?

54 But how then shall the scriptures be fulfilled, [a]that thus it must be?

55 In that same hour said Jesus to the multitudes, Are ye come out as against a [1]thief with swords and [2]staves for to take me? I sat daily with you teaching in the temple, and ye [3]laid no hold on me.

56 But all this was done, that the [a]scriptures of the prophets might be fulfilled. Then [b]all the disciples forsook him, and fled.

57 [a]And they that had laid hold on Jesus led *him* away to Caiaphas the high priest, where the scribes and the elders were assembled.

58 But [a]Peter followed him [1]afar off unto the high priest's [2]palace, and went in, and sat with the servants, to see the end.

59 Now the chief priests, and elders, and all the council, sought [a]false [1]witness against Jesus, to put him to death;

60 But found none: yea, though [a]many false witnesses came, *yet* found they none. At the last came [b]two false witnesses,

61 And said, This *fellow* said, [a]I am able to destroy the temple of God, and to build it in three days.

62 [a]And the high priest arose, and said unto him, Answerest thou nothing? what *is it which* these [1]witness against thee?

63 But [a]Jesus [1]held his peace. And the high priest answered and said unto him, [b]I adjure thee by the living God, that thou tell us whether thou be the Christ, the Son of God.

64 Jesus saith unto him, [1]Thou hast said: nevertheless I say unto you, [a]Hereafter shall ye see the Son of man [b]sitting on the right hand of power, and coming in the clouds of heaven.

65 [a]Then the high priest [1]rent his clothes, saying, He hath spoken blasphemy; what further need have we of witnesses? behold, now ye have heard his [b]blasphemy.

66 What think ye? They answered and said, [a]He is [1]guilty of death.

67 [a]Then did they spit in his face, and [1]buffeted him; and [b]others [2]smote *him* with [3]the palms of their hands,

68 Saying, [a]Prophesy unto us, thou Christ, Who is he that smote thee?

69 [a]Now Peter sat without in the palace: and a [1]damsel came unto him, saying, Thou also wast with Jesus of Galilee.

70 But he denied before *them* all, saying, I know not what thou sayest.

71 And when he was gone out [1]into the porch, another *maid* saw him, and said unto them that were there, This *fellow* was also with Jesus of Nazareth.

72 And again he denied with an oath, I do not know the man.

73 And after a while came unto *him* they that stood by, and said to Peter, Surely thou also art *one* of them; for thy [a]speech bewrayeth thee.

74 Then [a]began he to [1]curse and to [2]swear, *saying*, I know not the man. And immediately the [3]cock crew.

75 And Peter remembered the word of Jesus, which said unto him, [a]Before the cock crow, thou shalt deny me [1]thrice. And he went out, and wept bitterly.

## CHAPTER 27

WHEN the morning was come, [a]all the chief priests and elders of the people took counsel against Jesus to put him to death:

2 And when they had bound him, they led *him* away, and [a]delivered him to Pontius Pilate the governor.

3 [a]Then Judas, which had betrayed him, when he saw that he was condemned, [1]repented himself, and brought again the thirty [b]pieces of silver to the chief priests and elders,

4 Saying, I have sinned in that I have betrayed the innocent blood. And they said, What *is that* to us? see thou *to that.*

5 And he [1]cast down the pieces of silver in the temple, [a]and departed, and went and hanged himself.

### Cross References

26:45 [a] Matt. 17:22, 23; 20:18, 19
26:47 [a] Acts 1:16
26:48 [1] *seize him*
26:49 [a] 2 Sam. 20:9 [1] *Gr. rabbi*
26:50 [a] Ps. 41:9; 55:13
26:51 [a] John 18:10 [1] *cut*
26:52 [a] Rev. 13:10
26:53 [a] Dan. 7:10 [1] *provide me with*
26:54 [a] Is. 50:6; 53:2–11
26:55 [1] *robber* [2] *clubs* [3] *did not seize me*
26:56 [a] Lam. 4:20 [b] John 18:15
26:57 [a] John 18:12, 19–24
26:58 [a] John 18:15, 16 [1] *at a distance* [2] *courtyard*
26:59 [a] Ps. 35:11 [1] *testimony*
26:60 [a] Mark 14:55 [b] Deut. 19:15
26:61 [a] John 2:19
26:62 [a] Mark 14:60 [1] *testify*
26:63 [a] Is. 53:7 [b] Lev. 5:1 [1] *kept silent*
26:64 [a] Dan. 7:13 [b] [Acts 7:55] [1] *It is as you said*
26:65 [a] 2 Kin. 18:37 [b] John 10:30–36 [1] *tore*
26:66 [a] Lev. 24:16 [1] *deserving*
26:67 [a] Is. 50:6; 53:3 [b] Luke 22:63–65 [1] *beat* [2] *struck* [3] *Or rods*
26:68 [a] Mark 14:65
26:69 [a] John 18:16–18, 25–27 [1] *servant girl*
26:71 [1] *to the gateway*
26:73 [a] Luke 22:59
26:74 [a] Mark 14:71 [1] *call down curses* [2] *Swear oaths* [3] *rooster crowed*
26:75 [a] Matt. 26:34 [1] *three times*
27:1 [a] John 18:28
27:2 [a] Acts 3:13
27:3 [a] Matt. 26:14 [b] Matt. 26:15 [1] *felt remorse*
27:5 [a] Acts 1:18 [1] *threw down*

6 And the chief priests took the silver pieces, and said, It is not lawful for to put them into the treasury, because it is the price of blood.

7 And they took counsel, and bought with them the potter's field, to bury strangers in.

8 Wherefore that field was called, ªThe field of blood, unto this day.

9 Then was fulfilled that which was spoken by Jeremy the prophet, saying, ªAnd they took the thirty pieces of silver, the price of him that was ¹valued, whom they of the children of Israel did value;

10 And gave them for the potter's field, as the Lord ªappointed¹ me.

11 And Jesus stood before the governor: ªand the governor asked him, saying, Art thou the King of the Jews? And Jesus said unto him, ᵇThou¹ sayest.

12 And when he was accused of the chief priests and elders, ªhe answered nothing.

13 Then said Pilate unto him, ªHearest thou not how many things they ¹witness against thee?

14 And he answered him to never a word; insomuch that the governor marvelled greatly.

15 ªNow at *that* feast the governor was ¹wont to release unto the ²people a prisoner, whom they ³would.

16 And they had then a ¹notable prisoner, called Barabbas.

17 Therefore when they were gathered together, Pilate said unto them, Whom will ye that I release unto you? Barabbas, or Jesus which is called Christ?

18 For he knew that for ªenvy they had delivered him.

19 When he was set down on the judgment seat, his wife sent unto him, saying, Have thou nothing to do with that just man: for I have suffered many things this day in a dream because of him.

20 ªBut the chief priests and elders persuaded the multitude that they should ask Barabbas, and destroy Jesus.

21 The governor answered and said unto them, Whether of the twain will ye that I release unto you? They said, ªBarabbas.

22 Pilate saith unto them, What shall I do then with Jesus which is called Christ? *They* all say unto him, Let him be crucified.

23 And the governor said, ªWhy, what evil hath he done? But they cried out the more, saying, Let him be crucified.

24 When Pilate saw that he could ¹prevail nothing, but *that* rather a tumult was ²made, he ªtook water, and washed *his* hands before the mul-

titude, saying, I am innocent of the blood of this just person: see ye *to it*.

25 Then answered all the people, and said, ªHis blood *be* on us, and on our children.

26 Then released he Barabbas unto them: and when ªhe had ¹scourged Jesus, he delivered *him* to be crucified.

27 ªThen the soldiers of the governor took Jesus into the ¹common hall, and gathered unto him the whole ²band *of soldiers*.

28 And they ªstripped him, and ᵇput on him a scarlet robe.

29 ªAnd when they had ¹platted a crown of thorns, they put *it* upon his head, and a reed in his right hand: and they bowed the knee before him, and mocked him, saying, Hail, King of the Jews!

30 And ªthey spit upon him, and took the reed, and smote him on the head.

31 And after that they had mocked him, they took the robe off from him, and put his own ¹raiment on him, ªand led him away to crucify *him*.

32 ªAnd as they came out, ᵇthey found a man of Cyrene, Simon by name: him they compelled to bear his cross.

33 ªAnd when they were come unto a place called Golgotha, that is to say, a place of a skull,

34 ªThey gave him ¹vinegar to drink mingled with gall: and when he had tasted *thereof*, he would not drink.

35 ªAnd they crucified him, and ¹parted his garments, casting lots: that it might be fulfilled which was spoken by the prophet, ᵇThey ¹parted my garments among them, and upon my ²vesture did they cast lots.

36 ªAnd sitting down they ¹watched him there;

37 And ªset up over his head his accusation written, THIS IS JESUS THE KING OF THE JEWS.

38 ªThen were there two ¹thieves crucified with him, one on the right hand, and another on the left.

39 And ªthey that passed by ¹reviled him, wagging their heads,

40 And saying, ªThou that destroyest the temple, and buildest *it* in three days, save thyself. ᵇIf thou be the Son of God, come down from the cross.

41 Likewise also the chief priests mocking *him*, with the scribes and elders, said,

42 He ªsaved others; himself he cannot save. If he be the King of Israel, let him now come down from the cross, and we will believe him.

43 ªHe trusted in God; let him deliver him now, if he will have him: for he said, I am the Son of God.

27:8 ª Acts 1:19
27:9 ª Zech. 11:12
¹ priced
27:10 ª Jer. 32:6–9; Zech. 11:12, 13
¹ directed
27:11 ª Mark 15:2–5 ᵇ John 18:37 ¹ It is as *you say*
27:12 ª John 19:9
27:13 ª Matt. 26:62 ¹ testify
27:15 ª Luke 23:17–25 ¹ accustomed ² multitude ³ wished
27:16 ¹ notorious
27:18 ª Matt. 21:38
27:20 ª Acts 3:14
27:21 ª Acts 3:14
27:23 ª Acts 3:13
27:24 ª Deut. 21:6–8 ¹ accomplish ² rising
27:25 ª Josh. 2:19
27:26 ª [Is. 50:6; 53:5] ¹ flogged with a scourge
27:27 ª Mark 15:16–20 ¹ Gr. *praetorion*, the governor's headquarters ² cohort
27:28 ª John 19:2 ᵇ Luke 23:11
27:29 ª Is. 53:3 ¹ twisted
27:30 ª Matt. 26:67
27:31 ª Is. 53:7 ¹ clothes
27:32 ª Heb. 13:12 ᵇ Mark 15:21
27:33 ª John 19:17
27:34 ª Ps. 69:21 ¹ sour wine
27:35 ª Luke 23:34 ᵇ Ps. 22:18 ¹ divided ² clothing
27:36 ª Matt. 27:54 ¹ guarded
27:37 ª John 19:19
27:38 ª Is. 53:9, 12 ¹ robbers
27:39 ª Mark 15:29 ¹ blasphemed
27:40 ª John 2:19 ᵇ Matt. 26:63
27:42 ª [John 3:14, 15]
27:43 ª Ps. 22:8

44 [a]The [1]thieves also, which were crucified with him, cast the same in his teeth.

45 [a]Now from the sixth hour there was darkness over all the land unto the ninth hour.

46 And about the ninth hour [a]Jesus cried with a loud voice, saying, Eli, Eli, lama sabachthani? that is to say, [b]My God, my God, why hast thou forsaken me?

47 Some of them that stood there, when they heard *that,* said, This *man* calleth for Elias.

48 And straightway one of them ran, and took a spunge, [a]and filled *it* with vinegar, and put *it* on a reed, and gave him to drink.

49 The rest said, Let be, let us see whether Elias will come to save him.

50 [a]Jesus, when he had cried again with a loud voice, [b]yielded up the ghost.

51 And, behold, [a]the veil of the temple was [1]rent in twain from the top to the bottom; and the earth did quake, and the rocks [2]rent;

52 And the graves were opened; and many bodies of the saints which slept arose,

53 And came out of the graves after his resurrection, and went into the holy city, and appeared unto many.

54 [a]Now when the centurion, and they that were with him, [1]watching Jesus, saw the earthquake, and those things that were done, they feared greatly, saying, [b]Truly this was the Son of God.

55 And many women were there beholding afar off, [a]which followed Jesus from Galilee, ministering unto him:

56 [a]Among which was Mary Magdalene, and Mary the mother of James and Joses, and the mother of Zebedee's [1]children.

57 [a]When the [1]even was come, there came a rich man of Arimathaea, named Joseph, who also himself was Jesus' disciple:

58 He went to Pilate, and [1]begged the body of Jesus. Then Pilate commanded the body to be delivered.

59 And when Joseph had taken the body, he wrapped it in a clean linen cloth,

60 And [a]laid it in his own new tomb, which he had hewn out in the rock: and he rolled a great stone to the door of the sepulchre, and departed.

61 And there was Mary Magdalene, and the other Mary, sitting [1]over against the sepulchre.

62 Now the next day, that followed the day of the preparation, the chief priests and Pharisees came together unto Pilate,

63 Saying, Sir, we remember that that deceiver said, while he was yet alive, [a]After three days I will rise again.

64 Command therefore that the [1]sepulchre be made [2]sure until the third day, lest his disciples come by night, and steal him away, and say unto the people, He is risen from the dead: so the last [3]error shall be worse than the first.

65 Pilate said unto them, Ye have a [1]watch: go your way, make *it* as [2]sure as ye can.

66 So they went, and made the sepulchre [1]sure, [a]sealing the stone, and setting a [2]watch.

## CHAPTER 28

IN[1] the [a]end of the sabbath, as it began to dawn toward the first *day* of the week, came Mary Magdalene [b]and the other Mary to see the [2]sepulchre.

2 And, behold, there was a great earthquake: for [a]the angel of the Lord descended from heaven, and came and rolled back the stone from the door, and sat upon it.

3 [a]His countenance was like lightning, and his [1]raiment white as snow:

4 And for fear of him the [1]keepers did shake, and became as [a]dead *men.*

5 And the angel answered and said unto the women, Fear not ye: for I know that ye seek Jesus, which was crucified.

6 He is not here: for he is risen, [a]as he said. Come, see the place where the Lord lay.

7 And go quickly, and tell his disciples that he is risen from the dead; and, behold, [a]he goeth before you into Galilee; there shall ye see him: lo, I have told you.

8 And they departed quickly from the sepulchre with fear and great joy; and did run to bring his disciples word.

9 And as they went to tell his disciples, behold, [a]Jesus met them, saying, [1]All hail. And they came and held him by the feet, and worshipped him.

10 Then said Jesus unto them, Be not afraid: go tell [a]my brethren that they go into Galilee, and there shall they see me.

11 Now when they were going, behold, some of the [1]watch came into the city, and shewed unto the chief priests all the things that were done.

12 And when they were assembled with the elders, and had taken counsel, they gave [1]large money unto the soldiers,

13 Saying, Say ye, His disciples came by night, and stole him *away* while we slept.

14 And if this come to the governor's ears, we will persuade him, and [1]secure you.

15 So they took the money, and did as they were taught: and this saying is commonly reported among the Jews until this day.

16 Then the eleven disciples went away into Galilee, into a mountain [a]where Jesus had appointed them.

17 And when they saw him, they worshipped him: but some [a]doubted.

18 And Jesus came and spake unto them, saying, [a]All [1]power is given unto me in heaven and in earth.

19 [a]Go ye therefore, and [b]teach[1] all nations, baptizing them in the name of the Father, and of the Son, and of the Holy Ghost:

20 [a]Teaching them to observe all things whatsoever I have commanded you: and, lo, I am [b]with you alway, *even* unto the end of the world. Amen.

28:14 [1] *make you secure*
28:16 [a] Matt. 26:32; 28:7, 10
28:17 [a] John 20:24–29
28:18 [a] [Dan. 7:13, 14] [1] *authority*
28:19 [a] Mark 16:15 [b] Luke 24:47 [1] *make disciples of*

28:20 [a] [Acts 2:42] [b] [Acts 4:31; 18:10; 23:11]

# THE GOSPEL ACCORDING TO
# MARK

The message of Mark's gospel is captured in a single verse: "For even the Son of man came not to be ministered unto, but to minister, and to give his life a ransom for many" (10:45). Chapter by chapter, the book unfolds the dual focus of Christ's life: service and sacrifice.

Mark portrays Jesus as a Servant on the move, instantly responsive to the will of the Father. By preaching, teaching, and healing, He ministers to the needs of others even to the point of death. After the Resurrection, He commissions His followers to continue His work in His power—servants following in the steps of the perfect Servant.

The ancient title for this gospel was *Kata Markon*, "According to Mark." The author is best known by his Latin name *Marcus*, but in Jewish circles he was called by his Hebrew name *John*. Acts 12:12, 25 refer to him as "John, whose surname was Mark."

## CHAPTER 1

THE ªbeginning of the gospel of Jesus Christ, ᵇthe Son of God;

2 As it is written in the prophets, ªBehold, I send my messenger before thy face, which shall prepare thy way before thee.

3 ªThe voice of one crying in the wilderness, Prepare ye the way of the Lord, make his paths straight.

4 ªJohn did baptize in the wilderness, and preach the baptism of repentance for the ¹remission of sins.

5 ªAnd there went out unto him all the land of Judaea, and they of Jerusalem, and were all baptized of him in the river of Jordan, confessing their sins.

6 And John was ªclothed with camel's hair, and with a ¹girdle of a skin about his ²loins; and he did eat locusts and wild honey;

7 And preached, saying, ªThere cometh one mightier than I after me, the ¹latchet of whose ²shoes I am not worthy to stoop down and unloose.

8 ªI indeed have baptized you with water: but he shall baptize you ᵇwith the Holy Ghost.

9 ªAnd it came to pass in those days, that Jesus came from Nazareth of Galilee, and was baptized of John in Jordan.

10 ªAnd straightway coming up out of the water, he saw the heavens ¹opened, and the Spirit like a dove ᵇdescending upon him:

11 And there came a voice from heaven, *saying,* ªThou art my beloved Son, in whom I am well pleased.

12 ªAnd immediately the Spirit ¹driveth him into the wilderness.

13 And he was there in the wilderness forty days, tempted of Satan; and was with the wild beasts; ªand the angels ministered unto him.

14 ªNow after that John was put in prison, Jesus came into Galilee, ᵇpreaching the gospel of the kingdom of God,

15 And saying, ªThe time is fulfilled, and ᵇthe kingdom of God is ¹at hand: repent ye, and ²believe the gospel.

16 ªNow as he walked by the sea of Galilee, he saw Simon and Andrew his brother casting a net into the sea: for they were fishers.

17 And Jesus said unto them, Come ye after me, and I will make you to become ªfishers of men.

18 And straightway ªthey ¹forsook their nets, and followed him.

19 And when he had gone a little farther thence, he saw James the *son* of Zebedee, and John his brother, who also were in the ship mending their nets.

20 And straightway he called them: and they left their father Zebedee in the ship with the hired servants, and went after him.

21 ªAnd they went into Capernaum; and straightway on the sabbath day he entered into the ᵇsynagogue, and taught.

22 ªAnd they were astonished at his ¹doctrine: for he taught them as one that had authority, and not as the scribes.

23 And there was in their synagogue a man with an ªunclean spirit; and he cried out,

24 Saying, Let *us* alone; ªwhat have we to do with thee, thou Jesus of Nazareth? art thou come to destroy us? I ᵇknow thee who thou art, the ᶜHoly One of God.

25 And Jesus ªrebuked him, saying, ¹Hold thy peace, and come out of him.

26 And when the unclean spirit ªhad ¹torn him, and cried with a loud voice, he came out of him.

### Cross-references and notes

1:1 ª Luke 3:22
ᵇ Matt. 14:33
1:2 ª Mal. 3:1
1:3 ª Is. 40:3
1:4 ª Matt. 3:1
¹ forgiveness
1:5 ª Matt. 3:5
1:6 ª Matt. 3:4
¹ leather belt
² waist
1:7 ª John 1:27
¹ thong ² sandals
1:8 ª Acts 1:5; 11:16
ᵇ Is. 44:3
1:9 ª Matt. 3:13–17
1:10 ª Matt. 3:16
ᵇ Acts 10:38 ¹ torn open
1:11 ª Matt. 3:17; 12:18
1:12 ª Matt. 4:1–11
¹ sent him out
1:13 ª Matt. 4:10, 11
1:14 ª Matt. 4:12
ᵇ Matt. 4:23
1:15 ª [Gal. 4:4]
ᵇ Matt. 3:2; 4:17
¹ near ² believe in
1:16 ª Luke 5:2–11
1:17 ª Matt. 13:47, 48
1:18 ª [Luke 14:26]
¹ left
1:21 ª Luke 4:31–37 ᵇ Matt. 4:23
1:22 ª Matt. 7:28, 29; 13:54
¹ teaching
1:23 ª [Matt. 12:43]
1:24 ª Matt. 8:28, 29 ᵇ James 2:19
ᶜ Ps. 16:10
1:25 ª [Luke 4:39]
¹ Lit. Be muzzled
1:26 ª Mark 9:20
¹ convulsed

27 And they were all amazed, insomuch that they questioned among themselves, saying, What thing is this? what new doctrine *is* this? for with authority commandeth he even the unclean spirits, and they do obey him.

28 And immediately his ªfame spread abroad throughout all the region round about Galilee.

29 ªAnd forthwith, when they were come out of the synagogue, they entered into the house of Simon and Andrew, with James and John.

30 But Simon's wife's mother lay sick of a fever, and ¹anon they tell him of her.

31 And he came and took her by the hand, and lifted her up; and immediately the fever left her, and she ¹ministered unto them.

32 ªAnd at ¹even, when the sun did set, they brought unto him all that were diseased, and them that were possessed with ²devils.

33 And all the city was gathered together at the door.

34 And he healed many that were sick of ¹divers diseases, and ªcast out many ²devils; and ᵇsuffered not the ²devils to speak, because they knew him.

35 And ªin the morning, rising up a great while before day, he went out, and departed into a ¹solitary place, and there ᵇprayed.

36 And Simon and they that were with him ¹followed after him.

37 And when they had found him, they said unto him, ªAll *men* ᵇseek for thee.

38 And he said unto them, ªLet us go into the next towns, that I may preach there also: for ᵇtherefore came I forth.

39 ªAnd he preached in their synagogues throughout all Galilee, and ᵇcast out ¹devils.

40 ªAnd there came a leper to him, beseeching him, and kneeling down to him, and saying unto him, If thou ¹wilt, thou canst make me clean.

41 And Jesus, moved with ªcompassion, put forth *his* hand, and touched him, and saith unto him, I will; be thou clean.

42 And as soon as he had spoken, ªimmediately the leprosy departed from him, and he was cleansed.

43 And he ¹straitly charged him, and forthwith sent him away;

44 And saith unto him, See thou say nothing to any man: but go thy way, shew thyself to the priest, and offer for thy cleansing those things ªwhich Moses commanded, for a testimony unto them.

45 ªBut he went out, and began to ¹publish *it* much, and to ²blaze abroad the matter, insomuch that Jesus could no more openly enter into the city, but was ³without in desert places: ᵇand they came to him from every quarter.

## CHAPTER 2

AND again ªhe entered into Capernaum after *some* days; and it was ¹noised that he was in the house.

2 And straightway many were gathered together, insomuch that there was no room to receive *them,* no, ¹not so much as about the door: and he preached the word unto them.

3 And they come unto him, bringing one sick of ¹the ªpalsy, which was ²borne of four.

4 And when they could not come ¹nigh unto him for the ²press, they uncovered the roof where he was: and when they had broken *it* up, they let down the bed wherein the ³sick of the palsy lay.

5 When Jesus saw their faith, he said unto the ¹sick of the palsy, Son, thy sins be forgiven thee.

6 But there were certain of the scribes sitting there, and reasoning in their hearts,

7 Why doth this *man* thus speak blasphemies? ªwho can forgive sins but God only?

8 And immediately when Jesus perceived in his spirit that they so reasoned within themselves, he said unto them, Why reason ye these things in your hearts?

9 ªWhether is it easier to say to the ¹sick of the palsy, *Thy* sins be forgiven thee; or to say, Arise, and take up thy bed, and walk?

10 But that ye may know that the Son of man hath ¹power on earth to forgive sins, (he saith to the ²sick of the palsy,)

11 I say unto thee, Arise, and take up thy bed, and go thy way into thine house.

12 And immediately he arose, took up the bed, and went forth before them all; insomuch that they were all amazed, and ªglorified God, saying, We never saw ¹it on this fashion.

13 ªAnd he went forth again by the sea side; and all the multitude ¹resorted unto him, and he taught them.

14 ªAnd as he passed by, he saw Levi the *son* of Alphaeus sitting at the ¹receipt of custom, and said unto him, ᵇFollow me. And he arose and ᶜfollowed him.

15 ªAnd it came to pass, that, as Jesus ¹sat at meat in his house, many ²publicans and sinners sat also together with Jesus and his disciples: for there were many, and they followed him.

### Center notes

1:28 ª Matt. 4:24; 9:31
1:29 ª Luke 4:38, 39
1:30 ¹ *at once*
1:31 ¹ *served*
1:32 ª Matt. 8:16, 17 ¹ *evening* ² *demons*
1:34 ª Luke 13:32 ᵇ Acts 16:17, 18 ¹ *various* ² *demons*
1:35 ª Luke 4:42, 43 ᵇ Luke 5:16; 6:12; 9:28, 29 ¹ *deserted*
1:36 ¹ *searched for*
1:37 ª John 3:26; 12:19 ᵇ [Heb. 11:6]
1:38 ª Luke 4:43 ᵇ [Is. 61:1, 2]
1:39 ª Matt. 4:23; 9:35 ᵇ Mark 5:8, 13; 7:29, 30 ¹ *demons*
1:40 ª Luke 5:12–14 ¹ *are willing*
1:41 ª Luke 7:13
1:42 ª Matt. 15:28
1:43 ¹ *strictly*
1:44 ª Lev. 14:1–32
1:45 ª Matt. 28:15; Luke 5:15 ¹ *proclaim* ² *spread*

ᵇ Mark 2:2, 13; 3:7; Luke 5:17; John 6:2 ³ *outside*
2:1 ª Matt. 9:1 ¹ *heard*
2:2 ¹ *not even near*
2:3 ª Matt. 4:24; 8:6; Acts 8:7; 9:33 ¹ *paralysis* ² *carried by*
2:4 ¹ *near* ² *crowd* ³ *paralytic*
2:5 ¹ *paralytic*
2:7 ª Job 14:4; Is. 43:25; Dan. 9:9
2:9 ª Matt. 9:5 ¹ *paralytic*
2:10 ¹ *authority* ² *paralytic*
2:12 ª Matt. 15:31; [Phil. 2:11] ¹ *anything like this*
2:13 ª Matt. 9:9 ¹ *came*
2:14 ª Matt. 9:9–13; Luke 5:27–32 ᵇ Matt. 4:19; 8:22; 19:21; John 1:43; 12:26; 21:22 ᶜ Luke 18:28 ¹ *tax office*
2:15 ª Matt. 9:10 ¹ *was dining* ² *tax collectors*

16 And when the scribes and Pharisees saw him eat with [1]publicans and sinners, they said unto his disciples, How is it that he eateth and drinketh with [1]publicans and sinners?

17 When Jesus heard *it*, he saith unto them, [a]They that are whole have no need of the physician, but they that are sick: I came not to call the righteous, but sinners to repentance.

18 [a]And the disciples of John and of the Pharisees [1]used to fast: and they come and say unto him, Why do the disciples of John and of the Pharisees fast, but thy disciples fast not?

19 And Jesus said unto them, Can the [1]children of the bridechamber fast, while the bridegroom is with them? as long as they have the bridegroom with them, they cannot fast.

20 But the days will come, when the bridegroom shall be [a]taken away from them, and then shall they fast in those days.

21 No man also seweth a piece of [1]new cloth on an old garment: else the new piece that filled it up [2]taketh away from the old, and the [3]rent is made worse.

22 And no man putteth new wine into old [1]bottles: else the new wine doth burst the bottles, and the wine is spilled, and the bottles will be [2]marred: but new wine must be put into new bottles.

23 [a]And it came to pass, that he went through the [1]corn fields on the sabbath day; and his disciples began, as they went, [b]to pluck the [2]ears of corn.

24 And the Pharisees said unto him, Behold, why do they on the sabbath day that which is [a]not lawful?

25 And he said unto them, Have ye never read [a]what David did, when he had need, and was [1]an hungered, he, and they that were with him?

26 How he went into the house of God in the days of Abiathar the high priest, and did eat the shewbread, [a]which is not lawful to eat [1]but for the priests, and gave also to them which were with him?

27 And he said unto them, The sabbath was made for man, and not man for the [a]sabbath:

28 Therefore [a]the Son of man is Lord also of the sabbath.

## CHAPTER 3

A ND [a]he entered again into the synagogue; and there was a man there which had a withered hand.

2 And they [a]watched him, whether he would [b]heal him on the sabbath day; that they might accuse him.

3 And he saith unto the man which had the withered hand, [1]Stand forth.

4 And he saith unto them, Is it lawful to do good on the sabbath days, or to do evil? to save life, or to kill? But they [1]held their peace.

5 And when he had looked round about on them with anger, being grieved for the [a]hardness of their hearts, he saith unto the man, Stretch forth thine hand. And he stretched *it* out: and his hand was restored whole as the other.

6 [a]And the Pharisees went forth, and straightway [1]took counsel with [b]the Herodians against him, how they might destroy him.

7 But Jesus withdrew himself with his disciples to the sea: and a great multitude from Galilee followed him, [a]and from Judaea,

8 And from Jerusalem, and from Idumaea, and *from* beyond Jordan; and they about Tyre and Sidon, a great multitude, when they had heard what [a]great things he did, came unto him.

9 And he spake to his disciples, that a small ship should [1]wait on him because of the multitude, lest they should [2]throng him.

10 For he had healed [a]many; insomuch that they pressed [1]upon him for to [b]touch him, as many as had [2]plagues.

11 [a]And unclean spirits, when they saw him, fell down before him, and cried, saying, [b]Thou art the Son of God.

12 And [a]he [1]straitly charged them that they should not make him known.

13 [a]And he goeth up into a mountain, and calleth *unto him* whom he [1]would: and they came unto him.

14 And he [1]ordained twelve, that they should be with him, and that he might send them forth to preach,

15 And to have [1]power to heal sicknesses, and to cast out [2]devils:

16 And Simon [a]he [1]surnamed Peter;

17 And James the *son* of Zebedee, and John the brother of James; and he [1]surnamed them Boanerges, which is, The sons of thunder:

18 And Andrew, and Philip, and Bartholomew, and Matthew, and Thomas, and James the *son* of Alphaeus, and Thaddaeus, and Simon the Canaanite,

19 And Judas Iscariot, which also betrayed him: and they went into an house.

20 And the multitude cometh together again, [a]so that they could not so much as eat bread.

21 And when his [a]friends[1] heard *of it*, they went out to lay hold on him: [b]for they said, He is [2]beside himself.

22 And the scribes which came down from Jerusalem said, [a]He hath Beelzebub, and by the [b]prince[1] of the devils casteth he out devils.

23 [a]And he called them *unto him*, and said unto them in parables, How can Satan cast out Satan?

### Cross references (center column)

2:16 [1] *tax collectors*

2:17 [a] Matt. 9:12, 13; 18:11; Luke 5:31, 32; 19:10

2:18 [a] Matt. 9:14–17; Luke 5:33–38   [1] *were fasting*

2:19 [1] *friends of the bridegroom*

2:20 [a] Acts 1:9; 13:2, 3; 14:23

2:21 [1] *unshrunk* [2] *pulls away* [3] *tear*

2:22 [1] *wineskins* [2] *ruined*

2:23 [a] Matt. 12:1–8; Luke 6:1–5 [b] Deut. 23:25 [1] *grain* [2] *heads of grain*

2:24 [a] Ex. 20:10; 31:15

2:25 [a] 1 Sam. 21:1–6 [1] *hungry*

2:26 [a] Lev. 24:5–9 [1] *except*

2:27 [a] Deut. 5:14

2:28 [a] Matt. 12:8

3:1 [a] Luke 6:6–11

3:2 [a] Luke 14:1; 20:20 [b] Luke 13:14

3:3 [1] Lit. *Arise to the middle*

3:4 [1] *kept silent*

3:5 [a] Zech. 7:12

3:6 [a] Mark 12:13 [b] Matt. 22:16 [1] *plotted*

3:7 [a] Luke 6:17

3:8 [a] Mark 5:19

3:9 [1] *stand ready for* [2] *crush*

3:10 [a] Luke 7:21 [b] Matt. 9:21; 14:36 [1] *about* [2] *afflictions*

3:11 [a] Luke 4:41 [b] Matt. 8:29;

3:12 [a] Mark 1:25, 34 [1] *strictly warned*

3:13 [a] Luke 9:1 [1] *wanted*

3:14 [1] *appointed*

3:15 [1] *authority* [2] *demons*

3:16 [a] John 1:42 [1] *gave the name*

3:17 [1] *gave them the name*

3:20 [a] Mark 6:31

3:21 [a] Mark 6:3 [b] John 7:5; 10:20 [1] *own people* [2] *out of his mind*

3:22 [a] Matt. 9:34; 10:25 [b] [John 12:31; 14:30; 16:11] [1] *ruler of demons*

3:23 [a] Matt. 12:25–29

24 And if a kingdom be divided against itself, that kingdom cannot stand.

25 And if a house be divided against itself, that house cannot stand.

26 And if Satan rise up against himself, and be divided, he cannot stand, but hath an end.

27 [a]No man can enter into a strong man's house, and [1]spoil his goods, except he will first bind the strong man; and then he will [1]spoil his house.

28 [a]Verily I say unto you, All sins shall be forgiven unto the sons of men, and blasphemies wheresoever they shall blaspheme:

29 But he that shall blaspheme against the Holy Ghost hath never forgiveness, but is [1]in danger of eternal [2]damnation:

30 Because they [a]said, He hath an unclean spirit.

31 [a]There came then his [1]brethren and his mother, and, standing [2]without, sent unto him, calling him.

32 And the multitude sat about him, and they said unto him, Behold, thy mother and thy brethren [1]without seek for thee.

33 And he answered them, saying, Who is my mother, or my [1]brethren?

34 And he looked round about on them which [1]sat about him, and said, Behold my mother and my brethren!

35 For whosoever shall do the [a]will of God, the same is my brother, and my sister, and mother.

## CHAPTER 4

AND [a]he began again to teach by the sea side: and there was gathered unto him a great multitude, so that he entered into a ship, and sat in the sea; and the whole multitude was by the sea on the land.

2 And he taught them many things by parables, [a]and said unto them in his [1]doctrine,

3 Hearken; Behold, there went out a sower to sow:

4 And it came to pass, as he sowed, some fell by the way side, and the fowls of the air came and devoured it up.

5 And some fell on stony ground, where it had not much earth; and immediately it sprang up, because it had no depth of earth:

6 But when the sun was up, it was scorched; and because it had no root, it withered away.

7 And some fell among thorns, and the thorns grew up, and choked it, and it yielded no fruit.

8 And other fell on good ground, and did yield fruit that sprang up and increased; and brought forth, some thirty, and some sixty, and some an hundred.

### Center column references

3:27 [a] [Is. 49:24, 25] [1] plunder
3:28 [a] Luke 12:10
3:29 [1] subject to [2] condemnation
3:30 [a] Matt. 9:34
3:31 [a] Matt. 12:46–50 [1] brothers [2] outside
3:32 [1] are outside seeking
3:33 [1] brothers
3:34 [1] sat in a circle about
3:35 [a] Eph. 6:6
4:1 [a] Luke 8:4–10
4:2 [a] Mark 12:38 [1] teaching

4:10 [a] Luke 8:9
4:11 [a] [1 Cor. 2:10–16] [b] [Col. 4:5] [1] secret or hidden truths [2] outside
4:12 [a] Is. 6:9, 10; 43:8 [1] turn
4:13 [1] Understand
4:14 [a] Matt. 13:18–23
4:17 [1] tribulation [2] caused to stumble
4:19 [a] Luke 21:34 [b] 1 Tim. 6:9, 10, 17 [1] desires
4:20 [a] [Rom. 7:4]
4:21 [a] Matt. 5:15 [1] lamp [2] basket [3] lampstand
4:22 [a] Matt. 10:26, 27 [1] revealed [2] to light
4:23 [a] Matt. 11:15; 13:9, 43
4:24 [a] Matt. 7:2 [1] use
4:25 [a] Luke 8:18; 19:26
4:26 [a] [Matt. 13:24–30, 36–43] [1] upon

9 And he said unto them, He that hath ears to hear, let him hear.

10 [a]And when he was alone, they that were about him with the twelve asked of him the parable.

11 And he said unto them, Unto you it is given to [a]know the [1]mystery of the kingdom of God: but unto [b]them that are [2]without, all *these* things are done in parables:

12 [a]That seeing they may see, and not perceive; and hearing they may hear, and not understand; lest at any time they should [1]be converted, and *their* sins should be forgiven them.

13 And he said unto them, [1]Know ye not this parable? and how then will ye [1]know all parables?

14 [a]The sower soweth the word.

15 And these are they by the way side, where the word is sown; but when they have heard, Satan cometh immediately, and taketh away the word that was sown in their hearts.

16 And these are they likewise which are sown on stony ground; who, when they have heard the word, immediately receive it with gladness;

17 And have no root in themselves, and so endure but for a time: afterward, when [1]affliction or persecution ariseth for the word's sake, immediately they are [2]offended.

18 And these are they which are sown among thorns; such as hear the word,

19 And the [a]cares of this world, [b]and the deceitfulness of riches, and the [1]lusts of other things entering in, choke the word, and it becometh unfruitful.

20 And these are they which are sown on good ground; such as hear the word, and receive *it*, and bring forth [a]fruit, some thirtyfold, some sixty, and some an hundred.

21 [a]And he said unto them, Is a [1]candle brought to be put under a [2]bushel, or under a bed? and not to be set on a [3]candlestick?

22 [a]For there is nothing hid, which shall not be [1]manifested; neither was any thing kept secret, but that it should come [2]abroad.

23 [a]If any man have ears to hear, let him hear.

24 And he said unto them, Take heed what ye hear: [a]with what measure ye [1]mete, it shall be measured to you: and unto you that hear shall more be given.

25 [a]For he that hath, to him shall be given: and he that hath not, from him shall be taken even that which he hath.

26 And he said, [a]So is the kingdom of God, as if a man should cast seed [1]into the ground;

27 And should sleep, and rise night

and day, and the seed should spring and ᵃgrow up, he knoweth not how.

28 For the earth ᵃbringeth forth fruit of herself; first the blade, then the ear, after that the full ¹corn in the ear.

29 But when the fruit ¹is brought forth, immediately ᵃhe putteth in the sickle, because the harvest is come.

30 And he said, ᵃWhereunto shall we liken the kingdom of God? or with what ¹comparison shall we ²compare it?

31 *It is* like a grain of mustard seed, which, when it is sown in the earth, is ¹less than all the seeds that be in the earth:

32 But when it is sown, it groweth up, and becometh greater than all herbs, and shooteth out great branches; so that the ¹fowls of the air may lodge under ²the shadow of it.

33 ᵃAnd with many such parables spake he the word unto them, as they were able to hear *it*.

34 But without a parable spake he not unto them: and when they were alone, he ᵃexpounded¹ all things to his disciples.

35 ᵃAnd the same day, when the ¹even was come, he saith unto them, Let us ²pass over unto the other side.

36 And when they had sent away the multitude, they took him even as he was in the ship. And there were also with him other little ships.

37 And there arose a great storm of wind, and the waves beat into the ship, so that it was ¹now full.

38 And he was in the ¹hinder part of the ship, asleep on a pillow: and they awake him, and say unto him, ᵃMaster,² ᵇcarest thou not that we perish?

39 And he arose, and ᵃrebuked the wind, and said unto the sea, ᵇPeace,¹ be still. And the wind ceased, and there was a great calm.

40 And he said unto them, Why are ye so fearful? ᵃhow is it that ye have no faith?

41 And they feared exceedingly, and said one to another, ¹What manner of man is this, that even the wind and the sea obey him?

## CHAPTER 5

AND ᵃthey came over unto the other side of the sea, into the country of the Gadarenes.

2 And when he was come out of the ship, immediately there met him out of the tombs a man with an ᵃunclean spirit,

3 Who had *his* dwelling among the tombs; and no man could bind him, no, not with chains:

4 Because that he had been often bound with ¹fetters and chains, and the chains had been ²plucked asun-

---

4:27 ᵃ [2 Pet. 3:18]
4:28 ᵃ [John 12:24] ¹ *grain in the head*
4:29 ᵃ Rev. 14:15 ¹ *ripens*
4:30 ᵃ Matt. 13:31, 32 ¹ *parable* ² *picture*
4:31 ¹ *smaller*
4:32 ¹ *birds* ² *its shade*
4:33 ᵃ Matt. 13:34, 35
4:34 ᵃ Luke 24:27, 45 ¹ *explained*
4:35 ᵃ Luke 8:22, 25 ¹ *evening* ² *cross*
4:37 ¹ *already filling*
4:38 ᵃ [Matt. 23:8–10] ᵇ Ps. 44:23 ¹ *stern* ² *Teacher*
4:39 ᵃ Luke 4:39 ᵇ Ps. 65:7; 89:9; 93:4; 104:6, 7 ¹ Lit. *Silence*
4:40 ᵃ Matt. 14:31, 32
4:41 ¹ *Who can this be*
5:1 ᵃ Matt. 8:28–34
5:2 ᵃ Mark 1:23; 7:25
5:4 ¹ *shackles* ² *pulled apart*

¹ *shackles*
5:7 ᵃ Acts 19:13 ¹ *implore*
5:8 ᵃ Mark 1:25; 9:25
5:10 ¹ *begged him earnestly*
5:11 ᵃ Deut. 14:8 ¹ *near*
5:12 ¹ *demons* ² *begged*
5:13 ¹ *permission* ² *drowned*
5:14 ¹ *happened*
5:15 ᵃ Matt. 4:24; 8:16 ᵇ Luke 10:39 ᶜ [Is. 61:10] ¹ *demon*
5:16 ¹ *demon*
5:17 ᵃ Acts 16:39 ¹ *plead with* ² *region*
5:18 ᵃ Luke 8:38, 39 ¹ *demon begged*
5:19 ¹ *did not permit*
5:20 ᵃ Ps. 66:16 ᵇ Matt. 9:8, 33 ¹ *proclaim* ² Lit. *The Ten Cities*
5:21 ᵃ Luke 8:40 ¹ *crossed* ² *near*
5:22 ᵃ Matt. 9:18–26

---

der by him, and the ¹fetters broken in pieces: neither could any *man* tame him.

5 And always, night and day, he was in the mountains, and in the tombs, crying, and cutting himself with stones.

6 But when he saw Jesus afar off, he ran and worshipped him,

7 And cried with a loud voice, and said, What have I to do with thee, Jesus, *thou* Son of the most high God? I ᵃadjure¹ thee by God, that thou torment me not.

8 For he said unto him, ᵃCome out of the man, *thou* unclean spirit.

9 And he asked him, What *is* thy name? And he answered, saying, My name *is* Legion: for we are many.

10 And he ¹besought him much that he would not send them away out of the country.

11 Now there was there ¹nigh unto the mountains a great herd of ᵃswine feeding.

12 And all the ¹devils ²besought him, saying, Send us into the swine, that we may enter into them.

13 And forthwith Jesus gave them ¹leave. And the unclean spirits went out, and entered into the swine: and the herd ran violently down a steep place into the sea, (they were about two thousand;) and were ²choked in the sea.

14 And they that fed the swine fled, and told *it* in the city, and in the country. And they went out to see what it was that ¹was done.

15 And they come to Jesus, and see him that was ᵃpossessed with the ¹devil, and had the legion, ᵇsitting, and ᶜclothed, and in his right mind: and they were afraid.

16 And they that saw *it* told them how it befell to him that was possessed with the ¹devil, and *also* concerning the swine.

17 And ᵃthey began to ¹pray him to depart out of their ²coasts.

18 And when he was come into the ship, ᵃhe that had been possessed with the ¹devil prayed him that he might be with him.

19 Howbeit Jesus ¹suffered him not, but saith unto him, Go home to thy friends, and tell them how great things the Lord hath done for thee, and hath had compassion on thee.

20 And he departed, and began to ᵃpublish¹ in ²Decapolis how great things Jesus had done for him: and all *men* did ᵇmarvel.

21 ᵃAnd when Jesus was ¹passed over again by ship unto the other side, much people gathered unto him: and he was ²nigh unto the sea.

22 ᵃAnd, behold, there cometh one of the rulers of the synagogue, Jairus

by name; and when he saw him, he fell at his feet,

23 And ¹besought him greatly, saying, My little daughter lieth at the point of death: *I pray thee,* come and ªlay thy hands on her, that she may be healed; and she shall live.

24 And *Jesus* went with him; and ¹much people followed him, and thronged him.

25 And a certain woman, ªwhich had an ¹issue of blood twelve years,

26 And had suffered many things of many physicians, and had spent all that she had, and was ¹nothing bettered, but rather grew worse,

27 When she had heard of Jesus, came in the ¹press behind, and ªtouched his garment.

28 For she said, If I may touch but his clothes, I shall be whole.

29 And straightway the fountain of her blood was dried up; and she felt in *her* body that she was healed of that ¹plague.

30 And Jesus, immediately knowing in himself that ªvirtue¹ had gone out of him, turned him about in the ²press, and said, Who touched my clothes?

31 And his disciples said unto him, Thou seest the multitude thronging thee, and sayest thou, Who touched me?

32 And he looked round about to see her that had done this thing.

33 But the woman ªfearing and trembling, knowing what was done in her, came and fell down before him, and told him all the truth.

34 And he said unto her, Daughter, ªthy faith hath made thee whole; ᵇgo in peace, and be whole of thy ¹plague.

35 ªWhile he yet spake, there came from the ruler of the synagogue's *house certain* which said, Thy daughter is dead: why troublest thou the ¹Master any further?

36 As soon as Jesus heard the word that was spoken, he saith unto the ruler of the synagogue, Be not afraid, only ªbelieve.

37 And he ¹suffered no man to follow him, save Peter, and James, and John the brother of James.

38 And he cometh to the house of the ruler of the synagogue, and seeth the tumult, and them that ªwept and wailed greatly.

39 And when he was come in, he saith unto them, Why make ye this ¹ado, and weep? the ²damsel is not dead, but ªsleepeth.

40 And they laughed him to scorn. ªBut when he had put them all out, he taketh the father and the mother of the damsel, and them that were with him, and entereth in where the damsel was lying.

---

**Cross-references (center column):**

5:23 ª Acts 9:17; 28:8 ¹ *begged him earnestly*
5:24 ¹ *a great multitude*
5:25 ª Lev. 15:19, 25 ¹ *a flow*
5:26 ¹ *no better*
5:27 ª Matt. 14:35, 36 ¹ *crowd*
5:29 ¹ *affliction*
5:30 ª Luke 6:19; 8:46 ¹ *power* ² *crowd*
5:33 ª [Ps. 89:7]
5:34 ª Matt. 9:22 ᵇ Luke 7:50; 8:48 ¹ *affliction*
5:35 ª Luke 8:49 ¹ *Teacher*
5:36 ª [John 11:40]
5:37 ¹ *allowed*
5:38 ª Acts 9:39
5:39 ª John 11:4, 11 ¹ *commotion* ² Lit. *child*
5:40 ª Acts 9:40
5:41 ¹ *translated* ² *Little girl*
5:42 ª Mark 1:27; 7:37
5:43 ª [Matt. 8:4; 12:16–19; 17:9] ¹ *commanded* ² *strictly*
6:1 ª Matt. 13:54
6:2 ª Matt. 7:28 ᵇ John 6:42 ¹ *performed*
6:3 ª Matt. 12:46 ᵇ [Matt. 11:6] ¹ Or *Judas*
6:4 ª John 4:44 ¹ *relatives*
6:5 ª Gen. 19:22; 32:25 ¹ *except* ² *people*
6:6 ª Is. 59:16 ᵇ Matt. 9:35
6:7 ª Mark 3:13, 14 ᵇ [Eccl. 4:9, 10] ¹ *two by two* ² *authority*
6:8 ¹ *except* ² *bag* ³ *copper in their money belts*
6:9 ª [Eph. 6:15] ¹ *tunics*
6:10 ª Matt. 10:11
6:11 ª Matt. 10:14 ᵇ Acts 13:51; 18:6 ¹ *witness* ² or
6:13 ª [James 5:14] ¹ *demons*

---

41 And he took the damsel by the hand, and said unto her, Talitha cumi; which is, ¹being interpreted, ²Damsel, I say unto thee, arise.

42 And straightway the damsel arose, and walked; for she was *of the age* of twelve years. And they were ªastonished with a great astonishment.

43 And ªhe ¹charged them ²straitly that no man should know it; and commanded that something should be given her to eat.

## CHAPTER 6

AND ªhe went out from thence, and came into his own country; and his disciples follow him.

2 And when the sabbath day was come, he began to teach in the synagogue: and many hearing *him* were ªastonished, saying, ᵇFrom whence hath this *man* these things? and what wisdom *is* this which is given unto him, that even such mighty works are ¹wrought by his hands?

3 Is not this the carpenter, the son of Mary, ªthe brother of James, and Joses, and of ¹Juda, and Simon? and are not his sisters here with us? And they ᵇwere offended at him.

4 But Jesus said unto them, ªA prophet is not without honour, but in his own country, and among his own ¹kin, and in his own house.

5 ªAnd he could there do no mighty work, ¹save that he laid his hands upon a few sick ²folk, and healed *them.*

6 And ªhe marvelled because of their unbelief. ᵇAnd he went round about the villages, teaching.

7 ªAnd he called *unto him* the twelve, and began to send them forth ¹by ᵇtwo and two; and gave them ²power over unclean spirits;

8 And commanded them that they should take nothing for *their* journey, ¹save a staff only; no ²scrip, no bread, no ³money in *their* purse:

9 But ªbe shod with sandals; and not put on two ¹coats.

10 ªAnd he said unto them, In what place soever ye enter into an house, there abide till ye depart from that place.

11 ªAnd whosoever shall not receive you, nor hear you, when ye depart thence, ᵇshake off the dust under your feet for a ¹testimony against them. Verily I say unto you, It shall be more tolerable for Sodom ²and Gomorrha in the day of judgment, than for that city.

12 And they went out, and preached that men should repent.

13 And they cast out many ¹devils, ªand anointed with oil many that were sick, and healed *them.*

14 <sup>a</sup>And king Herod heard *of him;* (for his name <sup>1</sup>was spread abroad:) and he said, That John the Baptist was risen from the dead, and therefore <sup>b</sup>mighty works do <sup>2</sup>shew forth themselves in him.

15 <sup>a</sup>Others said, That it is Elias. And others said, That it is a <sup>b</sup>prophet, or as one of the prophets.

16 <sup>a</sup>But when Herod heard *thereof,* he said, It is John, whom I beheaded: he is risen from the dead.

17 For Herod himself had sent forth and laid hold upon John, and bound him in prison for Herodias' sake, his brother Philip's wife: for he had married her.

18 For John had said unto Herod, <sup>a</sup>It is not lawful for thee to have thy brother's wife.

19 Therefore Herodias <sup>1</sup>had a quarrel against him, and would have killed him; but she could not:

20 For Herod <sup>a</sup>feared John, knowing that he was a just man and an <sup>1</sup>holy, and <sup>2</sup>observed him; and when he heard him, he did many things, and heard him gladly.

21 <sup>a</sup>And when a convenient day was come, that Herod <sup>b</sup>on his birthday made a supper <sup>1</sup>to his lords, high <sup>2</sup>captains, and chief <sup>3</sup>*estates* of Galilee;

22 And when the daughter of the said Herodias came in, and danced, and pleased Herod and them that sat with him, the king said unto the damsel, Ask of me whatsoever <sup>1</sup>thou wilt, and I will give *it* thee.

23 And he sware unto her, <sup>a</sup>Whatsoever thou shalt ask of me, I will give *it* thee, unto the half of my kingdom.

24 And she went forth, and said unto her mother, What shall I ask? And she said, The head of John the Baptist.

25 And she came in straightway with haste unto the king, and asked, saying, I will that thou give me <sup>1</sup>by and by <sup>2</sup>in a charger the head of John the Baptist.

26 <sup>a</sup>And the king was exceeding sorry; *yet* for his oath's sake, and for their sakes which sat with him, he would not <sup>1</sup>reject her.

27 And immediately the king sent an executioner, and commanded his head to be brought: and he went and beheaded him in the prison,

28 And brought his head <sup>1</sup>in a charger, and gave it to the damsel: and the damsel gave it to her mother.

29 And when his disciples heard *of it,* they came and <sup>a</sup>took up his corpse, and laid it in a tomb.

30 <sup>a</sup>And the apostles gathered themselves together unto Jesus, and told him all things, both what they had done, and what they had taught.

31 <sup>a</sup>And he said unto them, Come ye yourselves <sup>1</sup>apart into a <sup>2</sup>desert place, and rest a while: for <sup>b</sup>there were many coming and going, and they had no leisure so much as to eat.

32 <sup>a</sup>And they departed into a <sup>1</sup>desert place by ship <sup>2</sup>privately.

33 And the <sup>1</sup>people saw them departing, and many <sup>2</sup>knew him, and ran afoot thither out of all cities, and <sup>2</sup>outwent them, and came together unto him.

34 <sup>a</sup>And Jesus, when he came out, saw <sup>1</sup>much people, and was moved with compassion toward them, because they were as <sup>b</sup>sheep not having a shepherd: and <sup>c</sup>he began to teach them many things.

35 <sup>a</sup>And when the day was now far spent, his disciples came unto him, and said, This is a desert place, and <sup>1</sup>now the time *is* far passed:

36 Send them away, that they may go into the country round about, and into the villages, and buy themselves bread: for they have nothing to eat.

37 He answered and said unto them, Give ye them to eat. And they <sup>1</sup>say unto him, <sup>a</sup>Shall we go and buy two hundred <sup>2</sup>pennyworth of bread, and give them to eat?

38 He saith unto them, How many loaves have ye? go and see. And when they <sup>1</sup>knew, they <sup>2</sup>say, <sup>a</sup>Five, and two fishes.

39 And he <sup>a</sup>commanded them to make all sit down by <sup>1</sup>companies upon the green grass.

40 And they sat down in ranks, by hundreds, and by fifties.

41 And when he had taken the five loaves and the two fishes, he <sup>a</sup>looked up to heaven, <sup>b</sup>and blessed, and brake the loaves, and gave *them* to his disciples to set before them; and the two fishes divided he among them all.

42 And they did all eat, and were filled.

43 And they took up twelve baskets full of the fragments, and of the fishes.

44 And they that did eat of the loaves were about five thousand men.

45 <sup>a</sup>And straightway he <sup>1</sup>constrained his disciples to get into the ship, and to go to the other side <sup>2</sup>before unto Bethsaida, while he sent away the <sup>3</sup>people.

46 And when he had sent them away, he <sup>a</sup>departed into a mountain to pray.

47 And when <sup>1</sup>even was come, the ship was in the <sup>2</sup>midst of the sea, and he alone on the land.

48 And he saw them toiling in rowing; for the wind was <sup>1</sup>contrary unto them: and about the fourth watch of the night he cometh unto them,

---

6:14 <sup>a</sup> Luke 9:7–9 <sup>b</sup> Luke 19:37 <sup>1</sup> had become well known <sup>2</sup> operate
6:15 <sup>a</sup> Matt. 16:14; Mark 8:28; Luke 9:19 <sup>b</sup> Matt. 21:11
6:16 <sup>a</sup> Matt. 14:2; Luke 3:19
6:18 <sup>a</sup> Lev. 18:16; 20:21
6:19 <sup>1</sup> held it against him
6:20 <sup>a</sup> Matt. 14:5; 21:26 <sup>1</sup> holy man <sup>2</sup> protected
6:21 <sup>a</sup> Matt. 14:6 <sup>b</sup> Gen. 40:20 <sup>1</sup> for his nobles <sup>2</sup> officers <sup>3</sup> Men
6:22 <sup>1</sup> you want
6:23 <sup>a</sup> Esth. 5:3, 6; 7:2
6:25 <sup>1</sup> at once <sup>2</sup> on a platter
6:26 <sup>a</sup> Matt. 14:9 <sup>1</sup> refuse
6:28 <sup>1</sup> on a platter
6:29 <sup>a</sup> 1 Kin. 13:29, 30; Matt. 27:58–61; Acts 8:2
6:30 <sup>a</sup> Luke 9:10
6:31 <sup>a</sup> Matt. 14:13 <sup>b</sup> Mark 3:20 <sup>1</sup> aside <sup>2</sup> deserted
6:32 <sup>a</sup> Matt. 14:13–21; Luke 9:10–17; John 6:5–13 <sup>1</sup> deserted <sup>2</sup> by themselves
6:33 <sup>a</sup> [Col. 1:6] <sup>1</sup> multitudes <sup>2</sup> arrived before them
6:34 <sup>a</sup> Matt. 9:36; 14:14; [Heb. 5:2] <sup>b</sup> Num. 27:17; 1 Kin. 22:17; 2 Chr. 18:16; Zech. 10:2 <sup>c</sup> [Is. 48:17; 61:1–3]; Luke 9:11 <sup>1</sup> a great multitude
6:35 <sup>a</sup> Matt. 14:15; Luke 9:12 <sup>1</sup> already the hour is late
6:37 <sup>a</sup> Num. 11:13, 22; 2 Kin. 4:43 <sup>1</sup> said <sup>2</sup> Gr. denarii
6:38 <sup>a</sup> Matt. 14:17; Luke 9:13; John 6:9 <sup>1</sup> found out <sup>2</sup> said
6:39 <sup>a</sup> Matt. 15:35; Mark 8:6 <sup>1</sup> in groups
6:41 <sup>a</sup> John 11:41, 42 <sup>b</sup> 1 Sam. 9:13; Matt. 15:36; 26:26; Mark 8:7; Luke 24:30
6:45 <sup>a</sup> Matt. 14:22–32; John 6:15–21 <sup>1</sup> compelled <sup>2</sup> before him <sup>3</sup> multitude
6:46 <sup>a</sup> Mark 1:35; Luke 5:16  6:47 <sup>1</sup> evening <sup>2</sup> middle
6:48 <sup>1</sup> against

walking upon the sea, and [a]would have passed by them.

49 But when they saw him walking upon the sea, they supposed it [1]had been a [a]spirit,[2] and cried out:

50 For they all saw him, and were troubled. And immediately he talked with them, and saith unto them, [a]Be[1] of good cheer: [2]it is I; be not [b]afraid.

51 And he went up unto them into the ship; and the wind [a]ceased: and they were [1]sore [b]amazed in themselves beyond measure, and [2]wondered.

52 For [a]they [1]considered not *the miracle* of the loaves: for their [b]heart was hardened.

53 [a]And when they had [1]passed over, they came into the land of Gennesaret, and [2]drew to the shore.

54 And when they were come out of the ship, straightway [1]they knew him,

55 And ran through that whole region round about, and began to carry about in beds those that were sick, where they heard he was.

56 And whithersoever he entered, into villages, or cities, or country, they laid the sick in the [1]streets, and [2]besought him that [a]they might touch if it were but the [b]border of his garment: and as many as touched him were made whole.

## CHAPTER 7

THEN [a]came together unto him the Pharisees, and certain of the scribes, which came from Jerusalem.

2 And when they saw some of his disciples eat bread with defiled, that is to say, with [a]unwashen,[1] hands, they found fault.

3 For the Pharisees, and all the Jews, except they wash *their* hands [1]oft, eat not, holding the [a]tradition of the elders.

4 And *when they come* from the market, except they wash, they eat not. And many other things there be, which they have received to hold, *as* the washing of cups, and [1]pots, brasen vessels, and of [2]tables.

5 [a]Then the Pharisees and scribes asked him, Why walk not thy disciples according to the tradition of the elders, but eat bread with unwashen hands?

6 He answered and said unto them, Well hath Esaias prophesied of you [a]hypocrites,[1] as it is written, [b]This people honoureth me with *their* lips, but their heart is far from me.

7 Howbeit in vain do they worship me, teaching [1]*for* doctrines the commandments of men.

8 For laying aside the commandment of God, ye hold the tradition of men, *as* the washing of [1]pots and cups: and many other such like things ye do.

9 And he said unto them, Full well ye [a]reject the commandment of God, that ye may keep your own tradition.

10 For Moses said, [a]Honour thy father and thy mother; and, [b]Whoso curseth father or mother, let him [1]die the death:

11 But ye say, If a man shall say to his father or mother, *It is* [a]Corban, that is to say, a [1]gift, by whatsoever thou mightest be profited by me; *he shall be free.*

12 And ye [1]suffer him no more to do [2]ought for his father or his mother;

13 Making the word of God of [1]none effect through your tradition, which ye have [2]delivered: and many such like things do ye.

14 [a]And when he had called all the [1]people *unto him,* he said unto them, Hearken unto me every one *of you,* and [b]understand:

15 There is nothing from [1]without a man, that entering into him can defile him: but the things which come out of him, those are they that [a]defile the man.

16 [a]If any man have ears to hear, let him hear.

17 [a]And when he was entered into the house [1]from the people, his disciples asked him concerning the parable.

18 And he saith unto them, [a]Are ye so without understanding also? Do ye not perceive, that whatsoever thing from without entereth into the man, *it* cannot defile him;

19 Because it entereth not into his heart, but into the belly, and [1]goeth out into the draught, [2]purging all meats?

20 And he said, [a]That which cometh out of the man, that defileth the man.

21 [a]For from within, out of the heart of men, [b]proceed evil thoughts, [c]adulteries, [d]fornications, murders,

22 Thefts, [a]covetousness, wickedness, [b]deceit, [c]lasciviousness,[1] an evil eye, [d]blasphemy, [e]pride, foolishness:

23 All these evil things come from within, and defile the man.

24 [a]And from thence he arose, and went into the [1]borders of Tyre and Sidon, and entered into an house, and would have no man know *it:* but he could not be [b]hid.

25 For a *certain* woman, whose young daughter had an unclean spirit, heard of him, and came and [a]fell at his feet:

26 The woman was a [1]Greek, a [2]Syrophenician by [3]nation; and she [4]besought him that he would cast forth the [5]devil out of her daughter.

27 But Jesus said unto her, Let the children first be filled: for it is not

### Cross-references (center column)

6:48 [a] Luke 24:28
6:49 [a] Matt. 14:26
[1] *was* [2] *ghost,* Gr. *phantasma*
6:50 [a] Matt. 9:2
[b] Is. 41:10 [1] *Take courage* [2] Lit. *I am*
6:51 [a] Ps. 107:29
[b] Mark 1:27;
2:12; 5:42; 7:37
[1] *greatly* [2] *marvelled*
6:52 [a] Mark 8:17, 18 [b] Mark 3:5; 16:14 [1] *understood*
6:53 [a] Matt. 14:34–36
[1] *crossed* [2] *anchored*
6:54 [1] The people
6:56 [a] Matt. 9:20
[b] Num. 15:38, 39
[1] *marketplaces* [2] *begged*
7:1 [a] Matt. 15:1–20
7:2 [a] Matt. 15:20
[1] *unwashed*
7:3 [a] Gal. 1:14 [1] *in a special way*
7:4 [1] *pitchers* [2] *couches*
7:5 [a] Matt. 15:2
7:6 [a] Matt. 23:13–29 [b] Is. 29:13
[1] *pretenders*
7:7 [1] *as*
7:8 [1] *pitchers*
7:9 [a] Prov. 1:25
7:10 [a] Ex. 20:12; Deut. 5:16 [b] Ex. 21:17 [1] *be put to death*
7:11 [a] Matt. 15:5; 23:18 [1] *Dedicated to the temple*
7:12 [1] *allow* [2] *anything*
7:13 [1] *no* [2] *handed down*
7:14 [a] Matt. 15:10 [b] Matt. 16:9, 11, 12 [1] *multitude*
7:15 [a] Is. 59:3 [1] *outside*
7:16 [a] Matt. 11:15
7:17 [a] Matt. 15:15 [1] *away from the crowd*
7:18 [a] [Heb. 5:11–14]
7:19 [1] *is eliminated* [2] *purifying all foods*
7:20 [a] Ps. 39:1
7:21 [a] Gen. 6:5; 8:21 [b] [Gal. 5:19–21] [c] 2 Pet. 2:14 [d] 1 Thess. 4:3
7:22 [a] Luke 12:15 [b] Rom. 1:28, 29 [c] 1 Pet. 4:3 [d] Rev. 2:9 [e] 1 John 2:16 [1] *licentiousness*
7:24 [a] Matt. 15:29 [b] Mark 2:1, 2 [1] *region* 7:25 [a] Mark 5:22; John 11:32; Rev. 1:17 7:26 [1] *Gentile* [2] A Syrian of Phoenicia [3] *birth* [4] *kept begging* [5] *demon*

[1]meet to take the children's bread,
and to cast *it* unto the [2]dogs.
28 And she answered and said unto
him, Yes, Lord: yet the [1]dogs under
the table eat of the children's crumbs.
29 And he said unto her, For this
saying go thy way; the [1]devil is gone
out of thy daughter.
30 And when she was come to her
house, she found the [1]devil gone out,
and her daughter laid upon the bed.
31 [a]And again, departing from the
[1]coasts of Tyre and Sidon, he came
unto the sea of Galilee, through the
midst of the [1]coasts of Decapolis.
32 And [a]they bring unto him one
that was deaf, and had an impediment in his speech; and they [1]be-
seech him to put his hand upon him.
33 And he took him aside from the
multitude, and put his fingers into
his ears, and [a]he spit, and touched his
tongue;
34 And [a]looking up to heaven, [b]he
sighed, and saith unto him, Ephpha-
tha, that is, Be opened.
35 [a]And straightway his ears were
opened, and the [1]string of his tongue
was loosed, and he spake plain.
36 And [a]he [1]charged them that they
should tell no man: but the more he
charged them, so much the more [2]a
great deal they [3]published *it;*
37 And were [a]beyond measure astonished, saying, He hath done all
things well: he [b]maketh both the deaf
to hear, and the [1]dumb to speak.

## CHAPTER 8

In those days [a]the multitude being
very great, and having nothing to
eat, Jesus called his disciples *unto
him,* and saith unto them,
2 I have [a]compassion on the multitude, because they have now been
with me three days, and have nothing to eat:
3 And if I send them away [1]fasting
to their own houses, they will faint
by the way: for [2]divers of them came
from far.
4 And his disciples answered him,
[1]From whence can a man satisfy
these *men* with bread here in the wilderness?
5 [a]And he asked them, How many
loaves have ye? And they said, Seven.
6 And he commanded the [1]peo-
ple to sit down on the ground: and
he took the seven loaves, and gave
thanks, and brake, and gave to his
disciples to set before *them;* and they
did set *them* before the [1]people.
7 And they had a few small fishes:
and [a]he blessed, and commanded to
set them also before *them.*
8 So they did eat, and were filled:
and they took up of the [1]broken *meat*
that was left seven baskets.

7:27 [1] Lit. *good* [2] *little dogs*
7:28 [1] *little dogs*
7:29 [1] *demon has*
7:30 [1] *demon*
7:31 [a] Matt. 15:29; Mark 15:37; Luke 23:46; 24:46; Acts 10:40; 1 Cor. 15:4 [1] *region*
7:32 [a] Matt. 9:32; Luke 11:14 [1] *begged*
7:33 [a] Mark 8:23; John 9:6
7:34 [a] Mark 6:41; John 11:41; 17:1 [b] John 11:33, 38
7:35 [a] Is. 35:5, 6 [1] *impediment*
7:36 [a] Mark 5:43 [1] *commanded* [2] *widely* [3] *proclaimed*
7:37 [a] Mark 6:51; 10:26 [b] Matt. 12:22 [1] *mute*
8:1 [a] Matt. 15:32–39; Mark 6:34–44; Luke 9:12
8:2 [a] Matt. 9:36; 14:14; Mark 1:41; 6:34
8:3 [1] *hungry* [2] *some*
8:4 [1] *How*
8:5 [a] Matt. 15:34; Mark 6:38; John 6:9
8:6 [1] *multitude*
8:7 [a] Matt. 14:19; Mark 6:41
8:8 [1] Fragments
8:10 [a] Matt. 15:39
8:11 [a] Matt. 12:38; 16:1; Luke 11:16; John 2:18; 6:30; 1 Cor. 1:22 [1] *dispute* [2] *testing*
8:12 [a] Mark 7:34 [b] Matt. 12:39
8:14 [a] Matt. 16:5 [1] Many mss. *they*
8:15 [a] Matt. 16:6; Luke 12:1 [1] *yeast*
8:17 [a] Mark 6:52; 16:14 [1] *is*
8:19 [a] Matt. 14:20; Mark 6:43; Luke 9:17; John 6:13
8:20 [a] Matt. 15:37
8:21 [a] [Mark 6:52]
8:22 [a] John 9:1 [b] Luke 18:15 [1] *begged*
8:23 [a] Mark 7:33 [1] *anything*
8:26 [a] Mark 5:43; 7:36
8:27 [a] Luke 9:18–20

9 And they that had eaten were
about four thousand: and he sent
them away.
10 And [a]straightway he entered
into a ship with his disciples, and
came into the parts of Dalmanutha.
11 [a]And the Pharisees came forth,
and began to [1]question with him,
seeking of him a sign from heaven,
[2]tempting him.
12 And he [a]sighed deeply in his
spirit, and saith, Why doth this generation seek after a sign? verily I say
unto you, There shall [b]no sign be
given unto this generation.
13 And he left them, and entering
into the ship again departed to the
other side.
14 [a]Now [1]*the disciples* had forgotten
to take bread, neither had they in the
ship with them more than one loaf.
15 [a]And he charged them, saying,
Take heed, beware of the leaven of
the Pharisees, and *of* the [1]leaven of
Herod.
16 And they reasoned among themselves, saying, *It is* because we have
no bread.
17 And when Jesus knew *it,* he
saith unto them, Why reason ye, because ye have no bread? [a]perceive ye
not yet, neither understand? [1]have ye
your heart yet hardened?
18 Having eyes, see ye not? and
having ears, hear ye not? and do ye
not remember?
19 [a]When I brake the five loaves
among five thousand, how many
baskets full of fragments took ye up?
They say unto him, Twelve.
20 And [a]when the seven among
four thousand, how many baskets
full of fragments took ye up? And
they said, Seven.
21 And he said unto them, How is it
that [a]ye do not understand?
22 And he cometh to Bethsaida;
and they bring a [a]blind man unto
him, and [1]besought him to [b]touch
him.
23 And he took the blind man by
the hand, and led him out of the
town; and when [a]he had spit on his
eyes, and put his hands upon him, he
asked him if he saw [1]ought.
24 And he looked up, and said, I see
men as trees, walking.
25 After that he put *his* hands again
upon his eyes, and made him look
up: and he was restored, and saw every man clearly.
26 And he sent him away to his
house, saying, Neither go into the
town, [a]nor tell *it* to any in the town.
27 [a]And Jesus went out, and his
disciples, into the towns of Caesarea
Philippi: and by the way he asked his
disciples, saying unto them, Whom
do men say that I am?

28 And they answered, ªJohn the Baptist: but some *say,* ᵇElias; and others, One of the prophets.

29 And he saith unto them, But whom say ye that I am? And Peter answereth and saith unto him, ªThou art the Christ.

30 ªAnd he charged them that they should tell no man of him.

31 And ªhe began to teach them, that the Son of man must suffer many things, and be ᵇrejected of the elders, and *of* the chief priests, and scribes, and be ᶜkilled, and after three days rise again.

32 And he spake that saying openly. And Peter ¹took him, and began to rebuke him.

33 But when he had turned about and looked on his disciples, he ªrebuked Peter, saying, Get thee behind me, Satan: for ¹thou savourest not the things that be of God, but the things that be of men.

34 And when he had called the people *unto him* with his disciples also, he said unto them, ªWhosoever will come after me, let him deny himself, and take up his cross, and follow me.

35 For ªwhosoever will save his life shall lose it; but whosoever shall lose his life for my sake and the gospel's, the same shall save it.

36 For what shall it profit a man, if he shall gain the whole world, and lose his own soul?

37 Or what shall a man give in exchange for his soul?

38 ªWhosoever therefore ᵇshall be ashamed of me and of my words in this adulterous and sinful generation; of him also shall the Son of man be ashamed, when he cometh in the glory of his Father with the holy angels.

## CHAPTER 9

AND he said unto them, ªVerily I say unto you, That there be some of them that stand here, which shall not taste of death, till they have seen ᵇthe kingdom of God ¹come with power.

2 ªAnd after six days Jesus taketh *with him* Peter, and James, and John, and leadeth them up into an high mountain apart by themselves: and he was transfigured before them.

3 And his ¹raiment became shining, exceeding ªwhite as snow; so as no ²fuller on earth can ³white them.

4 And there appeared unto them Elias with Moses: and they were talking with Jesus.

5 And Peter answered and said to Jesus, ¹Master, it is good for us to be here: and let us make three tabernacles; one for thee, and one for Moses, and one for Elias.

6 For he ¹wist not what to say; for they were ²sore afraid.

7 And there was a ªcloud that overshadowed them: and a voice came out of the cloud, saying, This is ᵇmy beloved Son: ᶜhear him.

8 And suddenly, when they had looked round about, they saw no man any more, ¹save Jesus only with themselves.

9 ªAnd as they came down from the mountain, he ¹charged them that they should tell no man what things they had seen, till the Son of man were risen from the dead.

10 And they kept that saying with themselves, questioning one with another ªwhat the rising from the dead ¹should mean.

11 And they asked him, saying, Why say the scribes ªthat Elias must first come?

12 And he answered and told them, Elias verily cometh first, and restoreth all things; and ªhow it is written of the Son of man, that he must suffer many things, and ᵇbe ¹set at nought.

13 But I say unto you, That ªElias is indeed come, and they have done unto him whatsoever they ¹listed, as it is written of him.

14 ªAnd when he came to *his* disciples, he saw a great multitude about them, and the scribes ¹questioning with them.

15 And straightway all the people, when they beheld him, were greatly amazed, and running to *him* ¹saluted him.

16 And he asked the scribes, What ¹question ye with them?

17 And ªone of the multitude answered and said, ¹Master, I have brought unto thee my son, which hath a ²dumb spirit;

18 And wheresoever he ¹taketh him, he ²teareth him: and he foameth, and gnasheth with his teeth, and ³pineth away: and I spake to thy disciples that they should cast him out; and they could not.

19 He answereth him, and saith, O ªfaithless generation, how long shall I be with you? how long shall I ¹suffer you? bring him unto me.

20 And they brought him unto him: and ªwhen he saw him, straightway the spirit ¹tare him; and he fell on the ground, and wallowed ²foaming.

21 And he asked his father, How long is it ago since this came unto him? And he said, ¹Of a child.

22 And ofttimes it hath cast him into the fire, and into the waters, to destroy him: but if thou canst do any thing, have compassion on us, and help us.

23 Jesus said unto him, ªIf thou canst believe, all things *are* possible to him that believeth.

### Center column references

8:28 ª Matt. 14:2
ᵇ Luke 9:7, 8

8:29 ª John 1:41; 4:42; 6:69; 11:27

8:30 ª Matt. 8:4; 16:20

8:31 ª Matt. 16:21; 20:19 ᵇ Mark 10:33 ᶜ Mark 9:31; 10:34

8:32 ¹ *took him aside*

8:33 ª [Rev. 3:19] ¹ *you are not mindful of*

8:34 ª Luke 14:27

8:35 ª John 12:25

8:38 ª Matt. 10:33 ᵇ 2 Tim. 1:8; 2:12

9:1 ª Luke 9:27 ᵇ [Matt. 24:30] ¹ *having come*

9:2 ª Matt. 17:1–8

9:3 ª Dan. 7:9 ¹ *clothing* ² *launderer* ³ *whiten*

9:5 ¹ Gr. *Rabbi*

9:6 ¹ *knew* ² *greatly*

9:7 ª Ex. 40:34 ᵇ Mark 1:11 ᶜ Acts 3:22

9:8 ¹ *except*

9:9 ª Matt. 17:9–13 ¹ *commanded*

9:10 ª John 2:19–22 ¹ *meant*

9:11 ª Mal. 4:5

9:12 ª Is. 53:3 ᵇ Phil. 2:7 ¹ *treated with contempt*

9:13 ª Luke 1:17 ¹ *wished*

9:14 ª Matt. 17:14–19 ¹ *disputing*

9:15 ¹ *greeted*

9:16 ¹ *discuss*

9:17 ª Luke 9:38 ¹ *Teacher* ² *mute*

9:18 ¹ *seizes* ² *throws him down* ³ *becomes rigid*

9:19 ª John 4:48 ¹ *bear with*

9:20 ª Mark 1:26 ¹ *convulsed* ² *foaming at the mouth*

9:21 ¹ *From childhood*

9:23 ª John 11:40

24 And straightway the father of the child cried out, and said with tears, Lord, I believe; [a]help thou mine unbelief.

25 When Jesus saw that the people came running together, he [a]rebuked the [1]foul spirit, saying unto him, *Thou* dumb and deaf spirit, I [2]charge thee, come out of him, and enter no more into him.

26 And *the spirit* cried, and [1]rent him [2]sore, and came out of him: and he was as one dead; insomuch that many said, He is dead.

27 But Jesus took him by the hand, and lifted him up; and he arose.

28 And when he was come into the house, his disciples asked him privately, Why could not we cast him out?

29 And he said unto them, This kind can come forth by nothing, but by [a]prayer and fasting.

30 And they departed thence, and passed through Galilee; and he [1]would not that any man should know *it*.

31 [a]For he taught his disciples, and said unto them, The Son of man [1]is delivered into the hands of men, and they shall [b]kill him; and after that he is killed, he shall [c]rise the third day.

32 But they understood [a]not that saying, and were afraid to ask him.

33 [a]And he came to Capernaum: and being in the house he asked them, What was it that ye [1]disputed among yourselves [2]by the way?

34 But they [1]held their peace: for by the way they had [a]disputed among themselves, who *should be* the [b]greatest.

35 And he sat down, and called the twelve, and saith unto them, [a]If any man desire to be first, *the same* shall be last of all, and servant of all.

36 And [a]he took a child, and set him in the midst of them: and when he had taken him in his arms, he said unto them,

37 Whosoever shall receive one of such children in my name, receiveth me: and [a]whosoever shall receive me, receiveth not me, but him that sent me.

38 [a]And John answered him, saying, [1]Master, we saw one casting out [2]devils in thy name, and he followeth not us: and we forbad him, because he followeth not us.

39 But Jesus said, Forbid him not: [a]for there is no man which shall do a miracle in my name, that can [1]lightly speak evil of me.

40 For [a]he that is not against us is on our [1]part.

41 [a]For whosoever shall give you a cup of water to drink in my name, because ye belong to Christ, verily I say unto you, he shall not lose his reward.

42 [a]And whosoever shall [1]offend one of *these* little ones that believe in me, it is better for him that a millstone were hanged about his neck, and he were cast into the sea.

43 [a]And if thy hand [1]offend thee, cut it off: it is better for thee to enter into life maimed, than having two hands to go into [2]hell, into the fire that never shall be quenched:

44 Where [a]their worm dieth not, and the fire is not quenched.

45 And if thy foot [1]offend thee, cut it off: it is better for thee to enter into [2]halt into life, than having two feet to be cast into [3]hell, into the fire that never shall be quenched:

46 Where [a]their worm dieth not, and the fire is not quenched.

47 And if thine eye [1]offend thee, pluck it out: it is better for thee to enter into the kingdom of God with one eye, than having two eyes to be cast into [2]hell fire:

48 Where their [a]worm dieth not, and the [b]fire is not quenched.

49 For every one shall be [a]salted[1] with fire, [b]and every sacrifice shall be [1]salted with salt.

50 [a]Salt *is* good: but if the salt have lost [1]his saltness, wherewith will ye season it? [b]Have salt in yourselves, and [c]have peace one with another.

## CHAPTER 10

AND [a]he arose from thence, and cometh into the [1]coasts of Judaea by the farther side of Jordan: and the people [2]resort unto him again; and, as he was [3]wont, he taught them again.

2 [a]And the Pharisees came to him, and asked him, Is it lawful for a man to [1]put away *his* wife? [2]tempting him.

3 And he answered and said unto them, What did Moses command you?

4 And they said, [a]Moses [1]suffered to write a bill of divorcement, and to [2]put *her* away.

5 And Jesus answered and said unto them, [1]For the hardness of your heart he wrote you this precept.

6 But from the beginning of the creation [a]God made them male and female.

7 [a]For this [1]cause shall a man leave his father and mother, and [2]cleave to his wife;

8 And they [1]twain shall be one flesh: so then they are no more twain, but one flesh.

9 What therefore God hath joined together, let not man [1]put asunder.

10 And in the house his disciples asked him again of the same *matter*.

9:24 [a] Luke 17:5
9:25 [a] Mark 1:25 [1] *unclean* [2] *command*
9:26 [1] *convulsed* [2] *severely*
9:28 [a] Matt. 17:19
9:29 [a] [James 5:16]
9:30 [1] *did not want any man to*
9:31 [a] Luke 9:44 [b] Matt. 16:21; 27:50 [c] 1 Cor. 15:4 [1] *is being delivered*
9:32 [a] Luke 2:50; 18:34
9:33 [a] Matt. 18:1–5 [1] *discussed* [2] *on the road*
9:34 [a] [Prov. 13:10] [b] Luke 22:24; 23:46; 24:46 [1] *kept silent*
9:35 [a] Luke 22:26, 27
9:36 [a] Mark 10:13–16
9:37 [a] Matt. 10:40
9:38 [a] Num. 11:27–29 [1] *Teacher* [2] *demons*
9:39 [a] 1 Cor. 12:3 [1] *soon afterward*
9:40 [a] [Matt. 12:30] [1] *side*
9:41 [a] Matt. 10:42
9:42 [a] Luke 17:1, 2 [1] *cause to stumble*
9:43 [a] Matt. 5:29, 30; 18:8, 9 [1] *makes you sin* [2] Gr. *gehenna*
9:44 [a] Is. 66:24
9:45 [1] *makes you sin* [2] *lame* [3] Gr. *gehenna*
9:46 [a] Is. 66:24
9:47 [1] *makes you sin* [2] Gr. *gehenna*
9:48 [a] Is. 66:24 [b] Jer. 7:20
9:49 [a] [Matt. 3:11] [b] Lev. 2:13 [1] *seasoned*
9:50 [a] Matt. 5:13 [b] Col. 4:6 [c] Rom. 12:18; 14:19 [1] *its flavour*
10:1 [a] Matt 19:1–9 [1] *region* [2] *gathered* [3] *accustomed*
10:2 [a] Matt. 19:3 [1] *divorce* [2] *testing*
10:4 [a] Deut. 24:1–4 [1] *permitted* [2] *dismiss her*
10:5 [1] *Because of*
10:6 [a] Gen. 1:27; 5:2
10:7 [a] Gen. 2:24 [1] *reason* [2] *be joined*   10:8 [1] *two*
10:9 [1] *separate*

11 And he saith unto them, <sup>a</sup>Whosoever shall <sup>1</sup>put away his wife, and marry another, committeth adultery against her.

12 And if a woman shall <sup>1</sup>put away her husband, and be married to another, she committeth adultery.

13 <sup>a</sup>And they brought young children to him, that he should touch them: and *his* disciples rebuked those that brought *them.*

14 But when Jesus saw *it*, he was much displeased, and said unto them, <sup>1</sup>Suffer the little children to come unto me, and forbid them not: for <sup>a</sup>of such is the kingdom of God.

15 Verily I say unto you, <sup>a</sup>Whosoever shall not receive the kingdom of God as a little child, he shall <sup>b</sup>not enter therein.

16 And he took them up in his arms, put *his* hands upon them, and blessed them.

17 <sup>a</sup>And when he was gone forth into the way, there came one running, and kneeled to him, and asked him, Good <sup>1</sup>Master, what shall I <sup>b</sup>do that I may inherit eternal life?

18 And Jesus said unto him, Why callest thou me good? *there is* none good but one, *that is,* <sup>a</sup>God.

19 Thou knowest the commandments, <sup>a</sup>Do not commit adultery, Do not <sup>1</sup>kill, Do not steal, Do not bear false witness, Defraud not, Honour thy father and mother.

20 And he answered and said unto him, <sup>1</sup>Master, all these have I <sup>a</sup>observed<sup>2</sup> from my youth.

21 Then Jesus beholding him loved him, and said unto him, One thing thou lackest: go thy way, <sup>a</sup>sell whatsoever thou hast, and give to the poor, and thou shalt have <sup>b</sup>treasure in heaven: and come, <sup>c</sup>take up the cross, and follow me.

22 And he was sad at that saying, and went away grieved: for he had great possessions.

23 <sup>a</sup>And Jesus looked round about, and saith unto his disciples, How <sup>1</sup>hardly shall they that have riches enter into the kingdom of God!

24 And the disciples were astonished at his words. But Jesus answereth again, and saith unto them, Children, how hard <sup>1</sup>is it for them <sup>a</sup>that trust in riches to enter into the kingdom of God!

25 It is easier for a camel to go through the eye of a needle, than for a <sup>a</sup>rich man to enter into the kingdom of God.

26 And they were astonished <sup>1</sup>out of measure, saying among themselves, Who then can be saved?

27 And Jesus looking upon them saith, With men *it is* impossible, but not <sup>a</sup>with God: for with God all things are possible.

---

10:11 <sup>a</sup> [Matt. 5:32; 19:9] <sup>1</sup> *divorce*
10:12 <sup>1</sup> *divorce*
10:13 <sup>a</sup> Luke 18:15–17
10:14 <sup>a</sup> [1 Pet. 2:2] <sup>1</sup> *Allow*
10:15 <sup>a</sup> Matt. 18:3, 4; 19:14 <sup>b</sup> Luke 13:28
10:17 <sup>a</sup> Matt. 19:16–30 <sup>b</sup> John 6:28 <sup>1</sup> *Teacher*
10:18 <sup>a</sup> 1 Sam. 2:2
10:19 <sup>a</sup> Ex. 20:12–16; Deut. 5:16–20 <sup>1</sup> *murder*
10:20 <sup>a</sup> Phil. 3:6 <sup>1</sup> *Teacher* <sup>2</sup> *kept*
10:21 <sup>a</sup> [Luke 12:33; 16:9] <sup>b</sup> Matt. 6:19, 20; 19:21 <sup>c</sup> [Mark 8:34]
10:23 <sup>a</sup> Matt. 19:23 <sup>1</sup> *hard it is for those*
10:24 <sup>a</sup> [1 Tim. 6:17] <sup>1</sup> *it is*
10:25 <sup>a</sup> [Matt. 13:22; 19:24]
10:26 <sup>1</sup> *beyond*
10:27 <sup>a</sup> Jer. 32:17

10:28 <sup>a</sup> Luke 18:28
10:29 <sup>1</sup> *brothers* <sup>2</sup> Lit. *fields*
10:30 <sup>a</sup> Luke 18:29, 30 <sup>b</sup> [1 Pet. 4:12, 13]
10:31 <sup>a</sup> Luke 13:30
10:32 <sup>a</sup> Matt. 20:17–19 <sup>b</sup> Mark 8:31; 9:31; Luke 9:22; 18:31
10:34 <sup>1</sup> *flog him with a Roman scourge*
10:35 <sup>a</sup> [James 4:3] <sup>1</sup> *Teacher*
10:38 <sup>a</sup> Matt. 26:39, 42; Mark 14:36; Luke 22:42; John 18:11 <sup>b</sup> Luke 12:50
10:39 <sup>a</sup> Matt. 10:17, 18, 21, 22; 24:9; John 16:33; Acts 12:2; Rev. 1:9 <sup>1</sup> *with*
10:40 <sup>a</sup> [Matt. 25:34; John 17:2, 6, 24; Rom. 8:30; Heb. 11:16]
10:41 <sup>a</sup> Matt. 20:24
10:42 <sup>a</sup> Luke 22:25 <sup>1</sup> *considered rulers* <sup>2</sup> *lord it over*
10:43 <sup>a</sup> Matt. 20:26, 28; Mark 9:35; Luke 9:48 <sup>1</sup> *desires to be* <sup>2</sup> *servant*

---

28 <sup>a</sup>Then Peter began to say unto him, Lo, we have left all, and have followed thee.

29 And Jesus answered and said, Verily I say unto you, There is no man that hath left house, or <sup>1</sup>brethren, or sisters, or father, or mother, or wife, or children, or <sup>2</sup>lands, for my sake, and the gospel's,

30 <sup>a</sup>But he shall receive an hundredfold now in this time, houses, and brethren, and sisters, and mothers, and children, and lands, with <sup>b</sup>persecutions; and in the world to come eternal life.

31 <sup>a</sup>But many *that are* first shall be last; and the last first.

32 <sup>a</sup>And they were in the way going up to Jerusalem; and Jesus went before them: and they were amazed; and as they followed, they were afraid. <sup>b</sup>And he took again the twelve, and began to tell them what things should happen unto him,

33 *Saying,* Behold, we go up to Jerusalem; and the Son of man shall be delivered unto the chief priests, and unto the scribes; and they shall condemn him to death, and shall deliver him to the Gentiles:

34 And they shall mock him, and shall <sup>1</sup>scourge him, and shall spit upon him, and shall kill him: and the third day he shall rise again.

35 <sup>a</sup>And James and John, the sons of Zebedee, come unto him, saying, <sup>1</sup>Master, we would that thou shouldest do for us whatsoever we shall desire.

36 And he said unto them, What would ye that I should do for you?

37 They said unto him, Grant unto us that we may sit, one on thy right hand, and the other on thy left hand, in thy glory.

38 But Jesus said unto them, Ye know not what ye ask: can ye drink of the <sup>a</sup>cup that I drink of? and be baptized with the <sup>b</sup>baptism that I am baptized with?

39 And they said unto him, We can. And Jesus said unto them, <sup>a</sup>Ye shall indeed drink of the cup that I drink of; and with the baptism that I am baptized <sup>1</sup>withal shall ye be baptized:

40 But to sit on my right hand and on my left hand is not mine to give; but *it shall be given to them* <sup>a</sup>for whom it is prepared.

41 <sup>a</sup>And when the ten heard *it,* they began to be much displeased with James and John.

42 But Jesus called them *to him,* and saith unto them, <sup>a</sup>Ye know that they which are <sup>1</sup>accounted to rule over the Gentiles <sup>2</sup>exercise lordship over them; and their great ones exercise authority upon them.

43 <sup>a</sup>But so shall it not be among you: but whosoever <sup>1</sup>will be great among you, shall be your <sup>2</sup>minister:

44 And whosoever of you ¹will be the chiefest, shall be servant of all.

45 For even ᵃthe Son of man came not to be ¹ministered unto, but to ²minister, and ᵇto give his life a ransom for many.

46 ᵃAnd they came to Jericho: and as he went out of Jericho with his disciples and a great ¹number of people, blind Bartimaeus, the son of Timaeus, sat by the ²highway side begging.

47 And when he heard that it was Jesus of Nazareth, he began to cry out, and say, Jesus, *thou* ᵃson of David, ᵇhave mercy on me.

48 And many ¹charged him that he should ²hold his peace: but he ³cried the more a great deal, *Thou* son of David, have mercy on me.

49 And Jesus stood still, and commanded him to be called. And they call the blind man, saying unto him, Be of good ¹comfort, rise; he calleth thee.

50 And he, ¹casting away his garment, rose, and came to Jesus.

51 And Jesus answered and said unto him, What wilt thou that I should do unto thee? The blind man said unto him, ¹Lord, that I might receive my sight.

52 And Jesus said unto him, Go thy way; ᵃthy faith hath made thee whole. And immediately he received his sight, and followed Jesus in the way.

## CHAPTER 11

AND ᵃwhen they came nigh to Jerusalem, unto Bethphage and Bethany, at the mount of Olives, he sendeth forth two of his disciples,

2 And saith unto them, Go your way into the village ¹over against you: and as soon as ye be entered into it, ye shall find a colt tied, whereon never man sat; loose him, and bring *him.*

3 And if any man say unto you, Why do ye this? say ye that the Lord hath need of him; and straightway he will send him hither.

4 And they went their way, and found the colt tied by the door ¹without ²in a place where two ways met; and they ³loose him.

5 And certain of them that stood there said unto them, What do ye, loosing the colt?

6 And they said unto them even as Jesus had commanded: and they let them go.

7 And they brought the colt to Jesus, and cast their garments on him; and he sat upon him.

8 ᵃAnd many spread their garments in the ¹way: and others cut down branches off the trees, and strawed *them* in the ¹way.

9 And they that went before, and they that followed, cried, saying, ᵃHosanna; Blessed *is* he that cometh in the name of the Lord:

10 Blessed *be* the kingdom of our father David, that cometh in the name of the Lord: ᵃHosanna in the highest.

11 ᵃAnd Jesus entered into Jerusalem, and into the temple: and when he had looked round about upon all things, ¹and now the eventide was come, he went out unto Bethany with the twelve.

12 ᵃAnd ¹on the morrow, when they were come from Bethany, he was hungry:

13 ᵃAnd seeing a fig tree afar off having leaves, he came, if ¹haply he might find any thing thereon: and when he came to it, he found nothing but leaves; for the time of figs was not *yet.*

14 And Jesus answered and said unto it, ¹No man eat fruit of thee hereafter for ever. And his disciples heard *it.*

15 ᵃAnd they come to Jerusalem: and Jesus went into the temple, and began to cast out them that sold and bought in the temple, and ¹overthrew the tables of the moneychangers, and the seats of them that sold ᵇdoves;

16 And would not ¹suffer that any man should carry *any* ²vessel through the temple.

17 And he taught, saying unto them, Is it not written, ᵃMy house shall be called ¹of all nations the house of prayer? but ᵇye have made it a den of thieves.

18 And ᵃthe scribes and chief priests heard *it,* and sought how they might destroy him: for they feared him, because ᵇall the people was astonished at his ¹doctrine.

19 And when ¹even was come, he went out of the city.

20 ᵃAnd in the morning, as they passed by, they saw the fig tree dried up from the roots.

21 And Peter calling to remembrance saith unto him, ¹Master, behold, the fig tree which thou cursedst is withered away.

22 And Jesus answering saith unto them, Have faith in God.

23 For ᵃverily I say unto you, That whosoever shall say unto this mountain, Be thou removed, and be thou cast into the sea; and shall not doubt in his heart, but shall believe that those things which he saith shall come to pass; he shall have whatsoever he saith.

24 Therefore I say unto you, ᵃWhat things soever ye desire, when ye pray, believe that ye receive *them,* and ye shall have *them.*

25 And when ye stand praying, [a]forgive, if ye have [1]ought against any: that your Father also which is in heaven may forgive you your trespasses.

26 But [a]if ye do not forgive, neither will your Father which is in heaven forgive your trespasses.

27 And they come again to Jerusalem: [a]and as he was walking in the temple, there come to him the chief priests, and the scribes, and the elders,

28 And say unto him, By what [a]authority doest thou these things? and who gave thee this authority to do these things?

29 And Jesus answered and said unto them, I will also ask of you one question, and answer me, and I will tell you by what authority I do these things.

30 The [a]baptism of John, was *it* from heaven, or of men? answer me.

31 And they reasoned [1]with themselves, saying, If we shall say, From heaven; he will say, Why then did ye not believe him?

32 But if we shall say, Of men; they feared the people: for [a]all *men* counted John, that he was a prophet indeed.

33 And they answered and said unto Jesus, We cannot tell. And Jesus answering saith unto them, Neither do I tell you by what authority I do these things.

## CHAPTER 12

A ND [a]he began to speak unto them by parables. A *certain* man planted a vineyard, and set [1]an hedge about *it,* and digged *a place for* the winefat, and built a tower, and [2]let it out to [3]husbandmen, and went into a far country.

2 And at [1]the season he sent to the [2]husbandmen a servant, that he might receive from the husbandmen [3]of the fruit of the vineyard.

3 And they [1]caught *him,* and beat him, and sent *him* away [2]empty.

4 And again he sent unto them another servant; and at him they cast stones, and wounded *him* in the head, and sent *him* away shamefully handled.

5 And again he sent another; and him they killed, and many others; [a]beating some, and killing some.

6 Having yet therefore one son, his wellbeloved, he sent him also last unto them, saying, They will [1]reverence my son.

7 But those [1]husbandmen said among themselves, This is the heir; come, let us kill him, and the inheritance shall be ours.

8 And they took him, and [a]killed *him,* and cast *him* out of the vineyard.

9 What shall therefore the [1]lord of the vineyard do? he will come and destroy the [2]husbandmen, and will give the vineyard unto others.

10 And have ye not read this scripture; [a]The stone which the builders rejected is become the [1]head of the corner:

11 This was the Lord's doing, and it is marvellous in our eyes?

12 [a]And they sought to lay hold on him, but feared the [1]people: for they knew that he had spoken the parable against them: and they left him, and went their way.

13 [a]And they send unto him certain of the Pharisees and of the Herodians, to catch him in *his* words.

14 And when they were come, they say unto him, [1]Master, we know that thou art true, and [2]carest for no man: for thou [3]regardest not the person of men, but teachest the [a]way of God in truth: Is it lawful to [4]give tribute to Caesar, or not?

15 Shall we [1]give, or shall we not give? But he, knowing their [a]hypocrisy, said unto them, Why [2]tempt ye me? bring me a [3]penny, that I may see *it.*

16 And they brought *it.* And he saith unto them, Whose *is* this image and [1]superscription? And they said unto him, Caesar's.

17 And Jesus answering said unto them, [1]Render to Caesar the things that are Caesar's, and to [a]God the things that are God's. And they marvelled at him.

18 [a]Then come unto him the Sadducees, [b]which say there is no resurrection; and they asked him, saying,

19 Master, [a]Moses wrote unto us, If a man's brother die, and leave *his* wife *behind him,* and leave no children, that his brother should take his wife, and raise up [1]seed unto his brother.

20 Now there were seven brethren: and the first took a wife, and dying left no [1]seed.

21 And the second took her, and died, neither left he any seed: and the third likewise.

22 And the seven had her, and left no [1]seed: last of all the woman died also.

23 In the resurrection therefore, when they shall rise, whose wife shall she be of them? for the seven had her to wife.

24 And Jesus answering said unto them, Do ye not therefore [1]err, because ye know not the scriptures, neither the power of God?

25 For when they shall rise from the dead, they neither marry, nor are given in marriage; but [a]are as the angels which are in heaven.

### Cross references (center column)

11:25 [a] Matt. 6:14; 18:23–35; Eph. 4:32; [Col. 3:13] [1] *anything*

11:26 [a] Matt. 6:15; 18:35

11:27 [a] Matt. 21:23–27; Luke 20:1–8

11:28 [a] John 5:27

11:30 [a] [Mark 1:4, 5, 8]; Luke 7:29, 30

11:31 [1] *among*

11:32 [a] Matt. 3:5; 14:5; Mark 6:20

12:1 [a] Matt. 21:33–46; Luke 20:9–19 [1] *a wall* or *fence* [2] *leased* [3] *tenant farmers*

12:2 [1] *vintage-time* [2] *tenant farmers* [3] *some of*

12:3 [1] *took* [2] *empty-handed*

12:5 [a] 2 Chr. 36:16

12:6 [1] *respect*

12:7 [1] *tenant farmers*

12:8 [a] [Acts 2:23]

12:9 [1] *owner* [2] *tenant farmers*

12:10 [a] Ps. 118:22, 23 [1] *chief cornerstone*

12:12 [a] Matt. 21:45, 46; Mark 11:18; John 7:25, 30, 44 [1] *multitude*

12:13 [a] Matt. 22:15–22; Luke 20:20–26

12:14 [a] Acts 18:26 [1] *Teacher* [2] *Court* no one's favour [3] Lit. *look not on the face of men* [4] *pay taxes*

12:15 [a] Matt. 23:28; Luke 12:1 [1] *pay* [2] *test* [3] Gr. *denarius*

12:16 [1] *inscription*

12:17 [a] [Eccl. 5:4, 5] [1] *Pay*

12:18 [a] Matt. 22:23–33; Luke 20:27–38 [b] Acts 23:8

12:19 [a] Deut. 25:5 [1] *offspring for*

12:20 [1] *offspring*

12:22 [1] *offspring*

12:24 [1] *go astray*

12:25 [a] [1 Cor. 15:42, 49, 52]

26 And [1]as touching the dead, that they [2]rise: have ye not read in the book of Moses, how in the bush God spake unto him, saying, [b]I *am* the God of Abraham, and the God of Isaac, and the God of Jacob?

27 He is not the God of the dead, but the God of the living: ye therefore [1]do greatly err.

28 [a]And one of the scribes came, and having heard them reasoning together, and perceiving that he had answered them well, asked him, Which is the [1]first commandment of all?

29 And Jesus answered him, The [1]first of all the commandments *is*, [a]Hear, O Israel; The Lord our God is one Lord:

30 And thou shalt [a]love the Lord thy God with all thy heart, and with all thy soul, and with all thy mind, and with all thy strength: this *is* the first commandment.

31 And the second *is* like, *namely* this, [a]Thou shalt love thy neighbour as thyself. There is none other commandment greater than [b]these.

32 And the scribe said unto him, [1]Well, Master, thou hast said the truth: for there is one God; [a]and there is none other but he:

33 And to love him with all the heart, and with all the understanding, and with all the soul, and with all the strength, and to love *his* neighbour as himself, [a]is more than all whole burnt offerings and sacrifices.

34 And when Jesus saw that he answered [1]discreetly, he said unto him, Thou art not far from the kingdom of God. [a]And no man after that [2]durst ask him *any question*.

35 [a]And Jesus answered and said, while he taught in the temple, How say the scribes that Christ is the son of David?

36 For David himself said [a]by the Holy Ghost, [b]The LORD said to my Lord, Sit thou on my right hand, till I make thine enemies thy footstool.

37 David therefore himself calleth him Lord; and whence is he *then* his [a]son? And the common people heard him gladly.

38 And [a]he said unto them in his [1]doctrine, [b]Beware of the scribes, which love to go in long [2]clothing, and [c]*love* salutations in the marketplaces,

39 And the [a]chief[1] seats in the synagogues, and the [2]uppermost rooms at feasts:

40 [a]Which devour widows' houses, and for a pretence make long prayers: these shall receive greater [1]damnation.

41 [a]And Jesus sat [1]over against the treasury, and beheld how the people cast money [b]into the treasury: and many that were rich cast in much.

42 And there came a certain poor widow, and she threw in two [1]mites, which make a [2]farthing.

43 And he called *unto him* his disciples, and saith unto them, Verily I say unto you, That [a]this poor widow hath cast more in, than all they which have cast into the treasury:

44 For all *they* did cast in of their [1]abundance; but she [2]of her want did cast in all that she had, [a]*even* [3]all her living.

## CHAPTER 13

AND [a]as he went out of the temple, one of his disciples saith unto him, [1]Master, see what manner of stones and what buildings *are here!*

2 And Jesus answering said unto him, Seest thou these great buildings? [a]there shall not be left one stone upon another, that shall not be thrown down.

3 And as he sat upon the mount of Olives [1]over against the temple, [a]Peter and [b]James and [c]John and [d]Andrew asked him privately,

4 [a]Tell us, when shall these things be? and what *shall be* the sign when all these things shall be fulfilled?

5 And Jesus answering them began to say, [a]Take heed lest any *man* deceive you:

6 For many shall come in my name, saying, I am *Christ;* and shall deceive many.

7 And when ye shall hear of wars and rumours of wars, be ye not troubled: for *such things* must needs be; but the end *shall* not *be* yet.

8 For nation shall rise against nation, and [a]kingdom against kingdom: and there shall be earthquakes in [1]divers places, and there shall be famines and troubles: [b]these *are* the beginnings of [2]sorrows.

9 But [a]take heed to yourselves: for they shall deliver you up to councils; and in the synagogues ye shall be beaten: and ye shall be brought before rulers and kings for my sake, for a testimony against them.

10 And [a]the gospel must first be published among all nations.

11 [a]But when they shall [1]lead *you,* and deliver you up, [2]take no thought beforehand what ye shall speak, neither do ye premeditate: but whatsoever shall be given you in that hour, that speak ye: for it is not ye that speak, [b]but the Holy Ghost.

12 Now [a]the brother shall betray the brother to death, and the father

---

12:26 [a] [John 5:25, 28, 29]; Acts 26:8; Rom. 4:17; [Rev. 20:12, 13] [b] Ex. 3:6, 15 [1] *concerning*

12:27 [1] *are greatly deceived*

12:28 [a] Matt. 22:34–40; Luke 10:25–28; 20:39 [1] *foremost*

12:29 [a] Deut. 6:4, 5; Is. 44:8; 45:22; 46:9; 1 Cor. 8:6 [1] *foremost*

12:30 [a] [Deut. 10:12; 30:6]; Luke 10:27

12:31 [a] Lev. 19:18; Matt. 22:39; Gal. 5:14; James 2:8 [b] [Rom. 13:9]

12:32 [a] Deut. 4:39; Is. 45:6, 14; 46:9; [John 1:14, 17; 14:6] [1] *Well said, Teacher*

12:33 [a] [1 Sam. 15:22; Hos. 6:6; Mic. 6:6–8; Matt. 9:13; 12:7]

12:34 [a] Matt. 22:46 [1] *wisely* [2] *dared*

12:35 [a] Matt. 22:41–46; Luke 20:41–44

12:36 [a] 2 Sam. 23:2 [b] Ps. 110:1

12:37 [a] [Acts 2:29–31]

12:38 [a] Mark 4:2 [b] Matt. 23:1–7; Luke 20:45–47 [c] Matt. 23:7; Luke 11:43 [1] *teaching* [2] *robes*

12:39 [a] Luke 14:7 [1] *best* [2] *best places*

12:40 [a] Matt. 23:14 [1] *condemnation*

12:41 [a] Luke 21:1–4 [b] 2 Kin. 12:9 [1] *opposite*

12:42 [1] Gr. *lepta,* small copper coins [2] Gr. *kodrantes,* a Roman coin

12:43 [a] [2 Cor. 8:12]

12:44 [a] Deut. 24:6 [1] *surplus* [2] *out of her poverty* [3] *whole livelihood*

13:1 [a] Luke 21:5–36 [1] *Teacher*

13:2 [a] Luke 19:44

13:3 [a] Matt. 16:18 [b] Mark 1:19 [c] Mark 1:19 [d] John 1:40 [1] *opposite*

13:4 [a] Matt. 24:3

13:5 [a] Eph. 5:6

13:8 [a] Hag. 2:22 [b] Matt. 24:8 [1] *various* [2] Lit. *birth pangs* 13:9 [a] Matt. 10:17, 18; 24:9 13:10 [a] Matt. 24:14 13:11 [a] Luke 12:11; 21:12–17 [b] Acts 2:4; 4:8, 31 [1] *arrest* [2] *do not worry* 13:12 [a] Mic. 7:6

the son; and children shall rise up against *their* parents, and shall cause them to be put to death.

13 <sup>a</sup>And ye shall be hated of all *men* for my name's sake: but <sup>b</sup>he that shall ¹endure unto the end, the same shall be saved.

14 <sup>a</sup>But when ye shall see the abomination of desolation, <sup>b</sup>spoken of by Daniel the prophet, standing where it ought not, (let him that readeth understand,) then <sup>c</sup>let them that be in Judaea flee to the mountains:

15 And let him that is on the housetop not go down into the house, neither enter *therein,* to take any thing out of his house:

16 And let him that is in the field not turn back again for to ¹take up his garment.

17 <sup>a</sup>But woe to them that are ¹with child, and to them ²that give suck in those days!

18 And pray ye that your flight be not in the winter.

19 <sup>a</sup>For *in* those days shall be ¹affliction, such as was not from the beginning of the creation which God created unto this time, neither shall be.

20 And except that the Lord had shortened those days, no flesh should be saved: but for the elect's sake, whom he hath chosen, he hath shortened the days.

21 <sup>a</sup>And then if any man shall say to you, Lo, here *is* Christ; or, lo, *he is* there; believe *him* not:

22 For false Christs and false prophets shall rise, and shall shew signs and <sup>a</sup>wonders, to ¹seduce, if *it were* possible, even the ²elect.

23 But <sup>a</sup>take ye heed: behold, I have foretold you all things.

24 <sup>a</sup>But in those days, after that tribulation, the sun shall be darkened, and the moon shall not give her light,

25 And the stars of heaven shall fall, and the powers that are in heaven shall be <sup>a</sup>shaken.

26 <sup>a</sup>And then shall they see the Son of man coming in the clouds with great power and glory.

27 And then shall he send his angels, and shall gather together his elect from the four winds, from the uttermost part of the earth to the uttermost part of heaven.

28 <sup>a</sup>Now learn a parable of the fig tree; When her branch is ¹yet tender, and putteth forth leaves, ye know that summer is near:

29 So ye in like manner, when ye shall see these things come to pass, know that ¹it is nigh, *even* at the doors.

30 Verily I say unto you, that this generation shall not pass, till all these things be done.

31 Heaven and earth shall pass away: but <sup>a</sup>my words shall ¹not pass away.

32 But of that day and *that* hour <sup>a</sup>knoweth no man, no, not the angels which are in heaven, neither the Son, but the <sup>b</sup>Father.

33 <sup>a</sup>Take ye heed, watch and pray: for ye know not when the time is.

34 <sup>a</sup>*For the Son of man is* as a man taking a far journey, who left his house, and gave <sup>b</sup>authority to his servants, and to every man his work, and commanded the ¹porter to watch.

35 <sup>a</sup>Watch ye therefore: for ye know not when the master of the house cometh, at ¹even, or at midnight, or at the cockcrowing, or in the morning:

36 Lest coming suddenly he find you sleeping.

37 And what I say unto you I say unto all, Watch.

## CHAPTER 14

**A**FTER <sup>a</sup>two days was *the feast of* the passover, and of <sup>b</sup>unleavened bread: and the chief priests and the scribes sought how they might take him by ¹craft, and put *him* to death.

2 But they said, Not on the feast *day,* lest there be an uproar of the people.

3 <sup>a</sup>And being in Bethany in the house of Simon the leper, as he sat ¹at meat, there came a woman having an alabaster ²box of ointment of spikenard very ³precious; and she brake the ⁴box, and poured *it* on his head.

4 And there were some that had indignation within themselves, and said, Why was this waste of the ¹ointment made?

5 For it might have been sold for more than three hundred <sup>a</sup>pence,¹ and have been given to the poor. And they <sup>b</sup>murmured² against him.

6 And Jesus said, Let her alone; why trouble ye her? she hath wrought a ¹good work on me.

7 <sup>a</sup>For ye have the poor with you always, and whensoever ye will ye may do them good: <sup>b</sup>but me ye have not always.

8 She hath done what she could: she is come ¹aforehand to anoint my body ²to the burying.

9 Verily I say unto you, Wheresoever this gospel shall be <sup>a</sup>preached throughout the whole world, *this* also that she hath done shall be spoken of for a memorial of her.

10 <sup>a</sup>And Judas Iscariot, one of the twelve, went unto the chief priests, to betray him unto them.

11 And when they heard *it,* they were glad, and promised to give him money. And he sought how he might conveniently betray him.

### Center reference column

13:13 <sup>a</sup> Luke 21:17
<sup>b</sup> Matt. 10:22;
24:13 ¹ *bear patiently*
13:14 <sup>a</sup> Matt. 24:15
<sup>b</sup> Dan. 9:27; 11:31;
12:11 <sup>c</sup> Luke 21:21
13:16 ¹ *get*
13:17 <sup>a</sup> Luke 21:23
¹ *pregnant* ² *with nursing babies*
13:19 <sup>a</sup> Dan. 9:26;
12:1 ¹ *tribulation*
13:21 <sup>a</sup> Luke 17:23;
21:8
13:22 <sup>a</sup> Rev. 13:13,
14 ¹ *deceive*
² *chosen ones*
13:23 <sup>a</sup> [2 Pet. 3:17]
13:24 <sup>a</sup> Zeph. 1:15
13:25 <sup>a</sup> Is. 13:10;
34:4
13:26 <sup>a</sup> [Dan. 7:13, 14]
13:28 <sup>a</sup> Matt. 24:32; Luke 21:29
¹ *already*
13:29 ¹ Or *he is near*
13:31 <sup>a</sup> Is. 40:8;
[2 Pet. 3:7, 10, 12]
¹ *by no means*
13:32 <sup>a</sup> Matt. 25:13
<sup>b</sup> Matt. 24:36;
Acts 1:7
13:33 <sup>a</sup> Matt. 24:42; 25:13;
Luke 12:40; 21:34;
[Rom. 13:11];
1 Thess. 5:6;
1 Pet. 4:7
13:34 <sup>a</sup> Matt. 24:45; 25:14
<sup>b</sup> [Matt. 16:19]
¹ *doorkeeper*
13:35 <sup>a</sup> Matt. 24:42, 44
¹ *evening*
14:1 <sup>a</sup> Matt. 26:2–5; Luke 22:1, 2; John 11:55;
13:1 <sup>b</sup> Ex. 12:1–27; Mark 14:12
¹ *trickery*
14:3 <sup>a</sup> Matt. 26:6;
Luke 7:37; John 12:1, 3 ¹ *at the table* ² *flask of oil*
³ *costly* ⁴ *flask*
14:4 ¹ *fragrant oil*
14:5 <sup>a</sup> Matt. 18:28; Mark 12:15 <sup>b</sup> Matt. 20:11; John 6:61
¹ Gr. *denarii* ² *criticized her*
14:6 ¹ *beautiful deed*
14:7 <sup>a</sup> Deut. 15:11;
Matt. 26:11; John 12:8 <sup>b</sup> [John 7:33; 8:21; 14:2, 12;
16:10, 17, 28]
14:8 ¹ *beforehand*
² *for burial*
14:9 <sup>a</sup> Matt. 28:19, 20; Mark 16:15;
Luke 24:47
14:10 <sup>a</sup> Ps. 41:9; 55:12–14; Matt. 10:2–4

12 [a]And the first day of unleavened bread, when they killed the passover, his disciples said unto him, Where [1]wilt thou that we go and prepare that thou mayest eat the passover?

13 And he sendeth forth two of his disciples, and saith unto them, Go ye into the city, and there shall meet you a man [1]bearing a pitcher of water: follow him.

14 And wheresoever he shall go in, say ye to the [1]goodman of the house, The [2]Master saith, Where is the guestchamber, where I shall eat the passover with my disciples?

15 And he will shew you a large upper room furnished *and* prepared: there make ready for us.

16 And his disciples went forth, and came into the city, and found as he had said unto them: and they made ready the passover.

17 [a]And in the evening he cometh with the twelve.

18 And as they sat and did eat, Jesus said, Verily I say unto you, [a]One of you which eateth with me shall betray me.

19 And they began to be sorrowful, and to say unto him one by one, *Is* it I? and another *said, Is* it I?

20 And he answered and said unto them, *It is* one of the twelve, that dippeth with me in the dish.

21 [a]The Son of man indeed goeth, as it is written of him: but woe to that man by whom the Son of man is betrayed! good were it for that man if he had never been born.

22 [a]And as they did eat, Jesus took bread, and blessed, and brake *it,* and gave to them, and said, Take, eat: this is my [b]body.

23 And he took the cup, and when he had given thanks, he gave *it* to them: and they all drank of it.

24 And he said unto them, This is my blood of the new testament, which is shed for many.

25 Verily I say unto you, I will drink no more of the fruit of the vine, until that day that I drink it new in the kingdom of God.

26 [a]And when they had sung [1]an hymn, they went out into the mount of Olives.

27 [a]And Jesus saith unto them, All ye shall be [1]offended because of me this night: for it is written, [b]I will [2]smite the shepherd, and the sheep shall be scattered.

28 But [a]after that I am risen, I will go before you into Galilee.

29 [a]But Peter said unto him, Although all shall be [1]offended, yet *will* not I.

30 And Jesus said unto him, Verily I say unto thee, That this day, *even* in this night, before the [1]cock crow twice, thou shalt deny me [2]thrice.

31 But he spake the more vehemently, If I should die with thee, I will [1]not deny thee in any wise. Likewise also said they all.

32 [a]And they came to a place which was named Gethsemane: and he saith to his disciples, Sit ye here, while I shall pray.

33 And he [a]taketh with him Peter and James and John, and began to be [1]sore amazed, and to be [2]very heavy;

34 And saith unto them, [a]My soul is exceeding sorrowful unto death: tarry ye here, and watch.

35 And he went forward a little, and fell on the ground, and prayed that, if it were possible, the hour might pass from him.

36 And he said, [a]Abba, Father, [b]all things *are* possible unto thee; take away this cup from me: [c]nevertheless not what I will, but what thou [1]wilt.

37 And he cometh, and findeth them sleeping, and saith unto Peter, Simon, sleepest thou? couldest not thou watch one hour?

38 [a]Watch ye and pray, lest ye enter into temptation. [b]The spirit truly *is* ready, but the flesh *is* weak.

39 And again he went away, and prayed, and spake the same words.

40 And when he returned, he found them asleep again, (for their eyes were heavy,) neither [1]wist they what to answer him.

41 And he cometh the third time, and saith unto them, [1]Sleep on now, and take *your* rest: it is enough, [a]the hour is come; behold, the Son of man [2]is betrayed into the hands of sinners.

42 [a]Rise up, let us go; lo, he that betrayeth me [1]is at hand.

43 [a]And immediately, while he yet spake, cometh Judas, one of the twelve, and with him a great multitude with swords and [1]staves, from the chief priests and the scribes and the elders.

44 And he that betrayed him had given them a [1]token, saying, Whomsoever I shall [a]kiss, that same is he; take him, and lead *him* away safely.

45 And as soon as he was come, he goeth straightway to him, and saith, [1]Master, master; and kissed him.

46 And they laid their hands on him, and took him.

47 And one of them that stood by drew a sword, and [1]smote a servant of the high priest, and cut off his ear.

48 [a]And Jesus answered and said unto them, Are ye come out, as against a [1]thief, with swords and *with* [2]staves to take me?

49 I was daily with you in the temple [a]teaching, and ye took me not: but [b]the scriptures must be fulfilled.

---

**Cross-references (center column):**

14:12 [a] Ex. 12:8; Matt. 26:17–19; Luke 22:7–13 [1] *do you want*

14:13 [1] *carrying*

14:14 [1] *master* [2] *Teacher*

14:17 [a] Matt. 26:20–24; Luke 22:14, 21–23

14:18 [a] Ps. 41:9; Matt. 26:46; Mark 14:42; John 6:70, 71; 13:18

14:21 [a] Matt. 26:24; Luke 22:22; Acts 1:16–20

14:22 [a] Matt. 26:26–29; Luke 22:17–20; 1 Cor. 11:23–25 [b] [1 Pet. 2:24]

14:26 [a] Matt. 26:30 [1] *Or hymns*

14:27 [a] Matt. 26:31–35 [b] Zech. 13:7 [1] *caused to stumble* [2] *strike*

14:28 [a] Mark 16:7

14:29 [a] John 13:37, 38 [1] *caused to stumble*

14:30 [1] *rooster* [2] *three times*

14:31 [1] *never deny thee*

14:32 [a] Luke 22:40–46

14:33 [a] Mark 5:37; 9:2; 13:3 [1] *greatly troubled* [2] *deeply distressed*

14:34 [a] John 12:27

14:36 [a] Gal. 4:6 [b] [Heb. 5:7] [c] John 5:30; 6:38 [1] *will*

14:38 [a] Luke 21:36 [b] [Rom. 7:18, 21–24]

14:40 [1] *knew*

14:41 [a] John 13:1; 17:1 [1] *Are you still sleeping and resting?* [2] *is being*

14:42 [a] John 13:21; 18:1, 2 [1] *has drawn near*

14:43 [a] Luke 22:47–53 [1] *clubs*

14:44 [a] [Prov. 27:6] [1] *signal*

14:45 [1] *Gr. Rabbi, rabbi*

14:47 [1] *struck the servant*

14:48 [a] Matt. 26:55 [1] *robber* [2] *clubs*

14:49 [a] Matt. 21:23 [b] Is. 53:7

---

50 ªAnd they all forsook him, and fled.

51 And there followed him a certain young man, having a linen cloth cast about *his* naked *body;* and the young men laid hold on him:

52 And he left the linen cloth, and fled from them naked.

53 ªAnd they led Jesus away to the high priest: and with him were ᵇassembled all the ᶜchief priests and the elders and the scribes.

54 And ªPeter followed him ¹afar off, even into the palace of the high priest: and he sat with the servants, and warmed himself at the fire.

55 ªAnd the chief priests and all the council sought for ¹witness against Jesus to put him to death; and found none.

56 For many bare ªfalse witness against him, but their ¹witness agreed not together.

57 And there arose certain, and bare false witness against him, saying,

58 We heard him say, ªI will destroy this temple that is made with hands, and within three days I will build another made without hands.

59 But ¹neither so did their ²witness agree together.

60 ªAnd the high priest stood up in the midst, and asked Jesus, saying, Answerest thou nothing? what *is it* which these ¹witness against thee?

61 But ªhe ¹held his peace, and answered nothing. ᵇAgain the high priest asked him, and said unto him, Art thou the Christ, the Son of the Blessed?

62 And Jesus said, I am: ªand ye shall see the Son of man sitting on the right hand of power, and coming in the clouds of heaven.

63 Then the high priest ¹rent his clothes, and saith, What need we any further witnesses?

64 Ye have heard the ªblasphemy: what think ye? And they all condemned him to be ¹guilty of ᵇdeath.

65 And some began to ªspit on him, and ¹to cover his face, and to ²buffet him, and to say unto him, Prophesy: and the ³servants did strike him with the palms of their hands.

66 ªAnd as Peter was ¹beneath in the ²palace, there cometh one of the maids of the high priest:

67 And when she saw Peter warming himself, she looked upon him, and said, And thou also wast with ªJesus of Nazareth.

68 But he denied, saying, I know not, neither understand I what thou sayest. And he went out into the porch; and the ¹cock crew.

69 ªAnd ¹a maid saw him again, and began to say to them that stood by, This is *one* of them.

---

14:50 ª Ps. 88:8
14:53 ª Matt. 26:57–68 ᵇ Mark 15:1 ᶜ John 7:32; 18:3; 19:6
14:54 ª John 18:15 ¹ *at a distance*
14:55 ª Matt. 26:59 ¹ *testimony*
14:56 ª Ex. 20:16 ¹ *testimonies*
14:58 ª John 2:19
14:59 ¹ *not even then* ² *testimonies*
14:60 ª Matt. 26:62 ¹ *testify*
14:61 ª Is. 53:7 ᵇ Luke 22:67–71 ¹ *kept silent*
14:62 ª Luke 22:69
14:63 ¹ *tore*
14:64 ª John 10:33, 36 ᵇ John 19:7 ¹ *deserving*
14:65 ª Is. 50:6; 52:14 ¹ *blindfolded* ² *beat* ³ *officers*
14:66 ª John 18:16–18, 25–27 ¹ *below* ² *courtyard*
14:67 ª John 1:45
14:68 ¹ *rooster crowed*
14:69 ª Matt. 26:71 ¹ *the servant girl*
14:70 ª Luke 22:59 ᵇ Acts 2:7 ¹ *accent shows*
14:71 ¹ *call down curses* ² *swear by oaths*
14:72 ª Matt. 26:75 ¹ *rooster crowed* ² *three times*
15:1 ª Ps. 2:2 ᵇ Acts 3:13 ¹ *Sanhedrin*
15:2 ª Matt. 27:11–14 ¹ *It is as you say*
15:3 ª John 19:9
15:4 ª Matt. 27:13 ¹ *testify*
15:5 ª Is. 53:7
15:6 ª Matt. 27:15–26 ¹ *used to release* ² *requested*
15:7 ¹ *who was chained*
15:8 ¹ *ask* ² *always*
15:10 ¹ *because of*
15:11 ª Acts 3:14 ¹ *stirred up*
15:12 ª Mic. 5:2
15:14 ª 1 Pet. 2:21–23
15:15 ª Matt. 27:26 ᵇ [Is. 53:8]

---

70 And he denied it again. ªAnd a little after, they that stood by said again to Peter, Surely thou art *one* of them: ᵇfor thou art a Galilaean, and thy ¹speech agreeth *thereto.*

71 But he began to ¹curse and to ²swear, *saying,* I know not this man of whom ye speak.

72 ªAnd the second time the ¹cock crew. And Peter called to mind the word that Jesus said unto him, Before the cock crow twice, thou shalt deny me ¹thrice. And when he thought thereon, he wept.

## CHAPTER 15

A ND ªstraightway in the morning the chief priests held a consultation with the elders and scribes and the whole ¹council, and bound Jesus, and carried *him* away, and ᵇdelivered *him* to Pilate.

2 ªAnd Pilate asked him, Art thou the King of the Jews? And he answering said unto him, ¹Thou sayest *it.*

3 And the chief priests accused him of many things: but he ªanswered nothing.

4 ªAnd Pilate asked him again, saying, Answerest thou nothing? behold how many things they ¹witness against thee.

5 ᵃBut Jesus yet answered nothing; so that Pilate marvelled.

6 Now ªat *that* feast he ¹released unto them one prisoner, whomsoever they ²desired.

7 And there was *one* named Barabbas, ¹*which lay* bound with them that had made insurrection with him, who had committed murder in the insurrection.

8 And the multitude crying aloud began to ¹desire *him to do* as he had ²ever done unto them.

9 But Pilate answered them, saying, Will ye that I release unto you the King of the Jews?

10 For he knew that the chief priests had delivered him ¹for envy.

11 But ªthe chief priests ¹moved the people, that he should rather release Barabbas unto them.

12 And Pilate answered and said again unto them, What will ye then that I shall do *unto him* whom ye call the ªKing of the Jews?

13 And they cried out again, Crucify him.

14 Then Pilate said unto them, Why, ªwhat evil hath he done? And they cried out the more exceedingly, Crucify him.

15 ªAnd *so* Pilate, ¹willing to content the people, released Barabbas unto them, and delivered Jesus, when he had ²scourged *him,* to be ᵇcrucified.

¹ *wanting to gratify the crowd* ² *flogged with a Roman scourge*

16 ᵃAnd the soldiers led him away into the hall, called Praetorium; and they call together the whole ¹band.

17 And they clothed him with purple, and ¹platted a crown of thorns, and put it about his *head,*

18 And began to salute him, Hail, King of the Jews!

19 And they ᵃsmote¹ him on the head with a reed, and did spit upon him, and bowing *their* knees worshipped him.

20 And when they had ᵃmocked him, they took off the purple from him, and put his own clothes on him, and led him out to crucify him.

21 ᵃAnd they compel one Simon a Cyrenian, who passed by, coming out of the country, the father of Alexander and Rufus, to bear his cross.

22 ᵃAnd they bring him unto the place Golgotha, which is, being interpreted, The place of a skull.

23 ᵃAnd they gave him to drink wine mingled with myrrh: but he received *it* not.

24 And when they had crucified him, ᵃthey ¹parted his garments, casting lots ²upon them, what every man should take.

25 And ᵃit was the third hour, and they crucified him.

26 And ᵃthe superscription of his accusation was written over, THE KING OF THE JEWS.

27 And ᵃwith him they crucify two ¹thieves; the one on his right hand, and the other on his left.

28 And the scripture was fulfilled, which saith, ᵃAnd he was numbered with the transgressors.

29 And ᵃthey that passed by railed on him, ᵇwagging their heads, and saying, Ah, ᶜthou that destroyest the temple, and buildest *it* in three days,

30 Save thyself, and come down from the cross.

31 Likewise also the chief priests ᵃmocking said among themselves with the scribes, He saved ᵇothers; himself he cannot save.

32 Let Christ the King of Israel descend now from the cross, that we may see and believe. And ᵃthey that were crucified with him reviled him.

33 And ᵃwhen the sixth hour was come, there was darkness over the whole land until the ninth hour.

34 And at the ninth hour Jesus cried with a loud voice, saying, Eloi, Eloi, lama sabachthani? which is, ¹being interpreted, ᵃMy God, my God, why hast thou forsaken me?

35 And some of them that stood by, when they heard *it,* said, Behold, he calleth Elias.

36 And ᵃone ran and filled a spunge full of ¹vinegar, and put *it* on a reed, and ᵇgave him to drink, saying, Let

alone; let us see whether Elias will come to take him down.

37 ᵃAnd Jesus cried with a loud voice, and ¹gave up the ghost.

38 And ᵃthe veil of the temple was ¹rent in twain from the top to the bottom.

39 And ᵃwhen the centurion, which stood ¹over against him, saw that he so cried out, and ²gave up the ghost, he said, Truly this man was the Son of God.

40 ᵃThere were also women looking on ᵇafar off: among whom was Mary Magdalene, and Mary the mother of James the less and of Joses, and Salome;

41 (Who also, when he was in Galilee, ᵃfollowed him, and ministered unto him;) and many other women which came up with him unto Jerusalem.

42 ᵃAnd now when the ¹even was come, because it was the preparation, that is, the day before the sabbath,

43 Joseph of Arimathaea, an ¹honourable counsellor, which also ᵃwaited for the kingdom of God, came, and went in boldly unto Pilate, and ²craved the body of Jesus.

44 And Pilate marvelled if he were already dead: and calling *unto him* the centurion, he asked him whether he had been ¹any while dead.

45 And when he ¹knew *it* of the centurion, he gave the body to Joseph.

46 ᵃAnd he bought fine linen, and took him down, and wrapped him in the linen, and laid him in a sepulchre which was hewn out of a rock, and rolled a stone unto the door of the sepulchre.

47 And Mary Magdalene and Mary *the mother* of Joses beheld where he was laid.

## CHAPTER 16

AND ᵃwhen the sabbath was past, Mary Magdalene, and Mary the *mother* of James, and Salome, ᵇhad bought sweet spices, that they might come and anoint him.

2 And very early in the morning the first *day* of the week, they came unto the sepulchre at the rising of the sun.

3 And they said among themselves, Who shall roll us away the stone from the door of the sepulchre?

4 And when they looked, they saw that the stone was rolled away: for it was very ¹great.

5 ᵃAnd entering into the sepulchre, they saw a young man sitting on the right side, clothed in a long white ¹garment; and they were ²affrighted.

6 ᵃAnd he saith unto them, Be not ¹affrighted: Ye seek Jesus of Nazareth,

### Center reference column

15:16 ᵃ Matt. 27:27–31 ¹ Lit. *cohort*
15:17 ¹ *twisted*
15:19 ᵃ [Is. 50:6; 52:14; 53:5] ¹ *struck*
15:20 ᵃ Luke 22:63; 23:11
15:21 ᵃ Matt. 27:32
15:22 ᵃ John 19:17–24
15:23 ᵃ Matt. 27:34
15:24 ᵃ Ps. 22:18 ¹ *divided* ² *for*
15:25 ᵃ John 19:14
15:26 ᵃ Matt. 27:37
15:27 ᵃ Luke 22:37 ¹ *robbers*
15:28 ᵃ Is. 53:12
15:29 ᵃ Ps. 22:6, 7; 69:7 ᵇ Ps. 109:25 ᶜ John 2:19–21
15:31 ᵃ Luke 18:32 ᵇ John 11:43, 44
15:32 ᵃ Matt. 27:44
15:33 ᵃ Luke 23:44–49
15:34 ᵃ Ps. 22:1 ¹ *translated*
15:36 ᵇ John 19:29 ᵇ Ps. 69:21 ¹ *sour wine*

15:37 ᵃ Matt. 27:50 ¹ *breathed his last*
15:38 ᵃ Ex. 26:31–33 ¹ *torn in two*
15:39 ᵃ Luke 23:47 ¹ *opposite* ² *breathed his last*
15:40 ᵃ Matt. 27:55 ᵇ Ps. 38:11
15:41 ᵃ Luke 8:2, 3
15:42 ᵃ John 19:38–42 ¹ *evening*
15:43 ᵃ Luke 2:25, 38; 23:51 ¹ *prominent council member* ² *asked for*
15:44 ¹ *a long time*
15:45 ¹ *learned*
15:46 ᵃ Matt. 27:59, 60
16:1 ᵃ John 20:1–8 ᵇ Luke 23:56
16:2 ᵃ Luke 24:1
16:4 ¹ *large*
16:5 ᵃ John 20:11, 12 ¹ *robe* ² *alarmed*
16:6 ᵃ Matt. 28:6 ¹ *alarmed*

which was crucified: he is risen; he is not here: behold the place where they laid him.

7 But go your way, tell his disciples and Peter that he goeth before you into Galilee: there shall ye see him, [a]as he said unto you.

8 And they went out quickly, and fled from the sepulchre; for they trembled and were amazed: [a]neither said they any thing to any *man;* for they were afraid.

9 Now when *Jesus* was risen early the first *day* of the week, he appeared first to Mary Magdalene, [a]out of whom he had cast seven [1]devils.

10 [a]*And* she went and told them that had been with him, as they mourned and wept.

11 [a]And they, when they had heard that he was alive, and had been seen of her, believed not.

12 After that he appeared in another form [a]unto two of them, as they walked, and went into the country.

13 And they went and told *it* unto the [1]residue: neither believed they them.

14 [a]Afterward he appeared unto the eleven as they sat [1]at meat, and [2]upbraided them with their unbelief and hardness of heart, because they believed not them which had seen him after he was risen.

15 [a]And he said unto them, Go ye into all the world, [b]and preach the gospel to every creature.

16 [a]He that believeth and is baptized shall be saved; [b]but he that believeth not shall be [1]damned.

17 And these [a]signs shall follow them that [1]believe; [b]In my name shall they cast out [2]devils; [c]they shall speak with new tongues;

18 [a]They shall take up serpents; and if they drink any deadly thing, it shall [1]not hurt them; [b]they shall lay hands on the sick, and they shall recover.

19 So then [a]after the Lord had spoken unto them, he was [b]received up into heaven, and [c]sat on the right hand of God.

20 And they went forth, and preached every where, the Lord working with *them,* [a]and confirming the word with [1]signs following. Amen.

**Cross references:**
16:7 [a] Matt. 26:32; 28:16, 17
16:8 [a] Matt. 28:8
16:9 [a] Luke 8:2 [1] demons
16:10 [a] Luke 24:10
16:11 [a] Luke 24:11, 41
16:12 [a] Luke 24:13–35
16:13 [1] rest
16:14 [a] 1 Cor. 15:5 [1] at the table [2] rebuked
16:15 [a] Matt. 28:19 [b] [Col. 1:23]
16:16 [a] [John 3:18, 36] [b] [John 12:48] [1] condemned
16:17 [a] Acts 5:12 [b] Luke 10:17 [c] [Acts 2:4] [1] believed [2] demons
16:18 [a] Acts 28:3–6 [b] James 5:14 [1] never
16:19 [a] Acts 1:2, 3 [b] Luke 9:51; 24:51 [c] [Ps. 110:1]
16:20 [a] [Heb. 2:4] [1] accompanying signs

# THE GOSPEL ACCORDING TO
# LUKE

Luke, a physician, writes with the compassion and warmth of a family doctor as he carefully documents the perfect humanity of the Son of Man, Jesus Christ. Luke emphasizes Jesus' ancestry, birth, and early life before moving carefully and chronologically through His earthly ministry. Growing belief and growing opposition develop side by side. Those who believe are challenged to count the cost of discipleship. Those who oppose will not be satisfied until the Son of Man hangs lifeless on a cross. But the Resurrection insures that His purpose will be fulfilled: "to seek and to save that which was lost" (19:10).

*Kata Loukan*, "According to Luke," is the ancient title that was added to this gospel at a very early date. The Greek name *Luke* appears only three times in the New Testament (Col. 4:14; 2 Tim. 4:11; Philem. 24).

## CHAPTER 1

FORASMUCH as many have taken in hand to set forth in order a ¹declaration of those ᵃthings which are most surely believed among us,

2 Even as they ᵃdelivered them unto us, which ᵇfrom the beginning were ᶜeyewitnesses, and ministers of the word;

3 It seemed good to me also, having ¹had perfect understanding of all things from ²the very first, to write unto thee ³in order, ᵃmost excellent Theophilus,

4 ᵈThat thou mightest know the certainty of those things, wherein thou hast been instructed.

5 There was ᵃin the days of Herod, the king of Judaea, a certain priest named Zacharias, ᵇof the ¹course of ᶜAbia: and his ᵈwife *was* of the daughters of Aaron, and her name *was* Elisabeth.

6 And they were both righteous before God, walking in all the commandments and ordinances of the Lord blameless.

7 And they had no child, because that Elisabeth was barren, and they both were *now* well ¹stricken in years.

8 And it came to pass, that while he ¹executed the priest's office before God in the order of his ²course,

9 According to the custom of the priest's office, ¹his lot was ᵃto burn incense when he went into the temple of the Lord.

10 ᵃAnd the whole multitude of the people were praying ¹without at the ²time of incense.

11 And there appeared unto him an angel of the Lord standing on the right side of ᵃthe altar of incense.

12 And when Zacharias saw *him*, ᵃhe was troubled, and fear fell upon him.

13 But the angel said unto him, Fear not, Zacharias: for thy prayer is heard; and thy wife Elisabeth shall

bear thee a son, and ᵃthou shalt call his name John.

14 And thou shalt have joy and gladness; and ᵃmany shall rejoice at his birth.

15 For he shall be ᵃgreat in the sight of the Lord, and ᵇshall drink neither wine nor strong drink; and he shall be filled with the Holy Ghost, ᶜeven from his mother's womb.

16 And many of the ¹children of Israel shall he turn to the Lord their God.

17 ᵃAnd he shall go before him in the spirit and power of Elias, to turn the hearts of the fathers to the children, and the disobedient to the wisdom of the just; to make ready a people prepared for the Lord.

18 And Zacharias said unto the angel, ᵃWhereby shall I know this? for I am an old man, and my wife well ¹stricken in years.

19 And the angel answering said unto him, I am ᵃGabriel, that stand in the presence of God; and am sent to speak unto thee, and to shew thee ¹these glad ᵇtidings.

20 And, behold, ᵃthou shalt be ¹dumb, and not able to speak, until the day that these things shall be performed, because thou believest not my words, which shall be fulfilled in their ²season.

21 And the people waited for Zacharias, and marvelled that he ¹tarried so long in the temple.

22 And when he came out, he could not speak unto them: and they perceived that he had seen a vision in the temple: for he beckoned unto them, and remained speechless.

23 And it came to pass, that, as soon as ᵃthe days of his ¹ministration were ²accomplished, he departed to his own house.

24 And after those days his wife Elisabeth conceived, and hid herself five months, saying,

---

*Marginal references:*

1:1 ᵃ John 20:31  ¹ *narrative*
1:2 ᵃ Heb. 2:3  ᵇ Acts 1:21, 22  ᶜ Acts 1:2
1:3 ᵃ Acts 1:1  ¹ Lit. *accurately followed*  ² Or *above*  ³ *an orderly account*
1:4 ᵃ [John 20:31]
1:5 ᵃ Matt. 2:1  ᵇ 1 Chr. 24:1, 10  ᶜ Neh. 12:4  ᵈ Lev. 21:13, 14  ¹ *division*
1:7 ¹ *advanced*
1:8 ¹ *served as priest*  ² *division*
1:9 ᵃ Ex. 30:7, 8  ¹ *he was chosen by lot*
1:10 ᵃ Lev. 16:17  ¹ *outside*  ² Lit. *hour*
1:11 ᵃ Ex. 30:1
1:12 ᵃ Luke 2:9

1:13 ᵃ Luke 1:57, 60, 63
1:14 ᵃ Luke 1:58
1:15 ᵃ [Luke 7:24–28]  ᵇ Num. 6:3  ᶜ Jer. 1:5
1:16 ¹ Lit. *sons*
1:17 ᵃ Mal. 4:5, 6; Matt. 3:2; 11:14
1:18 ᵃ Gen. 17:17  ¹ *advanced*
1:19 ᵃ Dan. 8:16  ᵇ Luke 2:10  ¹ *this good news*
1:20 ᵃ Ezek. 3:26; 24:27  ¹ *mute*  ² *own time*
1:21 ¹ *delayed*
1:23 ᵃ 2 Kin. 11:5  ¹ *service*  ² *completed*

840

25 Thus hath the Lord dealt with me in the days wherein he looked on *me*, to [a]take away my reproach among men.

26 And in the sixth month the angel Gabriel was sent from God unto a city of Galilee, named Nazareth,

27 To a virgin [a]espoused[1] to a man whose name was Joseph, of the house of David; and the virgin's name *was* Mary.

28 And the angel came in unto her, and said, [a]Hail,[1] *thou that art* highly favoured, [b]the Lord *is* with thee: blessed *art* thou among women.

29 And when she saw *him*, [a]she was troubled at his saying, and [1]cast in her mind what manner of [2]salutation this should be.

30 And the angel said unto her, Fear not, Mary: for thou hast found [a]favour with God.

31 [a]And, behold, thou shalt conceive in thy womb, and bring forth a son, and [b]shalt call his name JESUS.

32 He shall be great, [a]and shall be called the Son of the [1]Highest: and [b]the Lord God shall give unto him the [c]throne of his [d]father David:

33 [a]And he shall reign over the house of Jacob for ever; and of his kingdom there shall be no end.

34 Then said Mary unto the angel, How shall this be, seeing I [1]know not a man?

35 And the angel answered and said unto her, [a]The Holy Ghost shall come upon thee, and the power of the [1]Highest shall overshadow thee: therefore also that holy [2]thing which shall be born of thee shall be called [b]the Son of God.

36 And, behold, thy [1]cousin Elisabeth, she hath also conceived a son in her old age: and this is the sixth month with her, who was called barren.

37 For [a]with God nothing shall be impossible.

38 And Mary said, Behold the [1]handmaid of the Lord; be it unto me according to thy word. And the angel departed from her.

39 And Mary arose in those days, and went into the hill country with haste, [a]into a city of Juda;

40 And entered into the house of Zacharias, and [1]saluted Elisabeth.

41 And it came to pass, that, when Elisabeth heard the [1]salutation of Mary, the babe leaped in her womb; and Elisabeth was [a]filled with the Holy Ghost:

42 And she spake out with a loud voice, and said, [a]Blessed *art* thou among women, and blessed *is* the fruit of thy womb.

43 And [1]whence *is* this to me, that the mother of my Lord should come to me?

44 For, lo, as soon as the voice of thy salutation sounded in mine ears, the babe leaped in my womb for joy.

45 And [a]blessed *is* she [1]that believed: for there shall be a [2]performance of those things which were told her from the Lord.

46 And Mary said, [a]My soul doth [1]magnify the Lord,

47 And my spirit hath [a]rejoiced in [b]God my Saviour.

48 For [a]he hath regarded the [1]low estate of his [2]handmaiden: for, behold, from henceforth [b]all generations shall call me blessed.

49 For he that is mighty [a]hath done to me great things; and [b]holy *is* his name.

50 And [a]his mercy *is* on them that fear him from generation to generation.

51 [a]He hath shewed strength with his arm; [b]he hath scattered the proud in the imagination of their hearts.

52 [a]He hath put down the mighty from *their* [1]seats, and exalted [2]them of low degree.

53 He hath [a]filled the hungry with good things; and the rich he hath sent empty away.

54 He hath [1]holpen his [a]servant Israel, [b]in remembrance of *his* mercy;

55 [a]As he spake to our [b]fathers, to Abraham, and to his [c]seed for ever.

56 And Mary abode with her about three months, and returned to her own house.

57 Now Elisabeth's full time came that she should be delivered; and she brought forth a son.

58 And her neighbours and her [1]cousins heard how the Lord had shewed great mercy upon her; and they [a]rejoiced with her.

59 And it came to pass, that [a]on the eighth day they came to circumcise the child; and they called him Zacharias, after the name of his father.

60 And his mother answered and said, [a]Not *so;* but he shall be called John.

61 And they said unto her, There is none of thy kindred that is called by this name.

62 And they made signs to his father, how he would have him called.

63 And he asked for a writing table, and wrote, saying, His name is John. And they marvelled all.

64 And his mouth was opened immediately, and his tongue *loosed,* and he spake, and praised God.

65 And fear came on all that dwelt round about them: and all these [1]sayings were [2]noised abroad throughout all the hill country of Judaea.

66 And all they that heard *them* [a]laid[1] *them* up in their hearts, saying, What manner of child shall this be!

## Cross References

1:25 [a] Gen. 30:23
1:27 [a] Matt. 1:18
[1] betrothed
1:28 [a] Dan. 9:23
[b] Judg. 6:12
[1] Rejoice
1:29 [a] Luke 1:12
[1] considered
[2] greeting
1:30 [a] Luke 2:52
1:31 [a] Is. 7:14
[b] Luke 2:21
1:32 [a] Mark 5:7
[b] 2 Sam. 7:12,
13, 16 [c] 2 Sam.
7:14–17 [d] Matt. 1:1
[1] Most High
1:33 [a] [Dan. 2:44]
1:34 [1] *am a virgin*
1:35 [a] Matt. 1:20
[b] [Heb. 1:2, 8]
[1] Most High [2] one
1:36 [1] relative
1:37 [a] Jer. 32:17
1:38 [1] maidservant
1:39 [a] Josh. 21:9
1:40 [1] greeted
1:41 [a] Acts 6:3
[1] greeting
1:42 [a] Judg. 5:24
1:43 [1] why

1:45 [a] John 20:29
[1] who believed
that there [2] fulfillment
1:46 [a] 1 Sam. 2:1–10 [1] exalt
1:47 [a] Hab. 3:18
[b] 1 Tim. 1:1; 2:3
1:48 [a] Ps. 138:6
[b] Luke 11:27
[1] lowly state
[2] maidservant
1:49 [a] Ps. 71:19;
126:2, 3 [b] Ps. 111:9
1:50 [a] Ps. 103:17
1:51 [a] Ps. 98:1;
118:15 [b] [1 Pet. 5:5]
1:52 [a] 1 Sam. 2:7,
8 [1] thrones [2] the
lowly
1:53 [a] [Matt. 5:6]
1:54 [a] Is. 41:8
[b] [Jer. 31:3]
[1] helped
1:55 [a] Gen. 17:19
[b] [Rom. 11:28]
[c] Gen. 17:7
1:58 [a] [Rom. 12:15]
[1] relatives
1:59 [a] Gen. 17:12
1:60 [a] Luke
1:13, 63
1:65 [1] things
[2] discussed
1:66 [a] Luke 2:19
[1] kept them

841

And [b]the hand of the Lord was with him.

67 And his father Zacharias [a]was filled with the Holy Ghost, and prophesied, saying,

68 [a]Blessed *be* the Lord God of Israel; for [b]he hath visited and redeemed his people,

69 [a]And hath raised up an horn of salvation for us in the house of his servant David;

70 [a]As he spake by the mouth of his holy prophets, which have been [b]since[1] the world began:

71 That we should be saved from our enemies, and from the hand of all that hate us;

72 [a]To perform the mercy *promised* to our fathers, and to remember his holy covenant;

73 [a]The oath which he sware to our father Abraham,

74 That he would grant unto us, that we being delivered out of the hand of our enemies might [a]serve him without fear,

75 [a]In holiness and righteousness before him, all the days of our life.

76 And thou, child, shalt be called the [a]prophet of the Highest: for [b]thou shalt go before the face of the Lord to prepare his ways;

77 To give [a]knowledge of salvation unto his people by the [1]remission of their sins,

78 Through the tender mercy of our God; whereby the [1]dayspring from on high hath visited us,

79 [a]To give light to them that sit in darkness and *in* the shadow of death, to [b]guide our feet into the way of peace.

80 And [a]the child grew, and [1]waxed strong in spirit, and [b]was in the deserts till the day of his [2]shewing unto Israel.

## CHAPTER 2

AND it came to pass in those days, that there went out a decree from Caesar Augustus, that all the world should be [1]taxed.

2 (*And* this [1]taxing was first made when [2]Cyrenius was governor of Syria.)

3 And all went to be [1]taxed, every one into his own city.

4 And Joseph also went up from Galilee, out of the city of Nazareth, into Judaea, unto [a]the city of David, which is called Bethlehem; ([b]because he was of the [1]house and lineage of David:)

5 To be taxed with Mary [a]his [1]espoused wife, being great with child.

6 And so it was, that, while they were there, the days were [1]accomplished that she should be delivered.

7 And [a]she brought forth her firstborn son, and wrapped him in swad-

<!-- center column references -->
1:66 [b] Acts 11:21
1:67 [a] Joel 2:28
1:68 [a] 1 Kin. 1:48
     [b] Ex. 3:16
1:69 [a] Ps. 132:17
1:70 [a] Rom. 1:2
     [b] Acts 3:21 [1] Lit. *from the ages*
1:72 [a] Lev. 26:42
1:73 [a] Gen. 12:3; 22:16–18
1:74 [a] [Heb. 9:14]
1:75 [a] [Eph. 4:24]
1:76 [a] Matt. 3:3; 11:9 [b] Is. 40:3
1:77 [a] [Mark 1:4]
    [1] forgiveness
1:78 [1] Lit. *Dawn,* the Messiah
1:79 [a] Is. 9:2
    [b] [John 10:4; 14:27; 16:33]
1:80 [a] Luke
2:40 [b] Matt. 3:1 [1] *became* [2] *manifestation*
2:1 [1] registered
2:2 [a] Acts 5:37 [1] *registration, census* [2] *Quirinius*
2:3 [1] registered
2:4 [a] 1 Sam. 16:1 [b] Matt. 1:16 [1] family
2:5 [a] [Matt. 1:18] [1] betrothed
2:6 [1] completed
2:7 [a] Matt. 1:25

[1] feed trough
2:9 [a] Luke 1:12 [1] stood before [2] greatly
2:10 [a] Luke 1:13, 30 [b] Gen. 12:3
2:11 [a] Is. 9:6 [b] Matt. 1:21 [c] Acts 2:36
2:12 [1] cloths [2] feed trough
2:13 [a] Dan. 7:10
2:14 [a] Luke 19:38 [b] Is. 57:19 [c] [Eph. 2:4, 7]
2:18 [1] marvelled
2:19 [a] Gen. 37:11
2:20 [a] Luke 19:37
2:21 [a] Lev. 12:3 [b] [Matt. 1:21] [c] Luke 1:31 [1] completed
2:22 [a] Lev. 12:2–8 [1] completed
2:23 [a] Deut. 18:4 [b] Ex. 13:2, 12, 15
2:24 [a] Lev. 12:2, 8

dling clothes, and laid him in a [1]manger; because there was no room for them in the inn.

8 And there were in the same country shepherds abiding in the field, keeping watch over their flock by night.

9 And, lo, the angel of the Lord [1]came upon them, and the glory of the Lord shone round about them: [a]and they were [2]sore afraid.

10 And the angel said unto them, [a]Fear not: for, behold, I bring you good tidings of great joy, [b]which shall be to all people.

11 [a]For unto you is born this day in the city of David [b]a Saviour, [c]which is Christ the Lord.

12 And this *shall be* a sign unto you; Ye shall find the babe wrapped in swaddling [1]clothes, lying in a [2]manger.

13 [a]And suddenly there was with the angel a multitude of the heavenly host praising God, and saying,

14 [a]Glory to God in the highest, and on earth [b]peace, [c]good will toward men.

15 And it came to pass, as the angels were gone away from them into heaven, the shepherds said one to another, Let us now go even unto Bethlehem, and see this thing which is come to pass, which the Lord hath made known unto us.

16 And they came with haste, and found Mary, and Joseph, and the babe lying in a manger.

17 And when they had seen *it,* they made known abroad the saying which was told them concerning this child.

18 And all they that heard *it* [1]wondered at those things which were told them by the shepherds.

19 [a]But Mary kept all these things, and pondered *them* in her heart.

20 And the shepherds returned, glorifying and [a]praising God for all the things that they had heard and seen, as it was told unto them.

21 [a]And when eight days were [1]accomplished for the circumcising of the child, his name was called [b]JESUS, which was so named of the angel [c]before he was conceived in the womb.

22 And when [a]the days of her purification according to the law of Moses were [1]accomplished, they brought him to Jerusalem, to present *him* to the Lord;

23 ([a]As it is written in the law of the Lord, [b]Every male that openeth the womb shall be called holy to the Lord;)

24 And to offer a sacrifice according to that which is said in the law of the Lord, [a]A pair of turtledoves, or two young pigeons.

25 And, behold, there was a man in Jerusalem, whose name *was* Simeon; and the same man *was* just and devout, [a]waiting for the consolation of Israel: and the Holy Ghost was upon him.

26 And it was revealed unto him by the Holy Ghost, that he should not [a]see death, before he had seen the Lord's Christ.

27 And he came [a]by the Spirit into the temple: and when the parents brought in the child Jesus, to do for him after the custom of the law,

28 Then took he him up in his arms, and blessed God, and said,

29 Lord, [a]now lettest thou thy servant depart in peace, according to thy word:

30 For mine eyes [a]have seen thy salvation,

31 Which thou hast prepared before the face of all people;

32 [a]A light to [1]lighten the Gentiles, and the glory of thy people Israel.

33 And Joseph and his mother marvelled at those things which were spoken of him.

34 And Simeon blessed them, and said unto Mary his mother, Behold, this *child* is [1]set for the [a]fall and rising again of many in Israel; and for [b]a sign which shall be spoken against;

35 (Yea, [a]a sword shall pierce through thy own soul also,) that the thoughts of many hearts may be revealed.

36 And there was one Anna, a prophetess, the daughter of Phanuel, of the tribe of [a]Aser: she was of a great age, and had lived with an husband seven years from her virginity;

37 And she *was* a widow of about fourscore and four years, which departed not from the temple, but served *God* with fastings and prayers [a]night and day.

38 And she coming in that instant gave thanks likewise unto the Lord, and spake of him to all them that [a]looked for redemption in Jerusalem.

39 And when they had performed all things according to the law of the Lord, they returned into Galilee, to their own city Nazareth.

40 [a]And the child grew, and [1]waxed strong in spirit, filled with wisdom: and the grace of God was upon him.

41 Now his parents went to [a]Jerusalem [b]every year at the feast of the passover.

42 And when he was twelve years old, they went up to Jerusalem [1]after the [a]custom of the feast.

43 And when they had fulfilled the [a]days, as they returned, the child Jesus [1]tarried behind in Jerusalem; and Joseph and his mother knew not *of it.*

44 But they, supposing him to have been in the company, went a day's journey; and they sought him among *their* [1]kinsfolk and acquaintance.

45 And when they found him not, they turned back again to Jerusalem, seeking him.

46 And it came to pass, that after three days they found him in the temple, sitting in the midst of the [1]doctors, both hearing them, and asking them questions.

47 And [a]all that heard him were astonished at his understanding and answers.

48 And when they saw him, they were amazed: and his mother said unto him, Son, why hast thou [1]thus dealt with us? behold, thy father and I have sought thee [2]sorrowing.

49 And he said unto them, How is it that ye sought me? [1]wist ye not that I must be [a]about [b]my Father's business?

50 And [a]they understood not the saying which he spake unto them.

51 And he went down with them, and came to Nazareth, and was subject unto them: but his mother [a]kept all these sayings in her heart.

52 And Jesus [a]increased in wisdom and stature, [b]and in favour with God and man.

## CHAPTER 3

Now in the fifteenth year of the reign of Tiberius Caesar, [a]Pontius Pilate being governor of Judaea, and Herod being tetrarch of Galilee, and his brother Philip tetrarch of Ituraea and of the region of Trachonitis, and Lysanias the tetrarch of Abilene,

2 [a]Annas and Caiaphas being the high priests, the word of God came unto [b]John the son of Zacharias in the wilderness.

3 [a]And he came into all the [1]country about Jordan, preaching the baptism of repentance [b]for the remission of sins;

4 As it is written in the book of the words of Esaias the prophet, saying, [a]The voice of one crying in the wilderness, Prepare ye the way of the Lord, make his paths straight.

5 Every valley shall be filled, and every mountain and hill shall be brought low; and the [1]crooked shall be made straight, and the rough ways *shall be* made smooth;

6 And [a]all flesh shall see the salvation of God.

7 Then said he to the multitude that came forth to be baptized of him, [a]O [1]generation of vipers, who hath warned you to flee from the wrath to come?

8 Bring forth therefore fruits [a]worthy of repentance, and begin not to

---

2:25 [a] Mark 15:43
2:26 [a] [Heb. 11:5]
2:27 [a] Matt. 4:1
2:29 [a] Gen. 46:30
2:30 [a] [Is. 52:10]
2:32 [a] Acts 10:45; 13:47; 28:28
[1] bring *revelation to*
2:34 [a] [1 Pet. 2:7, 8] [b] Acts 4:2; 17:32; 28:22
[1] *destined*
2:35 [a] Ps. 42:10
2:36 [a] Josh. 19:24
2:37 [a] 1 Tim. 5:5
2:38 [a] Mark 15:43
2:40 [a] Luke 1:80; 2:52 [1] *became*
2:41 [a] John 4:20 [b] Deut. 16:1, 16
2:42 [a] Ex. 23:14, 15 [1] *according to*
2:43 [a] Ex. 12:15 [1] *lingered*

2:44 [1] *relatives*
2:46 [1] *teachers*
2:47 [a] Matt. 7:28; 13:54; 22:33
2:48 [1] *done this to us* [2] *anxiously*
2:49 [a] John 9:4 [b] [Luke 4:22, 32] [1] *knew*
2:50 [a] John 7:15, 46
2:51 [a] Dan. 7:28
2:52 [a] [Col. 2:2, 3] [b] 1 Sam. 2:26
3:1 [a] Matt. 27:2
3:2 [a] Acts 4:6 [b] Luke 1:13
3:3 [a] Mark 1:4 [b] Luke 1:77 [1] *region around*
3:4 [a] Is. 40:3–5
3:5 [1] *crooked places*
3:6 [a] Is. 52:10
3:7 [a] Matt. 3:7; 12:34; 23:33 [1] *brood or offspring*
3:8 [a] [2 Cor. 7:9–11]

say within yourselves, We have Abraham [1]to our father: for I say unto you, That God is able of these stones to raise up children unto Abraham.

9 And now also the axe is laid unto the root of the trees: [a]every tree therefore which bringeth not forth good fruit is hewn down, and cast into the fire.

10 And the people asked him, saying, [a]What shall we do then?

11 He answereth and saith unto them, [a]He that hath two [1]coats, let him [2]impart to him that hath none; and he that hath [3]meat, [b]let him do likewise.

12 Then [a]came also [1]publicans to be baptized, and said unto him, [2]Master, what shall we do?

13 And he said unto them, [a]Exact[1] no more than that which is appointed you.

14 And the soldiers likewise demanded of him, saying, And what shall we do? And he said unto them, [1]Do violence to no man, [a]neither accuse *any* falsely; and be content with your wages.

15 And as the people were in expectation, and all men [1]mused in their hearts of John, whether he were the Christ, or not;

16 John answered, saying unto *them* all, [a]I indeed baptize you with water; but one mightier than I cometh, the [1]latchet of whose [2]shoes I am not worthy to unloose: he shall [b]baptize you with the Holy Ghost and with fire:

17 Whose [1]fan *is* in his hand, and he will throughly [2]purge his [3]floor, and [a]will gather the wheat into his [4]garner; but the chaff he will burn with fire unquenchable.

18 And many other [1]things in his exhortation preached he unto the people.

19 [a]But Herod the tetrarch, being [1]reproved by him for Herodias his brother Philip's wife, and for all the evils which Herod had done,

20 Added yet this above all, that he shut up John in prison.

21 Now when all the people were baptized, [a]it came to pass, that Jesus also being baptized, and praying, the heaven was opened,

22 And the Holy Ghost descended in a bodily shape like a dove upon him, and a voice came from heaven, which said, Thou art my beloved Son; in thee I am [a]well pleased.

23 And Jesus himself [1]began to be [a]about thirty years of age, being (as was supposed) [b]the son of Joseph, which was *the son* of Heli,

24 Which was *the son* of Matthat, which was *the son* of Levi, which was *the son* of Melchi, which was *the son*

of Janna, which was *the son* of Joseph,

25 Which was *the son* of Mattathias, which was *the son* of Amos, which was *the son* of Naum, which was *the son* of Esli, which was *the son* of Nagge,

26 Which was *the son* of Maath, which was *the son* of Mattathias, which was *the son* of Semei, which was *the son* of Joseph, which was *the son* of Juda,

27 Which was *the son* of Joanna, which was *the son* of Rhesa, which was *the son* of [a]Zorobabel, which was *the son* of [1]Salathiel, which was *the son* of Neri,

28 Which was *the son* of Melchi, which was *the son* of Addi, which was *the son* of Cosam, which was *the son* of Elmodam, which was *the son* of Er,

29 Which was *the son* of Jose, which was *the son* of Eliezer, which was *the son* of Jorim, which was *the son* of Matthat, which was *the son* of Levi,

30 Which was *the son* of Simeon, which was *the son* of Juda, which was *the son* of Joseph, which was *the son* of Jonan, which was *the son* of Eliakim,

31 Which was *the son* of Melea, which was *the son* of Menan, which was *the son* of Mattatha, which was *the son* of [a]Nathan, [b]which was *the son* of David,

32 [a]Which was *the son* of Jesse, which was *the son* of Obed, which was *the son* of Booz, which was *the son* of Salmon, which was *the son* of Naasson,

33 Which was *the son* of Aminadab, which was *the son* of Aram, which was *the son* of Esrom, which was *the son* of Phares, which was *the son* of Juda,

34 Which was *the son* of Jacob, which was *the son* of Isaac, which was *the son* of Abraham, [a]which was *the son* of Thara, which was *the son* of Nachor,

35 Which was *the son* of Saruch, which was *the son* of [1]Ragau, which was *the son* of Phalec, which was *the son* of Heber, which was *the son* of [2]Sala,

36 [a]Which was *the son* of Cainan, which was *the son* of [b]Arphaxad, [c]which was *the son* of [1]Sem, which was *the son* of Noe, which was *the son* of Lamech,

37 Which was *the son* of Mathusala, which was *the son* of Enoch, which was *the son* of Jared, which was *the son* of Maleleel, which was *the son* of Cainan,

38 Which was *the son* of Enos, which was *the son* of Seth, which was *the son* of Adam, [a]which was *the son* of God.

---

**Cross-references and notes:**

3:8 [1] *as*

3:9 [a] Matt. 7:19

3:10 [a] [Acts 2:37, 38; 16:30, 31]

3:11 [a] 2 Cor. 8:14 [b] Is. 58:7 [1] *tunics* [2] *give* [3] *food*

3:12 [a] Luke 7:29 [1] *tax collectors* [2] *Teacher*

3:13 [a] Luke 19:8 [1] *Collect*

3:14 [a] Ex. 20:16; 23:1 [1] *intimidate*, lit. *shake down for money*

3:15 [1] *reasoned*

3:16 [a] Matt. 3:11, 12 [b] John 7:39; 20:22 [1] *strap* [2] *sandal*

3:17 [a] Matt. 13:24–30 [1] *winnowing fan* [2] *clean out* [3] *threshingfloor* [4] *barn*

3:18 [1] *exhortations he preached*

3:19 [a] Matt. 14:3; Mark 6:17 [1] *rebuked*

3:21 [a] Matt. 3:13–17; John 1:32

3:22 [a] Ps. 2:7; [Is. 42:1]; Matt. 3:17; 17:5; Mark 1:11; Luke 1:35; 9:35; 2 Pet. 1:17

3:23 [a] [Num. 4:3, 35, 39, 43, 47] [b] Matt. 13:55; John 6:42 [1] *began his ministry at about*

3:27 [a] Ezra 2:2 [1] *Shealtiel*, Ezra 3:8

3:31 [a] Zech. 12:12 [b] 2 Sam. 5:14; 7:12; 1 Chr. 3:5; 17:11; Is. 9:7; Jer. 23:5

3:32 [a] Ruth 4:18–22; 1 Chr. 2:10–12; Is. 11:1, 10

3:34 [a] Gen. 11:24, 26–30; 12:3; Num. 24:17; 1 Chr. 1:24–27

3:35 [1] *Reu*, Gen. 11:18 [2] *Shelah*, 1 Chr. 1:18

3:36 [a] Gen. 11:12 [b] Gen. 10:22, 24; 11:10–13; 1 Chr. 1:17, 18 [c] Gen. 5:6–32; 9:27; 11:10 [1] *Shem*, Gen. 10:1

3:38 [a] Gen. 5:1, 2

## CHAPTER 4

**A**ND [a]Jesus being full of the [1]Holy Ghost returned from Jordan, and [b]was led by the Spirit into the wilderness,

2 Being forty days [1]tempted of the devil. And [a]in those days he did eat nothing: and when they were ended, he afterward [2]hungered.

3 And the devil said unto him, If thou be the [a]Son of God, command this stone that it be made bread.

4 And Jesus answered him, saying, It is written, [a]That man shall not live by bread alone, but by every word of God.

5 And the devil, taking him up into an high mountain, shewed unto him all the kingdoms of the world in a moment of time.

6 And the devil said unto him, All this [1]power will I give thee, and the glory of them: for [a]that is delivered unto me; and to whomsoever I will I give it.

7 If thou therefore wilt worship me, all shall be thine.

8 And Jesus answered and said unto him, Get thee behind me, Satan: for it is written, [a]Thou shalt worship the Lord thy God, and him only shalt thou serve.

9 [a]And he brought him to Jerusalem, and set him on a pinnacle of the temple, and said unto him, If thou be the Son of God, cast thyself down from hence:

10 For it is written, [a]He shall give his angels charge over thee, to keep thee:

11 And [a]in *their* hands they shall bear thee up, lest at any time thou dash thy foot against a stone.

12 And Jesus answering said unto him, It is said, [a]Thou shalt not [1]tempt the Lord thy God.

13 And when the devil had ended all the [1]temptation, he departed from him [a]for[2] a season.

14 [a]And Jesus returned [b]in the power of the Spirit into [c]Galilee: and there went out [1]a [d]fame of him through all the region round about.

15 And he [a]taught in their synagogues, [b]being glorified of all.

16 And he came to [a]Nazareth, where he had been brought up: and, as his custom was, [b]he went into the synagogue on the sabbath day, and stood up for to read.

17 And there was delivered unto him the book of the prophet Esaias. And when he had opened the book, he found the place where it was written,

18 [a]The Spirit of the Lord *is* upon me, because he hath anointed me to preach the gospel to the poor; he hath sent me to heal the broken-hearted, to preach deliverance to the captives, and recovering of sight to

the blind, to [b]set at liberty them that are [1]bruised,

19 To preach the acceptable year of the Lord.

20 And he closed the book, and he gave *it* again to the [1]minister, and sat down. And the eyes of all them that were in the synagogue were fastened on him.

21 And he began to say unto them, This day is this scripture [a]fulfilled in your [1]ears.

22 And all bare him witness, and [a]wondered at the gracious words which proceeded out of his mouth. And they said, [b]Is not this Joseph's son?

23 And he said unto them, Ye will surely say unto me this proverb, Physician, heal thyself: whatsoever we have heard done in [a]Capernaum, do also here in [b]thy country.

24 And he said, Verily I say unto you, No [a]prophet is accepted in his own country.

25 But I tell you of a truth, [a]many widows were in Israel in the days of Elias, when the heaven was shut up three years and six months, when great famine was throughout all the land;

26 But unto none of them was Elias sent, save unto [1]Sarepta, *a city* of Sidon, unto a woman *that was* a widow.

27 [a]And many lepers were in Israel in the time of Eliseus the prophet; and none of them was cleansed, saving Naaman the Syrian.

28 And all they in the synagogue, when they heard these things, were [a]filled with [1]wrath,

29 [a]And rose up, and thrust him out of the city, and led him unto the brow of the hill whereon their city was built, that they might cast him down [1]headlong.

30 But he [a]passing through the midst of them went his way,

31 And [a]came down to Capernaum, a city of Galilee, and taught them on the sabbath days.

32 And they were [a]astonished at his [1]doctrine: [b]for his word was with [2]power.

33 [a]And in the synagogue there was a man, which had a spirit of an unclean [1]devil, and cried out with a loud voice,

34 Saying, Let *us* alone; what have we to do with thee, *thou* Jesus of Nazareth? art thou come to destroy us? [a]I know thee who thou art; [b]the Holy One of God.

35 And Jesus rebuked him, saying, [1]Hold thy peace, and come out of him. And when the [2]devil had thrown him in the midst, he came out of him, and hurt him not.

---

**4:1** [a] [Is. 11:2; 61:1]; Matt. 4:1–11; Mark 1:12, 13 [b] Ezek. 3:12; Luke 2:27
[1] *Holy Spirit*

**4:2** [a] Ex. 34:28; 1 Kin. 19:8 [1] *tested by* [2] *was hungry*

**4:3** [a] Mark 3:11; John 20:31

**4:4** [a] Deut. 8:3

**4:6** [a] [John 12:31; 14:30; Rev. 13:2, 7] [1] *authority*

**4:8** [a] Deut. 6:13; 10:20; Matt. 4:10

**4:9** [a] Matt. 4:5–7

**4:10** [a] Ps. 91:11

**4:11** [a] Ps. 91:12

**4:12** [a] Deut. 6:16 [1] *test*

**4:13** [a] [Heb. 4:15] [1] *testing* [2] *until an opportune time*

**4:14** [a] Matt. 4:12 [b] John 4:43 [c] Acts 10:37 [d] Matt. 4:24 [1] *news*

**4:15** [a] Matt. 4:23 [b] Is. 52:13

**4:16** [a] Mark 6:1 [b] Acts 13:14–16; 17:2

**4:18** [a] Is. 49:8, 9; 61:1, 2

[b] [Dan. 9:24] [1] *oppressed*

**4:20** [1] *attendant*

**4:21** [a] Acts 13:29 [1] *hearing*

**4:22** [a] [Ps. 45:2] [b] John 6:42

**4:23** [a] Matt. 4:13; 11:23 [b] Matt. 13:54

**4:24** [a] John 4:44

**4:25** [a] 1 Kin. 17:9

**4:26** [1] *Zarephath*, 1 Kin. 17:9

**4:27** [a] 2 Kin. 5:1–14

**4:28** [a] Luke 6:11 [1] *rage*

**4:29** [a] John 8:37; 10:31 [1] *over the cliff*

**4:30** [a] John 8:59; 10:39

**4:31** [a] Matt. 4:13

**4:32** [a] Matt. 7:28, 29 [b] [John 6:63; 7:46; 8:26, 28, 38, 47; 12:49, 50] [1] *teaching* [2] *authority*

**4:33** [a] Mark 1:23 [1] *demon*

**4:34** [a] Luke 4:41 [b] Ps. 16:10

**4:35** [1] Lit. *Be muzzled* [2] *demon*

---

36 And they were all amazed, and spake among themselves, saying, What a word *is* this! for with authority and power he commandeth the unclean spirits, and they come out.

37 And the ¹fame of him went out into every place of the country round about.

38 ªAnd he arose out of the synagogue, and entered into ¹Simon's house. And Simon's wife's mother was ²taken with a great fever; and they ᵇbesought him for her.

39 And he stood over her, and ªrebuked the fever; and it left her: and immediately she arose and ¹ministered unto them.

40 ªNow when the sun was setting, all they that had any sick with ¹divers diseases brought them unto him; and he laid his hands on every one of them, and healed them.

41 ªAnd ¹devils also came out of many, crying out, and saying, ᵇThou art Christ the Son of God. And ᶜhe rebuking *them* ²suffered them not to speak: for they knew that he was Christ.

42 ªAnd when it was day, he departed and went into a ¹desert place: and the people sought him, and came unto him, and ²stayed him, that he should not depart from them.

43 And he said unto them, I must ªpreach the kingdom of God to other cities also: for therefore am I sent.

44 ªAnd he preached in the synagogues of Galilee.

### CHAPTER 5

AND ªit came to pass, that, as the people ¹pressed upon him to ᵇhear the word of God, he stood by the lake of Gennesaret,

2 And saw two ships standing by the lake: but the fishermen were gone out of them, and were washing *their* nets.

3 And he entered into one of the ships, which was Simon's, and ¹prayed him that he would thrust out a little from the land. And he ªsat down, and taught the ²people out of the ship.

4 Now when he had ¹left speaking, he said unto Simon, ªLaunch out into the deep, and let down your nets for a ²draught.

5 And Simon answering said unto him, Master, we have toiled all the night, and have ¹taken ªnothing: nevertheless ᵇat thy word I will let down the net.

6 And when they had this done, they ¹inclosed a great multitude of fishes: and their net ²brake.

7 And they beckoned unto *their* partners, which were in the other ship, that they should come and help

---

4:37 ¹ *report about him*

4:38 ª Mark 1:29–31 ᵇ Mark 5:23 ¹ Peter's ² *afflicted*

4:39 ª Luke 8:24 ¹ *served*

4:40 ª Matt. 8:16, 17 ¹ *various*

4:41 ª Mark 1:34; 3:11 ᵇ Mark 8:29 ᶜ Mark 1:25, 34; 3:11 ¹ *demons* ² *did not allow them*

4:42 ª Mark 1:35–38 ¹ *deserted* ² *tried to restrain him*

4:43 ª [John 9:4]

4:44 ª Matt. 4:23; 9:35

5:1 ª Mark 1:16–20 ᵇ Acts 13:44 ¹ *crowded*

5:3 ª John 8:2 ¹ *asked him to* ² *multitudes*

5:4 ª John 21:6 ¹ *stopped* ² *catch*

5:5 ª John 21:3 ᵇ Ps. 33:9 ¹ *caught*

5:6 ¹ *caught* ² *was breaking*

5:8 ª 1 Kin. 17:18

5:9 ª Mark 5:42; 10:24, 26 ¹ *catch*

5:10 ª Matt. 4:19

5:11 ª Matt. 4:20; 19:27 ¹ *left behind*

5:12 ª Mark 1:40–44 ᵇ Lev. 13:14 ¹ *implored*

5:13 ª John 5:9

5:14 ª Matt. 8:4 ᵇ Lev. 13:1–3; 14:2–32 ¹ *make an offering*

5:15 ª Mark 1:45 ᵇ John 6:2 ¹ *the report*

5:16 ª Luke 9:10 ᵇ Matt. 14:23

5:17 ¹ *teachers*

5:18 ª Mark 2:3–12 ¹ *paralyzed*

5:19 ª Matt. 15:30 ¹ *bed*

5:21 ª Mark 2:6, 7 ᵇ Is. 43:25

5:22 ª John 2:25 ¹ *Why do you*

---

them. And they came, and filled both the ships, so that they began to sink.

8 When Simon Peter saw *it,* he fell down at Jesus' knees, saying, ªDepart from me; for I am a sinful man, O Lord.

9 For he was ªastonished, and all that were with him, at the ¹draught of the fishes which they had taken:

10 And so *was* also James, and John, the sons of Zebedee, which were partners with Simon. And Jesus said unto Simon, Fear not; ªfrom henceforth thou shalt catch men.

11 And when they had brought their ships to land, ªthey ¹forsook all, and followed him.

12 ªAnd it came to pass, when he was in a certain city, behold a man full of ᵇleprosy: who seeing Jesus fell on *his* face, and ¹besought him, saying, Lord, if thou wilt, thou canst make me clean.

13 And he put forth *his* hand, and touched him, saying, I will: be thou clean. And ªimmediately the leprosy departed from him.

14 ªAnd he charged him to tell no man: but go, and shew thyself to the priest, and ¹offer for thy cleansing, ᵇaccording as Moses commanded, for a testimony unto them.

15 But so much the more went there ¹a ªfame abroad of him: ᵇand great multitudes came together to hear, and to be healed by him of their infirmities.

16 ªAnd he withdrew himself into the wilderness, and ᵇprayed.

17 And it came to pass on a certain day, as he was teaching, that there were Pharisees and ¹doctors of the law sitting by, which were come out of every town of Galilee, and Judaea, and Jerusalem: and the power of the Lord was *present* to heal them.

18 ªAnd, behold, men brought in a bed a man which was ¹taken with a palsy: and they sought *means* to bring him in, and to lay *him* before him.

19 And when they could not find by what *way* they might bring him in because of the multitude, they went upon the housetop, and let him down through the tiling with *his* ¹couch into the midst ªbefore Jesus.

20 And when he saw their faith, he said unto him, Man, thy sins are forgiven thee.

21 ªAnd the scribes and the Pharisees began to reason, saying, Who is this which speaketh blasphemies? ᵇWho can forgive sins, but God alone?

22 But when Jesus ªperceived their thoughts, he answering said unto them, ¹What reason ye in your hearts?

23 Whether is easier, to say, Thy sins be forgiven thee; or to say, Rise up and walk?

24 But that ye may know that the Son of man hath power upon earth to forgive sins, (he said unto the [1]sick of the palsy,) [a]I say unto thee, Arise, and take up thy [2]couch, and go into thine house.

25 And immediately he rose up before them, and took up that whereon he lay, and departed to his own house, [a]glorifying God.

26 And they were all amazed, and they [a]glorified God, and were filled with fear, saying, We have seen strange things to day.

27 [a]And after these things he went forth, and saw a [1]publican, named Levi, sitting at the [2]receipt of custom: and he said unto him, [b]Follow me.

28 And he left all, rose up, and [a]followed him.

29 And Levi made him a great feast in his own house: and [b]there was a great company of [1]publicans and of others that sat down with them.

30 But their scribes and Pharisees [1]murmured against his disciples, saying, [a]Why do ye eat and drink with [2]publicans and sinners?

31 And Jesus answering said unto them, They that are [1]whole need not a physician; but they that are sick.

32 [a]I came not to call the righteous, but sinners to repentance.

33 And they said unto him, [a]Why do the disciples of John fast often, and make prayers, and likewise *the disciples* of the Pharisees; but thine eat and drink?

34 And he said unto them, Can ye make the [1]children of the bridechamber fast, while the [a]bridegroom is with them?

35 But the days will come, when the bridegroom shall be taken away from them, and then shall they fast in those days.

36 [a]And he spake also a parable unto them; No man putteth a piece of a new garment upon an old; if otherwise, then both the new maketh a [1]rent, and the piece that was *taken* out of the new [2]agreeth not with the old.

37 And no man putteth new wine into old [1]bottles; else the new wine will burst the bottles, and be spilled, and the bottles shall [2]perish.

38 But new wine must be put into new [1]bottles; and both are preserved.

39 No man also having drunk old *wine* straightway desireth new: for he saith, The old is better.

## CHAPTER 6

AND [a]it came to pass on the second sabbath after the first, that he went through the [1]corn fields; and his disciples plucked the [2]ears of corn, and did eat, rubbing *them* in *their* hands.

5:24 [a] Luke 7:14
[1] *paralyzed man*
[2] *bed*
5:25 [a] Acts 3:8
5:26 [a] Luke 1:65; 7:16
5:27 [a] Matt. 9:9–17  [b] John 12:26; 21:19, 22  [1] *tax collector*  [2] *tax office*
5:28 [a] Mark 10:28
5:29 [a] Matt. 9:9, 10; Mark 2:15  [b] Luke 15:1  [1] *tax collectors*
5:30 [a] Matt. 11:19; Luke 15:2; Acts 23:9  [1] *grumbled*  [2] *tax collectors*
5:31 [1] *healthy*
5:32 [a] Matt. 9:13; 1 Tim. 1:15
5:33 [a] Matt. 9:14; Mark 2:18; Luke 7:33
5:34 [a] John 3:29  [1] *friends of the bridegroom*
5:36 [a] Matt. 9:16, 17; Mark 2:21, 22  [1] *tear*  [2] *does not match*
5:37 [1] *wineskins*  [2] *be ruined*
5:38 [1] *wineskins*
6:1 [a] Matt. 12:1–8; Mark 2:23–28  [1] *grain*  [2] *heads of grain*
6:2 [a] Ex. 20:10
6:3 [a] 1 Sam. 21:6  [1] *hungry*
6:4 [a] Lev. 24:9
6:6 [a] Matt. 12:9–14; Mark 3:1–6; Luke 13:14; 14:3; John 9:16
6:7 [a] Luke 13:14; 14:1–6  [b] Luke 20:20  [1] *closely watched*
6:8 [a] Matt. 9:4; John 2:24, 25
6:9 [a] John 7:23
6:10 [1] *Many mss. him*
6:11 [1] *rage*  [2] *discussed*
6:12 [a] Matt. 14:23; Mark 1:35; Luke 5:16; 9:18; 11:1
6:13 [a] John 6:70  [b] Matt. 10:1
6:14 [a] John 1:42
6:15 [1] *the Zealot*
6:16 [a] Jude 1  [b] Luke 22:3–6  [1] *became*
6:17 [a] Matt. 4:25; Mark 3:7, 8  [1] *a level place*
6:18 [1] *tormented*
6:19 [a] Matt. 9:21; 14:36; Mark 3:10

2 And certain of the Pharisees said unto them, Why do ye that [a]which is not lawful to do on the sabbath days?

3 And Jesus answering them said, Have ye not read so much as this, [a]what David did, when himself was [1]an hungred, and they which were with him;

4 How he went into the house of God, and did take and eat the shewbread, and gave also to them that were with him; [a]which it is not lawful to eat but for the priests alone?

5 And he said unto them, That the Son of man is Lord also of the sabbath.

6 [a]And it came to pass also on another sabbath, that he entered into the synagogue and taught: and there was a man whose right hand was withered.

7 And the scribes and Pharisees [1]watched him, whether he would [a]heal on the sabbath day; that they might find an [b]accusation against him.

8 But he [a]knew their thoughts, and said to the man which had the withered hand, Rise up, and stand forth in the midst. And he arose and stood forth.

9 Then said Jesus unto them, I will ask you one thing; [a]Is it lawful on the sabbath days to do good, or to do evil? to save life, or to destroy *it?*

10 And looking round about upon them all, he said unto [1]the man, Stretch forth thy hand. And he did so: and his hand was restored whole as the other.

11 And they were filled with [1]madness; and [2]communed one with another what they might do to Jesus.

12 And it came to pass in those days, that he went out into a mountain to pray, and continued all night in [a]prayer to God.

13 And when it was day, he called *unto him* his disciples: [a]and of them he chose [b]twelve, whom also he named apostles;

14 Simon, ([a]whom he also named Peter,) and Andrew his brother, James and John, Philip and Bartholomew,

15 Matthew and Thomas, James the *son* of Alphaeus, and Simon called [1]Zelotes,

16 And Judas [a]*the brother* of James, and [b]Judas Iscariot, which also [1]was the traitor.

17 And he came down with them, and stood in [1]the plain, and the company of his disciples, [a]and a great multitude of people out of all Judaea and Jerusalem, and from the sea coast of Tyre and Sidon, which came to hear him, and to be healed of their diseases;

18 And they that were [1]vexed with unclean spirits: and they were healed.

19 And the whole multitude [a]sought

to ᵇtouch him: for ᶜthere went ¹virtue out of him, and healed *them* all.

20 And he lifted up his eyes on his disciples, and said, ᵃBlessed *be ye* poor: for yours is the kingdom of God.

21 ᵃBlessed *are ye* that hunger now: for ye shall be ᵇfilled.¹ ᶜBlessed *are ye* that weep now: for ye shall ᵈlaugh.

22 ᵃBlessed are ye, when men shall hate you, and when they ᵇshall separate you *from their company*, and shall ¹reproach *you*, and cast out your name as evil, for the Son of man's sake.

23 ᵃRejoice ye in that day, and leap for joy: for, behold, your reward *is* great in heaven: for ᵇin the like manner did their fathers unto the prophets.

24 ᵃBut woe unto you ᵇthat are rich! for ᶜye have received your consolation.

25 ᵃWoe unto you that are full! for ye shall hunger. ᵇWoe unto you that laugh now! for ye shall mourn and ᶜweep.

26 ᵃWoe unto you, when all men shall speak well of you! for so did their fathers to the false prophets.

27 ᵃBut I say unto you which hear, Love your enemies, do good to them which hate you,

28 ᵃBless them that curse you, and ᵇpray for them which ¹despitefully use you.

29 ᵃAnd unto him that smiteth thee on the *one* cheek offer also the other; ᵇand him that taketh away thy cloak forbid not *to take thy* ¹coat also.

30 ᵃGive to every man that asketh of thee; and of him that taketh away thy goods ask *them* not again.

31 ᵃAnd as ye would that men should do to you, do ye also to them likewise.

32 ᵃFor if ye love them which love you, what ¹thank have ye? for sinners also love those that love them.

33 And if ye do good to them which do good to you, what ¹thank have ye? for sinners also do even the same.

34 ᵃAnd if ye lend *to them* of whom ye hope to receive, what ¹thank have ye? for sinners also lend to sinners, to receive as much again.

35 But ᵃlove ye your enemies, and ᵇdo good, and ᶜlend, hoping for nothing ¹again; and your reward shall be great, and ᵈye shall be the children of the Highest: for he is kind unto the unthankful and *to* the evil.

36 ᵃBe ye therefore merciful, as your Father also is merciful.

37 ᵃJudge not, and ye shall not be judged: condemn not, and ye shall not be condemned: ᵇforgive, and ye shall be forgiven:

38 ᵃGive, and it shall be given unto you; good measure, pressed down,

6:19 ᵇ Mark 5:27, 28; Luke 8:44–47
ᶜ Mark 5:30; Luke 8:46 ¹ *power*
6:20 ᵃ Matt. 5:3–12; [11:5]
6:21 ᵃ Is. 55:1; 65:13 ᵇ [Rev. 7:16] ᶜ [Is. 61:3] ᵈ Ps. 126:5 ¹ *satisfied*
6:22 ᵃ 1 Pet. 2:19; 3:14; 4:14 ᵇ [John 16:2] ¹ *revile*
6:23 ᵃ James 1:2 ᵇ Acts 7:51
6:24 ᵃ James 5:1–6 ᵇ Luke 12:21 ᶜ Luke 16:25
6:25 ᵃ [Is. 65:13] ᵇ [Prov. 14:13] ᶜ James 4:9
6:26 ᵃ [John 15:19]
6:27 ᵃ Rom. 12:20
6:28 ᵃ Rom. 12:14 ᵇ Acts 7:60 ¹ *spitefully*
6:29 ᵃ Matt. 5:39–42 ᵇ [1 Cor. 6:7] ¹ *tunic*
6:30 ᵃ Deut. 15:7, 8
6:31 ᵃ Matt. 7:12
6:32 ᵃ Matt. 5:45 ¹ *credit*
6:33 ¹ *credit*
6:34 ᵃ Matt. 5:42 ¹ *credit*
6:35 ᵃ [Rom. 13:10] ᵇ Heb. 13:16 ᶜ Ps. 37:26 ᵈ Matt. 5:46 ¹ *in return*
6:36 ᵃ Matt. 5:48
6:37 ᵃ Matt. 7:1–5 ᵇ Matt. 18:21–35
6:38 ᵃ [Prov. 19:17; 28:27]

ᵇ Ps. 79:12
ᶜ James 2:13 ¹ The fold in a garment used as a pocket ² *use*
6:39 ᵃ Matt. 15:14; 23:16
6:40 ᵃ [John 13:16; 15:20] ¹ *teacher* ² *perfectly trained*
6:41 ᵃ Matt. 7:3 ¹ *speck* ² *plank*
6:42 ¹ *speck* ² *plank*
6:43 ᵃ Matt. 7:16–18, 20 ¹ *bad*
6:44 ᵃ Matt. 12:33
6:45 ᵃ Matt. 12:35 ᵇ Matt. 12:34
6:46 ᵃ Mal. 1:6
6:47 ᵃ James 1:22–25
7:1 ᵃ Matt. 8:5–13 ¹ *hearing*
7:3 ¹ *imploring*

and shaken together, and running over, shall men give into your ᵇbosom.¹ For ᶜwith the same measure that ye ²mete withal it shall be measured to you again.

39 And he spake a parable unto them, ᵃCan the blind lead the blind? shall they not both fall into the ditch?

40 ᵃThe disciple is not above his ¹master: but every one that is ²perfect shall be as his ¹master.

41 ᵃAnd why beholdest thou the ¹mote that is in thy brother's eye, but perceivest not the ²beam that is in thine own eye?

42 Either how canst thou say to thy brother, Brother, let me pull out the ¹mote that is in thine eye, when thou thyself beholdest not the ²beam that is in thine own eye? Thou hypocrite, cast out first the beam out of thine own eye, and then shalt thou see clearly to pull out the mote that is in thy brother's eye.

43 ᵃFor a good tree bringeth not forth ¹corrupt fruit; neither doth a ¹corrupt tree bring forth good fruit.

44 For ᵃevery tree is known by his own fruit. For of thorns men do not gather figs, nor of a bramble bush gather they grapes.

45 ᵃA good man out of the good treasure of his heart bringeth forth that which is good; and an evil man out of the evil treasure of his heart bringeth forth that which is evil: for ᵇof the abundance of the heart his mouth speaketh.

46 ᵃAnd why call ye me, Lord, Lord, and do not the things which I say?

47 ᵃWhosoever cometh to me, and heareth my sayings, and doeth them, I will shew you to whom he is like:

48 He is like a man which built an house, and digged deep, and laid the foundation on a rock: and when the flood arose, the stream beat vehemently upon that house, and could not shake it: for it was founded upon a rock.

49 But he that heareth, and doeth not, is like a man that without a foundation built an house upon the earth; against which the stream did beat vehemently, and immediately it fell; and the ruin of that house was great.

## CHAPTER 7

Now when he had ended all his sayings in the ¹audience of the people, he ᵃentered into Capernaum.

2 And a certain centurion's servant, who was dear unto him, was sick, and ready to die.

3 And when he heard of Jesus, he sent unto him the elders of the Jews, ¹beseeching him that he would come and heal his servant.

4 And when they came to Jesus, they [1]besought him instantly, saying, That he was worthy for whom he should do this:

5 For he loveth our nation, and he hath built us a synagogue.

6 Then Jesus went with them. And when he was now not far from the house, the centurion sent friends to him, saying unto him, Lord, trouble not thyself: for I am not worthy that thou shouldest enter under my roof:

7 Wherefore [1]neither thought I myself worthy to come unto thee: but [a]say in a word, and my servant shall be healed.

8 For I also am a man set under [a]authority, having under me soldiers, and I say unto one, Go, and he goeth; and to another, Come, and he cometh; and to my servant, Do this, and he doeth *it*.

9 When Jesus heard these things, he marvelled at him, and [1]turned him about, and said unto the people that followed him, I say unto you, I have not found so great faith, no, [2]not in Israel.

10 And they that were sent, returning to the house, found the servant [1]whole that had been sick.

11 And it came to pass the day after, that he went into a city called Nain; and many of his disciples went with him, [1]and much people.

12 Now when he came [1]nigh to the gate of the city, behold, there was a dead man carried out, the only son of his mother, and she was a widow: and [2]much people of the city was with her.

13 And when the Lord saw her, he had [a]compassion on her, and said unto her, [b]Weep not.

14 And he came and touched the [1]bier: and they that bare *him* stood still. And he said, Young man, I say unto thee, [a]Arise.

15 And he that was dead [a]sat up, and began to speak. And he [b]delivered him to his mother.

16 [a]And [1]there came a fear on all: and they [b]glorified God, saying, [c]That a great prophet is risen up among us; and, [d]That God hath visited his people.

17 And this [1]rumour of him went forth throughout all Judaea, and throughout all the region round about.

18 [a]And the disciples of John [1]shewed him of all these things.

19 And John calling *unto him* two of his disciples sent *them* to Jesus, saying, Art thou [1]he that should [a]come? or [2]look we for another?

20 When the men were come unto him, they said, John Baptist hath sent us unto thee, saying, Art thou [1]he that should come? or look we for another?

21 And in that same hour he cured many of *their* infirmities and [1]plagues, and of evil spirits; and unto many *that were* blind he gave sight.

22 [a]Then Jesus answering said unto them, Go your way, and tell John what things ye have seen and heard; [b]how that the blind [c]see, the lame [d]walk, the lepers are [e]cleansed, the deaf [f]hear, the dead are raised, [g]to the poor the gospel is preached.

23 And blessed is *he,* whosoever shall not be [1]offended [2]in me.

24 [a]And when the messengers of John were departed, he began to speak unto the [1]people concerning John, What went ye out into the wilderness for to see? A reed shaken with the wind?

25 But what went ye out for to see? A man clothed in soft [1]raiment? Behold, they which are gorgeously [2]apparelled, and live [3]delicately, are in kings' courts.

26 But what went ye out for to see? A prophet? Yea, I say unto you, and much more than a prophet.

27 [a]This is *he,* of whom it is written, [a]Behold, I send my messenger before thy face, which shall prepare thy way before thee.

28 For I say unto you, Among those that are born of women there is not a [a]greater prophet than John the Baptist: but he that is least in the kingdom of God is greater than he.

29 And all the people that heard *him,* and the [1]publicans, [2]justified God, [a]being baptized with the baptism of John.

30 But the Pharisees and [1]lawyers rejected [a]the counsel of God [2]against themselves, being not baptized of him.

31 And the Lord said, [a]Whereunto then shall I liken the men of this generation? and to what are they like?

32 They are like unto children sitting in the marketplace, and calling one to another, and saying, We have [1]piped unto you, and ye have not danced; we have mourned to you, and ye have not wept.

33 For [a]John the Baptist came [b]neither eating bread nor drinking wine; and ye say, He hath a [1]devil.

34 The Son of man is come [a]eating and drinking; and ye say, Behold a gluttonous man, and a [1]winebibber, a friend of [2]publicans and sinners!

35 [a]But wisdom is justified of all her children.

36 [a]And one of the Pharisees [1]desired him that he would eat with him. And

---

7:4 [1] *implored him earnestly*

7:7 [a] Ps. 33:9; 107:20 [1] *I did not even think*

7:8 [a] [Mark 13:34]

7:9 [1] *turned around* [2] *not even*

7:10 [1] *healthy*

7:11 [1] *a large crowd*

7:12 [1] *near* [2] *a large crowd*

7:13 [a] Lam. 3:32; John 11:35; [Heb. 4:15] [b] Luke 8:52

7:14 [a] Mark 5:41; Luke 8:54; John 11:43; Acts 9:40; [Rom. 4:17] [1] *open coffin*

7:15 [a] Matt. 11:5; Luke 8:55; John 11:44 [b] 1 Kin. 17:23; 2 Kin. 4:36

7:16 [a] Luke 1:65 [b] Luke 5:26 [c] Luke 24:19; John 4:19; 6:14; 9:17 [d] Luke 1:68 [1] *fear seized them all*

7:17 [1] *report about*

7:18 [a] Matt. 11:2–19 [1] *reported to*

7:19 [a] [Mic. 5:2; Zech. 9:9; Mal. 3:1–3] [1] *the coming one* [2] *are we to look*

7:20 [1] *the coming one*

7:21 [1] *afflictions*

7:22 [a] Matt. 11:4 [b] Is. 35:5 [c] John 9:7 [d] Matt. 15:31 [e] Luke 17:12–14 [f] Mark 7:37 [g] [Is. 61:1–3; Luke 4:18]

7:23 [1] *caused to stumble* [2] *because of*

7:24 [a] Matt. 11:7 [1] *multitudes*

7:25 [1] *garments* [2] *dressed* [3] *in luxury*

7:27 [a] Is. 40:3; Mal. 3:1; Matt. 11:10; Mark 1:2

7:28 [a] [Luke 1:15]

7:29 [a] Matt. 3:5; Luke 3:12 [1] *tax collectors* [2] *declared the righteousness of*

7:30 [a] Acts 20:27 [1] *experts in the law* [2] *for*

7:31 [a] Matt. 11:16

7:32 [1] *played the flute for you*

7:33 [a] Matt. 3:1 [b] [Matt. 3:4]; Luke 1:15 [1] *demon*

7:34 [a] Luke 15:2 [1] *wine drinker* [2] *tax collectors*
7:35 [a] Matt. 11:19 7:36 [a] Matt. 26:6; Mark 14:3; John 11:2 [1] *asked him to eat*

he went into the Pharisee's house, and sat down [2]to meat.

37 And, behold, a woman in the city, which was a sinner, when she knew that *Jesus* sat [1]at meat in the Pharisee's house, brought an alabaster [2]box of ointment,

38 And stood at his feet behind *him* weeping, and began to wash his feet with tears, and did wipe *them* with the hairs of her head, and kissed his feet, and anointed *them* with the [1]ointment.

39 Now when the Pharisee which had [1]bidden him saw *it,* he spake within himself, saying, [a]This man, if he were a prophet, would have known who and what manner of woman *this is* that toucheth him: for she is a sinner.

40 And Jesus answering said unto him, Simon, I have somewhat to say unto thee. And he saith, [1]Master, say on.

41 There was a certain creditor which had two debtors: the one owed five hundred [a]pence,[1] and the other fifty.

42 And when they had nothing to [1]pay, he [2]frankly forgave them both. Tell me therefore, which of them will love him most?

43 Simon answered and said, I suppose that *he,* to whom he forgave most. And he said unto him, Thou hast rightly judged.

44 And he turned to the woman, and said unto Simon, Seest thou this woman? I entered into thine house, thou gavest me no [a]water for my feet: but she hath washed my feet with tears, and wiped *them* with the hairs of her head.

45 Thou gavest me no [a]kiss: but this woman since the time I came in hath not ceased to kiss my feet.

46 [a]My head with oil thou didst not anoint: but this woman hath anointed my feet with [1]ointment.

47 [a]Wherefore I say unto thee, Her sins, which are many, are forgiven; for she loved much: but to whom little is forgiven, *the same* loveth little.

48 And he said unto her, [a]Thy sins are forgiven.

49 And they that sat [1]at meat with him began to say within themselves, [a]Who is this that forgiveth sins also?

50 And he said to the woman, [a]Thy faith hath saved thee; go in peace.

## CHAPTER 8

A ND it came to pass afterward, that he went throughout every city and village, preaching and [1]shewing the glad tidings of the kingdom of God: and the twelve *were* with him,

2 And [a]certain women, which had been healed of evil spirits and [1]infir-

mities, Mary called Magdalene, [b]out of whom went seven [2]devils,

3 And Joanna the wife of Chuza Herod's steward, and Susanna, and many others, which [1]ministered unto him of their [2]substance.

4 [a]And when [1]much people were gathered together, and were come to him out of every city, he spake by a parable:

5 A sower went out to sow his seed: and as he sowed, some fell by the way side; and it was [1]trodden down, and the fowls of the air devoured it.

6 And some fell upon a rock; and as soon as it was sprung up, it withered away, because it lacked moisture.

7 And some fell among thorns; and the thorns sprang up with it, and choked it.

8 And other fell on good ground, and sprang up, and bare fruit an hundredfold. And when he had said these things, he cried, [a]He that hath ears to hear, let him hear.

9 [a]And his disciples asked him, saying, What might this parable [1]be?

10 And he said, Unto you it is given to know the [1]mysteries of the kingdom of God: but to others in parables; [a]that seeing they might not see, and hearing they might not understand.

11 [a]Now the parable is this: The seed is the [b]word of God.

12 Those by the way side are they that hear; then cometh the devil, and taketh away the word out of their hearts, lest they should believe and be saved.

13 They on the rock *are they,* which, when they hear, receive the word with joy; and these have no root, which for a while believe, and in time of [1]temptation fall away.

14 And that which fell among thorns are they, which, when they have heard, go forth, and are choked with cares and [a]riches and pleasures of *this* life, and bring no fruit to [1]perfection.

15 But that on the good ground are they, which in [1]an honest and good heart, having heard the word, keep *it,* and bring forth fruit with [a]patience.

16 [a]No man, when he hath lighted a [1]candle, covereth it with a vessel, or putteth *it* under a bed; but setteth *it* on a [2]candlestick, that they which enter in may see the [b]light.

17 [a]For nothing is secret, that shall not be [b]made[1] manifest; neither *any thing* hid, that shall not be known and come [2]abroad.

18 Take heed therefore how ye hear: [a]for whosoever hath, to him shall be given; and whosoever hath not, from him shall be taken even that which he seemeth to [b]have.

### Center column references

7:36 [2] *at the table*
7:37 [1] *at the table* [2] *flask of fragrant oil*
7:38 [1] *fragrant oil*
7:39 [a] Luke 15:2 [1] *invited*
7:40 [1] *Teacher*
7:41 [a] Matt. 18:28; Mark 6:37 [1] Gr. *denarii*
7:42 [1] *repay* [2] *freely*
7:44 [a] Gen. 18:4; 19:2; 43:24; Judg. 19:21; 1 Tim. 5:10
7:45 [a] Rom. 16:16
7:46 [a] 2 Sam. 12:20; Ps. 23:5; Eccl. 9:8; Dan. 10:3 [1] *fragrant oil*
7:47 [a] [1 Tim. 1:14]
7:48 [a] Matt. 9:2; Mark 2:5
7:49 [a] Matt. 9:3; [Mark 2:7]; Luke 5:21 [1] *at the table*
7:50 [a] Matt. 9:22; Mark 5:34; 10:52; Luke 8:48; 18:42
8:1 [1] *proclaiming the good news*
8:2 [a] Matt. 27:55; Mark 15:40, 41; Luke 23:49, 55 [b] Matt. 27:56; Mark 16:9 [1] *sicknesses* [x] *demons*
8:3 [1] *provided* [2] *possessions*
8:4 [a] Matt. 13:2–9; Mark 4:1–9 [1] *a great multitude*
8:5 [1] *trampled*
8:8 [a] Matt. 11:15; Mark 7:16; Luke 14:35; Rev. 2:7, 11, 17, 29; 3:6, 13, 22; 13:9
8:9 [a] Matt. 13:10–23; Mark 4:10–20 [1] *mean*
8:10 [a] Is. 6:9; Matt. 13:14; Acts 28:26 [1] *Veiled or hidden teachings*
8:11 [a] Matt. 13:18; Mark 4:14; [1 Pet. 1:23] [b] Luke 5:1; 11:28
8:13 [1] *testing*
8:14 [a] Matt. 19:23; 1 Tim. 6:9, 10 [1] *maturity*
8:15 [a] [Rom. 2:7; Heb. 10:36–39; James 5:7, 8] [1] *a noble*
8:16 [a] Matt. 5:15; Mark 4:21; Luke 11:33 [b] Matt. 5:14 [1] *lamp* [2] *lampstand*
8:17 [a] Matt. 10:26; Luke 12:2; [1 Cor. 4:5] [b] [Eccl. 12:14;
2 Cor. 5:10] [1] *revealed* [2] *to light* 8:18 [a] Matt. 25:29 [b] Matt. 13:12

19 [a]Then came to him *his* mother and his [1]brethren, and could not come at him for the [2]press.

20 And it was told him *by certain* which said, Thy mother and thy brethren stand [1]without, desiring to see thee.

21 And he answered and said unto them, My mother and my brethren are these which hear the word of God, and do it.

22 [a]Now it came to pass on a certain day, that he went into a ship with his disciples: and he said unto them, Let us go over unto the other side of the lake. And they launched forth.

23 But as they sailed he fell asleep: and there came down a storm of wind on the lake; and they were [1]filled *with water,* and were in jeopardy.

24 And they came to him, and awoke him, saying, Master, master, we perish. Then he arose, and rebuked the wind and the raging of the water: and they ceased, and there was a calm.

25 And he said unto them, [a]Where is your faith? And they being afraid [1]wondered, saying one to another, [b]What manner of man is this! for he commandeth even the winds and water, and they obey him.

26 [a]And they [1]arrived at the country of the Gadarenes, which is [2]over against Galilee.

27 And when he went forth to land, there met him out of the city a certain man, which had [1]devils long time, and [2]ware no clothes, neither abode in *any* house, but in the tombs.

28 When he saw Jesus, he [a]cried out, and fell down before him, and with a loud voice said, [b]What have I to do with thee, Jesus, [c]*thou* Son of God most high? I [1]beseech thee, torment me not.

29 (For he had commanded the unclean spirit to come out of the man. For oftentimes it had [1]caught him: and he was kept bound with chains and [2]in fetters; and he brake the bands, and was driven of the [3]devil into the wilderness.)

30 And Jesus asked him, saying, What is thy name? And he said, Legion: because many [1]devils were entered into him.

31 And they [1]besought him that he would not command them to go out [a]into the [2]deep.

32 And there was there an herd of many [a]swine feeding on the mountain: and they [1]besought him that he would [2]suffer them to enter into them. And he [3]suffered them.

33 Then went the [1]devils out of the man, and entered into the swine: and the herd ran violently down a steep place into the lake, and [2]were choked.

34 When they that fed *them* saw what was done, they fled, and went and told *it* in the city and in the country.

35 Then they went out to see what was done; and came to Jesus, and found the man, out of whom the [1]devils were departed, [a]sitting at the [b]feet of Jesus, clothed, and in his [c]right mind: and they were afraid.

36 They also which saw *it* told them by what means he that was possessed of the devils was healed.

37 [a]Then the whole multitude of the country of the Gadarenes round about [b]besought[1] him to [c]depart from them; for they were [2]taken with great [d]fear: and he went up into the ship, and returned back again.

38 Now [a]the man out of whom the devils were departed [b]besought him that he might be with him: but Jesus sent him away, saying,

39 Return to thine own house, and shew how great things God hath done unto thee. And he went his way, and [1]published throughout the whole city how great things Jesus had done unto him.

40 And it came to pass, that, when Jesus was returned, the people *gladly* received him: for they were all waiting for him.

41 [a]And, behold, there came a man named Jairus, and he was a ruler of the synagogue: and he fell down at Jesus' feet, and [1]besought him that he would come into his house:

42 For he had one only daughter, about twelve years of age, and she lay [a]a dying. But as he went the [1]people thronged him.

43 [a]And a woman having [1]an [b]issue of blood twelve years, which had spent all her [2]living upon physicians, neither could be healed of any,

44 Came behind *him,* and [a]touched the border of his garment: and immediately her [1]issue of blood [2]stanched.

45 And Jesus said, Who touched me? When all denied, Peter and they that were with him said, Master, the multitude throng thee and press *thee,* and sayest thou, Who touched me?

46 And Jesus said, Somebody hath touched me: for I perceive that [a]virtue[1] is gone out of me.

47 And when the woman saw that she was not hid, she came trembling, and falling down before him, she declared unto him before all the people for what cause she had touched him, and how she was healed immediately.

48 And he said unto her, Daughter, be of good [1]comfort: [a]thy faith hath made thee [2]whole; [b]go in peace.

49 [a]While he yet spake, there cometh one from the ruler of the synagogue's *house,* saying to him, Thy

---

**Cross-references (center column):**

8:19 [a] Ps. 69:8; Matt. 12:46–50; Mark 3:31–35
[1] brothers
[2] crowd

8:20 [1] outside

8:22 [a] Matt. 8:23–27; Mark 4:36–41

8:23 [1] filling

8:25 [a] Luke 9:41
[b] Luke 4:36; 5:26
[1] marvelled

8:26 [a] Matt. 8:28–34; Mark 5:1–17 [1] sailed to
[2] opposite

8:27 [1] demons
[2] wore

8:28 [a] Mark 1:26; 9:26 [b] Mark 1:23, 24 [c] Luke 4:41
[1] beg

8:29 [1] seized
[2] shackles
[3] demon

8:30 [1] demons

8:31 [a] Rom. 10:7; [Rev. 20:1, 3]
[1] begged [2] Lit. abyss

8:32 [a] Lev. 11:7; Deut. 14:8
[1] begged [2] allow
[3] allowed

8:33 [1] demons
[2] drowned

8:35 [a] [Matt. 11:28] [b] Matt. 28:9; Mark 7:25; Luke 10:39; 17:16; John 11:32 [c] [2 Tim. 1:7]
[1] demons

8:37 [a] Matt. 8:34 [b] Mark 1:24; Luke 4:34 [c] Job 21:14; Acts 16:39 [d] Luke 5:26 [1] asked
[2] seized

8:38 [a] Mark 5:18–20 [1] begged

8:39 [1] proclaimed

8:41 [a] Matt. 9:18–26; Mark 5:22–43 [1] begged

8:42 [a] Luke 7:2 [1] multitudes

8:43 [a] Matt. 9:20 [b] Luke 15:19–22 [1] a flow [2] livelihood

8:44 [a] Mark 6:56; Luke 5:13 [1] flow [2] stopped

8:46 [a] Mark 5:30; Luke 6:19 [1] power

8:48 [a] Mark 5:34; Luke 7:50 [b] John 8:11 [1] cheer [2] well

8:49 [a] Mark 5:35

daughter is dead; trouble not the [1]Master.

50 But when Jesus heard *it,* he answered him, saying, Fear not: [a]believe only, and she shall be made whole.

51 And when he came into the house, he [1]suffered no man to go in, [2]save Peter, and James, and John, and the father and the mother of the maiden.

52 And all wept, and [1]bewailed her: but he said, [a]Weep not; she is not dead, [b]but sleepeth.

53 And they laughed him to scorn, knowing that she was dead.

54 And he put them all out, and took her by the hand, and called, saying, Maid, [a]arise.

55 And her spirit came again, and she arose straightway: and he commanded to give her [1]meat.

56 And her parents were astonished: but [a]he charged them that they should tell no man what was done.

## CHAPTER 9

THEN [a]he called his twelve disciples together, and [b]gave them power and authority over all [1]devils, and to cure diseases.

2 And [a]he sent them to preach the kingdom of God, and to heal the sick.

3 [a]And he said unto them, Take nothing for *your* journey, neither [1]staves, nor [2]scrip, neither bread, neither money; neither have two [3]coats apiece.

4 [a]And whatsoever house ye enter into, there abide, and thence depart.

5 [a]And whosoever will not receive you, when ye go out of that city, [b]shake off the very dust from your feet for a testimony against them.

6 [a]And they departed, and went through the towns, preaching the gospel, and healing every where.

7 [a]Now Herod the tetrarch heard of all that was done by him: and he was perplexed, because that it was said of some, that John was risen from the dead;

8 And of some, that Elias had appeared; and of others, that one of the old prophets was risen again.

9 And Herod said, John have I beheaded: but who is this, of whom I hear such things? [a]And he [1]desired to see him.

10 [a]And the apostles, when they were returned, told him all that they had done. [b]And he took them, and went aside privately into a [1]desert place belonging to the city called Bethsaida.

11 And the [1]people, when they knew *it,* followed him: and he received them, and spake unto them

of the kingdom of God, and healed them that had need of healing.

12 [a]And when the day began to [1]wear away, then came the twelve, and said unto him, Send the multitude away, that they may go into the towns and country round about, and lodge, and get [2]victuals: for we are here in a [3]desert place.

13 But he said unto them, [1]Give ye them to eat. And they said, We have no more but five loaves and two fishes; except we should go and buy [2]meat for all this people.

14 For they were about five thousand men. And he said to his disciples, Make them sit down by fifties in a [1]company.

15 And they did so, and made them all sit down.

16 Then he took the five loaves and the two fishes, and looking up to heaven, he [a]blessed them, and brake, and gave to the disciples to set before the multitude.

17 And they did eat, and were all [1]filled: and there was taken up of fragments that remained to them twelve baskets.

18 [a]And it came to pass, as he was alone praying, his disciples were with him: and he asked them, saying, Whom say the [1]people that I am?

19 They answering said, [a]John the Baptist; but some *say,* Elias; and others *say,* that one of the old prophets is risen again.

20 He said unto them, But whom say ye that I am? [a]Peter answering said, The Christ of God.

21 [a]And he [1]straitly charged them, and commanded *them* to tell no man that thing;

22 Saying, [a]The Son of man must suffer many things, and be rejected of the elders and chief priests and scribes, and be slain, and be raised the third day.

23 [a]And he said to *them* all, If any *man* [1]will come after me, let him deny himself, and take up his cross daily, and follow me.

24 [a]For whosoever [1]will save his life shall lose it: but whosoever [2]will lose his life for my sake, the same shall save it.

25 [a]For what is a man [1]advantaged, if he gain the whole world, and [2]lose himself, or [3]be cast away?

26 [a]For whosoever shall be ashamed of me and of my words, of him shall the Son of man be [b]ashamed, when he shall come in his own glory, and *in his* Father's, and of the holy angels.

27 [a]But I tell you of a truth, there be some standing here, which shall not taste of death, till they see the kingdom of God.

### Center column references

8:49 [1] *Teacher*
8:50 [a] [Mark 11:22–24]
8:51 [1] *permitted* [2] *except*
8:52 [a] Luke 7:13 [b] [John 11:11, 13] [1] *mourned for*
8:54 [a] Luke 7:14; John 11:43
8:55 [1] *food*
8:56 [a] Matt. 8:4; 9:30; Mark 5:43
9:1 [a] Matt. 10:1, 2; Mark 3:13; 6:7 [b] Mark 16:17, 18; [John 14:12] [1] *demons*
9:2 [a] Matt. 10:7, 8; Mark 6:12; Luke 10:1, 9
9:3 [a] Matt. 10:9–15; Mark 6:8–11; Luke 10:4–12; 22:35 [1] *staffs* [2] *bag* [3] *tunics*
9:4 [a] Matt. 10:11; Mark 6:10
9:5 [a] Matt. 10:14 [b] Luke 10:11; Acts 13:51
9:6 [a] Mark 6:12; Luke 8:1
9:7 [a] Matt. 14:1, 2; Mark 6:14
9:9 [a] Luke 23:8 [1] *sought*
9:10 [a] Mark 6:30 [b] Matt. 14:13 [1] *deserted*
9:11 [1] *multitudes*

9:12 [a] Matt. 14:15; Mark 6:35; John 6:1, 5 [1] *decline* [2] *provisions* [3] *deserted*
9:13 [1] *You give* [2] *food*
9:14 [1] *group*
9:16 [a] Luke 22:19; 24:30
9:17 [1] *satisfied*
9:18 [a] Matt. 16:13–16 [1] *crowds*
9:19 [a] Matt. 14:2
9:20 [a] John 6:68, 69
9:21 [a] Matt. 8:4; 16:20 [1] *strictly warned*
9:22 [a] Matt. 16:21; 17:22
9:23 [a] Matt. 10:38; 16:24 [1] *desires to*
9:24 [a] [John 12:25] [1] *desires to* [2] *loses*
9:25 [a] Mark 8:36 [1] *benefited* [2] *is destroyed* [3] *lost*
9:26 [a] [Rom. 1:16] [b] Matt. 10:33
9:27 [a] Matt. 16:28

28 ᵃAnd it came to pass about an eight days after these sayings, he took Peter and John and James, and went up into a mountain to pray.

29 And as he prayed, the ¹fashion of his countenance was altered, and his ²raiment *was* white *and* ³glistering.

30 And, behold, there talked with him two men, which were ᵃMoses and ᵇElias:

31 Who appeared in glory, and spake of his ¹decease which he ²should accomplish at Jerusalem.

32 But Peter and they that were with him ᵃwere heavy with sleep: and when they ¹were awake, they saw his glory, and the two men that stood with him.

33 And it came to pass, as they departed from him, Peter said unto Jesus, Master, it is good for us to be here: and let us make three ¹tabernacles; one for thee, and one for Moses, and one for Elias: not knowing what he said.

34 While he thus spake, there came a cloud, and overshadowed them: and they feared as they entered into the ᵃcloud.

35 And there came a voice out of the cloud, saying, ᵃThis is my beloved Son: ᵇhear him.

36 And when the voice ¹was past, Jesus was found alone. ᵃAnd they kept *it* ²close, and told no man in those days any of those things which they had seen.

37 ᵃAnd it came to pass, that on the next day, when they were come down from the hill, ¹much people met him.

38 And, behold, a man of the ¹company cried out, saying, ²Master, I ³beseech thee, look upon my son: for he is mine only child.

39 And, lo, a spirit ¹taketh him, and he suddenly crieth out; and it ²teareth him ³that he foameth again, and bruising him ⁴hardly departeth from him.

40 And I ¹besought thy disciples to cast him out; and they could not.

41 And Jesus answering said, O ¹faithless and ²perverse generation, how long shall I be with you, and ³suffer you? Bring thy son hither.

42 And as he was yet a coming, the ¹devil threw him down, and ²tare *him*. And Jesus rebuked the unclean spirit, and healed the child, and delivered him again to his father.

43 And they were all amazed at the ¹mighty power of God. But while they wondered every one at all things which Jesus did, he said unto his disciples,

44 ᵃLet these sayings sink down into your ears: for the Son of man shall be delivered into the hands of men.

45 ᵃBut they understood not this saying, and it was hid from them,

that they perceived it not: and they feared to ask him of that saying.

46 ᵃThen there arose a ¹reasoning among them, which of them should be greatest.

47 And Jesus, ᵃperceiving the thought of their heart, took a ᵇchild, and set him ¹by him,

48 And said unto them, ᵃWhosoever shall receive this child in my name receiveth me: and ᵇwhosoever shall receive me ᶜreceiveth him that sent me: ᵈfor he that is least among you all, the same shall be great.

49 ᵃAnd John answered and said, Master, we saw one casting out ¹devils in thy name; and we forbad him, because he followeth not with us.

50 And Jesus said unto him, Forbid *him* not: for ᵃhe that is not against us is for us.

51 And it came to pass, when the time was come that ᵃhe should be received up, he stedfastly set his face to go to Jerusalem,

52 And sent messengers before his face: and they went, and entered into a village of the Samaritans, to make ready for him.

53 And ᵃthey did not receive him, because his face was ¹as though he would go to Jerusalem.

54 And when his disciples ᵃJames and John saw *this*, they said, Lord, wilt thou that we command fire to come down from heaven, and consume them, even as ᵇElias did?

55 But he turned, and rebuked them, and said, Ye know not what manner of ᵃspirit ye are of.

56 For ᵃthe Son of man is not come to destroy men's lives, but to save *them*. And they went to another village.

57 ᵃAnd it came to pass, that, as they went in the way, a certain *man* said unto him, Lord, I will follow thee whithersoever thou goest.

58 And Jesus said unto him, Foxes have holes, and birds of the air *have* nests; but the Son of man ᵃhath ¹not where to lay *his* head.

59 ᵃAnd he said unto another, Follow me. But he said, Lord, ¹suffer me first to go and bury my father.

60 Jesus said unto him, Let the dead bury their dead: but go thou and preach the kingdom of God.

61 And another also said, Lord, ᵃI will follow thee; but let me first go bid them farewell, which are at home at my house.

62 And Jesus said unto him, No man, having put his hand to the plough, and looking back, is ᵃfit for the kingdom of God.

## CHAPTER 10

AFTER these things the Lord appointed other seventy also, and

### Cross references (center column)

9:28 ᵃ Mark 9:2–8
9:29 ¹ *appearance of his face* ² *robe* ³ *glistening*
9:30 ᵃ Heb. 11:23–29 ᵇ 2 Kin. 2:1–11
9:31 ¹ *Death*, lit. *departure* ² *was about to*
9:32 ᵃ Dan. 8:18; 10:9 ¹ *were fully awake*
9:33 ¹ *Temporary dwellings*
9:34 ᵃ Ex. 13:21
9:35 ᵃ [Matt. 3:17; 12:18] ᵇ Acts 3:22
9:36 ᵃ Matt. 17:9 ¹ *had ceased* ² *quiet*
9:37 ᵃ Mark 9:14–27 ¹ *a great multitude*
9:38 ¹ *multitude* ² *Teacher* ³ *beg*
9:39 ¹ *seizes* ² *convulses* ³ *so that he foams* at the mouth ⁴ *with great difficulty departs*
9:40 ¹ *implored*
9:41 ¹ *unbelieving* ² *perverted* ³ *bear with*
9:42 ¹ *demon* ² *convulsed*
9:43 ¹ *majesty*
9:44 ᵃ Matt. 17:22
9:45 ᵃ Mark 9:32

¹ *so that*

9:46 ᵃ Matt. 18:1–5 ¹ *dispute*
9:47 ᵃ Matt. 9:4 ᵇ Luke 18:17 ¹ *beside*
9:48 ᵃ Matt. 18:5 ᵇ John 12:44 ᶜ John 13:20 ᵈ Eph. 3:8
9:49 ᵃ Mark 9:38–40 ¹ *demons*
9:50 ᵃ Luke 11:23
9:51 ᵃ Mark 16:19
9:53 ᵃ John 4:4, 9 ¹ *set to journey to*
9:54 ᵃ Matt 3:17 ᵇ 2 Kin. 1:10, 12
9:55 ᵃ [2 Tim. 1:7]
9:56 ᵃ John 3:17; 12:47
9:57 ᵃ Matt. 8:19–22
9:58 ᵃ Luke 2:7; 8:23 ¹ *nowhere*
9:59 ᵃ Matt. 8:21, 22 ¹ *allow*
9:61 ᵃ 1 Kin. 19:20
9:62 ᵃ 2 Tim. 4:10

[a]sent them two [1]and two before his face into every city and place, whither he himself [2]would come.

2 Therefore said he unto them, [a]The harvest truly *is* great, but the labourers *are* few: [b]pray ye therefore the Lord of the harvest, that he would send forth labourers into his harvest.

3 Go your ways: [a]behold, I send you forth as lambs among wolves.

4 [a]Carry neither purse, nor [1]scrip, nor [2]shoes: and [b]salute[3] no man [4]by the way.

5 [a]And into whatsoever house ye enter, first say, Peace *be* to this house.

6 And if [1]the son of peace be there, your peace shall rest upon it: if not, it shall turn to you again.

7 [a]And in the same house remain, [b]eating and drinking such things as they give: for [c]the labourer is worthy of his [1]hire. Go not from house to house.

8 And into whatsoever city ye enter, and they receive you, eat such things as are set before you:

9 [a]And heal the sick that are therein, and say unto them, [b]The kingdom of God is come [1]nigh unto you.

10 But into whatsoever city ye enter, and they receive you not, go your ways out into the streets of the same, and say,

11 [a]Even the very dust of your city, which [1]cleaveth on us, we do wipe off against you: notwithstanding be ye sure of this, that the kingdom of God [2]is come nigh unto you.

12 But I say unto you, that [a]it shall be more tolerable in that day for Sodom, than for that city.

13 [a]Woe unto thee, Chorazin! woe unto thee, Bethsaida! [b]for if the mighty works had been done in Tyre and Sidon, which have been done in you, they [1]had a great while ago repented, sitting in sackcloth and ashes.

14 But it shall be more tolerable for Tyre and Sidon at the judgment, than for you.

15 [a]And thou, Capernaum, which art [b]exalted to heaven, [c]shalt be thrust down to [1]hell.

16 [a]He that heareth you heareth me; and [b]he that [1]despiseth you [1]despiseth me; [c]and he that [1]despiseth me [1]despiseth him that sent me.

17 And [a]the seventy returned again with joy, saying, Lord, even the [1]devils are subject unto us through thy name.

18 And he said unto them, [a]I beheld Satan as lightning fall from heaven.

19 Behold, [a]I give unto you [1]power to [2]tread on serpents and scorpions, and over all the power of the enemy: and nothing shall by any means hurt you.

20 Notwithstanding in this rejoice not, that the spirits are subject unto you; but rather rejoice, because [a]your names are written in heaven.

21 [a]In that hour Jesus rejoiced in [1]spirit, and said, I thank thee, O Father, Lord of heaven and earth, that thou hast hid these things from the wise and prudent, and hast revealed them unto babes: even so, Father; for so it seemed good in thy sight.

22 [a]All things are delivered to me of my Father: and [b]no man knoweth who the Son is, but the Father; and who the Father is, but the Son, and *he* to whom the Son [1]will reveal *him*.

23 And he [1]turned him unto *his* disciples, and said privately, [a]Blessed *are* the eyes which see the things that ye see:

24 For I tell you, [a]that many prophets and kings have desired to see those things which ye see, and have not seen *them;* and to hear those things which ye hear, and have not heard *them*.

25 And, behold, a certain [1]lawyer stood up, and [2]tempted him, saying, [a]Master,[3] what shall I do to inherit eternal life?

26 He said unto him, What is written in the law? how readest thou?

27 And he answering said, [a]Thou shalt love the Lord thy God with all thy heart, and with all thy soul, and with all thy strength, and with all thy mind; and [b]thy neighbour as thyself.

28 And he said unto him, Thou hast answered right: this do, and [a]thou shalt live.

29 But he, [1]willing to [a]justify himself, said unto Jesus, And who is my neighbour?

30 And Jesus answering said, A certain *man* went down from Jerusalem to Jericho, and fell among [1]thieves, which stripped him of his [2]raiment, and wounded *him,* and departed, leaving *him* half dead.

31 And by chance there came down a certain priest that way: and when he saw him, [a]he passed by on the other side.

32 And likewise a Levite, when he was at the place, came and looked *on him,* and passed by on the other side.

33 But a certain [a]Samaritan, as he journeyed, came where he was: and when he saw him, he had [b]compassion *on him,*

34 And went to *him,* and [1]bound up his wounds, pouring in oil and wine, and set him on his own beast, and brought him to an inn, and took care of him.

35 And on the [1]morrow when he departed, he took out two [a]pence,[2] and

---

**Center column references:**

10:1 [a] Mark 6:7 [1] *by* [2] *was about to go*
10:2 [a] John 4:35 [b] 2 Thess. 3:1
10:3 [a] Matt. 10:16
10:4 [a] Luke 9:3–5 [b] 2 Kin. 4:29 [1] *bag* [2] *sandals* [3] *greet* [4] *along the road*
10:5 [a] Matt. 10:12
10:6 [1] Many mss. *a son*
10:7 [a] Matt. 10:11 [b] 1 Cor. 10:27 [c] 1 Tim. 5:18 [1] *wages*
10:9 [a] Mark 3:15 [b] Matt. 3:2; 10:7 [1] *near to*
10:11 [a] Acts 13:51 [1] *clings to* [2] *has come near*
10:12 [a] Matt. 10:15; 11:24
10:13 [a] Matt. 11:21–23 [b] Ezek. 3:6 [1] *would have*
10:15 [a] Matt. 11:23 [b] Is. 14:13–15 [c] Ezek. 26:20 [1] Gr. *hades*
10:16 [a] John 13:20 [b] 1 Thess. 4:8 [c] John 5:23 [1] *rejects*
10:17 [a] Luke 10:1 [1] *demons*
10:18 [a] John 12:31
10:19 [a] Mark 16:18 [1] *authority* [2] *trample*
10:20 [a] [Ex. 32:32, 33]; Ps. 69:28; Is. 4:3; Dan. 12:1; Phil. 4:3; Heb. 12:23; Rev. 13:8
10:21 [a] Matt. 11:25–27 [1] *the Spirit*
10:22 [a] Matt. 28:18; John 3:35; 5:27; 17:2 [b] [John 1:18; 6:44, 46] [1] *wills to reveal*
10:23 [a] Matt. 13:16, 17 [1] *turned to*
10:24 [a] 1 Pet. 1:10, 11
10:25 [a] Matt. 19:16–19; 22:35 [1] *expert in the law* [2] *tested* [3] *Teacher*
10:27 [a] Deut. 6:5 [b] Lev. 19:18; Matt. 19:19
10:28 [a] Lev. 18:5; Neh. 9:29; Ezek. 20:11, 13, 21; Matt. 19:17; Rom. 10:5
10:29 [a] Luke 16:15 [1] *wanting*
10:30 [1] *robbers* [2] *clothing*
10:31 [a] Ps. 38:11
10:33 [a] John 4:9
[b] Luke 15:20   10:34 [1] *bandaged*   10:35 [a] Matt. 20:2
[1] *next day* [2] Gr. *denarii*

---

gave *them* to the ³host, and said unto him, Take care of him; and whatsoever thou spendest more, when I come again, I will repay thee.

36 Which now of these three, thinkest thou, was neighbour unto him that fell among the ¹thieves?

37 And he said, He that shewed mercy on him. Then said Jesus unto him,ª Go, and do thou likewise.

38 Now it came to pass, as they went, that he entered into a certain village; and a certain woman named ªMartha ¹received him into her house.

39 And she had a sister called Mary, ªwhich also ᵇsat at Jesus' feet, and heard his word.

40 But Martha was ¹cumbered about much serving, and came to him, and said, Lord, dost thou not care that my sister hath left me to serve alone? ²bid her therefore that she help me.

41 And Jesus answered and said unto her, Martha, Martha, thou art ¹careful and troubled about many things:

42 But ªone thing is needful: and Mary hath chosen that good part, which shall not be taken away from her.

## CHAPTER 11

A ND it came to pass, that, as he was praying in a certain place, when he ceased, one of his disciples said unto him, Lord, teach us to pray, as John also taught his disciples.

2 And he said unto them, When ye pray, say, ªOur Father which art in heaven, Hallowed be thy name. Thy kingdom come. Thy will be done, as in heaven, so in earth.

3 Give us day by day our daily bread.

4 And ªforgive us our sins; for we also forgive every one that is indebted to us. And lead us not into temptation; but deliver us from ¹evil.

5 And he said unto them, Which of you shall have a friend, and shall go unto him at midnight, and say unto him, Friend, lend me three loaves;

6 For a friend of mine in his journey is come to me, and I have nothing to set before him?

7 And he from within shall answer and say, Trouble me not: the door is now shut, and my children are with me in bed; I cannot rise and give thee.

8 I say unto you, ªThough he will not rise and give him, because he is his friend, yet because of his ¹importunity he will rise and give him as many as he needeth.

9 ªAnd I say unto you, Ask, and it shall be given you; ᵇseek, and ye shall find; knock, and it shall be opened unto you.

10 For every one that asketh receiveth; and he that seeketh findeth;

and to him that knocketh it shall be opened.

11 ªIf a son shall ask bread of any of you that is a father, will he give him a stone? or if *he ask* a fish, will he for a fish give him a serpent?

12 Or if he shall ask an egg, will he ¹offer him a scorpion?

13 If ye then, being evil, know how to give ªgood gifts unto your children: how much more shall *your* heavenly Father give the Holy Spirit to them that ask him?

14 ªAnd he was casting out a ¹devil, and it was ²dumb. And it came to pass, when the ¹devil was gone out, the ²dumb spake; and the ³people wondered.

15 But some of them said, ªHe casteth out ¹devils through ²Beelzebub the ³chief of the devils.

16 And others, ¹tempting *him,* ªsought of him a sign from heaven.

17 ªBut ᵇhe, knowing their thoughts, said unto them, Every kingdom divided against itself is brought to desolation; and a house *divided* against a house falleth.

18 If Satan also be divided against himself, how shall his kingdom stand? because ye say that I cast out ¹devils through Beelzebub.

19 And if I by Beelzebub cast out ¹devils, by whom do your sons cast *them* out? therefore shall they be your judges.

20 But if I ªwith the finger of God cast out devils, no doubt the kingdom of God is come upon you.

21 ªWhen a strong man ¹armed ²keepeth his ³palace, his goods are in peace:

22 But ªwhen a stronger than he shall come upon him, and overcome him, he taketh from him all his armour wherein he trusted, and divideth his ¹spoils.

23 ªHe that is not with me is against me: and he that gathereth not with me scattereth.

24 ªWhen the unclean spirit is gone out of a man, he walketh through dry places, seeking rest; and finding none, he saith, I will return unto my house whence I came out.

25 And when he cometh, he findeth *it* swept and ¹garnished.

26 Then goeth he, and taketh ¹*to him* seven other spirits more wicked than himself; and they enter in, and dwell there: and ªthe last *state* of that man is worse than the first.

27 And it came to pass, as he spake these things, a certain woman of the ¹company lifted up her voice, and said unto him, ªBlessed *is* the womb that bare thee, and the ²paps which thou hast sucked.

28 But he said, ¹Yea ªrather, blessed

---

**Center column references:**

10:35 ³ *innkeeper*
10:36 ¹ *robbers*
10:37 ª Prov. 14:21; [Matt. 9:13; 12:7]
10:38 ª John 11:1; 12:2, 3 ¹ *welcomed*
10:39 ª [1 Cor. 7:32–40] ᵇ Luke 8:35; Acts 22:3
10:40 ¹ *distracted with* ² *tell*
10:41 ¹ *worried*
10:42 ª [Ps. 27:4; John 6:27]
11:2 ª Matt. 6:9–13
11:4 ª [Eph. 4:32] ¹ *the evil one*
11:8 ª [Luke 18:1–5] ¹ *persistence*
11:9 ª [John 15:7] ᵇ Is. 55:6

11:11 ª Matt. 7:9
11:12 ¹ *give*
11:13 ª James 1:17
11:14 ª Matt. 9:32–34; 12:22, 24 ¹ *demon* ² *mute* ³ *multitudes marvelled*
11:15 ª Matt. 9:34; 12:24 ¹ *demons* ² Gr. *Beelzebul* ³ *ruler*
11:16 ª Matt. 12:38; 16:1 ¹ *testing*
11:17 ª Matt. 12:25–29 ᵇ John 2:25
11:18 ¹ *demons*
11:19 ¹ *demons*
11:20 ª Ex. 8:19
11:21 ª Mark 3:27 ¹ *fully armed* ² *guards* ³ *estate*
11:22 ª [Is. 53:12] ¹ *plunder*
11:23 ª Matt. 12:30
11:24 ª Matt. 12:43–45
11:25 ¹ *put in order*
11:26 ª [2 Pet. 2:20] ¹ *With*
11:27 ª Luke 1:28, 48 ¹ *crowd* ² *breasts which nursed you*
11:28 ª [Luke 8:21] ¹ *More than that*

*are* they that hear the word of God, and keep it.

29 [a]And when the [1]people were gathered thick together, he began to say, This is an evil generation: they seek a [b]sign; and there shall no sign be given it, but the sign of Jonas the prophet.

30 For as [a]Jonas was a sign unto the Ninevites, so shall also the Son of man be to this generation.

31 [a]The queen of the south shall rise up in the judgment with the men of this generation, and condemn them: for she came from the utmost parts of the earth to hear the wisdom of Solomon; and, behold, a [b]greater than Solomon *is* here.

32 The men of Nineve shall rise up in the judgment with this generation, and shall condemn it: for [a]they repented at the preaching of Jonas; and, behold, a greater than Jonas *is* here.

33 [a]No man, when he hath lighted a [1]candle, putteth *it* in a secret place, neither under a [b]bushel, but on a [2]candlestick, that they which come in may see the light.

34 [a]The [1]light of the body is the eye: therefore when thine eye is [2]single, thy whole body also is full of light; but when *thine eye* is [3]evil, thy body also *is* full of darkness.

35 Take heed therefore that the light which is in thee be not darkness.

36 If thy whole body therefore *be* full of light, having no part dark, the whole shall be full of light, as when the bright shining of a [1]candle doth give thee light.

37 And as he spake, a certain Pharisee [1]besought him to dine with him: and he went in, and sat down [2]to meat.

38 And [a]when the Pharisee saw *it*, he marvelled that he had not first washed before dinner.

39 [a]And the Lord said unto him, Now do ye Pharisees make clean the outside of the cup and the platter; but [b]your inward part is full of [1]ravening and wickedness.

40 *Ye* fools, did not [a]he that made that which is [1]without make that which is within also?

41 [a]But rather give alms of [1]such things as ye have; and, behold, all things are clean unto you.

42 [a]But woe unto you, Pharisees! for ye tithe mint and rue and all manner of herbs, and [b]pass over [1]judgment and the [c]love of God: these ought ye to have done, and not to leave the other undone.

43 [a]Woe unto you, Pharisees! for ye love the [1]uppermost seats in the synagogues, and greetings in the markets.

44 [a]Woe unto you, scribes and Pharisees, hypocrites! [b]for ye are as graves which [1]appear not, and the men that walk over *them* are not aware *of them.*

45 Then answered one of the [1]lawyers, and said unto him, [2]Master, thus saying thou reproachest us also.

46 And he said, Woe unto you also, *ye* lawyers! [a]for ye [1]lade men with burdens [2]grievous to be borne, and ye yourselves touch not the burdens with one of your fingers.

47 [a]Woe unto you! for ye build the sepulchres of the prophets, and your fathers killed them.

48 Truly ye bear witness that ye [1]allow the deeds of your fathers: for they indeed killed them, and ye build their sepulchres.

49 Therefore also said the wisdom of God, [a]I will send them prophets and apostles, and *some* of them they shall slay and persecute:

50 That the blood of all the prophets, which was shed from the foundation of the world, may be required of this generation;

51 [a]From the blood of Abel unto [b]the blood of Zacharias, which perished between the altar and the temple: verily I say unto you, It shall be required of this generation.

52 [a]Woe unto you, [1]lawyers! for ye have taken away the [1]key of knowledge: ye entered not in yourselves, and them that were entering in ye hindered.

53 And as he said these things unto them, the scribes and the Pharisees began to [1]urge *him* vehemently, and to [2]provoke him to speak of many things:

54 Laying wait for him, and [a]seeking to catch something out of his mouth, that they might accuse him.

## CHAPTER 12

IN [a]the mean time, when there were gathered together an innumerable multitude of people, insomuch that they [1]trode one upon another, he began to say unto his disciples first of all, [b]Beware ye of the [2]leaven of the Pharisees, which is hypocrisy.

2 [a]For there is nothing covered, that shall not be revealed; neither hid, that shall not be known.

3 Therefore whatsoever ye have spoken in darkness shall be heard in the light; and that which ye have spoken in the ear in [1]closets shall be proclaimed upon the housetops.

4 [a]And I say unto you [b]my friends, Be not afraid of them that kill the body, and after that have no more that they can do.

5 But I will forewarn you whom ye shall fear: Fear him, which after he

### Center references

11:29 [a] Matt. 12:38–42 [b] 1 Cor. 1:22 [1] *multitudes*

11:30 [a] Jon. 1:17; 2:10; 3:3–10

11:31 [a] 1 Kin. 10:1–9 [b] [Rom. 9:5]

11:32 [a] Jon. 3:5

11:33 [a] Mark 4:21 [b] Matt. 5:15 [1] *lamp* [2] *lampstand*

11:34 [a] Matt. 6:22, 23 [1] *lamp* [2] *good or clear* [3] *bad*

11:36 [1] *lamp*

11:37 [1] *asked* [2] *at the table*

11:38 [a] Mark 7:2, 3

11:39 [a] Matt. 23:25 [b] Titus 1:15 [1] *grasping or robbery*

11:40 [a] Gen. 1:26, 27 [1] *outside*

11:41 [a] [Luke 12:33; 16:9] [1] *Or what is inside*

11:42 [a] Matt. 23:23 [b] [Mic. 6:7, 8] [c] John 5:42 [1] *justice*

11:43 [a] Mark 12:38, 39 [1] *best, lit. first*

11:44 [a] Matt. 23:27 [b] Ps. 5:9 [1] *are not seen*

11:45 [1] *experts in the law* [2] *Teacher*

11:46 [a] Matt. 23:4 [1] *load* [2] *heavy to bear*

11:47 [a] Matt. 23:29

11:48 [1] *approve*

11:49 [a] Matt. 23:34

11:51 [a] Gen. 4:8 [b] 2 Chr. 24:20, 21

11:52 [a] Matt. 23:13 [1] *experts in the law*

11:53 [1] *assail* [2] *interrogate him about*

11:54 [a] Mark 12:13

12:1 [a] Mark 8:15 [b] Matt. 16:12 [1] *trampled* [2] *yeast*

12:2 [a] Matt. 10:26; [1 Cor. 4:5]

12:3 [1] *inner rooms*

12:4 [a] Is. 51:7, 8, 12, 13 [b] [John 15:13–15]

hath killed hath power to cast into [1]hell; yea, I say unto you, [a]Fear him.

6 Are not five sparrows sold for two [1]farthings, and [a]not one of them is forgotten before God?

7 But even the very hairs of your head are all numbered. Fear not therefore: ye are of more value than many sparrows.

8 [a]Also I say unto you, Whosoever shall confess me [b]before men, him shall the Son of man also confess before the angels of God:

9 But he that [a]denieth me before men shall be denied before the angels of God.

10 And [a]whosoever shall speak a word against the Son of man, it shall be forgiven him: but unto him that blasphemeth against the Holy Ghost it shall not be forgiven.

11 [a]And when they bring you unto the synagogues, and *unto* magistrates, and [1]powers, [2]take ye no thought how or what thing ye shall answer, or what ye shall say:

12 For the Holy Ghost shall [a]teach you in the same hour what ye ought to say.

13 And one of the [1]company said unto him, [2]Master, speak to my brother, that he divide the inheritance with me.

14 And he said unto him, [a]Man, who made me a judge or [1]a divider over you?

15 And he said unto them, [a]Take heed, and beware of covetousness: for a man's life consisteth not in the abundance of the things which he possesseth.

16 And he spake a parable unto them, saying, The ground of a certain rich man brought forth plentifully:

17 And he thought within himself, saying, What shall I do, because I have no room where to [1]bestow my fruits?

18 And he said, This will I do: I will pull down my barns, and build greater; and there will I [1]bestow all my [2]fruits and my goods.

19 And I will say to my soul, [a]Soul, thou hast much goods laid up for many years; take thine ease, [b]eat, drink, *and* be merry.

20 But God said unto him, *Thou* fool, this night [a]thy soul shall be required of thee: [b]then whose shall those things be, which thou hast provided?

21 So *is* he that layeth up treasure for himself, [a]and is not rich toward God.

22 And he said unto his disciples, Therefore I say unto you, [a]Take[1] no thought for your life, what ye shall eat; neither for the body, what ye shall put on.

23 The life is more than [1]meat, and the body *is more* than [2]raiment.

24 Consider the ravens: for they neither sow nor reap; which neither have storehouse nor barn; and [a]God feedeth them: how much more are ye better than the fowls?

25 And which of you [1]with taking thought can add to his stature one cubit?

26 If ye then be not able to do that thing which is least, why [1]take ye thought for the rest?

27 Consider the lilies how they grow: they toil not, they spin not; and yet I say unto you, that [a]Solomon in all his glory was not [1]arrayed like one of these.

28 If then God so clothe the grass, which is to day in the field, and to morrow is cast into the oven; how much more *will he clothe* you, O ye of [a]little faith?

29 And seek not ye what ye shall eat, or what ye shall drink, neither [1]be ye of doubtful mind.

30 For all these things do the nations of the world seek after: and your Father [a]knoweth that ye have need of these things.

31 [a]But rather seek ye the kingdom of God; and all these things shall be added unto you.

32 Fear not, little flock; for [a]it is your Father's good pleasure to give you the kingdom.

33 [a]Sell that ye have, and give [b]alms; [c]provide yourselves bags which [1]wax not old, a treasure in the heavens that faileth not, where no thief approacheth, neither moth [2]corrupteth.

34 For where your treasure is, there will your heart be also.

35 [a]Let your [1]loins be girded about, and [b]*your* [2]lights burning;

36 And ye yourselves like unto men that wait for their lord, when he will return from the wedding; that when he cometh and knocketh, they may open unto him immediately.

37 [a]Blessed *are* those servants, whom the [1]lord when he cometh shall find watching: verily I say unto you, that he shall gird himself, and make them to sit down to [2]meat, and will come forth and serve them.

38 And if he shall come in the second watch, or come in the third watch, and find *them* so, blessed are those servants.

39 [a]And this know, that if the [1]goodman of the house had known what hour the thief would come, he would have watched, and not have [2]suffered his house to be broken [3]through.

40 [a]Be ye therefore ready also: for the Son of man cometh at an hour when ye think not.

41 Then Peter said unto him, Lord,

speakest thou this parable unto us, or even to [1]all?

42 And the Lord said, [a]Who then is that faithful and wise steward, whom *his* lord shall make ruler over his household, to give *them their* portion of [1]meat in due season?

43 Blessed *is* that servant, whom his [1]lord when he cometh shall find so doing.

44 [a]Of a truth I say unto you, that he will make him ruler over all that he hath.

45 [a]But and if that servant say in his heart, My lord delayeth his coming; and shall begin to beat the menservants and [1]maidens, and to eat and drink, and to be drunken;

46 The lord of that servant will come in a [a]day when he looketh not for *him*, and at an hour when he is not aware, and will cut him [1]in sunder, and will appoint him his portion with the unbelievers.

47 And [a]that servant, which [b]knew his [1]lord's will, and prepared not *himself*, neither did according to his will, shall be beaten with many *stripes*.

48 [a]But he that knew not, and did commit things worthy of stripes, shall be beaten with few *stripes*. For unto whomsoever much is given, of him shall be much required: and to whom men have committed much, of him they will ask the more.

49 [a]I am come to send fire on the earth; and [1]what will I, [2]if it be already kindled?

50 But [a]I have a baptism to be baptized with; and how am I [1]straitened till it be [b]accomplished!

51 [a]Suppose ye that I am come to give peace on earth? I tell you, Nay; [b]but rather division:

52 [a]For from henceforth there shall be five in one house divided, three against two, and two against three.

53 The [a]father shall be divided against the son, and the son against the father; the mother against the daughter, and the daughter against the mother; the mother in law against her daughter in law, and the daughter in law against her mother in law.

54 And he said also to the [1]people, [a]When ye see a cloud rise out of the west, straightway ye say, There cometh a shower; and so it is.

55 And when ye see the [a]south wind blow, ye say, There will be [1]heat; and it cometh to pass.

56 *Ye* hypocrites, ye can discern the face of the sky and of the earth; but how is it that ye do not discern [a]this time?

57 Yea, and why even of yourselves judge ye not what is right?

58 [a]When thou goest with thine adversary to the magistrate, [b]*as thou*

---

12:41 [1] *all people*
12:42 [a] Matt. 24:45, 46; 25:21 [1] *food*
12:43 [1] *master*
12:44 [a] Matt. 24:47; 25:21
12:45 [a] 2 Pet. 3:3, 4 [1] *maidservants*
12:46 [a] 1 Thess. 5:3 [1] *in two*
12:47 [a] Deut. 25:2 [b] [James 4:17] [1] *master's*
12:48 [a] [Lev. 5:17]
12:49 [a] Luke 12:51 [1] *how I wish* [2] *it were*
12:50 [a] Mark 10:38 [b] John 12:27; 19:30 [1] *distressed*
12:51 [a] Matt. 10:34–36 [b] John 7:43; 9:16; 10:19
12:52 [a] Mark 13:12
12:53 [a] Matt. 10:21, 36
12:54 [a] Matt. 16:2, 3 [1] *multitudes*
12:55 [a] Job 37:17 [1] *hot weather*
12:56 [a] Luke 19:41–44
12:58 [a] Prov. 25:8; Matt. 5:25, 26 [b] [Ps. 32:6; Is. 55:6]

13:1 [1] *mixed*
13:2 [1] *more than*
13:4 [1] *debtors*
13:6 [a] Is. 5:2; Matt. 21:19
13:7 [1] *keeper* [2] *does it use up or waste*
13:8 [1] *Master* [2] *fertilize*
13:9 [a] [John 15:2]
13:11 [1] *bent over* [2] *raise*
13:12 [a] Luke 7:21; 8:2
13:13 [a] Mark 16:18; Acts 9:17
13:14 [a] [Luke 6:6–11; 14:1–6]; John 5:16 [b] Ex. 20:9; 23:12 [c] Matt. 12:10; Mark 3:2; Luke 6:7; 14:3
13:15 [a] [Matt. 7:5; 23:13]; Luke 14:5 [1] *donkey*
13:16 [a] Luke 19:9

---

*art* in the way, give diligence that thou mayest be delivered from him; lest he [1]hale thee to the judge, and the judge deliver thee to the officer, and the officer cast thee into prison.

59 I tell thee, thou shalt not depart thence, till thou hast paid the very last mite.

## CHAPTER 13

THERE were present at that season some that told him of the Galilaeans, whose blood Pilate had [1]mingled with their sacrifices.

2 And Jesus answering said unto them, Suppose ye that these Galilaeans were sinners [1]above all the Galilaeans, because they suffered such things?

3 I tell you, Nay: but, except ye repent, ye shall all likewise perish.

4 Or those eighteen, upon whom the tower in Siloam fell, and slew them, think ye that they were [1]sinners above all men that dwelt in Jerusalem?

5 I tell you, Nay: but, except ye repent, ye shall all likewise perish.

6 He spake also this parable; [a]A certain *man* had a fig tree planted in his vineyard; and he came and sought fruit thereon, and found none.

7 Then said he unto the [1]dresser of his vineyard, Behold, these three years I come seeking fruit on this fig tree, and find none: cut it down; why [2]cumbereth it the ground?

8 And he answering said unto him, [1]Lord, let it alone this year also, till I shall dig about it, and [2]dung *it*:

9 And if it bear fruit, *well*: and if not, *then* after that thou shalt [a]cut it down.

10 And he was teaching in one of the synagogues on the sabbath.

11 And, behold, there was a woman which had a spirit of infirmity eighteen years, and was [1]bowed together, and could in no wise [2]lift up *herself*.

12 And when Jesus saw her, he called *her to him*, and said unto her, Woman, thou art loosed from thine [a]infirmity.

13 [a]And he laid *his* hands on her: and immediately she was made straight, and glorified God.

14 And the ruler of the synagogue answered with indignation, because that Jesus had [a]healed on the sabbath day, and said unto the people, [b]There are six days in which men ought to work: in them therefore come and be healed, and [c]not on the sabbath day.

15 The Lord then answered him, and said, *Thou* hypocrite, [a]doth not each one of you on the sabbath loose his ox or *his* [1]ass from the stall, and lead *him* away to watering?

16 And ought not this woman, [a]being a daughter of Abraham, whom

Satan hath bound, lo, these eighteen years, be loosed from this bond on the sabbath day?

17 And when he had said these things, all his adversaries were ¹ashamed: and all the ²people rejoiced for all the glorious things that were ªdone by him.

18 ªThen said he, Unto what is the kingdom of God like? and whereunto shall I ¹resemble it?

19 It is like a grain of mustard seed, which a man took, and cast into his garden; and it grew, and ¹waxed a great tree; and the fowls of the air ²lodged in the branches of it.

20 And again he said, Whereunto shall I liken the kingdom of God?

21 It is like ¹leaven, which a woman took and hid in three ªmeasures² of meal, till the whole was leavened.

22 ªAnd he went through the cities and villages, teaching, and journeying toward Jerusalem.

23 Then said one unto him, Lord, are there ªfew that be saved? And he said unto them,

24 ªStrive to enter in at the ¹strait gate: for ᵇmany, I say unto you, will seek to enter in, and shall not be able.

25 ªWhen once the master of the house is risen up, and ᵇhath shut to the door, and ye begin to stand ¹without, and to knock at the door, saying, ᶜLord, Lord, open unto us; and he shall answer and say unto you, ᵈI know you not ²whence ye are:

26 Then shall ye begin to say, We have eaten and drunk in thy presence, and thou hast taught in our streets.

27 ªBut he shall say, I tell you, I know you not ¹whence ye are; ᵇdepart from me, all *ye* workers of iniquity.

28 ªThere shall be weeping and gnashing of teeth, ᵇwhen ye shall see Abraham, and Isaac, and Jacob, and all the prophets, in the kingdom of God, and you *yourselves* thrust out.

29 And they shall come from the east, and *from* the west, and from the north, and *from* the south, and shall sit down in the kingdom of God.

30 ªAnd, behold, there are last which shall be first, and there are first which shall be last.

31 The same day there came certain of the Pharisees, saying unto him, Get thee out, and depart hence: for Herod ¹will kill thee.

32 And he said unto them, Go ye, and tell that fox, Behold, I cast out ¹devils, and I ²do cures to day and to morrow, and the third *day* ªI shall be ³perfected.

33 Nevertheless I must ¹walk to day, and to morrow, and the *day* following: for it cannot be that a prophet ²perish out of Jerusalem.

34 ªO Jerusalem, Jerusalem, which killest the prophets, and stonest them that are sent unto thee; how often would I have gathered thy children together, as a hen *doth gather* her brood under *her* wings, and ye would not!

35 Behold, ªyour house is left unto you desolate: and verily I say unto you, Ye shall not see me, until *the time* come when ye shall say, ᵇBlessed *is* he that cometh in the name of the Lord.

## CHAPTER 14

AND it came to pass, as he went into the house of one of the chief Pharisees to eat bread on the sabbath day, that they ¹watched him.

2 And, behold, there was a certain man before him which had the dropsy.

3 And Jesus answering spake unto the ¹lawyers and Pharisees, saying, ªIs it lawful to heal on the sabbath day?

4 And they ¹held their peace. And he took *him,* and healed him, and let him go;

5 And answered them, saying, ªWhich of you shall have an ¹ass or an ox fallen into a pit, and will not straightway pull him out on the sabbath day?

6 And they could not answer him ¹again to these things.

7 And he put forth a parable to those which were ¹bidden, when he ²marked how they chose out the ³chief rooms; saying unto them,

8 When thou art bidden of any *man* to a ¹wedding, sit not down in the ²highest room; lest a more honourable man than thou be bidden of him;

9 And he that ¹bade thee and him come and say to thee, Give this man place; and thou begin with shame to take the lowest ²room.

10 ªBut when thou art bidden, go and sit down in the lowest ¹room; that when he that ²bade thee cometh, he may say unto thee, Friend, go up higher: then shalt thou have ³worship in the presence of them that sit at meat with thee.

11 ªFor whosoever exalteth himself shall be ¹abased; and he that humbleth himself shall be exalted.

12 Then said he also to him that ¹bade him, When thou makest a dinner or a supper, call not thy friends, nor thy brethren, neither thy kinsmen, nor *thy* rich neighbours; lest they also ²bid thee again, and a recompence be made thee.

13 But when thou makest a feast, call ªthe poor, the ¹maimed, the lame, the blind:

14 And thou shalt be ªblessed; for they cannot ¹recompense thee: for

### Center column references

13:17 ª Mark 5:19, 20 ¹ *put to shame* ² *multitude*
13:18 ª Matt. 13:31, 32; Mark 4:30–32 ¹ *compare*
13:19 ¹ *became* ² *nested*
13:21 ª Matt. 13:33 ¹ *yeast* ² Gr. *sata*
13:22 ª Matt. 9:35; Mark 6:6
13:23 ª [Matt. 7:14; 20:16]
13:24 ª [Matt. 7:13] ᵇ [John 7:34; 8:21; 13:33; Rom. 9:31] ¹ *narrow*
13:25 ª Is. 55:6 ᵇ Matt. 25:10 ᶜ Luke 6:46; 7:23 ᵈ Matt. 7:23; 25:12 ¹ *outside.* ² *where you are from*
13:27 ª [Matt. 7:23; 25:41] ᵇ Ps. 6:8 ¹ *where you are from*
13:28 ª Matt. 8:12; 13:42; 24:51 ᵇ Matt. 8:11
13:30 ª [Matt. 19:30; 20:16]
13:31 ¹ *wants to*
13:32 ª [Heb. 2:10; 5:9; 7:28] ¹ *demons* ² *perform* ³ *Resurrected*
13:33 ¹ *journey* ² *should perish outside of*
13:34 ª Matt. 23:37–39
13:35 ª Lev. 26:31, 32 ᵇ Ps. 118:26; Matt. 21:9
14:1 ¹ *closely watched*
14:3 ª Matt. 12:10 ¹ *experts in the law*
14:4 ¹ *kept silent*
14:5 ª [Ex. 23:5] ¹ *donkey*
14:6 ¹ *regarding these*
14:7 ¹ *invited* ² *noted* ³ *best places*
14:8 ¹ *wedding feast* ² *best place*
14:9 ¹ *invited* ² *place*
14:10 ª Prov. 25:6, 7 ¹ *place* ² *invited* ³ *glory*
14:11 ª Matt. 23:12 ¹ *humbled*
14:12 ¹ *invited* ² *invite you back*
14:13 ª Neh. 8:10, 12 ¹ *crippled*
14:14 ª [Matt. 25:34–40] ¹ *repay*

thou shalt be recompensed at the resurrection of the just.

15 And when one of them that sat ¹at meat with him heard these things, he said unto him, ªBlessed *is* he that shall eat bread in the kingdom of God.

16 ªThen said he unto him, A certain man made a great supper, and ¹bade many:

17 And ªsent his servant at supper time to say to them that were bidden, Come; for all things are now ready.

18 And they all with one ¹*consent* began to make excuse. The first said unto him, I have bought a piece of ground, and I must needs go and see it: I pray thee have me excused.

19 And another said, I have bought five yoke of oxen, and I go to ¹prove them: I pray thee have me excused.

20 And another said, I have married a wife, and therefore I cannot come.

21 So that servant came, and ¹shewed his lord these things. Then the master of the house being angry said to his servant, Go out quickly into the streets and lanes of the city, and bring in hither the poor, and the ²maimed, and the ³halt, and the blind.

22 And the servant said, Lord, it is done as thou hast commanded, and yet there is room.

23 And the lord said unto the servant, Go out into the highways and hedges, and compel *them* to come in, that my house may be filled.

24 For I say unto you, ªThat none of those men which were bidden shall taste of my supper.

25 And there went great multitudes with him: and he turned, and said unto them,

26 ªIf any *man* come to me, ᵇand hate not his father, and mother, and wife, and children, and ¹brethren, and sisters, ᶜyea, and his own life also, he cannot be my disciple.

27 And ªwhosoever doth not bear his cross, and come after me, cannot be my disciple.

28 For ªwhich of you, intending to build a tower, sitteth not down first, and counteth the cost, whether he have *sufficient* to finish *it?*

29 Lest ¹haply, after he hath laid the foundation, and is not able to finish *it,* all that behold *it* begin to mock him,

30 Saying, This man began to build, and was not able to finish.

31 Or what king, going to make war against another king, sitteth not down first, and ¹consulteth whether he be able with ten thousand to meet him that cometh against him with twenty thousand?

32 Or else, while the other is yet a great way off, he sendeth ¹an ambassage, and ²desireth conditions of peace.

14:15 ª Rev. 19:9
¹ *at the table*

14:16 ª Matt. 22:2–14 ¹ *invited*

14:17 ª Prov. 9:2, 5

14:18 ¹ Accord

14:19 ¹ *test*

14:21 ¹ *reported* ² *crippled* ³ *lame*

14:24 ª [Matt. 21:43; 22:8; Acts 13:46]

14:26 ª Deut. 13:6; 33:9; Matt. 10:37 ᵇ Rom. 9:13 ᶜ Rev. 12:11 ¹ *brothers*

14:27 ª Matt. 16:24; Mark 8:34; Luke 9:23; [2 Tim. 3:12]

14:28 ª Prov. 24:27

14:29 ¹ *perhaps*

14:31 ¹ *considers*

14:32 ¹ *a delegation* ² *asks for*

14:33 ª Matt. 19:27

14:34 ª Matt. 5:13; [Mark 9:50] ¹ *its flavour* ² *with what*

14:35 ¹ *rubbish heap*

15:1 ª [Matt. 9:10–15] ¹ *tax collectors*

15:2 ª Acts 11:3; Gal. 2:12 ¹ *welcomes*

15:4 ª Matt. 18:12–14; 1 Pet. 2:25

15:6 ª [Rom. 12:15] ᵇ [Luke 19:10; 1 Pet. 2:10, 25]

15:7 ª [Luke 5:32] ᵇ [Mark 2:17] ¹ *upright*

15:8 ¹ Gr. *drachma*, a valuable silver coin often worn in a ten-piece garland by married women ² *coin* ³ *lamp*

15:12 ª Mark 12:44 ¹ *livelihood*

15:13 ¹ *possessions* ² *wasteful* or *prodigal*

15:16 ¹ *gladly*

33 So likewise, whosoever he be of you that ªforsaketh not all that he hath, he cannot be my disciple.

34 ªSalt *is* good: but if the salt have lost ¹his savour, ²wherewith shall it be seasoned?

35 It is neither fit for the land, nor yet for the ¹dunghill; *but* men cast it out. He that hath ears to hear, let him hear.

## CHAPTER 15

THEN ªdrew near unto him all the ¹publicans and sinners for to hear him.

2 And the Pharisees and scribes murmured, saying, This man ¹receiveth sinners, ªand eateth with them.

3 And he spake this parable unto them, saying,

4 ªWhat man of you, having an hundred sheep, if he lose one of them, doth not leave the ninety and nine in the wilderness, and go after that which is lost, until he find it?

5 And when he hath found *it,* he layeth *it* on his shoulders, rejoicing.

6 And when he cometh home, he calleth together *his* friends and neighbours, saying unto them, ªRejoice with me; for I have found my sheep ᵇwhich was lost.

7 I say unto you, that likewise joy shall be in heaven over one sinner that repenteth, ªmore than over ninety and nine ¹just persons, which ᵇneed no repentance.

8 Either what woman having ten ¹pieces of silver, if she lose one ²piece, doth not light a ³candle, and sweep the house, and seek diligently till she find *it?*

9 And when she hath found *it,* she calleth *her* friends and *her* neighbours together, saying, Rejoice with me; for I have found the piece which I had lost.

10 Likewise, I say unto you, there is joy in the presence of the angels of God over one sinner that repenteth.

11 And he said, A certain man had two sons:

12 And the younger of them said to *his* father, Father, give me the portion of goods that falleth *to me.* And he divided unto them ªhis ¹living.

13 And not many days after the younger son gathered all together, and took his journey into a far country, and there wasted his ¹substance with ²riotous living.

14 And when he had spent all, there arose a mighty famine in that land; and he began to be in want.

15 And he went and joined himself to a citizen of that country; and he sent him into his fields to feed swine.

16 And he would ¹fain have filled his

belly with the [2]husks that the swine did eat: and no man gave unto him.

17 And when he came to himself, he said, How many hired servants of my father's have bread enough and to spare, and I perish with hunger!

18 I will arise and go to my father, and will say unto him, Father, [a]I have sinned against heaven, and before thee,

19 And am no [1]more worthy to be called thy son: make me as one of thy hired servants.

20 And he arose, and came to his father. But [a]when he was yet a great way off, his father saw him, and had compassion, and ran, and fell on his neck, and kissed him.

21 And the son said unto him, Father, I have sinned against heaven, [a]and in thy sight, and am no more worthy to be called thy son.

22 But the father said to his servants, Bring forth the best robe, and put *it* on him; and put a ring on his hand, and [1]shoes on *his* feet:

23 And bring hither the fatted calf, and kill *it;* and let us eat, and be merry:

24 [a]For this my son was dead, and is alive again; he was lost, and is found. And they began to be merry.

25 Now his elder son was in the field: and as he came and drew nigh to the house, he heard musick and dancing.

26 And he called one of the servants, and asked what these things meant.

27 And he said unto him, Thy brother is come; and thy father hath killed the fatted calf, because he hath received him safe and sound.

28 And he was angry, and would not go in: therefore came his father out, and [1]intreated him.

29 And he answering said to *his* father, Lo, these many years do I serve thee, neither transgressed I at any time thy commandment: and yet thou never gavest me a [1]kid, that I might make merry with my friends:

30 But as soon as this thy son was come, which hath devoured thy [1]living with harlots, thou hast killed for him the fatted calf.

31 And he said unto him, Son, thou art ever with me, and all that I have is thine.

32 It was [1]meet that we should make merry, and be glad: [a]for this thy brother was dead, and is alive again; and was lost, and is found.

## CHAPTER 16

AND he said also unto his disciples, There was a certain rich man, which had a steward; and the same was accused unto him that he had wasted his goods.

---

15:16 [2] *carob pods*
15:18 [a] Ex. 9:27; 10:16; Num. 22:34; Josh. 7:20; 1 Sam. 15:24, 30; 26:21; 2 Sam. 12:13; 24:10, 17; Ps. 51:4; Matt. 27:4
15:19 [1] *longer*
15:20 [a] [Jer. 3:12]; Matt. 9:36; [Acts 2:39; Eph. 2:13, 17]
15:21 [a] Ps. 51:4
15:22 [1] *sandals*
15:24 [a] Matt. 8:22; Luke 9:60; 15:32; Rom. 11:15; [Eph. 2:1, 5; 5:14; Col. 2:13; 1 Tim. 5:6]
15:28 [1] *begged*
15:29 [1] *young goat*
15:30 [1] *livelihood*
15:32 [a] Luke 15:24 [1] *right*

16:2 [a] [Rom. 14:12; 2 Cor. 5:10; 1 Pet. 4:5, 6]
16:3 [1] *master*
16:6 [1] Gr. *batos,* same as Heb. *bath;* 8 or 9 gallons each
16:7 [1] Gr. *koros,* same as Heb. *kor;* 10 or 12 bushels each [2] *eighty*
16:8 [a] [John 12:36; Eph. 5:8]; 1 Thess. 5:5 [1] *shrewdly* [2] Lit. *sons*
16:9 [a] Dan. 4:27; [Matt. 6:19; 19:21]; Luke 11:41; [1 Tim. 6:17–19] [1] Lit., in Aram., *wealth*
16:10 [a] Matt. 25:21; Luke 19:17
16:11 [1] *wealth*
16:12 [a] [1 Pet. 1:3, 4]
16:13 [a] Matt. 6:24; Gal. 1:10 [1] *wealth*
16:14 [a] Matt. 23:14 [1] *lovers of money* [2] Lit. *turned up the nose at*
16:15 [a] Luke 10:29 [b] [Matt. 6:2, 5, 16] [c] 1 Chr. 28:9; 2 Chr. 6:30; Ps. 7:9; Prov. 15:11; Jer. 17:10 [d] 1 Sam. 16:7; Ps. 10:3; Prov. 6:16–19; 16:5
16:16 [a] Matt. 3:1–12; 4:17; 11:12, 13; Luke 7:29 [1] *pressing*
16:17 [a] Ps. 102:26, 27; Is. 40:8; 51:6; Matt. 5:18; 1 Pet. 1:25 [1] The smallest stroke of a Heb. letter

---

2 And he called him, and said unto him, How is it that I hear this of thee? give an [a]account of thy stewardship; for thou mayest be no longer steward.

3 Then the steward said within himself, What shall I do? for my [1]lord taketh away from me the stewardship: I cannot dig; to beg I am ashamed.

4 I am resolved what to do, that, when I am put out of the stewardship, they may receive me into their houses.

5 So he called every one of his lord's debtors *unto him,* and said unto the first, How much owest thou unto my lord?

6 And he said, An hundred [1]measures of oil. And he said unto him, Take thy bill, and sit down quickly, and write fifty.

7 Then said he to another, And how much owest thou? And he said, An hundred [1]measures of wheat. And he said unto him, Take thy bill, and write [2]fourscore.

8 And the lord commended the unjust steward, because he had done [1]wisely: for the [a]children of this world are in their generation wiser than [a]the [2]children of light.

9 And I say unto you, [a]Make to yourselves friends of the [1]mammon of unrighteousness; that, when ye fail, they may receive you into everlasting habitations.

10 [a]He that is faithful in that which is least is faithful also in much: and he that is unjust in the least is unjust also in much.

11 If therefore ye have not been faithful in the unrighteous [1]mammon, who will commit to your trust the true *riches?*

12 And if ye have not been faithful in that which is another man's, who shall give you that which is your [a]own?

13 [a]No servant can serve two masters: for either he will hate the one, and love the other; or else he will hold to the one, and despise the other. Ye cannot serve God and [1]mammon.

14 And the Pharisees also, [a]who were [1]covetous, heard all these things: and they [2]derided him.

15 And he said unto them, Ye are they which [a]justify yourselves [b]before men; but [c]God knoweth your hearts: for [d]that which is highly esteemed among men is abomination in the sight of God.

16 [a]The law and the prophets *were* until John: since that time the kingdom of God is preached, and every man [1]presseth into it.

17 [a]And it is easier for heaven and earth to pass, than one [1]tittle of the law to fail.

18 <sup>a</sup>Whosoever <sup>1</sup>putteth away his wife, and marrieth another, committeth adultery: and whosoever marrieth her that is <sup>2</sup>put away from *her* husband committeth adultery.

19 There was a certain rich man, which was clothed in purple and fine linen, and <sup>1</sup>fared sumptuously every day:

20 And there was a certain beggar named Lazarus, which was laid at his gate, full of sores,

21 And desiring to be fed with the crumbs which fell from the rich man's table: moreover the dogs came and licked his sores.

22 And it came to pass, that the beggar died, and was carried by the angels into <sup>a</sup>Abraham's bosom: the rich man also died, and was buried;

23 And in <sup>1</sup>hell he lift up his eyes, being in torments, and seeth Abraham afar off, and Lazarus in his bosom.

24 And he cried and said, Father Abraham, have mercy on me, and send Lazarus, that he may dip the tip of his finger in water, and <sup>a</sup>cool my tongue; for I <sup>b</sup>am tormented in this flame.

25 But Abraham said, Son, <sup>a</sup>remember that thou in thy lifetime receivedst thy good things, and likewise Lazarus evil things: but now he is comforted, and thou art tormented.

26 And beside all this, between us and you there is a great gulf fixed: so that they which would pass from hence to you cannot; neither can they pass to us, that *would come* from thence.

27 Then he said, I pray thee therefore, father, that thou wouldest send him to my father's house:

28 For I have five brethren; that he may testify unto them, lest they also come into this place of torment.

29 Abraham saith unto him, <sup>a</sup>They have Moses and the prophets; let them hear them.

30 And he said, Nay, father Abraham: but if one went unto them from the dead, they will repent.

31 And he said unto him, <sup>a</sup>If they hear not Moses and the prophets, <sup>b</sup>neither will they be persuaded, though one rose from the dead.

## CHAPTER 17

THEN said he unto the disciples, <sup>a</sup>It is impossible but that <sup>1</sup>offences will come: but <sup>b</sup>woe *unto him,* through whom they come!

2 It were better for him that a millstone were hanged about his neck, and he cast into the sea, than that he should <sup>1</sup>offend one of these little ones.

3 Take heed to yourselves: <sup>a</sup>If thy brother trespass against thee, <sup>b</sup>rebuke him; and if he repent, forgive him.

16:18 <sup>a</sup> Matt. 5:32; 19:9; Mark 10:11; 1 Cor. 7:10, 11 <sup>1</sup> *divorces* <sup>2</sup> *divorced*
16:19 <sup>1</sup> *lived in luxury*
16:22 <sup>a</sup> Matt. 8:11
16:23 <sup>1</sup> Gr. *hades*
16:24 <sup>a</sup> Zech. 14:12 <sup>b</sup> [Is. 66:24; Mark 9:42–48]
16:25 <sup>a</sup> Job 21:13; Luke 6:24; James 5:5
16:29 <sup>a</sup> Is. 8:20; 34:16; [John 5:39, 45]; Acts 15:21; 17:11; [2 Tim. 3:15]
16:31 <sup>a</sup> [John 5:46] <sup>b</sup> John 12:10, 11
17:1 <sup>a</sup> [1 Cor. 11:19] <sup>b</sup> Matt. 18:6, 7; 26:24; Mark 9:42; Jude 11; [2 Thess. 1:6] <sup>1</sup> *stumbling blocks*
17:2 <sup>1</sup> *cause one of these little ones to stumble*
17:3 <sup>a</sup> [Matt. 18:15, 21] <sup>b</sup> Lev. 19:17; [Prov. 17:10; Gal. 6:1]; James 5:19, 20]

17:6 <sup>a</sup> Matt. 17:20; 21:21; [Mark 9:23; 11:23]; Luke 13:19 <sup>1</sup> *mulberry*
17:7 <sup>1</sup> *tending sheep* <sup>2</sup> *eat*
17:8 <sup>a</sup> [Luke 12:37] <sup>1</sup> *something for me to eat*
17:9 <sup>1</sup> *think*
17:10 <sup>a</sup> Job 22:3; 35:7; Ps. 16:2; Matt. 25:30; Rom. 3:12; 11:35; [1 Cor. 9:16, 17]; Philem. 11
17:11 <sup>a</sup> Luke 9:51, 52; John 4:4
17:12 <sup>a</sup> Lev. 13:46; Num. 5:2
17:14 <sup>a</sup> Lev. 13:1–59; 14:1–32; Matt. 8:4; Luke 5:14
17:15 <sup>a</sup> Luke 5:25; 18:43
17:16 <sup>a</sup> 2 Kin. 17:24; Luke 9:52, 53; John 4:9
17:19 <sup>a</sup> Matt. 9:22; Mark 5:34; 10:52; Luke 7:50; 8:48; 18:42
17:20 <sup>1</sup> *asked by*
17:21 <sup>a</sup> Luke 17:23 <sup>b</sup> [Rom. 14:17] <sup>1</sup> *in your midst*
17:22 <sup>a</sup> Matt. 9:15; Mark 2:20; Luke 5:35; [John 17:12]

4 And if he trespass against thee seven times in a day, and seven times in a day turn again to thee, saying, I repent; thou shalt forgive him.

5 And the apostles said unto the Lord, Increase our faith.

6 <sup>a</sup>And the Lord said, If ye had faith as a grain of mustard seed, ye might say unto this <sup>1</sup>sycamine tree, Be thou plucked up by the root, and be thou planted in the sea; and it should obey you.

7 But which of you, having a servant plowing or <sup>1</sup>feeding cattle, will say unto him by and by, when he is come from the field, Go and sit down to <sup>2</sup>meat?

8 And will not rather say unto him, Make ready <sup>1</sup>wherewith I may sup, and gird thyself, <sup>a</sup>and serve me, till I have eaten and drunken; and afterward thou shalt eat and drink?

9 Doth he thank that servant because he did the things that were commanded him? I <sup>1</sup>trow not.

10 So likewise ye, when ye shall have done all those things which are commanded you, say, We are <sup>a</sup>unprofitable servants: we have done that which was our duty to do.

11 And it came to pass, <sup>a</sup>as he went to Jerusalem, that he passed through the midst of Samaria and Galilee.

12 And as he entered into a certain village, there met him ten men that were lepers, <sup>a</sup>which stood afar off:

13 And they lifted up *their* voices, and said, Jesus, Master, have mercy on us.

14 And when he saw *them,* he said unto them, <sup>a</sup>Go shew yourselves unto the priests. And it came to pass, that, as they went, they were cleansed.

15 And one of them, when he saw that he was healed, turned back, and with a loud voice <sup>a</sup>glorified God,

16 And fell down on *his* face at his feet, giving him thanks: and he was a <sup>a</sup>Samaritan.

17 And Jesus answering said, Were there not ten cleansed? but where *are* the nine?

18 There are not found that returned to give glory to God, save this stranger.

19 <sup>a</sup>And he said unto him, Arise, go thy way: thy faith hath made thee whole.

20 And when he was <sup>1</sup>demanded of the Pharisees, when the kingdom of God should come, he answered them and said, The kingdom of God cometh not with observation:

21 <sup>a</sup>Neither shall they say, Lo here! or, lo there! for, behold, <sup>b</sup>the kingdom of God is <sup>1</sup>within you.

22 And he said unto the disciples, <sup>a</sup>The days will come, when ye shall desire to see one of the days of the Son of man, and ye shall not see *it.*

23 ªAnd they shall say to you, See here; or, see there: go not after *them,* nor follow *them.*

24 ªFor as the lightning, that ¹lighteneth out of the one *part* under heaven, shineth unto the other *part* under heaven; so shall also the Son of man be in his day.

25 ªBut first must he suffer many things, and be ᵇrejected of this generation.

26 ªAnd as it ᵇwas in the ᶜdays of ᵈNoe, so shall it be also in the days of the Son of man.

27 They did eat, they drank, they married wives, they were given in marriage, until the ªday that Noe entered into the ark, and the flood came, and ᵇdestroyed them all.

28 ªLikewise also as it was in the days of Lot; they did eat, they drank, they bought, they sold, they planted, they builded;

29 But ªthe same day that Lot went out of Sodom it rained fire and brimstone from heaven, and destroyed *them* all.

30 Even thus shall it be in the day when the Son of man ªis revealed.

31 In that day, he ªwhich shall be upon the housetop, and his ¹stuff in the house, let him not come down to take it away: and he that is in the field, let him likewise not return back.

32 ªRemember Lot's wife.

33 ªWhosoever shall seek to save his life shall lose it; and whosoever shall lose his life shall preserve it.

34 ªI tell you, in that night there shall be two ¹*men* in one bed; the one shall be taken, and the other shall be left.

35 ªTwo *women* shall be grinding together; the one shall be taken, and the other left.

36 Two *men* shall be in the field; the one shall be taken, and the other left.

37 And they answered and said unto him, ªWhere, Lord? And he said unto them, Wheresoever the body *is,* thither will the ¹eagles be gathered together.

## CHAPTER 18

A ND he spake a parable unto them *to this end,* that men ought ªalways to pray, and not to ¹faint;

2 Saying, There was ¹in a city a judge, which feared not God, neither ²regarded man:

3 And there was a widow in that city; and she came unto him, saying, ¹Avenge me of mine adversary.

4 And he would not for a while: but afterward he said within himself, Though I fear not God, nor regard man;

5 ªYet because this widow troubleth me, I will ¹avenge her, lest by her continual coming she weary me.

17:23 ª Matt. 24:23; Mark 13:21; [Luke 21:8]
17:24 ª Matt. 24:27 ¹ flashes
17:25 ª Mark 8:31; 9:31; 10:33 ᵇ Luke 9:22
17:26 ª Matt. 24:37–39 ᵇ [Gen. 6:5–7] ᶜ [Gen. 6:8–13] ᵈ 1 Pet. 3:20
17:27 ª Gen. 7:1–16 ᵇ Gen. 7:19–23
17:28 ª Gen. 19
17:29 ª Gen. 19:16, 24, 29
17:30 ª [2 Thess. 1:7]
17:31 ª Mark 13:15 ¹ possessions
17:32 ª Gen. 19:26
17:33 ª Matt. 10:39; 16:25
17:34 ª [1 Thess. 4:17] ¹ People
17:35 ª Matt. 24:40, 41
17:37 ª Matt. 24:28 ¹ vultures
18:1 ª Luke 11:5–10 ¹ lose heart
18:2 ¹ in a certain city ² respected
18:3 ¹ Vindicate me against
18:5 ª Luke 11:8 ¹ vindicate
18:7 ª Rev. 6:10 ¹ vindicate
18:8 ª Heb. 10:37 ¹ vindicate
18:9 ª Luke 10:29; 16:15
18:10 ¹ tax collector
18:11 ª Ps. 135:2 ᵇ Is. 1:15; 58:2 ¹ tax collector
18:13 ¹ tax collector ² beat
18:14 ª Luke 14:11
18:15 ª Mark 10:13–16
18:16 ª 1 Pet. 2:2 ¹ Allow
18:17 ª Mark 10:15
18:18 ª Matt. 19:16–29 ¹ Teacher
18:19 ª Ps. 86:5; 119:68
18:20 ª Ex. 20:12–16; Deut. 5:16–20 ᵇ Eph. 6:2; Col. 3:20 ¹ murder
18:21 ª Phil. 3:6
18:22 ª Matt. 6:19, 20; 19:21
18:24 ª Prov. 11:28; Matt. 19:23; Mark 10:23 ¹ hard it is for those ... to enter

6 And the Lord said, Hear what the unjust judge saith.

7 And ªshall not God ¹avenge his own elect, which cry day and night unto him, though he bear long with them?

8 I tell you ªthat he will ¹avenge them speedily. Nevertheless when the Son of man cometh, shall he find faith on the earth?

9 And he spake this parable unto certain ªwhich trusted in themselves that they were righteous, and despised others:

10 Two men went up into the temple to pray; the one a Pharisee, and the other a ¹publican.

11 The Pharisee ªstood and prayed thus with himself, ᵇGod, I thank thee, that I am not as other men *are,* extortioners, unjust, adulterers, or even as this ¹publican.

12 I fast twice in the week, I give tithes of all that I possess.

13 And the ¹publican, standing afar off, would not lift up so much as *his* eyes unto heaven, but ²smote upon his breast, saying, God be merciful to me a sinner.

14 I tell you, this man went down to his house justified *rather* than the other: ªfor every one that exalteth himself shall be abased; and he that humbleth himself shall be exalted.

15 ªAnd they brought unto him also infants, that he would touch them: but when *his* disciples saw *it,* they rebuked them.

16 But Jesus called them *unto him,* and said, ¹Suffer little children to come unto me, and forbid them not: for ªof such is the kingdom of God.

17 ªVerily I say unto you, Whosoever shall not receive the kingdom of God as a little child shall in no wise enter therein.

18 ªAnd a certain ruler asked him, saying, Good ¹Master, what shall I do to inherit eternal life?

19 And Jesus said unto him, Why callest thou me good? none *is* good, save ªone, *that is,* God.

20 Thou knowest the commandments, ªDo not commit adultery, Do not ¹kill, Do not steal, Do not bear false witness, ᵇHonour thy father and thy mother.

21 And he said, All ªthese have I kept from my youth up.

22 Now when Jesus heard these things, he said unto him, Yet lackest thou one thing: ªsell all that thou hast, and distribute unto the poor, and thou shalt have treasure in heaven: and come, follow me.

23 And when he heard this, he was very sorrowful: for he was very rich.

24 And when Jesus saw that he was very sorrowful, he said, ªHow ¹hardly

shall they that have riches enter into the kingdom of God!

25 For it is easier for a camel to go through a needle's eye, than for a rich man to enter into the kingdom of God.

26 And they that heard *it* said, Who then can be saved?

27 And he said, [a]The things which are impossible with men are possible with God.

28 [a]Then Peter said, Lo, we have left all, and followed thee.

29 And he said unto them, Verily I say unto you, [a]There is no man that hath left house, or parents, or brethren, or wife, or children, for the kingdom of God's sake,

30 [a]Who shall not receive [1]manifold more in this present time, and in the [2]world to come life everlasting.

31 [a]Then he took *unto him* the twelve, and said unto them, Behold, we go up to Jerusalem, and all things [b]that are written by the prophets concerning the Son of man shall be [1]accomplished.

32 For [a]he shall be delivered unto the Gentiles, and shall be mocked, and [1]spitefully entreated, and spitted on:

33 And they shall scourge *him,* and put him to death: and the third day he shall rise again.

34 [a]And they understood none of these things: and this saying was hid from them, neither knew they the things which were spoken.

35 [a]And it came to pass, that as he was come nigh unto Jericho, a certain blind man sat by the way side begging:

36 And hearing the multitude pass by, he asked what it meant.

37 And they told him, that Jesus of Nazareth passeth by.

38 And he cried, saying, Jesus, *thou* [a]son of David, have mercy on me.

39 And they which went before rebuked him, that he should [1]hold his peace: but he cried so much the more, *Thou* son of David, have mercy on me.

40 And Jesus [1]stood, and commanded him to be brought unto him: and when he was come near, he asked him,

41 Saying, What wilt thou that I shall do unto thee? And he said, Lord, that I may receive my sight.

42 And Jesus said unto him, Receive thy sight: [a]thy faith hath saved thee.

43 And immediately he received his sight, and followed him, [a]glorifying God: and all the people, when they saw *it,* gave praise unto God.

## CHAPTER 19

AND *Jesus* entered and passed through [a]Jericho.

2 And, behold, *there was* a man named Zacchaeus, which was [1]the chief among the publicans, and he was rich.

3 And he sought to [a]see Jesus who he was; and could not [1]for the press, because he was [2]little of stature.

4 And he ran before, and climbed up into a sycomore tree to see him: for he was to pass that *way.*

5 And when Jesus came to the place, he looked up, and saw him, and said unto him, Zacchaeus, [1]make haste, and come down; for to day I must [2]abide at thy house.

6 And he [1]made haste, and came down, and received him joyfully.

7 And when they saw *it,* they all [1]murmured, saying, [a]That he was gone to be guest with a man that is a sinner.

8 And Zacchaeus stood, and said unto the Lord; Behold, Lord, the half of my goods I give to the [a]poor; and if I have taken any thing from any man by [b]false accusation, [c]I restore *him* fourfold.

9 And Jesus said unto him, This day is salvation come to this house, forsomuch as [a]he also is [b]a son of Abraham.

10 [a]For the Son of man is come to seek and to save that which was lost.

11 And as they heard these things, he added and spake a parable, because he was [1]nigh to Jerusalem, and because [a]they thought that the kingdom of God should immediately appear.

12 [a]He said therefore, A certain nobleman went into a far country to receive for himself a kingdom, and to return.

13 And he called his ten servants, and delivered them ten [1]pounds, and said unto them, [2]Occupy till I come.

14 [a]But his citizens hated him, and sent a message after him, saying, We will not have this *man* to reign over us.

15 And it came to pass, that when he was returned, having received the kingdom, then he commanded these servants to be called unto him, to whom he had given the money, that he might know how much every man had gained by trading.

16 Then came the first, saying, Lord, thy pound hath gained ten pounds.

17 And he said unto him, [a]Well,[1] thou good servant: because thou hast been [b]faithful in a very little, have thou authority over ten cities.

18 And the second came, saying, Lord, thy pound hath gained five pounds.

19 And he said likewise to him, Be thou also over five cities.

20 And another came, saying, Lord, behold, *here is* thy pound, which I have kept laid up in a [1]napkin:

18:27 [a] Job 42:2; Jer. 32:17; Zech. 8:6; Matt. 19:26; Luke 1:37
18:28 [a] Matt. 19:27
18:29 [a] Deut. 33:9
18:30 [a] Job 42:10 [1] *many times* [2] *age*
18:31 [a] Matt. 16:21; 17:22; 20:17; Mark 10:32; Luke 9:51 [b] Ps. 22; [Is. 53] [1] *fulfilled*
18:32 [a] Matt. 26:67; 27:2, 29, 41; Mark 14:65; 15:1, 19, 20, 31; Luke 23:1; John 18:28; Acts 3:13 [1] *insulted*
18:34 [a] Mark 9:32; Luke 2:50; 9:45; [John 10:6; 12:16]
18:35 [a] Matt. 20:29–34; Mark 10:46–52
18:38 [a] Matt. 9:27
18:39 [1] *be quiet*
18:40 [1] *stood still*
18:42 [a] Luke 17:19
18:43 [a] Luke 5:26; Acts 4:21; 11:18
19:1 [a] Josh. 6:26; 1 Kin. 16:34
19:2 [1] *a chief tax collector*
19:3 [a] John 12:21 [1] *because of the crowd* [2] *small*
19:5 [1] *hurry* [2] *stay*
19:6 [1] *hurried*
19:7 [a] Matt. 9:11; Luke 5:30; 15:2 [1] *grumbled*
19:8 [a] [Ps. 41:1] [b] Luke 3:14 [c] Ex. 22:1; Lev. 6:5; Num. 5:7; 1 Sam. 12:3; 2 Sam. 12:6
19:9 [a] Luke 3:8; 13:16; [Rom. 4:16; Gal. 3:7] [b] [Luke 13:16]
19:10 [a] Matt. 18:11; [Luke 5:32; Rom. 5:8]
19:11 [a] Acts 1:6 [1] *near*
19:12 [a] Matt. 25:14–30; Mark 13:34
19:13 [1] Gr. *mna,* same as Heb. *minah,* each worth about three months' salary [2] *Do business*
19:14 [a] [John 1:11]
19:17 [a] Matt. 25:21, 23 [b] Luke 16:10 [1] *Well done*
19:20 [1] *handkerchief*

21 ᵃFor I feared thee, because thou art ¹an austere man: ²thou takest up ³that thou layedst not down, and reapest that thou didst not sow.

22 And he saith unto him, ᵃOut of thine own mouth will I judge thee, *thou* wicked servant. ᵇThou knewest that I was ¹an austere man, ²taking up ³that I laid not down, and reaping that I did not sow:

23 Wherefore then gavest not thou my money into the bank, that at my coming I might have required mine own with ¹usury?

24 And he said unto them that stood by, Take from him the pound, and give *it* to him that hath ten pounds.

25 (And they said unto him, ¹Lord, he hath ten pounds.)

26 For I say unto you, ᵃThat unto every one which hath shall be given; and from him that hath not, even that he hath shall be taken away from him.

27 But those mine enemies, which would not that I should reign over them, bring hither, and slay *them* before me.

28 And when he had thus spoken, ᵃhe went ¹before, ascending up to Jerusalem.

29 ᵃAnd it came to pass, when he was come nigh to Bethphage and ᵇBethany, at the mount called ¹*the* ᶜ*mount* of Olives, he sent two of his disciples,

30 Saying, Go ye into the village ¹over against *you;* in the which at your entering ye shall find a colt tied, whereon yet never man sat: loose him, and bring *him hither.*

31 And if any man ask you, Why do ye loose *him?* thus shall ye say unto him, Because the Lord hath need of him.

32 And they that were sent went their way, and found even ᵃas he had said unto them.

33 And as they were loosing the colt, the owners thereof said unto them, Why loose ye the colt?

34 And they said, The Lord hath need of him.

35 And they brought him to Jesus: ᵃand they ¹cast their garments upon the colt, and they set Jesus thereon.

36 And as he went, they spread their clothes ¹in the way.

37 And when he was come ¹nigh, even now at the descent of the mount of Olives, the whole multitude of the disciples began to ᵃrejoice and praise God with a loud voice for all the mighty works that they had seen;

38 Saying, ᵃBlessed *be* the King that cometh in the name of the Lord: ᵇpeace in heaven, and glory in the highest.

39 And some of the Pharisees from among the multitude said unto him, ¹Master, rebuke thy disciples.

40 And he answered and said unto them, I tell you that, if these should ¹hold their peace, ᵃthe stones would immediately cry out.

41 And when he was come near, he beheld the city, and ᵃwept over it,

42 Saying, If thou hadst known, even thou, at least in this ᵃthy day, the things *which* ᵇ*belong* unto thy ᶜpeace! but now they are hid from thine eyes.

43 For the days shall come upon thee, that thine enemies shall ᵃcast¹ a trench about thee, and ²compass thee round, and ³keep thee in on every side,

44 And ᵃshall ¹lay thee even with the ground, and thy children within thee; and ᵇthey shall not leave in thee one stone upon another; ᶜbecause thou knewest not the time of thy visitation.

45 ᵃAnd he went into the temple, and began to cast out them that sold therein, and them that bought;

46 Saying unto them, ᵃIt is written, My house is the house of prayer: but ye have made it a ᵇden of thieves.

47 And he ᵃtaught daily in the temple. But ᵇthe chief priests and the scribes and the ¹chief of the people sought to destroy him,

48 And could not find what they might do: for all the people were very attentive to ᵃhear him.

## CHAPTER 20

ᴀ ND ᵃit came to pass, *that* on one of those days, as he taught people in the temple, and preached the gospel, the chief priests and the scribes came upon *him* with the elders,

2 And spake unto him, saying, Tell us, ᵃby what authority doest thou these things? or who is he that gave thee this authority?

3 And he answered and said unto them, I will also ask you one thing; and answer me:

4 The ᵃbaptism of John, was it from heaven, or of men?

5 And they reasoned with themselves, saying, If we shall say, From heaven; he will say, Why then believed ye him not?

6 But and if we say, Of men; all the people will stone us: ᵃfor they be persuaded that John was a prophet.

7 And they answered, that they could not tell whence *it was.*

8 And Jesus said unto them, Neither tell I you by what authority I do these things.

19:21 ᵃ Matt. 25:24
¹ *a severe* ² *you collect* ³ *what you did not deposit*
19:22 ᵃ 2 Sam. 1:16; Job 15:6; [Matt. 12:37]
ᵇ Matt. 25:26 ¹ *a severe* ² *collecting* ³ *what I did not deposit*
19:23 ¹ *interest*
19:25 ¹ *Master*
19:26 ᵃ Matt. 13:12; 25:29; Mark 4:25; Luke 8:18
19:28 ᵃ Mark 10:32 ¹ *on ahead*
19:29 ᵃ Matt. 21:1; Mark 11:1 ᵇ Matt. 26:6; John 12:1 ᶜ John 8:1; Acts 1:12 ¹ *Olivet*
19:30 ¹ *opposite*
19:32 ᵃ Luke 22:13
19:35 ᵃ 2 Kin. 9:13; Matt. 21:7; Mark 11:7 ¹ *spread*
19:36 ¹ *on the road*
19:37 ᵃ Luke 13:17; 18:43 ¹ *near*
19:38 ᵃ Ps. 118:26; Luke 13:35 ᵇ Luke 2:14; [Eph. 2:14]
19:39 ¹ *Teacher*
19:40 ᵃ Hab. 2:11 ¹ *keep silent*
19:41 ᵃ Is. 53:3; John 11:35
19:42 ᵃ Ps. 95:7, 8; Heb. 3:13 ᵇ [Luke 1:77–79; Acts 10:36] ᶜ [Rom. 5:1]
19:43 ᵃ Is. 29:3, 4; Jer. 6:3, 6; Luke 21:20 ¹ *build an embankment* ² *surround* ³ *close you in*
19:44 ᵃ 1 Kin. 9:7, 8; Mic. 3:12 ᵇ Matt. 24:2; Mark 13:2; Luke 21:6 ᶜ [Dan. 9:24; Luke 1:68, 78; 1 Pet. 2:12] ¹ *level*
19:45 ᵃ Mal. 3:1; Matt. 21:12, 13; Mark 11:11, 15–17; John 2:13–16
19:46 ᵃ Is. 56:7 ᵇ Jer. 7:11
19:47 ᵃ Luke 21:37; 22:53 ᵇ Mark 11:18; Luke 20:19; John 7:19; 8:37 ¹ *leaders*
19:48 ᵃ Luke 21:38
20:1 ᵃ Matt. 21:23–27; Mark 11:27–33
20:2 ᵃ Acts 4:7; 7:27
20:4 ᵃ John 1:26, 31
20:6 ᵃ Matt. 14:5; 21:26; Mark 6:20; Luke 7:24–30

9 Then began he to speak to the people this parable; [a]A certain man planted a vineyard, and [1]let it forth to [2]husbandmen, and went into a far country for a long time.

10 And at [1]the season he [a]sent a servant to the [2]husbandmen, that they should give him [3]of the fruit of the vineyard: but the [2]husbandmen beat him, and sent *him* away [4]empty.

11 And again he sent another servant: and they beat him also, and [1]entreated *him* shamefully, and sent *him* away [2]empty.

12 And again he sent a third: and they wounded him also, and cast *him* out.

13 Then said the lord of the vineyard, What shall I do? I will send my beloved son: it may be they will [1]reverence *him* when they see him.

14 But when the [1]husbandmen saw him, they reasoned among themselves, saying, This is the [a]heir: come, [b]let us kill him, that the inheritance may be [c]ours.

15 So they cast him out of the vineyard, and [a]killed *him*. What therefore shall the [1]lord of the vineyard do unto them?

16 He shall come and destroy these [1]husbandmen, and shall give the vineyard to [a]others. And when they heard *it,* they said, [2]God forbid.

17 And he beheld them, and said, What is this then that is written, [a]The stone which the builders rejected, the same is become the [1]head of the corner?

18 Whosoever shall fall upon that stone shall be [a]broken; but [b]on whomsoever it shall fall, it will grind him to powder.

19 And the chief priests and the scribes the same hour sought to lay hands on him; [1]and they feared the people: for they [2]perceived that he had spoken this parable against them.

20 [a]And they watched *him,* and sent forth spies, which [1]should feign themselves just men, that they might [2]take hold of his words, that so they might deliver him unto the power and authority of the governor.

21 And they asked him, saying, [a]Master,[1] we know that thou sayest and teachest rightly, neither [2]acceptest thou the person *of any,* but teachest the way of God truly:

22 Is it lawful for us to [1]give tribute unto Caesar, or no?

23 But he perceived their craftiness, and said unto them, Why [1]tempt ye me?

24 Shew me a [1]penny. Whose image and [2]superscription hath it? They answered and said, Caesar's.

25 And he said unto them, [a]Render therefore unto Caesar the things which be Caesar's, and unto God the things which be God's.

26 And they could not [1]take hold of his words before the people: and they marvelled at his answer, and [2]held their peace.

27 [a]Then came to *him* certain of the Sadducees, [b]which deny that there is any resurrection; and they asked him,

28 Saying, [1]Master, Moses wrote unto us, If any man's brother die, having a wife, and he die without children, that his brother should take his wife, and raise up [2]seed unto his brother.

29 There were therefore seven brethren: and the first took a wife, and died without children.

30 And the second took her to wife, and he died childless.

31 And the third took her; and in like manner the seven also: and they left no children, and died.

32 Last of all the woman died also.

33 Therefore in the resurrection whose wife of them is she? for seven had her to wife.

34 And Jesus answering said unto them, The [1]children of this world marry, and are given in marriage:

35 But they which shall be [a]accounted worthy to obtain that [1]world, and the resurrection from the dead, neither marry, nor are given in marriage:

36 Neither can they die any more: for [a]they are equal unto the angels; and are the [1]children of God, [b]being the [1]children of the resurrection.

37 Now that the dead are raised, even Moses shewed at the [1]bush, when he calleth the Lord [a]the God of Abraham, and the God of Isaac, and the God of Jacob.

38 For he is not a God of the dead, but of the living: for [a]all live unto him.

39 Then certain of the scribes answering said, [1]Master, thou hast [2]well said.

40 And after that they [1]durst not ask him any *question at all.*

41 And he said unto them, [a]How say they that Christ is David's son?

42 And David himself saith in the book of Psalms, [a]The LORD said unto my Lord, Sit thou on my right hand,

43 Till I make thine enemies thy footstool.

44 David therefore calleth him Lord, [a]how is he then his son?

45 [a]Then in the [1]audience of all the people he said unto his disciples,

46 [a]Beware of the scribes, which desire to walk in long robes, and [b]love

---

20:9 [a] Ps. 80:8; Matt. 21:33–46; Mark 12:1–12 [1] leased it [2] tenant farmers
20:10 [a] 2 Kin. 17:13, 14; 2 Chr. 36:15, 16; [Acts 7:52; 1 Thess. 2:15] [1] vintage-time [2] tenant farmers [3] some of [4] empty-handed
20:11 [1] treated [2] empty-handed
20:13 [1] respect
20:14 [a] [Heb. 1:1–3] [b] Matt. 27:21–23 [c] John 11:47, 48 [1] tenant farmers
20:15 [a] Luke 23:33; Acts 2:22, 23; 3:15 [1] owner
20:16 [a] [John 1:11–13]; Rom. 11:1, 11; 1 Cor. 6:15; Gal. 2:17; 3:21; 6:14 [1] tenant farmers [2] Certainly not!
20:17 [a] Ps. 118:22; Matt. 21:42; 1 Pet. 2:7, 8 [1] chief corner stone
20:18 [a] Is. 8:14, 15 [b] [Dan. 2:34, 35, 44, 45]; Matt. 21:44
20:19 [1] but [2] knew
20:20 [a] Matt. 22:15 [1] pretended to be [2] catch him in
20:21 [a] Matt. 22:16; Mark 12:14 [1] Teacher [2] are you partial to any, lit. receive the face
20:22 [1] pay taxes
20:23 [1] test
20:24 [1] Gr. denarius [2] inscription
20:25 [a] Matt. 17:24–27; Rom. 13:7; [1 Pet. 2:13–17]
20:26 [1] catch him in [2] kept silent
20:27 [a] Matt. 22:23–33; Mark 12:18–27 [b] Acts 23:6, 8
20:28 [1] Teacher [2] offspring
20:34 [1] sons of this age
20:35 [a] Phil. 3:11 [1] age
20:36 [a] [1 Cor. 15:42, 49, 52; 1 John 3:2] [b] Rom. 8:23 [1] Lit. sons
20:37 [a] Ex. 3:1–6, 15 [1] burning bush
20:38 [a] [Rom. 6:10, 11; 14:8, 9]
20:39 [1] Teacher [2] spoken well  20:40 [1] dared
20:41 [a] Matt. 22:41–46  20:42 [a] Ps. 110:1
20:44 [a] Rom. 1:3; 9:4, 5  20:45 [a] Matt. 23:1–7 [1] hearing  20:46 [a] Matt. 23:5 [b] Luke 11:43; 14:7

greetings in the markets, and the
[1]highest seats in the synagogues, and
the [2]chief rooms at feasts;
47 [a]Which devour widows' houses,
and for a [b]shew[1] make long prayers:
the same shall receive greater [2]dam-
nation.

## CHAPTER 21

AND he looked up, [a]and saw the
rich men [1]casting their gifts into
the treasury.
2 And he saw also a certain [a]poor
widow casting in thither two [b]mites.[1]
3 And he said, Of a truth I say unto
you, [a]that this poor widow hath cast
in more than they all:
4 For all these have of their abundance cast in unto the offerings of
God: but she of her [1]penury hath cast
in [a]all the [2]living that she had.
5 [a]And as some spake of the temple, how it was adorned with goodly
stones and gifts, he said,
6 *As for* these things which ye
behold, the days will come, in the
which [a]there shall not be left one
stone upon another, that shall not be
thrown down.
7 And they asked him, saying,
[1]Master, but when shall these things
be? and what sign *will there be* when
these things shall come to pass?
8 And he said, [a]Take heed that ye
be not deceived: for many shall come
in my name, saying, I am *Christ;* and
the time draweth near: go ye not
therefore after them.
9 But when ye shall hear of [a]wars
and commotions, be not terrified: for
these things must first come to pass;
but the end [1]*is* not by and by.
10 [a]Then said he unto them, Nation
shall rise against nation, and kingdom against kingdom:
11 And great [a]earthquakes shall
be in [1]divers places, and famines,
and pestilences; and fearful sights
and great signs shall there be from
heaven.
12 [a]But before all these, they shall
lay their hands on you, and persecute
*you,* delivering *you* up to the synagogues, and [b]into prisons, [c]being
brought before kings and rulers [d]for
my name's sake.
13 And [a]it shall [1]turn to you for a
testimony.
14 [a]Settle *it* therefore in your hearts,
not to meditate before what ye shall
answer:
15 For I will give you a mouth and
wisdom, [a]which all your adversaries
shall not be able to [1]gainsay nor resist.
16 [a]And ye shall be betrayed both
by parents, and brethren, and kinsfolks, and friends; and [b]*some* of you
shall they cause to be put to death.
17 And [a]ye shall be hated of all *men*
for my name's sake.
18 [a]But there shall not an hair of
your head perish.
19 In your patience possess ye your
souls.
20 [a]And when ye shall see Jerusalem [1]compassed with armies, then
know that the desolation thereof is
[2]nigh.
21 Then let them which are in Judaea flee to the mountains; and let
them which are in the midst of it depart out; and let not them that are in
the [1]countries enter thereinto.
22 For these be the days of vengeance, that [a]all things which are
written may be fulfilled.
23 [a]But woe unto them that are
[1]with child, and to them that [2]give
suck, in those days! for there shall be
great distress in the land, and wrath
upon this people.
24 And they shall fall by the edge of
the sword, and shall be led away captive into all nations: and Jerusalem
shall be [1]trodden down of the Gentiles, [a]until the times of the Gentiles
be fulfilled.
25 [a]And there shall be signs in the
sun, and in the moon, and in the
stars; and upon the earth distress of
nations, with perplexity; the sea and
the waves roaring;
26 Men's hearts failing them [1]for
fear, and [2]for looking after those
things which are coming on the
earth: [a]for the powers of heaven shall
be shaken.
27 And then shall they see the
Son of man [a]coming in a cloud with
power and great glory.
28 And when these things begin to
come to pass, then look up, and lift
up your heads; for [a]your redemption
draweth [1]nigh.
29 [a]And he spake to them a parable;
Behold the fig tree, and all the trees;
30 When they now shoot forth, ye
see and know of your own selves that
summer is now [1]nigh at hand.
31 So likewise ye, when ye see
these things come to pass, know ye
that the kingdom of God is [1]nigh at
hand.
32 Verily I say unto you, This generation shall not pass away, till all be
fulfilled.
33 [a]Heaven and earth shall pass
away: but my [b]words shall not pass
away.
34 And [a]take heed to yourselves,
lest at any time your hearts be [1]over-
charged with [2]surfeiting, and drunkenness, and [b]cares of this life, and *so*
that day come upon you unawares.
35 For [a]as a snare shall it come on
all them that dwell on the face of the
whole earth.

20:46 [1] *best,* lit. *first* [2] *best places,* lit. *first places*
20:47 [a] Matt. 23:14 [b] [Matt. 6:5, 6] [1] *pretense* [2] *condemnation*
21:1 [a] Mark 12:41–44 [1] *putting*
21:2 [a] [2 Cor. 6:10] [b] Mark 12:42 [1] Small copper coins
21:3 [a] [2 Cor. 8:12]
21:4 [a] [2 Cor. 8:12] [1] *poverty* [2] *livelihood*
21:5 [a] Mark 13:1
21:6 [a] Luke 19:41–44
21:7 [1] *Teacher*
21:8 [a] Eph. 5:6
21:9 [a] Rev. 6:4 [1] *is not coming immediately*
21:10 [a] Matt. 24:7
21:11 [a] Rev. 6:12 [1] *various*
21:12 [a] [Rev. 2:10] [b] Acts 4:3; 5:18; 12:4; 16:24 [c] Acts 25:23 [d] 1 Pet. 2:13
21:13 [a] [Phil. 1:12–14, 28] [1] *be an occasion*
21:14 [a] Luke 12:11
21:15 [a] Acts 6:10 [1] *refute*
21:16 [a] Mic. 7:6 [b] Acts 7:59; 12:2
21:17 [a] Matt. 10:22
21:18 [a] Matt. 10:30
21:20 [a] Mark 13:14 [1] *surrounded* [2] *near*
21:21 [1] *country*
21:22 [a] [Dan. 9:24–27]
21:23 [a] Matt. 24:19 [1] *pregnant* [2] *are nursing babies*
21:24 [1] *trampled* [a] [Dan. 9:27; 12:7]
21:25 [a] [2 Pet. 3:10–12]
21:26 [a] Matt. 24:29 [1] *from* [2] *expectation of*
21:27 [a] Rev. 1:7; 14:14
21:28 [a] [Rom. 8:19, 23] [1] *near*
21:29 [a] Mark 13:28
21:30 [1] *near*
21:31 [1] *near*
21:33 [a] Matt. 24:35 [b] Is. 40:8
21:34 [a] 1 Thess. 5:6 [b] Luke 8:14 [1] *weighed down* [2] *carousing*
21:35 [a] Rev. 3:3; 16:15

36 <sup>a</sup>Watch ye therefore, and <sup>b</sup>pray always, that ye may be accounted <sup>c</sup>worthy to escape all these things that shall come to pass, and <sup>d</sup>to stand before the Son of man.

37 <sup>a</sup>And in the day time he was teaching in the temple; and <sup>b</sup>at night he went out, and <sup>1</sup>abode in the mount that is called <sup>2</sup>*the mount* of Olives.

38 And all the people came early in the morning to him in the temple, for to hear him.

### CHAPTER 22

Now <sup>a</sup>the feast of unleavened bread drew nigh, which is called the Passover.

2 And <sup>a</sup>the chief priests and scribes sought how they might kill him; for they feared the people.

3 <sup>a</sup>Then entered Satan into Judas surnamed Iscariot, being of the number of the <sup>b</sup>twelve.

4 And he went his way, and <sup>1</sup>communed with the chief priests and captains, how he might betray him unto them.

5 And they were glad, and <sup>a</sup>covenanted<sup>1</sup> to give him money.

6 And he promised, and sought opportunity to <sup>a</sup>betray him unto them in the absence of the multitude.

7 <sup>a</sup>Then came the day of unleavened bread, when the passover must be <sup>1</sup>killed.

8 And he sent Peter and John, saying, Go and prepare us the passover, that we may eat.

9 And they said unto him, Where wilt thou that we prepare?

10 And he said unto them, Behold, when ye are entered into the city, there shall a man meet you, bearing a pitcher of water; follow him into the house where he entereth in.

11 And ye shall say unto the <sup>1</sup>goodman of the house, The <sup>2</sup>Master saith unto thee, Where is the guestchamber, where I shall eat the passover with my disciples?

12 And he shall shew you a large upper room furnished: there make ready.

13 And they went, and <sup>a</sup>found as he had said unto them: and they made ready the passover.

14 <sup>a</sup>And when the hour was come, he sat down, and the twelve apostles with him.

15 And he said unto them, <sup>1</sup>With desire I have desired to eat this passover with you before I suffer:

16 For I say unto you, I will not any more eat thereof, <sup>a</sup>until it be fulfilled in the kingdom of God.

17 And he took the cup, and gave thanks, and said, Take this, and divide *it* among yourselves:

18 For <sup>a</sup>I say unto you, I will not drink of the fruit of the vine, until the kingdom of God shall come.

19 <sup>a</sup>And he took bread, and gave thanks, and brake *it,* and gave unto them, saying, This is my <sup>b</sup>body which is given for you: <sup>c</sup>this do in remembrance of me.

20 Likewise also the cup after supper, saying, <sup>a</sup>This cup *is* the new <sup>1</sup>testament in my blood, which is shed for you.

21 <sup>a</sup>But, behold, the hand of him that betrayeth me *is* with me on the table.

22 <sup>a</sup>And truly the Son of man goeth, <sup>b</sup>as it was determined: but woe unto that man by whom he is betrayed!

23 <sup>a</sup>And they began to enquire among themselves, which of them it was that should do this thing.

24 <sup>a</sup>And there was also a <sup>1</sup>strife among them, which of them should be <sup>2</sup>accounted the greatest.

25 <sup>a</sup>And he said unto them, The kings of the Gentiles exercise lordship over them; and they that exercise authority upon them are called benefactors.

26 <sup>a</sup>But ye *shall* not *be* so: <sup>b</sup>but he that is greatest among you, let him be as the younger; and he that is <sup>1</sup>chief, as he that doth serve.

27 <sup>a</sup>For <sup>1</sup>whether *is* greater, he that sitteth <sup>2</sup>at meat, or he that serveth? *is* not he that sitteth <sup>2</sup>at meat? but <sup>b</sup>I am among you as he that serveth.

28 Ye are they which have continued with me in <sup>a</sup>my <sup>1</sup>temptations.

29 And <sup>a</sup>I <sup>1</sup>appoint unto you a kingdom, as my Father hath <sup>2</sup>appointed unto me;

30 That <sup>a</sup>ye may eat and drink at my table in my kingdom, <sup>b</sup>and sit on thrones judging the twelve tribes of Israel.

31 And the Lord said, Simon, Simon, behold, <sup>a</sup>Satan hath desired *to have* you, that he may <sup>b</sup>sift *you* as wheat:

32 But <sup>a</sup>I have prayed for thee, that thy faith fail not: and when <sup>1</sup>thou art converted, <sup>b</sup>strengthen thy brethren.

33 And he said unto him, Lord, I am ready to go with thee, both into prison, and to death.

34 <sup>a</sup>And he said, I tell thee, Peter, the <sup>1</sup>cock shall not crow this day, before that thou shalt <sup>2</sup>thrice deny that thou knowest me.

35 <sup>a</sup>And he said unto them, When I sent you without purse, and <sup>1</sup>scrip, and <sup>2</sup>shoes, lacked ye any thing? And they said, Nothing.

36 Then said he unto them, But now, he that hath a purse, let him take *it,* and likewise *his* <sup>1</sup>scrip: and he that hath no sword, let him sell his garment, and buy one.

---

**Center column cross-references:**

21:36 <sup>a</sup> Matt. 24:42; 25:13
<sup>b</sup> Luke 18:1 <sup>c</sup> Luke 20:35 <sup>d</sup> [Eph. 6:13]

21:37 <sup>a</sup> John 8:1, 2 <sup>b</sup> Luke 22:39 <sup>1</sup> stayed <sup>2</sup> Olivet

22:1 <sup>a</sup> Matt. 26:2–5

22:2 <sup>a</sup> John 11:47

22:3 <sup>a</sup> Mark 14:10, 11 <sup>b</sup> Matt. 10:2–4

22:4 <sup>1</sup> conferred

22:5 <sup>a</sup> Zech. 11:12 <sup>1</sup> agreed

22:6 <sup>a</sup> Ps. 41:9

22:7 <sup>a</sup> Matt. 26:17–19 <sup>1</sup> Sacrificed

22:11 <sup>1</sup> master <sup>2</sup> Teacher

22:13 <sup>a</sup> Luke 19:32

22:14 <sup>a</sup> Mark 14:17

22:15 <sup>1</sup> I have earnestly desired

22:16 <sup>a</sup> [Rev. 19:9]

22:18 <sup>a</sup> Mark 14:25

22:19 <sup>a</sup> Matt. 26:26 <sup>b</sup> [1 Pet. 2:24] <sup>c</sup> 1 Cor. 11:23–26

22:20 <sup>a</sup> 1 Cor. 10:16 <sup>1</sup> covenant

22:21 <sup>a</sup> John 13:21, 26, 27

22:22 <sup>a</sup> Matt. 26:24 <sup>b</sup> Acts 2:23

22:23 <sup>a</sup> John 13:22, 25

22:24 <sup>a</sup> Mark 9:34 <sup>1</sup> rivalry <sup>2</sup> considered

22:25 <sup>a</sup> Mark 10:42–45

22:26 <sup>a</sup> [1 Pet. 5:3] <sup>b</sup> Luke 9:48 <sup>1</sup> leader

22:27 <sup>a</sup> [Luke 12:37] <sup>b</sup> Phil. 2:7 <sup>1</sup> who <sup>2</sup> at the table

22:28 <sup>a</sup> [Heb. 2:18; 4:15] <sup>1</sup> trials

22:29 <sup>a</sup> Matt. 24:47 <sup>1</sup> bestow upon <sup>2</sup> bestowed upon

22:30 <sup>a</sup> [Matt. 8:11] <sup>b</sup> [Rev. 3:21]

22:31 <sup>a</sup> 1 Pet. 5:8 <sup>b</sup> Amos 9:9

22:32 <sup>a</sup> [John 17:9, 11, 15] <sup>b</sup> John 21:15–17 <sup>1</sup> you have turned again

22:34 <sup>a</sup> John 13:37, 38 <sup>1</sup> rooster <sup>2</sup> three times

22:35 <sup>a</sup> Matt. 10:9 <sup>1</sup> bag <sup>2</sup> sandals

22:36 <sup>1</sup> bag

37 For I say unto you, that this that is written must yet be ¹accomplished in me, ªAnd he was reckoned among the transgressors: for the things concerning me have an end.

38 And they said, Lord, behold, here *are* two swords. And he said unto them, It is enough.

39 ªAnd he came out, and ᵇwent, as he was ¹wont, to the mount of Olives; and his disciples also followed him.

40 ªAnd when he was at the place, he said unto them, Pray that ye enter not into temptation.

41 ªAnd he was withdrawn from them about a stone's ¹cast, and kneeled down, and prayed,

42 Saying, Father, if thou be willing, remove this cup from me: nevertheless ªnot my will, but thine, be done.

43 And there appeared ªan angel unto him from heaven, strengthening him.

44 ªAnd being in an agony he prayed more earnestly: and his sweat was as it were great drops of blood falling down to the ground.

45 And when he rose up from prayer, and was come to his disciples, he found them sleeping for sorrow,

46 And said unto them, Why ªsleep ye? rise and ᵇpray, lest ye enter into temptation.

47 And while he yet spake, ªbehold a multitude, and he that was called ᵇJudas, one of the twelve, went before them, and drew near unto Jesus to kiss him.

48 But Jesus said unto him, Judas, betrayest thou the Son of man with a ªkiss?

49 When they which were about him saw what ¹would follow, they said unto him, Lord, shall we ²smite with the sword?

50 And ªone of them ¹smote the servant of the high priest, and cut off his right ear.

51 And Jesus answered and said, ¹Suffer ye thus far. And he touched his ear, and healed him.

52 ªThen Jesus said unto the chief priests, and captains of the temple, and the elders, which were come to him, ¹Be ye come out, as against a ᵇthief,² with swords and ³staves?

53 When I was daily with you in the ªtemple, ye ¹stretched forth no hands against me: but this is your ᵇhour, and the power of darkness.

54 ªThen took they him, and led *him*, and brought him into the high priest's house. ᵇAnd Peter followed afar off.

55 ªAnd when they had kindled a fire in the midst of the ¹hall, and were set down together, Peter sat down among them.

56 But a certain ¹maid beheld him as he sat by the fire, and ²earnestly

looked upon him, and said, This man was also with him.

57 And he denied him, saying, Woman, I know him not.

58 ªAnd after a little while another saw him, and said, Thou art also of them. And Peter said, Man, I am not.

59 ªAnd about the space of one hour after another confidently affirmed, saying, Of a truth this *fellow* also was with him: for he is a ᵇGalilaean.

60 And Peter said, Man, I know not what thou sayest. And immediately, while he yet spake, ¹the cock crew.

61 And the Lord turned, and looked upon Peter. And ªPeter remembered the word of the Lord, how he had said unto him, ᵇBefore the ¹cock crow, thou shalt deny me ²thrice.

62 And Peter went out, and wept bitterly.

63 ªAnd the men that held Jesus mocked him, and ᵇsmote¹ *him*.

64 And when they had blindfolded him, they ªstruck him on the face, and asked him, saying, Prophesy, who is it that ¹smote thee?

65 And many other things blasphemously spake they against him.

66 ªAnd as soon as it was day, ᵇthe elders of the people and the chief priests and the scribes came together, and led him into their ¹council, saying,

67 ¹Art thou the Christ? tell us. And he said unto them, If I tell you, ye will ᵇnot believe:

68 And if I also ask *you,* ye will not answer me, nor let *me* go.

69 ªHereafter shall the Son of man sit on the right hand of the power of God.

70 Then said they all, Art thou then the Son of God? And he said unto them, ªYe ¹say that I am.

71 ªAnd they said, What need we any further ¹witness? for we ourselves have heard of his own mouth.

## CHAPTER 23

AND ªthe whole ¹multitude of them arose, and led him unto ᵇPilate.

2 And they began to ªaccuse him, saying, We found this *fellow* ᵇperverting the nation, and ᶜforbidding to ¹give tribute to Caesar, saying ᵈthat he himself is Christ a King.

3 ªAnd Pilate asked him, saying, Art thou the King of the Jews? And he answered him and said, ¹Thou sayest *it.*

4 Then said Pilate to the chief priests and *to* the ¹people, ªI find no fault in this man.

5 And they were the more fierce, saying, He stirreth up the people, teaching throughout all ¹Jewry, beginning from ªGalilee to this place.

22:37 ª Is. 53:12
¹ *fulfilled*
22:39 ª John 18:1 ᵇ Luke 21:37
¹ *accustomed*
22:40 ª Mark 14:32–42
22:41 ª Matt. 26:39 ¹ *throw*
22:42 ª John 4:34; 5:30; 6:38; 8:29
22:43 ª Matt. 4:11
22:44 ª [Heb. 5:7]
22:46 ª Luke 9:32 ᵇ Luke 22:40
22:47 ª John 18:3–11 ᵇ Acts 1:16, 17
22:48 ª [Prov. 27:6]
22:49 ¹ *was going to happen* ² *strike*
22:50 ª Matt. 26:51 ¹ *struck*
22:51 ¹ *Permit even this*
22:52 ª Matt. 26:55 ᵇ Luke 23:32 ¹ *Have* ² *robber* ³ *clubs*
22:53 ª Luke 19:47, 48 ᵇ [John 12:27] ¹ *did not try to seize*
22:54 ª Matt. 26:57 ᵇ John 18:15
22:55 ª Mark 14:66–72 ¹ *courtyard*
22:56 ¹ *servant girl* ² *intently*
22:58 ª John 18:25
22:59 ª Mark 14:70 ᵇ Acts 1:11; 2:7
22:60 ¹ *a rooster crowed*
22:61 ª Matt. 26:75 ᵇ John 13:38 ¹ *rooster crows* ² *three times*
22:63 ª Ps. 69:1, 4, 7–9 ᵇ Is. 50:6 ¹ *beat*
22:64 ª Zech. 13:7 ¹ *struck*
22:66 ª Matt. 27:1 ᵇ Acts 4:26 ¹ *Sanhedrin*
22:67 ª Matt. 26:63–66 ᵇ Luke 20:5–7
22:69 ª Heb. 1:3; 8:1
22:70 ª Matt. 26:64; 27:11 ¹ *rightly say*
22:71 ª Mark 14:63 ¹ *testimony*
23:1 ª John 18:28 ᵇ Luke 3:1; 13:1 ¹ *assembly*
23:2 ª Acts 24:2

ᵇ Acts 17:7 ᶜ Matt. 17:27 ᵈ John 19:12 ¹ *pay taxes*
23:3 ª 1 Tim. 6:13 ¹ *It is as you say* 23:4 ª [1 Pet. 2:22] ¹ *crowd* 23:5 ª John 7:41 ¹ *Judea*

6 When Pilate heard of Galilee, he asked whether the man were a Galilaean.

7 And as soon as he knew that he belonged unto [a]Herod's jurisdiction, he sent him to Herod, who himself also was at Jerusalem at that time.

8 And when Herod saw Jesus, [a]he was exceeding glad: for he [1]was desirous to see him [2]of a long *season,* because [b]he had heard many things of him; and he hoped to have seen some miracle done by him.

9 Then he questioned with him in many words; but he answered him [a]nothing.

10 And the chief priests and scribes stood and vehemently accused him.

11 [a]And Herod with his men of war [1]set him at nought, and mocked *him,* and [2]arrayed him in a gorgeous robe, and sent him again to Pilate.

12 And the same day [a]Pilate and Herod [1]were made friends together: for before they were at enmity between themselves.

13 [a]And Pilate, when he had called together the chief priests and the rulers and the people,

14 Said unto them, [a]Ye have brought this man unto me, as one that [1]perverteth the people: and, behold, [b]I, having examined *him* before you, have found no fault in this man [2]touching those things whereof ye accuse him:

15 No, nor yet Herod: for I sent you to him; and, lo, nothing worthy of death is done [1]unto him.

16 [a]I will therefore chastise him, and release *him.*

17 [a](For of necessity he must release one unto them at the feast.)

18 And [a]they cried out all at once, saying, Away with this *man,* and release unto us Barabbas:

19 (Who for a certain [1]sedition made in the city, and for murder, was cast into prison.)

20 Pilate therefore, willing to release Jesus, spake again to them.

21 But they cried, saying, Crucify *him,* crucify him.

22 And he said unto them the third time, Why, what evil hath he done? I have found no [1]cause of death in him: I will therefore chastise him, and let *him* go.

23 And they were [1]instant with loud voices, requiring that he might be crucified. And the voices of them and of the chief priests prevailed.

24 And [a]Pilate gave sentence that it should be as they required.

25 [a]And he released unto them him that for [1]sedition and murder was cast into prison, whom they had [2]desired; but he delivered Jesus to their will.

26 [a]And as they led him away, they laid hold upon one Simon, a Cyrenian, coming out of the country, and on him they laid the cross, that he might bear *it* after Jesus.

27 And there followed him a great [1]company of people, and of women, which also bewailed and lamented him.

28 But Jesus turning unto them said, Daughters of Jerusalem, weep not for me, but weep for yourselves, and for your children.

29 [a]For, behold, the days are coming, in the which they shall say, Blessed *are* the barren, and the wombs that never bare, and the [1]paps which never gave suck.

30 Then shall they begin [a]to say to the mountains, Fall on us; and to the hills, Cover us.

31 [a]For if they do these things in a green tree, what shall be done in the dry?

32 [a]And there were also two other, [1]malefactors, led with him to be put to death.

33 And [a]when they were come to the place, which is called [1]Calvary, there they crucified him, and the [2]malefactors, one on the right hand, and the other on the left.

34 Then said Jesus, Father, [a]forgive them; for [b]they know not what they do. And [c]they [1]parted his raiment, and cast lots.

35 And [a]the people stood beholding. And the [b]rulers also with them [1]derided *him,* saying, He saved others; let him save himself, if he be Christ, the chosen of God.

36 And the soldiers also mocked him, coming to him, and offering him [a]vinegar,[1]

37 And saying, If thou be the king of the Jews, save thyself.

38 [a]And a superscription also was written over him in letters of Greek, and Latin, and Hebrew, THIS IS THE KING OF THE JEWS.

39 [a]And one of the [1]malefactors which were hanged [2]railed on him, saying, If thou be Christ, save thyself and us.

40 But the other answering rebuked him, saying, Dost not thou fear God, seeing thou art in the same condemnation?

41 And we indeed justly; for we receive the due reward of our deeds: but this man hath done [a]nothing [1]amiss.

42 And he said unto Jesus, Lord, remember me when thou comest into thy kingdom.

43 And Jesus said unto him, Verily I say unto thee, To day shalt thou be with me in [a]paradise.

44 [a]And it was about the sixth hour,

## Cross-references

23:7 [a] Luke 3:1; 9:7; 13:31
23:8 [a] Luke 9:9 [b] Matt. 14:1 [1] had desired [2] for
23:9 [a] John 19:9
23:11 [a] Is. 53:3 [1] treated him with contempt [2] dressed
23:12 [a] Acts 4:26, 27 [1] became
23:13 [a] Mark 15:14
23:14 [a] Luke 23:1, 2 [b] Luke 23:4 [1] misleads [2] concerning
23:15 [1] by
23:16 [a] John 19:1
23:17 [a] John 18:39
23:18 [a] Acts 3:13–15
23:19 [1] insurrection
23:22 [1] reason for
23:23 [1] insistent
23:24 [a] Mark 15:15
23:25 [a] Is. 53:8 [1] insurrection [2] requested
23:26 [a] Matt. 27:32
23:27 [1] multitude
23:29 [a] Matt. 24:19 [1] breasts which never nursed
23:30 [a] Hos. 10:8; Rev. 6:16, 17; 9:6
23:31 [a] [Jer. 25:29]
23:32 [a] Is. 53:9, 12 [1] criminals
23:33 [a] John 19:17–24 [1] Latin for Skull [2] criminals
23:34 [a] 1 Cor. 4:12 [b] Acts 3:17 [c] Matt. 27:35 [1] divided his garments
23:35 [a] Ps. 22:17 [b] Matt. 27:39 [1] sneered
23:36 [a] Ps. 69:21 [1] sour wine
23:38 [a] John 19:19
23:39 [a] Mark 15:32 [1] criminals [2] blasphemed
23:41 [a] [Heb. 7:26] [1] wrong
23:43 [a] [Rev. 2:7]
23:44 [a] Matt. 27:45–56

and there was a darkness over all the 'earth until the ninth hour.

45 And the sun was darkened, and ªthe vail of the temple was 'rent in the midst.

46 And when Jesus had cried with a loud voice, he said, ªFather, into thy hands I commend my spirit: ᵇand having said thus, he 'gave up the ghost.

47 ªNow when the centurion saw what 'was done, he glorified God, saying, Certainly this was a righteous man.

48 And all the 'people that came together to that sight, beholding the things which were done, ²smote their breasts, and returned.

49 ªAnd all his acquaintance, and the women that followed him from Galilee, stood afar off, beholding these things.

50 ªAnd, behold, *there was* a man named Joseph, a 'counsellor; *and he was* a good man, and a just:

51 (The same had not consented to the counsel and deed of them;) he *was* of Arimathaea, a city of the Jews: ªwho also himself waited for the kingdom of God.

52 This *man* went unto Pilate, and begged the body of Jesus.

53 ªAnd he took it down, and wrapped it in linen, and laid it in a sepulchre that was hewn in stone, wherein never man before was laid.

54 And that day was ªthe preparation, and the sabbath drew 'on.

55 And the women also, ªwhich came with him from Galilee, followed after, and ᵇbeheld the sepulchre, and how his body was laid.

56 And they returned, and ªprepared spices and 'ointments; and rested the sabbath day ᵇaccording to the commandment.

### CHAPTER 24

Now ªupon the first *day* of the week, very early in the morning, they came unto the 'sepulchre, ᵇbringing the spices which they had prepared, and certain *others* with them.

2 ªAnd they found the stone rolled away from the sepulchre.

3 ªAnd they entered in, and found not the body of the Lord Jesus.

4 And it came to pass, as they were much perplexed 'thereabout, ªbehold, two men stood by them in shining garments:

5 And as they were afraid, and bowed down *their* faces to the earth, they said unto them, Why seek ye the living among the dead?

6 He is not here, but is risen: ªremember how he spake unto you when he was yet in Galilee,

7 Saying, The Son of man must be ªdelivered into the hands of sinful men, and be crucified, and the third day rise again.

8 And ªthey remembered his words,

9 ªAnd returned from the sepulchre, and told all these things unto the eleven, and to all the rest.

10 It was Mary Magdalene, and ªJoanna, and Mary *the mother* of James, and other *women that were* with them, which told these things unto the apostles.

11 ªAnd their words seemed to them as idle tales, and they believed them not.

12 ªThen arose Peter, and ran unto the sepulchre; and stooping down, he beheld the linen clothes laid by themselves, and departed, wondering in himself at that which was come to pass.

13 ªAnd, behold, two of them went that same day to a village called Emmaus, which was from Jerusalem *about* threescore 'furlongs.

14 And they talked together of all these things which had happened.

15 And it came to pass, that, while they 'communed *together* and reasoned, ªJesus himself drew near, and went with them.

16 But ªtheir eyes were 'holden that they ²should not know him.

17 And he said unto them, What 'manner of communications *are* these that ye have one to another, as ye walk, and are sad?

18 And the one of them, ªwhose name was Cleopas, answering said unto him, Art thou 'only a stranger in Jerusalem, and hast not known the things which are come to pass there in these days?

19 And he said unto them, What things? And they said unto him, Concerning Jesus of Nazareth, ªwhich was a prophet ᵇmighty in deed and word before God and all the people:

20 ªAnd how the chief priests and our rulers delivered him to be condemned to death, and have crucified him.

21 But we 'trusted ªthat it had been he which ²should have redeemed Israel: and beside all this, to day is the third day since these things were done.

22 Yea, and ªcertain women also of our company made us astonished, which were early at the sepulchre;

23 And when they found not his body, they came, saying, that they had also seen a vision of angels, which said that he was alive.

24 And ªcertain of them which were with us went to the sepulchre, and found *it* even so as the women had said: but him they saw not.

23:44 ¹ *land*
23:45 ª Matt. 27:51 ¹ *torn in the middle*
23:46 ª Ps. 31:5 ᵇ John 19:30 ¹ *breathed his last*
23:47 ª Mark 15:39 ¹ *had happened*
23:48 ¹ *crowd* ² *beat*
23:49 ª Ps. 38:11
23:50 ª Matt. 27:57–61 ¹ *council member*
23:51 ª Luke 2:25, 38
23:53 ª Mark 15:46
23:54 ª Matt. 27:62 ¹ *near*
23:55 ª Luke 8:2 ᵇ Mark 15:47
23:56 ª Mark 16:1; Luke 24:1 ᵇ Ex. 20:10; Deut. 5:14 ¹ *fragrant oils*
24:1 ª Matt. 28:1–8; Mark 16:1–8; John 20:1–8 ᵇ Luke 23:56 ¹ *tomb*
24:2 ª Matt. 28:2; Mark 16:4
24:3 ª Mark 16:5
24:4 ª John 20:12; Acts 1:10 ¹ *about this*
24:6 ª Matt. 16:21; Mark 8:31; Luke 9:22
24:7 ª Hos. 6:1, 2; Luke 9:44; 11:29, 30; 18:31–33
24:8 ª Luke 9:22, 44; John 2:19–22
24:9 ª Matt. 28:8; Mark 16:10
24:10 ª Luke 8:3
24:11 ª Luke 24:25
24:12 ª John 20:3–6
24:13 ª Mark 16:12 ¹ Gr. *stadia*
24:15 ª [Matt. 18:20] ¹ *talked*
24:16 ª John 20:14; 21:4 ¹ *restrained* ² *would*
24:17 ¹ *kind of conversation*
24:18 ª John 19:25 ¹ *the only stranger*
24:19 ª Matt. 21:11; Luke 7:16; John 3:2; Acts 2:22 ᵇ Acts 7:22
24:20 ª Luke 23:1; Acts 13:27, 28
24:21 ª Luke 1:68; 2:38; [Acts 1:6] ¹ *were hoping* ² *would have*
24:22 ª Matt. 28:8; Mark 16:10; Luke 24:9, 10
24:24 ª Luke 24:12

25 Then he said unto them, O fools, and slow of heart to believe all that the prophets have spoken:

26 ªOught not Christ to have suffered these things, and to enter into his ᵇglory?

27 And beginning at ªMoses and ᵇall the prophets, he expounded unto them in all the scriptures the things concerning himself.

28 And they drew ¹nigh unto the village, whither they went: and ªhe made as though he would have gone further.

29 But ªthey constrained him, saying, ᵇAbide with us: for it is toward evening, and the day is far spent. And he went in to tarry with them.

30 And it came to pass, as ªhe sat ¹at meat with them, he took bread, and blessed *it,* and brake, and gave to them.

31 And their eyes were opened, and they knew him; and he vanished out of their sight.

32 And they said one to another, Did not our heart burn within us, while he talked with us by the way, and while he opened to us the scriptures?

33 And they rose up the same hour, and returned to Jerusalem, and found the eleven gathered together, and them that were with them,

34 Saying, The Lord is risen indeed, and ªhath appeared to Simon.

35 And they told what things *were done* in the way, and how he was known of them in breaking of bread.

36 ªAnd as they thus spake, Jesus himself stood in the midst of them, and saith unto them, Peace *be* unto you.

37 But they were terrified and ¹affrighted, and supposed that they had seen ªa spirit.

38 And he said unto them, Why are ye troubled? and why do ¹thoughts arise in your hearts?

24:26 ª Acts 17:2, 3; [Heb. 2:9, 10] ᵇ [1 Pet. 1:10–12]

24:27 ª [Gen. 3:15; 12:3; Num. 21:9; Deut. 18:15]; John 5:46 ᵇ [Ps. 16:9, 10; 22; 132:11; Is. 7:14; 9:6; Jer. 23:5; 33:14, 15; Ezek. 34:23; 37:25; Dan. 9:24]; Mic. 7:20; [Mal. 3:1; 4:2]; John 1:45; 5:39; [Rom. 1:1–6]

24:28 ª Gen. 32:26; 42:7; Mark 6:48 ¹ *near*

24:29 ª Gen. 19:2, 3; Acts 16:15 ᵇ [John 14:23]

24:30 ª Matt. 14:19; Mark 8:6; Luke 9:16 ¹ *at the table*

24:34 ¹ 1 Cor. 15:5

24:36 ª Mark 16:14

24:37 ª Mark 6:49 ¹ *frightened*

24:38 ¹ *doubts*

24:39 ª John 20:20, 27 ᵇ [1 Cor. 15:50]

24:41 ª Gen. 45:26 ᵇ John 21:5 ¹ *marvelled* ² *food*

24:43 ª Acts 10:39–41

24:44 ª Matt. 16:21; 17:22; 20:18

24:45 ª Acts 16:14

24:46 ª Acts 17:3 ¹ *was necessary for*

24:47 ª Acts 5:31; 10:43; 13:38; 26:18 ᵇ [Jer. 31:34]

24:48 ª [Acts 1:8]

24:49 ª Joel 2:28 ¹ *stay*

24:50 ª Acts 1:12

39 Behold my hands and my feet, that it is I myself: ªhandle me, and see; for a ᵇspirit hath not flesh and bones, as ye see me have.

40 And when he had thus spoken, he shewed them *his* hands and *his* feet.

41 And while they yet believed not ªfor joy, and ¹wondered, he said unto them, ᵇHave ye here any ²meat?

42 And they gave him a piece of a broiled fish, and of an honeycomb.

43 ªAnd he took *it,* and did eat before them.

44 And he said unto them, ªThese *are* the words which I spake unto you, while I was yet with you, that all things must be fulfilled, which were written in the law of Moses, and *in* the prophets, and *in* the psalms, concerning me.

45 Then ªopened he their understanding, that they might understand the scriptures,

46 And said unto them, ªThus it is written, and thus it ¹behoved Christ to suffer, and to rise from the dead the third day:

47 And that repentance and ªremission of sins should be preached in his name ᵇamong all nations, beginning at Jerusalem.

48 And ªye are witnesses of these things.

49 ªAnd, behold, I send the promise of my Father upon you: but ¹tarry ye in the city of Jerusalem, until ye be endued with power from on high.

50 And he led them out ªas far as to Bethany, and he lifted up his hands, and blessed them.

51 ªAnd it came to pass, while he blessed them, he was parted from them, and carried up into heaven.

52 ªAnd they worshipped him, and returned to Jerusalem with great joy:

53 And were continually ªin the temple, praising and blessing God. Amen.

24:51 ª Mark 16:19   24:52 ª Matt. 28:9   24:53 ª Acts 2:46

# THE GOSPEL ACCORDING TO
# JOHN

Just as a coin has two sides, both valid, so Jesus Christ has two natures, both valid. Luke presents Christ in His humanity as the Son of Man; John portrays Him in His deity as the Son of God. John's purpose is crystal clear: to set forth Christ in His deity in order to spark believing faith in his readers. John's gospel is topical, not primarily chronological, and it revolves around seven miracles and seven "I am" statements of Christ.

Following an extended eyewitness description of the Upper Room meal and discourse, John records events leading up to the Resurrection, the final climactic proof that Jesus is who He claims to be—the Son of God.

The title of the Fourth Gospel follows the same format as the titles of the synoptic Gospels: *Kata Ioannen*, "According to John." As with the others, the word "Gospel" was added later. *Ioannes* is derived from the Hebrew name *Johanan*, "Yahweh Has Been Gracious."

## CHAPTER 1

IN the beginning <sup>a</sup>was the Word, and the <sup>b</sup>Word was <sup>c</sup>with God, and the Word was <sup>d</sup>God.

2 <sup>a</sup>The same was in the beginning with God.

3 <sup>a</sup>All things were made by him; and without him was not any thing made that was made.

4 <sup>a</sup>In him was life; and <sup>b</sup>the life was the light of men.

5 And <sup>a</sup>the light shineth in darkness; and the darkness <sup>1</sup>comprehended it not.

6 There was a <sup>a</sup>man sent from God, whose name *was* John.

7 The same came for a <sup>a</sup>witness, to bear witness of the Light, that all *men* through him might <sup>b</sup>believe.

8 He was not that Light, but *was* sent to bear witness of that <sup>a</sup>Light.

9 <sup>a</sup>*That* was the true Light, which lighteth every man that cometh into the world.

10 He was in the world, and the world was made by him, and <sup>a</sup>the world knew him not.

11 <sup>a</sup>He came unto <sup>1</sup>his own, and <sup>2</sup>his own received him not.

12 But <sup>a</sup>as many as received him, to them gave he <sup>1</sup>power to become the <sup>2</sup>sons of God, *even* to them that believe on his name:

13 <sup>a</sup>Which were born, not of blood, nor of the will of the flesh, nor of the will of man, but of God.

14 <sup>a</sup>And the Word <sup>b</sup>was<sup>1</sup> made <sup>c</sup>flesh, and dwelt among us, (and <sup>d</sup>we beheld his glory, the glory as of the only begotten of the Father,) <sup>e</sup>full of grace and truth.

15 <sup>a</sup>John bare witness of him, and cried, saying, This was he of whom I spake, <sup>b</sup>He that cometh after me <sup>1</sup>is preferred before me: <sup>c</sup>for he was before me.

16 And of his <sup>a</sup>fulness have all we received, and grace for grace.

17 For <sup>a</sup>the law was given by Moses, *but* <sup>b</sup>grace and <sup>c</sup>truth came by Jesus Christ.

18 <sup>a</sup>No man hath seen God at any time; <sup>b</sup>the only begotten Son, which is in the bosom of the Father, he hath declared *him*.

19 And this is <sup>a</sup>the <sup>1</sup>record of John, when the Jews sent priests and Levites from Jerusalem to ask him, Who art thou?

20 And <sup>a</sup>he confessed, and denied not; but confessed, I am not the Christ.

21 And they asked him, What then? Art thou Elias? And he saith, I am not. Art thou <sup>a</sup>that prophet? And he answered, No.

22 Then said they unto him, Who art thou? that we may give an answer to them that sent us. What sayest thou of thyself?

23 He said, <sup>a</sup>I *am* the voice of one crying in the wilderness, Make straight the way of the Lord, as <sup>b</sup>said the prophet Esaias.

24 And they which were sent were of the Pharisees.

25 And they asked him, and said unto him, Why baptizest thou then, if thou be not that Christ, nor Elias, neither that prophet?

26 John answered them, saying, <sup>a</sup>I baptize with water: <sup>b</sup>but there standeth one among you, whom ye know not;

27 <sup>a</sup>He it is, who coming after me <sup>1</sup>is preferred before me, whose shoe's latchet I am not worthy to unloose.

28 These things were done <sup>a</sup>in Bethabara beyond Jordan, where John was baptizing.

---

1:1 <sup>a</sup> 1 John 1:1
<sup>b</sup> Rev. a19:13
<sup>c</sup> [John 17:5]
<sup>d</sup> [1 John 5:20]
1:2 <sup>a</sup> Gen. 1:1
1:3 <sup>a</sup> [Col. 1:16, 17]
1:4 <sup>a</sup> [1 John 5:11]
<sup>b</sup> John 8:12; 9:5; 12:46
1:5 <sup>a</sup> [John 3:19]
<sup>1</sup> apprehended
1:6 <sup>a</sup> Matt. 3:1–17
1:7 <sup>a</sup> John 3:25–36; 5:33–35
<sup>b</sup> [John 3:16]
1:8 <sup>a</sup> Is. 9:2; 49:6
1:9 <sup>a</sup> Is. 49:6
1:10 <sup>a</sup> Heb. 1:2
1:11 <sup>a</sup> [Luke 19:14]
<sup>1</sup> His own things or domain <sup>2</sup> His own people
1:12 <sup>a</sup> Gal. 3:26
<sup>1</sup> the right <sup>2</sup> Lit. children
1:13 <sup>a</sup> [1 Pet. 1:23]
1:14 <sup>a</sup> Rev. 19:13
<sup>b</sup> Gal. 4:4 <sup>c</sup> Heb. 2:11 <sup>d</sup> Is. 40:5
<sup>e</sup> [John 8:32; 14:6; 18:37] <sup>1</sup> became flesh
1:15 <sup>a</sup> John 3:32 <sup>b</sup> [Matt. 3:11] <sup>c</sup> [Col. 1:17]
<sup>1</sup> ranks higher than I
1:16 <sup>a</sup> Col. 1:19; 2:9
1:17 <sup>a</sup> [Ex. 20:1]
<sup>b</sup> [Rom. 5:21; 6:14]
<sup>c</sup> [John 8:32; 14:6; 18:37]
1:18 <sup>a</sup> Ex. 33:20
<sup>b</sup> 1 John 4:9
1:19 <sup>a</sup> John 5:33
<sup>1</sup> testimony
1:20 <sup>a</sup> Luke 3:15
1:21 <sup>a</sup> Deut. 18:15, 18
1:23 <sup>a</sup> Matt. 3:3

<sup>b</sup> Is. 40:3  1:26 <sup>a</sup> Matt. 3:11 <sup>b</sup> Mal. 3:1  1:27 <sup>a</sup> Acts 19:4
<sup>1</sup> ranks higher than I  1:28 <sup>a</sup> Judg. 7:24

**29** The next day John seeth Jesus coming unto him, and saith, Behold [a]the Lamb of God, [b]which taketh away the sin of the world.

**30** This is he of whom I said, After me cometh a man which [1]is preferred before me: for he was before me.

**31** And I knew him not: but that he should be made manifest to Israel, [a]therefore am I come baptizing with water.

**32** [a]And John bare [1]record, saying, I saw the Spirit descending from heaven like a dove, and it [2]abode upon him.

**33** And I knew him not: but he that sent me to baptize with water, the same said unto me, Upon whom thou shalt see the Spirit descending, and remaining on him, [a]the same is he which baptizeth with the Holy Ghost.

**34** And I saw, and [1]bare record that this is the [a]Son of God.

**35** Again the next day after John stood, and two of his disciples;

**36** And looking upon Jesus as he walked, he saith, [a]Behold the Lamb of God!

**37** And the two disciples heard him speak, and they [a]followed Jesus.

**38** Then Jesus turned, and saw them following, and saith unto them, What seek ye? They said unto him, Rabbi, (which is to say, being interpreted, [1]Master,) where [2]dwellest thou?

**39** He saith unto them, Come and see. They came and saw where he dwelt, and [1]abode with him that day: for it was about the tenth hour.

**40** One of the two which heard John *speak,* and followed him, was [a]Andrew, Simon Peter's brother.

**41** He first findeth his own brother Simon, and saith unto him, We have found the Messias, which is, [1]being interpreted, the [2]Christ.

**42** And he brought him to Jesus. And when Jesus beheld him, he said, Thou art Simon the son of Jona: [a]thou shalt be called Cephas, which is by interpretation, [1]A stone.

**43** The day following Jesus [1]would go forth into Galilee, and findeth [a]Philip, and saith unto him, Follow me.

**44** Now [a]Philip was of Bethsaida, the city of Andrew and Peter.

**45** Philip findeth [a]Nathanael, and saith unto him, We have found him, of whom [b]Moses in the law, and the [c]prophets, did write, Jesus [d]of Nazareth, the [e]son of Joseph.

**46** And Nathanael said unto him, [a]Can there any good thing come out of Nazareth? Philip saith unto him, Come and see.

**47** Jesus saw Nathanael coming to him, and saith of him, Behold [a]an Israelite indeed, in whom is no [1]guile!

**48** Nathanael saith unto him, [1]Whence knowest thou me? Jesus answered and said unto him, Before that Philip called thee, when thou wast under the fig tree, I saw thee.

**49** Nathanael answered and saith unto him, Rabbi, [a]thou art the Son of God; thou art [b]the King of Israel.

**50** Jesus answered and said unto him, Because I said unto thee, I saw thee under the fig tree, believest thou? thou shalt see greater things than these.

**51** And he saith unto him, Verily, verily, I say unto you, [a]Hereafter ye shall see heaven open, and the angels of God ascending and descending upon the Son of man.

## CHAPTER 2

AND the third day there was a [a]marriage in [b]Cana of Galilee; and the [c]mother of Jesus was there:

**2** And both Jesus was [1]called, and his disciples, to the marriage.

**3** And when they [1]wanted wine, the mother of Jesus saith unto him, They have no wine.

**4** Jesus saith unto her, [a]Woman, [b]what [1]have I to do with thee? [c]mine hour is not yet come.

**5** His mother saith unto the servants, Whatsoever he saith unto you, do *it.*

**6** And there were set there six waterpots of stone, [a]after[1] the manner of the purifying of the Jews, containing two or three [2]firkins apiece.

**7** Jesus saith unto them, Fill the waterpots with water. And they filled them up to the brim.

**8** And he saith unto them, [1]Draw out now, and [2]bear unto the [3]governor of the feast. And they bare *it.*

**9** When the [1]ruler of the feast had tasted [a]the water that was made wine, and knew not whence it was: (but the servants which drew the water knew;) the [1]governor of the feast called the bridegroom,

**10** And saith unto him, Every man at the beginning doth set forth good wine; and when men have well drunk, then that which is [1]worse: but thou hast kept the good wine until now.

**11** This [a]beginning of [1]miracles did Jesus in Cana of Galilee, [b]and [2]manifested forth his glory; and his disciples believed on him.

**12** After this he went down to [a]Capernaum, he, and his mother, and [b]his brethren, and his disciples: and they continued there not many days.

**13** [a]And the Jews' passover was at hand, and Jesus went up to Jerusalem,

**14** [a]And found in the temple those that sold oxen and sheep and doves, and the changers of money sitting:

1:29 [a] Rev. 5:6–14
[b] [1 Pet. 2:24]
1:30 [1] ranks higher than I
1:31 [a] Matt. 3:6
1:32 [a] Mark 1:10 [1] witness
[2] remained
1:33 [a] Matt. 3:11
1:34 [a] John 11:27 [1] testified
1:36 [a] John 1:29
1:37 [a] Matt. 4:20, 22
1:38 [1] Teacher [2] are you staying
1:39 [1] remained
1:40 [a] Matt. 4:18
1:41 [1] translated [2] Lit. Anointed One
1:42 [a] Matt. 16:18 [1] Peter
1:43 [a] John 6:5; 12:21, 22; 14:8, 9 [1] wanted to
1:44 [a] John 12:21
1:45 [a] John 21:2 [b] Luke 24:27 [c] [Zech. 6:12] [d] [Matt. 2:23] [e] Luke 3:23
1:46 [a] John 7:41, 42, 52
1:47 [a] Ps. 32:2; 73:1 [1] deceit

1:48 [1] How
1:49 [a] Matt. 14:33 [b] Matt. 21:5
1:51 [a] Gen. 28:12
2:1 [a] [Heb. 13:4] [b] Josh. 19:28 [c] John 19:25
2:2 [1] invited
2:3 [1] ran out of
2:4 [a] John 19:26 [b] 2 Sam. 16:10 [c] John 7:6, 8, 30; 8:20 [1] does your concern have to do with me
2:6 [a] [Mark 7:3] [1] according to [2] Gr. metretes
2:8 [1] Draw some out [2] take it [3] master
2:9 [a] John 4:46 [1] master
2:10 [1] inferior
2:11 [a] John 4:54 [b] [John 1:14] [1] signs [2] revealed
2:12 [a] Matt. 4:13 [b] Matt. 12:46; 13:55
2:13 [a] Deut. 16:1–6
2:14 [a] Mark 11:15, 17

15 And when he had made a ¹scourge of small cords, he drove them all out of the temple, and the sheep, and the oxen; and poured out the changers' money, and ²overthrew the tables;

16 And said unto them that sold doves, Take these things hence; make not ªmy Father's house an house of merchandise.

17 And his disciples remembered that it was written, ªThe zeal of thine house hath eaten me up.

18 Then answered the Jews and said unto him, ªWhat sign shewest thou unto us, seeing that thou doest these things?

19 Jesus answered and said unto them, ªDestroy this temple, and in three days I will raise it up.

20 Then said the Jews, Forty and six years was this temple in building, and wilt thou ¹rear it up in three days?

21 But he spake ªof the temple of his body.

22 When therefore he was risen from the dead, ªhis disciples remembered that he had said this unto them; and they believed the scripture, and the word which Jesus had said.

23 Now when he was in Jerusalem at the passover, in the feast *day,* many believed in his name, when they saw ªthe ¹miracles which he did.

24 But Jesus did not commit himself unto them, because he ªknew all *men,*

25 And needed not that any should testify of man: for ªhe knew what was in man.

## CHAPTER 3

THERE was a man of the Pharisees, named Nicodemus, a ruler of the Jews:

2 ªThe same came to Jesus by night, and said unto him, Rabbi, we know that thou art a teacher come from God: for ᵇno man can do these ¹miracles that thou doest, except ᶜGod be with him.

3 Jesus answered and said unto him, Verily, verily, I say unto thee, ªExcept a man be born ¹again, he cannot see the kingdom of God.

4 Nicodemus saith unto him, How can a man be born when he is old? can he enter the second time into his mother's womb, and be born?

5 Jesus answered, Verily, verily, I say unto thee, ªExcept a man be born of water and *of* the Spirit, he cannot enter into the kingdom of God.

6 That which is born of the flesh is ªflesh; and that which is born of the Spirit is spirit.

7 Marvel not that I said unto thee, Ye must be born again.

---

2:15 ¹ *whip*
² *overturned*
2:16 ª Luke 2:49
2:17 ª Ps. 69:9
2:18 ª Matt. 12:38
2:19 ª Matt. 26:61; 27:40
2:20 ¹ *raise*
2:21 ª [1 Cor. 3:16; 6:19]
2:22 ª Luke 24:8
2:23 ª [Acts 2:22]
¹ *signs*
2:24 ª Rev. 2:23
2:25 ª Matt. 9:4
3:2 ª John 7:50; 19:39 ᵇ John 9:16, 33 ᶜ [Acts 10:38]
¹ *signs*
3:3 ª [1 Pet. 1:23]
¹ Or *from above*
3:5 ª [Acts 2:38]
3:6 ª 1 Cor. 15:50

3:8 ª Eccl. 11:5
¹ *wishes*
3:9 ª John 6:52, 60
3:10 ¹ *teacher*
3:11 ª [Matt. 11:27]
ᵇ John 3:32; 8:14
¹ *what*
3:13 ª Eph. 4:9
3:14 ª Num. 21:9
ᵇ John 8:28; 12:34; 19:18
3:15 ª John 6:47
ᵇ John 3:36
3:16 ª Rom. 5:8
ᵇ [Is. 9:6]
3:17 ª Luke 9:56
3:18 ª John 5:24; 6:40, 47; 20:31
3:19 ª [John 1:4, 9–11] ¹ Lit. *the light*
3:20 ª Eph. 5:11, 13 ¹ *practises* ² *exposed*
3:21 ª 1 Cor. 15:10
3:22 ª John 4:1, 2 ¹ *remained*
3:23 ª 1 Sam. 9:4 ᵇ Matt. 3:5, 6
3:24 ª Matt. 4:12; 14:3
3:26 ª John 1:7, 15, 27, 34

---

8 ªThe wind bloweth where it ¹listeth, and thou hearest the sound thereof, but canst not tell whence it cometh, and whither it goeth: so is every one that is born of the Spirit.

9 Nicodemus answered and said unto him, ªHow can these things be?

10 Jesus answered and said unto him, Art thou a ¹master of Israel, and knowest not these things?

11 ªVerily, verily, I say unto thee, We speak ¹that we do know, and testify ¹that we have seen; and ᵇye receive not our witness.

12 If I have told you earthly things, and ye believe not, how shall ye believe, if I tell you *of* heavenly things?

13 And ªno man hath ascended up to heaven, but he that came down from heaven, *even* the Son of man which is in heaven.

14 ªAnd as Moses lifted up the serpent in the wilderness, even so ᵇmust the Son of man be lifted up:

15 That whosoever ªbelieveth in him should not perish, but ᵇhave eternal life.

16 ªFor God so loved the world, that he gave his only begotten ᵇSon, that whosoever believeth in him should not perish, but have everlasting life.

17 ªFor God sent not his Son into the world to condemn the world; but that the world through him might be saved.

18 ªHe that believeth on him is not condemned: but he that believeth not is condemned already, because he hath not believed in the name of the only begotten Son of God.

19 And this is the condemnation, ªthat ¹light is come into the world, and men loved darkness rather than light, because their deeds were evil.

20 For ªevery one that ¹doeth evil hateth the light, neither cometh to the light, lest his deeds should be ²reproved.

21 But he that doeth truth cometh to the light, that his deeds may be made manifest, that they are ªwrought in God.

22 After these things came Jesus and his disciples into the land of Judaea; and there he ¹tarried with them, ªand baptized.

23 And John also was baptizing in Aenon near to ªSalim, because there was much water there: ᵇand they came, and were baptized.

24 For ªJohn was not yet cast into prison.

25 Then there arose a question between *some* of John's disciples and the Jews about purifying.

26 And they came unto John, and said unto him, Rabbi, he that was with thee beyond Jordan, ªto whom thou barest witness, behold, the

same baptizeth, and all *men* [b]come to him.

27 John answered and said, [a]A man can receive nothing, except it be given him from heaven.

28 Ye yourselves bear me witness, that I said, [a]I am not the Christ, but [b]that I am sent before him.

29 [a]He that hath the bride is the bridegroom: but [b]the friend of the bridegroom, which standeth and heareth him, rejoiceth greatly because of the bridegroom's voice: this my joy therefore is fulfilled.

30 [a]He must increase, but I *must* decrease.

31 [a]He that cometh from above [b]is above all: [c]he that is of the earth is earthly, and speaketh of the earth: [d]he that cometh from heaven is above all.

32 And [a]what he hath seen and heard, that he [1]testifieth; and no man receiveth his testimony.

33 He that hath received his testimony [a]hath [1]set to his seal that God is true.

34 [a]For he whom God hath sent speaketh the words of God: for God giveth not the Spirit [b]by measure *unto him*.

35 [a]The Father loveth the Son, and hath given all things into his hand.

36 [a]He that believeth on the Son hath everlasting life: and he that believeth not the Son shall not see life; but the [b]wrath of God [1]abideth on him.

### CHAPTER 4

WHEN therefore the Lord knew how the Pharisees had heard that Jesus made and [a]baptized more disciples than John,

2 (Though Jesus himself baptized not, but his disciples,)

3 He left Judaea, and departed again into Galilee.

4 And he [1]must needs go through Samaria.

5 Then cometh he to a city of Samaria, which is called Sychar, near to the [1]parcel of ground that [a]Jacob [b]gave to his son Joseph.

6 Now Jacob's well was there. Jesus therefore, being wearied with *his* journey, sat thus on the well: *and* it was about the sixth hour.

7 There cometh a woman of Samaria to draw water: Jesus saith unto her, Give me to drink.

8 (For his disciples were gone away unto the city to buy [1]meat.)

9 Then saith the woman of Samaria unto him, How is it that thou, being a Jew, askest drink of me, which am a woman of Samaria? for [a]the Jews have no dealings with the [b]Samaritans.

10 Jesus answered and said unto her, If thou knewest the [a]gift of God, and who it is that saith to thee, Give me to drink; thou wouldest have asked of him, and he would have given thee [b]living water.

11 The woman saith unto him, Sir, thou hast nothing to draw with, and the well is deep: from whence then hast thou that living water?

12 Art thou greater than our father Jacob, which gave us the well, and drank thereof himself, and his children, and his [1]cattle?

13 Jesus answered and said unto her, Whosoever drinketh of this water shall thirst again:

14 But [a]whosoever drinketh of the water that I shall give him shall never thirst; but the water that I shall give him [b]shall be in him a [1]well of water springing up into everlasting life.

15 [a]The woman saith unto him, Sir, give me this water, that I thirst not, neither come hither to draw.

16 Jesus saith unto her, Go, call thy husband, and come hither.

17 The woman answered and said, I have no husband. Jesus said unto her, Thou hast well said, I have no husband:

18 For thou hast had five husbands; and he whom thou now hast is not thy husband: in that saidst thou truly.

19 The woman saith unto him, Sir, [a]I perceive that thou art a prophet.

20 Our fathers worshipped in [a]this mountain; and ye say, that in [b]Jerusalem is the place where men ought to worship.

21 Jesus saith unto her, Woman, believe me, the hour cometh, [a]when ye shall neither in this mountain, nor yet at Jerusalem, worship the Father.

22 Ye worship [a]ye know not what: we know what we worship: for [b]salvation is of the Jews.

23 But the hour cometh, and now is, when the true worshippers shall [a]worship the Father in [b]spirit [c]and in truth: for the Father seeketh such to worship him.

24 [a]God *is* a Spirit: and they that worship him must worship *him* in spirit and in truth.

25 The woman saith unto him, I know that Messias [a]cometh, which is called Christ: when he is come, [b]he will tell us all things.

26 Jesus saith unto her, [a]I that speak unto thee am *he.*

27 And upon this came his disciples, and marvelled that he talked with [1]the woman: yet no man said, What seekest thou? or, Why talkest thou with her?

28 The woman then left her waterpot, and went her way into the city, and saith to the men,

29 Come, see a man, [a]which told me all things that ever I did: [1]is not this the Christ?

30 Then they went out of the city, and [1]came unto him.

31 In the mean while his disciples [1]prayed him, saying, [2]Master, eat.

32 But he said unto them, I have [1]meat to eat that ye know not of.

33 Therefore said the disciples one to another, Hath any man brought him [1]ought to eat?

34 Jesus saith unto them, [a]My [1]meat is to do the will of him that sent me, and to [b]finish his work.

35 Say not ye, There are yet four months, and *then* cometh [a]harvest? behold, I say unto you, Lift up your eyes, and look on the fields; [b]for they are white already to harvest.

36 [a]And he that reapeth receiveth wages, and gathereth fruit unto life eternal: that [b]both he that soweth and he that reapeth may rejoice together.

37 And herein is that saying true, [a]One soweth, and another reapeth.

38 I sent you to reap that whereon ye [1]bestowed no labour: [a]other men laboured, and ye are entered into their labours.

39 And many of the Samaritans of that city believed on him [a]for the saying of the woman, which testified, He told me all that ever I did.

40 So when the Samaritans were come unto him, they [1]besought him that he would [2]tarry with them: and he [3]abode there two days.

41 And many more believed because of his own [a]word;

42 And said unto the woman, Now we believe, not because of thy saying: for [a]we have heard *him* ourselves, and know that this is indeed the Christ, the Saviour of the world.

43 Now after two days he departed thence, and went into Galilee.

44 For [a]Jesus himself testified, that a prophet hath no honour in his own country.

45 Then when he was come into Galilee, the Galilaeans received him, [a]having seen all the things that he did at Jerusalem at the feast: [b]for they also went unto the feast.

46 So Jesus came again into Cana of Galilee, [a]where he made the water wine. And there was a certain [1]nobleman, whose son was sick at Capernaum.

47 When he heard that Jesus was come out of Judaea into Galilee, he went unto him, and [1]besought him that he would come down, and heal his son: for he was at the point of death.

48 Then said Jesus unto him, [a]Except ye see signs and wonders, ye will not believe.

49 The nobleman saith unto him, Sir, come down [1]ere my child die.

50 Jesus saith unto him, Go thy way; thy son liveth. And the man believed the word that Jesus had spoken unto him, and he went his way.

51 And as he was now going down, his servants met him, and told *him,* saying, Thy son liveth.

52 Then enquired he of them the hour when he began to [1]amend. And they said unto him, Yesterday at the seventh hour the fever left him.

53 So the father knew that *it was* at the same hour, in the which Jesus said unto him, Thy son liveth: and himself believed, and his whole [1]house.

54 This *is* again the second [1]miracle *that* Jesus did, when he was come out of Judaea into Galilee.

## CHAPTER 5

AFTER [a]this there was a feast of the Jews; and Jesus [b]went up to Jerusalem.

2 Now there is at Jerusalem [a]by the sheep [1]*market* a pool, which is called in the Hebrew tongue Bethesda, having five porches.

3 In these lay a great multitude of [1]impotent folk, of blind, [2]halt, [3]withered, waiting for the moving of the water.

4 For an angel went down at a certain [1]season into the pool, and [2]troubled the water: whosoever then first after the troubling of the water stepped in was made whole of whatsoever disease he had.

5 And a certain man was there, which had an infirmity thirty and eight years.

6 When Jesus saw him lie, and knew that he had been now a long time *in that* [1]case, he saith unto him, [2]Wilt thou be made whole?

7 The [1]impotent man answered him, Sir, I have no man, when the water is [2]troubled, to put me into the pool: but while I am coming, another steppeth down before me.

8 Jesus saith unto him, [a]Rise, take up thy bed, and walk.

9 And immediately the man was made [1]whole, and took up his bed, and walked: and [a]on the same day was the sabbath.

10 The Jews therefore said unto him that was cured, It is the sabbath day: [a]it is not lawful for thee to carry *thy* bed.

11 He answered them, He that made me whole, the same said unto me, Take up thy bed, and walk.

12 Then asked they him, What man is that which said unto thee, Take up thy bed, and walk?

13 And he that was [a]healed [1]wist not who it was: for Jesus had [2]conveyed

### Cross references

4:29 [a] John 4:25
[1] could this be

4:30 [1] were coming

4:31 [1] urged  [2] Gr. Rabbi

4:32 [1] food

4:33 [1] Anything

4:34 [a] Ps. 40:7, 8; Heb. 10:9  [b] Job 23:12; [John 6:38; 17:4; 19:30]  [1] food

4:35 [a] Gen. 8:22  [b] Matt. 9:37; Luke 10:2

4:36 [a] Dan. 12:3; Rom. 6:22  [b] 1 Thess. 2:19

4:37 [a] 1 Cor. 3:5–9

4:38 [a] Jer. 44:4; [1 Pet. 1:12]  [1] have not laboured

4:39 [a] John 4:29

4:40 [1] urged  [2] stay  [3] stayed

4:41 [a] Luke 4:32; [John 6:63]

4:42 [a] John 17:8; 1 John 4:14

4:44 [a] Matt. 13:57; Mark 6:4; Luke 4:24

4:45 [a] John 2:13, 23; 3:2  [b] Deut. 16:16

4:46 [a] John 2:1, 11  [1] royal official

4:47 [1] implored

4:48 [a] John 6:30; Rom. 15:19; 1 Cor. 1:22; 2 Cor. 12:12; [2 Thess. 2:9]; Heb. 2:4

4:49 [1] before my child dies

4:52 [1] get better

4:53 [1] household

4:54 [1] sign

5:1 [a] Lev. 23:2; Deut. 16:16  [b] John 2:13

5:2 [a] Neh. 3:1, 32; 12:39  [1] Gate

5:3 [1] sick people  [2] lame  [3] paralyzed

5:4 [1] time  [2] stirred up

5:6 [1] Condition  [2] Do you want to be

5:7 [1] sick  [2] stirred up

5:8 [a] Matt. 9:6; Mark 2:11; Luke 5:24

5:9 [a] John 9:14  [1] well

5:10 [a] Ex. 20:10; Neh. 13:19; Jer. 17:21, 22; Matt. 12:2; Mark 2:24; Luke 6:2

5:13 [a] Luke 13:14; 22:51  [1] knew  [2] withdrawn

himself away, a multitude being in *that* place.

14 Afterward Jesus findeth him in the temple, and said unto him, Behold, thou art made whole: ªsin no more, lest a worse thing come unto thee.

15 The man departed, and told the Jews that it was Jesus, which had made him whole.

16 And ¹therefore did the Jews ªpersecute Jesus, and sought to slay him, because he had done these things on the sabbath day.

17 But Jesus answered them, ªMy Father worketh hitherto, and I work.

18 Therefore the Jews ªsought the more to kill him, because he not only had broken the sabbath, but said also that God was his Father, ᵇmaking himself equal with God.

19 Then answered Jesus and said unto them, Verily, verily, I say unto you, ªThe Son can do nothing of himself, but what he seeth the Father do: for what things soever he doeth, these also doeth the Son likewise.

20 For ªthe Father loveth the Son, and ᵇsheweth him all things that himself doeth: and he will shew him greater works than these, that ye may marvel.

21 For as the Father raiseth up the dead, and ¹quickeneth *them;* ªeven so the Son ¹quickeneth whom he will.

22 For the Father judgeth no man, but ªhath committed all judgment unto the Son:

23 That all *men* should honour the Son, even as they honour the Father. ªHe that honoureth not the Son honoureth not the Father which hath sent him.

24 Verily, verily, I say unto you, ªHe that heareth my word, and believeth on him that sent me, hath everlasting life, and shall not come into ¹condemnation; ᵇbut is passed from death unto life.

25 Verily, verily, I say unto you, The hour is coming, and now is, when ªthe dead shall hear the voice of the Son of God: and they that hear shall live.

26 For ªas the Father hath life in himself; so hath he given to the Son to have ᵇlife in himself;

27 And ªhath given him authority to execute judgment also, ᵇbecause he is the Son of man.

28 Marvel not at this: for the hour is coming, in the which all that are in the graves shall ªhear his voice,

29 ªAnd shall come forth; ᵇthey that have done good, unto the resurrection of life; and they that have done evil, unto the resurrection of ¹damnation.

30 ªI can of mine own self do nothing: as I hear, I judge: and my judgment is ¹just; because ᵇI seek not

mine own will, but the will of the Father which hath sent me.

31 ªIf I bear witness of myself, my witness is not ¹true.

32 ªThere is another that beareth witness of me; and I know that the witness which he witnesseth of me is true.

33 Ye sent unto John, ªand he bare witness unto the truth.

34 But I receive not testimony from man: but these things I say, that ye might be saved.

35 He was a burning and ªa shining ¹light: and ᵇye were willing for a ²season to rejoice in his light.

36 But ªI have greater witness than *that* of John: for ᵇthe works which the Father hath given me to finish, the same ᶜworks that I do, bear witness of me, that the Father hath sent me.

37 And the Father himself, which hath sent me, ªhath borne witness of me. Ye have neither heard his voice at any time, ᵇnor seen his ¹shape.

38 And ye have not his word abiding in you: for whom he hath sent, him ye believe not.

39 ªSearch¹ the scriptures; for in them ye think ye have eternal life: and ᵇthey are they which testify of me.

40 ªAnd¹ ye will not come to me, that ye might have life.

41 ªI receive not honour from men.

42 But I know you, that ye have not the love of God in you.

43 I am come in my Father's name, and ye receive me not: if another shall come in his own name, him ye will receive.

44 ªHow can ye believe, which receive honour one of another, and seek not ᵇthe honour that *cometh* from God only?

45 Do not think that I will accuse you to the Father: ªthere is *one* that accuseth you, *even* Moses, in whom ye trust.

46 For had ye believed Moses, ye would have believed me: ªfor he wrote of me.

47 But if ye believe ªnot his writings, how shall ye believe my words?

## CHAPTER 6

AFTER ªthese things Jesus went over the sea of Galilee, which is *the sea of*ᵇ Tiberias.

2 And a great multitude followed him, because they saw his ¹miracles which he did on them that were ªdiseased.

3 And Jesus went up into a mountain, and there he sat with his disciples.

4 ªAnd the passover, a feast of the Jews, was ¹nigh.

---

5:14 ª Matt. 12:45; [Mark 2:5]; John 8:11
5:16 ª Luke 4:29; John 8:37; 10:39 ¹ *for this reason*
5:17 ª [John 9:4; 17:4]
5:18 ª John 7:1, 19 ᵇ John 10:30; Phil. 2:6
5:19 ª Matt. 26:39; John 5:30; 6:38; 8:28; 12:49; 14:10
5:20 ª Matt. 3:17 ᵇ [Matt. 11:27]
5:21 ª [John 11:25] ¹ *gives life to*
5:22 ª [Acts 17:31]
5:23 ª 1 John 2:23
5:24 ª John 3:16, 18; 6:47 ᵇ [1 John 3:14] ¹ *judgment*
5:25 ª [Col. 2:13]
5:26 ª Ps. 36:9 ᵇ 1 Cor. 15:45
5:27 ª [Acts 10:42; 17:31] ᵇ Dan. 7:13
5:28 ª [1 Thess. 4:15–17]
5:29 ª Is. 26:19 ᵇ Dan. 12:2 ¹ *condemnation*
5:30 ª John 5:19 ᵇ Matt. 26:39 ¹ *righteous*

5:31 ª John 8:14 ¹ *valid as testimony*
5:32 ª [Matt. 3:17]
5:33 ª [John 1:15, 19, 27, 32]
5:35 ª 2 Pet. 1:19 ᵇ Mark 6:20 ¹ *lamp* ² *time*
5:36 ª 1 John 5:9 ᵇ John 3:2; 10:25; 17:4 ᶜ John 9:16; 10:38
5:37 ª Matt. 3:17 ᵇ 1 John 4:12 ¹ *form*
5:39 ª Is. 8:20; 34:16 ᵇ Luke 24:27 ¹ *You search*
5:40 ª [John 1:11; 3:19] ¹ *But*
5:41 ª 1 Thess. 2:6
5:44 ª John 12:43 ᵇ [Rom. 2:29]
5:45 ª Rom. 2:12
5:46 ª Deut. 18:15, 18
5:47 ª Luke 16:29, 31
6:1 ª Mark 6:32 ᵇ John 6:23; 21:1
6:2 ª Matt. 4:23; 8:16; 9:35; 14:36; 15:30; 19:2 ¹ *signs*
6:4 ª Deut. 16:1 ¹ *near*

5 [a]When Jesus then lifted up *his* eyes, and saw a great [1]company come unto him, he saith unto [b]Philip, Whence shall we buy bread, that these may eat?

6 And this he said to [1]prove him: for he himself knew what he would do.

7 Philip answered him, [a]Two hundred [1]pennyworth of bread is not sufficient for them, that every one of them may take a little.

8 One of his disciples, [a]Andrew, Simon Peter's brother, saith unto him,

9 There is a lad here, which hath five barley loaves, and two small fishes: [a]but what are they among so many?

10 And Jesus said, Make the men sit down. Now there was much grass in the place. So the men sat down, in number about five thousand.

11 And Jesus took the loaves; and when he had given thanks, he distributed to the disciples, and the disciples to them that were [1]set down; and likewise of the fishes as much as they [2]would.

12 When they were filled, he said unto his disciples, Gather up the fragments that remain, that nothing be lost.

13 Therefore they gathered *them* together, and filled twelve baskets with the fragments of the five barley loaves, which remained over and above unto them that had eaten.

14 Then those men, when they had seen the miracle that Jesus did, said, This is of a truth [a]that prophet [1]that should come into the world.

15 When Jesus therefore perceived that they [1]would come and take him by force, to make him a [a]king, he departed again into a mountain himself alone.

16 [a]And when [1]even was *now* come, his disciples went down unto the sea,

17 And entered into a ship, and went over the sea toward Capernaum. And it was now dark, and Jesus [1]was not come to them.

18 And the sea arose by reason of a great wind that blew.

19 So when they had rowed about five and twenty or thirty [1]furlongs, they see Jesus walking on the sea, and drawing [2]nigh unto the ship: and they were [a]afraid.

20 But he saith unto them, [a]It is I; be not afraid.

21 Then they willingly received him into the ship: and immediately the ship was at the land whither they [1]went.

22 The day following, when the people which stood on the other side of the sea saw that there was none other boat there, [1]save that one whereinto his disciples were entered, and that

Jesus went not with his disciples into the boat, but *that* his disciples were gone away alone;

23 (Howbeit there came other boats from Tiberias [1]nigh unto the place where they did eat bread, after that the Lord had given thanks:)

24 When the people therefore saw that Jesus was not there, neither his disciples, they also [1]took shipping, and came to Capernaum, [a]seeking for Jesus.

25 And when they had found him on the other side of the sea, they said unto him, Rabbi, when camest thou hither?

26 Jesus answered them and said, Verily, verily, I say unto you, Ye seek me, not because ye saw the [1]miracles, but because ye did eat of the loaves, and were filled.

27 [a]Labour not for the [1]meat which perisheth, but [b]for that [1]meat which endureth unto everlasting life, which the Son of man shall give unto you: [c]for him hath God the Father sealed.

28 Then said they unto him, What shall we do, that we might work the works of God?

29 Jesus answered and said unto them, [a]This is the work of God, that ye believe on him whom he hath sent.

30 They said therefore unto him, [a]What sign [1]shewest thou then, that we may see, and believe thee? what dost thou work?

31 [a]Our fathers did eat manna in the desert; as it is written, [b]He gave them bread from heaven to eat.

32 Then Jesus said unto them, Verily, verily, I say unto you, Moses gave you not that bread from heaven; but [a]my Father giveth you the true bread from heaven.

33 For the bread of God is he which cometh down from heaven, and giveth life unto the world.

34 [a]Then said they unto him, Lord, evermore give us this bread.

35 And Jesus said unto them, [a]I am the bread of life: [b]he that cometh to me shall never hunger; and he that believeth on me shall never [c]thirst.

36 [a]But I said unto you, That ye also have seen me, and believe [b]not.

37 [a]All that the Father giveth me shall come to me; and [b]him that cometh to me I will [1]in no wise cast out.

38 For I came down from heaven, [a]not to do mine own will, [b]but the will of him that sent me.

39 And this is the Father's will which hath sent me, [a]that of all which he hath given me I should lose nothing, but should raise it up again at the last day.

40 And this is the will of him that sent me, [a]that every one which seeth

## Cross References

6:5 [a] Matt. 14:14
[b] John 1:43
[1] *crowd*
6:6 [1] *test*
6:7 [a] Num. 11:21, 22 [1] Gr. *denarii*
6:8 [a] John 1:40
6:9 [a] 2 Kin. 4:43
6:11 [1] *sitting* [2] *wanted*
6:14 [a] Gen. 49:10; Deut. 18:15, 18; John 1:21; 7:40; Acts 3:22; 7:37 [1] *who is coming*
6:15 [a] [John 18:36] [1] *were about to come*
6:16 [a] Matt. 14:23; Mark 6:47 [1] *evening*
6:17 [1] *had*
6:19 [a] Matt. 17:6 [1] Gr. *stadia* [2] *near to*
6:20 [a] Is. 43:1, 2
6:21 [1] *were going*
6:22 [1] *except*
6:23 [1] *near*
6:24 [a] Mark 1:37; Luke 4:42 [1] *got into boats*
6:26 [1] *signs*
6:27 [a] Matt. 6:19 [b] John 4:14; [Eph. 2:8, 9] [c] Ps. 2:7; Is. 42:1; Matt. 3:17; 17:5; Mark 1:11; 9:7; Luke 3:22; 9:35; John 5:37; Acts 2:22; 2 Pet. 1:17 [1] *food*
6:29 [a] 1 Thess. 1:3; James 2:22; [1 John 3:23]; Rev. 2:26
6:30 [a] Matt. 12:38; 16:1; Mark 8:11; 1 Cor. 1:22 [1] *will you perform*
6:31 [a] Ex. 16:15; Num. 11:7; 1 Cor. 10:3 [b] Ex. 16:4, 15; Neh. 9:15; Ps. 78:24
6:32 [a] John 3:13, 16
6:34 [a] John 4:15
6:35 [a] John 6:48, 58 [b] John 4:14; 7:37; Rev. 7:16 [c] Is. 55:1, 2
6:36 [a] John 6:26, 64; 15:24 [b] John 10:26
6:37 [a] John 6:45 [b] [Matt. 24:24; John 10:28, 29]; 2 Tim. 2:19; 1 John 2:19 [1] *certainly not*
6:38 [a] Matt. 26:39; John 5:30 [b] John 4:34
6:39 [a] John 10:28; 17:12; 18:9
6:40 [a] John 3:15, 16; 4:14; 6:27, 47, 54

the Son, and believeth on him, may have everlasting life: and I will raise him up at the last day.

41 The Jews then ¹murmured at him, because he said, I am the bread which came down from heaven.

42 And they said, ªIs not this Jesus, the son of Joseph, whose father and mother we know? how is it then that he saith, I came down from heaven?

43 Jesus therefore answered and said unto them, ¹Murmur not among yourselves.

44 ªNo man can come to me, except the Father which hath sent me ᵇdraw him: and I will raise him up at the last day.

45 ªIt is written in the prophets, And they shall be all taught of God. ᵇEvery man therefore that hath heard, and hath learned of the Father, cometh unto me.

46 ªNot that any man hath seen the Father, ᵇsave he which is ¹of God, he hath seen the Father.

47 Verily, verily, I say unto you, ªHe that believeth on me hath everlasting life.

48 ªI am that bread of life.

49 ªYour fathers did eat manna in the wilderness, and are dead.

50 ªThis is the bread which cometh down from heaven, that a man may eat thereof, and not die.

51 I am the living bread ªwhich came down from heaven: if any man eat of this bread, he shall live for ever: and ᵇthe bread that I will give is my flesh, which I will give for the life of the world.

52 The Jews therefore ªstrove¹ among themselves, saying, How can this man give us *his* flesh to eat?

53 Then Jesus said unto them, Verily, verily, I say unto you, Except ªye eat the flesh of the Son of man, and drink his blood, ye have no life in you.

54 ªWhoso eateth my flesh, and drinketh my blood, hath eternal life; and I will raise him up at the last day.

55 For my flesh is ¹meat indeed, and my blood is drink indeed.

56 He that eateth my flesh, and drinketh my blood, ªdwelleth in me, and I in him.

57 As the living Father hath sent me, and I live by the Father: so he that eateth me, even he shall live ¹by me.

58 ªThis is that bread which came down from heaven: not ᵇas your fathers did eat manna, and are dead: he that eateth of this bread shall live for ever.

59 These things said he in the synagogue, as he taught in Capernaum.

60 ªMany therefore of his disciples, when they had heard *this,* said, This is ¹an hard saying; who can ²hear it?

61 When Jesus knew in himself that his disciples ¹murmured at it, he said unto them, Doth this offend you?

62 ª*What* and if ye shall see the Son of man ascend up where he was before?

63 ªIt is the spirit that ¹quickeneth; the ᵇflesh profiteth nothing: the ᶜwords that I speak unto you, *they* are spirit, and *they* are life.

64 But ªthere are some of you that believe not. For ᵇJesus knew from the beginning who they were that believed not, and who should betray him.

65 And he said, Therefore ªsaid I unto you, that no man can come unto me, except it were given unto him of my Father.

66 ªFrom that *time* many of his disciples went ¹back, and walked no more with him.

67 Then said Jesus unto the twelve, ¹Will ye also go away?

68 Then Simon Peter answered him, Lord, to whom shall we go? thou hast ªthe words of eternal life.

69 ªAnd we believe and ¹are sure that thou art that Christ, the Son of the living God.

70 Jesus answered them, ªHave not I chosen you twelve, ᵇand one of you is a devil?

71 He spake of ªJudas Iscariot *the son* of Simon: for he it was that should ᵇbetray him, being one of the twelve.

## CHAPTER 7

AFTER these things Jesus walked in Galilee: for he would not walk in ¹Jewry, ªbecause the Jews sought to kill him.

2 ªNow the Jews' feast of tabernacles was at hand.

3 ªHis brethren therefore said unto him, Depart hence, and go into Judaea, that thy disciples also may see the works that thou doest.

4 For *there is* no man *that* doeth any thing in secret, ¹and he himself seeketh to be known openly. If thou do these things, shew thyself to the world.

5 For ªneither did his ᵇbrethren believe in him.

6 Then Jesus said unto them, ªMy time is not yet come: but your time is alway ready.

7 ªThe world cannot hate you; but me it hateth, ᵇbecause I testify of it, that the works thereof are evil.

8 Go ye up unto this feast: I go not up yet unto this feast; ªfor my time is not yet full come.

9 When he had said these words unto them, he ¹abode *still* in Galilee.

---

6:41 ¹ grumbled
6:42 ª Matt. 13:55; Mark 6:3; Luke 4:22
6:43 ¹ Stop grumbling
6:44 ª Song 1:4 ᵇ [Phil. 1:29; 2:12, 13]
6:45 ª Is. 54:13 ᵇ John 6:37
6:46 ª John 1:18 ᵇ Matt. 11:27 ¹ from
6:47 ¹ [John 3:16, 18]
6:48 ª John 6:33, 35
6:49 ª John 6:31, 58
6:50 ª John 6:51, 58
6:51 ª John 3:13 ᵇ Heb. 10:5
6:52 ª John 7:43; 9:16; 10:19 ¹ quarreled
6:53 ª Matt. 26:26
6:54 ª John 4:14; 6:27, 40
6:55 ¹ food
6:56 ª [1 John 3:24; 4:15, 16]
6:57 ¹ because of
6:58 ª John 6:49–51 ᵇ Ex. 16:14–35
6:60 ª John 6:66 ¹ a difficult ² understand
6:61 ¹ grumbled
6:62 ª Acts 1:9; 2:32, 33
6:63 ª 2 Cor. 3:6 ᵇ John 3:6 ᶜ [John 6:68; 14:24] ¹ gives life
6:64 ª John 6:36 ᵇ John 2:24, 25; 13:11
6:65 ª John 6:37, 44, 45
6:66 ª Luke 9:62 ¹ away
6:67 ¹ Do you also want to
6:68 ª Acts 5:20
6:69 ª Luke 9:20 ¹ Lit. know
6:70 ª Luke 6:13 ᵇ [John 13:27]
6:71 ª John 12:4; 13:2, 26 ᵇ Matt. 26:14–16
7:1 ª John 5:18; 7:19, 25; 8:37, 40 ¹ Judea
7:2 ª Lev. 23:34
7:3 ª Matt. 12:46
7:4 ¹ while
7:5 ª Ps. 69:8 ᵇ Mark 3:21
7:6 ª John 9:4; 8:20
7:7 ª [John 15:19] ᵇ John 3:19   7:8 ª John 8:20
7:9 ¹ remained

10 But when his brethren were gone up, then went he also up unto the feast, not openly, but as it were in secret.

11 Then [a]the Jews sought him at the feast, and said, Where is he?

12 And [a]there was much murmuring among the people concerning him: for [b]some said, He is a good man: others said, Nay; but he deceiveth the people.

13 Howbeit no man spake openly of him [a]for fear of the Jews.

14 Now about the [1]midst of the feast Jesus went up into the temple, and [a]taught.

15 [a]And the Jews marvelled, saying, How knoweth this man letters, having never [1]learned?

16 Jesus answered them, and said, [a]My doctrine is not mine, but his that sent me.

17 [a]If any man will do his will, he shall know [1]of the doctrine, whether it be of God, or *whether* I speak of myself.

18 [a]He that speaketh of himself seeketh his own glory: but he that [b]seeketh his glory that sent him, the same is true, and [c]no unrighteousness is in him.

19 [a]Did not Moses give you the law, and *yet* none of you keepeth the law? [b]Why go ye about to kill me?

20 The people answered and said, [a]Thou hast a [1]devil: who goeth about to kill thee?

21 Jesus answered and said unto them, I have done one work, and ye all marvel.

22 [a]Moses therefore gave unto you circumcision; (not because it is of Moses, [b]but of the fathers;) and ye on the sabbath day circumcise a man.

23 If a man on the sabbath day receive circumcision, that the law of Moses should not be broken; are ye angry at me, because [a]I have made a man [1]every whit whole on the sabbath day?

24 [a]Judge not according to the appearance, but judge righteous judgment.

25 Then said some of them of Jerusalem, Is not this he, whom they seek to [a]kill?

26 But, lo, he speaketh boldly, and they say nothing unto him. [a]Do the rulers know indeed that this is the very Christ?

27 [a]Howbeit we know this man whence he is: but when Christ cometh, no man knoweth whence he is.

28 Then cried Jesus in the temple as he taught, saying, [a]Ye both know me, and ye know whence I am: and [b]I am not come of myself, but he that sent me [c]is true, [d]whom ye know not.

29 But [a]I know him: for I am from him, and he hath sent me.

30 Then [a]they sought to take him: but [b]no man laid hands on him, because his hour was not yet come.

31 And [a]many of the people believed on him, and said, When Christ cometh, will he do more [1]miracles than these which this *man* hath done?

32 The Pharisees heard that the people murmured such things concerning him; and the Pharisees and the chief priests sent officers to take him.

33 Then said Jesus unto them, [a]Yet a little while [1]am I with you, and *then* I [b]go unto him that sent me.

34 Ye [a]shall seek me, and shall not find *me:* and where I am, *thither* ye [b]cannot come.

35 Then said the Jews among themselves, Whither will he go, that we shall not find him? will he go unto [a]the [1]dispersed among the [2]Gentiles, and teach the Gentiles?

36 What *manner of* saying is this that he said, Ye shall seek me, and shall not find *me:* and where I am, *thither* ye cannot come?

37 [a]In the last day, that great *day* of the feast, Jesus stood and cried, saying, [b]If any man thirst, let him come unto me, and drink.

38 [a]He that believeth on me, as the scripture hath said, [b]out of his [1]belly shall flow rivers of living water.

39 ([a]But this spake he of the Spirit, which they that believe on him should receive: for the Holy Ghost was not yet *given;* because that Jesus was not yet [b]glorified.)

40 Many of the people therefore, when they heard this saying, said, Of a truth this is [a]the Prophet.

41 Others said, This is [a]the Christ. But some said, Shall Christ come out of Galilee?

42 [a]Hath not the scripture said, That Christ cometh of the seed of David, and out of the town of Bethlehem, [b]where David was?

43 So [a]there was a division among the people because of him.

44 And [a]some of them would have taken him; but no man laid hands on him.

45 Then came the officers to the chief priests and Pharisees; and they said unto them, Why have ye not brought him?

46 The officers answered, [a]Never man spake like this man.

47 Then answered them the Pharisees, Are ye also deceived?

48 Have any of the rulers or of the Pharisees believed on him?

49 But this [1]people who knoweth not the law are cursed.

---

7:11 [a] John 11:56
7:12 [a] John 9:16; 10:19 [b] Luke 7:16
7:13 [a] [John 9:22; 12:42; 19:38]
7:14 [a] Mark 6:34 [1] *middle*
7:15 [a] Matt. 13:54 [1] *studied*
7:16 [a] John 3:11
7:17 [a] John 3:21; 8:43 [1] *concerning*
7:18 [a] John 5:41 [b] John 8:50 [c] [2 Cor. 5:21]
7:19 [a] Deut. 33:4 [b] Matt. 12:14
7:20 [a] John 8:48, 52 [1] *demon*
7:22 [a] Lev. 12:3 [b] Gen. 17:9–14
7:23 [a] John 5:8, 9, 16 [1] *completely well*
7:24 [a] Prov. 24:23
7:25 [a] Matt. 21:38; 26:4
7:26 [a] John 7:48
7:27 [a] Luke 4:22
7:28 [a] John 8:14 [b] John 5:43 [c] Rom. 3:4 [d] John 1:18; 8:55

7:29 [a] Matt. 11:27
7:30 [a] Mark 11:18 [b] John 7:32, 44; 8:20; 10:39
7:31 [a] Matt. 12:23 [1] *signs*
7:33 [a] John 13:33 [b] [1 Pet. 3:22] [1] *I shall be*
7:34 [a] Hos. 5:6 [b] [Matt. 5:20]
7:35 [a] James 1:1 [1] *dispersion,* scattered Jews [2] *Greeks*
7:37 [a] Lev. 23:36 [b] [Is. 55:1]
7:38 [a] Deut. 18:15 [b] Is. 12:3; 43:20; 44:3; 55:1 [1] *heart*
7:39 [a] Is. 44:3 [b] John 12:16; 13:31; 17:5
7:40 [a] Deut. 18:15, 18
7:41 [a] John 4:42; 6:69
7:42 [a] Mic. 5:2 [b] 1 Sam. 16:1; 4
7:43 [a] John 7:12
7:44 [a] John 7:30
7:46 [a] Luke 4:22
7:49 [1] *crowd*

50 Nicodemus saith unto them, (ªhe that came ¹to Jesus by night, being one of them,)

51 ªDoth our law judge *any* man, before it hear him, and know what he doeth?

52 They answered and said unto him, Art thou also of Galilee? Search, and look: for ªout of Galilee ariseth no prophet.

53 And every man went unto his own house.

## CHAPTER 8

Jesus went unto the mount of Olives.

2 And early in the morning he came again into the temple, and all the people came unto him; and he sat down, and ªtaught them.

3 And the scribes and Pharisees brought unto him a woman ¹taken in adultery; and when they had set her in the midst,

4 They say unto him, ¹Master, this woman was ²taken in ªadultery, in the very act.

5 ªNow Moses in the law commanded us, that such should be stoned: but what sayest thou?

6 This they said, ¹tempting him, that they ªmight ²have to accuse him. But Jesus stooped down, and with *his* finger wrote on the ground, *as though he heard them not.*

7 So when they continued asking him, he ¹lifted up himself, and said unto them, ªHe that is without sin among you, let him first cast a stone at her.

8 And again he stooped down, and wrote on the ground.

9 And they which heard *it,* ªbeing convicted by *their own* conscience, went out one by one, beginning at the eldest, *even* unto the last: and Jesus was left alone, and the woman standing in the midst.

10 When Jesus had ¹lifted up himself, and saw none but the woman, he said unto her, Woman, where are those thine accusers? hath no man condemned thee?

11 She said, No man, Lord. And Jesus said unto her, ªNeither do I condemn thee: go, and ᵇsin no more.

12 Then spake Jesus again unto them, saying, ªI am the light of the world: he that ᵇfolloweth me shall not walk in darkness, but shall have the light of life.

13 The Pharisees therefore said unto him, ªThou bearest ¹record of thyself; thy ¹record is not ²true.

14 Jesus answered and said unto them, Though I bear ¹record of myself, *yet* my record is true: for I know whence I came, and whither I go; but ªye cannot tell whence I come, and whither I go.

15 ªYe judge ¹after the flesh; ᵇI judge no man.

16 And yet if I judge, my judgment is true: for ªI am not alone, but I ¹and the Father that sent me.

17 ªIt is also written in your law, that the testimony of two men is true.

18 I am one that bear witness of myself, and ªthe Father that sent me beareth witness of me.

19 Then said they unto him, Where is thy Father? Jesus answered, ªYe neither know me, nor my Father: ᵇif ye had known me, ye should have known my Father also.

20 These words spake Jesus in ªthe treasury, as he taught in the temple: and ᵇno man laid hands on him; for ᶜhis hour was not yet come.

21 Then ªsaid Jesus again unto them, I ¹go my way, and ªye shall seek me, and ᵇshall die in your ²sins: whither I go, ye cannot come.

22 Then said the Jews, Will he kill himself? because he saith, Whither I go, ye cannot come.

23 And he said unto them, ªYe are from beneath; I am from above: ᵇye are of this world; I am not of this world.

24 ªI said therefore unto you, that ye shall die in your sins: ᵇfor if ye believe not that I am *he,* ye shall die in your sins.

25 Then said they unto him, Who art thou? And Jesus saith unto them, Even *the same* that I ªsaid unto you from the beginning.

26 I have many things to say and to judge ¹of you: but ªhe that sent me is true; and ᵇI speak to the world those things which I have heard of him.

27 They understood not that he spake to them of the Father.

28 Then said Jesus unto them, When ye have ªlifted¹ up the Son of man, ᵇthen shall ye know that I am *he,* and ᶜ*that* I do nothing of myself; but ᵈas my Father hath taught me, I speak these things.

29 And ªhe that sent me is with me: ᵇthe Father hath not left me alone; ᶜfor I do always those things that please him.

30 As he spake these words, ªmany believed on him.

31 Then said Jesus to those Jews which believed on him, If ye ªcontinue¹ in my word, *then* are ye my disciples indeed;

32 And ye shall know the ªtruth, and ᵇthe truth shall make you free.

33 They answered him, ªWe be Abraham's ¹seed, and were never ²in bondage to any man: how sayest thou, Ye shall be made free?

34 Jesus answered them, Verily, verily, I say unto you, ªWhosoever committeth sin is the ¹servant of sin.

### Cross references

7:50 ª John 3:1, 2; 19:39　¹ Lit. *to him*
7:51 ª Deut. 1:16, 17; 19:15
7:52 ª [Is. 9:1, 2]
8:2 ª John 8:20; 18:20
8:3 ¹ *caught*
8:4 ª Ex. 20:14 ¹ *Teacher* ² *caught*
8:5 ª Lev. 20:10
8:6 ª Matt. 22:15 ¹ *testing* ² *have something of which to*
8:7 ª Deut. 17:7 ¹ *raised*
8:9 ª Rom. 2:22
8:10 ¹ *raised*
8:11 ª [John 3:17] ᵇ [John 5:14]
8:12 ª John 1:4; 9:5; 12:35 ᵇ 1 Thess. 5:5
8:13 ª John 5:31 ¹ *witness* ² *valid as testimony*
8:14 ª John 7:28; 9:29 ¹ *witness*
8:15 ª John 7:24 ᵇ [John 3:17; 12:47; 18:36] ¹ *according to*
8:16 ª John 16:32 ¹ *am with*
8:17 ª Deut. 17:6; 19:15
8:18 ª John 5:37
8:19 ª John 16:3 ᵇ John 14:7
8:20 ª Mark 12:41, 43 ᵇ John 2:4; 7:30 ᶜ John 7:8
8:21 ª John 7:34; 13:33 ᵇ John 8:24 ¹ *am going away* ² Lit. *sin*
8:23 ª John 3:31 ᵇ 1 John 4:5
8:24 ª John 8:21 ᵇ [Mark 16:16]
8:25 ª John 4:26
8:26 ª John 7:28 ᵇ John 3:32; 15:15 ¹ *concerning*
8:28 ª John 3:14; 12:32; 19:18 ᵇ [Rom. 1:4] ᶜ John 5:19, 30 ᵈ John 3:11 ¹ *Crucified*
8:29 ª John 14:10 ᵇ John 8:16; 16:32 ᶜ John 4:34; 5:30; 6:38
8:30 ª John 7:31; 10:42; 11:45
8:31 ª [John 14:15, 23] ¹ *abide*
8:32 ª [John 1:14, 17; 14:6] ᵇ [Rom. 6:14, 18, 22]
8:33 ª [Matt. 3:9] ¹ *descendants* ² *enslaved*
8:34 ª 2 Pet. 2:19 ¹ *slave*

35 And ᵃthe servant abideth not in the house for ever: *but* the Son abideth ¹ever.

36 ᵃIf the Son therefore shall make you free, ye shall be free indeed.

37 I know that ye are Abraham's ¹seed; but ᵃye seek to kill me, because my word hath no place in you.

38 ᵃI speak that which I have seen with my Father: and ye do that which ye have seen with your father.

39 They answered and said unto him, ᵃAbraham is our father. Jesus saith unto them, ᵇIf ye were Abraham's children, ye would do the works of Abraham.

40 ᵃBut now ye seek to kill me, a man that hath told you the truth, ᵇwhich I have heard of God: this did not Abraham.

41 Ye do the deeds of your father. Then said they to him, We be not born of fornication; ᵃwe have one Father, *even* God.

42 Jesus said unto them, ᵃIf God were your Father, ye would love me: ᵇfor I proceeded forth and came from God; ᶜneither came I of myself, but he sent me.

43 ᵃWhy do ye not understand my speech? *even* because ye cannot hear my word.

44 ᵃYe are of *your* father the devil, and the ᵇlusts¹ of your father ye will ᶜdo. He was a murderer from the beginning, and ᵈabode² not in the truth, because there is no truth in him. When he speaketh a lie, he speaketh ³of his own: for he is a liar, and the father of it.

45 And because I tell *you* the truth, ye believe me not.

46 Which of you ¹convinceth me of sin? And if I say the truth, why do ye not believe me?

47 ᵃHe that is of God heareth God's words: ye therefore hear *them* not, because ye are not of God.

48 Then answered the Jews, and said unto him, Say we not well that thou art a Samaritan, and ᵃhast a ¹devil?

49 Jesus answered, I have not a ¹devil; but I honour my Father, and ᵃye do dishonour me.

50 And ᵃI seek not mine own glory: there is one that seeketh and judgeth.

51 Verily, verily, I say unto you, ᵃIf a man keep my ¹saying, he shall never see death.

52 Then said the Jews unto him, Now we know that thou ᵃhast a ¹devil. ᵇAbraham is dead, and the prophets; and thou sayest, If a man keep my saying, he shall never taste of death.

53 Art thou greater than our father Abraham, which is dead? and the prophets are dead: ᵃwhom makest thou thyself?

54 Jesus answered, ᵃIf I honour myself, my honour is nothing: ᵇit is my Father that honoureth me; of whom ye say, that he is your God:

55 Yet ᵃye have not known him; but I know him: and if I should say, I know him not, I shall be a liar like unto you: but I know him, and ᵇkeep his ¹saying.

56 Your father Abraham ᵃrejoiced to see my day: ᵇand he saw *it,* and was glad.

57 Then said the Jews unto him, Thou art not yet fifty years old, and hast thou seen Abraham?

58 Jesus said unto them, Verily, verily, I say unto you, ᵃBefore Abraham was, ᵇI am.

59 Then ᵃtook they up stones to cast at him: but Jesus hid himself, and went out of the temple, ᵇgoing through the midst of them, and so passed by.

## CHAPTER 9

AND as *Jesus* passed by, he saw a man which was blind from *his* birth.

2 And his disciples asked him, saying, ¹Master, ᵃwho did sin, this man, or his parents, that he was born blind?

3 Jesus answered, Neither hath this man sinned, nor his parents: ᵃbut that the works of God should be ¹made manifest in him.

4 ᵃI must work the works of him that sent me, while it is ᵇday: the night cometh, when no man can work.

5 As long as I am in the world, ᵃI am the light of the world.

6 When he had thus spoken, ᵃhe spat on the ground, and made clay of the ¹spittle, and he ²anointed the eyes of the blind man with the clay,

7 And said unto him, Go, wash ᵃin the pool of Siloam, (which is ¹by interpretation, Sent.) ᵇHe went his way therefore, and washed, and came seeing.

8 The neighbours therefore, and they which ¹before had seen him that he was blind, said, Is not this he that sat and begged?

9 Some said, This is he: others *said,* He is like him: *but* he said, I am *he.*

10 Therefore said they unto him, How were thine eyes opened?

11 He answered and said, ᵃA man that is called Jesus made clay, and anointed mine eyes, and said unto me, Go to the pool of Siloam, and wash: and I went and washed, and I received sight.

12 Then said they unto him, Where is he? He said, I know not.

13 They brought to the Pharisees him that ¹aforetime was blind.

8:35 ᵃ Gal. 4:30
¹ *forever*
8:36 ᵃ Gal. 5:1
8:37 ᵃ John 7:19
¹ *descendants*
8:38 ᵃ [John 3:32; 5:19, 30; 14:10, 24]
8:39 ᵃ Matt. 3:9
ᵇ [Rom. 2:28]
8:40 ᵃ John 8:37
ᵇ John 8:26
8:41 ᵃ Is. 63:16
8:42 ᵃ 1 John 5:1
ᵇ John 16:27; 17:8, 25 ᶜ Gal. 4:4
8:43 ᵃ [John 7:17]
8:44 ᵃ Matt. 13:38
ᵇ 1 John 2:16, 17
ᶜ [1 John 3:8–10, 15] ᵈ [Jude 6]
¹ *desires* ² *stands*
³ *from his own*
nature
8:46 ¹ *convicts*
8:47 ᵃ 1 John 4:6
8:48 ᵃ John 7:20;
10:20 ¹ *demon*
8:49 ᵃ John 5:41
¹ *demon*
8:50 ᵃ John 5:41;
7:18
8:51 ᵃ John 5:24;
11:26 ¹ *word*
8:52 ᵃ John 7:20;
10:20 ᵇ Zech. 1:5
¹ *demon*
8:53 ᵃ John 10:33;
19:7

8:54 ᵃ John 5:31,
32 ᵇ Acts 3:13
8:55 ᵃ John 7:28,
29 ᵇ [John 15:10]
¹ *word*
8:56 ᵃ Luke 10:24
ᵇ Heb. 11:13
8:58 ᵃ Mic. 5:2
ᵇ Rev. 1:8
8:59 ᵃ John 10:31;
11:8 ᵇ Luke 4:30
9:2 ᵃ John 9:34
¹ *Rabbi*
9:3 ᵃ John 11:4
¹ *revealed*
9:4 ᵃ [John 4:34;
5:19, 36; 17:4]
ᵇ John 11:9, 10;
12:35
9:5 ᵃ [John 1:5, 9;
3:19; 8:12; 12:35,
46]
9:6 ᵃ Mark 7:33;
8:23 ¹ *saliva*
² *applied the clay*
*upon the eyes of*
*the blind man*
9:7 ᵃ Neh. 3:15
ᵇ 2 Kin. 5:14
¹ *translated*
9:8 ¹ *previously*
9:11 ᵃ John 9:6, 7
9:13 ¹ *formerly*

14 And it was the sabbath day when Jesus made the clay, and opened his eyes.

15 Then again the Pharisees also asked him how he had received his sight. He said unto them, He put clay upon mine eyes, and I washed, and do see.

16 Therefore said some of the Pharisees, This man is not of God, because he [1]keepeth not the sabbath day. Others said, [a]How can a man that is a sinner do such miracles? And [b]there was a division among them.

17 They say unto the blind man again, What sayest thou of him, that he hath opened thine eyes? He said, [a]He is a prophet.

18 But the Jews did not believe concerning him, that he had been blind, and received his sight, until they called the parents of him that had received his sight.

19 And they asked them, saying, Is this your son, who ye say was born blind? how then doth he now see?

20 His parents answered them and said, We know that this is our son, and that he was born blind:

21 But by what means he now seeth, we know not; or who hath opened his eyes, we know not: he is of age; ask him: he shall speak for himself.

22 These *words* spake his parents, because [a]they feared the Jews: for the Jews had agreed already, that if any man did confess that he was Christ, he [b]should be put out of the synagogue.

23 Therefore said his parents, He is of age; ask him.

24 Then again called they the man that was blind, and said unto him, [a]Give God the praise: [b]we know that this man is a sinner.

25 He answered and said, Whether he be a sinner *or no*, I know not: one thing I know, that, whereas I was blind, now I see.

26 Then said they to him again, What did he to thee? how opened he thine eyes?

27 He answered them, I have told you already, and ye did not [1]hear: [2]wherefore would ye hear *it* again? [3]will ye also be his disciples?

28 Then they reviled him, and said, Thou art his disciple; but we are Moses' disciples.

29 We know that God [a]spake unto [b]Moses: *as for* this *fellow*, [c]we know not from whence he is.

30 The man answered and said unto them, [a]Why herein is a marvellous thing, that ye know not from whence he is, and *yet* he hath opened mine eyes.

31 Now we know that [a]God heareth not sinners: but if any man be a wor-

shipper of God, and doeth his will, him he heareth.

32 Since the world began was it not heard that any man opened the eyes of one that was born blind.

33 [a]If this man were not of God, he could do nothing.

34 They answered and said unto him, [a]Thou wast altogether born in sins, and dost thou teach us? And they [1]cast him out.

35 Jesus heard that they had cast him out; and when he had [a]found him, he said unto him, Dost thou [b]believe on [c]the Son of God?

36 He answered and said, Who is he, Lord, that I might believe on him?

37 And Jesus said unto him, Thou hast both seen him, and [a]it is he that talketh with thee.

38 And he said, Lord, I believe. And he [a]worshipped him.

39 And Jesus said, [a]For judgment I am come into this world, [b]that they which see not might see; and that they which see might be made blind.

40 And *some* of the Pharisees which were with him heard these words, [a]and said unto him, Are we blind also?

41 Jesus said unto them, [a]If ye were blind, ye should have no sin: but now ye say, We see; therefore your sin remaineth.

## CHAPTER 10

V ERILY, verily, I say unto you, He that entereth not by the door into the sheepfold, but climbeth up some other way, the same is a thief and a robber.

2 But he that entereth in by the door is the shepherd of the sheep.

3 To him the [1]porter openeth; and the sheep hear his voice: and he calleth his own sheep by [a]name, and leadeth them out.

4 And when he putteth forth his own sheep, he goeth before them, and the sheep follow him: for they know his voice.

5 And a [a]stranger will they not follow, but will flee from him: for they know not the voice of strangers.

6 This [1]parable spake Jesus unto them: but they understood not what things they were which he spake unto them.

7 Then said Jesus unto them again, Verily, verily, I say unto you, I am the door of the sheep.

8 All that ever came before me are thieves and robbers: but the sheep did not hear them.

9 [a]I am the door: by me if any man enter in, he shall be saved, and shall go in and out, and find pasture.

10 The thief cometh not, [1]but for to steal, and to kill, and to destroy: I am

### Cross references (center column)

9:16 [a] John 3:2; 9:33 [b] John 7:12, 43; 10:19 [1] *observes*

9:17 [a] [John 4:19; 6:14]

9:22 [a] John 7:13; 12:42; 19:38; Acts 5:13 [b] John 16:2

9:24 [a] Josh. 7:19; 1 Sam. 6:5; Ezra 10:11; Rev. 11:13 [b] John 9:16

9:27 [1] *listen* [2] *why do you want to* [3] *do you also want to be*

9:29 [a] Ex. 19:19, 20; 33:11; 34:29; Num. 12:6–8 [b] [John 5:45–47] [c] John 7:27, 28; 8:14

9:30 [a] John 3:10.

9:31 [a] Job 27:9; 35:12; Ps. 18:41; Prov. 1:28; 15:29; 28:9; Is. 1:15; Jer. 11:11; 14:12; Ezek. 8:18; Mic. 3:4; Zech. 7:13; [James 5:16]

9:33 [a] John 3:2; 9:16

9:34 [a] Ps. 51:5; John 9:2 [1] Excommunicated him

9:35 [a] John 5:14 [b] John 1:7; 16:31 [c] Matt. 14:33; 16:16; Mark 1:1; John 10:36; 1 John 5:13

9:37 [a] John 4:26

9:38 [a] Matt. 8:2

9:39 [a] [John 3:17; 5:22, 27; 12:47] [b] Matt. 13:13; 15:14

9:40 [a] [Rom. 2:19]

9:41 [a] John 15:22, 24

10:3 [a] John 20:16 [1] *doorkeeper*

10:5 [a] [2 Cor. 11:13–15]

10:6 [1] *illustration*

10:9 [a] [John 14:6; Eph. 2:18]

10:10 [1] *except*

come that they might have life, and that they might have *it* more abundantly.

11 [a]I am the good shepherd: the good shepherd giveth his life for the sheep.

12 But he that is an [1]hireling, and not the shepherd, whose own the sheep are not, seeth the wolf coming, and [a]leaveth the sheep, and fleeth: and the wolf catcheth them, and scattereth the sheep.

13 The hireling fleeth, because he is an hireling, and careth not for the sheep.

14 I am the good shepherd, and [a]know my *sheep,* and [b]am known of mine.

15 [a]As the Father knoweth me, even so know I the Father: [b]and I lay down my life for the sheep.

16 And [a]other sheep I have, which are not of this fold: them also I must bring, and they shall hear my voice; [b]and there shall be one [1]fold, *and* one shepherd.

17 Therefore doth my Father [a]love me, [b]because I lay down my life, that I might take it again.

18 No man taketh it from me, but I lay it down of myself. I [a]have power to lay it down, and I have power to take it again. [b]This commandment have I received of my Father.

19 [a]There was a division therefore again among the Jews for these sayings.

20 And many of them said, [a]He hath a [1]devil, and is [2]mad; why hear ye him?

21 Others said, These are not the words of him that hath a [1]devil. [a]Can a [1]devil [b]open the eyes of the blind?

22 And it was at Jerusalem the feast of the dedication, and it was winter.

23 And Jesus walked in the temple [a]in Solomon's porch.

24 Then came the Jews round about him, and said unto him, How long dost thou [1]make us to doubt? If thou be the Christ, tell us plainly.

25 Jesus answered them, I told you, and ye believed not: [a]the works that I do in my Father's name, they [b]bear witness of me.

26 But [a]ye believe not, because ye are not of my sheep, as I said unto you.

27 [a]My sheep hear my voice, and I know them, and they follow me:

28 And I give unto them eternal life; and they shall never perish, neither shall any *man* [1]pluck them out of my hand.

29 [a]My Father, [b]which gave *them* me, is greater than all; and no *man* is able to [1]pluck *them* out of my Father's hand.

30 [a]I and *my* Father are one.

10:11 [a] Gen. 49:24; Is. 40:11; Ezek. 34:23; [Heb. 13:20]; 1 Pet. 2:25; 5:4; Rev. 7:17
10:12 [1] *hired man* [a] Zech. 11:16, 17
10:14 [a] 2 Tim. 2:19 [b] 2 Tim. 1:12
10:15 [a] Matt. 11:27 [b] [John 15:13; 19:30]
10:16 [a] Is. 42:6; 56:8 [b] Eph. 2:13–18 [1] *flock*
10:17 [a] John 5:20 [b] [Heb. 2:9]
10:18 [a] [John 2:19; 5:26] [b] [John 6:38; 14:31; 17:4; Acts 2:24, 32]
10:19 [a] John 7:43; 9:16
10:20 [a] John 7:20 [1] *demon* [2] *insane*
10:21 [a] [Ex. 4:11] [b] John 9:6, 7, 32, 33 [1] *demon*
10:23 [a] Acts 3:11; 5:12
10:24 [1] *keep us in suspense*
10:25 [a] John 5:36; 10:38 [b] Matt. 11:4
10:26 [a] [John 8:47]
10:27 [a] John 10:4, 14
10:28 [1] *snatch*
10:29 [a] John 14:28 [b] [John 17:2, 6, 12, 24] [1] *snatch*
10:30 [a] John 17:11, 21–24
10:31 [a] John 8:59
10:33 [a] John 5:18 [b] Matt. 9:3
10:34 [a] Ps. 82:6
10:35 [a] Matt. 5:17, 18 [b] 1 Pet. 1:25
10:36 [a] John 6:27 [b] John 3:17 [c] John 5:17, 18 [d] Luke 1:35
10:37 [a] John 10:25; 15:24
10:38 [a] John 5:36 [b] John 14:10, 11
10:39 [a] John 7:30, 44
10:40 [a] John 1:28 [1] *stayed*
10:41 [a] [John 1:29, 36; 3:28–36; 5:33] [1] *came to* [2] *sign*
11:1 [a] Luke 10:38, 39
11:2 [a] Matt. 26:7 [1] *fragrant oil*
11:6 [a] John 10:40 [1] *stayed*
11:8 [a] John 8:59; 10:31 [1] *Rabbi*
11:9 [a] John 9:4; 12:35 [b] Is. 9:2

31 Then [a]the Jews took up stones again to stone him.

32 Jesus answered them, Many good works have I shewed you from my Father; for which of those works do ye stone me?

33 The Jews answered him, saying, For a good work we stone thee not; but for [a]blasphemy; and because that thou, being a man, [b]makest thyself God.

34 Jesus answered them, [a]Is it not written in your law, I said, Ye are gods?

35 If he called them gods, [a]unto whom the word of God came, and the scripture [b]cannot be broken;

36 Say ye of him, [a]whom the Father hath sanctified, and [b]sent into the world, Thou blasphemest; [c]because I said, I am [d]the Son of God?

37 [a]If I do not the works of my Father, believe me not.

38 But if I do, though ye believe not me, [a]believe the works: that ye may know, and believe, [b]that the Father *is* in me, and I in him.

39 [a]Therefore they sought again to take him: but he escaped out of their hand,

40 And went away again beyond Jordan into the place [a]where John at first baptized; and there he [1]abode.

41 And many [1]resorted unto him, and said, John did no [2]miracle: [a]but all things that John spake of this man were true.

42 And many believed on him there.

## CHAPTER 11

Now a certain *man* was sick, *named* Lazarus, of Bethany, the town of [a]Mary and her sister Martha.

2 ([a]It was *that* Mary which anointed the Lord with [1]ointment, and wiped his feet with her hair, whose brother Lazarus was sick.)

3 Therefore his sisters sent unto him, saying, Lord, behold, he whom thou lovest is sick.

4 When Jesus heard *that,* he said, This sickness is not unto death, but for the glory of God, that the Son of God might be glorified thereby.

5 Now Jesus loved Martha, and her sister, and Lazarus.

6 When he had heard therefore that he was sick, [a]he [1]abode two days still in the same place where he was.

7 Then after that saith he to *his* disciples, Let us go into Judaea again.

8 *His* disciples say unto him, [1]Master, the Jews of late sought to [a]stone thee; and goest thou thither again?

9 Jesus answered, Are there not twelve hours in the day? [a]If any man walk in the day, he stumbleth not, because he seeth the [b]light of this world.

10 But [a]if a man walk in the night, he stumbleth, because there is no light in him.

11 These things said he: and after that he saith unto them, Our friend Lazarus [a]sleepeth; but I go, that I may awake him out of sleep.

12 Then said his disciples, Lord, if he sleep, he shall do well.

13 Howbeit Jesus spake of his death: but they thought that he had spoken of taking of rest in sleep.

14 Then said Jesus unto them plainly, Lazarus is dead.

15 And I am glad for your sakes that I was not there, to the intent ye may believe; nevertheless let us go unto him.

16 Then said [a]Thomas, which is called Didymus, unto his fellowdisciples, Let us also go, that we may die with him.

17 Then when Jesus came, he found that he had *lain* in the [1]grave four days already.

18 Now Bethany was [1]nigh unto Jerusalem, about fifteen [2]furlongs off:

19 And many of the Jews came [1]to Martha and Mary, to comfort them concerning their brother.

20 Then Martha, as soon as she heard that Jesus was coming, went and met him: but Mary sat *still* in the house.

21 Then said Martha unto Jesus, Lord, if thou hadst been here, my brother had not died.

22 But I know, that even now, [a]whatsoever thou wilt ask of God, God will give *it* thee.

23 Jesus saith unto her, Thy brother shall rise again.

24 Martha saith unto him, [a]I know that he shall rise again in the resurrection at the last day.

25 Jesus said unto her, I am [a]the resurrection, and the life: [b]he that believeth in me, though he [1]were [c]dead, yet shall he live:

26 And whosoever liveth and believeth in me shall never die. Believest thou this?

27 She saith unto him, Yea, Lord: [a]I believe that thou art the Christ, the Son of God, which should come into the world.

28 And when she had so said, she went her way, and called Mary her sister secretly, saying, The [1]Master is come, and calleth for thee.

29 As soon as she heard *that,* she arose quickly, and came unto him.

30 Now Jesus was not yet come into the town, but was in that place where Martha met him.

31 [a]The Jews then which were with her in the house, and comforted her, when they saw Mary, that she rose up [1]hastily and went out, followed

her, saying, She goeth unto the grave to weep there.

32 Then when Mary was come where Jesus was, and saw him, she [a]fell down at his feet, saying unto him, [b]Lord, if thou hadst been here, my brother had not died.

33 When Jesus therefore saw her weeping, and the Jews also weeping which came with her, he groaned in the spirit, and was troubled,

34 And said, Where have ye laid him? They said unto him, Lord, come and see.

35 [a]Jesus wept.

36 Then said the Jews, Behold how he loved him!

37 And some of them said, Could not this man, [a]which opened the eyes of the blind, have caused that even this man should not have died?

38 Jesus therefore again groaning in himself cometh to the [1]grave. It was a cave, and a [a]stone lay [2]upon it.

39 Jesus said, Take ye away the stone. Martha, the sister of him that was dead, saith unto him, Lord, by this time he stinketh: for he hath been *dead* four days.

40 Jesus saith unto her, Said I not unto thee, that, if thou wouldest believe, thou shouldest [a]see the glory of God?

41 Then they took away the stone *from the place* where the dead was laid. And Jesus lifted up *his* eyes, and said, Father, I thank thee that thou hast heard me.

42 And I knew that thou hearest me always: but [a]because of the people which stand by I said *it,* that they may believe that thou hast sent me.

43 And when he thus had spoken, he cried with a loud voice, Lazarus, come forth.

44 And he that was dead came forth, bound hand and foot with [a]graveclothes: and [b]his face was [1]bound about with a napkin. Jesus saith unto them, Loose him, and let him go.

45 Then many of the Jews which came to Mary, [a]and had seen the things which Jesus did, believed on him.

46 But some of them went their ways to the Pharisees, and [a]told them what things Jesus had done.

47 [a]Then gathered the chief priests and the Pharisees a council, and said, [b]What [1]do we? for this man doeth many miracles.

48 If we let him [1]thus alone, all *men* will believe on him: and the Romans shall come and take away both our place and nation.

49 And one of them, *named* [a]Caiaphas, being the high priest that same year, said unto them, Ye know nothing at all,

---

**Cross-references (center column):**

11:10 [a] John 12:35

11:11 [a] Deut. 31:16; [Dan. 12:2]; Matt. 9:24; Acts 7:60; [1 Cor. 15:18, 51]

11:16 [a] Matt. 10:3; Mark 3:18; Luke 6:15; John 14:5; 20:26–28; Acts 1:13

11:17 [1] *tomb*

11:18 [1] *near* [2] Gr. *stadia;* about 1/8 mile

11:19 [1] Lit. *to those around Martha*

11:22 [a] [John 9:31; 11:41]

11:24 [a] [Luke 14:14; John 5:29]

11:25 [a] John 5:21; 6:39, 40, 44; [Rev. 1:18] [b] John 3:16, 36; 1 John 5:10 [c] 1 Cor. 15:22; [Heb. 9:27] [1] *may die*

11:27 [a] Matt. 16:16; Luke 2:11; John 4:42; 6:14, 69

11:28 [1] *Teacher*

11:31 [a] John 11:19, 33 [1] *quickly*

11:32 [a] Mark 5:22; 7:25; Rev. 1:17 [b] John 11:21

11:35 [a] Luke 19:41

11:37 [a] John 9:6, 7

11:38 [a] Matt. 27:60, 66; Mark 15:46; Luke 24:2; John 20:1 [1] *tomb* [2] *against*

11:40 [a] [John 11:4, 23]

11:42 [a] John 12:30; 17:21

11:44 [a] John 19:40 [b] John 20:7 [1] *wrapped with a cloth*

11:45 [a] John 2:23; 10:42; 12:11, 18

11:46 [a] John 5:15

11:47 [a] Ps. 2:2; Matt. 26:3; Mark 14:1; Luke 22:2 [b] John 12:19; Acts 4:16 [1] *shall we do*

11:48 [1] *alone like this*

11:49 [a] Matt. 26:3; Luke 3:2; John 18:14; Acts 4:6

50 ªNor consider that it is expedient for us, that one man should die for the people, and that the whole nation perish not.

51 And this spake he not ¹of himself: but being high priest that year, he prophesied that Jesus should die for that nation;

52 And not ªfor that nation only, ᵇbut that also he should gather together in one the children of God that were scattered abroad.

53 Then from that day forth they ¹took counsel together for to ªput him to death.

54 Jesus ªtherefore walked no more openly among the Jews; but went thence unto a country near to the wilderness, into a city called ᵇEphraim, and there ¹continued with his disciples.

55 ªAnd the Jews' passover was ¹nigh at hand: and many went out of the country up to Jerusalem before the passover, to ᵇpurify themselves.

56 ªThen sought they for Jesus, and spake among themselves, as they stood in the temple, What think ye, that he will not come to the feast?

57 Now both the chief priests and the Pharisees had given a commandment, that, if any man knew where he were, he should ¹shew *it*, that they might ªtake² him.

## CHAPTER 12

THEN Jesus six days before the passover came to Bethany, ªwhere Lazarus was which had been dead, whom he raised from the dead.

2 ªThere they made him a supper; and Martha served: but Lazarus was one of them that sat at the table with him.

3 Then took ªMary a pound of ¹ointment of ᵇspikenard, very costly, and anointed the feet of Jesus, and wiped his feet with her hair: and the house was filled with the ²odour of the ointment.

4 Then saith one of his disciples, ªJudas Iscariot, Simon's *son*, which should betray him,

5 Why was not this ¹ointment sold for three hundred ²pence, and given to the poor?

6 This he said, not that he cared for the poor; but because he was a thief, and ªhad the ¹bag, and ²bare what was put therein.

7 Then said Jesus, Let her alone: ¹against the day of my burying hath she kept this.

8 For ªthe poor always ye have with you; but me ye have not always.

9 ¹Much people of the Jews therefore knew that he was there: and they came not for Jesus' sake only, but that they might see Lazarus also, ªwhom he had raised from the dead.

10 ªBut the chief priests ¹consulted that they might put Lazarus also to death;

11 ªBecause that by reason of him many of the Jews went away, and believed on Jesus.

12 ªOn the next day ¹much people that were come to the feast, when they heard that Jesus was coming to Jerusalem,

13 Took branches of palm trees, and went forth to meet him, and cried, Hosanna: ªBlessed *is* the King of Israel that cometh in the name of the Lord.

14 ªAnd Jesus, when he had found a young ¹ass, sat thereon; as it is written,

15 ªFear not, daughter of Sion: behold, thy King cometh, sitting on an ¹ass's colt.

16 These things ¹understood not his disciples at the first: ᵇbut when Jesus was glorified, ᶜthen remembered they that these things were written of him, and *that* they had done these things unto him.

17 The people therefore that was with him when he called Lazarus out of his grave, and raised him from the dead, bare ¹record.

18 ªFor this cause the people also met him, for that they heard that he had done this ¹miracle.

19 The Pharisees therefore said among themselves, ªPerceive¹ ye how ye ²prevail nothing? behold, the world is gone after him.

20 And there ªwere certain Greeks among them ᵇthat came up to worship at the feast:

21 The same came therefore to Philip, ªwhich was of Bethsaida of Galilee, and ¹desired him, saying, Sir, we would see Jesus.

22 Philip cometh and telleth Andrew: and again Andrew and Philip tell Jesus.

23 And Jesus answered them, saying, ªThe hour is come, that the Son of man should be glorified.

24 Verily, verily, I say unto you, ªExcept a ¹corn of wheat fall into the ground and die, it ²abideth alone: but if it die, it bringeth forth much fruit.

25 ªHe that loveth his life shall lose it; and he that hateth his life in this world shall keep it unto life eternal.

26 If any man serve me, let him ªfollow me; and ᵇwhere I am, there shall also my servant be: if any man serve me, him will *my* Father honour.

27 ªNow is my soul troubled; and what shall I say? Father, save me from this hour: ᵇbut for this ¹cause came I unto this hour.

28 Father, glorify thy name. ªThen came there a voice from heaven, *saying*, I have both glorified *it,* and will glorify *it* again.

### Center column references

11:50 ª John 18:14
11:51 ¹ *on his own authority*
11:52 ª Is. 49:6
ᵇ [Eph. 2:14–17]
11:53 ª Matt. 26:4
¹ *plotted to put*
11:54 ª John 4:1, 3; 7:1 ᵇ 2 Chr. 13:19
¹ *remained*
11:55 ª John 2:13; 5:1; 6:4 ᵇ Num. 9:10, 13; 31:19, 20
¹ *near*
11:56 ª John 7:11
11:57 ª Matt. 26:14–16 ¹ *report* ² *seize*
12:1 ª John 11:1, 43
12:2 ª Mark 14:3; Luke 10:38–41
12:3 ª John 11:2 ᵇ Song 1:12 ¹ *oil* ² *fragrance*
12:4 ª John 13:26
12:5 ¹ *fragrant oil* ² Gr. *denarii*
12:6 ª John 13:29 ¹ *money box* ² *used to take*
12:7 ¹ *for*
12:8 ª Mark 14:7
12:9 ª John 11:43, 44 ¹ *A great crowd*
12:10 ª Luke 16:31 ¹ *took counsel*
12:11 ª John 11:45; 12:18
12:12 ª Matt. 21:4–9 ¹ *a great multitude*
12:13 ª Ps. 118:25, 26
12:14 ª Matt. 21:7 ¹ *donkey*
12:15 ª Zech. 9:9 ¹ *donkey's*
12:16 ª Luke 18:34 ᵇ John 7:39; 12:23 ᶜ [John 14:26]
12:17 ¹ *witness*
12:18 ª John 12:11 ¹ *sign*
12:19 ª John 11:47, 48 ¹ *See* ² *accomplish*
12:20 ª Acts 17:4 ᵇ 1 Kin. 8:41, 42
12:21 ª John 1:43, 44; 14:8–11 ¹ *asked*
12:23 ª John 13:32
12:24 ª 1 Cor. 15:36 ¹ *grain* ² *remains*
12:25 ª Mark 8:35
12:26 ª [Matt. 16:24] ᵇ John 14:3; 17:24
12:27 ª [Matt. 26:38, 39] ᵇ Luke 22:53 ¹ *purpose*
12:28 ª Matt. 3:17; 17:5

29 The people therefore, that stood by, and heard *it*, said that it thundered: others said, An angel spake to him.

30 Jesus answered and said, ªThis voice came not because of me, but for your sakes.

31 Now is the judgment of this world: now shall ªthe ¹prince of this world be cast out.

32 And I, ªif I be ¹lifted up from the earth, will draw ᵇall *men* unto me.

33 ªThis he said, signifying what death he should die.

34 The people answered him, ªWe have heard out of the law that Christ abideth for ever: and how sayest thou, The Son of man must be lifted up? who is this Son of man?

35 Then Jesus said unto them, Yet a little while ªis the light with you. ᵇWalk while ye have the light, lest darkness come upon you: for ᶜhe that walketh in darkness knoweth not whither he goeth.

36 While ye have light, believe in the light, that ye may ¹be ªthe children of light. These things spake Jesus, and departed, and ᵇdid² hide himself from them.

37 But though he had done so many ªmiracles¹ before them, yet they believed not on him:

38 That the saying of Esaias the prophet might be fulfilled, which he spake, ªLord, who hath believed our report? and to whom hath the arm of the Lord been revealed?

39 Therefore they could not believe, because that Esaias said again,

40 ªHe hath blinded their eyes, and hardened their heart; ᵇthat they should not see with *their* eyes, nor understand with *their* heart, and be converted, and I should heal them.

41 ªThese things said Esaias, when he saw his glory, and spake of him.

42 Nevertheless among the chief rulers also many believed on him; but ªbecause of the Pharisees they did not ¹confess *him*, lest they should be put out of the synagogue:

43 ªFor they loved the praise of men more than the praise of God.

44 Jesus cried and said, ªHe that believeth on me, ᵇbelieveth not on me, ᶜbut on him that sent me.

45 And ªhe that seeth me seeth him that sent me.

46 ªI am come a light into the world, that whosoever believeth on me should not abide in darkness.

47 And if any man hear my words, and believe not, ªI judge him not: for ᵇI came not to judge the world, but to save the world.

48 ªHe that rejecteth me, and receiveth not my words, hath one that judgeth him: ᵇthe word that I have

---

12:30 ª John 11:42
12:31 ª [2 Cor. 4:4]
¹ ruler
12:32 ª John 3:14;
8:28 ᵇ [Rom.
5:18] ¹ Crucified
12:33 ª John
18:32; 21:19
12:34 ª Mic. 4:7
12:35 ª [John 1:9;
7:33; 8:12] ᵇ Eph.
5:8 ᶜ [1 John
2:9–11]
12:36 ª Luke
16:8 ᵇ John 8:59
¹ become sons
² was hidden
12:37 ª John 11:47
¹ signs
12:38 ª Is. 53:1
12:40 ª Is. 6:9, 10
ᵇ Matt. 13:14
12:41 ª Is. 6:1
12:42 ª John 7:13;
9:22 ¹ publicly
acknowledge
12:43 ª John
5:41, 44
12:44 ª Mark
9:37 ᵇ [John 3:16,
18, 36; 11:25, 26]
ᶜ [John 5:24]
12:45 ª [John
14:9]
12:46 ª John 1:4,
5; 8:12; 12:35, 36
12:47 ª John 5:45
ᵇ John 3:17
12:48 ª [Luke
10:16] ᵇ Deut.
18:18, 19
12:49 ª John 8:38
ᵇ Deut. 18:18 ¹ my
own authority
12:50 ª John 5:19;
8:28
13:1 ª Matt. 26:2
ᵇ John 12:23; 17:1
ᶜ John 15:9
13:2 ª Luke 22:3
¹ already
13:3 ª Acts 2:36
ᵇ John 8:42; 16:28
ᶜ John 17:11; 20:17
¹ was going
13:4 ª [Luke 22:27]
13:6 ª Matt. 3:14
¹ Lit. he ² are you
washing
13:7 ª John 12:16;
16:12 ᵇ John 13:19
¹ understandeth
13:8 ª [1 Cor. 6:11]
13:10 ª [John 15:3]
¹ bathed ² completely clean
13:11 ª John 6:64;
18:4 ¹ would
13:13 ª Matt. 23:8,
10 ¹ Teacher
13:14 ª Luke 22:27
ᵇ [Rom. 12:10]
¹ Teacher
13:15 ª [1 Pet.
2:21–24]
13:16 ª Matt. 10:24
¹ master

---

spoken, the same shall judge him in the last day.

49 For ªI have not spoken of ¹myself; but the Father which sent me, he gave me a commandment, ᵇwhat I should say, and what I should speak.

50 And I know that his commandment is life everlasting: whatsoever I speak therefore, even as the Father said unto me, so I ªspeak.

## CHAPTER 13

Now ªbefore the feast of the passover, when Jesus knew that ᵇhis hour was come that he should depart out of this world unto the Father, having loved his own which were in the world, he ᶜloved them unto the end.

2 And supper being ended, ªthe devil having ¹now put into the heart of Judas Iscariot, Simon's *son*, to betray him;

3 Jesus knowing ªthat the Father had given all things into his hands, and that he was ᵇcome from God, and ᶜwent¹ to God;

4 ªHe riseth from supper, and laid aside his garments; and took a towel, and girded himself.

5 After that he poureth water into a bason, and began to wash the disciples' feet, and to wipe *them* with the towel wherewith he was girded.

6 Then cometh he to Simon Peter: and ¹Peter saith unto him, Lord, ªdost² thou wash my feet?

7 Jesus answered and said unto him, What I do thou ªknowest¹ not now; ᵇbut thou shalt know hereafter.

8 Peter saith unto him, Thou shalt never wash my feet. Jesus answered him, ªIf I wash thee not, thou hast no part with me.

9 Simon Peter saith unto him, Lord, not my feet only, but also *my* hands and *my* head.

10 Jesus saith to him, He that is ¹washed needeth not save to wash *his* feet, but is ²clean every whit: and ªye are clean, but not all.

11 For ªhe knew who ¹should betray him; therefore said he, Ye are not all clean.

12 So after he had washed their feet, and had taken his garments, and was set down again, he said unto them, Know ye what I have done to you?

13 ªYe call me ¹Master and Lord: and ye say well; for *so* I am.

14 ªIf I then, *your* Lord and ¹Master, have washed your feet; ᵇye also ought to wash one another's feet.

15 For ªI have given you an example, that ye should do as I have done to you.

16 ªVerily, verily, I say unto you, The servant is not greater than his ¹lord;

neither he that is sent greater than he that sent him.

17 ªIf ye know these things, happy are ye if ye do them.

18 I speak not of you all: I know whom I have chosen: but that the ªscripture may be fulfilled, ᵇHe that eateth bread with me hath lifted up his heel against me.

19 ªNow I tell you before it come, that, when it is come to pass, ye may believe that I am *he.*

20 ªVerily, verily, I say unto you, He that receiveth whomsoever I send receiveth me; and he that receiveth me receiveth him that sent me.

21 ªWhen Jesus had thus said, ᵇhe was troubled in spirit, and testified, and said, Verily, verily, I say unto you, that ᶜone of you shall betray me.

22 Then the disciples looked one on another, ¹doubting of whom he spake.

23 Now ªthere was ¹leaning on Jesus' bosom one of his disciples, whom Jesus loved.

24 Simon Peter therefore beckoned to him, that he should ask who it should be of whom he spake.

25 He then ¹lying on Jesus' breast saith unto him, Lord, who is it?

26 Jesus answered, He it is, to whom I shall give a ¹sop, when I have dipped *it.* And when he had dipped the ¹sop, he gave *it* to ªJudas Iscariot, *the son* of Simon.

27 ªAnd after the sop Satan entered into him. Then said Jesus unto him, That thou doest, do quickly.

28 Now no man at the table knew for what ¹intent he spake this unto him.

29 For some *of them* thought, because ªJudas had the ᵇbag, that Jesus had said unto him, Buy *those things* that we have need of ²against the feast; or, that he should give something to the poor.

30 He then having received the ¹sop went immediately out: and it was night.

31 Therefore, when he was gone out, Jesus said, ªNow is the Son of man glorified, and ᵇGod is glorified in him.

32 If God be glorified in him, God shall also glorify him in himself, and ªshall ¹straightway glorify him.

33 Little children, yet a ªlittle while I am with you. Ye shall seek me: ᵇand as I said unto the Jews, Whither I go, ye cannot come; so now I say to you.

34 ªA new commandment I give unto you, That ye love one another; as I have loved you, that ye also love one another.

35 ªBy this shall all *men* know that ye are my disciples, if ye have love one to another.

36 Simon Peter said unto him, Lord, whither goest thou? Jesus answered him, Whither I ªgo, thou canst not follow me now; but ᵇthou shalt follow me afterwards.

37 Peter said unto him, Lord, why cannot I follow thee now? I will ªlay down my life for thy sake.

38 Jesus answered him, Wilt thou lay down thy life for my sake? Verily, verily, I say unto thee, The cock shall not ªcrow, till thou hast denied me thrice.

## CHAPTER 14

LET ªnot your heart be troubled: ye believe in God, believe also in me.

2 In my Father's house are many ¹mansions: if *it were* not *so,* I would have told you. ªI go to prepare a place for you.

3 And if I go and prepare a place for you, ªI will come again, and receive you unto myself; that ᵇwhere I am, *there* ye may be also.

4 And whither I go ye know, and the way ye know.

5 ªThomas saith unto him, Lord, we know not whither thou goest; and how can we know the way?

6 Jesus saith unto him, I am ªthe way, ᵇthe truth, and ᶜthe life: ᵈno man cometh unto the Father, ᵉbut by me.

7 ªIf ye had known me, ye should have known my Father also: and from henceforth ye know him, and have seen him.

8 Philip saith unto him, Lord, shew us the Father, and it ¹sufficeth us.

9 Jesus saith unto him, Have I been so long time with you, and yet hast thou not known me, Philip? ªhe that hath seen me hath seen the Father; and how sayest thou *then,* Shew us the Father?

10 Believest thou not that ªI am in the Father, and the Father in me? the words that I speak unto you ᵇI speak not of ¹myself: but the Father that dwelleth in me, he doeth the works.

11 Believe me that I *am* in the Father, and the Father in me: ªor else believe me for the very works' sake.

12 ªVerily, verily, I say unto you, He that believeth on me, the works that I do shall he do also; and greater *works* than these shall he do; because I go unto my Father.

13 ªAnd whatsoever ye shall ask in my name, that will I do, that the Father may be ᵇglorified in the Son.

14 If ye shall ask any thing in my name, I will do *it.*

15 ªIf ye love me, keep my commandments.

16 And I will pray the Father, and ªhe shall give you another ¹Comforter, that he may abide with you for ever;

### Cross-references

13:17 ª [James 1:25]
13:18 ª John 15:25; 17:12 ᵇ Ps. 41:9
13:19 ª John 14:29; 16:4
13:20 ª Matt. 10:40
13:21 ª Luke 22:21 ᵇ John 12:27 ᶜ 1 John 2:19
13:22 ¹ *perplexed about*
13:23 ª John 19:26; 20:2; 21:7, 20 ¹ *reclining at*
13:25 ¹ *leaning back*
13:26 ª John 6:70, 71; 12:4 ¹ *piece of bread*
13:27 ª Luke 22:3
13:28 ¹ *reason*
13:29 ª John 12:6 ¹ *money box* ² *for*
13:30 ¹ *piece of bread*
13:31 ª John 12:23 ᵇ [1 Pet. 4:11]
13:32 ª John 12:23 ¹ *immediately*
13:33 ª John 12:35; 14:19; 16:16–19 ᵇ [John 7:34; 8:21]
13:34 ª 1 Thess. 4:9
13:35 ª 1 John 2:5
13:36 ª John 13:33; 14:2; 16:5 ᵇ 2 Pet. 1:14
13:37 ª Mark 14:29–31
13:38 ª John 18:25–27
14:1 ª [John 14:27; 16:22, 24]
14:2 ª John 13:33, 36 ¹ Lit. *dwellings*
14:3 ª [Acts 1:11] ᵇ [John 12:26]
14:5 ª Matt. 10:3
14:6 ª [Heb. 9:8; 10:19, 20] ᵇ [John 1:14, 17; 8:32; 18:37] ᶜ [John 11:25] ᵈ 1 Tim. 2:5 ᵉ [John 10:7–9]
14:7 ª John 8:19
14:8 ¹ *will satisfy*
14:9 ª Col. 1:15
14:10 ª John 10:38; 14:11, 20 ᵇ John 5:19;
14:24 ¹ *my own authority*
14:11 ª John 5:36; 10:38
14:12 ª Luke 10:17
14:13 ª Matt. 7:7 ᵇ John 13:31
14:15 ª 1 John 5:3
14:16 ª Rom. 8:15 ¹ *Helper,* Gr. *Paraclete*

17 *Even* ªthe Spirit of truth; ᵇwhom the world cannot receive, because it seeth him not, neither knoweth him: but ye know him; for he dwelleth with you, ᶜand shall be in you.

18 ªI will not leave you ¹comfortless: ᵇI will come to you.

19 Yet a little while, and the world seeth me no more; but ªye see me: ᵇbecause I live, ye shall live also.

20 At that day ye shall know that ªI *am* in my Father, and ye in me, and I in you.

21 ªHe that hath my commandments, and keepeth them, he it is that loveth me: and he that loveth me shall be loved of my Father, and I will love him, and will ¹manifest myself to him.

22 ªJudas saith unto him, not Iscariot, Lord, how is it that thou wilt manifest thyself unto us, and not unto the world?

23 Jesus answered and said unto him, If a man love me, he will keep my words: and my Father will love him, ªand we will come unto him, and make our ¹abode with him.

24 He that loveth me not keepeth not my ¹sayings: and ªthe word which ye hear is not mine, but the Father's which sent me.

25 These things have I spoken unto you, being *yet* present with you.

26 But ªthe ¹Comforter, *which is* the Holy Ghost, whom the Father will ᵇsend in my name, ᶜhe shall teach you all things, and bring all things to your ᵈremembrance, whatsoever I have said unto you.

27 ªPeace I leave with you, my peace I give unto you: not as the world giveth, give I unto you. Let not your heart be troubled, neither let it be afraid.

28 Ye have heard how ªI said unto you, I go away, and come *again* unto you. If ye loved me, ye would rejoice, because I said, ᵇI go unto the Father: for ᶜmy Father is greater than I.

29 And ªnow I have told you before it come to pass, that, when it is come to pass, ye might believe.

30 Hereafter I will not talk much with you: ªfor the ¹prince of this world cometh, and hath ᵇnothing in me.

31 But that the world may know that I love the Father; and ªas the Father gave me commandment, even so I do. Arise, let us go hence.

## CHAPTER 15

I AM the ¹true vine, and my Father is the ²husbandman.

2 ªEvery branch in me that beareth not fruit he taketh away: and every *branch* that beareth fruit, he ¹purgeth it, that it may bring forth ᵇmore fruit.

---

14:17 ª [1 John 4:6; 5:7] ᵇ [1 Cor. 2:14] ᶜ [1 John 2:27]

14:18 ª [Matt. 28:20] ᵇ [John 14:3, 28] ¹ *orphans*

14:19 ª John 16:16, 22 ᵇ [1 Cor. 15:20]

14:20 ª John 10:38; 14:11

14:21 ª 1 John 2:5 ¹ *reveal*

14:22 ª Luke 6:16

14:23 ª Rev. 3:20; 21:3 ¹ *home*

14:24 ª John 5:19 ¹ *words*

14:26 ª Luke 24:49 ᵇ John 15:26 ᶜ 1 Cor. 2:13 ᵈ John 2:22; 12:16 ¹ *Helper, Gr. Paraclete*

14:27 ª [Phil. 4:7]

14:28 ª John 14:3, 18 ᵇ John 16:16 ᶜ [Phil. 2:6]

14:29 ª John 13:19

14:30 ª [John 12:31] ᵇ [Heb. 4:15] ¹ *ruler*

14:31 ª John 10:18

15:1 ¹ *genuine* ² *vinedresser*

15:2 ª Matt. 15:13 ᵇ [Matt. 13:12] ¹ *prunes*

15:3 ª [John 13:10; 17:17] ¹ Lit. *because of*

15:4 ª [Col. 1:23]

15:5 ª Hos. 14:8 ᵇ 2 Cor. 3:5

15:6 ª Matt. 3:10

15:7 ª 1 John 2:14 ᵇ John 14:13; 16:23 ¹ *for*

15:8 ª [Matt. 5:16] ᵇ John 8:31

15:9 ª John 5:20; 17:26 ¹ *abide*

15:10 ª John 14:15

15:11 ª 1 John 1:4

15:12 ª 1 John 3:11 ᵇ Rom. 12:9

15:13 ª 1 John 3:16

15:14 ª [Matt. 12:50; 28:20]

15:15 ª Gen. 18:17

15:16 ª John 6:70; 13:18; 15:19 ᵇ [Col. 1:6] ᶜ John 14:13; 16:23, 24 ¹ *appointed*

15:18 ª 1 John 3:13

15:19 ª 1 John 4:5 ᵇ John 17:14

15:20 ª John 13:16 ᵇ Ezek. 3:7

15:21 ª John 10:22; 24:9

---

3 ªNow ye are clean ¹through the word which I have spoken unto you.

4 ªAbide in me, and I in you. As the branch cannot bear fruit of itself, except it abide in the vine; no more can ye, except ye abide in me.

5 I am the vine, ye *are* the branches: He that abideth in me, and I in him, the same bringeth forth much ªfruit: for without me ye can do ᵇnothing.

6 If a man abide not in me, ªhe is cast forth as a branch, and is withered; and men gather them, and cast *them* into the fire, and they are burned.

7 If ye abide in me, and my words ªabide in you, ᵇye shall ask what ye will, and it shall be done ¹unto you.

8 ªHerein is my Father glorified, that ye bear much fruit; ᵇso shall ye be my disciples.

9 As the Father hath ªloved me, so have I loved you: ¹continue ye in my love.

10 ªIf ye keep my commandments, ye shall abide in my love; even as I have kept my Father's commandments, and abide in his love.

11 These things have I spoken unto you, that my joy might remain in you, and ªthat your joy might be full.

12 ªThis is my ᵇcommandment, That ye love one another, as I have loved you.

13 ªGreater love hath no man than this, that a man lay down his life for his friends.

14 ªYe are my friends, if ye do whatsoever I command you.

15 Henceforth I call you not servants; for the servant knoweth not what his lord doeth: but I have called you friends; ªfor all things that I have heard of my Father I have made known unto you.

16 ªYe have not chosen me, but I have chosen you, and ᵇordained¹ you, that ye should go and bring forth fruit, and *that* your fruit should remain: that whatsoever ye shall ask of the Father ᶜin my name, he may give it you.

17 These things I command you, that ye love one another.

18 ªIf the world hate you, ye know that it hated me before *it hated* you.

19 ªIf ye were of the world, the world would love his own: but ᵇbecause ye are not of the world, but I have chosen you out of the world, therefore the world hateth you.

20 Remember the word that I said unto you, ªThe servant is not greater than his lord. If they have persecuted me, they will also persecute you; ᵇif they have kept my saying, they will keep yours also.

21 But ªall these things will they do unto you for my name's sake, because they know not him that sent me.

22 [a]If I had not come and spoken unto them, they had not had sin: [b]but now they have no [1]cloke for their sin.

23 [a]He that hateth me hateth my Father also.

24 If I had not done among them [a]the works which none other man did, they had not had sin: but now have they both [b]seen and hated both me and my Father.

25 But *this cometh to pass,* that the word might be fulfilled that is written in their law, [a]They hated me without a cause.

26 [a]But when the [1]Comforter is come, whom I will send unto you from the Father, *even* the Spirit of truth, which proceedeth from the Father, [b]he shall testify of me:

27 And [a]ye also shall bear witness, because [b]ye have been with me from the beginning.

### CHAPTER 16

THESE things have I spoken unto you, that ye [a]should not be [1]offended.

2 [a]They shall put you out of the synagogues: yea, the time cometh, [b]that whosoever killeth you will think that he doeth God service.

3 And [a]these things will they do unto you, because they have not known the Father, nor me.

4 But these things have I told you, that when the time shall come, ye may remember that I told you of them. And these things I said not unto you at the beginning, because I was with you.

5 But now I [a]go my way to him that sent me; and none of you asketh me, Whither goest thou?

6 But because I have said these things unto you, [a]sorrow hath filled your heart.

7 Nevertheless I tell you the truth; It is [1]expedient for you that I go away: for if I go not away, the [2]Comforter will not come unto you; but [a]if I depart, I will send him unto you.

8 And when he is [a]come, he will [1]reprove the world of sin, and of righteousness, and of judgment:

9 [a]Of sin, because they believe not on me;

10 [a]Of righteousness, [b]because I go to my Father, and ye see me no more;

11 [a]Of judgment, because [b]the [1]prince of this world is judged.

12 I have yet many things to say unto you, [a]but ye cannot bear them now.

13 Howbeit when he, [a]the Spirit of truth, is come, [b]he will guide you into all truth: for he shall not speak [1]of himself; but whatsoever he shall hear, *that* shall he speak: and he will shew you things to come.

14 [a]He shall glorify me: for he shall receive [1]of mine, and shall [2]shew *it* unto you.

15 [a]All things that the Father hath are mine: therefore said I, that he shall take of mine, and shall shew *it* unto you.

16 A [a]little while, and ye shall not see me: and again, a little while, and ye shall see me, [b]because I go to the Father.

17 Then said *some* of his disciples among themselves, What is this that he saith unto us, A little while, and ye shall not see me: and again, a little while, and ye shall see me: and, Because I go to the Father?

18 They said therefore, What is this that he saith, A little while? we cannot [1]tell what he [2]saith.

19 Now Jesus knew that they were desirous to ask him, and said unto them, Do ye enquire among yourselves of that I said, A little while, and ye shall not see me: and again, a little while, and ye shall see me?

20 Verily, verily, I say unto you, That ye shall weep and [a]lament, but the world shall rejoice: and ye shall be sorrowful, but your sorrow shall be turned into [b]joy.

21 [a]A woman when she is in [1]travail hath sorrow, because her hour is come: but as soon as she [2]is delivered of the child, she remembereth no more the anguish, for joy that a [3]man is born into the world.

22 And ye now therefore have sorrow: but I will see you again, and [a]your heart shall rejoice, and your joy no man taketh from you.

23 And in that day ye shall ask me nothing. [a]Verily, verily, I say unto you, Whatsoever ye shall ask the Father in my name, he will give *it* you.

24 Hitherto have ye asked nothing in my name: ask, and ye shall receive, [a]that your joy may be [b]full.

25 These things have I spoken unto you in [1]proverbs: but the time cometh, when I shall no more speak unto you in [1]proverbs, but I shall [2]shew you [a]plainly of the Father.

26 At that day ye shall ask in my name: and I say not unto you, that I will pray the Father for you:

27 [a]For the Father himself loveth you, because ye have loved me, and [b]have believed that I came out from God.

28 [a]I came forth from the Father, and am come into the world: again, I leave the world, and go to the Father.

29 His disciples said unto him, Lo, now speakest thou plainly, and [1]speakest no proverb.

30 Now are we sure that [a]thou knowest all things, and needest not that any man should ask thee: by this

## Center reference column

15:22 [a] John 9:41;
15:24 [b] [James 4:17] [1] *excuse*
15:23 [a] 1 John 2:23
15:24 [a] John 3:2 [b] John 14:9
15:25 [a] Ps. 35:19; 69:4; 109:3–5
15:26 [a] Luke 24:49 [b] 1 John 5:6 [1] *Helper,* Gr. *Paraclete*
15:27 [a] Luke 24:48 [b] Luke 1:2
16:1 [a] Matt. 11:6 [1] *made to stumble*
16:2 [a] John 9:22 [b] Acts 8:1
16:3 [a] John 8:19; 15:21
16:5 [a] John 7:33; 13:33; 14:28; 17:11
16:6 [a] [John 16:20, 22]
16:7 [a] Acts 2:33 [1] *advantageous* [2] *Helper* or *Advocate,* Gr. *Paraclete*
16:8 [a] Acts 1:8; 2:1–4, 37 [1] *convict*
16:9 [a] Acts 2:22
16:10 [a] Acts 2:32 [b] John 5:32
16:11 [a] Acts 26:18 [b] [Luke 10:18] [1] *ruler*
16:12 [a] Mark 4:33
16:13 [a] [John 14:17] [b] John 14:26 [1] *on his own authority*
16:14 [a] John 15:26 [1] *what is mine* [2] *declare*
16:15 [a] Matt. 11:27
16:16 [a] John 7:33; 12:35; 13:33; 14:19; 19:40–42; 20:19 [b] John 13:3
16:18 [1] *understand* [2] *is saying*
16:20 [a] Mark 16:10 [b] Luke 24:32, 41
16:21 [a] Is. 13:8; 26:17; 42:14 [1] *labour* [2] *has given birth to* [3] *human being*
16:22 [a] 1 Pet. 1:8
16:23 [a] Matt. 7:7
16:24 [a] John 17:13 [b] John 15:11
16:25 [a] John 7:13 [1] *figurative language* [2] *tell*
16:27 [a] [John 14:21, 23] [b] John 3:13
16:28 [a] John 13:1, 3; 16:5, 10, 17
16:29 [1] *use no figures of speech*
16:30 [a] John 21:17

[b]we believe that thou camest forth from God.

31 Jesus answered them, Do ye now believe?

32 [a]Behold, the hour cometh, yea, is now come, that ye shall be scattered, [b]every man to [1]his own, and shall leave me alone: and [c]yet I am not alone, because the Father is with me.

33 These things I have spoken unto you, that [a]in me ye might have peace. [b]In the world ye shall have tribulation: but be of good cheer; [c]I have overcome the world.

## CHAPTER 17

THESE words spake Jesus, and lifted up his eyes to heaven, and said, Father, [a]the hour is come; glorify thy Son, that thy Son also may glorify thee:

2 [a]As thou hast given him [1]power over all flesh, that he should give eternal life to as many [b]as thou hast given him.

3 And [a]this is life eternal, that they might know thee [b]the only true God, and Jesus Christ, [c]whom thou hast sent.

4 [a]I have glorified thee on the earth: [b]I have finished the work [c]which thou gavest me to do.

5 And now, O Father, glorify thou me [1]with thine own self with the glory [a]which I had with thee before the world was.

6 [a]I have [1]manifested thy name unto the men [b]which thou gavest me out of the world: [c]thine they were, and thou gavest them [2]me; and they have kept thy word.

7 Now they have known that all things whatsoever thou hast given me are of thee.

8 For I have given unto them the words [a]which thou gavest me; and they have received *them*, [b]and have known surely that I came out from thee, and they have believed that [c]thou didst send me.

9 I pray for them: [a]I pray not for the world, but for them which thou hast given me; for they are thine.

10 And all mine are thine, and [a]thine are mine; and I am glorified in them.

11 [a]And now I am no [1]more in the world, but these are in the world, and I come to thee. Holy Father, [b]keep through thine own name those whom thou hast given me, that they may be one, [c]as we *are*.

12 While I was with them in the world, [a]I kept them in thy name: those that thou gavest me I have kept, and [b]none of them is [1]lost, [c]but the son of [2]perdition; [d]that the scripture might be fulfilled.

13 And now come I to thee; and

16:30 [b] John 17:8
16:32 [a] Matt. 26:31, 56 [b] John 20:10
[c] John 8:29 [1] *his own place*
16:33 [a] [Eph. 2:14] [b] 2 Tim. 3:12
[c] Rom. 8:37
17:1 [a] John 12:23
17:2 [a] John 3:35
[b] John 6:37, 39; 17:6, 9, 24
[1] *authority*
17:3 [a] Jer. 9:23, 24
[b] 1 Cor. 8:4 [c] John 3:34
17:4 [a] John 13:31
[b] John 4:34; 19:30
[c] John 14:31
17:5 [a] Phil. 2:6
[1] Lit. *alongside*
17:6 [a] Ps. 22:22
[b] John 6:37
[c] Ezek. 18:4 [1] *revealed* [2] *to me*
17:8 [a] John 8:28
[b] John 8:42; 16:27, 30 [c] Deut. 18:15, 18
17:9 [a] [1 John 5:19]
17:10 [a] John 16:15
17:11 [a] John 13:1 [b] [1 Pet. 1:5]
[c] John 10:30
[1] *longer*
17:12 [a] Heb. 2:13 [b] 1 John 2:19 [c] John 6:70 [d] Ps. 41:9; 109:0 [1] *destroyed* [2] *destruction*
17:14 [a] John 15:19
[b] John 8:23
17:15 [a] 1 John 5:18
[1] *evil one*
17:17 [a] [Eph. 5:26]
[b] Ps. 119:9, 142, 151
[1] *Set them apart*
17:18 [a] John 4:38; 20:21
17:19 [a] [Heb. 10:10]
17:21 [a] [Gal. 3:28]
[b] John 10:38; 17:11, 23
17:22 [a] 1 John 1:3
[b] [2 Cor. 3:18]
17:23 [a] [Col. 3:14]
17:24 [a] [1 Thess. 4:17] [b] John 17:5
[1] *desire*
17:25 [a] John 15:21
[b] John 7:29; 8:55; 10:15 [c] John 3:17; 17:3, 8, 18, 21, 23
17:26 [a] John 17:6
[b] John 15:9
18:1 [a] Mark 14:26, 32 [b] 2 Sam. 15:23
[1] *Kidron,* 2 Sam. 15:23
18:2 [a] Luke 21:37; 22:39 [1] *often met*
18:3 [a] Luke 22:47–53 [1] Lit. *cohort,* about 600 soldiers
18:4 [a] John 6:64; 13:1, 3; 19:28

these things I speak in the world, that they might have my joy fulfilled in themselves.

14 I have given them thy word; [a]and the world hath hated them, because they are not of the world, [b]even as I am not of the world.

15 I pray not that thou shouldest take them out of the world, but [a]that thou shouldest keep them from the [1]evil.

16 They are not of the world, even as I am not of the world.

17 [a]Sanctify[1] them through thy truth: [b]thy word is truth.

18 [a]As thou hast sent me into the world, even so have I also sent them into the world.

19 And [a]for their sakes I sanctify myself, that they also might be sanctified through the truth.

20 Neither pray I for these alone, but for them also which shall believe on me through their word;

21 [a]That they all may be one; as [b]thou, Father, *art* in me, and I in thee, that they also may be one in us: that the world may believe that thou hast sent me.

22 And the [a]glory which thou gavest me I have given them; [b]that they may be one, even as we are one:

23 I in them, and thou in me, [a]that they may be made perfect in one; and that the world may know that thou hast sent me, and hast loved them, as thou hast loved me.

24 [a]Father, I [1]will that they also, whom thou hast given me, be with me where I am; that they may behold my glory, which thou hast given me: [b]for thou lovedst me before the foundation of the world.

25 O righteous Father, [a]the world hath not known thee: but [b]I have known thee, and [c]these have known that thou hast sent me.

26 [a]And I have declared unto them thy name, and will declare *it:* that the love [b]wherewith thou hast loved me may be in them, and I in them.

## CHAPTER 18

WHEN Jesus had spoken these words, [a]he went forth with his disciples over [b]the brook [1]Cedron, where was a garden, into the which he entered, and his disciples.

2 And Judas also, which betrayed him, knew the place: [a]for Jesus [1]ofttimes resorted thither with his disciples.

3 [a]Judas then, having received a [1]band *of men* and officers from the chief priests and Pharisees, cometh thither with lanterns and torches and weapons.

4 Jesus therefore, [a]knowing all things that should come upon him,

went forth, and said unto them, Whom seek ye?

5 They answered him, [a]Jesus [1]of Nazareth. Jesus saith unto them, I am *he.* And Judas also, which [b]betrayed him, stood with them.

6 As soon then as he had said unto them, I am *he,* they [1]went backward, and fell to the ground.

7 Then asked he them again, Whom seek ye? And they said, Jesus of Nazareth.

8 Jesus answered, I have told you that I am *he:* if therefore ye seek me, let these go their way:

9 That the saying might be fulfilled, which he spake, [a]Of them which thou gavest me have I lost none.

10 [a]Then Simon Peter having a sword drew it, and [1]smote the high priest's servant, and cut off his right ear. The servant's name was Malchus.

11 Then said Jesus unto Peter, Put up thy sword into the sheath: [a]the cup which my Father hath given me, shall I not drink it?

12 Then the [b]band and the captain and officers of the Jews took Jesus, and bound him,

13 And [a]led him away to [b]Annas first; for he was father in law to [c]Caiaphas, which was the high priest that same year.

14 [a]Now Caiaphas was he, which gave counsel to the Jews, that it was [1]expedient that one man should die for the people.

15 [a]And Simon Peter followed Jesus, and *so did* [b]another[1] disciple: that disciple was known unto the high priest, and went in with Jesus into the [2]palace of the high priest.

16 [a]But Peter stood at the door [1]without. Then went out that other disciple, which was known unto the high priest, and spake unto her that kept the door, and brought in Peter.

17 Then saith the [1]damsel that kept the door unto Peter, Art not thou also *one* of this man's disciples? He saith, I am [a]not.

18 And the servants and officers stood there, who had made a fire of coals; for it was cold: and they warmed themselves: and Peter stood with them, and warmed himself.

19 The high priest then asked Jesus of his disciples, and of his doctrine.

20 Jesus answered him, [a]I spake openly to the world; I [1]ever taught [b]in the synagogue, and [c]in the temple, whither the Jews always [2]resort; and in secret have I said nothing.

21 Why askest thou me? ask [a]them which heard me, what I have said unto them: behold, they know what I said.

22 And when he had thus spoken, one of the officers which stood by

[a]struck[1] Jesus with the palm of his hand, saying, Answerest thou the high priest so?

23 Jesus answered him, If I have spoken evil, bear witness of the evil: but if well, why smitest thou me?

24 [a]Now Annas had sent him bound unto [b]Caiaphas the high priest.

25 And Simon Peter stood and warmed himself. [a]They said therefore unto him, Art not thou also *one* of his disciples? He denied *it,* and said, I am not.

26 One of the servants of the high priest, being *his* kinsman whose ear Peter cut off, saith, Did not I see thee in the garden with him?

27 Peter then denied again: and [a]immediately the [1]cock crew.

28 [a]Then led they Jesus from Caiaphas unto the [1]hall of judgment: and it was early; [b]and they themselves went not into the judgment hall, lest they should be defiled; but that they might eat the passover.

29 [a]Pilate then went out unto them, and said, What accusation bring ye against this man?

30 They answered and said unto him, If he were not a [1]malefactor, we would not have delivered him up unto thee.

31 Then said Pilate unto them, Take ye him, and judge him according to your law. The Jews therefore said unto him, It is not lawful for us to put any man to death:

32 [a]That the saying of Jesus might be fulfilled, which he spake, [b]signifying what death he should die.

33 [a]Then Pilate entered into the [1]judgment hall again, and called Jesus, and said unto him, Art thou the King of the Jews?

34 Jesus answered him, Sayest thou this thing of thyself, or did others tell it thee of me?

35 Pilate answered, Am I a Jew? Thine own nation and the chief priests have delivered thee unto me: what hast thou done?

36 [a]Jesus answered, [b]My kingdom is not of this world: if my kingdom were of this world, then would my servants fight, that I should not be delivered to the Jews: but now is my kingdom not from hence.

37 Pilate therefore said unto him, Art thou a king then? Jesus answered, Thou [1]sayest that I am a king. To this end was I born, and for this cause came I into the world, [a]that I should bear [b]witness unto the truth. Every one that [c]is of the truth [d]heareth my voice.

38 Pilate saith unto him, What is truth? And when he had said this, he went out again unto the Jews, and saith unto them, [a]I find in him no fault *at all.*

---

18:5 [a] Matt. 21:11
[b] Ps. 41:9 [1] Lit. *the Nazarene*
18:6 [1] *drew back*
18:9 [a] [John 6:39; 17:12]
18:10 [a] Matt. 26:51
[1] *struck*
18:11 [a] Matt. 20:22; 26:39
18:12 [1] *cohort*
18:13 [a] Matt. 26:57
[b] Luke 3:2 [c] Matt. 26:3
18:14 [a] John 11:50
[1] *advantageous*
18:15 [a] Mark 14:54
[b] John 20:2–5
[1] Some mss. *the other* [2] *courtyard*
18:16 [a] Matt. 26:69 [1] *outside*
18:17 [a] Matt. 26:34
[1] *servant girl*
18:20 [a] Luke 4:15 [b] John 6:59
[c] Mark 14:49
[1] *always* [2] *meet*
18:21 [a] Mark 12:37

18:22 [a] Jer. 20:2
[1] Lit. *gave Jesus a blow*
18:24 [a] Matt. 26:57 [b] John 11:49
18:25 [a] Luke 22:58–62
18:27 [a] John 13:38
[1] *rooster crowed*
18:28 [a] Mark 15:1
[b] Acts 10:28; 11:3
[1] Gr. *praetorion,* the governor's headquarters
18:29 [a] Matt. 27:11–14
18:30 [1] *evildoer*
18:32 [a] Matt. 20:17–19; 26:2
[b] John 3:14; 8:28; 12:32, 33
18:33 [a] Matt. 27:11
[1] Gr. *praetorion*
18:36 [a] 1 Tim. 6:13
[b] [Dan. 2:44; 7:14]
18:37 [a] [Matt. 5:17; 20:28] [b] Is. 55:4 [c] [John 14:6]
[d] John 8:47; 10:27
[1] *sayest* rightly
18:38 [a] John 19:4, 6

39 ªBut ye have a custom, that I should release unto you one at the passover: will ye therefore that I release unto you the King of the Jews?

40 ªThen cried they all again, saying, Not this man, but Barabbas. ᵇNow Barabbas was a robber.

## CHAPTER 19

THEN ªPilate therefore took Jesus, and ¹scourged *him*.

2 And the soldiers ¹platted a crown of thorns, and put *it* on his head, and they put on him a purple robe,

3 And said, Hail, King of the Jews! and they ªsmote¹ him with their hands.

4 Pilate therefore went forth again, and saith unto them, Behold, I bring him forth to you, ªthat ye may know that I find no fault in him.

5 Then came Jesus forth, wearing the crown of thorns, and the purple robe. And *Pilate* saith unto them, Behold the man!

6 ªWhen the chief priests therefore and officers saw him, they cried out, saying, Crucify *him,* crucify *him.* Pilate saith unto them, Take ye him, and crucify *him:* for I find no fault in him.

7 The Jews answered him, ªWe have a law, and by our law he ought to die, because ᵇhe made himself the Son of God.

8 When Pilate therefore heard that saying, he was the more afraid;

9 And went again into the judgment hall, and saith unto Jesus, ¹Whence art thou? ªBut Jesus gave him no answer.

10 Then saith Pilate unto him, Speakest thou not unto me? knowest thou not that I have ¹power to crucify thee, and have ¹power to release thee?

11 Jesus answered, ªThou couldest have no ¹power *at all* against me, except it were given thee from above: therefore ᵇhe that delivered me unto thee hath the greater sin.

12 And from thenceforth Pilate sought to release him: but the Jews cried out, saying, If thou let this man go, thou art not Caesar's friend: ªwhosoever maketh himself a king speaketh against Caesar.

13 ªWhen Pilate therefore heard that saying, he brought Jesus forth, and sat down in the judgment seat in a place that is called the Pavement, but in the Hebrew, Gabbatha.

14 And ªit was the preparation of the passover, and about the sixth hour: and he saith unto the Jews, Behold your King!

15 But they cried out, Away with *him,* away with *him,* crucify him. Pilate saith unto them, Shall I crucify

your King? The chief priests answered, ªWe have no king but Caesar.

16 ªThen delivered he him therefore unto them to be crucified. And they took Jesus, and led *him* away.

17 ªAnd he bearing his cross ᵇwent forth into a place called *the place* of a skull, which is called in the Hebrew Golgotha:

18 Where they crucified him, and ªtwo other with him, on either side one, and Jesus in the ¹midst.

19 ªAnd Pilate wrote a title, and put *it* on the cross. And the writing was, JESUS OF NAZARETH THE KING OF THE JEWS.

20 This title then read many of the Jews: for the place where Jesus was crucified was ¹nigh to the city: and it was written in Hebrew, *and* Greek, *and* Latin.

21 Then said the chief priests of the Jews to Pilate, Write not, The King of the Jews; but that he said, I am King of the Jews.

22 Pilate answered, What I have written I have written.

23 ªThen the soldiers, when they had crucified Jesus, took his garments, and made four parts, to every soldier a part; and also *his* ¹coat: now the ¹coat was without seam, woven from the top throughout.

24 They said therefore among themselves, Let us not ¹rend it, but cast lots for it, whose it shall be: that the scripture might be fulfilled, which saith, ªThey parted my ²raiment among them, and for my ³vesture they did cast lots. These things therefore the soldiers did.

25 ªNow there stood by the cross of Jesus his mother, and his mother's sister, Mary the *wife* of ᵇCleophas,¹ and Mary Magdalene.

26 When Jesus therefore saw his mother, and ªthe disciple standing by, whom he loved, he saith unto his mother, ᵇWoman, behold thy son!

27 Then saith he to the disciple, Behold thy mother! And from that hour that disciple took her ªunto his own *home.*

28 After this, Jesus knowing that all things were now accomplished, ªthat the scripture might be fulfilled, saith, I thirst.

29 Now there was set a vessel full of ¹vinegar: and ªthey filled a spunge with ¹vinegar, and put *it* upon hyssop, and put *it* to his mouth.

30 When Jesus therefore had received the ¹vinegar, he said, ªIt is finished: and he bowed his head, and gave up ²the ghost.

31 The Jews therefore, ªbecause it was the preparation, ᵇthat the bodies should not remain upon the cross on the sabbath day, (for that sabbath day

### Center column references

18:39 ª Luke 23:17–25

18:40 ª Acts 3:14
ᵇ Luke 23:19

19:1 ª Matt. 20:19; 27:26 ¹ *whipped him with a Roman scourge*

19:2 ¹ *twisted*

19:3 ª Is. 50:6
¹ *struck*

19:4 ª John 18:33, 38

19:6 ª Acts 3:13

19:7 ª Lev. 24:16
ᵇ Matt. 26:63–66

19:9 ª Is. 53:7
¹ *Where are you from?*

19:10 ¹ *authority*

19:11 ª [Luke 22:53] ᵇ Rom. 13:1
¹ *authority*

19:12 ª Luke 23:2

19:13 ª 1 Sam. 15:24

19:14 ª Matt. 27:62

19:15 ª [Gen. 49:10]

19:16 ª Luke 23:24

19:17 ª Mark 15:21, 22 ᵇ Num. 15:36

19:18 ª Is. 53:12
¹ *center*

19:19 ª Matt. 27:37

19:20 ¹ *near*

19:23 ª Luke 23:34
¹ *tunic*

19:24 ª Ps. 22:18
¹ *tear* ² *garments* ³ *clothing*

19:25 ª Mark 15:40 ᵇ Luke 24:18 ¹ *Gr. Clopas*

19:26 ª John 13:23; 20:2; 21:7, 20, 24 ᵇ John 2:4

19:27 ª John 1:11; 16:32

19:28 ª Ps. 22:15

19:29 ª Matt. 27:48, 50 ¹ *sour wine*

19:30 ª John 17:4
¹ *sour wine* ² *his spirit*

19:31 ª Mark 15:42
ᵇ Deut. 21:23

was an [c]high day,) [1]besought Pilate that their legs might be broken, and *that* they might be taken away.

32 Then came the soldiers, and brake the legs of the first, and of the other which was crucified with him.

33 But when they came to Jesus, and saw that he was dead already, they brake not his legs:

34 But one of the soldiers with a spear pierced his side, and [1]forthwith [a]came there out blood and water.

35 And he that saw *it* bare record, and his record is [a]true: and he knoweth that he saith true, that ye might [b]believe.

36 For these things were done, [a]that the scripture should be fulfilled, A bone of him shall not be broken.

37 And again another scripture saith, [a]They shall look on him whom they pierced.

38 [a]And after this Joseph of Arimathaea, being a disciple of Jesus, but secretly [b]for fear of the Jews, [1]besought Pilate that he might take away the body of Jesus: and Pilate gave *him* [2]leave. He came therefore, and took the body of Jesus.

39 And there came also [a]Nicodemus, which at the first came to Jesus by night, and brought a mixture of [b]myrrh and aloes, about an hundred [1]pound *weight*.

40 Then took they the body of Jesus, and [a]wound[1] it in linen [2]clothes with the spices, as the manner of the Jews is to bury.

41 Now in the place where he was crucified there was a garden; and in the garden a new [1]sepulchre, wherein was never man yet laid.

42 [a]There laid they Jesus therefore [b]because of the Jews' preparation *day;* for the sepulchre was [1]nigh at hand.

### CHAPTER 20

THE [a]first *day* of the week cometh Mary Magdalene early, when it was yet dark, unto the [1]sepulchre, and seeth the [b]stone taken away from the sepulchre.

2 Then she runneth, and cometh to Simon Peter, and to the [a]other disciple, [b]whom Jesus loved, and saith unto them, They have taken away the Lord out of the [1]sepulchre, and we know not where they have laid him.

3 [a]Peter therefore went forth, and that other disciple, and [1]came to the sepulchre.

4 So they ran both together: and the other disciple did outrun Peter, and came first to the sepulchre.

5 And he stooping down, *and looking in,* saw [a]the linen clothes lying; yet went he not in.

6 Then cometh Simon Peter follow-

19:31 [c] Ex. 12:16
[1] *asked*
19:34 [a] [1 John 5:6, 8] [1] *immediately*
19:35 [a] John 21:24
[b] [John 20:31]
19:36 [a] [Ex. 12:46; Num. 9:12]; Ps. 34:20
19:37 [a] Zech. 12:10; 13:6
19:38 [a] Luke 23:50–56 [b] [John 7:13; 9:22; 12:42]
[1] *asked* [2] *permission*
19:39 [a] John 3:1, 2; 7:50 [b] Matt. 2:11 [1] Gr. *litras*
19:40 [a] John 20:5, 7 [1] *bound* [2] *strips*
19:41 [1] *tomb*
19:42 [a] Is. 53:9 [b] John 19:14, 31 [1] *nearby*
20:1 [a] Matt. 28:1–8 [b] Matt. 27:60, 66; 28:2 [1] *tomb*
20:2 [a] John 21:23, 24 [b] John 13:23; 19:26; 21:7, 20, 24 [1] *tomb*
20:3 [a] Luke 24:12 [1] *were going to the tomb*
20:5 [a] John 19:40
20:7 [a] John 11:44 [1] *face cloth* [2] *folded*
20:8 [a] John 21:23, 24 [1] *tomb*
20:9 [a] Ps. 16:10 [1] *understood*
20:11 [a] Mark 16:5 [1] *outside*
20:14 [a] Matt. 28:9; Mark 16:9 [b] [Luke 24:16, 31]; John 21:4 [1] *around*
20:15 [1] *carried him away*
20:16 [a] John 10:3 [1] *Teacher*
20:17 [a] Mark 16:19; Luke 24:5; Acts 1:9; 2:34–36; Eph. 4:8–10; Heb. 4:14 [b] Ps. 22:22; Matt. 18:10; Rom. 8:29; Heb. 2:11 [c] John 16:28; 17:11 [d] Eph. 1:17 [1] *Do not cling to me*
20:18 [a] Matt. 28:10; Luke 24:10, 23
20:19 [a] Mark 16:14; Luke 24:36; John 14:27; 1 Cor. 15:5 [b] John 9:22; 19:38 [c] John 14:27; 16:16; Eph. 2:17
20:20 [a] Acts 1:3 [b] John 16:20, 22

ing him, and went into the sepulchre, and seeth the linen clothes lie,

7 And [a]the [1]napkin, that was about his head, not lying with the linen clothes, but [2]wrapped together in a place by itself.

8 Then went in also that [a]other disciple, which came first to the [1]sepulchre, and he saw, and believed.

9 For as yet they [1]knew not the [a]scripture, that he must rise again from the dead.

10 Then the disciples went away again unto their own home.

11 [a]But Mary stood [1]without at the sepulchre weeping: and as she wept, she stooped down, *and looked* into the sepulchre.

12 And seeth two angels in white sitting, the one at the head, and the other at the feet, where the body of Jesus had lain.

13 And they say unto her, Woman, why weepest thou? She saith unto them, Because they have taken away my Lord, and I know not where they have laid him.

14 [a]And when she had thus said, she turned [1]herself back, and saw Jesus standing, and [b]knew not that it was Jesus.

15 Jesus saith unto her, Woman, why weepest thou? whom seekest thou? She, supposing him to be the gardener, saith unto him, Sir, if thou have [b]borne him hence, tell me where thou hast laid him, and I will take him away.

16 Jesus saith unto her, [a]Mary. She turned herself, and saith unto him, Rabboni; which is to say, [1]Master.

17 Jesus saith unto her, [1]Touch me not; for I am not yet [a]ascended to my Father: but go to [b]my brethren, and say unto them, [c]I ascend unto my Father, and your Father; and *to* [d]my God, and your God.

18 [a]Mary Magdalene came and told the disciples that she had seen the Lord, and *that* he had spoken these things unto her.

19 [a]Then the same day at evening, being the first *day* of the week, when the doors were shut where the disciples were assembled for [b]fear of the Jews, came Jesus and stood in the midst, and saith unto them, [c]Peace *be* unto you.

20 And when he had so said, he [a]shewed unto them *his* hands and his side. [b]Then were the disciples glad, when they saw the Lord.

21 Then said Jesus to them again, Peace *be* unto you: [a]as *my* Father hath sent me, even so send I you.

22 And when he had said this, he breathed on *them,* and saith unto them, Receive ye the Holy Ghost:

20:21 [a] [Matt. 28:18–20]; John 17:18, 19; [2 Tim. 2:2]; Heb. 3:1

23 [a]Whose soever sins ye [1]remit, they are [2]remitted unto them; *and* whose soever *sins* ye retain, they are retained.

24 But Thomas, one of the twelve, [a]called Didymus, was not with them when Jesus came.

25 The other disciples therefore said unto him, We have seen the Lord. But he said unto them, Except I shall see in his hands the print of the nails, and put my finger into the print of the nails, and thrust my hand into his side, I will not believe.

26 And after eight days again his disciples were within, and Thomas with them: *then* came Jesus, the doors being shut, and stood in the midst, and said, Peace *be* unto you.

27 Then saith he to Thomas, Reach hither thy finger, and behold my hands; and [a]reach hither thy hand, and thrust *it* into my side: and be not [b]faithless,[1] but believing.

28 And Thomas answered and said unto him, My Lord and my God.

29 Jesus saith unto him, Thomas, because thou hast seen me, thou hast believed: [a]blessed *are* they that have not seen, and *yet* have believed.

30 And [a]many other signs truly did Jesus in the presence of his disciples, which are not written in this book:

31 [a]But these are written, that [b]ye might believe that Jesus [c]is the Christ, the Son of God; [d]and that believing ye might have life [1]through his name.

## CHAPTER 21

AFTER these things Jesus shewed himself again to the disciples at the [a]sea of Tiberias; and [1]on this wise shewed he *himself.*

2 There were together Simon Peter, and [a]Thomas called Didymus, and [b]Nathanael of [c]Cana in Galilee, and [d]the *sons* of Zebedee, and two other of his disciples.

3 Simon Peter saith unto them, I [1]go a fishing. They say unto him, We also go with thee. They went forth, and entered into [2]a ship immediately; and that night they caught nothing.

4 But when the morning was now come, Jesus stood on the shore: but the disciples [a]knew not that it was Jesus.

5 Then [a]Jesus saith unto them, Children, have ye any [1]meat? They answered him, No.

6 And he said unto them, [a]Cast the net on the right side of the ship, and ye shall find. They cast therefore, and now they were not able to draw it for the multitude of fishes.

7 Therefore [a]that disciple whom Jesus loved saith unto Peter, It is the

20:23 [a] Matt. 16:19; 18:18 [1] forgive [2] forgiven
20:24 [a] John 11:16
20:27 [a] Ps. 22:16; Zech. 12:10; 13:6; 1 John 1:1 [b] Mark 16:14 [1] unbelieving
20:29 [a] 2 Cor. 5:7; 1 Pet. 1:8
20:30 [a] John 21:25
20:31 [a] Luke 1:4 [b] John 19:35; 1 John 5:13 [c] Luke 2:11; 1 John 5:1 [d] John 3:15, 16; 5:24; [1 Pet. 1:8, 9] [1] Lit. *in*
21:1 [a] Matt. 26:32; Mark 14:28; John 6:1 [1] *in this way*
21:2 [a] John 20:24 [b] John 1:45–51 [c] John 2:1 [d] Matt. 4:21; Mark 1:19; Luke 5:10
21:3 [1] *am going* [2] Lit. *the*
21:4 [a] Luke 24:16; John 20:14
21:5 [a] Luke 24:41 [1] *food*
21:6 [a] Luke 5:4, 6, 7
21:7 [a] John 13:23; 20:2 [1] *put on* [2] *had removed it*
21:10 [1] *some of*
21:12 [a] Acts 10:41 [1] *eat breakfast* [2] *dared*
21:14 [a] John 20:19, 26
21:15 [a] Acts 20:28; 1 Tim. 4:6; 1 Pet. 5:2 [1] *eaten breakfast* [2] *have affection for*
21:16 [a] Matt. 2:6; Acts 20:28; Heb. 13:20; 1 Pet. 2:25; 5:2, 4 [b] Ps. 79:13; Matt. 10:16; 15:24; 25:33; 26:31 [1] *have affection for* [2] *Tend*
21:17 [a] John 2:24, 25; 16:30 [1] *do you have affection for me* [2] *have affection for*
21:18 [a] John 13:36; Acts 12:3, 4
21:19 [a] 2 Pet. 1:13, 14 [b] [Matt. 4:19; 16:24]; John 21:22
21:20 [a] John 13:23; 20:2 [b] John 13:25
21:21 [1] *what about this man*
21:22 [a] [Matt. 16:27, 28; 25:31; 1 Cor. 4:5; 11:26; Rev. 2:25; 3:11; 22:7, 20] [1] *remain*

Lord. Now when Simon Peter heard that it was the Lord, he [1]girt *his* fisher's coat *unto him,* (for he [2]was naked,) and did cast himself into the sea.

8 And the other disciples came in a little ship; (for they were not far from land, but as it were two hundred cubits,) dragging the net with fishes.

9 As soon then as they were come to land, they saw a fire of coals there, and fish laid thereon, and bread.

10 Jesus saith unto them, Bring [1]of the fish which ye have now caught.

11 Simon Peter went up, and drew the net to land full of great fishes, an hundred and fifty and three: and for all there were so many, yet was not the net broken.

12 Jesus saith unto them, [a]Come *and* [1]dine. And none of the disciples [2]durst ask him, Who art thou? knowing that it was the Lord.

13 Jesus then cometh, and taketh bread, and giveth them, and fish likewise.

14 This is now [a]the third time that Jesus shewed himself to his disciples, after that he was risen from the dead.

15 So when they had [1]dined, Jesus saith to Simon Peter, Simon, *son* of Jonas, lovest thou me more than these? He saith unto him, Yea, Lord; thou knowest that I [2]love thee. He saith unto him, [a]Feed my lambs.

16 He saith to him again the second time, Simon, *son* of Jonas, lovest thou me? He saith unto him, Yea, Lord; thou knowest that I [1]love thee. [a]He saith unto him, [2]Feed my [b]sheep.

17 He saith unto him the third time, Simon, *son* of Jonas, [1]lovest thou me? Peter was grieved because he said unto him the third time, [1]Lovest thou me? And he said unto him, Lord, [a]thou knowest all things; thou knowest that I [2]love thee. Jesus saith unto him, Feed my sheep.

18 [a]Verily, verily, I say unto thee, When thou wast young, thou girdedst thyself, and walkedst whither thou wouldest: but when thou shalt be old, thou shalt stretch forth thy hands, and another shall gird thee, and carry *thee* whither thou wouldest not.

19 This spake he, signifying [a]by what death he should glorify God. And when he had spoken this, he saith unto him, [b]Follow me.

20 Then Peter, turning about, seeth the disciple [a]whom Jesus loved following; [b]which also leaned on his breast at supper, and said, Lord, which is he that betrayeth thee?

21 Peter seeing him saith to Jesus, Lord, and [1]what *shall* this man do?

22 Jesus saith unto him, If I will that he [1]tarry [a]till I come, what *is that* to thee? follow thou me.

23 Then went this saying abroad among the brethren, that that disciple should not die: yet Jesus said not unto him, He shall not die; but, If I [1]will that he [2]tarry till I come, what *is that* to thee?

24 This is the disciple which [a]testifieth of these things, and wrote these

things: and we know that his testimony is true.

25 [a]And there are also many other things which Jesus did, the which, if they should be written [1]every one, [b]I suppose that even the world itself could not contain the books that should be written. Amen.

21:23 [1] *desire*
[2] *remain*
21:24 [a] John 19:35; 3 John 12

21:25 [a] John 20:30 [b] Amos 7:10 [1] *one by one*

# THE ACTS
## OF THE APOSTLES

Jesus' last recorded words have come to be known as the Great Commission: "Ye shall be witnesses unto me both in Jerusalem, and in all Judaea, and in Samaria, and unto the uttermost part of the earth" (1:8). The Book of Acts, written by Luke, is the story of the men and women who took that commission seriously and began to spread the news of a risen Savior to the most remote corners of the known world.

Each section of the book (1–7; 8–12; 13–28) focuses on a particular audience, a key personality, and a significant phase in the expansion of the gospel message.

As the second volume in a two-part work by Luke, this book probably had no separate title. But all available Greek manuscripts designate it by the title *Praxeis*, "Acts," or by an expanded title like "The Acts of the Apostles." *Praxeis* was commonly used in Greek literature to summarize the accomplishments of outstanding men. While the apostles are mentioned collectively at several points, this book really records the acts of Peter (1–12) and of Paul (13–28).

## CHAPTER 1

THE former treatise have I made, O ªTheophilus, of all that Jesus began both to do and teach,

2 ªUntil the day in which he ¹was taken up, after that he through the Holy Ghost ᵇhad given commandments unto the apostles whom he had chosen:

3 ªTo whom also he ¹shewed himself alive after his ²passion by many ³infallible proofs, being seen of them forty days, and speaking of the things pertaining to the kingdom of God:

4 ªAnd, being assembled together with *them,* commanded them that they should not depart from Jerusalem, but wait for the promise of the Father, which, *saith he,* ye have ᵇheard of me.

5 ªFor John truly baptized with water; ᵇbut ye shall be baptized with the Holy Ghost not many days hence.

6 When they therefore were come together, they asked of him, saying, Lord, wilt thou at this time restore again the kingdom to Israel?

7 And he said unto them, ªIt is not for you to ᵇknow the times or the seasons, which the Father hath put in his own ¹power.

8 ªBut ye shall receive power, ᵇafter¹ that the Holy Ghost is come upon you: and ᶜye shall be witnesses unto me both in Jerusalem, and in all Judaea, and in ᵈSamaria, and unto the ᵉuttermost part of the earth.

9 ªAnd when he had spoken these things, while they beheld, ᵇhe was taken up; and a cloud received him out of their sight.

10 And while they looked stedfastly toward heaven as he went up, behold, two men stood by them ªin white apparel;

11 Which also said, Ye men of Gal-

ilee, why stand ye gazing up into heaven? this same Jesus, which is taken up from you into heaven, ªshall so come in like manner as ye have seen him go into heaven.

12 ªThen returned they unto Jerusalem from the mount called Olivet, which is from Jerusalem a sabbath day's journey.

13 And when they were come in, they went up ªinto an upper room, where ¹abode both ᵇPeter, and James, and John, and Andrew, Philip, and Thomas, Bartholomew, and Matthew, James *the son* of Alphaeus, and ᶜSimon ²Zelotes, and ᵈJudas *the* ³brother of James.

14 ªThese all continued with one ¹accord in prayer and supplication, with ᵇthe women, and Mary the mother of Jesus, and with ᶜhis brethren.

15 And in those days Peter stood up in the midst of the disciples, and said, (the number ªof names together were about an hundred and twenty,)

16 Men *and* brethren, this scripture must needs have been fulfilled, ªwhich the Holy Ghost by the mouth of David spake before concerning Judas, ᵇwhich was guide to them that took Jesus.

17 For ªhe was numbered with us, and had obtained part of ᵇthis ministry.

18 ªNow this man purchased a field with ᵇthe ¹reward of iniquity; and falling headlong, he burst ²asunder in the midst, and all his bowels gushed out.

19 And it was known unto all the dwellers at Jerusalem; insomuch as that field is called in their ¹proper tongue, Aceldama, that is to say, The field of blood.

20 For it is written in the book of Psalms, ªLet his ¹habitation be ²des-

---

1:1 ª Luke 1:3
1:2 ª Mark 16:19 ᵇ Matt. 28:19 ¹ Ascended into heaven
1:3 ª Mark 16:12, 14 ¹ presented ² suffering ³ unmistakable
1:4 ª Luke 24:49 ᵇ [John 14:16, 17, 26; 15:26]
1:5 ª Matt. 3:11 ᵇ [Joel 2:28]
1:7 ª 1 Thess. 5:1 ᵇ Matt. 24:36 ¹ authority
1:8 ª [Acts 2:1, 4] ᵇ Luke 24:49 ᶜ Luke 24:48 ᵈ Acts 8:1, 5, 14 ᵉ Col. 1:23 ¹ when
1:9 ª Luke 24:50, 51 ᵇ Acts 1:2
1:10 ª John 20:12
1:11 ª Dan. 7:13
1:12 ª Luke 24:52
1:13 ª Acts 9:37, 39; 20:8 ᵇ Matt. 10:2–4 ᶜ Luke 6:15 ᵈ Jude 1 ¹ were staying ² the Zealot ³ son of
1:14 ª Acts 2:1, 46 ᵇ Luke 23:49, 55 ᶜ Matt. 13:55 ¹ purpose or mind
1:15 ª Rev. 3:4
1:16 ª Ps. 41:9 ᵇ Luke 22:47
1:17 ª Matt. 10:4 ᵇ Acts 1:25
1:18 ª Matt. 27:3–10 ᵇ Mark 14:21; Matt. 26:14, 15 ¹ wages of unrighteousness ² open
1:19 ¹ own language
1:20 ª Ps. 69:25 ¹ dwelling place ² deserted

olate, and let no man dwell therein: and ᵇhis ³bishoprick let another take.

21 Wherefore of these men which have ¹companied with us all the time that the Lord Jesus went in and out among us,

22 Beginning from the baptism of John, unto that same day that ᵃhe was taken up from us, must one ᵇbe ordained ᵇto be a witness with us of his resurrection.

23 And they ¹appointed two, Joseph called ᵃBarsabas, who was surnamed Justus, and Matthias.

24 And they prayed, and said, Thou, Lord, ᵃwhich knowest the hearts of all *men,* shew ¹whether of these two thou hast chosen,

25 ᵃThat he may take part of this ministry and apostleship, from which Judas by transgression fell, that he might go to his own place.

26 And they ¹gave forth their lots; and the lot fell upon Matthias; and he was numbered with the eleven apostles.

### CHAPTER 2

A ND when ᵃthe day of Pentecost was fully come, ᵇthey were all with one ¹accord in one place.

2 And suddenly there came a sound from heaven as of a rushing mighty wind, and ᵃit filled all the house where they were sitting.

3 And there appeared unto them ¹cloven tongues like as of fire, and it sat upon each of them.

4 And ᵃthey were all filled with the Holy Ghost, and began ᵇto speak with other tongues, as the Spirit gave them utterance.

5 And there were dwelling at Jerusalem Jews, ᵃdevout men, out of every nation under heaven.

6 Now when this ¹was noised abroad, the ᵃmultitude came together, and were ²confounded, because that every man heard them speak in his own language.

7 And they were all amazed and marvelled, saying one to another, Behold, are not all these which speak ᵃGalilaeans?

8 And how hear we every man in our own ¹tongue, wherein we were born?

9 Parthians, and Medes, and Elamites, and the dwellers in Mesopotamia, and in Judaea, and ᵃCappadocia, in Pontus, and Asia,

10 Phrygia, and Pamphylia, in Egypt, and in the parts of Libya about Cyrene, and ¹strangers of Rome, Jews and proselytes,

11 Cretes and Arabians, we do hear them speak in our tongues the wonderful works of God.

12 And they were all amazed, and

were ¹in doubt, saying one to another, What meaneth this?

13 Others mocking said, These men are full of new wine.

14 But Peter, standing up with the eleven, lifted up his voice, and said unto them, Ye men of Judaea, and all *ye* that dwell at Jerusalem, be this known unto you, and hearken to my words:

15 For these are not drunken, as ye suppose, ᵃseeing it is *but* the third hour of the day.

16 But this is that which was spoken by the prophet Joel;

17 ᵃAnd it shall come to pass in the last days, saith God, ᵇI will pour out of my Spirit upon all flesh: and your sons and ᶜyour daughters shall prophesy, and your young men shall see visions, and your old men shall dream dreams:

18 And on my servants and on my handmaidens I will pour out in those days of my Spirit; ᵃand they shall prophesy:

19 ᵃAnd I will shew wonders in heaven above, and signs in the earth beneath; blood, and fire, and vapour of smoke:

20 ᵃThe sun shall be turned into darkness, and the moon into blood, before that great and notable day of the Lord come:

21 And it shall come to pass, *that* ᵃwhosoever shall call on the name of the Lord shall be saved.

22 Ye men of Israel, hear these words; Jesus of Nazareth, a man ¹approved of God among you ᵃby miracles and wonders and signs, which God did by him in the midst of you, as ye yourselves also know:

23 Him, ᵃbeing delivered by the determinate counsel and foreknowledge of God, ᵇye have taken, and by ¹wicked hands have crucified and slain:

24 ᵃWhom God hath raised up, having ¹loosed the ²pains of death: because it was not possible that he should be ³holden of it.

25 For David speaketh concerning him, ᵃI foresaw the Lord always before my face, for he is on my right hand, that I should not be ¹moved:

26 Therefore did my heart rejoice, and my tongue was glad; moreover also my flesh shall rest in hope:

27 Because thou wilt not leave my soul in ¹hell, neither wilt thou suffer thine Holy One to see ᵃcorruption.

28 Thou hast made known to me the ways of life; thou shalt make me full of joy ¹with thy countenance.

29 Men *and* brethren, let me freely speak unto you ᵃof the patriarch David, that he is both dead and buried, and his ¹sepulchre is with us unto this day.

---

1:20 ᵇ Ps. 109:8 ³ Gr. *episkopen, office of overseer*
1:21 ¹ *accompanied*
1:22 ᵃ Acts 1:9 ᵇ Acts 1:8; 2:32 ¹ *become*
1:23 ᵃ Acts 15:22 ¹ *proposed*
1:24 ᵃ 1 Sam. 16:7 ¹ *which*
1:25 ᵃ Acts 1:17
1:26 ¹ *cast*
2:1 ᵃ Lev. 23:15 ᵇ Acts 1:14 ¹ *purpose or mind*
2:2 ᵃ Acts 4:31
2:3 ¹ *divided*
2:4 ᵃ Acts 1:5 ᵇ Mark 16:17
2:5 ᵃ Acts 8:2
2:6 ᵃ Acts 4:32 ¹ *sound occurred* ² *confused*
2:7 ᵃ Acts 1:11
2:8 ¹ *language or dialect*
2:9 ᵃ 1 Pet. 1:1
2:10 ¹ *visitors from*

2:12 ¹ *perplexed*
2:15 ᵃ 1 Thess. 5:7
2:17 ᵃ Joel 2:28–32 ᵇ Acts 10:45 ᶜ Acts 21:9
2:18 ᵃ 1 Cor. 12:10
2:19 ᵃ Joel 2:30
2:20 ᵃ Matt. 24:29
2:21 ᵃ Rom. 10:13
2:22 ᵃ John 3:2; 5:6 ¹ *attested by*
2:23 ᵃ Luke 22:22 ᵇ Acts 5:30 ¹ *lawless*
2:24 ᵃ [Rom. 8:11] ¹ *destroyed* ² Lit. *birth pangs* ³ *held by*
2:25 ᵃ Ps. 16:8–11 ¹ *shaken*
2:27 ᵃ Acts 13:30–37 ¹ Gr. *hades*
2:28 ¹ *in thy presence*
2:29 ᵃ Acts 13:36 ¹ *tomb*

30 Therefore being a prophet, [a]and knowing that God had sworn with an oath to him, that of the fruit of his loins, according to the flesh, he would raise up Christ to sit on his throne;

31 He seeing this before spake of the resurrection of Christ, [a]that his soul was not left in [1]hell, neither his flesh did see corruption.

32 [a]This Jesus hath God raised up, [b]whereof we all are witnesses.

33 Therefore [a]being by the right hand of God [b]exalted, and [c]having received of the Father the promise of the Holy Ghost, he [d]hath shed forth this, which ye now see and hear.

34 For David is not ascended into the heavens: but he saith himself, [a]The LORD said unto my Lord, Sit thou on my right hand,

35 Until I make thy foes thy footstool.

36 Therefore let all the house of Israel know assuredly, that God hath made that same Jesus, whom ye have crucified, both Lord and Christ.

37 Now when they heard this, [a]they were [1]pricked in their heart, and said unto Peter and to the rest of the apostles, Men and brethren, what shall we do?

38 Then Peter said unto them, [a]Repent, and be baptized every one of you in the name of Jesus Christ for the [1]remission of sins, and ye shall receive the gift of the Holy Ghost.

39 For the promise is unto you, and [a]to your children, and [b]to all that are afar off, even as many as the Lord our God shall call.

40 And with many other words did he testify and exhort, saying, Save yourselves from this [1]untoward generation.

41 Then they that gladly received his word were baptized: and the same day there were added unto them about three thousand souls.

42 [a]And they continued stedfastly in the apostles' doctrine and fellowship, and in breaking of bread, and in prayers.

43 And fear came upon every soul: and [a]many wonders and signs were done [b]by the apostles.

44 And all that believed were together, and [a]had all things common;

45 And sold their possessions and goods, and [a]parted[1] them to all men, as [2]every man had need.

46 [a]And they, continuing daily with one [1]accord [b]in the temple, and [c]breaking bread from house to house, did eat their [2]meat with gladness and [3]singleness of heart,

47 Praising God, and having favour with all the people. [a]And the Lord added to the church daily such as [1]should be saved.

---

2:30 [a] Ps. 132:11
2:31 [a] Ps. 16:10
[1] Gr. hades
2:32 [a] Acts 2:24
[b] Acts 1:8; 3:15
2:33 [a] [Acts 5:31]
[b] [Heb. 10:12]
[c] [John 14:26]
[d] Acts 2:1–11, 17; 10:45
2:34 [a] Ps. 68:18; 110:1
2:37 [a] Luke 3:10, 12, 14 [1] cut to the heart
2:38 [a] Luke 24:47 [1] forgiveness
2:39 [a] Joel 2:28, 32 [b] Eph. 2:13
2:40 [1] crooked
2:42 [a] Acts 1:14
2:43 [a] Acts 2:22 [1] through
2:44 [a] Acts 4:32, 34, 37; 5:2
2:45 [a] Is. 58:7 [1] distributed [2] anyone
2:46 [a] Acts 1:14 [b] Luke 24:53 [c] Acts 2:42; 20:7 [1] mind [2] food [3] simplicity
2:47 [a] Acts 5:14 [1] were being

3:1 [a] Acts 2:46 [b] Ps. 55:17
3:2 [a] Acts 14:8 [b] John 9:8
3:6 [a] Acts 4:10
3:8 [a] Is. 35:6
3:9 [a] Acts 4:16, 21
3:10 [a] John 9:8 [1] begging
3:11 [a] John 10:23 [1] held on to [2] amazed
3:12 [1] intently [2] godliness
3:13 [a] John 5:30 [b] John 7:39; 12:23; 13:31 [c] Matt. 27:2 [d] Matt. 27:20
3:14 [a] Mark 1:24 [b] Acts 7:52 [c] John 18:40
3:15 [a] Acts 2:24 [b] Acts 2:32 [1] Author
3:16 [a] Matt. 9:22 [1] Comes through Jesus
3:17 [a] Luke 23:34 [1] know
3:18 [a] Acts 26:22 [b] 1 Pet. 1:10 [1] foretold by

---

## CHAPTER 3

Now Peter and John went up together [a]into the temple at the hour of prayer, [b]being the ninth hour.

2 And [a]a certain man lame from his mother's womb was carried, whom they laid daily at the gate of the temple which is called Beautiful, [b]to ask alms of them that entered into the temple;

3 Who seeing Peter and John about to go into the temple asked an alms.

4 And Peter, fastening his eyes upon him with John, said, Look on us.

5 And he gave heed unto them, expecting to receive something of them.

6 Then Peter said, Silver and gold have I none; but such as I have give I thee: [a]In the name of Jesus Christ of Nazareth rise up and walk.

7 And he took him by the right hand, and lifted him up: and immediately his feet and ankle bones received strength.

8 And he [a]leaping up stood, and walked, and entered with them into the temple, walking, and leaping, and praising God.

9 [a]And all the people saw him walking and praising God:

10 And they knew that it was he which [a]sat [1]for alms at the Beautiful gate of the temple: and they were filled with wonder and amazement at that which had happened unto him.

11 And as the lame man which was healed [1]held Peter and John, all the people ran together unto them in the porch [a]that is called Solomon's, greatly [2]wondering.

12 And when Peter saw it, he answered unto the people, Ye men of Israel, why marvel ye at this? or why look ye so [1]earnestly on us, as though by our own power or [2]holiness we had made this man to walk?

13 [a]The God of Abraham, and of Isaac, and of Jacob, the God of our fathers, [b]hath glorified his Son Jesus; whom ye [c]delivered up, and [d]denied him in the presence of Pilate, when he was determined to let him go.

14 But ye denied [a]the Holy One [b]and the Just, and [c]desired a murderer to be granted unto you;

15 And killed the [1]Prince of life, [a]whom God hath raised from the dead; [b]whereof we are witnesses.

16 [a]And his name through faith in his name hath made this man strong, whom ye see and know: yea, the faith which [1]is by him hath given him this perfect soundness in the presence of you all.

17 And now, brethren, I [1]wot that [a]through ignorance ye did it, as did also your rulers.

18 But [a]those things, which God [1]before had shewed [b]by the mouth of

all his prophets, that Christ ²should suffer, he hath so fulfilled.

19 ªRepent ye therefore, and be converted, that your sins may be blotted out, when the times of refreshing shall come from the presence of the Lord;

20 And he shall send Jesus Christ, which before was preached unto you:

21 ªWhom the heaven must receive until the times of ᵇrestitution¹ of all things, ᶜwhich God hath spoken by the mouth of all his holy prophets since the world began.

22 For Moses truly said unto the fathers, ªA prophet shall the Lord your God raise up unto you of your brethren, like unto me; him shall ye hear in all things whatsoever he shall say unto you.

23 And it shall come to pass, *that* every soul, which will not hear that prophet, shall be destroyed from among the people.

24 Yea, and ªall the prophets from Samuel and those that follow after, as many as have spoken, have likewise foretold of these days.

25 ªYe are the ¹children of the prophets, and of the covenant which God made with our fathers, saying unto Abraham, ᵇAnd in thy seed shall all the ²kindreds of the earth be blessed.

26 Unto you ªfirst God, having raised up his ¹Son Jesus, sent him to bless you, ᵇin turning away every one of you from his iniquities.

## CHAPTER 4

A ND as they spake unto the people, the priests, and the captain of the temple, and the ªSadducees, came upon them,

2 Being ¹grieved that they taught the people, and preached through Jesus the resurrection from the dead.

3 And they laid hands on them, and put *them* in ¹hold unto the next day: for it was now ²eventide.

4 Howbeit many of them which heard the word believed; and the number of the men was about five thousand.

5 And it came to pass on the morrow, that their rulers, and elders, and scribes,

6 And ªAnnas the high priest, and Caiaphas, and John, and Alexander, and as many as were of the ¹kindred of the high priest, were gathered together at Jerusalem.

7 And when they had set them in the midst, they asked, ªBy what power, or by what name, have ye done this?

8 ªThen Peter, filled with the Holy Ghost, said unto them, Ye rulers of the people, and elders of Israel,

3:18 ² would
3:19 ª [Acts 2:38; 26:20]
3:21 ª Acts 1:11  ᵇ Matt. 17:11  ᶜ Luke 1:70  ¹ restoration
3:22 ª Deut. 18:15, 18, 19
3:24 ª Luke 24:25
3:25 ª [Rom. 9:4, 8]  ᵇ Gen. 12:3; 18:18; 22:18; 26:4; 28:14  ¹ sons  ² families
3:26 ª [Rom. 1:16; 2:9]  ᵇ Matt. 1:21  ¹ Or Servant
4:1 ª Matt. 22:23
4:2 ¹ greatly disturbed
4:3 ¹ custody  ² evening
4:6 ª Luke 3:2  ¹ family
4:7 ª Matt. 21:23
4:8 ª Luke 12:11, 12

4:9 ¹ are judged for  ² helpless
4:10 ª Acts 2:22; 3:6, 16  ᵇ Acts 2:24
4:11 ª Ps. 118:22  ¹ rejected by  ² chief cornerstone
4:12 ª [1 Tim. 2:5, 6]
4:13 ª [1 Cor. 1:27]  ¹ uneducated and untrained  ² realized that
4:14 ª Acts 3:11
4:16 ª John 11:47  ᵇ Acts 3:7–10  ¹ remarkable sign  ² known
4:17 ¹ severely
4:18 ª Acts 5:28, 40
4:19 ª Acts 5:29
4:20 ª Acts 1:8; 2:32  ᵇ [1 John 1:1, 3]
4:21 ª Acts 5:26  ᵇ Matt. 15:31  ᶜ Acts 3:7, 8  ¹ for which
4:22 ¹ had been performed
4:23 ª Acts 2:44–46; 12:12  ¹ Companions
4:24 ª Ex. 20:11
4:25 ª Ps. 2:1, 2  ¹ plot

9 If we this day ¹be examined of the good deed done to the ²impotent man, by what means he is made whole;

10 Be it known unto you all, and to all the people of Israel, ªthat by the name of Jesus Christ of Nazareth, whom ye crucified, ᵇwhom God raised from the dead, *even* by him doth this man stand here before you whole.

11 ªThis is the stone which was ¹set at nought of you builders, which is become the ²head of the corner.

12 ªNeither is there salvation in any other: for there is none other name under heaven given among men, whereby we must be saved.

13 Now when they saw the boldness of Peter and John, ªand perceived that they were ¹unlearned and ignorant men, they marvelled; and they ²took knowledge of them, that they had been with Jesus.

14 And beholding the man which was healed ªstanding with them, they could say nothing against it.

15 But when they had commanded them to go aside out of the council, they conferred among themselves,

16 Saying, ªWhat shall we do to these men? for that indeed a ¹notable miracle hath been done by them *is* ᵇmanifest² to all them that dwell in Jerusalem; and we cannot deny *it.*

17 But that it spread no further among the people, let us ¹straitly threaten them, that they speak henceforth to no man in this name.

18 ªAnd they called them, and commanded them not to speak at all nor teach in the name of Jesus.

19 But Peter and John answered and said unto them, ªWhether it be right in the sight of God to hearken unto you more than unto God, judge ye.

20 ªFor we cannot but speak the things which ᵇwe have seen and heard.

21 So when they had further threatened them, they let them go, finding nothing ¹how they might punish them, ªbecause of the people: for all *men* ᵇglorified God for ᶜthat which was done.

22 For the man was above forty years old, on whom this miracle of healing ¹was shewed.

23 And being let go, ªthey went to their own ¹company, and reported all that the chief priests and elders had said unto them.

24 And when they heard that, they lifted up their voice to God with one accord, and said, Lord, ªthou *art* God, which hast made heaven, and earth, and the sea, and all that in them is:

25 Who by the mouth of thy servant David hast said, ªWhy did the heathen rage, and the people ¹imagine vain things?

26 The kings of the earth ¹stood up, and the rulers were gathered together against the Lord, and against his Christ.

27 For ᵃof a truth against ᵇthy holy ¹child Jesus, ᶜwhom thou hast anointed, both Herod, and Pontius Pilate, with the Gentiles, and the people of Israel, were gathered together,

28 ᵃFor to do whatsoever thy hand and thy ¹counsel determined before to be done.

29 And now, Lord, behold their threatenings: and grant unto thy servants, ᵃthat with all boldness they may speak thy word,

30 By stretching forth thine hand to heal; ᵃand that signs and wonders may be done ᵇby¹ the name of ᶜthy holy ²child Jesus.

31 And when they had prayed, ᵃthe place was shaken where they were assembled together; and they were all filled with the Holy Ghost, ᵇand they spake the word of God with boldness.

32 And the multitude of them that believed ᵃwere of one heart and of one soul: ᵇneither said any *of them* that ¹ought of the things which he possessed was his own; but they had all things common.

33 And with ᵃgreat power gave the apostles ᵇwitness of the resurrection of the Lord Jesus: and ᶜgreat grace was upon them all.

34 Neither was there any among them that lacked: ᵃfor as many as were possessors of lands or houses sold them, and brought the ¹prices of the things that were sold,

35 ᵃAnd laid *them* down at the apostles' feet: ᵇand distribution was made unto every man according as he had need.

36 And Joses, who by the apostles was surnamed Barnabas, (which is, being interpreted, The son of ¹consolation,) a Levite, *and* of the country of Cyprus,

37 ᵃHaving land, sold *it*, and brought the money, and laid *it* at the apostles' feet.

## CHAPTER 5

B UT a certain man named Ananias, with Sapphira his wife, sold a possession,

2 And kept back *part* of the price, his wife also being ¹privy *to it*, and brought a certain part, and laid *it* at the apostles' feet.

3 ᵃBut Peter said, Ananias, why hath ᵇSatan filled thine heart to lie to the Holy Ghost, and to keep back *part* of the price of the land?

4 Whiles it remained, was it not thine own? and after it was sold, was

---

it not in thine own ¹power? why hast thou conceived this thing in thine heart? thou hast not lied unto men, but unto God.

5 And Ananias hearing these words ᵃfell down, and ¹gave up the ghost: and great fear came on all them that heard these things.

6 And the young men arose, ᵃwound¹ him up, and carried *him* out, and buried *him*.

7 And it was about the space of three hours after, when his wife, not knowing what was done, came in.

8 And Peter answered unto her, Tell me whether ye sold the land for so much? And she said, Yea, for so much.

9 Then Peter said unto her, How is it that ye have agreed together ᵃto ¹tempt the Spirit of the Lord? behold, the feet of them which have buried thy husband *are* at the door, and shall carry thee out.

10 ᵃThen fell she down ¹straightway at his feet, and ²yielded up the ghost: and the young men came in, and found her dead, and, carrying *her* forth, buried *her* by her husband.

11 ᵃAnd great fear came upon all the church, and upon as many as heard these things.

12 And ᵃby¹ the hands of the apostles were many signs and wonders ²wrought among the people; (ᵇand they were all with one accord in Solomon's porch.

13 And ᵃof the rest ¹durst no man join himself to them: ᵇbut the people ²magnified them.

14 And believers were ¹the more added to the Lord, multitudes both of men and women.)

15 Insomuch that they brought forth the sick into the streets, and laid *them* on beds and couches, ᵃthat at the least the shadow of Peter passing by might ¹overshadow some of them.

16 There came also a multitude *out* of the cities round about unto Jerusalem, bringing ᵃsick folks, and them which were ¹vexed with unclean spirits: and they were healed every one.

17 ᵃThen the high priest rose up, and all they that were with him, (which is the sect of the Sadducees,) and were filled with ¹indignation,

18 ᵃAnd laid their hands on the apostles, and put them in the common prison.

19 But ᵃthe angel of the Lord by night opened the prison doors, and brought them forth, and said,

20 Go, stand and speak in the temple to the people ᵃall the words of this life.

---

**4:26** ¹ *took their stand*

**4:27** ᵃ Luke 22:2; 23:1, 8 ᵇ [Luke 1:35] ᶜ John 10:36 ¹ *servant*

**4:28** ᵃ Acts 2:23; 3:18 ¹ *purpose*

**4:29** ᵃ Acts 4:13, 31; 9:27; 13:46; 14:3; 19:8; 26:26

**4:30** ᵃ Acts 2:43; 5:12 ᵇ Acts 3:6, 16 ᶜ Acts 4:27 ¹ *through* ² Or *servant*

**4:31** ᵃ Acts 2:2, 4; 16:26 ᵇ Acts 4:29

**4:32** ᵃ Acts 5:12; Rom. 15:5, 6; 2 Cor. 13:11; Phil. 1:27; 2:2; 1 Pet. 3:8 ᵇ Acts 2:44 ¹ *any*

**4:33** ᵃ [Acts 1:8] ᵇ Acts 1:22 ᶜ Rom. 6:15

**4:34** ᵃ [Matt. 19:21]; Acts 2:45 ¹ *proceeds*

**4:35** ᵃ Acts 4:37; 5:2 ᵇ Acts 2:45; 6:1

**4:36** ¹ *encouragement*

**4:37** ᵃ Acts 4:34, 35; 5:1, 2

**5:2** ¹ *aware of*

**5:3** ᵃ Num. 30:2; Deut. 23:21; Eccl. 5:4 ᵇ Matt. 4:10; Luke 22:3; John 13:2, 27

**5:4** ¹ *control*

**5:5** ᵃ Ezek. 11:13; Acts 5:10, 11 ¹ *breathed his last*

**5:6** ᵃ John 19:40 ¹ *wrapped*

**5:9** ᵃ Matt. 4:7; Acts 5:3, 4 ¹ *test*

**5:10** ᵃ Ezek. 11:13; Acts 5:5 ¹ *instantly* ² *breathed her last*

**5:11** ᵃ Acts 2:43; 5:5; 19:17

**5:12** ᵃ Acts 2:43; 4:30; 6:8; 14:3; 15:12; [Rom. 15:19]; 2 Cor. 12:12; Heb. 2:4 ᵇ Acts 3:11; 4:32 ¹ *through* ² *done*

**5:13** ᵃ John 9:22 ᵇ Acts 2:47; 4:21 ¹ *dared* ² *esteemed them highly*

**5:14** ¹ *increasingly*

**5:15** ᵃ Matt. 9:21; 14:36; Acts 19:12 ¹ *fall on*

**5:16** ᵃ Mark 16:17, 18; [John 14:12] ¹ *tormented by*

**5:17** ᵃ Matt. 3:7; Acts 4:1,

**2, 6** ¹ *jealousy*  **5:18** ᵃ Luke 21:12; Acts 4:3; 16:37  **5:19** ᵃ Matt. 1:20, 24; 2:13, 19; 28:2; Luke 1:11; 2:9; Acts 12:7; 16:26  **5:20** ᵃ [John 6:63, 68; 17:3; 1 John 5:11]

**21** And when they heard *that,* they entered into the temple early in the morning, and taught. [a]But the high priest came, and they that were with him, and called the council together, and all the [1]senate of the [2]children of Israel, and sent to the prison to have them brought.

**22** But when the officers came, and found them not in the prison, they returned, and [1]told,

**23** Saying, The prison truly found we shut with all [1]safety, and the keepers standing [2]without before the doors: but when we had opened, we found no man within.

**24** Now when the high priest and [a]the captain of the temple and the chief priests heard these things, they [1]doubted of them whereunto this would grow.

**25** Then came one and told them, saying, Behold, the men whom ye put in prison are standing in the temple, and teaching the people.

**26** Then went the captain with the officers, and brought them without violence: [a]for they feared the people, lest they should have been stoned.

**27** And when they had brought them, they set *them* before the council: and the high priest asked them,

**28** Saying, [a]Did not we [1]straitly command you that ye should not teach in this name? and, behold, ye have filled Jerusalem with your doctrine, [b]and intend to bring this man's [c]blood upon us.

**29** Then Peter and the *other* apostles answered and said, [a]We ought to obey God rather than men.

**30** [a]The God of our fathers raised up Jesus, whom ye slew and [b]hanged on a tree.

**31** [a]Him hath God exalted with his right hand *to be* [b]a Prince and [c]a Saviour, [d]for to give repentance to Israel, and forgiveness of sins.

**32** And [a]we are his witnesses of these things; and *so is* also the Holy Ghost, [b]whom God hath given to them that obey him.

**33** When they heard *that,* they were [a]cut[1] *to the heart,* and took counsel to slay them.

**34** Then stood there up one in the council, a Pharisee, named [a]Gamaliel, a [1]doctor of the law, [2]had in reputation among all the people, and commanded to put the apostles forth [3]a little space;

**35** And said unto them, Ye men of Israel, take heed to yourselves what ye intend to do as [1]touching these men.

**36** For before these days rose up Theudas, boasting himself to be somebody; to whom a number of men, about four hundred, joined

themselves: who was slain; and all, as many as [1]obeyed him, were scattered, and brought to [2]nought.

**37** After this man rose up Judas of Galilee in the days of the [1]taxing, and drew away much people after him: he also perished; and all, *even* as many as obeyed him, were dispersed.

**38** And now I say unto you, [1]Refrain from these men, and let them alone: for if this counsel or this work be of men, it will come to nought:

**39** [a]But if it be of God, ye cannot overthrow it; lest haply ye be found even [b]to fight against God.

**40** And to him they agreed: and when they had [a]called the apostles, [b]and beaten *them,* they commanded that they should not speak in the name of Jesus, and let them go.

**41** And they departed from the presence of the council, [a]rejoicing that they were counted worthy to suffer shame for his name.

**42** And daily [a]in the temple, [b]they ceased not to teach and preach Jesus [1]Christ.

## CHAPTER 6

**A**ND in those days, [a]when the number of the disciples was multiplied, there arose a murmuring of the [b]Grecians[1] against the Hebrews, because their widows were neglected [c]in the daily [2]ministration.

**2** Then the twelve called the multitude of the disciples *unto them,* and said, [a]It is not [1]reason that we should leave the word of God, and serve tables.

**3** Wherefore, brethren, [a]look[1] ye out among you seven men of honest report, full of the Holy Ghost and wisdom, whom we may appoint over this [b]business.

**4** But we [a]will give ourselves continually to prayer, and to the ministry of the word.

**5** And the saying pleased the whole multitude: and they chose Stephen, [a]a man full of faith and of the Holy Ghost, and [b]Philip, and Prochorus, and Nicanor, and Timon, and Parmenas, and [c]Nicolas a proselyte of Antioch:

**6** Whom they set before the apostles: and [a]when they had prayed, [b]they laid *their* hands on them.

**7** And [a]the word of God [1]increased; and the number of the disciples multiplied in Jerusalem greatly; and a great company [b]of the priests were obedient to the faith.

**8** And Stephen, full of faith and power, did great [a]wonders and miracles among the people.

**9** Then there arose certain of the synagogue, which is called *the synagogue* of the [1]Libertines, and Cyrenians, and Alexandrians, and of them

### Cross-references (center column)

5:21 [a] Acts 4:5, 6
[1] *council of elders*
[2] Lit. *sons*

5:22 [1] *reported*

5:23 [1] *security*
[2] *outside*

5:24 [a] Luke 22:4; Acts 4:1; 5:26
[1] *wondered*

5:26 [a] Matt. 21:26

5:28 [a] Acts 4:17, 18  [b] Acts 2:23, 36  [c] Matt. 23:35
[1] *strictly*

5:29 [a] Acts 4:19

5:30 [a] Acts 3:13, 15  [b] [1 Pet. 2:24]

5:31 [a] [Acts 2:33, 36]  [b] Acts 3:15  [c] Matt. 1:21  [d] Luke 24:47

5:32 [a] John 15:26, 27  [b] Acts 2:4; 10:44

5:33 [a] Acts 2:37; 7:54  [1] *furious*

5:34 [a] Acts 22:3
[1] *teacher*  [2] *held in respect by*  [3] *for a little while*

5:35 [1] *regarding*

5:36 [1] *followed*
[2] *nothing*

5:37 [1] *census*

5:38 [1] *Keep away*

5:39 [a] 1 Cor. 1:25  [b] Acts 7:51; 9:5

5:40 [a] Acts 4:18  [b] Matt. 10:17

5:41 [a] [1 Pet. 4:13–16]

5:42 [a] Acts 2:46  [b] Acts 4:20, 29  [1] *as the Christ*

6:1 [a] Acts 2:41; 4:4  [b] Acts 9:29; 11:20  [c] Acts 4:35; 11:29  [1] *Hellenists*  [2] *food distribution*

6:2 [a] Ex. 18:17  [1] *desirable*

6:3 [a] 1 Tim. 3:7  [b] 1 Tim. 3:8–13  [1] *seek*

6:4 [a] Acts 2:42

6:5 [a] Acts 6:3; 11:24  [b] Acts 8:5, 26; 21:8  [c] Rev. 2:6, 15

6:6 [a] Acts 1:24  [b] [2 Tim. 1:6]

6:7 [a] Acts 12:24  [b] John 12:42
[1] *spread*

6:8 [a] Acts 2:43; 5:12; 8:15; 14:3

6:9 [1] *Freedmen*

of Cilicia and of Asia, disputing with Stephen.

10 And ªthey were not able to resist the wisdom and the spirit by which he spake.

11 ªThen they ¹suborned men, which said, We have heard him speak blasphemous words against Moses, and *against* God.

12 And they stirred up the people, and the elders, and the scribes, and came upon *him,* and caught him, and brought *him* to the council,

13 And set up false witnesses, which said, This man ceaseth not to speak blasphemous words against this holy place, and the law:

14 ªFor we have heard him say, that this Jesus of Nazareth shall destroy this place, and shall change the customs which Moses delivered us.

15 And all that sat in the council, looking stedfastly on him, saw his face as it had been the face of an angel.

## CHAPTER 7

THEN said the high priest, Are these things so?

2 And he said, ªMen, brethren, and fathers, hearken; The ᵇGod of glory appeared unto our father Abraham, when he was in Mesopotamia, before he dwelt in ᶜCharran,

3 And said unto him, ªGet thee out of thy country, and from thy ¹kindred, and come into the land which I shall shew thee.

4 Then ªcame he out of the land of the Chaldeans, and dwelt in Charran: and from thence, when his father was ᵇdead, he removed him into this land, wherein ye now dwell.

5 And he gave him none inheritance in it, no, not *so much as* to set his foot on: ªyet he promised that he would give it to him for a possession, and to his seed after him, when *as yet* he had no child.

6 And God spake ¹on this wise, ªThat his ²seed should sojourn in a strange land; and that they ³should bring them into ᵇbondage, and ⁴entreat *them* evil four hundred years.

7 ªAnd the nation to whom they shall be in bondage will I ᵇjudge, said God: ᶜand after that shall they come forth, and serve me in this place.

8 ªAnd he gave him the covenant of circumcision: ᵇand so *Abraham* begat Isaac, and circumcised him the eighth day; ᶜand Isaac *begat* Jacob; and ᵈJacob *begat* the twelve patriarchs.

9 ªAnd the patriarchs, moved with envy, ᵇsold Joseph into Egypt: ᶜbut God was with him,

10 And delivered him out of all his afflictions, ªand gave him favour and wisdom in the sight of Pharaoh king

of Egypt; and he made him governor over Egypt and all his house.

11 ªNow there came a ¹dearth over all the land of Egypt and Chanaan, and great affliction: and our fathers found no sustenance.

12 ªBut when Jacob heard that there was ¹corn in Egypt, he sent out our fathers first.

13 And at the ªsecond *time* Joseph was made known to his brethren; and Joseph's kindred was made known unto Pharaoh.

14 ªThen sent Joseph, and called his father Jacob to *him,* and ᵇall his kindred, threescore and fifteen souls.

15 ªSo Jacob went down into Egypt, ᵇand died, he, and our fathers,

16 And ªwere carried over into Sychem, and laid in ᵇthe ¹sepulchre that Abraham bought for a sum of money of the sons of ²Emmor *the father* of Sychem.

17 But when ªthe time of the promise drew nigh, which God had sworn to Abraham, ᵇthe people grew and multiplied in Egypt,

18 Till another king ªarose, which knew not Joseph.

19 ªThe same dealt ¹subtilly with our ²kindred, and ³evil entreated our fathers, ªso that they ⁴cast out their young children, to the end they might not live.

20 ªIn which time Moses was born, and ᵇwas ¹exceeding fair, and nourished up in his father's house three months:

21 And ªwhen he was ¹cast out, ᵇPharaoh's daughter took him up, and nourished him ²for her own son.

22 And Moses was learned in all the wisdom of the Egyptians, and was ªmighty in words and in deeds.

23 ªAnd when he was full forty years old, it came into his heart to visit his brethren the children of Israel.

24 And seeing one *of them* suffer wrong, he defended *him,* and avenged him that was oppressed, and smote the Egyptian:

25 For he supposed his brethren would have understood how that God by his hand would deliver them: but they understood not.

26 And the next day he shewed himself unto them as they strove, and would have ¹set them at one again, saying, Sirs, ye are brethren; why do ye wrong one to another?

27 But he that did his neighbour wrong thrust him away, saying, ªWho made thee a ruler and a judge over us?

28 Wilt thou kill me, as thou diddest the Egyptian yesterday?

29 ªThen fled Moses at this saying, and was a ¹stranger in the land of Madian, where he ᵇbegat two sons.

### Center column references

6:10 ª Luke 21:15
6:11 ª 1 Kin. 21:10, 13 ¹ *bribed*
6:14 ª Acts 10:38; 25:8
7:2 ª Acts 22:1 ᵇ Ps. 29:3 ᶜ Gen. 11:31, 32
7:3 ª Gen. 12:1 ¹ *relatives*
7:4 ª Gen. 11:31; 15:17 ᵇ Gen. 11:32
7:5 ª Gen. 12:7; 13:15; 15:3, 18; 17:8; 26:3
7:6 ª Gen. 15:13, 14, 16; 47:11, 12 ᵇ Ex. 1:8–14; 12:40, 41 ¹ *in this way* ² *descendants* ³ *would* ⁴ *oppress them*
7:7 ª Gen. 15:14 ᵇ Ex. 14:13–31 ᶜ Ex. 3:12
7:8 ª Gen. 17:9–14 ᵇ Gen. 21:1–5 ᶜ Gen. 25:21–26 ᵈ Gen. 29:31– 30:24; 35:18, 22–26
7:9 ª Gen. 37:4, 11, 28 ᵇ Gen. 37:28 ᶜ Gen. 39:2, 21, 23
7:10 ª Gen. 41:38–44
7:11 ª Gen. 41:54; 42:5 ¹ *famine*
7:12 ª Gen. 42:1, 2 ¹ *grain*
7:13 ª Gen. 45:4, 16
7:14 ª Gen. 45:9, 27 ᵇ Deut. 10:22
7:15 ª Gen. 46:1–7 ᵇ Gen. 49:33
7:16 ª Josh. 24:32 ᵇ Gen. 23:16 ¹ *tomb* ² *Hamor,* Gen. 33:19
7:17 ª Gen. 15:13 ᵇ Ex. 1:7–9
7:18 ª Ex. 1:8
7:19 ª Ex. 1:22 ¹ *treacherously* ² *people* ³ *oppressed* ⁴ *exposed their babies*
7:20 ª Ex. 2:1, 2 ᵇ Heb. 11:23 ¹ *well pleasing to God*
7:21 ª Ex. 2:3, 4 ᵇ Ex. 2:5–10 ¹ *set* ² *as*
7:22 ª Luke 24:19
7:23 ª Ex. 2:11, 12
7:26 ¹ *reconciled them*
7:27 ª Ex. 2:14
7:29 ª Heb. 11:27 ᵇ Ex. 2:15, 21, 99; 4:90; 18:3 ¹ *sojourner*

30 ᵃAnd when forty years were expired, there appeared to him in the wilderness of mount Sina an angel of the Lord in a flame of fire in a bush.

31 When Moses saw *it,* he ¹wondered at the sight: and as he drew near to behold *it,* the voice of the Lord came unto him,

32 *Saying,* ᵃI *am* the God of thy fathers, the God of Abraham, and the God of Isaac, and the God of Jacob. Then Moses trembled, and ¹durst not behold.

33 ᵃThen said the Lord to him, ¹Put off thy ²shoes from thy feet: for the place where thou standest is holy ground.

34 ᵃI have seen, I have seen the affliction of my people which is in Egypt, and I have heard their groaning, and am come down to deliver them. And now come, I will ᵇsend thee into Egypt.

35 This Moses whom they refused, saying, ᵃWho made thee a ruler and a judge? the same did God send *to be* a ruler and a deliverer ᵇby the hand of the angel which appeared to him in the bush.

36 ᵃHe brought them out, after that he had ᵇshewed wonders and signs in the land of Egypt, ᶜand in the Red sea, ᵈand in the wilderness forty years.

37 This is that Moses, which said unto the children of Israel, ᵃA prophet shall the Lord your God raise up unto you of your brethren, like unto me; ᵇhim shall ye hear.

38 ᵃThis is he, that was in the ¹church in the wilderness with ᵇthe angel which spake to him in the mount Sina, and *with* our fathers: ᶜwho received the ²lively ᵈoracles to give unto us:

39 To whom our fathers ᵃwould not obey, but thrust *him* from them, and in their hearts turned back again into Egypt,

40 ᵃSaying unto Aaron, Make us gods to go before us: for *as for* this Moses, which brought us out of the land of Egypt, we ¹wot not what is become of him.

41 ᵃAnd they made a calf in those days, and offered sacrifice unto the idol, and ᵇrejoiced in the works of their own hands.

42 Then ᵃGod turned, and gave them up to worship ᵇthe host of heaven; as it is written in the book of the prophets, ᶜO ye house of Israel, have ye offered to me slain beasts and sacrifices *by the space of* forty years in the wilderness?

43 Yea, ye took up the tabernacle of Moloch, and the star of your god Remphan, ¹figures which ye made to worship them: and ᵃI will carry you away beyond Babylon.

44 Our fathers had the tabernacle of witness in the wilderness, as he had appointed, speaking unto Moses, ᵃthat he should make it according to the fashion that he had seen.

45 ᵃWhich also our fathers ¹that came after brought in with Jesus into the possession of the Gentiles, ᵇwhom God drave out before the face of our fathers, unto the ᶜdays of David;

46 ᵃWho found favour before God, and ᵇdesired¹ to find ²a tabernacle for the God of Jacob.

47 ᵃBut Solomon built him an house.

48 Howbeit ᵃthe most High dwelleth not in temples made with hands; as saith the prophet,

49 ᵃHeaven *is* my throne, and earth *is* my footstool: what house will ye build me? saith the Lord: or what *is* the place of my rest?

50 Hath not my hand ᵃmade all these things?

51 Ye ᵃstiffnecked¹ and ᵇuncircumcised² in heart and ears, ye do always resist the Holy Ghost: as your fathers *did,* so *do* ye.

52 ᵃWhich of the prophets have not your fathers persecuted? and they have slain them which ¹shewed before of the coming of ᵇthe Just One; of whom ye have been now the betrayers and murderers:

53 ᵃWho have received the law by the ¹disposition of angels, and have not kept *it.*

54 ᵃWhen they heard these things, they were ¹cut to the heart, and they gnashed ²on him with *their* teeth.

55 But he, ᵃbeing full of the Holy Ghost, looked up stedfastly into heaven, and saw the ᵇglory of God, and Jesus standing on the right hand of God,

56 And said, Behold, ᵃI see the heavens opened, and the ᵇSon of man standing on the right hand of God.

57 Then they cried out with a loud voice, and stopped their ears, and ran upon him with one accord,

58 And cast *him* out of the city, and stoned *him:* and ᵃthe witnesses laid down their clothes at a young man's feet, whose name was Saul.

59 And they stoned Stephen, ¹calling upon *God,* and saying, Lord Jesus, ᵃreceive my spirit.

60 And he kneeled down, and cried with a loud voice, ᵃLord, lay not this sin to their charge. And when he had said this, he fell asleep.

## CHAPTER 8

A ND Saul was consenting unto his death. And at that time there ¹was a great persecution against the church which was at Jerusalem; and ᵃthey were all scattered abroad

### Center column references

7:30 ᵃ Ex. 3:1–10
7:31 ¹ *marvelled*
7:32 ᵃ Ex. 3:6, 15
¹ *dared not look*
7:33 ᵃ Ex. 3:5,
7, 8, 10  ¹ *Take*
² *sandals*
7:34 ᵃ Ex. 2:24, 25
ᵇ Ps. 105:26
7:35 ᵃ Ex. 2:14
ᵇ Ex. 14:21
7:36 ᵃ Ex. 12:41;
33:1  ᵇ Ps. 105:27
ᶜ Ex. 14:21  ᵈ Ex.
16:1, 35
7:37 ᵃ Deut. 18:15,
18, 19  ᵇ Matt. 17:5
7:38 ᵃ Ex. 19:3
ᵇ Gal. 3:19  ᶜ Deut.
5:27  ᵈ Heb.
5:12  ¹ *assembly*
² *living sayings*
7:39 ᵃ Ps. 95:8–11
7:40 ᵃ Ex. 32:1, 23
¹ *know*
7:41 ᵃ Deut. 9:16
ᵇ Ex. 32:6, 18, 19
7:42 ᵃ [2 Thess.
2:11]  ᵇ 2 Kin. 21:3
ᶜ Amos 5:25–27
7:43 ᵃ Jer. 25:9–12
¹ *images*

7:44 ᵃ [Heb. 8:5]
7:45 ᵃ Josh. 3:14;
18:1; 23:9  ᵇ Ps.
44:2  ᶜ 2 Sam.
6:2–15  ¹ *having
received it in turn,
brought*
7:46 ᵃ 2 Sam.
7:1–13  ᵇ 1 Chr.
22:7  ¹ *asked*  ² *a
dwelling*
7:47 ᵃ 1 Kin. 6:1–
38; 8:20, 21
7:48 ᵃ 1 Kin. 8:27
7:49 ᵃ Is. 66:1, 2
7:50 ᵃ Ps. 102:25
7:51 ᵃ Ex. 32:9
ᵇ Lev. 26:41
¹ *stubborn*  ² *Impenitent*
7:52 ᵃ 2 Chr. 36:16
ᵇ Acts 3:14; 22:14
¹ *foretold*
7:53 ᵃ Ex. 20:1
¹ *direction*
7:54 ᵃ Acts 5:33
¹ *furious*  ² *at*
7:55 ᵃ Acts 6:5
ᵇ [Ex. 24:17]
7:56 ᵃ Matt. 3:16
ᵇ Dan. 7:13
7:58 ᵃ Acts 22:20
7:59 ᵃ Ps. 31:5  ¹ *as
he was calling*
7:60 ᵃ Matt. 5:44
8:1 ᵃ Acts 8:4;
11:19  ¹ *arose*

throughout the regions of Judaea and Samaria, except the apostles.

2 And devout men carried Stephen *to his burial*, and [a]made great lamentation over him.

3 As for Saul, [a]he made havock of the church, entering into every house, and [1]haling men and women committed *them* to prison.

4 Therefore [a]they that were scattered abroad went every where preaching the word.

5 Then [a]Philip went down to [1]the city of Samaria, and preached Christ unto them.

6 And the [1]people with one accord gave heed unto those things which Philip spake, hearing and seeing the miracles which he did.

7 For [a]unclean spirits, crying with loud voice, came out of many that were possessed *with them:* and many taken with [1]palsies, and that were lame, were healed.

8 And there was great joy in that city.

9 But there was a certain man, called Simon, which beforetime in the same city [a]used[1] sorcery, and [2]bewitched the people of Samaria, [b]giving out that himself was some great one:

10 To whom they all gave heed, from the least to the greatest, saying, This man is the great power of God.

11 And to him they [1]had regard, because that of long time he had [2]bewitched them with [3]sorceries.

12 But when they believed Philip [1]preaching the things [a]concerning the kingdom of God, and the name of Jesus Christ, they were baptized, both men and women.

13 Then Simon himself believed also: and when he was baptized, he continued with Philip, and [1]wondered, beholding the miracles and signs which were done.

14 Now when the [a]apostles which were at Jerusalem heard that Samaria had received the word of God, they sent unto them Peter and John:

15 Who, when they were come down, prayed for them, [a]that they might receive the Holy Ghost:

16 (For [a]as yet he was fallen upon none of them: only [b]they were baptized in [c]the name of the Lord Jesus.)

17 Then [a]laid they *their* hands on them, and they received the Holy Ghost.

18 And when Simon saw that through laying on of the apostles' hands the Holy Ghost was given, he offered them money,

19 Saying, Give me also this power, that on whomsoever I lay hands, he may receive the Holy Ghost.

20 But Peter said unto him, Thy money perish with thee, because

[a]thou hast thought that [b]the gift of God may be purchased with money.

21 Thou hast neither part nor [1]lot in this matter: for thy [a]heart is not right in the sight of God.

22 Repent therefore of this thy wickedness, and pray God, [a]if perhaps the thought of thine heart may be forgiven thee.

23 For I perceive that thou art [1]in [a]the gall of bitterness, and [2]*in* the bond of iniquity.

24 Then answered Simon, and said, [a]Pray ye to the Lord for me, that none of these things which ye have spoken come upon me.

25 And they, when they had testified and preached the word of the Lord, returned to Jerusalem, and preached the gospel in many villages of the Samaritans.

26 And the angel of the Lord spake unto [a]Philip, saying, Arise, and go toward the south unto the way that goeth down from Jerusalem unto Gaza, which is [1]desert.

27 And he arose and went: and, behold, [a]a man of Ethiopia, an eunuch of great authority under Candace queen of the Ethiopians, who had the charge of all her treasure, and [b]had come to Jerusalem for to worship,

28 Was returning, and sitting in his chariot read Esaias the prophet.

29 Then the Spirit said unto Philip, Go near, and join thyself to this chariot.

30 And Philip ran thither to *him,* and heard him read the prophet Esaias, and said, Understandest thou what thou readest?

31 And he said, How can I, except some man should guide me? And he [1]desired Philip that he would come up and sit with him.

32 The place of the scripture which he read was this, [a]He was led as a sheep to the slaughter; and like a lamb [1]dumb before his shearer, [b]so opened he not his mouth:

33 In his humiliation his [a]judgment[1] was taken away: and who shall declare his generation? for his life is [b]taken from the earth.

34 And the eunuch answered Philip, and said, I pray thee, of whom speaketh the prophet this? of himself, or of some other man?

35 Then Philip opened his mouth, [a]and began at the same scripture, and preached unto him Jesus.

36 And as they went on *their* way, they came unto a certain water: and the eunuch said, See, *here is* water; [a]what doth hinder me to be baptized?

37 And Philip said, [a]If thou believest with all thine heart, thou mayest. And he answered and said, [b]I believe that Jesus Christ is the Son of God.

---

**Cross references (center column):**

8:2 [a] Gen. 23:2
8:3 [a] Phil. 3:6 [1] *dragging off*
8:4 [a] Matt. 10:23
8:5 [a] Acts 6:5; 8:26, 30 [1] Lit. *a*
8:6 [1] *multitudes*
8:7 [a] Mark 16:17 [1] *paralysis*
8:9 [a] Acts 8:11; 13:6 [b] Acts 5:36 [1] *practised magic* [2] *astonished*
8:11 [1] *paid attention* [2] *astonished* [3] *magic arts*
8:12 [a] Acts 1:3; 8:4 [1] *as he preached*
8:13 [1] *was amazed*
8:14 [a] Acts 5:12, 29, 40
8:15 [a] Acts 2:38; 19:2
8:16 [a] Acts 19:2 [b] Matt. 28:19; Acts 2:38 [c] Acts 10:48; 19:5
8:17 [a] Acts 6:6; 19:6; Heb. 6:2

8:20 [a] 2 Kin. 5:16; Is. 55:1; Dan. 5:17; [Matt. 10:8] [b] [Acts 2:38; 10:45; 11:17]
8:21 [a] Jer. 17:9 [1] *portion*
8:22 [a] Dan. 4:27; 2 Tim. 2:25
8:23 [a] Heb. 12:15 [1] *poisoned by bitterness* [2] *bound by*
8:24 [a] Gen. 20:7, 17; Ex. 8:8; Num. 21:7; 1 Kin. 13:6; Job 42:8; James 5:16
8:26 [a] Acts 6:5 [1] *deserted*
8:27 [a] Ps. 68:31; 87:4; Is. 56:3; Zeph. 3:10 [b] 1 Kin. 12:20
8:31 [1] *asked*
8:32 [a] Is. 53:7, 8 [b] Matt. 26:62, 63; 27:12, 14; John 19:9 [1] *silent*
8:33 [a] Luke 23:1–25 [b] Luke 23:33–46 [1] *justice*
8:35 [a] Luke 24:27; Acts 17:2; 18:28; 28:23
8:36 [a] Acts 10:47; 16:33
8:37 [a] Matt. 28:19; [Mark 16:16; Rom. 10:9, 10] [b] Matt. 16:16; John 6:69; 9:35, 38; 11:27

38 And he commanded the chariot to stand still: and they went down both into the water, both Philip and the eunuch; and he baptized him.

39 And when they were come up out of the water, [a]the Spirit of the Lord caught away Philip, that the eunuch saw him no more: and he went on his way rejoicing.

40 But Philip was found at [1]Azotus: and passing through he preached in all the cities, till he came to [a]Caesarea.

### CHAPTER 9

A ND [a]Saul, yet breathing out threatenings and [1]slaughter against the disciples of the Lord, went unto the high priest,

2 And [1]desired of him [a]letters to Damascus to the synagogues, that if he found any of [2]this way, whether they were men or women, he might bring them bound unto Jerusalem.

3 And [a]as he journeyed, he came near Damascus: and suddenly there shined round about him a light from heaven:

4 And he fell to the earth, and heard a voice saying unto him, Saul, Saul, [a]why persecutest thou me?

5 And he said, Who art thou, Lord? And the Lord said, I am Jesus whom thou persecutest: it is hard for thee to kick against the [1]pricks.

6 And he trembling and astonished said, Lord, what wilt thou have me to do? And the Lord said unto him, Arise, and go into the city, and it shall be told thee what thou must do.

7 And [a]the men which journeyed with him stood speechless, hearing a voice, but seeing no man.

8 And Saul arose from the earth; and when his eyes were opened, he saw no man: but they led him by the hand, and brought him into Damascus.

9 And he was three days without sight, and neither did eat nor drink.

10 And there was a certain disciple at Damascus, [a]named Ananias; and to him said the Lord in a vision, Ananias. And he said, Behold, I am here, Lord.

11 And the Lord said unto him, Arise, and go into the street which is called Straight, and enquire in the house of Judas for one called Saul, [a]of Tarsus: for, behold, he prayeth,

12 And hath seen in a vision a man named Ananias coming in, and putting his hand on him, that he might receive his sight.

13 Then Ananias answered, Lord, I have heard by many of this man, [a]how much [1]evil he hath done to thy saints at Jerusalem:

14 And here he hath authority from

the chief priests to bind all [a]that call on thy name.

15 But the Lord said unto him, Go thy way: for [a]he is a chosen vessel unto me, to bear my name before [b]the Gentiles, and [c]kings, and the [d]children of Israel:

16 For [a]I will shew him how great things he must suffer for my [b]name's sake.

17 [a]And Ananias went his way, and entered into the house; and [b]putting his hands on him said, Brother Saul, the Lord, even Jesus, that appeared unto thee in the way as thou camest, hath sent me, that thou mightest receive thy sight, and [c]be filled with the Holy Ghost.

18 And immediately there fell from his eyes [1]as it had been scales: and he received sight [2]forthwith, and arose, and was baptized.

19 And when he had received [1]meat, he was strengthened. [a]Then was Saul certain days with the disciples which were at Damascus.

20 And straightway he preached Christ in the synagogues, that he is the Son of God.

21 But all that heard him were amazed, and said; [a]Is not this he that destroyed them which called on this name in Jerusalem, and came hither for that [1]intent, that he might bring them bound unto the chief priests?

22 But Saul increased the more in strength, [a]and confounded the Jews which dwelt at Damascus, proving that [1]this is very Christ.

23 And after that many days were fulfilled, [a]the Jews [1]took counsel to kill him:

24 [a]But their [1]laying await was known of Saul. And they watched the gates day and night to kill him.

25 Then the disciples took him by night, and [a]let him down by the wall in a basket.

26 And [a]when Saul was come to Jerusalem, he [1]assayed to join himself to the disciples: but they were all afraid of him, and believed not that he was a disciple.

27 [a]But Barnabas took him, and brought him to the apostles, and declared unto them how he had seen the Lord [1]in the way, and that [2]he had spoken to him, [b]and how he had preached boldly at Damascus in the name of Jesus.

28 And [a]he was with them coming in and going out at Jerusalem.

29 And he spake boldly in the name of the Lord Jesus, and [1]disputed against the [a]Grecians:[2] [b]but they [3]went about to slay him.

30 Which when the brethren knew, they brought him down to Caesarea, and sent him forth to Tarsus.

---

8:39 [a] Ezek. 3:12, 14
8:40 [a] Acts 21:8 [1] Ashdod, Josh. 11:22
9:1 [a] Acts 7:57; 8:1, 3; 26:10, 11 [1] murder
9:2 [a] Acts 22:5 [1] asked [2] the Way
9:3 [a] 1 Cor. 15:8
9:4 [a] [Matt. 25:40]
9:5 [1] goads
9:7 [a] [Acts 22:9; 26:13]
9:10 [a] Acts 22:12
9:11 [a] Acts 21:39; 22:3
9:13 [a] Acts 9:1 [1] harm

9:14 [a] Acts 7:59; 9:2, 21
9:15 [a] Eph. 3:7, 8 [b] Rom. 1:5; 11:13 [c] Acts 25:22, 23; 26:1 [d] Rom. 1:16; 9:1–5
9:16 [a] Acts 20:23 [b] 2 Cor. 4:11
9:17 [a] Acts 22:12, 13 [b] Acts 8:17 [c] Acts 2:4; 4:31; 8:17; 13:52
9:18 [1] something like [2] at once
9:19 [a] Acts 26:20 [1] food
9:21 [a] Gal. 1:13, 23 [1] purpose
9:22 [a] Acts 18:28 [1] this Jesus is the Christ
9:23 [a] 2 Cor. 11:26 [1] plotted
9:24 [a] 2 Cor. 11:32 [1] plot
9:25 [a] Josh. 2:15
9:26 [a] Acts 22:17–20; 26:20 [1] tried
9:27 [a] Acts 4:36; 13:2 [b] Acts 9:20, 22 [1] on the road [2] Jesus
9:28 [a] Gal. 1:18
9:29 [a] Acts 6:1; 11:20 [b] 2 Cor. 11:26 [1] spoke openly [2] Hellenists, Greek-speaking Jews [3] attempted

31 [a]Then had the churches rest throughout all Judaea and Galilee and Samaria, and were [b]edified; and walking in the [c]fear of the Lord, and in the [d]comfort of the Holy Ghost, were [e]multiplied.

32 And it came to pass, as Peter passed [a]throughout all [1]*quarters,* he came down also to the saints which dwelt at [2]Lydda.

33 And there he found a certain man named Aeneas, which had [1]kept his bed eight years, and was [2]sick of the palsy.

34 And Peter said unto him, Aeneas, [a]Jesus Christ maketh thee whole: arise, and make thy bed. And he arose immediately.

35 And all that dwelt at Lydda and [a]Saron[1] saw him, and [b]turned to the Lord.

36 Now there was at Joppa a certain disciple named Tabitha, which [1]by interpretation is called [2]Dorcas: this woman was full [a]of good works and [3]almsdeeds which she did.

37 And it came to pass in those days, that she was sick, and died: whom when they had washed, they laid *her* in [a]an upper chamber.

38 And forasmuch as Lydda was nigh to Joppa, and the disciples had heard that Peter was there, they sent unto him two men, [1]desiring *him* that he would not delay to come to them.

39 Then Peter arose and went with them. When he was come, they brought him into the upper chamber: and all the widows stood by him weeping, and shewing the [1]coats and garments which Dorcas made, while she was with them.

40 But Peter [a]put them all forth, and [b]kneeled down, and prayed; and turning *him* to the body [c]said, Tabitha, arise. And she opened her eyes: and when she saw Peter, she sat up.

41 And he gave her *his* hand, and lifted her up, and when he had called the saints and widows, presented her alive.

42 And it was known throughout all Joppa; [a]and many believed in the Lord.

43 And it came to pass, that he [1]tarried many days in Joppa with one [a]Simon a tanner.

## CHAPTER 10

THERE was a certain man in [a]Caesarea called Cornelius, a centurion of the [1]band called the Italian *band,*

2 [a]A devout *man,* and one that [b]feared God with all his house, which gave [1]much alms to the people, and prayed to God alway.

3 [a]He saw in a vision [1]evidently about [2]the ninth hour of the day an angel of God coming in to him, and saying unto him, Cornelius.

4 And when he looked on him, he was afraid, and said, What is it, Lord? And he said unto him, Thy prayers and thine alms are come up for a memorial before God.

5 And now [a]send men to Joppa, and call for *one* Simon, whose surname is Peter:

6 He lodgeth with one [a]Simon a tanner, whose house is by the sea side: [b]he shall tell thee what thou oughtest to do.

7 And when the angel which spake unto Cornelius was departed, he called two of his household servants, and a devout soldier of them that waited on him continually;

8 And when he had declared all *these* things unto them, he sent them to Joppa.

9 On the [1]morrow, as they went on their journey, and drew nigh unto the city, [a]Peter went up upon the housetop to pray about [2]the sixth hour:

10 And he became very hungry, and would have eaten: but while they made ready, he fell into a trance,

11 And [a]saw heaven opened, and a certain vessel descending unto him, as it had been a great sheet [1]knit at the four corners, and let down to the earth:

12 Wherein were all manner of fourfooted beasts of the earth, and wild beasts, and creeping things, and fowls of the air.

13 And there came a voice to him, Rise, Peter; kill, and eat.

14 But Peter said, Not so, Lord; [a]for I have never eaten any thing that is common or unclean.

15 And the voice *spake* unto him again the second time, [a]What God hath cleansed, *that* call not thou common.

16 This was done [1]thrice: and the vessel was received up again into heaven.

17 Now while Peter [1]doubted in himself what this vision which he had seen should mean, behold, the men which were sent from Cornelius had made enquiry for Simon's house, and stood before the gate,

18 And called, and asked whether Simon, which was surnamed Peter, were lodged there.

19 While Peter thought on the vision, [a]the Spirit said unto him, Behold, three men seek thee.

20 [a]Arise therefore, and get thee down, and go with them, doubting nothing: for I have sent them.

21 Then Peter went down to the men which were sent unto him from Cornelius; and said, Behold, I am he whom ye seek: what *is* the cause wherefore ye are come?

### Cross-references

9:31 [a] Acts 5:11; 8:1; 16:5 [b] [Eph. 4:16, 29] [c] Ps. 34:9 [d] John 14:16 [e] Acts 16:5

9:32 [a] Acts 8:14 [1] Parts of the country [2] *Lod,* 1 Chr. 8:12

9:33 [1] *been bedridden* [2] *paralyzed*

9:34 [a] [Acts 3:6, 16; 4:10]

9:35 [a] 1 Chr. 5:16; 27:29; Is. 33:9; 35:2; 65:10 [b] Acts 11:21; 15:19 [1] *Sharon,* Is. 35:2

9:36 [a] 1 Tim. 2:10; Titus 3:8 [1] *is translated* [2] Lit. in Gr., *Gazelle* [3] *charitable deeds*

9:37 [a] Acts 1:13; 9:39

9:38 [1] *imploring*

9:39 [1] *tunics*

9:40 [a] Matt. 9:25 [b] Luke 22:41; Acts 7:60 [c] Mark 5:41, 42; John 11:43

9:42 [a] John 11:45

9:43 [a] Acts 10:6 [1] *stayed*

10:1 [a] Acts 8:40; 23:23 [1] Lit. *cohort*

10:2 [a] Acts 8:2; 9:22; 22:12 [b] [Acts 10:22, 35; 13:16, 26] [1] *many charitable gifts*

10:3 [a] Acts 10:30; 11:13 [1] *clearly* [2] 3:00 P.M.

10:5 [a] Acts 11:13, 14

10:6 [a] Acts 9:43 [b] Acts 11:14

10:9 [a] Acts 10:9–32; 11:5–14 [1] *next day* [2] Noon

10:11 [a] Ezek. 1:1; Matt. 3:16; Acts 7:56; Rev. 4:1; 19:11 [1] *bound*

10:14 [a] Lev. 11:4; 20:25; Deut. 14:3, 7; Ezek. 4:14

10:15 [a] [Matt. 15:11; Mark 7:19]; Acts 10:28; [Rom. 14:14]; 1 Cor. 10:25; [1 Tim. 4:4; Titus 1:15]

10:16 [1] *three times*

10:17 [1] *wondered*

10:19 [a] Acts 11:12

10:20 [a] Acts 15:7–9

**22** And they said, Cornelius the centurion, a just man, and one that feareth God, and [a]of good report among all the nation of the Jews, was warned from God by an holy angel to send for thee into his house, and to hear words of thee.

**23** Then called he them in, and lodged *them*. And on the morrow Peter went away with them, [a]and certain brethren from Joppa accompanied him.

**24** And the morrow after they entered into Caesarea. And Cornelius waited for them, and had called together his [1]kinsmen and [2]near friends.

**25** And as Peter was coming in, Cornelius met him, and fell down at his feet, and worshipped *him*.

**26** But Peter [1]took him up, saying, [a]Stand up; I myself also am a man.

**27** And as he talked with him, he went in, and found many that were come together.

**28** And he said unto them, Ye know how [a]that it is an unlawful thing for a man that is a Jew to keep company, or come unto one of another nation; but [b]God hath shewed me that I should not call any man common or unclean.

**29** Therefore came I *unto you* without [1]gainsaying, as soon as I was sent for: I ask therefore for what [2]intent ye have sent for me?

**30** And Cornelius said, Four days ago I was fasting until this hour; and at the ninth hour I prayed in my house, and, behold, [a]a man stood before me [b]in bright clothing,

**31** And said, Cornelius, [a]thy prayer is heard, [b]and [1]thine alms are [2]had in remembrance in the sight of God.

**32** Send therefore to Joppa, and call hither Simon, whose surname is Peter; he is lodged in the house of *one* Simon a tanner by the sea side: who, when he cometh, shall speak unto thee.

**33** Immediately therefore I sent to thee; and thou hast well done that thou art come. Now therefore are we all here present before God, to hear all things that are commanded thee of God.

**34** Then Peter opened *his* mouth, and said, [a]Of a truth I perceive that God is [1]no respecter of persons:

**35** But [a]in every nation he that feareth him, and worketh righteousness, is [b]accepted with him.

**36** The word which *God* sent unto the [1]children of Israel, [2]preaching peace by Jesus Christ: ([b]he is Lord of all:)

**37** That word, *I say*, ye know, which was [1]published throughout all Judaea, and [a]began from Galilee, after the baptism which John preached;

**38** How [a]God anointed Jesus of Nazareth with the Holy Ghost and with power: who [b]went about doing good, and healing all that were oppressed of the devil; [c]for God was with him.

**39** And we are [a]witnesses of all things which he did both in the land of the Jews, and in Jerusalem; whom they [b]slew[1] and hanged on a tree:

**40** Him [a]God raised up the third day, and shewed him openly;

**41** [a]Not to all the people, but unto witnesses chosen before of God, *even* to us, [b]who did eat and drink with him after he rose from the dead.

**42** And [a]he commanded us to preach unto the people, and to testify [b]that it is he which was ordained of God *to be* the Judge [c]of quick and dead.

**43** [a]To him give all the prophets witness, that through his name [b]whosoever believeth in him shall receive [c]remission[1] of sins.

**44** While Peter yet spake these words, [a]the Holy Ghost fell on all them which heard the word.

**45** [a]And [1]they of the circumcision which believed were astonished, as many as came with Peter, [b]because that on the Gentiles also was poured out the gift of the Holy Ghost.

**46** For they heard them speak with tongues, and magnify God. Then answered Peter,

**47** Can any man forbid water, that these should not be baptized, which have received the Holy Ghost [a]as well as we?

**48** [a]And he commanded them to be baptized [b]in the name of the Lord. Then [1]prayed they him to [2]tarry certain days.

## CHAPTER 11

AND the apostles and brethren that were in Judaea heard that the Gentiles had also received the word of God.

**2** And when Peter was come up to Jerusalem, [a]they that were of the circumcision [1]contended with him,

**3** Saying, [a]Thou wentest in to men uncircumcised, [b]and didst eat with them.

**4** But Peter [1]rehearsed *the matter* from the beginning, and expounded *it* [a]by[2] order unto them, saying,

**5** [a]I was in the city of Joppa praying: and in a trance I saw a vision, A certain vessel descend, as it had been a great sheet, let down from heaven by four corners; and it came even to me:

**6** Upon the which when I had fastened mine eyes, I considered, and saw fourfooted beasts of the earth, and wild beasts, and creeping things, and fowls of the air.

Center column references:

10:22 [a] Acts 22:12
10:23 [a] Acts 10:45; 11:12
10:24 [1] relatives [2] close
10:26 [a] Acts 14:14, 15 [1] lifted
10:28 [a] John 4:9; 18:28 [b] [Acts 10:14, 35; 15:8, 9]
10:29 [1] objection [2] reason
10:30 [a] Acts 1:10 [b] Matt. 28:3
10:31 [a] Dan. 10:12 [b] Heb. 6:10 [1] your charitable gifts [2] remembered
10:34 [a] Deut. 10:17 [1] impartial
10:35 [a] [Eph. 2:13] [b] Ps. 15:1, 2
10:36 [a] Is. 57:19 [b] Rom. 10:12 [1] Lit. sons
10:37 [a] Luke 4:14 [1] proclaimed
10:38 [a] Luke 4:18 [b] Matt. 4:23 [c] John 3:2; 8:29
10:39 [a] Acts 1:8 [b] Acts 2:23 [1] killed by hanging on
10:40 [a] Acts 2:24
10:41 [a] [John 14:17, 19, 22; 15:27] [b] Luke 24:30, 41–43
10:42 [a] Matt. 28:19 [b] John 5:22, 27 [c] 1 Pet. 4:5
10:43 [a] Zech. 13:1 [b] Gal. 3:22 [c] Acts 13:38, 39 [1] forgiveness
10:44 [a] Acts 4:31
10:45 [a] Acts 10:23 [b] Acts 11:18 [1] The Jews
10:47 [a] Acts 2:4; 10:44; 11:17; 15:8
10:48 [1] 1 Cor. 1:14–17 [b] Acts 2:38; 8:16; 19:5 [1] asked [2] stay
11:2 [a] Acts 10:45 [1] disputed
11:3 [a] Acts 10:28 [b] Gal. 2:12
11:4 [a] Luke 1:3 [1] explained [2] in
11:5 [a] Acts 10:9

7 And I heard a voice saying unto me, Arise, Peter; slay and eat.

8 But I said, Not so, Lord: for nothing common or unclean hath at any time entered into my mouth.

9 But the voice answered me again from heaven, What God hath cleansed, *that* call not thou common.

10 And this was done three times: and all were drawn up again into heaven.

11 And, behold, immediately there were three men already come unto the house where I was, sent from Caesarea unto me.

12 And [a]the Spirit bade me go with them, nothing doubting. Moreover [b]these six brethren accompanied me, and we entered into the man's house:

13 [a]And he shewed us how he had seen an angel in his house, which stood and said unto him, Send men to Joppa, and call for Simon, whose surname is Peter;

14 Who shall tell thee words, whereby thou and all thy house shall be saved.

15 And as I began to speak, the Holy Ghost fell on them, [a]as on us at the beginning.

16 Then remembered I the word of the Lord, how that he said, [a]John indeed baptized with water; but [b]ye shall be baptized with the Holy Ghost.

17 [a]Forasmuch then as God gave them the like gift as *he did* unto us, who believed on the Lord Jesus Christ; [b]what was I, that I could withstand God?

18 When they heard these things, they [1]held their peace, and glorified God, saying, [a]Then hath God also to the Gentiles granted repentance unto life.

19 [a]Now they which were scattered abroad upon the persecution that arose about Stephen travelled as far as Phenice, and Cyprus, and Antioch, preaching the word to none but unto the Jews only.

20 And some of them were men of Cyprus and Cyrene, which, when they were come to Antioch, spake unto [a]the [1]Grecians, preaching the Lord Jesus.

21 And [a]the hand of the Lord was with them: and a great number believed, and [b]turned unto the Lord.

22 Then [1]tidings of these things came unto the ears of the church which was in Jerusalem: and they sent forth [a]Barnabas, that he should go as far as Antioch.

23 Who, when he came, and had seen the grace of God, was glad, and [a]exhorted[1] them all, that with purpose of heart they would [2]cleave unto the Lord.

24 For he was a good man, and [a]full of the Holy Ghost and of faith: [b]and much people was added unto the Lord.

25 Then departed Barnabas to [a]Tarsus, for to seek Saul:

26 And when he had found him, he brought him unto Antioch. And it came to pass, that a whole year they assembled themselves with the church, and taught much people. And the disciples were called Christians first in Antioch.

27 And in these days came [a]prophets from Jerusalem unto Antioch.

28 And there stood up one of them named [a]Agabus, and [1]signified by the Spirit that there should be great [2]dearth throughout all the world: which came to pass in the days of [b]Claudius Caesar.

29 Then the disciples, every man according to his ability, determined to send [a]relief unto the brethren which dwelt in Judaea:

30 [a]Which also they did, and sent it to the elders by the hands of Barnabas and Saul.

## CHAPTER 12

Now about that time Herod the king stretched forth *his* hands to [1]vex certain of the church.

2 And he killed James [a]the brother of John with the sword.

3 And because he saw it pleased the Jews, he proceeded further to [1]take Peter also. (Then were [a]the days of unleavened bread.)

4 And [a]when he had apprehended him, he put *him* in prison, and delivered *him* to four [1]quaternions of soldiers to keep him; intending after [2]Easter to bring him forth to the people.

5 Peter therefore was kept in prison: but prayer was made without ceasing of the church unto God for him.

6 And when Herod [1]would have brought him forth, the same night Peter was sleeping between two soldiers, bound with two chains: and the [2]keepers before the door kept the prison.

7 And, behold, [a]the angel of the Lord [1]came upon *him,* and a light shined in the prison: and he smote Peter on the side, and raised him up, saying, Arise up quickly. And his chains fell off from *his* hands.

8 And the angel said unto him, Gird thyself, and bind on thy sandals. And so he did. And he saith unto him, Cast thy garment about thee, and follow me.

9 And he went out, and followed him; and [a]wist[1] not that it was [2]true which was done by the angel; but thought [b]he saw a vision.

11:12 [a] [John 16:13]; Acts 10:19; 15:7 [b] Acts 10:23

11:13 [a] Acts 10:30

11:15 [a] Acts 2:1–4; 15:7–9

11:16 [a] Matt. 3:11; Mark 1:8; John 1:26, 33; Acts 1:5; 19:4 [b] Is. 44:3

11:17 [a] [Acts 15:8, 9] [b] Acts 10:47

11:18 [a] Is. 42:1, 6; 49:6; Luke 2:32; John 11:52; Rom. 10:12, 13; 15:9, 16 [1] *became silent*

11:19 [a] Acts 8:1, 4

11:20 [a] Acts 6:1; 9:29 [1] *Hellenists*

11:21 [a] Luke 1:66; Acts 2:47 [b] Acts 9:35; 14:1

11:22 [a] Acts 4:36; 9:27 [1] *news*

11:23 [a] Acts 13:43; 14:22 [1] *encouraged* [2] *continue with*

11:24 [a] Acts 6:5 [b] Acts 5:14; 11:21

11:25 [a] Acts 9:11, 30

11:27 [a] Acts 2:17; 13:1; 15:32; 21:9; 1 Cor. 12:28; Eph. 4:11

11:28 [a] John 16:13; Acts 21:10 [b] Acts 18:2 [1] *showed* [2] *famine*

11:29 [a] Rom. 15:26; 1 Cor. 16:1; 2 Cor. 9:1

11:30 [a] Acts 12:25

12:1 [1] *harass*

12:2 [a] Matt. 4:21; 20:23

12:3 [a] Ex. 12:15; 23:15; Acts 20:6 [1] *seize*

12:4 [a] John 21:18 [1] Gr. *tetrads,* squads of four [2] Lit. *the Passover*

12:6 [1] *was about to bring* [2] *guards*

12:7 [a] Acts 5:19 [1] *stood by*

12:9 [a] Ps. 126:1 [b] Acts 10:3, 17; 11:5 [1] *knew* [2] *real*

10 When they were past the first and the second ¹ward, they came unto the iron gate that leadeth unto the city; ªwhich opened to them of his own accord: and they went out, and passed on through one street; and forthwith the angel departed from him.

11 And when Peter was come to himself, he said, Now I know ¹of a surety, that ªthe Lord hath sent his angel, and ᵇhath delivered me out of the hand of Herod, and *from* all the expectation of the people of the Jews.

12 And when he had considered *the thing,* ªhe came to the house of Mary the mother of ᵇJohn, whose surname was Mark; where many were gathered together ᶜpraying.

13 And as Peter knocked at the door of the gate, a damsel came to ¹hearken, named Rhoda.

14 And when she knew Peter's voice, she opened not the gate for gladness, but ran in, and told how Peter stood before the gate.

15 And they said unto her, Thou art ¹mad. But she constantly affirmed that it was even so. Then said they, ªIt is his angel.

16 But Peter continued knocking: and when they had opened *the door,* and saw him, they were astonished.

17 But he, ªbeckoning unto them with the hand to ¹hold their peace, declared unto them how the Lord had brought him out of the prison. And he said, Go shew these things unto James, and to the brethren. And he departed, and went into another place.

18 Now as soon as it was day, there was no small stir among the soldiers, what was become of Peter.

19 And when Herod had sought for him, and found him not, he examined the ¹keepers, and commanded that *they* should be put to death. And he went down from Judaea to Caesarea, and *there* abode.

20 And Herod was ¹highly displeased with them of ªTyre and Sidon: but they came with one accord to him, and, having made Blastus the king's chamberlain their friend, desired peace; because ᵇtheir country was ²nourished by the king's *country.*

21 And upon a set day Herod, ¹arrayed in royal apparel, sat upon his throne, and made an ²oration unto them.

22 And the people ¹gave a shout, *saying,* It *is* the voice of a god, and not of a man.

23 And immediately the angel of the Lord ªsmote him, because ᵇhe gave not God the glory: and he was eaten of worms, and ¹gave up the ghost.

24 But ªthe word of God grew and multiplied.

25 And ªBarnabas and Saul returned from Jerusalem, when they had ᵇfulfilled *their* ministry, and ᶜtook with them ᵈJohn, whose surname was Mark.

## CHAPTER 13

Now there were ªin the church that was at Antioch certain prophets and teachers; as ᵇBarnabas, and Simeon that was called Niger, and ᶜLucius of Cyrene, and Manaen, which had been brought up with Herod the tetrarch, and Saul.

2 As they ministered to the Lord, and fasted, the Holy Ghost said, ªSeparate me Barnabas and Saul for the work ᵇwhereunto I have called them.

3 And ªwhen they had fasted and prayed, and laid *their* hands on them, they sent *them* away.

4 So they, being sent forth by the Holy Ghost, departed unto Seleucia; and from thence they sailed to ªCyprus.

5 And when they were at Salamis, ªthey preached the word of God in the synagogues of the Jews: and they had also ᵇJohn ¹to *their* minister.

6 And when they had gone through the isle unto Paphos, they found ªa certain sorcerer, a false prophet, a Jew, whose name *was* Bar-jesus:

7 Which was with the ¹deputy of the country, Sergius Paulus, ²a prudent man; who called for Barnabas and Saul, and ³desired to hear the word of God.

8 But ªElymas the sorcerer (for so is his name ¹by interpretation) ²withstood them, seeking to turn away the deputy from the faith.

9 Then Saul, (who also *is called* Paul,) ªfilled with the Holy Ghost, ¹set his eyes on him,

10 And said, O full of all ¹subtilty and all ²mischief, ªthou ³child of the devil, *thou* enemy of all righteousness, wilt thou not cease ⁴to pervert the ⁵right ways of the Lord?

11 And now, behold, ªthe hand of the Lord *is* upon thee, and thou shalt be blind, not seeing the sun for a ¹season. And immediately there fell on him a mist and a darkness; and he went about seeking some to lead him by the hand.

12 Then the deputy, when he saw what was done, believed, being astonished at the ¹doctrine of the Lord.

13 Now when Paul and his company ¹loosed from Paphos, they came to Perga in Pamphylia: and ªJohn departing from them returned to Jerusalem.

14 But when they departed from Perga, they came to Antioch in Pisidia,

### Center column references

12:10 ª Acts 5:19;
16:26 ¹ *guard posts*

12:11 ª [Ps. 34:7]
ᵇ Job 5:19 ¹ *for certain*

12:12 ª Acts 4:23
ᵇ Acts 13:5, 13;
15:37 ᶜ Acts 12:5

12:13 ¹ *answer*

12:15 ª [Matt. 18:10] ¹ *out of your mind*

12:17 ª Acts 13:16;
19:33; 21:40
¹ *keep silent*

12:19 ¹ *guards*

12:20 ª Matt.
11:21 ᵇ Ezek.
27:17 ¹ *very angry*
² *supplied with food*

12:21 ¹ *dressed*
² *speech*

12:22 ¹ *kept shouting*

12:23 ª 2 Sam.
24:16, 17 ᵇ Ps.
115:1 ¹ *died*

12:24 ª Acts 6:7;
19:20

12:25 ª Acts
11:30 ᵇ Acts 11:30
ᶜ Acts 13:5, 13
ᵈ Acts 12:12; 15:37

13:1 ª Acts 14:26
ᵇ Acts 11:22
ᶜ Rom. 16:21

13:2 ª Gal. 1:15; 2:9
ᵇ Heb. 5:4

13:3 ª Acts 6:6

13:4 ª Acts 4:36

13:5 ª [Acts 13:46]
ᵇ Acts 12:25;
15:37 ¹ *as their assistant*

13:6 ª Acts 8:9

13:7 ¹ *proconsul*
² *an intelligent*
³ *sought*

13:8 ª Ex. 7:11
¹ *translated*
² *opposed*

13:9 ª Acts 2:4;
4:8 ¹ *looked intently at*

13:10 ª Matt.
13:38 ¹ *deceit*
² *fraud* ³ *son*
⁴ *making crooked*
⁵ *straight*

13:11 ª 1 Sam. 5:6
¹ *time*

13:12 ¹ *teaching*

13:13 ª Acts 15:38
¹ *set sail*

and [a]went into the synagogue on the sabbath day, and sat down.

15 And [a]after the reading of the law and the prophets the rulers of the synagogue sent unto them, saying, *Ye* men *and* brethren, if ye have [b]any word of exhortation for the people, say on.

16 Then Paul stood up, and beckoning with *his* hand said, Men of Israel, and [a]ye that fear God, [1]give audience.

17 The God of this people of Israel [a]chose our fathers, and exalted the people [b]when they dwelt as strangers in the land of Egypt, and with [1]an high arm [c]brought he them out of it.

18 And [a]about the time of forty years [1]suffered he their manners in the wilderness.

19 And when he had destroyed [a]seven nations in the land of Chanaan, [b]he divided their land to them by lot.

20 And after that [a]he gave *unto them* judges about the space of four hundred and fifty years, [b]until Samuel the prophet.

21 [a]And afterward they desired a king: and God gave unto them [b]Saul the son of Cis, a man of the tribe of Benjamin, [1]by the space of forty years.

22 And [a]when he had removed him, [b]he raised up unto them David to be their king; to whom also he gave testimony, and said, [c]I have found David the *son* of Jesse, [d]a man after mine own heart, which shall fulfil all my will.

23 [a]Of this man's [1]seed hath God according [b]to *his* promise raised unto Israel [c]a Saviour, Jesus:

24 [a]When John had first preached before his coming the baptism of repentance to all the people of Israel.

25 And as John fulfilled his course, he said, [a]Whom think ye that I am? I am not *he.* But, behold, [b]there cometh one after me, whose [1]shoes of *his* feet I am not worthy to loose.

26 Men *and* brethren, [1]children of the [2]stock of Abraham, and [a]whosoever among you feareth God, [b]to you is the word of this salvation sent.

27 For they that dwell at Jerusalem, and their rulers, [a]because they knew him not, nor yet the voices of the prophets which are read every sabbath day, they have fulfilled *them* in condemning *him.*

28 [a]And though they found no cause of death *in him,* yet [1]desired they Pilate that he should be slain.

29 [a]And when they had fulfilled all that was written of him, [b]they took *him* down from the tree, and laid *him* in a [1]sepulchre.

30 [a]But God raised him from the dead:

31 And [a]he was seen many days of them which came up with him from Galilee to Jerusalem, who are his witnesses unto the people.

32 And we declare unto you glad tidings, how that [a]the promise which was made unto the fathers,

33 God hath fulfilled the same unto us their children, in that he hath raised up Jesus again; as it is also written in the second psalm, [a]Thou art my Son, this day have I begotten thee.

34 And as concerning that he raised him up from the dead, *now* no more to return to [1]corruption, he said on this wise, [a]I will give you the sure [2]mercies of David.

35 Wherefore he saith also in another *psalm,* [a]Thou shalt not suffer thine Holy One to see corruption.

36 For David, after he had served [1]his own generation by the will of God, [a]fell on sleep, and was laid [2]unto his fathers, and [3]saw corruption:

37 But he, whom God raised again, saw no [1]corruption.

38 Be it known unto you therefore, men *and* brethren, that [a]through this man is preached unto you the forgiveness of sins:

39 And [a]by him all that believe are justified from all things, from which ye could not be justified by the law of Moses.

40 Beware therefore, lest that come upon you, which is spoken of in the prophets;

41 [a]Behold, ye despisers, and [1]wonder, and perish: for I work a work in your days, a work which ye shall [2]in no wise believe, though a man declare it unto you.

42 And when the Jews were gone out of the synagogue, the Gentiles [1]besought that these words might be preached to them the next sabbath.

43 Now when the congregation was broken up, many of the Jews and religious [1]proselytes followed Paul and Barnabas: who, speaking to them, [a]persuaded them to continue in [b]the grace of God.

44 And the next sabbath day came almost the whole city together to hear the word of God.

45 But when the Jews saw the multitudes, they were filled with envy, and [a]spake[1] against those things which were spoken by Paul, contradicting and blaspheming.

46 Then Paul and Barnabas [1]waxed bold, and said, [a]It was necessary that the word of God should first have been spoken to you: but [b]seeing ye [2]put it from you, and judge yourselves unworthy of everlasting life, lo, [c]we turn to the Gentiles.

47 For so hath the Lord commanded us, [a]*saying,* I have set thee

13:14 [a] Acts 16:13
13:15 [a] Luke 4:16 [b] Heb. 13:22
13:16 [a] Acts 10:35 [1] *listen*
13:17 [a] Deut. 7:6–8 [b] Acts 7:17 [c] Ex. 14:8 [1] *an uplifted*
13:18 [a] Num. 14:34 [1] *he put up with their ways*
13:19 [a] Deut. 7:1 [b] Josh. 14:1, 2; 19:51
13:20 [a] Judg. 2:16 [b] 1 Sam. 3:20
13:21 [a] 1 Sam. 8:5 [b] 1 Sam. 10:20–24 [1] *for*
13:22 [a] 1 Sam. 15:23, 26, 28 [b] 1 Sam. 16:1, 12, 13 [c] Ps. 89:20 [d] 1 Sam. 13:14
13:23 [a] Is. 11:1 [b] Ps. 132:11 [c] [Matt. 1:21] [1] *descendants*
13:24 [a] [Luke 3:3]
13:25 [a] Mark 1:7 [b] John 1:20, 27 [1] *sandals*
13:26 [a] Ps. 66:16 [b] Matt. 10:6 [1] *sons* [2] *family*
13:27 [a] Luke 23:34
13:28 [a] Matt. 27:22, 23 [1] *they asked*
13:29 [a] Luke 18:31 [b] Matt. 27:57–61 [1] *tomb*
13:30 [a] Matt. 12:39, 40; 28:6
13:31 [a] Acts 1:3, 11
13:32 [a] [Gen. 3:15]
13:33 [a] Ps. 2:7
13:34 [a] Is. 55:3 [1] *the state of decay* [2] *blessings*
13:35 [a] Ps. 16:10
13:36 [a] Acts 2:29 [1] *in his* [2] *with* [3] His body decayed
13:37 [1] *decay*
13:38 [a] Jer. 31:34
13:39 [a] [Is. 53:11]
13:41 [a] Hab. 1:5 [1] *marvel* [2] *by no means*
13:42 [1] *begged*
13:43 [a] Acts 11:23 [b] Titus 2:11 [1] Gentile converts to Judaism
13:45 [a] 1 Pet. 4:4 [1] *opposed*
13:46 [a] Rom. 1:16 [b] Ex. 32:10 [c] Acts 18:6 [1] *grew* [2] *reject it*
13:47 [a] Is. 42:6; 49:6

to be a light of the Gentiles, that thou shouldest be for salvation unto the ends of the earth.

48 And when the Gentiles heard this, they were glad, and glorified the word of the Lord: [a]and as many as were ordained to eternal life believed.

49 And the word of the Lord was published throughout all the region.

50 But the Jews stirred up the devout and [1]honourable women, and the chief men of the city, and [a]raised persecution against Paul and Barnabas, and expelled them out of their [2]coasts.

51 [a]But they shook off the dust of their feet against them, and came unto Iconium.

52 And the disciples [a]were filled with joy, and [b]with the Holy Ghost.

## CHAPTER 14

AND it came to pass in Iconium, that they went both together into the synagogue of the Jews, and so spake, that a great multitude both of the Jews and also of the [a]Greeks believed.

2 But the unbelieving Jews stirred up the Gentiles, and made their [1]minds [2]evil affected against the brethren.

3 Long time therefore abode they speaking boldly in the Lord, [a]which gave testimony unto the word of his grace, and granted signs and [b]wonders to be done by their hands.

4 But the multitude of the city was [a]divided: and part held with the Jews, and part with the [b]apostles.

5 And when there was [1]an assault made both of the Gentiles, and also of the Jews with their rulers, [a]to [2]use *them* despitefully, and to stone them,

6 They [1]were ware of *it,* and [a]fled unto Lystra and Derbe, cities of Lycaonia, and unto the region that lieth round about:

7 And there they preached the gospel.

8 [a]And there sat a certain man at Lystra, [1]impotent in his feet, being a cripple from his mother's womb, who never had walked:

9 The same heard Paul speak: [1]who [2]stedfastly beholding him, and perceiving that he had faith to be healed,

10 Said with a loud voice, [a]Stand upright on thy feet. And he leaped and walked.

11 And when the people saw what Paul had done, they lifted up their voices, saying in the speech of Lycaonia, [a]The gods are come down to us in the likeness of men.

12 And they called Barnabas, [1]Jupiter; and Paul, [2]Mercurius, because he was the chief speaker.

13 Then the priest of [1]Jupiter, [2]which was before their city, brought oxen and garlands unto the gates, [a]and would have done sacrifice with the people.

14 *Which* when the apostles, Barnabas and Paul, heard *of,* [a]they [1]rent their clothes, and ran in among the people, crying out,

15 And saying, Sirs, [a]why do ye these things? [b]We also are men of like passions with you, and preach unto you that ye should turn from [c]these [1]vanities [d]unto the living God, [e]which made heaven, and earth, and the sea, and all things that are therein:

16 [a]Who in [1]times past [2]suffered all nations to walk in their own ways.

17 [a]Nevertheless he left not himself without witness, in that he did good, and [b]gave us rain from heaven, and fruitful seasons, filling our hearts with [c]food and gladness.

18 And with these sayings [1]scarce restrained they the [2]people, [3]that they had not done sacrifice unto them.

19 [a]And there came thither *certain* Jews from Antioch and Iconium, who persuaded the people, [b]and, having stoned Paul, [1]drew *him* out of the city, supposing he had been [c]dead.

20 Howbeit, as the disciples stood round about him, he rose up, and came into the city: and the next day he departed with Barnabas to Derbe.

21 And when they had preached the gospel to that city, [a]and [1]had taught many, they returned again to Lystra, and *to* Iconium, and Antioch,

22 [1]Confirming the souls of the disciples, *and* [a]exhorting them to continue in the faith, and that [b]we must through much tribulation enter into the kingdom of God.

23 And when they had [a]ordained[1] them elders in every church, and had prayed with fasting, they commended them to the Lord, on whom they believed.

24 And after they had passed throughout Pisidia, they came to Pamphylia.

25 And when they had preached the word in Perga, they went down into Attalia:

26 And thence sailed to Antioch, from whence they had been [1]recommended to the grace of God for the work which they fulfilled.

27 And when they were come, and had gathered the church together, [a]they [1]rehearsed all that God had done with them, and how he had [b]opened the door of faith unto the Gentiles.

28 And there they abode long time with the disciples.

13:48 [a] [Acts 2:47]
13:50 [a] 2 Tim. 3:11 [1] *prominent* [2] *region*
13:51 [a] Matt. 10:14
13:52 [a] John 16:22 [b] Acts 2:4; 4:8, 31; 13:9
14:1 [a] Acts 18:4
14:2 [1] Lit. *souls* [2] *bitter* or *angry*
14:3 [a] Heb. 2:4 [b] Acts 5:12
14:4 [a] Luke 12:51 [b] Acts 13:2, 3
14:5 [a] 2 Tim. 3:11 [1] *a violent attempt* [2] *abuse*
14:6 [a] Matt. 10:23 [1] *became aware*
14:8 [a] Acts 3:2 [1] *without strength*
14:9 [1] Paul [2] *intently observing*
14:10 [a] [Is. 35:6]
14:11 [a] Acts 8:10; 28:6
14:12 [1] *Zeus* [2] *Hermes*
14:13 [a] Dan. 2:46 [1] *Zeus* [2] *whose temple* was
14:14 [a] Matt. 26:65 [1] *tore*
14:15 [a] Acts 10:26 [b] James 5:17 [c] 1 Cor. 8:4 [d] 1 Thess. 1:9 [e] Rev. 14:7 [1] *useless things*
14:16 [a] Ps. 81:12 [1] *past generations* [2] *allowed*
14:17 [a] Rom. 1:19, 20 [b] Deut. 11:14 [c] Ps. 145:16
14:18 [1] *they could scarcely restrain* [2] *multitudes* [3] *from sacrificing to them*
14:19 [a] Acts 13:45, 50; 14:2–5 [b] 2 Cor. 11:25 [c] [2 Cor. 12:1–4] [1] *they dragged*
14:21 [a] Matt. 28:19 [1] *made many disciples*
14:22 [a] Acts 11:23 [b] [2 Tim. 2:12; 3:12] [1] *Strengthening*
14:23 [a] Titus 1:5 [1] *appointed*
14:26 [1] *commended*
14:27 [a] Acts 15:4, 12 [b] 2 Cor. 2:12 [1] *reported*

## CHAPTER 15

AND [a]certain men which came
down from Judaea taught the
brethren, *and said,* [b]Except ye be circumcised after the manner of Moses,
ye cannot be saved.
2 When therefore Paul and Barnabas had no small dissension and
[1]disputation with them, they determined that [a]Paul and Barnabas, and
certain other of them, should go up
to Jerusalem unto the apostles and
elders about this question.
3 And [a]being [1]brought on their way
by the church, they passed through
Phenice and Samaria, [b]declaring[2] the
conversion of the Gentiles: and they
caused great joy unto all the brethren.
4 And when they were come to
Jerusalem, they were received of
the church, and *of* the apostles and
elders, and they [1]declared all things
that God had done with them.
5 But there rose up certain of the
sect of the Pharisees which believed,
saying, That it was [1]needful to circumcise them, and to command
*them* to keep the law of Moses.
6 And the apostles and elders came
together for to consider of this matter.
7 And when there had been much
disputing, Peter rose up, and said
unto them, [a]Men *and* brethren, ye
know how that a good while ago God
made choice among us, that the Gentiles by my mouth should hear the
word of the gospel, and believe.
8 And God, [a]which knoweth the
hearts, bare them witness, [b]giving
them the Holy Ghost, even as *he did*
unto us;
9 [a]And [1]put no difference between
us and them, [b]purifying their hearts
by faith.
10 Now therefore why [1]tempt ye
God, [a]to[2] put a yoke upon the neck
of the disciples, which neither our fathers nor we were able to bear?
11 But [a]we believe that through
the grace of the Lord Jesus Christ we
shall be saved, [1]even as they.
12 Then all the multitude kept silence, and [1]gave audience to Barnabas and Paul, declaring [2]what
miracles and wonders God had
[a]wrought[3] among the Gentiles [4]by
them.
13 And after they had [1]held their
peace, [a]James answered, saying,
Men *and* brethren, hearken unto me:
14 [a]Simeon[1] hath declared how
God at the first did visit the Gentiles,
to take out of them a people for his
name.
15 And to this agree the words of
the prophets; as it is written,
16 [a]After this I will return, and will
build again the tabernacle of David,
which is fallen down; and I will build
again the ruins thereof, and I will set
it up:
17 That the [1]residue of men might
seek after the Lord, [2]and all the Gentiles, [3]upon whom my name is called,
saith the Lord, who doeth all these
things.
18 Known unto God are all his works
from [1]the beginning of the world.
19 Wherefore [a]my [1]sentence is, that
we trouble not them, which from
among the Gentiles [b]are turned to
God:
20 But that we [a]write unto them,
that they abstain [b]from [1]pollutions
of idols, and [c]*from* [2]fornication, [d]and
*from* things strangled, and *from* blood.
21 For Moses of old time hath in every city them that preach him, [a]being
read in the synagogues every sabbath day.
22 Then pleased it the apostles
and elders, with the whole church,
to send chosen men of their own
company to Antioch with Paul and
Barnabas; *namely,* Judas surnamed
[a]Barsabas, and Silas, chief men
among the brethren:
23 And they wrote [1]*letters* by them
after this manner; The apostles and
elders and brethren *send* greeting
unto the brethren which are of the
Gentiles in Antioch and Syria and
Cilicia:
24 Forasmuch as we have heard,
that [a]certain which went out from us
have troubled you with words, [b]sub-
verting[1] your souls, saying, *Ye must*
be circumcised, and keep the law: to
whom we gave no *such* commandment:
25 It seemed good unto us, being
assembled with one accord, to send
chosen men unto you with our beloved Barnabas and Paul,
26 [a]Men that have [1]hazarded their
lives for the name of our Lord Jesus
Christ.
27 We have sent therefore Judas
and Silas, who shall also tell *you* the
same things by [1]mouth.
28 For it seemed good to the Holy
Ghost, and to us, to lay upon you no
greater burden than these necessary
things;
29 [a]That ye abstain from [1]meats
offered to idols, and [b]from blood,
and from things strangled, and from
[c]fornication:[2] from which if ye keep
yourselves, ye shall do well. Fare ye
well.
30 So when they were [1]dismissed,
they came to Antioch: and when they
had gathered the multitude together,
they delivered the epistle:
31 *Which* when they had read, they
rejoiced for the [1]consolation.

15:1 [a] Gal. 2:12 [b] Phil. 3:2
15:2 [a] Gal. 2:1 [1] *dispute*
15:3 [a] Rom. 15:24 [b] Acts 14:27; 15:4, 12 [1] *sent* [2] *describing*
15:4 [1] *reported*
15:5 [1] *necessary*
15:7 [a] Acts 10:20
15:8 [a] Acts 1:24 [b] Acts 2:4; 10:44, 47
15:9 [a] Rom. 10:12 [b] Acts 10:15, 28 [1] *made no distinction*
15:10 [a] Matt. 23:4 [1] *test* [2] *by putting*
15:11 [a] Rom. 3:4; 5:15 [1] *in the same manner*
15:12 [a] Acts 14:27; 15:3, 4 [1] *listened* [2] *how many* [3] *worked* [4] *through*
15:13 [a] Acts 12:17 [1] *stopped speaking*
15:14 [a] Acts 15:7 [1] Or *Simon*
15:16 [a] Amos 9:11, 12
15:17 [1] *rest of mankind* [2] *even* [3] *who are called by my name*
15:18 [1] *eternity*
15:19 [a] Acts 15:28; 21:25 [b] 1 Thess. 1:9 [1] *judgment*
15:20 [a] Acts 21:25 [b] [1 Cor. 8:1; 10:20, 28] [c] [1 Cor. 6:9] [d] Lev. 3:17 [1] *things polluted by* [2] *sexual immorality*
15:21 [a] Acts 13:15, 27
15:22 [a] Acts 1:23
15:23 [1] *this* letter
15:24 [a] Titus 1:10, 11 [b] Gal. 1:7; 5:10 [1] *unsettling*
15:26 [a] Acts 13:50; 14:19 [1] *risked*
15:27 [1] *word of mouth*
15:29 [a] Acts 15:20; 21:25 [b] Lev. 17:14 [c] Col. 3:5 [1] *things* [2] *sexual immorality*
15:30 [1] *sent off*
15:31 [1] *encouragement*

**32** And Judas and Silas, being [a]prophets also themselves, [b]exhorted the brethren with many words, and [1]confirmed *them.*

**33** And after they had [1]tarried *there* [2]a space, they were [3]let [a]go in peace from the brethren unto the apostles.

**34** Notwithstanding it pleased Silas to abide there still.

**35** [a]Paul also and Barnabas continued in Antioch, teaching and preaching the word of the Lord, with many others also.

**36** And some days after Paul said unto Barnabas, Let us go again and visit our brethren in every city where we have preached the word of the Lord, *and see* how they do.

**37** And Barnabas determined to take with them [a]John, whose surname was Mark.

**38** But Paul thought not good to take him with them, [a]who departed from them from Pamphylia, and went not with them to the work.

**39** And the contention was so sharp between them, that they [1]departed asunder one from the other: and so Barnabas took Mark, and sailed unto [a]Cyprus;

**40** And Paul chose Silas, and departed, [a]being recommended by the brethren unto the grace of God.

**41** And he went through Syria and Cilicia, [a]confirming[1] the churches.

## CHAPTER 16

THEN came he to [a]Derbe and Lystra: and, behold, a certain disciple was there, [b]named Timotheus, [c]the son of a certain woman, which was a Jewess, and believed; but his father *was* a Greek:

**2** Which was well reported of by the brethren that were at Lystra and Iconium.

**3** Him would Paul have to go forth with him; and [a]took and circumcised him because of the Jews which were in [1]those quarters: for they knew all that his father was a Greek.

**4** And as they went through the cities, they delivered them the [a]decrees for to keep, [b]that were [1]ordained of the apostles and elders which were at Jerusalem.

**5** And [a]so were the churches [1]established in the faith, and increased in number daily.

**6** Now when they had gone throughout Phrygia and the region of [a]Galatia, and were forbidden of the Holy Ghost to preach the word in [1]Asia,

**7** After they were come to Mysia, they [1]assayed to go into Bithynia: but the Spirit [2]suffered them not.

**8** And they passing by Mysia [a]came down to Troas.

**9** And a vision appeared to Paul in the night; There stood a [a]man of Macedonia, and [1]prayed him, saying, Come over into Macedonia, and help us.

**10** And after he had seen the vision, immediately we endeavoured to go [a]into Macedonia, [1]assuredly gathering that the Lord had called us for to preach the gospel unto them.

**11** Therefore [1]loosing from Troas, we came with a straight course to [2]Samothracia, and the next *day* to Neapolis;

**12** And from thence to [a]Philippi, which is the [1]chief city of that part of Macedonia, *and* a colony: and we were in that city abiding certain days.

**13** And on the sabbath we went out of the city by a river side, where prayer was [1]wont to be made; and we sat down, and spake unto the women which [2]resorted *thither.*

**14** And a certain woman named Lydia, a seller of purple, of the city of [a]Thyatira, which worshipped God, heard *us:* whose [b]heart the Lord opened, [1]that she attended unto the things which were spoken of Paul.

**15** And when she was baptized, and her household, she [b]besought *us,* saying, If ye have judged me to be faithful to the Lord, come into my house, and abide *there.* And [a]she constrained us.

**16** And it came to pass, as we went to prayer, a certain damsel [a]possessed with a spirit of divination met us, which brought her masters [b]much gain by [1]soothsaying:

**17** The same followed Paul and us, and cried, saying, These men are the servants of the most high God, which shew unto us the way of salvation.

**18** And this did she many days. But Paul, [a]being [1]grieved, turned and said to the spirit, I command thee in the name of Jesus Christ to come out of her. [b]And he came out the same hour.

**19** And [a]when her masters saw that the hope of their gains was gone, they [1]caught Paul and Silas, and [b]drew[2] *them* into the marketplace unto the [3]rulers,

**20** And brought them to the magistrates, saying, These men, being Jews, [a]do exceedingly trouble our city,

**21** And teach customs, which are not lawful for us to receive, neither to observe, being Romans.

**22** And the multitude rose up together against them: and the magistrates [1]rent off their clothes, [a]and commanded to beat *them.*

**23** And when they had laid many stripes upon them, they cast *them* into prison, charging the jailor to keep them [1]safely:

**24** Who, having received such a charge, thrust them into the inner prison, and [1]made their feet fast in the stocks.

### Cross-references

15:32 [a] Eph. 4:11
[b] Acts 14:22; 18:23
[1] *strengthened*

15:33 [a] Heb. 11:31
[1] *stayed* [2] *for a time* [3] *sent back with greetings*

15:35 [a] Acts 13:1

15:37 [a] Acts 12:12, 25

15:38 [a] Acts 13:13

15:39 [a] Acts 4:36;
13:4 [1] *separated*

15:40 [a] Acts 11:23;
14:26

15:41 [a] Acts 16:5
[1] *strengthening*

16:1 [a] Acts 14:6
[b] Rom. 16:21
[c] 2 Tim. 1:5; 3:15

16:3 [a] [Gal. 2:3;
5:2] [1] *that region*

16:4 [a] Acts 15:19–
21 [b] Acts 15:28, 29
[1] *determined by*

16:5 [a] Acts 2:47;
15:41 [1] *strengthened*

16:6 [a] Gal. 1:1,
2 [1] The Roman province of Asia

16:7 [1] *tried* [2] *permitted*

16:8 [a] 2 Cor. 2:12

16:9 [a] Acts 10:30
[1] *pleaded with*

16:10 [a] 2 Cor. 2:13
[1] *concluding*

16:11 [1] *sailing* [2] Or *Samothrace*

16:12 [a] Phil. 1:1
[1] *foremost*

16:13 [1] *customarily*
[2] *met*

16:14 [a] Rev. 1:11;
2:18, 24 [b] Luke 24:45 [1] *to heed*

16:15 [a] Gen. 19:3;
33:11; Judg. 19:21;
Luke 24:29; [Heb. 13:2] [1] *begged*

16:16 [a] Lev. 19:31;
20:6, 27; Deut. 18:11; 1 Sam. 28:3, 7; 2 Kin. 21:6;
1 Chr. 10:13; Is. 8:19 [b] Acts 19:24
[1] *fortune-telling*

16:18 [a] Mark 1:25,
34 [b] Mark 16:17
[1] *greatly annoyed*

16:19 [a] Acts 16:16;
19:25, 26 [b] Matt. 10:18 [1] *seized*
[2] *dragged* [3] *authorities*

16:20 [a] 1 Kin.
18:17; Acts 17:8

16:22 [a] 2 Cor. 6:5;
11:23, 25; 1 Thess. 2:2 [1] *tore*

16:23 [1] *securely*

16:24 [1] *fastened their feet in*

25 And at midnight Paul and Silas [1]prayed, and sang praises unto God: and the prisoners heard them.

26 [a]And suddenly there was a great earthquake, so that the foundations of the prison were shaken: and immediately [b]all the doors were opened, and every one's [1]bands were loosed.

27 And the keeper of the prison awaking out of his sleep, and seeing the prison doors open, he drew out his sword, and would have killed himself, supposing that the prisoners had been fled.

28 But Paul cried with a loud voice, saying, Do thyself no harm: for we are all here.

29 Then he called for a light, and [1]sprang in, and came trembling, and fell down before Paul and Silas,

30 And brought them out, and said, [a]Sirs, what must I do to be saved?

31 And they said, [a]Believe on the Lord Jesus Christ, and thou shalt be saved, and thy [1]house.

32 And they spake unto him the word of the Lord, and to all that were in his house.

33 And he took them the same hour of the night, and washed *their* stripes; and was baptized, he and all his, straightway.

34 And when he had brought them into his house, [a]he set [1]meat before them, and rejoiced, believing in God with all his house.

35 And when it was day, the magistrates sent the [1]serjeants, saying, Let those men go.

36 And the keeper of the prison told this saying to Paul, The magistrates have sent to let you go: now therefore depart, and go in peace.

37 But Paul said unto them, They have beaten us openly uncondemned, [a]being Romans, and have cast *us* into prison; and now do they [1]thrust us out [2]privily? nay verily; but let them come themselves and fetch us out.

38 And the [1]serjeants told these words unto the magistrates: and they feared, when they heard that they were Romans.

39 And they came and besought them, and brought *them* out, and [a]desired[1] *them* to depart out of the city.

40 And they went out of the prison, [a]and entered into *the house of* Lydia: and when they had seen the brethren, they comforted them, and departed.

## CHAPTER 17

**N**ow when they had passed through Amphipolis and Apollonia, they came to [a]Thessalonica, where was a synagogue of the Jews:

16:25 [1] *were praying and singing hymns*
16:26 [a] Acts 4:31
[b] Acts 5:19; 12:7, 10 [1] *chains*
16:29 [1] *ran*
16:30 [a] Luke 3:10; Acts 2:37; 9:6; 22:10
16:31 [a] [John 3:16, 36; 6:47; Acts 13:38, 39; Rom. 10:9–11; 1 John 5:10] [1] *household*
16:34 [a] Matt. 5:4; Luke 5:29; 19:6
[1] *food*
16:35 [1] Lit. *rod-bearers*
16:37 [a] Acts 22:25–29 [1] *put* [2] *secretly*
16:38 [1] Lit. *rod-bearers*
16:39 [a] Matt. 8:34
[1] *asked*
16:40 [a] Acts 16:14
17:1 [a] Acts 17:11, 13; 20:4; 27:2; Phil. 4:16; 1 Thess. 1:1; 2 Thess. 1:1; 2 Tim. 4:10

17:2 [a] Luke 4:16; Acts 9:20; 13:5, 14; 14:1; 16:13; 19:8
[b] 1 Thess. 2:1–16
[1] *custom*
17:3 [a] Luke 24:26, 46; Acts 18:5, 28; Gal. 3:1 [1] *Explaining* [2] *demonstrating*
17:4 [a] Acts 28:24
[b] Acts 15:22, 27, 32, 40 [1] *were persuaded* [2] *joined*
17:5 [a] Acts 13:45
[b] Rom. 16:21
[1] *were not persuaded* [2] *evil men* [3] *marketplace* [4] *mob* [5] *attacked*
17:6 [a] [Acts 16:20] [1] *dragged*
17:7 [a] 1 Pet. 2:13
[1] *welcomed*
17:8 [1] *crowd*
17:9 [1] *rest*
17:10 [a] Acts 9:25; 17:14
17:11 [a] John 5:39
[1] *fair-minded*
17:13 [1] *crowds*
17:14 [a] Matt. 10:23
17:15 [a] Acts 18:5
17:16 [a] 2 Pet. 2:8
[1] *provoked within* [2] *full of idols*
17:17 [1] *he reasoned*

2 And Paul, as his [1]manner was, [a]went in unto them, and three sabbath days [b]reasoned with them out of the scriptures,

3 [1]Opening and [2]alleging, [a]that Christ must needs have suffered, and risen again from the dead; and that this Jesus, whom I preach unto you, is Christ.

4 [a]And some of them [1]believed, and [2]consorted with Paul and [b]Silas; and of the devout Greeks a great multitude, and of the chief women not a few.

5 But the Jews which [1]believed not, moved with [a]envy, took unto them certain [2]lewd fellows of the [3]baser sort, and gathered a [4]company, and set all the city on an uproar, and [5]assaulted the house of [b]Jason, and sought to bring them out to the people.

6 And when they found them not, they [1]drew Jason and certain brethren unto the rulers of the city, crying, [a]These that have turned the world upside down are come hither also;

7 Whom Jason hath [1]received: and these all do contrary to the decrees of Caesar, [a]saying that there is another king, *one* Jesus.

8 And they troubled the [1]people and the rulers of the city, when they heard these things.

9 And when they had taken security of Jason, and of the [1]other, they let them go.

10 And [a]the brethren immediately sent away Paul and Silas by night unto Berea: who coming *thither* went into the synagogue of the Jews.

11 These were more [1]noble than those in Thessalonica, in that they received the word with all readiness of mind, and [a]searched the scriptures daily, whether those things were so.

12 Therefore many of them believed; also of honourable women which were Greeks, and of men, not a few.

13 But when the Jews of Thessalonica had knowledge that the word of God was preached of Paul at Berea, they came thither also, and stirred up the [1]people.

14 [a]And then immediately the brethren sent away Paul to go as it were to the sea: but Silas and Timotheus abode there still.

15 And they that conducted Paul brought him unto Athens: and [a]receiving a commandment unto Silas and Timotheus for to come to him with all speed, they departed.

16 Now while Paul waited for them at Athens, [a]his spirit was [1]stirred in him, when he saw the city [2]wholly given to idolatry.

17 Therefore [1]disputed he in the synagogue with the Jews, and with

the [2]devout persons, and in the [3]market daily with them that [4]met with him.

18 Then certain philosophers of the Epicureans, and of the Stoicks, encountered him. And some said, What will this [1]babbler say? other some, He seemeth to be a [2]setter forth of strange gods: because he preached unto them [a]Jesus, and the resurrection.

19 And they took him, and brought him unto [1]Areopagus, saying, May we know what this new doctrine, whereof thou speakest, *is?*

20 For thou bringest certain strange things to our ears: we would know therefore what these things mean.

21 (For all the Athenians and [1]strangers which were there spent their time in nothing else, but either to tell, or to hear some new thing.)

22 Then Paul stood in the midst of [1]Mars' hill, and said, *Ye* men of Athens, I perceive that in all things ye are [2]too superstitious.

23 For as I passed by, and beheld your [1]devotions, I found an altar with this inscription, TO THE UNKNOWN GOD. Whom therefore ye [2]ignorantly worship, him declare I unto you.

24 [a]God that made the world and all things therein, seeing that he is [b]Lord of heaven and earth, [c]dwelleth not in temples made with hands;

25 Neither is worshipped with men's hands, as though he needed any thing, seeing he [a]giveth to all life, and breath, and all things;

26 And hath made of one blood all nations of men for to dwell on all the face of the earth, and hath determined the times before appointed, and [a]the bounds of their habitation;

27 [a]That they should seek the Lord, [1]if haply they might [2]feel after him, and find him, [b]though he be not far from every one of us:

28 For [a]in him we live, and move, and have our being; [b]as certain also of your own poets have said, For we are also his offspring.

29 Forasmuch then as we are the offspring of God, [a]we ought not to think that the [1]Godhead is like unto gold, or silver, or stone, [2]graven by art and man's [3]device.

30 And [a]the times of this ignorance God [1]winked at; but [b]now commandeth all men every where to repent:

31 Because he hath appointed a day, in the which [a]he will judge the world in righteousness by *that* man whom he hath ordained; *whereof* he hath given assurance unto all *men,* in that [b]he hath raised him from the dead.

32 And when they heard of the resurrection of the dead, some mocked:

and others said, We will hear thee again of this *matter.*

33 So Paul departed from among them.

34 Howbeit certain men [1]clave unto him, and believed: among the which *was* Dionysius [2]the Areopagite, and a woman named Damaris, and others with them.

## CHAPTER 18

AFTER these things Paul departed from Athens, and came to Corinth;

2 And found a certain Jew named [a]Aquila, born in Pontus, lately come from Italy, with his wife Priscilla; (because that Claudius had commanded all Jews to depart from Rome:) and came unto them.

3 And because he was of the same [1]craft, he abode with them, [a]and [2]wrought: for by their occupation they were tentmakers.

4 [a]And he reasoned in the synagogue every sabbath, and persuaded the Jews and the Greeks.

5 And [a]when Silas and Timotheus were come from Macedonia, Paul was [b]pressed[1] in the spirit, and testified to the Jews *that* Jesus [2]*was* Christ.

6 And [a]when they opposed [1]themselves, and blasphemed, [b]he shook *his* [2]raiment, and said unto them, [c]Your blood *be* upon your own heads; [d]I *am* clean: [e]from henceforth I will go unto the Gentiles.

7 And he departed thence, and entered into a certain *man's* house, named Justus, *one* that worshipped God, whose house [1]joined hard to the synagogue.

8 [a]And Crispus, the chief ruler of the synagogue, believed on the Lord with all his [1]house; and many of the Corinthians hearing believed, and were baptized.

9 Then [a]spake the Lord to Paul in the night by a vision, Be not afraid, but speak, and [1]hold not thy peace:

10 [a]For I am with thee, and no man shall [1]set on thee to hurt thee: for I have much people in this city.

11 And he continued *there* a year and six months, teaching the word of God among them.

12 And when Gallio was the [1]deputy of Achaia, the Jews [2]made insurrection with one accord against Paul, and brought him to the judgment seat,

13 Saying, This *fellow* persuadeth men to worship God contrary to the law.

14 And when Paul was now about to open *his* mouth, Gallio said unto the Jews, If it were a matter of wrong or wicked [1]lewdness, O *ye* Jews, [2]reason would that I should bear with you:

---

Center column notes:

17:17 [2] Gentile worshippers
[3] marketplace
[4] happened to be there

17:18 [a] 1 Cor. 15:12
[1] Lit. seed-picker, an idler who makes a living picking up scraps
[2] proclaimer

17:19 [1] Lit. the Hill of Ares, or Mars' Hill

17:21 [1] foreigners

17:22 [1] Gr. Areopagus [2] very religious

17:23 [1] objects of worship
[2] worship without knowing

17:24 [a] Acts 14:15
[b] Matt. 11:25
[c] Acts 7:48-50

17:25 [a] Is. 42:5

17:26 [a] Deut. 32:8

17:27 [a] [Rom. 1:20] [b] Jer. 23:23, 24 [1] in the hope that [2] grope for

17:28 [a] [Heb. 1:3]
[b] Titus 1:12

17:29 [a] Is. 40:18, 19 [1] Divine Nature [2] shaped [3] devising

17:30 [a] [Rom. 3:25] [b] [Titus 2:11, 12] [1] overlooked

17:31 [a] Acts 10:42
[b] Acts 2:24

17:34 [1] joined [2] Member of the Athenian Supreme Court

18:2 [a] 1 Cor. 16:19

18:3 [a] Acts 20:34
[1] trade [2] worked

18:4 [a] Acts 17:2

18:5 [a] Acts 17:14, 15 [b] Acts 18:28
[1] compelled by the Spirit [2] is the Christ

18:6 [a] Acts 13:45 [b] Neh. 5:13 [c] 2 Sam. 1:16
[d] [Ezek. 3:18, 19]
[e] Acts 13:46-48; 28:28 [1] Or him [2] garments

18:7 [1] was next door to

18:8 [a] 1 Cor. 1:14
[1] household

18:9 [a] Acts 23:11
[1] do not keep silent

18:10 [a] Jer. 1:18, 19
[1] attack

18:12 [1] proconsul [2] rose up

18:14 [1] crimes [2] there would be reason why

15 But if it be a ªquestion of words and names, and *of* your law, look ye *to it;* for I will be no judge of such *matters.*

16 And he drave them from the judgment seat.

17 Then all the Greeks took ªSosthenes, the chief ruler of the synagogue, and beat *him* before the judgment seat. And Gallio ¹cared for none of those things.

18 And Paul *after this* ¹tarried *there* yet a good while, and then took his leave of the brethren, and sailed thence into Syria, and with him Priscilla and Aquila; having ªshorn² *his* head in ᵇCenchrea: for he had a vow.

19 And he came to Ephesus, and left them there: but he himself entered into the synagogue, and reasoned with the Jews.

20 When they ¹desired *him* to ²tarry longer time with them, he consented not;

21 But bade them farewell, saying, ªI must by all means keep this feast that cometh in Jerusalem: but I will return again unto you, ᵇif God will. And he sailed from Ephesus.

22 And when he had landed at ªCaesarea, and ¹gone up, and ²saluted the church, he went down to Antioch.

23 And after he had spent some time *there,* he departed, and went over *all* the country of ªGalatia and Phrygia in order, ᵇstrengthening all the disciples.

24 ªAnd a certain Jew named Apollos, born at Alexandria, an eloquent man, *and* mighty in the scriptures, came to Ephesus.

25 This man was instructed in the way of the Lord; and being ªfervent in the spirit, he spake and taught ¹diligently the things of the Lord, ᵇknowing only the baptism of John.

26 And he began to speak boldly in the synagogue: whom when Aquila and Priscilla had heard, they took him unto *them,* and ¹expounded unto him the way of God more ²perfectly.

27 And when he was disposed to pass into Achaia, the brethren wrote, exhorting the disciples to receive him: who, when he was come, ªhelped them much which had believed through grace:

28 For he mightily ¹convinced the Jews, *and that* publickly, ªshewing by the scriptures that Jesus was Christ.

**CHAPTER 19**

AND it came to pass, that, while ªApollos was at Corinth, Paul having passed through the ᵇupper ¹coasts came to Ephesus: and finding certain disciples,

2 He said unto them, ¹Have ye received the Holy Ghost ²since ye believed? And they said unto him, ªWe

18:15 ª Acts 23:29; 25:19
18:17 ª 1 Cor. 1:1
¹ took no notice
18:18 ª Acts 21:24  ᵇ Rom. 16:1
¹ remained  ² had his hair cut off
18:20 ¹ asked  ² stay a
18:21 ª Acts 19:21; 20:16  ᵇ 1 Cor. 4:19
18:22 ª Acts 8:40
¹ To Jerusalem  ² greeted
18:23 ª Gal. 1:2  ᵇ Acts 14:22; 15:32, 41
18:24 ª Titus 3:1
18:25 ª Rom. 12:11  ᵇ Acts 19:3
¹ accurately
18:26 ¹ explained  ² accurately
18:27 ª 1 Cor. 3:6
18:28 ª Acts 9:22; 17:3; 18:5  ¹ refuted
19:1 ª 1 Cor. 1:12; 3:5, 6  ᵇ Acts 18:23  ¹ regions
19:2 ª 1 Sam. 3:7  ¹ Did you receive  ² when

19:3 ª Acts 18:25
19:4 ª Matt. 3:11
19:5 ª Acts 8:12, 16; 10:48
19:6 ª Acts 6:6; 8:17  ᵇ Acts 2:4; 10:46
19:8 ª Acts 17:2; 18:4  ᵇ Acts 1:3; 28:23  ¹ reasoning
19:9 ª 2 Tim. 1:15  ᵇ Acts 9:2; 19:23; 22:4; 24:14  ¹ some  ² the Way  ³ withdrew  ⁴ reasoning
19:10 ª Acts 19:8; 20:31
19:11 ª Mark 16:20  ¹ unusual
19:12 ª Acts 5:15
19:13 ª Matt. 12:27  ᵇ Mark 9:38  ᶜ 1 Cor. 1:23; 2:2  ¹ itinerant Jewish exorcists  ² Solemnly command
19:17 ª Luke 1:65; 7:16
19:18 ª Matt. 3:6
19:19 ¹ practised magic

have not so much as heard whether there be any Holy Ghost.

3 And he said unto them, Unto what then were ye baptized? And they said, ªUnto John's baptism.

4 Then said Paul, ªJohn verily baptized with the baptism of repentance, saying unto the people, that they should believe on him which should come after him, that is, on Christ Jesus.

5 When they heard *this,* they were baptized ªin the name of the Lord Jesus.

6 And when Paul had ªlaid *his* hands upon them, the Holy Ghost came on them; and ᵇthey spake with tongues, and prophesied.

7 And all the men were about twelve.

8 ªAnd he went into the synagogue, and spake boldly for the space of three months, ¹disputing and persuading the things ᵇconcerning the kingdom of God.

9 But ªwhen ¹divers were hardened, and believed not, but spake evil ᵇof ²that way before the multitude, he departed from them, and ³separated the disciples, ⁴disputing daily in the school of one Tyrannus.

10 And ªthis continued by the space of two years; so that all they which dwelt in Asia heard the word of the Lord Jesus, both Jews and Greeks.

11 And ªGod wrought ¹special miracles by the hands of Paul:

12 ªSo that from his body were brought unto the sick handkerchiefs or aprons, and the diseases departed from them, and the evil spirits went out of them.

13 ªThen certain of the ¹vagabond Jews, exorcists, ᵇtook upon them to call over them which had evil spirits the name of the Lord Jesus, saying, We ²adjure you by Jesus whom Paul ᶜpreacheth.

14 And there were seven sons of *one* Sceva, a Jew, *and* chief of the priests, which did so.

15 And the evil spirit answered and said, Jesus I know, and Paul I know; but who are ye?

16 And the man in whom the evil spirit was leaped on them, and overcame them, and prevailed against them, so that they fled out of that house naked and wounded.

17 And this was known to all the Jews and Greeks also dwelling at Ephesus; and ªfear fell on them all, and the name of the Lord Jesus was magnified.

18 And many that believed came, and ªconfessed, and shewed their deeds.

19 Many of them also which ¹used curious arts brought their books together, and burned them before all

*men:* and they counted the price of them, and found *it* fifty thousand *pieces* of silver.

20 <sup>a</sup>So mightily grew the word of God and prevailed.

21 <sup>a</sup>After these things were <sup>1</sup>ended, Paul <sup>b</sup>purposed in the spirit, when he had passed through <sup>c</sup>Macedonia and Achaia, to go to Jerusalem, saying, After I have been there, <sup>d</sup>I must also see Rome.

22 So he sent into Macedonia two of them that ministered unto him, <sup>a</sup>Timotheus and <sup>b</sup>Erastus; but he himself stayed in Asia for a <sup>1</sup>season.

23 And <sup>a</sup>the same time there arose no small stir about <sup>b</sup>that<sup>1</sup> way.

24 For a certain *man* named Demetrius, a silversmith, which made silver shrines <sup>1</sup>for <sup>2</sup>Diana, brought <sup>a</sup>no small <sup>3</sup>gain unto the craftsmen;

25 Whom he called together with the workmen of <sup>1</sup>like occupation, and said, Sirs, ye know that by this <sup>2</sup>craft we have our wealth.

26 Moreover ye see and hear, that not alone at Ephesus, but almost throughout all Asia, this Paul hath persuaded and turned away much people, saying that <sup>a</sup>they <sup>1</sup>be no gods, which are made with hands:

27 So that not only this our craft is in danger <sup>1</sup>to be set at nought; but also that the temple of the great goddess Diana <sup>2</sup>should be despised, and her magnificence should be destroyed, whom all Asia and the world worshippeth.

28 And when they heard *these sayings,* they were full of wrath, and cried out, saying, Great *is* Diana of the Ephesians.

29 And the whole city was filled with confusion: and having <sup>1</sup>caught <sup>a</sup>Gaius and <sup>b</sup>Aristarchus, men of Macedonia, Paul's companions in travel, they rushed with one accord into the theatre.

30 And when Paul would have entered in unto the people, the disciples <sup>1</sup>suffered him not.

31 And certain of the <sup>1</sup>chief of Asia, which were his friends, sent unto him, <sup>2</sup>desiring *him* that he would not <sup>3</sup>adventure himself into the theatre.

32 Some therefore cried one thing, and some another: for the assembly was confused; and the <sup>1</sup>more part knew not wherefore they were come together.

33 And they drew Alexander out of the multitude, the Jews putting him forward. And <sup>a</sup>Alexander <sup>b</sup>beckoned with the hand, and <sup>1</sup>would have made his defence unto the people.

34 But when they knew that he was a Jew, all with one voice about the space of two hours cried out, Great *is* Diana of the Ephesians.

35 And when the townclerk had <sup>1</sup>appeased the people, he said, *Ye* men of Ephesus, what man is there that knoweth not how that the city of the Ephesians is <sup>2</sup>a worshipper of the great goddess Diana, and of the *image* which fell down from <sup>3</sup>Jupiter?

36 Seeing then that these things cannot be spoken against, ye ought to be quiet, and to do nothing rashly.

37 For ye have brought hither these men, which are neither robbers of <sup>1</sup>churches, nor yet blasphemers of your goddess.

38 Wherefore if Demetrius, and the craftsmen which are with him, have a matter against any man, the <sup>1</sup>law is open, and there are <sup>2</sup>deputies: let them <sup>3</sup>implead one another.

39 But if ye enquire any thing concerning other matters, it shall be determined in a lawful assembly.

40 For we are in danger to be called in question for this day's uproar, there being no cause whereby we may give an account of this <sup>1</sup>concourse.

41 And when he had thus spoken, he dismissed the assembly.

## CHAPTER 20

AND after the uproar was ceased, Paul called unto *him* the disciples, and embraced *them,* and <sup>a</sup>departed for to go into Macedonia.

2 And when he had gone over those parts, and had given them much <sup>1</sup>exhortation, he came into <sup>a</sup>Greece,

3 And *there* <sup>1</sup>abode three months. And <sup>a</sup>when the Jews <sup>2</sup>laid wait for him, as he was about to sail into Syria, he purposed to return through Macedonia.

4 And there accompanied him into Asia Sopater of Berea; and of the Thessalonians, <sup>a</sup>Aristarchus and Secundus; and <sup>b</sup>Gaius of Derbe, and <sup>c</sup>Timotheus; and of Asia, <sup>d</sup>Tychicus and <sup>e</sup>Trophimus.

5 These <sup>1</sup>going before <sup>2</sup>tarried for us at <sup>a</sup>Troas.

6 And we sailed away from Philippi after <sup>a</sup>the days of unleavened bread, and came unto them <sup>b</sup>to Troas in five days; where we <sup>1</sup>abode seven days.

7 And upon <sup>a</sup>the first *day* of the week, when the disciples came together <sup>b</sup>to break bread, Paul <sup>1</sup>preached unto them, ready to depart <sup>2</sup>on the morrow; and continued his <sup>3</sup>speech until midnight.

8 And there were many lights <sup>a</sup>in the upper chamber, where they were gathered together.

9 And there sat in a window a certain young man named Eutychus, being fallen into a deep sleep: and as Paul <sup>1</sup>was long preaching, he sunk down with sleep, and fell down from the third <sup>2</sup>loft, and was taken up dead.

### Center reference column

19:20 <sup>a</sup> Acts 6:7; 12:24
19:21 <sup>a</sup> Rom. 15:25 <sup>b</sup> Acts 20:22 <sup>c</sup> Acts 20:1 <sup>d</sup> Rom. 1:13; 15:22–29 <sup>1</sup> accomplished
19:22 <sup>a</sup> 1 Tim. 1:2 <sup>b</sup> Rom. 16:23 <sup>1</sup> time
19:23 <sup>a</sup> 2 Cor. 1:8 <sup>b</sup> Acts 9:2 <sup>1</sup> the Way
19:24 <sup>a</sup> Acts 16:16, 19 <sup>1</sup> of <sup>2</sup> Gr. Artemis <sup>3</sup> profit
19:25 <sup>1</sup> similar <sup>2</sup> trade
19:26 <sup>a</sup> Is. 44:10–20 <sup>1</sup> are not
19:27 <sup>1</sup> of falling into disrepute <sup>2</sup> may
19:29 <sup>a</sup> Rom. 16:23 <sup>b</sup> Col. 4:10 <sup>1</sup> seized
19:30 <sup>1</sup> allowed
19:31 <sup>1</sup> officials <sup>2</sup> pleading <sup>3</sup> venture
19:32 <sup>1</sup> majority
19:33 <sup>a</sup> 1 Tim. 1:20; 2 Tim. 4:14 <sup>b</sup> Acts 12:17 <sup>1</sup> wanted to make
19:35 <sup>1</sup> quieted <sup>2</sup> temple guardian <sup>3</sup> heaven
19:37 <sup>1</sup> temples
19:38 <sup>1</sup> courts are <sup>2</sup> proconsuls <sup>3</sup> bring charges against
19:40 <sup>1</sup> disorderly gathering
20:1 <sup>a</sup> 1 Cor. 16:5; 1 Tim. 1:3
20:2 <sup>a</sup> Acts 17:15; 18:1 <sup>1</sup> encouragement
20:3 <sup>a</sup> Acts 9:23; 23:12; 25:3; 2 Cor. 11:26 <sup>1</sup> stayed <sup>2</sup> plotted against
20:4 <sup>a</sup> Acts 19:29; Col. 4:10 <sup>b</sup> Acts 19:29 <sup>c</sup> Acts 16:1 <sup>d</sup> Eph. 6:21; Col. 4:7; 2 Tim. 4:12; Titus 3:12 <sup>e</sup> Acts 21:29; 2 Tim. 4:20
20:5 <sup>a</sup> 2 Cor. 2:12; 2 Tim. 4:13 <sup>1</sup> having gone ahead <sup>2</sup> waited
20:6 <sup>a</sup> Ex. 12:14, 15 <sup>b</sup> Acts 16:8; 2 Cor. 2:12; 2 Tim. 4:13 <sup>1</sup> stayed
20:7 <sup>a</sup> 1 Cor. 16:2; Rev. 1:10 <sup>b</sup> Acts 2:42, 46; 20:11; 1 Cor. 10:16 <sup>1</sup> spoke <sup>2</sup> the next day <sup>3</sup> message
20:8 <sup>a</sup> Acts 1:13
20:9 <sup>1</sup> continued speaking <sup>2</sup> story

10 And Paul went down, and [a]fell on him, and embracing *him* said, [b]Trouble not yourselves; for his life is in him.

11 When he therefore was come up again, and had broken bread, and eaten, and talked a long while, even till break of day, so he departed.

12 And they brought the young man alive, and were not a little comforted.

13 And we went [1]before to ship, and sailed unto Assos, there intending to take [2]in Paul: for so had he [3]appointed, [4]minding himself to go afoot.

14 And when he met with us at Assos, we took him in, and came to Mitylene.

15 And we sailed thence, and came the next *day* over against Chios; and the next *day* we arrived at Samos, and tarried at Trogyllium; and the next *day* we came to Miletus.

16 For Paul had determined to sail by Ephesus, because he would not spend the time in Asia: for [a]he [1]hasted, if it were possible for him, [b]to be at Jerusalem [c]the day of Pentecost.

17 And from Miletus he sent to Ephesus, and called the elders of the church.

18 And when they were come to him, he said unto them, Ye know, [a]from the first day that I came into Asia, after what manner I have been with you at all [1]seasons,

19 Serving the Lord with all humility of mind, and with many tears, and [1]temptations, which befell me [a]by the [2]lying in wait of the Jews:

20 *And* how [a]I kept back nothing that was profitable *unto you,* but have shewed you, and have taught you publickly, and from house to house,

21 [a]Testifying both to the Jews, and also to the Greeks, [b]repentance toward God, and faith toward our Lord Jesus Christ.

22 And now, behold, [a]I go bound in the spirit unto Jerusalem, not knowing the things that shall befall me there:

23 [1]Save that [a]the Holy Ghost witnesseth in every city, saying that [2]bonds and afflictions [3]abide me.

24 But [a]none of these things move me, neither count I my life dear unto myself, [b]so that I might finish my course with joy, [c]and the ministry, [d]which I have received of the Lord Jesus, to testify the gospel of the grace of God.

25 And now, behold, I know that ye all, among whom I have gone preaching the kingdom of God, shall see my face no more.

26 Wherefore I [1]take you to record this day, that I *am* [a]pure[2] from the blood of all *men.*

27 For I have not shunned to declare unto you all [a]the counsel of God.

28 [a]Take heed therefore unto yourselves, and to all the flock, over the which the Holy Ghost [b]hath made you overseers, to [1]feed the church of God, [c]which he hath purchased [d]with his own blood.

29 For I know this, that after my departing [a]shall [1]grievous wolves enter in among you, not sparing the flock.

30 Also [a]of your own selves shall men arise, speaking perverse things, to draw away disciples after them.

31 Therefore watch, and remember, that [a]by the space of three years I ceased not to warn every one night and day with tears.

32 And now, brethren, I commend you to God, and [a]to the word of his grace, which is able [b]to build you up, and to give you [c]an inheritance among all them which are sanctified.

33 I have coveted no man's silver, or gold, or apparel.

34 Yea, ye yourselves know, [a]that these hands have [1]ministered unto my necessities, and to them that were with me.

35 I have shewed you all things, [a]how that so labouring ye ought to support the weak, and to remember the words of the Lord Jesus, how he said, It is more blessed to give than to receive.

36 And when he had thus spoken, he kneeled down, and prayed with them all.

37 And they all [a]wept [1]sore, and [b]fell on Paul's neck, and kissed him,

38 Sorrowing most of all for the words which he spake, that they should see his face no more. And they accompanied him unto the ship.

## CHAPTER 21

AND it came to pass, that after we [1]were gotten from them, and had [2]launched, we came with a straight course unto [3]Coos, and the *day* following unto Rhodes, and from thence unto Patara:

2 And finding a ship sailing over unto Phenicia, we went aboard, and set [1]forth.

3 Now when we had [1]discovered Cyprus, we [2]left it on the left hand, and sailed into Syria, and landed at Tyre: for there the ship was to [3]unlade her [4]burden.

4 And finding disciples, we [1]tarried there seven days: [a]who said to Paul through the Spirit, that he should not go up to Jerusalem.

5 And when we had [1]accomplished those days, we departed and went

### Center column references

20:10 [a] 1 Kin. 17:21; 2 Kin. 4:34 [b] Matt. 9:23, 24; Mark 5:39

20:13 [1] *ahead to the* [2] *on board* [3] *ordered* [4] *intending*

20:16 [a] Acts 18:21; 19:21; 21:4 [b] Acts 24:17 [c] Acts 2:1; 1 Cor. 16:8 [1] *was hurrying*

20:18 [a] Acts 18:19; 19:1, 10; 20:4, 16 [1] *times*

20:19 [a] Acts 20:3 [1] *trials* [2] *plotting*

20:20 [a] Acts 20:27

20:21 [a] Acts 18:5; 19:10 [b] Mark 1:15

20:22 [a] Acts 19:21

20:23 [a] Acts 21:4, 11 [1] *Except* [2] *chains* [3] *await*

20:24 [a] Acts 21:13 [b] 2 Tim. 4:7 [c] Acts 1:17 [d] Gal. 1:1

20:26 [a] Acts 18:6 [1] *testify to you* [2] *innocent*

20:27 [a] Luke 7:30

20:28 [a] 1 Pet. 5:2 [b] 1 Cor. 12:28 [c] Eph. 1:7, 14 [d] Heb. 9:14 [1] *shepherd*

20:29 [a] Matt. 7:15 [1] *savage*

20:30 [a] 1 Tim. 1:20

20:31 [a] Acts 19:8, 10; 24:17

20:32 [a] Heb. 13:9 [b] Acts 9:31 [c] [Heb. 9:15]

20:34 [a] Acts 18:3 [1] *provided for*

20:35 [a] Rom. 15:1

20:37 [a] Acts 21:13 [b] Gen. 45:14 [1] *freely*

21:1 [1] *had departed* [2] *set sail* [3] *Or Cos*

21:2 [1] *sail*

21:3 [1] *sighted* [2] *passed* [3] *unload* [4] *cargo*

21:4 [a] [Acts 20:23; 21:12] [1] *stayed*

21:5 [1] *come to the end of*

our way; and they all ²brought us on
our way, with wives and children,
till *we were* out of the city: and ªwe
kneeled down on the shore, and
prayed.

6 And when we had taken our leave
one of another, we took ship; and
they returned ªhome again.

7 And when we had finished *our*
¹course from Tyre, we came to Ptole-
mais, and ²saluted the brethren, and
³abode with them one day.

8 And the next *day* we that were of
Paul's ¹company departed, and came
unto ªCaesarea: and we entered into
the house of Philip ᵇthe evangelist,
ᶜwhich was *one* of the seven; and
abode with him.

9 And the same man had four
daughters, virgins, ªwhich did prophesy.

10 And as we ¹tarried *there* many
days, there came down from Judaea
a certain prophet, named ªAgabus.

11 And when he was come unto us,
he took Paul's ¹girdle, and bound his
own hands and feet, and said, Thus
saith the Holy Ghost, ªSo shall the
Jews at Jerusalem bind the man that
owneth this ¹girdle, and shall deliver
*him* into the hands of the Gentiles.

12 And when we heard these things,
both we, and they of that place, ¹besought him not to go up to Jerusalem.

13 Then Paul answered, ªWhat
mean ye to weep and to break mine
heart? for I am ready not to be bound
only, but also to die at Jerusalem for
the name of the Lord Jesus.

14 And when he would not be persuaded, we ceased, saying, ªThe will
of the Lord be done.

15 And after those days we ¹took up
our carriages, and went up to Jerusalem.

16 There went with us also *certain*
of the disciples of Caesarea, and
brought with them one Mnason of
Cyprus, an ¹old disciple, with whom
we should lodge.

17 ªAnd when we were come to
Jerusalem, the brethren received us
gladly.

18 And the *day* following Paul went
in with us unto ªJames; and all the
elders were present.

19 And when he had ¹saluted them,
ªhe ²declared particularly what
things God had wrought among the
Gentiles ᵇby his ministry.

20 And when they heard *it*, they
glorified the Lord, and said unto him,
Thou seest, brother, how many ¹thousands of Jews there are which believe;
and they are all ªzealous of the law:

21 And they are informed of thee,
that thou teachest all the Jews which
are among the Gentiles to forsake
Moses, saying that they ought not to

21:5 ª Acts 9:40;
20:36 ² accom-
panied
21:6 ª John 1:11
21:7 ¹ voyage
² greeted ³ stayed
21:8 ª Acts 8:40;
21:16 ᵇ Eph.
4:11 ᶜ Acts 6:5
¹ companions
21:9 ª Joel 2:28
21:10 ª Acts 11:28
¹ stayed
21:11 ª Acts 20:23;
21:33; 22:25 ¹ belt
21:12 ¹ begged
21:13 ª Acts
20:24, 37
21:14 ª Luke 11:2;
22:42
21:15 ¹ packed
21:16 ¹ early
21:17 ª Acts 15:4
21:18 ª Gal. 1:19;
2:9
21:19 ª Rom. 15:18,
19 ᵇ Acts 1:17;
20:24 ¹ greeted
² told in detail
21:20 ª Acts 15:1;
22:3 ¹ Lit. myriads

21:22 ¹ certainly
21:24 ª Acts
18:18 ¹ pay their
expenses
21:25 ª Acts
15:19, 20, 29
¹ concerning ² de-
cided ³ sexual
immorality
21:26 ª Acts 21:24;
24:18 ᵇ Num. 6:13
¹ announce the
expiration ² at
which time
21:27 ª Acts 20:19;
24:18 ᵇ Acts 26:21
21:28 ª Acts 6:13;
24:6 ¹ defiled
21:29 ª Acts 20:4
¹ previously
21:30 ª Acts
16:19; 26:21 ¹ dis-
turbed ² seized
³ dragged
21:31 ª 2 Cor.
11:23 ¹ news
² commander
³ cohort
21:32 ª Acts
23:27; 24:7
¹ commander
² stopped
21:33 ª Acts 24:7
ᵇ Acts 20:23; 21:11
¹ asked
21:34 ¹ truth
² because of
³ barracks

circumcise *their* children, neither to
walk after the customs.

22 What is it therefore? the multitude must ¹needs come together: for
they will hear that thou art come.

23 Do therefore this that we say to
thee: We have four men which have a
vow on them;

24 Them take, and purify thyself
with them, and ¹be at charges with
them, that they may ªshave *their*
heads: and all may know that those
things, whereof they were informed
concerning thee, are nothing; but
*that* thou thyself also walkest orderly, and keepest the law.

25 As ¹touching the Gentiles which
believe, ªwe have written *and* ²con-
cluded that they observe no such
thing, save only that they keep themselves from *things* offered to idols,
and from blood, and from strangled,
and from ³fornication.

26 Then Paul took the men, and the
next day purifying himself with them
ªentered into the temple, ᵇto ¹signify
the accomplishment of the days of
purification, ²until that an offering
should be offered for every one of
them.

27 And when the seven days were
almost ended, ªthe Jews which were
of Asia, when they saw him in the
temple, stirred up all the people, and
ᵇlaid hands on him,

28 Crying out, Men of Israel, help:
This is the man, ªthat teacheth all *men*
every where against the people, and
the law, and this place: and further
brought Greeks also into the temple,
and hath ¹polluted this holy place.

29 (For they had seen ¹before with
him in the city ªTrophimus an Ephe-
sian, whom they supposed that Paul
had brought into the temple.)

30 And ªall the city was ¹moved,
and the people ran together: and
they ²took Paul, and ³drew him out of
the temple: and forthwith the doors
were shut.

31 And as they went ªabout to kill
him, ¹tidings came unto the ²chief
captain of the ³band, that all Jerusalem was in an uproar.

32 ªWho immediately took soldiers
and centurions, and ran down unto
them: and when they saw the ¹chief
captain and the soldiers, they ²left
beating of Paul.

33 Then the ªchief captain came
near, and took him, and ᵇcommanded
*him* to be bound with two chains; and
¹demanded who he was, and what he
had done.

34 And some cried one thing, some
another, among the multitude: and
when he could not know the ¹cer-
tainty ²for the tumult, he commanded
him to be carried into the ³castle.

35 And when he ¹came upon the stairs, so it was, that he was ²borne of the soldiers ³for the violence of the ⁴people.

36 For the multitude of the people followed after, crying, ᵃAway with him.

37 And as Paul was to be led into the ¹castle, he said unto the ²chief captain, May I speak unto thee? Who said, Canst thou speak Greek?

38 ᵃArt not thou that Egyptian, which before these days ¹madest an uproar, and leddest out into the wilderness four thousand men that were ²murderers?

39 But Paul said, ᵃI am a man *which am* a Jew of Tarsus, *a city* in Cilicia, a citizen of no ¹mean city: and, I beseech thee, ²suffer me to speak unto the people.

40 And when he had given him ¹licence, Paul stood on the stairs, and ᵃbeckoned with the hand unto the people. And when there was made a great silence, he spake unto *them* in the ᵇHebrew ²tongue, saying,

## CHAPTER 22

MEN, ᵃbrethren, and fathers, hear ye my defence *which I make* now unto you.

2 (And when they heard that he spake in the ᵃHebrew ¹tongue to them, they kept the more silence: and he saith,)

3 ᵃI am verily a man *which am* a Jew, born in Tarsus, *a city* in Cilicia, yet brought up in this city ᵇat the feet of ᶜGamaliel, *and* taught ᵈaccording to the ¹perfect manner of the law of the fathers, and ᵉwas zealous toward God, ᶠas ye all are this day.

4 ᵃAnd I persecuted this ¹way unto the death, binding and delivering into prisons both men and women.

5 As also the high priest doth bear me witness, and ᵃall the ¹estate of the elders: ᵇfrom whom also I received letters unto the brethren, and went to Damascus, ᶜto bring them which were there ²bound unto Jerusalem, for to be punished.

6 And ᵃit came to pass, that, as I made my journey, and was come ¹nigh unto Damascus about noon, suddenly there shone from heaven a great light round about me.

7 And I fell unto the ground, and heard a voice saying unto me, Saul, Saul, why persecutest thou me?

8 And I answered, Who art thou, Lord? And he said unto me, I am Jesus of Nazareth, whom thou persecutest.

9 And ᵃthey that were with me saw indeed the light, and were afraid; but they heard not the voice of him that spake to me.

10 And I said, What shall I do, Lord? And the Lord said unto me, Arise, and go into Damascus; and there it shall be told thee of all things which are appointed for thee to do.

11 And when I could not see for the glory of that light, being led by the hand of them that were with me, I came into Damascus.

12 And ᵃone Ananias, a devout man according to the law, ᵇhaving a good report of all the ᶜJews which dwelt *there,*

13 Came unto me, and stood, and said unto me, Brother Saul, receive thy sight. And the same hour I looked up upon him.

14 And he said, ᵃThe God of our fathers ᵇhath chosen thee, that thou shouldest ᶜknow his will, and ᵈsee that Just One, and ᵉshouldest hear the voice of his mouth.

15 ᵃFor thou shalt be his witness unto all men of ᵇwhat thou hast seen and heard.

16 And now why ¹tarriest thou? arise, and be baptized, ᵃand wash away thy sins, ᵇcalling on the name of the Lord.

17 And ᵃit came to pass, that, when I was come again to Jerusalem, even while I prayed in the temple, I was in a trance;

18 And ᵃsaw him saying unto me, ᵇMake¹ haste, and get thee quickly out of Jerusalem: for they will not receive thy testimony concerning me.

19 And I said, Lord, ᵃthey know that I imprisoned and ᵇbeat in every synagogue them that believed on thee:

20 ᵃAnd when the blood of thy martyr Stephen was shed, I also was standing by, and ᵇconsenting unto his death, and ¹kept the raiment of them that slew him.

21 And he said unto me, Depart: ᵃfor I will send thee far hence unto the Gentiles.

22 And they ¹gave him audience unto this word, and *then* lifted up their voices, and said, ᵃAway with such a *fellow* from the earth: for it is not fit that ᵇhe should live.

23 And as they cried out, and cast off *their* clothes, and threw dust into the air,

24 The ¹chief captain commanded him to be brought into the ²castle, and ³bade that he should be examined by ⁴scourging; that he might know wherefore they cried so against him.

25 And as they bound him with thongs, Paul said unto the centurion that stood by, ᵃIs it lawful for you to ¹scourge a man that is a Roman, and uncondemned?

26 When the centurion heard *that,* he went and told the ¹chief captain,

### Center column references

21:35 ¹ reached
² carried by ³ because of ⁴ mob
21:36 ᵃ John 19:15
21:37 ¹ barracks
² commander
21:38 ᵃ Acts 5:36
¹ raised a revolt
² assassins
21:39 ᵃ Acts 9:11;
22:3 ¹ obscure
² permit
21:40 ᵃ Acts 12:17 ᵇ Acts 22:2
¹ permission
² language
22:1 ᵃ Acts 7:2
22:2 ᵃ Acts 21:40
¹ language
22:3 ᵃ 2 Cor. 11:22 ᵇ Deut. 33:3 ᶜ Acts 5:34 ᵈ Acts 23:6; 26:5 ᵉ Gal. 1:14 ᶠ [Rom. 10:2]
¹ strictness
22:4 ᵃ 1 Tim. 1:13
¹ Way
22:5 ᵃ Acts 23:14; 24:1; 25:15 ᵇ Luke 22:66 ᶜ Acts 9:2 ¹ council ² in chains
22:6 ᵃ Acts 9:3; 26:12, 13 ¹ near
22:9 ᵃ Acts 9:7

22:12 ᵃ Acts 9:17 ᵇ Acts 10:22 ᶜ 1 Tim. 3:7
22:14 ᵃ Acts 3:13; 5:30 ᵇ Acts 9:15; 26:16 ᶜ Acts 3:14; 7:52 ᵈ 1 Cor. 9:1; 15:8 ᵉ Gal. 1:12
22:15 ᵃ Acts 23:11 ᵇ Acts 4:20; 26:16
22:16 ᵃ Heb. 10:22 ᵇ Rom. 10:13 ¹ do you wait
22:17 ᵃ Acts 9:26; 26:20
22:18 ᵃ Acts 22:14 ᵇ Matt. 10:14 ¹ Hurry
22:19 ᵃ Acts 8:3; 22:4 ᵇ Matt. 10:17
22:20 ᵃ Acts 7:54–8:1 ᵇ Luke 11:48 ¹ guarded the clothes
22:21 ᵃ Acts 9:15
22:22 ᵃ Acts 21:36 ᵇ Acts 25:24 ¹ listened to him until
22:24 ¹ commander ordered ² barracks ³ said ⁴ whipping
22:25 ᵃ Acts 16:37 ¹ whip
22:26 ¹ commander

saying, Take heed what thou doest: for this man is a Roman.

27 Then the [1]chief captain came, and said unto him, Tell me, art thou a Roman? He said, Yea.

28 And the chief captain answered, With a great sum obtained I this freedom. And Paul said, But I was [1]*free* born.

29 Then straightway they departed from him which [1]should have examined him: and the [2]chief captain also was afraid, after he knew that he was a Roman, and because he had bound him.

30 On the morrow, because he [1]would have known the certainty [2]wherefore he was accused of the Jews, he loosed him from *his* [3]bands, and commanded the chief priests and all their council to appear, and brought Paul down, and set him before them.

## CHAPTER 23

AND Paul, earnestly beholding the council, said, Men *and* brethren, [a]I have lived in all good conscience before God until this day.

2 And the high priest Ananias commanded them that stood by him [a]to [1]smite him on the mouth.

3 Then said Paul unto him, God shall smite thee, *thou* [1]whited wall: for sittest thou to judge me [2]after the law, and [a]commandest me to be smitten contrary to the law?

4 And they that stood by said, [1]Revilest thou God's high priest?

5 Then said Paul, [a]I [1]wist not, brethren, that he was the high priest: for it is written, [b]Thou shalt not speak evil of the ruler of thy people.

6 But when Paul perceived that the one part were Sadducees, and the other Pharisees, he cried out in the council, Men *and* brethren, [a]I am a Pharisee, the son of a Pharisee: [b]of[1] the hope and resurrection of the dead I am [2]called in question.

7 And when he had so said, there arose a dissension between the Pharisees and the Sadducees: and the multitude was divided.

8 [a]For the Sadducees say that there is no resurrection, neither angel, nor spirit: but the Pharisees confess both.

9 And there arose a great cry: and the scribes *that were* of the Pharisees' part arose, and [1]strove, saying, [a]We find no evil in this man: but [b]if a spirit or an angel hath spoken to him, [c]let us not fight against God.

10 And when there arose a great dissension, the [1]chief captain, fearing lest Paul should have been pulled in pieces of them, commanded the soldiers to go down, and to take him by

force from among them, and to bring *him* into the [2]castle.

11 And [a]the night following the Lord stood by him, and said, Be of good cheer, Paul: for as thou hast testified of me in [b]Jerusalem, so must thou bear witness also at [c]Rome.

12 And when it was day, [a]certain of the Jews banded together, and bound themselves under [1]a curse, saying that they would neither eat nor drink till they had [b]killed Paul.

13 And they were more than forty which had [1]made this conspiracy.

14 And they came to the chief priests and [a]elders, and said, We have bound ourselves under a great [1]curse, that we will eat nothing until we have slain Paul.

15 Now therefore ye with the council [1]signify to the [2]chief captain that he bring him down unto you to morrow, as though ye would enquire something [3]more perfectly concerning him: and we, [4]or ever he come near, are ready to slay him.

16 And when Paul's sister's son heard of their [1]lying in wait, he went and entered into the [2]castle, and told Paul.

17 Then Paul called one of the centurions unto *him,* and said, Bring this young man unto the [1]chief captain: for he hath a certain thing to tell him.

18 So he took him, and brought *him* to the chief captain, and said, Paul the prisoner called me unto *him,* and [1]prayed me to bring this young man unto thee, who hath something to say unto thee.

19 Then the chief captain took him by the hand, and went *with him* aside privately, and asked *him,* What is that thou hast to tell me?

20 And he said, [a]The Jews have agreed to [1]desire thee that thou wouldest bring down Paul to morrow into the council, as though they would enquire somewhat of him more [2]perfectly.

21 But do not thou yield unto them: for there lie in wait for him of them more than forty men, which have bound themselves with an oath, that they will neither eat nor drink till they have killed him: and now are they ready, looking for a promise from thee.

22 So the chief captain *then* let the young man depart, and charged *him,* See thou tell no man that thou hast [1]shewed these things to me.

23 And he called unto *him* two centurions, saying, Make ready two hundred soldiers to go to [a]Caesarea, and horsemen [1]threescore and ten, and spearmen two hundred, at [2]the third hour of the night;

---

*Center column references:*

22:27 [1] commander

22:28 [1] born a citizen

22:29 [1] were about to examine [2] commander

22:30 [1] wanted to know for sure [2] why [3] bonds

23:1 [a] 2 Tim. 1:3

23:2 [a] John 18:22 [1] strike

23:3 [a] Lev. 19:35; Deut. 25:1, 2; John 7:51 [1] whitewashed [2] according to

23:4 [1] Do you revile

23:5 [a] Lev. 5:17, 18 [b] Ex. 22:28; Eccl. 10:20; 2 Pet. 2:10 [1] knew

23:6 [a] Acts 26:5; Phil. 3:5 [b] Acts 24:15, 21; 26:6; 28:20 [1] concerning [2] being judged

23:8 [a] Matt. 22:23; Mark 12:18; Luke 20:27

23:9 [a] Acts 25:25; 26:31 [b] John 12:29; Acts 22:6, 7, 17, 18 [c] Acts 5:39 [1] protested

23:10 [1] commander

23:11 [a] Acts 18:9; 27:23, 24 [b] Acts 21:18, 19; 22:1–21 [c] Acts 28:16, 17, 23

23:12 [a] Acts 23:21, 30; 25:3 [b] Acts 9:23, 24; 25:3; 26:21; 27:42; 1 Thess. 2:15 [1] an oath

23:13 [1] formed

23:14 [a] Acts 4:5, 23; 6:12; 22:5; 24:1; 25:15 [1] oath

23:15 [1] suggest [2] commander [3] further [4] before he comes

23:16 [1] ambush [2] barracks

23:17 [1] commander

23:18 [1] asked

23:20 [a] Acts 23:12 [1] ask [2] fully

23:22 [1] revealed

23:23 [a] Acts 8:40; 23:33 [1] seventy [2] 9:00 P.M.

24 And provide *them* [1]beasts, that they may set Paul on, and bring *him* safe unto Felix the governor.

25 And he wrote a letter after this manner:

26 Claudius Lysias unto the most excellent governor Felix *sendeth* greeting.

27 [a]This man was [1]taken of the Jews, and [2]should have been killed of them: then came I with [3]an army, and rescued him, having understood that he was a Roman.

28 [a]And when I [1]would have known the cause wherefore they accused him, I brought him forth into their council:

29 Whom I perceived to be accused [a]of questions of their law, [b]but to have nothing laid to his charge worthy of death or of [1]bonds.

30 And [a]when it was told me how that the Jews laid wait for the man, I sent straightway to thee, and [b]gave commandment to his accusers also to say before thee what *they had* against him. Farewell.

31 Then the soldiers, as it was commanded them, took Paul, and brought *him* by night to Antipatris.

32 On the morrow they left the horsemen to go with him, and returned to the [1]castle:

33 Who, when they came to [a]Caesarea, and delivered the [b]epistle to the governor, presented Paul also before him.

34 And when the governor had read *the letter,* he asked of what province he was. And when he understood that *he was* of [a]Cilicia;

35 [a]I will hear thee, said he, when thine accusers are also come. And he commanded him to be kept in [b]Herod's [1]judgment hall.

## CHAPTER 24

AND after [a]five days [b]Ananias the high priest [1]descended with the elders, and *with* a certain orator *named* Tertullus, who [2]informed the governor against Paul.

2 And when he was called forth, Tertullus began to accuse *him,* saying, Seeing that by thee we enjoy great [1]quietness, and [2]that very worthy deeds are done unto this nation by thy [3]providence,

3 We accept *it* always, and in all places, most noble Felix, with all thankfulness.

4 Notwithstanding, that I be not further tedious unto thee, I pray thee that thou wouldest hear us [1]of thy clemency a few words.

5 [a]For we have found this man *a* [1]pestilent *fellow,* and a [2]mover of sedition among all the Jews throughout the world, and a ringleader of the sect of the Nazarenes:

23:24 [1] *mounts*
23:27 [a] Acts 21:30, 33; 24:7 [1] *seized by* [2] *was about to be* [3] *the troops*
23:28 [a] Acts 22:30 [1] *wanted to know*
23:29 [a] Acts 18:15; 25:19 [b] Acts 25:25; 26:31 [1] *chains*
23:30 [a] Acts 23:20 [b] Acts 24:8; 25:6
23:32 [1] *barracks*
23:33 [a] Acts 8:40 [b] Acts 23:26–30
23:34 [a] Acts 6:9; 21:39
23:35 [a] Acts 24:1, 10; 25:16 [b] Matt. 27:27 [1] Gr. *praetorion*
24:1 [a] Acts 21:27 [b] Acts 23:2, 30, 35; 25:2 [1] *came down* [2] *gave evidence to*
24:2 [1] *peace* [2] *prosperity is being brought* [3] *foresight*
24:4 [1] *by your courtesy*
24:5 [a] 1 Pet. 2:12, 15 [1] *plague* [2] *creator of dissension*
24:6 [a] Acts 21:28 [b] John 18:31 [1] *seized*
24:7 [a] Acts 21:33; 23:10 [1] *commander*
24:8 [a] Acts 23:30 [1] *him yourself you may ascertain all these*
24:10 [1] *nodded*
24:11 [a] Acts 21:15, 18, 26, 27; 24:17 [1] *no more than*
24:12 [a] Acts 25:8; 28:17 [1] *inciting the crowd*
24:14 [a] Acts 9:2; 24:22 [b] 2 Tim. 1:3 [c] Acts 26:22; 28:23 [1] *according to the Way*
24:15 [a] Acts 23:6; 26:6, 7; 28:20 [b] [Dan. 12:2] [1] *accept*
24:16 [a] Acts 23:1 [1] *this being so, I myself strive* [2] *without*
24:17 [a] Rom. 15:25–28
24:18 [a] Acts 21:27; 26:21 [b] Acts 21:26
24:19 [a] [Acts 23:30; 25:16] [1] *anything*
24:21 [a] [Acts 23:6; 24:15; 28:20] [1] *statement* [2] *Concerning*

6 [a]Who also hath gone about to profane the temple: whom we [1]took, and would [b]have judged according to our law.

7 [a]But the [1]chief captain Lysias came *upon us,* and with great violence took *him* away out of our hands,

8 [a]Commanding his accusers to come unto thee: by examining [1]of whom thyself mayest take knowledge of all these things, whereof we accuse him.

9 And the Jews also assented, saying that these things were so.

10 Then Paul, after that the governor had [1]beckoned unto him to speak, answered, Forasmuch as I know that thou hast been of many years a judge unto this nation, I do the more cheerfully answer for myself:

11 Because that thou mayest understand, that there are [1]yet but twelve days since I went up to Jerusalem [a]for to worship.

12 [a]And they neither found me in the temple disputing with any man, neither [1]raising up the people, neither in the synagogues, nor in the city:

13 Neither can they prove the things whereof they now accuse me.

14 But this I confess unto thee, that [1]after [a]the way which they call heresy, so worship I the [b]God of my fathers, believing all things which are written in [c]the law and in the prophets:

15 And [a]have hope toward God, which they themselves also [1]allow, [b]that there shall be a resurrection of the dead, both of the just and unjust.

16 And [a]herein[1] do I exercise myself, to have always a conscience [2]void of offence toward God, and *toward* men.

17 Now after many years [a]I came to bring alms to my nation, and offerings.

18 [a]Whereupon certain Jews from Asia found me [b]purified in the temple, neither with multitude, nor with tumult.

19 [a]Who ought to have been here before thee, and object, if they had [1]ought against me.

20 Or else let these same *here* say, if they have found any evil doing in me, while I stood before the council,

21 Except it be for this one [1]voice, that I cried standing among them, [a]Touching[2] the resurrection of the dead I am [3]called in question by you this day.

22 And when Felix heard these things, having more [1]perfect knowledge of [2]*that* way, he [3]deferred them, and said, When [b]Lysias the chief captain shall come down, I will [4]know the uttermost of your matter.

[3] *being judged*   24:22 [a] Acts 9:2; 18:26; 19:9, 23; 22:4 [b] Acts 23:26; 24:7 [1] *accurate* [2] *the Way* [3] *adjourned the proceedings* [4] *make a decision on*

23 And he commanded a centurion to keep Paul, and to let *him* have liberty, and [a]that he should forbid none of his acquaintance to [1]minister or come unto him.

24 And after certain days, when Felix came with his wife Drusilla, which was a Jewess, he sent for Paul, and heard him concerning the [a]faith in Christ.

25 And as he reasoned [1]of righteousness, [2]temperance, and judgment to come, Felix [3]trembled, and answered, Go thy way for this time; when I have a convenient [4]season, I will call for thee.

26 He hoped also that [a]money should have been given him of Paul, that he might loose him: wherefore he sent for him the oftener, and communed with him.

27 But after two years Porcius Festus [1]came into Felix' room: and Felix, [a]willing [2]to shew the Jews a [3]pleasure, left Paul bound.

## CHAPTER 25

Now when Festus was come into the province, after three days he [1]ascended from [a]Caesarea to Jerusalem.

2 [a]Then the high priest and the chief of the Jews informed him against Paul, and [1]besought him,

3 And [1]desired favour against him, that he would send for him to Jerusalem, [a]laying[2] wait in the way to kill him.

4 But Festus answered, that Paul should be kept at Caesarea, and that he himself would depart shortly *thither.*

5 Let them therefore, said he, which among you [1]are able, go down with *me,* and accuse this man, [a]if there be any wickedness in him.

6 And when he had [1]tarried among them more than ten days, he went down unto Caesarea; and the next day sitting on the judgment seat commanded Paul to be brought.

7 And when he was come, the Jews which came down from Jerusalem stood round about, [a]and laid many and [1]grievous complaints against Paul, which they could not prove.

8 While he answered for himself, [a]Neither against the law of the Jews, neither against the temple, nor yet against Caesar, have I offended any thing at all.

9 But Festus, [a]willing to do the Jews a pleasure, answered Paul, and said, [b]Wilt thou go up to Jerusalem, and there be judged of these things before me?

10 Then said Paul, I stand at Caesar's judgment seat, where I ought to be judged: to the Jews have I done no wrong, as thou very well knowest.

11 [a]For if I be an offender, or have committed any thing worthy of death, I [1]refuse not to die: but if there be none of these things whereof these accuse me, no man may deliver me unto them. [b]I appeal unto Caesar.

12 Then Festus, when he had conferred with the council, answered, Hast thou appealed unto Caesar? unto Caesar shalt thou go.

13 And after certain days king Agrippa and Bernice came unto Caesarea to [1]salute Festus.

14 And when they had been there many days, Festus declared Paul's cause unto the king, saying, [a]There is a certain man left [1]in bonds by Felix:

15 [a]About whom, when I was at Jerusalem, the chief priests and the elders of the Jews informed *me,* [1]desiring *to have* judgment against him.

16 [a]To whom I answered, It is not the [1]manner of the Romans to deliver any man to die, before that he which is accused have the accusers face to face, and [2]have licence to answer for himself concerning the crime laid against him.

17 Therefore, when they were come hither, [a]without any delay [1]on the morrow I sat on the judgment seat, and commanded the man to be brought forth.

18 Against whom when the accusers stood up, they brought none accusation of such things as I supposed:

19 [a]But had certain questions against him of their own [1]superstition, and of one Jesus, which was dead, whom Paul affirmed to be alive.

20 And because I [1]doubted of such manner of questions, I asked *him* whether he would go to Jerusalem, and there be judged of these matters.

21 But when Paul had [a]appealed to be reserved unto the [1]hearing of Augustus, I commanded him to be kept till I might send him to Caesar.

22 Then [a]Agrippa said unto Festus, I [1]would also hear the man myself. To morrow, said he, thou shalt hear him.

23 And on the morrow, when Agrippa was come, and Bernice, with great pomp, and was entered into the [1]place of hearing, with the [2]chief captains, and [3]principal men of the city, at Festus' commandment [a]Paul was brought forth.

24 And Festus said, King Agrippa, and all men which are here present with us, ye see this man, about whom [a]all the multitude of the Jews have [1]dealt with me, both at Jerusalem, and *also* here, crying that he ought [b]not to live any longer.

25 But when I found that [a]he had committed nothing worthy of death, [b]and that he himself hath appealed

---

**Center column cross-references:**

24:23 [a] Acts 23:16; 27:3; 28:16 [1] *provide for*

24:24 [a] [Rom. 10:9]

24:25 [1] *about* [2] *self-control* [3] *was afraid* [4] *time*

24:26 [a] Ex. 23:8

24:27 [a] Acts 12:3; 23:35; 25:9, 14 [1] *succeeded Felix* [2] *wanting* [3] *favour*

25:1 [a] Acts 8:40; 25:4, 6, 13 [1] *went up*

25:2 [a] Acts 24:1; 25:15 [1] *petitioned*

25:3 [a] Acts 23:12, 15 [1] *asked* [2] *while they lay in ambush*

25:5 [a] Acts 18:14; 25:18 [1] *have authority*

25:6 [1] *remained*

25:7 [a] Mark 15:3; Luke 23:2, 10; Acts 24:5, 13 [1] *serious*

25:8 [a] Acts 6:13; 24:12; 28:17

25:9 [a] Acts 12:2; 24:27 [b] Acts 25:20

25:11 [a] Acts 18:14; 23:29; 25:25; 26:31 [b] Acts 26:32; 28:19 [1] *do not object to dying*

25:13 [1] *greet*

25:14 [a] Acts 24:27 [1] *a prisoner*

25:15 [a] Acts 24:1; 25:2, 3 [1] *asking for a*

25:16 [a] Acts 25:4, 5 [1] *custom* [2] *has opportunity*

25:17 [a] Matt. 27:19; Acts 25:6, 10 [1] *the next day*

25:19 [a] Acts 18:14, 15; 23:29 [1] *religion*

25:20 [1] *was uncertain*

25:21 [a] Acts 25:11, 12 [1] *decision*

25:22 [a] Acts 9:15 [1] *also would like to*

25:23 [a] Acts 9:15 [1] *auditorium* [2] *commanders* [3] *prominent*

25:24 [a] Acts 25:2, 3, 7 [b] Acts 21:36; 22:22 [1] *petitioned me*

25:25 [a] Acts 23:9, 29; 26:31 [b] Acts 25:11, 12

to Augustus, I have determined to send him.

26 Of whom I have no certain thing to write unto my lord. Wherefore I have brought him forth before you, and specially before thee, O king Agrippa, that, after examination [1]had, I might have [2]somewhat to write.

27 For it seemeth to me unreasonable to send a prisoner, and not withal to signify the crimes *laid* against him.

## CHAPTER 26

THEN Agrippa said unto Paul, Thou art permitted to speak for thyself. Then Paul stretched forth the hand, and answered for himself:

2 I think myself [a]happy, king Agrippa, because I shall answer [b]for myself this day before thee [1]touching all the things whereof I am [c]accused of the Jews:

3 Especially *because I know* thee to be expert in all customs and questions which are among the Jews: wherefore I beseech thee to hear me patiently.

4 My manner of life from my youth, which was [1]at the first among mine own nation at Jerusalem, know all the Jews;

5 Which knew me from the beginning, if they would testify, that after [a]the [1]most straitest sect of our religion I lived a Pharisee.

6 [a]And now I stand and am judged for the hope of [b]the promise made of God unto our fathers:

7 Unto which *promise* [a]our twelve tribes, [1]instantly serving *God* [b]day and night, [c]hope to [2]come. For which hope's sake, king Agrippa, I am accused [3]of the Jews.

8 Why should it be thought a thing incredible with you, that God should raise the dead?

9 [a]I verily thought with myself, that I ought to do many things contrary to the name of [b]Jesus of Nazareth.

10 [a]Which thing I also did in Jerusalem: and many of the saints did I shut up in prison, having received authority [b]from the chief priests; and when they were put to death, I [1]gave my voice against *them.*

11 [a]And I punished them [1]oft in every synagogue, and compelled *them* to blaspheme; and being exceedingly [2]mad against them, I persecuted *them* even unto [3]strange cities.

12 [a]Whereupon as I went to Damascus with authority and commission from the chief priests,

13 At midday, O king, I saw in the way a light from heaven, above the brightness of the sun, shining round about me and them which journeyed with me.

14 And when we were all fallen to the earth, I heard a voice speaking unto me, and saying in the Hebrew [1]tongue, Saul, Saul, why persecutest thou me? *it is* hard for thee to kick against the [2]pricks.

15 And I said, Who art thou, Lord? And he said, I am Jesus whom thou persecutest.

16 But rise, and stand upon thy feet: for I have appeared unto thee for this purpose, [a]to make thee a minister and a witness both of these things which thou hast seen, and of those things in the which I will [1]appear unto thee;

17 Delivering thee from the people, and *from* the Gentiles, [a]unto whom now I send thee,

18 [a]To open their eyes, *and* [b]to turn *them* from darkness to light, and *from* the power of Satan unto God, [c]that they may receive forgiveness of sins, and [d]inheritance among them which are [e]sanctified[1] by faith that is in me.

19 Whereupon, O king Agrippa, I was not disobedient unto the heavenly vision:

20 But [a]shewed first unto them of Damascus, and at Jerusalem, and throughout all the [1]coasts of Judaea, and *then* to the Gentiles, that they should repent and turn to God, and do [b]works [2]meet for repentance.

21 For these causes the Jews [1]caught me in the temple, and went about to kill *me.*

22 Having therefore obtained help of God, I continue unto this day, witnessing both to small and great, saying none other things than those [a]which the prophets and [b]Moses did say should come:

23 [a]That Christ should suffer, *and* [b]that he should be the first that should rise from the dead, and [c]should[1] shew light unto the people, and to the Gentiles.

24 And as he thus spake for himself, Festus said with a loud voice, Paul, [a]thou art beside thyself; much learning [1]doth make thee mad.

25 But he said, I am not [1]mad, most noble Festus; but speak forth the words of truth and [2]soberness.

26 For the king [a]knoweth of these things, before whom also I speak freely: for I am persuaded that none of these things are hidden from him; for this thing was not done in a corner.

27 King Agrippa, believest thou the prophets? I know that thou believest.

28 Then Agrippa said unto Paul, Almost thou persuadest me to be a Christian.

29 And Paul said, [a]I would to God, that not only thou, but also all that

---

### Center reference column

25:26 [1] *has taken place* [2] *something*
26:2 [a] [1 Pet. 3:14; 4:14] [b] [1 Pet. 3:15, 16] [c] Acts 21:28; 24:5, 6 [1] *concerning*
26:4 [1] *spent from the beginning*
26:5 [a] Phil. 3:5 [1] *strictest*
26:6 [a] Acts 23:6 [b] Acts 13:32
26:7 [a] James 1:1 [b] 1 Thess. 3:10 [c] Phil. 3:11 [1] *earnestly* [2] *attain* [3] *by*
26:9 [a] 1 Tim. 1:12, 13 [b] Acts 2:22; 10:38
26:10 [a] Acts 8:1–3; 9:13 [b] Acts 9:14 [1] *cast my vote*
26:11 [a] Acts 22:19 [1] *often* [2] *enraged* [3] *foreign*
26:12 [a] Acts 9:3–8; 22:6–11; 26:12–18
26:14 [1] *language* [2] *goads*
26:16 [a] Acts 22:15 [1] *reveal*
26:17 [a] Acts 22:21
26:18 [a] Is. 35:5; 42:7, 16 [b] 1 Pet. 2:9 [c] Luke 1:77 [d] Col. 1:12 [e] Acts 20:32 [1] *set apart*
26:20 [a] Acts 9:19, 20, 22; 11:26 [b] Matt. 3:8 [1] *region* [2] *befitting*
26:21 [1] *seized*
26:22 [a] Rom. 3:21 [b] John 5:46
26:23 [a] Luke 24:26 [b] 1 Cor. 15:20, 23 [c] Luke 2:32 [1] *would proclaim*
26:24 [a] [1 Cor. 1:23; 2:13, 14; 4:10] [1] *is driving*
26:25 [1] *out of my mind* [2] *reason*
96:96 [a] Acts 26:3
26:29 [a] 1 Cor. 7:7

hear me this day, were both almost, and altogether such as I am, except these bonds.

30 And when he had thus spoken, the king rose up, and the governor, and Bernice, and they that sat with them:

31 And when they were gone aside, they talked between themselves, saying, [a]This man doeth nothing worthy of death or of [1]bonds.

32 Then said Agrippa unto Festus, This man might have been set at [a]liberty, [b]if he had not appealed unto Caesar.

## CHAPTER 27

AND when [a]it was determined that we should sail into Italy, they delivered Paul and certain other prisoners unto *one* named Julius, a centurion of Augustus' [1]band.

2 And entering into a ship of Adramyttium, we [1]launched, meaning to sail [2]by the coasts of Asia; *one* [a]Aristarchus, a Macedonian of Thessalonica, being with us.

3 And the next *day* we [1]touched at Sidon. And Julius [a]courteously[2] entreated Paul, and gave *him* liberty to go unto his friends to refresh himself.

4 And when we had launched from thence, we sailed [1]under Cyprus, because the winds were contrary.

5 And when we had sailed over the sea of Cilicia and Pamphylia, we came to Myra, *a city* of Lycia.

6 And there the centurion found a ship of [a]Alexandria sailing into Italy; and he put us therein.

7 And when we had sailed slowly many days, and scarce were come over against Cnidus, the wind not [1]suffering us, we sailed [2]under [a]Crete, [3]over against Salmone;

8 And, [1]hardly passing it, came unto a place which is called The fair havens; nigh whereunto was the city *of* Lasea.

9 Now when much time was spent, and when sailing was now dangerous, [a]because [1]the fast was now already past, Paul admonished *them,*

10 And said unto them, Sirs, I perceive that this voyage will be with [1]hurt and much [2]damage, not only of the [3]lading and ship, but also of our lives.

11 Nevertheless the centurion believed the [1]master and the owner of the ship, more than those things which were spoken by Paul.

12 And because the haven was not [1]commodious to winter in, the [2]more part advised to depart thence also, if by any means they might attain to Phenice, *and there* to winter; *which is* an [3]haven of Crete, and [4]lieth toward the south west and north west.

13 And when the south wind blew softly, supposing that they had obtained *their* purpose, loosing *thence,* they sailed close by Crete.

14 But not long after there arose against it a tempestuous wind, called [1]Euroclydon.

15 And when the ship was caught, and could not [1]bear up into the wind, we let *her* [2]drive.

16 And running [1]under a certain island which is called Clauda, we had much work to [2]come by the boat:

17 Which when they had [1]taken up, they used [2]helps, undergirding the ship; and, fearing lest they should [3]fall into the quicksands, strake sail, and so were driven.

18 And we being exceedingly tossed with a tempest, the next *day* they lightened the ship;

19 And the third *day* [a]we cast out with our own hands the tackling of the ship.

20 And when neither sun nor stars in many days appeared, and no small tempest [1]lay on *us,* all hope that we should be saved was then taken away.

21 But after long [1]abstinence Paul stood forth in the midst of them, and said, Sirs, ye should have hearkened unto me, and not have loosed from Crete, and to have gained this [2]harm and loss.

22 And now I [1]exhort you to [2]be of good cheer: for there shall be no loss of *any man's* life among you, but of the ship.

23 [a]For there stood by me this night the angel of God, whose I am, and [b]whom I serve,

24 Saying, Fear not, Paul; thou must be brought before Caesar: and, lo, God hath given thee all them that sail with thee.

25 Wherefore, sirs, [1]be of good cheer: [a]for I believe God, that it shall be even as it was told me.

26 Howbeit [a]we must [b]be cast upon a certain island.

27 But when the fourteenth night was come, as we were driven up and down in Adria, about midnight the shipmen [1]deemed that they drew near to some [2]country;

28 And sounded, and found *it* twenty fathoms: and when they had gone a little further, they sounded again, and found *it* fifteen fathoms.

29 Then fearing lest we should [1]have fallen upon rocks, they cast four anchors out of the stern, and wished for the day.

30 And as the [1]shipmen were about to flee out of the ship, when they had let down the [2]boat into the sea, under [3]colour as though they would have cast anchors out of the [4]foreship,

---

*Center column notes:*

26:31 [a] Acts 23:9, 29; 25:25  [1] *chains*

26:32 [a] Acts 28:18  [b] Acts 25:11

27:1 [a] Acts 25:12, 25  [1] *regiment,* lit. *cohort*

27:2 [a] Acts 19:29  [1] *set sail*  [2] *along*

27:3 [a] Acts 24:23; 28:16  [1] *landed*  [2] *treated Paul kindly*

27:4 [1] *under the shelter of*

27:6 [a] Acts 28:11

27:7 [a] Acts 2:11; 27:12, 21; Titus 1:5, 12  [1] *permitting*  [2] *under the shelter of*  [3] *opposite*

27:8 [1] *with difficulty*

27:9 [a] Lev. 16:29–31; 23:27–29; Num. 29:7  [1] The Day of Atonement

27:10 [1] *disaster*  [2] *loss*  [3] *cargo*

27:11 [1] *pilot*

27:12 [1] *suitable*  [2] *majority*  [3] *harbour*  [4] *opens toward*

27:14 [1] A southeast wind that stirs up waves

27:15 [1] *head*  [2] *be driven*

27:16 [1] *under the shelter of*  [2] *secure the ship's skiff*

27:17 [1] *taken it on board*  [2] *cables*  [3] *run aground on the Syrtis Sands*

27:19 [a] Jon. 1:5

27:20 [1] *beat*

27:21 [1] From food  [2] *disaster*

27:22 [1] *urge*  [2] *take heart*

27:23 [a] Acts 18:9; 23:11; 2 Tim. 4:17  [b] Dan. 6:16; Rom. 1:9; 2 Tim. 1:3

27:25 [a] Luke 1:45; Rom. 4:20, 21; 2 Tim. 1:12  [1] *take heart*

27:26 [a] Acts 28:1  [1] *run aground*

27:27 [1] *sensed*  [2] *land*

27:29 [1] *run aground*

27:30 [1] *sailors*  [2] *skiff*  [3] *pretense*  [4] *prow*

31 Paul said to the centurion and to the soldiers, Except these abide in the ship, ye cannot be saved.

32 Then the soldiers cut off the ropes of the [1]boat, and let her fall off.

33 And while the day was coming on, Paul [1]besought *them* all to take [2]meat, saying, This day is the fourteenth day that ye have [3]tarried and continued [4]fasting, having [5]taken nothing.

34 Wherefore I pray you to take *some* [1]meat: for this is for your [2]health: for [a]there shall not an hair fall from the head of any of you.

35 And when he had thus spoken, he took bread, and [a]gave thanks to God in presence of them all: and when he had broken *it*, he began to eat.

36 Then were they all [1]of good cheer, and they also took *some* [2]meat.

37 And we were in all in the ship two hundred threescore and sixteen [a]souls.

38 And when they had eaten enough, they lightened the ship, and cast out the wheat into the sea.

39 And when it was day, they [1]knew not the land: but they discovered a certain [2]creek with a [3]shore, into the which they were minded, if it were possible, to thrust in the ship.

40 And when they had [1]taken up the anchors, they [2]committed *themselves* unto the sea, and loosed the rudder [3]bands, and hoised up the mainsail to the wind, and made toward shore.

41 And [1]falling into a place where two seas met, [a]they ran the ship aground; and the [2]forepart stuck fast, and remained immoveable, but the [3]hinder part was [4]broken with the violence of the waves.

42 And the soldiers' [1]counsel was to kill the prisoners, lest any of them should swim out, and escape.

43 But the centurion, [1]willing to save Paul, kept them from *their* purpose; and commanded that they which could swim should cast *themselves* first *into the sea*, and get to land:

44 And the rest, some on boards, and some on *broken pieces* of the ship. And so it came to pass, [a]that they escaped all safe to land.

## CHAPTER 28

AND when they were escaped, then they knew that [a]the island was called [1]Melita.

2 And the [a]barbarous[1] people shewed us [2]no little kindness: for they kindled a fire, and received us every one, because of the present rain, and because of the cold.

3 And when Paul had gathered a bundle of sticks, and laid *them* on

---

27:32 [1] skiff
27:33 [1] begged
[2] food [3] waited
[4] without food
[5] eaten
27:34 [a] 1 Kin. 1:52;
[Matt. 10:30; Luke
12:7; 21:18] [1] food
[2] survival
27:35 [a] 1 Sam.
9:13; Matt. 15:36;
Mark 8:6; John
6:11; [1 Tim. 4:3, 4]
27:36 [1] encouraged [2] food
27:37 [a] Acts 2:41;
7:14; Rom. 13:1;
1 Pet. 3:20
27:39 [1] did not
recognize [2] bay
[3] beach
27:40 [1] cast off
[2] left them in the
sea [3] ropes
27:41 [a] 2 Cor. 11:25
[1] striking [2] prow
[3] stern [4] being
broken
27:42 [1] plan
27:43 [1] wanting
27:44 [a] Acts
27:22, 31
28:1 [a] Acts 27:26
[1] Or Malta
28:2 [d] Col.
3:11 [1] natives
[2] unusual
28:4 [1] creature
[2] justice [3] allows
28:5 [a] Mark
16:18 [1] creature
[2] suffered
28:6 [a] Acts 12:22;
14:11 [1] expected
that
28:7 [1] region
[2] was an estate
[3] Magistrate
28:8 [a] [James
5:14, 15] [b] Mark
5:23; 6:5; 7:32;
16:18 [1] dysentery
28:10 [a] Matt.
15:6 [b] [Phil. 4:19]
[1] provided
28:11 [a] Acts 27:6
[1] figurehead [2] Gr.
Dioscouri, the
Twin Brothers
of Zeus
28:12 [1] stayed
28:13 [1] circled
around
28:14 [a] Rom. 1:8
[1] invited to stay
28:15 [1] Inns
28:16 [a] Acts
23:11; 24:25;
27:3 [1] permitted
[2] guarded
28:17 [a] Acts
23:29; 24:12, 13;
26:31 [b] Acts 21:33
[1] leaders
28:18 [a] Acts
22:24; 24:10; 25:8;
26:32 [1] wanted to

---

the fire, there came a viper out of the heat, and fastened on his hand.

4 And when the barbarians saw the *venomous* [1]beast hang on his hand, they said among themselves, No doubt this man is a murderer, whom, though he hath escaped the sea, yet [2]vengeance [3]suffereth not to live.

5 And he shook off the [1]beast into the fire, and [a]felt[2] no harm.

6 Howbeit they [1]looked when he should have swollen, or fallen down dead suddenly: but after they had looked a great while, and saw no harm come to him, they changed their minds, and [a]said that he was a god.

7 In the same [1]quarters [2]were possessions of the [3]chief man of the island, whose name was Publius; who received us, and lodged us three days courteously.

8 And it came to pass, that the father of Publius lay sick of a fever and of [1]a bloody flux: to whom Paul entered in, and [a]prayed, and [b]laid his hands on him, and healed him.

9 So when this was done, others also, which had diseases in the island, came, and were healed:

10 Who also honoured us with many [a]honours; and when we departed, they [1]laded *us* with such things as were [b]necessary.

11 And after three months we departed in a ship of [a]Alexandria, which had wintered in the isle, whose [1]sign was [2]Castor and Pollux.

12 And landing at Syracuse, we [1]tarried *there* three days.

13 And from thence we [1]fetched a compass, and came to Rhegium: and after one day the south wind blew, and we came the next day to Puteoli:

14 Where we found [a]brethren, and were [1]desired to tarry with them seven days: and so we went toward Rome.

15 And from thence, when the brethren heard of us, they came to meet us as far as Appii forum, and The three [1]taverns: whom when Paul saw, he thanked God, and took courage.

16 And when we came to Rome, the centurion delivered the prisoners to the captain of the guard: but [a]Paul was [1]suffered to dwell by himself with a soldier that [2]kept him.

17 And it came to pass, that after three days Paul called the [1]chief of the Jews together: and when they were come together, he said unto them, Men *and* brethren, [a]though I have committed nothing against the people, or customs of our fathers, yet [b]was I delivered prisoner from Jerusalem into the hands of the Romans.

18 Who, [a]when they had examined me, [1]would have let *me* go, because there was no cause of death in me.

19 But when the Jews spake against *it,* [a]I was [1]constrained to appeal unto Caesar; not that I had [2]ought to accuse my nation of.

20 For this cause therefore have I called for you, to see *you,* and to speak with *you:* because that [a]for the hope of Israel I am bound with [b]this chain.

21 And they said unto him, We neither received letters out of Judaea concerning thee, neither any of the brethren that came shewed or spake any [1]harm of thee.

22 But we desire to hear of thee what thou thinkest: for as concerning this sect, we know that every where [a]it is spoken against.

23 And when they had appointed him a day, there came many to him into *his* lodging, [a]to whom he [1]expounded and testified the kingdom of God, persuading them concerning Jesus, [b]both out of the law of Moses, and *out of* the prophets, from morning till evening.

24 And [a]some believed the things which were spoken, and some believed not.

25 And when they agreed not among

28:19 [a] Acts 25:11, 21, 25 [1] *compelled* [2] *anything*
28:20 [a] Acts 26:6, 7 [b] Eph. 3:1; 4:1;
6:20
28:21 [1] *evil*
28:22 [a] [1 Pet. 2:12; 3:16; 4:14, 16]
28:23 [a] Luke 24:27 [b] Acts 26:6, 22 [1] *explained*
28:24 [a] Acts 14:4; 19:9

28:26 [a] Is. 6:9, 10; Jer. 5:21; Ezek. 12:2; Matt. 13:14, 15; Mark 4:12; Luke 8:10; John 12:40, 41; Rom. 11:8
28:27 [1] *has grown dull*
28:28 [a] Is. 42:1, 6; 49:6; Matt. 21:41; Luke 2:32; Rom. 11:11
28:29 [1] *dispute*
28:30 [1] *rented*
28:31 [a] Acts 4:31; Eph. 6:19

themselves, they departed, after that Paul had spoken one word, Well spake the Holy Ghost by Esaias the prophet unto our fathers,

26 Saying, [a]Go unto this people, and say, Hearing ye shall hear, and shall not understand; and seeing ye shall see, and not perceive:

27 For the heart of this people [1]is waxed gross, and their ears are dull of hearing, and their eyes have they closed; lest they should see with *their* eyes, and hear with *their* ears, and understand with *their* heart, and should be converted, and I should heal them.

28 Be it known therefore unto you, that the salvation of God is sent [a]unto the Gentiles, and *that* they will hear it.

29 And when he had said these words, the Jews departed, and had great [1]reasoning among themselves.

30 And Paul dwelt two whole years in his own [1]hired house, and received all that came in unto him,

31 [a]Preaching the kingdom of God, and teaching those things which concern the Lord Jesus Christ, with all confidence, no man forbidding him.

# THE EPISTLE OF PAUL THE APOSTLE TO THE
# ROMANS

Romans, Paul's greatest work, is placed first among his thirteen epistles in the New Testament. While the four Gospels present the words and works of Jesus Christ, Romans explores the significance of His sacrificial death. Using a question-and-answer format, Paul records the most systematic presentation of doctrine in the Bible. Romans is more than a book of theology; it is also a book of practical exhortation. The good news of Jesus Christ is more than facts to be believed; it is also a life to be lived—a life of righteousness befitting the person, "justified freely by [God's] grace through the redemption that is in Christ Jesus" (3:24).

Although some manuscripts omit "in Rome" in 1:7, 15, the title *Pros Romaious*, "To the Romans," has been associated with the epistle almost from the beginning.

## CHAPTER 1

PAUL, a [1]servant of Jesus Christ, [a]called *to be* an apostle, [b]separated unto the gospel of God,

2 ([a]Which he had promised [1]afore [b]by his prophets in the holy scriptures,)

3 Concerning his Son Jesus Christ our Lord, which was [a]made[1] of the seed of David according to the flesh;

4 And [a]declared *to be* the Son of God with power, according [b]to the [1]spirit of holiness, by the resurrection from the dead:

5 By whom [a]we have received grace and apostleship, for [b]obedience to the faith among all nations, [c]for his name:

6 Among whom are ye also the called of Jesus Christ:

7 To all that be in Rome, beloved of God, [a]called *to be* saints: [b]Grace to you and peace from God our Father, and the Lord Jesus Christ.

8 First, [a]I thank my God through Jesus Christ for you all, that [b]your faith is spoken of throughout the whole world.

9 For [a]God is my witness, [b]whom I serve [1]with my spirit in the gospel of his Son, that [c]without ceasing I make mention of you always in my prayers;

10 Making request, if by any means now at [1]length I might [2]have a prosperous journey by the will of God to come unto you.

11 For I long to see you, that [a]I may impart unto you some spiritual gift, to the end ye may be established;

12 That is, that I may be [1]comforted together with you by [a]the mutual faith both of you and me.

13 Now I would not have you ignorant, brethren, that oftentimes I [1]purposed to come unto you, (but [a]was [2]let hitherto,) that I might have some [b]fruit among you also, even as among other Gentiles.

14 I am debtor both to the Greeks, and to the Barbarians; both to the wise, and to the unwise.

15 So, as much as in me is, I am ready to preach the gospel to you that are at Rome also.

16 For [a]I am not ashamed of the gospel of Christ: for [b]it is the power of God unto salvation to every one that believeth; [c]to the Jew first, and also to the Greek.

17 For [a]therein is the righteousness of God revealed from faith to faith: as it is written, [b]The just shall live by faith.

18 [a]For the wrath of God is revealed from heaven against all ungodliness and [b]unrighteousness of men, who [1]hold the truth in unrighteousness;

19 Because [a]that which may be known of God is [1]manifest [2]in them; for [b]God hath shewed *it* unto them.

20 For [a]the invisible things of him from the creation of the world are clearly seen, being understood by the things that are made, *even* his eternal power and [1]Godhead; so that they are without excuse:

21 Because that, when they knew God, they glorified *him* not as God, neither were thankful; but [a]became [1]vain in their [2]imaginations, and their foolish heart was darkened.

22 [a]Professing themselves to be wise, they became fools,

23 And changed the glory of the [a]uncorruptible [b]God into an image made like to [1]corruptible man, and to birds, and fourfooted beasts, and creeping things.

24 [a]Wherefore God also gave them up to uncleanness through the lusts of their own hearts, [b]to dishonour their own bodies [c]between themselves:

25 Who [1]changed [a]the truth of God [b]into[2] a lie, and worshipped and served

1:1 [a] 1 Tim. 1:11
[b] Acts 9:15; 13:2
[1] *slave*
1:2 [a] Acts 26:5
[b] Gal. 3:8 [1] *before*
1:3 [a] Gal. 4:4
[1] *born*
1:4 [a] Acts 9:20;
13:33 [b] [Heb. 9:14] [1] Or *Spirit*
1:5 [a] Eph. 3:8
[b] Acts 6:7 [c] Acts 9:15
1:7 [a] 1 Cor. 1:2, 24
[b] 1 Cor. 1:3
1:8 [a] 1 Cor. 1:4
[b] Rom. 16:19
1:9 [a] Rom. 9:1
[b] Acts 27:23
[c] 1 Thess. 3:10
[1] Or *in*
1:10 [1] *last* [2] *find a way in the will*
1:11 [a] Rom. 15:29
1:12 [a] Titus 1:4
[1] *encouraged*
1:13 [a] [1 Thess. 2:18] [b] Phil. 4:17 [1] *planned* [2] *hindered*
1:16 [a] Ps. 40:9, 10
[b] 1 Cor. 1:18, 24
[c] Acts 3:26
1:17 [a] Rom. 3:21;
9:30 [b] Hab. 2:4
1:18 [a] [Acts 17:30]
[b] 2 Thess. 2:10
[1] *suppress*
1:19 [a] [Acts 14:17;
17:24] [b] [John 1:9]
[1] *evident* [2] *among*
1:20 [a] Ps. 19:1–6
[1] *divine nature*
1:21 [a] Jer. 2:5 [1] *futile* [2] *thoughts*
1:22 [a] Jer. 10:14
1:23 [a] 1 Tim. 1:17;
6:15, 16 [b] Deut. 4:16–18 [1] *perishable*
1:24 [a] Eph. 4:18, 19
[b] 1 Cor. 6:18 [c] Lev. 18:22
1:25 [a] 1 Thess. 1:9 [b] Is. 44:20 [1] *exchanged* [2] *for the lie*

the creature [3]more than the Creator, who is blessed for ever. Amen.

26 For this cause God gave them up unto [a]vile affections: for even their women did [1]change the natural use [2]into that which is against nature:

27 And likewise also the [1]men, leaving the natural use of the [2]woman, burned in their lust one toward another; [1]men with [1]men working that which is [3]unseemly, and receiving in themselves that [4]recompence of their error which was [5]meet.

28 And even as they did not like to retain God in *their* knowledge, God gave them over to a [1]reprobate mind, to do those things [a]which are not [2]convenient;

29 Being filled with all unrighteousness, fornication, wickedness, covetousness, maliciousness; full of envy, murder, [1]debate, deceit, [2]malignity; whisperers,

30 Backbiters, haters of God, [1]despiteful, proud, boasters, inventors of evil things, disobedient to parents,

31 Without understanding, covenantbreakers, without natural affection, [1]implacable, unmerciful:

32 Who [a]knowing the [1]judgment of God, that they which commit such things [b]are worthy of death, not only do the same, but [c]have[2] pleasure in them that do them.

## CHAPTER 2

THEREFORE thou art [a]inexcusable, O man, whosoever thou art that judgest: [b]for wherein thou judgest another, thou condemnest thyself; for thou that judgest doest the same things.

2 But we are sure that the judgment of God is according to truth against them which commit such things.

3 And thinkest thou this, O man, that judgest them which do such things, and doest the same, that thou shalt escape the judgment of God?

4 Or despisest thou [a]the riches of his goodness and [b]forbearance and [c]longsuffering; [d]not knowing that the goodness of God leadeth thee to repentance?

5 But after thy hardness and impenitent heart [a]treasurest up unto thyself wrath against the day of wrath and revelation of the righteous judgment of God;

6 [a]Who will render to every man according to his deeds:

7 To them who by patient continuance in well doing seek for glory and honour and immortality, eternal life:

8 But unto them that are [1]contentious, and [a]do not obey the truth, but obey unrighteousness, indignation and wrath,

9 Tribulation and anguish, upon every soul of man that doeth evil, of the Jew [a]first, and also of the [1]Gentile;

10 [a]But glory, honour, and peace, to every man that worketh good, to the Jew first, and also to the [1]Gentile:

11 For [a]there is no respect of persons with God.

12 For as many as have sinned without law shall also perish without law: and as many as have sinned in the law shall be judged by the law;

13 (For [a]not the hearers of the law *are* just before God, but the doers of the law shall be justified.

14 For when the Gentiles, which have not the law, do by nature the things contained in the law, these, having not the law, are a law unto themselves:

15 Which shew the [a]work of the law written in their hearts, their [b]conscience also bearing witness, and *their* thoughts [1]the mean while accusing or else excusing one another;)

16 [a]In the day when God shall judge the secrets of men [b]by Jesus Christ [c]according to my gospel.

17 Behold, [a]thou art called a Jew, and [b]restest in the law, [c]and makest thy boast of God,

18 And [a]knowest *his* will, and [b]approvest the things that are more excellent, being instructed out of the law;

19 And [a]art confident that thou thyself art a guide of the blind, a light of them which are in darkness,

20 An instructor of the foolish, a teacher of babes, [a]which hast the form of knowledge and of the truth in the law.

21 [a]Thou therefore which teachest another, teachest thou not thyself? thou that preachest a man should not steal, dost thou steal?

22 Thou that sayest a man should not [1]commit adultery, dost thou commit adultery? thou that abhorrest idols, [a]dost thou commit sacrilege?

23 Thou that [a]makest thy boast of the law, through breaking the law dishonourest thou God?

24 For the name of God is [a]blasphemed among the Gentiles through you, as it is [b]written.

25 [a]For circumcision verily profiteth, if thou keep the law: but if thou be a breaker of the law, thy circumcision [1]is made uncircumcision.

26 Therefore [a]if the uncircumcision keep the [1]righteousness of the law, shall not his uncircumcision be counted for circumcision?

27 And shall not uncircumcision which is [1]by nature, if [2]it fulfil the law, [a]judge thee, who [3]by the letter and circumcision dost transgress the law?

---

### Center reference column

1:25 [3] *rather*
1:26 [a] Lev. 18:22
[1] *exchange* [2] *for*
1:27 [1] Lit. *males*
[2] Lit. *female*
[3] *shameful* [4] *penalty* [5] *due*
1:28 [a] Eph. 5:4
[1] *debased* [2] *fitting*
1:29 [1] *strife* [2] *evilmindedness*
1:30 [1] *violent*
1:31 [1] *unforgiving*
1:32 [a] [Rom. 2:2]
[b] [Rom. 6:21]
[c] Hos. 7:3 [1] *righteous judgment*
[2] *approve of*
2:1 [a] [Rom. 1:20]
[b] [Matt. 7:1–5]
2:4 [a] [Eph. 1:7, 18; 2:7] [b] [Rom. 3:25]
[c] Ex. 34:6 [d] Is. 30:18
2:5 [a] [Deut. 32:34]
2:6 [a] Ps. 62:12; Prov. 24:12
2:8 [a] [2 Thess. 1:8]
[1] *self-seeking*

2:9 [a] 1 Pet. 4:17
[1] Lit. *Greek*
2:10 [a] [1 Pet. 1:7]
[1] Lit. *Greek*
2:11 [a] Deut. 10:17
2:13 [a] [James 1:22, 25]
2:15 [a] 1 Cor. 5:1
[b] Acts 24:25 [1] *between themselves*
2:16 [a] [Matt. 25:31] [b] Acts 10:42; 17:31
[c] 1 Tim. 1:11
2:17 [a] John 8:33
[b] Mic. 3:11 [c] Is. 48:1, 2
2:18 [a] Deut. 4:8
[b] Phil. 1:10
2:19 [a] Matt. 15:14
2:20 [a] [2 Tim. 3:5]
2:21 [a] Matt. 23:3
2:22 [a] Mal. 3:8
[1] *rob temples*
2:23 [a] Rom. 2:17; 9:4
2:24 [a] Ezek. 16:27
[b] Is. 52:5; Ezek. 36:22
2:25 [a] [Gal. 5:3]
[1] *has become*
2:26 [a] [Acts 10:34] [1] *righteous requirements*
2:27 [a] Matt. 12:41
[1] *physical* [2] *he*
[3] *even with your written code*

28 For [a]he is not a Jew, which is one outwardly; neither *is that* circumcision, which is outward in the flesh:

29 But he *is* a Jew, [a]which is one inwardly; and [b]circumcision *is that* of the heart, [c]in the spirit, *and* not in the letter; [d]whose [1]praise *is* not of men, but of God.

## CHAPTER 3

WHAT advantage then hath the Jew? or what profit *is* [1]there of circumcision?

2 Much every way: chiefly, because that [a]unto them were committed the [1]oracles of God.

3 For what if [a]some did not believe? [b]shall their unbelief make the [1]faith of God without effect?

4 [a]God[1] forbid: yea, let [b]God be [2]true, but [c]every man a liar; as it is written, [d]That thou mightest be justified in thy sayings, and mightest overcome when thou art judged.

5 But if our unrighteousness [1]commend the righteousness of God, what shall we say? *Is* God unrighteous who [2]taketh vengeance? ([a]I speak as a man)

6 [1]God forbid: for then [a]how shall God judge the world?

7 For if the truth of God hath more abounded through my lie unto his glory; why yet am I also judged as a sinner?

8 And [1]not *rather,* (as we be slanderously reported, and as some affirm that we say,) [a]Let us do evil, that good may come? whose [2]damnation is just.

9 What then? are we better *than they?* [1]No, in no wise: for we have [2]before proved both Jews and [3]Gentiles, that [a]they are all under sin;

10 As it is written, [a]There is none righteous, no, not one:

11 There is none that understandeth, there is none that seeketh after God.

12 They are all gone out of the way, they are together become unprofitable; there is none that doeth good, no, not one.

13 [a]Their throat *is* an open [1]sepulchre; with their tongues they have used deceit; [b]the poison of asps *is* under their lips:

14 [a]Whose mouth *is* full of cursing and bitterness:

15 [a]Their feet *are* swift to shed blood:

16 Destruction and misery *are* in their ways:

17 And the way of peace have they not known:

18 [a]There is no fear of God before their eyes.

19 Now we know that what things soever [a]the law saith, it saith to them who are under the law: that [b]every mouth may be stopped, and all the world may become guilty before God.

2:28 [a] [Gal. 6:15]
2:29 [a] [1 Pet. 3:4]
[b] Phil. 3:3 [c] Deut. 30:6 [d] [1 Cor. 4:5] [1] A play on words—*Jew* is literally *praise.*
3:1 [1] *the circumcision*
3:2 [a] Deut. 4:5–8 [1] *sayings*
3:3 [a] Heb. 4:2 [b] [2 Tim. 2:13] [1] *faithfulness*
3:4 [a] Job 40:8 [b] [John 3:33] [c] Ps. 62:9 [d] Ps. 51:4 [1] *Certainly not* [2] *Found true*
3:5 [a] Gal. 3:15 [1] *demonstrates* [2] *inflicts wrath*
3:6 [a] [Gen. 18:25] [1] *Certainly not*
3:8 [a] Rom. 5:20 [1] *why not say* [2] *condemnation*
3:9 [a] Gal. 3:22 [1] *Not at all* [2] *previously charged* [3] Lit. *Greeks*
3:10 [a] Ps. 14:1–3; 53:1–3; Eccl. 7:20
3:13 [a] Ps. 5:9 [b] Ps. 140:3 [1] *grave*
3:14 [a] Ps. 10:7
3:15 [a] Prov. 1:16; Is. 59:7, 8
3:18 [a] Ps. 36:1
3:19 [a] John 10:34 [b] Job 5:16
3:20 [a] [Gal. 2:16]
3:21 [a] Acts 15:11 [b] John 5:46 [c] 1 Pet. 1:10 [1] *apart from*
3:22 [a] [Col. 3:11]
3:23 [a] Gal. 3:22 [1] *fall*
3:24 [a] [Eph. 2:8] [b] [Heb. 9:12, 15] [1] *without any cost*
3:25 [a] Lev. 16:15 [b] Col. 1:20 [c] Acts 14:16; 17:30 [1] *a mercy seat* [2] *demonstrate* [3] *passing over of*
3:27 [a] [1 Cor. 1:29]
3:28 [a] Gal. 2:16 [1] *declared righteous* [2] *apart from*
3:30 [a] [Gal. 3:8, 20]
3:31 [1] *Certainly not*
4:1 [a] Is. 51:2 [b] James 2:21
4:2 [a] Rom. 3:20, 27 [1] *boast*
4:3 [a] Gen. 15:6
4:4 [a] Rom. 11:6 [1] *according to*
4:5 [a] [Eph. 2:8, 9] [b] Josh. 24:2

20 Therefore [a]by the deeds of the law there shall no flesh be justified in his sight: for by the law *is* the knowledge of sin.

21 But now [a]the righteousness of God [1]without the law is manifested, [b]being witnessed by the law [c]and the prophets;

22 Even the righteousness of God *which is* by faith of Jesus Christ unto all and upon all them that believe: for [a]there is no difference:

23 For [a]all have sinned, and [1]come short of the glory of God;

24 Being justified [1]freely [a]by his grace [b]through the redemption that is in Christ Jesus:

25 Whom God hath set forth [a]*to be* [1]a propitiation through faith [b]in his blood, to [2]declare his righteousness for the [3]remission of [c]sins that are past, through the forbearance of God;

26 To declare, *I say,* at this time his righteousness: that he might be just, and the justifier of him which believeth in Jesus.

27 [a]Where *is* boasting then? It is excluded. By what law? of works? Nay: but by the law of faith.

28 Therefore we conclude [a]that a man is [1]justified by faith [2]without the deeds of the law.

29 *Is he* the God of the Jews only? *is he* not also of the Gentiles? Yes, of the Gentiles also:

30 Seeing [a]*it is* one God, which shall justify the circumcision by faith, and uncircumcision through faith.

31 Do we then make void the law through faith? [1]God forbid: yea, we establish the law.

## CHAPTER 4

WHAT shall we say then that [a]Abraham our [b]father, as pertaining to the flesh, hath found?

2 For if Abraham were [a]justified by works, he hath *whereof* to [1]glory; but not before God.

3 For what saith the scripture? [a]Abraham believed God, and it was counted unto him for righteousness.

4 Now [a]to him that worketh is the reward not reckoned [1]of grace, but [1]of debt.

5 But to him that worketh [a]not, but believeth on him that justifieth [b]the ungodly, his faith is [1]counted for righteousness.

6 Even as David also [a]describeth the blessedness of the man, unto whom God imputeth righteousness [1]without works,

7 *Saying,* [a]Blessed *are* they whose [1]iniquities are forgiven, and whose sins are covered.

[1] *imputed as*  4:6 [a] Ps. 32:1, 2 [1] *apart from*  4:7 [a] Ps. 32:1, 2 [1] *lawless deeds*

8 Blessed *is* the man to whom the Lord will not impute sin.

9 *Cometh* this blessedness then upon the circumcision *only,* or upon the uncircumcision also? for we say that faith was ¹reckoned to Abraham for righteousness.

10 How was it then reckoned? when he was in circumcision, or in uncircumcision? Not in circumcision, but in uncircumcision.

11 And ªhe received the sign of circumcision, a seal of the righteousness of the faith which *he had yet* being uncircumcised: that ᵇhe might be the father of all them that believe, though they be not circumcised; that righteousness might be imputed unto them also:

12 And the father of circumcision to them who are not of the circumcision only, but who also walk in the steps of that faith of our father ªAbraham, which *he had* being *yet* uncircumcised.

13 For the promise, that he should be the ªheir of the world, *was* not to Abraham, or to his seed, through the law, but through the righteousness of faith.

14 For ªif they which are of the law *be* heirs, faith is made void, and the promise made of none effect:

15 Because ªthe law worketh wrath: for where no law is, *there is* no transgression.

16 Therefore *it is* of faith, that *it might be* ªby¹ grace; ᵇto the end the promise might be sure to all the seed; not to that only which is of the law, but to that also which is of the faith of Abraham; ᶜwho is the father of us all,

17 (As it is written, ªI have made thee a father of many nations,) before him whom he believed, *even* God, ᵇwho ¹quickeneth the dead, and calleth those ᶜthings which be not as though they were.

18 Who ¹against hope believed in hope, that he might become the father of many nations, according to that which was spoken, ªSo shall thy seed be.

19 And being not weak in faith, ªhe considered not his own body now dead, when he was about an hundred years old, ᵇneither yet the deadness of Sarah's womb:

20 He ¹staggered not at the promise of God through unbelief; but was ²strong in faith, giving glory to God;

21 And being fully ¹persuaded that, what he had promised, ªhe was able also to perform.

22 And therefore ªit was imputed to him for righteousness.

23 Now ªit was not written for his sake alone, that it was imputed to him;

**Cross-references (center column):**

4:9 ¹ *imputed*
4:11 ª Gen. 17:10
  ᵇ Luke 19:9
4:12 ª Rom. 4:18–22
4:13 ª Gen. 17:4–6; 22:17
4:14 ª Gal. 3:18
4:15 ª Rom. 3:20
4:16 ª [Rom. 3:24]
  ᵇ [Gal. 3:22] ᶜ Is. 51:2 ¹ *according to*
4:17 ª Gen. 17:5
  ᵇ [Rom. 8:11]
  ᶜ Rom. 9:26
  ¹ *gives life to*
4:18 ª Gen. 15:5
  ¹ *contrary to*
4:19 ª Gen. 17:17
  ᵇ Heb. 11:11
4:20 ¹ *wavered*
  ² *strengthened*
4:21 ª [Heb. 11:19]
  ¹ *convinced*
4:22 ª Gen. 15:6
4:23 ª Rom. 15:4
4:24 ª Acts 2:24
4:25 ª Is. 53:4,
5 ᵇ [1 Cor. 15:17]
  ¹ *because of*
5:1 ª Is. 32:17
  ᵇ [Eph. 2:14]
5:2 ª [Eph. 2:18; 3:12] ᵇ 1 Cor. 15:1
  ᶜ Heb. 3:6
5:3 ª Matt. 5:11, 12 ᵇ James 1:3 ¹ *produces perseverance*
5:4 ª [James 1:12]
  ¹ *character*
5:5 ª Phil. 1:20
  ᵇ 2 Cor. 1:22 ¹ *does not disappoint*
  ² *has been poured out in*
5:6 ª [Rom. 4:25; 5:8; 8:32] ¹ *at the right time*
5:7 ¹ *perhaps*
5:8 ª [John 3:16; 15:13] ¹ *demonstrates his own*
5:9 ª Eph. 2:13
  ᵇ 1 Thess. 1:10
  ¹ *having been*
5:10 ª [Rom. 8:32] ᵇ 2 Cor.
5:18 ᶜ John 14:19
  ¹ *having been*
5:11 ª [Gal. 4:9]
  ¹ *reconciliation*
5:12 ª [1 Cor. 15:21]
  ᵇ Gen. 2:17
5:13 ª 1 John 3:4
5:14 ª [1 Cor. 15:21, 22] ¹ *likeness* ² *a type*
5:15 ª [Is. 53:11]
  ¹ *the free gift is not like the false step*
  ² *Adam*
5:16 ¹ *the gift is not like that which came through the one who sinned*

24 But for us also, to whom it shall be imputed, if we believe ªon him that raised up Jesus our Lord from the dead;

25 ªWho was delivered ¹for our offences, and ᵇwas raised again ¹for our justification.

## CHAPTER 5

Therefore ªbeing justified by faith, we have ᵇpeace with God through our Lord Jesus Christ:

2 ªBy whom also we have access by faith into this grace ᵇwherein we stand, and ᶜrejoice in hope of the glory of God.

3 And not only *so,* but ªwe glory in tribulations also: ᵇknowing that tribulation ¹worketh patience;

4 ªAnd patience, ¹experience; and experience, hope:

5 ªAnd hope ¹maketh not ashamed; ᵇbecause the love of God ²is shed abroad in our hearts by the Holy Ghost which is given unto us.

6 For when we were yet without strength, ¹in due time ªChrist died for the ungodly.

7 For scarcely for a righteous man will one die: yet ¹peradventure for a good man some would even dare to die.

8 But ªGod ¹commendeth his love toward us, in that, while we were yet sinners, Christ died for us.

9 Much more then, ¹being now justified ªby his blood, we shall be saved ᵇfrom wrath through him.

10 For ªif, when we were enemies, ᵇwe were reconciled to God by the death of his Son, much more, ¹being reconciled, we shall be saved ᶜby his life.

11 And not only *so,* but we also ªjoy in God through our Lord Jesus Christ, by whom we have now received the ¹atonement.

12 Wherefore, as ªby one man sin entered into the world, and ᵇdeath by sin; and so death passed upon all men, for that all have sinned:

13 (For until the law sin was in the world: but ªsin is not imputed when there is no law.

14 Nevertheless death reigned from Adam to Moses, even over them that had not sinned after the ¹similitude of Adam's transgression, ªwho is ²the figure of him that was to come.

15 But ¹not as the offence, so also *is* the free gift. For if through the offence of ²one many be dead, much more the grace of God, and the gift by grace, *which is* by one man, Jesus Christ, hath abounded ªunto many.

16 And ¹not as *it was* by one that sinned, *so is* the gift: for the judgment *was* by one to condemnation, but the free gift *is* of many offences unto justification.

17 For if by one man's offence death reigned by [1]one; much more they which receive abundance of grace and of the gift of righteousness shall reign in life by one, Jesus Christ.)

18 Therefore as by [1]the offence of one *judgment came* upon all men to condemnation; even so by [2]the righteousness of [a]one *the free gift came* [b]upon all men unto justification of life.

19 For as by one man's disobedience many were made sinners, so by the [a]obedience of one shall many be made righteous.

20 Moreover [a]the law entered, that the [1]offence might abound. But where sin abounded, grace did much [b]more abound:

21 That as sin hath reigned unto death, even so might grace reign through righteousness unto eternal life by Jesus Christ our Lord.

### CHAPTER 6

WHAT shall we say then? [a]Shall we continue in sin, that grace may abound?

2 [1]God forbid. How shall we, [2]that are [a]dead to sin, live any longer therein?

3 [1]Know ye not, that [a]so many of us as were baptized into Jesus Christ [b]were baptized into his death?

4 Therefore we are [a]buried with him by baptism into death: that [b]like[1] as Christ was raised up from the dead by [c]the glory of the Father, [d]even so we also should walk in newness of life.

5 [a]For if we have been [1]planted together in the likeness of his death, [2]we shall be also *in the likeness* of *his* resurrection:

6 Knowing this, that [a]our old man is crucified with *him*, that [b]the body of sin might be [1]destroyed, that henceforth we should not [2]serve sin.

7 For [a]he that is dead is freed from sin.

8 Now [a]if we [1]be dead with Christ, we believe that we shall also live with him:

9 Knowing that [a]Christ being raised from the dead dieth no more; death hath no more dominion over him.

10 For in that he died, [a]he died unto sin [1]once: but in that he liveth, [b]he liveth unto God.

11 Likewise [1]reckon ye also yourselves to be [a]dead indeed unto sin, but [b]alive unto God [2]through Jesus Christ our Lord.

12 [a]Let not sin therefore reign in your mortal body, that ye should obey it in the lusts thereof.

13 Neither [1]yield ye your [a]members *as* [2]instruments of unrighteousness unto sin: but [b]yield[1] yourselves unto

God, as those that are alive from the dead, and your members *as* [2]instruments of righteousness unto God.

14 For [a]sin shall not have dominion over you: for ye are not under the law, but under grace.

15 What then? shall we sin, [a]because we are not under [1]the law, but under grace? [2]God forbid.

16 Know ye not, that [a]to whom ye [1]yield yourselves servants to obey, his [2]servants ye are to whom ye obey; whether of sin unto death, or of obedience unto righteousness?

17 But God be thanked, that [1]ye were the [2]servants of sin, but ye have obeyed from the heart [a]that form of doctrine [3]which was delivered you.

18 Being then [a]made free from sin, ye became the servants of righteousness.

19 I speak [1]after the manner of men because of the [2]infirmity of your flesh: for as ye have [3]yielded your members [4]servants to uncleanness and to iniquity unto [5]iniquity; even so now [6]yield your members [4]servants to righteousness unto holiness.

20 For when ye were [a]the servants of sin, ye were free from righteousness.

21 [a]What fruit had ye then in those things whereof ye are now ashamed? for [b]the end of those things *is* death.

22 But now [a]being made free from sin, and become servants to God, ye have your fruit unto holiness, and the end everlasting life.

23 For [a]the wages of sin *is* death; but [b]the gift of God *is* eternal life [1]through Jesus Christ our Lord.

### CHAPTER 7

KNOW ye not, brethren, (for I speak to them that know the law,) how that the law hath dominion over a man as long as he liveth?

2 For [a]the woman which hath an husband is bound by the law to *her* husband so long as he liveth; but if the husband be dead, she is loosed from the law [1]of *her* husband.

3 So then [a]if, while *her* husband liveth, she be married to another man, she shall be called an adulteress: but if her husband be dead, she is free from that law; so that she is no adulteress, though she be married to another man.

4 Wherefore, my brethren, ye also are become [a]dead to the law by the body of Christ; that ye should be married to another, *even* to him who is raised from the dead, that we should [b]bring forth fruit unto God.

5 For when we were in the flesh, the [1]motions of sins, which were [2]by the law, [a]did work in our members [b]to bring forth fruit unto death.

---

**Center reference column:**

5:17 [1] *the one*
5:18 [a] [1 Cor. 15:21, 45] [b] [John 12:32] [1] Lit. *one false step* [2] *one righteous act*
5:19 [a] [Phil. 2:8]
5:20 [a] John 15:22 [b] 1 Tim. 1:14 [1] *sin*
6:1 [a] Rom. 3:8; 6:15
6:2 [a] [Gal. 2:19] [1] *Certainly not* [2] *who died*
6:3 [a] [Gal. 3:27] [b] [1 Cor. 15:29] [1] Lit. *Or know*
6:4 [a] Col. 2:12 [b] 1 Cor. 6:14 [c] John 2:11 [d] [Gal. 6:15] [1] *just*
6:5 [a] Phil. 3:10 [1] *united* [2] Lit. *certainly we*
6:6 [a] Gal. 2:20; 5:24; 6:14 [b] Col. 2:11 [1] *rendered inoperative* [2] *be slaves of*
6:7 [a] 1 Pet. 4:1
6:8 [a] 2 Tim. 2:11 [1] *died*
6:9 [a] Rev. 1:18
6:10 [a] Heb. 9:27 [b] Luke 20:38 [1] *once for all*
6:11 [a] [Rom. 6:2; 7:4, 6] [b] [Gal. 2:19] [1] *consider* [2] *in Christ Jesus*
6:12 [a] Ps. 19:13
6:13 [a] Col. 3:5 [b] 1 Pet. 2:24; 4:2 [1] *present* [2] Or *weapons*
6:14 [a] [Gal. 5:18]
6:15 [a] 1 Cor. 9:21 [1] *law* [2] *Certainly not*
6:16 [a] 2 Pet. 2:19 [1] *present* [2] *slaves*
6:17 [a] 2 Tim. 1:13 [1] *though ye* [2] *slaves* [3] *to which you were entrusted*
6:18 [a] John 8:32
6:19 [1] *in human terms* [2] *weakness* [3] *presented* [4] *slaves* [5] *lawlessness* [6] *present*
6:20 [a] John 8:34
6:21 [a] Rom. 7:5 [b] Rom. 1:32
6:22 [a] Rom. 6:18; 8:2
6:23 [a] Gen. 2:17 [b] 1 Pet. 1:4 [1] Lit. *in Christ Jesus*
7:2 [a] 1 Cor. 7:39 [1] *concerning*
7:3 [a] [Matt. 5:32]
7:4 [a] Gal. 2:19; 5:18 [b] Gal. 5:22
7:5 [a] Rom. 6:13 [b] James 1:15 [1] *passions* [2] *aroused by*

6 But now we are delivered from the law, ¹that being dead wherein we were held; that we should serve ªin newness of spirit, and not *in* in the oldness of the letter.

7 What shall we say then? *Is* the law sin? ¹God forbid. Nay, ªI ²had not known sin, but by the law: for I ²had not known ³lust, except the law had said, ᵇThou shalt not covet.

8 But ªsin, taking ¹occasion by the commandment, ²wrought in me all manner of ³concupiscence. For ᵇwithout⁴ the law sin *was* dead.

9 For I was alive without the law once: but when the commandment came, sin revived, and I died.

10 And the commandment, ªwhich *was ordained* to life, I found *to be* unto death.

11 For sin, taking occasion by the commandment, deceived me, and by it slew *me*.

12 Wherefore ªthe law *is* holy, and the commandment holy, and just, and good.

13 Was then that which is good made death unto me? ¹God forbid. But sin, that it might appear sin, ²working death in me by that which is good; that sin by the commandment might become exceeding sinful.

14 For we know that the law is spiritual: but I am ¹carnal, ªsold under sin.

15 For that which I do I ¹allow not: for ªwhat I ²would, that do I not; but what I hate, that do I.

16 If then I do that which I would not, I ¹consent unto the law that *it is* good.

17 Now then it is no more I that do it, but sin that dwelleth in me.

18 For I know that ªin me (that is, in my flesh,) dwelleth no good thing: for to will is present with me; but *how* to perform that which is good I find not.

19 For the good that I ¹would I do not: but the evil which I would not, that I do.

20 Now if I do that I would not, it is no more I that do it, but sin that dwelleth in me.

21 I find then a law, that, when I ¹would do good, evil is present with me.

22 For I ªdelight in the law of God ¹after ᵇthe inward man:

23 But ªI see another law in ᵇmy members, warring against the law of my mind, and bringing me into captivity to the law of sin which is in my members.

24 O wretched man that I am! who shall deliver me ªfrom ¹the body of this death?

25 ªI thank God through Jesus Christ our Lord. So then with the mind I myself serve the law of God; but with the flesh the law of sin.

## CHAPTER 8

THERE *is* therefore now no condemnation to them which are in Christ Jesus, who ªwalk not after the flesh, but after the Spirit.

2 For ªthe law of ᵇthe Spirit of life in Christ Jesus hath made me free from ᶜthe law of sin and death.

3 For ªwhat the law could not do, in that it was weak through the flesh, ᵇGod sending his own Son in the likeness of sinful flesh, and ¹for sin, condemned sin in the flesh:

4 That the ¹righteousness of the law might be fulfilled in us, who ªwalk not after the flesh, but after the Spirit.

5 For ªthey that are after the flesh ¹do mind the things of the flesh; but they that are after the Spirit ᵇthe things of the Spirit.

6 For ªto be carnally minded *is* death; but to be spiritually minded *is* life and peace.

7 Because ªthe carnal mind *is* enmity against God: for it is not subject to the law of God, ᵇneither indeed can be.

8 So then they that are in the flesh cannot please God.

9 But ye are not in the flesh, but in the Spirit, if so be that the Spirit of God dwell in you. Now if any man have not the Spirit of Christ, he is none of his.

10 And if Christ *be* in you, the body *is* dead because of sin; but the Spirit *is* life because of righteousness.

11 But if the Spirit of ªhim that raised up Jesus from the dead dwell in you, ᵇhe that raised up Christ from the dead shall also ¹quicken your mortal bodies ²by his Spirit that dwelleth in you.

12 ªTherefore, brethren, we are debtors, not to the flesh, to live after the flesh.

13 For ªif ye live after the flesh, ye shall die: but if ye through the Spirit do ᵇmortify¹ the deeds of the body, ye shall live.

14 For ªas many as are led by the Spirit of God, they are the sons of God.

15 For ªye have not received the spirit of bondage again ᵇto fear; but ye have received the ᶜSpirit of adoption, whereby we cry, ᵈAbba, Father.

16 ªThe Spirit itself beareth witness with our spirit, that we are the children of God:

17 And if children, then ªheirs; heirs of God, and joint-heirs with Christ; ᵇif so be that we suffer with *him*, that we may be also glorified together.

18 For I reckon that ªthe sufferings of this present time *are* not worthy *to be compared* with the glory which shall be revealed in us.

### Cross references

7:6 ª Rom. 2:29
¹ having died to what we were held by
7:7 ª Rom. 3:20
ᵇ Ex. 20:17; Deut. 5:21 ¹ Certainly not ² would not have known ³ covetousness
7:8 ª Rom. 4:15
ᵇ 1 Cor. 15:56
¹ opportunity ² produced ³ desire ⁴ apart from
7:10 ª Lev. 18:5
7:12 ¹ Ps. 19:8
7:13 ¹ Certainly not ² was producing
7:14 ª 2 Kin. 17:17
¹ fleshly
7:15 ª [Gal. 5:17]
¹ understand ² want to do
7:16 ¹ agree with
7:18 ª [Gen. 6:5; 8:21]
7:19 ¹ want to do
7:21 ¹ want to do
7:22 ª Ps. 1:2
ᵇ [2 Cor. 4:16]
¹ according to
7:23 ª [Gal. 5:17]
ᵇ Rom. 6:13, 19
7:24 ª [1 Cor. 15:51, 52] ¹ this body of death
7:25 ª 1 Cor. 15:57

8:1 ª Gal. 5:16
8:2 ª Rom. 6:18, 22 ᵇ [1 Cor. 15:45]
ᶜ Rom. 7:24, 25
8:3 ª Acts 13:39
ᵇ [2 Cor. 5:21] ¹ on account of
8:4 ª Gal. 5:16, 25 ¹ righteous requirement
8:5 ª John 3:6
ᵇ [Gal. 5:22–25]
¹ set their minds on
8:6 ª Gal. 6:8
8:7 ª James 4:4
ᵇ 1 Cor. 2:14
8:11 ª Acts 2:24
ᵇ 1 Cor. 6:14
¹ give life to ² Or because of
8:12 ª [Rom. 6:7, 14]
8:13 ª Gal. 6:8
ᵇ Eph. 4:22 ¹ put to death
8:14 ª [Gal. 5:18]
8:15 ª Heb. 2:15
ᵇ 2 Tim. 1:7 ᶜ [Is. 56:5] ᵈ Mark 14:36
8:16 ª Eph. 1:13
8:17 ª Acts 26:18
ᵇ Phil. 1:29
8:18 ª 2 Cor. 4:17

19 For [a]the earnest expectation of the [1]creature waiteth for the manifestation of the sons of God.

20 For [a]the [1]creature was made subject to [2]vanity, not willingly, but by reason of him who hath subjected *the same* in hope,

21 Because the [1]creature itself also shall be delivered from the bondage of [2]corruption into the glorious [a]liberty of the children of God.

22 For we know that the whole creation [a]groaneth and [1]travaileth in pain together until now.

23 And not only *they,* but ourselves also, which have [a]the firstfruits of the Spirit, [b]even we ourselves groan [c]within ourselves, [1]waiting for the adoption, *to wit,* the [d]redemption of our body.

24 For we are saved by hope: but [a]hope that is seen is not hope: for what a man seeth, why doth he yet hope for?

25 But if we hope for that we see not, *then* do we with [1]patience [2]wait for *it.*

26 Likewise the Spirit also helpeth our [1]infirmities: for [a]we know not what we should pray for as we ought: but [b]the Spirit itself maketh intercession for us with groanings which cannot be uttered.

27 And [a]he that searcheth the hearts knoweth what *is* the mind of the Spirit, because he maketh intercession for the saints [b]according to *the will of* God.

28 And we know that all things work together for good to them that love God, to them [a]who are the called according to *his* purpose.

29 For whom [a]he did foreknow, [b]he also did predestinate [c]*to be* conformed to the image of his Son, [d]that he might be the firstborn among many brethren.

30 Moreover whom he did predestinate, them he also [a]called: and whom he called, them he also [b]justified: and whom he justified, them he also [c]glorified.

31 What shall we then say to these things? [a]If God *be* for us, who *can be* against us?

32 [a]He that spared not his own Son, but [b]delivered him up for us all, how shall he not with him also freely give us all things?

33 Who shall [1]lay any thing to the charge of God's elect? [a]*It is* God that [2]justifieth.

34 [a]Who *is* he that condemneth? *It is* Christ that died, yea rather, that is risen again, [b]who is even at the right hand of God, [c]who also maketh intercession for us.

35 Who shall separate us from the love of Christ? *shall* tribulation, or distress, or persecution, or famine, or nakedness, or peril, or sword?

36 As it is written, [a]For thy sake we are killed all the day long; we are accounted as sheep for the slaughter.

37 [a]Nay, in all these things we are more than conquerors through him that loved us.

38 For I am persuaded, that neither death, nor life, nor angels, nor [a]principalities, nor powers, nor things present, nor things to come,

39 Nor height, nor depth, nor any other creature, shall be able to separate us from the love of God, which is in Christ Jesus our Lord.

## CHAPTER 9

I [a]SAY[1] the truth in Christ, I [2]lie not, my conscience also bearing me witness in the Holy Ghost,

2 [a]That I have great [1]heaviness and continual [2]sorrow in my heart.

3 For [a]I could wish that myself were accursed from Christ for my brethren, my kinsmen according to the flesh:

4 Who are Israelites; [a]to whom *pertaineth* the adoption, and [b]the glory, and [c]the covenants, and [d]the giving of the law, and [e]the service *of God,* and [f]the promises;

5 [a]Whose *are* the fathers, and of [b]whom as concerning the flesh Christ came, [c]who is over all, [1]God blessed for ever. Amen.

6 [a]Not as though the word of God hath taken none effect. For [b]they *are* not all Israel, which are of Israel:

7 [a]Neither, because they are the seed of Abraham, *are they* all children: but, In [b]Isaac shall thy seed be called.

8 That is, They which are the children of the flesh, these *are* not the children of God: but [a]the children of the promise are counted [1]for the seed.

9 For this *is* the word of promise, [a]At this time will I come, and Sarah shall have a son.

10 And not only *this;* but when [a]Rebecca also had conceived by one, *even* by our father Isaac;

11 (For *the children* being not yet born, neither having done any good or evil, that the purpose of God according to election might stand, not of works, but of [a]him that calleth;)

12 It was said unto her, [a]The elder shall serve the younger.

13 As it is written, [a]Jacob have I loved, but Esau have I hated.

14 What shall we say then? [a]*Is there* unrighteousness with God? [1]God forbid.

15 For he saith to Moses, [a]I will have mercy on whom I will have mercy, and I will have compassion on whom I will have compassion.

### Center reference column

8:19 [a] [2 Pet. 3:13]
[1] *creation*

8:20 [a] Gen.
3:17–19 [1] *creation*
[2] *futility*

8:21 [a] [2 Cor. 3:17]
[1] *creation* [2] *decay*

8:22 [a] Jer. 12:4,
11 [1] *suffers birth pangs*

8:23 [a] 2 Cor.
5:5 [b] 2 Cor. 5:2,
4 [c] [Luke 20:36]
[d] Eph. 1:14; 4:30
[1] *eagerly waiting*

8:24 [a] Heb. 11:1

8:25 [1] *perseverance* [2] *eagerly wait*

8:26 [a] Matt.
20:22 [b] Eph. 6:18
[1] *weaknesses*

8:27 [a] 1 Chr. 28:9
[b] 1 John 5:14

8:28 [a] 2 Tim. 1:9

8:29 [a] 2 Tim.
2:19 [b] Eph. 1:5,
11 [c] [2 Cor. 3:18]
[d] Heb. 1:6

8:30 [a] [1 Pet. 2:9;
3:9] [b] [Gal. 2:16]
[c] John 17:22

8:31 [a] Num. 14:9

8:32 [a] Rom. 5:6,
10 [b] [Rom. 4:25]

8:33 [a] Is. 50:8, 9
[1] *bring a charge against* [2] *declares righteous*

8:34 [a] John 3:18
[b] Mark 16:19
[c] Heb. 7:25; 9:24

8:36 [a] Ps. 44:22

8:37 [a] 1 Cor. 15:57

8:38 [a] [Eph. 1:21]

9:1 [a] 2 Cor. 1:23
[1] *tell* [2] *am not lying*

9:2 [a] Rom. 10:1
[1] *sorrow* [2] *grief*

9:3 [a] Ex. 32:32

9:4 [a] Ex. 4:22
[b] 1 Sam. 4:21
[c] Acts 3:25 [d] Ps.
147:19 [e] Heb. 9:1,
6 [f] [Acts 2:39;
13:32]

9:5 [a] Deut. 10:15
[b] [Luke 1:34, 35;
3:23] [c] Jer. 23:6
[1] *the eternally blessed God*

9:6 [a] Num. 23:19
[b] [Gal. 6:16]

9:7 [a] [Gal. 4:23]
[b] Gen. 21:12

9:8 [a] Gal. 4:28 [1] *as*

9:9 [a] Gen. 18:10, 14

9:10 [a] Gen. 25:21

9:11 [a] [Rom. 4:17;
8:28]

9:12 [a] Gen. 25:23

9:13 [a] Mal. 1:2, 3

9:14 [a] Deut. 32:4
[1] *Certainly not*

9:15 [a] Ex. 33:19

16 So then *it is* not of him that willeth, nor of him that runneth, but of God that sheweth mercy.

17 For [a]the scripture saith unto Pharaoh, [b]Even for this same purpose have I raised thee up, that I might shew my power in thee, and that my name might be declared throughout all the earth.

18 Therefore hath he mercy on whom he will *have mercy,* and whom he will he [a]hardeneth.

19 Thou wilt say then unto me, Why doth he yet find fault? For [a]who hath resisted his will?

20 Nay but, O man, who art thou that repliest against God? [a]Shall the thing formed say to him that formed *it,* Why hast thou made me thus?

21 Hath not the [a]potter power over the clay, of the same lump to make [b]one vessel unto honour, and another unto dishonour?

22 *What* if God, [1]willing to shew *his* wrath, and to make his power known, endured with much longsuffering [a]the vessels of wrath [b]fitted[2] to destruction:

23 And that he might make known [a]the riches of his glory on the vessels of mercy, which he had [b]afore[1] prepared unto glory,

24 Even us, whom he hath [a]called, [b]not of the Jews only, but also of the Gentiles?

25 As he saith also in Osee, [a]I will call them my people, which were not my people; and her beloved, which was not beloved.

26 [a]And it shall come to pass, *that* in the place where it was said unto them, Ye *are* not my people; there shall they be called the [1]children of the living God.

27 Esaias also crieth concerning Israel, [a]Though the number of the children of Israel be as the sand of the sea, [b]a remnant shall be saved:

28 For he will finish the work, and cut *it* short in righteousness: [a]because a short work will the Lord make upon the earth.

29 And as Esaias said before, [a]Except the Lord of Sabaoth had left us a seed, [b]we [1]had been as Sodoma, and been made like unto Gomorrha.

30 What shall we say then? [a]That the Gentiles, which followed not after righteousness, have attained to righteousness, [b]even the righteousness which is of faith.

31 But Israel, [a]which followed after the law of righteousness, [b]hath not attained to the law of righteousness.

32 [1]Wherefore? Because *they sought it* not by faith, but as it were by the works of the law. For [a]they stumbled at that stumblingstone;

33 As it is written, [a]Behold, I lay in

9:17 [a] Gal. 3:8
[b] Ex. 9:16
9:18 [a] Ex. 4:21
9:19 [a] 2 Chr. 20:6
9:20 [a] Is. 29:16
9:21 [a] Prov. 16:4
[b] 2 Tim. 2:20
9:22 [a] [1 Thess. 5:9] [b] [1 Pet. 2:8] [1] *wanting*
[2] *prepared for*
9:23 [a] [Col. 1:27]
[b] [Rom. 8:28–30]
[1] *beforehand*
9:24 [a] [Rom. 8:28] [b] Rom. 3:29
9:25 [a] Hos. 2:23
9:26 [a] Hos. 1:10
[1] *sons*
9:27 [a] Is. 10:22, 23
[b] Rom. 11:5
9:28 [a] Is. 10:23; 28:22
9:29 [a] Is. 1:9 [b] Is. 13:19 [1] *would have become*
9:30 [a] Rom. 4:11 [b] Rom. 1:17; 3:21; 10:6
9:31 [a] [Rom. 10:2–4] [b] [Gal. 5:4]
9:32 [a] [1 Cor. 1:23] [1] *Why*
9:33 [a] Is. 8:14; 28:16

[b] Rom. 5:5; 10:11
[1] *put to shame*
10:2 [a] Acts 21:20
[1] *witness* [2] *for*
10:3 [a] [Rom. 1:17]
[b] [Phil. 3:9]
10:4 [a] [Gal. 3:24; 4:5]
10:5 [a] Lev. 18:5
[1] *writes about*
10:6 [a] Deut. 30:12–14
10:7 [1] *abyss*
10:8 [a] Deut. 30:14
[1] *near*
10:9 [a] Luke 12:8
10:11 [a] Is. 28:16
[1] *put to shame*
10:12 [a] Rom. 3:22, 29 [b] Acts 10:36
[c] Eph. 1:7
10:13 [a] Joel 2:32
[b] Acts 9:14
10:14 [a] Titus 1:3
10:15 [a] Is. 52:7; Nah. 1:15
10:16 [a] Is. 53:1

Sion a stumblingstone and rock of offence: and [b]whosoever believeth on him shall not be [1]ashamed.

## CHAPTER 10

BRETHREN, my heart's desire and prayer to God for Israel is, that they might be saved.

2 For I bear them [1]record [a]that they have a zeal [2]of God, but not according to knowledge.

3 For they being ignorant of [a]God's righteousness, and going about to establish their own [b]righteousness, have not submitted themselves unto the righteousness of God.

4 For [a]Christ *is* the end of the law for righteousness to every one that believeth.

5 For Moses [1]describeth the righteousness which is of the law, [a]That the man which doeth those things shall live by them.

6 But the righteousness which is of faith speaketh on this wise, [a]Say not in thine heart, Who shall ascend into heaven? (that is, to bring Christ down *from above:*)

7 Or, Who shall descend into the [1]deep? (that is, to bring up Christ again from the dead.)

8 But what saith it? [a]The word is [1]nigh thee, *even* in thy mouth, and in thy heart: that is, the word of faith, which we preach;

9 That [a]if thou shalt confess with thy mouth the Lord Jesus, and shalt believe in thine heart that God hath raised him from the dead, thou shalt be saved.

10 For with the heart man believeth unto righteousness; and with the mouth confession is made unto salvation.

11 For the scripture saith, [a]Whosoever believeth on him shall not be [1]ashamed.

12 For [a]there is no difference between the Jew and the Greek: for [b]the same Lord over all [c]is rich unto all that call upon him.

13 [a]For whosoever shall call [b]upon the name of the Lord shall be saved.

14 How then shall they call on him in whom they have not believed? and how shall they believe in him of whom they have not heard? and how shall they hear [a]without a preacher?

15 And how shall they preach, except they be sent? as it is written, [a]How beautiful are the feet of them that preach the gospel of peace, and bring glad tidings of good things!

16 But they have not all obeyed the gospel. For Esaias saith, [a]Lord, who hath believed our report?

17 So then faith *cometh* by hearing, and hearing by the word of God.

18 But I say, Have they not heard?

Yes verily, [a]their sound went into all the earth, [b]and their words unto the ends of the world.

19 But I say, Did not Israel know? First Moses saith, [a]I will provoke you to jealousy by *them that are* [1]no people, *and* by a [b]foolish nation I will anger you.

20 But Esaias is very bold, and saith, [a]I was found of them that sought me not; I was made manifest unto them that asked not after me.

21 But to Israel he saith, [a]All day long I have stretched forth my hands unto a disobedient and [1]gainsaying people.

## CHAPTER 11

I SAY then, [a]Hath God cast away his people? [b]God[1] forbid. For [c]I also am an Israelite, of the seed of Abraham, *of* the tribe of Benjamin.

2 God hath not cast away his people which [a]he foreknew. [1]Wot ye not what the scripture saith of Elias? how he maketh intercession to God against Israel, saying,

3 [a]Lord, they have killed thy prophets, and [1]digged down thine altars; and I am left alone, and they seek my life.

4 But what saith the answer of God unto him? [a]I have reserved to myself seven thousand men, who have not bowed the knee to *the image of* Baal.

5 [a]Even so then at this present time also there is a remnant according to the election of grace.

6 And [a]if by grace, then *is it* no more of works: otherwise grace is no more grace. But if *it be* of works, then is it no more grace: otherwise work is no more work.

7 What then? [a]Israel hath not obtained that which he seeketh for; but the [1]election hath obtained it, and the rest were [b]blinded[2]

8 (According as it is written, [a]God hath given them the spirit of [1]slumber, [b]eyes that they should not see, and ears that they should not hear;) unto this day.

9 And David saith, [a]Let their table be made a snare, and a trap, and a stumblingblock, and a recompence unto them:

10 Let their eyes be darkened, that they may not see, and bow down their back alway.

11 I say then, Have they stumbled that they should fall? [1]God forbid: but *rather* [a]through their [2]fall salvation *is come* unto the Gentiles, for to provoke them to [b]jealousy.

12 Now if the [1]fall of them *be* the riches of the world, and the [2]diminishing of them the riches of the Gentiles; how much more their fulness?

13 For I speak to you Gentiles, inasmuch as [a]I am [1]the apostle of the Gentiles, I magnify [2]mine office:

14 If by any means I may provoke to [1]emulation *them which are* my flesh, and [a]might save some of them.

15 For if the casting away of them *be* the reconciling of the world, what *shall* the receiving *of them be,* [a]but life from the dead?

16 For if [a]the firstfruit *be* holy, the lump *is* also *holy:* and if the root *be* holy, so *are* the branches.

17 And if [a]some of the branches be broken off, and thou, being a wild olive tree, [1]wert graffed in among them, and with them partakest of the root and fatness of the olive tree;

18 [a]Boast not against the branches. But if thou boast, [1]thou bearest not the root, but the root thee.

19 Thou wilt say then, The branches were broken off, that I might be graffed in.

20 Well; because of [a]unbelief they were broken off, and thou standest by faith. Be not [1]highminded, but fear:

21 For if God spared not the natural branches, *take heed* lest he also spare not thee.

22 Behold therefore the goodness and severity of God: on them which fell, severity; but toward thee, goodness, [a]if thou continue in *his* goodness: otherwise [b]thou also shalt be cut off.

23 And they also, [a]if they abide not still in unbelief, shall be graffed in: for God is able to graff them in again.

24 For if thou [1]wert cut out of the olive tree which is wild by nature, and [1]wert graffed contrary to nature into a good olive tree: how much more shall these, which be the natural *branches,* be graffed into their own olive tree?

25 For I would not, brethren, that ye should be ignorant of this mystery, lest ye should be [a]wise in your own [1]conceits; that [b]blindness[2] in part is happened to Israel, [c]until the fulness of the Gentiles be come in.

26 And so all Israel shall be saved: as it is written, [a]There shall come out of Sion the Deliverer, and shall turn away ungodliness from Jacob:

27 [a]For this *is* my covenant unto them, when I shall take away their sins.

28 As concerning the gospel, *they are* enemies for your sakes: but [1]as touching the election, *they are* [a]beloved for the fathers' sakes.

29 For the gifts and calling of God *are* [a]without[1] repentance.

30 For as ye [a]in times past [1]have not believed God, yet have now obtained mercy through their [b]unbelief:

31 Even so have these also now not [1]believed, that through [2]your mercy they also may obtain mercy.

### Cross references (center column)

10:18 [a] Ps. 19:4
[b] 1 Kin. 18:10
10:19 [a] Deut. 32:21
[b] Titus 3:3 [1] *not a nation*
10:20 [a] Is. 65:1
10:21 [a] Is. 65:2
[1] *contrary*
11:1 [a] Jer. 46:28
[b] 1 Sam. 12:22
[c] 2 Cor. 11:22
[1] *Certainly not*
11:2 [a] [Rom. 8:29]
[1] *Know*
11:3 [a] 1 Kin. 19:10, 14 [1] *torn*
11:4 [a] 1 Kin. 19:18
11:5 [a] Rom. 9:27
11:6 [a] Rom. 4:4
11:7 [a] Rom. 9:31
[b] 2 Cor. 3:14
[1] *elect* [2] *hardened*
11:8 [a] Is. 29:10, 13
[b] Deut. 29:3, 4
[1] *stupor*
11:9 [a] Ps. 69:22, 23
11:11 [a] Is. 42:6, 7 [b] Rom. 10:19
[1] *Certainly not* [2] *trespass*
11:12 [1] *trespass* [2] *failure*
11:13 [a] Acts 9:15; 22:21 [1] Lit. *an* [2] *my ministry*

11:14 [a] 1 Cor. 9:22
[1] *jealousy*
11:15 [a] [Is. 26:16–19]
11:16 [a] Lev. 23:10
11:17 [a] Jer. 11:16
[b] [Eph. 2:12]
[1] *were*
11:18 [a] [1 Cor. 10:12] [1] *remember that you do not support the*
11:20 [a] Heb. 3:19
[1] *haughty*
11:22 [a] 1 Cor. 15:2
[b] [John 15:2]
11:23 [a] [2 Cor. 3:16]
11:24 [1] *were*
11:25 [a] Rom. 12:16 [b] 2 Cor. 3:14 [c] Luke 21:24 [1] *opinion* [2] *hardening*
11:26 [a] Is. 59:20, 21
11:27 [a] Is. 27:9
11:28 [a] Deut. 7:8; 10:15 [1] *concerning the*
11:29 [a] Num. 23:19 [1] *irrevocable*
11:30 [a] [Eph. 2:2] [1] *were disobedient to* [2] *disobedience*
11:31 [1] *obeyed* [2] *the mercy shown you*

32 For God hath [1]concluded them [a]all [2]in unbelief, that he might have mercy upon all.

33 O the depth of the riches both of the wisdom and knowledge of God! how unsearchable *are* his judgments, and his ways past finding out!

34 For who hath known the [a]mind of the Lord? or [b]who hath been his counsellor?

35 [a]Or who hath first given to him, and it shall be [1]recompensed unto him again?

36 For [a]of him, and through him, and to him, *are* all things: [b]to whom *be* glory for ever. Amen.

## CHAPTER 12

I [a]BESEECH you therefore, brethren, by the mercies of God, that ye present your bodies a [b]living sacrifice, holy, acceptable unto God, *which is* your [1]reasonable service.

2 And [a]be not conformed to this world: but [b]be ye transformed by the renewing of your mind, that ye may [c]prove what *is* that good, and acceptable, and perfect, will of God.

3 For I say, [a]through the grace given unto me, to every man that is among you, [b]not to think *of himself* more highly than he ought to think; but to think soberly, according as God hath dealt [c]to every man the measure of faith.

4 For [a]as we have many members in one body, and all members have not the same [1]office:

5 So [a]we, *being* many, are one body in Christ, and [1]every one members one of another.

6 Having then gifts differing according to the grace that is [a]given to us, whether prophecy, *let us* [b]prophesy according to the proportion of faith;

7 Or ministry, *let us wait* on *our* ministering: or [a]he that teacheth, on teaching;

8 Or [a]he that exhorteth, on exhortation: [b]he that giveth, *let him do it* with [1]simplicity; [c]he that ruleth, with diligence; he that sheweth mercy, [d]with cheerfulness.

9 [a]*Let* love be without [1]dissimulation. [b]Abhor that which is evil; [2]cleave to that which is good.

10 [a]*Be* kindly [1]affectioned one to another with brotherly love; [b]in honour [2]preferring one another;

11 Not [1]slothful in business; fervent in spirit; serving the Lord;

12 [a]Rejoicing in hope; [b]patient[1] in tribulation; [c]continuing[2] instant in prayer;

13 [a]Distributing to the [1]necessity of saints; [b]given to hospitality.

14 [a]Bless them which persecute you: bless, and curse not.

15 [a]Rejoice with them that do rejoice, and weep with them that weep.

16 [a]*Be* of the same mind one toward another. [b]Mind[1] not high things, but [2]condescend to men of low estate. Be not wise in your own [3]conceits.

17 [a]Recompense[1] to no man evil for evil. [b]Provide[2] things honest in the sight of all men.

18 If it be possible, as much as [1]lieth in you, [a]live peaceably with all men.

19 Dearly beloved, [a]avenge not yourselves, but *rather* give place unto wrath: for it is written, [b]Vengeance *is* mine; I will repay, saith the Lord.

20 [a]Therefore if thine enemy hunger, feed him; if he thirst, give him drink: for in so doing thou shalt heap coals of fire on his head.

21 Be not overcome of evil, but [a]overcome evil with good.

## CHAPTER 13

LET every soul be [a]subject unto the [1]higher [2]powers. For there is no [3]power but of God: the [2]powers that be are [4]ordained of God.

2 Whosoever therefore resisteth [a]the [1]power, resisteth the ordinance of God: and they that resist shall receive to themselves [2]damnation.

3 For rulers are not a terror to good works, but to the evil. [1]Wilt thou then not be afraid of the [2]power? [a]do that which is good, and thou shalt have praise of the same:

4 For he is the minister of God to thee for good. But if thou do that which is evil, be afraid; for he beareth not the sword in vain: for he is the minister of God, [1]a revenger to *execute* wrath upon him that doeth evil.

5 Wherefore [a]*ye* must needs be subject, not only [1]for wrath, [b]but also for conscience sake.

6 For for this cause pay ye [1]tribute also: for they are God's ministers, attending continually upon this very thing.

7 [a]Render therefore to all their dues: [1]tribute to whom [1]tribute *is due;* custom to whom custom; fear to whom fear; honour to whom honour.

8 Owe no man any thing, but to love one another: for [a]he that loveth another hath fulfilled the law.

9 For this, [a]Thou shalt not commit adultery, Thou shalt not [1]kill, Thou shalt not steal, Thou shalt not bear false witness, Thou shalt not covet; and if *there be* any other commandment, it is [2]briefly comprehended in this saying, namely, [b]Thou shalt love thy neighbour as thyself.

---

11:32 [a] [Gal. 3:22] [1] *confined* [2] *to disobedience*

11:34 [a] Is. 40:13; Jer. 23:18 [b] Job 36:22

11:35 [a] Job 41:11 [1] *repaid*

11:36 [a] Heb. 2:10 [b] Heb. 13:21

12:1 [a] 2 Cor. 10:1–4 [b] Heb. 10:18, 20 [1] *rational*

12:2 [a] 1 John 2:15, [b] Eph. 4:23 [c] [1 Thess. 4:3]

12:3 [a] Gal. 2:9 [b] Prov. 25:27 [c] [Eph. 4:7]

12:4 [a] 1 Cor. 12:12– 14 [1] *function*

12:5 [a] [1 Cor. 10:17] [1] *individually*

12:6 [a] [John 3:27] [b] Acts 11:27

12:7 [a] Eph. 4:11

12:8 [a] Acts 15:32 [b] [Matt. 6:1–3] [c] [Acts 20:28] [d] 2 Cor. 9:7 [1] *liberality*

12:9 [a] 1 Tim. 1:5 [b] Ps. 34:14 [1] *hypocrisy* [2] *cling*

12:10 [a] Heb. 13:1 [b] Phil. 2:3 [1] *affectionate* [2] *giving preference to*

12:11 [1] *lagging in diligence*

12:12 [a] Luke 10:20 [b] Luke 21:19 [c] Luke 18:1 [1] *persevering* [2] *steadfastly*

12:13 [a] 1 Cor. 16:1 [b] 1 Tim. 3:2 [1] *needs*

12:14 [a] [Matt. 5:44]

12:15 [a] [1 Cor. 12:26]

12:16 [a] [Phil. 2:2; 4:2] [b] Jer. 45:5 [1] *Do not set your mind on* [2] *associate with the humble* [3] *estimation*

12:17 [a] [Matt. 5:39] [b] 2 Cor. 8:21 [1] *Repay* [2] *Have regard for good things*

12:18 [a] Heb. 12:14 [1] *depends on*

12:19 [a] Lev. 19:18 [b] Deut. 32:35

12:20 [a] Prov. 25:21, 22

12:21 [a] [Rom. 12:1, 2]

13:1 [a] 1 Pet. 2:13 [1] *governing* [2] *authorities* [3] *authority* [4] *appointed by*

13:2 [a] [Titus 3:1] [1] *authority* [2] *judgment*    13:3 [a] 1 Pet. 2:14 [1] *Do you want to be unafraid* [2] *authority*    13:4 [1] *an avenger*    13:5 [a] Eccl. 8:2 [b] [1 Pet. 2:13, 19] [1] *because of*    13:6 [1] *taxes*    13:7 [a] Matt. 22:21 [1] *tax* 13:8 [a] [Gal. 5:13, 14]    13:9 [a] Ex. 20:13–17; Deut. 5:17–21 [b] Lev. 19:18 [1] *murder* [2] *summed up*

10 Love ¹worketh no ill to his neighbour: therefore ᵃlove *is* the fulfilling of the law.

11 And that, knowing the time, that now *it is* high time ᵃto awake out of sleep: for now *is* our salvation nearer than when we ¹believed.

12 The night is far spent, the day is at hand: ᵃlet us therefore cast off the works of darkness, and ᵇlet us put on the armour of light.

13 ᵃLet us walk ¹honestly, as in the day; ᵇnot in ²rioting and drunkenness, ᶜnot in ³chambering and ⁴wantonness, ᵈnot in strife and envying.

14 But ᵃput ye on the Lord Jesus Christ, and ᵇmake not provision for the flesh, to *fulfil* the lusts *thereof.*

## CHAPTER 14

H IM that ᵃis weak in the faith receive ye, *but* not to doubtful disputations.

2 For one believeth that he ᵃmay eat all things: another, who is weak, eateth ¹herbs.

3 Let not him that eateth despise him that eateth not; and ᵃlet not him which eateth not judge him that eateth: for God hath received him.

4 ᵃWho art thou that judgest another man's servant? to his own master he standeth or falleth. Yea, he shall be ¹holden up: for God is able to make him stand.

5 ᵃOne man esteemeth one day above another: another esteemeth every day *alike.* Let every man be fully ¹persuaded in his own mind.

6 He that ᵃregardeth¹ the day, regardeth *it* unto the Lord; and he that ¹regardeth not the day, to the Lord he doth not regard *it.* He that eateth, eateth to the Lord, for ᵇhe giveth God thanks; and he that eateth not, to the Lord he eateth not, and giveth God thanks.

7 For ᵃnone of us liveth to himself, and no man dieth to himself.

8 For whether we ᵃlive, we live unto the Lord; and whether we die, we die unto the Lord: whether we live therefore, or die, we are the Lord's.

9 For ᵃto this end Christ both died, and rose, and ¹revived, that he might be ᵇLord both of the dead and living.

10 But why dost thou judge thy brother? or why dost thou ¹set at nought thy brother? for ᵃwe shall all stand before the judgment seat of Christ.

11 For it is written, ᵃ*As* I live, saith the Lord, every knee shall bow to me, and every tongue shall confess to God.

12 So then ᵃevery one of us shall give account of himself to God.

13 Let us not therefore judge one another any more: but judge this

rather, that ᵃno man put a stumblingblock or an occasion to fall in *his* brother's way.

14 I know, and am persuaded by the Lord Jesus, ᵃthat *there is* nothing unclean of itself: but to him that ¹esteemeth any thing to be unclean, to him *it is* unclean.

15 But if thy brother be grieved ¹with *thy* ²meat, now walkest thou not charitably. ᵃDestroy not him with thy ²meat, for whom Christ died.

16 ᵃLet not then your good be evil spoken of:

17 ᵃFor the kingdom of God is not ¹meat and drink; but righteousness, and ᵇpeace, and joy in the Holy Ghost.

18 For he that in these things serveth Christ ᵃ*is* acceptable to God, and approved of men.

19 ᵃLet us therefore follow after the things which make for peace, and things wherewith ᵇone may ¹edify another.

20 ᵃFor ¹meat destroy not the work of God. ᵇAll things indeed *are* pure; ᶜbut *it is* evil for that man who eateth with offence.

21 *It is* good neither to eat ᵃflesh, nor to drink wine, nor *any thing* whereby thy brother stumbleth, or is offended, or is made weak.

22 Hast thou faith? have *it* to thyself before God. ᵃHappy *is* he that condemneth not himself in that thing which he ¹alloweth.

23 And he that doubteth is ¹damned if he eat, because *he eateth* not of faith: for ᵃwhatsoever *is* not of faith is sin.

## CHAPTER 15

W E ᵃthen that are strong ought to bear the ¹infirmities of the weak, and not to please ourselves.

2 ᵃLet every one of us please *his* neighbour for *his* good to ¹edification.

3 ᵃFor even Christ pleased not himself; but, as it is written, The ᵇreproaches of them that reproached thee fell on me.

4 For ᵃwhatsoever things were written ¹aforetime were written for our learning, that we through ²patience and comfort of the scriptures might have hope.

5 ᵃNow the God of patience and ¹consolation grant you to be likeminded one toward another according to Christ Jesus:

6 That ye may ᵃwith one mind *and* one mouth glorify God, even the Father of our Lord Jesus Christ.

7 Wherefore ᵃreceive ye one another, ᵇas Christ also received us to the glory of God.

8 Now I say that ᵃJesus Christ ¹was a minister of the circumcision for the

13:10 ᵃ [Matt. 7:12; 22:39, 40] ¹ *does no harm*
13:11 ᵃ [1 Cor. 15:34] ¹ *first believed*
13:12 ᵃ Eph. 5:11 ᵇ [Eph. 6:11, 13]
13:13 ᵃ Phil. 4:8 ᵇ Prov. 23:20 ᶜ [1 Cor. 6:9] ᵈ James 3:14 ¹ *properly* ² *revelry* ³ *licentiousness* ⁴ *lewdness*
13:14 ᵃ Gal. 3:27 ᵇ [Gal. 5:16]
14:1 ᵃ [1 Cor. 8:9; 9:22]
14:2 ᵃ [Titus 1:15] ¹ *only vegetables*
14:3 ᵃ [Col. 2:16]
14:4 ᵃ James 4:11, 12 ¹ *made to stand*
14:5 ᵃ Gal. 4:10 ¹ *Convinced*
14:6 ᵃ Gal. 4:10 ᵇ [1 Tim. 4:3] ¹ *observes*
14:7 ᵃ [Gal. 2:20]
14:8 ᵃ 2 Cor. 5:14, 15
14:9 ᵃ 2 Cor. 5:15 ᵇ Acts 10:36 ¹ *lived again*
14:10 ᵃ 2 Cor. 5:10 ¹ *despise*
14:11 ᵃ Is. 45:23
14:12 ᵃ 1 Pet. 4:5
14:13 ᵃ 1 Cor. 8:9
14:14 ᵃ 1 Cor. 10:25 ¹ *considers*
14:15 ᵃ 1 Cor. 8:11 ¹ *by* ² *food*
14:16 ᵃ [Rom. 12:17]
14:17 ᵃ 1 Cor. 8:8 ᵇ [Rom. 8:6] ¹ *food*
14:18 ᵃ 2 Cor. 8:21
14:19 ᵃ Rom. 12:18 ᵇ 1 Cor. 14:12 ¹ *build up*
14:20 ᵃ Rom. 14:15 ᵇ Acts 10:15 ᶜ 1 Cor. 8:9–12 ¹ *food*
14:21 ᵃ 1 Cor. 8:13
14:22 ᵃ [1 John 3:21] ¹ *approves*
14:23 ᵃ Titus 1:15 ¹ *condemned*
15:1 ᵃ [Gal. 6:1, 2] ¹ *weaknesses*
15:2 ᵃ 1 Cor. 9:22; 10:24, 33 ¹ *being built up*
15:3 ᵃ Matt. 26:39 ᵇ Ps. 69:9
15:4 ᵃ 1 Cor. 10:11 ¹ *beforehand* ² *perseverance*
15:5 ᵃ 1 Cor. 1:10 ¹ *comfort*
15:6 ᵃ Acts 4:24 15:7 ᵃ Rom. 14:1, 3 ᵇ Rom. 5:2
15:8 ᵃ Matt. 15:24 ¹ *became a servant*

truth of God, [b]to confirm the promises *made* unto the fathers:

9 And [a]that the Gentiles might glorify God for *his* mercy; as it is written, [b]For this cause I will confess to thee among the Gentiles, and sing unto thy name.

10 And again he saith, [a]Rejoice, ye Gentiles, with his people.

11 And again, [a]Praise the Lord, all ye Gentiles; and laud him, all ye people.

12 And again, Esaias saith, [a]There shall be a root of Jesse, and he that shall rise to reign over the Gentiles; in him shall the Gentiles trust.

13 Now the God of hope fill you with all [a]joy and peace in believing, that ye may abound in hope, through the power of the Holy Ghost.

14 And [a]I myself also am [1]persuaded of you, my brethren, that ye also are full of goodness, [b]filled with all knowledge, able also to admonish one another.

15 Nevertheless, brethren, I have written the more boldly unto you [1]in some sort, as [2]putting you in mind, [a]because of the grace that is given to me of God,

16 That [a]I should be [1]the minister of Jesus Christ to the Gentiles, ministering the gospel of God, that the [b]offering up of the Gentiles might be acceptable, being sanctified by the Holy Ghost.

17 I have therefore [1]whereof I may glory through Jesus Christ [a]in those things which pertain to God.

18 For I will not dare to speak of any of those things [a]which Christ hath not wrought by me, [b]to make the Gentiles obedient, by word and deed,

19 [a]Through mighty signs and wonders, by the power of the Spirit of God; so that from Jerusalem, and round about unto Illyricum, I have fully preached the gospel of Christ.

20 Yea, so have I [1]strived to preach the gospel, not where Christ was named, [a]lest I should build upon another man's foundation:

21 But as it is written, [a]To whom he was not spoken of, they shall see: and they that have not heard shall understand.

22 For which cause also [a]I have been much hindered from coming to you.

23 But now having no more place in these parts, and [a]having a great desire these many years to come unto you;

24 Whensoever I take my journey into Spain, I will come to you: for I trust to see you in my journey, [a]and to be [1]brought on my way thitherward by you, if first I [2]be somewhat [b]filled with your *company*.

15:8 [b] 2 Cor. 1:20
15:9 [a] John 10:16
  [b] 2 Sam. 22:50;
  Ps. 18:49
15:10 [a] Deut. 32:43
15:11 [a] Ps. 117:1
15:12 [a] Is. 11:1, 10
15:13 [a] Rom. 12:12; 14:17
15:14 [a] 2 Pet. 1:12
  [b] 1 Cor. 1:5; 8:1, 7,
  10 [1] *confident*
15:15 [1] on some points [2] *reminding you* [a] Rom. 1:5; 12:3
15:16 [a] Rom. 11:13
  [b] [Is. 66:20] [1] *a*
15:17 [a] Heb. 2:17;
  5:1 [1] *reason to glory*
15:18 [a] Acts 15:12; 21:19 [b] Rom. 1:5
15:19 [a] Acts 19:11
15:20 [a] [2 Cor. 10:13, 15, 16]
  [1] *aimed*
15:21 [a] Is. 52:15
15:22 [a] Rom. 1:13
15:23 [a] Acts 19:21; 23:11
15:24 [a] Acts 15:3 [b] Rom. 1:12
  [1] *helped* [2] *may enjoy your company for a while*

25 But now [a]I go unto Jerusalem to minister unto the saints.

26 For [a]it hath pleased them of Macedonia and Achaia to make a certain contribution for the poor saints which are at Jerusalem.

27 It hath pleased them verily; and their debtors they are. For [a]if the Gentiles have been made partakers of their spiritual things, [b]their duty is also to minister unto them in [1]carnal things.

28 When therefore I have performed this, and have sealed to them [a]this fruit, I will come [1]by you into Spain.

29 [a]And I am sure that, when I come unto you, I shall come in the fulness of the blessing of the gospel of Christ.

30 Now I beseech you, brethren, [1]for the Lord Jesus Christ's sake, and [a]for[2] the love of the Spirit, [b]that ye strive together with me in *your* prayers to God for me;

31 [a]That I may be delivered from them that do not believe in Judaea; and that [b]my service which *I have* for Jerusalem may be [1]accepted of the saints;

32 [a]That I may come unto you with joy [b]by the will of God, and may with you [c]be refreshed.

33 Now [a]the God of peace *be* with you all. Amen.

## CHAPTER 16

I COMMEND unto you Phebe our sister, which is a servant of the church which is at [a]Cenchrea:

2 [a]That ye receive her in the Lord, [b]as becometh saints, and that ye assist her in whatsoever business she hath need of you: for she hath been a [1]succourer of many, and of myself also.

3 Greet [a]Priscilla and Aquila my helpers in Christ Jesus:

4 Who have for my life [1]laid down their own necks: unto whom not only I give thanks, but also all the churches of the Gentiles.

5 Likewise *greet* [a]the church that is in their house. Salute my wellbeloved Epaenetus, who is [b]the firstfruits of Achaia unto Christ.

6 Greet Mary, who bestowed much labour on us.

7 [1]Salute Andronicus and Junia, my kinsmen, and my fellowprisoners, who are of note among the [a]apostles, who also [b]were in Christ before me.

8 Greet Amplias my beloved in the Lord.

9 Salute Urbane, our helper in Christ, and Stachys my beloved.

10 Salute Apelles approved in Christ. Salute them which are of Aristobulus' *household*.

15:25 [a] Acts 19:21
15:26 [a] 1 Cor. 16:1
15:27 [a] Rom. 11:17 [b] 1 Cor. 9:11
  [1] *material*
15:28 [a] Phil. 4:17
  [1] *by way of you*
15:29 [a] [Rom. 1:11]
15:30 [a] Phil. 2:1 [b] 2 Cor. 1:11
  [1] *through the Lord Jesus Christ* [2] *through*
15:31 [a] 2 Tim. 3:11;
  4:17 [b] 2 Cor. 8:4
  [1] *acceptable to*
15:32 [a] Rom. 1:10 [b] Acts 18:21
  [c] 1 Cor. 16:18
15:33 [a] 1 Cor. 14:33
16:1 [a] Acts 18:18
16:2 [a] Phil. 2:29 [b] Phil. 1:27
  [1] *helper*
16:3 [a] Acts 18:2, 18, 26
16:4 [1] *risked*
16:5 [a] 1 Cor. 16:19
  [b] 1 Cor. 16:15
16:7 [a] Acts 1:13, 26 [b] Gal. 1:22
  [1] *Greet, and so throughout the chapter*

11 Salute Herodion my kinsman. Greet them that be of the *household* of Narcissus, which are in the Lord.

12 Salute Tryphena and Tryphosa, who labour in the Lord. Salute the beloved Persis, which laboured much in the Lord.

13 Salute Rufus [a]chosen in the Lord, and his mother and mine.

14 Salute Asyncritus, Phlegon, Hermas, Patrobas, Hermes, and the brethren which are with them.

15 Salute Philologus, and Julia, Nereus, and his sister, and Olympas, and all the saints which are with them.

16 [a]Salute one another with an holy kiss. The churches of Christ salute you.

17 Now I beseech you, brethren, [1]mark them [a]which cause divisions and offences contrary to the doctrine which ye have learned; and [b]avoid them.

18 For they that are such serve not our Lord Jesus Christ, but [a]their own belly; and [b]by [1]good words and [2]fair speeches deceive the hearts of the [3]simple.

19 For [a]your obedience is [1]come abroad unto all *men*. I am glad there-

fore on your behalf: but yet I would have you [b]wise unto that which is good, and simple concerning evil.

20 And [a]the God of peace [b]shall [1]bruise Satan under your feet shortly. [c]The grace of our Lord Jesus Christ *be* with you. Amen.

21 [a]Timotheus my workfellow, and [b]Lucius, and [c]Jason, and [d]Sosipater, my kinsmen, salute you.

22 I Tertius, who wrote *this* epistle, salute you in the Lord.

23 [a]Gaius mine host, and of the whole church, saluteth you. [b]Erastus the [1]chamberlain of the city saluteth you, and Quartus a brother.

24 [a]The grace of our Lord Jesus Christ *be* with you all. Amen.

25 Now [a]to him that is [1]of power to [2]stablish you [b]according to my gospel, and the preaching of Jesus Christ, [c]according to the revelation of the mystery, [d]which was kept secret since the world began,

26 But [a]now is made manifest, and by the scriptures of the prophets, according to the commandment of the everlasting God, made known to all nations for [b]the obedience of faith:

27 To [a]God only wise, *be* glory through Jesus Christ for ever. Amen.

16:13 [a] 2 John 1
16:16 [a] 1 Cor. 16:20
16:17 [a] [Acts 15:1]
[b] [1 Cor. 5:9]
[1] note
16:18 [a] Phil.
3:19 [b] Col. 2:4
[1] smooth [2] flattering [3] innocent
16:19 [a] Rom. 1:8
[1] reported

16:20 [b] Matt. 10:16
16:20 [a] Rom.
15:33 [b] Gen.
3:15 [c] 1 Cor. 16:23
[1] crush
16:21 [a] Acts 16:1
[b] Acts 13:1 [c] Acts
17:5 [d] Acts 20:4
16:23 [a] 1 Cor.
1:14 [b] Acts 19:22
[1] treasurer
16:24 [a] 1 Thess.
5:28
16:25 [a] [Eph.
3:20] [b] Rom. 2:16
[c] Eph. 1:9 [d] Col.
1:26; 2:2; 4:3
[1] able [2] establish
16:26 [a] Eph. 1:9
[b] Rom. 1:5
16:27 [a] Jude 25

# THE FIRST EPISTLE OF PAUL THE APOSTLE TO THE
# CORINTHIANS

Corinth, the most important city in Greece during Paul's day, was a bustling hub of worldwide commerce, degraded culture, and idolatrous religion. There Paul founded a church (Acts 18:1–17), and two of his letters are addressed "Unto the church of God which is at Corinth" (1:2; 2 Cor. 1:1).

First Corinthians reveals the problems, pressures, and struggles of a church called out of a pagan society. Paul addresses a variety of problems in the lifestyle of the Corinthian church: factions, lawsuits, immorality, questionable practices, abuse of the Lord's Supper, and spiritual gifts. In addition to words of discipline, Paul shares words of counsel in answer to questions raised by the Corinthian believers.

The oldest recorded title of this epistle is *Pros Korinthious A*, in effect, the "First to the Corinthians." The *A* was no doubt a later addition to distinguish this book from Second Corinthians.

## CHAPTER 1

PAUL, [a]called *to be* an apostle of Jesus Christ [b]through the will of God, and [c]Sosthenes *our* brother,

2 Unto the church of God which is at Corinth, to them that [a]are sanctified in Christ Jesus, [b]called *to be* saints, with all that in every place call upon the name of Jesus Christ [c]our Lord, [d]both theirs and ours:

3 [a]Grace *be* unto you, and peace, from God our Father, and *from* the Lord Jesus Christ.

4 [a]I thank my God always [1]on your behalf, for the grace of God which is given you by Jesus Christ;

5 That in every thing ye are enriched by him, [a]in all utterance, and *in* all knowledge;

6 Even as [a]the testimony of Christ was confirmed in you:

7 So that ye come [1]behind in no gift; [a]waiting for the [2]coming of our Lord Jesus Christ:

8 [a]Who shall also confirm you unto the end, [b]*that ye may be* blameless in the day of our Lord Jesus Christ.

9 [a]God *is* faithful, by whom ye were called unto [b]the fellowship of his Son Jesus Christ our Lord.

10 Now I beseech you, brethren, by the name of our Lord Jesus Christ, [a]that ye all [1]speak the same thing, and *that* there be no [2]divisions among you; but *that* ye be perfectly joined together in the same mind and in the same judgment.

11 For it hath been declared unto me of you, my brethren, by them *which are of the house* of Chloe, that there are [1]contentions among you.

12 Now this I say, [a]that every one of you saith, I am of Paul; and I of [b]Apollos; and I of [c]Cephas; and I of Christ.

13 [a]Is Christ divided? was Paul crucified for you? or were ye baptized in the name of Paul?

14 I thank God that I baptized [a]none of you, but [b]Crispus and [c]Gaius;

15 Lest any should say that I had baptized in mine own name.

16 And I baptized also the household of [a]Stephanas: besides, I know not whether I baptized any other.

17 For Christ sent me not to baptize, but to preach the gospel: [a]not with wisdom of words, lest the cross of Christ should be made of none effect.

18 For the [1]preaching of the cross is to [a]them that perish [b]foolishness; but unto us [c]which are saved it is the [d]power of God.

19 For it is written, [a]I will destroy the wisdom of the wise, and will bring to nothing the understanding of the prudent.

20 [a]Where *is* the wise? where *is* the scribe? where *is* the [1]disputer of this world? [b]hath not God made foolish the wisdom of this world?

21 For after that in the [a]wisdom of God the world by wisdom knew not God, it pleased God by the foolishness of [1]preaching to save them that believe.

22 For the [a]Jews require a sign, and the Greeks seek after wisdom:

23 But we preach Christ crucified, [a]unto the Jews a stumblingblock, and unto the Greeks [b]foolishness;

24 But unto them which are called, both Jews and Greeks, Christ [a]the power of God, and [b]the wisdom of God.

25 Because the foolishness of God is wiser than men; and the weakness of God is stronger than men.

26 For [1]ye see your calling, brethren, how that [a]not many wise men after the flesh, not many mighty, not many noble, *are called:*

27 But [a]God hath chosen the foolish things of the world to [1]confound the

1:1 [a] Rom. 1:1 [b] 2 Cor. 1:1 [c] Acts 18:17
1:2 [a] [Acts 15:9] [b] Rom.
1:7 [c] [1 Cor. 8:6] [d] [Rom. 3:22]
1:3 [a] Rom. 1:7
1:4 [a] Rom. 1:8 [1] *concerning you*
1:5 [a] [1 Cor. 12:8]
1:6 [a] 2 Tim. 1:8
1:7 [a] Phil. 3:20 [1] *short* [2] *revelation*
1:8 [a] 1 Thess. 3:13; 5:23 [b] Col. 1:22; 2:7
1:9 [a] Is. 49:7 [b] [John 15:4]
1:10 [a] 2 Cor. 13:11 [1] Have a uniform testimony [2] *dissensions* or *schisms*
1:11 [1] *quarrels*
1:12 [a] 1 Cor. 3:4 [b] Acts 18:24 [c] John 1:42
1:13 [a] 2 Cor. 11:4
1:14 [a] John 4:2 [b] Acts 18:8 [c] Rom. 16:23
1:16 [a] 1 Cor. 16:15, 17
1:17 [a] [1 Cor. 2:1, 4, 13]
1:18 [a] 2 Cor. 2:15 [b] Acts 17:18 [c] [1 Cor. 2:14; 15:2] [d] Rom. 1:16 [1] *message,* lit. *word*
1:19 [a] Is. 29:14
1:20 [a] Is. 19:12; 33:18 [b] Job 12:17 [1] *debater*
1:21 [a] Dan. 2:20 [1] *the message preached*
1:22 [a] Matt. 12:38
1:23 [a] Luke 2:34 [b] [1 Cor. 2:14]

1:24 [a] [Rom. 1:4] [b] Col. 2:3   1:26 [a] John 7:48 [1] *consider*   1:27 [a] Matt. 11:25 [1] *put to shame*

wise; and God hath chosen the weak things of the world to ¹confound the things which are mighty;

28 And ¹base things of the world, and things which are despised, hath God chosen, *yea,* and things which are not, to bring to ²nought things that are:

29 That no flesh should glory in his presence.

30 But of him are ye in Christ Jesus, who of God ¹is made unto us wisdom, and ᵃrighteousness, and sanctification, and redemption:

31 That, according as it is written, ᵃHe that glorieth, let him glory in the Lord.

## CHAPTER 2

AND I, brethren, when I came to you, came not with excellency of speech or of wisdom, declaring unto you the testimony of God.

2 For I determined not to know any thing among you, ᵃsave¹ Jesus Christ, and him crucified.

3 And ᵃI was with you ᵇin weakness, and in fear, and in much trembling.

4 And my speech and my preaching ᵃ*was* not with ¹enticing words of man's wisdom, ᵇbut in demonstration of the Spirit and of power:

5 That your faith should not ¹stand in the wisdom of men, but in the ᵃpower of God.

6 Howbeit we speak wisdom among them that are ¹perfect: yet not the wisdom of this world, nor of the ²princes of this ³world, that come to ⁴nought:

7 But we speak the wisdom of God in a mystery, *even* the hidden *wisdom,* which God ¹ordained before the ²world unto our glory:

8 Which none of the ¹princes of this ²world knew: for ᵃhad they known *it,* they would not have ᵇcrucified the Lord of glory.

9 But as it is written, ᵃEye hath not seen, nor ear heard, neither have entered into the heart of man, the things which God hath prepared for them that love him.

10 But ᵃGod hath revealed *them* unto us by his Spirit: for the Spirit searcheth all things, yea, the deep things of God.

11 For what man knoweth the things of a man, ¹save the ᵃspirit of man which is in him? ᵇeven so the things of God knoweth no man, but the Spirit of God.

12 Now we have received, not the ¹spirit of the world, but ᵃthe spirit which is of God; that we might know the things that are freely given to us of God.

13 Which things also we speak, not in the words which man's wisdom teacheth, but which the Holy Ghost teacheth; comparing spiritual things with spiritual.

14 ᵃBut the natural man receiveth not the things of the Spirit of God: for they are foolishness unto him: neither can he know *them,* because they are spiritually discerned.

15 But he that is spiritual judgeth all things, yet he himself is judged of no man.

16 ᵃFor who hath known the mind of the Lord, that he may instruct him? ᵇBut we have the mind of Christ.

## CHAPTER 3

AND I, brethren, could not speak unto you as unto spiritual, but as unto carnal, *even* as unto ᵃbabes in Christ.

2 I have fed you with ᵃmilk, and not with ¹meat: ᵇfor ²hitherto ye were not able *to bear it,* neither yet now are ye able.

3 For ye are yet carnal: for whereas *there is* among you envying, and strife, and ¹divisions, are ye not ²carnal, and walk ³as men?

4 For while one saith, I am of Paul; and another, I *am* of Apollos; are ye not carnal?

5 Who then is Paul, and who *is* Apollos, but ᵃministers by whom ye believed, even as the Lord gave to every man?

6 ᵃI have planted, ᵇApollos watered; ᶜbut God gave the increase.

7 So then ᵃneither is he that planteth any thing, neither he that watereth; but God that giveth the increase.

8 Now he that planteth and he that watereth are one: ᵃand every man shall receive his own reward according to his own labour.

9 For ᵃwe are ¹labourers together with God: ye are God's ²husbandry, *ye are* ᵇGod's building.

10 ᵃAccording to the grace of God which is given unto me, as a wise masterbuilder, I have laid ᵇthe foundation, and another buildeth thereon. But let every man take heed how he buildeth thereupon.

11 For other foundation can no man lay than ᵃthat is laid, ᵇwhich is Jesus Christ.

12 Now if any man build upon this foundation gold, silver, precious stones, wood, hay, ¹stubble;

13 Every man's work shall ¹be made manifest: for the day ᵃshall declare it, because ᵇit shall be revealed by fire; and the fire shall ²try every man's work of what sort it is.

14 If any man's work ¹abide which he hath built thereupon, he shall receive a reward.

15 If any man's work shall be burned, he shall suffer loss: but he himself shall be saved; yet so as ¹by fire.

1:27 ¹ *put to shame*
1:28 ¹ *insignificant*
² *nothing*
1:30 ᵃ [2 Cor. 5:21]
¹ *became for us*
1:31 ᵃ Jer. 9:23, 24
2:2 ᵃ Gal. 6:14
¹ *except*
2:3 ᵃ Acts 18:1
ᵇ [2 Cor. 4:7]
2:4 ᵃ 2 Pet. 1:16
ᵇ Rom. 15:19
¹ *persuasive*
2:5 ᵃ 1 Thess. 1:5 ¹ *be*
2:6 ¹ *mature*
² *rulers* ³ *age*
⁴ *nothing*
2:7 ¹ *predetermined* ² *ages*
2:8 ᵃ Luke 23:34
ᵇ Matt. 27:33–50
¹ *rulers* ² *age*
2:9 ᵃ [Is. 64:4; 65:17]
2:10 ᵃ Matt. 11:25; 13:11; 16:17
2:11 ᵃ [James 2:26] ᵇ Rom. 11:33 ¹ *except*
2:12 ᵃ [Rom. 8:15]
¹ Or *Spirit*

2:14 ᵃ Matt. 16:23
2:16 ᵃ Is. 40:13
ᵇ [John 15:15]
3:1 ᵃ Heb. 5:13
3:2 ᵃ 1 Pet. 2:2
ᵇ John 16:12
¹ *solid food* ² *until now*
3:3 ¹ *dissensions*
² *fleshly* ³ Lit. *according to man*
3:5 ᵃ 2 Cor. 3:3, 6; 4:1; 5:18; 6:4
3:6 ᵃ Acts 18:4
ᵇ Acts 18:24–27
ᶜ [2 Cor. 3:5]
3:7 ᵃ [Gal. 6:3]
3:8 ᵃ Ps. 62:12
3:9 ᵃ 2 Cor. 6:1
ᵇ [Eph. 2:20–22]
¹ Lit. *God's fellow workers* ² *field*
3:10 ᵃ Rom. 1:5
ᵇ 1 Cor. 4:15
3:11 ᵃ Is. 28:16
ᵇ Eph. 2:20
3:12 ¹ *straw*
3:13 ᵃ 1 Pet. 1:7 ᵇ Luke 2:35
¹ *become evident*
² *test*
3:14 ¹ *endures*
3:15 ¹ *through*

16 [a]Know ye not that ye are the temple of God, and *that* the Spirit of God dwelleth in you?

17 If any man [1]defile the temple of God, him shall God destroy; for the temple of God is holy, which *temple* ye are.

18 [a]Let no man deceive himself. If any man among you seemeth to be wise in this [1]world, let him become a fool, that he may be wise.

19 For the wisdom of this world is foolishness with God. For it is written, [a]He taketh the wise in their own craftiness.

20 And again, [a]The Lord knoweth the thoughts of the wise, that they are [1]vain.

21 Therefore let no man glory in men. For [a]all things are yours;

22 Whether Paul, or Apollos, or Cephas, or the world, or life, or death, or things present, or things to come; all are yours;

23 And [a]ye are Christ's; and Christ *is* God's.

## CHAPTER 4

LET a man so [1]account of us, as of [a]the [2]ministers of Christ, [b]and stewards of the [3]mysteries of God.

2 Moreover it is required in stewards, that a man be found faithful.

3 But with me it is a very small thing that I should be judged of you, or of man's [1]judgment: yea, I judge not mine own self.

4 For I know nothing [1]by myself; yet am I not hereby justified: but he that judgeth me is the Lord.

5 [a]Therefore judge nothing before the time, until the Lord come, who both will bring to [b]light the hidden things of darkness, and will [1]make [c]manifest the [2]counsels of the hearts: and [d]then shall every man have praise of God.

6 And these things, brethren, I have [1]in a figure transferred to myself and *to* Apollos for your sakes; that ye might learn in us not to think of *men* above that which is written, that no one of you be [2]puffed up for one against another.

7 For who [1]maketh thee to differ *from another?* and [a]what hast thou that thou didst not receive? now if thou didst receive *it,* why dost thou glory, as if thou hadst not received *it?*

8 Now ye are full, [a]now ye are rich, ye have reigned as kings without us: and I [1]would to God ye did reign, that we also might reign with you.

9 For I think that God hath [1]set forth us the apostles last, as [2]it were appointed to death: for we are made a [a]spectacle unto the world, and to angels, and to men.

10 We *are* [a]fools for Christ's sake, but ye *are* wise in Christ; [b]we *are* weak, but ye *are* strong; ye *are* [1]honourable, but we *are* [2]despised.

11 Even unto this present hour we both hunger, and thirst, and are [1]naked, and are [2]buffeted, and [3]have no certain dwellingplace;

12 [a]And labour, working with our own hands: [b]being reviled, we bless; being persecuted, we [1]suffer it:

13 Being [1]defamed, we [2]intreat: [a]we are made as the filth of the world, *and are* the offscouring of all things unto this day.

14 I write not these things to shame you, but [a]as my beloved sons I warn *you.*

15 For though ye have ten thousand instructors in Christ, yet *have* ye not many fathers: for [a]in Christ Jesus I have begotten you through the gospel.

16 Wherefore I [1]beseech you, [a]be[2] ye followers of me.

17 For this cause have I sent unto you [a]Timotheus, [b]who is my beloved son, and faithful in the Lord, who shall bring you [c]into remembrance of my ways which be in Christ, as I [d]teach every where [e]in every church.

18 [a]Now some are [1]puffed up, as though I would not come to you.

19 [a]But I will come to you shortly, [b]if the Lord will, and will know, not the speech of them which are puffed up, but the power.

20 For [a]the kingdom of God *is* not in word, but in [b]power.

21 What [1]will ye? [a]shall I come unto you with a rod, or in love, and *in* the spirit of [2]meekness?

## CHAPTER 5

IT is [1]reported commonly *that there is* [2]fornication among you, and such fornication as is not so much as named among the Gentiles, that one should have his father's [a]wife.

2 And ye are [1]puffed up, and have not rather [b]mourned, that he that hath done this deed might be taken away from among you.

3 [a]For I verily, as absent in body, but present in spirit, have judged already, as though I were present, *concerning* him that hath so done this deed,

4 In the [a]name of our Lord Jesus Christ, when ye are gathered together, and my spirit, [b]with the power of our Lord Jesus Christ,

5 [a]To deliver such an one unto [b]Satan for the destruction of the flesh, that the spirit may be saved in the day of the Lord Jesus.

6 [a]Your glorying *is* not good. Know ye not that [b]a little leaven leaveneth the whole lump?

### Center column references

3:16 [a] 2 Cor. 6:16
3:17 [1] *destroys*
3:18 [a] Prov. 3:7
[1] *age*
3:19 [a] Job 5:13
3:20 [a] Ps. 94:11
[1] *futile*
3:21 [a] [2 Cor. 4:5]
3:23 [a] 2 Cor. 10:7
4:1 [a] Col. 1:25 [b] Titus 1:7 [1] *consider us* [2] *servants* [3] *hidden truths*
4:3 [1] Lit. *day*
4:4 [1] *against*
4:5 [a] Matt. 7:1 [b] Matt. 10:26 [c] 1 Cor. 3:13 [d] Rom. 2:29 [1] *reveal* [2] *motives*
4:6 [1] *figuratively* [2] *proud*
4:7 [a] John 3:27 [1] *distinguishes you*
4:8 [a] Rev. 3:17 [1] *wish you really did*
4:9 [a] Heb. 10:33 [1] *displayed* [2] *men condemned*
4:10 [a] Acts 17:18; 26:24 [b] 2 Cor. 13:9 [1] *distinguished* [2] *dishonoured*
4:11 [1] *poorly clothed* [2] *beaten* [3] *are homeless*
4:12 [a] Acts 18:3; 20:34 [b] Matt. 5:44 [1] *endure*
4:13 [a] Lam. 3:45 [1] *slandered* [2] *encourage*
4:14 [a] 1 Thess. 2:11
4:15 [a] Gal. 4:19
4:16 [a] [1 Cor. 11:1] [1] *urge* [2] *imitate me*
4:17 [a] Acts 19:22 [b] 1 Tim. 1:2, 18 [c] 1 Cor. 11:2 [d] 1 Cor. 7:17 [e] 1 Cor. 14:33
4:18 [a] 1 Cor. 5:2 [1] *arrogant*
4:19 [a] Acts 19:21; 20:2 [b] Acts 18:21
4:20 [a] 1 Thess. 1:5 [b] 1 Cor. 2:4
4:21 [a] 2 Cor. 10:2 [1] *do you want* [2] *gentleness*
5:1 [a] Lev. 18:6–8 [1] *actually reported that* [2] *sexual immorality*
5:2 [a] 1 Cor. 4:18 [b] 2 Cor. 7:7–10 [1] *proud*
5:3 [a] Col. 2:5
5:4 [a] [Matt. 18:20] [b] [John 20:23]
5:5 [a] 1 Tim. 1:20 [b] [Acts 26:18]
5:6 [a] 1 Cor. 3:21 [b] Gal. 5:9

7 [1]Purge out therefore the old leaven, that ye may be a new lump, as ye are unleavened. For even [a]Christ our [b]passover is sacrificed for us:

8 Therefore [a]let us keep the feast, [b]not with old leaven, neither [c]with the leaven of malice and wickedness; but with the unleavened *bread* of sincerity and truth.

9 I wrote unto you in an epistle [a]not to [1]company with [2]fornicators:

10 Yet not altogether with the fornicators of this world, or with the covetous, or extortioners, or with idolaters; for then must ye needs go [a]out of the world.

11 But now I have written unto you not to keep company, [a]if any man that is called a brother be a fornicator, or covetous, or an idolater, or a [1]railer, or a drunkard, or an extortioner; with such an one [b]no not to eat.

12 For what have I to do [1]to judge them also that are [2]without? do not ye judge them that are within?

13 But them that are [1]without God judgeth. Therefore [a]put away from among yourselves that wicked person.

## CHAPTER 6

D ARE any of you, having a matter against another, go to law before the [1]unjust, and not before the [a]saints?

2 Do ye not know that [a]the saints shall judge the world? and if the world shall be judged by you, are ye unworthy to judge the smallest matters?

3 Know ye not that we shall [a]judge angels? how much more things that pertain to this life?

4 If then ye have [1]judgments of things pertaining to this life, set them to judge who are least esteemed in the church.

5 I speak to your shame. Is it so, that there is not a wise man among you? no, not one that shall be able to judge between his brethren?

6 But brother goeth to law with brother, and that before the unbelievers.

7 Now therefore there is [1]utterly a fault among you, because ye go to law one with another. [a]Why do ye not rather [2]take wrong? why do ye not rather *suffer yourselves to* be defrauded?

8 Nay, ye do wrong, and defraud, and that [1]*your* brethren.

9 Know ye not that the unrighteous shall not inherit the kingdom of God? Be not deceived: [a]neither [1]fornicators, nor idolaters, nor adulterers, nor [2]effeminate, nor [3]abusers of themselves with mankind,

10 Nor thieves, nor covetous, nor drunkards, nor revilers, nor extortioners, shall inherit the kingdom of God.

11 And such were [a]some of you: [b]but ye are washed, but ye are [1]sanctified, but ye are [2]justified, in the name of the Lord Jesus, and by the Spirit of our God.

12 [a]All things are lawful unto me, but all things are not [1]expedient: all things are lawful for me, but I will not be brought under the power of [2]any.

13 [a]Meats[1] for the belly, and the belly for meats: but God shall destroy both it and them. Now the body *is* not for [b]fornication, but [c]for the Lord; [d]and the Lord for the body.

14 And [a]God hath both raised up the Lord, and will also raise up us [b]by his own power.

15 Know ye not that [a]your bodies are the members of Christ? shall I then take the members of Christ, and make *them* the members of an harlot? [1]God forbid.

16 What? know ye not that he which is joined to an harlot is one body? for [a]two, saith he, shall be one flesh.

17 [a]But he that is joined unto the Lord is one spirit.

18 [a]Flee fornication. Every sin that a man doeth is [1]without the body; but he that committeth fornication sinneth [b]against his own body.

19 What? [a]know ye not that your body is the temple of the Holy Ghost *which is* in you, which ye have of God, [b]and ye are not your own?

20 For [a]ye are bought with a price: therefore glorify God in your body, and in your spirit, which are God's.

## CHAPTER 7

N OW concerning the things whereof ye wrote unto me: [a]*It is* good for a man not to touch a woman.

2 Nevertheless, *to avoid* fornication, let every man have his own wife, and let every woman have her own husband.

3 [a]Let the husband render unto the wife due [1]benevolence: and likewise also the wife unto the husband.

4 The wife hath not [1]power of her own body, but the husband: and likewise also the husband hath not power of his own body, but the wife.

5 [a]Defraud[1] ye not one the other, except *it be* with consent for a time, that ye may give yourselves to fasting and prayer; and come together again, that [b]Satan tempt you not [2]for your [3]incontinency.

6 But I speak this by permission, [a]*and* not of commandment.

7 For [a]I would that all men were even as I myself. But every man hath his proper gift of God, one after this manner, and another after that.

### Cross references

5:7 [a] Is. 53:7
[b] John 19:14
[1] *Clean out*

5:8 [a] Ex. 12:15
[b] Deut. 16:3
[c] Matt. 16:6

5:9 [a] 2 Cor. 6:14
[1] *associate* [2] *sexually immoral people*

5:10 [a] John 17:15

5:11 [a] Matt. 18:17
[b] Gal. 2:12 [1] *reviler*

5:12 [1] *with judging* [2] *outside*

5:13 [a] Deut. 13:5; 17:7, 12; 19:19; 21:21; 22:21, 24; 24:7 [1] *outside*

6:1 [a] Dan. 7:22
[1] *unrighteous*

6:2 [a] Ps. 49:14

6:3 [a] 2 Pet. 2:4

6:4 [1] *courts*

6:7 [a] [Prov. 20:22]
[1] *an utter failure* [2] *accept*

6:8 [1] *To your*

6:9 [a] Gal. 5:21
[1] *the sexually immoral* [2] *homosexuals* [3] *sodomites*

6:11 [a] [1 Cor. 12:2]
[b] Heb. 10:22 [1] *set apart* [2] *declared righteous*

6:12 [a] 1 Cor. 10:23 [1] *helpful* [2] *anything*

6:13 [a] Matt. 15:17 [b] Gal. 5:19
[c] 1 Thess. 4:3
[d] [Eph. 5:23]
[1] *Foods*

6:14 [a] 2 Cor. 4:14
[b] Eph. 1:19

6:15 [a] Rom. 12:5
[1] *Certainly not*

6:16 [a] Gen. 2:24

6:17 [a] [John 17:21–23]

6:18 [a] Heb. 13:4
[b] Rom. 1:24
[1] *outside*

6:19 [a] 2 Cor. 6:16
[b] Rom. 14:7

6:20 [a] 2 Pet. 2:1

7:1 [a] 1 Cor. 7:8, 26

7:3 [a] Ex. 21:10
[1] *affection*

7:4 [1] *authority over*

7:5 [a] Joel 2:16
[b] 1 Thess. 3:5
[1] *Deprive* [2] *because of* [3] *lack of self-control*

7:6 [a] 2 Cor. 8:8

7:7 [a] Acts 26:29

8 I say therefore to the unmarried and widows, <sup>a</sup>It is good for them if they abide even as I.

9 But <sup>a</sup>if they cannot <sup>1</sup>contain, let them marry: for it is better to marry than to <sup>2</sup>burn.

10 And unto the married I command, *yet* not I, but the <sup>a</sup>Lord, <sup>b</sup>Let not the wife depart from *her* husband:

11 But and if she depart, let her remain unmarried, or be reconciled to *her* husband: and let not the husband <sup>1</sup>put away *his* wife.

12 But to the rest speak I, not the Lord: If any brother hath a wife that believeth not, and she be pleased to dwell with him, let him not <sup>1</sup>put her away.

13 And the woman which hath an husband that believeth not, and if he be pleased to dwell with her, let her not <sup>1</sup>leave him.

14 For the unbelieving husband is sanctified by the wife, and the unbelieving wife is sanctified by the husband: else <sup>a</sup>were your children unclean; but now are they holy.

15 But if the unbelieving depart, let him depart. A brother or a sister is not under bondage in such *cases:* but God hath called us <sup>a</sup>to peace.

16 For what knowest thou, O wife, whether thou shalt <sup>a</sup>save *thy* husband? or how knowest thou, O man, whether thou shalt save *thy* wife?

17 But as God hath distributed to every man, as the Lord hath called every one, so let him walk. And <sup>a</sup>so ordain I in all churches.

18 Is any man called being circumcised? let him not become uncircumcised. Is any called in uncircumcision? <sup>a</sup>let him not be circumcised.

19 <sup>a</sup>Circumcision is nothing, and uncircumcision is nothing, but <sup>b</sup>the<sup>1</sup> keeping of the commandments of God.

20 Let every man abide in the same calling wherein he was called.

21 Art thou called *being* a <sup>1</sup>servant? care not for it: but if thou mayest be made free, use *it* rather.

22 For he that is called in the Lord, *being* a servant, is <sup>a</sup>the Lord's freeman: likewise also he that is called, *being* free, is <sup>b</sup>Christ's servant.

23 <sup>a</sup>Ye are bought with a price; be not ye the servants of men.

24 Brethren, let every man, wherein he is called, therein abide with <sup>a</sup>God.

25 Now concerning virgins <sup>a</sup>I have no commandment of the Lord: yet I give my judgment, as one <sup>b</sup>that hath obtained mercy of the Lord <sup>c</sup>to be faithful.

26 I suppose therefore that this is good for the present distress, *I say,* <sup>a</sup>that *it is* good for a man so to be.

27 Art thou bound unto a wife?

7:8 <sup>a</sup>1 Cor. 7:1, 26
7:9 <sup>a</sup>1 Tim. 5:14
<sup>1</sup> *exercise self-control* <sup>2</sup> *burn with passion*
7:10 <sup>a</sup> Mark 10:6–10 <sup>b</sup> [Matt. 5:32]
7:11 <sup>1</sup> *divorce*
7:12 <sup>1</sup> *divorce her*
7:13 <sup>1</sup> *divorce*
7:14 <sup>a</sup> Mal. 2:15
7:15 <sup>a</sup> Rom. 12:18
7:16 <sup>a</sup> 1 Pet. 3:1
7:17 <sup>a</sup> 1 Cor. 4:17
7:18 <sup>a</sup> Acts 15:1
7:19 <sup>a</sup> [Gal. 3:28; 5:6; 6:15] <sup>b</sup> [John 15:14]
<sup>1</sup> *what matters is keeping*
7:21 <sup>1</sup> *slave*
7:22 <sup>a</sup> [John 8:36] <sup>b</sup> 1 Pet. 2:16
7:23 <sup>a</sup> 1 Pet. 1:18, 19
7:24 <sup>a</sup> [Col. 3:22–24]
7:25 <sup>a</sup> 2 Cor. 8:8 <sup>b</sup> 1 Tim. 1:13, 16 <sup>c</sup> 1 Tim. 1:12
7:26 <sup>a</sup> 1 Cor. 7:1, 8

seek not to be loosed. Art thou loosed from a wife? seek not a wife.

28 But and if thou marry, thou hast not sinned; and if a virgin marry, she hath not sinned. Nevertheless such shall have trouble in the flesh: but I spare you.

29 But <sup>a</sup>this I say, brethren, the time *is* short: it remaineth, that both they that have wives be as though they had none;

30 And they that weep, as though they wept not; and they that rejoice, as though they rejoiced not; and they that buy, as though they possessed not;

31 And they that use this world, as not <sup>a</sup>abusing *it:* for <sup>b</sup>the <sup>1</sup>fashion of this world passeth away.

32 But I would have you without <sup>1</sup>carefulness. <sup>a</sup>He that is unmarried careth for the things that belong to the Lord, how he may please the Lord:

33 But he that is married careth for the things that are of the world, how he may please *his* wife.

34 There is difference *also* between a wife and a virgin. The unmarried woman <sup>a</sup>careth for the things of the Lord, that she may be holy both in body and in spirit: but she that is married careth for the things of the world, how she may please *her* husband.

35 And this I speak for your own profit; not that I may <sup>1</sup>cast a snare upon you, but for that which is <sup>2</sup>comely, and that ye may attend upon the Lord without distraction.

36 But if any man think that he behaveth himself <sup>1</sup>uncomely toward his <sup>2</sup>virgin, if she pass the flower of *her* <sup>3</sup>age, and need so require, let him do what he will, he sinneth not: let them marry.

37 Nevertheless he that standeth stedfast in his heart, having no necessity, but hath power over his own will, and hath so decreed in his heart that he will keep his virgin, doeth well.

38 <sup>a</sup>So then he that giveth *her* in marriage doeth well; but he that giveth *her* not in marriage doeth better.

39 <sup>a</sup>The wife is bound by the law as long as her husband liveth; but if her husband be dead, she is at liberty to be married to whom she will; <sup>b</sup>only in the Lord.

40 But she is happier if she so abide, <sup>a</sup>after my judgment: and <sup>b</sup>I think also that I have the Spirit of God.

7:29 <sup>a</sup> 1 Pet. 4:7
7:31 <sup>a</sup> 1 Cor. 9:18 <sup>b</sup> [1 John 2:17]
<sup>1</sup> *form*
7:32 <sup>a</sup> 1 Tim. 5:5
<sup>1</sup> *concern*
7:34 <sup>a</sup> Luke 10:40
7:35 <sup>1</sup> *put a leash on* <sup>2</sup> *proper*
7:36 <sup>1</sup> *improperly* <sup>2</sup> Or *virgin daughter* <sup>3</sup> *youth*
7:38 <sup>a</sup> Heb. 13:4
7:39 <sup>a</sup> Rom. 7:2 <sup>b</sup> 2 Cor. 6:14
7:40 <sup>a</sup> 1 Cor. 7:6, 25 <sup>b</sup> 1 Thess. 4:8

8:1 <sup>a</sup> Acts 15:20 <sup>b</sup> Rom. 14:14 <sup>c</sup> Rom. 14:3 <sup>1</sup> *concerning* <sup>2</sup> *love* <sup>3</sup> *builds up*

## CHAPTER 8

Now <sup>a</sup>as <sup>1</sup>touching things offered unto idols, we know that we all have <sup>b</sup>knowledge. <sup>c</sup>Knowledge puffeth up, but <sup>2</sup>charity <sup>3</sup>edifieth.

2 And [a]if any man think that he knoweth any thing, he knoweth nothing yet as he ought to know.

3 But if any man love God, the same is known of him.

4 As concerning therefore the eating of those things that are offered in sacrifice unto idols, we know that [a]an idol *is* nothing in the world, [b]and that *there is* none other God but one.

5 For though there be that are [a]called gods, whether in heaven or in earth, (as there be gods many, and lords many,)

6 But [a]to us *there is but* one God, the Father, [b]of whom *are* all things, and we [1]in him; and [c]one Lord Jesus Christ, [d]by whom *are* all things, and [e]we [2]by him.

7 Howbeit *there is* not in every man that knowledge: for some [a]with conscience of the idol unto this hour eat *it* as a thing offered unto an idol; and their conscience being weak is [b]defiled.

8 But [a]meat[1] commendeth us not to God: for neither, if we eat, are we the better; neither, if we eat not, are we the worse.

9 But [a]take heed lest by any means this [1]liberty of yours become [b]a [2]stumblingblock to them that are weak.

10 For if any man see thee which hast knowledge [1]sit at meat in the idol's temple, shall not [a]the conscience of him which is weak be emboldened to eat those things which are offered to idols;

11 And [a]through[1] thy knowledge shall the weak brother perish, for whom Christ died?

12 But [a]when ye sin so against the brethren, and wound their weak conscience, ye sin against Christ.

13 Wherefore, [a]if [1]meat make my brother to [2]offend, I will eat no flesh while the world standeth, lest I make my brother to [2]offend.

## CHAPTER 9

A M [a]I not an apostle? am I not free? [b]have I not seen Jesus Christ our Lord? [c]are not ye my work in the Lord?

2 If I be not an apostle unto others, yet doubtless I am to you: for [a]the [1]seal of mine apostleship are ye in the Lord.

3 [1]Mine answer to them that do examine me is this,

4 [a]Have we not [1]power to eat and to drink?

5 Have we not [1]power to lead about a sister, a [2]wife, as well as other apostles, and *as* [a]the [3]brethren of the Lord, and [b]Cephas?

6 Or I only and Barnabas, [a]have not we [1]power to [2]forbear working?

7 Who [a]goeth [1]a warfare any time at his own [2]charges? who [b]planteth a vineyard, and eateth not of the fruit thereof? or who [c]feedeth[3] a flock, and eateth not of the milk of the flock?

8 Say I these things as a man? or saith not the law the same also?

9 For it is written in the law of Moses, [a]Thou shalt not muzzle the mouth of the ox that treadeth out the corn. [1]Doth God take care for oxen?

10 Or saith he *it* altogether for our sakes? For our sakes, no doubt, *this* is written: that [a]he that ploweth should plow in hope; and that he that thresheth in hope should be partaker of his hope.

11 [a]If we have sown unto you spiritual things, *is it* a great thing if we shall reap your [1]carnal things?

12 If others be partakers of *this* [1]power over you, *are* not we [2]rather? [a]Nevertheless we have not used this [1]power; but [3]suffer all things, [b]lest we should hinder the gospel of Christ.

13 [a]Do ye not know that they which minister about holy things live *of* the things of the [b]temple? and they which [1]wait at the altar are partakers with the altar?

14 Even so [a]hath the Lord [1]ordained [b]that they which preach the gospel should live of the gospel.

15 But [a]I have used none of these things: neither have I written these things, that it should be so done unto me: for [b]*it were* better for me to die, than that any man should make my [1]glorying void.

16 For though I preach the gospel, I have nothing to glory of: for [a]necessity is laid upon me; yea, woe is unto me, if I preach not the gospel!

17 For if I do this thing willingly, [a]I have a reward: but if against my will, [b]a [1]dispensation *of the gospel* is [2]committed unto me.

18 What is my reward then? *Verily* that, [a]when I preach the gospel, I may [1]make the gospel of Christ without charge, that I [b]abuse not my [2]power in the gospel.

19 For though I be [a]free from all *men*, yet have [b]I made myself servant unto all, [c]that I might [1]gain the more.

20 And [a]unto the Jews I became as a Jew, that I might [1]gain the Jews; to them that are under the law, as under the law, that I might [1]gain them that are under the law;

21 [a]To [b]them that are without law, as without law, ([c]being not without law to God, but under the law to Christ,) that I might gain them that are without law.

## Center column references

8:2 [a] [1 Cor. 13:8–12]

8:4 [a] Is. 41:24
[b] Deut. 4:35, 39; 6:4

8:5 [a] [John 10:34]

8:6 [a] Mal. 2:10
[b] Acts 17:28
[c] John 13:13
[d] John 1:3 [e] Rom. 5:11 [1] *for* [2] live *by*

8:7 [a] [1 Cor. 10:28]
[b] Rom. 14:14, 22

8:8 [a] [Rom. 14:17]
[1] *food*

8:9 [a] Gal. 5:13
[b] Rom. 12:13, 21
[1] Lit. *right* [2] *cause of offence*

8:10 [a] 1 Cor. 10:28
[1] *eating*

8:11 [a] Rom. 14:15, 20 [1] *because of*

8:12 [a] Matt. 25:40

8:13 [a] Rom. 14:21
[1] *food* [2] *stumble*

9:1 [a] Acts 9:15
[b] 1 Cor. 15:8
[c] 1 Cor. 3:6; 4:15

9:2 [a] 2 Cor. 12:12
[1] *certification*

9:3 [1] *My defence*

9:4 [a] [1 Thess. 2:6, 9] [1] *right*

9:5 [a] Matt. 13:55 [b] Matt.

8:14 [1] *right* [2] *a believing wife*
[3] *brothers*

9:6 [a] Acts 4:36
[1] *right* [2] *refrain from*

9:7 [a] 2 Cor. 10:4
[b] Deut. 20:6
[c] John 21:15 [1] *to war* [2] *expense*
[3] *shepherds*

9:9 [a] Deut. 25:4
[1] *Is it oxen God is concerned about?*

9:10 [a] 2 Tim. 2:6

9:11 [a] Rom. 15:27
[1] *material*

9:12 [a] [Acts 18:3; 20:33] [b] 2 Cor. 11:12 [1] *authority, right* [2] *even more*
[3] *endure*

9:13 [a] Lev. 6:16, 26; 7:6, 31 [b] Num. 18:8–31 [1] *serve*

9:14 [a] Matt. 10:10
[b] Rom. 10:15
[1] *commanded*

9:15 [a] Acts 18:3; 20:33 [b] 2 Cor. 11:10 [1] *boasting*

9:16 [a] [Rom. 1:14]

9:17 [a] 1 Cor. 3:8, 14; 9:18 [b] Gal. 2:7 [1] *stewardship*
[2] *entrusted*

9:18 [a] 1 Cor. 10:33
[b] 1 Cor. 7:31;
9:12 [1] *present*
[2] *authority*

9:19 [a] 1 Cor. 9:1 [b] Gal. 5:13 [c] Matt. 18:15 [1] *win*
9:20 [a] Acts 16:3; 21:23–26 [1] *win* 9:21 [a] [Gal. 2:3; 3:2]
[b] [Rom. 2:12, 14] [c] [1 Cor. 7:22]

22 ᵃTo the weak became I as weak, that I might gain the weak: ᵇI ¹am made all things to all *men*, ᶜthat I might by all means save some.

23 And this I do for the gospel's sake, that I might be partaker thereof with *you*.

24 Know ye not that they which run in a race run all, but one receiveth the prize? ᵃSo run, that ye may obtain.

25 And every man that ¹striveth for the mastery ²is temperate in all things. Now they *do it* to obtain a ³corruptible crown; but we ᵃan ⁴incorruptible.

26 I therefore so run, ᵃnot as uncertainly; so fight I, not as one that beateth the air:

27 ᵃBut I ¹keep under my body, and ᵇbring *it* into subjection: lest that by any means, when I have preached to others, I myself should be ᶜa² castaway.

## CHAPTER 10

MOREOVER, brethren, I ¹would not that ye should be ²ignorant, how that all our fathers were under ᵃthe cloud, and all passed through ᵇthe sea;

2 And were all baptized unto Moses in the cloud and in the sea;

3 And did all eat the same ᵃspiritual ¹meat;

4 And did all drink the same ᵃspiritual drink: for they drank of that spiritual Rock that followed them: and that Rock was Christ.

5 But with ¹many of them God was not well pleased: for they ᵃwere ²overthrown in the wilderness.

6 Now these things ¹were our examples, to the intent we should not lust after evil things, as ᵃthey also lusted.

7 ᵃNeither be ye idolaters, as *were* some of them; as it is written, ᵇThe people sat down to eat and drink, and rose up to play.

8 ᵃNeither let us commit ¹fornication, as ᵇsome of them committed, and ᶜfell in one day three and twenty thousand.

9 Neither let us ¹tempt Christ, as ᵃsome of them also tempted, and ᵇwere destroyed of serpents.

10 Neither murmur ye, as ᵃsome of them also murmured, and ᵇwere destroyed of ᶜthe destroyer.

11 Now all these things happened unto them for ensamples: and ᵃthey are written for our ¹admonition, ᵇupon whom the ends of the ²world are come.

12 Wherefore ᵃlet him that thinketh he standeth take heed lest he fall.

13 There hath no temptation ¹taken you but such as is common to man: but ᵃGod *is* faithful, ᵇwho will not

suffer you to be tempted above that ye are able; but will with the temptation also make a way to escape, that ye may be able to ²bear *it*.

14 Wherefore, my dearly beloved, ᵃflee from idolatry.

15 I speak as to ᵃwise men; judge ye what I say.

16 ᵃThe cup of blessing which we bless, is it not the ¹communion of the blood of Christ? ᵇThe bread which we break, is it not the ¹communion of the body of Christ?

17 For ᵃwe *being* many are one bread, *and* one body: for we are all partakers of that one bread.

18 Behold ᵃIsrael ᵇafter the flesh: ᶜare not they which eat of the sacrifices ¹partakers of the altar?

19 What say I then? ᵃthat the idol is any thing, or that which is offered in sacrifice to idols is any thing?

20 But *I say*, that the things which the Gentiles ᵃsacrifice, ᵇthey sacrifice to ¹devils, and not to God: and I would not that ye should have fellowship with devils.

21 ᵃYe cannot drink the cup of the Lord, and ᵇthe cup of ¹devils: ye cannot be partakers of the ᶜLord's table, and of the table of ¹devils.

22 Do we ᵃprovoke the Lord to jealousy? ᵇare we stronger than he?

23 All things are lawful for me, but all things are not ᵃexpedient:¹ all things are lawful for me, but all things ²edify not.

24 Let no man seek his own, but every man ᵃanother's ¹*wealth*.

25 ᵃWhatsoever is sold in the ¹shambles, *that* eat, asking no question for conscience sake:

26 For ᵃthe earth *is* the Lord's, and the fulness thereof.

27 If any of them that believe not bid you *to a feast*, and ye ¹be disposed to go; ᵃwhatsoever is set before you, eat, asking no question for conscience sake.

28 But if any man say unto you, This is offered in sacrifice unto idols, eat not ᵃfor his sake that ¹shewed it, and for conscience sake: for ᵇthe earth *is* the Lord's, and the fulness thereof:

29 Conscience, I say, not thine own, but of the other: for ᵃwhy is my liberty judged of another *man's* conscience?

30 For if I ¹by grace ²be a partaker, why am I evil spoken of for that ᵃfor which I give thanks?

31 ᵃWhether therefore ye eat, or drink, or whatsoever ye do, do all to the glory of God.

---

9:22 ᵃ Rom. 14:1; 15:1 ᵇ 1 Cor. 10:33 ᶜ Rom. 11:14 ¹ *have become*
9:24 ᵃ Gal. 2:2
9:25 ᵃ James 1:12 ¹ *competes for the prize* ² *has self-control* ³ *perishable* ⁴ *imperishable*
9:26 ᵃ 2 Tim. 2:5
9:27 ᵃ [Rom. 8:13] ᵇ [Rom. 6:18] ᶜ Jer. 6:30 ¹ *discipline* ² *disqualified*
10:1 ᵃ Ex. 13:21, 22 ᵇ Ex. 14:21, 22, 29 ¹ *do not want* ² *unaware*
10:3 ᵃ Ex. 16:4, 15, 35 ¹ *food*
10:4 ᵃ Ex. 17:5–7
10:5 ᵃ Num. 14:29, 37; 26:65 ¹ *most* ² *strewn*
10:6 ᵃ Num. 11:4, 34 ¹ *became*
10:7 ᵃ 1 Cor. 5:11; 10:14 ᵇ Ex. 32:6
10:8 ᵃ Rev. 2:14 ᵇ Num. 25:1–9 ᶜ Ps. 106:29 ¹ *sexual immorality*
10:9 ᵃ Ex. 17:2, 7 ᵇ Num. 21:6–9 ¹ *test*
10:10 ᵃ Ex. 16:2 ᵇ Num. 14:37 ᶜ Ex. 12:23
10:11 ᵃ Rom. 15:4 ᵇ Phil. 4:5 ¹ *instruction* ² *ages*
10:12 ᵃ Rom. 11:20
10:13 ᵃ 1 Cor. 1:9 ᵇ Ps. 125:3 ¹ *overtaken* ² *endure*
10:14 ᵃ 2 Cor. 6:17
10:15 ᵃ 1 Cor. 8:1
10:16 ᵃ Matt. 26:26–28 ᵇ Acts 2:42 ¹ Lit. *fellowship*
10:17 ᵃ 1 Cor. 12:12, 27
10:18 ᵃ Rom. 4:12 ᵇ Rom. 4:1 ᶜ Lev. 3:3; 7:6, 14 ¹ Lit. *sharers*
10:19 ᵃ 1 Cor. 8:4
10:20 ᵃ Lev. 17:7 ᵇ Deut. 32:17 ¹ *demons*
10:21 ᵃ 2 Cor. 6:15, 16 ᵇ Deut. 32:38 ᶜ [1 Cor. 11:23–29] ¹ *demons*
10:22 ᵃ Deut. 32:21 ᵇ Ezek. 22:14
10:23 ᵃ 1 Cor. 6:12 ¹ *helpful* ² *do not build up*
10:24 ᵃ Phil. 2:4 ¹ *Well-being*
10:25 ᵃ [1 Tim.

4:4] ¹ *meat market* 10:26 ᵃ Ps. 24:1 10:27 ᵃ Luke 10:7, 8 ¹ *desire to* 10:28 ᵃ [1 Cor. 8:7, 10, 12] ᵇ Ps. 24:1 ¹ *told you* 10:29 ᵃ Rom. 14:16 10:30 ᵃ Rom. 14:6 ¹ *with thanks* ² *partake* 10:31 ᵃ Col. 3:17

32 ªGive none offence, neither to the Jews, nor to the ¹Gentiles, nor to the church of God:

33 Even ªas I please all *men* in all *things,* not seeking mine own profit, but the *profit* of many, that they may be saved.

## CHAPTER 11

Bᴇ ªye ¹followers of me, even as I also *am* of Christ.

2 Now I praise you, brethren, that ye remember me in all things, and keep the ¹ordinances, as I delivered *them* to you.

3 But I would have you know, that ªthe head of every man is Christ; and ᵇthe head of the woman *is* the man; and ᶜthe head of Christ *is* God.

4 Every man praying or ªprophesying, having *his* head covered, dishonoureth his head.

5 But every woman that prayeth or prophesieth with *her* head uncovered dishonoureth her head: for that is ¹even all one as if she were ªshaven.

6 For if the woman be not covered, let her also be shorn: but if it be ªa shame for a woman to be shorn or shaven, let her be covered.

7 For a man indeed ought not to cover *his* head, forasmuch as ªhe is the image and glory of God: but the woman is the glory of the man.

8 For the man is not of the woman; but the woman ªof the man.

9 Neither was the man created for the woman; but the woman ªfor the man.

10 For this cause ought the woman to have ¹power on *her* head because of the angels.

11 Nevertheless ªneither is the man ¹without the woman, neither the woman ¹without the man, in the Lord.

12 For as the woman *is* of the man, even so *is* the man also by the woman; but all things of God.

13 Judge in yourselves: is it ¹comely that a woman pray unto God uncovered?

14 Doth not even nature itself teach you, that, if a man have long hair, it is a ¹shame unto him?

15 But if a woman have long hair, it is a glory to her: for *her* hair is given her for a covering.

16 But ªif any man seem to be contentious, we have no such custom, ᵇneither the churches of God.

17 Now in this that I declare *unto you* I praise *you* not, that ye come together not for the better, but for the worse.

18 For first of all, when ye come together in the church, ªI hear that there be divisions among you; and I partly believe it.

10:32 ª Rom. 14:13
¹ Lit. *Greeks*
10:33 ª Rom. 15:2
11:1 ª Eph. 5:1
¹ *imitators*
11:2 ¹ *traditions*
11:3 ª Eph. 1:22;
4:15; 5:23   ᵇ Gen.
3:16   ᶜ John 14:28
11:4 ª 1 Cor. 12:10
11:5 ª Deut. 21:12
¹ *one and the same*
11:6 ª Num. 5:18
11:7 ª Gen. 1:26,
27; 5:1; 9:6¹
11:8 ª Gen.
2:21–23
11:9 ª Gen. 2:18
11:10 ¹ *a symbol of authority*
11:11 ª [Gal. 3:28]
¹ *independent of*
11:13 ¹ *proper*
11:14 ¹ *dishonour*
11:16 ª 1 Tim. 6:4
ᵇ 1 Cor. 7:17
11:18 ª 1 Cor. 1:10–12; 3:3

11:19 ª 1 Tim.
4:1   ᵇ [Deut.
13:3]   ¹ *factions*
² *recognized*
11:21 ª Jude 12
¹ *ahead of others*
11:22 ª 1 Cor. 10:32
ᵇ James 2:6   ¹ The *poor*
11:23 ª 1 Cor. 15:3
ᵇ Matt. 26:26–28
11:25 ¹ *after supper*
11:26 ª John 14:3
¹ *proclaim*
11:27 ª [John 6:51]
¹ *in an unworthy manner*
11:28 ª 2 Cor. 13:5
11:29 ¹ *in an unworthy manner*
² *judgment*
11:30 ¹ Are *dead*
11:31 ª [1 John 1:9]
11:32 ª Ps. 94:12
11:33 ª 1 Cor. 14:26
¹ *wait*
11:34 ¹ *for judgment*
12:1 ª 1 Cor. 12:4;
14:1, 37
12:2 ª Eph. 2:11
ᵇ Ps. 115:5   ¹ *silent*

19 For ªthere must be also ¹heresies among you, ᵇthat they which are approved may be ²made manifest among you.

20 When ye come together therefore into one place, *this* is not to eat the Lord's supper.

21 For in eating every one taketh ¹before *other* his own supper: and one is hungry, and ªanother is drunken.

22 What? have ye not houses to eat and to drink in? or despise ye ªthe church of God, and ᵇshame ¹them that have not? What shall I say to you? shall I praise *you* in this? I praise *you* not.

23 For ªI have received of the Lord that which also I delivered unto you, ᵇThat the Lord Jesus the *same* night in which he was betrayed took bread:

24 And when he had given thanks, he brake *it,* and said, Take, eat: this is my body, which is broken for you: this do in remembrance of me.

25 After the same manner also *he took* the cup, ¹when he had supped, saying, This cup is the new testament in my blood: this do ye, as oft as ye drink *it,* in remembrance of me.

26 For as often as ye eat this bread, and drink this cup, ye do ¹shew the Lord's death ªtill he come.

27 Wherefore whosoever shall eat ªthis bread, and drink *this* cup of the Lord, ¹unworthily, shall be guilty of the body and blood of the Lord.

28 But ªlet a man examine himself, and so let him eat of *that* bread, and drink of *that* cup.

29 For he that eateth and drinketh ¹unworthily, eateth and drinketh ²damnation to himself, not discerning the Lord's body.

30 For this cause many *are* weak and sickly among you, and many ¹sleep.

31 For ªif we would judge ourselves, we should not be judged.

32 But when we are judged, ªwe are chastened of the Lord, that we should not be condemned with the world.

33 Wherefore, my brethren, when ye ªcome together to eat, ¹tarry one for another.

34 And if any man hunger, let him eat at home; that ye come not together ¹unto condemnation. And the rest will I set in order when I come.

## CHAPTER 12

Nᴏᴡ ªconcerning spiritual *gifts,* brethren, I would not have you ignorant.

2 Ye know ªthat ye were Gentiles, carried away unto these ᵇdumb¹ idols, even as ye were led.

3 Wherefore I give you to understand, that no man speaking by the

Spirit of God calleth Jesus [1]accursed: and [a]*that* no man can say that Jesus is the Lord, but by the Holy Ghost.

4 Now [a]there are [1]diversities of gifts, but [b]the same Spirit.

5 [a]And there are differences of [1]administrations, but the same Lord.

6 And there are diversities of [1]operations, but it is the same God [a]which worketh [a]all in all.

7 But the manifestation of the Spirit is given to every man to profit [1]withal.

8 For to one is given by the Spirit [a]the word of wisdom; to another [b]the word of knowledge by the same Spirit;

9 [a]To another faith by the same Spirit; to another [b]the gifts of healing by the same Spirit;

10 [a]To another the working of miracles; to another [b]prophecy; to another [c]discerning of spirits; to another [d]*divers* kinds of tongues; to another the interpretation of tongues:

11 But all these worketh that one and the selfsame Spirit, [a]dividing[1] to every man [2]severally [b]as he will.

12 For [a]as the body is one, and hath many members, and all the members of that one body, being many, are one body: [b]so also *is* Christ.

13 For [a]by one Spirit are we all baptized into one body, [b]whether *we be* Jews or [1]Gentiles, whether *we be* [2]bond or free; and [c]have been all made to drink into one Spirit.

14 For the body is not one member, but many.

15 If the foot shall say, Because I am not the hand, I am not of the body; is it therefore not of the body?

16 And if the ear shall say, Because I am not the eye, I am not of the body; is it therefore not of the body?

17 If the whole body *were* an eye, where *were* the hearing? If the whole *were* hearing, where *were* the smelling?

18 But now hath [a]God set the members every one of them in the body, [b]as it hath pleased him.

19 And if they were all one member, where [1]*were* the body?

20 But now *are they* many members, yet but one body.

21 And the eye cannot say unto the hand, I have no need of thee: nor again the head to the feet, I have no need of you.

22 Nay, much more those members of the body, which seem to be more [1]feeble, are necessary:

23 And those *members* of the body, which we think to be less honourable, upon these we bestow more abundant honour; and our [1]uncomely *parts* have more abundant [2]comeliness.

24 For our [1]comely *parts* have no need: but God hath [2]tempered the body together, having given more abundant honour to that *part* which lacked:

25 That there should be no [1]schism in the body; but *that* the members should have the same care one for another.

26 And [1]whether one member suffer, all the members suffer with it; or one member be honoured, all the members rejoice with it.

27 Now [a]ye are the body of Christ, and [b]members [1]in particular.

28 And [a]God hath [1]set some in the church, first [b]apostles, secondarily [c]prophets, thirdly teachers, after that [d]miracles, then [e]gifts of healings, [f]helps, [g]governments, [2]diversities of tongues.

29 *Are* all apostles? *are* all prophets? *are* all teachers? *are* all workers of miracles?

30 Have all the gifts of healing? do all speak with tongues? do all interpret?

31 But [a]covet[1] earnestly the best gifts: and yet shew I unto you a more excellent way.

## CHAPTER 13

THOUGH I speak with the tongues of men and of angels, and have not [1]charity, I am become *as* sounding brass, or a [2]tinkling cymbal.

2 And though I have *the gift of* [a]prophecy, and understand all mysteries, and all knowledge; and though I have all faith, [b]so that I could remove mountains, and have not [1]charity, I am nothing.

3 And [a]though I bestow all my goods to feed *the poor,* and though I give my body to be burned, and have not [1]charity, it profiteth me nothing.

4 [a]Charity[1] suffereth long, *and* is [b]kind; charity [c]envieth not; [1]charity [2]vaunteth not itself, is not [3]puffed up,

5 Doth not behave itself [1]unseemly, [a]seeketh not her own, is not easily provoked, [2]thinketh no evil;

6 [a]Rejoiceth not in iniquity, but [b]rejoiceth in the truth;

7 [a]Beareth all things, believeth all things, hopeth all things, endureth all things.

8 [1]Charity never faileth: but whether *there be* prophecies, they shall [2]fail; whether *there be* tongues, they shall cease; whether *there be* knowledge, it shall [2]vanish away.

9 [a]For we know in part, and we prophesy in part.

10 But when that which is [1]perfect is come, then that which is in part shall be done away.

12:3 [a] Matt. 16:17
[1] Gr. *anathema*

12:4 [a] Rom.

12:3–8 [b] Eph. 4:4
[1] *various kinds*

12:5 [a] Rom. 12:6
[1] *ministries*

12:6 [a] 1 Cor. 15:28
[1] *activities* [2] *all things* [a]

12:7 [1] All

12:8 [a] 1 Cor. 2:6, 7
[b] Rom. 15:14

12:9 [a] 2 Cor. 4:13
[b] Mark 3:15; 16:18

12:10 [a] Mark 16:17 [b] Rom.
12:6 [c] 1 John 4:1
[d] Acts 2:4–11

12:11 [a] Rom.
12:6 [b] [John 3:8]
[1] *distributing*
[2] *individually*

12:12 [a] Rom. 12:4, 5 [b] [Gal. 3:16]

12:13 [a] [Rom. 6:5]
[b] Col. 3:11 [c] [John 7:37–39] [1] Lit. *Greeks* [2] *slaves*

12:18 [a] 1 Cor. 12:28
[b] Rom. 12:3

12:19 [1] *would the body be*

12:22 [1] *weak*

12:23 [1] *unpresentable* [2] *modesty*

12:24 [1] *presentable* [2] *composed*

12:25 [1] *division*

12:26 [1] *if*

12:27 [a] Rom.
12:5 [b] Eph. 5:30
[1] *individually*

12:28 [a] Eph. 4:11
[b] [Eph. 2:20; 3:5]
[c] Acts 13:1 [d] 1 Cor.
12:10, 29 [e] 1 Cor.
12:9, 30 [f] Num.
11:17 [g] Rom. 12:8
[1] *appointed these*
[2] *varieties*

12:31 [a] 1 Cor. 14:1, 39 [1] *desire*

13:1 [1] *love*
[2] *clanging*

13:2 [a] 1 Cor.
12:8–10, 28; 14:1
[b] Matt. 17:20; 21:21
[1] *love*

13:3 [a] Matt. 6:1,
2 [1] *love*

13:4 [a] Prov. 10:12;
17:9 [b] Eph. 4:32
[c] Gal. 5:26 [1] *Love*
[2] *does not brag on* [3] *arrogant*

13:5 [a] 1 Cor. 10:24
[1] *rudely* [2] *keeps no accounts of evil*

13:6 [a] Rom. 1:32
[b] 2 John 4

13:7 [a] Gal. 6:2

13:8 [1] *Love*
[2] *cease*

13:9 [a] 1 Cor. 8:2; 13:12   13:10 [1] *complete*

11 When I was a child, I spake as a child, I understood as a child, I thought as a child: but when I became a man, I put away childish things.

12 For [a]now we see through a [1]glass, [2]darkly; but then [b]face to face: now I know in part; but then shall I know even as also I am known.

13 And now abideth faith, hope, [1]charity, these three; but the greatest of these *is* [1]charity.

## CHAPTER 14

FOLLOW after [1]charity, and [a]desire spiritual *gifts,* [b]but rather that ye may prophesy.

2 For he that [a]speaketh in an *unknown* tongue speaketh not unto men, but unto God: for no man understandeth *him;* howbeit in the spirit he speaketh mysteries.

3 But he that prophesieth speaketh unto men *to* [a]edification, and [b]exhortation, and comfort.

4 He that speaketh in an *unknown* tongue edifieth himself; but he that prophesieth edifieth the church.

5 I would that ye all spake with tongues, but [1]rather that ye prophesied: for greater *is* he that prophesieth than he that speaketh with tongues, except he interpret, that the church may receive [2]edifying.

6 Now, brethren, if I come unto you speaking with tongues, what shall I profit you, except I shall speak to you either by [a]revelation, or by knowledge, or by prophesying, or by [1]doctrine?

7 And even things without life giving sound, whether [1]pipe or harp, except they give a distinction in the sounds, how shall it be known what is piped or harped?

8 For if the trumpet give an uncertain sound, who shall prepare himself to the battle?

9 So likewise ye, except ye utter by the tongue words easy to be understood, how shall it be known what is spoken? for ye shall speak into the air.

10 There are, it may be, so many kinds of voices in the world, and none of them *is* without [1]signification.

11 Therefore if I know not the meaning of the voice, I shall be unto him that speaketh a [1]barbarian, and he that speaketh *shall be* a barbarian unto me.

12 Even so ye, forasmuch as ye are zealous of spiritual *gifts,* seek that ye may excel to the edifying of the church.

13 Wherefore let him that speaketh in an *unknown* tongue pray that he may [a]interpret.

14 For if I pray in an *unknown* tongue, my spirit prayeth, but my understanding is unfruitful.

15 What [1]is it then? I will pray with the spirit, and I will pray with the understanding also: [a]I will sing with the spirit, and I will sing [b]with the understanding also.

16 Else when thou shalt bless with the spirit, how shall he that occupieth the [1]room of the [2]unlearned say Amen [a]at thy giving of thanks, seeing he understandeth not what thou sayest?

17 For thou verily givest thanks well, but the other is not edified.

18 I thank my God, I speak with tongues more than ye all:

19 Yet in the church I had rather speak five words with my understanding, that *by my voice* I might teach others also, than ten thousand words in an *unknown* tongue.

20 Brethren, [a]be not children in understanding: howbeit in malice [b]be ye [1]children, but in understanding be [2]men.

21 [a]In the law it is [b]written, With *men of* other tongues and other lips will I speak unto this people; and yet for all that will they not hear me, saith the Lord.

22 Wherefore tongues are for a [a]sign, not to them that believe, but to them that believe not: but prophesying *serveth* not for them that believe not, but for them which believe.

23 If therefore the whole church be come together into one place, and all speak with tongues, and there come in *those that are* [1]unlearned, or unbelievers, [a]will they not say that ye are [2]mad?

24 But if all prophesy, and there come in one that believeth not, or *one* unlearned, he is convinced [1]of all, he is judged [1]of all:

25 And thus are the secrets of his heart made manifest; and so falling down on *his* face he will worship God, and report [a]that God is in you of a truth.

26 How is it then, brethren? when ye come together, every one of you hath a psalm, [a]hath a doctrine, hath a tongue, hath a revelation, hath an interpretation. [b]Let all things be done unto edifying.

27 If any man speak in an *unknown* tongue, *let it be* by two, or at the most *by* three, and *that* by course; and let one interpret.

28 But if there be no interpreter, let him keep silence in the church; and let him speak to himself, and to God.

29 Let the prophets speak two or three, and [a]let the other judge.

30 If *any thing* be revealed to another that sitteth by, [a]let the first [1]hold his peace.

31 For ye may all prophesy one by one, that all may learn, and all may be [1]comforted.

### Marginal references

13:12 [a] Phil. 3:12
[b] [1 John 3:2]
[1] *mirror* [2] *dimly*

13:13 [1] *love*

14:1 [a] 1 Cor. 12:31; 14:39 [b] Num. 11:25, 29 [1] *love*

14:2 [a] Acts 2:4; 10:46

14:3 [a] Rom. 14:19; 15:2 [b] 1 Tim. 4:13

14:5 [1] *even more* [2] *building up*

14:6 [a] 1 Cor. 14:26 [1] *teaching*

14:7 [1] *flute*

14:10 [1] *meaning*

14:11 [1] *foreigner*

14:13 [a] 1 Cor. 12:10

14:15 [a] Col. 3:16 [b] Ps. 47:7 [1] *is the conclusion*

14:16 [a] 1 Cor. 11:24 [1] *place* [2] *uninformed*

14:20 [a] Ps. 131:2 [b] [1 Pet. 2:2] [1] *babes* [2] *mature*

14:21 [a] John 10:34 [b] Is. 28:11, 12

14:22 [a] Mark 16:17

14:23 [a] Acts 2:13 [1] *uninformed* [2] *insane*

14:24 [1] *by*

14:25 [a] Is. 45:14

14:26 [a] 1 Cor. 12:8–10; 14:6 [b] [2 Cor. 12:19]

14:29 [a] 1 Cor. 12:10

14:30 [a] [1 Thess. 5:19, 20] [1] *keep silent*

14:31 [1] *encouraged*

32 And ᵃthe spirits of the prophets are subject to the prophets.

33 For God is not *the author* of ¹confusion, but of peace, ᵃas in all churches of the saints.

34 ᵃLet your women keep silence in the churches: for it is not permitted unto them to speak; but *they are commanded* to be ¹under obedience, as also saith the ᵇlaw.

35 And if they will learn any thing, let them ask their husbands at home: for it is a shame for women to speak in the church.

36 What? came the word of God ¹out from you? or came it unto you only?

37 ᵃIf any man think himself to be a prophet, or spiritual, let him acknowledge that the things that I write unto you are the commandments of the Lord.

38 But if any man be ignorant, let him be ignorant.

39 Wherefore, brethren, ᵃcovet¹ to prophesy, and forbid not to speak with tongues.

40 ᵃLet all things be done decently and in order.

## CHAPTER 15

MOREOVER, brethren, I declare unto you the gospel ᵃwhich I preached unto you, which also ye have received, and ᵇwherein ye stand;

2 ᵃBy which also ye are saved, if ye ¹keep in memory ²what I preached unto you, unless ᵇye have believed in vain.

3 For ᵃI delivered unto you first of all that ᵇwhich I also received, how that Christ died for our sins ᶜaccording to the scriptures;

4 And that he was buried, and that he rose again the third day ᵃaccording to the scriptures:

5 ᵃAnd that he was seen of ¹Cephas, then ᵇof the twelve:

6 After that, he was seen of above five hundred brethren at once; of whom the greater part remain unto this present, but some ¹are fallen asleep.

7 After that, he was seen of James; then ᵃof all the apostles.

8 ᵃAnd last of all he was seen of me also, as of one born out of due time.

9 For I am ᵃthe least of the apostles, that am not ¹meet to be called an apostle, because ᵇI persecuted the church of God.

10 But ᵃby the grace of God I am what I am: and his grace which *was* bestowed upon me was not in vain; but I laboured more abundantly than they all: ᵇyet not I, but the grace of God which was with me.

11 Therefore whether *it were* I or they, so we preach, and so ye believed.

12 Now if Christ be preached that he rose from the dead, how say some among you that there is no resurrection of the dead?

13 But if there be no resurrection of the dead, ᵃthen is Christ not risen:

14 And if Christ be not risen, then *is* our preaching ¹vain, and your faith *is* also vain.

15 Yea, and we are found false witnesses of God; because ᵃwe have testified of God that he raised up Christ: whom he raised not up, if so be that the dead rise not.

16 For if the dead rise not, then is not Christ raised:

17 And if Christ be not raised, your faith *is* ¹vain; ᵃye are yet in your sins.

18 Then they also which ¹are fallen ᵃasleep in Christ are perished.

19 ᵃIf in this life only we have hope in Christ, we are of all men most ¹miserable.

20 But now ᵃis Christ risen from the dead, *and* become ᵇthe firstfruits of them that ¹slept.

21 For ᵃsince by man *came* death, ᵇby man *came* also the resurrection of the dead.

22 For as in Adam all die, even so in Christ shall all ᵃbe made alive.

23 But ᵃevery man in his own order: Christ the firstfruits; afterward they that are Christ's at his coming.

24 Then *cometh* the end, when he shall have delivered up ᵃthe kingdom to God, even the Father; when he shall have put down all rule and all authority and power.

25 For he must reign, ᵃtill he hath put all enemies under his feet.

26 ᵃThe last enemy *that* shall be destroyed *is* death.

27 For he ᵃhath put all things under his feet. But when he saith all things are put under *him, it is* ¹manifest that he is excepted, which did put all things under him.

28 ᵃAnd when all things shall be subdued unto him, then ᵇshall the Son also himself be subject unto him that put all things under him, that God may be all in all.

29 Else what shall they do which are baptized for the dead, if the dead rise not at all? why are they then baptized for the dead?

30 And ᵃwhy stand we in jeopardy every hour?

31 I ¹protest by ᵃyour² rejoicing which I have in Christ Jesus our Lord, ᵇI die daily.

32 If after the manner of men ᵃI have fought with beasts at Ephesus, what advantageth it me, if the dead rise not? ᵇlet us eat and drink; for to morrow we die.

14:32 ᵃ 1 John 4:1
14:33 ᵃ 1 Cor. 11:16
¹ *disorder*
14:34 ᵃ 1 Tim. 2:11 ᵇ Gen. 3:16 ¹ *submissive*
14:36 ¹ *originally from*
14:37 ᵃ 2 Cor. 10:7
14:39 ᵃ 1 Cor. 12:31 ¹ *earnestly desire*
14:40 ᵃ 1 Cor. 14:33
15:1 ᵃ [Gal. 1:11] ᵇ [Rom. 5:2; 11:20]
15:2 ᵃ Rom. 1:16 ᵇ Gal. 3:4 ¹ *hold fast* ² *the word*
15:3 ᵃ 1 Cor. 11:2, 23 ᵇ [Gal. 1:12] ᶜ Ps. 22:15
15:4 ᵃ Ps. 16:9–11; 68:18; 110:1
15:5 ᵃ Luke 24:34 ᵇ Matt. 28:17 ¹ *Peter*
15:6 ¹ *Have died*
15:7 ᵃ Acts 1:3, 4
15:8 ᵃ [Acts 9:3–8; 22:6–11; 26:12–18]
15:9 ᵃ Eph. 3:8 ᵇ Acts 8:3 ¹ *worthy*
15:10 ᵃ Eph. 3:7, 8 ᵇ Phil. 2:13
15:13 ᵃ [1 Thess. 4:14]
15:14 ¹ *futile*
15:15 ᵃ Acts 2:24
15:17 ᵃ [Rom. 4:25] ¹ *futile*
15:18 ᵃ Job 14:12; Ps. 13:3 ¹ *Have died*
15:19 ᵃ 1 Cor. 4:9; 2 Tim. 3:12 ¹ *pitiable*
15:20 ᵃ Acts 2:24; 1 Pet. 1:3 ᵇ Acts 26:23; 1 Cor. 15:23; Rev. 1:5 ¹ *have fallen asleep, have died*
15:21 ᵃ Gen. 3:19; Ezek. 18:4; Rom. 5:12; 6:23; Heb. 9:27 ᵇ John 11:25
15:22 ᵃ [John 5:28, 29]
15:23 ᵃ [1 Thess. 4:15–17]
15:24 ᵃ [Dan. 2:44; 7:14, 27; 2 Pet. 1:11]
15:25 ᵃ Ps. 110:1; Matt. 22:44
15:26 ᵃ [2 Tim. 1:10; Rev. 20:14; 21:4]
15:27 ᵃ Ps. 8:6 ¹ *evident*
15:28 ᵃ [Phil. 3:21] ᵇ 1 Cor. 3:23; 11:3; 12:6
15:30 ᵃ 2 Cor. 11:26 15:31 ᵃ 1 Thess. 2:19 ᵇ Rom. 8:36 ¹ *affirm* ² *the boasting in you which* 15:32 ᵃ 2 Cor. 1:8 ᵇ Eccl. 2:24; Is. 22:13; 56:12; Luke 12:19

33 Be not deceived: [a]evil [1]communications corrupt good [2]manners.

34 [a]Awake to righteousness, and sin not; [b]for some have not the knowledge of God: [c]I speak *this* to your shame.

35 But some *man* will say, [a]How are the dead raised up? and with what body do they come?

36 *Thou* fool, [a]that which thou sowest is not [1]quickened, except it die:

37 And that which thou sowest, thou sowest not that body that shall be, but [1]bare grain, [2]it may chance of wheat, or of some other *grain:*

38 But God giveth it a body as it hath pleased him, and to every seed his own body.

39 All flesh *is* not the same flesh: but *there is* one *kind of* flesh of men, another flesh of beasts, another of fishes, *and* another of birds.

40 *There are* also [1]celestial bodies, and bodies [2]terrestrial: but the glory of the celestial *is* one, and the *glory* of the terrestrial *is* another.

41 *There is* one glory of the sun, and another glory of the moon, and another glory of the stars: for *one* star differeth from *another* star in glory.

42 [a]So also *is* the resurrection of the dead. It is sown in [1]corruption; it is raised [2]in incorruption:

43 [a]It is sown in dishonour; it is raised in glory: it is sown in weakness; it is raised in power:

44 It is sown a natural body; it is raised a spiritual body. There is a natural body, and there is a spiritual body.

45 And so it is written, [a]The first man Adam was made a living soul; [b]the last Adam *was made* [c]a [1]quickening spirit.

46 Howbeit that *was* not first which is spiritual, but that which is natural; and afterward that which is spiritual.

47 [a]The first man *is* of the earth, [b]earthy:[1] the second man *is* the Lord [c]from heaven.

48 As *is* the [1]earthy, such *are* they also that are earthy: [a]and as *is* the heavenly, such *are* they also that are heavenly.

49 And [a]as we have borne the image of the [1]earthy, [b]we shall also bear the image of the heavenly.

50 Now this I say, brethren, that [a]flesh and blood cannot inherit the kingdom of God; neither doth corruption inherit incorruption.

51 Behold, I shew you a mystery; [a]We shall not all sleep, [b]but we shall all be changed,

52 In a moment, in the twinkling of an eye, at the last [1]trump: [a]for the trumpet shall sound, and the dead shall be raised incorruptible, and we shall be changed.

53 For this corruptible must put on incorruption, and [a]this mortal *must* put on immortality.

54 So when this corruptible shall have put on incorruption, and this mortal shall have put on immortality, then shall be brought to pass the saying that is written, [a]Death is swallowed up in victory.

55 [a]O death, where *is* thy sting? O [1]grave, where *is* thy victory?

56 The sting of death *is* sin; and [a]the strength of sin *is* the law.

57 [a]But thanks *be* to God, which giveth us [b]the victory through our Lord Jesus Christ.

58 [a]Therefore, my beloved brethren, be ye stedfast, unmoveable, always abounding in the work of the Lord, forasmuch as ye know [b]that your labour is not [1]in vain in the Lord.

## CHAPTER 16

Now concerning [a]the collection for the saints, as I have given [1]order to the churches of Galatia, even so do ye.

2 [a]Upon the first *day* of the week let every one of you [1]lay by him in store, as *God* hath prospered him, that there be no [2]gatherings when I come.

3 And when I come, [a]whomsoever ye shall approve by *your* letters, them will I send to bring your [1]liberality unto Jerusalem.

4 [a]And if it be [1]meet that I go also, they shall go with me.

5 Now I will come unto you, [a]when I shall pass through Macedonia: for I do pass through Macedonia.

6 And it may be that I will abide, yea, and winter with you, that ye may [a]bring[1] me on my journey whithersoever I go.

7 For I will not see you now [1]by the way; but I trust to [2]tarry a while with you, [a]if the Lord permit.

8 But I will tarry at Ephesus until [a]Pentecost.

9 For [a]a great [1]door and effectual is opened unto me, and [b]there are many adversaries.

10 Now [a]if Timotheus come, see that he may be with you without fear: for [b]he worketh the work of the Lord, as I also *do.*

11 [a]Let no man therefore despise him: but [1]conduct him forth [b]in peace, that he may come unto me: for I [2]look for him with the brethren.

12 As [1]touching *our* brother [a]Apollos, I greatly [2]desired him to come unto you with the brethren: but his will was not at all to come at this time; but he will come when he shall have convenient time.

### Cross references

15:33 [a] [1 Cor. 5:6] [1] *company corrupts* [2] *habits*
15:34 [a] Rom. 13:11; Eph. 5:14 [b] [1 Thess. 4:5] [c] 1 Cor. 6:5
15:35 [a] Ezek. 37:3
15:36 [a] John 12:24 [1] *made alive*
15:37 [1] *mere* [2] *perhaps wheat*
15:40 [1] *heavenly* [2] *earthly*
15:42 [a] [Dan. 12:3; Matt. 13:43] [1] *a perishable state* [2] *imperishable*
15:43 [a] [Phil. 3:21; Col. 3:4]
15:45 [a] Gen. 2:7 [b] [Rom. 5:14] [c] John 5:21; 6:57; [Rom. 8:2; Phil. 3:21; Col. 3:4] [1] *life-giving*
15:47 [a] John 3:31 [b] Gen. 2:7; 3:19 [c] John 3:13 [1] *made of dust*
15:48 [a] Phil. 3:20 [1] *man of dust*
15:49 [a] Gen. 5:3 [b] Rom. 8:29 [1] *man of dust*
15:50 [a] [John 3:3, 5]
15:51 [a] [1 Thess. 4:15] [b] [Phil. 3:21]
15:52 [a] Matt. 24:31 [1] *trumpet*
15:53 [a] 2 Cor. 5:4
15:54 [a] Is. 25:8
15:55 [a] Hos. 13:14 [1] Gr. *hades*
15:56 [a] [Rom. 3:20; 4:15; 7:8]
15:57 [a] [Rom. 7:25] [b] [1 John 5:4]
15:58 [a] 2 Pet. 3:14 [b] [1 Cor. 3:8] [1] *futile*
16:1 [a] Gal. 2:10 [1] *orders*
16:2 [a] Acts 20:7 [1] *lay something aside, and store up* [2] *collections*
16:3 [a] 2 Cor. 3:1; 8:18 [1] *gifts*
16:4 [a] 2 Cor. 8:4, 19 [1] *fitting*
16:5 [a] 2 Cor. 1:15, 16
16:6 [a] Acts 15:3 [1] *send*
16:7 [a] James 4:15 [1] *on* [2] *stay*
16:8 [a] Lev. 23:15–22
16:9 [a] Acts 14:27 [b] Acts 19:9 [1] *and effective door*
16:10 [a] Acts 19:22 [b] Phil. 2:20
16:11 [a] 1 Tim. 4:12 [b] Acts 15:33 [1] *send* [2] *am waiting*
16:12 [a] 1 Cor. 1:12; 3:5 [1] *concerning* [2] *urged*

13 [a]Watch ye, [b]stand fast in the faith, [1]quit you like men, [c]be strong.

14 [1]Let all your things be done with [1]charity.

15 I beseech you, brethren, (ye know [a]the house of Stephanas, that it is [b]the firstfruits of Achaia, and *that* they have [1]addicted themselves to [c]the ministry of the saints,)

16 [a]That ye submit yourselves unto such, and to every one that [1]helpeth with *us,* and [b]laboureth.

17 I am glad of the coming of Stephanas and Fortunatus and Achaicus: [a]for that which was lacking on your part they have supplied.

18 [a]For they have refreshed my spirit and yours: therefore [b]acknowledge ye them that are such.

19 The churches of Asia [1]salute you. Aquila and Priscilla [1]salute you [2]much in the Lord, [a]with the church that is in their house.

20 All the brethren greet you. [a]Greet ye one another with an holy kiss.

21 [a]The salutation of *me* Paul with mine own hand.

22 If any man [a]love not the Lord Jesus Christ, [b]let him be [1]Anathema [c]Maranatha.[2]

23 [a]The grace of our Lord Jesus Christ *be* with you.

24 My love *be* with you all in Christ Jesus. Amen.

16:13 [a] Matt. 24:42 [b] Phil. 1:27; 4:1 [c] [Eph. 3:16; 6:10] [1] *be brave*
16:14 [a] [1 Pet. 4:8] [1] *love*
16:15 [a] 1 Cor. 1:16 [b] Rom. 16:5 [c] 2 Cor. 8:4 [1] *devoted*
16:16 [a] Heb. 13:17 [b] [Heb. 6:10] [1] *works*
16:17 [a] 2 Cor. 11:9
16:18 [a] Col. 4:8 [b] Phil. 2:29
16:19 [a] Rom. 16:5 [1] *greet* [2] *heartily*
16:20 [a] Rom. 16:16
16:21 [a] Col. 4:18    16:22 [a] Eph. 6:24 [b] Gal. 1:8, 9 [c] Jude 14, 15 [1] *Accursed* [2] *O Lord, come.*
16:23 [a] Rom. 16:20

# CORINTHIANS

Since Paul's first letter, the Corinthian church had been swayed by false teachers who stirred the people against Paul. They claimed he was fickle, proud, unimpressive in appearance and speech, dishonest, and unqualified as an apostle of Jesus Christ. Paul sent Titus to Corinth to deal with these difficulties, and upon his return, rejoiced to hear of the Corinthians' change of heart. Paul wrote this letter to express his thanksgiving for the repentant majority and to appeal to the rebellious minority to accept his authority. Throughout the book he defends his conduct, character, and calling as an apostle of Jesus Christ.

To distinguish this epistle from First Corinthians, it was given the title *Pros Korinthious B*, the "Second to the Corinthians." The *A* and *B* were probably later additions to *Pros Korinthious*.

## CHAPTER 1

PAUL, ªan apostle of Jesus Christ by the will of God, and ᵇTimothy *our* brother, unto the church of God which is at Corinth, ᶜwith all the saints which are in all Achaia:

2 ªGrace *be* to you and peace from God our Father, and *from* the Lord Jesus Christ.

3 ªBlessed *be* God, even the Father of our Lord Jesus Christ, the Father of mercies, and the God of all comfort;

4 Who ªcomforteth us in all our tribulation, that we may be able to comfort them which are in any ¹trouble, by the comfort wherewith we ourselves are comforted of God.

5 For as ªthe sufferings of Christ abound in us, so our ¹consolation also aboundeth by Christ.

6 And ¹whether we be afflicted, ª*it is* for your consolation and salvation, which is ²effectual in the enduring of the same sufferings which we also suffer: or whether we be comforted, *it is* for your consolation and salvation.

7 And our hope of you *is* stedfast, knowing, that ªas ye are partakers of the sufferings, so *shall ye be* also of the ¹consolation.

8 For we would not, brethren, have you ignorant of ªour ¹trouble which came to us in Asia, that we were ²pressed out of measure, above strength, insomuch that we despaired even of life:

9 But we had the sentence of death in ourselves, that we should ªnot trust in ourselves, but in God which raiseth the dead:

10 ªWho delivered us from so great a death, and doth deliver: in whom we trust that he will yet deliver *us;*

11 Ye also ªhelping together by prayer for us, that ᵇfor the gift ¹*bestowed* upon us by the means of many persons thanks may be given by many on our behalf.

1:1 ª 2 Tim. 1:1
ᵇ 1 Cor. 16:10
ᶜ Col. 1:2
1:2 ª Rom. 1:7
1:3 ª 1 Pet. 1:3
1:4 ª Is. 51:12;
66:13 ¹ *tribulation*
1:5 ª 2 Cor. 4:10
¹ *comfort*
1:6 ª 2 Cor.
4:15; 12:15 ¹ *if*
² *effective*
1:7 ª [Rom. 8:17]
¹ *comfort*
1:8 ª Acts 19:23
¹ *tribulation*
² *burdened*
1:9 ª Jer. 17:5, 7
1:10 ª [2 Pet. 2:9]
1:11 ª Rom. 15:30
ᵇ 2 Cor. 4:15; 9:11
¹ *given to*
1:12 ² 2 Cor. 2:17
ᵇ [1 Cor. 2:4]
¹ *boasting* ² The
opposite of
duplicity ³ *conducted ourselves*
1:13 ¹ *understand*
1:14 ª 2 Cor.
5:12 ᵇ Phil. 2:16
¹ *understood*
² *boast*
1:15 ª 1 Cor. 4:19
ᵇ Rom. 1:11; 15:29
1:16 ª 1 Cor. 16:3–6
¹ *helped*
1:17 ª 2 Cor. 10:2;
11:18 ¹ *planning this* ² *plan*
1:18 ª 1 John 5:20
¹ *faithful*
1:19 ª Mark
1:1 ᵇ 1 Pet.
5:12 ᶜ 2 Cor. 1:1
ᵈ [Heb. 13:8]
1:20 ª [Rom.
15:8, 9]
1:21 ª [1 John 2:20,
27] ¹ *establishes*
1:22 ª [Eph. 4:30]
ᵇ [Eph. 1:14]
¹ *down payment*
1:23 ª Gal. 1:20

12 For our ¹rejoicing is this, the testimony of our conscience, that in ²simplicity and ªgodly sincerity, ᵇnot with fleshly wisdom, but by the grace of God, we have ³had our conversation in the world, and more abundantly to you-ward.

13 For we write none other things unto you, than what ye read or ¹acknowledge; and I trust ye shall ¹acknowledge even to the end;

14 As also ye have ¹acknowledged us in part, ªthat we are your ²rejoicing, even as ᵇye also *are* ours in the day of the Lord Jesus.

15 And in this confidence ªI was minded to come unto you before, that ye might have ᵇa second benefit;

16 And to pass by you into Macedonia, and ªto come again out of Macedonia unto you, and of you to be ¹brought on my way toward Judaea.

17 When I therefore was ¹thus minded, did I use lightness? or the things that I ²purpose, do I purpose ªaccording to the flesh, that with me there should be yea yea, and nay nay?

18 But *as* God *is* ªtrue,¹ our word toward you was not yea and nay.

19 For ªthe Son of God, Jesus Christ, who was preached among you by us, *even* by me and ᵇSilvanus and ᶜTimotheus, was not yea and nay, ᵈbut in him was yea.

20 ªFor all the promises of God in him *are* yea, and in him Amen, unto the glory of God by us.

21 Now he which ¹stablisheth us with you in Christ, and ªhath anointed us, *is* God;

22 Who ªhath also sealed us, and ᵇgiven the ¹earnest of the Spirit in our hearts.

23 Moreover ªI call God ¹for a record upon my soul, ᵇthat to spare you I came ²not as yet unto Corinth.

24 Not for ªthat we have domination

ᵇ 1 Cor. 4:21 ¹ *as witness against* ² *no more unto*
1:24 ª [1 Pet. 5:3]

over your faith, but are ¹helpers of your joy: for ᵇby faith ye stand.

## CHAPTER 2

**B**UT I determined this with myself, ᵃthat I would not come again to you in ¹heaviness.

2 For if I make you ᵃsorry,¹ who is he then that maketh me glad, but the same which is made sorry by me?

3 And I wrote this same unto you, lest, when I came, ᵃI should have sorrow from them of whom I ought to rejoice; ᵇhaving confidence in you all, that my joy is *the joy* of you all.

4 For out of much affliction and anguish of heart I wrote unto you with many tears; ᵃnot that ye should be grieved, but that ye might know the love which I have more abundantly unto you.

5 But ᵃif any have caused grief, he hath not ᵇgrieved me, but in part: that I may not ¹overcharge you all.

6 Sufficient to such a man *is* this punishment, which *was inflicted* ᵃof many.

7 ᵃSo that contrariwise ye *ought* rather to forgive *him,* and comfort *him,* lest perhaps such a one should be swallowed up with overmuch sorrow.

8 Wherefore I beseech you that ye would ¹confirm *your* love toward him.

9 For to this end also did I write, that I might ¹know the proof of you, whether ye be ᵃobedient in all things.

10 To whom ye forgive any thing, I *forgive* also: for if I forgave any thing, to whom I forgave *it,* for your sakes *forgave I it* in the ¹person of Christ;

11 Lest Satan should get an advantage of us: for we are not ignorant of his devices.

12 Furthermore, ᵃwhen I came to Troas to *preach* Christ's gospel, and ᵇa¹ door was opened unto me of the Lord,

13 ᵃI had no rest in my spirit, because I found not Titus my brother: but taking my leave of them, I went from thence into Macedonia.

14 Now thanks *be* unto God, which always ¹causeth us to triumph in Christ, and maketh manifest the ²savour of his knowledge by us in every place.

15 For we are unto God ¹a sweet savour of Christ, ᵃin² them that are saved, and ᵇin² them that perish:

16 ᵃTo the one *we are* the ¹savour of death unto death; and to the other the ¹savour of life unto life. And ᵇwho *is* sufficient for these things?

17 For we are not as many, which ᵃcorrupt¹ the word of God: but as ᵇof sincerity, but as ²of God, in the sight of God speak we in Christ.

## CHAPTER 3

**D**O ᵃwe begin again to commend ourselves? or need we, as some *others,* ᵇepistles of commendation to you, or *letters* of commendation from you?

2 ᵃYe are our epistle written in our hearts, known and read of all men:

3 *Forasmuch as ye are* manifestly declared to be the epistle of Christ ᵃministered¹ by us, written not with ink, but with the Spirit of the living God; not ᵇin ²tables of stone, but ᶜin fleshy ²tables of the heart.

4 And such trust have we through Christ to God-ward:

5 ᵃNot that we are sufficient of ourselves to think any thing as of ourselves; but ᵇour sufficiency *is* of God;

6 Who also hath made us ¹able ᵃministers of ᵇthe new ²testament; not ᶜof the letter, but of the ³spirit: for ᵈthe letter killeth, ᵉbut the spirit giveth life.

7 But if ᵃthe ¹ministration of death, ᵇwritten *and* engraven in stones, was glorious, ᶜso that the children of Israel could not ²stedfastly behold the face of Moses for the glory of his countenance; which *glory* was ³to be done away:

8 How shall not ᵃthe ¹ministration of the ²spirit be ³rather glorious?

9 For if the ¹ministration of condemnation *be* glory, much more doth the ¹ministration ᵃof righteousness exceed in glory.

10 For even that which was made glorious had no glory in this respect, ¹by reason of the glory that excelleth.

11 For if that which is ¹done away *was* glorious, much more that which remaineth *is* glorious.

12 Seeing then that we have such hope, ᵃwe use great ¹plainness of speech:

13 And not as Moses, ᵃ*which* put a vail over his face, that the children of Israel could not ¹stedfastly look to ᵇthe end of that which ²is abolished:

14 But ᵃtheir minds were ¹blinded: for until this day remaineth the same vail untaken away in the reading of the old testament; which *vail* is done away in Christ.

15 But even unto this day, when Moses is read, the vail is upon their heart.

16 Nevertheless ᵃwhen ¹it shall turn to the Lord, ᵇthe vail shall be taken away.

17 Now ᵃthe Lord is that Spirit: and where the Spirit of the Lord *is,* there *is* ᵇliberty.

18 But we all, with ¹open face beholding ᵃas in a ²glass ᵇthe glory of the Lord, ᶜare ³changed into the same

### Center reference column

1:24 ᵇ Rom. 11:20
¹ fellow workers for

2:1 ᵃ 2 Cor. 1:23
¹ sorrow

2:2 ᵃ 2 Cor. 7:8
¹ sorrowful

2:3 ᵃ 2 Cor. 12:21
ᵇ Gal. 5:10

2:4 ᵃ [2 Cor. 2:9; 7:8, 12]

2:5 ᵃ [1 Cor. 5:1]
ᵇ Gal. 4:12 ¹ *be too severe with*

2:6 ᵃ 1 Cor. 5:4, 5

2:7 ᵃ Gal. 6:1

2:8 ¹ *reaffirm*

2:9 ᵃ 2 Cor. 7:15;
10:6 ¹ *put you to the test*

2:10 ¹ *presence*

2:12 ᵃ Acts 16:8
ᵇ 1 Cor. 16:9 ¹ An *opportunity*

2:13 ᵃ 2 Cor. 7:6, 13; 8:6

2:14 ¹ *leads us in*
² *fragrance*

2:15 ᵃ [1 Cor. 1:18]
ᵇ [2 Cor. 4:3]
¹ *the fragrance of* ² *among*

2:16 ᵃ Luke 2:34
ᵇ [1 Cor. 15:10]
¹ *aroma*

2:17 ᵃ 2 Pet. 2:3
ᵇ 2 Cor. 1:12 ¹ *peddle by trickery* ² *from*

3:1 ᵃ 2 Cor. 5:12;
10:12, 18; 12:11
ᵇ Acts 18:27

3:2 ᵃ 1 Cor. 9:2

3:3 ᵃ 1 Cor.
3:5 ᵇ Ex. 24:12;
31:18; 32:15 ᶜ Ps. 40:8 ¹ *cared for*
² *tablets*

3:5 ᵃ [John 15:5]
ᵇ 1 Cor. 15:10

3:6 ᵃ 1 Cor. 3:5
ᵇ Jer. 31:31 ᶜ Rom. 2:27 ᵈ Gal. 3:10
ᵉ John 6:63
¹ *sufficient as*
² *covenant* ³ Or *Spirit*

3:7 ᵃ Rom. 7:10
ᵇ Ex. 34:1 ᶜ Ex. 34:29 ¹ *ministry* ² *steadily* ³ *passing away*

3:8 ᵃ [Gal. 3:5]
¹ *ministry* ² Or *Spirit* ³ *more*

3:9 ᵃ [Rom. 1:17; 3:21] ¹ *ministry*

3:10 ¹ *because*

3:11 ¹ *passing*

3:12 ᵃ Eph. 6:19
¹ *boldness*

3:13 ᵃ Ex. 34:33–35 ᵇ [Gal. 3:23]
¹ *look steadily at* ² *was passing away*

3:14 ᵃ Acts 28:26 ¹ *made dull* 3:16 ᵃ Rom. 11:23
¹ *one* ᵇ Is. 25:7 3:17 ᵃ [1 Cor. 15:45] ᵇ Gal. 5:1, 13
3:18 ᵃ 1 Cor. 13:12 ᵇ [2 Cor. 4:4, 6] ᶜ [Rom. 8:29, 30]
¹ *unveiled* ² *mirror* ³ *being transformed*

image from glory to glory, *even* as by the Spirit of the Lord.

## CHAPTER 4

Therefore seeing we have this ministry, [a]as we have received mercy, we [1]faint [b]not;

2 But have renounced the hidden things of [1]dishonesty, not walking in craftiness, nor [2]handling the word of God deceitfully; but by manifestation of the truth [a]commending ourselves to every man's conscience in the sight of God.

3 But if our gospel be [1]hid, [a]it is hid to them that are [2]lost:

4 In whom [a]the god of this world [b]hath blinded the minds of them which believe not, lest [c]the light of the [1]glorious gospel of Christ, [d]who is the image of God, should shine unto them.

5 [a]For we preach not ourselves, but Christ Jesus the Lord; and [b]ourselves your servants for Jesus' sake.

6 For God, [a]who commanded the light to shine out of darkness, hath [b]shined in our hearts, to *give* the light of the knowledge of the glory of God in the face of Jesus Christ.

7 But we have this treasure in earthen vessels, [a]that the excellency of the power may be of God, and not of us.

8 *We are* [a]troubled[1] on every side, yet not [2]distressed; *we are* perplexed, but not in despair;

9 Persecuted, but not [a]forsaken; [b]cast[1] down, but not destroyed;

10 [a]Always bearing about in the body the dying of the Lord Jesus, [b]that the life also of Jesus might be made manifest in our body.

11 For we which live [a]are alway delivered unto death for Jesus' sake, that the life also of Jesus might be made manifest in our mortal flesh.

12 So then death worketh in us, but life in you.

13 We having [a]the same spirit of faith, according as it is written, [b]I believed, and therefore have I spoken; we also believe, and therefore speak;

14 Knowing that [a]he which raised up the Lord Jesus shall raise up us also by Jesus, and shall present *us* with you.

15 For [a]all things *are* for your sakes, that [b]the abundant grace might through the thanksgiving of many [1]redound to the glory of God.

16 For which cause we [1]faint [a]not; but though our outward man [2]perish, yet the inward *man* is [b]renewed day by day.

17 For [a]our light affliction, which is but for a moment, worketh for us a far more exceeding *and* eternal weight of glory;

4:1 [a] 1 Cor. 7:25
[b] 2 Cor. 4:16  [1] *do not lose heart*
4:2 [a] 2 Cor. 5:11
[1] *shame* [2] *adulterating the word of God*
4:3 [a] [1 Cor. 1:18]
[1] *veiled* [2] *perishing*
4:4 [a] John 12:31
[b] John 12:40
[c] [2 Cor. 3:8, 9] [d] [John 1:18]
[1] *gospel of the glory of*
4:5 [a] 1 Cor. 1:13
[b] 1 Cor. 9:19
4:6 [a] Gen. 1:3
[b] 2 Pet. 1:19
4:7 [a] 1 Cor. 2:5
4:8 [a] 2 Cor. 1:8; 7:5  [1] *hard-pressed* [2] *crushed*
4:9 [a] Ps. 37:24
[b] [Heb. 13:5]
[1] *struck*
4:10 [a] Phil. 3:10
[b] Rom. 8:17
4:11 [a] Rom. 8:36
4:13 [a] 2 Pet. 1:1
[b] Ps. 116:10
4:14 [a] [Rom. 8:11]
4:15 [a] Col. 1:24
[b] 2 Cor. 1:11
[1] *abound*
4:16 [a] 2 Cor. 4:1
[b] [Is. 40:29, 31]
[1] *do not lose heart*
[2] *is perishing*
4:17 [a] Rom. 8:18
4:18 [a] [Heb. 11:1, 13]
5:1 [a] Job 4:19
[b] Mark 14:58
[1] *Physical body*
[2] *tent* [3] *destroyed*
5:2 [a] Rom. 8:23
5:3 [a] Rev. 3:18
5:4 [a] 1 Cor. 15:53
[1] *tent*
5:5 [a] Rom. 8:23
[1] *prepared* [2] *this very* [3] *down payment*
5:7 [a] Heb. 11:1
5:8 [a] Phil. 1:23
5:9 [1] *make it our aim* [2] *well pleasing to*
5:10 [a] Rom. 2:16; 14:10, 12  [b] Eph. 6:8
5:11 [a] [Heb. 10:31; 12:29]
5:12 [a] 2 Cor. 3:1
[b] 2 Cor. 1:14
5:13 [a] 2 Cor. 11:1, 16; 12:11  [1] *if* [2] *for* [3] *of sound mind*
5:14 [a] [Rom. 5:15; 6:6]
5:15 [a] [Rom. 6:11]
5:16 [a] 2 Cor. 10:3
[b] [Matt. 12:50]
[1] *we regard*
[2] *according to*

18 [a]While we look not at the things which are seen, but at the things which are not seen: for the things which are seen *are* temporal; but the things which are not seen *are* eternal.

## CHAPTER 5

For we know that if [a]our [1]earthly house of *this* [2]tabernacle were [3]dissolved, we have a building of God, an house [b]not made with hands, eternal in the heavens.

2 For in this [a]we groan, earnestly desiring to be clothed upon with our house which is from heaven:

3 If so be that [a]being clothed we shall not be found naked.

4 For we that are in *this* [1]tabernacle do groan, being burdened: not for that we would be unclothed, but [a]clothed upon, that mortality might be swallowed up of life.

5 Now he that hath [1]wrought us for [2]the selfsame thing *is* God, who also [a]hath given unto us the [3]earnest of the Spirit.

6 Therefore *we are* always confident, knowing that, whilst we are at home in the body, we are absent from the Lord:

7 (For [a]we walk by faith, not by sight:)

8 We are confident, *I say,* and [a]willing rather to be absent from the body, and to be present with the Lord.

9 Wherefore we [1]labour, that, whether present or absent, we may be [2]accepted of him.

10 [a]For we must all appear before the judgment seat of Christ; [b]that every one may receive the things *done* in *his* body, according to that he hath done, whether *it be* good or bad.

11 Knowing therefore [a]the terror of the Lord, we persuade men; but we are made manifest unto God; and I trust also are made manifest in your consciences.

12 For [a]we commend not ourselves again unto you, but give you occasion [b]to glory on our behalf, that ye may have somewhat to *answer* them which glory in appearance, and not in heart.

13 For [a]whether[1] we be beside ourselves, *it is* [2]to God: or whether we be [3]sober, *it is* for your cause.

14 For the love of Christ constraineth us; because we thus judge, that [a]if one died for all, then were all dead:

15 And *that* he died for all, [a]that they which live should not henceforth live unto themselves, but unto him which died for them, and rose again.

16 [a]Wherefore henceforth [1]know we no man [2]after the flesh: yea, though we have known Christ after the flesh, [b]yet now henceforth know we *him* no more.

17 Therefore if any man [a]*be* in Christ, he is [b]a new [1]creature: [c]old things are passed away; behold, all things are become [d]new.

18 And all things *are* of God, [a]who hath reconciled us to himself by Jesus Christ, and hath given to us the ministry of reconciliation;

19 [1]To wit, that [a]God was in Christ, reconciling the world unto himself, not imputing their trespasses unto them; and hath committed unto us the word of reconciliation.

20 Now then we are [a]ambassadors for Christ, as though God did beseech *you* by us: we [1]pray *you* in Christ's [2]stead, be ye reconciled to God.

21 For [a]he hath made him *to be* sin for us, who knew no sin; that we might be made [b]the righteousness of God in him.

## CHAPTER 6

WE then, *as* [a]workers together *with him,* [b]beseech *you* also that ye receive not the grace of God in vain.

2 (For he saith, [a]I have heard thee in a time accepted, and in the day of salvation have I [1]succoured thee: behold, now *is* the accepted time; behold, now *is* the day of salvation.)

3 [a]Giving no offence in any thing, that the ministry be not blamed:

4 But in all *things* [1]approving ourselves [a]as the ministers of God, in much [2]patience, in afflictions, in necessities, in distresses,

5 [a]In stripes, in imprisonments, in tumults, in labours, in [1]watchings, in fastings;

6 By pureness, by knowledge, by longsuffering, by kindness, by the Holy Ghost, by love [1]unfeigned,

7 [a]By the word of truth, by [b]the power of God, by [c]the armour of righteousness on the right hand and on the left,

8 By honour and dishonour, by evil report and good report: as deceivers, and *yet* true;

9 As unknown, and [a]*yet* well known; [b]as dying, and, behold, we live; [c]as chastened, and not killed;

10 As sorrowful, yet alway rejoicing; as poor, yet making many [a]rich; as having nothing, and *yet* possessing all things.

11 O *ye* Corinthians, our mouth [1]is open unto you, [a]our heart is [2]enlarged.

12 Ye are not [1]straitened in us, but [a]ye are [1]straitened in your own [2]bowels.

13 Now [1]for a recompence in the same, (aI speak as unto *my* children,) be ye also [2]enlarged.

14 [a]Be ye not unequally yoked together with unbelievers: for [b]what [1]fellowship hath righteousness with [2]unrighteousness? and what [3]communion hath light with darkness?

5:17 [a] [John 6:63]
[b] [Rom. 8:9]
[c] Is. 43:18; 65:17
[d] [Rom. 6:3–10]
[1] *creation*
5:18 [a] Rom. 5:10
5:19 [a] [Rom. 3:24]
[1] *That is*
5:20 [a] Eph. 6:20
[1] *implore* [2] *behalf*
5:21 [a] Is. 53:6, 9
[b] [Rom. 1:17; 3:21]
6:1 [a] 1 Cor. 3:9
[b] 2 Cor. 5:20
6:2 [a] Is. 49:8
[1] *helped*
6:3 [a] Rom. 14:13
6:4 [a] 1 Cor. 4:1
[1] *commending*
[2] *endurance*
6:5 [a] 2 Cor. 11:23
[1] *sleeplessness*
6:6 [1] Lit. *without hypocrisy*
6:7 [a] 2 Cor.
7:14 [b] 1 Cor. 2:4
[c] 2 Cor. 10:4
6:9 [a] 2 Cor. 4:2;
5:11 [b] 1 Cor. 4:9, 11
[c] Ps. 118:18
6:10 [a] [2 Cor. 8:9]
6:11 [a] 2 Cor. 7:3
[1] *has spoken freely*
[2] *wide open*
6:12 [a] 2 Cor. 12:15
[1] *restricted by*
[2] *affections*
6:13 [a] 1 Cor. 4:14
[1] *in return for*
[2] *open*
6:14 [a] 1 Cor. 5:9
[b] Eph. 5:6, 7,
11 [1] *in common*
[2] *lawlessness*
[3] *fellowship*
6:15 [1] *accord*
[2] *unbeliever*
6:16 [a] [1 Cor. 3:16,
17; 6:19] [b] Lev.
26:12; Jer. 31:33;
32:38; Ezek.
37:26, 27
6:17 [a] Is. 52:11
6:18 [a] 2 Sam. 7:14
[b] [Rom. 8:14]
7:1 [a] [1 John 3:3]
7:2 [a] Acts 20:33
7:3 [a] 2 Cor. 6:11,
12 [1] *die together*
[2] *live together*
7:4 [a] 2 Cor. 3:12
[b] 1 Cor. 1:4 [c] Phil.
2:17 [1] *boasting on your behalf*
7:5 [a] 2 Cor. 2:13
[b] 2 Cor. 4:8
[c] Deut. 32:25
[1] *outside*
7:6 [a] Is. 49:13;
2 Cor. 1:3, 4
[b] 2 Cor. 2:13; 7:13
7:7 [1] *comfort*
[2] *zeal for me*
7:8 [a] 2 Cor.
2:2 [b] 2 Cor. 2:4
[1] *regret it* [2] *while*
7:9 [1] *according to*

15 And what [1]concord hath Christ with Belial? or what part hath he that believeth with an [2]infidel?

16 And what agreement hath the temple of God with idols? for [a]ye are the temple of the living God; as God hath said, [b]I will dwell in them, and walk in *them;* and I will be their God, and they shall be my people.

17 [a]Wherefore come out from among them, and be ye separate, saith the Lord, and touch not the unclean *thing;* and I will receive you,

18 [a]And will be a Father unto you, and ye shall be my [b]sons and daughters, saith the Lord Almighty.

## CHAPTER 7

HAVING [a]therefore these promises, dearly beloved, let us cleanse ourselves from all filthiness of the flesh and spirit, perfecting holiness in the fear of God.

2 Receive us; we have wronged no man, we have corrupted no man, [a]we have defrauded no man.

3 I speak not *this* to condemn *you:* for [a]I have said before, that ye are in our hearts to [1]die and [2]live with *you.*

4 [a]Great *is* my boldness of speech toward you, [b]great *is* my [1]glorying of you: [c]I am filled with comfort, I am exceeding joyful in all our tribulation.

5 For, [a]when we were come into Macedonia, our flesh had no rest, but [b]we were troubled on every side; [c]without[1] *were* fightings, within *were* fears.

6 Nevertheless [a]God, that comforteth those that are cast down, comforted us by [b]the coming of Titus;

7 And not by his coming only, but by the [1]consolation wherewith he was comforted in you, when he told us your earnest desire, your mourning, your [2]fervent mind toward me; so that I rejoiced the more.

8 For though I made you [a]sorry with a letter, I do not [1]repent, [b]though I did [1]repent: for I perceive that the same epistle hath made you sorry, though *it were* but for a [2]season.

9 Now I rejoice, not that ye were made sorry, but that ye sorrowed to repentance: for ye were made sorry [1]after a godly manner, that ye might [2]receive damage by us in nothing.

10 For [a]godly sorrow worketh repentance to salvation not to be [1]repented of: [b]but the sorrow of the world worketh death.

11 For behold this selfsame thing, that ye sorrowed after a godly [1]sort, what [2]carefulness it wrought in you, yea, *what* [a]clearing of yourselves, yea, *what* indignation, yea, *what* fear,

[2] *suffer loss from* 7:10 [a] 2 Sam. 12:13; Ps. 32:10; Matt.
26:75 [b] Prov. 17:22 [1] *regretted* 7:11 [a] Eph. 5:11 [1] *manner*
[2] *diligence*

yea, *what* vehement desire, yea, *what* zeal, yea, *what* [3]revenge! In all *things* ye have [4]approved yourselves to be [b]clear in this matter.

12 Wherefore, though I wrote unto you, *I did it* not for his cause that had done the wrong, nor for his cause that suffered wrong, [a]but that our care for you in the sight of God might appear unto you.

13 Therefore we were comforted in your comfort: yea, and exceedingly the more joyed we for the joy of Titus, because his spirit [a]was refreshed by you all.

14 For if I have boasted any thing to him of you, I am not ashamed; but as we spake all things to you in truth, even so our boasting, which *I made* before Titus, is found a truth.

15 And his inward affection is more abundant toward you, whilst he remembereth [a]the obedience of you all, how with fear and trembling ye received him.

16 I rejoice therefore that [a]I have confidence in you in all *things.*

### CHAPTER 8

Moreover, brethren, we [1]do you to wit of the grace of God bestowed on the churches of Macedonia;

2 How that in a great trial of affliction the abundance of their joy and [a]their deep poverty abounded unto the riches of their liberality.

3 For to *their* [1]power, I bear [2]record, yea, and beyond *their* power *they were* willing of themselves;

4 [1]Praying us with much [2]intreaty that we would receive the gift, and *take upon us* [a]the fellowship of the ministering to the saints.

5 And *this they did,* not as we hoped, but first [a]gave their own selves to the Lord, and unto us by the [b]will of God.

6 Insomuch that [a]we [1]desired Titus, that as he had begun, so he would also finish in you the same grace also.

7 Therefore, as [a]ye abound in every *thing, in* faith, and [1]utterance, and knowledge, and *in* all diligence, and *in* your love to us, *see* [b]that ye abound in this grace also.

8 [a]I speak not by commandment, but by [1]occasion of the forwardness of others, and to [2]prove the sincerity of your love.

9 For ye know the grace of our Lord Jesus Christ, [a]that, though he was rich, yet for your sakes he became poor, that ye through his poverty might be [b]rich.

10 And herein [a]I give *my* advice: for [b]this is [1]expedient for you, who have begun before, not only to do, [2]but also to be [c]forward a year ago.

7:11 [b] 2 Cor. 2:5–11
[3] vindication
[4] proved
7:12 [a] 2 Cor. 2:4
7:13 [a] Rom. 15:32
7:15 [a] 2 Cor. 2:9; Phil. 2:12
7:16 [a] 2 Cor. 2:3; 8:22; 2 Thess. 3:4; Philem. 8, 21
8:1 [1] make known to you
8:2 [a] Mark 12:44
8:3 [1] ability [2] witness
8:4 [a] Acts 11:29; 24:17; Rom. 15:25, 26; 1 Cor. 16:1, 3, 4; 2 Cor. 9:1 [1] Imploring [2] urgency
8:5 [a] [Rom. 12:1, 2] [b] [Eph. 6:6]
8:6 [a] 2 Cor. 8:17; 12:18 [1] urged
8:7 [a] [1 Cor. 1:5; 12:13] [b] 2 Cor. 9:8 [1] speech
8:8 [a] 1 Cor. 7:6 [1] the diligence of others [2] test
8:9 [a] Matt. 8:20; Luke 9:58; Phil. 2:6, 7 [b] Rom. 9:23; [Eph. 1:7; Rev. 3:18]
8:10 [a] 1 Cor. 7:25, 40 [b] [Prov. 19:17; Matt. 10:42; 1 Tim. 6:18, 19; Heb. 13:16] [c] 1 Cor. 16:2; 2 Cor. 9:2 [1] profitable [2] and were desiring to do a year ago
8:11 [1] But now you also must complete the doing [2] completion
8:12 [a] Mark 12:43, 44; Luke 21:3, 4; 2 Cor. 9:7
8:14 [1] lack
8:15 [a] Ex. 16:18
8:17 [1] diligent
8:18 [a] 1 Cor. 16:3; 2 Cor. 12:18
8:19 [a] 1 Cor. 16:3, 4 [b] 2 Cor. 4:15 [1] gift [2] Lord himself
8:20 [1] lavish gift
8:21 [a] Rom. 12:17 [1] honourable
8:23 [a] 2 Cor. 7:13, 14 [b] Phil. 2:25 [1] worker [2] Lit. apostles
8:24 [a] 2 Cor. 7:4, 14; 9:2
9:1 [a] Gal. 2:10
9:2 [a] 2 Cor. 8:10 [1] willingness [2] stirred up the majority
9:3 [a] 2 Cor. 8:6, 17

11 [1]Now therefore perform the doing *of it;* that as *there was* a readiness to will, so *there may be* a [2]performance also out of that which ye have.

12 For [a]if there be first a willing mind, *it is* accepted according to that a man hath, *and* not according to that he hath not.

13 For *I mean* not that other men be eased, and ye burdened:

14 But by an equality, *that* now at this time your abundance *may be a supply* for their [1]want, that their abundance also may be *a supply* for your [1]want: that there may be equality:

15 As it is written, [a]He that *had gathered* much had nothing over; and he that *had gathered* little had no lack.

16 But thanks *be* to God, which put the same earnest care into the heart of Titus for you.

17 For indeed he accepted the exhortation; but being more [1]forward, of his own accord he went unto you.

18 And we have sent with him [a]the brother, whose praise *is* in the gospel throughout all the churches;

19 And not *that* only, but who was also [a]chosen of the churches to travel with us with this [1]grace, which is administered by us [b]to the glory of the [2]same Lord, and *declaration of* your ready mind:

20 Avoiding this, that no man should blame us in this [1]abundance which is administered by us:

21 [a]Providing [1]for honest things, not only in the sight of the Lord, but also in the sight of men.

22 And we have sent with them our brother, whom we have oftentimes proved diligent in many things, but now much more diligent, upon the great confidence which *I have* in you.

23 Whether *any do enquire* of [a]Titus, *he is* my partner and [1]fellowhelper concerning you: or our brethren *be enquired of, they are* [b]the [2]messengers of the churches, *and* the glory of Christ.

24 Wherefore shew ye to them, and before the churches, the proof of your love, and of our [a]boasting on your behalf.

### CHAPTER 9

For as touching [a]the ministering to the saints, it is superfluous for me to write to you:

2 For I know the [1]forwardness of your mind, for which I boast of you to them of Macedonia, that Achaia was ready a [a]year ago; and your zeal hath [2]provoked very many.

3 [a]Yet have I sent the brethren, lest our boasting of you should be in vain in this behalf; that, as I said, ye may be ready:

4 Lest haply if they of Macedonia come with me, and find you unprepared, we ([1]that we say not, ye) should be ashamed in this same confident boasting.

5 Therefore I thought it necessary to exhort the brethren, that they would go [1]before unto you, and make up beforehand your [2]bounty, whereof ye had [3]notice before, that the same might be ready, as *a matter of* [4]bounty, and not as *of* [5]covetousness.

6 [a]But this *I say,* He which soweth sparingly shall reap also sparingly; and he which soweth [1]bountifully shall reap also [1]bountifully.

7 Every man according as he purposeth in his heart, *so let him give;* [a]not grudgingly, or of [1]necessity: for [b]God loveth a [2]cheerful giver.

8 [a]And God *is* able to make all grace abound toward you; that ye, always having all sufficiency in all *things,* may abound to every good work:

9 (As it is written, [a]He hath dispersed abroad; he hath given to the poor: his righteousness remaineth for ever.

10 Now [1]he that [a]ministereth[2] seed to the sower both [3]minister bread for *your* food, and multiply your seed sown, and increase the fruits of your [b]righteousness;)

11 Being enriched in every thing to all [1]bountifulness, [a]which causeth through us thanksgiving to God.

12 For the administration of this service not only [a]supplieth the [1]want of the saints, but is [2]abundant also by many thanksgivings unto God;

13 Whiles by the [1]experiment of this [2]ministration they [a]glorify God for [3]your professed subjection unto the gospel of Christ, and for *your* liberal [b]distribution[4] unto them, and unto all *men;*

14 And by their prayer for you, which [1]long after you for the exceeding [a]grace of God in you.

15 Thanks *be* unto God [a]for his [1]unspeakable gift.

## CHAPTER 10

Now [a]I Paul myself beseech you by the meekness and gentleness of Christ, [b]who in presence *am* [1]base among you, but being absent am bold toward you:

2 But I beseech *you,* [a]that I may not be bold when I am present with that confidence, wherewith I [1]think to be bold against some, which think of us as if we walked according to the flesh.

3 For though we walk in the flesh, we do not war [1]after the flesh:

4 ([a]For the weapons [b]of our warfare *are* not [1]carnal, but [c]mighty through

9:4 [1] *not to mention you*
9:5 [1] *on ahead* [2] *bountiful gift* [3] *promised* [4] *generosity* [5] *grudging obligation*
9:6 [a] Prov. 11:24; 22:9 [1] Lit. *in blessings*
9:7 [a] Deut. 15:7 [b] Rom. 12:8 [1] *compulsion* [2] *joyful*
9:8 [a] [Prov. 11:24]
9:9 [a] Ps. 112:9
9:10 [a] Is. 55:10 [b] Hos. 10:12 [1] *may he* [2] *supplies* [3] *supply*
9:11 [a] 2 Cor. 1:11 [1] *liberality*
9:12 [a] 2 Cor. 8:14 [1] *needs* [2] *abounding*
9:13 [a] [Matt. 5:16] [b] [Heb. 13:16] [1] *proof* [2] *ministry* [3] *the obedience of your confession* [4] *sharing*
9:14 [a] 2 Cor. 8:1 [1] *yearn for*
9:15 [a] [James 1:17] [1] *indescribable*
10:1 [a] Rom. 12:1 [b] 1 Thess. 2:7 [1] *lowly*
10:2 [a] 1 Cor. 4:21 [1] *intend*
10:3 [1] *according to*
10:4 [a] Eph. 6:13 [b] 1 Tim. 1:18 [c] Acts 7:22 [d] Jer. 1:10 [1] *of the flesh*
10:5 [a] 1 Cor. 1:19 [1] *arguments*
10:6 [a] 2 Cor. 13:2, 10 [b] 2 Cor. 7:15 [1] *punish*
10:7 [a] [John 7:24] [b] 1 Cor. 1:12; 14:37 [c] 1 Cor. 3:23 [1] *is convinced in*
10:8 [a] 2 Cor. 13:10 [b] 2 Cor. 7:14 [1] *building up*
10:10 [a] Gal. 4:13 [b] 2 Cor. 11:6
10:12 [a] 2 Cor. 5:12
10:13 [a] 2 Cor.
10:15 [1] *beyond* [2] *province* [3] *apportioned*
10:14 [a] 1 Cor. 3:5, 6
10:15 [a] Rom. 15:20 [1] *in our province*
10:16 [1] *province of accomplishment*
10:17 [a] Jer. 9:24
10:18 [a] Prov. 27:2 [b] Rom. 2:29
11:1 [a] 2 Cor. 11:4, 16, 19 [1] *you do bear*
11:2 [a] Gal. 4:17 [b] Hos. 2:19 [1] *betrothed*

God [d]to the pulling down of strong holds;)

5 [a]Casting down [1]imaginations, and every high thing that exalteth itself against the knowledge of God, and bringing into captivity every thought to the obedience of Christ;

6 [a]And having in a readiness to [1]revenge all disobedience, when [b]your obedience is fulfilled.

7 [a]Do ye look on things after the outward appearance? [b]If any man [1]trust to himself that he is Christ's, let him of himself think this again, that, as he *is* Christ's, even so *are* [c]we Christ's.

8 For though I should boast somewhat more [a]of our authority, which the Lord hath given us for [1]edification, and not for your destruction, [b]I should not be ashamed:

9 That I may not seem as if I would terrify you by letters.

10 For *his* letters, say they, *are* weighty and powerful; but [a]*his* bodily presence *is* weak, and *his* [b]speech contemptible.

11 Let such an one think this, that, such as we are in word by letters when we are absent, such *will we be* also in deed when we are present.

12 [a]For we dare not make ourselves of the number, or compare ourselves with some that commend themselves: but they measuring themselves by themselves, and comparing themselves among themselves, are not wise.

13 [a]But we will not boast of things [1]without *our* measure, but according to the measure of the [2]rule which God hath [3]distributed to us, a measure to reach even unto you.

14 For we stretch not ourselves beyond *our measure,* as though we reached not unto you: [a]for we are come as far as to you also in *preaching* the gospel of Christ:

15 Not boasting of things without *our* measure, *that is,* [a]of other men's labours; but having hope, when your faith is increased, that we shall be enlarged by you [1]according to our rule abundantly,

16 To preach the gospel in the *regions* beyond you, *and* not to boast in another man's [1]line of things made ready to our hand.

17 [a]But he that glorieth, let him glory in the Lord.

18 For [a]not he that commendeth himself is approved, but [b]whom the Lord commendeth.

## CHAPTER 11

Would to God ye could bear with me a little in [a]*my* folly: and indeed [1]bear with me.

2 For I am [a]jealous over you with godly jealousy: for [b]I have [1]espoused

you to one husband, <sup>c</sup>that I may present *you* <sup>d</sup>*as* a chaste virgin to Christ.

3 But I fear, lest by any means, as <sup>a</sup>the serpent <sup>1</sup>beguiled Eve through his <sup>2</sup>subtilty, so your minds <sup>b</sup>should be corrupted from the simplicity that is in Christ.

4 For if he that cometh preacheth another Jesus, whom we have not preached, or *if* ye receive <sup>1</sup>another spirit, which ye have not received, or <sup>a</sup>another<sup>1</sup> gospel, which ye have not accepted, ye might well bear with *him*.

5 For I <sup>1</sup>suppose <sup>a</sup>I was not <sup>2</sup>a whit behind the very chiefest apostles.

6 But though <sup>a</sup>*I be* <sup>1</sup>rude in speech, yet not <sup>b</sup>in knowledge; but <sup>c</sup>we have been throughly made manifest among you in all things.

7 Have I committed an offence in <sup>1</sup>abasing myself that ye might be exalted, because I have preached to you the gospel of God <sup>a</sup>freely?<sup>2</sup>

8 I robbed other churches, taking wages *of them*, to do you service.

9 And when I was present with you, and <sup>1</sup>wanted, <sup>a</sup>I was <sup>2</sup>chargeable to no man: for that which was lacking to me <sup>b</sup>the brethren which came from Macedonia supplied: and in all *things* I have kept myself from being burdensome unto you, and *so* will I keep *myself*.

10 <sup>d</sup>As the truth of Christ is in me, <sup>b</sup>no man shall stop me of this boasting in the regions of Achaia.

11 Wherefore? <sup>a</sup>because I love you not? God knoweth.

12 But what I do, that I will do, <sup>a</sup>that I may cut off <sup>1</sup>occasion from them which desire <sup>1</sup>occasion; that wherein they glory, they may be found even as we.

13 For such <sup>a</sup>*are* false apostles, <sup>b</sup>deceitful workers, transforming themselves into the apostles of Christ.

14 And no marvel; for Satan himself <sup>1</sup>is transformed into <sup>a</sup>an angel of light.

15 Therefore *it is* no great thing if his ministers also be transformed as the ministers of righteousness; <sup>a</sup>whose end shall be according to their works.

16 I say again, Let no man think me a fool; if otherwise, yet as a fool receive me, that I may boast myself a little.

17 That which I speak, <sup>a</sup>I speak *it* not after the Lord, but as it were foolishly, in this confidence of boasting.

18 Seeing that many glory after the flesh, I will glory also.

19 For ye <sup>1</sup>suffer fools gladly, <sup>a</sup>seeing ye *yourselves* are wise.

20 For ye <sup>1</sup>suffer, <sup>a</sup>if a man bring you into bondage, if a man devour *you*, if a man take *of you*, if a man exalt himself, if a man <sup>2</sup>smite you on the face.

11:2 <sup>c</sup> Col. 1:28
<sup>d</sup> Lev. 21:13
11:3 <sup>a</sup> Gen. 3:4, 13 <sup>b</sup> Eph. 6:24 <sup>1</sup> *deceived* <sup>2</sup> *craftiness*
11:4 <sup>a</sup> Gal. 1:6–8 <sup>1</sup> *a different*
11:5 <sup>a</sup> 2 Cor. 12:11 <sup>1</sup> *consider* <sup>2</sup> *at all inferior to*
11:6 <sup>a</sup> [1 Cor. 1:17] <sup>b</sup> [Eph. 3:4] <sup>c</sup> [2 Cor. 12:12] <sup>1</sup> *untrained*
11:7 <sup>a</sup> 1 Cor. 9:18 <sup>1</sup> *humbling* <sup>2</sup> *free of charge*
11:9 <sup>a</sup> Acts 20:33 <sup>b</sup> Phil. 4:10 <sup>1</sup> *in need* <sup>2</sup> *a burden*
11:10 <sup>a</sup> Rom. 1:9; 9:1 <sup>b</sup> 1 Cor. 9:15
11:11 <sup>a</sup> 2 Cor. 6:11; 12:15
11:12 <sup>a</sup> 1 Cor. 9:12 <sup>1</sup> *opportunity*
11:13 <sup>a</sup> Phil. 1:15 <sup>b</sup> Phil. 3:2
11:14 <sup>a</sup> Gal. 1:8 <sup>1</sup> *transforms himself*
11:15 <sup>a</sup> [Phil. 3:19]
11:17 <sup>a</sup> 1 Cor. 7:6
11:19 <sup>a</sup> 1 Cor. 4:10 <sup>1</sup> *put up with*
11:20 <sup>a</sup> [Gal. 2:4; 4:3, 9; 5:1] <sup>1</sup> *put up with it* <sup>2</sup> *strikes*
11:21 <sup>a</sup> 2 Cor. 10:10 <sup>b</sup> Phil. 3:4 <sup>1</sup> *shame*
11:22 <sup>a</sup> Phil. 3:4–6
11:23 <sup>a</sup> 1 Cor. 15:10 <sup>b</sup> Acts 9:16 <sup>c</sup> 1 Cor. 15:30
11:24 <sup>a</sup> Deut. 25:3 <sup>b</sup> 2 Cor. 6:5 <sup>1</sup> *minus*
11:25 <sup>a</sup> Acts 16:22, 23; 21:32 <sup>b</sup> Acts 14:5, 19 <sup>c</sup> Acts 27:1–44
11:26 <sup>a</sup> Acts 9:23, 24; 13:45, 50; 17:5, 13 <sup>b</sup> Acts 14:5, 19; 19:23; 27:42 <sup>1</sup> *Gentiles*
11:27 <sup>a</sup> Acts 20:31 <sup>b</sup> 1 Cor. 4:11 <sup>c</sup> Acts 9:9; 13:2, 3; 14:23 <sup>1</sup> *toil* <sup>2</sup> *sleeplessness*
11:28 <sup>a</sup> Acts 20:18 <sup>1</sup> *other things* <sup>2</sup> *deep concern for*
11:29 <sup>a</sup> [1 Cor. 8:9, 13; 9:22] <sup>1</sup> *made to stumble* <sup>2</sup> *do not burn with indignation*
11:30 <sup>a</sup> [2 Cor. 12:5, 9, 10] <sup>1</sup> *my weaknesses*
11:31 <sup>a</sup> 1 Thess.

21 I speak as concerning <sup>1</sup>reproach, <sup>a</sup>as though we had been weak. Howbeit <sup>b</sup>whereinsoever any is bold, (I speak foolishly,) I am bold also.

22 Are they <sup>a</sup>Hebrews? so *am* I. Are they Israelites? so *am* I. Are they the seed of Abraham? so *am* I.

23 Are they ministers of Christ? (I speak as a fool) I *am* more; <sup>a</sup>in labours more abundant, <sup>b</sup>in stripes above measure, in prisons more frequent, <sup>c</sup>in deaths oft.

24 Of the Jews five times received I <sup>a</sup>forty <sup>b</sup>*stripes* <sup>1</sup>save one.

25 Thrice was I <sup>a</sup>beaten with rods, <sup>b</sup>once was I stoned, thrice I <sup>c</sup>suffered shipwreck, a night and a day I have been in the deep;

26 *In* journeyings often, in perils of waters, *in* perils of robbers, <sup>a</sup>*in* perils by *mine own* countrymen, <sup>b</sup>*in* perils by the <sup>1</sup>heathen, *in* perils in the city, *in* perils in the wilderness, *in* perils in the sea, *in* perils among false brethren;

27 In weariness and <sup>1</sup>painfulness, <sup>a</sup>in <sup>2</sup>watchings often, <sup>b</sup>in hunger and thirst, in <sup>c</sup>fastings often, in cold and nakedness.

28 Beside those <sup>1</sup>things that are without, that which cometh upon me daily, <sup>a</sup>the <sup>2</sup>care of all the churches.

29 <sup>a</sup>Who is weak, and I am not weak? who is <sup>1</sup>offended, and I <sup>2</sup>burn not?

30 If I must needs glory, <sup>a</sup>I will glory of the things which concern <sup>1</sup>mine infirmities.

31 <sup>a</sup>The God and Father of our Lord Jesus Christ, <sup>b</sup>which is blessed for evermore, knoweth that I lie not.

32 <sup>a</sup>In Damascus the governor under Aretas the king kept the city of the Damascenes with a garrison, desirous to apprehend me:

33 And through a window in a basket was I let down by the wall, and escaped his hands.

## CHAPTER 12

IT is not <sup>1</sup>expedient for me doubtless to <sup>2</sup>glory. I will come to <sup>a</sup>visions and <sup>b</sup>revelations of the Lord.

2 I knew a man <sup>a</sup>in Christ above fourteen years ago, (whether in the body, I <sup>1</sup>cannot tell; or whether out of the body, I <sup>1</sup>cannot tell: God knoweth;) such an one <sup>b</sup>caught up to the third heaven.

3 And I knew such a man, (whether in the body, or out of the body, I <sup>1</sup>cannot tell: God knoweth;)

4 How that he was caught up into <sup>a</sup>paradise, and heard <sup>1</sup>unspeakable words, which it is not lawful for a man to utter.

2:5 <sup>b</sup> Rom. 9:5   11:32 <sup>a</sup> Acts 9:19–25   12:1 <sup>a</sup> Acts 16:9; 18:9; 22:17, 18; 23:11; 26:13–15; 27:23 <sup>b</sup> [Gal. 1:12; 2:2]
<sup>1</sup> *profitable* <sup>2</sup> *boast*   12:2 <sup>a</sup> Rom. 16:7 <sup>b</sup> Acts 22:17
<sup>1</sup> *do not know*   12:3 <sup>1</sup> *do not know*   12:4 <sup>a</sup> Luke 23:43
<sup>1</sup> *inexpressible*

5 Of such an one will I ¹glory: yet of myself I will not ᵃglory, but in mine infirmities.

6 For though I would desire to glory, I shall not be a fool; for I will say the truth: but *now* I ¹forbear, lest any man should think of me above that which he seeth me *to be,* or *that* he heareth of me.

7 And lest I should be exalted above measure through the abundance of the revelations, there was given to me a ᵃthorn in the flesh, ᵇthe messenger of Satan to ¹buffet me, lest I should be exalted above measure.

8 ᵃFor this thing I ¹besought the Lord ²thrice, that it might depart from me.

9 And he said unto me, **My grace is sufficient for thee: for my ¹strength is made perfect in weakness.** Most gladly therefore ᵃwill I rather glory in my ²infirmities, ᵇthat the power of Christ may rest upon me.

10 Therefore ᵃI take pleasure in infirmities, in reproaches, in necessities, in persecutions, in distresses for Christ's sake: ᵇfor when I am weak, then am I strong.

11 I am become ᵃa fool in ¹glorying; ye have compelled me: for I ought to have been commended of you: for ᵇin nothing am I behind the very chiefest apostles, though ᶜI be nothing.

12 ᵃTruly the signs of an apostle were wrought among you in all ¹patience, in signs, and ᵇwonders, and mighty ᶜdeeds.

13 For what is it wherein ye were inferior to other churches, except *it be* that I myself was not burdensome to you? forgive me this wrong.

14 ᵃBehold, the third time I am ready to come to you; and I will not be burdensome to you: for ᵇI seek not yours, but you: ᶜfor the children ought not to lay up for the parents, but the parents for the children.

15 And I will very gladly spend and be spent ᵃfor ¹you; though ᵇthe more abundantly I love you, the less I be loved.

16 But be it ¹so, ᵃI did not burden you: nevertheless, being crafty, I caught you with guile.

17 Did I ¹make a gain of you by any of them whom I sent unto you?

18 I ¹desired Titus, and with *him* I sent a ᵃbrother. Did Titus make a gain of you? walked we not in the same spirit? *walked we* not in the same steps?

19 ᵃAgain, think ye that we excuse ourselves unto you? ᵇwe speak before God in Christ: ᶜbut *we do* all things, dearly beloved, for your edifying.

20 For I fear, lest, when I come, I shall not find you such as I ¹would,

and *that* ᵃI shall be found ²unto you such as ye ¹would not: lest *there be* ³debates, envyings, wraths, ⁴strifes, backbitings, whisperings, ⁵swellings, tumults:

21 *And* lest, when I come again, my God ᵃwill humble me among you, and *that* I shall ¹bewail many ᵇwhich have sinned already, and have not repented of the uncleanness and ᶜfornication and ²lasciviousness which they have committed.

## CHAPTER 13

**T**HIS *is* ᵃthe third *time* I am coming to you. ᵇIn the mouth of two or three witnesses shall every word be established.

2 ᵃI told you before, and foretell you, as if I were present, the second time; and being absent now I write to them ᵇwhich heretofore have sinned, and to all ¹other, that, if I come again, ᶜI will not spare:

3 Since ye seek a proof of Christ ᵃspeaking in me, which to you-ward is not weak, but is mighty ᵇin you.

4 ᵃFor though he was crucified through weakness, yet ᵇhe liveth by the power of God. For ᶜwe also are weak in him, but we shall live with him by the power of God toward you.

5 Examine yourselves, whether ye be in the faith; prove your own selves. Know ye not your own selves, ᵃhow that Jesus Christ is in you, ¹except ye be ᵇreprobates?

6 But I trust that ye shall know that we are not reprobates.

7 Now I pray to God that ye do no evil; not that we should appear approved, but that ye should do that which is honest, though ᵃwe ¹be as reprobates.

8 For we can do nothing against the truth, but for the truth.

9 For we are glad, ᵃwhen we are weak, and ye are strong: and this also we ¹wish, ᵇ*even²* your perfection.

10 ᵃTherefore I write these things being absent, lest being present I should use sharpness, according to the ᵇpower which the Lord hath given me ¹to edification, and not ¹to destruction.

11 Finally, brethren, farewell. Be ¹perfect, ᵃbe of good comfort, be of one mind, live in peace; and the God of love ᵇand peace shall be with you.

12 ᵃGreet one another with an holy kiss.

13 All the saints ¹salute you.

14 ᵃThe grace of the Lord Jesus Christ, and the love of God, and ᵇthe ¹communion of the Holy Ghost, *be* with you all. Amen.

12:5 ᵃ 2 Cor. 11:30
¹ *boast*
12:6 ¹ *refrain*
12:7 ᵃ Ezek. 28:24
ᵇ Job 2:7 ¹ *beat*
12:8 ᵃ Matt. 26:44
¹ *pleaded with*
² *three times*
12:9 ᵃ 2 Cor. 11:30
ᵇ [1 Pet. 4:14]
¹ *power* ² *weak-nesses*
12:10 ³ [Rom. 5:3;
8:35] ᵇ 2 Cor. 13:4
12:11 ᵃ 2 Cor.
5:13; 11:1, 16;
12:6 ᵇ 2 Cor. 11:5
ᶜ 1 Cor. 3:7; 13:2;
15:9 ¹ *boasting*
12:12 ᵃ Rom.
15:18 ᵇ Acts 15:12
ᶜ Acts 14:8–10;
16:16–18; 19:11, 12;
20:6–12; 28:1–10
¹ *perseverance*
12:14 ᵃ 2 Cor. 1:15;
13:1, 2 ᵇ [1 Cor.
10:24–33] ᶜ 1 Cor.
4:14
12:15 ᵃ [2 Tim.
2:10] ᵇ 2 Cor. 6:12,
13 ¹ Lit. *your souls*
12:16 ᵃ 2 Cor. 11:9
¹ *as it may*
12:17 ¹ *take advantage*
12:18 ᵃ 2 Cor. 8:18
¹ *urged*
12:19 ᵃ 2 Cor. 5:12
ᵇ [Rom. 9:1, 2]
ᶜ 1 Cor. 10:33
12:20 ᵃ 1 Cor.
4:21 ¹ *wish* ² *by*
³ *contentions*
⁴ *selfish ambitions*
⁵ *conceits*
12:21 ᵃ 2 Cor.
2:1, 4 ᵇ 2 Cor.
13:2 ᶜ 1 Cor. 5:1
¹ *mourn* ² *licen-tiousness*
13:1 ᵃ 2 Cor. 12:14
ᵇ Deut. 17:6; 19:15
13:2 ᵃ 2 Cor. 10:2
ᵇ 2 Cor. 12:21
ᶜ 2 Cor. 1:23; 10:11
¹ *the rest*
13:3 ᵃ Matt. 10:20
ᵇ [1 Cor. 9:2]
13:4 ᵃ [1 Pet. 3:18]
ᵇ [Rom. 1:4; 6:4]
ᶜ [2 Cor. 10:3, 4]
13:5 ᵃ [Gal. 4:19]
ᵇ 1 Cor. 9:27
¹ *unless you don't stand the test*
13:7 ᵃ 2 Cor.
6:9 ¹ *may seem disqualified*
13:9 ᵃ 1 Cor. 4:10
ᵇ [1 Thess. 3:10]
¹ *pray* ² *that you may be made complete*
13:10 ᵃ 1 Cor. 4:21
ᵇ 2 Cor. 10:8 ¹ *for*
13:11 ᵃ Rom. 12:16,
18 ᵇ Rom. 15:33
¹ *complete* 13:12 ᵃ Rom. 16:16 13:13 ¹ *greet*
13:14 ᵃ Rom. 16:24 ᵇ Phil. 2:1 ¹ *fellowship*

# THE EPISTLE OF PAUL THE APOSTLE TO THE

# GALATIANS

The Galatians, having launched their Christian experience by faith, seem content to leave their voyage of faith and chart a new course based on works—a course Paul finds disturbing. His letter to the Galatians is a vigorous attack against the gospel of works and a defense of the gospel of faith.

Paul begins by setting forth his credentials as an apostle with a message from God: blessing comes from God on the basis of faith, not law. The law declares men guilty and imprisons them; faith sets men free to enjoy liberty in Christ. But liberty is not license. Freedom in Christ means freedom to produce the fruits of righteousness through a Spirit-led lifestyle.

The book is called *Pros Galatas*, "To the Galatians," and it is the only letter of Paul that is specifically addressed to a number of churches ("unto the churches of Galatia," 1:2). The name *Galatians* was given to this Celtic people because they originally lived in Gaul before their migration to Asia Minor.

## CHAPTER 1

PAUL, an apostle, (not of men, neither by man, but [a]by Jesus Christ, and God the Father, [b]who raised him from the dead;)

2 And all the brethren which are with me, unto the churches of Galatia:

3 Grace *be* to you and peace from God the Father, and *from* our Lord Jesus Christ,

4 [a]Who gave himself for our sins, that he might deliver us [b]from this present evil [1]world, according to the will of God and our Father:

5 To whom *be* glory for ever and ever. Amen.

6 I marvel that ye are so soon [1]removed [a]from him that called you into the grace of Christ unto [2]another gospel:

7 [a]Which is not another; but there be some [b]that trouble you, and [1]would [c]pervert the gospel of Christ.

8 But though [a]we, or an angel from heaven, preach any other gospel unto you than that which we have preached unto you, let him be [1]accursed.

9 As we said before, so say I now again, If any *man* preach any other gospel unto you [a]than that ye have received, let him be accursed.

10 For [a]do I now [b]persuade men, or God? or [c]do I seek to please men? for if I yet pleased men, I should not be the servant of Christ.

11 [a]But I [1]certify you, brethren, that the gospel which was preached of me is not [2]after man.

12 For [a]I neither received it of man, neither was I taught *it*, but [b]by the revelation of Jesus Christ.

13 For ye have heard of my [1]conversation in time past in the Jews' religion, how that [a]beyond measure I persecuted the church of God, and [b]wasted[2] it:

14 And [1]profited in the Jews' religion above many my [2]equals in mine own nation, [a]being more exceedingly zealous [b]of the traditions of my fathers.

15 But when it pleased God, [a]who separated me from my mother's womb, and called *me* by his grace,

16 [a]To reveal his Son in me, that [b]I might preach him among the [1]heathen; immediately I conferred not with [c]flesh and blood:

17 Neither went I up to Jerusalem to them which were apostles before me; but I went into Arabia, and returned again unto Damascus.

18 Then after three years [a]I went up to Jerusalem to see Peter, and [1]abode with him fifteen days.

19 But [a]other of the apostles saw I none, [1]save [b]James the Lord's brother.

20 Now the things which I write unto you, behold, before God, I lie not.

21 [a]Afterwards I came into the regions of Syria and Cilicia;

22 And was unknown by face unto the churches of Judaea which [a]were in Christ:

23 But they had [a]heard only, That he which [b]persecuted us in times past now preacheth the faith which once he destroyed.

24 And they [a]glorified God in me.

## CHAPTER 2

THEN fourteen years [1]after [a]I went up again to Jerusalem with Barnabas, and took Titus with *me* also.

2 And I went up [1]by revelation, and communicated unto them that gospel which I preach among the Gentiles, but [a]privately to them which were of reputation, lest by any means [b]I should run, or had run, in vain.

3 But neither Titus, who was with me, being a Greek, was compelled to be circumcised:

### Center reference column

1:1 [a] Acts 9:6
[b] Acts 2:24
1:4 [a] [Matt. 20:28]
[b] Heb. 2:5 [1] *age*
1:6 [a] Gal. 1:15; 5:8
[1] *turning away*
[2] *a different*
1:7 [a] 2 Cor.
11:4 [b] Gal. 5:10,
12 [c] 2 Cor. 2:17
[1] *want to*
1:8 [a] 1 Cor. 16:22
[1] Gr. *anathema*
1:9 [a] Deut. 4:2
1:10 [a] 1 Thess.
2:4 [b] 1 Sam. 24:7
[c] 1 Thess. 2:4
1:11 [a] 1 Cor. 15:1
[1] *make known to*
[2] *according to*
1:12 [a] 1 Cor. 15:1
[b] [Eph. 3:3–5]
1:13 [a] Acts 9:1
[b] Acts 8:3; 22:4, 5
[1] *conduct* [2] *tried*
to *destroy*

1:14 [a] Acts
26:9 [b] Jer. 9:14
[1] *advanced* [2] *contemporaries*
1:15 [a] Is. 49:1, 5
1:16 [a] [2 Cor.
4:5–7] [b] Acts
9:15 [c] Matt. 16:17
[1] *Gentiles*
1:18 [a] Acts 9:26
[1] *remained*
1:19 [a] 1 Cor. 9:5
[b] Matt. 13:55
[1] *except*
1:21 [a] Acts 9:30
1:22 [a] Rom. 16:7
1:23 [a] Acts 9:20,
21 [b] Acts 8:3
1:24 [a] Acts 11:18
2:1 [a] Acts 15:2
[1] *later*
2:2 [a] Acts 15:1–4
[b] Phil. 2:16 [1] *because of*

964

4 And that because of [a]false brethren [1]unawares brought in, who came in [2]privily to spy out our [b]liberty which we have in Christ Jesus, [c]that they might bring us into bondage:

5 To whom we [g]gave place by subjection, no, not for an hour; that [a]the truth of the gospel might continue with you.

6 But of these [a]who seemed to be somewhat, (whatsoever they were, it maketh no [1]matter to me: [b]God [2]accepteth no man's person:) for they who seemed *to be somewhat* [c]in conference added nothing to me:

7 But contrariwise, [a]when they saw that the gospel of the uncircumcision [b]was committed unto me, as *the gospel* of the circumcision *was* unto Peter;

8 (For he that [1]wrought effectually in Peter to the apostleship of the [a]circumcision, [b]the same [1]was [c]mighty in me toward the Gentiles:)

9 And when James, [1]Cephas, and John, who seemed to be [a]pillars, perceived [b]the grace that was given unto me, they gave to me and Barnabas the right hands of fellowship; [c]that we *should go* unto the [2]heathen, and they unto the circumcision.

10 Only *they would* that we should remember the poor; [a]the same which I also was [1]forward to do.

11 [a]But when Peter was come to Antioch, I [1]withstood him to the face, because he was to be blamed.

12 For before that certain came from James, [a]he did eat with the Gentiles: but when they were come, he withdrew and separated himself, fearing them which were of the circumcision.

13 And the other Jews [1]dissembled likewise with him; insomuch that Barnabas also was carried away with their [2]dissimulation.

14 But when I saw that they walked not uprightly according to [a]the truth of the gospel, I said unto Peter [b]before *them* all, [c]If thou, being a Jew, livest after the manner of Gentiles, and not as do the Jews, why compellest thou the Gentiles to live as do the Jews?

15 [a]We *who are* Jews by nature, and not [b]sinners of the Gentiles,

16 [a]Knowing that a man is not [1]justified by the works of the law, but [b]by the faith of Jesus Christ, even we have believed in Jesus Christ, that we might be justified by [2]the faith of Christ, and not by the works of the law: for [c]by the works of the law shall no flesh be justified.

17 But if, while we seek to be justified by Christ, we ourselves also are found [a]sinners, *is* therefore Christ the minister of sin? [1]God forbid.

18 For if I build again the things which I destroyed, I make myself a transgressor.

19 For I [a]through the law [b]am dead to the law, that I might [c]live unto God.

20 I am [a]crucified with Christ: nevertheless I live; yet not I, but Christ liveth in me: and the life which I now live in the flesh [b]I live [1]by the faith of the Son of God, [c]who loved me, and gave himself for me.

21 I do not [1]frustrate the grace of God: for [a]if righteousness *come* by the law, then Christ [2]is dead in vain.

## CHAPTER 3

O FOOLISH Galatians, who hath bewitched you, that ye should not obey the truth, before whose eyes Jesus Christ hath been [1]evidently set forth, crucified among you?

2 This only [1]would I learn of you, Received ye the Spirit by the works of the law, [a]or by the hearing of faith?

3 Are ye so foolish? [a]having begun in the Spirit, are ye now [1]made perfect by [b]the flesh?

4 [a]Have ye suffered so many things in vain? if *it be* yet in vain.

5 He therefore that [1]ministereth to you the Spirit, and worketh miracles among you, *doeth he it* by the works of the law, or by the hearing of faith?

6 Even as [a]Abraham believed God, and it was accounted to him for righteousness.

7 Know ye therefore that [a]they which are of faith, the same are the children of Abraham.

8 And [a]the scripture, foreseeing that God would justify the [1]heathen through faith, preached before the gospel unto Abraham, *saying*, [b]In thee shall all nations be blessed.

9 So then they which be of faith are blessed with [1]faithful Abraham.

10 For as many as are of the works of the law are under the curse: for it is written, [a]Cursed *is* every one that continueth not in all things which are written in the book of the law to do them.

11 But that no man is [1]justified by the law in the sight of God, *it is* evident: for, [a]The just shall live by faith.

12 And [a]the law is not of faith: but, [b]The man that doeth them shall live [1]in them.

13 [a]Christ hath redeemed us from the curse of the law, [1]being made a curse for us: for it is written, [b]Cursed *is* every one that hangeth on a tree:

14 [a]That the blessing of Abraham might come on the [b]Gentiles [1]through Jesus Christ; that we might receive [c]the promise of the Spirit through faith.

---

2:4 [a] Acts 15:1, 24 [b] Gal. 3:25; 5:1, 13 [c] Gal. 4:3; 9 [1] *secretly* [2] *by stealth*

2:5 [a] [Gal. 1:6; 2:14; 3:1] [1] *did not yield in*

2:6 [a] Gal. 2:9; 6:3 [b] Acts 10:34 [c] 2 Cor. 11:5; 12:11 [1] *difference* [2] *shows no partiality*

2:7 [a] Acts 9:15; 13:46; 22:21 [b] 1 Thess. 2:4

2:8 [a] 1 Pet. 1:1 [b] Acts 9:15 [c] [Gal. 3:5] [1] *worked effectively*

2:9 [a] Matt. 16:18 [b] Rom. 1:5 [c] Acts 13:3 [1] Peter [2] *Gentiles*

2:10 [a] Acts 11:30 [1] *eager*

2:11 [a] Acts 15:35 [1] *opposed*

2:12 [a] [Acts 10:28; 11:2, 3]

2:13 [1] *played the hypocrite* [2] *hypocrisy*

2:14 [a] Gal. 1:6; 2:5 [b] 1 Tim. 5:20 [c] [Acts 10:28]

2:15 [a] [Acts 15:10] [b] Matt. 9:11

2:16 [a] Acts 13:38, 39 [b] Rom. 1:17 [c] Ps. 143:2 [1] *declared righteous* [2] *faith in Christ*

2:17 [a] [1 John 3:8] [1] *Certainly not*

2:19 [a] Rom. 8:2 [b] [Rom. 6:2, 14; 7:4] [c] [Rom. 6:11]

2:20 [a] [Rom. 6:6] [b] 2 Cor. 5:15 [c] Eph. 5:2 [1] *by faith in*

2:21 [a] Heb. 7:11 [1] *set aside* [2] *died for nothing*

3:1 [1] *clearly*

3:2 [a] Rom. 10:16, 17 [1] *I want to*

3:3 [a] [Gal. 4:9] [b] Heb. 7:16 [1] *being made*

3:4 [a] Heb. 10:35

3:5 [1] *supplies*

3:6 [a] Gen. 15:6

3:7 [a] John 8:39

3:8 [a] Rom. 9:17 [b] Gen. 12:3; 18:18; 22:18; 26:4; 28:14 [1] *nations*

3:9 [1] *believing*

3:10 [a] Deut. 27:26

3:11 [a] Hab. 2:4 [1] *declared righteous*

3:12 [a] Rom. 4:4, 5 [b] Lev. 18:5 [1] *by*

3:13 [a] [Rom. 8:3] [b] Deut. 21:23 [1] *having become*

3:14 [a] [Rom. 4:1–5, 9, 16] [b] Rom. 3:29, 30 [c] Is. 32:15 [1] Lit. *in Christ Jesus*

15 Brethren, I speak after the manner of men; [a]Though *it be* but a man's covenant, yet *if it be* confirmed, no man disannulleth, or addeth thereto.

16 Now [a]to Abraham and his seed were the promises made. He saith not, And to seeds, as of many; but as of [b]one, And to thy seed, which is [c]Christ.

17 And this I say, *that* the covenant, that was confirmed before of God in Christ, the law, [a]which was four hundred and thirty years after, cannot disannul, [b]that it should make the promise of none effect.

18 For if [a]the inheritance *be* of the law, [b]*it is* no more of promise: but God gave *it* to Abraham by promise.

19 [1]Wherefore then *serveth* the law? [a]It was added because of transgressions, till the [b]seed should come to whom the promise was made; *and it was* [c]ordained by angels in the hand [d]of a mediator.

20 Now a mediator [1]is not *a mediator* of one, [a]but God is one.

21 *Is* the law then against the promises of God? [1]God forbid: for if there had been a law given which could have given life, verily righteousness should have been by the law.

22 But the scripture hath [1]concluded [a]all under sin, [b]that the promise by faith of Jesus Christ might be given to them that believe.

23 But before faith came, we were [1]kept under the law, [2]shut up unto the faith which should afterwards be revealed.

24 Wherefore [a]the law was our [1]schoolmaster *to bring us* unto Christ, [b]that we might be [2]justified by faith.

25 But after that faith is come, we are no longer under a [1]schoolmaster.

26 For ye [a]are all the [1]children of God by faith in Christ Jesus.

27 For [a]as many of you as have been baptized into Christ [b]have put on Christ.

28 [a]There is neither Jew nor Greek, [b]there is neither [1]bond nor free, there is neither male nor female: for ye are all [c]one in Christ Jesus.

29 And [a]if ye *be* Christ's, then are ye Abraham's [b]seed, and [c]heirs according to the promise.

## CHAPTER 4

NOW I say, *That* the heir, as long as he is a child, differeth nothing from a servant, though he be [1]lord of all;

2 But is under [1]tutors and governors until the time appointed of the father.

3 Even so we, when we were children, [a]were in bondage under the elements of the world:

4 But [a]when the fulness of the time was come, God sent forth his Son,

[b]made [c]of a woman, [d]made [1]under the law,

5 [a]To redeem them that were under the law, [b]that we might receive the adoption of sons.

6 And because ye are sons, God hath sent forth [a]the Spirit of his Son into your hearts, crying, [1]Abba, Father.

7 Wherefore thou art no more a servant, but a son; [a]and if a son, then an heir of God through Christ.

8 Howbeit then, [a]when ye knew not God, [b]ye did service unto them which by nature are no gods.

9 But now, [a]after that ye have known God, or rather are known of God, [b]how turn ye again to [c]the weak and beggarly elements, whereunto ye desire again to be in bondage?

10 [a]Ye observe days, and months, and [1]times, and years.

11 I am afraid [1]of you, [a]lest I have [2]bestowed upon you labour in vain.

12 Brethren, I beseech you, be as I *am*; for I *am* as ye *are*: [a]ye have not injured me at all.

13 Ye know how [a]through infirmity of the flesh I preached the gospel unto you at the first.

14 And my [1]temptation which was in my flesh ye despised not, nor rejected; but received me [a]as [2]an angel of God, [b]*even* as Christ Jesus.

15 Where is then the blessedness [1]ye spake of? for I bear you [2]record, that, if *it had been* possible, ye would have plucked out your own eyes, and have given them to me.

16 Am I therefore become your enemy, because I tell you the truth?

17 They [a]zealously [1]affect you, *but* not [2]well; yea, they [3]would exclude you, that ye might [4]affect them.

18 But *it is* good to be zealously affected always in *a* good *thing*, and not only when I am present with you.

19 [a]My little children, of whom I [1]travail in birth again until Christ be formed in you,

20 I desire to be present with you now, and to change my [1]voice; for I [2]stand in doubt of you.

21 Tell me, ye that desire to be under the law, do ye not hear the law?

22 For it is written, that Abraham had two sons, [a]the one by a [1]bondmaid, [b]the other by a freewoman.

23 But he *who was* of the bondwoman [a]was born [1]after the flesh; [b]but he of the freewoman *was* by promise.

24 Which things are [1]an allegory: for these are the two covenants; the one from the mount [a]Sinai, which [2]gendereth to bondage, which is Agar.

---

3:15 [a] Heb. 9:17
3:16 [a] Gen. 22:18
[b] Gen. 12:3,
7; 13:15; 24:7
[c] [1 Cor. 12:12]
3:17 [a] Ex. 12:40
[b] [Rom. 4:13]
3:18 [a] [Rom. 8:17]
[b] Rom. 4:14
3:19 [a] John 15:22
[b] Gal. 4:4 [c] Acts
7:53 [d] Ex. 20:19
[1] *What purpose*
3:20 [a] [Rom.
3:29] [1] *does not
mediate for one
only*
3:21 [1] *Certainly
not*
3:22 [a] Rom.
11:32 [b] Rom. 4:11
[1] *confined*
3:23 [1] *guarded*
[2] *confined*
3:24 [a] Rom. 10:4
[b] Acts 13:39 [1] *tutor, the guardian
responsible for
care and discipline* [2] *declared
righteous*
3:25 [1] *tutor*
3:26 [a] John 1:12
[1] Lit. *sons*
3:27 [a] [Rom. 6:3]
[b] Rom. 10:12;
13:14
3:28 [a] Col. 3:11
[b] [1 Cor. 12:13]
[c] [Eph. 2:15, 16]
[1] *slave*
3:29 [a] Gen.
21:10 [b] Rom. 4:11
[c] Rom. 8:17
4:1 [1] *master*
4:2 [1] *guardians
and stewards*
4:3 [a] Col. 2:8, 20
4:4 [a] [Gen. 49:10]
[b] [John 1:14]
[c] Gen. 3:15 [d] Luke
2:21, 27 [1] *born*
4:5 [a] [Matt.
20:28] [b] [John
1:12]
4:6 [a] [Rom.
5:5; 8:9, 15, 16]
[1] Aram. for *father*
4:7 [a] [Rom.
8:16, 17]
4:8 [a] Eph. 2:12
[b] Rom. 1:25
4:9 [a] [1 Cor. 8:3]
[b] Col. 2:20 [c] Heb.
7:18
4:10 [a] Rom. 14:5
[1] *seasons*
4:11 [a] 1 Thess. 3:5
[1] *for* [2] *laboured
for you*
4:12 [a] 2 Cor. 2:5
4:13 [a] 1 Cor. 2:3
4:14 [a] Mal. 2:7
[b] [Luke 10:16]
[1] *trial* [2] *a messenger*

4:15 [1] *you enjoyed* [2] *witness* 4:17 [a] Rom. 10:2
[1] *court* [2] *for good* [3] *want to* [4] *be zealous for them*
4:19 [a] 1 Cor. 4:15 [1] *labour* 4:20 [1] *tone* [2] *have doubts
about* 4:22 [a] Gen. 16:15 [b] Gen. 21:2 [1] *servant
woman* 4:23 [a] Rom. 9:7, 8 [b] Heb. 11:11 [1] *according to*
4:24 [a] Deut. 33:2 [1] *symbolic* [2] *gives birth*

25 For this Agar is mount Sinai in Arabia, and [1]answereth to Jerusalem which now is, and is in bondage with her children.

26 But [a]Jerusalem which is above is free, which is the mother of us all.

27 For it is written, [a]Rejoice, *thou* barren that bearest not; break forth and [1]cry, thou that [2]travailest not: for the desolate hath many more children than she which hath an husband.

28 Now [a]we, brethren, as Isaac was, are [b]the children of promise.

29 But as then [a]he that was born [1]after the flesh persecuted him *that was born* after the Spirit, [b]even so *it is* now.

30 Nevertheless what saith [a]the scripture? [b]Cast out the bondwoman and her son: for [c]the son of the bondwoman shall not be heir with the son of the freewoman.

31 So then, brethren, we are not children of the bondwoman, but of the free.

### CHAPTER 5

STAND[a] fast therefore in the liberty wherewith Christ hath made us free, and be not entangled again with the [b]yoke of bondage.

2 Behold, I Paul say unto you, that [a]if ye be circumcised, Christ shall profit you nothing.

3 For I testify again to every man that is circumcised, [a]that he is [1]a debtor to do the whole law.

4 [a]Christ[1] is become of no effect unto you, whosoever of you [2]are justified by the law; [b]ye are fallen from grace.

5 For we through the Spirit [a]wait[1] for the hope of righteousness by faith.

6 For [a]in Jesus Christ neither circumcision availeth any thing, nor uncircumcision; but [b]faith which worketh by love.

7 Ye [a]did run well; who did hinder you that ye should not obey the truth?

8 This persuasion *cometh* not of him that calleth you.

9 [a]A little leaven leaveneth the whole lump.

10 I have confidence in you [1]through the Lord, that ye will be none otherwise minded: but he that troubleth you shall bear his judgment, whosoever he be.

11 And I, brethren, if I yet preach circumcision, [a]why do I yet suffer persecution? then is [b]the offence of the cross ceased.

12 [a]I [1]would they [2]were even [3]cut off [b]which trouble you.

13 For, brethren, ye have been called unto liberty; only [a]*use* not liberty for an [b]occasion to the flesh, but [c]by love serve one another.

14 For [a]all the law is fulfilled in one word, *even* in this; [b]Thou shalt love thy neighbour as thyself.

15 But if ye bite and devour one another, take heed that ye be not consumed one of another.

16 *This* I say then, [a]Walk in the Spirit, and ye shall not fulfil the lust of the flesh.

17 For [a]the flesh lusteth against the Spirit, and the Spirit against the flesh: and these are contrary the one to the other: [b]so that ye cannot do the things that ye would.

18 But [a]if ye be led of the Spirit, ye are not under the law.

19 Now [a]the works of the flesh are [1]manifest, which are *these;* Adultery, fornication, uncleanness, [2]lasciviousness,

20 Idolatry, [1]witchcraft, hatred, [2]variance, [3]emulations, wrath, [4]strife, [5]seditions, heresies,

21 Envyings, murders, drunkenness, revellings, and such like: of the which I tell you before, as I have also told *you* in time past, that [a]they which do such things shall not inherit the kingdom of God.

22 But [a]the fruit of the Spirit is [b]love, joy, peace, longsuffering, [1]gentleness, [c]goodness, [d]faith,[2]

23 Meekness, [1]temperance: [a]against such there is no law.

24 And they that are Christ's [a]have crucified the flesh with [1]the affections and lusts.

25 [a]If we live in the Spirit, let us also walk in the Spirit.

26 [a]Let us not be [1]desirous of vain glory, provoking one another, envying one another.

### CHAPTER 6

BRETHREN, if a man be [1]overtaken in a fault, ye which are spiritual, restore such an one in the spirit of [a]meekness; considering thyself, lest thou also be tempted.

2 [a]Bear ye one another's burdens, and so fulfil [b]the law of Christ.

3 For [a]if a man think himself to be something, when [b]he is nothing, he deceiveth himself.

4 But [a]let every man [1]prove his own work, and then shall he have rejoicing in himself alone, and [b]not in another.

5 For [a]every man shall bear his own burden.

6 [a]Let him that is taught in the word [1]communicate unto him that teacheth in all good things.

7 Be not deceived; God is not mocked: for [a]whatsoever a man soweth, that shall he also reap.

4:25 [1] *corresponds*
4:26 [a] [Is. 2:2]
4:27 [a] Is. 54:1
[1] *shout* [2] *has no birth pangs*
4:28 [a] Gal. 3:29
[b] Acts 3:25
4:29 [a] Gen. 21:9 [b] Gal. 5:11
[1] *according to*
4:30 [a] [Gal. 3:8, 22] [b] Gen. 21:10, 12 [c] [John 8:35]
5:1 [a] Phil. 4:1
[b] Acts 15:10
5:2 [a] Acts 15:1
5:3 [a] [Rom. 2:25]
[1] *obligated to keep*
5:4 [a] [Rom. 9:31]
[b] Heb. 12:15 [1] *You have become estranged from Christ* [2] *attempt to be*
5:5 [a] Rom. 8:24
[1] *eagerly wait*
5:6 [a] [Gal. 6:15]
[b] 1 Thess. 1:3
5:7 [a] 1 Cor. 9:24
5:9 [a] 1 Cor. 5:6
5:10 [1] Lit. *in*
5:11 [a] 1 Cor. 15:30
[b] [1 Cor. 1:23]
5:12 [a] Josh. 7:25
[b] Acts 15:1, 2
[1] *wish* [2] *would* [3] *cut themselves off,* mutilate themselves
5:13 [a] 1 Cor. 8:9 [b] 1 Pet. 2:16
[c] 1 Cor. 9:19
5:14 [a] Matt. 7:12; 22:40 [b] Lev. 19:18
5:16 [a] Rom. 6:12
5:17 [a] Rom. 7:18, 22, 23; 8:5
[b] Rom. 7:15
5:18 [a] [Rom. 6:14; 7:4; 8:14]
5:19 [a] Eph. 5:3, 11
[1] *evident* [2] *licentiousness*
5:20 [1] *sorcery* [2] *contentions* [3] *jealousies* [4] *selfish ambitions* [5] *dissensions*
5:21 [a] 1 Cor. 6:9, 10
5:22 [a] [John 15:2] [b] [Col. 3:12–15] [c] Rom. 15:14 [d] 1 Cor. 13:7 [1] *kindness* [2] *faithfulness*
5:23 [a] 1 Tim. 1:9
[1] *self-control*
5:24 [a] Rom. 6:6
[1] *its passions*
5:25 [a] [Rom. 8:4, 5]
5:26 [a] Phil. 2:3
[1] *conceited*
6:1 [a] Eph. 4:2

[1] *caught* 6:2 [a] Rom. 15:1 [b] [James 2:8] 6:3 [a] Rom. 12:3 [b] [2 Cor. 3:5] 6:4 [a] 1 Cor. 11:28 [b] Luke 18:11 [1] *examine* 6:5 [a] [Rom. 2:6] 6:6 [a] 1 Cor. 9:11, 14 [1] *share with* 6:7 [a] [Rom. 2:6]

8 For he that soweth to his flesh shall of the flesh reap corruption; but he that soweth to the Spirit shall of the Spirit reap [a]life everlasting.

9 And [a]let us not be weary in well doing: for in due season we shall reap, [b]if we [1]faint not.

10 [a]As we have therefore opportunity, [b]let us do good unto all *men,* [c]especially unto them who are of the household of faith.

11 Ye see [1]how large a letter I have written unto you with mine own hand.

12 As many as desire to make a [1]fair shew in the flesh, they [2]constrain you to be circumcised; [a]only [3]lest they should suffer persecution for the cross of Christ.

13 For neither they themselves who

6:8 [a] [Rom. 6:8]
6:9 [a] 1 Cor. 15:58
[b] [James 5:7, 8]
[1] *do not lose heart*
6:10 [a] Prov. 3:27
[b] Titus 3:8 [c] Rom. 12:13
6:11 [1] *with what large letters*
6:12 [a] Gal. 5:11
[1] *good showing*
[2] *try to compel*
[3] *that they may not suffer*
6:14 [a] [1 Cor. 1:18]
[b] [Gal. 2:20]; Col. 2:20 [1] *except*
[2] *Or by which, the cross*
6:15 [a] [Rom. 2:26, 28]; 1 Cor. 7:19; [Gal. 5:6] [1] *creation*

are circumcised keep the law; but desire to have you circumcised, that they may glory in your flesh.

14 But God forbid that I should glory, [1]save in the [a]cross of our Lord Jesus Christ, [2]by whom the world is crucified unto me, and [b]I unto the world.

15 For [a]in Christ Jesus neither circumcision availeth any thing, nor uncircumcision, but a new [1]creature.

16 And as many as walk according to this rule, peace *be* on them, and mercy, and upon the Israel of God.

17 From henceforth let no man trouble me: for I bear in my body the marks of the Lord Jesus.

18 Brethren, the grace of our Lord Jesus Christ *be* with your spirit. Amen.

# THE EPISTLE OF PAUL THE APOSTLE TO THE
# EPHESIANS

Ephesians is addressed to a group of believers who are rich beyond measure in Jesus Christ, yet living as beggars, and only because they are ignorant of their wealth. Paul begins by describing in chapters 1–3 the contents of the Christian's heavenly "bank account": adoption, acceptance, redemption, forgiveness, wisdom, inheritance, the seal of the Holy Spirit, life, grace, citizenship—in short, every spiritual blessing. In chapters 4–6 the Christian learns a spiritual walk rooted in his spiritual wealth. "For we are his workmanship, created in Christ Jesus [1–3] unto good works, . . . that we should walk in them [4–6]" (2:10).

The traditional title of this epistle is *Pros Ephesious*, "To the Ephesians." Many ancient manuscripts, however, omit *en Epheso*, "at Ephesus," in 1:1. This has led a number of scholars to challenge the traditional view that this message was directed specifically to the Ephesians. The encyclical theory proposes that it was a circular letter sent by Paul to the churches of Asia. It is argued that Ephesians is really a Christian treatise designed for general use: it involves no controversy and deals with no specific problems in any particular church. Some scholars accept an ancient tradition that Ephesians is Paul's letter to the Laodiceans (Col. 4:16), but there is no way to be sure. If Ephesians began as a circular letter, it eventually became associated with Ephesus, the foremost of the Asian churches. Another plausible option is that this epistle was directly addressed to the Ephesians, but written in such a way as to make it helpful for all the churches in Asia.

## CHAPTER 1

PAUL, an apostle of Jesus Christ by the will of God, to the saints which are at Ephesus, and to the faithful in Christ Jesus:

2 Grace *be* to you, and peace, from God our Father, and *from* the Lord Jesus Christ.

3 ªBlessed *be* the God and Father of our Lord Jesus Christ, who hath blessed us with all spiritual blessings in heavenly *places* in Christ:

4 According as ªhe hath chosen us in him ᵇbefore the foundation of the world, that we should ᶜbe holy and without blame before him in love:

5 ªHaving predestinated us unto ᵇthe adoption ¹of children by Jesus Christ to himself, ᶜaccording to the good pleasure of his will,

6 To the praise of the glory of his grace, ªwherein he hath ¹made us accepted in ᵇthe beloved.

7 ªIn whom we have redemption through his blood, the forgiveness of sins, according to ᵇthe riches of his grace;

8 Wherein he hath abounded toward us in all wisdom and ¹prudence;

9 ªHaving made known unto us the mystery of his will, according to his good pleasure ᵇwhich he hath purposed in himself:

10 That in the dispensation of ªthe fulness of times ᵇhe might gather together in one ᶜall things in Christ, both which are in heaven, and which are on earth; *even* in him:

11 ªIn whom also we have obtained an inheritance, being predestinated according to ᵇthe purpose of him who worketh all things after the counsel of his own will:

12 ªThat we should be to the praise of his glory, ᵇwho first trusted in Christ.

13 In whom ye also *trusted,* after that ye heard ªthe word of truth, the gospel of your salvation: in whom also after that ye believed, ᵇye were sealed with that holy Spirit of promise,

14 ªWhich is the ¹earnest of our inheritance ᵇuntil the redemption of ᶜthe purchased possession, ᵈunto the praise of his glory.

15 Wherefore I also, ªafter I heard of your faith in the Lord Jesus, and love unto all the saints,

16 ªCease not to give thanks for you, making mention of you in my prayers;

17 That ªthe God of our Lord Jesus Christ, the Father of glory, ᵇmay give unto you the spirit of wisdom and revelation in the knowledge of him:

18 ªThe eyes of your understanding being enlightened; that ye may know what is ᵇthe hope of his calling, and what the riches of the glory of his inheritance in the saints,

19 And what *is* the exceeding greatness of his power to us-ward who believe, ªaccording to the working of his mighty power,

20 Which he wrought in Christ, when ªhe raised him from the dead,

---

1:3 ª 2 Cor. 1:3
1:4 ª Rom. 8:28
ᵇ 1 Pet. 1:2 ᶜ Luke 1:75
1:5 ª [Rom. 8:29] ᵇ John 1:12
ᶜ [1 Cor. 1:21] ¹ *as sons*
1:6 ª [Rom. 3:24] ᵇ Matt. 3:17 ¹ Lit. *bestowed grace (favour) upon us*
1:7 ª [Heb. 9:12] ᵇ [Rom. 3:24, 25]
1:8 ¹ *understanding*
1:9 ª [Rom. 16:25] ᵇ [2 Tim. 1:9]
1:10 ª Gal. 4:4 ᵇ 1 Cor. 3:22 ᶜ [Col. 1:16, 20]
1:11 ª Rom. 8:17 ᵇ Is. 46:10
1:12 ª 2 Thess. 2:13 ᵇ James 1:18
1:13 ª John 1:17 ᵇ [2 Cor. 1:22]
1:14 ª 2 Cor. 5:5 ᵇ Rom. 8:23 ᶜ [Acts 20:28] ᵈ 1 Pet. 2:9 ¹ *down payment or deposit*
1:15 ª Col. 1:4
1:16 ª Rom. 1:9
1:17 ª John 20:17 ᵇ Col. 1:9
1:18 ª Acts 26:18 ᵇ Eph. 2:12
1:19 ª Col. 2:12
1:20 ª Acts 2:24

969

and <sup>b</sup>set<sup>1</sup> *him* at his own right hand in the heavenly *places,*

21 <sup>a</sup>Far above all <sup>b</sup>principality, and power, and might, and dominion, and every name that is named, not only in this <sup>1</sup>world, but also in that which is to come:

22 And <sup>a</sup>hath put all *things* under his feet, and gave him <sup>b</sup>*to be* the head over all *things* to the church,

23 <sup>a</sup>Which is his body, <sup>b</sup>the fulness of him <sup>c</sup>that filleth all in all.

## CHAPTER 2

AND <sup>a</sup>you *hath he* <sup>1</sup>*quickened,* <sup>b</sup>who were dead in trespasses and sins;

2 <sup>a</sup>Wherein in time past ye walked according to the <sup>1</sup>course of this world, according to <sup>b</sup>the prince of the power of the air, the spirit that now worketh in <sup>c</sup>the children of disobedience:

3 <sup>a</sup>Among whom also we all <sup>1</sup>had our conversation in times past in <sup>b</sup>the lusts of our flesh, fulfilling the desires of the flesh and of the mind; and <sup>c</sup>were by nature the children of wrath, even as others.

4 But God, <sup>a</sup>who is rich in mercy, for his <sup>b</sup>great love wherewith he loved us,

5 <sup>a</sup>Even when we were dead in sins, hath <sup>b</sup>quickened<sup>1</sup> us together with Christ, (by grace ye <sup>2</sup>are saved;)

6 And hath raised *us* up together, and made *us* sit together <sup>a</sup>in heavenly *places* in Christ Jesus:

7 That in the ages to come he might shew the exceeding riches of his grace in <sup>a</sup>*his* kindness toward us <sup>1</sup>through Christ Jesus.

8 <sup>a</sup>For by grace <sup>1</sup>are ye saved <sup>b</sup>through faith; and that not of yourselves: <sup>c</sup>*it is* the gift of God:

9 Not of <sup>a</sup>works, lest any man should <sup>b</sup>boast.

10 For we are <sup>a</sup>his <sup>1</sup>workmanship, created in Christ Jesus <sup>2</sup>unto good works, which God hath before <sup>3</sup>ordained that we should walk in them.

11 Wherefore remember, that ye *being* in time past Gentiles in the flesh, who are called Uncircumcision by that which is called <sup>a</sup>the Circumcision in the flesh made by hands;

12 That at that time ye were without Christ, being aliens from the commonwealth of Israel, and strangers from the covenants of promise, having no hope, and without God in the world:

13 But now in Christ Jesus ye who <sup>1</sup>sometimes were far off are made nigh by the blood of Christ.

14 For <sup>1</sup>he is our peace, who hath made both one, and hath broken down the middle wall of <sup>2</sup>partition *between us;*

15 Having abolished in his flesh the enmity, *even* the law of command-

---

1:20 <sup>b</sup> Ps. 110:1
<sup>1</sup> *seated*

1:21 <sup>a</sup> Phil. 2:9, 10
<sup>b</sup> [Rom. 8:38, 39]
<sup>1</sup> *age*

1:22 <sup>a</sup> Ps. 8:6;
110:1 <sup>b</sup> Heb. 2:7

1:23 <sup>a</sup> Rom.
12:5 <sup>b</sup> Col. 2:9
<sup>c</sup> [1 Cor. 12:6]

2:1 <sup>a</sup> Col. 2:13
<sup>b</sup> Eph. 4:18
<sup>1</sup> *made alive*

2:2 <sup>a</sup> Col. 1:21
<sup>b</sup> Eph. 6:12 <sup>c</sup> Col.
3:6 <sup>1</sup> Lit. *age*

2:3 <sup>a</sup> 1 Pet. 4:3
<sup>b</sup> Gal. 5:16 <sup>c</sup> [Ps.
51:5] <sup>1</sup> *conducted ourselves*

2:4 <sup>a</sup> Rom. 10:12
<sup>b</sup> John 3:16

2:5 <sup>a</sup> Rom. 5:6,
8 <sup>b</sup> [Rom. 6:4, 5]
<sup>1</sup> *made us alive*
<sup>2</sup> *have been*

2:6 <sup>a</sup> Eph. 1:20

2:7 <sup>a</sup> Titus 3:4
<sup>1</sup> Lit. *in*

2:8 <sup>a</sup> [2 Tim.
1:9] <sup>b</sup> Rom. 4:16
<sup>c</sup> [John 1:12, 13]
<sup>1</sup> *you have been*

2:9 <sup>a</sup> Rom. 4:4, 5;
11:6 <sup>b</sup> Rom. 3:27

2:10 <sup>a</sup> Is. 19:25
<sup>1</sup> *creation* <sup>2</sup> *for*
<sup>3</sup> *prepared*

2:11 <sup>a</sup> [Col. 2:11]

2:13 <sup>1</sup> *once*

2:14 <sup>1</sup> *he himself*
<sup>2</sup> *division*

2:15 <sup>a</sup> Gal. 6:15
<sup>1</sup> *create* <sup>2</sup> *the two*

2:16 <sup>a</sup> [Col. 1:20–22] <sup>b</sup> [Rom. 6:6]
<sup>1</sup> *put to death*

2:18 <sup>a</sup> John 10:9
<sup>b</sup> 1 Cor. 12:13

2:20 <sup>a</sup> 1 Pet. 2:4
<sup>b</sup> Matt. 16:18
<sup>c</sup> 1 Cor. 12:28
<sup>d</sup> Ps. 118:22

2:21 <sup>a</sup> 1 Cor. 3:16,
17 <sup>1</sup> *being joined together*

2:22 <sup>a</sup> 1 Pet. 2:5
<sup>b</sup> John 17:23
<sup>1</sup> *being built*
<sup>2</sup> *dwelling place*

3:2 <sup>a</sup> Acts 9:15
<sup>1</sup> *stewardship*

3:3 <sup>a</sup> Acts 22:17,
21; 26:16 <sup>b</sup> [Rom.
11:25; 16:25]
<sup>1</sup> *hidden truth*
<sup>2</sup> *before*

3:6 <sup>a</sup> Gal. 3:28, 29

3:7 <sup>a</sup> Rom.
15:16 <sup>b</sup> Rom. 1:5
<sup>c</sup> Rom. 15:18 <sup>1</sup> *became* <sup>2</sup> *effective*

3:8 <sup>a</sup> [1 Cor.
15:9] <sup>b</sup> [Col. 1:27;
2:2, 3]

3:9 <sup>a</sup> Heb. 1:2

---

ments *contained* in ordinances; for to <sup>1</sup>make in himself of <sup>2</sup>twain one <sup>a</sup>new man, *so* making peace;

16 And that he might <sup>a</sup>reconcile both unto God in one body by the cross, <sup>b</sup>having <sup>1</sup>slain the enmity thereby:

17 And came and preached peace to you which were afar off, and to them that were nigh.

18 For <sup>a</sup>through him we both have access <sup>b</sup>by one Spirit unto the Father.

19 Now therefore ye are no more strangers and foreigners, but fellowcitizens with the saints, and of the household of God;

20 And are <sup>a</sup>built <sup>b</sup>upon the foundation of the <sup>c</sup>apostles and prophets, Jesus Christ himself being <sup>d</sup>the chief corner *stone;*

21 In whom all the building <sup>1</sup>fitly framed together groweth unto <sup>a</sup>an holy temple in the Lord:

22 <sup>a</sup>In whom ye also are <sup>1</sup>builded together for an <sup>b</sup>habitation<sup>2</sup> of God through the Spirit.

## CHAPTER 3

FOR this cause I Paul, the prisoner of Jesus Christ for you Gentiles,

2 If ye have heard of the <sup>1</sup>dispensation of the grace of God <sup>a</sup>which is given me to you-ward:

3 <sup>a</sup>How that by revelation <sup>b</sup>he made known unto me the <sup>1</sup>mystery; (as I wrote <sup>2</sup>afore in few words,

4 Whereby, when ye read, ye may understand my knowledge in the mystery of Christ)

5 Which in other ages was not made known unto the sons of men, as it is now revealed unto his holy apostles and prophets by the Spirit;

6 That the Gentiles <sup>a</sup>should be fellowheirs, and of the same body, and partakers of his promise in Christ by the gospel:

7 <sup>a</sup>Whereof I <sup>1</sup>was made a minister, <sup>b</sup>according to the gift of the grace of God given unto me by <sup>c</sup>the <sup>2</sup>effectual working of his power.

8 Unto me, <sup>a</sup>who am less than the least of all saints, is this grace given, that I should preach among the Gentiles <sup>b</sup>the unsearchable riches of Christ;

9 And to make all *men* see what *is* the fellowship of the mystery, which from the beginning of the world hath been hid in God, who <sup>a</sup>created all things by Jesus Christ:

10 <sup>a</sup>To the intent that now <sup>b</sup>unto the principalities and powers in heavenly *places* <sup>c</sup>might be known by the church the <sup>1</sup>manifold wisdom of God,

---

3:10 <sup>a</sup> 1 Pet. 1:12 <sup>b</sup> [1 Tim. 3:16] <sup>c</sup> Col. 1:16; 2:10, 15
<sup>1</sup> *many-sided*

11 ᵃAccording to the eternal purpose which he purposed in Christ Jesus our Lord:

12 In whom we have boldness and access ᵃwith confidence by ¹the faith of him.

13 ᵃWherefore I ¹desire that ye ²faint not at my tribulations for you, ᵇwhich is your glory.

14 For this cause I bow my knees unto the ᵃFather of our Lord Jesus Christ,

15 Of whom the whole family in heaven and earth is named,

16 That he would grant you, ᵃaccording to the riches of his glory, ᵇto be strengthened with might by his Spirit in ᶜthe inner man;

17 ᵃThat Christ may dwell in your hearts by faith; that ye, ᵇbeing rooted and grounded in love,

18 ᵃMay be able to ¹comprehend with all saints ᵇwhat *is* the ²breadth, and length, and depth, and height;

19 And to know the love of Christ, which passeth knowledge, that ye might be filled ᵃwith all the fulness of God.

20 Now ᵃunto him that is able to do exceeding abundantly ᵇabove all that we ask or think, ᶜaccording to the power that worketh in us,

21 ᵃUnto him *be* glory in the church by Christ Jesus throughout all ages, world without end. Amen.

## CHAPTER 4

I THEREFORE, the prisoner ¹of the Lord, beseech you that ye ᵃwalk worthy of the ²vocation wherewith ye are called,

2 With all lowliness and ¹meekness, with longsuffering, ²forbearing one another in love;

3 Endeavouring to keep the unity of the Spirit ᵃin the bond of peace.

4 ᵃ*There is* one body, and one Spirit, even as ye are called in one hope of your calling;

5 ᵃOne Lord, ᵇone faith, ᶜone baptism,

6 ᵃOne God and Father of all, who *is* above all, and ᵇthrough all, and in you all.

7 But ᵃunto every one of us is given grace according to the measure of the gift of Christ.

8 Wherefore he saith, ᵃWhen he ascended up on high, he led captivity captive, and gave gifts unto men.

9 (ᵃNow that he ascended, what is it but that he also descended first into the lower parts of the earth?

10 He that descended is the same also ᵃthat ascended up far above all heavens, ᵇthat he might ¹fill all things.)

11 And ¹he gave some, apostles; and some, prophets; and some, evangelists; and some, pastors and teachers;

12 For the ¹perfecting of the saints, for the work of the ministry, ᵃfor the edifying of ᵇthe body of Christ:

13 Till we all come ¹in the unity of the faith, ᵃand of the knowledge of the Son of God, unto ᵇa ²perfect man, unto the measure of the stature of the fulness of Christ:

14 That we *henceforth* be no more ᵃchildren, tossed to and fro, and carried about with every wind of doctrine, by the ¹sleight of men, *and* cunning craftiness, ᵇwhereby they lie in wait to deceive;

15 But speaking the truth in love, may grow up into him in all things, which is the ᵃhead, *even* Christ:

16 ᵃFrom whom the whole body fitly joined together and ¹compacted by that which every joint supplieth, according to the ²effectual working ³in the measure of every part, ⁴maketh increase of the body unto the edifying of itself in love.

17 This I say therefore, and testify in the Lord, that ye henceforth ᵃwalk not as other Gentiles walk, in the ¹vanity of their mind,

18 Having the understanding darkened, being alienated from the life of God ¹through the ignorance that is in them, because of the ᵃblindness² of their heart:

19 ᵃWho being past feeling ᵇhave given themselves over unto ¹lasciviousness, to work all uncleanness with greediness.

20 But ye have not so learned Christ;

21 If so be that ye have heard him, and have been taught by him, as the truth is in Jesus:

22 That ye ᵃput off concerning the former ¹conversation the old man, which is corrupt according to the deceitful lusts;

23 And ᵃbe renewed in the spirit of your mind;

24 And that ye ᵃput on the new man, which after God is created in righteousness and true holiness.

25 Wherefore putting away lying, ᵃspeak every man truth with his neighbour: for ᵇwe are members one of another.

26 ᵃBe ye angry, and sin not: let not the sun go down upon your wrath:

27 ᵃNeither give ¹place to the devil.

28 Let him that stole steal no more: but rather ᵃlet him labour, working with *his* hands the thing which is good, that he may have to give ᵇto him that needeth.

29 ᵃLet no corrupt communication proceed out of your mouth, but ᵇthat which is good to the use of edifying, ᶜthat it may minister grace unto the hearers.

### Cross references

3:11 ᵃ [Eph. 1:4, 11]
3:12 ᵃ Heb. 4:16; 10:19, 35 ¹ *faith in*
3:13 ᵃ Phil. 1:14 ᵇ 2 Cor. 1:6 ¹ *ask* ² *not lose heart*
3:14 ᵃ Eph. 1:3
3:16 ᵃ [Phil. 4:19] ᵇ Col. 1:11 ᶜ Rom. 7:22
3:17 ᵃ John 14:23 ᵇ Col. 1:23
3:18 ᵃ Eph. 1:18 ᵇ Rom. 8:39 ¹ *understand* ² *width*
3:19 ᵃ Eph. 1:23
3:20 ᵃ Rom. 16:25 ᵇ 1 Cor. 2:9 ᶜ Col. 1:29
3:21 ᵃ Rom. 11:36
4:1 ᵃ 1 Thess. 2:12 ¹ Lit. *in* ² *calling*
4:2 ¹ *gentleness* ² *bearing with*
4:3 ᵃ Col. 3:14
4:4 ᵃ Rom. 12:5
4:5 ᵃ 1 Cor. 1:13 ᵇ Jude 3 ᶜ [Heb. 6:6]
4:6 ᵃ Mal. 2:10 ᵇ Rom. 11:36
4:7 ᵃ [1 Cor. 12:7, 11]
4:8 ᵃ Ps. 68:18
4:9 ᵃ John 3:13; 20:17
4:10 ᵃ Acts 1:9 ᵇ [Eph. 1:23] ¹ *fulfil*
4:11 ¹ *he himself*
4:12 ᵃ 1 Cor. 14:26 ᵇ Col. 1:24 ¹ *equipping*
4:13 ᵃ Col. 2:2 ᵇ 1 Cor. 14:20 ¹ *into* ² *mature*
4:14 ᵃ 1 Cor. 14:20 ᵇ Rom. 16:18 ¹ *trickery*
4:15 ᵃ Eph. 1:22
4:16 ᵃ Col. 2:19 ¹ *knit together* ² *effective* ³ *of each part doing its share* ⁴ *causes growth*
4:17 ᵃ Eph. 2:2; 4:22 ¹ *futility*
4:18 ᵃ Rom. 1:21 ¹ *because of* ² *hardening*
4:19 ᵃ 1 Tim. 4:2 ᵇ 1 Pet. 4:3 ¹ *licentiousness*
4:22 ᵃ Col. 3:8 ¹ *conduct*
4:23 ᵃ [Rom. 12:2]
4:24 ᵃ [Rom. 6:4; 7:6; 12:2]
4:25 ᵃ Zech. 8:16 ᵇ Rom. 12:5
4:26 ᵃ Ps. 4:4; 37:8
4:27 ᵃ [Rom.
12:19] ¹ *an opportunity* 4:28 ᵃ Acts 20:35 ᵇ Luke 3:11
4:29 ᵃ Col. 3:8 ᵇ 1 Thess. 5:11 ᶜ Col. 3:16

30 And [a]grieve not the holy Spirit of God, whereby ye are sealed unto the day of redemption.

31 [a]Let all bitterness, and wrath, and anger, and clamour, and [b]evil speaking, be put away from you, [c]with all malice:

32 And [a]be ye kind one to another, tenderhearted, [b]forgiving one another, even as God [1]for Christ's sake hath forgiven you.

## CHAPTER 5

BE [a]ye therefore followers of God, as dear [b]children;

2 And [a]walk in love, [b]as Christ also hath loved us, and hath given himself for us an offering and a sacrifice to God [c]for a sweetsmelling [1]savour.

3 But fornication, and all [a]uncleanness, or [b]covetousness, let it not be once named among you, as becometh saints;

4 [a]Neither filthiness, nor [b]foolish talking, nor [1]jesting, [c]which are not [2]convenient: but rather [d]giving of thanks.

5 For this ye know, that no whoremonger, nor unclean person, nor covetous man, who is an idolater, hath any [a]inheritance in the kingdom of Christ and of God.

6 Let no man deceive you with [1]vain words: for because of these things cometh the wrath of God upon the [2]children of disobedience.

7 Be not ye therefore [a]partakers with them.

8 For ye were [1]sometimes darkness, but now *are ye* [a]light in the Lord: walk as children of light:

9 (For [a]the fruit of the Spirit *is* in all goodness and righteousness and truth;)

10 [a]Proving what is acceptable unto the Lord.

11 And have [a]no fellowship with the unfruitful works of darkness, but rather [1]reprove *them*.

12 [a]For it is a shame even to speak of those things which are done of them in secret.

13 But [a]all things that are [1]reproved are made manifest by the light: for whatsoever doth make manifest is light.

14 Wherefore he saith, [a]Awake thou that sleepest, and arise from the dead, and Christ shall give thee light.

15 [a]See then that ye walk [1]circumspectly, not as fools, but as wise,

16 [a]Redeeming the time, [b]because the days are evil.

17 [a]Wherefore be ye not unwise, but [b]understanding [c]what the will of the Lord *is*.

18 And [a]be not drunk with wine, wherein is [1]excess; but be filled with the Spirit;

---

4:30 [a] Is. 7:13
4:31 [a] Col. 3:8,
19 [b] James 4:11
[c] Titus 3:3
4:32 [a] 2 Cor. 6:10
[b] [Mark 11:25] [1] *in Christ forgave*
5:1 [a] Luke 6:36
[b] 1 Pet. 1:14–16
5:2 [a] 1 Thess. 4:9
[b] Gal. 1:4 [c] 2 Cor. 2:14, 15 [1] *aroma*
5:3 [a] Col. 3:5–7
[b] [Luke 12:15]
5:4 [a] Matt. 12:34, 35 [b] Titus 3:9 [c] Rom. 1:28 [d] Phil. 4:6
[1] *coarse jesting*
[2] *fitting*
5:5 [a] 1 Cor. 6:9, 10
5:6 [1] *empty*
[2] *sons*
5:7 [a] 1 Tim. 5:22
5:8 [a] 1 Thess. 5:5
[1] *once*
5:9 [a] Gal. 5:22
5:10 [a] [Rom. 12:1, 2]
5:11 [a] 2 Cor. 6:14
[1] *expose*
5:12 [a] Rom. 1:24
5:13 [a] [John 3:20, 21] [1] *exposed*
5:14 [a] [Is. 26:19; 60:1]
5:15 [a] Col. 4:5
[1] *carefully*
5:16 [a] Col. 4:5
[b] Eccl. 11:2
5:17 [a] Col. 4:5
[b] [Rom. 12:2]
[c] 1 Thess. 4:3
5:18 [a] Prov. 20:1;
23:31 [1] *dissipation*
5:19 [a] Acts 16:25
[b] James 5:13
5:20 [a] Ps. 34:1
[b] [1 Pet. 2:5]
5:21 [a] [Phil. 2:3]
5:22 [a] Col. 3:18–4:1
5:23 [a] [1 Cor. 11:3]
[b] Col. 1:18
5:24 [a] Titus 2:4, 5
5:25 [a] Col. 3:19
[b] Acts 20:28
5:26 [a] John 3:5
[b] [John 15:3; 17:17]
[1] *set it apart*
5:27 [a] Col. 1:22
[b] Song 4:7
5:28 [1] *their own wives*
5:30 [a] Gen. 2:23
5:31 [a] Gen. 2:24
[b] [1 Cor. 6:16]
5:33 [a] Col. 3:19
[b] 1 Pet. 3:1, 6
[1] *respects*
6:1 [a] Col. 3:20
6:2 [a] Deut. 5:16
6:4 [a] Col. 3:21
[b] Gen. 18:19

---

19 Speaking to yourselves [a]in psalms and hymns and spiritual songs, singing and making [b]melody in your heart to the Lord;

20 [a]Giving thanks always for all things unto God and the Father [b]in the name of our Lord Jesus Christ;

21 [a]Submitting yourselves one to another in the fear of God.

22 Wives, [a]submit yourselves unto your own husbands, as unto the Lord.

23 For [a]the husband is the head of the wife, even as [b]Christ is the head of the church: and he is the saviour of the body.

24 Therefore as the church is subject unto Christ, so *let* the wives *be* to their own husbands [a]in every thing.

25 [a]Husbands, love your wives, even as Christ also loved the church, and [b]gave himself for it;

26 That he might [1]sanctify and cleanse it [a]with the washing of water [b]by the word,

27 [a]That he might present it to himself a glorious church, [b]not having spot, or wrinkle, or any such thing; but that it should be holy and without blemish.

28 So ought men to love [1]their wives as their own bodies. He that loveth his wife loveth himself.

29 For no man ever yet hated his own flesh; but nourisheth and cherisheth it, even as the Lord the church:

30 For [a]we are members of his body, of his flesh, and of his bones.

31 [a]For this cause shall a man leave his father and mother, and shall be joined unto his wife, and they [b]two shall be one flesh.

32 This is a great mystery: but I speak concerning Christ and the church.

33 Nevertheless [a]let every one of you in particular so love his wife even as himself; and the wife *see* that she [b]reverence[1] *her* husband.

## CHAPTER 6

CHILDREN, [a]obey your parents in the Lord: for this is right.

2 [a]Honour thy father and mother; which is the first commandment with promise;

3 That it may be well with thee, and thou mayest live long on the earth.

4 And, [a]ye fathers, provoke not your children to wrath: but [b]bring them up in the [1]nurture and admonition of the Lord.

5 [a]Servants, be obedient to them that are *your* masters according to the flesh, [b]with fear and trembling, [c]in [1]singleness of your heart, as unto Christ;

---

[1] *training*   6:5 [a] [1 Tim. 6:1] [b] 2 Cor. 7:15 [c] 1 Chr. 29:17
[1] *sincerity*

6 [a]Not with eyeservice, as men-pleasers; but as the servants of Christ, doing the will of God from the heart;

7 With good will doing service, as to the Lord, and not to men:

8 [a]Knowing that whatsoever good thing any man doeth, the same shall he receive of the Lord, whether *he be* [1]bond or free.

9 And, ye masters, do the same things unto them, [1]forbearing threatening: knowing that your [a]Master also is in heaven; [b]neither is there respect of persons with him.

10 Finally, my brethren, be strong in the Lord, and in the power of his might.

11 [a]Put on the whole armour of God, that ye may be able to stand against the [1]wiles of the devil.

12 For we wrestle not against flesh and blood, but against [a]principalities, against powers, against [b]the rulers of the darkness of this [1]world, against [2]spiritual wickedness in high *places.*

13 [a]Wherefore [1]take unto you the whole armour of God, that ye may be able to withstand [b]in the evil day, and having done all, to stand.

14 Stand therefore, [a]having [1]your loins girt about with truth, and [b]having on the breastplate of righteousness;

15 [a]And your feet shod with the preparation of the gospel of peace;

16 Above all, taking [a]the shield of faith, wherewith ye shall be able to quench all the fiery darts of the [1]wicked.

17 And [a]take the helmet of salvation, and [b]the sword of the Spirit, which is the word of God:

18 [a]Praying always with all prayer and supplication in the Spirit, and [b]watching thereunto with all perseverance and [c]supplication for all saints;

19 And for me, that utterance may be given unto me, [a]that I may open my mouth boldly, to make known the [1]mystery of the gospel,

20 For which [a]I am an ambassador in [1]bonds: that therein I may speak boldly, as I ought to speak.

21 But that ye also may know my affairs, *and* how I do, [a]Tychicus, a beloved brother and [b]faithful minister in the Lord, shall make known to you all things:

22 [a]Whom I have sent unto you for the same purpose, that ye might know our affairs, and *that* he might [b]comfort your hearts.

23 Peace *be* to the brethren, and love with faith, from God the Father and the Lord Jesus Christ.

24 Grace *be* with all them that love our Lord Jesus Christ in sincerity. Amen.

---

**Cross-references (center column):**

6:6 [a] Col. 3:22
6:8 [a] Rom. 2:6
[1] *slave*
6:9 [a] Col. 4:1
[b] Rom. 2:11
[1] *giving up*
6:11 [a] [2 Cor. 6:7]
[1] *schemes*
6:12 [a] Rom. 8:38
[b] Luke 22:53
[1] *age* [2] *spiritual hosts of*
6:13 [a] [2 Cor. 10:4] [b] Eph. 5:16
[1] *take up*
6:14 [a] Is. 11:5 [b] Is. 59:17 [1] *girded your waist with*

6:15 [a] Is. 52:7
6:16 [a] 1 John 5:4
[1] *wicked one*
6:17 [a] 1 Thess. 5:8
[b] [Heb. 4:12]
6:18 [a] Luke 18:1
[b] [Matt. 26:41]
[c] Phil. 1:4
6:19 [a] Col. 4:3
[1] *hidden truth*
6:20 [a] 2 Cor. 5:20
[1] *chains*
6:21 [a] Acts 20:4
[b] 1 Cor. 4:1, 2
6:22 [a] Col. 4:8
[b] 2 Cor. 1:6

# THE EPISTLE OF PAUL THE APOSTLE TO THE
# PHILIPPIANS

Paul writes a thank-you note to the believers at Philippi for their help in his hour of need, and he uses the occasion to send along some instruction on Christian unity. His central thought is simple: Only in Christ are real unity and joy possible. With Christ as your model of humility and service, you can enjoy a oneness of purpose, attitude, goal, and labor—a truth which Paul illustrates from his own life, and one the Philippians desperately need to hear. Within their own ranks, fellow workers in the Philippian church are at odds, hindering the work in proclaiming new life in Christ. Because of this, Paul exhorts the church to "stand fast . . . be of the same mind . . . rejoice in the Lord alway . . . but in every thing by prayer and supplication with thanksgiving let your requests be made known . . . and the peace of God, which passeth all understanding, shall keep your hearts and minds through Christ Jesus" (4:1, 2, 4, 6, 7).

This epistle is called *Pros Philippesious*, "To the Philippians." The church at Philippi was the first church Paul founded in Macedonia.

## CHAPTER 1

PAUL and Timotheus, the servants of Jesus Christ, to all the saints in Christ Jesus which are at Philippi, with the ¹bishops and ªdeacons:

2 Grace *be* unto you, and peace, from God our Father, and *from* the Lord Jesus Christ.

3 ªI thank my God upon every remembrance of you,

4 Always in ªevery prayer of mine for you all making request with joy,

5 ªFor your fellowship in the gospel from the first day until now;

6 Being confident of this very thing, that he which hath begun ªa good work in you will ¹perform *it* until the day of Jesus Christ:

7 Even as it is ¹meet for me to think this of you all, because I have you in my heart; inasmuch as both in my ²bonds, and in the defence and confirmation of the gospel, ye all are ³partakers of my grace.

8 For God is my ¹record, how greatly I long after you all in the ²bowels of Jesus Christ.

9 And this I pray, that your love may abound yet more and more in knowledge and *in* all ¹judgment;

10 That ye may approve things that are excellent; that ye may be sincere and without offence till the day of Christ;

11 Being filled with the fruits of righteousness, ªwhich are by Jesus Christ, ᵇunto the glory and praise of God.

12 But I ¹would ye should understand, brethren, that the things *which happened* unto me have ²fallen out rather unto the furtherance of the gospel;

13 So that my ¹bonds in Christ are ²manifest ªin all the ³palace, and in ⁴all other *places;*

14 And ¹many of the brethren in the Lord, ²waxing confident by my ³bonds, are much more bold to speak the word without fear.

15 Some indeed preach Christ even of envy and strife; and some also of good will:

16 The one preach Christ of ¹contention, not sincerely, supposing to add affliction to my ²bonds:

17 But the other of love, knowing that I am ¹set for the defence of the gospel.

18 What then? notwithstanding, every way, whether in pretence, or in truth, Christ is preached; and I therein do rejoice, yea, and will rejoice.

19 For I know that ªthis shall turn to my salvation through your prayer, and the supply of the Spirit of Jesus Christ,

20 According to my earnest expectation and *my* hope, that in nothing I shall be ashamed, but *that* ªwith all boldness, as always, *so* now also Christ shall be magnified in my body, whether *it be* by life, ᵇor by death.

21 For to me to live *is* Christ, and to die *is* gain.

22 But if I live in the flesh, this ¹*is* the fruit of my labour: yet what I shall choose I ²wot not.

23 For I am ¹in a strait betwixt two, having a ªdesire to depart, and to be with Christ; which is ᵇfar better:

24 Nevertheless to abide in the flesh *is* more needful for you.

25 And having this confidence, I know that I shall abide and continue with you all for your ¹furtherance and joy of faith;

26 That ªyour rejoicing may be more abundant in Jesus Christ for me by my coming to you again.

27 Only ªlet your ¹conversation be as it becometh the gospel of Christ:

---

1:1 ª [1 Tim. 3:8–13] ¹ overseers
1:3 ª 1 Cor. 1:4
1:4 ª Eph. 1:16; 1 Thess. 1:2
1:5 ª [Rom. 12:13]
1:6 ª [John 6:29] ¹ complete
1:7 ¹ right ² chains ³ sharers
1:8 ¹ witness ² affection
1:9 ¹ discernment
1:11 ª [Eph. 2:10]; Col. 1:6 ᵇ John 15:8
1:12 ¹ want you to know ² turned out
1:13 ª Phil. 4:22 ¹ chains are for Christ ² Well known ³ palace guard, Gr. praetorion ⁴ all the rest

1:14 ¹ most ² becoming ³ chains
1:16 ¹ selfish ambition ² chains
1:17 ¹ appointed
1:19 ª Job 13:16, LXX
1:20 ª Eph. 6:19, 20 ᵇ [Rom. 14:8]
1:22 ¹ Will mean fruit from ² know
1:23 ª [2 Cor. 5:2, 8]; 2 Tim. 4:6 ᵇ [Ps. 16:11] ¹ hard-pressed between the two
1:25 ¹ progress
1:26 ª 2 Cor. 1:14
1:27 ª Eph. 4:1 ¹ conduct be worthy of

that whether I come and see you, or else be absent, I may hear of your affairs, that ye stand fast in one spirit, [b]with one mind [c]striving together for the faith of the gospel;

28 And in [1]nothing terrified by your adversaries: which is to them [2]an evident token of [3]perdition, but to you of salvation, and that of God.

29 For unto you [a]it is given in the behalf of Christ, [b]not only to believe on him, but also to [c]suffer for his sake;

30 [a]Having the same conflict [b]which ye saw in me, and now hear *to be* in me.

## CHAPTER 2

IF *there be* therefore any [1]consolation in Christ, if any [2]comfort of love, if any fellowship of the Spirit, if any [a]bowels[3] and mercies,

2 [a]Fulfil ye my joy, [b]that ye be likeminded, having the same love, *being* of [c]one accord, of one mind.

3 [a]Let nothing *be done* through strife or vainglory; but [b]in lowliness of mind let each esteem other better than themselves.

4 [a]Look not every man on his own things, but every man also on the [1]things of [b]others.

5 [a]Let this mind be in you, which was also in Christ Jesus:

6 Who, [a]being in the form of God, thought it not robbery to be equal with God:

7 [a]But made himself of no reputation, and took upon him the form [b]of a servant, and [c]was[1] made in the likeness of men:

8 And being found in [1]fashion as a man, he humbled himself, and [a]became [b]obedient unto death, even the death of the cross.

9 [a]Wherefore God also [b]hath highly exalted him, and [c]given him a name which is above every name:

10 [a]That at the name of Jesus every knee should bow, of [1]*things* in heaven, and [1]*things* in earth, and [1]*things* under the earth;

11 And [a]*that* every tongue should confess that Jesus Christ *is* Lord, to the glory of God the Father.

12 Wherefore, my beloved, [a]as ye have always obeyed, not as in my presence only, but now much more in my absence, [b]work out your own salvation with [c]fear and trembling.

13 For [a]it is God which worketh in you both to will and to do [b]of [1]*his* good pleasure.

14 Do all things [a]without [1]murmurings and [b]disputings:

15 That ye may be blameless and [1]harmless, the [2]sons of God, without [3]rebuke, in the midst of a crooked and perverse [4]nation, among whom ye shine as [a]lights in the world;

16 Holding [1]forth the word of life; that [a]I may rejoice in the day of Christ, that [b]I have not run in vain, neither laboured in [c]vain.

17 Yea, and if [a]I be [1]offered upon the sacrifice [b]and service of your faith, [c]I joy, and rejoice with you all.

18 For the same cause also do ye joy, and rejoice with me.

19 But I trust in the Lord Jesus to send [a]Timotheus shortly unto you, that I also may be [1]of good comfort, when I know your [2]state.

20 For I have no man [a]likeminded, who will [1]naturally care for your state.

21 For all seek their own, not the things which are Jesus Christ's.

22 But ye know [1]the proof of him, [a]that, as a son with the father, he hath served with me in the gospel.

23 Him therefore I hope to send [1]presently, so soon as I shall see how it will go with me.

24 But I trust in the Lord that I also myself shall come shortly.

25 Yet I supposed it necessary to send to you [a]Epaphroditus, my brother, and [1]companion in labour, and [b]fellowsoldier, [c]but your messenger, and [d]he that ministered to my [2]wants.

26 [a]For he [1]longed after you all, and was [2]full of heaviness, because that ye had heard that he had been sick.

27 For indeed he was sick nigh unto death: but God had mercy on him; and not on him only, but on me also, lest I should have sorrow upon sorrow.

28 I sent him therefore the more carefully, that, when ye see him again, ye may rejoice, and that I may be the less sorrowful.

29 Receive him therefore in the Lord with all gladness; and hold such in [1]reputation:

30 Because for the work of Christ he was nigh unto death, not regarding his life, [a]to supply your lack of service toward me.

## CHAPTER 3

FINALLY, my brethren, [a]rejoice in the Lord. To write the same things to you, to me indeed *is* not [1]grievous, but for you *it is* safe.

2 [a]Beware of dogs, beware of [b]evil workers, [c]beware of the [1]concision.

3 For we are [a]the circumcision, [b]which worship God in the [1]spirit, and rejoice in Christ Jesus, and have no confidence in the flesh.

4 Though [a]I might also have confidence in the flesh. If any other man thinketh that he hath whereof he might trust in the flesh, I [b]more:

### Center references

1:27 [b] Eph. 4:3
[c] Jude 3
1:28 [1] *no way* [2] *a proof* [3] *destruction*
1:29 [a] [Matt. 5:11, 12] [b] Eph. 2:8 [c] [2 Tim. 3:12]
1:30 [a] Col. 1:29; 2:1 [b] Acts 16:19–40
2:1 [a] Col. 3:12 [1] *encouragement* [2] *consolation* [3] *affection*
2:2 [a] John 3:29 [b] Rom. 12:16 [c] Phil. 4:2
2:3 [a] Gal. 5:26 [b] Rom. 12:10
2:4 [a] 1 Cor. 13:5 [b] Rom. 15:1, 2 [1] *interests*
2:5 [a] [Matt. 11:29]
2:6 [a] 2 Cor. 4:4
2:7 [a] Ps. 22:6 [b] Is. 42:1 [c] [John 1:14] [1] *emptied himself of his privileges*
2:8 [a] Matt. 26:39 [b] Heb. 5:8 [1] *appearance*
2:9 [a] Heb. 2:9 [b] Acts 2:33 [c] Eph. 1:21
2:10 [a] Is. 45:23 [1] *those*
2:11 [a] John 13:13
2:12 [a] Phil. 1:5, 6; 4:15 [b] John 6:27, 29 [c] Eph. 6:5
2:13 [a] Heb. 13:20, 21 [b] Eph. 1:5 [1] *according to*
2:14 [a] 1 Pet. 4:9 [b] Rom. 14:1 [1] *grumbling*
2:15 [a] Matt. 5:15, 16 [1] *innocent* [2] *children* [3] *fault* [4] *generation*
2:16 [a] 2 Cor. 1:14 [b] Gal. 2:2 [c] 1 Thess. 3:5 [1] *fast to*
2:17 [a] 2 Tim. 4:6 [b] Rom. 15:16 [c] 2 Cor. 7:4 [1] *poured out as a drink offering on the*
2:19 [a] Rom. 16:21 [1] *encouraged* [2] *condition*
2:20 [a] 2 Tim. 3:10 [1] *sincerely*
2:22 [a] 1 Cor. 4:17 [1] *his proven character*
2:23 [1] *at once*
2:25 [a] Phil. 4:18 [b] Philem. 2 [c] 2 Cor. 8:23 [d] 2 Cor. 11:9 [1] *fellow worker* [2] *need*
2:26 [a] Phil. 1:8
2:30 [a] 1 Cor. 16:17 [1] *high esteem*　　2:29 [1] *high esteem*　3:1 [a] 1 Thess. 5:16 [1] *tedious*
3:2 [a] Gal. 5:15 [b] Ps. 119:115 [c] Rom. 2:28 [1] *mutilation*
3:3 [a] Deut. 30:6 [b] Rom. 7:6 [1] *Or Spirit*　3:4 [a] 2 Cor. 5:16; 11:18 [b] 2 Cor. 11:22, 23

5 Circumcised the eighth day, of the stock of Israel, [a]of the tribe of Benjamin, [b]an Hebrew of the Hebrews; as touching the law, [c]a Pharisee;

6 Concerning zeal, [a]persecuting the church; touching the righteousness which is in the law, blameless.

7 But [a]what things were gain to me, those I counted loss for Christ.

8 Yea doubtless, and I count all things *but* loss [a]for the excellency of the knowledge of Christ Jesus my Lord: for whom I have suffered the loss of all things, and do count them *but* [1]dung, that I may win Christ,

9 And be found in him, not having [a]mine own righteousness, which is of the law, but [b]that which is through the faith of Christ, the righteousness which is of God by faith:

10 That I may know him, and the [a]power of his resurrection, and [b]the fellowship of his sufferings, being made conformable unto his death;

11 If by any means I might [a]attain[1] unto the resurrection of the dead.

12 Not as though I had already [a]attained,[1] either were already [b]perfect: but I [2]follow after, if that I may [3]apprehend that for which also I am apprehended of Christ Jesus.

13 Brethren, I count not myself to have [a]apprehended: but *this* one thing *I do,* [a]forgetting those things which are behind, and [b]reaching [9]forth unto those things which are [3]before,

14 [a]I press toward the [1]mark for the prize of [b]the [2]high calling of God in Christ Jesus.

15 Let us therefore, as many as be [a]perfect,[1] [b]be thus minded: and if in any thing ye be otherwise minded, [c]God shall reveal even this unto you.

16 Nevertheless, [1]whereto we have already [2]attained, [a]let us walk [b]by the same rule, let us [3]mind the same thing.

17 Brethren, [a]be[1] followers together of me, and [2]mark them which walk so as [b]ye have us for [3]an ensample.

18 (For many walk, of whom I have told you often, and now tell you even weeping, *that they are* [a]the enemies of the cross of Christ:

19 [a]Whose end *is* destruction, [b]whose God *is their* belly, and [c]*whose* glory *is* in their shame, [d]who [1]mind earthly things.)

20 For [a]our [1]conversation is in heaven; [b]from whence also we [c]look for the Saviour, the Lord Jesus Christ:

21 [a]Who shall change our vile body, that it may be fashioned [b]like unto his glorious body, [c]according to the working whereby he is able even to [d]subdue all things unto himself.

## CHAPTER 4

**T**HEREFORE, my brethren dearly beloved and [a]longed for, [b]my joy

and crown, so [c]stand fast in the Lord, *my* dearly beloved.

2 I beseech Euodias, and beseech Syntyche, [a]that they be of the same mind in the Lord.

3 And I intreat thee also, true [1]yokefellow, help those women which [a]laboured with me in the gospel, with Clement also, and *with* other my fellowlabourers, whose names *are* in [b]the book of life.

4 [a]Rejoice in the Lord alway: *and* again I say, Rejoice.

5 Let your [1]moderation be known unto all men. [a]The Lord *is* at hand.

6 [a]Be [1]careful for nothing; but in every thing by prayer and supplication with [b]thanksgiving let your requests be made known unto God.

7 And [a]the peace of God, which passeth all understanding, shall [1]keep your hearts and minds through Christ Jesus.

8 Finally, brethren, whatsoever things are [a]true, whatsoever things *are* [b]honest,[1] whatsoever things *are* [c]just, [d]whatsoever things *are* pure, whatsoever things *are* [e]lovely, whatsoever things *are* of good report; if *there be* any virtue, and if *there be* [2]any praise, [3]think on these things.

9 Those things, which ye have both learned, and received, and heard, and seen in me, do: and [a]the God of peace shall be with you.

10 But I rejoiced in the Lord greatly, that now at the last [a]your [1]care of me hath [2]flourished again; [3]wherein ye were also careful, but ye lacked opportunity.

11 Not that I speak in [1]respect of want: for I have learned, in whatsoever state I am, [a]*therewith* to be content.

12 [a]I know both how to [b]be abased, and I know how to [2]abound: every where and in all things I am instructed both to be full and to be hungry, both to abound and to suffer need.

13 I can do all things [a]through Christ which strengtheneth me.

14 Notwithstanding ye have well done, that [a]ye did [1]communicate with my affliction.

15 Now ye Philippians know also, that in the beginning of the gospel, when I departed from Macedonia, [a]no church [1]communicated with me as concerning giving and receiving, but ye only.

16 For even in Thessalonica ye sent once and again unto my necessity.

17 Not because I [1]desire a gift: but I [1]desire [a]fruit that may abound to your account.

3:5 [a] Rom. 11:1
[b] 2 Cor. 11:22
[c] Acts 23:6
3:6 [a] Acts 8:3;
22:4, 5; 26:9–11
3:7 [a] Matt. 13:44
3:8 [a] Jer. 9:23
[1] *rubbish*
3:9 [a] Rom. 10:3
[b] Rom. 1:17
3:10 [a] Eph. 1:19, 20
[b] [Rom. 6:3–5]
3:11 [a] Acts 26:6–8
[1] Lit. *arrive at*
3:12 [a] [1 Tim.
6:12, 19] [b] Heb.
12:23 [1] *obtained it* [2] *press on* [3] *lay hold of*
3:13 [a] Luke 9:62
[b] Heb. 6:1 [1] *laid hold of it* [2] *forward* [3] *ahead*
3:14 [a] 2 Tim. 4:7
[b] Heb. 3:1 [1] *goal*
[2] *upward*
3:15 [a] 1 Cor. 2:6
[b] Gal. 5:10 [c] Hos.
6:3 [1] *mature*
3:16 [a] Gal. 6:16
[b] Rom. 12:16; 15:5
[1] *to the degree that* [2] *arrived*
[3] *be of the same mind*
3:17 [a] [1 Cor. 4:16;
11:1] [b] Titus 2:7, 8
[1] *join in following my example*
[a] *note* [3] *a pattern*
3:18 [a] Gal. 1:7
3:19 [a] 2 Cor. 11:15
[b] 1 Tim. 6:5 [c] Hos.
4:7 [d] Rom. 8:5
[1] *set their mind on*
3:20 [a] Eph. 2:6, 19
[b] Acts 1:11 [c] 1 Cor.
1:7 [1] *citizenship*
3:21 [a] [1 Cor.
15:43–53] [b] 1 John
3:2 [c] Eph. 1:19
[d] [1 Cor. 15:28]
4:1 [a] Phil. 1:8
[b] 2 Cor. 1:14 [c] Phil.
1:27
4:2 [a] Phil. 2:2; 3:16
4:3 [a] Rom. 16:3
[b] Luke 10:20
[1] *companion*
4:4 [a] Rom. 12:12
4:5 [a] [James 5:7–
9] [1] *gentleness*
4:6 [a] Matt. 6:25
[b] [1 Thess. 5:17, 18]
[1] *anxious*
4:7 [a] [John 14:27]
[1] *guard*
4:8 [a] Eph. 4:25
[b] 2 Cor. 8:21
[c] Deut. 16:20
[d] 1 Thess. 5:22
[e] 1 Cor. 13:4–7
[1] *noble* [2] *anything praiseworthy*
[3] *meditate*
4:9 [a] Rom. 15:33
4:10 [a] 2 Cor.
11:9 [1] *concern*

[2] *revived* [3] *though you surely did care* 4:11 [a] 2 Cor. 9:8;
1 Tim. 6:6, 8; Heb. 13:5 [1] *regard of need* 4:12 [a] 1 Cor.
4:11 [1] *live humbly* [2] *live in prosperity* 4:13 [a] John 15:5
4:14 [a] Phil. 1:7 [1] *share in* 4:15 [a] 2 Cor. 11:8, 9 [1] *shared*
4:17 [a] Titus 3:14 [1] *seek*

18 But I [1]have all, and abound: I am full, having received of [a]Epaphroditus the things *which were sent* from you, [b]an [2]odour of a sweet smell, [c]a sacrifice acceptable, wellpleasing to God.

19 But my God [a]shall supply all your need according to his riches in glory by Christ Jesus.

4:18 [a] Phil. 2:25
[b] Heb. 13:16 [c] Rom. 12:1; 2 Cor. 9:12 [1] Or *have received all*
[2] *aroma*

4:19 [a] Ps. 23:1;
2 Cor. 9:8

4:20 [a] Rom. 16:27
4:21 [a] Gal. 1:2 [1] *Greet*
4:22 [1] *greet*
[2] *especially*

20 [a]Now unto God and our Father *be* glory for ever and ever. Amen.

21 [1]Salute every saint in Christ Jesus. The brethren [a]which are with me greet you.

22 All the saints [1]salute you, [2]chiefly they that are of Caesar's household.

23 The grace of our Lord Jesus Christ *be* with you all. Amen.

# THE EPISTLE OF PAUL THE APOSTLE TO THE
# COLOSSIANS

If Ephesians can be labeled the epistle portraying the "church of Christ," then Colossians must surely be the "Christ of the church." Ephesians focuses on the body; Colossians focuses on the Head. Like Ephesians, the little Book of Colossians divides neatly in half with the first portion doctrinal (1 and 2) and the second practical (3 and 4). Paul's purpose is to show that Christ is preeminent—first and foremost in everything—and the Christian's life should reflect that priority. Because believers are rooted in Him, alive in Him, hidden in Him, and complete in Him, it is utterly inconsistent for them to live life without Him. Clothed in His love, with His peace ruling in their hearts, they are equipped to make Christ first in every area of life.

This epistle became known as *Pros Kolossaeis*, "To the Colossians," because of 1:2. Paul also wanted it to be read in the neighboring church at Laodicea (4:16).

## CHAPTER 1

PAUL, ªan apostle of Jesus Christ by the will of God, and Timotheus *our* brother,

2 To the saints ªand faithful brethren in Christ which are at Colosse: ᵇGrace *be* unto you, and peace, from God our Father and the Lord Jesus Christ.

3 ªWe give thanks to God and the Father of our Lord Jesus Christ, praying always for you,

4 ªSince we heard of your faith in Christ Jesus, and of ᵇthe love *which ye have* to all the saints,

5 For the hope ªwhich is laid up for you in heaven, whereof ye heard before in the word of the truth of the gospel;

6 Which is come unto you, ªas *it is* in all the world; and ᵇbringeth forth fruit, as *it doth* also in you, since the day ye heard *of it,* and knew ᶜthe grace of God in truth:

7 As ye also learned of ªEpaphras our dear fellowservant, who is ¹for you ᵇa faithful minister of Christ;

8 Who also declared unto us your ªlove in the Spirit.

9 ªFor this cause we also, since the day we heard *it,* do not cease to pray for you, and to desire ᵇthat ye might be filled with ᶜthe knowledge of his will ᵈin all wisdom and spiritual understanding;

10 ªThat ye might walk worthy of the Lord ᵇunto all pleasing, ᶜbeing fruitful in every good work, and increasing in the ᵈknowledge of God;

11 ªStrengthened with all might, according to his glorious power, ᵇunto all patience and longsuffering ᶜwith joyfulness;

12 ªGiving thanks unto the Father, which hath ¹made us meet to be partakers of ᵇthe inheritance of the saints in ²light:

13 Who hath delivered us from ªthe

power of darkness, ᵇand hath ¹translated *us* into the kingdom of ²his dear Son:

14 ªIn whom we have redemption through his blood, *even* the forgiveness of sins:

15 Who is ªthe image of the invisible God, ᵇthe ¹firstborn ²of every creature:

16 For ªby him were all things created, that are in heaven, and that are ¹in earth, visible and invisible, whether *they be* thrones, or ᵇdominions, or ªprincipalities, or ³powers: all things were created ᶜby him, and for him:

17 ªAnd he is before all things, and ¹by him ᵇall things consist.

18 And ªhe is the head of the body, the church: who is the beginning, ᵇthe firstborn from the dead; that in all *things* he might have the preeminence.

19 For it pleased *the Father* that ªin him should all fulness dwell;

20 And, ªhaving made peace through the blood of his cross, ᵇby him to reconcile ᶜall things unto himself; by him, *I say,* whether *they be* things ¹in earth, or things in heaven.

21 And you, ªthat were sometime alienated and enemies in *your* mind ᵇby wicked works, yet now hath he ᶜreconciled

22 ªIn the body of his flesh through death, ᵇto present you holy and unblameable and unreproveable in his sight:

23 If ye continue in the faith ªgrounded and ¹settled, and *be* ᵇnot moved away from the hope of the gospel, which ye have heard, ᶜand which was preached to every creature which is under heaven; ᵈwhereof I Paul am made a minister;

1:1 ª Eph. 1:1
1:2 ª 1 Cor. 4:17 ᵇ Gal. 1:3
1:3 ª 1 Cor. 1:4; Eph. 1:16; Phil. 1:3
1:4 ª Eph. 1:15 ᵇ [Heb. 6:10]
1:5 ª [1 Pet. 1:4]
1:6 ª Matt. 24:14 ᵇ John 15:16 ᶜ Eph. 3:2
1:7 ª Col. 4:12; Philem. 23 ᵇ 1 Cor. 4:1, 2; 2 Cor. 11:23 ¹ *on your behalf*
1:8 ª Rom. 15:30
1:9 ª Eph. 1:15–17 ᵇ 1 Cor. 1:5 ᶜ [Rom. 12:2]; Eph. 5:17 ᵈ Eph. 1:8
1:10 ª Eph. 4:1 ᵇ 1 Thess. 4:1 ᶜ Heb. 13:21 ᵈ 2 Pet. 3:18
1:11 ª [Eph. 3:16; 6:10] ᵇ Eph. 4:2 ᶜ [Acts 5:41]
1:12 ª [Eph. 5:20] ᵇ Eph. 1:11 ¹ *qualified us to* ² *the light*
1:13 ª Eph. 6:12 ᵇ 2 Pet. 1:11 ¹ *transferred* ² Lit. *the Son of his love*
1:14 ª Eph. 1:7
1:15 ª 2 Cor. 4:4 ᵇ Rev. 3:14 ¹ *First in rank* ² *over*
1:16 ª Heb. 1:2, 3 ᵇ [Eph. 1:20, 21] ᶜ Heb. 2:10 ¹ *on* ² *rulers* ³ *authorities*
1:17 ª [John 17:5] ᵇ Heb. 1:3 ¹ Lit. *in him*
1:18 ª Eph. 1:22 ᵇ Rev. 1:5
1:19 ª John 1:16
1:20 ª Eph. 2:14

ᵇ 2 Cor. 5:18 ᶜ Eph. 1:10 ¹ *on* 1:21 ª [Eph. 2:1] ᵇ Titus 1:15 ᶜ 2 Cor. 5:18, 19 1:22 ª 2 Cor. 5:18 ᵇ [Eph. 5:27] 1:23 ª Eph. 3:17 ᵇ [John 15:6] ᶜ Col. 1:6 ᵈ Col. 1:25 ¹ *steadfast*

24 [a]Who now rejoice in my sufferings [b]for you, and fill up [c]that which is [1]behind of the afflictions of Christ in my flesh for [d]his body's sake, which is the church:

25 Whereof I am made a minister, according to [a]the [1]dispensation of God which is given to me for you, to fulfil the word of God;

26 *Even* [a]the [1]mystery which hath been hid from ages and from generations, [b]but now [2]is made manifest to his saints:

27 [a]To whom God [1]would make known what *is* [b]the riches of the glory of this mystery among the Gentiles; which is [c]Christ in you, [d]the hope of glory:

28 Whom we preach, [a]warning every man, and teaching every man in all wisdom; [b]that we may present every man perfect in Christ Jesus:

29 Whereunto I also labour, striving according to his working, which worketh in me [a]mightily.

## CHAPTER 2

FOR I [1]would that ye knew what great [a]conflict I have [2]for you, and *for* them at Laodicea, and *for* as many as have not seen my face in the flesh;

2 That their hearts might be [1]comforted, being knit together in love, [2]and unto all riches of the full assurance of understanding, to the [3]acknowledgement of the mystery of God, [4]and of the Father, and of Christ;

3 [a]In whom are hid all the treasures of wisdom and knowledge.

4 And this I say, [a]lest any man should [1]beguile you with [2]enticing words.

5 For [a]though I be absent in the flesh, yet am I with you in the spirit, joying and beholding [b]your [1]order, and the [c]stedfastness of your faith in Christ.

6 [a]As ye have therefore received Christ Jesus the Lord, *so* walk ye in him:

7 [a]Rooted and built up in him, and stablished in the faith, as ye have been taught, abounding therein with thanksgiving.

8 Beware lest any man [1]spoil you through philosophy and [2]vain deceit, [3]after [a]the tradition of men, [3]after the [b]rudiments[4] of the world, and not [3]after Christ.

9 For [a]in him dwelleth all the fulness of the Godhead bodily.

10 And ye are complete in him, which is the [a]head of all [1]principality and power:

11 In whom also ye are [a]circumcised with the circumcision made without hands, in [b]putting off the body of the sins of the flesh by the circumcision of Christ:

12 [a]Buried with him in baptism, wherein also ye are risen with *him* through [b]the faith of the operation of God, [c]who hath raised him from the dead.

13 And you, being dead in your sins and the uncircumcision of your flesh, hath he [1]quickened together with him, having forgiven you all trespasses;

14 [a]Blotting out the [1]handwriting of ordinances that was against us, which was contrary to us, and took it out of the way, nailing it to his cross;

15 *And* [a]having [1]spoiled [b]principalities and powers, he made a [2]shew of them openly, triumphing over them in it.

16 Let no man therefore [a]judge you in [1]meat, or in drink, or in respect [2]of an holyday, or of the new moon, or of the sabbath *days:*

17 [a]Which are a shadow of things to come; but the [b]body *is* of Christ.

18 Let no man [1]beguile you of your reward [2]in a voluntary humility and worshipping of angels, intruding into those things which he hath not seen, vainly puffed up by his fleshly mind,

19 And not [1]holding [a]the Head, from which all the body by joints and [2]bands having nourishment ministered, and knit together, [b]increaseth with the increase of God.

20 Wherefore if ye be [a]dead with Christ from the [1]rudiments of the world, [b]why, as though living in the world, are ye subject to [2]ordinances,

21 ([a]Touch not; taste not; handle not;

22 Which all are to perish with the using;) [a]after[1] the commandments and doctrines of men?

23 [a]Which things have indeed [1]a shew of wisdom in [2]will worship, and humility, and [3]neglecting of the body; [4]not in any honour to the satisfying of the flesh.

## CHAPTER 3

IF ye then be [a]risen with Christ, seek those things which are above, where [b]Christ sitteth on the right hand of God.

2 Set your [1]affection on things above, not on things on the [a]earth.

3 [a]For ye are dead, [b]and your life is hid with Christ in God.

4 [a]When Christ, *who is* [b]our life, shall appear, then shall ye also appear with him [c]in glory.

5 [a]Mortify[1] therefore [b]your members which are upon the earth; [c]fornication, uncleanness, [2]inordinate

1:24 [a] 2 Cor. 7:4 [b] Eph. 3:1, 13 [c] [2 Cor. 1:5; 12:15] [d] Eph. 1:23 [1] *lacking*
1:25 [a] Gal. 2:7 [1] *stewardship*
1:26 [a] [1 Cor. 2:7] [b] [2 Tim. 1:10] [1] *hidden truth* or *secret* [2] *has been revealed*
1:27 [a] 2 Cor. 2:14 [b] Rom. 9:23 [c] [Rom. 8:10, 11] [d] 1 Tim. 1:1 [1] *willed to*
1:28 [a] Acts 20:20 [b] Eph. 5:27
1:29 [a] Eph. 3:7
2:1 [a] Phil. 1:30 [1] *want you to know* [2] *on your behalf*
2:2 [1] *encouraged* [2] *and* attaining to [3] *knowledge* [4] *both*
2:3 [a] 1 Cor. 1:24, 30
2:4 [a] Rom. 16:18 [1] *deceive* [2] *persuasive*
2:5 [a] 1 Thess. 2:17 [b] 1 Cor. 14:40 [c] 1 Pet. 5:9 [1] *good order*
2:6 [a] 1 Thess. 4:1
2:7 [a] Eph. 2:21
2:8 [a] Gal. 1:14 [b] Gal. 4:3, 9, 10 [1] *plunder you* or *take you captive* [2] *empty* [3] *according to* [4] *basic principles*
2:9 [a] [John 1:14]
2:10 [a] [Eph. 1:20, 21] [1] *rule and authority*
2:11 [a] Deut. 10:16 [b] Rom. 6:6; 7:24
2:12 [a] Rom. 6:4 [b] Eph. 1:19, 20 [c] Acts 2:24
2:13 [1] *made alive*
2:14 [a] [Eph. 2:15, 16] [1] *certificate of debt with its decrees*
2:15 [a] [Is. 53:12] [b] Eph. 6:12 [1] *disarmed* [2] *spectacle*
2:16 [a] Rom. 14:3 [1] *food* [2] *to a feast day*
2:17 [a] Heb. 8:5; 10:1 [1] *substance*
2:18 [1] *defraud* [2] *by delighting in false humility*
2:19 [a] Eph. 4:15 [b] Eph. 1:23; 4:16 [1] *holding fast to* [2] *ligaments*
2:20 [a] Rom. 6:2–5 [b] Gal. 4:3, 9
[1] *basic principles* [2] *rules* 2:21 [a] 1 Tim. 4:3 2:22 [a] Titus 1:14 [1] *according to* 2:23 [a] 1 Tim. 4:8 [1] *an appearance* [2] *self-imposed religion* [3] *severe treatment* [4] *but are of no value against the indulgence of* 3:1 [a] Col. 2:12 [b] Eph. 1:20 3:2 [a] [Matt. 6:19–21] [1] *mind* 3:3 [a] [Rom. 6:2] [b] [2 Cor. 5:7] 3:4 [a] [1 John 3:2] [b] John 14:6 [c] 1 Cor. 15:43 3:5 [a] [Rom. 8:13] [b] [Rom. 6:13] [c] Eph. 5:3 [1] *Put to death* [2] *passion*

affection, evil ³concupiscence, and covetousness, ᵈwhich is idolatry:

6 ᵃFor which things' sake the wrath of God cometh on ᵇthe children of disobedience:

7 ᵃIn the which ye also walked some time, when ye lived in them.

8 ᵃBut now ye also put off all these; anger, wrath, malice, blasphemy, filthy communication out of your mouth.

9 Lie not one to another, seeing that ye have put off the old man with his deeds;

10 And have put on the new *man,* which ᵃis renewed in knowledge ᵇafter the image of him that ᶜcreated him:

11 Where there is neither ᵃGreek nor Jew, circumcision nor uncircumcision, Barbarian, Scythian, ¹bond *nor* free: ᵇbut Christ *is* all, and in all.

12 Put on therefore, ᵃas the elect of God, holy and beloved, ᵇbowels¹ of mercies, kindness, humbleness of mind, meekness, longsuffering;

13 ᵃForbearing¹ one another, and forgiving one another, if any man have a quarrel against any: even as Christ forgave you, so also *do* ye.

14 ᵃAnd above all these things ᵇ*put on* ¹charity, which is the ᶜbond of perfectness.

15 And let ᵃthe peace of God rule in your hearts, ᵇto the which also ye are called ᶜin one body; and ᵈbe ye thankful.

16 Let the word of Christ dwell in you richly in all wisdom; teaching and admonishing one another ᵃin psalms and hymns and spiritual songs, singing with grace in your hearts to the Lord.

17 And ᵃwhatsoever ye do in word or deed, *do* all in the name of the Lord Jesus, giving thanks to God and the Father by him.

18 ᵃWives, submit yourselves unto your own husbands, ᵇas it is ¹fit in the Lord.

19 ᵃHusbands, love *your* wives, and be not ᵇbitter against them.

20 ᵃChildren, obey *your* parents ᵇin all things: for this is well pleasing unto the Lord.

21 ᵃFathers, provoke not your children *to anger,* lest they be discouraged.

22 ᵃServants, obey in all things *your* masters according to the flesh; not with eyeservice, as menpleasers; but in ¹singleness of heart, fearing God:

23 ᵃAnd whatsoever ye do, do *it* heartily, as to the Lord, and not unto men;

24 ᵃKnowing that of the Lord ye shall receive the reward of the inheritance: ᵇfor ye serve the Lord Christ.

25 But he that doeth wrong shall receive for the wrong which he hath done: and ᵃthere is no respect of persons.

## CHAPTER 4

MASTERS,ᵃ give unto *your* servants that which is just and ¹equal; knowing that ye also have a Master in heaven.

2 ᵃContinue in prayer, and watch in the same ᵇwith thanksgiving;

3 ᵃWithal¹ praying also for us, that God would ᵇopen unto us a door ²of utterance, to speak ᶜthe mystery of Christ, ᵈfor which I am also in bonds:

4 That I may make it manifest, as I ought to speak.

5 ᵃWalk in ᵇwisdom toward them that are ¹without, ᶜredeeming the time.

6 Let your speech *be* alway ᵃwith grace, ᵇseasoned with salt, ᶜthat ye may know how ye ought to answer every man.

7 All my state shall ᵃTychicus declare unto you, *who is* a beloved brother, and a faithful minister and fellowservant in the Lord:

8 ᵃWhom I have sent unto you for the same purpose, that he might know your ¹estate, and comfort your hearts;

9 With ᵃOnesimus, a faithful and beloved brother, who is *one* of you. They shall make known unto you all things which *are done* here.

10 ᵃAristarchus my fellowprisoner ¹saluteth you, and ᵇMarcus, sister's son to Barnabas, (touching whom ye received commandments: if he come unto you, receive him;)

11 And Jesus, which is called Justus, who are of the circumcision. These only *are my* fellowworkers unto the kingdom of God, which have been a comfort unto me.

12 ᵃEpaphras, who is *one* of you, a servant of Christ, ¹saluteth you, always ᵇlabouring fervently for you in prayers, that ye may stand ᶜperfect and ²complete in all the will of God.

13 For I bear him ¹record, that he hath a great zeal for you, and them *that are* in Laodicea, and them in Hierapolis.

14 ᵃLuke, the beloved physician, and ᵇDemas, greet you.

15 ¹Salute the brethren which are in Laodicea, and Nymphas, and ᵃthe church which is in his house.

16 And when ᵃthis epistle is read among you, cause that it be read also in the church of the Laodiceans; and that ye likewise read the *epistle* from Laodicea.

17 And say to ᵃArchippus, Take heed to ᵇthe ministry which thou hast received in the Lord, that thou fulfil it.

18 ᵃThe salutation by ¹the hand of me Paul. ᵇRemember my ²bonds. Grace *be* with you. Amen.

# THE FIRST EPISTLE OF PAUL THE APOSTLE TO THE
# THESSALONIANS

**P**aul has many pleasant memories of the days he spent with the infant Thessalonian church. Their faith, hope, love, and perseverance in the face of persecution are exemplary. Paul's labors as a spiritual parent to the fledgling church have been richly rewarded, and his affection is visible in every line of his letter.

Paul encourages them to excel in their newfound faith, to increase in their love for one another, and to rejoice, pray, and give thanks always. He closes his letter with instruction regarding the return of the Lord, whose advent signifies hope and comfort for believers both living and dead.

Because this is the first of Paul's two canonical letters to the church at Thessalonica, it received the title *Pros Thessalonikeis A*, the "First to the Thessalonians."

## CHAPTER 1

**P**AUL, and [a]Silvanus, and Timotheus, unto the church of the [b]Thessalonians *which is* in God the Father and *in* the Lord Jesus Christ: Grace *be* unto you, and peace, from God our Father, and the Lord Jesus Christ.

2 [a]We give thanks to God always for you all, making mention of you in our prayers;

3 Remembering without ceasing [a]your work of faith, [b]and labour of love, and patience of hope in our Lord Jesus Christ, in the sight of God and our Father;

4 Knowing, brethren beloved, [a]your election [1]of God.

5 For [a]our gospel came not unto you in word only, but also in power, and [b]in the Holy Ghost, [c]and in much assurance; as ye know what manner of men we were among you for your sake.

6 And [a]ye became followers of us, and of the Lord, having received the word in much affliction, [b]with joy of the Holy Ghost:

7 So that ye were ensamples to all that believe in Macedonia and Achaia.

8 For from you [a]sounded out the word of the Lord not only in Macedonia and Achaia, but also [b]in every place your faith to God-ward is spread abroad; so that we need not to speak any thing.

9 For they themselves [1]shew of us [a]what manner of entering in we had unto you, [b]and how ye turned to God from idols to serve the living and true God;

10 And [a]to wait for his Son from heaven, whom he raised from the dead, *even* Jesus, which delivered us [b]from the wrath to come.

## CHAPTER 2

**F**OR yourselves, brethren, know our [1]entrance in unto you, that it was not in vain:

2 But even after that we had suffered before, and were [1]shamefully entreated, as ye know, at [a]Philippi, we were [b]bold in our God to speak unto you the gospel of God [2]with much contention.

3 [a]For our exhortation *was* not of [1]deceit, nor of uncleanness, nor in [2]guile:

4 But as [a]we were [1]allowed of God [b]to be put in trust with the gospel, even so we speak; [c]not as pleasing men, but God, [d]which [2]trieth our hearts.

5 For [a]neither at any time used we flattering words, as ye know, nor a cloak [1]of covetousness; [b]God *is* witness:

6 [a]Nor of men sought we glory, neither of you, nor *yet* of others, when [b]we might have [1]been [c]burdensome, [d]as the apostles of Christ.

7 But [a]we were gentle among you, even as a [1]nurse cherisheth her children:

8 So being affectionately [1]desirous of you, we were [2]willing [a]to have imparted unto you, not the gospel of God only, but also [b]our own souls, because ye were dear unto us.

9 For ye remember, brethren, our [a]labour and [1]travail: for labouring night and day, [b]because we would not be [2]chargeable unto any of you, we preached unto you the gospel of God.

10 [a]Ye *are* witnesses, and God *also,* [b]how [1]holily and justly and unblameably we behaved ourselves among you that believe:

11 As ye know how we exhorted and comforted and [1]charged every one of you, as a father *doth* his children,

12 [a]That ye would walk worthy of God, [b]who hath called you unto his kingdom and glory.

13 For this cause also thank we God [a]without ceasing, because, when ye

1:1 [a] 1 Pet. 5:12
[b] Acts 17:1–9
1:2 [a] Rom. 1:8
1:3 [a] John 6:29
[b] Rom. 16:6
1:4 [a] Col. 3:12 [1] *by*
1:5 [a] Mark 16:20
[b] 2 Cor. 6:6
[c] Heb. 2:3
1:6 [a] 1 Cor. 4:16;
11:1 [b] Acts 5:41;
13:52
1:8 [a] Rom. 10:18
[b] Rom. 1:8; 16:19
1:9 [a] 1 Thess.
2:1 [b] 1 Cor. 12:2
[1] *declare*
1:10 [a] [Rom. 2:7]
[b] Rom. 5:9
2:1 [1] *coming*
2:2 [a] Acts 14:5;
16:19–24 [b] Acts
17:1–9 [1] *spitefully
treated* [2] *in much
conflict*
2:3 [a] 2 Cor. 7:2
[1] *error* [2] *deceit*
2:4 [a] 1 Cor. 7:25
[b] Titus 1:3 [c] Gal.
1:10 [d] Prov. 17:3
[1] *approved by*
[2] *tests*
2:5 [a] 2 Cor. 2:17
[b] Rom. 1:9 [1] *for*
2:6 [a] 1 Tim.
5:17 [b] 1 Cor.
9:4 [c] 2 Cor. 11:9
[d] 1 Cor. 9:1 [1] *made
demands*
2:7 [a] 1 Cor. 2:3
[1] *nursing mother*
2:8 [a] Rom. 1:11
[b] 2 Cor. 12:15
[1] *longing for*
[2] *well pleased*
2:9 [a] Acts 18:3;
20:34, 35 [b] 2 Cor.
12:13 [1] *toil* [2] *a
burden*
2:10 [a] 1 Thess.
1:5 [b] 2 Cor. 7:2
[1] *devoutly*
2:11 [1] Many mss.
*implored*
2:12 [a] Eph. 4:1 [b] 1 Cor. 1:9   2:13 [a] 1 Thess. 1:2, 3

[b]received the word of God which ye heard of us, ye [1]received *it* [c]not *as* the word of men, but as it is in truth, the word of God, which [2]effectually [d]worketh also in you that believe.

14 For ye, brethren, became [1]followers [a]of the churches of God which in Judaea are in Christ Jesus: for [b]ye also have suffered like things of your own countrymen, even as they *have* of the Jews:

15 [a]Who both killed the Lord Jesus, and [b]their own prophets, and have persecuted us; and they please not God, [c]and are [1]contrary to all men:

16 [a]Forbidding us to speak to the Gentiles that they might be saved, [b]to [1]fill up their sins alway: [c]for the wrath is come upon them to the uttermost.

17 But we, brethren, being taken from you for a short time [a]in presence, not in heart, endeavoured the more abundantly to see your face with great desire.

18 Wherefore we [1]would have come unto you, even I Paul, once and again; but [a]Satan hindered us.

19 For [a]what *is* our hope, or joy, or [b]crown of rejoicing? *Are* not even ye in the [c]presence of our Lord Jesus Christ [d]at his coming?

20 For ye are our glory and joy.

## CHAPTER 3

WHEREFORE when we could no longer [1]forbear, we thought it good to be left at Athens alone;

2 And sent [a]Timotheus, our brother, and minister of God, and our fellowlabourer in the gospel of Christ, to establish you, and to [1]comfort you concerning your faith:

3 [a]That no man should be [1]moved by these afflictions: for yourselves know that [b]we are appointed thereunto.

4 [a]For verily, when we were with you, we told you before that we should suffer tribulation; [1]even as it came to pass, and ye know.

5 For this cause, when I could no longer [1]forbear, I sent to know your faith, [a]lest by some means the tempter have tempted you, and [b]our labour be in vain.

6 [a]But now when Timotheus came from you unto us, and brought us good [1]tidings of your faith and [2]charity, and that ye have good remembrance of us always, desiring greatly to see us, [b]as we also *to see* you:

7 Therefore, brethren, [a]we were comforted [1]over you in all our affliction and distress by your faith:

8 For now we live, if ye [a]stand fast in the Lord.

9 For what thanks can we render to God again for you, for all the joy wherewith we joy for your sakes before our God;

10 Night and day praying exceedingly that we might see your face, [a]and might perfect that which is lacking in your faith?

11 Now God himself and our Father, and our Lord Jesus Christ, [a]direct our way unto you.

12 And the Lord make you to increase and [a]abound in love one toward another, and toward all *men*, even as we *do* toward you:

13 [1]To the end he may stablish [a]your hearts unblameable in holiness before [2]God, even our Father, at the coming of our Lord Jesus Christ with all his saints.

## CHAPTER 4

FURTHERMORE then we [1]beseech you, brethren, and exhort *you* by the Lord Jesus, [a]that as ye have received of us how ye ought to walk and to please God, *so* ye would [b]abound more and more.

2 For ye know what commandments we gave you by the Lord Jesus.

3 For this is [a]the will of God, *even* [b]your sanctification, [c]that ye should abstain from [1]fornication:

4 [a]That every one of you should know how to possess his vessel in sanctification and honour;

5 [a]Not in the [1]lust of concupiscence, [b]even as the Gentiles [c]which know not God:

6 That no *man* [1]go beyond and defraud his brother in *any* matter: because that the Lord [a]is the avenger of all such, as we also have forewarned you and testified.

7 For God hath not called us unto uncleanness, [a]but unto holiness.

8 [a]He therefore that [1]despiseth, [1]despiseth not man, but God, [b]who hath also given unto us his holy Spirit.

9 But [1]as touching brotherly love ye need not that I write unto you: for [a]ye yourselves are taught of God [b]to love one another.

10 And indeed ye do it toward all the brethren which are in all Macedonia: but we beseech you, brethren, [a]that ye increase more and more;

11 And that ye [1]study to be quiet, and [a]to [2]do your own business, and [b]to work with your own hands, as we commanded you;

12 [a]That ye may walk [1]honestly toward them that are [2]without, and *that* ye may have lack of nothing.

13 But I would not have you to be ignorant, brethren, concerning them which [1]are asleep, that ye sorrow not, [a]even as others [b]which have no hope.

14 For [a]if we believe that Jesus died and rose again, even so [b]them also

---

**Cross references (center column):**

2:13 [b] Mark 4:20 [c] [Gal. 4:14] [d] [1 Pet. 1:23] [1] welcomed [2] *effectively*
2:14 [a] Gal. 1:22 [b] Acts 17:5 [1] *imitators*
2:15 [a] Acts 2:23 [b] Matt. 5:12; 23:34, 35 [c] Esth. 3:8 [1] Opposed
2:16 [a] Luke 11:52 [b] Gen. 15:16 [c] Matt. 24:6 [1] *fill up the measure of their*
2:17 [a] 1 Cor. 5:3
2:18 [a] Rom. 1:13; 15:22 [1] *wanted to*
2:19 [a] 2 Cor. 1:14 [b] Prov. 16:31 [c] Jude 24 [d] 1 Cor. 15:23
3:1 [1] *endure it*
3:2 [a] Rom. 16:21 [1] *encourage*
3:3 [a] Eph. 3:13 [b] Acts 9:16; 14:22 [1] *shaken*
3:4 [a] Acts 20:24 [1] *just*
3:5 [a] 1 Cor. 7:5 [b] Gal. 2:2 [1] *endure it*
3:6 [a] Acts 18:5 [b] Phil. 1:8 [1] *news* [2] *love*
3:7 [d] 2 Cor. 1:4 [1] *concerning*
3:8 [a] Phil. 4:1
3:10 [a] 2 Cor. 13:9
3:11 [a] Mark 1:3
3:12 [a] Phil. 1:9
3:13 [a] 2 Thess. 2:17 [1] *So that he* [2] *our God and Father*
4:1 [a] 1 Cor. 15:58 [b] Phil. 1:27 [1] *urge*
4:3 [a] [Rom. 12:2] [b] Eph. 5:27 [c] [1 Cor. 6:15–20] [1] *sexual immorality*
4:4 [a] Rom. 6:19
4:5 [a] Col. 3:5 [b] Eph. 4:17, 18 [c] 1 Cor. 15:34 [1] *passion of lust*
4:6 [a] 2 Thess. 1:8 [1] *should take advantage of*
4:7 [a] Lev. 11:44
4:8 [a] Luke 10:16 [b] 1 Cor. 2:10 [1] *rejects*
4:9 [a] [Jer. 31:33, 34] [b] Matt. 22:39 [1] *concerning*
4:10 [a] 1 Thess. 3:12
4:11 [a] 2 Thess. 3:11 [b] Acts 20:35 [1] *aspire to lead a quiet life* [2] *mind*
4:12 [a] Rom. 13:13 [1] *properly*

[1] *outside*  4:13 [a] Lev. 19:28 [b] [Eph. 2:12] [1] *have fallen asleep*, are dead  4:14 [a] 1 Cor. 15:13 [b] 1 Cor. 15:20, 23

which sleep in Jesus will God bring with him.

15 For this we say unto you [a]by the word of the Lord, that [b]we which are alive *and* remain unto the coming of the Lord shall not [1]prevent them which are [2]asleep.

16 For [a]the Lord himself shall descend from heaven with a shout, with the voice of the archangel, and with [b]the [1]trump of God: [c]and the dead in Christ shall rise first:

17 [a]Then we which are alive *and* remain shall be caught up together with them [b]in the clouds, to meet the Lord in the air: and so [c]shall we [1]ever be with the Lord.

18 [a]Wherefore comfort one another with these words.

## CHAPTER 5

BUT of [a]the times and the seasons, brethren, ye have no need that I write unto you.

2 For yourselves know perfectly that [a]the day of the Lord so cometh as a thief in the night.

3 For when they shall say, Peace and safety; then [a]sudden destruction cometh upon them, [b]as [1]travail upon a [2]woman with child; and they shall not escape.

4 [a]But ye, brethren, are not in darkness, that that day should overtake you as a thief.

5 Ye are all [a]the [1]children of light, and the [1]children of the day: we are not of the night, nor of darkness.

6 [a]Therefore let us not sleep, as *do* others; but [b]let us watch and be [1]sober.

7 For [a]they that sleep sleep in the night; and they that be drunken [b]are drunken in the night.

8 But let us, who are of the day, be sober, [a]putting on the breastplate of faith and love; and for an helmet, the hope of salvation.

9 For [a]God hath not appointed us to wrath, [b]but to obtain salvation by our Lord Jesus Christ,

10 [a]Who died for us, that, whether we wake or sleep, we should live together with him.

11 Wherefore [1]comfort [2]yourselves together, and [3]edify one another, even as also ye [4]do.

12 And we beseech you, brethren, [a]to [1]know them which labour among you, and are over you in the Lord, and [2]admonish you;

13 And to esteem them very highly in love for their work's sake. [a]*And* be at peace among yourselves.

14 Now we exhort you, brethren, [a]warn them that are [1]unruly, [b]comfort the [2]feebleminded, [c]support the weak, [d]be patient toward all *men*.

15 [a]See that none render evil for evil unto any *man;* but ever [b]follow that which is good, both among yourselves, and to all *men*.

16 [a]Rejoice evermore.

17 [a]Pray without ceasing.

18 In every thing give thanks: for this is the will of God in Christ Jesus concerning you.

19 [a]Quench not the Spirit.

20 [a]Despise not prophesyings.

21 [a]Prove all things; [b]hold fast that which is good.

22 Abstain from [1]all appearance of evil.

23 And [a]the very God of peace [b]sanctify you wholly; and *I pray God* your whole spirit and soul and body [c]be preserved blameless unto the coming of our Lord Jesus Christ.

24 [a]Faithful *is* he that calleth you, who also will [b]do *it*.

25 Brethren, pray for us.

26 Greet all the brethren with an holy kiss.

27 I charge you by the Lord that this [1]epistle be read unto all the holy brethren.

28 The grace of our Lord Jesus Christ *be* with you. Amen.

4:15 [a] 1 Kin. 13:17; 20:35 [b] 1 Cor. 15:51, 52 [1] *precede* [2] *Dead*
4:16 [a] [Matt. 24:30, 31] [b] [1 Cor. 15:52] [c] [1 Cor. 15:23] [1] *trumpet*
4:17 [a] [1 Cor. 15:51–53] [b] Acts 1:9 [c] John 14:3; 17:24 [1] *always*
4:18 [a] 1 Thess. 5:11
5:1 [a] Matt. 24:3
5:2 [a] [2 Pet. 3:10]
5:3 [a] Is. 13:6–9 [b] Hos. 13:13 [1] *labour pains* [2] *pregnant woman*
5:4 [a] 1 John 2:8
5:5 [a] Eph. 5:8 [1] *Lit. sons*
5:6 [a] Matt. 25:5 [b] [1 Pet. 5:8] [1] *self-controlled*
5:7 [a] [Luke 21:34] [b] Acts 2:15
5:8 [a] Eph. 6:14
5:9 [a] Rom. 9:22 [b] [2 Thess. 2:13]
5:10 [a] 2 Cor. 5:15
5:11 [1] *encourage* [2] *each other* [3] *build up* [4] *are doing*
5:12 [a] 1 Cor. 16:18 [1] *recognize* [2] *instruct*
5:13 [a] Mark 9:50
5:14 [a] 2 Thess. 3:6, 7, 11 [b] Heb. 12:12 [c] Rom. 14:1; 15:1 [d] Gal. 5:22 [1] *insubordinate* [2] *faint-hearted*
5:15 [a] Lev. 19:18 [b] Gal. 6:10
5:16 [a] [2 Cor. 6:10]
5:17 [a] Eph. 6:18
5:19 [a] Eph. 4:30
5:20 [a] 1 Cor. 14:1, 31
5:21 [a] 1 John

4:1 [b] Phil. 4:8   5:22 [1] *every form of*   5:23 [a] Phil. 4:9 [b] 1 Thess. 3:13 [c] 1 Cor. 1:8, 9   5:24 [a] [1 Cor. 10:13] [b] Phil. 1:6   5:27 [1] *letter*

# THESSALONIANS

Since Paul's first letter, the seeds of false doctrine have been sown among the Thessalonians, causing them to waver in their faith. Paul removes these destructive seeds and again plants the seeds of truth. He begins by commending the believers on their faithfulness in the midst of persecution and encouraging them that present suffering will be repaid with future glory. Therefore, in the midst of persecution, expectation can be high.

Paul then deals with the central matter of his letter: a misunderstanding spawned by false teachers regarding the coming day of the Lord. Despite reports to the contrary, that Day has not yet come, and Paul recounts the events that must first take place. Laboring for the gospel, rather than lazy resignation, is the proper response.

As the second letter in Paul's Thessalonian correspondence, this was entitled *Pros Thessalonikeis B*, the "Second to the Thessalonians."

## CHAPTER 1

PAUL, and Silvanus, and Timotheus, unto the church of the Thessalonians in God our Father and the Lord Jesus Christ:

2 [a]Grace unto you, and peace, from God our Father and the Lord Jesus Christ.

3 We are bound to thank God always for you, brethren, as it is [1]meet, because that your faith groweth exceedingly, and the [2]charity of every one of you all toward each other aboundeth;

4 So that [a]we ourselves [1]glory in you [2]in the churches of God [b]for your patience and faith [c]in all your persecutions and tribulations that ye endure:

5 *Which is* [a][1]manifest token of the righteous judgment of God, that ye may be counted worthy of the kingdom of God, [b]for which ye also suffer:

6 [a]Seeing *it is* a righteous thing with God to [1]recompense tribulation to them that trouble you;

7 And to you who are troubled [a]rest with us, when [b]the Lord Jesus shall be revealed from heaven with his mighty angels,

8 In flaming fire taking vengeance on them that know not God, and that obey not the gospel of our Lord Jesus Christ:

9 [a]Who shall be punished with everlasting destruction from the presence of the Lord, and [b]from the glory of his power;

10 When he shall come [a]to be [b]glorified in his saints, and to be admired in all them that believe (because our testimony among you was believed) in that day.

11 Wherefore also we pray always for you, that our God would [a]count you worthy of *this* calling, and fulfil all the good pleasure of *his* goodness, and [b]the work of faith with power:

12 [a]That the name of our Lord Jesus Christ may be glorified in you, and ye in him, according to the grace of our God and the Lord Jesus Christ.

## CHAPTER 2

NOW we [1]beseech you, brethren, [a]by[2] the coming of our Lord Jesus Christ, [b]and [2]*by* our gathering together unto him,

2 [a]That ye be not soon shaken in mind, or be troubled, neither by spirit, nor by word, nor by letter as from us, as that the day of Christ [1]is at hand.

3 Let no man deceive you by any means: for *that day shall not come,* [a]except there come a falling away first, and [b]that man of sin be revealed, [c]the son of perdition;

4 Who opposeth and [a]exalteth himself [b]above all that is called God, or that is worshipped; so that he as God sitteth in the temple of God, shewing himself that he is God.

5 Remember ye not, that, when I was yet with you, I told you these things?

6 And now ye know what [1]withholdeth that he might be revealed in his time.

7 For [a]the [1]mystery of [2]iniquity doth already *work:* only he who now [3]letteth *will let,* until he be taken out of the way.

8 And then shall that [1]Wicked be revealed, [a]whom the Lord shall consume [b]with the [2]spirit of his mouth, and shall destroy [c]with the brightness of his coming:

9 *Even him,* whose coming is [a]after the working of Satan with all power and [b]signs and lying wonders,

10 And with all [1]deceivableness of unrighteousness [2]in [a]them that perish; because they received not [b]the love of the truth, that they might be saved.

### Reference column

1:2 [a] 1 Cor. 1:3
1:3 [1] *fitting* [2] *love*
1:4 [a] 2 Cor. 7:4; [1] Thess. 2:19] [b] 1 Thess. 1:3 [c] 1 Thess.
2:14 [1] *boast of* [2] *among*
1:5 [a] Phil. 1:28 [b] 1 Thess. 2:14 [1] *plain evidence*
1:6 [a] Rev. 6:10 [1] *repay with*
1:7 [a] Rev. 14:13 [b] Jude 14
1:9 [a] Phil. 3:19 [b] Deut. 33:2
1:10 [a] Matt. 25:31 [b] John 17:10
1:11 [a] Col. 1:12 [b] 1 Thess. 1:3

1:12 [a] [Col. 3:17]
2:1 [a] [1 Thess. 4:15–17] [b] Matt. 24:31 [1] *ask* [2] *concerning*
2:2 [a] Matt. 24:4 [1] *had come*
2:3 [a] 1 Tim. 4:1 [b] Dan. 7:25; 8:25; 11:36 [c] John 17:12
2:4 [a] Is. 14:13, 14 [b] 1 Cor. 8:5
2:6 [1] *is restraining*
2:7 [a] 1 John 2:18 [1] *hidden truth* [2] *lawlessness* [3] *restrains will do so*
2:8 [a] Dan. 7:10 [b] Is. 11:4 [c] Heb. 10:27 [1] *Lawless One* [2] *breath*
2:9 [a] John 8:41 [b] Deut. 13:1
2:10 [a] 2 Cor. 2:15 [b] 1 Cor. 16:22 [1] *unrighteous deception* [2] *among*

11 And [a]for this cause God shall send them strong delusion, [b]that they should believe [1]a lie:

12 That they all might be [1]damned who believed not the truth, but [a]had pleasure in unrighteousness.

13 But we are [1]bound to give thanks alway to God for you, brethren beloved of the Lord, because God [a]hath [b]from the beginning chosen you to salvation [c]through sanctification of the Spirit and belief of the truth:

14 Whereunto he called you by our gospel, to [a]the obtaining of the glory of our Lord Jesus Christ.

15 Therefore, brethren, [a]stand fast, and hold [b]the traditions which ye have been taught, whether by word, or our epistle.

16 Now our Lord Jesus Christ himself, and God, even our Father, [a]which hath loved us, and hath given *us* everlasting consolation and [b]good hope through grace,

17 Comfort your hearts, [a]and stablish you in every good word and work.

## CHAPTER 3

FINALLY, brethren, [a]pray for us, that the word of the Lord may [1]have *free* course, and be glorified, even as *it is* with you:

2 And [a]that we may be delivered from unreasonable and wicked men: [b]for all *men* have not faith.

3 But [a]the Lord is faithful, who shall stablish you, and [b]keep *you* from [1]evil.

4 And [a]we have confidence in the Lord [1]touching you, that ye both do and will do the things which we command you.

5 And [a]the Lord direct your hearts into the love of God, and into the [1]patient waiting for Christ.

2:11 [a] Rom. 1:28
[b] 1 Tim. 4:1 [1] Lit. *the*

2:12 [a] Rom. 1:32
[1] *condemned*

2:13 [a] Eph. 1:4
[b] 1 Thess. 1:4
[c] [1 Pet. 1:2] [1] *under obligation*

2:14 [a] 1 Pet. 5:10

2:15 [a] 1 Cor. 16:13
[b] 1 Cor. 11:2

2:16 [a] [Rev. 1:5]
[b] 1 Pet. 1:3

2:17 [a] 1 Cor. 1:8

3:1 [a] Eph. 6:19
[1] Lit. *run*

3:2 [a] Rom. 15:31
[b] Acts 28:24

3:3 [a] 1 Cor. 1:9
[b] John 17:15 [1] *the evil one*

3:4 [a] 2 Cor. 7:16
[1] *concerning*

3:5 [a] 1 Chr. 29:18
[1] *patience of Christ*

3:6 [a] Rom. 16:17 [b] 1 Cor. 5:1
[c] 1 Thess. 4:11

3:8 [a] 1 Thess. 2:9
[1] *free of charge*
[2] *worked* [3] *toil*
[4] *a burden*

3:9 [a] 1 Cor. 9:4, 6–14 [1] *authority*

3:11 [a] 1 Tim. 5:13;
1 Pet. 4:15

3:12 [a] Eph. 4:28;
1 Thess. 4:11, 12

3:13 [a] 2 Cor. 4:1;
Gal. 6:9

3:14 [a] Matt. 18:17

3:15 [a] Lev. 19:17
[b] Titus 3:10 [1] *warn*

3:16 [a] John 14:27;
Rom. 15:33; Phil. 4:9

3:17 [a] 1 Cor. 16:21
[1] *sign*

6 Now we command you, brethren, in the name of our Lord Jesus Christ, [a]that ye withdraw yourselves [b]from every brother that walketh [c]disorderly, and not after the tradition which he received of us.

7 For yourselves know how ye ought to follow us: for we behaved not ourselves disorderly among you;

8 Neither did we eat any man's bread [1]for nought; but [2]wrought with [a]labour and [3]travail night and day, that we might not be [4]chargeable to any of you:

9 Not because we have not [a]power,[1] but to make ourselves an ensample unto you to follow us.

10 For even when we were with you, this we commanded you, that if any would not work, neither should he eat.

11 For we hear that there are some which walk among you disorderly, working not at all, but are [a]busybodies.

12 Now them that are such we command and exhort by our Lord Jesus Christ, [a]that with quietness they work, and eat their own bread.

13 But ye, brethren, [a]be not weary in well doing.

14 And if any man obey not our word by this epistle, note that man, and [a]have no company with him, that he may be ashamed.

15 [a]Yet count *him* not as an enemy, [b]but [1]admonish *him* as a brother.

16 Now [a]the Lord of peace himself give you peace always by all means. The Lord *be* with you all.

17 [a]The salutation of Paul with mine own hand, which is the [1]token in every epistle: so I write.

18 [a]The grace of our Lord Jesus Christ be with you all. Amen.

3:18 [a] Rom. 16:20, 24; 1 Thess. 5:28

# THE FIRST EPISTLE OF PAUL THE APOSTLE TO
# TIMOTHY

Paul, the aged and experienced apostle, writes to the young pastor Timothy who is facing a heavy burden of responsibility in the church at Ephesus. The task is challenging: false doctrine must be erased, public worship safeguarded, and mature leadership developed. In addition to the conduct of the church, Paul talks pointedly about the conduct of the minister. Timothy must be on his guard lest his youthfulness become a liability, rather than an asset, to the gospel. He must be careful to avoid false teachers and greedy motives, pursuing instead righteousness, godliness, faith, love, perseverance, and the gentleness that befits a man of God.

The Greek title for this letter is *Pros Timotheon A*, the "First to Timothy." *Timothy* means "honoring God" or "honored by God," and probably was given to him by his mother Eunice.

## CHAPTER 1

PAUL, an apostle of Jesus Christ by the commandment of God our Saviour, and Lord Jesus Christ, *which is* our hope;

2 Unto Timothy, [a]*my* [1]own son in the faith: [b]Grace, mercy, *and* peace, from God our Father and Jesus Christ our Lord.

3 As I [1]besought thee to abide still at Ephesus, [a]when I went into Macedonia, that thou mightest charge some [b]that they teach no other doctrine,

4 [a]Neither give heed to fables and endless genealogies, which [1]minister questions, rather than godly edifying which is in faith: *so do.*

5 Now [a]the [1]end of the commandment is [2]charity [b]out of a pure heart, and *of* a good conscience, and *of* [3]faith unfeigned:

6 From which some having [1]swerved have turned aside unto [a]vain[2] jangling;

7 Desiring to be teachers of the law; understanding neither what they say, nor whereof they affirm.

8 But we know that the law *is* [a]good, if a man use it lawfully;

9 Knowing this, that the law is not made for a righteous man, but for the lawless and disobedient, for the ungodly and for sinners, for unholy and profane, for murderers of fathers and murderers of mothers, for manslayers,

10 For [1]whoremongers, for [2]them that defile themselves with mankind, for [3]menstealers, for liars, for [4]perjured persons, and if there be any other thing that is contrary to sound doctrine;

11 According to the glorious gospel of the [a]blessed God, which was [b]committed to my trust.

12 And I thank Christ Jesus our Lord, who hath [a]enabled me, [b]for

that he counted me faithful, [c]putting me into the ministry;

13 [a]Who was before a blasphemer, and a persecutor, and [1]injurious: but I obtained mercy, because [b]I did *it* ignorantly in unbelief.

14 [a]And the grace of our Lord was exceeding abundant [b]with faith and love which is in Christ Jesus.

15 [a]This *is* a faithful saying, and worthy of all acceptation, that [b]Christ Jesus came into the world to save sinners; of whom I am chief.

16 Howbeit for this cause I obtained mercy, that in me first Jesus Christ might shew forth all longsuffering, for a pattern to them which should hereafter believe on him to life everlasting.

17 Now unto [a]the King eternal, [b]immortal, [c]invisible, [d]the only wise God, [e]*be* honour and glory for ever and ever. Amen.

18 This [1]charge I commit unto thee, son Timothy, according to the prophecies [2]which went before on thee, that thou by them mightest war a good warfare;

19 Holding faith, and a good conscience; which some having [1]put away concerning faith have [2]made shipwreck:

20 Of whom is [a]Hymenaeus and [b]Alexander; whom I have delivered unto Satan, that they may learn not to [c]blaspheme.

## CHAPTER 2

I EXHORT therefore, that, first of all, supplications, prayers, intercessions, *and* giving of thanks, be made for all men;

2 [a]For kings, and [b]*for* all that are in [1]authority; that we may lead a quiet and peaceable life in all godliness and [2]honesty.

3 For this *is* [a]good and acceptable in the sight [b]of God our Saviour;

1:2 [a] Titus 1:4
[b] Gal. 1:3 [1] *true*
1:3 [a] Acts 20:1,
3 [b] Gal. 1:6, 7
[1] *urged*
1:4 [a] Titus 1:14
[1] *cause disputes*
1:5 [a] Rom. 13:8–
10 [b] Eph. 6:24
[1] *purpose* [2] *love*
[3] *sincere faith*
1:6 [a] 1 Tim. 6:4, 20
[1] *strayed* [2] *idle talk*
1:8 [a] Rom. 7:12, 16
1:10 [1] *fornicators*
[2] *sodomites*
[3] *kidnappers*
[4] *perjurers*
1:11 [a] 1 Tim. 6:15
[b] 1 Cor. 9:17
1:12 [a] 1 Cor. 15:10
[b] 1 Cor. 7:25

[c] Col. 1:25
1:13 [a] Acts 8:3
[b] John 4:21
[1] *insolent*
1:14 [a] Rom. 5:20
[b] 2 Tim. 1:13; 2:22
1:15 [a] 2 Tim. 2:11
[b] Matt. 1:21; 9:13
1:17 [a] Ps. 10:16
[b] Rom. 1:23
[c] Heb. 11:27
[d] Rom. 16:27
[e] 1 Chr. 29:11
1:18 [1] *command*
[2] *previously made concerning you*
1:19 [1] *rejected*
[2] *suffered*
1:20 [a] 2 Tim. 2:17,
18 [b] 2 Tim. 4:14
[c] Acts 13:45
2:2 [a] Ezra 6:10
[b] [Rom. 13:1] [1] *a prominent place*
[2] *reverence*
2:3 [a] Rom. 12:2
[b] 2 Tim. 1:9

4 [a]Who [1]will have all men to be saved, [b]and to come unto the knowledge of the truth.

5 [a]For *there is* one God, and [b]one mediator between God and men, the man Christ Jesus;

6 [a]Who gave himself a ransom for all, to be testified in due time.

7 [a]Whereunto I am ordained a preacher, and an apostle, (I speak the truth in Christ, *and* lie not;) [b]a teacher of the Gentiles in faith and [1]verity.

8 I will therefore that men pray [a]every where, [b]lifting up holy hands, without wrath and doubting.

9 In like manner also, that [a]women adorn themselves in modest apparel, with [1]shamefacedness and [2]sobriety; not with broided hair, or gold, or pearls, or costly [3]array;

10 [a]But (which [1]becometh women professing godliness) with good works.

11 Let the woman learn in silence with all [1]subjection.

12 But [a]I [1]suffer not a woman to teach, nor to [2]usurp authority over the man, but to be in silence.

13 For Adam was first formed, then Eve.

14 And Adam was not deceived, but the woman being deceived was in the transgression.

15 Notwithstanding she shall be saved in childbearing, if they continue in faith and [1]charity and holiness with [2]sobriety.

## CHAPTER 3

THIS *is* a true saying, If a man [1]desire the office of [2]a bishop, he desireth a good work.

2 A bishop then must be blameless, the husband of one wife, [1]vigilant, [2]sober, of good behaviour, given to hospitality, [3]apt to teach;

3 Not [1]given to wine, [2]no striker, not greedy [3]of filthy lucre; but patient, not a brawler, not covetous;

4 One that ruleth well his own house, having his children in subjection with all [1]gravity;

5 (For if a man know not how to rule his own house, how shall he take care of the church of God?)

6 Not a [1]novice, lest being lifted up with pride he fall into the condemnation of the devil.

7 Moreover he must have a good [1]report of them which are [2]without; lest he fall into reproach and the [a]snare of the devil.

8 Likewise *must* the deacons *be* [1]grave, not doubletongued, [a]not given to much wine, not greedy of [2]filthy lucre;

9 Holding the [1]mystery of the faith in a pure conscience.

10 And let these also first be proved; then let them [1]use the office of a deacon, being *found* blameless.

11 Even so *must their* wives *be* [1]grave, not slanderers, [2]sober, faithful in all things.

12 Let the deacons be the husbands of one wife, ruling their children and their own houses well.

13 For they that have [1]used the office of a deacon [a]well [2]purchase to themselves a good [3]degree, and great boldness in the faith which is in Christ Jesus.

14 These things write I unto thee, hoping to come unto thee shortly:

15 But if I [1]tarry long, that thou mayest know how thou oughtest to [2]behave thyself in the house of God, which is the church of the living God, the pillar and [3]ground of the truth.

16 And without controversy great is the [1]mystery of godliness: [a]God was manifest in the flesh, [b]justified in the Spirit, [c]seen of angels, [d]preached unto the Gentiles, [e]believed on in the world, [f]received up into glory.

## CHAPTER 4

NOW the Spirit speaketh expressly, that in the latter times some shall depart from the faith, giving heed [a]to [1]seducing spirits, and doctrines of devils;

2 [a]Speaking lies in hypocrisy; having their conscience [b]seared with a hot iron;

3 Forbidding to marry, *and commanding* to abstain from [1]meats, which God hath created to be received with thanksgiving of them which believe and know the truth.

4 For every creature of God *is* good, and nothing to be refused, if it be received with thanksgiving:

5 For it is [1]sanctified by the word of God and prayer.

6 If thou put the brethren in remembrance of these things, thou shalt be a good minister of Jesus Christ, [a]nourished up in the words of faith and of good doctrine, whereunto thou hast [1]attained.

7 But [a]refuse [1]profane and old wives' fables, and [b]exercise thyself *rather* unto godliness.

8 For [a]bodily exercise profiteth little: but godliness is profitable unto all things, [b]having promise of the life that now is, and of that which is to come.

9 This *is* a faithful saying and worthy of all acceptation.

10 For therefore we both labour and suffer reproach, because we trust in the living God, [a]who is the Saviour of all men, specially of those that believe.

11 These things command and teach.

## Center column references

2:4 [a] Ezek. 18:23, 32 [b] [John 17:3] [1] *desires to*

2:5 [a] Gal. 3:20 [b] [Heb. 9:15]

2:6 [a] Mark 10:45

2:7 [a] Eph. 3:7, 8 [b] [Gal. 1:15, 16] [1] *truth*

2:8 [a] Luke 23:34 [b] Ps. 134:2

2:9 [a] 1 Pet. 3:3 [1] *propriety* [2] *moderation* [3] *clothing*

2:10 [a] 1 Pet. 3:4 [1] *is proper for*

2:11 [1] *submission*

2:12 [a] 1 Cor. 14:34 [1] *permit* [2] *have*

2:15 [1] *love* [2] *self-control*

3:1 [1] *aspires* [2] *overseer*

3:2 [1] *temperate* [2] *sober-minded* [3] *able*

3:3 [1] *addicted* [2] *not violent* [3] *for money*

3:4 [1] *reverence*

3:6 [1] *new convert*

3:7 [a] 2 Tim. 2:26 [1] *testimony among* [2] *outside*

3:8 [a] Ezek. 44:21 [1] *reverent* [2] *money*

3:9 [1] *hidden truth*

3:10 [1] *serve as*

3:11 [1] *reverent* [2] *temperate*

3:13 [a] Matt. 25:21 [1] *served as* [2] *obtain for* [3] *standing*

3:15 [1] *am delayed* [2] *conduct* [3] *foundation*

3:16 [a] [John 1:14; 1 Pet. 1:20; 1 John 1:2; 3:5, 8] [b] [Matt. 3:16; Rom. 1:4] [c] Matt. 28:2 [d] Acts 10:34; Rom. 10:18 [e] Rom. 16:26; 2 Cor. 1:19; Col. 1:6, 23 [f] Luke 24:51 [1] *hidden truth*

4:1 [a] 2 Tim. 3:13; Rev. 16:14 [1] *deceiving*

4:2 [a] Matt. 7:15 [b] Eph. 4:19

4:3 [1] *foods*

4:5 [1] *consecrated*

4:6 [a] 2 Tim. 3:14 [1] *carefully followed*

4:7 [a] 2 Tim. 2:16; Titus 1:14 [b] Heb. 5:14 [1] *reject*

4:8 [a] 1 Cor. 8:8 [b] Ps. 37:9

4:10 [a] Ps. 36:6

12 Let no man [1]despise thy youth; but be thou an [a]example of the believers, in word, in [2]conversation, in charity, in spirit, in faith, in purity.

13 Till I come, give attendance to reading, to exhortation, to [1]doctrine.

14 [a]Neglect not the gift that is in thee, which was given thee by prophecy, [b]with the laying on of the hands of the [1]presbytery.

15 Meditate upon these things; give thyself [1]wholly to them; that thy [2]profiting may [a]appear to all.

16 Take heed unto thyself, and unto the doctrine; continue in them: for in doing this thou shalt both save thyself, and them that hear thee.

## CHAPTER 5

REBUKE not an [1]elder, but [2]intreat *him* as a father; *and* the younger men as brethren;

2 The elder women as mothers; the younger as sisters, with all purity.

3 Honour widows that are widows indeed.

4 But if any widow have children or [1]nephews, let them learn first to shew piety at home, and [a]to [2]requite their parents: for that is good and acceptable before God.

5 Now she that is a widow indeed, and [1]desolate, trusteth in God, and continueth in supplications and prayers [a]night and day.

6 But she that liveth in [1]pleasure is dead while she liveth.

7 And these things [1]give in charge, that they may be blameless.

8 But if any provide not for his own, [a]and specially for those of his own [1]house, [b]he hath denied the faith, [c]and is worse than an [2]infidel.

9 Let not a widow be taken into the number under threescore years old, [1]having been the wife of one man,

10 Well reported of for good works; if she have brought up children, if she have lodged strangers, if she have washed the saints' feet, if she have relieved the afflicted, if she have diligently followed every good work.

11 But the younger widows [1]refuse: for when they have begun to [2]wax wanton against Christ, they [3]will marry;

12 Having [1]damnation, because they have cast off their first [2]faith.

13 And [1]withal they learn *to be* idle, wandering about from house to house; and not only idle, but [2]tattlers also and busybodies, speaking things which they ought not.

14 I will therefore that the younger women marry, bear children, [1]guide the house, give [2]none occasion to the adversary to speak reproachfully.

15 For some are already turned aside after Satan.

4:12 [a] Phil. 3:17; Titus 2:7; 1 Pet.
5:3 [1] *look down on* [2] *conduct*
4:13 [1] *teaching*
4:14 [a] 2 Tim. 1:6 [b] Acts 6:6; 1 Tim.
5:22 [1] *council of elders*
4:15 [1] *entirely* [2] *progress* [3] *be evident*
5:1 [1] *older man* [2] *exhort*
5:4 [a] Gen. 45:10 [1] *grandchildren* [2] *repay*
5:5 [a] Acts 26:7 [1] *left alone*
5:6 [1] *indulgence*
5:7 [1] *command*
5:8 [a] Is. 58:7; 2 Cor. 12:14 [b] 2 Tim. 3:5 [c] Matt. 18:17 [1] *household* [2] *unbeliever*
5:9 [1] *and not unless she has been*
5:11 [1] *Refuse to enroll* [2] *grow* [3] *desire to*
5:12 [1] *condemnation* [2] *promise*
5:13 [1] *besides* [2] *gossips*
5:14 [1] *manage* [2] *no opportunity*
5:16 [1] *assist* [2] *burdened*
5:18 [a] Deut. 25:4 [b] Luke 10:7 [1] *wages*
5:19 [a] Deut. 17:6; 19:15
5:20 [1] *in the presence of*
5:21 [a] Deut. 1:17 [1] *chosen* [2] *prejudice*
5:22 [a] Eph. 5:6, 7 [1] *hastily* [2] *share in*
5:23 [1] *frequent sicknesses*
5:24 [a] Gal. 5:19–21 [1] *clearly evident* [2] *preceding them* [3] *those of some men* [4] *later*
6:1 [a] Eph. 6:5
6:3 [a] 2 Tim. 1:13 [b] Titus 1:1 [1] *agree* [2] *teaching*
6:4 [1] *is obsessed with disputes* [2] *arguments over* [3] *reviling* [4] *suspicions*
6:5 [a] 2 Tim. 3:5 [1] *Useless wranglings* [2] *godliness is a means of gain*
6:6 [a] Heb. 13:5
6:7 [a] Job 1:21

16 If any man or woman that believeth have widows, let them [1]relieve them, and let not the church be [2]charged; that it may relieve them that are widows indeed.

17 Let the elders that rule well be counted worthy of double honour, especially they who labour in the word and doctrine.

18 For the scripture saith, [a]Thou shalt not muzzle the ox that treadeth out the corn. And, [b]The labourer *is* worthy of his [1]reward.

19 Against an elder receive not an accusation, but [a]before two or three witnesses.

20 Them that sin rebuke [1]before all, that others also may fear.

21 I charge *thee* before God, and the Lord Jesus Christ, and the [1]elect angels, that thou observe these things without [2]preferring [a]one before another, doing nothing by partiality.

22 Lay hands [1]suddenly on no man, neither [2]be [a]partaker of other men's sins: keep thyself pure.

23 Drink no longer water, but use a little wine for thy stomach's sake and thine [1]often infirmities.

24 Some men's sins are [a]open[1] beforehand, [2]going before to judgment; and [3]some *men* they follow [4]after.

25 Likewise also the good works *of some* are manifest beforehand; and they that are otherwise cannot be hid.

## CHAPTER 6

LET as many [a]servants as are under the yoke count their own masters worthy of all honour, that the name of God and *his* doctrine be not blasphemed.

2 And they that have believing masters, let them not despise *them,* because they are brethren; but rather do *them* service, because they are faithful and beloved, partakers of the benefit. These things teach and exhort.

3 If any man teach otherwise, and [1]consent not to [a]wholesome words, *even* the words of our Lord Jesus Christ, [b]and to the [2]doctrine which is according to godliness;

4 He is proud, knowing nothing, but [1]doting about questions and [2]strifes of words, whereof cometh envy, strife, [3]railings, evil [4]surmisings,

5 [1]Perverse disputings of men of corrupt minds, and destitute of the truth, supposing that [2]gain is godliness: from [a]such withdraw thyself.

6 But godliness with [a]contentment is great gain.

7 For we brought nothing into *this* world, *and it is* [a]certain we can carry nothing out.

8 And having food and [1]raiment let us be therewith [a]content.

9 But they that [1]will be rich fall into temptation and a snare, and *into* many foolish and [2]hurtful lusts, which drown men in [3]destruction and perdition.

10 For the love of money is the root of [1]all evil: [2]which while some coveted after, they have erred from the faith, and pierced themselves through with many sorrows.

11 But thou, O man of God, flee these things; and follow after righteousness, godliness, faith, love, patience, meekness.

12 Fight the good fight of faith, lay hold on eternal life, whereunto thou art also called, and hast [1]professed a good [2]profession before many witnesses.

13 I give thee charge in the sight of God, who [1]quickeneth all things, and *before* Christ Jesus, [a]who before Pontius Pilate witnessed a good confession;

14 That thou keep *this* commandment without spot, [1]unrebukeable, until the appearing of our Lord Jesus Christ:

15 Which in his times he shall [1]shew, *who is* the blessed and only Potentate, the King of kings, and Lord of lords;

16 Who only hath immortality, dwelling in the [a]light which no man can approach unto; [b]whom no man hath seen, nor can see: to whom *be* honour and power everlasting. Amen.

17 [1]Charge them that are rich in this [2]world, that they be not [3]highminded, nor trust in uncertain [a]riches, but in the living God, who giveth us richly all things [b]to enjoy;

18 That they do good, that they be rich in good works, ready to [1]distribute, willing to [2]communicate;

19 [a]Laying up in store for themselves a good foundation against the time to come, that they may lay hold on eternal life.

20 O Timothy, [a]keep that which is committed to thy trust, [b]avoiding profane *and* [1]vain babblings, and [2]oppositions of science falsely so called:

21 Which some professing have [1]erred concerning the faith. Grace *be* with thee. Amen.

---

6:8 [a] Prov. 30:8, 9
[1] clothing

6:9 [1] desire to be
[2] harmful [3] ruin
and destruction.

6:10 [1] all kinds of
[2] for which some
in their greedi-
ness have strayed
from the faith

6:12 [1] confessed
[2] confession

6:13 [a] John 18:36,
37 [1] gives life to

6:14 [1] blameless

6:15 [1] manifest

6:16 [a] Dan. 2:22
[b] John 6:46

6:17 [a] Jer. 9:23;
48:7 [b] Eccl. 5:18,
19 [1] Command
[2] present age
[3] haughty

6:18 [1] give
[2] share

6:19 [a] [Matt.
6:20, 21; 19:21]

6:20 [a] [2 Tim.
1:12, 14] [b] Titus
1:14 [1] empty talk
[2] contradictions
of knowledge

6:21 [1] strayed

# THE SECOND EPISTLE OF PAUL THE APOSTLE TO
# TIMOTHY

**P**rison is the last place from which to expect a letter of encouragement, but that is where Paul's second letter to Timothy originates. He begins by assuring Timothy of his continuing love and prayers, and reminds him of his spiritual heritage and responsibilities. Only the one who perseveres, whether as a soldier, athlete, farmer, or minister of Jesus Christ, will reap the reward. Paul warns Timothy that his teaching will come under attack as men desert the truth for ear-itching words (4:3). But Timothy has Paul's example to guide him and God's Word to fortify him as he faces growing opposition and glowing opportunities in the last days.

Paul's last epistle received the title *Pros Timotheon B*, the "Second to Timothy." When Paul's epistles were collected together the *B* was probably added to distinguish this letter from the first letter he wrote to Timothy.

## CHAPTER 1

**P**AUL, an apostle of Jesus Christ by the will of God, according to the ªpromise of life which is in Christ Jesus,

2 To Timothy, *my* dearly ªbeloved son: Grace, mercy, *and* peace, from God the Father and Christ Jesus our Lord.

3 I thank God, whom I serve ¹from *my* ªforefathers with pure conscience, that without ceasing I have remembrance of thee in my prayers night and day;

4 Greatly desiring to see thee, being mindful of thy tears, that I may be filled with joy;

5 When I call to remembrance ªthe ¹unfeigned faith that is in thee, which dwelt first in thy grandmother Lois, and ᵇthy mother Eunice; and I am persuaded that in thee also.

6 Wherefore I put thee in remembrance ªthat thou stir up the gift of God, which is in thee by the ¹putting on of my hands.

7 For ªGod hath not given us the spirit of fear; ᵇbut of power, and of love, and of a sound mind.

8 ªBe not thou therefore ashamed of ᵇthe testimony of our Lord, nor of me ᶜhis prisoner: but ¹be thou partaker of the afflictions of the gospel according to the power of God;

9 Who hath saved us, and called *us* with an holy calling, ªnot according to our works, but ᵇaccording to his own purpose and grace, which was given us in Christ Jesus ᶜbefore ¹the world began,

10 But ªis now made manifest by the appearing of our Saviour Jesus Christ, who hath abolished death, and hath brought life and immortality to light through the gospel:

11 ªWhereunto I am appointed a preacher, and an apostle, and a teacher of the Gentiles.

1:1 ª Titus 1:2
1:2 ª 1 Tim. 1:2; 2 Tim. 2:1; Titus 1:4
1:3 ª Acts 24:14
¹ *as* did
1:5 ª 1 Tim. 1:5; 4:6 ᵇ Acts 16:1
¹ *genuine*
1:6 ª 1 Tim. 4:14
¹ *laying*
1:7 ª John 14:27; Rom. 8:15; 1 John 4:18 ᵇ [Acts 1:8]
1:8 ª [Mark 8:38; Luke 9:26; Rom. 1:16]; 2 Tim. 1:12, 16 ᵇ 1 Tim. 2:6 ᶜ Eph. 3:1; 2 Tim. 1:16 ¹ *share with me in the sufferings*
1:9 ª [Rom. 3:20]; Eph. 2:8, 9 ᵇ Rom. 8:28 ᶜ Rom. 16:25; Eph. 1:4; Titus 1:2 ¹ *time*
1:10 ª Eph. 1:9
1:11 ª Acts 9:15

1:12 ª 1 Pet. 4:19 ¹ *until*
1:13 ª 2 Tim. 3:14; Titus 1:9 ᵇ Rom. 2:20; 6:17 ᶜ 1 Tim. 6:3
1:16 ª 2 Tim. 4:19 ¹ *often*
1:18 ª Matt. 6:4; Mark 9:41 ᵇ 2 Thess. 1:10 ᶜ Heb. 6:10 ¹ *ways*
2:1 ª 1 Tim. 1:2 ᵇ Eph. 6:10
2:3 ª 2 Tim. 4:5 ᵇ 1 Cor. 9:7; 1 Tim. 1:18 ¹ *hardship*
2:4 ª [2 Pet. 2:20]
2:5 ª [1 Cor. 9:25] ¹ *competes in athletics* ² *competes*

12 For the which cause I also suffer these things: nevertheless I am not ashamed: ªfor I know whom I have believed, and am persuaded that he is able to keep that which I have committed unto him ¹against that day.

13 ªHold fast ᵇthe form of ᶜsound words, which thou hast heard of me, in faith and love which is in Christ Jesus.

14 That good thing which was committed unto thee keep by the Holy Ghost which dwelleth in us.

15 This thou knowest, that all they which are in Asia be turned away from me; of whom are Phygellus and Hermogenes.

16 The Lord give mercy unto the ªhouse of Onesiphorus; for he ¹oft refreshed me, and was not ashamed of my chain:

17 But, when he was in Rome, he sought me out very diligently, and found *me*.

18 The Lord ªgrant unto him that he may find mercy of the Lord ᵇin that day: and in how many ¹things he ᶜministered unto me at Ephesus, thou knowest very well.

## CHAPTER 2

**T**HOU therefore, ªmy son, ᵇbe strong in the grace that is in Christ Jesus.

2 And the things that thou hast heard of me among many witnesses, the same commit thou to faithful men, who shall be able to teach others also.

3 Thou therefore ªendure ¹hardness, ᵇas a good soldier of Jesus Christ.

4 ªNo man that warreth entangleth himself with the affairs of *this* life; that he may please him who hath chosen him to be a soldier.

5 And ªif a man also ¹strive for masteries, *yet* is he not crowned, except he ²strive lawfully.

990

6 The [1]husbandman that laboureth must be first partaker of the [2]fruits.

7 Consider what I say; and the Lord [a]give thee understanding in all things.

8 Remember that Jesus Christ [a]of the seed of David [b]was raised from the dead [c]according to my gospel:

9 [a]Wherein I suffer trouble, as an evil doer, [b]*even* unto [1]bonds; [c]but the word of God is not [2]bound.

10 Therefore [a]I endure all things for the [1]elect's sakes, [b]that they may also obtain the salvation which is in Christ Jesus with eternal glory.

11 *It is* a faithful saying: For [a]if we be dead with *him*, we shall also live with *him:*

12 [a]If we [1]suffer, we shall also reign with *him:* [b]if we deny *him*, he also will deny us:

13 If we [1]believe not, *yet* he abideth faithful: he [a]cannot deny himself.

14 Of these things put *them* in remembrance, [a]charging *them* before the Lord that they strive not about words to no profit, *but* to the [1]subverting of the hearers.

15 [a]Study[1] to [2]shew thyself approved unto God, a workman that needeth not to be ashamed, rightly dividing the word of truth.

16 But shun profane *and* [1]vain babblings: for they will increase unto more ungodliness.

17 And their word will [1]eat as doth a [2]canker: of whom is [a]Hymenaeus and Philetus;

18 Who concerning the truth have [1]erred, [a]saying that the resurrection is past already; and overthrow the faith of some.

19 Nevertheless [a]the foundation of God standeth sure, having this seal, The Lord [b]knoweth them that are his. And, Let every one that nameth the name of Christ depart from iniquity.

20 But in a great house there are not only [a]vessels of gold and of silver, but also of wood and of [1]earth; and some to honour, and some to dishonour.

21 If a man therefore [1]purge himself from [2]these, he shall be a vessel unto honour, [3]sanctified, and [4]meet for the master's use, *and* [a]prepared unto every good work.

22 [a]Flee also youthful lusts: but [1]follow righteousness, faith, [2]charity, peace, with them that call on the Lord out of a pure heart.

23 But foolish and [1]unlearned questions avoid, knowing that they do [2]gender strifes.

24 And [a]the servant of the Lord must not [1]strive; but be gentle unto all *men*, [b]apt[2] to teach, [c]patient,

25 [a]In meekness [1]instructing those that [2]oppose themselves; [b]if God per-

adventure will give them repentance [c]to[3] the acknowledging of the truth;

26 And *that* they may [1]recover themselves [a]out of the snare of the devil, who are taken captive by him [2]at his will.

## CHAPTER 3

THIS know also, that [a]in the last days perilous times shall come.

2 For men shall be lovers of their own selves, [1]covetous, boasters, proud, blasphemers, disobedient to parents, unthankful, unholy,

3 Without natural affection, [1]trucebreakers, [2]false accusers, [3]incontinent, [4]fierce, despisers of [5]those that are good,

4 [a]Traitors, [1]heady, [2]highminded, lovers of pleasures [3]more than lovers of God;

5 [a]Having a form of godliness, but [b]denying the power thereof: [c]from such turn away.

6 For [a]of this sort are they which creep into houses, and lead captive silly women laden with sins, led away with divers lusts,

7 Ever learning, and never able [a]to come to the knowledge of the truth.

8 [a]Now as Jannes and Jambres withstood Moses, so do these also resist the truth: [b]men of corrupt minds, [c]reprobate[1] concerning the faith.

9 But they shall proceed no further: for their folly shall be manifest unto all *men*, [a]as theirs also was.

10 [a]But thou hast fully [1]known my doctrine, manner of life, purpose, faith, longsuffering, [2]charity, patience,

11 Persecutions, afflictions, which came unto me [a]at Antioch, [b]at Iconium, [c]at Lystra; what persecutions I endured: but [d]out of *them* all the Lord delivered me.

12 Yea, and [a]all that will live godly in Christ Jesus shall suffer persecution.

13 [a]But evil men and [1]seducers shall [2]wax worse and worse, deceiving, and being deceived.

14 But [a]continue thou in the things which thou hast learned and hast been assured of, knowing of whom thou hast learned *them;*

15 And that from a child thou hast known [a]the holy scriptures, which are able to make thee wise unto salvation through faith which is in Christ Jesus.

16 [a]All scripture *is* given by inspiration of God, [b]and *is* profitable for doctrine, for reproof, for correction, for instruction in righteousness:

---

2:6 [1] *farmer*
[2] *crops*
2:7 [a] Prov. 2:6
2:8 [a] Rom. 1:3,
4  [b] 1 Cor. 15:4
[c] Rom. 2:16
2:9 [a] Acts 9:16
[b] Eph. 3:1  [c] Acts
28:31 [1] *chains*
[2] *chained*
2:10 [a] Eph. 3:13
[b] 2 Cor. 1:6 [1] *chosen ones'*
2:11 [a] Rom. 6:5, 8
2:12 [a] [Rom. 5:17; 8:17]  [b] Matt. 10:33
[1] *endure*
2:13 [a] Num. 23:19
[1] *are faithless*
2:14 [a] Titus 3:9
[1] *ruin*
2:15 [a] 2 Pet. 1:10
[1] Lit. *Be diligent*
[2] *present*
2:16 [1] *worthless talk*
2:17 [a] 1 Tim. 1:20
[1] *spread* [2] *cancer*
2:18 [a] 1 Cor. 15:12
[1] *strayed*
2:19 [a] [1 Cor. 3:11]
[b] [Nah. 1:7]
2:20 [a] Rom. 9:21
[1] *clay*
2:21 [a] 2 Tim. 3:17
[1] *cleanse* [2] *the latter* [3] *set apart* [4] *useful*
2:22 [a] 1 Tim. 6:11
[1] *pursue* [2] *love*
2:23 [1] *ignorant disputes* [2] *generate*
2:24 [a] Titus 3:2
[b] Titus 1:9  [c] 1 Tim. 3:3 [1] *quarrel* [2] *able*
2:25 [a] Gal. 6:1  [b] Acts 8:22
[c] 1 Tim. 2:4
[1] *correcting* [2] *are in opposition* [3] *so they may know*
2:26 [a] 1 Tim. 3:7
[1] *come to their senses* [2] *to do*
3:1 [a] 1 Tim. 4:1
3:2 [1] *money lovers*
3:3 [1] *irreconcilable* [2] *slanderers* [3] *without self-control* [4] *brutal* [5] *good*
3:4 [a] 2 Pet. 2:10 [1] *reckless* [2] *haughty* [3] *rather than*
3:5 [a] Titus 1:16
[b] 1 Tim. 5:8
[c] 2 Thess. 3:6
3:6 [a] Matt. 23:14
3:7 [a] 1 Tim. 2:4
3:8 [a] Ex. 7:11, 12, 22; 8:7;
9:11 [b] 1 Tim. 6:5 [c] Rom. 1:28
[1] *disapproved*
3:9 [a] Ex. 7:11, 12; 8:18; 9:11 3:10 [a] 1 Tim. 4:6 [1] *followed* [2] *love* 3:11 [a] Acts 13:44–52 [b] Acts 14:1–6, 19 [c] Acts 14:8–20 [d] Ps. 34:19 3:12 [a] [Ps. 34:19] 3:13 [a] 2 Thess. 2:11 [1] *imposters* [2] *grow* 3:14 [a] 2 Tim. 1:13 3:15 [a] John 5:39 3:16 [a] [2 Pet. 1:20] [b] Rom. 4:23; 15:4

17 <sup>a</sup>That the man of God may be perfect, <sup>b</sup>throughly <sup>1</sup>furnished unto all good works.

## CHAPTER 4

I <sup>a</sup>CHARGE *thee* therefore before God, and the Lord Jesus Christ, <sup>b</sup>who shall judge the <sup>1</sup>quick and the dead at his appearing and his kingdom;

2 Preach the word; be <sup>1</sup>instant in season, out of season; <sup>a</sup>reprove, <sup>b</sup>rebuke, <sup>c</sup>exhort with all longsuffering and doctrine.

3 <sup>a</sup>For the time will come when they will not endure <sup>b</sup>sound doctrine; <sup>c</sup>but after their own lusts shall they heap to themselves teachers, having itching ears;

4 And they shall turn away *their* ears from the truth, and <sup>a</sup>shall be turned unto fables.

5 But watch thou in all things, <sup>a</sup>endure afflictions, do the work of <sup>b</sup>an evangelist, make full proof of thy ministry.

6 For <sup>a</sup>I am now ready to be offered, and the time of <sup>b</sup>my <sup>1</sup>departure is at hand.

7 <sup>a</sup>I have fought a good fight, I have finished *my* <sup>1</sup>course, I have kept the faith:

8 Henceforth there is laid up for me <sup>a</sup>a crown of righteousness, which the Lord, thc righteous <sup>b</sup>judge, shall give me <sup>c</sup>at that day: and not to me only, but unto all them also that love his appearing.

9 Do thy diligence to come shortly unto me:

10 For <sup>a</sup>Demas hath forsaken me, <sup>b</sup>having loved this present world, and is departed unto Thessalonica;

### Cross references

3:17 <sup>a</sup> 1 Tim. 6:11
<sup>b</sup> 2 Tim. 2:21
<sup>1</sup> *equipped*

4:1 <sup>a</sup> 1 Tim. 5:21
<sup>b</sup> Acts 10:42
<sup>1</sup> *living*

4:2 <sup>a</sup> Titus 2:15
<sup>b</sup> 1 Tim. 5:20
<sup>c</sup> 1 Tim. 4:13
<sup>1</sup> *ready*

4:3 <sup>a</sup> 2 Tim.
3:1 <sup>b</sup> 1 Tim. 1:10
<sup>c</sup> 2 Tim. 3:6

4:4 <sup>a</sup> 1 Tim. 1:4

4:5 <sup>a</sup> 2 Tim. 1:8
<sup>b</sup> Acts 21:8

4:6 <sup>a</sup> Phil. 2:17
<sup>b</sup> [Phil. 1:23]
<sup>1</sup> *Death*

4:7 <sup>a</sup> 1 Cor. 9:24–27 <sup>1</sup> *race*

4:8 <sup>a</sup> James 1:12 <sup>b</sup> John 5:22
<sup>c</sup> 2 Tim. 1:12

4:10 <sup>a</sup> Col. 4:14
<sup>b</sup> 1 John 2:15

4:11 <sup>a</sup> Acts 12:12, 25; 15:37–39

4:12 <sup>a</sup> Acts 20:4

4:14 <sup>a</sup> 1 Tim. 1:20

4:15 <sup>1</sup> *you beware*

4:16 <sup>a</sup> Acts 7:60
<sup>1</sup> *defence*

4:17 <sup>a</sup> Acts 23:11 <sup>b</sup> Acts 9:15
<sup>c</sup> 1 Sam. 17:37

4:18 <sup>a</sup> Ps. 121:7
<sup>b</sup> Rom. 11:36

4:19 <sup>a</sup> Acts 18:2
<sup>b</sup> 2 Tim. 1:16

4:20 <sup>a</sup> Rom. 16:23
<sup>b</sup> Acts 20:4; 21:29

Crescens to Galatia, Titus unto Dalmatia.

11 Only Luke is with me. Take <sup>a</sup>Mark, and bring him with thee: for he is profitable to me for the ministry.

12 And <sup>a</sup>Tychicus have I sent to Ephesus.

13 The cloke that I left at Troas with Carpus, when thou comest, bring *with thee,* and the books, *but* especially the parchments.

14 <sup>a</sup>Alexander the coppersmith did me much evil: the Lord reward him according to his works:

15 Of whom <sup>1</sup>be thou ware also; for he hath greatly withstood our words.

16 At my first <sup>1</sup>answer no man stood with me, but all *men* forsook me: <sup>a</sup>*I pray God* that it may not be laid to their charge.

17 <sup>a</sup>Notwithstanding the Lord stood with me, and strengthened me; <sup>b</sup>that by me the preaching might be fully known, and *that* all the Gentiles might hear: and I was delivered <sup>c</sup>out of the mouth of the lion.

18 <sup>a</sup>And the Lord shall deliver me from every evil work, and will preserve *me* unto his heavenly kingdom: <sup>b</sup>to whom *be* glory for ever and ever. Amen.

19 Salute <sup>a</sup>Prisca and Aquila, and the household of <sup>b</sup>Onesiphorus.

20 <sup>a</sup>Erastus abode at Corinth: but <sup>b</sup>Trophimus have I left at Miletum sick.

21 Do thy diligence to come before winter. Eubulus greeteth thee, and Pudens, and Linus, and Claudia, and all the brethren.

22 The Lord Jesus Christ *be* with thy spirit. Grace *be* with you. Amen.

# THE EPISTLE OF PAUL TO
# TITUS

Titus, a young pastor, faces the unenviable assignment of setting in order the church at Crete. Paul writes advising him to appoint elders, men of proven spiritual character in their homes and businesses, to oversee the work of the church. But elders are not the only individuals in the church who are required to excel spiritually. Men and women, young and old, each have their vital functions to fulfill in the church if they are to be living examples of the doctrine they profess. Throughout his letter to Titus, Paul stresses the necessary, practical working out of salvation in the daily lives of both the elders and the congregation. Good works are desirable and profitable for all believers.

This third Pastoral Epistle is simply titled *Pros Titon*, "To Titus." Ironically, this was also the name of the Roman general who destroyed Jerusalem in A.D. 70 and succeeded his father Vespasian as emperor.

## CHAPTER 1

PAUL, a servant of God, and an apostle of Jesus Christ, according to the faith of God's elect, and ᵃthe acknowledging of the truth ᵇwhich is ¹after godliness;

2 In hope of eternal life, which God, that ᵃcannot lie, promised before ¹the world began;

3 But hath in due times manifested his word through preaching, which is committed unto me according to the commandment of God our Saviour;

4 To ᵃTitus, ¹*mine* own son ²after the common faith: Grace, mercy, *and* peace, from God the Father and the Lord Jesus Christ our Saviour.

5 For this cause left I thee in Crete, that thou shouldest ᵃset in order the things that are ¹wanting, and ordain elders in every city, as I ²had appointed thee:

6 If any be blameless, the husband of one wife, ᵃhaving faithful children not accused of ¹riot or ²unruly.

7 For ¹a bishop must be blameless, as the steward of God; not selfwilled, not ²soon angry, ᵃnot given to wine, ³no striker, not ⁴given to filthy lucre;

8 But a lover of hospitality, a lover of ¹good men, ²sober, just, holy, ³temperate;

9 Holding fast the faithful word as he hath been taught, that he may be able by sound doctrine both to exhort and to ¹convince ²the gainsayers.

10 For there are many ¹unruly and vain ᵃtalkers and deceivers, specially they of the circumcision:

11 Whose mouths must be stopped, who subvert whole houses, teaching things which they ought not, ᵃfor ¹filthy lucre's sake.

12 ᵃOne of themselves, *even* a prophet of their own, said, The Cretians *are* alway liars, evil beasts, ¹slow bellies.

13 This witness is true. ᵃWherefore

1:1 ᵃ 2 Tim. 2:25
ᵇ [1 Tim. 3:16]
¹ *according to*
1:2 ᵃ Num. 23:19
¹ *time began*
1:4 ᵃ 2 Cor. 2:13;
8:23 ¹ *my true*
² *in our*
1:5 ᵃ 1 Cor. 11:34
¹ *lacking* ² *commanded*
1:6 ᵃ 1 Tim. 3:2–4
¹ *dissipation* ² *insubordination*
1:7 ᵃ Lev. 10:9 ¹ *an overseer* ² *quicktempered* ³ *not violent* ⁴ *greedy for money*
1:8 ¹ *what is good* ² *sober-minded* ³ *self-controlled*
1:9 ¹ *convict* ² *those who contradict*
1:10 ᵃ James 1:26 ¹ *insubordinate*
1:11 ᵃ 1 Tim. 6:5 ¹ *dishonest gain's*
1:12 ᵃ Acts 17:28 ¹ *lazy gluttons*
1:13 ᵃ 2 Cor. 13:10
1:14 ᵃ Is. 29:13
1:15 ᵃ 1 Cor. 6:12
1:16 ᵃ Matt. 7:20–23; 25:12 ᵇ [2 Tim. 3:5, 7] ᶜ Rom. 1:28 ¹ *disqualified*
2:1 ¹ *are proper for*
2:2 ¹ *reverent* ² *love*
2:3 ¹ *slanderers*
2:4 ¹ *admonish*
2:5 ᵃ 1 Tim. 5:14 ᵇ 1 Cor. 14:34 ᶜ Rom. 2:24 ¹ *homemakers*
2:7 ᵃ 1 Tim. 4:12 ᵇ Eph. 6:24 ¹ *integrity* ² *reverence* ³ *incorruptibility*
2:8 ¹ *an opponent*

rebuke them sharply, that they may be sound in the faith;

14 Not giving heed to Jewish fables, and ᵃcommandments of men, that turn from the truth.

15 ᵃUnto the pure all things *are* pure: but unto them that are defiled and unbelieving *is* nothing pure; but even their mind and conscience is defiled.

16 They profess that they ᵃknow God; but ᵇin works they deny *him*, being abominable, and disobedient, ᶜand unto every good work ¹reprobate.

## CHAPTER 2

BUT speak thou the things which ¹become sound doctrine:

2 That the aged men be sober, ¹grave, temperate, sound in faith, in ²charity, in patience.

3 The aged women likewise, that *they be* in behaviour as becometh holiness, not ¹false accusers, not given to much wine, teachers of good things;

4 That they may ¹teach the young women to be sober, to love their husbands, to love their children,

5 *To be* discreet, chaste, ¹keepers at ᵃhome, good, ᵇobedient to their own husbands, ᶜthat the word of God be not blasphemed.

6 Young men likewise exhort to be sober minded.

7 In all things shewing thyself a ᵃpattern of good works: in doctrine *shewing* ¹uncorruptness, ²gravity, ᵇsincerity,³

8 Sound speech, that cannot be condemned; that he that is ¹of the contrary part may be ashamed, having no evil thing to say of you.

9 *Exhort* ᵃservants to be obedient unto their own masters, *and* to please *them* well in all *things;* not answering ¹again;

10 Not ¹purloining, but shewing all good fidelity; that they may adorn

2:9 ᵃ 1 Tim. 6:1 ¹ *back* 2:10 ¹ *pilfering*

993

the doctrine of God our Saviour in all things.

11 For <sup>a</sup>the grace of God that bringeth salvation hath appeared to all men,

12 Teaching us that, denying ungodliness and worldly lusts, we should live soberly, righteously, and godly, in this present ¹world;

13 <sup>a</sup>Looking for that blessed <sup>b</sup>hope, and the glorious appearing of the great God and our Saviour Jesus Christ;

14 <sup>a</sup>Who gave himself for us, that he might redeem us from all iniquity, <sup>b</sup>and purify unto himself <sup>c</sup>a¹ peculiar people, zealous of good works.

15 These things speak, and <sup>a</sup>exhort, and rebuke with all authority. Let no man despise thee.

## CHAPTER 3

PUT them in mind <sup>a</sup>to be subject to ¹principalities and ²powers, to obey magistrates, <sup>b</sup>to be ready to every good work,

2 To speak evil of no man, to be ¹no brawlers, *but* gentle, shewing all meekness unto all men.

3 For <sup>a</sup>we ourselves also were sometimes foolish, disobedient, deceived, serving divers lusts and pleasures, living in malice and envy, hateful, *and* hating one another.

4 But after that <sup>a</sup>the kindness and love of <sup>b</sup>God our Saviour toward man appeared,

5 <sup>a</sup>Not by works of righteousness which we have done, but according

### Cross references (center column)

2:11 <sup>a</sup> [Rom. 5:15]
2:12 ¹ *age*
2:13 <sup>a</sup> 1 Cor. 1:7
<sup>b</sup> [Col. 3:4]
2:14 <sup>a</sup> Gal. 1:4
<sup>b</sup> [Heb. 1:3; 9:14]
<sup>c</sup> Ex. 15:16 ¹ *his own special*
2:15 <sup>a</sup> 2 Tim. 4:2
3:1 <sup>a</sup> 1 Pet. 2:13
<sup>b</sup> Col. 1:10 ¹ *rulers*
² *authorities*
3:2 ¹ *not contentious*
3:3 <sup>a</sup> 1 Cor. 6:11
3:4 <sup>a</sup> Titus 2:11
<sup>b</sup> 1 Tim. 2:3
3:5 <sup>a</sup> [Rom. 3:20]; Eph. 2:4–9
<sup>b</sup> John 3:3
¹ *poured out*
3:6 <sup>a</sup> Ezek. 36:25
3:7 <sup>a</sup> [Matt. 25:34]; Mark 10:17; [Rom. 8:17, 23, 24; Titus 1:2] ¹ *declared righteous*
3:8 <sup>a</sup> 1 Tim. 1:15
3:9 <sup>a</sup> 1 Tim. 1:4; 2 Tim. 2:23 ¹ *disputes* ² *useless*
3:10 <sup>a</sup> Matt. 18:17 ¹ *divisive*
3:11 ¹ *warped*
3:12 <sup>a</sup> Acts 20:4; Eph. 6:21; Col. 4:7; 2 Tim. 4:12
3:13 <sup>a</sup> Acts 18:24; 1 Cor. 16:12 ¹ *lacking*
3:14 ¹ *urgent needs*
3:15 ¹ *greet*

to his mercy he saved us, by <sup>b</sup>the washing of regeneration, and renewing of the Holy Ghost;

6 <sup>a</sup>Which he ¹shed on us abundantly through Jesus Christ our Saviour;

7 That being ¹justified by his grace, <sup>a</sup>we should be made heirs according to the hope of eternal life.

8 <sup>a</sup>This *is* a faithful saying, and these things I will that thou affirm constantly, that they which have believed in God might be careful to maintain good works. These things are good and profitable unto men.

9 But <sup>a</sup>avoid foolish ¹questions, and genealogies, and contentions, and strivings about the law; for they are unprofitable and ²vain.

10 A man that is ¹an heretick after the first and second admonition <sup>a</sup>reject;

11 Knowing that he that is such is ¹subverted, and sinneth, being condemned of himself.

12 When I shall send Artemas unto thee, or <sup>a</sup>Tychicus, be diligent to come unto me to Nicopolis: for I have determined there to winter.

13 Bring Zenas the lawyer and <sup>a</sup>Apollos on their journey diligently, that nothing be ¹wanting unto them.

14 And let ours also learn to maintain good works for ¹necessary uses, that they be not unfruitful.

15 All that are with me ¹salute thee. Greet them that love us in the faith. Grace *be* with you all. Amen.

# THE EPISTLE OF PAUL TO
# PHILEMON

**D**oes Christian brotherly love really work, even in situations of extraordinary tension and difficulty? Will it work, for example, between a prominent slave owner and one of his runaway slaves? Paul has no doubt! He writes a "postcard" to Philemon, his beloved brother and fellow worker, on behalf of Onesimus—a deserter, thief, and formerly worthless slave, but now Philemon's brother in Christ. With much tact and tenderness, Paul asks Philemon to receive Onesimus back with the same gentleness with which he would receive Paul himself. Any debt Onesimus owes, Paul promises to make good. Knowing Philemon, Paul is confident that brotherly love and forgiveness will carry the day.

Since this letter is addressed to Philemon in verse 1, it becomes known as *Pros Philemona,* "To Philemon." Like First and Second Timothy and Titus, it is addressed to an individual, but unlike the Pastoral Epistles, Philemon is also addressed to a family and a church (v. 2).

**P**AUL, a [a]prisoner of Jesus Christ, and Timothy *our* brother, unto Philemon our dearly beloved, and fellowlabourer,

2 And to *our* beloved Apphia, and [a]Archippus our fellowsoldier, and to the church in thy house:

3 Grace to you, and peace, from God our Father and the Lord Jesus Christ.

4 [a]I thank my God, making mention of thee always in my prayers,

5 [a]Hearing of thy love and faith, which thou hast toward the Lord Jesus, and toward all saints;

6 That the [1]communication of thy faith may become [2]effectual [a]by the acknowledging of [b]every good thing which is in you in Christ Jesus.

7 For we have great joy and [1]consolation in thy love, because the [2]bowels of the saints are refreshed by thee, brother.

8 Wherefore, though I might be much bold in Christ to [1]enjoin thee that which is [2]convenient,

9 Yet for love's sake I rather [1]beseech *thee,* being such an one as Paul the aged, and now also a prisoner of Jesus Christ.

10 I beseech thee for my son [a]Onesimus, whom I have begotten in my [1]bonds:

11 Which in time past was to thee unprofitable, but now profitable to thee and to me:

12 Whom I have sent [1]again: thou therefore receive him, that is, mine own [2]bowels:

13 Whom I [1]would have retained with me, that in thy [2]stead he might

have ministered unto me in [3]the bonds of the gospel:

14 But [1]without thy mind would I do nothing; [a]that thy [2]benefit should not be as it were of necessity, but willingly.

15 For perhaps he therefore departed for a season, that thou shouldest receive him for ever;

16 Not now as a servant, but [1]above a servant, a brother beloved, specially to me, but how much more unto thee, both in the [a]flesh, and in the Lord?

17 If thou count me therefore a partner, receive him as myself.

18 If he hath wronged thee, or oweth *thee* [1]ought, put that on mine account;

19 I Paul have written *it* with mine own [a]hand, I will repay *it:* albeit I do not say to thee how thou owest unto me even thine own self besides.

20 Yea, brother, let me have joy of thee in the Lord: refresh my [1]bowels in the Lord.

21 [a]Having confidence in thy obedience I wrote unto thee, knowing that thou wilt [1]also do more than I say.

22 But [1]withal prepare me also a lodging: for [a]I trust that [b]through your prayers I shall be given unto you.

23 There [1]salute thee [a]Epaphras, my fellowprisoner in Christ Jesus;

24 [a]Marcus, [b]Aristarchus, [c]Demas, [d]Lucas,[1] my fellowlabourers.

25 [a]The grace of our Lord Jesus Christ *be* with your spirit. Amen.

# THE EPISTLE TO THE
# HEBREWS

Many Jewish believers, having stepped out of Judaism into Christianity, want to reverse their course in order to escape persecution by their countrymen. The writer of Hebrews exhorts them to "go on unto perfection" (6:1). His appeal is based on the superiority of Christ over the Judaic system. Christ is better than the angels, for they worship Him. He is better than Moses, for He created him. He is better than the Aaronic priesthood, for His sacrifice was once for all time. He is better than the law, for He mediates a better covenant. In short, there is more to be gained in Christ than to be lost in Judaism. Pressing on in Christ produces tested faith, self-discipline, and a visible love seen in good works.

Although the title is sometimes given as "The Epistle of Paul the Apostle to the Hebrews," there is no early manuscript evidence to support it. The oldest and most reliable title is simply *Pros Ebraious*, "To Hebrews."

## CHAPTER 1

GOD, who ¹at sundry times and ᵃin ²divers manners spake in time past unto the fathers by the prophets,

2 Hath in these last days spoken unto us by *his* Son, whom he hath appointed heir of all things, by whom also he made the ¹worlds;

3 ᵃWho being the brightness of *his* glory, and the express ᵇimage of his person, and ᶜupholding all things by the word of his power, ᵈwhen he had by himself ¹purged our sins, ᵉsat down on the right hand of the Majesty on high;

4 Being made so much better than the angels, as ᵃhe hath by inheritance obtained a more excellent name than they.

5 For unto which of the angels said he at any time, ᵃThou art my Son, this day have I begotten thee? And again, ᵇI will be to him a Father, and he shall be to me a Son?

6 And again, when he bringeth in ᵃthe ¹firstbegotten into the world, he saith, ᵇAnd let all the angels of God worship him.

7 And of the angels he saith, ᵃWho maketh his angels spirits, and his ministers a flame of fire.

8 But unto the Son *he saith,* ᵃThy throne, O God, *is* for ever and ever: ¹a sceptre of righteousness *is* the sceptre of thy kingdom.

9 Thou hast loved righteousness, and hated ¹iniquity; therefore God, *even* thy God, ᵃhath anointed thee with the oil of gladness above thy ²fellows.

10 And, ᵃThou, Lord, in the beginning hast laid the foundation of the earth; and the heavens are the works of thine hands:

11 ᵃThey shall perish; but thou remainest; and ᵇthey all shall ¹wax old as doth a garment;

1:1 ᵃ Num. 12:6, 8 ¹ Or *in many portions* ² Lit. *many ways*
1:2 ¹ Or *ages*
1:3 ᵃ John 1:14 ᵇ 2 Cor. 4:4 ᶜ Col. 1:17 ᵈ [Heb. 7:27] ᵉ Ps. 110:1 ¹ *cleansed*
1:4 ᵃ [Phil. 2:9, 10]
1:5 ᵃ Ps. 2:7 ᵇ 2 Sam. 7:14
1:6 ᵃ [Rom. 8:29] ᵇ Deut. 32:43, LXX, DSS; Ps. 97:7 ¹ *firstborn*
1:7 ᵃ Ps. 104:4
1:8 ᵃ Ps. 45:6, 7 ¹ A *ruler's staff*
1:9 ᵃ Is. 61:1, 3 ¹ *lawlessness* ² *companions*
1:10 ᵃ Ps. 102:25–27
1:11 ᵃ [Is. 34:4] ᵇ Is. 50:9; 51:6 ¹ *grow*
1:12 ᵃ Heb. 13:8 ¹ *cloak*
1:13 ᵃ Ps. 110:1
1:14 ᵃ Ps. 103:20 ᵇ Rom. 8:17
2:1 ¹ *drift away*
2:2 ᵃ Acts 7:53 ᵇ Num. 15:30 ¹ *proved* ² *penalty*
2:3 ᵃ Heb. 10:28 ᵇ Matt. 4:17 ᶜ Luke 1:2
2:4 ᵃ Mark 16:20 ᵇ Acts 2:22, 43 ᶜ 1 Cor. 12:4, 7, 11 ᵈ Eph. 1:5, 9 ¹ *various*
2:5 ᵃ [2 Pet. 3:13]
2:6 ᵃ Ps. 8:4–6 ¹ *to take care of him*
2:7 ¹ Or *for a little while lower*
2:8 ᵃ Matt. 28:18

12 And as a ¹vesture shalt thou fold them up, and they shall be changed: but thou art the ᵃsame, and thy years shall not fail.

13 But to which of the angels said he at any time, ᵃSit on my right hand, until I make thine enemies thy footstool?

14 ᵃAre they not all ministering spirits, sent forth to minister for them who shall be ᵇheirs of salvation?

## CHAPTER 2

THEREFORE we ought to give the more earnest heed to the things which we have heard, lest at any time we should ¹let *them* slip.

2 For if the word ᵃspoken by angels ¹was stedfast, and ᵇevery transgression and disobedience received a just ²recompence of reward;

3 ᵃHow shall we escape, if we neglect so great salvation; ᵇwhich at the first began to be spoken by the Lord, and was ᶜconfirmed unto us by them that heard *him;*

4 ᵃGod also bearing *them* witness, ᵇboth with signs and wonders, and with ¹divers miracles, and ᶜgifts of the Holy Ghost, ᵈaccording to his own will?

5 For unto the angels hath he not put in subjection ᵃthe world to come, whereof we speak.

6 But one in a certain place testified, saying, ᵃWhat is man, that thou art mindful of him? or the son of man, that thou ¹visitest him?

7 Thou madest him ¹a little lower than the angels; thou crownedst him with glory and honour, and didst set him over the works of thy hands:

8 ᵃThou hast put all things in subjection under his feet. For in that he put all in subjection under him, he left nothing *that is* not put under

him. But now [b]we see not yet all things put under him.

9 But we see Jesus, [a]who was made [1]a little lower than the angels for the suffering of death, [b]crowned with glory and honour; that he by the grace of God should taste death [c]for every man.

10 For it [1]became him, [a]for whom *are* all things, and by whom *are* all things, in bringing many sons unto glory, to make the [2]captain of their salvation [b]perfect[3] through sufferings.

11 For [a]both he that [1]sanctifieth and they who are sanctified [b]*are* all of one: for which cause [c]he is not ashamed to call them brethren,

12 Saying, [a]I will declare thy name unto my brethren, in the midst of the [1]church will I sing praise unto thee.

13 And again, [a]I will put my trust in him. And again, [b]Behold I and the children which God hath given me.

14 Forasmuch then as the children are partakers of flesh and blood, he [a]also himself likewise [1]took part of the same; [b]that through death he might destroy him that had the power of [c]death, that is, the devil;

15 And deliver them who [a]through fear of death were all their lifetime subject to [1]bondage.

16 For verily he [1]took not on *him the nature of* angels; but he [2]took on *him* the seed of Abraham.

17 Wherefore in all things [1]it behoved him [a]to be made like unto *his* brethren, that he might be [b]a merciful and faithful high priest in things *pertaining* to God, to make [2]reconciliation for the sins of the people.

18 [a]For in that he himself hath suffered being tempted, he is able to [1]succour them that are tempted.

### CHAPTER 3

WHEREFORE, holy brethren, partakers of the heavenly calling, consider the Apostle and High Priest of our [1]profession, Christ Jesus;

2 Who was faithful to him that appointed him, as also [a]Moses *was faithful* in all his house.

3 For this *man* was counted worthy of more glory than Moses, inasmuch as [a]he who hath builded the house hath more honour than the house.

4 For every house is builded by some *man;* but [a]he that built all things *is* God.

5 [a]And Moses verily *was* faithful in all his house, as [b]a servant, [c]for a testimony of those things which were to be spoken [1]after;

6 But Christ as [a]a son over his own house; [b]whose house are we, [c]if we hold fast the confidence and the rejoicing of the hope firm unto the end.

7 Wherefore (as [a]the Holy Ghost saith, [b]To day if ye will hear his voice,

8 Harden not your hearts, as in the [1]provocation, in the day of [2]temptation in the wilderness:

9 When your fathers [1]tempted me, proved me, and saw my works forty years.

10 Wherefore I was [1]grieved with that generation, and said, They do always [2]err in *their* heart; and they have not known my ways.

11 So I sware in my wrath, They shall not enter into my rest.)

12 Take heed, brethren, lest there be in any of you an evil heart of unbelief, in departing from the living God.

13 But exhort one another daily, while it is called To day; lest any of you be hardened through the deceitfulness of sin.

14 For we [1]are made partakers of Christ, if we hold the beginning of our confidence stedfast unto the end;

15 While it is said, [a]To day if ye will hear his voice, harden not your hearts, as in the [1]provocation.

16 [a]For some, when they had heard, did [1]provoke: howbeit not all that came out of Egypt by Moses.

17 But with whom was he [1]grieved forty years? *was it* not with them that had sinned, [a]whose [2]carcases fell in the wilderness?

18 And [a]to whom sware he that they should not enter into his rest, but to them that [1]believed not?

19 So we see that they could not enter in because of [a]unbelief.

### CHAPTER 4

LET [a]us therefore fear, lest, a promise [1]being left *us* of entering into his rest, any of you should seem to come short of it.

2 For unto us was the gospel preached, as well as unto them: but the word preached did not profit them, not being mixed with faith in them that heard *it.*

3 For we which have believed do enter into rest, as he said, [a]As I have sworn in my wrath, [1]if they shall enter into my rest: although the works were finished from the foundation of the world.

4 For he spake in a certain place of the seventh *day* [1]on this wise, [a]And God did rest the seventh day from all his works.

5 And in this *place* again, [a]If[1] they shall enter into my rest.

6 Seeing therefore it remaineth that some must enter therein, and they to whom it was first preached entered not in because of [1]unbelief:

7 Again, he [1]limiteth a certain day, saying in David, To day, after so long a time; as it is said, [a]To day if ye

2:8 [b] 1 Cor. 15:25, 27
2:9 [a] Phil. 2:7–9 [b] Acts 2:33; 3:13 [c] [John 3:16] [1] Or *for a little while*
2:10 [a] Col. 1:16 [b] Heb. 5:8, 9; 7:28 [1] *was fitting for him* [2] *author* [3] *complete*
2:11 [a] Heb. 10:10 [b] Acts 17:26 [c] Matt. 28:10 [1] *sets apart*
2:12 [a] Ps. 22:22 [1] *congregation*
2:13 [a] 2 Sam. 22:3; Is. 8:17 [b] Is. 8:18
2:14 [a] John 1:14 [b] Col. 2:15 [c] 2 Tim. 1:10 [1] *shared*
2:15 [a] [Luke 1:74] [1] *slavery*
2:16 [1] Or *did not give aid to,* lit. *did not take hold of* [2] *takes hold of, gives aid to*
2:17 [a] Phil. 2:7 [b] [Heb. 4:15; 5:1–10] [1] *he had to be made* [2] *propitiation*
2:18 [a] [Heb. 4:15, 16] [1] *aid*
3:1 [1] *confession*
3:2 [a] Num. 12:7
3:3 [a] Zech. 6:12, 13
3:4 [a] [Eph. 2:10]
3:5 [a] Heb. 3:2 [b] Ex. 14:31 [c] Deut. 18:15, 18, 19 [1] *Afterward*
3:6 [a] Heb. 1:2 [b] [1 Cor. 3:16] [c] [Matt. 10:22]
3:7 [a] Acts 1:16 [b] Ps. 95:7–11
3:8 [1] *rebellion* [2] *trial*
3:9 [1] *tested*
3:10 [1] *angry* [2] *go astray*
3:14 [1] *have become*
3:15 [a] Ps. 95:7, 8 [1] *rebellion*
3:16 [a] Num. 14:2, 11, 30 [1] *rebel*
3:17 [a] Num. 14:22, 23 [1] *angry* [2] *corpses*
3:18 [a] Num. 14:30 [1] *obeyed*
3:19 [a] 1 Cor. 10:11, 12
4:1 [a] Heb. 12:15 [1] *remaining of*
4:3 [a] Ps. 95:11 [1] *they shall not*
4:4 [a] Gen. 2:2 [1] *in this way*
4:5 [a] Ps. 95:11 [1] *They shall not*
4:6 [1] *disobedience*
4:7 [a] Ps. 95:7, 8 [1] *designates*

will hear his voice, harden not your hearts.

8 For if ¹Jesus had ªgiven them rest, then ²would he not afterward have spoken of another day.

9 There remaineth therefore a rest to the people of God.

10 For he that is entered into his rest, he also hath ceased from his own works, as God *did* from his.

11 ªLet us ¹labour therefore to enter into that rest, lest any man fall after the same example of ²unbelief.

12 For the word of God *is* ªquick,¹ and powerful, and ᵇsharper than any ᶜtwoedged sword, piercing even to the dividing asunder of soul and spirit, and of the joints and marrow, and *is* ᵈa² discerner of the thoughts and ³intents of the heart.

13 ªNeither is there any creature that is ¹not manifest in his sight: but all things *are* ᵇnaked and opened unto the eyes of him with whom we ²have to do.

14 Seeing then that we have a great ªhigh priest, that is passed ¹into the heavens, Jesus the Son of God, ᵇlet us hold fast *our* profession.

15 For ªwe have not an high priest which cannot ¹be touched with ²the feeling of our infirmities; but ᵇwas in all points tempted like as *we are,* ᶜyet without sin.

16 ªLet us therefore come ¹boldly unto the throne of grace, that we may obtain mercy, and find grace to help in time of need.

### CHAPTER 5

FOR every high priest taken from among men ªis ¹ordained for men in things *pertaining* to God, that he may offer both gifts and sacrifices for sins:

2 Who can have compassion on the ignorant, and on them that are ¹out of the way; for that he himself also is ²compassed with ªinfirmity.

3 And by reason hereof he ¹ought, as for the people, so also for ªhimself, to offer for sins.

4 And no man taketh this honour unto himself, but he that is called of God, as ªwas Aaron.

5 ªSo also Christ glorified not himself to be made an high priest; but he that said unto him, ᵇThou art my Son, to day have I begotten thee.

6 As he saith also in another *place,* ªThou *art* a priest for ever after the order of Melchisedec.

7 Who in the days of his flesh, when he had ªoffered up prayers and supplications ᵇwith strong crying and tears unto ᶜthat that was able to save him from death, and was heard ᵈin¹ that he feared;

8 Though he were a Son, yet learned

he ªobedience by the things which he suffered;

9 And ªbeing made perfect, he became the author of eternal salvation unto all them that obey him;

10 Called of God an high priest after the order of Melchisedec.

11 Of whom ªwe have many things to say, and hard to ¹be uttered, seeing ye are ᵇdull of hearing.

12 For ¹when for the time ye ought to be teachers, ye have need that one teach you again which *be* the first principles of the ²oracles of God; and are become such as have need of ªmilk, and not of ³strong meat.

13 For every one that ¹useth milk *is* unskilful in the word of righteousness: for he is ªa babe.

14 But ¹strong meat belongeth to them that are ²of full age, *even* those who by reason of ³use have their senses ⁴exercised ªto discern both good and evil.

### CHAPTER 6

THEREFORE ªleaving the ¹principles of the doctrine of Christ, let us go on unto ²perfection; not laying again the foundation of repentance from ᵇdead works, and of faith toward God,

2 ªOf the doctrine of baptisms, ᵇand of laying on of hands, ᶜand of resurrection of the dead, ᵈand of eternal judgment.

3 And this will we do, if God permit.

4 For *it is* impossible for those who were once enlightened, and have tasted of ªthe heavenly gift, and ᵇwere made partakers of the Holy Ghost,

5 And have tasted the good word of God, and the powers of the ¹world to come,

6 If they shall fall away, to renew them again unto repentance; ªseeing they crucify to themselves the Son of God ¹afresh, and put *him* to an open shame.

7 For the earth which drinketh in the rain that cometh ¹oft upon it, and bringeth forth herbs ²meet for them by whom it is ³dressed, ªreceiveth blessing from God:

8 ªBut that which beareth thorns and briers *is* rejected, and *is* nigh unto ¹cursing; whose end *is* to be burned.

9 But, beloved, we are ¹persuaded better things ²of you, and things that accompany salvation, though we thus speak.

10 For ªGod *is* not unrighteous to forget ᵇyour work and labour of love, which ye have shewed toward his name, in that ye have ᶜministered to the saints, and do minister.

4:8 ª Josh. 22:4
¹ Joshua ² *he would not*
4:11 ª 2 Pet. 1:10
¹ *be diligent*
² *disobedience*
4:12 ª Ps. 147:15
ᵇ Is. 49:2 ᶜ Eph. 6:17 ᵈ 1 Cor. 14:24, 25 ¹ *living* ² *able to judge* ³ *intentions*
4:13 ª Ps. 33:13–15; 90:8 ᵇ Job 26:6 ¹ *hidden from* ² *must give account*
4:14 ª Heb. 2:17; 7:26 ᵇ Heb. 10:23 ¹ *through*
4:15 ª Is. 53:3–5 ᵇ Luke 22:28 ᶜ 2 Cor. 5:21 ¹ *sympathize* ² *our weaknesses*
4:16 ª [Eph. 2:18] ¹ *confidently*
5:1 ª Heb. 2:17; 8:3 ¹ *appointed*
5:2 ª Heb. 7:28 ¹ *going astray* ² *beset by weakness*
5:3 ª Lev. 9:7; 16:6 ¹ *is required*
5:4 ª Ex. 28:1
5:5 ª John 8:54 ᵇ Ps. 2:7
5:6 ª Ps. 110:4
5:7 ª Matt. 26:39, 42, 44 ᵇ Ps. 22:1 ᶜ Matt. 26:53 ᵈ Matt. 26:37 ¹ *because of his godly fear*
5:8 ª Phil. 2:8
5:9 ª Heb. 2:10
5:11 ª [John 16:12] ᵇ [Matt. 13:15] ¹ *explain*
5:12 ª 1 Cor. 3:1–3 ¹ *though by this time* ² *sayings* ³ *solid food*
5:13 ª Eph. 4:14 ¹ *partakes of*
5:14 ª Is. 7:15 ¹ *solid food* ² *mature* ³ *practise* ⁴ *trained*
6:1 ª Heb. 5:12 ᵇ [Heb. 9:14] ¹ *elementary discussion of* ² *maturity*
6:2 ª Acts 19:3–5 ᵇ [Acts 8:17] ᶜ Acts 17:31 ᵈ Acts 24:25
6:4 ª [John 4:10] ᵇ [Gal. 3:2, 5]
6:5 ¹ *age*
6:6 ª Heb. 10:29 ¹ *again*
6:7 ª Ps. 65:10 ¹ *often* ² *useful* ³ *cultivated*
6:8 ª Is. 5:6 ¹ *being cursed* 6:9 ¹ *confident of* ² *concerning* 6:10 ª Rom. 3:4 ᵇ 1 Thess. 1:3 ᶜ Rom. 15:25

11 And we desire that every one of you do shew the same diligence ᵃto the full assurance of hope unto the end:

12 That ye be not ¹slothful, but ²followers of them who through faith and patience ᵃinherit the promises.

13 For when God made promise to Abraham, because he could swear by no greater, ᵃhe sware by himself,

14 Saying, ᵃSurely blessing I will bless thee, and multiplying I will multiply thee.

15 And so, after he had patiently endured, he obtained the ᵃpromise.

16 For men verily swear by the greater: and ᵃan oath for confirmation *is* to them an end of all ¹strife.

17 Wherein God, ¹willing more abundantly to shew unto ᵃthe heirs of promise ᵇthe ²immutability of his counsel, confirmed *it* by an oath:

18 That by two ¹immutable things, in which *it was* impossible for God to ᵃlie, we might have a strong consolation, who have fled for refuge to lay hold upon the hope ᵇset before us:

19 Which *hope* we have as an anchor of the soul, both sure and stedfast, ᵃand which entereth ¹into that within the veil;

20 ᵃWhither the forerunner is for us entered, *even* Jesus, ᵇmade¹ an high priest for ever after the order of Melchisedec.

## CHAPTER 7

FOR this ᵃMelchisedec, king of Salem, priest of the most high God, who met Abraham returning from the slaughter of the kings, and blessed him;

2 To whom also Abraham gave a tenth part of all; first being ¹by interpretation King of righteousness, and after that also King of Salem, which is, King of peace;

3 Without father, without mother, without ¹descent, having neither beginning of days, nor end of life; but made like unto the Son of God; abideth a priest continually.

4 Now consider how great this man *was*, unto whom even the patriarch Abraham gave the tenth of the ¹spoils.

5 And verily ᵃthey that are of the sons of Levi, who receive the office of the priesthood, have a commandment to take tithes of the people according to the law, that is, of their brethren, though they come out of the loins of Abraham:

6 But he whose ¹descent is not ²counted from them received tithes of Abraham, ᵃand blessed ᵇhim that had the promises.

7 And ¹without all contradiction the less is blessed of the better.

8 And here men that die receive tithes; but there he *receiveth them,* ᵃof whom it is witnessed that he liveth.

9 And as I may so say, Levi also, who receiveth tithes, payed tithes ¹in Abraham.

10 For he was yet in the loins of his father, when Melchisedec met him.

11 ᵃIf therefore ¹perfection were by the Levitical priesthood, (for under it the people received the law,) what further need *was there* that another priest should rise after the order of Melchisedec, and not be called after the order of Aaron?

12 For the priesthood being changed, there is made of necessity a change also of the law.

13 For he of whom these things are spoken ¹pertaineth to another tribe, of which no man ²gave attendance at the altar.

14 For *it is* evident that ᵃour Lord sprang out of ᵇJuda; of which tribe Moses spake nothing concerning priesthood.

15 And it is yet far more evident: for that after the ¹similitude of Melchisedec there ariseth another priest,

16 Who ¹is made, not after the law of a ²carnal commandment, but after the power of an endless life.

17 For he testifieth, ᵃThou *art* a priest for ever after the order of Melchisedec.

18 For there is verily a ¹disannulling of the ²commandment going before for ᵃthe weakness and unprofitableness thereof.

19 For ᵃthe law made nothing perfect, but the bringing in of ᵇa better hope *did;* by the which ᶜwe draw ¹nigh unto God.

20 And inasmuch as not without an oath *he was made priest:*

21 (For those priests were made without an oath; but this with an oath by him that said unto him, ᵃThe Lord sware and will not ¹repent, Thou *art* a priest for ever after the order of Melchisedec:)

22 By so ¹much was Jesus made a ²surety of a ᵃbetter ³testament.

23 And they truly were many priests, because they were not ¹suffered to continue by reason of death:

24 But this *man*, because he continueth ever, hath an unchangeable priesthood.

25 Wherefore he is ᵃable also to save them to the uttermost that come unto God by him, seeing he ever liveth ᵇto make intercession for them.

26 For such an high priest ¹became us, ᵃ*who is* holy, ²harmless, undefiled, separate from sinners, ᵇand ³made higher than the heavens;

### Center column references

6:11 ᵃ Col. 2:2
6:12 ᵃ Heb. 10:36 ¹ *sluggish* ² *imitators*
6:13 ᵃ Gen. 22:16, 17
6:14 ᵃ Gen. 22:16, 17
6:15 ᵃ Gen. 12:4; 21:5
6:16 ᵃ Ex. 22:11 ¹ *dispute*
6:17 ᵃ Heb. 11:9 ᵇ Rom. 11:29 ¹ *determining* ² *unchangeableness*
6:18 ᵃ Num. 23:19 ᵇ [Col. 1:5] ¹ *unchangeable*
6:19 ᵃ Lev. 16:2, 15 ¹ *the Presence behind the veil*
6:20 ᵃ [Heb. 4:14] ᵇ Heb. 3:1; 5:10, 11 ¹ *having become*
7:1 ᵃ Gen. 14:18–20
7:2 ¹ *translated*
7:3 ¹ *genealogy*
7:4 ¹ *plunder*
7:5 ᵃ Num. 18:21–26
7:6 ᵃ Gen. 14:19, 20 ᵇ [Rom. 4:13] ¹ *genealogy* ² *derived*
7:7 ¹ *beyond*
7:8 ᵃ Heb. 5:6; 6:20
7:9 ¹ *through*
7:11 ᵃ Heb. 7:18; 8:7 ¹ *completion*
7:13 ¹ *belongs* ² *has officiated*
7:14 ᵃ Is. 1:1 ᵇ Matt. 1:2
7:15 ¹ *likeness*
7:16 ¹ *has come* ² *fleshly*
7:17 ᵃ Ps. 110:4
7:18 ᵃ [Rom. 8:3] ¹ *setting aside* ² *former commandment*
7:19 ᵃ [Acts 13:39] ᵇ Heb. 6:18, 19 ᶜ Rom. 5:2 ¹ *near*
7:21 ᵃ Ps. 110:4 ¹ *relent*
7:22 ᵃ Heb. 8:6 ¹ *much more Jesus has become* ² *guarantee* ³ *covenant*
7:23 ¹ *allowed*
7:25 ᵃ Jude 24 ᵇ Rom. 8:34
7:26 ᵃ Heb. 4:15 ᵇ Eph. 1:20 ¹ *was fitting for* ² *innocent* ³ *has become*

27 Who needeth not daily, as those high priests, to offer up sacrifice, first for his [a]own sins, and then for the people's: for this he did once, when he offered up himself.

28 For the law maketh men high priests which have [1]infirmity; but the word of the oath, which [2]was since the law, *maketh* the Son, who [3]is consecrated for evermore.

## CHAPTER 8

Now of the things which we have spoken *this is* the [1]sum: We have such an high priest, [a]who is set on the right hand of the throne of the Majesty in the heavens;

2 A minister of [a]the sanctuary, and of [b]the true tabernacle, which the Lord pitched, and not man.

3 For [a]every high priest is ordained to offer gifts and sacrifices: wherefore [b]*it is* of necessity that this man have somewhat also to offer.

4 For if he were on earth, he should not be a priest, seeing that there are priests that offer gifts according to the law:

5 Who serve unto the [a]example[1] and [b]shadow of heavenly things, as Moses was [2]admonished of God when he was about to make the tabernacle: [c]for, See, saith he, *that* thou make all things according to the pattern shewed to thee [3]in the mount.

6 But now [a]hath he obtained a more excellent ministry, [1]by how much also he is the mediator of a [b]better covenant, which was established upon better promises.

7 For if that [a]first *covenant* had been faultless, then should no place have been sought for the second.

8 For finding fault with them, he saith, [a]Behold, the days come, saith the Lord, when I will make a new covenant with the house of Israel and with the house of Judah:

9 Not according to the covenant that I made with their fathers in the day when I took them by the hand to lead them out of the land of Egypt; because they continued not in my covenant, and I [1]regarded them not, saith the Lord.

10 For this *is* the covenant that I will make with the house of Israel after those days, saith the [a]Lord; I will put my laws into their mind, and write them in their hearts: and [b]I will be to them a God, and they shall be to me a people:

11 And [a]they shall not teach every man his neighbour, and every man his brother, saying, Know ye the [b]Lord: for all shall know me, from the least to the greatest.

12 For I will be merciful to their unrighteousness, [a]and their sins and their [1]iniquities will I remember no more.

13 [a]In that he saith, A new *covenant,* he hath made the first [1]old. Now that which [2]decayeth and [3]waxeth old *is* ready to vanish away.

## CHAPTER 9

Then verily the first *covenant* had also ordinances of divine service, and [a]a[1] worldly sanctuary.

2 For there was a tabernacle made; the first, wherein *was* the [1]candlestick, and the table, and the shewbread; which is called the [2]sanctuary.

3 [a]And [1]after the second veil, the [2]tabernacle which is called the Holiest of all;

4 Which had the [a]golden [1]censer, and [b]the ark of the covenant overlaid round about with gold, wherein *was* [c]the golden pot that had manna, and [d]Aaron's rod that budded, and [e]the [2]tables of the covenant;

5 And [a]over it the cherubims of glory shadowing the mercyseat; of which we cannot now speak [1]particularly.

6 Now when these things were thus [1]ordained, [a]the priests went always into the first [2]tabernacle, accomplishing the service *of God.*

7 But into the second *went* the high priest alone [a]once every year, not without blood, which he offered for [b]himself, and *for* the [1]errors of the people:

8 The Holy Ghost this signifying, that [a]the way into the holiest of all was not yet made manifest, while as the first tabernacle was yet standing:

9 Which *was* [1]a figure for the time then present, in which were offered both gifts and sacrifices, [a]that could not make him that did the service perfect, [2]as pertaining to the conscience;

10 [1]*Which stood* only in [a]meats and drinks, and [b]divers[2] washings, [c]and [3]carnal ordinances, imposed *on them* until the time of reformation.

11 But Christ being come an high priest of [a]good things to come, by a greater and more perfect tabernacle, not made with hands, that is to say, not of this [1]building;

12 Neither [a]by the blood of goats and calves, but [b]by his own blood he entered in [c]once into the [1]holy place, [d]having obtained eternal redemption *for us.*

13 For if [a]the blood of bulls and of goats, and [b]the ashes of an heifer sprinkling the unclean, [1]sanctifieth to the purifying of the flesh:

14 How much more shall the blood of Christ, who through the eternal Spirit offered himself without [1]spot to God, [a]purge[2] your conscience from [b]dead works [c]to serve the living God?

### Center references

7:27 [a] Lev. 9:7; 16:6
7:28 [1] *weakness*
[2] *came after* [3] *has been perfected*
8:1 [a] Col. 3:1
[1] *main point*
8:2 [a] Heb. 9:8, 12
[b] Heb. 9:11, 24
8:3 [a] Heb. 5:1; 8:4
[b] [Eph. 5:2]
8:5 [a] Heb. 9:23, 24
[b] Col. 2:17 [c] Ex. 25:40 [1] *copy* [2] *divinely instructed* [3] *on the mountain*
8:6 [a] [2 Cor. 3:6–8] [b] Heb. 7:22
[1] *inasmuch as*
8:7 [a] Ex. 3:8; 19:5
8:8 [a] Jer. 31:31–34
8:9 [1] *disregarded them*
8:10 [a] Jer. 31:33
[b] Zech. 8:8
8:11 [a] Is. 54:13
[b] Jer. 31:34
8:12 [a] Rom. 11:27
[1] *lawless deeds*
8:13 [a] [2 Cor. 5:17]
[1] *obsolete* [2] *is becoming obsolete* [3] *growing*
9:1 [a] Ex. 25:8 [1] *an earthly*
9:2 [1] *lampstand* [2] *holy place*
9:3 [a] Ex. 26:31–35; 40:3 [1] *behind* [2] *part of the tabernacle*
9:4 [a] Lev. 16:12
[b] Ex. 25:10 [c] Ex. 16:33 [d] Num. 17:1–10 [e] Ex. 25:16; 34:29 [1] *altar of incense* [2] *tablets*
9:5 [a] Lev. 16:2 [1] *in detail*
9:6 [a] Num. 18:2–6; 28:3 [1] *prepared* [2] *part of the*
9:7 [a] Ex. 30:10
[b] Heb. 5:3 [1] *sins committed in ignorance*
9:8 [a] [John 14:6]
9:9 [a] Heb. 7:19
[1] *symbolic* [2] *in regard to*
9:10 [a] Col. 2:16
[b] Num. 19:7
[c] Eph. 2:15 [1] *Concerned only with foods* [2] *various baptisms* [3] *fleshly*
9:11 [a] Heb. 10:1
[1] *creation*
9:12 [a] Heb. 10:4
[b] Eph. 1:7 [c] Zech. 3:9 [d] [Dan. 9:24]
[1] *Most Holy Place*
9:13 [a] Lev. 16:14, 15
[b] Num. 19:2 [1] *sets apart*
9:14 [a] 1 John 1:7
[b] Heb. 6:1 [c] Luke 1:74 [1] *blemish* [2] *cleanse*

15 And for this cause [a]he is the mediator of the new [1]testament, that by means of death, for the redemption of the transgressions *that were* under the first [1]testament, [b]they which are called might receive the promise of eternal inheritance.

16 For where a testament *is,* there must also of necessity be the death of the testator.

17 For [a]a testament *is* of force after men are dead: otherwise it is of no strength at all while the testator liveth.

18 [a]Whereupon [1]neither the first [2]*testament* was dedicated without blood.

19 For when Moses had spoken every [1]precept to all the people according to the law, [a]he took the blood of calves and of goats, [b]with water, and scarlet wool, and hyssop, and sprinkled both the book, and all the people,

20 Saying, [a]This *is* the blood of the [1]testament which [b]God hath [2]enjoined unto you.

21 Moreover [a]he sprinkled with blood both the tabernacle, and all the vessels of the ministry.

22 And almost all things are by the law [1]purged with blood; and [a]without shedding of blood is no [2]remission.

23 *It was* therefore necessary that [a]the patterns of things in the heavens should be [1]purified with these; but the heavenly things themselves with better sacrifices than these.

24 For [a]Christ is not entered into the holy places made with hands, *which are* the [1]figures of [b]the true; but into heaven itself, now [c]to appear in the presence of God for us:

25 Nor yet that he should offer himself often, as [a]the high priest entereth into the [1]holy place every year with blood of others;

26 For then must he often have suffered since the foundation of the world: but now once in the end of the [1]world hath he appeared to put away sin by the sacrifice of himself.

27 [a]And as it is appointed unto men once to die, [b]but after this the judgment:

28 So [a]Christ was once [b]offered to bear the sins [c]of many; and unto them that [d]look[1] for him shall he appear the second time [2]without sin unto salvation.

## CHAPTER 10

FOR the law having a [a]shadow of good things to come, *and* not the very image of the things, [b]can never with those sacrifices which they offered year by year continually make the comers thereunto perfect.

2 For then would they not have ceased to be offered? because that the worshippers once [1]purged should have had no more [2]conscience of sins.

3 But in those *sacrifices there is* a remembrance again *made* of sins every year.

4 For [a]*it is* not possible that the blood of bulls and of goats should take away sins.

5 Wherefore when he cometh into the world, he saith, [a]Sacrifice and offering thou [1]wouldest not, but a body hast thou prepared me:

6 In burnt offerings and *sacrifices* for sin thou hast had no pleasure.

7 Then said I, Lo, I come (in the volume of the book it is written of me,) to do thy will, O God.

8 [1]Above when he said, Sacrifice and offering and burnt offerings and *offering* for sin thou [2]wouldest not, neither hadst pleasure *therein;* which are offered [3]by the law;

9 Then said he, Lo, I come to do thy will, O God. He taketh away the first, that he may establish the second.

10 [a]By the which will we are [1]sanctified [b]through the offering of the body of Jesus Christ once *for all.*

11 And every priest standeth [a]daily ministering and offering [1]oftentimes the same sacrifices, which can never take away sins:

12 [a]But this man, after he had offered one sacrifice for sins for ever, sat down [b]on the right hand of God;

13 From henceforth [1]expecting [a]till his enemies be made his footstool.

14 For by one offering he hath perfected for ever them that are sanctified.

15 *Whereof* the Holy Ghost also is a witness to us: for after that he had said before,

16 This *is* the covenant that I will make with them after those days, saith the [a]Lord, I will put my laws into their hearts, and in their minds will I write them;

17 And their sins and [1]iniquities will I remember no more.

18 Now where [1]remission of these *is, there is* no more offering for sin.

19 Having therefore, brethren, [a]boldness[1] to enter [b]into the holiest by the blood of Jesus,

20 By a new and [a]living way, which he hath consecrated for us, through the veil, that is to say, his flesh;

21 And *having* an high priest over the house of God;

22 Let us [a]draw near with a true heart [b]in full assurance of faith, having our hearts sprinkled from an evil conscience, and our bodies washed with pure water.

23 Let us hold fast the [1]profession of *our* [2]faith without wavering; (for [a]he *is* faithful that promised;)

9:15 [a] Rom. 3:25 [b] Heb. 3:1 [1] *covenant*
9:17 [a] Gal. 3:15
9:18 [a] Ex. 24:6 [1] *not even* [2] *Covenant*
9:19 [a] Ex. 24:5, 6 [b] Lev. 14:4, 7 [1] *commandment*
9:20 [a] [Matt. 26:28] [b] Ex. 24:3–8 [1] *covenant* [2] *commanded*
9:21 [a] Ex. 29:12, 36
9:22 [a] Lev. 17:11 [1] *cleansed* [2] *forgiveness*
9:23 [a] Heb. 8:5 [1] *cleansed*
9:24 [a] Heb. 6:20 [b] Heb. 8:2 [c] Rom. 8:34 [1] *copies*
9:25 [a] Heb. 9:7 [1] *Most Holy Place*
9:26 [1] *ages*
9:27 [a] Gen. 3:19 [b] [2 Cor. 5:10]
9:28 [a] Rom. 6:10 [b] 1 Pet. 2:24 [c] Matt. 26:28 [d] Titus 2:13 [1] *eagerly wait* [2] *apart from*
10:1 [a] Heb. 8:5 [b] Heb. 7:19; 9:9
10:2 [1] *cleansed* [2] *consciousness*
10:4 [a] Mic. 6:6, 7
10:5 [a] Ps. 40:6–8 [1] *did not desire*
10:8 [1] *Previously saying* [2] *did not desire* [3] *according to*
10:10 [a] John 17:19 [b] [Heb. 9:12] [1] *set apart*
10:11 [a] Num. 28:3 [1] *repeatedly*
10:12 [a] Col. 3:1 [b] Ps. 110:1
10:13 [a] Ps. 110:1 [1] *waiting*
10:16 [a] Jer. 31:33, 34
10:17 [1] *their lawless deeds*
10:18 [1] *forgiveness*
10:19 [a] [Eph. 2:18] [b] Heb. 9:8, 12 [1] *confidence*
10:20 [a] John 14:6
10:22 [a] Heb. 7:19; 10:1 [b] Eph. 3:12
10:23 [a] 1 Cor. 1:9; 10:13 [1] *confession* [2] *hope*

24 And let us consider one another to ¹provoke unto love and to good works:

25 ªNot forsaking the assembling of ourselves together, as the manner of some *is;* but exhorting *one another:* and ᵇso much the more, as ye see ᶜthe day approaching.

26 For ªif we sin wilfully ᵇafter that we have received the knowledge of the truth, there remaineth ᶜno more sacrifice for sins,

27 But a certain fearful looking for of judgment and ªfiery indignation, which shall devour the adversaries.

28 He that ¹despised Moses' law died without mercy under two or three ªwitnesses:

29 ªOf how much ¹sorer punishment, suppose ye, shall he be thought worthy, who hath ²trodden under foot the Son of God, and ᵇhath counted the blood of the covenant, wherewith he was sanctified, ³an unholy thing, ᶜand hath ⁴done despite unto the Spirit of grace?

30 For we know him that hath said, ªVengeance *belongeth* unto me, I will ¹recompense, saith the Lord. And again, ᵇThe Lord shall judge his people.

31 ª*It is* a fearful thing to fall into the hands of the living God.

32 But ªcall to remembrance the former days, in which, after ye were ¹illuminated, ye endured a great ²fight of afflictions;

33 Partly, whilst ye were made ªa ¹gazingstock both by reproaches and ²afflictions; and partly, whilst ᵇye became companions of them that were so ³used.

34 For ye had compassion of me ªin my ¹bonds, and ᵇtook joyfully the ²spoiling of your goods, knowing in yourselves that ᶜye have in heaven a better and an enduring ³substance.

35 Cast not away therefore your confidence, ªwhich hath great recompence of reward.

36 ªFor ye have need of ¹patience, that, after ye have done the will of God, ᵇye might receive the promise.

37 For ªyet a little while, and ᵇhe that shall come will come, and will not ¹tarry.

38 Now ªthe just shall live by faith: but if *any man* draw back, my soul shall have no pleasure in him.

39 But we are not of them ªwho draw back unto ¹perdition; but of them that ᵇbelieve to the saving of the soul.

## CHAPTER 11

Now faith is the ¹substance of things hoped for, the ²evidence ªof things not seen.

2 For by it the elders obtained a good report.

3 Through faith we understand that ªthe ¹worlds were ²framed by the word of God, so that things which are seen were not made of things which ³do appear.

4 By faith ªAbel offered unto God a more excellent sacrifice than Cain, by which he obtained witness that he was righteous, God testifying of his gifts: and by it he being dead yet ᵇspeaketh.

5 By faith ªEnoch was translated ¹that he should not see death; and was not found, because God had translated him: for before his translation he had this testimony, that he pleased God.

6 But without faith *it is* impossible to please *him:* for he that cometh to God must believe that he is, and *that* he is a rewarder of them that diligently seek him.

7 By faith ªNoah, being warned of God of things not seen as yet, moved with ¹fear, ᵇprepared an ark to the saving of his house; by the which he condemned the world, and became heir of ᶜthe righteousness which is by faith.

8 By faith ªAbraham, when he was called to go out into a place which he should after receive for an inheritance, obeyed; and he went out, not knowing ¹whither he went.

9 By faith he sojourned in the land of promise, as *in* a ¹strange country, ªdwelling in ²tabernacles with Isaac and Jacob, ᵇthe heirs with him of the same promise:

10 For he ¹looked for ªa city which hath foundations, ᵇwhose builder and maker *is* God.

11 Through faith also ªSara herself received strength to conceive seed, and ᵇwas¹ delivered of a child when she was past age, because she judged him ᶜfaithful who had promised.

12 Therefore sprang there even of one, and him as good as ªdead, *so many* as the ᵇstars of the sky in multitude, and as the sand which is by the sea shore innumerable.

13 These all died in faith, ªnot having received the ᵇpromises, but ᶜhaving seen them afar off, and were ¹persuaded of *them,* and embraced *them,* and ᵈconfessed that they were strangers and pilgrims on the earth.

14 For they that say such things ªdeclare plainly that they seek a ¹country.

15 And truly, if they had been mindful of ªthat *country* from whence they came out, they might have had opportunity to have returned.

16 But now they desire a better *country,* that is, an heavenly: wherefore God is not ashamed ªto be called

---

Marginal references:

10:24 ¹ *stir up*
10:25 ª Acts 2:42 ᵇ Rom. 13:11 ᶜ Phil. 4:5
10:26 ª Num. 15:30 ᵇ 2 Pet. 2:20 ᶜ Heb. 6:6
10:27 ª Zeph. 1:18
10:28 ª Deut. 17:2–6; 19:15 ¹ *has rejected*
10:29 ª [Heb. 2:3] ᵇ 1 Cor. 11:29 ᶜ [Matt. 12:31] ¹ *worse* ² *trampled* ³ *a common* ⁴ *insulted*
10:30 ª Deut. 32:35 ᵇ Deut. 32:36 ¹ *repay*
10:31 ª [Luke 12:5]
10:32 ª Gal. 3:4 ¹ *enlightened* ² *struggle with sufferings*
10:33 ª 1 Cor. 4:9 ᵇ Phil. 1:7 ¹ *spectacle* ² *tribulations* ³ *treated*
10:34 ª 2 Tim. 1:16 ᵇ Matt. 5:12 ᶜ Matt. 6:20 ¹ *chains* ² *plundering* ³ *possession*
10:35 ª Matt. 5:12
10:36 ª Luke 9:19 ᵇ [Col. 3:24] ¹ *endurance*
10:37 ª Luke 18:8 ᵇ Hab. 2:3, 4 ¹ *delay*
10:38 ª Rom. 1:17
10:39 ª 2 Pet. 2:20 ᵇ Acts 16:31 ¹ *destruction*
11:1 ª Rom. 8:24 ¹ *realization* ² *conviction*
11:3 ª Ps. 33:6 ¹ *Or ages* ² *prepared* ³ *are visible*
11:4 ª Gen. 4:3–5 ᵇ Heb. 12:24
11:5 ª Gen. 5:21–24 ¹ *so that*
11:7 ª Gen. 6:13–22 ᵇ 1 Pet. 3:20 ᶜ Rom. 3:22 ¹ *reverence*
11:8 ª Gen. 12:1–4 ¹ *where he was going*
11:9 ª Gen. 12:8; 13:3, 18; 18:1, 9 ᵇ Heb. 6:17 ¹ *foreign* ² *tents*
11:10 ª [Heb. 12:22; 13:14] ᵇ [Rev. 21:10] ¹ *was waiting*
11:11 ª Gen. 17:19; 18:11–14; 21:1, 2 ᵇ Luke 1:36 ᶜ Heb. 10:23 ¹ *bore*
11:12 ª Rom. 4:19 ᵇ Gen. 15:5;

22:17; 32:12 11:13 ª Heb. 11:39 ᵇ Gen. 12:7 ᶜ John 8:56 ᵈ Ps. 39:12 ¹ *assured* 11:14 ª Heb. 13:14 ¹ *homeland* 11:15 ª Gen. 11:31 11:16 ª Ex. 3:6, 15; 4:5

their God: for he hath [b]prepared for them a city.

17 By faith Abraham, [a]when he was [1]tried, offered up Isaac: and he that had received the promises offered up his only begotten *son,*

18 Of whom it was said, [a]That in Isaac shall thy seed be called:

19 Accounting that God [a]*was* able to raise *him* up, even from the dead; from whence also he received him in a [1]figure.

20 By faith [a]Isaac blessed Jacob and Esau concerning things to come.

21 By faith Jacob, when he was a dying, [a]blessed both the sons of Joseph; and worshipped, *leaning* upon the top of his staff.

22 By faith [a]Joseph, when he died, made mention of the [1]departing of the children of Israel; and gave commandment concerning his bones.

23 By faith [a]Moses, when he was born, was hid three months of his parents, because they saw *he was* a [1]proper child; and they were not afraid of the king's [b]commandment.

24 By faith [a]Moses, when he [1]was come to years, refused to be called the son of Pharaoh's daughter;

25 Choosing rather to suffer affliction with the people of God, than to enjoy the [1]pleasures of sin for a season;

26 Esteeming [a]the reproach of Christ greater riches than the treasures in Egypt: for he [1]had respect unto the [b]recompence of the reward.

27 By faith [a]he forsook Egypt, not fearing the wrath of the king: for he endured, as seeing him who is invisible.

28 Through faith [a]he kept the passover, and the sprinkling of blood, lest he that destroyed the firstborn should touch them.

29 By faith [a]they passed through the Red sea as by dry *land:* which the Egyptians [1]assaying to do were drowned.

30 By faith [a]the walls of Jericho fell down, after they were [1]compassed about seven days.

31 By faith [a]the harlot Rahab perished not with them that believed not, when [b]she had received the spies with peace.

32 And what shall I more say? for the time would fail me to tell *of* [a]Gedeon, and *of* [b]Barak, and *of* [c]Samson, and *of* [d]Jephthae; *of* [e]David also, and [f]Samuel, and *of* the prophets:

33 Who through faith subdued kingdoms, wrought righteousness, obtained promises, [a]stopped the mouths of lions,

34 [a]Quenched the violence of fire, escaped the edge of the sword, out of weakness were made strong, [1]waxed

valiant in [2]fight, turned to flight the armies of the aliens.

35 [a]Women received their dead raised to life again: and others were [b]tortured, not accepting deliverance; that they might obtain a better resurrection:

36 And others had trial of *cruel* mockings and scourgings, yea, moreover [a]of [1]bonds and imprisonment:

37 [a]They were stoned, they were sawn asunder, were tempted, were slain with the sword: [b]they wandered about [c]in sheepskins and goatskins; being destitute, afflicted, tormented;

38 (Of whom the world was not worthy:) they wandered in deserts, and *in* mountains, and [a]*in* dens and caves of the earth.

39 And these all, [a]having obtained a good [1]report through faith, received not the promise:

40 God having provided some better thing for us, that they [1]without us should not be [a]made [2]perfect.

## CHAPTER 12

WHEREFORE [1]seeing we also are [2]compassed about with so great a cloud of witnesses, [a]let us lay aside every weight, and the sin which doth so easily [3]beset *us,* and [b]let us run [c]with [4]patience the race that is set before us,

2 Looking unto Jesus the [1]author and [2]finisher of *our* faith; [a]who for the joy that was set before him [b]endured the cross, despising the shame, and [c]is set down at the right hand of the throne of God.

3 [a]For consider him that endured such [1]contradiction of sinners against himself, [b]lest ye be wearied and [2]faint in your [3]minds.

4 [a]Ye have not yet resisted unto [1]blood, striving against sin.

5 And ye have forgotten the exhortation which speaketh unto you as unto [1]children, [a]My son, despise not thou the [2]chastening of the Lord, nor [3]faint when thou art rebuked of him:

6 For [a]whom the Lord loveth he chasteneth, and scourgeth every son whom he receiveth.

7 [a]If ye endure chastening, God dealeth with you as with sons; for what [b]son is he whom the father chasteneth not?

8 But if ye be without chastisement, [a]whereof all are partakers, then are ye [1]bastards, and not sons.

9 Furthermore we have had fathers of our flesh which corrected *us,* and we gave *them* [1]reverence: shall we not much rather be in subjection unto [a]the Father of spirits, and live?

11:16 [b] [Rev. 21:2]
11:17 [a] James 2:21
　[1] tested
11:18 [a] Gen. 21:12
11:19 [a] Rom. 4:17
　[1] figurative sense
11:20 [a] Gen. 27:26–40
11:21 [a] Gen. 48:1, 5, 16, 20
11:22 [a] Gen. 50:24, 25 [1] Gr. exodus
11:23 [a] Ex. 2:1–3
　[b] Ex. 1:16, 22
　[1] beautiful
11:24 [a] Ex. 2:11–15
　[1] came of age
11:25 [1] passing pleasures of sin
11:26 [a] Heb. 13:13 [b] Rom. 8:18
　[1] looked
11:27 [a] Ex. 10:28
11:28 [a] Ex. 12:21
11:29 [a] Ex. 14:22–29 [1] attempting
11:30 [a] Josh. 6:20
　[1] encircled
11:31 [a] Josh. 2:9; 6:23 [b] Josh. 2:1
11:32 [a] Judg. 6:11; 7:1–25 [b] Judg. 4:6–24 [c] Judg. 13:24–16:31
　[d] Judg. 11:1–29; 12:1–7 [e] 1 Sam. 16; 17 [f] 1 Sam. 7:9–14
11:33 [a] Dan. 6:22
11:34 [a] Dan. 3:23–28 [1] became [2] battle
11:35 [a] 1 Kin. 17:22 [b] Acts 22:25
11:36 [a] Gen. 39:20 [1] chains
11:37 [a] 1 Kin. 21:13 [b] 2 Kin. 1:8 [c] Zech. 13:4
11:38 [a] 1 Kin. 18:4, 13; 19:9
11:39 [a] Heb. 11:2, 13 [1] testimony
11:40 [a] Heb. 5:9 [1] apart from [2] complete
12:1 [a] Col. 3:8 [b] 1 Cor. 9:24 [c] Rom. 12:12 [1] since [2] surrounded by [3] ensnare [4] perseverance
12:2 [a] Luke 24:26 [b] Phil. 2:8 [c] Ps. 110:1 [1] originator [2] perfector
12:3 [a] Matt. 10:24 [b] Gal. 6:9 [1] hostility [2] discouraged [3] Lit. souls
12:4 [a] [1 Cor. 10:13] [1] bloodshed
12:5 [a] Prov. 3:11, 12 [1] sons [2] discipline [3] be discouraged
12:6 [a] Rev. 3:19
12:7 [a] Deut. 8:5 [b] Prov. 13:24; 19:18; 23:13 12:8 [a] 1 Pet. 5:9 [1] illegitimate 12:9 [a] [Job 12:10] [1] respect

10 For they verily for a few days chastened *us* [1]after their own pleasure; but he for *our* profit, [a]that *we* might be partakers of his holiness.

11 Now no [1]chastening for the present seemeth to be joyous, but grievous: nevertheless afterward it yieldeth [a]the peaceable fruit of righteousness unto them which are [2]exercised thereby.

12 Wherefore [a]lift[1] up the hands which hang down, and the feeble knees;

13 And make straight paths for your feet, lest that which is lame be [1]turned out of the way; but let it rather be healed.

14 [a]Follow[1] peace with all *men,* and holiness, [b]without which no man shall see the Lord:

15 Looking diligently lest any man [a]fail[1] of the grace of God; lest any [b]root of bitterness springing up trouble *you,* and thereby many be defiled;

16 Lest there be any [a]fornicator, or [1]profane person, as Esau, [b]who for one morsel of [2]meat sold his birthright.

17 For ye know how that afterward, when he [1]would have inherited the blessing, he was [a]rejected: for he found no place of repentance, though he sought it carefully with tears.

18 For ye are not come unto [a]the mount that might be touched, and that burned with fire, nor unto blackness, and darkness, and tempest,

19 And the sound of a trumpet, and the voice of words; which *voice* they that heard [a]intreated[1] that the word should not be spoken to them any more:

20 (For they could not endure that which was commanded, [a]And if so much as a beast touch the mountain, it shall be stoned, or thrust through with [1]a dart:

21 And so terrible was the sight, *that* Moses said, [a]I exceedingly fear and quake:)

22 But ye are come unto mount Sion, and unto the city of the living God, the heavenly Jerusalem, and to an innumerable company of angels,

23 To the [1]general assembly and church of [a]the firstborn, [b]which are [2]written in heaven, and to God [c]the Judge of all, and to the spirits of just men [d]made perfect,

24 And to Jesus [a]the mediator of the new covenant, and to [b]the blood of sprinkling, that speaketh better things [c]than *that of* Abel.

25 See that ye refuse not him that speaketh. For [a]if they escaped not who refused him that spake on earth, much more *shall not* we *escape,* if we turn away from him that *speaketh* from heaven:

26 Whose voice then shook the earth: but now he hath promised, saying, [a]Yet once more I shake not the earth only, but also heaven.

27 And this *word,* Yet once more, signifieth the [a]removing of those things that are shaken, as of things that are made, that those things which cannot be shaken may remain.

28 Wherefore we receiving a kingdom which cannot be [1]moved, let us have grace, whereby we may [a]serve God acceptably with reverence and godly fear:

29 For [a]our God *is* a consuming fire.

## CHAPTER 13

LET [a]brotherly love continue.

2 [a]Be not forgetful to entertain strangers: for thereby [b]some have entertained angels unawares.

3 [a]Remember them that are [1]in bonds, [2]as bound with them; *and* them which [3]suffer adversity, as being yourselves also in the body.

4 [a]Marriage *is* honourable [1]in all, and the bed undefiled: [b]but [2]whoremongers and adulterers God will judge.

5 *Let your* [1]conversation *be* without covetousness; *and be* content with such things as ye have: for he hath said, [a]I will never leave thee, nor forsake thee.

6 So that we may boldly say, [a]The Lord *is* my helper, and I will not fear what man [1]shall do unto me.

7 Remember them which [1]have the rule over you, who have spoken unto you the word of God: whose faith follow, considering the [2]end of *their* [3]conversation.

8 Jesus Christ [a]the same yesterday, and to day, and for ever.

9 Be not carried about with [1]divers and strange [2]doctrines. For *it is* a good thing that the heart be established with grace; not with [3]meats, which have not profited them that have been occupied therein.

10 We have an altar, whereof they have no right to eat which serve the tabernacle.

11 For the bodies of those beasts, whose blood is brought into the sanctuary by the high priest for sin, are burned [1]without the camp.

12 Wherefore Jesus also, that he might [1]sanctify the people with his own blood, suffered [2]without the gate.

13 Let us go forth therefore unto him [1]without the camp, bearing [a]his reproach.

14 For here have we no continuing city, but we seek one to come.

15 [a]By him therefore let us offer [b]the sacrifice of praise to God continually, that is, [c]the fruit of *our* lips [1]giving thanks to his name.

### Cross references

12:10 [a] Lev. 11:44
[1] *as seemed* best to them
12:11 [a] James 3:17, 18 [1] *discipline*
[2] *trained*
12:12 [a] Is. 35:3
[1] *strengthen*
12:13 [1] Dislocated
12:14 [a] Ps. 34:14
[b] Matt. 5:8
[1] *Pursue*
12:15 [a] Heb. 4:1
[b] Deut. 29:18 [1] *fall short*
12:16 [a] [1 Cor. 6:13–18] [b] Gen. 25:33
[1] *godless* [2] *food*
12:17 [a] Gen. 27:30–40 [1] *wanted to inherit*
12:18 [a] Deut. 4:11; 5:22
12:19 [a] Ex. 20:18–26 [1] *begged*
12:20 [a] Ex. 19:12, 13
[1] *an arrow*
12:21 [a] Deut. 9:19
12:23 [a] [James 1:18] [b] Luke 10:20 [c] Ps. 50:6; 94:2 [d] [Phil. 3:12]
[1] *festive gathering*
[2] *registered*
12:24 [a] Heb. 8:6; 9:15 [b] Ex. 24:8
[c] Gen. 4:10
12:25 [a] Heb. 2:2, 3
12:26 [a] Hag. 2:6
12:27 [a] [Is. 34:4; 54:10; 65:17]
12:28 [a] Heb. 13:15, 21 [1] *shaken*
12:29 [a] Ex. 24:17
13:1 [a] Rom. 12:10
13:2 [a] Matt. 25:35 [b] Gen. 18:1–22; 19:1
13:3 [a] Matt. 25:36 [1] *in prison* [2] *as if chained* [3] *are mistreated*
13:4 [a] Prov. 5:18, 19 [b] 1 Cor. 6:9
[1] *among* [2] *fornicators*
13:5 [a] Deut. 31:6, 8; Josh. 1:5
[1] *conduct*
13:6 [a] Ps. 27:1; 118:6
[1] *can*
13:7 [1] *lead* [2] *outcome* [3] *conduct*
13:8 [a] Heb. 1:12
13:9 [1] *various* [2] *teachings* [3] *foods*
13:11 [1] *outside*
13:12 [1] *set apart* [2] *outside*
13:13 [a] 1 Pet. 4:14
[1] *outside*
13:15 [a] Eph. 5:20 [b] Lev. 7:12 [c] Hos. 14:2 [1] Lit. *confessing to*

16 ᵃBut to do good and to ¹communicate forget not: for ᵇwith such sacrifices God is well pleased.

17 ᵃObey them that ¹have the rule over you, and submit yourselves: for ᵇthey watch for your souls, as they that must give account, ²that they may do it with joy, and not with grief: for that *is* unprofitable for you.

18 ᵃPray for us: for we ¹trust we have ᵇa good conscience, in all things ²willing to live ³honestly.

19 But I beseech *you* the rather to do this, that I may be restored to you the sooner.

20 Now ᵃthe God of peace, ᵇthat brought again from the dead our Lord Jesus, ᶜthat great shepherd of

13:16 ᵃ Rom.
12:13 ᵇ Phil. 4:18
¹ *share*

13:17 ᵃ Phil. 2:29
ᵇ Ezek. 3:17 ¹ *lead*
² *let them do so*

13:18 ᵃ Eph. 6:19
ᵇ Acts 23:1 ¹ *are confident that*
² *desiring* ³ *honourably*

13:20 ᵃ Rom. 5:1, 2, 10; 15:33 ᵇ Rom. 4:24 ᶜ 1 Pet. 2:25; 5:4 ᵈ Zech. 9:11

13:21 ᵃ Phil. 2:13
¹ *complete*

13:22 ¹ *bear with*

13:24 ¹ *Greet*
² *lead*

the sheep, ᵈthrough the blood of the everlasting covenant,

21 Make you ¹perfect in every good work to do his will, ᵃworking in you that which is wellpleasing in his sight, through Jesus Christ; to whom *be* glory for ever and ever. Amen.

22 And I beseech you, brethren, ¹suffer the word of exhortation: for I have written a letter unto you in few words.

23 Know ye that *our* brother Timothy is set at liberty; with whom, if he come shortly, I will see you.

24 ¹Salute all them that ²have the rule over you, and all the saints. They of Italy ¹salute you.

25 Grace *be* with you all. Amen.

# THE GENERAL EPISTLE OF

# JAMES

Faith without works cannot be called faith. "Faith without works is dead" (2:26), and a dead faith is worse than no faith at all. Faith must work; it must produce; it must be visible. Verbal faith is not enough; mental faith is insufficient. Faith must be there, but it must be more. It must inspire action. Throughout his epistle to Jewish believers, James integrates true faith and everyday practical experience by stressing that true faith must manifest itself in works of faith.

Faith endures trials. Trials come and go, but a strong faith will face them head-on and develop endurance. Faith understands temptations. It will not allow us to consent to our lust and slide into sin. Faith obeys the Word. It will not merely hear and not do. Faith produces doers. Faith harbors no prejudice. For James, faith and favoritism cannot coexist. Faith displays itself in works. Faith is more than mere words; it is more than knowledge; it is demonstrated by obedience; and it overtly responds to the promises of God. Faith controls the tongue. This small but immensely powerful part of the body must be held in check. Faith can do it. Faith acts wisely. It gives us the ability to choose wisdom that is heavenly and to shun wisdom that is earthly. Faith produces separation from the world and submission to God. It provides us with the ability to resist the Devil and humbly draw near to God. Finally, faith waits patiently for the coming of the Lord. Through trouble and trial it stifles complaining.

The name *Iakobos* (James) in 1:1 is the basis for the early title *Iakobou Epistole*, "Epistle of James." *Iakobos* is the Greek form of the Hebrew name Jacob, a Jewish name common in the first century.

## CHAPTER 1

JAMES, [a]a servant of God and of the Lord Jesus Christ, to the twelve tribes which are scattered abroad, greeting.

2 My brethren, [a]count it all joy [b]when ye fall into [1]divers temptations;

3 [a]Knowing *this,* that the [1]trying of your faith [2]worketh patience.

4 But let patience have *her* perfect work, that ye may be perfect and [1]entire, [2]wanting nothing.

5 [a]If any of you lack wisdom, [b]let him ask of God, that giveth to all *men* liberally, and [1]upbraideth not; and [c]it shall be given him.

6 [a]But let him ask in faith, [1]nothing wavering. For he that [2]wavereth is like a wave of the sea driven with the wind and tossed.

7 For let not that man think that he shall receive any thing of the Lord.

8 [a]A double minded man *is* unstable in all his ways.

9 Let the [1]brother of low degree rejoice in [2]that he is exalted:

10 But the rich, in [1]that he is made low: because [a]as the flower of the grass he shall pass away.

11 For the sun is no sooner risen with a burning heat, but it withereth the grass, and the flower thereof falleth, and the [1]grace of the fashion of it perisheth: so also shall the rich man fade away in his [2]ways.

12 [a]Blessed *is* the man that endureth temptation: for when he [1]is

tried, he shall receive [b]the crown of life, [c]which the Lord hath promised to them that love him.

13 Let no man say when he is tempted, I am tempted of God: for God cannot be tempted with evil, neither tempteth he any man:

14 But every man is tempted, when he is drawn away of his own [1]lust, and enticed.

15 Then [a]when [1]lust hath conceived, it [2]bringeth forth sin: and sin, when it is [3]finished, [b]bringeth forth death.

16 Do not [1]err, my beloved brethren.

17 [a]Every good gift and every perfect gift is from above, and cometh down from the Father of lights, [b]with whom is no [1]variableness, neither shadow of turning.

18 [a]Of his own will begat he us with the [b]word of truth, [c]that we should be a kind of firstfruits of his creatures.

19 Wherefore, my beloved brethren, let every man be swift to hear, [a]slow to speak, [b]slow to wrath:

20 For the wrath of man [1]worketh not the righteousness of God.

21 Wherefore [a]lay apart all filthiness and [1]superfluity of [2]naughtiness, and receive with meekness the [3]engrafted word, [b]which is able to save your souls.

1:1 [a] Acts 12:17
1:2 [a] Acts 5:41 [b] 2 Pet. 1:6 [1] *various trials*
1:3 [a] Rom. 5:3–5 [1] *testing* [2] *produces*
1:4 [1] *complete* [2] *lacking*
1:5 [a] 1 Kin. 3:9 [b] Matt. 7:7 [c] Jer. 29:12 [1] *without reproach*
1:6 [a] [Mark 11:23, 24] [1] *not doubting* [2] *doubts*
1:8 [a] James 4:8
1:9 [1] *lowly brother* [2] *his exaltation*
1:10 [a] Job 14:2 [1] *his humiliation*
1:11 [1] *beautiful appearance* [2] *pursuits*
1:12 [a] James 5:11 [b] [1 Cor. 9:25] [c] Matt. 10:22 [1] *has been proved*
1:14 [1] *desires*
1:15 [a] Job 15:35 [b] [Rom. 5:12; 6:23] [1] *desire* [2] *gives birth to* [3] *full-grown*
1:16 [1] *be deceived*
1:17 [a] John 3:27 [b] Num. 23:19 [1] *variation*
1:18 [a] John 1:13 [b] [1 Pet. 1:3, 23] [c] [Eph. 1:12, 13]
1:19 [a] Prov. 10:19; 17:27 [b] Prov. 14:17; 16:32 1:20 [1] *does not produce* 1:21 [a] Col. 3:8 [1] *abundance* [2] *wickedness* [b] Acts 13:26 [3] *implanted*

22 But [a]be ye doers of the word, and not hearers only, deceiving your own selves.

23 For [a]if any be a hearer of the word, and not a doer, he is like unto a man [1]beholding his natural face in a [2]glass:

24 For he beholdeth himself, and goeth his way, and straightway forgetteth what manner of man he was.

25 But [a]whoso looketh into the perfect law of liberty, and continueth *therein,* he being not a forgetful hearer, but a doer of the work, [b]this man shall be blessed in [1]his deed.

26 If any man among you [1]seem to be religious, and [a]bridleth not his tongue, but deceiveth his own heart, this man's religion *is* [2]vain.

27 [a]Pure religion and undefiled before God and the Father is this, [b]To visit the fatherless and widows in their affliction, [c]*and* to keep himself unspotted from the world.

## CHAPTER 2

M Y brethren, [1]have not the faith of our Lord Jesus Christ, [a]*the Lord* of glory, with [b]respect[2] of persons.

2 For if there come unto your assembly a man with a gold ring, in [1]goodly apparel, and there come in also a poor man in [2]vile raiment;

3 And ye [1]have respect to him that weareth the [2]gay clothing, and say unto him, Sit thou here in a good place; and say to the poor, Stand thou there, or sit here [3]under my footstool:

4 [1]Are ye not then partial in yourselves, and are become judges [2]of evil thoughts?

5 Hearken, my beloved brethren, [a]Hath not God chosen the poor of this world [b]rich[1] in faith, and heirs of the kingdom [c]which he hath promised to them that love him?

6 But [a]ye have [1]despised the poor. Do not rich men oppress you, [b]and [2]draw you before the judgment seats?

7 Do not they blaspheme that [1]worthy name by the which ye are [a]called?

8 If ye fulfil the royal law according to the scripture, [a]Thou shalt love thy neighbour as thyself, ye do well:

9 But if ye [1]have respect to persons, ye commit sin, and are [2]convinced of the law as [a]transgressors.

10 For whosoever shall keep the whole law, and yet [a]offend[1] in one *point,* [b]he is guilty of all.

11 For he that said, [a]Do not commit adultery, said also, [b]Do not kill. Now if thou commit no adultery, yet if thou kill, thou art become a transgressor of the law.

12 So speak ye, and so do, as they that shall be judged by [a]the law of liberty.

1:22 [a] Matt. 7:21–28
1:23 [a] Luke 6:47 [1] *observing* [2] *mirror*
1:25 [a] James 2:12 [b] John 13:17 [1] *what he does*
1:26 [a] Ps. 34:13 [1] *thinks he is* [2] *useless*
1:27 [a] Matt. 25:34–36 [b] Is. 1:17 [c] [Rom. 12:2]
2:1 [a] 1 Cor. 2:8 [b] Lev. 19:15 [1] *hold* [2] *partiality*
2:2 [1] *fine* [2] *filthy clothes*
2:3 [1] *pay special attention* [2] *fine* [3] *at*
2:4 [1] *Have you not discriminated among* [2] *with*
2:5 [a] 1 Cor. 1:27 [b] Luke 12:21 [c] Ex. 20:6 [1] *to be rich*
2:6 [a] 1 Cor. 11:22 [b] Acts 13:50 [1] *dishonoured* [2] *drag you into the courts*
2:7 [a] 1 Pet. 4:16 [1] *noble or good*
2:8 [a] Lev. 19:18
2:9 [a] Deut. 1:17 [1] *show partiality* [2] *convicted*
2:10 [a] Gal. 3:10 [b] Deut. 27:26 [1] *stumble*
2:11 [a] Ex. 20:14; Deut. 5:18 [b] Ex. 20:13; Deut. 5:17
2:12 [a] James 1:25
2:13 [a] Job 22:6 [b] Prov. 21:13 [c] Mic. 7:18 [d] Rom. 12:8 [1] *triumphs over*
2:14 [a] Matt. 7:21–23, 26; 21:28–32
2:15 [a] Luke 3:11
2:16 [a] [1 John 3:17, 18]
2:18 [a] Heb. 6:10 [b] James 3:13
2:20 [1] *do you want to know* [2] *foolish*
2:21 [a] Gen. 22:9, 10, 12, 16–18
2:22 [a] Heb. 11:17 [b] John 8:39 [1] *was working* [2] *complete*
2:23 [a] Gen. 15:6 [b] 2 Chr. 20:7 [1] *accounted*
2:25 [a] Heb. 11:31
3:1 [a] [Matt. 23:8] [b] Luke 6:37 [1] *let not many of you be* [2] *teachers* [3] *stricter judgment*
3:2 [a] 1 Kin. 8:46 [b] Ps. 34:13

13 For [a]he shall have judgment without mercy, that hath shewed [b]no [c]mercy; and [d]mercy [1]rejoiceth against judgment.

14 [a]What *doth it* profit, my brethren, though a man say he hath faith, and have not works? can faith save him?

15 [a]If a brother or sister be naked, and destitute of daily food,

16 And [a]one of you say unto them, Depart in peace, be *ye* warmed and filled; notwithstanding ye give them not those things which are needful to the body; what *doth it* profit?

17 Even so faith, if it hath not works, is dead, being alone.

18 Yea, a man may say, Thou hast faith, and I have works: [a]shew me thy faith without thy works, [b]and I will shew thee my faith by my works.

19 Thou believest that there is one God; thou doest well: the devils also believe, and tremble.

20 But [1]wilt thou know, O [2]vain man, that faith without works is dead?

21 Was not Abraham our father justified by works, [a]when he had offered Isaac his son upon the altar?

22 Seest thou [a]how faith [1]wrought with his works, and by [b]works was faith made [2]perfect?

23 And the scripture was fulfilled which saith, [a]Abraham believed God, and it was [1]imputed unto him for righteousness: and he was called [b]the Friend of God.

24 Ye see then how that by works a man is justified, and not by faith only.

25 Likewise also [a]was not Rahab the harlot justified by works, when she had received the messengers, and had sent *them* out another way?

26 For as the body without the spirit is dead, so faith without works is dead also.

## CHAPTER 3

M Y brethren, [a]be[1] not many [2]masters, [b]knowing that we shall receive the [3]greater condemnation.

2 For [a]in many things we [1]offend all. [b]If any man [1]offend not in word, [c]the same *is* a perfect man, *and* able also to bridle the whole body.

3 Behold, [a]we put bits in the horses' mouths, that they may obey us; and we turn about their whole body.

4 Behold also the ships, which though *they be* so great, and *are* driven of fierce winds, yet are they turned about with a very small [1]helm, whithersoever the [2]governor listeth.

5 Even so [a]the tongue is a little member, and [b]boasteth great things. Behold, how great a [1]matter a little fire [2]kindleth!

[c] [Matt. 12:34–37] [1] *stumble* 3:3 [a] Ps. 32:9 3:4 [1] *rudder* [2] *pilot wants* 3:5 [a] Prov. 12:18; 15:2 [b] Ps. 12:3; 73:8 [1] *forest* [2] *sets on fire*

6 And [a]the tongue *is* a fire, a world of iniquity: [1]so is the tongue among our members, that it [b]defileth the whole body, and setteth on fire the course of [2]nature; and it is set on fire of [3]hell.

7 For every kind of beasts, and of birds, and of serpents, and of things in the sea, is tamed, and hath been tamed of mankind:

8 But the tongue can no man tame; *it is* an unruly evil, [a]full of deadly poison.

9 Therewith bless we God, even the Father; and therewith curse we men, which are made [a]after the [1]similitude of God.

10 Out of the same mouth proceedeth blessing and cursing. My brethren, these things ought not so to be.

11 Doth a fountain send forth at the same place sweet *water* and bitter?

12 Can the [a]fig tree, my brethren, bear olive berries? either a vine, figs? so *can* no fountain both yield salt water and fresh.

13 [a]Who *is* a wise man and [1]endued with knowledge among you? let him shew out of a good [2]conversation [3]his works with meekness of wisdom.

14 But if ye have [a]bitter envying and [1]strife in your hearts, [b]glory[2] not, and lie not against the truth.

15 [a]This wisdom descendeth not from above, but *is* earthly, sensual, [1]devilish.

16 For [a]where envying and [1]strife *is*, there *is* confusion and every evil work.

17 But [a]the wisdom that is from above is first pure, then peaceable, gentle, *and* [1]easy to be intreated, full of mercy and good fruits, [b]without partiality, [c]and without hypocrisy.

18 [a]And the fruit of righteousness is sown in peace of them that make peace.

### CHAPTER 4

FROM whence *come* [1]wars and fightings among you? *come they* not hence, *even* of your [2]lusts [a]that war in your members?

2 Ye lust, and have not: ye [1]kill, and [2]desire to have, and cannot obtain: ye fight and [3]war, yet ye have not, because ye ask not.

3 [a]Ye ask, and receive not, [b]because ye ask amiss, that ye may consume *it* upon your [1]lusts.

4 Ye adulterers and adulteresses, know ye not that the [a]friendship [1]of the world is enmity with God? [b]whosoever therefore [2]will be a friend of the world [3]is the enemy of God.

5 Do ye think that the scripture saith in vain, [a]The [1]spirit that dwelleth in us [2]lusteth to envy?

6 But he giveth more grace. Wherefore he saith, [a]God resisteth the proud, but giveth grace unto the humble.

---

3:6 [a] Prov. 16:27
[b] [Matt. 12:36; 15:11, 18] [1] *so set*
[2] *existence* [3] Gr. *gehenna*
3:8 [a] Ps. 140:3
3:9 [a] Gen. 1:26; 5:1; 9:6 [1] *likeness*
3:12 [a] Matt. 7:16-20
3:13 [a] Gal. 6:4
[1] *has understanding* [2] *conduct*
[3] *that his works are done in the*
3:14 [a] Rom. 13:13
[b] Rom. 2:17 [1] *self-seeking* [2] *do not boast*
3:15 [a] Phil. 3:19
[1] *demonic*
3:16 [a] 1 Cor. 3:3
[1] *self-seeking exist*
3:17 [a] 1 Cor. 2:6, 7 [b] James 2:1
[c] Rom. 12:9 [1] *willing to yield*
3:18 [a] Prov. 11:18
4:1 [a] Rom. 7:23 [1] *conflicts*
[2] *Desires for pleasure*
4:2 [1] *murder*
[2] *covet* [3] *battle*
4:3 [a] Job 27:8, 9 [b] [Ps. 66:18]
[1] *pleasures*
4:4 [a] 1 John 2:15 [b] Gal. 1:4
[1] *with* [2] *wants to* [3] *makes himself an enemy*
4:5 [a] Gen. 6:5 [1] *Or Spirit*
[2] *yearns jealously*
4:6 [a] Prov. 3:34
4:7 [a] [Eph. 4:27; 6:11]
4:8 [a] 2 Chr. 15:2
[b] Is. 1:16 [c] 1 Pet. 1:22 [1] *near*
4:9 [a] Matt. 5:4
[1] *Lament* [2] *gloom*
4:10 [a] Job 22:29
4:11 [a] 1 Pet. 2:1-3
[b] [Matt. 7:1-5]
4:12 [a] [Matt. 10:28] [b] Rom. 14:4
4:13 [1] *Come now*
[2] *make a profit*
4:14 [a] Job 7:7
4:15 [a] Acts 18:21
4:16 [a] 1 Cor. 5:6
[1] *boast* [2] *arrogance*
4:17 [a] [Luke 12:47]
5:1 [a] [Luke 6:24]
5:2 [a] Matt. 6:19
[b] Job 13:28 [1] *have rotted*
5:3 [a] Rom. 2:5
[1] *corroded* [2] *in*
5:4 [a] Lev. 19:13
[1] *wages* [2] *mowed*
[b] Deut. 24:15

---

7 Submit yourselves therefore to God. [a]Resist the devil, and he will flee from you.

8 [a]Draw [1]nigh to God, and he will draw [1]nigh to you. [b]Cleanse *your* hands, *ye* sinners; and [c]purify *your* hearts, *ye* double minded.

9 [a]Be[1] afflicted, and mourn, and weep: let your laughter be turned to mourning, and *your* joy to [2]heaviness.

10 [a]Humble yourselves in the sight of the Lord, and he shall lift you up.

11 [a]Speak not evil one of another, brethren. He that speaketh evil of *his* brother, [b]and judgeth his brother, speaketh evil of the law, and judgeth the law: but if thou judge the law, thou art not a doer of the law, but a judge.

12 There is one lawgiver, [a]who is able to save and to destroy: [b]who art thou that judgest another?

13 [1]Go to now, ye that say, To day or to morrow we will go into such a city, and continue there a year, and buy and sell, and [2]get gain:

14 Whereas ye know not what *shall be* on the morrow. For what *is* your life? [a]It is even a vapour, that appeareth for a little time, and then vanisheth away.

15 For that ye *ought* to say, [a]If the Lord will, we shall live, and do this, or that.

16 But now ye [1]rejoice in your [2]boastings: [a]all such rejoicing is evil.

17 Therefore [a]to him that knoweth to do good, and doeth *it* not, to him it is sin.

### CHAPTER 5

GO to now, *ye* [a]rich men, weep and howl for your miseries that shall come upon *you*.

2 Your [a]riches [1]are corrupted, and [b]your garments are motheaten.

3 Your gold and silver is [1]cankered; and the rust of them shall be a witness against you, and shall eat your flesh as it were fire. [a]Ye have heaped treasure together [2]for the last days.

4 Behold, [a]the [1]hire of the labourers who have [2]reaped down your fields, which [3]is of you kept back by fraud, [4]crieth: and [b]the cries of them which have reaped are entered into the ears of the Lord of sabaoth.

5 Ye have lived in pleasure on the earth, and [1]been wanton; ye have [2]nourished your hearts, as in a day of slaughter.

6 Ye have condemned *and* killed the just; *and* he doth not resist you.

7 Be patient therefore, brethren, unto the coming of the Lord. Behold, the [1]husbandman waiteth for the precious fruit of the earth, and hath

[3] *you have* [4] *cry out*   5:5 [1] *indulgence* [2] *fattened*
5:7 [1] *farmer*

long patience for it, until he receive the early and latter rain.

8 Be ye also patient; ¹stablish your hearts: for the coming of the Lord ²draweth nigh.

9 ¹Grudge not one against another, brethren, lest ye be condemned: behold, the judge standeth before the door.

10 ªTake, my brethren, the prophets, who have spoken in the name of the Lord, for an example of suffering affliction, and of ᵇpatience.

11 Behold, ªwe count them ¹happy which ᵇendure. Ye have heard of ᶜthe ²patience of Job, and have seen ᵈthe end ³of the Lord; that ᵉthe Lord is very ⁴pitiful, and of tender mercy.

12 But above all things, my brethren, ªswear not, neither by heaven, neither by the earth, neither by any other oath: but let your yea be yea; and *your* nay, nay; lest ye fall into ¹condemnation.

13 Is any among you ¹afflicted? let him ªpray. Is any ²merry? ᵇlet him sing psalms.

14 Is any sick among you? let him call for the elders of the church; and

let them pray over him, ªanointing him with oil in the name of the Lord:

15 And the prayer of faith shall save the sick, and the Lord shall raise him up; ªand if he have committed sins, they shall be forgiven him.

16 Confess *your* ¹faults one to another, and pray one for another, that ye may be healed. ªThe ²effectual ³fervent prayer of a righteous man availeth much.

17 Elias was a man ªsubject¹ to like passions as we are, and ᵇhe prayed earnestly that it might not rain: and it rained not on the ²earth by the space of three years and six months.

18 And he prayed ªagain, and the heaven gave rain, and the earth brought forth her fruit.

19 Brethren, if any of you do ¹err from the truth, and one ªconvert² him;

20 Let him know, that he which ¹converteth the sinner from the error of his way ªshall save a soul from death, and ᵇshall ²hide a multitude of sins.

# THE FIRST EPISTLE GENERAL OF

# PETER

Persecution can cause either growth or bitterness in the Christian life. Response determines the result. In writing to Jewish believers struggling in the midst of persecution, Peter encourages them to conduct themselves courageously for the Person and program of Christ. Both their character and conduct must be above reproach. Having been born again to a living hope, they are to imitate the Holy One who has called them. The fruit of that character will be conduct rooted in submission: citizens to government, servants to masters, wives to husbands, husbands to wives, and Christians to one another. Only after submission is fully understood does Peter deal with the difficult area of suffering. The Christians are not to think it "strange concerning the fiery trial which is to try you, as though some strange thing happened unto you" (4:12), but are to rejoice as partakers of the suffering of Christ. That response to life is truly the climax of one's submission to the good hand of God.

This epistle begins with the phrase *Petros apostolos Iesou Christou*, "Peter, an apostle of Jesus Christ." This is the basis of the early title *Petrou A*, the "First of Peter."

## CHAPTER 1

PETER, an apostle of Jesus Christ, to the [1]strangers [a]scattered throughout Pontus, Galatia, Cappadocia, Asia, and Bithynia,

2 [a]Elect [b]according to the foreknowledge of God the Father, [c]through sanctification of the Spirit, unto [d]obedience and [e]sprinkling of the blood of Jesus Christ: [f]Grace unto you, and peace, be multiplied.

3 [a]Blessed *be* the God and Father of our Lord Jesus Christ, which [b]according to his abundant mercy [c]hath begotten us again unto a [1]lively hope [d]by the resurrection of Jesus Christ from the dead,

4 To an inheritance incorruptible, and undefiled, and that fadeth not away, [a]reserved in heaven for you,

5 [a]Who are kept by the power of God through faith unto salvation ready to be revealed in the last time.

6 [a]Wherein ye greatly rejoice, though now [b]for a season, if need be, [c]ye are [1]in heaviness through manifold temptations:

7 That [a]the [1]trial of your faith, being much more precious than of gold that perisheth, though [b]it be [2]tried with fire, [c]might be found unto praise and honour and glory at the [3]appearing of Jesus Christ:

8 [a]Whom having not seen, ye love; [b]in whom, though now ye see *him* not, yet believing, ye rejoice with joy unspeakable and full of glory:

9 Receiving the end of your faith, *even* the salvation of *your* souls.

10 Of which salvation the prophets have enquired and searched diligently, who prophesied of the grace *that should come* unto you:

11 Searching what, or what manner

of time [a]the Spirit of Christ which was in them [1]did signify, when it testified beforehand the sufferings of Christ, and the glory that [2]should follow.

12 Unto whom it was revealed, that not unto themselves, but unto us they did minister the things, which are now reported unto you by them that have preached the gospel unto you with the Holy Ghost sent down from heaven; which things the [a]angels desire to look into.

13 Wherefore [1]gird up the loins of your mind, be sober, and [2]hope to the end for the grace that is to be brought unto you at the revelation of Jesus Christ;

14 As obedient children, not [a]fashioning[1] yourselves according to the former lusts in your ignorance:

15 [a]But as he which hath called you is holy, so be ye holy in all manner of [1]conversation;

16 Because it is written, [a]Be ye holy; for I am holy.

17 And if ye call on the Father, who [a]without [1]respect of persons judgeth according to every man's work, pass the time of your [2]sojourning *here* in fear:

18 Forasmuch as ye know that ye were not redeemed with [1]corruptible things, *as* silver and gold, from your [2]vain conversation *received* by tradition from your fathers;

19 But [a]with the precious blood of Christ, [b]as of a lamb without blemish and without spot:

20 [a]Who verily was foreordained before the foundation of the world, but was [1]manifest [b]in these last times for you,

---

1:1 [a] James 1:1
[1] *exiles of the dispersion in*
1:2 [a] Eph. 1:4
[b] [Rom. 8:29]
[c] 2 Thess. 2:13
[d] Rom. 1:5 [e] Heb. 10:22; 12:24
[f] Rom. 1:7
1:3 [a] Eph. 1:3
[b] Gal. 6:16
[c] [John 3:3, 5]
[d] 1 Cor. 15:20
[1] *living*
1:4 [a] Col. 1:5
1:5 [a] John 10:28
1:6 [a] Matt. 5:12 [b] 2 Cor. 4:17 [c] James 1:2
[1] *distressed*
1:7 [a] James 1:3 [b] Job 23:10
[c] [Rom. 2:7]
[1] *genuineness*
[2] *tested* [3] *revelation*
1:8 [a] 1 John 4:20
[b] John 20:29
1:11 [a] 2 Pet. 1:21
[1] *was indicating*
[2] *would*
1:12 [a] Eph. 3:10
1:13 [1] *Prepare your mind for action* [2] *rest your hope fully upon the grace*
1:14 [a] [Rom. 12:2]
[1] *conforming*
1:15 [a] [2 Cor. 7:1]
[1] *conduct*
1:16 [a] Lev. 11:44, 45; 19:2; 20:7
1:17 [a] Acts 10:34
[1] *partiality* [2] *stay*
1:18 [1] *perishable*
[2] *aimless conduct*
1:19 [a] Acts 20:28
[b] Ex. 12:5
1:20 [a] Rom. 3:25 [b] Gal. 4:4 [1] *revealed*

21 Who by him do believe in God, [a]that raised him up from the dead, and [b]gave him glory; that your faith and hope might be in God.

22 Seeing ye [a]have purified your souls in obeying the truth through the Spirit unto [1]unfeigned [b]love of the brethren, *see that ye* love one another with a pure heart fervently:

23 [a]Being born again, not of [1]corruptible seed, but of [2]incorruptible, [b]by the word of God, which liveth and abideth for ever.

24 For [a]all flesh *is* as grass, and all the glory of man as the flower of grass. The grass withereth, and the flower thereof falleth away:

25 [a]But the [1]word of the Lord endureth for ever. [b]And this is the word which by the gospel is preached unto you.

## CHAPTER 2

WHEREFORE [a]laying aside all malice, and all guile, and hypocrisies, and envies, and all evil speakings,

2 [a]As newborn babes, desire the [1]sincere [b]milk of the word, that ye may grow thereby:

3 If so be ye have [a]tasted that the Lord is gracious.

4 To whom coming, *as unto* a living stone, [a]disallowed[1] indeed of men, but chosen of God, *and* precious,

5 Ye also, as [1]lively stones, [2]are built up a spiritual house, an holy priesthood, to offer up spiritual sacrifices, acceptable to God by Jesus Christ.

6 Wherefore also it is contained in the scripture, [a]Behold, I lay in Sion a chief corner stone, [1]elect, precious: and he that believeth on him shall not be [2]confounded.

7 Unto you therefore which believe *he is* precious: but unto them which be disobedient, [a]the stone which the builders [1]disallowed, the same is made the [2]head of the corner,

8 [a]And a stone of stumbling, and a rock of offence, [b]*even to them* which stumble [1]at the word, being disobedient: [c]whereunto also they were appointed.

9 But ye *are* a chosen generation, a royal priesthood, an holy nation, [1]a peculiar people; that ye should [2]shew forth the praises of him who hath called you out of [a]darkness into his marvellous light:

10 [a]Which in time past *were* not a people, but *are* now the people of God: which had not obtained mercy, but now have obtained mercy.

11 Dearly beloved, I beseech *you* as strangers and pilgrims, abstain from fleshly lusts, [a]which war against the soul;

12 [a]Having your [1]conversation [2]honest among the Gentiles: that, whereas

they speak against you as evildoers, [b]they may by *your* good works, which they shall behold, glorify God in the day of visitation.

13 [a]Submit yourselves to every [1]ordinance of man for the Lord's sake: whether it be to the king, as supreme;

14 Or unto governors, as unto them that are sent by him for the punishment of evildoers, and for the praise of them that do well.

15 For so is the will of God, that with well doing ye may put to silence the ignorance of foolish men:

16 [a]As free, and not [b]using *your* liberty for a cloak of [1]maliciousness, but as the servants of God.

17 Honour all *men*. Love the brotherhood. Fear [a]God. Honour the king.

18 [a]Servants, *be* subject to *your* masters with all fear; not only to the good and gentle, but also to the [1]froward.

19 For this *is* [a]thankworthy,[1] if a man for conscience toward God endure grief, suffering wrongfully.

20 For [a]what glory *is it*, if, when ye be [1]buffeted for your faults, ye shall take it patiently? but if, when ye do well, and suffer *for it*, ye take it patiently, this *is* [2]acceptable with God.

21 For [a]even hereunto were ye called: because Christ also suffered for us, [b]leaving us an example, that ye should follow his steps:

22 [a]Who did no sin, neither was [1]guile found in his mouth:

23 [a]Who, when he was reviled, reviled not [1]again; when he suffered, he threatened not; but [b]committed *himself* to him that judgeth righteously:

24 [a]Who his own self bare our sins in his own body on the tree, [b]that we, being dead to sins, should live unto righteousness: [c]by whose [1]stripes ye were healed.

25 For [a]ye were as sheep going astray; but are now returned [b]unto the Shepherd and [1]Bishop of your souls.

## CHAPTER 3

LIKEWISE, [a]ye wives, *be* in subjection to your own husbands; that, if any obey not the word, [b]they also may without [1]the word [c]be won by the [2]conversation of the wives;

2 [a]While they behold your chaste [1]conversation *coupled* with fear.

3 [a]Whose adorning let it not be that outward *adorning* of [1]plaiting the hair, and of wearing of gold, or of putting on of [2]apparel;

4 But *let it be* [a]the hidden man of the heart, in that which is not corruptible, *even the ornament* of a [1]meek and quiet spirit, which is in the sight of God [2]of great price.

1:21 [a] Acts 2:24
[b] Acts 2:33
1:22 [a] Acts 15:9 [b] Heb. 13:1
[1] *sincere*
1:23 [a] John 1:13 [b] James 1:18 [1] *perishable* [2] *imperishable*
1:24 [a] Is. 40:6–8
1:25 [a] Is. 40:8 [b] [John 1:1] [1] *spoken word*
2:1 [a] Heb. 12:1
2:2 [a] [Matt. 18:3; 19:14] [b] 1 Cor. 3:2 [1] *pure*
2:3 [a] Heb. 6:5
2:4 [a] Ps. 118:22 [1] *rejected*
2:5 [1] *living* [2] *are being*
2:6 [a] Is. 28:16 [1] *chosen* [2] *put to shame*
2:7 [a] Ps. 118:22 [1] *rejected* [2] *chief cornerstone*
2:8 [a] Is. 8:14 [b] 1 Cor. 1:23 [c] Rom. 9:22 [1] *being disobedient to the word*
2:9 [a] [Acts 26:18] [1] *his own special people* [2] *proclaim*
2:10 [a] Hos. 1:9, 10; 2:23
2:11 [a] James 4:1
2:12 [a] Phil. 2:15 [b] Matt. 5:16; 9:8 [1] *conduct* [2] *honourable*
2:13 [a] Matt. 22:21 [1] *institution*
2:16 [a] Rom. 6:14, 20, 22 [b] Gal. 5:13 [1] *evil*
2:17 [a] Prov. 24:21
2:18 [a] Eph. 6:5–8 [1] *harsh*
2:19 [a] Matt. 5:10 [1] *commendable*
2:20 [a] Luke 6:32–34 [1] *beaten* [2] *commendable before*
2:21 [a] Matt. 16:24 [b] [1 John 2:6]
2:22 [a] Is. 53:9 [1] *deceit*
2:23 [a] Is. 53:7 [b] Luke 23:46 [1] *in return*
2:24 [a] [Heb. 9:28] [b] Rom. 7:6 [c] Is. 53:5 [1] *wounds*
2:25 [a] Is. 53:5, 6 [b] [Ezek. 34:23] [1] *Overseer*
3:1 [a] Eph. 5:22 [b] 1 Cor. 7:16 [c] Matt. 18:15 [1] *a* [2] *conduct*
3:2 [a] 1 Pet. 2:12; 3:6
3:3 [a] 1 Tim. 2:9 [1] *arranging* [2] *fine apparel*
3:4 [a] Rom. 2:29 [1] *gentle* [2] *precious*

5 For after this manner in the old time the holy women also, who trusted in God, adorned themselves, being in subjection unto their own husbands:

6 Even as Sara obeyed Abraham, [a]calling him lord: whose daughters ye are, as long as ye do well, and are not afraid with any [1]amazement.

7 [a]Likewise, ye husbands, dwell with *them* [1]according to knowledge, giving honour unto the wife, [b]as unto the weaker vessel, and as being heirs together of the grace of life; [c]that your prayers be not hindered.

8 Finally, *be ye* all of one mind, having compassion one of another, love as brethren, *be* [1]pitiful, *be* courteous:

9 [a]Not rendering evil for evil, or [1]railing for [1]railing: but contrariwise [b]blessing; knowing that ye are thereunto called, [c]that ye should inherit a blessing.

10 For [a]he that will love life, and see good days, [b]let him refrain his tongue from evil, and his lips that they speak no [1]guile:

11 Let him [a]eschew[1] evil, and do good; [b]let him seek peace, and [2]ensue it.

12 For the eyes of the Lord *are* over the righteous, [a]and his ears *are open* unto their prayers: but the face of the Lord *is* against them that do evil.

13 [a]And who *is* he that will harm you, if ye be followers of that which is good?

14 [a]But and if ye suffer for righteousness' sake, [1]happy *are ye:* [b]and be not afraid of their [2]terror, neither be troubled;

15 But [1]sanctify the Lord God in your hearts: and [a]*be* ready always to give [2]an answer to every man that asketh you a reason of the [b]hope that is in you with meekness and [3]fear:

16 [a]Having a good conscience; that, whereas they speak evil of you, as of evildoers, they may be ashamed that falsely accuse your good [1]conversation in Christ.

17 For *it is* better, if the will of God be so, that ye suffer for well doing, than for evil doing.

18 For Christ also hath once suffered for sins, the just for the unjust, that he might bring us to God, being put to death in the flesh, but [1]quickened by the Spirit:

19 By which also he went and preached unto the spirits in prison;

20 Which [1]sometime were disobedient, when once the longsuffering of God waited in the days of Noah, while the ark was [2]a preparing, wherein few, that is, eight souls were saved by water.

21 [a]The[1] like figure whereunto *even* baptism doth also now save us [b](not

---

3:6 [a] Gen. 18:12
[1] terror
3:7 [a] [Eph. 5:25]
[b] 1 Cor. 12:23
[c] Job 42:8 [1] *with understanding*
3:8 [1] *tenderhearted*
3:9 [a] [Prov. 17:13]
[b] Matt. 5:44
[c] Matt. 25:34
[1] *reviling*
3:10 [a] Ps. 34:12–16
[b] James 1:26
[1] *deceit*
3:11 [a] Ps. 37:27
[b] Rom. 12:18
[1] *turn away from*
[2] *pursue*
3:12 [a] John 9:31
3:13 [a] Prov. 16:7
3:14 [a] James 1:12
[b] Is. 8:12 [1] *blessed*
[2] *threats*
3:15 [a] Ps. 119:46
[b] [Titus 3:7] [1] *set apart* [2] *a defence*
[3] *reverential awe*
3:16 [a] Heb. 13:18
[1] *conduct*
3:18 [1] *made alive*
3:20 [1] *formerly*
[2] *being prepared*
3:21 [a] Eph. 5:26
[b] [Titus 3:5]
[1] *There is an antitype, namely baptism, which does*

[c] [Rom. 10:10]
3:22 [a] Ps. 110:1
[b] Rom. 8:38
4:2 [a] John 1:13
4:3 [1] *is enough for* [2] *done*
[3] *licentiousness*
[4] *drunkenness*
[5] *drinking parties*
4:4 [1] *dissipation*
4:5 [a] Acts 10:42
[1] *living*
4:6 [a] 1 Pet. 1:12;
3:19 [b] [Rom. 8:9, 13]
4:7 [a] Rom. 13:11
4:8 [a] [Prov. 10:12]
[1] *love*
4:9 [a] Heb. 13:2
[b] 2 Cor. 9:7
[1] *grumbling*
4:10 [a] Rom. 12:6–8 [b] 1 Cor. 4:1, 2
[c] [1 Cor. 12:4]
4:11 [a] Eph. 4:29
[b] [1 Cor. 10:31]
[1] *utterances*
4:13 [a] James 1:2
[b] 2 Tim. 2:12 [1] *to the extent that*
4:14 [a] Matt. 5:11
[b] Matt. 5:16 [1] *insulted* [2] *blessed*
[3] *blasphemed*

---

the putting away of the filth of the flesh, [c]but the answer of a good conscience toward God,) by the resurrection of Jesus Christ:

22 Who is gone into heaven, and [a]is on the right hand of God; [b]angels and authorities and powers being made subject unto him.

## CHAPTER 4

FORASMUCH then as Christ hath suffered for us in the flesh, arm yourselves likewise with the same mind: for he that hath suffered in the flesh hath ceased from sin;

2 That he no longer should live the rest of *his* time in the flesh to the lusts of men, [a]but to the will of God.

3 For the time past of *our* life [1]may suffice us to have [2]wrought the will of the Gentiles, when we walked in [3]lasciviousness, lusts, [4]excess of wine, revellings, [5]banquetings, and abominable idolatries:

4 Wherein they think it strange that ye run not with *them* to the same excess of [1]riot, speaking evil of *you:*

5 Who shall give account to him that is ready [a]to judge the [1]quick and the dead.

6 For for this cause [a]was the gospel preached also to them that are dead, that they might be judged according to men in the flesh, but [b]live according to God in the spirit.

7 But [a]the end of all things is at hand: be ye therefore sober, and watch unto prayer.

8 And above all things have fervent [1]charity among yourselves: for [a]charity[1] shall cover the multitude of sins.

9 [a]Use hospitality one to another [b]without [1]grudging.

10 [a]As every man hath received the gift, *even so* minister the same one to another, [b]as good stewards of [c]the manifold grace of God.

11 [a]If any man speak, *let him speak* as the [1]oracles of God; if any man minister, *let him do it* of the ability which God giveth: that [b]God in all things may be glorified through Jesus Christ, to whom be praise and dominion for ever and ever. Amen.

12 Beloved, think it not strange concerning the fiery trial which is to try you, as though some strange thing happened unto you:

13 But rejoice, [a]inasmuch[1] as ye are partakers of Christ's sufferings; that, [b]when his glory shall be revealed, ye may be glad also with exceeding joy.

14 If ye be [1]reproached for the name of Christ, [a]happy[2] *are ye;* for the spirit of glory and of God resteth upon you: on their part he is [3]evil spoken of, [b]but on your part he is glorified.

15 But let none of you suffer as a murderer, or *as* a thief, or *as* an

evildoer, or as a [1]busybody in other men's matters.

16 Yet if *any man suffer* as a Christian, let him not be ashamed; but let him glorify God on this [1]behalf.

17 For the time *is come* [a]that judgment must begin at the house of God: and if *it* first *begin* at us, [b]what shall the end *be* of them that obey not the gospel of God?

18 And [a]if the righteous scarcely be saved, where shall the ungodly and the sinner appear?

19 Wherefore let them that suffer according to the will of God [a]commit the keeping of their souls *to him* in well doing, as unto a faithful Creator.

## CHAPTER 5

THE elders which are among you I exhort, who am also an elder, and a [a]witness of the sufferings of Christ, and also a partaker of the [b]glory that shall be revealed:

2 [a]Feed[1] the flock of God which is among you, taking the oversight *thereof,* [b]not by constraint, but willingly; [c]not for [2]filthy lucre, but [3]of a ready mind;

3 Neither as [a]being lords over [b]*God's*[1] heritage, but [c]being ensamples to the flock.

4 And when [a]the chief Shepherd shall appear, ye shall receive [b]a crown of glory that fadeth not away.

5 Likewise, ye younger, submit yourselves unto the elder. Yea, [a]all *of you* be subject one to another, and be clothed with humility: for [b]God resisteth the proud, and [c]giveth grace to the humble.

6 Humble yourselves therefore under the mighty hand of God, that he may exalt you in due time:

7 Casting all your care upon him; for he careth for you.

8 Be sober, be vigilant; because your adversary the devil, as a roaring lion, walketh about, seeking whom he may devour:

9 Whom resist stedfast in the faith, knowing that the same afflictions are [1]accomplished in your brethren that are in the world.

10 But the God of all grace, [a]who hath called us unto his eternal glory by Christ Jesus, after that ye have suffered a while, make you perfect, [1]stablish, strengthen, settle *you.*

11 [a]To him *be* glory and dominion for ever and ever. Amen.

12 By [a]Silvanus, a faithful brother unto you, as I [1]suppose, I have written briefly, exhorting, and testifying [b]that this is the true grace of God wherein ye stand.

13 The *church that is* at Babylon, elected together with *you,* [1]saluteth you; and *so doth* [a]Marcus[2] my son.

14 Greet ye one another with a kiss of [1]charity. Peace *be* with you all that are in Christ Jesus. Amen.

### Center column references

4:15 [1] *meddler*
4:16 [1] *matter*
4:17 [a] Is. 10:12
[b] Luke 10:12
4:18 [a] Prov. 11:31
4:19 [a] 2 Tim. 1:12
5:1 [a] Matt. 26:37
[b] Rom. 8:17, 18
5:2 [a] Acts 20:28 [b] 1 Cor. 9:17 [c] 1 Tim. 3:3 [1] *Shepherd* [2] *dishonest gain* [3] *eagerly*
5:3 [a] Ezek. 34:4 [b] Ps. 33:12 [c] Phil. 3:17 [1] *those entrusted to you*
5:4 [a] Heb. 13:20 [b] 2 Tim. 4:8
5:5 [a] Eph. 5:21 [b] Prov. 3:34 [c] Is. 57:15
5:9 [1] *experienced by*
5:10 [a] 1 Cor. 1:9 [1] *confirm*
5:11 [a] Rev. 1:6
5:12 [a] 2 Cor. 1:19 [b] Acts 20:24 [1] *consider him*
5:13 [a] Acts 12:12, 25; 15:37, 39 [1] *greets* [2] *Mark*
5:14 [1] *love*

# THE SECOND EPISTLE GENERAL OF
# PETER

First Peter deals with problems from the outside; Second Peter deals with problems from the inside. Peter writes to warn the believers about the false teachers who are peddling damaging doctrine. He begins by urging them to keep close watch on their personal lives. The Christian life demands diligence in pursuing moral excellence, knowledge, self-control, perseverance, godliness, brotherly kindness, and selfless love. By contrast, the false teachers are sensual, arrogant, greedy, and covetous. They scoff at the thought of future judgment and live their lives as if the present would be the pattern for the future. Peter reminds them that although God may be longsuffering in sending judgment, ultimately it will come. In view of that fact, believers should live lives of godliness, blamelessness, and steadfastness.

The statement of authorship in 1:1 is very clear: "Simon Peter, a servant and an apostle of Jesus Christ." To distinguish this epistle from the first by Peter it was given the Greek title *Petrou B,* the "Second of Peter."

## CHAPTER 1

SIMON Peter, a servant and an ªapostle of Jesus Christ, to them that have obtained ᵇlike¹ precious faith with us through the righteousness of ²God and our Saviour Jesus Christ:

2 ªGrace and peace be multiplied unto you ¹through the knowledge of God, and of Jesus our Lord,

3 According as his ªdivine power hath given unto us all things that *pertain* unto life and godliness, through the knowledge of him ᵇthat hath called us ¹to glory and virtue:

4 ªWhereby are given unto us exceeding great and precious promises: that by these ye might be ᵇpartakers of the divine nature, having escaped the corruption that is in the world through lust.

5 ¹And beside this, ªgiving all diligence, add to your faith virtue; and to virtue ᵇknowledge;

6 And to knowledge ¹temperance; and to temperance ²patience; and to patience godliness;

7 And to godliness brotherly kindness; and ªto brotherly kindness ¹charity.

8 For if these things ¹be in you, and abound, they make *you that ye shall* neither *be* ²barren ªnor unfruitful in the knowledge of our Lord Jesus Christ.

9 But he that lacketh these things is ªblind, and ¹cannot see afar off, and hath forgotten that he was ²purged from his old sins.

10 Wherefore the rather, brethren, give diligence ªto make your calling and election sure: for if ye do these things, ye shall never ¹fall:

11 For so an entrance shall be ¹ministered unto you abundantly into the everlasting kingdom of our Lord and Saviour Jesus Christ.

12 Wherefore ªI will not be negligent to put you always in remembrance of these things, ᵇthough ye know *them,* and be established in the present truth.

13 Yea, I think it ¹meet, ªas long as I am in this ²tabernacle, ᵇto stir you up by putting *you* in remembrance;

14 ªKnowing that shortly I must ¹put off *this* my tabernacle, even as ᵇour Lord Jesus Christ hath shewed me.

15 Moreover I will endeavour that ye may be able after my ¹decease to have these things always in remembrance.

16 For we have not followed ªcunningly devised fables, when we made known unto you the ᵇpower and ᶜcoming of our Lord Jesus Christ, but were ᵈeyewitnesses of his majesty.

17 For he received from God the Father honour and glory, when there came such a voice to him from the excellent glory, ªThis is my beloved Son, in whom I am well pleased.

18 And this voice which came from heaven we heard, when we were with him in ªthe holy mount.

19 We have also ¹a more sure word of prophecy; whereunto ye do well that ye take heed, as unto a ªlight that shineth in a dark place, ᵇuntil the day dawn, and ᶜthe day star arise in your ᵈhearts:

20 Knowing this first, that ªno prophecy of the scripture is of any private ¹interpretation.

21 For ªthe prophecy came not in ¹old time by the will of man: ᵇbut holy men of God spake *as they were* moved by the Holy Ghost.

## CHAPTER 2

BUT there were false prophets also among the people, even as there

1:1 ª Gal. 2:8
ᵇ Eph. 4:5  ¹ *the same kind of*
² *our God and Saviour*
1:2 ª Dan. 4:1  ¹ *in*
1:3 ª 1 Pet. 1:5
ᵇ 1 Thess. 2:12  ¹ *by*
1:4 ª 2 Cor. 1:20; 7:1  ᵇ [2 Cor. 3:18]
1:5 ª 2 Pet. 3:18
ᵇ 1 Pet. 3:7  ¹ *But also for this very reason*
1:6 ¹ *self-control*  ² *perseverance*
1:7 ª Gal. 6:10  ¹ *love*
1:8 ¹ *are yours*  ª [John 15:2]  ² *useless*
1:9 ª 1 John 2:9–11  ¹ *short-sighted*  ² *cleansed*
1:10 ª 1 John 3:19  ¹ *stumble*
1:11 ¹ *supplied*
1:12 ª Phil. 3:1  ᵇ 1 Pet. 5:12
1:13 ª [2 Cor. 5:1, 4]  ᵇ 2 Pet. 3:1  ¹ *is right*  ² *tent, body*
1:14 ª [2 Tim. 4:6]  ᵇ John 13:36; 21:18, 19  ¹ *Die*
1:15 ¹ *death*
1:16 ª 1 Cor. 1:17  ᵇ [Eph. 1:19–22]  ᶜ [1 Pet. 5:4]  ᵈ Matt. 17:1–5
1:17 ª Matt. 17:5
1:18 ª Matt. 17:1
1:19 ª [John 1:4, 5, 9]  ᵇ Prov. 4:18  ᶜ Rev. 2:28; 22:16  ¹ Or *the prophetic word made more sure*
1:20 ª [Rom. 12:6]  ¹ Or *origin*  1:21 ª [2 Tim. 3:16]  ᵇ 2 Sam. 23:2  ¹ *any*

shall be [a]false teachers among you, who [1]privily shall bring in [2]damnable heresies, even denying the Lord that bought them, and bring upon themselves swift destruction.

2 And many shall follow their [1]pernicious ways; by reason of whom the way of truth shall be [2]evil spoken of.

3 And through covetousness shall they with [1]feigned words [2]make merchandise of you: whose judgment now of a long time [3]lingereth not, and their [4]damnation slumbereth not.

4 For if God spared not the angels that sinned, but cast *them* down to [1]hell, and delivered *them* into chains of darkness, to be reserved unto judgment;

5 And spared not the old world, but saved Noah the eighth *person,* a preacher of righteousness, bringing in the flood upon the world of the ungodly;

6 And turning the cities of [a]Sodom and Gomorrha into ashes condemned *them* [1]with an overthrow, making *them* an ensample unto those that [2]after should live ungodly;

7 And [a]delivered just Lot, [1]vexed with the filthy [2]conversation of the wicked:

8 (For that righteous man dwelling among them, [a]in seeing and hearing, [1]vexed *his* righteous soul from day to day with *their* unlawful deeds;)

9 [a]The Lord knoweth how to deliver the godly out of temptations, and to reserve the unjust unto the day of judgment to be punished:

10 But chiefly [a]them that walk [1]after the flesh in the lust of uncleanness, and despise [2]government. [b]Presumptuous *are they,* selfwilled, they are not afraid to speak evil of [3]dignities.

11 Whereas [a]angels, which are greater in power and might, bring not [1]railing accusation against them before the Lord.

12 But these, [a]as natural brute beasts, made to be [1]taken and destroyed, speak evil of the things that they understand not; and shall utterly perish in their own corruption;

13 [a]And shall receive the [1]reward of unrighteousness, *as* they that count it pleasure [b]to [2]riot in the day time. [c]Spots *they are* and blemishes, [3]sporting themselves with their own deceivings while [d]they feast with you;

14 Having eyes full of adultery, and that cannot cease from sin; [1]beguiling unstable souls: [a]an heart they have [2]exercised with covetous practices; cursed children:

15 Which have forsaken the right way, and are gone astray, following the way of [a]Balaam *the son* of [1]Bosor,

who loved the wages of unrighteousness;

16 But was rebuked for his iniquity: the dumb [1]ass speaking with man's voice [2]forbad the madness of the prophet.

17 [a]These are wells without water, clouds that are carried with a tempest; to whom the [1]mist of darkness is reserved for ever.

18 For when they speak great swelling *words* of [1]vanity, they allure through the lusts of the flesh, *through much* [2]wantonness, those that were [3]clean escaped from them who live in error.

19 While they promise them liberty, they themselves are the servants of corruption: [a]for of whom a man is overcome, of the same is he brought [1]in bondage.

20 For if after they [a]have escaped the pollutions of the world through the knowledge of the Lord and Saviour Jesus Christ, they are [b]again entangled therein, and overcome, the latter end is worse with them than the beginning.

21 For [a]it had been better for them not to have known the way of righteousness, than, after they have known *it,* to turn from the holy commandment delivered unto them.

22 But it is happened unto them according to the true proverb, [a]The dog [1]is turned to his own vomit again; and the sow that was washed to her wallowing in the mire.

## CHAPTER 3

THIS second epistle, beloved, I now write unto you; in *both* which [a]I stir up your pure minds by way of remembrance:

2 That ye may be mindful of the words [a]which were spoken before by the holy prophets, [b]and of the commandment of us the apostles of the Lord and Saviour:

3 Knowing this first, that there shall come in the last days [1]scoffers, [a]walking [2]after their own lusts,

4 And saying, Where is the promise of his coming? for since the fathers [1]fell asleep, all things continue as *they were* from the beginning of the [a]creation.

5 For this they willingly [1]are ignorant of, that [a]by the word of God the heavens were of old, and the earth [b]standing out of the water and in the water:

6 [a]Whereby the world that then was, being overflowed with water, perished:

7 But [a]the heavens and the earth, which are now, by the same word are kept in store, reserved unto [b]fire [1]against the day of judgment and [2]perdition of ungodly men.

### Center reference column

2:1 [a] 1 Tim. 4:1,
2 [1] *secretly*
[2] *destructive*

2:2 [1] *destructive*
[2] *blasphemed*

2:3 [1] *deceptive*
[2] *exploit* [3] *has not been idle*
[4] *destruction*

2:4 [1] Gr. *tartarus*

2:6 [a] Gen. 19:1–26
[1] *to destruction*
[2] *afterward*

2:7 [a] Gen. 19:16,
29 [1] *oppressed*
[2] *conduct*

2:8 [a] Ps. 119:139
[1] *tormented*

2:9 [a] Ps. 34:15–19

2:10 [a] Jude
4, 7, 8 [b] Jude
8 [1] *according to* [2] *authority*
[3] *dignitaries*

2:11 [a] Jude 9
[1] *reviling*

2:12 [a] Jude 10
[1] *caught*

2:13 [a] Phil. 3:19
[b] Rom. 13:13
[c] Jude 12 [d] 1 Cor.
11:20, 21 [1] *wages*
[2] *revel* [3] *reveling in*

2:14 [a] Jude
11 [1] *enticing*
[2] *trained*

2:15 [a] Num. 22:5,
7 [1] *Beor,* Num.
22:5

2:16 [1] *donkey*
[2] *restrained*

2:17 [a] Jude 12, 13
[1] *gloom*

2:18 [1] *emptiness*
[2] *licentiousness*
[3] *indeed*

2:19 [a] John 8:34
[1] *into*

2:20 [a] Matt. 12:45
[b] [Heb. 6:4–6]

2:21 [a] Luke 12:47

2:22 [a] Prov. 26:11
[1] *returns*

3:1 [a] 2 Pet. 1:13

3:2 [a] 2 Pet. 1:21
[b] Jude 17

3:3 [a] 2 Pet.
2:10 [1] *mockers*
[2] *according to*

3:4 [a] Gen. 6:1–7
[1] *Died*

3:5 [a] Gen. 1:6, 9
[b] Ps. 24:2; 136:6
[1] *forget*

3:6 [a] Gen. 7:11, 12,
21–23

3:7 [a] 2 Pet. 3:10,
12 [b] [2 Thess.
1:8] [1] *until* [2] *destruction*

8 But, beloved, be not ignorant of this one thing, that one day *is* with the Lord as a thousand years, and [a]a thousand years as one day.

9 [a]The Lord is not slack concerning his promise, as some men count slackness; but [b]is longsuffering to us-ward, [c]not willing that any should perish, but [d]that all should come to repentance.

10 But [a]the day of the Lord will come as a [1]thief in the night; in the which [b]the heavens shall pass away with a great noise, and the elements shall melt with fervent heat, the earth also and the works that are therein shall be burned up.

11 *Seeing* then *that* all these things shall be dissolved, what manner *of persons* ought ye to be [a]in *all* holy [1]conversation and godliness,

12 [a]Looking for and [1]hasting unto the coming of the day of God, wherein the heavens being on fire shall [b]be dissolved, and the elements shall [c]melt with fervent heat?

13 Nevertheless we, according to his promise, look for [a]new heavens and

a [b]new earth, wherein dwelleth righteousness.

14 Wherefore, beloved, seeing that ye look for such things, be diligent [a]that ye may be found of him in peace, without spot, and blameless.

15 And [1]account *that* [a]the longsuffering of our Lord *is* salvation; even as our beloved brother Paul also according to the wisdom given unto him hath written unto you;

16 As also in all *his* [a]epistles, speaking in them of these things; in which are some things hard to be understood, which they that are [1]unlearned and unstable [2]wrest, as *they do* also the [b]other scriptures, unto their own destruction.

17 Ye therefore, beloved, [a]seeing ye know *these things* [1]before, [b]beware lest ye also, being led away with the error of the wicked, fall from your own stedfastness.

18 [a]But grow in grace, and *in* the knowledge of our Lord and Saviour Jesus Christ. [b]To him *be* glory both now and for ever. Amen.

3:8 [a] Ps. 90:4
3:9 [a] Hab. 2:3
[b] Is. 30:18 [c] Ezek. 33:11 [d] [Rom. 2:4]
3:10 [a] Rev. 3:3; 16:15 [b] Ps. 102:25, 26 [1] robber
3:11 [a] 1 Pet. 1:15 [1] conduct
3:12 [a] 1 Cor. 1:7, 8 [b] Ps. 50:3 [c] Mic. 1:4 [1] hastening
3:13 [a] Is. 65:17; 66:22

b Rev. 21:1
3:14 [a] 1 Cor. 1:8; 15:58
3:15 [a] Rom. 2:4 [1] consider
3:16 [a] 1 Cor. 15:24 [b] 2 Tim. 3:16 [1] untaught [2] twist
3:17 [a] Mark 13:23 [b] Eph. 4:14 [1] beforehand
3:18 [a] Eph. 4:15 [b] 2 Tim. 4:18

# JOHN

God is light; God is love; and God is life. John is enjoying a delightful fellowship with that God of light, love, and life, and he desperately desires that his spiritual children enjoy the same fellowship.

God is light. Therefore, to engage in fellowship with Him we must walk in light and not in darkness. As we walk in the light, we will regularly confess our sins, allowing the blood of Christ to continually cleanse us. Two major roadblocks to hinder this walk will be falling in love with the world and falling for the alluring lies of false teachers.

God is love. Since we are His children we must walk in love. In fact, John says that if we do not love, we do not know God. Love is more than just words; it is actions. Love is giving, not getting. Biblical love is unconditional in its nature. Christ's love fulfilled those qualities and when that brand of love characterizes us, we will be free of self-condemnation and experience confidence before God.

God is life. Those who fellowship with Him must possess His quality of life. Spiritual life begins with spiritual birth which occurs through faith in Jesus Christ. Faith in Jesus Christ infuses us with God's life—eternal life.

Although the apostle John's name is not found in this book, it was given the title *Ioannou A*, the "First of John."

## CHAPTER 1

THAT [a]which was from the beginning, which we have heard, which we have [b]seen with our eyes, [c]which we have looked upon, and [d]our hands have handled, of the [e]Word of life;

2 (For [a]the life [b]was [1]manifested, and we have seen *it*, [c]and bear witness, and [2]shew unto you that eternal life, which was [d]with the Father, and was manifested unto us;)

3 That which we have seen and heard declare we unto you, that ye also may have fellowship with us: and truly our fellowship *is* [a]with the Father, and with his Son Jesus Christ.

4 And these things write we unto you, [a]that your joy may be full.

5 [a]This then is the message which we have heard of him, and declare unto you, that [b]God is light, and in him is no darkness at all.

6 [a]If we say that we have fellowship with him, and walk in darkness, we lie, and [1]do not the truth:

7 But if we [a]walk in the light, as he is in the light, we have fellowship one with another, and [b]the blood of Jesus Christ his Son cleanseth us from all sin.

8 If we say that we have no sin, we deceive ourselves, and the truth is not in us.

9 If we [a]confess our sins, he is [b]faithful and just to forgive us *our* sins, and to [c]cleanse us from all unrighteousness.

10 If we say that we have not sinned, we [a]make him a liar, and his word is not in us.

1:1 [a] [John
1:1] [b] John
1:14 [c] 2 Pet. 1:16
[d] Luke 24:39
[e] [John 1:1, 4, 14]
1:2 [a] John 1:4
[b] Rom. 16:26
[c] John 21:24
[d] [John 1:1, 18;
16:28] [1] *revealed*
[2] *declare*
1:3 [a] 1 Cor. 1:9
1:4 [a] John 15:11;
16:24
1:5 [a] 1 John 3:11
[b] [1 Tim. 6:16]
1:6 [a] [1 John
2:9–11] [1] *do not
practise the*
1:7 [a] Is. 2:5
[b] [1 Cor. 6:11]
1:9 [a] Prov. 28:13
[b] [Rom. 3:24–26]
[c] Ps. 51:2
1:10 [a] 1 John 5:10

## CHAPTER 2

MY little children, these things write I unto you, that ye [1]sin not. And if any man sin, [a]we have an [2]advocate with the Father, Jesus Christ the righteous:

2 And [a]he is the propitiation for our sins: and not for ours only, but [b]also for *the sins of* the whole world.

3 And hereby we do know that we know him, if we keep his commandments.

4 He that saith, I know him, and keepeth not his commandments, is a [a]liar, and the truth is not in him.

5 But [a]whoso keepeth his word, [b]in him verily is the love of God perfected: hereby know we that we are in him.

6 [a]He that saith he abideth in him [b]ought himself also so to walk, even as he walked.

7 Brethren, I write no new commandment unto you, but an old commandment which ye had [a]from the beginning. The old commandment is the word which ye have heard from the beginning.

8 Again, [a]a new commandment I write unto you, which thing is true in him and in you: [b]because the darkness is [1]past, and [c]the true light now shineth.

9 [a]He that saith he is in the light, and hateth his brother, is in darkness even until now.

10 [a]He that loveth his brother abideth in the light, and [b]there is [1]none occasion of stumbling in him.

11 But he that [a]hateth his brother is in darkness, and [b]walketh in darkness,

2:1 [a] Heb. 7:25;
9:24 [1] *may not
sin* [2] *intercessor,*
Gr. *paracletos*
2:2 [a] [Rom. 3:25]
[b] John 1:29
2:4 [a] Rom. 3:4
2:5 [a] John 14:21,
23 [b] [1 John 4:12]
2:6 [a] John 15:4
[b] 1 Pet. 2:21
2:7 [a] 1 John 3:11;
23; 4:21
2:8 [a] John 13:34;
15:12 [b] Rom. 13:12
[c] [John 1:9; 8:12;
12:35] [1] *passing
away*
2:9 [a] [1 Cor. 13:2]
2:10 [a] [1 John
3:14] [b] 2 Pet. 1:10
[1] *no cause for*

2:11 [a] [1 John 2:9; 3:15; 4:20] [b] John 12:35

and knoweth not whither he goeth, because that darkness hath blinded his eyes.

12 I write unto you, little children, because [a]your sins are forgiven you for his name's sake.

13 I write unto you, fathers, because ye have known him *that is* [a]from the beginning. I write unto you, young men, because ye have overcome the wicked one. I write unto you, little children, because ye have [b]known the Father.

14 I have written unto you, fathers, because ye have known him *that is* from the beginning. I have written unto you, young men, because [a]ye are strong, and the word of God abideth in you, and ye have overcome the wicked one.

15 [a]Love not the world, neither the things *that are* in the world. [b]If any man love the world, the love of the Father is not in him.

16 For all that *is* in the world, the lust of the flesh, [a]and the lust of the eyes, and the pride of life, is not of the Father, but is of the world.

17 And [a]the world passeth away, and the lust thereof: but he that doeth the will of God abideth for ever.

18 [a]Little children, [b]it is the last [1]time: and as ye have heard that [c]antichrist shall come, [d]even now are there many antichrists; whereby we know [e]that it is the last [1]time.

19 [a]They went out from us, but they were not of us; for [b]if they had been of us, they would *no doubt* have continued with us: but *they went out,* [c]that they might be made manifest that [1]they were not all of us.

20 But [a]ye have an [1]unction [b]from the Holy One, and [c]ye know all things.

21 I have not written unto you because ye know not the truth, but because ye know it, and that no lie is of the truth.

22 [a]Who is a liar but he that denieth that [b]Jesus is the Christ? He is antichrist, that denieth the Father and the Son.

23 [a]Whosoever denieth the Son, the same hath not the [b]Father: *[but]* [c]*he that acknowledgeth the Son hath the Father also.*

24 Let that therefore abide in you, [a]which ye have heard from the beginning. If that which ye have heard from the beginning shall remain in you, [b]ye also shall continue in the Son, and in the Father.

25 [a]And this is the promise that he hath promised us, *even* eternal life.

26 These *things* have I written unto you concerning them that [1]seduce you.

27 But the [a]anointing which ye have received of him abideth in you, and

2:12 [a] [1 Cor. 6:11]
2:13 [a] John 1:1
[b] [Rom. 8:15–17]
2:14 [a] Eph. 6:10
2:15 [a] [Rom. 12:2]
[b] James 4:4
2:16 [a] [Eccl. 5:10, 11]
2:17 [a] 1 Cor. 7:31
2:18 [a] John 21:5 [b] 1 Pet. 4:7 [c] 2 Thess. 2:3 [d] 2 John 7 [e] 1 Tim. 4:1 [1] *hour*
2:19 [a] Deut. 13:13 [b] Matt. 24:24 [c] 1 Cor. 11:19 [1] *none of them were*
2:20 [a] 2 Cor. 1:21 [b] Acts 3:14 [c] [John 16:13] [1] *anointing*
2:22 [a] 2 John 7 [b] 1 John 4:3
2:23 [a] John 15:23 [b] John 5:23 [c] 1 John 4:15; 5:1
2:24 [a] 2 John 6, 7 [b] John 14:23
2:25 [a] John 3:14–16; 6:40; 17:2, 3
2:26 [1] *try to deceive*
2:27 [a] [John 14:16; 16:13]

[h] [Jer. 31:33]
[c] [John 14:16]
2:28 [a] 1 John 3:21; 4:17; 5:14
2:29 [a] Acts 22:14 [b] 1 John 3:7, 10 [1] *practises*
3:1 [a] [1 John 4:10] [b] [John 1:12] [c] John 15:18, 21; 16:3 [1] Lit. *children*
3:2 [a] [Rom. 8:15, 16] [b] [Rom. 8:18, 19, 23] [c] Rom. 8:29 [d] [Ps. 16:11] [1] *children*
3:3 [a] 1 John 4:17
3:4 [a] Rom. 4:15 [1] *commits lawlessness* [2] *lawlessness*
3:5 [a] 1 John 1:2; 3:8 [b] John 1:29 [c] [2 Cor. 5:21]
3:7 [1] *practises*
3:8 [a] Matt. 13:38 [b] Luke 10:18 [1] *practises*
3:9 [a] John 1:3; 3:3 [b] 1 Pet. 1:23 [1] *practise*
3:11 [a] [John 13:34; 15:12]
3:12 [a] Gen. 4:4, 8 [1] *murdered*
3:13 [a] [John 15:18; 17:14]
3:15 [a] Matt. 5:21 [b] [Gal. 5:20, 21]

[b]ye need not that any man teach you: but as the same anointing [c]teacheth you of all things, and is truth, and is no lie, and even as it hath taught you, ye shall abide in him.

28 And now, little children, abide in him; that, when he shall appear, we may have [a]confidence, and not be ashamed before him at his coming.

29 [a]If ye know that he is righteous, ye know that [b]every one that [1]doeth righteousness is born of him.

## CHAPTER 3

BEHOLD, [a]what manner of love the Father hath bestowed upon us, that [b]we should be called the [1]sons of God: therefore the world knoweth us not, [c]because it knew him not.

2 Beloved, [a]now are we the [1]sons of God, and [b]it doth not yet appear what we shall be: but we know that, when he shall appear, [c]we shall be like him; for [d]we shall see him as he is.

3 [a]And every man that hath this hope in him purifieth himself, even as he is pure.

4 Whosoever committeth sin [1]transgresseth also the law: for [a]sin is [2]the transgression of the law.

5 And ye know [a]that he was manifested [b]to take away our sins; and [c]in him is no sin.

6 Whosoever abideth in him sinneth not: whosoever sinneth hath not seen him, neither known him.

7 Little children, let no man deceive you: he that [1]doeth righteousness is righteous, even as he is righteous.

8 [a]He that [1]committeth sin is of the devil; for the devil sinneth from the beginning. For this purpose the Son of God was manifested, [b]that he might destroy the works of the devil.

9 Whosoever is [a]born of God doth not [1]commit sin; for [b]his seed remaineth in him: and he cannot sin, because he is born of God.

10 In this the children of God are manifest, and the children of the devil: whosoever doeth not righteousness is not of God, neither he that loveth not his brother.

11 For this is the message that ye heard from the beginning, [a]that we should love one another.

12 Not as [a]Cain, *who* was of that wicked one, and [1]slew his brother. And wherefore slew he him? Because his own works were evil, and his brother's righteous.

13 Marvel not, my brethren, if [a]the world hate you.

14 We know that we have passed from death unto life, because we love the brethren. He that loveth not *his* brother abideth in death.

15 [a]Whosoever hateth his brother is a murderer: and ye know that [b]no

murderer hath eternal life abiding in him.

16 [a]Hereby perceive we the love *of God,* [b]because he laid down his life for us: and we ought to lay down *our* lives for the brethren.

17 But [a]whoso hath this world's [1]good, and seeth his brother have need, and shutteth up his [2]bowels *of compassion* from him, how dwelleth the love of God in him?

18 My little children, [a]let us not love in word, neither in tongue; but in deed and in truth.

19 And hereby we know [a]that we are of the truth, and shall [1]assure our hearts before him.

20 [a]For if our heart condemn us, God is greater than our heart, and knoweth all things.

21 Beloved, if our heart condemn us not, [a]*then* have we confidence toward God.

22 And [a]whatsoever we ask, we receive of him, because we keep his commandments, [b]and do those things that are pleasing in his sight.

23 And this is his commandment, That we should believe on the name of his Son Jesus Christ, [a]and love one another, as he gave us commandment.

24 And [a]he that keepeth his commandments [b]dwelleth in him, and he in him. And [c]hereby we know that he abideth in us, by the Spirit which he hath given us.

## CHAPTER 4

BELOVED, believe not every spirit, but [a]try[1] the spirits whether they are of God: because [b]many false prophets are gone out into the world.

2 Hereby know ye the Spirit of God: [a]Every spirit that confesseth that Jesus Christ is come in the flesh is of God:

3 And every spirit that confesseth not that Jesus Christ is come in the flesh is not of God: and this is that *spirit* of antichrist, whereof ye have heard that it should come; and even now already is it in the world.

4 Ye are of God, little children, and have overcome them: because greater is he that is in you, than [a]he that is in the world.

5 [a]They are of the world: therefore speak they of the world, and [b]the world heareth them.

6 We are of God: he that knoweth God heareth us; he that is not of God heareth not us. [a]Hereby know we the spirit of truth, and the spirit of error.

7 [a]Beloved, let us love one another: for love is of God; and every one that [b]loveth is born of God, and knoweth God.

8 He that loveth not knoweth not God; for God is love.

9 [a]In this was manifested the love of God toward us, because that God sent his only begotten [b]Son into the world, that we might live through him.

10 Herein is love, [a]not that we loved God, but that he loved us, and sent his Son [b]*to be* the propitiation for our sins.

11 Beloved, [a]if God so loved us, we ought also to love one another.

12 [a]No man hath seen God at any time. If we love one another, God dwelleth in us, and his love is perfected in us.

13 [a]Hereby know we that we dwell in him, and he in us, because he hath given us of his Spirit.

14 And [a]we have seen and do testify that [b]the Father sent the Son *to be* the Saviour of the world.

15 [a]Whosoever shall confess that Jesus is the Son of God, God dwelleth in him, and he in God.

16 And we have known and believed the love that God hath to us. God is love; and [a]he that [1]dwelleth in love [1]dwelleth in God, and God [b]in him.

17 Herein is [1]our love made perfect, that [a]we may have boldness in the day of judgment: because as he is, so are we in this world.

18 There is no fear in love; but perfect love casteth out fear: because fear [1]hath torment. He that feareth is not made perfect in love.

19 [a]We love him, because he first loved us.

20 [a]If a man say, I love God, and hateth his brother, he is a liar: for he that loveth not his brother whom he hath seen, how can he love God [b]whom he hath not seen?

21 And [a]this commandment have we from him, That he who loveth God love his brother also.

## CHAPTER 5

WHOSOEVER believeth that [a]Jesus is the Christ is [b]born of God: and every one that loveth him that begat loveth him also that is begotten of him.

2 By this we know that we love the children of God, when we love God, and [a]keep his commandments.

3 [a]For this is the love of God, that we keep his commandments: and [b]his commandments are not [1]grievous.

4 For [a]whatsoever is born of God overcometh the world: and this is the victory that [b]overcometh the world, *even* our faith.

5 Who is he that overcometh the world, but [a]he that believeth that Jesus is the Son of God?

6 This is he that came [a]by water and blood, *even* Jesus Christ; not by

### Center reference column

3:16 [a] [John 3:16]
[b] John 10:11; 15:13
3:17 [a] Deut. 15:7
[1] *goods* [2] *heart*
3:18 [a] Ezek. 33:31
3:19 [a] John 18:37
[1] *persuade*
3:20 [a] [1 Cor. 4:4, 5]
3:21 [a] [1 John 2:28; 5:14]
3:22 [a] Ps. 34:15
[b] John 8:29
3:23 [a] Matt. 22:39
3:24 [a] John 14:23
[b] John 14:21; 17:21
[c] Rom. 8:9, 14, 16
4:1 [a] 1 Cor. 14:29
[b] Matt. 24:5 [1] *test*
4:2 [a] 1 Cor. 12:3
4:4 [a] John 14:30; 16:11
4:5 [a] John 3:31
[b] John 15:19; 17:14
4:6 [a] [1 Cor. 2:12–16]
4:7 [a] 1 John 3:10, 11, 23 [b] 1 Thess. 4:9
4:9 [a] Rom. 5:8
[b] John 3:16
4:10 [a] Titus 3:5
[b] 1 John 2:2
4:11 [a] Matt. 18:33
4:12 [a] John 1:18
4:13 [a] John 14:20
4:14 [a] John 1:14
[b] John 3:17; 4:42
4:15 [a] [Rom. 10:9]
4:16 [a] [1 John 3:24] [b] [John 14:23] [1] *abides*
4:17 [a] 1 John 2:28
[1] *love made perfect among us*
4:18 [1] *involves*
4:19 [a] 1 John 4:10
4:20 [a] [1 John 2:4]
[b] 1 John 4:12
4:21 [a] [Matt. 5:43, 44; 22:37]
5:1 [a] 1 John 2:22; 4:2, 15 [b] John 1:13
5:2 [a] John 15:10
5:3 [a] John 14:15
[b] Matt. 11:30; 23:4
[1] *burdensome*
5:4 [a] John 16:33
[b] 1 John 2:13; 4:4
5:5 [a] 1 Cor. 15:57
5:6 [a] John 1:31–34; [Eph. 5:26, 27]

water only, but by water and blood. [b]And it is the Spirit that beareth witness, because the Spirit is truth.

7 For there are three that bear [1]record in heaven, the Father, [a]the Word, and the Holy Ghost: [b]and these three are one.

8 And there are three that bear witness in earth, [a]the Spirit, and the water, and the blood: and these three agree [1]in one.

9 If we receive [a]the witness of men, the witness of God is greater: [b]for this is the witness of God which he hath testified of his Son.

10 He that believeth on the Son of God [a]hath the witness in himself: he that believeth not God [b]hath made him a liar; because he believeth not the [1]record that God gave of his Son.

11 And this is the [1]record, that God hath given to us eternal life, and this life is in his Son.

12 [a]He that hath the Son hath [1]life; *and* he that hath not the Son of God hath not [1]life.

13 These things have I written unto you that believe on the name of the Son of God; that ye may know that ye have eternal life, and that ye may believe on the name of the Son of God.

14 And this is the confidence that we have in him, that, [a]if we ask any thing according to his will, he heareth us:

15 And if we know that he hear us, whatsoever we ask, we know that we have the petitions that we [1]desired of him.

16 If any man see his brother sin a sin *which is* not unto death, he shall ask, and [a]he shall give him life for them that sin not unto death. [b]There is a sin unto death: [c]I do not say that he shall pray for it.

17 [a]All unrighteousness is sin: and there is a sin not unto death.

18 We know that [a]whosoever is born of God sinneth not; but he that is begotten of God [b]keepeth[1] himself, and that wicked one toucheth him not.

19 *And* we know that we are of God, and [a]the whole world lieth in wickedness.

20 And we know that the [a]Son of God is come, and [b]hath given us an understanding, [c]that we may know him that is true, and we are in him that is true, *even* in his Son Jesus Christ. [d]This is the true God, [e]and eternal life.

21 Little children, keep yourselves from idols. Amen.

---

5:6 [b] [John 14:17]
5:7 [a] [John 1:1]
[b] John 10:30
[1] *witness*
5:8 [a] John 15:26
[1] *as*
5:9 [a] John 5:34, 37; 8:17, 18
[b] [Matt. 3:16, 17]; John 5:32, 37
5:10 [a] [Rom. 8:16]; Gal. 4:6; Rev. 12:17 [b] John 3:18, 33; 1 John 1:10 [1] *testimony*
5:11 [1] *testimony*
5:12 [a] [John 3:15, 36; 6:47; 17:2, 3] [1] Lit. *the life*
5:14 [a] [1 John 2:28; 3:21, 22]
5:15 [1] *asked*
5:16 [a] Job 42:8 [b] [Matt. 12:31] [c] Jer. 7:16; 14:11
5:17 [a] 1 John 3:4
5:18 [a] [1 Pet. 1:23]; 1 John 3:9 [b] James 1:27 [1] *guards*
5:19 [a] John 12:31; 17:15; Gal. 1:4
5:20 [a] 1 John 4:2 [b] Luke 24:45 [c] John 17:3; Rev. 3:7 [d] Is. 9:6
[e] 1 John 5:11, 12

# JOHN

"Let him that thinketh he standeth take heed lest he fall" (1 Cor. 10:12). These words of the apostle Paul could well stand as a subtitle for John's little epistle. The recipients, a chosen lady and her children, were obviously standing. They were walking in truth, remaining faithful to the commandments they had received from the Father. John is deeply pleased to be able to commend them. But he takes nothing for granted. Realizing that standing is just one step removed from falling, he hesitates not at all to issue a reminder: "love one another" (v. 5). The apostle admits that this is not new revelation, but he views it sufficiently important to repeat. Loving one another, he stresses, is equivalent to walking according to God's commandments.

John indicates, however, that this love must be discerning. It is not a naive, unthinking, open to anything and anyone kind of love. Biblical love is a matter of choice; it is dangerous and foolish to float through life with undiscerning love. False teachers abound who do not acknowledge Christ as having come in the flesh. It is false charity to open the door to false teaching. We must have fellowship with God. We must have fellowship with Christians. But we must not have fellowship with false teachers.

The "elder" of verse 1 has been traditionally identified with the apostle John, resulting in the Greek title *Ioannou B*, the "Second of John."

THE elder unto the [1]elect lady and her children, whom I love in the truth; and not I only, but also all they that have known [a]the truth;

2 For the truth's sake, which [1]dwelleth in us, and shall be with us for ever.

3 [a]Grace [1]be with you, mercy, *and* peace, from God the Father, and from the Lord Jesus Christ, the Son of the Father, in truth and love.

4 I [a]rejoiced greatly that I found [1]of thy children walking in truth, as we have received a commandment from the Father.

5 And now I beseech thee, lady, not as though I wrote a new commandment unto thee, but that which we had from the beginning, [a]that we love one another.

6 And [a]this is love, that we walk [1]after his commandments. This is the commandment, That, [b]as ye have heard from the beginning, ye should walk in it.

7 For [a]many deceivers are entered into the world, [b]who confess not that Jesus Christ is come in the flesh. [c]This is a deceiver and an antichrist.

8 [a]Look to yourselves, [b]that we lose not those things which we have [1]wrought, but that we receive a full reward.

9 [a]Whosoever transgresseth, and abideth not in the doctrine of Christ, hath not God. He that abideth in the doctrine of Christ, he hath both the Father and the Son.

10 If there come any unto you, and bring [a]not this doctrine, receive him not into *your* house, neither [b]bid him God speed:

11 For he that [b]biddeth him God speed [2]is partaker of his evil deeds.

12 [a]Having many things to write unto you, I [1]would not *write* with paper and ink: but I [2]trust to come unto you, and speak face to face, [b]that our joy may be full.

13 [a]The children of thy elect sister greet thee. Amen.

1:1 [a] Col. 1:5 · [1] *chosen*
1:2 [1] *abides*
1:3 [a] Rom. 1:7; 1 Tim. 1:2 · [1] *will be*
1:4 [a] 1 Thess. 2:19, 20; 3 John 3, 4 · [1] *some of*
1:5 [a] [John 13:34, 35; 15:12, 17]; 1 John 3:11; 4:7, 11
1:6 [a] John 14:15; 1 John 2:5; 5:3 · [b] 1 John 2:24 · [1] *according to*
1:7 [a] 1 John 2:19; 4:1 · [b] 1 John 4:2 · [c] 1 John 2:22
1:8 [a] Mark 13:9 · [b] Gal. 3:4 · [1] *worked for*
1:9 [a] John 7:16; 8:31; 1 John 2:19, 23, 24
1:10 [a] 1 Kin. 13:16; Rom. 16:17; 2 Thess. 3:6, 14; Titus 3:10 · [1] *give him a greeting*
1:11 [1] *greets him* · [2] *shares in*
1:12 [a] 3 John 13, 14 · [b] John 17:13 · [1] *do not wish* to write · [2] *hope*
1:13 [a] 1 Pet. 5:13

In Third John the apostle encourages fellowship with Christian brothers. Following his expression of love for Gaius, John assures him of his prayers for his health and voices his joy over Gaius's persistent walk in truth and for the manner in which he shows hospitality and support for missionaries who have come to his church.

But not everyone in the church feels the same way. Diotrephes's heart is one hundred and eighty degrees removed from Gaius's heart. He is no longer living in love. Pride has taken precedence in his life. He has refused a letter John has written for the church, fearing that his authority might be superseded by that of the apostle. He also has accused John of evil words and refused to accept missionaries. He forbids others to do so and even expels them from the church if they disobey him. John uses this negative example as an opportunity to encourage Gaius to continue his hospitality. Demetrius has a good testimony and may even be one of those turned away by Diotrephes. He is widely known for his good character and his loyalty to the truth. Here he is well commended by John and stands as a positive example for Gaius.

The Greek titles of First, Second, and Third John are *Ioannou A, B*, and *G*. The *G* is gamma, the third letter of the Greek alphabet; *Ioannou G* means the "Third of John."

THE elder unto the wellbeloved Gaius, [a]whom I love [1]in the truth.

2 Beloved, I [1]wish above all things that thou mayest prosper and be in health, even as thy soul prospereth.

3 For I [a]rejoiced greatly, when the brethren came and testified of the truth that is in thee, even as thou walkest in the truth.

4 I have no greater [a]joy than to hear that [b]my children walk in truth.

5 Beloved, thou doest faithfully whatsoever thou doest [1]to the brethren, and [1]to strangers;

6 Which have borne witness of thy [1]charity before the church: whom if thou [2]bring forward on their journey [3]after a godly sort, thou shalt do well:

7 Because that for his name's sake they went forth, [a]taking nothing [1]of the Gentiles.

8 We therefore ought to [a]receive such, that we might be fellowhelpers [1]to the truth.

9 I wrote unto the church: but Diotrephes, who loveth to have the preeminence among them, receiveth us not.

10 Wherefore, if I come, I will remember his deeds which he doeth, [a]prating[1] against us with malicious words: and not content therewith, neither doth he himself receive the brethren, and forbiddeth them that would, and [2]casteth *them* out of the church.

11 Beloved, [a]follow[1] not that which is evil, but that which is good. [b]He that doeth good is of God: but he that doeth evil hath not seen [c]God.

12 Demetrius [a]hath [1]good report of all *men,* and of the truth itself: yea, and we *also* bear [2]record; [b]and ye know that our [3]record is true.

13 [a]I had many things to write, but I will not with ink and pen write unto thee:

14 But I trust I shall shortly see thee, and we shall speak face to face. Peace *be* to thee. *Our* friends [1]salute thee. Greet the friends by name.

1:1 [a] 2 John 1 [1] Lit. *in truth*
1:2 [1] *pray that in all things*
1:3 [a] 2 John 4
1:4 [a] 1 Thess. 2:19, 20; 2 John 4 [b] [1 Cor. 4:15]
1:5 [1] *for*
1:6 [1] *love* [2] *send* [3] *in a manner worthy of God*
1:7 [a] 1 Cor. 9:12, 15 [1] *from*
1:8 [a] Matt. 10:40; Rom. 12:13; Heb. 13:2; 1 Pet. 4:9 [1] *for*
1:10 [a] Prov. 10:8, 10 [1] *talking nonsense* [2] *puts*
1:11 [a] Ps. 34:14; 37:27; Rom. 14:19; 1 Thess. 5:15; 1 Tim. 6:11; 2 Tim. 2:22 [b] [1 John 2:29; 3:10] [c] [1 John 3:10] [1] *do not imitate*
1:12 [a] Acts 6:3;

1 Tim. 3:7 [b] John 19:35; 21:24 [1] *a good testimony* [2] *witness* [3] *testimony* 1:13 [a] 2 John 12 1:14 [1] *greet*

# THE GENERAL EPISTLE OF
# JUDE

Fight! Contend! Do battle! When apostasy arises, when false teachers emerge, when the truth of God is attacked, it is time to fight for the faith. Only believers who are spiritually "in shape" can answer the summons. At the beginning of his letter Jude focuses on the believers' common salvation, but then feels compelled to challenge them to contend for the faith. The danger is real. False teachers have crept into the church turning God's grace into unbounded license to do as they please. Jude reminds such men of God's past dealings with unbelieving Israel, disobedient angels, and wicked Sodom and Gomorrah. In the face of such danger Christians should not be caught off guard. The challenge is great, but so is the God who is able to keep them from stumbling.

The Greek title *Iouda,* "Of Jude," comes from the name *Ioudas* which appears in verse 1. This name, which can be translated Jude or Judas, was popular in the first century because of Judas Maccabaeus (died 160 B.C.), a leader of the Jewish resistance against Syria during the Maccabean revolt.

JUDE, the servant of Jesus Christ, and ᵃbrother of James, to them that are ¹sanctified by God the Father, and ᵇpreserved in Jesus Christ, *and* ᶜcalled:

2 Mercy unto you, and ᵃpeace, and love, be multiplied.

3 Beloved, when I gave all diligence to write unto you ᵃof the common salvation, it was needful for me to write unto you, and exhort *you* that ᵇye should earnestly contend for the faith which was ¹once delivered unto the saints.

4 For there are certain men crept in ¹unawares, who were ²before of old ordained to this condemnation, ungodly men, turning the grace of our God into ³lasciviousness, and denying the only Lord God, and our Lord Jesus Christ.

5 I will therefore put you in remembrance, though ye once knew this, how that ᵃthe Lord, having saved the people out of the land of Egypt, afterward destroyed them that believed not.

6 And the angels which kept not their ¹first estate, but left their own habitation, he hath reserved in everlasting chains under darkness unto the judgment of the great day.

7 Even as ᵃSodom and Gomorrha, and the cities about them in like manner, giving themselves over to ¹fornication, and going after strange flesh, are set forth for an example, suffering the ²vengeance of eternal fire.

8 ᵃLikewise also these *filthy* dreamers defile the flesh, ¹despise dominion, and ᵇspeak evil of ²dignities.

9 Yet Michael the archangel, when ¹contending with the devil he ²disputed about the body of Moses, ³durst not bring against him a ⁴railing accusation, but said, ᵃThe Lord rebuke thee.

10 ᵃBut these speak evil of those things which they know not: but what they know naturally, as brute beasts, in those things they corrupt themselves.

11 Woe unto them! for they have gone in the way ᵃof Cain, and ᵇran greedily after the error of Balaam for ¹reward, and perished ᶜin the ²gainsaying of Core.

12 These are ¹spots in your ²feasts of charity, when they feast ³with you, feeding themselves without fear: clouds *they are* without water, carried about of winds; ⁴trees whose fruit withereth, without fruit, twice dead, plucked up by the roots;

13 ᵃRaging waves of the sea, ᵇfoaming ¹out their own shame; wandering stars, ᶜto whom is reserved the blackness of darkness for ever.

14 And Enoch also, the seventh from Adam, prophesied of these, saying, Behold, the Lord cometh with ten thousands of his saints,

15 To execute judgment upon all, and to ¹convince all that are ungodly among them of all their ungodly deeds which they have ²ungodly committed, and of all their ᵃhard³ *speeches* which ungodly sinners have spoken against him.

16 These are murmurers, complainers, walking after their own lusts; and their ᵃmouth speaketh great swelling *words,* ᵇhaving¹ men's persons in admiration because of advantage.

17 ᵃBut, beloved, remember ye the words which were spoken before ¹of the apostles of our Lord Jesus Christ;

18 How that they told you ᵃthere should be mockers in the last time, who should walk after their own ungodly lusts.

1:1 ᵃ Acts 1:13
ᵇ John 17:1
ᶜ Rom. 1:7 ¹ *set apart*
1:2 ᵃ 1 Pet. 1:2;
2 Pet. 1:2
1:3 ᵃ Titus 1:4
ᵇ Phil. 1:27 ¹ *once for all*
1:4 ¹ *unnoticed* ² *long ago marked out for* 3 *licentiousness*
1:5 ᵃ Ex. 12:51;
1 Cor. 10:5–10;
Heb. 3:16
1:6 ¹ *proper domain*
1:7 ᵃ Gen. 19:24
¹ *sexual immorality* ² *punishment*
1:8 ᵃ 2 Pet.
2:10 ᵇ Ex. 22:28
¹ *reject authority* ² *glorious ones*
1:9 ᵃ Zech. 3:2
¹ *disputing* ² *discussed* 3 *dared*
4 *reviling*
1:10 ᵃ 2 Pet. 2:12
1:11 ᵃ Gen. 4:3–8
ᵇ 2 Pet. 2:15
ᶜ Num. 16:1–3,
31–35 ¹ *profit* ² *rebellion*
1:12 ¹ *hidden reefs or stains* ² *love feasts* 3 *with you without fear, serving only themselves* 4 *late autumn trees without fruit*
1:13 ᵃ Is. 57:20
ᵇ [Phil. 3:19]
ᶜ 2 Pet. 2:17 ¹ *up*
1:15 ᵃ 1 Sam. 2:3
¹ *convict* ² *in an ungodly way* 3 *harsh things*
1:16 ᵃ 2 Pet.
2:18 ᵇ Prov.
28:21 ¹ *flattering people to gain advantage* 1:17 ᵃ 2 Pet. 3:2 ¹ *by* 1:18 ᵃ [1 Tim. 4:1]

19 These be they who ¹separate themselves, ²sensual, having not the Spirit.

20 But ye, beloved, ªbuilding up yourselves on your most holy faith, ᵇpraying in the Holy Ghost,

21 Keep yourselves in the love of God, ªlooking for the mercy of our Lord Jesus Christ unto eternal life.

22 And of some have compassion, making a ¹difference:

1:19 ¹ *cause divisions* ² *worldly*
1:20 ª Col. 2:7
ᵇ [Rom. 8:26]
1:21 ª Titus 2:13
1:22 ¹ *distinction*
1:23 ª Rom. 11:14
ᵇ Amos 4:11
ᶜ [Zech. 3:4, 5]
¹ *defiled*
1:24 ª [Eph. 3:20] ᵇ Col. 1:22
¹ *stumbling*

23 And others ªsave with fear, ᵇpulling *them* out of the fire; hating even ᶜthe garment ¹spotted by the flesh.

24 ªNow unto him that is able to keep you from ¹falling, and ᵇto present *you* faultless before the presence of his glory with exceeding joy,

25 To the only wise God our Saviour, *be* glory and majesty, dominion and power, both now and ever. Amen.

# THE
# REVELATION
## OF JESUS CHRIST

Just as Genesis is the book of beginnings, Revelation is the book of consummation. In it, the divine program of redemption is brought to fruition, and the holy name of God is vindicated before all creation. Although there are numerous prophecies in the Gospels and Epistles, Revelation is the only New Testament book that focuses primarily on prophetic events. Its title means "unveiling" or "disclosure." Thus, the book is an unveiling of the character and program of God. Penned by John during his exile on the island of Patmos, Revelation centers around visions and symbols of the resurrected Christ, who alone has authority to judge the earth, to remake it, and to rule it in righteousness.

The title of this book in the Greek text is *Apokalypsis Ioannou*, "Revelation of John." It is also known as the Apocalypse, a transliteration of the word *apokalypsis*, meaning "unveiling," "disclosure," or "revelation." Thus, the book is an unveiling of that which otherwise could not be known. A better title comes from the first verse: *Apokalypsis Iesou Christou*, "Revelation of Jesus Christ." This could be taken as a revelation which came from Christ or as a revelation which is about Christ—both are appropriate. Because of the unified contents of this book, it should not be called Revelations.

## CHAPTER 1

THE Revelation of Jesus Christ, [a]which God gave unto him, to shew unto his servants things which must [1]shortly come to pass; and [b]he sent and signified *it* by his angel unto his servant John:

2 [a]Who [1]bare record of the word of God, and of the testimony of Jesus Christ, and of all things [b]that he saw.

3 [a]Blessed *is* he that readeth, and they that hear the words of this prophecy, and keep those things which are written therein: for [b]the time *is* at hand.

4 JOHN to the seven churches which are in Asia: Grace *be* unto you, and peace, from him [a]which is, and [b]which was, and which is to come; [c]and from the seven Spirits which are before his throne;

5 And from Jesus Christ, [a]*who is* the faithful [b]witness, *and* the [c]first [1]begotten of the dead, and [d]the [2]prince of the kings of the earth. Unto him [e]that loved us, [f]and washed us from our sins in his own blood,

6 And hath [a]made us kings and priests unto God and his Father; [b]to him *be* glory and dominion for ever and ever. Amen.

7 Behold, he cometh with [a]clouds; and every eye shall see him, and [b]they *also* which pierced him: and all [1]kindreds of the earth shall [2]wail because of him. Even so, Amen.

8 [a][b]I am Alpha and Omega, the beginning and the ending, saith the Lord, which is, and which was, and which is to come, the [c]Almighty.

9 I John, who also am your brother, and [a]companion in [1]tribulation, and [b]in the kingdom, and [2]patience of Jesus Christ, was in the isle that is called Patmos, for the word of God, and for the testimony of Jesus Christ.

10 [a]I was in the Spirit on [b]the Lord's day, and heard behind me [c]a great voice, as of a trumpet,

11 Saying, I am Alpha and Omega, the first and the last: and, What thou seest, write in a book, and send *it* unto the seven churches which are in Asia; unto Ephesus, and unto Smyrna, and unto Pergamos, and unto Thyatira, and unto Sardis, and unto Philadelphia, and unto Laodicea.

12 And I turned to see the voice that spake with me. And being turned, [a]I saw seven golden [1]candlesticks;

13 [a]And in the midst of the seven [1]candlesticks [b]*one* like unto the Son of man, [c]clothed with a garment down to the foot, and [d]girt[2] about the [3]paps with a golden [4]girdle.

14 His head and [a]*his* hairs *were* white like wool, as white as snow; and [b]his eyes *were* as a flame of fire;

15 [a]And his feet like unto fine brass, as if they [1]burned in a furnace; and [b]his voice as the sound of many waters.

16 [a]And he had in his right hand seven stars: and [b]out of his mouth went a sharp twoedged sword: [c]and his countenance *was* as the sun shineth in his strength.

17 And [a]when I saw him, I fell at his feet as dead. And [b]he laid his right

---

1:1 [a] John 3:32
[b] Rev. 22:6
[1] *quickly* or *swiftly*
1:2 [a] 1 Cor. 1:6
[b] 1 John 1:1 [1] *bore witness*
1:3 [a] Luke 11:28
[b] James 5:8
1:4 [a] Ex. 3:14
[b] John 1:1 [c] [Is. 11:2]
1:5 [a] John 8:14
[b] Is. 55:4 [c] [Col. 1:18] [d] Rev. 17:14
[e] John 13:34
[f] Heb. 9:14 [1] *born*
[2] *ruler over*
1:6 [a] 1 Pet. 2:5, 9
[b] 1 Tim. 6:16
1:7 [a] Matt. 24:30
[b] Zech. 12:10–14
[1] *the tribes*
[2] *mourn*
1:8 [a] Is. 41:4
[b] Rev. 4:8; 11:17
[c] Is. 9:6
1:9 [a] Phil. 1:7
[b] [2 Tim. 2:12]
[1] *persecution*
[2] *perseverance*
1:10 [a] Acts 10:10
[b] Acts 20:7
[c] Rev. 4:1
1:12 [a] Ex. 25:37
[1] *lampstands*
1:13 [a] Rev. 2:1
[b] Ezek. 1:26
[c] Dan. 10:5 [d] Rev. 15:6 [1] *lampstands*
[2] *girded* [3] *chest*
[4] *band*
1:14 [a] Dan. 7:9
[b] Dan. 10:6
1:15 [a] Ezek. 1:7
[b] Ezek. 1:24; 43:2
[1] *were refined*
1:16 [a] Rev. 1:20; 2:1; 3:1 [b] Is. 49:2 [c] Matt. 17:2
1:17 [a] Ezek. 1:28 [b] Dan. 8:18; 10:10, 12

hand upon me, saying unto me, Fear not; [c]I am the first and the last:

18 [a]I *am* he that liveth, and was dead; and, behold, [b]I am alive for evermore, Amen; and [c]have the keys of [1]hell and of death.

19 Write the things which thou hast [a]seen, [b]and the things which are, [c]and the things which shall [1]be hereafter;

20 The [1]mystery of the seven stars which thou sawest in my right hand, and the seven golden [2]candlesticks. The seven stars are [a]the [3]angels of the seven churches: and [b]the seven [2]candlesticks which thou sawest are the seven churches.

## CHAPTER 2

UNTO the [1]angel of the church of Ephesus write; These things saith [a]he that holdeth the seven stars in his right hand, [b]who walketh in the midst of the seven golden [2]candlesticks;

2 [a]I know thy works, and thy labour, and thy [1]patience, and how thou canst not [2]bear them which are evil: and [b]thou hast [3]tried them [c]which say they are apostles, and are not, and hast found them liars:

3 And hast [1]borne, and hast patience, and for my name's sake hast laboured, and hast [a]not [2]fainted.

4 Nevertheless I have *somewhat* against thee, because thou hast left thy first love.

5 Remember therefore from whence thou art fallen, and repent, and do the first works; [a]or else I will come unto thee quickly, and will remove thy [1]candlestick out of his place, [2]except thou repent.

6 But this thou hast, that thou hatest the deeds of the Nicolaitanes, which I also hate.

7 [a]He that hath an ear, let him hear what the Spirit saith unto the churches; To him that overcometh will I give [b]to eat of [c]the tree of life, which is in the midst of the paradise of God.

8 And unto the angel of the church in Smyrna write; These things saith [a]the first and the last, which was dead, and is alive;

9 I know thy works, and tribulation, and poverty, (but thou art [a]rich) and *I know* the blasphemy of [b]them which say they are Jews, and are not, [c]but *are* [1]the synagogue of Satan.

10 [a]Fear none of those things which thou shalt suffer: behold, the devil shall cast *some* of you into prison, that ye may be [1]tried; and ye shall have tribulation ten days: [b]be thou faithful unto death, and I will give thee [c]a crown of life.

11 [a]He that hath an ear, let him hear what the Spirit saith unto the

churches; He that overcometh shall not be hurt of [b]the second death.

12 And to the [1]angel of the church in Pergamos write; These things saith [a]he which hath the sharp sword with two edges;

13 I know thy works, and where thou dwellest, *even* where Satan's [1]seat *is:* and thou holdest fast my name, and hast not denied my faith, even in those days wherein Antipas *was* my faithful martyr, who was slain among you, where Satan dwelleth.

14 But I have a few things against thee, because thou hast there them that hold the doctrine of [a]Balaam, who taught Balac to [1]cast a stumblingblock before the children of Israel, [b]to eat things sacrificed unto idols, [c]and to commit [2]fornication.

15 So hast thou also them that hold the doctrine of the Nicolaitanes, which thing I hate.

16 Repent; or else I will come unto thee quickly, and [a]will fight against them with the sword of my mouth.

17 He that hath an ear, let him hear what the Spirit saith unto the churches; To him that overcometh will I give to eat of the hidden [a]manna, and will give him a white stone, and in the stone [b]a new name written, which no man knoweth [1]saving he that receiveth *it.*

18 And unto the [1]angel of the church in Thyatira write; These things saith the Son of God, [a]who hath his eyes like unto a flame of fire, and his feet *are* like fine brass;

19 [a]I know thy works, and [1]charity, and service, and faith, and thy [2]patience, and thy works; and the last *to be* more than the first.

20 Notwithstanding I have a few things against thee, because [1]thou sufferest that woman [a]Jezebel, which calleth herself a prophetess, to teach and to [2]seduce my servants [b]to commit fornication, and to eat things sacrificed unto idols.

21 And I gave her [1]space [a]to repent of her fornication; and she repented not.

22 Behold, I will cast her into a [1]bed, and them that commit adultery with her into great tribulation, [2]except they repent of their deeds.

23 And I will kill her children with death; and all the churches shall know that I am he which [a]searcheth the [1]reins and hearts: and I will give unto every one of you according to your works.

24 But unto you I say, and unto the rest in Thyatira, as many as have not this [1]doctrine, and which have not known the [a]depths of Satan, as they

1:17 [c] Is. 41:4; 44:6; 48:12

1:18 [a] Rom. 6:9 [b] Rev. 4:9 [c] Ps. 68:20 [1] Gr. *hades*

1:19 [a] Rev. 1:9–18 [b] Rev. 2:1 [c] Rev. 4:1 [1] *take place*

1:20 [a] Rev. 2:1 [b] Zech. 4:2 [1] A hidden truth [2] *lampstands* [3] *messengers*

2:1 [a] Rev. 1:16 [b] Rev. 1:13 [1] *messenger* [2] *lampstands*

2:2 [a] Ps. 1:6 [b] 1 John 4:1 [c] 2 Cor. 11:13 [1] *perseverance* [2] endure [3] tested

2:3 [a] Gal. 6:9 [1] persevered [2] become weary

2:5 [a] Matt. 21:41 [1] *lampstand* [2] unless

2:7 [a] Matt. 11:15; Rev. 2:11, 17; 3:6, 13, 22; 13:9 [b] [Rev. 22:2, 14] [c] [Gen. 2:9; 3:22]

2:8 [a] Rev. 1:8, 17, 18

2:9 [a] Luke 12:21 [b] Rom. 2:17 [c] Rev. 3:9 [1] a congregation

2:10 [a] Matt. 10:22 [b] Matt. 24:13 [c] James 1:12 [1] tested

2:11 [a] Rev. 13:9 [b] [Rev. 20:6, 14; 21:8]

2:12 [a] Is. 49:2; Rev. 1:16; 2:16 [1] *messenger*

2:13 [1] *throne*

2:14 [a] Num. 31:16 [b] Num. 25; Acts 15:29; [1 Cor. 10:20]; Rev. 2:20 [c] 1 Cor. 6:13 [1] *put an enticement to sin* [2] *sexual immorality*

2:16 [a] Is. 11:4; 2 Thess. 2:8; Rev. 19:15

2:17 [a] Ex. 16:33, 34; [John 6:49, 51] [b] Is. 56:5; 62:2; 65:15; Rev. 3:12 [1] except

2:18 [a] Rev. 1:14, 15 [1] *messenger*

2:19 [a] Rev. 2:2 [1] *love* [2] *endurance*

2:20 [a] 1 Kin. 16:31; 21:25; 2 Kin. 9:7, 22, 30 [b] Ex. 34:15 [1] *you allow* [2] *beguile*

2:21 [a] Rom. 2:5; Rev. 9:20; 16:9, 11 [1] *time*

2:22 [1] sickbed

2:23 [a] Ps. 7:9; 26:2; 139:1; Jer. 11:20; 17:10; Matt. 16:27; Luke 16:15; Acts 1:24; Rom. 8:27 [1] *minds*

2:24 [a] 2 Tim. 3:1–9 [1] teaching

speak; [b]I will put upon you none other burden.

25 But [a]that which ye have *already* hold fast till I come.

26 And he that overcometh, and keepeth [a]my works unto the end, [b]to him will I give power over the nations:

27 [a]And he shall rule them with a rod of iron; as the vessels of a potter shall they be broken to [1]shivers: even as I received of my Father.

28 And I will give him [a]the morning star.

29 He that hath an ear, let him hear what the Spirit saith unto the churches.

## CHAPTER 3

AND unto the [1]angel of the church in Sardis write; These things saith he that [a]hath the seven Spirits of God, and the seven stars; I know thy works, that thou hast a name that thou livest, [2]and art dead.

2 Be watchful, and strengthen the things which remain, that are ready to die: for I have not found thy works [1]perfect before God.

3 [a]Remember therefore how thou hast received and heard, and hold fast, and [b]repent. [c]If therefore thou shalt not watch, I will come on thee [d]as a [1]thief, and thou shalt not know what hour I will come upon thee.

4 Thou hast [a]a few names even in Sardis which have not [b]defiled[1] their garments; and they shall walk with me [c]in white: for they are worthy.

5 He that overcometh, [a]the same shall be clothed in white [1]raiment; and I will not [b]blot out his name out of the [c]book of life, but [d]I will confess his name before my Father, and before his angels.

6 [a]He that hath an ear, let him hear what the Spirit saith unto the churches.

7 And to the [1]angel of the church in Philadelphia write; These things saith [a]he that is holy, [b]he that is true, [c]he that hath the key of David, [d]he that openeth, and no man shutteth; and [e]shutteth, and no man openeth;

8 [a]I know thy works: behold, I have set before thee [b]an open door, and no man can shut it: for thou hast a little strength, and hast kept my word, and hast not denied my name.

9 Behold, I will make [a]them of the synagogue of Satan, which say they are Jews, and are not, but do lie; behold, [b]I will make them to come and worship before thy feet, and to know that I have loved thee.

10 Because thou hast kept [1]the word of my patience, [a]I also will keep thee from the hour of [2]temptation, which shall come upon [b]all the world, to [3]try them that dwell [c]upon the earth.

11 Behold, [a]I come quickly: [b]hold that fast which thou hast, that no man take [c]thy crown.

12 Him that overcometh will I make [a]a pillar in the temple of my God, and he shall [b]go no more out: and [c]I will write upon him the name of my God, and the name of the city of my God, *which is* [d]new Jerusalem, which [e]cometh down out of heaven from my God: [f]and *I will write upon him* my new name.

13 [a]He that hath an ear, let him hear what the Spirit saith unto the churches.

14 And unto the [1]angel of the church of the Laodiceans write; [a]These things saith the Amen, [b]the faithful and true witness, [c]the beginning of the creation of God;

15 [a]I know thy works, that thou art neither cold nor hot: I [1]would thou [2]wert cold or hot.

16 So then because thou art lukewarm, and neither cold nor hot, I will [1]spue thee out of my mouth.

17 Because thou sayest, [a]I am rich, and [1]increased with goods, and have need of nothing; and knowest not that thou art wretched, and miserable, and poor, and blind, and naked:

18 I counsel thee [a]to buy of me gold [1]tried in the fire, that thou mayest be rich; and [b]white [2]raiment, that thou mayest be clothed, and *that* the shame of thy nakedness [3]do not appear; and anoint thine eyes with eyesalve, that thou mayest see.

19 [a]As many as I love, I rebuke and [b]chasten: be zealous therefore, and repent.

20 Behold, [a]I stand at the door, and knock: [b]if any man hear my voice, and open the door, [c]I will come in to him, and will [1]sup with him, and he with me.

21 To him that overcometh [a]will I grant to sit with me [1]in my throne, even as I also overcame, and am set down with my Father [1]in his throne.

22 [a]He that hath an ear, let him hear what the Spirit saith unto the churches.

## CHAPTER 4

AFTER this I looked, and, behold, a door *was* [a]opened in heaven: and the first voice which I heard *was* as it were of a [b]trumpet talking with me; which said, Come up hither, and I will shew thee things which must be hereafter.

2 And immediately [a]I was in the [1]spirit: and, behold, [b]a throne was set in heaven, and *one* sat on the throne.

2:24 [b] Acts 15:28
2:25 [a] Rev. 3:11
2:26 [a] [John 6:29] [b] [Matt. 19:28]
2:27 [a] Ps. 2:8, 9; Rev. 12:5; 19:15 [1] *pieces*
2:28 [a] 2 Pet. 1:19; Rev. 22:16
3:1 [a] Rev. 1:4, 16 [1] *messenger* [2] *but you are dead*
3:2 [1] *complete*
3:3 [a] 1 Tim. 6:20 [b] Rev. 3:19 [c] Matt. 24:42, 43; Luke 12:39 [d] [Rev. 16:15] [1] *robber*
3:4 [a] Acts 1:15 [b] [Jude 23] [c] Rev. 4:4; 6:11 [1] *stained*
3:5 [a] [Rev. 19:8] [b] Ex. 32:32 [c] Phil. 4:3 [d] Luke 12:8 [1] *garments*
3:6 [a] Rev. 2:7
3:7 [a] Acts 3:14 [b] 1 John 5:20 [c] Is. 9:7; 22:22 [d] [Matt. 16:19] [e] Job 12:14 [1] *messenger*
3:8 [a] Rev. 3:1 [b] 1 Cor. 16:9
3:9 [a] Rev. 2:9 [b] Is. 45:14; 49:23; 60:14
3:10 [a] 2 Pet. 2:9 [b] Luke 2:1 [c] Is. 24:17 [1] *my command to persevere* [2] *trial* [3] *test*
3:11 [a] Phil. 4:5 [b] Rev. 2:25 [c] [Rev. 2:10]
3:12 [a] 1 Kin. 7:21 [b] Ps. 23:6 [c] [Rev. 14:1; 22:4] [d] [Heb. 12:22] [e] Rev. 21:2 [f] [Rev. 2:17; 22:4]
3:13 [a] Rev. 2:7
3:14 [a] 2 Cor. 1:20 [b] Rev. 1:5; 3:7; 19:11 [c] [Col. 1:15] [1] *messenger*
3:15 [a] Rev. 3:1 [1] *wish* [2] *were*
3:16 [1] *spit or vomit*
3:17 [a] Hos. 12:8 [1] *have become wealthy*
3:18 [a] Is. 55:1 [b] 2 Cor. 5:3 [1] *refined* [2] *garments* [3] *may not be revealed*
3:19 [a] Job 5:17 [b] Heb. 12:6
3:20 [a] Song 5:2 [b] Luke 12:36, 37 [c] [John 14:23] [1] *dine*
3:21 [a] Matt. 19:28 [1] *on*
3:22 [a] Rev. 2:7
4:1 [a] Ezek. 1:1 [b] Rev. 1:10   4:2 [a] Rev. 1:10 [b] Is. 6:1 [1] Or *Spirit*

3 And he that sat was to look upon [a]like a jasper and a [1]sardine stone: [b]and *there was* a rainbow round about the throne, in [2]sight like unto an emerald.

4 [a]And round about the throne *were* four and twenty [1]seats: and upon the [1]seats I saw four and twenty elders sitting, [b]clothed in white [2]raiment; and they had on their heads crowns of gold.

5 And out of the throne proceeded [a]lightnings and thunderings and voices: [b]and *there were* seven lamps of fire burning before the throne, which are [c]the seven Spirits of God.

6 And before the throne *there was* [a]a sea of glass like unto crystal: [b]and in the midst of the throne, and round about the throne, *were* four [1]beasts full of eyes [2]before and behind.

7 [a]And the first beast *was* like a lion, and the second beast like a calf, and the third beast had a face as a man, and the fourth beast *was* like a flying eagle.

8 And the four beasts had each of them [a]six wings about *him;* and *they were* full of eyes within: and they [1]rest not day and night, saying, [b]Holy, holy, holy, [c]Lord God Almighty, [d]which was, and is, and is to come.

9 And when those [1]beasts give glory and honour and thanks to him that sat on the throne, [a]who liveth for ever and ever,

10 [a]The four and twenty elders fall down before him that sat on the throne, and worship him that liveth for ever and ever, and cast their crowns before the throne, saying,

11 [a]Thou art worthy, O Lord, to receive glory and honour and power: [b]for thou hast created all things, and [1]for [c]thy pleasure they are and were created.

## CHAPTER 5

A ND I saw in the right hand of him that sat on the throne [a]a [1]book written within and on the backside, [b]sealed with seven seals.

2 And I saw a strong angel proclaiming with a loud voice, [a]Who is worthy to open the book, and to loose the seals thereof?

3 And no man in heaven, nor in earth, neither under the earth, was able to open the [1]book, neither to look thereon.

4 And I wept much, because no man was found worthy to open and to read the book, neither to look thereon.

5 And one of the elders saith unto me, Weep not: behold, [a]the Lion of the tribe of [b]Juda, [c]the Root of David, hath [d]prevailed[1] to open the book, [e]and to loose the seven seals thereof.

---

4:3 [a] Rev. 21:11
[b] Ezek. 1:28
[1] *sardius* [2] *appearance*
4:4 [a] Rev. 11:16
[b] Rev. 3:4, 5
[1] *thrones* [2] *robes*
4:5 [a] Rev. 8:5; 11:19; 16:18 [b] Ex. 37:23 [c] [Rev. 1:4]
4:6 [a] Rev. 15:2
[b] Ezek. 1:5 [1] *living creatures* [2] *in front*
4:7 [a] Ezek. 1:10; 10:14
4:8 [a] Is. 6:2
[1] *cease* [b] Is. 6:3 [c] Rev. 1:8 [d] Rev. 1:4
4:9 [a] Rev. 1:18
[1] *living creatures*
4:10 [a] Rev. 5:8, 14; 7:11; 11:16; 19:4
4:11 [a] Rev. 1:6; 5:12
[b] Gen. 1:1 [c] Col. 1:16 [1] *by your will they exist*
5:1 [a] Ezek. 2:9, 10 [b] Is. 29:11 [1] *scroll*
5:2 [a] Rev. 4:11; 5:9
5:3 [1] *scroll*
5:5 [a] Gen. 49:9 [b] Heb. 7:14 [c] Is. 11:1, 10 [d] Rev. 3:21 [e] Rev. 6:1 [1] *overcome*

5:6 [a] [John 1:29]
[b] Zech. 3:9; 4:10
[c] Rev. 1:4; 3:1; 4:5
5:7 [a] Rev. 4:2
[1] *scroll*
5:8 [a] Rev. 4:8–10; 19:4 [b] Rev. 8:3
[1] *living creatures*
[2] *bowls* [3] *incense*
5:9 [a] Rev. 14:3
[b] Rev. 4:11 [c] John 1:29 [d] [Heb. 9:12]
[1] *scroll* [2] *tribe*
5:10 [a] Ex. 19:6
[b] Is. 61:6
5:11 [1] *living creatures*
5:13 [a] Phil. 2:10
[b] 1 Chr. 29:11
[c] Rev. 4:2, 3; 6:16; 20:11
5:14 [1] *living creatures*
6:1 [a] [Rev. 5:5–7, 12; 13:8] [b] Rev. 4:7 [1] *sound* [2] *living creatures*
6:2 [a] Zech. 1:8;
6:3 [a] Ps. 45:4, 5, LXX [c] Zech. 6:11 [d] Matt. 24:5
6:3 [a] Rev. 4:7
[1] *living creature*
6:4 [a] Zech. 1:8;
6:2 [b] Matt. 24:6, 7

---

6 And I beheld, and, lo, in the midst of the throne and of the four beasts, and in the midst of the elders, stood [a]a Lamb as it had been slain, having seven horns and [b]seven eyes, which are [c]the seven Spirits of God sent forth into all the earth.

7 And he came and took the [1]book out of the right hand [a]of him that sat upon the throne.

8 And when he had taken the book, [a]the four [1]beasts and four *and* twenty elders fell down before the Lamb, having every one of them harps, and golden [2]vials full of [3]odours, which are the [b]prayers of saints.

9 And [a]they sung a new song, saying, [b]Thou art worthy to take the [1]book, and to open the seals thereof: for thou wast slain, and [c]hast redeemed us to God [d]by thy blood out of every [2]kindred, and tongue, and people, and nation;

10 And hast made us unto our God [a]kings and [b]priests: and we shall reign on the earth.

11 And I beheld, and I heard the voice of many angels round about the throne and the [1]beasts and the elders: and the number of them was ten thousand times ten thousand, and thousands of thousands;

12 Saying with a loud voice, Worthy is the Lamb that was slain to receive power, and riches, and wisdom, and strength, and honour, and glory, and blessing.

13 And [a]every creature which is in heaven, and on the earth, and under the earth, and such as are in the sea, and all that are in them, heard I saying, [b]Blessing, and honour, and glory, and power, *be* unto him [c]that sitteth upon the throne, and unto the Lamb for ever and ever.

14 And the four [1]beasts said, Amen. And the four *and* twenty elders fell down and worshipped him that liveth for ever and ever.

## CHAPTER 6

A ND [a]I saw when the Lamb opened one of the seals, and I heard, as it were the [1]noise of thunder, [b]one of the four [2]beasts saying, Come and see.

2 And I saw, and behold [a]a white horse: [b]and he that sat on him had a bow; [c]and a crown was given unto him: and he went forth [d]conquering, and to conquer.

3 And when he had opened the second seal, [a]I heard the second [1]beast say, Come and see.

4 [a]And there went out another horse *that was* red: and *power* was given to him that sat thereon to [b]take peace from the earth, and that they should kill one another: and there was given unto him a great sword.

5 And when he had opened the third seal, [a]I heard the third [1]beast say, Come and see. And I beheld, and lo [b]a black horse; and he that sat on him had a pair of [c]balances[2] in his hand.

6 And I heard a voice in the midst of the four [1]beasts say, A [2]measure of wheat for a [3]penny, and three measures of barley for a [3]penny; and [a]*see* thou hurt not the oil and the wine.

7 And when he had opened the fourth seal, [a]I heard the voice of the fourth beast say, Come and see.

8 [a]And I looked, and behold a pale horse: and his name that sat on him was Death, and [1]Hell followed with him. And [2]power was given unto them over the fourth part of the earth, [b]to kill with sword, and with hunger, and with death, [c]and with the [3]beasts of the earth.

9 And when he had opened the fifth seal, I saw under [a]the altar [b]the souls of them that were slain [c]for the word of God, and for [d]the testimony which they held:

10 And they cried with a loud voice, saying, [a]How long, O Lord, [b]holy and true, [c]dost thou not judge and avenge our blood on them that dwell on the earth?

11 And [a]white robes were given unto every one of them; and it was said unto them, [b]that they should rest yet for a little [1]season, until their fellowservants also and their brethren, that should be killed as they *were,* should be fulfilled.

12 And I beheld when he had opened the sixth seal, [a]and, lo, there was a great earthquake; and [b]the sun became black as sackcloth of hair, and the moon became as blood;

13 [a]And the stars of heaven fell unto the earth, even as a fig tree [1]casteth her untimely figs, when she is shaken of a mighty wind.

14 [a]And the [1]heaven departed as a scroll when it is rolled together; and [b]every mountain and island were moved out of their places.

15 And the [a]kings of the earth, and the great men, and the rich men, and the chief captains, and the mighty men, and every [1]bondman, and every free man, [b]hid themselves in the [2]dens and in the rocks of the mountains;

16 [a]And said to the mountains and rocks, Fall on us, and hide us from the face of him that [b]sitteth on the throne, and from the wrath of the Lamb:

17 For the great day of his wrath is come; [a]and who [1]shall be able to stand?

## CHAPTER 7

AND after these things I saw four angels standing on the four corners of the earth, [a]holding the four winds of the earth, [b]that the wind should not blow on the earth, nor on the sea, nor on any tree.

2 And I saw another angel ascending from the east, having the seal of the living God: and he cried with a loud voice to the four angels, to whom it was given to hurt the earth and the sea,

3 Saying, [a]Hurt not the earth, neither the sea, nor the trees, till we have sealed the servants of our God [b]in their foreheads.

4 [a]And I heard the number of them which were sealed: *and there were* sealed [b]an hundred *and* forty *and* four thousand [c]of all the tribes of the [1]children of Israel.

5 Of the tribe of Juda *were* sealed twelve thousand. Of the tribe of Reuben *were* sealed twelve thousand. Of the tribe of Gad *were* sealed twelve thousand.

6 Of the tribe of Aser *were* sealed twelve thousand. Of the tribe of Nephthalim *were* sealed twelve thousand. Of the tribe of Manasses *were* sealed twelve thousand.

7 Of the tribe of Simeon *were* sealed twelve thousand. Of the tribe of Levi *were* sealed twelve thousand. Of the tribe of Issachar *were* sealed twelve thousand.

8 Of the tribe of Zabulon *were* sealed twelve thousand. Of the tribe of Joseph *were* sealed twelve thousand. Of the tribe of Benjamin *were* sealed twelve thousand.

9 After this I beheld, and, lo, [a]a great multitude, which no man could number, [b]of all nations, and [1]kindreds, and people, and [2]tongues, stood before the throne, and before the Lamb, [c]clothed with white robes, and [3]palms in their hands;

10 And cried with a loud voice, saying, [a]Salvation [1]to our God [b]which sitteth upon the throne, and unto the Lamb.

11 [a]And all the angels stood round about the throne, and *about* the elders and the four [1]beasts, and fell before the throne on their faces, and [b]worshipped God,

12 [a]Saying, Amen: Blessing, and glory, and wisdom, and thanksgiving, and honour, and power, and might, *be* unto our God for ever and ever. Amen.

13 And one of the elders answered, saying unto me, [1]What are these which are arrayed in [a]white robes? and whence came they?

14 And I said unto him, Sir, thou knowest. And he said to me, [a]These are they which came out of great tribulation, and have [b]washed their robes, and made them white in the blood of the Lamb.

6:5 [a] Rev. 4:7 [b] Zech. 6:2, 6 [c] Matt. 24:7 [1] *living creature* [2] *scales*
6:6 [a] Rev. 7:3; 9:4 [1] *living creatures* [2] Gr. *choinix* [3] Gr. *denarius*
6:7 [a] Rev. 4:7
6:8 [a] Zech. 6:3 [b] Ezek. 5:12, 17; 14:21; 29:5 [c] Lev. 26:22 [1] Gr. *hades* [2] *authority* [3] *wild animals*
6:9 [a] Rev. 8:3 [b] [Rev. 20:4] [c] Rev. 1:2, 9 [d] 2 Tim. 1:8
6:10 [a] Zech. 1:12 [b] Rev. 3:7 [c] Rev. 11:18
6:11 [a] Rev. 3:4, 5; 7:9 [b] Heb. 11:40 [1] *while*
6:12 [a] Matt. 24:7 [b] Joel 2:10, 31; 3:15
6:13 [a] Rev. 8:10; 9:1 [1] *drops its late figs*
6:14 [a] Is. 34:4 [b] Rev. 16:20 [1] *sky split apart*
6:15 [a] Ps. 2:2–4 [b] Is. 2:10, 19, 21; 24:21 [1] *slave* [2] *caves*
6:16 [a] Luke 23:29, 30 [b] Rev. 20:11
6:17 [a] Zeph. 1:14 [1] Lit. *is able*
7:1 [a] Dan. 7:2 [b] Rev. 7:3; 8:7; 9:4
7:3 [a] Rev. 6:6 [b] Rev. 22:4
7:4 [a] Rev. 9:16 [b] Rev. 14:1, 3 [c] Gen. 49:1–27 [1] Lit. *sons*
7:9 [a] Rom. 11:25 [b] Rev. 5:9 [c] Rev. 3:5, 18; 4:4; 6:11 [1] *tribes* [2] *languages* [3] *palm branches*
7:10 [a] Ps. 3:8 [b] Rev. 5:13 [1] *belongs to*
7:11 [a] Rev. 4:6 [b] Rev. 4:11; 5:9, 12, 14; 11:16 [1] *living creatures*
7:12 [a] Rev. 5:13, 14
7:13 [a] Rev. 7:9 [1] *Who*
7:14 [a] Rev. 6:9 [b] [Heb. 9:14]

15 Therefore are they before the throne of God, and serve him day and night in his temple: and he that sitteth on the throne shall [a]dwell among them.

16 [a]They shall hunger no more, neither thirst any more; [b]neither shall the sun [1]light on them, nor any heat.

17 For the Lamb which is in the midst of the throne [a]shall [1]feed them, and shall lead them unto living fountains of waters: [b]and God shall wipe away [2]all tears from their eyes.

## CHAPTER 8

AND [a]when he had opened the seventh seal, there was silence in heaven about the space of half an hour.

2 [a]And I saw the seven angels which stood before God; [b]and to them were given seven trumpets.

3 And another angel came and stood at the altar, having a golden censer; and there was given unto him much incense, that he should offer *it* with [a]the prayers of all saints upon [b]the golden altar which was before the throne.

4 And [a]the smoke of the incense, *which came* with the prayers of the saints, ascended up before God out of the angel's hand.

5 And the angel took the censer, and filled it with fire of the altar, and cast *it* [1]into the earth: and [a]there were [2]voices, and thunderings, [b]and lightnings, [c]and an earthquake.

6 And the seven angels which had the seven trumpets prepared themselves to sound.

7 The first angel sounded, [a]and there followed hail and fire mingled with blood, and they were cast [b]upon the earth: and the third part [c]of trees was burnt up, and all green grass was burnt up.

8 And the second angel sounded, [a]and as it were a great mountain burning with fire was cast into the sea: [b]and the third part of the sea [c]became blood;

9 [a]And the third part of the creatures which were in the sea, and had life, died; and the third part of the ships were destroyed.

10 And the third angel sounded, [a]and there fell a great star from heaven, burning as it were a [1]lamp, [b]and it fell upon the third part of the rivers, and upon the [2]fountains of waters;

11 [a]And the name of the star is called Wormwood: [b]and the third part of the waters became wormwood; and many men died of the waters, because they were made bitter.

12 [a]And the fourth angel sounded, and the third part of the sun was [1]smitten, and the third part of the moon, and the third part of the stars; so as the third part of them was darkened, and the day [2]shone not for a third part of it, and the night likewise.

13 And I beheld, [a]and heard an angel flying through the midst of heaven, saying with a loud voice, [b]Woe, woe, woe, to the inhabiters of the earth by reason of the [1]other voices of the trumpet of the three angels, which are [2]yet to sound!

## CHAPTER 9

AND the fifth angel sounded, [a]and I saw a star [1]fall from heaven unto the earth: and to him was given the key of [b]the [2]bottomless pit.

2 And he opened the [1]bottomless pit; and there arose a smoke out of the pit, as the smoke of a great furnace; and the [a]sun and the air were darkened by reason of the smoke of the pit.

3 And there came out of the smoke locusts upon the earth: and unto them was given power, [a]as the scorpions of the earth have power.

4 And it was commanded them [a]that they should not hurt [b]the grass of the earth, neither any green thing, neither any tree; but only those men which have not [c]the seal of God in their foreheads.

5 And to them it was given that [1]they should not kill them, [a]but that they should be tormented five months: and their torment *was* as the torment of a scorpion, when he striketh a man.

6 And in those days [a]shall men seek death, and shall not find it; and shall desire to die, and death shall flee from them.

7 And [a]the shapes of the locusts *were* like unto horses prepared unto battle; [b]and on their heads *were* as it were crowns like gold, [c]and their faces *were* as the faces of men.

8 And they had hair as the hair of women, and [a]their teeth were as *the teeth* of lions.

9 And they had breastplates, as it were breastplates of iron; and the sound of their wings *was* [a]as the sound of chariots of many horses running to battle.

10 And they had tails like unto scorpions, and there were stings in their tails: and their [1]power *was* to hurt men five months.

11 And they had a king over them, *which is* [a]the angel of the bottomless pit, whose name in the Hebrew tongue *is* [1]Abaddon, but in the Greek tongue hath *his* name [2]Apollyon.

12 [a]One woe is past; *and,* behold, there come two woes more hereafter.

7:15 [a] Is. 4:5, 6
7:16 [a] Is. 49:10 [b] Ps. 121:6 [1] *strike*
7:17 [a] Ps. 23:1 [b] Rev. 21:4 [1] *shepherd* [2] *every tear*
8:1 [a] Rev. 6:1
8:2 [a] [Matt. 18:10] [b] 2 Chr. 29:25–28
8:3 [a] Rev. 5:8 [b] Ex. 30:1
8:4 [a] Ps. 141:2
8:5 [a] Rev. 11:19; 16:18 [b] Rev. 4:5 [c] 2 Sam. 22:8 [1] *to* [2] *noises*
8:7 [a] Ezek. 38:22 [b] Rev. 16:2 [c] Rev. 9:4, 15–18
8:8 [a] Jer. 51:25 [b] Ex. 7:17 [c] Ezek. 14:19
8:9 [a] Rev. 16:3
8:10 [a] Is. 14:12 [b] Rev. 14:7; 16:4 [1] *torch* [2] *springs*
8:11 [a] Ruth 1:20 [b] Ex. 15:23
8:12 [a] Is. 13:10 [1] *struck* [2] *had no light*
8:13 [a] Rev. 14:6; 19:17 [b] Rev. 9:12; 11:14; 12:12 [1] *remaining blasts* [2] *about*
9:1 [a] Rev. 8:10 [b] Luke 8:31 [1] *which had fallen* [2] Lit. *shaft of the abyss*
9:2 [a] Joel 2:2, 10 [1] Lit. *shaft of the abyss*
9:3 [a] Judg. 7:12
9:4 [a] Rev. 6:6 [b] Rev. 8:7 [c] Rev. 7:2, 3
9:5 [a] [Rev. 9:10; 11:7] [1] The locusts
9:6 [a] Jer. 8:3
9:7 [a] Joel 2:4 [b] Nah. 3:17 [c] Dan. 7:8
9:8 [a] Joel 1:6
9:9 [a] Joel 2:5–7
9:10 [1] *authority*
9:11 [a] Eph. 2:2 [1] Lit. *Destruction* [2] Lit. *Destroyer*
9:12 [a] Rev. 8:13; 11:14

13 And the sixth angel sounded, and I heard a voice from the four horns of the [a]golden altar which is before God,

14 Saying to the sixth angel which had the trumpet, [1]Loose the four angels which are bound [a]in[2] the great river Euphrates.

15 And the four angels were loosed, which were prepared for [1]an hour, and a day, and a month, and a year, for to slay the [a]third part of men.

16 And [a]the number of the army [b]of the horsemen *were* two hundred thousand thousand: [c]and I heard the number of them.

17 And thus I saw the horses in the vision, and them that sat on them, having breastplates of [1]fire, and of [2]jacinth, and [3]brimstone: [a]and the heads of the horses *were* as the heads of lions; and out of their mouths issued fire and smoke and [4]brimstone.

18 By these three was the third part of men killed, by the fire, and by the smoke, and by the brimstone, which issued out of their mouths.

19 For their power is in their mouth, and in their tails: [a]for their tails *were* like unto serpents, and had heads, and with them they do hurt.

20 And the rest of the men which were not killed by these plagues [a]yet repented not of the works of their hands, that they should not worship [b]devils,[1] [c]and idols of gold, and silver, and brass, and stone, and of wood: which neither can see, nor hear, nor walk:

21 Neither repented they of their murders, [a]nor of their sorceries, nor of their fornication, nor of their thefts.

## CHAPTER 10

AND I saw another mighty angel come down from heaven, clothed with a cloud: [a]and a rainbow *was* upon [b]his head, and his face *was* as it were the sun, and [c]his feet as pillars of fire:

2 And he had in his hand a little book open: [a]and he set his right foot upon the sea, and *his* left *foot* on the [1]earth,

3 And cried with a loud voice, as *when* a lion roareth: and when he had cried, [a]seven thunders uttered their voices.

4 And when the seven thunders had uttered their voices, I was about to write: and I heard a voice from heaven saying unto me, [a]Seal up those things which the seven thunders uttered, and write them not.

5 And the angel which I saw stand upon the sea and upon the earth [a]lifted up his hand to heaven,

6 And sware by him that liveth for ever and ever, [a]who created heaven, and the things that therein are, and the earth, and the things that therein are, and the sea, and the things which are therein, [b]that there should be [1]time no longer:

7 But [a]in the days of the voice of the seventh angel, when he shall begin to sound, the mystery of God should be finished, as he hath declared to his servants the prophets.

8 And the voice which I heard from heaven spake unto me again, and said, Go *and* take the little book which is open in the hand of the angel which standeth upon the sea and upon the earth.

9 And I went unto the angel, and said unto him, Give me the little book. And he said unto me, [a]Take *it,* and eat it up; and it shall make thy belly bitter, but it shall be in thy mouth sweet as honey.

10 And I took the little book out of the angel's hand, and ate it up; [a]and it was in my mouth sweet as honey: and as soon as I had eaten it, [b]my belly was bitter.

11 And he said unto me, Thou must prophesy again before many peoples, and nations, and tongues, and kings.

## CHAPTER 11

AND there was given me [a]a [1]reed like unto a [2]rod: and the angel stood, saying, [b]Rise, and measure the temple of God, and the altar, and them that worship therein.

2 But [a]the court which is [1]without the temple leave out, and measure it not; [b]for it is given unto the Gentiles: and the holy city shall they [c]tread under foot [d]forty *and* two months.

3 And I will give *power* unto my two [a]witnesses, [b]and they shall prophesy [c]a thousand two hundred *and* [1]threescore days, clothed in sackcloth.

4 These are the [a]two olive trees, and the two [1]candlesticks standing before the God of the earth.

5 And if any man will hurt them, [a]fire proceedeth out of their mouth, and devoureth their enemies: [b]and if any man will hurt them, he must in this manner be killed.

6 These [a]have [1]power to shut heaven, that it rain not in the days of their prophecy: and have [1]power over waters to turn them to blood, and to smite the earth with all plagues, as often as they will.

7 And when they [a]shall have finished their testimony, [b]the beast that ascendeth [c]out of the bottomless pit [d]shall make war against them, and shall overcome them, and kill them.

8 And their dead bodies *shall lie* in the street of [a]the great city, which spiritually is called Sodom and Egypt, [b]where also our Lord was crucified.

9:13 [a] Rev. 8:3
9:14 [a] Rev. 16:12 [1] *Release* [2] *at*
9:15 [a] Rev. 8:7–9; 9:18 [1] *the*
9:16 [a] Dan. 7:10 [b] Ezek. 38:4 [c] Rev. 7:4
9:17 [a] Is. 5:28, 29 [1] *fiery red* [2] *hyacinth blue* [3] *sulphur yellow* [4] *burning sulphur*
9:19 [a] Is. 9:15
9:20 [a] Deut. 31:29 [b] 1 Cor. 10:20 [c] Dan. 5:23 [1] *demons*
9:21 [a] Rev. 21:8; 22:15
10:1 [a] Rev. 4:3 [b] Rev. 1:16 [c] Rev. 1:15
10:2 [a] Matt. 28:18 [1] *land*
10:3 [a] Ps. 29:3–9
10:4 [a] Dan. 8:26; 12:4, 9
10:5 [a] Dan. 12:7
10:6 [a] Rev. 4:11 [b] Rev. 16:17 [1] *delay*
10:7 [a] Rev. 11:15
10:9 [a] Jer. 15:16
10:10 [a] Ezek. 3:3 [b] Ezek. 2:10
11:1 [a] Ezek. 40:3–42:20 [b] Num. 23:18 [1] *measuring rod* [2] *staff*
11:2 [a] Ezek. 40:17, 20 [b] Ps. 79:1 [c] Dan. 8:10 [d] Rev. 12:6; 13:5 [1] *outside*
11:3 [a] Rev. 20:4 [b] Rev. 19:10 [c] Rev. 12:6 [1] *sixty*
11:4 [a] Zech. 4:2, 3, 11, 14 [1] *lampstands*
11:5 [a] 2 Kin. 1:10–12 [b] Num. 16:29
11:6 [a] 1 Kin. 17:1 [1] *authority*
11:7 [a] Luke 13:32 [b] Rev. 13:1, 11; 17:8 [c] Rev. 9:1, 2 [d] Dan. 7:21
11:8 [a] Rev. 14:8 [b] Heb. 13:12

9 [a]And they of the [1]people and [2]kindreds and [3]tongues and nations shall see their dead bodies three days and an half, [b]and shall not [4]suffer their dead bodies to be put in graves.

10 [a]And they that dwell upon the earth shall rejoice over them, and make merry, [b]and shall send gifts one to another; [c]because these two prophets tormented them that dwelt on the earth.

11 [a]And after three days and an half [b]the [1]Spirit of life from God entered into them, and they stood upon their feet; and great fear fell upon them which saw them.

12 And they heard a great voice from heaven saying unto them, Come up hither. [a]And they ascended up to heaven [b]in a cloud; [c]and their enemies beheld them.

13 And the same hour [a]was there a great earthquake, [b]and the tenth part of the city fell, and in the earthquake were slain of men seven thousand: and the remnant were affrighted, [c]and gave glory to the God of heaven.

14 [a]The second woe is past; *and,* behold, the third woe cometh quickly.

15 And [a]the seventh angel [1]sounded; [b]and there were great voices in heaven, saying, [c]The kingdoms of this world are become *the kingdoms* of our Lord, and of his Christ; [d]and he shall reign for ever and ever.

16 And [a]the four and twenty elders, which sat before God on their [1]seats, fell upon their faces, and [b]worshipped God,

17 Saying, We give thee thanks, O Lord God Almighty, [a]which[1] art, and wast, and art to come; because thou hast taken to thee thy great power, [b]and hast reigned.

18 And the nations were [a]angry, and [1]thy wrath is come, and the time of the [b]dead, that they should be judged, and that thou shouldest give reward unto thy servants the prophets, and to the saints, and them that fear thy name, small and great; and shouldest destroy them which destroy the earth.

19 And [a]the temple of God was opened in heaven, and there was seen in his temple the ark of his [1]testament: and [b]there were lightnings, and voices, and thunderings, and an earthquake, [c]and great hail.

## CHAPTER 12

AND there appeared a great [1]wonder in heaven; a woman clothed with the sun, and the moon under her feet, and upon her head a [2]crown of twelve stars:

2 And she being with child cried, [a]travailing[1] in birth, and [2]pained to be [3]delivered.

---

11:9 [a] Rev. 17:15
[b] Ps. 79:2, 3
[1] *peoples* [2] *tribes*
[3] *languages*
[4] *allow*
11:10 [a] Rev. 12:12
[b] Esth. 9:19, 22
[c] Rev. 16:10
11:11 [a] Rev. 11:9
[b] Ezek. 37:5, 9, 10
[1] *breath*
11:12 [a] Is. 14:13
[b] Acts 1:9 [c] 2 Kin. 2:1
11:13 [a] Rev. 6:12;
8:5; 11:19; 16:18
[b] Rev. 16:19 [c] Rev. 14:7; 16:9; 19:7
11:14 [a] Rev. 8:13;
9:12
11:15 [a] Rev. 8:2;
10:7 [b] Is. 27:13
[c] Rev. 12:10 [d] Ex. 15:18 [1] *blew his trumpet*
11:16 [a] Rev. 4:4
[b] Rev. 4:11; 5:9, 12, 14; 7:11 [1] *thrones*
11:17 [a] Rev. 16:5
[b] Rev. 19:6 [1] *who is and was and is*
11:18 [a] Ps. 2:1
[b] Dan. 7:10 [1] *your anger*
11:19 [a] Rev. 4:1;
15:5, 8 [b] Rev. 8:5
[c] Rev. 16:21 [1] *covenant*
12:1 [1] *sign* [a] *garland*
12:2 [a] Is. 26:17;
66:6–9 [1] *being in labour* [2] *in pain*
[3] *give birth*
12:3 [a] Rev. 13:1;
17:3, 7, 9 [1] *sign*
[2] *diadems*
12:4 [a] Rev. 9:10,
19 [b] Rev. 8:7, 12
[c] Dan. 8:10 [d] Rev. 12:2. [e] Matt. 2:16
[1] *give birth*
12:5 [a] Ps. 2:9
[b] Acts 1:9–11
[1] *male*
12:6 [a] Rev. 12:4,
14 [b] Rev. 11:3; 13:5
[1] *sixty*
12:7 [a] Dan. 10:13,
21; 12:1 [b] Rev. 20:2
12:8 [1] *a place found for them*
12:9 [a] John 12:31
[b] Gen. 3:1, 4 [c] Rev. 20:3 [d] Rev. 9:1 [1] *to*
12:10 [a] Rev. 11:15
[b] Zech. 3:1
12:11 [a] Rom. 16:20
[b] Luke 14:26
12:12 [a] Ps. 96:11
[b] Rev. 8:13 [c] Rev. 10:6
12:13 [a] Rev. 12:5
[1] *male*
12:14 [a] Ex. 19:4
[b] Rev. 12:6 [c] Rev. 17:3 [d] Dan. 7:25;
12:7

---

3 And there appeared another [1]wonder in heaven; and behold [a]a great red dragon, having seven heads and ten horns, and seven [2]crowns upon his heads.

4 And [a]his tail drew the third part [b]of the stars of heaven, [c]and did cast them to the earth: and the dragon stood [d]before the woman which was ready to [1]be delivered, [e]for to devour her child as soon as it was born.

5 And she brought forth a [1]man child, [a]who was to rule all nations with a rod of iron: and her child was [b]caught up unto God, and *to* his throne.

6 And [a]the woman fled into the wilderness, where she hath a place prepared of God, that they should feed her there [b]a thousand two hundred *and* [1]threescore days.

7 And there was war in heaven: [a]Michael and his angels fought [b]against the dragon; and the dragon fought and his angels,

8 And prevailed not; neither was [1]their place found any more in heaven.

9 And [a]the great dragon was cast out, [b]that old serpent, called the Devil, and Satan, [c]which deceiveth the whole world: [d]he was cast out [1]into the earth, and his angels were cast out with him.

10 And I heard a loud voice saying in heaven, [a]Now is come salvation, and strength, and the kingdom of our God, and the power of his Christ: for the accuser of our brethren is cast down, [b]which accused them before our God day and night.

11 And [a]they overcame him by the blood of the Lamb, and by the word of their testimony; [b]and they loved not their lives unto the death.

12 Therefore [a]rejoice, *ye* heavens, and ye that dwell in them. [b]Woe to the inhabiters of the earth and of the sea! for the devil is come down unto you, having great wrath, [c]because he knoweth that he hath but a short time.

13 And when the dragon saw that he was cast unto the earth, he persecuted [a]the woman which brought forth the [1]man *child*.

14 [a]And to the woman were given two wings of a great eagle, [b]that she might fly [c]into the wilderness, into her place, where she is nourished [d]for a time, and times, and half a time, from the face of the serpent.

15 And the serpent [a]cast[1] out of his mouth [2]water as a flood after the woman, that he might cause her to be carried away of the flood.

16 And the earth helped the woman, and the earth opened her mouth, and

---

12:15 [a] Is. 59:19 [1] *spewed* [2] *a river of water*

swallowed up the flood which the dragon cast out of his mouth.

17 And the dragon was [1]wroth with the woman, and went to make war with the [2]remnant of her seed, which keep the commandments of God, and have the testimony of Jesus Christ.

## CHAPTER 13

AND I stood upon the sand of the sea, and saw [a]a beast rise up out of the sea, [b]having seven heads and ten horns, and upon his horns ten crowns, and upon his heads [1]the [c]name of blasphemy.

2 And the beast which I saw was like unto a leopard, and his feet were as the feet of a bear, and his mouth as the mouth of a lion: and the [a]dragon gave him his power, and his [1]seat, and great authority.

3 And I saw one of his heads [a]as [1]it were wounded to death; and his deadly wound was healed: and [b]all the world [2]wondered after the beast.

4 And they worshipped the dragon which gave [1]power unto the beast: and they worshipped the beast, saying, [a]Who is like unto the beast? who is able to make war with him?

5 And there was given unto him [a]a mouth speaking great things and blasphemies; and power was given unto him to continue [b]forty and two months.

6 And he opened his mouth in blasphemy against God, to blaspheme his name, [a]and his tabernacle, and them that dwell in heaven.

7 And it was given unto him [a]to make war with the saints, and to overcome them: [b]and [1]power was given him over all [2]kindreds, and tongues, and nations.

8 And all that dwell upon the earth shall worship him, [a]whose names are not written in the book of life of the Lamb slain [b]from the foundation of the world.

9 [a]If any man have an ear, let him hear.

10 [a]He that leadeth into captivity shall go into captivity: [b]he that killeth with the sword must be killed with the sword. [c]Here is the patience and the faith of the saints.

11 And I beheld another beast [a]coming up out of the earth; and he had two horns like a lamb, and he spake as a dragon.

12 And he exerciseth all the [1]power of the first beast [2]before him, and causeth the earth and them which dwell therein to worship the first beast, [a]whose deadly wound was healed.

13 And [a]he doeth great [1]wonders, [b]so that he maketh fire come down

12:17 [1] enraged
[2] rest of her offspring
13:1 [a] Dan. 7:2, 7
[b] Rev. 12:3 [c] Rev. 17:3 [1] a blasphemous name
13:2 [a] Rev. 12:3, 9; 13:4, 12 [1] throne
13:3 [a] Rev. 13:12, 14 [b] Rev. 17:8
[1] if it had been
[2] marvelled at
13:4 [a] Rev. 18:18
[1] authority
13:5 [a] Dan. 7:8, 11, 20, 25; 11:36
[b] Rev. 11:2
13:6 [a] [Col. 2:9]
13:7 [a] Dan. 7:21
[b] Rev. 11:18 [1] authority [2] tribes
13:8 [a] Ex. 32:32
[b] Rev. 17:8
13:9 [a] Rev. 2:7
13:10 [a] Is. 33:1
[b] Gen. 9:6 [c] Rev. 14:12
13:11 [a] Rev. 11:7
13:12 [a] Rev. 13:3, 4
[1] authority [2] in his presence
13:13 [a] Matt. 24:24
[b] 1 Kin. 18:38
[1] signs
13:14 [a] Rev. 12:9 [b] 2 Thess. 2:9 [c] 2 Kin. 20:7
[1] was granted
13:15 [a] Rev. 16:2
[1] breath
13:16 [a] Rev. 7:3; 14:9; 20:4 [1] slave
13:17 [a] Rev. 14:9–11 [b] Rev. 15:2
[1] except
13:18 [a] Rev. 17:9
[b] [1 Cor. 2:14]
[c] Rev. 15:2 [d] Rev. 21:17
14:1 [a] Rev. 5:6
[b] Rev. 7:4; 14:3
[c] Rev. 7:3; 22:4
14:2 [a] Rev. 1:15; 19:6 [b] Rev. 5:8
14:3 [a] Rev. 5:9
[1] living creatures
14:4 [a] [2 Cor. 11:2] [b] Rev. 3:4; 7:17 [c] Rev. 5:9
[d] James 1:18
14:5 [a] Ps. 32:2
[b] Eph. 5:27
[1] deceit
14:6 [a] Rev. 8:13
[b] Eph. 3:9 [c] Rev. 13:7 [1] tribe
14:7 [a] Rev. 11:18 [b] Neh. 9:6
[1] springs

from heaven on the earth in the sight of men,

14 [a]And deceiveth them that dwell on the earth [b]by the means of those miracles which he [1]had power to do in the sight of the beast; saying to them that dwell on the earth, that they should make an image to the beast, which had the wound by a sword, [c]and did live.

15 And he had power to give [1]life unto the image of the beast, that the image of the beast should both speak, [a]and cause that as many as would not worship the image of the beast should be killed.

16 And he causeth all, both small and great, rich and poor, free and [1]bond, [a]to receive a mark in their right hand, or in their foreheads:

17 And that no man might buy or sell, [1]save he that had the mark, or [a]the name of the beast, [b]or the number of his name.

18 [a]Here is wisdom. Let him that hath [b]understanding count [c]the number of the beast: [d]for it is the number of a man; and his number is Six hundred threescore and six.

## CHAPTER 14

AND I looked, and, lo, a [a]Lamb stood on the mount Sion, and with him an [b]hundred forty and four thousand, having his Father's name [c]written in their foreheads.

2 And I heard a voice from heaven, [a]as the voice of many waters, and as the voice of a great thunder: and I heard the voice of [b]harpers harping with their harps:

3 And they sung as it were a new song before the throne, and before the four [1]beasts, and the elders: and no man could learn that song [a]but the hundred and forty and four thousand, which were redeemed from the earth.

4 These are they which were not defiled with women; [a]for they are virgins. These are they [b]which follow the Lamb whithersoever he goeth. These [c]were redeemed from among men, [d]being the firstfruits unto God and to the Lamb.

5 And [a]in their mouth was found no [1]guile: for [b]they are without fault before the throne of God.

6 And I saw another angel [a]fly in the midst of heaven, [b]having the everlasting gospel to preach unto them that dwell on the earth, [c]and to every nation, and [1]kindred, and tongue, and people,

7 Saying with a loud voice, [a]Fear God, and give glory to him; for the hour of his judgment is come: [b]and worship him that made heaven, and earth, and the sea, and the [1]fountains of waters.

8 And there followed another angel, saying, [a]Babylon is fallen, is fallen, that great city, because [b]she made all nations drink of the wine of the wrath of her fornication.

9 And the third angel followed them, saying with a loud voice, [a]If any man worship the beast and his image, and receive *his* [b]mark in his forehead, or in his hand,

10 The same [a]shall drink of the wine of the wrath of God, which is [b]poured out [1]without mixture into [c]the cup of his indignation; and [d]he shall be tormented with [e]fire and brimstone in the presence of the holy angels, and in the presence of the Lamb:

11 And [a]the smoke of their torment ascendeth up for ever and ever: and they have no rest day nor night, who worship the beast and his image, and whosoever receiveth the mark of his name.

12 [a]Here is the [1]patience of the saints: [b]here *are* they that keep the commandments of God, and the faith of Jesus.

13 And I heard a voice from heaven saying unto me, Write, [a]Blessed *are* the dead [b]which die in the Lord from henceforth: Yea, saith the Spirit, [c]that they may rest from their labours; and their works do follow [d]them.

14 And I looked, and behold a white cloud, and upon the cloud *one* sat like unto the Son of man, having on his head a golden crown, and in his hand a sharp sickle.

15 And another angel [a]came out of the temple, crying with a loud voice to him that sat on the cloud, [b]Thrust in thy sickle, and reap: for the time is come for thee to reap; for the harvest [c]of the earth is ripe.

16 And he that sat on the cloud thrust in his sickle on the earth; and the earth was reaped.

17 And another angel came out of the temple which is in heaven, he also having a sharp sickle.

18 And another angel came out from the altar, [a]which had power over fire; and cried with a loud cry to him that had the sharp sickle, saying, [b]Thrust in thy sharp sickle, and gather the clusters of the vine of the earth; for her grapes are fully ripe.

19 And the angel thrust in his sickle into the earth, and gathered the vine of the earth, and cast *it* into [a]the great winepress of the wrath of God.

20 And the [a]winepress was [1]trodden [b]without[2] the city, and blood came out of the winepress, [c]even unto the horse bridles, by the space of a thousand *and* six hundred [3]furlongs.

**Center column references:**

14:8 [a] Is. 21:9
[b] Jer. 51:7
14:9 [a] Rev. 13:14, 15; 14:11 [b] Rev. 13:16
14:10 [a] Ps. 75:8
[b] Rev. 18:6 [c] Rev.
[1] *full strength*
[e] 2 Thess. 1:7
14:11 [a] Is. 34:8–10
14:12 [a] Rev.
13:10 [b] Rev. 12:17
[1] *steadfastness*
14:13 [a] Eccl. 4:1, 2 [b] 1 Cor. 15:18
[c] Heb. 4:9, 10
[d] [1 Cor. 3:11–15; 15:58]
14:15 [a] Rev. 16:17
[b] Joel 3:13 [c] Jer. 51:33
14:18 [a] Rev. 16:8
[b] Joel 3:13
14:19 [a] Rev. 19:15
14:20 [a] Is. 63:3
[b] Heb. 13:12 [c] Is. 34:3 [1] *trampled*
[2] *outside* [3] Gr. *stadion*

15:1 [a] Rev. 12:1, 3
[b] Rev. 21:9 [c] Rev. 14:10
15:2 [a] Rev. 4:6
[b] [Matt. 3:11]
[c] Rev. 13:14, 15
[d] Rev. 13:17 [e] Rev. 5:8
15:3 [a] Ex. 15:1–21
[b] Rev. 15:3 [c] Deut. 32:3, 4 [d] Ps. 145:17
15:4 [a] Ex. 15:14
[b] Lev. 11:44 [c] Is. 66:23
15:5 [a] Num. 1:50
[1] *sanctuary*
15:6 [a] Ex. 28:6
[1] *sanctuary*
[2] *chests* [3] *bands*
15:7 [a] Rev. 4:6
[b] 1 Thess. 1:9
[1] *living creatures*
[2] *bowls*
15:8 [a] Ex. 19:18; 40:34 [b] 2 Thess. 1:9
16:1 [a] Rev. 15:1
[b] Rev. 14:10
[1] *bowls*
16:2 [a] Rev. 8:7
[b] Ex. 9:9–11 [c] Rev. 13:15–17; 14:9
[d] Rev. 13:14 [1] *foul and loathsome*
16:3 [a] Rev. 8:8; 11:6 [b] Ex. 7:17–21
[c] Rev. 8:9 [1] *bowl* [2] *creature*
16:4 [a] Rev. 8:10
[b] Ex. 7:17–20
[1] *bowl* [2] *springs*
16:5 [a] Rev. 15:3, 4
[b] Rev. 1:4, 8

**CHAPTER 15**

AND [a]I saw another sign in heaven, great and marvellous, [b]seven angels having the seven last plagues; [c]for in them is filled up the wrath of God.

2 And I saw as it were [a]a sea of glass [b]mingled with fire: and them that had gotten the victory over the beast, [c]and over his image, and over his mark, *and* over the [d]number of his name, stand on the sea of glass, [e]having the harps of God.

3 And they sing [a]the song of Moses the servant of God, and the song of the [b]Lamb, saying, [c]Great and marvellous *are* thy works, Lord God Almighty; [d]just and true *are* thy ways, thou King of saints.

4 [a]Who shall not fear thee, O Lord, and glorify thy name? for *thou* only *art* [b]holy: for [c]all nations shall come and worship before thee; for thy judgments are made manifest.

5 And after that I looked, and, behold, [a]the [1]temple of the tabernacle of the testimony in heaven was opened:

6 And the seven angels came out of the [1]temple, having the seven plagues, [a]clothed in pure and white linen, and having their [2]breasts girded with golden [3]girdles.

7 [a]And one of the four [1]beasts gave unto the seven angels seven golden [2]vials full of the wrath of God, [b]who liveth for ever and ever.

8 And [a]the temple was filled with smoke [b]from the glory of God, and from his power; and no man was able to enter into the temple, till the seven plagues of the seven angels were fulfilled.

**CHAPTER 16**

AND I heard a great voice out of the temple saying [a]to the seven angels, Go your ways, and pour out the [1]vials [b]of the wrath of God upon the earth.

2 And the first went, and poured out his vial [a]upon the earth; and [b]there fell a [1]noisome and grievous sore upon the men [c]which had the mark of the beast, and *upon* them [d]which worshipped his image.

3 And the second angel poured out his [1]vial [a]upon the sea; and [b]it became as the blood of a dead *man:* [c]and every living [2]soul died in the sea.

4 And the third angel poured out his [1]vial [a]upon the rivers and [2]fountains of waters; [b]and they became blood.

5 And I heard the angel of the waters say, [a]Thou art righteous, O Lord, [b]which art, and wast, and shalt be, because thou hast judged thus.

6 For <sup>a</sup>they have shed the blood <sup>b</sup>of saints and prophets, <sup>c</sup>and thou hast given them blood to drink; for <sup>1</sup>they are worthy.

7 And I heard another out of the altar say, Even so, <sup>a</sup>Lord God Almighty, <sup>b</sup>true and righteous *are* thy judgments.

8 And the fourth angel poured out his <sup>1</sup>vial <sup>a</sup>upon the sun; <sup>b</sup>and power was given unto him to scorch men with fire.

9 And men were scorched with great heat, and <sup>a</sup>blasphemed the name of God, which hath power over these plagues: <sup>b</sup>and they repented not <sup>c</sup>to give him glory.

10 And the fifth angel poured out his <sup>1</sup>vial <sup>a</sup>upon the <sup>2</sup>seat of the beast; <sup>b</sup>and his kingdom was full of darkness; <sup>c</sup>and they gnawed their tongues for pain,

11 And blasphemed the God of heaven because of their pains and their sores, and repented not of their deeds.

12 And the sixth angel poured out his <sup>1</sup>vial <sup>a</sup>upon the great river Euphrates; <sup>b</sup>and the water thereof was dried up, <sup>c</sup>that the way of the kings of the east might be prepared.

13 And I saw three unclean <sup>a</sup>spirits like frogs *come* out of the mouth of <sup>b</sup>the dragon, and out of the mouth of the beast, and out of the mouth of <sup>c</sup>the false prophet.

14 For they are the spirits of <sup>1</sup>devils, <sup>a</sup>working<sup>2</sup> miracles, *which* go forth unto the kings of the earth <sup>b</sup>and of the whole world, to gather them to <sup>c</sup>the battle of that great day of God Almighty.

15 <sup>a</sup>Behold, I come as a thief. Blessed *is* he that watcheth, and keepeth his garments, <sup>b</sup>lest he walk naked, and they see his shame.

16 <sup>a</sup>And he gathered them together into a place called in the Hebrew tongue <sup>1</sup>Armageddon.

17 And the seventh angel poured out his <sup>1</sup>vial into the air; and there came a great voice out of the temple of heaven, from the throne, saying, <sup>a</sup>It is done.

18 And <sup>a</sup>there were <sup>1</sup>voices, and thunders, and lightnings; <sup>b</sup>and there was a great earthquake, <sup>c</sup>such as was not since men were upon the earth, so mighty an earthquake, *and* so great.

19 And <sup>a</sup>the great city was divided into three parts, and the cities of the nations fell: and <sup>b</sup>great Babylon <sup>c</sup>came in remembrance before God, <sup>d</sup>to give unto her the cup of the wine of the fierceness of his wrath.

20 And <sup>a</sup>every island fled away, and the mountains were not found.

21 And there fell upon men a great hail out of heaven, *every stone* about

the weight of a talent: and men blasphemed God because of the plague of the hail; for the plague thereof was exceeding great.

## CHAPTER 17

A<sup>ND</sup> there came <sup>a</sup>one of the seven angels which had the seven <sup>1</sup>vials, and talked with me, saying unto me, Come hither; <sup>b</sup>I will shew unto thee the judgment of <sup>c</sup>the great <sup>2</sup>whore <sup>d</sup>that sitteth upon many waters:

2 <sup>a</sup>With whom the kings of the earth have committed fornication, and <sup>b</sup>the inhabitants of the earth have been made drunk with the wine of her fornication.

3 So he carried me away in the <sup>1</sup>spirit <sup>a</sup>into the wilderness: and I saw a woman sit <sup>b</sup>upon a scarlet coloured beast, full of <sup>c</sup>names of blasphemy, having seven heads and ten horns.

4 And the woman <sup>a</sup>was arrayed in purple and scarlet colour, <sup>b</sup>and <sup>1</sup>decked with gold and precious stones and pearls, <sup>c</sup>having a golden cup in her hand <sup>d</sup>full of abominations and filthiness of her fornication:

5 And upon her forehead *was* a name written, <sup>a</sup>MYSTERY, BABYLON THE GREAT, THE MOTHER OF HARLOTS AND ABOMINATIONS OF THE EARTH.

6 And I saw <sup>a</sup>the woman drunken <sup>b</sup>with the blood of the saints, and with the blood of <sup>c</sup>the martyrs of Jesus: and when I saw her, I <sup>1</sup>wondered with great <sup>2</sup>admiration.

7 And the angel said unto me, Wherefore didst thou marvel? I will tell thee the mystery of the woman, and of the beast that carrieth her, which hath the seven heads and ten horns.

8 The beast that thou sawest was, and is not; and <sup>a</sup>shall ascend out of the bottomless pit, and <sup>b</sup>go into <sup>1</sup>perdition: and they that <sup>c</sup>dwell on the earth <sup>d</sup>shall <sup>2</sup>wonder, <sup>e</sup>whose names were not written in the book of life from the foundation of the world, when they behold the beast that was, and is not, and yet is.

9 And <sup>a</sup>here *is* the mind which hath wisdom. <sup>b</sup>The seven heads are seven mountains, on which the woman sitteth.

10 And there are seven kings: five <sup>1</sup>are fallen, and one is, *and* the other is not yet come; and when he cometh, he must <sup>a</sup>continue a short <sup>2</sup>space.

11 And the <sup>a</sup>beast that was, and is not, even he is the eighth, and is of the seven, and goeth into <sup>1</sup>perdition.

12 And <sup>a</sup>the ten horns which thou sawest are ten kings, which have received no kingdom as yet; but receive <sup>1</sup>power as kings one hour with the beast.

---

16:6 <sup>a</sup> Matt. 23:34
<sup>b</sup> Rev. 11:18  <sup>c</sup> Is. 49:26  <sup>1</sup> *it is their just due*
16:7 <sup>a</sup> Rev. 15:3
<sup>b</sup> Rev. 13:10; 19:2
16:8 <sup>a</sup> Rev. 8:12
<sup>b</sup> Rev. 9:17, 18  <sup>1</sup> *bowl*
16:9 <sup>a</sup> Rev. 16:11
<sup>b</sup> Dan. 5:22  <sup>c</sup> Rev. 11:13
16:10 <sup>a</sup> Rev. 13:2
<sup>b</sup> Rev. 8:12; 9:2
<sup>c</sup> Rev. 11:10  <sup>1</sup> *bowl*
<sup>2</sup> *throne*
16:12 <sup>a</sup> Rev. 9:14
<sup>b</sup> Jer. 50:38  <sup>c</sup> Is. 41:2, 25; 46:11
<sup>1</sup> *bowl*
16:13 <sup>a</sup> 1 John 4:1  <sup>b</sup> Rev. 12:3,
9  <sup>c</sup> Rev. 13:11, 14; 19:20; 20:10
16:14 <sup>a</sup> 2 Thess. 2:9  <sup>b</sup> Luke 2:1
<sup>c</sup> Rev. 17:14; 19:19;
20:8  <sup>1</sup> *demons*
<sup>2</sup> *performing signs*
16:15 <sup>a</sup> Matt. 24:43
<sup>b</sup> 2 Cor. 5:3
16:16 <sup>a</sup> Rev. 19:19
<sup>1</sup> Lit. *Mount Megiddo*
16:17 <sup>a</sup> Rev. 10:6; 21:6  <sup>1</sup> *bowl*
16:18 <sup>a</sup> Rev. 4:5
<sup>b</sup> Rev. 11:13  <sup>c</sup> Dan. 12:1  <sup>1</sup> *noises*
16:19 <sup>a</sup> Rev. 14:8
<sup>b</sup> Rev. 17:5, 18
<sup>c</sup> Rev. 14:8; 18:5
<sup>d</sup> Is. 51:17
16:20 <sup>a</sup> Rev. 6:14; 20:11
17:1 <sup>a</sup> Rev. 1:1; 21:9
<sup>b</sup> Rev. 16:19  <sup>c</sup> Nah. 3:4  <sup>d</sup> Jer. 51:13
<sup>1</sup> *bowls*  <sup>2</sup> *harlot*
17:2 <sup>a</sup> Rev. 2:22;
18:3, 9  <sup>b</sup> Jer. 51:7
17:3 <sup>a</sup> Rev. 12:6, 14;
21:10  <sup>b</sup> Rev. 12:3
<sup>c</sup> Rev. 13:1  <sup>1</sup> Or *Spirit*
17:4 <sup>a</sup> Rev. 18:12, 16
<sup>b</sup> Dan. 11:38  <sup>c</sup> Jer. 51:7  <sup>d</sup> Rev. 14:8
<sup>1</sup> *adorned*
17:5 <sup>a</sup> 2 Thess. 2:7
17:6 <sup>a</sup> Rev. 18:24
<sup>b</sup> Rev. 13:15  <sup>c</sup> Rev. 6:9, 10  <sup>1</sup> *marvelled*
<sup>2</sup> *amazement*
17:8 <sup>a</sup> Rev. 11:7
<sup>b</sup> Rev. 13:10; 17:11
<sup>c</sup> Rev. 3:10  <sup>d</sup> Rev. 13:3  <sup>e</sup> Rev. 13:8
<sup>1</sup> *destruction*
<sup>2</sup> *marvel*
17:9 <sup>a</sup> Rev. 13:18
<sup>b</sup> Rev. 13:1
17:10 <sup>a</sup> Rev. 13:5
<sup>1</sup> *have*  <sup>2</sup> *time*
17:11 <sup>a</sup> Rev. 13:3,
12, 14; 17:8  <sup>1</sup> *destruction*
17:12 <sup>a</sup> Dan. 7:20  <sup>1</sup> *authority*

13 These have one mind, and shall give their power and ¹strength unto the beast.

14 ªThese shall make war with the Lamb, and the Lamb shall ᵇovercome them: ᶜfor he is Lord of lords, and King of kings: ᵈand they that are with him *are* called, and chosen, and faithful.

15 And he saith unto me, ªThe waters which thou sawest, where the ¹whore sitteth, ᵇare peoples, and multitudes, and nations, and tongues.

16 And the ten horns which thou sawest upon the beast, ªthese shall hate the whore, and shall make her ᵇdesolate ᶜand naked, and shall eat her flesh, and ᵈburn her with fire.

17 ªFor God hath put in their hearts to fulfil his will, and to ¹agree, and give their kingdom unto the beast, ᵇuntil the words of God shall be fulfilled.

18 And the woman which thou sawest ªis that great city, ᵇwhich reigneth over the kings of the earth.

## CHAPTER 18

AND ªafter these things I saw another angel come down from heaven, having great ¹power; ᵇand the earth was ²lightened with his glory.

2 And he cried mightily with a ¹strong voice, saying, ªBabylon the great is fallen, is fallen, and ᵇis become the habitation of ²devils, and ³the hold of every foul spirit, and ᶜa cage of every unclean and ⁴hateful bird.

3 For all nations ªhave drunk of the wine of the wrath of her fornication, and the kings of the earth have committed fornication with her, ᵇand the merchants of the earth ¹are waxed rich through the abundance of her ²delicacies.

4 And I heard another voice from heaven, saying, ªCome out of her, my people, that ye be not partakers of her sins, and that ye receive not of her plagues.

5 ªFor her sins have reached unto heaven, and ᵇGod hath remembered her iniquities.

6 ªReward her even as she rewarded you, and ¹double unto her double according to her works: ᵇin the cup which she hath filled ᶜfill to her double.

7 ªHow much she hath glorified herself, and lived ¹deliciously, so much torment and sorrow give her: for she saith in her heart, I sit a ᵇqueen, and am no widow, and shall see no sorrow.

8 Therefore shall her plagues come ªin one day, death, and mourning, and famine; and ᵇshe shall be utterly

burned with fire: ᶜfor strong *is* the Lord God who judgeth her.

9 And ªthe kings of the earth, who have committed fornication and lived ¹deliciously with her, ᵇshall ²bewail her, and lament for her, ᶜwhen they shall see the smoke of her burning,

10 Standing afar off for the fear of her torment, saying, ªAlas, alas that great city Babylon, that mighty city! ᵇfor in one hour is thy judgment come.

11 And ªthe merchants of the earth shall weep and mourn over her; for no man buyeth their merchandise any more:

12 ªThe merchandise of gold, and silver, and precious stones, and of pearls, and fine linen, and purple, and silk, and scarlet, and ¹all thyine wood, and all manner vessels of most precious wood, and of brass, and iron, and marble,

13 And cinnamon, and ¹odours, and ²ointments, and frankincense, and wine, and oil, and fine flour, and wheat, and ³beasts, and sheep, and horses, and chariots, and ⁴slaves, and ⁵souls of men.

14 And the fruits that thy soul ¹lusted after are departed from thee, and all things which ²were dainty and ³goodly are departed from thee, and thou shalt find them no more at all.

15 The merchants of these things, which were made rich by her, shall stand afar off for the fear of her torment, weeping and wailing,

16 And saying, Alas, alas ªthat great city, ᵇthat was clothed in fine linen, and purple, and scarlet, and ¹decked with gold, and precious stones, and pearls!

17 ªFor in one hour so great riches is come to ¹nought. And ᵇevery shipmaster, and all ²the company in ships, and sailors, and as many as trade by sea, stood afar off,

18 ªAnd cried when they saw the smoke of her burning, saying, ᵇWhat *city is* like unto this great city!

19 And ªthey cast dust on their heads, and cried, weeping and wailing, saying, Alas, alas that great city, wherein were made rich all that had ships in the sea by reason of her ¹costliness! ᵇfor in one hour is she made ²desolate.

20 ªRejoice over her, *thou* heaven, and *ye* holy apostles and prophets; for ᵇGod hath avenged you on her.

21 And a mighty angel took up a stone like a great millstone, and cast *it* into the sea, saying, ªThus with violence shall that great city Babylon be thrown down, and ᵇshall be found no more at all.

### Center reference column

17:13 ¹ authority
17:14 ª Rev. 16:14;
19:19 ᵇ Rev. 19:20
ᶜ 1 Tim. 6:15 ᵈ Jer. 50:44
17:15 ª Is. 8:7
ᵇ Rev. 13:7 ¹ harlot
17:16 ª Jer. 50:41
ᵇ Rev. 18:17, 19
ᶜ Ezek. 16:37, 39
ᵈ Rev. 18:8
17:17 ª 2 Thess. 2:11
ᵇ Rev. 10:7 ¹ be of one mind
17:18 ª Rev. 11:8;
16:19 ᵇ Rev. 12:4
18:1 ª Rev. 17:1,
7 ᵇ Ezek. 43:2
¹ authority ² illuminated
18:2 ª Is. 13:19;
21:9 ᵇ Is. 13:21;
34:11, 13–15 ᶜ Is. 14:23 ¹ loud ² demons ³ a prison for ⁴ hated
18:3 ª Rev. 14:8
ᵇ Is. 47:15 ¹ have become ² luxury
18:4 ª Is. 48:20
18:5 ª Gen. 18:20
ᵇ Rev. 16:19
18:6 ª Ps. 137:8
ᵇ Rev. 14:10 ᶜ Rev. 16:19 ¹ repay
18:7 ª Ezek. 28:2–8 ᵇ Is. 47:7, 8 ¹ luxuriously
18:8 ª Rev. 18:10
ᵇ Rev. 17:16 ᶜ Jer. 50:34
18:9 ª Ezek. 26:16;
27:35 ᵇ Jer. 50:46 ᶜ Rev. 19:3 ¹ luxuriously ² weep for
18:10 ª Is. 21:9
ᵇ Rev. 18:17, 19
18:11 ª Ezek. 27:27–34
18:12 ª Rev. 17:4
¹ every kind of citron wood
18:13 ª Ezek. 27:13
¹ incense ² fragrant oil ³ cattle ⁴ bodies
18:14 ¹ longed for ² are rich ³ splendid
18:16 ª Rev.
17:18 ᵇ Rev. 17:4
¹ adorned
18:17 ª Rev. 18:10
ᵇ Is. 23:14 ¹ nothing ² who travel by ship
18:18 ª Ezek. 27:30
ᵇ Rev. 13:4
18:19 ª Josh.
7:6 ᵇ Rev. 18:8
¹ wealth ² a wasteland
18:20 ª Jer. 51:48
ᵇ Luke 11:49
18:21 ª Jer. 51:63,
64 ᵇ Rev. 12:8;
16:20

22 [a]And the [1]voice of harpers, and musicians, and of [2]pipers, and trumpeters, shall be heard no more at all in thee; and no craftsman, of whatsoever craft *he be,* shall be found any more in thee; and the sound of a millstone shall be heard no more at all in thee;

23 [a]And the light of a [1]candle shall shine no more at all in thee; [b]and the voice of the bridegroom and of the bride shall be heard no more at all in thee: for [c]thy merchants were the great men of the earth; [d]for by thy sorceries were all nations deceived.

24 And [a]in her was found the blood of prophets, and of saints, and of all that [b]were slain upon the earth.

## CHAPTER 19

AND after these things [a]I heard a great voice of [1]much people in heaven, saying, Alleluia; [b]Salvation, and glory, and honour, and power, unto the Lord our God:

2 For [a]true and righteous *are* his judgments: for he hath judged the great [1]whore, which did corrupt the earth with her fornication, and [b]hath avenged the blood of his servants [2]at her hand.

3 And again they said, Alleluia. [a]And her smoke rose up for ever and ever.

4 And [a]the four and twenty elders and the four [1]beasts fell down and worshipped God that sat on the throne, saying, [b]Amen; Alleluia.

5 And a voice came out of the throne, saying, [a]Praise our God, all ye his servants, and ye that fear him, [b]both small and great.

6 [a]And I heard as it were the voice of a great multitude, and as the [1]voice of many waters, and as the [1]voice of mighty thunderings, saying, Alleluia: for [b]the Lord God omnipotent reigneth.

7 Let us be glad and rejoice, and give [1]honour to him: for [a]the marriage of the Lamb is come, and his wife hath made herself ready.

8 And [a]to her was granted that she should be arrayed in fine linen, clean and [1]white: [b]for the fine linen is the [2]righteousness of saints.

9 And he saith unto me, Write, [a]Blessed *are* they which are called unto the marriage supper of the Lamb. And he saith unto me, [b]These are the true sayings of God.

10 And [a]I fell at his feet to worship him. And he said unto me, [b]See *thou do it* not: I am thy [c]fellowservant, and of thy brethren [d]that have the testimony of Jesus: worship God: for the [e]testimony of Jesus is the spirit of prophecy.

11 [a]And I saw heaven opened, and behold [b]a white horse; and he that sat upon him *was* called [c]Faithful

and True, and [d]in righteousness he doth judge and make war.

12 [a]His eyes *were* as a flame of fire, and on his head *were* many crowns; [b]and he had a name written, that no man knew, but he himself.

13 [a]And he *was* clothed with a [1]vesture dipped in blood: and his name is called [b]The Word of God.

14 [a]And the armies *which were* in heaven followed him upon white horses, [b]clothed in fine linen, white and clean.

15 And [a]out of his mouth goeth a sharp sword, that with it he should [b]smite the nations: and [b]he shall rule them with a rod of iron: and [c]he treadeth the winepress of the fierceness and wrath of Almighty God.

16 And [a]he hath on *his* [1]vesture and on his thigh a name written, [b]KING OF KINGS, AND LORD OF LORDS.

17 And I saw an angel standing in the sun; and he cried with a loud voice, saying to all the [1]fowls that fly in the midst of heaven, [a]Come and gather yourselves together unto the supper of the great God;

18 [a]That ye may eat the flesh of kings, and the flesh of captains, and the flesh of mighty men, and the flesh of horses, and of them that sit on them, and the flesh of all *men, both* free and [1]bond, both small and great.

19 [a]And I saw the beast, and the kings of the earth, and their armies, gathered together to make war against him that sat on the horse, and against his army.

20 [a]And the beast was [1]taken, and with him the false prophet that [2]wrought miracles [3]before him, with which he deceived them that had received the mark of the beast, and [b]them that worshipped his image. [c]These both were cast alive into a lake of fire [d]burning with brimstone.

21 And the [1]remnant [a]were slain with the sword of him that sat upon the horse, which *sword* proceeded out of his mouth: [b]and all the [2]fowls [c]were filled with their flesh.

## CHAPTER 20

AND I saw an angel come down from heaven, [a]having the key of the bottomless pit and a great chain in his hand.

2 And he laid hold on [a]the dragon, that old serpent, which is the Devil, and Satan, and bound him a thousand years,

3 And cast him into the bottomless pit, and shut him up, and [a]set a seal upon him, [b]that he should deceive the nations no more, till the thousand years should be fulfilled: and after that he must be [1]loosed a little [2]season.

### Cross references

18:22 [a] Jer. 7:34; 16:9; 25:10
[1] sound   [2] flutists
18:23 [a] Jer. 25:10
[b] Jer. 7:34; 16:9
[c] Is. 23:8   [d] 2 Kin. 9:22   [1] lamp
18:24 [a] Rev. 16:6; 17:6   [b] Jer. 51:49
19:1 [a] Rev. 11:15;
19:6 [b] Rev. 4:11
[1] Lit. *a great multitude*
19:2 [a] Rev. 15:3; 16:7 [b] Deut. 32:43
[1] harlot [2] shed by her
19:3 [a] Is. 34:10
19:4 [a] Rev. 4:4, 6, 10 [b] 1 Chr. 16:36
[1] living creatures
19:5 [a] Ps. 134:1
[b] Rev. 11:18
19:6 [a] Ezek. 1:24 [b] Rev. 11:15
[1] sound
19:7 [a] [Matt. 22:2; 25:10] [1] glory
19:8 [a] Ezek. 16:10
[b] Ps. 132:9 [1] bright
[2] righteous acts
19:9 [a] Luke 14:15
[b] Rev. 22:6
19:10 [a] Rev. 22:8
[b] Acts 10:26
[c] [Heb. 1:14]
[d] 1 John 5:10
[e] Luke 24:27
19:11 [a] Rev. 15:5
[b] Rev. 6:2; 19:19,
21 [c] Rev. 3:7, 14
[d] Is. 11:4
19:12 [a] Rev. 1:14
[b] Rev. 2:17; 19:16
19:13 [a] Is. 63:2,
3 [b] [John 1:1, 14]
[1] robe
19:14 [a] Rev. 14:20
[b] Matt. 28:3
19:15 [a] Is. 11:4
[b] Ps. 2:8, 9 [c] Is. 63:3–6 [1] strike
19:16 [a] Rev. 2:17;
19:12 [b] Dan. 2:47
[1] robe
19:17 [a] Ezek. 39:17
[1] birds
19:18 [a] Ezek. 39:18–20 [1] slave
19:19 [a] Rev. 16:13–16
19:20 [a] Rev. 16:13
[b] Rev. 13:8, 12, 13
[c] Dan. 7:11 [d] Rev. 14:10 [1] captured
[2] worked signs
[3] in his presence
19:21 [a] Rev. 19:15
[b] Rev. 19:17, 18
[c] Rev. 17:16 [1] rest
[2] birds
20:1 [a] Rev. 1:18; 9:1
20:2 [a] 2 Pet. 2:4
20:3 [a] Dan. 6:17
[b] Rev. 12:9; 20:8,
10 [1] released
[2] while

4 And I saw ªthrones, and they sat upon them, and ᵇjudgment was given unto them: and I *saw* ᶜthe souls of them that were beheaded for the witness of Jesus, and for the word of God, and ᵈwhich had not worshipped the beast, ᵉneither his image, neither had received *his* mark upon their foreheads, or in their hands; and they ᶠlived and ᵍreigned with Christ a thousand years.

5 But the rest of the dead lived not again until the thousand years were finished. This *is* the first resurrection.

6 Blessed and holy *is* he that hath part in the first resurrection: on such ªthe second death hath no power, but they shall be ᵇpriests of God and of Christ, ᶜand shall reign with him a thousand years.

7 And when the thousand years are ¹expired, Satan shall be ²loosed out of his prison,

8 And shall go out ªto deceive the nations which are in the four quarters of the earth, ᵇGog and Magog, ᶜto gather them together to battle: the number of whom *is* as the sand of the sea.

9 ªAnd they went up on the breadth of the earth, and ¹compassed the camp of the saints about, and the beloved city: and fire came down from God out of heaven, and devoured them.

10 And the devil that deceived them was cast into the lake of fire and brimstone, ªwhere the beast and the false prophet *are,* and ᵇshall be tormented day and night for ever and ever.

11 And I saw a great white throne, and him that sat on it, from whose face ªthe earth and the heaven fled away; ᵇand there was found no place for them.

12 And I saw the dead, ªsmall and great, stand before God; ᵇand the books were opened: and another ᶜbook was opened, which is *the book* of life: and the dead were judged out of those things which were written in the books, ᵈaccording to their works.

13 And the sea gave up the dead which were in it; ªand death and ¹hell delivered up the dead which were in them: ᵇand they were judged every man according to their works.

14 And ªdeath and ¹hell were cast into the lake of fire. ᵇThis is the second death.

15 And whosoever was not found written in the book of life ªwas cast into the lake of fire.

## CHAPTER 21

A ND ªI saw a new heaven and a new earth: ᵇfor the first heaven and the first earth were passed away; and there was no more sea.

2 And I John saw ªthe holy city, new Jerusalem, coming down from God out of heaven, prepared ᵇas a bride adorned for her husband.

3 And I heard a great voice out of heaven saying, Behold, ªthe tabernacle of God *is* with men, and he will dwell with them, and they shall be his people, and God himself shall be with them, *and be* their God.

4 ªAnd God shall wipe away all tears from their eyes; and ᵇthere shall be no more death, ᶜneither sorrow, nor crying, neither shall there be any more pain: for the former things are passed away.

5 And ªhe that sat upon the throne said, ᵇBehold, I make all things new. And he said unto me, Write: for ᶜthese words are true and faithful.

6 And he said unto me, ªIt is done. ᵇI am Alpha and Omega, the beginning and the end. ᶜI will give unto him ¹that is athirst of the fountain of the water of life freely.

7 He that overcometh shall inherit all things; and ªI will be his God, and he shall be my son.

8 ªBut the ¹fearful, and unbelieving, and the abominable, and murderers, and ²whoremongers, and sorcerers, and idolaters, and all liars, shall have their part in ᵇthe lake which burneth with fire and brimstone: which is the second death.

9 And there came unto me one of ªthe seven angels which had the seven ¹vials full of the seven last plagues, and talked with me, saying, Come hither, I will shew thee ᵇthe bride, the Lamb's wife.

10 And he carried me away ªin the ¹spirit to a great and high mountain, and shewed me ᵇthat great city, the holy Jerusalem, descending out of heaven from God,

11 ªHaving the glory of God: and her light *was* like unto a stone most precious, even like a jasper stone, clear as crystal;

12 And had a wall great and high, *and* had ªtwelve gates, and at the gates twelve angels, and names written thereon, which are *the names* of the twelve tribes of the children of Israel:

13 ªOn the east three gates; on the north three gates; on the south three gates; and on the west three gates.

14 And the wall of the city had twelve foundations, and ªin¹ them the names of the twelve apostles of the Lamb.

15 And he that talked with me ªhad a golden reed to measure the city, and the gates thereof, and the wall thereof.

16 And the city ¹lieth foursquare, and the length is as large as the breadth:

## Cross References

20:4 ª Dan. 7:9
ᵇ [1 Cor. 6:2, 3]
ᶜ Rev. 6:9 ᵈ Rev. 13:12 ᵉ Rev. 13:15
ᶠ John 14:19
ᵍ Rom. 8:17
20:6 ª [Rev. 2:11; 20:14] ᵇ Is. 61:6
ᶜ Rev. 20:4
20:7 ¹ *completed* ² *released*
20:8 ª Rev. 12:9; 20:3, 10 ᵇ Ezek. 38:2; 39:1, 6
ᶜ Rev. 16:14
20:9 ª Ezek. 38:9, 16 ¹ *surrounded*
20:10 ª Rev. 19:20; 20:14, 15 ᵇ Rev. 14:10
20:11 ª 2 Pet. 3:7 ᵇ Dan. 2:35
20:12 ª Rev. 19:5 ᵇ Dan. 7:10 ᶜ Ps. 69:28 ᵈ Matt. 16:27
20:13 ª Rev. 1:18; 6:8; 21:4 ᵇ Rev. 2:23; 20:12 ¹ *Gr. hades*
20:14 ª ¹ Cor. 15:26 ᵇ Rev. 21:8 ¹ *Gr. hades*
20:15 ª Rev. 19:20
21:1 ª [2 Pet. 3:13] ᵇ Rev. 20:11

21:2 ª Is. 52:1
ᵇ 2 Cor. 11:2
21:3 ª Lev. 26:11
21:4 ª Is. 25:8
ᵇ 1 Cor. 15:26 ᶜ Is. 35:10; 51:11; 65:19
21:5 ª Rev. 4:2, 9; 20:11 ᵇ Is. 43:19
ᶜ Rev. 19:9; 22:6
21:6 ª Rev. 10:6; 16:17 ᵇ Rev. 1:8; 22:13 ᶜ John 4:10 ¹ *who thirsts*
21:7 ª Zech. 8:8
21:8 ª ¹ Cor. 6:9 ᵇ Rev. 20:14 ¹ *cowardly* ² *sexually immoral*
21:9 ª Rev. 15:1 ᵇ Rev. 19:7; 21:2 ¹ *bowls*
21:10 ª Rev. 1:10 ᵇ Ezek. 48 ¹ *Or Spirit*
21:11 ª Rev. 15:8; 21:23; 22:5
21:12 ª Ezek. 48:31–34
21:13 ª Ezek. 48:31–34
21:14 ª Eph. 2:20 ¹ *on*
21:15 ª Ezek. 40:3
21:16 ¹ *is laid out as a square*

and he measured the city with the
reed, twelve thousand [2]furlongs. The
length and the breadth and the height
of it are equal.
17 And he measured the wall
thereof, an hundred *and* forty *and*
four cubits, *according to* the measure
of a man, that is, of the angel.
18 And the [1]building of the wall of it
was *of* jasper: and the city *was* pure
gold, like unto clear glass.
19 [a]And the foundations of the wall
of the city *were* [1]garnished with all
manner of precious stones. The first
foundation *was* jasper; the second,
sapphire; the third, a chalcedony; the
fourth, an emerald;
20 The fifth, sardonyx; the sixth,
sardius; the seventh, [1]chrysolyte; the
eighth, beryl; the ninth, a topaz; the
tenth, a chrysoprasus; the eleventh, a
jacinth; the twelfth, an amethyst.
21 And the twelve gates *were* twelve
[a]pearls; every [1]several gate was of one
pearl: [b]and the street of the city *was*
pure gold, as it were transparent glass.
22 [a]And I saw no temple therein:
for the Lord God Almighty and the
Lamb are the temple of it.
23 [a]And the city had no need of the
sun, neither of the moon, to shine in
it: for the glory of God did [1]lighten it,
and the Lamb *is* the light thereof.
24 [a]And the nations of them which
are saved shall walk in the light of it:
and the kings of the earth do bring
their glory and honour into it.
25 [a]And the gates of it shall not be
shut at all by day: for [b]there shall be
no night there.
26 [a]And they shall bring the glory
and honour of the nations into it.
27 And [a]there shall in no wise enter
into it any thing that defileth, neither
*whatsoever* [1]worketh abomination,
or *maketh* a lie: but they which are
written in the Lamb's [b]book of life.

## CHAPTER 22

AND he shewed me [a]a pure river of
water of life, clear as crystal, pro-
ceeding out of the throne of God and
of the Lamb.
2 [a]In the [1]midst of the street of it,
and on either side of the river, *was*
*there* [b]the tree of life, which bare
twelve *manner of* fruits, *and* yielded
her fruit every month: and the leaves
of the tree *were* [c]for the healing of the
nations.
3 And [a]there shall be no more
curse: [b]but the throne of God and of
the Lamb shall be in it; and his [c]ser-
vants shall serve him:
4 And [a]they shall see his face; and
[b]his name *shall be* [1]in their foreheads.
5 [a]And there shall be no night
there; and they need no [1]candle, neither [b]light of the sun; for [c]the Lord
God giveth them light: [d]and they
shall reign for ever and ever.
6 And he said unto me, [a]These sayings *are* faithful and true: and the
Lord God of the holy prophets [b]sent
his angel to shew unto his servants the
things which must [c]shortly [1]be done.
7 [a]Behold, I come quickly: [b]blessed
*is* he that keepeth the sayings of the
prophecy of this book.
8 And I John saw these things, and
heard *them*. And when I had heard
and seen, [a]I fell down to worship
before the feet of the angel which
shewed me these things.
9 Then saith he unto me, [a]See *thou*
*do it* not: for I am thy fellowservant,
and of thy brethren the prophets, and
of them which keep the [1]sayings of
this book: worship God.
10 [a]And he saith unto me, Seal not
the [1]sayings of the prophecy of this
book: [b]for the time is at hand.
11 He that is unjust, let him be unjust still: and he which is filthy, let
him be filthy still: and he that is righteous, let him be righteous still: and
he that is holy, let him be holy still.
12 And, behold, I come quickly; and
[a]my reward *is* with me, [b]to give every
man according as his work shall be.
13 [a]I am Alpha and Omega, the beginning and the end, the first and the
last.
14 [a]Blessed *are* they that do his
commandments, that they may have
right [b]to the tree of life, [c]and may enter in through the gates into the city.
15 For [a]without[1] *are* [b]dogs, and
sorcerers, and [2]whoremongers, and
murderers, and idolaters, and whosoever loveth and [3]maketh a lie.
16 [a]I Jesus have sent mine angel to
testify unto you these things in the
churches. [b]I am the root and the offspring of David, *and* [c]the bright and
morning star.
17 And the Spirit and [a]the bride say,
Come. And let him that heareth say,
Come. [b]And let him that [1]is athirst
come. And whosoever [2]will, let him
take the water of life freely.
18 For I testify unto every man that
heareth the words of the prophecy of
this book, [a]If any man shall add unto
these things, God shall add unto him
the plagues that are written in this
book:
19 And if any man shall take away
from the words of the book of this
prophecy, [a]God shall take away his
part out of the book of life, and out
of the holy city, and *from* the things
which are written in this book.
20 He which testifieth these things
saith, Surely I come quickly. Amen.
Even so, come, Lord Jesus.
21 The grace of our Lord Jesus
Christ *be* with you all. Amen.

21:16 [2] Gr. *stadion*
21:18 [1] *construction*
21:19 [a] Is. 54:11 [1] *adorned*
21:20 [1] *chrysoprase*
21:21 [a] Matt. 13:45, 46 [b] Rev. 22:2 [1] *individual*
21:22 [a] John 4:21, 23
21:23 [a] Is. 24:23; 60:19, 20 [1] *illuminate*
21:24 [a] Is. 60:3, 5; 66:12
21:25 [a] Is. 60:11 [b] Is. 60:20
21:26 [a] Rev. 21:24
21:27 [a] Joel 3:17 [b] Phil. 4:3 [1] *causes an*
22:1 [a] Ezek. 47:1
22:2 [a] Ezek. 47:12 [b] Gen. 2:9 [c] Rev. 21:24 [1] *middle*
22:3 [a] Zech. 14:11 [b] Ezek. 48:35 [c] Rev. 7:15
22:4 [a] [Matt. 5:8] [b] Rev. 14:1 [1] *on*
22:5 [a] Rev. 21:23 [b] Rev. 7:15 [c] Ps. 36:9 [1] *lamp* [d] Dan. 7:18, 27
22:6 [a] Rev. 19:9 [b] Rev. 1:1 [c] Heb. 10:37 [1] *take place*
22:7 [a] [Rev. 3:11] [b] Rev. 1:3
22:8 [a] Rev. 19:10
22:9 [a] Rev. 19:10 [1] *words*
22:10 [a] Dan. 8:26 [b] Rev. 1:3 [1] *words*
22:12 [a] Is. 40:10; 62:11 [b] Rev. 20:12
22:13 [a] Is. 41:4
22:14 [a] Dan. 12:12 [b] [Prov. 11:30] [c] Rev. 21:27
22:15 [a] 1 Cor. 6:9 [b] Phil. 3:2 [1] *outside* [2] *sexually immoral* [3] *practises*
22:16 [a] Rev. 1:1 [b] Rev. 5:5 [c] Num. 24:17
22:17 [a] [Rev. 21:2, 9] [b] Is. 55:1; Rev. 21:6 [1] *thirsts* [2] *desires*
22:18 [a] Deut. 4:2; 12:32; Prov. 30:6
22:19 [a] Ex. 32:33

# THE MIRACLES OF JESUS CHRIST

| Miracle | Matthew | Mark | Luke | John |
|---|---|---|---|---|
| 1. Cleansing a Leper | 8:2 | 1:40 | 5:12 | |
| 2. Healing a Centurion's Servant (of paralysis) | 8:5 | | 7:1 | |
| 3. Healing Peter's Mother-in-Law | 8:14 | 1:30 | 4:38 | |
| 4. Healing the Sick at Evening | 8:16 | 1:32 | 4:40 | |
| 5. Stilling the Storm | 8:23 | 4:35 | 8:22 | |
| 6. Demons Entering a Herd of Swine | 8:28 | 5:1 | 8:26 | |
| 7. Healing a Paralytic | 9:2 | 2:3 | 5:18 | |
| 8. Raising the Ruler's Daughter | 9:18, 23 | 5:22, 35 | 8:40, 49 | |
| 9. Healing the Hemorrhaging Woman | 9:20 | 5:25 | 8:43 | |
| 10. Healing Two Blind Men | 9:27 | | | |
| 11. Curing a Demon-Possessed, Mute Man | 9:32 | | | |
| 12. Healing a Man's Withered Hand | 12:9 | 3:1 | 6:6 | |
| 13. Curing a Demon-Possessed, Blind and Mute Man | 12:22 | | 11:14 | |
| 14. Feeding the Five Thousand | 14:13 | 6:30 | 9:10 | 6:1 |
| 15. Walking on the Sea | 14:25 | 6:48 | | 6:19 |
| 16. Healing the Gentile Woman's Daughter | 15:21 | 7:24 | | |
| 17. Feeding the Four Thousand | 15:32 | 8:1 | | |
| 18. Healing the Epileptic Boy | 17:14 | 9:17 | 9:38 | |
| 19. Temple Tax in the Fish's Mouth | 17:24 | | | |
| 20. Healing Two Blind Men | 20:30 | 10:46 | 18:35 | |
| 21. Withering the Fig Tree | 21:18 | 11:12 | | |
| 22. Casting Out an Unclean Spirit | | 1:23 | 4:33 | |
| 23. Healing a Deaf and Dumb Man | | 7:31 | | |
| 24. Healing a Blind Paralytic at Bethsaida | | 8:22 | | |
| 25. Escape from the Hostile Multitude | | | 4:30 | |
| 26. Draught of Fish | | | 5:1 | |
| 27. Raising of a Widow's Son at Nain | | | 7:11 | |
| 28. Healing the Infirm, Bowed Woman | | | 13:11 | |
| 29. Healing the Man with Dropsy | | | 14:1 | |
| 30. Cleansing the Ten Lepers | | | 17:11 | |
| 31. Restoring a Servant's Ear | | | 22:51 | |
| 32. Turning Water into Wine | | | | 2:1 |
| 33. Healing the Nobleman's Son (of fever) | | | | 4:46 |
| 34. Healing an Infirm Man at Bethesda | | | | 5:1 |
| 35. Healing the Man Born Blind | | | | 9:1 |
| 36. Raising of Lazarus | | | | 11:43 |
| 37. Second Draught of Fish | | | | 21:1 |

# THE PARABLES OF JESUS CHRIST

| Parable | Matthew | Mark | Luke |
|---------|---------|------|------|
| 1. Lamp Under a Basket | 5:14–16 | 4:21, 22 | 8:16, 17; 11:33–36 |
| 2. A Wise Man Builds on Rock and a Foolish Man Builds on Sand | 7:24–27 | | 6:47–49 |
| 3. Unshrunk (New) Cloth on an Old Garment | 9:16 | 2:21 | 5:36 |
| 4. New Wine in Old Wineskins | 9:17 | 2:22 | 5:37, 38 |
| 5. The Sower | 13:3–23 | 4:2–20 | 8:4–15 |
| 6. The Tares (Weeds) | 13:24–30 | | |
| 7. The Mustard Seed | 13:31, 32 | 4:30–32 | 13:18, 19 |
| 8. The Leaven | 13:33 | | 13:20, 21 |
| 9. The Hidden Treasure | 13:44 | | |
| 10. The Pearl of Great Price | 13:45, 46 | | |
| 11. The Dragnet | 13:47–50 | | |
| 12. The Lost Sheep | 18:12–14 | | 15:3–7 |
| 13. The Unforgiving Servant | 18:23–35 | | |
| 14. The Laborers in the Vineyard | 20:1–16 | | |
| 15. The Two Sons | 21:28–32 | | |
| 16. The Wicked Vinedressers | 21:33–45 | 12:1–12 | 20:9–19 |
| 17. The Wedding Feast | 22:2–14 | | |
| 18. The Fig Tree | 24:32–44 | 13:28–32 | 21:29–33 |
| 19. The Wise and Foolish Virgins | 25:1–13 | | |
| 20. The Talents | 25:14–30 | | |
| 21. The Growing Seed | | 4:26–29 | |
| 22. The Absent Householder | | 13:33–37 | |
| 23. The Creditor and Two Debtors | | | 7:41–43 |
| 24. The Good Samaritan | | | 10:30–37 |
| 25. A Friend in Need | | | 11:5–13 |
| 26. The Rich Fool | | | 12:16–21 |
| 27. The Faithful Servant and the Evil Servant | | | 12:35–40 |
| 28. Faithful and Wise Steward | | | 12:42–48 |
| 29. The Barren Fig Tree | | | 13:6–9 |
| 30. The Great Supper | | | 14:16–24 |
| 31. Building a Tower and a King Making War | | | 14:25–35 |
| 32. The Lost Coin | | | 15:8–10 |
| 33. The Prodigal Son | | | 15:11–32 |
| 34. The Unjust Steward | | | 16:1–13 |
| 35. The Rich Man and Lazarus | | | 16:19–31 |
| 36. Unprofitable Servants | | | 17:7–10 |
| 37. The Persistent Widow | | | 18:1–8 |
| 38. The Pharisee and the Tax Collector | | | 18:9–14 |
| 39. The Minas (Pounds) | | | 19:11–27 |

# ONE YEAR READING PLAN

## JANUARY

| Date | MORNING | EVENING |
|---|---|---|
| | MATT. | GEN. |
| 1 | 1 | 1, 2, 3 |
| 2 | 2 | 4, 5, 6 |
| 3 | 3 | 7, 8, 9 |
| 4 | 4 | 10, 11, 12 |
| 5 | 5:1–26 | 13, 14, 15 |
| 6 | 5:27–48 | 16, 17 |
| 7 | 6:1–18 | 18, 19 |
| 8 | 6:19–34 | 20, 21, 22 |
| 9 | 7 | 23, 24 |
| 10 | 8:1–17 | 25, 26 |
| 11 | 8:18–34 | 27, 28 |
| 12 | 9:1–17 | 29, 30 |
| 13 | 9:18–38 | 31, 32 |
| 14 | 10:1–20 | 33, 34, 35 |
| 15 | 10:21–42 | 36, 37, 38 |
| 16 | 11 | 39, 40 |
| 17 | 12:1–23 | 41, 42 |
| 18 | 12:24–50 | 43, 44, 45 |
| 19 | 13:1–30 | 46, 47, 48 |
| 20 | 13:31–58 | 49, 50 |
| | | EX. |
| 21 | 14:1–21 | 1, 2, 3 |
| 22 | 14:22–36 | 4, 5, 6 |
| 23 | 15:1–20 | 7, 8 |
| 24 | 15:21–39 | 9, 10, 11 |
| 25 | 16 | 12, 13 |
| 26 | 17 | 14, 15 |
| 27 | 18:1–20 | 16, 17, 18 |
| 28 | 18:21–35 | 19, 20 |
| 29 | 19 | 21, 22 |
| 30 | 20:1–16 | 23, 24 |
| 31 | 20:17–34 | 25, 26 |

## FEBRUARY

| Date | MORNING | EVENING |
|---|---|---|
| | MATT. | EX. |
| 1 | 21:1–22 | 27, 28 |
| 2 | 21:23–46 | 29, 30 |
| 3 | 22:1–22 | 31, 32, 33 |
| 4 | 22:23–46 | 34, 35 |
| 5 | 23:1–22 | 36, 37, 38 |
| 6 | 23:23–39 | 39, 40 |
| | | LEV. |
| 7 | 24:1–28 | 1, 2, 3 |
| 8 | 24:29–51 | 4, 5 |
| 9 | 25:1–30 | 6, 7 |
| 10 | 25:31–46 | 8, 9, 10 |
| 11 | 26:1–25 | 11, 12 |
| 12 | 26:26–50 | 13 |
| 13 | 26:51–75 | 14 |
| 14 | 27:1–26 | 15, 16 |
| 15 | 27:27–50 | 17, 18 |
| 16 | 27:51–66 | 19, 20 |
| 17 | 28 | 21, 22 |
| | MARK | |
| 18 | 1:1–22 | 23, 24 |
| 19 | 1:23–45 | 25 |
| 20 | 2 | 26, 27 |
| | | NUM. |
| 21 | 3:1–19 | 1, 2 |
| 22 | 3:20–35 | 3, 4 |
| 23 | 4:1–20 | 5, 6 |
| 24 | 4:21–41 | 7, 8 |
| 25 | 5:1–20 | 9, 10, 11 |
| 26 | 5:21–43 | 12, 13, 14 |
| 27 | 6:1–29 | 15, 16 |
| 28 | 6:30–56 | 17, 18, 19 |
| 29 | 7:1–13 | 20, 21, 22 |

## MARCH

| Date | MORNING | EVENING |
|---|---|---|
| | MARK | NUM. |
| 1 | 7:14–37 | 23, 24, 25 |
| 2 | 8:1–21 | 26, 27 |
| 3 | 8:22–38 | 28, 29, 30 |
| 4 | 9:1–29 | 31, 32, 33 |
| 5 | 9:30–50 | 34, 35, 36 |
| | | DEUT. |
| 6 | 10:1–31 | 1, 2 |
| 7 | 10:32–52 | 3, 4 |
| 8 | 11:1–18 | 5, 6, 7 |
| 9 | 11:19–33 | 8, 9, 10 |
| 10 | 12:1–27 | 11, 12, 13 |
| 11 | 12:28–44 | 14, 15, 16 |
| 12 | 13:1–20 | 17, 18, 19 |
| 13 | 13:21–37 | 20, 21, 22 |
| 14 | 14:1–26 | 23, 24, 25 |
| 15 | 14:27–53 | 26, 27 |
| 16 | 14:54–72 | 28, 29 |
| 17 | 15:1–25 | 30, 31 |
| 18 | 15:26–47 | 32, 33, 34 |
| | | JOSH. |
| 19 | 16 | 1, 2, 3 |
| | LUKE | |
| 20 | 1:1–20 | 4, 5, 6 |
| 21 | 1:21–38 | 7, 8, 9 |
| 22 | 1:39–56 | 10, 11, 12 |
| 23 | 1:57–80 | 13, 14, 15 |
| 24 | 2:1–24 | 16, 17, 18 |
| 25 | 2:25–52 | 19, 20, 21 |
| 26 | 3 | 22, 23, 24 |
| | | JUDG. |
| 27 | 4:1–30 | 1, 2, 3 |
| 28 | 4:31–44 | 4, 5, 6 |
| 29 | 5:1–16 | 7, 8 |
| 30 | 5:17–39 | 9, 10 |
| 31 | 6:1–26 | 11, 12 |

## APRIL

| Date | MORNING | EVENING |
|---|---|---|
| | LUKE | JUDG. |
| 1 | 6:27–49 | 13, 14, 15 |
| 2 | 7:1–30 | 16, 17, 18 |
| 3 | 7:31–50 | 19, 20, 21 |
| | | RUTH |
| 4 | 8:1–25 | 1, 2, 3, 4 |
| | | 1 SAM. |
| 5 | 8:26–56 | 1, 2, 3 |
| 6 | 9:1–17 | 4, 5, 6 |
| 7 | 9:18–36 | 7, 8, 9 |
| 8 | 9:37–62 | 10, 11, 12 |
| 9 | 10:1–24 | 13, 14 |
| 10 | 10:25–42 | 15, 16 |
| 11 | 11:1–28 | 17, 18 |
| 12 | 11:29–54 | 19, 20, 21 |
| 13 | 12:1–31 | 22, 23, 24 |
| 14 | 12:32–59 | 25, 26 |
| 15 | 13:1–22 | 27, 28, 29 |
| 16 | 13:23–35 | 30, 31 |
| | | 2 SAM. |
| 17 | 14:1–24 | 1, 2 |
| 18 | 14:25–35 | 3, 4, 5 |
| 19 | 15:1–10 | 6, 7, 8 |
| 20 | 15:11–32 | 9, 10, 11 |
| 21 | 16 | 12, 13 |
| 22 | 17:1–19 | 14, 15 |
| 23 | 17:20–37 | 16, 17, 18 |
| 24 | 18:1–23 | 19, 20 |
| 25 | 18:24–43 | 21, 22 |
| 26 | 19:1–27 | 23, 24 |
| | | 1 KIN. |
| 27 | 19:28–48 | 1, 2 |
| 28 | 20:1–26 | 3, 4, 5 |
| 29 | 20:27–47 | 6, 7 |
| 30 | 21:1–19 | 8, 9 |

## MAY

| Date | MORNING | EVENING |
|---|---|---|
| | LUKE | 1 KIN. |
| 1 | 21:20–38 | 10, 11 |
| 2 | 22:1–20 | 12, 13 |
| 3 | 22:21–46 | 14, 15 |
| 4 | 22:47–71 | 16, 17, 18 |
| 5 | 23:1–25 | 19, 20 |
| 6 | 23:26–56 | 21, 22 |
| | | 2 KIN. |
| 7 | 24:1–35 | 1, 2, 3 |
| 8 | 24:36–53 | 4, 5, 6 |
| | JOHN | |
| 9 | 1:1–28 | 7, 8, 9 |
| 10 | 1:29–51 | 10, 11, 12 |
| 11 | 2 | 13, 14 |
| 12 | 3:1–18 | 15, 16 |
| 13 | 3:19–36 | 17, 18 |
| 14 | 4:1–30 | 19, 20, 21 |
| 15 | 4:31–54 | 22, 23 |
| 16 | 5:1–24 | 24, 25 |
| | | 1 CHR. |
| 17 | 5:25–47 | 1, 2, 3 |
| 18 | 6:1–21 | 4, 5, 6 |
| 19 | 6:22–44 | 7, 8, 9 |
| 20 | 6:45–71 | 10, 11, 12 |
| 21 | 7:1–27 | 13, 14, 15 |
| 22 | 7:28–53 | 16, 17, 18 |
| 23 | 8:1–27 | 19, 20, 21 |
| 24 | 8:28–59 | 22, 23, 24 |
| 25 | 9:1–23 | 25, 26, 27 |
| 26 | 9:24–41 | 28, 29 |
| | | 2 CHR. |
| 27 | 10:1–23 | 1, 2, 3 |
| 28 | 10:24–42 | 4, 5, 6 |
| 29 | 11:1–29 | 7, 8, 9 |
| 30 | 11:30–57 | 10, 11, 12 |
| 31 | 12:1–26 | 13, 14 |

## JUNE

| Date | MORNING | EVENING |
|---|---|---|
| | JOHN | 2 CHR. |
| 1 | 12:27–50 | 15, 16 |
| 2 | 13:1–20 | 17, 18 |
| 3 | 13:21–38 | 19, 20 |
| 4 | 14 | 21, 22 |
| 5 | 15 | 23, 24 |
| 6 | 16 | 25, 26, 27 |
| 7 | 17 | 28, 29 |
| 8 | 18:1–18 | 30, 31 |
| 9 | 18:19–40 | 32, 33 |
| 10 | 19:1–22 | 34, 35, 36 |
| | | EZRA |
| 11 | 19:23–42 | 1, 2 |
| 12 | 20 | 3, 4, 5 |
| 13 | 21 | 6, 7, 8 |
| | ACTS | |
| 14 | 1 | 9, 10 |
| | | NEH. |
| 15 | 2:1–21 | 1, 2, 3 |
| 16 | 2:22–47 | 4, 5, 6 |
| 17 | 3 | 7, 8, 9 |
| 18 | 4:1–22 | 10, 11 |
| 19 | 4:23–37 | 12, 13 |
| | | ESTH. |
| 20 | 5:1–21 | 1, 2 |
| 21 | 5:22–42 | 3, 4, 5 |
| 22 | 6 | 6, 7, 8 |
| 23 | 7:1–21 | 9, 10 |
| | | JOB |
| 24 | 7:22–43 | 1, 2 |
| 25 | 7:44–60 | 3, 4 |
| 26 | 8:1–25 | 5, 6, 7 |
| 27 | 8:26–40 | 8, 9, 10 |
| 28 | 9:1–21 | 11, 12, 13 |
| 29 | 9:22–43 | 14, 15, 16 |
| 30 | 10:1–23 | 17, 18, 19 |

# JULY

| Date | MORNING | EVENING |
|---|---|---|
| | ACTS | JOB |
| 1 | 10:24–48 | 20, 21 |
| 2 | 11 | 22, 23, 24 |
| 3 | 12 | 25, 26, 27 |
| 4 | 13:1–25 | 28, 29 |
| 5 | 13:26–52 | 30, 31 |
| 6 | 14 | 32, 33 |
| 7 | 15:1–21 | 34, 35 |
| 8 | 15:22–41 | 36, 37 |
| 9 | 16:1–21 | 38, 39, 40 |
| 10 | 16:22–40 | 41, 42 |
| | | PSS. |
| 11 | 17:1–15 | 1, 2, 3 |
| 12 | 17:16–34 | 4, 5, 6 |
| 13 | 18 | 7, 8, 9 |
| 14 | 19:1–20 | 10, 11, 12 |
| 15 | 19:21–41 | 13, 14, 15 |
| 16 | 20:1–16 | 16, 17 |
| 17 | 20:17–38 | 18, 19 |
| 18 | 21:1–17 | 20, 21, 22 |
| 19 | 21:18–40 | 23, 24, 25 |
| 20 | 22 | 26, 27, 28 |
| 21 | 23:1–15 | 29, 30 |
| 22 | 23:16–35 | 31, 32 |
| 23 | 24 | 33, 34 |
| 24 | 25 | 35, 36 |
| 25 | 26 | 37, 38, 39 |
| 26 | 27:1–26 | 40, 41, 42 |
| 27 | 27:27–44 | 43, 44, 45 |
| 28 | 28 | 46, 47, 48 |
| | ROM. | |
| 29 | 1 | 49, 50 |
| 30 | 2 | 51, 52, 53 |
| 31 | 3 | 54, 55, 56 |

# AUGUST

| Date | MORNING | EVENING |
|---|---|---|
| | ROM. | PSS. |
| 1 | 4 | 57, 58, 59 |
| 2 | 5 | 60, 61, 62 |
| 3 | 6 | 63, 64, 65 |
| 4 | 7 | 66, 67 |
| 5 | 8:1–21 | 68, 69 |
| 6 | 8:22–39 | 70, 71 |
| 7 | 9:1–15 | 72, 73 |
| 8 | 9:16–33 | 74, 75, 76 |
| 9 | 10 | 77, 78 |
| 10 | 11:1–18 | 79, 80 |
| 11 | 11:19–36 | 81, 82, 83 |
| 12 | 12 | 84, 85, 86 |
| 13 | 13 | 87, 88 |
| 14 | 14 | 89, 90 |
| 15 | 15:1–13 | 91, 92, 93 |
| 16 | 15:14–33 | 94, 95, 96 |
| 17 | 16 | 97, 98, 99 |
| | 1 COR. | |
| 18 | 1 | 100, 101, 102 |
| 19 | 2 | 103, 104 |
| 20 | 3 | 105, 106 |
| 21 | 4 | 107, 108, 109 |
| 22 | 5 | 110, 111, 112 |
| 23 | 6 | 113, 114, 115 |
| 24 | 7:1–19 | 116, 117, 118 |
| 25 | 7:20–40 | 119:1–88 |
| 26 | 8 | 119:89–176 |
| 27 | 9 | 120, 121, 122 |
| 28 | 10:1–18 | 123, 124, 125 |
| 29 | 10:19–33 | 126, 127, 128 |
| 30 | 11:1–16 | 129, 130, 131 |
| 31 | 11:17–34 | 132, 133, 134 |

# SEPTEMBER

| Date | MORNING | EVENING |
|---|---|---|
| | 1 COR. | PSS. |
| 1 | 12 | 135, 136 |
| 2 | 13 | 137, 138, 139 |
| 3 | 14:1–20 | 140, 141, 142 |
| 4 | 14:21–40 | 143, 144, 145 |
| 5 | 15:1–28 | 146, 147 |
| 6 | 15:29–58 | 148, 149, 150 |
| | | PROV. |
| 7 | 16 | 1, 2 |
| | 2 COR. | |
| 8 | 1 | 3, 4, 5 |
| 9 | 2 | 6, 7 |
| 10 | 3 | 8, 9 |
| 11 | 4 | 10, 11, 12 |
| 12 | 5 | 13, 14, 15 |
| 13 | 6 | 16, 17, 18 |
| 14 | 7 | 19, 20, 21 |
| 15 | 8 | 22, 23, 24 |
| 16 | 9 | 25, 26 |
| 17 | 10 | 27, 28, 29 |
| 18 | 11:1–15 | 30, 31 |
| | | ECCL. |
| 19 | 11:16–33 | 1, 2, 3 |
| 20 | 12 | 4, 5, 6 |
| 21 | 13 | 7, 8, 9 |
| | GAL. | |
| 22 | 1 | 10, 11, 12 |
| | | SONG |
| 23 | 2 | 1, 2, 3 |
| 24 | 3 | 4, 5 |
| 25 | 4 | 6, 7, 8 |
| | | IS. |
| 26 | 5 | 1, 2 |
| 27 | 6 | 3, 4 |
| | EPH. | |
| 28 | 1 | 5, 6 |
| 29 | 2 | 7, 8 |
| 30 | 3 | 9, 10 |

# OCTOBER

| Date | MORNING | EVENING |
|---|---|---|
| | EPH. | IS. |
| 1 | 4 | 11, 12, 13 |
| 2 | 5:1–16 | 14, 15, 16 |
| 3 | 5:17–33 | 17, 18, 19 |
| 4 | 6 | 20, 21, 22 |
| | PHIL. | |
| 5 | 1 | 23, 24, 25 |
| 6 | 2 | 26, 27 |
| 7 | 3 | 28, 29 |
| 8 | 4 | 30, 31 |
| | COL. | |
| 9 | 1 | 32, 33 |
| 10 | 2 | 34, 35, 36 |
| 11 | 3 | 37, 38 |
| 12 | 4 | 39, 40 |
| | 1 THESS. | |
| 13 | 1 | 41, 42 |
| 14 | 2 | 43, 44 |
| 15 | 3 | 45, 46 |
| 16 | 4 | 47, 48, 49 |
| 17 | 5 | 50, 51, 52 |
| | 2 THESS. | |
| 18 | 1 | 53, 54, 55 |
| 19 | 2 | 56, 57, 58 |
| 20 | 3 | 59, 60, 61 |
| | 1 TIM. | |
| 21 | 1 | 62, 63, 64 |
| 22 | 2 | 65, 66 |
| | | JER. |
| 23 | 3 | 1, 2 |
| 24 | 4 | 3, 4, 5 |
| 25 | 5 | 6, 7, 8 |
| 26 | 6 | 9, 10, 11 |
| | 2 TIM. | |
| 27 | 1 | 12, 13, 14 |
| 28 | 2 | 15, 16, 17 |
| 29 | 3 | 18, 19 |
| 30 | 4 | 20, 21 |
| | TITUS | |
| 31 | 1 | 22, 23 |

# NOVEMBER

| Date | MORNING | EVENING |
|---|---|---|
| | TITUS | JER. |
| 1 | 2 | 24, 25, 26 |
| 2 | 3 | 27, 28, 29 |
| 3 | PHILEM. | 30, 31 |
| | HEB. | |
| 4 | 1 | 32, 33 |
| 5 | 2 | 34, 35, 36 |
| 6 | 3 | 37, 38, 39 |
| 7 | 4 | 40, 41, 42 |
| 8 | 5 | 43, 44, 45 |
| 9 | 6 | 46, 47 |
| 10 | 7 | 48, 49 |
| 11 | 8 | 50 |
| 12 | 9 | 51, 52 |
| | | LAM. |
| 13 | 10:1–18 | 1, 2 |
| 14 | 10:19–39 | 3, 4, 5 |
| | | EZEK. |
| 15 | 11:1–19 | 1, 2 |
| 16 | 11:20–40 | 3, 4 |
| 17 | 12 | 5, 6, 7 |
| 18 | 13 | 8, 9, 10 |
| | JAMES | |
| 19 | 1 | 11, 12, 13 |
| 20 | 2 | 14, 15 |
| 21 | 3 | 16, 17 |
| 22 | 4 | 18, 19 |
| 23 | 5 | 20, 21 |
| | 1 PET. | |
| 24 | 1 | 22, 23 |
| 25 | 2 | 24, 25, 26 |
| 26 | 3 | 27, 28, 29 |
| 27 | 4 | 30, 31, 32 |
| 28 | 5 | 33, 34 |
| | 2 PET. | |
| 29 | 1 | 35, 36 |
| 30 | 2 | 37, 38, 39 |

# DECEMBER

| Date | MORNING | EVENING |
|---|---|---|
| | 2 PET. | EZEK. |
| 1 | 3 | 40, 41 |
| | 1 JOHN | |
| 2 | 1 | 42, 43, 44 |
| 3 | 2 | 45, 46 |
| 4 | 3 | 47, 48 |
| | | DAN. |
| 5 | 4 | 1, 2 |
| 6 | 5 | 3, 4 |
| 7 | 2 JOHN | 5, 6, 7 |
| 8 | 3 JOHN | 8, 9, 10 |
| 9 | JUDE | 11, 12 |
| | REV. | HOS. |
| 10 | 1 | 1, 2, 3, 4 |
| 11 | 2 | 5, 6, 7, 8 |
| 12 | 3 | 9, 10, 11 |
| 13 | 4 | 12, 13, 14 |
| | | JOEL |
| 14 | 5 | |
| | | AMOS |
| 15 | 6 | 1, 2, 3 |
| 16 | 7 | 4, 5, 6 |
| 17 | 8 | 7, 8, 9 |
| | | OBAD. |
| 18 | 9 | |
| | | JON. |
| | | MIC. |
| 19 | 10 | |
| 20 | 11 | 1, 2, 3 |
| 21 | 12 | 4, 5 |
| 22 | 13 | 6, 7 |
| | | NAH. |
| 23 | 14 | |
| | | HAB. |
| 24 | 15 | |
| | | ZEPH. |
| 25 | 16 | |
| | | HAG. |
| 26 | 17 | |
| | | ZECH. |
| 27 | 18 | 1, 2, 3, 4 |
| 28 | 19 | 5, 6, 7, 8 |
| 29 | 20 | 9, 10, 11, 12 |
| 30 | 21 | 13, 14 |
| 31 | 22 | MAL. |

# KJV CONCORDANCE

## A

### ABASE
*a* him that is high...... Ezek 21:26
he is able to *a*............ Dan 4:37
himself shall be *a*...... Matt 23:12
both how to be *a*........ Phil 4:12
*See* Job 40:11; 2 Cor 11:7

### ABIDE
*a* ye every man .......... Ex 16:29
*a* without the camp ... Num 31:19
shall not *a* with us......1 Sam 5:7
Lord, who shall *a*..........Ps 15:1
shall *a* under the shadow ...Ps 91:1
*a* among the wise ...... Prov 15:31
the earth *a* for ever.......Eccl 1:4
*a* in this land ...........Jer 42:10
no man shall *a* there ....Jer 49:18
thou shalt *a* for me....... Hos 3:3
who can *a* it ...............Joel 2:11
there *a* till ye go ....... Matt 10:11
*a* till ye depart..........Mark 6:10
there *a*................... Luke 9:4
wrath of God *a* on him...John 3:36
not his word *a* in you...John 5:38
Comforter, that
   he may *a* ........... John 14:16
*A* in me, and I in you ... John 15:4
He that *a* in me......... John 15:5
*a* in my love .......... John 15:10
If any man's work *a* .....1 Cor 3:14
now *a* faith, hope.......1 Cor 13:13

### ABILITY
They gave after their *a* ...Ezra 2:69
such as had *a* in them....Dan 1:4
his several *a* .......... Matt 25:15
*a* which God giveth......1 Pet 4:11
*See* Lev 27:8; Neh 5:8; Acts 11:29

### ABLE
give as he is *a*...........Deut 16:17
hath been *a* to stand ... Josh 23:9
*a* to stand before .....1 Sam 6:20
who is *a* to judge .......1 Kin 3:9
who is *a* to build .......2 Chr 2:6
who is *a* to stand........Prov 27:4
*a* to deliver ............ Dan 3:17
land is not *a* to bear ...Amos 7:10
God is *a*................. Matt 3:9
Believe ye that I am *a*... Matt 9:28
Are ye *a* to drink.......Matt 20:22
not *a* to do.............Luke 12:26
not *a* to resist..........Acts 6:10
had promised he was *a*...Rom 4:21
*a* to separate us ........ Rom 8:39
that ye are *a* ..........1 Cor 10:13
*a* ministers ............. 2 Cor 3:6
*a* to comprehend ....... Eph 3:18
Now unto him that is *a*... Eph 3:20
*a* even to subdue ....... Phil 3:21
he is *a* to keep .........2 Tim 1:12
*a* to succour them ...... Heb 2:18
*a* also to save ........... Heb 7:25
*a* to save ...............James 4:12
*a* to keep you............ Jude 24
was *a* to open the book ...Rev 5:3
who shall be *a* to stand...Rev 6:17
*See* Ex 18:21; Mark 4:33

### ABOMINATION
is an *a* unto the
   Egyptians ............Gen 43:32
every shepherd is an *a*...Gen 46:34
commit any of these *a* ...Lev 18:26
shalt thou bring an *a*... Deut 7:26
*a* of these nations ...... Deut 18:9
because of these *a* ..... Deut 18:12

unrighteously, are an *a*...Deut 25:16
the froward is *a* ........ Prov 3:32
wickedness is an *a* ......Prov 8:7
froward is *a* to the Lord ...Prov 11:20
an *a* to the Lord ........Prov 15:8
way of the wicked an *a*... Prov 15:9
wicked are an *a*........ Prov 15:26
of the wicked is *a*......Prov 21:27
his prayer shall be *a* .... Prov 28:9
residue thereof an *a* ...... Is 44:19
put away thine *a* ........Jer 4:1
they had committed *a*.... Jer 6:15
place the *a*..............Dan 11:31
the *a* of desolation .... Matt 24:15
shall see the *a* ........ Mark 13:14
is *a* in the sight ........ Luke 16:15
worketh *a*, or maketh ...Rev 21:27
*See* Lev 7:18; 11:41; Mal 2:11

### ABOVE
thou shalt be *a* only ... Deut 28:13
God is there from *a*.......Job 31:2
way of life is *a* .........Prov 15:24
The disciple is not *a*... Matt 10:24
from *a* is *a* all.........John 3:31
I am from *a*.............John 8:23
one day *a* another.......Rom 14:5
*a* that which ............ 1 Cor 4:6
Jerusalem which is *a*....Gal 4:26
a name which is *a* ....... Phil 2:9
things which are *a*........ Col 3:1
*See* Gen 48:22; James 1:17

### ABSTAIN
*a* from pollutions
   of idols ................Acts 15:20
ye *a* from meats........Acts 15:29
*A* from all.............1 Thess 5:22
*a* from fleshly lusts..... 1 Pet 2:11
*See* 1 Thess 4:3; 1 Tim 4:3

### ABUNDANCE
sound of *a* of rain ......1 Kin 18:41
*a* of his riches............. Ps 52:7
*a* of peace................. Ps 72:7
reveal unto them the *a*... Jer 33:6
loveth *a* with increase... Eccl 5:10
but the *a* of the rich .... Eccl 5:12
*a* of the heart ......... Matt 12:34
shall have more *a* .......Matt 13:12
and he shall have *a*....Matt 25:29
of the *a* of the heart ....Luke 6:45
in the *a* ................Luke 12:15
the *a* of their joy........ 2 Cor 8:2
*a* of the revelations..... 2 Cor 12:7
*See* Job 36:31; Rom 5:17; Rev 18:3

### ABUNDANT
distill upon man *a*......Job 36:28
*a* utter the memory ......Ps 145:7
for he will *a* pardon ........Is 55:7
have it more *a* ........John 10:10
I laboured more *a* ......1 Cor 15:10
in labours more *a* ...... 2 Cor 11:23
exceeding *a* above.......Eph 3:20
was exceeding *a*........ 1 Tim 1:14
Which he shed on us *a*... Titus 3:6
ministered unto you *a*... 2 Pet 1:11
*See* Ex 34:6; Is 55:7; 1 Pet 1:3

### ABUSE
use this world, as
   not *a* it ................1 Cor 7:31
that I *a* not my power....1 Cor 9:18
*See* 1 Sam 31:4; 1 Chr 10:4

### ACCEPT
shalt thou not be *a* .......Gen 4:7
*a* before the Lord........ Ex 28:38
been *a* in the sight ......Lev 10:19

*a* the work............. Deut 33:11
and he was *a* .......... 1 Sam 18:5
Lord thy God *a* thee...2 Sam 24:23
for him will I *a* ........... Job 42:8
the Lord also *a* Job ...... Job 42:9
to *a* the person .........Prov 18:5
I will not *a* them.........Jer 14:12
supplication ... be *a* .....Jer 37:20
will I *a* them.............Ezek 20:40
I will *a* you.............. Ezek 43:27
I will not *a* them.........Amos 5:22
should I *a* this...........Mal 1:13
No prophet is *a*..........Luke 4:24
righteousness, is *a*......Acts 10:35
be *a* of the saints ......Rom 15:31
we may be *a* ............. 2 Cor 5:9
behold, now is the
   *a* time .................2 Cor 6:2
*See* Ps 119:108; Eccl 12:10; Mal 1:8

### ACCEPTABLE
be *a* in thy sight, O Lord... Ps 19:14
proclaim the *a* year........Is 61:2
To preach the *a* year ... Luke 4:19
holy, *a* unto God.........Rom 12:1

### ACCESS
we have *a* by faith into
   this grace............. Rom 5:2
*a* by one Spirit........... Eph 2:18
*a* with confidence ....... Eph 3:12

### ACCORD
continued with one *a* in
   prayer ...................Acts 1:14
to God with one *a* .......Acts 4:24
the people with one *a*....Acts 8:6
love, being of one *a*...... Phil 2:2

### ACCORDING
*a* as he hath promised....Ex 12:25
*a* to his ways............Job 34:11
*a* to the fruit.............Jer 17:10
recompense them *a* to....Jer 25:14
*a* to his ways............Jer 32:19
every man *a* ........... Matt 16:27
*a* to the appearance .... John 7:24
*a* to his deeds............ Rom 2:6
*a* to his purpose........ Rom 8:28
*a* to the grace........... Rom 12:6
*a* to that a man......... 2 Cor 8:12
Lord reward him *a* to... 2 Tim 4:14
*See* Titus 3:5; 1 Pet 1:2

### ACCOUNT
they shall give *a*
   thereof .............. Matt 12:36
*a* of thy stewardship ... Luke 16:2
*a* worthy to obtain ...Luke 20:35
shall give *a* ............Rom 14:12
*a* to him ................ Gal 3:6
put that on mine *a* .....Philem 18
that must give *a*........Heb 13:17
*See* Job 33:13; 1 Pet 4:5

### ACCUSATION
thing from any man by
   false *a* ................. Luke 19:8
receive not an *a* ........1 Tim 5:19
not railing *a* ............2 Pet 2:11
a railing *a*................ Jude 9
*See* Matt 27:37; Mark 15:26

### ACCUSE
*A* not a servant unto his
   master................Prov 30:10
I will *a* you............. John 5:45
*See* Matt 12:10; Mark 3:2

### ACKNOWLEDGE
I *a* my sin unto thee.......Ps 32:5

I *a* my transgressions ..... Ps 51:3
all thy ways *a* him ...... Prov 3:6
Israel *a* us not ........... Is 63:16
he that *a* the Son ......1 John 2:23
See Hos 5:15; 1 Cor 14:37

## ACQUIT
thou wilt not *a* .........Job 10:14
all *a* the wicked...........Nah 1:3

## ACTIONS
by him *a* are weighed....1 Sam 2:3

## ADDICTED
they have *a*
themselves...........1 Cor 16:15

## ADMINISTER
are differences of *a*.....1 Cor 12:5
which is *a* by us ........2 Cor 8:19
abundance which is *a*..2 Cor 8:20
*a* of this service.........2 Cor 9:12

## ADMONISH
Paul *a* them .............Acts 27:9
able also to *a* ...........Rom 15:14
*a* one another ...........Col 3:16
Lord, and *a* you.......1 Thess 5:12
*a* him as ...............2 Thess 3:15
Moses was *a* of God .....Heb 8:5
See Eccl 4:13; 12:12; Jer 42:19

## ADMONITION
they are written
for our *a*..............1 Cor 10:11
*a* of the Lord..............Eph 6:4
second *a* reject .........Titus 3:10

## ADOPTION
ye have received the
Spirit of *a*.........Rom 8:15
waiting for the *a*.......Rom 8:23
whom pertaineth the *a*...Rom 9:4
receive the *a* of sons ......Gal 4:5
the *a* of children..........Eph 1:5

## ADORN
bride *a* herself.............Is 61:10
women *a* themselves ...1 Tim 2:9
*a* the doctrine ..........Titus 2:10
that outward *a* ..........1 Pet 3:3
*a* themselves ............1 Pet 3:5
*a* for her husband ........Rev 21:2
See Jer 31:4; Luke 21:5

## ADVERSARY
and an *a* unto thine *a* .. Ex 23:22
for an *a* against.........Num 22:22
vengeance to his *a* ....Deut 32:43
stirred up an *a*..........1 Kin 11:14
that mine *a*.............Job 31:35
are mine *a*..............Ps 38:20
*a* are all before thee ......Ps 69:19
how long shall the *a*......Ps 74:10
right hand of his *a*.......Ps 89:42
they are my *a*............Ps 109:4
the reward of mine *a*... Ps 109:20
mine *a* be clothed ......Ps 109:29
ease me of mine *a*..........Is 1:24
who is mine *a* ............Is 50:8
fury to his *a* .............Is 59:18
known to thine *a*.........Is 64:2
and all thine *a* ..........Jer 30:16
avenge him of his *a*......Jer 46:10
An *a* there shall be .....Amos 3:11
upon thine *a*.............Mic 5:9
vengeance on his *a*.......Nah 1:2
Agree with thine *a* ......Matt 5:25
goest with thine *a* .....Luke 12:58
*a* were ashamed........Luke 13:17
Avenge me of mine *a* ... Luke 18:3
there are many *a* ....... 1 Cor 16:9
terrified by your *a* ....... Phil 1:28
occasion to the *a* .......1 Tim 5:14
shall devour the *a* ......Heb 10:27
your *a* the devil...........1 Pet 5:8
See 1 Sam 2:10; Is 9:11; 11:13

## ADVERSITY
saved you out of all
your *a* ..............1 Sam 10:19
soul out of all *a*.........2 Sam 4:9
vex them with all *a*.....2 Chr 15:6
I shall never be in *a* .....Ps 10:6
from the days of *a*.......Ps 94:13
born for *a*..............Prov 17:17
in the day of *a* ........Prov 24:10
bread of *a*................Is 30:20
them which suffer *a*.....Heb 13:3
See Ps 31:7; 35:15

## ADVOCATE
an *a* with the Father, Jesus
Christ.................1 John 2:1

## AFFECTION
because I have set my *a*
to the..................1 Chr 29:3
up unto vile *a*.......... Rom 1:26
without natural *a* ...... Rom 1:31
Be kindly *a* one.......Rom 12:10
crucified ... with the *a*.. Gal 5:24
Set your *a* on things.......Col 3:2
inordinate *a* .............Col 3:5
Without natural *a* ... 2 Tim 3:3
See 2 Cor 7:15

## AFFLICT
ye shall *a* your souls.... Lev 16:29
hast thou *a* thy ........ Num 11:11
and ye shall *a*..........Num 29:7
Almighty hath *a* me.....Ruth 1:21
thou *a* them ............1 Kin 8:35
*a* the seed of David....1 Kin 11:39
thou dost *a* them..... 2 Chr 6:26
To him that is *a* pity.....Job 6:14
*a* the people................Ps 44:2
hear, and *a* them ........Ps 55:19
do justice to the *a* .........Ps 82:3
thou hast *a* us..........Ps 90:15
Before I was *a* ..........Ps 119:67
I have been *a* ...........Ps 119:71
the cause of the *a* ......Ps 140:12
days of the *a*............Prov 15:15
neither oppress the *a* . Prov 22:22
any of the *a*.............Prov 31:5
now this, thou *a*.........Is 51:21
smitten of God, and *a* .... Is 53:4
and he was *a* .............Is 53:7
thou *a*, tossed with.......Is 54:11
all their *a* he was *a* .......Is 63:9
the Lord hath *a* her......Lam 1:5
Lord hath *a* me..........Lam 1:12
he doth not *a* willingly...Lam 3:33
will *a* thee no more ......Nah 1:12
*a* and poor people...... Zeph 3:12
*a*, it is for your........... 2 Cor 1:6
relieved the *a*..........1 Tim 5:10
*a*, tormented............Heb 11:37
Be *a*, and mourn ......James 4:9
Is any among you *a* ...James 5:13
See Ex 1:11, 12; 22:22, 23

## AFFLICTION
the Lord hath looked
upon my *a*..........Gen 29:32
surely seen the *a* ..........Ex 3:7
the bread of *a*...........Deut 16:3
and looked on our *a*...Deut 26:7
*a* of thine handmaid ...1 Sam 1:11
in our *a*................. 2 Chr 20:9
in *a*, he besought......2 Chr 33:12
*a* cometh not forth.......Job 5:6
days of *a* have taken.... Job 30:16
days of *a* prevented.....Job 30:27
cords of *a* ...............Job 36:8
mine *a* and my pain......Ps 25:18
*a* of the righteous ........Ps 34:19
my comfort in my *a*....Ps 119:50
David, and all his *a*......Ps 132:1
water of *a*................Is 30:20
furnace of *a* ..............Is 48:10
In all their *a* .............Is 63:9

in the day of *a* ...........Jer 16:19
man that hath seen *a*.....Lam 3:1
in their *a* they ...........Hos 5:15
*a* or persecution........Mark 4:17
out of all his *a* ..........Acts 7:10
Canaan, and great *a*.....Acts 7:11
*a* of my people..........Acts 7:34
bonds and *a* abide..... Acts 20:23
much *a* and anguish ... 2 Cor 2:4
light *a*, which is .......2 Cor 4:17
great trial of *a* ..........2 Cor 8:2
add *a* to my bonds .......Phil 1:16
communicate with
my *a*.................. Phil 4:14
great fight of *a*.........Heb 10:32
*a* with the people.......Heb 11:25
widows in their *a*......James 1:27
See Col 1:24; James 5:10

## AFRESH
to themselves the Son
of God *a* ................Heb 6:6

## AGES
That in the *a* to come
he might.................Eph 2:7
Which in other *a* ........Eph 3:5
throughout all *a*.........Eph 3:21
hid from *a*................Col 1:26

## AGREE
except they be *a*........Amos 3:3
*A* with thine ............Matt 5:25
two of you shall *a* ..... Matt 18:19
witness *a* not..........Mark 14:56
did their witness *a* ....Mark 14:59
these three *a* ...........1 John 5:8
See Matt 20:2; Luke 5:36

## AGREEMENT
with hell are we at *a*...... Is 28:15
*a* hath the temple ......2 Cor 6:16

## AIR
the Lord in the *a* .....1 Thess 4:17

## ALIENATED
*a* from the life ...........Eph 4:18
that were sometime *a*.....Col 1:21

## ALIVE
he presented *a* before
the Lord...............Lev 16:10
went down *a* into ......Num 16:33
are *a* every one ........ Deut 4:4
I kill, and I make *a*.....Deut 32:39
The Lord .. maketh *a* . 1 Sam 2:6
save the souls *a* ........Ezek 13:18
heard that he was *a* ...Mark 16:11
dead, and is *a* again ... Luke 15:24
said that he was *a* .....Luke 24:23
shewed himself *a*........ Acts 1:3
Paul affirmed to be *a*...Acts 25:19
but *a* unto ...............Rom 6:11
*a* from the dead ........ Rom 6:13
all be made *a* .......... 1 Cor 15:22
we which are *a* .......1 Thess 4:15
I am *a* for evermore......Rev 1:18
See 2 Kin 5:7; Dan 5:19

## ALMIGHTY
by the name of God *A* ......Ex 6:3
*A* hath dealt............ Ruth 1:20
find out the *A*............Job 11:7
When the *A* was yet ..... Job 29:5
the voice of the *A*.......Ezek 1:24
*A* God when he
speaketh ...........Ezek 10:5
saith the Lord *A* ........2 Cor 6:18
is to come, the *A*..........Rev 1:8
holy, Lord God *A*......... Rev 4:8
O Lord God *A* ..........Rev 11:17
See Job 21:15; Ps 91:1

## ALMS
do not your *a* before
men ....................Matt 6:1

give *a* of such..........Luke 11:41
have, and give *a* ......Luke 12:33
*a* to the people .........Acts 10:2

## ALWAY
I would not live *a*.........Job 7:16
man that feareth *a* ....Prov 28:14
I am with you *a*.......Matt 28:20
in the Lord *a*.............Phil 4:4

## ALWAYS
My spirit shall not *a*
    strive with.............Gen 6:3
not *a* chide ................Ps 103:9
the poor with you *a* ....Mark 14:7
me ye have not *a* .......Mark 14:7
the poor *a* ye have....John 12:8

## AMBASSADOR
*a* for Christ ..........2 Cor 5:20
*See* Prov 13:17; Is 18:2

## ANGEL
The *A* which re-
    deemed me..........Gen 48:16
*a* of the Lord.............Ps 34:7
Man did eat *a* food .....Ps 78:25
shall give his *a*..........Ps 91:11
before the *a* .............Eccl 5:6
*a* of his presence .........Is 63:9
who hath sent his *a* .....Dan 3:28
he has power over *a*.....Hos 12:4
reapers are the *a* ......Matt 13:39
are as the *a* which.....Mark 12:25
equal unto the *a*......Luke 20:36
*a* charge over thee......Luke 4:10
there appeared an *a*..Luke 22:43
*a* went down ............John 5:4
It is his *a*..............Acts 12:15
we shall judge *a* .........1 Cor 6:3
an *a* of light............2 Cor 11:14
word spoken by *a* ....... Heb 2:2
the nature of *a*..........Heb 2:16
entertained *a* ..........Heb 13:2
*a* desire to look..........1 Pet 1:12
*See* Gen 19:1; Matt 25:41; Heb 2:7

## ANGER
Cursed be their *a*, for it was
    fierce .................. Gen 49:7
slow to *a*.................. Neh 9:17
not in thine *a*............. Ps 6:1
*a* endureth but a .........Ps 30:5
gracious, slow to *a*.......Ps 103:8
words stir up *a* .........Prov 15:1
deferreth his *a*.........Prov 19:11
*a* resteth in the bosom... Eccl 7:9
on them with *a*.........Mark 3:5
and wrath, and *a* ...... Eph 4:31
*a*, wrath, malice .........Col 3:8
your children to *a* .......Col 3:21
*See* Ps 37:8; 85:3; Prov 16:32

## ANGRY
God is *a* with the wicked...Ps 7:11
He that is soon *a* .......Prov 14:17
with an *a* man .........Prov 22:24
an *a* countenance .....Prov 25:23
well to be *a*.............Jon 4:4
*a* with his brother .... Matt 5:22
are ye *a* at me .........John 7:23
Be ye *a*, and sin not ...Eph 4:26
not soon *a* ...............Titus 1:7
*See* Gen 18:30; Prov 21:19

## ANOINT (*v.*)
shall not *a* thyself with
    the oil .............. Deut 28:40
Lord hath *a* thee.......1 Sam 10:1
*a* not thyself ....... 2 Sam 14:2
*a* the shield.................Is 21:5
the Lord hath *a* me.........Is 61:1
*a* my body ..............Mark 14:8
hath *a* me to preach.... Luke 4:18
thou didst not *a* .......Luke 7:46
*a* the eyes..............John 9:6

*a* the feet of Jesus ...... John 12:3
and hath *a* us............2 Cor 1:21
*a* thine eyes ..............Rev 3:18
*See* Judg 9:8; James 5:14

## ANOINTED (*n.*)
against the Lord's *a* ...1 Sam 26:9
Touch not mine *a* .......Ps 105:15
the Lord to his *a*...........Is 45:1

## APART
desert place *a* .........Matt 14:13
a mountain *a* to pray ...Matt 14:23
into an high
    mountain *a*.......... Matt 17:1
Come ye yourselves *a*... Mark 6:31
*See* Zech 12:12; James 1:21

## APPEAR
on the outward *a*......1 Sam 16:7
and *a* before God ........Ps 42:2
Let thy work *a*...........Ps 90:16
flowers *a* on the.........Song 2:12
they may *a* unto men....Matt 6:16
outwardly *a* righteous Matt 23:28
that it might *a* sin.......Rom 7:13
all *a* before the ........2 Cor 5:10
glory in *a* ...............2 Cor 5:12
who is our life, shall *a*.....Col 3:4
all *a* of evil............1 Thess 5:22
profiting may *a*.........1 Tim 4:15
the *a* of our Lord Jesus..1 Tim 6:14
the *a* of our Saviour ....2 Tim 1:10
that love his *a* .........2 Tim 4:8
the glorious *a*...........Titus 2:13
for him shall he *a*........Heb 9:28
glory at the *a* ..............1 Pet 1:7
*See* Ex 23:15; Matt 24:30

## APPOINT
*a* over this business......Acts 6:3
not *a* us to wrath.......1 Thess 5:9
*See* Job 14:13; Acts 17:31

## ARCHANGEL
with the voice of the *a*1 Thess 4:16
Michael the *a*..............Jude 9

## ARISE
*a* a little cloud out of
    the sea................1 Kin 18:44
*a* and build ..............Neh 2:20
Let God *a* ................Ps 68:1
dead *a* and praise ........Ps 88:10
there *a* light ..............Ps 112:4
children *a* up .........Prov 31:28
of righteousness *a*........Mal 4:2
*A*, and take up ..........Mark 2:11
I say unto thee, *A* .......Luke 7:14
saying, Maid, *a* .......Luke 8:54
I will *a* and go .........Luke 15:18
said, Tabitha, *a*.........Acts 9:40
*a* from the dead .........Eph 5:14
till the day star *a* .......2 Pet 1:19
*See* Is 26:19; Jer 2:27

## ARMOUR
but he put his *a* in
    his tent ............1 Sam 17:54
they washed his *a* ....1 Kin 22:38
in that day to the *a* ........Is 22:8
his *a* wherein...........Luke 11:22
the *a* of light...........Rom 13:12
*a* of righteousness....... 2 Cor 6:7
the whole *a* of God .....Eph 6:11

## ASCEND
Thou hast *a* on high......Ps 68:18
I will *a* into heaven........Is 14:13
angels of God *a*........John 1:51
no man hath *a* up to ... John 3:13
Son of man *a* up........John 6:62
I am not yet *a* .........John 20:17
shall *a* into heaven ..... Rom 10:6
he *a* up on high...........Eph 4:8
*a* up before God ........ Rev 8:4

they *a* up to heaven ..... Rev 11:12
*See* Ps 24:3; 139:8; Rev 17:8

## ASHAMED
shall no man make
    thee *a*....................Job 11:3
wait on thee be *a*.........Ps 25:3
let me never be *a* .........Ps 31:2
their faces were not *a* ....Ps 34:5
shall not be *a*.............Is 45:17
ye shall be *a* ..............Is 65:13
the thief is *a* .............Jer 2:26
they shall be *a* .........Jer 12:13
not *a* of the gospel .....Rom 1:16
hope maketh not *a* ...... Rom 5:5
shall not be *a* ......... Rom 9:33
I am not *a* ............. 2 Cor 7:14
*a* of the testimony.......2 Tim 1:8
not *a* of my chain........2 Tim 1:16
needeth not to be *a* ....2 Tim 2:15
not *a* to call them ........Heb 2:11
not *a* to be called ........Heb 11:16
let him not be *a* .........1 Pet 4:16
not be *a* before him.....1 John 2:28
*See* Gen 2:25; 2 Tim 1:12

## ASHES
which am but
    dust and *a*..........Gen 18:27
among the *a*................Job 2:8
like dust and *a*..........Job 30:19
and repent in dust
    and *a* ................. Job 42:6
*See* 2 Sam 3:19; Esth 4:1

## ASK
*A* of me, and I shall
    give thee .................Ps 2:8
*A* me of things to come.....Is 45:11
of them that *a* not...........Is 65:1
*A*, and it shall be given ...Matt 7:7
if his son *a* bread ........ Matt 7:9
them that *a* him .......Matt 7:11
ye shall *a* in prayer ....Matt 21:22
*a* of me whatsoever .....Mark 6:22
to them that *a* him .....Luke 11:13
whatsoever ye shall *a* ...John 14:13
abide in you, ye shall *a*...John 15:7
At that day ye shall *a*...John 16:26
let him *a* of God .......James 1:5
because ye *a* not.........James 4:2
every man that *a* you...1 Pet 3:15
whatsoever we *a* ......1 John 3:22
if we *a* any thing.......1 John 5:14
*See* Deut 32:7; John 4:9, 10

## ASLEEP
some are fallen *a* ...... 1 Cor 15:6
them which are *a*......1 Thess 4:13
the fathers fell *a* ...... 2 Pet 3:4
*See* Song 7:9; Matt 26:48

## ASSURANCE
quietness and *a* for ever ...Is 32:17
*a* of understanding........Col 2:2
and in much *a*.........1 Thess 1:5
the full *a* of hope .........Heb 6:11
in full *a* of faith...........Heb 10:22
*See* Deut 28:66; Acts 17:31

## ASTROLOGERS
Let now the *a*, the
    stargazers...............Is 47:13
magicians, and the *a* ... Dan 2:2
to bring in the *a* ......... Dan 5:7

## AUTHOR
God is not the *a* of
    confusion ........1 Cor 14:33
became the *a* of .........Heb 5:9
the *a* and finisher .......Heb 12:2

## AUTHORITY
taught them as one
    having *a*..............Matt 7:29
I am a man under *a* .....Matt 8:9
what *a* doest thou.....Matt 21:23

as one that had *a* ...... Mark 1:22
with *a* and power ..... Luke 4:36
am a man set under *a* ... Luke 7:8
power and *a* over all..... Luke 9:1
*a* over ten cities ........Luke 19:17
*a* to execute ............. John 5:27
all *a* and power......... 1 Cor 15:24
all that are in *a* ........1 Tim 2:2
nor to usurp *a* .......... 1 Tim 2:12
rebuke with all *a* ....... Titus 2:15
*a* and powers........... 1 Pet 3:22

## AVENGE

he will *a* the blood of his
  servants .............Deut 32:43
the people had *a* .......Josh 10:13
the Lord *a* me ... 1 Sam 24:12
God that *a* me ...... 2 Sam 22:48
to *a* themselves ....... Esth 8:13
*a* me of mine enemies ...Is 1:24
*A* me of mine .......... Luke 18:3
not God *a* his own..... Luke 18:7
*See* Gen 4:24; Lev 19:18

## AVOID

*A* it, pass not by it,...... Prov 4:15
*a* profane and vain .... 1 Tim 6:20
questions *a*........... 2 Tim 2:23
But *a* foolish............Titus 3:9
*See* Rom 16:17; 2 Cor 8:20

## AWAKE

when I *a*, with thy
  likeness.................Ps 17:15
*A*, *a*, put on ..............Is 51:9
*A*, ye drunkards.........Joel 1:5
*A*, O sword..........Zech 13:7
*a* out of sleep ..........Rom 13:11
*A* to righteousness .... 1 Cor 15:34
*A* thou that sleepest.... Eph 5:14
*See* Mark 4:38; John 11:11

--------- **B** ---------

## BABE

of the mouth of *b* and
  sucklings ................. Ps 8:2
*b* shall rule over them ......Is 3:4
them unto *b* .........Matt 11:25
the mouth of *b*.........Matt 21:16

## BACKSLIDER

*b* in heart shall be
  filled.............Prov 14:14
that which *b* Israel ........ Jer 3:6
*b* Israel committed ...... Jer 3:8
The *b* Israel hath .........Jer 3:11
Return, thou *b* Israel ..... Jer 3:12
perpetual *b*............. Jer 8:5
our *b* are many ...........Jer 14:7
as a *b* heifer............Hos 4:16
bent to *b* from me .......Hos 11:7
will heal their *b* ..........Hos 14:4
*See* Jer 2:19; 5:6; 31:22; 49:4

## BALM

Is there no *b* in Gilead....Jer 8:22
*See* Gen 37:25; 43:11; Jer 51:8

## BANDS

break their *b* asunder....... Ps 2:3
there are no *b*..............Ps 73:4
and break their *b* ....... Ps 107:14
with *b* of love ...........Hos 11:4
other I called *B* ..........Zech 11:7
the whole *b* ...........Matt 27:27
*See* Job 38:31; Eccl 7:26

## BAPTISM

the *b* that I am
  baptized with .......Matt 20:22
The *b* of John.......... Matt 21:25
*b* of repentance ........ Mark 1:4
The *b* of John, was it ... Mark 11:30
preaching the *b*..........Luke 3:3
with the *b* of John .....Luke 7:29

I have a *b* to be ........Luke 12:50
Beginning from the *b*.... Acts 1:22
knowing only the *b*.....Acts 18:25
Unto John's *b*........... Acts 19:3
buried with him by *b* .... Rom 6:4
one faith, one *b*........... Eph 4:5
with him in *b* ............ Col 2:12
Of the doctrine of *b*...... Heb 6:2
*See* Matt 3:7; 1 Pet 3:21

## BAPTIZE

I indeed *b* you
  with water ...........Matt 3:11
he shall *b* you...........Matt 3:11
I have need to be *b* .......Matt 3:14
Jesus, when he was *b* ....Matt 3:16
baptism that I am *b* ...Mark 10:39
believeth and is *b*..... Mark 16:16
to be *b* of him........... Luke 3:7
publicans to be *b* ....... Luke 3:12
*b* you with water ...... Luke 3:16
shall *b* you with ........ Luke 3:16
Jesus also being *b* ...... Luke 3:21
being *b* with the........ Luke 7:29
being not *b* ............Luke 7:30
I *b* with water ...........John 1:26
he that sent me to *b* ..... John 1:33
with them, and *b* ....... John 3:22
came and were *b* ....... John 3:23
*b* more disciples ..........John 4:1
Jesus himself *b* not........ John 4:2
John truly *b* with ........ Acts 1:5
Repent, and be *b* .......Acts 2:38
his word were *b* ........ Acts 2:41
*b*, both men............... Acts 8:12
*b* in the name........... Acts 8:16
hinder me to be *b*....... Acts 8:36
arose, and was *b*........ Acts 9:18
should not be *b* .........Acts 10:47
when she was *b* ........ Acts 16:15
was *b*, he and all........Acts 16:33
believed, and were *b* .... Acts 18:8
what then were ye *b*.... Acts 19:3
John verily *b* ........... Acts 19:4
be *b*, and wash away ... Acts 22:16
of us as were *b*.......... Rom 6:3
were ye *b* in the ....... 1 Cor 1:13
were all *b* unto Moses.. 1 Cor 10:2
all *b* into one body......1 Cor 12:13
*b* for the dead......... 1 Cor 15:29
been *b* into Christ ........ Gal 3:27
*See* Matt 28:19; John 1:25

## BATTLE

the fight, and shouted
  for the *b* ............ 1 Sam 17:20
the *b* is the Lord's ..... 1 Sam 17:47
to God in the *b*..........1 Chr 5:20
*b* is not yours ..........2 Chr 20:15
strength unto the *b*..... Ps 18:39
in peace from the *b*..... Ps 55:18
*b* to the strong............Eccl 9:11
sound of *b* is in .........Jer 50:22
*See* Job 39:25; 41:8; Ps 76:3

## BEAR (v.)

greater than I can *b*...... Gen 4:13
not *b* false witness ...... Ex 20:16
shall *b* his sin ............Lev 24:15
I am not able to *b*..... Num 11:14
to *b* you myself..........Deut 1:9
to *b* witness ........... 1 Kin 21:10
shall *b* thee up..........Ps 91:12
spirit who can *b* .......Prov 18:14
ye shall *b* the sins...... Ezek 23:49
not worthy to *b*......... Matt 3:11
hands they shall *b* ...... Matt 4:6
to *b* his cross .......... Matt 27:32
Rufus, to *b* his ........ Mark 15:21
Truly ye *b* witness..... Luke 11:48
not *b* his cross ........ Luke 14:27
that he might *b* it......Luke 23:26
to *b* witness ..............John 1:7
I *b* witness of myself ... John 5:31

I am one that *b*
  witness................ John 8:18
also shall *b* witness.... John 15:27
cannot *b* them now ... John 16:12
The Spirit itself *b* ....... Rom 8:16
*b* not the sword.........Rom 13:4
*b* the infirmities ........ Rom 15:1
be able to *b* it .........1 Cor 10:13
also *b* the image ..... 1 Cor 15:49
*B* ye one another's....... Gal 6:2
every man shall *b* his...... Gal 6:5
for I *b* in my body ........ Gal 6:17
offered to *b* the sins ....Heb 9:28
and *b* witness............ 1 John 1:2
*b* witness in earth ......1 John 5:8
*See* Ex 28:38; Prov 12:24

## BEAST

the life of his *b*..........Prov 12:10
above a *b* .............. Eccl 3:19
fought with *b*.......... 1 Cor 15:32
Every kind of *b* ......... James 3:7
as natural brute *b* ...... 2 Pet 2:12
*See* Lev 11:47; Ps 50:10

## BEAUTIFUL

*B* for situation, the joy
  of the...................Ps 48:2
*b* in his time ............Eccl 3:11
Thou art *b*, O my love ... Song 6:4
of the Lord be *b*............Is 4:2
put on thy *b* garments.....Is 52:1
*b* upon the mountains ....Is 52:7
Our holy and our *b* ......Is 64:11
thy *b* flock .............Jer 13:20
indeed appear *b* ....... Matt 23:27
which is called *B*........ Acts 3:2
alms at the *B* gate ...... Acts 3:10
How *b* are the feet......Rom 10:15

## BEAUTY

the Lord in the *b* of
  holiness .............. 1 Chr 16:29
the *b* of holiness........2 Chr 20:21
to *b* the house ..........Ezra 7:27
the *b* of the Lord.......... Ps 27:4
*b* to consume away....... Ps 39:11
perfection of *b*...........Ps 50:2
in the *b* of.............. Ps 110:3
*b* is vain ............... Prov 31:30
*See* 2 Sam 1:19; Zech 9:17

## BEGINNING

In the *b* God created the
  heaven ................ Gen 1:1
Though thy *b* was small...Job 8:7
*b* of wisdom ............ Ps 111:10
is true from the *b*......Ps 119:160
the *b* of knowledge....... Prov 1:7
Lord is the *b* ........... Prov 9:10
than the *b* thereof ........ Eccl 7:8
from the *b* ............ Matt 19:8
*b* at Moses ............. Luke 24:27
the *b* was the Word......John 1:1
This *b* of miracles .......John 2:11
*b* of our confidence ...... Heb 3:14
the *b* and the ending ......Rev 1:8
the *b* and the end......Rev 21:6
*See* 1 Chr 17:9; Prov 8:22, 23

## BEGOTTEN

*b* of the Father..........John 1:14
his only *b* Son .......... John 3:16
today have I *b* thee ....... Heb 5:5
*b* us again.............. 1 Pet 1:3
his only *b* Son .........1 John 4:9
*See* Job 38:28; Philem 10

## BEHIND

my sins *b* thy back.........Is 38:17
things which are *b*....... Phil 3:13
that which is *b*.......... Col 1:24
*See* 1 Kin 14:9; Neh 9:26

## BEHOLD

*b* the upright .............Ps 37:37
*b* the face .............. Matt 18:10

may *b* my glory........ John 17:24
*b* as in a glass........... 2 Cor 3:18
*See* Num 24:17; Ps 91:8; 119:37

**BELIEVE**
how long will it be ere
    they *b* me............. Num 14:11
*B* in the Lord......... 2 Chr 20:20
*b* his prophets ........ 2 Chr 20:20
they *b* not in God........Ps 78:22
*b* every word.......... Prov 14:15
as thou hast *b* ......... Matt 8:13
*B* ye that I am able...... Matt 9:28
did ye not then *b* him ...Matt 21:25
and we will *b* him ..... Matt 27:42
not afraid, only *b* ........Mark 5:36
If thou canst *b* ..........Mark 9:23
*b* that ye receive them...Mark 11:24
neither *b* they them ... Mark 16:13
most surely *b*............Luke 1:1
which for a while *b* ..... Luke 8:13
*b* only, and she shall....Luke 8:50
slow of heart to *b*......Luke 24:25
while they yet *b* ...... Luke 24:41
through him might *b*.....John 1:7
that *b* on his name ......John 1:12
they *b* the scripture ...John 2:22
how shall ye *b* .......... John 3:12
How can ye *b* .......... John 5:44
how shall ye *b* my
    words ............. John 5:47
seen me, and *b* not .....John 6:36
did his brethren *b* ....... John 7:5
Pharisees *b* on him..... John 7:48
*b* the works............John 10:38
to intent ye may *b* .....John 11:15
*B* thou this............John 11:26
thou wouldest *b* .....John 11:40
all men will *b* on him....John 11:48
*b* in the light............John 12:36
ye in God, *b* also.......John 14:1
the world may *b*......John 17:21
I will not *b* .............John 20:25
and yet have *b* ....... John 20:29
them that *b*.............Acts 4:32
by him all that *b* ......Acts 13:39
to eternal life *b* .......Acts 13:48
*B* on the Lord Jesus .... Acts 16:31
*b* in God with all his ....Acts 16:34
all them that *b*............Rom 4:11
against hope *b*.......... Rom 4:18
whosoever *b* on him.... Rom 9:33
how shall they *b*.......Rom 10:14
wife, that *b* not..........1 Cor 7:12
we also *b*................ 2 Cor 4:13
given to them that *b*.....Gal 3:22
all them that *b*........2 Thess 1:10
know whom I have *b*...2 Tim 1:12
*b* to the saving.......... Heb 10:39
must *b* that he is ........Heb 11:6
devils also *b* .........James 2:19
he that *b* on him........ 1 Pet 2:6

**BELLY**
upon thy *b* shalt
    thou go.............. Gen 3:14
goeth into the *b* ....... Matt 15:17
but into the *b*......... Mark 7:19
out of his *b* shall....... John 7:38
but their own *b*.......Rom 16:18
whose God is their *b*.... Phil 3:19

**BELOVED**
The *b* of the Lord
    shall dwell.........Deut 33:12
giveth his *b* sleep.........Ps 127:2
greatly *b* ................Dan 9:23
a man greatly *b* ........Dan 10:11
said, O man greatly *b*...Dan 10:19
This is my *b* Son.......Matt 3:17
Thou art my *b* Son.....Mark 1:11
Thou art my *b* Son.....Luke 3:22
they are *b*................Rom 11:28
accepted in the *b* ........ Eph 1:6

faithful and *b* brother .....Col 4:9
a brother *b*..............Philem 16
This is my *b* Son........2 Pet 1:17
*See* Neh 13:26; Song 2:16

**BENEVOLENCE**
render unto the
    wife due *b* ..............1 Cor 7:3

**BESOUGHT**
And Moses *b* the Lord
    his God .................. Ex 32:11
And I *b* the Lord.........Deut 3:23
the man of God *b* ....... 1 Kin 13:6
he *b* the Lord ..........2 Chr 33:12
and *b* the Lord..........Jer 26:19
the devils *b* him ........ Matt 8:31
they *b* him that he....... Matt 8:34
and he *b* him much..... Mark 5:10
And they *b* him ......... Luke 8:31
to him to depart..........Luke 8:32
I *b* the Lord thrice......2 Cor 12:8
*See* Gen 42:21; Esth 8:3

**BEST**
man at his *b* state .........Ps 39:5
the *b* gifts................1 Cor 12:31
*See* Gen 43:11; Deut 23:16

**BETTER**
to obey is *b* than
    sacrifice ............. 1 Sam 15:22
lovingkindness is *b* than ....Ps 63:3
Two are *b* than one....... Eccl 4:9
former days were *b* ...... Eccl 7:10
each esteem other *b*...... Phil 2:3
much *b* than the angels ....Heb 1:4
a *b* country ..............Heb 11:16
For it had been *b* ....... 2 Pet 2:21
*See* Eccl 2:24; Song 1:2; Jon 4:3

**BEWARE**
Take heed and *b*......... Matt 16:6
*b* of the leaven.......... Mark 8:15
*B* of the scribes .......Mark 12:38
*B* ye of the leaven....... Matt 16:11
*b* of covetousness ......Luke 12:15
*b* of evil workers....... Phil 3:2
*See* Deut 6:12; 8:11; 15:9

**BIND**
*B* them continually
    upon thine ..........Prov 6:21
*b* up the brokenhearted ....Is 61:1
shalt *b* on earth........ Matt 16:19
*b* on earth shall be..... Matt 18:18
*See* Num 30:2; Job 26:8; 38:31

**BIRD**
as a speckled *b*............ Jer 12:9
*See* Ps 11:1; 124:7; Eccl 10:20

**BIRTH**
whom I travail in *b* ....... Gal 4:19
*See* Eccl 7:1; Luke 1:14

**BISHOP**
If a man desire the
    office of *b*............. 1 Tim 3:1
*b* must be blameless .....Titus 1:7
Shepherd and *B* ...... 1 Pet 2:25
*See* Acts 1:20; Phil 1:1

**BITTERNESS**
I will speak in the *b* of
    my soul................Job 10:1
knoweth his own *b*......Prov 14:10
Let all *b*, and wrath...... Eph 4:31
lest any root of *b*........ Heb 12:15
*See* 1 Sam 15:32; Prov 17:25

**BLAME**
that the ministry
    be not *b*................ 2 Cor 6:3
that no man
    should *b* us.......... 2 Cor 8:20
he was to be *b* ............Gal 2:11
be holy and without *b*.....Eph 1:4

**BLAMELESS**
be *b* in the day of ........1 Cor 1:8
that ye may be *b* ........ Phil 2:15
*See* Matt 12:5; Phil 3:6; Titus 1:6, 7

**BLASPHEME**
the enemies of the
    Lord to *b* ........... 2 Sam 12:14
my name ... is *b*........... Is 52:5
themselves, This man *b*...Matt 9:3
*b* against the...........Mark 3:29
compelled them to *b* ... Acts 26:11
name of God is *b*....... Rom 2:24
*b* that worthy name ...... James 2:7
*See* 1 Kin 21:10; 1 Tim 1:20

**BLASPHEMY**
All manner of sin and *b*
    shall be................Matt 12:31
He hath spoken *b*.....Matt 26:65
Ye have heard the *b*....Mark 14:64
which speaketh *b*....... Luke 5:21
*See* 2 Kin 19:3; Ezek 35:12

**BLEMISH**
holy and without *b* ..... Eph 5:27
a lamb without *b* ........1 Pet 1:19
*See* Lev 21:17; Deut 15:21

**BLESS**
The Lord *b* thee, and
    keep thee..........Num 6:24
*B* shalt thou be .........Deut 28:3
thou wouldest *b* me.... 1 Chr 4:10
*B* is he whose..............Ps 32:1
I will *b* the Lord .........Ps 34:1
*B* the Lord, O my soul .... Ps 103:1
within me, *b* his holy..... Ps 103:1
the just is *b* .............Prov 10:7
*B* are ye that sow ........Is 32:20
*b* himself in the God..... Is 65:16
*B* are the poor in........ Matt 5:3
*b* them that curse ...... Matt 5:44
more *b* to give than.... Acts 20:35
*B* them which........... Rom 12:14
being reviled, we *b* .....1 Cor 4:12
*b* for evermore..........2 Cor 11:31
for that *b* hope.......... Titus 2:13
*B* are the dead .......... Rev 14:13
*See* Hag 2:19; James 3:9

**BLESSING**
thy God turned the curse
    into a *b* ...........Deut 23:5
the curse into a *b* ........ Neh 13:2
*b* of him that............ Job 29:13
*b* of the Lord............ Prov 10:22
shall abound with *b* ...Prov 28:20
for a *b* is in it............ Is 65:8
I will curse your *b* ........ Mal 2:2
pour you out a *b*......... Mal 3:10
the *b* of the gospel..... Rom 15:29
cup of *b* which......... 1 Cor 10:16
*b* and cursing.........James 3:10
and glory, and *b* .........Rev 5:12
*See* Gen 27:35; Deut 11:26, 29

**BLIND**
the gift *b* the wise ........ Ex 23:8
eyes of the *b* .............. Is 35:5
their minds were *b* ..... 2 Cor 3:14
of this world hath *b* ..... 2 Cor 4:4
darkness hath *b* ...... 1 John 2:11
*See* Deut 16:19; 1 Sam 12:3

**BLINDNESS**
because of *b* of
    their heart............ Eph 4:18
*See* Deut 28:28; Zech 12:4

**BLOOD**
Whoso sheddeth man's *b* ... his *b*
    be shed ............... Gen 9:6
is there in my *b*.......... Ps 30:9
precious shall their *b* ..... Ps 72:14
garments rolled in *b*........Is 9:5
*b* of the souls ............ Jer 2:34

land is full of *b*.......... Ezek 9:9
his *b* shall be upon ....Ezek 18:13
flesh and *b*............. Matt 16:17
the innocent *b*........ Matt 27:4
His *b* be on us ........ Matt 27:25
*b* of the new
  testament ..........Mark 14:24
new testament in
  my *b*.............. Luke 22:20
great drops of *b*.......Luke 22:44
not of *b*, or of ...........John 1:13
drinketh my *b*.......... John 6:54
my *b* is drink........... John 6:55
and from *b*..............Acts 15:20
made of one *b* .........Acts 17:26
with his own *b*........ Acts 20:28
from *b*, and from .......Acts 21:25
faith in his *b* ........... Rom 3:25
justified by his *b*........ Rom 5:9
the *b* of Christ ......... 1 Cor 10:16
new testament
  in my *b* ..............1 Cor 11:25
*b* of the Lord............1 Cor 11:27
flesh and *b*.............. 1 Cor 15:50
through his *b* ............Eph 1:7
without shedding of *b*...Heb 9:22
hath counted the *b* .....Heb 10:29
*b* of the everlasting.....Heb 13:20
precious *b* of Christ ....1 Pet 1:19
the *b* of the Lamb ........Rev 7:14
by the *b* of the Lamb .... Rev 12:11
*See* Gen 9:4; Ex 4:9; Rev 16:6

**BLOSSOM**
desert shall rejoice, and
  *b* as the rose..............Is 35:1
*See* Gen 40:10; Num 17:5; Is 27:6

**BLOT**
*b* me, I pray thee, out of
  thy book................ Ex 32:32
mercies *b* out my...........Ps 51:1
Let them be *b* out ....... Ps 69:28
your sins may be *b* ......Acts 3:19
*B* out the handwriting....Col 2:14
I will not *b* out..............Rev 3:5
*See* Deut 9:14; 2 Kin 14:27

**BOAST (n.)**
My soul shall make her *b*.. Ps 34:2
makest thy *b* of God .....Rom 2:17
that makest thy *b*.......Rom 2:23
Where is *b* then......... Rom 3:27

**BOAST (v.)**
trust in their wealth,
  and *b* ...................Ps 49:6
workers of iniquity *b* .....Ps 94:4
*B* not thyself..............Prov 27:1
I may *b* myself...........2 Cor 11:16
lest any man should *b*.....Eph 2:9
member, and *b* great ...James 3:5
*See* 2 Chr 25:19; Prov 20:14

**BODILY**
Holy Ghost descended
  in a *b* ..................Luke 3:22
but his *b* presence......2 Cor 10:10
of the Godhead *b* ..........Col 2:9
For *b* exercise............1 Tim 4:8

**BODY**
worms destroy this *b*... Job 19:26
thy flesh and thy *b*...... Prov 5:11
not that thy whole *b*.... Matt 5:29
The light of the *b* ...... Matt 6:22
nor yet for your *b* ...... Matt 6:25
she felt in her *b* .........Mark 5:29
neither for the *b* .......Luke 12:22
Wheresoever the *b* is...Luke 17:37
the temple of his *b* .....John 2:21
from his *b* were..........Acts 19:12
*b* of sin might be ........ Rom 6:6
*b* of this death ........... Rom 7:24
present your *b* a living ... Rom 12:1

many members
  in one *b*................Rom 12:4
*b* is the temple........... 1 Cor 6:19
I keep under my *b* ....... 1 Cor 9:27
*b* is not one member ...1 Cor 12:14
give my *b* to be burned...1 Cor 13:3
absent from the *b* .......2 Cor 5:8
the *b*, I cannot tell......2 Cor 12:2
I bear in my *b*............. Gal 6:17
unto his glorious *b* ...... Phil 3:21
own *b* on the tree....... 1 Pet 2:24
*See* Gen 47:18; Rom 12:5

**BOLD**
the *b* of his face shall be
  changed ................. Eccl 8:1
he speaketh *b*...........John 7:26
we have *b* and access.... Eph 3:12
therefore come *b* unto ... Heb 4:16
have *b* in the day ...... 1 John 4:17
*See* Prov 28:1; Acts 13:46

**BOND**
bitterness, and in
  the *b* of ................Acts 8:23
*b* of peace............... Eph 4:3
*b* of perfectness ........ Col 3:14
*See* Num 30:2; Ezek 20:37

**BOOK**
Seek ye out of the *b*....... Is 34:16
*b* of remembrance........Mal 3:16
the *b* of life ............... Phil 4:3
name out of the *b* ........Rev 3:5
not written in the *b* ....Rev 13:8
another *b* was opened ...Rev 20:12
written in the
  Lamb's *b*..............Rev 21:27
the words of the *b* ..... Rev 22:19
part out of the *b* ....... Rev 22:19
written in this *b* ........ Rev 22:19
*See* Ex 17:14; Ezra 4:15

**BORN**
man is *b* unto trouble .....Job 5:7
that is *b* of a woman.... Job 14:1
he which is *b* of a ....... Job 15:14
this man was *b* there ......Ps 87:4
unto us a child is *b* ......... Is 9:6
shall a nation be *b* .......Is 66:8
*b* King of the Jews....... Matt 2:2
Among them that
  are *b* ................. Matt 11:11
For unto you is *b* .......Luke 2:11
*b*, not of blood...........John 1:13
Except a man be
  *b* again.................John 3:3
is *b* of the Spirit .........John 3:8
*b* out of due time ........1 Cor 15:8
*b* again not of............1 Pet 1:23
loveth is *b* of God........1 John 4:7
Christ is *b* of God .......1 John 5:1
whatsoever is *b*
  of God .................1 John 5:4
*b* of God sinneth not...1 John 5:18
*See* Prov 17:17; Eccl 3:2

**BORNE**
he hath *b* our griefs........ Is 53:4
*See* Lam 5:7; Matt 20:12

**BOSOM**
into Abraham's *b* ......Luke 16:22
*b* of the Father..........John 1:18
leaning on Jesus' *b* ....John 13:23
*See* Ex 4:6; Deut 13:6; Job 31:33

**BOUGHT**
For ye are *b* .............1 Cor 6:20
Ye are *b* with a price.... 1 Cor 7:23
the Lord that *b* them .....2 Pet 2:1

**BOW**
unto me every knee
  shall *b* ................. Is 45:23
every knee shall *b* ...... Rom 14:11

**BOWELS**
his *b* did yearn upon his
  brother................Gen 43:30
the sounding of my *b*..... Is 63:15
in your own *b*.......... 2 Cor 6:12
*b* of mercies ............. Col 3:12
you all in the *b*...........Phil 1:8
if any *b* and mercies......Phil 2:1
*b* of compassion.......1 John 3:17
*See* Acts 1:18; Philem 12

**BRANCH**
tender *b* thereof will
  not cease ............... Job 14:7
flourish as a *b*..........Prov 11:28
*B* shall grow out ...........Is 11:1
David a righteous *B* ......Jer 23:5
lodge in the *b*......... Matt 13:32
*b* from the trees ........ Matt 21:8
*b* of palm trees ........ John 12:13
*See* Zech 3:8; John 15:2, 4, 6

**BREAD**
man doth not live by
  *b* only................... Deut 8:3
in giving them *b*......... Ruth 1:6
ravens brought him *b* ...1 Kin 17:6
her poor with *b* ..........Ps 132:15
*b* eaten in secret.........Prov 9:17
be satisfied with *b*...... Prov 12:11
have plenty of *b* ....... Prov 28:19
the *b* of idleness........Prov 31:27
Cast thy *b* upon..........Eccl 11:1
stones be made *b*........ Matt 4:3
shall not live by *b*....... Matt 4:4
this day our daily *b* .....Matt 6:11
that it be made *b* ....... Luke 4:3
ask *b* of any of you...... Luke 11:11
in breaking of *b*.......Luke 24:35
I am the *b* of life.........John 6:35
in breaking of *b*..........Acts 2:42
together to break *b* .....Acts 20:7
he took *b*, and gave......Acts 27:35
betrayed took *b*.........1 Cor 11:23
eat any man's *b* ....... 2 Thess 3:8
*See* Josh 9:5; Judg 7:13

**BREATH**
into his nostrils the *b*
  of life ................... Gen 2:7
wherein is the *b* ..........Gen 6:17
from man, whose *b*........ Is 2:22
cause *b* to enter ........ Ezek 37:5
*b* came into them...... Ezek 37:10
all life, and *b* ...........Acts 17:25
*See* Job 12:10; 33:4, Ps 146:4

**BREATHE**
he *b* on them ......... John 20:22

**BRETHREN**
all ye are *b* ...............Matt 23:8
or *b*, or sisters ........Mark 10:29
parents, or *b*...........Luke 18:29
faithful *b* in Christ......... Col 1:2
to call them *b*............Heb 2:11
we love the *b* ..........1 John 3:14
*See* Gen 42:28; John 7:5

**BRIDE**
prepared as a *b* ..........Rev 21:2
the Spirit and the *b*......Rev 22:17

**BRIDEGROOM**
to meet the *b* ...........Matt 25:1
of the *b* voice...........John 3:29
*See* Ps 19:5; Is 62:5; Matt 9:15

**BRIDLE**
a *b* for the ass.......... Prov 26:3
*b* not his tongue.........James 1:26
to *b* the whole body .....James 3:2
*See* 2 Kin 19:28; Is 37:29

**BRING**
*B* ye all the tithes
  into the................ Mal 3:10

if thou *b* thy gift ........ Matt 5:23
that it may *b* forth...... John 15:2

**BROKEN**
unto them that are of a
   *b* heart................... Ps 34:18
are a *b* spirit .............. Ps 51:17
*b* and a contrite heart ..... Ps 51:17
Reproach hath *b*........ Ps 69:20
cannot be *b*............ John 10:35
bone ... shall not
   be *b*................... John 19:36
*b* down the middle ...... Eph 2:14
*See* Job 17:11; Prov 25:19

**BROTHER**
*b* is born for adversity... Prov 17:17
is *b* to him ............... Prov 18:9
*b* offended is harder.... Prov 18:19
closer than a *b* ......... Prov 18:24
neither child nor *b*....... Eccl 4:8
*b* shall deliver.......... Matt 10:21
*b* goeth to law .......... 1 Cor 6:6
him as a *b*............2 Thess 3:15
*See* Gen 4:9; Matt 5:23

**BROTHERLY**
one to another with
   *b* love ................Rom 12:10
as touching *b* love .....1 Thess 4:9
Let *b* love continue.......Heb 13:1
*See* Amos 1:9; 2 Pet 1:7

**BRUISE** (*v.*)
*b* for our iniquities ........ Is 53:5
*See* Gen 3:15; Rom 16:20

**BUFFET**
they spit in his face
   and *b* him ...........Matt 26:67
and are *b*............... 1 Cor 4:11
of Satan to *b* me........ 2 Cor 12:7
when ye be *b* ........... 1 Pet 2:20

**BUILD**
labour in vain that *b*...... Ps 127:1
a time to *b* up............. Eccl 3:3
*b* the old waste .......... Is 58:12
I will *b* my church ..... Matt 16:18
able to *b* you up ....... Acts 20:32
should *b* upon
   another............... Rom 15:20
if any man *b* upon.......1 Cor 3:10
also are *b* together....... Eph 2:22
*See* 2 Chr 6:9; Eccl 2:4

**BUILDER**
the stone which the *b*
   refused ................ Ps 118:22
The stone which the *b*
   rejected............. Matt 21:42
at nought of you *b*.......Acts 4:11
*b* and maker is God.....Heb 11:10
stone which the *b* ........1 Pet 2:7
*See* 1 Kin 5:18; Ezra 3:10

**BUILDING**
husbandry, ye are
   God's *b* ............... 1 Cor 3:9
we have a *b* of God ...... 2 Cor 5:1
the *b* fitly framed........ Eph 2:21
the *b* of the wall .........Rev 21:18

**BURDEN**
Cast thy *b* upon
   the Lord............... Ps 55:22
shall be a *b*............ Eccl 12:5
my *b* is light .......... Matt 11:30
which have borne
   the *b*............... Matt 20:12
For they bind heavy *b*... Matt 23:4
with *b* grievous........ Luke 11:46
touch not the *b*....... Luke 11:46
one another's *b*........... Gal 6:2
shall bear his own *b* ....... Gal 6:5
*See* Num 11:11; 2 Cor 12:16

**BURN**
while I was musing the
   fire *b*...................... Ps 39:3
*B* lips and a wicked.... Prov 26:23
wickedness *b* as a .........Is 9:18
with everlasting *b*....... Is 33:14
shall *b* as an oven.......... Mal 4:1
in bundles to *b* ........ Matt 13:30
the chaff he will *b* .....Luke 3:17
and your lights *b* ...... Luke 12:35
Did not our heart *b*....Luke 24:32
He was a *b*............. John 5:35
my body to be *b* .........1 Cor 13:3
whose end is to be *b*...... Heb 6:8
lamps of fire *b*............Rev 4:5
*b* with brimstone....... Rev 19:20
*See* Gen 44:18; Ex 3:2; 21:25

**BURNT OFFERING**
as great delight in *b*....1 Sam 15:22
*b* and sin offering......... Ps 40:6
I hate robbery for *b*.........Is 61:8
*b* are not acceptable.....Jer 6:20
of God more than *b*...... Hos 6:6
more than *b* ...........Mark 12:33
*See* Gen 22:7; Lev 1:4; 6:9

**BURY**
dead *b* their dead.......Luke 9:60
we are *b* with him ....... Rom 6:4
he was *b* ................1 Cor 15:4
*B* with him in baptism ... Col 2:12
*See* Gen 23:4; 47:29; Matt 14:12

**BUSINESS**
diligent in his *b*.......... Rom 22:29
about my Father's *b*....Luke 2:49
Not slothful in *b* ....... Rom 12:11
to do your own *b* ..... 1 Thess 4:11
*See* Josh 2:14; Judg 18:7; Neh 13:30

---

# C

**CALL**
*c* ye upon him while he
   is near .................... Is 55:6
And why *c* ye me .......Luke 6:46
*c* of God.................Rom 11:29
in the same *c* ........... 1 Cor 7:20
the hope of his *c*.........Eph 1:18
prize of the high *c* ...... Phil 3:14
worthy of this *c*....... 2 Thess 1:11
with a holy *c*...........2 Tim 1:9
of the heavenly *c* .........Heb 3:1
make your *c* ............2 Pet 1:10
*See* Acts 7:59; 1 Cor 1:26

**CANDLE**
When his *c* shined upon
   my head ............... Job 29:3
thou wilt light my *c*......Ps 18:28
*c* of the Lord ......... Prov 20:27
lighted a *c*........ Luke 8:16; 11:33
*c* shall shine no more... Rev 18:23
need no *c* ................ Rev 22:5
*See* Job 18:6; 21:17; Prov 24:20

**CAPTIVITY**
into *c* to the law of sin ...Rom 7:23
bringing into *c*.......... 2 Cor 10:5
*See* Job 42:10; Ps 14:7

**CARE** (*n.*)
nation, that dwelleth
   without *c*.............. Jer 49:31
the *c* of this world .... Matt 13:22
with *c* and riches ....... Luke 8:14
and *c* of this life ...... Luke 21:34
Doth God take *c* ....... 1 Cor 9:9
*c* one for another ...... 1 Cor 12:25
the *c* of all............. 2 Cor 11:28
Casting all your *c* .........1 Pet 5:7
*See* 2 Kin 4:13; 2 Cor 7:12

**CAREFUL**
Be *c* for nothing ......... Phil 4:6

*c* with tears.............Heb 12:17
*See* Phil 4:10; Titus 3:8

**CARNAL**
*c*, sold under sin.........Rom 7:14
*c* mind is enmity ........Rom 8:7
but as unto *c*.............1 Cor 3:1
weapons ... are not *c* .. 2 Cor 10:4
*See* 1 Cor 9:11; Heb 7:16; 9:10

**CARRY**
Spirit of the Lord shall
   *c* thee.................1 Kin 18:12
*c* them in .................Is 40:11
*c* our sorrows............ Is 53:4
*c* them all the days ........ Is 63:9
men that *c* tales ........ Ezek 22:9
not *c* about .............. Heb 13:9
that are *c* ................2 Pet 2:17
*c* about of winds.......... Jude 12
*See* Ex 33:15; Num 11:12

**CAST**
Why art thou *c* down,
   O my soul................Ps 42:5
*C* thy burden upon .......Ps 55:22
lot is *c* into............. Prov 16:33
in no wise *c* out.........John 6:37
*C* down imaginations ... 2 Cor 10:5
*C* all your care ...........1 Pet 5:7
love *c* out fear ......... 1 John 4:18
*See* Ps 76:6; 3 John 10

**CAUGHT**
*c* up to the third ........ 2 Cor 12:2
be *c* up together........ 1 Thess 4:17
*See* Prov 7:13; Rev 12:5

**CEASE**
poor shall never *c*
   out of.................Deut 15:11
the wicked *c*.............Job 3:17
He maketh wars to *c* .....Ps 46:9
the strife *c*.............Prov 26:20
grinders *c*................ Eccl 12:3
I *c* not to warn........Acts 20:31
tongues, they shall *c*.... 1 Cor 13:8
Pray without *c*....... 1 Thess 5:17
hath *c* from sin ...........1 Pet 4:1
*See* Gen 8:22; Is 1:16; 2:22

**CELESTIAL**
There are also *c*
   bodies............... 1 Cor 15:40

**CHAFF**
burn up the *c* with
   unquenchable........ Matt 3:12
the *c* he will burn.......Luke 3:17
*See* Hos 13:3; Zeph 2:2

**CHANGE** (*v.*)
I am the Lord, I *c* not..... Mal 3:6
*c* the glory ..............Rom 1:23
we shall all be *c*.........1 Cor 15:51
*c* ... from glory ........ 2 Cor 3:18
*See* Job 17:12; Jer 2:36; 13:23

**CHARGE**
nor *c* God foolishly ......Job 1:22
angels he *c* with folly.....Job 4:18
sin to their *c*...........Acts 7:60
any thing to the *c*.......Rom 8:33
gospel ... without *c* .... 1 Cor 9:18
*c* some that they......... 1 Tim 1:3
I *c* thee before God .....1 Tim 5:21
*C* them that are rich .... 1 Tim 6:17
I *c* thee therefore ....... 2 Tim 4:1
be laid to their *c* ....... 2 Tim 4:16
*See* Ex 6:13; Ps 35:11; 91:11

**CHARITY**
put on *c*................... Col 3:14
the *c* of every one....... 2 Thess 1:3
the commandment is *c* ...1 Tim 1:5
faith, *c* ................. 2 Tim 2:22
sound in faith, in *c* ......Titus 2:2
*c* shall cover the .........1 Pet 4:8

## CHASTE (cont.)

brotherly kindness *c* .....2 Pet 1:7
your feasts of *c* .......... Jude 12
*See* 1 Cor 8:1; 13:1; Rev 2:19

**CHASTE**
present you as a *c*
  virgin..................2 Cor 11:2
discreet, *c*................Titus 2:5
your *c* conversation ....1 Pet 3:2

**CHASTEN**
as a man *c* his son.......Deut 8:5
neither *c* me.................Ps 6:1
man whom thou *c*........Ps 94:12
*C* thy son............Prov 19:18
as *c*, and not killed.....2 Cor 6:9
Lord loveth he *c* .........Heb 12:6
no *c* for the present ....Heb 12:11
I rebuke and *c* ...........Rev 3:19
*See* Ps 69:10; 73:14; 118:18

**CHASTISEMENT**
not seen the *c* of
  the Lord.................Deut 11:2
I have borne *c* ...........Job 34:31
the *c* of our peace.........Is 53:5

**CHEER**
maketh a *c* coun-
  tenance...............Prov 15:13
be of good *c*............John 16:33
sheweth mercy, with *c*...Rom 12:8
God loveth a *c* giver .....2 Cor 9:7
*See* Matt 9:2; 14:27; Mark 6:50

**CHIEF**
whosoever will be *c*
  among you.............Matt 20:27
the *c* corner stone .......Eph 2:20
of whom I am *c*.........1 Tim 1:15
when the *c* Shepherd....1 Pet 5:4

**CHILD**
a *c* is known by his ....Prov 20:11
Train up a *c* in the way ...Prov 22:6
in the heart of a *c*.....Prov 22:15
to us a *c* is born...............Is 9:6
*c* shall die an hundred....Is 65:20
What manner of *c* ......Luke 1:66
When I was a *c* ........1 Cor 13:11
*See* Eccl 4:13; 10:16, Heb 11:23

**CHILDREN**
weeping for her *c*.......Jer 31:15
*c* teeth are set ......... Ezek 18:2
take the *c* bread ....... Matt 15:26
Then are the *c* free .... Matt 17:26
Suffer little *c*.........Matt 19:14
little *c* to come........Mark 10:14
*c* of this world .......... Luke 16:8
*c* of the resurrection ...Luke 20:36
the *c* of light ...........John 12:36
we are the *c* of God ..... Rom 8:16
*c* of God by faith.........Gal 3:26
no more *c*................ Eph 4:14
*c* of disobedience........ Eph 5:6
walk as *c* of .............. Eph 5:8
*C*, obey your parents ..... Eph 6:1
cometh on the *c* ......... Col 3:6
Ye are all the *c* .........1 Thess 5:5
his *c* in subjection .......1 Tim 3:4
Behold I and the *c* ...... Heb 2:13
In this the *c*...........1 John 3:10
*See* Num 16:27; Esth 3:13

**CHOOSE**
*c* you this day whom ye
  will serve........... Josh 24:15
*C* rather to suffer ....... Heb 11:25

**CHOSEN**
people whom he hath *c*
  for his .................Ps 33:12
called, but few *c* ......Matt 20:16
but few are *c*.......... Matt 22:14
*c* that good part .......Luke 10:42
*c* out the chief rooms....Luke 14:7

Ye have not *c* me ...... John 15:16
he is a *c* vessel...........Acts 9:15
*c* in the Lord...........Rom 16:13
*c* the foolish things......1 Cor 1:27
despised, hath God *c*... 1 Cor 1:28
According as he hath *c* ....Eph 1:4
*c* of God.................1 Pet 2:4
a *c* generation ........... 1 Pet 2:9
*See* Ex 18:25; 1 Chr 16:13

**CHRIST**
Thou art the *C* ........ Matt 16:16
saying, I am *C*........ Matt 24:5
which is called *C*........John 4:25
is not this the *C*........John 4:29
thou art that *C*.........John 6:69
in due time *C* died...... Rom 5:6
*C* died for us ............ Rom 5:8
*C* liveth in me...........Gal 2:20
indeed preach *C*........Phil 1:15
*C* of contention ........Phil 1:16
me to live is *C*..........Phil 1:21
the Spirit of *C*.........1 Pet 1:11
Jesus is the *C* .......1 John 2:22
reigned with *C*......... Rev 20:4
of God and of *C* ........ Rev 20:6
*See* Matt 1:16; 2:4; Luke 2:26

**CHRISTIAN**
disciples were called
  *C* first.................Acts 11:26
me to be a *C* ..........Acts 26:28
man suffer as a *C*.......1 Pet 4:16

**CHURCH**
tell it unto the *c* .......Matt 18:17
added to the *c* daily .....Acts 2:47
the *c* in the wilderness...Acts 7:38
made havoc of the *c*.....Acts 8:3
elders in every *c* ......Acts 14:23
neither robbers of *c* ....Acts 19:37
feed the *c* of God .......Acts 20:28
greet the *c* that .........Rom 16:5
The *c* of Christ..........Rom 16:16
set some in the *c* ...... 1 Cor 12:28
silence in the *c*.....1 Cor 14:28, 34
with the *c* that..........1 Cor 16:19
I robbed other *c* ...... 2 Cor 11:8
the *c* is subject........ Eph 5:24
also loved the *c*.........Eph 5:25
the body, the *c*...........Col 1:18
which is the *c* ...........Col 1:24
care of the *c* of God.......1 Tim 3:5
*c* of the firstborn .......Heb 12:23
*See* Matt 16:18; Rev 1:4; 2:1

**CIRCUMCISE**
ye shall *c* the flesh...... Gen 17:11
Except ye be *c* ........Acts 15:1
though they be not *c* ....Rom 4:11
if ye be *c*, Christ........... Gal 5:2
*C* the eighth day ....... Phil 3:5
*See* John 7:22; Gal 2:3; Col 2:11

**CIRCUMCISION**
the covenant of *c* ........Acts 7:8
what profit is there of *c*... Rom 3:1
a minister of the *c* ......Rom 15:8
neither *c* ................. Gal 5:6
the *c*, which worship ..... Phil 3:3
*c* made without hands ....Col 2:11
*c* nor uncircumcision......Col 3:11
*See* Ex 4:26; John 7:22; Acts 7:8

**CITY**
there shall be six *c* for
  refuge ................Num 35:6
six *c* with .............. Josh 15:59
make glad the *c* of God ....Ps 46:4
a *c* of truth...............Zech 8:3
a *c* which hath..........Heb 11:10
*c* of the living God ......Heb 12:22
no continuing ..........Heb 13:14
the *c* of the nations......Rev 16:19
the beloved *c* ...........Rev 20:9
*See* Gen 4:17; 11:4; Jon 1:2

**CLAY**
formed out of the *c*......Job 33:6
out of the miry *c*..........Ps 40:2

**CLEAN**
bring a *c* thing out........Job 14:4
He that hath *c* hands......Ps 24:4
Create in me a *c* heart ....Ps 51:10
Is his mercy *c*...........Ps 77:8
*c* in his own eyes .......Prov 16:2
Wash you, make you *c*.....Is 1:16
be ye *c*, that bear .......Is 52:11
I sprinkle *c* water.......Ezek 36:25
canst make me *c*....... Matt 8:2
for ye make *c* .........Matt 23:25
Pharisees make *c*...... Luke 11:39
all things are *c*........Luke 11:41
Ye are not all *c* .........John 13:11
*c* through the word..... John 15:3
I am *c*...................Acts 18:6
linen, *c* and white ........Rev 19:8
*See* Josh 3:17; Prov 14:4

**CLEANSE**
*c* thou me from........... Ps 19:12
I have *c* my heart.........Ps 73:13
wound *c* away evil....Prov 20:30
*c* first that .............Prov 23:26
What God hath *c* ...... Acts 10:15
let us *c* ourselves .........2 Cor 7:1
*C* your hands .........James 4:8
his Son *c* us..............1 John 1:7
to *c* us...................1 John 1:9
*See* Ezek 36:25; Mark 1:44

**CLEAVE**
*c* unto the Lord
  your God ...........Josh 23:8
heart they would *c* .....Acts 11:23
*c* to that which ......... Rom 12:9
*See* Gen 2:24; Matt 19:5

**CLOTHE**
*c* himself with ...........Ps 109:18
*c* with righteousness ....Ps 132:9
shall *c* a man ..........Prov 23:21
household are *c* ........Prov 31:21
*c* the heavens............. Is 50:3
*C* me with the garments...Is 61:10
if God so *c* ..............Matt 6:30
shall we be *c* .......... Matt 6:31
Naked, and ye *c* me...Matt 25:36
naked and ye *c*
  me not................Matt 25:43
If then God so *c*........Luke 12:28
desiring to be *c* .........2 Cor 5:2
be *c* with humility ........1 Pet 5:5
that thou mayest be *c*....Rev 3:18
woman *c* with the sun ...Rev 12:1
*c* with a vesture.........Rev 19:13
*See* Ex 40:14; Esth 4:4

**CLOUD**
them by day in a pillar
  of a *c*...................Ex 13:21
fire and of the *c*.........Ex 14:24
ariseth a little *c*........ 1 Kin 18:44
was black with *c*....... 1 Kin 18:45
the pillar of the *c* ...... Neh 9:19
*c* drop down the dew... Prov 3:20
the *c* of heaven ..........Dan 7:13
a bright *c*
  overshadowed ........Matt 17:5
in the *c* of heaven
  with .................Matt 24:30
and coming in the
  *c* of ...................Matt 26:64
a *c* that overshadowed... Mark 9:7
man coming in the *c* ...Mark 13:26
a *c*, and
  overshadowed .......Luke 9:34
in a *c* with power...... Luke 21:27
fathers were under
  the *c* ...................1 Cor 10:1
caught up . . . in
  the *c* ................ 1 Thess 4:17

*c* that are carried with...2 Pet 2:17
*c* they are without water...Jude 12
he cometh with *c*...........Rev 1:7
and behold a white *c*....Rev 14:14
*See* Gen 9:13; Ex 24:15; 40:34

## COLD
cup of *c* water.........Matt 10:42
many shall wax *c*......Matt 24:12
in *c* and nakedness.....2 Cor 11:27
neither *c* nor hot.........Rev 3:15
*See* Job 24:7; Ps 147:17

## COME
Then said I, Lo, I *c*.........Ps 40:7
*c* ye to the waters...........Is 55:1
*C* unto me.............Matt 11:28
the Son of man is *c*...Matt 18:11
compel them to *c*......Luke 14:23
I will *c* again...........John 14:3
*c*, Lord Jesus............Rev 22:20

## COMFORT (n.)
*c* of the Holy Ghost......Acts 9:31
patience and *c*...........Rom 15:4
God of all *c*...............2 Cor 1:3
comforted in your *c*...2 Cor 7:13
be of good *c*...........2 Cor 13:11
if any *c* of love.............Phil 2:1
*See* Job 10:20; Ps 94:19

## COMFORT (v.)
staff they *c* me.............Ps 23:4
*C* ye, *c* ye my people........Is 40:1
the Lord hath *c*.....Is 49:13; 52:9
*c* all that mourn..........Is 61:2
whom his mother *c*......Is 66:13
they shall be *c*...........Matt 5:4
he is *c*..................Luke 16:25
to *c* them.............John 11:19
able to *c* them........2 Cor 1:4
*c* one another.........1 Thess 4:18
*c* yourselves
together.............1 Thess 5:11
*c* the feebleminded...1 Thess 5:14
*See* Gen 5:29; 18:5; 37:35

## COMFORTER
miserable *c* are ye all.....Job 16:2
looked... for *c*..........Ps 69:20
give you another *C*....John 14:16
when the *C* is come...John 15:26
*C* will not come.........John 16:7
*See* 2 Sam 10:3; 1 Chr 19:3

## COMMANDMENT
*c* are faithful..............Ps 119:86
*c* is exceeding broad.....Ps 119:96
I love thy *c*..............Ps 119:127
thy *c* are my delight...Ps 119:143
for doctrines the *c*.....Matt 15:9
according to the *c*....Luke 23:56
A new *c* I give.........John 13:34
*c* holy, and just.........Rom 7:12
and not of *c*............1 Cor 7:6
I speak not by *c*.........2 Cor 8:8
first *c* with promise......Eph 6:2
after the *c*................Col 2:22
end of the *c*............1 Tim 1:5
I write no new *c*.......1 John 2:7
I wrote a new *c*.........2 John 5
*See* Esth 3:3

## COMMEND
I *c* my spirit............Luke 23:46
God *c* his love
toward us.............Rom 5:8
*See* Eccl 8:15; Acts 20:32

## COMMIT
Thou shalt not *c*
adultery...............Ex 20:14
*C* thy way unto........Ps 37:5
have *c* two evils..........Jer 2:13
Jesus did not *c*.........John 2:24
hath *c* all judgment......John 5:22
*c* the oracles of God.....Rom 3:2

*c* unto us the word.....2 Cor 5:19
that which is *c*.........1 Tim 6:20
which I have *c*.........2 Tim 1:12
*c* himself to him.......1 Pet 2:23
*See* Job 5:8; Ps 31:5; 1 Cor 9:17

## COMMUNICATION
let your *c* be, Yea.......Matt 5:37
What manner of *c*.....Luke 24:17
evil *c* corrupt...........1 Cor 15:33
Let no corrupt *c*.........Eph 4:29
*See* 2 Kin 9:11; Philem 6

## COMMUNION
*c* of the blood of
Christ................1 Cor 10:16
*c* of the body of Christ...1 Cor 10:16
what *c* hath light.......2 Cor 6:14
*c* of the Holy Ghost....2 Cor 13:14

## COMPASSION
she should not have *c*....Is 49:15
his *c* fail not.............Lam 3:22
will he have *c*...........Lam 3:32
will have *c* upon us........Mic 7:19
he was moved with *c*...Matt 9:36
with *c* toward them...Matt 14:14
*c* on thy.................Matt 18:33
had *c* on them........Matt 20:34
Jesus, moved with *c*....Mark 1:41
Lord hath... had *c*....Mark 5:19
have *c* on us...........Mark 9:22
he had *c* on him.......Luke 10:33
saw him, and had *c*....Luke 15:20
will have *c* on whom....Rom 9:15
have *c* on the ignorant...Heb 5:2
one mind, having *c*......1 Pet 3:8
his bowels of *c*.........1 John 3:17
have *c*...................Jude 22
*See* Ps 78:38; 86:15; 112:4

## COMPEL
*c* thee to go a mile......Matt 5:41
*c* to bear his cross......Matt 27:32
they *c* one Simon......Mark 15:21
*c* them to come in.....Luke 14:23
*c* them to...............Acts 26:11
*See* 2 Cor 12:11; Gal 2:3

## COMPLETE
seven sabbaths
shall be *c*.............Lev 23:15
are *c* in him...............Col 2:10
perfect and *c* in all........Col 4:12

## COMPREHEND
doeth he, which we
cannot *c*................Job 37:5
and *c* the dust............Is 40:12
the darkness *c* it not......John 1:5
*c* with all saints..........Eph 3:18

## CONDEMN
I will say unto God, Do
not *c* me.................Job 10:2
drink the wine of the *c*...Amos 2:8
have *c* the guiltless......Matt 12:7
thou shalt be *c*..........Matt 12:37
and shall *c* it...........Matt 12:42
shall *c* him to death...Matt 20:18
he saw that he was *c*...Matt 27:3
all *c* him to.............Mark 14:64
*c* not, and ye shall......Luke 6:37
into the world to *c*.......John 3:17
believeth not is *c*.......John 3:18
hath no man *c* thee......John 8:10
Neither do I *c* thee......John 8:11
thou *c* thyself...........Rom 2:1
*c* sin in the flesh.........Rom 8:3
Who is he that *c*.......Rom 8:34
Happy is he that *c*......Rom 14:22
that cannot be *c*........Titus 2:8
Ye have *c* and killed....James 5:6
lest ye be *c*..............James 5:9
if our heart *c* us........1 John 3:21
*See* Job 9:20; 15:6; Matt 12:41

## CONDEMNATION
this is the *c*, that
light is................John 3:19
shall not come into *c*...John 5:24
administration of *c*......2 Cor 3:9
the *c* of the devil........1 Tim 3:6
lest ye fall into *c*.......James 5:12
ordained to this *c*.........Jude 4
*See* Luke 23:40; Rom 5:16; 8:1

## CONFESS
whoso *c* and
forsaketh them......Prov 28:13
*c* me before men......Matt 10:32
*c* that he was Christ....John 9:22
they did not *c* him......John 12:42
Pharisees *c* both........Acts 23:8
*c* with thy mouth........Rom 10:9
every tongue shall *c*....Rom 14:11
*c* that Jesus Christ.......Phil 2:11
*c* that they were.........Heb 11:13
*C* your faults...........James 5:16
if we *c* our sins..........1 John 1:9
Every spirit that *c*......1 John 4:2
*c* that Jesus is the......1 John 4:15
will *c* his name.........Rev 3:5
*See* 1 Kin 8:33; 2 Chr 6:24

## CONFESSION
Lord my God, and
made my *c*...............Dan 9:4
mouth *c* is made.......Rom 10:10
witnessed a good *c*.....1 Tim 6:13

## CONFIDENCE
the *c* of all the ends of
the earth................Ps 65:5
to put *c* in man...........Ps 118:8
to put *c* in princes......Ps 118:9
Lord shall be thy *c*......Prov 3:26
Lord is strong *c*.........Prov 14:26
in *c* shall be your.........Is 30:15
hath rejected thy *c*......Jer 2:37
*c* by the faith.............Eph 3:12
no *c* in the flesh..........Phil 3:3
might also have *c*........Phil 3:4
if we hold fast the *c*......Heb 3:6
beginning of our *c*.......Heb 3:14
therefore your *c*.......Heb 10:35
we may have *c*........1 John 2:28
have we *c* toward
God..................1 John 3:21
this is the *c* that we....1 John 5:14
*See* Job 4:6; Prov 25:19

## CONFIDENT
against me, in this will
I be *c*....................Ps 27:3
fool rageth, and is *c*....Prov 14:16
we are always *c*.........2 Cor 5:6
*c* of this very thing........Phil 1:6

## CONFIRM
*c* the feeble knees........Is 35:3
*c* the word.............Mark 16:20
*C* the souls of..........Acts 14:22
words, and *c* them......Acts 15:32
*c* the churches..........Acts 15:41
*c* the promises made.....Rom 15:8
*See* 2 Kin 15:19; 1 Cor 1:6

## CONFORM
to be *c* to the image of
his Son...............Rom 8:29
not *c* to this world......Rom 12:2
*c* unto his death.........Phil 3:10

## CONGREGATION
all the *c* said, Amen......Neh 5:13
nor sinners in the *c*........Ps 1:5
in the *c* will I bless.......Ps 26:12
the *c* of the dead.......Prov 21:16

## CONQUER
we are more than *c*
through him......Rom 8:37
he went forth *c*..........Rev 6:2

## CONSCIENCE
*c* void of offence........Acts 24:16
their *c* also bearing.......Rom 2:15
my *c* also bearing me.....Rom 9:1
also for *c* sake............Rom 13:5
shall not the *c* of him... 1 Cor 8:10
and wounded their
    weak *c*................ 1 Cor 8:12
question for *c* sake .... 1 Cor 10:25
and for *c* sake.......... 1 Cor 10:28
testimony of our *c*.......2 Cor 1:12
a good *c*.................. 1 Tim 1:5
faith, and a good *c*...... 1 Tim 1:19
in a pure *c* ...............1 Tim 3:9
*c* seared with a
    hot iron.................1 Tim 4:2
purge your *c* from ....... Heb 9:14
from an evil *c*...........Heb 10:22
we have a good *c* ....... Heb 13:18
Having a good *c*........1 Pet 3:16
*See* John 8:9; 2 Cor 4:2

## CONSIDER
When I *c* thy heavens ......Ps 8:3
my people doth not *c*........Is 1:3
*C* your ways............. Hag 1:5, 7
*C* the lilies of the........Matt 6:28
*c* not the beam .........Matt 7:3
*C* the ravens ........... Luke 12:24
*c* thyself, lest thou........ Gal 6:1
*c* the Apostle..............Heb 3:1
*c* how great this
    man was................ Heb 7:4
*c* one another..........Heb 10:24
*c* him that endured..... Heb 12:3
*c* the end of their ........ Heb 13:7
*See* Deut 32:29; 1 Sam 12:24

## CONSOLATION
Are the *c* of God small... Job 15:11
have received your *c*....Luke 6:24
of patience and *c* ........Rom 15:5
any *c* in Christ ..........Phil 2:1
everlasting *c*..........2 Thess 2:16
have a strong *c* ......... Heb 6:18
*See* Luke 2:25; Acts 4:36

## CONSUME
bush was not *c* .............Ex 3:2
God is a *c* fire ...........Deut 4:24
as a *c* fire he shall....... Deut 9:3
and *c* the burnt ........ 1 Kin 18:38
shall *c* him.................Job 20:26
*c* away like a moth........ Ps 39:11
that we are not *c*....... Lam 3:22
are not *c* ................... Mal 3:6
*c* them ...................Luke 9:54
heed that ye be not *c* ..... Gal 5:15
For our God is a *c*.......Heb 12:29
that ye may *c* it ........James 4:3
*See* Ex 32:10; 33:3; Josh 24:20

## CONSUMMATION
until the *c*, and that
    determined............Dan 9:27

## CONTAIN
heavens cannot *c* thee ...1 Kin 8:27
heavens cannot *c* him....2 Chr 2:6
itself could not *c*.......John 21:25
if they cannot *c*..........1 Cor 7:9

## CONTENT
willing to *c* the people...Mark 15:15
be *c* with your wages... Luke 3:14
therewith to be *c* ........Phil 4:11
godliness with *c*........1 Tim 6:6
to be therewith *c* .......1 Tim 6:8
be *c* with such things.... Heb 13:5
*See* Gen 37:27; Josh 7:7

## CONTINUE
as a shadow, and *c* not ...Job 14:2
shall be *c*................ Ps 72:17
that *c* until night ...........Is 5:11
may *c* many days ........ Jer 32:14

*c* all night.............. Luke 6:12
*c* with me in ..........Luke 22:28
if ye *c* in my word....... John 8:31
*c* ye in my love........... John 15:9
*c* with one accord........ Acts 1:14
they *c* steadfastly........Acts 2:42
they, *c* daily with .......Acts 2:46
Peter *c* knocking.........Acts 12:16
to *c* in the grace .......Acts 13:43
exhorting them to *c* ....Acts 14:22
I *c* unto this day ....... Acts 26:22
Shall we *c* in sin ........Rom 6:1
*c* instant in prayer......Rom 12:12
*c* not in all things........ Gal 3:10
If ye *c* in the faith.........Col 1:23
*C* in prayer, and watch..... Col 4:2
if they *c* in faith.........1 Tim 2:15
*c* in them ...............1 Tim 4:16
*c* thou in .................2 Tim 3:14
not suffered to *c*........ Heb 7:23
because he *c* ever........ Heb 7:24
Let brotherly love *c*......Heb 13:1
have we no *c* city ........ Heb 13:14
and *c* there a year......James 4:13
all things *c* ............. 2 Pet 3:4
no doubt have *c* .......1 John 2:19
*See* 1 Sam 12:14; 2 Sam 7:29

## CONTRITE
saveth such as be of a *c*
    spirit....................Ps 34:18
a broken and a *c* heart....Ps 51:17
of a *c* and humble .........Is 57:15
heart of the *c* ones.........Is 57:15
and of a *c* spirit............Is 66:2

## CONVERSATION
such as be of upright *c* ... Ps 37:14
ordereth his *c* aright..... Ps 50:23
*c* be as it becometh......Phil 1:27
our *c* is in heaven.......Phil 3:20
in *c*, in charity .......... 1 Tim 4:12
*c* be without .............Heb 13:5
the end of their *c* ........ Heb 13:7
in all manner of *c*....... 1 Pet 1:15
from your vain *c* ....... 1 Pet 1:18
your *c* honest.............1 Pet 2:12
with the filthy *c*......... 2 Pet 2:7
be in all holy *c* ..........2 Pet 3:11
*See* Eph 2:3; 4:22; James 3:13

## CONVERSION
declaring the *c* of the
    Gentiles ............... Acts 15:3

## CONVERT
perfect, *c* the soul ........ Ps 19:7
their heart, and *c* ......... Is 6:10
be *c*, and I should......Matt 13:15
Except ye be *c* .......... Matt 18:3
they should be *c* ........ Mark 4:12
when thou art *c* ....... Luke 22:32
and be *c* .................Acts 3:19
and one *c* him .........James 5:19
he which *c* ........... James 5:20
*See* Ps 51:13; Is 1:27; 60:5

## CONVICTED
being *c* by their own
    conscience ............John 8:9

## CORNER
become the head stone
    of the *c* ..............Ps 118:22
may be as *c* stones........Ps 144:12
precious *c* stone.......... Is 28:16
*c* of the streets........... Matt 6:5
not done in a *c* .........Acts 26:26
being the chief *c*.........Eph 2:20
a chief *c* stone ......... 1 Pet 2:6
four *c* of the earth ......... Rev 7:1
*See* Job 1:19; Prov 7:8; 21:9

## CORRECT
whom the Lord
    loveth he *c*.............Prov 3:12

*C* thy son................Prov 29:17
not be *c* by words...... Prov 29:19
*c* me, but with ...........Jer 10:24
I will *c* thee ............. Jer 30:11
but *c* thee in measure ...Jer 46:28
of our flesh which *c* us ... Heb 12:9
*See* Job 5:17; Ps 39:11; 94:10

## CORRECTION
rod of *c* shall drive..... Prov 22:15
they received no *c* ......Jer 2:30
refused to receive *c*........ Jer 5:3
nor receiveth *c*.......... Jer 7:28
she received not *c* ........Zeph 3:2
for reproof, for *c*....... 2 Tim 3:16
*See* Job 37:13; Prov 3:11; 7:22

## CORRUPT
Lest ye *c* yourselves .... Deut 4:16
ye will utterly *c*........Deut 31:29
and rust doth *c* ........ Matt 6:19
a *c* tree bringeth forth...Matt 7:17
make the tree *c* ........ Matt 12:33
not forth *c* fruit.........Luke 6:43
neither moth *c*.........Luke 12:33
communications *c* ... 1 Cor 15:33
which *c* the word....... 2 Cor 2:17
we have *c* no man ....... 2 Cor 7:2
your minds should
    be *c*....................2 Cor 11:3
old man, which is *c*......Eph 4:22
Let no *c* communi-
    cation .................Eph 4:29
men of *c* minds..........1 Tim 6:5
men of *c* minds .........2 Tim 3:8
your riches are *c*.......James 5:2
*See* Job 17:1; Prov 25:26

## CORRUPTION
suffer thine Holy One
    to see *c* .................Ps 16:10
and not see *c* ...........Ps 49:9
my life from *c*............. Jon 2:6
did see *c* ..............Acts 2:31
from the bondage of *c*...Rom 8:21
It is sown in *c*.......... 1 Cor 15:42
neither doth *c* ....... 1 Cor 15:50
of the flesh reap *c* .........Gal 6:8
the *c* that is in .......... 2 Pet 1:4
perish in their own *c* ... 2 Pet 2:12
*See* Lev 22:25; Is 38:17

## COUNSEL
*c* of the ungodly .............Ps 1:1
The *c* of the Lord ......... Ps 33:11
took sweet *c* together ....Ps 55:14
guide me with thy *c* ....Ps 73:24
at nought all my *c* .......Prov 1:25
Where no *c* is .......... Prov 11:14
Without *c* purposes .... Prov 15:22
the *c* of the Lord.......Prov 19:21
nor *c* against the Lord...Prov 21:30
I *c* thee..................... Eccl 8:2
wonderful in *c*.............Is 28:29
that take *c* ................Is 30:1
My *c* shall stand .......... Is 46:10
Great in *c* ...............Jer 32:19
ashamed of his own *c* ... Hos 10:6
took *c* with ..............Mark 3:6
took *c* together ........ John 11:53
determinate *c* ..........Acts 2:23
thy hand and thy *c*......Acts 4:28
all the *c* of God......... Acts 20:27
*c* of his own will ......... Eph 1:11
of his *c*....................Heb 6:17

## COUNSELLOR
multitude of *c* there is
    safety................. Prov 11:14
*c* of peace is joy........Prov 12:20
in the multitude of *c* ...Prov 15:22
called Wonderful, *C*........ Is 9:6

## COUNT
he *c* it to him for
    righteousness......... Gen 15:6

*c* as sheep. . . . . . . . . . . . . . .Ps 44:22
*c* unto him for . . . . . . . . . .Ps 106:31
is *c* wise. . . . . . . . . . . . . . .Prov 17:28
be *c* for a forest . . . . . . . . Is 32:15
because they *c* him. . . . .Matt 14:5
men *c* John . . . . . . . . . . Mark 11:32
and *c* the cost. . . . . . . . . Luke 14:28
that they were *c* . . . . . . . . . Acts 5:41
neither *c* I my light . . . . Acts 20:24
I *c* loss for. . . . . . . . . . . . . . Phil 3:7
I *c* all things . . . . . . . . . . . . Phil 3:8
I *c* not myself . . . . . . . . . . . Phil 3:13
may be *c* worthy. . . . . . . 2 Thess 1:5
God would *c* you
    worthy . . . . . . . . . . . . . 2 Thess 1:11
he *c* me faithful. . . . . . . . 1 Tim 1:12
well be *c* worthy. . . . . . . 1 Tim 5:17
*c* the blood. . . . . . . . . . . . .Heb 10:29
*c* it all joy . . . . . . . . . . . . .James 1:2
as some men *c* . . . . . . . . . . 2 Pet 3:9
*See* Num 23:10; Job 31:4

## COUNTENANCE
Look not on his *c* . . . . . . .1 Sam 16:7
of a beautiful *c*. . . . . . . .1 Sam 16:12
ruddy, and of a fair *c* . . .1 Sam 17:42
Why is thy *c* sad . . . . . . . . Neh 2:2
thou changest his *c*. . . . . Job 14:20
light of thy *c* . . . . . . . . . . . . .Ps 4:6
light of thy *c* . . . . . . . . . . . .Ps 44:3
in the light of *c* . . . . . . . . .Ps 89:15
maketh a cheerful *c* . . . .Prov 15:13
sharpeneth the *c* . . . . . . .Prov 27:17
the sadness of the *c* . . . . . .Eccl 7:3
their *c* doth witness . . . . . . . Is 3:9
of a sad *c*. . . . . . . . . . . . . Matt 6:16
*c* was like lightning. . . . .Matt 28:3
his *c* was altered. . . . . .Luke 9:29
his *c* was as the sun . . . . . .Rev 1:16
*See* Gen 4:5; Num 6:26; Judg 13:6

## COURAGE
Be strong and of a
    good *c* . . . . . . . . . . . . . Deut 31:6
be of good *c*. . . . . . . . . . . . . Ps 27:14
and took *c* . . . . . . . . . . .Acts 28:15
*See* Num 13:20; Josh 1:7; 2:11

## COURSE
that I might finish my *c*
    with joy . . . . . . . . . . . . Acts 20:24
may have free *c*. . . . . . 2 Thess 3:1
I have finished my *c* . . . .2 Tim 4:7
the *c* of nature. . . . . . . . .James 3:6
*See* Ps 82:5; Acts 13:25

## COVENANT
it is a *c* of salt for ever . . .Num 18:19
my *c* of peace . . . . . . . . Num 25:12
by a *c* of salt . . . . . . . . . . 2 Chr 13:5
his *c* for ever. . . . . . . . . . . .Ps 105:8
for them his *c*. . . . . . . . . Ps 106:45
mindful of his *c*. . . . . . . . . .Ps 111:5
*c* with death . . . . . . . . . . . . Is 28:18
they *c* with him. . . . . . . Matt 26:15
and *c* to give him. . . . . . Luke 22:5
*c* which God made. . . . . .Acts 3:25
glory, and the *c* . . . . . . . . Rom 9:4
the *c* of promise . . . . . . . . Eph 2:12
mediator of a better *c* . . . .Heb 8:6
mediator of the new *c*. . Heb 12:24
of the everlasting *c* . . . . .Heb 13:20
*See* Gen 9:15; Ex 34:28; Job 31:1

## COVER
depths have *c* them . . . . . . .Ex 15:5
*c* thee with my hand. . . . .Ex 33:22
*c* with a mantle. . . . . . 1 Sam 28:14
they *c* Haman's face . . . . .Esth 7:8
whose sin is *c*. . . . . . . . . . . .Ps 32:1
*c* them as a garment. . . . . .Ps 73:6
He shall *c* thee. . . . . . . . . . .Ps 91:4
Thou *c* it with . . . . . . . . . .Ps 104:6
violence *c* the mouth. . . Prov 10:6
love *c* all sins . . . . . . . . . .Prov 10:12

a prudent man *c*
    shame . . . . . . . . . . . . . .Prov 12:16
He that *c* a
    transgression . . . . . . . .Prov 17:9
He that *c* sins . . . . . . . . .Prov 28:13
no more *c* her slain. . . . . . Is 26:21
ship was *c* . . . . . . . . . . . . Matt 8:24
there is nothing *c*. . . . .Matt 10:26
whose sins are *c*. . . . . . . . .Rom 4:7
having his head *c*. . . . . .1 Cor 11:4
the woman be not *c* . . . .1 Cor 11:6
not to *c* his head. . . . . . . .1 Cor 11:7
charity shall *c*. . . . . . . . . . .1 Pet 4:8
*See* Gen 7:19; Ex 8:6; 21:33

## COVET
Thou shalt not *c*. . . . . . . . .Ex 20:17
He *c* greedily all
    the day . . . . . . . . . . . . Prov 21:26
him that *c* an evil. . . . . . . .Hab 2:9
*c* no man's silver. . . . . . .Acts 20:33
*c* earnestly. . . . . . . . . . . .1 Cor 12:31
while some *c* after. . . . . .1 Tim 6:10
*See* Ex 5:21; Rom 7:7

## COVETOUS
hateth *c* shall prolong
    his days. . . . . . . . . . . . .Prov 28:16
goeth after their *c* . . . .Ezek 33:31
Thefts, *c*, wickedness. . .Mark 7:22
beware of *c* . . . . . . . . . . .Luke 12:15
*c*, nor drunkards. . . . . . . 1 Cor 6:10
all uncleanness, or *c*. . . . . .Eph 5:3
nor *c* man. . . . . . . . . . . . . . .Eph 5:5

## CREATE
God *c* the heaven and
    the earth . . . . . . . . . . . . . Gen 1:1
So God *c* man in his . . . . .Gen 1:27
who hath *c* these . . . . . . . .Is 40:26
*c* him for my glory. . . . . . . .Is 43:7
I *c* new heavens . . . . . . . . .Is 65:17
hath *c* a new thing. . . . . . Jer 31:22
and *c* the wind. . . . . . . . Amos 4:13
one God *c* us. . . . . . . . . . . Mal 2:10
*c* for the woman . . . . . . . .1 Cor 11:9
*c* in Christ Jesus . . . . . . . . Eph 2:10
*c* in righteousness. . . . . . Eph 4:24
were all things *c*. . . . . . . . .Col 1:16
which God hath *c* . . . . . .1 Tim 4:3
for thou hast *c*. . . . . . . . . .Rev 4:11
*See* Gen 6:7; Deut 4:32; Ps 51:10

## CREATION
But from the beginning
    of the *c* . . . . . . . . . . . .Mark 10:6
beginning of the *c*. . . . . Mark 13:19
from the *c* . . . . . . . . . . . .Rom 1:20
whole *c* groaneth. . . . . . Rom 8:22

## CREATOR
Remember now thy *C* in
    the days . . . . . . . . . . . . .Eccl 12:1
the *C* of the ends . . . . . . . .Is 40:28
more than the *C*. . . . . . . .Rom 1:25
unto a faithful *C*. . . . . . . .1 Pet 4:19

## CREATURE
came the likeness of four
    living *c*. . . . . . . . . . . . . .Ezek 1:5
gospel to every *c*. . . . . . Mark 16:15
expectation of the *c* . . . .Rom 8:19
nor any other *c* . . . . . . . Rom 8:39
he is a new *c* . . . . . . . . . . 2 Cor 5:17
but a new *c* . . . . . . . . . . . . Gal 6:15
firstborn of every *c* . . . . . .Col 1:15
preached to every *c*. . . . . .Col 1:23
every *c* of God . . . . . . . . . .1 Tim 4:4
*See* Gen 1:20; 2:19; Ezek 1:20

## CROOKED
is *c* cannot be made
    straight. . . . . . . . . . . . . . .Eccl 1:15
which he hath made *c*. . .Eccl 7:13
the *c* shall be. . . . . . . . . . . .Is 40:4
*c* things straight . . . . . . . . Is 42:16

make the *c* places. . . . . . . . . Is 45:2
made them *c* paths. . . . . . .Is 59:8
hath made my paths *c*. . .Lam 3:9
*c* and perverse nation . . Phil 2:15
*See* Deut 32:5; Job 26:13

## CROSS
deny himself, and take
    up his *c* . . . . . . . . . . . .Matt 16:24
to bear his *c*. . . . . . . . . .Matt 27:32
come down from
    the *c* . . . . . . . . . . . . . .Matt 27:40
take up the *c*. . . . . . . . . .Mark 10:21
Rufus, to bear his *c* . . . .Mark 15:21
come down from
    the *c* . . . . . . . . . . . . . .Mark 15:30
take up his *c* daily . . . . . .Luke 9:23
they laid the *c* . . . . . . . .Luke 23:26
stood by the *c* . . . . . . . . John 19:25
the *c* of Christ. . . . . . . . . . 1 Cor 1:17
preaching of the *c* . . . . .1 Cor 1:18
offence of the *c* . . . . . . . . .Gal 5:11
persecution for the *c* . . . .Gal 6:12
glory, save in the *c*. . . . . . Gal 6:14
reconcile . . . by the *c* . . . . Eph 2:16
the death of the *c*. . . . . . . Phil 2:8
enemies of the *c* . . . . . . . .Phil 3:18
blood of his *c* . . . . . . . . . . .Col 1:20
nailing it to his *c*. . . . . . . . Col 2:14
endured the *c*. . . . . . . . . .Heb 12:2
*See* Matt 10:38; John 19:17, 19

## CROWN
taken the *c* from
    my head . . . . . . . . . . . . . .Job 19:9
*c* him with glory. . . . . . . . . .Ps 8:5
*c* the year with. . . . . . . . . Ps 65:11
*c* thee with loving-
    kindness. . . . . . . . . . . . . .Ps 103:4
a *c* of glory. . . . . . . . . . . . . Prov 4:9
woman is a *c* to her. . . . . .Prov 12:4
prudent are *c* . . . . . . . . .Prov 14:18
children are the *c* . . . . . .Prov 17:6
woe to the *c* of pride . . . . . .Is 28:1
platted a *c* of thorns. . . .Matt 27:29
corruptible *c*. . . . . . . . . . 1 Cor 9:25
my joy and *c* . . . . . . . . . . . .Phil 4:1
or *c* of rejoicing. . . . . . .1 Thess 2:19
not *c*, except he. . . . . . . . . 2 Tim 2:5
a *c* of righteousness . . . . 2 Tim 4:8
thou *c* him with . . . . . . . . . Heb 2:7
death, *c* with glory . . . . . .Heb 2:9
the *c* of life. . . . . . . . . . . . .James 1:12
a *c* of glory. . . . . . . . . . . . . .1 Pet 5:4
I will give thee a *c* . . . . . .Rev 2:10
no man take thy *c* . . . . . . . Rev 3:11
cast their *c* . . . . . . . . . . . . .Rev 4:10
head were many *c* . . . . . .Rev 19:12
*See* Ex 25:25; 29:6; Job 31:36

## CRUCIFY
all say unto him, let
    him be *c* . . . . . . . . . . . Matt 27:22
again, *C* him . . . . . . . . . . Mark 15:13
*C* him, *c* him . . . . . . . . .Luke 23:21
away with him, *c* him . . .John 19:15
wicked hands have *c* . . . .Acts 2:23
that our old man is *c* . . . . Rom 6:6
was Paul *c* for you. . . . . .1 Cor 1:13
we preach Christ *c*. . . . . .1 Cor 1:23
Jesus Christ, and him *c* . . .1 Cor 2:2
would not have *c* . . . . . . .1 Cor 2:8
though he was *c* . . . . . . . 2 Cor 13:4
I am *c* with Christ . . . . . . .Gal 2:20
*c* among you. . . . . . . . . . . . Gal 3:1
have *c* the flesh. . . . . . . . . Gal 5:24
the world is *c* unto me . . .Gal 6:14
*c* to themselves. . . . . . . . . .Heb 6:6
*See* Matt 20:19; 23:34; 27:31

## CUP
head with oil, my *c* run-
    neth over. . . . . . . . . . . . .Ps 23:5
*c* of cold water. . . . . . . Matt 10:42
drink of the *c* . . . . . . . . .Matt 20:22

## CURSE (n.)

the outside of the c.... Matt 23:25
he took the c.......... Matt 26:27
let this c pass ......... Matt 26:39
give you a c ............. Mark 9:41
And he took the c..... Mark 14:23
this c from me....... Mark 14:36
This c is the new ..... Luke 22:20
remove this c.........Luke 22:42
c which my Father.....John 18:11
c of blessing ........... 1 Cor 10:16
he took the c........... 1 Cor 11:25
ye ... drink this c......1 Cor 11:26
drink this c ........... 1 Cor 11:27
*See* Gen 40:11; 44:2; Prov 23:31

## CURSE (n.)

you this day a blessing
    and a c............... Deut 11:26
turned the c into ...... Deut 23:5
ye are cursed with a c .... Mal 3:9
ye c into ............... Matt 25:41
are under the c .......... Gal 3:10
no more c................ Rev 22:3
*See* Gen 27:12, Num 5:18

## CURSE (v.)

not c the deaf............Lev 19:14
How shall I c...........Num 23:8
c ye bitterly...........Judg 5:23
c God, and die ............Job 2:9
but they c inwardly........Ps 62:4
c your blessings ........ Mal 2:2
bless them that c ...... Matt 5:44
Then began he to c ..... Matt 26:74
tree which thou c......Mark 11:21
But he began to c...... Mark 14:71
them that c you.......Luke 6:28
the law are c............John 7:49
bless, and c not.......Rom 12:14
C is every one............ Gal 3:10
therewith c we men....James 3:9
*See* Gen 8:21; 12:3; Num 22:6

---

# D

## DAILY

sorrow in my heart d....... Ps 13:2
d loadeth us ..............Ps 68:19
I was d his delight......Prov 8:30
the d sacrifice ...........Dan 8:11
shall take away the d....Dan 11:31
our d bread...............Matt 6:11
take up his cross d......Luke 9:23
us day by day our d.......Luke 11:3
added to the church d...Acts 2:47
the d ministration........ Acts 6:1
increased in number d... Acts 16:5
the scriptures d.........Acts 17:11
I die d....................1 Cor 15:31
destitute of d food.....James 2:15
*See* Num 4:16; 28:24; Neh 5:18

## DAMNATION

can ye escape the d
    of hell................Matt 23:33
danger of eternal d ....Mark 3:29
resurrection of d .......John 5:29
to themselves d ........Rom 13:2
and drinketh d..........1 Cor 11:29
d slumbereth not...... 2 Pet 2:3
*See* Matt 23:14; Mark 12:40

## DAMNED

he that believeth not
    shall be d ........... Mark 16:16
doubteth is d .......... Rom 14:23
all might be d.........2 Thess 2:12

## DANGER

shall be in d of the
    judgment..............Matt 5:21
is in d of eternal .......Mark 3:29

## DARK

they grope in the d .....Job 12:25

---

open my d saying..........Ps 49:4
Let their eyes be d....... Ps 69:23
known in the d ........... Ps 88:12
their d sayings............ Prov 1:6
stars, be not d ......... Eccl 12:2
the windows be d ........ Eccl 12:3
be clear, nor d ......... Zech 14:6
shall the sun be d....... Matt 24:29
the sun shall be d......Mark 13:24
sun was d...............Luke 23:45
it was yet d ............ John 20:1
foolish heart was d...... Rom 1:21
understanding d......... Eph 4:18
*See* Ex 10:15; Joel 2:10

## DARKNESS

enlighten my d ..........Ps 18:28
that walketh in d ......... Ps 91:6
Such as sit in d ........ Ps 107:10
light in the d........... Ps 112:4
d and the light.......... Ps 139:12
in obscure d ...........Prov 20:20
light excelleth d ........ Eccl 2:13
fool walketh in d ....... Eccl 2:14
d be as the noon day ..... Is 58:10
d shall cover the earth.... Is 60:2
A day of d................ Joel 2:2
shall be full of d ...... Matt 6:23
out into outer d ........ Matt 8:12
What I tell you in d.... Matt 10:27
into outer d............. Matt 22:13
that sit in d ............ Luke 1:79
is full of d............. Luke 11:34
ye have spoken in d .... Luke 12:3
the power of d.........Luke 22:53
d over all the earth ....Luke 23:44
d comprehended it not...John 1:5
loved d rather than..... John 3:19
the light, lest d ...... John 12:35
from d to light........Acts 26:18
which are in d .......... Rom 2:19
the works of d..........Rom 13:12
hidden things of d....... 1 Cor 4:5
shine out of d...........2 Cor 4:6
hath light with d....... 2 Cor 6:14
works of d ................Eph 5:11
rulers of the d .......... Eph 6:12
the power of d............Col 1:13
night, nor of d .........1 Thess 5:5
out of d into ............ 1 Pet 2:9
into chains of d ........ 2 Pet 2:4
in him is no d.......... 1 John 1:5
and walk in d ......... 1 John 1:6
the d is past............1 John 2:8
hateth . . . is in d.......1 John 2:9
d hath blinded
    his eyes.............. 1 John 2:11
kingdom was full of d ...Rev 16:10
*See* Gen 1:2; 15:12; Ex 10:21

## DAY

old and full of d........ 1 Chr 23:1
our d on the earth ..... 1 Chr 29:15
d of an hireling ............ Job 7:1
d upon earth are..........Job 8:9
accomplish . . . his d ...... Job 14:6
stand at the latter d .... Job 19:25
d of destruction ........ Job 21:30
I said, D should speak ....Job 32:7
For length of d...........Prov 3:2
Length of d is in .......Prov 3:16
unto the perfect d.......Prov 4:18
what a d may bring......Prov 27:1
d of death................Eccl 7:1
while the evil d........Eccl 12:1
the d of the Lord ........Is 2:12
the d of visitation .......... Is 10:3
acceptable d............... Is 58:5
and the Ancient of d......Dan 7:9
for the d................Joel 1:15
the d of the Lord ........Joel 2:11
The great d .............Zeph 1:14
d of small things........Zech 4:10
d of his coming.......... Mal 3:2

---

great and dreadful d......Mal 4:5
Give us this d............Matt 6:11
d and hour knoweth...Matt 24:36
a d when he looketh...Matt 24:50
the d nor the hour..... Matt 25:13
of that d ...............Mark 13:32
that d come............Luke 21:34
again at the last d ......John 6:39
rejoiced to see my d ....John 8:56
while it is d............John 9:4
the d of Pentecost ...... Acts 2:1
great and notable d......Acts 2:20
d of wrath ............... Rom 2:5
esteemeth every d.......Rom 14:5
d of salvation............ 2 Cor 6:2
the d of Jesus Christ......Phil 1:6
d of the Lord..........1 Thess 5:2
children of the d.......1 Thess 5:5
d is with the Lord ....... 2 Pet 3:8
But the d of............ 2 Pet 3:10
*See* Gen 1:5; Job 1:4; Ps 77:5

## DAYSPRING

caused the d to know
    his place.............. Job 38:12
d from on high ........ Luke 1:78

## DAY STAR

d arise in your hearts....2 Pet 1:19

## DEAD

cuttings in your flesh
    for the d ............. Lev 19:28
dealt with the d.......... Ruth 1:8
forgotten as a d man ..... Ps 31:12
d praise not the Lord....Ps 115:17
the d are there..........Prov 9:18
which are already d ...... Eccl 4:2
d know not any thing .... Eccl 9:5
Thy d men shall live..... Is 26:19
Weep ye not for the d ... Jer 22:10
let the d bury ........... Matt 8:22
the d are raised up ...... Matt 11:5
God of the d ........... Matt 22:32
full of d men's bones .. Matt 23:27
the damsel is not d.....Mark 5:39
the rising from the d ...Mark 9:10
the d are raised........ Luke 7:22
For this my son was d...Luke 15:24
rose from the d ....... Luke 16:31
d shall hear ............John 5:25
and are d ...............John 6:49
though he were d...... John 11:25
he that was d .......... John 11:44
quick and d.............Acts 10:42
rise from the d........ Acts 26:23
that are d to sin........ Rom 6:2
if we be d with Christ... Rom 6:8
d indeed unto sin........Rom 6:11
d to the law...............Rom 7:4
Lord both of the d ..... Rom 14:9
the d rise not ...........1 Cor 15:15
How are the d raised....1 Cor 15:35
raiseth the d............ 2 Cor 1:9
then were all d.......... 2 Cor 5:14
through the law am d ... Gal 2:19
were d in trespasses.......Eph 2:1
arise from the d ........ Eph 5:14
firstborn from the d......Col 1:18
And you, being d ......... Col 2:13
if ye be d with Christ ....Col 2:20
d in Christ ........... 1 Thess 4:16
d while she liveth........1 Tim 5:6
we be d with him....... 2 Tim 2:11
quick and the d.........2 Tim 4:1
from d works ............ Heb 6:1
your conscience from d...Heb 9:14
being d yet speaketh .....Heb 11:4
again from the d........Heb 13:20
is d, being alone.......James 2:17
without works is d ... James 2:20
being d to sins........... 1 Pet 2:24
to them that are d........1 Pet 4:6
without fruit, twice d .... Jude 12

begotten of the *d* ......... Rev 1:5
liveth, and was *d* ........ Rev 1:18
and art *d* .................. Rev 3:1
Blessed are the *d* ....... Rev 14:13
rest of the *d* ............. Rev 20:5
the *d*, small ............. Rev 20:12
sea gave up the *d* ....... Rev 20:13
*See* Gen 23:3; Mark 9:26

## DEAF
shall the *d* hear ........... Is 29:18
the *d* hear ................ Matt 11:5
both the *d* to hear ....... Mark 7:37
dumb and *d* spirit ...... Mark 9:25

## DEATH
these men die the
  common of all .... Num 16:29
*d* of the righteous ..... Num 23:10
but *d* part thee ......... Ruth 1:17
When the waves of *d*.. 2 Sam 22:5
in *d* there is ............. Ps 6:5
the sleep of *d* ........... Ps 13:3
The sorrows of *d* ........ Ps 18:4
the shadow of *d* ......... Ps 23:4
our guide even unto *d*.... Ps 48:14
the issues from *d* ....... Ps 68:20
shall not see *d* ......... Ps 89:48
appointed to *d* ......... Ps 102:20
in the shadow of *d*...... Ps 107:10
precious ... is the *d* .... Ps 116:15
to the chambers of *d* ... Prov 7:27
that hate me love *d* .... Prov 8:36
hope in his *d* .......... Prov 14:32
drawn unto *d* ........ Prov 24:11
love is strong as *d* ...... Song 8:6
shadow of *d* ............. Is 9:2
He will swallow up *d* ..... Is 25:8
*d* cannot celebrate........ Is 38:18
rich in his *d* ............ Is 53:9
his soul unto *d* ......... Is 53:12
the shadow of *d* ........ Jer 2:6
*d* shall be chosen ...... Jer 8:3
pleasure in the *d* .. Ezek 18:32
*d* of the wicked ........ Ezek 33:11
O *d*, I will be ........ Hos 13:14
let him die the *d* ....... Matt 15:4
not taste of *d* ......... Matt 16:28
sorrowful, even
  unto *d* ............ Matt 26:38
at the point of *d* ...... Mark 5:23
sorrowful unto *d* ..... Mark 14:34
should not see *d*....... Luke 2:26
and to *d* ............ Luke 22:33
at the point of *d* ...... John 4:47
from *d* unto life......... John 5:24
shall never see *d* ...... John 8:51
never taste of *d* ....... John 8:52
sickness is not unto *d* .. John 11:4
signifying what *d*...... John 12:33
*d* he should glorify ... John 21:19
the pains of *d* .........Acts 2:24
worthy of *d* ........... Rom 1:32
by the *d* of his Son...... Rom 5:10
*d* by sin .............. Rom 5:12
*d* reigned from Adam.... Rom 5:14
likeness of his *d* ....... Rom 6:5
those things is *d* ....... Rom 6:21
wages of sin is *d* ....... Rom 6:23
law of sin and *d* ........ Rom 8:2
life, or *d* ............... 1 Cor 3:22
shew the Lord's *d* .... 1 Cor 11:26
by man came *d* ....... 1 Cor 15:21
O *d*, where is thy ...... 1 Cor 15:55
sting of *d* is sin ...... 1 Cor 15:56
sentence of *d* ......... 2 Cor 1:9
savour of *d* unto *d*..... 2 Cor 2:16
*d* worketh in us....... 2 Cor 4:12
frequent, in *d* oft ...... 2 Cor 11:23
*d*, even the........... Phil 2:8
flesh through *d* ......... Col 1:22
taste *d* for every man..... Heb 2:9
fear of *d* ................. Heb 2:15
bringeth forth *d* ...... James 1:15

have passed from *d* ...1 John 3:14
There is a sin unto *d*... 1 John 5:16
keys of hell and of *d* ..... Rev 1:18
be thou faithful unto *d*.. Rev 2:10
of the second *d* .......... Rev 2:11
sat on him was *D* ........ Rev 6:8
seek *d* ... and *d* ........ Rev 9:6
*d* and hell delivered up .. Rev 20:13
be no more *d* ...........Rev 21:4
*See* Prov 14:12; John 18:31

## DEBT
forgave him the *d* ..... Matt 18:27
*See* Matt 6:12; Rom 4:4

## DEBTOR
as we forgive our *d* ..... Matt 6:12
I am *d* both .............. Rom 1:14
*d* to do the whole law ..... Gal 5:3

## DECEIT
full of cursing and *d* ...... Ps 10:7
iniquity and *d* ........... Ps 36:3
*d* men shall not.......... Ps 55:23
the wicked are *d*........ Prov 12:5
Bread of *d* is sweet .... Prov 20:17
of an enemy are *d* ..... Prov 27:6
Favour is *d*............. Prov 31:30
the *d* of their heart ...... Jer 14:14
heart is *d* above ......... Jer 17:9
*d* of their own heart ..... Jer 23:26
work of the Lord *d* ..... Jer 48:10
of Israel with *d* ......... Hos 11:12
balances by *d* ......... Amos 8:5
with violence and *d* ..... Zeph 1:9
the *d* of riches ........ Matt 13:22
wickedness, *d* ......... Mark 7:22
they have used *d* ....... Rom 3:13
the word of God *d* ..... 2 Cor 4:2
*d* workers............... 2 Cor 11:13
the *d* lusts ............. Eph 4:22
vain *d*, after............. Col 2:8
*See* Ps 50:19; Prov 12:20

## DECEIVE
that your heart be
  not *d*.................. Deut 11:16
*d* and the deceiver are.... Job 12:16
whosoever is *d* ........ Prov 20:1
pride ... hath *d* thee...... Obad 3
no man *d* you.......... Matt 24:4
that *d* said ............. Matt 27:63
he *d* the people........ John 7:12
Are ye also *d* ........ John 7:47
Be not *d* ............... 1 Cor 6:9
*d*; evil communi-
  cations................ 1 Cor 15:33
as *d*, and yet true........ 2 Cor 6:8
Be not *d*; God is not ...... Gal 6:7
lie in wait to *d* .......... Eph 4:14
Let no man *d* you ....... Eph 5:6
*d* you by any means .. 2 Thess 2:3
Adam was not *d* ........ 1 Tim 2:14
*d*, and being *d* ...... 2 Tim 3:13
we *d* ourselves ......... 1 John 1:8
let no man *d* you ...... 1 John 3:7
*d* are entered into ........ 2 John 7
*See* Gen 31:7; Ezek 14:9

## DECENTLY
all things be done *d* ... 1 Cor 14:40

## DECISION
multitudes in the
  valley of *d* ............. Joel 3:14

## DECREASE
but I must *d* ............. John 3:30

## DEED
for our evil *d*............ Ezra 9:13
out my good *d*........ Neh 13:14
according to their *d* ...... Ps 28:4
According to their *d* ..... Is 59:18
*d* of your father...... Luke 11:48
due reward of our *d* ... Luke 23:41
mighty in *d* ......... Luke 24:19
because their *d* ........ John 3:19

Ye do the *d* of your ..... John 8:41
in words and in *d*........ Acts 7:22
by the *d* of the law..... Rom 3:20
faith without the *d* ..... Rom 3:28
the *d* of the body ....... Rom 8:13
old man with his *d* ..... Col 3:9
ye do in word or *d*....... Col 3:17
blessed in his *d* ....... James 1:25
in *d* and in truth....... 1 John 3:18
of his evil *d* ............. 2 John 11
their ungodly *d*.......... Jude 15
*See* Gen 44:15; Acts 19:18

## DEFENCE
the Almighty shall
  be thy *d*................ Job 22:25
My *d* is of God ......... Ps 7:10
for God is my *d* ..........Ps 59:9
he is my *d*................Ps 62:2
Lord is our *d*............Ps 89:18
the Lord is my *d* ...... Ps 94:22
wisdom is a *d*........... Eccl 7:12

## DEFEND
shout for joy, because thou
  *d* them.................Ps 5:11
*D* the poor ............. Ps 82:3
shall *d* them ............. Zech 9:15
*See* Ps 20:1; 59:1; Is 31:5

## DEFILE
*d* my sanctuary........ Ezek 23:38
they *d* it by their....... Ezek 36:17
would not *d* himself..... Dan 1:8
into the mouth *d* ...... Matt 15:11
they *d* the man...... Matt 15:18
the things which *d* ..... Matt 15:20
that *d* the man......... Mark 7:15
from within, and *d* ..... Mark 7:23
they should be *d*...... John 18:28
*d* the temple............ 1 Cor 3:17
being weak is *d*........1 Cor 8:7
that *d* themselves ...... 1 Tim 1:10
them that are *d* ........ Titus 1:15
conscience is *d* ........ Titus 1:15
thereby many be *d* .... Heb 12:15
filthy dreamers *d*........ Jude 8
which have not *d* ........Rev 3:4
*See* Lev 21:4; James 3:6

## DEFRAUD
*D* not, Honour........ Mark 10:19
yourselves to be *d*...... 1 Cor 6:7
*D* ye not one........... 1 Cor 7:5
*See* Lev 19:13; 1 Thess 4:6

## DELIGHT (n.)
Lord had a *d* in thy
  fathers................ Deut 10:15
great *d* in burnt....... 1 Sam 15:22
no *d* in thee.......... 2 Sam 15:26
*d* in the Almighty....... Job 22:26
his *d* is in the law......... Ps 1:2
in whom is all my *d* ....... Ps 16:3
Thy testimonies
  ... my *d*............... Ps 119:24
thy law is my *d* ......... Ps 119:77
commandments
  are my *d*.............. Ps 119:143
I was daily his *d* ....... Prov 8:30
my *d* were with......... Prov 8:31
fool hath no *d* ......... Prov 18:2
*D* is not seemly........ Prov 19:10
*See* Prov 11:1; 12:22; 15:8

## DELIGHT (v.)
Will he *d* himself in the
  Almighty .............. Job 27:10
*D* thyself also .......... Ps 37:4
*d* themselves in the ...... Ps 37:11
thou *d* not in burnt...... Ps 51:16
in whom my soul *d*....... Is 42:1
the Lord *d* in thee ...... Is 62:4
he *d* in mercy............ Mic 7:18
I *d* in the law ........... Rom 7:22
*See* Num 14:8; Prov 1:22; 2:14

# DELIVER

## DELIVER

am come down to *d* them... Ex 3:8
shall *d* thee ................Job 5:19
he *d* any ...................Ps 33:17
*d* my feet from............Ps 56:13
he shall *d* thee ............Ps 91:3
*d* David his servant.....Ps 144:10
forbear to *d* them......Prov 24:11
by his wisdom *d* .......Eccl 9:15
have I no power to *d* .....Is 50:2
with them to *d* thee.......Jer 1:8
*d* thee in that day........Jer 39:17
is able to *d* us...........Dan 3:17
*d* us from him............Matt 6:13
things are *d* unto me...Matt 11:27
being *d* by the ..........Acts 2:23
*d* for our offences ......Rom 4:25
we are *d* from the law...Rom 7:6
*d* from the bondage ... Rom 8:21
*d* unto death............2 Cor 4:11
*d* me from ............. 2 Tim 4:18
*See* 2 Cor 1:10; Gal 1:4

## DELIVERANCE

by a great *d*.............1 Chr 11:14
the songs of *d* ...........Ps 32:7
*d* to the captives........Luke 4:18

## DENY

lest ye *d* your God .....Josh 24:27
whosoever shall *d* .....Matt 10:33
let him *d* himself ....Matt 16:24
he cannot *d* himself ...2 Tim 2:13
in works they *d* him.... Titus 1:16
*See* 2 Tim 3:5; Titus 2:12

## DEPART

sceptre shall not *d*
from Judah........Gen 49:10
*d* from my God ...... 2 Sam 22:22
God, *D* from us ..........Job 21:14
to *d* from evil...........Job 28:28
*D* from me...............Ps 6:8
*D* from evil..............Ps 34:14
he may *d* from hell ....Prov 15:24
not *d* from it..........Prov 22:6
*d* from me ..............Matt 7:23
*D* from me, ye cursed ...Matt 25:41
*d* out of this world......John 13:1
not the wife *d* ..........1 Cor 7:10
desire to *d* ............Phil 1:23
*d* from the faith ........1 Tim 4:1
*d* from iniquity........2 Tim 2:19
*See* Mic 2:10; 2 Tim 4:6

## DESCEND

with them that *d* into
the pit................Ezek 26:20
Spirit of God *d*......... Matt 3:16
like a dove *d*........... Mark 1:10
king of Israel *d* .......Mark 15:32
the Holy Ghost *d* ....Luke 3:22
I saw the Spirit *d* ...... John 1:32
He that *d* is the ......... Eph 4:10
*d* from heaven........1 Thess 4:16
This wisdom *d* not ...James 3:15
*d* out of heaven.........Rev 21:10
*See* Gen 28:12; Ps 49:17; 133:3

## DESERT

the *d* shall rejoice...........Is 35:1
streams in the *d*........... Is 35:6
make straight in the *d*.....Is 40:3
rivers in the *d*........... Is 43:19
and was in the *d*........Luke 1:80
into a *d* place ...........Luke 9:10
eat manna in the *d* .....John 6:31
*See* Ex 5:3; 19:2; Is 51:3

## DESIRE (n.)

sought him with their
whole *d*.............. 2 Chr 15:15
of his heart's *d*...........Ps 10:3
*d* of thine heart........Ps 37:4
*d* of the wicked..........Ps 112:10
the *d* of the ...........Ps 140:8
satisfiest the *d*.........Ps 145:16

but the *d*...............Prov 10:24
*d* of the righteous ......Prov 11:23
*d* shall fail.............. Eccl 12:5
*d* of thine ..............Ezek 24:16
*d* of your eyes..........Ezek 24:21
the *d* of all nations ...... Hag 2:7
With *d* I have .........Luke 22:15
*d* of the flesh............ Eph 2:3
having a *d* to depart...... Phil 1:23
*See* Gen 3:16; Job 14:15; 31:16

## DESIRE (v.)

whatsoever thy
soul *d*................ Deut 14:26
as thy soul *d*........... 1 Sam 2:16
whom ye have *d*......1 Sam 12:13
*d* to reason with God ....Job 13:3
More to be *d*............ Ps 19:10
One thing have I *d*.......Ps 27:4
that *d* life ...............Ps 34:12
that I *d* beside .........Ps 73:25
things thou canst *d*........Prov 3:15
that may be *d* are....... Prov 8:11
soul of the sluggard *d* ...Prov 13:4
eyes *d* I kept ............Eccl 2:10
that we should *d* ......... Is 53:2
I *d* mercy............. Hos 6:6
my soul *d* the first........ Mic 7:1
O nation not *d*...........Zeph 2:1
If any *d* to be first ......Mark 9:35
ye *d*, when ye pray ... Mark 11:24
*d* spiritual gifts ........1 Cor 14:1
*d* to be clothed upon .... 2 Cor 5:2
*d* a better country ......Heb 11:16
and *d* to have ...........James 4:2
the angels *d*............ 1 Pet 1:12
as newborn babes *d*......1 Pet 2:2
petitions that we *d* ....1 John 5:15
*See* Gen 3:6; Job 7:2, Ps 51:6

## DESPISE

ye have *d* the Lord..... Num 11:20
he hath *d* the word ..... Num 15:31
that *d* me shall be ....1 Sam 2:30
thou wilt not *d* .........Ps 51:17
God hath *d* them .........Ps 53:5
not *d* their prayer........Ps 102:17
fools *d* wisdom..........Prov 1:7
*d* all my reproof ........Prov 1:30
heart *d* reproof ........Prov 5:12
Whoso *d* the word........Prov 13:13
A fool *d* his.............Prov 15:5
*d* his mother........Prov 15:20
*d* his own soul........Prov 15:32
wisdom is *d* ............Eccl 9:16
*d* the word of the .........Is 5:24
Because ye *d* this word... Is 30:12
to him whom man *d* ...... Is 49:7
He is *d* and rejected ....... Is 53:3
*d* among men...........Jer 49:15
*d* my judgments......Ezek 20:13
*d* mine holy things ..... Ezek 22:8
they have *d* the law..... Amos 2:4
who hath *d* the day..... Zech 4:10
we *d* thy name............Mal 1:6
and *d* the other........Matt 6:24
*d* not one of these ..... Matt 18:10
that *d* you *d* me....... Luke 10:16
and he that *d* me ......Luke 10:16
righteous, and *d*
others ................Luke 18:9
*d* thou the riches ...... Rom 2:4
things which are *d*..... 1 Cor 1:28
but we are *d* ...........1 Cor 4:10
*d* ye the church
of God ................1 Cor 11:22
Let no man ... *d* him... 1 Cor 16:11
*d* not man, but God...1 Thess 4:8
*D* not prophesyings ...1 Thess 5:20
Let no man *d* ..........1 Tim 4:12
Let no man *d* thee.... Titus 2:15
*d* the shame ...........Heb 12:2
ye have *d* the poor.....James 2:6
*See* Gen 16:4; 25:34; 2 Sam 6:16

## DESTROY

*d* the righteous with the
wicked.................Gen 18:23
he shall be utterly *d*..... Ex 22:20
that I may *d* them ...... Deut 9:14
to *d* him ....................Job 2:3
yet thou dost *d* me ......Job 10:8
He hath *d* me............Job 19:10
my skin worms *d*....... Job 19:26
seek after my soul
to *d* it ................Ps 40:14
the wicked will he *d*.....Ps 145:20
fools shall *d*..............Prov 1:32
is *d* for want of
judgment............Prov 13:23
that which *d* kings......Prov 31:3
one sinner *d* much ......Eccl 9:18
it is in his heart to *d*......Is 10:7
shall not hurt nor *d*....... Is 11:9
I will *d* the counsel........Is 19:3
but *d* them...............Jer 13:14
pastors that *d*............ Jer 23:1
with his *d* weapon.......Ezek 9:1
*d* souls.................Ezek 22:27
thou hast *d* thyself ...... Hos 13:9
not come to *d*..........Matt 5:17
him that is able to *d*.... Matt 10:28
art thou come to *d* us ... Mark 1:24
I will *d* this temple ......Mark 14:58
save life, or *d* it ....... Luke 6:9
is not come to *d* ........Luke 9:56
*D* this temple...........John 2:19
*d* with the
brightness.......... 2 Thess 2:8
*d* him .....................Heb 2:14
to save and to *d*...........James 4:12
*d* the works...............1 John 3:8
*See* Gen 6:17; Is 65:8; Rom 6:6

## DESTRUCTION

to his *d*...................2 Chr 22:4
heart was lifted up
to his *d* ..............2 Chr 26:16
be afraid of *d* ............Job 5:21
your *d* cometh...........Prov 1:27
Pride goeth before *d* ...Prov 16:18
seeketh *d*..............Prov 17:19
fool's mouth is his *d*....Prov 18:7
are appointed to *d*......Prov 31:8
the besom of *d* ...........Is 14:23
The city of *d* ...........Is 19:18
I will be thy *d*...........Hos 13:14
that leadeth to *d*........Matt 7:13
*D* and misery ...........Rom 3:16
fitted to *d*...............Rom 9:22
Whose end is *d* .........Phil 3:19
sudden *d* cometh.......1 Thess 5:3
with everlasting *d*.....2 Thess 1:9
drown men in *d* .........1 Tim 6:9
swift *d* ...................2 Pet 2:1
unto their own *d* ....... 2 Pet 3:16
*See* Job 21:20; Prov 10:29; 21:15

## DEVICE

be taken in the *d*..........Ps 10:2

## DEVIL

offer their sacrifices
unto *d* ................ Lev 17:7
tempted of the *d* ........Matt 4:1
two possessed with *d*... Matt 8:28
prepared for the *d*..... Matt 25:41
an unclean *d*...........Luke 4:33
*d* also came out......... Luke 4:41
went seven *d* ...........Luke 8:2
your father the *d* ......John 8:44
the *d* also believe......James 2:19
Resist the *d*............James 4:7
your adversary the *d* ....1 Pet 5:8
*See* Deut 32:17; Ps 106:37

## DEVOUT

the same man was
just and *d*.............Luke 2:25
Jews, *d* men ...........Acts 2:5

*d* men carried ...........Acts 8:2
*See* Acts 10:2; 13:50; 17:4, 17

## DIE
eatest thereof thou shalt
  surely *d*..................Gen 2:17
lest ye *d*....................Gen 3:3
thou shalt surely *d* ......Gen 20:7
that *d* of itself ............Lev 7:24
That which *d* of itself.... Lev 22:8
*d* the common death.... Num 16:29
let me *d* the death.....Num 23:10
that *d* of itself ..........Deut 14:21
that thou must *d* .......Deut 31:14
thou *d*, will I *d*..........Ruth 1:17
for thou shalt *d* .......2 Kin 20:1
*d* for his own sin.......2 Chr 25:4
curse God, and *d*.........Job 2:9
wisdom shall *d* .........Job 12:2
If a man *d*.................Job 14:14
*d* without instruction .. Prov 5:23
fools *d* for want.......Prov 10:21
a wicked man *d*......... Prov 11:7
how *d* the wise man.... Eccl 2:16
*d* before thy time......Eccl 7:17
they shall *d* ...............Eccl 9:5
worm shall not *d* ........Is 66:24
will ye *d*................. Jer 27:13
this year thou shalt *d*... Jer 28:16
Thou shalt *d* in peace ... Jer 34:5
Thou shalt surely *d*.... Ezek 3:18
it shall *d* ...............Ezek 18:4
why will ye *d* ..........Ezek 18:31
thou shalt surely *d* ....Ezek 33:8
let him *d* the death......Matt 15:4
Where their worm *d*....Mark 9:44
shall never *d*...........John 11:26
one man should *d* .....John 11:50
will one *d*...................Rom 5:7
sin revived, and I *d*.......Rom 7:9
It is Christ that *d* ......Rom 8:34
no man *d* to himself.....Rom 14:7
Christ both *d*, and rose...Rom 14:9
for whom Christ *d*....Rom 14:15
for whom Christ *d*......1 Cor 8:11
Christ *d* for our sins .....1 Cor 15:3
as in Adam all *d*........ 1 Cor 15:22
I *d* daily................1 Cor 15:31
except it *d* ...........1 Cor 15:36
if one *d* for all........... 2 Cor 5:14
and to *d* is gain ..........Phil 1:21
that Jesus *d*...........1 Thess 4:14
Who *d* for us..........1 Thess 5:10
here men that *d* ........ Heb 7:8
unto men once to *d* ... Heb 9:27
These all *d* in faith...... Heb 11:13
ready to *d*..................Rev 3:2
shall desire to *d*..........Rev 9:6
the dead which *d* .......Rev 14:13
*See* Job 14:10; Ps 118:17

## DIRECT
will I *d* my prayer ..........Ps 5:3
he shall *d* thy paths......Prov 3:6
shall *d* his way..........Prov 11:5
the Lord *d* his steps .... Prov 16:9
he *d* his way ........Prov 21:29
profitable to *d* .........Eccl 10:10
to *d* his steps ............Jer 10:23
*d* your hearts ......... 2 Thess 3:5
*See* Gen 46:28; Is 45:13; 61:8

## DISCERN
can I *d* between good
  and evil.............2 Sam 19:35
a wise man's heart *d* ..... Eccl 8:5
cannot *d* between .......Jon 4:11
*d* the face of the sky .... Matt 16:3
are spiritually *d*.........1 Cor 2:14
not *d* the Lord's body ...1 Cor 11:29
another *d* of spirits.....1 Cor 12:10
a *d* of the thoughts ...... Heb 4:12
to *d* both good..........Heb 5:14
*See* Gen 27:23; 2 Sam 14:17

## DISCIPLE
his twelve *d*..............Matt 10:1
The *d* is not above..... Matt 10:24
took the twelve *d*..... Matt 20:17
all the *d* forsook him ... Matt 26:56
tell his *d* that he is..... Matt 28:7
His *d* came by night .. Matt 28:13
Why do the *d* of John... Mark 2:18
all things to his *d* .......Mark 4:34
his *d* eat bread..........Mark 7:2
Why walk not thy *d*.... Mark 7:5
his *d* rebuked those ... Mark 10:13
passover with my *d* ... Mark 14:14
against his *d*............Luke 5:30
*d* of John fast..........Luke 5:33
unto him his *d*......... Luke 6:13
his eyes on his *d*........Luke 6:20
John also taught his *d*... Luke 11:1
he cannot be my *d*..... Luke 14:26
*d* began to rejoice .....Luke 19:37
*d* believed on him ......John 2:11
many of his *d*
  went back ...........John 6:66
*d* also may see........... John 7:3
are ye my *d* indeed .... John 8:31
will ye also be his *d*.... John 9:27
Thou art his *d* ..........John 9:28
to wash the *d* feet ...... John 13:5
known that ye are
  my *d*..................John 13:35
so shall ye be my *d* ..... John 15:8
and the *d*
  standing by.........John 19:26
being a *d* of Jesus ....John 19:38
came and told the *d*... John 20:18
*d* whom Jesus loved....John 21:7
seeth the *d*..............John 21:20
*d* should not die .......John 21:23
against the *d*..............Acts 9:1
to the *d*.................Acts 9:26
*d* were called ............Acts 11:26
the *d* came together.....Acts 20:7
to draw away *d*........Acts 20:30
*See* Matt 11:1; John 3:25; 18:1

## DISCOURAGE
*d* ye the heart of the
  children .............. Num 32:7
neither be *d*.............Deut 1:21
have *d* our heart........ Deut 1:28
lest they be *d* ...........Col 3:21
*See* Num 21:4; 32:9; Is 42:4

## DISEASE
put none of these *d*
  upon thee ..............Ex 15:26
who healeth all thy *d*.....Ps 103:3
it is an evil *d*..............Eccl 6:2
The *d* have ye not ...... Ezek 34:4
*See* Matt 4:23; 14:35; Luke 9:1

## DISHONOUR
son *d* the father ..........Mic 7:6
and ye do *d* me ....... John 8:49
another unto *d* ........ Rom 9:21
It is sown in *d* ......... 1 Cor 15:43
By honour and *d*........ 2 Cor 6:8
and some to *d* ........2 Tim 2:20
*See* Rom 1:24; 2:23; 1 Cor 11:4, 5

## DISOBEDIENCE
by one man's *d* .........Rom 5:19
the children of *d*.........Eph 2:2
the children of *d* ........ Eph 5:6
transgression and *d* ...... Heb 2:2

## DISOBEDIENT
*d* to the wisdom........Luke 1:17
not *d* unto
  the ... vision .........Acts 26:19
*d* to parents ........ Rom 1:30
the lawless and *d*........ 1 Tim 1:9
*d* to parents ......... 2 Tim 3:2
sometimes foolish, *d*.... Titus 3:3
unto them which be *d*....1 Pet 2:7

Which sometime
  were *d*................1 Pet 3:20
*See* 1 Kin 13:26; Rom 10:21

## DISORDERLY
every brother that
  walketh *d*........... 2 Thess 3:6
behaved not our-
  selves *d*..............2 Thess 3:7
walk among you *d*.... 2 Thess 3:11

## DISPENSATION
a *d* of the gospel is
  committed ............1 Cor 9:17
the *d* of the fullness ......Eph 1:10
*d* of the grace of God ..... Eph 3:2
to the *d* of God............ Col 1:25

## DISSOLVE
host of heaven shall be *d*....Is 34:4
and *d* doubts ............. Dan 5:16
this tabernacle were *d*... 2 Cor 5:1
things shall be *d*........2 Pet 3:11
shall be *d* ................ 2 Pet 3:12
*See* Job 30:22; Ps 75:3; Dan 5:12

## DISTRIBUTE
*d* unto the poor........Luke 18:22
*D* to the necessity ......Rom 12:13
as God hath *d*............1 Cor 7:17
your liberal *d* ...........2 Cor 9:13
*See* Josh 13:32; 2 Cor 10:13

## DIVERS
a garment of *d* sorts....Deut 22:11
in thy bag *d* weights...Deut 25:13
*D* weights..............Prov 20:10
with *d* diseases........ Matt 4:24
in *d* places ............. Matt 24:7
sick of *d* diseases ......Mark 1:34
earthquakes in *d*
  places ...............Mark 13:8
sick with *d* diseases ....Luke 4:40
shall be in *d*.............Luke 21:11
*d* kinds of tongues......1 Cor 12:10
led away with *d* lusts....1 Tim 3:6
serving *d* lusts...........Titus 3:3
into *d* temptations ......James 1:2
*See* Eccl 5:7; Heb 1:1; 13:9

## DIVIDE
but *d* not the hoof... Lev 11:4, 5, 6
*D* the living child .......1 Kin 3:25
the innocent shall *d* ....Job 27:17
Every kingdom *d* ......Matt 12:25
Satan, he is *d*........... Matt 12:26
if a kingdom be *d*.......Mark 3:24
and be *d*, he
  cannot stand.........Mark 3:26
*d* against itself..........Luke 11:17
If Satan also be *d*........Luke 11:18
five in one house *d*...... Luke 12:52
Is Christ *d* ..............1 Cor 1:13
*d* to every man .........1 Cor 12:11
rightly *d* the word ......2 Tim 2:15
the *d* asunder of soul.... Heb 4:12
*See* Dan 7:25; Matt 25:32

## DIVINATION
is there any *d* against
  Israel .................Num 23:23
a spirit of *d* ...........Acts 16:16
*See* Deut 18:10; 2 Kin 17:17

## DIVINE (*v.*)
I can certainly *d* ........ Gen 44:15
*d* unto me .............1 Sam 28:8
and that *d* lies .......... Ezek 13:9
they *d* a lie.......... Ezek 21:29
prophets thereof *d* ....... Mic 3:11
*See* Gen 44:5; Ezek 22:28

## DIVINE (*adj.*)
A *d* sentence is in the
  lips of the............Prov 16:10
of *d* service ..............Heb 9:1
as his *d* power hath.......2 Pet 1:3
the *d* nature .............2 Pet 1:4

## DIVINER

called for the priests
and the *d* .............. 1 Sam 6:2
and maketh *d* mad ....... Is 44:25
to your *d* ................... Jer 27:9
your prophets and
your *d* ...................Jer 29:8

## DIVISION

will put a *d* between my
people.................. Ex 8:23
Nay; but rather *d* ...... Luke 12:51
them which cause *d* ...... Rom 16:17
*See* 1 Cor 1:10; 3:3; 11:18

## DIVORCE

then let him write her a
bill of *d* ............... Deut 24:1
her that is *d*............. Matt 5:32
write a bill of *d* ........ Mark 10:4

## DO

to *d* good in his life...... Eccl 3:12
should *d* to you.......... Matt 7:12
this *d* ...................Luke 10:28
this *d* in
remembrance .......Luke 22:19
ye can *d* nothing........ John 15:5
that *d* I not ........... Rom 7:15
I can *d* all things......... Phil 4:13
and not a *d* ...........James 1:23
*See* John 6:38; 10:37; Rev 19:10

## DOCTRINE

I give you good *d* .........Prov 4:2
make to understand *d*..... Is 28:9
a *d* of vanities............. Jer 10:8
astonished at his *d* ..... Matt 7:28
the *d* of the Pharisees... Matt 16:12
what new *d* is this...... Mark 1:27
know of the *d*............John 7:17
in the apostles' *d* ......Acts 2:42
with your *d* ...........Acts 5:28
what this new *d* ........ Acts 17:19
form of *d* ................Rom 6:17
contrary to the *d* ......Rom 16:17
hath a *d*................ 1 Cor 14:26
every wind of *d*......... Eph 4:14
contrary to sound *d* .... 1 Tim 1:10
and of good *d*...........1 Tim 4:6
to exhortation, to *d*.... 1 Tim 4:13
and unto the *d*......... 1 Tim 4:16
fully known my *d*...... 2 Tim 3:10
profitable for *d* ....... 2 Tim 3:16
all longsuffering and *d* ..2 Tim 4:2
by sound *d*.............. Titus 1:9
become sound *d*........ Titus 2:1
adorn the *d* of God .....Titus 2:10
principles of the *d*....... Heb 6:1
Of the *d* of baptisms...... Heb 6:2
and strange *d*........... Heb 13:9
abideth in the *d* ....... 2 John 9
*See* Deut 32:2; Job 11:4

## DOMINION

let them have *d*.......... Gen 1:26
shall have *d*........... Num 24:19
*d* over the works.......... Ps 8:6
let them not have *d*...... Ps 119:13
He shall have *d* .........Ps 72:8
have *d* over me ........ Ps 119:133
*d* is an everlasting *d* ... Dan 4:34
his *d* shall be from sea...Zech 9:10
Gentiles exercise *d* ....Matt 20:25
death hath no more *d* .... Rom 6:9
sin shall not have *d* ..... Rom 6:14
law hath *d* over a man.... Rom 7:1
that we have *d* ........ 2 Cor 1:24
and *d*, and every name ...Eph 1:21
they be thrones or *d* .......Col 1:16
*See* Dan 6:26; Jude 25; Rev 1:6

## DOOR

sin lieth at the *d* ..........Gen 4:7
on the upper *d* post ....... Ex 12:7
ye everlasting *d*............Ps 24:7

opened the *d* of heaven ... Ps 78:23
the *d* of my lips........... Ps 141:3
*d* shall be shut............ Eccl 12:4
for a *d* of hope .......... Hos 2:15
shut the *d* for nought..... Mal 1:10
by the *d*................... John 10:1
the *d* is the shepherd... John 10:2
I am the *d*.............. John 10:7, 9
at the *d* ...................Acts 5:9
opened the *d* of faith... Acts 14:27
a great *d* ............... 1 Cor 16:9
a *d* was opened .......... 2 Cor 2:12
open unto us a *d* .........Col 4:3
standeth before the *d* ... James 5:9
thee an open *d* .......... Rev 3:8
I stand at the *d* ......... Rev 3:20
behold, a *d* was opened ... Rev 4:1
*See* Ex 21:6; Acts 5:19; 16:26

## DOUBLE

he shall restore *d*........Ex 22:4
let him pay *d* ..............Ex 22:7
a *d* portion................2 Kin 2:9
not of *d* heart............ 1 Chr 12:33
and with a *d* heart........ Ps 12:2
deacons not *d* tongued... 1 Tim 3:8
worthy of *d* honour .... 1 Tim 5:17
a *d* minded man......... James 1:8
*See* Gen 41:32; Is 61:7

## DOUBT

shall *d* come again........Ps 126:6
and dissolving of *d*...... Dan 5:12
didst thou *d* ...........Matt 14:31
and *d* not ...............Matt 21:21
shall not *d* ............. Mark 11:23
no *d* the kingdom ..... Luke 11:20
thou make us to *d*.....John 10:24
he that is damned... Rom 14:23
I stand in *d* of you.......Gal 4:20
without wrath and *d*.... 1 Tim 2:8
would no *d* ............. 1 John 2:19
*See* Luke 12:29; Acts 2:12

## DOVE

wings like a *d*..............Ps 55:6
descending like a *d*..... Matt 3:16
and harmless as *d* ..... Matt 10:16

## DRAW

*D* me not away ............Ps 28:3
*d* iniquity with cords.......Is 5:18
redemption *d* nigh ....Luke 21:28
except the Father
*d* him ..................John 6:44
will *d* all men
unto me ...............John 12:32
*d* near with .............Heb 10:22
but if any man *d* back... Heb 10:38
them who *d* back........ Heb 10:39
when he is *d* away..... James 1:14
*See* Acts 11:10; 20:30; Heb 7:19

## DREAM

shall fly away as a *d* .... Job 20:8
In a *d*, in a vision .......Job 33:15
As a *d* when one....... Ps 73:20
were like them that *d* ... Ps 126:1
a *d* cometh............... Eccl 5:3
prophet that hath a *d*....Jer 23:28
old men shall *d*
dreams .................Joel 2:28
filthy *d* defile ............. Jude 8
*See* Job 7:14; Is 29:8; Jer 27:9

## DRINK (n.)

Do not drink wine nor
strong *d* ...............Lev 10:9
wine and strong *d*...... Num 6:3
or for strong *d* ........Deut 14:26
wine or strong *d*........Deut 29:6
strong *d* is raging......Prov 20:1
Give strong *d* unto him.. Prov 31:6
*d* shall be bitter............ Is 24:9
erred through strong *d*.... Is 28:7
of strong *d*................ Mic 2:11

ye gave me *d*........... Matt 25:35
my blood is *d* indeed ...John 6:55
same spiritual *d* ........ 1 Cor 10:4
in meat or in *d*........... Col 2:16
*See* Gen 21:19; Is 5:11, 22

## DRINK (v.)

*d* of the river............... Ps 36:8
*d* the wine ................ Ps 60:3
vinegar to *d*...............Ps 69:21
givest them tears to *d*..... Ps 80:5
*d* yea, *d* abundantly .....Song 5:1
*d* the wine ............... Amos 2:8
they shall *d* .............Zech 9:15
shall give to *d*......... Matt 10:42
to *d* of the cup..........Matt 20:22
*D* ye all of it............Matt 26:27
day when I *d* it new ...Matt 26:29
except I *d* it............Matt 26:42
vinegar to *d* mingled... Matt 27:34
water to *d*............... Mark 9:41
can ye *d* of the cup ....Mark 10:38
I *d* it new ............Mark 14:25
*d* any deadly thing..... Mark 16:18
will not *d* of the .......Luke 22:18
Give me to *d*............ John 4:10
come unto me, and *d*... John 7:37
shall I not *d* it...........John 18:11
nor to *d* wine ...........Rom 14:21
did all *d* the same ...... 1 Cor 10:4
as oft as ye *d* it...........1 Cor 11:25
to *d* into one Spirit .....1 Cor 12:13
*See* Mark 2:16; Luke 7:33; 10:7

## DRUNK

and he made him *d*....2 Sam 11:13
himself .................. 1 Kin 20:16
stagger like a *d* man ...Job 12:25
I am like a *d* man........Jer 23:9
We have *d* our water ....Lam 5:4
makest him *d* also...... Hab 2:15
drink with the *d* ......Matt 24:49
and to be *d* ......... Luke 12:45
these are not *d* .......... Acts 2:15
another is *d*............. 1 Cor 11:21
*d* in the night .......... 1 Thess 5:7
*See* Eph 5:18; Rev 17:6

## DRUNKARD

he is a glutton,
and a *d* ..............Deut 21:20
*d* and the glutton...... Prov 23:21
hand of a *d*.............. Prov 26:9
nor *d*, nor revilers ...... 1 Cor 6:10
*See* Ps 69:12; Is 24:20; Joel 1:5

## DRUNKENNESS

to add *d* to thirst ......Deut 29:19
and not for *d*........... Eccl 10:17
filled with *d*...........Ezek 23:33
*See* Luke 21:34; Rom 13:13

## DUMB

who maketh the *d*......... Ex 4:11
the tongue of the *d*....... Is 35:6
as a sheep ... is *d*..........Is 53:7
they are all *d* dogs...... Is 56:10
a *d* man possessed .....Matt 9:32
blind, and *d*.............Matt 12:22
blind, *d*, maimed ....... Matt 15:30
the *d* to speak .......... Mark 7:37
hath a *d* spirit .......... Mark 9:17
*d* before his shearer ....Acts 8:32
*See* Ps 39:2; Luke 1:20; 11:14

## DUST

Lord God formed man
of the *d*................. Gen 2:7
*d* shalt thou eat.......... Gen 3:14
*d* thou art................ Gen 3:19
am but *d* and ashes..... Gen 18:27
into *d* again.............Job 10:9
turn again unto *d*.......Job 34:15
repent in *d* and ashes ... Job 42:6
the *d* praise thee ......... Ps 30:9
that we are *d* ...........Ps 103:14

return to their *d* ........ Ps 104:29
all are of the *d* ......... Eccl 3:20
*d* return to the earth .... Eccl 12:7
comprehended the *d* ..... Is 40:12
*d* shall be ................. Is 65:25
lick the *d*................ Mic 7:17
*d* of your feet ........ Matt 10:14
shake off the *d*......... Mark 6:11
shake off the very *d* .... Luke 9:5
*d* of your city ........ Luke 10:11
threw *d* into .......... Acts 22:23
*See* Ex 8:16; Num 23:10

**DUTY**
for this is the whole *d*
  of man................ Eccl 12:13
our *d* to do............Luke 17:10
their *d* is also ..........Rom 15:27
*See* Ex 21:10; 2 Chr 8:14

**DWELL**
cause his name to
  *d* there............... Deut 12:11
*d* between the.......... 1 Sam 4:4
will *d* in the house........Ps 23:6
thou *d* in the land ........Ps 37:3
than to *d* in tents........Ps 84:10
here will I *d*............Ps 132:14
brethren to *d* together ... Ps 133:1
shall *d* with the......... Is 33:14
He shall *d* on high ....... Is 33:16
I *d* in the high ...........Is 57:15
*d* in me .................John 6:56
Father that *d* in me.... John 14:10
for he *d* with you .......John 14:17
but sin that *d* in me .... Rom 7:17
*d* in your hearts......... Eph 3:17
all fullness *d*............Col 1:19
word of Christ *d* .........Col 3:16
*d* in the light............1 Tim 6:16
*d* righteousness ........ 2 Pet 3:13
how *d* the love......... 1 John 3:17
God *d* in us ............ 1 John 4:12
*See* 2 Cor 6:16; James 4:5

## E

**EAGLE**
how I bare you on
  *e* wings .................Ex 19:4
were swifter than *e*.... 2 Sam 1:23
renewed like the *e*........Ps 103:5
with wings as *e*........... Is 40:31
face of an *e*.............Ezek 1:10
A great *e* .............Ezek 17:3
the *e* be gathered......Matt 24:28
like a flying *e* .............Rev 4:7
*See* Dan 4:33; Rev 12:14

**EAR**
even into his *e*............Ps 18:6
his *e* are open............Ps 34:15
and incline thine *e*........Ps 45:10
stoppeth her *e*...........Ps 58:4
give *e*, O my people........ Ps 78:1
They have *e*............Ps 135:17
The *e* that heareth...... Prov 15:31
liar giveth *e*............Prov 17:4
*e* of the wise............Prov 18:15
hearing *e*...............Prov 20:12
stoppeth his *e* ..........Prov 21:13
bow down thine *e*........Prov 22:17
*e* of a foal ...............Prov 23:9
upon an obedient *e*...... Prov 25:12
a dog by the *e*...........Prov 26:17
nor the *e* filled........... Eccl 1:8
and make their *e* heavy ... Is 6:10
time that thine *e*.........Is 48:8
wakeneth my *e* to hear.... Is 50:4
incline your *e* ............ Is 55:3
nor his *e* heavy ............Is 59:1
*e* receive the word........Jer 9:20
a piece of an *e* .........Amos 3:12

their *e* are dull..........Matt 13:15
and your *e* ..............Matt 13:16
fingers into his *e*.......Mark 7:33
having *e*, hear ye not ... Mark 8:18
in heart and *e*...........Acts 7:51
things to our *e*.........Acts 17:20
and their *e* are dull.....Acts 28:27
nor *e* heard ............... 1 Cor 2:9
And if the *e* shall say ...1 Cor 12:16
having itching *e* ........ 2 Tim 4:3
*e* of the Lord............James 5:4
his *e* are open............1 Pet 3:12
*See* Matt 11:15; Mark 4:9

**EARNEST**
the *e* expectation........ Rom 8:19
covet *e* the best.........1 Cor 12:31
the *e* of the Spirit....... 2 Cor 1:22
given unto us the *e*..... 2 Cor 5:5
*e* of our inheritance ......Eph 1:14
*See* Heb 2:1; James 5:17

**EARTH**
While the *e* remaineth ... Gen 8:22
was the *e* divided....... Gen 10:25
Judge of all the *e* ...... Gen 18:25
*e* shall be filled......... Num 14:21
the *e* open her mouth... Num 16:30
Lord of all the *e*..........Josh 3:11
way of all the *e* .......Josh 23:14
man upon *e*..............Job 7:1
*e* is given................. Job 9:24
foundations of the *e*.... Job 38:4
inherit the *e* ..............Ps 25:13
the *e* is full................Ps 33:5
them from the *e*..........Ps 34:16
inherit the *e* ..............Ps 37:9
shall inherit the *e*.........Ps 37:11
blessed upon the *e* ........Ps 41:2
though *e* be removed......Ps 46:2
the *e* melted .............Ps 46:6
joy of the whole *e*.........Ps 48:2
made the *e* to tremble.... Ps 60:2
lower parts of the *e*.......Ps 63:9
the *e* shook ..............Ps 68:8
depths of the *e*..........Ps 71:20
that water the *e*...........Ps 72:6
none upon *e* that.........Ps 73:25
formed the *e* ............Ps 90:2
let the *e* rejoice ..........Ps 97:1
foundation of the *e*......Ps 102:25
the *e* is satisfied ........Ps 104:13
the *e* is full.............Ps 104:24
*e* hath he given .........Ps 115:16
a stranger in the *e* .......Ps 119:19
the *e* and heaven ......Ps 148:13
founded the *e*............Prov 3:19
or ever the *e* was .......Prov 8:23
foundations of the *e* ..... Prov 8:29
recompensed in the *e*...Prov 11:31
poor from off the *e* ..... Prov 30:14
the *e* abideth for ever......Eccl 1:4
downward to the *e* ...... Eccl 3:21
return to the *e* ...........Eccl 12:7
the *e* shall be full ........ Is 11:9
the *e* shall remove.........Is 13:13
the *e* to tremble .........Is 14:16
maketh the *e* empty......Is 24:1
*e* is clean dissolved ...... Is 24:19
circle of the *e* ...........Is 40:22
the ends of the *e*...........Is 40:28
foundation of the *e*....... Is 48:13
be joyful, O *e* ............Is 49:13
the *e* shall wax old........Is 51:6
the *e* is my footstool.......Is 66:1
Shall the *e* be made....... Is 66:8
and the *e* is burned........Nah 1:5
*e* shall be filled...........Hab 2:14
the *e* was full ............Hab 3:3
through the whole *e*.... Zech 4:10
Lord of all the *e*......... Zech 6:5
come and smite the *e* .... Mal 4:6
meek ... inherit the *e* ... Matt 5:5
treasures upon *e* ....... Matt 6:19

hath power on *e*......... Matt 9:6
to send peace on *e*.... Matt 10:34
shalt bind on *e*......... Matt 16:19
shall agree on *e*......... Matt 18:19
father upon the *e*...... Matt 23:9
on *e* peace ..............Luke 2:14
over all the *e*..........Luke 23:44
told you *e* things ....... John 3:12
of the *e* is earthly....... John 3:31
lifted up from the *e*... John 12:32
glorified thee on the *e*...John 17:4
taken from the *e*..........Acts 8:33
into all the *e*...........Rom 10:18
man of the *e* is *e*.......1 Cor 15:47
As is the *e*...............1 Cor 15:48
the image of the *e* .....1 Cor 15:49
in *e* vessels ............ 2 Cor 4:7
who mind *e* things ...... Phil 3:19
things on the *e* ...........Col 3:2
*e* which drinketh .........Heb 6:7
if he were on *e*.........Heb 8:4
pilgrims on the *e* .......Heb 11:13
that spake on *e* .........Heb 12:25
voice then shook
  the *e*.................Heb 12:26
but is *e*, sensual .......James 3:15
pleasure on the *e*........James 5:5
precious fruit of the *e* .. James 5:7
*e* brought forth .......James 5:18
the *e* also .................2 Pet 3:10
shall reign on the *e*.......Rev 5:10
Hurt not the *e* .............Rev 7:3
the *e* was lightened.......Rev 18:1
the *e* and heaven ........Rev 20:11
heaven and a new *e* .....Rev 21:1
*See* Gen 1:11; Ex 9:29

**EARTHQUAKE**
and after the wind
  an *e*....................1 Kin 19:11
*e*, and great noise...........Is 29:6
years before the *e* ..... Amos 1:1
the *e* in the days........Zech 14:5
*e*, in divers places....... Matt 24:7
saw the *e* .............Matt 27:54
there was a great *e* .....Acts 16:26
lightnings, and an *e* ...... Rev 8:5

**EAT**
the day that thou *e*
  thereof .................Gen 2:17
shall ye not *e* ...........Gen 9:4
not *e* anything ......... Lev 19:26
not *e* the blood ....... Deut 12:16
meek shall *e* .............Ps 22:26
hath *e* me up ...........Ps 69:9
*e* ashes like bread.........Ps 102:9
*e* of the fruit .............Prov 1:31
*e* to the satisfying ..... Prov 13:25
*e* the fruit...............Prov 18:21
*e* with a ruler ...........Prov 23:1
*e* thou honey .......... Prov 24:13
not good to *e* .......... Prov 25:27
honey shall he *e* ......... Is 7:15
the lion shall *e* straw ....... Is 11:7
come ye, buy, and *e* .......Is 55:1
my servants shall *e*..... Is 65:13
lion shall *e* straw ...... Is 65:25
*e* with publicans........Mark 2:16
dogs under the table *e*.. Mark 7:28
*e* such things ...........Luke 10:8
what ye shall *e*........Luke 12:22
let us *e*, and be
  merry................Luke 15:23
his flesh to *e*............John 6:52
may *e* all things..........Rom 14:2
*e*, *e* to the Lord .........Rom 14:6
who *e* with offence......Rom 14:20
neither to *e* flesh ....... Rom 14:21
not to *e* ..................1 Cor 5:11
*e* it as a thing offered....1 Cor 8:7
neither, if we *e*............1 Cor 8:8
I will *e* no flesh ......... 1 Cor 8:13
Have we not power to *e*...1 Cor 9:4

## EDIFY

all *e* the same........... 1 Cor 10:3
set before you, *e*...... 1 Cor 10:27
Whether therefore
ye *e*................... 1 Cor 10:31
that *e* and drinketh..... 1 Cor 11:29
should he *e*.......... 2 Thess 3:10
no right to *e*........... Heb 13:10
*e* of the tree of life........ Rev 2:7
*e* of the hidden manna ... Rev 2:17
*e* the flesh of kings ...... Rev 19:18
See Prov 31:27; Is 1:19; 65:4

## EDIFY

wherewith one may *e*
another................ Rom 14:19
his good to *e*............. Rom 15:2
charity *e*................. 1 Cor 8:1
all things *e* not......... 1 Cor 10:23
speaketh unto
men to *e*.............. 1 Cor 14:3
he that prophesieth *e* ... 1 Cor 14:4
for the *e* of the body..... Eph 4:12
See 2 Cor 10:8; 13:10; 1 Tim 1:4

## ELDER

before the *e* of my
people............... 1 Sam 15:30
among the *e* of the .... Prov 31:23
the tradition of the *e* .... Matt 15:2
the tradition of the *e* ... Mark 7:3
Let the *e* that rule ...... 1 Tim 5:17
ordain *e* in every ........ Titus 1:5
the *e* obtained........... Heb 11:2
the *e* of the church .... James 5:14
who am also an *e*........ 1 Pet 5:1
unto the *e*............... 1 Pet 5:5
See John 8:9; 1 Tim 5:2; 3 John 1

## ELECT

mine *e* in whom........... Is 42:1
mine *e* I have.............. Is 45:4
mine *e* shall inherit it ..... Is 65:9
mine *e* shall long enjoy... Is 65:22
for the *e* sake ......... Matt 24:22
deceived the very *e*.... Matt 24:24
gather together his *e* .... Matt 24:31
for the *e* sake ........ Mark 13:20
even the *e*............. Mark 13:22
God avenge his own *e*.... Luke 18:7
the charge of God's *e* ... Rom 8:33
as the *e* of God.......... Col 3:12
and the *e* angels........ 1 Tim 5:21
*E* according to the........ 1 Pet 1:2
a chief corner stone, *e*.. 1 Pet 2:6
See 2 Tim 2:10; Titus 1:1; 2 John 13

## ELECTION

of God according to *e*.... Rom 9:11
to the *e* of grace ........ Rom 11:5
your *e* of God .......... 1 Thess 1:4
calling and *e* sure....... 2 Pet 1:10

## END

The *e* of all flesh
is come................ Gen 6:13
at thy latter *e* .......... Deut 8:16
consider their latter *e*... Deut 32:29
what is mine *e*........... Job 6:11
thy latter *e* should........ Job 8:7
the wicked come to an *e* ... Ps 7:9
come to a perpetual *e*...... Ps 9:6
the *e* of that man......... Ps 37:37
years shall have no *e* .... Ps 102:27
an *e* of all ............. Ps 119:96
the *e* thereof are....... Prov 14:12
in the *e* of the earth .... Prov 17:24
be wise in thy latter *e* .. Prov 19:20
beginning to the *e*....... Eccl 3:11
no *e* of all his labour...... Eccl 4:8
no *e* of all the people .... Eccl 4:16
that is the *e* of all ........ Eccl 7:2
Better is the *e* of a ....... Eccl 7:8
the *e* of his talk ........ Eccl 10:13
there shall be no *e*........... Is 9:7
Declaring the *e* from ..... Is 46:10

will ye do in the *e*........ Jer 5:31
not her last *e*............. Lam 1:9
our *e* is near ............ Lam 4:18
time of the *e* shall ....... Dan 8:17
what shall be the *e* of.... Dan 12:8
endureth to the *e*..... Matt 10:22
harvest is the *e* of..... Matt 13:39
the *e* of the world...... Matt 24:3
shall endure unto
the *e*.............. Matt 24:13
from one *e* of
heaven to........... Matt 24:31
but hath an *e* ..........Mark 3:26
but the *e* shall not ..... Mark 13:7
there shall be no *e*...... Luke 1:33
them unto the *e* ........John 13:1
To this *e* was I born ... John 18:37
the *e* everlasting life.... Rom 6:22
Christ is the *e* of the.... Rom 10:4
upon whom the *e* of.... 1 Cor 10:11
Then cometh the *e* .... 1 Cor 15:24
Whose *e* is.............. Phil 3:19
the *e* of the ............ 1 Tim 1:5
whose *e* is to be ......... Heb 6:8
*e* of the world hath ...... Heb 9:26
the *e* of the Lord........ James 5:11
the *e* of your faith ....... 1 Pet 1:9
and hope to the *e*....... 1 Pet 1:13
*e* of all things............. 1 Pet 4:7
my works unto the *e* .... Rev 2:26
beginning and the *e*...... Rev 21:6
See Ps 19:6; Is 45:22; Jer 4:27

## ENDURE

but it shall not *e*.......... Job 8:15
But the Lord shall *e* ....... Ps 9:7
*e* for ever ................. Ps 19:9
weeping may *e* for a...... Ps 30:5
goodness of God *e*........ Ps 52:1
His name shall *e*........ Ps 72:17
his truth *e* to all ......... Ps 100:5
thou, O Lord, shalt *e*..... Ps 102:12
the Lord shall *e*
for ever ............ Ps 104:31
his mercy *e* for ever ...... Ps 106:1
his righteousness *e*....... Ps 111:3
judgments *e* for ever .... Ps 119:160
Thy name, O Lord, *e*.... Ps 135:13
thy mercy, O Lord, *e*.... Ps 138:8
and thy dominion *e* ..... Ps 145:13
and doth the crown *e*.. Prov 27:24
for his mercy *e*......... Jer 33:11
that *e* to the end....... Matt 10:22
But he that shall *e* ..... Matt 24:13
so *e* but for a time ...... Mark 4:17
*e* unto everlasting ...... John 6:27
*e* with much ........... Rom 9:22
*e* all things.............. 1 Cor 13:7
*e* hardness ............. 2 Tim 2:3
they will not *e* sound... 2 Tim 4:3
*e* afflictions............. 2 Tim 4:5
a better and *e*
substance .......... Heb 10:34
if ye *e* chastening........ Heb 12:7
the man that *e*........ James 1:12
them happy which *e*.. James 5:11
of the Lord *e* for ever .... 1 Pet 1:25
toward God *e* grief...... 1 Pet 2:19
See Heb 10:32; 11:27; 12:2, 3

## ENEMY

I will be an *e* unto
thine *e*................ Ex 23:22
all thine *e* perish........ Judg 5:31
mightest still the *e* ........ Ps 8:2
the presence of mine *e*.... Ps 23:5
mine *e* are lively.......... Ps 38:19
wiser than mine *e* ....... Ps 119:98
I count them mine *e*.... Ps 139:22
maketh even his *e* ...... Prov 16:7
when thine *e* falleth.... Prov 24:17
if thine *e* be hungry ... Prov 25:21
kisses of an *e* ............ Prov 27:6
and join his *e* ............. Is 9:11

to be their *e*............... Is 63:10
will cause the *e*.......... Jer 15:11
the wound of an *e*...... Jer 30:14
a man's *e* are the men..... Mic 7:6
and hate thine *e* ....... Matt 5:43
Love your *e*, bless ...... Matt 5:44
his *e* came and
sowed ............... Matt 13:25
An *e* hath done this.... Matt 13:28
The *e* that sowed.... Matt 13:39
Love your *e*............. Luke 6:27
thine *e* shall cast....... Luke 19:43
*e* of all righteousness... Acts 13:10
if when we were *e*....... Rom 5:10
they are *e* for your..... Rom 11:28
if thine *e* hunger....... Rom 12:20
therefore become
your *e*................ Gal 4:16
the *e* of the cross ........ Phil 3:18
were *e* in your mind....... Col 1:21
not as an *e*...........2 Thess 3:15
is the *e* of God ......... James 4:4
See Ps 110:1; Is 62:8; Jer 15:14

## ENJOY

therefore *e* pleasure....... Eccl 2:1
make his soul *e* good ... Eccl 2:24
and to *e* the good....... Eccl 5:18
all things to *e*........... 1 Tim 6:17
See Num 36:8; Is 65:22

## ENMITY

the carnal mind is *e*
against God ............ Rom 8:7
in his flesh the *e*........ Eph 2:15
having slain the *e*....... Eph 2:16
the world is *e*.......... James 4:4
See Gen 3:15; Num 35:21

## ENTER

*E* into his gates with
thanksgiving .......... Ps 100:4
may *e* in ............... Is 26:2
*e* into thy closet ......... Matt 6:6
*E* ye in ................... Matt 7:13
town ye shall *e* ........ Matt 10:11
thee to *e* into life ....... Matt 18:8
if thou wilt *e* into...... Matt 19:17
*e* thou into the joy..... Matt 25:21
that we may *e* into ..... Mark 5:12
for thee to *e* into....... Mark 9:43
*e* into temptation...... Mark 14:38
to *e* into them .......... Luke 8:32
*e* into the cloud........ Luke 9:34
whatsoever city ye *e*... Luke 10:8
Strive to *e* in........... Luke 13:24
*e* into his glory ........ Luke 24:26
can he *e* the second .... John 3:4
ye are *e* into .......... John 4:38
*e* not by the door ....... John 10:1
But he that *e*.......... John 10:2
sin *e* into the world..... Rom 5:12
*e* into the heart.......... 1 Cor 2:9
*e* into my rest.......... Heb 3:11
that they should not *e*... Heb 3:18
he that is *e* into.......... Heb 4:10
forerunner is for us *e*.... Heb 6:20
Christ is not *e*.......... Heb 9:12
See Ps 143:2; Matt 15:17

## ENTICE

if sinners *e* thee ......... Prov 1:10
with *e* words ............ 1 Cor 2:4
See Job 31:27; Prov 16:29

## ENVY

*e* slayeth the silly one ..... Job 5:2
*E* thou not.............. Prov 3:31
Let not thine heart *e* ... Prov 23:17
Be thou not *e* ........... Prov 24:1
*e* of his neighbour ........ Eccl 4:4
that for *e* they ......... Matt 27:18
delivered him for *e*.... Mark 15:10
moved with *e*........... Acts 7:9
were filled with *e*....... Acts 13:45

full of *e*, murder . . . . . . . . Rom 1:29
not in strife and *e* . . . . . Rom 13:13
*e*, and strife . . . . . . . . . . . . . 1 Cor 3:3
charity *e* not . . . . . . . . . . . . 1 Cor 13:4
*e*, wraths, strifes . . . . . . . 2 Cor 12:20
*E*, murders . . . . . . . . . . . . . . . Gal 5:21
*e* one another . . . . . . . . . . . . Gal 5:26
Christ even of *e* . . . . . . . . . Phil 1:15
whereof cometh *e* . . . . . . 1 Tim 6:4
in malice and *e* . . . . . . . . . Titus 3:3
lusteth to *e* . . . . . . . . . . . . James 4:5
*See* Ps 106:16; Ezek 31:9

**EPHOD**
they shall make the *e*
   of gold . . . . . . . . . . . . . . . . Ex 28:6
he made the *e* of gold . . . . Ex 39:2
And Gideon made
   an *e* . . . . . . . . . . . . . . . . Judg 8:27
an *e*, and teraphim . . . . . Judg 17:5

**EQUAL**
behold the things
   that are *e* . . . . . . . . . . . . . . . Ps 17:2
lame are not *e* . . . . . . . . . Prov 26:7
or shall I be *e* . . . . . . . . . . . Is 40:25
hast made them *e* . . . . . . Matt 20:12
*e* unto the angels . . . . . Luke 20:36
*e* with God . . . . . . . . . . . . John 5:18
not robbery to be *e* . . . . . . . Phil 2:6
just and *e* . . . . . . . . . . . . . . . Col 4:1
*See* Ex 36:22; 2 Cor 8:14

**ERR**
people that do *e* in
   their heart . . . . . . . . . . . . . Ps 95:10
do *e* from thy . . . . . . . . . . Ps 119:21
cause thee to *e* . . . . . . . . . . . Is 3:12
cause them to *e* . . . . . . . . . . Is 9:16
they *e* in vision . . . . . . . . . . . Is 28:7
shall not *e* . . . . . . . . . . . . . . Is 35:8
do *e*, not knowing . . . . . Matt 22:29
ye not therefore *e* . . . . Mark 12:24
have *e* from . . . . . . . . . . . . 1 Tim 6:10
have *e* concerning . . . . . 1 Tim 6:21
Do not *e* . . . . . . . . . . . . . . James 1:16
if any of you do *e* . . . . . James 5:19
*See* Is 29:24; Ezek 45:20

**ERROR**
Who can understand
   his *e* . . . . . . . . . . . . . . . . . Ps 19:12
it was an *e* . . . . . . . . . . . . . Eccl 5:6
an *e* which proceedeth . . Eccl 10:5
so the last *e* . . . . . . . . . . Matt 27:64
*e* of his way . . . . . . . . . . James 5:20
*e* of the wicked . . . . . . . . 2 Pet 3:17
the spirit of *e* . . . . . . . . 1 John 4:6
*See* Job 19:4; Rom 1:27; Heb 9:7

**ESCAPE**
they shall not *e* . . . . . . . . . Job 11:20
*e* with the skin . . . . . . . . . Job 19:20
shall not *e* . . . . . . . . . . . . Prov 19:5
pleaseth God shall *e* . . . . . Eccl 7:26
and how shall we *e* . . . . . . Is 20:6
*e* the damnation . . . . . . . Matt 23:33
worthy to *e* all . . . . . . . . . Luke 21:36
he *e* out of their . . . . . . John 10:39
they *e* all safe . . . . . . . . . Acts 27:44
*e* the sea . . . . . . . . . . . . . Acts 28:4
How shall we *e* . . . . . . . . . Heb 2:3
For if they *e* . . . . . . . . . . Heb 12:25
*e* the corruption . . . . . . . . . 2 Pet 1:4
*e* the pollutions . . . . . . . . 2 Pet 2:20
*See* Ps 124:7; 1 Cor 10:13

**ESTABLISH**
with thee will I *e* my
   covenant . . . . . . . . . . . . . . Gen 6:18
shall be *e* for ever . . . . . . Prov 12:19
*e* by righteousness . . . . . . Prov 16:12
Every purpose is *e* . . . . . Prov 20:18
hath *e* the world . . . . . . . . . Jer 10:12
yea, we *e* the law . . . . . . Rom 3:31
to *e* their own . . . . . . . . . Rom 10:3

to *e* you . . . . . . . . . . . . . . . 1 Thess 3:2
*See* Amos 5:15; Hab 2:12

**ETERNAL**
The *e* God is thy
   refuge . . . . . . . . . . . . . . Deut 33:27
an *e* excellency . . . . . . . . . . Is 60:15
may have *e* life . . . . . . . . . Matt 19:16
righteous into life *e* . . . Matt 25:46
is in danger of *e* . . . . . . . Mark 3:29
inherit *e* life . . . . . . . . . . Mark 10:17
but have *e* life . . . . . . . . . John 3:15
unto life *e* . . . . . . . . . . . . . John 4:36
ye have *e* life . . . . . . . . . . . John 5:39
of *e* life . . . . . . . . . . . . . . . John 6:68
give unto them *e* life . . . John 10:28
give *e* life to as many . . . John 17:2
ordained to *e* life . . . . . . Acts 13:48
immortality, *e* life . . . . . . Rom 2:7
unto *e* life . . . . . . . . . . . . . Rom 5:21
gift of God is *e* life . . . . . Rom 6:23
*e* weight of glory . . . . . 2 Cor 4:17
*e* in the heavens . . . . . . . 2 Cor 5:1
to the *e* purpose . . . . . . . . Eph 3:11
lay hold on *e* life . . . . . . . 1 Tim 6:12
In hope of *e* life . . . . . . . . . Titus 1:2
the hope of *e* life . . . . . . . . Titus 3:7
author of *e* salvation . . . . . Heb 5:9
and of *e* judgment . . . . . . . Heb 6:2
of *e* inheritance . . . . . . . . . Heb 9:15
unto his *e* glory . . . . . . . . 1 Pet 5:10
*e* life . . . . . . . . . . . . . . . . . 1 John 1:2
even *e* life . . . . . . . . . . . . 1 John 2:25
no murderer hath
   *e* life . . . . . . . . . . . . . . . 1 John 3:15
given to us *e* life . . . . . . 1 John 5:11
vengeance of *e* fire . . . . . . . . Jude 7
*See* Rom 1:20; 1 Tim 1:17

**ETERNITY**
lofty One that
   inhabiteth *e* . . . . . . . . . . . Is 57:15

**EVANGELIST**
entered the house of
   Philip the *e* . . . . . . . . . . Acts 21:8
and some, *e* . . . . . . . . . . . . . Eph 4:11
the work of an *e* . . . . . . . 2 Tim 4:5

**EVERLASTING**
an *e* priesthood . . . . . . . . . Ex 40:15
the *e* arms . . . . . . . . . . . . Deut 33:27
even from *e* to *e* . . . . . . . . Ps 90:2
lead me in the way *e* . . . . Ps 139:24
I was set up from *e* . . . . . Prov 8:23
an *e* foundation . . . . . . Prov 10:25
The *e* Father . . . . . . . . . . . . Is 9:6
Jehovah is *e* strength . . . . Is 26:4
dwell with *e* burnings . . . . Is 33:14
and *e* joy . . . . . . . . . . . . . . . Is 35:10
*e* salvation . . . . . . . . . . . . . Is 45:17
*e* joy shall be . . . . . . . . . . . Is 51:11
with *e* kindness . . . . . . . . . Is 54:8
an *e* sign . . . . . . . . . . . . . . Is 55:13
give them an *e* name . . . . . Is 56:5
an *e* light . . . . . . . . . . . . . Is 60:19
*e* joy shall . . . . . . . . . . . . . Is 61:7
an *e* name . . . . . . . . . . . . . Is 63:12
with an *e* love . . . . . . . . . Jer 31:3
some to *e* life . . . . . . . . . Dan 12:2
Art thou not from *e* . . . . . Hab 1:12
cast into *e* fire . . . . . . . . Matt 18:8
shall inherit *e* life . . . . . Matt 19:29
into *e* fire . . . . . . . . . . . . Matt 25:41
into *e* punishment . . . . Matt 25:46
into *e* habitations . . . . . Luke 16:9
to come life *e* . . . . . . . . . Luke 18:30
but have *e* life . . . . . . . . . John 3:16
up into *e* life . . . . . . . . . . John 4:14
endureth unto *e* life . . . . John 6:27
on him, may have
   *e* life . . . . . . . . . . . . . . . . John 6:40
commandment is
   life *e* . . . . . . . . . . . . . . . John 12:50
unworthy of *e* life . . . . . Acts 13:46

the end *e* life . . . . . . . . . . . Rom 6:22
reap life *e* . . . . . . . . . . . . . . Gal 6:8
with *e* destruction . . . . . 2 Thess 1:9
*e* consolation . . . . . . . . 2 Thess 2:16
in *e* chains . . . . . . . . . . . . . . Jude 6
having the *e* gospel . . . . . . Rev 14:6
*See* Dan 4:3; 7:27; 2 Pet 1:11

**EVIDENCE**
the *e* of things . . . . . . . . . . . Heb 11:1

**EVIL**
heart was only *e* con-
   tinually . . . . . . . . . . . . . . . Gen 6:5
*e* toward his brother . . . Deut 28:54
Depart from *e* . . . . . . . . . . Ps 34:14
rewarded me *e* . . . . . . . . . Ps 35:12
depart from *e* . . . . . . . . . . . Prov 3:7
*e* bow before the good . . . Prov 14:19
beholding the *e* . . . . . . . . . Prov 15:3
Whoso rewardeth *e* . . . . Prov 17:13
a seed of *e* . . . . . . . . . . . . . . Is 1:4
that call *e* good . . . . . . . . . . Is 5:20
to refuse the *e* . . . . . . . . . . Is 7:15
all manner of *e* . . . . . . . . Matt 5:11
day is the *e* . . . . . . . . . . . Matt 6:34
If ye then, being *e* . . . . . . Matt 7:11
An *e* and adulterous . . . Matt 12:39
lightly speak *e* . . . . . . . . . Mark 9:39
your name as *e* . . . . . . . . Luke 6:22
and to the *e* . . . . . . . . . . . Luke 6:35
deeds were *e* . . . . . . . . . . . John 3:19
If I have spoken *e* . . . . . John 18:23
not speak *e* . . . . . . . . . . . . Acts 23:5
the *e* which I would . . . . Rom 7:19
Abhor that which is *e* . . . Rom 12:9
overcome *e* with good . . . Rom 12:21
appearance of *e* . . . . . . . 1 Thess 5:22
the root of all *e* . . . . . . . . 1 Tim 6:10
every *e* work . . . . . . . . . . 2 Tim 4:18
speak *e* of no man . . . . . . . Titus 3:2
every *e* work . . . . . . . . . . James 3:16
rendering *e* for *e* . . . . . . . 1 Pet 3:9
*See* Prov 13:21; Is 45:7

**EXALT**
*e* as head above all . . . . . 1 Chr 29:11
vilest men are *e* . . . . . . . . . Ps 12:8
let us *e* his name . . . . . . . . . Ps 34:3
my horn shalt thou *e* . . . . Ps 92:10
*e* far above all gods . . . . . . . Ps 97:9
*E* her, and she shall . . . . . . Prov 4:8
Righteousness *e* . . . . . . Prov 14:34
*e* above the hills . . . . . . . . . . Is 2:2
Every valley shall be *e* . . . Is 40:4
*e* him that is low . . . . . . Ezek 21:26
and it shall be *e* . . . . . . . . . Mic 4:1
which art *e* . . . . . . . . . . . Matt 11:23
*e* himself . . . . . . . . . . . . . Luke 14:11
if a man *e* himself . . . . . 2 Cor 11:20
hath highly *e* him . . . . . . . Phil 2:9
*e* himself above . . . . . . . 2 Thess 2:4
that he may *e* you . . . . . . 1 Pet 5:6
*See* Luke 1:52; James 1:9

**EXAMINE**
*E* me, O Lord, and
   prove me . . . . . . . . . . . . . . Ps 26:2
If we this day be *e* . . . . . . Acts 4:9
*e* by scourging . . . . . . . . Acts 22:24
a man *e* himself . . . . . . . 1 Cor 11:28
*E* yourselves . . . . . . . . . . 2 Cor 13:5
*See* Ezra 10:16; Acts 24:8; 25:26

**EXAMPLE**
I have given you an *e* . . . . John 13:15
things were our *e* . . . . . . 1 Cor 10:6
for an *e* . . . . . . . . . . . . . . . Phil 3:17
ourselves an *e* . . . . . . . 2 Thess 3:9
be thou an *e* . . . . . . . . . . 1 Tim 4:12
leaving us an *e* . . . . . . . . 1 Pet 2:21
an *e* suffering the . . . . . . . . Jude 7
*See* Matt 1:19; 1 Cor 10:6

**EXCEEDING**
*e* glad with . . . . . . . . . . . . . Ps 21:6

## EXCELLENT (cont.)

God my *e* joy..............Ps 43:4
commandment is *e*......Ps 119:96
they are *e* wise........Prov 30:24
with *e* great joy........Matt 2:10
an *e* high mountain ....Matt 4:8
Rejoice, and be *e* glad...Matt 5:12
soul is *e* sorrowful.....Matt 26:38
*e* white as snow ........Mark 9:3
a far more *e*............2 Cor 4:17
am *e* joyful.............2 Cor 7:4
*e* zealous...............Gal 1:14
the *e* greatness........Eph 1:19
*e* riches of his grace ......Eph 2:7
able to do *e*
    abundantly..........Eph 3:20
faith groweth *e* ........2 Thess 1:3
*e* great and precious......2 Pet 1:4
with *e* joy..............Jude 24
*See* 1 Sam 26:21; Jon 3:3

## EXCELLENT
he is *e* in power, and in
    judgment............Job 37:23
how *e* is thy name........Ps 8:1, 9
speak of *e* things .......Prov 8:6
of an *e* spirit...........Prov 17:27
*e* things................Prov 22:20
he hath done *e* things.....Is 12:5
more *e* being ...........Rom 2:18
a more *e* way ..........1 Cor 12:31
*See* Song 5:15; Luke 1:3; Heb 1:4

## EXCEPT
*E* ye be converted ......Matt 18:3
*e* ye repent.............Luke 13:3
*E* a man be born again ...John 3:3
*e* they be sent..........Rom 10:15
*e* it die ................1 Cor 15:36
*See* Rom 7:7; 1 Cor 14:5; 15:27

## EXCHANGE
in *e* for his soul .......Matt 16:26

## EXHORT
he that *e*...............Rom 12:8
teach and *e* .............1 Tim 6:2
*e* and to convince.......Titus 1:9
*e* and rebuke............Titus 2:15
*e* one another daily......Heb 3:13
but *e* one another ......Heb 10:25
*See* 2 Cor 9:5; Titus 2:6, 9

## EXPECTATION
the *e* of the poor shall not
    perish ...............Ps 9:18
my *e* is from him ........Ps 62:5
the *e* of the wicked ....Prov 10:28
his *e* shall perish........Prov 11:7
the earnest *e*...........Rom 8:19
my earnest *e*............Phil 1:20
*See* Jer 29:11; Acts 3:5

## EXPEDIENT
Nor consider that it is *e*
    for us ...............John 11:50
It is *e* for you ........John 16:7
it was *e* that one man...John 18:14
things are not *e*........1 Cor 6:12

## EXPRESS
and the *e* image of his
    person................Heb 1:3

## EXPRESSLY
Spirit speaketh *e* ........1 Tim 4:1

## EXTOL
I will *e* thee.............Ps 30:1
*e* him that rideth ........Ps 68:4
*e* thee, my God..........Ps 145:1
*See* Ps 66:17; Is 52:13; Dan 4:37

## EYE
pleasant to the *e*........Gen 3:6
to us instead of *e* ......Num 10:31
lift up thine *e* .........Duet 3:27
right in his own *e*......Duet 12:8
doth blind the *e* .......Duet 16:19

---

apple of his *e* .........Duet 32:10
his *e* was not dim......Duet 34:7
right in his own *e*......Judg 17:6
*e* may be open ........2 Chr 6:20
the *e* of the Lord.......2 Chr 16:9
*e* see all the evil......2 Chr 34:28
thine *e* are upon me.....Job 7:8
the *e* of the wicked....Job 11:20
what do thy *e* wink at ....Job 15:12
mine *e* shall behold.....Job 19:27
I was *e* to the blind....Job 29:15
his *e* behold............Ps 11:4
enlightening the *e*........Ps 19:8
the *e* of the Lord.........Ps 33:18
before his *e* ...........Ps 36:1
Mine *e* fail .............Ps 119:82
sleep to mine *e* .........Ps 132:4
as smoke to the *e*......Prov 10:26
the seeing *e*.............Prov 20:12
redness of *e*............Prov 23:29
the *e* of man ...........Prov 27:20
The *e* that mocketh.....Prov 30:17
*e* is not satisfied .........Eccl 1:8
wise man's *e*............Eccl 2:14
sight of the *e*...........Eccl 6:9
for the *e* to behold......Eccl 11:7
hide mine *e* from you .....Is 1:15
hath closeth your *e*......Is 29:10
Thine *e* shall see.........Is 33:17
To open the blind *e*......Is 42:7
neither hath the *e* ........Is 64:4
which have *e* ...........Jer 5:21
mine *e* a fountain .......Jer 9:1
mine *e* shall weep ......Jer 13:17
Mine *e* do fail...........Lam 2:11
apple of thine *e*.........Lam 2:18
which have *e* ..........Ezek 12:2
desire of thine *e* ......Ezek 24:16
of purer *e* than...........Hab 1:13
*e* of the Lord...........Zech 4:10
if thy right *e* ...........Matt 5:29
Having *e*, see yo not .....Mark 8:18
their *e* were holden....Luke 24:16
which opened the *e* ...John 11:37
*E* hath not seen..........1 Cor 2:9
twinkling of an *e* ......1 Cor 15:52
your own *e*..............Gal 4:15
The *e* of your ...........Eph 1:18
*e* of the Lord............1 Pet 3:12
*e* of his majesty........2 Pet 1:16
the lust of the *e*........1 John 2:16
*See* Ezra 5:5; Matt 20:33

## EYESERVICE
Not with *e*, as
    menpleasers ..........Eph 6:6

---

# F

## FABLES
Neither give heed to *f* ...1 Tim 1:4
profane and old
    wives' *f*.............1 Tim 4:7
turned unto *f*...........2 Tim 4:4
to Jewish *f*.............Titus 1:14
cunningly devised *f* .....2 Pet 1:16

## FACE
from thy *f*.............Gen 4:14
seen God *f* to *f*.........Gen 32:30
unto Moses *f* to *f*......Ex 33:11
skin of his *f* shone......Ex 34:29
to confusion of *f*........Ezra 9:7
*f* to the ground ..........Neh 8:6
curse thee to thy *f*......Job 1:11
passed before my *f*......Job 4:15
hidest thou thy *f*........Job 13:24
thou hide thy *f*..........Ps 13:1
will behold thy *f*........Ps 17:15
Hide not thy *f*...........Ps 27:9
*f* were not ashamed .....Ps 34:5
*f* of thine anointed ......Ps 84:9
why hidest thou thy *f* ...Ps 88:14

---

Hide not thy *f* from me...Ps 102:2
*f* answereth to *f*........Prov 27:19
his *f* to shine.............Eccl 8:1
*f* of the poor .............Is 3:15
set my *f* like a flint.........Is 50:7
sins have hid his *f* ........Is 59:2
and not their *f*...........Jer 2:27
*f* harder than a rock ......Jer 5:3
all *f* are turned..........Jer 30:6
us confusion of *f*.........Dan 9:7
*f* as the appearance.......Dan 10:6
testify to his *f*...........Hos 5:5
*f* did shine as the sun....Matt 17:2
*f* of my Father .........Matt 18:10
before the *f* of all ......Luke 2:31
set his *f* to go ..........Luke 9:51
because his *f*............Luke 9:53
but then *f* to *f*...........1 Cor 13:12
vail over his *f* ...........2 Cor 3:13
all, with open *f* ..........2 Cor 3:18
And was unknown by *f*...Gal 1:22
withstood him to the *f*...Gal 2:11
his natural *f*............James 1:23
from whose *f*...........Rev 20:11
*See* 1 Kin 19:13; Dan 1:10

## FAIL
doth his promise *f*........Ps 77:8
my faithfulness to *f*.....Ps 89:33
his wisdom *f* him........Eccl 10:3
desire shall *f*............Eccl 12:5
the grass *f* ..............Is 15:6
of these shall *f* ..........Is 34:16
tongue *f* for thirst ........Is 41:17
truth *f*..................Is 59:15
their eyes did *f*..........Jer 14:6
as waters that *f*.........Jer 15:18
his compassions *f* not....Lam 3:22
every vision *f*...........Ezek 12:22
heavens that *f* not......Luke 12:33
that thy faith *f* not......Luke 22:32
Charity never *f*.........1 Cor 13:8
thy years shall not *f*......Heb 1:12
*See* Deut 31:6; Ps 40:12; 143:7

## FAITH
children in whom
    is no *f*..............Deut 32:20
O ye of little *f*..........Matt 6:30
found so great *f*.........Matt 8:10
thy *f* hath made .........Matt 9:22
O thou of little *f*........Matt 14:31
*f* as a grain .............Matt 17:20
if ye have *f*..............Matt 21:21
judgment, mercy,
    and *f* ..............Matt 23:23
have *f* in God ..........Mark 11:22
Thy *f* hath saved thee ...Luke 7:50
Where is your *f*.........Luke 8:25
Increase our *f*...........Luke 17:5
*f* on the earth...........Luke 18:8
that thy *f* fail not ......Luke 22:32
the *f* which ............Acts 3:16
a man full of *f*...........Acts 6:5
Holy Ghost and of *f*....Acts 11:24
had *f* to be healed .......Acts 14:9
opened the door of *f*....Acts 14:27
their hearts by *f* .........Acts 15:9
established in the *f*......Acts 16:5
*f* toward our Lord .......Acts 20:21
sanctified by *f*..........Acts 26:18
for obedience to the *f*...Rom 1:5
revealed from *f* to *f*......Rom 1:17
justified by *f*............Rom 3:28
*f* if counted ..............Rom 4:5
but was strong in *f*......Rom 4:20
we have access by *f*......Rom 5:2
the word of *f*............Rom 10:8
*f* cometh by hearing....Rom 10:17
the measure of *f*........Rom 12:3
not of *f* is sin...........Rom 14:23
though I have all *f*......1 Cor 13:2
And now abideth *f*.....1 Cor 13:13
your *f* is also vain.......1 Cor 15:14

stand fast in the *f*....1 Cor 16:13
dominion over your *f*... 2 Cor 1:24
same spirit of *f*.........2 Cor 4:13
we walk by *f*.............2 Cor 5:7
be in the *f*...............2 Cor 13:5
the *f* of Christ............Gal 2:16
*f* of the Son.............Gal 2:20
by the hearing of *f*........Gal 3:2
the law is not of *f*........Gal 3:12
justified by *f*.............Gal 3:24
*f* which worketh by love...Gal 5:6
of the household of *f*.....Gal 6:10
by the *f* of him............Eph 3:12
in your hearts by *f*........Eph 3:17
One Lord, one *f*..........Eph 4:5
in the unity of the *f*......Eph 4:13
taking the shield of *f*......Eph 6:16
for the *f*...................Phil 1:27
continue in the *f*..........Col 1:23
steadfastness of your *f*....Col 2:5
your work of *f*........ 1 Thess 1:3
the breastplate of *f*....1 Thess 5:8
and the work of *f*..... 2 Thess 1:11
all men have not *f*.... 2 Thess 3:2
son in the *f*............ 1 Tim 1:2
of *f* unfeigned ........... 1 Tim 1:5
if they continue in *f*.... 1 Tim 2:15
great boldness in the *f*... 1 Tim 3:13
shall depart from the *f*... 1 Tim 4:1
he hath denied the *f*..... 1 Tim 5:8
erred from the *f*........1 Tim 6:10
the unfeigned ........... 2 Tim 1:5
concerning the *f*......... 2 Tim 3:8
I have kept the *f*........2 Tim 4:7
not being mixed with *f*... Heb 4:2
of *f* toward God.......... Heb 6:1
through *f* and patience... Heb 6:12
in full assurance of *f*....Heb 10:22
*f* is the substance.........Heb 11:1
without *f* it is ...........Heb 11:6
These all died in *f*.......Heb 11:13
through *f* subdued ...... Heb 11:33
finisher of our *f*.........Heb 12:2
whose *f* follow...........Heb 13:7
trying of your *f*.........James 1:3
let him ask in *f*.........James 1:6
man say he hath *f*.....James 2:14
*f* if it hath not works....James 2:17
the prayer of *f*.........James 5:15
trial of your *f*.............1 Pet 1:7
the end of your *f*..........1 Pet 1:9
steadfast in the *f*..........1 Pet 5:9
even our *f*...............1 John 5:4
contend for the *f*..........Jude 3
your most holy *f*.........Jude 20
hast not denied my *f*.....Rev 2:13
patience and the *f*.......Rev 13:10
the *f* of Jesus ...........Rev 14:12
*See* Hab 2:4; 1 Tim 4:6

## FAITHFUL
a *f* witness in heaven.....Ps 89:37
commandments are *f*... Ps 119:86
righteous and very *f*.... Ps 119:138
a *f* spirit.................Prov 11:13
a *f* ambassador .........Prov 13:17
A *f* witness..............Prov 14:5
*f* man shall abound......Prov 28:20
a true and *f* witness ..... Jer 42:5
*f* and wise servant..... Matt 24:45
good and *f* servant .... Matt 25:21
*f* and wise steward .... Luke 12:42
*f* also in much ......... Luke 16:10
thou hast been *f*........Luke 19:17
judged me to be *f*..... Acts 16:15
man be found *f*.......... 1 Cor 4:2
*f* in the Lord............1 Cor 4:17
blessed with *f* Abraham ... Gal 3:9
and *f* minister ........... Eph 6:21
*f* minister in Christ ........Col 1:7
*F* is he that.............1 Thess 5:24
Lord is *f*................ 2 Thess 3:3
This is a *f* saying........ 1 Tim 1:15

*f* in all things.............1 Tim 3:11
thou to *f* man............ 2 Tim 2:2
It is a *f* saying...........2 Tim 2:11
yet he abideth *f*.........2 Tim 2:13
This is a *f* saying.........Titus 3:8
and *f* high priest......... Heb 2:17
*f* to him that appointed ... Heb 3:2
*f* that promised.........Heb 10:23
judged him *f*............Heb 11:11
as unto a *f* Creator.....1 Pet 4:19
he is *f*.................... 1 John 1:9
be thou *f* unto death .....Rev 2:10
my *f* martyr.............Rev 2:13
chosen, and *f*......... Rev 17:14
true and *f*..............Rev 21:5
*f* and true................ Rev 22:6
*See* Deut 7:9; Dan 6:4; Rev 1:5

## FAITHFULLY
doest *f* whatsoever...... 3 John 5

## FAITHFULNESS
no *f* in their mouth.........Ps 5:9
declared thy *f*............Ps 40:10
*f* the girdle..................Is 11:5
great is thy *f* ...........Lam 3:23
*See* 1 Sam 26:23; Ps 119:75

## FAITHLESS
O *f* and perverse
  generation ........... Matt 17:17
O *f* generation ..........Mark 9:19
and be not *f*............John 20:27

## FALL (n.)
haughty spirit before
  a *f*.....................Prov 16:18
great was the *f*........Matt 7:27
the *f* and rising .........Luke 2:34
if the *f* of them..........Rom 11:12
*See* Jer 49:21; Ezek 26:15

## FALL (v.)
let them *f*...................Ps 5:10
is *f* into the ditch .......... Ps 7:15
Though he *f* .............Ps 37:24
reproached are *f*.... Ps 69:9
kings shall *f* down .......Ps 72:11
A thousand shall *f*.........Ps 91:7
fool shall *f* ............. Prov 10:8
the people *f*........... Prov 11:14
riches shall *f*...........Prov 11:28
*f* into mischief ..........Prov 13:17
a perverse tongue *f*.... Prov 17:20
For a just man *f*......... Prov 24:16
shall *f* therein.......... Prov 26:27
alone when he *f*........ Eccl 4:10
diggeth a pit shall *f*..... Eccl 10:8
where the tree *f*........ Eccl 11:3
How art thou *f*............ Is 14:12
ye *f* down and worship... Dan 3:5
many shall *f* down...... Dan 11:26
and to the hills, *F*........ Hos 10:8
when I *f*..................Mic 7:8
*f* down and worship..... Matt 4:9
*f* on the ground........ Matt 10:29
*f* into the pit .......... Matt 12:11
*f* into the ditch..........Matt 15:14
*f* on the stone......... Matt 21:44
*f* from heaven .........Matt 24:29
they not both *f*.........Luke 6:39
temptation *f* away........ Luke 8:13
Satan as lightning *f*.... Luke 10:18
Whosoever shall
  *f* upon................Luke 20:18
*F* on us.................. Luke 23:30
he standeth or *f*..........Rom 14:4
occasion to *f*...........Rom 14:13
heed lest he *f*.........1 Cor 10:12
but some are *f* asleep... 1 Cor 15:6
*f* asleep in Christ ....1 Cor 15:18
ye are *f* from grace ...... Gal 5:4
*f* into..................... 1 Tim 3:6
*f* into reproach...........1 Tim 3:7
rich *f* into temptation ...1 Tim 6:9
lest any man *f*...........Heb 4:11

If they shall *f* away .......Heb 6:6
to *f* into the hands......Heb 10:31
when ye *f*...............James 1:2
flower thereof *f*.........James 1:11
*f* into condemnation... James 5:12
flower thereof *f* .........1 Pet 1:24
ye shall never *f* .........2 Pet 1:10
*f* from your own .........2 Pet 3:17
*F* on us....................Rev 6:16
*See* Is 21:9; Lam 5:16; Rev 14:8

## FALLING
have upholden him
  that was *f*................Job 4:4
my feet from *f*............Ps 56:13
a righteous man *f*..... Prov 25:26
a *f* away first........ 2 Thess 2:3
keep you from *f*...........Jude 24

## FALSE
Thou shalt not bear *f*
  witness................. Ex 20:16
raise a *f* report............ Ex 23:1
It is *f*...................2 Kin 9:12
hate every *f* way........Ps 119:104
thou *f* tongue...........Ps 120:3
a *f* witness..............Prov 6:19
A *f* balance............. Prov 11:1
a *f* witness deceit....... Prov 12:17
but a *f* witness.......... Prov 14:5
A *f* witness shall not.....Prov 19:5
Beware of *f* prophets....Matt 7:15
*f* Christs, and *f*........Matt 24:24
sought *f* witness........Matt 26:59
*f* prophets ............Mark 13:22
many bare *f* witness...Mark 14:56
by *f* accusation ......... Luke 19:8
found *f* witnesses ......1 Cor 15:15
are *f* apostles ......... 2 Cor 11:13
among *f* brethren...... 2 Cor 11:26
*f* accusers................ 2 Tim 3:3
not *f* accusers........... Titus 2:3
*See* 2 Pet 2:1; 1 John 4:1

## FAMILIAR
my *f* friends have for-
  gotten me.............Job 19:14
mine own *f* friend.........Ps 41:9

## FAMILY
shall all *f* of the earth be
  blessed ................ Gen 12:3
all the *f* of the earth .... Gen 28:14
*f* in heaven............. Eph 3:15
*See* Num 27:4; Amos 3:2

## FAMINE
pestilence, or *f*......... 2 Chr 20:9
alive in *f*.................Ps 33:19
the sword, the *f*......... Jer 24:10
evil arrows of *f*......... Ezek 5:16
there shall be *f*......... Matt 24:7
*f* and troubles ...........Mark 13:8
*f*, and pestilences ......Luke 21:11
*See* Luke 15:14; Rom 8:35

## FASHION
hands have made me
  and *f* me................Job 10:8
*f* us in the womb ........Job 31:15
He *f* their hearts.........Ps 33:15
the *f* of his .............Luke 9:29
*f* of this world ...........1 Cor 7:31
found in *f* as a man....... Phil 2:8
be *f* like ................. Phil 3:21
not *f* yourselves .........1 Pet 1:14
*See* Gen 6:15; Ezek 42:11

## FAST
Is not this the *f*........... Is 58:6
Sanctify ye a *f*..........Joel 1:14
did ye at all *f*.............Zech 7:5
when ye *f*.............. Matt 6:16
thy disciples *f* not ..... Matt 9:14
the children ... *f*....... Mark 2:19
*f* twice in the week .... Luke 18:12
*See* Matt 4:2; Acts 13:2

## FASTING

I humbled my soul
  with *f*.....................Ps 35:13
weak through *f*.........Ps 109:24
upon the *f* day............Jer 36:6
send them away *f*.......Mark 8:3
give yourselves to *f*.......1 Cor 7:5
in watchings, in *f*........2 Cor 6:5
in *f* often.................2 Cor 11:27
*See* Dan 6:18; 9:3; Matt 17:21

## FATHER

my *f* God..................Ex 15:2
iniquity of the *f*..........Ex 20:5
he that smiteth his *f*.....Ex 21:15
the God of thy *f*........1 Chr 28:9
God of our *f*..............Ezra 7:27
a *f* to the poor ..........Job 29:16
A *f* of the fatherless.....Ps 68:5
instruction of a *f*.........Prov 4:1
maketh a glad *f*.........Prov 10:1
the *f* of a fool ..........Prov 17:21
grief to his *f*.............Prov 17:25
The everlasting *F*..........Is 9:6
thou art our *f*............Is 63:16
thou art our *f*.............Is 64:8
My *f*, thou art ..........Jer 3:4
I am a *f* to Israel.........Jer 31:9
as the soul of the *f*.....Ezek 18:4
Have we not all one *f*....Mal 2:10
*F* which is in heaven....Matt 5:16
children of your *F* ......Matt 5:45
Our *F* which art......... Matt 6:9
for your heavenly *F*.....Matt 6:32
the will of my *F*.........Matt 7:21
go and bury my *f*.......Matt 8:21
the *f* the child..........Matt 10:21
He that loveth *f*.......Matt 10:37
Even so, *F* .............Matt 11:26
shall do the will
  of my *F*..............Matt 12:50
the face of my *F* .......Matt 18:10
not the will of your *F*..Matt 18:14
call no man your *f*.....Matt 23:9
Come, ye blessed
  of my *F*..............Matt 25:34
in the name of the *F*...Matt 28:19
he said, Abba, *F*......Mark 14:36
about my *F* business ...Luke 2:49
*F* also is merciful.......Luke 6:36
you that is a *f*..........Luke 11:11
your *F* knoweth ......Luke 12:30
your *F* good pleasure...Luke 12:32
*F*, I have sinned.........Luke 15:21
send him to my
  *f* house ..............Luke 16:27
*F*, if thou be willing....Luke 22:42
*F*, forgive them .......Luke 23:34
*F*, into thy hands.......Luke 23:46
begotten of the *F*......John 1:14
the *F* judgeth no man ..John 5:22
And the *F* himself ......John 5:37
All that the *F* giveth ....John 6:37
hath seen the *F*.........John 6:46
I and the *F* that sent....John 8:16
the *f* of it.................John 8:44
I honour my *F* ..........John 8:49
As the *F* knoweth me...John 10:15
I and my *F* are one ....John 10:30
*F*, save me ..............John 12:27
the *F* which sent me...John 12:49
unto the *F* ...............John 13:1
unto the *F*, but by me ...John 14:6
hath seen the *F*........John 14:9
And I will pray the *F*...John 14:16
the *F* which sent me...John 14:24
I go unto the *F*........John 14:28
my *F* is the
  husbandman...........John 15:1
ye shall ask of the *F* ...John 15:16
because I go to the *F*...John 16:16
pray the *F* for you ...John 16:26
the *F* is with me ......John 16:32

*F*, the hour is come ......John 17:1
I ascend unto my *F*....John 20:17
the God of my *f*......Acts 24:14
the *f* of all them ........Rom 4:11
we cry, Abba, *F* .........Rom 8:15
have ye not many *f*......1 Cor 4:15
*F* of mercies ............. 2 Cor 1:3
traditions of my *f*........Gal 1:14
appointed of the *f*........Gal 4:2
One God and *F* of all......Eph 4:6
*f*, provoke not your ......Eph 6:4
glory of God the *F* .......Phil 2:11
as a son with the *f*......Phil 2:22
it pleased the *f*........Col 1:19
entreat him as a *f*........1 Tim 5:1
I will be to him a *F* ......Heb 1:5
Without *f*................Heb 7:3
the *F* of spirits...........Heb 12:9
*F* of lights...............James 1:17
the *f* fell asleep ......... 2 Pet 3:4
is with the *F*.............1 John 1:3
an advocate with the *F*...1 John 2:1
the love of the *F* ......1 John 2:15
hath not the *F* .........1 John 2:23
of love the *F* hath.......1 John 3:1
the *F*, the Word .......1 John 5:7
*See* 1 Chr 29:10; Luke 11:2

## FAULTLESS

if that first covenant had
  been *f*....................Heb 8:7
and to present you *f*......Jude 24

## FEAR (n.)

the *f* of you and the
  dread of you............Gen 9:2
the *f* of God is not ...... Gen 20:11
and the *f* of thee........Deut 2:25
Is not this thy *f*..........Job 4:6
thou castest off *f* .........Job 15:4
The *f* of the Lord is ........Ps 19:9
I will teach you the *f*....... Ps 34:11
no *f* of God..............Ps 36:1
The *f* of the Lord .........Ps 111:10
when your *f* cometh.....Prov 1:26
not afraid of sudden *f*....Prov 3:25
*f* of the Lord ..........Prov 10:27
In the *f* of the Lord ....Prov 14:26
with the *f* of the Lord ...Prov 15:16
*f* of the Lord ........Prov 19:23
*f* of man bringeth.......Prov 29:25
and *f* shall be in..........Eccl 12:5
fear ye their *f*...............Is 8:12
and from thy *f*...............Is 14:3
*f* toward me is taught ....Is 29:13
of *f*, and not of peace ......Jer 30:5
I will put my *f*...........Jer 32:40
where is my *f*..............Mal 1:6
cried out for *f*........Matt 14:26
failing them for *f* ......Luke 21:26
openly of him for *f*......John 7:13
but secretly for *f*.......John 19:38
assembled for *f*.......John 20:19
*f* to whom *f*...........Rom 13:7
and in *f*, and in..........1 Cor 2:3
yea, what *f*.............2 Cor 7:11
with *f* and trembling ..... Eph 6:5
salvation with *f*........Phil 2:12
the spirit of *f*.............2 Tim 1:7
through *f* of death........Heb 2:15
moved with *f*.............Heb 11:7
reverence and godly *f*...Heb 12:28
themselves without *f*......Jude 12
others save with *f* ........Jude 23
*See* Ps 2:11; 1 Pet 2:18; 3:2

## FEAR (v.)

I know that thou *f* God ...Gen 22:12
and live; for I *f* God .....Gen 42:18
*F* ye not, stand still .......Ex 14:13
such as *f* God .............Ex 18:21
they may learn to *f* ......Deut 4:10
that they would *f* me ...Deut 5:29
*f* this glorious name ...Deut 28:58

*F* before him...........1 Chr 16:30
and *f* God above many ... Neh 7:2
Doth Job *f* God for
  nought ..................Job 1:9
I will *f* no evil...............Ps 23:4
whom shall I *f*........... Ps 27:1
*f* the Lord ...............Ps 34:9
not *f* what flesh..........Ps 56:4
all ye that *f* God..........Ps 66:16
is the man that *f*..........Ps 112:1
Ye that *f* the Lord........Ps 115:11
I will not *f* ...............Ps 118:6
They that *f* thee ........ Ps 119:74
*f* the Lord .................Prov 3:7
*f* thou the Lord ........Prov 24:21
the man that *f* always...Prov 28:14
but a woman that *f*.....Prov 31:30
that men should *f* .......Eccl 3:14
but *f* thou God...........Eccl 5:7
as he that *f* an oath.....Eccl 9:2
*F* God, and keep his .....Eccl 12:13
neither *f* ye their.........Is 8:12
Be strong, *f* not...........Is 35:4
*F* thou not .................Is 41:10
Let us now *f* the Lord ....Jer 5:24
Who would not *f* thee....Jer 10:7
shall *f* and tremble ......Jer 33:9
and *f* before the God.....Dan 6:26
Surely thou wilt *f* me....Zeph 3:7
they that *f* the Lord.....Mal 3:16
unto you that *f* my
  name ...................Mal 4:2
*f* him which is able ...Matt 10:28
whom ye shall *f*........Luke 12:5
*F* not, little flock.....Luke 12:32
judge, which *f* not God ...Luke 18:2
and one that *f* God......Acts 10:22
again to *f*...............Rom 8:15
not highminded, but *f*...Rom 11:20
But I *f* lest by ...........2 Cor 11:3
For I *f*, lest .............2 Cor 12:20
others also may *f* ....1 Tim 5:20
heard in that he *f*.........Heb 5:7
I will not *f* what man....Heb 13:6
no *f* in love...............1 John 4:18
*See* 1 Kin 18:12; Col 3:22

## FEED

fools *f* on foolishness...Prov 15:14
*f* me with food..........Prov 30:8
the lambs *f*...............Is 5:17
the bear shall *f*.............Is 11:7
there shall the calf *f*.....Is 27:10
He *f* on ashes...........Is 44:20
and the lamb shall *f*.....Is 65:25
*F* the flock of the ........Zech 11:4
heavenly Father *f*.......Matt 6:26
*F* my lambs.............John 21:15
He saith unto
  him, *F* my ...........John 21:16
Jesus saith unto
  him, *F* my ............John 21:17
hunger, *f* him ..........Rom 12:20
*F* the flock .............1 Pet 5:2
*See* Song 1:7; Acts 20:28

## FEET

lawgiver from be-
  tween his *f* ...........Gen 49:10
*f* was I to the lame.......Job 29:15
all things under his *f* .......Ps 8:6
my hands and my *f*......Ps 22:16
set my *f* upon a rock......Ps 40:2
thou deliver my *f*.........Ps 56:13
suffereth not our *f*.........Ps 66:9
and my *f* from falling....Ps 116:8
a lamp unto my *f*........Ps 119:105
Our *f* shall stand..........Ps 122:2
their *f* run to evil ........Prov 1:16
the path of thy *f* ........Prov 4:26
Her *f* go down to death...Prov 5:5
speaketh with his *f*......Prov 6:13
with his *f* sinneth........Prov 19:2
washed my *f*............Song 5:3

How beautiful are thy *f*...Song 7:1
he covered his *f*............ Is 6:2
even the *f* of the poor ..... Is 26:6
the *f* of him that ...........Is 52:7
place of my *f*............. Is 60:13
under his *f* all the...... Lam 3:34
stand upon thy *f*.........Ezek 2:1
set me upon my *f*....... Ezek 2:2
thy shoes upon thy *f*.. Ezek 24:17
stamped with the *f*.... Ezek 25:6
the waters with thy *f*... Ezek 32:2
the residue with
  your *f*................ Ezek 34:18
his *f* part of iron ......Dan 2:33
as the toes of the *f*.....Dan 2:42
his arms and his *f* ......Dan 10:6
And his *f* shall ..........Zech 14:4
them under their *f*...... Matt 7:6
the dust of your *f*.....Matt 10:14
two hands or two *f*.....Matt 18:8
dust under your *f*......Mark 6:11
guide our *f*.............. Luke 1:79
kissed his *f*.......... Luke 7:38
at the *f* of Jesus........Luke 8:35
dust from your *f*......... Luke 9:5
also sat at Jesus' *f* .....Luke 10:39
my hands and my *f*....Luke 24:39
and wiped his *f*.........John 11:2
anointed the *f*....... John 12:3
wash the disciples' *f*.... John 13:5
at the apostles' *f*........Acts 4:35
the *f* of them............Acts 5:9
the dust of their *f*..... Acts 13:51
*f* are swift to shed ......Rom 3:15
beautiful are the *f*......Rom 10:15
Satan under your *f* ...... Rom 16:20
the head to the *f*......1 Cor 12:21
enemies under his *f* ... 1 Cor 15:25
all things under his *f* .... Eph 1:22
your *f* shod .............. Eph 6:15
paths for your *f*......... Heb 12:13
*See* 2 Sam 4:4; 2 Kin 9:35

## FELL
his countenance *f* ........ Gen 4:5
Judas by
  transgression *f*........ Acts 1:25
*f* on sleep ...............Acts 13:36
the fathers *f* asleep ...... 2 Pet 3:4
of the nations *f*.........Rev 16:19
*See* Matt 13:4; Acts 10:44

## FELLOWSHIP
and *f,* and in breaking
  of bread ...............Acts 2:42
unto the *f* of his Son.......1 Cor 1:9
should have *f* with
  devils................1 Cor 10:20
what *f* hath ............. 2 Cor 6:14
see what is the *f* of ...... Eph 3:9
no *f* with the.............Eph 5:11
your *f* in the gospel.......Phil 1:5
if any *f* of the Spirit........Phil 2:1
the *f* of his ............... Phil 3:10
our *f* is with the ........ 1 John 1:3
we have *f* ................ 1 John 1:7
*See* Lev 6:2; 2 Cor 8:4

## FERVENT
being *f* in the spirit.....Acts 18:25
*f* in spirit.................. Rom 12:11
*f* prayer of a............James 5:16
a pure heart *f*............1 Pet 1:22
melt with *f* heat .......... 2 Pet 3:10
*See* 2 Cor 7:7; Col 4:12

## FEW
is of *f* days ...............Job 14:1
and *f* there be..........Matt 7:14
the labourers are *f*...... Matt 9:37
but *f* chosen ...........Matt 20:16
but *f* are chosen .......Matt 22:14
faithful over a *f*........ Matt 25:21
upon a *f* sick folk ........Mark 6:5
a *f* small fishes...........Mark 8:7

with *f* stripes .........Luke 12:48
*f* that be saved.........Luke 13:23
a *f* things against thee....Rev 2:14
*See* Deut 7:7; Ps 109:8

## FIERY
a *f* law for them.........Deut 33:2
a burning *f* furnace.......Dan 3:6
the *f* darts................ Eph 6:16
and *f* indignation....... Heb 10:27
the *f* trial................1 Pet 4:12
*See* Num 21:6; Deut 8:15

## FIGHT
The Lord shall *f* for you,
  and ye ..................Ex 14:14
he shall *f* for you........ Deut 1:30
he shall *f* for you........Deut 3:22
to *f* for you against .....Deut 20:4
he it is that *f*...........Josh 23:10
*f* the battles of.......1 Sam 25:28
would my servants *f*...John 18:36
to *f* against God..........Acts 5:39
not *f* against God ........Acts 23:9
so *f,* I, not as one.......1 Cor 9:26
without were *f*.......... 2 Cor 7:5
*f* the good *f* ...........1 Tim 6:12
fought a good *f* ........2 Tim 4:7
come wars and *f*........ James 4:1
*See* Zech 10:5; 14:14; Rev 2:16

## FILL
And I have *f* him with
  the spirit ................Ex 31:3
hath *f* him with...........Ex 35:31
shall be *f*................ Num 14:21
*f* my mouth with ........ Job 23:4
the whole earth be *f*.......Ps 72:19
and I will *f* it.............. Ps 81:10
they are *f* with good ....Ps 104:28
a fool when he is *f*.....Prov 30:22
for they shall be *f*........ Matt 5:6
be *f* with the
  Holy Ghost .............Luke 1:15
Elisabeth was *f* with....Luke 1:41
Zechariah was *f* with .. Luke 1:67
for ye shall be *f* ........ Luke 6:21
*f* all the house ...........Acts 2:2
Then Peter, *f* with .......Acts 4:8
and be *f* with the ........ Acts 9:17
Paul,) *f* with the ........Acts 13:9
*f* with all ................ Rom 1:29
*f* with all knowledge....Rom 15:14
that *f* all in all........... Eph 1:23
might be *f* with all...... Eph 3:19
be *f* with the Spirit ...... Eph 5:18
*f* with the fruits.......... Phil 1:11
*f* up that which ..........Col 1:24
be ye warmed and *f* ...James 2:16
in them is *f* up the........ Rev 15:1
*See* Dan 2:35; Luke 2:40; 15:16

## FIND
your sin will *f*
  you out...............Num 32:23
whoso *f* me, *f* life ....... Prov 8:35
Whoso *f* a wife *f* a ..... Prov 18:22
thy hand *f* to do .........Eccl 9:10
ye shall *f* rest .............. Jer 6:16
seek me, and *f* me ....... Jer 29:13
seek, and ye shall *f*.......Matt 7:7
few there be that *f* it.....Matt 7:14
shall *f* it.................Matt 10:39
his ways past *f* out .......Rom 11:33
and *f* grace to help.......Heb 4:16
*See* John 7:34; 2 Tim 1:18

## FINISH
the heavens and the
  earth were *f*.............Gen 2:1
thou hast *f*...........1 Chr 28:20
So the wall was *f* ....... Neh 6:15
and to *f* his work .......John 4:34
given me to *f* ...........John 5:36
have *f* the work........John 17:4

It is *f*...................John 19:30
I have *f* my course.......2 Tim 4:7
author and *f* of our ...... Heb 12:2
when it is *f*.............. James 1:15
*See* Dan 9:24; Rev 11:7; 19:7

## FIRE
bush burned with *f*.........Ex 3:2
there went out *f*.........Lev 10:2
pass through the *f*......Lev 18:21
pass through the *f*.... Deut 18:10
not in the *f*..............1 Kin 19:12
pass through the *f*.....2 Kin 17:17
from heaven by *f* ......1 Chr 21:26
the *f* burned ...............Ps 39:3
Lord in the *f*..............Is 24:15
walkest through the *f* ..... Is 43:2
I have seen the *f*..........Is 44:16
will come with *f*.......... Is 66:15
neither shall their *f*......Is 66:24
as a burning *f*..............Jer 20:9
a wall of *f* round ........ Zech 2:5
like a refiner's *f*........... Mal 3:2
and with *f*................Matt 3:11
into a furnace of *f* ..... Matt 13:42
into everlasting *f* ....... Matt 18:8
into everlasting *f* ...... Matt 25:41
the *f* that never ........Mark 9:43
come to send *f*.........Luke 12:49
*f* and brimstone from ...Luke 17:29
cast them into the *f* .... John 15:6
like as of *f*................Acts 2:3
yet so as by *f*...........1 Cor 3:15
In flaming *f*.............2 Thess 1:8
a flame of *f*...............Heb 1:7
the tongue is a *f* .......James 3:6
be tried with *f*...........1 Pet 1:7
reserved unto *f*......... 2 Pet 3:7
of eternal *f*.................Jude 7
out of the *f*................Jude 23
gold tried in the *f*.........Rev 3:18
and *f* came down.........Rev 20:9
into the lake of *f*........ Rev 20:10
with *f* and brimstone.....Rev 21:8
*See* Is 33:14; Jer 23:29

## FIRMAMENT
Let there be a *f* in
  the midst................Gen 1:6
the *f* sheweth his ..........Ps 19:1
likeness of the *f*.........Ezek 1:22
the brightness of the *f*... Dan 12:3

## FIRST
make me thereof a little
  cake *f*..................1 Kin 17:13
seek ye *f*...............Matt 6:33
*f* cast out the beam.......Matt 7:5
worse than the *f*........ Matt 12:45
Elijah must *f* come ..... Matt 17:10
is the *f* and great ......Matt 22:38
man desire to be *f*.......Mark 9:35
the *f* commandment ..Mark 12:28
let him *f* cast a stone ..... John 8:7
Christians *f* in .........Acts 11:26
the Jew *f* and also ....... Rom 2:9
the *f* of the Spirit ....... Rom 8:23
be the *f* among ......... Rom 8:29
if the *f* be holy ..........Rom 11:16
*f* apostles ..............1 Cor 12:28
let the *f* hold his ....... 1 Cor 14:30
and become the *f*...... 1 Cor 15:20
Christ the *f*.............1 Cor 15:23
*f* man Adam was
  made ................. 1 Cor 15:45
*f* gave their own ........2 Cor 8:5
if there be *f* a ........... 2 Cor 8:12
*f* commandment with.... Eph 6:2
*f* of every creature......Col 1:15
the *f* from the dead........Col 1:18
shall rise *f*.............1 Thess 4:16
a falling away *f* ....... 2 Thess 2:3
in me *f* Jesus.............. 1 Tim 1:16
Adam was *f* formed ....1 Tim 2:13

## FLAME

cast off their f faith ..... 1 Tim 5:12
f principles of ........... Heb 5:12
f for his own sins ........ Heb 7:27
church of the f ......... Heb 12:23
is f pure ................. James 3:17
and if it f begin ......... 1 Pet 4:17
he f loved us ........... 1 John 4:19
not their f estate ........... Jude 6
left thy f love ............. Rev 2:4
and do the f works ....... Rev 2:5
the f resurrection ....... Rev 20:5
f heaven and the f ...... Rev 21:1
See Ex 4:8; Num 18:13; John 12:16

## FLAME

f sword which turned
  every way ............. Gen 3:24
ascended in the f ..... Judg 13:20
and the f consumeth ..... Is 5:24
the f of devouring ........ Is 29:6
shall the f kindle ........... Is 43:2
with f of fire ........... Is 66:15
flaming f shall ........ Ezek 20:47
tormented in this f ... Luke 16:24
See Ps 29:7; Heb 1:7; Rev 1:14

## FLEE

he f also as a shadow ..... Job 14:2
F as a bird ................... Ps 11:1
The wicked f ............. Prov 28:1
f to the pit .............. Prov 28:17
the shadows f away .... Song 2:17
sighing shall f away ..... Is 35:10
mourning shall f .......... Is 51:11
f from the wrath ......... Matt 3:7
f into the ............... Matt 24:16
in Judea f to the ....... Mark 13:14
will f from him ........ John 10:5
F also youthful ........ 2 Tim 2:22
he will f from you ...... James 4:7
See 1 Cor 6:18; Rev 12:6, 14

## FLEECE

I will put a f of wool in
  the floor .............. Judg 6:37

## FLESH

and they shall be one f ... Gen 2:24
all f had corrupted ....... Gen 6:12
end of all f is come ..... Gen 6:13
all f died that moved ....Gen 7:21
life of all f is the blood ... Lev 17:14
cuttings in your f ....... Lev 19:28
spirits of all f ......... Num 16:22
yet in my f ............... Job 19:26
f is consumed away .... Job 33:21
my f also shall rest ........ Ps 16:9
shall all f come ......... Ps 65:2
thy f and thy body ...... Prov 5:11
troubleth his own f ..... Prov 11:17
riotous eaters of f ..... Prov 23:20
eateth his own f ........ Eccl 4:5
weariness of the f ..... Eccl 12:12
and all f shall see ........ Is 40:5
All f is grass .............. Is 40:6
upon all f ............... Joel 2:28
f and blood hath ....... Matt 16:17
shall be one f .......... Matt 19:5
no f be saved .......... Matt 24:22
the f is weak .......... Matt 26:41
no f should be ........ Mark 13:20
not f and bones ...... Luke 24:39
Word was made f ....... John 1:14
the bread ... is my f ... John 6:51
his f to eat .............. John 6:52
Whoso eateth my f ..... John 6:54
f profiteth nothing ...... John 6:63
Ye judge after the f ..... John 8:15
power over all f ......... John 17:2
infirmity of your f ...... Rom 6:19
condemned sin in the f ...Rom 8:3
live after the f ............ Rom 8:12
according to the f ....... Rom 9:3
provision for the f ......Rom 13:14
no f should glory ...... 1 Cor 1:29

shall be one f ........... 1 Cor 6:16
All f is not the same ... 1 Cor 15:39
f and blood ............ 1 Cor 15:50
a thorn in the f ......... 2 Cor 12:7
conferred not with f ...... Gal 1:16
live in the f ............... Gal 2:20
f lusteth ................. Gal 5:17
soweth to his f ............ Gal 6:8
two shall be one f ....... Eph 5:31
wrestle not against f ... Eph 6:12
confidence in the f ...... Phil 3:3
manifest in the f ....... 1 Tim 3:16
For all f is grass ........ 1 Pet 1:24
to death in the f ....... 1 Pet 3:18
come in the f .......... 1 John 4:2
dreamers defile the f ...... Jude 8
spotted by the f ........... Jude 23
See John 1:13; 3:6; Gal 5:19

## FLESHLY

not with f wisdom ....... 2 Cor 1:12
but in f tables ........... 2 Cor 3:3
by his f mind ............. Col 2:18
from f lusts ............. 1 Pet 2:11

## FLOCK

He shall feed his f like a
  shepherd ................ Is 40:11
f of my pasture ...... Ezek 34:31
O poor of the f ......... Zech 11:7
Fear not, little f ....... Luke 12:32
to all the f ............ Acts 20:28
the f of God ............ 1 Pet 5:2
See Mal 1:14; Matt 26:31

## FLOWER

shall die in the f of
  their age ............. 1 Sam 2:33
cometh forth like a f ..... Job 14:2
The f appear ............ Song 2:12
is a fading f ............... Is 28:1
as the f of the field ......... Is 40:6
See Job 15:33; 1 Cor 7:36

## FOLLOW

hath f me fully, him will
  I bring ................ Num 14:24
God, f him ............. 1 Kin 18:21
mercy shall f me ........... Ps 23:6
My soul f hard ............ Ps 63:8
the players ... f after ... Ps 68:25
f vain persons ........ Prov 12:11
f strong drink .............. Is 5:11
if we f on to ............. Hos 6:3
I f the flock ............ Amos 7:15
unto them, F me ....... Matt 4:19
I will f thee .......... Matt 8:19
and as they f ........... Mark 10:32
Lord, I will f thee ..... Luke 9:61
unto him, F me ......... John 1:43
and they f me ........... John 10:27
not f me now ........... John 13:36
f after the things ....... Rom 14:19
Rock that f them ....... 1 Cor 10:4
F after charity .......... 1 Cor 14:1
I f after ................. Phil 3:12
ever f that ............ 1 Thess 5:15
men they f after ........ 1 Tim 5:24
f after righteousness ... 1 Tim 6:11
f righteousness ....... 2 Tim 2:22
F peace with all ...... Heb 12:14
whose faith f ......... Heb 13:7
that should f .......... 1 Pet 1:11
that ye should f ....... 1 Pet 2:21
f the way ............... 2 Pet 2:15
which f the Lamb ...... Rev 14:4
works do f them ........ Rev 14:13
See Mark 9:38; 1 Pet 3:13

## FOLLOWER

Be ye therefore f of God ...Eph 5:1
but f of them ........... Heb 6:12

## FOOD

the tree was good for f ... Gen 3:6
her f, her raiment ........ Ex 21:10

in giving him f ......... Deut 10:18
Man did eat angels' f ..... Ps 78:25
f to all flesh ............. Ps 136:25
gathereth her f .......... Prov 6:8
she bringeth her f ..... Prov 31:14
bread for your f ......... 2 Cor 9:10
having f and raiment ... 1 Tim 6:8
destitute of daily f ..... James 2:15
See Gen 1:29; Lev 22:7

## FOOL

The f hath said ......... Ps 14:1
I said unto the f ........ Ps 75:4
f despise wisdom ........ Prov 1:7
the promotion of f ..... Prov 3:35
but a prating f ...... Prov 10:8, 10
f die for want ......... Prov 10:21
the f shall be servant ... Prov 11:29
way of a f is right ..... Prov 12:15
F make a mock at sin ... Prov 14:9
mouth of f poureth ... Prov 15:2
f will be meddling ..... Prov 20:3
A f uttereth all ........ Prov 29:11
the f walketh .......... Eccl 2:14
as the f ................. Eccl 2:16
A f also is full ........ Eccl 10:14
say, Thou f ............. Matt 5:22
ye f and blind ......... Matt 23:17
Thou f ................. Luke 12:20
O f, and slow of heart ... Luke 24:25
they became f .......... Rom 1:22
let him become a f ..... 1 Cor 3:18
We are f for Christ's ... 1 Cor 4:10
man think me a f ....... 2 Cor 11:16
a f in glorying ......... 2 Cor 12:11
not as f ................ Eph 5:15
See Prov 10:18; Eccl 10:3

## FOOLISH

O f people and unwise ...Deut 32:6
Forsake the f ........... Prov 9:6
A f woman is
  clamorous ............. Prov 9:13
f plucketh it down ...... Prov 14:1
A f son is a grief ....... Prov 17:25
neither be thou f ........ Eccl 7:17
my people is f .......... Jer 4:22
unto a f man ........... Matt 7:26
five were f ............. Matt 25:2
f heart was darkened .... Rom 1:21
made f the wisdom ..... 1 Cor 1:20
Are ye so f ............... Gal 3:3
nor f talking ........... Eph 5:4
f and hurtful lusts ...... 1 Tim 6:9
f and unlearned ....... 2 Tim 2:23
f questions ............. Titus 3:9
See Job 5:3; Lam 2:14; Ezek 13:3

## FOOLISHNESS

thou knowest my f ....... Ps 69:5
F is bound ............ Prov 22:15
thought of f is sin ...... Prov 24:9
them that perish f ...... 1 Cor 1:18
f of preaching ......... 1 Cor 1:21
f of God is wiser ........ 1 Cor 1:25
they are f unto him ..... 1 Cor 2:14
f with God ............. 1 Cor 3:19
See 2 Sam 15:31; Prov 27:22

## FOOTSTOOL

and the earth is my f ...... Is 66:1
for it is his f ........... Matt 5:35
be made his f .......... Heb 10:13

## FORBID

My lord Moses,
  f them ............... Num 11:28
F him not .............. Mark 9:39
f them not ........... Mark 10:14
f not to take ........... Luke 6:29
f to give tribute ....... Luke 23:2
Can any man f water ... Acts 10:47
f not to speak ......... 1 Cor 14:39
F to marry ............. 1 Tim 4:3
See Acts 16:6; 1 Thess 2:16

**FOREKNOW**
and *f* of God, ye
  have taken.............Acts 2:23
For whom he did *f*......Rom 8:29
people which he *f*.......Rom 11:2

**FOREORDAINED**
Who verily was
  *f* before...............1 Pet 1:20

**FORESEE**
A prudent man *f*
  the evil............... Prov 22:3
I *f* the Lord always ......Acts 2:25
*f* that God would .........Gal 3:8

**FORETELL**
behold, I have *f* you all
  things ...............Mark 13:23
have likewise *f*..........Acts 3:24
and *f* you ...............2 Cor 13:2

**FORGAVE**
loosed him, and *f* him
  the debt ........... Matt 18:27
I *f* thee all that debt ... Matt 18:32
he frankly *f* them.......Luke 7:42
he, to whom he
  *f* most .................Luke 7:43
if I *f* any thing .......2 Cor 2:10
even as Christ *f* you ......Col 3:13
*See* Ps 32:5; 78:38; 99:8

**FORGET**
lest thou *f* the things .... Deut 4:9
thou *f* not the Lord......Deut 8:11
of all that *f* God........Job 8:13
the nations that *f* God..... Ps 9:17
*f* not the humble .........Ps 10:12
*f* also thine own .........Ps 45:10
ye that *f* God.........Ps 50:22
and not *f* the works.......Ps 78:7
the land of *f*...........Ps 88:12
I will not *f* thy word .....Ps 119:16
*f* the covenant .........Prov 2:17
My son, *f* not my law ....Prov 3:1
they drink, and *f*........Prov 31:5
And *f* the Lord thy.......Is 51:13
that *f* my holy .........Is 65:11
cause my people to *f* ....Jer 23:27
*f* those things.........Phil 3:13
to *f* your work .........Heb 6:10
Be not *f* to entertain.....Heb 13:2
communicate *f* not.......Heb 13:16
*f* what manner........James 1:24
*See* Gen 41:51; Lam 5:20

**FORGIVE**
*f* iniquity............Ex 23:22
*f* iniquity............Num 14:18
thou hearest, *f*..........1 Kin 8:30
place, and *f*...........1 Kin 8:39
and will *f*...............2 Chr 7:14
transgression is *f*.........Ps 32:1
and ready to *f*.........Ps 86:5
Who *f* all...........Ps 103:3
*f* us our debts..........Matt 6:12
For if ye *f* men.........Matt 6:14
power on earth to *f* sins... Matt 9:6
and I *f*................Matt 18:21
from your hearts
  *f* not ...............Matt 18:35
who can *f* sins .........Mark 2:7
*f*, if ye have ought...... Mark 11:25
and ye shall be *f*........Luke 6:37
which are many, are *f*.....Luke 7:47
*f* us our sins ...........Luke 11:4
if he repent, *f* him .......Luke 17:3
Father, *f* them ......Luke 23:34
thine heart may be *f*.....Acts 8:22
whose iniquities are *f*.....Rom 4:7
ought rather to *f* .........2 Cor 2:7
To whom ye *f*.........2 Cor 2:10
*f* me this wrong ......2 Cor 12:13
hath *f* you................Eph 4:32

**FORGIVENESS**
there is *f* with thee .......Ps 130:4
hath never *f*...........Mark 3:29
and *f* of .................Acts 5:31
the *f* of sins .................Eph 1:7
even the *f* of sins .......Col 1:14
*See* Dan 9:9; Acts 13:38; 26:18

**FORGOTTEN**
*f* God that formed ..... Deut 32:18
not always be *f* ...........Ps 9:18
God hath *f* ................Ps 10:11
I am *f* ....................Ps 31:12
Why hast thou *f* me ......Ps 42:9
Hath God *f* to be ........Ps 77:9
shall all be *f*................Eccl 2:16
and they were *f*...........Eccl 8:10
the memory of them
  is *f*.......................Eccl 9:5
*f* the God................Is 17:10
thou shalt not be *f*........Is 44:21
my Lord hath *f* me .......Is 49:14
former troubles are *f*..... Is 65:16
my people have *f*.........Jer 2:32
they have the Lord ......Jer 3:21
thou hast *f* me...........Jer 13:25
my people have *f* me .....Jer 18:15
*f* the wickedness..........Jer 44:9
*f* their resting place......Jer 50:6
and hast *f* me.........Ezek 22:12
thou hast *f* me.........Ezek 23:35
had *f* to take bread ..... Matt 16:5
is *f* before God..........Luke 12:6
hath *f* that he was ....... 2 Pet 1:9
*See* Lam 2:6; Hos 4:6, 8:14

**FORMER**
rain, both the *f*............Jer 5:24
latter and *f* rain..........Hos 6:3
given you the *f*...........Joel 2:23
the *f* conversation ......Eph 4:22
for the *f* things............Rev 21:4
*See* Gen 40:13; Dan 11:13

**FORNICATION**
his wife, saving for the
  cause of *f*.............Matt 5:32
from *f*, and from......Acts 15:20
is not for *f* .................1 Cor 6:13
But *f* .......................Eph 5:3
should abstain from *f*...1 Thess 4:3

**FORSAKE**
he will not *f* thee ...... Deut 4:31
that thou *f* not.......... Deut 12:9
nor *f* thee ............... Deut 31:6
he *f* God which made....Deut 32:15
nor *f* thee ...............Josh 1:5
if thou *f* him ...........1 Chr 28:9
if ye *f* him ...........2 Chr 15:2
not *f* the house .........Neh 10:39
the house of God *f*......Neh 13:11
he *f* the fear...............Job 6:14
hath *f* the poor .........Job 20:19
why hast thou *f* me........ Ps 22:1
my mother *f* me .........Ps 27:10
seen the righteous *f*......Ps 37:25
judgment, and *f* not .....Ps 37:28
O *f* me not utterly ......Ps 119:8
*f* not the works .........Ps 138:8
and *f* not the law ........Prov 1:8
*f* the guide of her .......Prov 2:17
*F* her not..................Prov 4:6
friend, *f* not.............Prov 27:10
a great *f* in the midst ......Is 6:12
have I *f* thee ...........Is 54:7
the wicked *f* his way......Is 55:7
no more be termed *F*.....Is 62:4
A city not *f*............Is 62:12
have *f* me the fountain ... Jer 2:13

every city shall be *f*......Jer 4:29
they have *f* the Lord......Jer 17:13
every one that hath *f*... Jer 19:29
all the disciples *f*........Matt 26:56
they *f* their nets ........ Mark 1:18
And they all *f* him ....Mark 14:50
they *f* all ................Luke 5:11
you that *f* not all.......Luke 14:33
but not *f* .................2 Cor 4:9
Not *f* the .................Heb 10:25
By faith he *f* Egypt.......Heb 11:27
nor *f* thee .................Heb 13:5
*See* Ps 71:11; Is 49:14; Jer 5:7

**FORTRESS**
rock, and my *f*, and my
  deliverer..............2 Sam 22:2
my strength, and my *f*... Jer 16:19

**FORTY YEARS**
Israel did eat manna *f*....Ex 16:35
in the wilderness *f*.....Num 14:33
*F* long was I grieved......Ps 95:10
*See* Judg 3:11; 5:31; 8:28

**FOUGHT**
I have *f*................1 Cor 15:32
have *f* a good fight.......2 Tim 4:7

**FOUND**
when thou mayest be *f*....Ps 32:6
while he may be *f*.......... Is 55:6
but I *f* none............Ezek 22:30
and art *f* wanting........ Dan 5:27
iniquity was not *f*......... Mal 2:6
not *f* so great faith.......Matt 8:10
*f* one pearl of great .... Matt 13:46
they *f* fault..............Mark 7:2
I have *f* my sheep.......Luke 15:6
for I have *f* the piece.... Luke 15:9
was lost, and is *f*.......Luke 15:24
and was lost, and is *f*.... Luke 15:32
have *f* no fault.........Luke 23:14
have *f* the Messiah......John 1:41
was guile *f* in his ....... 1 Pet 2:22
*See* Gen 6:8; 2 Cor 5:3; Phil 3:9

**FOUNDATION**
whose *f* is in the..........Job 4:19
the *f* be destroyed..........Ps 11:3
the *f* of the earth..........Ps 82:5
thou laid the *f* of........Ps 102:25
an everlasting *f*.........Prov 10:25
in Zion for a *f*...........Is 28:16
the *f* of many .............Is 58:12
the *f* on a rock .........Luke 6:48
a *f* built an house.......Luke 6:49
upon another man's *f*... Rom 15:20
I have laid the *f*........1 Cor 3:10
other *f* can no man ....1 Cor 3:11
upon this *f* gold........1 Cor 3:12
in him before the *f*......Eph 1:4
a good *f* against........1 Tim 6:19
the *f* of God........... 2 Tim 2:19
from the *f* of the ........Heb 4:3
a city which hath *f*.......Heb 11:10
the city had twelve *f*.....Rev 21:14
*See* Matt 13:35; John 17:24

**FOUNTAIN**
were all the *f* of the
  great deep..............Gen 7:11
*f* also of the deep ......... Gen 8:2
of *f* and depths .........Deut 8:7
waters of the *f*........2 Chr 32:3
the *f* of life...............Ps 36:9
thy *f* be dispersed ......Prov 5:16
were no *f* abounding ... Prov 8:24
is a *f* of life.............Prov 13:14
at the *f*..................Eccl 12:6
*f* of living waters .......Jer 2:13
the *f* of living ............Jer 17:13
shall be a *f* opened ......Zech 13:1
a *f* send forth ..........James 3:11
no *f* both yield ..........James 3:12
unto living *f* of.............Rev 7:17

the *f* of waters ............. Rev 14:7
the *f* of the water ........ Rev 21:6
*See* Is 12:3; Joel 3:18; Mark 5:29

## FREE
tree of the garden thou
  mayest *f* eat ............ Gen 2:16
with thy *f* spirit............. Ps 51:12
*F* among the dead ......... Ps 88:5
let the oppressed go *f* ..... Is 58:6
I will love them *f* ........ Hos 14:4
*f* ye have received ...... Matt 10:8
are the children *f* ....... Matt 17:26
he shall be *f* ...........Mark 7:11
shall make you *f* ....... John 8:32
But I was *f* born ....... Acts 22:28
Being justified *f* ....... Rom 3:24
so also is the *f* gift ....... Rom 5:15
Being then made *f* ...... Rom 6:18
*f* from the law of sin.... Rom 8:2
am I not *f* ................1 Cor 9:1
though I be *f* from all... 1 Cor 9:19
we be bond or *f* ....... 1 Cor 12:13
neither bond nor *f* ....... Gal 3:28
Christ hath made us *f* ...... Gal 5:1
he be bond or *f* ......... Eph 6:8
the water of life *f* ......Rev 21:6
*See* Ex 21:2; Gal 4:22

## FRIEND
as a man speaketh
  unto his *f* ............. Ex 33:11
Abraham thy *f* ......... 2 Chr 20:7
he had been my *f* ......... Ps 35:14
familiar *f* in whom I ... Ps 41:9
Lover and *f* hast thou ....Ps 88:18
be surety for thy *f* ...... Prov 6:1
the rich hath many *f*... Prov 14:20
a *f* that sticketh closer... Prov 18:24
Wealth maketh many *f*... Prov 19:4
the wounds of a *f*....... Prov 27:6
this is my *f*............. Song 5:16
seed of Abraham my *f*......Is 41:8
and to all thy *f*........... Jer 20:4
Trust ye not in a *f*........ Mic 7:5
the house of my *f*....... Zech 13:6
his life for his *f*........ John 15:13
I have called you *f*.....John 15:15
the *F* of God ........... James 2:23
*f* of the world is the..... James 4:5
*See* Prov 22:24; Luke 14:10

## FRUIT
bringeth forth his *f*...... Ps 1:3
the *f* of the womb ........ Ps 127:3
*f* of the righteous....... Prov 11:30
his *f* was sweet .... Song 2:3
eat his pleasant *f* ....... Song 4:16
a basket of summer *f*....Amos 8:1
therefore *f* meet......... Matt 3:8
know them by their *f*....Matt 7:16
by their *f* ye shall ...... Matt 7:20
and his *f* good ........ Matt 12:33
also beareth *f*.......... Matt 13:23
bringeth forth *f*........Mark 4:28
the *f* of the vine.......Mark 14:25
therefore *f* worthy....... Luke 3:8
*f* unto life eternal.......John 4:36
bringeth forth much *f*... John 12:24
branch that beareth *f*... John 15:2
some *f* among you....... Rom 1:13
bring forth *f* unto God.....Rom 7:4
the *f* of your ............ 2 Cor 9:10
the *f* of the Spirit ....... Gal 5:22
*f* of the Spirit is in ...... Phil 1:11
*f* of righteousness ........ Phil 1:11
the *f* of my labour ....... Phil 1:22
I desire *f* that may........Phil 4:17
bringeth forth *f*............ Col 1:6
partaker of the *f*......... 2 Tim 2:6
peaceable *f* of............Heb 12:11
the *f* of our lips ........ Heb 13:15
of mercy and good *f*... James 3:17
the precious *f*...........James 5:7

trees whose *f* ............ Jude 12
yielded her *f* ............ Rev 22:2
*See* Gen. 30:2; Col 1:10

## FULFILL
will *f* the desire.......... Ps 145:19
that it might be *f* .......Matt 1:22
destroy, but to *f* .........Matt 5:17
all these things be *f*.... Matt 24:34
things shall be *f*........ Mark 13:4
be *f* in their season ..... Luke 1:20
the Gentiles be *f*....... Luke 21:24
be *f* in the kingdom ... Luke 22:16
joy therefore is *f*........John 3:29
might have my joy *f*...John 17:13
the law might be *f*...... Rom 8:4
is *f* in one word....... Gal 5:14
so *f* the law of Christ ...... Gal 6:2
*f* the desires of the........ Eph 2:3
*F* ye my joy ............ Phil 2:2
that thou *f* it.............. Col 4:17
*f* all the good.......... 2 Thess 1:11
If ye the royal .......James 2:8
*See* Ex 5:13; 23:26; Gal 5:16

## FULL
was *f* of the spirit...... Deut 34:9
and *f* of trouble........... Job 14:1
is *f* of cursing ............. Ps 10:7
is *f* of troubles .............Ps 88:3
is *f* of thy mercy ........ Ps 119:64
that hath his quiver *f*.... Ps 127:5
*f* soul loatheth ...........Prov 27:7
are never *f* ............. Prov 27:20
*f* of his praise ........... Hab 3:3
shall be *f* of light........ Matt 6:22
you that are *f* ........... Luke 6:25
be *f* of light .......... Luke 11:36
*f* of grace and truth...... John 1:14
joy might be *f*......... John 15:11
*f* of the Holy Ghost ...... Acts 6:3
*f* of the Holy Ghost ...... Acts 7:55
*f* of good works.......... Acts 9:36
*f* of the Holy Ghost .... Acts 11:24
is *f* of cursing ............Rom 3:14
*f* of goodness ......... Rom 15:14
Now ye are *f* ............. 1 Cor 4:8
both to be *f* ............. Phil 4:12
I am *f* ................... Phil 4:18
*f* proof of thy ministry ..2 Tim 4:5
that are of *f* ............... Heb 5:14
*f* of glory ...............1 Pet 1:8
joy may be *f*............. 1 John 1:4
*f* of the wrath of God ....Rev 15:7
*See* Lev 2:14; Amos 2:13

## FULLNESS
in thy presence is *f* of joy.....
of his *f* ................... John 1:16
much more their *f*.......Rom 11:25
the *f* of the time .......... Gal 4:4
the *f* of him ............. Eph 1:23
filled with all the *f*....... Eph 3:19
the *f* of Christ.......... Eph 4:13
should all *f* dwell ........Col 1:19
*f* of the Godhead bodily ... Col 2:9
*See* Num 18:27; Ps 96:11

---

# G

## GAIN
greedy of *g* troubleth...Prov 15:27
thou hast greedily *g* ... Ezek 22:12
the land for *g* ........... Dan 11:39
consecrate their *g* ....... Mic 4:13
*g* the whole world ..... Matt 16:26
*g* thy brother ......... Matt 18:15
*g* two other talents ... Matt 25:22
hath *g* ten pounds..... Luke 19:16
I might *g* the more ... 1 Cor 9:19
Did I make a *g* .......2 Cor 12:17
and to die is *g*............Phil 1:21
But what things were *g*....Phil 3:7

*g* is godliness ............1 Tim 6:5
*See* Job 27:8; James 4:13

## GARDEN
God planted a *g* eastward
  in Eden.................. Gen 2:8
as the *g* of the Lord..... Gen 13:10
*g* of the Lord.................Is 51:3
like a watered *g*...........Is 58:11
and as the *g*................Is 61:11
Eden the *g* of God ..... Ezek 28:13
The cedars in the *g*..... Ezek 31:8
is become like the *g* ...Ezek 36:35
*See* Gen 2:15; Amos 4:9; 9:14

## GARMENT
They part my *g* ...........Ps 22:18
wax old like a *g*......... Ps 102:26
wax old as a *g*............Is 50:9
put on thy beautiful *g* ......Is 52:1
*g* of praise ..................Is 61:3
the *g* of salvation .........Is 61:10
and not your *g*........... Joel 2:13
wear a rough *g*...........Zech 13:4
unto an old *g* ......... Matt 9:16
the hem of his *g* .......Matt 9:20
spread their *g* ...... Matt 21:8
on a wedding *g* ........Matt 22:11
parted his *g*........... Matt 27:35
and touched his *g* .....Mark 5:27
cast their *g* on him ......Mark 11:7
to take up his *g* ....... Mark 13:16
a piece of new *g* ....... Luke 5:36
border of his *g*......... Luke 8:44
they cast their *g* ...... Luke 19:35
let him sell his *g* ...... Luke 22:36
in shining *g* .......... Luke 24:4
your *g* are motheaten... James 5:2
hating even the *g*......... Jude 23
not defiled their *g* .......Rev 3:4
keepeth his *g* ........... Rev 16:15

## GATE
this is the *g* of heaven .. Gen 28:17
and on thy *g* ............. Deut 6:9
from the *g* of death...... Ps 9:13
Enter into his *g*.........Ps 100:4
*g* of righteousness ...... Ps 118:19
exalteth his *g* .......... Prov 17:19
known in the *g* ....... Prov 31:23
Open ye the *g*.......... Is 26:2
the *g* of the grave........ Is 38:10
the two leaved *g*.......... Is 45:1
thy *g* shall be open .......Is 60:11
and thy *g* Praise .........Is 60:18
for wide is the *g*........Matt 7:13
the *g* of hell............Matt 16:18
without the *g*........... Heb 13:12
And the *g* of it .......... Rev 21:25
*See* Ps 24:7; Is 28:6; Nah 2:6

## GAVE
she *g* me of the tree ..... Gen 3:12
Lord *g*, and the Lord ..... Job 1:21
thou *g* it him............. Ps 21:4
The Lord *g* the word ..... Ps 68:11
unto God who *g* it ....... Eccl 12:7
*g* his only begotten ...... John 3:16
as the Spirit *g*............. Acts 2:4
God *g* them over......... Rom 1:28
God *g* the increase........ 1 Cor 3:6
*g* gifts unto them......... Eph 4:8
he *g* some, apostles ......Eph 4:11
*g* himself for it..........Eph 5:25
Who *g* himself a
  ransom.................1 Tim 2:6
*See* 2 Cor 8:5; Titus 2:14

## GENERATION
one of these men of this
  evil.................. Deut 1:35
perverse and
  crooked *g*............. Deut 32:5
endure to every *g*...... Prov 27:24

One *g* passeth away ......Eccl 1:4
from *g* to *g*............... Is 34:10
O *g* of vipers...........Matt 3:7
judgment with this *g*...Matt 12:41
and perverse *g*........ Matt 17:17
ye *g* of vipers.........Matt 23:33
come upon this *g*...Matt 23:36
This *g* shall not pass...Matt 24:34
O faithless *g*...........Mark 9:19
in their *g* wiser.........Luke 16:8
rejected of this *g*...... Luke 17:25
This *g* shall not...... Luke 21:32
a chosen *g*............... 1 Pet 2:9
See Matt 1:1; Luke 11:30

## GENTILES
Go not into the way
  of the *G*.............. Matt 10:5
among the *G*............ John 7:35
before the *G* ............ Acts 9:15
*G* besought that .......Acts 13:42
lo, we turn to the *G*.... Acts 13:46
conversion of the *G*..... Acts 15:3
go unto the *G*........... Acts 18:6
also of the *G* .......... Rom 3:29
come unto the *G*....... Rom 11:11
apostle of the *G*....... Rom 11:13
named among the *G*....1 Cor 5:1
walk not as other *G*......Eph 4:17
teacher of the *G*........ 2 Tim 1:11
nothing of the *G*.........3 John 7
See 1 Pet 2:12; Rev 11:2

## GENTLE
we were *g* among you...1 Thess 2:7
but be *g* unto all....... 2 Tim 2:24
no brawlers, but *g*.......Titus 3:2
*g*, and easy...........James 3:17
the good and *g*...........1 Pet 2:18
See 2 Sam 18:5; 22:36; Gal 5:22

## GIFT
for the *g* blindeth
  the wise ............ Ex 23:8
neither take a *g*........ Deut 16:19
given us any *g*........2 Sam 19:42
nor taking of *g*......... 2 Chr 19:7
received *g* for men .......Ps 68:18
shall offer *g*...........Ps 72:10
givest many *g*.......... Prov 6:35
he that hateth *g* .......Prov 15:27
A *g* is as .............Prov 17:8
A man's *g* .............Prov 18:16
A *g* in secret ...........Prov 21:14
it is the *g* of God ........ Eccl 3:13
*g* destroyeth the heart.....Eccl 7:7
every one loveth *g*.........Is 1:23
bring thy *g*...........Matt 5:23
Leave there thy *g*....... Matt 5:24
give good *g* ............. Matt 7:11
casting their *g*.........Luke 21:1
the *g* of God.............John 4:10
thought that the *g*...... Acts 8:20
some spiritual *g*....... Rom 1:11
the *g* by grace..........Rom 5:15
the *g* of God............. Rom 6:23
the *g* and calling.......Rom 11:29
*g* differing according ... Rom 12:6
proper *g* of God...........1 Cor 7:7
diversities of *g*...........1 Cor 12:4
the best *g* .............1 Cor 12:31
desire spiritual *g* .........1 Cor 14:1
of spiritual *g*............1 Cor 14:12
his unspeakable *g* ...... 2 Cor 9:15
it is the *g* of God ........ Eph 2:8
gave *g* unto men.......... Eph 4:8
I desire a *g*............Phil 4:17
Neglect not the *g* .......1 Tim 4:14
stir up the *g* of God......2 Tim 1:6
Every good *g* ........... James 1:17
See Num 18:29; 1 Cor 13:2

## GLAD
he will be *g* in his heart....Ex 4:14
*g*, when they can ........ Job 3:22

my heart is *g*............... Ps 16:9
be *g* and rejoice........... Ps 31:7
hear thereof, and be *g*.....Ps 34:2
shall make *g* the city ......Ps 46:4
and be *g* ................. Ps 69:32
maketh *g* the heart ......Ps 104:15
I was *g* ................. Ps 122:1
whereof we are *g*........Ps 126:3
maketh a *g* father......Prov 10:1
not thine heart be *g* ....Prov 24:17
they are *g*................ Lam 1:21
merry, and be *g*....... Luke 15:32
saw it, and was *g* ......John 8:56
And I am *g* for your....John 11:15
that *g* received........... Acts 2:41
See Mark 6:20; 12:37; Luke 1:19

## GLADNESS
Also in the day of
  your *g* .............. Num 10:10
with *g* of heart........Deut 28:47
was very great *g* ......... Neh 8:17
put *g* in my heart........ Ps 4:7
the oil of *g*............. Ps 45:7
and *g* for the upright ..... Ps 97:11
obtain joy and *g* ......... Is 35:10
*g* and singleness....... Acts 2:46
See Ps 100:2; Prov 10:28

## GLASS
now we see through
  a *g* darkly.............1 Cor 13:12
beholding as in a *g* ...... 2 Cor 3:18
was a sea of *g*........... Rev 4:6
a sea of *g* mingled ........Rev 15:2

## GLORIFY
offereth praise *g* me..... Ps 50:23
I will *g* thy name .........Ps 86:12
I will *g* the house........ Is 60:7
I will be *g* ...............Ezek 28:22
and *g* your Father...... Matt 5:16
*g* the God of Israel......Matt 15:31
being *g* of all............ Luke 4:15
Jesus was not yet *g*.... John 7:39
Son of God might be *g*...John 11:4
but when Jesus was *g*...John 12:16
I have both *g* it .........John 12:28
God shall also *g* him...John 13:32
Herein is my Father *g* ... John 15:8
Son also may *g* thee....John 17:1
he should *g* God ....... John 21:19
*g* him not as God ........ Rom 1:21
that we may be also *g* ...Rom 8:17
them he also *g*........Rom 8:30
therefore *g* God.........1 Cor 6:20
And they *g* God in me .... Gal 1:24
*g* in his saints......... 2 Thess 1:10
Christ *g* not himself .... Heb 5:5
*g* God in the day ........1 Pet 2:12
See Is 25:5; Luke 7:16

## GLORIOUS
*G* things are spoken .......Ps 67:3
his rest shall be *g*......... Is 11:10
make thyself a *g* name ... Is 63:14
A *g* high throne..........Jer 17:12
stand in the *g* land ......Dan 11:16
*g* holy mountain........ Dan 11:45
*g* things..................Luke 13:17
*g* liberty................ Rom 8:21
in stones, was *g* ..... 2 Cor 3:7
spirit be rather *g*........2 Cor 3:8
light of the *g* gospel .... 2 Cor 4:4
to himself a *g* church.....Eph 5:27
like unto his *g* body ..... Phil 3:21
the *g* gospel.............1 Tim 1:11
the *g* appearing......... Titus 2:13
See Ex 15:1; 2 Sam 6:20

## GLORY
I beseech thee, shew
  me thy *g*...............Ex 33:18
be filled with the *g* .... Num 14:21
thy *g* above the heavens.... Ps 8:1

and the King of *g* .......... Ps 24:7
give grace and *g* ......... Ps 84:11
speak of the *g*........... Ps 145:11
shall inherit *g*........... Prov 3:35
the *g* of children.........Prov 17:6
the *g* of young men... Prov 20:29
the *g* of God............ Prov 25:2
their own *g* is not *g*.... Prov 25:27
is full of his *g* .............. Is 6:3
*g* to the righteous ........ Is 24:16
my *g* will I not give........ Is 42:8
created him for my *g* .......Is 43:7
the house of my *g* ..... Is 60:7
fill this house with *g*..... Hag 2:7
that they may have *g*.... Matt 6:2
the power, and the *g* ... Matt 6:13
his *g* was not ...........Matt 6:29
come in the *g*........... Matt 16:27
in the throne of his *g*... Matt 19:28
with power and
  great *g*...............Matt 24:30
great power and *g*.....Mark 13:26
*G* to God ............... Luke 2:14
come in his own *g*.....Luke 9:26
peace in heaven,
  and *g* .................Luke 19:38
power and great *g*.... Luke 21:27
to enter into his *g* ....Luke 24:26
we beheld his *g*........John 1:14
manifested forth his *g*...John 2:11
I seek not mine own *g*... John 8:50
see the *g* of God ....... John 11:40
with the *g* which I had ...John 17:5
they may behold
  my *g*................. John 17:24
gave not God the *g* ....Acts 12:23
come short of the *g*.... Rom 3:23
the *g* which shall be .... Rom 8:18
to whom be *g*...........Rom 11:36
no flesh should *g* ....... 1 Cor 1:29
to the *g* of God.........1 Cor 10:31
but the woman is the *g*...1 Cor 11:7
it is a *g* to her .........1 Cor 11:15
*g* of the celestial ....... 1 Cor 15:40
it is raised in *g*........1 Cor 15:43
the *g* of the Lord........ 2 Cor 3:18
I should *g*................ Gal 6:14
the Father of *g*............ Eph 1:17
Unto him be *g* .......... Eph 3:21
*g* is in their shame.......Phil 3:19
to his riches in *g*......... Phil 4:19
the hope of *g* ............. Col 1:27
appear with him in *g*......Col 3:4
the *g* of his power .....2 Thess 1:9
received up into *g* ......1 Tim 3:16
brightness of his *g*........Heb 1:3
many sons unto *g*......... Heb 2:10
worthy of more *g*......... Heb 3:3
full of *g* .................. 1 Pet 1:8
*g* that should follow ......1 Pet 1:11
the *g* of man.............1 Pet 1:24
the spirit of *g*............1 Pet 4:14
unto his eternal *g*.......1 Pet 5:10
from the excellent *g*..... 2 Pet 1:17
received *g* and honour ... Rev 4:11
and honour, and *g*.....Rev 5:12
Blessing, and *g* .........Rev 7:12
lightened with his *g* .....Rev 18:1
the *g* of God............. Rev 21:23
See Luke 17:18; James 2:1

## GLORYING
Your *g* is not good....... 1 Cor 5:6
should make my *g* void...1 Cor 9:15
great is my *g*............2 Cor 7:4
become a fool in *g*......2 Cor 12:11

## GNASH
shall be weeping and
  *g* of teeth............. Matt 8:12
and *g* of teeth...... Matt 13:42, 50
*g* with his teeth.........Mark 9:18
See Job 16:9; Ps 35:16

## GO

whither thou *g* .........Ruth 1:16
to *g* a mile ...............Matt 5:41
*G* ye therefore .........Matt 28:19
*g* unto my Father...... John 14:12
*See* Matt 8:9; 1 Cor 9:7

## GOD

And Enoch walked
  with *G* .................. Gen 5:22
and Noah walked
  with *G* .................. Gen 6:9
Thou *G* seest me......... Gen 16:13
thou power with *G* .....Gen 32:28
*G* shall be with you ..... Gen 48:21
*G* is not a man .........Num 23:19
What hath *G*
  wrought..............Num 23:23
*G* is there ............Deut 3:24
The eternal *G*..........Deut 33:27
that there is a *G*....... 1 Sam 17:46
If the Lord be *G*........1 Kin 18:21
The Lord, he is the *G* ...1 Kin 18:39
How doth *G* know ......Job 22:13
There is no *G* .............Ps 14:1
My *G*, my *G*, why hast...... Ps 22:1
for *G* is for me .............Ps 56:9
thou art *G* alone .........Ps 86:10
before *G:* for *G* is.......... Eccl 5:2
thou are the *G* ............Is 37:16
Is there a *G* .............Is 44:8
for I am *G*................. Is 45:22
for I am *G*................Hos 11:9
whose name is The *G* ...Amos 5:27
call upon thy *G* ...........Jon 1:6
walk humbly with thy *G*....Mic 6:8
is, *G* with us ............ Matt 1:23
*G* is not the *G* ........Matt 22:32
for there is one *G* ......Mark 12:32
that *G* is true..........John 3:33
*G* is a Spirit ...........John 4:24
from *G*, and went to *G*....John 13:3
to my *G* and your *G* .....John 20:17
let *G* be true ........... Rom 3:4
if *G* be for us ...........Rom 8:31
*G* is faithful ...............1 Cor 1:9
*G* is faithful .............1 Cor 10:13
that *G* is in you ........ 1 Cor 14:25
*G* is not the author .... 1 Cor 14:33
but *G* is one................Gal 3:20
*G* is not mocked ........ Gal 6:7
my *G* shall supply ...... Phil 4:19
all that is called *G*..... 2 Thess 2:4
he as *G* sitteth in the
  temple............... 2 Thess 2:4
*G* was manifest .........1 Tim 3:16
I will be to them a *G*..... Heb 8:10
to be called their *G* ......Heb 11:16
*G* the Judge of all ....... Heb 12:23
that *G* is light ...........1 John 1:5
*G* is love...............1 John 4:8
No man hath seen *G*...1 John 4:12
know that we are
  of *G*...................1 John 5:19
*G* himself shall be.........Rev 21:3
*G* shall wipe away ........Rev 21:4
I will be his *G* .............Rev 21:7
*See* Job 33:12; Ps 10:4

## GODHEAD

*G* is like unto gold ......Acts 17:29
eternal power and *G*.... Rom 1:20
fullness of the *G* bodily.... Col 2:9

## GODLINESS

great is the mystery
  of *g*....................1 Tim 3:16
thyself rather unto *g* ....1 Tim 4:7
supposing that gain
  is *g*.....................1 Tim 6:5
Having a form of *g* ..... 2 Tim 3:5
which is after *g* ...........Titus 1:1
unto life and *g*........... 2 Pet 1:3
and to patience *g*........ 2 Pet 1:6

conversation and *g*......2 Pet 3:11
*See* 1 Tim 2:2, 10; 6:6, 11

## GODLY

the *g* man ceaseth..........Ps 12:1
might seek a *g* seed ......Mal 2:15
simplicity and *g* .........2 Cor 1:12
*g* sorrow worketh ...... 2 Cor 7:10
live *g* in Christ Jesus....2 Tim 3:12
righteously, and *g* ...... Titus 2:12
and *g* fear...............Heb 12:28
deliver the *g* ............ 2 Pet 2:9
after a *g* sort ............ 3 John 6
*See* Ps 4:3; 2 Cor 7:9

## GONE

*g* like the shadow....... Ps 109:23
I have *g* astray.......... Ps 119:176
sheep have *g* astray ....... Is 53:6
her sun is *g* down ....... Jer 15:9
unclean spirit is *g* ..... Matt 12:43
lamps are *g* out........ Matt 25:8
They are all *g* ...........Rom 3:12
*g* in the way of Cain ......Jude 11
*See* Ps 89:34; Song 2:11

## GOOD (n.)

God meant it unto *g*... Gen 50:20
none that doeth *g* .........Ps 14:1
Withhold not *g* ........ Prov 3:27
there is no *g* in them .... Eccl 3:12
destroyeth much *g* ...... Eccl 9:18
went about doing *g* ...Acts 10:38
work together for *g*..... Rom 8:28
to thee for *g* .............Rom 13:4
*See* Job 5:27; Prov 11:17

## GOOD (adj.)

God saw the light, that
  it was *g*...............Gen 1:4
God saw that it was *g*.....Gen 1:10
the Lord is *g*...............Ps 34:8
*g* name is rather.........Prov 22:1
so is *g* news............. Prov 25:25
what is *g* for men......... Eccl 6:12
ye that which is *g*.......... Is 55:2
It is *g* that a man
  should................. Lam 3:26
It is *g* for a man......... Lam 3:27
*g* words ................Zech 1:13
to give *g* gifts ........... Matt 7:11
be of *g* comfort........ Matt 9:22
*G* Master, what *g*...... Matt 19:16
callest thou me *g* ...... Matt 19:17
thou *g* and faithful .... Matt 25:21
Salt is *g* ................Mark 9:50
*g* measure,
  pressed down ........Luke 6:38
chosen that *g* part.......Luke 10:42
Father's *g* pleasure.....Luke 12:32
Why callest thou
  me *g* ..................Luke 18:19
Can there any *g*......... John 1:46
I am the *g* shepherd...John 10:11
and just, and *g*.........Rom 7:12
dwelleth no *g* thing .....Rom 7:18
prove what is that *g*.....Rom 12:2
*g* neither to eat ....... Rom 14:21
*g* for the present........ 1 Cor 7:26
corrupt *g* manners .... 1 Cor 15:33
to every *g* work.........2 Cor 9:8
all *g* things................Gal 6:6
begun a *g* work in .........Phil 1:6
in every *g* work..........Col 1:10
that which is *g*........ 1 Thess 5:15
which is *g* .............1 Thess 5:21
the law is *g* .............1 Tim 1:8
he desireth a *g* work..... 1 Tim 3:1
creature of God is *g*..... 1 Tim 4:4
Fight the *g*............. 1 Tim 6:12
that are *g* .............. 2 Tim 3:3
a pattern of *g* works..... Titus 2:7
zealous of *g* works..... Titus 2:14
the *g* word..............Heb 6:5
it is a *g* thing............ Heb 13:9

Every *g* gift ............ James 1:17
but that which is *g* ......3 John 11
*See* 2 Thess 2:17; Titus 1:16

## GOODNESS

make all my *g* pass
  before thee............Ex 33:19
abundant in *g* and truth ...Ex 34:6
*g* extendeth not ...........Ps 16:2
Surely *g* and mercy......Ps 23:6
the *g* of the Lord.........Ps 27:13
earth is full of the *g*......Ps 33:5
the year with thy *g* ....... Ps 65:11
every one his own *g* ....Prov 20:6
your *g* is as a morning... Hos 6:4
how great is his *g* .......Zech 9:17
the riches of his *g*....... Rom 2:4
*See* Neh 9:25; Is 63:7; Gal 5:22

## GOSPEL

have the *g* preached
  to them................. Matt 11:5
my sake and the *g*......Mark 8:35
ashamed of the *g*...... Rom 1:16
preach the *g* of peace...Rom 10:15
But if our *g* be hid ...... 2 Cor 4:3
preach any other *g* ........ Gal 1:8
*g* of the uncircumcision ... Gal 2:7
the hope of the *g* ...... Col 1:23
to the glorious *g*..........1 Tim 1:11
the everlasting *g*........Rev 14:6
*See* Matt 4:23; Mark 16:15

## GOVERNMENT

the *g* shall be upon his
  shoulder............... Is 9:6
helps, *g*, diversities.... 1 Cor 12:28
and despise *g*........... 2 Pet 2:10

## GRACE

*g* is poured into............Ps 45:2
an ornament of *g*........Prov 1:9
but he giveth *g* unto.... Prov 3:34
spirit of *g* and of ....... Zech 12:10
full of *g* and truth.......John 1:14
*G* to you and peace ...... Rom 1:7
freely by his *g*........... Rom 3:24
not reckoned of *g*....... Rom 4:4
*g* did much more
  abound............... Rom 5:20
but under *g*............. Rom 6:14
the election of *g* ........ Rom 11:5
*G* be unto you..............1 Cor 1:3
*G* be to you .............. 2 Cor 1:2
the *g* of our Lord Jesus... 2 Cor 8:9
My *g* is sufficient ....... 2 Cor 12:9
into the *g* of Christ ...... Gal 1:6
and called me by his *g*.....Gal 1:15
ye are fallen from *g*....... Gal 5:4
by *g* ye are saved ....... Eph 2:5
is this *g* given............ Eph 3:8
the throne of *g*.......... Heb 4:16
the Spirit of *g*..........Heb 10:29
But he giveth more *g* .. James 4:6
and giveth *g* to ...........1 Pet 5:5
grow in *g*, and in the ... 2 Pet 3:18
*See* Acts 20:24; 2 Cor 6:1

## GRACIOUS

for I am *g* ................ Ex 22:27
*g* to whom I will ......... Ex 33:19
*g* and merciful........... Neh 9:17
forgotten to be *g* .........Ps 77:9
A *g* woman ........... Prov 11:16
he may be *g* unto....... Is 30:18
thou are a *g* God..........Jon 4:2
the *g* words.............Luke 4:22
the Lord is *g* .............1 Pet 2:3
*See* Ex 34:6; 2 Chr 30:9

## GRAVE (n.)

gray hairs with sorrow
  to the *g*...............Gen 42:38
sorrow to the *g* ......... Gen 44:31
goeth down to the *g* ....Job 7:9
in the *g* who shall ..........Ps 6:5

be silent in the *g*.......... Ps 31:17
the power of the *g*....... Ps 49:15
in the *g*.................. Eccl 9:10
the *g* cannot praise....... Is 38:18
his *g* with the wicked..... Is 53:9
O *g*, I will be ..........Hos 13:14
that are in the *g* .......John 5:28
to the *g* to weep ........John 11:31
O *g*, where is thy....... 1 Cor 15:55
*See* Matt 27:52; Rev 11:9

## GREAT
I will make of thee a *g*
    nation ................ Gen 12:2
*g* and mighty nation.... Gen 18:18
of these a *g* nation........ Gen 46:3
for *g* is our God ........ 2 Chr 2:5
how *g* is thy goodness.... Ps 31:19
how *g* are thy works....... Ps 92:5
O God! how *g* is the...... Ps 139:17
for *g* is your.............Matt 5:12
called *g* in the........... Matt 5:19
one pearl of *g* price.... Matt 13:46
*g* is thy faith ........ Matt 15:28
whosoever will be *g* ...Matt 20:26
the *g* commandment ...Matt 22:36
*g* is the mystery ........1 Tim 3:16
so *g* salvation.......... Heb 2:3
*See* Deut 9:2; Eccl 2:9; Rev 7:9

## GREATER
*g* than the temple ...... Matt 12:6
commandment
    *g* than ............. Mark 12:31
see *g* things than .... John 1:50
Art thou *g* than ......... John 4:12
*g* works than these ....John 5:20
*g* than our father........John 8:53
is *g* than all .............John 10:29
*g* works than these .... John 14:12
for my Father is *g*....... John 14:28
The servant is not *g*.... John 13:16
*G* love hath no man.... John 15:13
could swear by no *g* .... Heb 6:13
God is *g* than .......... 1 John 3:20
because *g* is he that ...1 John 4:4
I have no *g* joy.......... 3 John 4
*See* Gen 41:40; 48:19; Heb 9:11

## GREATEST
the *g* in the kingdom ....Matt 18:1
who should be the *g*....Mark 9:34
should be *g* .............Luke 9:46
but the *g* of .............1 Cor 13:13
*See* Job 1:3; Jer 31:34

## GRIEF
life is spent with *g*........ Ps 31:10
is much *g* ..............Eccl 1:18
acquainted with *g* ....... Is 53:3
*See* Jon 4:6; Heb 13:17

## GRIEVE
*g* for the hardness ....... Mark 3:5
And *g* not the holy......Eph 4:30
*See* Neh 2:10; 13:8; Ps 119:158

## GROW
*g* up before him ........... Is 53:2
both *g* together........ Matt 13:30
*g* unto a holy ........... Eph 2:21
may *g* up into him....... Eph 4:15
*g* in grace ............... 2 Pet 3:18
*See* 2 Kin 19:26; Jer 12:2

## GUIDE
he will be our *g*...........Ps 48:14
having no *g* ..............Prov 6:7
the Lord shall ............ Is 58:11
thou are the *g* of my....... Jer 3:4
*g* our feet into .......... Luke 1:79
he will *g* you........... John 16:13
*See* Gen 48:14; Prov 11:3

## GUILTY
clear the *g* ................Ex 34:7
clearing the *g*........... Num 14:18

become *g* before God... Rom 3:19
shall be *g* of.............1 Cor 11:27
he is *g* of all.............James 2:10
*See* Num 35:27; Prov 30:10

## ——— H ———

## HABITATION
Let their *h* be desolate ...Ps 69:25
into everlasting *h*...... Luke 16:9
let his *h* be desolate .....Acts 1:20
for a *h* of God ...........Eph 2:22
but left their own *h*....... Jude 6
*See* Prov 8:31; Acts 1:20

## HAIR
the *h* of mine head .......Ps 40:12
make one *h* white ..... Matt 5:36
the very *h* of your....... Matt 10:30
man have long *h* ........1 Cor 11:14
not with braided *h* ......1 Tim 2:9
of plaiting the *h* ..........1 Pet 3:3
*See* 2 Sam 14:26; Hos 7:9

## HALLOW
*H* be thy name........... Matt 6:9

## HAND
*h* for *h*....................Ex 21:24
Is the Lord's *h*........ Num 11:23
from his right *h*........Deut 33:2
*h* of God................1 Sam 5:11
*h* of the Lord.........2 Sam 24:14
In whose *h* is ..........Job 12:10
the *h* of God .............Job 19:21
at thy right *h*..............Ps 16:11
He that hath clean *h*.......Ps 24:4
the work of our *h*.......Ps 90:17
folding of the *h* ......... Prov 6:10
though *h* join in *h* .... Prov 11:21
hideth his *h*........... Prov 19:24
that strike *h* .......... Prov 22:26
the *h* of God .............Eccl 2:24
thy *h* findeth to do .......Eccl 9:10
withhold not thine *h* .....Eccl 11:6
hollow of his *h*............. Is 40:12
the Lord's *h* is not ...........Is 59:1
fill thine *h* .............. Ezek 10:2
wounds in thine *h*...... Zech 13:6
heaven is at *h*............. Matt 3:2
let not thy left *h* ........ Matt 6:3
if thy *h* or thy foot....... Matt 18:8
My time is at *h*.......... Matt 26:18
he is at *h* that.........Matt 26:46
thy *h* offend thee .......Mark 9:43
the right *h* of God...... Mark 16:19
not made with *h*.........2 Cor 5:1
The Lord is at *h*.......... Phil 4:5
Christ is at *h* ......... 2 Thess 2:2
lifting up holy *h* ........1 Tim 2:8
*h* of the living God....... Heb 10:31
Cleanse your *h*........James 4:8
the end ... is at *h*.........1 Pet 4:7
our *h* have handled......1 John 1:1
*See* Luke 9:62; Col 2:14

## HAPPY
*H* art thou ..............Deut 33:29
*h* is the man ...........Job 5:17
*h* shalt thou be ..........Ps 128:2
*H* is that people..........Ps 144:15
*h* is every one...........Prov 3:18
*h* is he...................Prov 14:21
are all they *h*...............Jer 12:1
call the proud *h*........Mal 3:15
*h* are ye ...............John 13:17
*H* is he that ...........Rom 14:22
we count them *h* ......James 5:11
*h* are ye ...............1 Pet 3:14
*See* Prov 29:18; 1 Cor 7:40

## HARDEN
but I will *h* his heart,
    that he....................Ex 4:21
will *h* the hearts ..........Ex 14:17

*H* not your heart............Ps 95:8
man *h* his face ..........Prov 21:29
he that *h* his heart..... Prov 28:14
being often reproved *h*...Prov 29:1
and *h* our heart..........Is 63:17
heart was *h* ...........Mark 6:52
your heart yet *h* .......Mark 8:17
and *h* their.............John 12:40
when divers were *h* .....Acts 19:9
he will be *h* ............Rom 9:18
*h* through the...........Heb 3:13
*See* Deut 15:7; Job 39:16

## HARDNESS
grieved for the *h* of their
    hearts ............... Mark 3:5
and *h* of heart ......... Mark 16:14
therefore endure *h* ..... 2 Tim 2:3
*See* Job 38:38; Mark 10:5

## HARVEST
seedtime and *h*..........Gen 8:22
the *h* is past...........Jer 8:20
the time of her *h*......... Jer 51:33
for the *h* is ripe.........Joel 3:13
The *h* truly is ...........Matt 9:37
Lord of the *h*...........Matt 9:38
and in the time of *h* ... Matt 13:30
because the *h* is come...Mark 4:29
*h* truly is great.......... Luke 10:2
white already to *h* ......John 4:35
the *h* of the earth.......Rev 14:15
*See* Josh 3:15; Matt 13:39

## HATE
not *h* thy brother.........Lev 19:17
*h* the righteous ........Ps 34:21
love the Lord, *h* evil ......Ps 97:10
and fools *h* knowledge... Prov 1:22
*h* is son ...............Prov 13:24
The poor is *h* ..........Prov 14:20
be that *h* reproof ......Prov 15:10
but he that *h* gifts ......Prov 15:27
Therefore I *h* life ........ Eccl 2:17
and a time to *h* .........Eccl 3:8
feasts my soul *h* ...........Is 1:14
I *h* robbery..................Is 61:8
*H* the evil.................Amos 5:15
Who *h* the good .........Mic 3:2
things that I *h* ...........Zech 8:17
I *h* Esau.................Mal 1:3
to them that *h* you ..... Matt 5:44
for either he will *h*...... Matt 6:24
we shall be *h*............ Matt 10:22
shall *h* one another..... Matt 24:10
men shall *h* you .......Luke 6:22
to them which *h*....... Luke 6:27
and *h* not his father .... Luke 14:26
*h* the light.................John 3:20
cannot *h* you .............John 7:7
he that *h* his life ....... John 12:25
If the world *h* you ..... John 15:18
both seen and *h* ....... John 15:24
Esau have I *h* ..........Rom 9:13
*h* his own flesh ..........Eph 5:29
*h* his brother............1 John 2:9
if the world *h* you....... 1 John 3:13
and *h* his brother .... 1 John 4:20
*See* Gen 27:41; Prov 6:16

## HAUGHTY
thine eyes are
    upon the *h*......... 2 Sam 22:28
my heart is not *h* .........Ps 131:1
and a *h* spirit ..........Prov 16:18
Proud and *h* scorner ....Prov 21:24
*h* shall be humbled....... Is 10:33
shalt no more be *h* ......Zeph 3:11
*See* Is 2:11; 13:11; Ezek 16:50

## HEAD
it shall bruise thy *h*...... Gen 3:15
be upon his *h*............Josh 2:19
Lift up your *h*...........Ps 24:7, 9
he lift up the *h*........... Ps 110:7

are upon the *h* . . . . . . . . . Prov 10:6
fire upon his *h* . . . . . . . . Prov 25:22
eyes are in his *h* . . . . . . . . Eccl 2:14
the whole *h* is sick. . . . . . . . . Is 1:5
joy upon their *h* . . . . . . . . . . Is 35:10
my *h* were waters . . . . . . . . . Jer 9:1
and covered their *h*. . . . . . Jer 14:3
the *h* of the poor. . . . . . . . Amos 2:7
lift up his *h* . . . . . . . . . . . . Zech 1:21
My *h* with oil . . . . . . . . . Luke 7:46
lift up your *h*. . . . . . . . . Luke 21:28
the *h* of every man . . . . . . 1 Cor 11:3
gave him to be *h*. . . . . . . . Eph 1:22
which is the *h* . . . . . . . . . . Eph 4:15
the husband is the *h*. . . . . Eph 5:23
the *h* of the body . . . . . . . . . Col 1:18
not holding the *H*. . . . . . . . Col 2:19
*See* Josh 7:6; Rev 13:1

### HEAL

for I am the Lord that
   *h* thee. . . . . . . . . . . . . . . . . Ex 15:26
I wound, and I *h*. . . . . . . Deut 32:39
the waters were *h* . . . . . . 2 Kin 2:22
I will *h* thee. . . . . . . . . . . . 2 Kin 20:5
O Lord, *h* me. . . . . . . . . . . . . Ps 6:2
*h* my soul . . . . . . . . . . . . . . . . Ps 41:4
*h* all thy diseases . . . . . . . . Ps 103:3
and *h* them . . . . . . . . . . . . . Ps 107:20
convert, and be *h*. . . . . . . . . Is 6:10
stripes we are *h*. . . . . . . . . . Is 53:5
refuseth to be *h*. . . . . . . . . Jer 15:18
*H* me, O Lord . . . . . . . . . . . . Jer 17:14
and he will *h* us. . . . . . . . . . Hos 6:1
*h* their backsliding. . . . . . . Hos 14:4
and to *h* all manner . . . . . Matt 10:1
*H* the sick. . . . . . . . . . . . . . Matt 10:8
lawful to *h*. . . . . . . . . . . . . . Matt 12:10
he would *h*. . . . . . . . . . . . . . Mark 3:2
*h* the brokenhearted . . . Luke 4:18
Physician, *h* thyself. . . . . Luke 4:23
present to *h* them . . . . . . Luke 5:17
*h* the sick . . . . . . . . . . . . . . Luke 10:9
faith to be *h*. . . . . . . . . . . . Acts 14:9
ye may be *h*. . . . . . . . . . . James 5:16
ye were *h* . . . . . . . . . . . . . . 1 Pet 2:24
deadly wound was *h* . . . . . Rev 13:3
*See* Eccl 3:3; Is 3:7; Matt 4:21

### HEALING

there is no *h* for us . . . . . . Jer 14:19
*h* in his wings. . . . . . . . . . . . Mal 4:2
*h* all manner. . . . . . . . . . . Matt 4:23
had need of *h* . . . . . . . . . . Luke 9:11
gifts of *h* . . . . . . . . . . . . . 1 Cor 12:9
then gift of *h*. . . . . . . . . . 1 Cor 12:28
*h* of the nations. . . . . . . . Rev 22:2
*See* Jer 30:13; Acts 4:22; 10:38

### HEAR

*H* the word . . . . . . . . . . 2 Kin 18:28
*h* with understanding . . . . Neh 8:2
Oh that one would *h*. . . . . Job 31:35
*H* me when I call . . . . . . . . . Ps 4:1
the Lord will *h*. . . . . . . . . . . Ps 4:3
thine ear to *h* . . . . . . . . . . Ps 10:17
*H* my prayer, O Lord. . . . . Ps 39:12
*H* my prayer, O God. . . . . . Ps 54:2
Lord will not *h* me. . . . . . . Ps 66:18
*h* what God . . . . . . . . . . . . . Ps 85:8
*H* my prayer, O Lord. . . . . Ps 102:1
but the poor *h* . . . . . . . . . Prov 13:8
before he *h* it . . . . . . . . . Prov 18:13
*h* the words. . . . . . . . . . . . Prov 22:17
be more ready to *h*. . . . . . . Eccl 5:1
better to *h* the rebuke . . . . Eccl 7:5
*H*, O heavens. . . . . . . . . . . . . . Is 1:2
shall the deaf *h* . . . . . . . . . Is 29:18
*H*, ye that are far off . . . . . Is 33:13
ye nations, to *h* . . . . . . . . . Is 34:1
I will not *h* thee. . . . . . . . . Jer 7:16
not *h* their cry . . . . . . . . . . Jer 14:12
yet will I not *h*. . . . . . . . . Ezek 8:18
*h* the prayer . . . . . . . . . . . . Dan 9:17

will *h* them . . . . . . . . . . . . Zech 10:6
whosoever *h* these . . . . . Matt 7:24
the deaf *h*. . . . . . . . . . . . . . Matt 11:5
*h* ye him . . . . . . . . . . . . . . . Matt 17:5
the deaf to *h* . . . . . . . . . . Mark 7:37
beloved Son: *h* him. . . . . . Mark 9:7
*h* my sayings. . . . . . . . . . . . Luke 6:47
the deaf *h*. . . . . . . . . . . . . . Luke 7:22
He that *h* you *h* me . . . . Luke 10:16
to *h* those things . . . . . . . Luke 10:24
*h* the voice of God . . . . . . John 5:25
who can *h* it . . . . . . . . . . . John 6:60
we know that God
   *h* not. . . . . . . . . . . . . . . . . John 9:31
thou *h* me always . . . . . John 11:42
any man *h* my words. . . . John 12:47
the word which ye *h*. . . John 14:24
*h* without a preacher . . Rom 10:14
world *h* them . . . . . . . . . . . 1 John 4:5
knoweth God *h* us. . . . . . 1 John 4:6
that he *h* us. . . . . . . . . . . 1 John 5:15
let him *h*. . . . . . . . . . . . . . . Rev 2:7
if any man *h* my voice . . . Rev 3:20
*See* 2 Kin 19:16; 2 Chr 6:21

### HEARD

And they *h* the voice of
   the Lord . . . . . . . . . . . . . . . Gen 3:8
And God *h* the voice . . . . . Gen 21:17
have *h* their cry . . . . . . . . . . Ex 3:7
and the Lord *h* it. . . . . . . Num 11:1
only ye *h* a voice. . . . . . . . Deut 4:12
*h* my supplication . . . . . . . . Ps 6:9
hast *h* the desire. . . . . . . . . Ps 10:17
and he *h* me . . . . . . . . . . . . Ps 34:4
hast *h* my vows. . . . . . . . . . Ps 61:5
hath *h* my voice . . . . . . . . . Ps 116:1
have ye not *h* . . . . . . . . . . . Is 40:21
hath *h*, such a thing . . . . . . Is 66:8
rumour that shall be *h* . . . Jer 51:46
be *h* for their. . . . . . . . . . . . Matt 6:7
thou hast *h* me . . . . . . . . John 11:41
*h* the word believed . . . . . Acts 4:4
we have seen and *h* . . . . Acts 4:20
they have not *h*. . . . . . . . Rom 10:14
nor ear *h* . . . . . . . . . . . . . . 1 Cor 2:9
and *h* unspeakable . . . . . 2 Cor 12:4
ye have *h* him. . . . . . . . . . Eph 4:21
received, and *h* . . . . . . . . . Phil 4:9
by them that *h*. . . . . . . . . . Heb 2:3
which we have *h*. . . . . . . . 1 John 1:1
we have seen and *h* . . . . 1 John 1:3
*See* John 5:37; Rev 19:6; 22:8

### HEARER

For not the *h* of the law
   are just . . . . . . . . . . . . . . Rom 2:13
grace unto the *h*. . . . . . . . Eph 4:29
and not *h* only. . . . . . . . . James 1:22

### HEARING

The *h* ear . . . . . . . . . . . . . Prov 20:12
ear filled with *h*. . . . . . . . . Eccl 1:8
*h* they hear not . . . . . . . . Matt 13:13
faith cometh by *h*. . . . . . Rom 10:17
where were the *h*. . . . . . . 1 Cor 12:17
ye are dull of *h*. . . . . . . . . . Heb 5:11
*See* Gal 3:2; 2 Pet 2:8

### HEART

with all your *h* . . . . . . . . . Deut 11:13
gave him another *h*. . . . 1 Sam 10:9
Lord looketh on the *h*. . . 1 Sam 16:7
an understanding *h* . . . . . 1 Kin 3:9
with all his *h*. . . . . . . . . . . 1 Kin 14:8
not of double *h* . . . . . . . . 1 Chr 12:33
triest the *h*. . . . . . . . . . . . 1 Chr 29:17
*h* was lifted up. . . . . . . . . 2 Chr 32:25
said in his *h*. . . . . . . . . . . . . Ps 10:6
rejoicing the *h*. . . . . . . . . . . Ps 19:8
*h* shall not fear . . . . . . . . . . Ps 27:3
*h* trusted in him . . . . . . . . . Ps 28:7
the *h*, is deep . . . . . . . . . . . . Ps 64:6
I had in mine *h* . . . . . . . . Ps 119:11
and know my *h* . . . . . . . . Ps 139:23

Keep thy *h* . . . . . . . . . . . . . Prov 4:23
The *h* knoweth . . . . . . . . Prov 14:10
thinketh in his *h*. . . . . . . . Prov 23:7
songs to a heavy *h*. . . . . Prov 25:20
*h* of her husband . . . . . . Prov 31:11
wise man's *h*. . . . . . . . . . . . Eccl 8:5
of a fearful *h*. . . . . . . . . . . . . Is 35:4
sing for joy of *h*. . . . . . . . . Is 65:14
reins and the *h* . . . . . . . . . Jer 11:20
The *h* is deceitful. . . . . . . . Jer 17:9
word was in mine *h* . . . . . Jer 20:9
will give them a *h* . . . . . . . Jer 24:7
the pride of thine *h* . . . . . Jer 49:16
take the stony *h* . . . . . . Ezek 11:19
make you a new *h* . . . . . Ezek 18:31
uncircumcised in *h*. . . . . Ezek 44:7
And rend your *h* . . . . . . . . . Joel 2:13
The pride of thine *h* . . . . . Obad 3
*h* of the fathers . . . . . . . . . Mal 4:6
the pure in *h*. . . . . . . . . . . . Matt 5:8
there will your *h* be. . . . . Matt 6:21
meek and lowly in *h*. . . . Matt 11:29
abundance of the *h*. . . . Matt 12:34
out of the *h*. . . . . . . . . . . . Matt 15:19
from your *h*. . . . . . . . . . . Matt 18:35
with all thy *h* . . . . . . . . . Matt 22:37
hardness of your *h* . . . . Mark 10:5
with all thy *h* . . . . . . . . . Mark 12:30
hardness of *h* . . . . . . . . . Mark 16:14
in her *h* . . . . . . . . . . . . . . . Luke 2:19
abundance of the *h*. . . . Luke 6:45
with all thy *h* . . . . . . . . . Luke 10:27
slow of *h*. . . . . . . . . . . . . Luke 24:25
our *h* burn within us . . Luke 24:32
Let not your *h* . . . . . . . . John 14:1
cut to the *h* . . . . . . . . . . . Acts 5:33
uncircumcised in *h*. . . . . Acts 7:51
were cut to the *h* . . . . . . Acts 7:54
with purpose of *h* . . . . . Acts 11:23
For with the *h* . . . . . . . . Rom 10:10
into the *h* of man. . . . . . . 1 Cor 2:9
tables of the *h* . . . . . . . . . 2 Cor 3:3
and not in *h* . . . . . . . . . . . 2 Cor 5:12
dwell in your *h* . . . . . . . . . Eph 3:17
making melody in
   your *h* . . . . . . . . . . . . . . . . Eph 5:19
from the *h*. . . . . . . . . . . . . . Eph 6:6
shall keep your *h* . . . . . . . . Phil 4:7
in singleness of *h*. . . . . . . . Col 3:22
Lord direct your *h* . . . . 2 Thess 3:5
intents of the *h* . . . . . . . . Heb 4:12
*h* be established . . . . . . . . Heb 13:9
strife in your *h*. . . . . . . . James 3:14
purify your *h* . . . . . . . . . James 4:8
hidden man of the *h*. . . . 1 Pet 3:4
God in your *h* . . . . . . . . . . 1 Pet 3:15
*See* Col 3:15; 2 Pet 1:19

### HEAVEN

is the gate of *h*. . . . . . . . . Gen 28:17
with you from *h* . . . . . . . Ex 20:22
the *h* of heavens. . . . . . . Deut 10:14
precious things of *h* . . . Deut 33:13
*h* and *h* of heavens . . . . . 1 Kin 8:27
make windows in *h* . . . . 2 Kin 7:2
When I consider thy *h*. . . . Ps 8:3
looked down from *h*. . . . . Ps 14:2
word is settled in *h*. . . . . Ps 119:89
he prepared the *h* . . . . . . Prov 8:27
God is in *h* . . . . . . . . . . . . . Eccl 5:2
I will shake the *h* . . . . . . . . Is 13:13
I create new *h* . . . . . . . . . . Is 65:17
the *h* were opened . . . . . Ezek 1:1
I will shake the *h* . . . . . . . Hag 2:6
the windows of *h*. . . . . . . Mal 3:10
the *h* were opened . . . . . Matt 3:16
Till *h* and earth pass. . . . Matt 5:18
*H* and earth shall . . . . . . Matt 24:35
he saw the *h* opened . . . Mark 1:10
the stars of *h*. . . . . . . . . Mark 13:25
angels which are in *h*. . . Mark 13:32
sinned against *h*. . . . . . Luke 15:18
shall see *h* open . . . . . . . John 1:51

true bread from *h* ......John 6:32
name under *h* given..... Acts 4:12
revealed from *h* .........Rom 1:18
eternal in the *h* ......... 2 Cor 5:1
which is from *h*.......... 2 Cor 5:2
an angel from *h*............ Gal 1:8
both which are in *h*.......Eph 1:10
family in *h* ............... Eph 3:15
Master also is in *h* .......Eph 6:9
conversation is in *h* ....Phil 3:20
a Master in *h*.............. Col 4:1
are written in *h*........... Heb 12:23
bear record in *h*........ 1 John 5:7
door was opened in *h* .... Rev 4:1
I saw a new *h*.............. Rev 21:1
*See* 1 Thess 4:16; 2 Thess 1:7

### HEAVENLY
a multitude of the
 *h* host................. Luke 2:13
your *h* Father............Luke 11:13
of *h* things ............. John 3:12
the *h* vision.............Acts 26:19
and as is the *h* ......... 1 Cor 15:48
in *h* places ................. Eph 1:3
together in *h* places ..... Eph 2:6
powers in *h* places....... Eph 3:10
of the *h* calling..........Heb 3:1
shadow of *h* things ...... Heb 8:5
but the *h* things .........Heb 9:23
that is, a *h* ............Heb 11:16
*See* 2 Tim 4:18; Heb 6:4; 12:22

### HEIR
This is the *h* .......... Matt 21:38
then *h*; *h* of God ........Rom 8:17
and *h* according .........Gal 3:29
then an *h* of God..........Gal 4:7
should be made *h* ...... Titus 3:7
whom ... appointed *h* ... Heb 1:2
the *h* of promise........ Heb 6:17
*h* of the righteousness ...Heb 11:7
*h* of the kingdom......James 2:5
*h* together .................1 Pet 3:7
*See* Mic 1:15; Rom 4:13

### HELL
shall burn unto the
 lowest *h* ...........Deut 32:22
The sorrows of *h* .....2 Sam 22:6
deeper than *h*.............Job 11:8
be turned into *h*.......... Ps 9:17
my soul in *h* ............ Ps 16:10
down quick into *h*........Ps 55:15
if I make my bed in *h*.....Ps 139:8
take hold on *h* ..........Prov 5:5
is the way of *h*..........Prov 7:27
the depths of *h* .........Prov 9:18
*H* and destruction...... Prov 15:11
he may depart from *h*...Prov 15:24
his soul from *h* ........ Prov 23:14
*H* and destruction..... Prov 27:20
*H* from beneath ............Is 14:9
and with *h* are we ... Is 28:15
cast him down to *h*.....Ezek 31:16
the midst of *h* .........Ezek 32:21
they dig into *h* .........Amos 9:2
the belly of *h*..............Jon 2:2
his desire as *h* .......... Hab 2:5
danger of *h* fire ......... Matt 5:22
be cast into *h* ........... Matt 5:29
soul and body in *h*...... Matt 10:28
brought down to *h* .....Matt 11:23
and the gates of *h* .... Matt 16:18
cast into *h* fire .......... Matt 18:9
more the child of *h* .... Matt 23:15
damnation of *h* ....... Matt 23:33
thrust down to *h* ...... Luke 10:15
to cast into *h*............ Luke 12:5
in *h* he lift up ..........Luke 16:23
not left in *h* ............Acts 2:31
on fire of *h*...........James 3:6
them down to *h* ........ 2 Pet 2:4
*See* Is 5:14; Rev 1:18; 20:13


### HELP
will make him a *h* meet
 for him ................. Gen 2:18
shield of thy *h* .........Deut 33:29
none to *h* .................. Ps 22:11
Lord: he is our *h*......... Ps 33:20
*h* of his countenance .....Ps 42:5
a very present *h* ...........Ps 46:1
whence cometh my *h* .....Ps 121:1
Our *h* is in the name.....Ps 124:8
in me is thine *h*.......... Hos 13:9
Lord, *h* me.......... Matt 15:25
*h* thou mine unbelief... Mark 9:24
find grace to *h* ........... Heb 4:16
*See* Rom 8:26; 1 Cor 1:24

### HELPER
Lord is my *h*, and I will
 not fear................ Heb 13:6

### HERESIES
there must be also *h*
 among you ...........1 Cor 11:19
strife, seditions, *h* ........Gal 5:20
in damnable *h* ............2 Pet 2:1

### HID
and the Lord hath *h* it
 from me.............. 2 Kin 4:27
for *h* treasures.............Job 3:21
have I not *h*.............. Ps 32:5
sins are not *h* .............Ps 69:5
Thy word have I *h* .......Ps 119:11
ye shall be *h* ........... Zeph 2:3
*h*, that shall............. Matt 10:26
there is nothing *h* ...... Mark 4:22
*h* from thine eyes.....Luke 19:42
the *h* wisdom.............1 Cor 2:7
if our gospel be *h* ....... 2 Cor 4:3
your life is *h* ............. Col 3:3
be the *h* man .............1 Pet 3:4
of the *h* manna .......Rev 2:17
*See* Matt 5:14; Mark 7:24

### HIDE
thou wouldest *h* me.....Job 14:13
when he *h* his face......Job 34:29
he *h* his face ..............Ps 10:11
*h* me under the shadow... Ps 17:8
the darkness *h* not ......Ps 139:12
I will *h* mine eyes........... Is 1:15
be as a *h* place .......... Is 32:2
God that *h* thyself ........Is 45:15
shall *h* a multitude ... James 5:20
*h* us from the face ....... Rev 6:16
*See* Prov 28:28; Amos 9:3

### HIGH
It is as *h* as heaven ....... Job 11:8
ascended on *h*............Ps 68:18
the heaven is *h* .......Ps 103:11
too *h* for me ...........Ps 131:1
Though the Lord be *h* ....Ps 138:6
it is *h*......................Ps 139:6
that which is *h*............Eccl 12:5
from on *h*................Is 32:15
He shall dwell on *h* ...... Is 33:16
make thy nest as *h* ......Jer 49:16
dayspring from on *h* ... Luke 1:78
power from on *h* ......Luke 24:49
Mind not *h* things ......Rom 12:16
it is *h* time...............Rom 13:11
*h* calling of God........ Phil 3:14
*See* Is 57:15; 2 Cor 10:5

### HIGHER
the heavens are *h* ... so
 are my ways *h*........ Is 55:9
Friend, go up *h* ........ Luke 14:10
unto the *h* powers.......Rom 13:1
*h* than the heavens ...... Heb 7:26

### HIGHEST
of the Lord: Hosanna
 in the *h* .............. Mark 11:10
the Son of the *H* ........ Luke 1:32


power of the *H*.......... Luke 1:35
prophet of the *H*........ Luke 1:76
Glory to God in the *h* ... Luke 2:14

### HILL
holy *h* of Zion................Ps 2:6
dwell in thy holy *h*..........Ps 15:1
ascend into the *h* .........Ps 24:3
upon a thousand *h* ......Ps 50:10
eyes unto the *h* ...........Ps 121:1
before the *h*............... Prov 8:25
from the *h* .................Jer 3:23
and to the *h*............... Hos 10:8
that is set on a *h*.........Matt 5:14
*See* Luke 4:29; 9:37; Acts 17:22

### HOLD
and *h* him in thine
 hand................... Gen 21:18
not *h* him guiltless ........Ex 20:7
*H* thou me up............Ps 119:117
*h* his peace............... Prov 11:12
a fool, when he *h* ......Prov 17:28
*h* thy right hand .........Is 41:13
*h* the truth...............Rom 1:18
let the first *h* ........... 1 Cor 14:30
*H* forth the word ....... Phil 2:16
And not *h* the Head......Col 2:19
*h* fast that which ..... 1 Thess 5:21
*H* faith .................1 Tim 1:19
*H* the mystery of .......1 Tim 3:9
*H* fast the form ......... 2 Tim 1:13
*H* fast the faithful ....... Titus 1:9
*h* the beginning.......... Heb 3:14
*h* fast our profession .... Heb 4:14
Let us *h* fast the
 profession............Heb 10:23
*h* fast my name..........Rev 2:13
*h* fast, and repent......... Rev 3:3
*See* Jer 2:13; 51:30; Ezek 19:9

### HOLIER
near to me; for I am *h*
 than thou................ Is 65:5

### HOLIEST
which is called the
 *H* of all................. Heb 9:3
into the *h* ............... Heb 10:19

### HOLINESS
who is like thee,
 glorious in *h*............ Ex 15:11
*H* to the Lord ............ Ex 28:36
in the beauty of *h*...... 1 Chr 16:29
remembrance of his *h*.....Ps 30:4
throne of his *h* ............Ps 47:8
*h* becometh thine house ... Ps 93:5
Thy way of *h*............... Is 35:8
habitation of thy *h*....... Is 63:15
the words of his *h* ......Jer 23:9
there shall be *h* ...........Obad 17
*H* unto the Lord ....... Zech 14:20
*h* and righteousness.....Luke 1:75
own power or *h*..........Acts 3:12
to the spirit of *h* .........Rom 1:4
your fruit unto *h* ....... Rom 6:22
perfecting *h* ..............2 Cor 7:1
and true *h* ............... Eph 4:24
unblameable in *h*..... 1 Thess 3:13
but unto *h* .............. 1 Thess 4:7
charity and *h* ...........1 Tim 2:15
as becometh *h* ..........Titus 2:3
partakers of his *h*....... Heb 12:10
*See* Ps 89:35; Is 23:18; Jer 2:3

### HOLY
place whereon thou
 standest is *h*...............Ex 3:5
a *h* nation.................Ex 19:6
to keep it *h*................ Ex 20:8
for it is *h*.................. Ex 31:14
*h* and unholy ............Lev 10:10
be ye *h* ................... Lev 20:7
and who is *h*............. Num 16:5
this is a *h* man...........2 Kin 4:9

*h* seed have . . . . . . . . . . . . . . . . Ezra 9:2
from his *h* heaven . . . . . . . . Ps 20:6
thou art *h* . . . . . . . . . . . . . . . . . . . Ps 22:3
for I am *h* . . . . . . . . . . . . . . . . . . Ps 86:2
worship at his *h* hill . . . . . . Ps 99:9
*h* in all his works . . . . . . . . Ps 145:17
that which is *h* . . . . . . . Prov 20:25
said, *H, h, h* . . . . . . . . . . . . . . . . Is 6:3
the *h* seed . . . . . . . . . . . . . . . . . Is 6:13
mine *h* things . . . . . . . . Ezek 22:26
between the *h* . . . . . . . . Ezek 22:26
child of the *H* Ghost . . . . . Matt 1:18
with the *H* Ghost . . . . . . . Matt 3:11
not that which is *h* . . . . . Matt 7:6
against the *H* Ghost . . . . Matt 12:31
but the *H* Ghost . . . . . . . Mark 13:11
The *H* Ghost shall . . . . . . Luke 1:35
the *H* Ghost
   descended . . . . . . . . . . . . . Luke 3:22
full of the *H* Ghost . . . . . . . Luke 4:1
the *H* Ghost shall . . . . . . Luke 12:12
with the *H* Ghost . . . . . . . John 1:33
the *H* Ghost was not . . . John 7:39
which is the *H* Ghost . . John 14:26
*H* Father . . . . . . . . . . . . . . . John 17:11
Receive ye the
   *H* Ghost . . . . . . . . . . . . John 20:22
*H* Ghost is come . . . . . . . . . . Acts 1:8
were all filled with
   the *H* . . . . . . . . . . . . . . . . . Acts 2:4
thy *h* child Jesus . . . . . . . . Acts 4:27
lie to the *H* Ghost . . . . . . . Acts 5:3
full of the *H* Ghost . . . . . . . Acts 6:3
resist the *H* Ghost . . . . . . Acts 7:51
receive the *H* Ghost . . . . . Acts 8:15
comfort of the *H* Ghost . . . Acts 9:31
the *H* Ghost fell . . . . . . . . Acts 10:44
received the *H* Ghost . . . Acts 10:47
giving them the
   *H* Ghost . . . . . . . . . . . . Acts 15:8
good to the *H* Ghost . . . Acts 15:28
*H* Ghost hath made . . . . Acts 20:28
the *h* scriptures . . . . . . . . . Rom 1:2
law is *h* . . . . . . . . . . . . . . . . . Rom 7:12
witness in the *H* Ghost . . . Rom 9:1
first fruit be *h* . . . . . . . . . . Rom 11:16
a living sacrifice, *h* . . . . . . Rom 12:1
joy in the *H* Ghost . . . . . . Rom 14:17
with a *h* kiss . . . . . . . . . . Rom 16:16
*H* Ghost teacheth . . . . . . . 1 Cor 2:13
temple of God is *h* . . . . . . 1 Cor 3:17
now are they *h* . . . . . . . . . 1 Cor 7:14
with a *h* kiss . . . . . . . . . . 2 Cor 13:12
we should be *h* . . . . . . . . . . Eph 1:4
unto an *h* temple . . . . . . . Eph 2:21
it should be *h* . . . . . . . . . . Eph 5:27
*h* and unblameable . . . . . . Col 1:22
*h* and beloved . . . . . . . . . . . Col 3:12
all the *h* brethren . . . 1 Thess 5:27
lifting up *h* hands . . . 1 Tim 2:8
an *h* calling . . . . . . . . . . . . 2 Tim 1:9
sober, just, *h* . . . . . . . . . . . Titus 1:8
renewing of the
   *H* Ghost . . . . . . . . . . . . Titus 3:5
Wherefore, *h* brethren . . . Heb 3:1
*H* Ghost sent down . . . . . 1 Pet 1:12
called you is *h* . . . . . . . . . 1 Pet 1:15
an *h* priesthood . . . . . . . . . 1 Pet 2:5
an *h* nation . . . . . . . . . . . . 1 Pet 2:9
the *h* women . . . . . . . . . . . 1 Pet 3:5
in the *h* mount . . . . . . . . . 2 Pet 1:18
*h* men . . . . . . . . . . . . . . . . . . 2 Pet 1:21
in all *h* conversation . . . 2 Pet 3:11
saith he that is *h* . . . . . . . . . Rev 3:7
saying, *H, h, h* . . . . . . . . . . . Rev 4:8
O Lord, *h* and true . . . . . . Rev 6:10
Blessed and *h* . . . . . . . . . . Rev 20:6
the *h* Jerusalem . . . . . . . . Rev 21:10
he that is *h* . . . . . . . . . . . . Rev 22:11
*See* 2 Tim 3:15; 1 Pet 1:16

## HONEST

in an *h* and good heart . . . Luke 8:15

men of *h* report . . . . . . . . . . Acts 6:3
*h* in the sight . . . . . . . . . . Rom 12:17
Let us walk *h* . . . . . . . . . . Rom 13:13
for *h* things . . . . . . . . . . . . 2 Cor 8:21
things are *h* . . . . . . . . . . . . . Phil 4:8
your conversation *h* . . . . 1 Pet 2:12
*See* 1 Thess 4:12; 1 Tim 2:2

## HONOUR (n.)

riches and *h* . . . . . . . . . . . . Prov 3:16
It is an *h* for a man . . . . . Prov 20:3
so *h* is not . . . . . . . . . . . . . . Prov 26:1
giveth *h* to a fool . . . . . . . Prov 26:8
riches, wealth, and *h* . . . . . Eccl 6:2
where is mine *h* . . . . . . . . . Mal 1:6
not without *h* . . . . . . . . . Matt 13:57
hath no *h* in his . . . . . . . . John 4:44
I receive not *h* . . . . . . . . . John 5:41
for glory and *h* . . . . . . . . . Rom 2:7
in *h* preferring . . . . . . . . . Rom 12:10
*h* to whom *h* . . . . . . . . . . Rom 13:7
worthy of double *h* . . . . . 1 Tim 5:17
some to *h* . . . . . . . . . . . . . 2 Tim 2:20
*h* unto the wife . . . . . . . . . 1 Pet 3:7
receive glory and *h* . . . . . . Rev 4:11
*See* Rev 5:13; 7:12; 19:1; 21:24

## HONOUR (v.)

*H* thy father and thy
   mother . . . . . . . . . . . . . . . Ex 20:12
but he *h* them . . . . . . . . . . . Ps 15:4
*H* the Lord . . . . . . . . . . . . . Prov 3:9
he that *h* himself . . . . . . . Prov 12:9
A son that *h* his father . . . . . Mal 1:6
*h* me with their lips . . . . Matt 15:8
that *h* not the Son . . . . . . John 5:23
*H* widows . . . . . . . . . . . . . . 1 Tim 5:3
*H* all men . . . . . . . . . . . . . . 1 Pet 2:17
*See* Is 29:13; 58:13; Acts 28:10

## HONOURABLE

were among thy *h*
   women . . . . . . . . . . . . . . . . . Ps 45:9
and the *h* man . . . . . . . . . . . Is 3:3
ancient and *h* . . . . . . . . . . . . Is 9:15
and make it *h* . . . . . . . . . . . Is 42:21
*See* Luke 14:8; 1 Cor 4:10

## HOPE (n.)

are spent without *h* . . . . . Job 7:6
the hypocrite's *h* . . . . . . . . Job 8:13
*h* hath he removed . . . . . . Job 19:10
shall rest in *h* . . . . . . . . . . Ps 16:9
my *h* is in thee . . . . . . . . . . Ps 39:7
*H* deferred . . . . . . . . . . . . Prov 13:12
righteous hath *h* . . . . . . . Prov 14:32
*h* of a fool . . . . . . . . . . . . Prov 26:12
living there is *h* . . . . . . . . . Eccl 9:4
whose *h* the Lord . . . . . . . . Jer 17:7
for we are saved by *h* . . . Rom 8:24
Rejoicing in *h* . . . . . . . . . . Rom 12:12
abideth faith, *h* . . . . . . . . 1 Cor 13:13
*h* of his calling . . . . . . . . . . Eph 1:18
having no *h* . . . . . . . . . . . . . Eph 2:12
the *h* of glory . . . . . . . . . . . Col 1:27
which have no *h* . . . . . . 1 Thess 4:13
the *h* of salvation . . . . . 1 Thess 5:8
*h* of eternal life . . . . . . . . . Titus 3:7
lay hold upon the *h* . . . . . Heb 6:18
unto a lively *h* . . . . . . . . . . 1 Pet 1:3
*See* Col 1:5; 1 John 3:3

## HOPE (v.)

didst make me *h* . . . . . . . . Ps 22:9
*h* in the Lord . . . . . . . . . . . Ps 31:24
will *h* continually . . . . . . . Ps 71:14
and *h* to the end . . . . . . . . 1 Pet 1:13
*See* Jer 3:23; Heb 11:1

## HOSPITALITY

necessity of saints;
   given to *h* . . . . . . . . . . . Rom 12:13
given to *h* . . . . . . . . . . . . . . 1 Tim 3:2
But a lover of *h* . . . . . . . . . Titus 1:8
*h* one to another . . . . . . . . 1 Pet 4:9

## HOUSE

none other but the *h*
   of God . . . . . . . . . . . . . . . Gen 28:17
thine *h* in order . . . . . . . . 2 Kin 20:1
*h* of God forsaken . . . . . . . Neh 13:11
to the *h* appointed . . . . . . Job 30:23
habitation of thy *h* . . . . . . Ps 26:8
the zeal of thine *h* . . . . . . : Ps 69:9
the *h* of the Lord . . . . . . . Ps 92:13
*h* of the righteous . . . . . . Prov 12:7
*H* and riches . . . . . . . . . . . Prov 19:14
*h* of mourning . . . . . . . . . . Eccl 7:2
join *h* to *h* . . . . . . . . . . . . . . Is 5:8
our beautiful *h* . . . . . . . . . . Is 64:11
your *h* is left . . . . . . . . . . Matt 23:38
if a *h* be divided . . . . . . . . Mark 3:25
upon that *h* . . . . . . . . . . . . Luke 6:48
my Father's *h* . . . . . . . . . . John 14:2
from *h* to *h* . . . . . . . . . . . . Acts 2:46
our earthly *h* . . . . . . . . . . . 2 Cor 5:1
those of his own *h* . . . . . . 1 Tim 5:8
*See* Matt 9:6; Luke 7:44; 19:5

## HOUSEHOLD

the *h* of faith . . . . . . . . . . . Gal 6:10
the *h* of God . . . . . . . . . . . Eph 2:19
*See* Gen 31:37; 47:12; 2 Sam 17:23

## HUMBLE

the cry of the *h* . . . . . . . . . . Ps 9:12
the *h* shall hear . . . . . . . . . Ps 34:2
of an *h* spirit . . . . . . . . . . . Prov 16:19
contrite and *h* spirit . . . . . . Is 57:15
therefore shall *h* . . . . . . . Matt 18:4
that *h* himself shall . . . . Luke 14:11
he *h* himself . . . . . . . . . . . . Phil 2:8
grace unto the *h* . . . . . . . James 4:6
*H* yourselves . . . . . . . . . . . 1 Pet 5:6
*See* Is 2:11; 5:15; Lam 3:20

## HUMBLY

to walk *h* with . . . . . . . . . . Mic 6:8

## HUMILITY

and before honour
   is *h* . . . . . . . . . . . . . . . . . Prov 15:33
By *h* and the fear . . . . . . . Prov 22:4
*See* Col 2:18, 23; 1 Pet 5:5

## HUNGER

They shall not *h* . . . . . . . . . Is 49:10
they which do *h* . . . . . . . . Matt 5:6
ye that *h* now . . . . . . . . . . Luke 6:21
shall never *h* . . . . . . . . . . . John 6:35
If thine enemy *h* . . . . . . . Rom 12:20
both *h*, and thirst . . . . . . . 1 Cor 4:11
And if any man *h* . . . . . . 1 Cor 11:34
shall *h* no more . . . . . . . . . Rev 7:16
*See* Matt 4:2; 12:1; Luke 15:17

## HUNGRY

filleth the *h* soul . . . . . . . . Ps 107:9
food to the *h* . . . . . . . . . . . Ps 146:7
if thine enemy be *h* . . . . Prov 25:21
to the *h* soul . . . . . . . . . . . Prov 27:7
filled the *h* with good . . . Luke 1:53
*See* Prov 6:30; Mark 11:12

## HUSBAND

a crown to her *h* . . . . . . . Prov 12:4
Her *h* is known . . . . . . . Prov 31:23
Maker is thine *h* . . . . . . . . Is 54:5
shalt save thy *h* . . . . . . . . 1 Cor 7:16
let them ask their *h* . . . 1 Cor 14:35
unto your own *h* . . . . . . . . Eph 5:22
*H*, love your wives . . . . . . Eph 5:25
*h* of one wife . . . . . . . . . . . 1 Tim 3:12
love their *h* . . . . . . . . . . . . Titus 2:4
to their own *h* . . . . . . . . . . Titus 2:5
*See* Ruth 1:11; Esth 1:17, 20

## HYPOCRITE

and the *h* hope shall
   perish . . . . . . . . . . . . . . . . Job 8:13
But the *h* in heart . . . . . . Job 36:13
for every one is an *h* . . . . . Is 9:17
as the *h* do . . . . . . . . . . . . Matt 6:2

be not, as the *h* ......... Matt 6:16
portion with the *h* ..... Matt 24:51
prophesied of you *h* ..... Mark 7:6
*See* Job 13:16; 27:8; Prov 11:9

---

## I

**IDLE**
and an *i* soul. ........... Prov 19:15
the bread of *i* ......... Prov 31:27
every *i* word ........... Matt 12:36
*i* in the marketplace.... Matt 20:3
*See* Eccl 10:18; 1 Tim 5:13

**IDOL**
all the gods of the
  people are *i*. ......... 1 Chr 16:26
joined to *i*. ............... Hos 4:17
pollutions of *i* ........ Acts 15:20
an *i* is nothing .......... 1 Cor 8:4
to God from *i* ........ 1 Thess 1:9
yourselves from *i*. ..... 1 John 5:21
*See* Gal 5:20; Col 3:5

**IGNORANCE**
that through *i* ye did .... Acts 3:17
the times of this *i*. ..... Acts 17:30
*i* that is in them ..... Eph 4:18
*i* of foolish men. ......... 1 Pet 2:15
*See* Lev 4:2; Num 15:24

**IGNORANT**
unlearned and *i* men.... Acts 4:13
For they being *i*. ........ Rom 10:3
if any man be *i*. ....... 1 Cor 14:38
for we are not *i* ........ 2 Cor 2:11
compassion on the *i*. ..... Heb 5:2
they willingly are *i*. .... 2 Pet 3:5
*See* Num 15:28; 1 Tim 1:13

**IMAGE**
said, Let us make man
  in our *i*. .............. Gen 1:26
into an *i* made .......... Rom 1:23
*i* of his Son. ............ Rom 8:29
same *i* from glory ...... 2 Cor 3:18

**IMAGINATION**
every *i* of the thoughts
  of his ............... Gen 6:5
the *i* of man's heart. ..... Gen 8:21
I walk in the *i* ......... Deut 29:19
*i* of the thoughts. ..... 1 Chr 28:9
*i* of his own heart. ...... Jer 23:17
vain in their *i* ......... Rom 1:21
Casting down *i* ........ 2 Cor 10:5
*See* Prov 6:18; Lam 3:60

**IMMORTALITY**
glory and honour and *i*...Rom 2:7
mortal must put on *i*.. 1 Cor 15:53
Who only hath *i* ....... 1 Tim 6:16
brought life and *i*. ..... 2 Tim 1:10

**IMPOSSIBLE**
With men this is *i* ..... Matt 19:26
it is *i*, but not with
  God ............... Mark 10:27
nothing shall be *i*. ..... Luke 1:37
things which are *i* ..... Luke 18:27
*See* Matt 17:20; Luke 17:1

**IMPUTE**
blood shall be *i* unto
  that man ........... Lev 17:4
Lord *i* not iniquity. ....... Ps 32:2
*i* this his power. .......... Hab 1:11
will not *i* sin ........... Rom 4:8
sin is not *i* ............ Rom 5:13
*See* 1 Sam 22:15; 2 Cor 5:19

**INCORRUPTIBLE**
corruptible crown; but
  we an *i* ............ 1 Cor 9:25
an inheritance *i*. .......... 1 Pet 1:4
*See* Rom 1:23; 1 Cor 15:42, 50

**INCREASE** (*n.*)
tithe all the *i*. .......... Deut 14:22
earth yield her *i*. .......... Ps 67:6
*i* of his government ........ Is 9:7
God gave the *i* ........... 1 Cor 3:6
*See* Jer 2:3; Eph 4:16; Col 2:19

**INCREASE** (*v.*)
Lord shall *i* you. ......... Ps 115:14
will *i* learning. ......... Prov 1:5
he that *i* knowledge. ..... Eccl 1:18
knowledge shall be *i* .... Dan 12:4
Jesus *i* in wisdom ..... Luke 2:52
*i* our faith. ............ Luke 17:5
word of God *i*. ........... Acts 6:7
*i* in number daily ........ Acts 16:5
*i* with goods ............ Rev 3:17
*See* Eccl 2:9; 5:11; Mark 4:8

**INFALLIBLE**
by many *i* proofs ......... Acts 1:3

**INFIRMITY**
Himself took our *i* ...... Matt 8:17
helpeth our *i*. ........... Rom 8:26
*See* Luke 5:15; 7:21; Heb 5:2

**INHERIT**
and they shall *i* it
  for ever. .............. Ex 32:13
seed shall *i*. ............ Ps 25:13
meek shall *i*. ............ Ps 37:11
simply *i* folly .......... Prov 14:18
*i* everlasting life ....... Matt 19:29
*i* the kingdom ........ Matt 25:34
*i* eternal life. ......... Mark 10:17
shall not *i*. .............. 1 Cor 6:9
cannot *i* the kingdom ... 1 Cor 15:50
*i* the blessing ........... Heb 12:17
*See* Heb 6:12; 1 Pet 3:9

**INHERITANCE**
The Lord is the portion
  of mine *i*. .............. Ps 16:5
earnest of our *i* ........ Eph 1:14
promise of eternal *i* ..... Heb 9:15
*See* Eph 5:5; Col 1:12; Heb 1:4

**INIQUITY**
visiting the *i* of the
  fathers. ............... Ex 20:5
forgiving *i* ............. Ex 34:7
that plow *i*. ............. Job 4:8
the *i* of my youth ....... Job 13:26
if I have done *i*. ........ Job 34:32
pardon mine *i* ......... Ps 25:11
imputeth not *i*. ......... Ps 32:2
I was shapen in *i* ....... Ps 51:5
forgiveth all thine *i*. ..... Ps 103:3
that soweth *i* ......... Prov 22:8
bruised for our *i*. ........ Is 53:5
not look on *i*. ........... Hab 1:13
*i* shall abound ........ Matt 24:12
the reward of *i*. ........ Acts 1:18
in the bond of *i* ......... Acts 8:23
to *i* unto *i*. ............ Rom 6:19
mystery of *i*. ........... 2 Thess 2:7
depart from *i* .......... 2 Tim 2:19
a world of *i* ........... James 3:6
*See* Ps 36:2; Ezek 3:18; 18:26

**INNOCENT**
*i* shall divide. ........... Job 27:17
shall not be *i*. ......... Prov 28:20
*See* Ex 23:7; Matt 27:24

**INSPIRATION**
the *i* of the Almighty .... Job 32:8
by *i* of God ............. 2 Tim 3:16

**INSTANT**
continuing *i* in prayer... Rom 12:12
be *i* in season. .......... 2 Tim 4:2

**INTERCESSION**
and made *i* for the
  transgressors. ......... Is 53:12
maketh *i* for us ......... Rom 8:26

to make *i* for them ...... Heb 7:25
*See* Jer 7:16; 27:18; 1 Tim 2:1

**INTERPRETATION**
the scripture is of any
  private *i* ............. 2 Pet 1:20

**INVISIBLE**
For the *i* things of him ...Rom 1:20
image of the *i* God. ........ Col 1:15
immortal, *i* .............. 1 Tim 1:17
him who is *i* ........... Heb 11:27

---

## J

**JEALOUS**
Lord thy God am
  a *j* God. ............... Ex 20:5
is a *j* God. ............... Ex 34:14
even a *j* God ............ Deut 4:24
am a *j* God .............. Deut 5:9
*j* God among you ....... Deut 6:15
he is a *j* God. ........... Josh 24:19
have been very *j*. ....... 1 Kin 19:10
*j* for my holy name .... Ezek 39:25
am *j* over you. ........... 2 Cor 11:2
*See* Joel 2:18; Zech 1:14; 8:2

**JEALOUSY**
For *j* is the ............ Prov 6:34
the Lord to *j* ........... 1 Cor 10:22
*See* Ps 78:58; 79:5; Is 42:13

**JESUS**
not the things which
  are *J* Christ's .......... Phil 2:21
*J* the Son of God ....... Heb 4:14
confess that *J*. .......... 1 John 4:15

**JOIN**
unto them that *j*. ........... Is 5:8
*j* to idols ............... Hos 4:17
God hath *j* together. ..... Matt 19:6
fitly *j* together ........... Eph 4:16
*See* Acts 8:29; 9:26; Eph 5:31

**JOY**
the *j* of the Lord ........ Neh 8:10
turned into *j*. ............ Job 41:22
fullness of *j* ............ Ps 16:11
but *j* cometh. ............ Ps 30:5
*j* of the whole earth. ....... Ps 48:2
*j* of thy salvation. ........ Ps 51:12
shall reap in *j* .......... Ps 126:5
It is *j* ................. Prov 21:15
everlasting *j*. ............ Is 51:11
*j* of the whole earth. ..... Lam 2:15
*j* of thy lord .......... Matt 25:21, 23
the word with *j*. ......... Luke 8:13
*j* shall be in heaven ...... Luke 15:7
believed not for *j* ...... Luke 24:41
this my *j* ............... John 3:29
*j* might be full .......... John 15:11
your *j* may be full. ...... John 16:24
Fulfil ye my *j*. .......... Phil 2:2
who for the *j*. ........... Heb 12:2
count it all *j* ........... James 1:2
rejoice with *j* ........... 1 Pet 1:8
with exceeding *j*. ........ 1 Pet 4:13
our *j* may be full ........ 2 John 12
*See* Gal 5:22; Phil 1:4

**JOYFUL**
Make a *j* noise ........... Ps 66:1
let us make a *j* noise. ...... Ps 95:1
prosperity be *j*. .......... Eccl 7:14
*j* in my house ........... Is 56:7
*See* 2 Cor 7:4; Heb 10:34

**JUDGE** (*n.*)
not the *J* of all the
  earth. ................ Gen 18:25
for God is *j* himself ...... Ps 50:6
a *j* of the widows ........ Ps 68:5
*j* of the earth. .......... Ps 94:2
*J* of quick ............. Acts 10:42
the righteous *j*. ......... 2 Tim 4:8

## JUDGE (v.)

God the *J* of all.........Heb 12:23
the *j* standeth..........James 5:9
*See* 2 Sam 15:4; James 4:11

## JUDGE (v.)

the Lord shall *j* .......Deut 32:36
*j* the fatherless.............. Is 1:17
*J* not.......................Matt 7:1
*J* not according........John 7:24
Who art thou that *j*......Rom 14:4
*See* John 16:11; Rom 2:16; 3:6

## JUDGMENT

for the *j* is God's ........ Deut 1:17
not stand in the *j* .......... Ps 1:5
every man's *j* .........Prov 29:26
bring thee into *j*..........Eccl 11:9
every work into *j* ...... Eccl 12:14
that executeth *j*............Jer 5:1
keep mercy and *j*...... Hos 12:6
danger of the *j*...........Matt 5:21
committed all *j*.........John 5:22
For *j* I am come........John 9:39
righteousness,
　　and of *j*...............John 16:8
*j* to come..............Acts 24:25
*j* seat of Christ........Rom 14:10
after this the *j* ..........Heb 9:27
*j* must begin...........1 Pet 4:17
*See* Heb 10:27; James 2:13

## JUST

habitation of the *j*...... Prov 3:33
The memory of the *j* ....Prov 10:7
The way of the *j* .......... Is 26:7
the *j* shall live............. Hab 2:4
rain on the *j* .......... Matt 5:45
of the *j*................Luke 14:14
*j* persons...............Luke 15:7
*j* and unjust.............Acts 24:15
*j* shall live by faith ...... Rom 1:17
*j* shall live by faith .......Gal 3:11
things are *j* ............. Phil 4:8
Now the *j* shall............Heb 10:38
the spirits of *j* men .....Heb 12:23
*j* for the unjust...........1 Pet 3:18
*See* Job 34:17; Acts 3:14

## JUSTICE

*J* and judgment...........Ps 89:14
judgment and *j*..........Jer 23:5
*See* Job 8:3; 36:17; Is 9:7; 56:1

## JUSTIFICATION

and was raised again
　　for our *j*..............Rom 4:25
offences unto *j* .........Rom 5:16

## JUSTIFY

mightest be *j* ............ Ps 51:4
Which *j* the wicked........ Is 5:23
But wisdom is *j*........Matt 11:19
wisdom is *j* ...........Luke 7:35
that believe are *j*........Acts 13:39
shall be *j* ...............Rom 2:13
shall no flesh be *j*........Rom 3:20
being *j* by faith ...........Rom 5:1
*j* by his blood ............ Rom 5:9
not *j* by the works ....... Gal 2:16
*j* in the Spirit ...........1 Tim 3:16
*j* by works...............James 2:21
*See* Is 50:8; Rom 4:5; 8:33

## JUSTLY

but to do *j*, and to
　　love mercy ............. Mic 6:8

---

## K

## KEEP

and *k* thee ...............Num 6:24
will *k* the feet............ 1 Sam 2:9
*K* me as the apple ...... Ps 17:8
time to *k*...................Eccl 3:6
*k* his commandments....Eccl 12:13
not *k* anger for ever ...... Jer 3:12

the earth *k* silence.......Hab 2:20
*k* his ordinance...........Mal 3:14
*k* the commandments ...Matt 19:17
of God, and *k* it ........ Luke 11:28
and *k* thee .............Luke 19:43
If a man *k* my saying ... John 8:51
will *k* my words .......John 14:23
Holy Father, *k* .......John 17:11
*k* themselves from .....Acts 21:25
I *k* under my body...... 1 Cor 9:27
to *k* the unity............. Eph 4:3
shall *k* your hearts.......Phil 4:7
*k* thyself pure...........1 Tim 5:22
*k* that which is.........1 Tim 6:20
to *k* himself..............James 1:27
*k* yourselves ...........1 John 5:21
*k* you from falling ........Jude 24
*k* thee from the hour .....Rev 3:10
*See* 1 Pet 1:5; Jude 6; Rev 3:8

## KEY

the *k* of the kingdom
　　of heaven............. Matt 16:19
*k* of knowledge .........Luke 11:52
have the *k* of hell ........Rev 1:18
*See* Is 22:22; Rev 3:7; 9:1

## KILL

A time to *k*............... Eccl 3:3
*k* the body .............Matt 10:28
that *k* the body ......... Luke 12:4
*k* all the day ............ Rom 8:36
letter *k*...................2 Cor 3:6
*See* Matt 23:37; Mark 12:5

## KIND

Charity ... is *k*...........1 Cor 13:4
*See* Eph 4:32; James 3:7

## KINDNESS

the law of *k* ...........Prov 31:26
with everlasting *k* ........ Is 54:8
*k* of thy youth............ Jer 2:2
*k*, humbleness of mind... Col 3:12
brotherly *k*................2 Pet 1:7
*See* Josh 2:12; Joel 2:13

## KING

God save the *k*........1 Sam 10:24
my *K*, and my God......... Ps 5:2
Lord is *K* for ever ...... Ps 10:16
O Lord of hosts, my *K* .....Ps 84:3
the *k* of the earth ........Ps 102:15
By me *k* reign...........Prov 8:15
Curse not the *k* ..........Eccl 10:20
a *k* shall reign............Is 32:1
an everlasting *k* ........ Jer 10:10
Blessed be the *K*.......Luke 19:38
Christ a *K* ...............Luke 23:2
to make him a *k* ....... John 6:15
Behold your *K* ........ John 19:14
unto the *K* eternal......1 Tim 1:17
*K* of *K*, and Lord .....1 Tim 6:15
*k* and priests.............Rev 1:6
thou *K* of saints.........Rev 15:3
*See* 1 Tim 2:2; 1 Pet 2:17

## KINGDOM

ye shall be unto me
　　a *k* of priests.............Ex 19:6
thine is the *k*...........1 Chr 29:11
the *k* is the Lord's ....... Ps 22:28
an everlasting *k* ..........Dan 4:3
gospel of the *k*..........Matt 4:23
For thine is the *k* ...... Matt 6:13
children of the *k*....... Matt 8:12
*k* divided................Matt 12:25
children of the *k*...... Matt 13:38
gospel of the *k*..........Matt 24:14
inherit the *k* ..........Matt 25:34
if a *k* be divided........Mark 3:24
Every *k* divided.........Luke 11:17
to give you the *k*.......Luke 12:32
appoint unto you a *k* ...Luke 22:29
My *k* is not............John 18:36
the *k* to Israel.............Acts 1:6

the *k* to God ...........1 Cor 15:24
us into the *k* ..............Col 1:13
his heavenly *k* ........ 2 Tim 4:18
heirs of the *k*............James 2:5
the everlasting *k*........ 2 Pet 1:11
*See* Rev 1:9; 11:15; 16:10; 17:17

## KISS

the *k* of an enemy ...... Prov 27:6
with a holy *k*...........Rom 16:16

## KNOCK

*k*, and it shall be opened
　　unto you................Matt 7:7
*k* at the door...........Luke 13:25
at the door, and *k*........ Rev 3:20

## KNOW

and *k* nothing ............Job 8:9
*k* that my redeemer ....Job 19:25
*k* that I am God..........Ps 46:10
and *k* my heart ........ Ps 139:23
*k* by his doings.........Prov 20:11
living *k* that...............Eccl 9:5
who can *k* it .............Jer 17:9
*K* the Lord .............Jer 31:34
shalt *k* the Lord..........Hos 2:20
left hand *k* ...............Matt 6:3
*k* the mysteries .........Matt 13:11
I *k* you not.............Matt 25:12
I *k* thee ...............Mark 1:24
to *k* the mystery........ Mark 4:11
If thou hadst *k*.........Luke 19:42
*k* of the doctrine........John 7:17
*k* my sheep ............ John 10:14
but thou shalt *k* ....... John 13:7
*k* the times.............Acts 1:7
we *k* that all things ..... Rom 8:28
he *k* them..............1 Cor 2:14
we *k* in part........... 1 Cor 13:9
to *k* the love .......... Eph 3:19
for I *k* whom..........2 Tim 1:12
*k* the holy scriptures ...2 Tim 3:15
saith, I *k* him .........1 John 2:4
we *k* that.............1 John 3:2
I *k* thy works...........Rev 2:2
*See* 2 Tim 2:19; 2 Pet 2:9

## KNOWLEDGE

*k* of thy ways ...........Job 21:14
teacheth man *k*.........Ps 94:10
Wise men lay up *k*.....Prov 10:14
increaseth *k* .............Eccl 1:18
by his *k* ...............Is 53:11
God gave them *k*.......Dan 1:17
*k* shall be increased ..... Dan 12:4
for lack of *k* ...............Hos 4:6
*k* of the glory ..........Hab 2:14
the key of *k* ...........Luke 11:52
having more
　　perfect *k*............. Acts 24:22
retain God in their *k*.... Rom 1:28
we all have *k*............1 Cor 8:1
*k* puffeth up.............1 Cor 8:1
*k*, it shall vanish ........ 1 Cor 13:8
the *k* of God.......... 1 Cor 15:34
which passeth *k* ........ Eph 3:19
*k* of Christ Jesus......... Phil 3:8
wisdom and *k* ...........Col 2:3
*k* of the truth ..........1 Tim 2:4
*k* of the truth ..........Heb 10:26
*See* 1 Sam 2:3; Hos 4:1

---

## L

## LABOUR (n.)

all *l* there is profit ..... Prov 14:23
man of all his *l*.........Eccl 2:22
All the *l* of man ..........Eccl 6:7
your *l* is not............1 Cor 15:58
and *l* of love ...........1 Thess 1:3
thy works, and thy *l* .....Rev 2:2
rest from their *l* .......Rev 14:13
*See* Gen 31:42; 2 Cor 6:5; 11:23

## LABOUR (v.)
Six days shalt thou *l*...... Ex 20:9
they *l* in vain.............. Ps 127:1
no end of all his *l*......... Eccl 4:8
The sleep of a *l* man..... Eccl 5:12
all ye that *l*................Matt 11:28
*L* not for... meat.......John 6:27
we are *l* together ........ 1 Cor 3:9
rather let him *l* .........Eph 4:28
know them which *l*...1 Thess 5:12
who *l* in the word ...... 1 Tim 5:17
*See* Matt 9:37; 20:1; Luke 10:2

## LAMB
dwell with the *l*.............Is 11:6
*l* to the slaughter.......Is 53:7
But I was like a *l*.........Jer 11:19
the *L* of God ...... John 1:29, 36
*l* without blemish ........1 Pet 1:19
blood of the *L*........... Rev 12:11
*See* Luke 10:3; John 21:15

## LAMP
Thy word is a *l* unto
   my feet .............. Ps 119:105
*l* of the wicked..........Prov 13:9

## LAST
and let my *l* end be
   like his............. Num 23:10
At the *l* it biteth....... Prov 23:32
*l* state of that man is ...Matt 12:45
first shall be *l*........ Matt 19:30
the *l* shall be first..... Matt 20:16
*l* which shall be.......Luke 13:30
at the *l* day...........John 6:39
*See* 2 Tim 3:1; 1 Pet 1:5

## LAUGH
I also will *l* at your
   calamity................Prov 1:26
a time to *l*..............Eccl 3:4
for ye shall *l*............ Luke 6:21
your *l* be turned .......James 4:9

## LAW
*l* is within my heart ...... Ps 40:8
thy *l* do I love.......... Ps 119:113
thy *l* is my delight ...... Ps 119:174
*l* of the wise .........Prov 13:14
destroy the *l*............Matt 5:17
by the deeds of the *l*.... Rom 3:20
the *l* is spiritual........Rom 7:14
what the *l* could not do ...Rom 8:3
the *l* was our..............Gal 3:24
all the *l* is fulfilled..... Gal 5:14
there is no *l*.............Gal 5:23
fulfill the *l* of Christ....... Gal 6:2
the *l* is good ............. 1 Tim 1:8
*l* of liberty ............James 1:25
fulfill the royal *l* .......James 2:8
*See* Ps 1:2; 19:7; Matt 7:12

## LAWFUL
is not *l* to do upon the
   sabbath day ...........Matt 12:2
All things are *l*.......... 1 Cor 6:12

## LEAN
*l* not unto thine own
   understanding ........Prov 3:5
*l* upon the Lord...........Mic 3:11

## LEARN
*L* to do well.................. Is 1:17
*l* war any more ..............Is 2:4
much *l* doth ........Acts 26:24
written for our *l*........Rom 15:4
yet *l* he obedience ....... Heb 5:8
*See* Matt 9:13; 11:29; Phil 4:11

## LEAST
these *l* commandments
   ... the *l* in the ........ Matt 5:19
is *l* in the kingdom ..... Matt 11:11
one of the *l* ...........Matt 25:40
*l* in the kingdom........ Luke 7:28
thing which is *l*........Luke 12:26

## LABOUR (v.)
that which is *l* ......... Luke 16:10
*l* of all saints.............. Eph 3:8
*See* Gen 32:10; 1 Cor 6:4

## LIBERTY
to proclaim *l*................ Is 61:1
*l* unto them................Jer 34:8
to set at *l* them ...... Luke 4:18
*l* of the children ........ Rom 8:21
this *l* of yours............ 1 Cor 3:9
there is *l* ................ 2 Cor 3:17
perfect law of *l* .......James 1:25
*See* Gal 5:13; 1 Pet 2:16

## LIE
is not a man, that he
   should *l*............. Num 23:19
that cannot *l*............. Titus 1:2
impossible for God to *l*.. Heb 6:18

## LIFE
into his nostrils the
   breath of *l* ............. Gen 2:7
the tree of *l* ............. Gen 2:9
the path of *l* ............Ps 16:11
strength of my *l* ......... Ps 27:1
fountain of *l* ............Ps 36:9
With long *l*............... Ps 91:16
*l* for evermore ...........Ps 133:3
*l* unto thy soul.......... Prov 3:22
findeth me findeth *l*..... Prov 8:35
The way of *l* ..........Prov 15:24
days of the *l* ............. Eccl 9:9
the way of *l* ............. Jer 21:8
thought for your *l* ..... Matt 6:25
to enter into *l* ......... Matt 18:8
enter into *l* maimed....Mark 9:43
for a man's *l* ..........Luke 12:15
The *l* is more ..........Luke 12:23
In him was *l* .............John 1:4
hath everlasting *l*.......John 5:24
ye might have *l*........John 5:40
everlasting *l*............John 6:47
I am that bread of *l*.....John 6:48
hath eternal *l*...........John 6:54
they might have *l*.......John 10:10
I lay down my *l*........John 10:15
and the *l*................ John 11:25
I will lay down my *l* ... John 13:37
the truth, and the *l*..... John 14:6
in newness of *l* ........ Rom 6:4
*l* from the dead....... Rom 11:15
*l* which I now live ....... Gal 2:20
alienated from the *l*.....Eph 4:18
your *l* is hid ..............Col 3:3
For what is your *l*.......James 4:14
*l* was manifested ....... 1 John 1:2
the pride of *l*........... 1 John 2:16
from death unto *l* ..... 1 John 3:14
to us eternal *l*........... 1 John 5:11
the tree of *l*...............Rev 2:7
river of water of *l*.........Rev 22:1
*See* Matt 10:39; Acts 5:20

## LIGHT
*l* of thy countenance ......Ps 4:6
The Lord is my *l*........... Ps 27:1
sins in the *l*............. Ps 90:8
*l* unto my path..........Ps 119:105
for thy *l* is come ......... Is 60:1
*l* of the world ..........Matt 5:14
Let your *l* so shine....... Matt 5:16
The *l* of the body ..... Matt 6:22
your *l* burning ........ Luke 12:35
children of *l*............ Luke 16:8
That was the true *L*...... John 1:9
that *l* is come ............ John 3:19
burning and a
   shining *l*..............John 5:35
is the *l* with you ....... John 12:35
from darkness to *l*.....Acts 26:18
*l* of the glorious......... 2 Cor 4:4
commanded the *l* ....... 2 Cor 4:6
an angel of *l* ...........2 Cor 11:14
dwelling in the *l*........1 Tim 6:16

## LABOUR (v.)
*l* that shineth............2 Pet 1:19
that God is *l*.............. 1 John 1:5
if we walk in the *l*...... 1 John 1:7
neither *l* of the sun...... Rev 22:5
*See* 2 Tim 1:10; Rev 7:16; 18:23

## LIKENESS
in the *l* of men..........Acts 14:11
*l* of his death........... Rom 6:5
his own Son in the *l* ..... Rom 8:3
in the *l* of men.......... Phil 2:7
*See* Gen 1:26; Deut 4:16

## LION
but the righteous are bold
   as a *l*...................Prov 28:1
the den of *l* .............. Dan 6:16
as a roaring *l*............1 Pet 5:8

## LIVE
he shall *l*................Lev 18:5
not *l* always.............Job 7:16
shall he *l* again ..........Job 14:14
not die, but *l*............Ps 118:17
make me to *l*........... Is 38:16
soul shall *l* ................. Is 55:3
he shall surely *l*........ Ezek 3:21
in thy blood, *L* ........ Ezek 16:6
he shall surely *l*....... Ezek 18:9
he shall even *l* ....... Ezek 20:11
he shall surely *l*....... Ezek 33:13
and we shall *l*........... Hos 6:2
*l* by his faith ........... Hab 2:4
not *l* by bread alone .... Matt 4:4
thou shalt *l*...........Luke 10:28
yet shall he *l*........... John 11:25
because I *l*............John 14:19
For in him we *l*........Acts 17:28
The just shall *l*.......... Rom 1:17
whether we *l* ......... Rom 14:8
gospel should *l* ........ 1 Cor 9:14
behold, we *l* ......... 2 Cor 6:9
might *l* unto God ....... Gal 2:19
If we *l* in the Spirit ...... Gal 5:25
me to *l* is Christ......... Phil 1:21
*l* godly in Christ .......1 Tim 3:12
we shall *l* ..............James 4:15
I am he that *l*........... Rev 1:18
name that thou *l* ........Rev 3:1
*See* 1 Tim 5:6; Rev 20:4

## LIVING
of life; and man became
   a *l* soul.................. Gen 2:7
land of the *l*............Job 28:13
light of the *l* ............Job 33:30
the book of the *l*........ Ps 69:28
well of *l* waters ......... Song 4:15
of *l* waters ............. Jer 2:13
that *l* waters ...........Zech 14:8
given thee *l* water ..... John 4:10
a *l* sacrifice ............. Rom 12:1
By a new and *l* way.....Heb 10:20
*See* Matt 22:32; 1 Cor 15:43

## LORD
The *L* our God ...........Deut 6:4
*L*, he is the God ....... 1 Kin 18:39
The *L* be with you ....... Ruth 2:4
God is the *L*.............Ps 33:12
This is the *L* doing....... Ps 118:23
O *L* our God............... Is 37:20
*L* shall be king .........Zech 14:9
saith unto me *L*, *L*....Matt 7:21
Son of man is *L*........Mark 2:28
why call ye me, *L*......Luke 6:46
both *L* and Christ........Acts 2:36
One *L*, one faith ......... Eph 4:5
*L* of peace............2 Thess 3:16
*See* 1 Cor 2:8; Rev 11:15

## LOSE
He that findeth his life
   shall *l* it.............. Matt 10:39
*l* his own soul.......... Matt 16:26
*l* himself ...............Luke 9:25
*See* Eccl 3:6; Luke 15:4, 8

## LOSS

**LOSS**
shall be burned, he
shall suffer l . . . . . . . . . . 1 Cor 3:15
l for Christ . . . . . . . . . . . . . . . Phil 3:7

**LOST**
I have gone astray like
a l sheep . . . . . . . . . . . . . Ps 119:176
hath been l sheep . . . . . . . .Jer 50:6
the l sheep . . . . . . . . . . . . . Matt 10:6
that which was l . . . . . . . Matt 18:11
that which was l . . . . . . Luke 19:10
none of them is l . . . . . . .John 17:12
See Deut 22:3; 2 Cor 4:3

**LOVE (n.)**
thy l to me was
wonderful . . . . . . . . . . . . 2 Sam 1:26
but l covereth . . . . . . . . . . Prov 10:12
where l is . . . . . . . . . . . . . . Prov 15:17
banner over me was l . . . Song 2:4
for l is strong . . . . . . . . . . . Song 8:6
an everlasting l . . . . . . . . . . Jer 31:3
with bands of l . . . . . . . . . Hos 11:4
the l of many . . . . . . . . . Matt 24:12
the l of God . . . . . . . . . . . John 5:42
l one to another . . . . . . . John 13:35
Greater l hath
no man . . . . . . . . . . . John 15:13
L worketh no ill . . . . . . . .Rom 13:10
the l of Christ . . . . . . . . 2 Cor 5:14
God of l and peace . . . 2 Cor 13:11
And to know the l . . . . . . Eph 3:19
l of money . . . . . . . . . . . 1 Tim 6:10
brotherly l continue . . . . Heb 13:1
l one another . . . . . . . . . . 1 John 4:7
for God is l . . . . . . . . . . . . 1 John 4:8
Herein is l . . . . . . . . . . . . 1 John 4:10
no fear in l . . . . . . . . . . . 1 John 4:18
left thy first l . . . . . . . . . . .Rev 2:4
See Gal 5:22; 1 Thess 1:3

**LOVE (v.)**
thou shalt l thy neighbour
as thyself . . . . . . . . . . Lev 19:18
l the Lord thy God . . . . . . Deut 6:5
to l the Lord thy God . . . Deut 19:9
I will l thee . . . . . . . . . . . . Ps 18:1
they that l his name . . . Ps 69:36
prosper that l thee . . . . .Ps 122:6
I l them that l me . . . . . . . Prov 8:17
friend l at all times . . . Prov 17:17
A time to l . . . . . . . . . . . . . Eccl 3:8
l them freely . . . . . . . . . . . Hos 14:4
l the good . . . . . . . . . . . . . Amos 5:15
to l mercy . . . . . . . . . . . . . . . Mic 6:8
L your enemies . . . . . . . . Matt 5:44
For if ye l . . . . . . . . . . . . . . Matt 5:46
L your enemies . . . . . . . Luke 6:27
l him most . . . . . . . . . . . . Luke 7:42
he whom thou l . . . . . . . . .John 11:3
That ye l one another . . .John 15:12
that I l thee . . . . . . . . . . . John 21:15
to l one another . . . . . . . Rom 13:8
l our Lord Jesus . . . . . . . . Eph 6:24
not seen, ye l . . . . . . . . . . 1 Pet 1:8
L the brotherhood . . . . . 1 Pet 2:17
We l him . . . . . . . . . . . . . . 1 John 4:19
As many as I l . . . . . . . . . . Rev 3:19
See John 14:31; 1 John 4:20, 21

**LOVINGKINDNESS**
Shew thy marvelous l . . . . .Ps 17:7
How excellent is thy l . . . . .Ps 36:7
thy l is better . . . . . . . . . . . . Ps 63:3
To shew forth thy l . . . . . . Ps 92:2
with l have I drawn . . . . . Jer 31:3

**LUST**
whatsoever thy soul
l after . . . . . . . . . . . . . . Deut 12:15
own hearts' l . . . . . . . . . . . . Ps 81:12
for I had not known l . . . .Rom 7:7
affections and l . . . . . . . . . Gal 5:24
and hurtful l . . . . . . . . . . .1 Tim 6:9

worldly l . . . . . . . . . . . . . . . Titus 2:12
of his own l . . . . . . . . . . . James 1:14
from fleshly l . . . . . . . . . . 1 Pet 2:11
l of the flesh . . . . . . . . . . 1 John 2:16
the l thereof . . . . . . . . . . . 1 John 2:17
after their own l . . . . . . . . . Jude 16
their own ungodly l . . . . . Jude 18
See Matt 5:38; 1 Cor 10:6

## — M —

**MAKER**
a man be more pure
than his m . . . . . . . . . . . . .Job 4:17
my m would . . . . . . . . . . . Job 32:22
Where is God my m . . . Job 35:10
righteousness to my M. . . Job 36:3
the Lord our m . . . . . . . . . Ps 95:6
reproacheth his M . . . . . Prov 14:31
the Lord is the m . . . . . . Prov 22:2
striveth with his M . . . . . . . Is 45:9
the Lord thy m . . . . . . . . . .Is 51:13
For thy M . . . . . . . . . . . . . . . . Is 54:5
whose builder and m . . . .Heb 11:10
See Is 1:31; 17:7; Hab 2:18

**MAN**
Let us make m in
our image . . . . . . . . . . . . Gen 1:26
imagination of m heart . . .Gen 8:21
God is not a m . . . . . . . . Num 23:19
Yet m is born . . . . . . . . . . . .Job 5:7
M that is born . . . . . . . . . . Job 14:1
m of the earth . . . . . . . . . . Ps 10:18
m obtaineth favour . . . . . .Prov 12:2
what is good for m . . . . . Eccl 6:12
Cease ye from m . . . . . . . . Is 2:22
it is not in m . . . . . . . . . . .Jer 10:23
I am God, and not m . . . .Hos 11:9
No m can serve two . . . . Matt 6:24
No m hath seen God . . . .John 1:18
outward m perish . . . . . 2 Cor 4:16
in fashion as a m . . . . . . . . Phil 2:8
the m Christ Jesus . . . . . 1 Tim 2:5
See 1 Cor 15:47; Eph 4:24

**MASTER**
can serve two m . . . . . . . Matt 6:24
not above his m . . . . . . . Matt 10:24
for one is your M . . . . . . Matt 23:8
can serve two m . . . . . . . Luke 16:13
Ye call me M and Lord . . .John 13:13
obey . . . your m . . . . . . . . . . Col 3:22
a M in heaven . . . . . . . . . . . Col 4:1
be not many m . . . . . . . . James 3:1
subject to your m . . . . . . 1 Pet 2:18
See Gen 24:12; Eccl 12:11

**MASTERY**
voice of them that
shout for m . . . . . . . . . . Ex 32:18
striveth for the m . . . . . . 1 Cor 9:25

**MEAT**
life more than m . . . . . . . Matt 6:25
have m to eat . . . . . . . . . . John 4:32
My m is to do . . . . . . . . . . John 4:34
the m which perisheth . . John 6:27
did eat their m . . . . . . . . . Acts 2:46
abstain from m . . . . . . . . Acts 15:29
with thy m . . . . . . . . . . . . . Rom 14:15
m destroy not . . . . . . . . . Rom 14:20
M for the belly . . . . . . . . 1 Cor 6:13
if m make my brother . . 1 Cor 8:13
same spiritual m . . . . . . 1 Cor 10:3
abstain from m . . . . . . . . .1 Tim 4:3
See Matt 3:4; Col 2:16

**MEDITATE**
went out to m in
the field . . . . . . . . . . . Gen 24:63
shalt m therein . . . . . . . . . Josh 1:8
his law doth he m . . . . . . . . Ps 1:2
m on thee . . . . . . . . . . . . . . Ps 63:6
I will m also . . . . . . . . . . . . Ps 77:12

m in thy word . . . . . . . . . .Ps 119:148
I m on all thy works . . . . . .Ps 143:5
Thine heart shall m . . . . . . Is 33:18
not to m before . . . . . . . . Luke 21:14
m upon these . . . . . . . . . . . 1 Tim 4:15
See Ps 19:14; 104:34; 119:97

**MEEK**
man Moses was
very m . . . . . . . . . . . . . . Num 12:3
the m shall eat . . . . . . . . . . Ps 22:26
The m will he guide . . . . . . .Ps 25:9
m shall inherit . . . . . . . . . . Ps 37:11
will beautify the m . . . . . . .Ps 149:4
m also shall increase . . . . . Is 29:19
tidings unto the m . . . . . . . . Is 61:1
Blessed are the m . . . . . . Matt 5:5
for I am m . . . . . . . . . . . . . . .Matt 11:29
ornament of a m . . . . . . . .1 Pet 3:4
See Ps 76:9; 147:6; Is 11:4

**MEMBER**
in thy book all my m
were written . . . . . . . . .Ps 139:16
yield ye your m . . . . . . . . . Rom 6:13
many m in one body . . . .Rom 12:4
the m of Christ . . . . . . . . 1 Cor 6:15
the m of an harlot . . . . . . 1 Cor 6:15
a little m . . . . . . . . . . . . . . . . James 3:5
war in your m . . . . . . . . . James 4:1
See Matt 5:29; Eph 4:25; 5:30

**MEMORY**
cut off the m of them . . . .Ps 109:15
utter the m . . . . . . . . . . . . . Ps 145:7
The m of the just . . . . . . Prov 10:7
for the m of them . . . . . . . Eccl 9:5

**MEN**
yourselves like m . . . . . . 1 Sam 4:9
to be but m . . . . . . . . . . . . . Ps 9:20
die like m . . . . . . . . . . . . . . Ps 82:7
strong m shall bow . . . . . Eccl 12:3
shew yourselves m . . . . . . . Is 46:8
I now persuade m . . . . . . . Gal 1:10
not as pleasing m . . . . . 1 Thess 2:4
See 1 Tim 2:4; 1 Pet 2:17

**MENTION**
will make m . . . . . . . . . . . . . Ps 71:16
m that his name . . . . . . . . .Is 12:4
m the lovingkindness . . . . . Is 63:7
m of you always . . . . . . . .Rom 1:9
making m of you . . . . . . 1 Thess 1:2
See Is 62:6; Ezek 18:22; 33:16

**MERCIFUL**
He is ever m . . . . . . . . . . . . .Ps 37:26
God be m unto us . . . . . . . . Ps 67:1
m man doeth good . . . . . Prov 11:17
m men are taken away . . . . .Is 57:1
for I am m . . . . . . . . . . . . . . Jer 3:12
Blessed are the m . . . . . . .Matt 5:7
m, as your Father . . . . . .Luke 6:36
m to me a sinner . . . . . . Luke 18:13
be a m and faithful . . . . . . Heb 2:17
See Ex 34:6; Joel 2:13

**MERCY**
shew m on whom I will
shew m . . . . . . . . . . . . . .Ex 33:19
for his m endureth . . . . 1 Chr 16:34
his m endureth for ever . . . Ezra 3:11
goodness and m shall . . . . .Ps 23:6
great is his m
toward them . . . . . . . . . Ps 103:11
full of thy m . . . . . . . . . . .Ps 119:64
m endureth for ever . . . . . . Ps 136:1
m on the poor . . . . . . . . . Prov 14:21
m and truth . . . . . . . . . . . .Prov 16:6
with great m . . . . . . . . . . . . .Is 54:7
and have no m . . . . . . . . . .Jer 6:23
of the Lord's m . . . . . . . . . Lam 3:22
and m to them . . . . . . . . . .Dan 9:4
no truth, nor m . . . . . . . . . .Hos 4:1
For I desired m . . . . . . . . . . Hos 6:6

fatherless findeth *m*..... Hos 14:3
to love *m*................. Mic 6:8
he delighteth in *m*...... Mic 7:18
in wrath remember *m*.... Hab 3:2
they shall obtain *m*......Matt 5:7
I will have *m*............ Matt 9:13
have *m* on whom....... Rom 9:15
by the *m* of God ....... Rom 12:1
that we may obtain *m*.. Heb 4:16
judgment without *m*... James 2:13
his abundant *m*..........1 Pet 1:3
*See* Dan 4:27; 1 Tim 1:2

## MIGHT
all thy soul, and with
all thy *m*............. Deut 6:5
do it with thy *m* ........Eccl 9:10
Not by *m*.................Zech 4:6
with all *m*...............Col 1:11
*See* 2 Pet 2:11; Rev 7:12

## MIGHTY
was a *m* hunter before
the Lord............... Gen 10:9
Thou hast a *m* arm.....Ps 89:13
the *m* One of Israel.........Is 1:24
*m* to save .................Is 63:1
*m* in work...............Jer 32:19
*m* works were done ...Matt 11:20
a rushing *m* wind........Acts 2:2
but *m* through God....2 Cor 10:4
*See* Eccl 6:10; Matt 3:11

## MILK
*m* and honey .............Ex 3:8
have need of *m* ......... Heb 5:12
*m* of the word ...........1 Pet 2:2
*See* Judg 4:19; Job 21:24

## MIND (*n.*)
whose *m* is stayed........ Is 26:3
carnal *m* .................Rom 8:7
same *m* one toward ....Rom 12:16
a willing *m* ............2 Cor 8:12
be of one *m* ............2 Cor 13:11
with one *m* ..............Phil 1:27
one accord, of one *m* .... Phil 2:2
Let this *m* be in you..... Phil 2:5
keep your hearts and *m* ..Phil 4:7
of corrupt *m*.............1 Tim 6:5
and of sound *m*....... 2 Tim 1:7
men of corrupt *m* ...... 2 Tim 3:8
*See* Rom 8:6; 1 Thess 5:14

## MIND (*v.*)
flesh do *m* the things
of the flesh ............ Rom 8:5
*M* not high things ......Rom 12:16
*m* the same thing........ Phil 3:16
who *m* earthly things ... Phil 3:19

## MINDFUL
What is man, that thou
art *m* of him..............Ps 8:4

## MINISTER (*n.*)
ye *m* of his................Ps 103:21
him *m* a flaming fire .....Ps 104:4
*M* of our God .............Is 61:6
the Lord's *m*............. Joel 1:9
let him be your *m* .....Matt 20:26
shall be your *m*.......Mark 10:43
is the *m* of God .........Rom 13:4
able *m* of the new .... 2 Cor 3:6
the *m* of sin............. Gal 2:17
I was made a *m*.......... Eph 3:7
faithful *m*.............. Eph 6:21
faithful *m* of Christ........Col 1:7
am made a *m*............Col 1:23
a faithful *m*................Col 4:7
shalt be a good *m*.......1 Tim 4:6
his *m* a flame of fire .....Heb 1:7
*See* 2 Cor 6:4; 1 Thess 3:2

## MINISTRY
and to the *m* of
the word................Acts 6:4

we have this *m* ..........2 Cor 4:1
*m* of reconciliation .....2 Cor 5:18
that the *m* ...............2 Cor 6:3
work of the *m* ...........Eph 4:12
Take heed to the *m*...... Col 4:17
proof of thy *m*........ 2 Tim 4:5
*See* Acts 1:17; 12:25; Rom 12:7

## MIRACLE
and where be all his *m* ...Judg 6:13
a *m* in my name ....... Mark 9:39
some *m* done..........Luke 23:8
beginning of *m*.........John 2:11
again the second *m*.....John 4:54
John did no *m*......... John 10:41
among you by *m*.......Acts 2:22
the working of *m*.......1 Cor 12:10
*See* Gal 3:5; Heb 2:4; Rev 13:14

## MOCK
God is not *m*.............. Gal 6:7
*See* 2 Kin 2:23; Matt 2:16

## MOCKER
there should be *m*........ Jude 18

## MODERATION
Let your *m* be known
unto all................. Phil 4:5

## MONEY
redeemed without *m*...... Is 52:3
the love of *m*...........1 Tim 6:10
*See* Gen 23:9; Mark 6:8; Luke 9:3;
Acts 4:37

## MORTAL
*m* man be more just
than God ............... Job 4:17
in your *m* body ........ Rom 6:12
this *m* must............ 1 Cor 15:53
*See* Deut 19:11; 2 Cor 4:11; 5:4

## MORTIFY
the Spirit do *m*
the deeds.............. Rom 8:13
*M* therefore............... Col 3:5

## MOTHER
Thou art my *m* .......... Job 17:14
to be a joyful *m*........ Ps 113:9
As one whom his *m* ...... Is 66:13
As is the *m*............. Ezek 16:44
Who is my *m* ........ Matt 12:48
and the *m* of Jesus ......John 2:1
*See* Gal 4:26; 1 Tim 1:9; 5:2

## MOURN
*m* at the last ............. Prov 5:11
all that *m* ................Is 61:2
turn their *m* ........... Jer 31:13
they that *m* .............. Matt 5:4
tribes of the earth *m* ...Matt 24:30
*See* Zech 7:5; James 4:9

## MOUTH
Out of the *m* of babes ......Ps 8:2
I will keep my *m*.......... Ps 39:1
open thy *m* wide ......... Ps 81:10
*m* of the foolish.........Prov 10:14
the fruit of his *m* .......Prov 13:2
Whoso keepeth his *m*...Prov 21:23
for his *m* ................ Eccl 6:7
was in his *m* .............. Mal 2:6
the *m* speaketh ........ Matt 12:34
a *m* and wisdom.......Luke 21:15
the *m* confession ...... Rom 10:10
*m* must be stopped......Titus 1:11
of the same *m* .........James 3:10
*See* John 19:29; 1 Pet 2:22

## MOVE
said in his heart, I shall
not be *m*................Ps 10:6
I shall not be *m*...........Ps 16:8
I shall never be *m* ........ Ps 30:6
we live, and *m*..........Acts 17:28
*See* Prov 23:31; Is 7:2

## MULTITUDE
shalt not follow a *m* to
do evil ................. Ex 23:2
In the *m* of words ......Prov 10:19
*m* of counsellors........ Prov 11:14
hide a *m* of sins....... James 5:20
cover a *m* of sins.........1 Pet 4:8
*See* Josh 11:4; Luke 2:13

## MUZZLE
not *m* the ox when he
treadeth .............. Deut 25:4
not *m* the mouth ....... 1 Cor 9:9
not *m* the ox............1 Tim 5:18

## MYSTERY
the *m* of the kingdom
of heaven.............. Matt 13:11
of God in a *m* .............1 Cor 2:7
I shew you a *m* ........1 Cor 15:51
This is a great *m*........ Eph 5:32

---

## N

## NAKED
they were both *n*, the
man and............... Gen 2:25
people were *n* ...........Ex 32:25
*N* came I.................. Job 1:21
*N*, and ye clothed.......Matt 25:36
thirst, and are *n* .......1 Cor 4:11
not be found *n*.......... 2 Cor 5:3
all things are *n*........... Heb 4:13
*See* John 21:7; Rev 3:17; 16:15

## NAME
in the *n* of our God .......Ps 20:5
declare thy *n*............. Ps 22:22
that love his *n*......... Ps 69:36
praise thy *n*................Ps 138:2
*n* of the wicked..........Prov 10:7
*n* of the Lord..........Prov 18:10
A good *n* is rather ......Prov 22:1
A good *n* is better.........Eccl 7:1
thy *n* is as ointment ..... Song 1:3
an everlasting *n* ........... Is 56:5
whose *n* is Holy ...........Is 57:15
by a new *n*............... Is 62:2
calleth upon thy *n*........ Is 64:7
*n* is great in might....... Jer 10:6
sworn by my great *n* ....Jer 44:26
fear my *n* ................ Mal 4:2
Hallowed be thy *n*...... Matt 6:9
in his *n*..................Matt 12:21
little child in my *n*...... Matt 18:5
together in my *n*...... Matt 18:20
for my *n* sake.......... Matt 19:29
come in my *n*........... Matt 24:5
My *n* is Legion........... Mark 5:9
children in my *n*.......Mark 9:37
a miracle in my *n*...... Mark 9:39
this child in my *n*.......Luke 9:48
your *n* are written......Luke 10:20
for my *n* sake ......... Luke 21:12
in my Father's *n*........John 5:43
shall ask in my *n*....... John 14:13
nothing in my *n* ...... John 16:24
his *n* through faith ...... Acts 3:16
there is none other *n* .... Acts 4:12
*n* that is named...........Eph 1:21
*n* which is above.......... Phil 2:9
at the *n* of Jesus ........ Phil 2:10
whose *n* are ............. Phil 4:3
*n* of the Lord Jesus ....... Col 3:17
a more excellent *n*.........Heb 1:4
*n* by the which..........James 2:7
holdest fast my *n*........Rev 2:13
a new *n* written .........Rev 2:17
his *n* shall be ............ Rev 22:4
*See* Ex 28:9; Is 45:3; John 10:3

## NATION
exalteth a *n*............ Prov 14:34
he sprinkle many *n*.......Is 52:15

For *n* shall rise.......... Matt 24:7
shall rise against *n* .... Luke 21:10
perverse *n* ................ Phil 2:15
*See* Deut 4:27; Jer 2:11; 4:2

## NATURAL
nor his *n* force abated... Deut 34:7
without *n* affection...... Rom 1:31
But the *n* man ........... 1 Cor 2:14
Without *n* affection .... 2 Tim 3:3
*See* Phil 2:20; James 1:23

## NATURE
Doth not even *n* itself
teach you............. 1 Cor 11:14
by *n* the children ........ Eph 2:3
the *n* of angels.......... Heb 2:16
of the divine *n*.......... 2 Pet 1:4
*See* Rom 1:26; Gal 2:15; 4:8

## NEAR
neighbour that is *n*.... Prov 27:10
come *n* to me............. Is 50:8
while he is *n*............. Is 55:6
day of the Lord is *n*.... Obad 15
great day ... is *n*........ Zeph 1:14
know that it is *n*....... Matt 24:33
summer is *n*............ Mark 13:28
*See* Ezek 11:3; 22:5; Rom 13:11

## NEGLECT
*N* not the gift .......... 1 Tim 4:14
*n* so great salvation ...... Heb 2:3

## NEIGHBOUR
love thy *n*............... Lev 19:18
truth to his *n* .......... Zech 8:16
love thy *n*............. Matt 19:19
And who is my *n* .....Luke 10:29
truth with his *n*......... Eph 4:25
*See* Lev 19:13; Rom 13:10

## NEVER
Hell and destruction
are *n* full............ Prov 27:20
are *n* satisfied ........ Prov 30:15
*n* have enough............ Is 56:11
I *n* knew you............ Matt 7:23
shall *n* thirst.......... John 4:14
shall *n* hunger.......... John 6:35
*N* man spake............. John 7:46
*n* see death............. John 8:51
they shall *n* perish.....John 10:28
shall *n* die............. John 11:26
*n* faileth................ 1 Cor 13:8
will *n* leave thee ........ Heb 13:5
*See* Judg 2:1; Dan 2:44

## NEW
But if the Lord make a
*n* thing................Num 16:30
a *n* song................. Ps 33:3
unto the Lord a *n*......... Ps 96:1
will sing a *n* song........ Ps 144:9
Is no *n* thing............. Eccl 1:9
create *n* heavens ......... Is 65:17
the *n* earth.............. Is 66:22
*n* every morning........ Lam 3:23
A *n* commandment.... John 13:34
he is a *n* creature ....... 2 Cor 5:17
one *n* man .............. Eph 2:15
put on the *n* man........ Eph 4:24
*n* and living way.......Heb 10:20
no *n* commandment ... 1 John 2:7
a *n* name written........ Rev 2:17
upon him my *n* name ....Rev 3:12
they sung a *n* song ...... Rev 5:9
were a *n* song............Rev 14:3
I saw a *n* heaven.......... Rev 21:1
make all things *n*........ Rev 21:5
*See* Is 24:7; 43:19; Acts 2:13

## NEWNESS
we also should walk in *n*
of life .................. Rom 6:4

## NIGH
word is very *n* ......... Deut 30:14

The word is *n* thee ..... Rom 10:8
are made *n* .............. Eph 2:13
*See* Joel 2:1; Heb 6:8

## NIGHT
songs in the *n* .......... Job 35:10
song in the *n* ............ Ps 77:6
all *n* in prayer........... Luke 6:12
the *n* cometh ............ John 9:4
walk in the *n*...........John 11:10
*n* is far spent...........Rom 13:12
a thief in the *n*........1 Thess 5:2
be no *n* there .......... Rev 21:25
*See* Ps 121:6; John 3:2

## NOBLE
but their *n* put not
their necks ......... Neh 3:5
*n* held their peace ...... Job 29:10
thee a *n* vine............. Jer 2:21
*n* have sent ............. Jer 14:3
were more *n*............Acts 17:11
not many *n* ........... 1 Cor 1:26
*See* Num 21:18; Eccl 10:17

## NONE
there is *n* righteous,
no, not one ........... Rom 3:10

## NUMBER (v.)
*n* ye the people ........2 Sam 24:2
Go, *n* Israel ........... 1 Chr 21:2
to *n* our days ............. Ps 90:12
wanting cannot be *n* .....Eccl 1:15
he was *n* ................ Is 53:12
very hairs ... are all *n*...Matt 10:30
no man could *n*..........Rev 7:9
*See* Job 14:16; Acts 1:17

## NURTURE
*n* and admonition of
the Lord.............. Eph 6:4

---
**O**
---

## OBEDIENCE
so by the *o* of one.......Rom 5:19
the *o* of faith........... Rom 16:26
*o* by the things ......... Heb 5:8
*See* 2 Cor 10:5; 1 Pet 1:2

## OBEDIENT
Lord ... said will we
do, and be *o*...........Ex 24:7
upon an *o* ear.......... Prov 25:12
willing and *o*............... Is 1:19
*o* in all things...........2 Cor 2:9
*o* to them that .......... Eph 6:5
became *o* unto death..... Phil 2:8
to be *o* ................... Titus 2:9
As *o* children............ 1 Pet 1:14
*See* Num 27:20; Titus 2:5

## OBEY
if ye *o* the
commandments .....Deut 11:27
voice will we *o*......... Josh 24:24
to *o* is better ........ 1 Sam 15:22
*o* my voice .............. Jer 7:23
ought to *o* God..........Acts 5:29
to whom ye *o*.......... Rom 6:16
*o* your parents .......... Eph 6:1
*o* in all things...........Col 3:22
*o* not the gospel .......2 Thess 1:8
*o* them that ............Heb 13:17
in *o* the truth ...........1 Pet 1:22
*o* not the gospel ....... 1 Pet 4:17
*See* Ex 5:2; 23:21; Dan 9:10

## OBSERVATION
of God cometh not
with *o* ............... Luke 17:20

## OBTAIN
and shall *o* favour of
the Lord............. Prov 8:35
they shall *o* joy .......... Is 35:10

shall *o* gladness........... Is 51:11
to *o* that world........Luke 20:35
*o* help of God .......... Acts 26:22
that ye may *o*........... 1 Cor 9:24
to *o* salvation ...........1 Thess 5:9
but I *o* mercy ........... 1 Tim 1:13
*o* the salvation......... 2 Tim 2:10
that we may *o* mercy.... Heb 4:16
*o* eternal redemption.... Heb 9:12
not *o* mercy.............1 Pet 2:10
that have *o*.............. 2 Pet 1:1
*See* Dan 11:21; Hos 2:23

## OFFENCE
for yielding pacifieth
great *o* .................. Eccl 10:4
a rock of *o*.................. Is 8:14
an *o* unto me .......... Matt 16:23
by whom *o* cometh ...Matt 18:7
that *o* will come ........Luke 17:1
and rock of *o*........... Rom 9:33
*See* Rom 5:15; 16:17; Gal 5:11

## OFFEND
A brother *o*.............Prov 18:19
if thy right eye *o* ........ Matt 5:29
not be *o* in me .........Matt 11:6
all things that *o*........Matt 13:41
shall *o* one of these..... Matt 18:6
eye *o* thee............... Matt 18:9
yet *o* in one point......James 2:10
*See* Jer 37:18; 2 Cor 11:29

## OFFER
the people willingly
*o* themselves .......... Judg 5:2
Whoso *o* praise ........ Ps 50:23
and *o* thy gift ......... Matt 5:24
*o* also the other........Luke 6:29
*o* unto idols...........1 Cor 8:1
*o* in sacrifice ......... 1 Cor 10:19
and if I be *o*............Phil 2:17
ready to be *o*......... 2 Tim 4:6
*o* to bear the sins ...... Heb 9:28
*See* Ezra 1:6; 2:68; Mal 1:8

## OIL
anointed thee with the
*o* of gladness ...........Ps 45:7
anointed with fresh *o* ....Ps 92:10
the *o* of joy..............Is 61:3
*See* Ex 27:20; Mic 6:7

## ONE
his wife; and they shall
be *o* flesh ............. Gen 2:24
I and my Father are *o*.. John 10:30
that they may be *o*......John 17:11
*o* in Christ Jesus........Gal 3:28
*o* Lord, *o* faith ............ Eph 4:5
*See* Mark 12:32; 1 Tim 2:5

## OPEN
and the earth
*o* her mouth..........Num 16:30
*o* thou mine eyes........ Ps 119:18
*o* thy mouth ...........Prov 31:8
To *o* the blind eyes ........Is 42:7
I will not *o* you .......... Mal 3:10
Lord, *o* to us...........Matt 25:11
*o* to us the scriptures... Luke 24:32
To *o* their eyes.........Acts 26:18
is *o* unto me ............ 1 Cor 16:9
*o* unto us a door.......... Col 4:3
*See* 2 Cor 2:12; Heb 4:13

## OPINION
How long halt ye
between two *o* .......1 Kin 18:21

## OPPRESS
neither vex a stranger,
nor *o* him................Ex 22:21
not *o* a stranger.......... Ex 23:9
not *o* one another .....Lev 25:14
fatherless and the *o* ......Ps 10:18
that *o* the poor .........Prov 14:31

*o* not the stranger ......... Jer 7:6
*o* not the widow ........Zech 7:10
*See* Mal 3:5; Acts 7:24; 10:38

## ORDAIN
thou *o* strength..............Ps 8:2
I *o* thee a prophet .........Jer 1:5
*o* twelve ................ Mark 3:14
and *o* you .........John 15:16
must one be *o* .......... Acts 1:22
was *o* of God.........Acts 10:42
*o* to eternal life .......Acts 13:48
*o* them elders..........Acts 14:23
*o* of the apostles........ Acts 16:4
*o* of God........... Rom 13:1
was *o* by angels......... Gal 3:19
*o* that we should......... Eph 2:10
and *o* elders ............. Titus 1:5
*o* to this................. Jude 4
*See* 1 Cor 2:7; 9:14; 1 Tim 2:7

## ORDER
set thine house in *o* ....2 Kin 20:1
*o* of Melchizedek ........ Ps 110:4
decently and in *o* ...... 1 Cor 14:40
set in *o* the things ....... Titus 1:5
rise after the *o* .......... Heb 7:11
*See* Ps 37:23; 1 Cor 15:23

## ORDINANCE
forsook not the *o* of
  their God ................ Is 58:2
have kept his *o* ..........Mal 3:14
the *o* of God...........Rom 13:2
contained in *o* ........... Eph 2:15
the handwriting of *o* ... Col 2:14
and carnal *o* .......... Heb 9:10
*See* Jer 31:36; 1 Pet 2:13

## OUTWARD
man looketh on the
  *o* appearance.......1 Sam 16:7
appear beautiful *o*..... Matt 23:27
*o* in the flesh.......... Rom 2:28
*o* man perish .......... 2 Cor 4:16
*See* Matt 23:28; 1 Pet 3:3

## OVERCOME
I have *o* the world .....John 16:33
Be not *o* of evil ........Rom 12:21
victory that *o* ...........1 John 5:4
*o* the world ............1 John 5:5
To him that *o* .............Rev 2:7
he that *o* ............... Rev 2:26
*See* Song 6:5; 2 Pet 2:19

---

# P

## PAIN
My heart is sore *p*
  within me ............... Ps 55:4
the *p* of hell.............. Ps 116:3
the *p* of death.........Acts 2:24
*See* Ps 73:16; 2 Cor 11:27

## PARDON
will not *p* your
  transgressions ........Ex 23:21
Lord *p* every one ......2 Chr 30:18
God ready to *p*.......... Neh 9:17
he will abundantly *p* .......Is 55:7
*See* Jer 33:8; Mic 7:18

## PARENTS
shall rise up against
  their *p* ............. Matt 10:21
or *p* or brethren ....... Luke 18:29
betrayed both by *p* .... Luke 21:16
this man or his *p* ....... John 9:2
disobedient to *p* ..... Rom 1:30
lay up for the *p* ...... 2 Cor 12:14
Children, obey your *p* .... Eph 6:1
obey your *p* in all........Col 3:20
disobedient to *p* ....... 2 Tim 3:2
*See* Luke 2:27; 8:56; 1 Tim 5:4

## PARTAKER
and hast been *p* with
  adulterers ..............Ps 50:18
made *p* of their........Rom 15:27
*p* of his hope............ 1 Cor 9:10
*p* with the altar ........ 1 Cor 9:13
for we are all *p*.........1 Cor 10:17
ye cannot be *p*..........1 Cor 10:21
neither be *p*.............1 Tim 5:22
*p* of the heavenly .........Heb 3:1
*p* of the Holy Ghost...... Heb 6:4
*p* of Christ's............1 Pet 4:13
a *p* of the glory ........1 Pet 5:1
might be *p*..................2 Pet 1:4
*See* Eph 3:6; Phil 1:7

## PASS
I see the blood, I will *p*
  over you.................Ex 12:13
cup *p* from me........Matt 26:39
world *p* away ...........1 Cor 7:31
which *p* knowledge ..... Eph 3:19
*p* all understanding ......Phil 4:7
the world *p* away ..... 1 John 2:17
*See* 2 Cor 5:17; Rev 21:2

## PASTOR
will give you *p* according
  to mine............... Jer 3:15
from being a *p*...........Jer 17:16
*p* that destroy ........... Jer 23:1
*p* and teachers...........Eph 4:11

## PASTURE
maketh me to lie down in
  green *p* ................Ps 23:2
the people of his *p*........Ps 95:7
sheep of his *p*.............Ps 100:3
in a good *p*............. Ezek 34:14
and find *p*............... John 10:9

## PATH
the *p* of life ................Ps 16:11
*p* in the great waters ..... Ps 77:19
a light unto my *p* ....... Ps 119:105
the *p* of the just.........Prov 4:18
walk in his *p*.................Is 2:3
make his *p* straight..... Matt 3:3
*See* Lam 3:9; Heb 12:13

## PATIENCE
In your *p* possess...... Luke 21:19
worketh *p* ........... Rom 5:3
ye have need of *p*......Heb 10:36
let us run with *p*.........Heb 12:1
faith worketh *p* ......... James 1:3
the *p* of Job............ James 5:11
to *p* godliness ............ 2 Pet 1:6
labour and thy *p*..........Rev 2:2
*p* of the saints ..........Rev 14:12
*See* Eccl 7:8; 1 Thess 5:14

## PATIENTLY
in the Lord, and wait *p*
  for him .................. Ps 37:7
waited *p* for the Lord......Ps 40:1
had *p* endured........... Heb 6:15
shall take it *p* ........... 1 Pet 2:20

## PATTERN
*p* to them which should
  hereafter ............. 1 Tim 1:16
*p* of good works ........ Titus 2:7
*p* shewed to thee ........ Heb 8:5
*p* of things...............Heb 9:23

## PEACE
and give thee *p* ........Num 6:26
my covenant of *p* ......Num 25:12
proclaim *p* unto it .....Deut 20:10
lay me down in *p*.......... Ps 4:8
end of that man is *p*.....Ps 37:37
and a time of *p* .......... Eccl 3:8
*p* been as a river......... Is 48:18
There is no *p* ............. Is 48:22
There is no *p* ...........Is 57:21
The way of *p*............... Is 59:8

saying P, *p* ................ Jer 6:14
shalt die in *p*............. Jer 34:5
they shall seek *p*....... Ezek 7:25
to send *p*................ Matt 10:34
*p* one with another.... Mark 9:50
the way of *p* ........... Luke 1:79
on earth *p* .............. Luke 2:14
*p* be to this house ..... Luke 10:5
P I leave with you ..... John 14:27
ye might have *p* ......John 16:33
*p* from God ............... Rom 1:7
the way of *p*..............Rom 3:17
we have *p* with God ......Rom 5:1
the gospel of *p*...........Rom 10:15
live in *p* .................2 Cor 13:11
For he is our *p*........... Eph 2:14
preached *p* to you ........Eph 2:17
the *p* of God .............Phil 4:7
the *p* of God rule.......... Col 3:15
*p* among yourselves....1 Thess 5:13
the Lord of *p*............2 Thess 3:16
King of *p* .............. Heb 7:2
Follow *p* with all men.....Heb 12:14
Depart in *p* .............James 2:16
let him seek *p*...........1 Pet 3:11
*p* be multiplied...........2 Pet 1:2
*See* John 20:19; Gal 6:16

## PEACEABLE
shall dwell in a *p*
  habitation............... Is 32:18
a quiet and *p* life........1 Tim 2:2

## PEACEABLY
live *p* with all ...........Rom 12:18

## PEOPLE
I will take you to
  me for a *p* ................Ex 6:7
*p* of inheritance ........Deut 4:20
O *p* saved by the
  Lord.................Deut 33:29
thy *p* Israel ............2 Sam 7:24
P which I knew not...2 Sam 22:44
happy is that *p* ....... Ps 144:15
a *p* not strong .........Prov 30:25
a *p* laden............... Is 1:4
*p* of no understanding .... Is 27:11
unto me for a *p* .......Jer 13:11
a *p* prepared...........Luke 1:17
a peculiar *p*.............Titus 2:14
*See* Rom 11:2; Heb 11:25

## PERCEIVE
Jesus *p* their........... Matt 22:18
*p* that virtue ..........Luke 8:46
I *p* that God...........Acts 10:34
*p* we the love ..........1 John 3:16
*See* Neh 6:12; Job 33:14

## PERDITION
of them is lost, but the
  son of *p*...............John 17:12
evident token of *p*...... Phil 1:28
draw back unto *p*.......Heb 10:39

## PERFECT
Noah was a just
  man and *p*............Gen 6:9
and be thou *p*............Gen 17:1
*p* with the Lord........Deut 18:13
his work is *p* ...........Deut 32:4
law of the Lord is *p*........Ps 19:7
Mark the *p* man .........Ps 37:37
unto the *p* day ........Prov 4:18
*p* in thy ways ........Ezek 28:15
Be ye therefore *p* .......Matt 5:48
If thou wilt be *p* ......Matt 19:21
may be made *p*........John 17:23
acceptable, and *p*......Rom 12:2
them that are *p*.......... 1 Cor 2:6
*p* in weakness ........ 2 Cor 12:9
Be *p*, be of ............2 Cor 13:11
unto a *p* man ......... Eph 4:13
were already *p*...........Phil 3:12
as many as be *p*........Phil 3:15

*p* in Christ Jesus.......... Col 1:28
*p* and complete.......... Col 4:12
man of God may be *p*...2 Tim 3:17
their salvation *p*........ Heb 2:10
not be made *p*......... Heb 11:40
men made *p*............ Heb 12:23
Make you *p*............ Heb 13:21
have her *p* work ........James 1:4
*p* gift is from above.... James 1:17
*p* law of liberty ........James 1:25
same is a *p* man ........James 3:2
made *p* in love.......1 John 4:18
*See* 2 Chr 8:16; Eph 4:12

## PERFECTION
find out the Almighty
   unto *p*................ Job 11:7
end of all *p*...............Ps 119:96
even your *p*........... 2 Cor 13:9
go on unto *p*............. Heb 6:1

## PERILOUS
the last days *p* times
   shall come............2 Tim 3:1

## PERISH
All flesh shall *p* .........Job 34:15
ungodly shall *p* ............. Ps 1:6
the wicked shall *p* ....... Ps 37:20
beasts that *p*...........Ps 49:12
They shall *p*............. Ps 102:26
the wicked *p*............Prov 11:10
ready to *p*...............Prov 31:6
that we *p* not ............. Jon 1:6
the sword shall *p* ......Matt 26:52
meat which *p*...........John 6:27
Thy money *p* ......... Acts 8:20
Which all are to *p*.........Col 2:22
that any should *p*........ 2 Pet 3:9
*See* Ps 2:12; John 10:28

## PERSECUTE
them that *p* me ...........Ps 7:1
doth *p* the poor...........Ps 10:2
hath *p* my soul ..........Ps 143:3
and *p* you............ Matt 5:11
and *p* you............... Matt 5:44
will also *p* you.......John 15:20
Saul, why *p* thou me .....Acts 9:4
being *p*..................1 Cor 4:12
*p* the church ..........1 Cor 15:9
*P*, but not forsaken ......2 Cor 4:9
*See* Acts 7:52; Rom 12:14

## PERSECUTION
or *p* ariseth because of
   the word.............Matt 13:21
*p* ariseth................. Mark 4:17
*p*, distresses ........... 2 Cor 12:10
shall suffer *p*............2 Tim 3:12
*See* Gal 6:12; 1 Tim 1:13

## PERSEVERANCE
with all *p* and
   supplication........... Eph 6:18

## PERSON
which regardeth
   not *p*..................Deut 10:17
respect any *p* ......... 2 Sam 14:14
a vile *p* is contemned...... Ps 15:4
followeth vain *p* ........ Prov 12:11
not the *p* of men........ Matt 22:16
in the *p* of Christ ....... 2 Cor 2:10
image of his *p* ............Heb 1:3
what manner of *p* ........2 Pet 3:11
*See* Mal 1:8; Jude 16

## PERSUADE
we will *p* him.......... Matt 28:14
thou *p* me to be ....... Acts 26:28
man be fully *p*............Rom 14:5
we *p* men................2 Cor 5:11
*p* better things......... Heb 6:9
*See* 2 Kin 18:32; 2 Tim 1:12

## PIECE
a *p* of bread............. Prov 6:26
thirty *p* of silver ........ Zech 11:12
*See* Luke 14:18; Acts 19:19

## PIERCE
whom they have *p*......Zech 12:10
*p* my hands................Ps 22:16
spear *p* his side........John 19:34
*p* themselves ...........1 Tim 6:10
*See* Is 27:1; Heb 4:12

## PILGRIMS
strangers and *p* on
   the earth ..............Heb 11:13
strangers and *p*........1 Pet 2:11

## PILLAR
and she became a *p*
   of salt................Gen 19:26
her seven *p* ..............Prov 9:1
seemed to be *p* .......... Gal 2:9
a *p* in the temple ........Rev 3:12
*See* Joel 2:30; Rev 10:1

## PIT
and cast him into
   some *p*..............Gen 37:20
open a *p* ................Ex 21:33
owner of the *p*..........Ex 21:34
into the *p*.............Num 16:30
alive into the *p* .......Num 16:33
down to the *p* .........Job 33:24
out of a horrible *p* ........Ps 40:2
women is a deep *p* .... Prov 22:14
woman is a narrow *p* .. Prov 23:27
into his own *p*........ Prov 28:10
*p* of corruption ............Is 38:17
it fall into a *p* .........Matt 12:11
ox fallen into a *p*........ Luke 14:5

## PLACE
*p* whereon thou standest
   is holy ....................Ex 3:5
art my hiding *p*...........Ps 32:7
our dwelling *p*...........Ps 90:1
a *p* of refuge ........... Prov 14:26
are in every *p* ...........Prov 15:3
All go unto one *p* ........Eccl 3:20
*p* of my rest.................Is 66:1
give *p* unto wrath ......Rom 12:19
*p* to the devil ...........Eph 4:27
no *p* of repentance ......Heb 12:17
no *p* for them..........Rev 20:11
*See* Ps 16:6; Is 40:4; Eph 1:3

## PLEASE
shalt thou be *p* .........Ps 51:19
Whatsoever the Lord *p*...Ps 135:6
When a man's ways *p* ...Prov 16:7
*p* themselves ............... Is 2:6
Yet it *p* the Lord .......... Is 53:10
that which I *p* ...........Is 55:11
Lord be *p* ...............Mic 6:7
will he be *p* with thee .....Mal 1:8
things that *p* him.......John 8:29
cannot *p* God ...........Rom 8:8
to *p* ourselves ..........Rom 15:1
it *p* God .................1 Cor 1:21
Even as I *p* all men ..1 Cor 10:33
I seek to *p* men........... Gal 1:10
impossible to *p* him.......Heb 11:6
*See* 1 Cor 7:32; 1 Thess 2:4

## PLEASURE
For what *p* hath he ......Job 21:21
*p* to the Almighty ....... Job 22:3
hand there are *p*..........Ps 16:11
Do good in thy good *p*...Ps 51:18
that do his *p* ...........Ps 103:21
Lord taketh *p*............Ps 147:11
that loveth *p* ..........Prov 21:17
no *p* in fools .............Eccl 5:4
no *p* in them..............Eccl 12:1
perform all my *p* .........Is 44:28
*p* of the Lord.............Is 53:10

*p* on my holy day .........Is 58:13
wherein is no *p*..........Jer 22:28
Have I any *p* ...........Ezek 18:23
no *p* in the death .......Ezek 33:11
I have no *p* in you .........Mal 1:10
*p* of this life.............. Luke 8:14
your Father's good *p*... Luke 12:32
*p* in infirmities ........ 2 Cor 12:10
*p* of his will ...............Eph 1:5
of his good *p*............. Phil 2:13
in *p* is dead ..............1 Tim 5:6
lovers of *p* ........... 2 Tim 3:4
no *p* in him .............Heb 10:38
enjoy the *p* of sin ...... Heb 11:25
after their own *p* ........ Heb 12:10
Ye have lived in *p*......James 5:5
and for thy *p*.............Rev 4:11
*See* Eccl 2:1; Titus 3:3

## PLOW
sluggard will not *p* .... Prov 20:4
*p* of the wicked .........Prov 21:4
swords into *p*................Is 2:4
Beat your *p* ............Joel 3:10
*p* shall overtake........ Amos 9:13
*See* Deut 22:10; 1 Cor 9:10

## POOR
*p* shall never cease ..... Deut 15:11
*p* of the earth ............ Job 24:4
a father to the *p* ........ Job 29:16
*p* committeth himself.... Ps 10:14
This *p* man cried .........Ps 34:6
I am *p* and needy.........Ps 40:17
rich and *p*...............Ps 49:2
am *p* and sorrowful ..... Ps 69:29
I am *p* and needy.........Ps 70:5
He becometh *p* ........Prov 10:4
the tillage of the *p* ..... Prov 13:23
The *p* useth ........... Prov 18:23
The rich and *p* meet.... Prov 22:2
or lest I be *p* ........... Prov 30:9
*p* and needy seek.......... Is 41:17
and the *p* ............... Amos 2:6
O *p* of the flock ........ Zech 11:7
the *p* in spirit ........ Matt 5:3
as *p*, yet making ........2 Cor 6:10
he became *p* ...........2 Cor 8:9
*See* James 2:2; Rev 3:17

## POSSESS
shall *p* the gate of his
   enemies.............. Gen 22:17
let thy seed *p* ...........Gen 24:60
Lord *p* me ........... Prov 8:22
all that I *p*.............. Luke 18:12
*p* ye your souls ......... Luke 21:19
*See* Luke 12:15; 2 Cor 6:10

## POSSESSION
Canaan, for an ever-
   lasting *p* ................Gen 17:8
sold their *p* ...............Acts 2:45
purchased *p* ...............Eph 1:14
*See* Lev 25:10; 1 Kin 21:15

## POSSIBLE
with God all
   things are *p*.......... Matt 19:26
if it were *p* ...........Matt 24:24
things are *p*............Mark 9:23
if it were *p* ...........Mark 13:22
are *p* unto thee .......Mark 14:36
are *p* with God......... Luke 18:27
*See* Acts 2:24; 20:16; Heb 10:4

## POUR
Hast thou not *p* me
   out as milk ............Job 10:10
grace is *p* ................Ps 45:2
*p* out your heart...........Ps 62:8
*p* out my spirit...........Prov 1:23
spirit be *p* upon us ...... Is 32:15
*p* out his soul.............Is 53:12
*p* out thine heart ........Lam 2:19
*p* out my spirit...........Joel 2:28

his fury is *p* out............Nah 1:6
I will *p* upon............Zech 12:10
*p* you out a blessing.....Mal 3:10
*p* it on his head........Matt 26:7
*p* out the................John 2:15
*p* out of my Spirit........Acts 2:17
*p* out in those days.....Acts 2:18
*p* out the gift............Acts 10:45
*See* 2 Sam 23:16; Rev 14:10; 16:1

## POWER

pride of your *p*.........Lev 26:19
God hath *p*...............2 Chr 25:8
*p* of the grave............Ps 49:15
*p* of thine hand.........Prov 3:27
*p* of the tongue.........Prov 18:21
hath given him *p*........Eccl 5:9
there is *p*................Eccl 8:4
*p* to the faint...........Is 40:29
had *p* with God..........Hos 12:3
I am full of *p*...........Mic 3:8
hiding of his *p*............Hab 3:4
nor by *p*................Zech 4:6
kingdom, and the *p*....Matt 6:13
*p* on earth..............Matt 9:6
of heaven with *p*.....Matt 24:30
All *p* is given........Matt 28:18
*p* of the Highest........Luke 1:35
*p* will I give thee........Luke 4:6
*p* of the Spirit..........Luke 4:14
hath killed hath *p*......Luke 12:5
a cloud with *p*.........Luke 21:27
*p* of darkness..........Luke 22:53
*p* from on high........Luke 24:49
*p* to become............John 1:12
*p* to lay it down.......John 10:18
*p* over all flesh........John 17:2
*p* to crucify thee......John 19:10
ye shall receive *p*.........Acts 1:8
by our own *p*.........Acts 3:12
Give me also this *p*.....Acts 8:19
the *p* of Satan.........Acts 26:18
even his eternal *p*......Rom 1:20
raised in *p*..............1 Cor 15:43
*p* of the air..............Eph 2:2
working of his *p*.........Eph 3:7
the *p* of his..............Phil 3:10
glory of his *p*..........2 Thess 1:9
of *p*, and of love.........2 Tim 1:7
denying the *p* thereof...2 Tim 3:5
the *p* of death...........Heb 2:14
the *p* of the world.......Heb 6:5
*p* of an endless life......Heb 7:16
will I give *p*............Rev 2:26
honour and *p*...........Rev 4:11
*See* Luke 22:69; Rom 1:16

## POWERFUL

The voice of the
  Lord is *p*..............Ps 29:4
is quick, and *p*...........Heb 4:12

## PRAISE (*n.*)

fearful in *p*, doing
  wonders................Ex 15:11
He is thy *p*.............Deut 10:21
*p* to the Lord God........Judg 5:3
blessing and *p*..........Neh 9:5
*p* to thy name.............Ps 9:2
the *p* of Israel..........Ps 22:3
My *p* shall be..........Ps 22:25
for *p* is comely........Ps 33:1
*p* glorifieth me..........Ps 50:23
sing and give *p*..........Ps 57:7
I sing *p* unto..........Ps 61:8
his *p* glorious..........Ps 66:2
I will sing *p*...........Ps 104:33
*p* of all his saints........Ps 148:14
a man to his *p*........Prov 27:21
thy gates *P*.............Is 60:18
garment of *p*...........Is 61:3
full of his *p*..........Hab 3:3
*p* among all people.....Zeph 3:20
Give God the *p*........John 9:24
*p* of men..............John 12:43

*p* is not of men.........Rom 2:29
*p* of the same...........Rom 13:3
have *p* of God............1 Cor 4:5
whose *p* is..............2 Cor 8:18
*p* of the glory............Eph 1:6
if there be any *p*........Phil 4:8
sacrifice of *p*...........Heb 13:15
for the *p* of them.......1 Pet 2:14
whom be *p*..............1 Pet 4:11
*See* 2 Chr 29:30; 1 Pet 2:9

## PRAISE (*v.*)

Shall the dust *p* thee.....Ps 30:9
shall yet *p* him............Ps 42:5
people *p* thee............Ps 45:17
my lips shall *p* thee........Ps 63:3
*p* thee, O God............Ps 67:3
will yet *p* thee more......Ps 71:14
daily shall he be *p*.......Ps 72:15
dead *p* not the Lord.....Ps 115:17
*p* thy works..............Ps 145:4
another man *p* thee.....Prov 27:2
her own works *p* her...Prov 31:31
he shall *p* thee...........Is 38:19
*See* Luke 2:13; Acts 2:47; 3:8

## PRAY

he shall *p* for thee.......Gen 20:7
I will *p* for you...........1 Sam 7:5
ceasing to *p* for you..1 Sam 12:23
and *p*, and seek.........2 Chr 7:14
*p* for the life..........Ezra 6:10
we *p* unto him...........Job 21:15
unto thee will I *p*..........Ps 5:2
at noon will I *p*.........Ps 55:17
*P* for the peace..........Ps 122:6
*p* unto a god...........Is 45:20
*p* not thou for...........Jer 7:16
*P* now unto the Lord.....Jer 37:3
*p* for us................Jer 42:2
*p* before the Lord......Zech 7:2
*p* for them.............Matt 5:44
to *p* standing..........Matt 6:5
therefore *p* ye.........Matt 6:7
mountain apart to *p*...Matt 14:23
go and *p* yonder......Matt 26:36
when ye stand *p*.....Mark 11:25
while I stand *p*.......Mark 14:32
teach us to *p*............Luke 11:1
men ought always
  to *p*....................Luke 18:1
will *p* the Father......John 14:16
*p* the Father for you...John 16:26
I *p* for them.............John 17:9
Neither *p* I.............John 17:20
Saul...he *p*...........Acts 9:11
we should *p*...........Rom 8:26
*p* with the spirit.......1 Cor 14:15
*P* always................Eph 6:18
*P* without ceasing....1 Thess 5:17
*p* everywhere..........1 Tim 2:8
let him *p*..............James 5:13
*p* one for another......James 5:16
shall *p* for it..........1 John 5:16
*See* Luke 9:29; 1 Thess 5:25

## PRAYER

unto the *p* that
  is made.................2 Chr 7:15
and restrainest *p*....Job 15:4
my *p* is pure...........Job 16:17
hear my *p*.................Ps 4:1
will I direct my *p*..........Ps 5:3
Lord will receive my *p*.....Ps 6:9
give ear unto my *p*........Ps 17:1
*p* returned..............Ps 35:13
Hear my *p*, O Lord.......Ps 39:12
O thou that hearest *p*......Ps 65:2
voice of my *p*...........Ps 66:19
*p* also shall..............Ps 72:15
give myself unto *p*........Ps 109:4
*p* of the upright.........Prov 15:8
when ye make many *p*.....Is 1:15
a house of *p*............Is 56:7
shutteth out my *p*.......Lam 3:8

the house of *p*..........Matt 21:13
shall ask in *p*...........Matt 21:22
make long *p*...........Matt 23:14
the house of *p*.........Mark 11:17
night in *p* to God.......Luke 6:12
the house of *p*........Luke 19:46
for a shew make
  long *p*..................Luke 20:47
the hour of *p*...........Acts 3:1
continually to *p*.........Acts 6:4
but *p* was made........Acts 12:5
where *p* was wont......Acts 16:13
*p* and supplication.......Phil 4:6
the *p* of faith..........James 5:15
*p* of a righteous man...James 5:16
watch unto *p*............1 Pet 4:7
the *p* of saints..........Rev 5:8
offer it with the *p*........Rev 8:3
*See* Ps 72:20; Col 4:2

## PREACH

prophets to *p* of thee at
  Jerusalem...............Neh 6:7
*p* good tidings..............Is 61:1
*p* unto it................Jon 3:2
Jesus began to *p*.........Matt 4:17
as ye go, *p*...............Matt 10:7
to teach and to *p*........Matt 11:1
gospel *p* to them........Matt 11:5
and he *p* the word......Mark 2:2
and *p* everywhere.....Mark 16:20
*p* the kingdom of God...Luke 9:60
*p* Christ unto them.......Acts 8:5
Israel, *p* peace.........Acts 10:36
*p* unto you............Acts 13:38
*p* unto them Jesus...Acts 17:18
that *p* a man............Rom 2:21
shall they *p*..........Rom 10:15
*p* of the cross..........1 Cor 1:18
of *p* to save............1 Cor 1:21
*p* Christ crucified........1 Cor 1:23
have *p* to others.........1 Cor 9:27
so we *p*................1 Cor 15:11
is our *p* vain...........1 Cor 15:14
For we *p* not..........2 Cor 4:5
*p* Christ................Phil 1:15
*P* the word.............2 Tim 4:2
the gospel *p*............Heb 4:2
*p* unto the spirits........1 Pet 3:19
*See* 2 Cor 11:4; Eph 2:17

## PRECIOUS

for the *p* things of
  heaven..............Deut 33:13
for the *p* things........Deut 33:16
be *p* in thy sight........2 Kin 1:13
*p* as gold................Ezra 8:27
their soul is *p*............Ps 49:8
*p* shall their blood be.....Ps 72:14
*P* in the sight...........Ps 116:15
more *p* than rubies......Prov 3:15
than *p* ointment.........Eccl 7:1
*p* than fine gold.........Is 13:12
a *p* corner stone........Is 28:16
*p* in my sight............Is 43:4
take forth the *p*.........Jer 15:19
The *p* sons of Zion.......Lam 4:2
more *p* than.............1 Pet 1:7
*p* blood of Christ........1 Pet 1:19
elect, *p*................1 Pet 2:6
like *p* faith...............2 Pet 1:1
and *p* promises..........2 Pet 1:4
*See* Matt 26:7; Mark 14:3

## PREDESTINATE

also did *p* to be
  conformed............Rom 8:29
whom he did *p*........Rom 8:30
Having *p* us..............Eph 1:5

## PRESENCE

Cain went out from
  the *p*................Gen 4:16
we die in thy *p*.........Gen 47:15
If thy *p* go not...........Ex 33:15

troubled at his *p*........Job 23:15
in thy *p* .....................Ps 16:11
forth from thy *p* ...........Ps 17:2
secret of thy *p* .............Ps 31:20
not away from thy *p*.......Ps 51:11
I flee from thy *p* .........Ps 139:7
*p* of a foolish man .......Prov 14:7
his *p* saved them ..........Is 63:9
you out of my *p*..........Jer 23:39
out from his *p* ............Jer 52:3
the *p* of the Lord.........Jon 1:3
*p* of the Lord God........Zeph 1:7
*See* Gen 16:12; Luke 15:10

## PRESENT
a very *p* help................Ps 46:1
yet *p* with you .........John 14:25
are we all here *p*.......Acts 10:33
for to will is *p*...........Rom 7:18
of this *p* time ..........Rom 8:18
ye *p* your bodies........Rom 12:1
for the *p* distress ....... 1 Cor 7:26
be *p* with the Lord.......2 Cor 5:8
*p* evil world................Gal 1:4
may *p* every man .......Col 1:28
this *p* world............ 2 Tim 4:10
*p* you faultless............Jude 24
*See* Ps 72:10; Matt 2:11

## PRESERVE
God face to face, and
    my life is *p*............Gen 32:30
to *p* life .................Gen 45:5
when God *p* me.........Job 29:2
thou *p* man and beast....Ps 36:6
*p* thee from all evil .......Ps 121:7
Lord shall *p*...............Ps 121:8
*p* the way ................Prov 2:8
Discretion shall *p*.......Prov 2:11
Mercy and truth *p* ....Prov 20:28
*p* them alive .............Jer 49:11
life shall *p* it ..........Luke 17:33
*See* Hos 12:13; Jude 1

## PREVAIL
one *p* against him .......Eccl 4:12
gates . . . shall not *p* ... Matt 16:18
the word of God,
    and *p* ................Acts 19:20
*See* Job 14:20; John 12:19

## PRICE
him again the *p* of his
    redemption ..........Lev 25:52
of thee at a *p*...........2 Sam 24:24
for the full *p* ............1 Chr 21:22
part of the *p* ...........Acts 5:2
bought with a *p* .........1 Cor 6:20
of great *p* .................1 Pet 3:4
*See* Deut 23:18; Zech 11:12

## PRIDE
thy presence from the *p*
    of man..................Ps 31:20
*p*, and arrogancy .......Prov 8:13
a rod of *p* .................Prov 14:3
Woe to the crown of *p*......Is 28:1
*p* of thine heart...........Jer 49:16
*See* Mark 7:22; 1 John 2:16

## PRIEST
*p* of the most high God...Gen 14:18
kingdom of *p* ..............Ex 19:6
a faithful *p*.............1 Sam 2:35
so with the *p* ........... Is 24:2
the *p* and the prophet.....Is 28:7
*P* of the Lord................Is 61:6
and the *p* ...............Jer 13:13
*p* unto God ................Rev 1:6
kings and *p* ...............Rev 5:10
be *p* of God ...............Rev 20:6
*See* Heb 2:17; 3:1; 4:15; 7:26

## PRIESTHOOD
shall surely be an
    everlasting *p* ..........Ex 40:15

seek ye the *p*...........Num 16:10
an everlasting *p* ......Num 25:13
an unchangeable *p* .....Heb 7:24
and holy *p* ................1 Pet 2:5
a royal *p* ................. 1 Pet 2:9
*See* Josh 18:7; Neh 13:29

## PRINCE
confidence in *p*...........Ps 118:9
*p* decree justice.........Prov 8:15
*p* of the devils .........Matt 9:34
*p* of this world........ John 12:31
*p* of this world........John 16:11
the *P* of life ..............Acts 3:15
a *P* and a Saviour.......Acts 5:31
*p* of this world........... 1 Cor 2:6
*p* of the power............Eph 2:2
*See* Is 3:4; Hos 7:5; Matt 20:25

## PRINCIPALITY
but against *p*, against
    powers .................Eph 6:12
to *p* and powers ........Titus 3:1
*See* Rom 8:38; Eph 1:21; 3:10

## PRISON
my soul out of *p* .........Ps 142:7
out of *p* ................Eccl 4:14
He was taken from *p* ......Is 53:8
opening of the *p*...........Is 61:1
I was in *p* ..............Matt 25:36
spirits in *p*...............1 Pet 3:19
*See* Jer 32:2; 39:14; Luke 3:20

## PRISONER
*p* of Jesus Christ...........Eph 3:1

## PROCLAIM
I will *p* the name of
    the Lord................Ex 33:19
*p* liberty ................Lev 25:10
*p* the acceptable year......Is 61:2
in *p* liberty...............Jer 34:15
shall be *p* ...............Luke 12:3
*See* Deut 20:10; Joel 3:9

## PROFANE
shalt thou *p* the name
    of thy God ............Lev 18:21
*p* not my holy name.....Lev 22:2
priest are *p* ...............Jer 23:11
the holy and *p* ........Ezek 22:26
*p* the sabbath...........Matt 12:5
to *p* the temple.........Acts 24:6
for unholy and *p*...........1 Tim 1:9
avoiding *p* and vain ... 1 Tim 6:20
But shun *p*............. 2 Tim 2:16
or *p* persons .............Heb 12:16
*See* Ps 89:39; Mal 1:12; 2:10

## PROFIT (*n.*)
What *p* hath a man .......Eccl 1:3
no *p* under the sun .......Eccl 2:11
and what *p* hath he......Eccl 5:16
is *p* to them...............Eccl 7:11
*See* Esth 3:8; 1 Tim 4:15

## PROFIT (*v.*)
It *p* a man.................Job 34:9
*p* nothing ................Prov 10:2
shall not *p* them...........Is 30:6
which doth not *p*.........Jer 2:11
they shall not *p*..........Jer 23:32
what is a man *p* .......Matt 16:26
shall it *p* a man .......Mark 8:36
shall *p* you nothing.......Gal 5:2
exercise *p* little ..........1 Tim 4:8
*See* Rom 2:25; 1 Cor 13:3

## PROFITABLE
Can a man be *p*
    unto God ..............Job 22:2
godliness is *p*............1 Tim 4:8
is *p* for doctrine ....... 2 Tim 3:16
*See* 2 Tim 4:11; Philem 11

## PROMISE (*n.*)
doth his *p* fail..............Ps 77:8

the *p* of my Father.....Luke 24:49
wait for the *p* .............Acts 1:4
the *p* is unto you .........Acts 2:39
the hope of the *p* .......Acts 26:6
*p* made of none effect...Rom 4:14
at the *p* of God.........Rom 4:20
and the *p* ..............Rom 9:4
children of the *p*.........Rom 9:8
all the *p* of God .........2 Cor 1:20
against the *p* of God.....Gal 3:21
are the children of *p*.....Gal 4:28
*p* of the life ...............1 Tim 4:8
the *p* of life ..............2 Tim 1:1
inherit the *p* .............Heb 6:12
the *p* of eternal .........Heb 9:15
might receive the *p*.....Heb 10:36
received the *p* .........Heb 11:13
and precious *p*...........2 Pet 1:4
*p* of his coming.........2 Pet 3:4
concerning his *p*........ 2 Pet 3:9
*See* Eph 1:13; Heb 4:1; 11:9

## PROMISE (*v.*)
according as he hath *p* ...Ex 12:25
the Lord hath *p*........Num 14:40
as he hath *p* you.........Deut 1:11
as he *p* thee.............Deut 15:6
your God *p* you .......Josh 23:15
as he *p* him .............2 Kin 8:19
what he had *p* ..........Rom 4:21
he is faithful that *p*.....Heb 10:23
faithful who had *p*...... Heb 11:11
that he hath *p* us .......1 John 2:25
*See* 1 Kin 8:24, 25; Ezek 13:22

## PROOF
his passion by many infal-
    lible *p*...............Acts 1:3
the *p* of you..............2 Cor 2:9
*p* of your love...........2 Cor 8:24
a *p* of Christ .......... 2 Cor 13:3
know the *p* of him.......Phil 2:22
make full *p* .............2 Tim 4:5

## PROPHECY
whether there be *p*.... 1 Cor 13:8
more sure word of *p*....2 Pet 1:19
the *p* came not ...........2 Pet 1:21
words of this *p* ...........Rev 1:3
sayings of the *p*........ Rev 22:7
*See* Neh 6:12; 1 Tim 4:14

## PROPHESY
spirit rested upon them,
    they *p*..................Num 11:25
*P* not unto us .............Is 30:10
prophets *p* falsely ....... Jer 5:31
which *p* of peace .........Jer 28:9
*P* unto the wind .......Ezek 37:9
daughters shall *p*........Joel 2:28
who can but *p* ..........Amos 3:8
*p* not again ..............Amos 7:13
I will *p* unto thee........ Mic 2:11
*P* unto us ...............Matt 26:68
unto him, *P* ...........Mark 14:65
*P*, who is it ............Luke 22:64
let us *p* according ...... Rom 12:6
we *p* in part............. 1 Cor 13:9
covet to *p* ..............1 Cor 14:39
Despise not *p*........ 1 Thess 5:20
*See* Amos 2:12; 1 Cor 11:5

## PROPHET
people were *p* ..........Num 11:29
a *p* among you..........Num 12:6
arise among you a *p*.....Deut 13:1
unto thee a *P* .........Deut 18:15
arose not a *p*...........Deut 34:10
also among the *p*..... 1 Sam 10:12
a *p* in Israel..............2 Kin 5:8
believe his *p* ..........2 Chr 20:20
no more any *p*............Ps 74:9
maketh himself a *p*.....Jer 29:26
the *p* is a fool ............ Hos 9:7
I was no *p* ............Amos 7:14

Beware of false *p* . . . . . . . Matt 7:15
in the name of a *p* . . . . . Matt 10:41
A *p* is not without . . . . . Matt 13:57
the tombs of the *p* . . . . . Matt 23:29
*p* of the Highest . . . . . . . Luke 1:76
No *p* is accepted . . . . . . . Luke 4:24
great *p* is risen up . . . . . Luke 7:16
a greater *p* than John . . . Luke 7:28
that a *p* perish . . . . . . . Luke 13:33
*p* mighty in deed . . . . . Luke 24:19
thou art a *p* . . . . . . . . . . John 4:19
a *p* hath no honour . . . . John 4:44
this is the *P* . . . . . . . . . . John 7:40
ariseth no *p* . . . . . . . . . John 7:52
are all *p* . . . . . . . . . . . 1 Cor 12:29
himself to be a *p* . . . . . . 1 Cor 14:37
the apostles and *p* . . . . . Eph 2:20
and some, *p* . . . . . . . . . . Eph 4:11
thy brethren the *p* . . . . . Rev 22:9
*See* 1 Kin 20:35; Neh 6:14

**PROPITIATION**
a *p* through faith in
    his blood . . . . . . . . . . . Rom 3:25
*p* for our sins . . . . . . . . 1 John 2:2

**PROSPER**
it shall not *p* . . . . . . . . Num 14:41
not *p* in thy ways . . . . . Deut 28:29
God made him to *p* . . . . 2 Chr 26:5
he will *p* us . . . . . . . . . . . Neh 2:20
he doeth shall *p* . . . . . . . . Ps 1:3
who *p* in his way . . . . . . . Ps 37:7
who *p* in the world . . . . . Ps 73:12
they shall *p* . . . . . . . . . . Ps 122:6
shall not *p* . . . . . . . . . . Prov 28:13
whether shall *p* . . . . . . . Eccl 11:6
of the Lord shall *p* . . . . . Is 53:10
thee shall *p* . . . . . . . . . . Is 54:17
shalt not *p* in them . . . . . Jer 2:37
way of the wicked *p* . . . . Jer 12:1
man that shall not *p* . . . Jer 22:30
Shall it *p* . . . . . . . . . . . Ezek 17:9
as God hath *p* him . . . . 1 Cor 16:2
as thy soul *p* . . . . . . . . . 3 John 2
*See* Prov 17:8; Dan 6:28; 8:12

**PROUD**
here shall thy *p* waves
    be stayed . . . . . . . . . . . Job 38:11
one that is *p* . . . . . . . . . Job 40:11
the *p* doer . . . . . . . . . . Ps 31:23
respecteth not the *p* . . . . . Ps 40:4
a reward to the *p* . . . . . . Ps 94:2
look and a *p* heart . . . . Ps 101:5
contempt of the *p* . . . . . Ps 123:4
the *p* he knoweth . . . . . Ps 138:6
A *p* look . . . . . . . . . . . . Prov 6:17
the house of the *p* . . . . Prov 15:25
is *p* in heart . . . . . . . . Prov 16:5
and a *p* heart . . . . . . . Prov 21:4
the *p* in spirit . . . . . . . . Eccl 7:8
he is a *p* man . . . . . . . . Hab 2:5
call the *p* happy . . . . . . Mal 3:15
the *p* in . . . . . . . . . . . . Luke 1:51
He is *p* . . . . . . . . . . . . . 1 Tim 6:4
God resisteth the *p* . . . . James 4:6
*See* Job 9:13; 26:12; 2 Tim 3:2

**PROVE**
ordinance, and there
    he *p* them . . . . . . . . . . Ex 15:25
let me *p* . . . . . . . . . . . Judg 6:39
he had not *p* it . . . . . . 1 Sam 17:39
came to *p* him . . . . . . . 1 Kin 10:1
to *p* Solomon . . . . . . . . 2 Chr 9:1
hast *p* mine heart . . . . . Ps 17:3
*p* me, and saw . . . . . . . Ps 95:9
*p* me now herewith . . . Mal 3:10
*p* your own selves . . . . 2 Cor 13:5
*P* all things . . . . . . . . 1 Thess 5:21
tempted me, *p* me . . . . Heb 3:9
*See* Eccl 2:1; 7:23; Dan 1:14

**PUNISH**
hast *p* us less than our
    iniquities . . . . . . . . . . . Ezra 9:13
*p* the just . . . . . . . . . . Prov 17:26
I will *p* the world . . . . . . . Is 13:11
*p* the inhabitants . . . . . . Is 26:21
shall *p* thee . . . . . . . . . . Jer 13:21
I *p* them oft . . . . . . . . . Acts 26:11
*p* . . . everlasting . . . . 2 Thess 1:9
judgment to be *p* . . . . . 2 Pet 2:9
*See* Lev 26:18; Prov 21:11

**PUNISHMENT**
My *p* is greater than I
    can bear . . . . . . . . . . . Gen 4:13
accept of the *p* . . . . . . . Lev 26:41
no *p* happen . . . . . . . . 1 Sam 28:10
*p* of his sins . . . . . . . . . . Lam 3:39
*p* of the iniquity . . . . . . Lam 4:6
*p* of thine iniquity . . . . . Lam 4:22
shall bear the *p* . . . . . . Ezek 14:10
into everlasting . . . . . . . Matt 25:46
Of how much sorer *p* . . . Heb 10:29
*p* of evildoers . . . . . . . . 1 Pet 2:14
*See* Prov 19:19; Amos 1:3; 2:1

**PURCHASE**
have I *p* to be my wife . . Ruth 4:10
hast *p* of old . . . . . . . . . Ps 74:2
man *p* a field . . . . . . . . Acts 1:18
be *p* with money . . . . . . Acts 8:20
*p* with his own blood . . . Acts 20:28
of the *p* possession . . . . . Eph 1:14
*p* to themselves . . . . . . 1 Tim 3:13
*See* Gen 49:32; Ex 15:16; Lev 25:33;
    Jer 32:11

**PURE**
drink the *p* blood of
    the grape . . . . . . . . . . . Deut 32:14
shew thyself *p* . . . . . . 2 Sam 22:27
a man be more *p* . . . . . . . Job 4:17
If thou wert *p* . . . . . . . . . . Job 8:6
My doctrine is *p* . . . . . . . Job 11:4
my prayer is *p* . . . . . . . Job 16:17
the stars are not *p* . . . . . Job 25:5
are *p* words . . . . . . . . . . Ps 12:6
of the Lord is *p* . . . . . . . . Ps 19:8
Thy word is very *p* . . . Ps 119:140
words of the *p* . . . . . . . Prov 15:26
*p* from my sin . . . . . . . . Prov 20:9
I count them *p* . . . . . . . Mic 6:11
a *p* language . . . . . . . . . Zeph 3:9
*p* from the blood . . . . . . Acts 20:26
indeed are *p* . . . . . . . . Rom 14:20
things are *p* . . . . . . . . . . Phil 4:8
in a *p* conscience . . . . . 1 Tim 3:9
keep thyself *p* . . . . . . . . 1 Tim 5:22
with *p* conscience . . . . . 2 Tim 1:3
all things are *p* . . . . . . . Titus 1:15
*P* religion . . . . . . . . . . James 1:27
is first *p* . . . . . . . . . . . James 3:17
your *p* minds . . . . . . . . 2 Pet 3:1
even as he is *p* . . . . . . . 1 John 3:3
*p* river of water . . . . . . . Rev 22:1
*See* Ezra 6:20; Mal 1:11

**PURIFY**
*p* unto himself a peculiar
    people . . . . . . . . . . . . . Titus 2:14
*p* your hearts . . . . . . . . James 4:8
*p* your souls . . . . . . . . . 1 Pet 1:22

**PURPOSE**
my *p* are broken off . . . . Job 17:11
*p* is established . . . . . . . Prov 20:18
hosts hath *p* . . . . . . . . . . Is 14:27
To what *p* . . . . . . . . . . Matt 26:8
with *p* of heart . . . . . . . Acts 11:23
according to his *p* . . . . . Rom 8:28
the *p* of God . . . . . . . . . Rom 9:11
*p* of him . . . . . . . . . . . . Eph 1:11
the eternal *p* . . . . . . . . . Eph 3:11
*See* 2 Tim 1:9; 1 John 3:8

**QUENCH**
cannot *q* love . . . . . . . . Song 8:7
It shall not be *q* . . . . . . . Is 34:10
shall he not *q* . . . . . . . . . Is 42:3
their fire be *q* . . . . . . . . Is 66:24
never shall be *q* . . . . . . Mark 9:43
fire is not *q* . . . . . . . . . Mark 9:44
*q* all the . . . . . . . . . . . . Eph 6:16
*Q* not the Spirit . . . . . . 1 Thess 5:19
*Q* the violence . . . . . . . Heb 11:34
*See* Ps 104:11; Amos 5:6

**QUICK**
and they go down *q*
    into the pit . . . . . . . . . Num 16:30
down *q* into hell . . . . . . . Ps 55:15
Judge of *q* . . . . . . . . . . Acts 10:42
shall judge the *q* . . . . . . 2 Tim 4:1
word of God is *q* . . . . . . . Heb 4:12
*See* Lev 13:10, 24; Ps 124:3

**QUICKEN**
sore troubles, shalt *q*
    me again . . . . . . . . . . . Ps 71:20
*q* us . . . . . . . . . . . . . . . Ps 80:18
*q* thou me . . . . . . . . . . Ps 119:25
word hath *q* me . . . . . . Ps 119:50
*q* your mortal . . . . . . . . Rom 8:11
sowest is not *q* . . . . . . 1 Cor 15:36
you hath he *q* . . . . . . . . . Eph 2:1
hath *q* us together . . . . . . Eph 2:5
hath he *q* . . . . . . . . . . . Col 2:13
*q* by the Spirit . . . . . . . 1 Pet 3:18
*See* John 5:21; 1 Tim 6:13

**QUICKLY**
thine adversary *q* . . . . . Matt 5:25
come unto thee *q* . . . . . . Rev 2:5
Behold, I come *q* . . . . . . Rev 3:11
Surely I come *q* . . . . . . . Rev 22:20
*See* Gen 18:6; 27:20; Luke 16:6

**QUIET**
be *q* from fear . . . . . . . Prov 1:33
study to be *q* . . . . . . . 1 Thess 4:11
may lead a *q* . . . . . . . . . 1 Tim 2:2
and *q* spirit . . . . . . . . . . 1 Pet 3:4
*See* 2 Kin 11:20; Job 3:13; 21:23

**RACE**
as a strong man to run a *r* . Ps 19:5
the *r* is not . . . . . . . . . . Eccl 9:11
which run in a *r* . . . . . . 1 Cor 9:24
*r* that is set . . . . . . . . . . Heb 12:1

**RAGE**
do the heathen *r* . . . . . . . . Ps 2:1
but the fool *r* . . . . . . . . Prov 14:16
*See* Prov 6:34; 29:9; Dan 3:13

**RAIN (*n.*)**
I will give you *r* in due
    season . . . . . . . . . . . . Lev 26:4
the *r* of heaven . . . . . . . Deut 11:11
shall drop as the *r* . . . . . Deut 32:2
shining after *r* . . . . . . . 2 Sam 23:4
abundance of *r* . . . . . . . 1 Kin 18:41
a time of much *r* . . . . . . Ezra 10:13
Who giveth *r* . . . . . . . . . Job 5:10
to the great *r* . . . . . . . . . Job 37:6
Hath the *r* a father . . . . . Job 38:28
come down like *r* . . . . . . . Ps 72:6
wind without *r* . . . . . . . Prov 25:14
wind driveth away *r* . . . Prov 25:23
as *r* in harvest . . . . . . . . Prov 26:1
sweeping *r* . . . . . . . . . . Prov 28:3
clouds be full of *r* . . . . . Eccl 11:3
return after the *r* . . . . . . Eccl 12:2
the *r* is over . . . . . . . . . Song 2:11
from storm and from *r* . . . . Is 4:6
the *r* cometh down . . . . . . Is 55:10

unto us as the *r*. . . . . . . . . . Hos 6:3
latter and former *r* . . . . . . Hos 6:3
*r* on the just . . . . . . . . . . . Matt 5:45
the *r* descended . . . . . . . . Matt 7:25
*See* Acts 14:17; 28:2; Heb 6:7

## RAIN (*v.*)

will *r* bread from heaven
  for you. . . . . . . . . . . . . . . . . . Ex 16:4
*r* it upon him . . . . . . . . . . Job 20:23
he shall *r* snares . . . . . . . . . . Ps 11:6
*r* down manna. . . . . . . . . . . Ps 78:24
He *r* flesh . . . . . . . . . . . . . . . Ps 78:27
*r* upon . . . . . . . . . . . . . . . . Ezek 22:24
*r* righteousness. . . . . . . . . Hos 10:12
*See* Gen 2:5; 7:4; Amos 4:7

## RAISE

God will *r* up unto
  thee a Prophet . . . . . . Deut 18:15
Lord *r* up judges. . . . . . . . Judg 2:16
*r* up all those . . . . . . . . . . . Ps 145:14
I have *r* him up . . . . . . . . . . . Is 45:13
he will *r* us up . . . . . . . . . . . Hos 6:2
*r* the dead. . . . . . . . . . . . . . Matt 10:8
the dead are *r*. . . . . . . . . . . Matt 11:5
be *r* again. . . . . . . . . . . . . . Matt 16:21
I will *r* it up . . . . . . . . . . . . John 2:19
*r* it up again . . . . . . . . . . . . John 6:39
whom God hath *r* up . . . . Acts 2:24
*r* from the dead. . . . . . . . . Acts 3:15
*r* from the dead. . . . . . . . . Acts 4:10
*r* up Jesus. . . . . . . . . . . . . . Acts 5:30
*r* up the third day. . . . . . Acts 10:40
But God *r* him . . . . . . . . . Acts 13:30
that he hath *r* him . . . . . Acts 17:31
God should *r* the dead. . Acts 26:8
was *r* again . . . . . . . . . . . . Rom 4:25
*r* up Jesus. . . . . . . . . . . . . . Rom 8:11
whom he *r* not up . . . 1 Cor 15:15
is not Christ *r*. . . . . . . . . 1 Cor 15:16
How are the dead
  *r* up. . . . . . . . . . . . . . . 1 Cor 15:35
is *r* in glory . . . . . . . . . . 1 Cor 15:43
which *r* the dead . . . . . . . 2 Cor 1:9
that he which *r* up. . . . . 2 Cor 4:14
Father, who *r* him . . . . . . Gal 1:1
when he *r* him. . . . . . . . . . Eph 1:20
hath *r* us up together. . . . Eph 2:6
able to *r* him up . . . . . . . Heb 11:19
*r* to life again . . . . . . . . . . Heb 11:35
shall *r* him up. . . . . . . . . James 5:15
*See* Luke 20:37; 2 Tim 2:8

## RANSOM

the *r* of his life . . . . . . . . . . Ex 21:30
a *r* for his soul . . . . . . . . . Ex 30:12
I have found a *r*. . . . . . . . Job 33:24
then a great *r* . . . . . . . . . . Job 36:18
nor give to God a *r*. . . . . . . Ps 49:7
*r* of a man's life . . . . . . . . Prov 13:8
the *r* of the Lord . . . . . . . . Is 35:10
Egypt for thy *r*. . . . . . . . . . Is 43:3
I will *r* them . . . . . . . . . . . Hos 13:14
give his life a *r* . . . . . . . Matt 20:28
*See* Prov 6:35; Is 51:10

## REAP

neither *r* that which
  groweth . . . . . . . . . . . . . Lev 25:11
shall *r* in joy . . . . . . . . . . . Ps 126:5
clouds shall not *r* . . . . . . . Eccl 11:4
but shall *r* thorns. . . . . . . Jer 12:13
*r* the whirlwind. . . . . . . . . Hos 8:7
*r* in mercy . . . . . . . . . . . . . Hos 10:12
thou shalt not *r*. . . . . . . . . Mic 6:15
neither do they *r* . . . . . . Matt 6:26
*r* where I sowed not. . . Matt 25:26
neither sow nor *r* . . . . . Luke 12:24
and *r* that thou . . . . . . . Luke 19:21
to *r* that whereon. . . . . . John 4:38
*r* your carnal things . . . . 1 Cor 9:11
*r* also sparingly. . . . . . . . 2 Cor 9:6
that shall he also *r*. . . . . . Gal 6:7

*r* down your fields. . . . . . James 5:4
*See* Is 17:5; John 4:36, 37

## REASON

choose out my words to *r*
  with him . . . . . . . . . . . . . Job 9:14
desire to *r* with God . . . . . Job 13:3
Should he *r* with. . . . . . . . Job 15:3
let us *r* together . . . . . . . . . Is 1:18
*r* among themselves. . . . . Matt 16:7
What *r* ye . . . . . . . . . . . . . Luke 5:22
communed to-
  gether and *r* . . . . . . . . Luke 24:15
*r* of righteousness. . . . . Acts 24:25
*See* 1 Sam 12:7; Mark 2:6; 12:28

## REBUKE (*n.*)

a day of trouble,
  and of *r*. . . . . . . . . . . . . 2 Kin 19:3
When thou with *r* . . . . . . . Ps 39:11
perish at the *r* . . . . . . . . . . Ps 80:16
At thy *r* they fled . . . . . . . Ps 104:7
poor heareth not *r*. . . . . . Prov 13:8
Open *r* is better. . . . . . . . . Prov 27:5
*r* of the wise . . . . . . . . . . . . Eccl 7:5
at the *r* of one . . . . . . . . . Is 30:17
I have suffered *r*. . . . . . . . Jer 15:15
without *r* . . . . . . . . . . . . . . Phil 2:15
*See* Deut 28:20; Is 25:8; 50:2

## REBUKE (*v.*)

O Lord, *r* me not in
  thine anger. . . . . . . . . . . . . Ps 6:1
O Lord, *r* me not. . . . . . . . . Ps 38:1
*r* a wicked man . . . . . . . . . Prov 9:7
*r* a wise man. . . . . . . . . . . . Prov 9:8
He that *r* a man. . . . . . . . Prov 28:23
*r* many people. . . . . . . . . . . Is 2:4
*r* strong nations . . . . . . . . Mic 4:3
The Lord *r* thee. . . . . . . . . Zech 3:2
*r* the devourer. . . . . . . . . . Mal 3:11
*r* the winds . . . . . . . . . . . Matt 8:26
began to *r* him. . . . . . . . . Matt 16:22
*r* the wind . . . . . . . . . . . . Mark 4:39
*r* the fever . . . . . . . . . . . . Luke 4:39
thee, *r* him. . . . . . . . . . . . . Luke 17:3
*r* thy disciples . . . . . . . . Luke 19:39
*R* not an elder . . . . . . . . . . 1 Tim 5:1
Them that sin *r*. . . . . . . . . 1 Tim 5:20
*r*, exhort with. . . . . . . . . . . 2 Tim 4:2
*r* them sharply. . . . . . . . . . Titus 1:13
exhort, and *r*. . . . . . . . . . . Titus 2:15
art *r* of him . . . . . . . . . . . . Heb 12:5
*See* Ruth 2:16; Amos 5:10

## RECEIVE

to *r* money, and to *r*
  garments. . . . . . . . . . . . 2 Kin 5:26
and mine ear *r*. . . . . . . . . . Job 4:12
*R*, I pray thee . . . . . . . . . . Job 22:22
Lord will *r* my prayer. . . . . Ps 6:9
he shall *r* me. . . . . . . . . . . Ps 49:15
*r* gifts for men . . . . . . . . . . Ps 68:18
*r* me to glory. . . . . . . . . . . . Ps 73:24
wilt *r* my words . . . . . . . . Prov 2:1
for she hath *r*. . . . . . . . . . . Is 40:2
they *r* no correction . . . . . Jer 2:30
shall *r* shame . . . . . . . . . . . Hos 10:6
*r* us graciously. . . . . . . . . . Hos 14:2
blind *r* their sight. . . . . . . Matt 11:5
if ye will *r* it. . . . . . . . . . . Matt 11:14
whoso shall *r* one . . . . . . Matt 18:5
let him *r* it . . . . . . . . . . . . Matt 19:12
believing, ye shall *r*. . . . Matt 21:22
he *r* it not. . . . . . . . . . . . . Mark 15:23
*r* up into heaven. . . . . . . Mark 16:19
This man *r* sinners . . . . . Luke 15:2
*R* thy sight. . . . . . . . . . . . . Luke 18:42
own *r* him not. . . . . . . . . . John 1:11
as many as *r* him . . . . . . . John 1:12
A man can *r* nothing. . . . John 3:27
and ye *r* me not. . . . . . . . . John 5:43
which *r* honour . . . . . . . . . John 5:44
ask, and ye shall *r* . . . . . John 16:24
*R* ye the Holy Ghost . . . . John 20:22

a cloud *r* him . . . . . . . . . . . Acts 1:9
*r* my spirit . . . . . . . . . . . . . Acts 7:59
*r* the Holy Ghost. . . . . . . . Acts 8:17
shall *r* remission. . . . . . . Acts 10:43
which I have *r* . . . . . . . . . Acts 20:24
*r* thy sight. . . . . . . . . . . . . Acts 22:13
*r* the atonement. . . . . . . . Rom 5:11
God hath *r* him . . . . . . . . Rom 14:3
as Christ also *r*. . . . . . . . . Rom 15:7
*r* his own reward . . . . . . . 1 Cor 3:8
I have *r* of the Lord. . . . . 1 Cor 11:23
as we have *r* mercy. . . . . . 2 Cor 4:1
*r* the things . . . . . . . . . . . . 2 Cor 5:10
*R* us. . . . . . . . . . . . . . . . . . . 2 Cor 7:2
*R* him therefore . . . . . . . . Phil 2:29
giving and *r*. . . . . . . . . . . . Phil 4:15
*r* Christ Jesus . . . . . . . . . . Col 2:6
*r* up into glory . . . . . . . . . 1 Tim 3:16
*r* with thanksgiving . . . . 1 Tim 4:4
we *r* of him . . . . . . . . . . . . 1 John 3:22
*See* Ezek 3:10; James 4:3

## REDEEM

Angel which *r* me
  from all evil . . . . . . . . . Gen 48:16
*r* you with . . . . . . . . . . . . . . Ex 6:6
thou hast *r*. . . . . . . . . . . . . Ex 15:13
shall be sold or *r*. . . . . . . . Lev 27:28
hath *r* my soul. . . . . . . . . 2 Sam 4:9
power to *r* them . . . . . . . . Neh 5:5
have *r* our brethren. . . . . . Neh 5:8
*r* thee from death. . . . . . . Job 5:20
*R* me from the hand. . . . . Job 6:23
*R* Israel, O God. . . . . . . . . Ps 25:22
Lord *r* the soul. . . . . . . . . Ps 34:22
and *r* us. . . . . . . . . . . . . . . Ps 44:26
*r* his brother . . . . . . . . . . . Ps 49:7
God will *r* my soul. . . . . . Ps 49:15
*r* their soul. . . . . . . . . . . . . Ps 72:14
Who *r* thy life . . . . . . . . . Ps 103:4
Let the *r* . . . . . . . . . . . . . . Ps 107:2
*r* Israel from all. . . . . . . . Ps 130:8
be *r* with judgment. . . . . . Is 1:27
*r* shall walk there. . . . . . . Is 35:9
for I have *r* thee . . . . . . . . Is 44:22
that it cannot *r* . . . . . . . . . Is 50:2
the *r* of the Lord. . . . . . . . Is 51:11
*r* without money. . . . . . . . Is 52:3
the year of my *r*. . . . . . . . . Is 63:4
I have *r* them . . . . . . . . . . Hos 7:13
I will *r* them . . . . . . . . . . . Hos 13:14
*r* his people. . . . . . . . . . . . Luke 1:68
have *r* Israel . . . . . . . . . . Luke 24:21
Christ hath *r* us. . . . . . . . . Gal 3:13
To *r* them. . . . . . . . . . . . . . Gal 4:5
he might *r* us . . . . . . . . . . Titus 2:14
not *r* with. . . . . . . . . . . . . . 1 Pet 1:18
and hast *r* us. . . . . . . . . . . Rev 5:9
*See* Num 18:15; Col 4:5

## REDEEMER

I know that my *r* liveth. . . Job 19:25
strength, and my *r*. . . . . . . Ps 19:14
high God their *r*. . . . . . . . . Ps 78:35
their *r* is mighty . . . . . . . Prov 23:11
As for our *r* . . . . . . . . . . . . Is 47:4
Saviour and thy *R* . . . . . . Is 49:26
*R* shall come to Zion. . . . . Is 59:20
our father, our *r* . . . . . . . . Is 63:16
*See* Is 41:14; 44:6; Jer 50:34

## REDEMPTION

ye shall grant a *r* for
  the land . . . . . . . . . . . . . Lev 25:24
*r* of their soul . . . . . . . . . . . Ps 49:8
*r* unto his people . . . . . . . Ps 111:9
is plenteous *r*. . . . . . . . . . Ps 130:7
the right of *r*. . . . . . . . . . . Jer 32:7
*r* in Jerusalem . . . . . . . . Luke 2:38
*r* draweth nigh . . . . . . . . Luke 21:28
*r* of our body. . . . . . . . . . . Rom 8:23
unto the day of *r*. . . . . . . . Eph 4:30
*See* Num 3:49; Heb 9:12

## REFRESH
seventh day he rested,
  and was *r*.............. Ex 31:17
that I may be *r*.......... Job 32:20
he *r* the soul ......... Prov 25:13
the times of *r* ........... Acts 3:19
*r* my spirit ...........1 Cor 16:18
*See* Is 28:12; 2 Cor 7:13; 13:7

## REGENERATION
the *r* when the Son of
  man shall........... Matt 19:28
the washing of *r* ........ Titus 3:5

## REIGN
Shalt thou indeed *r*
  over us ................ Gen 37:8
Lord shall *r* for ever ..... Ex 15:18
shall *r* over you .......Lev 26:17
*r* over many nations.... Deut 15:6
*R* thou over us........... Judg 9:8
Saul *r* over us..........1 Sam 11:12
a king shall *r*...........1 Sam 12:12
thou hast *r*............. 2 Sam 16:8
hypocrite *r* not ........ Job 34:30
God *r* over the ............. Ps 47:8
The Lord *r*............... Ps 93:1
that the Lord *r*...........Ps 96:10
The Lord *r*.............. Ps 97:1
By me kings *r*............Prov 8:15
a servant when he *r* ... Prov 30:22
he cometh to *r*.......... Eccl 4:14
*r* in righteousness...........Is 32:1
Thy God *r*...............Is 52:7
Shalt thou *r*.............. Jer 22:15
*r* and prosper.............Jer 23:5
shall *r* over them ......... Mic 5:4
to *r* over us ......... Luke 19:14
not that I should *r*..... Luke 19:27
death *r* from Adam......Rom 5:14
death *r* by one .......... Rom 5:17
sin hath *r* unto death....Rom 5:21
Let not sin ... *r*.......... Rom 6:12
to God ye did *r*.......... 1 Cor 4:8
For he must *r*.......... 1 Cor 15:25
also *r* with him .........2 Tim 2:12
*r* on the earth.............Rev 5:10
he shall *r* for ever....... Rev 11:15
God omnipotent *r*....... Rev 19:6
*See* Luke 1:33; Rev 20:4; 22:5

## REJECT
they have not *r* thee,
  but they have *r* me ... 1 Sam 8:7
*r* your God ...........1 Sam 10:19
thou hast *r* the word ...1 Sam 15:23
*r* him from reigning ....1 Sam 16:1
despised and *r* of men.... Is 53:3
*r* thy confidences......... Jer 2:37
the Lord hath *r* ......... Jer 7:29
have *r* the word........... Jer 8:9
utterly *r* Judah .......... Jer 14:19
hast utterly *r* us ....... Lam 5:22
hast *r* knowledge........ Hos 4:6
the builders *r*......... Matt 21:42
*r* the commandment ... Mark 7:9
lawyers *r* the counsel ... Luke 7:30
*r* of this generation... Luke 17:25
admonition *r*...........Titus 3:10
he was *r*................Heb 12:17
*See* Jer 6:19; Mark 6:26; 8:31

## REJOICE
shall *r* in all that ye put
  your hand .............Deut 12:7
*r* in every .............. Deut 26:11
will again *r* ...........Deut 30:9
*r* in thy salvation .......1 Sam 2:1
heart of them *r* ....... 1 Chr 16:10
saints *r* in goodness.... 2 Chr 6:41
*r* at the sound ......... Job 21:12
*r* because my wealth ....Job 31:25
*r* in his strength ........ Job 39:21
*r* with trembling............Ps 2:11
in thee *r* ..................Ps 5:11

*r* in thy salvation .......... Ps 9:14
*r* as a strong man.......... Ps 19:5
shall *r* in him .............Ps 33:21
adversity they *r*...........Ps 35:15
bones ... may *r*........... Ps 51:8
righteous shall *r*..........Ps 58:10
let them *r*.................Ps 68:3
*r* all the day...............Ps 89:16
Let the heavens *r*.........Ps 96:11
let the earth *r*............. Ps 97:1
*r* in his works............Ps 104:31
shall see it, and *r* .......Ps 107:42
Israel *r* in him ............Ps 149:2
Who *r* to do evil .........Prov 2:14
*r* with the wife............Prov 5:18
my heart shall *r*........ Prov 23:15
the righteous shall ... *r*Prov 23:24
*R* not when ..............Prov 24:17
the people *r*............. Prov 29:2
and she shall *r*.......... Prov 31:25
*r* in all my labour ........ Eccl 2:10
but for a man to *r*....... Eccl 3:12
to *r* in his labour......... Eccl 5:19
*R*, O young man ..........Eccl 11:9
shall *r* in the .............. Is 29:19
desert shall *r*............... Is 35:1
thy God *r* over thee........ Is 62:5
my servants shall *r* ..... Is 65:13
your heart shall *r* ........ Is 66:14
then thou *r* .............. Jer 11:15
I will *r* over them ........ Jer 32:41
that they may *r* ......... Jer 51:39
let not the buyer *r*.......Ezek 7:12
Ye which *r* ............. Amos 6:13
*R* not against me ..........Mic 7:8
will *r* in the Lord ........ Hab 3:18
he *r* more of ...........Matt 18:13
*r* at his birth .............Luke 1:14
*R* ye in that day........Luke 6:23
in this *r* not............Luke 10:20
Jesus *r* in spirit ........ Luke 10:21
*R* with me ............. Luke 15:6
to *r* in his light............John 5:35
*r* to see my day .........John 8:56
ye would *r* ............John 14:28
world shall *r*............John 16:20
your heart shall *r*......John 16:22
*r* in hope of ............. Rom 5:2
*R* with them ...........Rom 12:15
and they that *r*........ 1 Cor 7:30
*R* not in iniquity........ 1 Cor 13:6
I therein do *r* .............Phil 1:18
that I may *r*............. Phil 2:16
*r* in the Lord ...............Phil 3:1
*R* in the Lord alway ...... Phil 4:4
*R* evermore...........1 Thess 5:16
of low degree *r* ........ James 1:9
*r* against judgment.... James 2:13
ye *r* with joy ............1 Pet 1:8
*See* 1 Kin 1:40; 2 Kin 11:14

## REJOICING
laughing, and thy lips
  with *r*...................Job 8:21
his works with *r*.......Ps 107:22
The voice of *r*............ Ps 118:15
the *r* of my heart ...... Ps 119:111
come again with *r*.......Ps 126:6
*R* in the habitable .......Prov 8:31
Jerusalem a *r*............. Is 65:18
*r* of mine heart .......... Jer 15:16
is the *r* city.............. Zeph 2:15
*r* that they .............. Acts 5:41
*R* in hope ...............Rom 12:2
yet always *r*............ 2 Cor 6:10
or crown of *r*.........1 Thess 2:19
*See* Hab 3:14; James 4:16

## RELIGION
sect of our *r*..............Acts 26:5
in the Jews' *r* .............Gal 1:13
man's *r* is vain ........ James 1:26
Pure *r* and undefiled ... James 1:27

## REMEMBER
*R* the sabbath day ........ Ex 20:8
*r* all the
  commandments .... Num 15:39
*r* that thou wast ....... Deut 5:15
*R* the days of old....... Deut 32:7
*R* me, O my God ........Neh 13:14
he *r* them ................. Ps 9:12
*r* the name of ............. Ps 20:7
*R*, O Lord ................Ps 25:6
*R* not the sins ............ Ps 25:7
*r* not against us............Ps 79:8
*R* how short ............ Ps 89:47
*r* his covenant .......... Ps 105:8
I have *r* thy name........ Ps 119:55
*r* us in our .............. Ps 136:23
when we *r* Zion.......... Ps 137:1
*r* his misery no more .... Prov 31:7
*r* the days of his ........ Eccl 5:20
yet let him *r* ............. Eccl 11:8
*R* now thy Creator .......Eccl 12:1
*r* thy love .............. Song 1:4
*R* ye not................... Is 43:18
*R* the former things ....... Is 46:9
shall not be *r* .............Is 65:17
*r* the Lord afar off ...... Jer 51:50
in wrath *r* mercy ......... Hab 3:2
*r* me when thou
  comest .............Luke 23:42
should *r* the poor........ Gal 2:10
*R* my bonds............. Col 4:18
*R* without ceasing ..... 1 Thess 1:3
*R* them that are.......... Heb 13:3
*R* therefore from ........Rev 2:5
*See* Ps 88:5; 103:14; Matt 5:23

## REMEMBRANCE
bringing iniquity to *r*... Num 5:15
call my sin to *r*.........1 Kin 17:18
His *r* shall perish ........Job 18:17
no *r* of thee ................. Ps 6:5
*r* of his holiness ...........Ps 30:4
in everlasting *r* ........... Ps 112:6
*r* of former things ........ Eccl 1:11
no *r* of the wise........... Eccl 2:16
Put me in *r* ............. Is 43:26
set up thy *r* ................ Is 57:8
them still in *r* .......... Lam 3:20
calling to *r* ............ Ezek 23:19
a book of *r*...............Mal 3:16
this do in *r* ............. Luke 22:19
things to your *r* ........John 14:26
are had in *r* ............ Acts 10:31
do in *r* of me............1 Cor 11:24
I have *r* of thee ..........2 Tim 1:3
put them in *r* ...........2 Tim 2:14
*See* Heb 10:3; 2 Pet 1:12; 3:1

## REMISSION
is shed for many for
  the *r* of sins.......Matt 26:28
and *r* of sins .......... Luke 24:47
is no *r*....................Heb 9:22

## REMIT
Whose soever sins
  ye *r*.................. John 20:23

## REND
And *r* your heart ....... Joel 2:13
turn again and *r* you .... Matt 7:6
*See* Ps 7:2; Eccl 3:7; Jer 4:30

## RENDER
will *r* vengeance to
  mine enemies....... Deut 32:41
*r* to every man........1 Sam 26:23
he *r* unto him...........Job 34:11
*r* to them .................Ps 28:4
*r* evil for good.......... Ps 38:20
*r* unto our neighbours... Ps 79:12
*r* a reward ................Ps 94:2
I *r* unto the Lord........ Ps 116:12
*r* to every man........ Prov 24:12
can *r* a reason ........ Prov 26:16
so will we *r* .............. Hos 14:2

*r* me a recompense....... Joel 3:4
I will *r* double ......... Zech 9:12
*r* him the fruits.......Matt 21:41
*R* to Caesar ........... Mark 12:17
*R* therefore to all .......Rom 13:7
we *r* to God again.....1 Thess 3:9
*r* evil for evil.........1 Thess 5:15
*See* Num 18:9; Judg 9:56

## RENEW
Thou *r* thy witnesses
   against me ............Job 10:17
and my bow was *r*......Job 29:20
*r* a right spirit.............. Ps 51:10
thy youth is *r* ............Ps 103:5
thou *r* the face..........Ps 104:30
*r* their strength ........ Is 40:31
let the people *r*............ Is 41:1
*r* our days..............Lam 5:21
*r* day by day........... 2 Cor 4:16
be *r* in the spirit ........ Eph 4:23
is *r* in knowledge .........Col 3:10
to *r* them again............Heb 6:6
*See* 2 Chr 15:8; Titus 3:5

## REPAY
to the righteous good
   shall be *r*..............Prov 13:21
he will *r* him............ Deut 7:10
I will *r* thee ........Luke 10:35
is mine; I will *r* ........Rom 12:19
*See* Job 21:31; 41:11; Is 59:18

## REPENT
*r* the Lord that he had
   made man...............Gen 6:6
the people *r*................Ex 13:17
Lord *r* of the evil.........Ex 32:14
he should *r* ............Num 23:19
and *r* himself ..........Deut 32:36
not lie nor *r*........... 1 Sam 15:29
that he should *r* ..... 1 Sam 15:29
the Lord *r* him ........2 Sam 24:16
*r* in dust ..............Job 42:6
it *r* thee..................Ps 90:13
*r* according ..........Ps 106:45
and will not *r* ...........Ps 110:4
no man *r* him..........Jer 8:6
*r* of the evil ..............Jer 18:8
and the Lord will *r* .....Jer 26:13
the Lord *r* him ........Jer 26:19
was turned, I *r*........ Jer 31:19
*R* ye: for the............. Matt 3:2
*r* at the preaching ......Matt 12:41
but afterward he *r*... Matt 21:29
*r* himself ............. Matt 27:3
except ye *r*............. Luke 13:3
one sinner that *r*.......Luke 15:7
and if he *r*.............Luke 17:3
*R* therefore of...........Acts 8:22
and will not *r* ..........Heb 7:21
her space to *r*............Rev 2:21
*See* Acts 2:38; 17:30; Rev 2:5

## REPENTANCE
*r* shall be hid from
   mine eyes .............Hos 13:14
fruits meet for *r* ........ Matt 3:8
fruits worthy of *r*........ Luke 3:8
works meet for *r*.......Acts 26:20
leadeth thee to *r*........ Rom 2:4
are without *r*............Rom 11:29
sorrow worketh *r*....... 2 Cor 7:10
the foundation of *r*....... Heb 6:1
them again unto *r*........Heb 6:6
no place of *r* ............Heb 12:17
*See* Luke 15:7; Acts 20:21

## REPLENISH
multiply, and *r*
   the earth .............. Gen 1:28

## REPROVE
he *r* kings for
   their sakes............1 Chr 16:21
doth your arguing *r* ..... Job 6:25

He will surely *r* you......Job 13:10
Will he *r* thee.............Job 22:4
he that *r* God .............Job 40:2
I will not *r* ..............Ps 50:8
and let him *r* me.........Ps 141:5
*R* not a scorner .........Prov 9:8
one that *r* him ..........Prov 15:12
and *r* one that .........Prov 19:25
*r* hardeneth his neck ....Prov 29:1
lest he *r* thee...........Prov 30:6
*r* with equity ..............Is 11:4
shall *r* thee..............Jer 2:19
deeds should be *r* .....John 3:20
*r* the world of sin ....... John 16:8
*See* Luke 3:19; Eph 5:11, 13

## RESIST
at his right hand
   to *r* him............Zech 3:1
That ye *r* not evil ......Matt 5:39
to gainsay nor *r*.......Luke 21:15
*r* his will .................. Rom 9:19
*r* the ordinance..........Rom 13:2
God *r* the proud .......James 4:6
*R* the devil ............James 4:7
Whom *r* steadfast .......1 Pet 5:9
*See* Acts 6:10; 7:51; 2 Tim 3:8

## RESPECT (*n.*)
And the Lord had *r*
   unto Abel...............Gen 4:4
had *r* unto them..........Ex 2:25
have thou *r*.............1 Kin 8:28
Have *r* therefore........2 Chr 6:19
nor *r* of persons ........ 2 Chr 19:7
*r* unto the covenant ......Ps 74:20
*r* unto thy ways.......... Ps 119:15
*r* unto the lowly ........Ps 138:6
have *r* of persons ......Prov 24:23
To have *r* of persons... Prov 28:21
*r* to the Holy One ...........Is 17:7
*r* unto him.................Is 29:11
no *r* of persons .........Rom 2:11
in *r* of want ..............Phil 4:11
no *r* of persons .........Col 3:25
*See* Heb 11:26; James 2:1, 3, 9

## RESPECT (*v.*)
not *r* the person of
   the poor...............Lev 19:15
shall not *r* persons .....Deut 1:17
*r* not any..............Job 37:24
*See* Num 16:15; Lam 4:16

## REST (*n.*)
he saw that *r* was good...Gen 49:15
the sabbath of *r*...........Ex 31:15
and I will give thee *r*.....Ex 33:14
of *r* unto you............Lev 16:31
be a sabbath of *r*......... Lev 25:4
he giveth you *r* ........ Deut 12:10
weary be at *r* ............Job 3:17
thy *r* in safety............Job 11:18
and be at *r*...............Ps 55:6
enter into my *r* ..........Ps 95:11
Return unto thy *r*....... Ps 116:7
O Lord, into thy *r*........Ps 132:8
This is my *r* for ever ... Ps 132:14
not *r* in the night ........Eccl 2:23
*r* shall be glorious .........Is 11:10
whole earth is at *r*.........Is 14:7
I will take my *r* ...........Is 18:4
This is the *r*.............Is 28:12
returning and *r*...........Is 30:15
place of my *r*.............Is 66:1
*r* for your souls .........Jer 6:16
that are at *r*.............Ezek 38:11
is not your *r*...............Mic 2:10
and is at *r*................ Zech 1:11
I will give you *r*.........Matt 11:28
and ye shall find *r* ......Matt 11:29
seeking *r*................ Matt 12:43
and take your *r* ........Matt 26:45
of *r* in sleep.............John 11:13
churches *r* throughout... Acts 9:31
*See* Prov 29:17; 2 Thess 1:7

## REST (*v.*)
he *r* on the seventh day ... Gen 2:2
when the spirit *r* ......Num 11:25
shall *r* in hope ............Ps 16:9
*R* in the Lord .............. Ps 37:7
for anger *r* ..............Eccl 7:9
Lord shall *r* ................Is 11:2
I will not *r* ................Is 62:1
caused him to *r*...........Is 63:14
*r*, and be still.............Jer 47:6
thou shalt *r*............ Dan 12:13
and *r* a while.......... Mark 6:31
may *r* upon me ....... 2 Cor 12:9
they *r* not day ............ Rev 4:8
should *r* yet.............. Rev 6:11
that they may *r*.........Rev 14:13
*See* Prov 14:33; Song 1:7

## RESTORE
he shall *r* double.........Ex 22:4
*r* that which ..............Lev 6:4
and thou shalt *r* .......Deut 22:2
He *r* my soul.............Ps 23:3
*R* unto me the joy ...... Ps 51:12
I *r* that which...........Ps 69:4
I will *r* thy judges...........Is 1:26
*r* them to ..............Jer 27:22
*r* health unto thee ...... Jer 30:17
*r* the pledge............ Ezek 33:15
and *r* all things ..........Matt 17:11
I *r* him fourfold...........Luke 19:8
*r* again the kingdom...... Acts 1:6
*r* such an one ............Gal 6:1
*See* Ruth 4:15; Mark 8:25

## RETURN
dust shalt thou *r*......... Gen 3:19
*r* to their dust...........Ps 104:29
dog *r* to his vomit ......Prov 26:11
the dust *r* to the earth... Eccl 12:7
the ransomed ... shall *r*... Is 35:10
and shall not *r*...........Is 45:23
*r* unto me void............Is 55:11
If thou wilt *r*.............Jer 4:1
not *r* unto me..........Amos 4:6
if he will *r*...............Joel 2:14
will *r* unto you............Mal 3:7
*See* Gen 31:3; Lev 25:10

## REVEAL
A talebearer *r*........... Prov 11:13
*r* in mine ears............. Is 22:14
shall be *r*...................Is 40:5
righteousness to be *r*.......Is 56:1
He *r* the deep ..........Dan 2:22
he *r* his secret ...........Amos 3:7
shall not be *r* .........Matt 10:26
and hast *r* them ........Matt 11:25
blood hath not *r*.........Matt 16:17
hearts may be *r*......... Luke 2:35
Son of man is *r*.........Luke 17:30
the Lord been *r*.........John 12:38
God *r* from faith .........Rom 1:17
is *r* from heaven.........Rom 1:18
be *r* in us................ Rom 8:18
hath *r* them............. 1 Cor 2:10
be *r* by fire..............1 Cor 3:13
If any thing be *r* .......1 Cor 14:30
To *r* his Son................Gal 1:16
Jesus shall be *r* ...... 2 Thess 1:7
that man of sin be *r*... 2 Thess 2:3
shall that Wicked
   be *r*................ 2 Thess 2:8
ready to be *r*.............1 Pet 1:5
his glory shall be *r*.......1 Pet 4:13
glory that shall be *r*.......1 Pet 5:1
*See* Eph 3:5; 2 Thess 2:6

## REWARD (*n.*)
nor taketh *r*............Deut 10:17
the *r* of his work...........Job 7:2
there is great *r*..........Ps 19:11
*r* for the righteous........ Ps 58:11
the *r* of the wicked ........Ps 91:8
shall be a sure *r*........ Prov 11:18

a *r* in the bosom........Prov 21:14
shall be no *r* ..........Prov 24:20
have a good *r* ...........Eccl 4:9
they any more a *r*.......Eccl 9:5
followeth after *r* ..........Is 1:23
the wicked for *r*...........Is 5:23
his *r* is with him .........Is 40:10
thou givest a *r* ........Ezek 16:34
thy *r* to another........Dan 5:17
loved a *r* upon.............Hos 9:1
judge for *r* ...............Mic 3:11
judge asketh for a *r*......Mic 7:3
for great is your *r*.......Matt 5:12
what *r* have ye.........Matt 5:46
ye have no *r* ...........Matt 6:1
a prophet's *r*...........Matt 10:41
your *r* is great .........Luke 6:23
*r* shall be great........Luke 6:35
*r* of our deeds.......Luke 23:41
*r* of iniquity..............Acts 1:18
*r* not reckoned..........Rom 4:4
receive his own *r* .......1 Cor 3:8
What is my *r* then ......1 Cor 9:18
you of your *r*.............Col 2:18
receive the *r*...........Col 3:24
is worthy of his *r* .......1 Tim 5:18
recompense of *r*.........Heb 2:2
receive the *r* ........2 Pet 2:13
*See* 2 John 8; Jude 11; Rev 11:18

REWARD (v.)
Wherefore have ye *r*
evil for good............Gen 44:4
*r* them that ............Deut 32:41
hast *r* me good ........1 Sam 24:17
work shall be *r*.........2 Chr 15:7
he *r* him .................Job 21:19
and plentifully *r* .........Ps 31:23
They *r* me evil .........Ps 35:12
*r* us according ...........Ps 103:10
*r* evil for good..........Prov 17:13
Lord shall *r* thee......Prov 25:22
both *r* the fool .........Prov 26:10
work shall be *r*.........Jer 31:16
*See* 2 Sam 22:21; 2 Tim 4:14

RICH
and maketh *r*...........1 Sam 2:7
asked *r* for thyself .......1 Kin 3:11
earth for *r*..............1 Kin 10:23
Both *r* and honour ....1 Chr 29:12
not asked *r* .............2 Chr 1:11
He shall not be *r*......Job 15:29
swallowed down *r*......Job 20:15
The *r* man .............Job 27:19
Will he esteem thy *r*....Job 36:19
better than the *r*.........Ps 37:16
one is made *r*...........Ps 49:16
abundance of his *r*........Ps 52:7
if *r* increase..............Ps 62:10
full of thy *r*.............Ps 104:24
and *r* shall be .........Ps 112:3
*r* and honour ...........Prov 3:16
*R* and honour.........Prov 8:18
diligent maketh *r*.......Prov 10:4
*R* profit not...........Prov 11:4
yet hath great *r*........Prov 13:7
but the *r* answereth ... Prov 18:23
shall not be *r* ..........Prov 21:17
*r* man is wise .........Prov 28:11
poverty nor *r* ..........Prov 30:8
*r* kept for ................Eccl 5:13
curse not the *r*.........Eccl 10:20
and hidden *r*............Is 45:3
and with the *r* .........Is 53:9
glory in his *r*...........Jer 9:23
that getteth *r*.........Jer 17:11
because of thy *r*.......Ezek 28:5
I am become *r*..........Hos 12:8
for I am *r* ...............Zech 11:5
deceitfulness of *r*.....Matt 13:22
they that have *r*.......Mark 10:23
*r* cast in much .........Mark 12:41
the *r* he hath............Luke 1:53

that are *r*................Luke 6:24
with cares and *r*.......Luke 8:14
not *r* toward God.....Luke 12:21
thy *r* neighbours.......Luke 14:12
he was very *r* .........Luke 18:23
the *r* of his...............Rom 2:4
*r* of his glory ..........Rom 9:23
is *r* unto all .............Rom 10:12
*r* of the world...........Rom 11:12
depth of the *r*..........Rom 11:33
now ye are *r* .............1 Cor 4:8
yet making many *r* .....2 Cor 6:10
though he was *r*........2 Cor 8:9
*r* of his grace...........Eph 1:7
who is *r* in mercy........Eph 2:4
shew the exceeding *r*.... Eph 2:7
the unsearchable *r* ......Eph 3:8
to his *r* in glory ........Phil 4:19
the *r* of the glory ........Col 1:27
unto all *r*....................Col 2:2
that will be *r*.............1 Tim 6:9
Charge them that
are *r* .................1 Tim 6:17
*r* in good works.........1 Tim 6:18
greater *r* .................Heb 11:26
But the *r*.............James 1:10
*r* in faith ..............James 2:5
Your *r* are corrupted....James 5:2
but thou art *r*..........Rev 2:9
sayest, I am *r*...........Rev 3:17
mayest be *r*............Rev 3:18
power, and *r*............Rev 5:12
*See* Lev 25:47; Rev 6:15

RIGHT
which had led me in
the *r* way .............Gen 24:48
just and *r* is he...........Deut 32:4
good and the *r* way...1 Sam 12:23
them *r* judgments......Neh 9:13
are *r* words .............Job 6:25
more than *r*.............Job 34:23
of the Lord are *r*..........Ps 19:8
is a *r* sceptre.............Ps 45:6
and renew a *r* spirit ......Ps 51:10
by the *r* way ...........Ps 107:7
judgments are *r* .......Ps 119:75
in *r* paths ..............Prov 4:11
be *r* things ..............Prov 8:6
thoughts ... are *r*.......Prov 12:5
way of a fool is *r*.......Prov 12:15
way which seemeth *r* ... Prov 14:12
Every way of a
man is *r* ..............Prov 21:2
giveth a *r* answer.....Prov 24:26
us *r* things ...............Is 30:10
know not to do *r*.......Amos 3:10
whatsoever is *r*.........Matt 20:4
for this is *r* .............Eph 6:1
*See* Judg 17:6; 2 Pet 2:15

RIGHTEOUS
thee have I seen *r*
before me ................Gen 7:1
also destroy the *r*.......Gen 18:23
also a *r* nation ..........Gen 20:4
more *r* than I ..........Gen 38:26
words of the *r* ...........Ex 23:8
death of the *r*........Num 23:10
justify the *r*............Deut 25:1
more *r* than I .........1 Sam 24:17
two men more *r*........1 Kin 2:32
justifying the *r*..........2 Chr 6:23
*r* cut off.................Job 4:7
though I were *r*.........Job 9:15
The *r* also................Job 17:9
that thou art *r* ..........Job 22:3
said, I am *r* .............Job 34:5
congregation of the *r*.......Ps 1:5
for the *r* God trieth .......Ps 7:9
what can the *r* do.........Ps 11:3
The *r* cry ................Ps 34:17
that a *r* man hath........Ps 37:16
The *r* shall inherit ....Ps 37:29

salvation of the *r* ........Ps 37:39
*r* to be moved............Ps 55:22
reward for the *r*.........Ps 58:11
The *r* shall flourish ......Ps 92:12
the *r* shall be.............Ps 112:6
the lot of the *r* ..........Ps 125:3
*r* shall give thanks......Ps 140:13
Lord loveth the *r* ........Ps 146:8
wisdom for the *r*.........Prov 2:7
secret is with the *r* ......Prov 3:32
mouth of a *r* man......Prov 10:11
labour of the *r*..........Prov 10:16
*r* is an everlasting .....Prov 10:25
The *r* shall .............Prov 10:30
The *r* is delivered.......Prov 11:8
The thoughts of the *r*....Prov 12:5
A *r* man regardeth......Prov 12:10
*r* is more excellent.....Prov 12:26
but to the *r* good .......Prov 13:21
but the *r* hath hope....Prov 14:32
the way of the *r*........Prov 15:19
heart of the *r* ..........Prov 15:28
*R* lips are the ..........Prov 16:13
*r* runneth into it........Prov 18:10
*r* are bold as a lion.....Prov 28:1
*r* are in authority .......Prov 29:2
Be not *r* over much......Eccl 7:16
*r*, and the wise...........Eccl 9:1
one event to the *r* ......Eccl 9:2
Say ye to the *r* ...........Is 3:10
glory to the *r*............Is 24:16
*r* nation which..........Is 26:2
raised up the *r* man ......Is 41:2
shall my *r* servant........Is 53:11
*r* perisheth..............Is 57:1
shall be all *r*............Is 60:21
unto David a *r* Branch... Jer 23:5
heart of the *r* sad ......Ezek 13:22
they are more *r*........Ezek 16:52
righteousness of the *r*...Ezek 33:12
they sold the *r*.........Amos 2:6
between the *r* ..........Mal 3:18
to call the *r* ...........Matt 9:13
*r* men have desired.....Matt 13:17
*r* shine forth ..........Matt 13:43
appear *r* unto men ....Matt 23:28
sepulchres of the *r*....Matt 23:29
*r* into life eternal ......Matt 25:46
not to call the *r* ........Mark 2:17
both *r* before God .....Luke 1:6
that they were *r* ......Luke 18:9
this was a *r* man......Luke 23:47
judge *r* judgment.......John 7:24
There is none *r* .........Rom 3:10
scarcely for a *r* man .....Rom 5:7
many be made *r*........Rom 5:19
it is a *r* thing..........2 Thess 1:6
the *r* judge...........2 Tim 4:8
that he was *r*..........Heb 11:4
are over the *r*..........1 Pet 3:12
*r* scarcely be saved ......1 Pet 4:18
vexed his *r* soul.........2 Pet 2:8
Jesus Christ the *r*.......1 John 2:1
righteousness is *r* ......1 John 3:7
he that is *r*..............Rev 22:11
*See* Ezek 3:20; 1 Tim 1:9

RIGHTEOUSNESS
shall my *r* answer for me
in time................Gen 30:33
sacrifices of *r* .........Deut 33:19
every man his *r*......1 Sam 26:23
My *r* I hold fast..........Job 27:6
I put on *r* .............Job 29:14
My *r* is more ..........Job 35:2
ascribe *r* to my Maker ... Job 36:3
O God of my *r*..........Ps 4:1
judge the world in *r* .....Ps 9:8
and worketh *r* .........Ps 15:2
behold thy face in *r*.....Ps 17:15
in the paths of *r* ..........Ps 23:3
I have preached *r*.........Ps 40:9
lovest *r*...................Ps 45:7

declare his *r* .............. Ps 50:6
people with *r* .............. Ps 72:2
return unto *r* .............. Ps 94:15
*r* and judgment............. Ps 97:2
his *r* endureth ............. Ps 111:3
the gates of *r* ............. Ps 118:19
be clothed with *r* ........ Ps 132:9
riches and *r*............... Prov 8:18
but *r* delivereth........... Prov 10:2
*r* of the perfect .......... Prov 11:5
As *r* tendeth to life ..... Prov 11:19
way of *r* is life........... Prov 12:28
*R* exalteth a nation .... Prov 14:34
established by *r* ........ Prov 16:12
perisheth in his *r* ....... Eccl 7:15
*r* shall be the............... Is 11:5
will he not learn *r* ....... Is 26:10
shall reign in *r*........... Is 32:1
And the work of *r*........ Is 32:17
and his *r* ................. Is 59:16
shall see thy *r*........... Is 62:2
and all our *r* ............. Is 64:6
The Lord our *R* ......... Jer 23:6
Branch of *r*............... Jer 33:15
doth turn from his *r*.... Ezek 3:20
by their *r*................ Ezek 14:14
turneth away
  from his *r*........... Ezek 18:24
trust to his own *r*...... Ezek 33:13
thy sins by *r* ........... Dan 4:27
*r* belongeth unto thee.... Dan 9:7
bring in everlasting *r*... Dan 9:24
that turn many to *r*...... Dan 12:3
yourselves in *r*......... Hos 10:12
*r* as a mighty stream ... Amos 5:24
the fruit of *r* ........... Amos 6:12
seek *r*, seek meekness.... Zeph 2:3
Sun of *r* arise .......... Mal 4:2
fulfill all *r*............. Matt 3:15
thirst after *r* .......... Matt 5:6
persecuted for *r* sake... Matt 5:10
except your *r* .......... Matt 5:20
in the way of *r* ......... Matt 21:32
In holiness and *r* ...... Luke 1:75
of sin, and of *r* ........ John 16:8
and worketh *r* ......... Acts 10:35
enemy of all *r*.......... Acts 13:10
as he reasoned of *r*....Acts 24:25
therein is the *r*.......... Rom 1:17
commend the *r* of God....Rom 3:5
God imputeth *r*......... Rom 4:6
the gift of *r* ........... Rom 5:17
*r* unto God............. Rom 6:13
free from *r*............. Rom 6:20
life because of *r*........ Rom 8:10
followed not after *r*.....Rom 9:30
of the law for *r*......... Rom 10:4
believeth unto *r* ....... Rom 10:10
*r*, and peace.......... Rom 14:17
wisdom, and *r*.......... 1 Cor 1:30
Awake to *r*, and
  sin not................ 1 Cor 15:34
the *r* of God............ 2 Cor 5:21
the armour of *r*......... 2 Cor 6:7
fellowship hath *r* ...... 2 Cor 6:14
if *r* come by the law .... Gal 2:21
of *r* by faith ........... Gal 5:5
breastplate of *r*........ Eph 6:14
the fruits of *r* ......... Phil 1:11
not having mine own *r*... Phil 3:9
and follow after *r* ... 1 Tim 6:11
instruction in *r* ....... 2 Tim 3:16
a crown of *r*........... 2 Tim 4:8
Not by works of *r*....... Titus 3:5
a sceptre of *r*........... Heb 1:8
hast loved *r*........... Heb 1:9
in the word of *r*........ Heb 5:13
King of *r*.............. Heb 7:2
heir of the *r*........... Heb 11:7
wrought *r*............. Heb 11:33
peaceable fruit of *r*....Heb 12:11
not the *r* of God....... James 1:20

And the fruit of *r* .....James 3:18
should live unto *r* ...... 1 Pet 2:24
a preacher of *r*.......... 2 Pet 2:5
the way of *r*............. 2 Pet 2:21
dwelleth *r* ............. 2 Pet 3:13
that doeth *r*............ 1 John 2:29
*See* Is 54:14; 63:1; Zech 8:8

**RIGHTLY**
*r* dividing the word.....2 Tim 2:15

**RISE**
and ye shall *r* up early... Gen 19:2
a Sceptre shall *r* ...... Num 24:17
to *r* up early ............. Ps 127:2
She *r* also .............. Prov 31:15
*r* up at the voice ........ Eccl 12:4
Now will I *r* ........... Is 33:10
*r* in obscurity........... Is 58:10
glory of the Lord is *r*...... Is 60:1
*r* up early .............. Jer 7:13
and their *r* up.......... Lam 3:63
*r* on the evil........... Matt 5:45
be *r* again............... Matt 17:9
he shall *r* again ....... Matt 20:19
after I am *r* again...... Matt 26:32
*R*, let us be going .....Matt 26:46
*r* night and day ........ Mark 4:27
*r* from the dead....... Mark 9:9
the *r* from the dead..... Mark 9:10
*r* the third day ........ Mark 9:31
Be of good comfort, *r*... Mark 10:49
after that I am *r* ...... Mark 14:28
and *r* again ............ Luke 2:34
I cannot *r*................ Luke 11:7
*r* and pray ............. Luke 22:46
third day *r* again....... Luke 24:7
The Lord is *r* indeed...Luke 24:34
shall *r* again ........... John 11:23
*R*, Peter ............... Acts 10:13
*r*, and stand............ Acts 26:16
*r* from the dead....... Acts 26:23
that is *r* again.......... Rom 8:34
the dead *r* not ......... 1 Cor 15:15
*r* from the dead....... 1 Cor 15:20
be *r* with Christ......... Col 3:1
shall *r* first............ 1 Thess 4:16
*See* Is 60:3; Mark 16:2

**RIVER**
upon their streams,
  upon their *r* ........... Ex 7:19
poured me out *r* ....... Job 29:6
tree planted by the *r*....... Ps 1:3
There is a *r* ............ Ps 46:4
the *r* of God............ Ps 65:9
*R* of waters ........... Ps 119:136
By the *r* of Babylon..... Ps 137:1
*r* run into the sea......... Eccl 1:7
as *r* of water ............. Is 32:2
*r* in the desert .......... Is 43:19
peace been as a *r* ........ Is 48:18
to her like a *r* .......... Is 66:12
of *r* of oil.............. Mic 6:7
belly shall flow *r*....... John 7:38
shewed me a pure *r* ..... Rev 22:1
*See* Gen 41:1; Ex 1:22; Ezek 47:9

**ROCK**
I will put thee in a clift
  of the *r* ............. Ex 33:22
water out of this *r*....Num 20:10
thy nest in a *r*........ Num 24:21
the *r* of flint ......... Deut 8:15
He is the *R*............ Deut 32:4
*R* of his salvation ...... Deut 32:15
Of the *R* that ......... Deut 32:18
except their *R*........ Deut 32:30
The Lord is my *r*...... 2 Sam 22:2
The God of my *r* ...... 2 Sam 22:3
the *R* of Israel......... 2 Sam 23:3
embrace the *r* ......... Job 24:8
set me up upon a *r* ...... Ps 27:5
*r* and my fortress.......... Ps 31:3
my feet upon a *r*......... Ps 40:2

lead me to the *r*........... Ps 61:2
honey out of the *r* ....... Ps 81:16
he is my *r*............... Ps 92:15
houses in the *r* ....... Prov 30:26
clefts of the *r* ......... Song 2:14
a *r* of offence ............. Is 8:14
*r* of thy strength......... Is 17:10
shadow of a great *r*....... Is 32:2
founded upon a *r*....... Matt 7:25
upon this *r*.......... Matt 16:18
fell upon a *r*............. Luke 8:6
*r* of offence ............ Rom 9:33
that spiritual *R* ........ 1 Cor 10:4
a *r* of offence ........... 1 Pet 2:8
the mountains and *r* .... Rev 6:16
*See* Judg 6:20; 1 Sam 14:4

**ROOT**
*r* of the righteous........Prov 12:3
*r* shall be.................. Is 5:24
a *r* of Jesse............ Is 11:10
again take *r*............Is 37:31
*r* out of a dry ground ....... Is 53:2
for his *r* was ............ Ezek 31:7
*r* nor branch............. Mal 4:1
*r* of the trees......... Matt 3:10
they had no *r* ......... Matt 13:6
had no *r*................ Mark 4:6
dried up from the *r*.... Mark 11:20
these have no *r* ....... Luke 8:13
the *r* be holy........... Rom 11:16
*r* of all evil ........... 1 Tim 6:10
*r* of bitterness ......... Heb 12:15
plucked up by the *r*...... Jude 12
*r* and the offspring ..... Rev 22:16
*See* 2 Chr 7:20; Dan 4:15

**ROSE** (*n*.)
I am the *r* of Sharon......Song 2:1
blossom as the *r*...........Is 35:1

**ROSE** (*v*.)
over Penuel the sun *r*
  upon him............. Gen 32:31
*r* up upon a heap ........Josh 3:16
*r* from the dead........ Luke 16:31
both died, and *r* ........ Rom 14:9
that he *r* again........... 1 Cor 15:4
and *r* again ............ 2 Cor 5:15
*See* 1 Thess 4:14; Rev 19:3

**RULE** (*v*.)
light to *r* the day ... to *r*
  the night ................Gen 1:16
husband ...*r* over thee....Gen 3:16
*r* his spirit ............. Prov 16:32
The rich *r* over.......... Prov 22:7
*r* among fools............ Eccl 9:17
peace of God *r* ........... Col 3:15
*See* Dan 5:21; Zech 6:13

----------- S -----------

**SABBATH**
thou shalt number
  seven *s* of years ....... Lev 25:8
new moon, nor *s* .......2 Kin 4:23
she kept *s*.............2 Chr 36:21
but on the *s*............ Ezek 46:1
and the *s*.............. Amos 8:5
*s* was made for man....Mark 2:27
Lord also of the *s* ......Mark 2:28
of you on the *s*........ Luke 13:15
*See* Is 1:13; Matt 28:1

**SACKCLOTH**
your clothes, and gird
  you with *s* ......... 2 Sam 3:31
So they girded *s* ....... 1 Kin 20:32
and with *s* ..............Neh 9:1
on *s* with ashes ...... Esth 4:1
put off my *s*.............. Ps 30:11
my clothing was *s* ....... Ps 35:13
and put on *s* .............. Jon 3:5

## SACRIFICE (n.)

Jacob offered s upon
the mount............ Gen 31:54
s to the Lord.............. Ex 5:17
s of their gods ......... Num 25:2
better than s........... 1 Sam 15:22
s of righteousness.......... Ps 4:5
s of joy.................... Ps 27:6
S and offering ............ Ps 40:6
desirest not s ............ Ps 51:16
bind the s.............. Ps 118:27
s of the wicked.......... Prov 15:8
to the Lord than s ...... Prov 21:3
the s of fools............. Eccl 5:1
multitude of your s......... Is 1:11
nor your s sweet.......... Jer 6:20
by him the daily s........ Dan 8:11
take away the daily s .... Dan 11:31
and without a s......... Hos 3:4
mercy, and not s........ Hos 6:6
s every morning........ Amos 4:4
hath prepared a s........ Zeph 1:7
the blind for s.......... Mal 1:8
every s shall .......... Mark 9:49
offerings and s....... Mark 12:33
mingled with their s..... Luke 13:1
slain beasts and s...... Acts 7:42
would have done s ..... Acts 14:13
bodies a living s ...... Rom 12:1
in s unto idols .......... 1 Cor 8:4
is offered in s ......... 1 Cor 10:19
and a s to God ......... Eph 5:2
the s and service........ Phil 2:17
s acceptable .......... Phil 4:18
by the s of himself...... Heb 9:16
one s for sins .......... Heb 10:12
remaineth no more s...Heb 10:26
a more excellent s......Heb 11:4
s of praise to God...... Heb 13:15
with such s God is...... Heb 13:16
offer up spiritual s........1 Pet 2:5
See Ezra 6:10; Jon 1:16

## SACRIFICE (v.)

He that s unto any god ... Ex 22:20
we do s unto him........Ezra 4:2
will they s................ Neh 4:2
I will freely s............Ps 54:6
s their sons .............Ps 106:37
And let them s........Ps 107:22
him that s................Eccl 9:2
s in gardens.............. Is 65:3
They s flesh............. Hos 8:13
s unto their net..........Hab 1:16
our passover is ........1 Cor 5:7
they s to devils ........1 Cor 10:20

## SAFETY

multitude of
counsellors is s....... Prov 11:14
s is of the Lord.........Prov 21:31
Peace and s...........1 Thess 5:3
See Job 24:23; Ps 12:5; 33:17

## SAINTS

He will keep the feet
of his s................ 1 Sam 2:9
to which of the s..........Job 5:1
no trust in his s.........Job 15:15
But to the s ...........Ps 16:3
O ye s of his.............Ps 30:4
forsaketh not his s.......Ps 37:28
Gather my s...........Ps 50:5
congregation of the s......Ps 89:5
souls of his s............Ps 97:10
death of his s..........Ps 116:15
s shout for joy ..........Ps 132:9
have all his s ...........Ps 149:9
s of the most High....... Dan 7:18
one s speaking........... Dan 8:13
bodies of the s........ Matt 27:52
done to thy s.............Acts 9:13
called to be s............. Rom 1:7
intercession for the s... Rom 8:27

the necessity of s ......Rom 12:13
as becometh s ......... Rom 16:2
called to be s..............1 Cor 1:2
the s shall judge .......1 Cor 6:2
collection for the s.......1 Cor 16:1
ministry of the s.......1 Cor 16:15
inheritance in the s...... Eph 1:18
citizens with the s....... Eph 2:19
least of all s............Eph 3:8
perfecting of the s...... Eph 4:12
as becometh s .......... Eph 5:3
the s and faithful....... Col 1:2
with all his s ..........1 Thess 3:13
glorified in his s ......2 Thess 1:10
washed the s feet.......1 Tim 5:10
delivered unto the s...... Jude 3
the prayers of s......... Rev 5:8
See Phil 4:21; Rev 11:18; 13:7

## SAKE

cursed is the ground
for thy s................Gen 3:17
for man's s.............Gen 8:21
for thy s................Gen 12:13
for Jonathan's s........ 2 Sam 9:1
gently for my s........ 2 Sam 18:5
great mercies' s......... Neh 9:31
thy mercies' s............Ps 6:4
for his name's s..........Ps 23:3
thy name's s ...........Ps 25:11
righteousness' s .........Matt 5:10
the elect's s .........Matt 24:22
for the elect's s .......Mark 13:20
for my name's s........Luke 21:12
glad for your s .........John 11:15
for conscience s.........Rom 13:5
for Christ's s ............ 1 Cor 4:10
for conscience s ....1 Cor 10:25, 27
for his body's s.......... Col 1:24
for their work's s ....1 Thess 5:13
thy stomach's s .........1 Tim 5:23
filthy lucre's s...........Titus 1:11
For the truth's s ....... 2 John 2
See 2 Cor 8:9; 1 Thess 3:9

## SALVATION

I have waited for thy s,
O Lord................Gen 49:18
he is become my s.........Ex 15:2
Rock of his s ........... Deut 32:15
s in Israel ...........1 Sam 11:13
wrought this great s.. 1 Sam 14:45
great s for all........... 1 Sam 19:5
the tower of s........2 Sam 22:51
shew forth ... his s....1 Chr 16:23
be clothed with s ...... 2 Chr 6:41
the s of the Lord...... 2 Chr 20:17
S belongeth unto ........Ps 3:8
rejoice in thy s..............Ps 9:14
the s of Israel ............Ps 14:7
God of my s .............Ps 25:5
my light and my s ........Ps 27:1
I am thy s.................Ps 35:3
s of the righteous........Ps 37:39
shew the s of God........Ps 50:23
joy of thy s............... Ps 51:12
my rock and my s........Ps 62:2, 6
our God is the God of s ..Ps 68:20
working s ...............Ps 74:12
his s is nigh ..............Ps 85:9
the s of our God..........Ps 98:3
the cup of s ............Ps 116:13
is become my s ..........Ps 118:14
fainteth for thy s.........Ps 119:81
S is far from.............Ps 119:155
for thy s, O Lord .......Ps 119:174
he that giveth s.........Ps 144:10
the meek with s .........Ps 149:4
Behold, God is my s .......Is 12:2
our s also ................ Is 33:2
with an everlasting s ......Is 45:17
in a day of s have .......... Is 49:8
my s is gone forth ........Is 51:5
see the s of our God ...... Is 52:10

for my s is near ............Is 56:1
for s, but it is..............Is 59:11
helmet of s upon .........Is 59:17
call thy walls S.......... Is 60:18
the garments of s ........Is 60:10
is s hoped for ...........Jer 3:23
the s of the Lord...... Lam 3:26
S is of the Lord ..........Jon 2:9
thy chariots of s ........ Hab 3:8
the God of my s ........ Hab 3:18
and having s.......... Zech 9:9
horn of s for us ....... Luke 1:69
knowledge of s unto...Luke 1:77
have seen thy s ....... Luke 2:30
shall see the s of God ...Luke 3:6
This day is s come ...... Luke 19:9
for s is of the Jews....... John 4:22
is there s in any........ Acts 4:12
the way of s............. Acts 16:17
power of God unto s.....Rom 1:16
s nearer than when.....Rom 13:11
now is the day of s......2 Cor 6:2
repentance to s .........2 Cor 7:10
the gospel of your s.......Eph 1:13
the helmet of s ........ Eph 6:17
turn to my s ...........Phil 1:19
but to you of s ..........Phil 1:28
work out your own s ....Phil 2:12
the hope of s...........1 Thess 5:8
s by our Lord Jesus....1 Thess 5:9
make thee wise
unto s..................2 Tim 3:15
that bringeth s.......... Titus 2:11
be heirs of s.............Heb 1:14
neglect so great s ........Heb 2:3
captain of their s
perfect..................Heb 2:10
author of eternal s........Heb 5:9
that accompany s........Heb 6:9
without sin unto s.......Heb 9:28
through faith unto s......1 Pet 1:5
the s of your souls........1 Pet 1:9
of our Lord is s .........2 Pet 3:15
of the common s .........Jude 3
S to our God ...........Rev 7:10
See 1 Sam 2:1; Job 13:16

## SANCTIFY

ye shall therefore s
yourselves............. Lev 11:44
S yourselves against....Num 11:18
the people, S yourselves...Josh 3:5
s yourselves .......... 1 Sam 16:5
is holy shall be s ...........Is 5:16
commanded my s ones.....Is 13:3
they shall s my name..... Is 29:23
that s themselves........ Is 66:17
the womb I s thee ..........Jer 1:5
will be s in you ....... Ezek 20:41
be s... in the sight ..... Ezek 28:25
shall be s in you ...... Ezek 36:23
am s in them in the.... Ezek 39:27
S ye a fast..............Joel 1:14
the Father hath s ......John 10:36
S them through........John 17:17
sakes I s myself.........John 17:19
them which are s ......Acts 20:32
s by the Holy Ghost....Rom 15:16
are s in Christ Jesus ......1 Cor 1:2
but ye are s .............1 Cor 6:11
husband is s by the......1 Cor 7:14
he might s and...........Eph 5:26
of peace s you
wholly...............1 Thess 5:23
For it is s by the..........1 Tim 4:5
s, and meet for .........2 Tim 2:21
and they who are s ......Heb 2:11
we are s through ........Heb 10:10
them that are s .........Heb 10:14
he might s the ..........Heb 13:12
But s the Lord ...........1 Pet 3:15
them that are s by........Jude 1
See Gen 2:3; Ex 13:2; Job 1:5

## SATAN
S stood up against
  Israel ................... 1 Chr 21:1
and let S stand at ........ Ps 109:6
if S cast out S ......... Matt 12:26
Get thee behind
  me, S ............... Matt 16:23
S as lightning fall ...... Luke 10:18
hath S filled thine ....... Acts 5:3
power of S unto God ... Acts 26:18
messenger of S to ...... 2 Cor 12:7
of S with all .......... 2 Thess 2:9
delivered unto S ....... 1 Tim 1:20
turned aside after S .... 1 Tim 5:15
See Rom 16:20; 1 Cor 5:5

## SAVE
and to s your lives by
  a great .............. Gen 45:7
no man shall s thee ... Deut 28:29
people s by the Lord .. Deut 33:29
and s us ............... Josh 10:6
shall I s Israel .......... Judg 6:15
the Lord to s by ....... 1 Sam 14:6
but s his life ............ Job 2:6
and he shall s the ..... Job 22:29
God, which s the ....... Ps 7:10
Lord s his anointed ...... Ps 20:6
s such as be of a ...... Ps 34:18
own arm s them ........ Ps 44:3
s with thy right ........ Ps 60:5
s the children .......... Ps 72:4
and we shall be s ...... Ps 80:3
s thy servant ........... Ps 86:2
to s him from ......... Ps 109:31
S now, I beseech .... Ps 118:25
I am thine, s me ...... Ps 119:94
cried unto thee; s ... Ps 119:146
hand shall s me ....... Ps 138:7
and he shall s thee ... Prov 20:22
shall be s .......... Prov 28:18
will come and s ......... Is 35:4
and have s .......... Is 43:12
that cannot s .......... Is 45:20
and be ye s .......... Is 45:22
none shall s thee ..... Is 47:15
I will s thy children .... Is 49:25
that it cannot s ....... Is 59:1
mighty to s ........... Is 63:1
s thee in the time ...... Jer 2:28
and we are not s ...... Jer 8:20
shall not s them ...... Jer 11:12
that cannot s ......... Jer 14:9
for I am with thee to
  s thee .............. Jer 15:20
and I shall be s ...... Jer 17:14
I will s thee ........ Jer 30:10
to s thee ............. Jer 30:11
you to s you ......... Jer 42:11
I will s thee from .... Jer 46:27
Flee, s your lives ..... Jer 48:6
that could not s us ...... Jer 14:11
to s his life ......... Ezek 3:18
will I s my flock ..... Ezek 34:22
will s them by the ..... Hos 1:7
that may s thee in ..... Hos 13:10
and thou wilt not s .... Hab 1:2
he will s ............. Zeph 3:17
shall s his .......... Matt 1:21
the end shall be s ... Matt 10:22
whosoever will s his ... Matt 16:25
is come to s that ..... Matt 18:11
Who then can be s ... Matt 19:25
the same shall be s ... Matt 24:13
s thyself ........... Matt 27:40
himself he cannot s ... Matt 27:42
to s life, or to .......... Mark 3:4
S thyself, and come ... Mark 15:30
baptized shall be s ... Mark 16:16
to s life ............. Luke 6:9
faith hath s thee ..... Luke 7:50
believe and be s ..... Luke 8:12
but to s them ........ Luke 9:56
there few that be s .... Luke 13:23

seek and to s that ...... Luke 19:10
let him s himself ..... Luke 23:35
s thyself and us ...... Luke 23:39
him might be s ....... John 3:17
that ye might be s ..... John 5:34
he shall be s ......... John 10:9
but to s the world .... John 12:47
the Lord shall be s ..... Acts 2:21
such as should be s ... Acts 2:47
whereby we must be s .. Acts 4:12
ye cannot be s ........ Acts 15:1
must I do to be s ..... Acts 16:30
thou shalt be s ....... Acts 16:31
willing to s Paul ..... Acts 27:43
shall be s from ......... Rom 5:9
For we are s by hope ... Rom 8:24
a remnant shall be s ... Rom 9:27
they might be s ....... Rom 10:1
thou shalt be s ........ Rom 10:9
might s some of them .. Rom 11:14
all Israel shall be s .... Rom 11:26
us which are s ......... 1 Cor 1:18
preaching to s them .... 1 Cor 1:21
himself shall be s ..... 1 Cor 3:15
the spirit may be s .... 1 Cor 5:5
shalt s thy husband .... 1 Cor 7:16
by all means s some .. 1 Cor 9:22
them that are s ....... 2 Cor 2:15
by grace ye are s ...... Eph 2:5
by grace are ye s ...... Eph 2:8
the world to s sinners ... 1 Tim 1:15
all men to be s ....... 1 Tim 2:4
shalt both s thyself .... 1 Tim 4:16
to s him from death ..... Heb 5:7
s them to the
  uttermost ........... Heb 7:25
to the s of the soul ..... Heb 10:39
an ark to the s ......... Heb 11:7
to s your souls ....... James 1:21
can faith s him ....... James 2:14
who is able to s ...... James 4:12
faith shall s the ...... James 5:15
s a soul from death ... James 5:20
souls were s by water ... 1 Pet 3:20
scarcely be s ......... 1 Pet 4:18
others s with fear ....... Jude 23
See Matt 14:30; John 12:27

## SAVIOUR
tower, and my
  refuge, my s ........ 2 Sam 22:3
gave Israel a s ....... 2 Kin 13:5
forgat God their s ...... Ps 106:21
send them a s ......... Is 19:20
a just God and a S ...... Is 45:21
I the Lord am thy S ..... Is 49:26
so he was their S ........ Is 63:8
the s of the body ...... Eph 5:23
the S of all men ...... 1 Tim 4:10
God our S in all ....... Titus 2:10
and our S Jesus Christ ... Titus 2:13
only wise God our S ..... Jude 25
See Neh 9:27; Obad 21

## SCHOOLMASTER
law was our s to bring
  us unto .............. Gal 3:24

## SEARCH (v.)
that they may s the
  land of ............... Num 13:2
Lord s all hearts ...... 1 Chr 28:9
S me ... and know ...... Ps 139:23
Lord s the heart ....... Jer 17:10
Let us s and try
  our ways ............ Lam 3:40
S the scriptures ....... John 5:39
he that s the hearts ..... Rom 8:27
for the Spirit s ......... 1 Cor 2:10
and s diligently ....... 1 Pet 1:10
See Job 10:6, 28:3; 1 Pet 1:11

## SEE
Lord came down to s
  the city ............... Gen 11:5

when I s the blood ...... Ex 12:13
s the salvation ......... Ex 14:13
not s my face .......... Ex 33:20
shall I s God ........... Job 19:26
to s the goodness ....... Ps 27:13
s the works of God ...... Ps 66:5
s with their eyes ....... Is 6:10
eyes, and s not ......... Jer 5:21
they shall s God ....... Matt 5:8
shalt s greater ........ John 1:50
blind, now I s ........ John 9:25
we s Jesus ............ Heb 2:9
now ye s him not ...... 1 Pet 1:8
s him as he is ........ 1 John 3:2
See Matt 27:24; John 1:51

## SEEK
if thou s him .......... 1 Chr 28:9
heart to s God ......... 2 Chr 19:3
for we s your God ...... Ezra 4:2
I would s unto God ...... Job 5:8
them that s thee ....... Ps 9:10
not s after God ........ Ps 10:4
s out his wickedness .... Ps 10:15
understand, and s God ... Ps 14:2
them that s him ....... Ps 24:6
will I s after .......... Ps 27:4
S ye my face ......... Ps 27:8
do good; s peace ....... Ps 34:14
early will I s thee ..... Ps 63:1
live that s God ......... Ps 69:32
they may s thy name .... Ps 83:16
I will s thy good ...... Ps 122:9
shall s me early ....... Prov 1:28
s good procureth ...... Prov 11:27
that s death .......... Prov 21:6
to s mixed wine ...... Prov 23:30
I will s it ............ Prov 23:35
my heart to s ......... Eccl 1:13
to s out wisdom ....... Eccl 7:25
will s him ............ Song 3:2
s judgment ............ Is 1:17
shall s to the idols ..... Is 19:3
S ye out of the book .... Is 34:16
S ye me in vain ....... Is 45:19
ye shall s me ......... Jer 29:13
no man s after ....... Jer 30:17
soul that s him ...... Lam 3:25
they shall s peace ..... Ezek 7:25
to s by prayer ........ Dan 9:3
Israel, S ye me ....... Amos 5:4
S ye the Lord ........ Zeph 2:3
Should s the law ...... Mal 2:7
But s ye first ........ Matt 6:33
s, and ye shall find ..... Matt 7:7
evil ... generation s ... Matt 12:39
I come s fruit ........ Luke 13:7
and s diligently ....... Luke 15:8
s and to save ........ Luke 19:10
s ye the living ........ Luke 24:5
the Father s such ...... John 4:23
whom they s to kill ..... John 7:25
Ye shall s me ....... John 7:34, 36
if therefore ye s me ... John 18:8
that s after God ...... Rom 3:11
s after wisdom ........ 1 Cor 1:22
no man s his own ...... 1 Cor 10:24
s not her own ........ 1 Cor 13:5
I s not yours ......... 2 Cor 12:14
all s their own ....... Phil 2:21
s those things ......... Col 3:1
they s a country ...... Heb 11:14
s one to come ........ Heb 13:14
let him s peace ...... 1 Pet 3:11
s whom he may devour ... 1 Pet 5:8
shall men s death ...... Rev 9:6
See Jer 45:5; 1 Cor 10:33

## SEEN
I have s God face
  to face .............. Gen 32:30
whom ye have s ....... Ex 14:13
I have s an angel ...... Judg 6:22
mine eye hath s ....... Job 13:1

## SIT (continued)

The *s* in Zion are.......... Is 33:14
with publicans and *s* .... Matt 9:11
but *s* to repentance..... Matt 9:13
publicans and *s* ......... Matt 11:19
with publicans and *s* .... Mark 2:16
which was a *s* ........... Luke 7:37
were *s* above all ........ Luke 13:2
This man receiveth *s* ... Luke 15:2
heaven over one *s* ......Luke 15:7
merciful to me a *s* ..... Luke 18:13
a *s* do such miracles .... John 9:16
Whether he be a *s* ...John 9:25
While we were yet *s* ..... Rom 5:8
many were made *s* ......Rom 5:19
separate from *s* .......... Heb 7:26
*See* James 4:8; 1 Pet 4:18

## SIT

They that *s* in .............. Ps 69:12
to *s* on my right.......Matt 20:23
*See* Prov 23:1; Lam 3:63

## SLACK

The Lord is not *s* ........ 2 Pet 3:9

## SLAUGHTER

We are counted as sheep
for the *s*..............Ps 44:22
a lamb to the *s*.............Is 53:7
*See* Hos 5:2; Zech 11:4

## SLAY

Though he *s* me .........Job 13:15
*See* Gen 4:15; Ex 21:14

## SLEEP (n.)

a deep *s* from the
Lord .................. 1 Sam 26:12
lest I *s* .................... Ps 13:3
giveth his beloved *s* ...... Ps 127:2
and thy *s* shall .......... Prov 3:24
Yet a little *s* ............. Prov 6:10
Love not *s*, lest ........ Prov 20:13
*s* of a labouring .......... Eccl 5:12
may rejoice, and *s* ...... Jer 51:39
were heavy with *s* ...... Luke 9:32
of rest in *s* ..............John 11:13
awake out of *s* ........ Rom 13:11
*See* Dan 2:1; Acts 16:27

## SLEEP (v.)

I *s* in the dust............. Job 7:21
in peace, and *s*............. Ps 4:8
neither slumber nor *s* .... Ps 121:4
For they *s* not.......... Prov 4:16
when thou *s* ........... Prov 6:22
them that *s* in the ....... Dan 12:2
and many *s* ........... 1 Cor 11:30
We shall not all *s*....... 1 Cor 15:51
Awake thou that *s* ...... Eph 5:14
which *s* in Jesus ...... 1 Thess 4:14
let us not *s* ............ 1 Thess 5:6
*See* Gen 28:11; 1 Kin 18:27

## SLOW

*s* of speech................. Ex 4:10
*s* to anger .............. Neh 9:17
*s* to anger ............... Ps 103:8
He that is *s* ......... Prov 14:29
and *s* of heart to
believe............... Luke 24:25
*See* Acts 27:7; Titus 1:12

## SMITE

*S* a scorner............. Prov 19:25
my back to the *s* .......... Is 50:6
*s* the shepherd .........Zech 13:7
shall *s* thee on ......... Matt 5:39
*See* Luke 6:29; Acts 23:2

## SNARE

the *s* of death .........2 Sam 22:6
thee from the *s* of ........ Ps 91:3
*s* with the words....... Prov 6:2
the *s* of death ..........Prov 13:14
reproach and the *s* ..... 1 Tim 3:7
temptation and a *s* ..... 1 Tim 6:9
the *s* of the devil....... 2 Tim 2:26
*See* Ex 23:33; Deut 7:16

## SOBER

we be *s*.................. 2 Cor 5:13
watch and be *s*........1 Thess 5:6
one wife, vigilant, *s*..... 1 Tim 3:2
good men, *s* ............ Titus 1:8
That the aged men
be *s*...................Titus 2:2
women to be *s*...........Titus 2:4
be ye therefore *s* .........1 Pet 4:7
*See* Acts 26:25; Rom 12:3

## SON

the *s* of God saw the
daughters .............. Gen 6:2
the *s* of God came .........Job 1:6
all the *s* of God...........Job 38:7
Kiss the *S*............... Ps 2:12
*s* of thine handmaid ...... Ps 86:16
A wise *s* maketh ........Prov 10:1
wise *s* heareth ...........Prov 13:1
rule over a *s*..............Prov 17:2
foolish *s* is a grief........Prov 17:25
*s* is the calamity ..........Prov 19:13
the *s* of my womb ......Prov 31:2
unto us a *s* is given ....... Is 9:6
*s* of the morning...........Is 14:12
*s* of the house.............Jer 35:5
your *s* to pass........... Ezek 20:31
also caused their *s*.... Ezek 23:37
*s* of the living God .......Hos 1:10
spareth his own *s*........ Mal 3:17
man knoweth the *S*... Matt 11:27
the carpenter's *s*...... Matt 13:55
This is my beloved *S*...... Matt 17:5
whose *s* is he ..........Matt 22:42
the *s* of Mary ...........Mark 6:3
this Joseph's *s* ..........Luke 4:22
the *s* of peace ...........Luke 10:6
a *s* of Abraham ..........Luke 19:9
the *s* of God............John 1:12
the only begotten *S*......John 1:18
begotten *S* of God .......John 3:18
so the *S* quickeneth .....John 5:21
the *S* abideth ever .......John 8:35
*S*... make you free .......John 8:36
the *s* of perdition .......John 17:12
*s* of consolation...........Acts 4:36
gospel of his *S* ...........Rom 1:9
sending his own *S* ....... Rom 8:3
image of his *S* ......... Rom 8:29
spared not his own *S*.... Rom 8:32
as my beloved *s*.........1 Cor 4:14
the adoption of *s* ......... Gal 4:5
if a *s*, then an heir ........ Gal 4:7
the *s* of God............. Phil 2:15
of his dear *S*............Col 1:13
*s* of perdition ......... 2 Thess 2:3
in bringing many *s* ...... Heb 2:10
Though he were a *S* ...... Heb 5:8
the *s* of Pharaoh's ..... Heb 11:24
and scourgeth every *s* ... Heb 12:6
the Father and the *S*...1 John 2:22
the *s* of God............. 1 John 3:1
He that hath the *S* .....1 John 5:12
*See* 1 John 1:7; Rev 21:7

## SONG

*s* in the night ........... Job 35:10
*s* of deliverance .........Ps 32:7
Sing unto him a new *s*.....Ps 33:3
new *s* in my mouth........Ps 40:3
*s* of the drunkards ........Ps 69:12
remembrance my *s*.......Ps 77:6
have been my *s*.........Ps 119:54
sing the Lord's *s*.........Ps 137:4
that singeth *s*..........Prov 25:20
sing many *s*............. Is 23:16
to Zion with *s*........... Is 35:10
unto the Lord a new *s*.... Is 42:10
a very lovely *s*.........Ezek 33:32
the *s* of the temple ..... Amos 8:3
and spiritual *s* .......... Eph 5:19
*See* Song 1:1; Rev 5:9; 14:3

## SORROW

I will greatly
multiply thy *s* ......... Gen 3:16
eat the bread of *s* ........ Ps 127:2
all his days are *s* .........Eccl 2:23
*S* is better................. Eccl 7:3
a man of *s*................. Is 53:3
the beginning of *s* ...... Matt 24:8
For godly *s* worketh .... 2 Cor 7:10
that ye *s* not ........... 1 Thess 4:13
through with many *s*...1 Tim 6:10
*See* Prov 15:13; Hos 8:10

## SOUL

life; and man became a
living *s*.................. Gen 2:7
a ransom for his *s* ....... Ex 30:12
with all your *s* .......... Deut 11:13
as thine own *s* ......... Deut 13:6
with all thy *s* ...........Deut 30:2
his *s* was grieved ...... Judg 10:16
as his own *s*............1 Sam 18:1
with all their *s* ......... 1 Kin 8:48
your *s* to seek........ 1 Chr 22:19
the bitter in *s* ............Job 3:20
hand is the *s*...........Job 12:10
what his *s* desireth .....Job 23:13
a curse to his *s*.......... Job 31:30
his *s* draweth near......Job 33:22
*s* from death.............. Ps 33:19
Lord redeemeth the *s* ... Ps 34:22
redemption of their *s*...Ps 49:8
Truly my *s* waiteth ........ Ps 62:1
my *s* thirsteth............. Ps 63:1
*s* of thy turtledove ......... Ps 74:19
the Lord, O my *s* .........Ps 103:2
my *s* from death.......... Ps 116:8
Let my *s* live ........... Ps 119:175
The liberal *s*.............Prov 11:25
*s* be without
knowledge .............Prov 19:2
to a thirsty *s* ...........Prov 25:25
your *s* shall live ......... Is 55:3
the afflicted *s*............. Is 58:10
the *s* of the poor .........Jer 20:13
and their *s* shall.........Jer 31:12
the *s* that sinneth....... Ezek 18:4
they have devoured *s*... Ezek 22:25
against thy *s* ............ Hab 2:10
able to kill the *s*........ Matt 10:28
exchange for his *s* ..... Matt 16:26
My *s* is exceeding.....Matt 26:38
possess ye your *s* ...... Luke 21:19
and of one *s*............Acts 4:32
every *s* be subject .......Rom 13:1
and *s* and body .......1 Thess 5:23
an anchor of the *s* ...... Heb 6:19
for your *s* .............Heb 13:17
a *s* from death ........ James 5:20
war against the *s* .......1 Pet 2:11
keeping of their *s* .......1 Pet 4:19
unstable *s*............. 2 Pet 2:14
as thy *s* prospereth ..... 3 John 2
*See* Prov 3:22; Ezek 3:19

## SOUND (adj.)

He layeth up *s* wisdom...Prov 2:7
keep *s* wisdom..........Prov 3:21
A *s* heart ............... Prov 14:30
to *s* doctrine ........... 1 Tim 1:10
and of a *s* mind .......... 2 Tim 1:7
the form of *s* words.... 2 Tim 1:13
not endure *s* doctrine .. 2 Tim 4:3
able by *s* doctrine........ Titus 1:9
become *s* doctrine ........ Titus 2:1
*See* Ps 119:80; Titus 2:2, 8

## SPARE

*S* thy people ............Joel 2:17
*s* not his own Son ...... Rom 8:32
if God *s* not ............. Rom 11:21
God *s* not the angels..... 2 Pet 2:4
*See* Prov 17:27; Is 54:2; 58:1

**SPIRIT**

My *s* shall not always
  strive with. . . . . . . . . . . . . Gen 6:3
his *s* made willing . . . . . . . Ex 35:21
take of the *s*. . . . . . . . . . . . Num 11:17
another *s* with him . . . . . Num 14:24
*s* of all flesh. . . . . . . . . . . Num 16:22
and the *s* of God . . . . . . . Num 24:2
in whom is the *s* . . . . . . . Num 27:18
was there *s* in them . . . . . . Josh 5:1
and the *S* of God . . . . . . 1 Sam 10:10
there came forth a *s* . . . 1 Kin 22:21
thy *s* be upon me . . . . . . . 2 Kin 2:9
the *S* of God. . . . . . . . . . . .2 Chr 15:1
good *s* to instruct. . . . . . . . .Neh 9:20
Then a *s* passed. . . . . . . . . .Job 4:15
thy *s* against God . . . . . . . Job 15:13
*s* came from thee . . . . . . . Job 26:4
there is a *s* in man . . . . . . Job 32:8
I commit my *s* . . . . . . . . . . Ps 31:5
and in whose *s*. . . . . . . . . . .Ps 32:2
and renew a right *s* . . . . . . Ps 51:10
whose *s* was not. . . . . . . . . .Ps 78:8
maketh his angels *s* . . . . . .Ps 104:4
provoked his *s* . . . . . . . . . Ps 106:33
I go from thy *s* . . . . . . . . . Ps 139:7
Lord weigheth the *s* . . . . .Prov 16:2
and a haughty *s*. . . . . . . .Prov 16:18
be of a humble *s*. . . . . . . .Prov 16:19
he that ruleth his *s* . . . . Prov 16:32
the humble in *s*. . . . . . . .Prov 29:23
the *s* of man . . . . . . . . . . . Eccl 3:21
the patient in *s* . . . . . . . . . Eccl 7:8
to retain the *s*. . . . . . . . . . . Eccl 8:8
the way of the *s*. . . . . . . . .Eccl 11:5
the *s* shall return . . . . . . . Eccl 12:7
the *s* of judgment. . . . . . . . . .Is 4:4
*s* of the Lord . . . . . . . . . . . . . Is 11:2
his *s* it hath . . . . . . . . . . . . Is 34:16
put my *s* upon him . . . . . . .Is 42:1
I will pour my *s*. . . . . . . . . . Is 44:3
contrite and humble *s*. . . .Is 57:15
My *s* that is . . . . . . . . . . . . . Is 59:21
*S* of the Lord God. . . . . . . . . Is 61:1
the *s* lifted me up. . . . . .Ezek 3:14
a new *s* within you . . . . Ezek 11:19
and a new *s* . . . . . . . . . . .Ezek 18:31
I will pour out my *s*. . . . .Joel 2:28
man walking in the *s* . . . . . Mic 2:11
the *s* of grace . . . . . . . . .Zech 12:10
*S* of God descending. . . . Matt 3:16
*s* indeed is willing . . . . . Matt 26:41
the *S* like a dove . . . . . . . . Mark 1:10
the *s* driveth him . . . . . . Mark 1:12
sighed deeply in his *s*. . . Mark 8:12
in the *s* and power. . . . . . .Luke 1:17
came by the *S*. . . . . . . . . . Luke 2:27
in the power of the *S* . . . Luke 4:14
her *s* came again. . . . . . . . Luke 8:55
not what manner of *s* . . . Luke 9:55
Jesus rejoiced in *S*. . . . . Luke 10:21
for a *s* hath not . . . . . . . .Luke 24:39
the *S* descending . . . . . . . John 1:32
the *S* by measure . . . . . . .John 3:34
God is a *S* . . . . . . . . . . . . .John 4:24
*s* that quickeneth. . . . . . .John 6:63
Even the *S* of truth . . . . .John 14:17
the *S* of truth . . . . . . . . .John 15:26
the *S* gave them . . . . . . . . . Acts 2:4
the wisdom and the *s* . . .Acts 6:10
his *s* was stirred . . . . . . . Acts 17:16
neither angel, nor *s*. . . . .Acts 23:8
but after the *S* . . . . . . . . . Rom 8:1
the law of the *S* . . . . . . . . Rom 8:2
the *S* of him. . . . . . . . . . . . Rom 8:11
*S* itself beareth. . . . . . . . . Rom 8:16
*S* itself maketh. . . . . . . . . Rom 8:26
fervent in *s* . . . . . . . . . . . Rom 12:11
power of the *S* . . . . . . . . .Rom 15:19
of the *S*. . . . . . . . . . . . . . . . 1 Cor 2:4
for the *S* searcheth . . . 1 Cor 2:10
the *s* of meekness . . . . . 1 Cor 4:21
Lord is one *s*. . . . . . . . . . . 1 Cor 6:17

and in your *s*. . . . . . . . . . . .1 Cor 6:20
but the same *S*. . . . . . . . .1 Cor 12:4
discerning of *s* . . . . . . . . .1 Cor 12:10
in the *s* he speaketh . . . . .1 Cor 14:2
made a quickening *s* . . 1 Cor 15:45
the *s* giveth life . . . . . . . . .2 Cor 3:6
the *S* of the Lord is . . . . . 2 Cor 3:17
having begun in the *S* . . . Gal 3:3
Walk in the *S*. . . . . . . . . . . Gal 5:16
fruit of the *S* . . . . . . . . . . . .Gal 5:22
If we live in the *S* . . . . . . . Gal 5:25
soweth to the *S*. . . . . . . . . . Gal 6:8
the *s* of wisdom . . . . . . . . Eph 1:17
*s* that now worketh. . . . . . Eph 2:2
access by one *S* . . . . . . . . Eph 2:18
through the *S*. . . . . . . . . . . Eph 2:22
with might by his *S*. . . . . Eph 3:16
one body, and one *S*. . . . . Eph 4:4
be renewed in the *s*. . . . . Eph 4:23
grieve not the holy *S* . . . .Eph 4:30
the *S* is in all . . . . . . . . . . . Eph 5:9
filled with the *S*. . . . . . . . Eph 5:18
the sword of the *S* . . . . . Eph 6:17
stand fast in one *s* . . . . . . .Phil 1:27
fellowship of the *S*. . . . . . .Phil 2:1
your love in the *S*. . . . . . . . Col 1:8
with you in the *S*. . . . . . . . Col 2:5
Quench not the *S* . . . . 1 Thess 5:19
of the *S*. . . . . . . . . . . . . . .2 Thess 2:13
justified in the *S* . . . . . . . 1 Tim 3:16
*S* speaketh expressly . . . 1 Tim 4:1
be with thy *s*. . . . . . . . . . 2 Tim 4:22
all ministering *s* . . . . . . . .Heb 1:14
of soul and *s* . . . . . . . . . . . Heb 4:12
eternal *s* offered . . . . . . . . Heb 9:14
unto the Father of *s* . . . . . Heb 12:9
the *s* of just men. . . . . . . . Heb 12:23
body without the *s* . . . James 2:26
The *s* that dwelleth. . . . . .James 4:5
a meek and quiet *s* . . . . . .1 Pet 3:4
but quickened by the *S*. . . 1 Pet 3:18
the *s* in prison . . . . . . . . . . 1 Pet 3:19
to God in the *s*. . . . . . . . . . 1 Pet 4:6
*s* of glory. . . . . . . . . . . . . . .1 Pet 4:14
by the *S*. . . . . . . . . . . . . . .1 John 3:24
believe not every *s*. . . . . . 1 John 4:1
know ye the *S* of God . . .1 John 4:2
*s* that confesseth not . . .1 John 4:3
the *s* of truth. . . . . . . . . . .1 John 4:6
*S* that beareth
  witness. . . . . . . . . . . . . . .1 John 5:6
*s*, and the water . . . . . . . 1 John 5:8
having not the *S* . . . . . . . . Jude 19
I was in the *S* . . . . . . . . . . Rev 1:10
*S* saith unto. . . . . . . . . . . . Rev 2:7
I was in the *s* . . . . . . . . . . .Rev 4:2
the *S* of life. . . . . . . . . . . .Rev 11:11
Yea, saith the *S* . . . . . . . . Rev 14:13
*S* and the bride say . . . . .Rev 22:17
*See* Matt 8:16; John 3:5

**SPIRITUAL**

is a fool, the *s* man
  is mad . . . . . . . . . . . . . . . Hos 9:7
unto you some *s* gift. . . . Rom 1:11
that the law is *s*. . . . . . . . .Rom 7:14
of their *s* things. . . . . . . .Rom 15:27
comparing *s* things. . . . .1 Cor 2:13
But he that is *s*. . . . . . . . . .1 Cor 2:15
unto you as unto *s*. . . . . . .1 Cor 3:1
the same *s* meat . . . . . . . 1 Cor 10:3
concerning *s* gifts . . . . . .1 Cor 12:1
and desire *s* gifts . . . . . . 1 Cor 14:1
raised a *s* body. . . . . . . . . 1 Cor 15:44
which is *s* . . . . . . . . . . . . . 1 Cor 15:46
ye which are *s* . . . . . . . . . . Gal 6:1
hymns and *s* songs . . . . . . Eph 5:19
against *s* wickedness . . . . Eph 6:12
built up a *s* house. . . . . . . .1 Pet 2:5
*See* 1 Cor 9:11; Col 1:9; 3:16

**SPIRITUALLY**

but to be *s* minded
  is life. . . . . . . . . . . . . . . . . Rom 8:6

are *s* discerned . . . . . . . . . .1 Cor 2:14
which *s* is called . . . . . . . . .Rev 11:8

**STAND**

Fear ye not, *s* still, and
  see the. . . . . . . . . . . . . . . . Ex 14:13
how then shall we *s* . . . 2 Kin 10:4
*s* ye still . . . . . . . . . . . . . . .2 Chr 20:17
but it shall not *s* . . . . . . . .Job 8:15
he shall *s* at the. . . . . . . . .Job 19:25
nor *s* in the way . . . . . . . . . . .Ps 1:1
shall not *s*. . . . . . . . . . . . . . . . Ps 1:5
*S* in awe. . . . . . . . . . . . . . . . . Ps 4:4
Why *s* thou afar off . . . . . . Ps 10:1
or who shall *s* in . . . . . . . . . Ps 24:3
the Lord *s* for ever. . . . . . . Ps 33:11
*s* up for mine help. . . . . . . . Ps 35:2
and who may *s* in. . . . . . . . Ps 76:7
who will *s* up for . . . . . . . . Ps 94:16
*s* at the right hand. . . . . . . Ps 109:31
Our feet shall *s*. . . . . . . . . . Ps 122:2
who shall *s*. . . . . . . . . . . . . .Ps 130:3
who can *s* before . . . . . . . . Ps 147:17
shall *s* before . . . . . . . . . . Prov 22:29
but who is able to *s*. . . . . .Prov 27:4
*s* not in an evil. . . . . . . . . . . Eccl 8:3
It shall not *s* . . . . . . . . . . . . . .Is 7:7
I *s* . . . upon the . . . . . . . . . . .Is 21:8
hell shall not *s* . . . . . . . . . Is 28:18
our God shall *s*. . . . . . . . . . Is 40:8
*S* by thyself . . . . . . . . . . . . Is 65:5
*S* ye in the ways . . . . . . . . .Jer 6:16
*s* before me for ever . . . . . Jer 35:19
*s* in thy lot at the. . . . . . . . Dan 12:13
he shall *s* and feed. . . . . . . Mic 5:4
*S, s*, shall they. . . . . . . . . . . .Nah 2:8
Satan *s* at his . . . . . . . . . . .Zech 3:1
who shall *s* when. . . . . . . . . .Mal 3:2
itself shall not *s*. . . . . . . . Matt 12:25
be some *s* here. . . . . . . . Matt 16:28
that kingdom
  cannot *s* . . . . . . . . . . . .Mark 3:24
that house cannot *s* . . . .Mark 3:25
shall his kingdom *s*. . . . .Luke 11:18
grace wherein we *s*. . . . . . Rom 5:2
able to make him *s* . . . . .Rom 14:4
*s* in the wisdom of. . . . . . .1 Cor 2:5
*s* fast in the faith. . . . . . . .1 Cor 16:13
for I *s* in doubt. . . . . . . . . . .Gal 4:20
*S* fast therefore . . . . . . . . . .Gal 5:1
having done all, to *s* . . . . Eph 6:13
that ye *s* fast . . . . . . . . . . . .Phil 1:27
so *s* fast in the Lord . . . . . .Phil 4:1
if ye *s* fast. . . . . . . . . . . . .1 Thess 3:8
God *s* sure . . . . . . . . . . . . 2 Tim 2:19
the judge *s* before . . . . . .James 5:9
I *s* at the door. . . . . . . . . . . Rev 3:20
shall be able to *s*. . . . . . . . Rev 6:17
dead . . . *s* before God. . . Rev 20:12
*See* 1 Cor 10:12; Rev 15:2

**STILL**

and be *s*. . . . . . . . . . . . . . . . .Ps 4:4
beside the *s* waters. . . . . . .Ps 23:2
Be *s*, and know . . . . . . . . .Ps 46:10
that standeth *s* . . . . . . . . .Zech 11:16
Peace, be *s* . . . . . . . . . . . . .Mark 4:39
*See* Num 13:30; Ps 65:7

**STING**

where is thy *s*. . . . . . . . . . 1 Cor 15:55

**STIR**

eagle *s* up her. . . . . . . . . . . Deut 32:11
*s* up an adversary. . . . . . . . 1 Kin 11:14
*s* up the spirit. . . . . . . . . . . .1 Chr 5:26
Lord *s* up the spirit . . . . 2 Chr 36:22
*See* Song 2:7; 3:5; 8:4

**STONE**

foot against a *s* . . . . . . . . . Ps 91:12
*s* which the builders. . . . .Ps 118:22
that a *s* was cut. . . . . . . . .Dan 2:34
shall fall on this *s* . . . . . . Matt 21:44
one *s* upon another . . . . Matt 24:2

command this *s* ......... Luke 4:3
one *s* upon another ... Luke 19:44
interpretation, A *s* ...... John 1:42
cast a *s* at her ............ John 8:7
as lively *s*, are............1 Pet 2:5
*See* 1 Sam 30:6; 1 Cor 3:12

**STOREHOUSE**
Bring ye all the tithes
  into the *s* .............. Mal 3:10

**STRAIGHT**
make thy way *s* before
  my face................... Ps 5:8
look *s* before thee ...... Prov 4:25
cannot be made *s*..........Eccl 1:15
can make that *s*.......... Eccl 7:13
shall be made *s*............ Is 40:4
the crooked places *s*...... Is 45:2
make his paths *s*........ Matt 3:3
she was made *s*........ Luke 13:13
which is called *S*........ Acts 9:11
And make *s* paths ...... Heb 12:13
*See* Josh 6:5; 1 Sam 6:12

**STRANGER**
I am a *s* and a sojourner
  with you............Gen 23:4
I am a *s* with thee ........Ps 39:12
Lord preserveth the *s* ....Ps 146:9
I was a *s* ................Matt 25:35
save this *s*..............Luke 17:18
*s* from the covenants.... Eph 2:12
ye are no more *s*........ Eph 2:19
they were *s* ...........Heb 11:13
to entertain *s* .......... Heb 13:2
*See* Matt 17:25; 1 Pet 2:11

**STRENGTH**
The Lord is my *s*
  and song ................ Ex 15:2
trodden down *s* ........ Judg 5:21
hy *s* shall no man....... 1 Sam 2:9
the *S* of Israel......... 1 Sam 15:29
God is my *s* .......... 2 Sam 22:33
If I speak of *s* ............Job 9:19
is wisdom and *s* ........ Job 12:13
my God, my *s* ............. Ps 18:2
girded me with *s* ........Ps 18:32
Lord is the *s* ........... Ps 27:1
The Lord is my *s*.......... Ps 28:7
*s* unto his people ........ Ps 29:11
by much *s*................Ps 33:16
I may recover *s* ........Ps 39:13
God is our refuge and *s*.... Ps 46:1
Ascribe ye *s* unto God ... Ps 68:34
that giveth *s* ............ Ps 68:35
*s* of my heart............Ps 73:26
unto God our *s*.......... Ps 81:1
whose *s* is in thee ........Ps 84:5
*s* and beauty........... Ps 96:6
my *s* and song .......... Ps 118:14
with *s* in my soul ........Ps 138:3
the Lord is *s* .......... Prov 10:29
better than *s*...... Eccl 9:16
princes eat ... for *s*.... Eccl 10:17
Jehovah is my *s*............Is 12:2
a *s* to the poor ......... Is 25:4
he increaseth *s* ........Is 40:29
awake, put on *s*............Is 51:9
*s* of the kingdoms ...... Hag 2:22
He hath shewed *s*.......Luke 1:51
yet without *s* ............ Rom 5:6
and the *s* of sin ........ 1 Cor 15:56
thou hast a little *s* ....... Rev 3:8
*See* Job 21:23; 2 Cor 12:9

**STRENGTHEN**
*s* himself against the
  Almighty ...............Job 15:25
and *s* thee..............Ps 20:2
*s* man's heart ............ Ps 104:15
Wisdom *s* the wise ..... Eccl 7:19
*S* ye the weak hands....... Is 35:3
*s* thy brethren ........Luke 22:32

to be *s* with might ....... Eph 3:16
which *s* me .............. Phil 4:13
*S* with all might............Col 1:11
*See* Luke 22:43; 1 Pet 5:10

**STRIPES**
Forty *s* he may give
  him.................... Deut 25:3
by whose *s*.............. 1 Pet 2:24

**STRIVE**
My spirit shall not
  always *s* with man ..... Gen 6:3
*S* not with a man ....... Prov 3:30
*S* to enter ............Luke 13:24
*s* for masteries.......... 2 Tim 2:5
servant ... must not *s*..2 Tim 2:24
*See* Is 45:9; Jer 50:24

**STRONG**
Be *s*, and quit your-
  selves like ............ 1 Sam 4:9
be thou *s* therefore ...... 1 Kin 2:2
lo, he is *s*...................Job 9:19
rejoiceth as a *s* man ....... Ps 19:5
The Lord *s* and mighty....Ps 24:8
be thou my *s* rock ......... Ps 31:2
art my *s* refuge .............Ps 71:7
is his *s* city.............Prov 10:15
Lord is a *s* tower.......Prov 18:10
battle to the *s*............Eccl 9:11
be *s*, fear not............. Is 35:4
he is *s* in power.........Is 40:26
be *s*, yea, be *s* .......... Dan 10:19
a *s* man's house........ Matt 12:29
was *s* in faith .......... Rom 4:20
weak, but ye are *s* ...... 1 Cor 4:10
send them *s*
  delusion ............ 2 Thess 2:11
not of *s* meat ............ Heb 5:12
a *s* consolation ......... Heb 6:18
*See* Prov 14:26; Joel 3:10

**SUBJECT**
devils are *s* unto us.....Luke 10:17
*s* to the law of God.......Rom 8:7
made *s* to vanity.........Rom 8:20
every soul be *s*..........Rom 13:1
*s* to the prophets ...... 1 Cor 14:32
be *s* unto him.......... 1 Cor 15:28
*s* unto Christ.............. Eph 5:24
*s* to bondage............. Heb 2:15
*s* to like passions ...... James 5:17
*s* to your masters........1 Pet 2:18
powers being made *s*... 1 Pet 3:22
all of you be *s*...........1 Pet 5:5
*See* Luke 2:51; Titus 3:1

**SUBMIT**
Strangers shall *s*
  themselves.........2 Sam 22:45
*s* himself.............. Ps 68:30
Wives, *s* yourselves...... Eph 5:22
*S* yourselves .............James 4:7
*See* Rom 10:3; Eph 5:21

**SUBSTANCE**
with thy *s*................ Prov 3:9
increaseth his *s*......... Prov 28:8
wasted his *s* ........ Luke 15:13
faith is the *s* .............. Heb 11:1
*See* Prov 1:13; 6:31; 8:21

**SUFFER**
*s* the righteous ...........Ps 55:22
shall *s* hunger...........Prov 19:15
not *s* him to sleep ....... Eccl 5:12
*s* many things ............Matt 16:21
*S* little children ..........Matt 19:14
Son of man must *s* ..... Mark 8:31
*S* the little children ..... Mark 10:14
behooved Christ to *s* ... Luke 24:46
that Christ should *s* ..... Acts 3:18
we *s* with him ..........Rom 8:17
he shall *s* loss............1 Cor 3:15
one member *s* ......... 1 Cor 12:26

should *s* persecution ..... Gal 6:12
If we *s*...................2 Tim 2:12
shall *s* persecution .....2 Tim 3:12
to *s* affliction ........... Heb 11:25
Christ also *s*.............1 Pet 2:21
if ye *s* for..................1 Pet 3:14
Christ hath *s* for us .......1 Pet 4:1
*See* Phil 3:8; Heb 2:18; 5:8

**SUFFICIENT**
*S* unto the day .........Matt 6:34
*See* Deut 15:8; John 6:7

**SUN**
*S*, stand thou still upon
  Gibeon................ Josh 10:22
as the *s* when........... Judg 5:31
green before the *s* ........Job 8:16
may not see the *s*........Ps 58:8
a *s* and shield............. Ps 84:11
*s* shall not smite........... Ps 121:6
thing under the *s* ........ Eccl 1:9
to behold the *s*............Eccl 11:7
While the *s*.............. Eccl 12:2
the *s* hath looked........ Song 1:6
clear as the *s*............Song 6:10
her *s* is gone down ...... Jer 15:9
the *s* and the moon...... Joel 2:10
*S* of righteousness......... Mal 4:2
*s* to rise on.............. Matt 5:45
shine forth as the *s*... Matt 13:43
not the *s* go down .......Eph 4:26
*See* 1 Cor 15:41; Rev 7:16

**SUPPLICATION**
have heard thy prayer
  and thy *s*............... 1 Kin 9:3
*s* to my judge .............Job 9:15
Lord hath heard my *s* .......Ps 6:9
seek by prayer and *s*...... Dan 9:3
grace and of *s*...........Zech 12:10
all prayer and *s* ......... Eph 6:18
*s*, prayers ................ 1 Tim 2:1
*See* Ps 28:6; 31:22; Heb 5:7

**SUPPLY**
*s* all your need ........... Phil 4:19

**SWORD**
their tongue a sharp *s* .....Ps 57:4
shall not lift up *s*...........Is 2:4
The *s* is without .........Ezek 7:15
but a *s* ................. Matt 10:34
a *s* ... pierce ........Luke 2:35
beareth not the *s* ........Rom 13:4
*s* of the Spirit ............ Eph 6:17
any two-edged *s*....... Heb 4:12
a sharp two-edged *s*...... Rev 1:16
killeth with the *s* ........Rev 13:10
goeth a sharp *s* .........Rev 19:15
*See* Is 2:4; Joel 3:10; Mic 4:3

— T —

**TABERNACLE**
Lord, who shall abide
  in thy *t*...............Ps 15:1
In the secret of his *t* ..... Ps 27:5
How amiable are thy *t*..... Ps 84:1
a *t* that shall not.........Is 33:20
*See* Job 5:24; Prov 14:11

**TABLE**
Thou preparest a *t*
  before me ..............Ps 23:5
their masters' *t* ........Matt 15:27
dogs under the *t*........Mark 7:28
*See* Prov 3:3; Jer 17:1; Mal 1:7

**TAKE**
I will *t* you to me for a
  people...................Ex 6:7
*T* no thought ........... Matt 6:25
*t* no thought how...... Matt 10:19
*T* my yoke upon you....Matt 11:29
and said, *T*, eat........Matt 26:26

*t* thy coat also .........Luke 6:29
why *t* ye thought .....Luke 12:26
rather *t* wrong............1 Cor 6:7
*t* thy crown ...............Rev 3:11
*See* John 1:29; Rev 22:19

## TASTE
the *t* of it was as the *t*
    of fresh oil.............Num 11:8
there any *t*...............Job 6:6
mouth *t* his meat........Job 12:11
O *t* and see.................Ps 34:8
sweet . . . unto my *t*.....Ps 119:103
*t* remained in him........Jer 48:11
not *t* of death..........Matt 16:28
*t* of my supper.........Luke 14:24
never *t* of death.........John 8:52
Touch not; *t* not .........Col 2:21
should *t* death............Heb 2:9
and have *t* ...............Heb 6:4
ye have *t*..................1 Pet 2:3
*See* 1 Sam 14:43; 2 Sam 19:35

## TAUGHT
thou hast *t* me.............Ps 71:17
He *t* me also .............Prov 4:4
he *t* them as one........ Matt 7:29
for he *t* them .......... Mark 1:22
and thou hast *t* .......Luke 13:26
be all *t* of God...........John 6:45
as my Father hath *t*.....John 8:28
neither was I *t* it..........Gal 1:12
*t* in the word..............Gal 6:6
been *t* by him.......... Eph 4:21
ye have been *t* .......2 Thess 2:15
*See* 1 Thess 4:9; 1 John 2:27

## TEACH
and will *t* you............Ex 4:15
*t* their children ........ Deut 4:10
*t* them diligently .......Deut 6:7
And ye shall *t* them.....Deut 11:19
and *t* us..............Judg 13:8
I will *t* you............ 1 Sam 12:23
*t* the children of
    Judah................. 2 Sam 1:18
a *t* priest .............. 2 Chr 15:3
*T* me and I will .........Job 6:24
Shall not they *t* .........Job 8:10
they shall *t* thee .........Job 12:7
not *t* thou me.........Job 34:32
by his power: who *t* ....Job 36:22
*t* me thy paths..........Ps 25:4
will he *t* sinners ..........Ps 25:8
*T* me thy way.............Ps 27:11
will *t* you the fear.........Ps 34:11
I *t* transgressors..........Ps 51:13
*t* us to number our .......Ps 90:12
and *t* him out..........Ps 94:12
*t* with his fingers .......Prov 6:13
he will *t* us...............Is 2:3
shall teach *t* knowledge ......Is 28:9
and doth *t* him ...........Is 28:26
God which *t* thee .........Is 48:17
*t* your daughters........Jer 9:20
*t* my people............Ezek 44:23
thereof *t* for .............. Mic 3:11
and *t* all nations ....... Matt 28:19
Lord, *t* us to pray........Luke 11:1
Holy Ghost shall *t* ....Luke 12:12
dost thou *t* us..........John 9:34
he shall *t* you all ......John 14:26
ceased not to *t*..........Acts 5:42
or he that *t*..............Rom 12:7
*t* every where..........1 Cor 4:17
nature itself *t*..........1 Cor 11:14
my voice I might *t*......1 Cor 14:19
and *t* every man........Col 1:28
*t* and admonishing .......Col 3:16
*t* no other doctrine .... 1 Tim 1:3
apt to *t*..................1 Tim 3:2
things command
    and *t*.................. 1 Tim 4:11
*t* and exhort .............1 Tim 6:2

to *t* others also ......... 2 Tim 2:2
*t* things which...........Titus 1:11
*t* the young women .....Titus 2:4
*T* us that ...............Titus 2:12
*t* you again...............Heb 5:12
*See* Matt 22:16, Mark 6:34

## TEACHER
as the great, the *t* as
    the scholar ...........1 Chr 25:8
than all my *t* ...........Ps 119:99
the voice of my *t*........Prov 5:13
not thy *t* be removed.....Is 30:20
and a *t* of lies ............ Hab 2:18
*t* come from God ........John 3:2
a *t* of babes .......... Rom 2:20
are all *t*..................1 Cor 12:29
pastors and *t* ............Eph 4:11
*t* of the law .............1 Tim 1:7
*t* of good things..........Titus 2:3
*See* 1 Tim 2:7; 2 Tim 1:11

## TEARS
thy prayer, I have
    seen thy *t*..............2 Kin 20:5
They that sow in *t* .......Ps 126:5
wipe away *t*..............Is 25:8
covering . . . with *t*........Mal 2:13
wash his feet with *t* ....Luke 7:38
and with many *t*.........Acts 20:19
and day with *t* .........Acts 20:31
mindful of thy *t*..........2 Tim 1:4
*See* 2 Cor 2:4; Heb 5:7; 12:17

## TEMPLE
he did hear my voice
    out of his *t*...........2 Sam 22:7
within the *t*......... Neh 6:10
enquire in his *t* ..........Ps 27:4
in his *t* doth..............Ps 29:9
train filled the *t*............Is 6:1
songs of the *t*...........Amos 8:3
come to his *t*............Mal 3:1
greater than the *t*...... Matt 12:6
Destroy this *t*...........John 2:19
are the *t* of God ........ 1 Cor 3:16
body is the *t* ............1 Cor 6:19
*t* of the living God ......2 Cor 6:16
*See* Hos 8:14; Rev 7:15; 11:19

## TEMPORAL
the things which are
    seen are *t*.............2 Cor 4:18

## TEMPT
that God did *t* Abraham ...Gen 22:1
do ye *t* the Lord ...........Ex 17:2
and have *t* me ........Num 14:22
as ye *t* him...............Deut 6:16
they *t* God ...............Ps 78:18
I *t* the Lord ................Is 7:12
that *t* God................Mal 3:15
*t* the Lord thy God........Matt 4:7
said, Why *t* ye me...... Matt 22:18
and *t* him ...........Luke 10:25
to *t* the Spirit ...........Acts 5:9
why *t* ye God............Acts 15:10
you to be *t* ...............1 Cor 10:13
lest thou also be *t* ........ Gal 6:1
suffered being *t* ........ Heb 2:18
was in all points *t* ....... Heb 4:15
say when he is *t* ........James 1:13
*See* Matt 4:1; Mark 1:13

## TEMPTATION
lead us not into *t* ....... Matt 6:13
enter not into *t* ........ Matt 26:41
lest ye enter into *t* ......Mark 14:38
and in time of *t* ........Luke 8:13
no *t* taken you.........1 Cor 10:13
And my *t* which ..........Gal 4:14
fall into *t* ................1 Tim 6:9
fall into divers *t*.........James 1:2
the godly out of *t* ....... 2 Pet 2:9
*See* Luke 11:4; 1 Pet 1:6

## TEMPTER
And when the *t* came
    to him ................. Matt 4:3
*t* have tempted you....1 Thess 3:5

## TERRIBLE
a mighty God and *t* .....Deut 7:21
great and *t* things ..... Deut 10:21
the great and *t* God.........Neh 1:5
How *t* art thou.............Ps 66:3
O God, thou art *t*......... Ps 68:35
the hand of the *t*.........Jer 15:21
great and very *t*...........Joel 2:11
so *t* was the sight....... Heb 12:21
*See* Lam 5:10; Ezek 1:22; 28:7

## TERROR
the *t* of God was upon
    the cities .............. Gen 35:5
and *t* within ...........Deut 32:25
*t* of God ....................Job 6:4
*T* shall make.............. Job 18:11
*t* of the shadow..........Job 24:17
my *t* shall not............Job 33:7
the *t* of death............Ps 55:4
consumed with *t* ....... Ps 73:19
for the *t* by night ......... Ps 91:5
the *t* of the Lord........2 Cor 5:11
*See* Ezek 21:12; 1 Pet 3:14

## TESTIMONY
his *t* which he
    testified ..............2 Kin 17:15
Thy *t* are very sure .......Ps 93:5
I have kept thy *t* ........Ps 119:22
Thy *t* also ................Ps 119:24
will speak of thy *t* .......Ps 119:46
feet unto thy *t* ..........Ps 119:59
I love thy *t* ............. Ps 119:119
Thy *t* are wonderful.... Ps 119:129
Bind up the *t* .............Is 8:16
and to the *t* ...............Is 8:20
a *t* against them ....... Matt 10:18
to you for a *t*........... Luke 21:13
receiveth his *t* ..........John 3:32
his *t* is true ............John 21:24
*t* unto the word.......... Acts 14:3
the *t* of God..............1 Cor 2:1
*t* of our conscience ......2 Cor 1:12
ashamed of the *t* ........2 Tim 1:8
had this *t* ................Heb 11:5
*See* Rev 1:2; 6:9; 11:7

## THANK
I *t* thee, O Father .......Matt 11:25
God I *t* thee.............Luke 18:11
I *t* thee that.............John 11:41
he *t* God................Acts 28:15
I *t* my God always ........1 Cor 1:4
to *t* God always........2 Thess 1:3
I *t* Christ Jesus......... 1 Tim 1:12
*See* 1 Chr 23:30; Dan 2:23

## THANKS
companies of them
    that gave *t*........... Neh 12:31
and gave *t* .............Matt 26:27
gave *t* likewise..........Luke 2:38
he giveth God *t*.......... Rom 14:6
But *t* be to God ........1 Cor 15:57
Giving *t* always.........Eph 5:20
For what *t* can we .....1 Thess 3:9
*t* to him .................. Rev 4:9
*See* 2 Cor 1:11; Heb 13:15

## THANKSGIVING
may publish with the
    voice of *t* ............Ps 26:7
his presence with *t*......Ps 95:2
found therein, *t*............Is 51:3
a sacrifice of *t*..........Amos 4:5
supplication with *t* ...... Phil 4:6
in the same with *t*........ Col 4:2
be received with *t* .......1 Tim 4:3
*See* Neh 11:17; 12:8; 2 Cor 4:15

## THIEF

as a *t* in the
 night..... 1 Thess 5:2; 2 Pet 3:10
 *See* Prov 6:30; 29:24

## THIRST (v.)

My soul *t* for God...........Ps 42:2
my soul *t* for thee...........Ps 63:1
my soul *t* after thee........Ps 143:6
not hunger nor *t*.......... Is 49:10
Ho, every one that *t*......Is 55:1
*t* after righteousness.... Matt 5:6
him shall never *t*....... John 4:14
shall never *t*.............John 6:35
If any man *t*, let him.... John 7:37
saith, I *t*................John 19:28
neither *t* any more.......Rev 7:16
*See* Ex 17:3; Is 48:21

## THORN

and *t* in your sides.....Num 33:55
as *t* in your sides........ Judg 2:3
As the lily among *t*...... Song 2:2
a *t* in the flesh.......... 2 Cor 12:7
*See* Matt 13:7; 27:29

## THOUGHT (n.)

no *t* can be withholden....Job 42:2
in all his *t*..............Ps 10:4
and thy *t* which are........Ps 40:5
thy *t* are very deep.........Ps 92:5
the *t* of man ........... Ps 94:11
and know my *t* ......... Ps 139:23
*t* of the righteous .......Prov 12:5
and thy *t* shall be .......Prov 16:3
The *t* of foolishness .... Prov 24:9
unrighteous man his *t*......Is 55:7
For my *t* are not your......Is 55:8
the *t* of the Lord..........Mic 4:12
Take no *t* for your....... Matt 6:25
take no *t*, saying........ Matt 6:31
knowing their *t* said..... Matt 9:4
take no *t* how or what... Matt 10:19
Jesus knew their *t*..... Matt 12:25
proceed evil *t*..........Matt 15:19
proceed evil *t*........... Mark 7:21
take no *t* beforehand...Mark 13:11
*t* of many hearts.......Luke 2:35
perceived their *t*.......Luke 5:22
he knew their *t* .........Luke 6:8
the *t* of their heart.......Luke 9:47
knowing their *t*........Luke 11:17
take ye no *t* how or....Luke 12:11
*t* of thine heart.........Acts 8:22
the *t* of the wise ........1 Cor 3:20
*t* to the obedience ..... 2 Cor 10:5
the *t* and intents of...... Heb 4:12
*See* Gen 6:5; Jer 4:14

## THOUGHT (v.)

that *t* upon his name.....Mal 3:16
I *t* as a child............. 1 Cor 13:11
*t* it not robbery ...........Phil 2:6
*See* Gen 20:11; 50:20

## THRONE

the Lord's *t* is in heaven....Ps 11:4
the *t* of iniquity..........Ps 94:20
set *t* of judgment........Ps 122:5
and his *t* is.............Prov 20:28
The heaven is my *t*........Is 66:1
A glorious high *t*.........Jer 17:12
his *t* was like the.......... Dan 7:9
the *t* of his glory........ Matt 19:28
the *t* of his glory....... Matt 25:31
be *t*, or dominions.........Col 1:16
the *t* of grace ......... Heb 4:16
sit with me in my *t* .......Rev 3:21
a *t* was set in heaven ......Rev 4:2
*See* Rev 6:16; 7:9; 14:3; 19:4

## TIDINGS

He shall not be afraid of
 evil *t*.................... Ps 112:7
man who brought *t*......Jer 20:15

---

But *t* out of the ......... Dan 11:44
thee these glad *t*........Luke 1:19
good *t* of great joy..... Luke 2:10
glad *t* of the kingdom ... Luke 8:1
unto you glad *t*.........Acts 13:32
*t* of good things.......Rom 10:15
*See* Ex 33:4; 1 Kin 14:6

## TIME

the *t* drew nigh.........Gen 47:29
down out of *t*........... Job 22:16
the *t* of trouble ......... Job 38:23
pray unto thee in a *t*......Ps 32:6
in the evil *t* ............. Ps 37:19
in *t* of trouble............Ps 41:1
What *t* I am afraid........Ps 56:3
an acceptable *t* .........Ps 69:13
how short my *t* is........Ps 89:47
a *t* to every purpose ......Eccl 3:1
*t* and chance happeneth ...Eccl 9:11
an acceptable *t* have....... Is 49:8
hasten it in his *t* ........Is 60:22
and the *t* of their ........Jer 46:21
the *t* of love.............Ezek 16:8
until a *t* and *t* and ...... Dan 7:25
*t* to seek the Lord....... Hos 10:12
fruit before the *t*......... Mal 3:11
signs of the *t*............. Matt 16:3
the *t* of thy visitation... Luke 19:44
the *t* of refreshing .......Acts 3:19
the *t* of restitution.......Acts 3:21
high *t* to awake ......... Rom 13:11
the *t* is short.......... 1 Cor 7:29
is the accepted *t*.........2 Cor 6:2
Redeeming the *t*......... Eph 5:16
in *t* of need .............. Heb 4:16
of *t* the Spirit .............1 Pet 1:11
the *t* is at hand ..........Rev 1:3
should be *t* no longer.... Rev 10:6
*See* Prov 17:17; Eph 1:10

## TOGETHER

exalt his name *t* ...........Ps 34:3
the poor meet *t*........ Prov 22:2
Can two walk *t* ......... Amos 3:3
are gathered *t* .........Matt 18:20
God hath joined *t*....... Matt 19:6
work *t* for good........Rom 8:28
caught up *t* ......... 1 Thess 4:17
*See* Matt 19:6; Eph 2:21

## TO MORROW

Boast not thyself of *t*....Prov 27:1
drink; for *t* we shall die... Is 22:13
*t* shall be as this day...... Is 56:12
eat and drink; for *t* we...1 Cor 15:32
*See* Josh 5:12; 2 Kin 7:1

## TONGUE

he hid from the scourge
 of the *t*..................Job 5:21
it under his *t*............. Job 20:12
Keep thy *t* from..........Ps 34:13
*t* of the just ........... Prov 10:20
the *t* of the wise ........Prov 12:18
but a lying *t* is ..........Prov 12:19
A wholesome *t* is a .......Prov 15:4
the power of the *t* ......Prov 18:21
bridleth not his *t* ......James 1:26
the *t* is a fire ..........James 3:6
his *t* from evil...........1 Pet 3:10
in word, neither in *t*...1 John 3:18
*See* Ps 45:1; Luke 16:24

## TOOTH

Eye for eye, *t* for *t* .......Ex 21:24
is like a broken *t* .......Prov 25:19

## TRADITION

transgress the *t* of the
 elders..................Matt 15:2
*t* of the elders............ Mark 7:3
*t* of my fathers............Gal 1:14
the *t* of men ............. Col 2:8
received by *t*.............1 Pet 1:18

---

## TRANSFORMED

*t* by the renewing of
 your mind.............Rom 12:2
*t* themselves.............2 Cor 11:13
Satan himself is *t*.......2 Cor 11:14
*t* as ... ministers .......2 Cor 11:15

## TRANSGRESS

do ye *t* the
 commandment .....Num 14:41
Lord's people to *t*......1 Sam 2:24
If ye *t* .......................Neh 1:8
mouth shall not *t*......... Ps 17:3
that man will *t* ...... Prov 28:21
the pastors also *t*......... Jer 2:8
hast *t* against............ Jer 3:13
because he *t* by.......... Hab 2:5
*See* Matt 15:2; 1 John 3:4

## TRANSGRESSION

forgiving iniquity and *t* ...Ex 34:7
died for his *t*........... 1 Chr 10:13
because of the *t*.........Ezra 10:6
not pardon my *t*.........Job 7:21
my *t* and my sin ........Job 13:23
My *t* is sealed...........Job 14:17
If I covered my *t*...... Job 31:33
from the great *t* ....... Ps 19:13
nor my *t* ............... Ps 25:7
whose *t* is forgiven ..... Ps 32:1
blot out my *t*..............Ps 51:1
as for our *t*, thou..........Ps 65:3
because of their *t*........ Ps 107:17
a *t* seeketh love.........Prov 17:9
blotteth out thy *t* ....... Is 43:25
thy *t*.................... Is 44:22
wounded for our *t*...... Is 53:5
the *t* of my people......... Is 53:8
people their *t* ........... Is 58:1
All his *t* that ......... Ezek 18:22
For the *t* of Jacob......... Mic 1:5
*See* Rom 4:15; 5:14

## TRANSGRESSOR

way of *t* is hard.........Prov 13:15
a *t* from the womb ....... Is 48:8
numbered with the *t* ..... Is 53:12
reckoned among
 the *t* .................Luke 22:37
*See* Dan 8:23; Hos 14:9

## TRANSLATE

hath *t* us into ..............Col 1:13
Enoch was *t* ..............Heb 11:5

## TRAVAIL

the *t* of his soul............Is 53:11
and *t* in pain............ Rom 8:22
I *t* in birth again ........ Gal 4:19
*See* Job 15:20; Is 13:8

## TREASURE

a peculiar *t* unto me........Ex 19:5
thee his good *t*........ Deut 28:12
his peculiar *t*.............Ps 135:4
the peculiar *t* ........... Eccl 2:8
where your *t* is ......... Matt 6:21
shalt have *t* in heaven... Matt 19:21
*See* Deut 32:34; 33:19

## TREE

be like a *t* planted ......... Ps 1:3
The *t* of the Lord .......Ps 104:16
the *t* of Eden .......... Ezek 31:9
*See* Mark 8:24; Luke 21:29; Rev 22:2

## TREMBLE

and shall *t*, and be in
 anguish...............Deut 2:25
earth *t*, and the....... Judg 5:4
shook and *t*...........2 Sam 22:8
every one that *t*.........Ezra 9:4
pillars thereof *t*.......... Job 9:6
pillars of heaven *t* .......Job 26:11
rejoice with *t* .............Ps 2:11
the earth to *t* ............. Ps 60:2

the earth *t* ................ Ps 77:18
earth saw, and *t* .......... Ps 97:4
let the people *t* ............ Ps 99:1
the earth, and it *t*....... Ps 104:32
house shall *t*............. Eccl 12:3
the earth to *t* ............... Is 14:16
*t* at thy presence........... Is 64:2
*t* at his word ............... Is 66:5
*t* at my presence.......... Jer 5:22
shall fear and *t*........... Jer 33:9
not the land *t*.......... Amos 8:8
Felix *t*, and............. Acts 24:25
believe, and *t*.......... James 2:19
See Acts 9:6; 16:29

**TRESPASS**
what is my *t?* what is
  my sin............... Gen 31:36
*t* of thy servants ....... Gen 50:17
chief in this *t* .........Ezra 9:2
still in his *t*.............Ps 68:21
forgive men their *t* .... Matt 6:14
shall *t* against thee ....Matt 18:15
If thy brother *t*.........Luke 17:3
*t* unto them............. 2 Cor 5:19
who were dead in *t*.......Eph 2:1
forgiven you all *t* ....... Col 2:13
See Num 5:6; 1 Kin 8:31

**TRIAL**
laugh at the *t* of the
  innocent............... Job 9:23
great *t* of affliction ..... 2 Cor 8:2
See Ezek 21:13; Heb 11:36

**TRIBULATION**
shall be great *t*......... Matt 24:21
ye shall have *t* .......John 16:33
much *t* enter into.......Acts 14:22
that *t* worketh patience ...Rom 5:3
patient in *t*..............Rom 12:12
See 2 Cor 1:4; 7:4; Eph 3:13

**TRIED**
the word of the
  Lord is *t* ............2 Sam 22:31
for when he is *t*........ James 1:12

**TRIUMPH**
the Lord, for he hath *t*
  gloriously ............ Ex 15:1, 21
enemies *t* over me........Ps 25:2
I will *t* in the..............Ps 92:4
to *t* in Christ ............ 2 Cor 2:14
*t* over them in ............ Col 2:15
See 2 Sam 1:20; Job 20:5

**TROUBLE** (n.)
man is born unto *t* ........Job 5:7
and full of *t*............. Job 14:1
in the time of *t*............Ps 27:5
present help in *t*..........Ps 46:1
in the midst of *t*.........Ps 138:7
have *t* in the flesh ...... 1 Cor 7:28
See Prov 15:6; 25:19

**TRUE**
we are *t* men, thy
  servants ...............Gen 42:11
that which is *t* ...... 1 Kin 22:16
without the *t* God ...... 2 Chr 15:3
and *t* laws ...... Neh 9:13
Thy word is *t* ...........Ps 119:160
A *t* witness............Prov 14:25
is the *t* God ............ Jer 10:10
that thou art *t* ....... Matt 22:16
the *t* riches .............Luke 16:11
the *t* Light ............ John 1:9
the *t* worshippers .......John 4:23
witness is not *t* ........ John 5:31
you the *t* bread .........John 6:32
this man were *t*........John 10:41
I am the *t* vine.........John 15:1
the only *t* God ......... John 17:3
and yet *t* ................2 Cor 6:8
and *t* holiness ..........Eph 4:24

things are *t* ............. Phil 4:8
with a *t* heart.......... Heb 10:22
him that is *t* ........... 1 John 5:20
See Rev 3:7; 6:10; 15:3

**TRUST**
he slay me, yet will I *t*
  in him ................Job 13:15
Wilt thou *t* him.........Job 39:11
I *t* in thee ................. Ps 25:2
I *t* in the Lord............. Ps 31:6
*T* in the Lord............... Ps 37:3
shall *t* in the Lord ........Ps 40:3
I will *t* in thee............ Ps 55:23
I will *t* in thee............ Ps 56:3
*T* in him at all............ Ps 62:8
*t* thou in the Lord ........ Ps 115:9
It is better to *t*........... Ps 118:8
in thee do I *t*............ Ps 143:8
he in whom I *t*........... Ps 144:2
*T* in the Lord.............Prov 3:5
He that *t* in his......... Prov 28:26
let him *t* in the........... Is 50:10
thy widows *t* in me....... Jer 49:11
*T* ye not in a ............ Mic 7:5
that *t* in him ............. Nah 1:7
He *t* in God ..... Matt 27:43
which *t* in themselves....Luke 18:9
See Jer 17:5; 2 Cor 1:9

**TRUTH**
a God of *t* and without
  iniquity................ Deut 32:4
the *t* in his heart.......... Ps 15:2
thou desirest *t*........... Ps 51:6
his *t* ... be thy ........... Ps 91:4
the *t* of the Lord ......... Ps 117:2
the way of *t*............ Ps 119:30
Buy the *t*............. Prov 23:23
for *t* is fallen ............ Is 59:14
valiant for the *t*............ Jer 9:3
the *t* to his .............. Zech 8:16
The law of *t*.............. Mal 2:6
of grace and *t* .........John 1:14
know the *t*............. John 8:32
the *t*, and the life ....... John 14:6
the Spirit of *t* .......... John 16:13
thy word is *t*...........John 17:17
What is *t*.............John 18:38
the *t* in
  unrighteousness ...... Rom 1:18
sincerity and *t*.......... 1 Cor 5:8
against the *t* ......... 2 Cor 13:8
the *t* in love............. Eph 4:15
ground of the *t* ........1 Tim 3:15
the word of the *t* ........2 Tim 2:15
err from the *t*.........James 5:19
See 1 Cor 13:6; 2 Tim 3:7

**TRY**
God left him, to *t* him ...2 Chr 32:31
he hath *t* me.......... Job 23:10
*t* my reins and............Ps 26:2
*t* the spirits ............. 1 John 4:1
See Prov 17:3; Is 28:16

**TWINKLING**
in the *t* of an eye....... 1 Cor 15:52

-------- **U** --------

**UNBELIEF**
Lord, I believe; help
  thou mine *u*..........Mark 9:24
shall their *u*......... Rom 3:3
shall all in *u*........... Rom 11:32
evil heart of *u*.......... Heb 3:12
See Matt 13:58; Mark 6:6

**UNCLEAN**
not call any man
  common or *u*......Acts 10:28
nothing *u* of itself ......Rom 14:14
touch not the *u*......... 2 Cor 6:17

**UNDEFILED**
Blessed are the *u* in
  the way..................Ps 119:1
*u* before God..........James 1:27
incorruptible, and *u*......1 Pet 1:4
See Song 5:2; 6:9; Heb 7:26

**UNDERSTAND**
readeth, let him *u* ..... Matt 24:15
that they might *u*.....Luke 24:45
not *u* my speech........John 8:43
There is none that *u*.....Rom 3:11
not heard shall *u* ....... Rom 15:21
*u* all mysteries...........1 Cor 13:2
I *u* as a child ........... 1 Cor 13:11
See 1 Cor 14:2; 2 Pet 2:12; 3:16

**UNDERSTANDING**
of God, in wisdom,
  and in *u* ................ Ex 31:3
*u* in the sight ............ Deut 4:6
*u* to discern.............. 1 Kin 3:11
wisdom and *u*......... 1 Kin 4:29
*u* of the times.......... 1 Chr 12:32
who had *u* ...........2 Chr 26:5
counsel and *u* ..........Job 12:13
*u* of the aged.......... Job 12:20
heart from *u*............ Job 17:4
the place of *u* .......... Job 28:12
giveth them *u* ......... Job 32:8
praises with *u* ......... Ps 47:7
heart shall be of *u* ........Ps 49:3
Give me *u* ............... Ps 119:34
give me *u* ...............Ps 119:169
his *u* is infinite ........... Ps 147:5
*u* shall keep thee ....... Prov 2:11
unto thine own *u*........Prov 3:5
Get wisdom, get *u* .......Prov 4:5
thy getting get *u*.........Prov 4:7
in the way of *u*........... Prov 9:6
is of great *u* ............Prov 14:29
*U* is a wellspring....... Prov 16:22
him that hath *u*........Prov 17:24
he that keepeth *u* .......Prov 19:8
no wisdom nor *u* ...... Prov 21:30
not the *u* of a man..... Prov 30:2
riches to men of *u*.......Eccl 9:11
of wisdom and *u* ...........Is 11:2
the way of *u* ............. Is 40:14
with knowledge and *u* ... Jer 3:15
with thine *u* ......... Ezek 28:4
mine *u* returned........Dan 4:34
yet without *u*..........Matt 15:16
so without *u*........... Mark 7:18
and with all the *u*.....Mark 12:33
at his *u*............... Luke 2:47
opened he their *u* .....Luke 24:45
*u* of the prudent..........1 Cor 1:9
pray with the *u* .........1 Cor 14:15
be not children in *u* ... 1 Cor 14:20
the *u* darkened ..... Eph 4:18
passeth all *u* ..............Phil 4:7
See Col 1:9; 2:2; 1 John 5:20

**UNFAITHFUL**
and dealt *u* like their
  fathers...................Ps 78:57
in an *u* man........... Prov 25:19

**UNFRUITFUL**
the word and he
  becometh *u* ..... Matt 13:22
*u* works of darkness.....Eph 5:11
they be not *u* .......... Titus 3:14
*u* in the knowledge...... 2 Pet 1:8

**UNGODLINESS**
from heaven
  against all *u* .......Rom 1:18
shall turn away *u*.......Rom 11:26
unto more *u* .......... 2 Tim 2:16
denying *u*.............. Titus 2:12

**UNGODLY**
Shouldest thou
  help the *u* ......... 2 Chr 19:2

me to the *u* .............. Job 16:11
counsel of the *u* .............Ps 1:1
*u* shall perish .............. Ps 1:6
against an *u* nation........ Ps 43:1
An *u* man diggeth .....Prov 16:27
died for the *u* ............ Rom 5:6
*u* and the sinner........1 Pet 4:18
perdition of *u* men ...... 2 Pet 3:7
*See* 1 Tim 1:9; 2 Pet 2:5

**UNHOLY**
difference between
   holy and *u* .............Lev 10:10
for *u* and profane........ 1 Tim 1:9
unthankful, *u*........... 2 Tim 3:2
an *u* thing...............Heb 10:29

**UNITY**
brethren to dwell
   together in *u* .......... Ps 133:1
*u* of the Spirit............. Eph 4:3
*u* of the faith............. Eph 4:13

**UNJUST**
from the deceitful
   and *u* man............... Ps 43:1
the hope of *u* men....... Prov 11:7
*u* gain increaseth....... Prov 28:8
An *u* man ............... Prov 29:27
the *u* knoweth........... Zeph 3:5
and on the *u*........... Matt 5:45
the *u* judge saith ...... Luke 18:6
extortioners, *u*.........Luke 18:11
of the just and *u*........Acts 24:15
before the *u* ..............1 Cor 6:1
just for the *u*............1 Pet 3:18
He that is *u* ............Rev 22:11
*See* Ps 82:2; Is 26:10

**UNKNOWN**
this inscription, To
   the *u* God.............. Acts 17:23
in an *u* tongue...........1 Cor 14:2

**UNPROFITABLE**
Should he reason with
   *u* talk ..................Job 15:3
the *u* servant ..........Matt 25:30
We are *u* servants .....Luke 17:10
*See* Titus 3:9; Philem 11

**UNREPROVEABLE**
unblameable and *u* in
   his sight ................ Col 1:22

**UNRIGHTEOUS**
the wicked to be an *u*
   witness.................. Ex 23:1
*u* decrees ................. Is 10:1
and the *u* man..........Is 55:7
Is God *u*.................. Rom 3:5
God is not *u*............ Heb 6:10
*See* Deut 25:16; 1 Cor 6:9

**UNRIGHTEOUSNESS**
friends of the
   mammon of *u*........ Luke 16:9
hold the truth in *u*......Rom 1:18
but obey *u* ............... Rom 2:8
if our *u* commend ...... Rom 3:5
as instruments of *u* .... Rom 6:13
Is there *u* with God..... Rom 9:14
with *u* ................. 2 Cor 6:14
pleasure in *u* .........2 Thess 2:12
the reward of *u*........ 2 Pet 2:13
from all *u* .............1 John 1:9
All *u* is sin ...........1 John 5:17
*See* Lev 19:15; Jer 22:13

**UNSEARCHABLE**
doeth great things and *u* ..Job 5:9
greatness is *u*............Ps 145:3
how *u* are his ..........Rom 11:33
*u* riches of Christ ........ Eph 3:8

**UNSPEAKABLE**
Thanks be unto God for his
   *u* gift................. 2 Cor 9:15

and heard *u* words ..... 2 Cor 12:4
with joy *u*.................1 Pet 1:8

**UNSPOTTED**
to keep himself *u* from
   the world...........James 1:27

**UNTHANKFUL**
kind unto the *u* and to
   the evil ...............Luke 6:35
*u*, unholy ............... 2 Tim 3:2

**UNWISE**
O foolish people and *u* .Deut 32:6
he is an *u* son............Hos 13:13
wise, and to the *u* ......Rom 1:14
be ye not *u*...............Eph 5:17

**UNWORTHY**
*u* of everlasting life.....Acts 13:46
*u* to judge............... 1 Cor 6:2
of the Lord, *u*..........1 Cor 11:27

**UPHOLD**
and *u* me with thy free
   spirit..................... Ps 51:12
that *u* my soul............Ps 54:4
*U* me according......... Ps 119:116
*u* all that fall ........... Ps 145:14
I will *u* thee................Is 41:10
my servant, whom I *u*.....Is 42:1
was none to *u* ........... Is 63:5
*u* all things...............Heb 1:3
*See* Ps 37:17; 41:12; 63:8

**UPRIGHT**
just *u* man is laughed
   to scorn ................Job 12:4
*U* men shall be..........Job 17:8
then shall I be *u* ......... Ps 19:13
Good and *u* is the Lord....Ps 25:8
of *u* conversation........ Ps 37:14
*u* shall have..............Ps 49:14
that the Lord is *u*.........Ps 92:15
assembly of the *u*.........Ps 111:1
*u* shall dwell............ Prov 2:21
tabernacle of the *u* ..... Prov 14:11
the prayer of the *u*......Prov 15:8
the *u* shall have........ Prov 28:10
hath made man *u* ......Eccl 7:29
the *u* love thee...........Song 1:4
*See* Mic 7:2; Hab 2:4

**UPRIGHTNESS**
and in *u* of heart
   with thee.............. 1 Kin 3:6
pleasure in *u* .......... 1 Chr 29:17
the *u* of thy ways .........Job 4:6
unto man his *u* ........Job 33:23
and *u* preserve me ......Ps 25:21
the land of *u*............Ps 143:10
the paths of *u*...........Prov 2:13
*See* Ps 111:8; Prov 14:2

---

**V**

---

**VAIN**
thy God in *v*.................Ex 20:7
imagine a *v* thing.......... Ps 2:1
walketh in a *v* shew .....Ps 39:6
for *v* is the .................Ps 60:11
all men in *v* ............Ps 89:47
they labour in *v*.......... Ps 127:1
followeth *v* persons .... Prov 12:11
beauty is *v*............ Prov 31:30
his *v* life which he ......Eccl 6:12
Seek ye me in *v*........... Is 45:19
It is *v* to serve............Mal 3:14
use not *v* repetitions .... Matt 6:7
*v* they do worship ..... Matt 15:9
the sword in *v* ..........Rom 13:4
have believed in *v* ....1 Cor 15:2
grace of God in *v*........ 2 Cor 6:1
or had run, in *v* ...........Gal 2:2
*v* talkers and deceivers . Titus 1:10
man's religion is *v* .....James 1:26

*v* conversation...........1 Pet 1:18
*See* Prov 1:17; Rom 1:21

**VALUE**
ye are all physicians
   of no *v*.................Job 13:4
of more *v* .............. Matt 10:31
*See* Lev 27:16; Job 28:16

**VANISH**
shall *v* away ................Is 51:6
it shall *v*.................. 1 Cor 13:8
ready to *v* away.......... Heb 8:13

**VANITY**
I made to possess
   months of *v* .............Job 7:3
trust in *v*................Job 15:31
not hear *v*................Job 35:13
They speak *v* every ....... Ps 12:2
altogether *v*...............Ps 39:5
degree are *v* .............Ps 62:9
is like to *v*............. Ps 144:4
gotten by *v*............. Prov 13:11
far from me *v* ........... Prov 30:8
that increase *v*...........Eccl 6:11
youth are *v* ..............Eccl 11:10
the sieve of *v* ............Is 30:28
incense to *v*..............Jer 18:15
for very *v* .............. Hab 2:13
subject to *v*..............Rom 8:20
in the *v* of their..........Eph 4:17
swelling words of *v*..... 2 Pet 2:18
*See* Eccl 1:2; Jer 10:8

**VARIABLENESS**
with whom is no *v* .... James 1:17

**VEIL**
*v* of the temple was
   rent in twain ........Matt 27:51
within the *v* ............ Heb 6:19

**VENGEANCE**
To me belongeth *v* ....Deut 32:35
the day of *v* .............. Prov 6:34
the Lord's *v*.............. Is 34:8
garments of *v* for..........Is 59:17
the day of *v* ...............Is 61:2
the Lord's *v*.............. Jer 51:6
yet *v* suffereth...........Acts 28:4
suffering the *v*........... Jude 7
*See* Mic 5:15; Nah 1:2; Rom 2:19

**VESSEL**
he is a chosen *v*..........Acts 9:15
possess his *v*...........1 Thess 4:4
shall be a *v*..............2 Tim 2:21
the weaker *v*............1 Pet 3:7
*See* Is 52:11; 65:4

**VICTORY**
the *v* that day..........2 Sam 19:2
and the *v*............1 Chr 29:11
gotten him the *v*.......... Ps 98:1
judgment unto *v* ......Matt 12:20
the *v* that ............1 John 5:4
*See* Is 25:8; 1 Cor 15:54

**VILE**
his sons made
   themselves *v* ........ 1 Sam 3:13
*v* in your sight...........Job 18:3
I am *v*...................Job 40:4
*v* person is contemned.... Ps 15:4
The *v* person ............. Is 32:5
from the *v* .............Jer 15:19
I am become *v*...........Lam 1:11
stand up a *v* person .....Dan 11:21
and make thee *v*........ Nah 3:6
unto *v* affections ....... Rom 1:26
change our *v* body....... Phil 3:21
man in *v* raiment.......James 2:2
*See* 2 Sam 1:21; Job 30:8

**VIOLENCE**
the earth was filled
   with *v*..................Gen 6:11

## W

him that loveth *v* . . . . . . . . . . . Ps 11:5
I have seen *v* . . . . . . . . . . . . . . Ps 55:9
*v* of your hands . . . . . . . . . . . . Ps 58:2
from deceit and *v* . . . . . . . . . . Ps 72:14
*v* covereth them . . . . . . . . . . . Ps 73:6
drink the wine of *v* . . . . . Prov 4:17
but *v* covereth . . . . . . . Prov 10:6, 11
he had done no *v* . . . . . . . . . Is 53:9
*V* shall no more . . . . . . . . . . Is 60:18
the land with *v* . . . . . . . . . . Ezek 8:17
of thee with *v* . . . . . . . . Ezek 28:16
who store up *v* . . . . . . . . Amos 3:10
for spoiling and *v* . . . . . . . . Hab 1:3
one covereth *v* . . . . . . . . . . . Mal 2:16
heaven suffereth *v* . . . . . Matt 11:12
Do *v* to no man . . . . . . . . . Luke 3:14
*See* Mic 2:2; 6:12; Zeph 1:9

**VIRGIN**
a *v* shall conceive . . . . . . . . . . Is 7:14
O thou oppressed *v*,
  daughter of . . . . . . . . . . . . Is 23:12
O *v* daughter . . . . . . . . . . . . . . Is 47:1
man marrieth a *v* . . . . . . . . . Is 62:5
*v* daughter . . . . . . . . . . . . . . . Jer 14:17
a *v* shall be with child . . . Matt 1:23

**VIRTUE**
that *v* had gone out
  of him . . . . . . . . . . . . . . . Mark 5:30
*v* out of him . . . . . . . . . . . Luke 6:19
perceive that *v* . . . . . . . . . Luke 8:46
there be any *v* . . . . . . . . . . Phil 4:8
add to your faith *v* . . . . . . . 2 Pet 1:5

**VIRTUOUS**
know that thou art a
  *v* woman . . . . . . . . . . . . . Ruth 3:11
*v* woman is a crown . . . . Prov 12:4
can find a *v* woman . . . . Prov 31:10
daughters have done *v* Prov 31:29

**VISION**
chased away as a *v* of
  the night . . . . . . . . . . . . . Job 20:8
there is no *v* . . . . . . . . . . Prov 29:18
of the valley of *v* . . . . . . . . . . Is 22:1
they err in *v* . . . . . . . . . . . . . Is 28:7
no *v* from the Lord . . . . . . Lam 2:9
I have multiplied *v* . . . . Hos 12:10
men shall see *v* . . . . . . . . . Joel 2:28
one of his *v* . . . . . . . . . . . . Zech 13:4
the *v* to no man . . . . . . . . Matt 17:9
seen a *v* of angels . . . . . Luke 24:23
the heavenly *v* . . . . . . . . Acts 26:19
*See* Job 4:13; Ezek 1:1; 8:3

**VOCATION**
walk worthy of the *v* . . . . . Eph 4:1

**VOICE**
and obey his *v* . . . . . . . . . . Ex 23:21
*v* of God speaking . . . . . . Deut 4:33
a still small *v* . . . . . . . . . . 1 Kin 19:12
The *v* of him . . . . . . . . . . . . . Is 40:3
*v* of one crying . . . . . . . . . Matt 3:3
*v* of the Son of God . . . . John 5:25
for they know his *v* . . . . John 10:4
This *v* came not . . . . . . John 12:30
truth heareth my *v* . . . . John 18:37
*v* of the archangel . . . 1 Thess 4:16
if any man hear my *v* . . . Rev 3:20
*See* Gen 3:17; Ps 58:5

**VOID**
earth was without
  form, and *v* . . . . . . . . . . . Gen 1:2
*v* of counsel . . . . . . . . . . Deut 32:28
made *v* . . . covenant . . . . . Ps 89:39
made *v* thy law . . . . . . Ps 119:126
is *v* of wisdom . . . . . . . . . Prov 11:12
return unto me *v* . . . . . . . . Is 55:11
without form, and *v* . . . . Jer 4:23
make *v* the counsel . . . . . Jer 19:7
She is empty, and *v* . . . . . Nah 2:10
*v* of offence . . . . . . . . . . Acts 24:16
*See* Num 30:12; Rom 3:31; 4:14

**WAGES**
content with your *w* . . . . Luke 3:14
he . . . receiveth *w* . . . . . John 4:36
*w* of sin is death . . . . . . . Rom 6:23
loved the *w* . . . . . . . . . . . . 2 Pet 2:15
*See* Ezek 29:18; Mal 3:5

**WAIT**
I have *w* for thy
  salvation, O Lord . . . . . Gen 49:18
I *w* for the Lord . . . . . . . . 2 Kin 6:33
time will I *w* . . . . . . . . . . . . Job 14:14
when I *w* for light . . . . . . Job 30:26
*W* on the Lord . . . . . . . . . . Ps 27:14
Our soul *w* . . . . . . . . . . . . . Ps 33:20
Lord, and *w* patiently . . . . Ps 37:7
*w* on thy name . . . . . . . . . . Ps 52:9
my soul *w* upon God . . . . . Ps 62:1
Praise *w* for thee . . . . . . . . Ps 65:1
them that *w* on thee . . . . . Ps 69:6
soul *w* for the Lord . . . . . Ps 130:6
*w* on the Lord . . . . . . . . Prov 20:22
they that *w* . . . . . . . . . . . . Is 40:31
shall *w* for his law . . . . . . . Is 42:4
*w* for light . . . . . . . . . . . . . . Is 59:9
quietly *w* for the . . . . . . . Lam 3:26
he that *w* . . . . . . . . . . . . . Dan 12:12
*w* upon me . . . . . . . . . . . Zech 11:11
*w* for the kingdom . . . . Mark 15:43
*w* for their lord . . . . . . . Luke 12:36
*w* for the promise . . . . . . Acts 1:4
*w* for the adoption . . . . . Rom 8:23
we with patience *w* . . . . Rom 8:25
*w* for the hope . . . . . . . . . . Gal 5:5
*w* for his Son . . . . . . . . 1 Thess 1:10
*See* Num 3:10; Neh 12:44

**WALK**
*w* before me, and be thou
  perfect . . . . . . . . . . . . . . Gen 17:1
before whom I *w* . . . . . . Gen 24:40
Isaac did *w* . . . . . . . . . . . Gen 48:15
*w* in my law . . . . . . . . . . . . . Ex 16:4
I will *w* among you . . . . Lev 26:12
*w* in the midst . . . . . . . . Deut 23:14
and *w* by the way . . . . . . Judg 5:10
*w* all that night . . . . . . . 2 Sam 2:29
I *w* through the valley . . . . Ps 23:4
*w* in mine integrity . . . . . Ps 26:11
I may *w* before God . . . . . Ps 56:13
that *w* uprightly . . . . . . . . Ps 84:11
who *w* upon the wings . . Ps 104:3
*w* before the Lord . . . . . . Ps 116:9
I *w* in the midst . . . . . . . . Ps 138:7
he that *w* uprightly . . . . Prov 10:9
*w* with wise men . . . . . Prov 13:20
Whoso *w* uprightly . . . . Prov 28:18
fool *w* in darkness . . . . . . Eccl 2:14
let us *w* in the light . . . . . . . Is 2:5
that *w* in darkness . . . . . . . . Is 9:2
Isaiah hath *w* naked . . . . . Is 20:3
the way, *w* ye in it . . . . . . . Is 30:21
redeemed shall *w* there . . . Is 35:9
*w*, and not faint . . . . . . . . . Is 40:31
that *w* in darkness . . . . . . . Is 50:10
*w* in the light . . . . . . . . . . . Is 50:11
way, and *w* therein . . . . . . Jer 6:16
*w* to direct his steps . . . . Jer 10:23
that *w* in pride . . . . . . . . . . Dan 4:37
just shall *w* in them . . . . . Hos 14:9
to *w* humbly . . . . . . . . . . . . Mic 6:8
have *w* to and fro . . . . . . . Zech 1:11
*w* mournfully . . . . . . . . . . . Mal 3:14
he *w* on the water . . . . . Matt 14:29
Rise up and *w* . . . . . . . . . Luke 5:23
I must *w* today . . . . . . . . Luke 13:33
thy bed, and *w* . . . . . . . . . . John 5:8
not *w* in darkness . . . . . . John 8:12
any man *w* in the day . . John 11:9
rise up and *w* . . . . . . . . . . . Acts 3:6
also *w* in the steps . . . . . . Rom 4:12
*w* in newness of life . . . . . Rom 6:4

*w* not after the flesh . . . Rom 8:1, 4
For we *w* by faith . . . . . . . 2 Cor 5:7
*w* according to this . . . . . . Gal 6:16
in time past ye *w* . . . . . . . . Eph 2:2
we should *w* in them . . . . Eph 2:10
*w* worthy of the vocation . . . Eph 4:1
as other Gentiles *w* . . . . . . Eph 4:17
*w* circumspectly . . . . . . . . Eph 5:15
mark them which *w* . . . . . Phil 3:17
For many *w* . . . . . . . . . . . . . Phil 3:18
might *w* worthy . . . . . . . . . Col 1:10
which ye also *w* . . . . . . . . . Col 3:7
*w* worthy of God . . . . . 1 Thess 2:12
*w* and to please God . . . 1 Thess 4:1
*w* honestly
  toward them . . . . . . . 1 Thess 4:12
that *w* disorderly . . . . . 2 Thess 3:6
*w* in lasciviousness . . . . . . 1 Pet 4:3
*w* about, seeking . . . . . . . . 1 Pet 5:8
we *w* in the light . . . . . . . 1 John 1:7
also so to *w* . . . . . . . . . . . 1 John 2:6
*See* Gal 5:16; Eph 5:2

**WANT** (*v.*)
my shepherd; I shall
  not *w* . . . . . . . . . . . . . . . . Ps 23:1
Lord shall not *w* . . . . . . . . Ps 34:10
that *w* understanding . . . Prov 9:4
the wicked shall *w* . . . . Prov 13:25
so that he *w* nothing . . . . Eccl 6:2
none shall *w* . . . . . . . . . . . Is 34:16
have *w* all things . . . . . . Jer 44:18
*See* Eccl 1:15; Dan 5:27

**WAR** (*n.*)
the *w* was of God . . . . . . 1 Chr 5:22
though *w* should rise . . . . Ps 27:3
maketh *w* to cease . . . . . . Ps 46:9
*w* was in his heart . . . . . . Ps 55:21
that delight in *w* . . . . . . . Ps 68:30
good advice make *w* . . . Prov 20:18
a time of *w* . . . . . . . . . . . . Eccl 3:8
discharge in that *w* . . . . . Eccl 8:8
they learn *w* . . . . . . . . . . . . Is 2:4
shall see no *w* . . . . . . . . Jer 42:14
men averse from *w* . . . . . Mic 2:8
of *w* and rumours
  of *w* . . . . . . . . . . . . . . . Matt 24:6
*w* against another . . . . Luke 14:31
*w* and commotions . . . . Luke 21:9
*w* and fightings . . . . . . . James 4:1
was *w* in heaven . . . . . . . Rev 12:7
*See* Eccl 9:18; Dan 7:21

**WAR** (*v.*)
He teacheth my
  hands to *w* . . . . . . . . 2 Sam 22:35
people go out to *w* . . . . 2 Chr 6:34
they that *w* . . . . . . . . . . . . Is 41:12
*w* after the flesh . . . . . . . 2 Cor 10:3
*w* a good warfare . . . . . . 1 Tim 1:18
No man that *w* . . . . . . . . 2 Tim 2:4
*w* in your members . . . . . James 4:1
ye fight and *w* . . . . . . . . James 4:2
*w* against the soul . . . . . . 1 Pet 2:11
*See* 1 Kin 14:19; Rom 7:23

**WASH**
Go and *w* in Jordan
  seven times . . . . . . . . 2 Kin 5:10
may I not *w* in them . . . 2 Kin 5:12
If I *w* myself . . . . . . . . . . . Job 9:30
*w* away the filth . . . . . . . Job 14:19
When I *w* my steps . . . . . Job 29:6
I will *w* mine hands . . . . . Ps 26:6
*W* me thoroughly . . . . . . . Ps 51:2
and *w* my hands . . . . . . . Ps 73:13
yet is not *w* . . . . . . . . . . Prov 30:12
*w* with milk . . . . . . . . . . Song 5:12
*W* you, make you clean . . . . . Is 1:16
though thou *w* thee . . . . . Jer 2:22
*w* thine heart . . . . . . . . . . Jer 4:14
thou *w* in water . . . . . . . Ezek 16:4
and *w* thy face . . . . . . . . . Matt 6:17
*w* his hands . . . . . . . . . . Matt 27:24

except they w............ Mark 7:3
began to w his feet ..... Luke 7:38
w, and came seeing ..... John 9:7
w their stripes.......... Acts 16:33
w away thy sins........ Acts 22:16
but ye are w ............. 1 Cor 6:11
w with pure water...... Heb 10:22
sow that was w ........ 2 Pet 2:22
w us from our sins ...... Rev 1:5
and have w their robes ... Rev 7:14
*See* Neh 4:23; Titus 3:5

### WATCH (n.)
as a w in the night........ Ps 90:4
prevent the night w .... Ps 119:148
make the w strong ....... Jer 51:12
stand upon my w......... Hab 2:1
*See* Matt 14:25; Luke 2:8

### WATCH (v.)
the Lord w between me
    and thee.............. Gen 31:49
not w over my sin ....... Job 14:16
The wicked w............ Ps 37:32
w for the morning.......Ps 130:6
w for iniquity ............Is 29:20
All my familiars w .......Jer 20:10
will w to see ............. Hab 2:1
W therefore............ Matt 24:42
W and pray ............. Matt 26:41
W ye therefore........ Mark 13:35
Therefore w ...........Acts 20:31
w and be sober ........ 1 Thess 5:6
w for your souls ........Heb 13:17
w unto prayer ............ 1 Pet 4:7
*See* 1 Cor 16:13; 2 Tim 4:5; Rev 3:2

### WATER
Unstable as w............ Gen 49:4
land of brooks and w.... Deut 8:7
became as w........... Josh 7:5
and are as w .......... 2 Sam 14:14
drink no w ............. 1 Kin 13:22
with w of affliction... 1 Kin 22:27
poured out like w....... Ps 22:14
beside the still w ........ Ps 23:2
w that be above...........Ps 148:4
Drink w out of.......... Prov 5:15
Stolen w are sweet ..... Prov 9:17
is like deep w ........... Prov 20:5
w to a thirsty soul ..... Prov 25:25
bread upon the w........ Eccl 11:1
a well of living w ........ Song 4:15
w cannot quench love.... Song 8:7
shall w break out ......... Is 35:6
poor and needy seek w.... Is 41:17
passeth through the w .... Is 43:2
path in the mighty w ..... Is 43:16
w in the wilderness ...... Is 43:20
pour w upon him........... Is 44:3
come ye to the w .......... Is 55:1
fountain of living w ...... Jer 2:13
I sprinkle clean w .....Ezek 36:25
a thirst for w.............Amos 8:11
baptize you with w..... Matt 3:11
a cup of cold w ........ Matt 10:42
he took w, and
    washed.............. Matt 27:24
a cup of w to drink ..... Mark 9:41
filled with w ......... Luke 8:23
raging of the w ........ Luke 8:24
his finger in w ........ Luke 16:24
I baptize with w ....... John 1:26
man be born of w..... John 3:5
the moving of the w..... John 5:3
rivers of living w....... John 7:38
blood and w ........... John 19:34
baptized with w ....... Acts 1:5
indeed baptized
    with w............. Acts 1:16
in perils of w.......... 2 Cor 11:26
the washing of w........ Eph 5:26
were saved by w ....... 1 Pet 3:20
wells without w ........ 2 Pet 2:17

he that came by w......1 John 5:6
take the w of life.........Rev 22:17
*See* Ps 29:3; Jer 51:13; Ezek 32:2

### WAY
all flesh had
    corrupted his w ....... Gen 6:12
and prosper thy w.......Gen 24:40
thy w is perverse ......Num 22:32
to walk in his w.......... Deut 8:6
w of all the earth ..... Josh 23:14
the right w............ 1 Sam 12:23
his w is perfect ....... 2 Sam 22:31
I go the w............... 1 Kin 2:2
God, to walk in his w .... 1 Kin 2:3
them the good w ...... 2 Chr 6:27
a right w for us .......... Ezra 8:21
man whose w is hid ..... Job 3:23
he knoweth the w ...... Job 23:10
w of the righteous.......... Ps 1:6
perish from the w ......... Ps 2:12
Teach me thy w, O Lord...Ps 27:11
w that is not good ........Ps 36:4
Commit thy w ............. Ps 37:5
w is their folly ............Ps 49:13
thy w may be known ...... Ps 67:2
He made a w ........... Ps 78:50
not known my w .......... Ps 95:10
in a perfect w ........... Ps 101:2
walk in his w ........... Ps 119:3
my w were directed ...... Ps 119:5
the w of truth..........Ps 119:30
walketh in his w.........Ps 128:1
any wicked w in me .... Ps 139:24
w of his saints .......... Prov 2:8
w acknowledge him ...... Prov 3:6
the w of man ............Prov 5:21
consider her w...........Prov 6:6
the w of life............ Prov 6:23
The w of a fool......... Prov 12:15
w of the slothful man ... Prov 15:19
When a man's w
    please the ............Prov 16:7
a child in the w ........ Prov 22:6
heart in the w......... Prov 23:19
a lion in the w ........ Prov 26:13
w of the spirit............ Eccl 11:5
shall be in the w ........ Eccl 12:5
teach us of his w...........Is 2:3
a highway ... and a w ..... Is 35:8
My w is hid .............. Is 40:27
walk in his w ........... Is 42:24
direct all his w............ Is 45:13
are your w my w.......... Is 55:8
delight to know my w ..... Is 58:2
according to his w.......Jer 17:10
one heart, and one w....Jer 32:39
ask the w to Zion ....... Jer 50:5
from his wicked w......Ezek 3:18
The w of the Lord ..... Ezek 18:29
every one on his w ........ Joel 2:7
Lord hath his w.......... Nah 1:3
Consider your w ....... Hag 1:5, 7
shall prepare the w....... Mal 3:1
and broad is the w....... Matt 7:13
Go not into the w....... Matt 10:5
w of God in truth ...... Matt 22:16
faint by the w............. Mark 8:3
clothes in the w ...... Luke 19:36
teachest the w
    of God .............. Luke 20:21
up some other w ...... John 10:1
the w ye know.......... John 14:4
I am the w, the truth ... John 14:6
any of this w.............. Acts 9:2
the Lord in the w ...... Acts 9:27
the w of salvation ...... Acts 16:17
the w of God........... Acts 18:26
stir about that w........Acts 19:23
after the w............. Acts 24:14
a w to escape .......... 1 Cor 10:13
a more excellent w....1 Cor 12:31
the w into the holiest..... Heb 9:8

By a new and living w... Heb 10:20
unstable in all his w .... James 1:8
the error of his w ..... James 5:20
w of truth.............. 2 Pet 2:2
w of righteousness ..... 2 Pet 2:21
*See* Hos 2:6; Luke 10:31

### WEAK
then shall I be w........Judg 16:7
strengthened the w .......Job 4:3
O Lord; for I am w .........Ps 6:2
the w hands ............... Is 35:3
the flesh is w ......... Matt 26:41
support the w ......... Acts 20:35
not w in faith ......... Rom 4:19
w through the flesh ..... Rom 8:3
the w things ...........1 Cor 1:27
many are w and sickly... 1 Cor 11:30
presence is w ......... 2 Cor 10:10
Who is w............... 2 Cor 11:29
for when I am w ....... 2 Cor 12:10
to the w and beggarly ..... Gal 4:9
unto the w vessel......... 1 Pet 3:7
*See* Job 12:21; 1 Thess 5:14

### WEAKNESS
w of God is stronger
    than men...........1 Cor 1:25
I was with you in w...... 1 Cor 2:3
it is sown in w........ 1 Cor 15:43
*See* 2 Cor 12:9; 13:4; Heb 7:18

### WEALTH
the w which God ...... 1 Sam 2:32
asked riches, w .........2 Chr 1:11
their days in w ......... Job 21:13
not increase thy w........Ps 44:12
trust in their w ...........Ps 49:6
W in riches .......... Ps 112:3
filled with thy w........Prov 5:10
W gotten by vanity .... Prov 13:11
W maketh many
    friends................Prov 19:4
we have our w .........Acts 19:25
one another's w ....... 1 Cor 10:24
*See* Ruth 2:1; Ezra 9:12

### WEARY
the w be at rest.......... Job 3:17
soul is w of my life....... Job 10:1
neither be w............. Prov 3:11
lest he be w of thee..... Prov 25:17
None shall be w...........Is 5:27
but will ye w my God...... Is 7:13
cause the w to rest ....... Is 28:12
rock in a w land........... Is 32:2
run, and not be w ....... Is 40:31
him that is w ............. Is 50:4
I am w with repenting ... Jer 15:6
satiated the w soul ..... Jer 31:25
not w in well doing...2 Thess 3:13
*See* Judg 4:21; Hab 2:13

### WEEPING
w may endure .............Ps 30:5
fasting, and with w...... Joel 2:12
be w and gnashing ..... Matt 8:12
at the sepulchre w..... John 20:11
*See* Num 25:6; Mal 2:13

### WELL
is a w of life............. Prov 10:11
w of living waters ...... Song 4:15
the w of salvation .........Is 12:3
a w of water ........... John 4:14
w without water.........2 Pet 2:17
*See* Gen 21:19; 2 Sam 17:18

### WEPT
beheld the city, and w...Luke 19:41
Jesus w................ John 11:35
*See* 2 Sam 12:22; Ps 69:10

### WHATSOEVER
and w he doeth shall
    prosper................. Ps 1:3
w God doeth ........... Eccl 3:14

*w* is more ............... Matt 5:37
*w* ye would that men ....Matt 7:12
and *w* is right .......... Matt 20:4
*w* things are true ....... Phil 4:8
*See* John 15:16; Rom 14:23

## WHILE
Lord is with you, *w* ye be
  with him ............. 2 Chr 15:2
Seek ye the Lord *w* ....... Is 55:6
*w* it was yet day .......... Jer 15:9
*w* it is day ............... John 9:4
*See* 2 Sam 7:19; Acts 20:11

## WHITE
leprous, *w* as snow .... Num 12:10
garments be always *w* ....Eccl 9:8
My beloved is *w* ........ Song 5:10
be as *w* as snow .......... Is 1:18
not make one hair *w* ... Matt 5:36
*w* already to harvest.... John 4:35
give him a *w* stone ...... Rev 2:17
walk with me in *w*........Rev 3:4
*See* Dan 11:35; 12:10; Matt 17:2

## WHITER
I shall be *w* than snow .... Ps 51:7

## WHOLE
the *w* duty of man...... Eccl 12:13
be made *w* again ........ Jer 19:11
when it was *w* .......... Ezek 15:5
thy *w* body.............. Matt 5:29
that be *w* .............. Matt 9:12
gain the *w* world ...... Matt 16:26
They that are *w*........ Mark 2:17
*w* creation groaneth.... Rom 8:22
If the *w* body ......... 1 Cor 12:17
Put on the *w* armour .....Eph 6:11
your *w* spirit..........1 Thess 5:23
keep the *w* law .........James 2:10
sins of the *w* world .....1 John 2:2
the *w* world lieth ......1 John 5:19
*See* Matt 15:31; John 5:6; 7:23

## WICKED
destroy the righteous
  with the *w*........... Gen 18:23
in thy *w* heart........... Deut 15:9
*w* shall be silent ........ 1 Sam 2:9
the *w* cease from ........ Job 3:17
of the *w* shall come...... Job 8:22
If I be *w*................. Job 9:29
Wherefore do the *w* ...... Job 21:7
the *w* is reserved ...... Job 21:30
angry with the *w* ...........Ps 7:11
*w* shall be turned ......... Ps 9:17
*w* through the pride....... Ps 10:4
Upon the *w* he shall rain ....Ps 11:6
*w* walk on every side ..... Ps 12:8
not sit with the *w*........Ps 26:5
Evil shall slay the *w* ..... Ps 34:21
The *w* borroweth......... Ps 37:21
The *w* watcheth ......... Ps 37:32
*w* are estranged .......... Ps 58:3
*w* perish at the .......... Ps 68:2
shall the *w* triumph ......Ps 94:3
any *w* way in me......Ps 139:24
the *w* will he destroy....Ps 145:20
*w* shall fall by his ....... Prov 11:5
The *w* is driven away .....Prov 14:32
*w* flee when no man.....Prov 28:1
Be not over much *w*.....Eccl 7:17
I saw the *w* buried....... Eccl 8:10
evil, and the *w*............ Is 13:11
his grave with the *w*...... Is 53:9
Let the *w* forsake........... Is 55:7
the *w* are like ......... Is 57:20
and desperately *w*.........Jer 17:9
*w* man shall die......... Ezek 3:18
and give *w* counsel...... Ezek 11:2
that the *w* should die....Ezek 18:23
*w* restore the pledge ...Ezek 33:15
*w* shall do wickedly .... Dan 12:10
with the *w* balances ...... Mic 6:11

at all acquit the *w* ........Nah 1:3
spirits more *w*......... Matt 12:45
sever the *w* from ...... Matt 13:49
O thou *w* servant ....... Matt 18:32
Thou *w* and slothful... Matt 25:26
thou *w* servant ........ Luke 19:22
*w* hands have .............Acts 2:23
that *w* person............1 Cor 5:13
fiery darts of the *w* ...... Eph 6:16
by *w* works ................Col 1:21
then shall that *W* be....2 Thess 2:8
*See* Eccl 9:2; 2 Pet 2:7; 3:17

## WICKEDNESS
*W* proceedeth from ....1 Sam 24:13
iniquity, and sow *w* ........Job 4:8
Thy *w* may hurt a man .. Job 35:8
Oh let the *w* of the.......... Ps 7:9
*W* is in the midst ........ Ps 55:11
Yea, in heart ye work *w*....Ps 58:2
in the tents of *w* .........Ps 84:10
eat the bread of *w* ....... Prov 4:17
*w* is an abomination ....Prov 8:7
fall by his own *w* ....... Prov 11:5
but *w* overthroweth....Prov 13:6
his *w* shall be
  shewed..............Prov 26:26
know the *w* of folly...... Eccl 7:25
*w* burneth as the fire......Is 9:18
hast trusted in thy *w* ....Is 47:10
own *w* shall correct ..... Jer 2:19
repented him of his *w*.... Jer 8:6
*w* of your fathers ........Jer 44:9
turn not from his *w* .... Ezek 3:19
him out for his *w* ...... Ezek 31:11
*w* of their doings ...... Hos 9:15
treasures of *w* ........... Mic 6:10
he said, This is *w* ........ Zech 5:8
The border of *w* .........Mal 1:4
they that work *w* ........Mal 3:15
covetousness, *w*........ Mark 7:22
ravening and *w* ........ Luke 11:39
*w*, covetousness....... Rom 1:29
of malice and *w*........ 1 Cor 5:8
against spiritual *w*...... Eph 6:12
world lieth in *w*........1 John 5:19
*See* Gen 6:5; Ps 94:23

## WIFE
and rejoice with the
  *w* of thy youth.........Prov 5:18
Whoso findeth a *w* .... Prov 18:22
and a prudent *w*.......Prov 19:14
with the *w* whom thou... Eccl 9:9
I have married a *w* ....Luke 14:20
Remember Lot's *w* .... Luke 17:32
sanctified by the *w* ......1 Cor 7:14
the head of the *w*...... Eph 5:23
the Lamb's *w* ..........Rev 21:9
*See* 1 Tim 3:2; 5:9; Titus 1:6

## WILL
I *w*; be thou clean ....... Matt 8:3
so it is not the *w*........Matt 18:14
not as I *w*, but as ......Matt 26:39
shall do the *w* of God...Mark 3:35
*w* of the flesh ...........John 1:13
*w* of him that sent me... John 4:34
The *w* of the Lord ...... Acts 21:14
for to *w* is present.......Rom 7:18
both to *w* and to do ..... Phil 2:13
I *w* therefore ............1 Tim 2:8
whosoever *w* ...........Rev 22:17
*See* Rom 9:15; Eph 1:11; Heb 2:4

## WILLING
whosoever is of a
  *w* heart ................Ex 35:5
and with a *w* mind ....1 Chr 28:9
*w* to consecrate his.....1 Chr 29:5
people shall be *w*........ Ps 110:3
spirit indeed is *w*....... Matt 26:41
*w* rather to be ........... 2 Cor 5:8
first a *w* mind........... 2 Cor 8:12
*w* to communicate ....1 Tim 6:18

not *w* that any...........2 Pet 3:9
*See* Luke 22:42; Philem 14

## WIN
thought to *w* them for
  himself ................2 Chr 32:1
he that *w* souls ........Prov 11:30
that I may *w* Christ....... Phil 3:8

## WIND
is desperate, which
  are as *w*................. Job 6:26
my life is *w* ..............Job 7:7
shall inherit the *w* .....Prov 11:29
Prophesy unto the *w* .. Ezek 37:9
they have sown the *w* ... Hos 8:7
createth the *w* ......... Amos 4:13
shaken with the *w*..... Matt 11:7
The *w* bloweth where ... John 3:8
every *w* of doctrine..... Eph 4:14
*See* James 1:6; Jude 12

## WINGS
hide me under the
  shadow of thy *w*....... Ps 17:8
he did fly upon the *w*..... Ps 18:10
shadow of thy *w*......... Ps 36:7
had *w* like a dove ........ Ps 55:6
in the shadow of thy *w* ... Ps 57:1
in the covert of thy *w*..... Ps 61:4
*w* of a dove .............Ps 68:13
and under his *w* .......... Ps 91:4
the *w* of the morning... Ps 139:9
make themselves *w* .... Prov 23:5
mount up with *w*......... Is 40:31
healing in his *w*.......... Mal 4:2
*See* Zech 5:9; Matt 23:37

## WISDOM
they die, even
  without *w* ..............Job 4:21
*w* shall die with you......Job 12:2
*W* is the principal....... Prov 4:7
better is it to get *w* ....Prov 16:16
getteth *w* loveth........Prov 19:8
cease from thine
  own *w* ................ Prov 23:4
For in much *w*...........Eccl 1:18
and by my *w* .............Is 10:13
*w* of their wise men ...... Is 29:14
what *w* is in them ........ Jer 8:9
the man of *w* ............ Mic 6:9
But *w* is justified ....... Matt 11:19
with *w* of words .........1 Cor 1:17
and the *w* of God .......1 Cor 1:24
God is made unto
  us *w* ................... 1 Cor 1:30
we speak *w* among
  them................... 1 Cor 2:6
*w* of this world ......... 1 Cor 3:19
not with fleshly *w* .......2 Cor 1:12
his will in all *w*.......... Col 1:9
Walk in *w* toward them ... Col 4:5
any of you lack *w* ...... James 1:5
*w* that is from above .. James 3:17
and *w*, and strength......Rev 5:12
Here is *w*...............Rev 13:18
*See* Eccl 1:16; Rom 11:33

## WISE
to be desired to
  make one *w* ............ Gen 3:6
gift blindeth the *w*....... Ex 23:8
*w* and understanding ... Deut 4:6
O that they were *w* ....Deut 32:29
a *w* ... heart ............ 1 Kin 3:12
He is *w* in heart..........Job 9:4
vain man would be *w* .... Job 11:12
he that is *w* may be...... Job 22:2
men are not always *w*.... Job 32:9
Be *w* now therefore ..... Ps 2:10
making *w* the simple..... Ps 19:7
hath left off to be *w* ..... Ps 36:3
when will ye be *w* ........Ps 94:8
Whoso is *w* .............Ps 107:43
*w* man will hear ......... Prov 1:5

## WISER

*w* in thine own eyes......Prov 3:7
consider... and be *w*.... Prov 6:6
If thou be *w*..............Prov 9:12
winneth souls is *w*.....Prov 11:30
*w* in heart shall be.....Prov 16:21
A *w* king scattereth....Prov 20:26
my son, and be *w*...... Prov 23:19
be *w*, and make........ Prov 27:11
I said, I will be *w* ....... Eccl 7:23
righteous, and the *w* ..... Eccl 9:1
The words of the *w*.....Eccl 12:11
the *w* counsellors ......... Is 19:11
And they that be *w* ...... Dan 12:3
be ye therefore *w*...... Matt 10:16
things from the *w*...... Matt 11:25
both to the *w*............ Rom 1:14
Be not *w* in your own ...Rom 12:16
Where is the *w* ......... 1 Cor 1:20
ye are *w* in Christ....... 1 Cor 4:10
to make thee *w*.......2 Tim 3:15
*See* Is 5:21; Matt 25:2

## WISER

For he was *w* than
all men ...............1 Kin 4:31
*w* than the children .... Luke 16:8
God is *w* than men ......1 Cor 1:25

## WITCH

Thou shalt not suffer
a *w* to live ..............Ex 22:18
enchanter, or a *w*...... Deut 18:10

## WITHER

his leaf also shall not *w*..... Ps 1:3
The grass *w*............. Is 40:7, 8
the grass *w* ............1 Pet 1:24
trees whose fruit *w*....... Jude 12
*See* Joel 1:12; James 1:11

## WITHHOLD

*W* not thou thy tender
mercies................. Ps 40:11
*W* not good from them...Prov 3:27
*W* not correction ...... Prov 23:13
*w* not thine hand........Eccl 11:6
*See* Job 22:7; Joel 1:13

## WITHIN

God: yea, thy law is *w*
my heart............... Ps 40:8
right spirit *w* me.......... Ps 51:10
which is *w* the cup ....Matt 23:26
*See* Ps 45:13; Matt 3:9

## WITHSTAND

that I could *w* God.......Acts 11:17
*w* in the evil day ......... Eph 6:13
*See* Num 22:32; Esth 9:2

## WITNESS (*n.*)

God is *w* betwixt me
and thee................Gen 31:50
be a *w* unto us......... Josh 24:27
my *w* is in heaven .......Job 16:19
as a faithful *w* ...........Ps 89:37
*w* will not lie............Prov 14:5
given him for a *w* ...... Is 55:4
true and faithful *w* .......Jer 42:5
the world for a *w* ...... Matt 24:14
same came for a *w*......John 1:7
ye receive not our *w*....John 3:11
have greater *w* than ....John 5:36
himself without *w*...... Acts 14:17
also bearing *w*..........Rom 2:15
the *w* of God is.........1 John 5:9
the *w* in himself.........1 John 5:10
*See* Is 43:10; Luke 24:48

## WITNESS (*v.*)

I call heaven and
earth to *w* ...........Deut 4:26
countenance doth *w* ....... Is 3:9
the Holy Ghost *w* in ... Acts 20:33
being *w* by the law .....Rom 3:21
*w* a good confession....1 Tim 6:13
*See* 1 Sam 12:3; Matt 26:62

## WIZARD

or that is a *w*............ Lev 20:27

## WOMAN

men say not of me,
A *w* slew him .........Judg 9:54
as of a *w* in travail ........Ps 48:6
from the evil *w* ........ Prov 6:24
A foolish *w* is ...........Prov 9:13
virtuous *w* is a crown ...Prov 12:4
Every wise *w* buildeth... Prov 14:1
with a brawling *w*......Prov 21:9
find a virtuous *w* ......Prov 31:10
a *w* among all those .....Eccl 7:28
be in pain as a *w*.........Is 13:8
as the pangs of a *w* ........Is 21:3
as a *w* with child.........Is 26:17
as a *w* forsaken ...........Is 54:6
as of a *w* in travail ........Jer 6:24
lame, the *w* with child... Jer 31:8
A *w* shall compass.......Jer 31:22
be as the heart of a *w*... Jer 48:41
on a *w* to lust ....... Matt 5:28
*w*, great is thy faith.... Matt 15:28
last of all the *w* ........ Matt 22:27
Why trouble ye the *w* ... Matt 26:10
that this *w* hath
done................... Matt 26:13
*W*, what have I to do..... John 2:4
brought unto him a *w*... John 8:3
*W*, behold thy son .... John 19:26
this *w* was full of good ...Acts 9:36
natural use of the *w*.....Rom 1:27
not to touch a *w*......... 1 Cor 7:1
but the *w* is the glory.... 1 Cor 11:7
his Son, made of a *w* ..... Gal 4:4
I suffer not a *w* .........1 Tim 2:12
*w* being deceived........1 Tim 2:14
*See* Is 49:15; Luke 7:39; 13:16

## WOMEN

Blessed above *w*........ Judg 5:24
*w* answered one........1 Sam 18:7
the loving *w* ........2 Sam 1:26
thy honourable *w* .........Ps 45:9
thy strength unto *w* ....Prov 31:3
pitiful *w* have............Lam 4:10
that are born of *w* ...... Matt 11:11
*w* shall be grinding.... Matt 24:41
art thou among *w* ...... Luke 1:28
*w* keep silence....... 1 Cor 14:34
*w* adorn themselves.....1 Tim 2:9
the younger *w* marry....1 Tim 5:14
*w* laden with sins........ 2 Tim 3:6
The aged *w* likewise.... Titus 2:3
*W* received their........ Heb 11:35
*See* Acts 16:13; 1 Pet 3:5

## WONDERFUL

thy love to me was *w*... 2 Sam 1:26
things too *w* for me ..... Job 42:3
knowledge is too *w*......Ps 139:6
name shall be called *W*..... Is 9:6
*See* Deut 28:59; Jer 5:30

## WONDERFULLY

for I am fearfully and
*w* made................Ps 139:14

## WORD

by every *w* that
proceedeth out........ Deut 8:3
the *w* is very nigh......Deut 30:14
the *w* of my mouth....... Ps 19:14
The Lord gave the *w*...... Ps 68:11
the *w* of truth...........Ps 119:43
and a *w* spoken........ Ps 15:23
a *w* fitly spoken........Prov 25:11
every idle *w* that men ... Matt 12:36
*w* may be established ... Matt 18:16
*w* shall not pass away.... Matt 24:35
the *w* that I speak .......John 6:63
*w* of eternal life.........John 6:68
receiveth not my *w*......John 12:48
the *w* which ye hear ...John 14:24

*w* which thou
gavest me ............. John 17:8
*w* of exhortation........ Acts 13:15
remember the *w*....... Acts 20:35
the *w* of truth........ Acts 26:25
*w* is nigh thee........... Rom 10:8
with wisdom of *w*.......1 Cor 1:17
the kingdom ...
not in *w* ...............1 Cor 4:20
*w* easy to be
understood............ 1 Cor 14:9
our *w* toward you ...... 2 Cor 1:18
*w* of reconciliation ..... 2 Cor 5:19
By the *w* of truth ........ 2 Cor 6:7
fulfilled in one *w* ......... Gal 5:14
taught in the *w*......... Gal 6:6
heard the *w* of truth.......Eph 1:13
deceive you with vain *w*... Eph 5:6
the *w* of life............. Phil 2:16
the *w* of the truth..........Col 1:5
Let the *w* of Christ........ Col 3:16
unto you in *w*.......... 1 Thess 1:5
with these *w*..........1 Thess 4:18
in the *w* of faith ........1 Tim 4:6
they who labour
in the *w*............... 1 Tim 5:17
strive not about *w*......2 Tim 2:14
dividing the *w* ...........2 Tim 2:15
Preach the *w*............ 2 Tim 4:2
manifested his *w*........ Titus 1:3
the faithful *w*........... Titus 1:9
all things by the *w*.........Heb 1:3
the *w* spoken by angels ... Heb 2:2
*w* preached did not........ Heb 4:2
the *w* of God is quick .... Heb 4:12
*w* of righteousness ...... Heb 5:13
the good *w* of God........ Heb 6:5
but the *w* of the oath.... Heb 7:28
were framed by the *w*....Heb 11:3
spoken unto you the *w*...Heb 13:7
the *w* of truth.......... James 1:18
doers of the *w*.........James 1:22
man offend not in *w*....James 3:2
by the *w* of God..........1 Pet 1:23
milk of the *w* ...........1 Pet 2:2
stumble at the *w* ........ 1 Pet 2:8
if any obey not the *w*....1 Pet 3:1
sure of prophecy.......2 Pet 1:19
*w* which were spoken ... 2 Pet 3:2
by the same *w* are kept ...2 Pet 3:7
of the *W* of life..........1 John 1:1
But whoso
keepeth his *w* ........1 John 2:5
let us not love in *w* ....1 John 3:18
and hast kept my *w* ...... Rev 3:8
the *w* of my patience ....Rev 3:10
slain for the *w* of God..... Rev 6:9
*w* of the book........... Rev 22:19
*See* Is 8:20; Jer 20:9; Mic 2:7

## WORK (*n.*)

the seventh day God
ended his *w* .......... Gen 2:2
the *w* of their Lord ....... Neh 3:5
hast blessed the *w*........ Job 1:10
the *w* of a man........ Job 34:11
*w* of thy fingers............Ps 8:3
and all his *w* are done ...Ps 33:4
wonderful *w* which....... Ps 40:5
*w* that he hath done....... Ps 78:4
for his wonderful *w* ......Ps 107:8
The *w* of the Lord .......Ps 111:2
wonderful *w*..............Ps 111:4
practice wicked *w* ...... Ps 141:4
meditate on all thy *w*......Ps 143:5
Commit thy *w* ...........Prov 16:3
whether his *w*
be pure...............Prov 20:11
according to his *w*...... Prov 24:12
her own *w* praise her...Prov 31:31
have seen all the *w*...... Eccl 1:14
and for every *w*.......... Eccl 3:17
and destroy the *w* ........Eccl 5:6

unto every *w* .............Eccl 8:9
God now accepteth
thy *w* ...................Eccl 9:7
every *w* into judgment...Eccl 12:14
hasten his *w* ...............Is 5:19
performed his whole *w* ...Is 10:12
the *w* of men's hands.....Is 37:19
my *w* with my God ........Is 49:4
know their *w* .............Is 66:18
*w* of the hands............Jer 10:3
the *w* of the workman....Jer 10:9
and mighty in *w* ..........Jer 32:19
trusted in thy *w* .........Jer 48:7
any of their *w*...........Amos 8:7
for I will *w* ................Hab 1:5
many wonderful *w* .....Matt 7:22
ye after their *w* .........Matt 23:3
*w* they do for .........Matt 23:5
do no mighty *w*.........Mark 6:5
shew him greater *w* ...John 5:20
This is the *w* of God ...John 6:29
I have done one *w*......John 7:21
*w* of God should be......John 9:3
*w* that I do.............John 10:25
which of those *w*......John 10:32
the *w* that I do.......John 14:12
finished the *w* ..........John 17:4
wonderful *w* of God.... Acts 2:11
By what law? of *w* ...... Rom 3:27
righteousness
without *w* ..............Rom 4:6
not of *w*, but of him ....Rom 9:11
nor more of *w* ..........Rom 11:6
cast off the *w* ...........Rom 13:12
destroy not the *w*......Rom 14:20
man's *w* shall be.......1 Cor 3:13
ye my *w* in the Lord ...1 Cor 9:1
by the *w* of the law .......Gal 2:16
prove his own *w*..........Gal 6:4
Not of *w*, lest any .......Eph 2:9
*w* of the ministry........Eph 4:12
with the unfruitful *w*....Eph 5:11
by wicked *w* ...............Col 1:21
for their *w* sake ......1 Thess 5:13
good word and *w*.....2 Thess 2:17
according to our *w* ......2 Tim 1:9
the *w* of an evangelist....2 Tim 4:5
according to his *w*......2 Tim 4:14
but in *w* they deny .....Titus 1:16
by *w* of righteousness...Titus 3:5
repentance from
dead *w*..................Heb 6:1
conscience from
dead *w*..................Heb 9:14
her perfect *w* ...........James 1:4
faith without thy *w*...James 2:18
*w* that are therein ...... 2 Pet 3:10
*w* of the devil .........1 John 3:8
my *w* unto the end .......Rev 2:26
I know thy *w*............. Rev 3:8
and their *w* do follow....Rev 14:13
*See* Gal 5:19; 2 Thess 1:11

**WORK (v.)**
the Lord will *w* for us ...1 Sam 14:6
*w* evil in the ...........1 Kin 21:20
had a mind to *w* .........Neh 4:6
where he doth *w* .......Job 23:9
these things *w*........Job 33:29
ye *w* wickedness .........Ps 58:2
He that *w* deceit.........Ps 101:7
thee, Lord, to *w*.......Ps 119:126
I will *w*.....................Is 43:13
and *w* evil upon .........Mic 2:1
saith the Lord, and *w*.....Hag 2:4
that *w* wickedness.......Mal 3:15
Son, go *w* today .......Matt 21:28
Lord *w* with them ....Mark 16:20
My Father *w* ...........John 5:17
*w* the works of God....John 6:28
what dost thou *w*......John 6:30
when no man can *w*.....John 9:4
*w* righteousness........Acts 10:35

the law *w* wrath ........Rom 4:15
tribulation *w* patience... Rom 5:3
all things *w* together ... Rom 8:28
*w* with our own .........1 Cor 4:12
same God which *w* all...1 Cor 12:6
So then death *w* .......2 Cor 4:12
faith which *w* by love...... Gal 5:6
purpose of him who *w* ... Eph 1:11
spirit that now *w* .......Eph 2:2
to the power that *w* .....Eph 3:20
*w* with his hands .......Eph 4:28
*w* out your own..........Phil 2:12
and to *w* with.........1 Thess 4:11
doth already *w* .......2 Thess 2:7
if any would not *w*... 2 Thess 3:10
faith *w* patience ........James 1:3
*See* Ezek 46:1; Prov 11:18

**WORKMAN**
a *w* that needeth .......2 Tim 2:15

**WORKMANSHIP**
we are his *w* ............. Eph 2:10

**WORLD**
for the *w* is mine .........Ps 50:12
he hath set the *w*........Eccl 3:11
the face of the *w*..........Is 14:21
the *w*, and all things.......Is 34:1
kingdoms of the *w* ..... Matt 4:8
the light of the *w*.......Matt 5:14
the care of this *w* .....Matt 13:22
The field is the *w*.....Matt 13:38
the end of this *w*......Matt 13:40
gain the whole *w* .....Matt 16:26
Woe unto the *w* .........Matt 18:7
cares of this *w* .........Mark 4:19
and in the *w* to come...Mark 10:30
since the *w* began .......Luke 1:70
*w* should be taxed ........Luke 2:1
if he gain the whole *w*... Luke 9:25
the children of this *w*... Luke 16:8
in the *w* to come......Luke 18:30
children of this *w*..... Luke 20:34
to obtain that *w* ......Luke 20:35
He was in the *w* ........John 1:10
the sin of the *w* .........John 1:29
For God so loved the *w*...John 3:16
Saviour of the *w* ........John 4:42
light unto the *w* ........John 6:33
The *w* cannot hate you...John 7:7
I am the light of the *w*... John 8:12
judgment of this *w* .... John 12:31
to judge the *w* .........John 12:47
depart out of this *w* .....John 13:1
the *w* cannot receive ...John 14:17
not as the *w* giveth .... John 14:27
the prince of this *w*....John 14:30
If the *w* hate you .......John 15:18
In the *w* ye shall ......John 16:33
I pray not for the *w*..... John 17:9
They are not of the *w*...John 17:16
*w* may believe .........John 17:21
even the *w* itself......John 21:25
have turned the *w*.......Acts 17:6
all the *w* may become....Rom 3:19
conformed to this *w*......Rom 12:2
disputer of this *w*....... 1 Cor 1:20
the wisdom of this *w*...1 Cor 2:6
they that use this *w* ....1 Cor 7:31
the god of this *w*........2 Cor 4:4
the present evil *w* .......Gal 1:4
the *w* is crucified ........Gal 6:14
course of this *w* .........Eph 2:2
God in the *w*..........Eph 2:12
this present *w* .........2 Tim 4:10
*w* was not worthy ...... Heb 11:38
from the *w*..............James 1:27
a *w* of iniquity .........James 3:6
the friendship of
the *w* ................James 4:4
spared not the old *w* .... 2 Pet 2:5
Whereby the *w* that .....2 Pet 3:6
Love not the *w* .........1 John 2:15

the *w* knoweth us not....1 John 3:1
if the *w* hate you........1 John 3:13
Saviour of the *w* .......1 John 4:14
*w* lieth in
wickedness..........1 John 5:19
*See* 2 Sam 22:16; 1 Chr 16:30

**WORSHIP**
let us *w* and bow down....Ps 95:6
*w* him, all ye gods .........Ps 97:7
*w* at his footstool.........Ps 99:5
shall *w* the Lord in the ....Is 27:13
her cakes to *w* her .......Jer 44:19
them that *w* the host.....Zeph 1:5
fall down and *w* me .....Matt 4:9
in vain do they *w* me ... Matt 15:9
wilt *w* me.................Luke 4:7
men ought to *w* ........John 4:20
Ye *w* ye know not........John 4:22
that came up to *w* .....John 12:20
ye ignorantly *w*.........Acts 17:23
so *w* I the God .........Acts 24:14
and *w* and served.......Rom 1:25
he will *w* God ..........1 Cor 14:25
*See* Col 2:18; Heb 1:6; Rev 4:10

**WORTHY**
I am not *w* of the least
of all .................Gen 32:10
ye are *w* to die........1 Sam 26:16
himself a *w* man........1 Kin 1:52
shoes I am not *w*.......Matt 3:11
I am not *w* ............Matt 8:8
for the workman is *w*...Matt 10:10
more than me is
not *w* .................Matt 10:37
bidden were not *w* .....Matt 22:8
shoes I am not *w*......Mark 1:7
therefore fruits *w*.......Luke 3:8
he was *w* for whom .... Luke 7:4
for the labourer is *w*... Luke 10:7
things *w* of stripes....Luke 12:48
am no more *w*..........Luke 15:19
accounted *w* to .......Luke 20:35
latchet I am not *w*.......John 1:27
very *w* deeds ..........Acts 24:2
time are not *w*.......... Rom 8:18
that ye walk *w*...........Eph 4:1
walk *w* of the Lord ....... Col 1:10
walk *w* of God ......1 Thess 2:12
*w* of his reward........1 Tim 5:18
world was not *w*........ Heb 11:38
that *w* name............James 2:7
for they are *w*..........Rev 3:4
*See* Nah 2:5; Rev 4:11; 5:2

**WRATH**
I feared the *w*........Deut 32:27
to the day of *w*........ Job 21:30
the *w* of man .........Ps 76:10
and by thy *w*...........Ps 90:7
in the day of *w*.........Prov 11:4
The *w* of a king ........Prov 16:14
a fool's *w* is heavier ... Prov 27:3
much sorrow and *w* ..... Eccl 5:17
cruel both with *w*.........Is 13:9
In a little *w* I hid...........Is 54:8
and he reserveth *w*........Nah 1:2
in *w* remember mercy....Hab 3:2
day is a day of *w*.......Zeph 1:15
from the *w* to come ......Matt 3:7
unto thyself *w* ........... Rom 2:5
your children to *w*........Eph 6:4
appointed us to *w* .....1 Thess 5:9
without *w* and..........1 Tim 2:8
great day of his *w*........Rev 6:17
*See* James 1:19; Rev 6:16; 12:12

**WRITE**
unto Moses, W thou
these words...........Ex 34:27
thou shalt *w* them.......Deut 6:9
that *w* grievousness........Is 10:1
a child may *w* them .......Is 10:19
*W* ye this man ..........Jer 22:30

*W* thee all the words .....Jer 30:2
*w* it in their hearts...... Jer 31:33
*W* the vision ............. Hab 2:2
mind, and *w* them....... Heb 8:10
*See* Job 13:26; Rev 3:12

## WRITTEN
Oh that my words
    were now *w* ......... Job 19:23
*w* with the righteous .... Ps 69:28
and it was *w* within .... Ezek 2:10
are *w* in heaven.......Luke 10:20
What I have *w* ........John 19:22
they are *w* for..........1 Cor 10:11
*w* in our hearts .........2 Cor 3:2
*See* Is 4:3; Jer 17:1; Rev 2:17

---

## ———— Y ————

## YEAR
for seasons, and for
    days, and *y* ............Gen 1:14
once a *y*.................. Lev 16:34
it is a *y* of rest .......... Lev 25:5
each day for a *y*....... Num 14:34
forth *y* by *y* .......... Deut 14:22
the *y* of release ........ Deut 15:9
the *y* of tithing ........ Deut 26:12
*y* as man's days.........Job 10:5
and multitude of *y* ......Job 32:7
*y* as many generations ... Ps 61:6
*y* of ancient times ........ Ps 77:5
their *y* in trouble ........Ps 78:33
For a thousand *y* ......... Ps 90:4
The days of our *y* ....... Ps 90:10
*y* are throughout all ....Ps 102:24
*y* shall have no end......Ps 102:27
*y* of thy life .............Prov 4:10
*y* of the wicked ....... Prov 10:27

nor the *y* draw nigh .....Eccl 12:1
*y* of a hireling.............Is 21:16
*y* of the Lord................Is 61:2
the *y* of my redeemed..... Is 63:4
even the *y* of..............Jer 11:23
*y* of their iniquity....... Ezek 4:5
in the latter *y* ..........Ezek 38:8
*y* of liberty............ Ezek 46:17
and in the end of *y* ......Dan 11:6
to the *y* of many........Joel 2:2
calves of a *y* old.......... Mic 6:6
midst of the *y* .......... Hab 3:2
as in former *y*............ Mal 3:4
let it alone this *y* ...... Luke 13:8
times, and *y* ............ Gal 4:10
a thousand *y* ........... Rev 20:2
*See* Zech 14:16; James 4:13

## YESTERDAY
For we are but of *y* .......Job 8:9
years ... are but as *y* ..... Ps 90:4
same *y*, and today....... Heb 13:8

## YOKE
Take my *y* upon you....Matt 11:29
*y* together with......... 2 Cor 6:14
the *y* of bondage ..........Gal 5:1
are under the *y* .........1 Tim 6:1
*See* Job 1:3; 42:12; Lam 1:14

## YOUTH
man's heart is evil
    from his *y* ........ Gen 8:21
cattle from our *y* ......Gen 46:34
war from his *y*....... 1 Sam 17:33
whose son is this *y* ...1 Sam 17:55
thee from thy *y*........ 2 Sam 19:7
the Lord from my *y* ....1 Kin 18:12
iniquities of my *y*....... Job 13:26
the sin of his *y*...........Job 20:11
in the days of my *y* ...... Job 29:4

rise the *y*................ Job 30:12
to the days of his *y* ... Job 33:25
They die in *y*............ Job 36:14
the sins of my *y* .......... Ps 25:7
my trust from my *y* ...... Ps 71:5
taught me from my *y*......Ps 71:17
die from my *y* up........Ps 88:15
The days of his *y* ....... Ps 89:45
thy *y* is renewed..........Ps 103:5
the dew of thy *y* ....... Ps 110:3
children of the *y*.........Ps 127:4
afflicted me from my *y*... Ps 129:1
grown up in their *y*...... Ps 144:12
guide of her *y*...........Prov 2:17
wife of thy *y* ...........Prov 5:18
Rejoice, ... in thy *y*......Eccl 11:9
for childhood and *y* .....Eccl 11:10
days of thy *y*............Eccl 12:1
laboured from thy *y*......Is 47:12
shame of thy *y*............ Is 54:4
the kindness of thy *y*...... Jer 2:2
the guide of my *y* ....... Jer 3:4
thy manner from thy *y* .. Jer 22:21
the reproach of my *y* .... Jer 31:19
from their *y*..............Jer 32:30
the yoke in his *y*........Lam 3:27
from my *y* up even .....Ezek 4:14
the days of thy *y*...... Ezek 16:22
in the days of her *y*...... Hos 2:15
husband of her *y* .......Joel 1:8
cattle from my *y*........Zech 13:5
from my *y* up........Matt 19:20
observed from my *y* .. Mark 10:20
life from my *y* ..........Acts 26:4
despise thy *y* ...........1 Tim 4:12
*See* Prov 7:7; Is 40:30

## YOUTHFUL
Flee also *y* lusts ....... 2 Tim 2:22